Dictionary of **Southern Appalachian English**

Dictionary of Southern Appalachian English

MICHAEL B. MONTGOMERY &

JENNIFER K. N. HEINMILLER

Foreword by JOAN HOUSTON HALL

THE UNIVERSITY OF NORTH CAROLINA PRESS

Chapel Hill

This book was published in part with the support of the
W. L. EURY APPALACHIAN COLLECTION
at Appalachian State University; the Department of English, Linguistics, and Writing Studies at the University of Minnesota, Duluth; and Ricky Cox.

Manufactured in the United States of America
Designed by Richard Hendel
Set in Quadraat by Tseng Information Systems, Inc.

The University of North Carolina Press has been a member of the Green Press Initiative since 2003.

Cover illustration: *Great Smoky Mountains National Park at Oconaluftee Overlook*, © iStock.com/WerksMedia

Page i illustration by Jennifer K. N. Heinmiller

Library of Congress Cataloging-in-Publication Data
Names: Montgomery, Michael, 1950–2019, compiler. | Heinmiller, Jennifer K. N., compiler. | Hall, Joseph S. (Joseph Sargent), 1906–1992. | Montgomery, Michael, 1950–2019, Dictionary of Smoky Mountain English.
Title: Dictionary of Southern Appalachian English / Michael B. Montgomery and Jennifer K. N. Heinmiller.
Description: Chapel Hill : The University of North Carolina Press, [2021] | Includes bibliographical references and index.
Identifiers: LCCN 2020051338 | ISBN 9781469662541 (cloth ; alk. paper) | ISBN 9781469662558 (ebook)
Subjects: LCSH: English language—Dialects—Appalachian Region, Southern—Glossaries, vocabularies, etc. | Americanisms—Appalachian Region, Southern—Dictionaries. | Appalachians (People)—Languages. | Appalachian Region, Southern—Dictionaries. | LCGFT: Dictionaries. | Controlled vocabularies.
Classification: LCC PE2927.A6 M66 2021 | DDC 427/.975—dc23
LC record available at https://lccn.loc.gov/2020051338

This book is dedicated to the past, present, and future generations who call the mountains of Appalachia their home. It is intended as a token of the authors' appreciation for these communities, who share the beauty of their language, culture, and home with the world.

Contents

Figures and Tables

Figures

Tables

Foreword

The publication of the *Dictionary of Smoky Mountain English* (DSME) in 2004, edited by Michael B. Montgomery and based in large part on the historical collections of Joseph S. Hall, was an eagerly anticipated event in lexicographic, folkloric, and historical circles. It did not disappoint.

Lexicographers (especially my colleagues at the *Dictionary of American Regional English*) welcomed the documentation of words, phrases, and grammatical structures for which we often had tantalizingly little evidence; folklorists reveled in the elaboration—through well-chosen and detailed citations—of customs and traditions of a culture they understood and cherished; and historians found that excerpts from the diaries and letters of Civil War soldiers put a very human face on both the tragic and the quotidian aspects of the conflict. The DSME was clearly a landmark work giving serious and professional treatment to the language, culture, and history of a distinctive region.

The *Dictionary of Southern Appalachian English* (DSAE), a greatly enlarged, expanded, and augmented work, will be equally well received. The numbers of entry words and senses have been increased by thousands; the geographic range and the chronological scope of the citations have been expanded, with the documentation being increased by nearly 60 percent; and the inclusion of new source materials—many of them rare, in manuscript form, or disseminated only locally—adds extremely valuable evidence that is unavailable elsewhere.

Like the earlier work, the DSAE includes a detailed section explaining the many elements of morphology and syntax of southern mountain speech varieties that characterize them and set them off from other regional dialects. These include such widely recognized features as plural pronouns such as *y'all*, *you'uns*, *we'uns*, *us'ns*; possessive pronouns *hisn*, *hern*, *ourn*, *theirn*, *yourn*; superlatives like *fightingest*, *workingest*; multiple modals such as *may can*, *might could*, *might should ought*, *used to would*; nonstandard verb forms; *a*-prefixing, as in "He come a-runnin' and a-shoutin'"; postposed *one*, as in "He is in Tennessee or Kentucky, one"; and many other grammatical elements. These features are referenced in the entries themselves, and the "Grammar and Syntax of Southern Appalachian and Smoky Mountain English" section provides an overall account, with detailed and useful analysis.

For the DSAE, the decision to define "Southern Appalachia" as the area established by the Appalachian Regional Commission (encompassing parts of eight states from southern West Virginia to northeastern Alabama) was a pragmatic if not always comfortable one. Because it is much larger than the East Tennessee and western North Carolina region of the DSME, this area is inevitably more varied and less cohesive; but that also allowed an exploration of intraregional differences in language and culture, and it invited a more intensive investigation of traditional pastimes, occupations, and social customs.

Religious practices, such as the *camp meeting* (which is also called a *basket meeting*, *big meeting*, *brush meeting*, *grove meeting*, and *protracted meeting*) are given detailed treatment, as are the many kinds of *workings* (such as *barn raisings*, *house raisings*, *corn shuckings*, *log rollings*, and *quilting bees*) that are normally followed by a social event such as an *apple butter stirring*, *candy breaking*, or *molasses pull*. The entries for these traditional practices are accompanied by copious cross-references, making it easy for readers to search the *Dictionary* topic by topic. Unsurprisingly, entries for farming, fishing, hunting, milling, medicine, plants, and moonshining also receive full treatment. Amid them all are the colorful, innovative, expressive, and sometimes archaic lexical items that make the speech of Southern Appalachia one of the most widely recognized varieties of English in America.

As was true with the DSME, it is the citations that are the heart of the DSAE. Taken not just from novels, newspapers, histories, and biographies but also from diaries, letters, wills, church archives, and recordings such as those in Montgomery's Archive of Traditional Appalachian Speech and Culture, the quotations document the natural, unedited, unselfconscious speech of people throughout the region. A particularly valuable new resource for the DSAE was the ongoing Corpus of American Civil War Letters, which provided nearly two thousand citations.

The research for the expansion of the earlier work was begun shortly after its publication in 2004. As it became clear that the nature, number, and locations of excellent resources greatly exceeded the capacity of any one person to investigate them all, Montgomery invited his former student and research assistant, Jennifer Heinmiller, to be coeditor on the DSAE. Their very productive collaboration over the last decade has resulted in the first comprehensive dictionary of an American region based on historical principles. The DSAE will be valued not only by lexicographers and linguists but also by teachers, historians, oral historians, regional culture enthusiasts, and the many visitors to this distinctive region.

Sadly, Montgomery did not live to see publication of his magnum opus. Readers owe a huge debt to Heinmiller, whose dedication in shepherding it to completion makes it available now and in perpetuity.

JOAN HOUSTON HALL, Chief Editor Emerita,
Dictionary of American Regional English

Acknowledgments

This dictionary is a collaborative effort between the late Michael Montgomery and myself, as well as hundreds of others who have contributed directly or indirectly to the project over the years. In undertaking this project, we have strived to accurately document and record the speech of communities and individuals as a historical record, an academic and cultural resource, and a tribute to the men and women of this remarkable part of our country—those who came before us and those who carry on this vibrant legacy of a place unlike any other on this planet.

The volume you hold in your hands is the cumulative work of some eighty-five years of research. It began in the 1930s when a doctoral student from California named Joseph S. Hall was invited to conduct linguistic research in the Smoky Mountains. The project quickly exploded in scope, and Hall gathered invaluable written and audio data in the decades that followed, eventually becoming the foundation of his doctoral dissertation and several published books. His body of work provided the basis for the predecessor of this dictionary, the *Dictionary of Smoky Mountain English* (University of Tennessee Press, 2004). That volume was a massive project undertaken by the indefatigable Michael B. Montgomery (1951–2019), a professor emeritus of the University of South Carolina.

When I became the research assistant to Montgomery as a first-year graduate student in 2008, I had little idea that, slightly more than a decade later, I would be one of the two authors of such a work and, indeed, the sole surviving editor. For nearly eleven years, I had the privilege of crafting, compiling, editing, and editing again these pages alongside him. Together we spent countless hours researching, discussing, and occasionally arguing about lexicography and the trajectory of this book, which would come to occupy a huge part of both our lives. Dr. Montgomery considered the first edition of the dictionary something of an abridged version of what he truly wanted to accomplish, and he told me he knew almost immediately on its publication that he wanted to revise and expand the material to encompass a broader variety of terms in a more expansive region and to include a wider variety of sources. Together, we endeavored to do just that. This volume is approximately 30 percent larger in the number of example citations, and we have done our utmost to provide readers with a balanced selection of the most illustrative examples of the terms within.

Bringing the *Dictionary of Southern Appalachian English* to completion would not have been possible without the support of our many friends, family members, institutions, and well-wishers over the years. This dictionary, as well as the first edition of the dictionary, for which most research was completed by Dr. Montgomery in the 1990s, was made possible through the support of individuals from Southern Appalachia, our home institution at the University of South Carolina, and beyond. Among them are the research assistants assigned to Dr. Montgomery at the University of South Carolina from 1991 to 2002, who assisted in typing, researching, proofreading, and fact-checking material for the first edition, and many others from the University of South Carolina in the 1990s, 2000s, and 2010s. We are grateful to the following individuals from the University of South Carolina who provided years of technical and administrative support and assistance: Noreen Doughty, Eric Roman, Matthew Simmons, Homer Steedly, Timothy Stewart, Mila Tasseva, Errol Tisdale, and Zach White. A great number of the terms in this dictionary were attested to by consultants from the mountains of Tennessee and North Carolina, including Inez McCaulley Adams, Roy D. Brown, Florence Cope Bush, R. Glenn Cardwell, Michael E. Ellis, Loyal Jones, Ted R. Ledford, Pearl Mashburn Norris, Duane Oliver, and Jack Weaver. A warm thanks to our colleagues and friends who assisted with the background material and provided editorial and moral support, including Richard W. Bailey, Anthony Cavender, Allen Coggins, Joseph Earl Dabney, Bethany K. Dumas, Connie Eble, Harold Farwell, María García-Bermejo Giner, George Goebel, Rose Houk, Ellen Johnson, John M. Kirk, Jonathan L. Lighter, Houston Lowry, Judith McCulloh, Karl Nicholas, Thomas Nunnally, Lucinda Ogle, Larry Olsziewski, Dan Pittillo, Anita Puckett, Philip Robinson, Luanne von Schneidemesser, Mark Sohn, and Kathleen Curtis Wilson. I am grateful to have been afforded the opportunity to personally meet and work with some of these wonderful people and to build on the invaluable information they have provided.

I would like to especially thank Elizabeth Layman for her diligence and friendship over the years, and for her unfailing assistance to Dr. Montgomery. This work would not have come to light without her hard work, patience, and "mountaineer ears and sensibilities," in the words of Dr. Montgomery.

In bringing this dictionary to completion, I am indebted to Joan Houston Hall, Chief Editor Emerita of the *Dictionary of American Regional English*, for her guidance, advice, and proofreading over the past several years, and for her willingness to assist the project and propel it forward. I am also deeply grateful to Walt Wolfram of North Carolina State University for his enthusiasm and assistance in this project.

I am also grateful to the many friends and supporters I met along the way, as well as those who assisted Dr. Montgomery prior to my becoming part of the project. I speak for both of us in expressing our thanks to these individuals: Amber Cook, Amie Freeman, and other members of staff at the Interlibrary Loan Department and the circulation librarians at Thomas Cooper Library at the University of South Carolina; the staff at the East Tennessee Historical Society; the staff at the University of South Carolina Center for Digital Humanities; Joshua Morgan of Open Parks Network; the staff at the Great Smoky Mountains Association; the personnel at the Sugarlands Visitor Center at Great Smoky Mountains National Park in Gatlinburg, Tennessee; Appalachian State

University; Alice Lloyd College; Emory and Henry College; Lees Junior College; the South Caroliniana Library at the University of South Carolina; and the staff at the University of South Carolina Press. I would like to personally thank the following people, who contributed to the project in countless valuable ways: Bridget Anderson, the Atchley family, Barbara Bolt, Richard Brown, Don Casada, Jim Casada, Mark Cheslak, Michael Ellis, Karl Heinmiller, Kay Herbert, Kathy Wyly Mille, the Montgomery family, Tipper Pressley, Scott Elliott, Esq., and Tracey Weldon. A special thanks also to Michael's friends at First Presbyterian Church in Columbia, South Carolina. I wish to also express my thanks to the wonderful staff at the University of North Carolina Press for turning this ambitious vision into a reality.

My sincere gratitude to my many friends and family members who have provided support over the years, including my grandparents, Janet and Robert Richards and my grandfather, Ed Nelson, all of whom first made apparent the difference between regional varieties of American English and taught me to love them. And this work simply would not have been possible without the assistance and support of my mother and eternal champion, Kimberly Nelson, and my father, Mark Nelson. Without their support, patience, and generosity, none of this circumvengemous journey would have been possible.

JENNIFER KAY NELSON HEINMILLER
Asheville, North Carolina
February 2020

Authors' Note

While it has been the authors' intent from the beginning to base this work on language as it has historically been used in Appalachia and beyond, there are inevitably terms and ideas in the examples illustrating head words in this volume and its predecessor that do not reflect the authors' feelings, attitudes, or opinions. Although it is the obligation of the researcher to present information in a truthful way, there are ideologies that need not be perpetuated in text. As such, material of this nature has been largely removed from this volume. We are not proponents of censorship, but it is important to remember that, as modern readers, the lens through which we view historical language is vastly different from that of the speakers whose words are presented herein. Certain views expressed in works of that place and time are vastly different from those we as a community value today, and every attempt has been made to balance that authenticity with our educated, broader perspectives.

Aden Carver, who lived to be 101 years of age, joined the CCC in his nineties as a local master craftsman. In this photo, he is crossing a log over Bradley Fork at age ninety-one.

History of the Dictionary

This dictionary is an updated and revised edition of the *Dictionary of Smoky Mountain English* (University of Tennessee Press, 2004), a product of work undertaken by Michael Bryant Montgomery (1950–2019) and Joseph Sargent Hall (1906–92). Montgomery worked solo on the present edition from 2007 to 2009, and then with coeditor Jennifer K. N. Heinmiller from 2009 to early 2019. The project was brought to completion by Heinmiller following Montgomery's passing in July 2019. This dictionary, like its predecessor, is founded on material amassed by Hall, the pioneer researcher of the speech and culture of the Great Smoky Mountains.

Shortly after its formation, officials at Great Smoky Mountains National Park drew up plans for a permanent record of the culture of people remaining in the Smokies. In the spring of 1937, Roy Appleman, a historian with the National Park Service, invited Hall, then a graduate student at Columbia University in New York, to take a three-month assignment documenting mountain speech. That summer, Hall found himself in the Smokies for the first time. During that three-month period, he interviewed many people in the area but did not make audio recordings of the interviews; instead he concentrated on getting to know the individuals and the mountains that were their home. He filled four notebooks cover to cover with observations on expressions, pronunciations, and other details of locals' speech. In June 1939, with financial assistance from the Park Service and Columbia University, he returned to conduct research for a doctoral dissertation on Smokies pronunciation. With new audio equipment in tow, he began recording in earnest. He visited again in the summers of 1940, 1941, 1949, 1953, 1956, 1959, 1962, 1967, and 1976, usually spending several weeks to record and take notes, but also to visit friends and attend family gatherings and other events.

In 1939–40 he filled ten more field notebooks. With recording equipment, transportation, and an assistant provided by the park service and the Civilian Conservation Corps (CCC),[1] Hall located speakers throughout the Smokies. He used one CCC camp after another as a base from which to travel around and record conversations, stories, and music, including traditional ballads, folk songs, hymns, and popular songs of the era. Local men employed at each camp identified, and often introduced him to, "good talkers" in the neighborhood. In his early recordings he used two machines: a Garwick operated by cables hooked to the battery of a pickup truck, on which he made about ninety aluminum discs, and an Allied that ran on a battery pack, on which he made about seventy acetate discs.[2]

Hall's systematic gathering of data on Appalachian speech was the first by a linguist and marked the beginning of the most extensive collection on southern mountain language in existence, a collection of great historical significance (many of his interviewees were born in the mid-nineteenth century, at least two of

John Cable, Sam Sparks, Hubert Cable, and Fonz Cable, 1936. Photo by Charles S. Grossman.

them in the 1840s). To these early recordings he added forty tapes of stories, square dances, and other material of folkloric interest on his visits in the 1950s and 1960s to Smokies natives who were still residing just outside the park. He interviewed, or made observations on, more than two hundred mountain residents in the course of his work, noting as much personal information about them as possible.

In the beginning, Hall's primary interest was pronunciation, and his early field notes consisted largely of phonetic transcriptions of words.[3] It would be years before he began organizing his material into a form suggesting a glossary, much less a dictionary. Though originally focused on phonetics, Hall quickly found every aspect of Smokies speech intriguing, and even in his early notes an interest in vocabulary, local culture, and folk tales is apparent. His natural curiosity led him to continue collecting, and in later years he fashioned material into three popular volumes: *Smoky Mountain Folks and Their Lore* (1960), *Sayings from Old Smoky* (1972), and *Yarns and Tales from the Great Smokies* (1978).[4]

In 1972, Hall retired from Pasadena City College in California, where he had taught English for a quarter century. Four years later, he visited the Smokies for the last time and began concentrating his energies on a more thorough compilation of material from three and a half decades of notes and recordings.[5] Working with neither timetable nor explicit aim to publish, he extracted citations and prepared note cards for hundreds of vocabulary items and pronunciations. By 1990 his compilation had grown to over one thousand terms and had acquired the modest title "A Glossary of Some Smoky Mountain Words." In this way and others, Hall spent much of the final twenty years of his life putting his materials into a form for other scholars.[6] As he later explained to Montgomery, who had become acquainted with him

Man in front of herder's cabin, built by Frank Oliver, in 1935. Photo by Randolph A. Shields.

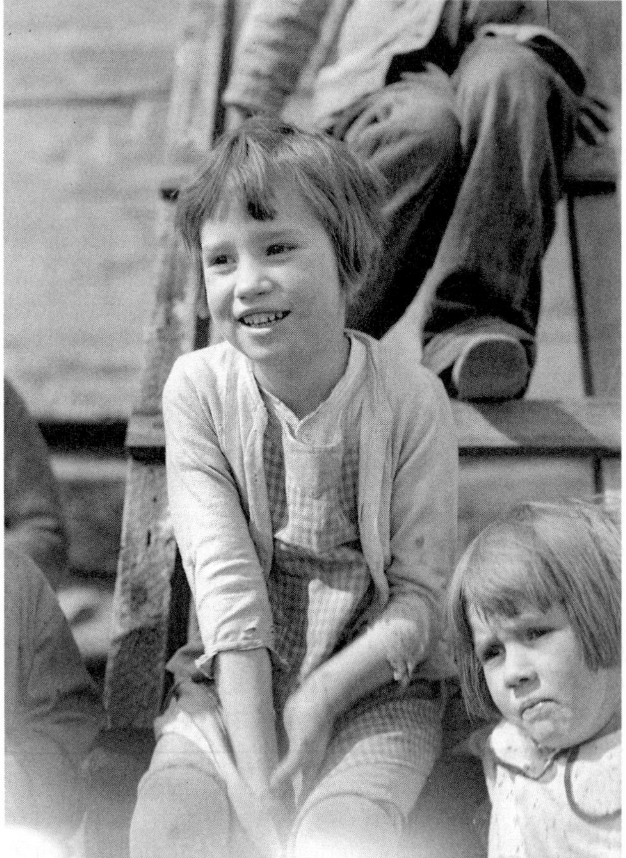

Pupils of the Little Greenbriar School, 1936. Photo by Edouard Exline.

through correspondence in the mid-1980s, he did this for the enlightenment and profit of future generations, to express his devotion to mountain people, and to open their world to others.

In 1990 Montgomery visited Hall and proposed to carry forward his work, persuading him to consider a full-length dictionary based on Hall's typescript and other material. In February 1992, upon Hall's death, Montgomery assumed sole direction of the project and began identifying the tasks that lay ahead for compiling a dictionary. He quickly concluded that the amount of other documentation and the lack of a comprehensive work on Smoky Mountain speech justified a full-scale reading program to supplement what he had inherited. Hall had been well aware of the limited topics covered in his recorded interviews, especially the early ones. He had most frequently asked men about hunting; women, who were sometimes reluctant to participate, had answered questions about cooking and home remedies. A disproportionate number of his citations pertain to these subjects, which he chose to focus on in his interviews because they would more predictably elicit longer, less-inhibited responses that often contained vivid narratives and recollections and more natural speech. His methodology, which allowed him to record the most colloquial speech possible, was ahead of its time for American linguistics, but it unfortunately left large areas of early twentieth-century Smokies culture poorly documented.

Montgomery's research program canvassed the full range of subject matter and types of literature, archival and published, from or about the Smokies. At the same time, it elaborated the approach employed by Hall. As shown in his 1942 work on Smokies phonetics and in his note cards and typescript glossary, Hall had sometimes sought substantiation of citations in the work of local color writers of fiction, studies in American folklore, and early modern English literature, especially Shakespeare's plays. Montgomery, a native of East Tennessee, would in his undertaking use to full advantage his familiarity with, and access to, local libraries and publications of which Hall, a Californian, could never have become aware. Wide-ranging inclusion of material from other sources often served to place Hall's citations in historical context while maintaining their centrality as the earliest tape-recorded evidence.

In the 1970s and 1980s, a librarian at Great Smoky Mountains National Park had made orthographic transcripts of hundreds of recorded interviews with speakers from the area. These included Hall's 1939 recordings (Hall had audited these for citations but had transcribed only those portions he considered of particular narrative or folkloric interest)[7] and two hundred hours of oral history interviews made by National Park Service personnel and volunteers between 1954 and 1985 (the majority of these date from the late 1960s or early 1970s).[8] Realizing the value of the Park Service interviews and their transcriptions (designated GSMNP in dictionary citations), Montgomery in 1994 read all of the transcriptions, audited them when warranted, and retranscribed many of them and Hall's interviews for greater accuracy and to form an electronic Corpus of Smoky Mountain English (CSME).

In 1994, Montgomery recruited a team of consultants native to the mountains and sought out specialists on various aspects

Lenard, Thelma, and Willie Ownby at Cherokee Orchard. Photo by Charles S. Grossman.

Mack Hannah, one of Hall's speakers, and Hiram Wilburn, an early advocate for preservation of mountain ways. This is one of the earliest photos of people native to the Smoky Mountains. Taken by Edouard Exline.

of mountain life to query on specific terms. Extensive one-on-one sessions in 1992–93 with two local authorities, A. Randolph Shields and Glenn Cardwell, demonstrated the many benefits of collaborating with consultants, which led to working with a larger team a year later. From 1994 to 1998 Montgomery sent six lengthy sets of queries to ten primary consultants, often following up responses with questions seeking clarification and elaboration. Montgomery queried consultants about these and terms from other sources that he anticipated for the Smokies. He consulted numerous other individuals about specific subjects.

That same year, Montgomery decided to expand the scope of the dictionary beyond the six counties of the Smoky Mountains proper. DARE's wider perspective suggests that terms rarely originated in, or were exclusive to, the Smokies. Far more often they were typical of Southern Appalachia or the broader South Midland region. For this reason and because a scholarly dictionary of Southern Appalachian English did not exist, the dictionary's coverage was broadened to encompass the Tennessee–North Carolina border region.

Following the publication of the *Dictionary of Smoky Mountain English* in 2004, Montgomery decided in 2007 to once again expand on the material and began work on a revised edition of the dictionary. For the new project, he envisioned widening the range of source material to include even more counties and states, with the goal of creating a more inclusive dictionary of Southern Appalachian English. To this end, he resumed his research program and began reading more publications and auditing more oral interviews, both for new terms and for citations to bolster terms existing in the first edition of the dictionary. Almost immediately he realized that, although he already had a solid foundation for the new project, it was a very large undertaking and he would need the assistance of another linguist. In 2008, he employed Jennifer K. N. Heinmiller, at the time a graduate student at the University of South Carolina, as a research assistant. For Heinmiller, a native of the Carolinas whose extended family had been situated in Appalachia for generations, the project held a natural interest. By that time, Montgomery had retired from his position at the University of South Carolina, but he had no intention of retiring from lexicographical work. He began training Heinmiller in lexicography and gave her a formal introduction to the study of Appalachian English, building on her preliminary education in varieties of American English. Although her area of focus was primarily in the study and documentation of endangered languages in the Okinawan archipelago of Japan, her interest in minority language varieties and her own North Carolina heritage made her an asset in editorial and research tasks. In 2011, Montgomery named Heinmiller coeditor of the dictionary. Montgomery wrote of Heinmiller in 2018, "Her natural lexicographical talents [were] clear. Her abilities to read, type, organize, and proof material as it evolved from printed and other sources to prospective citations and entries for the dictionary have been incomparable. As I read and marked texts, she prepared drafts and carried out many tasks beyond my power, including spending countless hours in the university library scouring microfiche." Montgomery and Heinmiller spent countless hours compiling, analyzing, and discussing material for the dictionary. Together they expanded the text to a volume that is approximately 30 percent larger than its predecessor and encompasses the entire Southern Appalachian region. Left with an unfinished manuscript upon Montgomery's unexpected death in July 2019, Heinmiller carried out the remainder of the project herself, carefully editing and working with consultants and finding a route to publication through the University of North Carolina Press to bring the revised and expanded dictionary to completion. As part of her work, she also launched a podcast, *Appalachian Words*, as a new platform from which to share the decades of research that have shaped the present dictionary.

User's Guide to the Dictionary

This guide provides an outline of the structure of the entries in the dictionary for ease of use. The format and notation of entries in this dictionary are designed to be as self-explanatory as possible. The entries follow the general principles of historical lexicography as enshrined in the *Oxford English Dictionary* (OED; 1888–1928), with modifications such as those introduced by the *Dictionary of American Regional English* (DARE), or as explained below. Except for one-line cross-references, each entry has at least three main divisions—the opening section, the definition, and the paragraph of supporting citations—and sometimes a fourth, an etymology. Within entries, abbreviations are kept to a minimum and are employed only in definitions, editorial notes, short titles, and etymologies. A list of these can be found at "Abbreviations Used in the Dictionary."

The Opening Section

The headword (the word or phrase that is the subject of a dictionary entry) appears at the beginning of each entry in bold type. Far more often than not, the headword appears in its conventional English spelling, but because this volume documents numerous speech-based forms, exceptions must be noted. Most of these are simply noted as "variant forms." In other cases, an unconventional spelling (e.g., *janders* "jaundice," *mushrat* "muskrat") heads an entry on the principle that it represents what a reader would find in literature from or about the region and thus would go in search of. This principle is impractical in cases where two or more variant forms are noted (e.g., *diamond*, *something*). Superscript numerals immediately following a headword differentiate two or more forms that have identical spellings but different origins (e.g., *low*¹, *low*², *low*³). Compound nouns and other compound forms (e.g., those beginning with *bear* or *in*) are normally entered as separate headwords and are not incorporated into a single entry with one base word as in some historical dictionaries. Headwords are arranged in alphabetical order regardless of whether their printed form is one word, two or more words joined by a hyphen, or two or more independent words. More often than not, compound nouns are spelled as one word, but compound verbs normally as two. Phrases are usually entered at what is judged to be their first significant element (e.g., *cut a dido* and *do a dido* are entered at *dido*). Two or more terms having identical meaning and closely related form and spelling (i.e., within the same letter of the alphabet) are often collapsed into one entry, with the alphabetically prior (e.g., *hen apple*), the derivationally more basic (e.g., *molasses pull*), or the more generally attested (e.g., *dog trot*) being the one chosen for the headword. In these cases, appropriate cross-references for the variant terms are found elsewhere in the dictionary and direct the user to the relevant entry. Other variant forms are presented in italics and placed in parentheses immediately following the headword. Two or more terms having identical meaning but unrelated forms are referred to one another by the notation "Same as." Forms that appear as headwords are always boldfaced; when cited elsewhere (as in defining another term), their appearance in bold indicates their status as headwords.

The second part of the headword line indicates the appropriate part of speech or word class and is given in italics. Because the phrasing of definitions is usually sufficient to indicate finer distinctions such as transitivity (e.g., *set to*), only in rare exceptions (e.g., *make*) is a transitive use of a verb distinguished from an intransitive one. The definition of a transitive verb (e.g., *destroy*, *tole*) will normally feature in parentheses a typical noun object that makes its transitivity clear.

Within an entry, variant forms are listed alphabetically early in the entry. However, occasionally a form occurring in a citation is not listed as a variant if it is judged to be contrived (e.g., *hes* "has," and *ove* "of" in works by George Washington Harris) or representing idiosyncratic usage judged lacking in linguistic interest. The dictionary's extensive use of nineteenth-century manuscripts by less-tutored writers (especially Civil War letters) has presented countless instances of forms to consider for inclusion. Thus, *something* has six variant forms deemed to be of interest, but could have had more. If an entry is devoted solely to documenting one or more variant forms (e.g., *ancient*, *camphor*, *garden*), these are given in the opening section of the entry, and the term is not defined. Otherwise, variant forms are listed in the first alphabetic paragraph (A) of an entry (e.g., *ballad*, *chance*), with subsequent paragraphs devoted to grammatical usages, meanings, and so on. At the appropriate alphabetic location, each variant form is entered and referenced to a headword where one or more citations can be found.

When an entry indicates the pronunciation of a term, this is usually presented in respellings, with capital letters for primary stress and small capitals for secondary stress (e.g., *confident*). Phonetic notation is employed in the definition line and also in some citations, but only when a respelling is not transparent or not sufficiently detailed. In these cases, the notation is presented in brackets using the conventions of the International Phonetic Alphabet (see the "Pronunciation Key"). Some forms found in citations (in addition to idiosyncratic ones from literary or manuscript sources) are not entered in the dictionary when they represent general tendencies of pronunciation in Appalachian speech (e.g., the alveolar nasal in words ending in *-ing*, usually spelled by dialect writers as *-in* or *-in'* ; or the raising of /ɛ/ to /ɪ/ before nasal consonants, as in *pen*, *hem*). Variant forms of morphological interest (e.g., verb principal parts at *see*) or syntactic interest (e.g., *forever*, *nobody*) are presented as thoroughly as the record permits and synoptically in the section "Grammar and Syntax of Southern Appalachian and Smoky Mountain English."

Definitions

Definitions are provided for one or more senses of terms, except in cases that have conventional meaning and are of interest only for their pronunciation or grammar. Definitions not only reflect the dated citations but may also be informed by other glossaries and dictionaries, by comments from consultants, or by the personal knowledge or experience of the editors. When, as is often the case, a citation already defines or explains a term in an entirely satisfactory manner or when it illustrates or elaborates on a term in an informative way, the instruction "See citation(s)" refers the reader to the paragraph below. Citations from nonfiction have proven extremely useful in defining and explaining many items.

Usage information of three types appears within definitions, often in parentheses. Details of a term's grammatical context may be cited (e.g., if the term is usually plural in form, as *druther*, or occurs only in negative clauses, as *abide* or *handily*). Social or pragmatic details may be supplied (in the form of a note), as from Joseph Hall's early observations or citing the currency (or lack thereof) in the editor's Archive of Traditional Appalachian Speech and Culture (ATASC), a compilation of transcribed oral history interviews. Usage labels are avoided because they are as likely to mislead as to inform and because they lend definitiveness that evidence rarely can justify. The designation *obsolete* no doubt applies to hundreds of items, but this is impossible to assess on a consistent basis, especially given that the dictionary's material often comes from the recollections of older individuals. A term may have continuing, if greatly reduced, currency in the present day beyond the lexicographer's ability to detect it.

The label *archaic* is also avoided, because what may be archaic in American English generally is often not so in Southern Appalachia, and what may be archaic in Southern Appalachia is often difficult to determine with confidence, even by asking native consultants. Some usage characterizations (e.g., "used as a derogatory term for") are very often implied within entries. The label *historical* is used occasionally, but with some confidence, because the cultural item or practice to which the term applies is itself obsolete. More often a definition uses the qualifiers *formerly* or *traditionally*. Where possible, technical information, such as the botanical Latinate names for flora, is cited in definitions, even though sources do not always provide this consistently.

At the end of a definition, extensive cross-referencing of two kinds serves to link to other entries that have complementary information for the same general semantic field as a headword: "Same as" identifies terms elsewhere in the dictionary having identical meaning; "See also" identifies terms elsewhere that are synonyms or are of related interest and expand the information found at an entry.

Dated Citations

The body of each entry is in large part made up of dated citations, which are examples of the headword in context or otherwise show evidence for its use. These citations are the foundation of the dictionary and reveal the wide-ranging, thorough collection programs undertaken by Joseph Hall, Michael Montgomery, and Jennifer Heinmiller. Each citation has been carefully selected in order to supply (1) the earliest evidence available at hand; (2) a chronological spread of evidence; (3) a definition that suffices for a word; (4) fuller descriptive information than is possible to include in an entry's definition; or (5) different contexts in which a term appears.

Citations are grouped into paragraph divisions according to their form, grammar, or meaning. These are designated by capital letters in alphabetical order, and a separate letter is used for each part of speech. Subsections that indicate specific forms or senses are presented in numbered sections within the alphabetic divisions. For example, at *blow*, section A deals with verb principal parts (subsection 1 with the past tense and 2 with the past participle), section B with senses of the verb, and section C with senses of the noun. The entry for *mind* has two sections: A for the word used as a noun (with two subsections) and B as a verb (five subsections). Some or all variant forms, in order to avoid repetition, may be illustrated not in section A of an entry but in subsequent sections pertaining to a certain use or sense of the term (e.g., *feisty*). In such cases, a cross-reference from A to the section below is included for easier navigation.

Each citation begins with a date in bold type. Sometimes this is nested within another date to indicate both the original occurrence or date of publication and its later republication. The date is followed by the author's or editor's surname in regular type, then an abbreviated title consisting of one to five words in italics, and then the page number or speaker for the citation, if available or relevant. These citation headers are included the dictionary's "Chronological List of Works Cited," where full bibliographic details for each title can be found.

Citations that do not employ the headword under which it is entered, but that provide useful supporting information for the term, appear within square brackets. Citations from a specific locale within a source (e.g., the *American Dialect Dictionary* or Joseph Hall's material) list that locale in parentheses before the citation; otherwise, the locale of a source can be found in the "Chronological List of Works Cited." Citations are normally presented as complete sentences and have sometimes had minor repetitions and such items as *you know* and *uh* edited out, especially for oral sources, in order not to proliferate ellipses within citations. Quotation marks are used only to set off quoted material. That is, if a citation occurs wholly within quotation marks in the original printed source, these marks are considered redundant and are omitted.

Priority is given to citations from audio recordings, especially for grammatical items. This is to emphasize the nature of the dictionary as a record of living speech patterns. The research for this dictionary included extensive efforts to consult oral history collections recorded since 1970, the overwhelming majority of which have been transcribed specifically for this dictionary. Many MA, MS, or MEd theses and PhD dissertations also provide examples documented directly from speech. All grammatical forms and syntactic patterns are faithfully maintained, and no spelling conventions are introduced to indicate pronunciation (except for some practices followed by Joseph Hall).

If more than one sense occurs for a term, these are arranged in terms of their apparent historical development, with functional relationships indicated within entries; for example, *blow* as a verb is defined and exemplified before *blow* as a noun. With only occasional exceptions, terms are supported by citations from oral or written sources, rather than by comments or confirmation by consultants alone.

Information from consultants, often derived from several years of querying by the editors, is compiled in data summaries introduced by "Montgomery *Coll*" or "Heinmiller *Coll*" following the date(s) of consultation. These summaries note responses that come from Montgomery's ten primary consultants, Heinmiller's consultants and fieldwork, and occasionally from other individuals. Montgomery and Heinmiller's consultants were asked to confirm recognition of a term and its meaning and, if possible, provide further information, such as furnishing an illustrative example, further details, or a comment about usage. Confirmations are presented first, then elaborations. For example, *candy roaster* was confirmed by three consultants and elaborated on by a fourth. In many cases (e.g., *barefoot*, *slow as Christmas*) consultants provide the richest material for an entry. Responses of consultants in the Montgomery collection are presented in alphabetical order by their surnames, unless eight or more consultants confirmed the item, in which case a numerical tally alone appears (e.g., *fidget*, *jaggedy*). Lack of familiarity by Montgomery's consultants is also explicitly noted: an item known to only one of them is identified as such (e.g., *bollyfox*, *shame briar*), and an item confirmed by none of them appears within brackets and identifies this as negative evidence. Citations from Montgomery's unsystematic observations of mountain speech are identified as "Montgomery *File*."

Etymologies

Etymologies are included to relate items to other stages and forms of the English language and to provide perspective on the character, sources, affiliations, and resources of the speech of Southern Appalachia. The dictionary does not give etymologies for entries when these are easily found in standard dictionaries, unless they are considered to be of particular interest. Etymologies are enclosed in square brackets at the end of an entry or at the end of the paragraph to which they pertain, rather than at the beginning of an entry, as is the practice of most dictionaries. They consist of one or more of three types of material:

1. Antecedents of an item (i.e., earlier forms and senses). Such historical and derivational information is most often taken from the *OED*. The symbol < ("derived from") precedes identification of a form from an earlier stage of English or other language from which a term has evolved (if this form differs from the headword of the entry or if its meaning differs from that in modern English). If relevant, the dates of currency of an item are also taken from the *OED*. Few words are traced back farther than their source in English. Within etymologies the etymon and other cited forms are given in italics.
2. Cross-references to other modern and historical dictionaries in which an item is treated. Evidence as found in the *English Dialect Dictionary* (*EDD*), *Scottish National Dictionary* (*SND*), *Concise Ulster Dictionary* (*CUD*), *The Hamely Tongue* (*HT*), and other works often identifies or suggests origins or semantic affinity with forms in historical varieties in the British Isles. In relating terms to usage at other times and places in the United States and the British Isles, these cross-references seek to put terms in historical and geographical context. When they show parallel usage elsewhere, these places cannot necessarily be taken to indicate a direct link.
3. Identification of the modern geographical range of an item, most often as indicated by *DARE* or *Webster's Third New International Dictionary* (*Web3*). When an etymology is taken from *DARE*, even when it cites the *OED* and other works on the language used in the present volume, this is indicated by attributing the information to *DARE*, as in the entry for *cobbled up*. In several cases, references to *DARE* etymologies cite revised versions of entries posted on the *DARE* website at http://dare.wisc.edu/words/quarterly-updates/all-updated-entries.

Pronunciation Key

The following symbols appear within brackets in dictionary entries to represent the pronunciation of words.

ˈ	primary stress on the following syllable
ː	slight elongation of a vowel
aɪ	vowel in *my*
æ	vowel in *rat*
aʊ	vowel in *cow*
aᵁ	same vowel as previous but slightly clipped
a	vowel intermediate between *cat* and *cot*
ɑ	vowel in *all* but slightly fronted and with lips unrounded
ɒ	vowel in *all* but slightly fronted and with lips rounded
ɔ	vowel in *all*
e	vowel in *ate*
ɛ	vowel in *net*
ɚ	"er" sound in *fur*
ɝ	"er" sound in *where*
i	vowel in *eat, see*
ɪ	vowel in *rib*
ə, ʌ	vowel in *rub*
o	vowel in *row*
u	vowel in *who*
ʊ	vowel in *pull*
b	consonant in *bee*
d	consonant in *do*
ʤ, ǰ	consonant in *joy*
f	consonant in *foe*
g	consonant in *go*
h	consonant in *hay*
k	consonant in *key, coo*
l	consonant in *lay*
m	consonant in *me*
n	consonant in *no*
ŋ	final consonant in *sung*
p	consonant in *pay*
r	consonant in *row*
s	consonant in *say*
ʃ	consonant in *shoe*
t	consonant in *tea*
ʧ	consonant in *chew, itch*
θ	initial consonant in *thin*
ð	consonant in *they*
v	consonant in *vie*
w	consonant in *way*
y	consonant in *you*
z	consonant in *zoo*
ʒ	middle consonant in *vision*

Abbreviations Used in the Dictionary

a	antedate
abbr	abbreviation
adj	adjective
adj phr	adjective phrase
adv	adverb
adv phr	adverb phrase
Amer	America
Anniv	Anniversary
Appal	Appalachian
appar	apparently
Archit	architecture
ATASC	Archive of Traditional Appalachian Speech and Culture
Atl	Atlantic
Autobio	Autobiography
Brit	British
c	century (as 16c)
Car	Carolina
CCC	Civilian Conservation Corps
cf	compare, confer
Chris	Christian
Cntry	Country
Co	County
Coll	Collection
Comm	Community
conj	conjunction
CSD	*Concise Scots Dictionary*, ed. Mairi Robinson et al. (Aberdeen: Aberdeen University Press, 1985)
CUD	*Concise Ulster Dictionary*, ed. Caroline Macafee (Oxford: Oxford University Press, 1996)
Cult	Culture
DAE	*Dictionary of American English*, ed. William Craigie and James Hulbert, 4 vols. (Chicago: University of Chicago Press, 1938–44)
DARE	*Dictionary of American Regional English*, ed. Frederic G. Cassidy et al., 6 vols. (Cambridge, MA: Belknap Press of Harvard University Press, 1985–2013)
def art	definite article
dem	demonstrative
DHE	*A Dictionary of Hiberno English*, ed. Terence P. Dolan (Dublin: Gill and MacMillan, 1998)
Dial	Dialect
Dict	Dictionary
DOST	*Dictionary of the Older Scottish Tongue*, ed. William Craigie and A. J. Aitken (Chicago: University of Chicago Press; and Oxford: Oxford University Press, 1937–2002).
DSAE	Dictionary of Southern Appalachian English
DSL	*Etymological Dictionary of the Scottish Language*, ed. John Jamieson (Edinburgh: Edinburgh University Press, 1808)
E	East
East	Eastern
EDD	*English Dialect Dictionary*, ed. Joseph S. Wright (Oxford: Henry Frowde, 1898–1905)
e.g.	for example
Eng	English
Engl	England
esp	especially
etym	etymology
exc	except
ext	extension
fig	figurative
freq	frequently
FWP	Federal Writers' Project
Geog	Geography
GSMNP	Great Smoky Mountains National Park
GSMNPOHP	Great Smoky Mountains National Park, Cooperative Oral History Project
High	Highlands, Highlanders
HT	*The Hamely Tongue: A Personal Record of Ulster-Scots in County Antrim*, ed. James Fenton (Belfast: Ullans Press, 2000)
Ibid.	ibidem (the same [e.g., same source as previous example])
i.e.	id est (that is)
influ	influence, influenced
interj	interjection
Irel	Ireland
LAGS	Linguistic Atlas of the Gulf States
LAMSAS	Linguistic Atlas of the Middle and South Atlantic States
Lex	Lexicon
Lg	Language
lit	literally
Med	Medieval
mEngl	English Midlands
Mon	Monitor
Ms	Manuscript
Mt	Mountain
Mtneers	Mountaineers
Mts	Mountains
N	North
Natl	National
NC	North Carolina
n.d.	no date
nEngl	northern England
nIrel	northern Ireland

n phr	noun phrase
N.p.: n.p.	no place (of publication): no publisher
NPS	National Park Service
Nth	Northern
OED	*Oxford English Dictionary*, ed. James Murray et al. (Oxford: Clarendon Press, 1888–1928)
OED2	*Oxford English Dictionary*, 2d ed., CD-ROM Version 3.1.2002 (New York: Oxford University Press, 2002).
OED3	*Oxford English Dictionary*, 3d ed. (New York: Oxford University Press, forthcoming), https://www.oed.com
orig	originally
past-part	past participle
Penn	Pennsylvania
perh	perhaps
pers pron	personal pronoun
phr	phrase
phrs	phrases
plur	plural
pred adj	predicate adjective
prep	preposition
present-part	present participle
prob	probably
pron	pronoun
pronc	pronunciation
Ques	Questionnaire
ref	reference
S	South
sAppalachians	Southern Appalachians
sb	substantive (noun)
Sci	Science
Scot	Scotland
SED	Survey of English Dialects
sEngl	southern England
sic	printed as in the original
sing	singular
Smok	Smokies
SND	*Scottish National Dictionary*, ed. William Grant and David Murison (Edinburgh: Scottish National Dictionary Association, 1931–76)
specif	specifically
spp	species and subspecies
Sthn	Southern
Sts	States
Tenn	Tennessee
Term	Terminology
TN	Tennessee
ts	typescript
ult	ultimately
uncert	uncertain
US	United States
usu	usually
v	verb
vbl n	verbal noun
Vocab	Vocabulary
wmEngl	English West Midlands
Web3	*Webster's Third New International Dictionary*, ed. Philip Gove (Springfield, MA: Merriam-Webster, 1961)
York	Yorkshire
yrs	years

Background and Context of the Dictionary

This dictionary is a revised and expanded edition of Michael B. Montgomery and Joseph S. Hall's *Dictionary of Smoky Mountain English* (University of Tennessee Press, 2004).[1] The original work presented the speech ways of a small region in the mountains of east Tennessee and western North Carolina that is known as the Great Smoky Mountains. At its heart is the Great Smoky Mountains National Park. The park was established in 1934 and currently enjoys the status of the most-visited national park in the United States, with more than 11 million visitors each year. This is more than double the second-most-visited national park, Grand Canyon National Park in Arizona. This continued popularity has made the region both a natural and a cultural reservoir, and it constitutes the most-studied, -described, and -documented area of the southern mountains of the eastern United States.

One of the challenges that the editors of the first edition faced was the lack of a convenient or natural boundary for the region, as regional dictionaries based on states, islands, or other designated areas have made use of. In addition, the currency and usage of terms in the first edition were not restricted to the Smoky Mountains. Like any language variety, Smoky Mountain English has quite a bit of overlap with other regions and communities and wider distribution of terms outside of the boundaries used by the original editors. Recognizing this, Montgomery endeavored to expand on the material in the first edition to include a much broader area, encompassing the entire Southern Appalachian region. Whereas the first edition of the dictionary focused primarily on terms gathered from the six core counties that comprise the Great Smoky Mountains (Blount, Cocke, and Sevier in

Alfred Dowdle cabin on Toe String Creek. Photo taken in 1937 by Joseph Hall.

Mr. Jones, the miller of Mingus Creek. Photo by Edouard Exline.

A ranger on horseback in the 1930s in Great Smoky Mountains National Park.

Tennessee; Haywood, Jackson, and Swain in North Carolina), the revised and expanded edition has gathered material from a much wider area. The Appalachian Regional Commission at the time of writing designates 420 counties in thirteen states as belonging to the region called Appalachia.[2] This dictionary includes material from nine of these states: Alabama, Georgia, Kentucky, Mississippi, North Carolina, South Carolina, Tennessee, Virginia, and West Virginia. This expansion entailed embarking on a reading and research program similar to the one undertaken by Montgomery for the publication of the *Dictionary of Smoky Mountain English*, including the reading of or listening to over one thousand primary sources, including but not limited to oral history projects produced by academic institutions, letters written by Civil War soldiers, newspaper and journal articles, memoirs, interviews, works of fiction, and more. Many older sources are long out of print, which required the editors to spend many hours examining microfilm and microfiche in university libraries each week for years. The new material has been painstakingly integrated with the material from the previous edition, and the old material has been revisited and carefully edited in order to create a more thorough reference. The result of this labor is the most complete record of Southern Appalachian English to date.

To understand the context of Southern Appalachian English, it is important to understand a bit about the linguistic and cultural history of the region. The English language was first brought to the Southern Appalachian mountains in the late eighteenth century, primarily by second- and third-generation Americans of Scotch-Irish, English, and German heritage. These groups came largely from the Piedmont region of North Carolina and southwestern Virginia to settle land that had long been held by the Cherokee. The settlers found the mountains a rough environment in which to carve out a life, and it took a generation to populate the fertile lowlands and foothills of the region. Only gradually were the more rugged, wooded uplands of Southern Appalachia settled and cultivated. The North Carolina mountains in particular had few white inhabitants before 1825. Since its settlement by those of European ancestry, the region has undergone a number of huge changes instigated primarily by the government and big business: namely, the establishment of Great Smoky Mountains National Park and the arrival of the logging and coal industries. On the creation of the national park, human inhabitants were gradually made to leave the area within its boundaries, forcing families off of lands they had held and worked for generations. Industry also triggered migration, both in forcing families and communities out and in enticing some locals to relocate to other communities for lucrative work.

Clementine Enloe, photo taken by Joseph Hall. Ms. Enloe said she would let Hall take the photo only if he gave her a can of snuff, which he agreed to. It can be seen in the photo, tucked into her dress above her belt.

Uncle Silas Messer, a tanner, dressing leather at Cove Creek, North Carolina, 1937. Photo by Edouard Exline.

James and Melissa Hannah at their cabin in Cataloochee, North Carolina. Created by Charles S. Grossman, 1935.

Scope and Sources of the Dictionary

The following is a revised version of material that originally appeared in the *Dictionary of Smoky Mountain English* (University of Tennessee Press, 2004). It is presented here largely in its original form to provide readers with the background information necessary for understanding how the original work was compiled and developed. The present dictionary built on the methods used for producing the first edition, although for this edition Montgomery and Heinmiller placed heavy emphasis on transcriptions of oral interviews, especially those produced by regional oral history projects undertaken by Alice Lloyd College and Lees Junior College in the 1970s, and more recent written material.

This dictionary presents the full range of regionally significant language of Southern Appalachia by identifying and illustrating words, phrases, and meanings from the past two centuries that meet one or more of six overlapping criteria that can be seen as the dictionary's guiding principles for inclusion:

1. That an item originated in, or is exclusive to, Southern Appalachia;
2. That an item is limited to the southern portion of Appalachia;
3. That an item has been found worthy of note and comment by outsiders and observers of Southern Appalachian speech;
4. That an item contrasts with general American usage, used significantly more often in Southern Appalachia, especially by less modern speakers;
5. That an item reflects an older stage of the English language and is old-fashioned, if not obsolete in general American usage; or
6. That an item reflects the traditional culture of the Southern Appalachian mountains. Often such an item is viewed as distinctive to southern mountain culture today but was once typical of a much broader region. It may have drawn comment, even from mountain people, who have seen their lifeways as increasingly different from the changing American mainstream.

These criteria qualify much of the language of and about the southern mountains for dictionary treatment. They give the dictionary a wide scope, encompassing terms for traditional medicine, farming, hunting, religion, social and community life, cooking, music, and many other domains and folkways. For no other variety of American English is there a more compelling case for broad presentation in dictionary form.

The dictionary excludes terms judged, by consulting other dictionaries and reference sources, to be general colloquial usage or slang. Using the above criteria, it seeks as complete and accurate a historical view of Southern Appalachian speech as possible, within the limitations discussed below. It follows four basic historical principles:

1. The dating of each citation, if possible
2. The chronological ordering of citations to give some indication of their currency and continuity
3. The ordering of subdivisions within entries, where possible or relevant, to show semantic or functional development of a term
4. The inclusion of pertinent etymological information

Because they are often hallmarks of Southern Appalachian English and are of much historical and comparative interest, grammatical forms and patterns are detailed with particular thoroughness. Information on morphology and syntax appears not only at individual entries but also in a comprehensive survey organized by parts of speech and grammatical categories (see the section "Grammar and Syntax of Southern Appalachian and Smoky Mountain English"). Unlike standard dictionaries, the work does not indicate the pronunciation of every item, most of which are obvious or of no interest, nor does it report all the evidence available on variant pronunciations. Rather, it presents selected forms through respellings, using phonetic notation (within brackets) only when necessary. These forms are to be regarded as representative of those to be found in mountain speech. They are frequently referenced in citations from Hall's 1942 monograph, but the dictionary does not repeat the material covered in that volume, which remains the best examination of phonetics in the Southern Appalachian mountains. Nor does the dictionary concern itself with general phonetic tendencies, pronunciations that are so ubiquitous in Southern Appalachian speech and elsewhere that it is unnecessary to include them as variants at individual entries.

Determining the parameters of the lexicon required consistent application of the six criteria above, along with a sense of proportion and the intrinsic interest of individual items. Applying the second criterion (that an item is limited to or of particular interest or unique usage in the southern portion of Appalachia) required the use of comprehensive sources that permit a comparative view of where a term does and does not occur.

The fifth criterion (that an item reflect an older stage of the English language and be considered old-fashioned or obsolete in general American usage) is somewhat less subjective than others, in that it relies on major historical dictionaries, especially the *Oxford English Dictionary*, to qualify an item for entry. The sixth criterion (that an item reflect the region's folk culture) justifies many lengthy, informative entries (e.g., *decoration day*, *serenade*). No other general reference work on Southern Appalachia presents, for example, the terminology of whiskey distilling. This includes technical terms that are found throughout Southern Appalachia and usually beyond, as well as others (especially descriptive terms for the beverage) that are almost certainly local to small communities or groups.

The popular nomenclature for flora (especially wildflowers) and fauna is a major component of the dictionary. The general practice has been to enter a plant name if the plant plays a role in traditional mountain pharmacopoeia or the name has inherent linguistic interest. Coverage is thus selective, not comprehensive. Inclusion does not imply that a plant or its name occurs only, or even principally, in Southern Appalachia, as, given the wide range of environments there, such narrow distribution would be unlikely.[1] Especially for plants, natural regionality influences usage more than linguistic regionality does, so it is reasonable that other considerations qualify a term for inclusion. Plant names exhibit much metaphorical language; some plants have three or more figurative or colloquial names within the region. Defining plants and identifying their Latin names often made them more challenging than any other subject matter. Additionally, technical works sometimes disagree about Latin names, and these names are also subject to revision from time to time. In addition, native speakers may apply a particular name to more than one plant, and they may disagree about whether two names are equivalent.

Types of Sources

The dictionary employs evidence from ten types of sources, the nature of which deserve discussion:

1. Recordings of speech
2. Manuscripts and historical documents
3. Commentaries by outsiders
4. Fiction set in the mountains
5. Scholarly and popular notes and glossaries
6. Local, historical, and other nonfiction literature
7. Dialect surveys
8. Archival collections
9. Responses from consultants
10. Personal observations of speech

Priority is given to citations from spoken sources when possible. Every reasonable effort has been made to go beyond the printed record for evidence from living speech or the knowledge of native speakers about local speech habits.

For an American dictionary this work employs an unprecedented amount of spoken and recorded audio material. Recordings of speech provide a perspective encompassing approximately 150 years. Of first importance are those made by Joseph Hall. Because most of his early work (1937–41) was with older individuals, the detailed list of his speakers in this volume can be used to identify usages that date to the mid-nineteenth century. Also of extraordinary importance are oral history interviews conducted under the auspices of the national park (made between 1954 and 1985), citations from which are designated GSMNP. These interviews also recorded older, old-fashioned speakers. Some of these interviews were made to document former settlements, buildings, cemeteries, and other sites, but most were recollections of life and activities from the days before the park's establishment, or shortly thereafter, and contain recalled cultural practices more often than contemporary ones. Their language reflects that of one to two generations earlier. These interviews were already transcribed, but Montgomery audited the tapes if there was any reason to do so (all citations are referenced to the page of the transcripts, which are archived at the library of the Great Smoky Mountains National Park). Thus, the date of a citation, indicating when a record was made, is often of more archival than linguistic relevance. The only middle-aged speakers participating in the oral history recordings were children of older informants who assisted with the interviews. The transcripts for these and other interviews conducted by park personnel employed spellings modified to represent pronunciations that have been regularized by Montgomery. However, spellings like *runnin'*, employed by Hall in his own transcriptions, are fewer and more conservative, and these are usually left unchanged, in deference to him.[2] Needless to say, quotations of written material throughout the dictionary maintain their original form, no matter how idiosyncratic or internally inconsistent it might be. More recent oral material includes forty hours of interviews conducted in 1978 and transcribed by Montgomery for his dissertation research in Jefferson County, Tennessee, in the Smokies foothills, as well as oral history projects undertaken by students at Alice Lloyd College and Lees Junior College in the 1970s.

Written sources are the most varied and provide the broadest time frame (more than two hundred years of documentation), but their evidence is less direct and sometimes more difficult to evaluate than recordings of speech. Manuscripts and historical documents written by local people before 1900 were sought and read for citations whenever possible.

Other pre–Civil War material includes commentaries and descriptions of mountain culture by travelers (e.g., Lanham 1849, Olmsted 1860). For more than a century and a half, outsiders who visited or moved to the southern mountains to live or teach wrote letters and records to explain the culture they observed and experienced. Very often they set apart terms they were not familiar with by placing them within quotation marks or by other methods.

The foremost commentator who sojourned in the mountains was Horace Kephart. (1869–1931). Our knowledge of Southern Appalachian and Smoky Mountain English would be far poorer without the pioneering work of this librarian who left St. Louis for western North Carolina in 1904. For two decades he observed mountain life closely and made the largest collection of material on speech before Hall. Best-known is his volume *Our Southern Highlanders* (1913; 2nd ed., 1922), whose chapter on mountain speech was the first general discussion of the subject and remained the most extensive one for several decades.[3] Farwell and Nicholas's *Smoky Mountain Voices: A Lexicon of Southern Appalachian Speech* (1993) has demonstrated that Kephart's volume and the more than two dozen scrapbooks he compiled on mountain life contained enough material on speech for a separate volume.[4] Kephart's influence has manifested itself in two generations of commentators and novelists who borrowed his material and often presented it as mountain speech, though they rarely acknowledged him as their source.

Fiction set in the Appalachian mountains that portrays local dialect began in the mid-nineteenth century. The works of two writers from Southern Appalachia that have been used extensively in the dictionary because of their early date are H. Taliaferro's *Fisher's River* (1859) and George Washington Harris's *Sut Lovingood Yarns* (1867). A tradition of representing southern mountain vernacular, often with extravagantly distorted spellings and a heavy infusion of eye dialect (i.e., words spelled in an unconventional way so as to reflect their regional pronunciation), is full-blown in Harris's work and has flourished since the 1880s, when Mary Murfree (writing under the name Charles Egbert Craddock) began publishing novels, the best-known of which was *The Prophet of the Great Smoky Mountains* (1885). Literary sources provide the principal (and occasionally the only) direct citation for some items, but it is not always easy to assess whether their dialect is firsthand knowledge. Depictions of mountain speech, especially by writers not native to the region, often contain forms of no lexicographic value or whose currency is doubtful (e.g., *bodacious*). Some of these have little or no basis of reality in the speech of the time and place represented and have either been perpetuated by literary tradition or are idiosyncratic attempts to represent the "quaintness" of mountain vernacular.

However accomplished professional writers of fiction may be, their purposes are literary, and the dictionary has used citations from literary dialogue only after confirming them with other sources. As a rule, the editors have cited only those writers whose nativity or longtime residence in the mountains has been verified. Citations from Murfree, who frequently set her work in the Smokies but apparently had little if any personal experience with the area or its people, are used only because of their early date or their unusual interest, and then only when substantiated by other sources. By contrast, the diction of Mildred Haun, May Justus, and Wilma Dykeman, writers native to the region, has been mined thoroughly.

Although little was written about the language of the Smoky Mountains before Joseph Hall's work, literature on Southern Appalachian speech, including by scholars, began appearing in the 1880s in the form of word studies and local glossaries that more often than not focused on archaisms. H. A. Edson and Edith M. Fairchild's "Tennessee Mountains in Word Lists" (1895)[5] was the first of several word lists and glossaries from the mountains that were compiled by American Dialect Society members for its journal *Dialect Notes* and that provide the earliest evidence for many terms. In giving a definition, usually a quotation indicating a term's linguistic context, occasionally identification of the locality in which it was observed, or even a note about its currency, such works provide substantial information. Like other written sources, glossaries are inferior to recordings in most ways. They are silent, and their accuracy cannot be double-checked, though it can often be confirmed by later native speakers. More problematic is that glossaries usually present terms as equally common and representative, when they may be precisely cited because they are unusual or rare. Popular glossaries of mountain speech, on the other hand, are often oriented toward the tourist market and produced in large part for entertainment. They are more prone to respell and otherwise distort and exaggerate mountain speech, but if produced by native speakers or longtime observers, they sometimes contain items a scholarly dictionary can usefully include.[6]

Until about a generation ago, both scholarly and popular writing on southern mountain speech was preoccupied with what were viewed as old-fashioned, archaic, or exotic usages. To be sure, many items have survived in mountain usage from earlier stages of the language while being superseded in general (especially written) British and American English in the modern day. Whether significantly more are found there than in other varieties of rural American English remains to be determined, however. Although lay researchers have argued for over a century that mountain speech is "Elizabethan," "Shakespearean," or even "Chaucerian," scholars have generally shied away from such descriptions. Hall discounted the idea early in his work: "Great Smokies speech is not Elizabethan English transplanted to America."[7] Among other things, this dictionary may contribute to a fuller and more accurate assessment of the linguistic sources of mountain speech, including its transatlantic ancestry, through information in its etymologies.

Put briefly, it appears that much of Appalachian English grammar is shared with Ulster and Scotland, while its pronunciation has a close affinity with that of southern England.[8] Though less so than many other parts of the country, the Southern Appalachians were a zone of linguistic contact from the beginning, mainly in the form of varieties of English originating in the British Isles. Modern-day Appalachian English has almost no discernible contribution from other languages with which English speakers have had contact. For reasons that demand explanation, the linguistic influence of German settlers (so pronounced in vernacular architecture and other domains)[9] is minute, limited to such words as *kraut* and *swinny*. Cherokee influence on mountain culture is manifest in some ways, particularly in medicinal applications,[10] but overt contributions to the local English appear to be detectable only in place-names.[11] Items of Gaelic ancestry are more numerous, but still not prominent, in mountain speech and were almost certainly brought by Ulster emigrants and are the product of earlier language contact. These include *brogan (shoe)*, *clabber*, *dauncy*, *dornick*, *striffin*, and *suggin*, some of which may ultimately derive from, or have been influenced by, Scottish Gaelic in addition to Irish Gaelic. As the dictionary makes clear, the archaisms are only part of what makes Appalachian speech distinctive today. Many of the remarkable items found in southern Appalachia are innovations rather than retentions from a former time.

DARE demonstrates that a survey using a standard questionnaire to gather data can establish both the existence and the comparative frequency of terms. Undertaking an entirely new survey project was not feasible for the present work, but the dictionary draws on extensive data from four geographically based projects that employed a questionnaire: the Linguistic Atlas of the Middle and South Atlantic States (LAMSAS); the Linguistic Atlas of the Gulf States (LAGS); the *Dictionary of American Regional English*; and Mary Newton's *Comparative Study of the Dialect Vocabularies of East Tennessee and Western North Carolina Using Selected Words*.[12] If a dictionary entry specifies only one form for a term, dictionary citations from the first three surveys often indicate only the county or locality in which that term was collected by one of these surveys. LAGS was useful in that one of its published volumes indicates the relative frequency of items in each of the sixteen sectors surveyed by the eight-state project.

Few efforts have been spared in seeking relevant material in archives to excerpt for the dictionary, regardless of the subject area. This included private collections such as those made by Horace Kephart deposited in the Hunter Library of Western Carolina University, Cullowhee, North Carolina (from the first two decades of the century), and by Edna Lynn Simms deposited in the Appalachian Collection at Berea College, Kentucky, compiled in Gatlinburg, Tennessee, in the 1930s.[13]

Use of Consultants

Although it continued through the end of the editorial process, the bulk of the reading and excerption program for the first edition of the dictionary was completed by the spring of 1995. As the gathering of citations slowed and work shifted to preparing entries, Montgomery became increasingly aware of matters requiring the assistance of native speakers from the mountains. However plentiful and rich were the oral and written sources employed, for many terms the reading program either provided insufficient or raised further issues. This led him to enlist consultants, a practice that Joseph Hall had employed informally, as reflected in the many reported usages that appeared on his note cards and citations. From 1937 Hall corresponded frequently with people he had met in the Smokies, and until shortly before his death he continued to query them by mail or phone. He was always concerned about precisely citing and defining terms that he had observed.[14]

Following successful sessions with two individuals in 1992–93, Montgomery recruited ten people to answer queries about specific terms from mountain speech on a regular basis. These primary consultants were natives of the mountains, five from North Carolina and five from Tennessee, and most were born in the 1920s or 1930s. Employed on a more limited basis were secondary consultants whose expertise was sought for terminology in such areas as weaving, wildflowers, farming, health and disease, mountain logging, and many other areas.

From personal acquaintance or by reputation from their writing, primary consultants were known to be experts on local history and culture. Collectively they formed an invaluable sample to determine whether (and how) terms found otherwise only in written sources were used in mountain speech, what the details of their usage were, and whether they were found in different parts of the mountains. These individuals were asked to respond to six sets of queries totaling well over one thousand items. Responses were sometimes followed up by phone calls or, when feasible, consultation in person. Generally consultants were called on to comment on particular items of vocabulary or to verify or revise definitions drafted by the editors. Their corrections, clarifications, and suggestions produced many fuller, more accurate definitions, and their familiarity with terms and meanings in mountain English often determined whether items would be entered at all. Consultants were not asked to suggest new terms for inclusion.

More specifically, primary consultants were asked to indicate their familiarity with items and, if they knew them, to comment on their meaning (including details of their pragmatics), their use (including their synonymy or overlap), or their currency. They were also asked to verify items that were attributed to local speech by outsiders or were poorly attested in other sources at hand; items with early citations, especially if these were the only citations for an entry, were routinely queried. Horace Kephart's 1913 book brought wide recognition to mountain English. He knew mountain people as individuals, but he usually wrote about them generically rather than individually, though with greater caution than most writers before and since. His material, mostly gathered in Swain County, North Carolina, between 1904 and 1907, has a prominent place in many entries and often constitutes the earliest citation. However, in some cases a quotation from Kephart is the only one for a term, making it difficult to know whether the term is a local one not found elsewhere, an obsolete one that passed away before others recorded it, an item noted by an especially keen observer, or possibly a misunderstanding on Kephart's part (he had no training in linguistics and must have had severely limited access to dictionaries). The first set of queries consisted of two hundred items from Kephart's book and were sent to consultants to discover their wider and later currency.

Consultants were equally important for substantiating anticipated items; that is, those that had no citation from the Smokies but for which there was good reason to suspect an existence there. *DARE* was not only used to exclude items, as noted earlier, but was also the principal source for identifying potential gaps in coverage. Items labeled "Appalachians" or "S Midland" in *DARE* for which no citation was at hand were systematically queried. Since *DARE* had been published only through the letter *O* at the time of publication for the first edition of this dictionary, Montgomery used the *American Dialect Dictionary* and primary sources cited in the first three volumes of *DARE* to identify items to query from the rest of the alphabet. Querying also permitted verification of items which were known to Montgomery from his personal experience in East Tennessee but for which there was also no Smokies citation.

Although some of their input is reflected in definitions, most information from consultants is compiled in citations in the form of data summaries introduced by "Montgomery Coll." In sum, information from consultants makes the dictionary a much fuller record of local speech and ensures that a more faithful reflection of their language will be found in it by mountain people, a group to whom the dictionary owes accountability. The ten primary consultants and their native counties were as follows:

Inez McCaulley Adams, Blount County, Tennessee
Roy Brown, Cocke County, Tennessee
Florence Cope Bush, Sevier County, Tennessee
R. Glenn Cardwell, Sevier County, Tennessee
Michael E. Ellis, Cherokee and Unicoi Counties, Tennessee

Loyal Jones, Cherokee and Clay Counties, North Carolina
Ted Ledford, Mitchell County, North Carolina
Pearl Mashburn Norris, Cherokee County, North Carolina
Duane Oliver, Haywood County, North Carolina
Jack Weaver, Ashe County, North Carolina

Limitations

Identifying the source of each citation gives the dictionary accountability by permitting a user to consult and evaluate any material it contains. However, two fundamental problems inherent to historical lexicography are that many written sources give artificial life to items and that a dictionary gives equivalent status to all citations included.

The large degree of spoken evidence in the dictionary offsets the artificial life given by print, but oral history recordings, the bulk of the spoken material used, are also meant to be recollections of the past and to provide material somewhat out of date, at least for lexical items. The dictionary has much more nineteenth-century material than is at first apparent, in that most speakers that Joseph Hall interviewed in 1937–41 had been born in the previous century. Even citations from written sources in the 1980s or 1990s often reflect speech recalled from childhoods that occurred decades earlier by older residents. This problem of an invisible time lag has been addressed to some extent by the querying of consultants, but they could hardly be expected to date their recollections or distinguish consistently between terms they use and ones they only recognize.

The user of this work is cautioned that from its pages a wholly reliable picture of contemporary Southern Appalachian speech cannot be gleaned. Mountain English is changing in many ways, and consultants could not be queried on everything.

Because it was impossible to undertake a formal survey specifically for this dictionary, subregional variation cannot be inferred from the evidence presented in it. Some items for which there are single citations are quite possibly coined terms of specific communities or even individuals, but this can rarely be known, as many items crop up in quite disparate places. Generally speaking, evidence from the oral material consulted for the dictionary indicates a striking uniformity of mountain speech with a much larger surrounding territory, which no doubt reflects settlement history and similar cultural networks that developed between mountain communities and nearby lowland areas.

Index of Joseph Hall Speakers from the Smoky Mountains

The following is a list prepared by Joseph Sargent Hall of the speakers he interviewed or observed between 1937 and 1972. Citations from many of these individuals are used in the text of the dictionary. During his years of more formal fieldwork, as well as later through querying people by mail and telephone, Hall sought to describe the linguistic material he collected and also to document social information on the individuals who produced it. He did so from a sense of professional accountability, assembling information that other scholars might find useful. He also felt obligated to recognize the contributions of individual mountain speakers to his work, both to prevent them from being viewed as a nameless or faceless mass and to acknowledge what they had provided to him and, by extension, to the outside world. In the text of the dictionary, citations and comments from these speakers are attributed to them by name.

Hall sought to ascertain the age and level of education attained by each speaker. Since he often did this unobtrusively, as by gleaning information from a casual conversation, from uncertain self-reports, or from third parties who knew the speakers, he sometimes had to estimate this information (if no figure appears in the respective column, he has supplied an appropriate comment). Information in the column "Level of Education" must in any case be considered advisedly, because many speakers growing up in the nineteenth century had only irregular formal education, spending at most three months a year in a one-room school. It is worth noting that Hall collected material from a broad range of people (including some with college education) who were born and reared in the mountains and who could recall their formative years.

Joseph Hall began collecting in 1937 under the auspices of the National Park Service, which hired him to document the speech and traditional culture that were being displaced by the park. He spent that first summer observing and becoming acquainted with mountain people, and in June 1939 he returned for nine months to make recordings of speech and music. From the beginning his speakers knew that what they told him would become part of a permanent record, and they routinely asked him to replay the recordings he made of them. Understanding his work to be that of a preservationist, most participated without evident reservations. For the most part, Hall found, they were independent-minded people who did not care what others thought of their language, but a handful declined to be recorded, thinking that their speech might be stereotyped or ridiculed. In his unpublished notes, Hall summarized his early fieldwork as follows:

> From my first days in the Smokies I listened carefully to all native people I met and noted down expressions that they used. During my first summer in the Smokies in 1937 I filled four secretarial notebooks with jotting from daily speech and notes from interviews. When I returned to the area in 1939 with Columbia's blessing and an appointment as Collaborator, I proceeded to fill more and larger notebooks and these plus those I made until 1972 as a private citizen gave me about 1,500 pages of material. Second to the notebooks were the phonographic recordings. . . . The topics of the recordings were anything the informant wished to talk about. Men talked about their farm, their crops, their cattle, and hunting. Women liked to tell recipes or talk about their interest in weaving and quilting and the like. . . . Most people were polite and cooperative and could see that the recordings were made for study and preservation as a historical record of aspects of Smokies life. A few speakers declined the microphone, not wishing "to be made light of." They were sensitive to "furriners" coming in to make fun of them.

Hall did not obtain explicit permission to make a permanent record of those he interviewed, but he did not disguise his purposes or record people without their tacit assent. Throughout his career he was committed to, and followed, the highest professional standards of respecting his subjects in the course of his fieldwork. If he had undertaken his work more recently, he would undoubtedly have had speakers sign release forms, but these were unknown in his day. Because none of these people are now living, so far as the first editor can discern, they cannot be asked to conform to the standards of a latter day by formally agreeing to being quoted in print. Hall's material is reproduced in this dictionary as closely as possible to the form in which he left it at his death in 1992. If more than one date is given, a speaker's age is based on the first date.

Table 1 Speakers Joseph Sargent Hall interviewed or observed, 1937–1972

Name	Age at time of first interview	Year interviewed	Education	Community	Occupation
Adams, Odus	21	1939	about 8 yrs	Wears Cove, TN	
Ayres, Ethel	32	1939	about 4 yrs	Smokemont, NC	grade-school teacher
Ball, Mrs. Will	85	1937		Cosby Creek, TN	
Barnes, Bill	95	1939	literate	Hartford, TN	deputy sheriff, farmer
Barnes, J. Lacy	c55	1959	college graduate	Hartford, TN	attorney
Baxter, Blanco	18	1937		Cosby, TN	
Baxter, Elizabeth	80	1937	prob illiterate	Catons Grove, TN	farm widow
Baxter, George	c23	1939	about 4 yrs	Cosby Creek, TN	CCC maintenance man
Bender, Ross	c50	1967	college graduate	Gatlinburg, TN	chief park naturalist
Benson, Cindy	c50	1937	illiterate	Cosby Creek, TN	
Benson, James	15	1937	illiterate	Cosby Creek, TN	farmhand
Bohanon, Levi	c30	1937	about 4 yrs	Emerts Cove, TN	farmer
Branton, R. L.	19	1939	about 8 yrs	Sevierville, TN	CCC clerk
Brown, Mrs. Bill	71	1939	about 4 yrs	Smokemont, NC	farm housewife
Bryson, Thad		1939, 1953		Bryson City, NC	
Burchfield, John	58	1939	8 yrs	Cades Cove, TN	farmer, stock herder
Burchfield, Lyddie	c80	1937	little education	Cades Cove, TN	farm widow
Cabe, Levada		1939		Bryson City, NC	
Cable, Acy	c10	1937		Cades Cove, TN	
Cable, Becky	89	1937, 1939	self-educated	Cades Cove, TN	farmer, store owner stock raiser
Cable, Dan	73	1939	prob illiterate	Proctor, NC	farmer, hunter
Cable, Fonze	59	1939	prob literate	Nine Mile Cr, TN	logging camp cook hunter
Cable, Milburn	45	1937	4 yrs	Cades Cove, TN	CCC employee
Cahorn, Delia	45	1956	about 8 yrs	Cades Cove, TN	farm housewife
Caldwell, Levi	65	1937, 1939	prob literate	Cataloochee, NC	CCC blacksmith
Caldwell, Mack	53	1939	self-educated	Mt. Sterling, NC	owner of country store
Calhoun, Granville	64	1939, 1953, 1956	self-educated	Hazel Creek, NC, later Bryson City, NC	owner of mountain store
Cambell, "Uncle" Tom	75	1937		Cataloochee, NC	
Campbell, Art	37	1965			
Campbell, Carlos C.	35	1937	college education	Knoxville, TN	insurance agent, member, GSM Conservation Assoc., lecturer, author
Cardwell, Bill	c45	1937	prob illiterate or little education	Emerts Cove, TN	farmer
Cardwell, Columbus	c20	1937	about 8 yrs	Emerts Cove, TN	CCC truck driver, manager, NPS maintenance shop
Carpenter, Bus		1939		Cataloochee, NC	
Carr, Jim	67	1956	5 yrs	Byrds Creek, TN	former deputy sheriff, farmer
Carver, Aden	91	1937	self-educated	Bradley Fork, NC	farmer, carpenter, millwright, stonemason, Baptist preacher
Carver, Mrs. Aden	45	1937	about 4 yrs	Bradley Fork, NC	farm housewife
Carver, David	45	1956	prob 8 yrs	Del Rio, TN	owner of large farm
Carver, Maxine	40	1956	prob 8 yrs	Del Rio, TN	farm housewife
Cathey, John	76	1953	literate	Bryson City, NC	logger
Cathey, Mark	54	1939, 1953	literate	Deep Creek, TN	logger, member of survey crew, farmer, hunter, hunting guide
Caton, Rhoda	90	1937	about 4 yrs	Catons Grove, TN	farm housewife

Table 1 (continued)

Name	*Age at time of first interview*	*Year interviewed*	*Education*	*Community*	*Occupation*
Clabo, Lewis	63	1956	about 12 yrs	Roaring Fork, TN	school teacher, owner of tearoom and tourist cabins
Clark, Perry	84	1937		Emerts Cove, TN	
Clark, Mrs. R. P.	77	1959, etc.	12 yrs	Newport, TN	wife of prosperous owner of country store
Coada, Mrs.	c40	1937	about 4 yrs	Cades Cove, TN	farm housewife
Cole, Sara	67	1953, 1956	prob illiterate	Gatlinburg, TN	farm widow
Cole, Steve	70	1939, 1940	some education, literate	Sugarlands, TN	farmer, hunter, logger
Collins, Ertman	21	1940, 1941	about 10 yrs	Morristown, TN	CCC trail crew
Collins, Jerry	23	1939, 1941	about 12 yrs	Morristown, TN	CCC cook; later army sergeant
Conner, D. F. "Doc"	84	1939	self-educated	Smokemont, NC	owner of country store
Conner, Jarvis S.		1939		Smokemont, NC	
Conner, Myrtle		1939		Gatlinburg, TN	
Crisp, Bert	47	1939		Smokemont, NC	CCC foreman
Crisp, Clara	55	1939	literate	Hazel Creek, NC	farm housewife
Crisp, Martha Jane	74	1937	prob illiterate	Mingus Creek, NC	farm widow
Crisp, Zeb	64	1939	prob literate	Hazel Creek, NC	farmer, logger
Crowson, Web	45	1939	prob literate	Wears Cove, TN	farmer
Dills, Alice Enloe		1939	little education	Sylva, NC	
Dodgen, E. W.	c67	1937, 1939	about 2–3 yrs	Gatlinburg, TN	farmer
Dorsey, "Hoss"	45	1937		Cosby, TN	
Dorsey, Roxie	45	1937		Cosby, TN	
Dowdle, Alfred	37	1937	about 4 yrs	Collins Creek, NC	CCC employee
Dowdle, Mrs. Alfred		1937		Collins Creek, NC	
Dowdle, John	30	1937		Collins Creek, NC	CCC foreman
Enloe, Mrs. Clem	84	1937	prob literate	Tight Run Branch, NC	farm widow
Evans, Lee	35	1937	about 8 yrs	Dellwood, NC	CCC employee
Evans, Tom	70	1937	prob illiterate	Newport, TN	retired farmer
Finger, John O.	40	1937	about 5–6 yrs	Jonathans Creek, NC	farmer, preacher
Fish, Marvin	20	1937	about 5–6 yrs	Emerts Cove, TN	farmhand
Fisher, Bud	50	1939	prob high school	Waynesville, NC	CCC foreman
Fowler, Lena	65	1953, etc.	prob high school	originally from Mt. Sterling, NC	schoolteacher
Fox, Robert L.	74	1939	prob 8 yrs	Waldens Creek, TN	farmer
Fox, Tillman		1939		Waldens Creek, TN	
Francis, Robert	64	1956	prob some college	Raccoon Creek, NC	owner of large farm
Gass, Florence	80	1937		Ravensford, NC	farm widow, wife of deputy sheriff, postmistress
Gibby, Grover	18	1939		Bryson City, NC	
Gregory, Jim		1937		Cades Cove, TN	
Grooms, James H.	64	1956	prob illiterate	Roostertown, TN	farmhand
Guilliams, Perry	50	1937	about 4 yrs	Emerts Cove, TN	farmer
Gunter, Pettibone	50	1937	prob could read and write	Emerts Cove, TN	constable
Hall, Americus	45	1937	about 3–4 yrs	Little Cataloochee, NC	farmer
Hall, Mrs. Americus	40	1937		Little Cataloochee, NC	farm housewife
Hambry, Billy	57	1937	prob illiterate	Big Creek, NC	farmer

Table 1 (continued)

Name	*Age at time of first interview*	*Year interviewed*	*Education*	*Community*	*Occupation*
Hammond, Mrs. Loyd	66	1956, 1959	prob high school	Murphy, NC	housewife
Hance, Mrs. Laurie	50	1956	prob 6–7 yrs	Newport, TN	widow
Hannah, Fannie	73	1939	about 4–5 yrs	Little Cataloochee, NC	farm housewife
Hannah, John		1939		Little Cataloochee, NC	
Hannah, Mack	81	1939	about 2–3 yrs	Little Cataloochee, NC	farmer
Hannah, Mark	55	1956	some college	Little Cataloochee, NC	NPS ranger
Hannah, Reva L.		1939		Mt. Sterling, NC	
Hannah, Steve		1956		Mt. Sterling, NC	
Haynes, Roxie	56			Bryson City, NC	
Henderson, Otto	60	1939	prob some high school	Waynesville, NC	CCC foreman
Henry, "Aunt" Sis	81	1937		Emerts Cove, TN	
Hicks, Letha	43	1956	prob illiterate	Big Bend, NC	housewife
Hicks, Lona	59	1956	about 8 yrs	Hurricane Creek, NC	farmer
Hicks, Oliver	46	1956	illiterate	Big Bend, NC	farmer
Hill, Millard	25	1937	about 6–7 yrs	Saunook, NC	farmhand
Hopkins, Crozier	c50	1939	prob 5–6 yrs	Mt. Sterling, NC	CCC employee
Hopkins, Lewis	79	1956	prob 5–6 yrs	Jones Cove, TN	farmer
Howell, Robert	79	1959	about 8 yrs	Jonathans Creek, NC	county commissioner
Huskey, Henry	56	1956		Wears Cove, TN	
Huskey, James	63	1956	about 8 yrs	Roaring Fork, TN	operator of small furniture-making shop
Jarrett, John		1937		Emerts Cove, TN	deputy sheriff
Jenkins, Roscoe		1956		Indian Camp Creek, TN	
Jenkins, Zora	55	1956	about 4–5 yrs	Indian Camp Creek, TN	farm housewife
Jennison, H. M.	60	1939	PhD	Knoxville, TN (at Univ. of Tennessee)	prof. of botany
Johnson, Arthur	22	1939, 1941	high school	Mitchell Co., NC	CCC truck driver
Johnson, Jack	60	1937, etc.	prob illiterate	Tuckaleechee Cove, TN	farmer, logger
Jones, John	70	1937	prob 4–5 yrs	Ravensford, NC	grist mill operator
Jones, Lawrence	35	1939	prob high school	Proctor, NC	NPS fire warden
King, Sheridan	20	1939	about 8 yrs	Wears Cove, TN	CCC trail worker
King, Wayne	20	1939		Byrds Creek, TN	CCC clerk
King, Wesley	50	1937	about 3–4 yrs	Wears Cove, TN	farmer
Lackey, Silvie	45	1939	prob 3–4 yrs	Mt. Sterling, NC	housewife
Lambert, Frank	38	1937, etc.	some grade school	Smokemont, NC	NPS employee, Cherokee Indian school
Lambert, Jess	50	1939	prob illiterate	Smokemont, NC	farmer
Large, Mrs. Field	50	1937	about 8 yrs	Cosby, TN	housewife
Lawson, Jim	c60	1937	self-educated, well read	Wears Cove, TN	unemployed, preacher
Leatherwood, Fay H.	30	1937, etc.	high school, much self-education	White Oak, NC	CCC company clerk, employee of engineering firm
Leatherwood, Sam		1939		Mt. Sterling, NC	
Ledbetter, Luke	30	1967	high school	Alcoa, TN	employee of Alcoa Aluminum
Ledbetter, Maynard	62	1967	prob 4–5 yrs	Townsend, TN (orig Cades Cove, TN)	
Lemons, George	85	1937	prob 3–4 yrs	Gumstand, TN	successful mountain farmer

Table 1 (continued)

Name	Age at time of first interview	Year interviewed	Education	Community	Occupation
Mahaffey, Frank	45	1939	prob 3–4 yrs	Maggie Valley, NC	CCC blacksmith, farmer, Baptist preacher
Maples, Sam	90	1937		Gatlinburg, TN	Civil War veteran
Mathis, Debbie	80	1937	prob literate	Mingus Creek, NC	widow on small farm
Mathis, Grady	50	1939		Tow String Creek, NC	
McClure, Boyd	50	1937	prob literate	Wears Cove, TN	farmer
McClure, Robert	23	1939	high school	Saunook, NC	CCC company clerk
McGaha, Burl	67	1956, etc.	prob 8 yrs	Newport, TN	logger
McGaha, Tom		1959		Mt. Sterling, NC	
McGaha, W. T.		1969		Big Bend, NC	
McMahan, Mollie	50	1956	prob illiterate	Hurricane Creek, NC	farm worker
McMahan, Ted					
McMillon, Rhoda	70	1939	prob 3–4 yrs	Madison Co., NC	
Medford, W. Clark	70	1956	some college	Waynesville, NC	writer for Waynesville Mountaineer
Mellinger, Edward		1939, etc.		Roaring Fork, TN	
Mellinger, Mrs. Edward		1959		Roaring Fork, TN	
Messer, Bessie	28	1937, 1939	high school	White Oak, NC	owner of farm
Messer, Brown	25	1939	high school	White Oak, NC	farmer, welder
Messer, Carl	21	1939	high school	White Oak, NC	farmer, hunter, trapper
Messer, James		1939		White Oak, NC	
Messer, W. D. "Doc"	77	1937, 1939	self-educated	Tobes Creek, TN	farmer
Messer, Mrs. W. D.	70	1937	about 6 yrs		
Metcalf, Fred	22	1956, etc.	high school	Del Rio, TN	farmer
Metcalf, Jack	21	1949	about 10 yrs	Del Rio, TN	farmer
Metcalf, Louisa	52	1949, etc.	some college	Del Rio, TN	
Metcalf, Paul	16	1967	11 yrs	Del Rio, TN	student, worked on family farm
Metcalf, Roy	35	1949	about 8 yrs	Del Rio, TN	farmhand
Metcalf, Vernell Jane	16	1967	10 yrs	Del Rio, TN	student
Metcalf, Wesley	55	1939, 1949	"could read big print, could barely scribble his name, attended maybe part of three month school"	Del Rio, TN	farmer, logger, coal miner
Metcalf, Wilford		1967, etc.		Del Rio, TN	
Miller, J. B.	21	1941	about 10 yrs	Waynesville, NC	CCC truck driver
Moody, Mollie	67	1937		Jonathans Creek, NC	
Moore, Ashley	52	1937	prob literate	Little Greenbrier, TN	farmer, hunter
Moore, William T.	21	1939, 1941	about 8 yrs	Saunook, NC	CCC truck driver, musician
Morris, Al	67	1939, 1953	3–4 yrs	Deep Creek, NC	farmer, logger, CCC employee
Myers, Cora	37	1937, 1939	about 5–6 yrs	Cades Cove, TN	
Myers, Dan	83	1937	prob literate	Cades Cove, TN	farmer, logger, cattle and hog raiser
Myers, Mrs. Dan		1939		Cades Cove, TN	
Myers, Earl	11	1937		Cades Cove, TN	
Myers, Labe	47	1937, 1956	4–5 yrs	Cades Cove, TN	NPS fire warden
Myers, Sherman	50	1937	self-educated	Cades Cove, TN	farmer, logger

Table 1 (continued)

Name	*Age at time of first interview*	*Year interviewed*	*Education*	*Community*	*Occupation*
Myers, Mrs. Sherman		1937		Cades Cove, TN	
Nelson, Jean	21	1941	high school	Jonathans Creek, NC	help tend farm, dry goods store clerk
Newman, Glenn	22	1937, 1938	high school	Gatlinburg, TN	helped on parents' farm
Nichols, Dinty	50	1939, 1941	4–5 yrs	Cataloochee, NC	CCC blacksmith
Noland, David	50	1940	college grad	Cataloochee, NC	CCC superintendent, engineer
Noland, Glenn	35	1956	college grad	Fines Creek, NC	schoolteacher, farmer
Noland, Mrs. Glenn	30		prob some college	Fines Creek, NC	
Oakley, Wiley	53	1939	about 4–5 yrs, some self-education	Gatlinburg, TN	owner of gift shop
Ogle, Dick	61	1937	prob 3–4 yrs	Emerts Cove, TN, later Roaring Fork, TN	farmer
Ogle, Mrs. Dick	63	1937	prob literate	Emerts Cove, TN, later Roaring Fork, TN	housewife
Ogle, Ellis	59	1950, 1956	prob illiterate	Roaring Fork, TN	farm helper, handyman
Ogle, Lewallen "Uncle Bud"	79	1939	prob 2–3 yrs	Roaring Fork, TN	farmer
Ogle, Noah	80	1939	some grade school	Emerts Cove, TN	farmer
Ogle, Wesley		1937			
Oliver, John	80	1962	grade school, business college	Cades Cove, TN, later Townsend, TN	mail carrier, Baptist preacher
Ownby, Dick		1937		Gatlinburg, TN	
Ownby, Lee "Swede"	30	1937	prob high school	Gatlinburg, TN	NPS fire warden, chief NPS stock clerk, Baptist preacher
Ownby, Newton	77	1939	prob 2–3 yrs	Wears Cove, TN	farmer, cattle raiser
Ownby, Mrs. Newton	78	1953	prob 4–5 yrs	Wears Cove, TN	housewife
Ownby, Steve	50	1937	prob 2–3 yrs	Elkmont, TN	farmer, hunter, trapper
Packett, Margaret	78	1939	prob illiterate	Big Bend, NC	farm housewife
Palmer, Charlie	45	1937		Cataloochee, NC	farmer, WWI veteran
Palmer, "Turkey" George	79	1937	2–3 yrs	Cataloochee, NC	
Palmer, Mrs. George	65	1939	3–4 yrs	Cataloochee, NC	
Palmer, Mary Alice	18	1939	high school	Cataloochee, NC	
Palmer, Vernon		1965		Cataloochee, NC	
Palmer, Vincent		1965		Cataloochee, NC	
Palmer, Will	65	1939, etc.	some grade school	Cataloochee, NC	farmer
Palmer, Mrs. Will	66	1939	prob high school	Cataloochee, NC, later Waynesville, NC	
Parris, John		1937, 1939		Sylva, NC	
Parris, Red	20	1939	about 7–8 yrs	Bryson City, NC	CCC employee
Parton, Jim	50	1956	about 8 yrs	Emerts Cove, TN	NPS fire warden
Parton, Margaret	77	1937, 1939	about 3–4 yrs	Copeland Creek, TN	farm widow
Phillips, George		1937		Big Creek, NC	
Phillips, Hobe	21	1940	about 8 yrs	Tobes Creek, TN	CCC employee
Phillips, Neil	70	1937	prob illiterate	Cosby, TN	farmer
Phillips, "Red"	20	1939	7–8 yrs	Saunook, NC	farmhand
Plott, John	70	1953	about 8 yrs, much self-education	Plott Creek, NC	farmer, hunter, breeder of bear hounds

Table 1 (continued)

Name	*Age at time of first interview*	*Year interviewed*	*Education*	*Community*	*Occupation*
Plott, Vaughn		1953		Plott Creek, NC	
Potter, Eli	60	1939	prob college	Smokemont, NC	NPS forester
Price, Bill		1937			
Price, Paul		1939		Sevierville, TN	
Proffitt, Bill	70	1937	prob literate	Upper Cosby Creek, TN	farmer
Queen, Rebecca	70	1939	about 3–4 yrs	Cherokee, NC	farm housewife
Ramsey, Bill		1937	unknown, prob little; alert and interested in affairs	Elkmont, TN	game warden
Ramsey, Carol	9	1937		Cosby, TN	
Ramsey, Lela	14	1937	8 yrs	Cosby, TN	student
Ramsey, Lorette	35	1937	about 8 yrs	Cosby Creek, TN	widow of CCC foreman
Ramsey, Phoebe	39	1956	about 8 yrs	Newport, TN	helped on parents' farm
Ramsey, Veenie	67	1937	term or two of school; "she could read good but she couldn't write much"	Cosby, TN	farm widow
Ray, Robert W.	22	1939	about 6–7 yrs	Jefferson City, TN	CCC truck driver, Hall's field trip assistant
Reagan, Amos	45	1939	about 8 yrs	Gatlinburg, TN	CCC foreman, owner of restaurant
Reagan, E. L.	63	1939	much self-education	Roaring Fork, TN	owner of furniture-making shop
Reagan, Elizabeth	60	1939	about 5–6 yrs	Gatlinburg, TN	widow
Reagan, Lee	c50	1939	about 3–4 yrs	Gatlinburg, TN	logger, helped father haul goods
Reagan, Lewis	30	1937, etc.	1 yr college	Gatlinburg, TN	NPS fire warden, owner of prosperous motel
Rolland, Mrs. Fred	50	1937	about 3–4 yrs	Smokemont, NC	farm housewife
"Sage"	70	1956, 1959	went to school; "can read and write"	Mt. Sterling, NC, later Hazelwood, NC	farmer, grist mill operator
Sharp, Joseph A.	55	1959	college graduate	Sevierville, TN	history teacher at Rule High, Knoxville, TN
Shook, Walter	70	1957		Clyde, NC	farmer
Shults, Glen	27	1937	high school	Emerts Cove, TN	clerk of park naturalist
Shults, Jake	70	1937	about 8 yrs	Cosby, TN	farmer
Shults, Joe	81	1937	prob 3–4 yrs	Emerts Cove, TN	unemployed
Shults, McDonald ("Don")	22	1956	high school	Newport, TN	farmhand, general work
Shults, Ralf	22	1937	high school	Emerts Cove, TN	farmer, other jobs
Shults, Will	50	1937, 1939	3–4 yrs	Emerts Cove, TN	farmer
Shults, Mrs. Will	45	1939	3–4 yrs	Emerts Cove, TN	
Siler, Albert	37	1939, 1949	prob high school	Dellwood, NC	CCC foreman, owner of gas station and store
Sisk, Levada				Cataloochee, NC	
Smith, Carl	21	1941	high school	Asheville, NC	CCC truck driver

Table 1 (continued)

Name	Age at time of first interview	Year interviewed	Education	Community	Occupation
Smith, Herman	22	1941	prob 4 yrs	Hot Springs, NC	CCC cook
Sparks, Bob	45	1937	about 6–7 yrs	Cades Cove, TN	CCC foreman
Sparks, Dave	77	1937	2–3 yrs, prob literate	Cades Cove, TN	farmer, logger
Stephenson, "Hub"	25	1939	prob 4–5 yrs	Saunook, NC	farmhand
Stinnett, Fannie		1957		Waynesville, NC	
Stinnett, Leona		1939		Emerts Cove, TN	
Stinnett, Will	70	1937	prob 4–5 yrs	Emerts Cove, TN	farmer
Stinnett, Mrs. Will	65	1937	about 4–5 yrs	Emerts Cove, TN	
Strickland, Boyd	20	1940	4–5 yrs	Spring Creek, NC	farmhand, musician
Stupka, Arthur		1937–40	college grad	Gatlinburg, TN	park naturalist
Styles, Mrs. Docia	66	1939	3–4 yrs	Indian Creek, NC	widow on farm
Styles, Sam	74	1956	3–4 yrs	Cosby, TN	farmer
Sutton, Eugene	43	1939	3–4 yrs	Cataloochee Creek, NC	farmer
Sutton, Jake	53	1939	7–8 yrs	Mt. Sterling, NC	NPS fire warden
Sutton, Jim	60	1939	3–4 yrs	Cataloochee, NC	CCC employee
Sutton, John Newton					
Sutton, Mitchell	65	1937, etc.		Gnat Camp, NC	
Sutton, Red		1937		Cataloochee, NC	
Sutton, Taylor		1937, etc.		Mt. Sterling, NC	
Sutton, Zilphie	70	1937, 1939		Big Creek, NC	
Swanninger, Aaron				Cades Cove, TN	
Teague, Lawson	60	1939	prob illiterate	White Oak, NC	farmer
Turner, Lizzie	70	1956	2–3 yrs; "could read but never did learn to write"	Sand Hill, TN	farm housewife
Valentine, Polly	80	1956	prob 2–3 yrs	Cosby, TN	farm housewife
Valentine, Willie	84	1956	about 8 yrs	Cosby Creek, TN	schoolteacher, owner of nursery
Vance, Nora Bell	30	1937	4–5 yrs	Emerts Cove, TN	farm housewife
Walker, John	60	1939	5 yrs	Tuckaleechee Cove, TN	logger, sawmill contracting, hunter
Walker sisters	50–60	1939	grade school	Little Greenbrier, TN	

Grammar and Syntax of Southern Appalachian and Smoky Mountain English

Introduction

This sketch surveys the elements of morphology and syntax—how words are formed and constructed into phrases and clauses—of the traditional English of the Smoky Mountains of North Carolina and Tennessee, one of the most widely recognized parts of Southern Appalachia.[1] Its traditional pronunciation has been treated extensively in Joseph Sargent Hall's *The Phonetics of Great Smoky Mountain Speech* (1942), and its word-stock and semantics are presented and illustrated in the *Dictionary of Smoky Mountain English* (Montgomery and Hall 2004). Much information on grammar appears in the latter work as well, but in piecemeal fashion at separate entries. Organizing the relevant material by traditional parts of speech and other categories permits a broad, synoptic picture of the grammar of Smoky Mountain English (SME), as well as attention to contextual details and analytical concerns not permissible in the confines of dictionary entries. Most features of Smokies speech are shared with types of English in nearby regions, but to date its grammar has received little consideration in the literature.[2]

The presentation here is contrastive: to identify and exemplify differences from "general American English" or "general usage" (terms that do not necessarily imply the existence of an invariant or national norm of American English).[3] Such an orientation permits only a limited view of Smoky Mountain speech, and the peculiarities of grammar cited will inevitably appear more numerous and prevalent than would ever occur in a conversation with a typical speaker. Likewise, it can convey the comparative currency of forms only by using such qualifying adverbs as "occasionally" or by specifying the one form among two or more that is the most common. The focus throughout is on structural contrast with general usage. The people whose grammar is presented here live or lived near the Tennessee/North Carolina border in the vicinity of the Great Smoky Mountains National Park, which encompasses an area roughly sixty miles long by thirty miles wide lying in approximately equal proportion in each state. The eight-hundred-square-mile area is itself no longer inhabited. The features presented here were not necessarily typical or used by all or even most speakers in the Smokies. That speakers of any variety fluctuate between forms is true no matter how small the community, as is usually the case within individuals as well. The scope of this survey permits only a qualitative view of variation, except for verb principal parts (§4.2).

Citations have been drawn from recordings, observations, or reports of the speech of the Smoky Mountain area as outlined below, with priority given to examples from recordings reviewed by Montgomery and Heinmiller whenever possible. This range of sources produces the fullest account of the subject to date, one that documents the language of rural speakers in the second and third quarters of the twentieth century. They were people of modest formal education living on the land in a largely self-sufficient agricultural economy.

Sources

This sketch is based largely on four types of sources:

A) Interviews recorded by Joseph Hall in 1939 and by personnel of and volunteers for the Great Smoky Mountains National Park between 1954 and 1983. These have been audited by the authors, who has transcribed and fashioned many of them into a computer-searchable Corpus of Smoky Mountain English (CSME). Hall's early material was drawn from nearly one hundred people reared in the mountains before the displacement brought by the national park in the 1930s.

B) Interviews recorded by Joseph Hall in the 1950s and observations made by him of mountain speech between 1937 and 1987. These materials produced numerous citations for the dictionary, but except for a few recordings, they have not been audited by the authors.

C) Material recorded by other investigators and reported in the scholarly literature. This includes surveys by the Linguistic Atlas of the Gulf States and studies by doctoral students, including the authors' own work in the Smokies foothills in Tennessee.[4]

D) Materials not tape-recorded but appearing in printed literature from reputable observers, especially local historians and commentators who were frequently native speakers of Smoky Mountain English. Though not equivalent in status to the first three sources, such materials are invaluable for attesting many infrequent and old-fashioned forms.

1 Nouns

Nouns are notable for the many ways in which their plurals differ from general usage.

1.1 Nouns of measure and weight like *mile*, *pound*, and *year* often lack plural *-s* when preceded by a numeral or another word expressing quantity. Such usage reflects the partitive genitive in the history of English.

> We had to walk ten *mile* to school.
> The bear weighed four hundred and seventy-five *pound*.
> [We] took that hide offen it and cut it into four *quarter*.
> I am nearly ten *year* older than my brother right over there.

1.2 Nouns interpreted in general usage as mass nouns (and thus unmarked for number) are sometimes construed in SME as count nouns. When this is the case, they may or may not take plural *-s* or an indefinite article:

Dan Myers has got lots of *beards* [i.e., a long, bushy beard].
Sometimes, you know, people would kill a *beef* or a sheep.
We killed a heap of *beeves*.
These *gravels* are hard on your feet.
Have you got any easing *powders*?
We had several *rock* on that trail and nothing to drill those *rock* with.

1.3 On the other hand, a count noun in general usage may be interpreted as a mass noun in the Smokies:

They scattered my *plank* on the ground. [perhaps by analogy with *lumber* or *timber*]

1.4 Some mass nouns and singular count nouns ending in *-s* or a similar consonant may be interpreted as plural in SME, sometimes producing singular forms through back-formation.

How did you go about cutting up that many *cabbage*?
Give me a hunk of them *cheese*.
I reckon most of the deal in getting your *licen* [i.e., a marriage license] is having the three dollars it takes to pay.
We like them *molasses*.
A panther is more of a dog *specie*, a lot bigger and way longer than a wild cat.

1.5 Plurals of nouns for animals are noteworthy in two respects. The lack of *-s* on *deer* may be extended to other nouns for other game animals:

He hunted *coon*, deer, [and] *bear*.
[There are] lots of *wildcat* here.

On the other hand, *-s* may be added to nouns that do not take the suffix in general usage:

[There] was *deers* and bears and all kinds of wild animals, I reckon.
Them *sheeps* would just eat that a sight in the world.
I caught a mess of *trouts* today.

1.6 Double Plurals. Nouns that are historically plural in English may be interpreted as singular in SME, taking an indefinite article and producing a double plural form:

We'uns come from educated *folkses*.
He didn't have a thing on but his *galluses* and his shoes. [original singular form *gallow*]
They built a little one-room house and had the Tow String *childrens* to go to school there a long time.
He was a good hand to break a *oxen*.
They had milk cows and *oxens* that they worked.

1.7 In SME nouns ending in *-sp*, *-st*, or *-sk* sometimes preserve the longer plural form *-es* that is inherited from earlier English:

waspes
Them *joistes* run through there.
The birds have built *nestes* in the spring house.
Over on the side of the mountains you will see a little house on stilts or *postes*.
He'd make [the tobacco leaves] up in these fancy little *twistes* of tobacco.

Other nouns follow the pronunciation tendency of adding a t after a final *s* sound (seen in *across* => *acrost*), to which the syllabic plural may be then added.

We have both men's and women's *clastes*.
She taken two *dostes* of medicine.

1.8 Regularized Plurals. A few nouns irregular in general usage may take regular plural forms in SME (*foremans*, *gentlemans*, *womans*). In religious discourse *sister* is occasionally pluralized as *sisteren*, by analogy with the more general *brother/brethren*.

1.9 Associative Plurals. In Smokies speech the phrases *and all*, *and them*, and *those* mean "and the rest, and (all) others" and are used after a noun to include associated people (i.e., group or family members) or things.

I carried roasting ears, sweet potatoes, Irish potatoes, tomatoes, cucumbers, cabbage, *and all*.
Pap *and them* was a-carrying the bear.
Helen *and those* were there.

2 Pronouns

2.1 Personal Pronouns. The nominative and objective forms of personal pronouns behave for the most part as in general American English, with the most noteworthy exception of *you'uns* (for *you ones*), *you all*, and *y'all* in the second-person plural and *hit* in the third-person singular.

Objective forms of personal pronouns occur as indirect objects, direct objects, and objects of prepositions. In the 1930s, Hall observed a few illiterate speakers using single objective pronouns in subject position, as in the following, but these do not appear on any recordings. However, the objective pronoun is often employed in subject position when conjoined with another pronoun or with a noun (in the latter case the personal pronoun usually comes first). This pattern with plural pronouns is very rare.

So *me* and four cousins began right then and there to lay our plans to go.
My daughter and *me* went over there.
Uncle Jim used to come up to home and *me and him* would bee hunt.
Her and Jess and the girl is all buried there on Caldwell Fork.
Him and one of his nephews went a-fishing one time, and they was up on what was called Desolation.
That mine *you* and Tom Graves found, how can you go to it?

2.1.1 First Person and Second Person Pronouns. *We'uns* may occur in the Smokies, but it is far less common than another form based on *ones*, *you'uns* (usually pronounced as two syllables). In Hall's observations *you'uns* occurred in traditional, familiar speech, whereas *you all* was more formal and used by better educated speakers. Though it remains current and is the

Table 2 Personal pronouns

NOMINATIVE CASE	
Singular	*Plural*
I, me	we, we'uns
you, ye/you, you'un	you'all, y'all, you all, ye
he, him	they
she, her	
hit, it	

OBJECTIVE CASE	
Singular	*Plural*
me	us
you, ye	you, you'uns, you'uns all, y'all, you all, ye
her, him, hit, it	them

Table 3 Possessive pronouns

Singular	*Plural*
my, mine	our, ours, ourn, ournses
your, yours, yourn	your, yours, yourn, your'unses, you'uns
his, hisn	their, theirs, theirn
her, hers, hern	
its, hits	

traditional periphrastic form in mountain speech, *you'uns* has been giving ground to *you all* (and less often to *y'all*) for at least two or three generations.

> *We'uns* come from educated folkses.
> *You'uns* set in front.
> *You all* may be need[ing] it one of these days.
> *Y'all* come back.

Ye (pronounced [yi] or [yɪ]) is a variant pronunciation of *you*, not a retention of the Early Modern English plural *ye* as found in the King James Bible and elsewhere. It occurs in both the singular and plural, usually in unstressed positions, as a direct object, an object of a preposition, or a subject when inverted in questions. It may also appear as a reflexive pronoun.

> [Boneset is] bitterer than quinine, and hit'll kill *ye* or cure *ye* one.
> If you call [a turkey] too much, you'll never get one to *ye*.
> You can see the ski lodge yander, can't *ye*?
> How old was *ye*?
> Get *ye* chairs.

2.1.2 In the third-person singular, *hit* (the older form of the pronoun) alternates with *it*, occurring most often in stressed positions (usually as a subject) and less often elsewhere.

Stressed

> Hit's been handed down to him, you see, so he's the third or fourth generation.
> Hit must have been in the thirties, in the twenty-nine, because I was up there on that river about eighteen year.

Unstressed

> I don't know how long hit's been.
> They had to raise the young one and take care of hit.

2.2 Possessive Pronouns

In attributive position possessive pronouns conform to general usage with only occasional infrequent exceptions like the following:

> That dog done *hits* best to break loose.
> I taken *you'uns* potion, for I had a misery.

In absolute or disjunctive position (e.g., at the end of a phrase or clause), possessive pronouns formed with *-n* (*hern*, *hisn*, etc.) rather than *-s* sometimes occur. Historically these developed by analogy with *mine* and *thine*, but many speakers today take them as deriving from a possessive pronoun + a reduction of *own* or *one*).

> The white mare is *hern*.
> I don't know just how he made *hisn*.
> [We] generally sold *ourn* to a man on Coopers Creek.
> The colts is *theirn*.
> Work them just like they was *yourn*.
> What did you'uns do with *yournses*?

2.3 Reflexive Pronouns

Reflexive pronouns in Smokies speech differ from general usage in four ways.

2.3.1 In a construction often known as the personal dative, personal pronoun forms are used rather than forms in *-self/-selves*, especially with the verbs *get* and *have*.

> Git *ye* chairs. [singular or plural]
> George built *him* a house up there.
> I had *me* a pair of crutches.
> They'd get *them* out honey.
> We had *us* a big fire made up at the root of the tree.
> Mary is fixing to make *her* some cotton dresses.

2.3.2 Plural reflexive pronouns are sometimes formed with *-self* or *-selfs*, in addition to *-selves*.

> We built another little barn *ourself*.
> We went by *ourselfs* to the head of Forneys Creek and fished.
> I said, "Dang you ones. If you want them out, get in and get them *yourself*."
> Step up here, boys, and he'p *you'unsself*.
> They'd all go and enjoy *themself*.

Table 4 Reflexive pronouns

Singular	*Plural*
me, myself	us, ourself, ourselfs, ourselves
you, ye, yourself	you, ye, yourself, yourselves, you'unsself
him, himself, hisself	
her, herself	them, theirself, theirselves, themself
it, itself	themselfs, themselves

I like to see young people try to make something of *themselfs*.
I've done forgot what they call *theirself*.

2.3.3 Following the pattern of *myself* and *yourself*, third-person reflexive pronouns sometimes add *-self* or *-selves* to a possessive rather than an objective form of a personal pronoun.

The little boy stayed there all night by *hisself*.
I've done forgot what they call *theirself*.
They even carded the wool *theirselves*.

2.3.4 *Own* is sometimes added to form an emphatic reflexive, which is always based on the possessive rather than the objective form.

Now that was an experience I experienced *my own self*.
They could prove you took a hand in it *your own self*.
He has a little kit to give *his own self* a shot.
Everybody took care of *their own self*.
People doctored *their own selfs*.
Most of them were blockaders *their own selves*.

2.4 Demonstrative Pronouns

These forms are used as demonstrative pronouns (and usually also as demonstrative adjectives) in SME. As in traditional English elsewhere, the distinction between proximate, intermediate, and distant is maintained (*this* vs. *that* vs. *yon*). *Yon/yan* and *yonder/yander* most often function as adverbs (see §13.4), but may also be demonstrative adjectives. A speaker who employs the three-way distinction may be able to express a further degree of physical and conceptual distance more economically than those with the two-way distinction. As in many other varieties of English, *them* occurs as a demonstrative pronoun and adjective in the Smokies. *This* and *that* and their plural forms may combine with *here*, *there*, or *'un*.

2.4.1 Demonstrative Pronouns

Them's not perch, *them's* bass.
This here's the old residenter bear hunter, Fonze Cable.
This here'un was made out of metal, you know. It had a lid, a little lever.
Maybe *this'un* had preaching first, and then they'd have Sunday school.
These here was on the inside there.
That there's Tom's boy, I guess.
We'll try another'un, being *that'un* paid off.

Table 5 Demonstrative pronouns

Singular	*Plural*
this, this here, this here'un, this'un (this one)	these, these here
that, that there, that'un (that one)	them, them there, those
yon/yan	yon/yan
yonder/yander	yonder/yander

2.4.2 Demonstrative Adjectives

Middlesboro is on *yan* side of Cumberland Gap.
You cross the big bridge going in *yander* way right there.
I'm afeared of *them* copperheads.
This here beadwood bark, make hit for tea.
He had one of *these here* hog rifles.
That there sawmill I worked at was there before I married.
Them there fellows come through here, stealing horses and things.

2.5 Indefinite Pronouns. Notable usages of indefinite pronouns in the Smokies include *ary/ary'un*, *nary/nary'un* (see §3.2) and the singular indefinite form *a body*.

We decided we'd go back in the sugar orchard to see if *ary'un* had come in there
We didn't see *nary'un*.
Could *a body* buy that there dog?
A body thought about it back then.

2.6 Interrogative pronouns, used to introduce direct or indirect questions, are noteworthy in several regards. SME has a set of forms that invert *ever* and the *wh-* element (see also §15.1).

We'll do *everwhat* Jim wants to do.
Everwhich one come nigh always come down to the house and stayed full half the night.
Everwho hears that will be surprised.

Interrogative pronouns may be combined with *all* in *who all*, *what all*, etc. (§2.7.2).

2.7 All. As suggested in §2.1, *all* can combine with other forms, usually to express inclusiveness. In these cases *all* takes secondary stress, making the constructions compounds rather than phrases.

2.7.1 Combining forms include personal and possessive pronouns (*they all*, *you all*, *your all*, *theirs all*, and *you'un(s) all*); in all of these the stress falls on the first element, not the second. Of these compounds, *you all* is the only one to have acquired properties of a personal pronoun).

Cades Cove nearly took *theirs all* to Gregory Bald.
It all doesn't mean anything.
Old man Lon and Will all, *they all* went with him.
You-all may be [needing] it one of these days.
Is this table *your all's*?

I want *you'un all* to come out to church next Sunday.
They'll catch *you-uns all*.

2.7.2 More often, *all* is combined with an interrogative pronoun to convey the inclusiveness and generality of a query or statement. Thus, *who all* is equivalent to both "All of whom?" and "Who in general?"

I don't know *where all* he sold it at.
I don't remember *all how* we used it.
What all kinds of herbs do you have on your porch?
I can remember *what all* happened, but I can't remember how old I was.
Who all was there?

Occasionally *all* is placed after a noun for the same reasons.

They'd shear the sheep, and she'd spin the wool, the thread, and make our britches and our shirts *all*.

2.8 *One*. The indefinite pronoun *one* is frequently contracted and reduced to *'un* (occasionally *'n*) when it is unstressed and follows a pronoun (§2.1) or an adjective.

We'uns can say nigh of two hundred would come a heap closer.
You'uns is talking about rough country.
We'll try *another'n*, being *that'un* paid off.
The *gooder'ns*'s all gone now!
This here'un is made out of metal.
What one didn't have *another'n* did.
Jack is an old hand to coon-hunt, but he never catches *nary'un*.
I don't recollect any of his *young'uns*.
They's all sizes from *little'uns* to *big'uns*.
If he killed *ary'un*, it was before my recollection.

(See §18.1 for *one* following *or* in coordinate constructions.)

2.9 Relative Pronouns. In Smokies English at least nine forms are used to introduce a relative clause (*that*, *'at*, *ø*, *which*, *as*, *what*, *thats*, *who*, *whose*). All of these are used in restrictive clauses, with *that* being far more common than any other form regardless of whether its head noun is human or nonhuman. Nonrestrictive clauses, less frequent than restrictive ones, are introduced by *which*, *who*, or *that*. In addition to *whose*, *thats* is attested as infrequent possessive form, but is extremely rare. Contrasting with general usage are the following:

that *(either restrictive or nonrestrictive)*:

Human Head Noun, Nonrestrictive Clause: Mister Wilson Queen, *that* lived there at the campground, he was a song leader when I was a little girl.

'at *(reduced form of* that*, only restrictive)*:

Nonhuman Head Noun, Restrictive Clause: And we had some old trained bear hounds *'at* turned off in the roughs.

ø: *The ellipsis of a pronoun (ø) occurs only in restrictive clauses and most often in existential constructions (see also §16.3). Unlike in general usage it may represent the subject of the verb in the relative clause.*

Human Head Noun: He was the crabbedest old feller ø ever I seed.
Human Head Noun: He come up to a party ø had been a-fighting a bear.
Nonhuman Head Noun: They was two wagon loads ø went out from there.

which:

Human Head Noun, Nonrestrictive Clause: Then he handed it down to Caleb, *which* was Eph's pa.

as *(only restrictive)*:

Nonhuman Head Noun, Restrictive Clause: They would mind rather than to take the punishment *as* I would put on them.
Human Head Noun, Restrictive Clause: Tom Sparks has herded more than any man *as* I've ever heard of.

what *(only restrictive). The relative pronoun* what*, common in literary portrayals of mountain speech, is virtually nonexistent in speech; Hall, for example, collected only one example of it.*

Human Head Noun, Restrictive Clause: I knowed the White Caps *what* done the murder.

thats *"whose" (only restrictive)*:

We need to remember a woman *thats* child has died.

3 Articles and Adjectives

(For demonstrative adjectives, see §2.4.)

3.1 Articles

3.1.1 The indefinite article *a* [ə] rather than *an* is often used before nouns beginning with a vowel sound in SME. Often it is partially absorbed by the following vowel.

We used to have *a* organ, and we don't have it there anymore.
[It] maybe might have been *a* epidemic of whooping cough or measles or something like that.
Just go on up to the Pole Mountain till you come to *a* ivy thicket.

3.1.2 In Smokies speech the definite article is employed in several notable contexts.

in place-names: *the Smoky* (= the main ridge of the Smoky Mountains), *the Pole Mountain*
in the phrase *in the bed*
with superlatives: *the best* "very well" (as "I always thought they got along the best")
to indicate possession: *the old lady* "my wife," *the woman* "my wife"
with an indefinite pronoun: *the both*, *the most*
with names of diseases and medical conditions: *the fever* "typhoid," *the sugar* "diabetes"

Before *other(s)* the definite article is occasionally reduced to *t'*, producing *t'other(s)*. With the function of *t'* as an article having been obscured, *t'other* may itself be modified by *the*.

One or *t'other* of them whupped the other one.
When one's gone *the t'other's* proud of it.

3.2 Indefinite Adjectives (see also §2.5). *Ary* "any" and *nary* "not a one, not any" occur in declarative clauses (occasionally in interrogative and conditional ones) and sometimes take an enclitic *'un* (< *one*) to form the indefinite pronouns *ary'un* ['ærən] and *nary'un* ['nærən]. Originally derived from *e'er a* (from *ever a*) and *ne'er a* (from *never a*), *ary* and *nary* in mountain speech preserve the adjective function of these constructions. According to Hall's observations in the 1930s, *ary* and *nary* were somewhat more emphatic than *any* and *none* and more likely to refer to singular things or units than to plural ones.

We didn't kill *ary* deer then.
We never seed *nary* another wolf.
If he killed *ary'un*, it was before my recollection.
I never seed a deer nor saw *nary'un's* tracks.

3.3 Comparatives. In the Smokies the comparative form of adjectives occasionally differs from general usage.

Nothin' [is] *gooder* than crumbled cornbread and milk.
You're *nearder* to the door than I am.

Double comparatives such as the following are characteristic of Smokies speech:

I'd say I was *more healthier* back then than I am now.
I was getting closer and *more closer* with every step I took.
I think there are *worser* things than being poor.

3.4 Superlatives. Double superlative forms also occur in Smokies speech.

Newport, though, is one of the *most liveliest* towns that I know of.
Doc was the *most wealthiest* man [in] this part of the country for to buy at that time.

The superlative suffix *-est* is sometimes added redundantly, including on adjectives that are historically superlative or absolute.

She could make the *bestest* [sweetbread] in all the country, we thought.
Who got there *firstest?*
Who got there *secondest?*
Who growed the *mostest* corn?

The superlatives suffix *-est* may be added to adjectives of two or more syllables that in general speech take the modifier *most*.

Tom Barnes was the *completest* hunter I was ever acquainted with.
He's the *disablest* one of the family.
All my family thought that was the *wonderfullest* thing ever was.

3.4.1 In Smokies speech, present participles of verbs used as attributive adjectives sometimes take the superlative suffix *-est*.

That's the *cheatin'est* place at the fair!
Daddy said he was the gamest and *fightingest* little rascal he ever hunted.
These are the *singin'est* children I have ever seen!
Ad said Barshia was the *thinkin'est* boy in the world.
He had told somebody she was the *workingest* girl in the country.
She's the *aggravatin'est* calf I've ever had.

Some of these forms have more than one possible interpretation. To say that someone is "the workingest" person ever seen may mean that person works very long ("the most"), very well ("the best"), or very hard. Likewise, *singingest* can be paraphrased as "sings better than anyone else," "enjoys singing more than anyone else," or "sings more than anyone else."[5] For *best* "most," see §13.2.

3.5 Anomalous Comparatives and Superlatives. In Smokies speech a form of *big* together with the noun it modifies is equivalent to *most*. *Big* may appear in its positive, comparative, or superlative form and modify any of several nouns, but the meaning of the construction remains the same ("most" or perhaps more loosely, "major").

A *big majority* of the people went to church pretty regular.
My father did the *big part* of the farming.
They done the *bigger majority* of their logging on Laurel Creek.
He rode a horse the *bigger part* of the time.
The *biggest half* of the people does it.
The *biggest majority* down there, they care.
[The county] went Democratic, *biggest part* of the time.
[The] *biggest portion* of people didn't have lumber.

Other unusual superlative forms include *onliest* "only" and *upperest* "situated on the highest ground, farthest up" (from *upper* "on high ground").

She treated it as if it was the *onliest* one she had.
Turkey George Palmer was in the *upperest* house on Indian Creek.

3.6 All The. The adjective phrase *all the* has the sense "the only" (as in general usage), but in addition to mass nouns it can modify singular count nouns or the indefinite pronoun *one*.

It was just a sled road but it was *all the* way you could take anything up there.
I reckon that's *all the* name she had.
That's *all the* one they got here.

All the can also modify the positive, comparative, or superlative form of an adjective to express extent.

That's *all the far* I want to go. [= as far as]
This is *all the further* we can go. [= as far as]
Is that *all the best* you can do? [= as good/well as]

4 Verbal Morphology

Verb inflections in Smokies English to mark agreement and tense are usually the same as in general usage in form, but they are often used in different contexts and follow different rules.

4.1 Subject-Verb Agreement. In his notes from the 1930s Joseph Hall observed that less-educated speakers used *-s* outside the third-person singular (as "if you wants to go"; "I knows them when I sees them"; "they says he done it") and that *-s* was in some cases absent from the third-person singular (as "Who want to know?" and "He still do live here"). However, such usages do not occur on his recordings or in other sources. Verbs in the third-person singular conform to general usage in nearly all respects. The most common exception is *don't* in the third-person singular. Occasionally *it seems* appears as *seem*, with the subject pronoun omitted ("Seem like I've heard it"). Verbs ending in *-st* sometimes take a syllabic suffix (parallel to nouns, shown in §1.7).

> That water freezes on the bark and *bustes* [i.e., bursts] it.
> Hit *costes* too much.
> It *disgustes* me now to drive down through this cove.

For subject-verb agreement the principal difference between Smoky Mountain English and general American English lies in third-person plural contexts. In these, *-s* occurs frequently on verbs having any subject other than a personal pronoun (as in *people knows*, *some goes*, etc.), but very rarely with the pronoun *they* (except when expressing the historical present, §7.4). This pronoun/nonpronoun pattern follows a rule that can be traced to Scotland as far back as the fourteenth century and that also operates for the verbs *be* and *have*.[6]

> They settled up there and entered all that land up back across the river over there where Steve Whaley and them *lives*.
> This comes from people who *teaches* biology.
> Some *thinks* it might be a mineral that causes it.
> It's where people *gathers* up and *shucks* corn in the fall when they get the corn gathered.
> That's the way cattle *feeds*. They *feed* together.

A pattern following the same rule involves verbs with a personal pronoun subject not adjacent to the verb. This pattern is attested in old letters written from the Smoky Mountains, but apparently did not survive into the twentieth century:

> I am very glad to hear that you have saved my foder and *is* doing with my things as well as you are. [1862 letter]
> We have some sickness in camp of mumps and *has* had some of fever. [1862 letter]
> I am now Volenteard to gow to texcas against the mexicans and *Expecks* to start the last of September or the first of October. [1836 letter]

For use of the suffix *-s* to express the historical present, see §7.4.

4.2 Verb Principal Parts

4.2.1 Regular verbs. Parallel with the noun plural and verbal agreement suffixes (§1.7 and §4.1), a syllabic variant of the tense suffix is occasionally added to verbs ending in *-st* when general usage does not.

> It never *costed* me one red [cent].

Smokies English exhibits much variation in the principal parts of both regular and irregular verbs. Verbs that are regular in general usage are often irregular in the mountains, and vice versa. More often verbs are irregular in both varieties but differ in their past-tense or past-participle forms. Table 6 identifies verbs whose principal parts vary in SME. Where variation occurs in the Corpus of Smoky Mountain English, the frequency of each form is indicated for the CSME, in order to present a quantitative view of this important area of grammar. At the same time, for each verb the type of source (identified at the introduction earlier as A, B, C, or D) in which each form is attested is indicated. Gaps in the list indicate that no form occurred in the material consulted, not that one is not found in speech.

The nearly one hundred verbs listed in table 6 vary considerably in their patterning, but most variant forms are centuries old and traceable to Early Modern English, if not earlier. Many may be usefully grouped according to how their past tense is formed.

4.2.2 Verbs with Variable Irregular Forms. In some cases (e.g., *climb*, *help*) older, irregular past-tense and past-participle forms have tended to be replaced by regular forms more slowly in SME than in general usage. In other cases (e.g., *took*) one irregular form has tended to dominate in SME for both the past tense and past participle.

> begin, began/begin/begun, begin/begun
> climb, clim/climbed/clome/clum, clim/climbed/clombed/clum
> come, came/come, came/come
> do, did/done, did/done
> drink, drank/drunk, drank/drunk
> drive, driv/drived/drove/druv, driv/driven/drove/druv
> eat, ate/eat/et, ate/eat/et
> give, gave/gin/give, gave/gin/give/given
> run, ran/run, ran/run
> take, taked/taken/took/tuck, taken/took/tooken/tuck

4.2.3 Some verbs that are irregular in general usage have both irregular and regular forms in SME.

> blow, blew/blowed, blowed/blown
> catch, catched/caught, catched/caught
> draw, drawed/drew, drawed/drawn
> grow, grew/growed, growed/grown
> know, knew/knowed, knowed/known
> see, saw/seed, seed/seen
> teach, teached/taught, teached/taught
> throw, threw/throwed, throwed/thrown

4.2.4 Some of the verbs in §4.2.2 have been leveled almost entirely to one form in traditional SME.

Table 6 Regular verbs

Verb	*Past-tense form(s)*	*Past-participle form(s)*	*Source*
arrive	arriv, arrove	arrove	C
ask	ask, ax	ask, ax	B
bang	bung	bunged	C
bear	bore	bore	D
become	became 16, become 2	become	A
begin	began 5, begin 37, begun 2	begin 1, begun 1	A
bite	bit	bit 5, bitten 8	A
blow	blew 2, blowed 16, blown 1	blowed 4, blown 3	A
break	broke	broke 11, broken 3	A
bring	brought 82, brung 1	brought	A
	brought	brung	C
buy	bought	boughten, boughtened	D
catch	catched 2, caught 15	caught 6	A
	cotch, cotched	catched	C
	caught	cotch, cotched	D
climb	clim 4, climbed 1, clum 7	climbed	A
	clome	clim, climbed	B
	climbed	clum	C
	climbed	clombed	D
come	came 53, come 747	came 1, come 29	A
cost	cos-ted		B
creep	crope	crept	C
dive	div	div, dived, dove	C
do	did 455, done 126	done	A
		did	C
drag	dragged 0, drug 4	dragged 0, drug 2	A
draw	drawed 10, drew 1		A
	drawed, drew	drawed, drawn	C
dream	dreamp, dreampt	dreamed	CD
drink	drank 2, drunk 12	drank 2, drunk 7	A
	drink	drank, drunk	B
	drinked	drank, drunk	C
drive	driv 8, drived 0, drove 15	driv 0, driven 1, drove 5	A
	driv, druv	driven, drove	B
	driv	druv	CD
drop		drapped	B
	drap		C
drown	drownded	drownded	B
eat	ate 1, eat 51	eat 8, eaten 2	A
	ate, et		D
		eaten, et	CD
fall	fell	fallen 0, fell 6	A
		fellen	D
fetch	fotch, fotched		CD
		fotch, fotched	D
fight	fit 5, fought 10	fit 1, fought 1	A
	faut		C
		foughten	D
fling	flang		C
forget	forgot	forgot 8, forgotten 3	A
forgive	forgave	forgive	B
	forgive	forgave	C

Table 6 (continued)

Verb	*Past-tense form(s)*	*Past-participle form(s)*	*Source*
freeze	froze	friz, froze, frozen	B
	friz		C
get	got	got 111, gotten 1	A
give	gave 7, give 108	gave 2, give 9, given 1	A
	gin	gin	D
go	went	gone 12, went 49	B
grow	grew 8, growed 43	grew 1, growed 28, grown 25	A
hear	heard 44, heared 72	heard 32, heared 24	A
	heard, heared, hearn	heard, heared	B
	heard, heared	hearn	C
heat	heated, het	heated, het	C
help	helped 30, holp 7, holped 6	helped 1	A
	hept, holp, holped	holp, holped	B
		holpen	C
hide	hid	hid 6, hidden 0	A
hold	held 20, helt 2	held	A
		helt	C
		holden	D
hunt	hunt		B
hurt	hurted		C
kill	kilt		C
		kilt	B
know	knew 63, knowed 121	knowed 6, known 18	A
lean	leaned, lent	leaned, lent	B
learn	learned, learnt	learned, leart	B
mistake	mistook	mistook	C
overheat		overhet	C
oversee	oversee		B
rake	roke, ruck, rucked, ruke		C
		ruck	D
reach	reached, retch, retched	reached, retch	B
ride	rid 1, rode 9	rode 2	A
	rode	rid	B
ring	rung		BC
rise	riz 2, rose 0		A
run	ran 6, run 25	run 8	A
	riz		D
rive	riv		C
	ran	ran	B
		runned	C
scratch	scrutch		B
scream	screampt		C
see	saw 71, see 3, seed 26, seen 46	saw 13, see 1, seed 2, seen 39	A
send	sont		C
set	sot	set	B
	set	sot	C
shake	shuck	shuck	B
shine	shun		C
sing		sang 2, sung 6	A
sit	sat, sit, sot	sat	B
		sit	C

Table 6 (continued)

Verb	*Past-tense form(s)*	*Past-participle form(s)*	*Source*
skin	skinned, skint, skun, skunt	skinned, skun	B
		skin, skint, skunt	C
slink	slunk		CD
snow	snew, snewed		CD
speak	spoke	spoke 5, spoken 0	A
spoil	spoilt		BC
spring	sprung		B
squat	squat		B
squeeze	squez, squoz		CD
stab	stob, stobbed		B
stall	stallded		C
stay	stay		B
steal		stold	B
		stole	D
strew	strowed		B
strike	strook, struck	strook, struck	B
swear	swore	swore 2, sworn 2	A
sweat	sweat	sweat	B
swell	swole	swelled, swole	B
swim	swimmed, swum		B
take	taked 1, taken 5, took 362	taken 4, took 28	A
	tuck	took, tuck	B
		tooken	C
teach	taught 24, teached 2	taught 3	A
	taught	teached	B
tear	tore	tore 9, torn 4	A
tell	told	tell, told	B
think	thought, thunk	thought	C
throw	threw 2, throwed 19	threw 0, throwed 4	A
touch	totch, touched	touched	B
wake		woked	B
	woked	woked	C
wave	wove	wove	B
wear	wore	wore 5, worn 0	A
weave		wove	B
weed	wed	wed	C
wrap	wrop		B
	wropped, wropt	wropped	C
write	wrote	written 9, wrote 4	A
	writ	writ	C
yell	yelded, yelt		C

The numbers listed in the two middle columns indicate the frequency of each form in the Corpus of Smoky Mountain English where variation occurs there. The items listed in the "Source" column are listed under "Sources" near the beginning of this "Grammar and Syntax" section.

come, come, come
eat, eat, eat
give, give, give
run, run, run

4.2.5 Regular verbs that have lost their *-ed* suffix (perhaps by analogy with *put/put/put*, etc.) include *hunt* and *squat*.

We *hunt* one night up on Scratch Britches Mountain and dark come along.
They moved out and come on up here and *squat* up there in Gatlinburg.

5 The Verb *Be*

5.1 Inflected Forms of *Be* in the Present Tense Indicative. There are no instances of *we is* or *you is* in the sources, and only one of *I's* (contraction of I + *is*, in "I's diggin' seng right now"). Thus, of inflected forms in the present tense, only those in the third person require discussion. In the third-person singular, *are* occurs occasionally in existential clauses with a singular subject:

They *are* another one down the street.
It seems like they used to be more water in the streams than they *are* now.

In the third-person plural, variation between *are* and *is* follows the subject-type rule discussed for other verbs (§4.1).

The bears *is* getting very gentle.
The rocks *is* still there yet.

With the expletive *there* (commonly pronounced *they*), *is* or *'s* generally prevails whether the following subject of the clause is singular or plural:

There's lots of mountains.
They's about six or seven guitar players here.

5.2 Uninflected *Be*. Although frequently employed by writers of fiction set in the mountains, finite, uninflected *be* in main clauses has been obsolescent in Smokies speech since the early twentieth century, if not earlier. It was not observed by Joseph Hall in the 1930s or later. When it occurs, *be* does not express habitual or repeated actions as in African American English. It is found most often in subordinate clauses introduced by *if*, *until*, or *whether*, contexts that are historically subjunctive.

If it *be* barn-cured tobacco, you have a different thing.
He would . . . leave [the tobacco] until it *be* so hard when it would come out it would never get dry and crum[b]ley.
. . . whether it *be* just providing materials so that you wouldn't have to ship cargo from way off.

Finite *be* also occurs in main clauses, regardless of the number and person of the subject.

Many *be* the time . . .
Them *be* all right to ride in, but you'll find out they ain't good to hike in.

Table 7 Inflected forms of *be* in the present tense indicative

Singular	Plural
am, 'm, 's (once)	are
are	are
is, are	are, is

Table 8 Past indicative forms of *be*

Singular	Plural
I was, were	we was, were
you was, were	you was, were
he/she/it was, were	they was, were

I *be* too old for such tomfoolery.
Be you one of the Joneses?

5.3 Past Indicative Forms of *Be*. In traditional Smokies speech, *was* and *were* may be used for either singular or plural, but there is today and has long been a strong preference for *was* in all persons and numbers. The use of *were* in the singular has a historical basis in the dialects of southern England, but its use in the mountains may be due in part to speakers who no longer distinguish between *was* and *were* in the plural and fluctuate between the two in the singular from insecurity.

I stayed there from the time I *were* about fifteen years old.
There *weren't* even a sprig of fire in his place! The fire *were* plumb out.
The moon *were* shining bright.
He *weren't* no hunter neither.

Was occurs frequently with plural subjects of all types:

They come from Ireland. They *was* Scot Irish.
You had to work the roads six days a [year] after you *was* twenty-one years old.
We *was* poor folks and hired out [to] get enough money to buy cloth to make me a dress.
The older people *was* inclined that way.

Was is occasionally contracted with I to form *I's* or with *they* or *there* in existential clauses.

I knowed *I's* a new duck.
They's two coons up the tree. We shot them out.

5.4 Negative Forms. In negative clauses contracted forms of *am*, *is*, and *are* are the norm in SME, but patterns with negation vary from general usage in several ways. The verb form may contract with either the subject ("He's not") or with *n't* ("He isn't"; see §11.6). In all persons and numbers *ain't* is a common alternative to forms of *be* in the present tense. *Hain't* also occurs, especially but not exclusively at the beginning of a clause.

With ten brothers and sisters, he *ain't* a gonna get lonesome.
It *ain't* half as big as it used to be.
Hain't no use to tell you anything about my sickness, Dr. Abels. I *ain't* got no money.
They *hain't* a-going to do that.

To negate a verb, *don't* is occasionally added to *be*, especially in an imperative clause with a following progressive verb form.

Don't be a-takin' it down till I tell you a little.
Don't be wearing your good clothes out to play in.

6 The Verb *Have*

6.1 Inflected forms of *have* in the present tense parallel those of *be*. *Have* occurs in the third-person singular, but rarely and apparently only in existential clauses.

They'*ve* been a big change.

In the third-person plural, variation between *have* and *has* follows the same variable subject-type rule for other verbs (§4.1) and for *be* (§5.1). *Has* is often used with plural nouns, but not with *they*.

The young folks *has* left that place.
They actually *have* folks here . . . some of them *has* their grandmother and grandfather.

6.2 Perfective Uses. In Smokies speech *has been* frequently occurs with adverbials that take the simple past tense in general usage, especially phrases that include the form *ago*.

It'*s been* twenty year ago they offered me a house and land.
This *has been* along back just a few years ago, before the park took over the Hazel Creek boundary . . .
That'*s been* a way back yonder.
It'*s been* a good while back, because I read it.

In the Smokies *have* and *had* are sometimes separated from their past participle by a direct object.

After we *had* all our work *done* up and *eaten* a good camp supper, I told Mark let's organize for the hunt tomorrow.

6.3 Infinitives after *Have*: see §10.3.

6.4 Negative Forms. In negative contexts *have* and *has* may be contracted to their subject. Alternatively, a contracted *not* may be attached to the verb form ("She's not" or "She *hasn't*"; see §11.6). In all persons and numbers *ain't* is a common alternative for *have* in the present tense, and it occasionally occurs in the past tense. Especially, but not exclusively, at the beginning of a clause the variant *hain't* sometimes occurs.

It'*s not* been very lucky to get railroads there.
You'*ve not* met him, I don't guess.
I *ain't* seen nothin' of him.
It *ain't* been long ago.
They *hain't* found it yet.
Hain't nobody never set it for any bears since; that's been thirty years ago.

6.5 Deletion and Addition of *Have*. Auxiliary *have* and *had* are sometimes elided in Smokies speech, especially before *been* or between a modal verb and a past participle. This pattern is based in part on phonology. See also §8.2.

[Q: How you getting along now?]: A: I ø been a-farmin' a little along.
I was done supposed to ø been there.
You ought to ø seen us all a-jumping and running.
He must've died in the forties. It must ø been forties whenever he died.
You wouldn't ø ever thought about kids a-comin' out of them hollers and hills.

Have of '*ve* may occur as a superfluous form in conditional clauses (perhaps by analogy with *would*).

Had that not *have* happened, there would have been somebody come in here with a lot of money.
I wish I had'*ve* kept all my old books

7 Other Verb Features

7.1 Progressive forms are frequently employed for stative verbs of mental activity, especially *want*, in the process giving the verbs a dynamic interpretation.

Was you *wantin'* to go to town?
That's not what I was *a-wantin'* to hear.
We was *liking* you just fine.

Present participles frequently take the prefix *a-* (see §9).

7.2 Perfective Aspect. To express completed action, sometimes to stress that completion, *did* or *done* is often used. In negative clauses *did* usually occurs with an infinitive form and with *n't* (as in general English), but sometimes with *never* (thus, "I *never did* see" = "I have never seen" or "I never saw"). The emphasis of such constructions is shown by the stress placed on both *never* and *did*, sometimes also with the following verb and other verb phrase elements.

I *never did see* Grandma do any work of any kind.
I *never did know* what caused it.
I *never did live* in a place where they was no meetings or no singings.

Auxiliary *done* expresses completion and is roughly equivalent to "already," "completely," or both. It most often precedes a past participle and may be accompanied by a form of *have* or *be*. Occasionally it is followed by an adjective, an adverbial, by *and*, or by a past-tense verb.

I already *done* seed three.
We stayed there till the bears *done* eat all the honey.
He got a job there hewing cross-ties for that railroad, as I've *done* said.
We thought pa and ma had *done* gone to church.
Herdin' was *done* stopped before the park come in.
The older ones was *done* through school and married.

Uncle John Mingus was *done* dead.
She's *done* and brought her second calf.

7.3 Ingressive or Inchoative Verbs. The beginning of an action or an action just begun may be expressed by any of several constructions involving a verb followed by an infinitive or verbal noun. While these are generally equivalent to "begin" or "start," they may vary in their nuances, some indicating one action followed immediately by another. Some are no doubt pleonastic, but others make action more graphic and vivid and are commonly used in storytelling.

begin to + verbal noun: Then next day everybody *begin to* wondering what caused the blast to go off.
break to + infinitive: It was a bear a-coming, and so he *broke to* run.
come on to + infinitive: I went in the house when it *come on to* rain.
commence to + infinitive: I *commenced to* train a yoke of oxen.
commence to + verbal noun: He went back up to the tree and *commenced to* barking.
fall in to + verbal noun: Mr. Huff said to me, "Wiley, *fall in to* eating and eat plenty, for you boys may haf to stay out all night."
fall to + verbal noun: I *fell to* shooting [the bear] and shot him ten times then before I killed him.
get + verbal noun: He said them men *got* hollering at him, and he give them a pumpkin.
get to + verbal noun: They *got to* deviling us about sparking. Later on the Indians *got to* burying their dead east to west.
go + verbal noun: He'd just get a little out of his bottle and just *go* putting that on there.
go in to + verbal noun: We just broke to it as quick as we could, and all *went in to* skinning that bear.
go to + verbal noun: One night he heard that hog *go to* squealing and hollering.
let in to + verbal noun: Then he *let in to* fussing at me because I let her go over there to spend two weeks with Amy.
set in to + verbal noun: Hit *set in to* raining about dark.
start in + verbal noun: Brother Franklin *started in* telling stories.
start in to + infinitive: I got so I *started in to* read it by heart.
start in to + verbal noun: So we *started in to* fishing near the Chimney Tops.
start off to + verbal noun: They *started off to* hunting.
start to + verbal noun: Then we'd all *start to* shelling [the corn].
take + verbal noun: He made a dive at my brother Richard, and he *took* running off.
take to + verbal noun: I was hoein' my field beans when somebody *tuck to* shootin' over in the pine patch.

7.4 Historical Present. In the recounting past events, especially in narrative style, a speaker may vicariously shift closer to the action by adding *-s*, usually to *say*.

They *comes* back and Scott *says* he was a-coming over to their house when Lester come back.
She turned over against the wall and she *says*, "Lord, let me live."
I *thinks* to myself I'll just slide down there and see if he'd make me holler.
So she *gets* up and started to go around the house to look for him to tell him what she thought.

8 Modal and Semimodal Auxiliary Verbs

8.1 Modal Verbs. Except for *mought*, an obsolescent variant of *might*[7] ("They *mought* have done it"; "That *mought* be what makes them so sour"), modal auxiliaries in Smokies speech differ from general usage only in usage, not in form. As in other southern varieties of American English, *might* or sometimes *may* (rarely another modal) may combine with another modal to express possibility or condition on one hand and indirectness (and thus politeness) on the other. These "double modals" tend to occur in certain types of face-to-face interactions, when one person is proposing or arranging something with another.

One of them *might could* tell a man where her grave is at.
If you give me thirty minutes, I *mighta coulda* thought of some names.
We finally decided we *might ought to* stop and ask at a service station.
I *might can* go with you tomorrow.
They say I *could might* have lived to make it to the hospital.
Used to can combine with a modal verb or another auxiliary.
The drummers *would used to* come from Morristown.
You *used to could* look from Grandpa's door to the graveyard and the church house where we attended church.
We *used to didn't* have nearly so many houses.
The children *used to would* kind of stay in the background.

8.2 Semi-auxiliary Verbs. In the Smokies several phrases occur in a fixed position before a verb and modify the principal action or statement of the verb. These include older forms such as *liked to* and such American innovations as *fixing to*. Some phrases can be inflected for tense, but others are more adverbial in their properties.

belong to "*to be obligated or accustomed to, deserve*":

That train don't *belong to* come till 12:15.
He *belongs to* come here today.

fix to/fixing to "*to prepare or get ready to, be about to, intend to*":

The base form of the phrase (*fix to*) is the source for the progressive, but it has become recessive, while the latter has achieved wide currency in the Smokies and throughout the southern United States.

I *fixed to* stay a week to bear hunt.
Better *fix to* come with us.
I'm *fixing to* leave now.
He looked around and he saw a large panther a-laying on a log *fixing to* jump on him.
It was *a-fixin' to* come a storm.

like(d) to *"almost, nearly" (originally* had liked to *or* was like to *followed by an infinitive form, often* have*)*

In Smokies speech today there is usually no evidence of a following *have* and often only the vestige *'d* of a preceding *had*. The final consonant of *liked* is normally elided with the following *to*.

He'd *like to* tuck a hard fit. (= He almost had a violent fit of anger.)
I *like to* have bled to death.
I stayed in the tree all night and *liked to* froze to death.
I *like to* never in the world got away.
He was the mayor the year they *like to* went broke down there.

need *(followed by a past-participle form)*

They started before sunup and worked to after sundown, if you had a job that *needed* finished.
There were men and women living in the Sugarlands with talent and the ability to do most anything *needed* done in the community.
That thing *needs* washed.
He'd bring that old jack that needed shoed, you know, and he was hard to shoe.

up and *"suddenly, immediately"*

They didn't *up and* take me and run to the doctor.
I got to thinking maybe she didn't know it, so I *upped and* told her that night.

used to *"formerly" (in combination with* could, did, would, *etc.): see* §8.1.

9 *a*-Prefixing

A prominent feature of traditional Appalachian English is the prefixing of *a*-, especially on present participles of verbs. Historically this form usually derived from the preposition *an* or *on*. Today the prefix is only a relic without meaning of its own, but it may lend a slight dramatic effect in storytelling, which it may occur in a series. The prefix is also well-known in ballad lyrics.

It just took somebody all the time *a*-working, *a*-keeping that, because it was *a*-boiling.
I got out there in the creek, and I went to slipping and *a*-falling and *a*-pitching.

The prefix occurs on verbs of all semantic and most structural types, as on compound verbs and on verbs in the middle voice (i.e., active verbs whose subjects receive the action).

Way back I guess forty year ago, there was a crowd of us going up Deep Creek *a*-deer driving.
People will up with their guns and go out *a*-rabbit hunting, *a*-bird hunting.
. . . while supper was *a*-fixing.
Something happened to the child when he was *a*-borning.

Much less often the prefix occurs on a past-tense or past-participle form of a verb (this form of the prefix has a different historical source from the use on present participles).

I just *a*-wondered.
You were *a*-scared of that place.
I would get them [= oxen] *a*-gentled up, and then I put the yoke on them.

The prefix may occasionally appear on a preposition, adverb of time or place, adverb, or adjective (see §14.2).

10 The Infinitive

10.1 *For To.* In Smokies speech an infinitive is sometimes introduced by *for* + *to* when general usage has only *to*. In some cases (especially after *like*) this construction has an intervening noun that functions as the subject of the infinitive. In others the verb introduced by *for to* has the implied subject of the higher clause, in which case it usually expresses a purpose and is equivalent to "in order to."

I'd like *for* you *to* give me help here whenever your time allows.
I sent them up here to serve a warrant on you, and I mean *for* it *to* be served!
I had to pick sang and pick up chestnuts *for to* buy what we had to wear.
Little River got to wanting the cables *for to* take to skid with 'em somewhere.
Doc was the most wealthiest man [in] this part of the country *for to* buy at that time.
They'd turn the sap side up and they'd use that *for to* spread the fruit on.
He's lookin' *for to* quit.

10.2 An apparently recent, American development of the infinitive is its use to express the "specification" or respect in which something is true. This type of infinitive follows certain nouns or adjectives. When it follows an adjective (e.g., "He was *bad to* drink"), the subject of the higher clause expresses as the subject of the infinitive. The use of *bad* and *awful* + infinitive often, but not always, implies unfavorable judgment on the part of the speaker (i.e., that a person spoken of has an unfortunate, excessive, or undesirable habit, inclination, or tendency).

He was awful *bad to* drink. [= He was a hard drinker.]
He was a *bad man to* drink. [= He was a hard drinker.]
[Bears] were *bad to* kill sheep, but not so *bad to* kill the hogs.
She was the *worst* I've ever seen *to* tell stories.
He's *awful to* tell stories.
The Queen family was all of them *good to* sing.
She's an *awful hand to* fish. [= She's crazy about fishing; she fishes a lot.]
He was no *hand to* hunt. [= He didn't like to hunt, he was a poor hunter.]

10.3 Infinitives with *Have*. An overt infinitive with *to* can follow *have* and its direct object, to express either causation or the occurrence or experiencing of a process or condition.

They'd make sassafras tea, you know, and *have* us *to* drink it.
He *had* my uncle *to* make a road.

I'd *have* my mustache *to* freeze till I couldn't hardly git my breath.
We *had* a little white dog *to* go mad.

10.4 Elliptical Infinitives. *Want* is often followed by a preposition and has an elliptical infinitive, as *want* (to get, go) *in*, *want* (to be) *out*.

All I *wanted out* of it was a little bucket of honey.
That dog doesn't know whether he *wants in* or *out*.

11 Negation

11.1 Multiple Negation. The negative markers *never*, *no*, and *not*/*n't* may occur in the same clause with other negative forms (*none*, *nary*, *nothing*, etc.) or followed by other words of negative value such as *hardly* in the same clause. Redundant negation is natural in English; it has roots in Old English and is found in every stage of the language and in all vernacular varieties.

They *ain't* a-bitin' to do *no* good.
I've *not never* heared of that
I *hain't* seen *nothing* of him.
Did he *not* get *none* of it?
Hit didn't scare me *nary* a speck *nor* a spark.
The snow *never hardly* got off the ground.
They [= there] *wasn't hardly* any at all.

11.2 Negative Concord. Smokies speech generally follows the rule of negative concord, whereby all indefinite elements in a clause with *not* or *never* conform in being negative.

We *didn't* have *no* use for it *noways*.
We *ain't* starvin' *none*.
There's an old house up here, but *don't nobody* live in it, *not noway*.
They *wasn't never nobody* moved back down there.
None of us *wasn't* real singers *nor nothin'* like that.
He *wouldn't never* charge *nobody* a dime for *nothing* like that.

However, there are occasional exceptions to this pattern:

I *never* did go *hardly any*.
I *never* did see Grandma do *any* work of *any* kind.
We *ain't* got *any* mill at all in there any more except a little hand mill.

11.3 *Never*. Smoky Mountain English uses *never* in two ways differing from general usage. First, the form can negate a past-tense verb referring to a single event or an event with a definite stopping point. Thus, *never saw* and *never seen* are equivalent to "didn't see," and Smokies speech has an alternative to the general English pattern of inserting *did* to negate a verb in the simple past tense, for a one-time, punctual event.

We *never* seen it then.
I *never* saw him while he lived.
[We thought] we'd a got all of them [= the bears], but we *never* done it.
She *never* died then.

In another pattern, *never* is followed by *did* and the base form of a verb. Thus, *never did see* is equivalent to "didn't ever see," "never saw," or "have/had never seen."

I *never did* live in a place where they was no meetin's nor singin's.
I *never did* see Grandma do any work of any kind.
I *never did* know what caused it.

11.4 As in general usage, *nor* follows *neither* in correlative constructions (*neither . . . nor*), but in SME it also occurs without *neither*. *Nor* may conjoin clauses and be equivalent to "and." In these cases *nor* more often than not follows *not* or *n't* and can be seen as adhering to negative concord.

Lightning *nor* thunder *nor* a good sousing *nor* anything else didn't keep him from going.
I didn't take any toll off any orphans *nor* widows.
I didn't ask him when to go *nor* where to go *nor* nothing.
She won't bother me, *nor* she won't bother anybody else.

11.5 Negative Inversion. A negated verb form such as *don't*, *didn't*, *ain't*, *hain't*, or *can't* may invert with the subject of a clause (see also §18.3).

There's an old house up here, but *don't nobody* live in it.
Didn't nobody up in there in Greenbrier know nothin' about it till they run up on it.
Ain't nary one of 'em married.
Hain't nobody never set [the trap] for any bears since.
The house is so far up in the hills that when me and my old woman fuss, *can't* nobody hear us.

11.6 Contraction with *Not*. In Smokies English a form of *be* or *have* or modal verb *will* or *would* may contract with its subject (more often with a pronoun than a noun), preserving the full form of *not*. Thus, *that's not* varies with *that isn't*, and so on.

That's *not* a cow brute's skull. That's a human skull.
There's *not* near so many as [there] were at the time we came here.
Now my memory's *not* as good as it used to be.
No, they said, that's *not* a bear. It's a wildcat.
I've *not* tasted of it yet.
You've *not* met him, I don't guess.
I'd *not* yet learned how wary those fish were.
We've *not* had a warm enough winter this year.
I'll *not* say that I'm going to buck it.
I'd *not* care to drive a car.

12 Direct and Indirect Objects

12.1 Where general American speech prefers the reflexive pronoun forms when an indirect object is coreferential with the subject of its clause, Smokies speech often uses simple personal pronoun forms. In these cases, the pronouns tend to be redundant.

I got *me* a little arithmetic and learned the multiplication table.

I got *me* a stick and was about to kill them [= black snakes], get shed of them.
I had got big enough to trade *me* in two or three pistols.
You can catch *you* a mole.
He put *him* a turnip hull on the end of his rifle gun so that he could see the darkness of the bear.
He wouldn't eat but two messes out of a big'un and then kill *him* another'n.
Well, they'd get *them* a preacher and let him preach a while. Then they'd change and get *them* another.

12.2 The pleonastic "accusative of inner object" occurs with a wider variety of verb than in general usage.

A man that ground-hogs *it* is a man that cain't help hisself.
I guess you fellers are behavin' *it* all right, aren't you?
They tried to run *it* over him.
John Lewis Moore's boy can pick *it* on the guitar.

13 Adverbs and Adverbials

13.1 The suffix *-s* may be added to some adverbs of place and time in Smoky Mountain English.

I don't imagine it was any worse than *anywheres* else in the mountains.
We learned we had to call him a long time *beforehands*.
They keep all over that mountain *everywheres* up there.
I get close around four hundred dollars a month, and it don't go *nowheres*.
They'd pull [the trains] in and take track up and put it *somewheres* else.

13.2 Adverbs (principally ones of manner or degree) without the suffix *-ly* are common in Smokies speech.

a *awful* ill teacher [= a very bad-tempered teacher]
I think it was a lady, if I'm not *bad* fooled.
There's not *near* so many as were at the time we came here.
We would hike the mountains ten or fifteen miles a day, searching *careful* as we went.
I have been *powerful* bothered for several days.
They don't like it *real* genuine. [i.e., very much]
Some of that country is *terrible* rough.
My family done *tolerable* well.

By the same token, *good* is a variant of *well* in adverbial contexts:

He knows [the song] *good*.
She could pull a crosscut [saw] as *good* as a boy.

Best, the superlative form of the adverb *good*, may take the definite article.

I've enjoyed it *the best* so far. (= very much)
I always thought they got along *the best*.

13.3 Intensifying Adverbs. Smokies speech has many adverbs to express "very" or "extremely." In his investigations Hall found that the force of *very* had apparently weakened—that is, "I'm very well" was reported to mean "I am fairly well"—and this semantic process may account in part for the numerous alternatives that occur.

Me and my brother went a-coon-huntin', but we never done *any* much good.
We had a *awful* rough, bad winter years ago.
That water isn't *bad* cold.
Newport's a *mighty* fine place for a young man to go.
Is that road *much* steep?
They said he never was *much* stout after that.
I used to trap for 'em, [but] never got so *powerful* many.
He was *right* young. He was just a boy.
It's a *terrible* bad place.

Smokies speech also has many ways to express "all the way" or "completely."

The bullet went *clean* through his leg.
My cattle run *clear* to Silers Bald.
Uncle John Mingus was *done* dead.
They was *plumb* sour, and they would keep *plumb* on till spring.
They owned all this, *plumb* up to the gap.
I'll be covered *slam* up.
We worked till *slap* dark.
He was *smack* drunk.

13.4 Locative Adverbs. Smokies English has many constructions not found in general usage to indicate position, distance, or direction. These are most often employed as adverbs, but some may also function as adjectives to modify nouns.

thataway "that way": When you're coming down *thataway*, they ain't many places to stop.
thisaway "this way": I'll go around down *thisaway* below him, and you go down in on him; I was a-laying on the bank watching them bees just out *thisaway* from where the mud hole was.
yon/yan "over there": I says, "Yon's the White Caps now"; She's in the field, up *yan*, gittin' roughness.
yonder/yander "over there": They was some trees that stood all up here and *yonder* about in the orchard; I sneaked up in here with a horse from down *yander* where I showed you mine.

13.5 Other adverbs differing from general American English include the following.

afore "before": I done what you told me *afore*, and it holp me some.
along (followed by a prepositional phrase) "approximately, somewhere, sometime": *Along* in nineteen and thirty-three I went into a southern [CCC] camp; He had two brothers that was hid *along* down on the road that they had to go.
along "continuously, steadily, regularly": We'd kill game *along*

all the time; [He] probably might have sold a few apples *along*.

anymore "nowadays, at present" (in positive sentences): *Anymore*, of course, they use more or less sugar in the mash; Things changes so much *anymore*.

anymore (in negative clauses) "again, from then on": He never remarried *anymore*.

anyways "to any degree or extent, at all": Well, if you was *anyways* near to a bear, he would charge you.

anyways "in any case, at any rate": Sometimes you would get more and sometimes less, but *anyways* from ten to fifteen dollars.

edgeways "edgewise": Let's leave time for people to get a word in *edgeways*. [similarly, *lengthways* "lengthwise"]

everly "always": He was *everly* going down to the store.

noways "in any way, at all": We didn't have no use for it *noways*.

right "immediately, exactly": You find that *right* today.

sometime "sometimes, from time to time": *Sometime* it takes about a couple of minutes for 'em to come up.

someway "somehow, in some manner": *Someway* Martha rolled a big rock loose, and it hit our big hog.

used to "formerly" (placed before the subject of a clause having a past-tense verb): *Used to* we didn't have as many cars around as we do nowadays; *Used to*, you know, there wasn't very much working on Sundays.

13.6 Miscellaneous Adverbial Features. In the Smokies *ago* often occurs with a present-perfect verb rather than one in the simple past (see §6.2). *Yet* retains its usage from older English in affirmative clauses (rather than, as in modern English, in only negative, conditional, or interrogative contexts). It is roughly equivalent to, but sometimes co-occurs with, *still*, in which case *still* always precedes *yet*.

The rocks is *still* there *yet*.
I have got the old collar up there *yet* that I used on him.
Some people *still* might use the signs *yet*.
I believe that old good book will do to live by *yet*.

13.7 Adverb Placement. The qualifying adverbs *about*, *much*, *mostly*, and *nearly* sometimes come after the construction they modify.

We had all kinds of apples anywhere you went *about*. [i.e., almost anywhere]
Well, they were all kinfolks *just about*, you see. [i.e., nearly all]
You been sleepin' all day *near about*, and you done broke a sweat, and that's good for you.
The weather never got any colder up there *much* than it did here.
They didn't have anything *much* to doctor with. [i.e., much of anything]
They'd set fires every fall *mostly*.
They'd all moved out *nearly* when I got big enough to recollect anything.
I'm always at home *nearly*.

14 Prepositions and Particles

The dialectal character of Smokies speech is conspicuous in the use of prepositions.

14.1 Prepositions with Verbs of Sensation and Mental Activity. Hall found that traditional speakers sometimes used *of* after verbs of sensation (*smell*, *feel*, and *taste*) and mental activity (*fear*, *recollect*, *remember*), but the preposition added little if any semantic nuance.

Feel *of* it now.
Smell *of* it.
He said he tasted *of* everything he had ever killed, every varment, even a buzzard.
I ain't a-fearin' *of* this man, nor no man that walks on two laigs.
I can recollect *of* him a-going to school.
I can remember *of* seeing the soldiers at the close of the Civil War.

14.2 Prepositions Differing from General Usage. *a-* (historically a reduction of the preposition *on*, this is attached to a variety of forms in Smokies English as an empty, redundant prefix):

present-participle forms of verbs (§9): a-going, *etc.*

past-tense and past-participle forms of verbs (§9).

prepositions: aback, anear, anext, anigh, apast, atoward(s), *etc.*:

I'll shoot if he comes *a-nigh* me.
Just *apast* the river there they made a bend in the mountain . . .
And the bear, it made a pass *a-toward* him.

nouns, especially to form adverbs or adverbial phrases of time, place, or manner:

I went back down *a-Sunday*.
It was *away* in the night when I got in to camp.
I didn't do it *a-purpose*.

adverbs of position, direction, or manner:

I've often thought how many preachers, as you say, would ride *a-horseback* as far as Gregory did from Cades Cove.
They went ahead there and went to running *a-backwards* and forwards.
He was *a-just* tearing that window open.

adjectives:

Most of my people lived to be up in years, but I had some to die off *a-young*, too.

abouten "about": I never knowed a thing *abouten* it.

afore "before": I allowed he'd return *afore* this.

afteren "after": He never give me his check before, just what was left over.

after'en he had been out with the boys.

against/again "by the time of, before": He'll be in town *against* nine o'clock; He didn't make it back *again* the night.

anent "close to, beside": I fell back into the river and just took up right up in the water and was wet all over and got up *anent* them.

being of "because of": *Bein' of* that, Mr. Hood, I just can't take anything from you for the death of Bill.

beside of "beside": She came over and set *beside of* me. [*of* here represents a reduction of the original phrase *by the side of*]

enduring "during, through": Did he stay *enduring* the night?

excepting "except": Faultin' others don't git you nowhere, *exceptin'* in trouble.

for "because of, on account of": I couldn't see across that log *for* the fog.

fornent "opposite, beside": He lived over *fornent* the store; The bear went up a tree *ferninst* us.

in "within": They was *in* three hundred yards of the top of Smoky.

offen "off, off of": [We] took that hide *offen* it and cut it into four quarter.

on (after a verb to express an unfortunate, unforeseen, or uncontrollable occurrence): When my cow up and died *on* me, hit wuz a main blow.

on "of, about": He was never heard *on* no more.

outen "out of": He frailed the hell *outen* him.

owing to "according to, depending on": It's *owing to* who you're talking to, of course.

till "to" (in expressions of time): . . . quarter *till* five.

to "at": Clay said he's afraid I'd be rotten spoiled did he get me everything all *to* once; I belong *to* home with your Ma.

to "for": That bear was small *to* his age.

to "in": Ever' bone [of a man's body allegedly murdered] was *to* its place but one.

to "of": He was a brother *to* my grandpa Whaley; They were men *to* the community.

withouten "without": I seed him throw a steer once and tie him up *withouten* any help.

14.3 Prepositions and Particles in Dialectal Phrases and Idioms. Smokies English uses prepositions in numerous ways that differ from general English.

14.3.1 With verbs (to form phrasal verbs):

cut down/off/on/up "turn down/off/on/up"

give out "announce": They *give* it *out* that there would be some preachin'.

lay off "plan for a considerable time": I *laid off* and *laid off* to visit Aunt Phoebe, but never got around to it.

leave out "depart": Moonshining is just about *left out*.

listen at "listen to": *Listen at* that pack of hounds!

read after "read, read about"; Of a writer [they say], "He's the best I *read after*"; I *read after* it last week.

study about/on/out/over/up: I hadn't *studied* anything much *about* it; I *studied on* it.

study after "study under, follow after": He never went to college. He just *studied after* Dr. Massey.

throw off on "belittle, disparage": She was *throwing off on* me.

top out "come to the top of [a ridge or mountain]"; I went on and *topped out* at the Bear Pen.

14.3.2 With adjectives:

awful to, *bad to* (see §10.2)

stout to "stout for, strong for": Aunt Sis is *stout to* her age.

thick of "thick with": It was *thick of* houses, *thick of* people up there.

14.3.3 With nouns:

book of "book about": I have a *book of* him.

brother to "brother of": Ephraim was a *brother to* John Mingus.

14.4 Particles Extending or Intensifying Verbal Action. In some cases a verbal particle serves less as an intrinsic element of a phrasal verb than it does to intensify or extend the basic action of the verb. For example, in "he topped out" *out* strengthens the idea in the verb and gives it a perfective aspect (i.e., the notion of an action being completed), but it also specifies the meaning to "reach the top of a mountain or ridge." The forms which appear most frequently in such contexts are *up* (as in general American speech), *in*, *on*, *out*, and *down*.

up: The storm scared us *up*; He was all liquored *up*; They've got it [a town] renewed *up*.

in: We dressed the bear and carried him *in* home. [Here *in* has both a durative and perfective force.][8]

on: Well, I'll come *on*; I started *on* up through the jungles.

out: Study it *out* [i.e., think it over] while you are bringing in the water; They *left out* of here. [= They departed]

down: I shot the bear in the mouth and killed him *down*; Quieten *down* a little!

14.5 Combination of Forms. A remarkable characteristic of Smokies speech is the use of two or more locative forms in a single phrase that both introduces a preposition and modifies the action of the preceding verb and thus may be viewed as either a compound preposition or as an adverbial phrase. Most convey physical movement. Rather than being pleonastic, they suggest a speaker's attention to the terrain and the adaptation of the language to the speakers and their environment. A hunter who says, "I started on up through the jungles" means every word he speaks. In saying "started on" he means that he resumed his course after having stopped. He adds *up* to indicate the direction of his progress and *through* because he was proceeding through thickets and woods.

I went right *down in on* him and give him another shot.

The bear run *down under* the mountain.

They was several houses *on up around up on* Mill Creek and *up in there* and *on up next to* Fork of the River back *up in* there.

The dogs was a-fighting the bear right *in under* the top of Smoky, pretty close *up to* the top.

An uncle of mine and a cousin [were] making liquor *in above* my home.

Later on, in a few weeks or months after that, they found a dead pant'er *in across at* the river bluffs down to the end of the Smoky Mountain in there.

Bradburn had a stack [of wheat] just *in behind* the schoolhouse out here at Shoal Creek.

We started wooding there, along not far from Polls Gap and a-going back *in on toward* Heintoga, behind the timber cutting.

It was just down where that road comes around, *on down in below* where that road comes around.

[I] carried two dogs part of the way *out back down to* where I could get to the truck to them.

He turned them loose [and] *down through* the sugar orchard they went *out up across over on* Enloe, back *around to* the big branch, *out across* the head of hit *over on* Three Fork.

There come one [bear] right *up in above* where he lived over there on Catalooch'.

The old tom cat went *up in under* the chair.

14.6 Prepositions are occasionally omitted in Smoky Mountain English, often following another preposition.

Back [in] old times.

He could count [in] Dutch and read Dutch.

She lived several years after his death, and she's buried out [at] Waynesville.

She lives over [at] what they call Corn Pone, Cascades.

14.7 Prepositional Phrases for Habitual Activity. A temporal prepositional phrase with *of* (especially with a singular indefinite noun as the object) indicate regular, frequent, or habitual activity, in one of three patterns.

of a + *singular noun:*

We would gather our apples in *of a day* and peel our apples *of a night* and put them out on a scaffold.

He farmed *of a summertime*, growed a crop of vegetables, corn, potatoes.

We would have singing *of a night* and *of a Sunday*.

He would go up there *of a mornin'* . . . and then come back that evenin'.

We could put anything in that you wanted to *of a winter*.

of the + *singular noun:*

Sometimes I take a nap and then come back *of the evening*.

They don't have no one to rely on *of the night*.

of + *plural noun:*

My grandfather was troubled *of nights* in his sleep with what was called nightmares.

15 Conjunctions

15.1 Uses of Subordinate Conjunctions. Many subordinating conjunctions in the Smokies either do not occur in general American speech or occur with different functions there.

afore "before": That happened *afore* I left the Smoky [i.e., the Smoky Mountains].

against "by the time that, before": We'd oughta do plenty of fishin' *against* the season closes; I was repairin' the tire *agin* you came.

as "than": I'd rather work *as* go to school.

as "that": I don't know *as* they ever took him to a doctor.

as how "that, whether": He reckoned *as how* he would stop by; I don't know *as how* I can finish it today.

being, being as, being that "because, seeing that": We'll try another'n, *being* that'un paid off; *Being as* you weren't at the meeting, you don't get to vote; *Being that* the president was sick, the vice-president adjourned the meeting.

everhow "however": He leased *ever how* many cars he needed.

evern "whenever, if ever": *Evern* you do that, you'll come home and find a cold supper.

everwhen "when": *Everwhen* we got there, Jack reached for his gun.

everwhere "wherever": They had to get their breakfasts, eat, and be in the field or *everwhere* they were working.

how come (see §17.2).

how soon "that . . . soon": I hope *how soon* he comes.

iffen "if": Come into the fire *iffen* you-ones wants to.

lessen "unless": But some of them were awful sully—wouldn't ever talk *lessen* there was need.

like that "like, that": It seems *like that* your best land is the most suitable land to build houses on.

nor "than"; He's a better fiddler *nor* me.

that (redundant after other forms, as in *because that, how that*, etc.; see §15.4)

till "so that, with the result that, to the point that": The bean beetle got so bad *till* we stopped growing [beans] here; He liked it so strong *till* you could slice it.

to where "to the extent that, to the point that": The coons was hung up *to where* they froze up and was alright; I got them *to where* they would mind what I'd say to them.

until "so that, with the result that": I've done this *until* they could take and interpret the pictures.

whenever "of a single event: when, at the moment that": What did they do with you *whenever* you killed that man two or three year ago?

whenever "as soon as, at the earliest point that": *Whenever* you get to Big Catalooch, it's just across the mountain to Caldwell Fork.

whenever "of a process or extended period: throughout or during the time that": My mother, *whenever* she was living, she just told you one time.

whenevern "of a periodic or intermittent event: when": Whenevern it was snowin', you couldn't get half the logs out of that brush.

whenevern "of a one-time event: as soon as": Whenevern we got married, we went on back to Marks Cove.

without "unless": You couldn't cow him [= a dog] *without* you whipped him.

withouten "unless": I won't go *withouten* you do.

15.2 Southern Appalachian English features two types of tenseless clause, both introduced by subordinate conjunctions. One involves the usage of a verbless absolute introduced by *and*, interpretable as having an elliptical form of *be*, being subordinate to a preceding finite clause, and having the sense "what with" or "at a time that." The *OED3* attests this usage, which ultimately has a basis in Irish or Scottish Gaelic, from 1500 and characterizes it as now regional (chiefly Irish English).

They all wore Mother Hubbard dresses, *and* them loose.
That woman is doing too much work, *and* her in a family way.
He would steal the hat off your head, *and* you a-lookin' at him.
Dan Abbott . . . just spoke in there a while ago, *and* all the congregation standing there.
We had nothing to do, only just pick it [= the gun] up and start for home, and Jack naked, all but his britches on.

The second pattern, introduced by *how come*, is discussed in §17.2.

15.3 Omission of Conjunctions in Clauses of Time Sequence. Rather than one being subordinated to another, two clauses sometimes occur consecutively, with no conjunction (especially when one clause has a causal relation to the other).

The first I seed him, he was placin' his feet to jump on me.
I allowed this corn was planted in the new of the moon, it grew so tall.
We didn't make any beans last year, ø hit was so dry.
Hit [= a hog] could eat the guts out of a pumpkin through a hole in the fence, ø its nose is so long.

Ellipsis of a conjunction introducing the complement of a verb occurs after *want*.

Child, I want ø ye should think about it all yer days!
They want ø you should use the hickory on some of them rough boys.

15.4 A redundant *that* is sometimes used after *where*, *what*, and similar combinations to introduce subordinating conjunctions.

Not just *because that* I'm born and raised here, but I'm just telling ye what other people tells me.
Tell us *how that* you would find and get the sheep in.
I don't remember exactly *when that* they started building in White Pine.
He brought him out, down to *where that* they could get him in a car.
Maybe you can explain then *why that* it does do that.

16 Existentials

Existential clauses in Smokies speech display variation from general usage in three principal respects: the form of the introductory existential element (the "expletive"); subject-verb agreement; and the presence of a relative pronoun.

16.1 Forms of the Expletive. Existential clauses are usually introduced by *there* or its related form *they*. Occasionally *it* introduces such clauses, although its existential force cannot always be distinguished from its pronominal one. (See also §18.3.)

They is something bad wrong with her.
I believe *they* is a cemetery there too, ain't *there*?
If you'd have seen what I made it with, *it* would be a lot of people would faint.
They got back there and *it* come a big snowstorm.
There was one bedroom upstairs, wasn't *it*?

16.2 Agreement in Existential Clauses. In the present tense *is* (usually contracted to *'s*) typically occurs with either a singular or plural subject. Likewise, *was* (sometimes contracted to *'s*) occurs in the past tense. Occasionally *are* appears with a singular subject.

They *is* not so many there now.
They *are* another one down the street.
They*'s* all sizes from little'uns to big'uns.
I knowed I*'s* a new duck.

16.3 In existential clauses the relative pronoun is often omitted in a variety of functions, including as the subject of a following verb.

They is six trees ø would have made anybody a good dwelling house.
They is people ø gets lost in these Smoky Mountains.

17 Compound and Complex Sentences

17.1 Indirect yes/no questions sometimes take the word order of direct questions, with inversion of the subject and auxiliary verb and with the tense conforming to that of the main clause.

Somebody asked me was that Jim Ike's truck.
We finally asked would they help us.

17.2 Indirect *wh*-questions usually pattern as in general usage except for a striking construction involving *how come*. As in general American English, the phrase is usually equivalent to "why" (but sometimes "how") and may introduce a clause marked for tense. However, in Smokies speech it may introduce a tenseless clause consisting of a noun or a personal pronoun in the objective case followed by a verbal infinitive. Thus, *that's how come me to fall* is equivalent to "that's how I came to fall" and *how come it* to "how it happened." The sequences *how come me* and *how come it* do not represent simple inversion of *come* with its subject.

I suppose *how come* him to come here.
So that's *how come* this particular branch here in Haywood County to be called Raccoon Creek.
That's *how come* it to be called the Devil's Courthouse.
That's *how come* us to leave there, you know.

17.3 The subject and verb of conditional clauses are sometimes inverted, with the omission of *if*, either by the fronting of an auxiliary verb or by the insertion of a form of *do*.

Could I lay my hands on them, I'd gut them like bantams.
Can we make it through this winter, I'll get the spring crops in the ground for you.

Do we reach the house-place before dark, we'd better get back onto our path.
Did they know who the renegades were, they'd never tell me.

18 Other Patterns

18.1 Postposed *One*. To identify alternatives, Smokies speakers employ not only *or* or *either . . . or*, but three other forms that may be placed after the second of two alternative elements: *either*, *either one*, or simply *one* (the last is the most common) and that may coordinate different parts of speech or types of phrases, most often nouns. Despite formal similarity to the other usages, postposed *one* is most likely derived from the phrase *one or the other*. Related negative constructions that follow conjoined elements include *neither* and *neither one*.

You never had any trouble out of them people, from Big Catalooch or Little Catalooch *either*.
It was just about as steep as a yoke cattle could go up or come down *either one*.
She found out how to get moonshine without making it or buying it *either one*.
He was in Tennessee or Kentucky *one*.
[Boneset is] bitterer than quinine, and hit'll kill ye or cure ye *one*.
I'm going home [and] see Emerts Cove or hell *one* before daylight.
They had [revival] meeting morning and evening or morning and night *one* all the time.
The first settlers come in here in the eighteen-thirties or the -forties *one*.
I was taught to respect elderly people, and we were to refer to them as aunt or uncle *one*, if they were old.
They [= bears] wouldn't run far. They'd set down and climb a tree or pick a fight *one*.
Soon it all died down and they never made mention of Meady nor Burt *neither*.
I didn't think about Eloyd nor Enzor *neither one* to be there.

18.2 Left Dislocation. Often a noun or noun phrase is moved from its usual position to the beginning (or "leftmost" position) of a clause, to be replaced by a simple personal pronoun in the original position.

Mister Wilson Queen that lived there at the campground, he was a song leader when I was a little girl.
Miss Hathaway, that lives here now in Gatlinburg, she taught the older children up there when I went to school.
The [hunters] that went the other way into the mountain, they'd killed them turkeys.

18.3 Interposed Pronouns. An indefinite pronoun or pronoun phrase coreferential with the subject of a clause may appear in the verb phrase, after a form of *be* or *do* or after a modal auxiliary verb.

The Queen family was *all of them* good to sing.
We don't *any of us* need anything.
They were *both of them* in the first religious organization that was ever held in Cades Cove.
They can *every one* sing.
They may *ever' one of them* be down [= sick] up there.
They wouldn't *nary one of them* go.
We don't *nobody* know how long we have.

A similar pattern involves the adverbial phrase *all the time*:

We're *all the time* going around saying, "I didn't understand you."
They was *all the time* arguing over who was the best candidate.

Sometimes the interposed pronoun phrase appears in an existential sentence, a pattern that may be the basis of clauses with negative inversion (§11.5).

They didn't *none of us* ever get snakebit, but their work animal did.
They'd *some* go to the stands, you know, and generally two of us drove all the time.
There'd *somebody* come around with a truck once in a while.
They was *some of them* higher than others.

19 Prefixes and Suffixes

Two prefixes and a number of suffixes in Smoky Mountain speech are of interest.

19.1 Prefixes

a- *(on verbs, see §9, §14.2).*

un-, on-, in-. *The prefixes* un- *(also* on- *in traditional speech) and* in- *are sometimes interchangeable:* inusual/unusual; inconvenient/unconvenient; impossible/unpossible.

19.2 Suffixes

-ed excrescent or pleonastic on verbs: *drownded*, *gallded*, *tosted*.
-ed to form the past-tense and past-participle of verbs: *blowed*, *drawed*, *growed*, *knowed*, *teached*, *throwed*. See also §4.2.3.
-en redundantly on prepositions and subordinate conjunctions: *abouten*, *iffen*, *withouten*.
-en (alteration of *of*) to form prepositions: *offen*, *outen*.
-en on adjectives to form verbs: *hotten* "to heat."
-en redundantly on verb past participles: *bloodshotten*.
-er to make regularized comparative forms: *gooder*.
-er redundantly on comparative forms: *worser*.
-er redundantly on adjectives modified by *more*: I was getting closer and *more closer* with every step I took.
-es to form the plural of nouns ending in *-sp*, *-st*, or *-sk*: *beastes*, *deskes*, *postes*, *waspes*, etc.
-es to nouns after excrescent -t to form syllabic plurals: *clastes*, *dostes*.
-es redundantly to form double plurals: *folkses*.
-es to form the third-person singular of verbs: *costes*.
-est to form superlatives of words of two or more syllables, especially -ing participles: *aggravatingest*, *bear huntingest*, *beatingest*, *cheatingest*, etc.

-est to form redundant superlatives: *firstest, bestest.*

-est redundantly on adjectives modified by *most*: *most wealthiest*, etc.

-ified on nouns and adjectives to form adjectives: *fightified, fitified, girlified, prettified, talkified, townified.*

-ify on verbs redundantly or on nouns to form verbs: *argufy, blamify, speechify.*

-like on adjectives and adverbs: *careful-like, careless-like, easy-like, fresh-like, sudden-like.*

-like on nouns and pronouns: *baker like, such-like, young man like.*

-s on verbs to indicate vicarious action in the past (especially with *say*). See §7.4.

-s on verbs to indicate agreement with a third-person plural noun subject. See §4.1.

-s on adverbs of place and time: *anywheres, beforehands, everywheres, somewheres.*

-some on adjectives: *darksome, gladsome.*

-some to form adjectives from verbs: *blundersome, boresome, troublesome.*

-y to form adjectives from verbs: *costy, haunty, jolty, lasty, resty, scary, yieldy.*

-y redundantly on adjectives: *fainty, floweredy, jaggedy, mingledy, raggedy, ramshacklety, shackledty, stripedy.*

-y to form adjectives from nouns: *strengthy, thickety, twisty.*

Notes

History of the Dictionary

1. The CCC had twenty-two camps in the Smokies, employing four thousand local men to clear land and build the roads, trails, campgrounds, and other infrastructure that turned the landscape into a national park. This included five hundred miles of hiking trails.

2. It is unclear how many discs Hall recorded; his records indicate different counts.

3. Hall used material from his notebooks and early speech recordings to produce his 1941 Columbia University dissertation. This was published in monograph form as *The Phonetics of Great Smoky Mountain Speech*, American Speech Reprints and Monographs no. 4 (Morningside Heights, NY: King's Crown Press, 1942).

4. These books were published by Cataloochee Press in Asheville, North Carolina, a press that Hall established to give his work local distribution. He published no further work on pronunciation or other technical analysis of Smokies speech after his 1942 monograph on phonetics, primarily because of an early professional adversity. A highly unfavorable, indeed hostile, review in *Language*, the leading linguistics journal of the day, by Raven I. McDavid Jr. (*Language* 19 [1943]: 184–95). McDavid, then at Yale and a proponent of the "more scientific" and "methodologically sound" Linguistic Atlas paradigm of research, had little sympathy for Hall's Columbia-based research and his informal approach to collecting data. History has vindicated Hall's work as more suitable for collecting natural speech and material useful for comparative purposes, but the attack caused Hall to lose faith in the linguistic value of his work. For the remainder of his career he never sought publication by a linguistics journal or press. While he did publish a popular lexicon of phrases and proverbs, *Sayings from Old Smoky* (1972), his fieldwork shifted largely to folklore when he returned to the Smokies after World War II.

5. Hall's contact with native speakers did not cease after his retirement. In later years he frequently phoned or wrote friends in the mountains to keep up with them and to double-check the definitions he was drafting.

6. Hall donated a copy of his note cards to the *Dictionary of American Regional English* for its use and a copy of his recordings, typescripts, and note cards to the American Folklife Center of the Library of Congress for consultation by other scholars. Following his death, his family donated much of his library and his original material to the Archives of Appalachia at East Tennessee State University, where it forms a special collection in his name.

7. Hall's 1960 and 1978 books were compilations of such excerpts.

8. These transcripts, produced by Mary Ruth Chiles, have been deposited in the library of Great Smoky Mountains National Park at the Sugarlands Visitor Center in Gatlinburg, Tennessee. In addition to the early Hall interviews and the Great Smoky Mountains National Park oral history collection, they include interviews by Lloyd Foster on the Walker Valley (1970), Weaver McCracken on mountain logging (1974–75), Mary Lindsay on grassy balds (1976), and Charlotte Pyle on CCC work in the Smokies (1983). Only the Hall and oral history interviews had the original recordings on deposit to consult.

Background and Context of the Dictionary

1. The 2004 *Dictionary of Smoky Mountain English* was the culmination of work that spanned nearly fifteen years and was based around the field notes and publications by Joseph S. Hall. For more information on Hall's works, see the Works Cited lists at the back of this dictionary.

2. Counties in Appalachia, 2020, Appalachian Regional Commission website, https://www.arc.gov/appalachian_region/CountiesinAppalachia.asp.

Scope and Sources of the Dictionary

1. Plants native to southern Appalachia are also found throughout the eastern United States: the varied climate in the region encompasses zones with climatic conditions analogous to those in latitudes ranging from Georgia to southern Canada.

2. Montgomery sometimes altered the punctuation of Hall's citations to give them consistency.

3. Horace Kephart, "The Mountain Dialect," in *Our Southern Highlanders* (New York: Macmillan, 1913), 276–304.

4. Harold Farwell and J. Karl Nicholas, *Smoky Mountain Voices: A Lexicon of Southern Appalachian Speech* (Lexington: University Press of Kentucky, 1993). The scrapbooks form part of the Horace Kephart Collection at the Hunter Library of Western Carolina University, Cullowhee, North Carolina.

5. H. A. Edson and Edith M. Fairchild, "Tennessee Mountains in Word Lists," *Dialect Notes* 1: 370–77.

6. Typical popular glossaries are Paul M. Fink, *Bits of Mountain Speech Gathered between 1910 and 1965 along the Mountains Bordering North Carolina and Tennessee* (Boone, NC: Appalachian Consortium, 1974); and Vic Weals, *Hillbilly Dictionary (Revised): An Edifying Collection of Mountain Expressions* (Gatlinburg, TN: privately printed, c. 1959).

7. Joseph S. Hall, *Mountain Speech in the Great Smokies*, NPS Popular Study Series no. 5 (Washington, DC: US Department of the Interior, National Park Service, 1941), 12.

8. See especially Michael Montgomery, "How Scotch-Irish Is Your English?," *Journal of East Tennessee History* 67 (1995): 1–33; and Michael Montgomery, "The Scotch-Irish Influence on Appalachian English: How Broad? How Deep?," *Ulster and North America: Transatlantic Perspectives on the Scotch-Irish*, ed. Curtis Wood and Tyler Blethen (Tuscaloosa: University of Alabama Press, 1997), 189–212.

9. See Henry Glassie, *Pattern in the Material Folk Culture in the Eastern United States* (Philadelphia: University of Pennsylvania Press, 1968).

10. Paul D. Hamel and Mary Ulmer Chiltoskey, *Cherokee Plants and Their Use* (Sylva, NC: Herald, 1975).

11. This is contrary to what one might think because of numerous Amerindian terms borrowed (and usually modified in form) into American English, e.g., *skunk*, *squash*. The absence of items directly from Cherokee may have resulted from the relative lateness of contact or another reason. On the other hand, Appalachian speech may hold many loan translations, especially in plant names, that can be identified only through careful etymological research by a person bilingual in Cherokee and English, an endeavor beyond the capacity of the editors.

12. Newton's work is an unpublished undergraduate thesis at Maryville College, Maryville, Tennessee.

13. For a number of years Mrs. Simms operated a private museum in Gatlinburg, Tennessee, where she displayed furniture, tools, and other artifacts. She also collected mountain expressions on index cards (see North Callahan, *Smoky Mountain Country* [Sevierville, TN: Smoky Mountain Historical Society, 1952], 222–23, for a brief account). After her death her children sold the Simms collection to the Appalachian Museum at Berea College, where most of it, including the note cards, remained in storage until Montgomery tracked them down in 1994.

14. In his 1972 book and especially in his 1942 published dissertation, Hall often indicated whether a usage was general or was old-fashioned or restricted in some other way. In the latter work he always indicated when he had documentation of only a single instance and could not confirm an item's more general currency.

Grammar and Syntax of Southern Appalachian and Smoky Mountain English

1. This sketch is based in part on an unpublished typescript by Joseph Sargent Hall in the 1950s.

2. Walt Wolfram and Donna Christian's *Appalachian Speech* (Arlington, VA: Center for Applied Linguistics, 1976) is the only other work broadly focusing on the subject. That study is based on interviews conducted in the mid-1970s in southern West Virginia, approximately 150 miles north of the Smokies.

3. All examples are found in the *Dictionary of Smoky Mountain English*, where the reader can identify their source and assess their status.

4. This study, conducted in White Pine, Tennessee, recorded forty natives whose parents or grandparents were born in the Smokies or the foothills of the Smokies. See Michael Montgomery, "A Discourse Analysis of Expository Appalachian English," PhD diss., University of Florida, 1979.

5. For further discussion of this area of grammar, see Michael Montgomery, "A Superlative Complex in Appalachian English," *Southeastern Journal of Linguistics* 23 (1999): 1–14.

6. For the history of this pattern, see Michael Montgomery, "The Evolution of Verb Concord in Scots," in *Studies in Scots and Gaelic: Proceedings of the Third International Conference on the Languages of Scotland*, ed. Alexander Fenton and Donald A. MacDonald, 81–95 (Edinburgh: Canongate Academic, 1994).

7. George O. Curme, *Syntax* (New York: D. C. Heath, 1931).

8. I.e., down the mountainside, out of view.

Dictionary of **Southern Appalachian English**

A

a[1] *indefinite article* (usually [ə]).

1 preceding a word beginning with a vowel sound.

1789 *Big Pigeon Church Minutes* 3 Whearas the times looking very Deficualt in respect of the Indians being so troubelsom and in Case the Church should be Disolv.d under such a unhappy sircumstance the Church Doth heareby impower Abram McKay as Clark of sd Church to give any Ordily Member as Disolv.d A letter of Dismition in behalf of sd. Church. **1813** Hartsell *Memora* 124 we made a Erley Start. **1859** (in **1974** Harris *High Times* 248) The sun aint more nor a our high. **1862** *Reese CW Letters* (Sept 29) I Sent you A lct tcr By hand to Elxander and I wae wating to git A answer from yu. **1862** *Walker CW Letters* (n.d.) lett us be a undevided famely in that Hapy land whear parten will Be nonen on mar and all our trubels may have a end. **1901** Harben *Westerfelt* 2 John Westerfelt has done you exactly as he has many a other gal. **1922** *TN CW Ques* 231 (Knox Co TN) Land sold at one dollar a acar. [**1931** Combs *Lg Sthn High* 1321 *An* is rarely employed, even before a word beginning with a vowel.] **1937** Hall *Coll* Grandfather came here on a ox wagon. [Other examples:] in a oven. There's a old hoss. **1939** Hall *Coll* (Saunook NC) The bear sort of made a ugly fuss, and finally he hollered pretty loud to try to scare the bear away. **1961** *Coe Ridge OHP*-334A Uncle Cal was at a election over there at one time. **1969** GSMNP-44:27 The powder would flash, and then they was a instant before the gun would fire. **1972** *AOHP/ALC*-276 When they got out there, the chickens was in a tree, you know, a apple tree. **1975** GSMNP-59:33 [It] maybe might have been a epidemic of whooping cough or measles or something like that. **1983** *Dark Corner OHP*-4A A old sow, you have to wait till they get up about eight or ten months old before you breed them. **1989** *Matewan OHP*-7 She was a expert on shooting a rifle. **1997** *Dante OHP*-14 I picked up a almanac and a calendar, too.

2 In phrase *a half a* = one-half, half of a.

1862 *Dalton CW Letters* (Feb 21) the orders was giv fall in that the yankeys was right hear we throan on Hour coutrements and fel in And march about a half a mile And forme aline of battle. **1863** *Click CW Letters* (July 17) I got in to the fight a half a hour or such a matter before the boys was taken. **1939** Hall *Coll* (Cataloochee NC) They run [the bear] off I guess for a half a mile before they got up with it and treed it. **1954** GSMNP-19:30b He said, "Get ye about a half a gallon of moonshine and a half a gallon of this mountain honey." **1961** *Coe Ridge OHP*-336B They was a whole load of shots that didn't cover a spot bigger than a half a dollar. **1974** *AOHP/ALC*-802 I never seen a half a dozen [mine inspections] in all my life. **1998** *Dante OHP*-69 They'd put a half a gallon of moonshine up there in that car.

a[2] *auxiliary verb* [Editor's note: The usages below cannot always be distinguished from those at **a- A6**.]

1 reduced form of *have*.

1861 *Hanes CW Letters* (Oct 7) tel Jim that I would A liked mity to a helpt him a shucked his corn but it was so I couldent. **1861** (in **1992** Jackson *Surry Co Soldiers* 258) (Jan 13) I would a went to the doctor and a stayed. **1936** (in **2009** Powell *Shenandoah Letters* 77) He must not a got my letter. **1941** Stuart *Men of Mts* 112 If he'd a-tried to a-come back, he'd be sleepin' in the same place Pa is sleepin'. **c1945** Haun *Hawk's Done* 226 Ma just said, "Cathey's bounden to a-learnt sech from her Ma." **1962** Dykeman *Tall Woman* 15 Could I a-brushed every tangle-bramble and stumble-stone out of your way, I'd have crawled to do it ere this. **1969** GSMNP-28:63 They couldn't a raised their family. **1973** GSMNP-88:5 They like to never a found her. **1989** *Matewan OHP*-33 I had close calls. The good Lord was with me or I'd a done been gone.

2 superfluous syllable, especially after *had* analyzed falsely as *would* when the latter is contracted to *'d*. See also **have B5**.

1813 Hartsell *Memora* 104 I shold [have] shot in aminit if he head not aspoock and shold [have] kiled him without axsedent. **1859** Taliaferro *Fisher's River* 90 The poor 'oman fainted away, and we liked to a nuver a fotched her to. **1862** *Epperly CW Letters* (Aug 2) it would a went hard with me if I had a bin at home but it is a gratedeel worse the way it is. **1864** (in **1976** Lawson *Hammontrees Fight* 117) (May 31) you think that I could not Set up neather would I if I had a beene at my home. **1895** *Mt Baptist Sermon* 14 They haint never aben no time an' place. **1923** Greer-Petrie *Angeline Doin' Society* 3–4 Lum 'lowed if Mis' Seelback had just a-thought to leave the front door onlatched ... we could tip-toe in r'al easy. **1939** Hall *Coll* (Hazel Creek NC) If I'd a knowed you fellows been a-coming and had studied up, why [I] could have give you fellows a whole lot of news. **1971** *AOHP/ALC*-260 I'd a have to wait till the train runned to bring that message back. **1978** Montgomery *White Pine Coll* I-1 VI-1 If they had a been anything said up there, at that time, anything would have got a bunch of folks killed. **1998** *Dante OHP*-48 Lawson If I'd a gone to Kingsport I never would have come back here.

a[3] *transitional syllable* See also **any which way**, **every which away**, **thataway**, **thisaway**, **whichaway**.

1910 Weeks *Barbourville Word List* 457 *that-a, this-a* = that, this: "You should not talk that-a-way." **1989** *Matewan OHP*-9 Someday another you might be able to see it, that if this a-world don't end before that.

a- *preposition/prefix* preceding or attached to various other forms. [Editor's note: Historically such a form as seen in paragraphs **A1–A4** represents a verbal noun developing into a present participle. Now functioning as a prefix, this form slowly developed from the prepositions *on* and *in*; today it is conventionally spelled with a hyphen or as joined solid to the following word, and spellings are grouped together here; some citations may reflect phonotactic processes for rhythmic effect, also exhibited in **a**[3]. See also **of 4** and Grammar and Syntax §9, §14.2.

A Preceding a verb form.

1 The present-participle form of a simple verb, especially in a narrative.

1774 *Dunmore's War* 41 He was informed, before he left Holston, that there was 2 or 3 Indians there a hunting. **1780** Donelson *Journal* (March 2) The same afternoon Reuben Harrison went out a hunting and did not return that night, though many guns were fired to fetch him in. **1798** *Big Pigeon Church Minutes* 31 theare is a report in Circulation that Henry Stiers is apt to drink too Excess and has been a gambeling. **1834** Crockett *Narrative* 159 I determined to get home to them, or die a-trying. **1844** Willnotah Ms 15 he exclaimed to his friends to come and see what that was a going up into the sky. **1862** *Gilley CW Letters* (July 3) we ar in farfax County a persuing the yankes. **1862** *Robinson CW Letters* (Dec 9) thare is a heep of gorgia boys a deserting & going home but not meny out of our Regt. **1863** (in **1992** Heller and Heller *Confederacy* 82) they have bin a fixing a road on the north side of the river like they aim to cross at Rockoon ford and they have bin a marching troops down the river like they was a going to cross at fort roal. **1863** *Warrick CW Letters* (July 26) it gave me much pleasure & satisfaction to here from you but I am sarow to here that you are a ameing to com here. **1864** Wilson *Confederate Private* 37 (March 8) father was a complaining of his fall little yet. **1889** *Cole Letters* 72 I want you all to try and meet me in heaven for I am A going to try and meet Jesus in heaven. **1928** (in **1952** Mathes *Tall Tales* 50) Here's the Good Book a-talkin' tonight, a-talkin' louder than the wind a-roarin' out yander an' the thunder a-poppin'. **1937** Hall *Coll* (Cades Cove TN) He did that just to be a-doin' [said to be a common phrase in the Smokies]. **1939** Hall *Coll* (Little Cataloochee NC) Johnny ran down the hill a-aimin' to go to his uncle's. *Ibid.* (Saunook NC) I went down to the branch where [a bear] had a been a-using. **1955** Ritchie *Singing Family* 243 Her chuffing and screaming like something had give her a mortal wound. Bells a-clanging, men a-hollern, women and children a-screaming, young boys a-laughing. **1956** GSMNP-22:15 It was a copperhead and a blacksnake a-fighting. **1961** *Coe Ridge OHP-333A* They kept on just a-aggravating them. **1964** Williams *Prep Mt Speech* 53 Not always clearly a preposition, however, *a* is sometimes used for what would seem to be rhythmical purposes: "and me a not a-knowin' a thang about it and a nuver a-cyurin' much." **1975–76** Wolfram/Christian *WV Coll* 83 He [= a dog] kept a-begging and a-crying and a-wanting to go out. **1978** Montgomery *White Pine Coll* III-2 It just took somebody all the time a-working, a-keeping that, because it was a-boiling. *Ibid.* V-3 Some had jobs a-carrying it or a-hauling it from the still to where they hid it to sell it later. **1981** Williams *Storytelling* We retain the beautiful Middle English "a-" in front of "-ing" words, so that if we have a string of those "-ing" words separated with the "a-"s, the result is indeed musical, lilting, of excellent aesthetic quality, so that our speech is indeed beautiful, partly because we did things our own stubborn way. **1989** Landry *Smoky Mt Interviews* 194 I got out there in the creek, and I went to slipping and a-falling and a-pitching. **2001** Joslin *Appal Bounty* 218 There's a lot of people from off goes down in those old boats afishing. **2012** *Blind Pig* (Jan 31) To me, there's a big difference between the following sentences: "There's a storm coming" and (more emphatically) "There's a storm a-comin'!" **2012** Milnes *Signs Cures Witchery* He'd see the person that was a-bewitching the other person. *Ibid.* If you don't believe in it, you ain't a-believing the Bible.

[< Middle English *a*, *on* < Old English *on*, *an*; OED3 *a* prep[1] 11 now archaic and regional; DARE *a* prep 5 throughout the U.S. but especially frequent Midland, Southwest, less frequent South, New England]

2 The present-participle form of a compound verb.

1861 (in **1938** Taliaferro *Carolina Humor* 14) When I were a boy, I useter go with daddy a squirrel huntin. **1863** *Warrick CW Letters* (Jan 29) I hope that I will git home beefore long and I shall wann to go a posom hunting. **1864** *Watkins CW Letters* (June 9) Me and Morgan and Edine verner has bin asquierl huntin this morning. **1904–20** Kephart *Notebooks* 4:739 Guess that's somebody a-tooth-brush-huntin'. **1939** Hall *Coll* (Deep Creek NC) Way back I guess forty year ago, there was a crowd of us going up Deep Creek a-deer driving. *Ibid.* (Hazel Creek NC) We went over there a-chestnut hunting and took our women with us, leave them there. **1940** Oakley *Roamin'/Restin'* 22 Traped [sic] in a forest fire one night my older brother and two other boys and I went a-possam hunting. **1959** Hall *Coll* I was about fifteen years old, and I went a-coon huntin'. **1974–75** McCracken *Logging* 5:56 I was a-water jackin' on a section. **1975** *AOHP/ALC-903* We had a truck mine up here, me and some fellows a-gang working. **1978** Montgomery *White Pine Coll* IV-2 People will up with their guns and go out a-rabbit hunting, a-bird hunting. **1984** High *Titan Rock* 35 A lot of us would go a boat riding whenever we took a fancy on those long streams of water. **1989** Landry *Smoky Mt Interviews* 181 Then we might have some leisure and go a-ground hog huntin'. *Ibid.* 194 I never went a-turkey hunting in my life. I never went a-deer hunting in my life. **1992** Seeger *Talking Feet* 43 If they hadn't ever invented the [TV] tube, Fred Moody and myself would still be a-square dancing. **2007** (in **2012** McQuaid *Interface* 269) We go up in West Virginia a lot a-train-riding and stuff.

3 A present-participle form used with passive meaning, especially *borning*.

1928 (in **1952** Mathes *Tall Tales* 55) "Sister Tollett," he began, "if ever'body was a-ponderin' the Book thataway, they'd be souls a-bornin' ever' night." **1940** Still *River of Earth* 237 "If they's pennies needed," he told Uncle Jolly, "that's some in the clock. I got me four a-saving." **1962** Dykeman *Tall Woman* 53 The baby was twenty-four hours a-borning. **1966** West *Dialect Sthn Mts* 32 While supper was a-fixin'. **1995** Montgomery *File* Something happened to the child when he was a-bornin' (85-year-old man, Greenbrier TN).

4 A present participle form followed by redundant *of*. See also **of B**. [Editor's note: Such constructions represent verbal nouns in the process of becoming present participles.]

1858 (in **1974** Harris *High Times* 140) Thar I stood a fixin' of my laigs tu run. **1881** Atkinson *After Moonshiners* 153 About a year ago they bought a still, and have been a runnen of it ever since on our place. **1892** Doak *Wagonauts Abroad* 82 This man's a guyin' of me; and ef he be, he's a dead man. **1913** Combs *KY Highlander* 23 Gentlemen! whenever you see a great big over-grown buck sitting at the mouth of some holler, or at the forks of some road—with a big slouch hat on, a blue collar, a celluloid, artificial rose on his coat lapel, and a banjo strung across his breast, and a-pickin' of Sourwood Mountain, fine that man, gentlemen, fine that man! **1940** Vincent *Us Mt Folks* 14 Now Lord, I ain't a-fearin' of this man, nor no man that walks on two laigs. **1996** Woodring *Times Gone By* 6 He said he took his rifle, and took a drink of liquor, and went on a huntin of em.

[OED3 *a*[1] 11 now archaic and regional]

5 The past-tense form of a verb.

1956 Hall *Coll* (Byrds Creek NC) I just a-wondered. **1969** *Burton-Manning Coll*-93A They's about three of them a-lived in that house. **1973** *AOHP/ASU*-69 There was a old soldier that a-lived here, old man Mac Norris over yonder. **1998** *Dante OHP*-71 He just a-looked at me.

6 The past-participle form of a verb. See also **a**[2], **a-scared.**

1913 Kephart *Our Sthn High* 225 Ike Morgan Pringle's a-been horse-throwed down the clift, and he's in a manner stone dead. **c1940** Padelford *Notes* He's a-treated her mean as pizen. **c1940** Simms *Coll* Well hit now looks as if we'uns air steppin' right into the pages ov history, with all that bein' a-written about us in the papers and magazine-books. **1954** *GSMNP*-19:6 Now they's people gets lost in these Smoky Mountains specially before the park has a-opened up so many bridle trails. **1969** *GSMNP*-46:1 I would get them a-gentled up and then I put the yoke on them. **1972** *AOHP/ALC*-355 They's a few new'uns a-being a-built. **1989** *Matewan OHP*-2 Nitro Hunter was the name of [the shotgun], and I'd a had it a-bored ... out for a sixteen gauge. **1989** *Matewan OHP*-89 I had four [children], and one baby, you know, a-borned dead. **1998** *Dante OHP*-12 They had done a-drove those mines through the mountain and come out on Chaney Creek.

[perhaps ultimately < Middle English *y*- < Old English *ge*- prefix to form past participles, now a relic form in southwestern England; cf OED2 *a*- prep 7 and *a*- particle]

B Preceding a preposition. See **a-back of**, **a-below**, **a-front of**, **a-near**, **a-next**, **a-nigh**, **a-past**, **a-towards.**

C Preceding a noun.

1 See **a-hold**, **a-plenty**.

2 Used in an expression of time such as a date or day of the week.

1790 *Lenoir Papers* a Tuesday Evening I got up to Mr. Davidsons and a Wednesday went to George Davidsons and stayd there tell Friday. **c1841** Shane (in **1998** Perkins *Border Life* 197) We never travelled a Sunday. **1862** *Griffin CW Letters* (March 11) we went out on picket a Sunday night and stood all night in the Rain. **1865** *Larue CW Letters* (Jan 5) you and John ou[gh]t to bin at home a christmas for ther was a grait meny Marrings. **1905** Miles *Spirit of Mts* 51 Anyhow, we'll all go together to the feet-washin' a-Sunday. **1923** Furman *Mothering* 185 Them's the good times I allus seed a-Christmas. **1939** Hall *Coll* (Deep Creek NC) I went back down a-Sunday. *Ibid.* (Little Cataloochee NC) Red, I went a-bear-huntin' onst a Fourth of July. **1957** Broaddus *Vocab Estill Co KY* 1 I got some pretty ones "a Christmas." **1963** Edwards *Gravel* 103 "Well," I said, "if you want me to see Gabe, I will. I'll go a Sunday." **1971** *AOHP/ALC*-33 We'd put one [dress] on on Monday, and we would take and wear hit till Thursday, and then we'd have the other one cleaned to wear a-Friday. **1977** Weals *Cove Folk* Let's go down here a-Monday mornin' and work that crop out. **1978** *Horsetrading* 47 I'll mail that eight dollars a Tuesday and you'll get it a Wednesday. **1995** Harrison *Smoke Rings* 165 "The moon newed a-Saturday" is a hillbilly way of saying there was a new moon the previous Saturday.

[OED3 *a* prep[1] 3a now Eng[lish] regional, Scot[tish], and Irish English]

3 Used to express place or position. See **abed**, **a-horseback.**

4 Used to express manner. See **a-purpose.**

[OED3 *a* prep[1] 9]

D Preceding a predicate adjective. See also **a-loose**, **a-scared.**

1859 Taliaferro *Fisher's River* 135 I soon got a-hongry, which I allers had a rantankerous appertite. **1940** Still *River of Earth* 142 They're a-liable to get off somewhere and drop stone down dead, only the buzzards seeing where. **1950** Justus *Luck for Lihu* 53 Little Lihu was a-weary with playing the music box by now. **1967** *DARE Survey* (Gatlinburg TN) The collar smelled a-funky. **1974** *AOHP/ASU*-204 I don't think anybody's any scardier of snakes than I was, black snakes, when I was a-little. **1975–76** Wolfram/Christian *WV Coll* 30 If she was a-jealous of me, she would want to go see where [the other women] was coming. **1983** *Dark Corner OHP*-5A She had nine [piglets], I believe it was, and every one of them [was] a-laying there a-dead.

E Preceding an adverb of position, direction, manner, or time. See also **away.**

1939 Hall *Coll* (Tow String Creek NC) They went ahead there and went to running a-backwards and forwards, bum cigarettes, from one company there to another. **1941** Still *Troublesome Creek* 22 We saw the man afar off on the road. **1973** *Foxfire Interviews* A-73-86 That place they call the mines is back over there a-yet. **1973** *GSMNP*-86:17 When I first caught up with myself a-not a-being as good a man as my father? **1983** *Dark Corner OHP*-5A 27A They'd come up here on Beaver Dam Creek over on twenty-five way up a-yonder and then get back to the office. **1996** *GSMNPCOHP* I told her this story and she looked a-straight at me and said, "I know the name of this baby."

a-b-abs (also *a-b-ab*) *noun* The ABCs (i.e., letters of the alphabet); figuratively, the most rudimentary elements of knowledge.

[**1835** Crockett *Account* 86 As far as my learning went, I would stand over it, and spell a strive or two with any of them, from *a-b-ab* to *crucifix*, which is where I left off at school.] **1903** Fox *Little Shepherd* 38 Learn yo' a-b-abs like a man now. **1938** Stuart *Dark Hills* 393 SweetBird don't know a letter of the A, B, abs.

a-back of (also *a-back to*) *phrasal preposition* Behind. Same as **back of 2.** See also **in back of**

1939 Hall *Coll* (Deep Creek NC) They was out of hearing a-going out just a-back of Round Top. **1975** Gainer *Speech Mtneer* 6 The well is a-back of the house. **1979** *Big South Fork OHP*-10/2 [The pole road] come out there a-back to Stockton. **1996–97** Montgomery *Coll*: *a-back of* (known to Brown, Cardwell, Ellis, Oliver).

[OED3 *aback of* (at *aback* adv P5) in later use chiefly Scotland, England regional, U.S. regional, and Caribbean]

a-back to See **a-back of.**

abed *adverb* Confined to bed, usually because of an illness or injury.

1934–47 LAMSAS (Swain Co NC). **1940** Still *River of Earth* 126 It plagued her to lie abed, helpless. **1955** Parris *Roaming Mts* 98 Here I was a-bed and could hardly move, but he said he would carry me. **1962** Dykeman *Tall Woman* 312 Just a year past, she come up on Stony Ridge and nursed me five days when I was abed. **1977** Arnow *Old Burnside* 31 I never lay abed listening very long before our mother was calling us from the foot of the stairs. **2009** Holbrook *Upheaval* 14 She lay abed, unable to shut her eyes.

[OED3 *abed* adv somewhat archaic]

a-below *preposition* Below.

1963 Edwards *Gravel* 154 On this side of the mountain in abelow the Carr Gap.

abide *verb* To tolerate, endure with patience or difficulty (usually expressed in the negative).

1895 Murfree *Phantoms* 196 She said she "couldn't abide a fiddle jes sawed helter-skelter." **1923** Furman *Mothering* 251 I was not surprised to hear from Hen later that he "had heared Dilsey tell Philip at recess she couldn't abide raggeddy boys." **1975** Gainer *Speech Mtneer* 6 I can't abide lazy people. **1984** Woods *WV Was Good* 230 *Abide* rarely ever was used to mean *to dwell*, but it not infrequently was employed as a substitute for *stand* or *endure*, or *tolerate*. (I just can't abide a man like that.) **2002** Rash *Foot in Eden* 87 He'd want to tarry and talk after but I wouldn't abide it.

able *adjective* Well-to-do.

1941 Still *Troublesome Creek* 12 I'm a-mind to buy a whole wooden kit o' mackerel. We'll be able. **c1960** Wilson *Coll* = rich, well-to-do. **2008** *Rosie Hicks* 4 I ain't able enough to take care of a girl.

a body See **body**.

aboon *preposition* Above.

1944 Wilson *Word-List* 38 = above, to think oneself superior. "That 'omern's aboon her own kinnery." **1998** Montgomery *Coll* (known to Brown, Bush).

[< Middle English *aboven* < Old English *abufan*/*onbofan*; OED3 *aboon* 16c; EDD *aboon* prep 2 Scot, nIrel, nEngl; SND *aboon*/*abune*; DARE *aboon* prep, adv western NC]

aboust See **about A**.

about See also **abouts**.

A Variant form *aboust*.

c1982 Young *Colloquial Appal* 1.

B *adverb*

1 Nearly, approximately (occurring after the construction modified). See also **just about**, **nearabout**.

1939 Hall *Notebooks* 13:45 (White Oak NC) Everybody about says July [for Julius]. **1956** Hall *Coll* I could walk it in about. **1999** Landry *Smoky Mt Interviews* We had all kinds of apples anywhere you went about.

2 Alternately; see **time about**, **weekends about**.

[OED3 *about* adv A3 "in turn, in succession . . . alternately," now U.S. regional]

abouten

A (also *'bouten*, *'bout'n*) *preposition* About.

1885 Murfree *Prophet* 8 He ain't studyin' 'bout'n me. **1886** Smith *Sthn Dialect* 350 Forms [such] as . . . *abouten* . . . bear the stamp of antiquity. **1957** Wise *Mt Speech* 307 *'bouten* for *about* [occurs] probably on the analogy of *outen*. **1971** Dwyer *Dict for Yankees* 23 I never knowed a thing 'bouten it. **1996** Montgomery *Coll*: *abouten* (known to Brown, Oliver); I never knowed a thing abouten it (Ledford).

B (also *aboutn*) *adverb* Nearly.

1957 Combs *Lg Sthn High: Word List* 1 *aboutn* = about. The excr[escent] N is puzzling; possibly a survival of the O[ld] E[nglish] and M[iddle] E[nglish] *en* ending. Ex: "Boys, I'm aboutn petered out." **2007** McMillon *Notes* It's abouten time.

[*about* + *-en* suffix; cf **-en**[1]]

about like common See **common 1**.

aboutn See **abouten B**.

abouts *adverb* About.

1975 *AOHP/ALC*-1128A Every coal company just abouts had a movie house. You'd go see a movie. **2008** *Rosie Hicks* 6 He worked just abouts anything you ax him he could do.

about to die *adjective phrase* Gravely ill.

1966 Frome *Strangers* 251 As nurse Helen Phyllis Higinbotham, of the Pi Beta Phi Settlement School at Gatlinburg during the early twenties, wrote, "I have had to get used to getting most of a woman's symptoms from her husband, and not having heart failure when a messenger comes with the news that so-and-so is 'bad off'—'about to die' or 'got the fever.'"

[DARE *about to die* adj phr chiefly South, South Midland]

above one's bend *adverb phrase* Beyond one's power or abilities.

1835 Crockett *Account* 44 I shall not attempt to describe the curiosities here; it is above my bend.

above one's raising See **raise A1**.

abroad *adjective*, *adverb* Away from home, out of the house.

1774 *Dunmore's War* 194 I am Obliged frequently to be abroad, to provide Provision for the Men on Duty and to stir up others for the Service. **1864** *Chapman CW Letters* (May 10) good helth is a good thing at home or a brod. **1937** (in **2009** Powell *Shenandoah Letters* 122) Ever Since the work has bin closed out up at big meadows my man hasent worked a day no where home nor a broad. **1940** Still *River of Earth* 238 At eleven o'clock Nezzie Crouch came for Father, sending him abroad into the camp. **1992** Brooks *Sthn Stuff* 9 = outside the mountains. "Our younguns cain't wait to grow up so's they can go abroad and work in the flatlands."

acause (also *a'cause*) *conjunction* Because.

1950 Dalton *Wordlist Sthn KY* 22 "Why did you do that?" "Jist acause." **1989** *Matewan OHP-28* Whether they need me or not, they'd a hired me just acause I had the papers. **1997** Andrews *Mountain Vittles* 82 Some folks called the little varmints whistle pigs a'cause of the noise they make.

[EDD *acause* conj English dialect]

accident *noun* Variant pronunciation with secondary stress on the last syllable. For similar forms, see **-ment A**.

1942 Hall *Phonetics Smoky Mts* 71 The suffixes *-dent* and *-ment* (except in *independent*) in most instances have secondary stress: *accident, confident, devilment, instrument, monument, payment, settlement, testament*, etc.

according to my conscience See **conscience**.

account *noun* See also **no-count**.

A Variant forms *acont* [see **1863** in **B**], *count* [see **1937** in **B**].

B Value, worth.

1863 *Brown CW Letters* (Nov 10) the socks we draw ant mutch acont. **1865** *Epperly CW Letters* (March 4) they have taking all the men or tride to take all that is any acont. **1867** Harris *Sut Lovingood* 106 I'm no count, no how. **1891** Swearingen *Letters* 166 Prof. wanted me to get up an essay and I didn't have time to write one that was any account. **1937** Hyatt *Kiverlid* 52 The last time I tried to scutch some hands that war raised a few yeer back hit war so bresh hit's no manner o'count. **1959** Pearsall *Little Smoky* 64 Some seem to have become completely discouraged, for "Uncle" Eli remembers that his father "never was much account after the war." **1973** *GSMNP-76:23* [The boots] was all right to ride with or all right to sit in house with. They ain't no count hiking. **1979** Carpenter *Walton War* 149 Women folks hain't much account now-a-days, they have tendered themselves too much. **2009** Williams *Maw Surry* She wasn't much count—a cussing, fussing, fighting old woman. **2018** *Blind Pig* (Nov 15) One day the friend [from Maryland] was talking about eating lunch down the road. Chitter said to her "Was the food any count?" The friend said "What? I don't understand what you're asking me."

ache (also *ache up*) *verb, verb phrase* To cause to hurt or have pain.

1924 Buffum *Shakespearean Survivals* 13 I have often heard, "My head aches me." **1978** Head *Mt Moments* Mom still says "my head aches me" when she has a headache. **2001** Lowry *Expressions* 18 Those breathing pills ache up my heart when I take them. **2004** Fisher *Kettle Bottom* 51 The cold aches me.

[in American usage, perhaps influenced by German; OED3 *ache* v 3 obsolete, rare, but cf CUD *ache* v "cause to ache"; Web3 *ache*[1] archaic]

acid timber (also *acid wood*) *noun* Chestnut, oak, and other trees whose bark is rich in tannic acid, harvested and sold for tanning leather. See also **tanbark**.

1939 Hall *Coll* (Indian Creek NC) During a hard crop year the . . . company would allow us to get out acid wood, telephone poles, and so on. **1954** Miller *Pigeon's Roost* (Jan 7) The acid timber is now almost gone. **1963** Hooper *Unwanted Boy* 232 Up in the morning old Joe Mayfield came down the Carson Road, driving a truck-load of acid wood to the extract plant. He had laboriously cut and snaked this wood from the mountain. **1975** *GSMNP-62:12* The biggest money we made was cutting acid wood and hauling it down there to the road and railroad and loading it on a car. **1983** Aiken *Mt Ways* 148 Tanbark was any species of tree bark rich in tannic acid and the wood itself was often called "acid wood" when being worked for the bark. **1984** Trout *Gatlinburg* "Acid wood"—chestnut, chestnut oak, and hemlock—tanned the hides of the leather industry.

ackempucky *noun* See citations.

c1928 (in **1944** Wentworth *ADD* 5) (wcWV) = a food of jellylike consistency, as gelatine. *Ibid.* = any food mixture of unknown ingredients.

acknowledge *verb* See citation.

1976 Thompson *Touching Home* 18 = to introduce: "He acknowledged his wife to me."

acknowledge the corn *verb phrase* To admit the truth, confess a mistake.

1881 Atkinson *After Moonshiners* 155 If you want the more sensible man of the two, I suppose I must acknowledge the corn, I'm the man. **1927** Woofter *Dialect from WV* 347 = to admit that one has made a mistake. "He acknowledged the corn about losing my knife."

[DARE *acknowledge the corn* v phr formerly widespread, now chiefly Midland]

acknowledgment See **make one's acknowledgment(s)**.

acont See **account**.

acorn tree *noun* An oak tree.

1954 Roberts *Bought a Dog* 19 A acorn had fallen in the horse's back and made a acorn tree.

across *adverb, preposition* Variant forms *acrost, acrostes, crost*.

1864 *Odell CW Letters* (Nov 6) The report is that old hood Is acrost tennessee river this morning. **1891** Brown *Dialect in TN* 172 In *oncet, twicet, acrost, dost*, and *clost*, we have a final t added. **1913** Kephart *Our Sthn High* 277 Although the hillsmen save some breath in this way, they waste a good deal by inserting sounds where they do not belong. Sometimes it is only an added consonant: gyarden, acrost. **1930** (in **1952** Mathes *Tall Tales* 180) Hit ain't but forty mile acrost the mountains yander to whar I live at, an' the walkin's good. **1963** Edwards *Gravel* 131 That spring fore plantin time I wuz avisitin one of my neighbors over crost the ridge a piece. *Ibid.* 154 He's gone, may have follered a mountaineer or a miner acrost the mountain. **1971** *AOHP/ALC-129* [He] just turn around and come back home and made me [a] rope ladder and put wood acrostes here. **1974** Fink *Bits Mt Speech* 1 They live *acrost* the river. **2005** Williams *Gratitude* 143 She could aim it cler acrost th' stall and hit where ever she wanted to.

[*across* + excrescent t]

across the waters *prepositional phrase* Overseas. [Editor's note: In the Smoky Mountains in the late 1930s this phrase was commonly used by older people to identify where their ancestors originated.]

1937 Hall *Coll* (Cosby TN) My granpaw came to this country from across the waters about the time of the Old War [= the Revolution].

acrost, acrostes See **across.**

act a fool (also *act the fool*) *verb phrase* To act up, play the clown.

1901 Harben *Westerfelt* 130 It's the feller mighty nigh ever' whack that acts the fool. **1937** Hall *Coll* (Cosby Creek TN) I was just actin' the fool. **1981** GSMNP-117:10 Her and some girl was in the back [of the] schoolhouse a-runnin', cuttin' up, and actin' the fool. **1989** *Matewan OHP*-56 The people come in, and I'll talk to them and act a fool with them. **1990** Merriman *Moonshine Rendezvous* 40 About halfway across [the creek] silly me started actin' the fool by pullin' back on his ears and spurrin' him like a horse. **1991** Weals *Last Train* 108 We all worked just alike, scuffled and cut up and acted the fool.

[DARE (at *act* v B1) chiefly South, Midland]

act big Ike See **big Ike.**

actiously *adverb* See citation.

2005 Williams *Gratitude* 476 = actually.

act the fool See **act a fool.**

Adam-and-Eve *noun* Puttyroot, an orchid (usually of the genus *Arethusa*), formerly used in conjuring to make a love potion.

1901 Lounsberry *Sthn Wild Flowers* 96 Another curious point is that when the plant is uprooted there are found to be as in a chain several old corms attached in succession to the one of the present season. It was perhaps a young plant which had borne but two which suggested to the donor of its popular name, Adam and Eve, hand in hand. **1939** Jennison *Flora Great Smokies* 293 Adam and Eve (*Aplectrum hyemale*) is common but not conspicuous. **1957** Broaddus *Vocab Estill Co KY* 2 = a medicinal herb "for after a woman gets you know how." [**1971** Krochmal et al. *Medicinal Plants Appal* 48 [The root of] the plant is reputed to have value in treating bronchial ailments.] **1972** Cooper *NC Mt Folklore* 18 [Love doctors] helped the forlorn in love by furnishing them Adam and Eve roots, John the Conqueror root, various love powders, and secret formulas to be recited at bedtime. **1989** Still *Rusties and Riddles* [10] = tuber of the puttyroot orchid. Before log fires on winter evenings young and old roasted Irishmen, chestnuts, and Adam-and-Eves.

Adam's ale *noun* Water (as a drink).

1939 Farr *TN Mt Regions* 89 = water: "I drink nothin' but Adam's Ale."

[OED3 *Adam's ale* n 1643]

Adam's apple *noun* See citation. Same as **Indian turnip.**

1957 Combs *Lg Sthn High: Word List* 2 = the Indian turnip, or jack-in-the-pulpit, known for its acrid, pungent taste.

Adam's fool, Adam's housecat See **Adam's off-ox.**

Adam's needle *noun* A yucca plant (*Yucca filamentosa* or *Y. smalliana*). Same as **bear grass.**

1940 Caton *Wildflowers of Smokies* 65. **1964** Stupka *Trees Shrubs Vines* 32 During some years Adam's needle begins to bloom at the end of May.

[from the sharp points of the yucca plant; OED3 1730→]

Adam's off-ox (also *Adam's fool, Adam's housecat*) *noun* A person one does not know or cannot identify (especially in phrase *know from* ___). [Editor's note: The phrase *know* ___ *from Adam* is widespread in the US.]

1931 Combs *Lg Sthn High* 1304 I didn't know him from Adam's off-ox. **1956** McAtee *Some Dial NC* 2 I wouldn't know him from Adam's house-cat. **1966–68** *DARE Survey* (Brasstown NC, Gatlinburg TN) I wouldn't know him from Adam's housecat; I wouldn't know him from Adam's fool. **1974–75** McCracken *Logging* 16:37 I didn't know Alec Jackson from Adam's off-ox. **1991** Still *Wolfpen Notebooks* 118 I said, "Oscar, do you know me?" "Shore I know you." He didn't know me from Adam's off-ox. **1991** Williams *Homeplace* 6–7 After all, she "didn't know me from Adam's housecat." But she had invited me in, and I doubt if she had any real intention of changing her ways.

[extension of *know from Adam*; DARE (at *Adam's off-ox* n 1) Variant of *Adam* n "the first man, the archetypal man," chiefly west of Appalachians]

adder See **after.**

adder's tongue *noun* A dogtooth violet (*Erythronium americanum/albidium*). Same as **lamb('s) tongue, trout lily.**

1970 Campbell et al. *Smoky Mt Wildflowers* 96 Few plants have such a widely accepted incorrect name, often being called dogtooth violet though a lily and not a violet . . . Other common names include adder's tongue and fawn lily. **1981** Brewer *Wonderment* 22 Lamb's tongue, Randy said, is trout lily. Or dogtooth violet, or adder's tongue, or fawn lily.

admire *verb* (+ *infinitive*) To desire, be pleased to, take pleasure in.

1939 Bond *Appal Dialect* 104 = to like: "I'd admire to go to town." **1971** Dwyer *Dict for Yankees* 23 = take pleasure in. "I sure would admire to have you go with me." **1974** Fink *Bits Mt Speech* 1 = to be pleased. "I'd shorely *admire to* see him agin." **1976** Weals *Two Minus* I'd sure admire to set a spell. **1988** Smith *Fair and Tender* 25 You and Mister Brown have made a tree and hanged it with playprettys I wuld [sic] admire to see it so.

[OED3 *admire* v 3 chiefly U.S. colloq; DARE *admire* v B1 chiefly New England, South Midland, and settlement areas]

adopt *verb* To contract (a disease or malady) or feign doing so.

1913 Kephart *Our Sthn High* 222 Sooner or later he "adopts a rheumatiz" and the adoption lasts till he dies. **1994** Montgomery *Coll* (known to Bush); He adopted laziness (Cardwell).

afeard (also *afeared, afeered, afyered, feard, feared, feered*) *predicate adjective* Afraid. [Editor's note: Joseph Hall found that in the Smoky Mountains in the late 1930s *afeard* was the form universally used in preference to *afraid*.]

1845 (in **1974** Harris *High Times* 47) She hugged me mity tite she was *"so feered of fallin off that drated poney."* **1847** (in **1870** Drake *Pioneer Life KY* 82) I was ever afterward "afeard" of wild and wicked horses. **1859** Taliaferro *Fisher's River* 209 I'm afeered you'll fall from grace ef you shout too soon, Sol. **1863** Hill *CW Letters* (Jan 1) I am all most feard to send [the money] in a letter. **1875** King *Great South* 536 He volunteered to direct us to the falls, though he "was powerful afeard of snakes. **1913** Kephart *Our Sthn High* 288 When the mountaineer boy challenges his mate: "I dar ye—I ain't afeared!" his verb and participle are of the same ancient and sterling rank [as Chaucer and Layamon]. **1924** Raine *Saddlebags* 97–98 *Afeared* is more logical than afraid, and was preferred by Lady MacBeth. **1929** Chapman *Speech Sthn Highlands* 619 "I am afeard" is quite as good English as "I am afraid." Better, in fact—*afeard* being the regular participle of the verb "affear," and "afraid" the very irregular participle of "affray," an inexplicable variant of "affright." **1937** Hall *Coll* (Cades Cove TN) I'm afeared of them copperheads. *Ibid.* (Kirklands Creek NC) I ain't nary bit afeared of him. **1938** Bowman *High Horizons* 46 Nearly all of the older people use the Elizabethan "afeared" while the children usually say "afraid," I have noticed. **1941** Hall *Coll* (Cataloochee NC) Pretty nearly all these old people say "afeared." **1956** Hall *Coll* (Cades Cove TN) My mother heared them old witch tales. She was afeared she'd see a witch. **1967** Hall *Coll* (Townsend TN) My daddy wasn't afeared of them hogs. Hit come up and hit stood right on his breast, looking right down on his face. **1978** Montgomery *White Pine Coll* I-3 They'd been feared of them. **1989** Smith *Flyin' Bullets* 244 That Charles had a lot of nerve, he wasn't afeared of them in the least bit. **2005** Williams *Gratitude* 476 *afyered.*

[ultimately < Old English *afæred*, past participle of *afæran*; OED3 *afeard* past-part/adj obsolete or dialect c1000→; EDD *afeard* adj in general dialect use in Scot, Irel, Engl; SND *afeard/afeart* rare since 1700; CUD *afeard* (also *afeart*); Web3 *afeard* adj now dialect; DARE *afear(e)d* adj once widespread, now chiefly South, Midland]

afeered See **afeard.**

affected *adjective* Infected.

1937 Hall *Coll* (Emerts Cove TN) His hand got affected. **1996–97** Montgomery *Coll* (known to Brown, Cardwell, Norris, Oliver).

affection *noun* Disease, ailment.

1863 *Apperson CW Letters* (Nov 18) [The doctor] said it was affection of Liver that caus my side to be in this condition. **1863** *Vance Papers* (July 13) I have not Been able to make a Support in the last four years, from a fatta [= fatty] tumor on my Right shoulder and a Dropsical affection of the Legs, and old age has broken me down.

[OED3 *affection* n[1] 7, a1398→]

afflicted *adjective* Mentally unbalanced, feeble-minded.

1952 Wilson *Folk Speech NC* 513 = idiotic. **1994–97** Montgomery *Coll* (known to nine consultants from the Smoky Mountains); A bunch of those Cables were afflicted (Shields).

[DARE *afflicted* ppl adj chiefly South, Midland]

Affrilachian *adjective* Of a loose group of poets and artists: African American and having a historical affinity for Appalachia.

2006 *Encycl Appalachia* 246 The term *Affrilachian* refers to a person of African descent residing in or originating from a multiracial community within the Appalachian region. By creating and using this term in his 1991 poem "Affrilachia," poet Frank X Walker challenged the common definition of an Appalachian—a white resident of the mountains—by making visible the black and multiracial individuals of Appalachia and their contributions to the region, as well as their communities of origin. The term [rebukes] the idea that one cannot claim both an African American and an Appalachian identity. [**2011** Spriggs *Walker Exemplar* 21 The term "Affrilachia" was originally coined by [Frank X. Walker], and, as a cultural landscape, has become integral to his identity as a multi-disciplinary artist and arts enthusiast.]

afinaciously See **finacious.**

a-finally See **finally 2.**

afore

A *adverb* Before.

1849 Lanman *Alleghany Mts* 89 Now, the way the thing happened was this, and I reckon you never heard sich like afore. **1861** *Hileman CW Letters* (Sept 21) I think it is some healthyer tha[n] it has been yet afore. **1875** Reid *Land of Sky* 80 He hadn't no doubt the professor had tried to go down to Caney Valley by a trail they two had followed thirteen years afore. **1889** Brown *Dialect Survivals in TN* 206 *Afore* . . . is found frequently enough in Shakespeare and Ben Johnson [sic]. . . . It is used constantly by [Murfree's] mountaineers. "It air toler'ble high,—higher'n I ever see it afore." **1904–20** Kephart *Notebooks* 4:725 Seems to me like I heered that name afore. **1913** Kephart *Our Sthn High* 288 Afore, atwixt, awar, heap o' folks . . . all these everyday expressions of the backwoods were contemporary with the *Canterbury Tales*. **1939** Walker *Mtneer Looks* 1 We ain't like nobody they ever seed afore. **1975** Chalmers *Better* 37 I 'lowed I'd send fer you, but I done what you told me afore, and it holp me some. **2007** Preece *Leavin' Sandlick* 19 I ain't never set up with the dead afore.

[OED3 *afore* adv now archaic and regional]

B *conjunction* Before, before the time that.

1859 Taliaferro *Fisher's River* 53 'Twasn't long afore I run out'n my shot-bag. **1867** Harris *Sut Lovingood* 20 We hed tu wait ni ontu seventeen days fur 'im tu thaw afore we cud skin 'im. **1873** Smith *Peace Papers* 94 Three of the dinged things stung me afore I could rise. **1924** Abernethy *Moonshine* 117 It were a hole year afore I'd look at nary nother woman. **1937** Hall *Coll* (Cosby TN) That happened afore I left the Smoky. **1962** Dykeman *Tall Woman* 123 I reckon he plans to gobble up the whole valley afore he's done. **1973** GSMNP-83:26 I was special deputy afore I was deputy under [the] high sheriff of Sevier County two year. **1988** Mashburn *Mt Summer* 55 As they started to shovel the dirt in on top, Sam struggled to his feet and said, "Don't you fellers think we'ns ought ter say a few words over that poor ol' cow afore you kiver her up?" **1997** Montgomery *Coll* It rained afore we had a chance to plow (Norris).

[OED3 *afore* conj now archaic and regional]

C *preposition* Before, in front of.

1867 Harris *Sut Lovingood* 73 He's in a hurry tu git thru, es he hes *yu* tu kill an' salt down afore day. **1883** Zeigler and Grosscup *Heart of Alleghanies* 50 "The way them curs crawl up to the blaze," said Wid Medfore, "is a shore sign thet hits goin' ter be cold nuff ter snow afore mornin'." **1936** (in **1952** Mathes *Tall Tales* 202) I'm goin' in thar with my dogs at crack o' day tomorrer, an' I'm goin' to have Ol' Slewfoot's hide stretched up on my cow shed afore sundown! **1937** Hall *Coll* (Cades Cove TN) I allowed he'd return afore this. **1954** Arnow *Dollmaker* 33 Whatever kind a luck comes, good or bad, it has already come to somebody afore us. **1979** Carpenter *Walton War* 166 He's a ridin' fer the town and a hopin' to git there afore dusky dark.

[represents Old English *on* + *foran* "in front of"; OED3 *afore* prep now archaic and regional; EDD *afore* adv/conj/prep in general dialect use in Scot, Irel, Engl; Web3 *afore* adv/conj/prep chiefly dialect; DARE *afore* adv, conj, prep once widespread, now chiefly South, Midland]

a-front of *phrasal preposition* In front of, before.

1986 Helton *Around Home* 380 = preceding. **1996–97** Montgomery *Coll* (known to Brown, Ellis, Norris, Oliver); Oscar always walked afront of his wife (Cardwell).

after

A *conjunction, preposition* Variant forms *adder, arter, ater, a'ter, atter*.

1859 Taliaferro *Fisher's River* 51 True, he had many obstinate competitors, but he distanced them all farther than he did the numerous snakes that "run arter him." **1873** Smith *Peace Papers* 111 He ki[c]ked him atter he was down, and throwd mud on him. **1904** Fox *Christmas Eve* 123 Atter a while the boys lets Dave come back, to take keer o' his ole mammy. **1913** Kephart *Our Sthn High* 278 Many say atter or arter. **1924** Bacheller *Happiest Person* 7 A'ter a while my sister broke down an' I tuk her five little uns. **1937** Wilson *Folklore SE KY* 30 *arter*. **c1945** Haun *Hawk's Done* 296 "I'll go ater Old Heif," Jake said. **1956** Hall *Coll* (Newport TN) They asked the boys what was wrong, and they said the devil was atter 'em. **1973** AOHP/ALC-259 Anything they could get money out of, why they'd about go atter it. **1979** *Big South Fork OHP*-21 I went back atter I got grown and eat another meal with them. **1989** Landry *Smoky Mt Interviews* 194 Atter we got our wheat sowed and everything in the cove is when we done our bear hunting. **2013** Venable *How to Tawlk* 1 I told Maw I'd fix the roof adder turkey season.

B *preposition* redundant following certain verbs. See **read after, study after.**

[DARE *after* prep B2 chiefly South Midland]

C *adjective* Latter. See also **fore part.**

1989 Landry *Smoky Mt Interviews* 181 Those big possums wouldn't come out in the fore part of the night. They'd come out in the after part. **1995** Peterson *Ginseng Hunter* 55 Thus, the hunter must first dig the root in order to determine the age and value of the sang because "the stalk dies down every fall, and where it perishes away from the neck of the root, it leaves a scar which remains to tell the age of the plant in after years."

D *adverb* Later in time, afterward.

1799 (in **2008** Ellison *High Vistas* 37) After We run the line between the State of N.C. & T. on the extreme height of the Stone Mn to our camp at the upper Rye Patch. **1863** *Hogg CW Letters* (July 2) John Adams Randals sone fell in to a hot troft of Still Slop and burnt him so he dide [= died] in some three weaks after. **1916** Combs *Old Early English* 288 *After* is used adverbially of time, e.g. "They ride into town, and *after* ride out again." **1973** GSMNP-86:40 I didn't never use no doctor medicine till after, just here for the last late years. **2004** Fisher *Kettle Bottom* 53 After, them four was out on the back porch drinking. **2008** *Rosie Hicks* 4 Hit must have did after.

afterdamp *noun* See citation. See also **black damp.**

1994 Crissman *Death and Dying* 190 The terms *blackdamp* (a mixture of carbon dioxide and nitrogen) and *afterdamp* (carbon monoxide) are used when the air in a mine becomes oxygen deficient to the extent that the workers can be asphyxiated or suffocate. The gases are propelled rapidly through the passageways of a mine following the detonation of methane gas or coal dust.

afterdinner *noun* The afternoon.

1997 Montgomery *Coll* (known to Brown, Bush); This afterdinner we'll go pay a visit (Oliver).

[Web3 *afterdinner* n obsolete; DARE *afterdinner* n chiefly South Midland]

afteren *conjunction* After.

1989 Smith *Flyin' Bullets* 120 He never give me his check before, just what was left over after'en he had been out with the boys, and this time there weren't no money left over. **1996** Montgomery *Coll* (known to Cardwell).

[*after* + -*en* suffix; cf **-en**[1]]

afterward(s) *adverb* Variant forms *arterards, arterward, attererds, atterwards*.

1867 Harris *Sut Lovingood* 22 I arterards foun' out, he were a-studyin how tu play the kar-acter ove a hoss puffectly. **1884** Murfree *In TN Mts* 253 A good while arterward. **1917** Kephart *Word-List* 407 I et me a bait o' ramps, and tasted them for a week atterwards. **1939** Hall *Coll* (Roaring Fork TN) He lived for years atterwards. **1964** Roberts *Hell-Fer-Sartin* 99 They went back and they saw Dirty Jack in a day or two atterwards. **1976** Garber *Mountain-ese* 5 Attererds, we all went fishin'.

afterwhile *adverb* In a little while, later on.

1862 *Bradshaw CW Letters* (April 13) he fell a sleepe and his capt tried to wake him upe but he could not and after while he woke him self. **1873** Smith *Peace Papers* 90 I rekon we'll git em all back atter while. **1907** Dugger *Balsam Groves* 30 He'll come home uv his own accord atter while, and bring George on his back ef he'll gist set there. **1939** Hall *Coll* (Cataloochee NC) After while a, an old one [= bear] run out, and she just run off. **1973** GSMNP-73 After while they just kept building and kept building. **2001** House *Clay's Quilt* 229 "Surely to God you ain't hungry after that big meal," Clay said. "Naw, but I will be after while."

[DARE *afterwhile* adv chiefly South, Midland]

afyered See **afeard**.

again See **against A**.

against

A Variant forms *again*, *aginst* [see **1974** in **C**], *agin*, *gin*.

1863 *Tesh CW Letters* (June 15) you had better take half of it but I tell You it goes mightly a gin the Grain. **1913** Kephart *Our Sthn High* 77 I've seed hit blow here on top of Smoky till a hoss couldn't stand up agin it. **1921** Weeks *Speech of KY Mtneer* 9 Again is often used in the old fashioned sense of against, "I'll be ready against you are"; "I'll saddle your mule again your goin' into town this evenin"; (agin or 'gin are more common). **1939** Hall *Coll* (Cataloochee NC) He stepped up, and I put the gun right agin [the bear's] head and fired. *Ibid.* (Wears Cove TN) It's strictly agin the law to set a trap out in a trail. **1955** Parris *Roaming Mts* 177 I never had no objection to meetin' a varmint in a square stand-up fight—his nails again my knife. **1969** GSMNP-27:7 That scared them bears and they tore loose and they just run agin that door. **1978** Montgomery *White Pine Coll* X-2 I haven't got anything agin it, but I wouldn't know. **1989** Landry *Smoky Mt Interviews* 195 They would want the dirt to go over right agin the plant. **1997** *Dante OHP*-14 I leaned up agin the wall in the courthouse and got married.

B *conjunction* By the time that, before.

1813 (in **1956** Eliason *Tarheel Talk* 258) (Burke Co NC) I expecte to get up the two Lower fiedds against you gite these fewe Lines. **c1830** (in **2007** Dunkerly *Kings Mt* 97) As we marched up the mountain it was dark again we got the prisoners under guard. **1859** Taliaferro *Fisher's River* 120 Against I pulled down the fence and got my hoss over, Sally and 'Gius was away yender. **1862** *Sullivan Co in CW* I 32 Tell Philip and Tom and John and William to get together all the chestnuts they can against we come home. **1864** *Poteet CW Letters* (Aug 30) [They] would not bee fit to eat again I got well. **1911** Shearin *E KY Word-List* 537 I'll get there against you do. **1937** Hall *Coll* (Dellwood NC) I was repairin' the tire agin you came. *Ibid.* (Collins Creek NC) We'd oughta do plenty of fishin' against the season closes. **1949** Kurath *Word Geog East US* 79 The greater part of the Midland and the South ... have retained in their folk speech the expression *agin I get there* ... *Agin* is most common in the Appalachians, but it has considerable currency among the simple folk, white and black, in the Southern piedmont and along the coast as well. **1953** Hall *Coll* (Hazel Creek NC) Hit come out from the mouth of the hole, again I could get my dogs loose. **1962** Dykeman *Tall Woman* 269 Again Professor Duncan comes back, you'll be ready to take that examination for going into college. **1970** GSMNP-26:11 He took his knife and cut him ... just cut him till he liked to bled to death again they could get him home. **1976** GSMNP-113:10 Gin he got to me it was summer. **1979** Slone *My Heart* 36 Most everybody has been married a long time, agin they are that old. **1981** GSMNP-122:55 Gin we'd get there the other'un would ring.

[OED3 *against* conj B now England regional and U.S. regional; Web3 *against* conj 1 now chiefly dialect; DARE *again* (at *again* conj D) chiefly South, Midland, *against* conj C1 chiefly southern Appalachians, Ozarks, *gin* conj[2] South, South Midland]

C *preposition* By the time of, before, in time for.

1774 *Dunmore's War* 58 I have requested of Capt. Crockett & Doack one half of their Men to meet against next Tuesday or sooner at the Town House. **1796** *Big Pigeon Church Minutes* 23 John Mulkey a Deligate to the Association report that he had no Minutes to present to the Church but will have them ready against next meeting. **1805** *Globe Creek Church Minutes* 20 [The] letter to be wrought & brought forred against our next meeting to be inspected. **1842** *Elijoy Church Minutes* 45 church met ... took a charge against Malden Delosier for disorder & John Tipton & Vincent Rogers to labour with him against next meeting. **1861** *Shipman CW Letters* (June 28) I am Coming home next Saturday I want you to hav me a good horse aganst then. **1927** Woofter *Dialect from WV* 347 Mr. Jones will hold the cattle against your arrival. **1939** Hall *Coll* (White Oak NC) He'll be in town against nine o'clock. **1973** GSMNP-87:2:28 He didn't make it back again the night. **1974** Fink *Bits Mt Speech* 1 = by the time of. "I'll be home *aginst* dark."

[OED3 (at *again* B10) "against the time that, before the" obsolete; Web3 *against* prep 11 dialect; DARE (at *again* prep C2) chiefly Midland]

age *noun* In phrases *get (an) age on*, *have age on* = to be or become very old.

1939 Hall *Coll* (Waynesville NC) He has a right smart of an age on him. **1967** Hall *Coll* (Del Rio TN) Bruce is gettin' age on him. **1976** Carter *Little Tree* 35 He was gittin' age on him, and when he liquored up would ofttimes git addled in the head and wander off.

ageable *adjective*

1 Of a person: aged.

c1940 Aswell *Glossary TN Idiom* 1 = old. "My daddy lived to be quite ageable." **1971** Dwyer *Dict for Yankees* 23 = old. "She's gettim' too ageable to marry." **1997** Montgomery *Coll* (known to Bush, Hooper).

2 Of wine or whiskey: mature for consumption.

1997 Montgomery *Coll* (known to Brown).

ageep *interjection* Come! (used as a call to pigs). Same as **goop**. See also **gooee**, **pig-ee**.

1990 Oliver *Cooking Hazel Creek* 17 The way the settlers called their hogs was not "sooie" as we might think, but to yell "ageep" which brought them running. **2002** Oliver *Cooking and Living* 68

To call [hogs] for feeding, the settlers did not yell "sooie," but "ageep," a word of ancient Scottish origin.

ager See **ague**.

agey *adjective* Of a person: aged.

1939 Hall *Coll* (Cosby Creek TN) Ellen's a-gettin' a little agey too. **1967** Hall *Coll* (Del Rio TN) Bruce is bound to be gettin' agey. **1976** Lindsay *Grassy Balds* 175 I'm getting a little agey. **1976** Still *Pattern of Man* 90 Two or three [people] got to be a hundred or so, so agey they looked like dried cushaws.

[OED3 *agey* adj variant of *agy*, archaic]

agg[1] See **egg**.

agg[2] (also *agg up*) *verb, verb phrase* To provoke, goad, egg on.

1917 Kephart *Word-List* 407 Both sides *agged* it up. **c1940** Aswell *Glossary TN Idiom* 1 *agg* = stir up trouble. **1994** Montgomery *Coll*: *agg up* (known to Cardwell).

[EDD (at *hag(g)* 1) "to incite, provoke, urge, irritate"; CUD *agg someone up* (at *egg* v) "egg someone on"]

aggervate See **aggravate**.

aggie forties See **aqua fortis**.

aggravate *verb*

A Variant form *aggervate*, also variant present-participle forms with secondary stress on the last syllable: *AG-gra-va-ting-est* [see **c1959**, **1994** in **B**].

1923 Greer-Petrie *Angeline Doin' Society* 1 Hit was aggervatin' fur Desdimony to whirl on him like a panter, atter he'd tried to he'p her. **1942** Hall *Phonetics Smoky Mts* 61 There is substitution of [d] for [r] in *aggravate*. **1994** McCarthy *Jack Two Worlds* 13 You get your ass away from h'yer . . . you've [sic] ag-gra-*va*-tin' me.

B To annoy, vex, cause trouble or difficulty (for); hence participial adjective *aggravating* = annoying, troublesome, *aggravatingest* = most troublesome. For other present-participle forms with *-est*, see Grammar and Syntax §3.4.1.

1864 *Councill CW Letters* (Nov 30) the body lise is a nuff to aggrevate any man to deth. **1873** Smith *Peace Papers* 84 A luxuryous lady with aggravatin curls had okkupide neerly all of a seet. **c1959** Weals *Hillbilly Dict* 2 = *aggervatingest* = most annoying; irksome. **1975** *AOHP/ALC-961* They'd keep you aggravated to death. **1975** *Logging* 177 That was the aggravatingest thing's ever been in the world. **1976** Garber *Mountain-ese* 1 *aggravatingest* = most irksome. "John has the most aggervatin'est wife in the whole Newnited States." **1994** Montgomery *Coll* She's the aggravatin'est calf I've ever had (Cardwell). **2005** Williams *Gratitude* 36 They [= the shoes] was awful heavy when they was wet too, and was the aggervatin'est thangs in the world t'try t'wring out. **2008** *Rosie Hicks* 1 She'd do everything to aggravate me.

[DARE *aggravate* v B "to annoy" scattered, but especially South, South Midland, *aggravated* especially frequent in South, Midland, *aggravating* widespread, though especially South, South Midland]

aggravate the devil *verb phrase* See citation.

1967 *DARE Survey* (Maryville TN) = to tease.

aggravatingest See **aggravate**.

agg up See **agg**[2].

agin, **aginst** See **against A**.

ago *adverb* Used with a present perfect or, rarely, present-tense verb or verb phrase, especially *has been*. See also **have B4**.

1801 Huskey *Rogers Papers* 12 I have no more at present to communicate but I have had a dam sore ass some time ago which almost took my life. **1863** *Reese CW Letters* (March 27) I hav studied it All over long A go. **1864** *Chapman CW Letters* (April 12) I have bin vaxionated a few days agow and my arm hurts me verry bad at this time. **1896** Fox *Last Stetson* 188 I don't know why I hain't killed thet spyin' skunk long ago. **1937** Conner *Ms* 19 Some one, No doubt has made a souveneer out of it, long ago. **1939** Hall *Coll* (Bradley Fork NC) It's been twenty year ago they offered me a house and land. **1953** Hall *Coll* (Plott Creek NC) It's been a number of years ago. I was only a young man at that time. . . . This has been along back just a few years ago, before the park took over the Hazel Creek boundary, game preserve. **1961** Miller *Pigeon's Roost* (Oct 5) We have had two light frosts scattered here and there about two weeks ago, but didn't do any damage to the late growing crops. **1973** Foster *Walker Valley* 9:83 I disremember who told me that, but it ain't been long ago. **1979** Slone *My Heart* 28 That has been almost fifty years ago, but I still recall it all.

a-God's plenty See **a-plenty**.

agonies *noun* See citations.

1976 Garber *Mountain-ese* 1 = sickness, ailment. "Mary hain't been doin' her work since she's been sufferin' with the agonies." **1998** Montgomery *Coll* = menstrual pains, also called *monthly agonies* (Brown), = menstrual pains (Cardwell), = generally applied to sickness and ailments (Weaver).

agreement *noun* variant pronunciation with secondary stress on the last syllable. For similar forms, see **-ment A**.

1969 Hannum *Look Back* 29 Sometimes it is an arbitrary accent on the single word that gives the rhythmic effect, as: "agreement, hostile."

ague *noun* See also **bear ague**, **buck ague**.

A Variant form *ager* ['ægɚ] [see **1925** in **B**].

B The fever and chills of malaria, influenza, or other ailment (sometimes expressed in the plural).

1824 (in **1912** Doddridge *Notes on Settlement* 83) The fort consisted of an assemblage of small hovels, situated on the margin of a large and noxious marsh, the effluvia of which gave the most of the women and children the fever and ague. **1864** *Carson CW Letters* (July 16) i have been quite porley with the ager tho I have gote them Stoped on mee and I thinke that I will bee all rite in a

Short time. **1867** Harris *Sut Lovingood* 80 My hans tuck the ager, an' my hart felt hot an onsatisfied like. **1896** Fox *Last Stetson* 184 "Whut ye mean, boy," he said, sharply, "reskin' the fever an' ager this way?" **1925** Dargan *Highland Annals* 46 There's shumake for a swelled throat, an' boneset for the ager . . . an' a lot more I'll show you if you go home with me some time. **1957** Broaddus *Vocab Estill Co KY* 2 *agers* = chills.

agueweed *noun*

1 A gentian wildflower (*Gentiana quinquefolia*), from which is made a tonic to treat a fever. Also called **gallflower**.

1901 Lounsberry *Sthn Wild Flowers* 428 The stiff gentian, a quaintly pretty one among them all, grows in either dry or moist soil and often ascends to a considerable height in the mountains. . . . In these parts of the country the mountain people call it the gall-flower because its juices are so bitter, and ague-weed on account of the extract they make from its roots and employ in curing fever. **1982** Stupka *Wildflowers* 88 Of all the various gentians in the southern mountains this species is readily recognized by the small size of the individual flowers and by the profusion of blossoms on a single plant. . . . Such local names as "ague-weed" and "gall-weed" relate to its former use as a tonic. **1997** Montgomery *Coll* (known to Cardwell).

2 A **boneset.**

1971 Krochmal et al. *Medicinal Plants Appal* 118 Ague-weed . . . in Appalachia, a tea made of the leaves is used to treat coughs and consumption, and it is used as a laxative.

ah (also *er*) *interjection* A high-pitched syllable articulated ingressively at the end of a phrase or breath group or at the beginning of one, used especially when a preacher reaches an intensely emotional juncture of a spontaneous sermon or public prayer, adding a rapid, melodic, quasi-chant quality to the message. Same as **uh**. See also **holy tone, huh.**

1881 Pierson *In the Brush* 73–74 My brief address was followed by a sermon entirely different from those of the preacher I have already described, and deserves notice as a type of thousands that are preached to the people in the Brush. Scarcely a sentence in the sermon was uttered in the usual method of speech. It was drawled out in a sing-song tone from the beginning to the end. The preacher ran his voice up, and sustained it at so high a pitch that he could make but little variation of voice upward. The air in his lungs would become exhausted, and at the conclusion of every sentence he would "catch" his breath with an "ah." As he proceeded with his sermon, and his vocal organs became wearied with this most unnatural exertion, the "ah" was repeated more and more frequently, until, with the most painful contortions of face and form, he would with difficulty articulate, in his sing-song tone: "Oh, my beloved brethren-ah, and sisters—ah, you have all got to die—ah, and be buried—ah, and go to the judgment—ah, and stand before the great white throne—ah, and receive your rewards—ah, for the deeds—ah, done in the body—ah." From the beginning to the end of his sermon, which occupied just an hour and ten minutes by my watch, I could not see the slightest evidence that he had any idea what he was going to say from one sentence to another. While "catching his breath," and saying "ah," he seemed to determine what he would say next. There was no more train of thought or connection of ideas than in the harangue of a maniac. And yet many hundreds of such sermons are preached in the Brush, and I am sorry to add that thousands of the people had rather hear these sermons than any others. This "holy tone" has charms for them not possessed by any possible eloquence. As the preacher "warms up" and becomes more animated in the progress of his discourse, the more impressible sisters begin to move their heads and bodies, and soon all the devout brethren and sisters sway their bodies back and forth in perfect unison, keeping time, in some mysterious manner, to his sing-song tone. **1895** *Mt Baptist Sermon* 13 Solomon he built a temple-ah! an' he hed all the work done way off-ah! so they warn't no sound of hammer to be heerd at the building-ah! An' the timber war ahewed-ah an'asquared-ah! an' aplumbed-ah, way out in the mountings-ah! **1901** McClintock *KY Mts* 21 Good wind is certainly a necessary qualification for a successful mountain preacher, for he is expected to preach as long as the "speerit" lasts—generally hours. He throws in a little aspirate like *er* and *ah*, when he warms up, which produces the "holy tone." An old minister one day was exhorting his brethren to repentance. "Oh, brethren," said he, "repent ye, and repent ye of your sins, er; for if you don't, er, the Lord, er, he will grab yer by the seat of yer pants, er, and hold yer over hell fire." **1931** Combs *Lg Sthn High* 1303 Intensely hortatory and polemic, the preacher's words are spoken rapidly and often incoherently. In a sing-song fashion, *-ah* is added at the end of most clauses and sentences. **1979** Melton *'Pon My Honor* 40 "Brothers and sisters, ah!" the preacher thundered, "I'm a-preaching the pure gospel to you'ens, ah! And iffen I throw out anything, ah! that you'ens ah! cant swaller ah! jest hand it back to me, ah!" IT IS!

a half a See **a**[1] **2.**

a heap See **heap B.**

ahind

A Variant forms *ahine* [see **1867** in **C**], *ahint* (rhymes with *pint*) [see **1884** in **C**].

B *adverb* Behind, late.

2009 Benfield *Mt Born* 120 = behind, or late, with something. "I cain't do that now; I'm ahind with my canning."

C *preposition* Behind.

1867 Harris *Sut Lovingood* 268 The tupentine lit up a bright road ahine him, kivered wif broke down an' tore up briars. **1884** Murfree *In TN Mts* 250 He war a-ridin' a-hint him. **1904–20** Kephart *Notebooks* 2:603 *ahind*. **1964** Glassie *Mt Jack Tales* 97 He run ahind the bed and got that harp. **1978** Hiser *Quare Do's* 51 There jist ahind them they could hear IT, amongst last year's dead dried beech leaves. **1996–97** Montgomery *Coll*: *ahind* (Cardwell, Shields); *ahint* (Cardwell). **2007** McMillon *Notes* Look ahind you.

[*a-* (reduced form of *at*) + *-hind*; EDD *ahind* prep/adv Scot, nIrel, nEngl; SND *ahint*; CUD *ahind/ahine/ahint/ahin* adv, prep "behind"; Web3 *ahind* prep dialect; DARE *ahind* prep, adv chiefly New England, South, South Midland]

ahine, ahint See **ahind.**

ah law See **eh la.**

a-hold (also *aholt, a-holt*) *noun* Possession, a firm grasp.

1861 *Patton CW Letters* (May 26) we expect to make the yankeys fly if we get a holt of them. **1862** *Walker CW Letters* (March 16) tell the boys ther not to let the calery [cholera] git aholt of them. **1901** Harben *Westerfelt* 14 Somehow he got ahold of it an' cut it out. **1932** Dargan *Call Home* 20 I kain't git aholt o' her. **1940** Haun *Hawk's Done* 57 I took a-hold of his neck and watched his foot. **1964** Stokely *Harvest* 153 [I w]isht I could find some way to git a-holt of some money. **1972** *AOHP/ALC*-355 Hard times was so hard that you couldn't get ahold of a nickel no way. **1979** *Preacher Cook* 192 The people that I'd called hypocrites back when I was a sinner were the first I got a'hold to. **1989** *Matewan OHP*-45 Me and him had got down there and got ahold of that hog. **1998** *Dante OHP*-69 I tried to get ahold of them down there at Erwin and I couldn't get ahold of L. J. or Bill, either one.

[Web3 *ahold* n dialect]

aholt See **a-hold.**

a-horseback *adverb* On horseback.

1864 *Apperson CW Letters* (Jan 6) tell brother henry to bring the pervision to me & the bes way is to come a horse back. **1957** GSMNP-23:2:1 [Francis Asbury] rode a-horseback all the time, and he figured it up one time to see how many times, how much he'd rode, so he figured up I think around the world once and a half. **1980** GSMNP-115:30 I've often thought how many preachers, as you say, would ride a-horseback as far as Gregory did from Cades Cove. **1991** Thomas *Sthn Appal* 131 I've went off on a trip a time ur two, a-horse-back.

aig See **egg.**

aih Lord See **eh la.**

ail

A *verb* variant past-tense form *ailded.*

1927 Woofter *Dialect from WV* 347 *ailded* = used only as the past tense of the verb *ail.* "Sally didn't know what ailded her mother." **c1960** Wilson Coll What ailed (or ailded) him?

B *noun* variant plural form *ailses.*

1975 *AOHP/ALC*-1128 Men back then was very hardy. They didn't have some of the ailses we have now.

aily *adjective* Ailing, incapacitated, with a chronic ailment.

1952 Wilson *Folk Speech NC* 514 = not well, ailing, complaining. **1994–97** Montgomery Coll (known to Brown, Cardwell); He's an aily fellow (Ledford).

aim on See **aim to.**

aim to (also *aim on, be aimed to*) *verb phrase* To intend (to), have one's mind set to (or on.)

1864 *Harrill CW Letters* (Aug 4) I can say to you that I aim to stop at the election an vote to day fore vance. **1889** *Cole Letters* 77 I guess you are ameing to go to the faire at Newport this fall. **1895** Edson and Fairchild *TN Mts* 370 She *aims* to go to-morrer. **1913** Kephart *Our Sthn High* 297 The woman's aimin' to go to meetin'. **1937** Haun *Cocke Co* 2 Folks still tote their turns of meal to mill in pokes and aim on raising a yieldy crap of corn next year. **1939** Hall Coll (Copeland Creek TN) I didn't aim to pay no notice to 'em. *Ibid.* (Deep Creek NC) I went on up and was a-aiming to get around above the tree and shoot the bear's brains out. **1961** *Coe Ridge OHP*-341B George was aimed to kill Cal. **1974** GSMNP-50:1:13 They took one of the log houses down there and put it up. Pa was aiming to move in it. **1984** Woods *WV Was Good* 227 He don't aim to be bad. (*Aim* could refer to intent or purpose.) **1985** Irwin *Alex Stewart* 69 I didn't aim to cut them down—just deaden them. **1989** *Matewan OHP*-56 They didn't intend to question him. They was aiming to shoot him. They was aiming to use some pretense to get him to do something. **2008** McKinley *Bear Mt* 67 Back then, we "aimed on" plantin' several big fields of corn ever year.

[DARE *aim* v formerly widespread, now chiefly South, South Midland]

aingern See **onion.**

aint See **aunt A.**

ain't *verb, auxiliary verb* See also **hain't** and Grammar and Syntax §5.4, §6.4.

A Variant forms *ant* [see **1862** in **B**], *an't* [see **1834** in **B**].

B = negative forms of present-tense *be.*

1 = *am not, are not, is not.*

1834 Crockett *Narrative* 124 I an't glad, for example, that the "government" moved the deposites. **c1844** Beckner *Shane Interview* 226 Oh, Caty! Ain't you most done? **1862** *Warrick CW Letters* (July 4) ther ant no danger of a fite here there ant no yenkis here. **1862** *Watters-Curtis CW Letters* (Jan 17) thank god iam A fre Man and ther ant any body that Can hender Mee from living with you. **1864** *Poteet CW Letters* (Aug 19) I am thankful that I aint in this fight. **1890** Fruit *KY Words* 67 *aint* = for *am not, is not, are not,* as "I aint goin'"; "He aint goin'"; "We or you aint goin'." Well nigh universally used here and farther south. **1895** Edson and Fairchild *TN Mts* 370 Well, I wish I may never, if you aint the beatenest boy ever I see (saw). **1922** *TN CW Ques* 237 (Surrey Co NC) I Filled this out myself an't much of a scooler. **1939** Hall Coll (Hazel Creek NC) They ain't one dog in a hundred would run a panther. **1940** Hall Coll (White Oak NC) I ain't for sure (said to be a "common expression"). **1955** Ritchie *Singing Family* 184 Don't look so all-fired mad, I ain't going to ask you to shoot yer granny. **1957** Combs *Lg Sthn High: Idioms* 12 She ain't a-carin' effn (if) ye do do it. **1963** Edwards *Gravel* 13 You must be blind as well as deaf if you ain't seed that Giles ain't never home on Sunday. **1971** Foster *Walker Valley* 3:9 You take a fellow with ten brothers and sisters—he ain't a gonna get lonesome. **1973** GSMNP-76:7 [The cattle] couldn't get a drink of water out of that creek. [There's a] lot of water in there now, but it ain't half as big as it used to be. **1985** Irwin *Alex Stewart* 105 Every horse ain't natured alike. **1987** Young *Lost Cove* 60 "Iffin he ain't the huntingest hound that ever tracked a rabbit" can be heard even today in the Lost Cove. **2009** Burton *Beech Mt Man* 94 If you get in them bars, it's rock and roll anymore—ain't bluegrass or nothin', ain't even country.

2 Used in statements with inversion of the subject and verb.

1977 *Shenandoah OHC* 136 Ain't none of us could play.

[OED2 *ain't/an't* v contraction of *are* + *not* dialect and colloquial 1778→]

C = negative forms of *have*.

1 = *has not, have not.*

1861 Sutton *CW Letters* (Oct 17) I aint got time to write anymore at this time. **1862** *Councill CW Letters* (Feb 4) I am well at this Time but I ant bin well for the last da an nite. **1895** Dromgoole *Humble Advocate* 330 Ye ain't got as much gumption as that thar chile thar this minute. **1913** Kephart *Our Sthn High* 355 "Borned in the kentry and ain't never been out o' hit" is all that most of them can say for themselves. **1931** Goodrich *Mt Homespun* 57 Laws, child, ain't you seen pokeweed a growin' up in the summertime, and then in the winter nothing left of it but a gray rag you couldn't kinnle a fire with? **1941** Stuart *Men of Mts* 68 Well it ain't allus been a wilderness. **1967** Hall *Coll* (Townsend TN) I ain't a hoof. **1969** GSMNP-27:20 You've set possum pens, ain't you, back when you was a boy? **1973** GSMNP-87:2:2 We ain't figured that out yet. **1989** *Matewan OHP*-45 I guess you've heared of him, ain't you? **1998** *Dante OHP*-61 I ain't got a thing agin the Union.

[OED2 *ain't/an't* v 2 variant of *hain't* dialect and vulgar 1845→]

2 = *had not.*

c1950 (in **2000** Oakley *Roamin' Man* 42) They had a watermellon like I aint never eat before. **1975** *AOHP/LJC*-384 If they ain't got burnt up, they'd have been right here. **2008** *Rosie Hicks* 6 = We ain't got even settled down.

D = negative form of *do*. [Editor's note: The speaker portrayed in the following citation is black; this usage does not occur in ATASC.]

1989 Millner *Letcher* 13 They ain't have no special ties to the Almighty that could give me that.

ain't it *exclamatory phrase* Isn't it? Isn't that right?

1992 Morgan *Potato Branch* 90 Them twins and that baby make a lot of work, ain't it, Deller?

ain't much See **much B1**.

aintney over See **Antony-over**.

air[1] (variant of **are**) See **be D1**.

air[2] See **ever a A**.

air[3] See **there**.

airish *adjective*

1 Of the atmosphere or temperature: brisk, cool to unpleasantly or unexpectedly windy and chilly.

1919 Combs *Word-List South* 36 *arsh* = cool, brisk (of the air). **1957** Broaddus *Vocab Estill Co KY* 2 = cool. **c1959** Weals *Hillbilly Dict* 2 = drafty, breezy, cool. "Shet the door. It feels sorta airish in here." **1971** Fox *Mouth of Mtneer* 4 = drafty: "It shore is airish in this room." **1974** Fink *Bits Mt Speech* 1 = windy, cool. "Hit's plumb *airish* out." **1986** Pederson et al. *LAGS* (Knox Co TN) Ooh, it's kind of airish out this morning. **1996–97** Montgomery *Coll* The night feels a bit airish (Brown); It was an awful airish day, wasn't it? (Cardwell). **2013** Venable *How to Tawlk* 1 = chilly: "Hit shore has turned airish fer July!"

[EDD *airish* adj Scot and Yorkshire; SND *airish* adj "cool, chilly"; DARE *airish* adj 1 formerly widespread, later chiefly South, South Midland]

2 Pompous, putting on airs.

1929 Kephart *Smoky Mt Magic* 119 Her airish pertness was gone. She was awed and humble now. **1995** Montgomery *Coll* (known to Adams, Cardwell, Weaver) **1996** Montgomery *File* She come in with an airish attitude (85-year-old man, Greenbrier TN).

[DARE *airish* adj 2 formerly widespread, later chiefly South, Midland]

airn See **ary one A**.

air shot *noun* See citation.

1973 Preston *Bituminous Term* 25 = [in coal mining] a weak explosion in which the end of the drill hole has been expanded so that a pocket of air surrounds the charge.

airy See **ary A**.

akin (also *akinned*) *adjective* Related, kin; hence noun *akin* = (a) relative. See also **kin**[1].

1937 Hall *Coll* I told the German doctor that we was akinned. **1942** Hall *Phonetics Smoky Mts* 92 [d] is added by most elderly speakers to *akin* and *born*: [əkɪnd], [bornd]. **1988** *Augusta Heritage* 153 They ain't no a-kin to me.

akinned See **akin**.

akyfortis See **aqua fortis**.

alcohol *noun*

A Variant form pronounced AL-*ky-hol*.

1942 Hall *Phonetics Smoky Mts* 60 A few words are generally sounded with [ɪ]: alcohol, dynamite, miracle, sassafras, spectacles, sycamore. In some of the words [ɪ] may be pinched or raised to or toward [i]: for example, [ˈælkihɔl]. **1973** *Gathered Together* 26 I's still under the influence a'alkyhol.

B Same as **first shot(s)**.

1956 Hall *Coll* (Waynesville NC) Then [the still] run alkyhol, run alkyhol so long. Then it breaks from alkyhol to whiskey, and then it'd run along and we'd measure it, measure it up, and third it down. **1959** Hall *Coll* (Mt Sterling NC) When liquor first come off [out of the still], it was alkyhol, and then hit'd break, and then you'd run your backin's as long as they was sweet, until they got sour.

alibi *verb* See citation.

1966 DARE *Survey* (Cherokee NC) = to excuse oneself speciously.

alky *noun* See citation.

1974 Maurer and Pearl *KY Moonshine* 113 1) illegal beverage alcohol. Not in general use among moonshiners, but used by bootleggers and wholesalers who distribute illegal liquor. 2) A grade of moonshine which, although of poor quality, is high-proof stuff to be cut by an equal amount of water. Used especially by those operators with experience during Prohibition.

alkyhol See **alcohol**.

alkyrub *noun* See citation.

1973 Miller *English Unicoi Co* 143 = rubbing alcohol.

all *pronoun*

1 compounded with a personal pronoun. See **they all**, **we all**, **you all**, and Grammar and Syntax §2.7.1.

2 compounded with an interrogative form. See **all how**, **how all**, **what all**, **where all**, **who all**, **why all**, and Grammar and Syntax §2.7.2.

3 compounded with a noun or noun phrase.

1834 *Seal Letter* my wife is very stout of her age and wants to see you and so does Zeally too and so does the children all. **1862** *Shifflet CW Letters* (March 11) I am in good helth at this time and I hope you and the children all is. **1862** *Spainhourd CW Letters* (Nov 24) I reseive one [letter] from Susan and the rest of them all. **1864** Wilson *Confederate Private* 60 (July 16) the wheat all is short in the valey. **1939** Hall *Coll* (Wears Cove TN) They'd shear the sheep, and she'd spin the wool, the thread, and make our britches and our shirts all. **1954** Roberts *Bought a Dog* [6] I knowed I couldn't kill the geese and the ducks all, and the snake. **1969** GSMNP-42:10 Old man Lon and Will all, they all went with him. **1973** *Foxfire Interviews* A-73-86 Then Stella and Eunice and them all, they all three went over there. **1994** Montgomery *Coll* They feed me enough for me and Fay and Oliver all (Cardwell).

allas, allays See **always**.

all-day singing *noun* A daylong community gathering featuring the singing of hymns, with a break for **dinner on the grounds**, held usually in connection with **homecoming** or **association**. See also **singing**.

1958 Morgan *Gift from Hills* 38 It's a great pity that these all-day singings are gradually being discontinued, for nothing really takes the place of them. Radio and TV cannot compare, certainly not socially. They were tremendous occasions, eagerly looked forward to. People would plan and prepare for days ahead of time, baking and cooking. Sometimes a family would take a whole trunkful of food. Nobody ever attended a singing convention in our country without getting his fill of food as well as song. When the morning of the great day arrived, the choirs, the congregations and the visitors from hither and yon began to gather at the appointed church. The choirs were assigned their turns, the first choir would take its position and the all-day singing would be off to a melodious start. They began to have competitions and one choir would be voted best for the year, but after a time this competition detracted from the sheer joy of the singing and the fellowship and it was discontinued. **1995** Williams *Smoky Mts Folklife* 42 A singing master would make a circuit through rural communities during the summer. The singing schools in this region typically lasted two weeks, and frequently the singing master's circuit would culminate in an all-day singing in the early fall. **2008** Malone *All-Day Singings* 163 The practice of combining food and religious music long ago gave rise to the phrase "all-day singing with dinner on the grounds," which describes one of the most common events in the rural South.

Allegheny servicetree See **service B1**.

alleluia *noun* The common wood sorrel (*Oxalis acetosella*). Same as **mountain shamrock**, **mountain sorrel**, **sheep sorrel**, **wood shamrock**.

1901 Lounsberry *Sthn Wild Flowers* 288 White wood-sorrel . . . Even in some places it is known by the delightful name of "Alleluia." **1932** Hines *Wildflowers Appal* 62.67 One of the Appalachian wild plants, known locally as Alleluia, is none other than the White Wood Sorrel. **1997** Montgomery *Coll* (known to Andrews, Bush).

[perhaps so named because it flowers in the Easter season; OED3 *alleluia* n² c1425→; DARE *alleluia* n chiefly southern Appalachians]

allers See **always**.

all fire and tow See **fire and tow**.

all-fired See also **hell-fire(d)**.

A *adjective* Complete, utter, thorough.

1913 Kephart *Our Sthn Highlander* 91 Guess I run her half a mile through all-fired thickets. **1981** Whitener *Folk-Ways* 82 An obliging native son seated at the end of the counter spoke up: "Excuse me, ma'am, but since you're in such a allfard hurry I'd be right proud to trade with you." **1985** Edwards *Folksy Sketches* 46 The all-firedest rattling of metal and iron pieces took place inside the store that you ever heard tell of.

B *adverb* Completely, utterly, excessively.

1864 Gilmore *Down in TN* 109 Thar I lied fur two all-fired long nights—in the mud up ter my knees. **1886** Smith *Sthn Dialect* 349 There are still others [= terms] which have not, so far as I know, the authority of Old English: all-fired (very, exceedingly). **1896** Fox *Vendetta* 162 I'd agot Jas myself ef he hadn't been so allfired quick o' trigger. **1955** Ritchie *Singing Family* 184 Don't look so all-fired mad, I ain't going to ask you to shoot yer granny. I just want to be friendly like. **1972** *Graham County* 138 Hit made me so all fired mad that I concluded I would jest kick that cat up the chimney. **1995–97** Montgomery *Coll* (known to nine consultants from the Smoky Mountains).

[euphemistic variant of *hell-fired*; OED3 *all-fired* adj/adv chiefly in U.S.]

all fire in tow See **fire and tow.**

all get-out (also *all git-out*) *noun* Something extreme in degree or intensity.

1963 Edwards *Gravel* 104 Now I'll be dad-blamed if that don't beat all get-out. **1984** *Six Hill'n Holler* 2 Hit was as big as All-git-out. **2013** Venable *How to Tawlk* 2 = a high level, usually involving volatile emotion: "Jabbo was sadder'n all git out when his boy got kilt in the war."

all-gone feeling *noun* See citation.

1940 Bowman *KY Mt Stories* 233 = feeling as though one would faint or die.

all how *conjunction* How, all the ways in which.

1952 Wilson *Folk Speech NC* 514 = how, completely how. "He told *all how* he beat that fellow up." **1978** Montgomery *White Pine Coll* IV-4 I don't remember all how we used it. **1988** Smith *Fair and Tender* 199 He knows all how to do it, too.

all in *adjective phrase* Fatigued, exhausted.

1927 Woofter *Dialect from WV* 347 = exhausted. "The men were all in when the fire was under control." **c1960** Wilson *Coll* I'm all in after working at the mill. **1976** Garber *Mountain-ese* 3 Atter walkin' home from work, I'm about all-in. **1986** Helton *Around Home* 378 = exhausted. **1995** Montgomery *Coll* (known to Cardwell, Shields).

all is *adverb phrase* All things considered, in any case (used to introduce and qualify statements).

1931 Hannum *Thursday April* 108 All is, hit'll be a heap sight better'n havin' him make cheer bottoms the rest of his days. **1981** GSMNP-117:27 "Now, all is," he said, "I don't care if you go if your parents don't care."

[DARE *all is* adv phr chiefly New England, Appalachians]

all-overs (usually *the all-overs*) *noun* Nervousness, the shivers, uneasy anticipation.

1917 Kephart *Word-List* 407 Every time I go to studyin' about it I git the *all-overs*. **1929** (in **1952** Mathes *Tall Tales* 136) "Git away! Don't tetch me! Hit gives me the all overs," the old lady shouted hysterically. **c1940** Aswell *Glossary TN Idiom* 1 = shivery feeling. **1952** Wilson *Folk Speech NC* 514 = nervousness, uneasiness. **1961** Seeman *Arms of Mt* 94 He shore had the all-overs that time. **1968** Wilson *Folklore Mammoth Cave* 41 Nervous fit[s], often suspected as hardly genuine . . . were *duck fits, conniption fits, jeeminy fits, the all-overs*, and, very recently, the *heebie-jeebies*, or the *whitty-jiggers*. **1975** Jackson *Unusual Words* 158 If he has a nervous disorder, he has the *all-overs* or is *loose all over*. **1998** Hyde *My Home* 46 An unusually nervous person was said to have the "all overs." **2001** Lowry *Expressions* 9 I've got the all-overs. **2016** *Blind Pig* (Oct 8) When I get the all-overs, I feel like someone I can't see is watching me and the little hairs on the back of my neck all stand to attention.

[DARE *all-overs* n pl chiefly South, South Midland]

all-overest (also *all-overst*) *adjective* Worst, most extreme or outlandish (used as a generalized intensive with the sense of "best of all" or "worst of all").

1937 Hall *Coll* (White Oak NC) It was the all-overst sight I ever seed. **1939** Hall *Coll* (Saunook NC) [Reported examples]: It was the all-overst achin' I ever had; It was the all-overst rain I ever seen; the all-overst [= most worthless] cow I ever seen. **1972** Hall *Sayings* 36 "He's the all-overst fellow I ever saw," said of one "who's full of fun, a practical joker"; can also mean, "there's no one like him." **1992** Davis *Jack Tales* 143 Why, that is the all-overest big tale that I have ever heard!

allow *verb*

A Variant form *'low* [see **1900** in **B**].

B [Editor's note: The senses below cannot always be differentiated, especially senses 1 and 3. The interpretation is highly nuanced and ranges from mock agreement to grudging admission to outright concurrence and assertion.]

1 To think, suppose, believe. See also **expect B, reckon B.**

1849 Lanman *Alleghany Mts* 89 Now, I allow this pond, in a common way, is nigh onto half a mile long. **1860** Olmsted *Back Country* 229 Whittling away, he addressed me: "'Low yer minin'" (searching for ore-beds). **1862** *Zimmerman CW Letters* (Sept 4) some of J W Banners things was in the Box we allowed you would know them apart. **1900** Harben *N GA Sketches* 56 They 'lowed I was jest homesick an' wanted a' excuse to come back. **1937** Hall *Coll* (Cosby Creek TN) I allowed this corn was planted in the new of the moon, it grew so tall. **1939** Hall *Coll* (Nine Mile TN) I looked up a tree. I allowed [the bear] might have had some cubs there and whooped them up a tree. **c1945** Haun *Hawk's Done* 254 "I allowed you was done already a Christian," she said. **1957** Combs *Lg Sthn High: Word List* 3 = suppose, think; usually contracted to 'low. Ex.: "I 'lowed he'd come." **1967** Fetterman *Stinking Creek* 133 I allowed my dogs'd already jumped at least a rabbit by now. **1973** GSMNP-81:10 I allowed they was two Dans [is] the reason they called him Smoker Dan. **1997** Montgomery *Coll* I 'lowed Susy would fly all over a daisy field and settle on a cow pile [in hunting a husband] (Brown).

[DARE *allow* v 1 chiefly South, Midland]

2 To plan, intend, purpose.

1863 *Penland CW Letters* (May 8) [I] allowed to get a permit to day and go to see him but there was no chance to get a permit to day. **1897** *Incidents* 31 "I don't never 'low to be out-clevered," he said, "and I don't like to be out-rascaled." **1904–20** Kephart *Notebooks* 2:461 I 'lowed to git me a plug o' tobacco. **1913** Kephart *Our Sthn High* 297 I 'low to go to town to-morrow. **1977** Shackelford et al. *Our Appalachia* 96 A big mink had a little hole dug through that cliff. I allowed I'd catch him for sure.

[DARE *allow* v 4 chiefly South, Midland]

3 To state, declare.

1901 Harben *Westerfelt* 118 She 'lowed ef we'd 'a' made you stay with us you'd not 'a' been apt to 'a met Wambush that day. **1923** Furman *Mothering* 138 [By the] time the rest of the Lusks got up from their wounds, they allowed paw was a mean enough man to leave alone. **1923** Greer-Petrie *Angeline Steppin' Out* 1 Lum 'lowd he'd heerd of writin' letters, and gittin' 'em, but he be dad burned if dictatin' 'em wan't a new one on him. **1923** Montague *Today Tomorrow* 160 Then he dosed him some, and 'lowed he'd be all right to-morrow. **1937** Thornburgh *Great Smoky Mt* 132 I lowed to him I never dreamt they'd believe a yarn like that. **1955** Ritchie *Singing Family* 123 We came to the crossroads where two forks of the little branch rolled in together and made one. He stopped and 'lowed that this was the place to say good-by. **1974** Murray *Down to Earth* 62 "Singing for nickels and dimes beats sitting around doing nothing" allows Billy as he strums his guitar under the awning of a five-and-ten. **2009** Benfield *Mt Born* 121 If a person allowed something, he was admitting or declaring it to be so.

4 In phrase *allow as how* = to acknowledge, concede, assert.

1940 Haun *Hawk's Done* 20 He allowed as how he would kill her and Joe both if she ever slipped off and went with him again. **1969** Miller *Raising Tobacco* 30 Studying on it, he might allow as how a feller might find it right handy—some other feller. **1992** Davis *Jack Tales* 75 Jack allowed as how he wasn't much for trying contests like this. **2000** Morgan *Mts Remember* 56 I allowed as to how his ma and pa must have been happy to see him.

allow as how See **allow B4**.

all's *pronoun* All that.

1985 Williams *Role of Folklore* 301 All's I got's what I'm wearin'. **1998** Montgomery *Coll* All's I know Jim taught me (Brown); All's I have is yours (Cardwell); All's I have is in the kitchen (Norris). **2009** Burton *Beech Mt Man* 97 All's they do is ax you to dance. **2012** *Blind Pig* (May 12) We use all's in place of all that: "All's I know is I did what she told me to do. And if that ain't good enough then I don't know what else a body could do." The grammar usages above are all very common in my area of Appalachia—and in my household.

[probably contraction of *all* + *as*]

all the *adjective phrase*

1 The only (preceding a singular count noun or the indefinite pronoun *one*).

1814 Hartsell *Memora* 143 he was all the purson that Dyed out of our ridgement yet. **1862** *Robinson CW Letters* (April 6) all the chance is to take Some body elses & jest Rip a head. **1862** *Lockmiller CW Letters* (July 18) he sed ... I was all the girl he seed that he cerd iney thinge ab oute looken at. **1863** *Warrick CW Letters* (Dec 10) they takend or kild green hinds and some mor but he is all the one that you no any thing A bout in this Compay. **1864** *Blair CW Letters* (April 30) I ansuerd your leter of the 17th inst whitch is all the lete[r] I hav received from home yet. **1915** Dingus *Word-List VA* 180 = the only, as "all the friend I've got." **1928** (in **1952** Mathes *Tall Tales* 44) Ye're all the child Tommy had, an' yer mammy died the night ye was borned. **1939** Hall *Coll* (Deep Creek NC) The old blue back speller was all the study we had, just study. **1940** Oakley *Roamin'/Restin'* 14 All the thing that I could think of was some great animal had come around and scared the dogs away and it must be a bear or some other dangurous animal. **1959** Hall *Coll* (Newport TN) He had about eight or ten on [the string], speckled trout—that's all the kind they was back in what they called Laurel Creek. **1972** *AOHP/ALC-241* That was all the way I traveled the most of the time. **1973** *GSMNP-74:14* In Sugarlands that's all the one I know anything about. **1978** Burton *Ballad Folks* 53 Them's all the kind that's pretty. **1989** *Matewan OHP-9* That's all the way they had to cross the river. **1993** *Stories 'neath Roan* 58 We raised wheat for our bread. That was all the way you could get any flour back then. **1997** Andrews *Mountain Vittles* 30 That was all the life the mountain women knew ... the hard work of taking care of their families.

[SND *all the one* (at *all* adj/adv (4) only for Ulster; CUD *all the* (at *all*) "the only"; HT *a' the yin* "the only one, the only one available"; DARE *all the* (at *all* adj[1] 1) formerly scattered New England, South, South Midland, now chiefly southern Appalachians]

2 Used to modify the positive form of an adjective to express extent (thus *all the far* = as far as, all the distance that, etc.).

1891 Brown *Dialect in TN* 175 All has a peculiar usage in examples like the following: "That's all the high (or higher) he can jump," "all the far you can throw." **1895** Murfree *Phantoms* 219 That's 'bout all the fur my school-larnin' kerried me, an' yourn didn't reach ter the nex' mile-post. **c1960** Wilson *Coll* "That's all the fast this horse can run." "That's all the further I can go." *As far* ... is probably less common than *all the far* or *all the further*. **1975** Montgomery *File* That's all the far I want to go. **1983** *Dark Corner OHP-5A* When the first gun was fired, I remember her a-asking, "Is that all the loud it's going to be?" **1997** Montgomery *Coll* (known to Brown).

[HT *a' the far* "all the distance"; DARE *all the* adv phr chiefly South, South Midland]

3 Used to modify the comparative form of an adjective to express extent (thus *all the faster* = as fast as).

[See **1891** in **2**]. **1946** Woodard *Word-List VA/NC* 3 = as far as: "That's all the farther I went." **1956** McAtee *Some Dial NC* 2 Is that all the faster you can run? **1957** Combs *Lg Sthn High: Syntax* 6 The conjunctival adverbial *as ... as* may be expressed by *all the*, but the comparative form of the following word must be used instead of the positive: "That's all the further I'm a-goin'." **1966** Dakin *Vocab Ohio River Valley* 306–7 The expressions *all the farther* and *all the further*, although sometimes characterized as "old-fashioned," are quite common in the speech of the more educated and in cultivated speech, especially in Kentucky. **1968** *DARE Survey* (Brasstown NC) This is all the further we can go. **1996–97** Montgomery *Coll* (known to Brown, Bush, Cardwell, Hooper, Jones, Ledford, Oliver).

4 to modify the comparative form of an adjective to express extent or superlative degree.

1927 Woofter *Dialect from WV* 347 = used with comparatives, such as *all the smaller*, *all the bigger*, with the meaning as small as, as big as. "These are all the bigger apples we have." **1957** Combs *Lg Sthn High: Word List* 3 = used superlatively, as in: "Them's all the littler pigs we have." (Those are the smallest pigs we have.)

5 to modify the superlative form of an adjective to express extent (thus *all the best* = as good as).

1996–97 Montgomery Coll (known to Brown, Bush, Hooper, Jones, Ledford, Oliver); Is that all the best you can do? (Cardwell).

all the far See **all the 2**.

all the farther See **all the 3**.

all the time *adverb phrase* Always, frequently (variant syntactic position within the predicate).

1859 Taliaferro *Fisher's River* 117–18 I staid away fur some time, and 'Gius was all the time knittin' away. **1863** *Epperly CW Letters* (Aug 1) it is unsurtain how long we will Stay at a plase they keep us all the time runing backwoard and forwards on The Railroade. **1864** *Love CW Letters* (July 8) us and the yanks is from two to 7 hundred yards apart We are all the time Sharp Shooting and Shelling each other. **1898** Elliott *Durket Sperret* 52 Was you all the time adoin' that. **c1945** Haun *Hawk's Done* 276 He was all the time learning her something. **1978** Montgomery *White Pine Coll* VIII-1 They was all the time arguing over who was the best candidate. . . . He's all the time hollering at me. **1989** *Matewan OHP*-45 He liked fishing. He was all the time fishing. **1998** *Dante OHP*-61 She's all the time wanting me to do something. **2009** Burton *Beech Mt Man* 91 He's all the time shadow boxin'. He'd run up, just hit in the air, you know, just kick, and jump. **2015** Holbrook *Something* 150 Miranda's all the time sick.

[DARE *all (the) time* adv phr chiefly South, South Midland]

all to *phrasal preposition* Except for.

1862 *Epperly CW Letters* (July 10) Joseph is well all to the toothache he had it very bad last night and has it yet he is well all to that. **1862** *Ingram CW Letters* (Oct 4) I now take my pen in hand to let you Know that I [am] tolable well all to a hurtin in my hip and Sholders. **1864** *Warrick CW Letters* (June 11) I am Still in the lan of liv yet an I am well all to A bad coof.

all to flinders See **flinders**.

all to once *adverb phrase* All at once. See also **to 4**.

1931 Combs *Lg Sthn High* 1321 *To* is used for *at* in: "He broke out all to onct." **1934** Cushman *Swing Mountain Gal* 100 We used to study, all to once't, out loud, and you couldn't hear what you was a-thinkin' fur the row! **1962** Dykeman *Tall Woman* 188 "It don't have a movable hot-water reservoir like Mrs. Nelson's," Sue Thurston added, "but Clay said he's afraid I'd be rotten spoiled did he get me everything all to once."

all to pieces *noun phrase, adjective phrase* See citations.

1990 Cavender *Folk Medical Lex* 17 = an expression used to describe an acute state of anxiety. **1994** Montgomery Coll = a state of acute illness (Shields). **2001** Lowry *Expressions* 10 My nerves is all to pieces.

allus See **always**.

almanac *noun* variant forms *almanick, alminick*.

1768 (in **1912** Chalkley *Augusta Co VA* 1.462) (DARE) 2 alminicks, 1 alminick. **1913** Kephart *Our Sthn High* 252 When a friend came to visit me, the landlady giggled an aside to her husband: "Git the almanick and see when that feller'll full!" (as though she were bidding him to look to see when the moon would be full). **1994** Montgomery Coll: *alminick* (Cardwell).

[DARE (at *almanac* n) chiefly New England, South Midland]

almanick See **almanac**.

almighty *adverb* Extremely, exceedingly.

1913 Kephart *Our Sthn High* 106 He crossed through the laurel on the Devil's Court House and tuk down an almighty steep place. **c1960** Wilson Coll "It's almighty hot today." Almost a cuss-word. **1982** Powers and Hannah *Cataloochee* 368 He had that all-mighty fine fiddle which set them to jigging just to hear it. **1994** Montgomery Coll (known to Cardwell).

Almighty be *interjection* Used as a mild oath.

1966 Dykeman *Far Family* 205 Almighty be! A piano? Of course we ought to have a piano for all these girls.

alminick See **almanac**.

along *adverb*

1 (also *'long*) Approximately, somewhere, sometime (usually with temporal reference and followed by a preposition or adverb, most often *about, back*).

1910 Cooke *Power and Glory* 15 Uncle Pros he got a revelation 'long 'bout midnight as to just whar that thar silver mine is. **1939** Hall Coll (Indian Creek NC) He tuck the whooping cough along about Christmas time and was out of school for a month, and then he tuck a back set and was out of school again. *Ibid.* (Hazel Creek NC) Along towards the last, a year or two before we quit, why we kept a man there with them all the time. *Ibid.* (Saunook NC) Along about twelve o'clock, why we found them. *Ibid.* (Sugarlands TN) Along back about the time the park started in here, why this country round here where I'm a-living now was just settled up thick. **1953** Hall Coll (Plott Creek NC) This has been along back just a few years ago, before the park took over the Hazel Creek boundary, game preserve. **1954** GSMNP-19:18 I went up one night with them to go a-fox hunting along in the autumn. **1964** Roberts *Hell-Fer-Sartin* 36 Along that evening he said, says, "How much will you give me to stay tonight up there?" **1975** GSMNP-59:17 He had two brothers that was . . . hid along down on the road that they had to go, and that was why that he knowed that they wouldn't get out with him. **1978** Montgomery *White Pine Coll* IX-2 They built the Douglas and the Cherokee [dams] about the same time, along two or three years apart maybe. **1979** *Big South Fork OHP*-11 Rob lived over there at where Bill Powells lives, along out across from Virgil's place. **1990** Wigginton *Foxfire Christmas* 79 We had a bunch of cousins that came to visit us along just before Christmas one time. **1997** *Dante OHP*-14 A lawyer along in St. Paul told me "if you're indicted," he said, "I'll defend."

2 Continuously, steadily, regularly, occasionally.

1864 Chapman *CW Letters* (May 29) I have been bying something to eat a long once and a whil and it takes money to by with. **1868** *Kendrick CW Letters* (June 28) I havent sold that brandie yet only a fiew quarts along once and a while. **1874** Swearingen *Letters* 165 I would like to have a few lines from her occasionally along. **1939** Hall *Coll* (Wears Cove TN) We'd kill game along all the time. **1966** Dykeman *Far Family* 296 Law, that was a sight, how Mama sold those two big boundaries of timber to the tannery and Mr. Austin's pulp mill and we got payments along to meet some of Papa's debts and interest and taxes. **1973** *Foxfire Interviews* A-73-86 I stayed away from home right smart along, working for people along at times when they needed it. **1978** Montgomery *White Pine Coll* X-2 I was for the Dodgers along when I first got to watching them on television. **1997** Andrews *Mountain Vittles* 24 Along, add more water for plenty a juice. **2003** LaLone et al. *Farming Life* 305 We have added a little bit [of land] along.

along of *phrasal preposition*

1 (also *long of*) Because of.

1931 Owens *Speech Cumberlands* 91 I came early long of wantin' to get it done afore the rain. **1936** Morehouse *Rain on Just* 79 Not one of us ought to be at licker. . . . Rease just now buried. Dead along of that same poison.

[DARE *along of* 1 chiefly New England, Midland, South]

2 (also *long o'*, *'long of*) With, beside.

1864 Gilmore *Down in TN* 108 I war a livin' long uv dad, over thar in Bladsoe. **1895** Dromgoole *Fiddling to Fame* 50 Some few sided long o' me, but most war tuk to Alf. **1937** Campbell *KY Mt Community* 530 You bile [the greens] up with pork and you orter have onions to eat 'long of the sallet. **1957** Combs *Lg Sthn High: Word List* 3 = along with. Ex.: "I'll go along o' you."

alongst *preposition* Along, alongside of.

1930 Armstrong *This Day and Time* 201 You 'ull git took up alongst with the balance of 'em. **1964** Williams *Prep Mt Speech* 54 Telescoped clusters of prepositions are discernible in . . . *alongst* (alongside of).

a-loose *adjective* Loose (used predicatively).

1901 Harben *Westerfelt* 83 Let it aloose, I tell you, or I'll mash your skull! **1961** *Coe Ridge OHP-334B* The good skiff broke a-loose, and Uncle C—said, told, says "some of you boys catch that skiff." **1972** *AOHP/LJC-104* [The mule]'d take a-loose from the plow and take the singletrees from it. **1983** *Dark Corner OHP-5A* You'll have you two hens and a gobbler. . . . Just take them over there and turn them a-loose. **2008** *Rosie Hicks* 1 I turned a-loose of it and started to the house.

[DARE perhaps reanalysis of *a loose*; *aloose* adj originally scattered, now chiefly South, South Midland]

al's See **always**.

alter *verb* To castrate or spay (an animal). See also **change**, **cut B2**, **trim**.

1862 *Wesson CW Letters* (March 12) hav the pig[s] Spaid and alterd in may. **1934–47** *LAMSAS* (Madison Co NC, Swain Co NC). **1975** Gainer *Speech Mtneer* 6 = to castrate an animal. "The sign is not right to alter the hogs." **1986** Pederson et al. *LAGS* (Blount Co TN). **1999** Montgomery *Coll* = also to spay (Cardwell).

altogether *adverb* Completely, exclusively, entirely (placed after a plural noun).

1953 Hall *Coll* (Bryson City NC) We used them altogether if we could. Sometimes we'd get ahold of other breeds of dogs. . . . The bloodhound made a cold nose for tracking up cold tracks, and that was one of the advantages in getting that into the Plott hound, and then we used that altogether as near as possible. **1973** *AOHP/ASU-111* When I was born, back that far now, they was no doctor around. They was midwives altogether. **1975** *GSMNP-59:29* The first five or six years there they used horses altogether. **1982** Powers and Hannah *Cataloochee* 360 We used shape-note songbooks altogether. **1985** Dabney *More Mt Spirits* 66 Back in them old days they used copper pots altogether, too.

[OED3 *altogether* C adv 1 now colloq. and regional (chiefly Irish English); cf DHE perhaps ultimately influenced by Irish Gaelic *ar fad*]

always *adverb* variant forms *allas*, *allays*, *allers*, *allus*, *al's*.

1859 (in **1974** Harris *High Times* 244) Thar's the ole billy goat allers had the name ove a minnit man. **1892** Doak *Wagonauts Abroad* 189 "They allus carried fishing tackle," he said, when we showed him our sporting outfit. **1923** (in **1952** Mathes *Tall Tales* 8) I'd allus heared him preachin' in his big roarin' voice, but that day he was plumb gentle, and his voice was soft and easy-like. **1931** Goodrich *Mt Homespun* 76 She was allays a workin' at suthin' and I recollect when she was at this. **c1940** Simms *Coll* Hit 'pears water air allus a-tryin' to be level. **1959** Roberts *Up Cutshin* 44 Any more I allas tell the truth. **1974** Fink *Bits Mt Speech* 1 He's *allers* late. **c1979** Chiles *Glossary* 1 *allers, al's, allus*. **1986** Helton *Around Home* 377 *allus*.

always-ago *adverb phrase* A long time ago.

1914 Furman *Sight* 70 [He] beseeched of her to forgive and forgit . . . which of course, being Marthy, she had already done allus-ago. **1917** Davis *A Bornin'* 705 Oh, that's been done by midwives sence allers ago; I heered it from my mammy. **1931** Combs *Lg Sthn High* 1320 "Always ago" (long ago) is corrupted into "allus-ago," or "allers (sharp s) ago." **1941** Still *Troublesome Creek* 104 Allus ago we fit, and nary a one could whoop. **1955** Ritchie *Singing Family* 9 Mo's voice would crack out like thunder on the Judgment Day, "Good Land! These young uns ought to've been asleep allus ago." [**1995–97** Montgomery *Coll* (unknown to consultants from the Smoky Mountains).]

[DARE *always-ago* adv eastern KY]

a many, **a many of** See **many**.

ambeer (also *ambia*, *ambier*, *ambure*) *noun* Spittle colored brown by chewing tobacco.

1878 Coale *Wilburn Waters* 50 Just then a man behind me spirted a mouthful of ambier all around [my hat]. **1886** Smith *Sthn Dialect* 349 There are still others [= terms] which have not, so far as I know, the authority of Old English: . . . ambia or ambeer (tobacco juice). **1904–20** Kephart *Notebooks* 2:438 Hit doesn't look nice to see a woman cuddin' this home-made tobacco, that's strong enough to kill a snake, and squirtin' ambeer around everywhere. **1962** Dykeman *Tall Woman* 187 The big yard, sloping down to the river, was filled with clusters of men standing in awkward, mid-week leisure, spitting ambeer, talking together with hats pushed on the backs of their heads. **1973** *Words and Expressions* 133 *ambure* = snuff or tobacco juice. **1978** Hiser *Quare Do's* 38 She laughed at me, and put ambeer on my bruised behind [to treat the pain]. **1984** Woods *WV Was Good* 221 *ambeer* = the spittal of a person chewing tobacco, probably a corruption of the word *amber*, which describes the color of tobacco juice. **2008** *Rosie Hicks* 1 He'll come and spit ambeer in my eyes.

[alteration of *amber*, perhaps influenced by *beer*; Web3 *ambeer* n South and Midland; DARE *ambeer* n 2 chiefly South, South Midland]

amber bell *noun* A bead lily (*Clintonia borealis*). Also called **balsam bell**.

1943 Stupka *Through the Year* 265 Many are the herbaceous plants which are at home in both places—clintonia (the "blue-bead lily" of the north woods; the "amber bell" of the southern highlands).

[from the color and shape of the flower]

amber days See **ember days**.

ambia, **ambier** See **ambeer**.

ambitious *adjective*

1 Especially of a horse: high-spirited, frisky, unruly, vicious.

1863 *Matthews CW Letters* (May 2) My Poney Stud hir Tripp verry well & is as ambissious Ass She can bee. **1886** Smith *Sthn Dialect* 349 There are still others [= terms] which have not, so far as I know, the authority of Old English: . . . ambitious (of a horse, spirited). **1919** Combs *Word-List South* 33 = applied to an "ambitious" (fiery) horse. **1931** Combs *Lg Sthn High* 1310 An "ambitious" horse is an unruly horse. **1952** Wilson *Folk Speech NC* 514 = vicious. "That dog is mighty *ambitious*."

[DARE *ambitious* adj South, Midland]

2 Especially of a child: lively, energetic.

c1960 Wilson *Coll* (DARE) = energetic rather than trying to dominate. **1996–97** Montgomery *Coll* (known to Brown); Quit being so ambitious or you'll get a whipping (Cardwell).

ambure See **ambeer**.

ambuscade *noun* A disagreement.

1895 Edson and Fairchild *TN Mts* 370 Him and me had several little *ambuscades*. **1996** Montgomery *Coll* (known to Brown) = usually physical rather than verbal (Oliver).

amen brethering *noun* See citation. See also **amen corner**, **brother**.

2014 Montgomery *Doctrine* 68–69 = these Brethering, typically deacons of various classes, sit together on the front benches during service. . . . If a speaker in the stand makes an especially impressive point they rally together better than cheerleaders at a Friday night football game and loudly AMEN!!! the fella.

amen corner *noun* The area usually at the right front of a church sanctuary and at the side of the pulpit, in which sit older men (occasionally women) of the congregation (deacons if they are Baptist, elders if Methodist, etc.) to reinforce and encourage the preacher by punctuating the sermon and prayers with calls of "Amen!" and other exhortations. See also **amen row**.

1928 Justus *Betty Lou* 76 They sang the last song, "Oh, Zion Haste Thy Mission High Fulfilling," and then the folks from the "Amen corner" came up and shook hands with Professor Poget and told him what they thought of his talk. **1938** Justus *No-End Hollow* 198 He would make a joke, I do believe, right in the Amen corner of the meeting house, if he had half a chance! **1968** Wilson *Folklore Mammoth Cave* 40 = the side in the *church-house* to the left of the preacher where sat the old men of the congregation, who often "amened" what the preacher had said. The opposite corner, where the older women sat, was, humorously, called the "awomen-corner." **c1975** Lunsford *It Used to Be* 173 The "Amen corner" means the corner of the church where most of the older members sat and cried "Amen" when they wanted to give encouragement to the minister, or the one leading the congregation in prayer. **1976** Braden *Grandma Was Girl* 75–76 The pulpit was at the other end, and on each side of the pulpit were long seats, or pews, where the older people sat. The women sat on the preacher's left; the men on his right. This area, we called the "Amen Corner." **c1980** Roberts *Olden Times* 61 The camp meetings were held in the forests with a temporary platform pulpit which always had a section to the right of the pulpit reserved for the local exhorters who punctuated the long and vigorous sermons with shouts of "Amen" and "Hallalujah" and "Praise the Lord," a chorus to keep both audience and preacher keyed to a high pitch. From this practice has come the term "amen corner."

[DARE *amen corner* n 1 chiefly South, Midland]

amen row *noun* A row or bench in the **amen corner**.

1925 Dargan *Highland Annals* 255 I reckon he wuz the furdest from the Amen row right then that he ever wuz in his life. **1995** Montgomery *Coll* (known to Shields, but not to other consultants from the Smoky Mountains).

a-mind *phrase* in phrases *be a-mind*, *be a-minded* = to have in mind, be disposed to. See also **mind B2**.

1863 *Tesh CW Letters* (March 15) Mr Hardin Sayes he will pay half of that money if You are a mine to You may go and get it. **1864** *Proffit CW Letters* (June 20) If you are a mind to bee flustrated a bout sutch a beeing as I am. **1875** Carpenter *Diary* I 151 Margit Carpenter . . . war good womin war good to the pore when she war amind. **1938** Justus *No-End Hollow* 242 Are you a-minded to tell the folks all that has happened today? **1978** Reese *Speech NE Tenn* 44 He was a-minded to marry me.

[perhaps reduction of *of a mind (to)* or reanalysis of *of mind*; cf EDD *mind* sb[1] 1(1)]

ancient *adjective* variant form *ann-cient* ['ænʃənt].

1935 Sheppard *Cabins in Laurel* 4 The mountain people call these first miners, whose identity is shrouded in mystery, "the ann-cients," and let it go at that. **1942** Hall *Phonetics Smoky Mts* 18 *Ancient* [is] heard only with the vowel [æ].

[DARE *ancient* adj A South Midland]

and *conjunction*

1 Used to conjoin verb phrases to express simultaneous initiative and the action of the second verb. See **go and**, **send and**, **take and**.

[OED3 *and* conj[1] 10]

2 What with, while, because, despite the fact that (used to introduce an absolute clause following a finite one and containing a present participle or interpretable as having an ellipted *being*, but no finite verb). See also Grammar and Syntax §15.2.

1861 *Hileman CW Letters* (Aug 23) Last night their was a sort of a stir in camp we was called out about 9 Oclock P M and it Raining to Boot. **1862** *Robinson CW Letters* (Sept 4) tha[y] will Steal the bread out of your haversacks & it hung to your Side. **1864** *Dalton CW Letters* (Dec 15) Last Sun day ourer regment had A little scrumish with the yankeys and it Asnowing jest as hard as I ever saw it in my life. **1867** Harris *Sut Lovingood* 32 I felt like I'd crowded intu a ole bee-gum, an' hit all full ove pissants. **1916** Schockel *KY Mts* 121 Then if the soil won't produce, I'd have to come back, an' them set agin me. **1939** Hall *Coll* (Sylva NC) That woman is doing too much work, and her in a family way. **1940** Haun *Hawk's Done* 25 Old Man Brock didn't want her, and him her own grandpa. **1956** Hall *Coll* (Del Rio TN) He would steal the hat off your head, and you a-looking at him. **1971** *AOHP/ALC*-4 He worked on for years, loaded coal, and him [in] awful bad shape. **1971** Foster *Walker Valley* 3:48 He's as close to that till he grabbed it by the back leg and it a straddle of that log. **1973** *Florence and Lawton* 194 [We would] get out an' throw'em from [one] t'th'other an' catch'em an' throw'em back, an' them a-fire! **1985** Irwin *Alex Stewart* 70 I ain't staying here and his nose all turned up at me. *Ibid.* 254 He come running and pulled out a .38 pistol and shot that dog right through the head and me a holding him. **1989** *Matewan OHP*-28 I've only missed one service in my life at church a-going on down here, and me being at home, and I missed one. **1994** Schmidt and Hooks *Whistle* 140 She took that pig out and hugged that pig and it just a-squealin' like one thing.

[probably from influence of Irish Gaelic/Scottish Gaelic *agus*; OED3 *and* conj 9b, a1500→, now regional (chiefly Irish English); cf EDD *and* conj 2 "to introduce a nominative absolute, sometimes with ellipsis of verb"; cf DHE]

3 Used in dates, to separate numbers, especially hundreds from tens.

1852 *Chapman CW Letters* (Dec 21) Dear uncle I can Give you my age and you can Judg whether I am old Enough to marry or not Jason Chapman was Born March the 7 eighteen hundred and Thirty I have bin Looking out for a companion but cant Find none to Soot me. **1939** Hall *Coll* (Deep Creek NC) The summer of nineteen and twenty-eight there came a fellow down here from New York City and wanted to go a-fishing. *Ibid.* (Tow String Creek NC) Along in nineteen and thirty three I went into a southern [CCC] camp, and then I went from there to a company of fifteen, that's northern camp. **1969** *GSMNP*-44:12 I turned in my resignation on the third Sunday in February, nineteen and thirty-nine, and moved straight on next week to Haywood County, and I've been there ever since. **1973** *Garland Willis* 76 [It's] been three years on May seventh and twentieth. **1974** *GSMNP*-51:11 I worked some on that church. That was built about nineteen and hundred. **1975** Woolley *We Be Here* 84 We're having to patch up what we've lost of what we won back in the nineteen and thirties. **1983** *Dark Corner OHP*-27A I resigned and I retired in sixty-three, I believe it was, April the first, nineteen and sixty-three. **1997** *Dante OHP*-14 He's born in nineteen and four.

[DARE *and* conj B2 chiefly South, Midland]

andirons *noun* variant forms *andyirons, handirons.*

1958 Wood *Words from TN* 6 *andy irons.* **1962** Clark *Folk Speech NC* 311 *handirons.* **1992–95** Montgomery *Coll*: *andyirons* (Cardwell); *handirons* (Shields).

and such *conjunctive phrase* And other like or similar things. See also **and them**, **and those**, **such A**.

1971 *AOHP/ALC*-505 I've walked from here to town plenty of times, plus a big load of chickens and eggs and such. **1972** Hall *Coll* (Emerts Cove TN) We entered the Depression with nothing and we come out of it with nothin', but we never remember bein' hungry. In fact, we lived purty high on the hog, with potato dumplin's 'n sich, foddered beans, [liver] mush fried in the mornin' for breakfast with molasses, brown-eyed peas, pickled cucumbers. **1991** Haynes *Haywood Home* 44 Barn and house raisings, corn shuckings, quiltings, log rollings and such were not only community labor sharing projects, but were also social occasions. **1997** Andrews *Mountain Vittles* 22 Foller this 'un fer all yer other jellies—apple, blackberry, and sech. **1999** Hodges *Tough Customers* 14 They even look at his supply books with me and ask him questions about what would work best for them and such.

and them (also *'nm*) *conjunctive phrase* And everyone else, other associated people, usually members of a family (consultants from the Smoky Mountains agree that this term is more common than *and those*). See also **and such**, **and those**.

1862 *Lockmiller CW Letters* (July 18) yew can let him hav the mool and the cow if yew want to if hyram dont let yew have corn for her and them. **1961** *Coe Ridge OHP*-333A [He] was Uncle Cephas' and Aunt Molly and them's father. **1969** *GSMNP*-42:3 When they come here, why, the Floyds entered that place up there. Floyd's daddy and old man John Mingus and Uncle Abe and them entered what we call the Floyd place. **1974–75** McCracken *Logging* 11:83 That's where old Charlie Lawson and them lived, if I ain't mistaken. **1989** Landry *Smoky Mt Interviews* 194 Pap and them was a-carrying the bear. . . . Laura Antley and them was raised right down there. **1991** Williams *Homeplace* 78 My granddaddy and them, they had two chimneys to their house. And kept a fire in both houses. **1998** *Dante OHP-12* I guess you've probably got a picture of the house here, where Ann and them was born. **2013** Venable *How to Tawlk* 33 = common term meaning "everyone else, all others": "Ast Bill 'nm if they'd like to eat dinner with us."

and those *conjunctive phrase* And the rest, other associated people. See also **and such, and them.**

1952 Wilson *Folk Speech NC* 515 = used after another substantive to mean one or more persons. "Helen *and those* were there." **1996** Montgomery *Coll* (known to Cardwell) = less common than *and them* (Jones).

and which *conjunctive phrase* And in this regard, and for that matter. See also **but B2, which B2.**

1858 *Zion Church Minutes* 43 Also the door of the church was opened for the reception of members & which Valentine Tipton joined by experience. **1983** *Dark Corner OHP-9A* My parents built back just a few hundred yards up behind here, and which this house burned some years ago, but I grew up there. **1989** *Matewan OHP-39* I belong to the Kiwanis Club. That's a civic organization and which is I think is one of the best civic organization there is. **1998** *Dante OHP-53* They elected a man and he goes up and has it changed back till they can have, get paid compensation for their injuries, and which rock dust is terrible. Silicosis [is] what it was. **2008** *Rosie Hicks* 1 I didn't go to school till about six, I guess, because we had to walk, and which I didn't finish that year up.

andyirons See **andirons.**

andy over See **Antony-over.**

a-near *preposition* Near, close to.

1863 *Bradshaw CW Letters* (Feb 27) [The small pox] are a dangers complaint dont go a near them . . . tell Father to not let Frankling and John nor non of the rest go a near them fur tha[y] are easy Caut. **1961** *Coe Ridge OHP-336A* He killed this man a-near a pond. **1972** Cooper *NC Mt Folklore* 41 "Be sure," said Aunt Viddie, "not to bury my old man anear his pap." **1975** Gainer *Speech Mtneer* 6 The well is a-near the house. **1995** Montgomery *Coll* (known to Cardwell).

[probably reduction of *of* + *near*; Web3 *anear* prep now chiefly dialect]

anent *preposition* Close to, near, beside.

1895 Edson and Fairchild *TN Mts* 370 It was *anent* two houses. **1939** Hall *Coll* (Deep Creek NC) I fell back into the river and just took up right up in the water and was wet all over and got up anent them. **1974** Fink *Bits Mt Speech* 1 = close to or by. "His house stood *anent* the church house."

[ultimately < Old English *on efen*; OED3 *anent* prep 7 archaic or dialect, now literary but old-fashioned]

a-next *preposition* Next, close.

1976 Garber *Mountain-ese* 3 We live anext-to the high school. **1995–97** Montgomery *Coll* (known to Brown, Bush, Cardwell, Weaver).

[perhaps *a* transitional syllable + *next* or by analogy with **a-near**]

aney wheares See **anywheres.**

angel biscuit *noun* A buttermilk biscuit made from yeast dough, kneaded and left to rise before baking. See 1998 citation.

1996 Houk *Foods and Recipes* 83 Richer biscuits were made with cream or even whipping cream. Some were so heavenly they earned the name "angel biscuits." **1998** Dabney *Smokehouse Ham* 117 Sometimes called "high biscuits" or "cream biscuits," angel biscuits are small-scale tender biscuits that have many qualities of a yeasty roll. That's because yeast is added and the dough is allowed to rise before placing it in the oven.

angel fingers *noun* See citation.

1973 *Foxfire II* 30 The sourwood tree, in early July, is covered with drooping racemes of waxy white bell-shaped blossoms that perfume the air and call all the honeybees in the neighborhood. Flowers are called "angel-fingers," and the sourwood is also known as "sorrel-tree" or "lily-of-the-valley tree."

angern See **onion.**

angling *adverb* Across, moving at a diagonal or angle.

1939 Hall *Coll* (Waldens Creek TN) The pitcher th'ows the ball anglin'. (As explained by another speaker, "It means the ball comes at an angle across the plate. It used to be used away back. Old timers might use it." The reference is to the game of **bull pen.**) **1986** Pederson et al. *LAGS* (Barrow Co GA, Campbell Co TN, Sullivan Co TN).

angry *adjective* Of a sore or wound: inflamed.

1934–47 *LAMSAS* (Swain Co NC). **1962** Dykeman *Tall Woman* 182 A good scab had formed over the wound, but the flesh around it was still bruised and angry.

[DARE *angry* adj chiefly New England, Midland]

a-nigh *preposition* Near, near to.

1892 Dromgoole *Dan to Beersheba* 82 Mely hev set herse'f up ter be sech a saint ez sinners sech ez I be can't come a-nigh her. **1925** Dargan *Highland Annals* 67 Some say this cave's ha'nted, an' won't come anigh it. **1961** Williams *Rhythm and Melody* 9 Let a chicken git in the gyarden, an' ye can howl yer head off fer a dog, but won't nary one on the place come a-nigh ye. **1974** Fink *Bits Mt Speech* 1 I'll shoot if he comes *a-nigh* me.

[perhaps *a* transitional syllable + *nigh* (patterned on **a-near**); EDD *anigh* adj nEngl, sEngl; DARE *anigh* prep especially South, South Midland]

animal *noun*

A Variant forms *animile, animule.*

1927 Mason *Lure of Smokies* 228 As for spillin' the blood of animiles, I ain't got no conscience agin it. **1928** (in **1952** Mathes *Tall Tales* 70) I ain't goin' to bother with feedin' no animile that looks like yer ol' grandsir Bluenose an' acts like a poodle. **1939** Hall *Notebooks* 13:6 (White Oak NC) *animile* (a jocular pronunciation). **c1960** Wilson Coll: *animule* = animal.

B Used as a euphemism for *bull*. See also **bull A1**.

c1960 Wilson Coll [The term *bull* is] rarely used in mixed company. Brute, animal, beast, male-cow are often substituted.

animile, animule See **animal.**

ann-cient See **ancient.**

anniover See **Antony-over.**

another *pronoun*

A Variant forms *nother, nuther.*

c1815 (in **2007** Davis *Co Line Baptist* 111) I hated that a brother should lie under that Character & thought it not amiss to mention to one brother what nother was impeached with. **1924** Abernethy *Moonshine* 117 It were a hole year afore I'd look at nary nother woman. **1925** Dargan *Highland Annals* 57 You scootle from here, Dan Goforth; don't you tech nary nuther tater in this patch! **1940** Haun *Hawk's Done* 85 She said she somehow or nother felt like she had to then. **1973** Foster *Walker Valley* 9:33 It must have surely been back in that, eighteen something or nother. **1982** Ginns *Snowbird Gravy* 131 Never did nary nother one come back.

B in phrases *one thing another, someday another, somehow another, something another, someway another.*

1862 *Watters-Curtis CW Letters* (May 22) Let me know all about wone thing another and tell mee all about the times up there. **1865** *Hill CW Letters* (Jan 19) I am Stil in hops of geting home a gain Some time a nother. **1973** *Gathered Together* 21 It may be someday they might throw me in a den a'lions or somethin'another. **1974** *AOHP/ALC-834* Someway another I cleaned up early and walked out. **1974** Roberts *Sang Branch* 27 She wanted us around close through the week so she could keep in touch with us, afeared we might get into something another. Something or the other. **1979** *Big South Fork OHP-10* The engineer's watch had stopped or something another had happened to it. **1989** *Matewan OHP-9* Someday another you might be able to see it, that is if this a-world don't end before that. **1991** Thomas *Sthn Appal* 120 I kain't keep him a-goin' without him bangin' up th' anvil, ur sump'n another. *Ibid.* 238 I pray to th' good Lord I won't fall an' injure me in some way a-nother. *Ibid.* 248 Somehow another, I didn't git that fer. **1998** *Dante OHP-71* People would come from Erwin or something another to work up here. **2008** *Rosie Hicks* 1 I guess I was kindly about six or something another maybe.

another'un (also *another'n*) *pronoun* Another one. See also **one 1, other'un, tothern.**

1901 Harben *Westerfelt* 3 He didn't care a hill o' beans fer no gal, but was out o' sight out o' mind with one as soon as another un struck his fancy. **1942** Hall *Phonetics Smoky Mts* 86 *which'un, that'un, next'un, big'un, another'un.* **c1945** Haun *Hawk's Done* 224 Then she would catch anothern, just walk up to the clover blossom it was lighted on and say out loud, as she wove her finger round and round it in circles. **1963** Edwards *Gravel* 123 Fast as Pap would finish one he'd throw it out of the shop door with the tongs and git busy on anothern. **1977** Weals *Cove Folk* Nobody wanted, or needed for nothin'. What one didn't have another'n did. **1994** Schmidt and Hooks *Whistle* 140 She took that pig out and hugged that pig and it just a-squealin' like one thing and she wanted to know if they had another'n that she could buy. **1997** Landry Coll We'll try another'n, being that'un paid off.

ant, an't See **ain't.**

ant bug *noun* See citation.

1944 Combs *Word-List Sthn High* 17 = the ant. A survival of the O[ld] E[nglish] fondness for compounds.

ante over See **Antony-over.**

antic

A (also *anticky*) *adjective* Animated or frisky, especially in a clownish or prankish way.

1917 Kephart *Word-List* 407 He's as *antic* as a jay bird when he takes the notion. **1937** Haun *Cocke Co* 2 Piedy cows sometimes get contrarious, and calves pert-nigh always have on antic spells. **1942** Justus *Step Along* 14 Once in awhile [the dog] would bark and look back as if to say, "See what a speedy dog I am to keep ahead of you!" And Jerry Jake and Step-Along would laugh at the anticky pup. **1944** Combs *Word-List Sthn High* 17 *antic* = given to fun, capers, pranks. "Old Lige is feeble, but he's plumb *antic*." **c1945** Haun *Hawk's Done* 260 Long Boy got to looking puny and not being very anticky. **1974** Fink *Bits Mt Speech* 1 He was an *antic* sort of fellow.

[DARE *antic* adj 2 chiefly South Midland]

B *noun* A comical or mischievous person.

1895 Edson and Fairchild *TN Mts* 370 Ab Deel's a *natchul* (natural) *antic*. **1966** Frome *Strangers* 154 Much has been made of words or expressions carried over from old English, undoubtedly with some justification . . . antic for a comical person. **1975** Chalmers *Better* 65 A child is a natural antic if he is lively and full of mischief.

[DARE *antic* n South Midland]

C *verb* To joke, play pranks.

1976 Garber *Mountain-ese* 3 Jim ain't too serious, he likes to antic with the boys. **1996–97** Montgomery Coll (known to Brown, Bush, Cardwell, Hooper, Oliver).

anticky See **antic A.**

anti-godlin (also *anti-goglin(g), anti-sidling, anti-sigodlin(g)*) *adjective, adverb* Out of line, askew; lopsided. See also **catawampus[2] B, cater-corner B, si-godlin.**

1917 Kephart *Word-List* 417 *antigodlin'*. **1944** Combs *Word-List Sthn High* 17 *antigodlin, antigoglin, antisigodlin* = out of plumb or square, slanting. **1952** Wilson *Folk Speech NC* 515 *antigodlin* = leaning, not parallel. **1955** Parris *Roaming Mts* 22 Slaunchways means slanting, and si-godlin or anti-sigodling is out of plumb or out of square. **1960** Cooper *Jularker Bussed* He just sets with his mouth pooched out (stuck out) since he discivered (discovered) he built the walls antigodlin (not plumb). **1986** Pederson et al. *LAGS* (Cocke Co TN, Sevier Co TN) *anti-godlin*. **1992–95** Montgomery *Coll*: *anti-godlin* (known to Jones, Norris, Oliver); *anti-gogling* (known to Brown, Bush, Hooper, Jones, Norris, Oliver, Shields); *anti-sidling* (known to Norris); *anti-sigodling* (Brown, Cardwell, Hooper, Ledford, Oliver). **2007** McMillon *Notes*: *antigodling*, *antigogling* (the latter is the more common term) = lopsided.

[Web3 *antigodlin/antigoglin* adv "at angles, crosswise" chiefly Midland; DARE *antigodlin* adj, adv 1, *anti-gogling* < *anti-* "against, counter" + *goggling* participial adjective < *goggle* "to shake, tremble" (EDD, SND); *anti-gogling* South, South Midland, West]

antiovers See **Antony-over.**

anti-sidling, **anti-sigodlin(g)** See **anti-godlin.**

ant'ney over, **antni over**, **ant'ny over** See **Antony-over.**

Antony-over (also *aintney over, andy over, ante-over, antiovers, ant'ney over, antni over, ant'ny over, handyover*) *noun* A game in which two teams are positioned on one side of a house or other building and alternate in throwing a ball over for the other team to catch; hence, the call teams shout to signal the throwing of the ball (see citations for different accounts).

1914 Arthur *Western NC* 288 A game almost universal with the children of that day was called "Ant'ny Over." Sides were chosen, one side going to one side of the house and the other to the other. A ball was tossed over the roof by one side, the problem being whether it would reach the comb of the roof and fall on the other side. If it did so and was caught by one on that side, that side ran around the house and tried to hit somebody on the other side with the ball. If they succeeded, the one hit had to join the other side, and the side catching the ball had to throw it over the house and so on until one side lost all children. The rule was for the side tossing the ball to cry "Ant'ny!" as they were ready to throw the ball and when the other side hollered "Over!" the ball was thrown. **1966–68** DARE *Survey* (Brasstown NC, Burnsville NC) *antni over*; (Gatlinburg TN) *andy over* = call made when the ball is thrown to a player on the other side; (Spruce Pine NC) *handyover* = call in game. **1973** GSMNP-4:42 We used to play what we called antiovers . . . throwing balls across the house, all the way across, see, and you don't know where that ball is going to come, whether on this end or on that end over yonder, but you'd better not let it touch the ground. **1973** GSMNP-6:14 Then [in] andyover, we'd throw something across the top of the house, and the one that could go round and get it the quickest was the leader for the next time. **1984** Smith *Enduring Memories* 28 The team with the ball would yell, "Ante-Over." Someone would throw the ball over the house and the opponents would try to catch it on the fly. If the receiving team failed to catch the ball before it hit the ground they would in return yell, "Ante-Over," and throw the ball back over the house. We would try to prevent the opponent from catching the ball by rolling it over or throwing very hard or at angles. Likewise we would spread our players out to cover as much area as possible to try to catch the ball. When it was caught, one of the players on the receiving team would hold the ball behind his back (all the other players would hold their hands behind their backs also) and the team would run around the house and try to hit as many players on the other team with the ball as possible. Each player hit by the ball before he could run around to the other side of the house was required to join that team. The team that ended up with all the players was the winner. **2002** Morgan *Mt Born* 116 The game began when one of the players on the team whose member had the ball called out "aintney" loud enough for the team on the other side of the house to hear it clearly. To signal that they were ready, they all sang out "over!" [and] the person with the ball then threw it over the roof of the house to those on the other side. The immediate object was for someone to catch the ball in the air. Assuming that someone did this, the object of the game now came into focus. Using deceptive yells of "aintney" and then silence, the person with the ball now ran around the house and tried to throw the ball and hit one of the players on the other team before they could run to the reverse side of the dwelling! Any player so struck was "put out," or eliminated from the game. The rest of the ball thrower's teammates gathered with him on the other side of the domicile, and the process was repeated.

[OED3 *Anthony over* chiefly U.S.; DARE *Antony-over* n probably of Scottish origin, chiefly southern Appalachians]

antymar See **antymire.**

antymire (also *antymar, antypismire, antypissmire*) *noun* A small black ant, better known as a **pissant.**

1930s (in **1944** Wentworth *ADD* 23) (eWV) *antymire*. Also *antypissmire*. **1931** Combs *Lg Sthn High* 1321 Them antymars (pissmires), the little hatefuls. **1996** Montgomery *Coll*: *antypismire* = a small black ant (Ledford).

[DARE *antymire* n chiefly North Atlantic, Central Atlantic, southern Appalachians]

antypismire, **antypissmire** See **antymire.**

anxious bench (also *anxious seat*) *noun* Same as **mourners' bench.**

1963 Hooper *Unwanted Boy* 16 Finally when fifteen years old I went up to the "anxious seat" or "mourner's bench," as it was frequently called, and after much prayer and much instruction from my friends, I professed faith in Christ. **1993** Montell *Cumberland Country* 91 In most early churches, salvation was sought either at the altar or at the mourner's bench, as it was generally called. Sometimes called the "anxious seat," this particular pew is located near the pulpit. It is here that the sinner goes to repent, pray, and wait for salvation, head buried all the while on an arm folded across the back of the pew. It is generally felt that this process of "praying one's way through to salvation" takes from seven to ten days. When salvation comes, the seeker sits erect on the mourner's bench, either crying from joy or smiling, thus announcing to others present what has happened. **1998** Montgomery *Coll*: *anxious bench* (Jones); *anxious seat* = also applies to the defendant's box at a trial (Brown).

[DARE *anxious bench* n 1 chiefly North Atlantic, South, South Midland]

anymore *adverb*

1 Now, nowadays, at present (in affirmative, declarative contexts).

1931 Malone *Any More* [In Bluefield WV] people used to shop a lot in the morning, but any more the crowd comes in about three o'clock; Any more the high school pupils are such babies nobody goes to their entertainments; My customers have to see me by appointment any more. **1932** Cox *Affirm Any More* 236 The term appears to be rather widely known, though sparingly used, in the northern part of West Virginia. Composition teachers tell me that occasionally it creeps into papers written by students.... The following examples are typical ... "He goes there a good deal any more." "The teacher didn't use to call on me, but any more I have to recite every day." **1941** Stuart *Men of Mts* 14 [You] got to take a little sweet terbacker with the home-made any more. **1942** (in **1944** Wentworth *ADD* 25) (WV) That seems to be easy to do any more. **1946** Moore *Affirm Any More* 301 The fairly high incidence of *any more* in the mountains of Eastern Kentucky has been known to me for twenty years.... The highland folk of English-Scotch-Irish descent have generally employed the form more extensively than people of other regions. **1956** Hall *Coll* (Hazelwood NC) Anymore of course they use more or less sugar in the mash.... Well, [the method is] pretty much the same only ... it's sugared anymore. **1959** Roberts *Up Cutshin* 44 I've been a Christian for nineteen year and don't tell any more of them big tales. Any more I allas tell the truth. **1977** *Shenandoah OHC* 136 A lot of the sisters and brothers [are] dead. Maybe three sisters are living any more, and we hardly ever see each other. **1978** Montgomery *White Pine Coll* III-1 Politics moves so fast and in such mysterious ways anymore, it's hard to keep up with it. *Ibid.* III-2 Since we've got freezers anymore, we put them in the freezer.... I declare, I'm so no-account anymore. **1982** Ginns *Snowbird Gravy* 16 We called it "hog" all the time. Anymore, they call it "pork." **1986** Pederson et al. *LAGS* (Roane Co TN) I forgot how fast I work anymore; (Claiborne Co TN) So many things are in bags anymore; (Johnson Co TN) They use them to dig grave[s] with anymore; (Sevier Co TN) They quit building two-story houses anymore for living houses; (Sullivan Co TN) Most people use a setter anymore; (Washington Co TN) I guess the Baptist [is] the largest denomination anymore. **1982** Ginns *Snowbird Gravy* 16 We called it "hog" all the time. Anymore, they call it "pork." **1989** Landry *Smoky Mt Interviews* 191 Things changes so much anymore. **1996** Montgomery *File* Anymore I want Christmas to be a quiet time (70-year-old woman, Gatlinburg TN). **1997** *Dante OHP*-14 [You] set half the day or all day sometimes to see the doctor. About everwhere you go anymore it's like that. **1997** Miller *Brier Poems* 84 When we kept cattle, I always locked up. But anymore, what's to keep in or out? **2009** Burton *Beech Mt Man* 67 Anymore, all you do is buy 'em a beer.

[perhaps ultimately influenced by Irish Gaelic source, but apparently unattested in Irish English]

2 Of an event or action: (once) again, from now on or then on (in negative or conditional contexts). See also **no more**.

1795 *Sinking Creek Church Minutes* II:3 The Reference from Last meeting concerning Brother Tipton was brought Forward and Setled and [will] not be Revived any more Except on new ground. **1834** Crockett *Narrative* 23 He persuaded me to stay with him, and not return any more to my father. **1861** *J Love CW Letter* (Nov 10) I Dont fere the yankeys tho they may Slay mee if they was to I would never hav to Dy any more. **1862** *Watters-Curtis CW Letters* (April 12) they are Sure to handle them both Rough if they Catch them anymore. **1915** Hall *Autobiog Claib Jones* 34 He left the state and fled to Virginia, so we never met any more. **1939** Hall *Coll* (Nine Mile TN) He [= a bear] walked out, got away from me. I never did get up with him anymore. **1939–42** Adams *Tales* 92 They all went back home and had plenty [to] eat from then on. They never did see the woman any more. *Ibid.* 125 It come a-running back just a yelping and hollering like it was about to die and run under the floor and they couldn't much it out anymore. **1944** Justus *Billy and Bones* 21 Mr. Bones [= a dog] kept close behind them as if he meant never to lose sight of them any more. **1969** *GSMNP*-28:39 He never remarried anymore. **a1975** Lunsford *It Used to Be* 32 He never did come back to the fox hunt any more. **1989** *Matewan OHP*-1 I never worked anymore until after Bobby got through high school. **c1999** Sutton *Me and Likker* 46 I never did see him any more and I am damn glad I ain't. **2007** Preece *Leavin' Sandlick* 35 If Paw never sees ye heer anymore in this life, I hope to see ye in Heaven someday on them sunny banks of fair deliverance.

any much *adjective phrase, adverb phrase* Very much. See also **much C1**, **none much**.

1922 *TN CW Ques* 9 (Jefferson Co TN) I dident have the oppertunity of attending any mutch [school]. **1939** Hall *Coll* Me and my brother went a-coon-huntin', but we never done any much good. *Ibid.* (Smokemont NC) We had to help them at home, and we didn't look out to ever need any much education. **1973** *GSMNP*-88 We had two sisters. They didn't work on the farm any much, though.

any'un *pronoun* Any one.

1979 Slone *My Heart* 29 No, he would never whup any'un.

anyways

A *adverb* To any degree or extent; at all.

1863 *Lister CW Letters* (Nov 28) I have no news to right that wood be eny ways interresting for you to Read. **1901** Harben *Westerfelt* 273 Goodness knows yo're showin' mighty little int'rust in the meetin' anyways. **1916** Combs *Old Early English* 288 Is he any ways hurt? **1937** (in **2009** Powell *Shenandoah Letters* 135) I am willing to do any thing that is any ways right. **1955** Ritchie *Singing Family* 45 Teacher didn't even try to hold us, he was grinning and patting, too, and having the hardest kind of time standing anyways still. **1975** *GSMNP*-62:17 If you was anyways near to a bear, he would charge you [a fine].

B *conjunction, adverb* In any case, at any rate.

1862 *Copenhaver CW Letters* (Aug 13) Thare is not much probibility of a fight hear any ways shortly. **1973** GSMNP-5:20 Sometimes you would get more and sometimes less, but anyways from ten to fifteen dollars. **1979** *Big South Fork OHP*-10/1 Oh law, we was worried to death anyways. **1989** *Matewan OHP*-88 Anyways, they wasn't working and they wasn't at home. **1995** Adams *Come Go Home* 42 There's probably not much left down there anyways. **1997** Andrews *Mountain Vittles* 54 Anyways as a little'un and being a little older I have had to wait through October when there wuz already morning frosts on the ground. **2003** LaLone et al. *Farming Life* 275 Right here is an old bucket. . . . Anyways, the milk goes into that and then you carried it and poured it into the tank.

[*any* + *ways* adverbial genitive; OED3 *anyways* B conj]

anywhars See **anywheres**.

anywheres *adverb*

A Variant forms *aney wheares* [see **1813** in **B**], *anywhars* [see **1901** in **B**], *anywhores*.

2013 Venable *How to Tawlk* 10 You kin buy a co-Cola anywhores in the world!

B Anywhere, in any place. See also **everywheres**, **nowheres**, **somewheres**.

1813 Hartsell *Memora* 134 Capt hambleton Signed his name to the paper, Readey to goo aney wheares. **1901** Harben *Westerfelt* 135 He's jest about the porest ketch anywhars about. **1913** Kephart *Our Sthn High* 122 The law wunt let us hav liquor shipped to us from anywhars in the State. **1931** Goodrich *Mt Homespun* 56 "Poor sister ain't fit to go anywheres till that neck of hers gets swaged down, but I'm aimin' to go and see for myself, come Sunday," said Hannah. **1940** Haun *Hawk's Done* 125 They had a hundred acres of as good land as can be found anywheres. **1953** Hall Coll (Bryson City NC) He didn't want the dogs to get hold of the little bear and tear it up anywheres. **1973** GSMNP-3:12 I don't imagine it was any worse than anywheres else in the mountains. **1978** Montgomery *White Pine Coll* II-3 There's a lot of just honest-to-goodness, down-to-earth normal people, just like anywheres else. You have two extremes in Cocke County. **1994** Landry Coll I can rest easier in the woods than anywheres. **1998** *Dante OHP*-71 Now when I go anywheres, Mommy wants to go.

[*anywhere* + -*s* adverb-forming suffix; cf **-s**[5]]

any which way *adverb* In any direction, anywhere. See also **a**[3], **every which away**, **whichaway**.

1940 Haun *Hawk's Done* 110 I couldn't move toward the door. I couldn't move any which way. **1993** Burchill et al. *Ghosts and Haunts* 62 Clem said he let the mule go any which way he wanted to go then.

anywhores See **anywheres**.

a-past

A (also *a-past of*) *preposition* Beyond.

1867 Harris *Sut Lovingood* 106 When the dorgs cum up, he were a-pas' prayin fur, at leas' ha'f a mile. **1895** Edson and Fairchild *TN Mts* 370 I don't put that shootin' any *apast* him. **1910** Cooke *Power and Glory* 67 I was goin' a-past the door. **1952** Wilson *Folk Speech NC* 515 *apast* = after, beyond. "It's a little *apast* mealtime." **1967** Hall Coll (Newport TN) Tell Lena I can't come. I'm apast of traveling. **1973** GSMNP-90:12 He'd picked up the mail at the post office in Gatlinburg, and he went up around Cherokee Orchard Road and down a-past our house. **1999** GSMNPCOHP-1:5 Just apast the river there they made a bend in the mountain where they were going to start digging.

B *adjective* Finished.

1941 Stuart *Men of Mts* 176 It [= winter] is something apast.

[*a* transitional syllable + *past* < Middle English *apassed*, past part of *apassen*; OED3 *apast* past-part/adj obsolete c1314→; cf EDD *apast* prep; DARE *apast* prep chiefly Midland]

ape oil *noun* See citation.

1940 Farr *More TN Expressions* 446 = liquor: "Sallie's man likes his ape oil."

apern See **apron**.

a-plenty (also *a-God's plenty*) *adjective phrase, adverb* (following a noun or adjective it modifies) Enough, abundantly. See also **plenty 1**.

1862 *Dalton CW Letters* (Jan 8) i have got monney A plenty. **1864** *Watkins CW Letters* (July 20) We have had rain a plenty so fur. **1939** Hall Coll (Mt Sterling NC) [The teacher] was rough a-plenty. **1941** Stuart *Men of Mts* 84 You either hump to it or I'll smear your baulk with weeds and weeds a-God's plenty. **1965** GSMNP-49:4 [We had] corn, Irish potatoes, wheat, rye, cabbage, all garden vegetables, apple trees a plenty.

[*a* transitional syllable (or perhaps preposition) + *plenty*]

Appalachia *noun* Usually pronounced *ap-uh-LAT-cha* by natives of the region, who often view the pronunciation *ap-uh-LAY-cha* as affected.

1986 Ivey *Damned Brier* 55 What I finally came to understand is that AppaLAYcha does not exist. At least, it doesn't exist in the real world. The AppaLATCHans exist; even AppaLATCHa exists. But AppaLAYcha is a fiction. It is an idea created by politicians and reporters. It has no more physical reality than Edgar Rice Burroughs' Africa or Ray Bradbury's Mars. . . . Every time we say AppaLAYcha or AppaLAYchan, we are strengthening that image of poor, dirty, stupid, lazy hillbillies, both in our own mind and in the minds of outsiders. **2000** Puckett *Pronunciation* 25 This student is subscribing to a belief among many native-born residents, especially in Central and Southern Appalachia: They are certain they can readily categorize individuals as "one of us" or "not one of us" based on how they say the word *Appalachia*. Those falling into the "one of us" group pronounce the word *Appalachia* with a short a in the stressed third syllable. The "not one of us" people say the word . . . with a long a in the same spot. Certainly this categorization of individuals by native-born Appalachians is a form of stereotyping. **2002** Williams *Appalachia* 14 As if the varying boundaries weren't enough, there is no fundamental agreement even about how to pronounce the word "Appalachia." Residents of southern and central Appalachia pronounce the term with a short *a* (æ) in the stressed third syllable; further north, the same *a* is given a long pronunciation, as in "Appal-*ay*-chia." Most of the experts and bureaucrats who came from Washington and elsewhere to fix the region's problems beginning in the 1960s adopted the northern pronunciation, while resident experts favor the southern—which led to a situation, according to one commentator, wherein "people who said AppaL'AYchia were perceived as outsiders who didn't know what they were talking about but were more than willing to tell people from the mountains what to do and how they should do it." Finally, while a majority of both long and short *a* users crunch the third syllable as though it were spelled Appal-*atch*-yuh, in New England—where the term "Appalachian" first came into widespread use by nongeologists thanks to the Appalachian Mountain Club and the development of the Appalachian Trail—a variant pronunciation uses "sh" rather than "ch," as in *Appal-ay-shuh*.

Appalachian *noun* A native of the Appalachian region, used as a quasi-ethnic term for one who self-identifies or is identified by others as a native of Appalachia. [Editor's note: The earlier currency of this usage is unclear, but it has become widespread as a result of national focus on the region from the 1960s, migration to form neighborhoods in the urban Midwest, and perhaps other factors. It is increasingly used by natives as a marker of self-identity to express affinity or solidarity.]

1970 Drake *Federal Union* 46 Probably most Appalachians opposed the adoption of the Constitution of 1787. One well known scholar has suggested that the Constitution was largely the work of a mall minority, perhaps no more than 100,000 people. **1971** Diehl *Stripping Myths* 6 Most Appalachians also realize that much of the region's natural wealth (land, lumber and minerals), and the means of production are owned by outsiders. By answering the question: Who is most responsible for the stripping of Appalachia, those opposing stripping may be better prepared to act more effectively in stopping strip mining. **1973** Primack *ARC* 6 The Appalachian Regional Commission itself came under fire during many of the speeches, especially because the ARC spends a large proportion of money and talks about roads, but not about clinics or other services badly needed by most Appalachians. **1976** Brandes and Brewer *Dialect Clash* 277 Some Appalachians vary their usage, sometimes employing a "standard" form and sometimes an Appalachian form. When asked about the extent to which the forms below apply to them, Appalachians will often respond in two ways: they may say that they themselves never employ these usages, but that they have acquaintances who do; or they may contend that they used to say a few. **1981** Philliber et al. *Invisible Minority* 2 Appalachians turned to urban areas outside the region in an effort to provide for themselves. In the twenty-year span from 1950 through 1969, 3.3 million Appalachians migrated to other areas. **1985** Williams *Role of Folklore* xii I wanted to collect personal experience narratives about the differences between mountain and city life and the problems of Appalachians in the urban culture. *Ibid.* 185 Right on this street there's people from Jackson County, Kentucky; Harlan County; Leslie County; McCreary County; people from Hazard and Perry County; people from Hawkins County, Tennessee; there's people from Hancock County, Tennessee, and a lot of 'em, they're Appalachians; I don't got no idea where they're from, but they're from all varied places. **1987** Obermiller *Labeling* 35 The stereotyping of rural Appalachians is a persistent phenomenon which has been documeted extensively. **1989** Cheek *Go Home* 9 My husband and I moved to Mars Hill, N.C., and chose to identify ourselves as Appalachians. . . . Because I identified intensely with my paternal grandparents, who lived in the Brushy Mountain foothills, I internalized the values of their way of life. This included, to me, a sense of place, a closeness to family and community, mutuality with nature, the Bible, independence, loyalty, work, frugality, ingenuity, story telling, handicrafts and music. Since these have often been termed Appalachian, I felt that I might qualify on the basis of heritage. **1996** Isserman *People in Appal* 14 I've been told by many of my students [at West Virginia University] that they don't consider themselves Appalachians. Appalachians are always people from further down South. **1996** Lewis *People in Appal* 14 I didn't know I was an Appalachian until the Appalachian Regional Commission came along and told us all that we were. **1999** Fisher *Stepchild* 189 As Mike Maloney puts it, if your parents, grandparents, and great-grandparents were from Appalachia, then you, too, are an Appalachian, if you want to be . . . I have a right to the label "Appalachian." But in inserting my identity as an Appalachian, I have had to rethink my and reinterpret my relationship with my kin from both sides of the family. **2000** Clark *Don't Mess* 30 "That's an interesting Appalachian dialect you have there," he said, pronouncing it "Appa-lay-shun." Whenever I hear the pronunciation, I feel as though the speaker is trying to assert his or her own sophistication, a sophistication that our area is presumed to lack. For a true Appalachian, it's equivalent to fingernails on a chalkboard. **2011** Garretson *Barefoot Hillbillies* 4 I'm going to go to college. I'm going to make something of myself, and when I do, I will still be proud to be an Appalachian with lots and lots of shoes. **2012–13** House *Spotlight* 26 One of the main ten[ets] of being an Appalachian is preservation. We like to preserve everything: stories, quilts, photographs, relationships . . . even our food, since we take such great pride in our canning and such. Appalachians have been told for over a hundred years that we're "a vanishing people" or "a disappearing culture." So I think that makes us hold on with white knuckles.

Appalachian basket *noun* See citation. Same as **rib basket**. See also **Aunt Lydia basket**.

1995 Williams *Smoky Mts Folklife* 83 The rib basket, with its thin splits woven on a foundation of curved ribs, is the form most frequently associated with the region and is sometimes known as the "Appalachian basket." Frances Louisa Goodrich found this to be the most common form in the Laurel Country of Madison County, North Carolina.

Appalachian dulcimer *noun* Same as **mountain dulcimer**. See also **dulcimer**.

[**1975** *Foxfire III* 188 There is no standard-sized or -shaped dulcimer. Every maker has the one he likes best. I use the same general pattern and vary the type of wood, or number of strings. Kentucky, Mountain, and Appalachian are all names for the plucked dulcimer, which may have any number of strings. Mountain people call them "dulcymores" or "delcymores."] **1995** Williams *Smoky Mts Folklife* 48 The only instrument generally associated with the home-based ballad tradition is the Appalachian dulcimer. However, there is little evidence that the dulcimer actually existed in the Great Smoky Mountains region until the mid-twentieth century. **2006** *WV Encycl* 205 The dulcimer has spread beyond Appalachia. Modern instruments are sometimes built with four or more strings, and musicians have developed techniques for playing a wide range of music. Today the dulcimer is often called the "Appalachian dulcimer" to distinguish it from the unrelated "hammered dulcimer," a many-stringed trapezoidal instrument played with small hand-held mallets.

appearant *adjective* Apparent.

1952 Wilson *Folk Speech NC* 515 = apparent. **1972** Cooper *NC Mt Folklore* 89.

[Web3 *appearant* adj chiefly Midland]

appearantly *adverb* Apparently.

1915 Dingus *Word-List VA* 180. **1956** Hall Coll (Roaring Fork TN) She was a big woman and awful scary appearantly. **1957** Combs *Lg Sthn High: Word List* 4 = apparently. A form "appearantly" more sensible and logical than *apparently*. **1994** Montgomery Coll (known to Shields).

[cf SND *appearandly* adv; DARE *appearently* adv chiefly Midland]

apple butter stir See **apple butter stirring**.

apple butter stirring (also *apple butter stir*) *noun* A community activity to make apple butter, combining work and socializing in the harvest season. Also called **butter stirring**.

1955 Parris *Roaming Mts* 151 An old timer is one who remembers . . . when the social calendar swirled around corn-shuckin's, sewing bees, quiltin' frolics, bean stringin's, apple butter stirrin's, and molasses pulls. **1997** Johnson *Melungeon Heritage* 86 Every year most of the households around the mountain had apple butter "stirs." This was mostly a woman's job, but all hands helped peel apples and took turns stirring the apple butter. It was an all-day job. **1997** Montgomery Coll: *apple butter stirring* (known to Brown, Ellis).

apple cutting (also *apple paring, apple peeling*) *noun* A gathering of family or neighbors in late summer or early fall to peel and slice apples in preparation for drying them for winter consumption. Like many similar events, it combines work and socializing. See also **schnitzing**.

1930 Armstrong *This Day and Time* 184 I reckon I 'ull git to make my apple butter next week, I've laid off to have me a apple parin'. **1959** Hall Coll (Hartford TN) We had what we called an apple peeling to cut up, can, dry, make [apples] into apple sauce. **1972** Cooper *NC Mt Folklore* 21 Corn-shuckings, bean-stringings, apple-cutting and molasses-boilings came in the early autumn and were always festive occasions, when gaiety made labor exciting and thrilling. **1975** *Shenandoah OHC* 121 Our family would get together. They['d] have what they called apple peeling. Now this is where the neighbors come in. Now they would walk for miles, you know, just to get together and peel apples, get things ready for the apple butter boiling . . . cut 'em up and get 'em ready . . . get up early on the morning that they was going to make apple butter . . . it would be an all-day job, boiling apple butter and packing cans and things. **1988** Dyer *Farmstead Yards* 27 October was usually the month for "apple peelings," another community social event.

[DARE *apple peeling* n chiefly Midland]

apple flat brandy *noun* Apple brandy.

1985 Dabney *More Mt Spirits* 52 A "flake stand" (condenser) spews out a "run" of "apple-flat" brandy. And the quality is good, the still being charged with pure apple "pummies," with relatively little sugar being added to the mash. Pure, "straight brandy" is virtually passé. **1990** Speer *Appal Photographs* 75 Whatever the title, you can get for yourself around twenty cases of twelve half-gallons of singlefoot likker or apple flat brandy, whichever you might be runnin', for a night of hunkering down around your worm box.

apple fruit *noun* Apples stewed or cooked, especially into applesauce. See also **fruit**.

1908 Smith *Reminiscences* 421 Even in the dialect of the people one is often reminded of Homeric speech. For example, the mountaineer says not simply "doctor" or "widow," but "doctor-man," "widow-woman," "cow-brute," "apple-fruit," just as the Homeric man three thousand years ago spoke of a "healer-man." **1974** Fink *Bits Mt Speech* 1 = cooked apples. "Pass the apple fruit." **2008** McKinley *Bear Mt* 127 The can house was stocked for the winter ahead. The shelves were packed with row after row of jars . . . "applefruit" (as they called applesauce).

[a redundancy, since *fruit* in traditional mountain speech often has the sense "apples"]

apple knocker *noun* The throat.

1986 Pederson et al. *LAGS* (Hamilton Co TN).

apple maul *noun* A large, heavy wooden hammer-like implement used to beat apples to a pulp prior to pressing them for juice in a **cider mill**.

1957 Parris *My Mts* 143 An old man in a weather-stained old hat, a hickory apple-mall [sic] in his hands, bends over a cider mill. **1995–97** Montgomery Coll (known to Brown, Bush, Cardwell, Shields).

apple out *verb phrase* See citation.

1962 Miller *Pigeon's Roost* (Aug 16) Here is an old saying that has been handed down by my grandfather Allen Miller, which says that if a vine crop such as pumpkin, cushaws and candy roasters began to "apple out," that is shed their bloom and the vine crop began to grow during the month of August, that it will make itself all right. To add a little more to this saying is to pinch off the end of the vine along about the 6th of August and this helps the vines to shed their bloom and go to "apple out."

apple paring See **apple cutting**.

apple peeler *noun* A pocketknife.

1862 *Bell CW Letters* (Aug 17) I wrote & sent by John Reid one hundred & fifty also an apple peeler of which you have never sayd whether you have recd or not. **1955** Parris *Roaming Mts* 151 An old timer is one who remembers—when a pocketknife was called an apple-peeler. **1995–97** Montgomery *Coll* (known to Brown, Hooper, Shields) = jocular, especially in speaking of another person's pocketknife, as in *let me borrow your apple peeler for a minute* (Ellis).

apple peeling See **apple cutting**.

apple press *noun* Same as **cider mill**. See also **press 1**.

1992 Davis *Jack Tales* 60 Then they cut [the apples] up and Jack and the farmer squeezed them in the apple press while the farmer's wife gathered up the jugs she had saved to put the cider in.

apple pummy See **pomace**.

apple rash *noun* A children's skin rash caused by prolonged wearing of unsanitary underwear in wintertime.

1964 Wright *Mt Medicine* 9 That old story of sewing children into their winter underclothes was no figment of some wag's imagination. They WERE sewed in, and many a seam was ripped open by the Doc to make a hole big enough for the entrance of the stethoscope. Tears flowed, and little clutching hands tried vainly to prevent this desecration, while the Doc listened to the heart and made note of the scabies lines across the skin. APPLE RASH it was called. I suppose the name started because the time when apples ripened was the time when the old winter clothes were taken out for school wear. And in the old winter clothes lurked last winter's scabies.

apple sanker *noun* A deep-dish apple pie. See also **sonker**.

1934–47 *LAMSAS Appal* = attested by 2/37 speakers (5.4%) from NC.

appointedly *adverb* See citation. See also **pointedly**.

1915 Dingus *Word-List VA* 180 *appintedly* = assuredly, positively: "I appintedly aint goin' to do it."

apricot, apricot vine See **wild apricot**.

April *noun* variant form with secondary stress on the second syllable.

1939 Hall *Notebooks* 13:48 (White Oak NC). **1942** Hall *Phonetics Smoky Mts* 72 *April* was ['eɪpraɪl] in the speech of a young man of Emerts Cove; a high-school girl of Cosby said that this is her grandmother's pronunciation. **2010** *Blind Pig* (June 15) A funny thing she [= my grandmother] did was in her pronunciation of April . . . she said "Ape-rile."

apron *noun*

A Variant form *apern*.

1942 Hall *Phonetics Smoky Mts* 71. **1944** Combs *Word-List Sthn High* 17. **2005** Williams *Gratitude* 72 You could pull up your apern tail, double it up and use it to pick up a hot pan [and] gether it up at the corners to carry a settin' of eggs.

B A dress worn by infants, regardless of gender.

1997 Nelson *Country Folklore* 110 The babies, regardless if they were boys or girls, wore dresses, called aprons. **1998** Montgomery *Coll* = a handmade protective dress from the neck to the knees, with a string looped around the neck and tied behind (Brown), = always small, checkered, and buttoned at the back (Norris).

a-purpose *adverb* Intentionally.

1861 *Martin CW Letters* (Dec 19) I pead 75 cts for the two [maps] A perpous for you. **1863** *Walker CW Letters* (May 22) they say wee are dismounted an sent there apurpose for heavy artillerymons. **1867** Harris *Sut Lovingood* 53 Now yu see, George, I'd cotch seven ur eight big pot-bellied lizzards, an' hed 'em in a littil narrer bag, what I had made a-purpus. **1913** Kephart *Our Sthn High* 282 Sis' blouses her waist a-purpose to carry a pistol. **1935** Sheppard *Cabins in Laurel* 71 They put him in with all blood marks a-purpose, so he could be thinkin' on what he done. **1939** Hall *Coll* (Cosby Creek TN) He came down a-purpose to kill him. **1978** Montgomery *White Pine Coll* X-2 I didn't do it a-purpose.

[*a-* (reduced form of *on*) + *purpose*; OED3 (at *purpose* n 1) now archaic and regional]

aqua fortis (also *aggie forties, akyfortis, aquafotis*) *noun* Originally, nitric acid drunk as a fortifying agent; by extension, any strong drink, especially alcohol.

1867 Harris *Sut Lovingood* 31 I'se pizen proof my sef; fur thuty dullars, I jis' let a sluice ove aquafotis run thru me fur ha'f a day, an' then live tu spen' the las' durn cent, fur churnbrain whiskey; ef I warnt (holding up his flask and peeping through it,) I'd dun been ded long ago. **1944** Wilson *Word-List* 38 *aggie forties* = anything very strong, generally used in reference to something to drink. **1962** Williams *Metaphor Mt Speech I* 12 If the vintage is raw and fiery it is said to be "as strong as akyfortis," but if it has mellowed in the moonlight it is sometimes referred to sweetly as "sankumsuly." [**1995** Montgomery *Coll* (unknown to consultants from the Smoky Mountains).]

[cf DARE *aggie forti(e)s* n chiefly South, South Midland]

aquafotis See **aqua fortis**.

ara See **ary**.

arbor *noun* An open structure of leafy branches spread across upright poles, in which is held an outdoor religious service. Same as **brush arbor**. See also **arbor meeting, meeting ground**.

1955 Dykeman *French Broad* 323 The heart of the meeting ground was the "arbor," an open-air structure with a roof supported by stout locust posts, and no sides at all. **1968** Wilson *Folklore Mammoth Cave* 40 (or *brush/bresh arbor*) = a temporary gathering place for religious services, made with a framework of poles covered with tree branches with their leaves on, to give shade.

[DARE *arbor* n B1 South, Midland]

arbor meeting (also *brush arbor meeting*) *noun* An outdoor religious service, usually a revival, held under an **arbor** or **brush arbor**. Same as **brush meeting**.

1943 Justus *Bluebird* 107 "They'll think we're having an arbor meeting, I reckon," Dovie laughed. **2016** *Blind Pig* (April 6) Many a new church was started with a brush arbor meeting and a traveling pastor. *Ibid.* In today's Appalachia the brush arbor revival has been replaced by tent revivals. They usually have a rather large one in Andrews [NC] each year. Even though the service is held in a tent, I still hear folks refer to it as the brush arbor meeting.

are See **be D**.

arey See **ary**.

argefy See **argufy**.

argufy (also *argefy*) *verb* To haggle, contend, especially in a petty or persistent way.

1895 Dromgoole *Fiddling to Fame* 50 Sometimes he'd say which beat in argufyin', but he mostly allus went with Alf. **1905** Miles *Spirit of Mts* 113 One time when the gals and their mother was argifyin' with a drunk man that had come in and aimed to stay, whether they wanted him or not, old man bein' away from home, old Nance she jist slapped him good and pulled him right out o' doors by the nose. **c1945** Haun *Hawk's Done* 229 Abe and George took to argufying back and forth and fussing with one another and got dubious of one another and sullen. **1963** Hooper *Unwanted Boy* 231 Of course, a husband gains nothing by arguing with his wife, especially if she has two or three different streaks of argufying blood in her veins. **1976** Garber *Mountain-ese* 4 = to argue, haggle. "John Henry is about the worst I ever see to argefy."

[*argue* + *-ify* verb-forming suffix; OED3 *argufy* v 2 colloquial; DARE *argufy* v 2 now chiefly South, South Midland]

argument (also *argymint*) *noun* variant pronunciation with secondary stress on the last syllable. For similar forms, see **-ment A**.

1867 Harris *Sut Lovingood* 62 The argymint fotch him, purticularly the spotted fawn part ove hit.

argy *verb* To argue.

1928 (in **1952** Mathes *Tall Tales* 57) "Mis' Tollett," said Gabe Mumpower rising, "I didn't come to argy with ye." **c1959** Weals *Hillbilly Dict* 2 Let's not argy any more 'bout this.

[DARE *argue* v A chiefly South, Midland]

argymint See **argument**.

arish See **Irish potato**.

ark *noun* See citations.

1954 Blackhurst *Riders of Flood* 79 The somewhat smaller horse arks, each carrying two teams of horses with their drivers, could navigate this far up the stream. The main ark, a floating bunkhouse, and a separate cook ark would be waiting two or three miles down. *Ibid.* 94 The ark was built on a heavy platform of logs. The heavy logs laid side by side formed a raft sixty feet long and twenty-four feet wide. **1964** Clarkson *Lumbering in WV* 355 = name applied in West Virginia to the floating houses used for cooking, eating, or sleeping, in river driving. There was usually a single ark used for the cookhouse and dining room, one for the bunkhouse, and one for the horses. The latter was called a horse-flat. **2006** *WV Encycl* 431 [In mining camps] "arks" from 70 to 100 feet long and 18 feet wide were built. The bunkhouse ark contained double-decked bunks and a large stove to keep the men warm; the cooking and dining hall occupied a second ark.

arm *noun*

1 An extension of a mountain or a mountain ridge; also used in place-names, as in *Long Arm* (TN) and *Crooked Arm* (TN) in the Smoky Mountains.

1751 (in **1940** McJimsey *Topo Terms in VA* 151) Four hundred Acres . . . on the Top of a Mountain an Arm of the blue Ledge. **1939** Hall *Coll* (Wears Cove TN) [We] herded them [= cattle] along on Smoky Mountain in part of the time and part of the time on what we call the Long Arm. **1956** Fink *That's Why* 4 Ridges, particularly those running down from a high peak or standing out like buttresses from the main divide, have various designations. Ridge is the most common, but there are others in frequent use, like Rocky Spur and Long, Crooked or Bent Arm. **1958** GSMNP-110:3 One [= a logging camp] of them was at the mouth of Marks Creek, and the other one was somewhere close to Long Arm.

2 A segment of a church congregation that branches off to form its own local congregation (i.e., not by schism). See also **arm off**.

1791 *Bent Creek Church Minutes* 10 Br Philip Hale chosen uppon trial to the office of a deacon in the arm of this church on Lick Creek. **1931** Burns *Coves Blount Co* 50 This church as well as the one in Tuckaleechee, was probably constituted as an arm or a creation of the Forks of Pigeon Church, now Sevierville. **1931–33** (in **1987** Oliver and Oliver *Sketches* 24, 25 The arm held regular meetings for two years to a month, June 20, 1829, when the arm was organized into a church of her own body and has always been known as the Cades Cove Church of Primitive Baptist. **1989** Ownby *Forks Little Pigeon* 13 Around 1804 an "arm" of the Forks of Little Pigeon Church was established on the East Fork of Little Pigeon River.

arm baby *noun* The smallest child in the family, one not yet able to leave its mother's arms. See also **knee baby, lap baby, set-along child**.

1939 *FWP Guide NC* 98 The boy, or "chap," may be called a little "shirttail boy" to distinguish him from her "arm baby and her knee baby." **1952** Wilson *Folk Speech NC* 516 = a baby small enough to hold in the arms. **1960** Cooper *Jularker Bussed* The littlest-un (least one) is an arm-baby (baby held in the arms), but they also have a lap-child (child held in the lap), a knee-child (child tall as one's knee) and a shirt-tail (wearing shirts) boy.

[DARE *arm baby* n especially NC]

armload *noun* The amount of wood or other material a person can carry at one time. Also called **load**. See 1949 citation. [Editor's note: The term *armful* is widespread in the US.] See also **grist B**, **turn B2**.

1949 Kurath *Word Geog East US* 29 The term *armful* stands by the side of *arm load* in the North Midland. *Arm load* and *load* are distinctive Midland expressions for an armful of wood. *Arm load* predominates in the North Midland, *load* in the South Midland. **1966** Dakin *Vocab Ohio River Valley* 148 *Arm load* is generally more common than simple *load*. Both are found throughout the [Ohio] Valley, but the characteristic South Midland *load* is more common along the Ohio between the Muskingum and the Big Sandy (as it also is on the West Virginia side of the river) and in the eastern Kentucky Mountains. **1997** Andrews *Mountain Vittles* 42 Momma sent me to the field a many of a time to pull an arm load a roastnears.

[DARE *armload* n widespread, but least frequent in North]

arm off *verb phrase* See citation. See also **arm 2**.

1995 McCauley *Mt Religion* 485 "Armed off" is an expression stemming from early Baptist revival culture during the Great Awakening in the South. It means that a church or association, called a "mother" church or association, constitutes or "arms off" "daughter" churches or associations. The expression is very common in the Appalachian region.

armstrong machine (also *armturn machine*) *noun* A machine operated by hand rather than mechanically.

1913 Kephart *Our Sthn High* 291 In some places to-day we still find the ancient quern or hand-mill, jocularly called an armstrong machine. **1992** Montgomery *Coll*: *armturn machine* (Shields, but neither term known to other consultants from the Smoky Mountains).

armturn machine See **armstrong machine**.

arn See **iron**.

arove See **arrive**.

arrangement *noun* variant pronunciation with secondary stress on the last syllable. For similar forms, see **-ment A**.

1943 Chase *Jack Tales* 5 We'll make arrange-ments about the work after we eat.

arriv See **arrive**.

arrive *verb* Principal parts.

1 variant past-tense forms *arriv*, *arove*.

1813 Hartsell *Memora* 128 Sence we arove he understood we war onley three monthes Volenteers and was not furnished to stay longer. **1863** (in **1999** Davis *CW Letters* 92) as Soon as I arov[e] here I droped you a few lines concerning our march. **1873** Smith *Peace Papers* 90 We finally arriv in the presinkts of our luvly hoam. **1923** Greer-Petrie *Angeline Steppin' Out* 10 We arriv' 'arly, and I had plenty of time to turn clean around and see everything that was a-gwine on. **1998** Montgomery *Coll*: *arriv* (Brown, Bush, Jones, Oliver); *arrove* I arrove too late to help (Cardwell).

2 variant past-participle forms *arriv*, *arove*, *arrove*.

1859 Taliaferro *Fisher's River* 24 The hour of muster have arrove. **1862** (in **1999** Davis *CW Letters* 76) Robert Welch has arove home, who reports Mathias is well. **1927** Mason *Lure of Smokies* 222 I had just arriv' when hit appears ter me I hears somep'n comin' the contrary way from the Sam's Creek side. **1998** Montgomery *Coll*: *arriv* (Brown, Bush, Jones, Oliver).

[These forms are not attested for either principal part in the OED3 after the 15th century.]

arrove See **arrive**.

arrowwood *noun*

1 A burning bush (*Euonymus americanus* or *E. atropurpurea*). Also called **strawberry bush**. See also **hearts bustin', spindle bush, wahoo 1**.

1970 Campbell et al. *Smoky Mt Wildflowers* 102 Common names include strawberry bush, swamp dogwood, spindle bush, arrowwood, wahoo, and a dozen others.

2 A black haw plant (*Viburnum prunifolium*) with medicinal uses.

2006 Howell *Medicinal Plants* 46–47 Historically, the straight, smooth branches were used to make arrows, hence the common name, arrow-wood. In the late summer, small dark blue-black berries or "haws" appear. Black haw was a common ingredient in formulas for women's "monthly troubles" and was used to relieve menstrual cramps, prevent miscarriage and as a labor tonic during the last few weeks of pregnancy. It was an ingredient in one of the best selling herbal remedies of all times, "Lydia Pinkham's Vegetable Compound for Females." Black haw was also used to relieve nervousness, stomach cramps, and tics or spasm.

arsafetida See **asafetida**.

arsh potato, **arsh tater** See **Irish potato**.

arsiplas See **bone arsiplas**.

arter See **after**.

arterards, **arterward** See **afterward(s)**.

article *noun*

A Variant pronunciation with stress on both the first and second syllables: *AR-TIC-le*.

1891 Brown *Dialect in TN* 175 *Article* is accented on the second syllable. **1940** [see in **B**]. **1996** Montgomery *Coll* I want to tell you about an ar-ticle that was in the paper this last week (Cardwell).

[DARE *article* n South, South Midland]

B A legal document.

1940 Stuart *Trees of Heaven* 48 He might make a good renter . . . but a man would have to bind him up mighty tight with a ar-tickle. **1968** Clarke *Stuart's Kentucky* 165 The landlord and the renter, or share cropper, signed a contract which they pronounced *ar-tickle*, including such details as allowing one of the children to work for cash during certain seasons, forbidding moonshining and the like, as well as declaring the amount of the cash or grain rent. **1971** Dwyer *Dict for Yankees* 23 I've got a ar-tickle drawed up by a lawyer! **1999** Montgomery *Coll* We've got all our ar-ticles drawn up by a lawyer (Cardwell).

article school *noun* A type of **subscription school**.

1988 Dunn *Cades Cove* 150 Before 1836, article schools were common in the cove. A schoolmaster took subscriptions, or "articles of agreement," from the people to teach school in the community.

ary See also **ary one**, **nary**, **nary one**.

A Variant forms *airy* [see **1985** in **B**], *ara* [see **1867** in **B**], *arey* [see **1862** in **B**], *ery* [see **1864** in **B**].

B *adjective* Any, a single. See also Grammar and Syntax §3.2.

1862 *Robinson CW Letters* (July 28) She sayes that She ant going to try arey nother. **1864** *D Walker CW Letters* (Aug 20) I am riten this morning in more pain then I have rot ery letter yet tho I think that pan will Soon war off. **1867** Harris *Sut Lovingood* 24 He lit ontu his hans agin, an kick'd strait up onst, then he rar'd, an' fotch a squal wus nur ara stud hoss in the State. **1913** Kephart *Our Sthn High* 81 My dogs can follow ary trail, same's a hound. **1939** Hall *Coll* (Wears Cove TN) It was a brother of mine that found [the remains of a dead man]. We never tetched the bones. We got a jury before we moved him ary bit. **1955** Ritchie *Singing Family* 85 I'm a mean, cranky old woman, but if it had a-been ary nother soul but you I wouldn't have cared. **1973** *GSMNP-90:15* If they's ary safe place in this house, I want to get in it. **1985** Irwin *Alex Stewart* 231 Back then if you was airy bit sick, why they'd light a pine torch and come to see about you. **1997** *Dante OHP-14* They wasn't ary high school, only at Council. That one was miles away, over in Buchanan County.

C *pronoun* Any (at all), a single one.

1999 Montgomery *Coll* I don't have ary (Cardwell).

[< *e'r a* < *ever* + *a*; DARE *ary* adj 1 throughout US, but especially South, Midland]

ary one *pronoun phrase* See also **ary**, **nary**, **nary one**. See also Grammar and Syntax §3.2.

A Variant forms *airn* [see **1957** in **B**], *ary'un* [see **1981** in **B**].

[DARE *ary* pron South, South Midland]

B Any one, a single one.

1862 *Lockmiller CW Letters* (Aug 23) I didnot think there wood be ari one take [the bounty money to re-enlist]. **1939** Hall *Coll* (Smokemont NC) My father said they were lots of deers. If he killed ary'un, it was before my recollection. **1957** Combs *Lg Sthn High: Word List* 3 *airn* = one, a one, any one . . . Ex. "I got two hats; you got airn?" **1975** Jackson *Unusual Words* 150 An object may be a *lillun*, a *bad'n*, a *big'n*, or a *new'n* or an individual may remark, "I ain't seen nair'n," or "I ain't got air'n." **1981** *GSMNP-122:51* Now let's see if I've left ary'un out. **1989** *Matewan OHP-89* I don't think they lack ary one of sweeping [old politicians from] the courthouse. **2003** Carter *Mt Home* 95 Daddy never did promise ary one of them he would vote for them.

[< *e'r a* < *ever a* + *one*; DARE *ary* adj 1 throughout US, but especially South, Midland]

as

A *conjunction*

1 Than (following *rather*).

1862 *Lockmiller CW Letters* (July) I would rather See you as to git a letter. **1863** *Brown CW Letters* (Sept 13) i wold rather hear from you now as any time senc i left. **1891** Primer *Studies in WV* 169 Would you rather have this as that? **1895** Edson and Fairchild *TN Mts* 376 I would rather see you as him. **1910** Cooke *Power and Glory* 104 There ain't anybody in this room I'd rather go by as by you. **1925** Furman *Glass Window* 57 I'd ruther pay for the window myself as to have the women pay for it, though. **1937** Hall *Coll* (Emerts Cove TN) I'd rather work as go to school. **1941** Hall *Coll* (Cosby TN) I'll betcha two-thirds of the boys here say "as" [instead of "than"]. **1953** Hall *Coll* (Deep Creek NC) They would rather have them as to have a chicken. **1968** Miller *Pigeon's Roost* (Aug 8) This farmer wanted this to be made plain that he would rather have one black snake take up at his barn to stay as to have a half dozen cats around it. **1976** *GSMNP-114:3* I'd rather have a mess of clay peas as white beans. **1983** Page and Wigginton *Aunt Arie* 197 I'd rather see younguns come as t'eat sugar. **1989** *Matewan OHP-102* She said she'd rather see them dead as to see them go to war. **1996** Harrell *Fetch It* 133–34 He would rather read and watch television on a snowy day as to be out in the snow.

[OED3 *as* conj B5 now English regional, Sc[ottish] regional, Irish English (north.) and U.S. regional; DARE *as* conj B3 chiefly Midland, South]

2 That, whether (following negative expressions with the verb *know*). See also **as how**, **so's**.

1774 *Dunmore's War* 221 I don't know as Col. Armstrong or Wright is to be trusted. **1863** *Warrick CW Letters* (Sept 5) my furlough will be out next Sunda but I dont no as I will be a ble [sic] to go back then or not. **1864** *Wright CW Letters* (April 8) I do not know as I have any thing else to write at present. **1883** Bonner *Dialect Tales* 134 Silence. Some young men shrugged their shoulders. One drawled out at last that he "didn't know as anybody keered three jumps of a louse for Jim Peters or his threatenin's." **1901** Harben *Westerfelt* 28 I don't know as I blame you much or harbor much resentment. **1939** Hall *Coll* (Deep Creek NC) I've been in several little bear fights. I don't know as I ever killed one myself, but I've been along when they was several of them killed. **1961** *Coe Ridge OHP-336B* [I] don't know as they ever did. **1970** *GSMNP-26:12* I don't know as they ever took him to a doctor. **1983** Pyle *CCC*

50th Anniv B:2:19 I don't know as I've been any benefit to the park service. **1996** Woodring *Times Gone By* 5 He didn't know as he had a murder warrant on his head.

[OED3 *as* conj 28 now Eng[lish] regional (south) and U.S. regional]

B *relative pronoun* That, who.

1859 (in **1974** Harris *High Times* 247) Them as had wings,—the buzzards, owls, chickenhawks, crows, bats and beetles, arter the ruff cum off jist went up-ards intu the gloom ove the storm. **1862** *Chapman CW Letters* (Dec 21) Father has six of his children with him yiet as is single they are all Grone. **1883** Bonner *Dialect Tales* 168 You don't feel as if you could give him up, my girl, for me as loves you so much, much more? **1897** *Incidents* 27 These eddicated preachers can't do no good alongise o' one of us fellers as is taught by the sperit. **1913** Kephart *Our Sthn High* 170 You wunt find ary critter as has a good word to say for the revenue. **1927** Mason *Lure of Smokies* 40 These fellers as sets b'ar traps 'thout markin' 'em is jest doin' the general public a injury. **1944** Wilson *Word-List* 39 Them as thinks they can whup me jest come ahead. **1969** GSMNP-46:12 They would mind rather than to take the punishment as I would put on them. **1972** Parris *Storied Mts* 23 "When I was young," Granville said, "folks as carried rifles to get something for supper never come home suckin' the barrel." **1978** Montgomery *White Pine Coll* VI-3 Some of the farmers as had to give up their farms, they just raised all kinds of sass about that. **1989** Landry *Smoky Mt Interviews* 194 Tom Sparks has herded more than any man as I've ever heard of. **1998** *Dante OHP*-58 He put Buster in the warmest water as he thought the baby could stand.

[DARE *as* pron D, formerly widespread, now chiefly Midland, South]

as a feller says See **fellow B1**.

asafetida *noun*

A Variant forms *asafidity* [see **1929** (Mathes) in **B**], *asfidity* [see **1973** in **B**], *arsafetida* [see **1997** in **B**], *asphidity* [see **1991** in **B**], *fidity* [see **1989** in **B**], *fitiddy* [see **2007** in **B**], *fittidy*.

2005 Williams *Gratitude* 344 *fittidy*.

B A wild plant (*Ferula foetida/rubicaulis*) from whose roots a resinous, brownish gum is extracted for a small sack that children wear around the neck to counter contagious disease [see **1979**], or taken in a liquid concoction to settle the stomach [see **c1999**]. Also called **devil's dung, rumptafetida**.

1929 (in **1952** Mathes *Tall Tales* 108) He says wearin' a lump of asafidity round yer neck an' takin' a little balsam ile ever-day will keep off might' nigh any sickness. **1929** Sanders *Medical Lore* 10 The asafoetida . . . was often sewed up in little bags and tied around our necks when there were any "catching" diseases in the neighborhood. **1969** Doran *Folklore White Co* 143 Asafoetida, an amulet for some people, was also worn around the neck or chewed or held in the mouth several times a day to kill germs. **1973** GSMNP-4:30 I remember seeing little kids would wear something like a bead that was asafetida, what they would call "asfidity." A small kid would have that around its neck. I guess that was to keep the germs or something, keep them from taking colds a lot. **1979** Smith *White Rock* 19 Normally, we didn't fear contagious illnesses very much because all of us were armed with an asafetida bag which we wore around all winter long. Mama put the brown gummy substance into small cloth bags into which shredded smoking tobacco had been sold in stores. She tied the bags around our necks and we spent the whole winter surrounded by their aura. Asafetida bore a striking resemblance in odor to garlic. **1989** *Matewan OHP*-9 They had a little box of fidity, and they'd roll it up in a little ball and tie it and put it in a rag and tie it around your neck, claimed that kept you from catching any disease. **1991** Thomas *Sthn Appal* 215 Then, another thing that got me worse 'an ennything: this ol' asphidity. She'd make us tie that around our necks, to keep th' diseases away, when we went to school. An' we had t' wear them rascals. That's th' way we done, instid of havin' to go to th' doctor. **1997** Montgomery *Coll* = facetiously known as *arsafetida* (Andrews). **c1999** Sutton *Me and Likker* 65 They kept asafetida and white likker as a stomach medicine, sick stomach or stomach hurting, more like Tagamet pills today. **2007** McMillon *Notes*: *fitiddy*.

asafidity See **asafetida**.

a-scared *adjective*

A Variant forms *a-scairt* [see **1969** in **B**], *a-skairt* [see **1986** in **B**], *a-skeart* [see **1924** in **B**].

B Frightened, afraid (for similar forms, see also **a- A3**).

1924 Greer-Petrie *Angeline Gits Eyeful* 8 We wuz a-skeart if she wuz to git married off ag'in, hit might thow Betty . . . out of a home. **1937** Hall *Coll* You were a-scared of that place? **c1950** (in **2000** Oakley *Roamin' Man* 71) She is for flying in a airplane to git there in a hurry but I am ascared to fly and I tell her I am not in that big of a hurry. **1969** Roberts *Greasybeard* 48 Now Big Jim was a-scairt but he warn't going to show it to the bird and, besides, he had a brain a-working like greased lightning. **1972** *AOHP/ALC*-241 I know I was a-scared of them. **1986** Rader *Mt Legacy* 19 Don't be askairt, Boy. **1989** *Matewan OHP*-102 I knew there was something wrong, and he was really a-scared about that.

[*a*- perhaps by analogy with *afeard*; DARE *ascared* adj formerly widespread, now especially Midland, South]

asfidity See **asafetida**.

ashamed *adjective*

A Variant form *shamed* [**1975** in **B**].

B Bashful, timid.

1921 Campbell *Sthn Highlander* 145 A young man "talking to" a young woman . . . is paying attention to her, and the young woman may be "ashamed" without having anything to be ashamed of—she is merely bashful. **1924** Raine *Saddlebags* 104 The littl'un's *ashamed* (bashful). She hasn't much manners. **1957** Combs *Lg Sthn High: Word List* 5 = bashful, timid. Ex.: "When company's around, that child's ashamed." **1975** Chalmers *Better* 65 He is shamed, rather than shy. **1994** Montgomery *Coll* She was ashamed to come out (Shields).

[DARE *ashamed* adj chiefly Midland]

ash-barrel baby *noun* See citation.

1949 McDavid *Grist* 106 (Clarke Co GA) = bastard.

ashcake (also *ashpone*) *noun* A small cake of cornbread shaped by hand and baked in the hot ashes of an open fire. See also **hoe-cake, jo cake.**

1853 Ramsey *Annals* 719 Mixed with cold water, [cornmeal] is, at once, ready for the cook—covered with hot ashes, the preparation is called the ash-cake. **1926** Thomas *Hills and Mts of KY* 154 Another way of baking or cooking bread was the ash cake, which was as follows: The dough was shaped into round or globular forms, without salt or soda, and placed in hot ashes, covered well with hot coals; this remained sufficiently long for complete baking, then the ashes were removed and the bread was ready to serve. **1949** Kurath *Word Geog East US* 39 From the Chesapeake Bay to the western parts of Virginia and the Carolinas, *ash cake* and *hoe cake* are used or remembered as words for hand-shaped corn cakes baked before an open fire. [**1960** Arnow *Seedtime* 395 Long a favorite in the farm home was the cake baked in front of the fire on a slanted board, usually of carefully smoothed ash, kept for the purpose. The board was sloped toward the fire so that the cake cooked first on top, and no small art was required to turn and get it back onto the sloping board without spilling it into the ashes.] **1966** Dakin *Vocab Ohio River Valley* 316 Kentucky alone has *ash cake* (occasionally *ash pone*), *egg bread*, *fatty bread*, *(corn) batter cakes*. *Hobby*, *fatty bread*, and *shortening bread* are rare outside the Mountains. **1972** *AOHP/ALC-355* Ash cakes is just a thick dough made up out of corn meal, cause nobody hardly had wheat and flour in them days, and they'd make that cornmeal real thick and pat it down on their hand and then lay it down on them red embers and then pour hot ashes out over them, and they'd lay there till they'd bake, and then they'd blow them ashes off and eat it, and that's what they called a ash cake. **1975** *Hartley I* 168 Mr. Hartley, you won't believe it, but my dad and I lived on ash pones. **1990** Oliver *Cooking Hazel Creek* 10 Ash cakes were made of a very stiff dough and were baked on the hearth in the ashes. When they were done, the ashes were, as much as possible, blown & brushed off.

[DARE *ashcake* n 1 chiefly South, South Midland]

ash catch *noun* A compartment underneath a wood-burning stove to catch ashes from the fire.

1962 Dykeman *Tall Woman* 188 This-here's the firebox, and under it there's this ash catch to keep your floor from getting gaumed up when you clean out the ashes.

ash hopper *noun* A barrel or hopper with a trough or spout for making lye by pouring water through ashes. See 1995 citation.

1848 (in **1870** Drake *Pioneer Life KY* 96) Our most important manufacture (I mean mother's and mine) was soap-making. Father constructed the "ash-hopper" which was composed of clapboards, arranged in an inverted pyramid. In the bottom were thrown some husks, or straw, or dried buffalo grass, to act as a strainer. It was filled with ashes, on the broad surface of which the water was, from time to time, poured by the bucketful. A trough beneath received the lye which, over a fire in the yard, was boiled down till it was strong enough to float an egg. The fat was then added, and the boiling continued until the soap came. **1972** Cooper *NC Mt Folklore* 37 Soap was made from grease and lye. The lye had been manufactured by allowing water to run through wood ashes in an ash hopper in the yard. **1973** Irwin *Arnwine Cabin* 30–31 The ash hopper was a familiar scene at almost every frontier cabin. Throughout the long winter months, the hardwood ashes were carried from the fireplace in the cabin and placed in the ash hopper. A log trough at the bottom of the hopper caught the lye water as it leached through the ashes. This lye water was used to make soap, hominy, to preserve meat and for other purposes such as an insecticide. [**1989** *Matewan OHP-102* [My father] made a little old building about four feet wide and maybe about six or eight feet high, and he would save wood ashes. They call this a hopper, and they'd pour them wood ashes up in the top of this. . . . He had a place where hit could drain out down at the bottom, and . . . they made their own lye, and they used that [for soap].] **1995** *Smokies Guide* (Autumn) 1 The first step [in soap making] was leaching lye from wood ashes by pouring water through the family "ash hopper." The lye was then mixed with kitchen grease and scraps of fat and boiled. Sassafras was added by some for its scent. The resulting soap was used for laundry, dishwashing, shampoo, and even poison ivy medication.

[DARE *ash hopper* n 1a chiefly South, Midland]

as how *conjunctive phrase* That.

1866 Smith *So Called* 34 A spiritual medium in our camp, says as how old Lucifer is preparing a factory. **1904** Fox *Christmas Eve* 122 Rosie kep' her mouth shet fer a long while; an' I reckon as how the feller 'lowed she wasn't goin' to tell. **1911** Shearin *E KY Word-List* 537 = that, e.g., "I heard as how there was a quarrel." **1931** Combs *Lg Sthn High* 1321 He told me as how he done it. **1940** Haun *Hawk's Done* 20 He allowed as how he would kill her and Joe both if she ever slipped off and went with him again. **1980** Matthews *Appal Physician* 67 He reckoned as how he would stop by. **1995–99** Montgomery Coll: *reckon as how* (Cardwell), I don't know as how I can finish it today (Cardwell).

[DARE *as how* conj phr chiefly South, Midland]

ashpone See **ashcake.**

ashtater See **Irish potato.**

ashy *adjective* Angry, worked up, vexed.

1891 Brown *Dialect in TN* 172 *Ashy* is used as a synonym for *angry*. **1923** Greer-Petrie *Angeline Steppin' Out* 13 As pretty a white gal as you'd want to see had run off and married him ag'inst her pap's wishes, and the old man was plum ashy about hit. **1934–47** LAMSAS (Swain Co NC).

[DARE *ashy* adj chiefly South, South Midland]

aside *preposition* Next to.

1976 Garber *Mountain-ese* 4 In the classroom the boys were often seated aside the girls. **1987** Young *Lost Cove* 26 Jace wasn't a bit afraid of work. He could lie down aside it and go to sleep. **2008**

Rosie Hicks 1 There was Santa standing right there aside the chimley. **2009** Burton *Beech Mt Man* 92 I was workin' aside this guy, and he said, "Be ready, 'cause here he come."

[*a-* (reduced form of *on*) + *side*]

ask *verb*

A Forms [Editor's note: Both *ast* and *ax* have occurred in all three functions below, and *ax* has been in continuous use from Old English, which had *acsian* and *ascian*; Joseph Hall observed *ax* and *axed* to be common among older speakers in the Smoky Mountains in the late 1930s; for commentary on the regional dimensions of *ax*, see the 1953 citation below; for its history, see the 1897 citation below and the etymology.]

1 variant base/present-tense forms *acks, aks, ast, ax*.

1817 (in **1969** Royall *Letters from AL* 81) Whenever my old man would go out, he would be a axin me how many neighbors I had, how many were in each family, and how far distant the country was inhabited around us. **1859** Taliaferro *Fisher's River* 117 Last I made out to ax Sally ef she'd have me. **1861** *Hileman CW Letters* (Aug 23) If you ever come back again. Just come out to our Camp [and] never aks for a pass. **1862** *Watson CW Letters* (March 8) I must rite Something a bout times here they acks Seventy five cts for corn here bacon 12½ cts a pound Salt 20 dollars a Sack. **1883** Zeigler and Grosscup *Heart of Alleghanies* 60 I heered the dogs a-comin' an knowed without axin' thet the bar war afore 'em. **1897** Brown *Dialectal Survivals* 139 *Ax* for *ask* is still common . . . it has an unbroken history from Anglo-Saxon days down to the present time. The Anglo-Saxon verb is *acsian* and *axian* as well as *ascian*. **1904–20** Kephart *Notebooks* 4:738 Run, Kit, back to Medderses, and ax what air they. **1937** Hall *Coll* (Cades Cove TN) I told the preacher if he was goin' to ax a blessin' he had to do it while we was gettin' the grub out [because a thunderstorm was approaching]. **1941** Stuart *Men of Mts* 124 Atter today I'm astin' to jine your family. **1952** Wilson *Folk Speech NC* 516 *ast* = present tense, past tense, and participle of *ask*. **1953** Atwood *Verbs East US* 5 The present form *ax* /æks/ does not occur north of the Pa.-Md. Boundary, and is found only at few isolated points in W.Va., Md., and Va. . . . In N.C. this form becomes much more common, reaching considerable concentration in the western one-fourth of the state, where nearly all of the Type I [= older, having little formal education] informants use it. . . . Those who use the present *ax* nearly always inflect it regularly (i.e. /ækst/), though there are four instances of the leveled combination: *ax* : *ax*. **1961** *Coe Ridge OHP-341A* I aimed to ast him about that. **1971** *AOHP/ALC-183* I want to ast you a question if you ain't too busy. **1974** Fink *Bits Mt Speech* 1 *ax* = ask. "You ax 'im." **1989** *Matewan OHP-28* I never would ast if you was working for me. **2008** Hicks 4 There's a black-headed girl up there axing about you.

2 variant third-person-singular forms *askes, ast* [see **1952** in **A1**], *axes*.

1867 Harris *Sut Lovingood* 36 Now George, ef a red-heded 'oman wif a reel foot axes yu tu marry her, yu may du hit. **1895** Murfree *Witch-Face* 213 He's been taught ez much ez any man ez ever held the office he axes ter be 'lected ter. **1923** (in **1952** Mathes *Tall Tales* 5) As sure as this Good Book's true from kiver to kiver, they's goin' to come a time when ye got to answer the Jedge when he axes ye, "Why ain't ye got on a weddin-garment"—ah? **1973** *Foxfire Interviews* A-73-86 That one place is all I've ever heared of [that] people always axes to buy. **1980** *GSMNP-122:65* They's the most people axes me where the sign's about 'em. **2006** Shelby *Appal Studies* 66 People askes me that.

3 variant past-tense forms *aks, ast, asted, axed, axsed, axt*.

1864 *Whitaker CW Letters* (March 22) I applide to Gen Longstreet & ast a trial. **1895** Dromgoole *Logan's Courtship* 148 Black-eyed Mandy axed him if he didn't think a sprinklin' now'n' then wuz healthy, he bein' Methodist. **1925** Greer-Petrie *Angeline Hill Country* 83 They hain't very fr'en'ly in Louisville, fur nobody axt us in thar house. **1937** Conner *Ms* 40 I aks the Dr. if he bought this farm? **c1945** Haun *Hawk's Done* 266 "Is that all that has took place?" I ast her. **1961** *Coe Ridge OHP-340B* He enjoyed singing that just as well as if you axed him to sing every Christian song there ever was. **1974** *AOHP/ALC-728* They axed him, said, "well, you been here?" **1974** *AOHP/ASU-204* Sam went and axsed Grandma about digging the grave. **1979** *Big South Fork OHP-1* [If] you ast a fellow now anything about working, about the first thing he's going to want to know is how much you're going to pay. **1983** *Dark Corner OHP-20A* They called me . . . the night before that and axed me did I know Big John. **2005** Williams *Gratitude* 16 We knowed to keep our mouth shet if anybody besides Dad or Mom asted us any questions about any thing. **2012** *Blind Pig* (Nov 29) A relative from W. VA does say *ax* every time. She said, "I axed him why he never brung no deer home when he went hunting."

4 variant past-participle form *axed*.

1859 Taliaferro *Fisher's River* 41 Brethering and sistering, one and all, I'll give you my 'pinion, though not axed fur it.

[cf EDD (at *ax* v) in general dialect use in Scot, Irel, Engl; DARE *ask* v A1a formerly especially New England, now chiefly South, Midland]

B Syntax.

1 Followed by an embedded yes/no question that maintains inversion of the subject and verb (thus *ask can you* = ask whether/if you can). See also **know C1**, **see B1**, **wonder 3**.

1924 Raine *Saddlebags* 77 He axed had anybody died suddintly. **1935** (in **2009** Powell *Shenandoah Letters* 59) I am asking you could I have some of these old buildings. **1954** Arnow *Dollmaker* 103 Th woman is asken you is they anything you want to know. **1970** *Foxfire Interviews* A-70-5 He asked Betty could she come back with him on Thursday. **1983** [see **A3**]. **1985** Irwin *Alex Stewart* 100 Old man Alder, he was sort of the boss over it, he asked Pap would he bottom them chairs. **1989** *Matewan OHP-28* They asked me did I see anything. **1991** Thomas *Sthn Appal* 177 She'd ask 'um had they been to dinner. **2007** Shelby *Molly Whuppie* 45 One day she went and asked her mommy and daddy didn't they reckon it was time for her to go off on her own and live and do by herself.

2 Followed by an embedded *wh*-question that maintains inversion of the subject and verb (thus *ask what did they think* = ask what they thought). See also **know C2**, **wonder 4**.

1904–20 Kephart *Notebooks* 4:738 Run, Kit, back to Medderses, and ax what air they. **1948** Chase *Grandfather Tales* 52 He called his girls, asked 'em what did they want him to bring 'em. **1954** Arnow

Dollmaker 37 She kept asken Granma Nevels when was Uncle Jesse comen home. **1985** Irwin *Alex Stewart* 120 He was up here and he worked and worked on a mouth bow and finally got it done and asked me what did I think of it. **1989** *Matewan OHP*-56 I was going to ask you what do you remember about the Fourth of July.

a-skairt, a-skeart See **a-scared**.

ask the blessing *verb phrase* To say a prayer at the beginning of a meal (used in preference to "say the blessing" on the premise that only God can grant a blessing).

1881 Pierson *In the Brush* 54–55 The method of extending an invitation to "ask a blessing" before a meal is quite as peculiar. **1939** Hall *Coll* (Dellwood NC) "Return thanks" is [becoming] most common . . . "Ask the blessing" is more old-fashioned. **1951** Justus *Lucky Penny* 14 They all bowed their heads while Grandpappy asked the blessing.

as lief See **lief B**.

asparagus *noun* variant forms *spargrass, spargus, sparrowgrass, sparegrass, spire grass*.

1892 Doak *Wagonauts Abroad* 41 Antique words, forms, and expressions, and the grammar and pronunciation of the illiterate may be found, but no dialect, scarcely even patois . . . "sparrowgrass," "settlement," with accent on the final syllable. **c1960** Wilson *Coll* We had spar'gus. **1975** Jackson *Unusual Words* 150 With oral transmission primary in the community . . . Spire grass is not a grass at all but rather the vegetable that is known to most as asparagus. **1979** Slone *My Heart* 69 Asparagus was only grown as a shrub in the yard, never eaten. The full-grown bush, with its green fernlike leaves and bright seed pod, is very beautiful. I have heard the old folks say, "You know, there are folks who eat 'sparegrass' when the sprouts are little." **1997** Andrews *Mountain Vittles* 41 The old timers said, "Spargus." **1997** Montgomery *Coll*: *spargrass* (known to Bush, Oliver, Weaver).

asphidity see **asafetida**.

aspireen *noun* Aspirin.

1986 Helton *Around Home* 377. **1987** Young *Lost Cove* 79 [The drummer] would rattle off in a monotone staccato the names of hundreds of items that Wess might need. "Aspireens, axle grease, carpet tacks, caster oil, cole cream, cotton bats, crowbars." **1998** Montgomery *Coll* (known to Cardwell).

aspite (also *aspite of*) *preposition* In spite of.

c1959 Weals *Hillbilly Dict* 2 = despite, in spite of. **1971** Fox *Mouth of Mtneer* 4 = despite, in spite of: "Aspite of all she said I still like her."

aspite of See **aspite**.

ass-dip *noun* See citation.

1957 Combs *Lg Sthn High: Word List* 5 = a small, slender bird which frequents creeks and small streams . . . so-called from the swaying motion of the bird's body backward and forward.

assle (also *assle around*) *verb, verb phrase* See citations.

1967 Wilson *Folkways Mammoth Cave* 27 = to be lazy and aimless. **2000** Wilcox *Shaped Notes* 39 He'd see them every one in hell before paying good wages for such assling around. **2013** Venable *How to Tawlk* 3 = foolish waste of time: "Walter assled around so long he missed his ride to the store."

association *noun* An organized body of churches in a district; also in phrase *association time* = the regular session of this body, especially for Baptists, held annually or (more recently) quarterly for two or more days to provide a time for preaching, conducting business, and sharing fellowship.

1797 *French Broad Church Minutes* 35 Agreed that our next Association be held at the forkes of little pigeon the Second friday in August 1798 and that Jon Mulkey open the same by Sermon in case of faillure Isaac barton. **1799** *Globe Creek Church Minutes* 7 On motion made it is agreed that bro[the]r George Brown be delegated to attend the holston ass[ociation] as corrispondent messenger. **1826** *Whitten Letter* Then there is the Regular Baptists enough in this purchase to form an association called the Forked Deer association. **1864** *Poteet CW Letters* (Oct 6) the Assosiation has past over there was 14 or 15 preachers there. **1889** Mooney *Folk Carolina Mts* 97 The great occasion of religious awakening is the "association," which takes place in the fall. **1968** Clarke *Stuart's Kentucky* 77 The Baptist *Association* held annually throughout the denomination had a particular social significance in the hill communities. Baptists from one or more counties met to report on the year's work and make plans for the coming year; they fellowshiped together, listened to budget reports and long sermon, ate much fried chicken, and gloried in being Baptists. **1977** Shackelford et al. *Our Appalachia* 46 Once a year they'd have what they called an Association, or the annual meeting, and they'd have dinner on the grounds. The Associations were held first [at] one church, then another. There were five, six, or seven churches, and a whole bevy of [preachers]. *Ibid.* 44 In the mountains an "Association" is the governing body of a group of Baptist churches in one locale or county that share common beliefs. For many years Association meetings were the largest and most important annual public gatherings. **1982** Ginns *Snowbird Gravy* 96 Now, that 'sociation was when all the Prims met up. . . . They come in over here and got started. Built that little church. All them preachers would come, and they would have a meeting sometimes for a month. 'Sociation, they called it. **1989** Dorgan *Regular Baptists* 134 In Old Regular country, the months of August and September are devoted to "association time," the annual three-day sessions during which the various associations combine business, worship, and fellowship into wonderful amalgams of fun, politics, and spirituality. Ranging in attendance from the forty or fifty delegates and visitors that the tiny Mud River Association (only three churches) can muster to the three thousand to four thousand participants of a New Salem Association annual gathering, these events become the culmination of a church year and capture in both their significance and size a degree of excitement that makes them irresistible to the typical Old Regular member—so irresistible, in fact, that large numbers of people regularly return from homes in Michigan, Illinois, Indiana, Ohio, North Carolina, Georgia, Florida, and points in between to reestablish their roots in Old Regular country. Thus these events are the homecomings of Old Regular tradition, drawing the faithful to their sites for large dinners-on-the-ground, spirited preaching and singing, exciting deliberations of the association delegates, and the annual reinstitution of social ties. **1996** Montgomery *Coll* = traditionally a week-long gathering in late summer, when the business of the denomination was conducted and preaching was held daily (Cardwell). **2014** Montgomery *Doctrine* 75 = a confederation of churches that associate together for the general purpose of correspondence and fellowship. Each church in an Association will call the other churches "Sister Churches." The Association will hold one large meeting a year, said meeting is also known as "The Sosation."

association time See **association.**

ast See **ask.**

as the feller said/says See **fellow B1.**

asthma dog *noun* See citation.

1966 Wilson *Coll* = Mexican hairless or other dog that one sleeps with as a cure for asthma.

as what See **what C.**

at

A *pronoun, conjunction* See **that A.**

B *preposition*

1 Reduced form in linkage to a following word beginning with a vowel sound (thus *at all* => *a tall* or *tall*).

1862 *Parris CW Letters* (July 3) [The bodies of dead soldiers] is laying in piles and not bered a tall. [**1922** *TN CW Ques* 1386 (Wilkes Co NC) I ond no property tall. **1939** Hall *Coll* (Deep Creek NC) He's not a tome (said of an animal). *Ibid.* (Gatlinburg TN) They was't any hardly a tall.] **1966** Dykeman *Far Family* 24 If he had just come to see me before going to Sheriff Doggett, we wouldn't have had anything a-tall to worry about. **1989** Smith *Flyin' Bullets* 40 They just might come in the middle of the night . . . and drag ye out of bed, and take ye out to kill ye, fer no reason a'tall. **2007** Preece *Leavin' Sandlick* 23 I couldn't do it a tall.

2 To. See also **listen at, quarrel at.**

1970 *Burton-Manning Coll*-93A They brought her to the undertakers and, and took him down at the railroad shop. **1983** *Dark Corner OHP*-5A It was on one Sunday morning, and I went out there to get it [= the ham] and went at the meat house. **1989** *Matewan OHP*-94 You went down there at Hatfield, Kentucky. **2007** McMillon *Notes* "They ain't nothing at 'im" = There is nothing significant to him.

3 Used redundantly following *where* or *wherever.*

1939 Hall *Coll* (Cataloochee NC) They jumped the bear and the bear come to the stand where we was at, and I gave him two good shots. *Ibid.* (Cable Branch NC) He thought it was Fonze, you know, come in from the cattle to where he was at. **1961** *Coe Ridge OHP*-336B [I] wanted to see where at he was killed. **1971** *AOHP/ALC*-276 Do you know where most of them's at today? **1975** *Another Look* 139 They know where every one of 'em's at before they ever come here. **1978** *Horsetrading* 43 I'll tell you where you might trade him at. **1981** *GSMNP*-118 He tuck up with another woman and married and raised a family, wherever it was at. **1983** *Dark Corner OHP*-9A I don't remember exactly where it was at, around the Spartanburg somewhere.

at air See **that there.**

at all[1], a tall See **at B1.**

at all[2] *adverb phrase* Of all.

1936 Lyman *WV Idioms* Common use of *at all* without a negative (We had the best time at all).

[DARE *at all* adv chiefly South, Midland]

at a smidgen See **smidgen.**

ate See **eat A3.**

ater, a'ter See **after.**

athout See **without A.**

at-it *noun* See citation.

1963 White *Marbles E KY* 61 = the marbles of an individual being played for in a game.

at oneself *adjective phrase* In one's normal senses or health, alert.

1915 Dingus *Word-List VA* 180 = in good health: "He has not been at hisself for several weeks." **1925** Furman *Glass Window* 5 I can tell you pine-blank where hit's a-wandering to. Hit's them quare women. You hain't been at yourself sence they come in. **c1960** Wilson *Coll* He certainly was at himself when he married that girl of his. **1993** Ison and Ison *Whole Nother Lg* 3 *at himself* = is fully awake and is thinking all right. **1999** Montgomery *Coll* = refers to health as well as presence of mind (Cardwell). **2000** Morgan *Mts Remember* 128 That one time in my life I was not at myself.

[EDD (at *at* VI(11); DARE *at oneself* adj phr chiefly South, Midland]

a-towards *preposition* In the direction of.

1939 Hall *Coll* (Gatlinburg TN) We run that bear about one mile right a-towards home.

attack *noun* variant form *attact*; *verb* variant base forms *attackt, attact,* producing variant past-tense and past-participle forms *attackted, attacted.*

1862 *Davis CW Letters* (May 25) whether our Generals intend to attackt them behind their fortifications or not I cant Say. **1862** Merriman *CW Letters* (Nov 21) we left Jackson and went up to Grenada a distance of 126 miles they expecting an attact from the enemy at that place. **1863** *Watters-Curtis CW Letters* (Dec 12) I was attacted by the gurillars once on my trip one mile and a half from the Tennessee line. **1891** Brown *Dialect in TN* 172 In *drownded, stallded, attackted*, etc., there may be an error as to what is the present tense of the verb. **1901** Harben *Westerfelt* 131–32 My legs is one solid sore streak from my heels up, an' now it's beginnin' to attact my spinebone. **1919** Combs *Word-List South* 36 *attacted*. **1964** Roberts *Hell-Fer-Sartin* 167 They got fire and started back. They got about half way on their journey and they's a painter attackted them on the way.

attact, attakt, attackted, attacted See **attack**.

atter See **after**.

attererds See **afterward(s)**.

atterwards See **afterward(s)**.

atween *preposition* Between. See also **atwixt and atween**.

1867 Harris *Sut Lovingood* 37 This critter look't like a cross atween a black snake an' a fireman's ladder. **1913** Kephart *Our Sthn High* 225 Right sensibly atween the shoulders I've got a pain. **1954** Arnow *Dollmaker* 128 I cain't let a piece o[f] land come atween a woman an her man an her people. **1994–97** Montgomery *Coll* (known to Brown, Cardwell, Ellis, Jones, Oliver, Weaver).

[OED3 *atween* prep A archaic and dialect; SND *atween* prep/adv; Web3 *atween* prep/adv now dialect]

atwixt (also *atwix*) *preposition* Between. See also **atwixt and atween**.

1867 Harris *Sut Lovingood* 35 The hide, har, an' paste were about ekally devided atwix me an' hit. **1884** Murfree *In TN Mts* 222 Her brother . . . tried ter keep the peace atwixt 'em. **1904–20** Kephart *Notebooks* 4:853 They had a gredge atwixt them. **c1960** Wilson *Coll* I'll be there atwixt two and four. **1974** Roberts *Sang Branch* 30 In London Bridge two would hold their hands up, you know, like a bridge, and they would go around atwixt them under their arms. **1997** Montgomery *Coll*: *atwixt* (known to Cardwell).

[OED3 *atwixt* prep, archaic or dialect, c1374→; Web3 *atwixt* prep dialect; DARE *atwixt* prep chiefly South Midland]

auger-eyed *adjective* Of an animal or person: having sharp eyes; hence noun *auger eyes* = sharp eyes.

1952 Wilson *Folk Speech NC* 517 = having sharp eyes. **1957** Broaddus *Vocab Estill Co KY* 4 = sharp-eyed. **1996–97** Montgomery *Coll* (known to Brown, Bush, Hooper) He looked at me with his auger eyes, but they didn't bother me (Cardwell), = having dark, piercing eyes (Hooper).

[DARE *auger-eyed* adj South Midland]

aunt *noun*

A Variant form *aint*.

1942 Hall *Phonetics Smoky Mts* 24. **1944** Williams *Word-List Mts* 30 We are a-goin' to set up with Aint Hanner she is *a-lookin' to die*. **1972** *AOHP/ALC-276* "Why, Aint," I said, "everything that ever breathes the breath of life has to die." **1973** Miller *English Unicoi Co* 97 *aint* attested by 3 of 5 speakers. **1994** Montgomery *Coll* (known to Cardwell).

[DARE *aunt* n A2 chiefly South Midland, less frequent South]

B Used as a quasi-honorific to express courtesy, familiarity, or respect for an older woman in the community not necessarily related to the speaker, often prefaced by *old* and the woman's name, to address or in third-person reference. See also **dad, granny A1, old aunt, old uncle, uncle.**

1878 Guild *Old Times TN* 213 Young persons were her delight, and she always had her house filled with them—clever young women and clever young men—all calling her affectionately, "Aunt Rachel." **1943** Justus *Bluebird* 119 She wasn't near kin, but was called "Aunt" by every one on Little Twin Mountain because she was an old-like person—nobody knew her age. **1962** Williams *Mtneers Mind Manners* 21 Children address by first names contemporaries of their parents, but they address people belonging to the generation of their grandparents as aunt and uncle without regard for blood kinship. **1973** *GSMNP-48*:8 I was taught to respect elderly people, and we were to refer to them as aunt or uncle one, if they were old. **1985** Wear *Lost Communities* 4 He was not my real uncle, but for respect we children were taught to call all old people uncle and aunt. **1991** Haynes *Haywood Home* 8 "Aunt" Ellie Beasley was the cook and lived with them for so long that she became the same as one of the family. *Ibid.* 70 He was not really our uncle. He was no kin to us that I know of. But the young of my time were taught to address older people as uncle or aunt whether they were any kin or not. It was respectful. **1994** Parton *Dolly* 4 We called her Aunt Marth, even though she wasn't related to us. **2005** Williams *Gratitude* 13 Back then, it was a sign of respect to call older folks "Aunt" and "Uncle," when they were friends too close to be called "Mister" and "Missus." **2013** Lyon *Voiceplace* 186 I wrote down a story she told me of Old Aunt Martha Money who could cure the summer complaint. **2017** *Blind Pig* (Oct 12) When I first went to a country church in my community (almost fifty years ago), my friend was introducing me to different people like "Aunt Hilda," "Uncle Clea," "Aunt Bessie," etc. I thought she was kin to every person in the congregation. *Ibid.* When I was young, adults were Aunt and Uncle if they were close to the family or neighbors, otherwise Miz and Mr.

Aunt Lydia basket (also *Lydia basket*) *noun* See 1937 citation.

1930 Perry *Handicraft Art* And when she reached the age when most people quit work and sit in a cozy corner, Lydia, who could still climb to the tops of her tallest trees, started making willow and split baskets with such original designs that they became famous around Gatlinburg as "Lydia baskets." **1937** Eaton *Handicrafts* 170 A Tennessee basket that still retains the name of its inventor is the Aunt Lydia Basket, which originated with Mrs. Lydia Whaley of Gatlinburg many years ago. . . . Her basket, which is one of the handsomest in the mountains, is round and made of strips of willow bark worked over unpeeled, smooth willow with a handle of a larger switch. It is noted for its exceptional design and soft reddish-brown color of the inside bark of the willow splint. **c1950** Whaley *Aunt Lydia* The "Aunt Lydia Basket" is round in shape with a peculiar indention in each side and is woven from willow bark which she prepares herself. She said her father brought this style of basket from Scotland with him and that the design of weaving had been in the family for three generations.

author *noun* Authority, a person or document considered authoritative.

c1940 Aswell *Glossary TN Idiom* 3 = authority. "William Jennings Bryan was my *author* on this evolution business." **1996–97** Montgomery Coll (known to Brown, Bush) The Bible's my author on that (Oliver).

[OED3 *author* n 5 now Sc[ottish] and archaic]

awar *adjective* Aware.

1913 Kephart *Our Sthn High* 288 Afore, atwixt, awar . . . all these everyday expressions of the backwoods were contemporary with the *Canterbury Tales*. **1994** Montgomery Coll (known to Cardwell).

[cf SND *awaur* adj]

away *adverb* Far (off), by a considerable distance or time. See also **away back, way.**

1892 Dromgoole *Dan to Beersheba* 77 From away down among the orange-lands came rumors of the white frosts that had breathed upon the tender fruit until it lay in pitiful heaps upon the ground. **1910** Cooke *Power and Glory* 99 "I come from away up in the mountains," she said softly. **1939** Hall Coll (Gatlinburg TN) [The bear] tore loose from the dogs and run away on down the flat and treed up another tree. *Ibid.* (Cataloochee NC) It was away in the night when I got in to camp. **1956** Hall Coll (Roaring Fork TN) I looked away up on the mountain. **1969** GSMNP-37:2:2 Thad Watson, he lived away yonder on Mingus Creek. She lived up on Yoncey's Fork, away up there next to where the school is now. **1972** AOHP/ALC-355 She lived up on Yoncey's Fork, away up there next to where the school is now. **1974** GSMNP-50 He carried the mail away after that . . . after the government established rural routes. **1979** *Big South Fork OHP-11* You went away off down in under the railroad. **1983** *Dark Corner OHP-27A* We got the radio away up in the forties. **1991** Thomas *Sthn Appal* 252 I'd a' been a way after night a-gittin' home if you hadn't picked me up. **1996** GSMNPCOHP-1:1 Dig a-way down deep. Now [the kraut]'s better in the bottom of the barrel. **2012** Milnes *Signs Cures Witchery* There at that house they were having a great big time that night, away late in the night.

away back (also *away back years ago, away back yonder, away years back*) *adverb phrase* Remote in place or past time. See also **a**³, **a- E, away, back A.**

1901 Harben *Westerfelt* 135 Somebody told 'er some'n Liz said away back when you fust started to fly around 'er. **1937** Hall Coll (Cosby TN) They bought [the land] away back. **1957** GSMNP-23:1:9 That was my great granddaddy, the old ancestors away back yonder. **1963** Edwards *Gravel* 54–55 I imagined he was somehow like the wildcats that roamed the mountain back toward the Kentucky line, away back in the deep hollows toward the mines. **1967** Hall Coll (Townsend TN) Hit come a storm away back years ago. **1991** Thomas *Sthn Appal* 161 I bought them shoes at th' Coffee store, a-way back there, then.

[perhaps a transitional syllable + *way back*; cf DARE *back yonder* adv chiefly South Midland]

away yander See **yonder B3.**

away years back See **away back.**

away yonder See **yonder B3.**

awful *adjective* Good, superb, extraordinary (often applied to a person with a fondness, propensity, or skill for performing a certain activity); hence *awfullest* = best, greatest, most extraordinary or intense. See also **awful to.**

1931 Goodrich *Mt Homespun* 56 They do say it's the awfullest meetin' ever heard of. **1939** Hall Coll (Cataloochee NC) My daddy one time—he's an awful horse trader—he had an old wind sucker. One morning he got on him, he said "I'll trade that thing if I don't get a bull yearling." *Ibid.* (Roaring Fork TN) We would have the awfullest time in the world. . . . He had the awfullest sight of apples I ever saw. *Ibid.* (Waldens Creek TN) He was the awfullest singer ever I heared. **1956** Hall Coll (Big Creek NC) His granddaddy was an awful hunter. He hunted bear a lot. **1968** Clarke *Stuart's Kentucky* 190 A similar show of bounty prevailed at the basket dinner . . . the awfulest lot of cooking included turkey, squirrel, several kinds of pickles, preserves, and similar articles to those listed above. **1969** Medford *Finis* 78 Oh what "awful sermonts" he could preach—"awful" was the term usually used. *Ibid.* 149 After they had gone on a few days, someone told me they wanted me to come, that they were having an "awful meetin'." **1973** GSMNP-88 Uncle Witt had an awful home here, hit was I'd say one as good of homes as they was in Cades Cove. **1976** GSMNP-113:7 She was a awful worker. . . . She picked peas and made such as that, you know. Lord a mercy. **1978** Parris *Mt Cooking* 12 I was an awful boy for dumplings. Didn't care so much for turkey meat, but I sure loved dumplings. **1981** Whitener *Folk-Ways* 40 "An awful generation of young'uns" = a large family. **1989** *Matewan OHP-33* [Mother Jones] was a speaker, man . . . the awfullest gangs you ever seen come to hear Mother Jones. **1991** Thomas *Sthn Appal* 204 When-ever'n I was a right young man . . . they'ud have some of the awfulest times.

[DARE *awful* adj 2 southern Appalachians]

awful to *adjective phrase* Having an unfortunate, unhealthy, or extreme disposition or tendency to (do a certain thing); hence noun phrases *awful hand to, awful man to, awful woman to*. The terms express a range of emotion from disapproval to admiration. For similar patterns with *to*, see Grammar and Syntax §10.2. See also **bad to, good to, great to, poor to.**

1935 Sheppard *Cabins in Laurel* 50 My daddy was an awful man to drink by spells. **1937** Hall Coll (Ravensford NC; said of the legendary Mrs. Clem Enloe, who fished in the Great Smoky

Mountains National Park year round despite rules prohibiting this) She's an awful hand to fish. **1953** Hall *Coll* (Bryson City NC) We had an old dog that come to the camp there, and we never knowed whose he was. He took up there and stayed, and he was awful to find snakes. **1956** Hall *Coll* (Roaring Fork TN) He's awful to tell stories. He does it a-purpose to get a laugh. **1981** GSMNP-121:35 I was an awful boy to hunt. **1990** *Matewan OHP*-73 I remember my grandmother was the awfullest woman to make tea ever was. **1997** Andrews *Mountain Vittles* 43 Use to be corn was awful to stick burning right to the bottom of the pot.

[DARE *awful* adj 3 South, South Midland]

a-winding See **winding**.

awkward *adverb* variant form *awkerd*.

c1900 (in **1997** Stoddart *Quare Women* 126) I'm allers sayin' sumpin' awkerd. **1942** Hall *Phonetics Smoky Mts* 88.

awomen corner *noun* See citations.

1968 Wilson *Folklore Mammoth Cave* 40 = the side in the *church-house* to the left of the preacher where sat the old men of the congregation, who often "amened" what the preacher had said. The opposite corner, where the older women sat, was, humorously, called the "awomen-corner." **2014** Montgomery *Doctrine* 70 = where certain sisters would sit and wait for the moment in the sermon that lent itself to such good feelings that they would begin to wail and shout. Some would raise their hands in glorious rapture; some would stand and begin to sway while moaning and shouting. This was more or less confined to Appalachia and the Southeast and by the late 20th century the awomen corner has been phased out even in those vicinities.

ax, **axed** See **ask**.

axe helve See **ax helve**.

ax helve (also *axe helve*) *noun* The handle of an ax, a haft.

1905 Miles *Spirit of Mts* 20 When a man has not only the living to provide, but many of his farm implements and much of his furniture—tables, chairs, axe-helves, bread-bowls, cupboards, cradles, even looms and wagons to make with the help of a few neighbors—perhaps his own shoemaking and blacksmithing to do, and certainly fuel to haul and a crop to raise—where is his time for bathing? **1957** Parris *My Mts* 80 "Not many folks make ax helves any more," Henry said. "Most of 'em buy turned or store-bought helves."

[< Middle English *helve* < Old English *hielfe*]

axle tree *noun* The spindle of a cart or wagon wheel.

1939 Hall *Coll* (Gumstand TN) The axle-tree of tarpole wagons [was] made out of hickory, [with] no skeins over it.

[OED3 *axle-tree* 1400→]

ay (also *aye*, *ey*, *i*) *interjection* Used as a mild exclamation or oath to express a range of emotion (affirmation, surprise, acknowledgment, regret, consternation, etc.), usually as a combining form, as in *aye God*, *aye gonnies*, *aye grain*, *aye grannies*, *aye jallus*, *aye jucks*, *ey God*, *ey gonnies*, *I God*, *I golly*, *I gonnies*, *I grannies*, *I growneys*. See also **by**, **dad-**, **eh la**.

1873 Smith *Peace Papers* 203 I golly, there aint many of us can say that. **1913** Kephart *Our Sthn High* 287–88 Ey God, a favorite expletive, is the original of egad, and goes back to Chaucer. **1931** Combs *Lg Sthn High* 1308 "Cuss-words" expressions of surprise and intense expressions [include] I (by) gonnies. **1935** Sheppard *Cabins in Laurel* 299 When we got back to Hector's, aye jallus, he'd done gone. **1939** Hall *Coll*: *ey gonnies* = said to be a common by-word of some people. *Ibid*. (Deep Creek NC) The coon went to coughing. Mark says "Aye God, he's a-givin' trouble, ain't he?" **1939** Hall *Notebooks* 9:41 (Saunook NC) One of his by-words is "I grannies." **c1950** Haun *When the Wind* 12 I God, I said where to? **1952** Wilson *Folk Speech NC* 557 *Igonnies* . . . Mild oath. **1961** Medford *History Haywood Co* 186 I grannies—I can dance a jig, and me over a hundred. **1973** GSMNP-91:31 Oh, aye, that's what caused this thumb stiff here. **1975** *AOHP/ALC*-903 Aye Lord . . . people just had it in for him. **1995–97** Montgomery *Coll* Aye gonnies, I ain't gonna do it (Cardwell); *aye jucks* (known to Cypher). **1997** Nelson *Country Folklore* 43 If someone would ask him for credit he would say, "Doggone, I growneys, Honey, I have so much on my book now." **2003** Onchuck *Mud Pie Memories* 128 [Daddy] prefaced many sentences with "I gracious," which I never did figure out why. I can still hear him say, "I gracious, Neve" (his pet name for Mama), "I'ma gonna tell you." **2007** McMillon *Notes*: *aye grain*, *aye grannies*, sometimes used as a sort of resignation to events, a fatalistic expression.

[cf OED3 *ay* interj 1 now the common northern exclamation of surprise, invocation, earnestness) 1340→, *aye* interj perhaps from *ay* "ever, always" 1576→; SND *ay* interj 6(3); DARE i prep chiefly South, South Midland]

aye god, **aye gonnies**, **aye grain**, **aye grannies**, **aye jallus**, **aye jucks** See **ay**.

ay-la See **eh la**.

aynion See **onion**.

B

ba'ar See **bear**[1].

Babdist See **Baptist.**

babe *noun* A pet name for a boy or young man.

1915 Dingus *Word-List VA* 180 = used as a pet name for a lad. The youngest son, though grown, is often called the baby. **1976** *DARE File* (wNC) = a pet name for a boy. In the South it often precedes the family name, as in Babe Johnson, Babe Brown. **1983** *Dark Corner OHP-24A* She was Babe Durham's daughter.

[DARE *babe* n South]

Babtist See **Baptist.**

baby catcher (also *baby snatcher*) *noun* A midwife, obstetrician. See also **baby catching, catch B1.**

1961 Williams *Content Mt Speech* 14 She's the best "baby snatcher" that ever attended a "granny racket" and "a great hand to set up with the dead." **1997** King *Mt Folks* 75 He was called "the baby catcher." **1999** Montgomery *Coll*: *baby catcher* = midwife (Brown).

baby catching *verbal noun* See citation. Same as **child catching.** See also **baby catcher, catch B1.**

2007 McMillon *Notes* = serving as a midwife in delivering a child.

baby-cradle *n* A cradle for an infant.

1952 Wilson *Folk Speech NC* 517.

[redundant compound]

baby mouth *noun* Same as **thrush.**

2009 Miller *Nigh Gone* 93 "Baby mouth" or "thrush" was an infection of the mouth or throat of a nursing infant. Usually someone in the village would have a reputation of being able to cure this by breathing into the infant's mouth. There were other remedies for this common condition.

baby powder *noun* Construed as a singular count noun; hence plural *baby powders*. For similar forms, see **powder A.**

1968 *Faith Healing* 63 I just draw the fire out of [the wound] and take common old baby powders—talcum powders they used t'call 'em—baby powders that they used t'put on a baby.

baby powders See **baby powder.**

baby snatcher See **baby catcher.**

babytear *noun* A bluet (*Houstonia* spp). See also **eyebright 1, innocence, Quaker lady.**

1956 Stuart *Year Rebirth* 100 They were picking the wild flowers that are so often called babytears here, though many call them bluets. **1997** Montgomery *Coll* (known to Brown, Bush).

bacca, baccer, baccow, baccy See **tobacco.**

bach (also *batch, batch it*) *verb, verb phrase* Usually of a man: to keep house temporarily or in crude conditions in the absence or without the benefit of a woman; to live by oneself temporarily.

1860 *Love CW Letters* (Oct 2) H M Hutcheson & E W Townsend is going to Bach on A while yet. **c1926** Bird *Cullowhee Wordlist*: *batch* = to live in a house temporarily and under primitive or crude conditions. "I batched in that house for more'n a month." **1937** White *Highland Heritage* 33–34 The places where they lived are not really human habitations. They may be deserted sawmill shacks or just any old building long since too dilapidated for use as a house. Perhaps the family will tell you that they are just "batching" here (whole families "batch," not just men). And it may really be that they are merely stopping here for some special reason, or you may find to your surprise that they have been here for years. **1976** GSMNP-113:10 I was batchin' and he come over there, said I had to stay with him or Fred one. **1981** Weals *Farmers* After several years away from his father, the late Thomas Cooper, they became lonesome for one another, and finally Bill rejoined his father. They "batched," in Bill's language, wherever Tom found employment. **1988** Kosier *Maggie* 101 He rented a trailer and "batched-it" on his own, driving home whenever he could. **1992** Giardina *Unquiet Earth* 19 There's no money for your train ticket at Christmas. Can you batch it here? **2006** Shumate *Bridge Crew* 40 That summer Mom had a sick spell and had to spend a few days in the hospital. Uncle Paul and I learned the meaning of "batching it." It was not so bad, cold cereal for breakfast, peanut butter and bread for lunch and Miss Hattie's for supper.

[shortening of *bachelor*]

back

A *adverb*

1 (also *back in*) Used to express remoteness in time. See also **away back.**

1975 *AOHP/ALC-961* Did everybody back live in company houses, all miners? **1977** Weals *Cove Folk* My father in his time, back in before me, he made the coffins, the caskets, for people that died in that place. **1992** Oxford *Ray Hicks* 88 There wasn't no stock laws back in when my daddy and them grew up. **2012** Milnes *Signs Cures Witchery* That's how us younger knowed from by our relations back.

2 Used to express remoteness in space (especially preceding a prepositional phrase).

1939 Hall *Coll* (Maggie Valley NC) We was right out after him, went back in on Stillwell and we was a-tracking him. **1957** GSMNP-23:2:10 They was several houses on up, around up on Mill Creek and up in there and on up next to Fork of the River back up in there. **1969** GSMNP-25:1:21 He came from across there on Little Dudley, back over down in that section, you know, down in where they come across in there. **1970** *Hunting Stories* 35 We took off back down toward Mulberry Gap. **1972** *Raising Sheep* 101 When the sheep got too far back, then the wild cats got'em. **1974–75** McCracken *Logging* 23:32 We started wooding there, along not far from Polls Gap and a-going back in on toward Heintoga, behind the timber cutting.

3 Of the wind: in a reverse direction, in one's face.

1972 Miller *Pigeon's Roost* (May 4) One farmer said that he was not looking for many tobacco plants this year as when he sowed his seeds, the wind was blowing so back that he was afraid that most of them was blowed across the fence.

B *verb*

1 To write an address on (a letter or envelope). [Editor's note: This term originated prior to envelopes, when letters were folded and the address written on the back side for mailing.]

1863 *Lister CW Letters* (Oct 23) I rote you a letter and give you diretion how to back your leters and laid you in paper and stamps. **1864** *Millican CW Letter* (Aug 9) I put your letter in a small white envelope and sealed it well and backed it to you and requested Mrs. G. to hand it to you. **1864** *D B Walker CW Letters* I rot one [= letter] yeasterdia Started it with this one I backed it to Cleavelon Tenn. **1913** Kephart *Our Sthn High* 32 In the group that gathered at mail time I often was solicited to "back" envelopes. **1939** Hall *Coll* (Saunook NC) I'm goin' to let you back that letter. **1956** Hall *Coll* (Hartford TN) If a letter comes to my mailbox, if it ain't backed "Lying John Sutton," I won't have it. **1988** Kosier *Maggie* 25 Sometimes they would "back" letters for customers—letters were folded over and addressed on the back when there were no envelopes.

[OED3 *back* v 12b Scot and U. S.; SND *back* 2(4) "to address a letter"; Web3 *back* vt 5 dialect; DARE *back* v 3 formerly more widespread, now chiefly South, South Midland]

2 See citation.

1957 Combs *Lg Sthn High: Word List* 7 = to mount (a horse).

3 To redistill whiskey.

1975 *Another Look* 134 [In] one of them [= stills], you just keep backing it and proofing it to what you want, and then you cut it off, and that's it.

C *interjection* (often *back! back!*) Move back! (used as a command to livestock). See also **ho back, whoa back.**

1996 Montgomery *Coll* (known to Adams, Jones, Ledford, Oliver) = a command given to a horse or to a cow at milking time, often accompanied by a hand to guide the movement of the animal (Cardwell).

[DARE *back* v 6 especially South Midland]

back and forth *verb phrase* To go from and return to the same place repeatedly, especially with minimal result or purpose.

1916 Combs *Old Early English* 294 Numerous other anomalous compounds and semi-hybrids are found, for example: *backing-and-forthing*. **1931** Combs *Lg Sthn High* 1307 He kep' a backin' an' a-forthin' all day. **1940** Haun *Hawk's Done* 158 What time Wilbur wasn't toting empty boxes or rolling a box of glass around somewhere on a cart, she had him backing and forthing to the post office with a pack of letters. **1971** Dwyer *Dict for Yankees* 24 *backing and forthing* = going back and forth or engaging in some futile exercise. "Congress jest keeps a'backin' and a'forthin' all year. **1981** Whitener *Folk-Ways* 40 The purist notes . . . a substitution of one part of speech for another ("a-backin' and a-forthin'").

[DARE *back and forth* v phr 1 South Midland]

back'ard, backards, back'ards See **backward.**

back assards See **backasswards.**

backasswards (also *back assards*) *adverb* Backwards, backside to the front.

c1982 Young *Colloquial Appal* 1 *backassards*. **2017** *Blind Pig* (Feb 28) I have heard "hindside first" used but my folks would say "back assards." *Ibid.* Turn it around back assards and it'll fit better.

back back See **back C.**

back cuss *verb phrase* To curse in reply to someone else's cursing. See also **backjaw.**

1976 *Hartley III* 4 Whenever they got too tough with me, I could back-cuss just as big as they could.

backdoor trots *noun* Overactive bowels.

1957 Neel *Backwoodsman* 5 = diarrhoea. **1990** Cavender *Folk Medical Lex* 17 = diarrhea. **1997** Montgomery *Coll* (known to Cardwell, Weaver). **2003** Cooper *Gathering Memories* 44 For running off at the bowels (or "back-door trots"), make a tea of lettuce and drink it.

backed up *adjective phrase* Constipated.

1995 Montgomery *Coll* (known to Cardwell).

[DARE *backed up* adj phr South Midland]

backer[1] See **tobacco.**

backer[2] *noun* One who finances and pays **a bootlegger** to deliver homemade whiskey to market.

1974 Maurer and Pearl *KY Moonshine* 73 Obviously, the moonshine whiskey industry makes demands on capital that are not common in most legitimate industries. . . . The backer, needless to say, never associates himself publicly with any phase of the industry, though it is not unknown. **1990** Merriman *Moonshine Rendezvous* 62 By 11:15 p.m., I shut off the engine at the backer's barn and started countin' money, while Warren watched from my car.

backerd(s), back'erds See **backward.**

backhand *noun* See citation.

1991 Thomas *Sthn Appal* 144 At th' start I liked th' work of coalminin' fine. I got my start. I worked with an old—it'ud be called a "backhand." If you'uz a greenhand, didn't know how to shoot coal, ur nothin', you'd be called a greenhand until you learned to shoot coal.

back-hill *adjective* Of a person: unsophisticated, as if raised in the hills.

1949 Arnow *Hunter's Horn* 234 Suse flushed; already the new teacher would take her for a little back-hill fool for staring so.

back house (also *backy, backy house*) *noun* An outhouse, privy. See also **johnny**.

1934–47 LAMSAS (Madison Co NC) *back house*. **1949** McDavid *Grist* 106 (Elbert Co GA) *backy, backy house* = privy. **1964** Reynolds *Born of Mts* 78 There were once plenty elsewhere, called outhouses on the farms, and back houses when back of the village houses. **1970** Mull *Mt Yarns* 23 A lot of fun was derived from the simplest situations . . . the "out house" or "back house" was the target of many jokes. **1986** Pederson et al. *LAGS*: *back house* = attested by 5/60 interviewees (8.3%) from E TN; 5/37 of all LAGS interviewees (13.5%) attesting term were from Appalachia. **1994** Montgomery *Coll* (known to Andrews, Cardwell, Shields). **1998** *Dante OHP-24* Everything up through here the company owned, and they wasn't nothing but back houses they called it.

backie See **tobacco**.

backie horse *adverb phrase* Riding piggyback.

1999 Montgomery *Coll* Let's go backie horse (Cardwell).

[cf EDD *backie* sb^3 in phrase *to give a backie* or *backie-up* Scot; cf SND *backie* n^1 "a hoist on the back"]

back in See **back A1**.

backing *noun* (usually *backings*) In making liquor, the weaker alcohol at the end of an initial distillation **run**, too low in proof to be considered whiskey. It is either put back in the still as **singlings** and run again or mixed with the stronger liquor produced at the start of the **run** (see **thump**). See also **fried backing**.

1917 Kephart *Word-List* 407 *backings* = liquor produced by continuing distillation after whiskey is made. **1949** Maurer *Argot of Moonshiner* 7 *backings* = low-proof liquor, not containing enough alcohol to be considered whiskey; usually low-proof distillate at the end of a run. **1959** Hall *Coll* (Mt Sterling NC) When liquor first come off [out of the still], it was alkyhol and then hit'd break, and then you'd run your backin's as long as they was sweet, until they got sour. In fact, when they got sour, it loses strength. **1967** Williams *Moonshining* 14 However, a few gallons of liquid with little or no alcoholic content (referred to as "backins") are placed in a churn or barrel for use in establishing uniform proof of the run later. . . . The whiskey with high alcoholic content is cut with "backins" until the total run is approximately 100 proof (50 per cent alcohol). **1972** *Foxfire I* 316 = what results after beer [= fermented mash] is run through a thumperless operation once. **a1975** Lunsford *It Used to Be* 81 Singlings are the same thing as backin's, or low wine. In other words, if you were to start without borrowing some backings or having some on hand anyway, you'd first run off, and that would not be high proof whiskey, that would be singlings. You set that back and then you mash in again and you double back! You put in your singlings, then "run off and run out." **1984** High *Titan Rock* 49 I took a cup and got into the backings. That's when it's half whiskey and half beer—before it's run off in its final state. **1992** Gabbard *Thunder Road* 67 When the alcohol quits runnin', what you get is backin's. If you got three cans of alcohol, you get three cans of backin's to cut it with and you put the rest of the backin's into the condenser. *Ibid.* 155 The first shots was over a hundard [sic] proof. If you wanted to make it eighty or ninety proof, you'd have to run so many jars of backin's to weaken it down. Then you could take a jar of it and shake it [to test the bead].

[OED3 *backings* (at *backing* n 11) "refuse of wool or flax, or what is left after dressing it"; cf SND *backings* n pl "refuse of tow, wool, etc."; DARE *backings* n South Midland]

backings party *noun* See citations. See also **backing**.

1976 Lindsay *Grassy Balds* 97 At the end of a runoff they would usually bring the backin's in out of the stillhouse to someone's house and have a backin's party. **1977** Shields *Cades Cove* 79 It was sort of a custom to have a party after a "run off" of moonshine whiskey. Sometimes called backins parties, these featured a quantity of the mash "backins" or spent beer, heated with spices and served along with food. . . . The alcoholic content of the drink is not high, but enough of it can elevate the drinkers' spirits.

backjaw (also *back sass*)

A *verb* To reply disrespectfully (to). Same as **jaw back**. See also **back cuss**.

1976 Dwyer *Southern Sayin's* 5 *backjaw* = to talk back. "Don't you back-jaw me." **1994–97** Montgomery *Coll*: *backjaw* (known to Adams, Bush, Oliver); Quit your back sassing or you'll get some hickory tea (Shields).

B *noun* Backtalk, impertinent or disrespectful replies. See also **back cuss**.

1936 Stuart *Head of Hollow* 36 Don't ever give me anymore of your back sass. **1952** Wilson *Folk Speech NC* 517 Don't give me no *backjaw*, big boy!

[EDD *backjaw* v "retort, altercate, abuse" Scot; cf SND *backjaw* n, v; CUD *back jaw* (at *back* adv) "impertinent replies"]

back of *phrasal preposition*

1 (also *the back of*) Of location: beyond, behind. Same as **a-back of, in back of.**

1862 *Dalton CW Letters* (Aug 22) I have went a bout thrity mils back of richmon we ar going to pedert burg to meat the yankes and I expect we will have big fite. **1939** Hall *Coll* (White Oak NC) Mountaineers don't say "in back of." They say "the back of." **1966** Dakin *Vocab Ohio River Valley* 51 Scattered speakers elsewhere in Ohio, Indiana, and Kentucky east of the Green-Barren River also say only (*in*) *back of*. **1970** GSMNP-26:4 The way the road runs now, the road comes back of the Ephraim house, but it did come in front of it. **1973** GSMNP-78:12 Part of the time a little creek run down the back of the house. She would lay her clothes on that and take a board and beat them, beat the dirt out. **1989** *Matewan OHP-*

33 [The jail] was over the back of the railroad down there where the station used to be.

2 Of time: before, earlier than.

1969 GSMNP-42:9 I heared him say back of that . . . way back a few years before that you could get four acres for a dollar. **1969** GSMNP-46:5 Back of that, he just minded every word I said to him. **1983** *Dark Corner OHP*-11A I don't think I would remember anything back of two years [old].

back out

A *verb phrase* To challenge or dare (someone).

1911 Shearin *E KY Word-List* 537 = to dare or challenge; e.g., "I'll back you out to do it." **1957** Combs *Lg Sthn High: Word List* 7 = to wager, e.g.: "I'll back ye out a-jumpin' over that log." **1973** GSMNP-79:1:22 I told the other two or three of the cousins, I said, "I'll back you out a-taking a chew of Grandpaw's tobacco."

B *noun* Cowardice, a tendency to withdraw or retreat from a challenge or dare.

1953 Hall *Coll* (Plott Creek NC) There's hardly any back out on one of [a Plott bear dog], for he'll fight anything from a woods mouse to a grizzly bear

[DARE *back-out* n Midland]

back parent *noun* An ancestor. See also **foreparent, forepeople.**

1978 Burton *Ballad Folks* 14 One of the songs her mother used to sing "a'ter supper," one which her mother in turn learned "from her back parents," is "Pretty Corina."

backpiece See **backstick.**

back-ridge *verb* See citation.

1957 Hall *Bear Stories* 71 We just put our dogs in atter one of the yearlin's [= bears]. And they [= dogs] run hit and treed it. . . . Everwhen we got there, why, I back-ridged [= went back along the ridge], got Jack's gun.

back room *noun* The main bedroom of a house.

1986 Pederson et al. *LAGS* (Greene Co TN) = the bedroom, for sleeping. **2009** Benfield *Mt Born* 28 Most often the room called a "back room" was a bedroom, depending on the size of the family. Bedrooms had a bed, a nightstand, and a bureau with mirror atop.

back sass See **backjaw.**

backscratcher *noun* Apparently a ruffian.

1983 *Dark Corner OHP*-3A Folks who lived out in there . . . I call them backscratchers and murderers and road killers, you understand, back there then.

backset *noun* A relapse during convalescence (especially in phrase *take a backset*).

1863 *Warrick CW Letters* (May 26) I will be as stowt as ever in a few days if I take no back set. **1864** *Lister CW Letters* (Feb 27) I want you to take good cear of your self When you haf to go apon your crutches and if it takes eny back set send and get Mrs Bolews gall to stay with you. **1889** Murfree *Broomsedge Cove* 366 I wur a-tryin' ter git over that backset. **1939** Hall *Coll* (Indian Creek NC) He tuck the whooping cough along about Christmas time and was out of school for a month, and then he tuck a back set and was out of school again. **1969** Madden and Jones *Walker Sisters* 29 Despite this expert care, the convalescing sister said, "I like to took a backset when I got to knockin' about," that is, when she got on her feet again. **1978** *Bird Traps* 74 The doctor told him to stay in, but he went to work anyway. He took a backset, and never got over it. **1985** Irwin *Alex Stewart* 33 It was cold and they was snow on the ground and I took a back-set and went as blind as if I'd never had an eye in my head. **1996** GSMNPCOHP-1:4 They'd get up too early and try to take care of somebody and take a backset.

[SND *backset* n 1; CUD *backset* 2 (at back adv) "reverse in illness"; DARE *backset* n 1b chiefly South, South Midland]

backside outwards *adverb phrase* See citation. See also **get up backwards.**

1937 Hall *Coll* (Cosby Creek TN) I put on my dress that morning backside out'ards [explaining jocularly why things went amiss during the day].

backstick (also *backpiece*) *noun* A large log put at the rear of a fireplace, especially one to throw light and heat into a room and keep a fire alive overnight or longer. Also called **night stick.** [Editor's note: The term *backlog* is widespread in the US.]

1934–47 *LAMSAS Appal*: *backstick* = attested by 4/148 speakers (2.7%) from WV, 9/20 (45%) from VA, 7/37 (18.9%) from NC, 7/14 (50%) from SC, and 10/12 (83.3%) from GA. **1949** McDavid *Grist* 106 (Greenville Co SC) *back piece.* **1963** Edwards *Gravel* 92 The dull glow on the back-stick played on his spectacles. **1966–68** *DARE Survey* (Brasstown NC, Gatlinburg TN, Spruce Pine NC) *backstick* = the big log behind the others in the back of the fireplace. **1977** Shields *Cades Cove* 32 A back-stick was a fire log placed at the back of the fireplace to force the burning logs toward the front and aid in reflecting heat to the room. *Ibid.* 33 A good hickory back-stick would last several days. **1978** Reese *Speech NE Tenn* 30 *backstick* = attested by 6/12 (50%) speakers. **1986** Pederson et al. *LAGS*: *backstick* = attested by 12/60 interviewees (20%) from E TN and 10/35 (28.6%) from N GA; 22/129 of all LAGS interviewees (17.0%) attesting term were from Appalachia. **2004** Myers and Boyer *Walker Sisters* 17 In the back of the large fireplace was a back-stick, a large log used to force the burning logs to the front to reflect heat into the room. This back-stick burned and required a replacement about once a week. If any of the previous back-stick remained, they pulled it to the front and placed it on the dog irons to give room to the new back-stick.

[DARE *backstick* n 2 chiefly southern Appalachians, Gulf States]

backswitch *noun* A sharp angle in a trail or road to permit a vehicle to climb a steep grade.

1939 Hall *Coll* (Gatlinburg TN) [There is a] cemetery above the

Sugarlands . . . at the first backswitch people there [are] buried over a hundred year. **1973** GSMNP-70:12 I knowed some Ogles that lived up there where you went through the Sugarlands and made a backswitch back here on top of the ridge.

[reversed form of *switchback*]

backward (also *backwards*)

A *adjective, adverb* variant forms *back'ard, backards, back'ards, backerd, backerds, back'erds.*

1863 *Watkins CW Letters* (March 4) I have got so I can go backerds and foreds from the horse pittle to the companey. **1867** Harris *Sut Lovingood* 166 He shot his belly forwards an' his shoulders back'ards, like ontu a 'oman shettin the nex' tu the top drawer ove a beauro. **1925** Dargan *Highland Annals* 152 Now I say it back'ards. **1937** Hall *Coll* (Cosby TN) He was jest a-walkin' back'erds n' forwards. **1973** Jones *Cades Cove TN* 102 *backerds*. **1989** *Matewan OHP*-28 I knowed the way backerd and forwards through the mountain. **1993** Burleson *Aunt Keziah* 2 The way abody sets a Dumb Supper, you git a bunch of single gals and git supper, but you do hit all backards, even to setting the table.

[DARE *backward(s)* adj, adv, n A especially South, Midland]

B *adjective*

1 Shy, hesitant, reluctant.

1861 *Huntley CW Letters* (Dec 3) tell pap if he needs hit [= the money] I dont Waunt him to be Backward about spending it fer I never expect to need it. **1862** (in **1999** Davis *CW Letters* 49) if that should be the result after a thorough acquaintance, I shall not be backward in making it known to you. **1900** Harben *N GA Sketches* 193 Do as I tell you, brother. Don't be back'ard. You can't hide nothin'. **1923** Greer-Petrie *Angeline Steppin' Out* 7 If any of 'em was backerd about larnin', me and him could take 'em thoo the sets ontell they got the hang of the thing. **1950** Wood *Sure of Life* 60 Eat all you want, and don't be backwards none. **1969** GSMNP-38:95 They'd tell you right at once what they believed. They wasn't a bit backward about talking. **1999** Montgomery *File* A lot of mountain people are kind of backward, but I don't care to talk to nobody (40-year-old woman, Del Rio TN). **2005** Williams *Gratitude* 478 *backerds* = bashful, not very polished and smooth in the social graces. **2016** *Blind Pig* (March 18) I was so backward when I was a child. I'd hide behind Granny or Pap's legs if somebody tried to talk to me. **2018** *Blind Pig* (Oct 16) I recall backward being used if the person was "painfully" shy.

2 Of a crop or growing season: late or slow in developing.

1831 *McLean Diary* (May 19) Warm Showers of Rain Vigitation Backward. **1863** *Warrick CW Letters* (June 10) Crops is verry Backwards her. **1864** *Chapman CW Letters* (April 10) It is the backardes Spring I have ever seen this is 12 day of aprile and thare is no sine of crop yet.

backwards See **backward.**

backwards and forwards *adverb phrase* To and fro, especially traveling to a destination and then returning home.

1989 *Matewan OHP*-9 Charlie and John wouldn't have bothered them. They's just going backwards and forwards home. *Ibid.* 94 We can't pay your travel expense backwards and forwards from down there to Logan.

backwater *verb* To reverse one's course, retreat or attempt to retreat from an obligation or predicament. Same as **take backwater.**

1952 Wilson *Folk Speech NC* 517 = to retreat, to change front. **1967** Wilson *Folkways Mammoth Cave* 27 = to retreat from some position or plan. **1987** Young *Lost Cove* 123 Oldtimers said that he wouldn't *back water* from even the biggest man, and once pulled a knife on Bad Straub when he called him a dirty Democrat. **1995–97** Montgomery *Coll* (known to Brown, Bush, Oliver, Weaver); He got up on stage and backwatered for a whole hour (Cardwell).

[from nautical use]

back word *noun* A spiteful or disrespectful response.

2002 Ogle *Remembrances* 18 Here comes Mrs. Duffield, our matron, with what looks like a quart of caster oil and a big spoon. I swallowed mine without a back word.

backy, backy house See **back house.**

back yonder See **back A1, A2.**

bacon and eggs *noun* Same as **butter and eggs.**

1998 Montgomery *Coll* (Cardwell).

bacon meat *noun* Bacon.

1952 Wilson *Folk Speech NC* 517. **1998** Montgomery *Coll* = old-fashioned usage (Cardwell). **1999** *Foxfire XI* 236 We didn't know what it was to go to the store and buy bacon or sausage or anything like that. We made our own sausage and dried our own bacon meat.

bacon up *verb phrase* See citations.

1917 Kephart *Word-List* 407 = to make bacon of. "Reckon I'll haffter kill that hog and "*bacon it up*." **1996** Montgomery *Coll* How much of the hog are you going to bacon up? (Cardwell).

bad

A Variant comparative forms *worser, wuss, wusser.*

1898 Elliott *Durket Sperret* 38 Don't you go to makin' her wuss mad 'an is needful. **1913** Kephart *Our Sthn High* 77 Hit's gettin' wusser. **1927** Bolton *Mt Girl Speaks* 4 We are always worser off, but 'taint no need of telling us sich 'cause we come more harder to it. **1955** Washburn *Country Doctor* 63 She's been ailin' off an' on fer more'n a year, but she's had three real bad attacks in less'n two weeks; an' ever' time the pain in 'er side an' shoulder gets wuss an' wusser. **1973** GSMNP-79:2:3 I think there are worser things than being poor. **1977** Shackelford et al. *Our Appalachia* 240 Conditions got worser and worser until it was nearly unbearable. **1989** Smith *Flyin' Bullets* 202 It's worser than a sight. **1993** Burton *Take Up Serpents* 19 We need to learn how to worship God worser than anything in the world. **2009** Burton *Beech Mt Man* 37 I walked down there, and it's gettin' worse and worse and worser.

B Variant superlative forms *worstest, wust.*

1913 Kephart *Our Sthn High* 75 This is the wust coggled-up fire I ever seed, to fry by. **1938** Bowman *High Horizons* 46 As a rule the mountain girl or boy who attends school says, "first" and "worst," whereas their parents say "fust" and "wust." **1942** Hall *Phonetics Smoky Mts* 42, 89. **2008** Salsi *Ray Hicks* 75 On the worstest, coldest days, we'd all stay inside.

C *adjective*

1 See **bad for, bad to.**

2 Ailing, in pain or seriously ill health. See also **bad sick, take bad, take down, take sick.**

1852 *Carson Letter* 146 John was very bad all night and on Wednesday I took sick. **1862** *Reese CW Letters* (Oct 29) I am un well and has Bin vary sick an yester day I was vary Bad. **1891** Swearingen *Letters* 165 Huse and High were awful bad awhile but Huse is dead. **1908** Smith *Reminiscences* 410 The baby was *bad* with a bealin' on its neck. **1963** Edwards *Gravel* 105 Hey, Doc, git up as soon as ye can and go to Mark Lane's. His wife is awful bad. **1973** GSMNP-88:12 Used to here, when they'd have bad sickness and people real bad and all, they'd go in and set up with them. **1998** *Dante OHP-71* All the time she was a-living, when she'd get real bad and everything, he would always come here to the house and check Ada out. **2012** Milnes *Signs Cures Witchery* Rose was bad, you know, laying here in bed.

D *adverb* Very, seriously, badly. See also **bad off, bad sick.**

1834 Crockett *Narrative* 63 Whenever a fellow gets bad lost, the way home is the way he don't think it is. **1836** *Sullivan Co Soldiers* Daniel's mare got bad hurt but is getting better. **1862** *Warrick CW Letters* (April 1) I am verry bad behind hand with my crop. **1937** Hall *Coll* (Cosby Creek TN) This water's not bad cold. **1954** Arnow *Dollmaker* 26 I was bad worried. **1969** GSMNP-46:10 I shod them twice, and their feet was a-getting bad out of shape. **1974–75** McCracken *Logging* 21:12 I think it was a lady if I'm not bad fooled. **1978** Parris *Mt Cooking* 138 She knew that there was something mighty bad wrong with Grandpa when he couldn't eat apple pie. **1983** McDermitt *Boy Named Jack* 21 There's somebody hurt bad. **2007** Shelby *Molly Whuppie* 7 I am bad put out with you, Molly Whuppie. **2015** Holbrook *Something* 150 Go ahead and tell me how bad injured you are.

bad ailment *noun* Presumably syphilis. See also **bad blood 2, bad disease.**

1985 Irwin *Alex Stewart* 136 Well, she got the bad ailment and she'd slip off to the doctors, but it just got worse and worse till her face got in a solid sore.

(as) bad as a crippled pup *adverb phrase* With an intense or painful desire but no capacity (to achieve a certain thing).

1940 Haun *Hawk's Done* 29 She wanted to play as bad as a crippled pup.

bad blood *noun* [Editor's note: The sense "ill feeling, bitterness between people" is widespread in the US.]

1 Inferior ancestry (to explain a mental or behavioral deficiency apparently running in a family).

1988 Carden *Looking Out* 8 My grandfather observed that I did not bear any resemblance to any member of my father's family. That . . . led my grandfather to conclude that I was totally a product of my mother's side of the family and therefore doomed. Bad blood, he called it. **1990** Cavender *Folk Medical Lex* 17 = used in reference to contemptible behavioral traits believed to be inherited from one generation to the next. "I wouldn't trust him because his family's got bad blood." **1994** Montgomery *Coll* (known to Cardwell) = inherited propensity for violence or meanness: "Uncle Art had bad blood" (Ogle).

2 Syphilis. See also **bad ailment, bad disease.**

2000 Lowry *Folk Medical Term* = syphilis. **2013** Reed *Medical Notes* = syphilis.

bad disease *noun* A venereal disease, usually syphilis. See also **bad ailment, bad blood 2.**

1862 *Lockmiller CW Letters* (April 18) we want you to quit huging the women for that is a bad practice for men to follow a way from home for we have a nuff of bad dis eases in our country all reddy. **1958** Wood *Words from TN* 7 Syphilis is always referred to as the bad disease. **1996** Montgomery *Coll* (known to Adams, Ledford, Oliver); He died with a bad disease (Cardwell). **2003** Cavender *Folk Medicine* 134 Syphilis was euphemistically known as "the disease," "the bad disease," or "bad blood." **2007** Myers *Smoky Mt Remedies* 9 = syphilis (with vocal emphasis on the word *bad*).

bad for *adjective phrase* Having an unfortunate, undesirable, or dangerous tendency for, prone to. See also **bad to.**

1973 GSMNP-76:21 I wore a pair of boots. That old Brushy Mountain was bad for snakes. **1978** Montgomery *White Pine Coll* V-3 Cocke County used to be bad for that, and still right down to this day it's bad for it. **1984** Page and Wigginton *Foxfire Cookery* 171 I'm bad for wild salads [greens].

bad laurel *noun* A thicket in which a person may easily become trapped or lost. See also **laurel, laurel bed.**

1917 Kephart *Camping and Woodcraft* 2:25 These men were not lost at all. In a "bad laurel" (heavily timbered), not very far from this, an old hunter and trapper who was born and bred in these mountains, was lost for three days, although the maze was not more than a mile square.

(the) bad man *noun*

1 The Devil; a demon or hobgoblin, especially one used to warn children and make them behave. Same as **black man.** See also **booger A1.**

c1950 Adams *Grandpap* 172 I'll tell you right now, hit was an awful plan. The old Badman hi'self couldn't a-thought up a meaner one. **1952** Wilson *Folk Speech NC* 517–18 = the devil. Usually to children to induce good behavior. "If you don't stop crying the (old) *bad man* will get you." **1958** Newton *Dialect Vocab* = attested by 4 of 36 speakers from E TN mountains. **1977** Hamilton *Mt Memories* 56 When Leona and I fussed, we would often say, "I know you'll go to the Bad Place," or "The Bad Man will get you for that." **1994–97** Montgomery *Coll* (known to Adams, Brown, Bush, Cardwell, Jones, Oliver, Weaver).

[SND *bad man* n "a child's name for the devil"; CUD (at *bad* "hell"); DARE *bad man* n 2 chiefly South, South Midland]

2 A man incorrigibly outside the law and given to violence and brutality, living either alone or as the leader of an extended family.

1926 Thomas *Hills and Mts of KY* 168 This dreadful feud was fought by heartless and fearless men on both sides. In not only this but in all the other feuds which I have mentioned, I could give the names of many of the men whom we commonly call bad men. But for the respect I have for both the living and the dead I will leave that part off. **1977** Shackelford et al. *Our Appalachia* 57 In pioneer communities throughout the nation, disputes easily got out of hand because there was often no recognized law enforcement structure. If one man committed a crime against another it was usually left to the injured person's family to take action in the absence of any outside law enforcer. It is not surprising, then, that the job of righting local wrongs, or at least of temporarily quieting them, sometimes fell to a small group of people who came to be known as "badmen." These men were acknowledged to be good with guns, good at looking out for themselves, and good at protecting their kinfolks and friends. They generally answered to no one. By prosecuting wrongdoers with gunfire or threats, they acted as law enforcers; by stirring up unnecessary trouble they were breaking the law themselves. **2009** Reed *Preface* xiii–xiv The Bad Man may not be bad in all ways (and is only usually a man—there is a female version), but this is definitely someone you don't want to cross or even seriously annoy, because he may respond with abrupt, brutal, or overwhelming violence. . . . It should go without saying that Bad Men exist on the fringes of groups made up, for the most part, of hard-working, churchgoing, respectable people and grotesquely exaggerate otherwise admirable values—a tradition of honor, for example, or an ethic of self-reliance developed in response to a hostile and dangerous environment.

bad man to *noun phrase* One who has a negative or unfortunate habit to (do something). For other patterns with *to*, see Grammar and Syntax §10.2. See also **bad to**.

1937 Hall Coll (Cosby TN) Old Sam McGaha was a bad man to drink. He said he eat a piece of panter. **1941** Stuart *Men of Mts* 111 Your Pa was a bad man to fight.

bad off (also *bad off sick*) *adjective phrase* Seriously ill, ailing, in poor health or circumstances. See also **bad C2**, **bad sick**.

1862 Sutton *CW Letters* (Nov 8) i heard that you had gone home and was very bad off. **1864** *Chapman CW Letters* (June 11) Tell Wm Mc Culy his sister Jane has got the White sweling and is verry bad off. **1867** Harris *Sut Lovingood* 104 He am powerful bad off; made his will, a-cuttin off old Sock wif a shillin, leaving Sicily an' me his maladickshuns. **1917** Kephart *Word-List* 407 The old man was right *bad off*. **1929** (in **1952** Mathes *Tall Tales* 111) Well, ye see, doc's grandson, "Little" Linky, has got some quare sickness. He's turrible bad off. **1969** Hannum *Look Back* 36 Les Alden got "bad off sick" and someone of the family sent for the coffin-maker. **1971** *AOHP/ALC-137* He got so bad off. He had to go get the doctor, he liked to died. **1974** Fink *Bits Mt Speech* 2 = in serious condition. "His woman is *bad off*." **1985** Irwin *Alex Stewart* 177 When we got there his wife was bad off, right at the point of death. **1988** Russell *It Happened* 86 A doctor was sent for only if someone was "bad off." **1998** *Dante OHP-58* He got so bad off that they stopped at Abingdon and put him in the hospital there.

[EDD (at *bad* adv 8[3]); DARE *bad off* adj phr 2 widespread, but especially South, South Midland]

(the) bad place *noun* Hell, especially as a term used to warn children and make them behave.

1915 Dingus *Word-List VA* 180 = hell. **c1950** Adams *Grandpap* 125 The old Devil, he didn't like that. He wanted 'em all to go to the bad place. **c1960** Wilson *Coll* He's not afraid of the bad place or he wouldn't talk thataway. **1977** Hamilton *Mt Memories* 56 "Hell" was always called the "Bad Place" . . . So when Leona and I fussed, we would often say, "I know you'll go to the Bad Place," or "The Bad Man will get you for that." **1993** Cunningham *Sthn Talk* 12 Grown folks and preachers call it hell, but children are not allowed to say that; they have to call it the bad place.

[cf SND *bad place* n; CUD (at *bad* "hell"); HT; DARE *bad place* n chiefly South, Midland]

bad row of stumps *noun phrase* See 1890 citation.

1890 Fruit *KY Words* 66 "He is in a bad row of stumps," means to be in trying places. [This expression] comes from the trouble one has in plowing a stumpy land. **1962** Weatherford and Brewer *Life and Religion* 117 If they are not ready they would be in a bad row of stumps.

bad sick *adjective phrase* Seriously ill; hence noun *bad sickness* = a serious illness. See also **bad C2**, **bad off**.

1940 Haun *Hawk's Done* 25 It was just three weeks after Bessie was born that Sadie Brock come running down here one evening late and said Tiny was bad sick. **1962** Dykeman *Tall Woman* 170 "Well, you claim assafoetida around a body's neck keeps away bad sickness," Lydia laughed. **1969** Doran *Folklore White Co* 99 I jist cain't git straightened out since that bad sick spell. Both *the* and *bad* are redundant. **1973** GSMNP-70:1:6 A half-sister that lived over there got sick and was very bad sick. **1973** GSMNP-88:12 Used to here, when they'd have bad sickness and people [were] real bad and all, they'd go in and set up with them. **1998** *Dante OHP-51* Missus Noe's father was really bad sick, and they just thought he might die. **2006** Shelby *Appal Studies* 39 After she got real bad sick he'd sit at the foot of the bed and cry like a baby. **2013** Venable *How to Tawlk* 5 = exceedingly ill: "Liz tuck bad-sick, and thar fer the longest time I thought she was a goner."

[DARE *bad sick* adj phr chiefly South, South Midland, but especially Inland South]

bad to *adjective phrase* Having an unfortunate, undesirable, or excessive habit, inclination, reputation, or weakness to (do something); prone to engage in annoying, detrimental, or troublesome behavior. The term usually expresses a speaker's disapproval or disparagement, but may lend only emphasis to a statement (thus "She was awful bad to talk" = She had a tendency or liked to talk a great deal). Hence comparative form *worse to* and superlative form *worst to*. See 1959 citation. See also **awful to**, **bad for**, **bad man to**, **good to**, **great to**, **poor to**, **terrible to**. For similar patterns with *to*, see Grammar and Syntax §10.2.

1904–20 Kephart *Notebooks* 4:847 He used to be bad to drink, but he's kinder tapered off. **1925** Carter *Mt White Tales* 349 The varmints weren't bad to try to come in of a day—always at night. **1937** Hall *Coll* He was awful bad to drink. She was awful bad to talk. *Ibid.* (Cosby TN) He was bad to hunt coon. **1939** Hall *Coll* (Hazel Creek NC) Little John Cable was purty bad to cuss. "By God," he says, "we've got 'im." **1956** Hall *Coll* (Roaring Fork TN) People was purty bad to stay all night with each other and tell stories. **1959** Stubbs *Mountain-Wise* (Aug–Sept) 6 Among the frequently used expressions when describing another is that he or she is "bad to" do something. "Bad" as thus used really means that the person described is addicted to a certain habit or possesses a certain trait. For example, a man may be "bad to go to church"—which does not infer that church-going is wrong, but—quite the reverse—that the man so described is a consistent church goer. But a man may also be "bad to drink" or "bad to smoke." One day I met a woman who told me that her mother was ill in bed with an aching rheumatic knee. I told her that hot compresses might bring relief and asked if she had tried them. She replied, "No, my mother is bad to not want no heat put on any part of her body." And, I might personally add that a lot of my neighbors are "bad to go fishing." **1968** *Faith Healing* 63 [The fire in the wound] just keeps burnin' deeper and makes it worse to sore. An' if you c'n draw that fire out, you don't have no sore. **1973** GSMNP-57:68 He wasn't too bad to grumble. **1976** Lindsay *Grassy Balds* 208 [Bears] were bad to kill sheep, but not so bad to kill the hogs. **1978** Montgomery *White Pine Coll* III-1 The North is especially bad to make fun of people when they don't know a damn thing about speaking the English language themselves. **1979** Melton *'Pon My Honor* 40 The preacher was plumb bad to chew tobacco, and he'd clean forgot and got up to preach with a big cud of it in his mouth. **1981** Dumas *Appal Glossary* 16 The phrase occurs in inflected forms, also, as in "She was the *worst* I've ever seen *to* tell stories." **1985** Irwin *Alex Stewart* 185 [Bees are] not bad to sting when they're swarming. **1996** Montgomery *Coll* He was worse to drink than ever (Cardwell). **2001** Lowry *Expressions* 5 I'm the worst to freeze. **2002** Ogle *Remembrances* 81 Watch especially for snakes [during the Dog Days of summer], they are shedding and ill natured and worse to bite at this time. **2017** *Blind Pig* (Jan 19) I'm bad to leave stuff at home I need for work.

[DARE *bad* adj B4 chiefly Appalachians, especially western NC, East TN]

bad top *noun* See citation.

1987 (in **2015** Yarrow *Voices* 25) = where a roof fall [in a coal mine] is more likely. "I've worked in bad top, but I tell the guys I don't have sense enough to be scared."

bait

A *noun*

1 (also *bate*) A portion or serving (of food), especially an ample one; a full meal, plenty.

c1859 Taliaferro *Fisher's River* 125 I toddled down to the sea-shore to git a bait uv oysters. **1862** *Robinson CW Letters* (July 18) I went back to the camp & got a big oven & cook them that evning I eat the master bate you ever Saw. **1864** *Chapman CW Letters* (March 28) to day is easter I useto when I was at home on easter morning have a good bait of egg for breakfast. **1917** Kephart *Word-List* 407 = a full meal. "I et me a *bait* o' ramps, and tasted them for a week atterwards." **1957** Parris *My Mts* 111 "I reckon," he used to say, "one good bait of bear meat a winter is about all a man can ask for" = a serving of food. **c1960** Wilson *Coll* (DARE) = all the food one can hold, a big meal or snack: "I sure got a bait at his house." **1974** Fink *Bits Mt Speech* 2 = food, generally a large amount. "He ate a real *bait* o'greens." **1994** Montgomery *Coll* I took a big bait this Sunday [i.e. we had a big meal] (Shields).

[Web3 *bait* n 6 chiefly South; DARE *bait* n[1] 1d chiefly South, South Midland]

2 An overly generous portion, a surfeit, one's fill.

1851 (in **1956** Eliason *Tarheel Talk* 258) (Haywood Co NC) Cousin Sophia has been taking a bait of kine pox. **1963** Arnow *Flowering* 150 Even by my childhood the wonderful word *bait*, when used in connection with food, was a noun only and considered a crude word; to eat a great bait or even a bait meant the person had taken more food than he should have. **1976** Dykeman *Time to Build* "Bait"—meaning a full meal for a person or an animal; an amount or lot of anything. **1976** Still *Pattern of Man* 38 Dee Buck blustered, "I've had a bait of you fellows." **1997** Montgomery *Coll* I've had a bait of that [i.e. to have one's fill of an activity or the speech or behavior of someone the speaker does not like or approve of] (Ellis).

[DARE *bait* n[1] 2 South, South Midland]

3 In a logging camp, food generally.

2006 Farwell *Logging Term* 1021 Provisions were "bait," beans "firecrackers," and biscuits "cat heads."

B *verb* To feed an ample portion to.

1891 Moffat *Mtneers Middle TN* 318 If, after the colloquy is over, the guest refuses all invitations to the next meal, or to stay all night, the horse is brought around, "baited" and resaddled, and the visitor mounts and rides off, not forgetting to invite the whole family to "drap in ef there a passin' his way."

bait worm *noun* An earthworm used for fish bait (less common than **redworm** and **fishing worm**, according to consultants from the Smoky Mountains).

1949 Kurath *Word Geog East US* 74 *Fish bait* and *bait worm* occupy smaller areas within the extensive *fishworm* and *fishing worm* areas of the Midland and South, namely . . . south-central Pennsylvania and adjoining parts of Maryland and . . . the western piedmont of North Carolina and adjoining parts of Virginia. **1958** Wood *Words from TN* 7. **c1960** Wilson *Coll*: *baitworm* = worm used in fishing; heard occasionally. **1996–97** Montgomery *Coll* (known to Adams, Brown, Cardwell, Oliver).

[DARE *baitworm* n 2 chiefly Midland, South]

bake See **bakie**.

baker (also *baker and lid*, *baker oven*) *noun* Same as **Dutch oven**.

1937 Hall *Coll* (Emerts Cove TN) Corn bread [was] baked in a hoe-cake baker over the coals, not in a stove. **1939** Hall *Coll* (Cable Branch NC) We didn't have no stove. We just cooked in a baker like. **1952** Callahan *Smoky Mt Country* 87 When mealtime approached, the housewife would rake out on the hearth a glowing mass of embers, and place over them the covered cast-iron oven known as a "baker." **1957** Combs *Lg Sthn High: Word List* 7 *baker* = a flat, round iron pan for baking corn bread in the pone. The baker is covered with a heavy lid, upon which white-hot coals are poured, in the fireplace or on the hearth. **1966** Dakin *Vocab Ohio River Valley* 121 In the southeastern Mountains [of KY] the name *baker* (once *baker and lid*) is common, and at least in some instances = *skillet and lid*. *Baker*, however, more often seems to be the name for a somewhat deeper utensil with straight sides, short legs (usually), a lid, and no handle. In the Mountain counties north of the *baker* area and scattered elsewhere, throughout Kentucky, Illinois, and Indiana the same vessel seems to be called simply *oven*, or rarely *oven and lid*, *bake(r) oven*, and *bread oven*. **1981** Weals *Older Cows* All cooking was done in the fireplace, in iron kettles, frying pans, or in a "baker and lid," a utensil more often called a Dutch oven. **1986** Pederson et al. *LAGS*: *baker* = attested by 19/60 interviewees (31.7%) from E TN; 19/47 of all LAGS interviewees (46.4%) attesting term were from E TN. **1981** Weals *Older Cows* All cooking was done in the fireplace, in iron kettles, frying pans, or in a "baker and lid," a utensil more often called a Dutch oven. **1991** Thomas *Sthn Appal* 49 We didn't call 'um ovens, back them days. They'uz jist ol' bakers—ol'-time bakers.

baker oven See **baker**.

bakie (also *bake*) *noun* A baking squash.

1976 Garber *Mountain-ese* 5 We raised ten bushels uv bakies in our garden this year. **1991** Thomas *Sthn Appal* 44 They got to raisin' these old "bakes," now, an' you can keep those all year. Some calls 'um bakies. **1997** Montgomery *Coll* = the acorn squash, which will preserve much longer than other squashes (Andrews).

baking powder *noun* Construed as a count noun; hence plural form *baking powders*. For similar forms, see **powder A**.

1913 Kephart *Our Sthn High* 297 Tomato, cabbage, molasses and baking powder are always used as plural nouns . . . "How many bakin'-powders has you got?" **1935** Sheppard *Cabins in Laurel* 182 Baking powders (commonly used in the plural) hurt me if I eat 'em regular. **1978** Parris *Mt Cooking* 151 In the old days when I used plain flour, I had to mix in baking powders and soda and salt and lard and buttermilk. **1981** Dumas *Appal Glossary* 16. **1994–97** Montgomery *Coll* (known to Brown, Jones, Ledford, Oliver). **2008** *Rosie Hicks* 1 You'd have to put your salt and soda, or baking powders or whatever, in your meal.

[DARE *baking powders* n chiefly southern Appalachians, Ozarks]

bald

A *adjective* See citations.

1824 (in **1912** Doddridge *Notes on Settlement* 71) [The wild strawberry] grew on poor land, on which there was no timber. There were many such places of small extent on the points of hills along the creeks. They were denominated bald knobs. **1950** King and Stupka *Geology and Natural History* 41 Although most of the Great Smoky Mountains are forested, small areas on some of the summits are bare of trees, or "bald," as they are locally described.

B *noun* A treeless area surrounded by forest on a mountain summit or slope, either a **grass bald** or **heath bald**; also used in place-names, as in *Silers Bald* (NC/TN) and *Gregory Bald* (TN). See 1960 citation. Also called **devil's footprint**. See also **shrub bald**, **sods**.

1890 Carpenter *Thunderhead Peak* 139 The mountains are entirely wooded, except on a few summits, called "balds," where the treeless tracts are covered with luxuriant grass and patches of bush breast-high. **1913** Kephart *Our Sthn High* 42 The best pasturage is high up in the mountains, where there are "balds" covered with succulent wild grass that resembles Kentucky blue grass. **1960** Stupka *Great Smoky Mts* 18 There are treeless areas on some of the higher mountaintops and ridges. Owing to their lack of forest cover, such places are called balds. That designation, however, is a relative one since other plants form a dense carpet over the balds. If these plants are largely shrubs belonging to the heath family, such balds are known as heath balds; if grasses and sedges prevail, the balds are termed grass balds. **1961** Stubbs *Mountain-Wise* (Aug–Sept) 10–11 The two highest mountains in Georgia are both called "Balds." Brasstown Bald is the higher of the two. The second, which dominates the landscape here, is Rabun Bald. Why "Bald" anyway? The answer is simple: "Bald-headed,"—no trees at the top. The mountains unlike New Hampshire's were not subject to the effects of glaciation, so we have vegetation most of the way up. But the very tops of some of them are bald, exposed rock. **1968** Powell *NC Gazetteer* 454 Silers Bald (on Welch Ridge and on the state line in Great Smoky Mountains National Park). Named for Jesse Richardson Siler (1793–1876) of Franklin, who owned this mountain and kept large herds of cattle on it. **1991** Walker *Great Smoky* 32 The Great Smoky Mountains National Park has two different types of balds, grassy balds and heath balds. The grassy variety is predominantly grass-covered, while the heath balds, or laurel slicks as they are sometimes called, appear to be grassy from a distance but upon closer contact it is apparent that it is an extremely dense thicket of shrub.

[DARE *bald* n chiefly South Midland, especially southern Appalachians, Ozarks]

baldface (also *baldfaced whiskey*, *baldface whiskey*) *noun* Poor-quality whiskey, usually unaged; hence the nickname *old Bald-face*.

1843 (in **1974** Harris *High Times* 28) I have been so *monstrous* busy, riding about, making speeches, soliciting votes, cajoling the husbands, shaking hands with the wives, kissing the children, and giving them dimes and half dimes, treating temperance men to watermelons, and topers to *old Bald-face*. **1955** Parris *Roaming Mts* 152 An old timer is one who remembers . . . when peartening juice fresh from the still was called baldface whiskey. **1972** Cooper *NC Mt Folklore* 89 *bald-faced whiskey* = whiskey fresh from the still.

[DARE *baldface* n 3 chiefly South, Midland]

Baldwin thug (also *Baldwin-Felts thugs*) *noun* See citations. See also **gun thug, thug.**

1969 Lee *Bloodletting* 11 In southern West Virginia, these pseudo-officers, called "Baldwin-Felts thugs" by the miners, were employees (called "operatives") of the Baldwin-Felts Detective Agency, an anti-union, labor-baiting, strikebreaking organization headed by William G. Baldwin and Thomas R. Felts, with headquarters in Bluefield. Their ostensible purpose, said the operators, was to preserve law and order in the coal camps. In reality, however, they were fearless mountain gunmen, many with criminal records, whose chief duties were to keep the miners intimidated, to beat up, arrest, jail, and even kill if necessary, any worker or visitor suspected of union activities around the camps. **1990** *Matewan* OHP-73 Instead of state police, they was called Baldwin thugs, and they was sent in here . . . to try to stop the fighting, you know what I mean, trying to quieten everything down.

baldy *adjective* Bald-headed.

1941 Still *Troublesome Creek* 81 I saw the baldy drummer show you where my playhouse is.

balk *noun* A small ridge or strip of ground of varying width between two rows of a crop. See also **chop.**

1956 Hall *Coll* (Big Bend NC) She'd hoe a row of corn and then weed a row of corn first, and then go back and chop the balks out, the weeds out of the balk. **1957** Broaddus *Vocab Estill Co KY* 5 = the space between the rows of corn. **1976** Garber *Mountain-ese* 5 = space between rows. "When you hoe the corn you also chop the weeds outta the balk." **1991** Still *Wolfpen Notebooks* 85 The balk between the corn rows should be the width of a mule's rump. **1997** Montgomery *Coll* = the area between rows of crops, especially corn, from which weeds are chopped for neatness and to facilitate access (Weaver).

[ultimately < Old English *balca* "ridge, bank"]

ballad *noun*

A Variant forms *ballat* [see **1947** in **B1**], *ballet*, *ballit* [see **1978** in **B2**].

1939 Hall *Recording Speech* 7 *Ballet* for *ballad* was the common sixteenth-century pronunciation (although Shakespeare has *ballad*), but it flourished also in the seventeenth century, being used by Pepys, among others.

[OED3 *ballet* (at *ballad* n^2) England regional, *ballette* obsolete form of *ballad*; EDD *ballet* sb 1]

B Senses.

1 (also *ballad song*) Any secular song (i.e., not only a traditional or Child ballad). See also **devil's ditty, love ballad, mountain song, song-ballad B1.**

1913 Kephart *Our Sthn High* 82 Other songs followed, with utter irrelevance—mere snatches from "ballets" composed, mainly, by the mountaineers themselves, though some dated back to a long-forgotten age when the British ancestors of these Carolina woodsmen were battling with lance and long-bow. **1915** Campbell *Songs and Ballads* 372 The term "ballad" is misleading, however. In the mountain country, it by no means applies only to the song that tells a story, or even to that which is really old or has been passed down by word of mouth for a number of generations. Almost any song is a "ballad," and Barbara Allen and the Casket of Old Letters may equally be referred to as "ballets" or "song-ballets," the singer having little idea of their comparative worth. **1947** Gamble *Heritage* 95 Hill folk are noted for making up "ballats" about local events. But the only way to get those is to live awhile with them long enough to make friends. **1957** Justus *Other Side* 54 Finally someone called for a ballad, or a "ballad song," as they said it. **1975** Chalmers *Better* 63 His children and their children learned the "ballets" at his knee and the touch of the strings at his guidance.

2 A manuscript copy or the written words for a song. See also **song-ballad B2.**

1927 Woofter *Dialect from WV* 348 She has promised to write me the ballet of that song. **1932** Sharp *Folk Songs* xxviii None of the singers whom I visited possessed any printed song-sheets, but some of them presented written copies, usually made by children, which they called "ballets," a term which the English singer reserves for the printed broadsides. **1939** Hall *Coll* (Cataloochee NC) I wish I had a ballet of that song. **1954** GSMNP-19: 17 I can't think of [the words of the song]. I ain't got the ballad. **1967** Combs *Folk-Songs* 49 It is not a "ballet" if it has not been written down, and most of the traditional songs of the Highlands are circulated by oral transmission, and are termed "old songs." **1974** GSMNP-54:2 I bet you've got the ballad with you someplace. *Ibid.* 13 I don't know the tune of it. I've got the ballad. **1977** Wolfe *TN Strings* 7 Many old ballad singers possessed handwritten texts, or "ballets," of their songs. Sometimes these ballets were pasted or copied into books passed down through the family. There have been few instances of singers actually singing from these ballets, but these texts were available for reference if need be. **1978** Burton *Ballad Folks* 1 It was in this box that she kept the "ballits" or words written down of "the lovesongs or mountain songs, old people's songs"—the songs she had learned through the years.

[DARE *ballad* n B chiefly South Midland]

ballad book (as *ballet book*) *noun* See citation.

1943 Niles *Folk Ballad* 236 In the backwoods of the mountains—in the really isolated places—many of the singers will possess a so-called "ballet book." This will be a store-bought blank book containing hand-written verses of the ballads, carols, and folk songs known in the family. The tunes are not written down.

ballad box (also *ballit box*) *noun* A small container in which handwritten copies of song lyrics are stored.

1978 Burton *Ballad Folks* 1 Mrs. Rena kept a "ballit" box. It wasn't a fancy one, rather it was a lap-sized cardboard box she had whipstitched along one edge for a hinge. It was in this box that she kept the "ballits" or words written down of "the lovesongs or mountain songs, old people's songs"—the songs she had learned through the years. **1994** Crissman *Death and Dying* 157 Many of the songs and ballads in central Appalachian society were brought by settlers from Scotland, Ireland, Germany, England, and Wales.... Some highlanders kept these in a ballad, or "ballit," box and handed them down to future generations. **2008** Salsi *Ray Hicks* 149 During that time, she got to where she'd lost the gift of the songs. She'd talk about rememberin' when she was young and she'd sing with her mama and daddy. Mama decided to write down the words she remembered and made it like a job. She sat and wrote down as many as she could. She fixed a box out of cardboard and called it her ballad box.

ballad card (as *ballet card*) *noun* See citation.

1977 Wolfe *TN Strings* 8 In the Kentucky-Tennessee area, many of the songs were printed on small cards about the size of a post-card (still called "ballet cards") by old-timers, usually signed by the composer or singer; rural minstrels wandered through the mountains singing at rural courthouses and making some money by selling their ballet cards for a penny or nickel each. These musicians were probably the first professional (or semiprofessional) musicians of country music; many of them were blind, and the music was the only way for them to earn their living.

ballad song See **ballad B1**.

ballat, **ballet** See **ballad A**.

ballhoot

A Variant form *bell hoop* [see **1964** in **B**].

B *verb*

1 To slide, roll, pull, or shoot (a log) down an incline, sometimes using a **skidder** along a **skid road** or **skidway**; (of a log) to slide freely down a slope. See also **ballhooter**.

1929 Carpenter *Evolution of Dialect* 28 Anyone who has frequented logging operations has heard . . . *ball-hootin'* logs . . . shooting logs down over a steep incline to a lower level. **1953** Hall *Coll* (Plott Creek NC) I went out on an incline where they used to ballhoot logs off.... What I mean by ballhootin' logs on this grade—that's a place where they pull 'em out and nothin' but a bear or somep'n like 'at can go. They turn 'em loose and roll 'em maybe a mile down the mountain. **1954** Blackhurst *Riders of Flood* 172 Where enough drop was found, a "ballhootin'" slide could be used. On steep ground these were often mere dirt tracks leading straight down to water. On lesser slopes regular trough slides of logs could be used. On the "ballhootin," or running slide, as it was also called, no horsepower was needed. The logs were simply put into the slide and went hurtling down on the momentum of gravity. **1964** Stubbs *Mountain-Wise* (June–July) 10 There would be no difficulty getting his logs down to a point where his tractor could reach them. He would "bell hoop" them down the trace, he said, that is, the way down being steep and straight, they would slide themselves. **1974–75** McCracken *Logging* 11:53 The rest of this down here now was cut, ballhooted, and skidded with a groundhog skidder. *Ibid.* 24:21 = a term that originated on Allens Creek, North Carolina; a steep place where you just shove the log endways and let it slide. **1975** *GSMNP-56:3* The logs were pulled down by horses to the top of that ridge. Then it was too steep from the top of that ridge down to where they could be picked up with a truck or train or something, for anything to stay ahead of them, so they just turned them loose on their own and they ballhooted down to where they were picked up. **1991** Weals *Last Train* 26 When a tree was cut on a very steep slope, they would peel the logs and nose them, round one end so that once a log was started sliding it would "ballhoot" to the foot of the slope by its own momentum. [**2002** Hayler *Sound Wormy* 210 The practice of sending cut logs down a steep slope by their ends first in an uncontrollable slide, was commonly used on slopes that were too steep for a team to work or when ice or rain made the slope too dangerous for skidding. Usually the end of the log was slightly rounded with an ax to keep it from digging in.]

2 See citation.

2006 Farwell *Logging Term* Some of the loggers' slang also lingers in other contexts, like *ball-hootin'*, which referred to the dangerous practice of rolling cut timber downhill, but is now used by some teenagers to describe speeding around in cars on mountain roads: "He was ball-hootin' down 107."

C *interjection* Look out! (a warning shouted when a log is released down an incline, to alert workers below).

1963 Lord *Blue Ridge* 17D Shouting the warning "ball-hoot!," men dug their canthooks into the logs and sent them sliding and crashing into a "jack-pot" of logs in the hollow below. **1975** *GSMNP-56:3* The word "ballhoot" meant to a person moving the logs out about the same thing that "timber" would mean to a person falling a tree.... When they turned a log over to ballhoot, that is, on its own to go down a steep place, why they holler "ballhoot." **1981** Brewer *Wonderment* 124 A lookout on a high stump below would holler, "BALL HOOT!" **2008** Salsi *Ray Hicks* 15 Those on the top hollered out as loud as they could, "B-a-l-l H-o-o-t." Those below 'ud hear the hollerin'. If not, they'd hear the trees crashin' down the mountain makin' a noise like a freight train. Everybody knowed to run for cover.... That big timber 'ud take down everything in its path. It'd take huge trees along as it gained speed and strength.

ballhooter *noun* A logger whose job is to **ballhoot**.

1913 Kephart *Our Sthn High* 195 I have had a drunken "ballhooter" (log-roller) from the lumber camps fire five shots around my head. **1967** Parris *Mt Bred* 133 A ballhooter is a fellow who rolls or slides logs down a hillside and a chickadee is a man who looks after the logging roads.

ballit See **ballad**.

ballit box See **ballad box**.

ballygilly See **balm of Gilead**.

bally hack *verb phrase* See citation.

1952 Wilson *Folk Speech NC* 518 = to impose on.

balm *noun* variant form *bam* [bæm].

1942 Hall *Phonetics Smoky Mts* 104 As for *balm* and *calm*, older speakers say [bæm] and [kæm]. **c1960** Wilson *Coll*: *balm* [bæm].

balm of Gilead *noun*

A Variant forms *ballygilly* [see **1939** in **B**], *bamagilia* [see **1982** in **B**], *bamagilly* [see **1971** in **B**], *bam-be-gilly* [see **1967** in **B**], *bam b'gilly* [see **1967** in **B**], *bamgillion* [see **1997** in **B**], *bammygilly* [see **1939** in **B**], *bomgillion* [see **1981** in **B**].

B A small poplar tree (usually *Populus gileadensis* or *P. balsamifera*) whose buds have medicinal uses, especially when made into a salve to treat burns and other skin problems; a salve made from the buds of this tree. Also called **gilly balm**.

1939 Hall *Coll* (Catons Grove TN) Ballygilly buds is good for to make salves. The best salve I ever used was made out of bammygilly buds. Take it and fry them in the fresh butter or sheep's tallow, and then make some life everlasting tea, about a half a teacupful full, and put in with it and boil it down and strain it. **1955** Dykeman *French Broad* 253 The balm of Gilead (or "gilly b'am"), ingredient of healing ointments, especially for earache, is left for winter. **1967** Jones *Peculiarities Mtneers* 66 Balm of Gilead (pronounced "bam-be-gilly" by the mountaineers) buds steeped in whiskey was used as a remedy for colds. *Ibid.* 72 "Bam b'gilly" (Balm of Gilead) buds, when cooked in mutton tallow, was used for burns, abrasions and hemorrhoids. **1971** *AOHP/ALC-147* If we got burnt, why she would take bamagilly buds and fry it in taller, and she would use that then to cure the burns. **1978** Montgomery *White Pine Coll* IX-1 He said, "You get some of those balm of Gilead buds and beat them up and put them in a bottle and put some whiskey on them and bathe with that." **1981** Whitener *Folk-Ways* 37 I was thinking about a substance which my father called Bomgillion, which is correctly pronounced *Balm of Gilead*. It was produced from the buds of balsam poplar tree and used with mutton tallow (taller), which when heated together on the back of the old wood-burning cook stove produced a salve which was used for chapped hands and other medical purposes. **1982** Powers and Hannah *Cataloochee* 284 They used to have a salve they'd make out of that bamagilia. Now it used to break some people out. I know some people it wouldn't even help. **1997** Landry *Coll* Her face was scarred and scruffalous. It was treated with bamgillion.

balsam *noun*

1 (also *balsam fir, balsam pine*) An evergreen tree, either one of two firs (*Abies fraseri* or *A. balsamea*) or the red spruce (*Picea rubra*), popular as a Christmas tree but now an endangered species in many areas due to infestation of the balsam woolly adelgid. Also called **blister pine, healing balsam, he-balsam, lashhorn, mountain balsam, she-balsam.**

1799 (in **2008** Ellison *High Vistas* 38) we spent the Sabbath day on taking observations from the high spur we crossed, In gathering the fir from [th]e Balsam Pine which is found on this mountain. **1851** (in **1956** Eliason *Tarheel Talk* 259) The Balsam is of two kinds, the He and She (or Blister). The latter has blisters in the bark, which alone contain the balsam. Nearly half a tea spoon can be obtained from one blister. **1908** Britton *N Amer Trees* 76 This southern fir, called ... Balsam fir ... occurs in the higher mountains of Virginia and West Virginia to North Carolina and Tennessee, where it sometimes forms forests, and reaches a maximum height of 25 meters. **1960** Stupka *Great Smoky Mts* 11 The Fraser fir, or "balsam" which comprises the bulk of the Great Smokies forests in mountains exceeding 6,000 feet appears very similar to the balsam fir or northern New England and Canada. Botanically the two species are distinct. **1964** Stupka *Trees Shrubs Vines* 22 The Fraser fir, also known as "balsam," is readily distinguished from the red spruce with which it often occurs. The fir is the only evergreen with upright cones. **2005** Cantrell *Clingman's Dome* 9 [In addition to the Fraser fir] the other dominant evergreen is the red spruce. Both are colloquially known as "balsams." Red spruce can be easily distinguished from the Fraser fir, which has flat blunt needles and resin blisters on its bark. Red spruce has needles with sharp ends and reddish-brown bark with resin blisters.

2 A mountainous area, especially one in the Balsam Mountain range of western North Carolina, dominated by fir or spruce; also used in place-names, as in *Cataloochee Balsam* (NC) and *Plott Balsam* (NC).

1943 Peattie *Indian Days* 40–41 A balsam is a mountain crowned by balsam fir or spruce or both. **1953** Hall *Coll* (Plott Creek NC) Several years ago, my father and some old man was a-trappin' out here close to Plott Balsam, trapping for bear with a pen. **1956** Hall *Coll* (Big Creek NC) ["Turkey" George Palmer] hunted on the ledge over toward Swain [Co] and on the Balsam.

balsam bell *noun* A bead lily (*Clintonia borealis*). Same as **amber bell**.

1939 Jennison *Flora Great Smokies* 292 The balsam bell (*Clintonia borealis*), a truly boreal form, is abundant on the floor of the spruce-fir forests, which clothe the mountain tops of the Great Smokies.

balsam fir See **balsam 1**.

balsam oil (also *balsam sap*) *noun* Sap from a balsam tree, made into a medicinal salve to treat cuts and wounds, sometimes gathered and sold for cash.

1929 (in **1952** Mathes *Tall Tales* 108) He says wearin' a lump of asafidity round yer neck an' takin' a little balsam ile ever-day will keep off might' nigh any sickness. **1939** Hall *Coll* (Roaring Fork TN) Gathering [balsam] sap on top of LeConte, Oscar Ogle would get three dollars a pint. [It was] good kidney medicine, also good for sores caused by dew poisoning.

balsam pine See **balsam 1**.

balsam sap See **balsam oil**.

bamagilia, bamagilly, bam-be-gilly, bam b'gilly See **balm of Gilead.**

bamboo brier *noun* A greenbrier (*Smilax* spp). See also **cat brier, saw brier.**

1901 Lounsberry *Sthn Wild Flowers* 63 *S. rotundifolia*, green brier, cat brier, or common bamboo, grows often in thickets, or where the soil is moist, and is prone to climb as high as thirty or forty feet. **1937** Thornburgh *Great Smoky Mts* 23 A few of the more common vines you may encounter along almost any trail are ... green brier, which is also called saw brier, cat brier, and bamboo brier. **1998** Montgomery *Coll* = usually known as the common greenbrier (Cardwell).

bamgillion, bammygilly, bam-be-gilly See **balm of Gilead.**

band mill *noun* A large, mechanized sawmill driven by a band saw rather than by a circular saw. See 2002 citation.

1953 Hall *Coll* (Bryson City NC) They built a railroad up from the main Southern line up into Hazel Creek and built a big double-band mill up in there and built a little town. That's what they call Proctor. **1973** GSMNP-83:11 We had a big band mill here at Townsend, you know, that took care of everything. **1977** Stanley *Tough* 30 The band mill means a band saw, a continuous band of steel going around two pulleys with teeth on it, driven by a large engine of some sort, the steam engine. They sawed the logs, and that kind of sawmill is opposed to a more modern type of mill which is just a circular blade saw. And the band saw had the advantage of being able to saw much larger logs, logs of much larger diameter. **1994** Lambert *Sawmills* 44 With the coming of the railroad, large band mills replaced many of the small saw mills. **2002** Hayler *Sound Wormy* 207–8 = a saw mill that uses a band saw as its head saw, or head rig. A band saw is a machine that uses a blade made of a continuous toothed steel ribbon. The size of a band is determined by the diameter of its top pulley, or head wheel.

band up *verb phrase*

1 See citation.

1917 Kephart *Word-List* 407 *banded up* = bandaged: "I was banded up for about three weeks."

2 See citation.

1960 Westover *Highland Lg* 19 = gather together.

bandy-shanked *adjective* Bow-legged, with thin, crooked legs.

1859 Taliaferro *Fisher's River* 47 Come here, you bandy-shanked rascal, and take my hoss. [**1930** *Herald-Advertiser* A lad is usually "old man Jones' boy" instead of being his son. When he grows up ... if very slender, [he] may bear the happy sobriquet "Banjer-Shanks."] **a1975** Lunsford *It Used to Be* 174 "Bandyshanked" means having thin, crooked shanks, bowlegged. **1996–97** Montgomery *Coll*: *bandy-shanked* (known to Brown, Bush, Hooper, Oliver).

[cf OED3 *bandy-legged* (at *bandy* adj 1); DARE *bandy-shanked* adj probably South, South Midland]

bang *verb* variant past-tense form *bung*.

1982 Hurst *Appal Words* 99 They also transformed bang into bung (He bung his finger), stalk into "staug" (to staug around), and crouch into "scruch."

banged *interjection* Used as a mild oath.

1939 Still *Ploughing* 776 Banged if I know.

bangest (also *banginest*) *adjective* Most extraordinary.

1955 Washburn *Country Doctor* 42 He's the *banginest* man—he is a remarkable man. **1957** Combs *Lg Sthn High: Word List* 8 *bangest* = the worst possible. Ex.: "That's the bangest nag I ever yit seed."

banginest See **bangest.**

banjer *noun* A banjo. See also **hell's banjo.**

1895 Edson and Fairchild *TN Mts* 375. **1903** Fox *Little Shepherd* 49 Who was that a-pickin' that banjer? **1917** Kephart *Word-List* 408. **1942** Hall *Phonetics Smoky Mts* 80. **1961** *Coe Ridge OHP*-340B Garner was the jailer, and he had his banjer kept in there. **1963** Edwards *Gravel* 156 The fiddle and banjer, of course, he had heard; they were a part of the life of the country people among whom he was raised. **1973** GSMNP-5 The scouts come in and killed ... two Grooms boys, and this. They was on this side of the gap at Mount Sterling, and they made them play the fiddle, pick the banjer, and then when they heard all the music they wanted, they had shot them, and that's called today the Grooms Boys Branch. **1994** Montgomery *Coll* (known to Cardwell). **1997** *Dante OHP*-14 My brother picked the banjer, too. **2008** Salsi *Ray Hicks* 3 Till he died in the 1980s, he was famous for his handmade groundhog hide banjers and lap dulcimers.

[DARE *banjer* (at *banjo* n A) South, Midland]

bank See **coal bank.**

bank barn *noun* A barn built into a hillside, permitting entrance on two levels.

1946 Nixon *Glossary VA Words* 10 = a barn erected on sloping ground, with three sides of the bottom story enclosed by earth ... [a term used] in northern part of the Blue Ridge. **2006** *WV Encycl* 43 As sawn boards became available, large, timer-framed bank barns, with their multi-level entrances, dotted the countryside in areas where people of German descent settled. **2007** Milnes *Signs Cures Witches* 55 German motifs were carved into furniture and painted on chests and barns and the like, including many painted and decorated "Pennsylvania" or German-Swiss "bank barns." The most common are ones painted red with decorative white bordering, and some have "devil doors" (painted arches over the doors) and white stars painted on the doors.

[DARE *bank barn* n chiefly PA, OH, MD, VA, IN]

bank car *noun* See citation.

1973 Preston *Bituminous Term* 42 = coal haulage vehicle.

bank clothes *noun* Clothing worn by coal miners, such as chambray shirts, denim pants and coats, heavy shoes, etc.

1941 Stuart *Men of Mts* 267 I was dressed in my bank clothes. **1968** Clarke *Stuart's Kentucky* 170 The men wore heavy shoes, bank clothes (heavy blue work shirts, jackets and pants of strong denim or some other coarse cloth), and bank caps with carbite (carbide) lamps on the front to give them light to work by a mile or more back inside the mine.

[from *coal bank* "a shallow hillside mine"]

bank posting *noun* The heavy timbers in a **coal bank** supporting the roof of the entryway and the area where miners dig coal.

1941 Stuart *Men of Mts* 267 So much of this bank postin' . . . it's that what cuts our average o' coal diggin' down.

bannock bread *noun* A hard bread made from flour and fried in a pan, common in logging camps in the Smoky Mountains.

1982 *Smokies Heritage* 37 A special camp bread of flour and sugar, bannock bread, was most often baked in Dutch ovens. **1997** Montgomery *Coll* (known to Bush).

[related to Irish Gaelic *bannach*/Scottish Gaelic *bannoch* and Old English *bannuc*, all ultimately < Latin *paniculum* "little bread"; EDD *bannock* sb Scot, Irel, Engl; CUD *bannock* n "originally an oatcake baked on a griddle"]

banter

A *verb* To dare, challenge, taunt.

1855 *Paw Paw Hollow Church Minutes* 161 Arming himself with a revolver and bantering and dunning his brother to go into a fight with him. **1903** Fox *Little Shepherd* 26 At the top of the hill both turned with bantering yells, derisive wriggling of their fingers at their noses, and with other rude gestures. **1924** (in **1952** Mathes *Tall Tales* 25) "That's a plumb good idy, boys," he said. "I'll banter him to do hisself proud this time, an' then I've jest thought of a brand-new drag I'll git off on him." **1944** Wilson *Word-List* 40 = to dare, to challenge. **1974** Fink *Bits Mt Speech* 2 John *bantered* him for a race.

[Web3 *banter* v 4 Midland; DARE *banter* v 2 chiefly South, Midland]

B *noun* A dare, challenge, taunt. See also **whet a banter**.

1834 Crockett *Narrative* 57 I couldn't help thinking, that she intended what she had said as a banter for me to court her!

[DARE *banter* n 1a chiefly South, Midland]

banterlick *noun* See citations.

a1975 Lunsford *It Used to Be* 16 They had what they called the banter lick. When a fellow felt pretty good and he thought he could beat the other fellows cutting wheat, he would whet the banter lick and then he would start out to cut. The other fellows would start in behind him. Sometimes they might be able to cut around him—that is, go right on ahead. They'd have to cut pretty far around so as not to hit anybody. *Ibid.* 164 The "banterlick" is a lick used in whetting a scythe, and when a person is in the harvest field and others are there with their scythes and cradles ready to go, and the man feels like he can cut around them or lead the entire group, he will whet the banterlick, that is, strike the blade first on one side and then on the other, and drops back and hits the blade twice as he comes out and drops back on the other side. That's the "banterlick" in the harvest field.

bantling *noun* A small child, infant.

1936 Farr *Folk Speech* 275 The bantling is in the cradle. **1944** Wilson *Word-List* 40 = a child. **1996–97** Montgomery *Coll* (known to Brown).

banty *noun* A type of miniature chicken. See also **bunty**.

1977 Still *Wonder Beans* 24 Bring me my little banty hen that lays gold eggs. **1989** *Matewan OHP*-9 You can call some of these fellows "Reverend," and they walk off like a little banty rooster. **1990** Fisher *Preacher Stories* 16 Our two small boys received one Christmas week a beautiful bantam rooster and five "banty" hens. . . . We were glad to get the banties. The boys enjoyed them as pets, and the hens supplied eggs for a long time. Finally, the only survivor was the little banty rooster. **1996** Montgomery *File* = variety of small chicken (85-year-old man, Greenbrier TN). **1998** Hyde *My Home* 80 The other Banty rooster, not yet advanced enough to give rise to a crow, looked on with curiosity and some envy, it seemed.

[alteration of *bantam*]

bapsouse *verb* To baptize by immersion.

1992 Brooks *Sthn Stuff* 16 = humorous for baptize.

Baptises, Baptistes See **Baptist**.

Baptist *noun* variant singular forms *Babdis(t)*, *Babtis(t)*, plural forms *Baptises*, *Baptistes*.

1895 *Mt Baptist Sermon* 13 Now brethering, they haint no more harm in the doctorings of the ole Hardshell Babtist church-ah! than they is in thet ole stump. **1923** (in **1952** Mathes *Tall Tales* 9) These here deep-water Babtists [are] a-puttin' their trust in goin' under the water instid o' gittin' under the blood! **1927** Woofter *Dialect from WV* 347 My mother was a Babdist. **1936** Coleman *Dial N GA* 26 "Baptises" [is used] for "Baptists." **1961** Murry *Salt* 71 Now that ole man was a turble Bab-dis an' didn' want to keep no Mormons. **1967** *Revival* 9 Last spring we attended a revival held at the tiny Joy Babtist [sic] Church below Wiley, Georgia. **1972** *AOHP/ALC*-241 Really I believe there's more Baptistes in the lower part of Long Fork. **1973** Miller *English Unicoi Co* 108 *Babdist* attested by 1 of 6 speakers, *Babdis* by 2 of 6. **1978** Hiser *Quare Do's* 6 My dad's old Hardshell Babtist Church held a meeting at the head of Lonesome once a month.

[DARE *Babdis(t)*, *Babtis(t)* (at *Baptist* n) especially South, Midland]

Baptist pallet (also *Old Baptist pallet*) *noun* See citations. Same as **pallet**. See also **Methodist pallet**.

1902 Grime *Middle TN Baptists* 284 This scribe well remembers when during the sitting of an Association he had about one hundred guests. . . . At night "Baptist pallets" were spread on all available space in the house. **1992** Brooks *Sthn Stuff* 16 = a make-do bed spread on the floor (named, no doubt, by a member of an opposing denomination). **2002** Myers *Best Yet Stories* 15 = a bed roll, used on the floor when there are too many guests and not enough beds. These pallets were necessary in many early homes. **2011** *Blind Pig* (June 8) In my family, a pallet for extra company was sometimes called a "Baptist pallet": i.e., "We'll make you a Baptist pallet." **2014** Montgomery *Doctrine* 154 = a small temporary bed comprised of quilts and blankets often made on the floor and used to sleep overnight guests during a large meeting. . . . Using the Old Baptist Pallet it is possible to house 20 to 30 guests in a modest home. Comfort is not the issue. Fellowship is.

baptizing *noun* A baptismal ceremony by immersion, traditionally held outdoors at the edge of a stream or river.

1923 (in **1952** Mathes *Tall Tales* 3) When "Preacher Ike" Gallaher hobbled down the valley to preach in the Hardshell meetinghouse, or perhaps to "hold a babtizin'" in the dark pool at the edge of the churchyard, the old man came with no soft gospel of compromise or tolerance toward the "onscriptural teachin's of these here Methodis' people up the creek." **1948** Chase *Grandfather Tales* 101 In a bend in the river . . . they were fixin' to have a big baptizin' the next day. **1969** GSMNP-37 They'd just call for mourners, and they'd go up there and confess and have baptizing. **1973** GSMNP-81:20 They had a baptizing, and of course everybody always took along a little food to these great ceremonies. **a1975** Lunsford *It Used to Be* 85 At that time when they'd have their baptizings, they would gather those who were to be baptized close to the bank, have someone, when they called for the candidate, to extend their hand and lead them out into the stream. **1980** GSMNP-115 They'd have baptizing in the winter time just the same as the summer. They didn't dread the water when they was wanting to jine the church and be baptized. **1995** McCauley *Mt Religion* 86–87 Baptizings . . . take place in a pool of water, or in the deepest part of a creek, or in a river, no matter what the season of the year.

bar See **bear**[1], **boar**.

bardy grease See **vordegrease**.

bare See **bear**[1].

barefoot (also *barefooted*) *adjective* Of a drink or food: having no added ingredients; undiluted or unmixed, most often applied to coffee without sugar or cream/milk, but also to foods made of only basic ingredients. See 1992–97 citations. See also **with socks on**.

1957 Combs *Lg Sthn High: Word List* 8 *barefooted* = fac[etious] for *au naturel*, straight, as in: "I'll take my coffee barefooted" (without sugar or cream). **1975** Dwyer *Thangs* 19 *barefoot bread* = a hard corn bread made without shortening. **1978** Reese *Speech NE Tenn* 30 *barefoot(ed)* = attested by 2/12 (16.7%) speakers. **1979** Slone *My Heart* 65 A "barefoot dumpling" was when the balls of dough were cooked in boiling water, containing only salt and lard. Of course, they were better in chicken broth or fresh meat "sop." **1986** Pederson et al. *LAGS*: *barefooted* = attested by 12/60 interviewees (20%) from E TN; 12/47 of all LAGS interviewees (25.5%) attesting term were from Appalachia; (Blount Co TN) *barefooted coffee* = just as black as you can make it; (Cumberland Co TN) *barefoot coffee* = nothing in it/no sugar and cream. **1992–97** Montgomery *Coll*: *barefoot* = any food made with basic ingredients (Bush); *barefoot bread* = hard bread, lacking such ingredients as eggs or lard, also *barefoot coffee* (Brown); I'll take my coffee barefoot (Shields); *barefooted coffee* (Brown); I like my coffee barefooted (Cardwell); *barefoot dumpling* = made from water, grease, and salt (Brown); *barefoot moonshine* He drinks his shine barefoot (Brown).

[cf SND *bar(e)fit broth* (at *barefit* adj) "broth made without meat"; cf CUD *barefoot* adj 2 "hungry, empty"]

bare-naked *adjective* Completely naked.

1944 Laughlin *Word-list Buncombe Co* 24 = naked. **c1960** Wilson *Coll* = redundant for naked.

bar hog *noun* A castrated hog; by extension, a man who is infertile.

1941 Stuart *Men of Mts* 345 We see crates of chickens . . . bar hogs . . . and bulls. **c1982** Young *Colloquial Appal* 2 = castrated hog. **2013** Crawford *Mt Memories* 80 Ed Cross here can't get no babies. He's a "bar hog." He can't make no lit'lens.

[DARE *bar* n[3] chiefly South, Midland, and northern New York]

bark

A *noun* A person's or potato's skin.

1940 Still *Love Rooster* 16 These clodhoppers I'm wearing have wore a half acre o' bark off my heels. **1941** Stuart *Men of Mts* 235 We get roasted taters from the ashes—peel the bark from them.

B *verb*

1 To kill (especially a squirrel) by shooting into the tree nearby. See 1996 citation.

1883 Zeigler and Grosscup *Heart of Alleghanies* 97 The crack marksman with a rifle generally barks his squirrel. **1940** Still *River of Earth* 5 He had barked them, firing at the tree trunk beside the animals' heads, and bringing them down without a wound. [**1941** Stuart *Men of Mts* 141 Pap would shoot under or over the squirrel—never touch the squirrel—just hit the bark beside it and kill the squirrel.] **1982** DeArmond *So High* 40 Robert showed his skill in "barking" a squirrel. **1996** Casada *Gospel Hook* 27 Cathey could "bark" squirrels with remarkable consistency. This was a technique where he aimed at the tree trunk or limb immediately underneath the bushytail, as opposed to actually taking a bead on the squirrel. If he was on target, the shock of flying bits of bark would stun or kill the squirrel without damaging the meat at all. It was a technique originally used by prudent frontiersmen firing muzzleloaders who wanted to retrieve and recycle the lead ball, and all Cathey was doing was "barking" with a modern weapon.

[DARE *bark* v[2] 1 chiefly South Midland]

2 To cut a ring of bark from the girth of a tree in order to prevent its sap from rising and kill it.

1963 Medford *Mt People* 34 The common pole axe was used not only in felling trees, cutting up the meat; it was also used for splitting rails, driving stakes, shaping handles, "barking" trees, and killing hogs—also to an extent in cutting up the meat, as a branding iron, and the handle as a two-foot measure. **1968** Connelly *Discover Appal* 159 He knew how to clear away his land for planting. If his mountain farm were surrounded by hickory, he only "barked" these trees by cutting a ring of bark. Soon the trees would die. Several hefty strokes with an axe were required to kill a stubborn walnut, and an oak took even more chopping.

3 See citation. See also **barker**.

1993 Stuart *Daughter* 228 *barking logs* = removing the bark from logs.

bark box (also *bark basket, bark bucket*) *noun* A simple, cuplike makeshift container fashioned from bark peeled off a tree, especially the tulip poplar.

2007 Alexander *Forgotten Basket* 7 Bill calls the baskets he makes "Mountain Berry Baskets," but they go by many different names like "poplar bark baskets," "berry pouches," "bark boxes" or "bark buckets." This style of basket could be made using a pocket knife and found material. A wide strip of bark was removed from a tulip poplar tree using a pocket knife. The basket was formed using this piece of poplar bark by scoring a "cat's eye" shape in the center of the strip of bark and folding the two ends together. It could be held together with a stick through all four corners, tied at the top with a vine, a piece of leather or with a small snip of poplar bark or hickory bark. The results would look very much like a modern day McDonald's french fry box. **2009** Waldvogel *Bark Baskets* 19 Old-timers around here called them berry barks, or berry baskets, named for their most common use—berry picking. Rather than carry metal buckets up the hill or if they just happened on a batch of wild blackberries, they would make a container on the spot with what they found. Back home, with the luscious contents transferred to a kitchen bowl, they threw the bark bucket on the woodpile, its use as a berry bucket over.

bark crew *noun* See citations.

1998 Farwell *Logging Terms* It had to be a snake-proof crew . . . they would dry that bark out generally. They spudded all the bark off and laid it down flat, because bark curls naturally whenever you just take it off the logs. They packed it all up in big packs, put rocks on top of it, whatever, to hold it down flat. So when they went back to get a load out, it was full of copperheads or rattlesnakes. So the guys would simply have to be snake-proof and be snake-wise. Most people didn't like to fool with the bark. You had to be hungry because you were always fighting snakes. . . . You need teamsters for a bark [crew]. They loaded it on sleds. It was mostly sledded out. **2006** Farwell *Logging Term* 1021 Bark crews had "spudders" and "rawhiders," who removed and stacked bark from felled trees.

barker *noun* See citation. See also **bark B3**.

1967 Parris *Mt Bred* 133 A barker is [a member of a logging crew] who peels bark in gathering tanbark.

bark spudder *noun* A logging worker whose job is to remove especially **tanbark** using a **spud**. Also called **spudder**. See also **spud A1**.

1955 Parris *Roaming Mts* 152 An old timer is one who remembers . . . when a timberman who peeled bark from logs was known as a bark spudder.

bark tree(d) *verb phrase* Of a hunting dog: to signal by barking that a pursued animal has been driven up a tree or cornered. See also **tree 1, tree bark**.

1953 Hall *Coll* (Plott Creek NC) I hustled right on and turned the other dogs loose. I heard 'em stop and bark "tree." **1968** Clarke *Stuart's Kentucky* 118 He knew how to interpret his dog's barking from cold-trailing to barking treed. **1997** Miller *Brier Poems* 42 He heard only . . . the remembered baying of coonhounds barking treed.

Barlow knife *noun* Usually a type of single-bladed pocket knife; occasionally a two-bladed knife; see 1997 citation.

1848 (in **1870** Drake *Pioneer Life KY* 112) Behold, then, the whole family arranged on chairs and stools around the great undressed hearthstone, each with a pewter plate in their lap and an iron fork, a "Barlow" knife or the sharp of an old pair of scissors in the right hand. **1864** *Lance CW Letters* (Aug 2) tell little Marcus I have got a little Barlow knife for him if I ever git Back. **1864** *Misemer CW Letters* (May 2) I send charley and Bud a barlow knife a peace with Each o[f] their names cut on the handle. **1939** Hall *Coll* (Deep Creek NC) [The deer] jumped right into a deep hole an' I jumped right on it and cut its throat with a Barlow knife. *Ibid.* (Tuckaleechee Cove TN) We had a Barlow knife and got it ready. It made two jumps at him, and he stopped it with a knife. The moon was shinin' bright, and he thought it was a panther. **1967** Wilson *Folkways Mammoth Cave* 17 There was a time when a man was known by his knife. And every man who wanted to be highly regarded owned a Russell Barlow knife; and every boy longed for the day when he would be old enough to own one and to join the group of whittlers at the country store. **1997** Montgomery *Coll* = an inexpensive but fairly heavy and strongly constructed jack or pocket knife, commonly having two blades opening from the same end, the larger-sized variety being called a "Daddy Barlow" (Ellis).

barn *noun*

A Variant forms *barnd, barned*.

1939 Walker *Mtneer Looks* 4 *Barnd* is said for *barn*, *bornd* for *born*. **1967** *DARE Survey* (Gatlinburg TN) *barnd owl*.

B One of the two main sections of a double barn under one roof.

1939 Hall *Coll* (Smokemont NC) They come a big rain and washed the old foot bridge plumb into the hallway between the barns.

barn boss *noun* The person in charge of the stables in a logging camp.

1998 Robbins *Logging Terms*.

barnd, barned See **barn A**.

barn dance See **bran dance**.

barn litter See **litter**.

barn loft *noun* See citations.

1966 Dakin *Vocab Ohio River Valley* 67 North of the Kentucky River and west of the Mountains, in Indiana south of the Till Plain, and in Illinois east of the Kaskaskia, the usual word is simple *loft* [for the upper part of a barn]. Commonly in the southern Knobs and Mountains and in scattered instances elsewhere, some say *barn loft* quite possibly because of *loft* = "attic" of a house in these same areas. **2014** Graves *Basin Ghosts* 56 The work of summer jobs finished, / tobacco leaves strung up in barn lofts to dry, / hay bales twined and rolled under tarp.

barn loom *noun* See citations.

1999 Montgomery *Coll* = a large, cumbersome, homemade loom used to weave coverlets, counterpanes, and clothing material (Wilson). **2001** Wilson *Textile Art* viii The hand loom, sometimes referred to as a "barn loom," was a piece of equipment that an ordinary carpenter built out of timber found on the farm and fitted with metal gears constructed by a local blacksmith.

barn lot (also *barnyard lot*) *noun* A fenced enclosure next to or surrounding a barn in which livestock are held; a barnyard. See also **lot A.**

1883 Jones *Highlands N Carol* 380 It leads us by a water-fall under thick hemlocks, and then out into a corn-field, and through the yard and barn-lot of a mountaineer's home. **1934–47** LAMSAS (Madison Co NC, Swain Co NC) *barn lot*. **1949** Kurath *Word Geog East US* 40 From the Rappahannock southward lot, *barn lot*, *stable lot* . . . are the usual terms for the barnyard, and these expressions are current in all of the South Midland as well as in parts of northern West Virginia, but not in the Shenandoah Valley. In West Virginia north of the Kanawha *barnyard lot* occurs beside the Southern lot. **1966** Dakin *Vocab Ohio River Valley* 87 West of Ohio and south of the river (*barn*) *lot* (or the other terms with *lot*), and an 8 to 1 majority in Kentucky [i.e. in contrast to *barnyard*, etc]. **1968** DARE *Survey* (Brasstown NC) *barnyard lot*. **1986** Pederson et al. LAGS: *barn lot* = attested by 22/60 interviewees (31.7%) from E TN; 22/73 of all LAGS interviewees (29%) attesting term were from E TN. **1996** GSMNPCOHP-1:4 4:19 They had what they call a barn lot. It was fenced in out around [the barn]. Usually it was where they could get to water, where they'd turn them out of the barn in that barn lot and get water anytime they wanted it.

[DARE *barn lot* n chiefly Midland, South]

barn martin *noun* The barn swallow (*Hirundo erythrogaster*), which nests in barns and similar structures.

1998 Montgomery *Coll* (known to Cardwell).

[DARE *barn martin* n especially KY, MO, TN]

barn raising *noun* Traditionally, an organized work activity of neighbors and kin to help a family erect a barn. See also **house covering, house raising, log raising.**

1939 Hall *Coll* (Cataloochee NC) We had log rollin's, house raisin's, barn raisin's, and corn shuckin's. **1971** *Corn Shuckin's* 100 We had a house raisin' t'raise this house, and we had a barn raisin' t'raise the barn. . . . Th'house ain't hard t'raise like th'barn. See, th'house is made out'a little logs, and th'barn is made out'a big logs. And th'barn's got four big stalls in it—maybe more. It took eight men for four stalls. You hardly ever got a barn raised in one day. **1991** Thomas *Sthn Appal* 175 For certain important activities in the mountains one man always required help. One was the erection of a building such as a house or barn. Commonly, when a man had cut and trimmed all the logs needed to build a new house, barn or other outbuilding, and had those logs dragged to the site, he would invite his neighbors to his house- or barn-raising.

barn scald *noun* See citations.

1967 Key *Tobacco Vocab* 33 A general darkening of the curing leaf caused by excessive moisture in the barn . . . barn burn, barn scald. **1969** Miller *Raising Tobacco* 36 Hanging tobacco too close in the barn, or in a barn that lacked adequate ventilation during especially hot, humid weather might result in *barn-scald*.

barnyard lot See **barn lot.**

barr See **borrow A.**

barrel *noun* See citation.

c1960 Wilson *Coll*: = a measure, usually five bushels.

[DARE *barrel* n B1 chiefly Midland, South]

barrel Baptist *noun* See citation.

2014 Montgomery *Doctrine* 82 = someone who has a barrel rather than a cup. They attend services and fill up their barrel so they don't have to come back for 3 to 4 weeks.

base See **baseborn.**

baseborn (also *base*) *adjective* Born out of wedlock.

1904 Fox *Christmas Eve* 161 A "baseborn" child toddled toward me. **1921** Campbell *Sthn Highlander* 132 There is not, moreover, the same stigma put upon the "baseborn" child as in other sections. **1949** Kurath *Word Geog East US* 77 On Chesapeake Bay, especially on the Eastern Shore, we find *base born (child)*, and this term appears here and there in the Appalachians (but not in the intervening Virginia Piedmont). **1966** Dakin *Vocab Ohio River Valley* 441 It seems also that *baseborn child*, commonly mentioned in the Kentucky Mountains but unknown elsewhere in the Valley, must be an even older expression which largely lost out to *woods colt* as veiled and semi-playful or neutral terms developed to supplant the blunter or more pejorative ones. **1973** Miller *English Unicoi Co* 143 *base child* = illegitimate child. **1986** Pederson et al. LAGS (Johnson Co TN, Carter Co TN) *baseborn*. **1997** Montgomery *Coll*: *baseborn baby* (Bush). **2008** Salsi *Ray Hicks* 73 Mama'd say the rowdy ones was probably base born, meanin' their mama's born them outside of marriage.

[OED3 *base-born* adj 2; DARE *baseborn* adj chiefly Delmarva, western NC]

basement *noun* See citations.

1974 Fink *Bits Mt Speech* 2 = basin. "A little *basement* between the hills." **1999** Montgomery *Coll* = a small area of rocky but productive ground along a stream (Brown).

basket dinner *noun* A meal, usually at a regular time of year, to which the members of a community or church congregation bring food to share at an outdoor meal. Formerly, the event was held on the occasion of a visiting preacher, but more recently it has taken place following a church service at a **homecoming** or **decoration day** observance or a **basket meeeting**. The term has generally been superseded by **dinner on the ground(s)**. See also **basket meeting**.

1946 Stuart *Plum Grove Hills* 41 He was a great church member—took in all the basket dinners and footwashin's. **1968** Clarke *Stuart's Kentucky* 79 A more frequent and popular church social was the basket dinner, or dinner on the grounds. When an all-day service made it practical, the women of the church prepared abundant food on Saturday for dinner on the church grounds preceding the evening preaching services. **1984** Wilder *You All Spoken* 85 = vittles packed in oak split baskets for serving at all-day church functions with dinner on the grounds. **1995** Montgomery *Coll* = *dinner on the grounds*, but a less common term (Adams), = held after morning preaching service and on special occasions, now held indoors and replaced by *covered dish dinner/supper* (Cardwell).

basket meeting *noun* A special church service or short series of services, as over a weekend or on the occasion of a visiting preacher, during which is shared a **basket dinner** with food that church members have brought. See also **camp meeting**.

1881 Pierson *In the Brush* 60–61 Religious meetings, popularly denominated "basket-meetings," were known and recognized as established institutions in the Brush. They were among the assemblages that had resulted from the sparseness of the population in those regions. . . . These meetings . . . could often be held where such a meeting would be impossible. They were usually not as large, and did not continue as many days. They were called "basket-meetings" from the fact that those from a distance brought their provisions, already cooked, in large baskets, and in quantities sufficient to last them during the continuance of the meeting. They put up no tents or cabins on the ground. They did not cook or sleep there. They most frequently commenced on Saturday, and continued through the Sabbath. They generally had a prayer-meeting and preaching on Saturday forenoon, and then adjourned for an hour or two. During this intermission the greater part of the people dispersed in groups among the trees, and took their dinner after the manner of a picnic. Those living in the immediate vicinity returned to their homes for dinner, taking with them as many of those inattendance as they could possibly secure. **1984** Wilder *You All Spoken* 180 = two or three days of religious services with "dinner on the grounds an' preachin' all around." So called because participants bring baskets of food. **1995** McCauley *Mt Religion* 384–85 "Basket meetings" were somewhat of a cross between "a big meeting" or a short-term revival held over Saturday and Sunday and "dinner on the ground" after Sunday worship.

[DARE *basket meeting* n South, South Midland]

basket oak (also *basket tree*) *noun* A white oak (*Quercus michauxii* or *Q. alba*), from whose logs **splits** of wood are stripped to make baskets and other handcrafted objects.

c1940 Simms *Coll*: *basket tree* = white oak, suitable for baskets. **1940** Still *River of Earth* 240 I never figure spring's in for shore till the basket oaks sprout buds. **1991** Law and Taylor *Oak Basketmaking* 31 Common regional names for the swamp chestnut oak include "basket oak" and "cow oak." Both swamp chestnut oak and O. alba have light ash-gray bark with flaky scales. **2004** Rehder *Appal Folkways* 271 [The] shape is believed to be designed to rest on the hip of a woman walking or riding horseback. The most durable and widely used material for Appalachian basketry was split white oak, Quercus alba, also appropriately called basket oak.

basket tree See **basket oak**.

bastard fashion *adverb phrase* See citation.

1969 GSMNP-38:180 All timber's got grooves or layers. Well, you can split it one way of the wood, and it'll rot out and leave these streaks solid. But this was all split the other way, what they called bastard fashion, like hauling it off from the outside.

bat[1]

A *verb* To blink (one's eye).

1923 Montague *Today Tomorrow* 159 The hands they was all jest carried away by the sight; but that kid, he never batted a eye. **1931** Combs *Lg Sthn High* 1304 When the doctor looked at him he batted his eyes like a toad in a hail storm. **1937** Hall *Coll* (Hartford TN) The bear was batting its eyes when the master hunter found him. **1966–68** *DARE Survey* (Cherokee NC, Gatlinburg TN, Maryville TN) = to open and close the eyes quickly.

[DARE *bat* v[2] widespread, but chiefly South, Midland]

B *noun* A wink or blink of one's eyes; a very short period of time.

1956 Hall *Coll* (Roaring Fork TN) When I said that by-word [= "God damn"], it was right when [a light] flashed up. It was just like the bat of your eye.

[*bat* "to wink" probably alteration of *bate* "to flutter (as a hawk)"; OED3 *bat* v[2] 2 originally dialect and U.S.]

bat[2] *verb* To nail strips of wood over cracks between boards or logs, as on the side of a cabin, to insulate it.

1943 Stuart *Private Tussie* 261 We . . . nailed a plank roof on the sheetin and batted the cracks. **1994** Montgomery *Coll* (known to Shields).

[shortening of *batten*; DARE *bat* v[3] southern Appalachians]

batch, batch it See **bach**.

bate See **bait**.

bath *verb* To bathe.

1976 Garber *Mountain-ese* 6 I'll be ready to go with you jist as soon as I bath the baby. **1989** *Matewan OHP*-28 I'd loaded coal in the coal mines, and I'd come in and bath in a wash tub. **1995–97** Montgomery *Coll* (known to Brown, Ledford, Norris, Oliver); We're going to have to bath the baby (Cardwell).

[DARE *bath* v chiefly South, South Midland]

batler, **batlet** See **battle**.

batter cake (also *batty cake*) *noun* See citations.

1934–47 LAMSAS Appal: *battercake* attested by 10/14 speakers (71.4%) from SC and 4/12 (33.3%) from GA. **1963** Wilson *Regional Words* 79 Though [*pancake*] has long been known and used, older people called these quickies of cooking *fritters* (*flitters*), *batter cakes*, or *flapjacks*. Small children often called them *batty-cakes*, to rhyme with *patty-cakes*. **1966** Dakin *Vocab Ohio River Valley* 326 The Southern *batter cake* [is] used on all social levels everywhere in this state [= KY] and is still far from being supplanted by *pancake*. **1992** Montgomery Coll: *batter cake* = a large, thin pancake, made from somewhat weaker batter than normal (Shields).

[DARE *battercake* n 1 chiefly South, South Midland]

battern *noun* See citation.

1917 Kephart *Word-List* 408 = in weaving, the arm that knocks in the thread.

[variant of *batten*; cf OED3 *batten* n² "movable bar or arm in a silk-loom"]

battle

A (also *batler, batlet, battling stick, beating stick*) *noun* Formerly, a heavy stick or long-handled paddle beaten on clothing to dislodge dirt from it after it is soaked, soaped, and placed on a **battling bench**. Also called **trouble stick**.

1913 Kephart *Our Sthn High* 246 Near by stands the great iron kettle for boiling clothes, making soap, scalding pigs, and a variety of other uses. Alongside of it is the "battlin' block" on which the family wash is hammered with a beetle ("battlin' stick") if the woman has no washboard, which is very often the case. **1915** Dingus *Word-List VA* 180 *battle* = a beetle (for battling clothes): "The washwoman broke the battle handle." **1924** Raine *Saddlebags* 11 Upon [the battling bench] lies the batler or batlet. **1959** Hall Coll (Mt Sterling NC) [We used a] wash pot, block, and battlin' stick, and homemade soap. **1973** *Foxfire Interviews* A-73-43 Then we'd wash the wash, and then I'd have to beat them [= clothes] with that blamed old beating stick. **1975** *Hartley I* 169 All them battling sticks . . . was made of red maple. Now you might wonder why red maple? Well, red maple is a fine grain, and in battling on them clothes the grain stays smooth. **1997** King *Mt Folks* 76 She used the old time scrub board and boiled the white clothes, and she scrubbed the colored clothes and took her battling stick to loosen the dirt in them. Everybody had a battling stick and a battling board. It usually took the whole day to do the washing and a day to do the ironing.

[EDD *battle* sb²; DARE *battling stick* n South, South Midland]

B *verb*

1 To use such an implement on a **battling bench** or **battling block** to beat soiled clothing that has been soaked and soaped in boiling water, in order to dislodge dirt. Same as **troubling**.

1895 Edson and Fairchild *TN Mts* 370 = to beat. **c1926** Cox *Cullowhee Wordlist* = to [wash] clothes with a paddle. **1956** Hall Coll (Roaring Fork TN) We'd battle the clothes with the battlin' stick. **1971** *AOHP/ALC-260* She'd dip them clothes down in that water in that trough and lay them up there, and I took a battling stick and battled them, and I'd bat them until they'd dry, and then we'd put them back in the water and battle them again.

[*battle* originally the frequentative form of *bat* (cf OED3 *battle* v⁴ obsolete); EDD *battle* sb², v¹; DARE *battle* v 1 chiefly South, South Midland]

2 See citation.

1983 Broaddus *Estill Co KY Word List* 30 *battle it out* = to beat the grain off the stalks of wheat.

battle spelling *noun* See citation.

1989 Still *Rusties and Riddles* [58] = open spelling contest.

battling bench (also *battling block, battling board, battling log, beatling block, paddling bench*) *noun* Formerly, a slab, stand, or other flat, wooden surface on which clothing soaked and soaped is beaten with a **battle** to dislodge dirt and thus to make it clean.

1913 Kephart *Our Sthn High* 246 Near by stands the great iron kettle for boiling clothes, making soap, scalding pigs, and a variety of other uses. Alongside of it is the "battlin' block" on which the family wash is hammered with a beetle ("battlin' stick") if the woman has no washboard, which is very often the case. **1925** Furman *Glass Window* 20 What a notion you tuck to have one, when you got the very finest battling-log and wash-trough in the country. **1961** Medford *History Haywood Co* 93 The thick beatlin' block (some called it battlin' block) was made of a heavy puncheon-like slab or split log smoothed off, which stood up on peg-legs nearly waist high. Or it was, sometimes, just a big log-cut, sawed off some 30 inches long, and stood up on one end. Here the boiled clothes were brought from the kettle to go through the beating process—with a hardwood stick or heavy paddle, some three inches wide. Wham-wham-wham! the battlin' stick rang out. [**1971** *AOHP/ALC-260* We had a big trough that was hewed out and [a] hole bored on the bottom of it, and a peg went up in there just to stop that water from running out, and on the end of it was flat, and she'd dip them clothes down in that water in that trough and lay them up there, and I took a battling stick and battled them . . . the trough had four legs to it, bored a hole in the bottom there and put four legs up like that to the floors, so hit'd be up.] **1974** Fink *Bits Mt Speech* 2 *battling block* = a smooth wooden block on which clothes are beaten with a battling stick while being washed. **a1975** Lunsford *It Used to Be* 45 They used what they called a "battling stick" and a "battling bench." They had a big, wooden log, trimmed off on top very smoothly, with holes in the bottom where they put the legs like a table. It had to be a firm table, of course, so that's the reason they used the log. **1982** Slone *How We Talked* 18 A battlin' board [was] a long, shallow, hollowed half of a split log, used to wash clothes. One end was left flat, a place to lay soaked clothes one at a time to beat out the dirt with a "battlin' stick." The hollow end was to hold the water. **1986** Lauterer *Runnin' on Rims* 204 We had what we called a paddling bench with a paddle and when we washed 'em a little, we put 'em on that bench and paddle[d] 'em and that helped to get the dirt out. Then we'd put 'em in a pot and boil 'em.

[DARE *battling block* n chiefly South Midland]

battling block, battling board, battling log See **battling bench.**

battling stick See **battle A.**

batty cake See **batter cake.**

bawbee *noun* Any item of little value.

1866 Smith *So Called* 115 I don't care a bobee about his being free, if I can subjugate him.

[from Scots *bawbee* half-penny]

bawdacious See **bodacious.**

bawl

A *verb*

1 Of an animal: to cry out loudly, as in alarm or distress; of a calf: to cry for its mother.

1926 Hunnicutt *Twenty Years* 183 We had not gone far until I heard the bear bawl. **1934–47** LAMSAS (Madison Co NC, Swain Co NC) = of a calf. **1939** Hall *Coll* (Hartford TN) That bear [after being stabbed with a knife] shrunk down and bawled, he said, like a calf. **1956** Hall *Coll* (Jones Cove TN) Then he heared a cub bear go to bawlin'. Then he saw the old she bear come runnin' out of the laurel. **1963** Hooper *Unwanted Boy* 227 A calf must be weaned in the dark of the moon. If you'll wean a calf when the sign is low, I'll guarantee it will bawl mighty few bawls. **1978** Montgomery *White Pine Coll* Dad never would wean a calf when the sign was in the head. He said it'd bawl itself to death. . . . He never did have calves to bawl. **1986** Pederson et al. *LAGS*: (of a calf) = attested by 39/60 interviewees (65%) from E TN and 15/35 (42.9%) from N GA; 54/210 of all LAGS interviewees (25.7%) attesting term were from Appalachia. **1999** Morgan *Gap Creek* 218 The cow bawled inside her stall and something banged against the barn like a log or floating outhouse.

[DARE *bawl* v 2 widespread, but chiefly Midland, West]

2 (also *bawl out*) Of a hunting dog: to yelp or howl when a trail of prey becomes hot; hence noun *bawler* a dog who barks in this way. Same as **bugle.** See also **bawl mouth.**

1926 Hunnicutt *Twenty Years* 23 Old Trail bawled again and then one of Ed Hyatt's dogs opened up his voice. *Ibid.* 47 Old Muse had gone on ahead and by the time we got in hearing of Little Cove, I heard Old Muse "ball [sic] out" very shrilly. **1989** Dorgan *Regular Baptists* 97 The quality and characteristics of this baying might be the very factor making a dog especially attractive to its owner. I listened with some initial confusion, and then with some amusement, to one elderly gentleman who asserted quite vehemently—at least three times—that he didn't want any "bawler on a tree." Any good coon hound, he asserted, should "bawl" on the trail but "chop" on the tree. He reserved particular disdain for any hound of such poor breeding that it would reverse these responses.

B *noun* The cry of an animal, especially a calf.

1963 Hooper *Unwanted Boy* 227 If you'll wean a calf when the sign is low [in the body], I'll guarantee it will bawl mighty few bawls. **1966–67** *DARE Survey* (Cherokee NC, Maryville TN) = noise made by a calf that's taken away from its mother. **1986** Pederson et al. *LAGS* (Blount Co TN, Cocke Co TN, Jefferson Co TN, Sevier Co TN). **2009** Prewitt *Coon Hounds* 273 Coon hunters often describe the sound of their trailing dogs as a "bugle" or a "bawl."

bawl baby *noun* A cry baby.

1943 Justus *Bluebird* 55 No use to be a bawl baby about bad luck. **1973** Kahn *Hillbilly Women* 69 She's a bawl baby and I ain't gonna work on her. **1997** Montgomery *Coll* Don't be such a bawl baby [= used especially among children] (Ellis).

bawler See **bawl A2.**

bawl mouth (also *bawl-mouthed dog*) *noun* See citation. See also **bawl A2.**

2007 Plott *Story Plott Hound* 179 = a term used to describe a hound's bark. The bawl mouth barks with a long, drawn-out voice, usually deep, or bass, in texture. Plott hounds typically bawl on cold tracks and chop as the trail warms up. A bawl mouth is appreciated by many pleasure hunters for its value and is generally regarded by hunters to be the most beautiful of all hound voices. It is important to note, however, that while Plott dogs bark both ways, most hounds tend to be classified as one or the other—a chop-mouthed or bawl-mouthed dog. And some hunters or owners value one more than the other based on personal preference.

bawl-mouthed dog See **bawl mouth.**

bawl out See **bawl A2.**

bay *verb* Of a hunting dog: to keep (an animal) treed or cornered by fierce barking, usually with a deep, throaty howl. See also **bay dog.**

1949 Hall *Coll* (Del Rio TN) Bay, that's when [the dogs] get him [= a pursued animal] cornered. He hasn't got a chance to get away or get up a tree. They just keep him bayed on the ground. **1953** Hall *Coll* (Plott Creek NC) The other pack of dogs had brought [a bear] out, run him out and bayed him on top of what's known as the Locust Knob, and he was a very large bear and had a real fight.

bay dog *noun* See citation.

2007 Plott *Story Plott Hound* 180 = term used in bear hunting to describe the dogs that bay or contain the bear while treed or on the ground. The bay dog is generally more aggressive and not as good a tracker or as cold-nosed as the strike dog.

bay horse sense (also *bay hoss sense*) *noun* Common sense. See also **horse sense.**

1910 Essary *TN Mtneers* 11 Happy's early education, like that of many of his fellows, had been sadly neglected, and still he was endowed with a reasonable amount of "bay horse sense" and native wit common in the hill country. **1955** Dykeman *French Broad* 235 What sense I have is common, mountain, bay-horse sense, and I'm proud of that too. **1967** Hall *Coll* (Del Rio TN) He had good common bay hoss sense. **1967** Hall *Coll* (Del Rio TN) He had common bay hoss sense.

bay sop *noun* Same as **red-eye gravy.**

1994–95 Montgomery *Coll* (known to Cardwell, Shields).

be *verb* See also **ain't**, **hain't**, and Grammar and Syntax §5.

A *be*.

1 In a main clause or nominal subordinate clause.

a Used as a finite verb in a declarative context, regardless of the number or person of the subject. [Editor's note: Although sometimes found in fiction set in the southern mountains, this form in finite clauses had become at best old-fashioned and rare in 20th-century speech. It was unknown to most of Joseph Hall's consultants from the Smoky Mountains and not observed by him in the 1930s or later. It does not occur in ATASC, nor is there evidence that it expresses habitual or other verbal aspect, as in some other varieties of English.] **1883** Zeigler and Grosscup *Heart of Alleghanies* 298 Thar be a power o'hants hyar. **1887** (in **1985** *Walker Bible Record* 61) The Locusts be here this year, it being the year of our Lord 1885. Their last apearence here before this was the year of our Lord 1868 makeing a Period of 17 years between. **1916** Combs *Old Early English* 292 *Be* is used . . . also after verbs of thinking, as in "I *think* you *be* right." These uses of *be* are rare, however. **1931** Goodrich *Mt Homespun* 67 "You-all ain't as used to it as I be," she continued, after a pause filled with constant dipping. **1936** Justus *Honey Jane* 19 I've dosed him up many and many be the time for fust one thing and then another. **c1950** Matthews *Smokey Hills* 31 Many *be* the time this story has been told by the fireside and it has become legendary, even though there is no possibility that it is true. **1957** Combs *Lg Sthn High: Word List* 8 = is, are . . . Use of the infinitive for an inflected form is not common, except in pseudo-dialect stories of the Highlanders. **1962** Dykeman *Tall Woman* 145 There be those that fall like an oak. *Ibid.* You be a sight for sore eyes. **1973** GSMNP-5:6 Many be the time. **1973** GSMNP-76 Now them [= shoes] be all right to ride in, but you'll find out they ain't good to hike in. **1976** Carter *Little Tree* 46 Mind ye've little to meet it [= the future] with . . . but the mountains'll not change on ye, and ye kin them; and we be honest men with our feelings. **1996–97** Montgomery *Coll* He be sick, I be too old for such tomfoolery (Oliver). **1996** Woodring *Times Gone By* 10 I heered Dave Maines's wife a telling over there at the Agby cemetery when Clarence be hung [that] they put him back in jail.

[OED2 "*Be* continued in concurrent use [with *am*, *are*, *is*] till the end of the [16th] century (see Shakespeare, and Bible of 1611) and still occurs as a poetic archaism, as well as in certain traditional expressions and familiar quotations of 16th century origin as 'the powers that be'. . . . Southern and eastern dialect speech [in Britain] retains *be* both in singular and plural"; DARE *be* v B1a chiefly Northeast, South]

b As a finite verb *beant* or *ben't* in negative clauses. [Editor's note: Although once occasionally found in fiction set in the mountains, this usage is not found in ATASC.]

1892 Dromgoole *Dan to Beersheba* 83 Father, I say! Ben't ye goin' ter the still ternight? **c1900** (in **1997** Stoddart *Quare Women* 80) Beant you the women that passed through the mountains last Summer and gave out purty picture books? **1921** Campbell *Sthn Highlander* 127 "Then you ben't married," said the weary mountain mother of many children to [an unmarried] teacher from a distant church school, "and you don't look like you minded it nuther."

c As a nonfinite verb, especially in an imperative clause. [Editor's note: This usage does not occur in ATASC.]

1939 Hall *Coll* Don't be a-tellin' me that! . . . Don't be a-kickin' my locker around. **c1950** (in **2000** Oakley *Roamin' Man* 58) Dont be biting a nacked fish hook that a dum fish wont. **1963** Weals *Old-timers* Don't be losing any more fingers. **1967** Williams *Subtlety Mt Speech* 14 Don't ye be a-openin' that thar poke whilest I'm gone. **1973** GSMNP-74:34 Don't be a-takin' it down till I tell you a little. **1983** Pyle *CCC 50th Anniv* B:2:13 When you go to Deep Creek . . . you don't quite be over at the ranger station. **1995** Adams *Come Go Home* 19 Don't be callin' this no account, poor excuse for a beast of labor Little Pete. **1996** Montgomery *Coll* Don't be wearing your good clothes out to play in (Ellis).

d In an non-negative interrogative clause. [Editor's note: This usage does not occur in ATASC.]

1883 Zeigler and Grosscup *Heart of Alleghanies* 146 Who be you uns? **c1900** (in **1997** Stoddart *Quare Women* 63–64) One charm of the people is their lack of self-consciousness. . . . They are very frank and the first questions they asked us were "How old be ye?" "Be ye married?" **1916** Combs *Old Early English* 292 *Be* is used in questions, as "Where *be* the horses?" . . . These uses of *be* are rare, however. **1939** Walker *Mtneer Looks* 10 Be ye whut they call the Mormons? **1941** Still *Troublesome Creek* 38 Be them boys amongst the Crownovers? I'm a-mind to play with one. **1957** Combs *Lg Sthn High: Word List* 8 = is, are. Ex.: "Be ye the stranger that rode by yistiddy?" **c1960** Wilson *Coll* "Be you going?" Said by a few elderly folks. **1962** Dykeman *Tall Woman* 63 Be you holding in your mind what I think is there? **1970** Mull *Mt Yarns* 13 "How be ye?"—How are you? **1986** Pederson et al. *LAGS* (Sullivan Co TN) *how be you?* = expression used by grandmother. **1997** Montgomery *Coll* Be you one of the Joneses? (Jones).

2 In a subordinate clause following *if*, *till*, *unless*, *until*, or *whether*.

1792 *Richland Church Minutes* 144 therefore We Do not Except Sd Commetees Advice Respecting McGees excommunication till their alegations be proven. **1861** *Huntley CW Letters* (Dec 29) I want you to Right soon and tell all my friends if Their Be any to Right. **1862** Tesh *CW Letters* (Oct 13) their haint no chance to get a Furlow now unless a man be sick. **1863** *Walker CW Letters* (Aug 20) wheather it be so or not I am not abel to Say. **1913** Kephart *Our Sthn High* 297 I'll name it to Newt, if so be he's thar. **1931–34** Oliver *Sketches* 36 He would fill up a gum with twists and set it under his log prise and let it down on his tobacco, and then put a sled load of rocks on his beam and leave it until it be so hard when it would come out it would never get dry and crumley. **a1975** Lunsford *It Used to Be* 27 If it be barn cured tobacco, you have a different thing. **1978** Montgomery *White Pine Coll* I-3 We could get some industry in here to initially support jobs, whether it be just providing materials so that you wouldn't have to ship cargo from way off. **1989**

Matewan OHP-28 We've not as much as heard whether there be a Holy Ghost or not.

3 Preceding infinitive.

1937 Campbell *KY Mt Community* 535 This old un was plenty good 'nough but Sally would be to have a stove what was purty and would git hotted up more quicker. **1941** Still *Troublesome Creek* 39 I be not to play with water-heads. **c1950** Adams *Grandpap* 49 If you will be to go, wrap up a chunk of fire an' pull the door after you.

B *am* used in a perfective verb phrase (= *have*). See also **be D3**, **E6**.

1865 *Love CW Letters* (Feb 9) I am not got Stout yet but I think I will soon be all rite again. **1895** Dromgoole *Humble Advocate* 323 Am I got ter wait all day fur a mouffull o' cole victuals? **1936** (in **2009** Powell *Shenandoah Letters* 72) I am got fether [= farther] to walk than any of them that ar working on the Same jobe. **1969** Hannum *Look Back* 98 I'm about decided to raise fightin' cocks instead of botherin' with another woman. **1996** Isbell *Last Chivaree* 116 Mama'[d] say "Ray, you ought to clean up some," and [he'd] say, "No, I'm quit, I'm give up."

C *is*.

1 Used to indicate agreement with a third-person-plural subject, except if that subject is a single adjacent personal pronoun. See also **be C2**, **have A1**, **-s³ 1**. See also Grammar and Syntax §4.1.

1774 *Dunmore's War* 136 Please give me instructions how the Forts is to be provided with Provisions. **1798** *French Broad Church Minutes* 44 John brigs and his wife is living in disorder. **1804** *Globe Creek Church Minutes* 19 he aught to be caushened—agin takeing heed to all words that is spoken. **1815** (in **1920** DeWitt *Sevier Journal* 58) (June 29) It is said that the goods is since ordered to be given over to Genl. Jackson for to be distributed as presents. **1841** *Elijoy Church Minutes* 43 The church passed an act against all kinds of plays that is against the word of God. **1842** *McLean Diary* (Dec 31) Times is hard and more scarce. **1859** Taliaferro *Fisher's River* 95 You see, Miss Yeasley, folks is gittin' too smart—too big fur thar britches. **1860** *Elijoy Church Minutes* 101 the Church concluded . . . that his tales is conflicting. **1860** *Love CW Letters* (Oct 2) I take my pen in hand to let you know I and all is well. **1861** (in **1992** Heller and Heller *Confederacy* 31) we have bi[s]cets that is so hard i could nock a bull down with one. **1862** (in **1999** Davis *CW Letters* 78) we allwill get back home when the Yankees is whipt back. **1888** *Greene Letters* 152 let us know [how] you & children is getting along. **1913** Kephart *Our Sthn High* 102 Bears is almost human, anyhow. **1939** Hall *Coll* (Gatlinburg TN) I have now different kind of stories to tell. I have some true and some is not true. *Ibid.* (Smokemont NC) Our lands is turned over to the Smoky Mountain National Park. **1956** Hall *Coll* (Bryson City NC) Sometimes we'd get ahold of other breeds of dogs, but mostly used for bear dogs is what we call Plott hound. **1970** *Burton-Manning Coll-94A* They have new songs, and they're right pretty, some of them is, but I still hold to the old songs. **1973** *AOHP/ALC-505* Is any of them still living? **1975** *GSMNP-62:4* Squirrels is the best, though, eating of any of them. **1979** Carpenter *Walton War* 163 Them gals is purty, but they're crazy as Junebugs. **1983** Pyle *CCC 50th Anniv* B:2:15 I know a lot that has gone on, and lots that is a-livin' yet. **1986** (in **2000** Puckett *Seldom Ask* 29) Is these Sheryl's keys? **1998** *Dante OHP-25* Some of them boarding houses is still standing over there at Kaiser. **2008** *Rosie Hicks* 6 mullein leaves is good for colds.

[DARE *be* v B3b chiefly South, South Midland]

2 Used to indicate agreement with a personal pronoun subject that is in the first or second person or in the third-person plural and that is not adjacent to its verb. See also **be C1**, **have A2**, **-s³ 2**.

1793 (in **1919** DeWitt *Sevier Journal* 16) (Oct 19) You will make War, & then is afraid to fight. **1808** Huskey *Rogers Papers* 21 I recived a letter from you Directed to my brother Robert Crockett and my self and is surprised to hear there is like to be a dispute about your land. **1861** (in **1980** Clark *Civil War Diary* 26) We are campt on the right of the road in the timber Sept 1st marched to Pikeville and rested 4 hours and is now reddy to start across the mountain. **1861** (in **1992** Heller and Heller *Confederacy* 39) I myself is in good health at this time. **1861** *Huntley CW Letters* (Nov 22) they [= the tents] Will not leak One drop and is vary Warm. **1863** *Chapman CW Letters* (Aug 12) There is agreat force in Kentucky They it seems is moving towards Tennessee. **1885** *Bayless Letters* 117 I have been sick for several days but is able to write to you (this) day and to inform you that winter hasn't broken up here yet.

3 Used with *I* as the subject, usually contracted to *I's*.

1867 Harris *Sut Lovingood* 126–27 I'se sorter fear'd tu try tu tell yu, George, the devilment that cussed infunel fool cow beaste wer a-doin. **1942** Hall *Phonetics Smoky Mts* 86. **1956** Hall *Coll* (Hurricane Creek NC) I's a-diggin' seng right now. **1994** Schmidt and Hooks *Whistle* 66 Goddam ya', if ya' don't quit comin' through here like y'er beatin' hell out of a tanbark tree, and killin' my chickens, I's gonna kill ya'!

4 Used with *we*, *you*, or *they* as the immediately adjacent subject.

1858 (in **1974** Harris *High Times* 128) They's fools about papermills only, for here they goes on a trot, like piss-ants afore a rain. **1860** *Zion Church Minutes* 48 Whar as Sister Annie Laws and Sister Susannah Dayton joined another church not of our own faith and order therefore we say thes [i.e. they is] no mour of us. **1862** *Parris CW Letters* (July 3) the[y] is laying in piles and not bered a tall. **1864** *Blair CW Letters* (April 27) they is goin home. **1939** Hall *Coll* (Proctor NC) [Bears] generally cross over the highest knob they is in reach of. They don't go through a gap like deer. **1971** *AOHP/ALC-33* They wasn't thick settled like they is now. **1973** *GSMNP-88* The old man Nathie Sparks lived just across the road on the other side of the road from right where we is at now. **1979** *Big South Fork OHP-11* If you is through, I'll go see if I can find them pictures. **1983** Page and Wigginton *Aunt Arie* 33 It's a wonder they ain't been killed if they is still as mean as they was. **2009** Burton *Beech Mt Man* 112 I'll hang around 'em to see if they is that mean.

D *are*.

1 Variant form *air* [æɚ].

1813 Hartsell *Memora* 120 these Remarks . . . air Just and trew as Can be ascertained by me. **1862** *Lockmiller CW Letters* (Aug 14) they say that they air going to offer [bounty money] too us. **1864** *Chapman CW Letters* (May 29) next weak we air going to work over our little truck patches. **1890** Fruit *KY Words* 67 *are* = pronounced like *air* by a few who have not forgotten their "old field school" training of thirty years ago. **1891** Brown *Dialect in TN* 172 We hear also . . . *air* for *are*. **1910** Cooke *Power and Glory* 7 Air ye afeared to go over as far as my house right now? **1937** Hall *Coll* (Cades Cove TN) How air ye? **c1940** Simms *Coll* These Smokies air here to stay. **1942** Hall *Phonetics Smoky Mts* 30 Many speakers (including, it is said, a number of younger people) still pronounce *are* as [æə˞]. **1957** Combs *Lg Sthn High: Word List* 3 *air*. **c1960** Wilson *Coll* [ær] = very old people. **1963** Edwards *Gravel* 13 "You ain't married yet, air you, Giles?" said Uncle Emmett.

[DARE *be* v A1 (pronunciation *air*) formerly widespread, now chiefly South, South Midland]

2 Used with a singular subject, especially in a clause beginning with *there* or *they*.

1790 *Lenoir Papers* I have got over the Grammar once and are now a Reviseing it. **1863** (in **1992** Heller and Heller *Confederacy* 110) I embrace the opport. of wrighting you a few lines that will in form you that i am not in good health But ar able to stay with my command. **1864** *Reese CW Letters* (July 9) tell Rebecky that I still air trying to surv my god. **1864** Wilson *Confederate Private* 49 (May 16) I donte now when I will get to valey for thay are sow much horse steling go on round her. **1865** (in **1983** *CW Harlan Co* 26) The Sheriff are unable to serve process or arrest the Gurillas and cannot in a greater portion of the county collect the State Revenue. **1892** Doak *Wagonauts Abroad* 144 "Stranger, is this Cosby?" "I recken hit ar," replied the woodchopper, cutting us off with a surly tone, without looking up. **1895** Dromgoole *Fiddling to Fame* 46 The boy air comin' ter no good. **1916** Combs *Old Early English* 285 I aren't called to preach a sarmon. **1936** (in **2009** Powell *Shenandoah Letters* 74) They are a press built in the house. **c1940** Simms *Coll* Hit 'pears water air allus a-tryin' to be level; Hit shore air hard to have a doctor tell a man that his woman will never be any good to him agin on this earth. **1953** Hall *Coll* (Deep Creek NC) I catched a lot of coons. Maybe stay out a week and catch eight or ten. I like coon better than any wild meat they are. **1954** Roberts *Bought a Dog* There are enough wood in that tree to last a whole year. **1970** Mull *Mt Yarns* 12 He air a good boy. **1972** *AOHP/ALC-342* [The farmer]'s the lowest class man they are, and he's the least took care of of every man they are, and he's the backbone. **1973** *GSMNP-88* I think this is one of the beauty spots there are in Cades Cove. **1974** Dabney *Mt Spirits* 126 [Speaker A:] Is steamer whiskey superior to copper pot double and twisted whiskey?: [Speaker B:] Shore is, It's the best they are. **1974** Roberts *Sang Branch* 215 They are a big jug of rum under the floor. **1977** Shackelford et al. *Our Appalachia* 269 If it hadn't been for the union, we'd just have been slaves right on; that's all there are to it. **1978** Montgomery *White Pine Coll* III-1 There are a big waste in it, you know. There are a great influx of people into the teaching profession, but they're not staying. **1994** Montgomery *File* They are another one down the street (30-year-old man, Gatlinburg TN). **1998** *Dante OHP-71* He would go in and ask the family "are they something the union can do for you?" **2007** McMillon *Notes* Go get some milk if they are any.

[DARE *be* v B 4a chiefly South Midland]

3 Used in a perfective verb phrase (= *have*). See also **be B**.

1863 *Love CW Letters* (Aug 18) thear was seveuerel mor sevier caces tho tha[y] aire all got well a gaine. **1919** Combs *Word-List South* 36 = have. The hillsmen of eastern Tennessee sometimes twit the hillsmen of northern Georgia, crediting them with the word: "You-uns ain't got ary auger, *air ye*?" **1941** Still *Troublesome Creek* 97 Air you been dranking John Corn?

4 Omitted after a plural personal pronoun.

1974 *AOHP/ASU-204* They too many people that can. **1978** Reese *Speech NE Tenn* 196 I said "you the fool asking me such a question." **1991** Thomas *Sthn Appal* 171 Th' ship's crew don't know whur we goin', they's sump'n up . . . I said, "Whur in th' world we goin'?" **2001** House *Clay's Quilt* 18 They way better than a full one. *Ibid.* 156 You my brother, but I'll shoot you if I have to.

E *was*.

1 Variant contracted forms in the negative: *wadn't, want, wan't, wa'nt, wa'n't, wont, wor'n't, wouldn't, wudden, wudent, wudn't, wutn't*. For *warn't*, see **be F1**.

1864 *Watkins CW Letters* (July 2) I rec[ei]ved a letter last thur but it want mine. **1864** Wilson *Confederate Private* 61 (July 28) wheat crop was very good hur but they wont eny corn rased hur a tol. **1886** Smith *Sthn Dialect* 348 He had hyeard ther might be a war 'twixt the Republicans and Dimercrats, but, as he hadn't hyeard any mo' about it, he reckined ther wan't gwine ter be none. **1890** Fruit *KY Words* 69 He said he wa'n't goin' to do it. **1910** Essary *TN Mtneers* 18 He's done been tried and sent to the pen for twenty years, and it was jest, too, wor'n't it, boys? **1913** Kephart *Our Sthn High* 101 He wa'n't hurt a bit. **1926** Montague *Big Music* 424 Aw no, Tony, that wan't me. You know what it was. **1935** Sheppard *Cabins in Laurel* 303 But, aye jallus, it wa'nt no time till out come some more and pretty quick they was all walking too. **c1950** Adams *Grandpap* 23 It wudden long till he was good an' dry. **1962** Williams *Verbs Mt Speech* 17 *Wasn't* often becomes *wudn't*. **1969** Roberts *Greasybeard* 95 Her stepmother and stepsister come in just a-talking and carrying on, "Oh, wouldn't she something now, and dancing with the King's Son." **1973** Joines *Twister Tales* 7 That cat run forty foot in the air before he even noticed that pole wadn't there. **1974** Dabney *Mt Spirits* Back in my day, they wan't any government likker. **1989** *Matewan OHP-86* I really wouldn't worried about it . . . really wouldn't worried, because something had to be done. **1991** Thomas *Sthn Appal* 24 They wudent enny saw-mills around, much. **2001** House *Clay's Quilt* 166 I wouldn't here when he come them times, though, I knowed we shouldn't have come here. **2005** Williams *Gratitude* 22 Dad was an intelligent man who could do almost any kind of work and was a hard worker, but they wutn't no studdy (steady) work to be found. **2009** Burton *Beech Mt Man* 65 He wadn't the kind of man that would hurt you—all he was, was a drunk.

2 Used with a plural noun or pronoun subject.

c1788 (in **1989** Fink *Jonesborough* 41) One of the strangers said that all ware at the taking of Sevier was Damd Scoundrels or words to that purpose and that Sevier was the preservation of the country. **1799** *Globe Creek Church Minutes* 6 then the several Letters was read & fild & the different Churches & delegates Names was enrolled. **1815** (in **1920** DeWitt *Sevier Journal* 59) (June 18) When the Cherokees was called on in behalf of Blackburn to make compensation for the Robbery, they excused themselves by saying the

Creeks was the owners of the land & could do as they pleased in their own country. **1820** (in **2003** *TN Petitions I* 117) The above named Claments Was in the Actual possession and occupency of Said Several Claims on the 6th day of February 1796. **1840** *Zion Church Minutes* 22 [The Church Conference] opened the door for the reception of members and Barbery Bennett, Anna Ayers and Moses Ayers all came forward and offered by experience and was received. **1862** *Griffin CW Letters* (July 31) they was not secessioners for they was for the younion. **1862** *Love CW Letters* (July 21) the 1 of july is the time we was in the Big fight and I hav not got time to tell you A Bout hit. **1866** *Elijoy Church Minutes* 110 the meeting lasted 16 days & nights during which time there was 27 baptised & there was 48 Joined the church. **1910** Cooke *Power and Glory* 227 they might have passed here while we was standin' back there talkin' to Roxy. **1939** Hall Coll (Cataloochee NC) We went over and put us up a still, and we was a-making some awful good [liquor]. It was so good you could taste the gal's feet in it that hoed the corn it was made out of. *Ibid.* (Little Cataloochee NC) They was ignorant, raised up in ignorance, no Sunday school, no church, nor nothing, nor no one to lead them on right in the right way. **1953** Hall Coll (Bryson City NC) Next morning the boys was to play a trick on them before they got up. **1969** GSMNP-44:12 They come from Ireland. They was Scot Irish. **1972** *AOHP/ALC-413* You were born in the year nineteen hundred, wasn't you? **1979** *Big South Fork OHP-5* We was hauling logs out through Mason over there before we was married. **1989** *Matewan OHP-001* We was lucky to have those. **1998** *Dante OHP-45* I'd leave many of a time [when] the stars was a-shining. **2008** *Rosie Hicks* 4 They say they was ghosts down there in the basement.

[DARE *be* v B 5b chiefly Midland, South]

3 Contracted to *'s*; hence *I's*, *they's*, etc.

1925 Dargan *Highland Annals* 94 We's well up Smoky, an' the coldest wind ablowin' that ever made an i-shickle out of a man's gizzard. **1938** Bowman *High Horizons* 48 My paw tuck land 'round old Blanket Mountain yander when I'se jist a little shaver, back atter the Civil War, an' we've been rooted as the trees ever since. **1939** Hall Coll (Cataloochee NC) I's up above the den, and he says, "come here, Steve." *Ibid.* (Maggie Valley NC) I knowed I's a new duck. **1941** Stuart *Men of Mts* 99 Ma would take the top of the house off if she's to see you come in at this gate! *Ibid.* 231 I looked every minute to see fire flash from a gun when we's getting them bees. **1961** *Coe Ridge OHP-333A* We's down there a few days ago. *Ibid.* He was killed before I's born. **1973** *AOHP/ASU-160* They was no hospital then for the babies to be born in. They's born at home. **1979** *Big South Fork OHP-10* They [= the schools] took a few weeks off when you's a-helping the folks gather their stuff. **1983** *Dark Corner OHP 9A* That was three years that's awful hard on me when I was about, when I was ten, eleven, and twelve years old. *Ibid.* 343A When I's a girl and lived on Marrowbone, we'd go to Glasgow, and [if] it come a rain you's just out of the luck. **1985** Irwin *Alex Stewart* 58 I'd be voting against him yet if he's a living. **1989** *Matewan OHP-33* He'd grab that laundry and you's hollering, "Wait a minute, wait a minute." **1997** *Dante OHP-14* I've went to church ever since I's a baby. **2008** *Rosie Hicks* 1 When I come up, I think they's almost dead then.

[DARE *be* v B 5a especially Midland, South]

4 In an inverted construction expressing a condition.

1941 Still *Troublesome Creek* 75 She'd skulp me, was I to trade. *Ibid.* 76 Was a feller to eat wild fruit, a dram o' that tonic would cuore the pizen.

5 As a negative to introduce a verbal complement, with inversion of the subject.

1930 Armstrong *This Day and Time* 211 Wasn't neither one of 'em worth the ammunition hit took to kill 'em. **1971** *Kenny Runnion* 130 [They] had to walk it, an' wadn't nobody goin' t'do that. **1983** *Dark Corner OHP-13A* After my husband died, why wasn't anybody here to tend [the land], so I just let it grow up. **1991** Thomas *Sthn Appal* 247 Course, wasn't ennything wrong with his wife.

6 As an auxiliary verb in a transitive construction. See also **be B, D3**.

2008 Salsi *Ray Hicks* 70 Bessie was finished her schoolin', Lewis was in year seven, Mae was ten.

F *were.*

1 Variant forms *wair*, *war*, *ware*, *warn't* (with either a singular or a plural subject).

1792 *Big Pigeon Church Minutes* 10 they both being present Made satesfation to the Church and ware receivd into fellowship. **1813** Hartsell *Memora* 104 the[y] war Creeks, and when the[y] Came I went to See them, and they wair Stout high men and Straight bilt men. **1842** Carpenter *Diary I* 148 Frank Davis ag 72 dide [= died] july 29 1842 ware fin man but mad sum brandy that warnt no good. **1849** Lanman *Alleghany Mts* 89 At this time they were draining the pond, and it warn't so very large. **1863** *Vance Papers* (March 31) while I war at home the Company wear exChanged to go to the Strawbury plains to thomases legon. **1867** Harris *Sut Lovingood* 23 He allers were a mos' complikated durned ole fool, and mam sed so when he warnt about. **1883** Zeigler and Grosscup *Heart of Alleghanies* 60 I heered the dogs a-comin' an knowed without axin' thet the bar war afore 'em. **1913** Kephart *Our Sthn High* 284 There are many corrupt forms of the verb, such as . . . war (was or were—the *a* as in far). **1940** Bowman *KY Mt Stories* 240 *hit war* = it was. **1941** Stuart *Men of Mts* 266 Warn't no standin' back and shirkin' when Lefty took holt o' a thing. **1956** Hall Coll (Gatlinburg TN) Quite a few rhododendron bushes had grown along the trail, and they'd just chopped these off and the snags war a-sticking up. **1970** *Foxfire Interviews* A-70-5 We never missed a day to where we warn't popping popcorn. **1981** Henry *Alex Stewart* 49 I seed it warn't a fire-coal.

[DARE *be* v B6 chiefly South Midland]

2 Contracted to *'re*.

2008 *Rosie Hicks* 1 We just kindly, you know, stayed where we're living.

3 With a singular subject in both affirmative and negative constructions.

1792 *Big Pigeon Church Minutes* 10 At a calld Meeting by a request of some of the Breathren Br.o Samuel Mathes Came before the Church and gave satesfaction for his transgration and ware receivd into union Again. **1861** *Kendrick CW Letters* (Dec 21) he stated that ther wer a talk of them having to go to kentucky. **1862** *Bradshaw CW Letters* (Oct 28) you dont now how glad I wer to hear from you and to hear that John had got home. **1862** (in **1999** Davis *CW Letters* 83) I were highly grattifide to hear you were all as well as common. **1875** Reid *Land of Sky* 80 "We brought [the body of Professor Elisha Mitchell] in a sheet slung to the top of stout poles. . . . Then it were carried down to Asheville, and then brought up again and buried there"—he nods to the peak [i.e. Mount Mitchell] above us. **1922** *TN CW Ques* 378 (Hancock Co TN) I lost my arm in a skirmish in Resaca Ga. And were in the hospitale one year and was not able to help myself for nine months time. **1924** (in **1952** Mathes *Tall Tales* 18) I were on one side of the water an' he were on the other. **1937** Hall *Coll* (Cades Cove TN) Dad gone it, there weren't even a sprig of fire in his place! The fire were plumb out. *Ibid.* (Cosby TN) He weren't no hunter nuther. **1939** Hall *Coll* Back when I were just a young man. . . . The moon were shining bright. . . . Hit were loaded, I'll be a son of a bitch! **1954** Roberts *Bought a Dog* They weren't no way for me to ex-cape out through it. **1957** Broaddus *Vocab Estill Co KY* 84 *were* = used in third person singular. **1972** *AOHP/LJC*-205 She were a Combs, and then old man Lish Clay, he was a Clay. **1976** Lindsay *Grassy Balds* 115 There weren't no money, much. **1978** Reese *Speech NE Tenn* 46 She were a mean, sweet thing. **1983** Pyle *CCC 50th Anniv* A:2:25 I'd never been given the job to do it myself, you see, because I were really too young. **1997** *GSMNPCOHP*-4:19 There were one in the upper end of the cove up towards where the picnic area is at. **2009** Burton *Beech Mt Man* 61 They weren't nary a grave been dug in that graveyard.

[DARE *be* v B6 chiefly South, South Midland]

G *been* used elliptically. See citation.

1939 Hall *Coll* [Come in and eat somethin' with us.] No, I been [i.e., I've already eaten].

be- *prefix* See citation.

1964 Williams *Prep Mt Speech* 54 The prepositional prefix *be-* (pronounced bi) . . . in mountain speech . . . appears in quaint verbal constructions, little used outside the highlands today: *besmeared*, *begommed*, *bedamned*, *besprinkled*, *beknownst*, *bedeviled*, *bedogged*, *bedraggled*, *bediked* (over dressed), *bespecked* (by fleas), *befouled*, *begrudged*, etc.

bead

A *noun* See 1949, 1973 citations.

1917 Kephart *Word-List* 408 = in moonshine whiskey, iridescent bubbles that form when the liquor is shaken up. **1935** Sheppard *Cabins in Laurel* 190 The commonest test for quality is to shake the jar and watch the bead that forms. **1949** Maurer *Argot of Moonshiner* 8 = the little bubbles which form along the meniscus of liquor when shaken in a bottle. The proof and quality of the liquor are judged by experienced moonshiners with great accuracy. "This stuff holds a good bead." **1973** Wellman *Kingdom of Madison* 158 Their test for alcoholic content, used in modern times, was accomplished by pouring a small amount into a bottle or vial, tilting and shaking it, then watching for small bubbles to rise in a collar at the upper surface. They called this the "bead." Both distiller and customer judged strength and quality by appearance and persistence of the bead. **1974** Dabney *Mt Spirits* xix = the bubbles that form when you shake liquor. An experienced distiller can evaluate the proof of the liquor by the size and position of the bubbles on the surface and whether it is pure corn whiskey or a combination of corn and sugar.

B *verb* See citations.

1972 *Foxfire I* 333 We use what we call "mule feed" for malt, and we add beading oil to make it bead good. **1974** Maurer and Pearl *KY Moonshine* 113 = to form bubbles and hold them around the surface periphery, as liquor tends to do. "This don't bead so good." **1985** Irwin *Alex Stewart* 162 They'd get old car batteries and take the water out of them and put it in their liquor. That would make it bead. **1990** Merriman *Moonshine Rendezvous* 41 Four or five minutes later, he walked toward us holdin' a quart jar. "Give it a good shake and see if it don't bead like the queen's pearls."

bead bush *noun* A small, deciduous tree (*Hamamelis virginiana*) that is a variety of witch-hazel.

1954 Miller *Pigeon's Roost* (Dec 16) The small trees known locally in the Pigeon Roost section as "bead-bush" blooms in the late fall. It is said the tree is called "bead bush," and the presence of the seed pods which resemble beads in appearance gave it that name. The trees have a number of other names such as "wych-hazel" or witch-hazel, "snapping hazel," [and] more appropriate of them all, "winterbloom." The forked twigs of the "bead-bush" trees are sometimes used as divining rods in efforts to locate buried treasures and underground water. The dried green leaves of "bead-bush" are sold on the local herb market.

beading oil *noun* See citations.

1949 Maurer *Argot of Moonshiner* 8 = oil added to low-proof liquor to make the bead appear as if the liquor were 100 proof. This practice, a survival from prohibition days, is frowned upon by both moonshiners and bootleggers: "When the bootleggers get it, they'll slip a little beading oil in it and two parts water." **1955** Dykeman *French Broad* 244 One man tells about going to a house on a creek and finding the family all sitting around a great tin wash tub "proofing the whiskey." This meant they were mixing the first jar or two of the run, which would be exceedingly high proof, with the rest of the run which was progressively lesser proof, and then they were spiking the whole thing with their alcohol "beading oil." **1974** Dabney *Mt Spirits* xix = a cooking oil used by modern moonshiners to create a false bead on low-grade whiskey and give the impression that it has a high proof.

be a-doing *verb phrase* To be engaged in an activity merely for diversion.

1937 Hall *Coll* (Cades Cove TN) He said that just to be a-doin'. **1956** Hall *Coll* (Mt Sterling NC) They'd know no one was up there just blowing a fox horn in daytime just to be a-doing, or they'd know that no one was out a-shooting a shotgun just to be a-doing. **1956** McAtee *Some Dial NC* 25 *just to be a doin'* = to be idly employed or to kill time.

beadwood *noun* Witch hazel (*Hamamelis virginiana*), the bark of which is used in making a poultice, a medicinal tea, and a dye.

1937 Hall *Coll* (Catons Grove TN) [Homemade clothes were] colored with bark. Take bark [of one of several trees] and bile it: beadwood, chestnut, oak, hickory and walnut. *Ibid.* (Cosby TN) To cure blood poison, use catnip and beadwood bark biled together and made into a poultice for blood pizen. **1961** Miller *Pigeon's Roost* (Oct 12) It is reported that the most kind of the one herb that has been collected here for the Botanical market this season that is now closing appears to be the beadwood (witch hazel) leaves. **1966** *DARE Survey* (Linville NC) *beadwood tea* = a spring tonic. **1992** Bush *Dorie* 114 Just to be sure she was right, she gave me a cup of beadwood tea to drink. **1998** Montgomery *Coll* = the bark was used to make beadwood tea, which was used by women for nerves and the cramping, aching feeling present at childbirth (Bush). **1999** Isbell *Keepers* 5 Now witch-hazel leaf—beadwood we call it—they're buying that, and I can get it plenty . . . Ted dried leaves and sometimes its bark. Drug companies use it to produce liniments. **2003** *Appal Journal* 30.291 Then the witch hazel, now we was teached to call it beadwood. Its seed on it looked like a bead, kind of. And the beadwood bark, here's something now, with me. I had a fever blister on my lip some years ago . . . There was a beadwood bush up there. I'd never known no people in the mountains using it for nothing. It'll draw in your mouth. "I'm gonna chew me some of it." It cured that fever blister well in three days.

beal *verb* Of a sore, especially one of the ear: to fester, become infected, inflamed, or abscessed; hence noun *bealing* = an abscess or boil, especially one on the ear.

1824 (in **1956** Eliason *Tarheel Talk* 259) (Haywood Co NC) your . . . woman Easther has been verry bad with a bealing on her brest. **1886** Smith *Sthn Dialect* 349 They all have the authority of old or dialect English, or many of them belong to all parts of the South, if not elsewhere . . . bealing (a swelling). **1908** Smith *Reminiscences* 410 The baby was bad with a bealin' on its neck. **1924** Greer-Petrie *Angeline Gits Eyeful* 20 I wuz li'ble to ketch cold in my years and start 'em to beelin' (running). **1927** Woofter *Dialect from WV* 348 = a suppurating sore; the act of suppurating. "He has a bad bealing on his hand." "The place went to bealing this morning." **1967** *DARE Survey* (Gatlinburg TN) "His head's bealed" = he has pus come out of his ear; (Jonesborough TN, Richwood WV) *bealing* = a swelling under the skin, bigger than a pimple, that comes to a head. **1974** Fink *Bits Mt Speech* 2 *bealing* = a boil or abscess. "Mary had a *bealing* on her neck." **1984** Woods *WV Was Good* 221 = to become festered and break out with pus, especially a bealed ear of a child. **1986** Helton *Around Home* 377 = abscess or boil. **1994–95** Montgomery *Coll* = also swollen up, as after creeling one's ankle (Cardwell); I got a bealing under my arm (Shields). **2006** Cavender *Medical Term* 1022 Variant forms of *beal* refer to an infected sore ("My ear is bealed") or a boil ("I've got a bealin' on the back of my neck").

[probably ultimately a variant of *boil*; OED3 *beal* v obsolete or dialect; CUD v "of a sore: fester, become septic"; HT *beal* "suppurate"; DARE *beal* v chiefly Appalachians, PA, OH; *bealed* ppl adj chiefly Appalachians, wPA, OH; *bealing* n formerly more widespread, now chiefly Appalachians, OH]

bealing See **beal**.

bean bread (also *bean dumpling*, *Cherokee bean bread*) *noun* A coarse bread made from usually dried beans (especially pintos) crushed and mixed with cornmeal, originally made by the Cherokee. Also called **Indian bean bread**. See also **bean cake**.

1939 Hall *Coll* (Cataloochee NC) Lots of people made chestnut bread and bean bread. They mix dried beans and corn meal. **1951** Ulmer and Beck *Cherokee Cooklore* 44 To prepare meal to make Bean Bread one uses flour corn. This corn is skinned with wood ashes. . . . To make Bean Bread, boil dry beans in plain water until tender. Pour boiling beans and some of the soup into the cornmeal and stir until mixed. Have a pot of plain water on the fire boiling. If you want bean dumplings, just make mixture out in balls and cook in the pot of plain water, uncovered, until done. Eat these dumplings plain, with butter, meat grease (the Indian's favorite), wild game, hot or cold, as suits one's fancy. **1997** Montgomery *File*: *bean bread* = made from October beans, which are cooked first and then put in hot dough, wrapped, and cooked in hot water for approximately twenty minutes (80-year-old man, Cherokee NC). **2003** Duncan and Riggs *Cherokee Trails* 58 The unique Cherokee bean bread is formed from unbolted corn meal and cooked pinto beans, then wrapped in corn husks and boiled like a dumpling, resulting in a solid cake. **2006** Sauceman *Place Setting* 38–39 JoAnn Kolanaheskie makes bean dumplings the way her mother and grandmother did. She cooks up a mess of soup beans, kneads the beans into a paste with cornmeal, and drops the dumplings into a pot of boiling water. **2016** Netherland *Appal Cooking* 73 Occasionally, my mother would drop some dumplings into the bean broth [of soup beans] and we would eat bean dumplings. The beans were always seasoned with some cured pork meat, such as streaky lean, sidemeat, fatback or hog jowl, and occasionally some meaty ham hock.

bean-breaking *noun* See 1982 citation.

1982 Powers and Hannah *Cataloochee* 161 Once we were having a great time in a bean-breaking. Everyone was working hard and getting a large pile of those green beans ready for pickling. . . . Some of the girls would be stringing. . . . Others would be breaking the green beans into pieces about 3/4 inches in length. **2000** Puckett *Seldom Ask* 252 Women generally perform tasks alone or as independent activities done communally, such as quilting or bean breaking.

bean cake *noun* See citation. See also **bean bread**.

1989 *Matewan OHP-28* My mom, see, would fry what you call bean cakes. She'd cook beans and then she'd take the beans after we'd eat from them, and she'd mash them up and make bean cakes out of them.

bean dumpling See **bean bread**.

bean flip *noun* A homemade slingshot. Same as **flip 1**.

1997 Landry *Coll* I call it a bean flip. **1998** Montgomery *Coll* (known to Cardwell).

bean gravy *noun* See citation.

2018 *Blind Pig* (Aug 31) Mom made something we called "bean gravy" which was leftover pinto beans mashed and mixed with cornmeal.

bean hulling (also *bean shelling, bean shelling bee*) *noun* Formerly, a family or community work activity to shell such beans as **Octobers**, allowed to dry on the vine before picking.

1941 Justus *Kettle Creek* 19 They saw through Noah's scheme in having this bean shelling bee! **c1960** Wilson *Coll*: *bean hulling* = a community "working" or "bee" once common. **1971** *AOHP/ALC-4* In the fall of the year they would have bean stringings and bean hullings, and then after they got the work done, why, they would make candy and sometimes they'd dance and have a good time after they got their work done. **1979** *Big South Fork OHP* 37 My grandmother used to tell about them having log-rollings and corn shuckings and bean shellings and all like that, but we didn't [have them]. **1999** Montgomery *Coll*: *bean shelling* (Cardwell).

bean shelling, bean shelling bee See **bean hulling**.

bean stringing *noun* Formerly, a neighborhood or family work activity to remove the strings from beans in preparing them for pickling, canning, or most often, drying by threading or stringing and hanging them, as on the porch, in the rafters, near a fireplace, or on a scaffold. Once dried, they are called **leather britches** or **shuck beans**. Often dancing and entertainment followed completion of work.

1908 Fox *Lonesome Pine* 289 There was a "bean-stringing" at the house that day. **1939** Campbell *Play Party* 18 Clearings, log-rollings, house-raisings, corn-shuckings, bean stringings, apple peelings, 'lasses stir-offs, and quiltings, though said to be not as common as they once were, still survive. **1956** Hall *Coll* (Roaring Fork TN) After the close of those corn shellings, bean stringings, they would have play . . . sometimes they would have a dance and drink corn whiskey. [**1978** Slone *Common Folks* 247 The beans were poured in the floor in the middle of the room. After all the work was "done up," and us girls had "spruced up," then the neighbors began to arrive, bringing their darning needles with them. At first, everyone would "snout" the beans (pull the strings off). When a good supply was ready, some would begin to put them on the twine. Of course, the boys and girls would pair off in couples and work together. Some boy, or man, would bring a banjo or fiddle and play music. **1986** Pederson et al. *LAGS* = attested by 4/60 interviewees (6.7%) from E TN; 4/4 of all LAGS interviewees (100%) attesting term were from Appalachia. **1986** Tyson *Reflections* 33 When we kids were growing up there wasn't much that we could do to pass the time. The only entertainment we had was when some of the neighbors would have a bean stringing. They would pick their greenbeans when they were ready to can and to put up for pickle beans. Sometimes they would have eight to ten bushels piled in the floor and they would invite all they could get to come in at night and help string the beans. When we would get done we would clean up the floor and have banjo and fiddle music. **2006** *Encycl Appalachia* 955 A bean stringing was a popular social event in the first part of the twentieth century, providing a way for neighbors to socialize while doing important work. Word would go out to neighbors that a bean stringing was to take place, and neighbors and acquaintances would assemble, with someone usually bringing a guitar, fiddle, or banjo to provide music.

[DARE *bean stringing* n chiefly southern Appalachians, especially eastern KY]

beant See **be A1b**.

bean wagon *noun* See citation.

1980 Riggleman *WV Mtneer* 126–27 [Loggers] usually had nicknames for everybody and everything around the camp. . . . A supply train was a "bean wagon."

bear[1] *noun* variant forms *ba'ar, bar* [bɑr] (rare and not heard by Joseph Hall in the Smoky Mountains), *bare* [bær], *bire*.

1934 Parke *Bear Hunt* 25 In this here mountain . . . is a mighty sight easier to carry a ba'ar. **1942** Hall *Phonetics Smoky Mts* 24 Oldtimers of a former day may have said [bær] for *bear*, n., but I have never heard it. It is perhaps [æ] that some dialect writers seek to represent by the spelling *b'ar*. **c1960** Wilson *Coll*: *bear* [bɑr] rare among the very old. **1978** Williams *Appal Speech* 175 In "bear," for example, as soon as *b* is articulated, blending begins. The result is a diphthong peculiar to mountain speech, which outsiders spell and pronounce "bar." However, it is not "bar," which, for the mountaineer is a castrated pig. Instead of a broad *a*, as the outsider would have it, the diphthong becomes vowelized in a glide from schwa to *r*. **2013** Venable *How to Tawlk* 6 *bire* = large black furry animal often seen in the Smokies, usually mispronounced "bar" by ignorant Yankees and Hollywood scriptwriters hoping to impress the natives: "Bire season opens next weekend."

[DARE *bear* n A first two forms chiefly South, Midland]

bear[2] *verb* Variant past-participle form *bore*. See also **born**.

1789 *French Broad Petitions* 216 We suffered many Injuries and losses by sd Indians Which were bore without resentment until the Began to murder. **1928** (in **1952** Mathes *Tall Tales* 57) Ye're a good woman an' ye've bore a heap in your time.

bear ague *noun* Nervous excitement of a hunter in shooting at a bear. See also **buck ague**.

1927 Mason *Lure of Smokies* 216 Ye've heerd o' buck aguer? Well, right thar's whar I got *b'ar-aguer*! I shivered and I shook so I couldn't load my gun an' I reckon I poured powder all over the ground tryin' to hit the muzzle. I had to set down awhile. I was too eager.

bearberry (also *bear huckleberry*) *noun* A high-bush cranberry (*Gaylussacia ursina*) from whose leaves a medicinal tea is made.

1848 Gray *Illustrations* 49 Although so long overlooked by botanists, this species [= *Gaylussacia ursina*] is very common through the mountains near the southwestern borders of North Carolina, where the fruit is known to the inhabitants by the name of *Bear-*

berry, or *Bear Huckleberry*. **1982** Powers and Hannah *Cataloochee* 354 What has happened to the Cataloochee sweets of yore. . . . Where are the pokeberry and bearberry jellies, pumpkin butters and corncob syrups? **1991** Haynes *Haywood Home* 66 Lower back pain was treated with tea made from Bearberry leaves. **1998** Montgomery Coll = sometimes made into jelly (Pittillo).

bear cabbage (also *bear corn*, *bear potato*) *noun* A small parasitic plant (*Conopholis americana*) that usually grows at the foot of oak trees. Same as **squaw corn**.

1971 Brewer *Your Community* In all the previous literature Larry read on bear eating habits, he found no mention of squawroot . . . But he says mountain people already evidently knew it. For they sometimes call squawroot by such names as "bear potato" or "bear cabbage." **1982** Stupka *Wildflowers* 108 The resemblance of this plant to a pine cone is indicated by its generic name, from the Greek *conos*, "cone," and *pholis*, "scale." . . . The stout stalks are covered by stiff overlapping scales instead of leaves. Squaw-root is also called "bear-corn" and "cancer-root." It is a fairly common parasite on the roots of oaks and other trees. **1997** Montgomery Coll: *bear cabbage* (Cardwell).

beard *noun* Construed as a count noun; hence plural form *beards* = whiskers. See also **hair 2**, **moustache**.

1937 Hall Coll (Cades Cove TN) Dan Myers has got lots of beards.

bear dog (also *bear hound*) *noun* A dog adept at tracking or attacking a bear, especially one bred for the purpose such as a **Plott** or a **black and tan hound**, breeds that are large, solidly built, and able to give and withstand punishment.

1913 Kephart *Our Sthn High* 80 I've been told that the Plott hounds are the best beardogs in the country. **1926** Hunnicutt *Twenty Years* 105 I had just finished saying this when old Drum went on one of the "pot-lickers," and then the bear hounds each picked out a dog and we had a fight between the bear dogs and the "pot-lickers." **1939** Hall Coll (Cataloochee NC) We had some dogs, some bear dogs, and we went on and we trailed, cold-trailed 'em right onto the side of Shanty Mountain. *Ibid.* (Deep Creek NC) We had some old trained bear hounds 'at turned off into the roughs, the laurel on the Bear Creek side, and picked up a cold trail. . . . It was one of our bear hounds, a black and tan hound, and he was just eat up, bloody all over. **1956** Hall Coll (Roaring Fork TN) He was give up to be the best bear dog in this country. **1970** Mull *Mt Yarns* 61 Now "bear" dogs in the mountains are so called, regardless of breed, because of their bravery, tenacity, and size.

bear drive *noun* An organized effort by hunters to encircle an area wherein bears are believed to roam, in order to **start** and **drive** one through a place (in the Smoky Mountains frequently a **gap** on a ridge) where a **stander** waits to shoot it. See also **deer drive**, **drive B2**, **driver**, **stand B1**, **stander**.

1926 Hunnicutt *Twenty Years* 41 The next morning there was a good snow on the ground and my oldest brother wanted to make a bear drive that day, but I told him we could not drive in the snow. **1939** Hall Coll (Deep Creek NC) So we started out the next morning for the bear drive and . . . they put it on me to place the standers.

beardy *adjective* Bearded.

1941 Stuart *Men of Mts* 207 Pa wiped his beardy face with his hands. **c1950** Adams *Grandpap* 51 He was a beardy lookin' sight an' she asked him if he didn't want a shave. **1994** McCarthy *Jack Two Worlds* 37 Long about twelve o'clock or one o'clock in the morning, come an old beardy man along all bent over. **2007** McMillon *Notes* = bearded.

bear fight (also *bear scrape*) *noun* An encounter between a bear and a hunter with his dogs who have tracked the bear. See also **scrape A**.

1926 Hunnicutt *Twenty Years* 41 We had a good time that night talking about our bear fight. **1953** Hall Coll (Bryson City NC) You run [a dog] and get him hot and get his blood hot all day in a bear fight. *Ibid.* (Plott Creek NC) Now that was a real bear fight. . . . We had a wonderful bunch of dogs. But this bear was some fighter. He bit up the dogs. **1956** Hall Coll (Roaring Fork TN) *Bear scrapes* = bear fights, i.e. fights with dogs to kill a "hemmed bear."

bear grass *noun* A yucca plant (*Yucca filamentosa* or *Y. smalliana*). Also called **Adam's needle**, **graveyard lily**. See also **Spanish bayonet**.

1970 Campbell et al. Smoky Mt Wildflowers 34 Known as the Spanish bayonet because of its tough sword-shaped leaves, it is also one of several plants commonly called beargrass. **1996–98** Montgomery Coll = used to hang hams in the meat house (Stupka), = an introduced species, used for decorations (Pittillo).

bear ground *noun* An area where bears tend to roam and feed.

1925 Dargan *Highland Annals* 81 They come down from the bear-ground on Smoky oncet in a while. **1997** Montgomery Coll = any area where natural food can be had by bears (Brown).

bear gun *noun* A high-caliber rifle. See 1941 citation.

1937 Hall Coll (Cosby TN) Tobe Phillips used a large rifle, a real bear gun. **1941** Kendall *Rifle-Making* 22 The calibre of the mountain rifles deserves a word of mention. Strictly speaking, these rifles had no calibre in the ordinary sense of the word. Usually, however, four kinds of rifles were made: one of about .35 calibre (0.35 inch) which was called a squirrel gun; one about .40 calibre (0.40 inch) called a turkey rifle; one about .45 calibre (0.45 inch) called a deer rifle; and one of approximately .50 calibre (0.50 inch) called a bear gun.

bear hobble *noun* Same as **dog hobble**.

1939 Hall Coll (Deep Creek NC) Pretty soon I found where the bear had went through the laurel and the bear hobble in the direction of the other fork of the creek, 'cross the Wooly Head Ridge.

bear hound See **bear dog**.

bear huckleberry See **bearberry.**

bear hug (also *bear walk*) *verb phrase* To shinny up a tree. See also **hug A1.**

1968 *DARE Survey* (Brasstown NC) *bear walk* = to climb the trunk of a tree by holding on with one's legs while pulling oneself up with the hands. **1996–97** Montgomery *Coll*: *bear hug* (Bush, Hooper, Ledford, Oliver).

[DARE *bear-hug* v chiefly South Midland]

bear hunt *verb phrase* To go hunting for bears. For similar compound forms, see **hunt B.**

1939 Hall *Coll* (Indian Creek NC) He was no hand to hunt. He made a few trips to bear hunt. *Ibid.* (Saunook NC) Red, I went a-bear-huntin onst a Fourth of July, and I went down to the branch where one had been a-usin'. *Ibid.* (Sugarlands TN) Him and his brother-in-law one night back years ago went out a-bear huntin'. **1989** Landry *Smoky Mt Interviews* 194 I've bear hunted a right smart.

bear-huntingest *adjective* Most inclined or proficient at hunting bears. See also **-est 1** and Grammar and Syntax §3.4.1.

1957 Parris *My Mts* 57 From the beginning, the Wilsons were destined to become the bear-huntin'est family in all the land.

bear jam *noun* Traffic congestion caused by one or more motorists stopping along a narrow mountain road to watch or photograph a bear; this term has arisen in recent decades as tourist traffic has escalated in areas like Great Smoky Mountains National Park after the park adopted a policy of roadside garbage cans that attracted bears.

1954 *Tennessean* (Nashville TN) 30 May sec C 18/1 (newspapers.com) The appearance of a bear family on a Sunday afternoon on a park highway is sure to result in what rangers call a "bear jam." **1977** *Smoky Vistas* (July 3) George West is a ranger on the North Carolina side of the park. He spends a lot of his time on road patrol breaking up "bear jams"—the mile or so back-up of honking cars and camera-clicking enthusiasts that results whenever a bear takes up its station along the road. **1979** Horton *Natural Heritage* 21 [The bear's] presence also results in "bear jams," when tourists see these animals, especially cubs, near US 441, a highway through the park. **1991** Rennicke *Black Bear* 29 Bears along the road will back traffic up for miles in what the rangers call "bear jams." As many as eight bear jams have been reported in the park at the same time.

bear lettuce *noun* An edible wild green (*Micranthes micranthidifolia* or *S. michauxii*) relished by cattle and bears, often gathered for human consumption in the early spring. Also called **branch lettuce, lettuce saxifrage, mountain lettuce.**

1977 Shields *Cades Cove* 19 After a winter with only stored, dried, or canned vegetables and fruits, the fresh wild greens of the spring were a welcome change. These included the wild cresses of the fields, the "bear" lettuce of the mountain streams, the toothwort of the moist stream banks, and, most abundant of all, the wild leek, or ramp, of the northern slopes. **1991** Weals *Last Train* 15 The cattle relished the first greens of spring—the ramps, bear lettuce, turkey mustard, lamb's tongue, and crow's foot—after their winter diet of hay. **1997** *GSMNPCOHP-1:2* I never did like bear lettuce, tasted too much like grass. . . . Now that bear lettuce would grow mostly on rocks or on the creek.

bear pen *noun* A log trap of the dead-fall type to catch a bear (see 1939 citation for mode of construction); place-names of the type *Bear Pen Branch* (Swain Co NC), *Bear Pen Creek* (Haywood Co NC), *Bear Pen Gap* (Sevier Co TN, Swain Co NC), *Bear Pen Hollow* (Sevier Co TN), and *Bear Pen Ridge* (Blount Co TN, Swain Co NC) suggest widespread use of such traps before the steel-built type became popular. See also **pen[1] 1, turkey pen.**

1845 *Johnston v. Shelton* On the 30th day of August, 1842, the plaintiffs made their entries, in the office of the entry-taker of vacant land in the County of Haywood. The first was, "No. 1440, for 640 acres of land, beginning on the line dividing the Counties of Haywood and Macon, at a point at or near Lowe's Bear-pen on the Hogback Mountain." **1939** Hall *Coll* (Smokemont NC) Then they decided they'd build a bear pen. They went and cut them some logs, floored it, built one log high. Then they built a lid for it, took triggers, set that bear trap, baited it with a piece of beef. And the bear come, throwed the trap. They never caught him. **1956** Hall *Coll* (Jones Cove TN) A fellow of the name of Styles raised John Sutton. They used to bear-hunt together and built bear pens, pens to catch bear. They had to . . . stay till night [at their camp] to go to the bear pens. **1957** *GSMNP-23:1:21* I don't think a man could catch a man in a bear pen, in a bear trap, and not tell it. **1968** Powell *NC Gazetteer* 30 [There are eleven entries of place-name *Bear Pen Branch* in western NC; USGS map has Bear Pen Gap on Blanket Mt., Bear Pen Ridge near Noland Divide, Bear Pen Branch in the Deep Creek area.]

bear pillar *noun* See citation.

2006 Hicks *Mt Legacy* 145 They mine it [= coal] crisscross and this causes huge blocks of coal to be left resembling a city with main streets. . . . Each solid block of downtown (without alleys) is called a Bear Pillar.

bear potato See **bear cabbage.**

bear race *noun* Pursuit of a bear by a hunter with dogs.

1926 Hunnicutt *Twenty Years* 54 I told the boys in the morning we would have a coon race or a bear race one. **1960** Burnett *My Valley* 152 The dogs responded, bringing to the nearby hunters excitement such as they had rarely, if ever, experienced in a bear race.

bear scrape See **bear fight.**

bear sign *noun* Any indication of a bear's recent presence, specifically droppings, torn bushes or limbs, footprints, etc., used by hunters to track a bear or gauge its proximity. See also **bear tree, sign 1.**

1904–20 Kephart *Notebooks* 4:749 Le's santer around in the laurel and see if we find any bear signs. **1926** Hunnicutt *Twenty Years* 40 My brother who had just come asked me if we had found any bear signs; I told him just plenty of them. **1959** Hall Coll (Newport TN) Miss McSwain or some of them axed him how he could tell bear sign. He said, "Shit and tracks, madam." **1960** Burnett *My Valley* 22–23 Scouts went out to locate bear signs, and wherever bears are there are plenty of signs. As he travels in search of food the bear leaves his readily recognized tracks. Overturned rocks and demolished and torn-to-pieces logs line his routes of travel. He relishes grubs and honey. He is on the lookout for yellow jacket nests, and you may see where he digs for groundhogs. He likes to add grubs and honey and fresh meat to his diet of nuts. So, if he is using a given area or territory, he is sure to leave plenty of signs.

bears in the weeds *noun* A children's hiding game, presumably similar to hide-and-go-seek.

1971 *AOHP/ALC*-147 We played bears in the weeds a-hiding from each other.

bear's paw *noun* A shield fern (*Dryopteris filix-mas*) with medicinal uses.

1941 *FWP Guide WV* 140 Bear's-paw root tea is considered good to cure a cold or a fever, although the remark is made that "it takes a good nerve" to drink it because of its "dark bitterness." **1968** Clarke *Stuart's Kentucky* 40 Bear's paw was taken "fer the stummick" and yellow root "fer bellyache and sore mouth."

bear tale *noun* An account of an encounter with a bear, especially an exaggerated or fantastic account. See also **panther tale**, **snake tale**, **wild hog tale**.

1939 Hall Coll A fellow would come in and tell a little extra story a little out of line, like he'd had an extra drink or something. We'd call that a bear tale. It meant his story was a little exaggerated in places. **1953** Hall Coll (Bryson City NC) Bear tale . . . meant a story that was . . . a little exaggerated in places, maybe, and that's the name we give to such stories as that. . . . For instance we had a man by the name of Henchley, stayed all night with us, and we was tellin' different huntin' stories. So he set there and told a great long story about what he done trappin' and how many bears he killed in one season. [It] mounted up to around fifty or somethin' like that. **1973** *GSMNP*-79:28 That was some of the pastime of the mountain people, a-telling scary stories and Indian stories and bear tales as they'd call them.

bear trail *noun* A narrow pathway made or frequented by bears.

1939 Hall Coll (Proctor NC) I went up thar and the old dog was settin' in one of them big bear trails. *Ibid.* (Wears Cove TN) It's strictly agin the law to set a trap in a trail. The trap was right in a bear trail.

bear tree *noun* A tree whose bark has been scraped or torn away, presumably by a bear to mark its territory. See 1975 citation. See also **bear sign**.

1975 Fink *Backpacking* 61 The black bear has a way of making his presence known in the neighborhood by rearing on his hind legs beside a balsam tree, then reaching back over his shoulder, tearing off a strip of bark with his teeth. Often he will add a stroke or two with his front claws. Maybe the height of the marks above the ground is his way of telling other bears his size, and warning the smaller ones to watch their step. Not infrequently a larger bear will chance by, and tear off a bit of bark higher than the first. On this day we saw a score of trees bearing marks of trees and claws, even three on a single tree. **1991** Rennicke *Black Bear* 40–41 Perhaps the most mysterious sign of bears, however, is the "bear tree." For reasons no one can say with certainty, some trees are clawed and bitten by bears. Some are marked once and never touched again. Others are marked year-after-year, scratched and clawed so deeply that it kills the tree. Bear trees are often on ridges or on a game trail. Pitch pine, red maple, Eastern hemlock, oaks, sourwood, even Fraser fir at the higher elevations all have displayed bear marks.

bear walk See **bear hug**.

bear wallow *noun* A shallow depression made or thought to be made by bears wallowing in the dirt. See also **hen wallow**, **hog wallow**, **use**.

1833 (in **1940** McJimsey *Topo Terms in VA* 155) At a double chesnut near a Bear Wallow on the top of the mountain. **1927** Mason *Lure of Smokies* 22 This retaining under-clay, characteristic of the high secluded ridges, makes ideal bathtubs for the black bear. Mountaineers call them "b'ar wallers," i.e. "bear-wallows." **1937** Hall Coll (Cataloochee NC) [There's a] bear waller in a swag under Spruce Mountain Tower where they use. **1960** Burnett *My Valley* 57 Daddy explained that during the summer season bears spent most of their time wallowing in the deep pools of the stream and mentioned the location of any number of "bear-wallows" on the watershed.

beaslings *noun*

A Variant forms *beastings* [see **1984** in **B**], *beazlings* [see **1984** in **B**], *beezlin's* [see **1984** in **B**].

B The first milk given by a cow after calving.

1936 Morehouse *Rain on Just* 37 Sukey's calf still born; Sukey herself with a corruption in her tit, and her milk still partly beazlings. **1984** Wilder *You All Spoken* 135 *beezlin's*, *beastings* = breast milk, colostrum, the first breast milk let down by cows and other animals after birthing. The milk is loaded with antibodies, vitamins, and a morphine-like substance, and cleans out the intestines of the young. **1998** Montgomery Coll (known to Ledford).

[ultimately < Old English biesting]

beast *noun*

A Variant plural forms of two syllables: *beast-es*, *beast-ies*, *beast-is*.

1859 (in **1974** Harris *High Times* 238) Ise studied the nater ove beastes mons[tr]ous well, particular the mean kind ove varmints. **1895** Edson and Fairchild *TN Mts* 374 I got a right smart little bit of roughness in for the beastis. **1913** Kephart *Our Sthn High* 285

The ancient syllabic plural is preserved in beasties (horses), nesties, posties, trousies (these are not diminutives). **1930** (in **1952** Mathes *Tall Tales* 182) I've had to chop the wood, tend to the beast-es, plow the corn an' tobacker an' mow the br'ars till I'm naterly werried an' wore out. **1940** Bowman *KY Mt Stories* 16 Even two of my high school students always pronounced "beasts" as "beastes." **2007** McMillon *Notes: beastes.*

[DARE *beast* n A chiefly South Midland, occasionally New England]

B Senses.

1 A horse. Also called **horse beast**.

1834 (in **1956** Eliason *Tarheel Talk* 259) (Haywood Co NC) work Beast [i.e. draft horse]. **1863** *Karnes CW Letters* (March 15) I have had aplesent ride this morning I come about forty miles be fore breakfast i have bin to see about kestersons beast I come down on the cars. **1913** Kephart *Our Sthn High* 295 Critter and beast are usually restricted to horse and mule. **1974** Fink *Bits Mt Speech* 2 = horse. "He had four head o' *beastes.*" **1994–97** Montgomery *Coll* (known to Jones, Ledford, Oliver) = a term found only in old wills (Cardwell).

[DARE *beast* n B1 South, South Midland, New England]

2 Used as a euphemism for bull. See also **cow brute, male brute**.

c1960 Wilson *Coll* = male, usually uncastrated, animal: "That old beast chased Pappy across the pasture field."

[DARE *beast* n B2 chiefly South, South Midland, occasionally New England]

beastings See **beaslings A**.

beat

A *verb* To win.

1895 Dromgoole *Fiddling to Fame* 50 Sometimes he'd say which beat in argerfyin', but he mostly allus went with Alf. **1931** Combs *Lg Sthn High* 1305 Who got to beat in that deal? **1938** Justus *No-End Hollow* 26 "We'll fill our buckets in no time. Let's see who beats!" cried Jessie. **1989** *Matewan OHP-7* [We'd] have a target setting out in a bottom and had everybody shooting at it, seeing who could beat. **1997** Montgomery *Coll* "I beat" is common among children (Ellis).

B *noun* (usually *the beat*) The better (of), someone or something that surpasses all others. See also **beatenest**.

1889 Murfree *Broomsedge Cove* 80 Wall, sir, eatin' supper by a tallow dip—whoever hearn the beat? **1930** (in **1952** Mathes *Tall Tales* 162) By grab, Nathes, did ye ever see the beat? **1952** Wilson *Folk Speech NC* 519 *the beat* = that which or who surpasses something or someone else. "I've never seen *the beat of* him." **1961** Murry *Salt* 62 Will says you never saw the beat of the way them ladies' eyes bugged out. **1963** Edwards *Gravel* 134 Doggon my hide if I ever seed the beat. **1980** Still *Run for Elbertas* 77 "It's blizzardy the hills over," Father chuffed edgily. "I don't recollect the beat." **1985** Irwin *Alex Stewart* 240 I never heard the beat, or anything like it in my life. **2001** Lowry *Expressions* 7 I never seen the beat.

beat a buck *verb phrase* See citations.

1940 Haun *Hawk's Done* 61 Enzor did beat a buck at slipping around and seeing when Eloyd was here. **1996** Montgomery *Coll* = to be crafty at slipping around and spying (Cardwell).

beat a hen a-pecking (also *beat a hen a-rooting*) *verb phrase* To do something to a supreme, unusual, accelerated, or unbelievable degree. See also **beat the devil, like a hen a-pecking**.

1904–20 Kephart *Notebooks* 2:625 I slep' last night to beat a hen-a peckin'. **1972** Hall *Sayings* 83 That beats a hen a-rootin'. **1994** Montgomery *Coll: beat a hen a-peckin'* (Bush, Weaver); That beat a hen a-peckin' (Cardwell).

beaten biscuit *noun* See citations. See also **biscuit 1**.

2006 *Encycl Appalachia* 918 The beaten biscuit was common in the mid-nineteenth century and throughout the Civil War. Comparable to the modern-day cracker—hard, flat, and crispy—this biscuit was valued for its storage longevity and not for its taste. Served plain or with very thin slices of aged country ham, these biscuits were so named because they were beaten with a rolling pin or mallet during preparation. **2014** Sauceman *Buttermilk* 53 Two centuries ago, however, long before mechanization and chemistry took over, biscuit making involved vigorous labor—clubbing dough until arms throbbed. The result was the beaten biscuit, with a shelf life of about a month.

[DARE *beaten biscuit* n chiefly South, South Midland, especially KY, MD, VA]

beatenest See **beatingest**.

beat hair *verb phrase* See citation.

1930 Pendleton *Wood-Hicks Speak* 86 = to [drive] a team of horses.

beatinest See **beatingest**.

beatingest (also *beatenest, beatinest*) *adjective* Most extreme, unusual, or astonishing, greatest or finest, surpassing all others. See also **beat B, -est 1**, and Grammar and Syntax §19.2.

1892 Fruit *KY Words* 229 *beatenest* = not to be beaten (in the superlative): "He is the beatenest man I ever saw"; "That is the beatenest trick I ever heard of." **1895** Edson and Fairchild *TN Mts* 370 Well, I wish I may *never*, if you ain't the *beatenest* boy ever I *see* (saw). **1913** Kephart *Our Sthn High* 72 A herdsman who was out at the time, and narrowly escaped a similar fate, assured me that "that was the beatenest snow-storm ever I seen." **1927** Woofter *Dialect from WV* 348 = that which cannot be beaten or excelled. "We had the beatenist time at the party last night." **1939** Walker *Mtneer Looks* 2–3 There are few words so characteristic as *beatin'est* and *workin'est*, which in politer society would be *strangest* and *most industrious*. **1940** Haun *Hawk's Done* 98 Of course, a Dunkards' supper is the beatinest place in the world for a boy and girl to start sparking. **1957** Combs *Lg Sthn High: Word List* 9 *beatenest* = best, most unusual or uncommon. Such irregular comparatives and superlatives, formed on the pres[ent] part[iciple], are common. Ex.: "He's the beatin'est hand at corn-shuckin' I ever seed, but I am a corn-hoeiner man than him." **c1960** Wilson *Coll*: *beatenest* = unusual: "He made the beatenest speech you ever heard." **1995** South *What It Is* 15 Yeah, Johnny, that Freddy shore is the beatenest!

[*beatin(g)* present participle of *beat* "to surpass" + *-est*]

beating stick See **battle A**.

beatling block See **battling bench**.

beat one's gums *verb phrase* See citations.

c1982 Young *Colloquial Appal* 2 = talk rapidly. **1988** Still *Hunting Hindman* 14 I'm wasting my time listening to you beat your gums.

beat out *adjective phrase* Worn out, exhausted.

1943 Hannum *Mt People* 128 There still is the North Carolina woman who "got so plumb beat out with the no-account ways of her fam-il-ee, that she was tuck to bed and stayed thar, year in and year out." **1974** Fink *Bits Mt Speech* 2 = exhausted. "I'm plumb *beat out*."

beat the devil *adverb phrase* To an extreme, remarkable, or superlative degree. See also **beat a hen a-pecking**.

1917 Kephart *Word-List* 408 The little feller tumbled down and benastied to beat the devil. **1994–97** Montgomery *Coll* (known to eight consultants from the Smoky Mountains); He could play that banjo to beat the devil (Shields).

beat the devil around the bush (also *beat the devil around the stump*) *verb phrase* To be evasive, not get to the point, "beat around the bush."

1933 Thomas *Traipsin' Woman* 170 There's no use beatin' the devil around the bush no longer. If this body sees fitten to larn a body to read and write evenin's when court is over, hit's her own business. **1940** Haun *Hawk's Done* 59 Amy vowed she didn't want to marry anybody at all. She said she didn't see the use in beating the devil around the stump or talking about it—she just didn't want to. **1994–97** Montgomery *Coll*: *beat the devil around the stump* (known to Adams, Bush, Cardwell, Jones, Oliver, Shields, Weaver); Preacher shore did beat the devil around the bush today (Brown).

beat the devil around the stump *verb phrase*

1 See **beat the devil around the bush**.

2 See citation.

c1960 Wilson *Coll* = to overcome someone by using his own tricks.

beat time *verb phrase* To kill or waste time on a job.

c1926 Bird *Cullowhee Wordlist* He can beat time the best I ever saw. **1996** Montgomery *Coll* (known to Cardwell).

[cf DARE *beat in time* v phr Midland]

beaves See **beef**.

beazlings See **beaslings A**.

became See **become A2**.

becase, beca'se See **because**.

because *conjunction*

A Variant forms *becase, beca'se, becaze, bekase, bekaze, kase, kaze* [kez]. See also **acause**.

1859 Taliaferro *Fisher's River* 231 I ain't that! Not becaze I'm a Dimmicrat, but on anuther account. **1867** Harris *Sut Lovingood* 49 But, I spect ait dullers won't fetch me, nither wud ait hundred, bekase thar's nun ove 'em fas' enuf tu ketch me, nither is thar hosses by the livin jingo! **1884** Murfree *In TN Mts* 253 I knowed it war the track o' Jeremiah Stubbs . . . 'kase his old shoe jes' fit the track. **1895** Dromgoole *Old Hickory* 19 His wife [was] a-cryin' becase the ward'n war 'bleeged ter lock her out. **1900** Harben *N GA Sketches* 137 I'm one that don't, nur never did, believe you meant to steal Williams's hoss, kase you was too drunk to know what you was a-doin'. **1927** Mason *Lure of Smokies* 228 I don't hunt as much as I useter, beca'se the Lord wanted me fer to be a hunter an' fisher o' men. **1934–47** *LAMSAS* (Swain Co NC) *bekaze*. **1939** Walker *Mtneer Looks* 5 The standard American vowels can hardly be recognized . . . *beca'se* for *because*. **1942** Hall *Phonetics Smoky Mts* 32–33 *kaze*. **1961** Kurath and McDavid *Pron Engl Atl Sts* 162 *Because* with the vowel /e/ of eight occurs in the folk speech of the South and South Midland; it is sharply recessive. **1969** *GSMNP*-37:2:6 I believe that his daddy used to live on Coopers Creek, for becaze after my brother married, my oldest one, by God, he moved up there and they called it Grandpaw's place.

[CUD *becase/bekase*; DARE pronunciations at *because* conj South, South Midland]

B In order that.

1916 Combs *Old Early English* 288 *Because* sometimes has a future use, e.g. "He took hook and line *because* he might catch some fish." **1979** *Big South Fork OHP*-1 I quit it because I could be at home.

because of *conjunctive phrase* Because.

1970 *Foxfire Interviews* A-70-5 Now I can't walk that way, cause of the road's growed up. **2008** *Rosie Hicks* 4 It wouldn't have been April Fool on us, 'cause of we wouldn't let them have it.

because that *conjunctive phrase* Because; for similar forms with *that*, see **that C** and Grammar and Syntax §15.4.

1921 Weeks *Speech of KY Mtneer* 9 We ignore your very existence because that you have offered us some deep insult. **1954** Hall *Coll* (Gatlinburg TN) So not just because that I'm born and raised here, but I'm just telling ye what other people tells me. **1974** *AOHP/ALC*-728 They's been sections [of coal mines], certain parts or sections closed down because that they didn't fix them. **1982** Ginns *Snowbird Gravy* 91 It's just as much glory to him because that if they'd look at it like that, it proves to 'em that it's not me. **1989** *Matewan OHP-23* [The price of gas] went up during the war, I guess, because that you couldn't get it.

becaze See **because.**

become *verb*

A Principal parts.

1 Variant past-tense forms *become, bekum.*

1834 (in **1996** Edmondson *Crawford Memoirs* 127) They moved from Indiana into Anderson County and lived there awhile and Nancy become in a family way, and when brought to bed the child was born but Nancy died in a short time. **1862** *Hundley CW Letters* (Dec 8) rite what become of the conscripts that were left at home. **1873** Smith *Peace Papers* 81–82 We bekum konverted over to the doktrin of squatter suvrinty. **1956** Hall *Coll* (Mt Sterling NC) They'd boil that down till it become a syrup. **1969** GSMNP-46:16 He just become rich there at Pigeon Forge. **1989** *Matewan OHP-9* I become a member of the Church of Christ, and when it all started out with a meeting house over here on the point. **2011** COROH (Brannon) Then he become a police sergeant with the TVA Police Department.

2 Variant past-participle form *became.*

1988 Kosier *Maggie* 113 He had gradually became more weak and "peaked."

B To come.

1939 Hall *Coll* (Saunook NC) When I became to be sixteen years old I joined the CCC. **1964** Roberts *Hell-Fer-Sartin* 103 Now you can spend this gold piece anywhere you want to and it'll become right back to your pocket.

bed

A *noun* in phrase *in the bed* = in bed.

1946 Dudley *KY Words* 270 "I was so tired I was in the bed before eight o'clock." This use of the definite article may derive from the time when one house normally contained one bed. **1969** GSMNP-27:7 We was all in the bed asleep and he come up. He knocked and knocked on the door and nobody answered him. **1973** GSMNP-85:2:9 Well in few days he took down sick and him and Bud was in the bed, in the same bed, you know, sick. **1989** *Matewan OHP-9* The next family lived above us was all in the bed with the flu. **2005** Williams *Gratitude* 537 Git yenses' feet washed and git in the bed.

[CUD (at the 1e); DARE *bed* n A2 chiefly South, South Midland]

B *verb*

1 (usually *bed it*) To lie in bed; to send (one) to bed. For the *it*, see also **behave it, go B2, run it over.**

1913 Kephart *Our Sthn High* 282 In mountain vernacular many words that serve as verbs are only nouns of action, or adjectives, or even adverbs . . . "I ain't goin' to bed it no longer" (lie abed). **1944** Wilson *Word-List* 40 = to cause one to go to bed, to lie in bed. "If you fool with me, I'll bed you"; "He's bedding late today." **1994–97** Montgomery *Coll* (known to Bush, Cardwell, Oliver).

2 To provide a bed for, furnish bedding for.

1937 Conner *Ms* 8 Those mountaineer's [sic] could feed, and bed a fellow nice, most any time. **1963** Edwards *Gravel* 94 After they had supper the farmer said, "We ain't got enough bed room to bed all of you, but you and one of your men," he said to the head drover, "can sleep in the only spare room we have."

bedabs (also *bedad, bedads, be-doggie, be-dom*) *interjection* Used to form mild oaths. See also **b'gad, by, dad-, I'll be dog.**

c1844 Beckner *Shane Interview* 236 "Be dad," said Yeager, "I was fresh, and no run-down Indians couldn't catch me." **1925** Carter *Mt White Tales* 343 Bedads, I'll go over and skin it. **1940** Still *River of Earth* 147 "Be dom," he said. "I thought pine-blank you was a mountycat about to spring." **1941** Still *Troublesome Creek* 71 Bedads, if the whole gin-works hain't got the punies. Even the mare tuck a spell today. *Ibid.* 98 "Be-doggie," Jimp swore, "Rant swore I was the only one to know." **1983** McDermitt *Boy Named Jack* 10 Bedad, I can try cuttin it. **2007** Cave *Recollections: bedabs/bydabs* = a mild oath heard in Swain County [NC] in the 1980s.

bedad, bedads See **bedabs.**

bed blanket *noun* A blanket for a bed.

1952 Wilson *Folk Speech NC* 519. **1968** Wilson *Folklore Mammoth Cave* 33 = one of many tautological expressions. **1998** Montgomery *Coll* (known to Jones) = any blanket used on a bed as opposed to a horse, buggy, etc. (Brown).

bedfast *adjective* Bedridden, confined to bed because of weakness or sickness.

1863 *Hanes CW Letters* (Nov) he went down to the manasa Junction to see his son that was in the army and was taken sick and was halled back home and he bed fast until he died. **1927** Dingus *Appal Mt Words* 468 = confined to bed; bed-ridden. **1939** Krumpelmann *WV Peculiarities* 155 = bedridden, confined to bed. "His father had been *bedfast* since the accident.". . . . This expression is current in the Tri-State region. Although the word is listed in Webster, it seems to be unknown in most sections of the East and South. **1971** *AOHP/ALC-147* He was able to get around until in November after his birthday, before he got bedfast. **1980** Berry and Repass *Grandpa Says* 18 = sick and confined to bed: "She's been bedfast for years." **1996** Woodring *Times Gone By* 3 I'uz askin about Clarence an' he said he 'uz bedfast at that time.

[DARE *bedfast* adj chiefly Midland, West]

bed it See **bed B1.**

be-doggie, be-dom See **bedabs.**

bedroom safe *noun* A chest of drawers, a freestanding cabinet for storing clothes or bedding. See also **safe B.**

1986 Pederson et al. *LAGS* (Johnson Co TN) = some with doors, some with drawers.

bedside coffin *noun* A coffin one in failing health readies for use by having it set nearby.

1975 Montell *Ghosts Cumberland* 217 = a container, generally made of wood, which was designed to rest on a stand by the bed of the deceased or in the parlor.

bedstid *noun* A bedstead.

1863 Hall *CW Letters* (March 30) I have raised Robert Hall and learnt him his trade he is Well Skild in the trad he can make plans [= woodworking planes] hoes axes knives Spinning Wheels reals Bedstids. **1979** Carpenter *Walton War* 164 The younguns was all scrootched up in the bedstid.

[DARE (at *bedstead* n) chiefly South, South Midland]

bed tick *noun* Same as **tick**.

1858 (in **1974** Harris *High Times* 148) His britches wer es big es a bedtick, with two meal-bags sowed tu hit fur laigs. **1862** *Martin CW Letters* (Feb 7) I also will Say if you have got any old bedticks to Send Me one if you pleas. **1943** Stuart *Private Tussie* 190–91 After supper we slept on our shuck bed ticks on the schoolhouse floor. **1974** *Death and Burial* 60 There were other [burial] practices with more or less superstitious characteristics—the burning of a bed tick on which a person had died (if made of straw) and waiting a considerable time for airing and cleaning (if feather tick). **1977** Shields *Cades Cove* 22 All the old straw was dumped out and the bed tick was washed and dried and stuffed anew with the fresh straw.

beebalm *noun* A horsemint (*Monarda didyma*) with medicinal uses and a sweet fragrance. Same as **oswego tea**.

1937 Thornburgh *Great Smoky Mts* 22 Summer flowers most frequently encountered include . . . the busy red flowers of the bee balm, member of the mint family. **1971** Hutchins *Hidden Valley* 189 For elimination of internal worms, infusions made from the bark of mountain maple, butternut, ambrosia (Chenopodium), bee balm, Indian pink, and oil from the oil nut were employed. **1980** *Smokies Heritage* 176 Hidden on the streambanks are beds of crimson bee balm, their red-fringed flowers nestled in mint leaves. Also called red horsemint, it is a flower of shady creeks, found in elevations up to 6500 feet where spruce and balsam grow. **1982** Stupka *Wildflowers* 99 Few of our wild flowers are as showy as the brilliantly colored Oswego tea or "bee-balm."

[from the plant's sweet fragrance, which attracts bees]

beech mast *noun* Fallen beechnuts serving as forage for bears, hogs, and other animals. See also **chestnut mast**, **mast**.

1915 Bohannon *Bear Hunt* 461–62 In all the creek bottoms there was no chestnut mast, but of beech there was plenty, both in feeding grounds which lay on the North Carolina side of the main ridge and the lying grounds which are on the Tennessee side. **1926** Hunnicutt *Twenty Years* 24 We had not gone far until we found where coons had been rooting for beech mast. **1953** Hall Coll (Bryson City NC) They is an awful lot of sign where [raccoons] had eaten the beech mast. . . . There's not much mast on that side of the mountain except some beech mast.

beef

A *noun* A head of cattle, especially fattened for slaughter (construed as a count noun; hence plural forms *beaves*, *beefs*, *beeves*).

1774 *Dunmore's War* 199 We are Stop'd a day to Get what Beaves and Cattles we can pick up. **1794** (in **1919** DeWitt *Sevier Journal* 173) (Dec 4) clear and cold[.] Killed a beef. **1813** Hartsell *Memora* 108 ther was severale Beeves kiled on the same day and brough[t] on the ground. **1844** Crosby *Journal/Account Book* 107 Mr Eldrige got half of a Small Beef 19th of Octr. **1863** *Coggin CW Letters* (July 19) when we would Camp in Penn we Just Burnt all the fencing that was any where Near to us and turn[ed] all the horses and Beaves into the wheat and Corn. **1937** Hall *Coll* (Catons Grove TN) We killed a heap of beeves. **1965** Miller *Pigeon's Roost* (Jan 7) Used to, all beefs was fixed that way. **1966** Medford *Ol' Starlin* 43 They killed beeves, muttons, and chickens; baked loaf and biscuit, gingerbread and cake, also brought out jars of preserves and canned goods a plenty! **1972** AOHP/ALC-298 [We] raised the hogs, fattened the hogs, beef, cured a beef now and then. **1979** *Big South Fork OHP-19* They killed beeves and killed sheep and hogs. **1983** *Dark Corner OHP-4A* Do you know how to skin a beef? **1993** *Stories 'neath Roan* 58 We killed beeves and hogs back then.

[OED3 *beef* n 3b as a singular noun now chiefly U.S.]

B *noun* Bear meat. See also **middling C**, **wild pork**.

1953 Hall Coll (Bryson City NC) He cut [the bear] open and had him a piece of beef cut out and was gonna broil and eat it.

C *verb* To hit, strike. See also **biff**.

1938 Stuart *Dark Hills* 66 They said he shore beefed him. Hit him right under the eye.

beefing *noun* The slaughter and parceling out among families of the meat of a bovine animal.

c1982 Young *Colloquial Appal* 2 = local slaughter of a beef. **1987** Young *Lost Cove* 24 *Beef-meat* made for powerful good eating in late summer and autumn. *Beefings* were always held on Friday afternoons. The meat was parceled out among the various families who were in on the cooperative endeavor.

beef meat *noun* See citations.

1941 Korson *Black Land* 23 In normal times, the Appalachian miner had "ham-meat," "pork-meat," or "beef-meat," always with gravy, a canned vegetable or fruit, hot "biscuit-bread," and a "miner's cup" of coffee. **c1982** Young *Colloquial Appal* 2 = meat of cattle. **1987** Young *Lost Cove* 148 Somebody tried to help out and scattered the beef-meat clean across the table.

beefs See **beef**.

beef shoot *noun* A marksmanship competition with muzzle-loading guns and a steer as a prize for the winner. See Ellis 1997 citation. See also **chicken shoot**, **turkey shoot**.

1937 Hall Coll (Little Greenbrier TN) My daddy was in most of them shoots. He driv many a beef off on foot. He was ruled out of the shoots [because he won so often]. **1954** *Waynesville Mtneer* Aug 2 Muzzle-loaders Cocked and Primed for Cataloochee Beef Shoot [headline] . . . immediate target a piece of charred wood, and their ultimate goal a quarter of beef. The shoot is open to "mountaineers" and "furriners" alike, but the "shooting-iron" must be a long-barrelled muzzleloader. . . . Many of the rifles are prized family heirlooms, some made in the Cataloochee area. Others are the famous "Lancasters" from Pennsylvania. Locally they are all called "hawg rifles." **1972** Cooper *NC Mt Folklore* 36 Beef and turkey shoots and rooster fights were great recreational events. **1997** Montgomery Coll = a shooting competition in which a steer was divided up among the winners, with hindquarters going to the first and second shooters, forequarters for numbers three and four, and hide-and-tallow for number five. An alternative distribution was both hindquarters for first place, forequarters for second, and hide-and-tallow for third. Beef shoots appear to be a thing of the past . . . although turkey (and ham) shoots were common . . . beef shoots were usually conducted with rifles, while modern turkey shoots usually are conducted with shot guns. The rules and methods of scoring are also different (Ellis).

bee gum *noun*

1 Originally, a section of a blackgum tree, which naturally hollows, especially for housing a swarm of bees; hence a beehive fashioned from a section of the tree; more generally, any beehive. See 1926 citation. Also called **gum A2**, **log gum**, **plank gum**.

1864 *C A Walker CW Letters* (April 19) every bee gum every hog chicken goose duck and every thing to eat is taken. **1883** Zeigler and Grosscup *Heart of Alleghanies* 101 A line of bee gums on the sagging upper porch had already been observed by our forager, and consequently he was not taken by surprise when a swarm of bees alighted on his head and shoulders. **1926** Willy *Great Smoky Natl Park* 54 Mr Ogle was pleased to show us his "bee gums," as he called them. They were the native style of beehive. "Bee gum" seems to be the name given them because, originally the first settlers caught and kept their swarms in hollow gum trees, which is done to this day. . . . These are hollow tree trunks sawed to about twenty inches in height. **1935** Thomas *Song Festival* 36 Mountain people sang their ballads at the plow, the spinning wheel, beside the sleeping *least uns* in the bee gum crib. **1991** Haynes *Haywood Home* 42 Most people referred to their stands of bees as "bee-gums." That was more literal than not. We didn't use all the fancy stuff beekeepers use nowadays. People kept their bees in hives made from sections of hollow logs. Blackgum trees were bad to go hollow if they got to be any size and they were most often used to make bee hives. The hives were, then, really bee gums.

[DARE *bee gum* n 1a chiefly South, South Midland]

2 See citation.

1939 *FWP Guide NC* 505 In this section any high hat is called a "beaver," or, in derision, a "bee gum."

bee gum stand (also *bee stand*) *noun* A hive of bees. Same as **stand B2**.

1861 Hedgecock *Diary* 99 Next morning I looked over the enormous number of his bee stands. The honey was furnished us in unsparing quantity. **1978** Montgomery *White Pine Coll* III-2 My dad's brother that lives up Del Rio in Cocke County, he had about twenty or twenty-five bee stands, we called it, gums of bees. **1985** *Smokies Anniv Book* 30 The average farm consisted of a cabin or house, barn, corn crib, smokehouse, springhouse and pig pen. Specialty buildings might include an apiary or "bee gum stand," a blacksmith shop or a small tub mill. **1994–97** Montgomery Coll: *bee stand* (known to eight consultants from the Smoky Mountains).

[DARE *bee stand* n chiefly South Midland]

bee hunt *verb phrase* To search for a **bee tree**, especially to **course** a returning swarm of bees to its hive, in order to cut the tree down and steal the honey or capture the colony of bees.

1984 GSMNP-153:32 Uncle Jim used to come up to home and me and him would bee hunt, and the way he'd bee hunt is, he'd go 'round the hog pen and where them bees was getting what is called bee bread to feed their little ones, and he'd watch 'em when they flew through a free, open place. Then the next day he'd take him a bucket lid with some honey in it and he'd set it on a post, you know, on a little farther, and get them bees to work it after that. Then he kept watching 'em and watching 'em, maybe it'd take us a week to find a bee tree, but he always looked up into the taller trees and watched for holes in the tree where the bees would go in and out. He had a pretty sharp eye, you know, towards seeing them bees.

bee hunter *noun* Apparently a man who evaded conscription during the Civil War. See also **bushwhacker**, **scout C**, **tory**.

1927 Mason *Lure of Smokies* 173 Many of the rifle "experts" aforementioned were among the "scouts" and "bee-hunters" who roamed the woods to escape conscription in a war which they claimed was unjust and of no concern to them.

beeler *noun* See 1957 citation.

1957 Broaddus *Vocab Estill Co KY* 6 = a wooden maul for splitting rails. **1994** Montgomery Coll (known to Shields).

bee martin *noun* The Eastern kingbird (*Tyrannus tyrannus*).

1940 Haun *Hawk's Done* 75 He said he was sure Pairlee's Spirit flew as straight to Heaven as a bee martin to its gourd. **1991** Alsop *Birds of Smokies* 69 This large flycatcher is a fairly common summer resident in the park. A bird of open areas, the "bee martin" as the locals know it, finds little suitable habitat in these forested mountains. **1996** Montgomery Coll (known to Cardwell, Stupka).

[DARE *bee martin* n 1 chiefly South, South Midland]

been away *noun* See citation.

2015 *Blind Pig* (July 21) A year or two ago a lifelong friend of mine and I were discussing some issues in Swain County [NC] which troubled both of us. She noted that our voices on the matters might not be heard or heeded because both of us were what her father often described as "been aways." That is to say, we had been away from the mountains and thereby somehow had been tainted a bit.

beer *noun* In the making of whiskey, the fermented **mash** solution produced during the first stage of distillation, sometimes drunk but more often distilled. Also called **corn beer**, **distiller's beer**, **still beer**.

1913 Kephart *Our Sthn High* 134 [After the conversion of sour mash into carbonic acid and alcohol] the resulting liquid is technically called the "wash," but the blockaders call it "beer." **1973** Wellman *Kingdom of Madison* 157 The "sweet mash," so called, was fermented until, to use the phrase of the knowledgeable, "it could stand on its own legs." It produced a liquid mixture of alcohol and carbon dioxide, called "wash" by professional distillers, "beer" by mountaineers—a brew that would intoxicate, but with a forbiddingly sour taste. **1990** Aiken *Stories* 199 The malt was mixed with ground cornmeal and water, then cooked to become "mash." The mash was allowed to ferment and produce a "beer." The beer was then distilled to become "moonshine." **2009** Webb et al. *Moonshining* 330 The fermented mixture [of water, yeast, ground grain, etc.], called "beer" was poured into the pot and heated over a wood fire.

[DARE *beer* n 1 chiefly southern Appalachians]

beer still *noun* See citation. See also **beer**.

1974 Maurer and Pearl *KY Moonshine* 114 = the still in which the beer is cooked to separate the spirits (low-proof alcohol) from the residue. In some areas this same still is then used to redistill the spirits to make whiskey. "We just got one more charge of beer. You put it in the beer still while I . . ."

bees swarm *phrase* Used in expressions having reference to the arrival of a baby. See also **mind one's bees, watch one's bees**.

[**1939** Hall *Coll* (Saunook NC) Minding or watching his bees (used of a man whose wife is expecting a baby): "Well, John, when are your bees going to swarm?"] **1960** Hall *Smoky Mt Folks* 65 "Watchin' his bees" or "waitin' for his bees to swarm" are euphemisms for expecting a baby. **1975** Gainer *Speech Mtneer* 7 They're expectin' the bees to swarm over at the Daly's. **1997** Miller *Brier Poems* 116 If George's wife is going to have a baby, his bees are about to swarm.

[DARE *bees swarm* phr South Midland]

bee stand See **bee gum stand**.

beeswax *noun* See 1960 citation. See also **stick A3**.

1960 Hall *Smoky Mt Folks* 52 If a widower said "beeswax" to a widow whom he had been "sparkin'," he was proposing marriage. If she wished to marry him, she answered "sticks." **1996** Montgomery *Coll* (known to Cardwell).

[alteration of *business*]

bee sweeting *noun* Honey.

1978 Parris *Mt Cooking* 210 White sugar was scarce. Folks had to look for substitutes. And usually, you would find on the table tree sweeting, bee sweeting, and sorghum—that is, maple sugar, honey, and molasses.

beetle bug *noun* See citation.

1957 Combs *Lg Sthn High: Word List* 9 = beetle; any coleopterous insect.

beetleweed *noun* Same as **galax B**.

[**1901** Lounsberry *Sthn Wild Flowers* 402 = *Galax aphylla* . . . In the mountainous parts of North Carolina I saw them . . . spreading over acres.] **1995** Montgomery *Coll* = another name of galax (Shields).

[DARE *beetleweed* n chiefly South Midland]

bee tree *noun* A hollow tree in which a colony of wild bees nests and stores its honey. Such a tree is hunted and felled to obtain its honey or to capture the colony. See also **bee hunt**.

1834 Crockett *Narrative* 119 While we were gone, two of our mess had been out, and each of them had found a bee tree. **1939** Hall *Coll* (Deep Creek NC) They found a bee tree one evening. Some boys wanted to cut it and did cut it, I reckon. **1954** GSMNP-19:23b My daddy had teach me how to find these wild bee trees. He'd give us some honey because he had plenty at home. I'd use a little of it and go out and catch the bees off of the flowers and then watch which way it'd go, and then I'd follow them up and cut down my bee tree.

beeves See **beef**.

beezlin's See **beaslings A**.

be for See **for[2] B2**.

before day *noun phrase* The period of light immediately before sunrise.

1967 *DARE Survey* (Jonesborough TN). **1996–97** Montgomery *Coll* (known to Brown, Cardwell, Jones, Oliver).

[DARE *before-day* n chiefly South, South Midland]

beforehands *adverb* Beforehand. See also **anywheres, somewheres**, etc.

1940 Haun *Hawk's Done* 40 We learned we had to call him a long time beforehands.

before that *conjunctive phrase* Before; for similar forms with *that*, see **that C** and Grammar and Syntax §15.4.

1985 Williams *Role of Folklore* 316 I went down there to see her again before that we left there. **1989** *Matewan OHP-102* Then the war ended before that my daddy had to go.

be fresh See **fresh C1**.

began See **begin A2**.

begaum *verb* To smear with a sticky or messy substance; to soil or make a mess of. See also **gaum**.

1859 Taliaferro *Fisher's River* 172 All the litigants begaumed her house with tobacco-juice. **1932** Creal *Quaint Speech* = to smear. **1992** Jones and Miller *Sthn Mt Speech* 66 = to make dirty, make a mess of. **1996–97** Montgomery *Coll* (known to Brown, Cardwell, Ellis, Jones, Oliver).

beggar bear *noun* A bear habituated to human food, as a result of which its diet is poor; it approaches humans rather than searching for food in the wild, and it endangers both itself and unwary humans. Also called **garbage bear**.

1977 *Smoky Vistas* (June) 2 Although roadside or "beggar" bears are still a problem in the front-country, bear proof garbage cans have greatly reduced the chance of a bear incident at a frontcountry campground. **1998** *Smokies Guide* (Summer) 7 When bears become habituated to eating human-related food, they lose their fear of people and their premature demise is all but certain. These "garbage" or "beggar" bears are often shot by poachers or hunters, killed by vehicles, or die from ingesting plastics or toxins from garbage cans.

beggar's button *noun* A burdock, a plant of the forest (*Arctium lappa*) with a burrlike seed that attaches easily to a passing object, such as to human clothing or animal fur.

2002 Myers *Best Yet Stories* 200 Those cockle burrs, known as beggar's buttons, had hundreds of shreds or hairs growing from a center. Each shred had a hook on the end of it that caused great entanglement.

beggar('s) lice (also *beggar tick*) *noun* Any of several plants (as of the *Desmodium* and *Bidens* genera) whose burrlike seed pods attach easily to passing objects, such as human clothing or animal fur. See also **hitch hiker**, **Spanish needle**, **stickerweed**.

1919 Combs *Word-List South* 35 *beggar lice* = a bothersome, flat, triangular shaped little burr. **1951** Pyle *Gatlinburg* 22 You know those little two-pronged stickers that come off onto your clothes by the hundreds when you walk through the weeds in the fall. . . . Here in the mountains they call them "beggar's lice." **1966–68** *DARE Survey* (Brasstown NC, Spruce Pine NC, Gatlinburg TN) *beggar lice*; (Burnsville NC, Spruce Pine NC) beggar's lice. **1966** Dykeman *Far Family* 273 She walked on through the abandoned orchard, bedraggling her skirts with beggar-lice and Spanish needles and all sorts of weed dust. [**1975** Hamel and Chiltoskey *Cherokee Plants* 30 Take this and other "stick-on" plants, drink decoction every four days for bad memory.] **1982** Stupka *Wildflowers* 59 [The naked-flower tick-trefoil] is one of a number of "stick-tights" or "beggar-ticks" growing in the southern mountains. **1994–98** Montgomery Coll (Cardwell and Pittillo agree that *beggar's lice* usually refers to *Desmodium* and *beggar tick* to *Bidens*).

beggar tick See **beggar('s) lice**.

begin *verb*

A Principal parts.

1 Variant past-tense forms *begin*, *beginned*, *begun*.

1780 (in **1853** Ramsey *Annals* 267) You know you begun the war by listening to the bad counsels of the King of England, and the falsehoods told you by his agents. **1813** Hartsell *Memora* 115 then the Deferent Companeys begun to form plat toons. **1845** (in **1974** Harris *High Times* 51) I begin to look about for a man I could lick and no mistake! **1861** *Griffin CW Letters* (Nov 24) I had to give him A spon off of whiskey Evry hour and he begun to git beter. **1864** *C A Walker CW Letters* (April 26) they would fire at us and directly the[y] begin to leave their brest works and we poured it into them. **1913** Kephart *Our Sthn High* 283–84 In mountain vernacular the Old English strong past tense still lives in begun, drunk, holped, rung, shrunk, sprung, stunk, sung, sunk, swum. **1939** Hall Coll (Bradley Fork NC) I beginned with the association, and in seven year I had a Baptist Church built there. *Ibid.* (Deep Creek NC) The birds begin to whistle, and we heard the gobbler gobbling across the far side of the right-hand fork of Indian Creek. **1956** Hall Coll (Raccoon Creek NC) The dogs begin running the coons. **1961** *Coe Ridge OHP-340* Yeah, that's what beginned it on. **1971** *AOHP/ALC-139* They had mines that begin to come in here by that time. **1991** Thomas *Sthn Appal* 122 Then he took that out, an' beginned to dry the hubs off of a night. **1998** *Dante OHP-24* When work picked up and begin to run, I was in about five hundred dollars in debt with the company.

[DARE *begin* v A1 chiefly South, South Midland]

2 Variant past-participle forms *began*, *begin*.

1941 Stuart *Men of Mts* 148 "I'd begin to think," he says, "my eyes weren't what they used to be." **1961** *Coe Ridge OHP-334A* They'd begin to curse at one another and abuse one another. **1973** GSMNP-79:9 Of course they always had the fireplace, which so many of the other homes had now begin to add heaters. **1977** *Jake Waldroop* 160 The fog had began to go up a little bit and we could tell where we was a going. **1983** Pyle *CCC 50th Anniv* A:2:1 One reason the people didn't have jobs then [is that] the Depression had begin. It'd a been a-goin' quite some time. **1997** GSMNPCOHP-1:5 Most people had begin to move out of the cove.

[DARE *begin* (at *begin* v A2) chiefly South, South Midland]

B in phrase *begin to* + *verbal noun* = to start.

1930 Justus *Foot Windy Low* 54 One morning Miss Annie was getting the children's ages to put down in a book, and they all began to talking about birthdays. **1939** Hall Coll (Mt Sterling NC) Then next day everybody begin to wondering where, what caused the blast to go off. **1961** *Coe Ridge OHP-334A* They begin to drifting away, and they finally quit that stuff [= moonshining]. **1964** Roberts *Hell-Fer-Sartin* 94 Soon the wind began to blowing and in came a young man and he took a seat by the third girl. **1972** *AOHP/ALC-226* We didn't have any coal or anything to build a fire with, and it was snowing. It begin to snowing. **2002** Magowan *Beech Mt Tales* 101 They begun to making fun of Jack.

beg on *verb phrase* To plead with.

1942 Campbell *Cloud-Walking* 6 Squire and the Little Teacher begged on her to sing again. **2008** *Rosie Hicks* 4 I kept a-begging on you and everything.

begone *interjection* Go away! Get off! (used to drive children or dogs away).

1953 Davison *Word-List Appal* 8 = Away! Used in speaking to dogs only. **1963** Edwards *Gravel* 19 "Now begone with you!" He kept pushing me around so that there was one pocket of his overalls I never got my hand into. **1966–69** *DARE Survey* (Barbourville KY, London KY, Pensacola NC, Cumberland Gap TN, Spencer WV) = expression used to drive away children.

[DARE *begone* v chiefly South Midland]

begun See **begin A1**.

behappen *verb* To happen to.

1862 *Thompson CW Letters* (Jan 24) doo the best yew can til i come home whitch I have confidence I will if no bad Axident be happens mee.

behaps *adverb* Perhaps.

1963 Williams *Metaphor Mt Speech II* 51 He prophesies a dire fate for the gangling boy who charges past the gate yelling like "wald Injun" and "behaps, a-shootin' off that 'ar old bulldog pistol o' hisn" besides.

behave it *verb phrase* To behave. For the *it*, see also **bed B1**, **go B2**, **run it over**.

1939 Hall *Coll* I guess you fellers are behavin' it all right, aren't you?

behind *preposition* variant forms *behint* [bɪ'haɪnt], *hine*. See also **ahind**.

1867 Harris *Sut Lovingood* 257 I'd swore tu a herearter. Yes, two herearters, by golly: one way up behint that ar black cloud wif the white bindin fur sich as her; the tuther herearter needs no wings nor laigs ither tu reach. **1958** Morgan *Gift from Hills* 18 Then hit was me en that calf down the hill, me a-runnin' to keep up, becuz I had my neck in that thar yoke en hit was either keep up or leave my neck behint. **1960** Hall *Smoky Mt Folks* 27 She was up behint a man on a mule. **1996–97** Montgomery *Coll*: *hine* (known to Cardwell, Oliver).

behind a dime *adverb phrase* In the least, at all.

1997 Montgomery *Coll* (known to Bush, Hooper); I wouldn't trust him behind a dime (Brown).

[DARE *behind a dime* adv phr chiefly South, South Midland, especially Middle Atlantic]

behindhand *adverb* Behind, late.

1862 *Warrick CW Letters* (April 1) I am verry bad behind hand with my crop.

behind of *phrasal preposition* Behind.

1972 *AOHP/LJC-203* I was up behind of her.

behint See **behind**.

beholden to *adjective phrase*

A Variant form *beholding*.

1934–47 *LAMSAS* (Swain Co NC).

B Obligated or indebted (to).

1913 Combs *KY Highlander* 16 Shakespearean English [terms still in use include] *beholden to* (King John I, Scene 1, l. 239). **1940** Haun *Hawk's Done* 146 He didn't want to be beholden to anybody. **1962** Dykeman *Tall Woman* 249 "Iffen you've helped save Old Thunder, I'll be beholden to you," Morgan Bludsoe said. **1974** Fink *Bits Mt Speech* 2 I'm not beholden to him. **1986** Pederson et al. *LAGS*: *beholden* = attested by 7/60 interviewees (11.7%) from E TN and 2/35 (5.7%) from N GA; 9/47 of all LAGS interviewees (19.1%) attesting term were from Appalachia. **2008** Terrell *Mt Lingo* As a thank you, mountain folks would say, "I'm beholden to you," and as a statement of fact, "I hain't beholden to nobody."

[originally the past participle of *behold*; DARE *beholden* adj now chiefly South, South Midland]

beholding See **beholden to A**.

be in for See **for[2] B2**.

being (also *being as*, *beings*, *beings as how*, *beings that*, *being that*, *bein's*, *benz*) *conjunction*, *conjunctive phrase* Because, seeing that.

1862 *Patton CW Letters* (July 24) I will send fifty Dollars by Mr Merrell being it is a good chance. **1863** *Gilley CW Letters* (June 16) I may not get the letter being as we ar marching. **1864** *Chapman CW Letters* (May 29) I don know what to rite so I will quit for the present being that I am tired of riting. **1892** Fruit *KY Words* 229 Bein's it's you, I will take a dollar for it. **1900** Harben *N GA Sketches* 20 Bein' as they say he's so fixy, I'm a-goin' to fetch in the lookin'-glass. **1944** Laughlin *Word-List Buncombe Co* 26 Being I can't go with him, I won't wait. **1952** Wilson *Folk Speech NC* 519 (Dellwood NC) *being* = since, because. **1956** McAtee *Some Dial NC* 4 *being* = seeing that. "Bein' it's you, the price is nothin'. **1964** Roberts *Hell-Fer-Sartin* 95 Now Jack always wanted to know everything, and being his cur'osity was up he walked up this road and after a while he come to the top of the hill. . . . He looked down and saw what looked like a party doings, and beings as how his cur'osity was up a right smart more he ambled down to see what was coming off. **1975–76** Wolfram/Christian *WV Coll* 83 I love her married, but being as she married before she got through school, that's what hurt me. **1976** Carter *Little Tree* 86 Grandpa said, that even being that we went to a hard-shell Baptist church, he would sure hate to see the hard-shells git control. **1987** Young *Lost Cove* 32 Beings that he was a church-going man, he cast his burden to the Lord. **1990** Fisher *Preacher Stories* 69 I just happen to recollect, being as you speak of sheep, that my ram died last month. **1998** Montgomery *Coll*: *being* (Adams, Bush, Ellis, Jones, Norris, Oliver, Weaver); Being that the president was sick, the vice-president adjourned the meeting (Brown); Being you're a teacher, what are you going to do this summer? (Cardwell); Being as you weren't at the meeting, you don't get to vote (Ledford); *beings* (Norris). **2013** Venable *How to Tawlk* 6 Benz how yore a'goan to Gatlinburg in the first place, do you care to buy me a few boxes of taffy?

[DARE *being* conj 1 chiefly South, South Midland, New England]

being as, **beings**, **beings as how**, **beings that**, **being that**, **bein's** See **being**.

bekase, **bekaze** See **because**.

bekum See **become**.

believe on *verb phrase* To believe, put trust in.

1937 Thornburgh *Great Smoky Mts* 131 Believe on me, off yander there is more mountains than I knowed were in the world. **1996–97** Montgomery *Coll* (known to Bush, Oliver); You can believe on his word (Brown); Believe on the Good Book (Hooper).

bell *verb* Of a dog: to bay.

1951 Giles *Harbin's Ridge* 56 There was something about the stilly night, and the belling of the hounds . . . that excited and quickened him. **1973** Davis *'Pon My Honor* 26 Them dogs a belling and whining at that deer made such a ruckus that the lawman couldn't hear his ears. **1978** Hiser *Quare Do's* 26 There, around the tallest cornstalk, stood all our dogs prancing and belling in a circle, pimeblank like they'd treed a coon up the cornstalk.

bell boy *noun* A type of logging worker. See citations.

1975 GSMNP-56:10 They had what was called a "bell boy" that touched two wires together that had batteries and a bell at the skidder. And when he'd touch these two wires together, it would ring the bell much the same as the telephone bell with a crank system. And they had different rings for different things to do—to slack off, pick up, go ahead, and things like that. **2009** Lloyd *Walker Valley* 38 It was the job of the bellboys to communicate to the engineer by hollering signals over long distances in the woods. **2010** Owenby *Trula Ownby* 12–13 The bell-boy would be stationed back up on the mountain, and when the crew got logs ready to come down the mountain the bell-boy rang a bell signaling the skidder operator they were ready.

bell cow *noun* See 1952 citation.

1952 Wilson *Folk Speech NC* 519 = the lead cow of a herd, the one that wears the bell; figuratively, a leader. **1998** Montgomery *Coll* (known to Bush, Cardwell); She's the bell cow of the women's group (Jones).

[DARE *bell cow* n 1 especially South, South Midland]

bell crowd See **belling**.

beller *verb, noun* To bellow.

1867 Harris *Sut Lovingood* 99 He wer the wust lookin cow brute, in the face, yu ever seed, an' hit made his bellerin soun like he hed the rattils. **1927** Mason *Lure of Smokies* 220 "B'ars bellers," he stated laconically, "sometimes when you shoot another of their kind." **1957** Broaddus *Vocab Estill Co KY* 6 = the noise a cow makes when its calf is being weaned. **1964** Roberts *Hell-Fer-Sartin* 95 No sooner had he got settled when he heard a furious bellering down the valley.

bell hoop See **ballhoot**.

bell house *noun* See citations.

c1960 Wilson *Coll* = the small house on a church or school roof in which the large bell is housed, a belfry. **1969** *DARE Survey* (Hindman KY).

belling *noun* A raucous celebration given newlyweds on their wedding night, usually at their new residence; hence *bell crowd* = the revelers who conduct such a celebration. Same as **serenade**, **shivaree**.

1946 Nixon *Glossary VA Words* 11 *belling* = serenade after a wedding . . . [a term used] in the northern part of the Blue Ridge. **1949** Kurath *Word Geog East US* 79 *Belling* [is used] in large parts of the Midland . . . Pennsylvania is doubtless the home of *belling* in the New World. **1964** Clarke *Stuart's Writing* 160–61 *belling* = ringing of cowbells, rattling of pans, beating on a wash tub, shooting, and noise-making in general just outside the dwelling of a newlywed couple; usually the couple serve refreshments—often including whisky—and invite the serenaders in for square dancing or play-party games. The practice has declined since World War II. **1966** Dakin *Vocab Ohio River Valley* 494 Outside of Ohio, however, *belling* is rare. It is apparently unknown in Kentucky except in the northeastern Mountain section which shares other terms with the Hanging Rock region of Ohio and with West Virginia (where *belling* is common). **1977** Simpkins *Culture* 44 The "bell crowd" was one in which the neighbors got together and located where the couple was the first night they were married so everybody came with all the noisemakers they could to keep them awake all night long and keep them from going to bed. The expected pattern was the young husband had to come out and bribe them to go home and leave them alone if he had the money. **2007** Milnes *Signs Cures Witches* 63 Belling, a practice sometimes known elsewhere as shivaree, from the French charivari, is still practiced in rural West Virginia. The word belling refers to the common use of cowbells to make a disturbing racket. All kinds of mischief [are] involved, most predicated on the effort to disrupt the new couple's wedding night. Grooms are commonly rode [sic] on a rail and brides are set in a tub of ice water, practices with sexual connotations. A Tucker County family has a rail on which is carved the initials of all the grooms who have been ridden on it. I was told of cables being stretched tight between a tree and the house, the cables rosined and played with a board, causing the whole house to vibrate with an unearthly noise. Clapper boxes are cranked with a handle creating an annoying racket. At a house burning coal or wood, if the couple fails to make an appearance, a sack of feed is put on top of the chimney and the couple is "smoked out."

[DARE *belling* vbl n now chiefly wPA, WV, OH, IN, MI]

bellows *noun*

A Variant form *bellowses*.

1867 Harris *Sut Lovingood* 76–77 Three ove her smiles when she wer a tryin ove hersef, taken keerfully ten minutes apart, wud make the gran' captin ove a temprunce s'iety so durn'd drunk, he wudn't no his britches frum a par ove bellowses, ur a pledge frum a-a-warter-pot. **1942** Hall *Phonetics Smoky Mts* 98.

[DARE *bellows* n A2 especially South Midland]

B Shortness of breath in a horse.

1995 Montgomery *Coll* The horse had the bellows (Shields).

bellowses See **bellows**.

bell-tail *noun* A rattlesnake.

1907 Dugger *Balsam Groves* 79 The braver of them return to the onset and pelt the poor bell-tail to death. **1917** Kephart *Word-List* 408 = rattlesnake. **1982** Powers and Hannah *Cataloochee* 382 A lovely name for rattlesnakes in Cataloochee was "bell-tails," called so with good reason, for they rang out, or were supposed to ring out, their warning. **1995–97** Montgomery *Coll* (known to Brown, Cardwell).

[DARE *bell-tail* n chiefly sAppalachians, GA, northern FL]

bell tree *noun* See citation.

1921 Campbell *Sthn Highlander* 109–10 It had been the practice in the neighborhood to leave a jug in a brush heap with a cup. The patron, watched from some secure vantage point, would take what he wished and leave payment in the cup. In other places there would be a bell-tree, or a hollow trunk, which yielded its store when the bell was rung. In the case in point, circumstantial evidence was strong, but the difficulties in getting convincing proof were many.

bellwood *noun* A common deciduous tree (*Halesia carolina*) in the region. Same as **peawood**.

1883 Zeigler and Grosscup *Heart of Alleghanies* 111 In the forests which belt the streams, the bell-wood is white with blossoms, and every dog-wood white with flowers. **1974–75** McCracken *Logging* 15:11 I call it a bellwood, but then the right name would have been a silverbell or in that time I guess peawood is what we would know it by. **1982** Powers and Hannah *Cataloochee* 438, Pink and white silverbells, called "bellwood" locally, embroidered the middle slopes.

belly band *noun* A strip of cloth tied around a newborn's waist, commonly used into the 20th century to protect the navel as the end of the umbilical cord shrivels away.

2003 Cavender *Folk Medicine* 131 The baby's navel area was thought to have a weakness that would result in a rupture; to prevent this, a "belly band" made from a piece of cloth was tied tightly around the baby's waist for six weeks. **2005** Williams *Gratitude* 52 A belly band was a strip of white knit cloth about four inches wide that they pinned good and tight around its belly.

belong *verb* (+ *infinitive*) To be obliged, deserve.

1911 Shearin *E KY Word-List* 537 = an auxiliary indicating duty or obligation; e.g., "Do I belong to chop the wood?" = "Must I (shall I) chop the wood?" **1913** Bruce *Terms from TN* 58 = should, ought to. "It *belongs* to be here." **1917** Kephart *Word-List* 408 = to be due. "That train don't *belong to* come till 12:15." **1952** Wilson *Folk Speech NC* 519 = to deserve, to behoove, to be appropriate, should. "He *belongs* to come here today." **1958** Campbell *Tales* 23 A song-ballet belongs to be sung and listened to and remembered and sung again. **2009** Benfield *Mt Born* 124 To "belong" to do something is to know that it is suitable, the right thing. Something which, by all accounts, should be accomplished. . . . If one man owes money to another, he belongs to pay it back. If a bus is scheduled to leave Craggy at 4:15 p.m., it belongs to do so. **2016** *Blind Pig* (June 9) "You don't belong to do that" meaning you shouldn't do that.

[DARE *belong* v B South, South Midland]

Belsnickel (also *Belsnickle, Pelsnickel, Pelznickel*) *noun* A person in masquerade who goes from house to house at the Christmas season sometimes to play pranks, beg for treats, but especially to query the good behavior of children; such a figure used by parents to warn children and make them behave; hence noun *belsnickling* = this custom, *belsnickler* = one who practices this custom, verb *pelse* = to approach a person's house with the intention to engage in this custom, nouns *pelse, pelsing* = this custom. See also **Kris Kringle**, **Santa Clausing**.

c1915 (in **1997** Blaustein *Pelznickel*) He said, "the Pelznickel will be here if you don't hush!!" And about that time I heard tapping on the door. He said, "you lay down, quiet down! The Pelznickel's here!" And you know, I hushed crying. **1995** Milnes *Old Christmas* 28 The custom of belsnickling in West Virginia is of dressing up in disguise, old clothes, or rags with masks and going from house to house. Belsnickles generally got involved in making mischief. **1995** Suter *Shenandoah Folklife* 31 You'd just go outside and holler and holler till they'd come to the door and invite you in. Just holler "Pelsnickels! Pelsnickels! Pelsnickels!" *Ibid.* 31 The words *belsnickel* and *kriskringle* are derived from German: *Belsnickel* contains the words Pelz (fur) as well as Saint Nicholaus [sic] (Santa Claus). . . . Santa Claus, *Belsnickel* and Kriskringle are thus essentially the forerunners of our present-day Christmas customs. *Ibid.* 34 We're going to have to stop at Mr. Spicher's house, we want to pelse him. So we pulled up in his driveway, my daddy and my uncle, they go up to the door and knock and holler, "Would you like to see a pelse?" **2006** *Encycl Appalachia* 850 In the mountains of Pennsylvania, eastern West Virginia, and the Great Valley region of Virginia, where substantial numbers of Germans settled, some communities practice the old German custom of belsnickling. Over time, the belsnickle, from the German Pelz Nichol, or "Saint Nicholas in fur," evolved from a dark figure who threatened and admonished children to be good to a friendly character recognizable in the modern-day Santa Claus. In some Appalachian communities, belsnickles still visit neighbors at Christmas and, in much the same way as carolers, are rewarded by gifts or food. **2006** *WV Encycl* 51 Of German origin, belsnickling is similar to mumming traditions as found in Anglo-Celtic countries (England, Scotland, Ireland). The term is an Anglicized version of two German words: Pels (fur) and Nicholas (St. Nicholas). Over time, pels Nicholas came to be pronounced belsnickle, and it simply means a furry St. Nicholas. . . . The practice of belsnickling (also called "pelsing") in West Virginia involves a group, dressed in masquerade, going from house to house visiting neighbors and having the inhabitants guess who they are. Sometimes mischief is involved, and often the belsnickles were given seasonal treats such as cider and cake. Some older people remember that they, as belsnickles, carried a switch and switched the hands of children who reached for the candy they offered. The belsnickle figure sometimes represented this darker presence, and it was common for parents to warn children to "be good or the belsnickle will get you." **2007** Milnes *Signs Cures Witches* 185 An examination of the terminology shows that the words shooters, mummers, belsnicklers, guisers, fantasticals, Fastnacht observers, and shanghais once described more clearly defined activities and character traits in their Old World forms but have since melded into the aggregate forms found in the Appalachian countryside. *Ibid.* 186 To people in the Potomac Highlands, belsnickling is the action of going from house to house in masquerade, with residents guessing the belsnicklers' identities. . . . Sometimes treats were offered to the belsnicklers, and sometimes the belsnicklers offered treats to the household. The custom is strong in living memory among older people in areas of eastern West Virginia, and the practice itself persists. . . . Belsnickling is still practiced in Grant County [WV]. Somehow, against great odds, this custom has found a way to continue into the twenty-first century in West Virginia. . . . The word anglicizes the German term Pelz Nicholas—pelz meaning "fur" or "pelt," and Nicholas as in St. Nicholas, combining to mean St. Nicholas in fur. The "Nicholas cult," as scholars term it, draws upon ancient legend to personify Santa Claus, originally St. Nicholas, who became the jolly old elf with whom many of us were familiarized as children. *Ibid.* 190 Belsnickling is a ritual tradition so strong that you can not find an older Pendleton Countian [of WV] who did not participate in, or is at least well acquainted with, the practice. Belsnickles were once dark characters, as Robert Simmons remembered, who carried switches and caused children to be warned, "Be good or the belsnickle will get you." The transfer of this once solitary character, the foreboding belsnickle, to a group mentality and group activity (belsnickling), as in the informal visit, is generally attributed to the influence of mumming traditions in Pennsylvania. The process of going from house to house in masquerade, sometimes begging, eases a primeval urge to act out in a ritualistic way during the darkest period of the year. . . . In West Virginia, people have not solidified a common pronunciation for the character, indicating that he is still a folk figure with much variation, even in terminology, and has not been typeset through popular media and become a commonly known and pronounced entity like Santa Claus. In Pendleton County, the figure is the belsnickle.

[DARE *Belsnickel* n 2 German settlement areas; *belsnickeling* vbl n German settlement areas, especially PA]

benasty *verb* To soil or befoul. See also **nasty B.**

1913 Kephart *Our Sthn High* 283 The little feller fell down and benastied himself to beat the devil. **1960** Cooper *Jularker Bussed* Such talk benasties a child's mind. **1973** Watkins and Watkins *Yesterday* 171 I throwed up twice on the floor, and I was so sick that I benastied my feet and my clothes in the mess. **1995–97** Montgomery *Coll* (known to Brown, Cardwell, Ellis, Jones, Norris, Oliver).

[DARE *benasty* v especially South Midland]

bench *noun*

1 A relatively level expanse of land, sometimes cultivated, on a mountainside or mountaintop; a shelf of land below a ridge or cliff. Also called **upland.** See also **bench field.**

1913 Morley *Carolina Mts* 241 The valleys that run up into the mountains hold little nests of houses, and here and there, far up on the mountain-side, in a cove or on a fertile "bench," one may find a clearing with its lonely cabin and its cornfield, to be reached only by a trail through the forest. **1923** (in **1952** Mathes *Tall Tales* 10) And Grandad's stick rapped smartly on the stones as he turned toward his cottage nestling on a "bench" of the mountain, a hundred yards above the road. **1939** Hall *Coll* (Proctor NC) = a piece of land that lays flat up on a hill, also called upland. Most people would call it a bench. There can be a bench also in a flat, wooded area. You don't hear upland used so very much. You hear bench much more. *Ibid.* (Sevierville TN) = a level place on top of a mountain. **c1950** Adams *Grandpap* 219 The house that we moved into was a little one-room split-log cabin. . . . It stood on a little bench of land about five hundred yards, up the hollow. **1957** Broaddus *Vocab Estill Co KY* 7 = a stretch of level land at the base of a cliff. **1963** Lord *Blue Ridge* 26D In the high regions of the Southern Appalachians, "levels" and "benches" frequently cover extensive areas at or near the crestline. **1980** Still *Run for Elbertas* 95 We climbed to the first bench of the knob and paused to catch our breaths. **1993** Brewer *Great Smoky Mts* 21 Some [settlers] found little flat areas on the hillsides, which they called "benches," where they planted tiny cornfields. After all the flatland was taken, some started cultivating the hillsides, which was disastrous, for the rains came and washed away the disturbed topsoil. **1996** Montgomery *Coll* = a comparatively level "shelf" on the side of a mountain, named after the owner of the land, the type of trees growing, etc. (Cardwell). **1999** Morgan *Gap Creek* 13 I figured if I could get to the bench on the mountain where Riley's spring was we could rest and give Masenier a drink of cold water.

2 See citation. See also **bench mining, highwall.**

2002 Armstead *Black Days* 241 = [the] bottom part of a coal seam after the coal above is mined.

bench field *noun* An open, flat expanse of cultivated land on the side of a mountain or hill. See also **bench.**

1940 Still *River of Earth* 138 He had brought a dozen down from the bench field and cornsilks were scattered about like brown locks of a woman's hair. **1949** McDavid *Grist* 106 (Fannin Co GA) = level field on hillside. **1956** Hall *Coll* (Roaring Fork TN) We had a big bench field away up on the mountain.

bench-legged *adjective* Of a dog: bow-legged, with forelegs spread wide apart.

1866 Smith *So Called* 159 He'd have his soul transmigrated to a bench-leg'd fice. **1937** Hall *Coll* (Wears Cove TN) A beagle [is] a bench-legged feist. **1938** Hall *Coll* (Emerts Cove TN) = having legs like those of bulldogs, short and spread apart.

[DARE *bench-legged* adj chiefly South, South Midland]

bench mining *noun* Same as **contour mining.** See also **highwall.**

2006 Mooney *Lg Coal Mining* 1028 In "contour mining," also known as "bench mining" or "highwall mining," workers follow the contour or direction of a seam along a mountainside, cutting straight down to remove the overburden and expose the seam.

2012 Portelli *They Say* 417 The "bench" and the "highwall" are the flat and the vertical cuts created by strip mining.

bench walker *noun* Same as **Holy Roller**.

1998 Montgomery *Coll* (known to Oliver).

bendified *adjective* Bent.

1919 Combs *Word-List South* 36 Zeke 'lowed ez how he'd been called to give his dream at the meetin', a-tellin' 'em how he'd dremp of drappin' down on his bendified knees in the cornfield, and a-makin' the masterest moanin' you ever hear. **1957** Combs *Lg Sthn High: Word List* 10 = bended. Ex.: "The preacher was down on his bendified knees."

ben-hicky-my-funker (also *hicky-my-funker*) *noun* See citation.

1944 Combs *Word-List Sthn High* 17 = a term of disparagement. "He's a pyore ben-hicky-my-funker." Also hicky-my-funker.

benighted *adjective* Overtaken by darkness, detained by nightfall.

1846 (in **1974** Harris *High Times* 59–60) Seeing as how I was a benighted boy, he reckoned I mought just lite. **1883** Zeigler and Grosscup *Heart of Alleghanies* 114 Not a column of smoke curls upward through the trees, unless it be from the open fire before the temporary shelter of a benighted cattle-herder, or a party of bear-hunters. **1963** Edwards *Gravel* 67 They would come back long after dark; and then it was indeed a sad sound to hear the benighted wagons rattling and banging over the rough stones. **1974** Fink *Bits Mt Speech* 2 = detained after nightfall. "John figured he'd be home by sundown, but he was *benighted*." **1995–97** Montgomery *Coll* (known to Brown, Bush, Jones, Oliver).

[DARE *benighted* ppl adj formerly widespread, now chiefly South Midland]

bent *noun* See citations.

1892 Fruit *KY Words* 229 = the timbers of one side of a barn as they stand framed together. **1957** Broaddus *Vocab Estill Co KY* 7 = a section of a barn between the rows of beams that form the framework of the barn.

ben't See **be A1b**.

benz See **being**.

bereft *adjective* Confused, crazy.

1944 Combs *Word-List Sthn High* 17 = crazy, "touched." "Air ye plumb bereft, ye fool?" **1994** Montgomery *Coll* (known to Brown, Bush, Cardwell, Jones, Oliver).

[shortening of *bereft of reason* (or *sense*)]

berry *verb* To gather wild berries; hence verbal noun *berrying*.

1930 Armstrong *This Day and Time* 98 I've been a-berryin' a many a time on your pap's mountain land. **1944** Justus *Billy and Bones* 52 The crops on Little Twin Mountain were laid by. It was time for folks to go berrying. **1964** Reynolds *Born of Mts* 10 When berrying, insect repellent should be put on the socks, and afterwards one should bathe or change clothing. *Ibid.* 17 When berrying, overalls are a good protection against briers and to some degree against snakes which may be there, but are rarely seen as with most wildlife. **1984** Woods *WV Was Good* 226 Bill put at me to go berryin' with him that morning.

berry canning *noun* Formerly, a neighborhood work activity in the fall, when berries and other fruits are preserved for the winter, with the work often followed by merrymaking.

1959 Hall *Coll* (Hartford TN) For social life back in the mountains when I was very young, it was mostly confined to working parties. We would have the apple peeling, the berry canning, the molasses making, and corn husking ... these seasonal affairs that the older people would let the younger people gather and do the seasonal canning or processing of food and promise them that afterward they could have a little social life in the form of doing the buck [and] wing or the hoedown.

berrying See **berry**.

berry sass *noun* See citation.

1978 Slone *Common Folks* 308 Berry sass (sauce) was a breakfast dish. The boiling berries were thickened with a little flour and water, not quite as heavy as for a pie filling, sweetened and served like a pudding.

berry stemming *noun* Formerly, a late-summer family or community work activity to remove stems from gathered wild berries.

1977 Shields *Cades Cove* 35 Berry stemmings occurred in late August or early September when the "gooseberries," sometimes called deerberries and related to the blueberries, were harvested.

be shet of, be shut of See **shut B**.

beside of (also *side of*) *phrasal preposition* Next to, alongside.

1892 Dromgoole *Dan to Beersheba* 77 Jake Marlow said that even the "big snow-winter" of forty years back, "ware a mighty small pertater side o' this here col' snap." **1939** Hall *Coll* She came over and set beside of me. **1955** Ritchie *Singing Family* 194 One of them would be standing beside of his girl, patting his foot and clapping and waiting his time to dance out. **1972** *AOHP/ALC-388* I took these half a gallons of whiskey out, laid them down right in beside of the tomato plants, and took the hoe and raked the dirt up over them just like a fresh-hoed tomato plant. **1979** *Big South Fork OHP-11* He got on that horse and rid him up beside of the porch, and I slid off on him. **1989** *Matewan OHP-9* [On Christmas Eve] we'd hang our sock up beside of the chimley. **1996** Woodring *Times Gone By* 7 He said he uz shootin at a porch post right there next beside of him. **2001** Montgomery *File* Let me put the bag down beside of you (60-year-old man, Blount Co TN).

beside oneself *adjective phrase* Disoriented, confused.

1939 Hall *Coll* (White Oak NC) He's kindly beside himself = "kind of off a little bit." **1997** Montgomery *Coll* (known to Ellis, Hooper).

bess bug (also *bessie bug*, *Betsy bug*, *Betty bug*) *noun* A large black beetle (family Passalidae), whose blood is sometimes said to have curative power.

1901 Price *KY Folk-Lore* 32 If you take a "Bess bug" (a large black beetle) and cut off his head one drop of blood will flow, this will cure the earache every time. **c1960** Wilson *Coll*: *Betty* (or *Betsy*) *bug*—any large beetle: "Jimmy caught a Betsy bug and put it down my back." **2003** Cooper *Gathering Memories* 45 If your child has an earache, catch a bessie bug and put a drop of its blood into the child's ear.

[DARE (at *Betsy bug*) chiefly South, South Midland]

best *adverb* Most. See also **bestest**, **(the) best kind**, **(the) best**.

1926 Hunnicutt *Twenty Years* 76 He had given the bear a dead shot and was the best pleased boy I ever saw. **1939** Hall *Coll* (Hazel Creek NC) I got the best tickled I ever was in life. We all went back up there [bear hunting].

the best *adverb phrase* Very well, the most. See also **best**, **the 5**, **the best kind**.

1939 Hall *Coll* (Saunook NC) I always thought they got along the best. . . . I've enjoyed [my job] the best so far. **1975** GSMNP-62:2 We possum hunted and we coon hunted and we hog hunted and we done a little of this and a little of that out here, but the main joy part of it was hog hunting and coon hunting, you know, to have some fine races of coons and hogs, and we enjoyed that about the best of anything in the hunting line. **1978** Hiser *Quare Do's* 12 They got along the best, like two families of mice in the same fodder shock.

[cf CUD *the best* 1 (at *best*) "very well"]

bestest *adjective* Best. See also **-est 3**.

1961 *Coe Ridge OHP-334B* They made the bestest song about that ever you seen. **1981** Brewer *Wonderment* 34 We dozen Oakley children would get out of bed at the crack of day and run half a mile down the road to get "Christmas gift" on our Great Aunt Lindy (Ogle) because she made the "bestest" sweetbread. **1986** Ogle *Lucinda* 44 What we called "Sweetbread" she could make the bestest in all the country we thought. **2009** Sutton *Me and Likker II* 199 I had the bestest daddy in the world, at least I think so!

best hand to See **hand A3**.

the best in the world See **(the) best kind**.

the best kind (also *the best in the world*, *the best upon earth*) *adverb phrase* Very well, more than anything else. See also **best**, **(the) best**, **(the) finest kind**.

1861 *Martin CW Letters* (Oct 13) I am enjoying my self the best in the world. **1862** *Love CW Letters* (March 20) I would like the Best kind to be at home. **1862** *Proffit CW Letters* (May 11) We are geting along the best kind. **1862** *Watters-Curtis CW Letters* (May 22) I woud like to see you the Best apon earth But i cant. **1864** *Councill CW Letters* (July 20) Aunt I would like to see you all the Best in the world. **1889** *Cole Letters* 77 I would like to be there the best in the world. **1905** Miles *Spirit of Mts* 132 I'd like the best in the world to see you and your folks, but I've done promised to go home with Sister 'Lectar Fetridge. **1948** Chase *Grandfather Tales* 116 Yes, I'd like that the best in the world! **1966** Dykeman *Far Family* 66 He did like strawberries the best in the world. **1990** Whitener *Thrice-Told* I would like to see you all the best in the world and Set down with you to breakfast and drink some milk and coffee and eat Some butter and porck [sic] and many other things.

best liver See **good liver**.

beth root *noun* The erect trillium (*Trillium erectum*), from which an extract is used medicinally to promote childbirth and for other purposes. Same as **wake robin**.

2006 Howell *Medicinal Plants* 40 Bethroot is an important part of the diverse American Indian apothecary of herbs used as labor tonics. The common name "bethroot" is derived from the more accurate name, birthroot, because it was often combined with black cohosh . . . and blue cohosh (*Caulophyllum thalictroides*) to stimulate uterine contractions and promote labor. Bethroot also has a long history of use as a folk remedy for treating chronic respiratory problems including coughs, congestion, breathing difficulties, and asthma. It was used as an astringent to relieve diarrhea, hemorrhage, and excessive mucus secretions. A poultice of fresh leaf and root was applied to tumors, slow healing ulcers, insect bites, and gangrenous conditions.

[alteration of *birthroot*]

Betsy bug See **bess bug**.

Betsy sop *noun* Flour gravy. Same as **Hannah sop**.

1989 Hannah *Reflections* 4 They both agreed that he needed something hot, so they made him a run of that Betsy sop. **1997** Montgomery *File* = flour gravy, as "That Betsy sop was a life saver; if it wasn't for that, I wouldn't be here talking to you" (70-year-old man, Maggie Valley NC).

bettern *auxiliary verb* Shouldn't.

1913 Kephart *Our Sthn High* 283 We better git some wood, bettern we? **1952** Wilson *Folk Speech NC* 520 We'd better go, *better'n we?* **1994–97** Montgomery *Coll* (known to Bush, Cardwell, Oliver).

[apparently a contraction of *better* + *not*]

Betty bug See **bess bug**.

betwixt *preposition*

A Variant form *twixt*. See also **atween**, **atwixt**. [See **1886** in **B**.]

1925 (in **1935** Edwards *NC Novels* 79) *twixt*. **1953** Davison *Word-List Appal* 14 *twixt* = still in use in extremely isolated sections of the mountains of Kentucky. **1976** GSMNP-114 You can see back twixt that house and that tree.

B Between.

1783 *Washington Co Petition* . . . thence running a North Course to the dividing Line Betwixt Sullivan and Washington Counties, thence along sd line to the Chimney top Mountain. **1794** *Bent Creek*

Church Minutes 18 a Dificulty subsisting Betwixt sister Maryann Coffman and sister Lydia Keel Being submitted to a committee is thereby adjested. **1862** *Love CW Letters* (Sept 10) we haft to drill one [h]our be fore break first and one our be tweixt that and dinner. **1864** *Chapman CW Letters* (May 15) I am in hopes this war will wind up betwixt now and next winter. **1886** Smith *Sthn Dialect* 348 He had hyeard ther might be a war 'twixt the Republicans and Dimercrats, but, as he hadn't hyeard any mo' about it, he reckined ther wan't gwine ter be none. **1928** (in **1952** Mathes *Tall Tales* 56) He said they'd told him what was writ on Tom's monument stone, an' them words kep a-risin' up betwixt him an' his Maker. **1976** *GSMNP*- 114:27 It's down here betwixt here and Walland.

[OED3 *betwixt* prep 1a now somewhat archaic; DARE *betwixt* prep scattered, but chiefly South, South Midland]

beyance, **beyanst**, **beyant** See **beyond**.

beyond *preposition* Variant forms *beyance*, *beyanst*, *beyant*.

1859 Taliaferro *Fisher's River* 52 I had a hog claim over beyant Moor's Fork. **1928** (in **1952** Mathes *Tall Tales* 67) A feller told me t'other day the ol' varmint has been a-usin' back in Huggins' Hell beyant the Alum cave. **1959** Cooper *Corpse Could Sleep* My old man jist shut his eye peaceful-like and passed out as his speerit leapt beyant the furder bank of Jordan. **1963** Williams *Metaphor Mt Speech II* 53 A sharp-tongue matriarch [will] take the offender "daoun a peg or two fer a-tryin' to get beyanst her raisin'." **1987** Young *Lost Cove* 74 Back beyance Wolf Ridge, Little Cove Creek had gathered up a dozen branches while it was hurrying to hook on with the other streams below the Chestnut Flat.

[DARE (at *beyond* prep, adv) chiefly South, South Midland]

B from a bull's bag, **not to know** (also *B from bull foot, not to know*; *B from bull's foot, not to know*) *verb phrase* Not to know anything at all.

1895 Murfree *Phantoms* 263 Never hearn afore ez enny o' the Yerbys knowed B from bull-foot. **1927** Woofter *Dialect from WV* 359 That driver doesn't know B from a bull's bag about loading his wagon. **1978** Hiser *Quare Do's* 39 They didn't neither one know b from bull's foot, as they said back then.

[DARE *B from (a) bull's foot, not to know* now chiefly South, Midland]

b'gad *interjection* Used as a mild oath. See also **bedabs**, **by**, **dad-**, **i**, **I'll be dod**.

1943 Stuart *Private Tussie* 78 B'Gad if I'll be cornswoggled into anything more.

[alteration of *by God*]

Bible book *noun* The Bible.

1940 Haun *Hawk's Done* 51 A little while before dinner he told Amy to fetch him the Bible Book. **1941** Still *Troublesome Creek* 148 I wouldn't believe Bot Shedders and him on a steeple o' Bible-books. **1952** Wilson *Folk Speech NC* 520 = Bible. **1998** Montgomery *Coll* I believe on the Bible book (Cardwell).

Bible bug *noun* Same as **pharaoh**.

1969 *DARE Survey* (Tompkinsville KY) = [There are] billions of 'em every 8–10 years, holler[ing] "Pharaoh" over and over.

Bible reader *noun* A preacher.

1931 Combs *Lg Sthn High* 1311 = a preacher.

biddable *adjective* Obedient, well-behaved, compliant.

1886 Smith *Southernisms* 36 = obedient, tractable; *biddableness* = [having a] disposition to obey: I have been familiar with the word in this sense in South Carolina all my life, and it is so used in East Tennessee, Georgia, and no doubt elsewhere. **1914** Furman *Sight* 71 I hain't only got these fine store-teeth and a tamed and biddable stummick. **c1940** Simms *Coll* Nice dog, as biddable as a child. **1957** Combs *Lg Sthn High: Word List* 10 = strong, good, as in: "He's got a biddable stomach." **1996–97** Montgomery *Coll* (known to Bush, Oliver, Weaver).

[EDD *biddable* adj Scot, Irel, nEngl; SND *biddable* adj "obedient"; CUD *biddable* (at *bid* v) "of a child: obedient, willing"; DARE *biddable* adj chiefly South, South Midland]

biddie See **biddy**.

biddie peck *verb phrase* Of a woman: to nag (her busband) mildly.

1957 Parris *My Mts* 112 While they may biddie-peck and fault their yokemate behind the door, they'll go through thick and thin for him without asking why. **1995–97** Montgomery *Coll* (known to Brown, Cardwell).

biddy (also *biddie*) *noun* A baby chicken; used as an affectionate term for a hen. Also *interjection* Come! (used as a call to chickens). See also **deedie**, **dibbler**, **diddle**[2] **A**, **widdie**.

1934–47 *LAMSAS* (Madison Co NC, Swain Co NC). **1948** Still *Nest* 54 She saw herself hiding in the coophouse, to play with newly hatched biddies as she had done the day before. **1978** Reese *Speech NE Tenn* 30 *biddy* = attested by 2/12 (16.7%) speakers; *biddie-biddie* = attested by 2/12 (16.7%) speakers. **1996** Montgomery *Coll* (known to Adams, Cardwell, Norris). **1998** Hyde *My Home* 81 [The rooster] moved with dispatch to protect his image and to quell this young upstart who would dare foment disruption to the Kingdom. For that could confuse the hens, distract the pullets, create general unrest and even lead the young biddies into ways foreign to the accepted sovereignty.

[OED3 *biddy* n^2 obsolete except dialect; DARE *biddy* n^1, n^3 probably coalescence of *biddy* and *beedie* of African origin, akin to Kongo *bidibidi* "a bird"]

biff *verb* To strike, deliver a blow to (someone). See also **beef C**.

1904 Fox *Christmas Eve* Captain Wells descended with no little majesty and "biffed" him. **c1950** Adams *Grandpap* 129 Now that made Will mad. He said, "If you do that again, Granddaddy, I'll biff you!" **1962** Williams *Mtneers Mind Manners* 19 Woe to the daring swain who attempts to "buss" [a girl] unawares if he is not prepared to be "biffed one on the snoot."

[probably imitative; DARE *biff* v scattered, but especially South, South Midland]

big

A *adjective*

1 See **big old**.

2 Pregnant, far advanced in pregnancy. See also **break one's leg 1**.

1929 Duncan and Duncan *Sayings* 234 A woman that's big musn't look at nothin' or she'll mark hit [= the child]. **1961** Williams *Content Mt Speech* 15 Her pap cussed the top of the house off when he larnt she was a-gittin' big. **1978** Hiser *Quare Do's* 152–53 There I was with three younguns and me so big I couldn't hardly walk with anothern. **1994–97** Montgomery *Coll* (known to Adams, Ledford, Norris, Oliver, Weaver), = not avoided in mixed company (Brown), = like *pregnant*, this term is not used in mixed company (Cardwell).

[DARE *big* adj 1 chiefly South, South Midland]

3 Of a river: high.

1973 GSMNP-79:12 We'd go down [to]what we called the sluice. That's where the water in the river after it gets so big runs.

4 In phrases *a big majority, the big part* = most.

1978 Montgomery *White Pine Coll* IX-1 My father did the big part of the farming. **1997** GSMNPCOHP-3:13 A big majority of the people went to church pretty regular. Of course it wasn't anything else to do.

5 in comparative phrases *the bigger majority, the bigger part* = most. See also **greater part**.

1960 McCaulley *Cades Cove* I'd make that casket. It'd take me a day and a part of the night, the bigger part of the night with a helper, to make one. **1974–75** McCracken *Logging* 6:102 They done the bigger majority of their logging on Laurel Creek.

6 in superlative phrases *the biggest half, the biggest majority, (the) biggest part, the biggest portion* = the most, largest.

1922 *TN CW Ques* 1402 (Grundy Co TN) I was arenter [sic] had in 20 acars in corn lost the bigest part of that. **1944** Hayes *Word-List NC* 34 The *biggest half* of the people does it. **1969** GSMNP-37:2:26 The biggest part of them was Democrats. It went Democratic, biggest part of the time. **1973** GSMNP-57:75 The biggest portion of people didn't have lumber. **1974** Dabney *Mt Spirits* 120 Sometimes we'd put a shelter over it, but the biggest part of the time we just had something to cover up the boxes to keep the mash from getting wet and the rest of the things was open. **1977** Shackelford et al. *Our Appalachia* 160 The biggest majority of them [coal miners who had emigrated from Hungary] were Catholic people [and] they didn't go to the American church. **1978** Montgomery *White Pine Coll* IV-2 I'd say this bonded whiskey has cut the biggest portion of [moonshining] out. **1982** *Foxfire VII* 208 He wouldn't say he could [stop blood] but you'd tell him an animal or a person was bleeding and the biggest part of the time it'd soon stop. **1983** Smith *Recollections of Blue Ridge* 23 I never spoke back to Mama or Papa in my life; the biggest majority of mountain children were brought up to respect their parents. **1985** Williams *Role of Folklore* 69 I got to noticin' that the biggest part of the people that used "you all" is movies stars on TV.

[DARE *big* adj 2 chiefly South Midland]

B *adverb* To a great or extreme degree.

1939 Hall *Coll* I'll divide big with you. **1940** Haun *Hawk's Done* 106 The Shin-bone branch is up so big I can't go after Ma. **1957** GSMNP-23:1:19 He said he didn't know whether it was all true or not when he'd yodel big, but if [it] was true, he wouldn't never yodel.

C *verb*

1 To make pregnant (a term often avoided in polite or mixed company); hence participial adjective *bigged* pregnant.

1917 Kephart *Word-List* 408 = to get with child. "Doc, Orr *bigged* Sis' Posey." **1939** Hall *Coll* (Proctor NC) [A poor woman is one] that's bigged, in a family way, in other words, pregnant. I've heard it used a few times. Just old timers used it. **1994–97** Montgomery *Coll* (known to Brown, Cardwell, Norris); He bigged her and had to marry her (Jones); He bigged his girlfriend (Cardwell). **2004** Adams *Old True Love* 98 "Don't pay me no never mind," I said to Larkin. "I am just some woman who is bigged."

[DARE *big* v 1 chiefly South, South Midland]

2 To exaggerate, enlarge.

1943 Hannum *Mt People* 148 He was biggin' and biggin' the story. **1972** Cooper *NC Mt Folklore* 90 Bigging and bigging it = exaggerating.

big church *noun* See citation.

1967 Fetterman *Stinking Creek* 137 This is the "big church," a church in the open, under a tree or under the open sky. Many mountain people will tell you, "I married in the big church." Or, "My daddy and momma were married in the big church." The big church at the Sizemore burying place is a natural amphitheater, sloping gently upward from the huge beech tree.

big dinner *noun* See citation.

2014 *WV Talk* = church reunion, "dinner on the ground."

big doing(s) *noun* A lively get-together, important social occasion.

c1960 Wilson *Coll*: *big-doings* = great occasion of some sort, like a party, a reunion, a marriage, or even a funeral. **1979** Slone *My Heart* 120 There was going to be some "big doing" at the school that night. All the community had been invited to come. **1997** Montgomery *Coll* We had a big doin's on Decoration Day (Brown).

big dope *noun* Any carbonated drink. See citations. Same as **dope 2**.

2002 Myers *Best Yet Stories* 77 = carbonated drink. **2009** Koontz *Guide to Smokies* 88 = a carbonated beverage, typically a 12-ounce Coke, Pepsi, or (if you're really Southern) RC Cola.

bigetty See **biggety**.

big eye (also *the big eye*) *noun* Insomnia, wakefulness; hence adjective *big-eyed* = afflicted with insomnia, wide awake. See also **moon eye**.

1956 Still *Burning of Waters* 56 Lying big-eyed in the dark I heard Father say to Mother, "That fire puzzles me tee-totally." **1960** Westover *Highland Lg* 19 *big eye* = insomnia. **1976** Garber *Mountain-ese* 8 The chilurn allers git the big-eye on Christmas night. **1980**

Berry and Repass *Grandpa Says* 18 *big-eyed* = wide awake, insomnia: "I had the big-eye last night." **1994–97** Montgomery *Coll* (known to Adams, Cardwell, Jones, Ledford, Ogle, Oliver, Weaver).

big-eyed *adjective*

1 See **big eye**.

2 Wild, unrestrained, thoroughgoing.

1940 Still *Snail Pie* 209 Without a line of big-eyed lies he couldn't have sold gnat balls and devil's snuff boxes. **1989** *Matewan OHP*-56 I was always all around them boys. We'd all of us have a big-eyed time. **2009** Williams *Maw Surry* Everybody always had a big-eyed time, the men and the women, the kids and the old timers.

big-foot *noun* Same as **hickory chicken**.

2007 Farr *My Appalachia* 107–8 One of the treats of springtime in the mountains was when Dad found hickory chickens. . . . In Appalachia, besides being called "hickory chickens" as my dad did, they are known as "dry land fish," "markels" (Morchella esculent), and "big-foot."

bigger majority, **bigger part** See **big A5**.

biggest half, **biggest majority** See **big A6**.

biggest'n, **biggest one** See **big one B**.

biggest part, **biggest portion** See **big A6**.

biggest way See **get in a big way**.

biggety (also *bigetty*, *biggity*, *bigity*) *adjective* Conceited, snobbish, impudent, "stuck up."

1884 Smith *Scrap Book* 79 The modern boy is entirely too biggity. **1939** Hall *Coll* (White Oak NC) Said of one who has "got the big head." **1941** Justus *Kettle Creek* 4 An outlander teacher with a lot o' bigetty ways. **1977** Hamilton *Mt Memories* 87 Them biggity Waltons over thar wouldn't say "howdy," if they met him in the big road! **1982** *Smokies Heritage* 66 = acting snobbishly.

[perhaps *big* + *-ity* "quality, state" or *bigot* n + *-y*; DARE *biggity* adj chiefly South, South Midland]

biggity See **biggety**.

biggurn See **big one**.

big gut See **cut a big figure**.

big hominy (also *whole hominy*) *noun* Hominy prepared from kernels of corn soaked in lye to remove the hulls. Also called **lye hominy**. See also **little hominy**.

1918 Steadman *NC Word List* 18 = lye hominy of whole corn; contrasted with little hominy, or grits. **1982** Powers and Hannah *Cataloochee* 353 Big hominy's the whole grain, corn, the kernel. **1998** Dabney *Smokehouse Ham* 316 [Mountain people] called grits "small hominy" in contrast to what they had eaten down through the years—whole-grain "big hominy," "whole hominy," or, the really traditional name, "lye hominy." The latter came from the pioneers' practice of boiling the whole grains of corn in their washpots after leaching off the bran with lye.

[DARE *big hominy* n chiefly South, South Midland]

big house (also *big room*) *noun* The main or living quarters of a dwelling; in days of two-room **log houses** it was often detached and doubled as sleeping quarters, but more recently has served as the living room. See 1956, 1991 citations. Also called **house 2**, **main house**. See also **new house**.

1879 Jones *Backwoods Carolina* 751 In bad weather the family made a rush from the "big house" to the kitchen, accepting without protest an inconvenience which they seemed to regard as irremediable. **1919** Combs *Word-List South* 32 *big house* = (1) the large, or living house, as opposed to the summer kitchen, "smoke house," etc., located away from the living house; (2) in a house of two or more rooms, the largest one is thus designated. House is synonymous with room, and a dwelling of more than one room is often called "houses." Knott Co [KY]. **1938** Bowman *High Horizons* 37 The larger room in the Walker cabin is referred to by them in the old way, as the "big house" or "settin' room." . . . Two tiny windows are hewn through the logs on either side of the fireplace in the "big house." **1949** Kurath *Word Geog East US* 37 In Western North Carolina simple folk call the living room in their homes the *big-house*. . . . [This expression is] not found elsewhere in the Eastern States. **1952–57** (in **1973** McDavid and McDavid *Vocab E KY* 155) *big house* = attested by 11/52 (21.1%) of E KY speakers for the Linguistic Atlas of the North Central States; *big room* = attested by 22/52 (42.3%) of E KY speakers for the Linguistic Atlas of the North Central States. **1956** Hall *Coll* (Bryson City NC) *big house* = the main or living room of the house. In the old log houses the rooms were built separately (and detached) as the family needed more room, but were covered usually with a common roof. Often an open hallway (variously called a breezeway etc.) separated two such linked log houses. **1966** Dakin *Vocab Ohio River Valley* 32 In the Kentucky Mountains and the southern and eastern Knobs *big-house*, *old-house* (sometimes simply *the house*), and *big-room* are common. These old terms (still found also, in the Carolina mountains and piedmont and on the Eastern Shore of Virginia) are used conversationally but are recognized as old terms by some informants. They are being replaced by *living room*. **1968** Wilson *Folklore Mammoth Cave* 38 *big room* = a living room. **1976** Ledford *Folk Vocabulary* 279 *Living room, gutters, mantel* . . . have completely replaced *big house, eaves trough, fireboard* . . . throughout the area. **1986** Pederson et al. *LAGS* (Cocke Co TN, Gilmer Co GA) *big house*; (Claiborne Co TN, Morgan Co TN, Hall Co GA) *big room*. **1987** Williams *Rethinking House* 176–78 Older people who speak of a single-pen house often refer to it as a "big house" or (more frequently "big house and kitchen"). Why would anyone call such a small house "big"? The term is not used in jest. While possible linguistic antecedents do exist, those who use "big house" think it makes sense: "it was a large, large room, usually accommodated two or three beds, double beds, plus chairs." . . . It was a room for conceptualizing and household chores, for sleeping and sitting, and for many it was also a room for cooking and eating. . . . Despite the role as a sleeping room, the big house is primarily associated, however, with its function as the center of social and family activity. . . . As the acceptance of the single-pen plan declined, so did the use of the term "big house," which expressed a positive evaluation of the plan. People under the age of 70 tend not to know the meaning of the term. **1991** Williams *Homeplace* 38–42 "Big house," used in reference to the architecture of the American South, usually conjures up images of antebellum plantations. In southwestern North Carolina, the term is applied, not to mansions, but to the smallest type in the regional repertoire of folk house forms, the single pen plan. "Big house" refers not as much to the specific house type, however, as to the concept of spatial use which it embodies. . . . "Well, they, people back then called the living room, the big house. Big house and the kitchen," commented Ellen Garrett, although she has known smaller and larger single pen houses during her life. . . . The various subplans possible among single pen houses account for some variety in the way the term "big house" is used. While the kitchen, if it existed, was not part of the big house, the upstairs or smaller room on the ground floor of the partitioned house may or may not be considered a part of the big house. Often an individual would define the big house as both the main dwelling unit (as opposed to the kitchen) and as the individual room in which the majority of living took place. In an unpartitioned single pen house that is only one story in height, there would be no conflict in these two ways of using the term. . . . In all these cases, big house refers to the room or physical unit where the majority of domestic activity took place.

[DARE *big house* n 2 chiefly South Midland]

bigified *adjective* See citation.

1968 Wilson *Folklore Mammoth Cave* 40 = another term for being *stuck-up* or *smart-alec*. This word does not appear in any standard dialect dictionary that I have consulted, but it ought to, to match *dignified, citified, countryfied*.

big Ike *noun* An arrogant or self-important person (as in phrase *act big Ike*).

1905 Miles *Spirit of Mts* 115 There was a feller she'd called a cymblin'-headed fool that tried to act big-Ike and sass her back. **1927** Bird *Among Highlanders* 26 The only way you can meet them big Ikes is by bein' their servant. **1957** Combs *Lg Sthn High: Word List* 11 = a "Smart-Alec," or one very important in his own estimation. **1995–97** Montgomery *Coll* (known to eight consultants from the Smoky Mountains).

[DARE *big Ike* n chiefly South, South Midland]

bigity See **biggety**.

big laurel *noun* Same as **rosebay rhododendron** (*Rhododendron maximum*); a thicket of such plants, sometimes quite expansive.

1853 Kennedy *Blackwater Chronicle* 89 This dale is girt round . . . by a broad belt of the *Rhododendron*—commonly called the *big laurel* out here [= WV] **1921** Campbell *Sthn Highlander* 123 Close by is the branch, slipping through growth of "big" and "little" laurel and set with "holly-bush" and groups of towering "spruce-pine." **1944** Hayes *Word-List NC* 32. **1970** *Hunting* 10 I am afraid to stay out of a night by myself—especially in th' big laurels around Nantahaly. **1982** Wells *Remarkable Flora* 5 Forming an understory in this magnificent forest are innumerable shrubs, among the most prominent being the white flowered rhododendron or "big laurel." **2006** *WV Encycl* 616 The rhododendron maximum, more commonly called great rhododendron or big laurel, was designated the official state flower of West Virginia, January 29, 1903, after being recommended by the governor and voted on by students in the public schools.

big lot *noun phrase* A great deal, large amount or number.

1899 Fox *Mt Europa* 27 Thar used to be a big lot o' moonshinin' done in these parts, 'n' a raider come hyeh to see 'bout it. **1941** Stuart *Men of Mts* 171 I'm growing up to be a man like Wilburn some day and have a big lot of foxhounds and drive a lot of cattle. **1964** Roberts *Hell-Fer-Sartin* 48 Nippy stold the old man's horses and brought 'em back to that other man and he paid him a big lot. . . . The man said he had some fine big horses and if he'd go get them horses he'd pay him a big lot more money. **1979** *Big South Fork OHP-1* [The brickyard] used to work a big lot of folks. **1998** *Dante OHP-71* They didn't make a whole big lot of money.

big majority See **big A4**.

big mamma *noun* A grandmother.

1984 Head *Brogans* 124 Grandmother Morgan, whom we affectionately called "Big Mamma," had a variety of [aprons] which she wore daily until she died.

[DARE *big mamma* chiefly South]

big meeting *noun* Traditionally, a series of religious revival services or an **association** running several days or longer, especially in the late summer or fall; hence *big meeting time* = the season when such services are usually held. See also **camp meeting, protracted meeting, revival meeting.**

1861 *Martin CW Letters* (Oct 31) I havbeen at three Big Meeting in this Month. **1862** *Neves CW Letters* (May 1) I am looking for Unke[l] Bery and aunt Frankey up the 10 . . . 11 of this month to a big meeting. **1913** Kephart *Our Sthn High* 269 "Big meetin' time" is a gala week, if there be any such thing at all in the mountains—its attractiveness is full as much secular as spiritual to the great body of the people. **1933** Hooker *Religion in Highlands* 183 The "big meetin'" is the big event of the year. Young people away at work plan to take their vacations at that time. Old residents come back, and visiting relatives swell the size of many families. Meetings are held both morning and evening for a week, ten days, two weeks, three or, in rare instances, longer. Attendance is large, averages of 200 or even 300 not being rare for the evening services. **1939** Burnett *Gap o' Mountains* 13 During the regular yearly two weeks of "Big Meeting" the mourners' bench was an institution. **1967**

Wilson *Folkways Mammoth Cave* 27 = may also mean a meeting of a Baptist Association of churches in a district. **1974** Russell *Hillbilly* 31 During revivals, or "big meetins," both morning and night services were held despite the poor lighting. **1975** Kroeger *WV Farm Life* 39 They would go for miles to attend a big meeting. There would be so many sometimes the church wouldn't hold them all, and there was so many more people then in the country than there is now, and they all liked to go to church. **1988** Russell *It Happened* 45 During the "big meetins" groups would walk some distance to attend—especially young men and women.

[DARE *big meeting* n chiefly South, South Midland]

big meeting time See **big meeting**.

big'n, **bigon** See **big one**.

big old *adjective phrase* (usually with stress on *big*) Large (with *old* adding little other than perhaps a slight dramatic effect and a tone varying from familiarity to uncommonness to nostalgia). See also **great big old**, **little old**.

1939 Hall Coll (Proctor NC) This big old coon come down about fifteen steps from where we was at. *Ibid.* (Nine Mile TN) He had a big old oxen. *Ibid.* (Gatlinburg TN) I up with this here, big old hog rifle cap and ball gun, and I took good bead at him, and I hit him right where I missed him before. **1969** GSMNP-25:1:16 In the little old hollow there, [there was a] big old chestnut tree that had fell, laying right across the hollow. **1971** *AOHP/ALC-139* [The school] was a frame building, painted, outside not inside, and of course a good roof and a big old stove you know in the middle of the room. **1989** *Matewan OHP-33* That was the time that they had that big old Mother Jones, she was a woman that made speeches all the time. **1997** Andrews *Mountain Vittles* 17 Serve with a big old spoon. **1998** *Dante OHP-51* They had this big old sergeant standing there and he says, "Knock your feet off, soldier."

big one *pronoun phrase*

A Variant forms *biggurn* [see **2013** in **B**], *big'n*, *bigon*, *big un* [see **1915** in **B**], *big'un*. See also **one 1**.

1861 *Proffit CW Letters* (Sept 10) I told them to fix a pockut in my over coat a bigon behind and fill up with aples tarts. **1942** Hall *Phonetics Smoky Mts* 86 [ˈbɪgən]. **1983** Page and Wigginton *Aunt Arie* 132 [The thrash doctor would] rench out his mouth and take his two hands and open up a child's mouth—a big'n 'r a little'n whichever one—hold it open and he'd blow in it. **1997** *Dante OHP-14* I had some big'uns and some little-sized ones.

B (also *biggest'n*) A large or supreme example, especially an exaggerated tale. See also **big A3**, **C2**.

1915 Dingus *Word-List VA* 181 = an incredible story; whopper. "Now tell us a big un, the biggest'n." **1939** Hall Coll (Gatlinburg TN) He told [tourists] great big'uns. **1976** GSMNP-113:5 Lord, no, they's great big uns. **1978** Hall *Yarns and Tales* 8 Hog-killin' time on cold days of early winter when families assembled for the myriad jobs involved were once great occasions for jokes, brags, and "big'uns" (tall tales). **2013** Venable *How to Tawlk* 6 = anything large, preferably of a game or fish nature: "Roy's walleye shore was a biggurn!"

big part See **big A4**.

big recess *noun* The main break in the school day, an hour for the midday meal at noon.

1903 Fox *Little Shepherd* 42 At noon—"big recess"—Melissa gave Chad some corn-bread and bacon, and the boys gathered around him. **1978** Hiser *Quare Do's* 43 I recollect the big boys a talkin about it while we played Antny Over acrost the top of the schoolhouse enduring big recess that noon with a red yarn ball Ellie here had wound out of her pap Uncle Pleas Bowlin's wore-out socks she'd unraveled.

big ring *noun* A marble game using a large circle drawn on the ground.

1938 Still *Bat Flight* 12 A boy named Leth came up to me and said, "Let's me and you play big ring," and he loaned me two marbles.

big road *noun* A main road, highway.

1834 Crockett *Narrative* 25 I had to guess at my way to the big road, which was about half a mile from my house. **1885** Murfree *Prophet* 232 Insisting that his unshod steed should keep straight up the rocky big road. **1892** Doak *Wagonauts Abroad* 294 I stood in amazement, wondering at this Terpsichorean feat, and Blane lectured him on the undignity of the display there in the "big road." **1915** Dingus *Word-List VA* 181 = a public drive-way. **1941** Stuart *Men of Mts* 229 I walk down the hollow to the big road. **1963** Edwards *Gravel* 165 Now that Ford and Macadam had invaded our section, the Big Road was to be made a state highway, which meant, we were soon to learn, that it would be possible to travel it. **1977** Hamilton *Mt Memories* 2 The "big road" as we called the public highways, was rather far from our house but near the barns.

[DARE *big road* n chiefly South, Midland]

big room See **big house**.

Big Smokies (also *Big Smoky*, *Big Smoky Mountain*, *Big Smoky Mountains*) *noun* The higher reaches of the Great Smoky Mountains, especially the main ridge that follows the TN/NC boundary; the terms appear to have had currency mainly by outsiders, especially in earlier days. See also **mountain B**, **Old Smoky**, (**the**) **Smoky**, **top of Smoky**.

1821 (in **2018** *Davenport Survey* 19) If there ever is a wagon road through the Big Smokies it must go through this gap. **1888** Alexander *Hiking Big Smokies* Where are the Big Smoky mountains? The name is given especially to that part of the range whose topmost ridge forms the dividing line between North Carolina and Tennessee, which lies between the French Broad and Little Tennessee Rivers. **1889** *Hogs* My guide and I crossed the Big Smoky mountain in Swain County, one of the least populated and wildest counties in the State, early in the morning. **1926** Morgan *Smoky Mts* 461

The range consists mainly of a main ridge which forms the divide between Tennessee and North Carolina. Oft times the spurs and peaks leading away from the main line of "Big Smokies" . . . attain a greater height than the main ridge. **1977** Hamilton *Mt Memories* 94 Rena was busy trying to keep our old home presentable while dreaming about a future life with Bert beyond the Big Smokies.

big spruce *noun* The eastern hemlock tree (*Tsuga canadensis*). Same as **spruce pine**.

1960 (in **2002** Weals *Legends*) 40 Back then we called those trees the *big spruce*, but now we call it *hemlock*.

big sticker *noun* A long-bladed knife, as one to finish killing a hog. See also **frogstick, sticker 1**.

1995–97 Montgomery *Coll* (known to Bush, Cardwell, Shields, Weaver).

big time *noun* A noisy party or celebration, sometimes with much consumption of alcohol.

1862 *Neves CW Letters* (Jan 9) I recon you had a big time we had noe Christmas up hear at taul. **1864** *Watters-Curtis CW Letters* (Jan 24) I Exspect to go home about the First of March on a Furlow I Shall Exspect to Have a big time then as I have not Been at Home for over tuo years. **1956** Hall *Coll* (Cades Cove TN) They used to have some pretty tough times [at a notorious house on Tab Cat Creek, south of Cades Cove]. They used to fiddle and dance. They've been several killed at those big times. **1977** Shackelford et al. *Our Appalachia* 161 They named it Happy Hill because the people there would have big times, and blowouts, and things. **1979** *Big South Fork OHP*-1 They had a platform out from hit where they made music and danced and had a big time. **1991** Williams *Homeplace* 86 Us young'uns in the wintertime, we'd all gather round in this bedroom, fireplace, and pop corn, and have a big time.

[DARE *big time* n widespread, but especially South, South Midland]

big top *noun* A mountain summit, high point on a mountain ridge. Same as **high top, top A1**.

1986 Rader *Mt Legacy* 18 Later in his kitchen, while sharing a cup of scalding coffee and giant slices of applesauce stackcake with Uncle Dave and his wife, I discovered why they had moved out of the "Big Tops" of the Smokies to this smaller fifty-acre farm.

big un, big'un See **big one**.

bile See **boil**.

biler See **boiler**.

biling See **boiling**.

bilious fever *noun* Yellow fever, characterized by general weakness. Formerly it was thought to be symptomatic of a liver disorder and connected with the bile.

1937 Hall *Coll* (Wears Cove TN) = yellow fever, a scourge of the population in times past.

bill *noun* A person's nose.

1967 *DARE Survey* (Maryville TN).

[DARE *bill* n[1] 2 chiefly South, South Midland]

Bill Seldom *noun* See citation.

1968 Wilson *Folklore Mammoth Cave* 18 One very old man said that, in his youth, cornbread was called *John Constant*; biscuits were called *Bill Seldom*.

Billy Hell (also *Old Billy Devil, Old Billy Hell*) *noun* Used as a nickname for the Devil; hell. See also **(the) Old Scratch**.

1904 Fox *Christmas Eve* 132 Thar was Daws on one side o' the meetin' house an' Mace on t'other, an' both jes awatchin' fer t'other to make a move, an' thar'd 'a' been billyhell to pay right thar! **1941** Stuart *Men of Mts* 46 Well, old billy-hell—you work for me on this farm! **1966** Dakin *Vocab Ohio River Valley* 520 Kentuckians say "old Billy hell." **1969** *DARE Survey* (Tompkinsville KY) He's meaner than old billy hell. **1980** Still *Run for Elbertas* 83 Mother threw up her hands. "You're as stubborn as Old Billy Devil!" she cried. **1983** Broaddus *Estill Co KY Word List* 7 *Old Billy Hell* = Satan.

bind (also *bine*) *noun* A bundle of grain cut and tied to be put in a **shock**.

1864 *Chapman CW Letters* (March 13) the soldiers tuck about 70 bushels of corn & fifty bushels of wheat & 200 pounds of bacon & 600 bines of fodder and the two Loads of oats. **1966** Dakin *Vocab Ohio River Valley* 304 Several speakers in the Mountains and southern Kentucky use the relic term *bind*.

[DARE *bind* n chiefly South Midland, TX]

(the) binds *noun* Constipation.

1990 Cavender *Folk Medical Lex* 18 She's got a bad case of the binds. **1994–97** Montgomery *Coll* (known to Brown, Bush, Cardwell, Jones, Norris, Weaver).

bine See **bind**.

birch still *noun* An operation that distills an extract from the sweet birch tree.

2018 *Smoky Mt News* (April 4) The sweet birch (Betula lenta) [is] also known as black, cherry, or mahogany birch. They serve as a reminder that moonshine stills weren't the only kind of stills that once proliferated in the region. Indeed, there was a time more than a century ago when birch stills were more common than moonshine stills. They weren't illegal and didn't need to be hidden. Birch stills rendered an extract known as either "birch oil" or "oil of wintergreen."

birch tea *noun* See citations. See also **hickory B2, peach-tree limb tea**.

2003 Triplett *Mt Roots* 59 Usually when a neighbor gave you "birch tea" (a whipping with a small birch tree branch) and a parent found out, you got another at home. **2005** Williams *Gratitude* 480 Since it was common to use a birch limb to give a youngun a whuppin', a parent would threaten to *give it a doast of birch tea.*

bird *noun* Possessive form *bird* used in compounds. See also **hen.**

c1960 Wilson *Coll*: *bird egg* is regular; *bird's egg* sounds foreign. **1970** Campbell et al. *Smoky Mt Wildflowers* 14 Birdfoot violet.

[DARE *bird* n A2 chiefly South, South Midland]

-bird *noun* Compounded with the names of specific birds. See 1944 citation.

1909 Bascom *Ballads and Songs* 241 [The songbook] contains the regular ballad refrain, the question and answer stanzas typical of ballads of this kind, and at the same time employs such objects of every-day life as sparrer-birds, turtle-doves, honey-bees, shoes, trees, and fish. **1941** Stuart *Men of Mts* 32 He hopped over the tater ridges toward the barn-lot like a sparrow-bird. **1944** Combs *Word-List Sthn High* 18 = suffix added redundantly after the names of birds: *sparrow-bird*, *wren-bird*, etc. **c1950** (in **2000** Oakley *Roamin' Man* 38) We saw one ravin bird and so meny little birds we couldent count them. **1998** Montgomery *Coll*: *quail-bird*, *sparrow-bird* (Cardwell).

[DARE *bird* n B2 chiefly South, South Midland]

bird-foot violet See **bird('s)-foot violet.**

bird's eye cannel *noun* See citation.

2006 Mooney *Lg Coal Mining* 1028 Many coal-mining] terms make use of analogies to nature or to animals. . . . "Bird's eye cannel" is a type of bituminous or "soft" coal (versus anthracite or "hard" coal) that is imprinted with small concretions said to resemble a bird's eye.

bird('s)-foot violet *noun* A perennial violet (*Viola pedata*). Same as **crowfoot violet.**

1941 Walker *Story of Mt* 46 There are some wild flowers which seem to have such good dispositions that they pay no attention to altitudes, and would as freely climb to a mountain's top as to remain and prosper in the valley. Among this class of flowers is heartsease, or field pansy, birdfoot violet, and harebell. **1970** Campbell et al. *Smoky Mt Wildflowers* 14 Birdfoot violet . . . blooms from March through June, and is identified by the leaves, which somewhat resemble the shape of a bird's foot. **1982** Stupka *Wildflowers* 67 The leaves [of the pansy violet] have three main divisions, but the lateral ones are divided again into slender or widened segments, which account for the names "bird's-foot" or "crowfoot violet."

[from the shape of the leaf]

bird's toe *noun* An edible green with a small, white root and pink blossom that grows in rocky places.

1952 Ritchie and Pickow *Swapping Song* 78 Jack and Judy and Joy go into the woods and gather wild flowers to make May baskets for their friends. Fire pinks, black-eyed susies, . . birds-toe, sweet-smelling arbeauty blossoms. **1956** Still *Burning of Waters* 58 We ate branch lettuce and ragged breeches and bird's-toe and swamp mustard. **1969** *DARE Survey* (Hazard KY) = [has] small white root, pink blossom, grows in rocky places.

[DARE *bird's toe* n southern Appalachians]

bire See **bear**[1].

birth *verb*

1 To give birth to.

1932 (in **1935** Edwards *NC Novels* 92) Annie birthed twins. **1958** Campbell *Tales* 53 The way some folks tell the tale, the mother died when she birthed little Snow White. **1960** Cooper *Jularker Bussed* She birthed three young-uns. (She gave birth to three babies.) **1999** Montgomery *Coll* (known to Cardwell).

[OED3 *birth* v 2 chiefly dialect and U.S. dialect; DARE *birth* v chiefly South, South Midland]

2 To deliver (a baby).

1984 Smith *Oral History* 58 Rosa Hibbitts had got to where she has about took over from me in birthing babies.

birthing *noun* The act of giving birth.

1949 Arnow *Hunter's Horn* 111 She had borne her first lamb; King Devil had stolen that . . . and scared her in the birthing of the second. **1978** Hiser *Quare Do's* 36–37 Eb Deaton had paid Granny [corn] when she went there to a birthing a couple of weeks before. **2003** Smith *Orlean Puckett* 39 The things she did, going to birthings and sometimes staying for days, and he didn't question her.

[DARE *birthing* vbl n chiefly South, South Midland]

biscuit *noun*

1 (also *biscuit bread*) Heavy bread made from wheat flour. See also **biscuit pone, light bread.**

1863 *Warrick CW Letters* (May 26) I could interest you if you would giv mee som butter milk to drink and som butter and buscuit to eat as it is about dinner time. **1884** Smith *Scrap Book* 73 By the 4th of July will have wheat bread and biskit and blackberry pies. **1940** Haun *Hawk's Done* 150 He didn't want to let him know he didn't have any biscuit bread to bring to school. **1957** Combs *Lg Sthn High: Word List* 11 *biscuit bread* = biscuits. **1957** Justus *Other Side* 11 No wheat could be grown on the mountainside, for it was too steep and rocky. That was why corn pone was the daily bread, with biscuit on rare occasions. **1966** *DARE Survey* (Cherokee NC) = bread made with wheat flour. **1986** Pederson et al. *LAGS*: *biscuit bread* = attested by 3/60 interviewees (5%) from E TN and 2/35 (5.7%) from N GA; 5/23 of all LAGS interviewees (21.7%) attesting term were from Appalachia.

[DARE *biscuit* n B1 chiefly South, South Midland; *biscuit bread* n chiefly South Midland]

2 A woman's hairdo. See citations.

1957 Broaddus *Vocab Estill Co KY* 7 = a small bun or roll of hair. When a woman wears two or more buns, they are called "biscuits." **c1960** Wilson *Coll* = hair done up in a small knot; a bun. Usually said of some elderly woman who has very little hair—or style.

biscuit bread See **biscuit 1**.

biscuit eater *noun* See citation.

2000 Miller *Looneyville* 39 = large breed of hunting dogs characterized by long droopy ears, short hair and a deep-throated bark. Leftover home made biscuits and *pon'* were always fed to the hunting dogs: "That old red and white biscuit eater is the best dog that I own."

biscuit pone *noun* Biscuit bread baked in a **pone**. See 2015 citation.

1956 Stuart *Year Rebirth* 363 For breakfast, we had two big pans of biscuits and a small pan of spare "biscuit pone" so we wouldn't run out of bread. My father, brother, and I ate ten biscuits each. **1994–97** Montgomery *Coll* (known to Cardwell, Shields). **2008** Riddle *All There Is* 39 We heard his father stabbed his mother to death in '64 because she burned the biscuit pone. **2015** Montgomery *File* If you want a Biscuit Pone (really one really big biscuit) then mix a batch of your favorite biscuit dough a little thick and don't overwork it.

bit See **bite 1**.

bit and grain See **every bit and grain**.

bitch link *noun* In logging, a pear-shaped link on the end of a chain, larger and heavier than other links, used to hold a chain in place.

1974–75 McCracken *Logging* 20:42 On the end of the cable that came down from the skidder that hooked to the logs, there was a big link on it that they called the "bitch link." I don't know what give it the name. At the ends of these chokers were just loops, plaited into the cable. And you'd take the choker, hook it around the log, and just run one loop through the other one and then this other loop is what fit in this bitch link. **1978** Weals *Two Locomotives* The jolt of the eight loaded cars against the engine, after the brakes had been eased off to take the slack out of the "bitch link" that anchored the log loader [started the accident].

bite *verb* Principal parts.

1 Variant past-participle form *bit*.

1913 Kephart *Our Sthn High* 101 Coaly fit again, all right, and got his tail bit. **1956** GSMNP-22:3 Verdie McCarter got bit, too. **1986** Pederson et al. *LAGS* (Cocke Co TN, Sevier Co TN). **1994** Walker *Life History* 122 Bob Tipton's dog went running across the road in front of me, and he had bit me the day before.

2 past-participle form *-bit* in compound verbs (as *dog-bit*).

1862 *Robinson CW Letters* (June 28) I Resevd 2 letters from you this weak one was Rote the day after you got Spider bit. **1864** *Brown CW Letters* (Jan 20) a great meny of the boyes has got heir feat frost bit. **1892** Doak *Wagonauts Abroad* 168 Jinny got copperhead bit and like to a died five year ago, an' I don't b'lieve she'll ever git over likin' a drop o' liquor for that old snake bite. **1920** Ridley *Sthn Mtneer* 85 "Guess I know when I'm dog-bit," said the complainant, "an' yore dog done it." **1939** Hall *Coll* (Tobes Creek NC) He got dog-bit in Asheville. **c1950** Adams *Grandpap* 192 She said that I might get copperhead bit if I got off in the tangle of weeds and vines by myself. **1953** Atwood *Verbs East US* 6 An interesting geographical phenomenon is the combination *dogbit* ("he was dog-bit," or "he got dogbit"), which covers the South Midland and adjoining parts of the South. . . . In W.Va. south of the Kanawha and in s.w. Va. it is practically universal. **1978** Slone *Common Folks* 208 Not even my father could have touched [the guarded quilt] without getting dog bit. **1985** Irwin *Alex Stewart* 265 As luck would have it, he didn't bite through my overalls, but I'll tell you, I come might near getting rattlesnake bit. **1993** Burton *Take Up Serpents* 58 Jean remembers once in Ooltewah when she was about twelve years old that her father was serpent bit.

bite up *verb phrase* To chew up, injure badly by biting. See also **eat up**.

1953 Hall *Coll* (Plott Creek NC) Now that was a real bear fight. . . . We had a wonderful bunch of dogs. But this bear was some fighter. He bit up the dogs.

biting *adjective* Of an animal: prone to bite.

1921 Greer-Petrie *Angeline Seelbach* 2 He was afeard Miss Seelback might have some bad bitin' dogs that would resh out and grab aholt of us. **1941** Stuart *Men of Mts* 230 "Don't be afraid, boys," says Big Aaron. "He ain't no bitin' dog. He's one of them barkin' dogs that never bites." **1963** Edwards *Gravel* 153 He had the reputation of being a biting-dog. **1968** Wilson *Coll*: *biting sow* = dangerously angry sow. "There's a biting sow in that 'ere field." Often used in phr "mad as a biting sow."

[DARE *biting* ppl adj South Midland]

bitter

A *adjective* Of milk: tainted, tasting of a plant that the cow has eaten, especially ragweed or wild onions. See also **bitterweed milk**.

1966 DARE *Survey* (Spruce Pine NC) = having a taste from something the cow ate in the pasture. **1995** Montgomery *Coll* (known to Cardwell, Shields).

[DARE *bitter* adj a scattered, but chiefly South, South Midland]

B *noun* (usually plural in form but construed as singular) A medicinal tea made from crushed herbs or other plant matter, often mixed with whiskey.

1956 Hall *Coll* (Hurricane Creek NC) [Asked if she prepared teas of different herbs and used them for different illnesses]: I fix a bitter of [all different types of herbs] and use it for everything. **1971** *AOHP/ALC*-147 The way she made her bitters, she would dig yellow dock and north and south roots, and then she dug what's called yellow sarsparilla and then a red sassafras, and she put that all in together, and she boiled hit down, and then she would put whiskey in it to preserve it, to keep it from souring, and she used it as bitters then. **1973** GSMNP-4:29 They would take what they call bitters, you know. They would take liquor that they would make and they would put a lot of cherry tree bark and stuff like that in it and set it on the fireboard, and they would come along and drink every night, maybe before they went to bed they would get them a drink of that. **1974** *No Sang* 4 They used to take ginseng and three or four herbs all together and put it in a quart of whiskey and shake it up and let it sit there awhile and then they'd take'em a drink of that every day. And they called it "bitters." . . . They didn't tell no crooked tale about them being bitter. **1983** *Dark Corner* OHP-5A All the old people back them days, they used all kind of bitters. They called it bitters, you know. They'd take whiskey and get all kinds of herbs and roots and barks, you know, and chinaberries and the wild cherries and all that and put it in the whiskey, and rat's vein, and make the medicine. **2003** Cavender *Folk Medicine* 65 Combinations of bitter-tasting plants like goldenseal, dandelion, and boneset were used to make a "bitters," which was thought good for promoting digestion, increasing appetite, and cleaning blood.

bitter oak *noun* A red oak such as *Quercus ilicifolia* or *Quercus pumila*, whose acorns are bitter in taste.

1937 Hall *Coll* (Cades Cove TN) Acorns were eaten by wild hogs [also bears, turkeys, and domestic hogs allowed to range in the woods], the nuts of white oak, chestnut oak, and in the winter bitter oak, called mast. **1997** Montgomery *Coll* = any oak but the white oak, which was the only oak species from which the acorn could be ground to make oak bread (Cardwell).

bitters See **bitter B**.

bitterweed *noun* Same as **hogweed**.

1982 Stupka *Wildflowers* 124 Common ragweed, also called "Roman worm-wood," "hog-weed," and "bitter-weed," has deeply divided fernlike leaves and inconspicuous heads of green flowers.

bitterweed milk *noun* Freshly given milk tainted by onions, ragweed, or another plant a cow has eaten. When the plant is known, the milk is sometimes called **ragweed milk**, **wild onion milk**, etc. See also **bitter A**, **weedy**.

1994–97 Montgomery *Coll* (known to Shields), = tainted by wild onions or dock (Brown), = tainted by ragweed or wild onions (Cardwell).

[DARE *bitterweed milk* n chiefly South, South Midland]

blab school *noun* An elementary school at which students recite lessons aloud in unison. See also **hollering school**, **shouting school**.

1888 Brown *Peculiar People* 507 Until recent years a system of what was locally known as "blabschools," wherein was much in vogue, each pupil studied his lesson aloud. The teacher, perched on a high stool with long hickory in hand, kept a watchful eye out for any one who for one moment suspended the nasal drawl required of all as audible evidence that he or she "war a-gittin' of that thar lesson." **1985** Kiser *Life and Times* 5 The schools were called "blab" schools. All the students were permitted to study aloud. **1998** Still *Appal Mother Goose* [4] The one-room schools were taught by masters of limited learning, and the custom was to recite lessons in a chorus of voices. Thus they were called Blab Schools. **2006** *Encycl Appalachia* 1527 Blab schools—so called because students studied lessons by repeating, or "blabbing," them aloud in unison or individually—were common throughout America in pioneer times and continued longer in Appalachia than in other parts of the country. The supporting pedagogical belief was that children learned better by doing lessons aloud. Because schools were usually confined to one room, the teacher had several age groups studying different subjects at the same time. While the teacher was involved with one group, the other children were directed to recite their lessons aloud, thus assuring the teacher that they were studying.

black and tan (also *black and tan hound*) *noun* A type of hound renowned in hunting game, especially bears.

1867 Harris *Sut Lovingood* 41 She thort, too, that four hundred black an' tan hound dorgs were cumpassin her etarnal ruin. **1939** Hall *Coll* (Deep Creek NC) I heard something a-coming down through the leaves, and when he come up to me, it was one of our bear hounds, a black and tan hound, and he was just eat up, bloody all over [from a bear fight]. **1960** Burnett *My Valley* 146 Pot Lickers, Blue Ticks, Black and Tans, sometimes just any old shabby-looking breed or cross-breed meet the requirements and mixed breeds of old-fashioned cur and hound often make outstanding bear dogs. **2009** Prewitt *Coon Hounds* 273 Nowadays, the black and tan, the redbone, the bluetick, the English, the treeing Walker, and the Plott are among the standard breeds that hunters say can potentially make good coon hounds.

[DARE *black and tan* n chiefly South, South Midland]

blackberry-blossom storm See **blackberry winter**.

blackberry dumpling *noun* A baked dessert pastry. See Norris citation.

1996 Montgomery *Coll* (known to Adams, Brown, Cardwell, Jones, Ledford, Oliver), = berries were placed in a small circle of dough and butter was added, the dough was folded over and the edges were crimped with a fork; then the dumpling was deep fried (Norris).

blackberry spell, **blackberry storm**, **blackberry summer** See **blackberry winter**.

blackberry winter (also *blackberry-blossom storm*, *blackberry summer*, *blackberry spell*, *blackberry storm*) *noun* A late frost or period of freezing weather, especially in May when blackberries have begun to bloom, that may kill buds, blossoms, and new plantings. For other terms describing a similar phenomenon, see **catbird winter**, **dogwood winter**, **Easter winter**, **foxgrape winter**, **martin winter**, **redbud winter**, **service winter**, **sick bird winter**, **whippoorwill winter**, **white oak winter**.

1913 Morley *Carolina Mts* 43 At their bloomingtime in April or early May comes a cold storm called the "blackberry-blossom storm," as a similar spell of bad weather in the North when the apple trees are out is called the "apple-blossom storm." **1918** Steadman *NC Word List* 18 *blackberry winter* = cold weather in spring when blackberries are in bloom. **1940** *Charleston Gazette* (WV) (June

23, 4/7) Charleston's "blackberry summer" weather continued last night after the temperature had hit a low of 46 degrees. . . . Unseasonal coolness at the time of the summer solstice's beginning was given the name "blackberry summer" when oldtimers in the Virginias noted that this brand of weather seemed to hit the same [time] summer blackberries are best. **1952** Wilson *Folk Speech NC* 520–21 *blackberry storm* = the cold season that sometimes comes when blackberries are in bloom. **1962** Dykeman *Tall Woman* 14 After the cold spell, when dogwoods bloomed, there would be whippoorwill winter and blackberry winter. "Dogwood winter" happens in April, but it is soon followed by another spell of cold called "blackberry winter," which occurs in May when blackberry briars put out their delicate flowers. **1995–97** Montgomery *Coll*: *blackberry winter* (Adams, Brown, Ledford, Norris), = occurs in latter half of May (Cardwell); *blackberry spell* (Norris).

[DARE *blackberry storm* n chiefly South, South Midland, *blackberry winter* n chiefly South, South Midland]

black Betsy See **black Betty**.

black Betty (also *Black Betsy*) *noun* A bottle of whiskey; whiskey itself.

1823 Doddridge *Logan* 42–43 (DARE) He that got first to the bride's house, got black betty, which was the name they called the bottle. . . . Every boy and gal, old and young . . . must kiss black betty; that is to take a good slug of a dram. **1957** McMeekin *Old KY Country* 64 Pretty late in the night someone would remind the company that the new couple must stand in need of some refreshments: "Black Betty," which was the name of the bottle, did not go along. **1974** Dabney *Mt Spirits* 24 Frontiersmen of the 1700s and 1800s referred to corn whiskey as "tiger spit," "black betsy," and "forty-rod."

[DARE *black betty* n chiefly Midland]

black Christmas *noun* A snowless period in late December.

1938 Stuart *Dark Hills* 337 It was a black Christmas last year. It takes a white Christmas for a good crop year. **1968** Clarke *Stuart's Kentucky* 38 A black Christmas was considered the sign of a poor crop year; a white Christmas, the sign of a good crop year.

[by analogy with *white Christmas*]

black cohosh *noun* A bugbane (*Cimicifuga racemosa*), a perennial wild shrub whose roots and rhizomes have many medicinal uses, especially in making a tonic. Also called **black joint, black snakeroot, blue ginseng, fairy candles, headache berry, mountain bugbane, rattletop.**

1971 Hutchins *Hidden Valley* 180 [White snakeroot] should not be confused with black snakeroot (Cimicifuga racemosa), also known as "bugbane" and "black cohosh." [**1971** Krochmal et al. *Medicinal Plants Appal* 98 The roots and rhizomes are considered valuable in treating chronic rheumatism. . . . In Appalachia, a tea made from the root is used to treat sore throat.] **1972** Cooper *NC Mt Folklore* 12 Yellow dock, mandrake, poke root, blood root and black cohosh were used as alternatives to tone up the system and establish a healthy condition. **2006** Howell *Medicinal Plants* 43 American Indians soaked black cohosh roots in alcohol to make a remedy for rheumatic pain. It was also used to treat coughs and colds, bring on delayed menses, and to help babies sleep.

black damp *noun* See citations. Also called **choke damp**. See also **afterdamp**.

1973 Preston *Bituminous Term* 26 = a combination of gases found in a mine after a fire or firedamp explosion, chiefly composed of carbon dioxide and nitrogen. **c1975** *Miners' Jargon* 1 = a term generally applied to carbon dioxide. Strictly speaking, it is a mixture of carbon dioxide and nitrogen. It is also applied to an atmosphere depleted by oxygen, rather than having an excess of carbon dioxide. **1989** Giardina *Storming Heaven* 26 One of my jobs in the mine was to keep an eye on our canary. We were always in danger from black damp, an odorless poison gas that collected in pockets where we blasted. We kept the bird in a small wooden cage at our place. If we hit a pocket of black damp the bird would fall over dead, and we would know to run. **1994** Crissman *Death and Dying* 190 The terms *blackdamp* (a mixture of carbon dioxide and nitrogen) and *afterdamp* (carbon monoxide) are used when the air in a mine becomes oxygen deficient to the extent that the workers can be asphyxiated or suffocate. The gases are propelled rapidly through the passageways of a mine following the detonation of methane gas or coal dust. **1997** *Dante OHP-53* They's what they call that black damp in those mines. . . . It's a stale air. It's poisonous air, and it will kill you, put you to sleep. That kills a lot of people. [If] they go in a mine that don't have any ventilation in it, that's the first thing that they hit. **2004** Fisher *Kettle Bottom* 72 I have seen a whole trip car of men drug by a mule through a pocket of black damp.

black dark *noun, adjective* Complete nightfall; completely dark. See also **dusk dark, gray dark.**

1939 Hall *Coll* (White Oak NC) = when it's so dark you can't see nothin'. **1955** Ritchie *Singing Family* 58 It was one of them black dark nights when you couldn't see hand fore your face, no moon, and clouds kivering the stars up solid. **1962** Dykeman *Tall Woman* 153 A year ago you couldn't a told me I'd go out in the black dark and try to kill me a bear.

[DARE *black dark* n probably South, South Midland]

Black Dutch *noun* Darker-skinned people whose origin is uncertain but widely conjectured.

1939 Hall *Coll* (Waldens Creek TN) = a local type of people of Germanic (?) extraction. The Foxes are known as "black Dutch. Pennsylvania is as far back as we can trace them. They are low, not tall, small and have black features." **1960** Hall *Smoky Mt Folks* 27 "One of my grandpaws was part Black Dutch and part Irish." . . . Just who the Black Dutch were originally seems to be a mystery, though the term is well-known in the mountains. **1992** Bush *Dorie* 9 The Woodruff family was Black Dutch (= combination of Spanish and Belgian ancestry from the Low Countries). **1992** Montgomery *Coll* = an amalgamation of Spanish (or Moor) and Dutch (Shields). **2007** Milnes *Signs Cures Witches* 131 People such as the "colored Moats" are often called Black Dutch (a mixture of black African and Caucasian German people). But this widely used term has many other definitions. For instance, the Melungeons of Appalachia have called themselves Black Dutch, and Gypsies, mulattos, and mixed race Native Americans have borrowed the term. One plausible theory has it that the true Black Dutch are thought to be the "Schwarzer Deutsch" or "Black Germans" who are found in Germany, including in areas along the Danube and, especially, the Rhine River.

[DARE *black Dutch* n especially South, South Midland]

black-eyed Susie *noun* Same as **yellow daisy**.

1968 DARE *Survey* (Brasstown NC) = a bright yellow daisy with a dark center that grows along roadsides in late summer. **1996** Montgomery *Coll* (known to Jones, Ledford, Norris).

[DARE *black-eyed Susie* n chiefly South, South Midland]

black garter See **blackguard D**.

blackguard

A Variant forms *blackgyard* [see **1955** in **B**], *blackgyuard* [see **1940** in **C**], *blaggard*.

c1960 Wilson *Coll*: *blaggard*.

B *noun* One who uses abusive or obscene language or is disreputable or untrustworthy; such language itself.

1930 Pendleton *Wood-Hicks Speak* 86 = a foul-mouthed person; an excessive user of profanity. **1955** Ritchie *Singing Family* 82 [She] wouldn't think a thing of calling the President of the United States a blackgyard if she felt like he was one. **1996–97** Montgomery *Coll* (known to nine consultants from the Smoky Mountains), = also a crook or liar (Brown). **1997** Johnson *Melungeon Heritage* 47 When people used obscenities, they were told they had a "blackguard mouth" or that they were being "blackguardish." **2007** McMillon *Notes* = a person who uses obscene language.

C *verb* To use abusive, insulting, or foul language; to insult, revile, or behave abusively toward (someone).

1864 *Misemer CW Letters* (May 2) some times S F catches it for blackguarding and telling bigg tales. **1904–20** Kephart *Notebooks* 4:853 They was a-blackgyardin' one another. **1930** Armstrong *This Day and Time* 91 I don't thank no man, Alf Bunts, to blackguard me. **1940** Haun *Hawk's Done* 155 The boys that stayed there were the kind that would blackgyuard a chicken roost. **1969** Medford *Finis* 102 This reminds us of what a certain illiterate and blackguarding fellow is reported to have said: "You jist wait. I'm a-gonna soon have enough money to buy me one o' them hills—then I'll show 'em; I'll move up an be one of 'em." **1980** Berry and Repass *Grandpa Says* 19 "I heard you been blackguardin' me." = insulting. **1994–97** Montgomery *Coll* (known to ten consultants from the Smoky Mountains). **2005** Williams *Gratitude* 480 = to *handle* (speak) filthy talk, especially around women and children.

[DARE *blackguard* v C2 chiefly South Midland]

D (also *black garter*) *adjective* Characterized by abusive or obscene language, disreputable, crude; hence *blackguard mouth*, *blackguard tale*. See also **blackguardish**.

1834 *Elijoy Church Minutes* 27 George Cagle & George Smith not coming forward to the church sd Cagle swaring George Smith singing blackguard songs & both getting drunk.—Excludes them. **1958** Campbell *Tales* 182 He had no use for women who either told or listened to what he called "blackguard tales." When one of the tales he was telling me got to the point where he considered it unfit for me to hear, he stopped right there and explained why he was not finishing the story. **1976** Thompson *Touching Home* 12 *black garter word* = cuss word. **1997** Johnson *Melungeon Heritage* 47 When people used obscenities, they were told they had a "blackguard mouth" or that they were being "blackguardish." **1997** Montgomery *Coll* I never heard anyone use such blackguard language (Cardwell). **2003** Onchuck *Mud Pie Memories* 128 Daddy especially had different words for everything. He referred to foul language as "blackguard."

[DARE *blackguard* adj D chiefly South Midland]

blackguardish

A Variant form *blackgyardish*.

B *adjective* Disgraceful, characterized by dirty or abusive language. See also **blackguard D**.

1997 Montgomery *Coll* He was just plain blackguardish (Cardwell).

C *adverb* In an abusive or obscene manner.

1940 Haun *Hawk's Done* 168 He made them shut up their mouths when they went to talking blackgyuardish in front of me and trying to jest me.

blackguard mouth, **blackguard tale** See **blackguard D**.

blackgum *noun* A deciduous tree, the tupelo (*Nyssa sylvatica*), which tends to rot and hollow out quickly while its exterior remains hard, so that sections can be cut into blocks for beehives. See also **bee gum**, **gum A1**, **A2**.

1941 Stuart *Men of Mts* 230 My bee gum is a cut of a hollow log with boards nailed on the top and bottom. It is black gum and it is heavy. **1993** Bansemer *Mts in Mist* 29 Hives were often made from hollow logs, usually black gum trees. It has a tendency to rot quickly on the inside, yet remain very hard on the outer edges, ideal for a hollow hive. Notches were cut at the bottom as an entrance for the bees. Slats of wood would be placed inside and the honey would be removed from these top layers leaving the bottom of the hive undisturbed.

[DARE *black gum* n 1 chiefly South, South Midland]

blackgum ooze *noun* A medicinal preparation made from the bark of the blackgum tree (*Nyssa sylvatica*). See citation.

a1975 Lunsford *It Used to Be* 67 The blackgum ooze is a wonderful medicine for kidney infection. Often I've seen men doctor horses by getting the bark off a blackgum tree or a blackgum root. They'd take off the rougher part using only the sappy side of the bark, and boil that until it's kind of a ropy black ooze. I've seen them administer that to a sick horse, and the horse would get well immediately.

blackgyard, **blackgyuard** See **blackguard**.

blackgyuardish See **blackguardish**.

blackjack (also *blackjack oak, black oak*) *noun* An inferior or scrub oak (especially *Quercus marilandica*). See citations. Same as **jack oak.**

1831 (in **1956** Eliason *Tarheel Talk* 260) (Rutherford Co NC). **1881** Pierson *In the Brush* 16 The country was rough and broken, with light, sandy soil, sparsely covered with small, scrubby oak-trees, called "black-jacks," and the region of country was known as the "Barrens." **1930** Armstrong *This Day and Time* 6 A cabin stood out against a steep snowy knobside that was bare of trees except for some scattered blackjacks. **1941** Walker *Story of Mt* 63–64 The better kinds [of oak] were cut for lumber, beginning at the top of the list where stands the white oak, and then on down to the lowest in commercial value, known as the common black jack, which finds a use for fuel. **c1960** Wilson *Coll*: *blackjack* = a Scrub Oak (*Quercus marilandica*), a very common tree on thin-soiled ridges, and worthless except for wood. "Why, that land won't grow nothing but blackjacks." **1985** Irwin *Alex Stewart* 205 You want to use hickory and blackjack oak for your fire. That'll hold about the same temperature and it'll hold the heat longer. You don't want to get it too hot or you'll burn whatever you're drying. **1994–97** Montgomery *Coll*: *blackjack oak, black oak* = grows on poorer land, especially in dry, barren, sandy to clay soil. Its wood is heavy, hard and strong, hence lends to making mauls, wooden hammers, and hand jacks (Cardwell); *blackjack oak* = usually grows on river and creek bottoms (Shields).

[DARE *blackjack oak* n chiefly South, South Midland]

black jacket *noun* A dark-colored wasp known for its viciousness.

1966 *DARE Survey* (Burnsville NC) = a stinging insect. **1973** Miller *English Unicoi Co* 143 = a large, very dark, shiny insect of the wasp family. **1974–75** McCracken *Logging* 6:104 Now you ain't never been stung by nothin' till you get stung by a black jacket. **1996** Montgomery *Coll* = a type of wasp larger and more vicious than a yellow jacket, sometimes confused with a hornet (Brown); Be thankful it was only a yellow jacket and you weren't stung by a black jacket (Cardwell). **1997** Montgomery *File* They're ill little fellows, them black jackets is (60-year-old man, Maggie Valley NC).

black joint *noun* A bugbane (*Cimicifuga racemosa*). Same as **black cohosh.**

1996 Montgomery *File* (known to 82-year-old man, Gatlinburg TN).

black man *noun* See citations. Same as **(the) bad man 1.**

1915 Dingus *Word-List VA* 180 = the Devil. **c1960** Wilson *Coll* = the Devil.

black mountain *noun* See citation.

1950 King and Stupka *Geology and Natural History* 41 The spruce and fir forests form a dark, somber growth that has earned for the ridges that bear them the local denomination of "black mountain."

black oak See **blackjack.**

black oat grass *noun* See citation.

1941 Walker *Story of Mt* 49–50 Black oat grass thrives in the open woodlands on the mountain. Its seed when ripe clings to the clothing and by a cork-screwlike device . . . works its way through until it strikes the flesh. The piercing pain that follows causes one to halt, unwind the hobo and toss it to the earth, thus accomplishing precisely that which nature designed from the beginning.

black pot *noun* See citations. Also called **submarine.**

1980 Crewdson *Revenuers* Illegal whisky is made these days in "black pots"—800-gallon wood and galvanized sheet vats shaped like a one-man submarine with a "port hole" in the top to draw off the alcohol vaporized by large burners, fueled by bottled gas. **2009** Webb et al. *Moonshining* 330 Southern moonshiners eventually began using the "blackpot" method for running for submarine stills. Instead of allowing mash to ferment in boxes or barrels and then transferring the mash to the pot, the still hands poured the ingredients directly into the pot. They then placed a second smaller container of mash between the primary worm and the boiler to generate more alcohol.

black powder See **powder B.**

black satchel *noun* A small locomotive used in the logging industry.

1976 Ferrell *Tweetsie Country* 217 In service on the Boone Fork Lumber Company's six miles of trackage were several Shays and a Class A Climax, locally known as a "Black Satchel." **1996** Cole *Forney's Creek* 62 While Ledford admits that this claim is perhaps a mild exaggeration, he points out that the small Climax locomotives, or "black satchels" as they were commonly called, often operated under very rugged conditions.

black sheep *verb phrase* See citation.

1927 Woofter *Dialect from WV* 348 *black sheep one* = to obtain another person's job: "Will Henry blacksheeped me while my father was sick and they needed me at home."

black snakeroot *noun* A bugbane (*Cimicifuga racemosa*), a perennial wild shrub whose roots and rhizomes have medicinal uses, especially in a bitter tea as a tonic or antidote for snakebite. Same as **black cohosh.**

1937 Haun *Cocke Co* 2 Folks still have the maw ache from eating too much sallet, and blacksnake root is the only thing that will cyore it. **1939** Hall *Coll* (Catons Grove TN) Blacksnake root, that's one of the best remedies I ever saw used for hives, isn't it? . . . Blacksnake root's real good for weeding the breast. **1941** Walker *Story of Mt* 48 Among the wild plants once employed as antidotes for the bites of poisonous reptiles, are rattlesnake-master, black snakeroot, rattlesnake-weed, Samson snakeroot or scurfy (whose tough fleshy root has long been used for tooth brushes), Virginia snakeroot, button snakeroot, and rattlesnake-root. **1956** Hall *Coll* (Sand Hill TN) My mom never had no doctors. She just doctored herself. She would get herself some root out in the woods and make a tea. I liked black snakeroot the worst. Hit was so bitter. Hit'd break the fever. [**1971** Krochmal et al. *Medicinal Plants Appal* 98 The roots and rhizomes are considered valuable in treating chronic rheumatism. . . . In Appalachia, a tea made from the root is used to treat sore throat.] **1982** Stupka *Wildflowers* 34 Attractive in appearance but disagreeable in the odor of its white flowers, black snakeroot displays its long, wandlike stalk of blooms in rich woodlands from June to August.

blackstrap

A (also *black straps*) *noun* Strong, crude molasses, usually dark in color.

1962 Clark *Folk Speech NC* 304 *black-straps* = molasses. **1998** Montgomery *Coll* = usually molasses that has boiled longer and has a darker color (Cardwell), = darker, stronger molasses (Ellis), = a type of molasses that was very dark in color and strong in flavor (Norris), = extremely dark molasses (Oliver).

B *verb* In logging, to lubricate a **slide** or **skid road** to ease logs down an incline to a landing.

1994 Schmidt and Hooks *Whistle* 42 To avoid the entanglement in other trees, stumps or brush, the slide was constructed of logs or cut lumber partly buried in the ground to form a V-shaped trough down the slope. Sometimes the slides were "black-strapped" with crude oil, grease, or another lubricant to facilitate continuous movement to the landing at the bottom.

[from similarity of the lubricant to molasses in color]

black tongue *noun* A disease affecting deer and cattle.

1937 Hall *Coll* (Bradley Fork NC) [What happened to the deer?]: I allowed they might a tuck the black tongue and died, just like it tuck the cattle. There was no cure.

[DARE *blacktongue* n chiefly South, South Midland]

Black Water See **Black Waterite**.

Black Waterite (also *Black Water*) *noun* A member of a triracial ethnic group in Eastern Kentucky.

1947 Dunlap and Weslager *Tri-racial Groups* 82 [Triracial mixed-blood groups] Black Waterites, or The Black Waters. (A division of the Melungeons.) *Ibid*. 86 = named for a nearby stream known as the Black Water, the bed of which is covered with dark slate rock. **1963** Berry *Almost White* 35 In Eastern Kentucky the mixed-bloods are called Black Waterites, because they live along the Black Water Creek.

[DARE *Black Waterite* n chiefly eastern KY]

blade *noun*

1 The leaf of a cornstalk. Same as **corn blade**. See also **blade fodder**, **fodder**, **roughness**.

1943 Stuart *Private Tussie* 271 It would look like livin to be able to walk through the corn in September when the fodder blades start a-turnin. **1966** Guthrie *Corn* 90 Others pulled fodder. They pulled the leaves (blades) from the plants and left them between the rows to be tied up when dampness made them pliable.

[DARE *blade* n 1 chiefly South, South Midland]

2 The stalk of a green onion.

1995–96 Montgomery *Coll* (known to Adams, Cardwell, Ledford, Oliver). **2009** Sohn *Appal Home Cooking* 294 *blades* = colloquial for onion or corn leaves. Mountaineers eat onion blades in the spring.

[DARE *blade* n 2 chiefly South, South Midland]

blade fodder *noun* The dried leaves of a cornstalk, collected to feed livestock. See also **blade 1**, **cut tops**, **fodder**, **fodder pulling time**, **roughness**, **top A2**.

1931 Goodrich *Mt Homespun* 54 The children were in the fields, stripping off the lower leaves of the corn for "blade fodder" while the larger boys and the men were "topping" the stalks; cutting the "top fodder" with a quick, dexterous slash of the knife. **1995** Montgomery *Coll* = the blades of corn were called fodder or blade fodder, and if the tops were cut above the last ear of corn and harvested for feed, then they were referred to as cut tops (Ledford).

[DARE *blade fodder* n chiefly South Midland]

blame(d) *adjective*, *adverb* Used as a mild oath or as an intensifier.

1873 Smith *Peace Papers* 95 It's blamed lu[c]ky, Bill, that I didn't go to Andersonville. **1895** Dromgoole *Fiddling to Fame* 52 Then he give the word ez he'd vote aginst me same's he would any other blamed Dimercrat. **1900** Harben *N GA Sketches* 77 You've been in Georgia, an' you know how blamed hard it is fer a feller to make his salt back thar. **1913** Kephart *Our Sthn High* 231 That is some more "blamed foolish'ness"—their adherence to old ways is stubborn, sullen, and perverse to a degree that others cannot comprehend. **1928** (in **1952** Mathes *Tall Tales* 72) He was brung up on the ol'-time hawg rifle, which it took a coon's age to load the blame thing, an' he jest had to git his b'ar the fust shot. **1969** Medford *Finis* 60 Yore mule's blame nigh as old as this hoss is; then the mule's not got the size on 'im, not big a-nuff to trade well. **1972** GSMNP-93:5 I remember there was snow about six inches deep up and down this blamed creek every day. **1984** Burns *Cold Sassy* 28 Doc Slaughter said blamed if he knew what it was. **1999** Carver *Branch Water Tales* 43 It was blamed near as long as he was tall. **2010** Owenby *Trula Ownby* 16 We got up the next morning and fed [the mule] a good breakfast and blamed if they didn't come get it before we could put the gears on it.

[OED3 *blamed* past-part/adj, adv dialect and U.S.]

blamify *verb* See citations.

1972 Cooper *NC Mt Folklore* 90 = to eternally blame without reason. **1997** Montgomery *Coll* (known to Brown); I'll be blamified if I'll tell you (Cardwell).

[*blame* + *-ify* verb-forming suffix]

blanket bed *noun* A bed for a small child or infant.

1979 *Smokies Heritage* 278 Martha put the baby into his blanket bed, then busied herself gathering dry sticks for the fire. **1997** Montgomery *Coll* (known to Andrews).

blare *verb* To open the eyes wide, stare wildly; hence adjective *blare-eyed*.

1970 *Hunting* 16 When they [= raccoons] first come out an' hit th' fresh air, they'll just blare their mouth like a possum grinnin' an' they'll fall over. **1973** *Foxfire II* 304 Aunt Arie told us . . . of a neighbor who was shot during a fight and died with his eyes open "blared," she called it. "And you could see th'devil in 'em fightin', y'know." **1990** Clouse *Wilder* 20 Lacey stood there on the porch looking all blare-eyed as old Aunt Mazy.

[DARE *blare* v 3 chiefly South]

blare-eyed See **blare**.

blasphemious *adjective* Blasphemous.

1925 Furman *Glass Window* 170 Peace to your blasphemious tongue!

blate

A *noun* The cry of a sheep or calf; a similar sound or a device that makes such a sound. See also **horn blate**.

1859 Taliaferro *Fisher's River* 92 I made me a blate (hunters split a stick, put a leaf into it, and by blowing it can imitate the bleating of deer so as to deceive them), went out to the laurel and ivy thicket whar I'd killed the doe, blated, and the fawn answered me. **1966–68** *DARE Survey* (Brasstown NC, Burnsville NC, Maryville TN) = noise made by a sheep. **1967** Wilson *Folkways Mammoth Cave* 24 = almost universal [rather than *bleat*]. **1994** Montgomery *Coll* (known to Shields).

[DARE *blate* n A1 chiefly South, South Midland]

B *verb* Of sheep (and by extension of people): to whine.

1859 [see **A** above]. **1895** Murfree *Phantoms* 216 He jes sets thar ez pitiful ez a lost kid, fairly ready ter blate aloud. **1995** Montgomery *Coll* She blated around all day long (Cardwell). **1996** Johnson *Lexical Change* 138 *blate* = statistically more common in the mountains of South Carolina and Georgia than in the Piedmont and Coastal Plain c1990.

blatherskite *noun* One who talks nonsense.

1957 Justus *Other Side* 39 Glory always laughed at this speech, and so did Mammy and Grandy, although Grandy called it "tomfoolery," and Matt a "blatherskite."

[alteration of *bletherskate*; OED3 *blether* v + *skate* n in Scots used contemptuously, *bletherskate* a, b dialect and U.S. colloquial; cf SND n 1 *bladderskate* "silly, foolish person"]

bleach *verb*

1 To treat (fruit, especially sliced apples) with the fumes of burning sulfur before drying them for later consumption. See 1996 citation.

1937 Hall *Coll* (Mingus Creek NC) After I was raised I got to bleachin' apples. Never knowed nothin' about canning fruits and vegetables when I was a girl. **1969** *Mt Recipes* 26 Several people in the area still remember the days when fruit was "bleached" with sulfur for preservation. . . . "Everybody nearly bleached fruits. And it was the sulfur [that] whited the apples, and they had a little sulfur flavor." **1996** Cole *Forney's Creek* 66 Kelly Cole explained how fruit used to be "bleached." First, sliced fruit was placed in a basket. Then the basket would be hung in a large barrel that was covered over with a quilt. Near the bottom of the barrel a hole was cut large enough so that a piece of iron, like an old plowshare, could be inserted. The piece of iron was heated red-hot and then sulfur was put on it and it was placed in a barrel. The smoke from the sulfur would rise up through the fruit and "bleach" it. The fruit could then be stored in a barrel for the winter. "You could just go into it any time you wanted to and have fresh cooked fruit."

2 See citation.

1957 Broaddus *Vocab Estill Co KY* 8 = to keep growing celery white by covering it.

bleed *verb* To sweat heavily.

1990 Merriman *Moonshine Rendezvous* 60 I kept both eyes peeled for that Buick, but to this day I've never spotted it. My guess is that they gave up at the pickup and tractor area. When I crossed the Trousdale-Smith County line, my palms stopped "bleeding."

[DARE *bleed* v chiefly South, South Midland]

bleed the lizard *verb phrase* See citation.

1957 Combs *Lg Sthn High: Idioms* 13 It's time to bleed the lizard (urinate, just before going to bed).

bless (also *bless out*) *verb, verb phrase* To castigate, scold sharply or unmercifully, "tell off."

1862 Robinson *CW Letters* (Dec 9) I went to the Sargent for [salt] in a very mild manner & he blesed me that if I was not thare to git it I would have to do withe out. **1967** *DARE Survey* (Gatlinburg TN) *bless out* = to give a very sharp scolding. **1971** Costner *Song of Life* 130 She blessed me out and told me to stand where I was until she and Alan got the hen back. **1976** Weals *It's Owin'* = scold, rebuke, bawl out. "She blessed him out for being late for the wedding." **2015** *Blind Pig* (Aug 25) He blessed me out up one side and down the other.

[DARE *bless out* v chiefly South, South Midland]

bless my time *interjection* Used as an exclamation of surprise. See also **help my time**, **save my time.**

2017 *Blind Pig* (June 10) I've heard variations, including "bless my time" and "save my time," although "help my time" is more common.

bless out See **bless**.

blind cabin *noun* See 1913 citation.

1913 Kephart *Our Sthn High* 248–49 Hundreds of backwoods families, large ones at that, exist in "blind" cabins that remind one somewhat of Irish hovels. . . . Such a cabin has but one room for all purposes. In rainy or gusty weather, when the two doors must be closed, no light enters the room save through the cracks in the wall and down the chimney. **1996–97** Montgomery *Coll* (known to Brown), = still found in the 1930s but were no longer used for living (Bush).

blind cat *noun* A bat-and-ball game of former days, apparently similar to baseball. See also **bull pen**, **cat 1**, **town ball**, **two-eyed cat**.

1939 Hall *Coll* (Waldens Creek TN) Blind cat [was] another ball game. The ball was throwed from one point to another across there. A fellow would bat.

blinder *noun* See citation.

a1975 *Miners' Jargon* 1 = a streak of impurity in a coal seam.

blind staggers *noun* Dizziness of a person or animal resulting from a natural condition (such as an inner-ear disorder), intoxication, or consumption of certain plants.

1981 Whitener *Folk-Ways* 59 Unlike corn silks, however, the rabbit tobacco burned so stubbornly that one pipeful pretty well exhausted a box of kitchen matches so that one sucked in almost as much match as tobacco smoke and after suffered the blind staggers when he attempted to walk. **1990** Cavender *Folk Medical Lex* 18 = a feeling of dizziness or light-headedness; an inability to walk due to intoxication. **1994** Montgomery *Coll* (known to Cardwell).

blind tiger *noun* A site for the illegal sale of whiskey, especially one where the customer never sees the dealer, in which the transaction takes place at a shed (where the customer puts cash into a drawer or other small opening and receives the purchase through the same), into a hollow tree (in which a customer leaves cash and returns later to find a filled bottle), or at a similar setup. See also **hollowing tree**, **rat house**.

1895 Wiltse *Moonshiners* 36 There recently appeared in an open sedge field, upon Indian Creek, Fentress county, Tennessee, a rudely constructed box just about large enough to render it possible for a man and a demijohn to dwell together in unity within. No door, window, or other place of entrance or exit was visible. Upon its side was inscribed in crude letters: "Drop in a 50c piece in open slot." When a thirsty mortal ventured to the place and heeded the injunction, a small drawer was drawn inward, the aperture apparently closed itself, and in a short time some invisible agency caused another drawer to be projected from another part of the magic "blind tiger," in which was always found a half pint bottle full of whiskey which was entirely innocent of revenue, rectification, color or previous condition of servitude. **1899** Crozier *White-Caps* 172 Jap and Joe Jenkins were conducting a livery stable in the lower end of town, also a "blind tiger," so the horses and liquor were at hand. **c1950** Adams *Grandpap* 182 When we reached the blind tiger, Pap reined the mare up to the side of the building and, without dismounting, leaned sideways and pulled out a little drawer. "A pint of corn whiskey!" he said, dropping a half-dollar into the drawer and pushing it back in. **1957** Combs *Lg Sthn High: Word List* 11 *blind tiger* = small, windowless log hut where whiskey is sold illegitimately. The "rat" dispenses it by means of a drawer, which one pulls out, and into which the money for the whiskey is placed. The "rat" pulls in the drawer, takes the money therefrom, puts the whiskey into the drawer, then pushes it out to the thirsty customer. **1977** Pederson *Randy Sons* 112 Extending out from a hole in the wall, a board made a sliding counter upon which $2.50 was placed by the purchaser, the board then being drawn in by an unseen treadle and returned with a gallon of corn liquor.... No one ever saw the operators of the blind tiger (as such an enterprise is called). **1985** Irwin *Alex Stewart* 155 He had a pretty slick way of selling his whiskey. He called his system the "blind tiger".... He had a little room fixed up where all you could see was a drawer. You'd pull it out and put your money and your empty bottle in it. Then you'd tap it a couple of times and push the drawer back. We'd put in whatever amount of liquor they'd paid for, and we'd shove the drawer out, and they never seed who was doing the selling. We never spoke a word and they couldn't turn us in. **1994** Montgomery *File: blind tiger* = an outlet selling moonshine on a state or county border so as to avoid the jurisdiction of one agency and to provide a quick escape (Weals). **1997** Montgomery *Coll: blind tiger* = also a house of prostitution, or sometimes just a false front for illegal activities (Brown).

[DARE *blind tiger* n 1 chiefly South, West Midland]

blink

A *verb* Of milk: to turn sour or begin to do so.

[See **1946** in **B.**] **c1960** Wilson *Coll* = to turn sour: "That milk is beginning to blink." [See **1969** in **B.**] **1986** Pederson et al. *LAGS* (Sevier Co TN) *hit'll blink* = [the milk will] curd/clabber; *hit blinked* = the milk began to turn. **1997** *GSMNPCOHP*-1:2 The milk was put in the spring house to keep the milk cool. If you didn't, it'd blink on you.

[OED3 *blink* v I originally "to deceive, elude, turn away" c1616→, v 7.b "to turn slightly sour" a1665→; EDD *blink* v[8] Scot, Irel, nEngl; SND *blink* v 3 1(a) "to glance at with the evil eye, to bewitch" (often as participial adj *blinkit* "bewitched; turned sour"); Web3 *blink* vt 1 "cause to sour" obsolete; DARE *blink* v 1 "from *blink* to exercise an evil influence, bewitch, hence to sour (souring of milk being formerly ascribed to witchcraft)"; chiefly Midland]

B (also *blinked*, *blinky*) *adjective* Of milk, vinegar, or mash: beginning to turn sour or otherwise foul.

1895 Edson and Fairchild *TN Mts* 370 The vinegar is *blinky*. **1939** Bond *Appal Dialect* 104 *blinky* = soured, spoiled: "That popskull mash went blinky on me." **1946** Matthias *Speech Pine Mt* 188 *blinky* = slightly sour: "This milk is blinky." Blinky has been found as an adjective in middle Tennessee also, and as a noun meaning "milk slightly soured" in western North Carolina. An explanation of the word may be found in the EDD, which gives as one of the meanings of the verb blink, "to exercise an evil influence, bewitch, overlook; hence, to turn anything sour." Blinked is therefore "bewitched, soured, spoiled." **1961** Seeman *Arms of Mt* 38 We are a long way from a cow; besides, without ice, the local milk turns "blinky" almost at once. **1966** Dakin *Vocab Ohio River Valley* 341 Scattered speakers in ... eastern Kentucky say that milk just turning sour is *blink(y) milk* or *blinked milk*, and use *blink* = "turn sour" as a verb. **1969** Dial *Dialect Appal People* 466 Many of our people refer to sour milk as *blinked* milk. This usage goes back at least to the early 1600's when people still believed in witches and the power of the evil eye. One of the meanings of the word *blink* back in those days was "to glance at"; if you glanced at something, you *blinked* at it, and thus sour milk came to be called blinked due to the evil machinations of the witch. **1986** Pederson et al. *LAGS*: *blink(ed)* = attested by 18/60 interviewees (30%) from E TN, 18/27 of all LAGS interviewees (66.7%) attesting term were from E TN; *blink(ing)* = fixing to sour (Cocke Co TN); *blinky* = attested by 4/60 interviewees (6.7%) from E TN; 4/11 of all LAGS interviewees (36.4%) attesting term were from E TN. **1995** Weber *Rugged Hills* 37 I realized that when she said "blinked milk" she meant milk that had gone a little sour. "My father truly enjoyed blinked milk," Ruby-Noah told me. "He'd put it on a big piece of corn bread for supper." **2017** *Blind Pig* (Jan 12) I grew up in a family that used the word blinked for describing milk that had gone bad. Pap and Granny both used the word to describe milk that had spoiled or just had a funny taste to it.

C (also *blinked, blind milk, blinky*) *noun* Milk beginning to turn sour.

1895 *Word-Lists* 384 = sour milk; Montgomery Co, Va. **1917** Kephart *Word-List* 408 *blinky* = milk slightly soured. **1967** *DARE Survey* (Gatlinburg TN) *blinked, blinky* = milk just beginning to become sour. **1986** Pederson et al. *LAGS* (Sevier Co TN) *blink* = turning milk. **2014** *WV Talk*: *blink milk* = sour milk. **2017** *Blind Pig* (Jan 12) I used to milk the cows for my granny and great-uncle as a kid. Our kin always used the word blinky for milk that was to be churned.

[DARE *blink* n[1] chiefly South Midland]

blinked, blink milk, blinky See **blink B, C.**

blinky-blue *noun* See citation. Same as **blue john 2.**

1944 Wilson *Word-List* 40 = sour skimmed milk.

blister pine *noun* The Fraser fir (*Abies fraseri*). Same as **balsam 1.**

1894 Bergen *Plant Names III* 99 *Abies balsamea* . . . blister pine . . . West Va. **2006** *WV Encycl* 695 Blister Swamp in Pocahontas County was named after the original balsam fir, commonly called "blister pine," but the species was eliminated from the site by grazing.

blixen, blixy See **cold as blixen.**

blizzard *noun* See citation.

c1960 Wilson *Coll* = common name for a severe cold spell, especially with snow.

[DARE *blizzard* n chiefly South, South Midland]

block

A *verb* To make illegal liquor. Same as **blockade B2.**

1917 Kephart *Word-List* 409 He's *blockin'* over in Hell's Holler. **1997** Montgomery *Coll* (known to Hooper, but not to other consultants from the Smoky Mountains).

B *noun* One who hauls illegal liquor.

1997 Montgomery *Coll* He's a block [i.e. he transports whiskey] (Hooper).

blockade

A *noun*

1 Originally, a fence or other barrier, such as one on the movement of animals; later, any government restriction on the transport and sale of illicit or contraband goods.

1981 GSMNP-122:3 They used to run their cattle in there, you know, and they had a place there they called the blockade, built a fence built out of poles, you know. The cattle couldn't get back out. They called it the blockade. **1996** Montgomery *Coll* (known to Cardwell).

2 (also *blockade juice, blockade liquor, blockade whiskey*) Homemade whiskey on which no tax has been paid. [Editor's note: Although still remembered in the Smoky Mountains, the term *blockade* was apparently no longer common when Joseph Hall began work there in 1937, having been replaced by **liquor**, **moonshine**, and others. According to one consultant from the Smokies in the 1990s, the term has had currency only in law-enforcement circles in recent decades.]

1881 Atkinson *After Moonshiners* 25 I have known several of the very best and bravest revenue officers to be killed while seizing blockade liquors on a public highway. **1897** Pederson *Mtneers Madison Co* 825 Extreme poverty and the fact that they looked upon whiskey as one of the necessities of life, led many mountaineers into the illicit and dangerous business of making "blockade" whiskey. **1913** Morley *Carolina Mts* 203 As the country became more thickly settled, the struggle for existence harder, and the officers of the law more vigilant, whiskey-making became a special rather than a general occupation, and was carried on by the boldest and most executive spirits of the region, who called their illicit product "blockade," thus attaching to themselves something of the respectability and even the heroism of a man running a blockade against an enemy in a just cause. **1935** Sheppard *Cabins in Laurel* 190 Most of the stills are run by people who have been making blockade for years and are proud of the flavor of their product as good housewives are proud of the flavor of their butter. **1967–70** *DARE Survey* (Pensacola NC, Westminster SC) *blockade*, (Dillard GA) *blockade juice*, (Maryville TN) *blockade liquor*, (Cherokee NC) *blockade whiskey* = Illegally made whiskey. **1978** *Smoky Vistas* (July–Sept) 3 The "blockade liquor" institution was not unlike any other aspect of mountain life in times gone by. . . . "Blockade whiskey" could then be sold for cash or used in higher value trading, thus making the original corn much more valuable to the subsistence of the farmer.

B *verb*

1 To block (one's path), cut off access to.

1937 Hall *Coll* (Mingus Creek NC) They've got me blockaded [a complaint made by Debbie Mathis because the Park engineers blocked her use of the road in order to install new water pipes, which meant she couldn't get to the milk gap to milk her cows]. **1939** Hall *Coll* (Cataloochee NC) [If] she'd just have blockaded the hole, we'd have got all of them [said of a mother bear and her cubs].

2 To make liquor without paying the tax on it; hence noun *blockading* = the making of such liquor. Same as **block A.**

1883 Zeigler and Grosscup *Heart of Alleghanies* 141 Blockading, or "moonshining" as it is sometimes called, because the distiller works by the light of the moon, is not as prevalent in these mountains as is generally supposed; and, besides, it is growing less with every year. **1913** Kephart *Our Sthn High* 126 Here an illicit distiller is called a blockader, his business is blockading, and the product is blockade liquor. **1939** *FWP Guide NC* 467 The making of illicit liquor, locally called "blockading," contributed to the feuds that have given this region its old name of "Bloody Madison [Co NC]." **1973** Wellman *Kingdom of Madison* 160 [After the Civil War] stills moved from back yards to tangled fastnesses where they would be hard to find, harder to approach. A new term for the old profession was blockading, a colorful analogy to the Confederate cargo-runners. Liquor kept right on trickling out of the worm, though it was harder to make now. **1982** Absher *Wilkes County* 68 Distillers had to purchase state licenses and tax stamps; and revenue agents, popularly called "brandy gaugers," went around and collected tax on each distiller's inventory in his warehouse (usually his wellhouse). But, because the whisky's tax nearly equalled its going price, almost always a portion of each run was put back out of sight to be "blockaded"—sold, that is, without benefit of the government tax stamp.

3 To sell untaxed whiskey, seeking to elude law-enforcement officers trying to prevent it.

1914 Arthur *Western NC* 273 Blockading is usually applied to the illegal selling of moonshine whiskey or brandy. **1967** Williams *Moonshining* 12 The whiskey produced was "blockaded" to illicit markets.

blockade juice, blockade liquor See **blockade A2**.

blockader (also *blockade runner*) *noun* Originally, one who makes and transports untaxed liquor; more recently, one who transports it by running a **blockade** of law-enforcement officials in order to sell it. For its historical development, see 1974 citation.

1883 Zeigler and Grosscup *Heart of Alleghanies* 141 Had we paid any attention to the opinion that, in the wilderness, we would be taken for revenue officers, and, as such, shot on sight by blockaders, we would have ridden uneasily. **1912** Mason *Raiding Moonshiners* 199 The splendid 50-gallon wild-cat outfit of this young "blockader," as he called himself, costing days of labor and representing an outlay of over a hundred dollars in cash, was soon rolling upward in smoke. **1921** Campbell *Sthn Highlander* 104–5 The moonshiner, as he is called without the mountains, or blockader, as he is more commonly known within them, is one who engages in the illicit distilling of spirituous liquors. Secrecy is necessary for this practice, and he is called moonshiner because it is supposed that he engages in his illicit traffic on moonlight nights when there is enough light to make work easy and enough darkness to make him secure. To dispose of the product of his still, he or his confederates must run the blockade thrown about the sale of liquor by government officials. He is, therefore, regarded as a blockade runner, or "blockader." **1964** Reynolds *Born of Mts* 81 Blockader was the most respectable of these names, for it indicated one who heroically ran the fully imposed blockade. **1968** *DARE Survey* (Brasstown NC) *blockader* = person who makes illegal liquor. **1974** Dabney *Mt Spirits* xv Pioneer moonshiners were called "blockaders" and the product "blockade whiskey." In all likelihood, the term derived from the blockade-running prior to and during the Revolutionary War, the War of 1812, and the Civil War, when contraband was rammed through coastal blockades. **2007** Alexander *Moonshiners Gone* 30 So it came to be that local moonshiners began to band together to fill orders from larger towns and cities, using one or more so-called "blockade runners." Making regular pickups, these blockaders would truck "made up" loads of white lightning into northern markets, reaping profits for all.

[DARE *blockader* n chiefly South Midland]

blockade runner See **blockader**.

blockade still *noun* See citation.

1971 Gordon *Moonshining in GA* 57 The basic parts of the blockade still are the still itself, the furnace (which is built around the still), the cap and cap stem, the thump post and thump barrel, the headache piece, the pre-heater box and trough, the slide connections, the flake stand and the condenser.

blockade whiskey See **blockade A2**.

blockading See **blockade B2**.

block-and-tackle *noun phrase* Homemade whiskey.

1981 Morrell *Mirth* 29 No narrative of the Great Smokies would be complete without at least one story about "Moonshine" whiskey, also known as "Splo," "panther sweat," "tangle-foot," and "block and tackle liquor." (You take a drink and walk a block, and by that time you are ready to tackle anything.) **1997** Montgomery *File* (known to 65-year-old man, Maggie Valley NC).

block setter *noun* See citation.

1994 Farwell and Buchanan *Logging Terms* = a member of a logging crew who set up the cuts for the boards that are to be sawed.

blocky *adjective* Of an animal: stocky, sturdily built.

1967 Fetterman *Stinking Creek* 70 She's a four year old blocky cow. I wouldn't sell her for no kind of money. **1995** Mullins *Road Back* 11 I don't see many people to talk to, especially in the winter when the weather is blocky like this.

bloober See **blubber A**.

blood bread *noun* Blood pudding, made from the blood of hogs.

1997 Andrews *Mountain Vittles* 80 Jeff [= a member of the Eastern Band of the Cherokee] said that around his house anybody who kills hogs saves the blood and makes blood bread. They mix it right in the meal and bake it.

blood builder (also *blood medicine, blood purifier, blood restorer, blood toner, blood tonic*) *noun* Any of several traditional medicines derived from plants and made into a tea drunk to "clean" or "improve" the blood. See also **sassafras B**, **spring tonic**, **strenghthening tonic**, **sulfur and molasses.**

1937 Hall Coll (Cades Cove TN) *blood tonic* = ginseng. **1937** Haun *Cocke Co* 4 Sarsasparilla bitters is a fine blood tonic. **1985** Irwin *Alex Stewart* 143 A lot of people don't know it but rhubarb is a good blood medicine too. Yes, sir, hit'll purify your blood right quick. **1997** Montgomery Coll: *blood medicine* = a mixture of many herbs boiled or steeped together, still used (Brown), = sassafras (Cardwell), = ginseng (Norris). **2001** Joslin *Appal Bounty* 112 Medicinally, clover, especially the red variety, has been an important part of the pharmacopeia for centuries. As a tea, it is used as a blood purifier and to relieve bronchial problems. **2003** Cavender *Folk Medicine* 124 In the spring the blood's invigorating properties were restored by taking a tonic, variously called a "blood builder," "blood restorer," "blood toner," or "spring tonic." The most popular tonic in Southern Appalachia was sulfur and molasses, which some thought was also good for cleaning the blood. **2006** *Encycl Appalachia* 867 Thin blood was treated through eating various foods (poke sallet, meat, eggs) or taking a "blood toner" or tonic. Sulfur and molasses constituted one of the more popular tonics. **2011** Lix *Medicine Women* 29 Come springtime, "blood builders" or "blood purifiers" were often used to restore health and vigor after the lean winter months. Molasses and sulfur was a popular combination, as was taking the dried and powdered leaves of lady's slipper orchids, mixing them with water, and drinking a spoonful of the mixture three times a day.

blood doctor (also *blood stopper*) *noun* See citations. See also **faith doctor**, **fever doctor**, **stop blood**.

1972 Cooper *NC Mt Folklore* 16 Usually there was only one person—commonly a woman—in each community who had sufficient faith to be a Blood Doctor and able to stop profuse bleeding from nose or cut by reading or reciting in a loud, clear and confident tone to the patient the sixth verse of the Sixteenth Chapter of Ezekiel. *Ibid.* 77 The *blood doctor* . . . stood before the patient and recited several times, if the usual three did not stop the bleeding, in a loud, clear voice Ezekiel 16:6: "And when I passed by thee, and saw thee polluted in thine own blood, I said unto thee when thou wast in thy blood, Live!" **2000** Montgomery Coll (known to Cardwell). **2003** Cavender *Folk Medicine* 203 *blood stopper* = a folk healer who has the ability to stop bleeding.

blood kin *noun* A blood relative, as distinct from relatives by marriage.

1925 (in **1935** Edwards *NC Novels* 94) *blood-kin*. **1941** Stuart *Men of Mts* 223 He would be proud of his blood kin. **1955** Ritchie *Singing Family* 96 He's your own blood kin and it's a sight what all he's collected up in his mind about the family. **1964** Thomas and Kob *Ballad Makin'* 9 Year after year in my travel through the mountains of Kentucky, on one mission or another, I "set down" all sorts of ballads and tunes, many of which the mountain minstrel, or his "own blood kin," claimed to have "made up right out of his head." **1968** *DARE Survey* (Brasstown NC) = general term for others related by blood. **1996** Montgomery Coll (known to Adams, Brown, Cardwell, Jones, Norris, Oliver).

[DARE *blood kin* n chiefly South, South Midland]

blood leather *noun* See citation.

1975 Hamel and Chiltoskey *Cherokee Plants* 6 Some of the lichens became known as blood leather from their use in stopping the flow of blood from wounds.

blood medicine See **blood builder.**

blood pizen See **blood poison.**

blood poison *noun*

A Variant form *blood pizen* [see **1937** in **B**].

B Blood poisoning.

1937 Hall Coll (Cosby TN) Catnip and beadwood bark [are] biled together and made into a poultice for blood pizen. **1939** Hall Coll (Big Creek NC) They was a weed that they call wild indigo. You can take hit, and it'll stop blood poison. Take the roots and beat it up, put sweet milk in it, and put it on [the wound], and it'll draw it white and cure it up.

blood purifier, **blood restorer** See **blood builder.**

bloodroot *noun* A perennial wild plant (*Sanguinaria canadensis*) with a root whose red juice is made into a medicinal tea and used as a dye. Also called **coonroot**, **puccoon**, **red Indian paint**, **red root 1.**

1824 (in **1912** Doddridge *Notes on Settlement* 116) Indian physic, or bowman root, a species of epicacuanha, was frequently used for a vomit, and sometimes the pocoon or blood root. **1937** Hyatt *Kiverlid* 99 In them days most persons got poke berry juice fer writin' with, or sometimes they'd use puccoon root—blood root they called it—but hit would soon fade down. **1940** Caton *Wildflowers of Smokies* 2 It derives its name from the fact that the juice of both stem and root is reddish, the stems "bleeding" when broken. **1971** Krochmal et al. *Medicinal Plants Appal* 226 [The juice] is an emetic, laxative, and emmenagogue; and because of its expectorant qualities, it has been used to treat chronic bronchitis. This plant is used both as a pain reliever and a sedative. When combined with oak bark, the roots give a red dye. In Appalachia, a piece of bloodroot is sometimes carried as a charm to ward off evil spirits. **1982** Stupka *Wildflowers* 39 The rootstock that gives this plant its name is ½–1 in. thick and up to 4 in. long, and contains a bright orange-red juice, said to have been used medicinally as a tonic and stimulant. . . . Among its other names are "puccoon-root" and "red Indian paint."

bloodshotten *adjective* Bloodshot.

1963 Watkins and Watkins *Yesterday* 39 The hot fire baked the blood in the front of the girls' legs, and they looked bloodshotten or piedidy. **1971** Dwyer *Dict for Yankees* 24 His eyes was bloodshotten. **1996–97** Montgomery Coll (known to Brown, Jones, Ledford, Norris, Oliver); He came in with bloodshotten eyes (Cardwell).

[*blood* + *shotten* obsolete past participle of *shoot*; OED3 *bloodshotten* adj U.S. regional and rare; Web3 *bloodshotten* adj now dialect; DARE *bloodshotten* adj chiefly South Midland, South]

blood stopper See **blood doctor.**

blood stopping See **stop blood.**

blood toner, blood tonic See **blood builder.**

bloody flux *noun* Hemorrhagic diarrhea; dysentery. See also **(the) flux.**

1904–20 Kephart *Notebooks* 2:469. **1962** Dykeman *Tall Woman* 68 She saw the figure of her least'un that had been buried years before during an awful siege of the bloody flux. **1977** Hamilton *Mt Memories* 15 Before they came, Lela told me Tim had "bloody flux" and she just knew he would die. **1982** Powers and Hannah *Cataloochee* 244 I was trying to decide what was the bloody flux. **1994** Montgomery *Coll* (known to Cardwell), = usually associated with typhoid fever (Shields).

bloom *noun* Blossoms of a tree or plant collectively.

1938 (in **2005** Ballard and Chung *Arnow Stories* 102) She'ull like th wahoo an th ivy bloom. **1959** Hall *Coll* (Newport TN) [Uncle Bill Barnes] had a lot of bees. They was plenty of bloom up there for 'em to make honey on. **1961** Miller *Pigeon's Roost* (June 22) Some old timers said there is the heaviest poplar bloom that they had seen in several years and it is an old timey sign that when there is a big poplar bloom, there will be plenty of rain while the bloom stays on the trees. **1981** Brewer *Wonderment* 197 He remembers chestnut honey, and he said oldtime beekeepers always claimed the bees "got a heep iller, would sting you quicker," when they were working on chestnut bloom. **1997** Montgomery *Coll* (known to Adams, Brown, Bush, Cardwell, Jones, Ledford).

[DARE *bloom* n[1] 1 chiefly South, South Midland]

bloom for the grave (also *blossom for the grave*) *verb phrase* To have one's hair turn white in old age.

1931 Combs *Lg Sthn High* 1305 Old Spence's head is a-blossomin' fer the grave. **1981** Whitener *Folk-Ways* 41 Those whose heads were bloomin' for the grave. **1998** Montgomery *File*: *bloom for the grave* (known to 85-year-old man, Greenbrier TN).

bloomy *adjective* Of hair: gray.

1940 Farr *More TN Expressions* 446 = gray hair: "Lillie's hair is bloomy."

blossom *noun*

1 A halo around the moon.

1973 *GSMNP*-57:91 They'd be a circle around the moon. My daddy always called that a blossom around the moon.

2 See citation.

a1975 *Miners' Jargon* 1 = the decomposed outcrop of a coal bed.

blossom cap *noun* See citation. Same as **cap A2.**

1968 *Best Was Made* 104 You can tell when [moonshine is] ready to run by studying the cap that has formed over the beer. Sometimes this cap will be two inches thick. Sometimes it will only be a half-inch thick, and sometimes it will just be suds and blubber (called a "blossom cap").

blossom for the grave See **bloom for the grave.**

blossom out *verb phrase*

1 See citation. See also **bud out.**

1994 Montgomery *Coll* = of a girl: to show physical signs of sexual maturation, to reach puberty (Ogle).

2 See citation.

1994 Montgomery *Coll* = to turn red, usually from an allergy, as "She blossomed out all over" (Ogle).

blow

A *verb* Principal parts.

1 Variant past-tense forms *blowed, blown.* [Editor's note: In the Smoky Mountains in the late 1930s Joseph Hall observed that *blowed* was in near-universal use.]

1834 Crockett *Narrative* 150 In the morning we concluded to go on with the boat to where a great harricane crossed the river, and blowed all the timber down into it. **1862** *Robinson CW Letters* (May 25) I Stood picket last Wensday in the hardest hail Storm I ever Saw it blowed down the timber all Round us. **1864** *Forgotten Ancestors* (Jefferson Co TN) 1 We got back to the regiment the other morning gest [= just] as they blowed the beugle for to get up. **1934–47** *LAMSAS Appal*: *blowed* = attested by 33/148 speakers (22.2%) from WV, 15/20 (75%) from VA, 29/37 (78.4%) from NC, 4/14 (28.6%) from SC, and 9/12 (75%) from GA. **1939** Hall *Coll* (Mt Sterling NC) [The dynamite] blowed Mister Sullivan for something like a hundred yards, I suppose, slapped him up again the face of another cliff. . . . So that's about the story, I expect, of the dynamite that blown up at that time. **1953** Atwood *Verbs East US* 6 As we proceed southward from Pa. *blowed* becomes more and more frequent until in N.C. it is used by more than nine tenths of Type I [i.e. older speakers having little formal education] and about four fifths of Type II [= younger speakers having more formal education]. **1973** *GSMNP*-80:6 The wind blowed a sight in the world hard up there. **1974–75** McCracken *Logging* 11:44 I showed you where it [= the blowdown fire] blowed off of the top of the mountain, blowed across on the Defeat Ridge. **1979** *Big South Fork OHP*—18 Fidelity had a explosion there and it blowed stuff out of the mines and killed two in a fire in the night at the Pine Ridge. **1998** *Dante OHP*-58 Somebody shot that power line down, took dynamite and blowed the poles down and it was all laying down.

[OED3 *blowed* 16c]

2 Variant past-participle forms *bload, blowed.*

1799 (in **2008** Ellison *High Vistas* 38) The wind has such a power on the top of his mountain that the ground is blowed in deep holes all over the northeast sides. **1862** *Warrick CW Letters* (Oct 28) by midnight our tents was blowed down an every thing rin[g]ing wet. **1863** *Brown CW Letters* (Oct 2) imust close the bugle has bload to water horse. **1939** Hall *Coll* (Mt Sterling NC) [It was] nineteen and seven, December the fifteenth, when all those boys got blowed up on Big Creek on this logging job. *Ibid.* (Nine Mile TN) Directly the gun fired, and when it fired, he fell just the same as if it'd blowed his head off. **1973** *GSMNP-79*:8 We'd take a pail or a sack and go out through the woods after the warm winds had blowed through the night. **1980** Miles *Verbs in Haywood Co* 88 The snow had blowed in the door. **1981** Weals *Becky Rewards* She said she was going the way a big spruce pine had blowed down. It made her a pretty open route. **1989** *Matewan OHP-56* That gun crew got blowed up. **1998** *Dante OHP-24* It's a wonder a lot of people hadn't got blowed up and killed.

[OED3 *blowed* 16c; DARE *blow* v¹ A3 chiefly South, South Midland, scattered North]

B *verb* Senses.

1 To pause (or cause to pause) to rest in the midst of strenuous exertion, pant or catch one's breath.

1867 Harris *Sut Lovingood* 49 Lite, lite, ole feller an' let that roan ove yourn blow a litil, an' I'll 'splain this cussed misfortnit affar: hit hes ruinated my karacter es a pius pusson in the s'ciety roun' yere, an' is a spreadin faster nur meazils. **1892** Doak *Wagonauts Abroad* 97 Now the road grows steep and craggy as we rise to the backbone of some bold ridge, and walk and push and scotch and "blow" our good team of smoking horses. **1924** (in **1952** Mathes *Tall Tales* 26) He was might'-nigh give out when he got to camp, but he said he'd foller us back as soon as he blowed a spell. **1948** Chase *Grandfather Tales* 198 When they got up in the gap the old man thought he'uld let her blow a spell 'fore he started down. **1963** Edwards *Gravel* 171 "Light, boys; light and rest yer nags," said Doc. . . . "Light and blow awhile." **1975** Fink *Backpacking* 5 Here we had to stop and blow a number of times before we emerged into the open, cultivated fields on top, to get our first clear view of Big Bald, across the valley of South Indian Creek.

[SND (at *blaw* I.4) "to recover one's breath"; DARE *blow* v¹ B1 especially West, Midland]

2 To boast, brag; to seek to deceive (one).

1859 Taliaferro *Fisher's River* 205 That ended Davis's bullyin', puffin', and blowin' about his manhood. **c1945** Haun *Hawk's Done* 218 He wouldn't be blowing when he told his boys how he fit for the woman he got. **1975** Jackson *Unusual Words* 153 If one man says of another, "Hay-lo, you gotta watch 'im; he'll blow you," the listener is being warned about an excessive bragger. **1995–97** Montgomery *Coll* (known to Ledford), = trick, tease, tell tall tales, mix fact and fiction, as "He blows a lot" = he brags or talks a lot (Cardwell).

[SND (at *blaw* II.1) "to boast, brag; to exaggerate"; CUD *blow* v 2 "boast, brag"]

3 To leave hurriedly.

1968 *DARE Survey* (Brasstown NC) = hurry. "I'm late; I'll have to blow."

4 See citation.

c1960 Wilson *Coll* = to treat: "He blowed us all to a bottle of pop."

C *noun*

1 A braggart.

1915 Dingus *Word-List VA* 181 = boaster: "That feller is nothing but a big blow." **1976** Thompson *Touching Home* 17 He was a big blow. **1995–97** Montgomery *Coll* (known to Adams, Brown, Cardwell, Jones, Norris, Oliver, Shields); He's just a big blow [i.e. one who misleads by false promises or exaggerations] (Ledford).

[DARE *blow* n² 2 scattered, but especially Midland]

2 A pause to rest or catch one's breath.

1928 (in **1952** Mathes *Tall Tales* 69) An hour later they stopped for a brief blow at Brackens' Cabin, where a little-used trail branches off to the left of the old road to Luftee Gap and follows the meanderings of Alum Cave Creek into the very jaws of Huggins' Hell.

3 (usually plural) An extended period of time.

1940 Farr *More TN Expressions* 446 I haven't seen him in blows. **1996** Montgomery *Coll* (known to Cardwell, Jones).

[DARE *blow* n² 3 chiefly South, South Midland]

4 A storm with high winds.

1913 Kephart *Our Sthn High* 79 Durn this blow, anyhow! No bear'll cross the mountain sich a night as this. **1994–97** Montgomery *Coll* (known to Adams, Brown, Cardwell, Jones, Weaver). **2007** McMillon *Notes* = a strong wind that levels trees. **2008** Salsi *Ray Hicks* 182 A big blow 'ud come over from Grandfather Mountain and we'd have snow when we thought we was gonna plant.

blow a foghorn *verb* See citation.

1980 Riggleman *WV Mtneer* 126–27 [Loggers] usually had nicknames for everybody and everything around the camp. . . . If he smoked a pipe, he "blew a foghorn."

blow breath *verb phrase* To exhale. See also **draw breath**.

1937 Hall *Coll* (Wears Cove TN) = the old expression for "to exhale."

blow doctor *noun* One purportedly able to heal rashes, burns, and other conditions by blowing on the affected area. Also called **fire blower**. See also **blow fire**.

1993 Montell *Cumberland Country* 104 "Blow doctors" were known for their ability to kill rashes and the like.

blowdown *noun*

1 A fierce wind that flattens trees and other vegetation.

1970 Campbell et al. *Smoky Mt Wildflowers* 26 Blackberries are among the first plants to become established after forest fires, "blow-downs," or other disturbances.

2 An area (as a *blowdown field* or *blowdown section*) wherein trees and vegetation have been uprooted or flattened by strong wind. The one on Thunderhead Mountain in Blount County on the TN-NC border, caused by a fierce windstorm in 1875, is enormous in extent.

1926 Hunnicutt *Twenty Years* 210 We got even with Sam's creek and then went up through what is known as the blowdown cross . . . to an old field known as the blow-down field. **1951** Giles *Harbin's Ridge* 74 By the light we could tell we were in a blowdown, with tree laps all around us. **1971** Hall *Coll* (Townsend TN) I didn't know any of them Walkers. They lived in the Blowdown Section, upper end. [What do they mean by the "Blowdown Section"?]: Hit come a storm in there one time and blowed all the timber down, and hit went by Blowdown ever since. Hit just tore everything down. **1975** Broome *Out under Smokies* 21 Everywhere I have gone in the mountains this spring I have found numerous blowdowns. **1975** Fink *Backpacking* 222 A quarter of the way down we ran full into the marks of a terrific windstorm of some years before, a "blowdown" where trees by the hundreds had been blown up by the roots by the tornado and pitched around like jackstraws. **c1980** Campbell *Memories of Smoky* 85 The thing that really slowed our progress, and caused a tremendous lot of heavy chopping on the part of Mr. Lewis, was that we encountered more than 20 "blow-downs" that were so big we could neither ride across them nor even find a good detour around them, so Al chopped openings big enough to permit us to pass.

blowed See **blow A1**, **A2**.

blow fire (also *blow fire out*, *blow out fire*) *verb phrase* To treat a burn by blowing on the affected area of skin, usually employing an incantation and ceremony. See also **blow doctor**, **draw B3**, **take out a burn**, **talk fire out**.

1939 Hall *Coll* (Hazel Creek NC) My uncle Wes can blow out fire and it won't blister. [He] blows all over it. **1956** Hall *Coll* (Big Bend NC) Katie Grooms used, before she died, she blowed fire out. One of my sisters, my baby sister, she got burnt pretty bad, and Maurie, my sister, took her to Katie, and she blowed the fire out of her arm. [**1968** *Faith Healing* 15 [The healers'] theory is that when a person has been burned, the fire continues flame inside the wound until it has been "blown out" or "drawn." If this is not done, they claim, the fire continues to burn inside the flesh until it reaches the bone.] **2007** Milnes *Signs Cures Witches* 102 Some German American curers claimed they could "blow" the fires out of burns while invoking Scripture.

[DARE *blow fire (out)* v phr South, South Midland]

blowing viper (also *blow serpent*) *noun* A hognose snake (*Heterodon platirhinos*). Also called **spread adder**, **spreading viper**.

1941 Still *Proud Walkers* 111 A blow-sarpent couldn't quile to your saw marks. **1941** Stuart *Men of Mts* 164 Never saw nothin but a blowin viper snake and a couple of crows. **1994–97** Montgomery *Coll* (known to Cardwell, Shields). **2007** Milnes *Signs Cures Witches* 87 Other curious snakelore among country people concerns the native hog-nosed snake, often called a puff adder or, in West Virginia, a "blowin' viper." This is because, like toads, it is thought to blow poison. People believe that it can not bite you because "God locked its jaws." It flattens its head like a cobra and it hisses and blows at you when you get near it. If that does not scare off what it perceives as danger, it rolls on its back, plays dead, and a red syrupy liquid flows from its mouth.

[DARE *blowing viper* n chiefly Appalachians]

blow-off *noun* A braggart. See also **blow B2**.

c1960 Wilson *Coll* = a boaster, braggart. **2008** Miller *Curse of Collar* 155 That Willard Lee, he's jest a blow off; he's always makin' up stories jest to make his daddy think he's workin'.

blow out fire See **blow fire**.

blows See **blow C3**.

blow snow *noun* See citation.

1944 Hayes *Word-List NC* 32 = a combination of wind and snow.

blowth *noun* Blooms, blossoms collectively.

1924 Raine *Saddlebags* 198 I prayed all night under yan plum tree, and at the first streak of dawn, I got peace, and afore sun-up, I tell ye, that old plum tree were jest one solid blowth o' blossoms. **c1940** Simms *Coll* You should see this country when the blowth (blooming of flowers and shrubs) is laid down. **1957** Combs *Lg Sthn High: Word List* 12 = blossoms, flowers, etc. that blow. Not so bad, etymologically, when one considers the etymon, *blow*. From *weal*, we make *wealth*; from *steal*, *stealth*; and from *spill*, *spilth*. [**1995** Montgomery *Coll* (unknown to consultants from the Smoky Mountains).]

[OED3 *blowth* n obsolete except dialect, by analogy with *growth*; Web3 *blowth* n now dialect]

blow up *verb phrase* See citation. See also **blow B2**.

1939 Hall *Coll*: *blow someone up* = to flatter a person.

blubber

A (also *bloober*) *noun* A bubble, mass of bubbles.

1943 Chase *Jack Tales* 24 One day the bull put his head down to drink out of a spring and a lot of blue blubbers came up in the water. **1968** *End of Moonshining* 100 = the bubbles which result when the moonshine in the proof vial is shaken violently. **2002** Magowan *Beech Mt Tales* 109 "Here's a drinking glass." He said, "If anybody's gonna die, get it half or a third full of water. And the blubbers, if they stay to the bottom, they're gonna die. And if they come to the top, they gonna live." **2005** Williams *Gratitude* 480 = bubbles. **2007** McMillon *Notes* (also *bloober*) = bubble.

[DARE *blubber* n chiefly South, South Midland]

B *verb* To bubble.

1971 *Arie's Egg Custard* 95 It will "blubber up"—or bubble, and then the bubbles will settle.

[DARE *blubber* v chiefly South, South Midland]

blue back(ed) speller *noun* An elementary spelling book authored by Noah Webster and first published in 1783, still in use in the Smokies in the early twentieth century. See also **red back speller**.

1939 Burnett *Gap o' Mountains* 16 The conquering of Webster's Blueback speller was the first ambition of all students, and this was no easy task. **1957** GSMNP-23:1:17 I used to be able to spell every word in the old blue back speller. **1963** Hooper *Unwanted Boy* 222 He delighted in displaying the book-larnin' he had acquired in his three-month course in Webster's old Blue-back Speller. **1969** Hall *Coll* (Mt Sterling NC) I never did get furder than Baker in the Blue Back Speller. **1999** Spencer *Memory Lane* II:5 In their declining years they often spoke of the "Blue Backed Speller." It contained so much information other than spelling.

blue beagle See **blue tick.**

Blue Bill *noun* A member of a group of citizens organized in Sevier County TN in the 1890s with the tacit sanction of local officials to counter activities of the **White Caps**, which had been intimidating and punishing citizens it deemed to have violated public order and morality.

1894 *Alexandria Gaz.* (VA) 29 Oct 1/2, For two years there has existed in Sevier county, Tenn., a large organization of white caps. They have committed many outrages on defenceless citizens, especially women. . . . Several weeks ago another gang was organized in opposition, which is known as "blue bills." It is said to be composed of the better element of citizens, and was organized to wipe out the white caps. **1899** Crozier *White-Caps* 186 Shortly after this occurrence an organization sprang up known as "Blue Bill's," so called by the White-caps, the purpose of which was to defeat the plan of the White-caps . . . they took no oath and wore no masks. They did not care to cover their faces to put down a crime like that of white-capping. The term "Blue Bill" applied not only to those who joined that organization, but any good citizen who had courage enough to denounce white-capism, was by the White-caps called a "Blue Bill." **1939** Hall Coll (Copeland Creek TN) I never did say anything about this at all till after the white caps was done put out. The blue bills cut them out. **1976** *Sevier Co Saga* 19 As the White Caps became too powerful for the law, another organization known as the "Blue Bills" was formed to oppose the actions of the White Caps. Their purpose was to encounter the White Caps and stop their attacks. **1985** *Sevier Settler* 4:16 The Blue Bills were organized to impede White-Capping. They differed very much from the White Caps. They had no bylaws or constitutions, no officers, no oath or obligations, and the members never wore masks. The purpose of the Blue Bills was to find out what particular night the White-Caps were to make a raid and the persons to be attacked. After this, the Blue Bills notified their members who were thoroughly armed against their enemy at the designated time and place. There were from six hundred to fifteen hundred White-Caps in Sevier County, but there were only approximately two hundred Blue Bills.

blue cohosh (also *blue ginseng*) *noun* A perennial wildflower (*Caulophyllum thalictroides*) whose rhizomes have medicinal uses. Also called **papoose root**.

[**1901** Lounsberry *Sthn Wild Flowers* 189 All about, it is known by the native people, whose belief it is that it does good to all young creatures, the faith, no doubt, transmitted to them by the Indians who dosed with it their papooses. In the autumn, therefore, they gather its rhizomes and prepare a decoction, held in reserve throughout the year.] **1957** Broaddus *Vocab Estill Co KY* 8 = a medicinal herb "for run-down nerves." **1968** *Sang Signs* 48 Blue cohosh . . . is sometimes collected as . . . "blue ginseng."

blue-devil (also *blueweed*) *noun* The viper's bugloss wildflower (*Echium vulgare*).

1982 Stupka *Wildflowers* 95 Viper's bugloss, also called "blueweed" and "blue-devil," grows in poor soil and dry, waste places, especially along roadsides.

bluefishy land *noun* See citation.

1986 Pederson et al. *LAGS* (Jefferson Co TN) = poor soil that seeps water.

blue George *noun* See citation.

1989 Still *Rusties and Riddles* [94] = metal cover for encouraging a draft in a fireplace.

blue ginseng *noun*

1 See **blue cohosh.**

2 Same as **black cohosh.**

1971 Krochmal et al. *Medicinal Plants Appal* 96 *Cimicifuga racemosa* . . . blue ginseng.

blue hound See **blue tick.**

blue john *noun*

1 (also *blue milk*) Milk from which the cream has been skimmed, giving it a faint bluish tint.

1927 Woofter *Dialect from WV* 349 *blue John* = milk deficient in butter fat, so that it has a blue tinge. "I don't like this old blue John we buy from the milkman." **1937** Hyatt *Kiverlid* 110 Milk that ever drap o' cream has been scum off'n, you might say [is] jist the puore [= pure] blue-john. **1955** Dykeman *French Broad* 281 I'd tease him later on when I was old enough. "There's some say that the folks that went out [to Texas] and stayed got rich as cream. Rest of us back in the hills got blue-john." **1989** Trent *Sequel to Lore* 79–80 The whole milk is poured into a big bowl and the crank [of the cream separator] is turned by hand to spin and spin. The separated cream comes out one spout and the milk (blue john) comes out the other. . . . The blue john was fed to the hogs and the cream was sold to the dairy. **1994–98** Montgomery *Coll*: *blue john* (Cardwell, Jones, Oliver, Weaver), = sometimes contemptuous (known to Ellis); *blue milk* (Bush, Cardwell, Norris).

2 (also *blue johnny, blue milk*) Skim milk beginning to sour. Also called **blinky-blue.**

1891 Brown *Dialect in TN* 174 *Blue-john* is a thin blue milk that has been skimmed, that is "sour sweet milk." **1944** Dennis *Word-List* 6 *blue-Johnny* = milk skimmed (hence blue) and slightly sour.

[DARE *blue john* n 1 and 2 both senses chiefly South, South Midland]

blue johnny See **blue john 2.**

blue laurel *noun* An evergreen rhododendron shrub (*Rhododendron catawbiense*) that usually has purplish flowers. Same as **catawba rhododendron**. See also **laurel, rhododendron.**

1901 Lounsberry *Sthn Wild Flowers* 379 So great is the diversity of opinion concerning colour [of the flower] that we find the greater number of natives through these parts calling the plant "blue laurel." **1982** Powers and Hannah *Cataloochee* 436 Cataloochans called rhododendron "laurel"—the purple variety being known as "blue l'arl."

blue milk See **blue john 1, 2.**

blue pot *noun* See citations.

1968 Connelly *Discover Appal* 131 Basically, the mountain people relied on two basic colors and two plants from which to obtain them. These colors were blue and red, which were obtained from indigo and madder, respectively. As late as the 1930's, the "blue pots" of the southern Appalachians were still fairly common. These kettles of blue dye were obtained from indigo growing wild in patches or cultivated in hillside gardens. The plant was brewed in a "blue pot" which brewed constantly behind the kitchen stove or on the fireplace hearth. **1973** *AOHP/ASU-111* She colored [the clothes that she wove]. She had an old-fashioned blue pot they call it, and she used indigo and madder that had to go with it, and color clothes. **1976** Bullard *Crafts TN Mts* 76 Honors for the oldest known system of natural dyeing must go to the "blue pot," a mysterious blend of indigo used as early as 3000 B.C. Blue pots were found in the Southern Highlands as late as the 1920's.

blue snow *noun* See citations.

1968 *DARE Survey* (Brasstown NC) = a very light fall of snow. **1998** Montgomery *Coll* = fine, powdery snow, very cold (Cardwell).

blue-speckled hound See **blue tick.**

blue tick (also *blue beagle, blue hound, blue-speckled hound, blue tick hound*) *noun* A hunting dog with bluish-gray markings on a white coat, used especially in hunting squirrels, raccoons, and other small animals.

1940 Oakley *Roamin'/Restin'* 99 This puppy dog was called blue beagle hound dog so I asked the man what would he want for the dog in money. **1960** Burnett *My Valley* 146 Pot Lickers, Blue Ticks, Black and Tans, sometimes, just any old shabby-looking breed or cross-breed meet the requirements and mixed breeds of old-fashioned cur and hound often make outstanding bear dogs. **1978** Hiser *Quare Do's* 25 I have a five dollar gold piece in my pocket says my blue hounds can tree more coons from seven o'clock to ten at night, twicet as many, as yourn. **1979** *Swapped That Dog* 42 [I] used t'coon hunt a whole lot. I had a blue speckled hound. **1994** Walker *Life History* 78 A real coon dog and a blue tick didn't seem to show much interest in the panther. **2006** *Encycl Appalachia* 872 Blue Ticks, Black and Tans, and Redbones have been popular coon dogs. **2009** Prewitt *Coon Hounds* 273 Nowadays, the black and tan, the redbone, the bluetick, the English, the treeing Walker, and the Plott are among the standard breeds that hunters say can potentially make good coon hounds.

[*blue* + *tick* "a dot, speck"; DARE *bluetick* n South, Midland]

blue tick hound See **blue tick.**

blueweed See **blue-devil.**

bluff (also *bluff out*) *verb, verb phrase* To disconcert, frighten, scare off.

1920 (in **2008** Bailey *Matewan* 2) Felts observed that at Paint Creek he had been shot at from ambush but had refused to be "bluffed out." **1941** Still *Proud Walkers* 112 Nevertheless, be on hand and show you're not bluffed out. **1941** Stuart *Men of Mts* 16 Son, that (his neighbor's digging his own grave) kindly bluffs me. *Ibid.* 236 "You can't lock from a thief," says Pa, "and you can't bluff one with bullets." **1994** McCarthy *Jack Two Worlds* 13 [She] thought it'd bluff him.

blundersome *adjective* Of a person: awkward, tending to blunder.

c1945 Haun *Hawk's Done* 312 "Awkward," she would say, "and blundersome as a blind buzzard."

blunt *noun* Blame, consequences.

1939 Hall *Coll* The poor old driver . . . always bore the blunt. **1969** *DARE Survey* (Viper KY).

[alteration of *brunt*; DARE *blunt* n² chiefly South Midland]

boar

A *noun* A male animal, usually a hog kept for breeding purposes; the term was traditionally avoided in polite or mixed company in favor of the euphemisms *hog* or *male*. See also **brute, bull A1.**

1967 *DARE Survey* (Maryville TN). **1986** Pederson et al. *LAGS* (Sevier Co TN).

B *adjective* used attributively to refer to a male animal.

1915 Dingus *Word-List VA* 181 *boar cat* = tom-cat. **1941** Stuart *Men of Mts* 299 [He] said he didn't want to sweat around on all these old hills and hoe corn and bring up a family—I told Locum—no use for him to talk about a family—and him like a boar-hog. **1957** Combs *Lg Sthn High: Word List* 12 *boar* = boar; *boar cat* = tom cat. **1987** Young *Lost Cove* 154 He was traveling sort of side ways like a boar hog walks after he has been cut. **1996** Montgomery *Coll* (known to eight consultants from the Smoky Mountains). **2007** McMillon *Notes* He's as horny as a boar mink.

[DARE *boar* n b chiefly South, South Midland]

C *verb* Of a sow: to be in heat.

1986 Pederson et al. *LAGS* (Sevier Co TN).

board *noun*

1 A thin slab of wood, especially one riven or sawed from oak, used for roofing a house, barn, etc. (especially 2 to 4 feet long, ½ to 1 inch thick, variable in width). See also **roof board, shake B.**

1886 Smith *Sthn Dialect* 349 There are still others [= terms] which have not, so far as I know, the authority of Old English: . . . board (shingle or plank). **1914** Arthur *Western NC* 258 [It was necessary] to rive out their shingles or "boards" for their roof covering and puncheons for their door and window "shutters" and their flooring. **1950** Woody *Cataloochee Homecoming* 14 The shingles and "boards" for the roof were made by hand from choice trees. **1982** Powers and Hannah *Cataloochee* 316 Shakes or "boards" for a roof were best rived with a froe out of Northern red oak. **1992**

Toops *Great Smoky Mts* 81 Roofing "boards" would be rived from white oak.

[DARE *board* n chiefly South, South Midland]

2 A similar piece of wood used to side a house. See also **board house**.

1990 Williams *Pride and Prejudice* 220 In interviewing people who grew up in rural southwestern North Carolina in the late nineteenth and early twentieth centuries, the question, "Was your childhood home frame or log?" sometimes evokes the answers, "No, it was plank," or "No, it was board." (The terms *plank* and *board* are used interchangeably in this region.)

3 A meal table.

1881 Pierson *In the Brush* 54–55 Being seated at the table, the host, turning to the preacher, says, "Will you make a beginning, sir?"—all at table reverently bowing their heads as he extends the invitation, and while the blessing is being asked. So, too, I have "made a beginning" at many a hospitable board in many different States. **2007** McMillon *Notes* = table: "Put it on the board, Maw!"

[Web3 *board* n 4b archaic]

board dog *noun* See citation.

1994 Farwell and Buchanan *Logging Terms* = in logging, an implement that held boards until they were sawed.

board house *noun* See citation. See also **boxed house**.

1990 Williams *Pride and Prejudice* 220 Well, you take a board house—take the board—they ain't got framing in it. They just built the whole plate around and nail the board down here up. And just slat it over. See, a frame house, it got two by fours in it, put the weatherboarding on the outside like this and ceiling on the inside. Boxed house ain't got it.

board light *noun* A large pine knot that can be used to set a fire or as a crude lamp.

1971 *Boogers* 46 "I'll make you a board light." There wadn't such a thing as a lantern or a light or a flashlight. . . . That 'uz just a big ol' pine knot, y'know, and they just keep a'burnin' and a'goin'.

board tree *noun* A tree large and straight enough to be sawed or split into **boards** or planks.

1878 Guild *Old Times TN* 117 The first was interrogated very closely as to the cutting of some rail-timber and its value; the second, as to the cutting of five board trees. **1925** Dargan *Highland Annals* 20 In choosin' a board-tree you've got to 'low so much for what you don't see. **1957** Broaddus *Vocab Estill Co KY* 9 = a straight grained tree, good for riving into boards. **1960** Arnow *Seedtime* 263 In early 1780 we can be certain Amos Eaton and other seasoned woodsmen were out hunting board trees, and they could, like Mr. Casada, avoid the wind-shaken tree, and tell by the lay of the bark whether or not the wood would split straight and true. The board tree, different from those for the walls, needed to be of a good size; a length of white oak or cedar log, three or even four feet in diameter would when split and rived yield a number of boards, wide if need be almost as the radius of the tree, and of quite uniform thickness. **1976** GSMNP-114:36 When I was a young man, my daddy sold some land up here that my granddaddy bought it from somebody. They's two big oaks there for board trees, excepted for board trees. **1994–95** Montgomery *Coll* (known to Cardwell, Shields).

[DARE *board tree* n chiefly South Midland]

boar's nest *noun* See citations.

1927 Woofter *Dialect from WV* 349 = a camp of laborers where there are no women. "We are all staying at the boar's nest this winter." **1997** Farwell *Logging* = An unsanitary area, especially a lumber camp bunkhouse, infested with lice and other vermin. "[It was] a place full of lice or something. You know, somebody didn't do a good job housekeeping. . . . A lot of lumbercamps . . . they had men cooks and generally the living quarters were taken care of by a bunch of loggers. So they came in at the end of the day, and . . . they didn't have a place to take a bath or anything like that, unless there was a creek somewhere . . . it got pretty raunchy staying in it several months at a time."

boat tide *noun* See citation. Same as **coal boat tide**. See also **tide A**.

1915 Dingus *Word-List VA* 181 = a freshet sufficient to float laden boats.

bobble *noun* A mistake, misstep, blunder.

1900 Harben *N GA Sketches* 171 I am powerful afraid I'll make a bobble of the whole thing from start to finish. **1915** Dingus *Word-List VA* 181 = a slight mistake: "He made only one little bobble." **1931** Goodrich *Mt Homespun* 52 There were no "bobbles" in it, nor uneven places nor broken selvedges. **1944** Laughlin *Word-List Buncombe Co* 24 = a mistake, especially a slight mistake. **1992** Gabbard *Thunder Road* 121–22 Dwight said, "He can't catch us as long as we are behind him, and when he makes a bobble, we're goin' to get in front of him."

[DARE *bobble* n[1] 1 chiefly South, South Midland]

bob-jacks *noun* See 1957 citation.

1927 *Louisville Courier-Journal* (Oct 2) (Junior sec 3/2) [Letter from Twila KY] We are both in the eighth grade. We enjoy all sports. Our best sports are basketball, tennis, Bobjacks and reading books or poems. **1957** Combs *Lg Sthn High: Word List* 12 = the game of jack-stones; also the pieces. **2017** *Salyersville Independent* (KY) (Aug, of 1960s) We played jacks a lot in school. We called them Bob-jacks. I had a set that most likely came from my winning stocking.

bobtail check *noun* See citations.

1986 Page *Daughter of Hills* 107 Little enough figuring we might need to be doing, for after Graball checked off the carbide and explosive a miner had to take on account, groceries and such, there was not much left but a neat row of ciphers on a bobtail check. **1998** Miller and Sharpless *Kingdom of Coal* 142 Prices in these "pluck me" stores, as the miners sometimes called them, were often set artificially high. After charges at the store had been deducted from a miner's pay, he sometimes received what was called a "bobtail check," a stub indicating that rent and the cost of supplies added up to the total of wages due. **2006** *WV Encycl* 644 Miners often received pay envelopes marked with a curling line across them, a symbol miners called the "bobtail check" or the "snake." It meant no wages due.

bodacious (also *bawdacious*) *adjective* Excellent, extraordinary, thorough; audacious, unrestrained. [Editor's note: This term has had questionable currency in Appalachia (but see 2007 citation); it was attested by only two (of ten) consultants from the Smoky Mountains in the 1990s and then only in jocular usage, while others were familiar with it only as fanciful usage by outsiders, especially in comic or literary portrayals of mountain speech (not represented here).]

1896 Pool *In Buncombe County* 239 I'm er bawdacious fool. **1992** Brooks *Sthn Stuff* 22 = 1. Extraordinary or remarkable. 2. Audacious. "I hired me some bodacious handyman today. He wouldn't even stop working long enough to catch his breath." **1997** Montgomery *Coll* (known to Adams, Norris). **2007** McMillon *Notes* = used seriously by many old timers, with the first syllable rhyming with *body*.

[perhaps blend of *bold* + *audacious*; cf EDD *boldacious* adj Devonshire, Cornwall; DARE *bodacious* adj 1, 2 chiefly South, South Midland]

bodaciously (also *bodyaciously*) *adverb* Extraordinarily, supremely, entirely; audaciously, unrestrainedly. Like **bodacious**, this term has questionable currency in Appalachia and is mainly confined to comic or literary portrayals of mountain speech (not represented here).

1896 *Word-List* 413 *bodaciously* = bodily. "Picked her up *bodaciously*, and carried her off." **1913** Kephart *Our Sthn High* 294 Bodaciously means bodily or entirely: "I'm bodaciously ruint" (seriously injured). **1929** (in **1952** Mathes *Tall Tales* 104) I've knowed of cases whar eddicated folks has plumb bodaciously busted their intelleck. **1957** Combs *Lg Sthn High: Word List* 12 *bodaciously* = bodily, entirely. Ex.: "I throwed him bodaciously off the clift." **1974** Fink *Bits Mt Speech* 3 *bodaciously* = completely, totally. "I'm most *bodaciously* wore out." **1992** Brooks *Sthn Stuff* 22 *bodaciously* = bodily, entirely. "He bodaciously beat the livin' daylights out'n thet bully."

[DARE *bodaciously* adv 1 chiefly South, South Midland]

body *noun*

1 (usually *a body*) Anyone, a person (often with implied reference to oneself). [Editor's note: The combining form *-body* is more prevalent than *-one* to form indefinite pronouns, as in *anybody, everybody, nobody, somebody*.]

1774 *Dunmore's War* 230 Paddy Brown is an Old Weaver Body, that lives with one of the Doughertys. **1860** *Week in Smokies* 125 I do declare I believe a body might larn a lawyer something, if he would only use his own eyes and sense. **1863** *Tesh CW Letters* (Aug 24) a body would be in adread for fear tha[y] would be punisht or killd or something else a body could not stand. **1866** Smith *So Called* 18 A body can't disperse until you put a stop to such unruly conduct. **1869** (in **1974** Harris *High Times* 219) Powerful provokin critters am wimmen, powerful provokin indeed. I can't raley hate 'em tho', for they do leave a good taste in a body's mouth, sometimes. **1895** Edson and Fairchild *TN Mts* 370 A *body* can't git along here. **1924** Spring *Lydia Whaley* 2 To know when soap is finished you cool it till a body can keep a finger in it. **1937** Hall *Coll* (Cosby TN) Fever weed breaks the fever on a body. **1940** Haun *Hawk's Done* 48 There wasn't anything a body could say to Barshia that would do him any good. **1954** Arnow *Dollmaker* 167 A body cain't git along in this town thout a car. **1969** *GSMNP-25:1:30* A body thought about it back then. **1970** *GSMNP-26* You took a turn, we called it a turn of corn, which would run about a bushel maybe, what a body could pretty well carry. **1973** *AOHP/ALC-987* [It's] the way we been used to living. A body just can't get away hardly from how they was raised and lived all their life. **1989** Smith *Flyin' Bullets* 40 "A body never knowed when they just might come in the middle of the night," Delia said, "and drag ye out of bed, and take ye out to kill ye, fer no reason a'tall." **1997** Montgomery *Coll* Could a body buy that there dog? How can a body live on such piddlin's? (Brown). **2009** Holbrook *Upheaval* 11 If a body can work, he ought to.

[cf Scottish usage: "If a body meet a body coming through the Rye"; DARE *body* n B1 widespread, but especially Midland]

2 (also *body waist*) A child's or woman's undershirt. See also **underbody**.

1952 Wilson *Folk Speech NC* 521 = a child's underwaist.—Alexander county. **c1960** Wilson *Coll* (or *body-waist*) = a child's under-waist, to which was buttoned his drawers. "Mammy bought me a new body yesterday." **1992** Brooks *Sthn Stuff* 23 = a bodice or undershirt. "To keep warm, she had to wear a flannel body under her shirtwaist."

[DARE *body waist* n chiefly South, South Midland]

bodyaciously See **bodaciously**.

body-waist See **body 2**.

bof See **both A**.

bog *noun* A relatively level area with poor drainage and often thick vegetation, found at all elevations of the Smoky Mountains and even on some **balds**. Same as **swamp A**.

1998 Montgomery *Coll* (known to Cardwell).

boggan, boggin See **toboggan**.

bogieman, bogieman See **booger A1**.

bohunk *noun* See citations.

1930 Pendleton *Wood-Hicks Speak* 86 = a heavy, short-handled hammer carried at the hames of a horse. **1964** Clarkson *Lumbering in WV* 356 = a hammer carried on the harness hames by means of a loop. It was used by the teamster to cut the trail of logs when out of sight of the grab driver.

boil

A *verb, noun* Variant form *bile*.

1862 *Robinson CW Letters* (July 18) we put on our chickens to bile & we Jest got them dun before we had to march. **1864** *Brown CW Letters* (July 26) i ama fraid I cant ride to morow for I have a bila comen and I cant hardley set down this eav[n]ing. **1883** Zeigler and Grosscup *Heart of Alleghanies* 91 The characters of most interest to all present were two good-natured-looking young men dressed in "biled" shirts, green neckties, "store-boughten" coats, and homespun pantaloons. **1913** Kephart *Our Sthn High* 120 Thar's plenty o' men and women grown, in these mountains, who don't know that the Government is ary thing but a president in a biled shirt who commands two-three judges and a gang o' revenue officers. **1934–47** *LAMSAS* (Madison Co NC). **1937** Hall *Coll* (Cosby TN) Saint John weeds with dew on 'em makes sores, not biles and risin's. **1942** Hall *Phonetics Smoky Mts* 46. **1975** Brewer *Valley So Wild* 239 We'd beat the clothes with a battling stick and bile 'em till they were white. **1991** Thomas *Sthn Appal* 41 They'd have what we needed, a big pot to bile water in.

[represents the older form, common in Early Modern English; DARE *boil* n[1], v A especially South, South Midland, New England]

B *verb* Principal parts.

1 variant past-tense form *biled*.

1867 Harris *Sut Lovingood* 31 She imejuntly sot in, an' biled a big pot ove paste. **2013** Venable *How to Tawlk* 42 Yeah, but she biled 'em 'taters 'til they's plum runt!

2 Variant past-participle forms *biled*, *b'ilt*, *boilt*. See also **boiled shirt**.

1861 Hileman *CW Letters* (Sept 22) [Every] few days I have a mess of Boilt Onions. **1867** Harris *Sut Lovingood* 219 Her eyes swelled tu the size an' looks ove hard-biled aigs [see **1883** in **A**]. **1904** Johnson *Highways South* 137 The sweet oil was an ingredient for one of these medicines, and he mentioned also using "mullein and evergreen biled together" and "a yearb called golden seal." **1937** Hall *Coll* (Cosby TN) To cure blood poison, use catnip and beadwood bark biled together and made into a poultice for blood pizen. **1953** Atwood *Verbs East US* 6 The form with voiceless suffix, *boilt* /bawlt/ or (occasionally among Type I informants [i.e. older speakers with little formal education]) /bailt/, is most characteristic of the Midland area (s. Pa., w. Md. and W.Va., reaching its greatest frequency in W.Va. where about three fifths of all informants use it). **1963** Edwards *Gravel* 18 I didn't come for to eat your dad-blasted hen but if she's well b'ilt and they's plenty of dumplins cooked with her I might take a leetle taste just to see if I remember how chicken tastes. **1978** Reese *Speech NE Tenn* 172 boilt = attested by 6/12 (50%) speakers. **1979** Melton *'Pon My Honor* 64 When he started home that night, he was not only three sheets in the wind, he was drunk as a "biled owl."

C (also **boil up**) *verb, verb phrase* Of clouds, a storm, etc.: to gather, swirl about.

1937 Hall *Coll* (Cades Cove TN) Hit's a-bilin' thar on them mountains. **1939** Hall *Coll* (Nine Mile TN) The bear run on and the snow a-boilin' and the dogs a-fightin' and run across the Anthony Ridge over onto what we call the Little Spruce Ridge. **1961** *Coe Ridge OHP*-341B They's a little cloud boil up, you see, and it come flying over. Well, it just come a pour-down. **1981** GSMNP-121:31 That must have been between thirty and thirty-one and the old red brick a-falling and the dust a-boiling up.

boiled shirt *noun* A man's starched dress shirt.

1883 Zeigler and Grosscup *Heart of Alleghanies* 91 The characters of most interest to all present were two good-natured-looking young men dressed in "biled" shirts, green neckties, "store-boughten" coats, and homespun pantaloons. **1913** Kephart *Our Sthn High* 120 Thar's plenty o' men and women grown, in these mountains, who don't know that the Government is ary thing but a president in a biled shirt who commands two-three judges and a gang o' revenue officers. **1967** Wilson *Folkways Mammoth Cave* 27 = a humorous reference to a laundered shirt, a Sunday-go-to-meeting shirt.

boiler *noun*

A Variant form *biler* [see **1982** in **B**].

B Senses.

1 A metal container in which water is heated to a boil for making coffee or whiskey. Also called **steam barrel**.

1936 Stuart *Head of Hollow* 73 You cannot go until I make a biler of hot coffee. **1937** Hall *Coll* (Cades Cove TN) The boiler of a still [is] the large metal tank in which the liquid of the mash is vaporized. **1968** Clarke *Stuart's Kentucky* 185 On it was a teakettle full of hot water, and the biler of coffee was usually filled several times during the day. **1974** Maurer and Pearl *KY Moonshine* 114 = an enclosed vessel in which water is boiled to generate steam for a steam still. It may be anything from an old oil drum, with crude fittings, to a standard upright, factory-made steam boiler with gauges. . . . "Boiler blowed up and kilt three of 'em." **1982** Slone *How We Talked* 62 When coffee was first introduced into Appalachia, it came to us green, in one-hundred pound sacks. It had to be roasted or "browned" in the oven in a bread pan, then ground by hand in a coffee grinder, boiled in a coffee "biler" and served hot and black. No one ever used sugar or cream.

2 See citation.

1980 Riggleman *WV Mtneer* 126–27 [Loggers] usually had nicknames for everybody and everything around the camp. . . . Cooks were called "boilers."

boiling *noun* See also **molasses boil**.

A Variant forms *bilin'* [see **1917** in **B**], *biling*. See also **kit and boiling**.

1940 Still *River of Earth* 14 "I figure they're fair ready for biling," he would say. "Time we had a mess."

B A crowd, collection, the entire lot.

1859 Taliaferro *Fisher's River* 144 I put on my studyin' cap to find out the best plan to make a smash uv the whole bilin' on 'um. **1917** Kephart *Word-List* 408 *boiling* = crowd. "The hull [whole] kit an' bilin' of 'em." [**1992** Montgomery *Coll* (unknown to consultants from the Smoky Mountains.)]

[DARE *boiling* n "a mass of material boiled together at one time" chiefly South, South Midland, New England]

boil up See **boil C**.

bold

A *adjective* Of the flowing of a spring: free and bountiful.

1878 Coale *Wilburn Waters* 25 Game was abundant, and the clear, bold springs afforded a plentiful supply of trout and other excellent varieties of fish. **1891** Primer *Studies in WV* 167 Bold is used in the sense of strong, vigorous; as, a bold spring is one whose waters bubble up strongly. **1943** Chase *Jack Tales* 91 Jack took that walkin' stick and went on to where there was a very bold spring comin' out the ground. **1974** Dabney *Mt Spirits* 14–15 He had his copper pots made by a skilled still-maker. Then he selected a secluded spot beside a "bold" stream of water and built up a furnace from rocks gathered from the water bed. **1986** *Back Home Blount Co* 49 The original preaching site, according to tradition, was under a spreading beech tree near a "bold spring of crystal water" in a clearing which served as the camping ground near the War Path. **1995** Weber *Rugged Hills* 118 When a spring is particularly good, it's called a "bold spring." **2003** Cooper *Gathering Memories* 24 The Appalachian family usually chose a place near a large stream or a "bold spring," which provided water year-round, and never ran dry.

B *adverb* Of the flowing of a spring: freely and bountifully.

1895 Edson and Fairchild *TN Mts* 370 The spring don't flow as *bold* as it did. **1996–97** Montgomery *Coll* (known to Brown, Bush, Cardwell, Hooper, Jones, Oliver).

bold hives *noun*

1 (also *boll hives, bone hives, bull hives, red hives, stretch hives*) A rash afflicting infants that is sometimes viewed according to folk belief as symptomatic of a potentially fatal internal disorder. Also called **hives**.

1949 Arnow *Hunter's Horn* 286 Sue Annie said that he would get no better until she got the hives broke out on him, and hinted, when she came in the late afternoon with a bottle of freshly made rattleroot tea, that she was afraid the hives were working in on him instead of out, or ever going into the boll hives. **1971** *Granny Women* 252 Mrs. Andy Webb told us . . . "It looks sort'a like th'measles, but it ain't measles. Them's bold hives . . . Th'bold hives works around th'heart . . . They'll have'em after they're born, and if them hives don't break out on 'em—it's the bone hives—it'll kill'em. You got to do something to clear the liver up. **1994–97** Montgomery *Coll* (known to Cardwell, Jones, Shields), = in the old days a rash babies always had at birth, for which they were given catnip tea (Adams). **1996** Cavender *Bold Hives* 18 The treatment for *bull hives* is identical to that for *bold hives*, an indication that descriptors are likely phonetic variants, as is *boll hives* in the Ozarks, of a common source term . . . probably *bowel hives*. **2003** Cavender *Folk Medicine* 203 = an infant-specific and potentially fatal illness caused by hives remaining inside the body; also known as "stretch hives" and "red hives." **2006** *Encycl Appalachia* 868 "Bold hives," an infant-specific illness introduced by the Scots and Scots-Irish, is a good example. Many believed that all newborns have a mysterious entity within them known as the hives. Infants were administered a tea, often made of catnip or ground ivy, to induce the hives out of the body. If not treated, the hives would "turn inward," causing damage to the heart and lungs and ultimately death.

[DARE *bold hives* n 2 chiefly South Midland]

2 A lung disease, perhaps croup.

1824 (in **1912** Doddridge *Notes on Settlement* 116) The croup, or what was then called the bold hives, was a common disease among the children, many of whom died of it. For the cure of this, the juices of roasted onions or garlic was given in large doses. **1975** Jackson *Unusual Words* 159 *Bold hives* was apparently related to pneumonia, but the exact nature of the illness is unknown. **2006** Cavender *Medical Term* 1022 The term *bold hives* . . . might be interpreted by a physician as urticaria, a skin disease caused by an allergic reaction to certain foods, drugs, or other agents. For some Appalachians, however, it refers to an infant-specific folk illness commonly known as the "croup."

bold sage *noun* A coarse, prickly perennial wild plant (*Solanum carolinense*) from whose roots is made a medicinal tea and whose berries also have medicinal uses. Also called **bull nettle**.

1956 Hall *Coll* (Big Bend NC) They used to use catnip for little babies and ground ivy and bold sage for hives. **1962** Hall *Coll* (Gatlinburg TN) Bold sage is the same as bull nettle root, good for the kidneys and good for dogs that have fits. Boil it and make a tea. Human beings drink the tea. Soak bread in it to give to dogs.

boll hives See **bold hives 1**.

bollyfox *verb* To idle, waste time, procrastinate. See also **pollyfox**.

c1940 Aswell *Glossary TN Idiom* 4 I'm just sort of *bollyfoxing* around this afternoon. **1996** Montgomery *Coll* = to poke around, mosey around (known to Cardwell, but not to other consultants from the Smoky Mountains).

bomgillion See **balm of Gilead**.

bone (also *bone coal*) *noun* See citations. See also **bone pile**.

1941 Stuart *Men of Mts* 268 Look at all th' bone and slate we got to cart out and dump over th' hill. **1973** Preston *Bituminous Term* 27 *bone coal* = a coal particularly high in slate or slate content, not marketable. **a1975** *Miners' Jargon* 1 *bone* = slaty coal found in the coal seam. **2006** Mooney *Lg Coal Mining* 1029 The miner then cleaned his working room of waste rock, called "gob" or "bone" and eventually hauled outside and added to a massive "slag pile" and then headed home for the day.

bone arsiplas *noun* Erysipelas.

1956 Hall *Coll* (Big Bend NC) One time [Aunt Nancy] had bone arsiplas. Old man Joe Packett started to get some red oak bark to make some ooze to draw her arm.

bone felon *noun* Same as **felon**.

c1960 Wilson *Coll* = paronychia or whitlow, an inflammation often said to be sore to the bone: "Aunt Sally's got a bone felon on her finger." **1966–68** DARE *Survey* (Brasstown NC, Burnsville NC, Spruce Pine NC) = the hard, painful swelling, especially on a finger, that seems to come from deep under the skin. **1996** Montgomery *Coll* (known to Cardwell, Jones, Ledford, Norris).

[a redundancy: *bone* + *felon* "whitlow"; DARE *bone felon* n chiefly South, South Midland]

bone hives See **bold hives**.

bone idle *adjective phrase* Habitually or utterly lazy.

1931 Hannum *Thursday April* 81 Joe would have been content to let the boy sit about the house bone idle. **1995–97** Montgomery *Coll* (known to Brown, Oliver, Weaver); Why do you want to marry that bone-idle fellow? (Cardwell).

[DARE *bone idle* adj (i.e. to the bone, bone tired) "extremely, utterly" + *idle*; chiefly South Midland]

bone orchard *noun* A cemetery.

c1960 Wilson *Coll* = humorous name for graveyard. **1968** *DARE Survey* (Marlinton WV, Milton WV, Westover WV).

[DARE *bone orchard* especially North, Midland]

bone pile *noun* See citation. Same as **gob heap**. See also **bone**.

1971 Lee *My Appalachia* 100 At each mine is the necessary but unsightly bone pile. It is waste composed of slate and rock to which more or less coal adheres. This refuse, called bone, is brought from the interior of the mine and hauled to the bone pile. In many instances these piles of waste are as large as small hills, contrasting somberly with the bright green mountains which form their backgrounds. Eventually, spontaneous combustion ignites the coal deep down in these heap wastes. Such fires cannot be extinguished, but smoulder and burn for years.

boneset *noun* A perennial wild plant (*Eupatorium* spp) from whose leaves is made a tea drunk to treat colds, coughs, influenza, fevers, and other ailments. See also **agueweed 2**, **iron blood**, **Joe-Pye weed**, **kill ye or cure ye**, **queen-of-the-meadow**, **white snake-root**.

1863 Lister *CW Letters* (Oct 10) I want you to send me some bone set and get me some red peper. **1901** Lounsberry *Sthn Wild Flowers* 498 From time almost immemorial, boneset has been utilised to make a strengthening tea. It is something that the "yarb doctor" never forgets. As about borage and vervain, an old superstition exists that it will not thrive far away from human habitations. **1937** Hall *Coll* (Bradley Fork NC) Boneset [tea is] bitterer than quinine. Hit'll kill ye or cure ye, one. *Ibid.* (Mingus Creek NC) For pneumony fever, black snake root and bone-set will break up the fever. **1939** Hall *Coll* (Catons Grove TN) Boneset's a good remedy for typhoid fever and flu and all sorts of fevers, colds. **1957** Parris *My Mts* 2 Boneset tea was the conventional remedy for a cough, and a cup of this bitter concoction, even if it did not cure, was calculated to make the patient forget all else for a time at least. **1964** Smith et al. *Germans of Valley* 129 Boneset . . . was one of the most commonly used plant medicines. The plant grows on low ground and is often found along streams and in swamps. It gets its name because it was once believed to bring rapid union of broken bones . . . the leaves were used in a tea, which has a very bitter taste. It was used to bring out a sweat and for colds. **1967** Jones *Peculiarities Mtneers* 72 For chills and fever or any sort of ague boneset tea was recognized as a prime relief and permanent remedy. [**1971** Krochmal et al. *Medicinal Plants Appal* 118 This plant is used as a stimulant to promote digestion, strengthen the viscera, and restore body tone. . . . In Appalachia tea made of the leaves is used to treat coughs and consumption, and it is used as a laxative.] **1978** Montgomery *White Pine Coll* III-2 Everybody had their home remedies. Children, if they took a cold, they'd make them some boneset tea. Old-time people gathered their boneset in the summer and had it ready to make their tea. . . . I dreaded to take it, it'd get so hot, that, that boneset would, but mother would make us some boneset tea and sweeten it, make it taste good to us. We didn't mind other than just the after effect of it, but it really done the work. **2006** Howell *Medicinal Plants* 60–61 Boneset has a long history of use in both European and American Indian herbal practice. The common name "boneset," refers to its analgesic properties in treating fever symptoms. Patients given boneset reported that the herb seemed to relieve aching in the bones that accompanied many types of fever. American Indians used boneset to treat respiratory infections, fevers, poor digestion, and rheumatic pains.

bonny clabber *noun* Milk that has soured and begun to thicken and curdle. Same as **clabber B**, the more common term.

1824 Knight *Letter from KY* 96 Bonny-clabber, in its season, is with *some* a favourite cooling drink. **1934–47** *LAMSAS Appal* = attested by 5/148 speakers (3.3%) from WV, 2/20 (10%) from VA, and 4/37 (10.8%) from NC. **1949** Kurath *Word Geog East US* 70 *Bonny-clabber* appears in scattered fashion in central and western Pennsylvania and from there southward to North Carolina, an area in which it has largely been replaced by other terms. **1997** Montgomery *Coll* (known to Andrews, Bush, Oliver), = soured milk ready to churn (Brown). **2007** Milnes *Signs Cures Witches* 77 Country butter, in West Virginia, is made after the cream has been allowed to sour or has become "bonnyclabber," as Dovie would say. Then it is churned into a white-colored sweet butter with a bit of a cultured taste to it.

[< Irish Gaelic *bainne clabair* "thick sourmilk"]

booby bush See **bubby bush A**.

boodget See **budget A**.

booger

A *noun*

1 (also *bogeyman, boogerbear, boogerman, boogeyman, boogieman, bugger, buggerbear*) A ghost or demon, especially a hobgoblin used to warn children and make them behave. See also **catawampus**[1], **Melungeon 2**, **rawhide**, **river man**.

1866 Smith *So Called* 78 They can't sleep for imagining that the screech owl is screaming, and . . . that their bones are to bleach in some gully, or to rot in some thicket far, far away, where ghosts and boogers go dodging around. **1913** Kephart *Our Sthn High* 24 My Goddamighty, Mam, thar's the boogerman—I done seed him! **1944** Hayes *Word-List NC* 32 *boogey-man* = the devil. **1944** Williams *Word-List Mts* 28 *booger* = a demon with which to frighten children; not to be confused with the devil or Satan. **1956** Hall *Coll* (Cosby TN) I've been all through them mountains, and I never have seen any boogers. *Ibid.* (Gatlinburg TN) A calf come out of a graveyard and my husband thought it was a booger. They rocked that calf for a half an hour. They poured the rocks to it. **1958** Miller *Pigeon's Roost* (Sept 11) Oxen are about as afraid of bugger bears as a horse is. If an oxen ever got scared, he would run away. **1958** Newton *Dialect Vocab*, *boogerman* = attested by 13 of 36 speakers from E TN mountains; *boogeyman* = attested by 5 of 36 speakers from East TN mountains. **c1960** Wilson *Coll*: *boogerman* = an imaginary Nemesis of childhood: "The boogerman will get you if you don't quit crying and go to sleep." **1966–68** DARE *Survey* (Brasstown NC) *boogerman* = name for the devil; (Spruce Pine NC, Gatlinburg TN) *boogerman* = hobgoblin used to threaten children; (Burnsville NC) *boogeyman* = hobgoblin used to threaten children. **1970** Hall *Witchlore* 32 "Rocking" (that is, throwing rocks at) was mentioned in two tales as the treatment for cows thought to be boogers or ghosts. **1973** GSMNP-5:11 They said what do you want to be. I says I want to be the boogerman. *Ibid.* 12 They would put me in the front room, and so if any boogers come they would get me first. **1977** Hamilton *Mt Memories* 56 The "Devil" was the "Booger-man," or the "Old Scratch." **1979** Slone *My Heart* 95 My father did not, nor would he let us believe in ghosts. We called them "haunts" or "buggers," but many of our neighbors would "sware right down to ye" that they had "seed things." **1992** Bush *If Life* 82 In the latter part of the 19th century, thieving murderers who terrorized the lower Appalachians were derisively called, "buggers." **1995–97** Montgomery *Coll*: *boogerbear* (Adams, Brown, Cardwell, Norris, Shields, Weaver). **1999** Montgomery *Coll* = usually pronounced ['bʌgɚ]. **2007** McMillon *Notes*: *boogerman* = a spirit, poltergeist; *the bogeyman* = the Devil; *booger* = anything frightening to children. **2016** *Blind Pig* (June 9) A boogieman is just something people use to try to keep their children in line. The Boogerman is Satan himself. He doesn't jump out and get you. He creeps into your heart. Not little children but adults and especially governments.

[alteration of *boggart* < *buggard* < Middle English *bugge* "ghost, hobgoblin"; Web3 *boogeyman* n dialect; DARE *booger* n 1a chiefly South, Midland; *boogerbear* n 1 chiefly South, Midland; *boogerman* n 1 chiefly South, Midland]

2 Used as an affectionate term for a small child; also used as a deprecatory term for an animal.

1940 Haun *Hawk's Done* 25 Bessie was a pretty little booger though. **1967** Wilson *Folkways Mammoth Cave* 27 *booger* = a term of endearment. "Come here, you little booger, and kiss your Grandma." **1978** Hiser *Quare Do's* 40 The little boogers was adriving me and their ma mad, a trackin foxes to their dens barefooted in this snow and chokin um with their naket hands, and such devilment. **1983** *Dark Corner OHP-4A* [The pig]'d just go out and root for them peas and eat them, you know, and that little bugger got so fat. **2005** Williams *Gratitude* 481 *booger* = word used to refer to a child, pet, or something little, as: "He's a cute little *booger*."

3 (also *boogerman*) A head louse.

1957 Combs *Lg Sthn High: Word List* 13 *boogers* (also *booger men*) = lice. **c1960** Wilson *Coll*: *booger* = head louse: "Them new kids in school has got boogers."

4 A mistake, misstep.

1970 *Hunting Stories* 35 He was just about ready t'fire, an' he moved or somethin'—or they made a booger.

5 Someone who causes trouble or problems.

1941 Stuart *Men of Mts* 97 He's a hard booger to kill. **1984** Burns *Cold Sassy* 37 I got rid of that old booger.

B *verb* Of an animal: to become frightened or shy, act skittishly. See also **booger up**.

1896 *Word-List* 413 = to shy, be frightened. "That horse *boogers* a little at pigs." **1969** Doran *Folklore White Co* 111 = usually of horses: to act skittish or startled. **1976** *Bear Hunting* 288 [The bear pens] were covered over with branches and leaves and moss to "disfigure them so bears wouldn't booger at them." **2005** Williams *Gratitude* 481 (also *get boogered at*) = become wary or afraid of, as: "The mule *got boogered at* the new gate." **2007** McMillon *Notes* = to frighten, startle.

[DARE *booger* v 1 chiefly South, South Midland, Southwest]

booger barker *noun* See citation. See also **booger barking**.

2007 Plott *Story Plott Hound* 180 = a dog that barks and remains a safe or comfortable distance from their prey, rather than more aggressively pursuing it.

booger barking *noun* See citation. See also **booger barker**.

2008 Salsi *Ray Hicks* 66 We called scairt dogs that are still a barkin' "booger barkin'."

boogerbear See **booger A1**.

booger dance *noun* See citation.

1989 Woodside *Hungry for Dance* 23–24 They tried to cope with the intrusion of outsiders through a fascinating form that straddled dance and drama, the Booger dance. Originally, the Native Americans performed the Booger dance as a way of driving away illness and death by ridiculing the witches that brought them. Later, outsiders—whites, blacks and alien Indian tribes—took the place of witches as the carriers of evil. . . . In the Booger dance, the audience, gathered together in a house, sang special songs as the Boogers outfitted themselves in special disguises, complete with masks made out of buckeye.

booger holler *noun* See citations. Same as **dark corner**.

1995–97 Montgomery *Coll* = rough terrain or a place where something bad had happened (Adams), = a wooded or dark hollow that is "hainted" with spirits, unusual noises, or boogers (Brown), = an area thought to be haunted, the term having no social connotation about the status of its residents (Cardwell), = a secluded, haunted hollow (Ledford), = a place far back in the mountains that is hard to get to, usually dark and scary in its remoteness, often used for moonshining (Oliver). **2007** McMillon *Notes* = any holler said to be hainted or inhabited by an undefined creature.

boogerish *adjective*

1 Of an animal: easily frightened.

1975 Jackson *Unusual Words* 159 A *skittish* or *boogerish* horse scares easily.

2 See citation. See also **boogerous**, **boogery**.

1996 Montgomery *Coll* = place or something that is scary (Oliver).

boogerman See **booger A1**.

boogerous *adjective* Having a spooky or frightening appearance. See also **boogerish 2**, **boogery**.

1930 (in **1952** Mathes *Tall Tales* 167) His big black whiskers looked plumb boog'rous to a youngun.

booger tale (also *bugger tale*) *noun* A ghost story.

1971 *Boogers* 28 My grandmother always used the times to the best advantage by telling ghost stories or "booger" tales. **1973** *AOHP/ASU-160* When I was a kid, I used to sit down and loved to hear people tell bugger tales we'd call them, and I don't know what has become of all the haunting places that they used to be. They disappeared somehow, that people used to tell, this old house that nobody didn't live in it. **1979** Slone *My Heart* 95 When we would hear some "bugger tale" from one of our schoolmates and come home and repeat it to him, he would make a fanning motion with his arms and a blowing with his lips and say, "Now, there, you see, I have blowed it all away. No more bugger."

booger up *verb phrase* To damage, tear up.

1940 Haun *Hawk's Done* 161 One thing that nigh made him puke, though, was that nearly everybody they met was boogered up in some way. **2005** Williams *Gratitude* 481 He *boogered up* the side of his car when he sideswiped the bridge.

boogery *adjective*

1 Of undergrowth: thick, especially with hemlock; hence of a place: hideous, threatening, with a ghostlike character or appearance.

1956 McAtee *Some Dial NC* 6 = buggery-looking: ugly, forbidding or scary-looking. **1997** Montgomery *Coll* (known to Adams, Brown, Cardwell, Ledford, Norris, Oliver).

2 Of a man's appearance: unkempt, unshaven, frightening. See also **boogerous**.

1997 Montgomery *Coll* (known to Cardwell, Ledford, Norris).

boogeyman, **boogieman** See **booger A1**.

boogle *verb* Apparently, to be deceived or "spooked."

1949 Arnow *Hunter's Horn* 44–45 It was uncommon for King Devil to run a straight race with no tricks and no foolery for so long. Maybe Zing was pressing him so hard he couldn't backtrack, for not once in the long running had Zing boogled or fumbled or given anything except the happy anger of his war cry when on the scent of the big red fox.

book *noun* Any bound, printed item, including a magazine.

1917 Kephart *Word-List* 408 = applied to magazines and pamphlets. **1937** Hall *Coll* (Cosby Creek TN) I saw where you strowed books on the floor.

book larnin' See **book learning A**.

book learning (also *book schooling*) noun

A Variant form *book larnin'* [see **1883** in **B**].

B Formal education from reading and classroom instruction, traditionally sometimes considered of uncertain value or use.

1883 Zeigler and Grosscup *Heart of Alleghanies* 51 He possesses a standard type of common sense; an abundance of native wit, unstrengthened by even the slightest "book-larnin'," is a close observer, a perfect mimic, and a shrewd judge of character. **1897** Pederson *Mtneers Madison Co* 825 Although lamentably lacking in "book larnin'" in general, the missionary is constantly surprised at the knowledge of "The Book," which these ignorant people have acquired. **1913** Kephart *Our Sthn High* 271 The mountain clergy, as a general rule, are hostile to "book larnin'," for "there ain't no Holy Ghost in it." **1924** Raine *Saddlebags* 163 "Book-larning" is not of such immediate importance as skill with an ax and gun, courage in danger, and resourcefulness in meeting the severe conditions of pioneer life. **1938** Justus *No-End Hollow* 40 I guess I've got enough book learning. I can read and write—and that's more than Pap can do, or Grandpap either. **1952** Wilson *Folk Speech NC* 521 *book schooling* = education. **1963** Hooper *Unwanted Boy* 222 He delighted in displaying the book-larnin' he had acquired in his three-month course in Webster's old Blue-back Speller. **1979** *Smokies Heritage* 149 Where education and "book learning" were lacking, it seems, common sense and ingenuity flourished.

book-read (also *book-smart*) *adjective* See citations.

c1959 Weals *Hillbilly Dict* 2 *book-read* = well informed; well educated. **1984** Six *Hill'n Holler* 3 *book-read* = well informed, well educated. Also *book smart*. **2003** Triplett *Mt Roots* 48 The parents, if they had enough book learning or [were] "book read," would help with the lessons.

books

A *noun* Time spent by school children reading, studying and reciting lessons from books; hence verb phrase *take up books* = (for a teacher or children) to begin recitation hours at school.

1853 Ramsey *Annals* 723 The good wishes of the season obliterate all recollection of past differences between [school]master and boys; and when, on the next Monday, "books" is called, each one quietly and cheerfully resumes his proper position in the school-house. **1878** Guild *Old Times TN* 332 On next Monday, "books" is called, [and] each one quietly and cheerfully resumes his proper position in the school-house. **1940** Haun *Hawk's Done* 19 Books were called and Basil got in her seat. **1941** Still *Troublesome Creek* 132 They got a leetle sheepbell to ring in the schoolhouse before and betwixt "books." **1951** Giles *Harbin's Ridge* 29 Books took up at eight o'clock. **1955** Ritchie *Singing Family* 184 I tried to hide my red face with the geography book. Cleve peeped over the edge. He had to whisper because it was in time of books. **c1970** Handlon *Ol' Smoky* 50 I felt that I wanted my pupils to have fun as well as "Books," the mountain word for school. **1983** Broaddus *Estill Co KY Word List* 58 *take up books* = to begin recitation hours at school.

[DARE *books* n pl chiefly South, South Midland]

B (also *it's books!*) *interjection* Schooltime! (Used as a teacher's call for children to come into the schoolroom and begin or resume lessons); hence *books away!* = Schooltime is out; hence verb phrase *call books* = for the teacher to summon children to come in at the beginning of the school day or after recess.

1931 Goodrich *Mt Homespun* 48 Shadrach's "ten" were in the schoolyard every morning when school "took up" and when Lois, for lack of a bell, pounded on the side of the door, calling "Books!" **1951** Giles *Harbin's Ridge* 37 He was always the first one out the door when the teacher called, "books away" at the end of the day. **1953** Hall *Coll* (Tuckaleechee Cove TN) Various calls were said to be used by teachers to call students into the school building, like "Books! It's books!" **1959** Pearsall *Little Smoky* 152 Today the teacher "calls books" in a larger room with separate desks, and he carries no pointer. **1978** Hiser *Quare Do's* 43 Mr. Kidd came to the schoolhouse door and clapped his hands and hollered Books! Books! to signal us recess was over.

[DARE *books* n chiefly South, South Midland]

books away See **books B**.

book schooling See **book learning**.

book-smart See **book-read**.

boolk See **bulk**.

boom[1]

A *noun* See 1964 citation. Also called **log boom**. See also **boom pole 1**.

1964 Clarkson *Lumbering in WV* 356 = logs fastened together end-to-end and used to hold floating logs until ready for sawing. **1973** Foster *Walker Valley* 9:1–2 When you start to put your lines out, the first thing [is that] you guy your boom off. **1973** Schulman *Logging Terms* 35 = tree-length logs linked together with chain dogs and used to keep logs floating in a creek from being lost.

B *verb* To collect or confine floating logs with a boom.

1994 Farwell and Buchanan *Logging Terms* = to get stray logs together in the river. **2006** Farwell *Logging Term* Where rivers could be used, the timber was bound or *boomed* into *cribs* and floated downstream like rafts by *drivers*.

boom[2] *verb* To make loud, persistent noise, as does the **boomer 1**.

1964 Reynolds *Born of Mts* 13 Mention should also be made of the Boomer, so-called in the mountains, simply because they scold or boom away at one. **1996** Montgomery *Coll* I wish you'd get out of here and stop your booming (Cardwell).

[echoic]

boomer *noun*

1 A diminutive red squirrel (*Tamiasciurus hudsonicus*) known for its noisy chattering. Also called **ferrididdle, mountain boomer 1**.

1883 Zeigler and Grosscup *Heart of Alleghanies* 64 The most curious noise of these forests is that of the boomer, a small red squirrel, native to the Alleghanies. **1913** Kephart *Our Sthn High* 90 Incessantly came the chip-chip-cluck of ground squirrels, the saucy bark of the grays, and the great chirruping among the "boomers." **1926** Hunnicutt *Twenty Years* 113 Old Riley was not tied and he was behind after a flying squirrel or a boomer. **1964** Reynolds *Born of Mts* 13 Mention should also be made of the Boomer, so-called in the mountains, simply because they scold or boom away at one. **c1984** Dennis *Smoky Mt Heritage* 39 Red squirrels are a northern species; here they live primarily at higher elevations. Because they chatter so insistently at intruders, they are called "boomers." **1986** Pederson et al. *LAGS* = attested by 11/60 interviewees (18.3%) from E TN; 11/11 of all LAGS interviewees (100%) attesting term were from Appalachia.

[< *boom* echoic of the squirrel's loud chattering; DARE *boomer* n[1] 1 chiefly southern Appalachians, especially East Tennessee, western NC]

2 By extension = a person native to or resident in the mountain woods, especially one who is loud and provocative in behavior. Same as **mountain boomer 2**.

1932 Strong *Great Smokies* 28–31 Stan was later to learn that "boomers" were the little gray [sic] squirrels that inhabited only the highest peaks of the Smokies. Sometimes the mountaineers referred to themselves as boomers. **1934–47** *LAMSAS* (Swain Co NC) = a person out in the woods. **1986** Pederson et al. *LAGS* (Sevier Co, Morgan Co TN, Rabun Co GA). **1994–97** Montgomery *Coll* (known to Adams, Bush, Jones, Ledford, Norris, Oliver, Weaver), = also a person who is behaving like a squirrel, i.e. talking loudly and provocatively.

boom log See **boom pole 1**.

boom pole *noun*

1 (also *boom log, boom stick*) See 1964 citation. See also **boom**[1].

1964 Clarkson *Lumbering in WV* 356 *boom log, boom pole, boom stick* = a timber which forms part of a boom. **1981** Henry *Alex Stewart* 54 A boom-pole was cut and secured across the mouth of the creek. The boom-pole kept the logs from floating out into the river and being lost. Logs were cut during the winter and put into the creek behind the boom-pole. The several loggers put their identifying marks on their logs.

2 See citation.

1983 Broaddus *Estill Co KY Word List* 58 = a log fastened on top of a load of hay in a wagon to hold the hay down.

boom stick See **boom pole 1**.

boosh See **bush**.

boot *noun*

1 Something extra (especially cash asked for or given to equalize a sale or exchange), a bonus or premium.

1800 (in **1920** DeWitt *Sevier Journal* 23) (Jan 30) Memo. Swaped horses with Colo. Hanly who is to give 20 dollars boot. **1863** *Bradshaw CW Letters* (Feb 27) wedont aske him eny boot so dont be oneasy a bout us. **c1945** Haun *Hawk's Done* 344 "We've got money in the treasury to pay the boot," he said. **1957** Parris *My Mts* 234 It ain't so much in just swappin' knife for knife. It's the boot you get. Takes a lot of talkin' to end up with the boot. **1969** Miller *Raising Tobacco* 30 My grandfather would probably never have owned a mechanical hand-setter had he not got it as *boot* in a trade of fox-hounds. **1973** GSMNP-57:64 We swapped a good milk cow for a organ and give, I think, a little boot, maybe ten or twelve dollars. **1990** Merriman *Moonshine Rendezvous* 25 I can't recall how much boot I had to give them and my '37 [Ford]. **1998** Hyde *My Home* 74 Dad would trade one horse or mule or cow for an older one and get boot in the trade—five or ten dollars in cash. Sometimes he got even more boot than that.

[Web3 *boot* n[1] 2 now chiefly dialect; DARE *boot* n[1] 1a chiefly South, Midland]

2 The trunk of a stagecoach.

1843 *Knoxville Register* (Nov 29) We learn from the Jonesborough Sentinel that a trunk was stolen from the boot of a Blountville and Abingdon Stage on the night of the 13th inst . . . containing about 200 dollars in specie, besides various articles of clothing, and some valuable papers.

bootlag See **bootleg**.

bootleg

A Variant forms *bootlag* [see **1959** in **C**], *lag* [see **1974** in **C**], *leg* [see **1972** in **C**].

B *noun* Homemade whiskey. See also **saddlebag A2**.

1966 *DARE Survey* (Spruce Pine NC) = illegally made whiskey. **1973** GSMNP-88:90 They had been a few men killed and a few men caught for making whiskey and bootleg and such as that.

C (also *bootlag*, *lag*) *verb* To make and sell homemade whiskey; hence noun *bootlegging*.

1937 Hall *Coll* (Little Greenbrier TN) I kept good liquor. [I did some] bootleggin'. It used to be made in the slicks, made later in the flats. . . . I often sold it for six dollars a gallon. **1959** Roberts *Up Cutshin* 28 I had a living to make for myself. Got into whisky making and bootlagging. **1972** Hall *Sayings* 86 *bootleggin'*, *bootlaggin'* = making bootleg (moonshine) liquor. Sometimes shortened to *'leggin'*. **1974** Roberts *Sang Branch* 92 *lag* = short for bootleg: "I didn't 'lag myself. My business was farmin'." **1978** Montgomery *White Pine Coll* VI-2 I believe we've never had no bootlegging much, very little moonshining. **1989** *Matewan OHP-33* He bootlegged and he said he'd hide that liquor all over the hillside. Then hit'd get dark [and] he'd get you a half a gallon at a time. **1995** Williams *Smoky Mts Folklife* 105 "Bootlegging," the marketing of illegal alcohol, was generally a separate profession [from the manufacturing].

[from the practice of hiding containers of the liquor in one's boot]

bootleg bonnet *noun* See citations.

1974 Dabney *Mt Spirits* 11 Although most modern moonshiners shun filters, many makers of earlier days used "bootleg bonnets," to strain the fresh whiskey. They would tack the hats across the top of the keg under the worm. **2007** Rowley *Moonshine!* 160 = a felt hat used as a strainer to filter moonshine as it emerges from the condenser.

bootlegger (also *legger*) *noun* Originally, one who made and sold homemade whiskey; more recently, one who transports the product to markets or distributors, usually after purchasing it from the **moonshiner** who made it. See also **bootleg C**.

1952 Callahan *Smoky Mt Country* 176 The 'legger had to move. He went to Union County, where he resumed his occupation of making moonshine. **1967** Williams *Moonshining* 12–13 One who dispensed the contraband product, which had to be concealed on one's person, was referred to as a "bootlegger," from the practice at first of concealing bottles in the legs of loosely fitting boots. **1977** Shackelford et al. *Our Appalachia* 247 We sold whiskey by the gallon to the bootleggers and the bootleggers sold it out by the bottle. **1985** Irwin *Alex Stewart* 163 Back then most all the men wore boots. They'd tie their britches around their leg and their boot with a string, and that way they could put a bottle in the top of their boot, and nobody would notice it. They'd go around where they was holding court or where an election was being held and sell it. When they wanted to get their bottle, they'd slip around behind a building and untie that string and get it out. **1989** Smith *Flyin' Bullets* 111 Bootleggers and moonshiners could be very rough people to deal with. . . . Bootleggers, carrying illegal moonshine, whisky, or bonded whisky, into dry counties where it was illegal to have it, drove with the threat of having the car confiscated, as well as facing jail terms. . . . Bootleggers and moonshiners, working on a large scale, were organized, many working for someone with contacts. Large sums of money exchanged hands which is evidenced by [the fact] that cars were easily replaced as they were confiscated by the law.

bootlegging See **bootleg C**.

bore *verb*

1 See **bear**[2].

2 See citation.

c1960 Wilson *Coll*: *bored [to tears]* = embarrassed rather than tired of things.

[DARE *bore* v[1] 1 chiefly Midland]

bore for the simples *verb phrase* To drill a hole in (a person, a person's head) as a (facetious) cure for foolishness.

1923 Greer-Petrie *Angeline Doin' Society* 18 If the Sennater paid sich a outlandish price as that, he orter have his head bored for the simples. **1927** Woofter *Dialect from WV* 349.

boresome *adjective* Boring, tiresome.

1966 *DARE Survey* (Cherokee NC). **1996** Montgomery *Coll* (known to Brown, Cardwell, Norris, Oliver).

[DARE *boresome* adj chiefly South, South Midland]

born *verb*

A Variant past participial forms *bornded*, *borned*, *bornt*.

1831 McLean *Diary* (July 7) William Pickens daughter Mary Elen borned. **1862** Huntley *CW Letters* (June 3) for my giving you a name for the new Borned I dont suppose I can give any Better a name than you can. **1864** Williams *CW Letters* (March 24) Elmira has two fine Boys which was Borned the 19 of this month. **1887** (in **1985** *Walker Bible Record* 61) Fannie Martin Walker was borned Dec. 13 1886. **1913** Kephart *Our Sthn High* 284 There are many corrupt forms of the verb, such as gwine for gone or going . . . borned, hurted, dremp. *Ibid.* 355 "Borned in the kentry and ain't never been out o' hit" is all that most of them can say for themselves. **1925** Furman *Glass Window* 118–19 [Animals] know better than humans when Jesus was bornded; and I have heared 'em at their lowing and praying, and have scratched the snow off'n the elders and seed the greenshoots the next morning. **1930** Greer-Petrie *Angeline Outsmarts* 28 You air supposed to take [the prescription] to a store down on the cornder, and giv' it to a white-coated fellow that was bornt without a conscience. **1939** Hall *Coll* (Big Creek NC) I was borned up here in the foot of the Chestnut Mountain, in Tennessee. **1942** Hall *Phonetics Smoky Mts* 92 [d] is added by most elderly speakers to *akin* and *born*. **1961** *Coe Ridge OHP*-343B I's bornded in eighteen and eight-five. **1969** *GSMNP*-38:39 She wasn't borned in this house. **1975–76** Wolfram/Christian *WV Coll* 83 I was bornt and raised at Elkins in West Virginia, mountains town. **1978** Montgomery *White Pine Coll* X-2 I was bornded in Cocke County. **1989** *Matewan OHP*-39 I was borned at Coal Run, Kentucky, below Pikesville, Kentucky. **1998** *Dante OHP*-45 He was the last one [of the family] borned in Wise County.

[DARE *borned* (at *born*) chiefly South, South Midland]

B Senses.

1 Especially of a baby: to be given birth, be delivered (usually expressed in the progressive); hence noun *borning* = birth. See also **a- A3**

1910 Essary *TN Mtneers* 22 Two of the brightest pages in the pages of forensic debate was blotted out by Judge Jones with a single stroke of his judicial power, and two great speeches "died abornin." **1917** Davis *A Bornin'* 704 The nurse made haste to accept the invitation in the hope of being present at a "bornin." **1928** (in **1952** Mathes *Tall Tales* 55) "Sister Tollett," he began, "if ever'body was a-ponderin' the Book thataway, they'd be souls a-bornin' ever' night." **1940** Still *River of Earth* 31 I seed you run away when the colt was a-borning. **1962** Dykeman *Tall Woman* 53 The baby was twenty-four hours a-borning. **1976** Carter *Little Tree* 60 There's spring storms like a baby borning in blood and pain. **1995** Montgomery *File* Something happened to the child when he was a-borning (85-year-old man, Greenbrier TN).

[DARE *born* v 1 chiefly South, South Midland]

2 Of a female animal or a mother (figuratively, a progenitor): to give birth to.

1924 Vollmer *Sun-Up* 78 I reckon these here hills that borned me, and nursed me kin take keer of me fer a little while. **1942** Campbell *Cloud-Walking* 16 To leave them at Sary's till Marthy was done borning her baby. **1957** Combs *Lg Sthn High: Word List* 13 = to give birth to (of animals). Ex.: "The mare borned a colt." **1996** Isbell *Last Chivaree* 32 Obviously at each [occasion], he talks of oxen, banjo making, the "barning" [sic] of babies, and of cars whose masters have died. **1996** Montgomery *Coll* (known to Brown, Cardwell, Oliver), = not as commonly used as a verb as is *birth* (Weaver).

[DARE *born* v 1, 2 both senses chiefly South, South Midland]

3 Of a midwife: to supervise and assist at the birth of (a child).

1939 *FWP Guide KY* 429 "Borning" was the job of a woman usually a grandmother whose qualification was the number of children and grandchildren she had "borned." **1951** Giles *Harbin's Ridge* 6 She had been a granny woman most of her days and had borned all the younguns up and down the ridge. **2003** Smith *Orlean Puckett* 91 She said that a lot of times she wished that she had kept a account of how many babies she had born, but she didn't.

[DARE *born* v 3 chiefly South, South Midland]

born days (also *borned days*) noun in the phrase *all my born(ed) days* = my entire lifetime.

1859 Taliaferro *Fisher's River* 55 I cum right plum upon one uv the curiousest snakes I uver seen in all my borned days. **c1960** Wilson *Coll* I've never seen the like of that in all my borned days. **1983** Davis *Multi-lingual Mule* 50 He fidgeted, seemed to search for a word, then said, "Nope, never in all my born days have I seen the like of this anywhere." **1988** Moore *Mt Voices* 11 I've never been so scared in all my born days. What made it really worse, I think, than it would've been, I had my baby. **2013** Venable *How to Tawlk* 7 = the entirety of one's life: "In all my borned days, I ain't never seed a wommin 'at purty!"

bornded, borned See **born A.**

borned days See **born days.**

borning See **born B1.**

bornt See **born A.**

borrey, borrie See **borrow.**

borrow

A Variant forms *borrey, borrie, borry.*

1861 Martin *CW Letters* (Oct 9) I think if you hant got the money to pay the fraite borry it and when I have the chance I wil send you some money. **1864** *Teague CW Letter* (March 8) yo[u] can borrey the money and i will pay it back when yo[u] come. **1873** Smith *Peace Papers* 131 If we are a State, we can borry munny in Augusty. **1910** Cooke *Power and Glory* 4 While you borryin' why cain't ye borry whole things that don't need mendin'? **1938** (in **2005** Ballard and Chung *Arnow Stories* 102) Now don't be afeard. She'ull borrie a light. **1954** Arnow *Dollmaker* 184 Did you want to borry th basket to look at? **1972** *AOHP/ALC*-342 I borried ten dollars off my dad and married. **1973** *Foxfire Interviews* A-73-46 You could always go to the bank, you know, and borry a little money if you had any credit. **1998** Hyde *My Home* 83 "We could borrie one," Walt said. **2007** McMillon *Notes* Did ye come to borry a chunk of fire?

B *verb* To lend.

1904–20 Kephart *Notebooks* 4:731 Will you borry me some sugar? **1922** Kephart *Our Sthn High* 235 They had the book, and they borried it to us to read. **1994–97** Montgomery *Coll* (known to Brown, Cardwell, Ledford).

C *noun* A borrowed item.

1975 Chalmers *Better* 66 When she has finished with them, she will "bring back my borries" so another may have them in time of need.

borrow a chunk of fire, borrow a coal of fire See **borrow fire 2.**

borrowed days *noun* The first three days of April, said to have been taken from March because they often have stormy weather.

1824 (in **1912** Doddridge *Notes on Settlement* 55) It was a common saying that we must not expect spring until the borrowed days, that is, the three first days of April were over.

borrow fire *verb phrase*

1 To obtain burning coals from a neighbor to rekindle one's own fire. See also **light a rag.**

1937 Hall *Coll* (Gatlinburg TN) People used to "borry far" when I was a small boy. **1948** Chase *Grandfather Tales* 115 They had to have fire, so they sent the oldest one of the girls over there to borrow some fire. **1954** Miller *Pigeon's Roost* (Jan 7) I have known many a person to come to our house early in the morning bringing two boards to "borrow" fire. [**1979** Slone *My Heart* 40 Many times when the fire had gone out, one of the kids would be sent to the neighbor to borrow some burning pieces of wood.] **1985** Irwin *Alex Stewart* 31 Before he got matches, they'd have to keep fire all the time. If they let the fire go out they'd come to our house and borrow fire. . . . They've come many a time at daylight to borrow fire to get breakfast with.

2 (also *borrow a chunk of fire, borrow a coal of fire*) To pay only a brief visit. See also **come to borrow fire.**

1977 Shackelford et al. *Our Appalachia* 70 If for any reason the fire [went] out I would have to go a mile or so to get fire, what we call "borrowing fire." Now a lovely [saying] came out of that: "Well, what'd you come for, a chunk of fire?" If you'd come for a chunk of fire you'd dash right off to get that fire back home and preserve it so that you could start your fire for cooking. **1984** Woods *WV Was Good* 17 Going away back beyond the time of matches is the humorous admonition to someone in a hurry, "Don't act like you came to borrow a coal of fire." **2007** McMillon *Notes* Did ye come to borry a chunk of fire?

borry See **borrow.**

boss-man *noun* A supervisor on a work crew.

1939 Hall *Coll* (Bradley Fork NC) The boss man couldn't get it into his head right that they got me to go there, and I went there.

[DARE *boss-man* n 1 chiefly South, Southern Appalachians]

both

A *pronoun* Variant form *bof.*

1867 Harris *Sut Lovingood* 103 Hit warn't eny use, George, fur they bof went outen site, jis' bustin the river plum open. **2007** Preece *Leavin' Sandlick* 16 I hope that ole busybidy that has a tongue loose at bof ends won't be thar. **2013** Venable *How to Tawlk* 7 Bofus [i.e. both of us] are fixin' to go a'fishin' on Saturday.

B *adjective* in phrase *the both*. See **the 6.**

bother

A verb

1 (also *bother up*) To confuse, upset (someone). See also **botherate.**

1926 Hunnicutt *Twenty Years* 51 Old Muse trailed up the creek to the falls and there she got bothered very badly. **1940** Haun *Hawk's Done* 35 I somehow didn't feel all bothered up inside. **1954** GSMNP-19:6 I've never exactly been lost, but I've been bothered for two or three days a few times.

2 (also *bother around*) To snoop around.

1923 Furman *Mothering* 104 Bad as he hated to do it, circumstances was such that he would have to fire on 'em if they kep' bothering around; that he had the living to make for the family, and no time to spend setting around enjoying hisself in jail. **1926** Hunnicutt *Twenty Years* 148 They went up the creek a little ways and bothered a little.

B *noun* in phrase *make a little bother*, especially of dogs in fox hunting: to put forth sounds of being confused or uncertain for a brief period of time.

1926 Hunnicutt *Twenty Years* 25 Just as we caught up with them at Roaring Branch the dogs made a little bother. **a1975** Lunsford *It Used to Be* 165 The word "bother" is a term used in talking about fox hunting and listening to the dogs as they are running. You can tell maybe at a certain place where they get tangled up and seem to scatter and get quiet. One man will say to the other, "Well, I believe he made a little bother right there." That means that the fox did something that would tend to throw the dogs off of the scent and so he "made a little bother." **1994** Montgomery *Coll* (known to Shields).

bother around See **bother A2.**

botherate *verb* To trouble, annoy. See also **bother A.**

1953 Davison *Word-List Appal* 9. **1995** Montgomery *Coll* (known to Cardwell, but not to other consultants from the Smoky Mountains).

[back-formation from *botheration*; DARE *botherate* v especially South Midland]

botheration

A *noun* Used as a nuisance, source of worry or annoyance.

1849 Lanman *Alleghany Mts* 55 This water-spout story has always been a great botheration to me. **1864** *Chapman CW Letters* (May 27) I had Declined the notion of marrying as wiming is onely a Botheration and children is a great Plague. **1927** Woofter *Dialect from WV* 349 = an annoyance or a nuisance. "You are such a botheration to me." **1938** Justus *No-End Hollow* 35 Jessie is a botheration, making fun the way she does, and Granny fusses at the noise. **1970** Vincent *More of Best* 41 He does have one little botheration now. **1994** Montgomery *Coll* He's a botheration (Shields).

B *interjection* Used as an expression of annoyance or vexation.

1927 Woofter *Dialect from WV* 349 Botheration! Why don't you let me alone? **1933** Thomas *Traipsin' Woman* 91 Botheration on old Aunt Hanner! **1998** Montgomery *Coll* (known to Cardwell).

botherment *noun* A nuisance, worry.

1912 Perrow *Songs and Rhymes* 139 Suffixes are still alive: we hear such formations as pushency, botherment, and even footback. **1931** Goodrich *Mt Homespun* 41 Up here I ain't got no botherments at all. **1957** Parris *My Mts* 61 Abody just couldn't be devilled with a lot of botherments if they was aiming to do a piece of weaving. **1983** Page and Wigginton *Aunt Arie* 53 I reckon that was a botherment. **1995–97** Montgomery *Coll* (known to Brown, Cardwell, Ledford, Shields).

bother up See **bother A1**.

both of them (also *both of us*) *pronoun phrase* Coreferent with the subject of the clause but having syntactic position within the predicate. See also Grammar and Syntax §18.3.

1923 Greer-Petrie *Angeline Doin' Society* 26 Terectly I seed Lum's eyes a-gittin' heavy, and pon my honor if me and him didn't both of us drap off to sleep right thar. **1931–33** (in **1987** Oliver and Oliver *Sketches* 24) They were both of them in the first religious organization that was ever held in Cades Cove in the month of June, the 16th, 1827. **2009** Holbrook *Upheaval* 117 They were both of them afraid like that.

bottled-in-the-barn *noun phrase* Homemade whiskey.

1940 Farr *More TN Expressions* 446 *bottled-in-the-barn* = liquor: "Bottled in the barn is hard on the nerves." **1941** Hall *Coll* (Cataloochee NC) = homemade, bootleg whiskey, not bonded whiskey.

[perhaps ironic contrast to *bottled in bond*, i.e. whiskey that bears an official government bond or seal]

bottle lamp *noun* See citation.

1953 Davison *Word-List Appal* 9 = a lamp made by putting kerosene into a bottle, with a homemade wick in the opening. Such a lamp is often used when a lantern is not available.

bottom *noun*

1 (also *bottom land, bottoms*) A stretch of low-lying, well-drained, usually fertile land formed by alluvial deposits along a river or stream; also used in place-names, as in *Metcalf Bottoms* in the Little River TN area, *Round Bottoms* (NC) in the northeast Smokies, and *Walker Bottoms* near Mt. Sterling NC. See also **branch bottom, creek bottom, river bottom(s)**.

1780 Donelson *Journal* (March 29) Gathered some herbs on the bottoms of Cumberland, which some of the Company called Shawne Salad. *Ibid.* (March 30) Our progress at present is slow. Camped at night near the mouth of a little river at which place and below there is a handsome bottom of rich land. **c1798** *Jefferson Co Wills II* 237 I give to my Daughter Rebekah Sellers and to my son Edward George all of my bottom Land to be equally divided between them. **1824** (in **1912** Doddridge *Notes on Settlement* 72) Our fall fruits were winter and fall grapes; the former grew in the bottom lands. **1834** Crockett *Narrative* 111 It was very dark, and the river was so full that it overflowed the banks and the adjacent low bottoms. **1862** *Martin CW Letters* (Feb 17) I have not Commenced sowing oats yet I want sow in our old Bottem. **1864** *C A Walker CW Letters* (April 24) We are camped in a cedar thicket on high ground and it will produce far better than Valley River bottoms. **1883** Zeigler and Grosscup *Heart of Alleghanies* 185 Its shallow channel is bordered by alluvial bottoms—deposits carried from the mountain slopes—varying in width from a few rods to five miles, making, with a background of mountains rising massively in the distance, a landscape of surpassing beauty. *Ibid.* 188 There is nothing like a continuous stretch of bottom along its affluents. **1910** Cooke *Power and Glory* 22 She had seen the shoestring creek bottoms between the endless mountains among which she was born and bred. **1931** Burns *Coves Blount Co* 47 Cade's [sic] Cove is remarkable for its rich bottoms and its meadow-like features. **1934–47** *LAMSAS Appal*: *bottoms* = attested by 2/148 speakers (1.4%) from WV, 5/20 (25%) from VA, 2/37 (5.4%) from NC, and 10/14 (71.4%) from SC; *bottom* = attested by 89/148 speakers (60.1%) from WV, 9/20 (45%) from VA, 22/37 (59.5%) from NC, 9/14 (64.3%) from SC, and 4/12 (33.3%) from GA. **1943** Peattie *Indian Days* 41 Level alluvial land among the mountains is usually a bottom. **1949** Kurath *Word Geog East US* 61 In the Midland and the South *bottom lands* and *bottoms* are the most common expressions for low-lying flat meadow lands and fields along large and small watercourses. *Bottom lands* is more common in the North Midland, *bottoms* in the South and South Midland. **1960** Stupka *Great Smoky Mts* 54 Farming was done along the narrow bottomlands, in the wider coves, and, often enough, on fairly steep hillsides. **1973** *GSMNP-70*:3 [The house] was right out in the middle of a little bottom. **1989** *Matewan OHP-9* Them big bottoms made good places for, to play ball, all smooth. **1997** King *Mt Folks* 12 "You ought to call this Caney Creek, because there's a little (sorghum) cane patch in about every flat bottom up through here," a man once told folks there. **1999** Coggins *Place Names Smokies* 163 *bottom(s)* = relatively flat terrain, particularly along a stream. The low, well-drained bottom land soils are often fertile and productive, but can also be submerged by floodwaters part of the year, and be nonproductive.

[SED nEngl; DARE *bottomland* n chiefly South, Midland]

2 See citations.

2002 Armstead *Black Days* 241 = the floor of a mining entry, heading, or room. **2007** *Mining Terms* = floor or underlying surface of an underground excavation [in a coal mine].

bottom land, bottoms See **bottom 1**.

boughten, boughtened See **buy**.

bound See also **bounden**.

A *verb* Variant past-tense form *bount*.

1962 Williams *Verbs Mt Speech* 17 The *-d* and *-ed* endings of past forms of verbs are frequently pronounced -t . . . A few such examples are *bound, bount*. **1981** Williams *Storytelling* I reckon a body's bount and compelt to do what he thinks he has to.

B *verb* Senses.

1 To wager, guarantee.

1963 Edwards *Gravel* 116 Many of 'em had a lot of truth in 'em too, I'll bound ye. **1998** Montgomery *Coll* (known to Brown).

2 In phrase *I'll be bound* = I swear.

1895 Murfree *Phantoms* 237 Ef I git ye home wunst more, I'll be bound I'll leave ye thar. **1952** Justus *Children* 53 He'll be no-account, I'll be bound, a traipsing good-for-nothing, just like his mammy. **1997** Montgomery *Coll* "I'll be bound you're right" [i.e. I'll have to admit it] (Cardwell).

C *noun* An obligation, responsibility, necessity, irreversible desire.

1924 Greer-Petrie *Angeline Gits Eyeful* 3 Them new p'inted-toed shoes of his'n got to pinchin' his corns so bad, he had a bound to set down and rest his feet fur awhile. **1925** Furman *Glass Window* 130 "I jest got a bound to hold it, Cindy," she cried, "seems like I never pined for nothing so bad in all my days!" **1942** Thomas *Blue Ridge* 155 He's got a-bound to act like a man, now. **1975** *AOHP/LJC-384* The sheriff had to [carry out the hanging]. He had a bound to do it. He stepped right on that thing and he hacked that rope. **1995** Montgomery *Coll* (known to Cardwell).

[< *bind* "to subject to an obligation"]

bound and compelled (also *bound and obliged*) *adjective phrase* Obligated, determined.

1943 Justus *Jerry Jake* 32 That 'tater crop is bound and obliged to be dug. **1981** Williams *Storytelling* I reckon a body's bount and compelt to do what he thinks he has to. **1987** Young *Lost Cove* 137 Harrison was *bound and compelled* to set a fire in [the fireplace] to see how it behaved and to take the autumn chill off the room.

boundary *noun* A large tract of land, especially one that is timbered.

1881 (in **1940** McJimsey *Topo Terms in VA* 158) In the Clinch Mountain are large boundaries of chestnut, chestnut oak, with hickory, etc. **1899** Frost *Sthn Mts* 9 The landless, luckless "poor white" . . . is far removed in spirit from the narrow-horizoned but proud owner of a mountain "boundary." **1913** Combs *KY Highlander* 23 More than a century ago, Virginia granted great boundaries of land [in what would become Kentucky] to various parties, and these grants lap and over-lap each other. **1917** Kephart *Word-List* 408 = a farm; a fenced-in field; a large, unfenced estate, such as a tract of timber land. **1937** Hall *Coll* (Little Cataloochee NC) Love owned a great big boundary of land. He let people have the land at two dollars an acre. **1953** Hall *Coll* (Plott Creek NC) We could buy a boundary of timber from a man, cut it, log it, and saw it. . . . This boundary [on Hazel Creek owned by a Smoky Mountain hunting club] was, and could be yet, one of the best boundaries I'd ever seen. . . . This [hunt] has been along back just a few years ago, before the park took over the Hazel Creek boundary game preserve. **1960** Mason *Memoir* 91 I was confident that I could obtain a sub contract from Mr. Holland if I could only buy a boundary of cross-tie timber. **1973** *AOHP/LJC-317* He was over the Kentucky Union land there for so many boundaries. **1989** Landry *Smoky Mt Interviews* 191 Right here we enter the Smoky Mountains National Park. It's a boundary of land bought and set aside for future generations.

[Web3 *boundary* n 3 Midland; DARE *boundary* n 1 chiefly South Midland]

bounded gut *noun* Constipation.

1994–96 Montgomery *Coll* (known to Adams, Cardwell, Ellis, Jones, Ledford, Norris, Oliver).

bounded up See **bound up.**

bounden (also *bounded*) *participial adjective* Obligated, required, certain. See also **bound.**

1 As an attributive adjective = obligatory.

1862 *Carter CW Letters* (May 6) I intend to contend for yourn and my childrens Rights as long as I can raise my hand for I feell that hit is my bounden duty a debt that I owe to you and the children. **c1940** Aswell *Glossary TN Idiom* 4 *bounded duty* = inescapable duty.

2 As a predicate adjective = indebted, under obligation (to a person).

1896 Fox *Vendetta* 111 I'll hev ye understan' that I don't want to be bounden to you, nor none o' yer kin.

3 As a predicate adjective = obliged, determined, certain, highly likely (to do something).

1921 Weeks *Speech of KY Mtneer* 7 "He was bounden to keep his promise" [is] on everyone's tongue. **c1945** Haun *Hawk's Done* 226 Ma just said, "Cathey's bounden to a-learnt sech from her Ma." **1952** Wilson *Folk Speech NC* 522 *bounden* = to be sure, to be obliged. In the passive form. "He'll be *bounden* to go to see her."

[DARE *bounden* adj chiefly South Midland]

bound to See **bound C.**

bound up (also *bounded up*) *adjective phrase* Constipated.

1966–68 *DARE Survey* (Burnsville NC, Spruce Pine NC, Gatlinburg TN, Maryville TN) *bound up* = constipated. **1995** Montgomery *Coll*: *bounded up* (known to Shields).

'bouten, 'bout'n See **abouten A.**

bow *noun* See citation. See also **Jew's harp, mouth bow.**

1985 Irwin *Alex Stewart* 120 Grandpap Stewart learnt me to make them when I was just small. He was getting out some cedar timber to make some churns one day, and he rived off a big splinter but it was too thin to make a stave. I was setting right on the end of the bench from him, and he picked it up and said, "Hebbins, I'll make you a purty out of that." And he made a bow. He went in the house and got a flax and tow string to put on it, and took English resin and rubbed the string and showed me how to play it. I soon caught on. The sound comes from your mouth, and in order to play a tune you've got to work your mouth right. I could shore play back yonder, but I've lost my teeth and I can't play half so good. Grandpap said he learned that from the Indians. Said they would set around of a night and play music on their hunting bows. They'd put one end in their mouth and pluck the string and they'd get a tune on them. Sort of like playing the Jew's harp.

bowel complaint *noun* Chronic diarrhea.

1862 *Ingram CW Letters* (Aug 28) I am not very Well at pesant I have got the Bowel complaint and Soar throat. **1863** *Chapman CW Letters* (Aug 12) I have had my health very well since i have been hear with the xception of a bad cold and a bowel complaint but I am well of that now. **1939** *Hall Coll* (Big Creek NC) Poke bark, they'd make hit for tea, for a bowel complaint. **1998** Montgomery *Coll* (known to Cardwell).

bow out *verb phrase* To curve or stretch out stiffly in the shape of a bow. Also called **bow up 1**.

1940 Haun *Hawk's Done* 52 He said he was going to bow out some little limbs like ribs and make a sort of frame of a horse, and then stretch Old Maud's hide over it.

[*bow* "to bend into a curve or arch" + *out*]

bow up *verb phrase*

1 Same as **bow out**.

1956 Hall *Coll* (Big Bend NC) Aunt Martha Packett brought Oliver into the world. He was crooked as a fish hook. He was so bowed up in his back. **1971** *Boogers* 34 M'horse got scared and wouldn't budge nary a inch. Just bowed right up, front legs stiff like boards.

2 To work in earnest, "buckle down."

1939 Farr *TN Mt Regions* 89 Mose will have to bow up if he improves his job. **1976** Dwyer *Southern Sayin's* 28 = to improve: "Bow up if you want to hold your job."

[DARE *bow up* v phr 2 chiefly South, West Midland, TX]

3 To assert oneself, express anger; to stand up (to someone).

1941 Stuart *Men of Mts* 159 He did bow up to Lead the other day when Lead snapped him through the ear and left a tiny hole. **1964** Roberts *Hell-Fer-Sartin* 121 He went down there and he bowed up to fight. **1994** Weals *Coll* He just bowed up and jowered at me. (Reported from Pete Monroe, c1948). **1995** Montgomery *Coll* (known to Cardwell), = to get angry, as "He bows up when he catches kids in his watermelon patch" (Shields).

4 To balk, stop abruptly.

2005 Williams *Gratitude* 481 = just quit and do nuthin'. As: "That old mule just *bowed up* and woutn't pull that plow another step." **2018** *Blind Pig* (Sept 13) If I was a mule or horse going round and round pulling the grinding apparatus, I'd bow-up like a donkey.

[DARE *bow up* v phr 3 chiefly southern Appalachians]

box *noun*

1 A coffin.

1937 Hall *Coll* (Cades Cove TN) Graves in Cades Cove [were] four feet deep, or three feet down to the box. The coffins [were] made by hand. **c1960** Wilson *Coll* = coffin: "He'll never do any such thing until he's in his box." **1967** Fetterman *Stinking Creek* 75 We put Ned in the box and moved him up to a good place on the hill, out of the way of the new road coming through. **1979** Melton *'Pon My Honor* 58 When the doctor said that [the hanged man] was dead, they cut him down and put him in his box. **2008** Cain *Wake Forest* 138 I can even remember back when babies died, someone in the community, a carpenter, would make the box and they would drape it with cloth.

[DARE *box* n 3 chiefly South, South Midland]

2 Any stringed musical instrument, usually a guitar.

1925 Greer-Petrie *Angeline Hill Country* 54 He could a-let him come out and pick the box. **1952** Wilson *Folk Speech NC* 522 = a stringed musical instrument, generally a guitar. **c1960** Wilson *Coll* = guitar: "Joe can surely play on his box." **a1975** Lunsford *It Used to Be* 178 "Box" is the name of a guitar and sometimes a fiddle or a banjo. It's a stringed instrument you carry around to make music on. **1996** Montgomery *Coll* (known to consultants from the Smoky Mountains only in compound *gitbox* = guitar).

[DARE *box* n 2 South, South Midland]

3 Same as **spring box**.

1997 Ownby *Big Greenbrier* I:23 Someone had made a box and placed it in the spring branch. We kept our milk and butter in it to keep it cool.

4 In phrase *off one's box* = mistaken, foolishly misled.

1996–97 Montgomery *Coll* (known to Brown, Bush, Cardwell).

box around *verb phrase* To play around, "hang out."

1967 Fetterman *Stinking Creek* 133 Some Sundays I got things to do. Run the dogs. Go to the head of the holler and box around with a friend.... We just cut up and talk.

boxcar *noun* See citations.

1963 White *Marbles E KY* 58 *box-cars* = large marbles. **1966–68** DARE *Survey* (Buckhannon VA) = the big one [= a marble] that's used to knock others out of the ring.

boxed house (also *box house*) *noun* A small, single-walled house of simple design in the shape of a box, with outer walls of vertical plank siding or **boxing**. See 1990, 1995 citations.

1939 Hall *Coll* (Gatlinburg TN) It was an old boxed up store house. It was a sight.... A boxed house [is made with] lumber [that was] sawed in a mill. **1973** *GSMNP-87*:12 No, a box house runs up and down, planks do, and your weatherboarded houses runs this way (i.e. horizontally). **1990** Morgan *Log House E TN* 102–4 In addition to balloon framing, another building innovation, "box" construction, contributed greatly to the decline of log construction in Blount County. Box construction, consisting of a single wall of vertical planks rather than the conventional double-wall technique, was much easier and cheaper to build than balloon framing. In typical box construction, "sills are placed on a foundation, wide boards are nailed on vertically at each corner, and a two-by-four [wall plank] is nailed on horizontally along the tops of those vertical boards.... Additional vertical boards are attached to form a single-thickness wall ... narrow strips of wood are nailed on outside over the cracks to produce board-and-batten siding" ... by the turn of the century it was the "prevailing house type" in Appalachia. It is not known when box construction first appeared in East Tennessee, but a few such houses may have been built in Blount County in the late 1870s. Box houses became common in the county in the 1880s, and larger numbers were erected in the 1890s and early 1900s. **1995** Williams *Smoky Mts Folklife* 70 Up until 1900, log and frame were the two construction options for most dwellings built in the Great Smoky Mountains. However, after the turn of the century, a third possibility began to appear in many communities in the region. While vertical-planked, known regionally as "boxed," construction is considered by many a type of frame construction, local builders always distinguished a boxed house from a frame house based on its single wall construction and minimal amount of framing. **1999** Bishir et al. *Archit W NC* 421 *boxed* = a method of construction using vertical planks without a frame, to form a wooden box. Sometimes also referred to as plank construction. The structure consists of sills to which planks were nailed at the corners to form corner posts, which then supported a headboard. More vertical planks were nailed to the upper and lower bands to form the walls. A common-rafter roof completed the structure. Window and door openings were sawn out. The vertical planks are thus structural and visible inside as well as out. Sometimes battens are nailed over the interstices between the planks. Some boxed houses were subsequently weatherboarded. In western N.C. boxed construction was widely employed in the late 19th and early 20th centuries, once sawmills were established, and in some areas into the mid-20th c. Boxed houses were common in lumber villages and other industrial communities; but they were also built as farmhouses, and they often succeeded traditional log construction as a building method. From the exterior, boxed construction is easily mistaken for board and batten, which has vertical boards applied to a frame. Early 20th-c. photographs show the frequency of boxed construction for the region's houses, for both white and Cherokee residents. Although the method was not considered as durable as frame construction, numerous examples still stand.

[DARE *box house* n 1 chiefly South Midland, especially Ozarks]

boxed supper See **box supper**.

boxing *noun* Vertical plank siding for houses, consisting of planks and battens. See also **boxed house**.

1943 Stuart *Private Tussie* 256 In one week we had the framework up, the boxin nailed to the framework, the winders and doors sawed. **1966–68** *DARE Survey* (Brasstown NC, Spruce Pine NC) = vertical strips of wood that cover the outside of a frame house. **1994–95** Montgomery *Coll* (known to Cardwell, Shields).

[DARE *boxing* n 1 chiefly South, South Midland]

box knocker *noun* See citation.

1939 Farr *TN Mt Regions* 89 = banjo player: "Beesley's a first-rate box knocker."

box social See **box supper**.

box supper (also *boxed supper, box social*) *noun* Formerly, a community social event to raise funds for a school, church, or other worthy cause. See also **pie supper**, **poke supper**.

1913 Morley *Carolina Mts* 167 In the villages there are the ordinary amusements of young people: parties, dancing, picnics, "box suppers," where the girls fill the boxes with fried chicken, bread, and cake, and the boys buy them; and of course there is music, the violin and guitar being the most popular instruments. **1955** Parris *Roaming Mts* 17 Most times after a gander-pull there was a box-supper. A feller who had won the gander-pull was fresh meat for the losers. They'd see to it that he had to bid way up to get his girl's box. **1967** Jones *Peculiarities Mtneers* 91 When money was needed to promote any worthy cause of improvement like rebuilding the school house steps, mending the watering trough or buy[ing] a new rope for the school bell, the promoters would arrange for a "box supper." Every unmarried woman in the community would be asked to prepare a nice tasty lunch for two—for herself and whatever boy should buy her box at auction. At times when there was keen rivalry for the favors of a certain girl the prices paid for these boxes were sometimes fabulous. Often a boy would go hopelessly into debt to his friends for borrowed money rather than permit another boy to eat with the girl of his choice. **1970** Smith *Folk Customs* 57 The young people also got together at ice cream socials, pie suppers, and box socials. At box socials each girl prepared a box lunch for two and placed her name inside the box. The box was sold to a boy, who shared the lunch with the girl whose name he found inside. **1989** Smith *Flyin' Bullets* 54 The social events were boxed lunch suppers. Girls brought a boxed lunch for a boy to bid on to make up money for the school. The girl had to sit with the boy and eat the lunch with him. Boys tried to guess which lunch belonged to the girl he was "sweet on" as girls connived to find a way to get a certain boy to bid on her lunch. After the biddings came the teasings. The boys, red-faced, half embarrassed and half proud, the girls blushing and shy. The same went for pie suppers. **1996** Montgomery *Coll*: *boxed supper* = an occasion when single girls would decorate boxes, such as shoe boxes, with paper flowers and ribbons and put their best-cooked dish in the box. The single men tried to figure out which box belonged to which girl. The boxes were sold to the highest bidder, who got the box of food and ate with the girl who prepared it (Norris).

box with five red nails *noun phrase* See citation.

1927 Woofter *Dialect from WV* 349 = a slap with the open hand. "I will give you a box with five red nails."

boy *noun* A son. See also **grandboy**.

1863 *Joyce CW Letters* (April 6) Francis I sent you name for our boy and for fear that you would not get the letter I sent it in I will send it in another. **1863** *Whitaker CW Letters* (Aug 2) green woods boy had beter come to camps the first chance. **1938** (in **2009** Powell *Shenandoah Letters* 143) Herman come and got him an[d] Albert Nichols boy. **c1950** Adams *Grandpap* 35 He met up with Jack an' he asked Jack whose boy he was. **1963** Edwards *Gravel* 21 I wisht I had me a boy like you, Tad. **1973** *Foxfire Interviews* A-73-46

My boy was carrying in a load just when he was six year old. **1983** *Dark Corner OHP-24A* Do you know Woodrow, Jud Bishop's boy? **1989** *Matewan OHP-9* I was working for Brother Harrison and his boy a-running a mines and I was dumping coal for them, and that [doctor] told Brother Harrison not to let me work nary another day, said my heart was in too bad of shape to do it. **2005** Williams *Gratitude* 481 = son, regardless of age: "He's Aunt Marthey's *boy*." **2012** Jourdan *Medicine Men* 114 Boy, you have done took the cake with this'n.

boy Dixie *noun* A simple type of **turner** plow.

1917 Goddard *Thirty Years* 64 The day of the Boy Dixie plow and the little tow-headed mule is rapidly passing. **1961** Medford *History Haywood Co* 28 In those days when farmers gave little attention to crop rotation; plowed their land with a bull-tongue, shovel plow or boy Dixie (about 2 1/2 inches deep); had no improved grasses to cover crops to keep his hillsides from washing away—just what could he do?

boys *interjection* Used as an exclamation of mild excitement or pleasure, often to punctuate a narrative.

1913 Kephart *Our Sthn High* 101 Boys, them dogs' eyes shined like new money. **1939** *Hall Coll* (Gatlinburg TN) Boys, you'uns [are] talkin' about rough country, but I'm gonna tell you one time the roughest country I was in. It was so steep the people had to look up the chimley to see if the cows was still in the pasture. **1993** Ison and Ison *Whole Nother Lg* 7 = [used] when prefacing a statement.

boys' britches *noun* The kernel of a walnut.

1940 Haun *Hawk's Done* 32 Effena was standing there eating a walnut and Bessie said, "I want the boys' britches out of that walnut." **c1945** Haun *Hawk's Done* 231 "Do you want some of these?" Ma said. And handed him some picked-out boy's britches. **1997** *Montgomery Coll* = the tip of a walnut kernel that joins the two sides together (Brown).

brag

A *adjective* Of a possession: superlative, first-rate. See also **brag dog**.

2007 McMillon *Notes* = the best I have known: "William Riley Schultz was the brag ballad singer in these parts."

[DARE *brag* adj chiefly South, Midland]

B *verb* To assert boastfully.

1949 Arnow *Hunter's Horn* 54 Men would forget he had spotlighted and shot the fox he had bragged to catch.

brag dog *noun* One's favorite dog; by extension = a pampered, self-important person. See citation.

1998 *Montgomery Coll* (known to Adams, Brown, Bush), = said of one's pride and joy, as "A brag dog can go bad easily," "Better be careful or a brag dog will get its tail cut off" (Cardwell).

[DARE *brag* adj chiefly South, Midland]

braggety *adjective* Boastful, self-important.

1943 Justus *Bluebird* 66 Bud cocked his sandy head in a smart-alecky fashion and sang his answers in a boastful and braggety way.

[perhaps by analogy with *biggety*]

brag on *verb phrase* To praise, boast about.

1863 *Shifflet CW Letters* (March 15) I Shode him the likenes and he bragged on them mitely. **1942** Campbell *Cloud-Walking* 28 Preaching Jim Speaks never done chopping and heaving logs enough to brag on. **1978** Montgomery *White Pine Coll-III:2* They give it a good name, and you hear people bragging on White Pine a-being a fine place. **1985** Irwin *Alex Stewart* 91 His brother come to see me and bragged on how handy I was and what a good job I could do. **1991** Still *Wolfpen Notebooks* 95 Gosh dog! Don't say that. Hit's bad luck to brag on something that hasn't happened. **1998** *Montgomery Coll* (known to all consultants from the Smoky Mountains); He brags on his new hound dog like it's one of a kind (Cardwell).

[DARE *brag on* v phr chiefly Midland]

brags See **make one's brags**.

brain fever *noun* Encephalitis or meningitis.

1862 *Bell CW Letters* (Jan 1) Russel is better this morning he has the Brain fever the doctor ses he will get well now if he will take care of him self but our doctors dont now much he cant set up but what he fants. **1862** *Reese CW Letters* (Nov 10) thair is A heep of Sickness hear with the Brane feaver we hav lost thirteen men out of this Rigment Sence we hav Bin hear. **1995–97** *Montgomery Coll* (known to Adams, Brown, Jones, Oliver, Weaver); He had brain fever when he was a child, so he's not right (Cardwell).

brake[1] See **canebrake**.

brake[2] *verb* Variant past-tense form *broke*.

1977 Moore *Jenks* 29 The man that was runnin' the motor [of a car in a coal mine] that killed him was Charlie Lander. I broke for him a many day. And nipped for him a many day. As you know, a nipper takes care of the cable, you see—where the motor has to go where there ain't no trolley wire, he used a nip and a cable. There was a stirrup on the motor that the nipper—they called him a nipper. He has to stay in that stirrup and in case the cable hangs up he's got to get it loose, you see. And I've nipped for Charlie and then I broke for him. He was a good motorman.

brakemens *noun* Brakemen.

1975 *AOHP/ALC-903* If it had been some of them brakemens, he'd been picking up. He'd have killed them. **1989** *Matewan OHP-28* What got most [men injured] of anything was brakesmens getting killed.

branch *noun* A tributary of a stream or creek, often named after a family originally occupying its land (as Becks Branch NC, Byrds

Branch TN), and sometimes so small that its flow is intermittent or seasonal; the general pattern in the Smokies from smallest to largest watercourse is spring => branch => creek => fork/prong => river. A river may have two or more **forks** or **prongs**. A **spring branch** originates from a spring or **drain** and becomes the headwaters of a creek.

1796 Dunlap *Will* To son John Dunlap—the lower end of my land, as follows: run a straight line across the creek to the upper end of my field, then run up the branch 30 poles. **1800** (in **1920** DeWitt *Sevier Journal* 31) (Nov 6) We discovered . . . fine springs and branches on the headwaters of mile creek. **1815–18** (in **2007** Dunkerly *Kings Mt* 61) [They] rode like fox hunters, as fast as their horses could run, through rough woods, across branches and ridges without any person that had any knowledge of the woods to guide them. **1843** Crosby *Journal/Account Book* 101 Sowd One Bushel of the Common Oats 27 of Feby Near the Pear Trees on the Branch at Rawleigh. **1863** *Reese CW Letters* (Oct 27) I want you to git A nuf of wheat if you can to sow the ground on the fur Cide of the Branch. **1863** *Tesh CW Letters* (March 15) I taken One of my new shirts down to the branch to get it washed and the wind blew verry Hard and a spark blown on it and burnt it clean up. **1899** Frost *Ancestors* 315 The mountain world is mapped out by "forks," "creeks," and "branches." This double isolation produces many marked variations in social conditions. It may happen, for example, that one of two leading families on the "branch"—the pillars of the narrow society—die out, or move out, and the social state, left unsupported, collapses. **1937** Hall *Coll* (Sylva NC) A branch may have branches runnin' into it. **1938** (in **2009** Powell *Shenandoah Letters* 143) Most of the logs and lumber is just around a little hill across the creek, up the branch, and up to his place. **1939** Hall *Coll* (Hazel Creek NC) It's been called the Rowan Branch ever since I was a young'un. **1949** Kurath *Word Geog East US* 40 Other expressions that are used throughout the South and the South Midland are *pallet*, *waiter*, *branch*, and the well-known *you-all*. . . . In West Virginia . . . there is a rather clear line of demarcation between the [Southern] *branch* and the [Midland] *run* area. Here *branch* is regular south of the Kanawha, *run* to the north of it. **1963** Arnow *Flowering* 139 Even when the old term was kept, it often knew a change of meaning, as in the case of creek, in England a narrow arm of the sea touched by the tides, but to us of the South, pronounced the same as the creak of a rusty hinge, it was bigger than a branch and smaller than a river. . . . We had many sizes of branch—spring branches were little, but creek branches were big. **1966** Dakin *Vocab Ohio River Valley* 209 The residents of Indiana, Illinois, and Kentucky rarely say anything but the *branch* of the South and South Midland. **1973** GSMNP-78:29 We went up this branch and across and come in above the Timmels and hunted all under them rocks. **1983** *Dark Corner OHP*-12A There was a little white feist dog that would appear and follow him till he got to a branch, and when he got there the little dog would disappear. **1989** *Matewan OHP*-28 This branch used to run big all the time, had plenty of water. **1998** *Dante OHP*-69 He come after me about when he moved down here on Honey Branch.

[OED3 *branch* n 2b U.S. 1624→; DARE *branch* n 1 chiefly South, South Midland]

branch bottom *noun* Low-lying land along a stream or **branch**. See also **bottom**.

1963 Edwards *Gravel* 69 Every time she bucked he sworped her over the head with his big white cowboy hat, and up and down and around and around they went all over the little branch-bottom field near the barn.

branch head *noun* The spring or other source of a **branch** of water; hence adjective = of a person from a remote or more distant area who may be knowledgeable in woods lore at the expense of formal education. See also **branch water mountaineer**.

1955 Parris *Roaming Mts* 24 Some of the branch-head boys were gathered on the porch at Ed Bumgarner's lodge here in the hills above Wilmot where there is always good talk and good food. **1984** Wilder *You All Spoken* 57 They were in ferment. "Well," one of the group said, taunting the newcomer, "what do you think of your man Scott now?" Shifting his cud and eyeballing his questioner, the branch-head boy replied: "Anything my dog trees, I'll eat." **1995–97** Montgomery *Coll* (known to Brown).

branch lettuce *noun* A golden saxifrage, an edible wild green (*Chrysosplenium americanum*) that tends to grow along streams and springs; it is relished by cattle and bears and often gathered for human consumption in the early spring. Same as **bear lettuce**. See also **killed lettuce**.

1899 *US Comm Fish and Fisheries Report for 1897–1898* 24.lxix (neTN) (DARE) The principal aquatic plant known in this region is the so-called branch lettuce, which spreads its roots under the shallow water or in wet mud. This remains green throughout the winter. During the cold season its leaves lie flat on the water, like lily pads, but in summer the seed stalks rise to the height of 2 feet. The submerged leaves and branches serve as nurseries for periwinkle and other lesser forms of animal life. **1958** Miller *Pigeon's Roost* (May 1) Good ol' branch lettuce picking time has rolled around again at least here on Pigeon Roost. Many folks are scouring the damp, deep hollers where flows the scattered stream of the little branches where they are looking for branch lettuce, which is the earliest of all wild salads that is called here just plain old sallet. The branch lettuce crop is also likened unto the foliage in the forests getting green; it was late this season in growing large enough to pick. **1973** Wellman *Kingdom of Madison* 8 Among these mountains and nowhere else on earth, at Easter time and never long before or after, can be found branch lettuce. It is always far off from anywhere, on the brink of a tumbling creek or rooted where water seeps down a broad face of stone. Sliced away in crisp handfuls, washed and drained and then scalded with hot bacon fat, it is a supreme joy to eat. Maybe it can be called spicy, maybe pungent, tangy. But nobody can tell you the taste if you've never tasted. **1978** Parris *Mt Cooking* 162 As for branch lettuce, it's mighty good but it's hard to come by. Not like poke. Grows only in the winding hollows where the water comes warm from the earth, or in and near the edge of a branch where the soil is dark and damp. **2005** Ellison *Mt Passages* 52 Branch lettuce (*Saxifraga micranthidifolia*), sometimes called wild lettuce, bear lettuce, or lettuce saxifrage, grows on wet banks and in seepage areas and streams.

Each basal rosette contains several toothed leaves from four to twelve inches long. Eat with a salad dressing. It's also good with a little vinegar and chopped onions. To make it really good, drizzle on some hot bacon grease to wilt the greens. The Cherokees often boil and then fry their branch lettuce with ramps.

branch lizard *noun* Any small salamander.

1956 Miller *Pigeon's Roost* (April 12) Some young citizens here have recently been catching several branch lizards to sell on the live fish bait market. But some of the people after they caught the lizards, they crowded them in tubs filled with water and many of them died before the truck came to get them. **1996** Huheey *Variant Names* = any small salamander.

branch walker *noun* A person who scours the banks of mountain streams for signs of illegal **stills** and reports findings to law enforcement authorities, usually for a bounty.

1973 Watkins and Watkins *Yesterday* 107 It was against the code to report a still to the revenue agents. But there were snoopers, branch-walkers, who received ten dollars for each still they reported to the revenue officers.

branch water *noun* Fresh water taken from a stream or **branch**, distinguished from well water, tap water, or a strong-tasting drink such as coffee (see 1968 citation).

1862 *Spainhourd CW Letters* (Sept 8) the water is bad hit is as warm as the branch water is a bout hear. **1873** Smith *Peace Papers* 33 [They] swear by the ghost of Calhoun they will eat roots and drink branch water the balance of the time. **1904–20** Kephart *Notebooks* 10:82 Stingy—him? He wouldn't drink the branch water until there's a flood. **1943** Hannum *Mt People* 117–18 If it is branch water they drink, it must come from some stream running in laurel and rock, or filtered by the hemlocks dipping in their shadow, so that the water comes sparkling to the sun, achingly cold in its purity. **1955** Dykeman *French Broad* 294 The town politician sets his glass half full of bourbon and "plain ole branch-water" on the weatherbeaten desk in front of him and props his feet up on either side of the glass. **1963** Lord *Blue Ridge* 8 Ever heard tell of branch water? Nothin' like it. Comes fresh out of a spring and then sort of branches into a bigger waters. **1968** Wilson *Folklore Mammoth Cave* 40 = a symbol of being weak, lacking in strength; hence coffee might be as *weak as branch water* or as *strong as lye*, an old man suffering with *rheumatiz* might also be as weak as *branch water*. **1976** GSMNP-114:22 Whenever you wanted a drink, you went out there with a cup, caught you [some] branch water. **1992** Montgomery *Coll* I believe I'll have branch water (Shields).

branch water mountaineer (also *branch water people*) *noun* One who lives on poorer land and a smaller stream in a higher elevation and who supplements farming by hunting and other means. See also **branch head**.

1913 Kephart *Our Sthn High* 249 We still shall find dire poverty the rule rather than the exception among the multitude of "branch-water people." **1972** Williams *Sthn Mtneers* 180 Branch-water mountaineers . . . live for the most part up the branches in the coves, on the ridges, and in the inaccessible parts of the mountain region. They are the small holders of usually poor land, or tenants, or squatters who move from abandoned tract to abandoned tract. **1999** Montgomery *Coll*: *branch water people* (known to Brown).

bran dance (also *barn dance*) *noun* A community event involving group dancing held on a surface sprinkled with wheat bran or other substance to create a resilient surface; a dance performed at such an event.

1883 Bonner *Dialect Tales* 152 They're goin' to have a bran dance to-morrer over in the settlement. [*Ibid.* 155 We found the dancers in a rustic arbor. . . . Floor there was none save the smooth earth covered three inches deep with wheat-bran. Slightly dampened, it was pleasant to dance on; but Heaven preserve them when they danced it dry.] **1942** Clark *Kentucky* 127 After the hand sticks and axes were put away, or the eave logs of a cabin laid, there was a frolic. No man could give a working and ignore the entertainment. Usually the party, if it followed the building of a cabin, was a bran dance. **1948** Dick *Dixie Frontier* 131 One type of dance was known as a bran dance. Modern usage in an attempt to recall bygone days has mouthed this into "barn dance." It was often held in a newly completed cabin if the floor was smooth enough. Otherwise it was held in the woods. A plot of ground was smoothed off and a quantity of bran or sawdust was spread over it to make it more elastic. People came early and stayed long at these frolics or "hops," as they were called. **c1960** Wilson *Coll* = an old-fashioned solo dance, done on an open space at the country store or or on a barn [floor] properly sprinkled with bran or sand.

brand-fire(d) new (also *bran-fire(d) new*) *adjective phrase* Utterly new and unused. See also **fire new**.

1834 Crockett *Narrative* 145 I therefore gave up all I had, and took a bran fire new start. **1911** Shearin *E KY Word-List* 537 = very; used only before "new": "His hat is branfired new." **c1945** Haun *Hawk's Done* 349 She twisted herself up to the piano like she thought she was something specially screwed together, all dyked out in a brand fired new dress—blue silk—bought for the show-off. And it did show off her hind end. **1995–97** Montgomery *Coll*: *brand-fired new* (known to Cardwell, Jones, Ledford, Shields).

[DARE *brand-fire-new* adj phr chiefly South Midland]

brandy *noun* A type of apple used in making apple brandy.

1939 Wilburn *Notes* 23 (Sylva NC) The old apple trees at the old Wes Enloe home are "brandies," the fruit used for making brandy (Alice Enloe Dills).

bran-fire(d) new See **brand-fire(d) new**.

brank *verb* Of milk: to turn sour.

1966 Wilson *Coll*: *branking* = said of milk. **1983** DARE *File* (csKY) I recall a cousin from that area using brank for milk which was "blinky," or "blue" (though "blue" milk usually meant milk from which all butterfat had been extracted—today's popular lo-fat beverage). In those days, the late 'forties, blue milk was more likely than other varieties to go blinky or "brank"; I recall the giggles over her use of the inappropriate term, used in the collocation "to go _____."

brash

A See **brush**.

B (also *brashy*) *adjective* Brittle.

1968 *Crafts* 8 The trees that grew on the high ground were said to be too "brash," or too brittle. They broke up too easily [to make basket splints]. **1986** Aiken *Mt Ways Two* 6 To make the "splits" he had to find just the right kind of white oak sapling—one that was clear of limbs or knots and would split easily and be flexible, not "brashy."

brashy See **brash B**.

braysh See **brush**.

bread

A *noun* Cornbread; figuratively = corn.

1917 Kephart *Word-List* 408. **1924** Raine *Saddlebags* 105 Bread may mean corn-bread, or simply corn. "I'm clearin' a field to raise my bread." **2006** *Encycl Appalachia* 926 Corn bread was the daily staff of life to such an extent that in the mountain South it was often referred to simply as "bread," with "light bread" signifying the common wheat loaves bought at the store.

[DARE *bread* n B1 chiefly South, South Midland]

B *verb* To supply with bread.

1860 Olmsted *Back Country* 230 No, [we] haint got much corn but a little that we want for ourselves, only just enough to bread us till corn comes again. **1917** Kephart *Word-List* 408 = to provide with daily bread. "He's got enough corn to *bread* his family all winter." **1974** Fink *Bits Mt Speech* 3 He raised enough corn to *bread* his family. **1994–96** Montgomery *Coll* (known to Cardwell); This crop will bread his family (Jones). **1995** Harrison *Smoke Rings* 165 "I've got enough corn to bread me for a year," one hillsman says to another. He means he has enough grain to supply his family with bread for one year.

[DARE *bread* v chiefly Midland, especially South Midland]

bread and butter (also *bread and cheese*) *noun* Same as **butter and eggs**.

1998 Montgomery *Coll bread and butter, bread and cheese* (known by Cardwell).

bread and cheese See **bread and butter**.

bread and with it *noun phrase* See citation.

a1975 Lunsford *It Used to Be* 162 "Bread and with it" means nothing but bread, as "I had bread and with it for breakfast."

bread is not done, one's *phrase* See citation.

1940 Farr *More TN Expressions* 446 = to indicate that a person is mentally dull or feeble-minded: "Henry's bread is not done."

bread rock *noun* A millstone.

1936 Ogden *Rescue Work* [There] are four millstones or "bread rocks" from ancient watermills. **c1940** Simms *Coll* = millstone.

bread safe *noun* A freestanding, ventilated cabinet in which bread and other food are kept fresh. See also **kitchen safe**, **pie safe**, **safe B**.

1999 Morgan *Gap Creek* 131 I put the cornbread and collards and ribs into the bread safe.

bread wagon *noun* Thunder. Also called **Lord's bread wagon**.

1915 Dingus *Word-List VA* 181 = thunder clap: "I heard a bread-wagon this morning." **1931** Combs *Lg Sthn High* 1304 Listen at that bread wagon (thunder). **1937** Hall *Coll* (White Oak NC) "That's the old bread wagon!" [is] sometimes said when thunder is heard because the rain makes the corn and wheat grow. **1998** Montgomery *File* The bread wagon is coming for a mess of potatoes (85-year-old man, Greenbrier TN).

break

A *verb* Principal parts.

1 Variant past-tense form *bruk*.

1884 Murfree *In TN Mts* 249 [I] slipped on a icy rock, an' bruk my ankle-bone. **1913** Kephart *Our Sthn High* 91 I fired a shoot as she riz in the air, but only bruk her wing. *Ibid.* 188 Examples of a strong preterite with dialectical change of the vowel are bruk, brung. **1994** Montgomery *Coll* (known to Cardwell).

2 Variant past-participle forms *breaked, brock, brok, broke, bruk*.

1840 *Pawpaw Hollow Church Minutes* 93 the Church being informed that John and Elizabeth Qualls and Susannah Cate has unconstusionally broke off from this Baptist Church and joined another Church that is not of the United Baptist we concider them no more members of this Church. **1861** *Chapman CW Letters* (Feb 2) Dear cosin i would write more but i am ritin with a stick and a brok on[e] at that. **1863** (in **1992** Miller *CW Campbell Co* 85) On Friday Nov. 13, 1863 Several rounds of cannon was fired on each side. One of our cannoniers had his legges brock by cannon ball of the Rebs. **1864** *Reese CW Letters* (March 31) I Am un Easey A Baut my left Arme it is Brok out on the El Bow Joint vary Bad. **1892** Dromgoole *Dan to Beersheba* 82 She only desired to show her power; "ter do somethin' gre't, an' hev it norated over the mount'n ez she hev bruk up Joe Brady's still." **1923** Furman *Mothering* 117 Nucky ran in to-night from shinny, to have a "broke" ankle tied up. **1934–47** *LAMSAS Appal*: *broke* = attested by 57/148 speakers (38.5%) from WV, 13/20 (65%) from VA, 24/37 (64.9%) from NC, 10/14 (71.4%) from SC, and 7/12 (58.3%) from GA. **1954** GSMNP-19:1 He told me the other day that a cow rolled out of the pasture field and fell into the highway and I don't know how many has done that around here . . . one or two has broke their neck. **1973** GSMNP-5:19 Both hips are broke now. **1977** McGreevy *Breathitt KY Grammar* 93 *breaked* = attested by 1 speaker. **1980** Miles *Verbs in Haywood Co* 97 Now they've got it all broke down. **1983** *Dark Corner OHP-23A* He had broke out [of prison] over there and kidnapped a doctor and somebody else. **1989** *Matewan OHP-7* I never did have a broke bone in all that time. **1997** Montgomery *Coll* Law, law, Bob got his leg broke (Brown). **1998** *Dante OHP-12* I got my foot broke, and when they turned me loose to go back to work, I quit.

B *verb* See also **breakdown, break one's leg, break out, break up.**

1 (also *break to run*) To bolt, dart, go in haste.

1834 Crockett *Narrative* 55 We heard some guns fired, and in a very short time after a keen whoop, which satisfied us, that wherever it was, there was war on a small scale. With that we all broke, like quarter horses, for the firing. **1939** Hall *Coll* (Hartford TN) We just broke to it as quick as we could, and all went into skinning that bear, skun it all out, took that hide offen it, and cut it into four quarter. *Ibid.* (Mt Sterling NC) He jumped and broke to run, and the panther took after him, and he still had his fish pole in his hand. *Ibid.* I broke and run, and the bear took after me. *Ibid.* (Cataloochee NC) The dogs broke when we got pretty close to a bear's den. Why, we couldn't do nothin' with our dogs. They just broke. **1956** Hall *Coll* (Big Bend NC) She looked around and there was a string had come acrost to the fence away from her a-holding her dress there, and she broke to run and run to the house and fell in the door dead. **2007** McMillon *Notes*: *break to run* = to take off quickly.

2 To soften (water).

1848 (in **1870** Drake *Pioneer Life KY* 94) Much [of the water] had to be brought from the spring and broke with ashes.

3 (also *break up*) Of a religious service, court session, a school day or term, etc.: to come to an end, finish.

1851 (in **1956** Eliason *Tarheel Talk* 261) (Forsyth Co NC) Our court broke on Wednesday. **1863** *Love CW Letters* (Aug 18) it did not seame to me like a camp meating it brok up last Monday. **1896** *Word-List* 413 *broke* = terminated. "Church is *broke*." **1912** De Long *Troublesome* Every man on the street carried his Winchester, and when congregations "broke up" the men picked up their hats in one hand and their guns with the other. **1935** Sheppard *Cabins in Laurel* 172 When a mountain boy slips up beside the girl he likes after "preachin' has broke" and escorts her up the road home, her friends says she is "talkin' to him." **1940** Haun *Hawk's Done* 65 Meeting broke the next Wednesday night and he wasn't there then. **1969** GSMNP-44:6 I was a-preaching on the Indian reservation, having a revival . . . when service broke up he says, "I've got some papers if you will sign." **1974** Fink *Bits Mt Speech* 3 Has meeting *broke* yet?

[DARE *break* v C3 chiefly South Midland]

4 (also *break at the coil, break at the worm*) Of liquor: to drop to a lower proof during the distilling process, marking the end of the first run. See also **singling(s)**.

1949 Maurer *Argot of Moonshiner* 8 *break at the coil* = used of a distillate. To drop to a low proof, indicating that the beer is becoming exhausted in the still. The moonshiner often says that the liquor "breaks at the coil" since he becomes aware of the drop of proof at this point. **1959** Hall *Coll* (Mt Sterling NC) When liquor first come off [out of the still], it was alkyhol and then hit'd break, and then you'd run your backin's as long as they was sweet, until they got sour. In fact, when they got sour, it loses strength. **1972** *Foxfire I* 316 *breaks at the worm* = an expression used at the moment when the whiskey coming out of the flake stand turns less than 100 proof, and thus will no longer hold a bead.

5 In phrase *break flax*. See also **flax brake, hackle.** *Old-fashioned.*

1922 *TN CW Ques* 1386 (Wilkes Co NC) I worke on the farm plowing . . . thrashing with a frail braking [sic] flax. **1931** Greve *Tradition Gatlinburg* 71 She raised the flax, "broke" it, spun and wove that, as well as the wool she carded (and sometimes sheared), into the linen, jeans and linsey-woolseys she and her husband and children wore . . . Some of the older men today tell of helping their mothers break the flax in their childhood; it was macerated in water until soft, the tough, outer fiber stripped and twisted into rope, the next layer, not quite so coarse, woven into stout material for meal bags and ticking for the beds, while the fine inner parts were spun into soft thread for weaving sheets and dresses and other articles of clothing.

6 To open (a will) after a person's death.

1969 GSMNP-42:11 They broke the will after he died.

7 Of a church congregation: to fall apart, disintegrate.

1998 *Dante OHP-71* When Harry gave [his pastoring] up, [the church] just broke.

8 (also *break down*) To change markedly for the worse physically, grow old or decline in health or vigor; to exhaust.

1864 Hill *CW Letters* (Sept 30) I can tel you that I am broke down my feete is all bliste[re]d and my legs is stiff and I hav Sufferd more than I ever did. **1864** *Watkins CW Letters* (July 2) J. W. Williams & G. E. Verner is gone to the sick camp but neither of them is verry bad off only broke Down by fatieuge. **1891** Moffat *Mtneers Middle TN* 318 He makes . . . perhaps a delicate allusion to the past charms of the matron, "Why, Mizz—, how you hev broke sence I wuz yer last." **1924** Bacheller *Happiest Person* 7 A'ter a while my sister broke down an' I tuk her five little uns 'gin she got better. **1949** Arnow *Hunter's Horn* 51 Her proudness and her prettiness were breaking; her face looked gray and pinched for a woman not yet twenty-one. **1952** Wilson *Folk Speech NC* 522 *break* = to age, to become weak as one grows older. **1973** GSMNP-76:29 They took him back to the house. He didn't live much longer. [He] broke down and then his wife. **1975** Gainer *Speech Mtneer* 7 *break* = change for the worse in physical condition. "Will has broke a lot since I last saw him." **1976** Brandes and Brewer *Dialect Clash* 303 "She's abreakin'" or "She's broke[n]" (her good looks and/or good health are disappearing). **1976** Thompson *Touching Home* 12 *broke* = to age suddenly: "Hasn't he broke?" **1990** Aiken *Wiley Oakley* Faith is what's left in you atter you're plum broke down and give out.

9 (also *break up*) To clear an area of trees and brush so it can be cultivated. See also **clean off, grub 1, new ground.**

1862 *Lockmiller CW Letters* (March 30) [We] have got the old grond brok up and the new grond purteni [= pretty nigh] cland of[f]. **1939** Hall *Coll* (Saunook NC) After breakin' new land, it's new ground and is not called such after two or three years. Sprouts of sassafras, locust, and running briers come up during that time, and you have to keep 'em cut down. **1981** Whitener *Folk-Ways* 26 Sometimes a mountain farmer could hear his neighbor plowing or breaking up.

C *noun* See citation.

c1960 Wilson *Coll* = an inappropriate act or word, a faux pas.

break a leg See **break one's leg 1.**

break at the coil, **break at the worm** See **break B4**.

break daylight *verb phrase* [with primary accent on both *day* and *light*] To become light in the early morning.

1937 Hall Coll (Smokemont NC) [By the] time we got the tree cut down, it was day, just breakin' daylight. **1939** Hall Coll (Proctor NC) We just stood there till it went to breakin' daylight and got to snowin'. *Ibid.* (Indian Creek NC) When it begin to break daylight till she could see to walk, she took her two little kids and went on in home.

breakdown *noun*

1 A boisterous dance party.

1942 Robertson *Red Hills* 125 A whole strain of kinfolks . . . spent their time fiddling at breakdown dances. **1948** Dick *Dixie Frontier* 131 The usual type of dance was the square dance commonly known as a hoedown or breakdown. **1995–97** Montgomery Coll (known to Cardwell, Shields, Weaver).

[DARE *breakdown* n chiefly South, South Midland, occasionally New England]

2 A fast-paced fiddle tune or dance.

1995–97 Montgomery Coll = fiddle tune (known to Jones). **2015** Jamison *Hoedowns* 201 = traditional rural Southern step dancing; fast Southern dance tune.

breaked See **break A2**.

breakfast *noun* Variant plural forms of three syllables: *breakfastes*, *breakfusses*.

1961 *Coe Ridge OHP*-342A When they got the breakfastes, they called grandmammy out. **1975** Dwyer *Thangs* 19 Have you had your BREAKFUSSES yet?

breakfast bacon (also *breakfast meat*) *noun* Sliced, smoke-cured bacon.

1934–47 LAMSAS Appal: *breakfast bacon* = attested by 38/148 speakers (25.6%) from WV, 13/20 (65%) from VA, 20/37 (54.1%) from NC, 8/14 (57.1%) from SC, and 6/12 (50%) from GA. **1949** Kurath *Word Geog East US* 70 In Virginia and southern West Virginia and adjoining parts of North Carolina *breakfast bacon* is the usual term, and this extension is current also in Maryland and northern West Virginia beside the simple bacon. **1957** Broaddus *Vocab Estill Co KY* 10 = sliced bacon bought at the store. **1966** Dakin *Vocab Ohio River Valley* 337 Indiana, Illinois, and most of Ohio have no special term for sliced bacon, but Kentuckians usually eat *breakfast bacon* or *sliced bacon*. Some older Mountain people also speak of *breakfast meat*; and bacon sliced and fried is *friedmeat*—perhaps the best example of the fact that for many simple folk in the Ohio Valley *meat* = *pork*. **1986** Pederson et al. *LAGS* = attested by 18/60 interviewees (30%) from E TN and 4/35 (11.4%) from N GA; 22/93 of all LAGS interviewees (23.6%) attesting term were from Appalachia. **1998** Montgomery Coll (known to Cardwell).

[DARE *breakfast bacon* chiefly Middle and South Atlantic]

break flax See **break B5**.

break one's leg *verb phrase*

1 (also *break a leg*, *break one's leg above the knee*) Of an unwed woman: to become pregnant and give birth to an illegitimate child. See also **big A2**

1952 Wilson *Folk Speech NC* 559 *break a leg* = to give birth to an illegitimate child. **1964** Cooper *History Avery Co* 16 They told each other ghost tales and witch stories. When nothing else seemed appropriate, they praised the Lord that no girl for many miles around had "broke her leg above the knee" (had given birth to an illegitimate baby). **1970** Mull *Mt Yarns* 115 Two expressions that were common in describing an unmarried girl who became pregnant were "breaking her leg above the knee" and "planting the corn before the fence was built." **1996** Montgomery Coll: *break one's leg* (Oliver).

2 To jilt, reject (one) in courtship.

1940 Oakley *Roamin'/Restin'* 36, 37 I thought to myself this is one time I had made a mistake in casting sheep eyes at this girl and I was so afraid that Dorothy would tell all the other girls for miles around and I would be ruined for life and no other girl would ever go with me again as the news would go out Dorothy had broken my leg . . . She dident say a word but up and give me a kick on my leg and then she went on her way so then I had another broken leg as is the saying of the young people. [**1995** Montgomery Coll = this sense unknown to consultants from the Smoky Mountains.]

3 To be jilted in courtship.

2004 Myers and Boyer *Walker Sisters* 73 If a boy asked a girl out and she gave him a sour look, she did not have to say anything. If she kicked him in the shins, that too told him "no." It was called "breaking your leg" among the boys. **2007** McMillon *Notes* He broke his leg on that girl.

break out *verb phrase*

1 Of a disease (such as measles): to peak and leave the body, as shown by disruptions on the skin and the lowering of one's fever. See also **bring out**, **burn**.

1976 *GSMNP*-114 He caught the measles. He told me them measles wouldn't break out on him. He was just about dead. *Ibid.* 114 [The doctor said], "there ain't a thing in the world wrong with you but the measles, [and] they won't break out." **1984–85** *Sevier Settler* 3:19 Sulfur and honey would make the measles break out.

2 To cause a disease (such as measles) to peak and leave one's body, as shown by disruptions on the skin and the lowering of one's fever.

1937 Hall Coll (Bradley Fork NC) To break out the hives, [use] catnip tea. **1966** Frome *Strangers* 248 Sheep dung, or "bullets," boiled down and sweetened, was sometimes used to "break out" measles. **1982** Slone *How We Talked* 70 A stew or hot toddie [was] a mixture of whiskey, water, sugar and ginger, heated and drank [sic] hot to help cure a cold or cough, and to make measles, chicken pox or hives "break out." Drink just before going to bed to sleep; it will cause you to sweat, thus getting rid of the fever.

break over *verb phrase* To violate a promise or rule.

1944 Wentworth *ADD* 74 (WV) Once in a while you got to break over & read a whole book . . . I broke over & smoked a cigaret . . . I made a resolution not to smoke, but I'll break over just once.

break stick *noun* See citations. Same as **mash stick**.

1985 Williams *Role of Folklore* 284 You break it [= mash] out with a break stick. . . . They put them little rods through 'em, make 'em out of wood, and as you pull 'em through there, that mash, and you put malt in it, you know, you break that mash up. **2011** Shearer *Moonshine Trade* 18 [In the process of distilling], cut a small sapling for stirring the meal when it is being poured in hot water. Cut the sapling four or five feet in length with three or four prongs, six to eight inches on one end. This is called the "break stick."

break through

A *verb phrase* To experience religious conversion or euphoria. See also **come through**, **pray through**, **pull through**, **through C1**.

1967 Giles *40 Acres* 13 The Appalachian is saved when, in public meeting, through the leading of the Spirit, there is no doubt left in him that God is speaking to him, that he has "broken through." He makes a public confession of his sins, followed by a public confession of his faith.

B *noun* See citations.

1986 (in **1991** Shifflett *Coal Towns* 85) On both sides of the tunnel are solid walls of coal, really pillars left to support the roof. Close to the face of the tunnels, these solid walls are broken by "break-throughs" or "cross-cuts," narrower tunnels cut by the miner for ventilation and to communicate with one another. *Ibid.* In the room-and-pillar system, miners worked in small parallel "rooms" set off from the main entry and connected to each other by "breakthroughs."

break to run See **break B1**.

break up *verb phrase*

1 See **break B3**, **B9**.

2 To ruin financially.

1930 (in **1952** Mathes *Tall Tales* 164) They was a young captain up in Virginny—I disremember his name—that was broke up right atter the Civil War an' had to sell his furnishments. **1936** Stuart *Head of Hollow* 23 I aim to give the poor people a chance since I am a poor man. My family has broke me up. **1973** GSMNP-85:1:16 He was wealthy and they broke him up. **c1982** Young *Colloquial Appal* 3 *broke up* = financially ruined. **2008** *Rosie Hicks* 1 He broke hisself up because he's just so good to kids.

breast

A *noun* Variant plural form *breast-es*.

1972 AOHP/ALC-276 She went and laid down just with her back towards the fireplace, you know, let the little baby nurse one of her breastes.

B *verb* To divulge, reveal.

1969 GSMNP-27:11 He was the one noticed them, of course. We never breasted it.

breast baby *noun* The youngest child in a family when nursing.

1970 Mull *Mt Yarns* 118–19 Babies were generally classified as "Breast Babies," "Lap Babies," or "Knee Babies." **a1975** Lunsford *It Used to Be* 179 The "breast baby" is the last one that's come into the home.

breast complaint (also *breast disease*) *noun* Pulmonary tuberculosis.

1862 *Reese CW Letters* (Oct 10) Send word to his wife if you Can he died with A Brest Complant. **1881** Atkinson *After Moonshiners* 152 One of the gals in the neighborhood was sick with the breast complaint, and another was down with the yaller janders. **1914** Furman *Sight* 33 She died of the breast-complaint; some calls it the galloping consumpt'. **1931** Owens *Speech Cumberlands* 92 *breast complaint* = tuberculosis: "Poor Cora pindled along for a year after Jim wuz took with the breast-complaint afore she died."

breath *noun* A moment of time.

1917 Kephart *Word-List* 408 = a moment. "I'll be there in just a *breath*." **1939** Hall *Coll* (Proctor NC) That feist, he was just a-yelping like he was looking at it [= a bear]. I says to Van, "He's gonna catch it directly." About that time just in a breath or two, why that feist went to hollering just like he was a-dying. **c1960** Wilson *Coll* We expected to fall down at every breath as we run away from the vicious hog.

breath harp *noun* A harmonica. Same as **French harp**.

1946 Woodard *Word-List VA/NC* 7 = a harmonica, a mouth harp. **1995–97** Montgomery *Coll* (known to Brown, Cardwell).

[DARE *breath harp* n 1 chiefly South, South Midland]

breetherin See **brother A**.

bresh See **brush**.

bretheren, **brethering**, **brethern** See **brother A**.

briar See **brier**.

brickle *adjective*

1 (also *brickley*, *brickly*) Brittle, easily broken. See also **work-brittle**.

1917 Kephart *Word-List* 408 *brickle* = brittle. **1925** Dargan *Highland Annals* 99 He had took off the muffler when he thought he was goin' to shave, an' the next minute his ears looked so brickle I could 'a' knocked 'em off with a stick. **1969** Miller *Raising Tobacco* 33 However, in this condition leaves were *brickle* (brittle) and shattered easily. **1974** Fink *Bits Mt Speech* 3 *brickley* = brittle. "That bread is awful *brickley*." **1975** Jackson *Unusual Words* 158 Old timers are careful to point out that the *brickle* black birch is unsuitable; only the tough white birch is wanted. **1987** Carver *Regional Dialects* 166 Some of the "folksiness" [of Upper South speech] comes from the old-fashioned or relic nature of many of the expressions, such as *brickle* and *brickly* meaning brittle or fragile. These variants of *bruckle*, which still has currency in Scotland, probably came to America with the Scotch-Irish. **1994** Montgomery *Coll* Handle this easy. It's brickle (Shields).

[< Middle English *bruchel* + (-*y*); OED3 *brickle* adj 1 "liable to break, easily broken," obsolete or English regional; SND *bruckle* adj "brittle, easily broken, crumbling"; cf CUD *bruckle* adj 1 "brittle, easily broken"; DARE *brickle* adj 1 chiefly South, Midland]

2 Changeable.

1861 *Thompson CW Letters* (Oct 30) times is verry brickle here we cant tell hoo will live or dye.

brickley, brickly See **brickle 1**.

bride of the woods *noun* The snowy dogwood tree.

1930 Edgerton and Mattoon *Sthn Forest Study* 216 The dogwood is sometimes referred to in books as the "flowering dogwood," although the showy white petals are really petal-like bracts.... So magical is the effect that sentimental people refer to this tree as the "bride of the woods." **1951** Barnwell *Our Mt Speech* Often they call our snowy dogwood "bride of the woods."

brier (also briar) *noun*

1 (also *brier hopper*) Used as a derogatory term for a native of southern or central Appalachia, especially one who migrated to the Midwest in the mid-twentieth century.

1937 Leybourne *Urban Adjustments* 241 [Mountain people] are popularly called "hill-billies," "briers," and "ridge-runners." **1940** Farr *More TN Expressions* 447 = dirt farmer. "Tillman's jist a plain brier hopper." **1973** Kahn *Hillbilly Women* 109 All you have to do is tell them you're from Kentucky and that's it. They act like you're so stupid you don't know what you're doing. Whenever the buckeyes get mad at you the first thing they can think is to say,... "you ain't nothin' but a briarhopper." **1975** Carawan and Carawan *Voices from Mt* 77 We no longer vote in Kentucky, nor do we pay taxes there. But being native-born "Briars," we can't get Kentucky out of our blood. **1976** Maloney *Appal Culture* 189 Hillbilly ... is used, along with other such terms as ridge-runner, briar-hopper, in either a friendly way or as a racial slur. Mountain people often apply these terms to each other or to themselves in a friendly way. **1976** Mathias *Briars* 2 Most large Midwestern cities accumulated over 100,000 of these migrants, numbers of them now going into their second and third generations.... The migrant was soon to feel the sting of hostility, some of it deserved, but most of it coming from blind ignorance. A much nastier development came when some civic leaders manipulated this hostility into channels benefitting the Establishment. The migrants, derisively called "Briars," were and are lumped together anytime the need arises to explain away city shortcomings. **1997** Miller *Brier Poems* 70 They said we were trash, said we were Briers. **1998** Montgomery *Coll* (consultants from the Smoky Mountains view term as sometimes derogatory, but most often as jocular). **2011** Tabler *Hillbilly Highway* Briars, first off, are what (some) Ohioans call workers transplanted from Appalachia. In the mid-twentieth century, Dayton was the port of entry for many Appalachians migrating from KY, TN, and VA looking for jobs as the coal mines were dwindling.

[DARE *brier hopper* n OH, TN, KY]

2 See citations.

1964 Clarkson *Lumbering in WV* 357 = a crosscut saw. **1967** Parris *Mt Bred* 132 "That," said the woodhick, "is a misery whip or a brier." He pointed to a seven-foot crosscut saw hanging on the wall. "It was designed for sawin' the huge logs of the virgin forest," he explained. **1980** Riggleman *WV Mtneer* 126–27 [Loggers] usually had nicknames for everybody and everything around the camp.... A crosscut saw was a "briar." **2006** Farwell *Logging Term* 1021 Sawyers with their crosscut saws, called "misery whips" or "briars," formed [logging] crews with "buckers," who sawed timber in lengths.

3 In phrases *keen as a brier, sharp as a brier* = quick-witted, sly.

1940 Still *River of Earth* 34 "Keen as a brier," Uncle Jolly said. **1996–97** Montgomery *Coll*: *sharp as a brier* (known to Adams, Brown, Cardwell, Jones, Oliver).

[DARE (at *brier* n 2) especially South Midland]

brier blade See **brier hook**.

brier hook (also *brier blade, brier scythe, brier snath*) *noun* A handheld reaping hook for cutting weeds or undergrowth.

1967–70 *DARE Survey* (Ball Ground GA) *brier blade*; (Cumberland Gap TN) *brier hook*; (Cumberland Gap TN, Jasper TN, Maryville TN) *brier scythe*; (Rogersville TN) *brier snath*. **1994–97** Montgomery *Coll* (known to Cardwell, Shields). **1996** Spurlock *Glossary* 391 *brier scythe* = long curved blade attached at a right angle to a long wooden shaft on which are two handles.

[DARE *brier hook* n chiefly South, South Midland]

brier hopper See **brier 1**.

brier scythe, brier snath See **brier hook**.

briggaty (also *brigaty, brigetty, briggity*) *adjective* Headstrong, sassy, conceited.

1895 *Word-Lists* 385 *brigetty* = smart and forward. **1911** Shearin *E KY Word-List* 537 *briggity* = headstrong, stubborn, "bigoted." **1913** Kephart *Our Sthn High* 94 You'uns won't be so feisty and brigaty atter this! ... When I say that Doc Jones thar is brigaty among women-folks, hit means that he's stuck on hisself and wants to show off. **1929** (in **1952** Mathes *Tall Tales* 105) All I've got to say is, these here briggaty town doctors, with their dude clo'es an' their fancy contraptions, is a-killin' a sight of people. **1965–70** *DARE Survey* (Hindman KY) *briggity* = a reckless person, one who takes foolish chances. **1984** Wilder *You All Spoken* 11 *brigaty* = self-important; wants to show off; haughty; arrogant. **2007** Preece *Leavin' Sandlick* 15 You quit ackin so briggity. **2014** *WV Talk* I often heard my mother refer to a girl or young woman who was showing off or flirty as "briggity."

[perhaps alteration of *biggety*; DARE *briggity* adj chiefly southern Appalachians]

briggilty *adjective* See citation.

1977 Howard *Fifty Years* 10 = one who changes his mind very often: "John is so briggilty that I do not know what he will do next."

[cf SND *breeghle* "to fiddle, to make little progress notwithstanding much bustling"]

briggle *verb* See citation.

1930s (in **1944** Wentworth *ADD* 75) (eWV) = to busy oneself without purpose, potter; meddle: "Stop brigglin' with that." Common.

[cf SND *breeghle* "to fiddle, to make little progress notwithstanding much bustling"; DARE *briggle* v chiefly North Midland]

bright *noun* Polish, especially on a new object.

1917 Kephart *Word-List* 409 = polish. "The bright sorta wore off." **1957** Combs *Lg Sthn High: Word List* 15 = polish, brightness. Ex.: "The bright's plum' wore offn his pistol." **1995–97** Montgomery *Coll* (known to Brown, Cardwell, Norris, Oliver).

bright around *verb phrase* See citation.

1957 Broaddus *Vocab Estill Co KY* 11 = to act biggity.

bright up *verb phrase* To illuminate.

1924 (in **1952** Mathes *Tall Tales* 44) Honey, fetch the lantern an' let's bright up the globe while we're settin'. [**1995** Montgomery *Coll* (unknown to consultants from the Smoky Mountains).]

brigsome *adjective* See citation.

2005 Williams *Gratitude* 482 = feelin' your oats; wantin' to go a-courtin' . . . *feelin' brigsome*.

brile See **broil**.

bring *verb*

A Principal parts.

1 Variant past-tense forms *bringed, brung*.

1824 Knight *Letter from KY* 106–7 Some words are used, even by genteel people, from their imperfect education, in a new sense; and others, by the lower classes in society, pronounced very uncouthly . . . I brung. **1863** *Brown CW Letters* (Sept 20) i sent one [letter] by the same man that brung my likness and ten dolars. **1864** *Poteet CW Letters* (Aug 30) the thing[s] that Pery Walker brung I haint never seen them and I dont expect to see them. **1913** Kephart *Our Sthn High* 284 Examples of a strong preterite with dialectical change of the vowel are bruk, brung. **1940** Haun *Hawk's Done* 190 He picked the letter up and brung it to the house. **1962** Williams *Verbs Mt Speech* 17 Verbs which retain either the strong preterites of Middle English or variant preterites of the English dialects [include] *bring* (present), *brung* (past), *brung* (past participle). **1969** GSMNP-25:1:15 I reckon they cut that up and brung it out during the war. **c1979** Chiles *Glossary* 1 bringed. **1989** *Matewan OHP-9* I'll make a new covenant with the house of Judah and the house of Israel, not like the covenant that I made with their fathers when I brung them up out of the land of Egypt. **2001** House *Clay's Quilt* 217 Anyway, she brung me in, flopped me on the bed. **2013** Venable *How to Tawlk* 29 TVA brung us the lectrick in 1943.

2 Variant past-participle forms *brong, broughten, brung*.

1861 (in **1992** Heller and Heller *Confederacy* 32) tha[y] was 74 yankees brong hear today tha[y] was capture near hatters fort on Saudrday. **1864** *Sexton CW Letters* (March 18) five of our company runway on the 14 day of March and on the 17. day of March tha[y] was brong Back and put in the gard house. **1923** (in **1952** Mathes *Tall Tales* 17) "Friends and neighbors," he began, "you-uns all know what has brung us out here today." **1938** Bowman *High Horizons* 38 We are used to it here and wouldn't want to leave from where we wuz born and brung up. **1961** *Coe Ridge OHP-343A* I saw them broughten down here, one or two of them [= rattlesnakes] for me to see. **1973** Jones *Cades Cove TN* 85 Many times I have brung it. **1995** Adams *Come Go Home* 46 I've brung him to give to Mama. She needs a good dawg to sort of look about her.

B Senses.

1 Of livestock: to give birth to (offspring), bear.

1957 Broaddus *Vocab Estill Co KY* 11 = to give birth to a calf. **1967** Fetterman *Stinking Creek* 64 That sow brought seven of the prettiest pigs I ever saw.

[DARE *bring* v C4 chiefly South, South Midland]

2 To assist in the delivery of (a newborn).

1949 Arnow *Hunter's Horn* 134 They's many a woman a sayen now that I'm gitten too old to bring babies any more. **1966** Dykeman *Far Family* 99 Old Tildy brought us and she didn't charge anything but board and room, although counting all the bellyaching and bossing she did that was a God's plenty.

bringed See **bring A1**.

bring out *verb phrase* To alleviate (a fever or ailment), cause (it) to leave the body. See also **break out 1**, **burn**.

1962 Dykeman *Tall Woman* 213 During days and nights of their fretfulness and fever, she gave the sick children hot brews Aunt Tildy had taught her would "bring out" the measles and keep them from "turning in." **c1984** Dennis *Smoky Mt Heritage* 7 Brew a weak catnip tea and give to newborn babies to bring out the hives.

britches *noun*

1 Trousers, pants. See also **britches baby**, **keep one's britches on**, **leather britches**, **wear the britches**.

1859 Taliaferro *Fisher's River* 47 This rich man, Taliaferro, [has] got too big fur his britches, and won't let me stay all night with him. **1862** *Ingram CW Letters* (Oct 4) I sold my Briches that I draw from old Jef Davis. **1863** *Revis CW Letters* (Feb 24) my britches is giting tolereble bad but I think I can make them do me til I come home. **1939** Hall *Coll* (Wears Cove TN) They'd shear the sheep, and she'd spin the wool, the thread, and make our britches and our shirts all. **1952** Taylor and Whiting *Proverbs and Sayings* 375 Don't get too big for your britches. Too big for his breeches. **1963** Edwards *Gravel* 103 A feller can get too big for his britches sometimes. That's all I got to say, too big for his britches! **1972** *Anna Howard* 54 They put on their britches just th'same as your daddy puts his on. **1985** Irwin *Alex Stewart* 86 I just rolled my britches legs as high up as I could and come on across. **1997** *Dante OHP-12* The foreman . . . wore a pair of khaki britches, yaller khaki britches, and leggings. **2007** Preece *Leavin' Sandlick* 39 Just don't forget ye raisin', Son, and get too big fer ye britches.

[variant of *breeches*; DARE *britches* n pl chiefly South, South Midland]

2 Part of a horse's harness.

1973 *Words and Expressions* 133 = harness for a mule.

britches baby *noun* A breech baby.

1984 Smith *Oral History* 47 Marylou Harkins had a britches-baby, taken it two days to come. **1988** Smith *Fair and Tender* 133 Beulah had him in a real medical way which was a good thing too as he come out a britches baby and Doctor Gray had to cut her and then stitch her up some. I hope my baby will not be a britches baby. Beulah is not feeling too good yet, either.

britheren See **brother A**.

broad *noun* A trip or journey.

1864 *Dalton CW Letters* (Dec 15) if you go yoer brod crismus tell cousin Lis ragdal hoddy for me and tell her that I Love her better then enny bod dy that I ever saw. **1921** Greer-Petrie *Angeline Seelbach* 25 I was sorry the Jedge was in sich a swivvit to git back to Louisville, bekase I didn't half git my broad out.

[reanalysis of *abroad* as *a broad*; DARE *broad* n especially South Midland]

broad ax *noun* An ax with a single wide blade and usually a short handle, used for rough smoothing of split logs, as for benches. Also called **hewing ax**. See also **felling ax**.

1937 Conner *Ms* 43 Some expert men with broad ax [went] to hewing plank we called puncheon's as the pioneer's had no saw mills in those day'es. **1971** *AOHP/ALC-33* They'd take a log, great big log, and they would split it. See, they'd . . . had big mauls back then and things they split it with, and they would split it wide open in the middle, and then they would, had a big hewing ax they called it, broad ax. They called it a broad ax, and then they would hew that all down with that broad ax till hit would be slick here on top, make seats out of. **1973** GSMNP-70:5 He got a job hewing them logs with that broad axe to make the tow boards and pen logs. **1979** *Big South Fork OHP-19* They used old broad axes, you know, to hew the logs, but I built mine [i.e. his house from] round, just notched. **c1995** *Cades Cove* 6 The round logs were *scored* first along their entire length with a felling axe, then *hewn* with a broad axe.

broad form deed *noun* See citation.

1982 Eller *Miners* 55 Some buyers . . . offered to purchase only the minerals under the land, leaving the surface to the ownership and use (and tax liability) of the farmer. The land would be disturbed at some future date, but it was difficult for the mountaineer to envision the scale and impact of the industrial change. These "broad form deeds," as they were known in Eastern Kentucky, effectively transferred to the land agents all of the mineral wealth and the right to remove it by whatever means necessary, while leaving the farmer and his descendants with the semblance of land ownership.

broadgy *adjective* Of livestock: tending to wander. See also **brogue[2] 2.**

1978 Hiser *Quare Do's* 51 Rushie was a lone widow with nothing but little gal younguns, no un to chase down a broadgy cow.

[probably from **brogue[2]** 2]

brock See **break A2.**

brogan *noun*

A Variant form with stress on both syllables: BRO-GAN.

1942 Hall *Phonetics Smoky Mts* 57. **1967** *DARE Survey* (Gatlinburg TN).

B (also *brogan shoe*) A coarse, heavy, high-topped, leather work shoe tied with thongs, often homemade and on the same last, so that one shape fitted either foot.

1843 (in **1974** Harris *High Times* 30) The mirth becomes uproarious, the men jump high, "cut the pigeon wing," and crack their heels together; the women shed their brogans. **1937** Hall *Coll* (Emerts Cove TN) *brogans* = heavy work shoes, strong enough to cut the mud. **1943** Hannum *Mt People* 142 There were no rights and lefts to those homemade brogans, square cut from tanned hide. . . . Gradually they wore to shape. **1956** Hall *Coll* (Roaring Fork TN) Back then when we didn't make our shoes, my dad would buy us one pair a year and it was a brogan shoe, called 'em brogans, of course, heavy leather, and if we wore the shoe out, we went barefooted. **1972** *AOHP/ALC-226* Me being a girl didn't make no difference. I wore brogans just like the boys. They called them brogans. They was rough leather on the outside. **1974** Roberts *Sang Branch* 9–10 If my dad went to the railroad in the late summer, he would bring us back our only pair of shoes for the year. They was old brogans, went by the name of Tennessee Ties. Wear 'em from the first frost till barefoot time in the spring. Never needed half-soling, about the only thing to keep handy was some mutton or beef tallow to keep 'em greased—till you could get 'em on—and off. **1976** Braden *Grandma Was Girl* 60 Shoes were heavy leather, and had high tops. Sometimes the toes had copper caps on them to make them last longer. These heavy shoes were called "brogans." **2018** *Blind Pig* (Jan 12) Over the years the word *brogan* has changed to mean heavy work boots . . . is still fairly common in Cherokee County NC.

[diminutive form of Irish Gaelic *bróg* "shoe"; cf SND *brogue[1]*; DARE *brogan* n 1 widespread, but especially South, South Midland]

brogan shoe See **brogan B.**

brogue[1] *noun* A distinctive local accent or habit of speech (with no reference to perceived Irish or Scottish characteristics).

1978 Montgomery *White Pine Coll* III-2 He's a Tennessean. I can tell by his brogue. **1996** Montgomery *File* He's just got an old mountain brogue.

[cf CUD *brogue* n 3 "a strong Irish accent (from the idea of having a shoe in your mouth)"; cf DHE "There is a view that Irish people used to speak English unintelligibly (as a result of linguistic contamination from Irish syntax and vocabulary), and the effect was as if they had a shoe on their tongue"; see also entry for *brogan*]

brogue[2] *verb*

1 To sole (a shoe, especially a moccasin) with leather.

1859 Taliaferro *Fisher's River* 153 Instead of shoes, he wears hog-skin moccasins brogued with sole-leather. **1959** Hall *Coll* (Mt Sterling NC) That Indian was settin' there broguin' his moccasins. Broguin' [means] puttin' soles on.

2 (also *brogue about*, *brogue it*) To go about on foot, especially to wander or walk aimlessly; to trudge. See also **broadgy**.

1883 Zeigler and Grosscup *Heart of Alleghanies* 51 I've brogued it through every briar patch an' laurel thicket, an' haint I bin with Guyot, Sandoz, Grand Pierre, and Clingman over every peak from hyar to the South Caroliny an' Georgy lines? **1913** Kephart *Our Sthn High* 203 I'm jest broguin' about. **1932** Creal *Quaint Speech* Such words as santering for sauntering, trafficking, prodjecting, all used to indicate walking, are as general as the words broguing, cootering, spudding, or toddling, descriptive of methods of getting about: to go in brogues, to trifle along, to totter or go carelessly, to traipse or trudge. **1962** Williams *Mtneers Mind Manners* 123 If the guest is not spending the night, he rises at the proper moment and "reckons" he'd "better be broguin' down the road." **1966** Medford *Ol' Starlin* 66 "Brogued it" (to travel in brogans) is another [expression not in the dictionary]. **1969** *DARE Survey* (Rome GA) = to walk heavily, making a lot of noise.

[DARE *brogue* v folk-etymology of *bogue* verb influenced by *brogue* "a heavy, coarse shoe," from the activity being done in the heavy shoe; chiefly southern Appalachians]

brogue about, **brogue it** See **brogue**[2] **2**.

broil *verb* Variant form *brile*.

1863 *Levi CW Letters* (April 24) Wee made the Canteens into grittirs to grate our corn and wee Bril[e]d our meat on the Coals and travaid on to the ohio river. **1864** *Watters-Curtis CW Letters* (July 18) she says it would make me Brile to see sam Burton waring paps hat and coat and she says if I dont beleve it Just Rite to the neigh Bors. **1883** Zeigler and Grosscup *Heart of Alleghanies* 52 Jist tend ter brilin' your bacon, Jonas, an' let me travel ter suit my own legs. **1913** Kephart *Our Sthn High* 288. **1974** Roberts *Sang Branch* 64–65 They had 'em some of that bear meat br'ile for supper, and then they laid down. **1979** Slone *My Heart* 42 As soon as the liver was removed from the hog, great chunks were thrown into the fire to "brile."

brok See **break A2**.

broke See **brake**[2], **break A2**.

broken stick *noun* See citations.

1957 Neel *Backwoodsman* 7 = an unreliable person: "If you're countin' on him, you're countin' on a broken stick." **c1960** Wilson *Coll* = something or somebody undependable or inadequate.

broke up *adjective* Distressed over an unfortunate occurrence.

1952 Wilson *Folk Speech NC* 523 = distressed over some misfortune. "She's all *broke up* over the death of her son." **1996–97** Montgomery *Coll* (known to eight consultants from the Smoky Mountains).

bronchial *adjective* Variant forms *bronchical*, *bronical*.

1946 Woodard *Word-List VA/NC* 7 *bronical* = bronchial. "I had bronical trouble." **1967** *DARE Survey* (Gatlinburg TN) *bronical* = the kind of cough that comes with bronchitis. **1978** Hiser *Quare Do's* 56 He had had a *bronchical* trouble as he got older and would cough and clear his throat and spit. **2001** Lowry *Expressions* 4 *bronical*.

bronchical See **bronchial**.

brong See **bring 1**.

bronical See **bronchial**.

brookie *noun* The brook or speckled trout (*Salvelinus fontinalis*), a fish native to the Smokies. Also called **spec**.

1977 *Smoky Vistas* (Winter) 2 The native Southern Appalachian Brook Trout was here long before the brown and rainbow trout. Since the arrival of the invaders, "brookies" have decreased in alarming numbers. Now occupying less than half the territory that they did in the 1930's, the brook trout are being pushed further upstream as the tougher rainbow trout overtakes their domain. **1979** Cantu *Great Smoky Mts* 20 There are three species of trout in the park, but only one of them is native, the Southern Appalachian brook trout, called affectionately "spec" or "brookie" by local folks. **1993** Brewer *Great Smoky Mts* 35 Fishermen used to catch brook trout in Smokies streams, but fishing for brookies is banned now because the population of the lovely little fish grew dangerously low.

broomcane *noun* Broom corn, a variety of cultivated sorghum (*Sorghum vulgare*) grown for its stiff, straw-like tassels, which are bound and made into brooms and brushes once the seeds are removed; its corn-like stalk can be tied around the handles of such implements. See also **broom sedge**, **corn broom**.

1982 DeArmond *So High* 31 The small amount of flat land was used for vegetables, sugar cane, broom cane, tobacco, and cotton. **1995** Trout *Historic Buildings* 42 Many farmers grew broom corn, a stiff variety of sorghum used to make bristles that were tied around a wooden handle.

broom sage See **broom sedge**.

broom sedge (also *broom straw*) *noun*

A Variant form *broom sage* [see **c1960** at **B**].

[probably a folk etymology]

B A coarse wild grass (*Andropogon virginicus*) that is dried, cut, and tied with twine into brooms, baskets, and other objects. It often grows in open woods and abandoned fields. Same as **sedge grass**. See also **hearth broom, sedge broom**.

1900 Harben *N GA Sketches* 136 He's a-courtin' of 'er like a broom-sedge field afire. **1939** Hall *Coll* (Proctor NC) *broom sedge* = same as sage-grass. Old timers used to use it for brooms to sweep off yards with. The best thing I saw it used for was hens' nests. It's the most dangerous fire hazard in the [National] Park. **c1960** Wilson *Coll*: *broom sage* = universally used; *broom sedge* is known, but is literary. Also called *sage grass*. **1968** Wilson *Local Plants* 322 Andropogon sp. Broomsage tea was a specific for whooping cough.

[DARE *broom sedge* n chiefly South, South Midland]

broomstick *noun*

1 See **broomstick marriage, jump the broom.**

2 See citation.

1939 Farr *TN Mt Regions* 89 = a wife: "Sally's been my broomstick for goin' on forty year."

broomstick marriage *noun* A common-law marriage, sanctioned by the community (and sometimes celebrated at a *broomstick shindig*) but not having the certification of a marriage bond or license obtained from the county. See also **jump the broom**.

1997 Montgomery *Coll*: *broomstick shindig* = a community gathering where a couple exchanged vows, joined hands, jumped over a broom, and received the full support of the community in which they lived, if a preacher could be found with enough courage to marry the couple without a license issued by the county government. The couple was then said to be "married by Grace, by a broomstick and by God" (Brown); *broomstick marriage* = figurative use only, did not involve actual broomstick (Bush), = a term not used by the couple but by others to describe a marriage not solemnized by clergy, also used by children for a mock or play marriage ceremony (Cardwell).

broomstick shindig See **broomstick marriage.**

brother *noun* See also **sister**.

A Variant plural forms *breetherin, brethering, brethern, brethren, brethrens, britheren, brotheren, brutherin, bruthering, bruthern, bruthring.*

c1807 (in **2007** Davis *Co Line Baptist* 114) we send our beloved brethering John hall David watson & John acuff Messengers to petition In our behalf. **1850** *Pawpaw Hollow Church Minutes* 144 The Brethering that was apointed to atend at Rocky Valley Church reports that after hearing the matter red and due consideration be thought to have nothing to do with the matter. **1852** (in **1998** Bueker *Head Letters* 17) I will fother inform you that the brotheren and Sisters of Wottager and Stoney Creek Senses ther best respects and well wishes to you. **1859** Taliaferro *Fisher's River* 208 Bruthering and sisters, sing a mighty sperritul hyme, and lift up yer hearts in prayer. **1890** Fruit *KY Words* 67 *bretheren* = for brethren. Sometimes pronounced "britheren" and "brutherin" and "breetherin"; "I tell you, breetherin and sisterin." **1899** Frost *Ancestors* 317 There may be some in other churches as don't know no better, and the Lord may, now an' then, take pity on some of 'em. But, brethering, mine's the reg'lar way. **1950** Bray *Disappearing Dialect* "Hunderd," "brethern," and "childern" are highland survivals of the pronunciations used by the best English speakers of the seventeenth and eighteenth centuries. **1989** *Matewan OHP*-9 The Bible says, "Call the older ones Elder and the younger ones Brethrens." **2007** McMillon *Notes*: *brethering, bruthern, bruthring.*

B Senses.

1 A male fellow church member (often but not necessarily one who is licensed to preach). The term is used as a title or as a form of address with either the given name or the surname, often to express solidarity and spiritual kinship.

1799 *Globe Creek Church Minutes* 3 No Member of the Church Shall Address another M[ember by] Any other term or Appelation but the title of brother or sister. **1837** (in **1990** Bush *Ocona Lufta Baptist* 22) We admit of no other title than brother or sister in addresses to each other while ingaged in business. **1881** Pierson *In the Brush* 6 That is our devoted and beloved young Brother [C]. His soul is all on fire with love for his Master. **1941** Stuart *Men of Mts* 90 [I] don't think they'll be any terbacker raised there if old Brother Toady Leadingham is right. **1973** GSMNP-86:23 The only thing I know is what I hear from a fellow like Brother Stinnett here. *Ibid.* 86:34 Brother Dan Abbott . . . just spoke in there a while ago, and all the congregation standing there. **1973** *Serpents* 38 I told'em not t'bring'em in because these brothers in th'church had a little disagreement an' weren't a'feelin' good towards each other. **1990** Bush *Ocona Lufta Baptist* 34 Brother Conner moved his membership to the Shoal Creek Baptist Church in 1850 and was licensed to preach the Gospel in July 1858. . . . Known to everyone as Brother Henry, he and his wife, Rachel Gibson, were servants of God at Lufty Baptist from 1860 until the time of their deaths. **2002** Carter *Chaney Creek* 11 It has been an honor to have Brother Clyde behind the pulpit of Mt. Pleasant Baptist Church and preach to our people. **2009** Callahan *Work and Faith* 44 Members of mountain churches referred to each other as "brother" and "sister" suggesting that church membership was considered an extension of membership and a form of fictive kinship, tying the church community to the home community and structures of authority. **2017** *Blind Pig* (Oct 12) He was a Deacon in a church where near everyone was called Brother or Sister, even the local postman or service station attendant.

2 Especially a preacher, usually an unpaid one; the term is used as a title with either the given name or the surname or used in direct address.

1860 *Toe Valley Church Minutes* 48 Ordered by the church that Brother Robbert McCracking bea invited to our next meeting. **1881** Pierson *In the Brush* 19 I was introduced by my host to Brother M, the "preacher in charge," and received from him an old itinerant's cordial shake of the hand and welcome to his circuit. **1901** Harben *Westerfelt* 276 It was all the Lord's doin's, Brother Tim said, to show him the true light. **1942** Posey *Frontier Baptist* 7 A church member based his opposition [to a paid ministry] on the reason that God had ordained that the Gospel be dispensed free of charge, and that even though Brother Barnes had ridden a long way to preach he should have no pay, for others had ridden just as far to hear him.

c1960 Wilson *Coll* We're a-goin' to build a bresh arbor for Brother Jones to preach in. *Ibid.* = title for an unprofessional or part-time lay preacher. **1982** *Foxfire VII* 279 Brother Cookman introduces the evangelist, Brother Clendennon, who is from Texas. **1989** *Matewan OHP-28* You'd say, "Brother Richard, should I go to the doctor?" I'd say, "now that's up to you." **1990** Bush *Ocona Lufta Baptist* 34 Brother Conner moved his membership to the Shoal Creek Baptist Church in 1850 and was licensed to preach the Gospel in July 1858. . . . Known to everyone as Brother Henry, he and his wife, Rachel Gibson, were servants of God at Lufty Baptist from 1860 until the time of their deaths. **1998** *Dante OHP-61* Brother Losloe Edwards and Fred Edwards is holding the awfullest revival over at the little old church in Castlewood I reckon ever was.

[DARE *brother* n B1 = preacher, chiefly South, South Midland]

brotheren See **brother A**.

brother to See **to 4**.

brought-on *adjective* Same as **fotch-on**.

1 (also *brung-on*) Of bread, clothes, or other goods brought from outside the mountains: commercially produced rather than homemade. See also **store A**, **store-bought**.

1895 Edson and Fairchild *TN Mts* 370 The clothes you have on I see are *brought on*. **1911** Shearin *E KY Word-List* 537 *brung-on* = newly arrived or imported; applied to new-comers, or to styles and methods lately introduced; e.g., "a brung-on suit of clothes": "Is he brung-on or is he a citizen?" **1917** Kephart *Word-List* 409 This here *brought-on* meat ain't noways as good as home-made meat. **1937** Eaton *Handicrafts* 60 The "brung on" cotton warp and woolen yarn were inferior to the old homespun. **1940** Bowman *KY Mt Stories* 235 *brought on* = goods manufactured or brought from town. **1957** Broaddus *Vocab Estill Co KY* 11 *brought-on bread* = bread bought at the store. **1966** Dakin *Vocab Ohio River Valley* 320 Mountain people from the headwaters of the Licking and the Kentucky southward use the distinctive expression *brought-on (bread)*. *Brought-on* is not used only or even primarily for bread, but is a descriptive phrase applied to many things if purchased rather than homemade. Several speakers report hearing, but do not admit using, *fotched-on*. **1971** Fetterman *People Cumberland Gap* 596 "Little things, I make them myself," he said, "No use for brought-on tools." "Brought on" means store-bought, and on farms such as John Caldwell's 300 steep acres, things like hoes, plow blades, rakes, hinges, knives, even furniture, are usually made as the need arises. **1974** Roberts *Sang Branch* 60 When they had more of any commodity than they needed for themselves, they sold it for money to pay taxes and to buy "brought on" necessities. **a1975** Lunsford *It Used to Be* 68 However, it [= wages] did help the man who cut the tan bark, or maybe the man who furnished the tree, to get a little salt, and maybe granulated sugar, or maybe shoes for his children, or things that had to be "brought on," that could not be produced on the farm. **1982** Slone *How We Talked* 14 Something "brought on" was anything coming from outside the hills. Anything not made at home was called "brought on."

[DARE *brought-on* ppl adj 1 chiefly South Midland]

2 Of a person: coming from outside the hills.

[See **1911** in **1**.] **1923** Furman *Mothering* 217 I asked them what they meant by "Old Christmas." "You brought-on women," said Taulbee, "thinks New Christmas is real Christmas; but it haint. Real Christmas comes to-morrow, on the sixth of January; and to-night is right Christmas Eve." **1938** Justus *No-End Hollow* 49 Granny continued to be suspicious of the brought-on teacher and her outlander notions, but regarded her much more highly when the children came home and told her about Rufe Farley getting switched for abusing a little boy. **1982** Slone *How We Talked* 14 Anyone coming from outside the hills was called a "brought on" person.

[DARE *brought-on* ppl adj 2 chiefly South Midland]

brow *noun* See citation.

2007 *Mining Terms* = a low place in the roof of a [coal] mine, giving insufficient headroom.

brown Beth *noun* The erect trillium (*Trillium erectum*). Same as **wake robin**.

1940 Caton *Wildflowers of Smokies* 18.

brown doper *noun* See citation. See also **dope 2**.

1981 Dumas *Appal Glossary* 17 I want a *brown doper* (Coca-Cola).

brown gravy *noun* A gravy made with broth or stock rather than milk.

2006 *Encycl Appalachia* 934 The majority of the common gravies are starch-bound, using either flour or cornmeal as a thickener. Most are also "white" as opposed to "brown" gravies, using milk instead of meat broth or stock as their liquid component.

brownie *noun* A penny.

1939 Hall *Coll* (Saunook NC) He hasn't got a brownie to his name. **1960** Stubbs *Mountain-Wise* (April–May) 11 He's so tight I couldn't get a brownie out of him. **1989** *Matewan OHP-9* [It] wouldn't be worth a brownie to you nor nobody else. **2008** Salsi *Ray Hicks* 24 We didn't mind the long walk to the Mast store when we knowed we could trade our spikes and come home with a stick of candy and a few brownies a jinglin' in our pocket.

brown lung *noun* See citation.

1973 Kahn *Hillbilly Women* 188 All she has to show for those years in the mill is brown lung, a serious respiratory disease known medically as byssinosis. Like the coal miner's black lung, brown lung is caused by unclean working conditions. Cotton mill workers' lungs are gradually filled with the fine dust that comes off the cotton as it is carded and wound and spun into cotton fabric which is used to make clothing.

bruise around *verb phrase* To go about.

1952 Wilson *Folk Speech NC* 523 = to go around slowly, with no particular aim. **c1960** Wilson *Coll*: *bruising around* = going with, associating with: "Ed has been bruising around among the women." **1997** Montgomery *Coll* (known to Brown).

[DARE *bruise* v 1 chiefly South, South Midland]

bruk See **break A1, A2.**

brung See **bring A.**

brung-on See **brought-on 1.**

brush

A Variant forms *brash, braysh, bresh.*

1824 Knight *Letter from KY* 106–7 Some words are used, even by genteel people, from their imperfect education, in a new sense; and others, by the lower classes in society, pronounced very uncouthly . . . bresh. **1862** *Spainhourd CW Letters* (Nov 10) we lie onder a bresh tent. **1863** *Reese CW Letters* (Jan 10) I send you A hair Bresh for the galls to keep slick hair and tha[y] must let Brug hav it to Bresh his Curls. **1913** Kephart *Our Sthn High* 278 Any other vowel may do for u: braysh or bresh (brush). *Ibid.* 331 He removed to Pineville, in another county, under guard of the two armed men, both of whom were shot dead "from the bresh." **1934–47** *LAMSAS* (Madison Co NC, Swain Co NC) *bresh.* **1939** Hall *Coll* (Little Cataloochee NC) The little bresh cracked above him, and he looked around and saw the bear. **1967** Hall *Coll* (Townsend TN) They used to have a brash fence. **1970** *Burton-Manning Coll*-94A He'd sow him a little bit of tobacco in there and throw some old pine brash on it. **1978** Slone *Common Folks* 303 We pronounce the word brush, meaning these limbs and twigs, as "brash."

[DARE *brash* (at *brush* n A2) chiefly South Midland, *bresh* (at *brush* A1) chiefly South, South Midland]

B *noun*

1 A small limb, especially one used to switch a child.

1940 Stuart *Trees of Heaven* 255 I jest got me a bresh and I whupped Boliver. **c1950** Adams *Grandpap* 149 She just grabbed up a brash an' hit at it. **1994** Montgomery *Coll* I'll take a brush to you (Shields).

[DARE *brush* n B3 chiefly South, South Midland]

2 See citation.

1930 Pendleton *Wood-Hicks Speak* 86 = greens served on the table.

brush arbor (also *brush harbor*) *noun* An improvised shelter at a clearing constructed of vertical poles secured in the ground or to trees, providing a framework over which leafy branches are piled for a roof, furnishing a temporary site especially for worship during the revival season. Same as **arbor, bush house.** See also **arbor meeting, brush meeting, meeting ground.**

1962 Dykeman *Tall Woman* 274 Mark believed he had found an answer on that Friday night in August under Gentry Caldwell's brush arbor. **1968** Miller *Pigeon's Roost* (July 25) I recall the last brush harbor meeting I now can think of was held in the upper section of Pigeon Roost Creek years and years ago. The public school building number two that had always been used for a preaching place too and when public school was no longer held in the building, it was sold to the highest bidder and torn down and all contents moved away. . . . At first the brush harbor was intended to have only day meetings in it but the interest right from the start was so great that there was several people because of their jobs could attend a night service that could not be there in the daytime. **1970** Mull *Mt Yarns* 65 A brush arbor would be built in a cleared area to keep off the sun and rain, and the whole countryside would convene in their wagons, buggies, on horseback, or on foot, complete with quilts, dogs, and vittles for an old fashioned "camp meeting." **1987** Trent *Yesteryear* 201 As a usual thing they were held in the open air, in tents or brush arbors (the latter being bowers of vines or branches of latticework covered with climbing shrubs or vines). This temporary structure kept off the sun but not the rain.

[DARE *brush arbor* n chiefly South, Midland]

brush arbor meeting See **arbor meeting.**

brush a road *verb phrase* See citation.

1964 Clarkson *Lumbering in WV* 357 = to cover with brush the mudholes and swampy places in a skid road, to make it solid.

brush broom *noun* A large broom usually of bundled twigs tied to the end of a handle, used to sweep the yard, clean a hay loft, etc.

1943 Justus *Bluebird* 135 Glory found herself a big brush broom and started to work beside Dovie, sweeping back the leaves and twigs—anything that could burn, leaving the ground bare. **1963** Watkins and Watkins *Yesterday* 38 Ma kept the bare clay yard swept clean with a brush broom. **1984** Wilder *You All Spoken* 32 = a yard broom made of dogwood boughs.

[DARE *brush broom* n[1] South, South Midland]

brush fence *noun* A makeshift fence of piled brush or tree branches or of cut brush high enough to deter cattle from leaving a pasture.

1962 Wilson *Folkways Mammoth Cave* 11 The most primitive sort of fence was made by chopping nearly down some small trees and bushes and arranging them in a sort of row, to make the *brush / bresh/* fence, which sometimes sprouted and grew and thus made itself even stronger. **a1975** Lunsford *It Used to Be* 59 A brush fence can't be made just anywhere. Where there's a good many saplings standing pretty thickly on the ground and the edge of woods or in the thicket, you can make a brush fence pretty readily. This is done by hacking down the saplings about three or four feet from the ground, let them lean over, and then cut another one a little ways from it. You have a fence that will last for some little while.

brush harbor See **brush arbor.**

brush horse *noun* A large limb used as a makeshift sled for dragging objects.

1957 Justus *Other Side* 92 It cheered her to hear Matt's cheery "halloo" as he approached with his brush horse, a slender young pine sapling with a thick and brushy top. . . . With Matt's help, Glory found a seat among the softest branches, and placed her feet among the crotches of the limbs which were most convenient for her. Then she seized a stout branch and held on tight with both hands, while Matt pulled the whole thing along as carefully as he could go. **1997** Montgomery *Coll*: *brush horse* (Brown, Bush).

brushing *verbal noun* See citation.

2007 *Mining Terms* = digging up the bottom or taking down the top [of a passageway in a coal mine] to give more headroom in roadways.

brush meeting *noun* An outdoor religious service held in a **brush arbor**. Same as **arbor meeting**.

1905 Miles *Spirit of Mts* 132 Far more picturesque are the "brush meetings," held in some charming nook of the woods.

brush whiskey *noun* Homemade whiskey.

1892 Dromgoole *Dan to Beersheba* 81 I air not honin' ter keep warm on bresh whiskey. **1913** Morley *Carolina Mts* 66 For corn is not only the principal food of the mountaineer, but supplies as well that important beverage, variously known as "corn-juice," "moonshine," "mountain-dew," "blockade," "brush whiskey," and in the outer world, "corn-whiskey," which is extracted from the grain and surreptitiously distributed. **1935** Murray *Schoolhouse* 75 For months he went in and out of Dawyer with brush whiskey masquerading as buttermilk.

[with reference to its manufacture in woods and thickets]

brute (also *brute beast*) *noun* Used as a euphemism for bull; also a male bear, etc. See also **boar B**, **cow brute**, **he-brute**, **male brute**, **stock brute**.

1892 Smith *Farm and Fireside* 55 [They were] running as fast as they could to get ahead of the brutes. **1913** Kephart *Our Sthn High* 295 Critter and beast are usually restricted to horse and mule, and brute to a bovine. A bull or boar is not to be mentioned as such in mixed company, but male-brute and male-hog are used as euphemisms. **1934** Parke *Sthn Highlander* 10 "Sometimes [the bears] do come down the valleys and kill brutes," here he referred to cattle. **1939** Hall *Coll* (Hazel Creek NC) [I] never did know a cow or brute [= a bull] caught in my life up there by a bear. *Ibid.* (Smokemont NC) [The hunt] was more fun to us than anybody would think because we was so interested in getting that brute [= a bear] that was a-killing our cattle up. **1949** Arnow *Hunter's Horn* 97 I allus say "brute" at school in class, but [in] th agriculture book it says "bull." **1949** Kurath *Word Geog East US* 37 In Western North Carolina . . . *brute* is the polite word for a bull. . . . [This expression is] not found elsewhere in the Eastern States. **1968** Wilson *Folklore Mammoth Cave* 14 [*Buck* is a] euphemism for the name of a male animal; some others are *brute*, *brute beast*, *daddy*, *he*, *male*, *old animal*, and *papa-cow*. **1980** *Smokies Heritage* 224 The mountain folks' name for a young steer [is a] "brute." **1996** Montgomery *Coll* (known to Ledford).

[DARE *brute* n chiefly South Midland, occasionally New England]

brutherin, **bruthering**, **bruthern**, **bruthring** See **brother A**.

bubby blossom See **bubby bush**.

bubby bush *noun*

A Variant form *booby bush*.

1994 Montgomery *Coll*: *booby bush* (Cardwell).

B A sweet shrub (*Calycanthus floridus*) whose reddish-brown flowers have a fruit-like fragrance and is so named from the custom of women putting it into their bosom as a perfume; hence *bubby blossom* = the flower of this plant; *bubby pod* = the seed pod of this plant. See also **Carolina allspice**, **sweet bubby**.

1893 Bergen *Plant Names II* 141 *Calycanthus glaucus*, bubby-bush. [**1913** Morley *Carolina Mts* 47 Another shrub that belongs to us and eastern Asia and that tempts one to nibble is what the people here call "sweet bubbies." It appears in old-fashioned Northern gardens under the name of sweet-scented or flowering or strawberry shrub.] **1943** Peattie *Men Mt Trees* 172 [An unimaginable plant] is strawberry shrub, with its dark red nipple-form flowers (called "bubby blossoms" by the mountain folk) and its strange odor, something like fermenting strawberries. **1964** Campbell *Great Smoky Wildflowers* 50 Shrubs up to 6 or 8 feet tall bear a profusion of deep maroon or brownish flowers. . . . This shrub [*Calycanthus floridus*] usually has a spicy fragrance. . . . It generally grows on stream banks and moist, wooded slopes at elevations below 3,500 feet. Other names [of sweet shrub] are bubby-bush and Carolina allspice. **1973** *GSMNP-78*:7 Bubby pod was a little pod that growed on a little bush. It wasn't a tree. It was actually a bush, and this little bubby pod was very poison to animals, of course the bigger the animal, the more the bubby pod, the pod had lots of little seeds, on the inside of the pod, and they claimed seven of these seeds would kill a sheep. **1980** *Smokies Heritage* 153 We called sweet shrub "bubby bush" back then, "bubbies" being our mountain word for bosom. **1994–96** Montgomery *Coll* (known to Jones, Ledford, Oliver), = a fragrant flower, often put in a woman's bosom, always pronounced *booby bush* (Cardwell).

[DARE "from resemblance of the flower to a *bubby* 'woman's breast'"; *bubbybush* n southern Appalachians]

bubby pod See **bubby bush B**.

buccaneer *noun* Same as **copper pot**.

1985 Dabney *More Mt Spirits* 154 The copper pot "mother still" is found in three configurations—the "turnip," round and fat; the "half turnip," and the upright copper pot, shaped like a metal drum and placed vertically in the furnace. It is also called the Buccaneer, the Blockade Still and the "mountain teapot." The American copper pot is very similar to the "poit du" (black pot) stills on display in the Highland Folk Museum in Scotland and the Poteen stills in Ireland.

buck *verb*

1 (also *buck up*) See citations. See also **bucker**.

1964 Clarkson *Lumbering in WV* 357 = to cut a tree into logs of suitable length after it has been felled. **1973** Schulman *Logging Terms* 35 *bucking* = cutting a tree-length log into transportable lengths. On the Upper Cumberland [River] logs were bucked into lengths ranging from ten to thirteen feet. **1998** Farwell *Logging Terms* = to cut the limbs from a felled tree. To slow a log down, brush might be hooked up to it the same way as it was before it was cut, before it was bucked up. . . . They might have a buckin' saw that they used to buck with.

2 See citation.

1890 Fruit *KY Words* 63 *buck a fellow* = to take a boy and swing him against a tree.

[DARE *buck* v[1] B 6c chiefly South Midland]

buck agger(s) See **buck ague**.

buck ague *noun*

A Variant forms *buck agger(s)* ['ægɚ(z)], *buck aguer* [see **1927** in **B1**], *buck akers* ['ækɚ(z)], *buck-eggers* [see **1941** in **B1**].

1934–47 LAMSAS (Swain Co NC) *buck agger*. **1942** Hall *Phonetics Smoky Mts* 79 *buck agger, buck akers*.

B Senses.

1 (also *buck fever*) Nervous excitement of a hunter (especially an inexperienced one) at the sight of game, especially in firing a gun at a deer. See also **bear ague**.

1883 Zeigler and Grosscup *Heart of Alleghanies* 159 Jake Rose had selected for him an excellent stand; admonished him to keep his eyes peeled, his gun cocked, and not take the "buck-ague" if a deer shot by him. **1927** Mason *Lure of Smokies* 169 He'd shoot like he had the buck aguer an' thet's the wust thing I c'd imagine a feller being plagued with! **1939** Hall *Coll* (White Oak NC) He had the buck aggers. He missed his shot at the squirrel. **1941** Stuart *Men of Mts* 144 "I killed seventy-two mallard ducks," he says, "in one hour and forty-five minutes. I took the buck-eggers." **1966–68** *DARE Survey* (Brasstown NC, Burnsville NC, Maryville TN) *buck ague* = excitement of hunter who can't shoot when he sees game. **1996–97** Montgomery *Coll*: *buck ague* (known to Bush); *buck fever* (known to nine consultants from the Smoky Mountains).

2 The chills and fever of malaria. See also **ague B**.

1960 Hall *Smoky Mt Folks* 60. **1967** Stuart *New Wine* 20 When settlers swarmed into this area, up from the seaboards of Virginia and North Carolina and down from the East, from New England and Pennsylvania, they settled in the low valleys. They didn't stay in the valleys long. They were afflicted with what they called the "Buckaggers," an ague, which came in three stages: chills, fever and sweating. The "buckaggers" they thought was caused by the cool damp air and not enough sunlight in the valleys. They chilled until their bones rattled and they had to go to bed. These men and women filled with pioneer spirit, people who had the will not to be whipped, people without Government handouts, took to the high ground where they built new homes from large trees they cut on clearings. They made roads of a sort, perhaps good enough for a joltwagon or a hugmetight in the dry seasons of the year. In winter they were usually closed in without access to a local village or town. They were fleeing from the dreaded "buckaggers." For this dreaded disease, they put spirits which they had distilled from their corn in boneset tea (often more spirits than tea), drank it as hot as the patient could stand, went to bed, under a pile of quilts. This was called breaking the spell of the "buckaggers." The "buckaggers" turned out later to be a form of malaria fever. **1960** Hall *Smoky Mt Folks* 60.

[*buck* "male deer" + *ague* "a fit of shivering, as from a fever"]

buck aker(s) See **buck ague**.

buck and wing, buck and wing dancer See **buckdance**.

buckberry *noun* Any of various small, fruit-bearing shrubs whose tart berries are made into jams and jellies.

1824 (in **1912** Doddridge *Notes on Settlement* 72) An indifferent kind of fruit, called buckberries, used to grow on small shrubs on poor ridges. This fruit has vanished from the settled parts of the country. **1901** Lounsberry *Sthn Wild Flowers* 396 About the juicy, acrid taste of the buckberry's fruit there seems to be some diversity of opinion. Many regard it as more delicious than any other of the genus. . . . Again it is thought to be a trifle "puckery." **1929** Kephart *Smoky Mt Magic* 43 On the ridges huckleberry and buckberry and thornless gooseberry bushes grew thick as hair on a dog's back. **1977** Hamilton *Mt Memories* 52 Then there was a berry growing in our woods that we had never seen before. It was called "buckberry" and grew on a bush a little like a big huckleberry bush. The berries were smooth, round, black, and very sour, but they made good jelly.

buckdance (also *buck and wing, buck dancing*) *noun* Traditionally, a style of improvisational solo step dancing performed with music (but occasionally without, as at interludes between sets of square dancing), its duration depending on the inspiration of the dancer. It is performed variously on the ball of the foot, on the toes, or on the heels, with feet close to the floor, the torso usually straight, and the arms often swinging loosely at the side. See 1983 and 1993–94 citations; hence verb phrase *buck dance* = to perform such a dance, nouns *buck dancer, buck and wing dancer* = a performer of the dance. See 1983 and 1993–94 citations. See also **clogging, flatfoot**.

1959 Hall *Coll* (Hartford TN) The older people would let the younger people gather and do the seasonal canning or processing of food and promise them that afterward they could have a little social life in the form of doing the buck [and] wing or the hoedown. **1975** *Fiddle Making* 309 Sometimes somebody'd jump out there an' buck dance a little, anybody who could buck dance. **1983** Matthews *Cutting a Dido* 32 From the early days of square dance to the present, a special time has been set aside for the virtuoso dancers of the community to dance alone, uninhibited by the group maneuvers of the square dance. These solo dancers are called buckdancers or buck and wing dancers, and they usually dance in a traditional style with their feet low to the ground with minimal movement from the waist up. . . . Buckdancers can be male or female. *Ibid.* 51 The cue for a buck dance occurs when the musicians, playing banjo, fiddle, guitar and almost any other instrument the band wants to play, even snare drum, begin to make music yet the caller does not call for a square dance. The music that is being played is clearly square, not round, dance music. Usually five or six dancers will come up as close to the music as they can and stand in a loose approximation of a circle. One dancer at a time will take the lead and move toward the center of the circle "strutting his stuff" while the other members of the circle will tone down their dance in a manner similar to that of a jazz riff. . . . Each dancer in the circle gets his/her chance to shine and is encouraged in a non-competitive manner by the other dancers. *Ibid.* 87 The buck dance is also an old style dance, stylistically identical to the old-time square dance, with the exception that the buck dance is performed outside the square dance context as a virtuoso solo dance. Buckdance is performed in relationship with other people, small groups gathered without holding hands, in a loose approximation of a circle, to best each other, but never with physical contact such as group figures. Buckdancing also sometimes is performed in competition, in which case dancers do not play off of one another, taking turns showing off, but rather line up and each is allowed a few minutes to dance alone. There is no caller for a buckdance. Each community is resplendent with square dancers, but only the best dancers, the smoothest, most versatile dancers with a wide variety of "steps" to show off, get up to dance during a buckdance. *Ibid.* 107 They just called it buck and wing, a toe dance, you know. Up on your toes pretty well with it. The buckdancing was up on your toes, 'cause a little shuffle went along with it. **1992** Seeger *Talking Feet* 9 Most dancers will agree that "flatfoot" is just a group of steps closer to the ground than "buck," but some will say that "buck" consists of certain steps done only up on the toes. *Ibid.* 42 John accepts local terminology for his dance: buck and wing. In this style, the person is up on their toes and the upper body shouldn't move very much. In a buck and wing, from the waist down should move. From the waist up actually shouldn't if you was in competition. In other words, you should hold your body pretty well straight if you were doing strictly the buck and wing. **1993–94** Jamison *Jubilant Spirit* 17 The first square dance teams starting in the late 1920s were made up of buckdancers, who kept a beat together, with each dancer doing his or her own steps. When precision dance teams started up in the 1950s, dancers began to synchronize their footwork, thus moving away from traditional Buckdancing and toward modern Clogging. . . . I think of Buckdancing as individual free-style dancing. No two dancers look the same or do the same steps. By definition, it is impossible to teach it to someone else. As they say, "it's caught, not taught." In both Buckdance and Flatfoot dance, the dancers seem to be sliding over the surface of the floor; in Buckdance up on the toes, and in Flatfoot, with more of a sliding appearance. **1995** Williams *Smoky Mts Folklife* 54 Flatfoot and the more high-step buck dancing existed as a solo dance form long before clogging came on the scene. . . . Within the competitive atmosphere of [Bascom Lamar] Lunsford's festival, the styles of flatfoot and buck dancing were married in the group formations of square dancing, and team clogging was born. **2009** Burton *Beech Mt Man* 94, 95 That's buck dance, flat foot, or whatever they call it—no partner. You just get up there and burn it up. Sometimes, others will join you. Sometimes, if you take anybody with you—if they can dance like that—they would join in. . . . He claimed he buck danced, but he did a lot of that fancy footwork. That ain't buck dancin', that's more cloggin' than it is buck dancing—he just didn't have taps on. He'd pick up his feet and do them circles with his feet, and buck dancing you don't do that. In buck dance you keep your feet right on the floor. And in flatfoot, you pick 'em up, but you don't do fancy footwork. **2009** *TN Encycl* The traditional dances of clogging and buckdancing are popular forms of percussive dancing that originated in the southern Appalachian mountains. . . . The leg is generally raised a little more than six inches off the ground in clogging, while the feet stay close to the ground in traditional buckdancing. **2014** Hicks *Driving* 41 After a nip of shine, Pap cut loose a buck and wing.

[DARE *buck-and-wing* n especially South, South Midland]

buck dancer, **buck dancing** See **buckdance**.

buck-eggers See **buck ague**.

bucker *noun* See citations. See also **buck 1**.

1964 Clarkson *Lumbering in WV* 357 = one who saws felled trees into logs. **2006** Farwell *Logging Term* 1021 Sawyers with their crosscut saws, called "misery whips" or "briars," formed [logging] crews with "buckers," who sawed timber in lengths.

buckeye *noun* A native of Ohio.

1973 Kahn *Hillbilly Women* 99 He's a buckeye but he acts just like a hillbilly. *Ibid.* 109 Whenever the buckeyes get mad at you the first thing they can think is to say . . . "you ain't nothin' but a briarhopper."

buckeye bark whiskey See **buckeye liquor**.

buckeye chestnut *noun* The buckeye (*Aesculus* spp), a large deciduous tree whose nut is carried purportedly to prevent arthritis and bring good luck.

[**1971** Krochmal et al. *Medicinal Plants Appal* 38 The bark is reported to have value as a tonic and febrifuge. Traditionally, people of Appalachia have carried a nut to prevent arthritis.] **1994–97** Montgomery *Coll* = so called to differentiate the tree from the chestnut, i.e. *Castanea* (Cardwell), = buckeye (Shields).

buckeye flat *noun* A relatively open, level area in the mountains in which **buckeye chestnut** trees once thrived. Same as **chestnut flat(s)**. See also **flat**, **flatwoods**.

1981 *Smokies Heritage* 26:11 Old-timers contend that the best places to search for ramps are in buckeye flats where the woods are rich and damp; near little creeks always lying in the shade, or within moist woods where the maple tree abounds. **1996** Montgomery *Coll* (known to Cardwell).

buckeye liquor (also *buckeye bark whiskey*, *buckeye whiskey*) *noun* See 1997 citation.

1856 *Athens Post* (TN) 4 July [2]/1 For ourselves, we have every confidence in these assurances, and protest against the practice of crediting cholera with what in most cases belong to a too free use of logwood brandy and buckeye whiskey. **1940** Haun *Hawk's*

Done 118 [He] kept on drinking till he got too much of Ad's old buckeye liquor. **1997** Montgomery *Coll*: *buckeye bark whiskey* = inferior whiskey whose process of fermentation has been hastened by putting buckeyes, an inedible mountain nut, into the corn mash (Ledford).

buckeye log See **jump the buckeye log**.

buckeye whiskey See **buckeye liquor**.

buck fever See **buck ague B1**.

buckle up to See **buck up to 1**.

buck oak *noun* Same as **chestnut oak**.

1972 *Hide Tanning* 182 In the spring of the year when the sap was up, they would strip bark off chestnut oaks (or "buck oaks" as R. M. Dickerson called them), and haul it to the place where the hides were to be tanned.

buck swamper *noun* See citation. See also **swamp, swamper**.

1994 Farwell and Buchanan *Logging Terms* = in logging, the boss of a crew cutting trees and brush off a new road being built.

buck tongue See **deer-tongue**.

buck up See **buck 1**.

buck up to *verb phrase*

1 (also *buckle up to, buck up against*) To defy, stand up to.

1859 Taliaferro *Fisher's River* 176 [He] buckled up to the 'squire, like a little dog does to a big one when he wants to show out. *Ibid.* 177 I tell you the train-ile [= perspiration] streamed out'n both on us, but Sol buckled up ter me like a man. **1957** Baughan *Tarheel Talk* 285 To *buck up to* somebody means to talk or act as good or as big as that somebody, hence "act big dog." **c1960** Wilson *Coll* = to defy, tell off: "He just bucked up to that big boy who hit him." **1971** *AOHP/ALC*-33 Did any of the students ever try to buck up against the teacher? **1987** Young *Lost Cove* 194 The blasted machine [i.e. an early automobile] wheezed, sneezed, snorted and threw blue smoke all over town. Hound dogs that would buck up to a bear tucked their tails between their hind legs and ran for dear life. **1996–97** Montgomery *Coll* (known to Brown, Bush, Cardwell, Cypher, Hooper).

2 See citation.

c1960 Wilson *Coll* = to "pay court to."

buck vine *noun* A trailing evergreen plant (*Mitchella repens*) whose roots have medicinal uses.

1971 *AOHP/ALC*-147 For the hives on a baby, you used the wild rosy roots or what's called a buck vine. It grows on rocks, has a little tiny red berry in the winter, and hit would cure that. **2006** *Encycl Appalachia* 849 Baby berry, often called buck vine or partridge berry, and tea made from cotton roots, ginger, or mayapple were said to induce premature labor.

buckwheat *verb* See citation.

1967 Parris *Mt Bred* 133 The word Buckwheat to a logger means "to hang up" or fell a tree so that it catches against another instead of falling to the ground.

buckwheat cake *noun* A pancake made from buckwheat flour.

1957 Parris *My Mts* 109 They are memories of buckwheat cakes with sorghum molasses and fresh home-made sausage of a winter morning, of Grandpa sitting at the big table in the kitchen and bowing his head and saying the blessing. **1995** Montgomery *Coll* (known to Cardwell), = the usual term for a pancake. In the early days pancakes were often made of buckwheat (Oliver).

[DARE *buckwheat cake* n chiefly Great Lakes, Appalachians]

buckwheater *noun* See citation.

1905 Pinchot *Logging Terms* 31 A novice at lumbering. **1905** *Pittsburgh Post* 32 On the other hand, to be a "buckwheater" is to be scorned of men, for the term is applied in the Appalachians to the novice.

buckwheat note *noun* Same as **shape note**.

[**1933** Jackson *White Spirituals* 419 The shape-noters have from the beginning had to defend their practices. When it was a matter merely of one notation against another, the controversy took the form of mutual ridicule. The adherents to the traditional notation called the rural innovation "buck-wheat grains."] **1957** Parris *My Mts* 204 He was a wandering troubador of the shaped-notes, sometimes referred to as "buckwheat notes" because in his own song book the heads of the various shapes were somewhat suggestive of buckwheat kernels. **1984** Allison *Character Notes* 86 Compared to other folk customs, this use of shape-notes to learn tunes and provide music for the church services had a very short existence—a little more than enough to span three or four generations. So, one can understand why the term "buckwheat" notes and its progeny have not evoked the response from the professional recorders of history. **1995** Montgomery *Coll* (known to Ledford). **2002** Goff *Sthn Gospel* 307 Another derivative was "buckwheat note," also derisive and supposedly named from the diamond shape of the character note "mi."

[from the shape of the musical notes]

Bud[1] *noun* See citation.

1915 Dingus *Word-List VA* 181 = often used instead of the Christian name: "Uncle Bud's a comin' to our house."

bud[2] *verb* Of an animal: to feed upon (the buds of trees); to feed an animal (the buds of trees).

1937 Hyatt *Kiverlid* 9 He knew what time of day fish would bite, and the kind of weather the squirrels would be "budding" the trees. **1964** Cooper *History Avery Co* 11 The fact that most of the land for more than a hundred years was "open"—unfenced—made for cheap grazing of cattle and sheep and the raising of hogs. When there was no fodder for the cattle in winter and early spring, they were "budded" by letting them eat the tender tips of the branches of felled linden trees.

budget

A Variant form *boodget* ['b®wt].

1993 Ison and Ison *Whole Nother Lg* 8 *boodget.*

B *noun* A pouch; a bundle or parcel, especially one of clothes tied together for travel.

1913 Kephart *Our Sthn High* 295 Some highland usages that sound odd to us are really no more than the original and literal meanings, as budget for a bag or parcel. **1931** Owens *Speech Cumberlands* 90 = a little bundle of clothing tied up in a bandanna or in a breakfast shawl: "There comes Aunt Rachel Fry with her little budget." **1940** Haun *Hawk's Done* 148 One day she came out with a budget under her arm and said, "Wilbur, I'm a-sending something to your Ma." **c1950** Adams *Grandpap* 59 She got up out of the chair an' started gatherin' up her things. An' she got 'em all together an' tied 'em up in a little budget. **1966** Frome *Strangers* 240 He remembered the story of how his grandfather came across the mountain from Car'liny, toting a "budget" of clothes on his hog rifle. **1981** Williams *Storytelling* Then she fixed him a little budget of grub [to] last him about three days. **1997** Miller *Brier Poems* 41 He'd break a little garden ground in spring, leave the tending to his wife and younguns, and in the slack time strike out with a little budget and work a spell in timber.

[OED3 *budget* n 1 obsolete except dialect; Web3 *budget* n 1 now dialect; DARE *budget* n 1 chiefly Appalachians]

bud out *verb phrase* Of a girl: to begin to show signs of puberty. See also **blossom out 1**.

1994 Montgomery *Coll* (known to Cardwell, Ogle).

Buffalo head *noun* See citation.

1983 Irwin *Guns and Gun-Making* 28 When I first saw this tool many years ago, I was told that it was a dumb anvil, a term I have heard several times since. My friend and fellow collector, W.G. Lenoir, refers to it as a buffalo head, but I suppose the more correct name is a "Swage block." It, of course, is used to shape various-sized rods and bars by hand, as well as to make spoons and ladles in the round and oval depressed areas.

buffalo nut *noun* The oilnut (*Pyrularia pubera*), a parasitic shrub. Same as **tallow nut**.

1901 Lounsberry *Sthn Wild Flowers* 148 Not until the buffalo-nut had been experimented with at Biltmore was it successfully propagated. **1982** Stupka *Wildflowers* 22 This is a common shrub in the southern Appalachian forest, especially where oaks are dominant at elevations up to 4,000 feet. . . . "Tallow-nut" and "buffalo-nut" are other names for it. **2010** *BearPaw* 3 Buffalo-nut (Pyrularia pubera) [is] a common resident of low and mid-elevations in the Smokies and throughout the Appalachians from Alabama to Pennsylvania. Buffalo-nut is typically found in dry oak woods and sometimes cove hardwood forests, where it parasitizes a range of tree roots, including hemlocks. To many people it may appear more like a sapling than a full-grown plant. . . . Early Cherokees called the plant "colic ball" in reference to the medicinal roots they found for it. There are other common names aplenty, including oil nut, elk nut, mountain coconut, rabbit-wood—even mother-in-law nut. This latter name refers to the poison that a beleaguered husband may have fed to his nemesis. "Buffalo-nut" likely comes from early white settlers who witnessed woodland bison eating the fruits in winter.

bug *verb* To rid (a plant) of insect pests.

1917 Kephart *Word-List* 409 = to kill bugs on. "Jim's out *buggin'* taters." **c1926** Cox *Cullowhee Wordlist* = to kill bugs, as on potatoes. **1994–97** Montgomery *Coll* (known to nine consultants from the Smoky Mountains).

bugaboo *noun* See citation.

c1960 Wilson *Coll* = ghost or some nonsensical fear: "She's always scared of some bugaboo."

[DARE *bugaboo* n 1 especially South, South Midland]

bug day *noun* See citations.

1939 *FWP Guide NC* 98 Pa was a-plantin' his potatoes when Alex come along and says, "Mr. Jones, stop right where you are. Them 'taters won't git a chanct to make. The bugs'll git 'em. This here is bug day." Naturally Pa stops and waits till bug day has passed. **1972** Cooper *NC Mt Folklore* 90 = days which should be avoided when planting potatoes to prevent bugs from destroying the green leaves.

bug dust *noun*

1 A highly volatile, flour-like carbon dust lingering after coal is blown free from a wall being mined.

1940 Still *River of Earth* 35 I wouldn't work in a coal mine if there was gold tracks running in. I'll be buried a-plenty when I'm dead. Don't want bug-dust in my face till then. **1959** Roberts *Up Cutshin* 17 Safety crews install fans and test the air gas, and lay down rock dust to keep the bugdust from exploding. **1973** Preston *Bituminous Term* 29 = particles of coal and other material that result from cutting, drilling, and shooting [a seam of coal]. **a1975** *Miners' Jargon* 1 = the fine particles of coal or other material resulting from the boring or cutting of the coalface by drill or machine. **1977** Shackelford et al. *Our Appalachia* 236 We'd take a long-handled shovel and shovel this "bug dust" out from under the coal. [Bug dust is] the fine coal, or the cuttings from the machine that crossed your face. It's what they call "carbon coal": they fire steam furnaces with it. **2002** Armstead *Black Days* 242 = fine particles of coal dust produced by cutting machines, continuous miners, and the longwall. **2006** Mooney *Lg Coal Mining* 1028 Many [coal-mining] terms make use of analogies to nature or to animals. . . . "Bug dust" refers to the fine particles of coal dust left lingering in the air after a section of coal is "shot from the face."

[DARE *bug dust* n 1 chiefly Midland coal-mining areas]

2 See citation.

1936 Farr *Folk Speech* 275 = cheap smoking tobacco: "Watch him puff the bug dust."

buggerbear See **booger A1**.

bugle *noun* Of a hunting dog: a yelp or howl when the trail of game becomes hot, a sound said to be distinctive for individual dogs; hence verb = to make such a cry. Same as **bawl A2**.

1972 Carson and Vick *Cookin* 2 58 Every man knowed his hound's voice, and when there was a chorus of bugling notes, men would say, "Thar goes Belle." **2009** Prewitt *Coon Hounds* 273 Coon hunters often describe the sound of their trailing dogs as a "bugle" or a "bawl."

bugleweed *noun* A water horehound (*Lycopus virginicus*). See citation.

1985 Dabney *More Mt Spirits* 41 Buck Carver of Rabun County, Georgia, on the other side of the Blue Ridge mountains, also attests to the flavor and popularity of fruit beer, which he sipped through the hollow weeds that he called "bugle weed." . . . Buck said mountain people would cut bugle weeds and use them as whistles.

bug light *noun* See citation.

a1975 *Miners' Jargon* 1 = flame safety light.

(**the**) **bugs** *noun* See citation.

1966 *DARE Survey* (Cherokee NC) = tuberculosis.

bug-wood (also *bug-wood chestnut*) *noun* See 1995 citation. Same as **wormy chestnut**.

1961 Seeman *Arms of Mt* 118 Thar hain't enough dead chestnut left worth gittin' even fer bug-wood. **1995** Montgomery *Coll* Bug-wood chestnut or wormy chestnut was sought for furniture because it gave a very attractive appearance, the small holes caused by bugs or worms disappearing during the finishing process (Shields).

buhr (also *burr*) *noun* A millstone.

1892 Doak *Wagonauts Abroad* 90 Here and there some quaint old mill, of a kind found only in the mountains, and of a type as old as settlements in these valleys, sat deep down in the rocky gorge, with wheel something after the turbine pattern, and arrangement with reference to the water, and an upright, perpendicular shaft conveying the power to the buhrs. **1944** Hayes *Word-List NC* 32 *buhr* = a millstone, the buhrstone (Buncombe County). **1945** O'Dell *Old Mills* 1 After the fanning process the wheat was washed and spread out to dry. Next it was ground on the "burr" or rock, after which it was sifted by hand through a sifter made of muslin stretched over a hoop. This was called a "sarch." **1981** Alderman *Tilson Mill* 29 Some types of grain, such as wheat and barley, required very hard stones for the best results; and burrstone rocks were often secured for this purpose. Then gradually all mill rocks used for grinding grain became commonly known as "burrs." **1991** *Smokies Guide* 13 The tub mill ground meal by means of two stone wheels or "burrs" which were water-driven by a hand-made wooden turbine wheel. **2006** *WV Encycl* 304 These mills commonly used rough circular revolving stones, called "buhrs" or "burrs," to grind grain, although a few crushed the grain with rollers or hammers. Most were erected on streams and used overshot water wheels.

[OED3 (at *burr* n[5]) c1330→]

build *verb* Variant past-tense and past-participle forms *builded*, *builted*.

1973 *AOHP/ASU-69* It was builted about nineteen and, hit was built about nineteen hundred and twenty-one. **1973** *Foxfire Interviews* A-73-86 They got their church finally builted. **1977** McGreevy *Breathitt KY Grammar* 93 *builded* = attested by 4 speakers. **1978** Slone *Common Folks* 237 [To wash our clothes] the water was either carried from the creek, or drawn from the well or spring. A wash tub or "mink" kettle was placed on two rocks, with a space between them where the fire was "builded."

building house *noun* A dwelling, in contrast to an outbuilding.

1944 Wright *Query* 10 Miss Nathalia Wright, in connection with some research on Lanier in the Montvale district, came across an old farmer who referred to a "building house" that had stood near there at one time.

bulger *noun*

1 A very large or remarkable thing.

1835 Crockett *Account* 37 [We] soon came in sight of the great city of New York, and a bulger of a place it is.

2 See citation.

1939 Hall *Coll* (Big Creek NC) I was eight year old when the Scottish Company came in. They logged on sleds and what they called bulgers. Bulgers are black gum logs.

3 (also *bulger wagon*) A wagon with wooden wheels, especially ones made for children's play. See 1989 citation.

1978 Dykeman and Stokely *Highland Homeland* 122 Boys such as these [in a photograph] in Happy Valley, Tennessee, still built and raced "bulger wagons." Every family had one or several of them. The wheels usually were made of black gum because that wood doesn't crack easily. **1985** *Pittman Comm* 140 Home made "bulger wagons," sleds, whistles, and slingshots were the delight of many boys. **1989** Smith *Flyin' Bullets* 52 A bulger-wagon had wooden wheels. They were sawed out and had a hole drilled through them. We'd put cold gravy on the axle and spin the wheel around a few times. We didn't have grease to grease the axle so we used gravy!—it would outrun any of them! **1997** King *Mt Folks* 35 Children made bulger wagons (a board with wooden wheels that was guided by placing the feet on the front axle and ridden down slopes).

bulger wagon See **bulger 3**.

bulk *noun*

A Variant form *boolk* [bulk].

1942 Hall *Phonetics Smoky Mts* 40 *Bulge* and *bulk* are always sounded with [u].

B The shape, outline, or size (of a person, animal, or object, especially one obscured or disguised).

1931 Combs *Lg Sthn High* 1304 Old Shade's nearly blind, but he can discern the bulk of a person. **1937** Hall *Coll* (Emerts Cove TN) I keep my pistol in my pocket so as to hide the bulk of it. **1939** Hall *Coll* (Proctor NC) John says "No, it's a bear . . . I can see the bulk of it." *Ibid.* (Hartford TN) The moon was a-shinin' bright. I seed somethin' squat down in the road, looked to be a good-sized bulk of something. **1953** Hall *Coll* (Bryson City NC) He said the bear come down the tree till it got where he could see the bulk of it. **1963** Edwards *Gravel* 105 The doctor could see the bulk of the rider sitting his mount just outside the bedroom window. **1979** *Big South Fork OHP-4* I could just see the bulk of him. He was about half bent.

bull

A *noun*

1 A male bovine (the term was traditionally avoided in polite or mixed company in the mountains in preference to such euphemistic usages as **animal B**, **beast B2**, **brute**, **cow brute**, **father cow**, **gentleman cow**, **he-brute**, **herd sire**, **jock**, **major**, **male**, **male brute**, **papa cow**, **steer**, **stock brute**). See also **boar B**.

1922 Kephart *Our Sthn High* 295 A bull or boar is not to be mentioned as such in mixed company, but male-brute and male-hog [are] used as euphemisms. **1939** Hall *Coll* (Saunook NC) "Cow brute" [was] used for a bull. [It is] still bad form in the Great Smoky Mountains to use the word "bull" in the presence of ladies. **1949** Kurath *Word Geog East US* 62 The plain term *bull* is current everywhere, and in the North Midland and New York State other expressions are rare. In New England, the South, and the South Midland, however, the plain term is not used by older folk of one sex in the presence of the other. Even many of the younger generation prefer the veiled expressions of the Victorian era. **1963** Arnow *Flowering* 144 Not many years ago some back-hill mothers who would have blushed at the word *bull*, saying *cow-brute* instead, used the four letter words of Shakespeare in discussing the bodily functions of their babies or the farm animals. **1963** Wilson *Regional Words* 81 A male of the cattle family was, only among men, a bull; elsewhere he was a *yearling* (regardless of his age), an *old animal*, a *steer*, or a *male-cow* (by very modest people). **1986** Pederson et al. *LAGS* = attested by 29/60 interviewees (48.3%) from E TN and 8/35 (22.7%) from N GA; 37/241 of all LAGS interviewees (15.3%) attesting usage were from Appalachia.

[DARE *bull* n 1 formerly often avoided as a taboo word especially in South, South Midland]

2 (also *bull of the woods*) See citations. See also **bull roar 2**.

1930 Pendleton *Wood-Hicks Speak* 86 *bull*, *bull of the woods* = a bully, a "tough guy." **1979** Carpenter *Walton War* 123 There was a "Woods Boss"—sometimes called the "Bull-of the-Woods," who was in charge of all the work, a cook who was responsible for the food (which Norton said was as good or better than any of the men had at home); and there was a man known as the "Lobby-hog." **2003** Triplett *Mt Roots* 59 "The Bull of the Woods" was the strongest, meanest, risk taking dominant man in the log camp. **2006** Farwell *Logging Term* 1021 Records indicate [logging] camp language was richly metaphoric. The boss, called a "bull," had to be tough, a "bull-roarer," or driver of men.

B *verb* Of a cow: to be in heat and to act like a bull.

1956 Hall *Coll* (Del Rio TN) That cow is a-bullin'. **1957** Broaddus *Vocab Estill Co KY* 12 When a cow is in heat, she puts her fore legs on the back of another cow and pretends she is a bull. This is called "bulling." **2005** Williams *Gratitude* 143 When a cow got to bullin' (come in heat), one of the boys'd have to go borry a bull, or take the cow . . . to get her bred. **2009** Wiles and Wiles *Location* 127 Since there were no bulls on the farm, the cows were driven up the road to breed with Grandpa James' bull. The cows would indicate their readiness to breed by "bullin"—mounting other cows in imitation of a bull.

[OED3 *bull* v[1] obsolete; DARE *bull* v chiefly South Midland]

bull bat *noun* The nighthawk (*Chordeiles minor*).

1939 Hall *Coll* = not the same as whippoorwill; ain't got the whiskers that the whippoorwill has. **1941** Still *Proud Walkers* 111 I recollect bull-bats soared overhead when we reached Shoal Creek in the late afternoon.

[DARE *bullbat* n 1 chiefly South Atlantic, Gulf States, Southwest, scattered South Midland]

bulldog *verb* See citation.

1949 Maurer *Argot of Moonshiner* 8 (also *dog*) = to heat used barrels by setting them against a large oil drum in which a fire is built in order to sweat out the whisky which has soaked into the barrel staves: ". . . bull-dog them barrels and get ten gallons of likker."

bulldog gravy *noun* See citations.

1932 (in **2012** Portelli *They Say* 185) "The principal food of the miners," Jim Garland testified, "is potatoes, beans and bacon—salt pork. Then, they make gravy. We call it 'bull dog gravy'": a mixture of water, salt, flour and grease, eaten with beans or with a "water sandwich" (bread soaked in lard and water). **1939** *FWP Guide KY* 436 The customary diet of the miner and his family consists chiefly of beans—and more beans—corn bread made without milk, and "bulldog gravy," a mixture of flour, water, and a little grease. **1969** *DARE Survey* (Honeybee KY) = joking name for thickened gravy made with meat juice and flour.

[DARE *bulldog gravy* n KY]

bullet *noun*

1 A pellet of sheep dung boiled to make a medicinal tea. See also **sheepball tea**.

1966 Frome *Strangers* 248 Sheep dung, or "bullets," boiled down and sweetened, was sometimes used to "break out" measles. **2004** Myers and Boyer *Walker Sisters* 54 Boiled or sweetened sheep dung, or "bullets," was supposed to "break out" measles.

2 See citations.

1981 Dumas *Appal Glossary* 16 = the developed bean pod (as opposed to the hull) of any bean that might be eaten shelled. "Cook 'em until the bullets'll mash" [i.e. be well done, tender]. **1996–97** Montgomery *Coll* (known to Brown, Bush), = pertains to any dried bean, not string beans (Cardwell).

bull fiddle *noun*

1 A type of noisemaker. See citation.

1964 Smith et al. *Germans of Valley* 102 Some men carried big saws, cow bells and occasionally a device they called a bull fiddle which made an unusual noise that could be heard a long distance.

2 A bass viol.

1994 Bluestein *Poplore* 127 Of course, they call it a fiddle but they really do a lot of violin stuff on it and add to that the big bull fiddle.

bull gang *noun* A crew of manual workers. See also **gin gang.**

1938 Stuart *Dark Hills* 138 My first work was with the gin gang. The "bull gang" it was called by many. We cleaned out manholes and laid sewer lines from the new privies the firm was building. We unloaded coke and coal by the trainload. We picked up scraps of rusty steel and sent it in on trucks to be worked over again. We pulled ragweed and crab grass from beside the long bright metal sheds with tops of glass. We worked ten hours each day. **1946** Stuart *Plum Grove Hills* 66 Crushing limestone rock at the quarry where my job was helping the other three on the "bull-gang" use the hand drill.

bullgrass *noun* A grass of the genus *Paspalum.*

1941 Stuart *Men of Mts* 66 Funny about the two little rocks down there in that corn balk with the bull-grass growing between them.

[DARE *bullgrass* n 1 chiefly South, South Midland]

bull grinder *noun* Same as **smoke grinder.**

1980 Wigginton *Foxfire VI* 161 Of course, bull grinders are the only name it had. I've heard them called do nothings and smoke grinders.

bull harrow *noun* Same as **gee whiz.**

1983 *Dark Corner OHP-4A* You'd plow it four or five times. The first time you'd take a little bull harrow, "gee whiz," they called it, and just scratch it, you know, little corn about that high, kill that little crab grass.

bull hives See **bold hives 1.**

bull hooker *noun* See citation.

1975 GSMNP-56:21 This "bull hooker" is the boss of the choker gang [in logging]. He was the one that gathered up the ends of the chokers and hooked to this link that lifted them up to the overhead cable.

bull nettle *noun* Same as **bold sage.**

1962 Hall *Coll* (Gatlinburg TN) = same as bold sage, used for the kidneys. [**1971** Krochmal et al. *Medicinal Plants Appal* 236 The berries, when properly prepared, have been used as diuretics, antispasmodics, anodynes ... and for epilepsy.]

bullnose *verb* To round off the end of (a log).

2008 Salsi *Ray Hicks* 15 Those who come to help bull nosed one end of each tree and skinned the bark off the underside so it'd slide off the mountain easy not catchin' too many snags.

bullnoser *noun* A bulldozer; hence verb *bullnoze* = to bulldoze.

1968 Ferrell *Bear Tales* 10 They are hacked out by bulldozers (called "bullnosers" in the mountains) and both roads and bridges are designed for the heavy-duty work of carrying loaded logging trucks. **1975** Gainer *Speech Mtneer* 7 They can make a sight of a road with that bullnozer. **1996** Woodring *Times Gone By* 8 I think some of them Sluder boys over there bullnozed the grave. **2000** Morgan *Mts Remember* 156 You could hear the bullnoser up there, working somewhere on the Knob.

bull of the woods *noun*

1 A foreman or top hand in a logging camp; see **bull A2.**

2 Hence a self-important person.

1994–95 Montgomery *Coll* (known to Cardwell, Shields).

[DARE *bull of the woods* n 2 = "self-important person" chiefly South, South Midland, Pacific]

bull pen *noun*

1 An outdoor children's game with one player on each of four corners who tries to hit players inside this area with a ball. See also **blind cat, cat 1, town ball, two-eyed cat.**

1915 Dingus *Word-List VA* 181 = a kind of ball game. **1972** Cooper *NC Mt Folklore* 61 The game of bull pen was played by any number of children, four of whom occupied bases forming a square, the others in the pen. After the ball was passed several times to allow it to become *hot* a player tried to hit one in the pen. Failing to do so, the unhit player took the thrower's base. [**1980** Wigginton *Foxfire VI* 278 You'd have at least eight players: four on a side. The game was played with a ball made of yarn, and we got our mother to sew around it to keep it from unraveling. If the ball was too light, sometimes we'd wrap the yarn around a core like a piece of wood to give it extra weight. The object of the game is to get all the men out on one team by hitting each one of them with the ball. One team of four players mans the bases, and the other players get in the center or in the bullpen.] [**1995–97** Montgomery *Coll* (unknown to consultants from the Smoky Mountains).]

2 A temporary jail for detaining individuals who have been arrested. Also called **pen[1] 2.**

1969 Lee *Bloodletting* 33 No "congregating" by the strikers was permitted. A military court was set up at the village of Pratt [WV] and a nearby freight house was converted to a temporary jail, which the strikers called a "Bull Pen."

[DARE *bullpen* n chiefly Midland]

3 See citation.

1964 Clarkson *Lumbering in WV* 357 = part of a sawmill just past the cut-off saws. Here timber is graded and tallied, then sorted on trucks for transport to the proper dock or dry kiln for stacking.

bull roar (also *bull roarer*) *noun*

1 A toy consisting of a wooden slat attached to a string that makes a loud hum or buzz when whirled in the air. See 1996–97 citations.

1972 Cooper *NC Mt Folklore* 34 For many decades and until stores became plentiful, the children's Christmas toys and gifts were mainly homemade. There were dolls, yarn balls, whistles, geehaw whimmydiddles or ziggerboos, rattle traps, noisemakers or bull roars and flipperdingers. **1996–97** Montgomery *Coll*: *bull-*

roarer = a whistle, whittled from wood or a green bark tree with a length of string tied to a springy green sprout, then swung around overhead (Brown), = a flat, elongated piece of wood attached to a string that, when whirled around, twisted and made a dull, loud noise (Jones).

[DARE *bull-roarer* n 1a chiefly South Midland]

2 Hence a loud braggart, domineering person.

1995–97 Montgomery *Coll* (known to Cardwell, Jones, Ledford). **2006** Farwell *Logging Term* The boss, called a *bull*, had to be tough, a *bull-roarer*, or driver of men.

bull's eye *noun*

1 A common field daisy (*Chrysanthemum leucanthemum*). Same as **ox-eye daisy**.

1937 Hall *Coll* (Cades Cove TN) = ox-eye daisy.

2 See citations.

1914 Arthur *Western NC* 263, When the logs were being placed in position they were lifted into place on the higher courses by means of what were called "bull's-eyes." These were made of hickory saplings whose branches had been plaited into rings and then slipped over the logs, their stems serving as handles for pulling, etc. **1969** Ferrell *Bear Tales* 34 In house raisings, higher logs were lifted into place by means of "bull's eyes" described by an early writer as being made of "Hickory saplings whose branches had been plaited into rings and then slipped over the logs, their stems (trunks) serving for handles for pulling."

bull snake *noun* The pine snake (*Pituophis melanoleucus*).

1967 Huheey and Stupka *Amphibians and Reptiles* 65 Some of the people residing in the adjacent farming areas know this serpent as the "Bull Snake."

bull-strong *adjective* Of a fence: sturdy enough to restrain a bull.

1942 Robertson *Red Hills* 209 "Boys," he shouted, "you got to keep your fences horse-high, bull-strong, and pig-tight."

[DARE *bull-strong* adj chiefly Midland]

bull toad *noun* A bullfrog.

1967 *DARE Survey* (Maryville TN).

bull tongue (also *bull tongue plow*) *noun* A simple one-horse plow using a single plow point or shovel that stirs but does not turn the soil, used especially on hillsides; the shovel of such a plow. See 1967 citation. Also called **hillside plow**. See also **boy Dixie**, **double-foot plow**, **laying-off plow**, **scooter plow**, **shovel plow**, **single foot A**, **three-foot(ed) plow**, **turner**.

1860 Olmsted *Back Country* 249 Where it [= the ground] becomes mossy, weedy, and thin, it is often improved by harrowing or scarifying with a small "bull-tongue," or coulter-plow, and meadows thus made and occasionally assisted, are considered "permanent." **1878** Coale *Wilburn Waters* 126 Little grubbing was done, and the roots were left in the ground to be torn up by the "bull-tongue" which was the first implement honored with the privilege of preparing the virgin soil for a crop. Often might be seen in one of these "clearings" a sovereign with his mule and bull-tongue, toiling, swearing and sweating, as his rude implement, striking a hidden root, would toss him into the air. **1897** Pederson *Mtneers Madison Co* 830 The mountaineer merely scratches the soil with a "bull-tongue" or single-shovel plow, and then drops his seed in the shallow furrows, a prey to the dry weather of mid-summer. **1913** Kephart *Our Sthn High* 37 The common plow was a "bull-tongue," which has aptly been described as "hardly more than a sharpened stick with a metal rim." *Ibid.* 42 For the rough work of cultivating the hillsides a single steer hitched to the "bull-tongue" was better adapted. **1966** Guthrie *Corn* 87 The simplest plow was the bull-tongue. This was made either by the farmer himself or by a neighboring blacksmith. It had a wooden beam or tongue, wooden curved handles, and a wooden foot with a wide iron point attached. . . . Once the soil was prepared for planting, the bull-tongue was used again to lay off the rows. **1972** GSMNP-93:39 Bull tongue, you know, that you put on your single foot. They was a shovel plow. In hard land you use that bull tongue and lay off your ground or loosen that to where it would be. A shovel plow they called it. Big wider plow maybe wasn't quite as big as a bull tongue, or three times as wide. **1973** GSMNP-4:10 I've plowed that with a bull tongue plow, all of it, with one horse, and raised a crop with what they call a bull tongue plow. It wasn't a turning plow, you know. It's just a straight, most people call layoff plow now. **1986** Pederson et al. *LAGS*: *bull tongue plow* = attested by 13/60 interviewees (21.7%) from E TN and 2/35 (5.7%) from N GA; 15/46 of all LAGS interviewees (32.6%) attesting term were from Appalachia. **1987** Carver *Regional Dialects* 167 Two types of plows he might use in setting his crop are a *double shovel plow*, which is simply a plow with two shovels or blades, and a *bull tongue plow*, which has a shovel shaped something like a tongue. Both terms have been in use since the early nineteenth century. **1995** Weber *Rugged Hills* 119 A bull-tongue plow looks like a spade turned backward. One pass with the turning plow and two with the bull-tongue and we had a pretty good ditch to lay pipe in. **1996** Spurlock *Glossary* 391 = a single-shovel plow [whose] shovel is small (6″ × 10″) and shaped similarly to a large tongue. A coulter (knife-like blade) is mounted to the beam of the plow in front of the shovel and functions to slice soil and roots in advance of the shovel.

[DARE *bull tongue* n 1 chiefly South, South Midland]

bullwhacker *noun* A driver of oxen that pull heavy objects, especially logs.

1984 Wilder *You All Spoken* 161 From drovers with bullwhips there was a progression in the language to "bullwhackers"—drovers who handled teams of oxen hitched to freight wagons. Their bullwhips usually had lashes a dozen feet long, and an expert with a bullwhip could flick the ear of a lead ox or mule, or a cigarette from the mouth of a girl performing in a sideshow. A duel between bullwhackers using bullwhips was a "lapjacket." **1991** *Smokies Guide* (Winter) 14 Employees with a variety of skills worked for the companies. There were woodhicks (loggers), gut robbers (cooks), bullwhackers (oxen drivers), engineers, blacksmiths, doctors, and other specialists. **2006** Farwell *Logging Term* 1021 "Hayburners," or horses, their "teamsters," and oxen driven by their "bullwhackers," all became outmoded, as did "crosspoling" logs across trails to make them sturdy and "swamping," or cutting, new trails to "snake" logs out of the forest.

bumberry *noun* See citation.

1982 Ginns *Snowbird Gravy* 116 There was an old name now, "bumberry." I wouldn't know what they call it anymore. They was bumberry briars up there, and they don't grow any blackberries. You can build a fence with 'em. It ain't nothing can get through 'em, that kind of briers.

[DARE *bumberry* n probably a variant of *brambleberry*]

bumblebee

A *noun* See citation.

1966 *DARE Survey* (Cherokee NC) = cockleburr.

B *adjective* Of a crop (especially corn): severely stunted in growth.

1919 Combs *Word-List South* 40 *bumblebee cotton* = cotton so low that the bees can lie on their back and suck the juice from the blooms. **1941** Stuart *Men of Mts* 14 Look at the corn . . . Bumblebee corn—a bumble-bee can't suck the tassels without his starn-end rubbing the ground! **1966** *DARE Survey* (Salem WV) [What's bumblebee corn?] Well, that's real short corn, where the bumble bees wear the ground out a-sitting on their hind ends and a-sucking on the tassels.

[DARE *bumblebee* adj South, South Midland]

bumblebee corn, bumblebee cotton See **bumblebee B**.

bumblebee whiskey *noun* See 1998 citation.

1867 Harris *Sut Lovingood* 33 I tuck me a four finger dost ove bumble-bee whisky. **1998** Montgomery *Coll* = cheap moonshine, made with blackstrap molasses, buckwheat, wheat shorts, dairy feed, even cotton seed meal (Brown).

bumble-headed *adjective* See citation.

1995 Montgomery *Coll* = of a person: from the remote parts of the mountains and therefore less refined in behavior (Norris).

bumblings *noun* Poor-grade, homemade whiskey (used as a term of derision referring to the effects of its consumption, especially a violent headache).

1913 Kephart *Our Sthn High* 137 Such decoctions are known in the mountains by the expressive terms "pop-skull," "bust-head," "bumblings" ("they make a bumbly noise in a feller's head"). **1997** Montgomery *Coll* (known to Brown, Bush).

bumbly *adjective* See citations.

1917 Kephart *Word-List* 409 = buzzing. "Hit makes a *bumbly* noise in a feller's head." **1995–97** Montgomery *Coll* (known to Brown, Bush, Cardwell, Shields).

bum bread *noun* Poor-quality bread.

1910 Essary *TN Mtneers* 70 For breakfast, he had bacon of the "swift" variety, "bum bread" and black coffee, while the same menu was served at the evening hour and produced his "nightmares" by night. **1980** *Smokies Heritage* 63 By and by, storekeepers started selling loaves of white bread, too. Folks around here called it "bum bread." Dad said it was because people would keep a slice or two to give out when folks knocked on the door asking for food. **1986** Pederson et al. *LAGS* (Washington Co TN) = store-bought bread; (Sevier Co TN) = week-old bread. **1997** Montgomery *Coll* = apparently a local term used in the Sugarlands (TN) area (Cardwell).

bumfuddle (also *bumfuzzle*) *verb* To confuse; hence participial adjective *bumfuddled* (also *bumfuzzled*) = confused.

1915 Dingus *Word-List VA* 181 *bumfuzzled* = confused. **1938** Stuart *Dark Hills* I didn't know you was that sharp after the way you bumfuzzled the Superintendant's office. **1987** Carver *Regional Dialects* 171 Two expressions from the lexicon [of Inland South speech] probably came from Pennsylvania with the Scotch-Irish. The humorous sounding *bumfuzzled* meaning "confused, perplexed, or flustered" may be related to Scots "bumbazed" (= stupefied). **1990** Cavender *Folk Medical Lex* 19 *bumfuddled* = having a confused mental state; also used as "bumfuzzled." **1993** Ison and Ison *Whole Nother Lg* 9 *bumfuzzled* = all mixed up about events or confused about directions. **1994** Montgomery *Coll*: *bumfuzzled* (Cardwell).

[DARE *bumfuddled* ppl adj, *bumfuddle* alteration of *bumfuzzle*, probably influenced by *befuddle*; DARE *bumfuzzle* v chiefly South, South Midland]

bumfuzzle(d) See **bumfuddle**.

bump

A *verb* See citation.

1997 Farwell *Logging* = to trim knots off a log after the tree is felled. "They had a fellow who trimmed knots off the log . . . he bumped knots."

B *noun*

1 A violent shifting of the wall, ceiling, or floor of a coal mine. Same as **mountain bump**.

1991 Shifflett *Coal Towns* 103–4 In Harlan County, Kentucky, in the early 1930s, a phenomenon called "bumps," caused by irresponsible pulling of pillars, emerged; pillars would be left standing in areas where coal was thin, while all those around them were removed, thus causing shifts in weight distribution and pressure and "a sudden, violent expulsion of coal from one or more pillars accompanied by a loud report and earth tremors." **1997** *Dante OHP*-53 I had a brother that was in that bump. He was braking on a motor for Marion Hardy. *Ibid.* 71 You never know when a big bump was going to come or a big fall out or something. **2006** Hicks *Mt Legacy* 146 The coal that shot out from a bump could hurt you badly. I saw piles of coal after a bump occurred close by. **2006** Lalone *Coal Camps* 150 Mining injuries due to slate falls, mine "bumps," or equipment/machinery accidents were common for individual miners, and mine explosions could take the lives of many men at one time. **2007** *Mining Terms* = a violent dislocation of the mine workings which is attributed to severe stresses in the rock surrounding the workings.

2 See citations.

1956 McAtee *Some Dial NC* 7 = pimple. **c1960** Wilson *Coll* = pimple, boil, hickey.

[DARE *bump* n 1 chiefly South, South Midland]

bunch bean *noun* Any green bean tending to grow in bunches. See also **pole bean**, **runner bean**, **stick bean**.

1946 Matthias *Speech Pine Mt* 189 = bush string beans. The explanation given by the mountain people is that these beans grow in bunches on the plant, or that one picks them in bunches. **1956** Hall *Coll* (Gatlinburg TN) [What are the different kinds of beans?]: Bunch beans, cornfield beans, stick beans, shuck beans (leather britches). **1957** Broaddus *Vocab Estill Co KY* 12 = green beans from the type of bean plant that grows to about two feet high and stands alone, as opposed to stick beans. **1994–97** Montgomery *Coll* (known to Shields), = the basic distinction between various kinds of green beans seemed to be pole beans, running beans (including corn-field beans), and bunch (or the newer term "bush") beans (Ellis).

[DARE *bunchbean* n especially South, Midland]

bunch in (also *bunch up*) *verb phrase* To gather, assemble; to collect into a group.

1939 Hall *Coll* (Sugarlands TN) Back at that time when a person would get sick, we had good neighbors in here. They'd bunch up if you was sick and come work your corn for you and make quiltings and roll logs and grubbings, one thing and another and help you when you was sick and disabled. **1957** Broaddus *Vocab Estill Co KY* 13 *bunch dishes up* = to remove dishes from the table after a meal. **1973** *Gardening* 251 If they was a family sick an' th'crops needed gatherin', th'neighbors'ud bunch in an' do it free of charge for'em. **1984** Page and Wigginton *Foxfire Cookery* 156 We'd get our corn gathered in the fall of the year, and then we'd have corn shuckings. We'd ask in ten or fifteen men. We'd get in women folks, too, and they'd bunch in and get supper. **1998** *Dante OHP-25* We'd bunch up like this. We'd all go to the crossing from here up there, and them people up yonder, they'd come down to the road where he could pick us up.

bundlesome *adjective* Bulky, cumbersome.

1940 Stuart *Trees of Heaven* 149 The women from the hills dressed in tattered dresses, bundlesome coats. **1944** Wentworth *ADD* 83 (WV) The dresses women wore to the parties in the country were not only warm but also very bundlesome. **1976** Bullard *Crafts TN Mts* 17 His homemade [potters'] kick-wheel was heavy and cumbersome ("bundlesome" is the mountain word).

bung See **bang**.

bunged up *participial adjective*

1 Constipated.

2005 Williams *Gratitude* 53 The big youngens and grown people got Black Draught™ (Drawft) when they was bunged up.

2 Bruised, injured.

1988 Jackson *Commodities* 31 She is all bunged up, her arm is in a sling. **2009** Holbrook *Upheaval* 31–32 It'd be his own woman laying bunged up in the back room, her holding a butcher knife, cussing him with one breath and begging us not to take him off with the next.

bungersome (also *bunglesome*) *adjective* Awkward, clumsy.

c1960 Wilson *Coll*: *bunglesome* = clumsy. **1973** Davis *'Pon My Honor* 69 The Devil crossed Mr. Vance up one day, and got him in such a bungersome fix that it made the old sinner see the light and get religion.

bungle up *verb phrase* To mangle, injure severely.

1973 Davis *'Pon My Honor* 11 Cousin Matt got all bungled up and died three days later.

bunkhouse lawyer *noun* See citation.

1967 Parris *Mt Bred* 133 A bunkhouse lawyer is the logger who orates to his mates, asserting his knowledge on all subjects.

bunty *adjective* Short and squat, stumpy (especially *bunty hen* = a type of tailless fowl). See also **banty**.

1858 (in **1974** Harris *High Times* 132) [The chunk of coal] went straight an' strong right inter the muzzle ove his durn'd bunty Connecticut gun, busted out the breech-pin, an' then lodged ontu the bull-curl in his forrid. **1941** Still *Stir-Off* 4 A tailless fowl. Peep Eye stood pretty as a bunty bird. **1956** McAtee *Some Dial NC* 7 My little bunty hen. **1994** Montgomery *Coll*: *bunty* (Brown, Ledford, Oliver). **1997** Montgomery *File*: *bunty* (85-year-old man, Greenbrier TN).

[EDD *bunty* sb 2 Scot; DARE (at *bunty* n) chiefly Appalachians]

bunty hen See **bunty**.

burfine See **burr vine**.

burn *verb* See citation. See also **break out 1**.

2003 Cavender *Folk Medicine* 85 The primary therapeutic locus for influenza, however, was fever. As for a cold, the central objective was to "burn" (sweat) the fever out of a body. This was done by administering a variety of hot teas, many of which were powerful diaphoretics like boneset, horsemint, and mustard seed, often in combination with other interventions such as onion poultices and "jackets" (poultices on the chest and back).

burn doctor *noun* See citations. Same as **fire doctor**. See also **blow fire**, **take out a burn**, **talk fire out**.

2003 Cavender *Folk Medicine* 203 = a folk healer who has the ability to treat burns; also known as a "fire doctor." **2006** *Encycl Appalachia* 868 Burn doctors "talked the fire" out of burns and promoted quick healing by moving a hand across and slightly above the burn while reciting the following: "There came an angel from the east bringing fire and frost. In frost, out fire, in the name of the Father, the Son, and the Holy Ghost." **2007** Myers *Smoky Mt Remedies* 9 = one who blows fire out of a burn or performs the burn ceremony.

burner *noun* See citation.

1949 Maurer *Argot of Moonshiner* 8 = a kerosene or gasoline heating unit for cooking mash or distilling liquor: "That old burner roars till I can't hear what you're saying."

burning worm *noun* Same as **packsaddle, stinging worm**.

2009 Wiles and Wiles *Location* 104 It was necessary to wear long-sleeved shirts and bandanas around their necks to keep from being slashed by the sharp edges of the corn leaves. This also protected them from being stung by the "burning worms" that were always in the corn.

burn its own smoke (also *burn their smoke*) *verb phrase* To disguise a distilling operation by sending it back into the **still**; of a furnace of a moonshining operation: to recirculate heat and thus avoid smoke.

1968 *End of Moonshining* 44 Others [= moonshiners], however, worried about the problem, "burn their smoke." A worm or pipe which runs out the side of the furnace and back into the firebox recirculates the smoke and makes it invisible. **1971** Gordon *Moonshining in GA* 58 A duck nest furnace of the type Doc builds, by recirculating its heat, is said to "burn its own smoke." This lessens the danger of dicovery of the [moonshining] operation.

burnout *noun* A destructive fire, usually a house fire.

1937 Hall Coll (Tobes Creek NC) They had a burnout at the city hall. **c1940** Simms Coll None of us know at what time we might have a burn out. **1961** Seeman *Arms of Mt* 157 If any family has a "burnout," everybody sends something to help them get started again.

[DARE *burnout* n 1 South Midland]

burn-out dog *noun* See citation.

1968 Clarke *Stuart's Kentucky* 120 The burn-out dogs began fast and tired the fox, but also tired quickly themselves; the cutter, or cuttin' dogs, cheated by taking the long circles around the mountain and along the ridges; stay-dogs that had the endurance to remain long in the chase.

burn their own smoke See **burn its own smoke**.

burn the wind *verb phrase* To move rapidly, hurry.

1946 Wilson *Fidelity Folks* 180 When something went fast in the older days, we said it "burned the wind." **1956** McAtee *Some Dial NC* 7 = go fast. **1963** Edwards *Gravel* 181 If someone is seen walking rapidly, as if in a great hurry to get somewhere in the shortest time possible, people unacquainted with Speedwell sayings would say he is "burning the wind," or wasting no time.

burn up squirrelly *verb phrase* To go very fast.

1963 Edwards *Gravel* 146 The Duffer was throwing gravels from under the soles of his shoes burning up squirrely back down the hill toward Uncle John's house.

burr See **buhr**.

burr vine (also *burfine*) *noun* A vervain (especially *Verbena stricta/urticifolia*), whose roots have various medical uses.

1941 *FWP Guide WV* 140 Burfine root is excellent for coughs and the flu. **1968** *DARE Survey* (Buchanan VA) = used for stomach cramps. **1973** *AOHP/ALC-259* For a bad cold they'd get what they call burr vine, a weed that grows here, and they'd boil the root and make a tea, and they claim that can break the cold.

burry See **bury**.

burst *verb* Variant past-tense form *bursted*.

1862 *Mangum CW Letters* (June 16) I saw whar the yankes bursted the tin of[f] ove the top of a house top with thir bums and bursted in to a house with one it opined a very good winder in it. **1862** *Neves CW Letters* (Aug 14) [They] throad a shell at us but it never bursted. **1939** Hall *Coll* **1968** *Faith Healing* 23 There's twenty-six stitches took up and down there, and a blood vessel bursted over here. **1975–76** Wolfram/Christian *WV Coll* 40 A vein in his nose bursted, and he went to hemorrhaging. Her leg bursted, and it run out in the bed, she was very sick all summer.

bury *verb* Variant form *burry* ['bʌri].

1864 *Chapman CW Letters* (July 21) We Burried him in the town Burrying ground. **1972** *AOHP/ALC-355* He'd go and haul apples in and beat them up and have his little barrels there. He'd burry the pomace. **1973** *GSMNP-79:1:1* She always talked about her people, some of 'em a-being burried on a little graveyard. **1995** Montgomery Coll = always pronounced [burr-y] (Cardwell).

burying (and variants) *noun* The interment of a deceased person and the accompanying graveside ceremony if one is held; formerly, the funeral service could follow much later to accommodate family members and preachers and could last much of the day. See also **funeral, funeralize, preaching funeral, memorial**.

1814 Hartsell *Memora* 128 It was the Stilest beriang that I ever Saw in my life, all but the firing of the platoons that was fired. *Ibid.* 137 ther heas binn a berion everey Sunday Sence we have binn heare. **1862** *Barkley CW Letters* (Sept 27) James B Willson wife is died [= died] She dide 27 that was last friday georg went to the berien And Com by to day from thar. **1898** Elliott *Durket Sperret* 116 I jawed Hannah . . . kase she wouldn't holler at the buryin'. **1913** Morley *Carolina Mts* 218 It happens that upon the death of a person in a remote district, although the actual "burying" takes place at once, one may be invited weeks or months or even a year or more afterward to attend the "funeral," a very important ceremony which is frequently deferred until the presence of some favorite preacher is obtainable. **1940** Mathes *Jeff Howell* 20 The keening of the women at the "wake" that night was made more harrowing by the foreboding of mothers, sisters, and wives over what was likely to happen at the burying on the morrow. **1957** Broaddus *Vocab Estill Co KY* 13 At a burying there would be no sermon, but perhaps a few songs would be sung. The funeral, if any, would be held at a later date. **1983** *Dark Corner OHP-5A* I remember when we went to the funeral, to the burying rather. **1985** Irwin *Alex Stewart* 261 She just let him lay there for two days, until some of the neighbors found him. She never went to the burying. **1991** Joslin *Mt People I* 115 Whether raising a house as a carpenter, pasturing his cows as a dairyman, planning a "burying" as a preacher or a class as a carpentry teacher, he's had to work with the weather to adjust to its changing conditions.

[DARE *burying* n South, South Midland]

burying ground (also *burying point*) *noun* A cemetery.

1817 (in **1995** Creekmore *TN Extracts*) At this place, on Wednesday evening last, the 12th inst of a short and very severe illness, Thomas Jackson Esqr, a native of Pennsylvania, and for many years a respected inhabitant of Hawkins County . . . Presbyterian burying-ground. **1862** *Williams CW Letters* (Oct 28) he died on the 24th of October in the morning about 6 Oclock and we had a coffin made for him and buried him in the Masonic Buring ground. **1864** *Chapman CW Letters* (July 21) We Burried him in the town Burrying ground. **1913** Kephart *Our Sthn High* 78 I mind about that time, Doc; but I disremember which buryin'-ground theyall buried ye in. **1927** Furman *Lonesome Road* 9 What about my five babes that lays on the burying pint yander, that vanished away, one after tother, with the choking-disease and the pneumony-fever? **1976** Garber *Mountain-ese* 36 We put a new grave rock at Uncle Penn's grave in the buryin' ground. **1982** Slone *How We Talked* 76 *burin'* [sic] *ground* = cemetery, or graveyard. **1996** Montgomery *Coll*: *burying ground* = usually a cemetery, not a makeshift burial plot (Cardwell)

burying point See **burying ground**.

bush

A *noun* Variant form *boosh*.

1969 Dial *Dialect Appal People* 486 You can hear many characteristic Scottish pronunciations. *Whar, thar, dar* (*where, there,* and *dare*) are typical. So also are *poosh, boosh, eetch, deesh* (*push, bush, itch, dish,* and *fish*).

B *verb* To drive (a hunted animal) into a thicket.

1939 Hall *Coll* (Deep Creek NC) "They [= the dogs] have bushed him [= a bear], Winston," I said, "I'll go on and see."

bush army *noun* The Civilian Conservation Corps, a federal program created in 1933 under President Franklin Delano Roosevelt. By the end of the decade there were twenty-two CCC camps in the Smokies, and their workers built the roads, trails, and other infrastructure of what is now Great Smoky Mountains National Park. Same as **Peckerwood Army**.

1967 Hall *Coll* (Del Rio TN) Out of all I was in the Bush Army with, I never did see but one [CCC member] while I was in the U.S. Army, and that was a little cotton-headed boy that stayed in Mount Sterling Tower.

bush ax (also *bush blade*) *noun* A small ax with a thin, curved blade for cutting roots and brush.

1958 Stuart *Plowshare* 210 He took the bush blades, sprouting hoes, new files, and scythe rocks. **1964** Clarke *Stuart's Writing* 163 Bush blades may have handles like a scythe and a blade somewhat broader and shorter than that of a scythe or they may have handles like those of a mattock or an ax and a blade thinner and broader, not unlike the blade attached to the scythe type of handle. **1968** *DARE Survey* (Brasstown NC) *bush axe, bush blade* = a tool used for cutting underbrush and digging out roots.

[DARE *bush ax* n chiefly South, South Midland, especially Middle Atlantic]

bush baby *noun* An illegitimate child.

1994–97 Montgomery *Coll* (known to Brown, Bush, Cardwell, Jones, Weaver).

[DARE *bush baby* n South]

bush bean *noun* See citations.

2006 *Encycl Appalachia* 935 Bush beans are short, bushy, and usually self-supporting. **2011** Best *Bean Terminology* = as a general rule, bush beans have tougher hulls than cornfield beans, which lessens their desirability. They also produce far fewer beans. . . . Depending on variety, they can be broken and cooked when full or while pods are still tender if they are varieties which become tough when full . . . as with cornfield beans, they can eaten as shelly or dry beans as well.

bush blade See **bush ax**.

bushel *noun* Variant plural form without -*s* following a numeral.

1861 *Martin CW Letters* (Oct 1) I am done geathring corn I made about 24 loads I think Ill have 200 hundred bushel I want to shuck tomorw. **1864** *Chapman CW Letters* (April 12) we have sold a bout forty bushel of Cloversead and has got enoug left to sow the Calf lot next spring. **1960** McCaulley *Cades Cove* That corn was sewed up in a canvas, seven bushel, and he laid it on his back and carried it up that ridge to the top. **1971** *AOHP/ALC-260* If I took me twenty bushel of apples over there, and that, with my beans and other stuff that I had to take, I'd come back with a little money. **1989** *Matewan OHP-9* I'd take an old mule and take two or three bushel of beans and take fried chickens and take eggs. **1998** *Dante OHP-45* I raised three bushel [of potatoes] last year.

bushel cook *noun* See citation.

1975 GSMNP-56:21 At these company-owned [logging] camps, the cooks were called "bushel cooks." They operated the camps according to the number of people that was working there. They got so much for each one and they were called "bushel cooks."

bush hacking *noun* See citation. See also **bushwhack A1**, **clean off**, **clearing**.

1911 Shearin *E KY Word-List* 537 = a social gathering upon invitation to assist the host in clearing new land of trees or underbrush, he in turn providing a feast, dance, or other diversion for his helpers.

bush hog

A *noun* A type of rotary mower for trimming or removing brush and other vegetation.

1986 Pederson et al. *LAGS* (Campbell Co TN, Lumpkin Co GA).

[originally a trade name; DARE *bush hog* n chiefly South, South Midland]

B To use such a machine to clear brush from (an area).

1983 *Dark Corner OHP-10A* We needed to have some cleared area bushhogged off, 'cause it'd just grown up over the years.

[DARE *bush hog* v chiefly South, South Midland]

bush house *noun* Same as **brush arbor**.

1936 Farr *Folk Speech* 275 The meetin' is being held in a bush house.

bushwhack

A *verb* [Editor's note: Senses cannot always be discriminated.]

1 To cut brush from a road in order to clear a path for another purpose; to pile brush on (a road); in Civil War times, to set brush on a road in order to obstruct travel; hence verbal noun *bushwhacking*.

1861 Hedgecock *Diary* 104–5 The road being so much obstructed and our travel with so much caution rendered necessary by bushwhacking by citizens and rebel troops, our progress was slow. **1940** Still *River of Earth* 121 Aus bushwhacked the road, waylaying Boone as he came home from Whitesburg. **1962** Stubbs *Mountain-Wise* (Aug–Sept) 8 We were bushwacking, clearing out undergrowth, "saw-briars," and saplings which were growing in the wrong places. **1988** *Smokies Guide* (Summer) 5 In some places rhododendron intertwines with other shrubs in dense thickets called "slicks" or "hells." If you have ever tried to bushwhack through one of these areas, you'll understand the origin of the latter term. **1996** Montgomery *Coll* We had to bushwhack through the forest (Cardwell).

2 To ambush (a person or animal) from the brush along a road or pathway.

1863 *Rector CW Letters* (May 20) a man was fooling with his gun last night drunk the pin went off shot him through the body he died immediately after he was shot another man went too the Still house and was bushwhack[ed] I havent hird whether he is dead of not. **1953** Hall *Coll* (Bryson City NC) I follered them back up, and they was a fellow in there [who] had bushwhacked our bear. **1974–75** McCracken *Logging* 1:11 He aimed to bushwhack him and kill him. **1985** Irwin *Alex Stewart* 260 Old George was afraid of Little George, so he hid out and bushwacked him. **1994** Montgomery *Coll* (known to Shields).

3 In Civil War times: to live in the brush, sometimes marauding and preying on civilians from the backwoods; to hide in the brush and attack (civilians); hence verbal noun *bushwhacking*. See also **bushwhacker**.

1926 Harris *WV Hand Book* 428 (DARE) At the outbreak of the war, in these mountains sentiment was divided. Great numbers of young men immediately volunteered and entered the regular army, some on one side and some on the other. But there were large numbers of men who were gathered into hostile groups of armed defenders, who were never recognized as regular soldiers. They were referred to generally as home guards and were dreaded and feared by the people far more than the regular armies. There were two State governments and civil affairs were in a chaotic condition. This section has never entirely recovered from the terrible experiences. A word was coined that makes us wince yet. It is a West Virginia word of local origin. Bushwhacker. The dictionary says that it is a guerrilla that beats through the bushes. But that is not the way we understand it. It refers to the man who strikes from the concealment of the leafy growth. And when the leaden ball sang from the foliage covering the hill, the word was bushwhacking. **1973** Wellman *Kingdom of Madison* 88 The Franklins upheld the Confederacy, although none of the boys enlisted in the southern army. However, they gave trouble to neighbors who bushwhacked on the Union side. Whenever fighting broke out in their part of the world, the Franklin boys turned out with rifles, sometimes firing volleys alongside Confederate soldiers. **1975** Brewer *Valley So Wild* 166 "Bushwhacking" became the scourge of these last years. Both armies soon learned conventional lines of battle did not work for mountain fighting. **1988** Trotter *Bushwhackers* 221 When an officer finds himself and men bushwhacked from behind every shrub, tree, or projection from every side of the road, only severe measures will stop it. **2006** *WV Encycl* 94 In West Virginia, some took advantage of the Civil War to settle personal grievances or pursue personal gain or other nonmilitary ends. They were called bushwhackers from their habit of ambushing or "bushwhacking" their adversaries from under cover. Usually they claimed to be attached to one side in the struggle, often the South.

B *noun* See **bushwhacker**.

bushwhacker (also *bushwhack*) *noun* In Civil War times, a deserter or evader of conscript (from either side), a local partisan ostensibly having sympathies (with either side), or an outlaw, one often taking refuge in rough, hilly, but familiar local terrain, marauding and preying on civilians. See 1955, 1975 citations. See also **bee hunter**, **bushwhack A3**, **jayhawker**, **outlier**, **scout C**, **tory**.

1863 *Walker CW Letters* (July 31) sence them bush whacers has took fathers horses i have felt more like fighting than ever did in my life. **1865** *Wax Letter* 39 I have lost four good horses since I have been living at Hill Hill [sic] besides the other things the Bushwhackers have took from me four they plundered every place cut off nearly every saddle skirt off they could get there hands on. **1926** [see **bushwhack A3**]. **1955** Dykeman *French Broad* 113 Bushwhackers and renegades they all were, with belief in no "side" but their own skins, and serving no command but their own lawlessness. Their hideouts were caves along the river or in shaley mountainsides far from the settlements. Horses and food were their prime necessities and these they stole frequently. **1974** Underwood *Madison Co* 38 The most tragic experience for Madison people were the results of bushwacking. These "bushwackers" fought for neither side but were mainly a group of vandals. **1975** Brewer *Valley So Wild* 166–67 "Bushwhacking" became the scourge of these last years. Both armies soon learned conventional lines of battle did not work for mountain fighting. They put a premium on the vicious type of guerilla marksmen who could strike from ambush, and organized them into small bands. At first bushwhackers fought under pretense of military discipline.

But as both armies resorted to living off the land all rules went out the window. They degenerated into predatory outlaws warring against anyone who had provisions and against rival bands. **1983** Whiteaker *Enemy Is Brother* 37 Although the generals on both sides usually ignored the upper Cumberland, hundreds of residents of the area adopted one banner or the other and carried out their own civil war. These were the pro-Confederacy or pro-Union guerrillas who, at least in their own minds, were fighting for a good cause. Joining the guerrillas in the perpetration of violence and destruction were others who, under the guise of military service, seized the opportunity that the war provided to rob and destroy, settle personal grievances, and murder. These were the Upper Cumberland's notorious "bushwhackers." **2007** Ballard and Weinstein *Neighbor* 73 The term Bushwhacker is not widely used. It was once current among men, women and children in the North Western part of North Carolina, the North Eastern part of Tennessee and a few adjacent counties across the Virginia border. To those unfamiliar with the word, Bushwhacker, it might be well to say that in time of war men who profess to be neutral and refuse to join either side, openly, but as individuals, or in small bands, using ambush tactics, attack, kill or plunder the homes of those unable to defend themselves are called by this name.

bushwhacking See **bushwhack A1, A3.**

bus-left *adjective phrase* Left behind by a bus.

1967 *DARE Survey* (nwSC) I got bus-left. [Used mostly by schoolchildren.] **1975** *DARE File* (neGA) I was late to class because I was bus-left.

[DARE (at *-left* suff) South Atlantic]

buss

A *verb*

1 To kiss.

1913 Combs *KY Highlander* 16 Shakespearean English [terms still in use include] *buss* (kiss, King John III Scene 10, l. 35). **1924** Raine *Saddlebags* 103 The venerable word *buss* (to kiss) has fallen into disrepute in the dictionaries. But it is still uncontaminated in the Mountains. **1962** Williams *Mtneers Mind Manners* 19 Woe to the daring swain who attempts to "buss" [a girl] unawares if he is not prepared to be "biffed one on the snoot."

[Web3 *buss* n probably of imitative origin; DARE *buss* v[1] chiefly South Midland]

2 To take a swallow from (a vessel).

1859 Taliaferro *Fisher's River* 180 He poured out a cupful, and gin it to the 'squire fust, who bussed the cup a little, and then I bussed it.

B *noun* A kiss.

1934–47 *LAMSAS* (Madison Co NC, Swain Co NC). **c1960** Wilson *Coll* = a loud kiss. **1967–68** *DARE Survey* (Brasstown NC, Gatlinburg TN). **1986** Pederson et al. *LAGS* = attested by 5/60 interviewees (8.3%) from E TN and 2/35 (5.7%) from N GA; 7/22 of all LAGS interviewees (31.8%) attesting term were from Appalachia. **1996–97** Montgomery *Coll* (known to Brown, Cardwell, Jones, Norris, Oliver).

[OED3 *buss* v[1] and n[2] 1 chiefly archaic and regional; cf SND *boose* n[2] "mouth"; DARE *buss* n chiefly Midland]

bussy *noun* A sweetheart.

1895 Edson and Fairchild *TN Mts* 370 Ef you'd a ben thar you mout (might) a got a *bussy*. **1924** Raine *Saddlebags* 103 = a sweetheart. **1996–97** Montgomery *Coll* (known to Brown, Cardwell, Jones).

[DARE *bussy* n chiefly southern Appalachians]

bust *verb* Variant of *burst*.

A Variant third-singular form of two syllables: *bust-es*. See also **-es**[2].

1997 Montgomery *File* That water freezes on the bark and bustes it (60-year-old man, Maggie Valley NC).

B Variant past-tense and past-participle form of two syllables: *bust-ed*.

1863 Robinson *CW Letters* (Jan 2) at 4 in the morning tha[y] comenst thowing thare bums at us tha[y] fell & busted all Round & over us but no body hurt. **1863** *Walker CW Letters* (Jan 7) the bum [i.e. bombs] and grape and minny com like hale stone from the north the bum busted over us and all A round us. **1969** *Burton-Manning Coll*-89B The Perkins brothers operated till they went busted. **1997** Montgomery *Coll* He got so mad he busted a hamestring (Cardwell). **2001** Lowry *Expressions* 18 Back in the winter my ear busted and run out my nose and everywhere.

C Senses.

1 (also *bust up*) To chop or split (a rock, a log for firewood or posts, or another object or material); to break open.

1959 Pearsall *Little Smoky* 74 "Busting" logs and piling the "chunks" are important masculine activities, especially in the fall. **1969** GSMNP-42:7 We just had it up there, a-busting these stakes ... and putting this fence around. **1972** GSMNP-93:30 Them black gums, them won't bust hardly. You can't hardly bust one up for wood.

2 (also *bust out*) To break (ground), as with a plow (especially in phrase *bust the middle[s]*).

1894 Murfree *Vanished Star* 98 Luther with a bull-tongue plow was industriously engaged in "bustin' out the middles" since the land had been planted ... without the preliminary "breaking out." **1966** Guthrie *Corn* 89 The plow then was driven once or twice through the balk between the rows to bust the middle and kill weeds there. **1995** Montgomery *File*: *bust the middles* = to plow earth between the rows of a crop (85-year-old man, Greenbrier TN).

[DARE *bust* v 1 "to break ground," chiefly South, South Midland]

bust a hame string *verb phrase* See 1927 citation. See also **hame**.

1927 Woofter *Dialect from WV* 349 = to break some essential part of the equipment with which you are working by subjecting it to unnecessary strain. "Father busted a hamestring when he put so much load on that wagon." **1944** Combs *Word-List Sthn High* 19 = to make an extreme effort. **1996–97** Montgomery *Coll* = to suddenly become angry, "he got so mad he busted a hamestring" (Cardwell).

busted See **bust B.**

buster *noun* See citations.

c1960 Wilson *Coll* (DARE) = Something large for its expected size. **1984** Burns *Cold Sassy* 120 I do recollect seein' thet feller somewheres before. Ain't he a buster though!

[DARE *buster* n 1 especially Midland]

bustes See **bust A.**

busthead *noun*

1 (also *bust-skull*) Homemade whiskey of an inferior quality (used as a term of derision referring to the effects of its consumption, especially a violent headache). Also called **old busthead, popskull.** See also **rotgut.**

1864 Gilmore *Down in TN* 185 They obtain plentiful supplies of a vile fluid, which is compounded of log-wood, strychnine, juniper berries, and alcohol, and "circulates" among them under the appropriate names of "Tangle-foot," "Blue-ruin," "Red-eye," "Bust-head," and "Knock-'em-stiff." **1913** Kephart *Our Sthn High* 137 As for purity, all of the moonshine whiskey used to be pure, and much of it still is; but every blockader knows how to adulterate, and when one of them does stoop to such tricks he will stop at no halfway measures. . . . Such decoctions are known in the mountains by the expressive terms "pop-skull," "bust-head." **c1960** Wilson *Coll* (or *bust-skull*) = illicit, and usually strong whiskey. **1968** *End of Moonshining* 101 "Busthead" and "Popskull" are names applied to whiskey which produces violent headaches due to various elements which have not been removed during the stilling process. **1992** Montgomery *Coll* (known to Shields).

[DARE *busthead* n 1 chiefly South, South Midland]

2 See citation.

1939 Farr *TN Mt Regions* 90 = headache: "I've got a killing bust head."

bust out

A *verb phrase*

1 See **bust C2.**

2 (also *bust out to*) *verb phrase* (+ present participle) To start suddenly or energetically.

1937 Campbell *KY Mt Community* 547 Maybe you never wanted me to bust out singing like I done, but talking about women following their men minded me of that song ballet. **c1950** Adams *Grandpap* 59 She cried so hard that her nose busted out to bleedin' an' it bled three drops of blood on the bear's back. **1991** Thomas *Sthn Appal* 219 He busted out t' cryin', jist a-weepin' out lo-o-oud. **1999** Morgan *Gap Creek* 106 One of his suspenders broke and I busted out laughing. **2007** Shelby *Molly Whuppie* 4 This made Poll and Betts feel so sorry for themselves they busted out a-crying.

B *noun*

1 A sudden, destructive surge of water from rain, a flash flood.

1961 Seeman *Arms of Mt* 21 Gathering water comes leaping down the gullies in "bust-outs." **1997** Montgomery *Coll* (known to Brown, Bush, Cardwell, Weaver).

2 A landslide.

1993 *Stories 'neath Roan* 5 The land was cleared, where the bust-out was, up as fur as hit went. **2004** Adams *Old True Love* 142 They had what they called a bust-out on further north of us. . . . They said this woman was in her house cooking supper with two of her young'uns and all at once it come the biggest clap of thunder she'd ever heard but it did not come from the natural place. It come from under her *feet* and everything went perfectly black and then everything started to slide. They found the house at the bottom of the mountain and it took them over an hour to dig them out. **2008** Salsi *Ray Hicks* 139 The earth got so full it couldn't hold no more moisture. Water seeped through the rocks and a pressure built up. The ground finally exploded bringin' rocks, and boulders, and water rushin' down. Lewis and I seed a bust-out straight up the mountain. As all the mud and rocks and trees headed down toward our house, we were fixed to the spot.

bust-out bean See citation. See also **cutshort.**

2011 Best *Bean Terminology* = a type of bean where the seeds outgrow the hulls and lock the developing seeds against one another. This makes them appear square, rectangular, triangular, or even trapezoidal in form. . . . They are sometimes called bust-out beans because the dried hulls will often split apart vigorously after the bean pods have dried out and then become wet again by rain or even a heavy dew. This is nature's way of scattering.

bust out to See **bust out A2.**

bust-skull See **busthead 1.**

bust the middles See **bust C2.**

bust up See **bust C1.**

but[1]

A *adverb* (usually in negative contexts) Only, even, more than.

1774 *Dunmore's War* 204 Meat is but scarce on Clinch. *Ibid.* 245 This unlucky affair happened when there were but few men in the Fort. **c1841** Shane (in **1998** Perkins *Border Life* 199) We had moved down to McConnel's station but about a week, and shot him. **1862** *Epperly CW Letters* (July 27) I beleave I will press a furlow and come aney how they cant but take my life from me if I doo. **1863** *Revis CW Letters* (July 13) thare is but very few that has got over thare corn but twice yet and some has jest got over the first time. **1864** *Chapman CW Letters* (March 28) I am not dressing any my self nor don't expect to dress but very Little if any. **1922** *TN CW Ques* 886 I worked as a smith from my youth never did but little farm work. **1961** *Coe Ridge OHP*-334A He didn't live but about a mile away. **1971** *AOHP/ALC*-33 They wouldn't be but that [many students]. **1978** *Horsetrading* 52 Out of the whole bunch, there wasn't but six that would work a'tall. **2007** McMillon *Notes* My great-granny Rhody McMillon knew all [these things], but I never learned but a few.

B *conjunction*

1 (+ *relative pronoun*) (Anything) except (that).

1861 *Carden CW Letter* (Oct 6) they did not know but what they boath belonged to the same Army. **1864** *Warrick CW Letters* (April 8)

I hant Seen but one or too but what has Eat there breakfast this morning. **1900** Harben *N GA Sketches* 139 I don't know railly but what she may have promised him. **1919** Combs *Word-List South* 32 = transposed, as in "Corn bread? Shucks! that's jist what we ain't got nothin' else of but." **1964** Glassie *Mt Jack Tales* 95 I don't know but what it will be pretty hard to get. **1982** *Foxfire VII* 202 I've never been to a Holiness communion but what we didn't wash feet—all but one of them and that was down yonder at Gainesville. **1983** Page and Wigginton *Aunt Arie* 48 I never set down at th'table but what I want th'blessin' asked. **1999** Morgan *Gap Creek* 8 I didn't know but what Masenier had a catching sickness. **2008** *Rosie Hicks* 4 I didn't know I'd end up with him, but which I did. *Ibid.* 6 I had to go by the sixth, but which I say my birthday is March the second.

2 Variant syntactic position at the end of the second of two conjoined independent clauses. [Editor's note: All of the examples below are from West Virginia.]

1988 *Augusta Heritage* 153 [Speaker A:] We haven't put needles into the old winded-up one [= a phonograph], where they played just as clear as a crystal. [Speaker B:] Oh yeah, they'd play on that. A: We haven't tried it but. *Ibid.* [Speaker A:] Is he dead? [Speaker B:] No, he's living yet but. **1989** *Matewan OHP-2* I worked at Red Jacket Junior. Well, I worked at some of the other mines after that, but. *Ibid.* 9 They was another doctor, but I can't think of his name, worked with Hodge a long time there but. *Ibid.* 88 She beat him over the head with her umbrella after he kept on shooting him. Its a wonder he hadn't shot her but. They really, it was a made-up deal but. **1990** *Matewan OHP-73* We didn't have no phone. They would walk but.

[OED3 *but* adv B3 colloquial (chiefly Austral., Irish English, and Sc.); CUD *but*[1] conj 2 "used at the end of an utterance in recognition of a speaker's actual or potential doubts"]

but[2] See **butt**.

butt (also *but*) *noun* [rhymes with *putt*] An abrupt, often blunt end of a ridge or mountain; also used in place-names, as in *Mollies Butt* (NC) at the end of Mollies Ridge in the Smoky Mountains; hence verb phrase *butt off* = of the end of a mountain, to come to an abrupt end.

1803 (in **2004** *TN Petitions III* 27) Along the Extream hight of the mountain that Lays between Stonay Creek and the Holston River to the Ritch butt. **1829** (in **1940** McJimsey *Topo Terms in VA* 162) To two white Oaks on a but of the river mountain. **1849** (in **2003** *TN Petitions I* 133) We the undersigned citizens of Sevier and Knox Counties in the State of Tennessee Respectfully represent that the line dividing the said counties of Sevier and Knox, from what is called the "Butt" of Bays Mountain to the boundary of Jefferson County not far from McBee's Ferry cannot be discovered. **1922** Kephart *Our Sthn High* 374 Big Butt is what Westerners call a butte. **1939** Hall *Coll* (Mt Sterling NC) He lived in what we know as the Hickory Butt, next to Pigeon River. **1956** Fink *That's Why* 4 There are not formations like mesas here, and the occasional term *butt* is in no wise a variant of butte. Instead, it is where the end of a ridge or mountain breaks away sharply to the valley below, or in the mountain phrase, "butts off." **1982** Weals *Hog or Cow Brute* In the Smokies one definition of a *butt* is that it is the sudden, blunt lower end of a ridge.

[cf OED3 *butt* n[5] "a hillock, mound" obsolete except dialect, and *butt* n[8] "a headland, promontory" obsolete except in local names; DARE *butt* n[2] especially southern Appalachians]

butt cut (also *butt log*) *noun* The first portion cut above the stump of a felled tree, especially in reference to this as a section cut by loggers.

1927 Woofter *Dialect from WV* 349 *butt cut* = the part of the log nearest the stump of the tree. "The butt cut will make sixteen ties." **1964** Clarkson *Lumbering in WV* 357 *butt log* = the first log above the stump. **1974** GSMNP-50:1:1 We logged trees there. They was eight foot through. The butt cut was eight through. **1991** Weals *Last Train* 74 Brackin remembered the diameter of the "butt cut," or first log, as being "nearly eight feet."

butt down *verb phrase* To end in a butt.

1853 Kennedy *Blackwater Chronicle* 6 A large spur—apparently the Backbone itself—keeps straight to the south, and butts down on the Cheat.

butter and eggs *noun* A yellow-flowered toadflax flower (*Linaria vulgaris*), which has yellow and orange blossoms. Also called **bacon and eggs, bread and butter, chopped eggs**

1965 Shelton *Pioneer Comforts* 9 Butter and Eggs [was made into a tea for] Constipation. **1968** *DARE Survey* (Brasstown NC) = a large violet with a yellow center and small ragged leaves, comes up early in spring.

butter and eggs day *noun* See citation.

1975 Montell *Ghosts Cumberland* 217 = a local expression derived from the days of a barter economy when farm families took home-produced items to town to exchange for groceries and notions. Saturday was the traditional butter and eggs day in the Kentucky foothills until livestock markets were opened in the county seat towns in the 1920s; after that, the day of the livestock auction tended to become the butter and eggs day.

butter bean *noun* A small lima bean.

1949 Kurath *Word Geog East US* 73 *Butter beans* is a common expression for *lima beans* in all of the Southern area. Many people in this section differentiate between the large *lima beans* and the smaller *butter beans*. **1962** Wilson *Folkways Mammoth Cave* 14 The butter bean, a small, flat bean grown all over the South and called by many names, can be taken as a sort of test word for the region; to call it a *Lima bean* would still subject you to questioning as to where you *live at*, for Limas beans are *fetch-on*, either dried, as in former times, or frozen, as now.

[DARE *butter bean* 1 chiefly South, Midland]

buttercup *noun* A daffodil (*Narcissus* spp). Also called **Easter flower 3, March flower**.

1958 Wood *Words from TN* 8 In our early days . . . we fought over *buttercups* as opposed to *daffodils* or *jonquils*. We still say *buttercup* for the early variety that grows everywhere. **1968** Wilson *Folklore Mammoth Cave* 15 = daffodil . . . Called also *Easter flowers*, *jonquils*, *March flowers*. **1996** Montgomery Coll (known to eight consultants from the Smoky Mountains).

[from the color of the flower; DARE *buttercup* n 4 especially southern Appalachians]

butterfly root (also *butterfly weed*) *noun* Same as **pleurisy root**.

1862 *Huntley CW Letters* (Feb 10) i waunt you to send me some kind of sweating medicin . . . that Would Be good For the Fever or to sweat I think the Butterfly Root Would Be good. **1939** Jennison *Flora Great Smokies* 280 A little later roses bloom in profusion, and are succeeded by such striking things as the trumpet-creeper and a bright-colored milkweed called the "butterfly-weed" (*Asclepias tuberosa*). [**1971** Krochmal et al. *Medicinal Plants Appal* 70 This plant has been used as an expectorant, diaphoretic, and emetic, and to treat rheumatism. Indians of Appalachia made a tea of the leaves to induce vomiting.] **1981** *Smokies Heritage* 28:50–51 Butterfly weed produces brilliant orange flower clusters, but a watery juice instead of milk. . . . As usual, though, the common names are more attractive, and butterfly weed aptly describes the predilection of these insects for the sweet nectar in the flower.

buttermilk cheese *noun* See citation.

1949 McDavid *Grist* 106 (Oconee Co SC) = cottage cheese.

butternut *adjective* Dyed with butternut hulls.

1847 (in **1870** Drake *Pioneer Life KY* 74) My equipments were a substantial suit of butternut-linsey, a wool hat.

butter one's nose *verb phrase* To smear butter or another substance on a person's nose in mock celebration of that person's birthday, usually by slipping up on him or her.

[**1981** Eiler et al. *Blue Ridge Harvest* 100 During the evening [of her birthday] David slipped up and surprised his mother by smearing butter on her nose. The custom is well-known in the [Blue Ridge] region, and Janet said it even happened with some frequency at the high school: "The kids do it in the lunchroom. Every once in a while you'll hear a "Happy Birthday" burst out and someone will have found—whether it's butter or something similar—to smear on noses. And of course the element of surprise is supposed to be there."] **2011** *DSAE Internet File* How many of you have ever heard of getting your nose buttered on your birthday? When I was growing up in the Floyd/Patrick/Carroll counties area of Virginia, it was traditional to attempt to sneak up on the birthday person and smear butter on their nose. Even our teachers in elementary school would get in on the action, going to the cafeteria and getting the butter. I just assumed that this was a common practice until several years ago, when I mentioned something about it to a co-worker here in Roanoke. They looked at me like I was insane! Then, I started asking everyone that I knew here if they had ever heard of this tradition. No one had. Then, I asked my husband if he had ever heard of it. He grew up in Scott County, Virginia. While he had not heard of that tradition, they would get soot from the chimney and smear it on the birthday person's nose.

butter pie *noun* See citation.

c1982 Young *Colloquial Appal* 4 = cornbread and melted butter.

butter stirring *noun* Same as **apple butter stirring**.

1886 *Bayless Letters* 120 I was at a big butterstirring last Tuesday night and made about 7 gallons at Dick Hardwoods. Jack, we had some good old fun. Butterstirrings is just coming in whack.

butt heading *noun* See citation.

1991 Shifflett *Coal Towns* 86 It was also common, if not uniform, to make two openings in the initial penetration of [a] coal seam, ten to twelve feet wide and about thirty feet apart. These openings or "butt headings," were driven parallel to one another, and sometimes they advanced gradually as rooms were tunneled at right angles to them.

butt log See **butt cut**.

butt off See **butt**.

button

A *noun*

1 The rattle from a rattlesnake's tail.

1975 Purkey *Madison Co* 55 When a rattler was killed, the boys removed the "buttons" from the snake's tail to carry home as a trophy for all the family to see and admire.

2 Formerly, an inside door latch consisting of a strip of leather which fitted over a peg or button to keep the door closed.

1941 Hall Coll (Dellwood NC) There was a button on the [out]-house door.

B *verb* See citations.

1937 Hall Coll (Gatlinburg TN) *button the door* = latch the door. **2008** *Rosie Hicks* 6 If she got the tendency, she'd button the door.

button snakeroot *noun* The blazing star (*Liatris spicata*), a perennial wildflower reputed to produce an antidote for the poison of a snakebite. See also **fairy wand**, **rattlesnake master 2**, **rattlesnake root 1**, **snakeroot tea**.

1941 Walker *Story of Mt* 48 Among the wild plants once employed as antidotes for the bites of poisonous reptiles, are rattlesnake-master, black snakeroot, rattlesnake-weed, Samson snakeroot or scurfy (whose tough fleshy root has long been used for tooth brushes), Virginia snakeroot, button snakeroot, and rattlesnake-root. **1982** Stupka *Wildflowers* 119 [One] name for this handsome plant is "button-snakeroot," from its globular roots.

but which *conjunctive phrase* But in this regard, and for that matter. See also **and which**, **which B2**.

1983 Page and Wigginton *Aunt Arie* 48 I never set down at th'table but what I want th'blessin asked. **2008** *Rosie Hicks* 4 I didn't know I'd end up with him, but which I did. *Ibid.* 6 I had to go by the sixth, but which I say my birthday is March the second.

buy *verb* variant past-participle forms *boughten, boughtened*; hence participial adjective *boughten* = store-bought rather than homemade or homegrown. See also **store-bought**.

1848 (in **1870** Drake *Pioneer Life KY* 92) Those who labor through the week in coarse and dirty clothes can estimate the cheering influence of a clean face and feet, a clean shirt, and "boughten" clothes on a Sabbath morning. **1917** Kephart *Camping and Woodcraft* 1:110 He has learned, too, how to fashion on the spot many substitutes for many "boughten" things that we consider necessary at home. **1934–47** *LAMSAS Appal: boughten bread* = attested by 8/148 speakers (5.4%) from WV. **1941** Still *Troublesome Creek* 11 "I need me a shirt," I said. "A boughten shirt." **1957** Broaddus *Vocab Estill Co KY* 10 *boughten* = bought, as opposed to home made. **1972** *AOHP/LJC-104* They didn't have much boughten lye like any other kind now. **1978** *Smokies Heritage* 192 Every bit of good had to be drained from the material that had been boughten at the store. **1983** *Dark Corner OHP-13A* It looked just like a mattress that you'd boughten. **1990** Aiken *Stories* 42 For one thing the steers were cheaper, could graze more and need less expensive grain or "boughten" hay than a horse. **1997** Andrews *Mountain Vittles* 25 Nowadays, the women make cobblers with two crusts and them boughtened. In the ol' timey cobblers the women jest poured the fruit right in the pan and put the crust in with it or on top er it. **2003** Carter *Mt Home* 13 When he could get it, he chawed store boughten twist.

[DARE *boughten* adj 1 chiefly North, North Midland]

buying gingerbread *verbal noun* See citation.

1977 Shackelford et al. *Our Appalachia* 36 In the past, mountain politicians often bought gingerbread cakes from elderly women and distributed them to people in the hope of gaining a few extra votes. By doing this, candidates earned the goodwill of the gingerbread bakers and of the people who received a free piece of cake. The practice has almost died now and today "buying gingerbread" is usually a euphemism for vote buying.

buzzard *noun* See citation.

1962 Clark *Folk Speech NC* 305 = one who carries the intestines at hog-killing time.

buzzard bait *noun* Bait to attract buzzards; figuratively, a thin, sickly-looking animal; by extension = a person with such an appearance.

1984 Woods *WV Was Good* 225 He is too ornery for buzzard bait. **1996–97** Montgomery *Coll* (known to Adams, Brown, Jones, Ledford, Norris, Oliver).

[DARE *buzzard bait* n especially South Midland]

buzzard wing *noun* See citation.

1997 Montgomery *Coll* = the wing of a turning plow (Brown).

by *interjection* Used as a quasi-prefix to form a mild oath (e.g. *bydabs, bydads, by gonnies, by juckers*) expressing a wide variety of sentiments, especially disgust or surprise. See 1915, 1969 citations. See also **ay, bedabs, b'gad, by-word, dad-**.

1859 Taliaferro *Fisher's River* 36 No, by juckers! **1915** Dingus *Word-List VA* 181 = in mild imprecations used merely for emphasis, as by Dad, Drot, George, Golly, Gonny, Gosh, Hawker, Shot. **1923** Furman *Mothering* 189 "We like you all right," he said; "but, by grab, a fellow's got to see some fun!" **1928** (in **1952** Mathes *Tall Tales* 73) "Hit's a hot trail, by gonnies!" Birdeye panted as he toiled on. **c1940** Hall *Coll: by jollies* = an exclamation expressing various emotions. **1940** Still *River of Earth* 178 "By juckers," he said. "First tree ever I saw lay eggs." **1964** Williams *Prep Mt Speech* 55 That possum's hide is wuth a round dollar if hits wuth ary red pinny under the sun, by Jacks! **1969** Doran *Folklore White Co* 108–9 Several mild expletives let off verbal steam respectably. People, unless they avoid "slangy words," use such expressions as these: "Land's sakes"; "For gosh sakes"; "Land's smuffin"; "Land-o-Goshins"; "Gosh darn it"; "Confound it"; "By Doggies"; "By grab"; "By cracky"; "By gum"; "Dad gum it"; "I'll be goll-durned"; "Good golliwogs"; "Plag on it"; "Plag take it"; "Geewhillikin"; "That son-of-a-billy goat"; and "Shoot fire and save matches." **1971** *Granny Women* 257 By grannies, she'd took that young'un and went down there and stayed. **1984** Woods *WV Was Good* 231 A common byword was the term *bygonnies. Bydad* was another. **1985** Irwin *Alex Stewart* 137 Well, by-ginneys, if you'll let me have some corn, I'll make you some medicine. **1991** Thomas *Sthn Appal* 27 He said "By jacks, I'll jist take and build a hotel." An' he did. **1995** Prince *Quill Rose* 27 Quill quipped, "I kept some [= distilled whiskey] for three months—and by godlings, it aint so." **1996–98** Montgomery *Coll: by doggies* (Ledford); *by gonnies* (Cardwell). **1999** Hodges *Tough Customers* 72 But, then I thought, no, by grab, my father founded this church, and I will not be run off by some preacher who doesn't want to be called a preacher. **2000** Miller *Looneyville* 40 *by dad* = an exclamation of amusement, surprise or disgust depending on a person's tone of voice: "Bydad, I didn't expect you so soon!" **2007** Cave *Recollections: bedabs/bydads* = a mild oath heard in Swain County [NC] in the 1980s.

bydabs, bydads, by gonnies, by juckers See **by**.

by my lone See **lone**.

by Ned *interjection* Used as a mild oath. See also **by**.

1923 Furman *Mothering* 61 "You women," he continued, severely, "think you know so much, and lay down so many laws, and, by Ned, you don't even know how to bile beans!" **1960** Mason *Memoir* 81 You have to buy your medicine and by ned I've got enough sense to make mine. **1963** Edwards *Gravel* 30 By Ned! he'd buy Peggy Mullins's pie, so he would, if he had to pay twenty dollars for it! **1983** *Smokies Guide* (Fall) He tries to explain the attraction: "Well, I don't rightly know, but—by Ned—there's people that come here from all parts of the country; and, as sure as they come once, they'll be back." **1992** Morgan *Potato Branch* 98 "There ain't never no cuss words on Marshall Gregg's lips," Aunt Carrie told me. "No swear words. The worst he'll say is 'by Ned.' I've seen him miss a nail and hit his thumb with a hammer and all he'll say is 'by Ned, that hurts.'"

by one's lone, by one's lone self, by one's lonesome See **lone**.

by sun *adverb phrase* After sunrise or before sunset (as a way of specifying time). See 1956 citation.

1834 Crockett *Narrative* 91 It was about an hour by sun in the morning, when we got near the fort. **1862** *Robinson CW Letters* (July 18) we marcht all nite we got back about 1 hour by Sun in the morning. **1886** Smith *Southernisms* 45 an hour by sun = before sunset. **1903** Fox *Little Shepherd* 93 "Don't get into trouble, my boy," said the Major, "an' come back here an hour or two by sun." **1935** Murray *Schoolhouse* 63 The only times of day that mountain folk know are variously expressed by "soon" (early in the morning), "late"; "about an hour, or two hours, by sun" (meaning after sunrise or before sunset); and they can make a tolerably good guess at noon when the sun is shining. **1956** McAtee *Some Dial NC* 5 = the time before sundown estimated by the height of the sun above the horizon; "an hour by sun." **1997** Montgomery *Coll* (known to Brewer, but not to other consultants from the Smoky Mountains).

[DARE *by* prep 4 chiefly South, South Midland]

by the littles *adverb phrase* Gradually, a little at a time.

1940 Haun *Hawk's Done* 20 The Old Man and Ad kept easing off by the littles till finally they went on away and didn't show themselves again that night. *Ibid.* 46 Dona kept telling me things by the littles. Every time I would see her. **1969** *DARE Survey* (Hardshell KY).

by-word *noun* A favorite expression of an individual, especially a mild oath or exclamation used to avoid profanity. [Editor's note: Examples collected by Joseph Hall in the Smoky Mountains in 1937 include *aye the gosh*, *by gosh*, *dad burn it*, *dad gone it*, *laws a massy*, *laws a mercy*, *lord have mercy*, *lordy yes*, *mercy*, *my country alive*, *why law yes*, and *yes lord*.] See also **by**, **i**.

1863 (in **1992** Heller and Heller *Confederacy* 102) the soldiers has a by word when any body dies or anything lost saying its gone up the spout. tell Washington that I say the *Confederacy* is on her way up the spout. **1937** Hall *Coll* (Emerts Cove TN) By-words [are] slang, like "hell!," "dame" [= damn ye]; not cussin', takin' the Lord's name in vain. **1939** Hall *Notebooks* 9:41 (Saunook NC) One of his by-words is "I grannies." **1940** Haun *Hawk's Done* 76 His byword was, "God, He knows." **1956** Hall *Coll* (Roaring Fork TN) When I said that by-word, it was right when [a light] flashed up. It was just like the bat of your eye. **1963** Edwards *Gravel* 27 As he liked to say himself, as a sort of by-word, he was the "genuwine stuff." *Ibid.* 180 My Uncle Ben . . . had a by-word which many people remember. It was nearly a cuss-word but Uncle Ben intended it only as a by-word, which was allowable. "Dom"—that was it. **1975** Carter *Gospel Truth* When he really meant to cuss, he did it out by the barn or down by the granary. Around womenfolk he was usually more gentle. Restraint was part of the pride in him, but he often softened words as if he were a bit ashamed. He used "by words" instead of cuss words. "By damn" was acceptable. **1975** *Hartley II* 381 He had a by-word, "by gracious." He said, "By gracious, I had to go up to the spring and fix [the spout back] so my wife could get some water." **1984** Woods *WV Was Good* 231 A common byword was the term *bygonnies*. *Bydad* was another. **1998** Ownby *Big Greenbrier* III:12 We were never allowed to use any kind of a "by-word" or accuse each other of telling a lie. **1999** Milnes *Play of Fiddle* 94 Another common oral tradition in West Virginia is the byword. Most tale tellers mimic the actual speaking voices of the characters, including the identifying byword(s) interjected throughout the tale. For instance, Eddie Hammons's byword was "Upon my honor," with which he apparently started almost every sentence. In most tellings, this gets shortened to just "'Pon my honor," or, "My honor." Maggie Hammons Parker remembered an old-timer whose bywords were "I'll eat hell." A common one is preceding a sentence with "I hope I may die," which comes out "hope-ma-die" and is shortened from "I hope I may die if this isn't the truth." **2005** Ebel *Orville Hicks* 17 A lot of people had by-words. Daddy's was "buddy, buddy." **2008** Salsi *Ray Hicks* 142 He'd say, "Just help to rid us of it." He was always a sayin', "just." It was his by-word.

[OED3 *by-word* n 3 "a word or phrase of frequent occurrence in speech" obsolete; DARE *byword* n chiefly South Midland]

C

ca- See **ker-**.

cabbage

A *noun* Variant plural form without *-s*.

1913 Kephart *Our Sthn High* 297 Tomato, cabbage, molasses and baking powder are always used as plural nouns . . . "I'll have a few more of them cabbage." **1934–47** LAMSAS (Madison Co NC, Swain Co NC) *them cabbage*. **1956** Hall Coll (Del Rio TN) How did you go about cutting up that many cabbage? **1973** GSMNP-80:14 You know what we chopped them cabbage up with? **1976** GSMNP-114:7 He just raise them cabbage. I don't think he ever had a tomato plant there, just cabbage. **1981** Williams *Storytelling* She built the fire in the morning and cooked the meals and scoured the pots and washed the dishes and hoed the cabbage and gathered them. **1994** Montgomery Coll Them cabbage weren't fit (Cardwell).

[DARE *cabbage* n A2a South Midland, New England]

B (also *cabbage on to*) *verb, verb phrase* To steal, take possession of.

1952 Wilson *Folk Speech NC* 524 *cabbage* = to take possession of, to steal. **1956** McAtee *Some Dial NC* 7 *cabbage onto* = steal. **a1975** Lunsford *It Used to Be* 158 The word "cabbage" means to take possession of, as "he cabbaged on to all the rent collected." **c1982** Young *Colloquial Appal* 4 *cabbaged* = nabbed, captured. **2005** Williams *Gratitude* 483 = to steal. "He didn't buy it, he cabbaged it."

cabbage on to See **cabbage B**.

cableway skidder *noun* See citation. Same as **overhead skidder**. See also **groundhog skidder, skidder**.

1994 Schmidt and Hooks *Whistle* 156 = a machine to skid logs by suspending them from cables.

cackleberry *noun* A hen's egg. Same as **hen apple**.

1983 Pyle *CCC 50th Anniv* A:3:2 When he wanted a dozen eggs, he'd say, "Bring me up a dozen cackleberries." **1984** Woods *WV Was Good* 193 None of us ever got too much cholesterol from eggs for the plain reason that we seldom got to eat "cackleberries." Eggs always were a salable commodity at the stores. **1994–97** Montgomery Coll (known to Cardwell, Shields, Weaver).

cacky *noun* Human excrement.

1886 Smith *Southernisms* 37 = "alvum exonerare." Webster gives to cack in this sense from Pope. It may still be heard in East Tennessee.

caddi-did *noun* See citation.

1978 Reese *Speech NE Tenn* 41 = cicada.

caddy (also *catty*) *adjective* Lively, active, spry, strong.

1938 Hall Coll (Emerts Cove TN) *catty* = active, lively, not still a minute. **1939** Hall Coll (White Oak NC) *caddy* = rather spry. **1956** Hall Coll (Big Creek NC) He was a terribly strong man and terribly caddy. *Ibid.* (Emerts Cove TN) I'd have fights in school. Ever once in a while [they'd] have to whup me. I was caddy for a little feller. **1982** Ginns *Snowbird Gravy* 94 He was just as young and catty as a young man.

[cf EDD *caddy* adj 1 "hale, hearty, in good health or spirits"]

cadgy *adjective*

A Variant forms *cagey* [see **1927** in **B2**], *caigy*.

1913 Kephart *Our Sthn High* 280 A few words, caigy (cadgy), coggled, fernent, gin for it, needcessity, trollop, almost exhaust the list of distinct Scotticisms.

B Senses.

1 High-spirited, excited.

1955 Parris *Roaming Mts* 177 The dogs are cagey. They are born to taunt rather than fight.

2 Sexually aroused, lusty.

1917 Kephart *Word-List* 409 *caigy* = full of sexual desire. **1927** Woofter *Dialect from WV* 350 = full of sexual desire and usually used in referring to males. "The stallion was so cagey as I rode past that mare I could hardly hold him." **1976** Garber *Mountain-ese* 13 = sexually adventurous. "Pa, that Ellie May is so cagey she's agoin' to get into trouble." **1994** Montgomery Coll: *caigy* (known to Brown, Cardwell). **1994** Walker *Life History* 30 [A powder was] used to make the animals "cagey" and reproduce.

[OED3 *cadgy* adj 1 "wanton, lustful, amorous," Scot and north dialect; EDD *cadgy* adj 1 "in good spirits, sportive"; Scot, Irel, nEngl; SND *cadgy* adj "cheerful; dotingly amorous"; CUD *cadgy* adj "cheerful, playful; active"; HT *caigy* "lively; full of energy"; DARE *cadgy* adj both senses chiefly South Midland]

cag See **keg**.

cagey See **cadgy**.

caggey bumps *noun* See citation.

1982 Slone *How We Talked* 105 Pimples [were] thought to be worms under the skin that eat your body after death. Also called "caggey bumps." They were thought to come on the face when a person got old enough to have sexual desires.

caigy See **cadgy**.

Cain corn *noun* Homemade whiskey.

1952 McCall *Cherokees and Pioneers* 101 If you are invited to share a little something, whether it be called moonshine, corn juice, nubbin booze, Cain corn, white mule, stump juice, white lightning, Old Nick, hoot owl, O be joyful, or mountain dew, you should be warned that the thing meant is that powerful rank pizen what cheers the heart of even a man with a nagging wife.

[from Cain, character in the Old Testament book of Genesis]

Cain's reed grass *noun* See citation.

1967 Campbell *Memories of Smoky* 134 It was on that day that Dr. Cain found a species of grass that, up to that time, was unknown to science. It was growing on the steep west face of Cliff Top, and found when Dr. Cain crawled up through the dense vegetation. Not being familiar with the species, Dr. Cain sent a sample to the nation's leading authority on grasses. It was verified as an entirely new species and was named by the grass specialist in honor of Dr. Cain. The name is *Calamagrostis canii*, with the common name of "Cain's reed grass."

cain't See **can**[1] **A2**.

cain't see to cain't see See **can see to can't see**.

cake *noun* See citation.

1958 Combs *Archaic English in KY* 32 = loaf: "Buy a cake of bread."

cakewalking *noun* A social event, as one held at a **box supper** or **pie supper**, in which participants march around seats until music stops, at which moment one standing at a given spot wins a cake. [Editor's note: The form *cakewalk* is widespread in the US.]

1940 Haun *Hawk's Done* 19 Joe took Tiny to a cake-walking over at Holiways church house one night.

calaboose *noun* A jail.

1908 Fox *Lonesome Pine* 198 Did you git board in the calaboose? **1984** Burns *Cold Sassy* 353 Come git us and put us in the calaboose. **2005** Williams *Gratitude* 483 = jail. "They put the thievin' rascal in the calaboose."

[< Spanish *calabozo* n "dungeon"; DARE *calaboose* n scattered, but chiefly South, West]

calabosh *noun* The entire crowd.

1952 Wilson *Folk Speech NC* 524 = the entire crowd. **1995–97** Montgomery *Coll* (known to Brown, Oliver).

calarip See **calarrup**.

calarrup (also *calarip*) *verb* Same as **larrup B**.

1878 Guild *Old Times TN* 168 I wished to give him rope, so I could "calarip" him. *Ibid.* 388 In my early day, no lawyer wore a ring. He dared not do it, for some of us would come along and "calarrup" him, sure.

[*ca-* variant of *ker-* + *larrup*]

calf lot *noun* An outdoor enclosure or pen for calves, often near a barn. See also **lot A**.

1864 *Chapman CW Letters* (April 12) we have sold a bout forty bushel of Cloversead and has got enoug left to sow the Calf lot next spring. **1973** GSMNP-78:1 We had us a fence around the pasture, between the barn and the house, which we called the calf lot. **1997** Montgomery *Coll* = a fenced lot for keeping calves separated from their mothers until feeding and milking time.

calf rope *interjection* Enough! I give in! (used as a cry signaling good-natured surrender in a contest, especially in wrestling or children's games). Also called **gate post**.

1955 Parris *Roaming Mts* 40 Nathan was judged the winner in bout after bout, with his opponents shouting "calf-rope," the mountain equivalent of enough. **1966–67** *DARE Survey* (Burnsville NC, Cherokee NC, Gatlinburg TN) = call to quit by one who is losing a fight, most often in wrestling. **1967** Wilson *Folkways Mammoth Cave* 27 = a rope used to tie a calf away from its mother at milking time. Since the calf would make some raucous noise, "calf rope" came to mean "I give up" when two boys were wrestling. **1993** Cunningham *Sthn Talk* 27 This time I ain't gonna let you up till you call calf rope loud enough for ever'body to hear. **1995–97** Montgomery *Coll* (known to Adams, Brown, Ledford, Norris). **2005** Williams *Gratitude* 483 = the words a person hollers out that means "I give up," as in wrestling. City speech is "Cry Uncle." **2014** *WV Talk* We said "calf rope" rather than "uncle" to give up in a wrestling match.

[DARE *calf rope, holler* v phr chiefly South Midland, Gulf States]

calf slobbers *noun* Meringue.

1993 Cunningham *Sthn Talk* 27 Jane's lemon pie allus has about two inches of calf slobbers on it. **2013** Venable *How to Tawlk* 9 = meringue, also any kind of thick pastry icing: "I bet the calf slobbers on 'at lemon pie was two inches tall!"

[DARE *calf slobbers* n 2 chiefly South Midland, Southwest]

calico *verb* See citation.

1915 Dingus *Word-List VA* 181 = to pass one's time with ladies, "fuss": "He's out a calicoin' every Sunday."

calico bush *noun* The mountain laurel tree (*Kalmia latifolia*), usually known as **ivy** or **mountain ivy** in the region.

1913 Morley *Carolina Mts* 56 Like the New Englander they call [laurel] "calico-bush," a comfortable name suggesting Sunday starch and fresh young girls. **1940** Haun *Hawk's Done* 7 The calico bushes all over the Lead Hill with their white, closed-up blossoms that open up when they feel a bee light on them. **1982** Stupka *Wildflowers* 80 Usually the attractive pink or white-saucered blossoms are so abundant that the mountain laurel in full bloom is one of our most spectacular plants. . . . "Ivy" and "calico-bush" are among its other names. **1982** Wells *Remarkable Flora* 5 Forming an understory in this magnificent forest are innumerable shrubs, among the most prominent being . . . the true laurel or calico bush with its pink spotted flowers.

call

A *verb*

1 To mention or state (a name).

1917 Kephart *Word-List* 409 Ain't you never heard Tommy *call* my name? **1919** Combs *Word-List South* 32 = used in inquiring after one's name, as, "How did ye say ye *called* yer name?" Knott Co [KY]. **1973** GSMNP-76 He called her name. She lived on Indian Creek there where the ranger's cabin is. **1984** GSMNP-154 He went by a man's house, which I'll not call his name, and picked up a little bottle of whiskey. **1994** Montgomery *Coll* (known to Cardwell). **1998** *Dante OHP*-69 I don't think I've ever heard his name called.

2 To recall (especially a name).

1939 Hall Coll (Copeland Creek TN) The man's name was Teague. I can't call his other name, of course, but his first name was Teague. **1967** Fetterman *Stinking Creek* 80 We had good young uns, but to tell you the truth I don't call all their ages. I could study on it awhile and come pretty dern close. **1972** GSMNP-73 John Dockery and two other men . . . I can't call their names.

[DARE *call* v 12 chiefly South, South Midland]

3 (also *call for*) To summon or seek the notice of (occupants of a dwelling) when approaching.

1901 Harben *Westerfelt* 156 I called Bill out in his shift on the porch. **1974** Roberts *Sang Branch* 243–44 [He] come to a house and he called and wanted something to eat. **1983** *Dark Corner OHP*-28A They come over there [and] called for him, and he went to the door. **2013** Pierce *Corn in Jar* 85 Cline and others went to the man's house, called him out, and "talked to him long enough for neighbors to notice."

4 in the passive phrase *be called* = to die.

1987 Young *Lost Cove* 83 When he was *called*, and they put his body in the ground atop the little knoll above the store, none of the oldtimers had the heart to come to the store for nearly a week.

B *noun* A reason, occasion, duty (especially in phrases *no call for, no call to*).

1891 Moffat *Mtneers Middle TN* 317 I ain't a feelin' no call to make dog meat outen myself this time in the mornin'. **1904–20** Kephart *Notebooks* 4:853 He had no call to do it. **1913** Kephart *Our Sthn High* 296 Many common English words are used in peculiar senses by the mountain folk, as call for name or mention or occasion. **1944** Combs *Word-List Sthn High* 18 = to intend, to have a mind to: "I hev a call to go to town today." **1956** Hall Coll (Big Creek NC) He had no call to practice [reading and writing]. **1957** Combs *Lg Sthn High: Word List* 17 *to hev (have) a call* = to intend, have in mind to. Ex: "I hev a call to go to town to-day." **1962** Dykeman *Tall Woman* 85 There'll be no call for you to do anything you don't want to do.

[DARE *call* n 8a "duty, need, occasion, right"]

call by *verb phrase* See citations.

1946 Woodard *Word-List VA/NC* 8. **c1960** Wilson Coll = come to visit, even for a brief time.

[DARE *call by* v phr probably South Midland]

call down *verb phrase* To reprimand, scold, castigate.

1941 Still *Troublesome Creek* 164 I hate like rip to call the old man down. **c1960** Wilson Coll = to scold severely. **2014** Montgomery *Doctrine* 68–69 = if (God forbid!) said preacher should preach some false doctrine or even something that *sounds* fishy, these good Bretheren [i.e. in the "amen corner"] are likely to call him down.

[DARE *call down* v phr chiefly North, Midland]

called out in meeting, be *verb phrase* Formerly of a couple intending to marry: to have their intentions announced publicly at a church service.

1939 *FWP Guide KY* 438 A couple contemplating marriage is "called out in meetin'" at least once prior to the marriage ceremony.

called to straw *adjective phrase* Pregnant, in childbed. See also **go to straw**.

1931 Combs *Lg Sthn High* 1307 Maggie's been called to straw. (She is pregnant.) **1940** Haun *Hawk's Done* 117 She was two months called to straw and easy to upset. **1996–97** Montgomery Coll (known to Brown, Jones). **1999** Russell and Barnett *Granny Curse* 25 She was born during a thunderstorm. Her mother was called to straw when the storm first started down Gregory Bald Mountain.

[DARE *called to straw* adj South Midland]

call figures *verb phrase* See citation.

1927 Woofter *Dialect from WV* 350 = to call the changes for a square dance. "Can any one here call figures?"

call for See **call A3**.

call off *verb phrase*

1 To list from memory. See also **call A2**.

1990 *Matewan OHP*-73 I can't call them off because I am forgetful.

2 To insult, curse.

1975 *AOHP/ALC*-903 I called him off in a mean name.

call out *verb phrase* To seek, pursue (payment).

1939 Hall Coll (Bradley Fork NC) I never called out no pension. I went through by my work.

call up *verb phrase* To entice (a hunted animal, especially a turkey), by imitating its call.

1939 Hall Coll = to call an animal imitatively; to attract so as to shoot: "They couldn't call 'em up. That is calling, the way of calling up a turkey gobbler, calling with my mouth." *Ibid.* (Deep Creek NC) Some of the Luftee fellows had told me about this gobbler a-gobbling there and they couldn't call him up, and I hardly ever failed back then on calling up a turkey. It's the way you call that brings them. If you call too much, you'll never get one to ye.

calm *adjective, verb* Variant forms *cam, ca'm* [kæm] or [kɑm].

1813 Hartsell *Memora* 112 that shet ther mouthes Close and the[y] goot verey Cam. **1873** Smith *Peace Papers* 127 Our wimmen are advised to be cam and serene. **1923** Montague *Today Tomorrow* 166 That ca'med the Sulivan feller, but Big Henry said he'd as leave go thar fighting, as to go any other way. **1933** Carpenter *Sthn Mt Dialect* 23 CALM is quite commonly pronounced in the old way, that is sounded to rhyme with SAM, south of West Virginia, but only occasionally to the north. **1942** Hall *Phonetics Smoky Mts* 104 As for *balm* and *calm*, older speakers say [bæm] and [kæm]; others say [bɑm], [kɑm]. **c1959** Weals *Hillbilly Dict* 4 Now hesh up and ca'm down. **1961** Kurath and McDavid *Pron Engl Atl Sts* 141 *Calm* with the vowel /æ/ of *bag* has extensive currency in the Midland and the South, except in cultivated speech. It is the predominant folk pronunciation throughout this far-flung area, being nearly universal outside of eastern Pennsylvania and parts of South Carolina. **1996** Montgomery Coll (known to Cardwell).

[DARE *calm* n, adj, v [kæm] especially South, Midland, infrequently New England]

calm daylight (also *calm of day, calm of the day*) *noun* Full daylight following or preceding darkness.

1939 *FWP Guide NC* 98 Daylight is "calm daylight" or "calm of day." **1972** Cooper *NC Mt Folklore* 126 Anyway, I've riz at calm of the day too many times over the years just to watch the sunshine play with the fog in them woods to consider selling a foot of that land. **1998** Montgomery *Coll*: *calm of day* (Bush, Cardwell); *evening calm of the day* = sunset to dusk; *morning calm of the day* = daylight to sunrise (Brown).

cam See **calm**.

came See **come A2**.

camfire See **camphor**.

campaign liquor *noun* A small portion of liquor distributed as a gratuity by a candidate during an election campaign.

[**1966** Caudill *My Appalachia* 2 If a Republican candidate for state office thought it worth his time to campaign in the mountain counties, his visit was the occasion of a big spread of home-cooked victuals provided by Republican wives for menfolks only and liquor provided by the candidate—also for menfolks only.] **1997** Montgomery *Coll* In the past at election time, candidates would often hand out half-pint or pint bottles of moonshine . . . this was known as campaign liquor (Ellis).

Campbellite *noun* A follower of Alexander Campbell, a revivalist preacher of the early nineteenth century. See also **newlight**.

1862 *Warrick CW Letters* (Oct 6) We have had some good preaching here in our Camps of late One was baptised yesterday morning by a missionary from Montgomery Ala. and 3 were baptised last night by a Campbellite preacher he was One of the Fort Donalson prisoners he was or is a good preacher. **1909** Godfrey *Autobiog* 119 [Alexander] Campbell's doctrine took better in Kentucky than in any other state in the Union. It is a notorious fact that the Campbellite Church was built up in Kentucky by taking in the children of the Methodists and Baptists. **1915** Bradley *Hobnobbing* 92 Again we lost our way and were forced to spend a night on the road—this time at the house of a "Campbellite" preacher—a bearded, patriarchal figure, who was also the local storekeeper. **2005** Sparks *Famous Preacher* 110 In the "Campbellite communities" of the Kentucky/West Virginia border country the Reformation/Disciple movement has had a venerable history, and more than once I have heard mild criticism from eastern Kentuckians.

campfire See **camphor**.

camphor *noun, verb* Variant forms *camfire, campfire*.

1867 Harris *Sut Lovingood* 145 Well, arter they'd tuck the ole 'oman up stairs an' camfired her to sleep, things begun tu work agin. **1907** Dugger *Balsam Groves* 159 Git the camp-fire quick! Yer pap's fell out uv the loft an' killed hisself! **1917** Kephart *Word-List* 412 That ain't got no bad taste; it has a leetle farewell to it as though it had campfire in it. **1920** Ridley *Sthn Mtneer* 103 Git me turpentine an' oil an' the campfire, an' that blamed lin'ment we used on the mule. **1942** Hall *Phonetics Smoky Mts* 91 *Camphor* as [kæmfaɪr] is probably a popular etymology. **1998** Montgomery *Coll* (known to Bush, Cardwell, Oliver).

[DARE *camphor* n A especially South Midland]

camp meeting *noun* Traditionally, an annual series of outdoor religious services, held usually (especially by Methodists) in late summer at an encampment with families from a wide area gathered, often under a **brush arbor**, to hear itinerant preachers, sing and pray, and socialize. After the middle of the 19th century, the event in most areas evolved into a denominational **association** meeting or a nondenominational **protracted meeting**, held in a local church or, more recently, under a tent (and called a *tent meeting* or simply a *revival*). Through the 20th century their prevalence continued to wane steadily, but they may still occasionally be found, sponsored by Baptists, Methodists, or the Church of God. Also called **grove meeting**. See also **big meeting, protracted meeting, revival meeting**.

1862 *Neves CW Letters* (Aug 6) We will not tent at camp meeting this year there is a sociation close by but I will not get to go as Bery is not at home. **1863** *Love CW Letters* (Aug 18) i was fixing for the camp meating we had a fine meating but it did not seame to me like a camp meating. **1881** Pierson *In the Brush* 13 I preached in a log meeting-house, or at a "stand" erected in a grove at some cross-roads, or at a camp-meeting, or wherever else I should be able to meet and address the people. **1948** Dick *Dixie Frontier* 199–200 As a frontier institution the camp-meeting developed a standard pattern during the first few years of the nineteenth century. A forest area was selected near a sparkling stream with plenty of shade and grass for hundreds of horses. A large square clearing was made and over this was constructed an immense brush arbor or, as a camp-ground became permanent, a long shed covered with clapboards. The logs were laid end to end in rows lengthwise, and rough slabs, split from other logs with wedges, were laid across these in tiers the full length of the arbor. At one end was a high platform, known as "the pulpit-stand," made of poles or poles and slabs. At the foot of the stand was a straw-floored enclosure about thirty feet square, known as "the altar" or "penitent's pen." A rail fence was built down the center of the arbor to separate the men from the women. Forming a quadrangle or large ellipse of about two acres including the arbor, and some distance from it, were the dwelling-places of the worshippers. These were called "the tents," although in a permanent camp they were often pole pens covered with clapboards. Many, however, were tents made of tow, or improvised tents made by stretching quilts, sheets, and counterpanes around and over crude pole frames. On the fourth side of the quadrangle, behind the pulpit-stand, were the dwelling-places of the ministers. **1955** Dykeman *French Broad* 322 The third or fourth week in August, when crops were "laid by" and "garden truck" was at its most plentiful, families within a radius of many miles put finishing touches on their arrangement to attend camp meetings. **c1980** Roberts *Olden Times* 61 The camp meetings were held in the forests with a temporary platform pulpit which always had a section to the right of the pulpit reserved for the local exhorters who punctuated the long and vigorous sermons with shouts of "Amen" and "Hallalujah" and "Praise the Lord" a chorus to keep both audience and preacher keyed to a high pitch. **1982** *Foxfire VII* 14 The camp meeting, anchored firmly in the American past, continues as a reality in West Virginia, Georgia, the Carolinas, and throughout the Bible Belt of the American heartland. *Ibid.* 271 We have a good camp meeting each year. The district sends several preachers out here for the week and we have several services each day. There are over fifty tent holders and on Friday and Saturday nights, this arbor is full. The camp meeting is something out of the past that has continued on and on. **1990** Brown *Oldest Camp Meeting* 253 The 1794 outdoor revival at Daniel Asbury's Rehobet [sic] Methodist Church in Lincoln County, North Carolina, has been considered as the first camp meeting ever held . . . the evidence indicates that this meeting, commonly called "Grassy Branch Camp Meeting," and now listed on the national register of Methodist sites, was indeed one of the very first camp meetings. **1998** Montgomery *Coll* = still held by Church of God and by Baptists (Adams), = most were nondenominational, usually lasting 3 or 4 days, but I knew one to go 30 days, nowadays they are usually called tent meeting (Brown), = held by Baptists and Methodists (Bush), = mostly Baptists and Methodists held camp meeting, later called revivals. Camp meetings were held inside a tent (Cardwell). **2004** Maynard *Churches of Smokies* 4 Camp meetings usually lasted three to four days, but sometimes extended to a week or more and became known as "protracted meetings." At the camp a shelter was constructed for preaching, the sacraments, and worship. In the early years the sheds were brush arbors built of logs supporting a roof of leafy branches. Later, some of those sheds became large permanent wooden structures capable of holding a thousand or more. **2004** Whitaker *Saints Sinners* 51 By the 1810s, [Methodists] had turned the spontaneous camp meeting into the organized camp meeting that became the main means for Methodist recruitment for the next half century. After the Civil War, the church gradually turned the camp meeting into a "protracted meeting" (or revival), in which people no longer camped at the site, but came to hear preaching for several nights in a row. This kind of revival became the model for membership used by Methodists, Baptists, Presbyterians, and other denominations in the region.

[DARE *camp meeting* n chiefly South, Midland]

can[1] *auxiliary verb*

A Forms.

1 Variant form *kin*.

1860 Taliaferro *Ducktown* 341 Do yer reckin I kin get thar tonight? **1864** *Warrick CW Letters* (Jan 3) I done hope that you kin get to come home this mounth for I had rotha see you com than to hear you Say that you are a coming and not Com home. **1886** Smith *Sthn Dialect* 348 When we asked for dinner, the man said, "Well, boys, hit's mighty rough, but ef you-uns kin eat it you're mo'n welcome ter it." **1923** Greer-Petrie *Angeline Steppin' Out* 4 Now, childern, all I ax you is, kin you beat that, when hit comes to cuttin' a rusty? **1940** Still *River of Earth* 18 I seed a brash o' blossoms on them vines. In a leetle time you'll have all you kin eat. **1953** Wharton *Dr Woman Cumberlands* 75 I kin take ye there a nigh way, cross country. **1970** Roberts and Roberts *Time Stood Still* 31 "So when you see one of them signs up here about a landslide," says Mr. Wright, "remember they kin be destructious." **2013** Venable *How to Tawlk* 10 = a famous brand of soft drink: "You kin buy a Co-Cola anywhores in the world!"

2 Variant negative forms *cain't*, *cayn't*, *kain't*.

1861 *Martin CW Letters* (Sept 29) I dont want you to ever volinteer in the world for you caint stan it. **1899** Frost *Ancestors* 317 I hain't a-sayin' that God cayn't let in a truly repentant sinner that don't come up to this yere standard. **1913** Kephart *Our Sthn High* 80 A plumb cur, of course, cain't follow a cold track—he just runs by sight. **1932** Dargan *Call Home* 20 I kain't git aholt o' her. **1937** Hall *Coll* (Little Greenbrier TN) Granddaddy kept bear meat, tastes like pork. Lots of people cain't tell it from pork meat. **c1959** Weals *Hillbilly Dict* 4 I hate I cain't help ye. **1973** Miller *English Unicoi Co* 92 *cain't* attested by 6 of 6 speakers. **1982** Powers and Hannah *Cataloochee* 93 (The Park) has rernt this country. They have us hemmed in, 'n you cain't kill a thing.

[DARE *can* v[1] b especially South, South Midland]

3 Variant negative form *coutn't*.

2005 Williams *Gratitude* 142 A family just about coutn't make it 'thout a cow.

B Syntax.

1 *can't*, *couldn't* inverted with the subject in a negative statement.

See Grammar and Syntax §11.5.

1924 (in **1952** Mathes *Tall Tales* 32) Can't nary one of us read no kind of writin' ner printin', but we can recollec' the main idy of it if you'll read it off, like. **1939** Burnett *Gap o' Mountains* 57 "Caint nobody deny that old Spot was glad to see you," said Mose: "his antics shore proved he was a dog." **1948** Chase *Grandfather Tales* 165 [The cave] just was big enough for them [i.e. children] to crawl in, and couldn't no grown person get in at all. **1959** Stubbs *Mountain-Wise* (Aug–Sept) 6 Can't no woman live on a gallon of tea and two bird bites a day. **1972** Ensor *Tales of Supernatural* 71 Thar're places on that mountain, big rock ledges that can't nobody get to. **1973** *AOHP/ASU-106* The top one [= a bed cover] would come down on you. Couldn't no air get to you. **1977** Shackelford et al. *Our Appalachia* 62 They had the funeral at the house and couldn't many people get inside the house. **1979** *Big South Fork OHP-18* They couldn't nobody do that. **1989** Giardina *Storming Heaven* 246 Hit's like water running and cant nobody hold it back. **2004** Fisher *Kettle Bottom* 11 Mostly it is a big lot of nothing cant nobody use. *Ibid.* 29 [The] Company says couldn't nobody have lived. **2007** Shelby *Molly Whuppie* 66 When they got up there, they saw that the tree had no limbs on it: "Can't nobody climb a tree like that," said Jack.

2 In phrases *ask can*, *know can*, *see can*, *wonder can*. See **ask B1**, **know C1**, **see B1**, **wonder 3**.

3 In phrase *could I* = if I could. See also **do A1**, **A4c**. See also

Grammar and Syntax §17.3. [Editor's note: This usage does not occur in ATASC.]

1802 (in **1941** Rothert *McDowell Letters*) (Sept 25) I am satisfyed could I have stayed 10 or 12 or 14 days I would have got clear of the deficulty in my Eyes. **1913** Kephart *Our Sthn High* 233 I lay thar an' think o' the spring branch runnin over the root o' that thar poplar; an' I say, could I git me one drink o' that water I'd be content to lay me down and die. **1941** Still *Troublesome Creek* 36 Could I lend a hand, 'twould be a satisfaction. **1962** Dykeman *Tall Woman* 41 Could I lay my hands on them, I'd gut them like bantams. **1976** Still *Pattern of Man* 58 Aye, could I stack Roaring's votes on top of Salt Springs I'd be as good as elected.

4 (also *could*) combined with another auxiliary verb. See also **may B1**, **B2**, **B3**, **used to B1**, **will A4**.

1884 Smith *Scrap Book* 66 I used to could plow, but it looks like I have lost the lick [= skill]. **1930s** (in **1944** Wentworth *ADD* 92) (WV) "He'll not kin go" . . . Always in combination *'ll not kin* or *'ll never kin*: "She'll never kin catch a mouse now." Said when a pet cat became crippled. **1934–47** *LAMSAS* (Swain Co NC) *may can*, *might can*. **1937** Hall *Coll* (Wears Cove TN) You might could ask somebody along the road (from woman of whom Joseph Hall was asking directions). **1953** Atwood *Verbs East US* 35 Type I informants [i.e. older speakers with little formal education] offer [*might could*] with hardly any exceptions, and it is also used by from two thirds (Va.) to practically all (N.C.) of Type II informants [i.e. younger speakers with more formal education] as well. . . . A good many informants in the S[outh] A[tlantic] S[tates] use the form *mought* rather than *might* in this phrase. **1961** *Coe Ridge OHP-336A* Some of the rest of them could might give you more information about this than I can. **1974–75** McCracken *Logging* 9:3 If I think about it, I might could tell you. **1978** Montgomery *White Pine Coll* VIII-2 They say I could might have lived to make it to the hospital. **1986** Pederson et al. *LAGS* (Hawkins Co TN) You might could get up here and help me; (Johnson Co TN) Now I might can tell you something; (Sevier Co) [I] used to couldn't slaughter [hogs]; (Johnson Co TN) I used to could work all day. **1988** Dickey and Bake *Wayfarer* 24 You might could sit up a little bit, if you feel like it. **2001** Montgomery *File* I may can get it out tomorrow (54-year-old woman, Jefferson Co TN).

can[2]

A *noun* See citation.

1949 Maurer *Argot of Moonshiner* 8 = in the Southern mountains, a half-gallon fruit jar . . . in other districts, a five- to ten-gallon wood-covered metal container. A postwar addition is the G.I. can, one of the Army's five-gallon gasoline cans adapted to distilling needs: "Set that can of likker over here."

B *verb* See citations.

1956 McAtee *Some Dial NC* 7 = tie an empty can to the tail of a cat or dog in thoughtless abuse. **c1960** Wilson *Coll* = to tie a tin can to a dog's tail; formerly regarded as very funny, esp. at the country store.

candle board *noun* The horizontal shelf or ledge over a fireplace.

1949 McDavid *Grist* 107 (Greenville Co SC) = mantel.

candle fly *noun*

1 See citation. Same as **miller**.

1973 Miller *English Unicoi Co* 144 = a moth or miller, a small winged insect with dusty wings.

[DARE *candle fly* n 1 chiefly South, Midland]

2 A firefly.

1968 *DARE Survey* (Lexington VA).

candlelight *noun*

1 A candle.

1922 *TN CW Ques* 1386 (Wilkes Co NC) Mother and my sisters coked washed scowerd, carded spun wove picked wool cotin with fingers by the old candell lites.

2 (also *candle-lighting time*) Dusk. See also **early candlelight**.

1803 (in **1956** Eliason *Tarheel Talk* 263) (Haywood Co NC) They did not depart for home . . . till some time after Candle Light. **c1940** Simms *Coll*: *candlelight* = the time [of day] for lighting candles. **1967** Wilson *Folkways Mammoth Cave* 13 Houses were lighted by kerosene or coal-oil lamps. This time, along about dusky dark, when the lamps were lighted, became for everyone a very poetic time. . . . Very old people speak of it as *candle-lighting time*.

candlelighter *noun* See citation.

1980 Riggleman *WV Mtneer* 5 To light the lamp or lantern we used "candlelighters," which were made by rolling up pages of magazines or newspapers. . . . To light the lamp, the end of a candlelighter was lit in the fireplace and touched to the wick of the lamp.

candle-lighting time See **candlelight 2**.

candy ankle *noun* A weak or effeminate man.

1938 Stuart *Dark Hills* 148 When we catch a candy-ankle going between the sheds a couple or three of us fellars grab him and away we take him to a barrel of oil. We souse him under too. **1996** Spurlock *Glossary* 392 = someone considered "soft" by another who considers himself "rough and tough."

candy breaking (also *candy pulling*) *noun* Formerly, an early fall gathering and party following a **molasses boil** at which young people make stick candy from freshly boiled **sorghum molasses**, as by a girl and a boy taking a handful of hot molasses and then pulling and stretching candy as it cools and hardens into breakable pieces. See 1975, 1977 citations. Also called **molasses pull**, **taffy pull**.

1912 Perrow *Songs and Rhymes* 143 At "Square" Murray's, near the head of Wildcat, there is pretty sure to be, before many weeks pass, . . . a "pea-hullin'." **a1975** Lunsford *It Used to Be* 38 Some of that molasses they have left aside, and they boil it and boil it and boil it until it gets to be a kind of candy. And then's when you have the "candy-pulling." The young people get together, and, after all the work around the place has been done, they get this candy ready. The more you pull it, the brighter it gets and the better it gets. You pull it in this sort of way: you take a wisp of this candy—

it looks like the golden hair of some blonde—and two young people face each other. You put your left hand on the end of this roll of soft and stretchy candy, and you put your right hand about two-thirds of the way down on it. The other party facing you—boy or girl—does just exactly the same thing. Each one pulls and brings his hands together and then they twist. That puts it in four different strands. You twist that around, twist it around, pull it out again, and bring it out just like they did with the same motion. And, of course, they carry that on till the small hours of the morning. We've often heard the question, "when are we going to have the next candy pullin'?" **1977** Hamilton *Mt Memories* 88 At the "candy pullings," the molasses would be boiled down to a certain thickness and set aside to cool. When it cooled enough to handle, a girl and boy would wash and grease their hands, dig out a ball of the stuff, and start to pull, hand over hand. When the candy turned from a dark molasses color to a beautiful taffy shade, it was spread out on a greased surface to get cold. Then the long strands would be cut into sticks. It was very good since candy of any kind was a rarity. Most of all, the boys and girls had enjoyed being together. **1978** Montgomery *White Pine Coll* III-2 The only recreation we'd have would be if somebody had a candy pulling. . . . In fact, that's where I met my husband was at a candy pulling. **1990** Wigginton *Foxfire Christmas* 38 We'd have what they called a candy pulling—the girls and boys would. We'd get us a girl and pull candy. The more we worked it, the better it'd be. Made it harder and stiffer. I remember boiling the syrup down, and it'd turn white as we pulled on it. **1993** Montell *Cumberland Country* 66 Candy breakings were social gatherings sometimes held for mercenary reasons by the host. Sticks of candy were identified individually, each bearing the name of one of the girls present. The candy was then auctioned off, as was done at pie and box suppers, with the fellow making the highest bid getting both the candy stick and the girl. Most of the time, however, candy breakings were scheduled so that the area's young people could just come together and have a good time. Sometimes the candy stick was broken in two so that both boy and girl could each have half a stick. Other times the couple would sit face to face eating away at the unbroken stick of candy. Naturally, their lips would touch as they partook of the last bite. Candy breakings were always followed by music and games.

[DARE *candy breaking* n South Midland, *candy pulling* scattered, but chiefly South, South Midland, New England, California]

candy drawing *noun* See citations.

1973 *Foxfire II* 374 They'd have a dishpan fulla stick candy broke up into little pieces. . . . And th'pan was covered. And a girl and boy would pair off and go and reach under there and get a piece a'candy. If they each got a piece alike [the same color], why they could keep it, but if they didn't, they had t'put it back. **1979** *Daddy Oakley* 178 We had lots of candy drawings. They'd bake the candy, and we had two different kinds. Then they'd break it up into short pieces. Somebody would be holding a cloth with a pan over it and a boy and a girl would each draw a piece. The girl would run her hand under the cloth first and draw a stick and then the boy would draw. If they got pieces alike, they got to keep it and if not, they had to put it back. . . . They would keep drawing till they ran out of candy.

candy knocking *noun* See citations.

1963 Watkins and Watkins *Yesterday* 105 At a candy knocking a piece of candy was tied to a string hanging from the ceiling. One person was blindfolded and handed a stick of wood. If he swung at the candy and hit it, he was given a stick of candy. **1998** Dabney *Smokehouse Ham* 43 [She] recalled going to a "candy knocking" in the Faucette Lake district of Dawson County, Georgia, where she grew up. "It was at the John Turner place. A whole crowd of young folks was there, including a big crowd of Turner children. . . . Candy was tied up in the loft, and you marched around there and they gave you a stick to knock it down with."

candy pulling See **candy breaking**.

candy roaster *noun* A large squash similar in color to a pumpkin, but sweeter (or sweetened), cooked into pies and cakes or made into a sauce.

1925 Dargan *Highland Annals* 50 I went calmly through the orchard, picking my way over the fallen fruit that no hand would rescue from decay; looked unwistfully at the pumpkins, cushaws, and "candy-roasters" that would feed nothing but the frost. **1973** Miller *English Unicoi Co* 144 = a variety of squash of which the edible part is preserved by canning. **1996–97** Montgomery *Coll* (known to Adams, Brown, Ledford), = a large squash used to make pies, larger and sweeter than a pumpkin, about the size and shape of a small watermelon, the skin of which is similar in color and texture to a butternut squash (Ellis), = a large squash, 12–24 inches long, colored like a pumpkin, ripens in the fall, and is cooked like a pumpkin (Oliver). **1997** Andrews *Mountain Vittles* 61 Grandpa Jim Cagle shor' did love candy roasters. They are sort of like a pumpkin. Mountain folks like 'em cause they cook a sauce a lot smoother and sweeter than a pumpkin. You can put it on yer toast or waffles ever' mornin'. Grandpa Cagle always did say the green 'uns were better.

candy stew *noun* A party at which candy is made.

1835 (in **1956** Eliason *Tarheel Talk* 263) (Wilkes Co NC) We had a candy stew . . . last night. **1858** Webb *Letter* 109 There has been a Candy stew every other night in this settlement since Christmas as three nights in a week at John Stipe's and of all dancing you ever heard of this is the place for it. **1982** Ginns *Snowbird Gravy* 147 We'd have a candy stew—we called it a candy stew—or we'd have a corn shucking or some event, such as grinding molasses, to get together. At the candy stew, we'd make up a bunch of chocolate candy [from] milk, chocolate, sugar, what have you. Everybody would get around and tell tales, play games.

[DARE *candy stew* n KY, NC, VA]

canebrake *noun* A thicket of river cane (*Arundinaria gigantea*), a species of bamboo that grows along streams and rivers in stalks as high as thirty feet; such thickets once covered extensive tracts of the southeastern United States.

1769 (in **1940** McJimsey *Topo Terms in VA* 162) As we ascended the brow of a small hill, a number of Indians rushed out of a thick cane brake. **1814** Hartsell *Memora* 146 we went about two miles twolow whare we Struck a large Cain brack. **1824** Knight *Letter from KY* 88 In the southern parts of this state, there were, formerly, extensive cane-brakes, which were evergreen, when other herbage was sere and brown; and in which cattle went to browse in the winter. **1834** Crockett *Narrative* 172 My apology is, that I want the world to understand my true history, and how I worked along to rise from a cane-brake to my present station in life. **1939** Hall *Coll* (Wears Cove TN) This bottomland below here was in canebrakes. They's lots of it here yet. They was wildernesses of canebrake then. **1969** Hall *Coll* (Mt Sterling NC) There was a big canebrake [in the Big Bend]. They'd cut canes and make baskets. **1999** Fulcher *Raising Cane* 11 The canebrakes—untidy, infuriating, and foreboding swaths to many visitors—were a conspicuous feature of the landscape on the "wild frontier," and Crockett was happy to take them as his emblem. **2007** *Smokies Guide* (Spring) 11 River cane (*Arundinaria gigantea*) is a close relative to Asian bamboo that grows up to 20 feet tall and once covered miles of fertile riverside land in dense thickets called cane breaks [sic]. It's native to the southeastern United States, occurring from northern Florida to east Texas to southern Ohio. Cane [brakes] were haven to a variety of wildlife—bison, black bear, white-tailed deer, Wild Turkey, and warblers. The Cherokee and other American Indians used canes for everything from arrow shafts and blow guns to baskets and flutes.

[*cane* + *-brake* < Middle English *brake*, akin to Old English *brecan* "to break"]

cane mill (also *cane press, cane press mill*) *noun* A small boxlike device for pressing the stalks of **sorghum** for their juice, which is made into molasses. Now mechanized, the process was long carried out by grinding raw stalks fed into the mill, which was driven by a lever attached to the harness of a horse or mule, which encircled a ring for hours. Such a mill was often owned by one person in the community and, though sometimes portable, was often the site of a neighborhood **molasses boil** in the early fall. Also called **grinder, horse-around, molasses mill, press 1, sorghum gin.**

1945 O'Dell *Old Mills* 2–3 The cane mill was powered by a horse, but it was nevertheless a mill, and it figured large in pioneer life. For from the cane mill came the juice that was made into sorghum molasses, and sorghum molasses when made properly was a favorite "sweetening." The cane mill consisted of two large iron rollers mounted near the top of a mill four or five feet high. A lever was attached to the top of the mill in such a way that, when a horse was attached to the lever and driven around the mill, it set the rollers in motion. The cane was hand-fed into the rollers, and the juice ran through a cloth into a tube. The ground cane was thrown into the pathway for the horses to walk on.... Each mill [in Cocke County] served a radius of about twenty miles. Each owner charged fifty cents a day for the use of the mill. This was usually paid in molasses. **1977** *Smoky Vistas* (Fall) 3 Few mountain settlers could afford the cane mills necessary to squeeze the juice out of the cane. A man who owned one allowed his neighbors to use it. His land was alive with activity during sorghum season, as families came to grind the cane and make the syrup, and of course, to socialize. Each person brought his cane and enough wood to fire the boiler and cook his sorghum juice. In payment for the use of the cane mill the man and his helpers usually received every fourth gallon of molasses. **1984** Smith *Enduring Memories* 15 The cane press mill was always mounted about 30 or 40 feet from the pan and on higher ground, so that as the cane was pressed producing its juice, the liquid would flow down hill to the pan. Plenty of wood was necessary to cook the juice and assure a good even fire under the pan which was usually about twelve feet long and four feet wide. The cane had to be stripped by pulling all the leaves off the stalks, then the stalks were cut and hauled to the mill. A mule was used to turn the mill and compress the cane, forcing the juice out. The juice would flow from the hollow of the mill into a 90 gallon holding barrel. A one-inch pipe ran from the bottom of the barrel underground to the front section of the cooking pan. The fire would be started and the experienced molasses maker would move the molasses from the front to the back in the four or five sections of the pan as the juice cooked, driving off the water and becoming molasses. By the time it reached the last section of the pan it was ready to be placed in containers for keeping. Usually eight-gallon lard stands were used. The good molasses maker knew how to stir and skim the molasses and exactly when to move the juice along in the pan. It was not something you could get from a book, and a farmer that could make good molasses was the pride of the community. Usually only one mill would serve a large community and the farmers would haul their cane by wagons for several miles to get the good molasses maker to process their cane. **1988** Lambert *Kinfolks Custard Pie* 100 The cane mill was operated usually by mule power. It required a mule hooked to a long pole to walk in endless circles; the other end of the pole was attached to the mill and caused the upright wheels in the mill to turn. Someone sat near the mill, low enough not to get hit by the turning pole, and fed the cane into the mill. There it was crushed by the wheels, and the juice ran out the bottom into a pan. **1997** *Smokies Guide* (Autumn) 13 The molasses was made from the juice inside the cane. To extract the juice, the stalks were fed between the turning rollers of a cane mill. Power for a mill was provided by a horse or mule harnessed to the end of a long pole that was attached to the top of one of the rollers.... It was customary for families to take their cane to a neighboring farmer who had a mill and cooker. In return, the owner of the cane mill received a portion of the molasses, usually one out of every eight or 12 gallons. **2001** Cooper and Cooper *New River* 147 My dad had an oxen and a cane press. As the oxen was led around and around, another person was shoving in the cane after the leaves had been stripped off. **2003** LaLone et al. *Farming Life* 322–23 One fellow in the community had what they called a cane mill. That was the part that ground cane. Stick it in, then grind it, squish it, make the juice run out into a little trough that catches the juice, and that's what you made the molasses out of.... You'd have to go in and strip all the leaves off of [the cane stalk], then cut it. And this particular fellow had a cane mill and he would take it from farm to farm because most of us couldn't have bought a cane mill. . . . He charged you so much molasses for use of his cane mill. You hooked a horse to it and the horse went round and round in a ring just like this. It had a long pole that turned the cane mill as you fed it in, the juice ran out into a little trough and the rest of the cane went on through on the other side. Then you had to have a large vat you cooked it in, boil it down till [it became] molasses.

cane molasses See **molasses B.**

cane press mill See **cane mill.**

cane pummies See **pomace.**

cane stripping *noun* Traditionally, a family or community work activity to strip leaves and tops off **sorghum cane** before taking the stalks to a **cane mill** for pressing.

1991 Haynes *Haywood Home* 59 We'd have apple peelings, pumpkin cuttings, bean stringings to make leatherbritches, corn shuckings, cane strippings, quiltings and log rollings to name only a few. **1993** Page and Smith *Foxfire Toys and Games* 69 If you could get the kids to work you could make a big cane patch. Work hard and then have a cane strippin' that fall. After you got the cane stripped you'd have a big dance.

can house *noun* A cellar, pantry, or outbuilding, sometimes built partially below ground, in which canned fruits and vegetables, jellies, and other foods are stored, especially for winter consumption.

1973 Miller *English Unicoi Co* 144 = a small wood or stone building for storing canned foods and dried fruits and vegetables. **1975** Jackson *Unusual Words* 155 Women would dry apple slices and beans and store them in the loft of the house or in the *sass hole*, also known as the *root cellar* or *can house*, and they would be ready for use during the winter. **1982** *Smokies Heritage* 19 A squat log structure built over icy flowing water, the springhouse served as a storeroom for milk, butter, and cheese, crocks of kraut, and cans of jellies and jam. (It was also called a "can house.") **1986** Pederson et al. *LAGS* = attested by 4/60 interviewees (6.7%) from E TN; 4/4 of all LAGS interviewees (100%) attesting term were from Appalachia; (Carter Co TN, Greene Co TN, Cocke Co TN) = old term for a pantry. **1996** Houk *Foods and Recipes* 8 The Mason jar was patented in 1858, and once the glass "cans," or jars, became available in the mountains, women put up gallons upon gallons of fruits and vegetables and lined them up in neat rows in the "can house" or cellar. **1996–97** Montgomery *Coll* (known to Brown), = a structure partly recessed into a bank so that the contents would not freeze (Jones), = a small structure that was built partially underground to put canned food in so that it wouldn't freeze (Cardwell). **1999** Postell *Traditions* 11–12 Once the food is "put up," it is stored in the canhouse—a small well built structure made out of rock, wood, cement blocks, etc., usually built somewhere close to the main house. Many times the structure is built so that it will go back into the mountainside.

canned heat *noun* See citation.

1939 Farr *TN Mt Regions* 90 = corn liquor: "He's full of canned heat."

canoodle *verb* To fondle one another; to engage in behind-doors behavior.

1973 (in **2018** Montgomery *DSAE File*) Committee chairman Sam Ervin was skeptical, contending that the White House and Haldeman had done some "canoodling together" to leak a sanitized version of the tapes in the hearings while keeping the originals from the committee's scrutiny. **2012** *Blind Pig* (Aug 12) Nana, Papaw, my aunt, and whatever "goober" friend Papaw brought would go out each Friday, and according to my aunt, Nana and Papaw would be "canoodling" while she and the goober friend sat there awkwardly.

can see to can't see (also *cain't see to cain't see*, *can to can't*, *kin-see to kain't-see*) *noun phrase* Dawn to dusk, the entire day long.

1939 *FWP Guide NC* 98 From *kin-see to kain't-see* is a full day's work. **1952** Wilson *Folk Speech NC* 556 *kin-see to* (till) *can't see* = from early morning (the time one "can see") till dark (the time one "can't see"). "I work from *kin-see to can't see.*" **1978** *Smokies Heritage* 106 A day of workin' can to can't (daylight to dusk) in the cornfields had a way of taking the red out of even a young rooster's comb. **1979** Carpenter *Walton War* 167 I've worked all my life from Can-see to Can't-see, jist to keep soul and body together. **1992** Brooks *Sthn Stuff* 25 *cain't-see to cain't-see* = from before dawn to after dusk. "Them labor unions are awright if you ast me. They got a lot o' rights for us workin' folks. I know 'cause you're talkin' to somebody c'n still recollect when his ma and pa worked up there in the mill nigh on most o' their lived from cain't-see to cain't-see. **1995–97** Montgomery *Coll* (known to Brown, Cardwell). **2007** Alexander *Moonshiners Gone* 127 The usual workday always lasted from "can til can't." Which means every day from the time you could see at daylight until dark thirty when you could no longer see.

[DARE *can to can't, from* v phr chiefly South, Midland]

can't See **can[1] B1.**

cantakerious *adjective* See citation.

1982 Slone *How We Talked* 29 = mean, hateful.

cant dog (also *cant hook*) *noun* See citations. See also **peavey.**

1964 Clarkson *Lumbering in WV* 358 *cant dog* = a tool similar to peavey but having a toe-ring and lip at the end instead of a pike. Used to roll and lift logs. This term was often used in West Virginia to denote a peavey. **1998** Farwell *Logging Terms: cant hook* = an implement used to turn cants [i.e. logs already sawed on one or more sides]. **2006** Farwell *Logging Term* 1020–21 Old terms such as *cant hooks*, which refers to long poles topped with a hook for turning logs, are still in use for loggers' tools.

cantdog man *noun* See citation.

1967 Parris *Mt Bred* 133 A bullwhacker is a driver of oxen and a cantdog man is a fellow who uses a short-handled peavey.

cant hook See **cant dog**.

cantilever barn *noun* A barn with second-floor counterweighted overhangs on two or four sides, found in the United States mainly in Sevier and Blount Counties, TN.

1993 Moffett and Wodehouse *E TN Barns* xiii For many people in East Tennessee, the Tipton barn [in Cades Cove] is probably the most prominent example of a cantilever barn, an unusual form peculiar to this region. Its base story is composed of two log cribs erected on the foundation stones similar to the cabins and other outbuildings constructed in the cove and elsewhere. Above the ground floor, however, the similarity to other barns ceases. The topmost crib logs extend out to the barn's side ends to become the *primary cantilevers*, and upon these rest a series of *secondary cantilevers*, which protect front to back, establishing the width of the barn. These cantilevers support the loft floor and become the base for a heavy timber loft frame, which completes the barn and unites the separate structures of the two cribs. *Cantilever* is the structural name for the characteristic overhanging hewn beams, and *cantilever barn* is the term used to describe the building type. **1995** Trout *Historic Buildings* 47–48 Practically all cantilever barns fell into one of two categories: two-pen or four-pen. These groups were further subdivided into ones with overhang on the front and rear only, and those with a four-way overhang. . . . Getting two pens aligned and level was a necessity, and very difficult if the site was on a slope or uneven ground. Building four pens multiplied the chances that something wouldn't turn out just right. Assuming all went well with the pens, the hayloft framing was begun. It rested on the huge cantilever beams that were laid across the tops of the cribs, in one direction only for the front and rear overhang and at right angles to each other for four-way overhang. The bottom surface of each overhanging beam was hewn so that it tapered toward the tip. This was done to reduce the beam's own weight so that it would not sag at the tip. The cantilever principle is a simple one, regardless of how and to what it is applied. The end of any beam that sticks out over a support can hold up some weight as long as there is an equal or greater weight holding down the other end. If both ends of the same beam project over opposite walls of a building, and the weight on each end is about the same, then all is in equilibrium, as with a balanced seesaw. **1997** Morgan *Barn in SW VA* 276–78 The typical cantilever barn in Blount and Sevier Counties in Tennessee is a double-pen or double-crib structure, with a pen simply being a four wall unit of simple horizontal construction. The barn consists of level log cribs and an overhanging frame upper floor supported by log beams or cantilevers. The log cribs are usually separated by a central passage or runway. A majority of the barns have overhangs on all four sides, with most of the remaining structures having overhangs on front and rear only. Lower cribs were used as animal stalls and the upper floor was a hayloft. Perhaps the most important function of the overhang was to provide a dry area in which to feed barnyard animals, especially cattle.

can to can't See **can see to can't see**.

cap

A *noun*

1 See 1974 citation. Same as **still cap**.

1967 Williams *Moonshining* 13 A copper bucket to which a length of copper tubing has been soldered will serve as a good cap. **1968** *End of Moonshining* 49 = the top third of the still. It is removable so that the still can be filled after a run. **1974** Maurer and Pearl *KY Moonshine* 115 = the cover, usually of copper, that is placed over the opening in the top of the still through which vapor passes via the connections to the condenser. "You put the cap on and I'll put the paste to her." **a1975** Lunsford *It Used to Be* 80 Then there's the cap. That's the part that goes on top of the still that's connected with the worm. It carries the steam out and the cool water causes it to congeal. It comes out of the worm into a vessel. **1982** Slone *How We Talked* 68 *cap* = the lid or top, which was used to seal the top of the copper drum in which the mash was cooked. It was sealed on with paste made from water and flour.

2 See citation. Same as **blossom cap**.

1974 Maurer and Pearl *KY Moonshine* 115 = the frothy formation on top of the vat of fermenting beer that finally clears away, settling through the beer. "It ain't ready to run. The cap ain't broke."

3 (also *cap bundle, capsheaf, capstone, sheaf cap*) The sheaf or pair of sheaves broken and placed on top of a stack (or **shock**) of grain or hay to deflect rain; also used figuratively.

1867 Harris *Sut Lovingood* 38 [He] got rich, got forty maulins fur his nastiness, an' tu put a cap sheaf ontu his stack ove raskallity, got religion, an' got to Congress. **1957** Broaddus *Vocab Estill Co KY* 14 *cap* = the bundles of wheat put on the top of a wheat stack. **c1960** Wilson *Coll*: *cap* or *cap-sheaf* = the bundle or bundles of grain turned bottom upwards on a shock to protect the shocked bundles from getting wet. **1986** Pederson et al. *LAGS*: *cap* = attested by 7/60 interviewees (11.7%) from E TN; 7/7 of all LAGS interviewees (100%) attesting term were from Appalachia; *cap bundle* = attested by 5/60 interviewees (8.3%) from E TN; 5/5 of all LAGS interviewees (100%) attesting *cap bundle* were from Appalachia. **1997** Montgomery *Coll*: *cap* (known to Brown, Cardwell, Jones, Ledford, Weaver); *cap bundle* (Cardwell); *sheaf cap* (Brown, Cardwell); *capstone* (Weaver).

[DARE *cap bundle* n especially Midland]

4 The green top removed from a strawberry before it is eaten.

c1960 Wilson *Coll* = the green part that pulls off the vine with the berry (strawberry, usually). **1966–68** *DARE Survey* (Brasstown NC, Burnsville NC).

[DARE *cap* n 5 chiefly South, South Midland]

5 (also *cap corn, capping corn*) Popcorn. See also **cap B4**, **capper**.

1946 Dudley *KY Words* 270 *caps* = popcorn. **1980** Still *Run for Elbertas* 51 One house stood yellow as capping corn, and new-painted. **1982** Slone *How We Talked* 33 *cap corn* = popcorn.

6 Same as **eye**.

[**1950** Stuart *Hie Hunters* 51 Arn walked to the flat-topped cookstove [and] lifted the top from the firebox with the cap-lifter.] **1977** *Foxfire IV* 128 [The step-stove]'s an iron stove up on four legs—a little flat feller. They's two caps . . . down here, and then it raises up a little and they's two caps up here.

[DARE *cap* n 2a chiefly South Midland, South]

B *verb*

1 To remove the green top of (a strawberry or other berry).

1895 Edson and Fairchild *TN Mts* 370 Hit's mighty slow, pickin' and cappin' berries. **1925** Dargan *Highland Annals* 67 I'd never fill my bucket if I stopped to cap them. **1997** Andrews *Mountain Vittles* 21 My Momma of course picked any leaves and stems out the berries and she capped 'em.

[DARE *cap* n 5 South, South Midland]

2 See citation.

c1999 Sutton *Me and Likker* 55 You put 2 gallons [of wheat bran] on each barrel on top—that is what you call capping [the whiskey being distilled]. Keeps it warm, keeps it from evaporating and it will start to work within 15 minutes of adding sugar to it.

3 See 1957 citation; by extension = to "beat all."

1957 Broaddus *Vocab Estill Co KY* 14 = to put the cap on a stack of wheat. **2003** Carter *Mt Home* 16 She laughed as she carried the ice cream pan in, "If that don't cap the stack, that dausted dog has gobbled up ever bite!"

4 To pop (dried kernels of corn). See also **cap A5**, **capper**.

1946 Dudley *KY Words* 270 = to pop (corn). **1976** Still *Pattern of Man* 121 *cap corn* = [to] heat corn until it bursts. **1980** Berry and Repass *Grandpa Says* 19 = pop: "I'm going to cap some corn."

capacitated *adjective* See citation.

1960 Westover *Highland Lg* 19 = had the ability to.

cap and ball gun *noun* A long-barreled rifle that uses a percussion cap to fire its charge. See also **hog rifle**, **squirrel gun**.

1939 Hall *Coll* (Gatlinburg TN) I had this old cap and ball gun. Well, I was just a little bit choicey, and I didn't want to just shoot one and all the rest of the flock would fly away. **1960** Burnett *My Valley* 48 She was a splendid shot, and even after her husband and hunting sons had acquired modern rifles, she used her old cap and ball muzzle-loading rifle. **1983** Irwin *Guns and Gun-Making* 8 The early Kentucky rifles were of the flintlock type, requiring a mechanism which struck a piece of flint against a steel plate called a frizzen, or battery, providing a spark of fire which ignited the powder in the pan, which in turn fired the powder inside the barrel. (This technique was developed by the French in the early 1600's.) Early in the 1800's the percussion cap was invented and soon thereafter most of the Kentucky rifles were converted to the cap-and-ball type. After about 1830–1840 most Kentucky rifles were made using the percussion (cap-and-ball) ignition system. **cap arm** *noun* See citations.

1968 *End of Moonshining* 49 = the copper pipe connecting the cap with the next section of the still—conveys steam to this section. **2007** Rowley *Moonshine!* 160 = a pipe extending from the head of the still that conveys alcoholic vapors to the thump keg or directly to the condenser.

cap bundle, **capsheaf**, **cap stone** See **cap A3**.

cap corn See **cap A5**, **B4**.

cape *noun* See citations.

1972 *Foxfire I* 315 = the bulge in the main body of the [moonshine] still. It is the point of greatest circumference. *Ibid.* 319 The sides of the furnace touched the still at only one point, and that was above the cape at the point where the sides of the furnace tapered in.

capper *noun* A popcorn popper. See also **cap A5**, **B4**.

1958 Stuart *Plowshare* 62 He watched sister Nell put another capper of popcorn over the fire. **1976** Braden *Grandma Was Girl* 110 = popcorn popper. **1993** Stuart *Daughter* 228 *capper of corn* = a wire basket with a long handle attached, used for popping popcorn over an open fire.

capping corn See **cap A4**.

cap rock *noun* See citation.

2002 Armstead *Black Days* 242 = a two- to six-inch layer of rock, mixed with coal or carboniferous rock, located between a coal seam and the solid rock roof of a mine.

captain *noun*

1 Someone or something excellent or exemplary, one who is skillful.

1904–20 Kephart *Notebooks* 4:761 He's a captain on the floor to dance. **1917** Kephart *Word-List* 409 = one who excels. "He's a *captain* to tell a tale." **1939** Hall *Coll* (White Oak NC) "It's a captain" describes a tough road. **1957** Combs *Lg Sthn High: Word-List* 17 = one who is skilled in his profession or trade. **1960** Hall *Smoky Mt Folks* 64 = one who excels.

[DARE *captain* n B3 chiefly South Midland]

2 An amusing or mischievous person, a prankster (also as a sardonic form of address).

1937 Hall *Coll* (Cades Cove TN) John McCaulley's a great talker. Old McCaulley's a captain. *Ibid.* (Emerts Cove TN) = comical person, full of fun, full of mischief. **1939** Hall *Coll* (Cades Cove TN) He was a captain to talk. He told some of the masterest stories. *Ibid.* (White Oak NC) Some of the local people address a stranger as "captain." Older people will call little kids "captain." The term is used of children who cut up and get into mischief, as "he's a captain." **1957** Combs *Lg Sthn High: Word-List* 17 = one who is good at jokes, pranks, etc. **1967** Hall *Coll* (Del Rio TN) He was a captain. He was a cutter-up.

car *noun*

A Variant forms *cyar*, *keyar*, *kyah*.

1895 Edson and Fairchild *TN Mts* 375 The front variety of *g* and *k* are used as in other parts of the South, giving the pronunciation represented by *kyah*, *gya(r)den*, etc. **1930** Thomas *Death Knell* Often syllables ending in an "r" sound have a "y" inserted in front of them, as cyar (car), gyarden, pyore (poor). **1937** Wilson *Folklore SE KY* 31 *cyar*. **1939** Walker *Mtneer Looks* 5 Only a few mountaineers say *cyar* for *car* and *gyarden* for *garden*, but it would be an impossibility for most of them to pronounce *cow* any other way than *cyow*, or *care* any other way than *kyeer* or *kyer*. **1942** Hall *Phonetics Smoky Mts* 94 In the speech of older people this glide [j] is very common after [k] or [g] before [ɑ]; for example, *car*. **1970** Broome *Earth Man* 62 Once we druv a cyar through a creek and wet its shassy and then came a big freeze and froze it to the ground. **1984** Woods *WV Was Good* 230 Many old people said . . . *keyar* for *car*. **1993** Burleson *Aunt Keziah* 6 They'd git the poe-lease cyar to haul him to one store in town.

[DARE *car* n[1] especially South Midland]

B A type of portable house used in logging camps. See also **car shack.**

1991 Weals *Last Train* 98 While the Fosters lived in a board-and-batten house built at the site, most of the families lived in what were called "cars" or "set-off houses."

car box *noun* A railroad box car.

1942 Hall *Coll* (Cataloochee NC). **1949** McDavid *Grist* 107 *car-boxes* = box cars. **1976** Hall *Coll* (Gatlinburg TN).

[inversion of elements, as in *backswitch*, *cover under man*]

carboy *noun* See citation.

2013 Pierce *Corn in Jar* 61 Sugar-liquor was usually shipped out in five-gallon glass jars called carboys or in steel cans.

carcass *noun* Variant form *cyarcass*.

1927 Furman *Lonesome Road* 33 I hated them, and their old cruel religion, and their old black sunbonnets and dresses, looking like a passel of buzzards setting round a cyarcass.

card

A *noun*, *verb* Variant forms *ceard*, *cyard*.

1913 Kephart *Our Sthn High* 277 I gotta me a deck o' cyards. **1916** Combs *Old Early English* 296 "Palatal influence." When these words are "broken" we have: "cy-ard." **1942** Hall *Phonetics Smoky Mts* 94 In the speech of older people this glide [j] is very common after [k] or [g] before [ɑ]; for example . . . *card*. **1960** Hall *Smoky Mt Folks* 27 (Copeland Creek TN) When I was a little girl, we'd have to pick a pint of cottonseed before goin' to bed, while Mother 'ud set and cyard. **1970** *Burton-Manning Coll*-93B We wove, spun, and made, cyarded and spun and made our cloth with looms them times what we had to wear. **1981** Williams *Storytelling* Some old-timers in Appalachia still say *cyard* and *gyarden*. **1987** Young *Lost Cove* 101 I'm a telling you that all ceard playing, be it poker, set-back, or rook, is a mortal sin. **1996** Isbell *Last Chivaree* 29 She sent me a cyard. Would I come? Tell stories to her class.

[DARE *card* n[1] especially South Midland]

B *verb* To move, hasten.

1952 Wilson *Folk Speech NC* 525 = to go home, to move on. "Well, I'd better be *carding*." **1996** Montgomery *Coll* = to move quickly, be in a hurry (Ledford).

care

A *noun*, *verb* Variant forms *cear*, *ceer*, *keer*.

1862 *Lockmiller CW Letters* (Feb 14) i Want if you cant get to come home iwant you to try to tak good ceer of your self. **1863** *Revis CW Letters* (June 6) Sereptia I want you to take good cear of your self tell all the folks howdey for mee. **1867** Harris *Sut Lovingood* 56 Brethren, brethren, take keer ove yerselves, the Hell-sarpints *hes got me!* **1883** Bonner *Dialect Tales* 134 [He] didn't know as anybody keered three jumps of a louse for Jim Peters or his threatenin's. **1903** Fox *Little Shepherd* 6 I don't keer ef I did. **1942** Hall *Phonetics Smoky Mts* 24 [kæɚ], 25 [kɪɚ].

B in participial adjective phrase *caring for* = fond of.

2008 *Rosie Hicks* 1 I wasn't all that caring for meat really.

C *verb* (in negative constructions) To be willing or pleased (usually in response to a suggestion or invitation).

1862 (in **1999** Davis *CW Letters* 83) I dont care if we get to Stay here during the war for I am highly pleased with our Situation. **1862** *Patton CW Letters* (July 6) I would not care if you could send me a strong pare of janes pants and a pare of sox. **1864** *D Walker CW Letters* (June 19) I wold not Car if yow wold Send me your lik-nesses. **1910** Weeks *Barbourville Word List* 456 (with a negative) = to be willing: "If I had a horse and carriage I wouldn't care to take you to Boring." **1921** Weeks *Speech of KY Mtneer* 16 When my friend in the Cumberlands says, "Now if I jest had a horse and carriage, I wouldn't care to take you to Camp Ground to-day," I understand him to say that it would be no care or trouble, but only a pleasure for him to take me anywhere I wanted to go. The family jolt-wagon and mules were at my service, however, and the ride was one to remember. **1931** Hannum *Thursday April* 52 "Come and set?" "I wouldn't keer to." The rising inflection of the guest's voice indicated her willingness, so together they dropped down in the cool grass. **1937** Hall *Coll* (Cosby TN) He didn't care to lay down anywhere [i.e. he didn't care where he lay down, would lie down anywhere he felt like it]. **1939** Hall *Recording Speech* 7 Examples of *not to care to* for *not to mind*, as in a sentence spoken by an Emerts Cove man, "She don't care to talk," meaning "She doesn't mind talking," are found in both the sixteenth and seventeenth centuries. **c1959** Weals *Hillbilly Dict* 5 When a mountaineer says, "I don't keer to work," what he means is that he doesn't object to working, that he's used to working, and that he accepts the fact that a man must work to live. **1961** *Coe Ridge OHP*-342B [Speaker A:] Did these . . . boys ever sit around and laugh about how they outwitted the revenue men or anything? [Speaker B:] Why yeah, they didn't care for telling it, no. **1969** *Burton-Manning Coll*-94A I wouldn't care if they'd make me a record made of them. **1975** Duncan *Mt Sayens* Two of my friends, from the Midwest, left a little old lady standing in the road because she replied "I don't care to" to their offer of a ride. **1978** Montgomery *White Pine Coll* V-3 They said, "If you fellows are deer hunting up in there, now watch about shooting down on us because we'll be up there making liquor." They didn't care to tell it. **1981** *GSMNP*-117:27 He said, "I don't care if you goin' if your parents don't care." **1986** (in **2000** Puckett *Seldom Ask* 89) If you don't care to, Sue, would you fix me a sandwich? **1990** Clouse *Wilder* 146 If you could be at the aid station, I reckon they wouldn't care to take it from you. **1994** Dumas *Care To* Gosh, I thought everyone KNEW. Throughout Southern Appalachia, the phrase "don't care to" means . . . either "don't mind" (neutral to positive) or "want to" (quite positive). When we talk about this pattern in my introductory linguistics courses, I can see the light dawn on the part of non-Appalachian speakers. **1998** Brewer *Words of Past* Another East Tennesseeism is the practice, when asking somebody to do something, of adding "if you don't care to" when the meaning is exactly opposite of the plain English. An example would be, "Would you carry me to work, if you don't care to?" **1998** *Dante OHP-71* I didn't care to say what I wanted to to my dad cause I was married and all. **1999** Montgomery *File* A lot of mountain people are kind of backward, but I don't care to talk to nobody (40-year-old woman, Del Rio TN). **2005** Bailey *Henderson County* 32 Now and then he pushed his wilted felt hat to the back of his head and wiped away beads of perspiration that gleamed on his brow. Yet he never slackened his pace and his eyes charted the road ahead as he walked with determined steps. Then someone he knew eased up alongside him. "I'm on my way to town, Will," the fellow said. "Want to ride wi' me?" Will looked into the familiar face, and feeling in no way compelled to prove his independence, he answered, "I wouldn't care to." Because the driver knew that, in mountain lingo, "I wouldn't care to" means "I don't mind if I do," he waited for Will to open the door and climb in.

[DARE *care* v B1 chiefly Midland]

care-akter See **character**.

careen *verb*

A Variant form *creen* [see 1917 in **B**].

B Of an object: to lean or bend sideways, away from vertical position. See also **creel**. [Editor's note: The sense "to sway or lurch from side to side" is widespread in the US.]

1917 Kephart *Word-List* 410 = to bend the body to one side. "I noticed a ketch in my back ever' time I *c'reened*." **c1960** Wilson *Coll* = to lean awry. **1995–96** Montgomery *Coll* (known to Cardwell, Shields).

[DARE *careen* v 1 chiefly South Midland]

careful *adverb* Carefully.

c1950 (in **2000** Oakley *Roamin' Man* 14) We would hike the mountains 10 or 15 miles a day, searching careful as we went.

careless (also *careless weed*) *noun* Amaranth (*Amaranthus hybridus*), an annual wildflower having medicinal uses that populates barnyards and cultivated fields and that is considered a weed.

1941 Stuart *Men of Mts* 152 In his area the careless is a non-succulent weed with a notched oval leaf. "It (the blue-tick pig) likes ragweeds, pusley, careless, and horseweeds." **1957** Combs *Lg Sthn High: Word-List* 17 *careless* = a tender, red-stemmed plant or weed (Amaranthus/hybridus). **1968** Wilson *Folklore Mammoth Cave* 15 *careless* = the red-rooted pigweed (*Amaranthus*, sp.), very common in gardens and other places with rich soil. The name apparently came from the carelessness shown by the gardener in allowing the weed to grow. [**1971** Krochmal et al. *Medicinal Plants Appal* 44 Because of its astringent quality, this plant has been used in treating dysentery, ulcers, and hemorrhage of the bowel].

[DARE *careless weed* n 1 chiefly west Midland, Southwest]

carn See **carrion**.

Carolina allspice *noun* A sweet shrub (*Calycanthus floridus*), whose aromatic leaves are used as a perfume. Same as **sweet bubby**. See also **bubby bush**.

1970 Campbell et al. *Smoky Mt Wildflowers* 70 Other names [of the sweet shrub] are the bubby bush and Carolina allspice. **1975** Hamel and Chiltoskey *Cherokee Plants* 58 = roots are strong emetics.

Carolina pine *noun* A pine (*Tsuga caroliniana*) native to western North Carolina and neighboring territory, found at elevations between 2,000 and 4,000 feet.

1907 Dugger *Balsam Groves* 88.

Carolina rhododendron *noun* An evergreen rhododendron shrub (*Rhododendron carolinianum*) that usually has pinkish flowers. See citation.

2006 Ellison *Nature Journal* 34–35 Carolina rhododendron—also called dwarf or piedmont rhododendron, as well as deer-tongue laurel—is the evergreen rhododendron with which people are least familiar. As a straggling upright shrub, it grows in the higher elevations with its Catawba cousin or in the lower elevations with its rosebay cousin. The flowers are magenta in color. The leaves are short and rough, with conspicuous brown scales on the undersides.

car pecker *noun* See citation.

1994 Farwell and Buchanan *Logging Terms* = a member of a logging crew who built parts for logging cars.

carpenter's-herb *noun* Self-heal, a perennial plant (*Prunella vulgaris*) with medicinal uses. Same as **heal-all**.

1982 Stupka *Wildflowers* 97 This common and very widespread mint is thought to have been a native plant but has also been naturalized from Europe and Asia. In Europe, old-time herb doctors used [heal-all] in the treatment of throat ailments and other afflictions, whereby it acquired its common name and other names as "self-heal" and "carpenter's herb."

carpet *noun*

A Variant forms *cyarpet, keerpet*.

1900 Harben *N GA Sketches* 296 The new house is jest splendid—green blinds to the winders, an' cyarpets on the floors. **c1940** Simms *Coll* Why [the growth of flowers] kivers the mountains like cyarpets (carpets) and is a heap sight purty. **1975** Gainer *Speech Mtneer* 12 Grandma wove a keerpet for the little room.

B in phrase *on the carpet* = courting, eager to marry.

1915 Dingus *Word-List VA* 181 = in the field to get married. **1952** Wilson *Folk Speech NC* 225 Well, I hear he's *on the carpet* again, and his wife ain't been dead more'n a year. **1996** Montgomery *Coll* Kinsey was on the carpet when his wife was still alive (Cardwell).

[DARE *carpet, on the* adj phr South, South Midland, especially NC, TX, AR]

carrion *noun* variant forms *carn, cyarn, cyarne, kaeron, kyarn.*

1913 Kephart *Our Sthn High* 277 Occasionally a word is both added to and clipped from, as cyarn (carrion). **1937** Wilson *Folklore SE KY* 31 *cyarn.* **1939** Hall *Notebooks* 13:44 (White Oak NC) *kaeron, kyarn* = carrion. **1942** Hall *Phonetics Smoky Mts* 94 In the speech of older people this glide [j] is very common after [k] or [g] before [ɑ]; for example . . . *carrion.* **1970** *Hunting* 15–16 Many shunned possum, polecat, and other "nasty" animals that sometimes feed on carrion ("carn"). **1974** Roberts *Sang Branch* 204 It's nothing but just a raven flying over the house with a piece of cyarne in its mouth. **1996** Montgomery *Coll: carn* (Adams).

[DARE *carrion* n A especially South Midland]

carrion crow *noun* The black vulture (*Coragrips atratus*); by extension = a reprehensible person.

1957 Combs *Lg Sthn High: Word-List* 57 *kyarn crow* = term of opprobrium. **1962** Wilson *Folkways Mammoth Cave* 8 The black vulture, often called a *carrion crow*, was a /kyarn/ crow.

carriony *adjective, adverb* Disgusting; in a disgusting or wretched manner.

1991 Still *Wolfpen Notebooks* 118 If he treated me that carriony, I'd kick his rump till his nose bled. **2014** *Blind Pig* (Aug 29) = used as an adjective to describe something that smells horrible.

carry *verb*

1 To take, bring.

1864 *Tesh CW Letters* (Feb 18) I gave your socks to Mr Macy he sed he would carry them to you. **1967** Hall *Coll* I'd buy him grub from the stores, you know, and I'd carry this grub to him over there.

[DARE *carry* v B2 chiefly South, South Midland]

2 To escort, accompany.

1861 *Neves CW Letters* (Sept 13) the Boys arrived according to promise on their was to muster and to carry me home. **1862** *Councill CW Letters* (April 27) I tole you beefor I lefet home that if [you] was not sades fide that I would Cary you a way. **1913** Kephart *Our Sthn High* 296 When a mountain swain "carries his gal to meetin'" he is not performing so great an athletic feat. **1939** Hall *Coll* (Hazel Creek NC) I toted him in and laid him on the bed. . . . After he got better I carried him out on a bear hunt. **1949** Kurath *Word Geog East US* 80 The well-known Southern *carry you home* is heard from Annapolis, Maryland, southward. **1957** Combs *Lg Sthn High: Word-List* 17 = to escort, conduct. Not common in the Highlands, but due to Lowland (especially in Virginia) influence. **1973** GSMNP-1They went up there and picked them up and carried them back to where the graves is now. **1974** Fink *Bits Mt Speech* 4 I have to *carry* my woman to the doctor tomorrow. **1984** Burns *Cold Sassy* 245 I'll carry you home. In the car. **1989** Landry *Smoky Mt Interviews* 181 They had to lead us and carry us home.

[DARE *carry* v B1 now chiefly South, South Midland]

3 To lead, conduct (especially a horse).

1860 *Foust CW Letters* (Dec 14) they capture every white woman that they could find alone carry them off to be thier wives. **1861** *Neves CW Letters* (Sept 3) I found Jack Dill and Thomas there trying to trade for a horse and they carried off William Neves mule. **1881** Pierson *In the Brush* 38 Ho! boy, carry this horse to the stable and take good care of her. D'ye hear?

[DARE *carry* v B4 chiefly South]

4 To haul, transport in a vehicle.

1969 GSMNP-37 I carried roasting ears, sweet potatoes, Irish potatoes, tomatoes, cucumbers, cabbage, and all. I had a horse and buggy. **1973** GSMNP-1 I can remember when they carried it [= the mail] in a buggy . . . and then later on they carried it horseback.

[DARE *carry* v B3 formerly Middle Atlantic, now widespread]

carry a corner (also *carry up corners*) *verb phrase* See c1960 citation.

1878 Guild *Old Times TN* 160 The principal workmen in making notches in the logs (carrying up corners), were Hon John Bell and Dr. Boyd McNairy. **1945** Wilson *Passing Institutions* 47 It took skill to carry a corner. Only the most agile young men could do this. The rabble could tote logs and push them up the skids. **c1960** Wilson *Coll: carry a corner* = to notch logs and fit them in situ, at a house- or barn-raising; a very skillful job.

carry-log *noun* Two wheels connected by an axle under which a log can be suspended for dragging.

1892 Smith *Farm and Fireside* 52 A ride on the carrylog tongue would suit me pretty well.

[DARE *carry-log* n 1 South]

carry tales *verb phrase* To spread gossip.

1904 Fox *Christmas Eve* 131 Abe Shivers . . . was a-carryin' tales from one side to t'other an' a-stirrin' up hell ginerally. **2007** McMillon *Notes* = to spread gossip.

carry up corners See **carry a corner**.

car shack *noun* A small, portable dwelling used by loggers or their families at a logging camp. Same as **set-off house**. See also **car B**.

n.d. *Tremont Logging* 6–7 Some [structures] were permanent houses built on site, but many were pre-fabricated, portable houses referred to as "car shacks." Car shacks were about 12′ × 12′ and could easily be lifted on and off flat cars by a loader. As logging operations moved, car shacks could be picked up and moved to the new site and set off along the track. Usually several shacks were joined together to form a house or bunkhouse. More shacks could be added if the family was large or the crew was increased. **2008** McCaulley *Cove Childhood* 71 Workers and their families lived in an early version of manufactured housing—tiny units called "car shacks" that were hauled to the camps in sections on the railroad that also carried the logs out. Several units could be put together to make a dormitory, a meeting hall or extra housing for a large family. They were lifted off by a crane mounted on a flatbed, so they had to be set close by the tracks. People just got used to living in a dwelling that shook when the train went by.

car shed *noun* A garage.

1932 (in **1944** Wentworth *ADD* 242–43) (WV) Car shed is often used instead [of garage]. **1936** (in **2009** Powell *Shenandoah Letters* 76) I lost everything I had by fire, a few people give me some things and I moved in a car shed.

[DARE *car shed* n chiefly South, South Midland]

cart *noun* variant form *cyart*.

1942 Hall *Phonetics Smoky Mts* 94 In the speech of older people this glide [j] is very common after [k] or [g] before [ɑ]; for example . . . *cart*. **1963** Ritchie *Dulcimer Book* 7 Dad says that it would be a common sight, when he was a little slip of a "chap," "to see Thomas' dulcimer cyarts go up and down the creek roads in the summertime."

carton-box *noun* See citation.

1946 Dudley *KY Words* 270 = a characteristic reduplication.

cartridge *noun*

1 variant forms *caterige, catirge, catridge* [see **1911** in **2**], *catterag, catterge*.

1862 *Shifflet CW Letters* (March 18) I dred the trip for I hav my nap sack to carry and two blankets and three shirts and a par of drowers and my over Coat and gun and caterige box. **1863** *A B Walker CW Letters* (Jan 7) they throd ever thing as they run they throd ther guns napsack haversack catterag box coffey pot blan[k]cts and ever els. **1942** Hall *Phonetics Smoky Mts* 30 [ˈkjætrɪdʒ, ˈkjɑtɚdʒ]. **1957** Combs *Lg Sthn High: Word-List* 17 *catirge* = metathesized form of *cartridge*. **1963** Watkins and Watkins *Yesterday* 25 Aw, Pa, I just drapped a few little old catterges in the heater to hear them pop.

2 variant plural form *cartridge*.

1911 Shearin *E KY Word-List* 37 *cartridge*; also used as a collective: "How many catridge have you?"

carve *noun* variant form *cyarve*.

1928 Justus *Betty Lou* 46 That was already in the bark. All I had to do was to cyarve around that grin and make his face to match. **1931** Thomas *Ditties* 10 He scraped and cyarved out o' warnut a fine pretty music box. **1942** Hall *Phonetics Smoky Mts* 94 In the speech of older people this glide [j] is very common after [k] or [g] before [ɑ]; for example . . . *carve*.

case *noun*

1 See citation.

c1999 Sutton *Me and Likker* 103 = 6 gallon of likker in gallon glass jugs or 12 half gallon jars. Any one who puts likker in plastic milk jugs shows their likker is not worth a damn.

2 In phrase *in case* = of tobacco leaves: sufficiently moist and pliable to be stripped from the plant.

1950 Stuart *Hie Hunters* 95 They knew this vapor was carried by the wind among the drying tobacco plants in the wall-less tobacco barns and it moistened them and put them in case. **1957** Broaddus *Vocab Estill Co KY* 43 = moist enough to handle without crumbling (cured tobacco). **1969** *DARE Survey* (Adams KY) After a rain or the weather's damp enough . . . it'll get in case till it's flexible and you won't damage or break it up when you're trying to strip it. **2007** McMillon *Notes* = when the weather is humid enough to hand off tobacco.

case hardened *adjective* Of a knife: having a blade tempered and hardened in the smithy; by extension = of a person: indifferent to reproof or shame, unchangeable in character, set in one's ways.

1973 Davis *'Pon My Honor* 94 = unchangeable; not sensitive; no sense of shame. **1995–97** Montgomery *Coll* (known to Adams, Brown, Jones, Norris, Oliver, Weaver); He's a case-hardened fellow; you can't change him (Cardwell).

case knife *noun* A table knife, usually a serrated one; also, a pocket-knife originally manufactured by the Case Company.

1858 (in **1974** Harris *High Times* 152) I hilt on with fork an teeth, an tried tu saw off a bite with a case knife. **1864** *Stepp CW Letters* (May 21) [I] rote aletter to you by D burnet i sent Some little things by him to you . . . one case knife half quire of paper and some envalopes. **1940** Haun *Hawk's Done* 6 Joe cut it out with a case knife. **c1960** Wilson *Coll* = a table knife: "Mammy broke one of her best case knives yesterday." **1984** Head *Brogans* 22 Before we walked a half a mile, Pappy pulled out a "twist" of tobacco and cut off a chew with an old Case knife he always carried. **2005** Williams *Gratitude* 484 We had *case knifes*, like you eat with, an'en we had cuttin' knifes, like a pocket knife, parin' knife, [and] butcher knife. **2013** *Blind Pig* (Feb 7) A Case knife . . . actually refers to a long-established and revered brand of knives, one that ranks right alongside of Barlow, Remington, and Buck among collectors and knife aficionados.

[DARE *case knife* n 1 "from its originally being carried in a case"; especially frequent Midland]

cash dollar See **cash money**.

cash money (also *cash dollar*) *noun* Currency in the form of bills and coins rather than credit, money order, check, or goods for barter; money in hand or available.

1913 Kephart *Our Sthn High* 123 Corn juice is about all we can tote around over the country and get cash money for. **1924** Raine *Saddlebags* 9 Men take out logs, go to the monthly Court at the county seat, drive cattle, and occasionally go to earn some "cash money" at "public works." **1938** (in **2009** Powell *Shenandoah Letters* 138) i am writing you a few lines to ask you if you would give me thouse if i move it i have cash money in the buiden. **1944** Hayes *Word-List NC* 32 *cash money* = ready money. **1966** Caudill *My Appalachia* 31 We had heard rumors that cash money jingled in the pockets of some mountaineer up the river who had sold a patch of land to an outlander. **1971** *AOHP/ALC-137* They dug ginseng to get money, you know, cash money. **1978** *Smokies Heritage* 107 In an area where most work was of the swap-out variety (you help me and I'll help you), nothing was harder to come by than cash money. **1989** Aiken *Tragedy* 8 The chestnuts also produced actual cash for the settlers, and "cash money" was all too hard to come by. **1991** Haynes *Haywood Home* 79 Hardly any tenant paid cash money rent. **1997** Hufford *American Ginseng* 9 The people would come out of the hollows in the fall and sell him their ginseng and they would buy their shoes and salt and staples and so forth and he in turn sold it to exporters in New York or a broker, and that sent some cash dollars back here.

[Web3 *cash money* n South and Midland; DARE *cash money* n chiefly South, South Midland]

cask *noun* variant plural form of two syllables: *cask-es*.

1939 Hall *Notebooks* 13:42 (White Oak NC) *cask-es* = plural of *cask*.

caskes See **cask**.

cat *noun*

1 (also *catball*) A rudimentary form of baseball played by children. See also **blind cat**, **bull pen**, **kitty wants a corner**, **town ball**, **two-eyed cat**.

1890 Fruit *KY Words* 63 = a game at ball. In two-cornered cat, a boy with bat stands at each corner; there is a catcher behind each boy. If a batter is "caught out," or "crossed out," he gives up his bat. He is "crossed out" when the ball is thrown between him and the corner to which he is running. **c1960** Wilson *Coll*: *cat-ball* = a simple ball game, usually played with two batters and a certain number of strikes before the batters change places. **1993** Page and Smith *Foxfire Toys and Games* 8 Catball. One-eyed Cat: Each team has a pitcher, a catcher, and a batter. There is a home plate and one base. Any additional players are in the field. Rotation for batting: the batter goes to field, the fielder to pitcher, the pitcher to catcher, and the catcher to bat. The batter tries to hit the ball and run to the base and back to home plate. He can either be thrown out at home plate or tagged out during his run to or from the base. The batter continues until he either strikes out (three strikes) or is thrown out or if his hit is caught on the fly or first bounce. Each successful "run," from home plate to base and back, counts one point. The winner is the player with the most points.

[DARE *cat* n 3c chiefly South, South Midland]

2 A catfish.

1915 Dingus *Word-List VA* 181 = catfish, as *blue cat*, *channel cat*, or *mud cat*.

cata-cornered See **cater-corner**.

cat-a-gogling *present participle/adjective* See citation. See also **anti-godlin**, **si-godlin**.

1939 Farr *TN Mt Regions* 90 = walking side ways or angling: "He's cat-a-gogling."

catamount *noun* A lynx (*Lynx* spp). See also **panther**.

1953 Hall *Coll* (Bryson City NC) A wild cat is smaller and has a lot of stripes around his legs, and this catamount has a big muff on his jaws . . . and he's got a master big head. He's somethin' between a wild cat and a panter. . . . They decided it was a catamount or a panter from the looks of its track. **1969** *DARE Survey* (Sawyer KY). **2016** Ellison *Excursions* 108 Another common name for the lynx is "catamount." Bobcats are also called "wildcats."

[DARE *catamount* n 1 chiefly South, South Midland, Northeast]

cat-and-clay (also *cats and clay*) *noun* Clay mixed with sticks, straw, poles, or occasionally stone, used as building material for a chimney; the chimney itself. See also **stick-and-clay chimney**.

1847 (in **1870** Drake *Pioneer Life KY* 21) [He resided] in the same original log cabin, which in course of time acquired a . . . chimney carried up with "cats and clay" to the height of the ridge-pole. These "cats and clay" were pieces of small poles, well embedded in mortar. **1917** (in **1944** Wentworth *ADD* 99) (sWV) *cat-and-clay* = of a chimney: built of mud and sticks. **1933** Thomas *Traipsin' Woman* 18 Now and then we passed a log cabin with a feeble stream of smoke curling out of a "cat and clay" chimney; low chimneys they were of mud and sticks and stones which often reached only to the bristling shingled roof of the windowless cabin. **1948** Dick *Dixie Frontier* 28 The chimney was made of sticks and clay, known as "cats and clay." The sticks were well embedded to keep the fire from burning them. The fireplace itself was made of clay.

[cf EDD *cat* sb 13 "a piece of soft clay mixed with straw, thrust in between the laths in building mud walls" Scot, nIrel, nEngl; cf SND *cat* n[3] 2 "a handful of straw, mixed with soft clay, and used in building mud walls"; DARE *cat-and-clay* n South Midland]

cat-ar See **catarrh**.

cat around *verb* See citation. Same as **tomcat (around)**.

2009 Benfield *Mt Born* 129 *catting around* = running around with women. Most often a married man is doing this. "Steve's been catting around on her for years."

catarrh *noun*

A Variant form with primary stress on the first syllable: *cat-ar*, *cat-tar* [see **1974** in **B**].

1930 Thomas *Death Knell* The disease catarrh is cat-ar, with first syllable accented.

B Originally, a head cold, with inflammation of the upper respiratory tract; more generally, any sore or abscess, including one in the intestines.

1862 *Hamblen CW Letters* 65 I am well with the exception of a cottarr on the joint of my Rist. **1974** Roberts *Sang Branch* 80 His dad had a cat-tar in his head, he called it. The doctors claimed, or the nurse—they didn't have no doctors then—his nose was bleeding out of both nose-holes just about as free as it could bleed. **1979** *Big South Fork OHP-9* They had a disease called catarrh [of] the head. You remember that? **1992** Bush *Dorie* 76 Dr. Cogdill said I had catarrh of the stomach (gastritis), and I couldn't have anything to eat for a few days. **1997** Montgomery *Coll* = gastritis or any severe stomach ache, even typhoid fever (Bush).

catawampous See **catawampus**[2].

catawampus[1] (also *catawampus cat*, *cattywampus*) *noun* An imaginary, fearsome cat-like creature of indeterminate size, a figure used to intimidate and warn children to behave; a hobgoblin. See also **booger**, **saugus cat**, **wampus B**.

1866 Smith *So Called* 54 It is a thing that plots, and plans, and schemes for a few weeks, and then suddenly pokes its head out like a catawampus and says *Booh!* **c1960** Wilson Coll (or *catawampus cat*) = one of the folk animals, or *wampus cat*. **1976** Garber *Mountain-ese* 14 = vicious beast. "You'd better be keerful, there's a catawampus loose in them mountains." **1994–97** Montgomery Coll (known to Adams, Brown, Cardwell, Jones, Ledford, Weaver), = same as *wampus* (Oliver). **2019** *Blind Pig* (Feb 22) I too heard catty-wampus instead of wampus cat.

[probably alteration of *catamount*; Web3 *catawampus* n "an imaginary fierce, wild animal" dialect; DARE *catawampus* n 1 chiefly South, South Midland]

catawampus[2]

A Variant forms *catawampous* [see **1891** in **B**], *cattywampus* [see **1975** in **B**], *catty-whumpus* [see **1976** in **B**].

B *adjective*

1 Set at or moving in a diagonal manner, crossways; out of position or shape, lopsided, not straight. See also **anti-godlin**(**g**), **cater-corner**, **si-godlin**, **slanchways**.

1891 Brown *Dialect in TN* 173 *catawampous* . . . means twisted or careened to one side, although [it] seems to have the idea of the diagonal prominent in it; for instance, we might call a rhombus a *catawampous* square. **1917** Kephart *Word-List* 409 *catawampus* = mixed up; all awry. **1937** Wilson *Folklore SE KY* 7 It may have been "catawampus" or "si-waddlin," with many imperfections in architecture; but the mountain cabin held happiness and the opposite with a distinct way of expressing both. **1975** Jackson *Unusual Words* 159 Four terms suggest something out of line or out of plumb: *catty-cornered*, *cattywampus*, *slaunchways*, or *sigodlin* (also pronounced *si-goglin*). **1976** Thompson *Touching Home* 13 *catty-whumpus* = lop-sided. **1992–97** Montgomery Coll: *catawampus* (known to nine consultants from the Smoky Mountains), = cobbled out (Cardwell).

[Web3 *catawampus2* adj "askew, awry, catercorner" dialect; DARE *catawampus* adj alteration of *cater-* "diagonally" + *wumpus*, *wampous*, perhaps related to Scots *wampish* "to wriggle, twist, or swerve about"]

2 See citation.

1972 Cooper *NC Mt Folklore* 90 = big and fine.

C *adverb* Crosswise, out of line.

2011 Coonfield *Varmits* 80 Holding the corn holders, just run the corn catawampus (a word common to my upbringing that meant "crosswise" or "out of line" but one I have no earthly idea how to spell) across a stick of butter creating a nice little corn-size well in the butter for others to use.

catawampus around *verb phrase* To live in a carefree or careless manner.

1994 Montgomery Coll He was catawampusing around (known to Cardwell).

catawba *noun* A deciduous tree (*Catalpa spp*) with large, heart-shaped leaves.

1939 *FWP Guide TN* 19 This region is the natural habitat of the catalpa or "catawba," a fast-growing tree with purple, yellow, and white flowers and large heart-shaped leaves.

[< Choctaw *Katápa* "separated (i.e. from the main body of the Siouan peoples")]

catawba rhododendron *noun* An evergreen shrub (*Rhododendron catawbiense*) that usually has purplish flowers and is one of the two dominant rhododendron species along the Tennessee–North Carolina border, growing at elevations above 3,500 feet. Also called **blue laurel**, **crimson laurel**, **mountain rosebay**, **red laurel**. See also **rhododendron**, **rosebay rhododendron**.

1964 Stupka *Trees Shrubs Vines* 116 The Catawba, with its profusion of purplish-pink blossoms, is, when in flower, the most spectacular and the greatest favorite with the visiting public. . . . It is abundant on high-altitude (above 4,000 ft.) ridges where it is one of the major components of the heath balds ("laurel slicks"). **1988** *Smokies Guide* (Summer) 5 The two main types of rhododendron in the Smokies are rosebay and catawba. Catawba rhododendron is the first to bloom and lives mostly in the Park's higher elevations. Its rose-colored flowers begin opening at the mid-elevations in early June and spread up the mountains until early July. Only in the southern Appalachians does the catawba occur. . . . Both the catawba and rosebay are somewhat unusual for keeping their large green leaves through the winter. **2006** Ellison *Nature Journal* 34 The showiest of the evergreen rhododendrons is the purple rhododendron. The leaves are four to six inches long with rounded tips. It grows as a compact shrub on rocky slopes, ridges and balds above three thousand feet. It is also called Catawba rhododendron. According to legend, the Catawba Indians once challenged all of the other Indian nations to a great battle in the mountains in early summer. After many days of battle, the Catawbas were victorious—but in the fighting they shed so much precious blood that these rhododendrons have bloomed red ever since in mute tribute to their sacrifice.

[DARE *catawba* n B1 chiefly South, South Midland, Ohio, Indiana]

catball See **cat 1**.

catbird winter *noun* A late spring cold spell associated with the return of migrating catbirds. See citations. For terms describing a similar phenomenon, see **blackberry winter**.

1954 *Asheville Citizen-Times* (May 17) Since Pink Baldwin quit us, we can't rightly say whether this is the "dogwood winter," "blackberry winter," or "catbird winter," but it falls short of any kind of pleasant spring weather for a fact. **1961** Stubbs *Mountain-Wise* (April–May) 9 A cold spell in the late spring caused us to enquire of a neighbor: "What kind of winter is this we're having? 'Blackberry winter' is over and it's too early for 'dogwood winter'?" He replied: "This is 'cat-bird winter.' You'll notice all the cat-birds come back each year in just such a cold spell as this." **1962** Miller *Pigeon's Roost* (May 17) An old timer the other day told me about a catbird winter. First time I ever heard of it. He said that's what that cold pinching spell was about two weeks ago, "Catbird winter spell." Really, it was about the time the first catbirds arrived back from their winter's staying place. **1967** Stubbs *Mountain-Wise* (April–May) 9) The catbird, that devastator of fruits and berries, is much with us, but not until after the first spring windstorm—"blown in," so they say. Then there is a cold snap locally called "catbird winter." Suddenly they appear in droves.

[DARE *catbird winter* n chiefly southern Appalachians]

cat brier *noun* A greenbrier (*Smilax rotundifolia*). See also **bamboo brier**.

1901 Lounsberry *Sthn Wild Flowers* 63 *S. rotundifolia*, green brier, cat brier, or common bamboo, grows often in thickets, or where the soil is moist, and is prone to climb as high as thirty or forty feet. **1937** Thornburgh *Great Smoky Mts* 23 A few of the more common vines you may encounter along almost any trail are . . . green brier, which is also called saw brier, cat brier, or bamboo brier.

catch

A *verb* Principal parts. [Editor's note: The forms *cotch* and *cotched* do not occur in ATASC.]

1 variant infinitive/base forms *cotch*, *ketch*.

1862 *Shifflet CW Letters* (Feb 28) I under Stood to day that tha [= the Confederates] had left nash ville and gon Still futher on So I dont think we ever will ketch them. **1863** *Woody CW Letter* (May 3) I go A fishing evry day or So and ketch some fish. **1864** *Love CW Letters* (April 2) I and Erven had a fine time ketching Rabbits we caught 12 we had Rashtions a plenty while they lasted. **1913** Kephart *Our Sthn High* 81 Then we-uns ketches up and finishes him. *Ibid.* 322 Thirty cents for each witness he cotches. **1930** Thomas *Death Knell* Verbs especially have undergone many changes for the worse, such as seed for saw and seen, cotch (in all tenses) for catch, fotch, chaw, clem, wed (weeded), bile, borned, and drempt. **1937** Hall Coll (Emerts Cove TN) I knowed I'd cotch him. **1942** Hall *Phonetics Smoky Mts* 26 For *catch*, [kɛč] is usual, [kač] rare. **1967** Fetterman *Stinking Creek* 88 He was a midwife doctor. He went out on nights wasn't fit for stock to be out to cotch a baby. He was the best midwife doctor in the state of Kentucky. **1991** Thomas *Sthn Appal* 52 He was awful to hunt. He'd go coon-huntin'. He'd ketch two or three coons in one night.

2 variant past-tense forms *catched*, *cotch*, *cotched*, *ketched*, *kotch*, *kotched*.

1863 *Revis CW Letters* (May 13) we cotch atory as we came on and kild him and the tories shot at our boys and shot one threw the hat. **1873** Smith *Arp Peace Papers* 94 I roled some twenty feet into the edge of the woods, and kotch up agin a old pine stump that wer full of yaller jackets. **1895** Dromgoole *Fiddling to Fame* Then I ketched ole Jube Turner's eye. **1901** Harben *Westerfelt* 117 He said they'd ketched the men right whar you left 'em. **1904–20** Kephart *Notebooks* 4:855 I cotch hell from the woman. **1937** Thornburgh *Great Smoky Mts* 135 I wouldn't go back but I waited till they kotched up with me. **1939** Hall Coll (Copeland Creek TN) He'd kill Carl Miller if he ever catched him. **1953** Atwood *Verbs East US* 8 The form *cotch* /kY"/ occurs a few times around Chesapeake Bay and in w. N.C. and in s. W.Va . . . *Catched* . . . becomes considerably more common in the South and South Midland, occurring in nearly half the communities investigated in W.Va. and N.C. [**1967** See **B** below.]. **1969** GSMNP-38:148 Where he catched that sheep you could hear them talk about that ridge today. **1969** Roberts *Greasybeard* 42 About that time I looked up and saw a freight coming down the tracks making ninety miles an hour. I retch up and kotched her. **1978** Reese *Speech NE Tenn* 185 There's people come in there and catched them snakes. **1985** Irwin *Alex Stewart* 257 He catched me gone and come up to my house one day, drinking and raising cain, and slapped Margie and the kids around. **2008** *Rosie Hicks* 1 We went with him, catched some minners to put on the hook for him to fish.

3 variant past-participle forms *catched* (in near-universal use among older speakers observed by Joseph Hall in the Smoky Mountains in 1937–41), *cotch*, *cotched*, *ketched*, *kotch*.

1862 *Patton CW Letters* (Sept 8) you could not of catched us if you had a tride. **1863** *Tesh CW Letters* (Dec 5) I wanto know if You and John Ketches anny Rabits these days or not and how many You have Kotch. **1901** Harben *Westerfelt* 146 He said they'd ketched the men right whar you left 'em. **1937** Hall Coll I've killed lots of deer and lots of turkey and catched lots of fish. **c1945** Haun *Hawk's Done* 256 There she was—with her petticoat all cotched on the barbed wire. **1957** GSMNP-23:1:21 I never could believe Art would have catched him in a bear pen . . . lots of people did but I didn't believe it. **1966** Medford *Ol' Starlin* 119 Enny way, if my name had a bin Paul, you'de a never kotch me at a show like that. **1972** *AOHP/ALC*-298 Now Chris hasn't catched, caught this one down here. **1985** Irwin *Alex Stewart* 196 That turkle had catched him by the leg. **1987** Young *Lost Cove* 192 Lem Tucker is as solemn as a judge as he tells about the time that Simon Street got his galluses "cotch" up in a thrashing machine, and how it warped him against the ground 'til he was as limber as a dishrag. **1995** Prince *Quill Rose* 29 In 1918, when Quill was 77, he broke his 11th Commandment, "Never get ketched."

B *verb* Senses.

1 Especially of a midwife: to assist in the delivery of (a child). See also **baby catcher**, **baby catching**.

1917 Davis *A Bornin'* 704 The crucial moment arrived! The baby was "kotched," and its face wiped off with a corner of the apron. **1931** Hannum *Thursday April* 19 I'm expectin' you to catch me a boy! **1939** Hall Coll (Chestnut Branch NC) I catched them in Middlesboro, and I catched them Cumberland Gap, and I catched them at this place out here. *Ibid.* (Roaring Fork TN) They's an old woman here. She's caught four or five hundred. She'd stay with the mother a week or two weeks before birth, and then after. They'd charge about a dollar a week for stayin' and a dollar for other work. **1955** Dykeman *French Broad* 333 Law, child, I've had to be strong. I'm eighty-four years old now and I've catched babies ever since I was twenty. **1957** Parris *My Mts* 255 "I think her time is about to come," she said. "You get over there and get ready to catch the baby. I'll tell you what to do." **1967** Fetterman *Stinking Creek* 88 "My dad cotched four hundred children," Charley said with a welling of pride. "He was a midwife doctor." **1972** Cooper *NC Mt Folklore* 14 In her fervor to serve her neighbors she was content in knowing that all she had cotch belonged to the rare breed of men who lived in the Appalachian Mountains of North Carolina and who would grow up to be tall in the sight of God. **1989** *Matewan OHP*-11 I think five dollars was her price for catching a baby then.

2 (also *catch up*) To harness (a horse or mule).

1939 Hall *Coll* (Cataloochee Creek NC) A couple of old gentlemen raised in this country here . . . went down to the barn one morning to catch a mule. **1942** Campbell *Cloud-Walking* 16 He pulled on his britches to go catch up the nag for Sary.

[DARE *catch* v B10 chiefly South, South Midland]

3 See citation.

1946 Matthias *Speech Pine Mt* 189 = to have: "If you don't watch out careful, you'll catch a fall."

4 See citation. See also **catch fire**, **catch out 2**.

1957 Combs *Lg Sthn High: Word-List* 17 = to strike, or cause to ignite, as of a match.

C *noun*

1 (also *catch pain*) A sudden, sharp pain, especially in the side.

1863 Wilson *Confederate Private* 10 (March 11) I stil have that pane in my back and sholders and catch in my neck that I cant hardly turn my head a tol. **1957** Broaddus *Vocab Estill Co KY* 15 = a sudden, sharp pain in the side. **c1960** Wilson *Coll*: *catch* = a sudden muscular contraction in the back. **1998** Montgomery *Coll*: *catch pain* (known to Brown, Bush).

[SND *catch-pain* (at *catch* II2) "a sharp pain"; DARE *catch-pain* n chiefly South, South Midland]

2 See citation. Same as **stove catch**.

1957 Combs *Lg Sthn High: Word-List* 17 = a lifter for stove caps.

catch can *noun* See citation.

1974 Maurer and Pearl *KY Moonshine* 115 = the receptacle that receives the distillate from the terminal of the flakestand. Usually a five-gallon can or bucket.

catch dog *noun* See citations.

1970 *Hunting* 13 Traditionally the mountain people kept several different kinds of dogs around their homes. . . . Since cows and hogs were grazed on open range, mountain families also trained "ketch dogs." Their job was to help round up the stock when the time came to bring it in for slaughtering or for sale. **1997** Montgomery *Coll* = a dog trained to run alongside a hog that has been allowed to range and fatten in the mountains, catch it by the ear, then swing around a small tree, and hold the hog until a man could tie a rope around one of the hog's rear legs, to be driven out of the mountains (Brown). **2006** *Encycl Appalachia* 1373 Dogs used to bring a bear to bay are called "catch dogs." These are aggressive, agile dogs that physically challenge a bear, fighting it and keeping it from escaping until hunters arrive. Breeds other than hounds, such as Airedale terriers, are sometimes used as catch dogs. **2007** Plott *Story Plott Hound* 180 = a term used mostly in hog hunting to describe a more aggressive hound used to fight and catch or bay game. In hog hunting, the catch dog literally does just that: it bites and catches or holds onto the hog's leg or ear. The catch dog is usually not as good a trailing canine as a strike dog, and it is usually released to follow the strike dog once it has established the game trail. In western states many Plott owners use the term "cut" dog to describe a catch dog. **2009** Plott *Legendary Hunters* 61 Leroy is my catch dog, my bear fighting dog, he will take the fight to the bear or hog.

catched See **catch A2, A3**.

catch fire *verb phrase* See citation.

1985 Irwin *Alex Stewart* 30 When the frontiersmen struck a piece of flint-stone with his knife, it caused a spark of fire which he quite literally "caught" in a bunch of cotton. The spark ignited the cotton, which had a little gunpowder sprinkled on it. From this frontier term, our present day expression "catching fire" is doubtless derived.

catchfly *noun* A perennial wildflower (*Silene* spp) with a star-shaped blossom and medicinal uses. Same as **fire pink**.

[**1971** Krochmal et al. *Medicinal Plants Appal* 50 This plant, which is extremely poisonous, is a cardioactive drug. It has been used also as a tonic, diuretic, and purgative.] **1982** Stupka *Wildflowers* 26 Beneath the 5-petal flower is a sticky, elongated calyx, which explains the name "catch-fly" sometimes given this wildflower.

catch learning *verb phrase* See citation.

1940 Bowman *KY Mt Stories* 241 = to become educated; learn something.

catch out *verb phrase*

1 (also *catch up*) To rope or snare (a mule, horse, calf, etc.).

1963 Edwards *Gravel* 175 On another occasion Uncle Eph caught up a dog which belonged to his neighbor and used his sharp knife on him. **1991** Thomas *Sthn Appal* 35 We 'ud ketch up them ca'ves. **1997** Montgomery *Coll*: *catch out* (known to Bush, Cardwell, Weaver).

[DARE *catch* v B10 chiefly South, South Midland]

2 Of a fire: to break out, spread.

1939 Hall *Coll* (Tow String Creek NC) I still want you to fight it still harder, for a fire is hard to protect when it catches out.

catch pain See **catch C1**.

catch up See **catch out 1**.

cater-corner

A Variant forms *caddy-cornering* [see **1961** in **B**], *catacornered* [see **c1945** in **B**], *caticorner'd* [see **1867** in **B**], *catty-corner(ed)* [see **c1926**, **1940** in **B**], *kittycorner* [see **2007** in **B**].

B *adjective, adverb* Slantwise, off center, at a diagonal (as buildings across a street), askew or at an angle (as furniture). See also **anti-godlin**, **catawampus**[2], **si-godlin**, **slanchways**.

1867 Harris *Sut Lovingood* 92 The nex tail fus' experdishun wer made aginst the caticorner'd cupboard, outen which he made a perfeck momox. **c1926** Bird *Cullowhee Wordlist* He went kinder catty-cornered across the field. **1940** Still *River of Earth* 44 Mother set pans where the roof leaked. We pushed the beds catty-corner, away from the drips. **c1945** Haun *Hawk's Done* 281 In the middle of the paper, at the top, he made a flag, red with broad blue stripes running catacornered and crossing in the middle; and in the blue stripes he put thirteen stars—one big one in the middle where the stripes come together to make a square and three little ones running four directions out from it. **1961** *Coe Ridge OHP-337B* The house was built, was right across, caddy-cornering across the fields from the house that I lived in forty-one years. **1975** Jackson *Unusual Words* 159 Four terms suggest something out of line or out of plumb: *catty-cornered, cattywampus, slaunchways,* or *sigodlin* (also pronounced *si-goglin*). **1995** Montgomery Coll He set the chair catty corner to the stove (Cardwell). **2007** McMillon Notes: *kittycorner*.

[OED3 *cater-cornered* adj/adv "diagonal, diagonally" U.S. and dialect; EDD *cater* adv 2 "diagonally" + *corner*; Web3 *catercorner* adv from obsolete *cater* "four spot" + *corner*; DARE *catercorner* adj, adv A1a = "askew" chiefly South, South Midland]

caterige See **cartridge**.

cat-eyed *adjective* See citation.

1967 DARE Survey (Maryville TN) = having sharp and piercing eyes.

cat fit *noun* A burst of emotion, most often anger. See also **duck fit**.

1957 Broaddus *Vocab Estill Co KY* 14 = a severe fit, tantrum. **c1960** Wilson Coll = a fit of anger or joy: "When she got his letter, she had a cat fit." **1968** Wilson *Folklore Mammoth Cave* 41 = nervous fit[s], often suspected as hardly genuine . . . were *duck fits, conniption fits, jeeminy fits, the allovers,* and, very recently, the *heebie-jeebies*, or the *whitty-jiggers*.

cat fur *noun* See citation.

1966 Wilson Coll = answer to [a child's] question "What's that fer?" "Cat fur to make kitten britches, d'you want a pair?" **2017** *Blind Pig* (Nov 14) My mother used to answer "cat fur to make kitten britches" after repeated "what for" or "what fur" questions. Too many "what" questions might elicit "chicken squat, pick it up and see what you've got."

cat-head (also *cat-head biscuit*) *noun* A large biscuit.

1960 Hall *Smoky Mt Folks* 7 It was a novel experience to eat "cat heads" (biscuits) or corn pone three times a day. **1991** Weals *Last Train* 56 His biscuits were what Mary called cat-head biscuits because of their size, cut from dough with the end of an empty tin can. **1994** Huskey *County Squire* 26 We had plenty of biscuits. Mother would make them so big! When they were that size, the folks in the mountains called them "cat heads." **2005** Williams *Gratitude* 484 *cat head biscuits* = big ol' biscuits, big as a cat's head. They are so light you have to watch or they'll float off the plate. They're also what we call "choked out," or "choked off" biscuits because the amount of dough for a biscuit is choked off between the thumb and index finger. **2009** Sohn *Appal Home Cooking* 294 = large, uneven, hand-pulled drop biscuits. . . . Other biscuits are uniformly formed with a biscuit cutter.

[DARE *cathead* n 1 South, South Midland]

cathole *noun* See citation.

1992 Jones and Miller *Sthn Mt Speech* 65 = a hole where chinking has fallen out of a cabin wall.

cati-corner'd See **cater-corner**.

catirge See **cartridge**.

cat race *noun* Pursuit of a wildcat with dogs, in a hunt.

1977 *Jake Waldroop* 153 We'd turn the dog loose an' have a cat race and kill a wild cat.

catridge See **cartridge**.

cats and clay See **cat-and-clay**.

cat shaking (also *shake the cat*) *noun* See citations.

1932 Dugger *War Trails* 240–41 Mary Clawson, who was a good match-maker, called from the big house door: "Come in here, boys. We're goin' to have a cat shakin' before dinner." The quilt had been quilted and taken out of the frames. It had been spread out on the floor with the cotton bats grinning around the edges between the top and the lining. Each boy and girl stooped and gripped the rim of the quilt with both hands and raised it up as they straightened. Mrs. Clawson now threw the cat over into the center of the quilt and all began to shake up and down. The poor cat was perfectly bewildered. For a moment its eyes pleaded with the shakers in vain. Then they bleared with wild excitement, as it rolled from side to side on the quilt. When it tried to leap over on one side, they hurled it back to the other; when it was wriggling to get on its feet, they whirled it over on its back. The wilder the cat's excitement the harder they shook and the louder they laughed and hallooed; and the greater their glee the wilder the cat became. At last with all its reserved strength reinforced by terrible fright, it made a grand leap for liberty, but just as it reached the border of the quilt it was tossed heels up towards the ceiling, but fell on its feet outside the quilt and went out at the door into the woods with such terrible speed that it looked more like a streak of cat than a cat, and did not come home for three days. **1969** Hannum *Look Back* 47 They called it cat shakin'—and poor cat! A quilt was laid out on the floor; all courting-age young bent down, took firm hold of its edges with both hands, and raised up with it. Then the cat was thrown in and the boys would try to shake it out toward their best girl. That was the idea of the game; whichever girl the wild-eyed tabby leaped nearest to would marry first. The shakers laughed and yelled as they tossed the oracle of their fate from one to another, and high in the air. [**1977** Shackelford et al. *Our Appalachia* 20 There'd be a lot of girls there, seventeen- and eighteen-year-old, helping them quilt. We all would come in of an evening, and we'd want to shake the cat. Four girls—one at each corner—would get a hold of that quilt and another one would throw the cat in, and they got to shaking it as hard as they could shake and whichever one that cat jumped toward was going to get married first. . . . It happened all over this country at all the workings.] [**2011** Houk *Quilts* 12 Quilts are cloaked in superstition too, like "shake the cat" for example. When a quilt came off the frame, the unmarried women went outdoors, put a wary feline in the center of the quilt, held onto the corners and bounced the nervous animal into the air. Whoever the cat landed closest to would be the next to wed.]

cat's paw *noun* A burning bush (*Euonymus americanus*). Same as **hearts bustin'**.

1937 Thornburgh *Great Smoky Mts* 25 The seeds of some shrubs are more spectacular than their flowers. This is true of one of the showiest shrubs in the Great Smokies, the euonymous, wahoo or spindlebush. It is especially lovely in October when its seed-pod bursts open, displaying orange-colored seeds in its glowing red heart. It has many descriptive local names—swamp willow, strawberry bush, catspaw, jewel-box, but most descriptive of all is the name given by a mountain man of, "Heart's-bustin'-with-love."

catterag, catterge See **cartridge**.

cat-tracks *noun* See citations.

1919 Combs *Word-List South* 33 = trachoma, "sore-eyes," ... This figure is perhaps derived from the red spots and streaks seen in the eyes. **1923** Combs *Addenda KY* 242 = any disease of the eyes.

catty See **caddy**.

cattycorner(ed) See **cater-corner**.

cattywampus, cattywhumpus See **catawampus**[1].

cattywampus, cattywhumpus See **catawampus**[2].

caucus *verb*

A Variant form *corkus*.

1913 Kephart *Our Sthn High* 277 The hillmen ... [insert] sounds where they do not belong. Sometimes it is only an added consonant: gyarden, acrost, corkus (caucus); sometimes a syllable: loaferer, musicianer, suddenty.

B To converse; talk idly.

1932 Creal *Quaint Speech* "I want to corkus with younse a minute" means "I want to consult you." **1974** Fink *Bits Mt Speech* 4 = to talk idly. "They set around and *caucused* all day." **1995** Montgomery *Coll* (known to Cardwell).

caution *noun* A great wonder, startling or alarming event, thing, or person.

1895 Dromgoole *Humble Advocate* 327 I declar' ter goodness, Mis' Gary, it ware a plumb caution the way they-uns talked. **1899** Fox *Mt Europa* 29 The way he lighted inter the furriners was a caution. He 'lowed he was a-goin' to fight cyard-playin' and dancin' ez long ez he hed breath. **1957** Combs *Lg Sthn High: Word-List* 18 = a curiosity, sight; also a term of approval, as in: "That feller's a caution!" **c1960** Wilson *Coll* = a sort of half-complimentary name for a person who is unlike most of his acquaintances. **1963** Edwards *Gravel* 62 Teacher Bowers was what the people in our community would call "a case" or "a caution." "Now he's a case, I tell you"; or "He's a caution, from all the children say." **1979** Slone *My Heart* 18 "It will be a caution of beans ye'll have, if'n the blooms don't fall off too soon," Cindy remarked. **1982** Slone *How We Talked* 30 = a great wonder or great sight (a "caution" to see). **1998** Montgomery *File* "That boy's a caution" meant that you just never knew what he might do ... liable to do anything (51-year-old woman, Jefferson Co TN).

cave *verb* To rave, rage, grumble.

1949 Arnow *Hunter's Horn* 352 It was good to know why Nunn cursed so; he might quarrel and rave and cave all through supper, but at least it wouldn't be for her. **1957** Combs *Lg Sthn High: Word-List* 18 = to grumble constantly, or "chew the rag." Ex.: "He's been a-cavin' aroun' all day."

[Web3 *cave* v 2 "to be noisily and demonstrably angry"; DARE *cave* v chiefly Midland]

cawk *verb* Of a hunter: to imitate the call (of a wild turkey).

1939 Hall *Coll* (Cataloochee NC) He hollowed a bone out of a turkey's wing. He could cawk just like one.

cayn't See **can**[1] **A2**.

cazen (also *kazen*) *noun, verb* variants of *cause*.

1911 Shearin *E KY Word-List* 537 Câzen, v. tr. To cause; e.g., "You cazened me to do it" ... n. Cause, e.g., "You are the cazen of all the trouble." **1931** Combs *Lg Sthn High* 1307 "Kazen," v. and n. is also heard.

cear, ceer See **care A**.

ceard See **card A**.

ceer See **care A**.

cemetery vine *noun* The common periwinkle (*Vinca minor*). Same as **grave vine**.

[**1964** Stupka *Trees Shrubs Vines* 134 This exotic, trailing shrub was "often planted in cemeteries and gardens" ... where the plants have persisted.] **1980** *GSMNP-115:51* We call it in the park, and I've heard older people call it, cemetery vine. It was brought over here from England for putting around banks and cemeteries.

cent *noun* variant plural form without -s following a numeral.

1862 *Robinson CW Letters* (May 7) I have to pay ... 1 dollar per quier for paper & 75 cent for invelops by the pack. **1863** *Reese CW Letters* (March 1) tha[y] air seling flouer at three dollars pur hundred and shugar at ten Cents pur pound and Coffey at fifty Cent pur pound. **1973** *AOHP/ASU-71* We'd buy a hundred pound of salt for sixty cent then. **1983** *Dark Corner OHP-10A* If you had a team of mules, you could earn as much as fifty cent a day with that team of mules. **1989** *Matewan OHP-23* I worked for a dollar and eighty cent [a day].

ceremony *noun* A prescribed, repetitive incantation or ritualistic formula uttered by a **blood doctor**, **fire doctor**, or other healer. See also **charm doctor**, **conjure doctor**, **faith doctor**, **fever doctor**, **stop blood**, **wart doctor**.

1901 Price *KY Folk-Lore* 32 To "take out fire" (cure burns) [a healer] wet his forefinger with spittle, and gently rubbed over the burned places, repeating some "ceremony." **1939** Hall *Coll* (Hazel Creek NC) "Tell me his full name and how old he is, and I'll stop the blood," he said over some ceremony. He [= folk healer] can tell three women, and a woman can tell eight men. **1974** Roberts *Sang Branch* 71 Mat said some kind of ceremony and made some kind of noise, and the deer was coming through there just like a gang of sheep. **1985** Irwin *Alex Stewart* 139 She could lay her hand on you and say a sort of ceremony, and that would cure the scrofula.

certain

A *adjective, adverb, noun variant forms sartain, sartin, surtin* [see **1864** in **B**].

1797 *Sinking Creek Church Minutes* II:6 this Church doth Excommunicate John Carr on Sartain Chargis Lade in by the Church. **1859** Taliaferro *Fisher's River* 49 You'll see how it will go with us on that day, sartin. **1895** Murfree *Phantoms* 233 Nothin' is sartin in this vale o' tears. **1934–47** *LAMSAS Appal* (Madison Co NC, Swain Co NC) *sartain*. **1961** Williams *Rhythm and Melody* 9 They'll be larrupin' good fer sartain shore. **1969** Hannum *Look Back* 30 "I thought shorely undoubtedly of a sartin hit war so," you will hear, perhaps of a rumor believed in and found in relief not to be true.

[DARE *certain* adj, adv A especially Northeast, South, South Midland]

B *adverb* Certainly.

[See **1859** in **A**.] **1864** *Apperson CW Letters* (Jan 6) I neede it very bad surtin.

certain and declare *interjection* I'll declare for sure!

1970 *Hunting Stories* 78 He said, "Certain'n'declare no. I don't believe I ever did."

certain sure *adjective phrase, adverb phrase* Unquestionable; unquestionably with absolute confidence.

1864 (in **2003** Watford *Civil War in NC* 154) they was lots of men that told us that it was surtin shure for they said that they had seen the wounded men a going to the horse pital and they told them that they got hirt. **1910** Cooke *Power and Glory* 112 Hit's [= a disease] sartin shore to go through 'em like it would go through a family. **1952** Justus *Children* 36 I reckon I owe it to you, certain-sure. **2002** Rash *Foot in Eden* 94 He'll be back and he'll certain sure have some words with you.

cha cha *noun* See citation.

1944 Wilson *Word-List* 41 = the katydid.

chaff piler *noun* An early grain-threshing machine.

c1980 Roberts *Olden Times* 110 The threshing machines of earlier days, often called a "shuffler" or "chaff piler," were quite different from those of a generation or so ago. The earlier machines did not move from farm to farm, but instead were stationed at certain barns which had a "threshing floor"—loft floor without cracks upon which the threshed grain and the chaff could be spread. After the threshing was finished the grain and the chaff was then put through the windmill seed cleaners turned by hand. This blew the chaff from the heavier grain. Farmers from nearby brought their grain to the threshing floor to have it threshed and cleaned.

chafted *adjective* See citation.

2005 Williams *Gratitude* 484 *chafted* = chapped; made sore by rubbing, as in riding a horse. *Galded* is a worse condition than *chafted*.

chain *noun* The warp of a web of cloth in weaving. See also **linsey**.

1931 Goodrich *Mt Homespun* 6 When all the bouts are completed, she ties the "crosses"—the crossed threads—in such a way as to keep them apart at that point, and then takes the warp from the bars, looping it onto itself to make a chain of heavy, soft, white links, and the onlooker understands why the warp is called, in the mountains, the "chain." **1937** Hall *Coll* (Big Creek NC) Linsey—a cloth for underwear, all wool but the chain, cotton thread put into the loom to weave with.

chaince See **chance A**.

chain dog *noun* See citation.

1973 Schulman *Logging Terms* 35 = a device made up of two iron spikes joined together by a chain of three to five links. The chain dogs were used in the rafting of hardwood logs.

chainy See **china**.

chair *noun variant forms cheer, chur*.

1826 Royall *Sketches* 58 [They say] "put them *cheers*," (chairs) out of the road. **1835** *McLean Diary* 34 Widow peterough sail baught half Dozen Churs price five Dollars. **1861** *Martin CW Letters* (Nov 16) wee are nerly as weel fixt as wee wer at hom wee hav baurowrs tables cheers chis & boxes. **1883** Zeigler and Grosscup *Heart of Alleghanies* 146 Now lite, go to the house, and take cheers while we stable the nags. **1897** *Incidents* 27 An my frens, you all can't help ahavin' bad thoughts kum inter yer heads, but ye hain't got no necessity fer ter set 'em a cheer. **1913** Kephart *Our Sthn High* 197 If you-uns can stand what we-uns has ter, w'y come right in and set you a cheer. **1937** Hall *Coll* (Cades Cove TN) Come up and git ye a cheer [= common, polite way of asking a person to join others on the porch]. **c1959** Weals *Hillbilly Dict* 3 Draw up a cheer and set a spell. **1971** *AOHP/ALC-33* They made their cheers out of hickory wood. **1997** Nelson *Country Folklore* 13 In the downstairs room were beds (bedsteads), dressers (bureaus), straight chairs (cheers), and two sewing machines. **2002** Morgan *Mt Born* 163 *chur*.

[DARE *cheer* (at *chair* n) South, South Midland, scattered Pennsylvania, New England]

chalk *verb* To work through (a crop) cutting weeds.

1996 Montgomery *Coll* I've got to chalk the corn (known to Cardwell).

chalk-eye *noun* In coal mining, a type of subcontractor; hence verb = to work in such a role and verbal noun *chalk-eyeing* = working in such a role.

1957 Hewes *Boxcar* 78 Poverty-ridden mountain folk worked to erect new buildings on their new homesteads; their labor time at about thirty cents an hour was credited in lieu of cash toward ownership. During the construction phase they received cash grants for food and other essentials. Soon they organized a racket, hiring substitute laborers at five cents an hour and paying the substitutes out of their own cash grants; these substitutes were the "chalk eyes" colloquially named for their starvation-ravaged countenances. **1973** Kahn *Hillbilly Women* 47 I went to another man and he put down that he chalk-eyed for Ab in mines for ten years or more. That's where, like a man has a great big place in the mines with different rooms and they hire these men to load coal for them. They call it chalk-eyeing. **1974** *AOHP/ALC-802* Some men had a whole entry [= passage in a coal mine] maybe, or maybe they'd hire eight or ten men ... what you'd call a chalk eye was a man that had maybe a whole entry, and he can hire as many men as he wanted to to help him, and ... he paid them.

chalk up *verb phrase* See citation.

c1975 *Miners' Jargon* 2 *chalking up* = reporting higher production than actually achieved.

chamber lye *noun* See citations.

c1960 Wilson *Coll* = a term now very rarely heard. **2003** Cavender *Folk Medicine* 112 In eastern Tennessee, a sow bug emulsion or chamber-lye (urine accretion scraped from a chamber pot) was applied.

[DARE *chamber lye* n chiefly South, South Midland, West]

chameleon *noun* The green angle lizard (*Angois carolinensis*).

1967 Huheey and Stupka *Amphibians and Reptiles* 49 This so-called "Chameleon" is not uncommon along the western boundary [of Great Smoky Mountains National Park].

chance *noun*

A Variant forms *chaince, chancet, chanct*.

1863 *Coggin CW Letters* (Jan 10) I Dont No that thar is Any Chaince for me to git afurlough if the Company was all together I think that the chaince would Bee Better. **1863** *Walker CW Letters* (April 15) tell them All to writ to me you Must write ever chaince you have. **1913** Kephart *Our Sthn High* 85 Your chanct is ruined. **1931** Goodrich *Mt Homespun* 40 Aunt Liza said I did "mighty well for the chaince" I'd had in my "raising." **1963** Edwards *Gravel* 118 "I'll gi' you one more chanct to speak howdy," said Zeke, "and if you don't, I'll blow you into flinders wi' this shot gun." **1971** *AOHP/ALC-260* They've got a chancet to get money to go to school on that we didn't have, and hit's a lot better. **1991** Thomas *Sthn Appal* 6 His only chaince wuz t' plunge into that river, an' git away from 'um.

[DARE *chaince* (at *chance* n A) especially southern Appalachians]

B Senses. [Editor's note: The senses below cannot always be differentiated.]

1 A portion or quantity, usually a large one, especially of a crop.

1834 Crockett *Narrative* 89–90 found a fine chance of potatoes in [the cellar], and hunger compelled us to eat them. **1863** *Tesh CW Letters* (Aug 24) I have nice potatoes and some onions to and if it rains some I shall have a fine chance of cabage. **1881** Pierson *In the Brush* 259 He couldn't stan' it no longer, he told the boys if any of 'em would go down and lick that big feller he'd give him his gal, and a right smart chance of plunder. **1939** Hall *Coll* (Smokemont NC) Back some years ago we had a good chance of fine mountain range. *Ibid.* (White Oak NC) A chance of wheat or corn means fifty or more bushels. **c1940** Aswell *Glossary TN Idiom* 5 = portion, number, quantity. "A right smart *chance* of people." **1952** Wilson *Folk Speech NC* 526 I have a nice *chance* of potatoes this season.

[OED3 *chance* n 4b U.S. dialect; DARE *chance* n B1 chiefly South, South Midland]

2 An opportunity, prospect, example.

1862 *Epperly CW Letters* (July 20) wee ar now about 12 mild from Richmond and have A bad chanse to get our letters. **1863** *Walker CW Letters* (May 31) i hope i will git hom with you all som tim but it looke like a bad chanc at this time. **1907** Dugger *Balsam Groves* 31 "We want to stay all night with you, Mr. Toddy," said the elderly gentleman. "It's a mighty poor chance; we're not fixed to keep nobody hur." **1917** Kephart *Word-List* 409 A poor chance of a place to spend the night. **1956** Hall *Coll* (Big Bend NC) That's about all the chance I have of makin' a livin'—from the cattle and the 'baccer in the fall. **1974** Fink *Bits Mt Speech* 4 = prospect. "A good *chance* of corn." **1990** Whitener *Thrice-Told* I want him to write to me and excuse him for not writing to him for my chance is very bad and i am a bad Scribe at best.

chancet, chanct See **chance A**.

chancy *adjective* Lucky, bringing good fortune. [Editor's note: The sense "risky, doubtful" is widespread in the US.]

1971 Dwyer *Dict for Yankees* 24 = lucky. "I know a chancy place to fish." **1996** Montgomery *Coll* It's a chancy place to fish (Cardwell).

[OED3 *chancy* adj 1 "lucky ... auspicious," Scot[tish], obsolete; SND *chancy* adj 1 "lucky; auspicious"]

change *verb* To castrate (an animal, especially a boar pig); to spay. See also **alter, cut B2, trim**.

1966 Dakin *Vocab Ohio River Valley* 245 *Trim* ... is fairly common (but no less so than other terms) in the Mountains but rare farther west in Kentucky and unused west of the Kentucky River. In the Kentucky Mountains the most common term, and the only one used by numerous informants, is *change*. *Change* is almost completely a Mountain expression now being unknown elsewhere in Kentucky, in Ohio, and in Illinois. **1976** Ledford *Folk Vocabulary* 281 To *change* (in both noun and participial usage) was once standard in Western North Carolina for castration of a boar pig. **1985** Irwin *Alex Stewart* 106 I've been wanting them changed (castrated) for a long time. **1996–97** Montgomery *Coll* (known to Jones, Ledford), = both to castrate and spay (Brown).

[DARE *change* v chiefly South, southern Appalachians]

change baby *noun* A baby born when a woman is approaching menopause.

1952 Giles *40 Acres* 39 Kenneth is what is called around here a "change baby." Long after Miss Bessie thought her childbearing days were over he made an unexpected and it may be even an unwelcome appearance, but that was only temporary. He became the darling of the family at once.

chap *noun* A child, especially (but not necessarily) a boy.

1863 *Bartlett CW Letters* (Jan 4) my hole Studdy is about you and my little chaps. **1865** *Hill CW Letters* (March 5) I am well and harty at presant hoping this few lins may find you and your little Chaps all well. **1939** *FWP Guide NC* 98 The boy, or "chap," may be called a little "shirttail boy" to distinguish him from her "arm baby and her knee baby." **1940** Still *River of Earth* 118 The kiver was opened and thar the chap was, hits little face red and wrinkled. *Ibid.* 128 I recollect your ma when she was a chap. **1953** Wharton *Dr Woman Cumberlands* 55, 57 "My little chap's got a sore throat and is mighty puny." . . . On the pillow, to my surprise, was the face of a beautiful little girl. I had imagined a boy, since the man had said "chap." **1963** Ritchie *Dulcimer Book* 7 Dad says that it would be a common sight, when he was a little slip of a "chap," "to see Thomas' dulcimer cyarts go up and down the creek roads in the summertime." **1966** Dykeman *Far Family* 180 "Don't want no chaps around," the short, bearded man growled. "Better send him home, Tom." **1982** Ginns *Snowbird Gravy* 102 Now it ain't wrong to steal if you get to where you have to for food. If you got a little bunch of chaps, and you go and ask for it first. **1996–97** Montgomery *Coll* (known to Brown, Cardwell, Ellis, Jones, Norris, Oliver).

[DARE *chap* n 1 chiefly South, South Midland]

chapel *noun* A church, as one named after a local family or a landowner who donated the property on which it was built, or more recently, one that has acquired the redundant designation *church*, as *Murphy's Chapel Church*, *Anderson Chapel Church*.

1823 (in **2003** *TN Petitions II* 206) We pray you therefore in your wisdom to . . . and convey Specially to the trustees of the methodist meeting house pine chappel. **1937** Hall *Coll* (Copeland Creek TN) The first church house on Webb's Creek was Evans Chapel. *Ibid.* (Wears Cove TN) [There are] two Dutch centers—Byrds Chapel and Fox schoolhouse. **1963** Edwards *Gravel* 47 She belonged to the Baptist Church at Hennessey's Chapel, and she attended regularly, taking her children, all in clean, well-ironed clothes. **1973** *AOHP/ALC* Our little church, about a half a mile to Bells Chapel Church, we had special prayer services there for the boys. **1991** Headrick *Headrick's Chapel* 207 The present Harp singing at Headrick's Chapel actually began at the Primitive Baptist Church of Townsend about 1920 when it was known as the Coker Hill Old Harp Singing. **1998** *Dante OHP-69* Carl was one of the first Deacons in the Freewill Baptist in Mills Chapel Church.

character *noun* variant pronunciation with primary stress on the second syllable: *care-akter*, *cha-racter*, *char-ac-ter*, *char-rack-ter*, *charreckter*, *kar-acter*.

1867 Harris *Sut Lovingood* 22 I arterards foun' out, he were a-studyin how tu play the kar-acter ove a hoss puffectly. **1939** Hall *Notebooks* 9:34 (Saunook NC). **1952** Wilson *Folk Speech NC* 526. **1955** Washburn *Country Doctor* 45 She's quite a cha-racter; in fac' she's a sight in this worl'. **1961** Williams *R in Mt Speech* 7 *charreckter*. **1962** Wilson *Folkways Mammoth Cave* 9 The secondary accent is really a second primary accent, fully as strong as the supposedly main one. Mammoth Cave people spoke of . . . *character* as /CHAR-AC-ter/. **1997** Andrews *Mountain Vittles* 88 I know sitting along the road and up the mountains in the hollers and coves they have a lot of char-rack-ter but, I've seen snow sift through the walls and from the roof in wintertime and water frozen solid in the face pan. **2013** Venable *How to Tawlk* 9 *care-akter* = a delightful, humorous person: "Ol' Barney is such a care-akter! Everbidy in town loves him."

character note *noun* Same as **shape note**.

1984 Allison *Character Notes* 86 Compared to other folk customs, this use of shape-notes to learn tunes and provide music for the church services had a very short existence—a little more than enough to span three or four generations. So, one can understand why the term "buckwheat" notes and its progeny have not evoked the response from the professional recorders of history. **2009** *TN Encycl* Shape-note singing, a predominantly rural, Protestant, Anglo-American music tradition, involves singing from hymnals or "tunebooks" having shaped notes (aka "character notes," "buckwheat notes," or "patent notes") as opposed to the standard "round notes."

charge

A *verb*

1 To exhort, instruct.

1983 Page and Wigginton *Aunt Arie* 167 A man and a woman come here th'other day and th'man charged me not t'go into that garden.

2 See citation.

1949 Maurer *Argot of Moonshiner* 8 = to fill the still with beer.

B *noun* See citation.

1949 Maurer *Argot of Moonshiner* 8 = one filling of the still from the fermenter vats. This beer is boiled until the alcohol has evaporated, when another charge is put into the still. "We only lacked one charge of being through"; "We can run a charge an hour."

charge it to the dust/sand and let the rain settle it *verb phrase* See citations.

1946 Woodard *Word-List VA/NC* 35 *charge it to the sand (dust) and let the rain settle it* = charge it on the books but it may not be paid. (Generally said jokingly.) **1966** Dykeman *Far Family* 99 "Let's charge that account to the dust and let the rain settle it," Ivy said. **1967** Hall *Coll* (Del Rio TN) = said in dismissing a loan when it is small, unimportant, or impossible to collect. **1984** *DARE File* (wNC) *charge it to the dust and let the rain settle it* = in my experience, this phrase asserts the futility of charging (i.e. recording a debt) in a particular case. No actual debt-recording occurs because such action is considered a waste of effort.

charivari See **shivaree.**

Charley liniment *noun* See citations.

1977 Madden and Jones *Mt Home* 31–32 The mainstay of the Walker sisters' healing potions was "Charley linament," a "soothing balm" of secret ingredients concocted by Uncle Charley Walker. It was an herb mixture that used Indian Turnip and May apple root along with many others, and is remembered as being "hot as hell's hinges" and "mighty powerful." For headache or fainting, it was rubbed on the temples. Charley linament on the chest helped coughs, colds, and other lung ailments, and stiffness eased by rubbing it into the muscle. In fact, it was used practically every way except internally. **1997** *BearPaw* 5 An herb garden with medicinals and teas grew behind the house and the sisters were well known as "herb doctors." Using catnip, boneset, and Charley liniment, a concoction of secret ingredients created by Uncle Charley Walker, the sisters treated everything from fevers and pneumonia, to stiff joints and sore muscles.

charm doctor *noun* A person reputedly able to stop bleeding, remove warts, or perform other healing by a verbal formula (for stopping blood, usually reciting Ezekiel 16:6). See also **blood doctor, ceremony, conjure doctor, faith doctor, fever doctor, power doctor, wart doctor.**

1863 *Earnest CW Diary* 84 [I] had a charm doctor to work on my warts. He made quite an exhibition of his mystic arts. **1927** Furman *Lonesome Road* 17 Jared was thrilled indeed. Old Aunt Emmaline! Not only the old granny-woman that brought babies to the creeks around, but also the charm-doctor, the witch-doctor of whom he had heard such wonderful tales. **1956** Hall *Coll* (Roaring Fork TN) The old mountain people believed that there was a charm doctor in every community. Wes Rayfield's boy was cuttin' wood and cut an artery. Mrs. Rayfield, she was a doctor. She charmed it, but it just bled on. She got excited and missed a word. When she got in the house and off to herself, she thought of the word and said the rhyme over and the blood stopped. Wes said it was the first time his wife ever failed. She was scared. **1985** Irwin *Alex Stewart* 123 I went to see an old charm doctor once to have her to take some warts off my hand, and she was setting there playing one of them dulcimers and that was the first one I ever heard. **1988** Brown *Beech Creek* 177 A few low-class and intermediate-class [people] even went to a "charm doctor" on Coon Creek when sick. (Most who did this were reluctant to admit they believed in charms.)

charm stick *noun* A forked stick used to dowse for underground water, a divining rod. Same as **witching stick.**

1967 *DARE Survey* (Gatlinburg TN) = a forked stick that shows water underground.

char-rack-ter, charreckter See **character.**

chart *noun* In weaving, a plan or diagram showing how to make a given design. See also **draft 1.**

1959 Hall *Coll* (Cataloochee NC) A chart on the loom for the pattern [showed] how many times to tramp the treadles. The different draft you wove by would make the flower different.

chart class *noun* Formerly, the most basic class in elementary formal education, involving the learning of the alphabet, numerals, etc.

1949 Stuart *Thread* 4 I had pupils from the chart class to and including the eighth grade.

chatterack *noun* A noisy insect such as a cicada or katydid.

1883 Zeigler and Grosscup *Heart of Alleghanies* 321 These woods were filled with insects termed "chatteracks" by the natives. **1953** Miller *Pigeon's Roost* (Aug 27) It is reported that chatteracks began hollering here the first of this month. The old saying is it will frost within six weeks after they start their noise. **1995** Adams *Come Go Home* 75–76 I can remember the sounds: the rustle of hymn books that were being used as fans, young'uns fussing and being told to hush, the hum of chatteracks outside the open, screenless windows. **1996–97** Montgomery *Coll* (known to Brown), = any small noisy insect such as a jarfly or katydid that makes a sound like "chatterack" (Oliver).

[echoic]

chaw See **chew.**

chaw stick *noun* A twig chewed and frayed at one end to be used to apply snuff under one's lip or beside one's gum. Same as **toothbrush 1.**

1998 Joslin *Living Heritage* 77 At a black gum tree, you read that twigs from this species are used as "chaw sticks" by mountain folks to place snuff behind their lips.

cheatingest *adjective* Characterized by much cheating. For similar present-participle forms taking *-est*, see **-est A.**

1939 Hall *Coll* (Bryson City NC) That's the cheatin'est place here at the [Cherokee Indian Fair].

cheating stick See **cheat stick.**

cheat stick (also *cheating stick*) *noun* In logging, the rule stick with which a scaler computes the amount of lumber in a group of logs.

1964 Clarkson *Lumbering in WV* 358 *cheating stick* = scale-rule. Syn. Thieving rod. **1998** Buchanan *Logging Terms: cheat stick.*

check[1] *noun* A snack, light meal.

1949 Kurath *Word Geog East US* 36 Two sections of the South Midland, the Kanawha and Western North Carolina, have some interesting local expressons. On the Kanawha we find *check* and *jack-bite* . . . beside the Southern *snack* for a bite between meals. **1952** Wilson *Folk Speech NC* 526 = a light meal.

[cf SND *chack* n[3] "a snack; a casual, slight or hurried meal": Web3 *check* n[1] 9 dialect; DARE *check* n[2] Appalachians]

check[2] *noun*

1 A playing piece in the game of checkers; hence noun *checks* = the game of checkers.

c1960 Wilson *Coll*: *Checkers* [is often called] *checks*. **2007** McMillon *Notes* = a playing piece; hence noun *checks* = the game of checkers.

[DARE *check* n[3] 3 South, South Midland]

2 A crossing point of furrows plowed at right angles to mark planting points.

2002 Ogle *Remembrances* 61 We were renting from Ephraim Ogle so I would have to go in the spring time to help him plant corn. He would say, Wiley bring that oldest girl to drop it in the checks. She don't scatter it.

3 In phrases *check in one's checks*, *hand in one's checks*, *turn in one's checks* = to die.

1927 Woofter *Dialect from WV* 356 *hand in your checks*. **1968** DARE *Survey* (Laurel Fork VA) *turned in his checks*; (Wytheville VA) *checking in his checks*.

check cloth *noun* A fabric with a pattern of squares in alternating colors, used for clothing.

1963 Watkins and Watkins *Yesterday* 5 A week or two before school began, mothers bought calico cloth to make new dresses for the girls and "check cloth" to make a blue-and-white striped shirt for the boys.

checkedy (also *checkerdy*) *adjective* Checked.

1949 Arnow *Hunter's Horn* 269 She lingered too long admiring the pretty checkerdy coats. **1968** *End of Moonshining* 42 I seed that checkedy sole print in the soft ground. **2014** *Blind Pig* (Oct 4) Personally I was never much for flowerdy or stripedy. I am more of a checkerdy type myself.

checkerbacker *noun* The downy woodpecker (*Dryobates pubescens*).

1917 Kephart *Word-List* 409 = downy woodpecker.

checkerberry *noun* The teaberry, a low evergreen shrub (*Gaultheria procumbens*) that produces bright berries in the fall and winter and whose oil is used as a flavoring and as medicine. Same as **mountain tea**.

1970 Campbell et al. *Smoky Mt Wildflowers* 80 Other common names [of the teaberry] are checkerberry, wintergreen, and mountain tea. **1982** Stupka *Wildflowers* 83 Teaberry, often called "wintergreen" or "checkerberry," is an old-time remedy, used as a diuretic.

checkerdy See **checkedy**.

checkline *noun* A checkrein, the ropes or leathers that the driver of a wagon holds to guide a horse or team of horses.

1941 Stuart *Men of Mts* 28 "Yes-sir, Mr. Mennix," says Pewee holdin' to the leather check-lines and lookin' straight ahead at the road. **1963** Edwards *Gravel* 72 Having said "Whoa," Dad put the brake on tight, wrapped the check-lines securely about the brake handle, and jumped down off the wagon. **1964** Reynolds *High Lands* 7 Rescuers had to go back a mile to get some check lines off some horses to use as ropes which proved not long enough, and also had to detour along a narrow ledge to the point of the accident. **1986** Pederson et al. *LAGS*: *checkline(s)* = attested by 13/60 interviewees (21.7%) from E TN and 1/35 (2.9%) from N GA; 14/29 of all LAGS interviewees (48.2%) attesting term were from Appalachia. **1987** Carver *Regional Dialects* 167 When hitched to a draft animal, the leathers or ropes used to guide it are often called *checklines*, in standard usage "checkreins." **1996–97** Montgomery *Coll*: *checklines* (known to Adams, Brown, Cardwell, Ledford, Norris, Oliver, Weaver), = sometimes known as *checkreins* (Jones).

[DARE *checkline* n 2 chiefly South Midland]

check-off *noun* See citations.

1943 Korson *Coal Dust* 73 Deductions made from wages, or "check-offs," kept the mine worker in perpetual indebtedness. There were two kinds of deductions: those for occupational supplies and services, which in nearly every other industry were furnished free by the employer, and those for household goods obtained at the company store. **1969** Lee *Bloodletting* 12 Always, the miners asserted that they sought . . . to enforce the "check off," whereby the operators deduct union dues from workers' wages and pay them directly to the union.

checkreins See **checkline**.

check tag *noun* See citation.

2011 *Massey Report* 37 There is no safety precaution more fundamental than maintaining a system that tells operators who is in a coal mine at a given time. Throughout the 19th and 20th centuries, operators used a "tag-in" system. Each miner was assigned a number with a corresponding metal check tag that was moved to an "in" position hook by the miner as he entered the mine. When he left the mine after his shift, the miner moved the tag to an "out" position.

chee See **cheese**.

cheep *verb* To utter or reveal (a secret); to betray a confidence.

1900 Harben *N GA Sketches* 273 It got out, an' me nur Sally narry one never cheeped it, fer we wuz ashamed. **1923** Greer-Petrie *Angeline Steppin' Out* 17 We got away from thar as soon as Lum's bruises would let us, and we never even cheeped hit to the Jedge. **1940** Haun *Hawk's Done* 22 I never did cheep it to Joe. I thought it best not to. **1952** Wilson *Folk Speech NC* 528 = to reveal confidential matter. "Don't you dast *cheep* what I just told you." **c1960** Wilson *Coll* = to betray a secret: "He didn't cheep until I told him he could talk."

[DARE *cheep* v chiefly South Midland]

cheer See **chair**.

cheese *noun* Construed as a plural; hence singular form *chee* through back-formation.

1863 Sexton *CW Letters* (Nov 12) tell Jo to fetch me Some onions a couple of cheese and Some Molasses Some butter and a hat if you can git it. **1895** Edson and Fairchild *TN Mts* 376 *chee.* **1972** AOHP/LJC-104 I was thirteen years old ever before I eat any cheese, and that day we eat them. **1974** Fink *Bits Mt Speech* 4 Them *cheese.* **1995** Montgomery Coll Give me a hunk of them cheese (Cardwell).

[DARE *cheese* n A chiefly South Midland]

Cherokee ball *noun* Same as **stickball.**

1916 Canby *Top Smoky* 579 The boys, when free from tasks, play "Cherokee ball"—a kind of lacrosse—on a green meadow beneath the school buildings, with queer, shrill cries.

Cherokee bean *noun* See citation.

1955 Boone *Folk Names* 234 The Cherokee Bean (*Erythrina herbacea*) . . . was used both as a food and as an ornament by the Cherokee Indians; it is still used in some parts of Florida as a Christmas tree decoration.

Cherokee bean bread See **bean bread.**

Cherokee rose *noun* A white-flowered evergreen rose (either *Rosa laevigata* or *R. bractiata*).

2001 House *Clay's Quilt* 212 At each turn he was sure that he saw a clearing where sunlight fell in a wide block on the ground, where the trees stepped back to make way for a field full of Cherokee roses, Queen Anne's lace, jonquils, jack-in-the pulpits, black-eyed Susans, purple daisies. **2002** Quasha *Draw Georgia* 16 The Cherokee rose became Georgia's state flower on August 18, 1916. The Cherokee rose is not native to the United States. In fact, it came from China and was brought to America by English settlers in the 1700s. The flower, however, got its name from the Cherokees, Native Americans who planted it throughout the state.

[DARE *Cherokee rose* n South]

Cherokee sallet *noun* Same as **poke**[2].

1998 Dabney *Smokehouse Ham* 265 Called "Cherokee sallet" in some parts of east Tennessee—poke is described by many as a gourmet dish of majestic proportions.

cherry bird *noun* The cedar waxwing (*Bombycilla cedrorum*).

1913 Morley *Carolina Mts* 67 No sooner does the fruit turn red on the few [cherry] trees lovingly watched by their owners than there appear upon the scene a large and happy flock of cedar waxwings, for no slight reason named "cherry-birds." **1996–97** Montgomery Coll (known to Andrews, Brown, Cardwell, Stupka).

chest *noun* variant forms *chis, chist,* variant plural form of two syllables: *chest-es.*

1863 *Love CW Letters* (May 12) I sent my coat and chist and a few more litle things by bill Ruth. **1867** Harris *Sut Lovingood* 97e [sic] Thar wur Sicily a flingin out bed qilts outen a big chist. **1891** Brown *Dialect in TN* 172 *Chist* is heard for *chest.* **1914** Arthur *Western NC* 260 On the tops of boxes or trunks, usually called "chists," were folded and piled in neat order the extra quilts, sheets and counterpanes. **1973** GSMNP-88:75–76 He left a lot of his books and chists. . . . They used to have these big old chistes. **1975** Chalmers *Better* 12 There were hand wrought iron implements for farming and for fire place cookery, candle molds, wooden "piggen," heavy "chist," and a bread tray scooped out of a log. **1993** Cunningham *Sthn Talk* 29 Willodeene's hope chist is slam full.

[CUD *chist* n; DARE *chist* n especially frequent New England, Midland]

chest consumption *noun* Same as **consumption.**

1999 Morgan *Gap Creek* 4 During the terrible winter when Papa took the chest consumption, we didn't hardly get off the mountain, and we almost run out of cornmeal.

chestes See **chest.**

chestnut bake *noun* Formerly, a festive event at which gathered chestnuts were roasted in the fire and eaten.

1973 GSMNP-79:9 We always had to go to Grandmaw's house to have a good chestnut bake. Cut a little gap out in the chestnut and rake out a place in the coals in the fireplace and pile it full of chestnuts and then rake the coals back over them. And bake them maybe seven to eight minutes. And they rake them all in and dust the ashes off. And boy talk about something good to eat. Us kids will never forget our good old chestnut bakes in the Sugarlands.

chestnut bread *noun* A heavy bread made originally by the Cherokee from nuts of the now-blighted American chestnut tree (*Castanea dentata*).

1939 Hall Coll (Cataloochee NC) Lots of people made chestnut bread and bean bread. They mix dried beans and corn meal. **1955** Parris *Roaming Mts* 210 One of the ancient dishes of the Cherokee Indians was chestnut bread. **1995–97** Montgomery Coll (known to Cardwell, Norris, Shields). **2015** Seidl *New Roots* Paul Dillman of Qualla Boundary makes traditional Cherokee chestnut bread. But he says he's never tasted an American chestnut. . . . Chestnut bread is a variation of bean bread, a traditional staple food among the Cherokee. It's prepared much the same way, just substituting chestnuts for pinto beans. . . . The American chestnuts (Castanea dentata) that formerly served as the base for this dish were largely wiped out by the chestnut blight, Cryphonectria parasitica, a pathogenic fungus brought to this country by imported Asian chestnuts in the late 19th century. . . . Dillman uses Chinese chestnuts (Castanea mollissima) in his chestnut bread, which he says are larger than the American variety.

chestnut burr *noun* The hard shell of a chestnut.

1956 Hall Coll (Roaring Fork TN) I could crack chestnut burrs with my [bare] heels as easy as with my shoe heel. I've cracked a many a one with my naked heel. **1959** Hall Coll (Newport TN) I can crack chestnut burrs with my heel [= a common boast of one's hardihood in childhood or said by elderly people in reminiscence].

chestnut flat(s) *noun* A relatively level, open area in the mountains where chestnut trees once thrived. Same as **buckeye flat**. See also **flat, flatwoods 1**.

1960 Burnett *My Valley* 8 Frederic figured the panther had been following him downwind from the time he left the chestnut flats. **1973** GSMNP-6:2 My grandfather, after he had married and came there with his bride, had been hewing logs out of the chestnut flat back there, the big poplar logs, to make him a home. **1985** Kiser *Life and Times* 59 In the days before the chestnut blight, there were plenty in the woods. Almost every farmer had a "chestnut flat." That was a flat place upon the hill where nothing much grew but chestnut trees.

chestnut hunt See **hunt B**.

chestnut mast *noun* Fallen nuts of the now-blighted American chestnut tree (*Castanea dentata*), which serve as a source of food for animals, especially wild hogs and bears.

1915 Bohannon *Bear Hunt* 461–62 In all the creek bottoms there was no chestnut mast, but of beech there was plenty, both in feeding grounds which lay on the North Carolina side of the main ridge and the lying grounds which are on the Tennessee side. **1956** Hall *Coll* (Emerts Cove TN) I fenced up my woodlands till I could keep hogs. The chestnut mast was good for 'em. They'd grow fat. **1989** Oliver *Hazel Creek* 24 Since they were the major source of meat, hogs (razor-back or ridge-rooters) were raised first, and allowed to run wild around the farms, fattening on acorn and chestnut mast.

chestnut oak *noun* Any of several oaks that often replaced the American chestnut when the latter was decimated by blight in the early twentieth century. It is the principal source of **tanbark**.

1884 Murfree *In TN Mts* 60 Now and again the forest quiet was broken by the patter of acorns from the chestnut oaks. **1937** Hall *Coll* (Cades Cove TN) Acorns were eaten by wild hogs [also by bears, turkeys, and domestic hogs allowed to range in the woods], the nuts of white oak, chestnut oak, and in the winter bitter oak, called mast. **1941** Walker *Story of Mt* 64 Among the trees that have furnished crossties, the chestnut oak perhaps leads. Its bark was long sought for use in tanning leather. **1964** Stupka *Trees Shrubs Vines* 50 Lambert remarked that during the logging era the chestnut oak was the largest contributor to the tanbark industry in the Southern Appalachian area. **1997** Montgomery *Coll* = so called because its leaves have a shape similar to a chestnut's (Cardwell).

[so called from the shape of the leaf]

chestnut orchard *noun* A grove of the now-blighted American chestnut tree (*Castanea dentata*), the nuts of which were considered a delicacy and were gathered to be sold for cash.

1955 Parris *Roaming Mts* 210 Folks who didn't have chestnut orchards would get up parties and get a covered wagon or two and go off into the hills where there was a good stand of chestnut. **1991** Haynes *Haywood Home* 50 Just about every farm on Fines Creek and Crabtree had a chestnut orchard even though chestnut trees grew wild everywhere. **1995** Montgomery *Coll* (known to Cardwell, Shields).

chestnut pudding *noun* See citation.

1997 Montgomery *Coll* = made from chestnuts mixed with huckleberries, persimmons, etc., sweetened with molasses and baked (Brown).

chestnut soil *noun* See citation.

1927 Woofter *Dialect from WV* 350 = thin soil on northern exposures: "That farm has too much chestnut soil."

chev-a-robe See **chifforobe**.

chew

A *verb, noun* variant form *chaw*.

1862 *Robinson CW Letters* (May 7) I have to pay 50 cents per plug fore tobacco littel bits of pluges I can chaw 1 a week. **1873** Smith *Arp Peace Papers* 25 Do you chaw tobakker? **1898** Elliott *Durket Sperret* 115 If I jest could box her ears oncest, she'd not chaw none fur a-while. **1913** Kephart *Our Sthn High* 81 They'll run right in on the varmint, snappin' and chawin' and worryin' till he gets so mad you can hear his tushes pop a half mile. **1934–47** *LAMSAS Appal* (Madison Co NC, Swain Co NC). **1956** Hall *Coll* (Del Rio TN) He would steal a chaw of terbacker out of your mouth an' you a-lookin' at him. **1975** GSMNP-62:3 We had a three-quarter English and quarter bulldog, and when he got to a hog, he chawed him. **1997** Montgomery *Coll* I need a chaw of tobacco (Cardwell). **2003** Carter *Mt Home* 13 When he could get it, he chawed store boughten twist.

B *verb*

1 In phrase *chew up* = to injure by biting.

1928 (in **1952** Mathes *Tall Tales* 78) Ye durn nigh got both of us chawed plumb up! **1955** Parris *Roaming Mts* 48 He was a master brute and would have chawed them dogs up if he'd had any teeth.

2 (also *chew up*) To embarrass, offend.

1881 Pierson *In the Brush* 258 The old feller, Saul, the gineral, he felt more chawed up and meaner than the sogers, and, when he couldn't stan' it no longer, he told the boys if any of 'em would go down and lick that big feller he'd give him his gal, and a right smart chance of plunder. **1953** Davison *Word-List Appal* 9 That compliment sort of chawed me. **1971** Dwyer *Dict for Yankees* 24 *chawed up* = embarrassed. "I was sure chawed up when I heard that." **1997** Montgomery *Coll* (known to Brown, Bush, Cardwell).

3 To be stingy. See also **chew one's tobacco twice**.

1927 Woofter *Dialect from WV* 350 = to be stingy. "Mr. Thompson does not buy much tobacco, because he always chaws it twice."

C *noun*

1 A hold, an attachment.

1895 Edson and Fairchild *TN Mts* 370 = of a flirt. "She's tryin' to git a *chaw* on a feller." **1997** Montgomery *Coll* (known to Bush, Cardwell, Jones).

2 A bite of chewing tobacco.

1879 Jones *Backwoods Carolina* 754 The men had worked out their road-tax, and had exchanged "chaws" of tobacco and a vast lot of petty neighborhood gossip. **1941** Stuart *Men of Mts* 89 Well, Red Callihan was there and he pulled out a twist and offered me a chaw. **1997** Montgomery *Coll* I need a chaw of tobacco (Cardwell).

2003 Cavender *Folk Medicine* 101 Tobacco juice obtained from a dab of snuff or a bit of "chaw" (chewed tobacco) taken directly from the mouth was applied to an insect bite or sting.

chew of tobacco, not worth a *adjective phrase* See citation.

1927 Woofter *Dialect from WV* 350 *chaw of tobacco, not worth a . . .* entirely worthless: "Don't buy that cow. She's not worth a chaw of tobacco."

chew one's bits *verb phrase* See citation.

1939 Farr *TN Mt Regions* 90 = [have] a fit of anger: "John's chewing his bits."

[DARE *chew one's bits* v phr chiefly South, South Midland]

chew one's (own) tobacco *verb phrase*

1 To speak.

1984 Wilder *You All Spoken* 146 *I chew my tobacco* = I've spoken my piece; I've done said it.

2 To fend for oneself.

1997 Montgomery *Coll*: *chew one's own tobacco* (known to Adams, Brewer, Brown, Bush, Jones, Weaver).

[DARE *chew one's tobacco* v phr 1 chiefly South, South Midland]

chew one's tobacco thin *verb phrase* See citation.

1961 Williams *Content Mt Speech* 14 People who are living hard are said to be "chawin' their terbaccer thin."

chew one's tobacco twice *verb phrase*

1 See citation.

1927 Woofter *Dialect from WV* 350 = to consider for a long time before acting. "He will chaw his tobacco twice on that proposition."

2 To repeat what one has said.

1961 Williams *Content Mt Speech* 14 The peppery old man with the vigorous mustache may retort, when asked to repeat what he has said, "I don't chaw my terbaccer twicet, young man." **1981** Whitener *Folk-Ways* 19 The first speaker, in humorous exchange, replied: "I don't chew my tobacco twice."

[DARE *chew one's tobacco* v phr both senses chiefly South, South Midland]

chew up See **chew B1**, **B2**.

chickadee *noun* Same as **road monkey**.

1967 Parris *Mt Bred* 133 A ballhooter is a fellow who rolls or slides down a hillside and a chickadee is a man who looks after the logging roads. **1989** Oliver *Hazel Creek* 65 The fellows responsible for keeping the logging road in proper condition were called "Chickadees" or "road monkeys." **2006** Farwell *Logging Term* 1021 *Swampers* built roads maintained by *chickadees* and *grease monkeys*, who kept them slick.

chickamy chickamy craney crow *noun* A children's game in which one player tries to catch others who are being protected by another player.

1953 Brewster *Amer Nonsinging Games* 71 *Chickamy Chickamy Craney Crow* = one player is the hawk, another is the hen, and the rest are chickens.

[DARE *chickamy chickamy craney crow* chiefly South, South Midland]

chick, chick, chick(ie) (also *chick, chick, chickoo*; *chickie, chickie, chickie*; *chicky, chicky, chicky*; *tcheeky, tcheeky*) *interjection* Come! (used as a call, often in a falsetto voice, to chickens at feeding time, with one word repeated two or more times; for further details, see 1966–68 citation). See also **chickeroo**.

1884 Smith *Arp Scrap Book* 73 Over 200 [chickens] now respond to my old 'oman's call every mornin, as she totes around the bread-tray a-singin tcheeky, tcheeky. **1966–68** *DARE Survey* (Burnsville NC, Cherokee NC) *chicky chicky chicky*; (Spruce Pine NC) *chick chick chick* = a call is long [and] drawn out, with rising pitch on the first word and then two fast ones. **1978** Head *Mt Moments* My grandfather Morgan called his animals this way: "Sook cow" for his milker; "chick, chick, chickie" for poultry; and "piuggy" for hogs. **1978** Reese *Speech NE Tenn* 30 *chick-chick* = attested by 6/12 (50%) speakers; *chickie-chickie* = attested by 4/12 (33.3%) speakers. **1986** Pederson et al. *LAGS*: *chicky chicky chicky* (Blount Co TN, Cocke Co TN, Jefferson Co TN, Sevier Co TN). **1996–97** Montgomery *Coll*: *chick, chick, chickoo* (known to Brown, Cardwell); *chicky chicky chicky* (known to Norris, Oliver). **1997** King *Mt Folks* 67 With an apron full of corn and a "here, chickie, chickie, chickie," she gives the chickens at her feet their morning feed.

[DARE *chickie* n 1 widespread, but especially frequent Midland, South; *chickoo* interj South, South Midland]

chicken crow *noun* Dawn.

1940 Haun *Hawk's Done* 66 I knowed they wouldnt be back till chicken crow. Somehow I wished they wouldn't go. **1982** Slone *How We Talked* 30 = early morning; daylight.

[DARE *chicken crow* n South Midland]

chickenest-pecked *adjective* Of a man: the most hen-pecked (by his wife).

1959 Stubbs *Mountain-Wise* (Aug–Sept) 6 Hereabouts the husband and father occupies a dominant position in the household. One who fails to maintain such a position is held in disregard. Such a man was described to me by one who knew him well: "He was the chickenest-pecked fellow I have ever seen."

chicken fight *noun* Any of several violets (*Viola* spp) used in a children's competition. See citations. Same as **rooster A2**. See also **rooster fight**.

c1960 Wilson *Coll*: *Chicken-fights* = violets, or a contest with them to see which head can be pulled off first. Called also *rooster-fighters*. **1996** Montgomery *Coll* = stems were curled around each other and pulled by children, with the child having the stem which broke being the loser. Typically each child would pick five flowers and try to win three of the five pulls. Winners of each round would meet in a tournament-style competition until a grand winner was declared (Cardwell).

[DARE *chicken fight* n 1 chiefly South Midland, especially KY, MD]

chickenhouse divorce *noun* See citations.

1982 Slone *How We Talked* 43 = a divorce so that a woman can get government aid through the child welfare program. The husband would live close by in a small house. **1999** Montgomery *Coll* = the separation of two people who had been living together, the divorce consisting of dividing the chickens and other property (Brown).

chicken ladder *noun* See citation.

1941 Stuart *Men of Mts* 257 It had one of them pole ladders—we call them chicken ladders—just one straight pole with little tiny steps nailed across it.

chicken lot *noun* A fenced enclosure for chickens.

1981 Whitener *Folk-Ways* 45 Jim Pruitt fell out of bed and headed for the chicken lot, a basket of feed in one hand, a gun in the other. **1984** *Sevier Settler* 1:9 She went to fetch her basket and feed; then she headed for the chicken lot. **1986** Pederson et al. *LAGS* = (Hamilton Co TN).

chicken mustard *noun* Any of several early spring edible mustards (genus *Brassica*) or cresses (of genera *Cardamine, Barbarea, Arabis*). See also **crowsfoot, turkey foot mustard**.

1967 *DARE Survey* (Gatlinburg TN) = a troublesome weed. **1998** Montgomery *Coll* = so called because it often grows around the chicken house and chickens frequently nibble at it when it comes up in the spring, also called pepper grass, because it produces pods of tiny seeds (Cardwell).

chicken sense *noun* Minimal common sense.

1940 Hall *Coll* (White Oak NC).

chicken shoot *noun* See citation. See also **beef shoot, turkey shoot**.

2009 Fields *Growing Up* 30 The rules of the Chicken Shoot were that each gentleman that took a shot at the chicken had to pay a nickel per miss. If the marksman hit the fowl, it was his to keep and he didn't have to pay. If he missed, he would just pay up, adjust his aim, and wait for his next turn. Usually about twenty men lined up to take their turns at shooting. The fowl being shot at was always tied down to a metal stake near a big tree.

chickentoe *verb* A wild spring green.

2009 Sohn *Appal Home Cooking* 294 = the common name for tangle-gut and spring-beauty, *Claytonia virginica*. An early wild spring green that foragers add to salads and serve with soup beans.

chicken wobble *noun* Formerly, a party, usually of men, at which stolen chickens are cooked and there was drinking, music making, tale-telling, and other revelry. See citations. See also **goat wobble**.

1971 Costner *Song of Life* 79–80 Few may have heard of a Chicken Wobble. It is a feast without the dance and is an outdoor affair, ladies barred. The chickens had to come from someone represented there, and they made the rounds choosing them from the different roosts. No one knew just when he was eating his own chicken, as they were stolen very quietly early in the evening.... It was shortly after crops and fodder pulling time and we had had very little fun that summer, and some of the men working hard in the lumber camp. This was our first big get-together in many weeks. When I arrived at the place most of the fellows were there. They had a great fire going, the kettle boiling, and three fat hens stretched out on a log, two of them were already unfeathered. . . . Squire Joe, Bill and Hoopie Roe were thrumming and sawing on their instruments, tuning up they said. And Milem Butters, who could sing and dance as well without music as with, was getting in tune also. **1973** *GSMNP*-4:1:37–38 About every Saturday night we would have a square dance and a chicken wobble.... Most of the times they'd be a bunch of the boys, you know, would go out and steal a chicken or something and bring it in and cook it. **2001** Montgomery *Coll* = when I was a child (in the 30's) the men (and sometimes women) thought it was great fun on a Saturday night to steal a chicken or two, go to someone's house, cook the bird, and have a party. Any alcohol was consumed out of the presence of the women, however. It was great fun to steal a man's chicken and feed it to him without his knowledge! (Ledford).

[*wobble* perhaps from stirring of the chicken]

chickeroo *interjection* Come! Used as a call to chickens. See also **chick, chick, chick(ie)**.

1940 Still *River of Earth* 170 We raised thirty-six dommers. They scarcely pecked at the bran we threw out, for there was such a plenty of food in the fields and patches. You could holler "chickeroo" the day long and they wouldn't come.

[DARE (at *chickoo*) South, South Midland]

chick(ie), chickoo, chicky See **chick, chick, chick(ie)**.

chief *verb* Among the Eastern Band of the Cherokee in western North Carolina, to engage in the modern practice of donning a full-feathered headdress and other regalia traditional to Plains tribes rather than the Cherokee in order to entice photographs and monetary tips from tourists at souvenir shops and roadside sites.

1991 Finger *Cherokee Americans* 161–62 For those who "look" Indian with copper skins, raven-black hair, and hawk noses, and appropriate costuming, "chiefing" can be very profitable. Henry Lambert has been at it for years, as well as Joseph George and other regulars along the federal highways. They make money from photographs and tips and also lure customers to the particular souvenir shop they represent. That their Plains regalia and tepees are quite un-Cherokee bothers them not at all. **1998** Olson *Blue Ridge Folklife* 137 Some Cherokee made money by donning the elaborate headdresses seen in Hollywood movies and posing for tourists' photographs in front of Sioux tepees. Called "chiefing," this was, of course, an inauthentic depiction of traditional Cherokee culture.

chifforobe (also *chev-a-robe*) *noun* A tall piece of bedroom furniture usually of two sides, consisting of a chest of drawers (sometimes topped by a mirror) and hanging space for clothes, with doors on one or both sides; a movable closet, especially for storage. See also **clothes press, press 3**.

1984 Head *Brogans* 138 The contents of the trunk were moved to one of the huge drawers in the chest. We called the chest a "chev-a-robe," a term not used today. **1994–97** Montgomery *Coll* (known to eight consultants from the Smoky Mountains). **2005** Williams *Gratitude* 485 = a moveable closet in which to store clothes—a separate piece of furniture. Usually there were two doors, behind which were drawers on one side and a place to hang clothes on the other.

[blend of *chiffonier* + *wardrobe*; DARE *chifforobe* n especially frequent South, South Midland]

chigger *noun* A mite (*Trombicula* spp) that burrows under the skin and causes intense itching. [Editor's note: This term predominates in the Upper South and in Appalachia, while its equivalent *redbug* is found mainly in the Deep South.]

1966–68 DARE *Survey* (Brasstown NC, Spruce Pine NC, Gatlinburg TN, Maryville TN). **1974** Cate et al. *Sthn Appal Heritage* 86 There was the fear of snakes as well as the certainty of having numerous chigger bites which would itch for days. Sometimes kerosene was rubbed around the ankles to ward off these pesky red mites. If chigger bites became too uncomfortable, they were rubbed with salt or sometimes the greasy inside of a salty meat skin. Either method was supposed to relieve the itching. **1986** Ogle *Lucinda* 65 After picking our buckets full of blackberries or huckleberries we would stop on our way at this beautiful water fall and drown the chiggers (red bugs) by going swimming. **1986** Pederson et al. *LAGS* = attested by 48/60 interviewees (80%) from E TN and 21/35 (60%) from N GA; 69/407 of all LAGS interviewees (16.9%) attesting term were from Appalachia. **1992** Bush *Dorie* 25 The pinpoint-sized red devil—the chigger—was subdued by thick, brown tobacco juice, too. **2003** LaLone et al. *Farming Life* 317 Do you know how to get rid of chiggers? Get you some lard [and] mix it up real good with salt and rub it all over you where them chiggers are and go to bed that night and you get up the next morning you won't have no chiggers.

[Web3 *chigger* n of African origin]

chigger flower *noun* A black-eyed Susan wildflower (*Rudbeckia fulgida/hirta*). Same as **yellow daisy**.

1968 Wilson *Folklore Mammoth Cave* 16 = the black-eyed Susan.

chigger's uncle *noun* See citation.

1968 Wilson *Folklore Mammoth Cave* 18 = used humorously to indicate small or insignificant.

chiggerweed *noun* Same as **butterfly root**.

1970 Campbell et al. *Smoky Mt Wildflowers* 74 The stiff plant, up to about 2 feet high, is also known as chigger weed and orange milkweed. **1982** Stupka *Wildflowers* 90 Not many of the native wildflowers are as conspicuous or as radiant as this one, and it appears to have a particular attraction for butterflies. Yet in many localities, where it is known as "chigger-weed," people have an unfounded prejudice against it. **1994** Montgomery *Coll* (known to Cardwell).

[so called from the belief that it harbors chiggers; DARE *chiggerweed* n 2 chiefly South Midland]

child

A *noun* variant plural forms.

1 forms with r metathesis: *childering, childern, chillern, chilurn*.

1859 Taliaferro *Fisher's River* 250 Hence, you could see the ox-carts coming in ... and the "childering" walking. **1863** Epperly *CW Letters* (May 12) the childern is both as fat as litle pigs and your Fathers family is all well. **1886** Smith *Arp Peace Papers* 69 Sheep wer blatin, childern were kryin, wagginers wer kussin, whips wer poppin, and hosses stallin. **1923** Greer-Petrie *Angeline Steppin' Out* 4 Now, childern, all I ax you is, kin you beat that, when hit comes to cuttin' a rusty? **1924** Spring *Lydia Whaley* 4 It's easier to have chilurn on the toes than on the heart. **1939** Hall *Coll* (Cataloochee NC) Don't you childern act so rowdy. **1959** Roberts *Up Cutshin* 7 They raised I think it was eight chillern and has taken in one or two to raise. **1972** *AOHP/ALC-342* Anyone that wasn't able to work might have needed stuff, like a widder woman with a few chillern. **1975** Purkey *Madison Co* 19 Maybe I am pushin' the chillern out o' the nest too soon. **1979** *Big South Fork OHP-4* They was his chillern. **1985** Williams *Role of Folklore* 295 I went down there and told her I don't want them childern in my house. **1998** Montgomery *Coll*: *childering* (known to Brown). **2007** Preece *Leavin' Sandlick* 43 Betty Sue and Mat'll be here soon, and I don't want no big-eyed time in front of the childern.

[DARE *child* n A2 chiefly South, South Midland]

2 forms without r: *chillen, chillun(s)*.

1859 Taliaferro *Fisher's River* 97 Nur shall my chillun talk it. **1898** Elliott *Durket Sperret* 90 They must speck to hev chilluns like young Dave; an' only God knows who them chilluns'll marry. **1910** Cooke *Power and Glory* 4 I knowed in reason she'd have baby clothes that she couldn't expect to wear out on her own chillen. **1975** *AOHP/ALC-961* I had about three chillen, and through the biggest part of this Depression that they talk about I was on a salary driving a store truck.

[DARE (at *child* n A2) chiefly South, South Midland]

3 forms without d: *chillen, chillern, chillun, chilurn, chirren*.

[See **1859** in **2**.] **1886** Smith *Sthn Dialect* 348 He did confess that "the mountain was a bad place ter raise chillern; no school, nor Sunday-school, nor meetin', nor nothin', and the chillern jest as wild as they could be." [See **1910** in **2**.] [See **1924**, **1975** in **1**.] **1979** *Big South Fork OHP-4* We had six chirren, and they're all scattered and gone.

[DARE *chirren* (at *child* n A2) chiefly South, South Midland]

4 Other forms: *childer, childring*.

1854 (in **1956** Eliason *Tarheel Talk* 308) (Burke Co NC) *childring*. **1863** Hall *CW Letters* (May 24) we all think of you ofton an talk of you the childring talks about granpap an gram hall. **1863** *Vance Papers* (July 20) I hav a vary larg famly a 11 and the most Smal childer and my ag is 41 one yers and the malish[a] off[ic]ers has in rold my nam with the concripes thru a mistak. **1928** (in **1952** Mathes *Tall Tales* 167–68) They's too many women an' childer nowadays a-rippin' an' a-tearin', a-runnin' hither an' yon a-pleasurin' theirselves. **2007** McMillon *Notes*: childring.

5 double plural forms: *childrens, chillens.*

1972 *AOHP/ALC-355* It wasn't nothing for people to do, chillens to do. **1975** GSMNP-62:5 Right about just on this side of our church they built a little one room house and had Tow String childrens to go to school there a long time. **1975** Woolley *We Be Here* 82 The childrens was there, and the wives was there, and just about everybody in Verda was right there. **2008** *Rosie Hicks* 1 Papa said, "Childrens, you don't know what hungry is."

[DARE *childrens* (at *child* n A3) South, South Midland]

B *verb* To be pregnant, give birth; hence verbal noun *childing* = giving birth.

1943 Hannum *Mt People* 115 Whatever the hazards of "childing"—as Shakespeare and the mountain people put it—the new baby itself is the most welcome thing on earth. *Ibid.* 149 "[C]hilding" [means] to be pregnant. **1950** Wood *Sure of Life* 49 Our women do their childing in the bed. **1972** Cooper *NC Mt Folklore* 89 *a-childing* = gestating; pregnant. [**1995** Montgomery *Coll* (unknown to consultants from the Smoky Mountains).]

[cf OED3 *childing* n now archaic]

childbed fever (also *childbirth fever*) *noun* A serious infection, fever, or trauma associated with giving birth to a child. See 2003 citation. See also **milk leg**.

1955 Washburn *Country Doctor* 74 She's most allus sick an' she's had chile-bed fever rail bad two times. **1971** *Granny Women* 241 Mothers could and did die from what we called "childbed fever," puerperal sepsis. **1989** Smith *Flyin' Bullets* 41 In October 1899, Polly gave birth to a daughter and died of "childbirth fever." **1997** Montgomery *Coll* (known to Adams, Brown, Bush, Ledford, Oliver, Weaver). **2003** Cavender *Folk Medicine* 131 Childbed fever (puerperal fever) is a bacterial infection of the endometrium caused by unsanitary birthing procedures and conditions. Some midwives thought it could be prevented by having the mother remain in bed after her afterbirth for a few hours or several days.

child catching (also *child fetching*) *verbal noun* Assisting in the delivery of a baby. Same as **baby catching**. See also **catch C**.

1931 Hannum *Thursday April* 7 Godamighty, Thursday April! I hain't no hand with child-fetchin'. **1942** Campbell *Cloud-Walking* 15 Sary was a right good hand at child-fetching. **1995–97** Montgomery *Coll*: *child catching* (known to Cardwell); *child fetching* (known to Brown).

[DARE *child fetching* vbl n southern Appalachians]

childer, childering, childern See **child A**.

child fetching See **child catching**.

child fever *noun* Same as **milk leg**.

1986 Ogle *Lucinda* 54 Soon as Granny saw Momie she said "She has got child fever." (Now called phlebitis, I think. Or it is called milk leg by some old folks.)

childing See **child B**.

childrens, childring See **child A**.

chill bumps *noun* Gooseflesh.

c1960 Wilson *Coll* = goose pimples. **2009** Sutton *Me and Likker II* 202 I would listen to him pick that Gibson Banjo and it would sound so good and keen it would make me have chill bumps.

[DARE *chill bumps* n chiefly South, South Midland]

chillen, chillern, chillens, chilurn See **child A**.

chimbley, chimbly, chimley See **chimney**.

chimney *noun*

A Variant forms *chimbley, chimbly, chimley*.

1858 (in **1956** Eliason *Tarheel Talk* 309) (Burke Co NC) *chimley*. **1862** *Dalton CW Letters* (Feb 5) mother wee have chimley to hourer [= our] tent but the weather is verry Coal. **1862** *Love CW Letters* (Feb 9) we hav our tents fix up chimleys to them so we can keep Dry as A pouder house all the time. **1898** Elliott *Durket Sperret* 116 I busted my pipe 'ginst the chimbly back. [See **1913** in **B1**.] **1934–47** *LAMSAS Appal*: *chimley* = attested by 75/148 speakers (50.6%) from WV, 11/20 (55%) from VA, 37/37 (100%) from NC, 1/14 (7.1%) from SC, and 9/12 (75%) from GA. **1939** Hall *Coll* (Gatlinburg TN) Boys, you'uns [are] talkin' about rough country, but I'm gonna tell you one time the roughest country I was in. It was so steep the people had to look up the chimley to see if the cows was still in the pasture. **1942** Hall *Phonetics Smoky Mts* 91–92 *chimley* = the common form; *chimbley* = rare. **1969** GSMNP-38:62 They had it about all finished except the chimbley. **1975** *Foxfire III* 244 I wished I just had one little rock from that old chimbley. **1989** *Matewan OHP-39* We was all learnt to run under the floor and get behind the chimleys [when the shooting started]. **1998** *Dante OHP* 51 It wasn't anywhere close to the chimley. **2008** *Rosie Hicks* 1 There was Santa standing right there aside the chimley.

[SND *chimbley, chimley* (at *chimley* n); CUD *chimbley, chimley*; DARE *chimney* n *chimbley* chiefly South, Midland]

B Senses.

1 A fireplace, hearth.

1913 Kephart *Our Sthn High* 249 You can set by the fire and spit out through the chimbly. **1939** Hall *Coll* (Proctor NC) Beans and fruit were dried in the chimley. **1953** Hall *Coll* (Bryson City NC) [We] built a big stack chimley in the middle [of the cabin] for heatin' purposes. **1975** Purkey *Madison Co* 6 The house on Lost Creek, in Madison County, was a typical mountain one, with its scalped logs and mud daubed "chimley."

[OED3 *chimney* n 1a "a fireplace or hearth" obsolete except dialect; DARE *chimney* n B1 chiefly South, South Midland]

2 by extension = a rock formation on a mountain peak resembling the tower of a chimney, which often has a natural updraft; also used in the place-name *Chimney Tops* (Sevier Co TN). See 1956 citation.

1913 Morley *Carolina Mts* 347 There are "chimneys" over the edge of the precipice, whose tops have been conquered by brave little fir trees, and mossy things and a few flowers. **1956** Fink *That's Why* 16 One of the most widely known and photographed features of the Smokies is the spectacular twin-topped pinnacle called the Chimney Tops, or more simply, the Chimneys. Mountain idiom has long used the term chimneys for tall rock spires or towering cliffs.

chimney corner law *noun* A principle or agreement that is informal and unwritten, but nonetheless strictly adhered to.

1982 Slone *How We Talked* 51 = unstated customs that were more strictly kept and observed than the real laws made by the government. **1996–97** Montgomery *Coll* (known to Brown, Bush, Ledford), = literally, an agreement made outside the house and behind the chimney—thus an informal, unwritten one (Hooper).

chimney shelf *noun* A mantelpiece (the most common term for this in traditional mountain speech is **fireboard**).

1930 Armstrong *This Day and Time* 151 Uncle Jake's clock [was] on the chimney-shelf, the table extending almost from door to door, beautiful in the white cloth Shirley had given her. **1986** Pederson et al. *LAGS* (Blount Co). **1996–97** Montgomery *Coll* (known to Brown, Cardwell, Jones, Norris, Oliver).

[Web3 *chimney shelf* n dialect]

chimney sweep (also *chimney sweeper, chimbly swift*) *noun* The chimney swift (*Chaetura pelagica*), a small, dark-colored bird that often nests in chimneys.

1957 Combs *Lg Sthn High: Word-List* 19 *chimbly swift* = The American chimney sweep (Chaetura pelagica) [is] a bird similar to the swallow, which builds in the chimneys of houses. **1961** Miller *Pigeon's Roost* (Sept 28) We always call the chimney swift birds the chimney sweepers. The towhees, jorees; phoebee, pewees; turkey vultures, turkey buzzards; nighthawks, bullbats; and wood thrush, wood thrashers. **1967** *DARE Survey* (Maryville TN) *chimney sweep*. **1996–97** Montgomery *Coll*: *chimney sweep* (known to Adams, Cardwell, Jones, Ledford, Norris, Oliver); *chimney sweeper* (known to Brown, Oliver).

[DARE *chimney sweep* n chiefly South, South Midland]

chin (also *chin music*) *noun* Foolish or excessive talk; hence verb *chin* = to talk excessively.

1926 Lunsford *Folk-Lore* 13 When a boy I remember hearing him "call the house to order" at a political speaking in Buncombe where the late Governor Craig and the Honorable Virgil S. Lusk were to measure swords in a political debate. He began by saying, "All right gentlemen, get quiet as soon as possible for we are soon going to start up the 'chin music.'" **1927** Woofter *Dialect from WV* 350 *chin music* = foolish or senseless talk. "I don't want to hear any more chin music about this." **c1960** Wilson *Coll*: *chin* = idle talking or talk. **1992** Brooks *Sthn Stuff* 29 *chinnin'* = talking to; gabbing with. "She's been chinnin' on the phone all mornin'." **1998** Montgomery *Coll*: *chin music* = talk (Brown), = idle, meaningless, or insincere talk (Ledford). **2017** *Blind Pig* (April 28) *chin music* = [an] expression used in Monroe County [TN] for a wife complaining or nagging.

china *noun* variant forms *chainy, chiny*.

1927 Camak *June of Hills* 36 The children used tin plates and cups, while June and McDowell were served in "chiny"—cheap, yellow crockery. **1965** *Dict Queen's English* 5 She set out her finest *chainy* for the dinner. I wouldn't do that for all the tea in *Chainy*. **1982** Hurst *Appal Words* 99 *chainy*.

[cf CUD *chiny* n; DARE *china* n especially South, South Midland]

China egg *noun* A false egg made of porcelain, placed in a hen's nest to induce her to lay. See also **cymling B**, **nest egg**, **setting egg**.

1986 Pederson et al. *LAGS* (Cocke Co TN, Jefferson Co TN, Sevier Co TN). **1996** Montgomery *Coll* (known to Cardwell). **1999** Morgan *Gap Creek* 144 The steps to the loft was outside the feed room, and as I climbed the steps I seen two dusty china eggs on the shelf by the harness.

chink See also **daub**.

A *noun*

1 A hole, crack, or other opening between logs or planks on the inside of a house or cabin.

2000 Robbins *Mt Museum* 5 Unlike many log houses, Davis chose to seal the chink, or crack, between the logs with hand-split board instead of clay. **2004** Rehder *Appal Folkways* 84 Chinks are the cracks between logs in a log-walled house, and we will want to fill them in with chinking.

[Web3 probably alteration of Middle English *chin* "crack"]

2 (also *chinking*) Sticks, slabs of wood, etc. (sometimes **daubed** with mud, lime, clay, or similar material) to cover such an opening and serve as crude insulation.

1944 Blair *Tall Tale America* 66 In the spring, when the dogwood came out, they'd knock away the chinks so that light and air could come into the cabin. **1957** Broaddus *Vocab Estill Co KY* 16 *chinking* = pieces of wood driven into the chinks between the logs during the construction of a log house. **1982** Rives *Blue Ridge* 22 Once the logs were in place, the spaces between were filled with mixtures of mud and lime called "chinking." **2004** Rehder *Appal Folkways* 84 Chinking can be mud, clay, stone, bits of wood, rags, paper—just about anything that might slow the winter wind.

B *verb* To cover (such an opening in an inside wall) to prevent drafts and preserve heat.

1748 (in **1912** Chalkley *Augusta Co VA* 1.35) (DARE) Presentment vs. Court House . . . built of logs, chinked with mud, but cracks 4 to 5 inches wide. **1878** Guild *Old Times TN* 50 In the winter we "chinked" the cracks between the logs, and in the summer we knocked out the chinking, which afforded light and ventilation to the cabin. **1889** Mooney *Folk Carolina Mts* 96 His house is a log cabin, chinked with mud in the cracks, and generally consisting of two small rooms and a loft, the latter used as a sleeping room and reached by a ladder. **1914** Arthur *Western NC* 258 The walls of these log houses were "chinked and daubed." That is, the spaces between the logs were filled with blocks or scraps of wood and the interstices left were filled with plain, undisguised mud—lime being too expensive to be used for that purpose. **1922** *TN CW Ques* 1098 (Hamilton Co TN) The logs were hune very smothe great broad logs the cracks were chinked with lime marter and daubing was wite washed with lime. **1937** Conner *Ms* 126 [T]hen we would chink all crack's [sic] between the log's [sic], with split timber, and daub with clay morter. **1972** *AOHP/ALC-413* It [= the wall of a **double log house**] was chinked with slabs of wood and mud [that were] hung in there, tucked in there at an angle shape, and [they] cracked and then daubed it with blue mud . . . most everybody had the chinked [sic] and daubing. **1991** Haynes *Haywood Home* 38 The spaces between the logs were chinked and daubed. To chink between the logs, Daddy would cut tall, slender saplings, hewed [sic] them so that they would not quite fit into the cracks and hammered them so that they wedged tightly into the spaces between the logs from the inside.

[DARE *chink* v chiefly South, South Midland]

chinkapin, **chinkepin**, **chinkypin** See **chinquapin**.

chinking See **chink A2**.

chinquapin *noun*

A Variant forms *chinkapin* [see **1997** in **B1**], *chinkepin*, *chinkypin* [see **1981** in **B1**].

1867 Harris *Sut Lovingood* 285 There I seed the bald aind ove Squire Hanley's ole Sunday hoss, a-pushin hits way thru the chinkepin bushes.

B Senses.

1 A shrub-like tree (*Castanea pumila*) related to the American chestnut and killed by the same fungus in the early twentieth century; its small, round, dark brown nut was edible and also used by children to make necklaces; for use of the term in a common simile, see 1981 citation.

1964 Reynolds *Born of Mts* 55 The chinquapin, a dwarf chestnut tree, yet exists, but the nuts are often wormeaten, and it is said that it too now has the blight. **1977** Hamilton *Mt Memories* 49 We had chinquapin trees in our pastures. It was a sort of a dwarf chestnut. The nut was the color of a chestnut but the size of a big bead. We would boil them and string them to wear around our necks to school. Each child wanted to own the longest string and sometimes they would be doubled and tripled around the neck. **1979** Smith *White Rock* 33 Chinquapins were another nut which we enjoyed eating as well as using for ornamentation. The tiny round nut was black and had a flavor much like that of the chestnut. Chinquapins grew on small shrubs or bushes which were of the beech family and resembled the chestnut in looks, but which were tiny dwarfs compared to the giant chestnut tree. **1981** Whitener *Folk-Ways* 41 [U]gly as a mud fence daubed with chinkypins. **1983** *Dark Corner OHP-5A* There's a few little old chinkapin trees around about in this country. [There] used to be some of them right down here below my old home place, right behind Skinner's, around the edge of that hill, a few little old chinkapin trees all along there when I was growing up. **1997** King *Mt Folks* 2 The round chinkapins (of the chestnut family) are threaded on a string and worn the same as beads around children's necks. The Rolens and their neighbors [would] wear them to school to snack on during the day. **2005** Williams *Gratitude* 485 = a native tree bearing small round nuts covered with a burr which opens when mature to allow the nut to drop out. The round nuts are a little bigger than a large pearl and have a taste similar to a chestnut. They are close to the same color and texture as a chestnut, and have a similar skin and burr covering. The tree is more like a large shrub, however—nothing like the size of a chestnut tree.

[DARE *chinquapin* n B1 chiefly South, South Midland]

2 See citation.

1973 Miller *English Unicoi Co* 144 = a small red squirrel that feeds on [chinquapin] nuts.

3 See citation.

1973 *Words & Expressions* = change, as in dimes, quarters, etc.

chinquapin eyes *noun* See citation.

1968 *DARE Survey* (Brasstown NC) = eyes that are very round. **2011** Woodall *Not My Mt* 35 Bea had Dad's chinquapin eyes that melted Moma's heart, managing to get just about anything she wanted.

chinquapin money *noun* Pocket change.

1920 De Long *Fiddler John* I allus have a leetle chinkapin money in my pocket.

chiny See **china**.

chipper *noun* A member of a logging crew. See citations.

1960 Mason *Memoir* 110–11 It was the responsibility of the chipper to decide the most desirable direction in which to fall the tree. **1974–75** McCracken *Logging* 14 = the guy that would put the lead in the tree. He determined which way the tree would fall. And he measured off the logs. **1994** Schmidt and Hooks *Whistle* 156 = one of a three-man falling crew who undercuts a standing tree to force a direction of fall.

chipper dog *noun* See citation.

1994 Farwell and Buchanan *Logging Terms* = an implement that chipped slabs, producing chips used for fuel and paper pulp.

chippy (also *chippy-bird*) *noun* A sparrow (usually *Spizella passerina*).

1940 Still *River of Earth* 143, 144 A chippy sat on a fence post in the yard, cocking his head. . . . I could see as far as a chippy-bird could fly between daylight and dark.

[DARE (at *chipping sparrow*) chiefly North, North Midland]

chirk up *verb phrase* To become more cheerful or energetic.

1954 Arnow *Dollmaker* 153 Chirk up. You'll have th littil uns feelin bad. **1969** Hannum *Look Back* 177 Davey chirked up and had himself a good feed. **1992** Brooks *Sthn Stuff* 30 *chirk up* = to cheer up and show some life. **2003** Williams *Coming of Age* 118 If they could just come in and warm by the fire for a few minutes and have a glass of milk and any leftovers from supper they would be chirked up and the little young'ens would have better hearts for travel in the cold night.

chirky *adjective* Cheerful, energetic.

1944 Justus *Lizzie* 46 He looks as chirky as if he had taken ten doses of medicine!

chirren See **child A.**

chis See **chest.**

chisel down *verb phrase* To cause (someone) to succumb through continual pressure, as to reduce the price of an object for sale.

1917 Kephart *Word-List* 409 = beat down. "I *chiseled him down* right smart on the coffee business." **1995–97** Montgomery *Coll* (known to Brown, Bush, Cardwell, Hooper, Ledford, Norris).

chisel-faced *adjective* See citation.

1957 Combs *Lg Sthn High: Word-List* 19 = of sharp physiognomic features; term of contempt.

chist, chistes See **chest.**

chitlins *noun* Chitterlings, the small intestines and sometimes stomach of a hog, prepared as food by frying to a crisp.

1934–47 *LAMSAS Appal* (Swain Co NC) *chitlins*. **1956** Hall *Coll* (Gatlinburg TN) Chitlins come from the stomach, tripe from the intestines. Chitlins, they're crisp. They crackle when you cook 'em. **1969** Hall *Coll* (Del Rio TN) [At hog-killing time] wives [were] cookin', makin' sausages. They'd take all the fat off, wash 'em good. That's the real chitlin's. Fry 'em. The most use we made for 'em was in shortnin' bread.

[*DARE chitlins* (at *chitterlings* n pl 1) chiefly South, South Midland]

chittam *noun* A large deciduous tree (*Cotinus obovatus*) that grows at middle elevations of the mountains. Same as **yellowwood.**

1967 *DARE Survey* (Maryville TN) *chittam* = yellowwood. **1970** Campbell et al. *Smoky Mt Wildflowers* 40 Other common names [of the yellowwood] are chittum [sic] and gopherwood, which legend tells us was used by Noah in building his ark.

chittydid *noun* See citation.

2007 McMillon *Notes* = katydid.

chivalree, chivalry, chivaree See **shivaree.**

chivvy out *verb phrase* To lure (an animal) from its den or place of hiding.

1925 Dargan *Highland Annals* 77 I could 'a' chivvied that fox out if I had gone after him; but if a man don't sleep he's weak at the ploughhandles. **1997** Montgomery *Coll* (known to Brown); Jim chivvied the groundhog right out of that old hollow (Andrews).

[*OED3 chivvy* v[1] "to harry, harass, trouble, worry" variant of *chevy*; *CUD chivvy* (at *cheevy* v) "chase, harass"]

choicey (also *choicy*) *adjective* Choosy, fussy, particular.

1936 (in **2009** Powell *Shenandoah Letters* 95) I am a willing worker and willing to do anything. I am not choicey at all. **1939** Hall *Coll* (Gatlinburg TN) I had this old cap and ball gun. Well I was just a little bit choicey, and I didn't want to just shoot one and all the rest of the flock would fly away. **1967** *DARE Survey* (Jonesborough TN) = of somebody eating a meal [who] takes little bits of food and leaves most of it on his plate. **1974** Fink *Bits Mt Speech* 4 = particular, fastidious. "You needn't be so *choicey* about it." **2005** Bailey *Henderson County* 30 When a person has "fared sumptious" the appetite has done full justice to the meal, but a "timid eater" is too "choicy" to make the efforts of the cook worthwhile.

choke damp *noun* Same as **black damp.**

1943 Korson *Coal Dust* 221 From the manner in which it killed its victims, blackdamp was nicknamed chokedamp.

choked off (also *choked out*) *adjective phrase* See citation.

2005 Williams *Gratitude* 484 [Cat-head biscuits are] big ol' biscuits, big as a cat's head. They are so light you have to watch or they'll float off the plate. They're also what we call "choked out," or "choked off" biscuits because the amount of dough for a biscuit is choked off between the thumb and index finger.

choker *noun* In logging, a loop of wire rope or cable hooked either to secure a chain or around a log to pull it. See 1975 citation. See also **choker hooker.**

1964 Clarkson *Lumbering in WV* 358 = a loop of cable used in skidding logs with a steam skidder. **1973** Foster *Walker Valley* 9:10 Just anywhere you could get a choker around a log, that's where you hooked him. **1974–75** McCracken *Logging* 14:5 On this buggy or carriage that ran on the big cable they were called chokers. They was made out of half-inch cable. They went around the logs and they had two hooks on the end that lapped over. *Ibid.* 21 Chokers [are] short steel ropes to put around the logs. Then [you] hook them to the bull hooks or bitch links, whichever they were using. **1975** GSMNP-56:18 There was a special link on the end of the cable that dropped down to the logs that you could hook other short pieces of cable into. These shorter pieces were called "chokers." It was lengths of cable with an eye spliced into either end, and the choker hookers would just wrap this small piece of cable or choker around the log, loop it through itself and then tie or put the other loop into this special link that was on the end of the cable that dropped down from the overhead cable to the operation on the ground.

choke-rag *noun* See citation.

1973 *Words & Expressions* 133 = necktie.

choker hooker *noun* See citation. See also **choker.**

2009 Lloyd *Tremont* 35 A skidder team included a bell boy, a fireman, a landing jack, two choker hookers, a jangle ball hooker, an engineer, and a foreman.

choking *noun* A method of fishing whereby fish are jerked out of the water before they can fully swallow the bait on a fishing line.

2006 *Encycl Appalachia* 872 Since fishhooks were often unaffordable, early mountaineers used the fishing method known as "choking," which involved tying suitable bait to a length of string and dropping it into the water. If a trout took it, the angler attempted to jerk the fish onto the bank quickly before it had a chance to expel the bait. According to old-timers, many a meal of fresh trout came to the table as a result of choking fish.

choking disease *noun* Diphtheria.

1912 De Long *Troublesome* Typhoid is very prevalent and the "chokin' disease" (diphtheria) and "the breast complaint" (consumption) take heavy tolls. **1927** Furman *Lonesome Road* 8 What about my five babes that lays on the burying pint yander, that vanished away, one after tother, with the choking-disease and the pneumony-fever?

choog See **chug 2.**

choose *verb*

A Variant past-tense forms *choosed, chused.*

1812 *Globe Creek Church Minutes* 36 The Church met . . . chused Bro[the]r Elijah Chambers for an ordain preacher of the ghospel. **1976** Miller *Mts within Me* 83 Another common characteristic is the use of regular construction of irregular verbs in the past tense. This would be evident in the use of . . . "choosed" instead of chose and the like. **1991** Thomas *Sthn Appal* 72 I choosed th' first 'un that fought that mornin'—matched 'im. **2000** Morgan *Mts Remember* 34 I knowed the rest of my life would depend on what I choosed.

B Sense. See citation.

1915 Dingus *Word-List VA* 181 = to desire, care for; usually negative in declining food: "I wouldn't choose any."

chop

A (also *chop out*) *verb, verb phrase* To cut (vegetation) with a hoe or other implement; to hoe a piece of land. See also **chopping.**

1844 *McLean Diary* 88 Charle Scoot helpt me Chopt with too hand one Day. **1956** *Hall Coll* (Big Bend NC) She'd hoe a row of corn and then weed a row of corn first, and then go back and chop the balks out, the weeds out of the balk. **c1960** *Wilson Coll*: *chop* = to hoe, not necessarily to chop out or thin the plants, as of corn. **1963** Hooper *Unwanted Boy* 229 I must chop out that gyarden—hit's getting mighty "filthy." **1969** GSMNP-38 They hoed lots of corn, chopped the weeds out of it and worked in the fields, but they never did plow none. **1973** AOHP/ASU-89 People would work all the summer, and then when winter come they gathered in their crops themself. Then they chopped a new ground, and, well, hit's about all they done then that winter. **1997** GSMNPCOHP-5:19 I chopped out the corn. It seemed like the weeds growed more in the corn.

[DARE *chop* v B1 chiefly South, Midland]

B *noun* See citation.

2003 Smith *Orlean Puckett* 65 Neighbors traded buckets of ground wheat, known as "chop," with Orlean for her cow's milk.

[DARE *chop* n^{1} 1 now chiefly South, Midland]

chop mouth *noun* See citation.

2007 Plott *Story Plott Hound* 181 = another term used to describe a Plott hound's bark. The chop mouth hound barks with a sharp staccato, or quick cadence resembling the sound of an axe chopping wood. The chop mouth hound is generally perceived to be faster on the track, or trail, than a bawl mouth dog. Most hounds bawl mouth bark while trailing and chop mouth bark when their prey is treed or bayed. Some Plott experts feel that the old-time Plott hound was strictly a solid chop mouth dog.

chop out See **chop A.**

chopped eggs *noun* Same as **butter and eggs.**

1998 Montgomery *Coll* (Cardwell).

chopper *noun* See citations. Same as **knot bumper.**

1998 Buchanan *Logging Terms* = the man who clears limbs off trees. In a cutting crew of four, one would be the chopper. **1998** Farwell *Logging Terms* = knot bumper.

chopping *noun* Formerly, a work activity to clear underbrush and trees from a parcel of land; the parcel of land itself.

1842 *McLean Diary* 80 [I] had a Chopi̇ng and quiltin. **1964** Cooper *History Avery Co* 7 In those days, the spots of human habitation which did not have the status of "Place" or "Settlement" were known as "Improvements," "Clearings," and "Choppings."

chopping fodder *noun* See citation.

2014 Montgomery *Doctrine* 98 = an expression meaning the sermon was not quite up to snuff and the poor preacher couldn't preach a lick.

chopping frolic *noun* See citation.

1853 Ramsey *Annals* 720 The bugle, the violin, the fife and drum, furnished all the musical entertainments. These were much used and passionately admired. Weddings, military trainings, house-raisings, chopping frolics, were often followed with the fiddle, and dancing, and rural sports.

chopsack *noun* A large, heavy fabric bag for carrying **chop B.** Same as **tow sack.**

1973 Miller *English Unicoi Co* 144 = burlap bag.

chounse *verb* To freshen (a pillow) by shaking.

c1960 *Wilson Coll* = to shake up as one shakes a pillow.

[variant of *jounce*; Web3 *chounse* v South and Midland; DARE *chounse* v 1 South, Midland]

Christmas Eve gift *interjection* Used as a greeting in a ritual similar to **Christmas gift**, sometimes in mock imitation of the latter. See also **New Year's Eve gift**.

1949 McDavid *Grist* 107 (Fannin Co GA) = a greeting. **1968** Wilson *Folklore Mammoth Cave* 41 Some families had "Christmas Eve Gift," used just as soon as the sun went down on Christmas Eve. Many people expected or pretended to expect a gift if they got your "Christmas Gift" first. **1990** Wigginton *Foxfire Christmas* 143 We would say to each other, "Christmas gift!" So they would have to run and get a piece of candy, an orange, or an apple. Everybody said it to each other all the time on Christmas Day. Sometimes we would say "Christmas Eve Gift," and let us know it wasn't time to have "Christmas gift." It lasted only one day, but as I remember it was a jolly good time.

Christmas gift (also *Christmas give*) *interjection* Merry Christmas! Used in a Christmas Day ritual formerly in which the first person to use this expression was usually, but now not necessarily, owed a small gift or a sign of affection (such as a hug or kiss) from the person(s) greeted; hence noun = this ritual involving such a gift. Formerly, in some areas children would roam from house to house to awaken neighbors and claim a treat. See 1942, 1981 citations. See also **Christmas Eve gift**, **New Year's Eve gift**, **serenade**.

1861 Griffin *CW Letters* (Dec) Dear sisters a few lins to you as brother has Claim A Christmas gifte I think I might have one to I Claim one from gorge and from Joseph you Can tell them to have it for me when I come home If I live. **1861** *Rector CW Letters* (Dec 8) if you have any Christmas send some down heare we are not going to have any heare this year get all the boys Christmas Gift for me. **1915** Dingus *Word-List VA* 181 = used as a greeting on Christmas morning. Whoever says it first may claim a present in return: "I got your Christmas gift. Now what are you goin' to gi' me?" **1931** Thomas *Ditties* 17 [They shouted] good-naturedly to those indoors until the man came out and welcomed them in. With shouts of "Christmas Gift!" they brushed past their host, and everyone made out he was surprised. **1934–47** *LAMSAS Appal* (Madison Co NC, Swain Co NC) *Christmas gift*. **1942** Thomas *Blue Ridge* 159 The young folks of the community go from home to home, bursting in with a cheery "Christmas gift!" Those who have been taken unaware, though it happens the same way each year, forgetting, in the pleasant excitement of the occasion, to cry the greeting first, must pay a forfeit of something good to eat—cake, home-made taffy, popcorn, apples, nuts. **1966** Dakin *Vocab Ohio River Valley* 522 This common Southern and South Midland expression is still regularly used by many older speakers in Kentucky . . . and in this state a fairly common comment by younger people is that outsiders are greeted with *Merry Christmas!* but that within the family and among intimates the greeting is *Christmas Gift!* **1968** Wilson *Folklore Mammoth Cave* 41 *Christmas Gift* = a regular greeting, a long time ago and still. Some families had "Christmas Eve Gift," used just as soon as the sun went down on Christmas Eve. Many people expected or pretended to expect a gift if they got your "Christmas Gift" first. **1973** GSMNP-61:8 We were out before daylight and if you could get Christmas gift on them, they had to give you something, which was usually apples or stick candy. **1974** Ogle *Memories* 58 Christmas morning, the folks would let me get up any time I wanted to and go to someone's house and holler, "Christmas—Give!" The first person to the house who hollered, "Christmas—Give," got candy. **1974** Russell *Hillbilly* 48 We were pleased upon arising, if we could be the first to say, "Christmas gift" to other members of the family, even though we knew we wouldn't receive the gift that was supposed to be forthcoming. **1975** Purkey *Madison Co* 63 Mama had a zest for living. She got us children up early on Christmas morning and we would steal out to our nearest neighbor's house and "serenade" them by banging pots and pans together and setting off firecrackers, which my oldest brothers somehow always contrived to get. Then we all yelled in unison, "Christmas Gift!" **1981** Brewer *Wonderment* 34 If you said "Christmas gift" to somebody on Christmas morning before they said it to you, they had to give you a present before the end of the day. **1986** Pederson et al. *LAGS* (Cocke Co TN, Sevier Co TN); *Christmas give* (Blount Co TN, Cocke Co TN, Cumberland Co TN, Jefferson Co TN, Knox Co TN) *Christmas gift*. **1990** Wigginton *Foxfire Christmas* 143 We would wear that little saying, "Christmas gift," out every time. We would say to each other, "Christmas gift!" So they would have to run and get a piece of candy, an orange, or an apple. Everybody said it to each other all the time on Christmas Day.

[DARE *Christmas gift* exclam chiefly South, South Midland]

Christmas give See **Christmas gift**.

Christmas poke *noun* Formerly, a small bag of treats that schoolchildren would exchange for Christmas. See also **poke**[1].

2006 Lalone *Coal Camps* 159 They [= the children] would draw names, of course, and have Christmas pokes, what they call Christmas poke. Alright, a Christmas poke, they usually consisted of an orange and an apple, and a bar of candy, and some hard Christmas candy, and a little trinket of some sort.

Christmas trick *noun* An act or prank performed rarely, such as once a year at Christmas.

1855 (in **1956** Eliason *Tarheel Talk* 265) (Wilkes Co NC) Papa waded the river for his Christmas trick. **1862** *Neves CW Letters* (Jan 9) I woold be glad to see you & hear you tell some of your christmas trick as you have taken it wher you did never beforure I recon you had a big time.

chronical *noun* A chronic disease, especially one that runs in the family.

1957 Broaddus *Vocab Estill Co KY* 17 = tuberculosis that runs in the family.

chuck-full (also *chug full*) *adjective phrase* Chock-full.

1915 Dingus *Word-List VA* 182 *chug full* = chock full. **1937** Hall *Coll* (Bradley Fork NC) When I was a boy the woods was chuck full of deer, panter, and wolves. **c1960** Wilson *Coll*: *chug full* = very full, even crammed or stuffed. Also *chuckfull*. **1994** Montgomery *Coll*: *chug full* (known to Shields).

[CUD *chuck-full* adj "full to the brim"]

chuck hole (also *chug hole, chunk hole*) *noun* A deep hole, often muddy, in a dirt road; a rut in a road of any kind of surface.

1916 Schockel *KY Mts* 117 The road leads over a mountain, and is full of chuck holes. In the spring time, when our heavy traffic must be carried on, the wheels sink axle-deep in the holes. **1938** Stuart *Dark Hills* 94 There were many chug-holes the drivers couldn't miss. **c1960** Wilson *Coll*: *chug hole* = a hole in the road with steep sides, giving a vehicle a jerk when it plunges into it. **1967–68** *DARE Survey* (Gatlinburg TN) *chuck hole* = a rough place in an unpaved road; (Berea KY, Clayhole KY) *chughole* = a sudden short dip in the road. **1985** Irwin *Alex Stewart* 90 We'd bust them rocks up and put them in them big deep ruts, and in the chug holes, so you could sorta get over the roads with a wagon and team. **1994–97** Montgomery *Coll*: *chug hole* (known to nine consultants from the Smoky Mountains); *chuck hole* = more common term (Ellis). **2004** Adams *Old True Love* 179 We've hunted all through there so I knowed the placement of every rock and chug-hole.

[cf OED2 *chuck* v² (originally *chock*); DARE *chughole* n 1 chiefly South Midland, especially KY]

chuck-will's-widow *noun* A whippoorwill (*Antrostomus carolinensis*), a brownish-gray, nocturnal bird.

1971 Hutchins *Hidden Valley* 101 This valley is, indeed, remote and secluded, and now, as if to emphasize this fact, the voice of a chuck-will's-widow drifts through the forest. **1997** Montgomery *Coll* (known to Brewer, Brown, Cardwell, Jones, Ledford).

[echoic]

chuckwood *noun* A woodpecker. See also **peckerwood 1**, **sapsucker**, **woodchuck**.

1966 Dakin *Vocab Ohio River Valley* 395 In Kentucky, however, *peckerwood* [for a woodpecker] is common among older speakers everywhere and is regular in the southwest. In the Mountains and the eastern Knobs older speakers commonly say *woodchuck* (once *chuckwood* in Johnson County).

chuffy *adjective* Of a person: short and stocky.

1939 Hall *Coll* (Saunook NC) She's all right, but she's a little chuffy. **1974** Fink *Bits Mt Speech* 4 = short, stout. "He's a *chuffy* sort of boy." **1982** Slone *How We Talked* 34 = short and stocky; fat. **1995** Montgomery *Coll* (known to Cardwell). **2005** Williams *Gratitude* 485 A person who was a little overweight was described as being chunky or chuffy, as a chunky gal. A more overweight person was described as being "flashy" (fleshy).

[OED3 *chuff* n² "a cheek swollen or puffed with fat" + *-y*; Web3 perhaps from *chuff* "fat, chubby, swollen; proud, elated, satisfied" + *-y*; DARE *chuffy* adj² chiefly South Midland]

chug *verb*

1 To strike, punch.

1891 Brown *Dialect in TN* 174 We also *chug* a man in the short ribs with the fist. **1996–97** Montgomery *Coll* Get out of here or I'll chug you one (Cardwell).

[DARE *chug* v 1 chiefly South, South Midland]

2 (also *choog*) See citation.

1891 Brown *Dialect in TN* 174 *Chug* (*choog*) is the verb used to denote the act of casting anything into the water when special attention is directed toward the noise which it makes in coming in contact with the surface of the water.

chug full See **chuck-full**.

chug hole See **chuck hole**.

chug up *adverb phrase* Close, next.

1859 Taliaferro *Fisher's River* 119 At last we cum chug up to a fence that had no draw-bars nur gate. **1998** Montgomery *Coll* (known to Adams, Bush), = close to those in front of you (Brown); We came chug up to a fence and then had to stop (Oliver). **2007** McMillon *Notes* = right up.

chune See **tune**.

chunk

A *noun*

1 A piece of wood, especially firewood. See also **chunk stove**.

1937 Eaton *Handicrafts* 185 He likes to whittle out of chunks of "popple" (poplar) and other soft woods that grow around his cabin. **1959** Pearsall *Little Smoky* 74 "Busting" logs and piling the "chunks" are important masculine activities, especially in the fall.

2 (also *chunk of fire*) A burning coal in or from a fire, an ember. See also **fire chunk**.

1867 Harris *Sut Lovingood* 97f-g [sic] I know'd that I hed planted a big skeer an that hit would bar fruit afore moon down, so I jist snatched up a chunk ove fire ofen the hath an toch off the powder onder the tail ove the ole hoss. **1940** Still *River of Earth* 198 A chunk of fire burned in the grate. **1958** *GSMNP-110*:34 The big chunks burnt out, and it looked like a small spark wouldn't catch. **c1960** Wilson *Coll*: *chunk of fire* = a burning brand or some coals borrowed to start a new fire. **1977** Shackelford et al. *Our Appalachia* 70 If for any reason the fire [went] out I would have to go a mile or so to get fire, what we call "borrowing fire." Now a lovely [saying] came out of that: "Well, what'd you come for, a chunk of fire?" If you'd come for a chunk of fire you'd dash right off to get that fire back home and preserve it so that you could start your fire for cooking.

[DARE *chunk of fire* n chiefly South Midland]

3 In phrases *chunk of a boy, chunk of a dog*, etc. = a noteworthy or promising specimen; one of good size but not fully grown. See also **sprout of a boy, strip of a boy**.

1823 Doddridge *Logan* [39] (DARE) I was then a thumpin chunk of a boy, may be ten or a dozen years old. **1873** Smith *Arp Peace Papers* 93 The old man had a chunk of a nag that worked in a slide. **1881** Pierson *In the Brush* 240 A "chunk of a boy," as his father called him, about a dozen years old, who was placed in the bed between us, with his head at our feet, and ex necessitate his feet not far from my head. **1903** Fox *Little Shepherd* 106 I've knowed him sence he was a chunk of a boy, but I don't rickollect ever hearin' his last name. **1913** Kephart *Our Sthn High* 70 He arrested Tom Hayward, a chunk of a boy, that was scared most fitified and never resisted more'n a mouse. **1937** Hall *Coll* (Cosby TN) [I was] just a chunk of a boy when my father killed his last panther. **1953** Hall *Coll* (Deep Creek NC) I just walked up on a bear . . . a bear and two cubs, the cubs as big as a good chunk of a dog. **1957** Combs *Lg Sthn High: Word-List* 20 = of good size, as in: "Jude's a great big chunk of a gal." **1991** Still *Wolfpen Notebooks* 61 Look at them little chunks of boys playing in the creek and having a wild time and not knowing what's ahead of them when they grow up. **1996** Montgomery *Coll* = 10–16 years of age (Cardwell).

B *verb*

1 To throw or cast (a solid object).

1948 Chase *Grandfather Tales* 100 They chunked some rocks at him, knocked him down. **1974** Fink *Bits Mt Speech* 4 *Chunk* me the ball. **1992** Davis *Jack Tales* 74 All night long there would be old boys whistling from the yard, chunking little rocks on top of the house, even peeking on the windows, trying to get that girl to come out of the house so they could court her for a little while.

2 (also *chunk up*) To feed (a fire) by adding fresh wood.

1906 Haney *Mt People KY* 69 Several times he has carried wood and "chunked up" the fire under a "moonshine still." **1939** Hall *Coll* (Cataloochee NC) My brother, he was chunking fire that day, blowed the cap off it. **c1945** Haun *Hawk's Done* 249 I chunked up the fire and put another piece of wood on. **1963** Edwards *Gravel* 92 If you ain't [had enough to eat], I'll chunk up the far a bit and we'll roast a tater here in the ashes and eat it before we go to bed. **1972** *Foxfire I* 339 Chunk the fire easy, starting slowly, and gradually building it up in intensity. **1983** Helsly *Country Doctor* 19 In the winter, Papa would "chunk" up the open fire to warm the bedroom, which was used both as a family sitting room and bedroom as well as the reception room for patients who came to the house for medication. **1989** Hannah *Reflections* 4 The boys chunked up the fire to thaw out his feet. **2005** Williams *Gratitude* 485 To *chunk up* a fire is to add more firewood (chunk of wood) to the fire.

[OED3 *chunk* apparently a modification of *chuck* n[1], colloquial and dialect]

chunk floater (also *chunk washer*) *noun* A heavy rain.

c1961 Cooper *Nairy a Word*: *chunk washer* = a heavy rainfall. **1996–97** Montgomery *Coll*: *chunk floater* (known to Brown, Bush, Norris); *chunk washer* (known to Brown, Bush).

[DARE *chunk floater* n chiefly South, South Midland]

chunk of a boy/dog/girl See **chunk A3**.

chunk of fire See **chunk A2**.

chunk rack *noun* See citation.

2000 Strutin *Gristmills* 5–6 The millrace channels water into the 200-foot-long wooden flume that rides atop a bed of low cribbing—a romantic sight, now bedecked with orange jewelweed in summer. A watergate on the flume regulates flow, a "chunk rack" holds leaves, twigs, and other debris, and a box in the bottom of the flume catches sand that could ruin the turbine.

chunk stove *noun* A wood-burning stove. See also **chunk A1**.

c1970 Handlon *Ol' Smoky* 63 It was cool weather so we had a little fire going in the chunk stove.

chunk up See **chunk B2**.

chunk washer See **chunk floater**.

chur See **chair**.

church *verb* See also **de-church**, **exclude**, **put out 4**, **turn out 2**, **unchurch**.

1 To try (a church member) before church authorities or the congregation, to consider discipline or punishment (usually to suspend membership) for violating standards of church or biblical conduct.

1945 Williams *Comment* 9 To church, as I have known the term, means to call before local church authorities for some offense. The penalty is not necessarily expulsion but may be censure or some form of penance—or even acquittal. **1974** Fink *Bits Mt Speech* 4 = to put on trial before the congregation. "They *churched* him for drinking."

2 To convict and expel a church member for such violation (see 1990 citation for examples).

1900 Harben *N GA Sketches* 136 He up an' said some'n about folks bein' churched in his settlement fer the mistreatment o' widows. **1913** Kephart *Our Sthn High* 370 Sometimes a man is "churched" for breaking the Sabbath. **1938** Simms *Coll* Why, they'd a-lawed us as well as churched us, if we'd a gone about in such garbs (shorts, slacks, bathing suits, etc.) as they now shamelessly strut about Gatlinburg. **1939** Hall *Coll* (Proctor NC) Walt Proctor was an old timer, deacon of the church, and superintendent of the Sunday school. One day he got drunk, and he was called before the church. When they put a member out, they called a meeting of the whole church. At that time he said, "I took about thirty drams too many." They didn't church him when they give him the trial. **c1945** Haun *Hawk's Done* 241 After that they fussed at her all the time and threatened to have her churched, claiming she wasn't good enough to be a member. **1960** Sutherland *Folk Speech* 13 They'll church you if you jine the Odd-Fellows. **1963** Edwards *Gravel* 81 The church trial, not an infrequent happening, smacks of human, earthly things resembling in a simple way the trials heard at the regular meeting of the county criminal court, except, of course, that the sentence is not to be jailed but to be "churched"—that is, turned out of the church, deprived of membership. **1963** Medford *Mt People* 70 Oftentimes liquor entered into these otherwise innocent mountain "parties"—that's why the churches in those days were so much opposed to them, and sometimes "churched" their members for attending them. **1990** Bush *Ocona Lufta Baptist* 4 In earlier times people were "churched" or removed from the body of the church if there was no reconciliation between the factions or if the board found enough evidence to call for dismissal or exclusion. At times, leaders or members of other Baptist churches came in to give impartial judgements on the complaints. Some of the offenders were put under the "watch care" of the church members. In effect, [they were] taking the Biblical question: "Am

I my brother's keeper?" to heart. They tried to keep each other on the straight and narrow paths of righteousness. Charges leveled against Lufty members ranged from telling falsehoods, gossiping, stealing (from handkerchiefs to land or cows), playing cards, drinking, profanity, general misconduct, and causing strife in the family to the more serious charges—sins of the flesh. **2002** Morgan *Mt Born* 40–41 Union Hill Church had an elected, standing committee whose purpose was somewhat analogous to the Spanish Inquisition of the Middle Ages. Its sole purpose was to investigate all members who allegedly had been involved in a "gross" sin: drinking alcoholic beverages, using profanity, fighting, etc. At the convening of this special session, a vote was taken as to whether or not to authorize the investigating committee to look into the matter. When the investigation was completed, the church was again called into plenary session to hear the report and to decide the issue. At the next called special session the committee's report was presented. If it was favorable to the person in question, the matter was dropped. If the report was unfavorable, the committee was authorized to notify the "accused" of the time and date to present himself/herself before the entire congregation. If the person appeared at the appointed time, "pleaded guilty," and asked for forgiveness, he/she was automatically continued in full fellowship. If the person showed up and denied the charges, his story was heard and the evidence to the contrary was presented. If the person refused to comply, that is, refused to come to the church, a vote was taken whether or not to continue the miscreant in full membership. If the result was negative, the person's name was stricken from the membership roll. It was said that the person had been "churched." **2004** Maynard *Churches of Smokies* 25 Soon after the log building was raised [in 1837], a controversy over missions, temperance societies, and Sunday schools caused a split among the young Baptist church. In 1839, thirteen members were expelled (or "churched") from the fellowship. Those thirteen formed the Missionary Baptist Church and the remaining group took on the name of the Primitive Baptist Church to denote their perceived allegiance to the doctrine of the early (primitive) church of the New Testament.

[DARE *church* v 1 chiefly South Midland]

3 To attend church.

1968 Vincent *Best Stories* 99 She liked for him to look nice when they churched on Sunday, liked to be proud of him. **1994** Montgomery *Coll* (known to Cardwell).

church-chain *noun* See citation.

1996 Thompson *Link in Chain* 18 The UPC grew out of prayer chains found at individual churches, or "church-chains" as Anderson refers to them. A typical church chain is centered in one house of worship and has 10 to 14 members, including a prayer chain coordinator. Usually, it is a member of the congregation who gives a prayer request to a church-chain member, who then forwards the request to the rest of the members of the chain.

church dulcimer *noun* A type of **mountain dulcimer**.

1999 Milnes *Play of Fiddle* 136 Other names I have heard for dulcimers in central West Virginia are . . . church dulcimer (which was used to describe a large, six-stringed dulcimer in Nicholas County).

church house *noun* A building in which religious services with preaching are held (i.e. in contrast to *church* in the sense of the larger institution or denomination of members). Same as **meeting house**.

1861 (in **1980** Clark *Civil War Diary* 30) We went 14 miles and came close to a creek on the right of the rode at a church house. **1868** *Carter CW Letters* (June 5) the 12 of may on Sunday evening at 4 oclock in the north part of this state was the awfulist storm I ever herd of thare was a church house Blown all to peaces. **1874** *Elijoy Church Minutes* 130 Church met & . . . Apointed Jacob Tipton H H gamble & Willoughby Rogers a Committa for the Purpous of geting up means & to imploy Some Person to keep the Church house in order keep the windows and doors Shut also to keep fire lights & water. **1913** Morley *Carolina Mts* 90 From the lonely little "church-house" a path guides you to the top of Glassy Rock, whose steep front shines like glass when wet—which is much of the time. **1937** Hall *Coll* (Copeland Creek TN) The first church house on Webb's Creek was Evans Chapel. **1939** Hall *Coll* (Bradley Fork NC) I went to work cutting wood to put up a church house. *Ibid.* (Little Cataloochee NC) There's grown children there that never had been in a church house, till they come up here. **1940** Haun *Hawk's Done* 19 Joe took Tiny to a cake-walking over at Holiways church house one night. **1971** *AOHP/ALC-33* They was a little log cabin there. They built it out of logs, and they hewed logs out and put them inside for people to sit on, and it was built on the dirt, and that was the first little church house that I ever knowed of. **1973** *GSMNP-84:24* At the old church house where I used to go to church, they was a traveling preacher holding a revival meeting. **1989** *Matewan OHP-23* They had the revivals at their church, at the church house. **2004** House *Coal Tattoo* 88 I can't live my life inside a church house.

[DARE *church house* n chiefly South Midland, South]

churn-jar *noun* A churn.

1961 Stubbs *Mountain-Wise* 11 Other double words are "poker-stick" for poker; "pick-sack" for use in picking apples; "churn-jar" for churn.

[a redundant form]

cider *verb* To derive cider from.

1962 Williams *Verbs Mt Speech* 18 [The mountaineer] "ciders" his apples (when he doesn't "brandy" them).

cider mill (also *cider press*) *noun* A small barrel-like container in which apples are crushed to extract the juice to make cider. Also called **apple press**, **grinder**. See also **press 1**.

1955 Parris *Roaming Mts* 169 The cider-mill and the ash hopper are only memories. **1985** Dabney *More Mt Spirits* 59 In my day back near the Amicalola River in Dawson County, I had a neighbor who had a big apple orchard. He had a cider mill and he'd grind 'em apples up and pour 'em up in 50 gallon barrels and pour enough of the cider in to come to the top. **1994–97** Montgomery *Coll*: *cider* mill (known to Brown, Cardwell, Ellis, Ledford, Norris, Oliver, Shields); *cider press* (known to Adams, Cardwell, Ellis, Ledford, Norris, Weaver).

cider press See **cider mill.**

Cincinnati chicken *noun* See citation.

2006 *Encycl Appalachia* 950 The Kentucky writer James Still recalled hard times when all his family had in the way of meat was salt pork (also known as white bacon or side meat), which was sometimes dredged in flour or cornmeal before frying. Thus upgraded, the dish became "Cincinnati chicken"—a humorous nod to its packinghouse place of origin.

ciphen See **cipher A.**

cipher

A (also *ciphen*) *noun*

1 The zero.

1891 Moffat *Mtneers Middle TN* 315 Why, ther ciphers, ain't they? **1983** Broaddus *Estill Co KY Word List* 35 *ciphen* = a cipher, zero.

[DARE *cipher* n 1 chiefly North, Midland]

2 Any numeral.

1940 Stuart *Trees of Heaven* 170 They [= bankers] have everything down in ciphers and in the word [= in writing] in big books.

3 (as *ciphers*) A letter or word (or by extension, handwriting) difficult or impossible to make out.

1968 *DARE Survey* (Warm Springs VA) *ciphers* = joking names for handwriting that's hard to read.

B *verb*

1 (also *cipher out*) To figure (out), perform arithmetic calculations; hence noun *ciphering* = elementary arithmetic, calculation.

1848 (in **1870** Drake *Pioneer Life KY* 150) My first studies in "Cyphering" were here, and my voice and fluency enabled me to say the multiplication, in the style of a real declaimer. **1879** Jones *Backwoods Carolina* 752 The younger children, bending over to shade their eyes from the light, pored over some schoolbook or "ciphered" on their slates. **1899** Temple *E TN Civil War* 73–74 There are few of the younger generation who can not read and write, and cipher, too. **1926** Thomas *Hills and Mts of KY* 158 My father told the commissioner that he wanted to teach school. "Well, all right, Green," responded the commissioner. "Can you write? can you spell? can you cipher?" **1937** Eaton *Handicrafts* 222 [The family] often work together around the rug frame, deciding among themselves just how to fill in certain parts of the pattern which had been left for them to "cipher out." **1940** Still *River of Earth* 67 These chaps ought to be in school. Ought to be larning to read and cipher. **c1960** Wilson *Coll*: *ciphering* = older name of arithmetic: "Reading, writing, and ciphering to the Rule of Three." **1987** Young *Lost Cove* 81 Wess filled her order, then ciphered out what the eggs and butter came to. **1994–97** Montgomery *Coll*: *ciphering* (known to Jones, Oliver, Weaver), = common term for arithmetic, = the formal school term for arithmetic (Cardwell); I have to do my reading and my ciphering (Norris). **1999** Morgan *Gap Creek* 79 It was a portent, but we didn't know how to cipher it. **2008** Salsi *Ray Hicks* 70 I stayed at home times I should've been in school. Yet, it was better for me to learn about farmin', even though I managed to learn some spellin' and cipherin'.

[DARE *ciphering* vbl n chiefly South Midland]

2 See citation.

1957 Broaddus *Vocab Estill Co KY* 17 = to loaf.

cipher down *verb phrase* Of one team of students: to defeat (a rival team) in a **ciphering match** in solving problems in arithmetic. See also **spell down A.**

1927 Woofter *Dialect from WV* 350 = to turn an opponent down at a ciphering match. "We had three men left on our side when the other side was ciphered down." **c1960** Wilson *Coll*: *cipher down* = to defeat in an arithmetic match . . . (old usage; now rarely heard or known).

ciphering See **cipher B1.**

ciphering match *noun* A classroom competition between two teams of students, conducted like a spelling match and testing accuracy and speed of solving problems in arithmetic.

1927 Woofter *Dialect from WV* 350 = a contest in which sides are chosen for the purpose of testing accuracy and speed in arithmetic. "There will be a ciphering match at the Hardman School Thursday night." **c1960** Wilson *Coll* = a quick drill in arithmetic, usually done on a slate; the first one getting the correct answer won.

cipher out See **cipher B1.**

ciphers See **cipher A3.**

circle saw, **circle saw mill** See **fight a circle saw.**

circuit preacher See **circuit rider.**

circuit rider (also *circuit preacher*) *noun* Traditionally, an itinerant Methodist, Baptist, or other minister responsible for more than one church congregation, often over a large area, each tended on a weekly, monthly, or other regular basis (but less regularly for smaller churches or ones in a less populated area). The last of such ministers in the vicinity of the Smokies died in the early 1990s. See also **circuit-riding.**

1863 *Tesh CW Letters* (Aug 24) I must tell you about the two days meeting we had up at union last Thursday and Friday the sircuit preacher had. **1867** Harris *Sut Lovingood* 89 She married ole Clapshaw, the suckit rider. **1881** Pierson *In the Brush* 173–74 Such was the devout character and spirit of the young circuit-rider whom I accompanied on his week-day visit to Rocky Creek. **1884** Murfree *In TN Mts* 232 The dancing party at Harrison's Cove would be a text for the bloody-minded sermons of the circuit-rider for all time to come. **1908** Smith *Reminiscences* 412 The primitive or "foot-washing" Baptists still have their churches in the mountain coves, where their shepherds feed their flocks on sound and fury and nonsense; but the missionary Baptist and the circuit-rider follow steadily in the wake of the schoolmaster, and the sect in ignorance is already doomed. **1941** Justus *Kettle Creek* 59 As if there were not enough hip-and-hurrah going on already to keep all tongues a-wag, some folks on Little Twin had the notion to get up a pounding for the Circuit Rider. **1974** Cate et al. *Sthn Appal Heritage* 44 There were few churches and even fewer preachers. Often the remote coves were served by a circuit rider whose visits were infrequent, often many months apart. He visited families along his route during the week and preached at a central point on Sunday. People came from great distances for the important and happy occasion. **1974** Raulston and Livingood *Sequatchie* 104–5 [In the early days] circuit riders came not to serve established congregations but to find scattered Methodists from older communities, create some organization among them, and to make converts. Covering hundreds of lonely miles, he rode horseback around circuits which required from four to six weeks to complete. Often the preacher's saddlebag was as lean as his horse; it contained, at best, a change of clothes, a Bible, and a hymnbook. He lived in the homes of the people, who welcomed him for his social companionship and for the role he could play in delayed funeral or wedding ceremony. The circuit rider preached whenever and wherever he could find a few to listen. When the word went out that services would be held, people walked or rode for miles to attend. They gathered in a cabin, at a tavern, outdoors, or any other spot that was available if no chapel had been built in the neighborhood. If preaching was scheduled on a weekday, it generally began at noontime, mainly because on a clear day everyone without a watch or clock could tell when it was twelve o'clock. Wedding ceremonies, baptisms, and funeral services had to be planned for a time when the circuit rider was in the vicinity. **1978** Montgomery *White Pine Coll* VI-2 Them old circuit riders had seven or eight churches, them Methodists did. Maybe this'un had preaching first, and then they'd have Sunday school, and then he'd go down here and preach. **c1980** Roberts *Olden Times* 61 Apparently realizing that the people needed the Gospel long before they were able to erect church buildings, the Methodists sent to the frontier missionaries known as circuit riders whose objective was to find the people and to conduct religious services in their homes. They then organized "classes" of about 12 persons who were to meet weekly in their homes for prayer and to hear a simple sermon by the local leader or exhorter, and to pay tithes. Whenever several classes were organized within an area, a congregation was organized and usually a church soon was erected. The practical approach to a pressing problem resulted in the Methodist Church becoming the most numerous in many sections of the frontier. **1991** Haynes *Haywood Home* 39 The Methodists had Sunday School every Sunday and preaching only when the Circuit-Preacher came through. Sometimes, when the Circuit-Preacher was a long time in coming, Methodists would have preaching with a Lay-preacher presiding. **2006** *Encycl Appalachia* 1330 The circuit rider often provided services other than purely spiritual ones: news from afar; perhaps an application of some remedy from John Wesley's *Primitive Physic* (1747), a volume on herbal medicines; the sanctification of a common law marriage; the memorialization of a death; or the passing along of some domestic skill or agricultural knowledge enjoyed elsewhere.

circuit-riding *adjective* Serving several churches (as a minister) or places (as a lawyer or judge) in a district on a weekly, monthly, or other prescribed rotation.

1980 *Smokies Heritage* 153 Now sarvis always blooms in the spring, and signaled it was the time for the circuit-riding preacher to make his rounds. He'd preach the funerals of all those who'd died during the winter . . . and marry those couples who ought to have been married. **1982** Powers and Hannah *Cataloochee* 373 The eloquent circuit-riding lawyer, Allen Davidson, said [the Cherokee language] was the most beautiful sound in the world. **1993** Parris *Folklore* 469 The Old Man talked about the circuit riding judges and circuit riding preachers and when crackers were shipped in barrels and folks sat around the cracker barrel at the country store and spun yarns.

[back-formation from *circuit rider*]

circular saw See **fight a circle saw.**

circumscribed *adjective* See citation.

2000 Lowry *Folk Medical Term* = circumcised.

[folk etymology]

circumstance *noun*

A Variant form *sarcumstance.*

1867 Harris *Sut Lovingood* 67 Sarcumstances turn about pow'ful fas', an' all yu kin du is tu think jis' es fas es they kin turn, an' jis' es they turn, an' ef yu du this, I'm durnd ef yu don't git out sumhow. **1883** Zeigler and Grosscup *Heart of Alleghanies* 60 Jist figger to yerself the weight of an animal under sich sarcumstances. **1913** Kephart *Our Sthn High* 297 Reckon Pete was knowin' to the sarcumstance?

B in phrase *no/not a circumstance (to)* = not comparable to.

1873 Smith *Arp Peace Papers* 55 A kno-nothin convention ain't a circumstance to it. **1901** Harben *Westerfelt* 276 Job an' all he went through, b'iles an' all, wasn't a circumstance, an' it was all the Lord's doin's, Brother Tim said, to show him the true light. **1931** Combs *Lg Sthn High* 1308 Josh ain't no sarcumstance to Bud. (Josh can't be compared to Bud.) **1941** Still *Troublesome Creek* 42 House and neighbors hain't a circumstance to getting a crop and the garden planted. **c1960** Wilson *Coll* She's not a circumstance (that is, not to be compared with) to Mary.

circumvengemous *adverb* See citations.

1927 Woofter *Dialect from WV* 350 = in a roundabout manner: "Mother told the story very circumvengemous." **1977** Howard *Fifty Years* 10 = in a roundabout manner.

circus veins *noun* Varicose veins.

1968 *DARE Survey* (Brasstown NC) = blue, swollen veins a woman gets on her legs when expecting a baby.

citizen *noun* A local resident or native (in contrast to an outsider or newcomer, who is often called a **foreigner**); hence *citizens* = the local population.

1862 *Couch CW Letters* (Aug 9) I have been staying for the last five days in a citizens house in taswell. **1864** *C A Walker CW Letters* (April 28) The Yankees went back down the road They told the Citizens that they killed about half of our Legion. **1901** Harben *Westerfelt* 185 "I've done all that kin be done," he said. "I've been round among the citizens." **1911** Shearin *E KY Word-List* 537 = a native of a locality, as distinguished from a new-comer. **1917** Kephart *Word-List* 409 = a native; as distinguished from *furriner*. **1939** Hall Coll (Emerts Cove TN) There isn't anyone stays in Greenbrier Cove now except a few rangers and a few fire guards. There isn't any citizens that lives there at all now. *Ibid.* (Roaring Fork TN) Citizens lived in Gatlinburg years and years before this creek was settled. **1957** Combs *Lg Sthn High: Word-List* 20 = native, as opposed to an outsider. Used especially to differentiate a lowlander from a mountaineer. For example, one may be from Louisville, but to the Highlander he is not a citizen. However, a North Carolina Highlander is to the Kentucky Highlander a citizen. The resident of Louisville is termed a *ferriner*. **1958** GSMNP-110:16 It was fine timber up Jakes Creek, but those citizens had cut out a whole lot of it and took out and sold it. **1975** *AOHP/ALC-1128* Most people was of a local people in them mountains here [and] was the same citizens as when the mines was opened up. **1991** Thomas *Sthn Appal* 105 I covered a pretty big territory, but I soon found out where to stay. I usually knew th' kinds of citizens that lived in each community.

city bug *noun* See citation.

1936 Farr *Folk Speech* 275 = a person who lives in the city.

civer See **cover**.

civet (also *civet cat, civvy cat*) *noun* Usually the small spotted skunk (*Spilogale putorius*).

1971 Linzey and Linzey *Mammals of Smoky* 65 The Spotted Skunk, or the "civet," is a handsome member of the Park fauna, there being no other mammal with a similar color pattern. This skunk has a white spot on its forehead, one under each ear, and four broken white stripes along the neck, back, and sides. **1994–97** Montgomery Coll: *civet cat* (known to Adams, Brown, Cardwell, Jones, Ledford, Weaver); *civvy cat* (known to Adams, Brown, Cardwell, Oliver). **2006** Ellison *Nature Journal* 79 Sometimes referred to as a civet, the spotted skunk is black with a white spot on its forehead and under each ear. There are also four broken white stripes along its neck, back and sides, as well as a white-tipped tail.

civil *adjective* Courteous, considerate, polite.

1936 Skidmore *Lift Up Eyes* 57 Don't you go gitten smart-alecky, Nat Cutlip. I was jist asken a civil question. **1944** Wilson *Word-List* 41 = respectable, considerate of others. **1957** Combs *Lg Sthn High: Word-List* 20 = nice, quiet, obedient (of children). When company is present, and when one of the small children becomes noisy: "Be civil!" **1992** Offutt *KY Straight* 44 Owl's just being civil until he knows you better.

[DARE *civil* adj 1 chiefly South, South Midland]

civilly *adverb* See citations.

1919 Combs *Word-List South* 33 = certainly, positively, indeed. "I jist *civilly* had to git up an' light a rag fer home." Knott and Perry counties [KY]. **1923** Combs *Addenda KY* 242 = intensive for *certainly, surely*. "I civilly just had to hand him my hardware (gun)."

civil party *noun* See citation. See also **play, twistification**.

1973 *AOHP/ASU-111* They could have what they called civil parties. It was a get-together of the young people who would play funny little games and things like that.

civvy cat See **civet**.

clabber

A Variant forms *clabby* [see **1966–67** in **B**], *clobber* [see **1997** in **C1**].

B (also *clabbered milk, clabber milk*) *noun* Milk that has thickened and begun to sour and curdle and thus is used to form cottage cheese or be churned into butter. Also called **bonny clabber**. See also **clabber cheese, curd cheese**.

1934–47 *LAMSAS Appal*: *clabber* = attested by 27/148 speakers (18.2%) from WV, 7/20 (35%) from VA, 16/37 (43.2%) from NC, and 2/12 (16.7%) from GA; *clabber milk* = attested by 25/148 speakers (16.8%) from WV, 6/20 (30%) from VA, 15/37 (40.5%) from NC, 2/14 (14.3%) from SC, and 4/12 (33.3%) from GA; *clabbered milk* = attested by 8/148 speakers (5.4%) from WV, 3/20 (15%) from VA, 4/37 (10.8%) from NC, 1/14 (7.1%) from SC, and 1/12 (8.3%) from GA. **1949** Kurath *Word Geog East US* 36 Another South Midland expression is *clabber milk, clabbered milk*, which is here more common than the simple Southern *clabber*. It is found as far north as the northern watershed of the Kanawha. **1958** Newton *Dialect Vocab* In E TN mountains, *clabber* was preferred by 3 of 36 speakers, *clabber milk* by 11 of 36, and *clabbered milk* by 16 of 36. **1966–67** *DARE Survey* (Cherokee NC) *clabby*. **1986** Pederson et al. *LAGS*: *clabbered (milk)* = attested by 16/60 interviewees (26.7%) from E TN and 4/35 (11.4%) from N GA; 20/64 of all LAGS interviewees (31.2%) attesting term were from Appalachia. **1997** Montgomery Coll: *clabber* (known to Adams, Jones, Oliver), = cream allowed to thicken, ready to churn for butter and buttermilk (Brown). **1999** Nelson *Aroma and Memories* 16 We girls helped to churn the clabbered milk until it turned into butter and buttermilk.

[DARE *clabber* n[1] 1 chiefly South, Midland, West]

C *verb*

1 Of milk: to turn sour and thicken, curdle. Same as **turn B1**.

1984 Page and Wigginton *Foxfire Cookery* 59 Let [the cream] stay where it's warm till it sours, and then it'll clabber and be thick. Then it's ready to churn. **1985** Irwin *Alex Stewart* 200 If you wanted to make your milk clabber quicker, just drop a pod or two in, and in a few hours it would commence to clabber. **1997** Montgomery Coll This milk is clabbered; this milk will clabber if you set it in a warm place (Ledford); Milk has to clobber before you churn it (Norris). **1997** Nelson *Country Folklore* 62 Churning was a children's job. The milk had set by the kitchen stove in a crock jar, getting clabbered and ready to churn. Mama or Grandma placed it in the churn, and we pushed the dash up and down until we had butter and buttermilk. **2005** Williams *Gratitude* 143 When it [= the milk] first started to turn (sour), it was called blinked milk, then it set up thick and clabbered.

2 (also *clabber up*) Of weather: to become heavily clouded, threaten to rain.

1921 Campbell *Sthn Highlander* 146 Asking the morning wayfarer as to the weather prospects, one is surprised to hear him call the mackerel sky "clabbered" until its appropriateness flashes upon him. **1988** Russell *It Happened* 36 Other expressions that I remember are "It's like looking for a needle in a haystack." "It's clobberin' up to rain." **2005** Williams *Gratitude* 486 An old saying, said in fun (usually) to a youngun was, "I'm gonna *clabber up* and rain all over you." **2009** Benfield *Mt Born* 130 *clobbering up to rain* = clouds are gathering before a rain.

[< Irish Gaelic *clábar* "mud"]

clabber cheese (also *clabbered cheese, clabber milk cheese*) *noun* Cottage cheese. See also **clabber B.**

1946 Nixon *Glossary VA Words* 15 *clabber cheese* = cheese made of the drained curd of sour milk . . . [a term used] in the Blue Ridge, the northern Piedmont, and the Southern Neck. **1949** Kurath *Word Geog East US* 43 *Clabber-cheese* . . . for cottage cheese . . . also has some currency in the westernmost part of Virginia and in West Virginia by the side of the Midland *smear case*. **c1960** Wilson *Coll*: *clabber cheese* = formerly the commonest name; few people made this cheese and [they] regarded it as cheap stuff anyway. **1966** Dakin *Vocab Ohio River Valley* 343–44 *Clabber cheese* (occasionally *clabber milk cheese*), primarily a South Midland and Southern term, is common in north-central and northeastern Kentucky (Bluegrass, northern Pennyroyal and northern Mountains). *Curds, curd cheese*, and *home-made cheese*, also Southern and South Midland terms, compete with *clabber cheese* in the northeast and are more common in southern Kentucky from the Mountains to the Mississippi. **1966–67** *DARE Survey* (Maryville TN) *clabbered cheese*. **1986** Pederson et al. *LAGS*: *clabbered* = attested by 16/60 interviewees (26.7%) from E TN and 4/35 (11.4%) from N GA; 20/64 of all LAGS interviewees (31.2%) attesting term were from Appalachia.

[DARE *clabber cheese* n chiefly South, South Midland]

clabbers will get you (also *clavers will get you*) *phrase* See citations.

1908 *Mt Life* 9 The traveler stopping at a lonely cottage may hear the mother quiet an unruly child by saying—"Behave now, son, or Clavers will get you!" It is doubtful whether the woman knows anything about the bogey she conjurs [sic] up to "haud the wretch in order" but she is really referring to Claverhouse, the Scotch rough rider who harried the Covenanter in ancient days! **1910** Bolton *Scotch-Irish Pioneers* 300 The illiterate mother in the hills of Kentucky today passes on her burden of tradition when she exclaims: "Behave yourself, or Clavers will get you!" To her Clavers is but a bogey; to her ancestors Graham of Claverhouse was a very real cause for terror. **1952** Wilson *Folk Speech NC* 527 *the Clavers will get you* = this would appear to be a threat, like *lay-overs to catch meddlers*. [**1995** Montgomery *Coll* (unknown to consultants from the Smoky Mountains).] **1996** Landry *Coll* The Clabbers'll get you.

[perhaps originally a reference to John Graham of Claverhouse, sent by King Charles II to Scotland to suppress Covenanter Presbyterians in the early 1680s]

clabber up See **clabber C1.**

clabby See **clabber A.**

clacker *noun* A private currency issued by a coal company, negotiable only at the company's store. Same as **scrip.**

1943 Korson *Coal Dust* 72 The same colloquial terms were used for scrip and store orders, such as "stickers," "clackers," "flickers," and "drag." **2006** Mooney *Lg Coal Mining* 1029 Every two weeks or month the miner collected his pay, often in the form of company money called "scrip" or "clacker" that had to be spent in the company store or "pluck me store" as miners called it because of inflated prices.

clair See **clear.**

clapperclaw *noun, verb* See citation.

2009 Benfield *Mt Born* 130 = your hands. To clapperclaw a thing is to grab, claw at, or take with the hands. "Keep your clapperclaws offen my rocking chair."

clar, cl'ar See **clear.**

clarify *verb* See citations.

1860 *Week in Smokies* 123 She told me that her "old man," as she called her husband, once, when she was sick, had bought some "store sugar," "but, Mister, when I got well," said she, "I clarified some of it, and you can't think what a power of nastiness I got out of it." **1997** Montgomery *Coll* = to reboil molasses or syrup in order to skim off impurities (Brown), = to drain off impurities (Bush).

clart *verb, noun* See citation.

1944 Williams *Word-List Mts* 28 = to defecate. Also *noun* = feces.

[OED3 *clart* v now Scots and northern dialect; SND *clart* v[1] "to besmear; to spread thickly, to dirty"]

clarty *noun* Of soil: muddy, sticking to the plow.

1997 Montgomery *Coll* (known to Ledford, but not to other consultants from the Smoky Mountains).

[cf OED3 *clart* n a "sticky or claggy dirt" Scot and north dialect; EDD *clart* sb Scot, Irel, nEngl]

class *noun* variant plural form of two syllables: *clas-tes*.

1996 Montgomery *File* We have both men's and women's clastes [in Sunday school] (45-year-old man, Gatlinburg TN).

clastes See **class.**

clatterment *noun*

1 Noise, especially loud conversation.

c1950 Adams *Grandpap* 50 He hadn't got but a little piece when he heard a clatterment behind him. **1996** Montgomery *Coll* = a talkative person's conversation (Adams), = only talk, as "I've never heard such clatterment in all my life" (Cardwell), = noise in the house (Jones), = noise, "I never heared such a clatterment" (Norris).

2 (usually plural; also *klediments*) Belongings.

1895 Edson and Fairchild *TN Mts* 371 *clatterments* = belongings, accoutrements. "Sam, what did you do with all of the clatterments that belong to the mowin' scythes and the harness?" **1979** Cash *Among Klediments* 12 (DARE) A klediment can be almost anything that has earned a right to be a part of things close to you. It can be precious antique furniture gathered from grandmother, pieces of china, little handmade doilies, the straw mats on your floor, or the priscilla curtains you made yourself. A klediment can be a thing you love. . . . A klediment can be a thing you just won't throw away. . . . A klediment can be a person dear to you. **1996** Montgomery *Coll*: *clatterments* (known to Adams, Brown, Jones, Oliver). **2007** McMillon *Notes*: *klediments* = belongings.

[DARE *clatterment* n cf Scots *clatter-trap*, *clutterment*, see also OED3 *cladment* n "a garment, dress" obsolete, rare]

clavers will get you See **clabbers will get you**.

claw bar *noun* See citation.

1957 Broaddus *Vocab Estill Co KY* 17 = a crow bar.

clay-bank *adjective, noun* Of a horse: yellowish brown to dirty white in color; a horse of such a color.

1892 Dromgoole *War of Roses* 481 He issued invitations in the good old way, that is, by mounting his clay-bank mare, and striking off across the mountain, calling from door to door, that on Thursday, October the 15th, there would be a corn-shucking at his place down at the Ford. **1927** Mason *Lure of Smokies* 240 Abe was swearing profoundly at the lead horses, one a blind, wind-broken beast; the other, a thin, yellow "clay-bank" with a narrow strip of soft leather over his nose in lieu of a bridle. **1966–67** *DARE Survey* (Spruce Pine NC, Maryville TN) = a horse of a dirty white color. **1969** Foust *Kingdom of Wilkes* 39 One day Father came home with a little "claybank" horse which was proudly presented to the "womenfolks" for our very own. I was delighted. He was handsome with shapely body, black mane and tiny feet, and so gentle—much safer than the playful calves—and soon I was riding him all over the place. **1996–97** Montgomery *Coll* (known to Brown, Bush).

[DARE *claybank* adj now chiefly South, South Midland]

clay dummy *noun* See citation.

2006 Mooney *Lg Coal Mining* 1029 After kneeling or lying on his side and "undercutting" the seam (which had to be further supported with short timbers or "sprags"), the miner drilled blasting holes with a "breast auger," used a "tamping rod" to pack his black powder, inserted a "clay dummy" for proper repercussion of the explosion, lit the fuse, and yelled "Fire in the hole!" or perhaps "Shootin' coal!" to warn other miners of the impending blast.

clay pea *noun* Apparently a type of black-eyed pea.

1971 *Corn Shuckin's* 101 Ever'body planted these old clay peas. I ain't seen 'em in over twenty years. Th'seeds of 'em's about t'run out. People used t'always plant 'em in their corn field. **1976** GSMNP-113 You could git all them old clay peas picked on the halves, and he sowed them clay peas. . . . That's what kept the ground up. . . . Clay peas, now, they cook them. I'd rather have a mess of clay peas as white beans. **1994** Montgomery *Coll* = black-eyed pea (Cardwell). **1999** Perry *Clinch River* Dad started growing "clay peas" in the corn. Vines would climb up the stalk and they would have to be picked and shelled.

clean

A *verb* variant past-tense forms *cleant*, *clen*.

1930 Greer-Petrie *Angeline Outsmarts* 2–3 He spit on his handkercher and cleant his cellyloid collar with hit. **1938** Bowman *High Horizons* 46 These antique words, such as "engern" for onion, "vigrous" for vigorous, "holpt" for helped, "atter" for after, and "clen" for cleaned, although plentiful, do not form the whole fabric of the mountaineer's daily speech as some people seem to think. **1997** Montgomery *Coll*: *clen* (known to Brown, Bush).

B *adverb* All the way, completely. See also **plumb B2**.

1863 *Reese CW Letters* (Dec 6) ouer Batter[ie]s Cood play on the yankeys Clean over us. **1863** *Tesh CW Letters* (March 15) I taken One of my new shirts down to the branch to get it washed and the wind blew verry Hard and a spark blown on it and burnt it clean up. **1866** Smith *So Called* 128 You feel like throwing yourself clean away for your country. **1901** Harben *Westerfelt* 195 I reckon they've run Toot Wambush clean off. **1921** Combs *Slang Survivals* 116 = quite, entirely: "He's clean finished his house." **1935** Sheppard *Cabins in Laurel* 51 She grabbed my sister's hand and run for the Hoppas cabin that stood clean over the mountain in what's the Jase Burleson orchard now. **c1940** Padelford *Notes* Clean to the cove I've rid today. **1969** GSMNP-27 They went out of our sight up over the fence when they clean clumb the fence and went out. **1975** Chalmers *Better* 66 One who is discouraged is clean out of heart, his nerves may be all tore up, or he is merely tired and whupped out. **1975** Gainer *Speech Mtneer* 8 = entirely, completely. "The bullet went clean through his leg." "The horses pulled the wagon clean to the top of the hill." **1989** *Matewan OHP*-22 I got me a taxi all the way from Williamson clean up this Red Jacket Hollow.

clean as a hound's tooth *adjective phrase* Extremely clean.

1927 Woofter *Dialect from WV* 357 = very clean. "Her kitchen is as clean as a hound's tooth."

clean off (also *clean up*) *verb phrase* To remove trees and brush from (a piece of land) in preparing for cultivation. See also **break B9**, **grub 1**, **log rolling**, **new ground**.

1836 *McLean Diary* 41 [I] Commenst Cleening up my Corn ground Warm for the Season. **1847** *Ibid.* 98 [I] Cleand of[f] our field for Corn. **1899** Fox *Mt Europa* 57 Thar used to be prime huntin' in these parts when my dad cleared off this spot more'n fifty year ago, but the varmints hev mostly been killed out. **1975** GSMNP-59 The earliest [people that] come in, of course, they kind of cleaned up the ground, you know, and made. They done the farming, raised corn. **1985** Irwin *Alex Stewart* 69 He leased me a piece of ground up there and give me seven dollars a acre for cleaning it up, and he give me the first crop. **1991** Thomas *Sthn Appal* 30 Ye'd git t' tend it three years, ye know, after ye cleaned it up. . . . Maybe ye'd have some tol'ble level land with trees on it . . . ye'd didn't clean up po'r land. It wouldn't pay ye.

clean one's plow *verb phrase* To whip or punish someone (a threat often used to an unruly child or other malefactor).

1953 Hall *Coll* (Del Rio TN) I'll clean your plow for that. **1957** Combs *Lg Sthn High: Word-List* 21 = to give one a whipping. A lazy boy is thus handled, when he claims that he can't plow because his plow is heavy with damp soil, or full of weeds, turf, etc. **1984** Wilder *You All Spoken* 48 *clean his plow* = tell him off; give him what for; thrash him. **1994** Montgomery *Coll* (known to Shields). **2005** Williams *Gratitude* 486 If somebody tells you they aim to clean your plow, you better either run or git ready to fight.

[DARE *clean one's plow* v phr chiefly South, South Midland]

cleant See **clean A.**

clean up See **clean off.**

clear

A Variant forms *clair, clar, cl'ar, cler, clur.*

1813 Hartsell *Memora* 104 the General on axamination clared him and sent him to his post. **1838** *McLean Diary* 57 Clar and warm Sumer Sets in. **1856** (in **1956** Eliason *Tarheel Talk* 309) (Caldwell Co NC) *clar.* **1913** Kephart *Our Sthn High* 36 I've cl'ared me a patch and grubbed hit out. **1940** Oakley *Roamin'/Restin'* 30 When they got a few acors claired up on the dark night of the moon in March they would plant airish potatoes. **c1959** Weals *Hillbilly Dict* 3 The weather's a-cl'arin' some. **1973** GSMNP-57:66 [You] work and clur the fields and ditch the land and pile the rocks and build you a cellar. **1991** Thomas *Sthn Appal* 116 He clured ten thousand dollars in th' root an' herb bizness one year. **2005** Williams *Gratitude* 486 = completely, totally: "I *cler light* forgot about it."

[DARE *clar* (at *clear* n, v, adv, adj A) chiefly South, South Midland]

B (also *clear off*) *verb, verb phrase* Of **beer** in **moonshining**: to settle and become clear at the end of the fermentation stage of liquor making, indicating it is ready to be distilled; hence noun *clearing off* = this process.

1949 Maurer *Argot of Moonshiner* 8 *clear off* = used of the cap of meal on top of the fermenter. To break and settle to the bottom, leaving the beer relatively clear. *Ibid.* 9 *clear* = for the cap of meal on top of the fermenter to break and settle to the bottom, leaving the beer relatively clear: "Quick as that beer clears, we'll run it." **1959** Hall *Coll* They would add about fifty pounds of sugar to each barrel and leave it around eight days . . . before it would stop bubbling and working and it all settled down. They called that the process of clearing off.

clearing *noun* Formerly, a community work activity in which neighbors help a family rid an area of brush and trees so that it can be cultivated. Also called **ground clearing.** See also **bush hacking, chopping, hacking.**

1859 Taliaferro *Fisher's River* 218 Corn-shuckings were conducted in the same way; nor could a man clear a piece of ground without inviting his neighbors, and having a "clearin'." **1939** Campbell *Play Party* 18 Clearings, log-rollings, house-raisings, corn-shuckings, bean stringings, apple peelings, 'lasses stir-offs, and quiltings, though said to be not as common as they once were, still survive.

[DARE *clearing* South Midland]

clear light *adverb phrase* Entirely, completely.

1943 Justus *Jerry Jake* 22 [I] reckon Grandpappy clear light forgot. **2005** Williams *Gratitude* 486 = completely, totally: "I *cler light* forgot about it."

clear off *verb phrase*

1 See **clear B.**

2 Of weather: to clear up, become bright and cloudless. Same as **fair off.**

1862 *Neves CW Letters* (Jan 12) We have had warm cloudy weather for some days. it looks alittle like clearing off now but it is too warm to say clear any time. **1864** *Mangum CW Letters* (June 4) it has bin raning ever since may and it has bin a auful time to Cook I havent bin dry in a week til last night I think it is goin to clear off. **1926** Hunnicutt *Twenty Years* 54 After supper we skinned the other coon and by the time we had it skinned it had cleared off. **1934–47** *LAMSAS Appal* (Swain Co NC). **1953** Hall *Coll* (Bryson City NC) It snowed all the day nearly, but during the night it cleared off. **1967–68** *DARE Survey* (Gatlinburg TN, Maryville TN) = when clouds begin to decrease. **1986** Pederson et al. *LAGS* (Cocke Co TN).

cleat *noun* See citation.

c1975 *Miners' Jargon* 2 = the vertical cleavage of coal seams. The main-set of joints along which coal breaks when mined.

clen See **clean A.**

cler See **clear A.**

clever *adjective*

1 Neighborly, generous, obliging, accommodating. See c1959 citation.

1796 Cunningham *Letter* Jas. Cunningham is living on the Cataba River yet, and is maried to a mighty clever widow woman and is right full in the world. **1834** Crockett *Narrative* 61 When I got there I found her father a very clever old man, and the old woman as talkative as ever. **c1844** Beckner *Shane Interview* 233 The Yocums were clever neighbors; great for log-rolling. **1864** *Chapman CW Letters* (July 13) I am Staying at A private house on Cumberlin River about 2½ miles South of Gallatin with as Clever A Famley as any one would wish to be with. **1902** Hubbard *Moonshiner at Home* 238 This is the home of Garret Heddon, a man feared by revenue officials and mountaineers alike, yet loved, too, by the latter, for, as they say, he is "clever," and will do anything in the world for a friend, a fact which was emphasized when his defense of a comrade made him a fratricide. **1913** Kephart *Our Sthn High* 296 Many common English words are used in peculiar senses by the mountain folk, as . . . clever for obliging. **1925** Greer-Petrie *Angeline Hill Country* 83 We're pore, but clever, as the sayin' is. **1937** Conner *Ms* 83 I once knew a man called Joel Conner-senior, he sure was one of the cleverest men you ever looked in the face of, his door's [sic] was alwayes spread wide-open, regardless of name, rank, or occupation, he met everybody with a smile, he met shelter to the strainger, and food to the hungry, without charge. **1937** Hall *Coll* = in general use, as in "clever folks." **c1959** Weals *Hillbilly Dict* 3 Clever folks are the kind that make you feel at home, feed you well, make your visit enjoyable with good conversation. **1964** Roberts *Hell-Fer-Sartin* 28 Once upon a time there were two little boys. One was clever and the other was stingy. **1967** Wilson *Folkways Mammoth Cave* 22 = well-mannered, engaging. **1987** Young *Lost Cove* 47 Even the most frugal families were clever with their table. Anyone who happened to be around at mealtime was obliged to eat. "Sit yourself down and have a little bit, such as it is," was the usual invitation. **1994** Jones *Appal Values* 69 No greater compliment could be paid a mountain family than that they were "clever folks," meaning that they were quick to invite you to visit and generous with the food.

[OED3 adj 8 c "good-natured, well-disposed, amiable" U.S. colloquial; DARE *clever* adj 3 now chiefly South, South Midland]

2 Good at talking.

1979 Carpenter *Walton War* 144 It states the obvious, but no doubt contributed to the speaker's reputation for being "clever"; that is, a good talker. **1994–97** Montgomery *Coll* (known to Brown).

cleverly *adverb*

1 Fully, thoroughly.

1917 Kephart *Word-List* 409 = fully. "He wasn't *cleverly* grown—just a slick-faced boy." **1925** Dargan *Highland Annals* 87 I went cleverly all over it. **1995** Montgomery *Coll* (known to Oliver).

[OED3 *cleverly* adv 5 now dialect and U.S.; Web3 *cleverly* adv 2 dialect]

2 Barely, only.

1919 Combs *Word-List South* 33 = barely. "'Lish's Rob's jist *cleverly* begun to crap (farm)." Knott Co [KY]. **1923** Combs *Addenda KY* 242 = only; just: "Spark's jist cleverly begun to farm."

cliff *noun* variant form *clift*; variant plural forms *clift-es*, *clivs*, *clivves*. See also **rock cliff**, **rock house**.

1862 *Leigh CW Letters* (Oct 17) [We] have cool nights now but no frost yet we killed a large rattle snake this evening on the clift. **1913** Kephart *Our Sthn High* 225 Ike Morgan Pringle's been a-horse-throwed down the clift. **1928** (in **1952** Mathes *Tall Tales* 70) Ol' Lucky's been hunted so much he ain't goin' to run past them stands, an' we'll have to git him right up at the head of this holler under them big rock cliftes. **1942** Hall *Phonetics Smoky Mts* 92 Many speakers pronounce the following words with excrescent final t: *Cliff, trough*. **1946** Dudley *KY Words* 270 *clivs* = cliffs. **1953** Hall *Coll* (Bryson City NC) He told Cope to look out, he says, "there's a rock clift here." **1964** Roberts *Hell-Fer-Sartin* 167 They made beds out of moss and leaves and so on, and built their fires of log heaps under the clivves. **1972** *AOHP/ALC-276* They took them saddlebags and all his papers in them and took them to a big clift on Cumberland Mountain and hid them. **1998** *Dante OHP-69* They would just run you off against a clift!

[cliff + excrescent t]

clim See **climb 1**, **2**.

climb *verb* Principal parts.

1 variant past-tense forms *clim* (the form most often observed by Joseph Hall in the Smoky Mountains from 1937 to 1941), *clomb*, *clombed*, *clome*, *cloom*, *clum*, *clumb*.

1861 *Mason CW Letter* 177 The yankes threw t[h]er guns down and some clum trees. **1886** Smith *Sthn Dialect* 350 A language might deteriorate any time from such causes in the way of such forms as . . . *clomb* . . . bear the stamp of antiquity. **1913** Kephart *Our Sthn High* 106 The bear clim a tree purty fur. **1921** Weeks *Speech of KY Mtneer* 7 The preterite of climb is, with older people clomb, but more often by everyone corrupted to climb [sic] and clumb. **1934–47** *LAMSAS Appal* (Madison Co NC, Swain Co NC) *clim*. **1939** Hall *Coll* (Deep Creek NC) So I crossed the river and clim out on the east side of the river and came out, I guess, a half a mile and couldn't hear nothing. *Ibid.* (Hartford TN) It clumb right up, and I heared it hit the ground two or three times. **1940** Oakley *Roamin'/Restin'* 116 Once two men from the state of Ohio clombed the Chimneys tops up on Sugar land mountain not very long ago 3 or 4 years ago. **1942** Hall *Phonetics Smoky Mts* 44–45 For *climbed*, pret. and ptc., [klɪm] flourishes in the speech of older people, and [klʌm] may sometimes be heard. Other reported variants are [kloʊm] and [klum], now apparently obsolete. **1953** Atwood *Verbs East US* 9 In the rest of Pa., as in N.J., w. Md., W.Va., and the Shenandoah Valley of Va., the form *clum* /klʌm/ is heavily favored, though in some communities *clim* likewise occurs . . . in inland North Carolina *clum* and *clim* are about equally distributed, and there are a few instances of *clome*. **1953** Hall *Coll* (Bryson City NC) [A bear] went around the hill, clim up a birch tree. **1969** *Burton-Manning Coll-89B* I clumb up on the boom on the derrick 'cause I didn't want them to get ahold of me. **1972** Cooper *NC Mt Folklore* 90 *clim, cloom*. **1973** *GSMNP-81:2* He's the man clumb the tree. **1978** Reese *Speech NE Tenn* 172 *clim* = attested by 6/12 (50%) speakers; *clum* = attested by 3/12 (25%) speakers. **1984** Six *Hill 'n Holler* 4 *clum* = past tense of climb: "He clum this here hillside last week."

2 variant past-participle forms *clim*, *clomb*, *clum*, *clumb*.

1834 Crockett *Narrative* 181–82 On examining more closely, I discovered that a bear had clomb the tree. **1942** Hall *Phonetics Smoky Mts* 44–45 For *climbed*, pret. and ptc., [klɪm] flourishes in the speech of older people, and [klʌm] may sometimes be heard. **c1960** Wilson *Coll* *clim* or *clumb* = past participle of *climb*. **1978** Reese *Speech NE Tenn* 173 *clim* = attested by 6/12 (50%) speakers; *clum* = attested by 3/12 (25%) speakers.

[DARE *clomb*, *clome* past and past participle (at *climb* v 2c) chiefly

Midland, especially VA, NC; *cloom* past and past participle (at *climb* v 2e) especially VA, NC]

climb the wall *verb phrase* See citation.

2013 Landry *Tellin' It* Connie explained . . . "Maw had to climb the wall." . . . All these old cabins, we learned, had lofts, and Connie was referring to climbing up the side of the cabin into the loft by way of an opening between the floors. Usually, the opening was along the wall. Short poles or long pegs were driven into the logs and stuck out from the wall. They were used as rungs, like you would use a ladder.

cling peach (also *clingstone, clingstone peach*) *noun* A peach whose flesh adheres to the seed. See also **freeseed peach**, **open peach**.

1949 Kurath *Word Geog East US* 72 Both *cling-stone peach* and *cling peach* are common in Greater New York City and in western North Carolina. **1966–68** *DARE Survey* (Brasstown NC, Burnsville NC, Spruce Pine NC) = a type of peach in which the hard center is tight to the flesh. **1982** Slone *How We Talked* 67 We grew a small variety of peaches that we called "cling stones" because they had to be cut from the stone. They were smaller than the size of an egg. We peeled these and canned them whole in sugar. Sometimes we pickled them. **1996** Johnson *Lexical Change* 138 *cling, clingstone* = statistically more common in the mountains of South Carolina and Georgia than in the Piedmont and Coastal Plain c1990.

clingstone (peach) See **cling peach**.

clink *noun* A fragment of impure matter left after coal is burned.

1984 Head *Brogans* 28 After leaving the office building, I walked over a mile to my employer to care for his furnace. I had to remove the "clinks," dead and burned out lumps of coal.

clinker *noun* See citations.

1895 Edson and Fairchild *TN Mts* 371 = insect. "These clinkers are mighty thick in this yere cabin." **1998** Montgomery *Coll*: *clinkers* = gnats, mosquitoes, heel flies, etc. (Brown).

clivs, clivves See **cliff**.

clobber See **clabber A**.

clodbuster *noun*

1 A large, heavy work shoe. Same as **clodhopper 2**.

1940 Still *Love Rooster* 62 Reckon I'll just make these clodbusters I got on do. **2005** Williams *Gratitude* 486 *clodbusters* = heavy work shoes, like one would wear while plowing. **2017** Kinsler *Take Girl* 71 *clodhoppers* = farmer's work shoes.

2 (also *clod soaker*) A heavy rain.

1969 Doran *Folklore White Co* 104 A heavy rain is a "clod soaker" and a "gully washer." **1996–97** Montgomery *Coll*: *clod buster* (known to Brown, Cardwell, Jones, Shields).

[DARE *clod buster* n 1 especially South, South Midland]

3 See citation.

1969 Miller *Raising Tobacco* 29 In addition, my grandfather often used a *clodbuster*, a home-made drag consisting of boards nailed overlapping to the bottom of sled runners, weighted down with rocks (and children) and *drug* (dragged) by horses and mules over the patch.

clodhopper *noun*

1 (also *clodjumper*) A rustic, poor farmer.

1943 Korson *Coal Dust* 4–5 Farmers and farm-hands also hired themselves out to coal operators as miners during the winter season. Since digging and loading coal was only temporary work for them, they were less likely to be interested in efforts to raise wages and improve working conditions than professional miners . . . Full-time miners naturally resented them and expressed their distrust by calling them "winter diggers," "wheats," "corncrackers," "hay johns," pumpkin rollers," "clodhoppers." **c1960** Wilson *Coll* = a rustic, a yokel. Less common is *clod-jumper*. **1966** Dakin *Vocab Ohio River Valley* 452 *Clod hopper* has currency in the Bluegrass in the Kentucky River valley. This term also appears along the upper Kentucky within the Mountains and farther south in Whitley County. **1968** Wilson *Folklore Mammoth Cave* 41 *clodhopper* = a humorous or sarcastic reference to a farmer, now falling into innocuous desuetude since the tractor and other machinery do the clodhopping. **1976** Smith and Smith *Sthn Words* [9] = field hand.

2 (also *clodhopper shoe*) A large, heavy shoe, especially one for work in the field. Same as **clodbuster 1**.

1940 Still *Love Rooster* 16 These clodhoppers I'm wearing have wore a half acre o' bark off my heels. **1976** Smith and Smith *Sthn Words* [9] = heavy work shoe. **2003** Carter *Mt Home* 13 He wore long sleeved faded blue denim shirts, even in the summertime, and faded over-hall britches that he turned up a time or two along with brown leather clod hopper shoes.

clodhopper shoe See **clodhopper 2**.

clodjumper See **clodhopper 1**.

clod soaker See **clodbuster 2**.

clogging *noun* A type of heavy-heeled dance performed on the toes and heels, often employing taps or heavy shoes to produce percussive, rhythmic effects. Of its two styles, freestyle and precision (or synchronized), the former is more recent, developing around 1930, and is often featured in team competitions and performances. See also **buckdance**, **flatfoot**.

1977 Nevell *Time to Dance* 180 Today clogging is a synthesis of two old-time arts, the traditional Appalachian square dance, the Big Circle figures, combined with the footwork of buckdancin'. *Ibid*. 199 A clogging routine is the same as a Big Circle dance during which the dancers are constantly "clogging"—that is, stamping their feet in a rhythmic pattern with or without taps on. **1983** Matthews *Cutting a Dido* 29 The term "clogging," however, has only recently become a part of Haywood County's vocabulary and therefore post dates the dance in western North Carolina. **1992** Seeger *Talking Feet* 10 The word "clog," which is used widely by the general public to describe any kind of foot dancing to Southern string music, was not used by any of our older traditional dancers to describe their style. This term has been used occasionally in western North Carolina since about 1930, primarily to describe dances done in teams by competition or performance. Most of our dancers said that they first heard the term after about 1970. **1993–94** Jamison *Jubilant Spirit* 16 In reference to mountain dancing, the earliest use of the word "Clog" that I have found in print was at the first Galax Fiddlers Convention in 1935 . . . I did not find the term "clogging team" in print until 1950. *Ibid.* 17 Group dancing is usually called "clogging," and "precision," or "modern" cloggers perform sequences of steps that have been choreographed and memorized. . . . When precision dance teams started up in the 1950s, dancers began to synchronize their footwork, thus moving away from traditional Buckdancing and toward modern Clogging. . . . Clogging steps . . . tend to have a stomping feel to them. They are heavier on the heels and harder on the knees, as the body weight tends to go up and down more. **1995** Williams *Smoky Mts Folklife* 54 Flatfoot and the more high-step buck dancing existed as a solo dance form long before clogging came on the scene. . . . Within the competitive atmosphere of [Bascom Lamar] Lunsford's festival, the styles of flatfoot and buck dancing were married in the group formations of square dancing, and team clogging was born. **2009** TN *Encycl* The traditional dances of clogging and buckdancing are popular forms of percussive dancing that originated in the southern Appalachian mountains. . . . The leg is generally raised a little more than six inches off the ground in clogging, while the feet stay close to the ground in traditional buckdancing. **2015** Jamison *Hoedowns* 147 During the twentieth century, Appalachian step dancing also became known as clogging, and this is the most common term used today. This name was adopted from stage clog dances based on the English Lancashire Clog, which became popular in America in the 1840s. Like the earlier English hornpipes, these step dances involved percussive sounds made by striking the toes and heels on the floor, and they were performed in stiff, wooden-soled shoes called "clogs" (hence the name).

[cf OED3 *clog* n derivation obscure, originally "a thick piece of wood" c1440→]

clomb See **climb 1, 2.**

clombed, clome See **climb 1.**

clomp *verb* See 1957 citation.

1957 Broaddus *Vocab Estill Co KY* 18 = to walk heavily. **2005** Hicks *Blood and Bone* 54 Rabbits . . . bounce / from scrub cedars to honeysuckle thickets / and briar-tangled warrens, laughing / under their breath at clomping / bipedal pursuit.

[alteration of *clump*]

cloom See **climb 1.**

close

A *adjective, adverb* variant forms *clost* [klost], *clus, cluss;* hence comparative form *closter,* superlative form *clostest.*

1862 Gilley *CW Letters* (June 3) some of them said the yankes was coming closter an I left their an come out of the road and lay their all night an then come to the camp. **1863** Griffin *CW Letters* (July 15) it is the first time I have bin clost to eny corn. **1864** Gilmore *Down in TN* 85 Yer takin' it powerful cool, bein's yer in a purty clus fix. **1869** (in **1974** Harris *High Times* 218) You see them jist keep a comein a lettle closter, an' a lettle closter—thar eyes half shut. **1891** Brown *Dialect in TN* 172 In *oncet, twicet, acrost, clost,* and *clost,* we have a final t added. **1913** Kephart *Our Sthn High* 103 You're so crooked a man cain't lay cluss enough to you to keep warm! **1937** Thornburgh *Great Smoky Mts* 133 I left whar I was and went up whar the men wuz, and stayed thar and watched them clost as I could. **1941** Stuart *Men of Mts* 95 If he'd a-been ten yards closter to me I'd a-been a gone-goslin. **1942** Hall *Phonetics Smoky Mts* 92 Many speakers pronounce the following words with excrescent final t: *close, dose.* **1964** Roberts *Hell-Fer-Sartin* 101 When you are out traveling if anyone meets you at the crossroad and tells you it will be closter to your home if you take the left, you must never do that. **1967** Hall *Coll* (Townsend TN) They had [Decoration Day] the clostest day to the thirtieth. **1971** *AOHP/ALC-147* I wouldn't know where the clostest doctor [was]. **1989** *Matewan OHP-22* When he got there, he drove the wagon just clost up to the house as he could.

B *adverb* Closely.

1961 *Coe Ridge OHP-335B* He looked after me very clost.

close akin *adjective phrase* See citation.

2005 Williams *Gratitude* 486 = nearly, almost, as: "*clost akin* to bein' naked" or "*clost akin* to tellin' a lie."

clost, closter, clostest See **close.**

clothes pack *noun* See citation.

2005 Williams *Gratitude* 39 We had a clothes pack, or clothes shelf, in there on the wall next to the quilt pack. They was planks nailed up to make shelfs that we put our clothes on after we got 'em ironed and doubled up. Ever'body had their own place and knowed where their clothes went in the clothes pack.

clothes press *noun* A tall, movable enclosure for hanging and storing clothes, a clothes closet. See also **chifforobe, press 3.**

1934–47 *LAMSAS Appal* = attested by 33/148 speakers (22.2%) from WV, 4/20 (20%) from VA, 3/37 (8.1%) from NC, 4/14 (28.6%) from SC, and 3/12 (25%) from GA. **1966** Dakin *Vocab Ohio River Valley* 45 In Kentucky scattered informants know (*clothes*) *press* or have heard others use it, but it apparently has had little currency other than in the northeastern Mountain region settled by expansion from the Big Sandy and more closely related to adjoining West Virginia (where *clothes press* is fairly common along the Ohio). **1986** Pederson et al. *LAGS* = attested by 2/60 interviewees (3.3%) from E TN and 5/35 (14.3%) from N GA; 7/28 of all LAGS interviewees (25%) attesting term were from Appalachia; (Sequatchie Co TN) = between a chifforobe and dresser, (Cherokee Co GA) = more like a trunk. **1988** Russell *It Happened* 7 A small middle room housed two clothes presses (cabinets), the baby cradle with rockers, Pa's trunk, many nails on the wall for hanging clothes (We had no wire or wooden clothes hangers), and in one corner were two shotguns and a hog rifle. **1993** Stuart *Daughter* 229 = usually had two upright doors and two horizontal drawers at the bottom and were sometimes lined with cedar for moth prevention.

[Web3 *clothes press* n 2 South and Midland]

clothes ward *noun* See citation.

1973 Miller *English Unicoi Co* 145 = a wardrobe or chifforobe.

cloud *noun*

1 See **gray cloud**, **silver cloud**.

2 See citation.

2006 Childs *Texana* 18 The Indians, I found out later on, were also prejudiced people. And they referred to blacks as clouds. You'd come down the street, this is what the older ones tell me, they see you coming, they would refer to you as a cloud, like a cloud going by.

cloudbust *noun* A sudden heavy rain. [Editor's note: The form *cloudburst* is widespread in the US.]

1939 Hall Coll (Deep Creek NC) They'd been a water spout, a cloudbust put there in time and run in, just a lot, awful lot of spruce and timber. **1983** Broaddus *Estill Co KY Word List* 35 = a rain heavier than a *pour down*, lighter than a *gulley washer.*

clout *noun* A small piece of cloth (especially one used as a diaper), a rag or patch. See also **dish clout**.

c1940 Simms Coll = baby diaper. **1958** Combs *Archaic English in KY* 33 = rag: "The baby wore a clout." **1967** *DARE Survey* (Gatlinburg TN) = diaper. **1995** Montgomery Coll = a rag for cleaning (Cardwell), = a patch (Hooper). **2007** McMillon *Notes* = a diaper; also a piece of cloth.

[EDD *clout* sb 3 Scot, Engl; CUD *clout*^{2} 3 "a rag, patch of cloth"; DARE *clout* n^1 1 especially Midland]

clout pin *noun* See citation.

1957 Combs *Lg Sthn High: Word-List* 22 = safety pin.

clove *noun* A unit of weight of approximately eight pounds.

1863 Wilson *Confederate Private* 1 (Feb 1) Mr. Kitts brak out six cloves of flax last Monday There is a bout a nuf for two cloves to brake yet.

[cf OED3 *clove* n^3 "a weight formerly used for wool and cheese, equal to 7 or 8 lbs. avoirdupois"]

club fist *noun* A children's game played by interlocking the fists.

c1945 Haun *Hawk's Done* 268 He was all the time learning her something. How to ... play ... club fist as his own ma had showed him when he was little.

[DARE *club fist* n especially Appalachians]

clum, clumb See **climb 1, 2.**

clur See **clear.**

clus, cluss See **close.**

co- See **ker-.**

coach-ann, coachie-ann See **cochan.**

coal bank (also *bank*) *noun* See 1973 citation.

1946 Stuart *Plum Grove Hills* 122 "You didn't have any business goin' in that coal mine on Bill Sexton," Grandma answered. "You went in that coal bank to whop him." [**1973** Preston *Bituminous Term* 42 *bank* = all the buildings, grounds, and underground passages associated with a particular coal mining operation.] **1978** Slone *Common Folks* 207 I can "recollect" following my father everywhere he went, playing in his "chair-shop"; waiting on the outside of a coal bank while he "picked out a coffee sackful" of coal. **2001** Liftig *Lessons* 13 Ganderbill swings right by the mouth of the "coal bank" in front of my house—where my dad and his dad and on and on back generations have dug out the family's winter coal for their stoves and fireplaces.

coal bloom *noun* A seam of coal near ground level, marked by a depression or discoloration.

2006 Hicks *Mt Legacy* 30 None of us kids knew what a bloom was, but Dad showed us where to dig and shovel so we would find out.... Sure enough, after about two hours of work, the brown clay dirt and shale started to turn a color of gray. "That's a coal bloom," said Dad.

coal boat tide *noun* A surge of a river or stream after spring rains, producing a water level sufficient to float coal barges past rapids downstream. Same as **boat tide**. See also **tide A.**

1993 Montell *Cumberland Country* 14 [Miners] dumped coal into wooden barges that were sent downstream to Burnside when rains afforded the [Cumberland] river with a "coal boat tide."

coal buggy *noun* A small mechanized car used to haul coal out of a mine. [Editor's note: The 1995 citation is from southern IL.]

1938 Stuart *Dark Hills* 31 It was great fun to ride in a coal buggy back into the darkness under a hill. **1941** Stuart *Men of Mts* 281 His shoulders looked nearly as wide as th' coal-buggy and his powerful big muscled legs fell limp over th' end o' th' buggy. **1995** Horrell and Russell *Coal Portfolio* xv The continuous miners merged these four steps into one; a broad drum with carbide-tipped teeth, now ripped the coal from the seam and passed it along a conveyor past the operator and into a waiting shuttle car (or "coal buggy"); the coal buggy then carried the coal to a coal car or a moving conveyer belt, which carried the coal out of the mine.

coal hod *noun* A coal scuttle.

1986 Pederson et al. *LAGS* = attested by 4/60 interviewees (6.7%) from E TN; 4/17 of all LAGS interviewees (23.5%) attesting term were from Appalachia.

coal house *noun* A shed for storing coal.

1986 Pederson et al. *LAGS* = attested by 3/60 interviewees (5%) from E TN; 3/13 of all LAGS interviewees (23.0%) attesting term were from Appalachia. **1989** *Matewan OHP-11* Missus Hoskins, the teacher, hid one of the detectives in her coalhouse in the back of her home.

coal kill *noun* An outdoor furnace made of hardwood and covered by turf in which charcoal is made.

1859 Taliaferro *Fisher's River* 176 He was sweatin' like a coal-kill. [alteration of *coal kiln*]

coal miner's steak *noun* See citation.

2000 Goode *Being Appalachian* 82 The next morning at 4 a.m. she would finish with some sandwiches made with plain white bread and "coal miners' steak"—thick slices of King Cole Bologna.

coal oil *noun* Same as **lamp oil**.

1934–47 *LAMSAS Appal* (Madison Co NC, Swain Co NC). **1937** Hall *Coll* (Cades Cove TN) [Along with whiskey and turpentine] coal oil was recommended . . . for a snake bite. **1949** Kurath *Word Geog East US* 34 [*Coal oil*] has spread far to the south [of PA], doubtless as a trade word, beginning with the 1860's . . . [it appears] on the upper reaches of the Potomac in West Virginia, in the Shenandoah Valley, and on the Rappahannock in Virginia; furthermore, in southern Ohio and adjoining parts of West Virginia, beside the more common *lamp oil*. **1958** Wood *Words from TN* 8 We said *coal oil* but we knew it was *kerosene*. **1974** Cate et al. *Sthn Appal Heritage* 63 Father was checking to be sure that adequate supplies of food and extra harness parts were loaded into the wagon and that the lantern was well-filled with coal oil. **c1984** Dennis *Smoky Mt Heritage* 7 Bad Cuts: Keep saturated with coal-oil (kerosene).

coal oil light *noun* A kerosene lamp.

1978 Montgomery *White Pine Coll* IV-2 We had them coal oil lights and them old wood burning stoves, and maybe your money would run short, you didn't have money, you can buy a quart of coal oil to fill up that lamp with. Well, you'd pour water down in there and that'd bring the oil up for the wick to catch it and bring it up.

coal tattoo *noun* Coal dust embedded under the skin, forming permanent marks.

2004 Fisher *Kettle Bottom* 77 I did not hold John's hands, speckled with coal tattoos. **2004** House *Coal Tattoo* 157 He has a coal tattoo. . . . It's a sign of survival. . . . My brother has one, from being in a mine cave-in, when the chunks of coal fell on his arm. He never could get rid of that blue mark it left. . . . When the coal breaks the skin, it becomes a part of you. *Ibid.* 167 My uncle had a coal tattoo . . . right there, just a faint little hint of blue, like a permanent bruise.

cob *verb*

1 To pelt with corncobs, especially in children's play. See also **cob battle**.

1962 Hall *Coll* (Canton NC) Then we'd get around the barn and play. . . . We'd call it cobbing each other. We'd break corn cobs and th'ow them at each other. We'd peep around and catch one, why, we'd th'ow and try to hit 'im. **1996** Montgomery *Coll* (known to Cardwell).

2 See citation.

1940 Farr *More TN Expressions* 447 = to embarrass: "Maria's bussy cobbed her."

cob battle (also *corncob battle, corncob fight*) *noun* A mock battle in which children throw corncobs at one another. See also **cob 1**.

1946 Lassiter *Games Played* 18–19 A favorite game which was usually for boys only was a cob battle. The opposing sides armed themselves with a good supply of cobs and then the battle was on. The game usually went along all right until someone wanting to make some special gains began using cobs which had been well soaked in water. It took only a few of these to register a knockout blow. [**1974** Ogle *Memories* 37 Their big game[s] was cob fighting and pitching horse shoes.] **1989** Landry *Smoky Mt Interviews* 195 Then we would have what we called corn-cob fights on Sunday afternoons . . . we'd throw those cobs back and forth at each other. **1991** Haynes *Haywood Home* 56 On rainy days, in any season, older boys would have corncob battles around the crib and barn. **1997** King *Mt Folks* 1 Corn cobs will make great ammunition for corn cob fights or for the Rolens to use with chicken feathers—just to watch them twirl and drop to the ground.

cobbled up (also *coggled [up]*) *adjective, adjective phrase* Rickety, constructed poorly, hastily, or clumsily.

1913 Kephart *Our Sthn High* 280 A few words, caigy (cadgy), coggled, fernent, gin for if, needcessity, trollop, almost exhaust the list of distinct Scotticisms [in mountain speech]. **1917** Kephart *Word-List* 409 = rickety, wobbly. "That's the most *coggled up* far [= fire] I ever seed." **1974** GSMNP-50:2:13 He left there and went to Greenbrier and lived there in some old cobbled up log houses until he built his new house. **1994–97** Montgomery *Coll*: *cobbled up* (known to Cardwell, Hooper); *coggled up* (known to Brown, Bush, Cardwell, Norris). **2005** Williams *Gratitude* 486 *cobbled up* = botched; made a mess out of a job (usually carpentry).

[OED3 *coggle* n (known only from 14th c); possibly from a root **kug-* with the sense "rounded lump," cf German *Kugel*, Dutch *kogel*; but this is doubtful]

cobbler *noun* A type of white potato. Same as **Irish cobbler**.

1986 Pederson et al. *LAGS* = attested by 7/60 interviewees (11.7%) from E TN, 7/16 of all LAGS interviewees (43.7%) attesting term were from E TN.

cobbler pie *noun* A deep-dish fruit pie with no bottom crust. Same as **family pie**. [Editor's note: The form *cobbler* is widespread in the US.]

1986 Pederson et al. *LAGS* = (Claiborne Co TN, Cherokee Co GA, Habersham Co GA).

cob pipe (also *corncob pipe*) *noun* A pipe for smoking tobacco whose bowl is made from a corncob, most often from the butt.

1881 Pierson *In the Brush* 120–21 I have met some people who were so ignorant in regard to rustic manufactures that they did not know what a "cob"-pipe was. For the sake of any that may be similarly uninformed, I will describe one. It is made by taking a section off a common corn-cob some two or three inches in length, and boring or burning out with a hot iron the pith of the cob some two thirds of its length, and then boring or burning a small hole transversely through the cob to the base of the bowl already made, and inserting in this a small hollow reed or cane for a stem. These pipe-stems are long or short, from a few inches to two or three feet, according to the preference of those who are to use them. **1924** Greer-Petrie *Angeline Gits Eyeful* 21 If hit wuz the fashion fur rich wimmen to smoke seeg'rets, shorely and undoubtedly hit wuz all right fur us country hunks to . . . smoke our cob pipes. **1957** Parris *My Mts* 155 Back in the jean-britches and wool-hat era when the corncob pipe was all the go. **1973** GSMNP-80:9 We got her old cob pipe and broke it. She kept it in the chimney, you know, laying up in the chimney crack.

Coca-cola *noun*

A variant form *Co-cola.*

2008 McKinley *Bear Mt* 111 A "Co'-Cola" was 6 cents; Pepsi and R.C. Cola were only a nickel—and the bottles were bigger. **2013** Venable *How to Tawlk* 10 = a famous brand of soft drink: "You kin buy a Co-Cola anywhores in the world!"

B Any carbonated drink.

c1960 Wilson Coll (or *coke*) = the name for any carbonated drink. **1984** Six *Hill 'n Holler* 4 = soft drink, sometimes referred to as a Coke. **2005** Williams *Gratitude* 139 Back then, they called all soft dranks [sic] "Co-coalies" or "dopes."

[DARE *coca-cola* B chiefly South, South Midland, Southwest]

cochan (also *coach-ann, coachie-ann*) *noun* An edible wild green (*Rudbeckia laciniata*). Same as **sochan**.

1973 *Foxfire II* 90 Tall coneflower (*Rudbeckia laciniata*) . . . (cochan, coach-ann) . . . Mrs. Hershel Keener said, "There's a plant that grows along this branch called coachie-ann; now I don't know how you spell it, and it's got such an odor when it's cooking." **1984** Page and Wigginton *Foxfire Cookery* 172, 174 Cochan grows all up and down these branches, and *people'd eat that* . . . Cochan is a wild [plant]. You'd say it was a weed. . . . But it grows out on the branch banks and on real rich ground. It has a forked leaf, and it's always great long. After it gets grown it has a yellow flower on it like this Golden Glow. Some people likes it [to eat], and some don't.

cock[1] *noun* The female genitals.

1863 *Click CW Letters* (Aug 11) You stated in your letter that a feller cold get more fat cock then he knowed what to doo with up thare. **1944** Combs *Word-List Sthn High* 18 = pudenda muliebra. Always a vulgar term among the highlanders, no matter what it is used for. In the vulgar sense it is always applied to females, never to males. **1996** Montgomery Coll (known to Cardwell).

[DARE *cock* n[1] 1 chiefly South, South Midland]

cock[2] *noun* A small pile of hay in the field. Same as **haycock.**

1832 *McLean Diary* 14 [I] finished stacking my hay thare was 80 Cocks on the meadow. **1949** Kurath *Word Geog East US* 54 The Midland *cock*, however, is still common in the Valley of Virginia, not uncommon in Western North Carolina, and relics of it have survived in central West Virginia.

[DARE *cock* n[2] chiefly North, North Midland]

cockleburr *noun* variant forms *cuckceld bur, cuckleburr, cuclebur.*

1803 (in **1920** DeWitt *Sevier Journal* 36) (Jan 5) Cuckceld bur leaves boiled in new milk good for a snake bite. **1841** Donaldson (in **1934** Smith *Tennessean's Pronunciation* 263) *cuclebur*s. **1884** Smith *Arp Scrap Book* 72 Then there is briars and nettles and tread safts and smartsweed and pison oak and Spanish needles and cuckle burrs and dog fennel and snakes. **1967** *DARE Survey* (Maryville TN) *cuckleburr* = wild bush with bunches of round, prickly seeds. **1991** Thomas *Sthn Appal* 215 I've drunk cuckleburr tea. You go pick ye cuckleburrs when they're dry, an' clean 'um. Git th' dried ones. An' when one ov us 'ud take a cold, mother thought that'uz the best thang fer a cold that ever wuz, wuz cuckleburr tea. And she'd make it so-o-o strong that it looked like a cuckleburr. Yes, sir, I've drunk that a menny a time. **1996–97** Montgomery Coll (known to Brown, Cardwell, Ellis, Jones, Ledford, Norris, Oliver).

[DARE at *cockleburr* n 1 chiefly South, South Midland, Southwest]

Co-cola See **Coca-cola.**

cod *noun* A testicle.

1939 Hall Coll (Saunook NC) Cod—what you've got in your britches. **1956** Hall Coll (Townsend TN) That long-codded mule. **1957** Combs *Lg Sthn High: Word-List* 22 = the scrotum. Inelegant in Highland parlance, as elsewhere, although as old as Anglo-Saxon. **c1960** Wilson Coll He won't play fair; he's always trying to kick someone in the cods. **c1980** Campbell *Memories of Smoky* 39 The ten-year-old lad, who was obviously more familiar with the anatomy of farm animals than with camera equipment, turned to his father and remarked: "Oh, look! It's got a cod."

[OED3 *cod* n[1] 4 < Old English *cod(d)*; DARE *cod* n[1] 1 chiefly South Midland]

coffeepot boiler *noun* In logging, the boiler of a steam-powered engine used to load logs onto waiting flatcars of narrow-gauge railways.

1998 Robbins *Logging Terms.*

coffee sack *noun* A large, heavy fabric bag or sack. Same as **tow sack.**

1915 Hall *Autobiog Claib Jones* 17 They had baked [the corn bread] in a salt kettle and were carrying it in a coffee sack. **1952–57** (in **1973** McDavid and McDavid *Vocab E KY* 155) = attested by 31/52 (59.6%) of E KY speakers for the Linguistic Atlas of the North Central States. **1966** Dakin *Vocab Ohio River Valley* 137 West of the *coffee sack* region of eastern Kentucky, but appearing side by side with this name in the southern Mountains and the southern and western Knobs and Bluegrass margins, are two terms common in the East. These are *grass sack* (never *sea-grass sack* in the Ohio Valley)—common around Chesapeake Bay and along the coast from Delaware to northern North Carolina—and *tow sack*—the North Carolina name. **1982** Slone *How We Talked* 26 = a burlap bag. **1989** *Matewan OHP*-28 I'd take a . . . coffee sack, a feed sack, and I'd go to the store and buy the stuff, back through the mountain. [DARE *coffee sack* n chiefly KY]

coffin (also *coffin box*) *noun* A plain wooden container, often widened at the shoulders, in which a person is buried (in traditional mountain speech preferred to *casket*, which is often considered a pretentious term).

1957 Broaddus *Vocab Estill Co KY* 14 [*Casket* is] a "newer" term for a coffin. **1965** Stubbs *Mountain-Wise* (Aug–Sept) 12 [That cliff] could be blasted out deep and wide enough for a coffin box. Then the hole could be filled up with some real hard cement. **1974** GSMNP-51:25 My daddy had lumber there. He kept it all the time to make, we called them coffins then. **1975** Montell *Ghosts Cumberland* 217 *coffin* = the chest-like container in which a corpse is interred. The folk primarily used this term rather than casket. **1980** Riggleman *WV Mtneer* 49 There were no caskets in our community. They were all homemade and were called "coffins." There was always someone in the community who would make coffins whenever someone would pass away. **1982** Ginns *Snowbird Gravy* 110 When someone died, they hauled 'em in a wagon. Just put 'em in a coffin—not a casket, now. A coffin is a different thing. It's just a wooden box, made bigger up across the shoulders. There was a man that made 'em and sold 'em. **1995** Montgomery *Coll*: *coffin* = the usual term, rarely *casket* (Cardwell).

coffin maker *noun* Formerly, a designated person in a mountain community who kept boards ready to construct a coffin of needed dimensions at short notice, because burial usually took place the day following a death.

1959 Cooper *Corpse Could Sleep* In those days, before the undertaking establishment had become an integral part of most communities of the state, most rural families depended upon their relatives and friends to give the deceased a decent burial. That was why each neighborhood had two or three men who were known as "coffin-makers." They kept dried boards especially for the purpose, together with a supply of casket necessities, and within an hour after death they went to work with plane, saw and hammer to form the casket with remarkable speed.

coffin-nail *noun* See citation.

1964 Clarkson *Lumbering in WV* 358 *coffin-nails* = cigarettes.

coffin racket *noun* See citation.

1971 Lee *My Appalachia* 78 A practice of the operators, closely related to the burial fund, was what the miners called the "coffin racket." Most of the operators carried a stock of cheap, pine-box coffins. They were covered with black cloth, lined with muslin and probably cost about $20 or $25 dollars each. When needed, they furnished one of these to a bereaved family, and charged as much as $200 dollars against the burial fund.

coffin still *noun* See citation. Same as **deadman still**.

1974 Maurer and Pearl *KY Moonshine* 116 = a small still designed to fit over two burners of a gasoline or kerosene stove.

coggled (**up**) See **cobbled up**.

Cohee (also *Coohee*, *Kohee*) *noun* Formerly, an inhabitant of or from west of the Blue Ridge Mountains, especially in Virginia.

1789 (in **1873** May *Journal* 144) (DARE) My little log hut was filled with two boats' crews of Yankees from Marietta, and a number of Kohees, belong to the [Wheeling, WV] settlement. **1815** (in **1956** Eliason *Tarheel Talk* 126) The back country people [of VA] are called "Cohees" from some of the back country people using frequently the term "quote he" and "quote she" or as they usually speak it "coo he" and "coo she." **1817** (in **1975** Higgs and Manning *Voices* 65) This snug little rivalry is beginning to bud vigorously in Virginia. The people of whom I am now writing call those east of the mountain Tuckahoes, and their country Old Virginia. They themselves are the Cohees, and their country New Virginia. **1899** Green *VA Word-Book* 96 *Coohees* = of Scotch origin "Quo'he," *Coohees* was the nickname applied to people in western Virginia, while those in the east were called "Tuckahoes." **1929** Phillips *Life and Labor* 354 J. K. Paulding noted while in the Shenandoah about 1815: "The people of whom I am now writing call those east of the mountain Tuckahoes, and their country Old Virginia. They themselves are the Cohees, and their country New Virginia" (*Letters from the South*, I, 111). He set forth at some length the contrasting cults of elegance by the one and plainness by the other. **2000** Inscoe *Appalachians and Race* 16 Forty-five years ago one of the most prominent historians of the Old South, Thomas Jefferson Wertenbaker of the University of Virginia, claimed that one of the most significant struggles in American history was played out within southern society as Appalachian backwoodsmen—"Cohees," as he called them and as they called themselves—attempted to stop the march of plantation society across a line that proceeded southward from Winchester, Virginia, to Chattanooga, Tennessee. **2006** Montgomery *Ulster to America* 41 Originally a phrase used in oral narration in some parts of Ireland (apparently especially in Donegal), whereby a person reports another's speech by "quo he," "quo she," "quo I," etc. (literally "he said," etc.) In the 18th century this habit was brought to American colonies, where it was applied to rural, less-cultivated persons in the backwoods from Virginia to the Carolinas and became a nickname for them. In the U.S. the term has only this latter sense.

coil

A *verb, noun* variant forms *querl, querril, quile, quirl, quorl*.

1867 Harris *Sut Lovingood* 53 Then he turned ontu the wommen: tole 'em how [the snakes would] quile intu thar buzzims, an' how they *wud* crawl down onder thar frock-strings, no odds how tite they tied 'em. **1895** Edson and Fairchild *TN Mts* 375 *quile*. **1913** Kephart *Our Sthn High* 278 The word coil is variously pronounced quile, querl, or quorl. **1917** Kephart *Word-List* 416 *quorl* = coil, whorl. "The *quorl* of sang roots." "That snake quorled over on its back." **1930** Thomas *Death Knell* Coil is pronounced coil, quile, or querl to suit the meaning. A metal spring coils, a snake fixing to strike quiles, and corn blades in dry weather querl. **1937** Hall *Coll* (Emerts Cove TN) The bear was all quiled up and dead. **1982** Hurst *Appal Words* 99 *quile*. **1994** Montgomery *Coll*: *quorl* (known to Cardwell). **1999** Isbell *Keepers* 9 "The 'sang roots can look like a little man," says Ted. "Got two legs, sometimes two arms, and a 'quirl' that looks like a head." **2002** Oliver *Cooking and Living* 48 At the top of the ripening watermelon is a curled stem, which the settlers called a "querril."

[perhaps influenced by *curl*; DARE *coil* v chiefly South, South Midland]

B *noun* In distilling, the long, usually spiral-shaped, copper tubing attached to the **cap** of a **still** or **cooker** and submerged in cold water, in which vaporized alcohol condenses. Same as **worm 1**.

1949 Maurer *Argot of Moonshiner* 8 = a type of condenser, usually made of twenty to forty feet of copper tubing coiled within a barrel of cold water. **1956** Hall *Coll* (Mt Sterling NC) The coils is set into what's called the flake stand, the cooling stand.

Coke See **Coca-cola B**.

cold as blixen (also *cold as blixy*) *adjective phrase* Very cold.

1966 Wilson *Coll* = very cold. **1998** *Dante OHP*-58 We opened at eleven, and it was cold as blixy. It was wintertime.

cold as blixy See **cold as blixen**.

cold-cut *adverb* See citation.

1939 Bond *Appal Dialect* 105 = really; sure enough; used intensively: "He was cold-cut tired."

colder 'n kraut *adjective phrase* See citation.

2009 Benfield *Mt Born* 130 = It's very, very cold outside. The kraut referenced here is made by fermenting cabbage in a churn. It was called "kraut," short for sauerkraut. It was canned, kept, and served cold. This expression was used almost exclusively to weather.

cold medicine *noun* Homemade whiskey See also **headache medicine**, **snakebite medicine**.

1996 Casada *Gospel Hook* 26 One of the party, "Poley" Bryson, proffered the jug and said "Mark, you need a nip of this cold medicine."

cold-nosed *adjective* Of a hunting dog: having a sensitive nose for detecting and following the faint or stale scent of an animal. See also **cold trailer**, **hot-nosed**.

1953 Hall *Coll* (Plott Creek NC) My dog is a cold-nosed dog. [My brother] John's dog is a hot-nosed dog. **1994** Montgomery *File* (known to 85-year-old man, Greenbrier TN). **2007** Plott *Story Plott Hound* 181 = term used to describe the trailing abilities of a hound. The cold-nosed dog has the capability to "strike" (or find) older, colder trails. Some of these trails could be hours, or even days old, yet the cold-nosed hound has the ability to often find it.

[DARE (at *cold nose* n) southern Appalachians]

cold pie *noun* A dish of leftover biscuits cooked in a shallow pan, split and layered with berries and sugar and then left to sit so the biscuits can absorb the sweet juice.

1996 Houk *Foods & Recipes* 84 The biscuits were layered with berries and sugar and set out overnight for "cold pie," perfectly permissible for breakfast the next morning.

cold track See **cold trail A**.

cold trail

A (also *cold track*) *noun* The track of a hunted animal whose scent has grown faint or stale.

1894 Wingfield *Big Buck* 400 The nearest we came to a deer was a cold trail. **1939** Hall *Coll* (Deep Creek NC) So they just turned [the dogs] loose as they usually did and picked up a cold trail. *Ibid.* (White Oak NC) *cold trail* = one that's been made the night before. **1953** Hall *Coll* (Plott Creek NC) What I mean by a cold track—the animal or varmint's been gone maybe eight, ten, twelve hours. **1975** GSMNP-62:3 He could trail a cold track as well as any hound. He'd open on a coon's track in daytime, just go right on with it.

B *verb phrase* Of a hunting dog: to follow (a hunted animal) by picking up and following a stale or faint scent.

1939 Hall *Coll* (Deep Creek NC) We had some dogs, some bear dogs, and we went on and we trailed, cold-trailed 'em, right onto the side of Shanty Mountain. **1960** Burnett *My Valley* 147 Later, he would go along with the cold-trailing pack until the trail became fresher, and somewhat suddenly he seemed to understand what it was all about.

[DARE *cold-trail* v 1 chiefly South Midland]

cold trailer *noun* A hunting dog that can pick up a **cold trail** and quietly follow the scent of a hunted animal. See also **cold-nosed**, **trail dog**.

1939 Hall *Coll* (Cataloochee NC) A cold trailer won't make any noise. *Ibid.* (White Oak NC) Some cold trailers can follow trails two or three days old. Some cold trailers won't bark hardly ever. They're not plumb silent. They'll bark once in a while.

colic *noun* Appendicitis. Same as **cramp colic 1**.

1986 Pederson et al. *LAGS* = attested by 3/60 interviewees (5%) from E TN and 1/35 (2.9%) from N GA; 4/13 of all LAGS interviewees (30.8%) attesting term were from Appalachia.

colic ball *noun* The fruit of the **buffalo nut**.

1975 Hamel and Chiltoskey *Cherokee Plants* 27 Buffalo nut, colic ball, oilnut . . . Chew nut to make vomit for colic.

collar

A *noun* See citation.

1968 *End of Moonshining* 49 = the connection for the cap and the body of the still.

B *verb* Same as **dead C**. See also **dead ring**.

1980 Brewer *Hit's Gettin'* Several acres of "collared" or "girdled" trees is a "deadening."

collarmoggis *noun* A joking name for diarrhea (i.e. cholera morbus).

1968 Clarke *Stuart's Kentucky* 188 The abundant apples tempted *younguns* to eat too many when they were too green, sometimes causing summer complaint or collarmoggis.

collogue *verb* To conspire, intrigue, discuss confidentially or surreptitiously.

1904–20 Kephart *Notebooks* 2:457. **a1954** Adams *Word-List* = [to] conspire. **1996–97** Montgomery *Coll* (known to Bush, Oliver).

[perhaps < French *colloque* "conference, consultation"; CUD *collogue* v "talk privately and confidentially, often implying scheming and conspiring"; DARE *collogue* v 1 chiefly South Midland]

colored pine *noun*.

1986 Pederson et al. *LAGS* (Cumberland Co TN).

coltsfoot *noun* Same as **galax**.

1894 Bergen *Plant Names III* 94 (Banner Elk NC). **1975** Broome *Out under Smokies* 214 Some of the mountain people call the galax "coltsfoot," in a vivid reference to the shape of its leaves. **a1975** Lunsford *It Used to Be* 69 When you go pretty far back in the coves there's a vocation that is peculiar to the high reaches of the Blue Ridge Mountains, and that's the gathering of an unusual plant called galax. There's a place up in Virginia close to the North Carolina line called Galax,—Galax, Virginia. Following the Blue Ridge clear on through Mt. Mitchell, on the higher elevations this plant is found. The old folk name for it would be "coltsfoot." The higher up you go into the Blue Ridge, the larger the leaves, and, in colder weather and in the spring, they turn bronze. They're used for decorations and so on in many places. In the Blue Ridge section especially they're gathered by mountaineers along with locothia, locothia spray or dog-hobble, and other evergreens, and shipped.

[from the shape of the leaf]

column *noun* variant forms *colyum, colyumn, kolyum*.

c1960 Wilson *Coll* = often *colyum*. **1966** Medford *Ol' Starlin* 119 Mr. J. H. Trantham, of Shee-cawgo, informs Unkle Abe that there wuz 2 mis-spelled wurds in this kolyum week before last. **1978** Montgomery *White Pine Coll* I-1. **2013** Venable *How to Tawlk* 10 Sam Venable's colyumn in the *News Sentinel* runs Tuesdays, Thursdays, Fridays and Sundays.

colyum, colyumn See **column**.

comb *noun* The crest of a roof; the pole along this crest. See also **cone**.

1824 (in **1912** Doddridge *Notes on Settlement* 136) The roof was formed by making the end logs shorter, until a single log formed the comb of the roof. **1886** Smith *Southernisms* 37 *Comb* of a house, i.e. "apex of a roof," the ridge ... is very common in the South. **1939** Siler *Cherokee Lore* 17 Members of the third, fourth, and fifth generation are today living under the board roof upheld with long and slender poplar poles which are fastened together in the "comb" by wooden pins. **1959** Hall *Coll* (Murphy NC) She heard her mother say that the panthers would sit on the comb of the house and holler. **1978** Glassie *Sthn Mt Cabin* 402 The cabin's gabled roof is formed with simple rafters butted at the ridge—the "comb"—either on each other or on a plank ridge pole—both of these roof framing methods were common in medieval England; the latter was usual in Scotland and Ireland.

[DARE *comb* n B2 (Scots and nEngl dialect) chiefly Midland, occasionally South]

comb grave *noun* See citations.

1993 Montell *Cumberland Country* 117 Stone grave coverings include the rectangular "box grave," resembling an above-ground vault. Grave houses of this variety are often termed "peaked graves," "slab graves," "sandstone graves," "cattle rocks," "hog troughs," and "comb graves." Although they are sparsely located in certain parts of Alabama, Arkansas, and Texas, these traditional prismatic grave structures more than any other single cultural feature lend uniqueness to the folk cemeteries in the Upper Cumberland Valley. **2014** Finch *TN Comb Graves* 1–2 A "Comb grave" is a burial that features a grave cover made, normally, of two rectangular slabs of two stones leaned together to form a gable roof over the grave. The term "comb" signifies the "crest or ridge of a roof" (OED, 1971). . . . "Comb grave" is the name used by stonecutters and known users of this traditional style of grave cover, and its essential form is that of a gable roof set directly on the grave, with no supporting walls. The above-ground space beneath the "roof" is normally that of a simple triangular prism. Most comb graves feature a headstone that is separate from the comb structure, and some have both head and footstones. . . . In Tennessee, over 3,250 combs are found in 400 cemeteries scattered along a NNE-SSW-trending band paralleling the western front of the Cumberland Plateau.

comb one's hair/wool *verb phrase* To scold severely.

1927 Woofter *Dialect from WV* 351 *comb his wool* = to find fault with; to scold: "Your mother will comb your wool well when she hears of this." **1938** Stuart *Dark Hills* 281 I promised her I'd be back ... by nine o'clock. It's nearly ten now. She'll comb my hair, Jesse.

com'd See **come**.

come *verb*

A Principal parts.

1 variant past-tense forms *com, com'd, come, comed*.

1790 *Lenoir Papers* [I] stayd there tell Friday and then i come to M[r]. Benj. Birds. **1826** Royall *Sketches* 58 But, to return to my Grison Republic; [they say] "the two ens of it comed loose." **1834** Crockett *Narrative* 156 I put in, and waded on till I come to the channel, where I crossed that on a high log. **c1841** Shane (in **1998** Perkins *Border Life* 197) We come to Lexington in October. **1862** *Epperly CW Letters* (May 12) the ball went in near his mouth and com out just befar his ear. **1863** *Bradshaw CW Letters* (Feb 2) he aught to have given the rest of us furlows and let him a wated untill his turn come. **1881** Pierson *In the Brush* 261 All them chil'en of Israel fellers jest shouted and chased 'em clean over the mountain into a valley, and then com'd back and got all their camp-plunder. **1910** Cooke *Power and Glory* 82 We had to find money for the undertaker, when he come to lay her out. **1939** Hall *Coll* (Cataloochee NC) He just laid his gun down, went right in with the dogs, and here come the bear down the tree just jumping down thataway. **1954** GSMNP-19:5 All at once something come dashing in a dark thicket. It may have been a bear, but I thought it was a wolf or something or other. I heard some funny scream, and I went up a tree. **1961** *Coe Ridge OHP-343A* His father come from North Carolina after the Civil War. **1972** *AOHP/ALC-355* They comed and helped me a little bit. **1973** GSMNP-5:12 These women [and] children would all bunch at one place, and they would put me in the front room, and so if any boogers come they would get me first. **1977** McGreevy *Breathitt KY Grammar* 93 *comed* = attested by 1 speaker. **1990** *Matewan OHP-73* They wasn't no doctors that come out. **2007** McMillon *Notes* They comed.

2 variant past-participle forms *came, comed*.

1787 *Sinking Creek Church Minutes* I:2 Sum of the Churches had not came to the Rules that Sum of you that Sum among you Desire they Should Come to all. **1862** *Robinson CW Letters* (Sept 24) we are driving them through Caintuckey & we have came in 8 miles of them. **1864** *McGill CW Letters* (May 22) I have came to the conclusion That you wer all gon back north. **1939** Hall *Coll* (Deep Creek NC) There had came a water spout. **1961** *Coe Ridge OHP-337B* He'd comed in about, his grandfather wouldn't cut the wood. **1978** Montgomery *White Pine Coll* V-2 He could have just came from a party. **1989** *Matewan OHP-22* People had came out of the south and different places.

B Syntax.

1 with inversion of the verb and the subject, thus *come snow* = when or if snow arrives or arrived; the verb in such a usage may be viewed as a quasi-preposition = by, about.

1913 Kephart *Our Sthn High* 78 You remember the big storm three year ago, come grass, when the cattle all huddled up a-top o' each other and friz in one pile, solid. **1935** Sheppard *Cabins in Laurel* 64 Two of us children was Democrats and two Republicans, so we just killed each other's votes regular, come election. **1941** Still *Troublesome Creek* 30 "Come that time" Mother said, "maybe we'll have plenty saved for a house." **1956** Hall *Coll* (Big Bend NC) In the fall we fatten [hogs] on corn. We kill 'em in November when it gets good and cold, maybe come a snow. **1974** Fink *Bits Mt Speech* 4 = by or about. "They'll git here *come* night." **1976** Lindsay *Grassy Balds* 37 Them fellers out of Cades Cove [would] go up and feed 'em [= cattle] come a snow. **2004** Fisher *Kettle Bottom* 80 It was a law among the roof miners that, come a roof fall, you run.

[DARE *come* v B5 especially South Midland]

2 in an existential clause (with or without the overt marker *there* or *it*).

1937 Hall *Coll* (Cades Cove TN) I had a good barn there [at the Spence Place on top of Smoky] until come a wind storm and blowed it down. *Ibid.* (Copeland Creek TN) When come a snow, I run from Mother's to the first house in my bare feet. **1939** Hall *Coll* (Hazel Creek NC) In the spring of the year come a spell of snow and it covered the cattle up, lots of 'em, nearly covered 'em up with snow, and they was lots of 'em died. *Ibid.* (Smokemont NC) They come a big rain and washed the old foot bridge plumb into the hallway between the barns. **1961** *Coe Ridge OHP-343A* [If] it come a rain you's just out of the luck. **1982** Weals *Andy Greer* I was with him when it came that snow. **1983** *Dark Corner OHP-4A* [When] it come a ordinary rain, it wouldn't get wet in there and mold it. **1999** Morgan *Gap Creek* 159 There was a pause and the fire popped and whined, like it was coming a rain or even snow.

3 in conjunctive phrases *how come it, how come me*, etc. See **how come.**

C Senses.

1 To approach (an age).

c1960 Wilson *Coll*: *coming twenty* (or some other age) = about to be, especially of animals.

2 To develop.

1991 Thomas *Sthn Appal* 133 After ye git ye clay, wy, ye haff to git ever—if they'uz a grit in it as big as a corn grain, it'ud cause ye ware to come a crack in it.

come a little bit of (also *come a little to, come an ace of, come as nigh as a p, come as nigh as pease, come in a bean, come in a one, come in a pea, come in one, come nigh as a pea, come within one of*) *verb phrase* To come very close to or barely miss (doing something).

1901 Harben *Westerfelt* 131 Marthy come as nigh as pease a-doin' of it, her maw said. **1931** Combs *Lg Sthn High* 1304 He come as nigh as a p gittin' thar. **1938** Stuart *Dark Hills* 388 "I've come in a one havin' a lot of fights over you." **1940** Stuart *Trees of Heaven* 107 You come in one gittin lost. **1959** Roberts *Up Cutshin* 14 You talk about white-eyeing on the job[,] I come in a pea a-doing it on my first job in the mines. **c1960** Wilson *Coll*: *come in* (or *within*) *one of* = to come close to doing something that would have been embarassing or worse. **1968** Clarke *Stuart's Kentucky* 103 In "One of the Lost Tribe" a boy closely resembling Jesse Stuart at the age killed a snake with his bare hands, choked a groundhog that come nigh as a pea tearing his guts out. **1975** *AOHP/ALC-903* I just come a little to whipping him in that restaurant. **1989** *Matewan OHP-23* I come a little bit of beating him. **2005** Williams *Gratitude* 149 [The mother hen] come in a bean a-drowndin' herself a-tryin' t'take kyerr a them diddles. **2014** Williams *Coll*: *I come an ace of hitting that dog* = "I almost hit that dog."

come a little to See **come a little bit of.**

come along (also *come on, come up*) *verb phrase* Of a person: to grow up.

1939 Hall *Coll* (Smokemont NC) I've been here in these mountains ever since I reared up, just come up. **1957** Parris *My Mts* 55 It was a right peart community back sixty years ago when I come along. *Ibid.* 70 When I was comin' along our table had just as much on it at breakfast as dinner, which was a heap. *Ibid.* 154 Back when I was comin' on matches was scarce. Cost a heap of money too. **1973** GSMNP-83:5 I come up the hard way. **1983** McDermitt *Boy Named Jack* 5 I learned the tales as I come up. **1994–97** Montgomery *Coll*: *come on* (known to Brown, Ellis, Jones, Ledford,

Oliver); *come up* (known to Cardwell). **2007** McMillon *Notes: come on* = to grow up. **2008** *Rosie Hicks* 1 When I come up, I think they's almost dead then.

[DARE *come up* v phr 4 both chiefly South, South Midland]

come an ace of See **come a little bit of.**

come and go along See **come and go home with me.**

come and go home with me (also *come and go along, come go home with me, come go with us, come home with me*) *phrase* Come see me (used as an invitation to visit, issued by a guest when departing). See also **go home with us, stay all night, you'uns come.**

1925 Greer-Petrie *Angeline Hill Country* 83 Down in Happy Oaks, we alluz ax everyone presint to "Come go home with us!" **1933** Thomas *Traipsin' Woman* 20 Then flicking the rope bridle on the neck of the mule, he spoke in a low, matter-of-fact voice, "You all," including me with a look of his sad eyes, "you all best come home with me." He pressed his knees against the muddy sides of the mule and rode slowly on his sorrowful mission. **1957** Neel *Backwoodsman* ix While the mountaineer may appear shy, reserved and inhospitably cold around a stranger, he is all warmth and hospitality with his own kind. No matter how brief the chance meeting with another, he will likely say in parting: "Come and go along. He does not expect you to accompany him, but he gives the invitation—even when his destination is secret. He may say: "You fellers come!" That is, you are invited to visit him in his home. "Fellers" is all-inclusive, and means your entire family. **1959** Pearsall *Little Smoky* 153 Smaller groups [going home from school] turn off at each side trail with the customary parting invitation, "Come go home with us." **1959–60** Stubbs *Mountain-Wise* (Dec–Jan) 7 There is always a show of hospitality. The newcomer is invariably invited to come into the house or to take a chair on the porch. The stock expression on departure: "Come go home with me," does not mean that I expect you to do so now, but rather: "Come when you can." **1993** Ison and Ison *Whole Nother Lg* 11 *come and go home with me* = expression of departure, usually not a serious invitation. **2003** Onchuck *Mud Pie Memories* 127 It was just common courtesy to let guests know their visit had been appreciated. Protesting their leaving was considered good manners and I can still recall how the visitors would then reciprocate with a homey reply, "Ya otta jest come go with us." **2010** *Blind Pig* (June 10) Two "goodbyes" that we've heard all our lives [are] "Come go home with me" (said by the folks who are leaving) and "You ought to just spend the night" (said by the folks who you've been visiting with).

come as nigh as a p, come as nigh as pease See **come a little bit of.**

come back on *verb phrase* Of a person: to return in order to provoke (one).

1939 Hall *Coll* (Big Creek NC) Don't never come back on me no more.

come by *verb phrase*

1 To obtain, acquire.

1924 (in **1952** Mathes *Tall Tales* 25) He had not come by his sobriquet "Draggin' Ellick" by accident. **1957** Parris *My Mts* 154 Nobody much bothered with store-bought tobacco in them days. Fact was, it was hard to come by at stores hereabouts. **1978** *Smokies Heritage* 107 In an area where most work was of the swap-out variety (you help me and I'll help you), nothing was harder to come by than cash money.

[DARE *come by* v phr 1 chiefly South Midland]

2 To pay a brief visit.

1989 *Matewan OHP-86* They come by and asked me one time about a job. **1998** *Dante OHP-25* Doctor McNeil come by you know off of a call and he knocked on the door. **2013** Shedlarz *Rosa Hicks* 4 [The] weather was a little rough, you know. We didn't have many people to come by.

[DARE *come by* v phr 2 chiefly South, South Midland]

come-by-chance (also *come-by-chance child*) *noun* Usually of a child: one of doubtful legitimacy.

1835 Crockett *Account* 89 Squire Williams, my neighbor, said he didn't think so: [nullification] was a kind of come-by-chance, that was too wicked to know its own kin. **1868** (in **1974** Harris *High Times* 191) I dusent suckil cum by chance childer. **1995–97** Montgomery *Coll* (known to Brown, Cardwell).

[DARE *come-by-chance* n chiefly New England, South, South Midland]

come-by-chance child See **come-by-chance.**

come clear *verb phrase* To be freed of or escape legal conviction, be exonerated.

1861 *Watson CW Letters* (Oct 29) S I Calhoun came clare of killing crane. **1863** *Sexton CW Letters* (Nov 12) if he will come rite on he will come clear for bad Robert Mccar mick has come and has come clear and is out of the guard House. **1913** Kephart *Our Sthn High* 193 He will "come clear" in court because every fellow on the jury feels he would have done the same thing himself under similar provocation. **1973** *AOHP/ASU-69* He took an appeal to the [NC] Supreme Court for a new trial, and they granted him a new trial, and the next trial he come clear. **1989** *Matewan OHP-23* [The judge] said, "Well, I'm going to hold that against you. If you ever do anything else, I'm going to give you double time," so I come clear. **1994–97** Montgomery *Coll* (known to eight consultants from the Smoky Mountains).

comed See **come A1, A2.**

come down dusky *verb phrase* Of daylight: to come to an end.

1937 Hall *Coll* (Cosby TN) Hit began to come down dusky. The sun was a-settin. **1992** Montgomery *Coll* (known to Shields).

come fresh See **fresh C1.**

come go home with me See **come and go home with me.**

come grass See **grass.**

come home with me See **come and go home with me.**

come honest by *verb phrase* To inherit legitimately.

1940 Bowman *KY Mt Stories* 236 = to inherit.

come in *verb phrase* Of a cow: to calve and therefore to begin producing milk. See also **fresh C1, D.**

1915 Dingus *Word-List VA* 182 = to calve. **1963** Watkins and Watkins *Yesterday* 79 Most quarrels were soon forgotten, and the next time the cow of one of the two "went dry," the other kept him in milk until the cow had a calf and "come in." **1968** *DARE Survey* (Brasstown NC) = when a cow has a calf, "She's come in." **1996** Johnson *Lexical Change* 138 *come in, come in fresh* = statistically more common in the mountains of South Carolina and Georgia than in the Piedmont and Coastal Plain c1990. **1996** Montgomery *Coll* My cow will come in soon (known to Cardwell). **2005** Williams *Gratitude* 486 When a cow gave birth, or "come in," she was said to have *found a calf*, or *come in frash* (*fresh, frush*).

come in a bean, come in a one, come in a pea See **come a little bit of.**

come in fresh See **fresh C1.**

come in one See **come a little bit of.**

come it *verb phrase* To manage, be able to do something.

1917 Kephart *Word-List* 411 I love strong coffee, but when I get on the down-go, I cain't hardly come it. **1956** McAtee *Some Dial NC* 9 = to be able to eat. "I can't come it." **1972** Cooper *NC Mt Folklore* 93 *I can't come it* = I can't eat more. **c1982** Young *Colloquial Appal* 4 *can't come it* = can't do it. **2008** Terrell *Mt Lingo* Someone who had eaten his fill might refuse more food by simply saying "I can't come it."

come nigh as a pea See **come a little bit of.**

come-off *noun* A result, outcome, especially an unfortunate or unexpected one.

1938 Justus *No-End Hollow* 65 "That's just a come-off for you," she said. "You never let on what ails you." **1943** Justus *Bluebird* 45 Well, if that's not a come-off for certain! **1979** Carpenter *Walton War* 175 Hit was a sorry repayment fer all I had done fer him and I told him hit was a poor come off. **1999** Morgan *Gap Creek* 49 "This is a fine come off," Mama said, "after your Papa died in the spring."

[DARE *come-off* n 1 South, South Midland]

come on *verb phrase*

1 See **come along.**

2 Of a person: to proceed (with redundant *on*; see also **on C1**).

1861 *Lance CW Letters* (Nov 10) I thought he was comeing on all the time. **1939** Hall *Coll* (Deep Creek NC) He come on up, and the first word he said to me, "Well," he says, "Cathey," he says. *Ibid.* (Smokemont NC) We decided we'd make our way back to the house, and as we come on in, we met up with two more fellows ... then we come on in home and dressed them up and laid down and took a nap ... we shot [the raccoon] off, come on about a half a mile or three quarter and dogs struck. **1963** Edwards *Gravel* 104 When dinner was ready Gabe yelled for us to wash our hands and faces at the spring and come on to dinner. **1969** *GSMNP-42*: 38 Well, they come on down there then to next house ... old man Wilson come on out there [and] Aunt Rosie. **1975** Screven *John B Wright* 14 I come on down until it got a little louder, till I could hear it. **1989** *Matewan OHP-11* Then my father decided we'd just take number seven and come on to Williamson and we stayed here with my Uncle, Jacob Shine. **1998** *Dante OHP-29* I come on out and went on down to the doctor's office.

3 Of the weather or a specified event: to arrive, become prevalent. See also **come C2, come on for.**

1913 Kephart *Our Sthn High* 297 I had in head to plow to-day, but hit's come on to rain. **1940** Haun *Hawk's Done* 42 When cold weather come on he would tell me to move his chair up in front of the fireplace. **1958** Campbell *Tales* 65–66 He don't wear no shoes but when it comes on cold [weather]. **1962** Hall *Coll* (Cades Cove TN) [Uncle Noah Burchfield] was one of the most highly honored men of this county because of his integrity, character. [He was] hard down on lawlessness.... He was ten year old when the Civil War came on. **1974** Fink *Bits Mt Speech* 4 I went in the house when it *come on to* rain. **1978** Parris *Mt Cooking* 210 Until lemons come on here in the mountains, folks used vinegar instead of lemon juice [in making cough syrup]. **1983** *Dark Corner OHP-26A* That war come on, and up there on the Shankle place beyond where the school was ... they [= the army] shot them big, great big shells, four-inch [shells for artillery practice]. **1994** Montgomery *Coll* (known to Cardwell). **1997** Montgomery *Coll* My chickens are coming on with eggs (Brown).

4 To fare, manage; to feel (usually in the greeting "How do you come on?").

c1863 (in **1992** Jackson *Surry Co Soldiers* 251) Let me know how all my friends is coming on. **1863** *Sexton CW Letters* (March 24) Write how all the connection are coming on. **1873** Smith *Arp Peace Papers* 25 How do you come on with your stone fleet? **1895** Edson and Fairchild *TN Mts* 371 *come on*: for do. (Most common salutation.) "How do you come on?" **1925** Greer-Petrie *Angeline Hill Country* 84 Lum, thinkin' he was the Sennater, shuck his hand and axt him how he come on? **1937** Hyatt *Kiverlid* 35 "How do you come on this evenin' Granny?" inquired Nancy, as she entered the big house. **1967** *DARE Survey* (Cumberland Gap TN) How do you come on today? **1996** Montgomery *Coll* How do you come on today? (Cardwell).

[DARE *come on* v phr 3 chiefly South Midland]

come on for *verb phrase* To advance or develop (adverse or unfavorable weather). See also **come C2, come on 3.**

1988 Smith *Fair and Tender* 32 Yesterdy when I was the one hauling the water, it was coming on for dark.

come out the little end of the horn *verb phrase* See citation.

1931 Combs *Lg Sthn High* 1307 He come out o' the leetle end o' the horn. (Unsuccessful in a trade.)

[DARE (at *horn* n B8b) southern Appalachians]

come through *verb phrase* To experience spiritual or religious conversion, show religious enthusiasm (as by shouting), profess religious experience, especially at a revival service. See also **break through**, **mourners' bench**, **pray through**, **pull through**, **through C1**.

1895 Edson and Fairchild *TN Mts* 371 Here's a mourner just *come through*, an' wants to give his experience before the church. **1924** Raine *Saddlebags* 197 Then, after prolonged and sometimes intense wrestling in prayer, he "comes through," receiving assurance of salvation, preferably by some notable or strange token. **1948** Dick *Dixie Frontier* 190 Hand-shaking or kissing was very cordial when someone was converted, or "came through," as they called it. **1959** Pearsall *Little Smoky* 113 The meeting was winding up with singing and general participation, some weeping, others shouting and happy, repeating "Sweet name of Jesus." . . . Finally two penitents "came through for Jesus," and all rose, happy, gay, laughing, greeting fellow Christians as the group began to disperse. **1974** Fink *Bits Mt Speech* 4 Did John *come through* at the meetin' last night? **1994** Montgomery *Coll* (known to Shields).

[DARE *come through* v phr 1 chiefly South, South Midland]

come to borrow a chunk of fire, **come to borrow fire coals**, **come to fetch fire** See **come to borrow fire**.

come to borrow fire (also *come to borrow a chunk of fire*, *come to borrow fire coals*, *come to fetch fire*) *verb phrase* To pay a brief visit, be impatient to leave.

1904–20 Kephart *Notebooks* 4:723 "Did ye come to bory firecoals?" That's the common word with us when a body 'pears to be in a hurry. **1931** Combs *Lg Sthn High* 1307 Have you come to borry far (fire) that ye're in sech a hurry? **1976** Dwyer *Southern Sayin's* 5 *come to fetch fire* = to come and leave at once. **1995–97** Montgomery *Coll*: *come to borrow fire* (known to Adams, Brown, Bush, Ledford, Norris, Weaver); What's the hurry? Have you come to borrow fire? (Cardwell); *come to fetch fire* (Adams, Brown, Bush, Weaver). **2007** McMillon *Notes* Did ye come to borry a chunk of fire?

[DARE *fire, come to borrow* v phr especially South Midland]

come to one's milk *verb phrase* See citation.

1927 Woofter *Dialect from WV* 351 = to do what must be done, either willingly or unwillingly through the force of necessity: "That boy will come to his milk soon."

come up *verb phrase*

1 See **come along**.

2 To move; to urge a draft animal on (as an imperative).

1949 Kurath *Word Geog East US* 43 We find the regional call *come up!* from the Virginia Piedmont westward and southward, but not on the Southern coast. **1966** *DARE Survey* (Cherokee NC) = to make a horse go faster. **1994** Montgomery *Coll* (known to Shields). **2005** Bailey *Henderson County* 83 Bub slapped the reins across the backs of the mules, and "Come up, Bill, John!" signaled the start of his long, slow return to Pinnacle Mountain.

[DARE *come up* v phr 1 chiefly South, South Midland]

comfort *noun*

1 A heavy bedcover, often a quilt, with a cotton filling, a comforter.

1862 *Tesh CW Letters* (Nov 2) Tell Miss Rebeca Brann I want her to make me a Knit Comfort. **1949** Kurath *Word Geog East US* 61 The thick cotton-padded quilt is known as a *comfort* in the Midland and the South, as a *comforter* or as a *comfortable* in the North. **1952–57** (in **1973** McDavid and McDavid *Vocab E KY* 152) *comfort* = heavy tied quilt. **1967** *DARE Survey* (Gatlinburg TN) = a padded covering used on a bed, mostly for warmth. **1968** Wilson *Folklore Mammoth Cave* 34 (or *comforter* or *tacked quilt*) = all these terms were used for a bed cover that was filled with cotton and tacked rather than quilted in a set pattern; usually it was of solid cloth and not "pieced."

[DARE *comfort* n 1 chiefly South, South Midland]

2 (also *comforter*) A woolen scarf. Same as **neck comfort**.

1862 *Shockley CW Letters* (March 21) my other comfort and gloves will last another winter unless I wear them more than I have this. **1862** *Watters-Curtis CW Letters* (Feb 15) the doctor giv me that cumpfort that mr Burger braut you and a blanket and i thought i Would Send it to you. **1901** Harben *Westerfelt* 290 Peter smiled grimly and went to the mantelpiece for his foul-smelling comforter.

comforter See **comfort 2**.

commence (+ *to* + *verbal noun*) *verb phrase* To begin, start. [Editor's note: This verb followed by either an infinitive or a simple verbal noun is widespread in the US, but is probably old-fashioned.]

1939 Hall *Coll* (Deep Creek NC) The dogs come in behind him and commenced to catching him [= a bear]. **1961** *Coe Ridge OHP-340B* He commenced to calling his mother and all of them. **1969** *GSMNP-27:10* He [= my father] was a-climbing that hill just like one thing, he says, when he commenced to cussing up a storm. **1973** *AOHP/LJC-296* I commenced to mining in sixteen at Riverside. **1983** *Dark Corner OHP-5A* I commenced to shooting, went around [the house].

commencement party *noun* A wedding shower.

2004 Mays *Passion* 76 When word got around about the upcoming marriage, all the members of the traveling group decided to give them a "commencement party," or wedding shower.

common *adjective*

1 Usual, ordinary, average (usually in phrases about one's health or well-being: thus, *as well as common* = as well as usual, (about) *like common* = like usual; *past common* = beyond the usual).

1842 *McLean Diary* 75 The River has Bin higher than Comon. **1861** *Sutton CW Letters* (Oct 17) James Turpin and Allen are both with us and they are both in common health. **1862** *Kendrick CW Letters* (Sept 29) I am as well as common onley tierd from the fatigue of my long trip. **1864** Poteet *CW Letters* (Aug 21) I am only in Comon health at this time. **1900** Harben *N GA Sketches* 60 I hope you are as well as common, Henry? **1908** Smith *Reminiscences* 435 This far it had been, as Husky said, "cooler'n common, plumb cool for the season o' the year." **1925** Dargan *Highland Annals* 189 She came in one day to tell me of an incident that had amused her "past common." **1949** Hall Coll They are feeling as well as common. **1975** Chalmers *Better* 66 If her health was about as usual, she would say she was "sortie like common." **1976** Garber *Mountainese* = in average health. "How air ye Jed?" "Oh, I'm jist common Seth, jist common." **2005** Williams *Gratitude* 487 = usual. The question, "How are you?" is usually answered with, "About like common."

[Web3 *common* adj 4c Midland; DARE *common* adj 2 chiefly South Midland, occasionally New England]

2 Especially of a person: unpretentious, approachable, down to earth. [Editor's note: The sense "uncultured, ill-bred" in reference to a person is not unknown in Southern Appalachia, but is primarily found in the Deep South.]

1913 Morley *Carolina Mts* 175 When you hear one of your friends spoken of by a highlander as being "common" you are puzzled, to say the least, until you learn that the word is the most complimentary possible, retaining its original meaning as understood when we speak of the "common people," the "common good." **1924** Raine *Saddlebags* 105 "He's a mighty *common* man" (affable, mingles with folk as an equal). **1931** Owens *Speech Cumberlands* 90 = friendly, hospitable: "I like to go to Taylors'; they're sich common folks." **c1945** Haun *Hawk's Done* 211 There hain't no commoner man living than old man Fuller. **1956** Hall Coll (Waynesville NC) There's a millionaire, but he's just as common as a shoe. **1970** Roberts and Roberts *Time Stood Still* For a lawyer or a banker or, indeed, anyone to succeed here, his door must be open. "He's a mighty common man" is the local way of saying that a man mingles with others as an equal. Mountain people are quick to recognize affectation. **1978** Montgomery *White Pine Coll* X-2 He has a little farm there and raised them up, very, very common boys. **1984** Wilder *You All Spoken* 9 = unassuming; without put-on or airs; ordinary. "When you come right down to it, our governor is jist as common as you and me." **1986** Pederson et al. *LAGS* = attested by 13/60 interviewees (21.7%) from E TN and 2/35 (5.7%) from N GA; 15/77 of all LAGS interviewees (19.4%) attesting term were from Appalachia. **2005** Bailey *Henderson County* 36 The best way to get into the community where Will Benton lived was to be born there, unless, by nature, you were in such complete accord with the inhabitants that they found you "common." **2007** McMillon *Notes* = said of a person who will do anything for you.

[DARE *common* adj 1 chiefly South Midland]

common school *noun* A free public school.

1973 *AOHP/ASU-69* [Our children] just got a common-school education coming up. **1983** Jones *Sin-Eater* v-vi After the formation of the state of West Virginia, laws were passed for the establishment of a free public school system and for compulsory attendance of school-age children who lived within two miles of a school. Because of the deplorable means of transportation and communication at that time, little effort was made by state officials for several years to implement the legislation with any uniform enforcement procedures. Nevertheless, within a few decades what became known as common schools, or one-room rural schools, rose literally by the hundreds throughout the region.

communion meeting *noun* Same as **sacrament meeting**.

1843 *Paw Paw Hollow Church Minutes* 117 Church ordered that Elders I Kimbrough Layman Tipton Langford and Hodges be invited to our communion meeting to be protracted in October. **1995** McCauley *Mt Religion* 177 The initial divisions of the early seventeenth-century "sacramental season" or communion meeting were a penitential fast on Thursday, preparatory sermons on Saturday, distribution of the communion elements (which could continue for up to twelve hours) on Sunday, and a thanksgiving service on Monday.

companion *noun* A wife.

1939 Hall Coll = wife. **1967** *DARE Survey* (Greenville SC) [He] got himself a companion.

company room *noun* The living room of a dwelling.

1984 Burns *Cold Sassy* 25 At first Miss Love stayed at Granny and Grandpa's house, in their company room.

completest *adjective* Best, most complete.

1937 Hall Coll (Little Cataloochee NC) Tom Barnes was the completest hunter I was ever acquainted with.

co-nan, **coo-nannie**, **coo-sheepie** See **co-sheep**.

concern *verb* variant form *consarn*; hence past participle/adjective *consarned* = damned.

1792 *Richland Church Minutes* 144 the Church met and after prayer to God . . . held a conference consarning the matter in hand with Bro Magee. **1859** Taliaferro *Fisher's River* 133 My old inimy were perfectly satisfied with me, and let me truckle off and save my bacon, so fur as he were consarned. **1891** Murfree *Stranger People* 130 I never knowed you-uns ter be consarned in sech ez moonshinin'. **1925** Furman *Glass Window* 52 I'm that consarned to keep a breath of air from getting to her. **1950** Dalton *Wordlist Sthn KY* 23 Keep your nose out of things that don't consarn you. **1985** Jones *Travail* That sallet ain't as good as that we used to get down there where they put in that consarned road.

conclude (also *konclude*) *verb* To decide, calculate.

1863 *Hundley CW Letters* (July 19) As I have an opportunity I have concluded to write you a few lines. **1873** Smith *Arp Peace Papers* 19 A few of us boys have koncluded to write you, and ax for a little more time. **1937** Hall Coll (Emerts Cove TN) He concluded he'd have to get to stay there. **1972** *Graham County* 138 Hit made me so all fired mad that I concluded I would jest kick that cat up the chimney. **1994** McCarthy *Jack Two Worlds* 36 He found out where the Old Rich Man kept his money, and he concluded he's going to help hisself to some of it.

condenser *noun* See citations.

1949 Maurer *Argot of Moonshiner* 9 = copper tubing used to condense alcohol vapor. Sometimes one tube enclosed within another of larger diameter. In some localities, a copper pipe laid lengthwise in a trough of spring water: "That condenser acts like they ain't no baffles in it." **a1975** Lunsford *It Used to Be* 83 The "condenser" is where the water runs around the worm, condenses it.

cone *noun* The crest of a roof. See also **comb**.

1957 Broaddus *Vocab Estill Co KY* 19.

[DARE *cone* n 1 chiefly West Midland]

Confederate War *noun* The American Civil War. Same as **War between the States**.

1939 Hall *Coll* (Cherokee NC) We lived there till in the time of the Confederate War. It was the last of the Confederate War. **1963** Stubbs *Mountain-Wise* (April–May) 9 Did you know it was three North Carolinians that lost the Confederate War? **1973** Kahn *Hillbilly Women* 118 He lived to be ninety-six years old. And he fought in the Confederate War. **1986** Pederson et al. *LAGS* (Habersham Co GA, Towns Co GA, Hamilton Co TN, Knox Co TN). **1996–97** Montgomery *Coll* (known to Adams, Bush, Cypher, Hooper, Oliver, Weaver). **1999** Morgan *Gap Creek* 89 Since I was a little girl I'd heard stories about the Confederate War. **2002** Rash *Foot in Eden* 10–11 I took a right turn and passed another field where men once laid horses during what folks up here still spoke of as the Confederate War.

[DARE *Confederate War* n chiefly South Atlantic]

confidence *verb* To trust, believe in. Same as **confident B**.

1917 Kephart *Word-List* 410 = to place confidence in. "I don't *confidence* these dogs much." **1931–33** (in **1987** Oliver and Oliver *Sketches* 24) He was sincere in all things and was confidenced by all who knew him. **c1940** Simms *Coll* He's a listenable man; I'll harken to his prattle, but I don't confidence what he says. **1968** *Expressions* 24 "You can confidence me," means "You can trust me." Also, "Can I confidence you?" **1972** Cooper *NC Mt Folklore* 90 *can't confidence* = can't trust or believe.

[DARE *confidence* v chiefly South Midland]

confident *verb*

A variant pronunciation with secondary stress on the last syllable: CON-fi-DENT. For similar forms, see **-ment A**.

1942 Hall *Phonetics Smoky Mts* 62.

B To trust, believe in. Same as **confidence**.

1937 Hall *Coll* (Mt Sterling NC) I don't confident the story. **1973** *GSMNP-84:26* I didn't think that would be any of my business and didn't want to interfere with him since other people confidented in him.

[DARE *confident* v perhaps back-formation from *confidence* v, understood as *confidents* v 3rd sing]

conjure *verb* To invoke a spell or magical agent, as by an incantation or an herb; to bewitch, effect a cure, treat (a condition such as warts, etc.); hence noun = such practice. According to consultants from the Smoky Mountains, the term was applied to practitioners in white, Cherokee, and African American communities, but most often to the last, especially in recent times. See also **conjure doctor, wart doctor**.

1937 Hall *Coll* (Ravensford NC) The Indians will conjure two or three days before a ball game. The night before a game they'll have a dance and conjure all night long. **c1960** Wilson *Coll* = to place someone under a spell; very rare, largely now [used in] a joke. **1968** *DARE Survey* (Brasstown NC) We had 'em [= warts] conjured. **1996–97** Montgomery *Coll* (known to Adams, Brown, Bush, Jones, Oliver, Weaver). **2007** McMillon *Notes* = any kind of "witchment," not just the raising of a spirit or demon.

conjure ball *noun* Same as **hair ball**. See also **witch ball**.

1970 Hall *Witchlore* 3–4 "Russ Maynor's mother was said to be a witch. Wads of hair were found in her straw bed when she died." [She was referring to the hair or conjure balls thrown at intended victims to bring sickness or death.]

conjure doctor (also *conjure man, conjurer, conjure woman, conjuring man*) *noun* One who practices the arts of invoking a spell or magical agent, as by an incantation or an herb, to bewitch, effect a cure, treat a condition such as warts, divine the future, etc.; this person was a respected member of the community. See also **conjure, herb doctor, Indian doctor, wart conjurer, witch doctor**.

1959 Pearsall *Little Smoky* 130 The only major differentiation of roles is between "man" and "woman," although some may in addition be "preacher," "grannywoman" (midwife), or "conjure doctor" by virtue of possessing more of certain kinds of folk knowledge than their fellows. **1966** Frome *Strangers* 142 The native wild tobacco, or "old tobacco," when fixed by a conjureman in a little black cloth, is like a little witch. **1967** Jones *Peculiarities Mtneers* 48 A popular remedy for headaches used by these "conjure doctors," as they were called, was to take a few hairs from the sufferer's head and hide them in a secret place under a rock where no one would ever find them for at least seven days. Generally the headache would have run its course before the conjure charm could work or become effective. Little serious attention was paid to such alleged cures, but the "conjure doctors" did give the serious minded mountain people cause for many chuckles and some hearty laughs. **1969** Parris *Uncle Smart Carter* Uncle Smart Carter was a conjurin' man. He slept with a necklace of bear-claws about his throat to keep the ha'nts away. He wore a belt of rattlesnake skin to keep off rheutamism . . . he could make a charm or weave a spell. He made love potions from herbs he grew in his little garden and sold them to folks for a pretty penny. **1990** Kline *Cherokee Songs and Ceremonies* 27 Big Cove would get the conjure man and they would do the dance. The conjure man would conjure for the ball players. I know the song they sung while the conjure man was working—The Ball Dance Song. **1996–97** Montgomery *Coll* (known to Adams, Brown), = one who removes warts and such (Jones). **1999** Lane *Chattooga* 52 A conjure woman used to wander out of the Chattooga hills once a year and make her predictions. **2003** Cavender *Folk Medicine* 169 Mark Norman is quite different from the conventional Cherokee healer, known as a "conjurer" or "medicine man." The conjurer works in a clandestine manner. He not only treats illness but finds lost objects, restores lost affection, brings harm to enemies, and provides other services as well. His three basic tools are burning tobacco, recitation of "sacred formulae," and use of herbs.

conjure man, conjurer, conjure woman, conjuring man See **conjure doctor.**

connection(s) *noun* Relative(s), familial relations collectively.

1862 *Martin CW Letters* (Feb 17) I want him to write me & also tell howdy for I have not [heard] from our connections in Anderson for Some time. **1863** *Sexton CW Letters* (March 24) Write how all the connection are coming on. **1882** Winstadt *Letter* The rest of the connection is all well as fur as I no. **1899** Fox *Mt Europa* 27 She's a sort o' connection o' mine. Me and Bill married cousins.

consarn See **concern.**

conscience *noun* Opinion, judgment (apparently only in phrase *according to my conscience*).

1939 Hall Coll (Mt Sterling NC) That was the best version I've read, according to my conscience. **1996–97** Montgomery Coll: *according to my conscience* (known to Adams, Brown, Cardwell, Jones, Oliver).

consentable *adjective* Willing, agreeable.

1914 Arthur *Western NC* 266 [We] also say "plague" for tease, and when we are willing, we say we are "consentable." **1997** Montgomery Coll (known to Adams, Brown, Bush, Cardwell, Norris).

considerably *adverb* See citation.

1917 Kephart *Word-List* 410 = for the most part. "My parents were *considerably* Scotch."

(the) consumption *noun* Tuberculosis.

1861 *Click CW Letters* (Aug 19) georg is got the consumtion I think he looks verry bad we have bin trying to send him home but have not suckseaded in getting him off. **1862** *Dalton CW Letters* (Aug 22) you rote to me what I thougt was the matter with Amos I will tell you jest what I think he is broke Down and I beleave he has got the consumtion.

continuous loader See **continuous miner.**

continuous miner (also *continuous loader*) *noun* See citations.

1973 *AOHP/EH-79* A man that was on the cutting machine or loader would get more dust. Then a man that's operating a "Joy" machine or one of these new continuous loaders that they use now mostly, they'll get more dust that way. **1993** Moore *Dark and Deep* 81 We turned up to the coal face. Ahead sat the big-daddy of the mine's machines, the continuous miner. It dwarfed the working space. At the front end was the ripperhead, a cylindrical drum that was fitted with steel teeth that spun into the coal seam to cut the coal. In the giant's belly, mechanical claws pushed the cut coal onto an internal conveyor that dumped it, by way of a boom, into the five-ton bed of a waiting shuttlecar. **2002** Armstead *Black Days* 242 = [a] mining machine with sharp bits attached to a revolving drum or to rotating arms. One miner can mine up to eighty tons in an hour.

contour mining *noun* See citation. Same as **bench mining.** See also **highwall.**

2006 Mooney *Lg Coal Mining* 1028 In "contour mining," also known as "bench mining" or "highwall mining," workers follow the contour or direction of a seam along a mountainside, cutting straight down to remove the overburden and expose the seam.

contracted meeting *noun* A series of special religious services featuring a visiting preacher who has been "contracted" to lead them; a revival. See also **protracted meeting.**

1995 Montgomery Coll (known to Brown, Cardwell).

contrarious (also *contrarisome*) *adjective* Perverse, obstinate, cantankerous.

1886 Smith *Southernisms* 38 Even the adj. contrarisome, which [John] Jamieson gives [in *An Etymological Dictionary of the Scottish Language*, Edinburgh, 1840–41], may be heard. **1924** Raine *Speech of Land* 234 When a lad calls a cow contrarious, he has the authority of Milton. **c1945** Haun *Hawk's Done* 251 She told as how her pa was an ill-tempered, contrarious man and how she took after him when she was a youngon and paid no heed to things her ma said to her. **1952** Justus *Children* 54 It would take leading and driving too, to get the contrarious cow back home. **1978** Burns *Our Sthn Mtneers* 12 Like Milton, he may speak of a "contrarious cow."

[*contrary* + *-ous*; DARE *contrarious* adj chiefly southern Appalachians]

contrarisome See **contrarious.**

contrary

A variant pronunciation with primary stress on the second syllable.

1824 Knight *Letter from KY* 106–7 Some words are used, even by genteel people, from their imperfect education, in a new sense; and others, by the lower classes in society, pronounced very uncouthly . . . contráry. [See **1886** in **C** below.] **1891** Primer *Studies in WV* 167 *Contrary* when it means perverse, froward, wayward, always has the accent on the penultimate [syllable]. **1942** Hall *Phonetics Smoky Mts* 57 *Contrary* is never stressed on the initial syllable as in general American, always being pronounced [kɑn'træri].

[cf CUD *contrairy* adj "perverse, stubborn, ill-natured"]

B *adjective* Stubborn, cantankerous.

1864 *Brown CW Letters* (May 28) i have a horse and sadle the horse is Contra[r]y When i git on him i cant ceap him still and he wont go fard [= forward] by him Self. **1899** Fox *Mt Europa* 127 She used to be mighty wilful 'n' contrary, but as soon as you come I seed at oncet that a change was comin' over her. **1937** Hall Coll (Emerts Cove TN) He was very contrary and quare-turned. **c1950** Adams *Grandpap* 36 She was the contrariest old woman you ever seed. **1955** Dykeman *French Broad* 341 After you once get hogs broke to the road, you can't get them off, no matter how contrary they were at the start. **1969** GSMNP-38:120 This old Kit now was the contrariest old mule I ever seen in my life. **1973** AOHP/ASU-160 All children gets contrary and parents get irritated, and I don't think people's strict enough. **1982** DeArmond *So High* 63 I guess that contrary mule brought out the worst in Robert. **1999** Morgan *Gap Creek* 101 "He's contrary as an old mule," Ma Richards said. **2009** Holbrook *Upheaval* 22 Her own sister, Rilla . . . was so contrary she could barely stand anybody's company but her own.

C *verb* To contradict, oppose, disobey, vex, provoke (someone); to act contrary.

1862 *Councill CW Letters* (Feb 4) the officers like me vary well so far as I now I like them so far as I have had them they all seem vary kind to ward me an I will try to please them Just as long as I can I ant a gont to Contrary to them. **1886** Smith *Sthn Dialect* 349 They all have the authority of old or dialect English, or many of them belong to all parts of the South, if not elsewhere . . . contra'ry (to oppose, provoke). **1913** Kephart *Our Sthn High* 283 I didn't do nary thing to contrary her. **1928** (in **1952** Mathes *Tall Tales* 780 "Mis' Collins," said Jeter Clegg admiringly, "I'd shore hate to git that man o' yourn agin me an' have to contrary him." **1937** Hyatt *Kiverlid* 67 "Eh well," put in Granny, "don't be so tetchus, Marthy Lou, gittin' your self all in a dither, jist ain't no use contraryin' the young-un that away." **c1945** Haun *Hawk's Done* 300 Ma was sick and I couldn't afford to contrary her too much. **1946** Woodard *Word-List VA/NC* = to disobey, said of children. **1972** Cooper *NC Mt Folklore* 96 = to vex or anger.

[DARE *contrary* v chiefly South Midland]

contypin See **counterpane**.

conversation fluid *noun* Homemade whiskey.

1968 *End of Moonshining* 101 Various names given moonshine include: . . . conversation fluid.

coo-chick *interjection* Come! (used as a call to chickens).

1966 Dakin *Vocab Ohio River Valley* 288 Two speakers in Kentucky mention the use of *coo-chick!*, a call used in the Virginia Piedmont and Tidewater.

[DARE *co-chick* v phr chiefly VA]

cook (also *cook off*) *verb, verb phrase* In making whiskey: to distill, i.e., the beer produced from fermented mash is heated to vaporize the alcohol, which is then condensed to produce whiskey; hence verbal noun *cooking*.

1913 Kephart *Our Sthn High* 131 Here many a dismal hour of the night is passed when there is nothing to do but to wait on the "cooking." **1939** Hall Coll The mash after cooking is often fed to the hogs. A still hog is a hog that hangs around a still for the resultant mixture. **1959** Hall Coll (Mt Sterling NC) [Silver cloud is] whiskey that has been made in a big process and . . . they're making it on zinc, on tin, on everything they can get in other words to hold their mash while they cook it . . . and it is very dangerous to drink.

cookee *noun* An assistant cook in a logging camp.

1954 Blackhurst *Riders of Flood* 52 When the men had come from the woods, they had found the cook and his assistant, the cookee, preparing the mess. **1994** Farwell and Buchanan *Logging Terms* = in logging, a kitchen hand who often cleaned up after a meal in addition to helping with the cooking. **2006** Farwell *Logging Term* 1021 A "gut bell" announced the meals, which the cook, called a "gut robber," had prepared with the help of "cookees."

cooker *noun* In making liquor: a **still B** or **whiskey still**.

1949 Maurer *Argot of Moonshiner* 5 These stills . . . do not depend on the old-time copper pot, but have a metal boiler . . . from which steam is piped into one or more large *cookers*, sometimes built of staves and demountable, where vaporization takes place. *Ibid.* 8 = the beer still proper. **1968** *End of Moonshining* 49 = the container into which the beer is placed for boiling. Also called Evaporator or Boiler. **1974** Maurer and Pearl *KY Moonshine* 116 = the beer still proper . . . A tank or box to precook beer.

cooking See **cook**.

cooking bee *noun* A community work activity.

1977 Shields *Cades Cove* 44 Saturday was a mass cooking bee.

cook off See **cook**.

cookroom *noun* A kitchen, especially one separated from the house.

1904 Johnson *Highways South* 135 It was fully twice as commodious as the average houses of the region and had four rooms in the body of the house, and a cook-room in a semi-detached ell. **1940** Bandy *Folklore Macon Co TN* 58 The kitchen is in most homes the "cook-room." **1996–97** Montgomery Coll (known to Brown, Cardwell, Jones, Norris, Oliver).

[DARE *cookroom* n chiefly South, South Midland]

cooling board *noun* A broad plank on which a newly deceased person is laid to be prepared for burial; traditionally, it is set up in the home of the deceased while a carpenter makes the coffin and burial arrangements are set. Same as **laying-out board**. See also **lay out 2**.

1944 Wilson *Word-List* 41 = a large board used to lay a dead person on before *rigor mortis* sets in. In w. N.C. it is regarded as bad luck to allow a corpse to lie in any position other than straight. **1988** Russell *It Happened* 50 Usually a board or wide plank was used to place the body on overnight or for several hours and was called a "cooling board." **1997** Davis *Cataloochee Valley* 85 Cataloochee did not have a funeral home or any way to embalm a body. When a person died, some of the family or friends would bathe the body and lay it out on a cooling board and lay coins on the eyes to keep them closed. **2006** *WV Encycl* 92 Planks, tables, or even ironing boards were used as cooling boards.

[DARE *cooling board* n South, Midland]

cooling stand (also *cooling tub*) *noun* See citations. Same as **flake stand**.

1956 Hall *Coll* (Waynesville NC) They'd usually just have a little vessel, you see, and it'd set down here at the end where it'd come out, come out at the end of the cooling stand here, and you'd just catch it maybe in it, or maybe it'd be a gallon or two gallons it'd hold, and they'd catch alcohol from that and into the worm. **1968** Connelly *Discover Appal* 118 This worm rested in a cooling tub through which a stream of water constantly poured from a nearby branch or creek. This cooling process condensed the steam which fell into the "singling keg." For a higher-proofed whisky, the liquid was boiled again and passed through the copper tubing. **c1999** Sutton *Me and Likker* 104 = what your worm or condenser sets in with cold water piped to the bottom to push the hot water off the top to keep it cool.

cooling tub See **cooling stand**.

coolwort *noun* A foamflower (*Tiarella cordifolia*), a perennial plant with creamy white blossoms and medicinal uses. See also **nancy-over-the-ground**.

1901 Lounsberry *Sthn Wild Flowers* 217 With its masses of handsome flowers and usually attractive foliage the coolwort, as the mountaineers call the plant, is one of the early bloomers. **1940** Caton *Wildflowers of Smokies* 26. [**1971** Krochmal et al. *Medicinal Plants Appal* 250 This herb is reputed to be useful as a tonic and diuretic.]

coon

A *noun* common form of *raccoon*; variant plural form *coon*.

1937 Hall *Coll* (Little Greenbrier TN) He traps for coon and minks. . . . A coon can wear a dog out. It can cut a dog all to pieces. **1953** Hall *Coll* (Bryson City NC) We went about a quarter of a mile along the top of the mountain and caught seven coon that they shook out of the beech bushes and all. **1991** Thomas *Sthn Appal* 86 They was plenty of coon.

B *noun* A rascal, especially a crafty, unpredictable old man.

1937 Hall *Coll* (Gumstand TN) [General Morgan] fit there at Greeneville. He was a bad old coon. He was a fighter. **1939** Hall *Coll* (Cataloochee NC) "He's a bad old coon"—lots of old people use that. **1956** Hall *Coll* (Big Creek NC) "Coon" [is] a common nickname for a crafty man, as in "Coon" McMillen [a resident of Catons Grove TN]. **1999** Montgomery *Coll*: *old coon* = an old man of questionable reputation or morals, not to be trusted (Cardwell).

[DARE *coon* n^1 1 "a person, fellow; especially a rustic" chiefly South, South Midland, West]

C *verb*

1 (also *coon it*) To crawl on all fours, as across a **foot-log** or fallen tree, in the manner of a raccoon; to crawl across (a log).

1917 Kephart *Word-List* 410 *coon* = to creep like a coon, clinging close. "I *cooned* acrost on a log." **1952** Wilson *Folk Speech NC* 528 *coon a log* = to crawl on a log on all fours like a coon. **1961** Medford *History Haywood Co* 198 "What do you mean by 'cooned' it, Wid?" said somebody. "Why, just like this, down on yore hands and feet—just like you'd do ef you made it across on a log." **1974–75** McCracken *Logging* 1:3 I started up that tree. I got up to a place where there wasn't no limbs, and they was about twenty foot there that I had what we call cooning it. I just had to hold to it with my legs and arms and keep going up by little jerks. **c1978** Trout and Watson *Piece of Smokies* 112 Crossing rivers and creeks on a footlog was tricky. Upright if you were young; "cooning it" at ninety-one.

[DARE *coon* v 1 chiefly South, South Midland]

2 (also *coon up*) To climb (a tree) in the manner of a raccoon; to scramble upward as a raccoon would.

1969 Hall *Coll* (Big Bend NC) An old chestnut tree that had fell against a big oak [was] just slantin' enough so I could coon it up. **1974–75** McCracken *Logging* 1:3 I started up that tree. I got up to a place where there wasn't no limbs, and they was about twenty foot there that I had what we call cooning it. I just had to hold to it with my legs and arms and keep going up by little jerks. **1980** Riggleman *WV Mtneer* 4 When it was time for bed, mother always stood at the corner and counted us as we "cooned" up [into the attic to sleep]. **1991** Haynes *Haywood Home* 80 His nimble legs 'cooned up many a tree to shake out whatever his dogs had treed.

[DARE *coon* v 2 chiefly South, Midland]

3 To pilfer, steal.

1917 Kephart *Word-List* 410 = to steal. "I had to *coon* an ace of hearts." **1944** Laughlin *Word-List Buncombe Co* 25 = to pilfer, not applied to serious theft. "Let's go and *coon* some watermelons." **1997** Montgomery *Coll* (known to Brown, Bush).

coo-nan, coo-nannie See **co-sheep**.

coon dog (also *coon hound*) *noun* A dog trained specifically to hunt raccoons. See also **black and tan**, **blue tick**, **Walker**.

1939 Hall *Coll* (Cataloochee NC) We went up Nettle Creek. We had a coon dog. He treed a coon in the cliff. **1975** *GSMNP-62*:3 He'd circle around and directly, he'd come back and set down, and he'd go barking every breath up the tree. He was a good coon dog. **1989** Dorgan *Regular Baptists* 96 Each man felt compelled, it seemed, to make a trip out to the hounds, inspecting the lot with a critical eye of an experienced runner of coon dogs. I also made my trip and in the process was told something about coon hounds, the differences, for example, between blueticks, black-and-tans, and walkers. *Ibid.* 97 Any good coon hound, he asserted, should "bawl" on the trail but "chop" on the tree. He reserved particular disdain for any hound of such poor breeding that it would reverse these responses. **2006** *Encycl Appalachia* 872 Blue Ticks, Black and Tans, and Redbones have been popular coon dogs. **2009** Prewitt *Coon Hounds* 273 Nowadays, the black and tan, the redbone, the bluetick, the English, the treeing Walker, and the Plott are among the standard breeds that hunters say can potentially make good coon hounds. **2017** Kinsler *Take Girl* 42 My Uncle Coob owned specialty bred dogs called coonhounds. . . . These dogs were trained to follow the scent of a raccoon's pelt and once mastered it was taken to the woods by itself or with other dogs.

[DARE *coon dog* n^1 chiefly South, South Midland]

coon hunt *verb phrase* To go hunting for raccoons (a construction used rather than the phrase *hunt for coons*; see **hunt** for similar compounds). See also **coon race**.

1937 Hall Coll (Cataloochee NC) There's more real sport in coon huntin' than in bear huntin'. Hit takes only one man to coon hunt. When you tree a coon, you've got him. [**1939** Hall Coll (Tuckaleechee Cove TN) Me and my brother-in-law one time left the White Oak . . . and went a-coon huntin' one night.] **1975** GSMNP-62:2 We possum hunted and we coon hunted and we hog hunted and we done a little of this and a little of that out here, but the main joy part of it was hog hunting and coon hunting, you know, to have some fine races of coons and hogs, and we enjoyed that about the best of anything in the hunting line. **1979** *Swapped That Dog* 42 [I] used t'coon hunt a whole lot. I had a blue speckled hound.

[perhaps back-formation from *coon hunter* or *coon hunting*; DARE *coon hunt* v chiefly South Midland]

coon oil *noun* Oil rendered from the fat of a raccoon.

1937 Hall Coll (Cataloochee NC) Oil from coons is worth more than lard. Coon oil has most the same taste as lard.

coon race *noun* Pursuit of a raccoon with dogs.

1926 Hunnicutt *Twenty Years* 54 I told the boys in the morning we would have a coon race or a bear race one.

coonroot *noun* Same as **bloodroot**.

1937 Eaton *Handicrafts* 153 [One chairmaker's] favorite color is orange made from "coon root," an abbreviation of puccoon, the Indian name for bloodroot. **1964** Hall Coll = puccoon. **1991** Haynes *Haywood Home* 75 In early spring, Nance dug 'Coon Root, Burdock, Yellow Dock and Narrow-leaf Dock.

[shortening of *puccoon* + *root*; DARE *coon root* n chiefly southern Appalachians]

coon skinner *noun* See citations; hence *coonskinning*.

1930 Pendleton *Wood-Hicks Speak* 86 = a peeler of tanbark; a woodsman who cuts by the thousand feet, cutting very close, almost literally by "skinning" the land. *Ibid.* 87 *coon skinning* = peeling tanbark, or cutting [trees] . . . by the thousand feet, cutting very close, almost literally "skinning" the land. **1964** Clarkson *Lumbering in WV* 358 = a subcontractor cutting timber.

coonskinning See **coon skinner**.

coon up See **coon C2**.

coon yarn *noun* A vivid account of hunting raccoons.

1895 Dromgoole *Fiddling to Fame* 63 Can't ye tell a good coon yarn, Bob?

coo-sheepie See **co-sheep**.

cooter[1] *noun* A freshwater turtle of various kinds.

1996–97 Montgomery Coll (known to Bush, Cardwell), = used especially for a small turtle that lives in water (Ellis).

[of African origin]

cooter[2] (also *cooter along*, *cooter around*, *cooter off*) *verb*, *verb phrase* To saunter, go about aimlessly.

1913 Kephart *Our Sthn High* 203 I'm just cooterin' around. **1952** Wilson *Folk Speech NC* 529 *cooter around* = to travel aimlessly. **1966** *DARE Survey* (Burnsville NC) *cootering around* = doing little, unimportant things. **1968** *Asheville Citizen* (NC, 10 Mar) (*DARE*) These news-spreaders and news-gatherers had a way of trying to cover up their mission by saying they were "jes' cooterin' around." **1974** Fink *Bits Mt Speech* 5 = spend time idly. "He *cootered* around all day." **1987** Young *Lost Cove* 161 He slowly got to his feet and cootered off toward home. *Ibid.* 84 Morefield Hopson cootered over to where Fonzer was meditating. **2009** Benfield *Mt Born* 131 *cooter along* = moseying around, ambling about mostly out of curiosity.

[DARE *cooter* v 1 cf SND *cuiter/couther* v 1 "to nurse . . . to pamper . . . nurse oneself" and *queeter* v "to work lazily . . . waste time," chiefly southern Appalachians]

cooter along, **cooter around**, **cooter off** See **cooter**[2].

coot up *verb phrase* See 1917 citation.

1917 Kephart *Word-List* 410 = to revive. "After the rope broke they *cooted* him up and hung him sure enough the next time." **1997** Montgomery Coll (known to Brown).

cope (also *c-u-u-u-p*, *cwup*, *koop*, *kope*, *kuop*, *kwope*, *kwopie*, *kwup*, *quoby*, *quope*, *quopy*, *quowa*, *quup*) *interjection* Come! (used as a call to a horse or horses at pasture).

1915 Dingus *Word-List VA* 188 *kuop* = call to a horse. Also quopy, quoby, quowa. **1934–47** *LAMSAS Appal* (Madison Co NC, Swain Co NC) *cope*. **1957** Broaddus *Vocab Estill Co KY* 46 *kwup* = a call to make a horse come to you. **1957** Combs *Lg Sthn High: Word-List* 25 *c-u-u-u-p* = call to a horse. Also *cwup*. Contraction of come up. **c1960** Wilson Coll: *quope*, *quup* = to call horses. **1962** Wilson *Folkways Mammoth Cave* 10 "Quope, quope" or "Quup, quup" should bring a horse from the pasture, especially if you use his name after each call. **1966** Dakin *Vocab Ohio River Valley* 276 South of the [Ohio] river [the call] is *kwope!* or *kwopie!* No variations of *kope!* appear in Kentucky, but *kobe!*, *koke!*, *ko-boy!*, *ko!* plus a whistle *ke-babe!* [sic], and *koop!* [kōp] [sic] all are attested to in the north. Only the variant of the type [kōp] [sic] appears more than once or twice. **1966–67** *DARE Survey* (Spruce Pine NC, Maryville TN) *cope* = to get horses in from pasture. **1986** Pederson et al. *LAGS*: *cope* = attested by 6/60 interviewees (10%) from E TN; 6/14 of all LAGS interviewees (42.9%) attesting term were from E TN. **1987** Carver *Regional Dialects* 167 The Upper South is distinguished by *co-sheep(ie)* or *cu-sheep(ie)*, used to bring sheep in from the pasture, and *cope* or *kwope*, the corresponding call to horses. Both expressions have the nearly universal, abbreviated form of "come": co-, cu-, or kwo-, the latter call, *cope*, probably deriving from *come up*.

copper *noun*

1 Copper components of a **moonshine pot**. See also **copper pot**, **cut up copper**.

1949 Maurer *Argot of Moonshiner* 9 = the still pot [and] all copper parts of the moonshiner's equipment: "Pull out the copper and leave the rest be."

2 (also *copper snake*) A copperhead snake.

1964 Reynolds *Born of Mts* 50 This is the snake that Timberlake in exploring these mountains in 1765 refers to as the copper snake, and of which a native in killing is apt to say, "Well, that's one more copperhead less." **1998** Montgomery *Coll* (known to Adams, Bush, Weaver); We saw a copper on the trail (Cardwell).

copperhead-bit *adjective phrase* Bitten by a copperhead snake. For similar forms, see **bite A2**.

1892 Doak *Wagonauts Abroad* 168 Jinny got copperhead bit and like to a died five year ago, an' I don't b'lieve she'll ever git over likin' a drop o' liquor for that old snake bite. **c1950** Adams *Grandpap* 192 She said that I might get copperhead bit if I got off in the tangle of weeds and vines by myself.

copper pot (also *copper pot still, copper still*) *noun* A type of **still** used in making whiskey. See 1974 citations. Also called **buccaneer**, **kettle B**, **mountain teapot**, **pot still**. See also **gray cloud**, **half-turnip**, **pot still**, **silver cloud**, **turnip B2**.

1883 Zeigler and Grosscup *Heart of Alleghanies* 362 While the men worked in the light of the furnace fire, and talked in loud tones above the noise of the running water flowing down troughs into the hogshead, through which wound the worm from the copper still, I listened and "j'ined" in at intervals. **1939** Hall *Coll* (Gatlinburg TN) [It was] copper stills on Cosby, steel stills in the Sugarlands and Wears Valley. **1956** Hall *Coll* (Del Rio TN) Vordegrease comes from the copper still. It comes from the pot ordinarily, which is very poisonous. **1974** Dabney *Mt Spirits* xxi Sometimes called a "copper," or kettle, this still, with roots going back to Scotland and Ireland, was a favorite along the Appalachians and can still be found in isolated spots in the hills. It has three forms—the "turnip" round and fat; the "half turnip"; and the upright copper pot, shaped like a metal drum and placed vertically in the furnace. *Ibid.* xxi Doubling liquor [is] whiskey run through a copper pot still twice, which produces a proof of well over 100. Sometimes known as high wines or "doubled and twisted whiskey." **1985** Dabney *More Mt Spirits* 154 The copper pot "mother still" is found in three configurations—the "turnip," round and fat; the "half turnip," and the upright copper pot, shaped like a metal drum and placed vertically in the furnace. It is also called the Buccaneer, the Blockade Still and the "mountain teapot." The American copper pot is very similar to the "poit du" (black pot) stills on display in the Highland Folk Museum in Scotland and the Poteen stills in Ireland.

copper pot still See **copper pot**.

copper snake See **copper 2**.

copper still See **copper pot**.

corduroy road *noun* See citations. Same as **pole road**. See also **plank road**.

1927 Woofter *Dialect from WV* 351 = a road made by laying poles or slabs of logs over the muddy places. "The corduroy road is rough traveling." **1964** Clarkson *Lumbering in WV* 358 = a road built over soft ground by laying small poles across it at right angles to the line of travel. **1995** Weber *Rugged Hills* 83 When the ground was flat, it was hard for the team to pull the logs. So we made what we called a "corduroy road." We cut a bunch of short, small logs about 6 or 8 inches in diameter and laid them on the ground about 2 foot apart. They acted like rollers.

cork *noun* A calk embedded into the sole of a boot to provide traction.

1954 Blackhurst *Riders of Flood* 15 The bottoms [of loggers' shoes], both sole and heel, were studded with three circuits of sharp, half-inch-long caulks, or as Brake had called them, "corks." **1964** Clarkson *Lumbering in WV* 359 *corks* = short, sharp, metal spikes placed in the soles of loggers' boots to prevent slipping when walking on logs, ice, etc. **1991** Weals *Last Train* 117 The calks were also pronounced "corks," but by any name they were dozens of sharp steel points embedded in the sole and heel of each boot.

corkus See **caucus**.

corn

A *noun* Whiskey made from ground sprouted corn. Same as **corn juice**, **straight corn**.

1939 *FWP Guide TN* 426 Under the leaves in the hollows they stashed (cached) away the fresh corn [moonshine] in ten-gallon kegs and let it charter (char) for months. **1949** Maurer *Argot of Moonshiner* 4 So-called "corn whisky" is still made, although the pure corn or straight corn of older days is now practically nonexistent. **1963** Edwards *Gravel* 106 When the doctor got near the top of this ridge, he took another heavy drink from the bottle of corn to help defeat the inclement weather.

B *verb* To plant (a field) in corn.

1940 Stuart *Trees of Heaven* 129 I'd corn this land three years, then I'd sow it in wheat and orchard grass. **1961** Williams *Content Mt Speech* 16 He's got a good little piece of crappin' land there, but he won't corn it ner hay it nuther. **1962** Williams *Verbs Mt Speech* 17 He grasses a field after he has corned it for a few years.

corn beads *noun* Same as **Job('s) tears**.

1972 Miller *Pigeon's Roost* (May 11) Amanda Arrowood of Tipton Hill section planted her crop of Job tears or corn beads last week. Several folks in lower Mitchell County area grow Job tears to make homemade beads out of them. Some of the folks who grow Job tears sell them. **1979** Slone *My Heart* 51 Mountain people grew "corn beads" or "Job's tears." The seeds are very pretty, with a hole through the center, and can be strung like beads. They decorated beautiful "comb cases" and picture frames for the walls of their homes with these beads.

corn beer *noun* Same as **beer**.

1939 Hall *Coll* = *beer*: fermented mash which is distilled in the making of whiskey. **1974** Dabney *Mt Spirits* 5 The mash bubbles so much that it starts rolling, literally, and keeps on for a day or two days. When the bubbles stops rising, and the cap disappears, the mash, now called "corn beer" or distiller's beer, becomes a soupy yellow and is ready to be distilled.

[DARE *corn beer* n chiefly South]

corn bin *noun* See citations.

c1960 Wilson *Coll* = a place to store corn, usually shelled corn. **1967** *DARE Survey* (Brasstown NC) = a structure for storing shelled corn.

[DARE *corn bin* n chiefly South, Midland]

corn blade *noun* A leaf of the corn stalk, usually stripped, dried and used as **fodder**. Same as **blade 1**.

1835 *McLean Diary* 35 frost this morning Scorched the Corn blaids a Littel. **1957** Justus *Other Side* 33 The corn blades made a whispering sound, as if they were talking together, and their tassels far above her head showered golden dust down upon her. **1986** Tyson *Reflections* 19 I would start to the barn with about six bundles of fodder and lose about half of it. The corn blades were dry. They would break off in my hands. Although I did the best that I could, I would always go back and find the bundles of fodder I had dropped. **1995–96** Montgomery *Coll* (known to Adams, Cardwell, Jones, Ledford, Oliver).

corn box *noun* See citation.

1998 Hamby *Grassy Creek* 113 Sometimes they would plan a hay ride when it snowed. The young men would take the farm sled and put the slatted "corn box" on it. The box was about six feet long and four feet wide with a floored bottom, but with slatted sides and ends to allow air to circulate through if the husked corn had been left in it overnight before hauling it to the granary, or if the unhusked corn had been hauled to the barn hallway for a corn husking. The three foot high box would be filled to the top with hay, but after six or seven people sat down on the hay it was considerably less high.

corn bread *noun* [with accent on *bread*]. See also **cornmeal**.

1994 Landry *Coll* It's more flavorable if you like corn bread.

corn broom *noun* A broom made from the tops of **broomcorn**.

1964 Smith et al. *Germans of Valley* 148 Take a corn broom and sweep the horse all over with it and he'll get better [from colic]. **1968** *DARE Survey* (Brasstown NC).

corn cake *noun* See citations. Same as **dodger**. See also **hoecake**.

1958 Wood *Words from TN* 8 = a large flat cake of cornbread usually fried in a griddle. **c1960** Wilson *Coll* = a griddle cake made of cornmeal. **1966** Dakin *Vocab Ohio River Valley* 316 The names *corn cake*, *hoe cake*, *corn (bread)*, *dodger* (occasionally *dodge bread* in Kentucky), *johnny cake* (only in Ohio and eastern Indiana), and (very rarely) *hobby* are used above the river as well as in Kentucky. **1998** Montgomery *Coll* (known to Brown, Bush, Cardwell, Ellis, Jones, Oliver).

[DARE *corn cake* n chiefly South, Midland]

corncob battle, corncob fight See **cob battle**.

corncob jelly (also *corncob syrup*) *noun* A heavy, sometimes congealed topping made from the juice of boiled corncobs. It is now sold in tourist shops as a novelty item.

1982 Powers and Hannah *Cataloochee* 354 What has happened to the Cataloochee sweets of yore. . . . Where are the pokeberry and bearbelly jellies, pumpkin butters and corncob syrups? **1996–97** Montgomery *Coll* (known to Jones, Oliver), = the recipe is as follows: cook red corncobs (for color) and Winter John apples, strain, add sugar, honey, or molasses, and then boil until jelled (Brown), = generally made only when other sources had a bad year, but is now available in specialty shops (Bush).

corncob pipe See **cob pipe**.

corncob syrup See **corncob jelly**.

corn cracker *noun*

1 Formerly, a small, hand-operated mill for grinding corn into meal.

1883 Zeigler and Grosscup *Heart of Alleghanies* 130 The man who, with a bushel of meal over his shoulders, is coming on foot from the nearest "corn-cracker." **1982** Powers and Hannah *Cataloochee* 311 When the first small settlement of Cataloochee was formed, the settlers had only a hand-operated corncracker which took twelve hours to grind a bushel of corn.

2 A farmer hired to mine coal only in colder months of the year.

1943 Korson *Coal Dust* 4–5 Farmers and farm-hands also hired themselves out to coal operators as miners during the winter season. Since digging and loading coal was only temporary work for them, they were less likely to be interested in efforts to raise wages and improve working conditions than professional miners. . . . Full-time miners naturally resented them and expressed their distrust by calling them "winter diggers," "wheats," "corncrackers."

cornder See **corner**.

corn dodger *noun* Same as **dodger**. See also **corn pone**.

1883 Zeigler and Grosscup *Heart of Alleghanies* 98 Between each bite you take of a smoking piece of corn-dodger, you can look up at the shadowed front of the Anderson Roughs (for long since the western wall has intercepted the sunlight from pouring on it), and watch how the shadows thicken, while still the sky is bright and clear above. **1946** Nixon *Glossary VA Words* 16 = a hard, hand-shaped cake of cornbread . . . [a term used] west of the Blue Ridge. **1949** Kurath *Word Geog East US* 68 In the South Midland (most of western Virginia, Western North Carolina) . . . the *corn dodger* is applied to a small corn cake (two or three in one pan). **1970** Justus *Tales* 23 She might make hoe-cakes, which were round and flat. She might make corn dodgers, round and fat. She might make corn pone, round and even fatter. **1976** Ledford *Folk Vocabulary* 283 Griddle cakes were sometimes called *corn dodger*, and that term was frequently applied to corn bread baked in pones. **2005** Williams *Gratitude* 487 = a cake of cornbread, regardless of size.

[DARE *corn dodger* n 1 chiefly South, South Midland]

corn dumpling *noun* See 1967 citation.

1967 *DARE Survey* (Brasstown NC) = a cornmeal dumpling steamed or boiled with meat or vegetables. **1998** Montgomery *Coll* (known to Brown, Bush, Cardwell, Oliver).

corner *noun* variant forms *cornder, cyorner*.

1890 Fruit *KY Words* 64 *cornder*: for *corner*. **1925** Greer-Petrie *Angeline Hill Country* 136 One of 'em whirled 'round a cornder, when we wa'n't lookin', and knocked Lum a-wyndin'. **1963** Williams *Metaphor Mt Speech II* 51 I'd be willin' . . . to bet ye a double handful of hullgull ches'nits he couldn't hem a blind pig in a fence cyorner.

corner man *noun* Formerly, in the constructing a log house or barn, one who notched the ends of logs so that they locked tightly and accurately at the corners. See also **house raising**.

1824 (in **1912** Doddridge *Notes on Settlement* 107) In the morning of the next day the neighbors collected for the [house] raising. The first thing to be done was the election of four corner men, whose business it was to notch and place the logs. The rest of the company furnished them with the timbers. **1913** Kephart *Our Sthn High* 240 The mountain home of to-day is the log cabin of the American frontier . . . a pen that can be erected by four "corner men" in one day and is finished by the owner at his leisure. **1924** Raine *Saddlebags* 208 Even on the outskirts of towns the man with little money today cuts down suitable trees, hews two sides of each log flat, notches the ends, and invites his neighbors to help with the house-raising. The corner-men fit the notches together as the logs are lifted or slid up to the top of the walls. After the top sills are laid, the rafters are put in place, and the owner can finish the house himself. **1995** Moffett *Cantilever Barns* 15 In the backcountry virtually everyone had basic wood-construction skills, and old-timers recalled that particular individuals in the community were once known as good corner men, meaning that they worked in pairs to cut the log notches that kept the log rounds rising level and consistently.

corn-fed *adjective*

1 See citation.

1936 Farr *Folk Speech* 275 = [of] one who lives in the country: "She is a corn fed girl."

2 See citation.

1972 Cooper *NC Mt Folklore* 90 = husky; strong.

cornfield bean *noun* A running green bean planted next to a corn plant so that it will climb the stalk as it grows. See 2011 citation.

c1960 Wilson *Coll* = a variety of common bean planted with corn, especially in the later "rosenear" patches. **1968** *DARE Survey* (Brasstown NC) = a type of bean that is eaten in the pod before being dried. **1982** Powers and Hannah *Cataloochee* 199 There was always a pot of cornfield beans with bacon cooking on the stove when the children came in. **1986** Pederson et al. *LAGS* = attested by 11/60 interviewees (18.3%) from E TN and 6/35 (17.4%) from N GA; 17/32 of all LAGS interviewees (53.1%) attesting term were from Appalachia. **2006** *Encycl Appalachia* 421 Heirloom beans are described in terms of three general characteristics. Cut-shorts are beans packed so tightly in the hulls that the ends are squared off; that is, they cannot grow to full length inside the hull and are "cut short." Greasies do not have the fuzzy skins common to other beans but are shiny, or greasy, in appearance. One of the "three sisters" recognized by Native Americans, cornfield beans are climbing beans traditionally grown in corn along with pumpkins or squash, a technique that raises efficiency by fostering a symbiotic relationship among the plants. Beans can be any combination of these three types. For example, a particular bean might be described as a speckled long greasy cut-short cornfield bean. **2011** Best *Bean Terminology* = any climbing bean. Corn patches traditionally served as the poles which beans used for climbing. **2016** *Blind Pig* (June 8) A cornfield bean doesn't always have to grow among the corn, but it usually does; the bean is much larger than a white half runner and seems more filling when cooked.

cornfield pea *noun* A black-eyed pea. Also called **roasting ear pea**.

1895 Murfree *Witch-Face* 157 I would n't hev trested him with a handful o' cornfield peas. **1974** *AOHP/ALC-708* We raised corn, we raised cotton, and we raised cornfield peas and cornfield beans. **1994–97** Montgomery *Coll* (known to Adams, Jones, Norris, Oliver, Weaver), = same as clay pea (Brown, Cardwell).

[DARE *cornfield pea* n South, South Midland]

corn fritter *noun* Same as **fritter B**.

1960 Burnett *My Valley* 25 Corn fritters were good eating beside the campfires. **1995–97** Montgomery *Coll* = sometimes topped with sorghum, served as a snack (Cardwell).

corn gathering *noun* A time in the fall for gathering corn from the field during which school was dismissed so that children could help with the work. See also **fodder pulling time**.

1953 Hall *Coll* (Tuckaleechee Cove TN) We had to [stop] school for fodder pullin', pea pickin', and corn gatherin', maybe two weeks at a time.

corn grinder *noun* See comments at 1997 citation.

1940 Oakley *Roamin'/Restin'* 74 I fond many airow heads, speer heads. skinning knives. tommy halks. and corn grinders. **1997** Montgomery *Coll* = stone mallet to pound grains of corn into meal in a depression in a rock (Brown), = a stone shaped to grind corn, used by Indians (Cardwell), = a hollowed-out rock in which corn was placed and ground with another rock or stake [= mortar and pestle] (Oliver), = a smooth stone two by three inches in diameter, six by twelve inches long, ground in a rock bowl by Indians (Weaver).

corn grits *noun* Ground sprouted corn used to make **sweet mash** in the production of homemade liquor; grains of such corn.

1976 Miller *Mts within Me* 115 The sprouted corn then was dried in the sun or on the hearth before an open fire, after which it was ground into a coarse meal called "corn grits" or "chop." Most mountain families owned or bartered use of a tubmill for this process, and it was possible, if the moonshiner had a wife and several sons with strong arms, to turn out up to two bushels of ground corn a day. Great care was taken to see that the "grits" were kept absolutely dry. "Corn grits" were converted into "sweet mash" by putting them in an oak barrel and adding hot water in the proportion called for by the recipe used, usually half a barrel of pure spring water for each bushel of ground corn. Sufficient room had to be left in the barrel to allow for the expansion that came with fermentation.

corn ground *noun* A cornfield.

1834 McLean *Diary* 27 [I] finished Plowin my Corn Ground. **1862** *Tesh CW Letters* (Jan 26) we have very nice weather now our folks has begun to break up there corn ground. **1865** *Hill CW Letters* (Jan 6) I want him [to] brake up all of his corn groun if the wether is nice and fix for a big corn crope. **1886** Smith *History KY* 367 (DARE) Uncle Ben . . . plowed the corn-ground. **1949** McDavid *Grist* 107 (Fannin Co GA) = cornfield.

corn juice (also *corn likker, corn liquor, corn oil, corn whiskey*) *noun* Illegal whiskey made from ground sprouted corn and cornmeal. Also called **corn**, **straight corn**. See also **mash**[2] **B**.

1845 (in **1974** Harris *High Times* 46) He can belt six shillins worth of corn-juice at still-house rates and travel—can out shute and out lie any feller from the Smoky Mounting to Noxville. **1864** *Chapman CW Letters* (May 10) if I only had a little of the good old corn oil that I once had it would go mity well. **1881** Atkinson *After Moonshiners* 57 [Stills are] just where you'd least expect to find them, generally between hills and mountains, near a murmuring rill, water of course being a necessary element in the making of "cornjuice." **1913** Kephart *Our Sthn High* 123 You can see for yourself that corn can't be shipped outen hyar. . . . Corn juice is about all we can tote around over the country and git cash money for. **1922** *TN CW Ques* 18 Father . . . made some apple and peach brandy and corn whiskey. **1931** Owens *Speech Cumberlands* 92 *corn-liquor* = whiskey made from malted corn: "Since prohibition there's not any corn-liquor in the mountains." **1949** Maurer *Argot of Moonshiner* 4 So-called "corn whisky" is still made, although the pure corn or straight corn of older days is now practically nonexistent. Some corn malt (prepared by burying sacks of corn under damp leaves in the woods, drying, and then grinding the sprouted grain) is used, along with barley malt, rye malt, or other grains similarly prepared; principally, however, corn malt is used to flavor whisky made from molasses or commercial sugar, which then passes for "corn whisky." *Ibid.* 9 *corn liquor* = among moonshiners, used to mean liquor made with some corn, usually from one peck to one bushel per barrel of mash, the rest of the mash being sugar or, more rarely, some other grain. . . . [In] selling, [the term] used to mean liquor made from "pure" corn (100 percent corn), which is rare indeed . . . "You got any corn likker?" "This ain't sugar likker, this is corn likker"; "Shore, that's corn likker." Intonation often reflects the degree to which corn is actually used. **1982** Slone *How We Talked* 68 We no longer have many men that make moonshine whiskey, and those that do don't make the real corn whiskey like our old-timers did. The stuff they make now is more harmful. The real "corn likker" was made from corn, no sugar added. It wouldn't hurt you, nor make you crazy drunk. It was used for medicine as well as just to drink. Even the preachers drank it.

corn light bread *noun* See citation.

1978 Parris *Mt Cooking* 117 Corn light bread is something to make your mouth water. It's made with yeast and molasses, and you've got to make it up the night before, so it will rise overnight and be ready for baking the next day. Molasses is put in the butter.

corn likker, **corn liquor** See **corn juice**.

cornmeal *noun* [with accent on *meal*]. See also **corn bread**.

1973 GSMNP-4:19 [Take] just like you buy at the store, corn meal, and cook it and put, I believe, about fifty pounds of sugar to a barrel, a sixty-gallon barrel [in the production of corn whiskey].

cornmeal gravy *noun* A heavy gravy made with cornmeal, most often called **sawmill gravy**.

1978 *Smokies Heritage* 203 Corn ground at a nearby mill provided meal for the cornbread, mush and cornmeal gravy that made up a large part of the winter diet in the mountains.

corn medicine *noun* Homemade whiskey.

1965 Ferrell *Bear Tales* 38 I heard no small amount of talk about bringing the "corn medicine" out from under a bunk and passing it around, but I never saw any.

corn mill *noun* A mill (such as an **overshot mill** or a **tub mill**) for grinding corn but not wheat, the latter taken to a mill with finer-grained stones. Also called **grit mill**. See also **moonshine mill**.

1939 Hall *Coll* (Emerts Cove TN) In eighteen hundred and seventy two I visited Newport. There were two stores. There was a corn mill and an old-fashioned jump up and down sash saw that sawed lumber. **1969** GSMNP-43:4 Yes, they had quit growing wheat. He didn't run the wheat mill at all. He just run the corn mill.

corn night *noun* October 30th as a night for pranks.

1989 Still *Rusties and Riddles* [60] Fool's Day in April and Corn Night in October were opportunities for pulling rusties, both for fair and foul.

[DARE *corn night* n chiefly N Midl; also Appalachians]

corn oil See **corn juice**.

corn patty *noun* Same as **dodger**. See also **corn pone**.

1994–97 Montgomery *Coll* (known to Cardwell, Norris, Oliver, Shields), = the recipe is as follows: combine fresh corn with meal, add buttermilk, salt, and pepper, and fry in butter (Brown).

[DARE *corn patty* n chiefly South, South Midland]

corn pone *noun* Corn bread fashioned into various shapes, especially into a small, oval cake or **pone** with the hands and baked (in the past especially in a **Dutch oven** in the coals of a fire); also a large cake of corn bread (see 1997 citation). See also **corn cake**, **corn dodger**, **pone A1**.

1905 Miles *Spirit of Mts* 32 First the oven and its lid are brought out and heated on the fire to be filled with corn-pones—each oval pone with a hand-print conspicuous in its surface. **1927** Justus *Peter Pocket* 66 She shaped the corn dough into three soft corn pones and popped them quickly into the oven. **1934–47** *LAMSAS Appal* = attested by 51/148 speakers (34.4%) from WV, 3/20 (15%) from VA, 4/37 (10.8%) from NC, 7/14 (50%) from SC, and 1/12 (8.3%) from GA. **1937** Hall *Coll* (Gatlinburg TN) Corn pone! Come and get her or leave her alone! (a "husband call" to dinner, a winning entry in a calling contest held at an Old Timers' Day). **1949** Kurath *Word Geog East US* 67 In the valley of the Susquehanna, in all of Pennsylvania lying to the west of it, and in all the Atlantic states south of Pennsylvania *pone*, *corn pone*, and *pone bread* are widely used. **1969** Medford *Finis* 125 The corn pone was rather hard (but fairly good bread); the bacon and gravy rather salty, the sorghum molasses, average, and the coffee black and strong. **1996** Johnson *Lexical Change* 138 = statistically more common in the mountains of South Carolina and Georgia than in the Piedmont and Coastal Plain c1990. **1997** Nelson *Country Folklore* 56 In the oven pan we made huge cakes of corn pone. The cakes of bread were about four or five inches thick. Coals were placed around and on top of the lid. What delicious corn pone it was.

corn shelling *noun* Formerly, a family or community work activity at which the grains are removed from ears of corn dried in a corn crib, with the shelled grains taken to mill to be ground.

1955 Ritchie *Singing Family* 72 The corn crop we planted in spring, hoed in summer, and gathered in the fall would just make bread for the hungry family and feed the mule, the cow, the twenty or thirty chickens, and the two or three pigs during the winter months. The bread from our corn was good. We would get almost to the bottom of the meal barrel, and then would come an evening to have a corn shelling. Sometimes the family did this alone if there were enough of us to shell a turn for the mill in a few minutes but more often the Brashear cousins from across the branch and the Engle cousins from up the holler would come in and we'd shell enough for three or four turns ahead. **1956** Hall *Coll* (Roaring Fork TN) After the close of those corn shellings [and] bean stringings, they would have play . . . sometimes they would have a dance and drink corn whiskey. **1971** *AOHP/ALC-147* They'd have bean stringings, and then they'd have apple peelings and corn shellings.

corn shock *noun* See citation.

1996 Spurlock *Glossary* 394 = dried corn stalks cut and leaned vertically against a "horse," made by tying together the tops of four uncut stalks. The stalks are secured by a stout string tied around the top, making the shock resemble a tepee. Ears of corn are harvested from the stalks at a later date and dried stalks (fodder) fed to livestock.

corn shuck *noun* Same as **shuck[2] A1**.

1989 Oliver *Hazel Creek* 18 Bed ticks were filled with, at first, dry grass and later with corn shucks (noisy and lumpy) or with straw. **1997–98** *Smokies Guide* (Winter) 13 While a less frugal society might simply dispose of the green sheaths which protect corn ears, old-time farmers found over a dozen practical uses. All told, rural folks probably had more uses for shucks than the corn itself. Boiled corn shucks were stripped and stuffed into mattresses and pillows for a soft, sweet-smelling sleep many old-timers remember fondly. Farmers braided shucks into mule and horse collars as well as bridles and rope. Corn shuck mops and doormats were said to be functional and long-lived.

corn-shuck doll *noun* A homemade doll fashioned from husks of corn. Also called **shuck doll**. See also **corn-stalk doll**.

1974 *Cornshuck Dolls* 78 The cornshuck dolls are usually made for doll collectors more than for toys now. **1975** Dwyer *Thangs* 16 Corn-shuck dolls are a traditional folk art of the southern Appalachian mountains. These dolls, small and large (from two to eight inches tall), were made by mountain women as a pastime and to entertain small children. With today's interest in folk art, the older mountain corn-shuck dolls have become museum pieces and collector's items. . . . This basic doll will use about ten pieces of dried husks or shucks. **1993** Page and Smith *Foxfire Toys and Games* 95 Although the cornstalk animals . . . were very popular among children years ago, not as many people remembered making or playing with the cornshuck doll. Today the cornshuck doll has become a popular item for doll collectors.

corn shucking *noun* Traditionally, a festive community work activity, often culminating in dancing and merry-making. Typically a family invites neighbors to help husk a pile of newly harvested corn, sometimes also to help pick it, with the host sometimes placing a bottle of whiskey underneath and the finder either winning it as a prize or having the right to the first drink. Also called **shucking 1**, **shucking bee**, **shuck pulling**. See also **shuck[2] B1**.

[**1843** (in **1974** Harris *High Times* 30) The way they do things in Morgan pleases me, especially deer hunting and corn-shucking, and corn-shucking in particular. All the corn on the farm is gathered and heaped at the crib, and then gather the maids and men. They are divided into companies, and the corn into as many heaps. At it they go—hurrah, men, women, boys and girls, for a race! Singing, talking, betting, drinking, shucking, or husking, as you call it; and last, though not least, kissing who, when, and where they please, and as often as they wish for the red ears.] **1861** *Martin CW Letters* (Nov 15) Mr B—s had a cotting picking last week and corn shucking at night and afrolick after that. **1862** *Tesh CW Letters* (July 4) Tell John and Sam I want them to make all the corn They can so they can have a big corn shucking this Fall. [**1892** Dromgoole *War of Roses* 482 Corn-shucking is a courtesy, however, as sacred to the mountaineer as assisting at a funeral, or "sittin' up with a corpse."] **1924** Abernethy *Moonshine* 132 They never went anywhere; that is to say, the women went wherever there was a "quiltin'" or birth in the neighborhood; the men went to "corn-shuckin's," "log-rollin's," and, on every fifth Sunday, to the meetin'-house. **1954** GSMNP-19:9 A corn shucking . . . it's where people gathers up and shucks corn, in the fall when they get the corn gathered. **1964** Greve *Story of Gatlinburg* 62 "Corn-shuckings" afforded occasions for jollity at harvest time, the men assembling in the barn to shuck the ripe corn that had been brought in; and great was the hilarity over the speed contests, when men vied with each other to see who could shuck a bushel of corn in the shortest time. **1969** GSMNP-37:2:24 They'd have corn shucking, you know, and a jug of liquor hid in the back of the shed where they had the corn throwed in. They'd shuck till they come to that liquor. Then they'd clean up. They'd have it all shucked out by the time they found it, and they'd clean up the shucks and put them in the barn loft and they'd dance from that till daylight. **1972** GSMNP-93:14 You folks would call it husking bees. But we called it corn shuckings. **1986** Pederson et al. *LAGS* = attested by 5/60 interviewees (8.3%) from E TN and 1/35 (2.9%) from N GA; 6/6 of all LAGS interviewees (100%) attesting term were from Appalachia.

[DARE *corn shucking* n 1 chiefly South, South Midland]

cornsilk *noun* One of many silk-like threads hanging in a tassel from an ear of corn. Also called **silk**.

1940 Still *River of Earth* 138 He had brought a dozen [ears of corn] down from the bench field and cornsilks were scattered about like brown locks of a woman's hair. **1941** Stuart *Men of Mts* 174 Summer is the trail of beauty, growth, and fragrant smells of devil-shoestring blossoms, corn silks, and corn tassels.

corn squeezings *noun* Homemade corn whiskey.

1959 Hall Coll (Del Rio TN) You double it back and you run it again. Then you get your good whiskey, which the old people called "corn squeezin's." **c1960** Wilson Coll = home-made whiskey. **1968** *End of Moonshining* 101 Various names given moonshine include . . . corn squeezin's. **1975** Carter *Gospel Truth* Whiskey was "ruckus juice" or "corn squeezins."

[DARE *corn squeezings* n especially Midland]

corn-stalk doll (also *corn-stalk horse*, etc.) *noun* A children's toy made of corn stalks. See also **corn-shuck doll**.

c1945 Haun *Hawk's Done* 223 He would make cornstalk dolls when she told him to make them and would rock them to sleep in his arms and try to sing the songs she told him to sing. **1953** Hall Coll (Mt Sterling NC) He would take a length of corn stalk between two joints. He made corn-stalk horses for toys. **1986** Tyson *Reflections* 18 We kids did have fun and enjoyed ourselves even if we didn't have the toys kids have today. The only toys we had were rag dolls or cornstalk horses. [**1997** Montgomery Coll Dolls were made of cornstalk (for arms and legs), corn silk (for hair), and cornshuck for the body (Cardwell); Stalks were used for making horses, cabins, and animals (Jones); Horses, fiddles, and dolls were made from cornstalks (Brown).]

corn whiskey See **corn juice**.

corpse flower (also *corpse plant*) *noun* A white, leafless wildflower (*Monotropa uniflora*) with a single, pipe-shaped blossom and a pale appearance due to a lack of chlorophyll; fresh juice derived from the plant has medicinal uses. Also called **ghostflower**, **Indian pipe**.

1901 Lounsberry *Sthn Wild Flowers* 376 Its small nodding flowers are shaped like a pipe, and its look is ghost-like, the plant being entirely without the grains of chlorophyll, which produce the green colouring matter we are so accustomed to seeing in foliage. **1971** Hutchins *Hidden Valley* 146 Sometimes these peculiar plants are also called "ghostflowers" or "corpse flowers," both names being quite descriptive. **1982** Stupka *Wildflowers* 77 Indian pipe . . . is also called "ghost flower" and "corpse plant."

[because of its colorless appearance and its tendency to turn black when handled]

corpse money *noun* See citation.

1967 Jones *Peculiarities Mtneers* 77 Some mountain families owned what was called "corpse money." This usually consisted of two silver half dollars that had been used to close the eye lids of some deceased member of the family. These coins were carefully preserved and used again in subsequent deaths. It was considered very bad luck to permit any but family members to use the coins.

corpse-yard *noun* A cemetery.

1937 Thornburgh *Great Smoky Mts* 94 She's buried in the corpse-yard yander. **1997** Montgomery Coll (known to Brown).

corruption *noun* Pus from a sore, boil, or wound.

1915 Dingus *Word-List VA* 182 = pus. **1934–47** LAMSAS Appal (Madison Co NC, Swain Co NC). **1966** Dakin *Vocab Ohio River Valley* 480 *Corruption* and *matter* appear with about equal frequency and both are heard from the Tennessee border to the National Road. *Corruption* is the more common term in Kentucky, however, and was unquestionably the predominant usage among those who came into the Ohio Valley from the south. **2000** Lowry *Folk Medical Term* = purulent material. **2005** Williams *Gratitude* 487 = purulent drainage . . . a sure sign of infection in a wound.

[OED3 *corruption* n 3 obsolete except dialect; DARE *corruption* n 1 chiefly South, South Midland]

co-sheep (also *coo-nan, coo-nannie, coo-sheepie, co-sheepie, cu-sheep, cu-sheepie*, and variants) *interjection* Come! (used as a call to sheep, sometimes uttered in a repetition of the last part). See also **sheepie**, **sheep-i-nan**.

1903 Fox *Little Shepherd* 37 "Coo-oo-sheep! Coo-oo-sh'p-cooshy-cooshy-coo-oo-sheep!" The sheep were answering. They were coming down a ravine, and Chad's voice rang out above. **1915** Dingus *Word-List VA* 182 *coo-sheep* = a call to sheep. Also *coo-sheepy, coo-nan, coo-nannie.* **1949** Kurath *Word Geog East US* 30 In the Appalachians south of the Kanawha the Virginia Piedmont call *co-sheep* now competes with the Midland call [*Sheep! Sheepie!*]. *Ibid.* 42 The *co-sheep!* of the Appalachians south of the Kanawha may be due to Virginia [Piedmont] influence. **1957** Broaddus *Vocab Estill Co KY* 19 *coo sheep, coo sheep, coo sheep* = the way sheep are called. **1962** Wilson *Folkways Mammoth Cave* 10 "Cu-sheep, cu-sheep" or just "Sheep, sheep, sheepie" should attract the attention of all the woolly ones. **1978** Reese *Speech NE Tenn* 32 *coo-nan* = attested by 1/12 (8.3%) speakers; *co-sheep* = attested by 8/12 (66.7%) speakers. **1987** Carver *Regional Dialects* 167 The Upper South is distinguished by *co-sheep(ie)* or *cu-sheep(ie)*, used to bring sheep in from the pasture, and *cope* or *kwope*, the corresponding call to horses. Both expressions have the nearly universal, abbreviated form of "come": *co-*, *cu-*, or *kwo-*, the latter call, *cope*, probably deriving from *come up*. **1995** Montgomery *Coll*: *co-sheep* (known to Cardwell).

[DARE *co-sheep(ie)* v phr chiefly South Midland]

co-sheepie See **co-sheep**.

cosses See **cost A1**.

cost

A *verb*

1 variant third-singular forms of two syllables: *coss-es, cost-es.* See also **-es**[2].

[See **1895** in **B**.] **1939** Burnett *Gap o' Mountains* 55 "Before I'll be bamboozled by that old buzzard," Mose declared, "I'll carry it to the Supreme Court of the United States if it costes me my farm." **1942** Hall *Phonetics Smoky Mts* 81. **1953** Atwood *Verbs East US* 28 A variation from the usual inflectional pattern (/s/ after voiceless consonants) is seen in the form *costes* . . . which occurs occasionally in the Chesapeake Bay area, s. W.Va., N.C., S.C., and Ga. All together, 54 informants (51 of them in Type I [= older speakers with little formal education]) use this form. A similar form, *cosses*, . . . is used by nine additional Southern informants. **1974** Fink *Bits Mt Speech* 5 Hit *costes* too much.

[DARE *cost* v A1 especially South Midland]

2 variant past-tense form of two syllables: *cost-ed.*

1956 Hall *Coll* (Hurricane Creek NC) It never costed me one red cent. **1972** *Burial Customs* 19 You never could get kicked out, but it costed you so much to belong to it. **1979** *Big South Fork OHP-2* They costed from three to five hundred dollars a mule. **1984–86** *Sevier Settler* 3:7 I had to go swear out the marriage license, which costed me six dollars, and I bought a piece of chocolate pie for lunch for ten cents. **2008** Salsi *Ray Hicks* 71 The smooth white paper they sold costed a lot.

B *noun* variant plural form of two syllables: *cost-es.*

1895 Edson and Fairchild *TN Mts* 375 The most interesting thing . . . is the use of a vowel in plurals and the third singular of verbs, giving such forms as *costes, vestes, postes, nestes.*

costed See **cost A2**.

costes See **cost A1**, **B**.

costivity *noun* Expense.

1928 (in **1952** Mathes *Tall Tales* 53) They kep' hands off an' let the law handle John when a lot of folks would 'a' saved the state the costivity of tryin' that feller, an' then feedin' an' clothin' him. **1996** Montgomery *Coll* (known to Oliver, but not to other consultants from the Smoky Mountains).

costy *adjective* Expensive, costly.

1962 Dykeman *Tall Woman* 243 It can be mighty costy to a feller. **1991** Still *Wolfpen Notebooks* 104 When coffee gets more costy than likker, I'm drinking likker.

[*cost* n + *-y* adjective-forming suffix; OED3 *costy* adj obsolete]

cotch See **catch A1**, **A2**, **A3**.

cotched See **catch A2**, **A3**.

cotee *verb* See citation.

1982 Slone *How We Talked* 76 = repeat a phrase from the Bible, giving chapter and verse, from memory. Many of our old folks could "cotee" large portions of the Bible correctly.

cottage meeting *noun* See citation. See also **meeting**.

1984 High *Titan Rock* 40 Back years ago in the Gorge they'd have what we'd call cottage meetings. They would go from house to house like they did in olden times, breaking bread like the Bible tells us.

cottonheaded *adjective* Fair-headed.

c1960 Wilson *Coll*: *cotton-headed* = with light-colored hair, tow-headed. **1995** Montgomery *Coll*: *cottonheaded* (known to Cardwell); There were a lot of cotton-headed kids around (Shields).

[DARE *cottonhead* n 1 especially South, South Midland]

cough *verb* To cause to cough.

2001 Lowry *Expressions* 17 I get a little tickle in my throat and it coughs me.

coughweed *noun* A perennial ragwort (*Senecio aureus*) used medicinally. Same as **squaw-weed**.

1960 Price *Root Digging in Appal* 9 The common names more often suggest medicinal uses, among them . . . coughweed. **1971** Krochmal et al. *Medicinal Plants Appal* 234 *Senecio aureus* . . . As the common name, "coughweed," would indicate, the herb is an expectorant. **1999** Montgomery *Coll* (known to Cardwell).

could See **can**[1].

counterpane *noun*

A variant forms *contypin* [see **1863** in **B**], *counterpin, countypin* [see **1931** in **B**].

1917 Kephart *Word-List* 410 *counterpin* = variant of *counterpane.*

B Usually a white cotton bed cover woven on a loom; more generally, a bedspread. See also **cover B1**, **coverlet.**

1863 *Brown CW Letters* (Oct 2) her Sister had dide [= died] and left her a fine quilt and a Contypin and her likeness to rember her. **1931** Goodrich *Mt Homespun* 10 The "Countypin" drafts, for weaving white cotton counterpanes, are rather different from the drafts for the coverlets. **1934–47** *LAMSAS Appal* (Madison Co NC) *counterpin*; (Madison Co NC, Swain Co NC) *countypin.* **1937** Eaton *Handicrafts* 112–13 Sometimes the term "counterpane" is applied to the coverlet, but with Highland weavers there is a distinction. **1959** Hall *Coll* (Waynesville NC) I wove a web of coverlids and a web of counterpins. **1966** Frome *Strangers* 241 She knew how to make "ooze" out of barks, roots, and weeds and could explain every step in the making of "county pins" (counterpanes, in the outside world), from the raising of sheep, through shearing, washing, spinning, twisting, and dyeing of wool to making of such old patterns as the "Rattlesnake" and "Gentleman's Fancy." **2001** Wilson *Textile Art* 104 = an all white cotton bedcover made in a variety of styles and methods, including those that require weaving, knitting, crocheting, and candlewicking techniques.

[DARE *counterpin* n "bedspread" chiefly South, South Midland]

counterpin See **counterpane.**

counting stick *noun* Formerly, a primitive device for adding sums.

1950 Justus *Luck for Lihu* 65 The "counting stick" was a stick full of notches on which the Linders counted up the prices of different things.

country *noun* The immediate vicinity or district in which one resides or is situated.

1835 Crockett *Account* 45 If you was to talk that way to a man in my country, he'd give you first-rate hell. **1864** *C A Walker CW Letters* (April 24) this is a great deal better a country than Cherokee Co. **1864** *Chapman CW Letters* (March 6) yo wanted to now how times was in this Cuntry. **1939** Hall *Coll* (Bradley Fork NC) I removed my mill on the waters of Flat Creek, Tennessee, Sevier County, and there I stayed a year, and I never was in such a law breaking country in my life. It was no count, and I decided to leave. *Ibid.* (Smokemont NC) Ask Will Elmore where he is. [He] knows everbody in that country. **1957** *GSMNP*-23:2:10 I can tell you every man [who] entered land in this country around here. **1979** *Big South Fork OHP*-10 He sawed this whole country out here for years, cutting logs. **1991** Thomas *Sthn Appal* 216 They come a diphtheria outbreak through here one time, an' killed all th' children, nearly, in th' country. **1998** *Dante OHP*-25 We've held revivals all over this country at school houses and everywhere.

[DARE *country* n B1 especially South Midland]

country bank *noun* See citation. Same as **doghole.**

1943 Korson *Coal Dust* 4 Some farmers . . . operated small mines variously called "country banks," "wagon mines," "dog holes," "gopher holes," or "father-and-son" mines.

country butter *noun* Homemade butter from cow's milk, as distinct from margarine and commercially produced butter. See also **cow butter.**

1984 Head *Brogans* 34 Sometimes, in addition to the milk, we bought a pound of butter, which was called "country butter," to distinguish it from the margarine sold in stores. Country butter is a product of churned milk. **1997** Montgomery *Coll* (known to Adams, Bush, Ellis, Jones, Ledford, Norris, Weaver); He is as plain as country butter (Cardwell).

country jake *noun* Same as **jake A1.**

1891 Brown *Dialect in TN* 173 If his clothes are *tacky* and he appears to be from the backwoods, he is called a *country-jake*, and is said to look *jakey.* **1962** Wilson *Folkways Mammoth Cave* 45 To put a person in his place, or *take him down a button-hole*, you call him a *clodhopper*, *a hick*, *a country jake.*

[DARE (at *country*) n 2a scattered, but chiefly West Midland]

country legs *noun* Lower legs with red and white blotches from having sat close to the fire. See also **fire-blossomed**, **pieded 2.**

1996 Montgomery *File* (known to 75-year-old woman, Newport TN).

countryman *noun* A person who resides in or belongs to a rural region, a rustic.

1901 Harben *Westerfelt* 215 Worthy was weighing a pail of butter for a countryman in a slouch hat and a suit of brown jeans. **c1950** Adams *Grandpap* 85 He had the reputation of driving hard bargains with countrymen who brought in their stuff to trade. **1963–64** Stubbs *Mountain-Wise* (Dec–Jan) 13 This feller . . . came both mornin' and evenin' and every time he bought two hammers for a dollar and a half apiece. The store man became puzzled and asked him, "What are you a-doin' with all those hammers?" The countryman said, "A-sellin' 'em." **1964** Stubbs *Mountain-Wise* (Oct–Nov) 13 Once a countryman stormed into a local store and remarked, "Hit's too danged cold to snow." Then he turned to the storekeeper and asked, "Have you got a Grier's Almanac?" The latter said he had one. "Well," said the countryman, "give me one then, for I've got tired of a-takin' the weather as hit comes."

[DARE (at *country* n B 2d) chiefly South Atlantic]

country round-up *noun* A lively party with square dancing.

1973 *GSMNP*-5:7 They could pick and play the fiddle, and we would go and just have a time, running old country roundup. **1996–97** Montgomery *Coll* (known to Bush, Oliver).

country sager Same as **sager.**

1949 McDavid *Grist* 107 (DeKalb Co GA) = a rustic. **1986** Pederson et al. (Chattanooga Co GA).

county *noun* variant forms *ceounty*, *cyounty.*

1913 Kephart *Our Sthn High* 394 She's got, I reckon, about the toughest deestric in the ceounty, which is saying a good deal. **1994** Montgomery *Coll*: *cyounty* (known to Cardwell).

county law *noun* A county-level law-enforcement officer. See also **law**[2].

1975 Woolley *We Be Here* 27 If the county law and all his deputies, and the state polices and Governor Ford ain't gonna see that we get justice, they's going to drive us into the mountains.

county pin See **counterpane.**

county site (also *county town*) *noun* A county seat.

1841 Donaldson (in **1934** Smith *Tennessean's Pronunciation* 263). **1862** *Alexander CW Letters* (May 28) This is in my opinion a healthy county a high roling mountainous place we are located in a half mile of Clinton the county site of Anderson County. **1910** Essary *TN Mtneers* 12 Happy was a regular attender on all of the courts of his county town, although he never had any special business except to meet the boys and get a few drinks of the joyful, which the more fortunate always had on such occasions. **1913** Kephart *Our Sthn High* 322 I'd haffter walk nineteen miles out to the railroad, pay seventy miles round-trip to the county-site, pay my board thar fer mebbe a week, and then a witness don't git no fee at all onless they convict. **1994–97** Montgomery *Coll* (known to Brown, Cardwell).

[DARE *county site* n chiefly southern Appalachians]

county town See **county site.**

courage *noun* Male sexual desire or vigor.

1983 Broaddus *Estill Co KY Word List* 36 = sexual desire. **2003** Cavender *Folk Medicine* 203 = sexual drive, as in, "My husband's lost his courage." **2007** Myers *Smoky Mt Remedies* 9 = sex drive. "Her husband has lost his courage."

course *verb*

1 To trace or follow (wild bees) to their tree by observing their direction of flight; to direct (a colony of wild bees) into a hive.

1926 Hunnicutt *Twenty Years* 73 I told him I was going to course the bees. **1950** Woody *Cataloochee Homecoming* 13 He could "course" a bee with an unerring eye, and he seldom got a sting. **1952** Stuart *Christmas in Valley* 81 Trace a bee to its hive by following its observed direction of flight. "Once I watched the wild bees in the warm sand . . . she (Grandma) told me how to "course" them. I went to a place as far as my eye could follow them from the stream. I stood at this place and, keeping the bees between me and the sun so they would look bigger, just as Grandma told me, I watched them in a white oak on Grandma's farm. **1976** Carroll and Pulley *Little Cataloochee* 18 He was an expert in searching out bee trees and had the ability to course bees into hives for the purpose of producing honey. **1991** Thomas *Sthn Appal* 58 Th' hardest bunch of bees that I ever tried to find was back over here. Folks had course 'um th' year before. An' ever tree in th' woods there had been looked. An' they come after me, an' wonted me to go over there, an' see if I could find 'um. **2007** Farr *My Appalachia* 59 To fill his new bee gums, Dad would go "coursing" the wild bees. He put corncobs soaked in honey in a cleared spot in the woods, sat down nearby, and waited for the bees to find the bait. Soon dozens of bees were attracted to the spot. When they rose up to fly home, he noted the direction and followed. It might take several baits placed out before he could find the bee tree.

2 To ascertain the path of (hunted game).

2013 Venable *How to Tawlk* 10 = to follow, usually by sound: "'At turkey gobbled at everthank: crows, thunder, jaybirds. Hit was rail easy to course him."

court *verb*

1 To attend court proceedings; hence verbal noun *courting*.

1904–20 Kephart *Notebooks* 4:887 He puts in most of his time a-courtin' [i.e. in court]. **1917** Kephart *Word-List* 410 = attending court, litigating. "Bill, are they *courtin'* up there yit?" **1927** Woofter *Dialect from WV* 352 *courting* = attending the circuit court. "My brother has been at courting for two weeks." **1997** Montgomery *Coll* (Brown, Hooper).

2 To sue, take legal actions against (someone).

1974 Fink *Bits Mt Speech* 5 = to sue at law. "Jones *courted* Smith over a horse." **1997** Montgomery *Coll* (known to Brown).

[DARE *court* v chiefly southern Appalachians]

court around *verb phrase* To spend time at a county courthouse during sessions of court hoping to be empaneled on a jury (and thereby earn a fee).

1994–97 Montgomery *Coll* (known to Brown, Cardwell).

courting dulcimer *noun* See citations. Same as **double dulcimer.**

1983 *Dark Corner OHP-24A* I built what is called a courting dulcimer. It's got strings on two sides, and what it would be is when the young man would come to court, he would bring this double or courting dulcimer with two sets of strings, and he and the young lady would sit outside on the porch, and the parents figured as long as they could hear two sets of strings playing, everything was all right, and that if one would play one part and the woman would play the other part, and if they could play well together, that was a good sign that the marriage might work. So it was called a double or a courting dulcimer. **2006** *Encycl Appalachia* 181 In some parts of the region, especially in eastern Kentucky, a young couple might be allowed to visit without parental supervision if they jointly played the "courting dulcimer," an Appalachian instrument possessing two fretboards. As long as the nearby parents could hear both sets of strings being strummed, they could leave the couple unobserved, knowing that the young man and woman were properly preoccupied.

coutn't See **can**[1] **A3.**

cove *noun* A relatively level valley, chiefly or entirely enclosed by hills or mountains, with arable land and a single drainage outlet; also used in place-names, especially in the Smoky Mountains, as in *Cades Cove* (TN), *Big Cove* (NC).

1762 (in **1940** McJimsey *Topo Terms in VA* 167) On the ridges and in the Coves of a mountain. **1774** *Dunmore's War* 3 This day I leave this neighborhood to go towards the Rye Coves. **1860** *Week in Smokies* 124 I saw scarcely any calico, and of course crinoline has never penetrated these coves of the mountains. **1864** *Brown CW Letters* (Aug 22) the twelth india[na] caverly gite whip every time they go in the Cove but we have bin over thare twice and they dont show them selves and if we were to se them i dont think we wold run with loded guns. **1890** Carpenter *Thunderhead Peak* 140 A "cove" is a valley that lies between two mountain ridges, generally ending in a point like a cove on the sea-shore. **1908** Smith *Reminiscences* 405 The mountaineers in all this region dwell in the valleys or "coves," only herders straying from spring until fall, their cattle on the heights. **1931** Burns *Coves Blount Co* 46 In the southern part of Sevier [County], and in Blount County, there is a group of three large and very interesting coves. They lie completely imbedded among the mountains. The first two are surrounded by these ridges which occur in the space between the main Unaka Range and the outlier-Chilhowee Mountain; the third lies immediately at the base of the main range. They all have nearly the same dimensions, ranging from five to six miles in length, and from one and a half to two miles in breadth. **1937** Hall *Coll* (Wears Cove TN) Only the enclosed valleys are called "coves." "Cove" is originally a nautical term. **1959** Pearsall *Little Smoky* 28 Everywhere in the mountains there are sections of lower and smoother land that can be placed under profitable cultivation, but they are scattered across the map in a patchwork arrangement along stream valleys and in basins and "coves." **a1975** Lunsford *It Used to Be* 70 A cove is a place in the mountains where two ridges go up to the top of the mountain, and between the two ridges the waters coursed. There would be a spring near the top of the mountain. Some of those fields would be cleared up, and the hollow, or cove,—that would be the smaller cove—and there could be a cove with many smaller ridges, or smaller coves in it, but it'd be a larger range coming down, and that would make the bigger cove, all of it steep land. **1977** Shields *Cades Cove* 2 A mountain cove, similar to its aquatic counterpart, is a low area, surrounded by mountains and having a single drainage outlet. **1986** *Back Home Blount Co* 91 The Chilhowee Mountains, which are the outlying front of the Great Smoky Mountains over-thrust fault, shield the approach to areas known as "coves": Miller's Cove, Tuckaleechee Cove, and Cades Cove. In the overlying Precambrian-Cambrian rocks, which are dominated by shales, sandstone, and graywacke, these "coves" are geological windows through which the younger Ordovician limestones have been exposed by millions of years of erosion. This overthrust dates to the extensive mountain building Permian period of the Paleozoic era some 220 to 270 million years ago. **1988** Moore *Roadside Guide* 29 In several areas [of the Great Smoky Mountains] erosion has weathered through the older Precambrian rocks, exposing the younger Paleozoic rocks beneath the thrust fault. Areas where the Paleozoic limestones and shales have been exposed have formed mountain coves such as Cades Cove and Wears Cove. These coves are surrounded by older and topographically higher rock strata to form "windows" down into the younger (limestone) strata of the cove. The fertile, deep soils produced by the weathering of the limestone made the coves attractive places for pioneers to settle and farm. **2005** Fisher *CW in Smokies* 16 The other sites favored by the settlers were the numerous Smoky Mountain coves, including Weir, Tuckaleechee, and Jones coves in Sevier County, Miller and Cades in Blount, and Big and Little Cataloochee in Haywood. Coves offered their own substantial advantages: level and fertile land for farming, rich pastures for cattle on the mountain slopes and balds, and protection from the extremes of both summer and winter.

[by analogy with the marine counterpart; DARE *cove* n[1] 3, especially South Midland]

coveite (also *covite*) *noun* An inhabitant of the hills, a rustic (especially in the vicinity of Sewanee TN).

1898 Elliott *Durket Sperret* 79 "If you should ask a Covite that question," he answered, "he would very soon show you that he did not consider your condition any better than his own." **1963** Edwards *Gravel* 7 He is a ridge-runner and a cove-ite all kneaded into one, with gravel in his shoes. **1994** (in DSAE file) In my 33rd year, I heard one [= a nickname for a person from Appalachia] that was new to me. A woman from around Ashland, KY (in the northeastern "corner" of the state) said of a man we both knew "Oh he's a cove-ite." I knew immediately what she meant by this and didn't ask her about the term's provenance. **2006** Lang *Conversations* 275 They [= people in Sewanee TN] called me a coveite because they surmised that I came from a cove. The people living in the area were referred to in the same way, and they weren't welcome in the university chapel.

[DARE *coveite* n southern Appalachians, especially east TN]

cove juice *noun* Homemade whiskey.

1952 Wilson *Folk Speech NC* 530 = whisky. **1968** *End of Moonshining* 101 Various names given moonshine include . . . cove juice.

cover

A *noun, verb* variant forms *civer, kiver, kivver*.

1862 *Robinson CW Letters* (Sept 4) one [bomb] struck close to a woman & child & civerd the child nearley up with the dirt. **1862** *Willis CW Letters* (Aug 31) we make a bed on the ground & kiver with our blankets. **1873** Smith *Arp Peace Papers* 23 The yaller leaves of autum have kivered the ground. **1904–20** Kephart *Notebooks* 2:399 I got lots o' bed-kivers. We'll jest make a pallet on the floor. **c1926** Bird *Cullowhee Wordlist* You ain't got enough kiver on the bed. **c1940** Simms *Coll* Why [the growth of flowers] kivers the mountains like cyarpet (carpets) and is a heap sight purty. **1944** Justus *Billy and Bones* 48 It's good luck . . . to sleep under a new kivver, I've always heard tell. **1969** GSMNP-37:2:4 I says, "I'd rather just fill [the hole] back up and kiver it up like it was a grave." **1970** Mull *Mt Yarns* 7 "Snaking the kivvers," that is removing all the bed clothes from beds before retiring and shaking them good, became essential. **1971** *AOHP/ALC-129* Hit's kivered up deep in the mine by a mine fall. **1984** *Six Hill 'n Holler* 9 *kiver* = quilt, blanket or the like.

[DARE *cover* n, v A South, Midland, occasionally New England]

B *noun*

1 A bedspread, usually a **coverlet**. See also **counterpane B.**

1901 McClintock *KY Mts* 27 The "kivers" are made of a cotton warp and the wool has two shuttles, one carrying the white cotton and the other the wool. These "kivers" are the favorite product of the loom. They are heavy coverlets, handed down from generation to generation, and constitute a point in social distinction. **1913** Kephart *Our Sthn High* 245–46 In many homes you will still find the ancient spinning-wheel, with a hand loom on the porch and in the loft there will be a set of quilting frames for making "kivers." **2012** Houk *Weaving in Smokies* 40 The traditional Appalachian coverlet, or "kivver," was produced in a weaving style called overshot (a "shot" being one row).

2 The front or back surface of a book, especially the Bible. Same as **lid 1**.

1923 (in **1952** Mathes *Tall Tales* 5) An' as sure as this Good Book's true from kiver to kiver, they's goin' to come a time when ye got to answer the Jedge when he axes ye, "Why ain't ye got on a weddin-garment"—ah? **1939** Hall *Coll* Preachers boast of reading the Bible from kiver to kiver, lid to lid. **1995** Stone *Smoky Mt Women* 70 Ogle said Lydia was a "good little Christian" who could quote the Bible from "kiver to kiver."

3 A roof.

1939 Hall *Coll* (Cataloochee NC) A cover would be an old board roof made of split boards. It's used by old people lots. *Ibid.* (Saunook NC) That's an old-timey kiver on that house. Kiver is used for roof by old people. You never hear it from the young generation.

covered up *participial adjective phrase* Inundated (with work), made or caused to be busy or crowded.

1962 Stubbs *Mountain-Wise* (Aug–Sept) 8 A man who operated an automobile repair shop in the vicinity was described thus: "He needs a mechanic to help him. He's *all covered up* with work." **1971** *Corn Shuckin's* 106 We had th'whole place covered up with young people. **1998** Montgomery *Coll* I'll be covered slam up (Andrews); He's been covered up with work (Cardwell).

coverhauls *noun* A one-piece article of men's clothing, consisting of overalls with sleeves. See also **unionalls 1**.

1986 Pederson et al. *LAGS* (Cumberland Co TN, Stephens Co GA).

[apparently a blend of *coveralls* + *overhalls*]

coverlet *noun*

A variant forms *covalid* [see **1862** Councill in **B**], *cover lead* [see **1862** Dalton in **B**], *coverled* [see **1934–47** in **B**], *coverlid* [see **1914** in **B**], *coverlit* [see **1966–68** in **B**], *kiverlid* [see **1975** in **B**], *kiverlit* [see **c1945** in **B**], *kivirlid* [see **1866** in **B**].**B** A bedspread, often a fancy one kept on top of the bed only for decoration. See also **counterpane B**, **cover B1**.

1862 Councill *CW Letters* (Feb 4) I wosch I had my Covalid at home fore I have got as mutch as I can tote. **1862** Dalton *CW Letters* (Jan 8) i have got monney A plenty if i hade a cover lead or a bed quilt i[t] wood do. **1866** (in **1974** Harris *High Times* 287) Yet still onder that black velvit kivirlid, inside that iron coffin, atwix the fine linen an' that shrivil'd hide ove his'n, is that ball ove dirt. **1891** Brown *Dialect in TN* 173 We sleep under a *counterpin* instead of a *counterpane* and call it a *coverlet* until we learn that we ought to say *lid* instead of *led*; then we call it a *coverlid*. **1914** Arthur *Western NC* 260 Some of these counterpanes or "coverlids" were marvels of skill and beauty in color and design and all were woven in the loom which stood at one end of the porch or shed in front of the house. **1931** Goodrich *Mt Homespun* 4–5 Of all the fabrics, the coverlets were the most interesting. They were of lighter weight than those in the North, as befitted the milder climate, and were almost all in overshot designs. In very old ones the cotton was hand spun. Later, thread was bought from small country mills under the name of "bunch thread." **1934–47** *LAMSAS Appal* (Madison Co NC) *coverled*. **c1945** Haun *Hawk's Done* 292 I told him I could spin and knit and weave, and about the Gentleman's Fancy kiverlit I had wove and how warm they would be to sleep under at nighttime. **1966** Dakin *Vocab Ohio River Valley* 192 In the Mountains and eastern Knobs of Kentucky *coverlid* is common and the most frequently used older term. A number of older speakers mention no other. **1966–68** *DARE Survey* (Brasstown NC) *coverlet*; (Spruce Pine NC) *coverlit*; (Gatlinburg TN) *coverlid*. **1975** Chalmers *Better* 12 It had been made a museum of sorts, with hand made dresser and corner cupboards, rope beds with straw ticks and hand woven "kiverlids." **2001** Wilson *Textile Art* 1 In practical usage, a coverlet usually refers to a bed cover woven on a handloom (without power) by individuals not working in a factory setting. Coverlets cover the top and sides of the bed, while bedspreads spread over the mattress to the floor at the sides and end of the bed. Older southern Appalachians continue to use the words cover, coverlid, counterpin and county pin, and counterpane to describe their handwoven bedding, but the word "coverlet" is regarded as the acceptable name for handwoven, wool and cotton material used as a bed cover.

coverlid, **coverlit** See **coverlet**.

cover-under man *noun* A detective.

1937 Hall *Coll* (Cosby Creek TN) I axed if you was a cover-under man, and he said you wasn't.

[inversion of word order]

covey dirt *noun* See citation.

1967 *DARE Survey* (Gatlinburg TN) = loose, dark soil.

covite See **coveite**.

cow *noun* variant form *cyow*.

1939 Walker *Mtneer Looks* 5 Only a few mountaineers say *cyar* for *car* and *gyarden* for *garden*, but it would be an impossibility for most of them to pronounce *cow* any other way than *cyow*, or *care* any other way than *kyeer* or *kyer*. **1942** Hall *Phonetics Smoky Mts* 46. **1994** Montgomery *Coll* (known to Cardwell).

cow beast See **cow brute**.

cow brute (also *cow beast*, *cow critter*) *noun* A cow or bull, used especially as a euphemism for the latter (traditionally a taboo term often not used in mixed or polite company). Same as **beast B2**, **brute**, **male brute**. See also **mammy cow brute**.

1867 Harris *Sut Lovingood* 126–27 I'se sorter fear'd tu try tu tell yu, George, the devilment that cussed infunel fool cow beaste wer a-doin. **1886** Smith *Sthn Dialect* 350 There are still others [= terms] which have not, so far as I know, the authority of Old English: . . . cow-beast or cow-brute (cow). **1889** Murfree *Broomsedge Cove* 126 Ye had better lay off ter milk the cow-critters. **1937** (in **1952** Mathes *Tall Tales* 218) It was hard to understand his mumbling jargon when he would accost a neighbor, but sooner or later he would make it clear that he was wanting to buy, sell, or swap a cow-brute or a beef-critter. **1939** Hall *Coll* (Saunook NC) It is still not good form to use the word "bull" in the presence of women. "Cow brute" is used instead. **1943** Justus *Bluebird* 47 No doubt it was hard for a cow beast to understand the reason why one piece of pasture isn't as free for her as for another. **1956** Hall *Coll* (Roaring Fork TN) They'd split rails and build rail fences to protect their crops, and the law was to build it five rails high, and if a cow brute broke over that and hit five rails high, the owner of the brute had to pay for the damage, but if it was under that, the damage was his loss. **c1960** Wilson *Coll*: *cow critter* = any member of the cattle family—usually humorous. **1963** Arnow *Flowering* 144 Not many years ago some back-hill mothers who would have blushed at the word *bull*, saying *cow-brute* instead, used the four letter words of Shakespeare in discussing the bodily functions of their babies or the farm animals. **1969** GSMNP-46:7 I can just about tell his age on a steer or cow brute, but now a horse, I can just tell an old one and young one apart. **1997** Montgomery *Coll*: *cow beast* = found only in old wills (Oliver).

[redundant forms; DARE *cowbrute* n Midland, Southwest, *cow critter* chiefly South Midland]

cow butter *noun* Homemade butter from cow's milk, as distinct from margarine. See also **country butter**.

1863 *Neves CW Letters* (March 26) tha[y] give us apple buter & cow butter to Eat up hear. **1975–76** *Wolfram/Christian WV Coll* 85 They had old butter, you know, old cow butter. **1976** Garber *Mountainese* 18 = homemade butter. "We allers serve real cow butter atter the cows cum fresh." **1994–97** Montgomery *Coll* (known to Adams, Brown, Cardwell, Ledford, Norris, Weaver).

cow cousins *noun* See citation.

1944 Hayes *Word-List NC* 33 = cousins weaned on the milk of the same cow.

cow critter See **cow beast**.

cowcumber See **cucumber**.

cowcumber tree See **cucumber tree**.

cow cushion *noun* A patty of dried cow manure.

1984 Burns *Cold Sassy* 66 He and I had us a great manure war then, throwing dry cow cushions and sheep pills and horse biscuits at each other and dying laughing.

cow doctor *noun*

1 A person who treats animal ailments and diseases, a veterinarian.

1973 GSMNP-76:31 Old Dave Plemmons was a cow doctor. **1981** Whitener *Folk-Ways* 27 The word veterinarian was never used when I was growing up. We had one local cow-doctor and he made his rounds through each community, de-horning and doctoring cattle. **1996–98** Montgomery *Coll* (known to Brown, Ledford, Oliver, Weaver).

2 A self-taught doctor, often one not very capable.

1998 Montgomery *Coll* (known to Brown, Cardwell, Jones, Weaver).

co-wench *interjection* Come! (used as a call to cows).

1978 Reese *Speech NE Tenn* 30 = attested by 2/12 (16.7%) speakers.

[DARE *co-wench* v phr chiefly South Atlantic]

cow gap *noun* Same as **milk gap**.

1986 Pederson et al. *LAGS* (Carter Co TN).

cow grease *noun* Butter.

1930 Pendleton *Wood-Hicks Speak* 87 = butter. **1936** Farr *Folk Speech* 275 = butter. **1957** Neel *Backwoodsman* 11 = butter. **1998** Montgomery *Coll* Pass me the cow grease [= old-fashioned usage] (Cardwell).

[DARE *cow grease* n chiefly Midland]

cow-itch (also *cow-itch vine*) *noun* A woody vine (*Mucuna pruriens*) with stiff hairs that when touched can cause intense itching.

1938 *Facts and Legends of Cullowhee* 13 The vine climbing high on the corner of Joyner Building, bearing large red flowers in summer, is the trumpet creeper, bignonia, or *Tecoma radicans*, a native plant also known by the less attractive name of "cow itch." **1941** Walker *Story of Mt* 56–57 Trumpet creeper appears in many situations, ascending trees as well as stumps and posts. Its foliage is deciduous and its large red trumpet-shaped flowers are marvelously beautiful. The native countryman, however, can scarcely appreciate this vine since it proves a pest in his cultivated fields, where it is known by the undignified name of cow-itch vine. **1970** Campbell et al. *Smoky Mt Wildflowers* 60 When the plant is wet, it is mildly poisonous to some people; hence another common name, the cow-itch vine.

cow lot *noun* An enclosed yard or pen, usually adjacent to or near a barn, where cattle are kept. See also **lot A**.

1900 Harben *N GA Sketches* 95 She's out thar at the cow-lot a-milkin'. She tuk 'er bucket an' the feed fer Brindle jest now. **1934–47** *LAMSAS Appal* (Madison Co NC). **1966** Dakin *Vocab Ohio River Valley* 90 [In the Ohio Valley] *Cow lot* occurs more frequently [than *cow pen*], but is common only in eastern Kentucky and immediately along the Ohio above the Big Sandy. **1966** *DARE Survey* (Burnsville NC) = place near the barn with a fence around it where livestock are kept. **1966** Medford *Ol' Starlin* 64 Let's follow him out to his log stable—where there is also a rail fence cow lot, and see what he does. **1990** Aiken *Stories* 12 Early of a morning the current Atchley Cowboy would make the rounds of town and open the gate to the cow lot and the resident cow would join the herd being conducted to the grazing ground out Hardin Lane way.

[DARE *cow lot* n chiefly South, Midland]

cow pea *noun* A black-eyed pea.

1942 Robertson *Red Hills* 65 I never heard this invocation varied except once when one of our cousins, who did not care for cowpeas and fat back, bowed his head and said: "Good God, look at this." **1984** Wilder *You All Spoken* 72 We got a right good chance of cow peas.

[DARE *cow pea* n chiefly South, Midland]

cow's pocketbook *noun* See citation.

2011 Woodall *Not My Mt* 41 Cornfields grew right up to the yard's edge. A pole fence surrounded the yard to keep out the cows' manure that she called "cow pocketbooks."

cow stomp *noun* See citations. See also **stomp B**.

1952 Wilson *Folk Speech NC* 530 = a cool, shaded place where cows seek refuge during the heat of the day and "stomp" when attacked by flies.—West. **1961** Niles *Ballad Book* 29 = a cool, dusty place under a tree where cows rest in summer and stamp at flies. **1984** Wilder *You All Spoken* 193 = a shady place where cows take refuge from sunshine and heat and stomp their hooves to discourage flies.

crab *noun* See citation.

1952 Breckinridge *Neighborhoods* 174 The logs for the second story of the Big House, and for the attic, were raised by means of a contraption called a "crab," with a pulley system used on the branches of the giant beeches.

crack

A *verb* Of a **moonshine still**: to issue sounds indicating that the whiskey is ready to **run**.

1976 Miller *Mts within Me* 115 The cover was replaced on the barrel and it was allowed to stand for several more days with continued care to maintain the proper temperature, during which time the "sweet mash" became "sour mash" as the sugar was changed to alcohol and carbonic acid through fermentation. When the cap "cracked," the experienced moonshiner knew by the sound that the contents were "ripe" and ready to run. The cracking sound has been described as being "like rain on a tin roof" or "old ned frying in the pan."

B (also *cracker, crackerjack*) *noun* An amusing or comical person, joker.

1954 GSMNP-19:25 I'm going to tell ye a story about a moonshiner one time. He was a regular crack. **1956** Hall *Coll* (Byrds Creek NC) Old Isaac, he was a crackerjack, the old big hat he wore and the way he acted. **1996–97** Montgomery *Coll*: *crack* = a character or joker (Bush); *cracker* = a joker, amusing person (Brown); *crackerjack* (Brown); *crackerjack* = a person full of hot air or one full of energy, also a joker, a person who is a good entertainer (Cardwell).

cracker See **crack B**.

crackerjack

A *noun* See **crack B**.

B *adjective* Superlative, exceptional.

1976 Garber *Mountain-ese* 18 Jake is shore a crackerjack shot when it comes to squirrel huntin'. **1996** Montgomery *Coll* (known to Adams, Ellis, Jones, Ledford, Norris, Weaver).

Crackers' Neck *noun* A derogatory term for a community considered rural and thus of lower class or status.

1976 Braden *Grandma Was Girl* 89 Another old lady who just came to spend the night, I remember well. She was Aunt Jane Hatmaker. I didn't like her much. She lived out in the Island Ford community, which some people spoke of rather slightingly as "Crackers' Neck." Once my tongue slipped when I was asking Aunt Jane a question, and I said "Crackers' Neck." She really put me in my place for saying it.

crackledy *adjective* Crackly.

1984 Burns *Cold Sassy* 88 I knew by the crackledy voice that Miss Alice Ann Boozer was one of them.

crackling *noun* (usually plural) A fragment of the rind or fat of a hog (rarely of another animal) from which lard has been rendered, used as flavoring, especially when fried to a crisp and baked in cornmeal to make **crackling bread**. See 1990 citation; also used figuratively.

1834 Crockett *Narrative* 106 I looked like a pretty cracklin ever to get to Congress!!! **1900** Harben *N GA Sketches* 137 She said she was afeered her cracklin's would burn, but I'll bet she seed you down the road. **1939** Hall *Coll* (Cataloochee NC) We cooked that coon and all lay down to sleep and the coon cooked into cracklin's. We didn't have anything but cracklin's and a pot of grease next morning. **1974** Russell *Hillbilly* 57 The lard was rendered from the skins and used for cooking; the remaining "cracklins" were sometimes used to make cracklin bread or fed to the chickens. **1977** Shields *Cades Cove* 28 Cracklings, the remains from the lard rendering process, were used to flavor many dishes, including corn bread—called cracklin' bread in Cades Cove. It was a rich but delicious bread, especially if the cracklings were crisp. **1984** Smith *Enduring Memories* 13 Cracklings were used to flavor cornbread and other dishes on the farm. Cracklings were made by boiling the fat scraps cut from the middlings, shoulders, hams, etc., of the hog and the fat meat pulled from the intestines. The fat scraps were placed in a large kettle and boiled until the animal fat (called lard) was rendered out. The scraps were cooked like bacon or sausage and when they were light brown the cooking stopped. The solid pieces (cracklings) left were canned or stored to be used later. **1990** Oliver *Cooking Hazel Creek* 18 Leaf fat and fat from intestines was rendered for lard; that is, it was boiled in a large pot to release the lard or grease. This fat then became cracklins which, coarsely ground, were delicious when mixed with corn meal and baked as cracklin bread.

[OED3 *crackling* n 2 "crisp skin or rind of roast pork" 1708→; CUD *cracklins* n pl; DARE *crackling* n 1 chiefly South, Midland]

crackling bread *noun* Corn bread with **cracklings** baked inside. Also called **fatty bread, shortened bread**.

1862 Spainhourd *CW Letters* (Dec 8) I Would like to be at home to eat Som God crackling bred and Wold like to take crismas With you. **1949** Kurath *Word Geog East US* 39 From the Chesapeake Bay to the western parts of Virginia and the Carolinas, *ash cake* and *hoe cake* are used or remembered as words for hand-shaped corn cakes baked before an open fire. *Egg bread* for a special kind of corn bread is current in the same area, and so is *cracklin bread* for corn bread containing *cracklins* (crisp bits of rendered pork fat). **1976** Braden *Grandma Was Girl* 40 The fat scraps were saved to make lard for seasoning. We did that by putting the scraps into the wash kettle over a low fire until the fat was rendered out by melting. The small scraps of meat left in the melted lard were strained out. These small scraps were called "cracklings," and we used them in cornbread. Such "crackling bread" was very good. **1988** Russell *It Happened* 68 Occasionally we made crackling bread after hog-killing time, Ma rendered the lard from quite a bit of the fat back and the crisp cracklings that remained were sometimes used in the bread.

[DARE *crackling bread* n chiefly South, South Midland]

crack of day *noun* Daybreak.

1970 *Hunting Stories* 35 We pulled out before day an' went up above Barker's Creek there a piece, an' got up there before crack a' day. **1972** Cooper *NC Mt Folklore* 90 *crack of day*. **1981** Brewer *Wonderment* 34 We dozen Oakley children would get out of bed at the crack of day and run half a mile down the road to get "Christmas gift" on our Great Aunt Lindy (Ogle).

[DARE *crack of day* n chiefly South]

cradle

A *noun* An implement with curved wooden fingers attached to a scythe and used for harvesting wheat and other grains. See 1997 citation. Also called **wheat cradle**.

1838 *McLean Diary* 58 [I] made a Cradel and Cut my Wheet. **1863** *Vance Papers* (July 13) ther is [a] Woman in this Settle Ment that had to take the cr[a]dle and cut ther wheat. **1922** *TN CW Ques* 18 (Cocke Co TN) In the early young manhood we cut wheat with a cradle and sych [sic]. [**1939** Hall *Coll* (White Oak NC) [It has] five fingers and a blade, a farm implement like a scythe.] **1957** Broaddus *Vocab Estill Co KY* 20 = a scythe with a frame on it to catch the grain as it is cut. **1960** Mason *Memoir* 16 The chief tools were the ax, saw, eyed-hoe, scooter plow, mowing blade and cradle. **a1975** Lunsford *It Used to Be* 14 The scythe-and-cradle has a scythe about three-and-a-half feet long on the side of the sneed, which was the handle that had two things to hold by. **1987** Wear *Sevierville* 98 His father cut wheat with an old time cradle and mowed hay by using a team of horses and a mowing machine with a long blade. **1997** Montgomery *Coll* = a farm tool with a metal cutting blade and a number of curved, wood fingers attached to a curved wood handle; it was hefted by a strong man and swung into standing, small ripe grain, the metal blade cutting the grain and the fingers cutting the cut grain stalks for tying into bunches or sheaves (Brown). **2009** Wiles and Wiles *Location* 106 A cradle was used to cut wheat, oats, and buckwheat. The wooden cradle consisted of a long handle, a cutting blade with five fingers above the blade to hold the straws of grain as they were cut. The cradling was always done from left to right and if on a hill, from bottom to top. Since the blade cut only a five-foot swath, two inches deep, it was a long process to cut an entire field.

B *verb* To cut (grain) with such an implement.

1973 *AOHP/EH* 66 Sometimes old man Mitch Carico had some work hired out. He'd have some of them to cradle some oats. **1973** GSMNP-76:27 They used to come up here from down in the country and get people to go and help them cradle the wheat in them big fields. **a1975** Lunsford *It Used to Be* 14 When I grew older, I would go down and take part in that and cradle wheat or oats.

cramp-colic *noun*

1 Appendicitis. Same as **colic**.

1862 Shockley *CW Letters* (Feb 13) A J Tolbert one of my mess mates is verry sick he was taken with cramp cholic and has not got over it yet. **1937** Thornburgh *Great Smoky Mts* 160. **1967** Jones *Peculiarities Mtneers* 71 A tobacco leaf poultice was credited with relieving the pains of appendicitis, which was called "cramp colic" at that time. **1973** *Foxfire II* 382 I never heard tell of 'pendicitis till I was growed. . . . I didn't know there was such a thing. People called it th' cramp colic. **1996** Montgomery *Coll* (known to Adams, Cardwell, Norris, Oliver).

2 Stomach cramps, as from eating green apples.

1894 Bergen *Plant Names III* 112 Rattlesnake venom cures cramp-colic. **1997** Montgomery *Coll* (known to eight consultants from the Smoky Mountains).

[DARE *cramp-colic* n both senses scattered South, South Midland]

cranesbill *noun* A geranium (*Geranium maculatum*) with medicinal uses.

[**1901** Lounsberry *Sthn Wild Flowers* 285 As its leaves grow old they turn yellow, or become blotched, or spotted with white, which peculiarity in connection with the long crane-like beak of its young carpels is the significance of one of its English names.] [**1971** Krochmal et al. *Medicinal Plants Appal* 134 In Appalachia, a tea made from the whole plant is used to treat dysentery and sore throat.] **1982** Stupka *Wildflowers* 61 The long-beaked fruit accounts for another common name, "cranesbill," from the Greek *geranos*, meaning crane.

cranksided *adjective* Lopsided, twisted.

1891 Brown *Dialect in TN* 173 *Cranksided* means twisted or careened to one side; and *catawampous* means something near the same thing, although the latter seems to have the idea of the diagonal prominent in it.

[DARE *crank-sided* adj chiefly South]

crap See **crop.**

crawdab, crawdabber See **crawdad.**

crawdad (also *crawdab, crawdabber, crawdadder, crawdaddy, crow dabber*) *noun* A crayfish. [Editor's note: The form *crawfish* is widespread in the US.]

1929 Rainey *Animal Plant Lore* 8 When I came down to Kentucky, this faithful companion of my student and teaching life became a crawdad. **1957** Combs *Lg Sthn High: Word-List* 24 *crawdab, crawdabber* = var[iants] of "crawdad." **1967** Fetterman *Stinking Creek* 27–28 Hundreds of streams bear biological poisons that kill the wildlife and plants they touch. "There ain't even a crawdad around here," an old-timer observed. **1982** Slone *How We Talked* 44 *crawdad* (also *crow dabber*) = crawfish. **1986** Pederson et al. *LAGS crawdab* = attested by 7/60 interviewees (11.7%) from E TN; 1/35 interviewees (2.9%) from N GA; 8/9 of all LAGS interviewees (88.9%) attesting term were from Appalachia; *crawdad* = attested by 16/60 interviewees (26.7%) from E TN and 4/35 (11.4%) from N GA; 20/160 of all LAGS interviewees (12.5%) attesting term were from Appalachia; *crawdaddy* (Bradley Co TN, Hamilton Co TN). **1991** Still *Wolfpen Notebooks* 59 Us boys used to chase minnows and crawdadders in the branch waters all summer.

[DARE *crawdab* n scattered Midland, now especially Appalachians; *crawdad* n 1 chiefly west of Appalachians]

crawdadder, crawdaddy See **crawdab.**

crawdad backwards See **crawfish A.**

crawfish [Editor's note: *Crawfish* as a noun occurs widely in the US.]

A (also *crawdad backwards*) *verb, verb phrase* To back off or away from a commitment or position, seek to withdraw; to be evasive.

1900 Harben *N GA Sketches* 277 No man, I reckon, has a moral right to act so as to make his family miserable. I crawfished, I know, an' on short notice; but law me! **1946** Stuart *Foretaste Glory* 132 When he put the marriage proposition to one [woman] she "crawdaded backwards." **1957** Neel *Backwoodsman* 11 *crawfish* = to back down on an agreement. **c1982** Young *Colloquial Appal* 6 *crawfish* = renege, back out of. **1994–97** Montgomery *Coll: crawfish* (known to Adams, Brown, Jones, Ledford, Weaver); Quit your crawfishin', He saw he was wrong, so he started to crawfish (Cardwell).

[DARE *crawfish* v 2 chiefly South, West Midland, Pacific Northwest]

B (also *crawfishy*) *adjective* Of land: low, wet, mushy, with porous soil.

1984 Wilder *You All Spoken* 134 *crawfishy land* = porous soil. **1986** Pederson et al. *LAGS: crawfish* = attested by 4/60 interviewees (6.7%) from E TN and 1/35 (2.9%) from N GA; 5/22 of all LAGS interviewees (22.7%) attesting term were from Appalachia; *crawfishy land* = attested by 10/60 interviewees (16.7%) from E TN; 10/23 of all LAGS interviewees (43.4%) attesting term were from Appalachia. **1994** Montgomery *Coll* (known to Shields).

[DARE *crawfish* adj chiefly South, South Midland]

crawfishy See **crawfish B.**

crawl over *verb phrase* To rebuke, reprove.

1996 Montgomery *Coll: crawl all over* (known to Adams, Brown, Cardwell, Jones, Ledford, Norris, Oliver).

[DARE (at *crawl* v) chiefly South, South Midland]

(as) crazy as a bed bug *adjective phrase* Insane, drunk, unpredictable or erratic in behavior.

1940 Oakley *Roamin'/Restin'* 41 I plug the bear through and stood by an old pine tree that was ded and the bark was starting to shed off this bear tuck up this tree crazy as a bed bug. **1999** Montgomery *Coll* = behaving in an unpredictable manner, as "He come in crazy as a bed bug" [= drunk] (Cardwell). **2005** Rains *Appal Mt Stories* 51 Why, ain't nothing wrong with her, except she is crazy as a bed bug.

creaseback (also *creasyback*) *noun* A green bean with a large, crescent-shaped pod. See 2011 citation. Same as **greasy-back bean.**

1983 Montell *Don't Go Up* 27 In their gardens, frontier families grew . . . black crease-back beans. **1990** Fisher *Preacher Stories* 61 When we went over and took the lid off that little round pot, we found it full of creasyback beans. A creasyback is a bean somewhat like a Kentucky Wonder. **1996** Houk *Foods & Recipes* 47 Smoky Mountain horticulture includes a lengthy litany of legumes—creaseback, cutshort, cornfield beans, bunch beans, pink or peanut beans, greasy beans, sulfur beans, and half runners. **2011** Best *Bean Terminology* = a type of heirloom bean that has a crease in the outer portion of the bean hull. They are sometimes called creasy beans (not to be confused with greasy beans).

creases, creasies, creasy (greens) See **cress.**

creature *noun*

A variant forms *creatur, creetur, creter, cre'tur* [see **1883** in **B1**], *critter.*

1863 *Fuller CW Letters* (March 9) i wood giv hur enney thing that i hav in this world if it wood mak hur happey for poor creter she has a hard time of it. **1867** Harris *Sut Lovingood* 37 Well, this critter look't like a cross atween a black snake an' a fireman's ladder. **1901** Harben *Westerfelt* 278 She was the happiest creetur God ever made. **1923** Furman *Mothering* 238 The pore little creetur just whimps and pines for him continual, and won't scacely tech the food its pap gives it. **1942** Hall *Phonetics Smoky Mts* 79 [krɪtɚ]. **c1960** Wilson *Coll: creature* is sometimes *critter* or *creatur*; chiefly now humorous. **1969** GSMNP-43 Do you remember such critters in the Park? **2007** McMillon *Notes: creetur.*

[OED3 *critter* (variant of *creature* 1815→); DARE *creature* n A South, South Midland, New England]

B Senses.

1 Any animal, domesticated or wild, especially one that has pesty, unsavory, or unruly qualities; by extension = a person who looks or behaves like an animal, as in jocular usage applied to a child. See also **cow critter.**

1883 Murfree *Old Sledge* 556 "Ye're a pore leetle cre'tur," he said, with scathing contempt. **1913** Kephart *Our Sthn High* 43 Jerseys, and other blooded cattle thrive in the valleys, where there are no free ranges, but the backwoodsman does not want "critters that haffter to be gentled and hand-fed." **1924** Raine *Saddlebags* 29 I reckon I have rid a bigger critter than ary one of you fellers ever seed. **1939** Hall *Coll* (Jefferson City TN) He was a ugly old critter. *Ibid.* (in yelling at a mule) You durn critter. **1965** Ferrell *Bear Tales* 17 Their hound was told to run the critter back to where it belonged. **1972** Cooper *NC Mt Folklore* 90 *critter* = a wild or vicious animal. **1992** Brooks *Sthn Stuff* 35 = anything that twists and turns. **1997** Montgomery *Coll* = can refer to wild and domesticated animals as well as people (Brown), = used usually of small animals, both wild and domestic, and in the collective (Ellis). **1997** Ownby *Big Greenbrier* 1:21 Nothing could get across the fence. He did this to keep out the chickens and all the other critters. **2007** Stryk *Groundhog Brood* 43 Mike ... raises "beagle pups" in chicken wire curled around his shed, and clears unwanted "critters" for the neighborfolk.

2 A horse.

1790 (in **1956** Eliason *Tarheel Talk* 267) (Wilkes Co NC) I shall go home if I can Get a Creature to Ride. **1890** Fruit *KY Words* 64 *critter* = used for horse by old people: "My critter got foundered last week"; "I went to church critter-back." **1913** Kephart *Our Sthn High* 295 Critter and beast are usually restricted to horse and mule, and brute to a bovine. **1952** Wilson *Folk Speech NC* 612 Git down and rest your critter. **1968** Wilson *Folklore Mammoth Cave* 16 *critter* = derogatory and humorous term for an ornery or worthless horse. **1972** Cooper *NC Mt Folklore* 90 = a riding mare. **1977** Still *Wonder Beans* 7 He went up the road and down the road, aiming for to sell the critter.

[OED3 *creature* n 3b "a farm animal" chiefly U.S. regional]

creeces See **cress**.

creek *noun*

A variant form *crick* [Editor's note: This form was rarely observed by Joseph Hall in the Smoky Mountains in the late 1930s.]

1787 (in **1956** Eliason *Tarheel Talk* 309) (Stokes Co NC) *crick*. **1813** Hartsell *Memora* 101 then ther came a large crick into the river, which we had to run up with the botes be fore we cold land. **1867** Harris *Sut Lovingood* 27 What wer agwine on at the cabin, this side the crick, when yu pass'd thar? **1939** Hall *Notebooks* 13:9 (White Oak NC) = almost non-existent. **1941** Stuart *Men of Mts* 103 I took up the crick the way I'd come. **1952–57** (in **1973** McDavid and McDavid *Vocab E KY* 153) The North Midland *run* "small stream" is practically confined to the Ohio Valley, as is the pronunciation of *creek* ... riming [sic]with *lick*. **2007** McMillon *Notes*: = never pronounced *crick* south of central West Virginia.

[DARE *creek* n especially Inland North, North Midland, West]

B See citation.

1940 Bowman *KY Mt Stories* 237 = larger stream fed by the branches.

creek bottom *noun* A low-lying area of land along a creek. See also **bottom**.

1915 Bohannon *Bear Hunt* 461–62 In all the creek bottoms there was no chestnut mast, but of beech there was plenty, both in feeding grounds which lay on the North Carolina side of the main ridge and the lying grounds which are on the Tennessee side. **1940** Still *River of Earth* 20–21 I walked into the creek bottom. Bloodroot blossomed under the oaks and I sat down there. **1960** Mason *Memoir* 4 Along the creek bottoms, great hemlocks went towering toward the heavens. **a1975** Lunsford *It Used to Be* 33 He had a good creek-bottom farm, and he was a leader in the Newfound Baptist Church. **1994** Montgomery *Coll* = lowlands having a creek (Shields). **1996** Cole *Forney's Creek* 19 He found the rich but usually narrow river valleys occupied by whites, who also had drifted up the creek bottoms and even settled coves far back in the mountains.

creeker (also *cricker*) *noun* A white person from the backwoods or a working-class community.

1991 Egerton *Dispatches* 29 Urbane Charlestonians [of WV] ... often treat West Virginian as a synonym for hillbilly—tend to put the greatest possible distance between themselves and the mountain folk around them. At best, the rural, hill-and-hollow residents of Kanawha County have been ignored; at worst, they have been ridiculed, scorned, and exploited. They are, in local parlance, "the creekers"—coal miners, truck drivers, factory workers. **1998** Giardina *No Scapin* I30 I still lived in a holler, but I fled each Sunday to a local Episcopal church to worship with people who disdained the ways of "crickers." **1999** Fisher *Stepchild* 187 There was little interaction in the [junior high] school between the middle-class whites from the suburbs, inner-city blacks, and the "hillbillies" or "creekers" from the surrounding hollows. I didn't fit. The [middle-class] suburban kids knew from my dress, accent, and mannerisms that I wasn't one of them, the blacks knew I wasn't white, and the "creekers" knew only that I wasn't from the [middle-class] suburbs. **2012** Pittman *Proud Creekers* x If you talk to anyone who grew up in these parts you will probably hear them refer to themselves as "Creekers." We will let you know that we all consider ourselves "Creekers" to this day.

creel *verb* To wrench, sprain (one's leg, ankle, etc.); in verb phrase *creel over* = to collapse. See also **careen**.

1917 Kephart *Word-List* 410 = to wrench. "I *creeled* my knee (neck, back)." **1974** Fink *Bits Mt Speech* 5 = to reel, give way or fall. "His leg *creeled* under him." **1975** Chalmers *Better* 34 Splinters and briars, a "risin'" to incise for drainage, a "creeled foot" strapped to relieve strained muscles. **1983** Broaddus *Estill Co KY Word List* 36 *creel* = to sprain (an ankle). **1994–97** Montgomery *Coll*: *creel* = to sprain (Shields); *creel over* (known to Brown, Cardwell, Jones, Ledford, Oliver).

[cf EDD *creel* v² 1 "to bend"; DARE *creel* v South Midland]

creel over See **creel**.

creen See **careen**.

creep *verb*

1 variant past-tense forms *crope, crup.*

1886 Smith *Sthn Dialect* 350 A language might deteriorate any time from such causes in the way of such forms as . . . *crope* . . . [which] bear the stamp of antiquity. **1904–20** Kephart *Notebooks* 2:489 *crope.* **c1960** Wilson *Coll* He crup up behind me. **1974** Fink *Bits Mt Speech* 5 I *crope* up on a deer. **1994–97** Montgomery *Coll: crope* (known to Brown, Cardwell, Shields).

2 variant past-participle form *crope.*

1898 Elliott *Durket Sperret* 114 Now they've done crope inter Durket's farm.

[DARE *creep* v A, both forms chiefly South, South Midland]

creeping cedar *noun* A lush green clubmoss (*Lycopodium clavatum/complanatum*). Also called **running pine**.

1999 McNeil *Purchase Knob* 65–66 At eye level, in the brittle grass of an old road bank, I suddenly noticed a lush green ground cover spreading about under a mountain laurel. Its miniature, cedar-like fronds made springy green nests wherever they ran. The moss had the endearing quality of making you want to pet it. . . . "Creeping cedar" or "running pine" the mountain people call it, completely inaccurate but appealing "folk names." Lycopodium is not even vaguely related to pines or cedars. No doubt its evergreen, frond-like texture inspired such titles.

cress (also *creases, creasies, creasy (greens), creeces, cressy greens*) *noun* An early spring wild green of the mustard family, especially wintercress (*Nasturtium officinale* or *Barbarea vulgaris*), eaten boiled or in salads. See also **dryland cress, land cress, watercreases, wintercress.**

1937 Hyatt *Kiverlid* 79 We picked wild mustard . . . an' I don't know what all I think maybe some creeces, too. **c1945** Haun *Hawk's Done* 251 She seed that he was hungry and she set him down to the best she had—corn bread and cress sallet. **1963** Watkins and Watkins *Yesterday* 79 Food was plentiful in the spring; creases grew in the creek bottom, and the "salet" of creases boiled with a piece of fat meat was good. **1974** Fink *Bits Mt Speech* 5 *cresses* = water cress or a field salad, always in the plural. **1977** Shields *Cades Cove* 19 After a winter with only stored, dried, or canned vegetables and fruits, the fresh wild greens of the spring were a welcome change. These included the wild cresses of the fields, the "bear" lettuce of the mountain streams, the toothwort of the moist stream banks, and, most abundant of all, the wild leek, or ramp, of the northern slopes. **1979** Smith *White Rock* 34 Cress grew on land too and we ate these "creasy greens" boiled like spinach. **1983** Patterson *Cooking* 20 "Greens" enthusiasts will search dales as early as February hoping to find a "mess" of Winter Cress greens (also known as Land Cress and Cressy Greens). **1992** Brooks *Sthn Stuff* 35 *creases* = watercress or ground cress, a spicy green eaten boiled or in salads. **1998** Dabney *Smokehouse Ham* 268 The very first greens to appear—and a sign that spring was on its way—was wild watercress, more familiarly known as "creases," "creasy greens," "field cress," or "cresses." The wild creases exhibit a more full-bodied flavor than cultivated watercress. **2001** Joslin *Appal Bounty* 1, 3 In late winter, although snow still lies in sheltered coves and temperatures sink below freezing at night, the first of spring's free-handed bounty has pushed up through the frozen soil. Creasy greens are ready for gathering, cooking, and eating. Part of the fun is gathering the creasies. I take my children out to the pasture and garden spot to get them as soon as the snow melts in late February or early March. The bright green plants are easy to spot and to harvest. . . . Gathering the plant is as simple as sowing. You take a knife and cut the head from the root. When you have a poke full, you're ready to clean the greens and prepare them for cooking. Pauline's recipe is simple. You cut the core out of the plant, then rinse the leaves well. Boil them until tender, then fry in grease. They are also easy to save. After electricity came up Greasy Creek, Pauline would take her creasy greens, boil them by the sackful, then save them in the freezer. **2007** McMillon *Notes: creases.* **2012–13** *Smokies Guide* 10 Cresses, often called "creasies" or "creasy greens," were among a very few wild greens available in winter. A non-native plant in the genus *Barbarea*, cresses grow along streams and in fallow fields. . . . In the southern Appalachians, creases were harvested throughout the winter and were extremely high in vitamin C and A. In fact, one nickname for the plant was "scurvy grass," because its high vitamin content could ward off the disease. Cresses are similar in appearance to spinach, and could be eaten in similar ways. They could be washed thoroughly and used fresh in salads or cooked the old-fashioned way either by boiling with salt pork or sauteing in bacon grease. **2016** Lundy and Autry *Victuals* 55 Creasy greens, known elsewhere as "land cresses," is a type of mustard that grows both wild and cultivated in the mountains. Similar in flavor to watercress, creasies are both strong in taste and firm in texture.

[DARE *cress* n *crease* (at *creece*) chiefly South Midland, *cress* chiefly Appalachians, especially western VA]

cresses, cressy greens See **cress**.

crib *noun*

1 A slatted or barred compartment in a barn, used to store dried corn ears, corn husks, apples, etc. [Editor's note: This term in reference to an outbuilding with the same function is widespread in the US.] See 1965 citations. See also **log crib, shuck pen.**

1949 Kurath *Word Geog East US* 54 The simplex *crib* is characteristic of all of North Carolina and adjoining parts of Tidewater Virginia (south of the James), and of westernmost Virginia. **1965** Glassie *Old Barns* 21 From this ancient rectangular construction unit, usually in the mountains called a "crib" or a "pen," developed, partially in Europe and partially in America, most if not all of the traditional barn types found today in the Southern Mountains. *Ibid.* 28 In the general area of the Blue Ridge and particularly the Great Smokies . . . the log double-crib barn-type II is found with a large frame loft overhanging in front and back on all sides by means of the cantilever principle.

[DARE *crib* n[1] 1 "structure in a barn" mainly West Midland, Gulf States]

2 The catchment area below a **splash dam** in which logs are gathered to be floated downstream.

2006 Farwell *Logging Term* 1021 Where rivers could be used, the timber was "boomed," or "bound," into "cribs" and floated downstream by "drivers."

3 See citation.

1969 Lee *Bloodletting* 187 From the beginning coal was brought from the interior of the mines in small cars designed to hold a specified weight of coal. But the companies "cribbed" their miners by building a "crib" or frame around the top of these cars until they held from 500 to 1,000 pounds more coal than the miners were paid for mining.

crick See **creek**.

cricker See **creeker**.

crimpy *adjective* Of weather: cold and unpleasant.

1983 Broaddus *Estill Co KY Word List* 36 = cool (referring to the weather). **1995–97** Montgomery *Coll* (known to Brown, Cardwell, Norris, Oliver, Weaver).

[DARE *crimpy* adj especially South Midland]

crimson laurel *noun* Same as **catawba rhododendron**.

2007 McMillon *Notes*.

cripple *verb* To limp, hobble.

1963 Edwards *Gravel* 123 Wal, they come cripplin on up to fernent the shop and the cap'm said "Halt."

[DARE *cripple* v South Midland]

crippledy *adjective* Crippled.

1972 Ensor *Tales of Supernatural* 69 He told her, says, "In the morning, I'm a-burying you next to the baby." Says, "You crippledy thing."

crisp *noun* variant plural form *crispers*.

1973 *Hair Singed* 50 There was another man one time that said he could handle that fire and he got his hands burnt to two big crispers.

critter See **creature**.

crocus bag (also *crocus sack*) *noun*

A variant forms *croaker sack* [see **1975** in **B**], *crocker sack* [see **1942** in **B**], *croker sack* [see **1993** in **B**], *crokass bag* [see **1790** in **B**].

B A large sack made of coarse, loosely woven fabric, a gunny sack, the usual term for which in the mountains is **tow sack**.

1790 (in **1912** Chalkley *Augusta Co VA* 1.509) (DARE) James McPheeters opened a . . . grave and took therefrom the body, in order to dissect the same . . . and after doing so, did sew him up in a crokass bag and put him in the cave within mentioned. **1942** Robertson *Red Hills* 226 Whole families would appear with crocker sacks slung over one shoulder—old and young would take to the cotton patch. **1958** Wood *Words from TN* 9 *crocus sack* = a burlap bag. **1975** Brewer *Valley So Wild* 266 "I filled the croaker sacks and he brought them down," Mrs. Stedman said. **1993** Page and Smith *Foxfire Toys and Games* 75 What you did was take a boy and get him out about dark and tell him he's going snipe hunting. And of course nobody would give it away. You'd get you a big croker sack or tow sack to carry along and a lantern and we'd take this boy off in the woods far enough away to circle him around to make him think he's five miles from home. **1996** Johnson *Lexical Change* 138 *crocus bag, crocus sack, croker sack* = statistically more common in the mountains of South Carolina and Georgia than in the Piedmont and Coastal Plain c1990. **1996** Montgomery *Coll*: *crocus sack* (known to Jones, Ledford, Norris).

[DARE *crocus sack* n probably from use of the material for sacks in which crocus, saffron, (etc.) was shipped]

croker sack See **crocus bag**.

crooked rail fence *noun* Same as **worm fence**.

c1960 Wilson *Coll* = the ordinary, zigzag type, the rail fence par excellence. **2006** *Encycl Appalachia* 433 The "crooked rail" fence typical of Appalachia during that time was almost exclusively made from chestnut, as was the "paling," or picket fence used around yards and gardens to keep poultry out.

crookedy *adjective, adverb* Crooked.

1962 Williams *Metaphor Mt Speech* I 12 If the stubborn wife persists in her "jarrin' and mouthin'," the irate husband is "like to commence a-foulin' one hock and a-rubbin' it on t'other" before he roars, "Shet up yer big mouth before I knock ye hell-western crookedy!" **1986** Still *Wolfpen Poems* 18 Thick hoofs are striking fire on the crookedy trail. **1992** Brooks *Sthn Stuff* 35 = anything that twists and turns. "This is the crookedyest danged road I ever seed in my life."

crop

A *noun, verb* variant form *crap* [kræp].

1834 Crockett *Narrative* 154 Having laid by my crap, I went home, which was a distance of about a hundred and fifty miles. **1852** *Chapman CW Letters* (July 22) we have raised the Best crap of cabbages and turnups Potatoes that we Ever maid before. **1860** Olmsted *Back Country* 260 Folks that have farms of their own, they do put in their craps and tend 'em. **1900** Harben *N GA Sketches* 84 I tol' 'em they was welcome to my intrust in the crap, an that I had had all I could stand up under. **1921** Weeks *Speech of KY Mtneer* 8 If you will "stop by" when you are in the mountains, we will cheerfully crop for you a handful of our choicest flowers. Crop is Anglo-Saxon, but if you prefer, we will crap them for you, and thus prove to you the Scotch strain in our blood. **1937** Haun *Cocke Co* 2 Folks still tote their turns of meal to mill in pokes and aim on raising a yieldy crap of corn next year. **1942** Hall *Phonetics Smoky Mts* 29. **1960** Hall *Smoky Mt Folks* 32 Uncle Dave was faithfully cultivating his cornfield, "layin' by his crap" (hoeing the ground for the last time), and seemed glad to stop for a "spell" to talk with me, but not for long. **1961** Kurath and McDavid *Pron Engl Atl Sts* 143 The /æ/ of *cat* appears in *crop* in the folk speech of two areas: (1) the Atlantic coast from Chesapeake Bay to the Neuse River in North Carolina, and (2) the Appalachians south of the Kanawha River. **1967** Wilson *Folkways Mammoth Cave* 24 = an older pronunciation now used largely for fun. **1969** GSMNP-46 We just have to pick up the craps.

[DARE *crop* n chiefly South, South Midland]

B *verb* To farm, raise a crop (also in phrase *crop it*; hence verbal noun phrase *cropping it*).

1835 Click *Departed Voice* Mr. Click has been croping it with aman the name of Hugh Henry ever since we left Tennysie. **1866** Smith *So Called* 95 Our nearest neighbor cropped it over some seven hundred acres of scattering land, situated from six to ten inches under water. **1919** Combs *Word-List South* 33 Lish's Rob's jist cleverly begun to crap (farm). **1961** Williams *Content Mt Speech* 16 He's got a good little piece of crappin' land there, but he won't corn it ner hay it nuther.

[DARE *crop* v 3 South Midland]

crope See **creep 1, 2.**

crop it See **crop B.**

crop one's wing *verb phrase* See citation.

1960 Westover *Highland Lg* 19 = to punish children.

cropper *noun* A sharecropper who tends all or part of a farm's crops, using his employer's equipment and livestock and paying an agreed portion of the produce each year. See also **renter.**

1942 Robertson *Red Hills* 164 In our state only a third of the farmers owned their own land. A third were renters, a third were croppers. **c1960** Wilson *Coll* = a tenant farmer who uses the implements and stock of his employer and gets a certain percentage of the crops for his own, the rest going as rent. Usually he is distinguished from the renter, who uses his own tools and stock.

cross *verb* variant form *crost*, third-person-singular form *crost-es*.

1928 (in **1952** Mathes *Tall Tales* 69) You know whar the main trail crostes over t'wards Mingus.

crossbar hotel *noun* See citation.

1989 Still *Rusties and Riddles* [78] = jail.

crossbench spelling, crossbench spelling bee, crossbench spelling match See **cross spelling.**

cross-cornered *adverb* See citation.

1973 Miller *English Unicoi Co* 145 = catty-cornered or diagonally.

cross-cut *noun* See citation.

1991 Shifflett *Coal Towns* 85 On both sides of the tunnel are solid walls of coal, really pillars left to support the roof. Close to the face of the tunnel, these solid walls are broken by "breakthroughs" or "cross-cuts," narrower tunnels cut by the miner for ventilation and to communicate with one another.

cross(ed) questions and (or) crooked answers *noun phrase* A parlor guessing game in which the participants, often a dozen or more, are divided into two rows standing opposite each other. The leader of the game gives those on one side questions and those on the other side answers, the latter usually humorous and unrelated to the questions; after a participant asks the assigned question the one opposite to him or her gives the assigned answer, and because the randomly distributed questions and answers might pertain to personal traits of participants, much laughter and amusement followed.

1941 Hall *Party Games* 69 "Cross Questions and Crooked Answers" was similar. Each player was provided in advance with a question and with an answer to his partner's question. Each question and answer were repeated three times, the idea being not to laugh at the humorous and sometimes embarrassing incongruities which would develop. **1990** Wigginton *Foxfire Christmas* 139 We had games we'd play, too. We'd play "pleased or displeased" and we'd play "crossed questions or crooked answers." That's so funny. You line up a bunch of girls on one side and a bunch of boys on the other, and three people tell *them* separately what they're supposed to ask and answer. Neither one of those three know what the others said. We usually got a man to tell the boys something. They might ask, "Will you marry me?" Well, no one else knew what the boy was going to ask the girl, and the girls had answers they were supposed to give like, "Come see me sometime," or "I'll meet you at the wash place" [the creek or branch where the clothes were washed].

crosslegged snow *noun* See citation.

2019 *Blind Pig* (Jan 30) A cross-legged snow will be deep [where] the snow is one where wind is in play, driving the snow flakes this way and that. The connection with a deep snow makes sense, because such winds are usually associated with strong fronts.

cross over *verb phrase* To die.

c1940 Simms *Coll* Do you know whose [i.e. who's] crossed over? **1990** Cavender *Folk Medical Lex* 20 When did your brother cross over? **1994** Montgomery *Coll* (known to Cardwell).

cross questions and (or) crooked answers See **cross(ed) questions and (or) crooked answers.**

cross spelling (also *crossbench spelling*, *crossbench spelling bee*, *crossbench spelling match*) *noun* A school spelling competition, sometimes conducted by teams lined up and facing one another on benches.

1905 Miles *Spirit of Mts* 8 Or the excitement of "cross-spelling" is asked for, an exercise in which all but the babes take part. **1977** Hurst and Lewis *Roaring Fork* 23 Every Friday afternoon the class would divide in half and take part in the cross-bench spelling bee. The teacher would choose a girl and a boy to take turns choosing who they wanted on their side. Then she'd give us our words and if you spelled it right, you'd cross over to the bench on the other side of the room. Then the teacher would tally the score to see who had crossed over the most times and the one who had was the winner. **1978** *Smokies Heritage* 257 We called it cross bench spelling mainly because that's what it was. If a speller from one side missed a word the speller on the opposite bench was given a chance. **1986**

Tyson *Reflections* 29 We looked forward to Fridays. Most of the time we would get to have a cross bench spelling match. We put four benches together and the teacher would give out the word and if the one that sat by you misspelled the word and you could spell it you took their place and on that way 'til you got to the end of the bench. If you spelled the word, you crossed to the next bench and made one talley.

cross-tie *verb* See citation.

1962 Williams *Verbs Mt Speech* 18 The ease with which mountain folk convert nouns and adjectives to verbs has long fascinated outsiders. . . . He cradles his oats and . . . "cross-ties" his white oaks.

crossways (also *crosswise*) *adjective* Hard to get along with, ill-tempered; hence *crossways of* (or *to*) *one another* = at odds, in disagreement, at cross purposes.

1863 *Patton CW Letters* (Feb 22) our Colonel . . . was a little crossways: but we told him of the accidents on the road and it was all right. **c1960** Wilson *Coll* (or *crosswise*) = frustrated, ill-tempered, hard to get along with. **1973** *Words & Expressions* 133 *crossways of each other* = to be in disagreement or to disagree. **1976** Thompson *Touching Home* 13 = two people disagreeing. **1995–97** Montgomery *Coll* (known to Adams, Brown, Jones, Ledford, Norris, Oliver); They're crossways to each other on politics (Cardwell).

[DARE *crossways* adj 1, 2 chiefly South, South Midland]

crossways of one another, crossways to one another See **crossways.**

crosswise See **crossways.**

crost See **across, cross.**

crostes See **cross.**

crowd *verb* Of a hunting dog: to pursue (game) closely.

1950 Stuart *Hie Hunters* 36 Then they heard Shooting Star barking every breath on a warm track: "He's crowdin' somethin'," Sparkie shouted: "Be ready any time to hear him tree."

crow dabber See **crawdab.**

crowfoot violet *noun* Same as **bird('s) foot violet.**

1982 Stupka *Wildflowers* 67 The leaves [of the pansy violet] have three main divisions, but the lateral ones are divided again into slender or widened segments, which account for the names "bird's-foot" or "crowfoot violet."

crowhop *verb* See citations.

1927 Woofter *Dialect from WV* 351 = to take an unfair advantage in the start of any sort of athletic contest: "He crowhopped on the other men, and the judges set him back three feet." **1963** White *Marbles E KY* 64 = [to try] to get a closer shot by placing the hand in a position nearer to the marble being shot at.

crown *noun* See citations. Also called **death crown, feather crown.**

1961 *DARE File* Feather pillows on which children died were often ripped open and searched for "crowns," little whorls of feathers forming a circle, which were considered to symbolize the fact that the child was in Heaven. **2002** Myers *Best Yet Stories* 57 Years ago when someone died, a relative immediately split their feather pillow open searching for a woven mass of feathers resembling a bun. It was soft to the touch but quite heavy. It was fascinating how the feathers were sometimes woven into a perfect circle. Many believed that a crown of feathers in a pillow was proof that the deceased was going to an eternal reward in heaven. If they found a "crown," everyone rejoiced.

crowsfoot (also *crow's foot*) *noun* An early spring edible wild green, a toothwort (*Cardamine concatenata*). Same as **turkey foot mustard.** See also **chicken mustard.**

c1950 Adams *Grandpap* 193 Sanging our way back home, in the cool of the afternoon, we'd gather Mammy's apron full of crowsfoot and redworms and Mammy would wilt them down in hot grease for our supper . . . we had to be careful not to get any staggerweed in with the crowsfoot when we were pulling it. The two plants are very much alike in leaf-form and manner of growth. But staggerweed is deadly poison, particularly so if you happen to get some of the root. **1973** GSMNP-85:2:8 It tastes like mustard . . . crowsfoot we call it. **1988** Dyer *Farmstead Yards* 25 In a recent interview, Inez Adams recalled the folk names of her mother's favorite wild greens (which, presumably, fall into Shields' "field cresses" category): "crowsfoot," "freckleface," "gravy leg," and "narrow dock." **1991** Weals *Last Train* 15 The cattle relished the first greens of spring—the ramps, bear lettuce, turkey mustard, lamb's tongue, and crow's foot—after their winter diet of hay. **1997** Montgomery *Coll* = could deaden the nerve of a tooth and stop tooth ache; also its leaves were often used in sandwiches and salads (Cardwell).

crow to pick, have a *verb phrase* To have a grievance or dispute to settle.

1927 Woofter *Dialect from WV* 361 We have a crow to pick over that affair.

[DARE *crow to pick, have a* v phr chiefly South, Midland]

cruddle *verb* Of milk: to curdle, coagulate.

1930s (in **1944** Wentworth *ADD* 146) (eWV) *cruddle.*

[SND *crudle* v 1; CUD *crudle* v]

cruise *verb* In logging, to survey (a specified area) to assess the amount and value of timber that might be harvested.

1964 Clarkson *Lumbering in WV* 359 = to estimate the amount and value of standing timber. **1978** Weals *Mules* Champion was building a lodge below the gap, beside the Indian trail and at the very headwaters of Deep Creek, for one reason, to house the men who were "cruising" timber in that area, measuring the potential board feet in the trees still standing, in order to affirm the value of the tracts being transferred to the national park.

crumbled in *noun* See citations.

1958 Wood *Words from TN* 9 = biscuits in sweetened coffee. **1996–97** Montgomery *Coll* (known to Bush, Hooper, Jones).

crumble in (also *crumble up*, *crumbly*, *crumb up*) *noun* See citations. Also called **soppy crumbs**.

1952 Callahan *Smoky Mt Country* 88 Often [corn bread] was simply crumbled into a glass of milk and eaten with a spoon, this delectable dish being called "crumble up" and often serving as the sole item in a full evening meal by the mellow fire. **1958** Wood *Words from TN* 9 *crumb up* = cornbread soaked in sweet milk. **1982** Slone *How We Talked* 90 *crumble in* = large pieces of corn bread and crust were soaked in milk. This is what most kids took to school for their lunch, in an empty lard bucket, a spoon to eat it with in their pocket. **1994–97** Montgomery *Coll*: *crumble in* (known to Oliver); *crumble up* (known to Cardwell, Shields). **1998** Hamby *Grassy Creek* 84 I remember the children of one family that once or twice brought "crumbly" (corn bread broken up in milk in a tin syrup bucket with lid). They had brought spoons and gathered around the pail and ate their crumbly. **2006** *Encycl Appalachia* 927 Hot corn bread accompanied the other dishes at the main meal of the day, and a light supper was often made on corn bread alone, crumbled into a tall glass and covered with sweet milk or buttermilk. In some southern recipes of the mountains, this dish is called "crumble-in."

crumble up, **crumbly**, **crumb up** See **crumble in**.

crumpled horn (also *crumply cow*, *crumply horn*) *noun* A cow with twisted horns.

1885 Murfree *Prophet* 70 In the corner of the rail fence was the "crumply cow," chewing her cud. **1996–97** Montgomery *Coll*: *crumpled horn* (known to Brown, Bush, Jones, Norris, Oliver); *crumply horn* (known to Brown, Bush, Norris).

crumply cow, **crumply horn** See **crumpled horn**.

crup See **creep**.

crust *noun* variant plural form of two syllables: *crust-es*.

1964 Glassie *Mt Jack Tales* 97 You've got pie crustes in your eyes.

cry off *verb phrase* To announce (the results of an electoral contest, at the voting venue).

1977 Shackelford et al. *Our Appalachia* 28 They counted the vote and came to the door and cried the vote off and I carried the precinct pretty good. *Ibid.* 30 Most of the time it would be ten or eleven o'clock at night before they would get through and they would cry off the vote at the door and show how many each candidate got.

crystial *noun* Crystal.

1944 Hayes *Word-List NC* 33. **1946** Dudley *KY Words* 270.

cry tad *noun* A crybaby, whiner.

2012 Williams *Coll* Dad will say "cry tad" as a unit.... He said that she would say something like "You ain't nothin but a little cry tad." Maybe I'm wrong (or maybe I just haven't heard it used enough), but it seems to be used affectionately.

cry up *verb phrase* See citation.

1936 Lyman *WV Idioms* 63 He was given up (cried up, reputed) to be a good writer.

cub up *verb phrase* To live cosily.

1997 Montgomery *Coll* = to live cosily, as a bear cub in a den (Oliver).

cuckceld bur See **cockleburr**.

cuckle See **cuckold**.

cuckleburr See **cockleburr**.

cuckol' See **cuckold**.

cuckold *verb* [Editor's note: This term as a noun is widespread in the US.]

A variant forms *cuckle*, *cuckol'*.

1942 Hall *Phonetics Smoky Mts* 92 [d] is frequently unsounded after [n] or [l], as in ... *cuckold*.

[DARE *cuckold* A chiefly southern Appalachians]

B To betray (someone) by being unfaithful to one's mate or partner; to go out with another fellow's girlfriend.

1895 Edson and Fairchild *TN Mts* 371 "She cuckold 'em"—of an unscrupulous but pretty woman, who made fools of neighbors' husbands. **1939** Hall *Coll* = used jocularly by CCC boys; for example, when one boy goes out with another boy's girl. The unlucky boy may ask, "You didn't cuckold me last night, did you?" **1945** Williams *Comment* 9–10 In the Kentucky mountains *cuckol'* is used mainly as a verb. Used literally, it means that one man makes a cuckol' of another by having carnal knowledge of the latter's wife: "Hank *cuckol'ed* John seven year." Sometimes the verb may refer to the conduct of the wife who has been unfaithful to her husband. Used figuratively, it means to reach the wrong conclusion through faulty reason or prejudice. As a noun, the word means the husband who has been abused as above. **1969** DARE *Survey* (WV) = to go out with another fellow's girl friend is to cuckold him. No actual sexual activity is necessary or implied. (Among young people of high-school, or "dating," age.)

[DARE *cuckold* v B1 chiefly southern Appalachians, Ozarks]

cuclebur See **cockleburr**.

cucumber *noun* variant form *cowcumber*. Now often jocular.

1863 *Warrick CW Letters* (June 4) I Could of Cooled him of Cool as a Cow Cumber. **1930** Armstrong *This Day and Time* 100 Your cowcumbers ain't a-lookin' so extry. **1942** Hall *Phonetics Smoky Mts* 38. **1955** Ritchie *Singing Family* 180 She'd never stop until she got to the top of the ridge, then she'd stand still and puff a little, fanning herself with a cowcumber leaf and looking all around her. **1986** Pederson et al. LAGS = attested by 10/60 interviewees (16.7%) from E TN; 10/36 of all LAGS interviewees (27.7%) attesting term were from E TN. **1997** Andrews *Mountain Vittles* 39 Soon as the cowcumber—that's what we mostly call 'em—were big enough to slice momma always had a dishful on the table, along with sliced maters.

[EDD *cowcumber* sb in general use in Scot, Irel, Engl; CUD (at *cowcumber*)]

cucumber magnolia tree See **cucumber tree.**

cucumber tree (also *cowcumber tree, cucumber magnolia tree*) *noun* A large deciduous tree (*Magnolia* spp). Same as **Indian bitter 2, mountain magnolia, umbrella tree, wahoo 2, wild cucumber tree, yellow linn.**

1883 Zeigler and Grosscup *Heart of Alleghanies* 49 Numerous cucumber trees are scattered on the slopes. These with the beech, water birch, black birch or mountain mahogany, black gum, red maple, and hickory, form the forests from the mountain bases to the line of the balsams. **1913** Morley *Carolina Mts* 21 There are several varieties of these "cucumber" and "umbrella" trees, as the people call them. **1934–47** LAMSAS *Appal* (Madison Co NC, Swain Co NC) *cowcumber tree*; (Madison Co NC) *cucumber tree*. **1961** Douglas *My Wilderness* 172 Here were cucumber magnolia trees whose pale yellow, fragrant flowers bring the woods to life, come springtime, and turn to dark red cucumbers that break open at maturity and expose the seeds on their surface. **1964** Stupka *Trees Shrubs Vines* 59 In the Greenbrier district, at 3050 elevation on Kalanu Prong, stands a venerable cucumber tree that measures 18 ft. 4 inches—a record size for this species. **1971** Hutchins *Hidden Valley* 104 On my first hike over it I saw numerous Fraser magnolias, known locally as "cucumber" trees, probably because of their large leaves. **1986** Pederson et al. LAGS: *cucumber tree* = attested by 7/60 interviewees (11.7%) from E TN; 7/15 of all LAGS interviewees (46.7%) attesting term were from Appalachia. **2001** Liftig *Lessons* 16 One of my childhood favorites was the "cowcumber" tree (cucumber magnolia or *Magnolia acuminata*), which looked like an umbrella, with its whorl of 12- to 15-inch leaves coming off a common center that at times was a blooming flower and, at other times, a red seed pod. **2011** *Smoky Mt Times* (May 18) The cucumber tree is so-named because of the clasping greenish-yellow petals it produces that tend to blend with the leaf and stem colors. It fruits—often in exotic asymmetrical forms—in August and September.

cud *noun* A chew cut from a plug or a portion taken from a pouch of chewing tobacco.

c1926 Cox *Cullowhee Wordlist* = quid. "Have a cud of baccy, ma'am." **1963** Edwards *Gravel* 20 Put your cud on a chip, Jeems. **1966–67** *DARE Survey* (Cherokee NC, Maryville TN) = portion of tobacco used at one time. **1979** Melton *'Pon My Honor* 40 The preacher was plumb bad to chew tobacco, and he'd clean forgot and got up to preach with a big cud of it in his mouth. **1996** Montgomery *Coll* (known to Cardwell, Ellis, Jones, Ledford, Norris, Oliver). **2005** Williams *Gratitude* 488 = enough chewin' tobacco to make a "chaw."

cudweed *noun* Same as **rabbit tobacco.**

1982 Stupka *Wildflowers* 124 It is sometimes called "poverty weed" and "old-field balsam," because it thrives in dry areas and waste places. Names such as "sweet balsam" and "sweet everlasting" refer to its fragrance. Other names are "rabbit tobacco" and "cudweed."

cull

A *verb* To reject in courtship.

2017 *Blind Pig* (June 9) She's been courting him for a few weeks, but after that shine he pitched at the dance I'd say she'll cull him now.

B *noun* A woman who, because of her age, is considered to have been rejected in courtship or too old for a marriage proposal. See also **cull list.**

c1900 (in **1997** Stoddart *Quare Women* 19) Both Pettit and Stone found some of the assumptions of patriarchal society amusing including the notion that, as single women over twenty, they were "culls."

cullion *noun* A wild green onion. See citation.

1968 Wilson *Folklore Mammoth Cave* 16 = a name used all over the region for *volunteer* or *winter onions*, which usually grow, without cultivation, around the edges of the garden.

cull list, on the *adjective phrase* Of a woman: presumed to be rejected in marriage or too old to marry. See also **cull.**

1921 Campbell *Sthn Highlander* 133 A girl is a spinster by eighteen, and on the "cull list" by twenty. [**1925** Furman *Glass Window* 15 First thing you know, you'll maybe fetch you a man, and be tuck off the cull-list.] **1951** Craig *Singing Hills* 111 A nicer-turned woman we never saw than you, but you'll be on the cull list if you don't get yourself a man soon. **1952** Wilson *Folk Speech NC* 531 = to be no longer on the marriage list. [**1967** *DARE Survey* (Gatlinburg TN) *cull list* = unmarried girls over twenty. Old-fashioned term used by the country people around here.]

[DARE *cull list, on the* adj phr South Midland]

cullowhee *noun* A wild lily. See citations.

[**1953** Greene and Blomquist *Flowers South* 14 (DARE) *Zephyranthes Atamasco* . . . The Cherokee Indian name for this lily was Cullowhee for which the town of Cullowhee, N.C. was named.] **1970** *DARE Survey* (wNC) Cullowhee was thought to mean "valley of the lilies." Now the usual translation is "swampy hunting ground." The lilies are rather rare in this part of North Carolina.

Culver's root *noun* A tall perennial plant (*Veronicastrum virginicum*) whose root has medicinal uses as a tonic, laxative, etc. Also called **gulver.**

1937 Hall *Coll* (Catons Grove TN) = also known as *gulver root*. [**1971** Krochmal et al. *Medicinal Plants Appal* 268 The rhizome is reputed to be a laxative, emetic, chologogue, and tonic.] **1985** Irwin

Alex Stewart 143 Black root, some people call it culvers, is good for your blood and a lot of things.

[from Doctor Culver, early American physician]

Cumberland River Rule *noun* See citation.

1983 Montell *Don't Go Up* 90 The device used to measure the logs and determine how many board feet each one contained was the Cumberland River Rule, a long measuring stick with a hook at the end that caught under the log. This rule was designed to measure logs in the water rather than on land, as did the Doyle and Scribner's rules. The Cumberland River Rule [whose origin is unknown] was used only on the river which gave it its name. Each end of the log was measured, and then an average was taken of the two.

cumfluttered *adjective* Excited, flustered.

1933 Chapman *Glen Hazard* 297 = flustered, excited. **1952** Wilson *Folk Speech NC* 531 = excited. **1995** Montgomery Coll (known to Cardwell, but not to other consultants from the Smoky Mountains).

[DARE *cumfluttered* adj Scots *cum-* intensive + *flutter* "to show agitation" + *-ed*]

cuore See **cure.**

cup *verb*

1 Of wood: to curl up, warp.

1955 Dykeman *French Broad* 53 Instead of boards, sometimes called "shakes," there would be shingles for this roof. They might be made of poplar, chestnut, white oak, or white pine. If they were oak, it was believed they could not be laid when the moon was light or they would "cup," that is, curl up at the exposed end. **1991** Thomas *Sthn Appal* 247 They's a lot of people goes with signs, to do thangs. Now, it'ull show quicker on a board roof than enny other thing. If ye put one side fer a roof when th' sign's down, that roof 'ull stay flat. Then, if ye put th' other side on when th' sign's up, wy, it jist keeps cuppin' up.

2 To draw a small amount of blood from (a person) by slitting the skin and catching the blood in a cup or glass, as a medical treatment; hence verbal noun *cupping*.

1992 Joslin *Mt People II* 269 Now cupping, you slit a cross with a knife, light a match to a paper and catch it in a glass, and put that on the slit to suck the blood out; [they] thought there was too much blood or something. **1996** Harrell *Fetch It* 132 She had a sore throat, and now I think she had what the doctors call strep throat. She was a sick girl. My parents went and asked Uncle Wylie Harrell, who was the oldest man in the community, to come over and "bleed" or "cup" Helen. Here is what they did. They turned the little girl over on her stomach and on her bare back, about half way down the spine, they cut with a straight razor two tiny slits in the form of a cross, one right across the other, deep enough so each of them bled a little bit—not a great deal, but a little bit. Then, Uncle Wylie took a lighted match, held a drinking glass upright and dropped that match in that drinking glass. When that match had just about gone out (it had apparently burned up what oxygen was in the glass), he turned that glass upside down and put that glass over the cut spot on Helen's back. The vacuum formed by that match burning up the oxygen pulled the blood out of Helen's back. This process was called either cupping or bleeding.

cupping See **cup 2.**

cur See **ker-.**

curb (also *curbing*) *noun* The rim around the mouth of a well.

1977 *Foxfire IV* 372 There's a well up here in town where me and my daddy walled it up to the top and put a rock curbing on it. *Ibid.* 368 [Caption:] Note the wooden curb built up over the hole to keep things from the surface from falling into it.

curd cheese (also *curds*) *noun* Cottage cheese.

1966 Dakin *Vocab Ohio River Valley* 343–44 Curds, *curd cheese*, and *home-made cheese*, also Southern and South Midland terms, compete with *clabber cheese* in the northeast and are more common in southern Kentucky from the Mountains to the Mississippi.

cur dog *noun* A dog of mixed or uncertain breed, especially one that is worthless.

1941 Stuart *Men of Mts* 201 He brought a cur dog that would run a human being like a polecat. **2012** Jourdan *Medicine Men* 74 When she ran out through the automatic doors, a little cur dog ran in on three legs.

[DARE *cur dog* n chiefly South, South Midland]

curds See **curd cheese.**

cure *verb* variant forms *cuore, cyor, cyore, keyor, kyor.*

1901 Harben *Westerfelt* 171 [We'll] put some turkey red calico stripes on that broad back o' yorn, an' rub in some salt and pepper to cuore it up. **1904** Johnson *Highways South* 137 I golly, I've cyored a heap with them medicines. **1937** Wilson *Folklore SE KY* 31 *cyor*. **1941** Still *Troublesome Creek* 76 Was a feller to eat wild fruit, a dram o' that tonic would cuore the pizen. **1942** Hall *Phonetics Smoky Mts* 37. **c1945** Haun *Hawk's Done* 259 Big Sam cyored him. **1969** Miller *Raising Tobacco* 33 Some farmers claimed burley "just naturally *kyored* (cured) up prettier" if it was stuck or scaffolded before it was dried. **1991** Haynes *Haywood Home* 76 "I see ye went an' keyord (cured) yerself," he'd say with a laugh.

[DARE *cure* n, v chiefly South, South Midland]

cure-all *noun* Self-heal, a perennial plant (*Prunella vulgaris*) with medicinal uses. Same as **heal-all.**

1997 Montgomery Coll = used for teas and for salves to put on cuts and the chest (Cardwell).

cured-out See **cure out.**

cure out (also *cure up*) *verb phrase* Of tobacco, meat, etc.: to become usable or edible by drying, aging, etc; hence participial adjective phrase *cured-out* properly dried.

1941 Stuart *Men of Mts* 49 Got some cured-out burley out there in the barn-shed. **1966–69** *DARE Survey* (Tompkinsville KY) It [= tobacco] hangs there till it all cures out, the . . . water all leaves it, and the leaf matures; (Maryville TN) I like dry weather to kill hogs . . . because the meat cures out better; (Westover WV) Then you have to hang it in what they call a tobacco barn and let it cure out. **1991** Weals *Last Train* 13 When the hams cured out, they would put them in what we would call bran sacks—cotton sacks.

[DARE *cure out* v phr South, South Midland]

cure up *verb phrase*

1 See **cure out.**

2 To cure (a person or an ailment) completely.

1939 Hall *Coll* (Big Creek NC) They was a weed that they call wild indigo. You can take hit, and it'll stop blood poison. Take the roots and beat it up, put sweet milk in it, and put it on it, and it'll draw it white, and cure it up. **1953** Wharton *Dr Woman Cumberlands* 60 No use to go fer the doctor if'n the granny woman an' the yarbs an' sich as that can cure them up. **1968** *Faith Healing* 18 I doctored them and cured 'em up.

curiosity *noun*

A variant forms *cur'osity, kurosity, kyurosty.*

1873 Smith *Arp Peace Papers* 150 Our peepul ain't a notisin you, only out of kurosity. **1930** (in **1952** Mathes *Tall Tales* 179) Folks will spend a power o' money anyhow to see a nacheral cur'osity like a peetrified woman or a five-legged calf. **1939** Hall *Notebooks* 13: 45 (White Oak NC) *kyurosty*. **1964** Roberts *Hell-Fer-Sartin* 95 Now Jack always wanted to know everything, and being his cur'osity was up he walked up this road and after a while he come to the top of the hill.

[DARE *curiosity* n especially South, South Midland]

B See citation.

1957 Combs *Lg Sthn High: Word-List* 25 = something, or some one amusing or exciting. Ex.: "It was a curiosity to look at that man." "He's a pyore curiosity."

curious *adjective* variant forms *curis, curous, cur'us.*

1862 Gilley *CW Letters* (Aug 3) the last letter that some body rote for will Cox was a mity curous rote leter. **1892** Dromgoole *Dan to Beersheba* 81 Gals is cur'us critters. **1924** Montague *Betsy Beaver* 228 She went on a-singing to him in that curous voice of hers that sounded more like running water and trees and birds, than it sounded human. **1963** Edwards *Gravel* 131 Well, that sorty made me curis, and I got to lookin at them shucks and shuckin out the years.

[DARE *curious* adj chiefly South, South Midland, New England]

curis See **curious.**

curledy *adjective* Having curls.

1954 Arnow *Dollmaker* 46 Mom, make her a curledy dress.

curly birch (also *curly maple, curly poplar, curly timber, curly tree, curly wood*) *noun* A tree whose wood has a distinctive figured and curled grain, making it prized for its appearance for furniture. See also **figured wood.**

1942 Robertson *Red Hills* 104 Our beautiful curly maple and solid walnut furniture was made by hand. **1960** Burnett *My Valley* 82 My Father and Uncle Dan, both of whom were lumbermen, knew of only one curly poplar tree left in the entire Valley, and it was standing near the head of the Left-Hand Fork—only a mile or so below the Balsam Gap. **1974–75** McCracken *Logging* 6:88 He could look at the side of that mountain over there [and] pick out ever' piece of curly wood there was on it. **1976** Lindsay *Grassy Balds* 40 A feller from Johnson City come here, helped 'em with a carload of curlywood. . . . He'd go in these mountains and cut those curly trees and bring 'em down there. **1982** Powers and Hannah *Cataloochee* 116 A death in the family meant that the best curly maple and walnut wood . . . was put into the hands of a good carpenter, who fashioned a simple coffin. **1991** Thomas *Sthn Appal* 151 My father dealt in what was called "curly birch." This yellow birch that growed up in under th' Roan Mount'n, there. They ewst to be quite a bit of it. An' in that birch, a lot of it was figured, or curly. . . . I ewst to work in th' curly timber bizness. Some called it "figured wood." It's what ye call curly maple. An' it brought a high price. **1997** Montgomery *Coll*: *curly tree* = either a wind-blown tree or one with a gnarled grain (Cardwell).

curly poplar, curly timber, curly tree, curly wood See **curly birch.**

curnet *noun* See citation.

c1982 Young *Colloquial Appal* 6 = gooseberry.

curous, cur'us See **curious.**

cushaw *noun* A large crookneck squash (*Cucurbita mixta*) with pale-yellow, edible flesh.

1797 Imlay *Western Terr* 240 (DARE) Cushas; cucurbita melopepo; squashes, a kind of pumpkin. **1924** Raine *Saddlebags* 28 When I asked an old man why he preferred "cushaws" (a large crook-neck squash) to pumpkins, he spat reflectively and answered, "If we growed punkins up in yan cove, they'd break loose and roll down and kill somebody." **1989** Still *Rusties and Riddles* [57] = winter squash. **1992** Brooks *Sthn Stuff* 37 = a crooked-neck squash; the "neck punkin.'" **2006** *Encycl Appalachia* 927 One of the older squash varieties eaten today is cushaw, a large, smooth, hard-skinned winter squash. It is Appalachia's dominant squash because of its size and because it has long been adaptable to the mountain climate. **2009** Sohn *Appal Home Cooking* 295 This smooth-skinned, hard-shelled winter squash is shaped like a yellow crookneck summer squash.

[of Algonquian origin; DARE *cushaw* n chiefly South, South Midland]

cushaw butter *noun* See citation.

1978 Slone *Common Folks* 313 The solid-shelled [gourds] were peeled, sliced, cooked, and mashed, sugar and spices added and called "cushaw butter."

cu-sheep, cu-sheepie See **co-sheep.**

cuss *noun* A perverse, mean, or irascible person or creature; a person to avoid.

1858 (in **1974** Harris *High Times* 120) It wer about layin by corn time when she married that hard faced, meaty fisted, groanin ole cuss. **1896** Fox *Last Stetson* 213 Some triflin' cuss took old Steve Brayton's [cause] jes to cross the river. **1913** Kephart *Our Sthn High* 91 [The bear is] a foxy cuss. **1923** Montague *Today Tomorrow* 159 Well, *sirs!* Tony he cert'nly is a great cuss! **1924** Abernethy *Moonshine* 118 The hired help were so cussed no-count, that after a-tarryin' at the throne like wrastlin' Jacob with the angel, I had a sorter hunch that the Lord were willin' fer me to go a-courtin' Widder Jinkins. **1963** Edwards *Gravel* 117 He was known among his neighbors as about the wickedest ole cuss that ever drawed the breath of life. **1979** Melton *'Pon My Honor* 43 Old Tom Bailey, who was as ornery an old cuss as ever run the river, was one of the biggest loggers and rafters in Clay County. **1984** Woods *WV Was Good* 228 He was a strappin' big cuss. (*Strapping* meant both large in size and *stalwart.*) **2005** Ellison *Mt Passages* 32 Wild boars are independent cusses that made the transition from one continent to another with admirable ease.

cussed *adjective* (pronounced as two syllables: *cuss-ed*) Willfully perverse, mean, infernal.

1862 *Love CW Letters* (Feb 9) they was Some caveldry men on picket close to Beaufort and the cused yankes com A cross the river one night and Shot 2 of them and killed them and then run Back on the other. **1865** *Parlier CW Letters* (Jan 11) I think this cussed ware will end soon and in the way I have thought all the time. **1867** Harris *Sut Lovingood* 126–27 I'se sorter fear'd tu try tu tell yu, George, the devilment that cussed infunel fool cow beaste wer a-doin. **1901** Harben *Westerfelt* 109 Thar are Folks in this cussed Settlement mean enough to begrudge her the grave Lot she has becase of what she was driv to. **1939** Hall *Coll* (Cataloochee NC) Confound it, that cussed old cat scratched my horse and he's tee-totally ruined him.

cussedness *noun* Willful perversity, irascibility.

1892 Doak *Wagonauts Abroad* 270 Coming up, we see a big rough mountaineer with a hangdog look and a general air of "pure cussedness," holding a long rifle at a recover. **1959** Pearsall *Little Smoky* 19 When an element of human "cussedness" is added, the problem becomes insurmountable. **1964** Stubbs *Mountain-Wise* (June–July) 10 The mule refused to cooperate, from pure "cussedness," we believe. **2004** Rehder *Appal Folkways* 296 = meanness: "Hits jus' pure cussedness that makes Jack kick the dawg."

cuss fight (also *cussing fight*) *noun* A loud and angry quarrel, especially one with much profane and obscene language.

1904–20 Kephart *Notebooks* 4:853 Him and Sam fell out and had a cuss-fight. **1913** Kephart *Our Sthn High* 36 By that time the land will be so poor hit wouldn't raise a cuss-fight. **1966–68** *DARE Survey* (Brasstown NC, Burnsville NC, Cherokee NC, Spruce Pine NC, Gatlinburg TN) = a fight between two people with words. **1973** *AOHP/EH* 66 I've heard a lot of cussing fights, and they'd get it broke up before it got real bad. **1976** Garber *Mountain-ese* 19 = exchange of profanity. "They had the dangedest cussfight you ever seed." **1987** Carver *Regional Dialects* 168 Upper Southerners, especially older and rural ones, are likely to call an argument or verbal fight a *cuss fight*.

[DARE *cuss-fight* n chiefly South, South Midland]

cussingest *adjective* Cursing the most, most inclined to curse. See also **-est 1** and Grammar and Syntax §3.4.1.

1924 (in **1952** Mathes *Tall Tales* 23) Dave would have the floor, with one of his homely romances, whether of the tallest hemlock, the biggest band-mill, the pullin'est team of hosses, the cussin'est boss, or the luckiest hand of cards that ever was on land or sea. **1968** Vincent *Best Stories* 81 Little Sam was the highest-tempered, and the cussingest young fellow in the whole neighborhood, and his mammy and pappy felt awful about it.

cussing fight See **cuss fight.**

custom mill *noun* A water-driven commercial mill that grinds wheat and corn for individual customers, as for a **toll.**

c1978 Trout and Watson *Piece of Smokies* 92 Some families had their own tiny tub mills, but most people took their grain to the local "custom mill." **1988** *Smokies Guide* (Summer) 7 As isolated farms merged into communities, a few of the larger and more romantic custom mills were built locally. These ground wheat as well as corn and often had a sawmill operation powered by the same water-driven wheel. During the years when custom mills ran, most local people existed on a nearly cashless economy. Millers extracted one-eighth of each client's grain as a fee for grinding. The millers then sold their toll grain to widows or lumbermen or others who did not raise their own crops. Custom mills were social centers too. Even the biggest mills only ground about four bushels of corn per hour, leaving the customer with plenty of time to catch up on news, do some horse trading or just listen to the cool, burbling waters and the humming of the wheels. **1990** *Smokies Guide* (Summer) 13 Bigger still were the custom mills that ground corn and wheat as a business. Farmers without their own tub mills would have their grain processed for about 12% toll. Both the Cable and Mingus custom mills have been preserved in the park. **c1995** *Mingus Mill* All through the years the [Mingus mill] was a "custom mill," one that ground to each customer's taste. . . . Corn was received by the miller, ground to the texture preferred by the customer (thus, "custom milling"), and the meal returned to him, minus a toll (usually one-eighth). The miller could sell it for cash or trade it at the store.

cut

A *verb* variant past-participle form *cutted*.

1989 *Matewan OHP-9* [I] first went to work just to bring that cutted coal, and [it] didn't differ if it took us till eleven o'clock that night, [you had to] bring that cutted coal or bring your tools, either one. *Ibid.* 87 Nowadays they could put one [= an ear] back that, they got it cutted off and [would] sew it back on and made it work.

B Senses.

1 To stab or slash with or as with a knife. See also **cutting scrape.**

1904–20 Kephart *Notebooks* 4:785 Bob sot thar pale as a corpse—it cut him to the gizzard—and soon he went upstairs lookin' like a sheep-killin' dog. **1915** Hall *Autobiog Claib Jones* 14 Lewis caught me and held me and Kelse cut me thirteen times with a knife. **1941** Stuart *Men of Mts* 232 He was cutting at me with a corn knife. **1970** GSMNP-26:11 He took his knife and cut him, a little switchblade knife with a short blade . . . just cut him till he liked to bled to death again they could get him home. **1989** *Matewan OHP*-23 He got into it with them, and he was cut all to pieces with knives.

[DARE *cut* v 1 chiefly South, South Midland]

2 To castrate (a male domestic animal). See also **alter**, **change**, **trim.**

1934–47 LAMSAS *Appal* (Madison Co NC). **1940** Haun *Hawk's Done* 188 The menfolks mostly just laughed about it and the womenfolks all whispered in one another's ears and said an old dog like that ought to be cut. **1957** Broaddus *Vocab Estill Co KY* 21 = to castrate. **1985** Irwin *Alex Stewart* 106 Why Lord yeah, I've cut many a brute. **1987** Young *Lost Cove* 154 He was traveling sort of side ways like a boar hog walks after he has been cut.

3 (also *cut on*) Of a squirrel: to crack and eat the nuts from (a tree); to crack and eat (nuts).

1944 Hall *Coll* (Del Rio TN) The squirrels sure are cutting the boxwood trees now, and they are easy killed on them. **1963** Edwards *Gravel* 141 "Gonna kill some squirrels, I 'spect," ventured Uncle Stevey. "Yes, Alvis Hale says they're cuttin on hickory nuts now."

4 (also *cut down*, *cut up*) To destroy (an illegal distilling operation); to stop (a person) from running such an operation. See also **cut up copper.**

1904 Fox *Christmas Eve* 135 One night somebody guides the revenoos in on Hell fer Sartain, an' they cuts up four stills. **1969** Parris *Hard Likker* As a still-hunter, he's cut down a passel of whisky-making outfits in the past eight years in Haywood county hills. **1977** *Ben Chappell* 233 He run [the still] a month and by God, and ol' John Beck Dockins went in there and cut him down. **1983** *Dark Corner OHP*-27A We have cut as high as forty-six distilleries in one month. **1989** Smith *Flyin' Bullets* 333 The "silver cloud" stills were big aluminum pots that held five or six hundred gallons. They just ran whiskey off on one worm. We would bring all the copper stills in but we cut down and destroy [sic] all the silver clouds. **1992** Gabbard *Thunder Road* 119 From then on, ever time we got cut, we'd just put back. Sometimes we'd run three or four rounds, sometimes we'd lose the sweet mash. 'Course, I had a pretty good sponsor. I could go see Daddy and tell him we'd got cut, and he'd give us enough money and enough sugar to get started back.

5 To go directly, head.

1939 Burnett *Gap o' Mountains* 18 I was aridin' bareback on Beck, my little gray mule, and when I seed Shorty Randolph agittin' on that hoss, I cut for home.

6 To dilute (freshly distilled whiskey) in order to reduce its proof and make it drinkable.

1992 Gabbard *Thunder Road* 65 When the alcohol quits runnin', what you get is backin's. If you got three cans of alcohol, you get three cans of backin's to cut it with and you put the rest of the backin's into the condenser. **2007** Alexander *Moonshiners Gone* v The raw liquid was too high in alcohol content to drink and [it] had to be thinned down or "cut." *Ibid.* 202 Ethel was a local expert in cutting raw whiskey down "jest right."

C *noun*

1 (also *cut-off*, *cut-out*) A passageway through the mountains, by trail, road, or rail; a "short cut." See also **near cut**, **new cut**, **nigh cut.**

1866 Smith *So Called* 127 Leavin my wagin with a widder woman, I took it afoot across the country by a settlement road they called the "cut-off." **1883** Jones *Highlands N Carol* 380 This is a "cut-off" and we take it to save distance. **1926** Hunnicutt *Twenty Years* 26 Andy said if we can get in a little cut-out I know of, we can get to Rock Stop. Finally we got into this little cut-out and soon got on top of the mountain at the Rock Stop. *Ibid.* 207 When we got to the cut-out we could see tracks where he had gone to the cut-out, where the trail was cut through the laurel across the Cage Drive Ridge. **1994** Montgomery *Coll*: *cut off* (known to Shields). **1999** Perry *Clinch River Crossing* to the South side of the bridge was "the cut," where an unpaved road turned left up the River Road on our side.

2 A portion of cultivated land.

1844 Crosby *Journal/Account Book* 103 Began to Plant Corn 13th of April and Planted the first Cut above the New Barn 3rd Week of Apl. **1890** Fruit *KY Words* 64 With tobacco-raisers *cut* means a portion of a tobacco field: "Did you finish worming that cut you were on?" **1999** Montgomery *Coll* When old Joe died, he gave the upper cut to his daughter and the lower cut to his son (Cardwell).

[DARE *cut* n 2 "portion of land" chiefly South, South Midland]

3 See 1973 citation.

1973 Preston *Bituminous Term* 52 = the amount of coal dislodged by the explosion [set off to loosen coal at the **face** of a mine]. **1977** Shackelford et al. *Our Appalachia* 266 If you can't clean the cut, take your tools; the other man can.

cut a big figure (also *cut a big gut*) *verb phrase* To behave wildly, act ostentatiously or foolishly.

1939 Farr *TN Mt Regions* 90 *cut a big gut* = to act foolish or appear ridiculous. "He cut a big gut at the dance." **1939** Hall *Coll* (Smokemont NC) [The bear] went back into the laurel hung with this trap . . . he was cuttin' a big figure an' a-growlin' and so on. **1995** Montgomery *Coll*: *cut a big figure* (known to Cardwell); *cut a big gut* (known to Cardwell, Oliver).

cut a big gut See **cut a big figure.**

cut a choagie See **cut a shuck.**

cut a dido See **dido 1, 2.**

cut a rusty (also *cut some rusty*) *verb phrase* To caper or perform a prank, have an outburst of exuberance or wit drawing attention to oneself or creating a scene; to throw a fit or tantrum.

1923 Greer-Petrie *Angeline Steppin' Out* 4 Now, childern, all I ax you is, kin you beat that, when hit comes to cuttin' a rusty? **1946** Stuart *Plum Grove Hills* 113 The last spell I took was one night I's out with the men fox huntin' . . . I cussed and laughed. I called my dogs. I tooted my fox horn. I cut some rusty. **1961** Williams *Content Mt Speech* 15 She jist said she reckoned all them thar shines and rusties the old man had cut had marked Lil's baby. **1976** Garber *Mountain-ese* 18 The dog really cut a rusty when we gave him a big juicy bone. **1989** Still *Rusties and Riddles* [60] = turn of wit or common prank. **1992** Brooks *Sthn Stuff* 131 *rusty* = a show-off action. "You cut one of your rusties while we're visiting the Perkinses, boy, you'll catch what-for when we get home." **1994–97** Montgomery Coll (known to seven consultants from the Smoky Mountains, who agree that the phrase can have all three senses).

[DARE *cut a rusty* v phr (at *rusty* n 1) chiefly South, South Midland]

cut a shine (also *cut up a shine*) *verb phrase* To make a commotion or display, throw a fit, misbehave, play a prank. See also **shine C1.**

1858 (in **1974** Harris *High Times* 103) Well, you'd a dam soon foun' the fac' out, if you'd a cut up any shines roun' yere. **1901** Harben *Westerfelt* 271 Don't cut up any o' yore shines with these Christian women who are tryin' to do good. **1953** Davison *Word-List Appal* 13 = to behave in an unseemly manner; to display anger: "When I git mad I sure cut a shine." **1955** Ritchie *Singing Family* 202 I raced through the woods like a deer, swinging on grapevines and tree limbs, and laughing and making speeches on top of high rocks, and cutting such a shine that I was ashamed of myself. **1956** Hall Coll (Bryson City NC) The dog's run out and cut a big shine. *Ibid.* (Indian Camp Creek NC) [A heifer with calf itch] would cut the awfullest shine I've ever heared. **c1960** Wilson Coll = to behave in a bad or untactful way. **1967** Hall Coll (Del Rio TN) A calf would cut a shine when it sees its mommy if it had been lost or somethin'. **1985** Irwin *Alex Stewart* 145 Whiskey is about the best for that. Hit's good for a lot of things. Of course it'll make you cut a shine if you drink too much of it. **1989** *Matewan OHP-23* They like to tore that schoolhouse down a-laughing, and I tell you, man, they cut a shine. **1995** Weber *Rugged Hills* 92 A few hours later, I was awakened when I heard a chicken really "cutting a shine."

cut a shuck (also *cut a choagie*) *verb phrase* Same as **light a rag.**

2016 *Blind Pig* (Dec 8) I've heard and used "cut a shuck," which means to proceed in great haste just as "light a rag" and "light a shuck." Another term I've heard and used is "cut a choagie," which means the same.

cut a skive *verb phrase* See citation.

1957 Combs *Lg Sthn High: Word-List* 25 = to prance about (as of a horse).

cut a through See **through C1.**

cut down *verb phrase*

1 See **cut B4.**

2 To reduce (the volume, pace, or intensity of). See also **cut up 2.**

1939 Hall Coll (Hartford TN) I cut down my horse a little bit. **1999** Montgomery File Cut down the lights.

3 (also *cut out, cut slip*) To take aim and shoot or throw; (with *on*) to aim and strike (someone) with a rock or gun. See also **drive B3.**

1939 Hall Coll (Nine Mile TN) He says, "Riley, knock its damn teeth out of there," and he cut down with a rock and right in the mouth [the bear] tuck it. *Ibid.* (Cataloochee NC) George studied hisself agin the saplin' and cut down and just busted that bear's head wide open. **1953** Hall Coll (Deep Creek NC) He cut down and shot it. **1957** Combs *Lg Sthn High: Word-List* 26 *cut slip* = to throw, or shoot quickly. Ex: "I cut slip and knocked him in the head with a rock." **1961** *Coe Ridge OHP-334B* Aunt Mary cut out on him with a rock and hit him on the arm and went and knocked the pistol down. *Ibid.* 336B He had an old cap and ball pistol, and he cut down on Scarborough and killed him. **1970** *Hunting Stories* 28 When a hunter says, "I cut down on him," he means he opened fire. **1979** *Daddy Oakley* 176 I cut down with the pitchfork and killed [the hen] as dead as a hammer. **1989** *Matewan OHP-39* Somebody had cut down on them offen the mountain there, and he shot one of these state policemans in the thigh. **2005** Williams *Gratitude* 488 *cut down at, cut down on* = if throwin' rocks, means you let 'em fly as hard, as fast, and as clost as you can throw 'em. If shootin' a gun, means you drawed a bead and shot right fast.

cut drive See **drive B3.**

cute as a speckled pup See **speckled pup.**

cut loose *verb phrase* To let go or start suddenly or energetically; to act, speak, shoot, etc. without restraint. See also **take loose.**

1939 Hall Coll (Wears Cove TN) Bowles says, "I'll shoot it if it catches us both." I says, "Cut loose, I'll take care of myself and you take care of yourn." **1954** GSMNP-19:18 While they was sitting there all at once a rattlesnake cut loose to singing. **1969** Roberts *Greasybeard* 30 When they all got fixed the way the mule said, he give the signal and they all cut loose to yelling. The mule hee-hawed, the dog barked and snarled, and the cat meowed, and the rooster crowed. **2007** Shelby *Molly Whuppie* 10 This one giant, he got him a big hunk of hog meat and was just about to put it on his fork when Molly Whuppie cut loose with a rock.

cut off

A *verb phrase*

1 To lay (a person) off work. Same as **cut out A2.**

1977 Shackelford et al. *Our Appalachia* 276 Trade a little more at the company store or we'll have to cut you off. **1989** *Matewan OHP-94* In nineteen and fifty-two [with] the lull in the coal industry, they had several people that was cut off in the offices over there.

1998 *Dante OHP-61* We got cut off in fifty-nine, and I've been in a little bit of everything ever since then.

2 To leave in a hurry, dash away.

2014 Williams *Coll* You cut off like you're going to Bad Branch Falls.

B *noun* See **cut C1**.

cut one's eye down *verb phrase* See citation.

1927 Woofter *Dialect from WV* 352 = to blacken one's eye: "Several of the boys got their eyes cut down at the fair."

cut one's eye-teeth *verb phrase* See citation.

1921 Combs *Slang Survivals* 116 In England, the "cutting of one's eye-teeth" was supposed evidence of sharpness, intelligence; in the hills it means to humiliate, or cause chagrin. E.g., "Samp greened him out (beat him) in that deal, and it cut his eye-teeth.'"

cut one's foot *verb phrase* See citation.

1931 Combs *Lg Sthn High* 1307 He cut his foot (stepped in excrement) behind the barn.

[DARE *cut one's foot* v phr especially South Midland]

cut out

A *verb phrase*

1 See **cut down 3**.

2 (as *cut out of*) To lay a person off work from (a workplace). Same as **cut off A1**.

1975 Screven *John B Wright* 13 I was on electrician's job when I was cut out of the mines. **1989** *Matewan OHP-89* I run a business out here, a beer garden, a tavern for forty-five years, and raised my children on that 'cause Roland was cut out of the mines.

B *noun* See **cut C1**.

cut-out tree *noun* See citation.

2007 McMillon *Notes* = a tree with a limb cut out as a marker or boundary.

cut-over *adjective* Of land: cleared of marketable timber.

1962 Dykeman *Tall Woman* 304 I've always thought the ivy was about the prettiest thing growing here, the way it clings to the mountains, the way it comes in the cutover places and covers up the scars with blooms in spring. **1975** Broome *Out under Smokies* 149 The old fields, cut-over lands, and roadsides began to explode with color.

cutshort *noun* A small **running bean**, usually a **half-runner**.

1957 Broaddus *Vocab Estill Co KY* 21 = a type of green beans. **c1960** Wilson *Coll* = a variety of pole beans that has seeds, crowded in a short pod; often raised as a cornfield bean. **1977** Farthing *Food Customs* 41 To make leather breeches, green beans are strung on heavy thread, whole or in broken pieces, and then hung in the sun to dry. "Greasy backs" and "cut shorts" are two often used varieties. **2011** Best *Bean Terminology* = a type of bean where the seeds outgrow the hulls and lock the developing seeds against one another. This makes them appear square, rectangular, triangular, or even trapezoidal in form. . . . They are sometimes called bust-out beans because the dried hulls will often split apart vigorously after the bean pods have dried out and then become wet again by rain or even a heavy dew. This is nature's way of scattering.

cut slip See **cut down 3**.

cut some rusty See **cut a rusty**.

cutted See **cut A**.

cutter *noun*

1 (also *cutter boot*) See citation.

1991 Weals *Last Train* 117–18 Calked boots could be a deadly weapon when the men who wore them fought, if one got the other down and stomped him. The calks . . . were dozens of sharp steel points embedded in the sole and heel of each boot. . . . They were called "cutter boots," or cutters, as often as they were called calked boots, and many men thought of them as an investment.

2 A type of fox-hound that tries to anticipate the path of a fox rather than follow its scent.

1950 Stuart *Hie Hunters* 14 "What do you mean by a good cutter?" "She won't track with the other hounds. She knows these fox woods and foxes so well she makes for the places where the foxes cross the ridges and the low gaps. . . . Fleet not only gits ahead of the other dogs, but she gits ahead of the fox and she sits and waits on 'im. And when he gits close she gives him a sight chase."

3 (also *cutter plow*) A heavy plow with a knife-like blade tearing up roots. Also called **root-cutter plow**.

1941 Stuart *Men of Mts* 174 He was a giant ox and he pulled the cutter plow through the earth and tore out the stumps in the corn rows. **1983** Broaddus *Estill Co KY Word List* 37 *cutter* = a plow with a thin, knife-like blade for cutting roots.

[DARE *cutter*[1] n 8 chiefly South Midland]

4 See citation.

1977 Shackelford et al. *Our Appalachia* 35 (Knott Co KY) Somebody that didn't want me to be elected would put on somebody they knew that could take some votes. . . . Such candidates are called "cutters" in mountain political circles.

cutter boot See **cutter 1**.

cutter plow See **cutter 3**.

cut the blood out of (also *cut the britches off of*) *verb phrase* To punish (someone) severely by whipping.

1953 Davison *Word-List Appal* 10 = to whip severely. "Pa cut the blood out of Bill when he laid out of school." **1997** Montgomery *Coll*: *cut the blood out of* (known to ten consultants from the Smoky Mountains). **1998** *Dante OHP-71* You talk about a boy getting a whipping. Now he [= the teacher] about cut the britches off of him. He went out to a big ole tree in the yard . . . they'd go and cut switches and cut rings around it so they would break.

cut the buck *verb phrase*

1 To engage in a **buckdance.**

1924 Greer-Petrie *Angeline Gits Eyeful* 17 They gallivanted all over the country, here and thar, dancin', and playin' kyards, and cuttin' the buck gin'rally.

2 See citation.

1927 Woofter *Dialect from WV* 352 = to accomplish any effort: "He was not able to cut the buck that time."

cut the pigeon wing See **pigeon('s) wing.**

cut the short dog *verb phrase* See citation.

1946 Woodard *Word-List VA/NC* 11 = to caper and frisk around when tipsy . . . Occasional among bons vivants.

cutting scrape *noun* A knife fight. See also **cut B1, scrape A.**

1970 GSMNP-26:11 He got into a scraping and cutting scrape with a fellow and cut him up till the other fellow didn't die, but he was never stout after it. **1983** Jones *Sin-Eater* 13 Practically all men there, at that time, carried handguns and knives for their real or imagined protection and, as a result, shooting and cutting scrapes occurred almost daily.

cut tops

A *verb phrase* To remove the **tops** of corn stalks for use as feed; hence verbal noun *cutting tops*. See 1939 citation. See also **blade fodder, fodder, roughness, top B1.**

1939 Hall *Coll* (Saunook NC) Cutting tops is the same as taking roughness. Cut the stalk from the ear of corn up. Then shock the tops up in a field, about thirty stalks to the shock. To pull fodder, one man [can work] between rows, takin' two rows at a time. Get the fodder (blades) in a small bundle and hang it on the stalk after the tops have been cut. Tie a bunch of blades with two or three blades, hang it on the stalk. Then put the bundles on stalks about fifteen feet apart. Then haul all the roughness (or tops) and fodder out. Take a big old long rope, tie about a hundred bundles of fodder together and carry it out. Put the roughness (tops) in one stack and the fodder (blades) in another, each around a pole. Make the stacks about eighteen or twenty feet high. Some farmers, mostly dairies, take the roughness and fodder and put it in a silo. **1966** Guthrie *Corn* 90 As a means of conserving feed, some people *cut tops* after the corn was fairly mature but while the plant was still green. The tops of the corn plants were cut off just above the ears, tied into *shocks*, and later hauled in for feed. **1973** *Gardening* 240 We'd always cut our tops an' pull our fodder long about September. **1991** Haynes *Haywood Home* 48 Harvesting corn was a lot of extra work compared to how it's done today. First, we cut tops and stripped the fodder. Cutting tops is cutting the stalk just above the ear and tying them in little bundles which were shocked and dried in the field. When dry, tops were gathered and stacked in the stackyards near the barn.

B *noun* The tops of corn stalks cut off for use as feed.

1996 Montgomery *Coll* If the top were cut above the last ear of corn and harvested for feed, then they were referred to as cut tops (Cardwell).

cut up *verb phrase*

1 See **cut B4.**

2 To turn up, increase (the volume or intensity of). See also **cut down 2.**

1995 Montgomery *File* Let's see if we can cut up the heat (48-year-old man, White Pine TN).

cut up a shine See **cut a shine.**

cut up copper *verb phrase* See citation. See also **cut B5.**

1917 Kephart *Word-List* 410 = to destroy a still: "Last winter there come a revenue in here and cut up a lot of copper on Jones' Creek."

cut up jack *verb phrase* To be boisterous or in high spirits; to cause a disturbance. See also **jack**[1], **tear up jack.**

1941 Still *Troublesome Creek* 127 Spring lizards were cutting up jack, and the hills were the color of greenback money.

[DARE (at *jack* n[1] 14) chiefly South, Midland]

c-u-u-u-p, cwup See **cope.**

cyar See **car.**

cyarcass See **carcass.**

cyard See **card.**

cyarn, cyarne See **carrion.**

cyarpet See **carpet.**

cyart See **cart.**

cyarve See **carve.**

cymbling See **cymling.**

cymling *noun*

A variant forms *cymbling* [see **1886** in **B**], *simblin* [see **c1844** in **B**], *simlin* [see **1886** in **B**].

B (also *cymling squash*) A small, inedible summer squash with an egg-like shape, sometimes put in a nest to encourage a hen to lay; *simlin* [see **1886** in **B**].

c1844 Beckner *Shane Interview* 237 [He] had gone out to get simblins at a pit the outside of the station yard. **1864** Poteet *CW Letters* (Aug 19) I has a mess of simblins for supper dont you wish you had some. **1886** Smith *Southernisms* 38 *cymbling* or *simlin* = a "variety of squash." This and not squash is the universal name for the fruit in the South, as a professor at Vanderbilt University, from New York, found out when he ordered a *squash* and failed utterly to make the huckster understand. **1906** Weir *Hot Springs* 25 One man reproving the "preacher" for some offense said, "If you talk that-a-way, you are no better than soundin' brass, and tinklin' cymlings" (a small gourd). **1957** Broaddus *Vocab Estill Co KY* 69 *simlin* =

a flat squash with scalloped edges. **1968** Wilson *Folklore Mammoth Cave* 16 = a summer squash, usually of the pattypan type (*Cucurbita pepo*). In one community this vegetable is called a *ten-toed squash*. **1986** Pederson et al. *LAGS* (as a false egg) = attested by 3/60 interviewees (5%) from E TN; 3/8 of all LAGS interviewees (37.5%) attesting term were from Appalachia. **2002** Oliver *Cooking and Living* 59 Pattypan or cymling squash was raised, and anyone who was hard-headed, or rather dense, was often called a cymlin' head.

[DARE *cymling* n 1 chiefly South, South Midland]

cymling head *noun* A small round head; a person with such a head; hence adjective *cymling-headed* = hard-headed, dumb.

1905 Miles *Spirit of Mts* 115 There was a feller she'd called a cymblin'-headed fool that tried to act big-Ike and sass her back. **1968** *DARE Survey* (Brasstown NC) = having a small head. **1996** Montgomery *Coll* (known to Adams, Brown, Cardwell, Jones, Oliver). **2002** Oliver *Cooking and Living* 59 Pattypan or cymling squash was raised, and anyone who was hard-headed, or rather dense, was often called a cymlin' head.

[DARE *cymling-head* n chiefly South, South Midland]

cyor, cyore See **cure.**

cyorner See **corner.**

cyounty See **county.**

cyow See **cow.**

D

dabble *verb* To wash oneself.

1939 (in **1944** Wentworth *ADD* 152) (eWV) I want to dabble and go to bed. **1941** Stuart *Men of Mts* 38 You fellars dabble in the pan and git ready to eat.

dad *noun* Used as a term of respect for an older man unrelated to the speaker, in both direct address and third-person reference. See also **aunt B, granny A1, old aunt, old uncle, uncle.**

1927 Mason *Lure of Smokies* 8 [He] used to be fond of relating a tale of one "Dad" Bivins, a mountaineer who lived alone in the high hills . . . "Mornin', Dad!" **1931** Stuart *Yarb Doctor* 4 "Hello, dad!" I said softly. "How-do-ye-do, young man, and who may ye be?" came the instant reply, and "Ain't ye most lost in these here parts?" **1988** *Augusta Heritage* 153 He looked at me and said, "Dad, I had an itching to buy that red car today." *Ibid.* He's working back in there, and he come in to me and said, "Dad, I'm looking to buy that, get that old wrecked car."

dad- (also *dag-, dod-*) *interjection* Used as a euphemism for *damn* or *God*, especially to combine with a verb past-participle, as in *dad-busted, dad-gone*, etc. See also **bedabs, b'gad, by, dog[1], I'll be dod.**

1859 Taliaferro *Fisher's River* 201 I'll be dadsamped ef one good butt ain't wuth two knocks. It knocks the wind out'n you quick as thunder. **1866** Smith *So Called* 47 I'll be dad-swamp'd if the commissary didn't keep his flour in 'em. **1867** (in **1974** Harris *High Times* 185) Oh! You be dadrabbited. **1868** (in **1974** Harris *High Times* 87) Now, Mister, dod durn me if I haint made all the apology necessary, an' more too. **1890** Fruit *KY Words* 64 *dad, dod*, for God, in certain curses. Thus: "Dad-drat your hide"; "Dad-drot you"; "Dod-rot you," "Dad burn"; "Drat it" is also used. **1913** Kephart *Our Sthn High* 101 Then the dad-burned gun wouldn't stand roostered (cocked); the feather-spring had jumped out o' place. **1922** Cobb *KY Mt Rhymes* 6 Nowadays-folks can't blow that [gourd] horn; / Blow, and they puff, puff, and they blow, / And swar the dad-busted thing won't go. **1937** Hall *Coll* (Cades Cove TN) Dad gone it, there weren't even a sprig of fire in his place! The fire were plumb out. **1942** Robertson *Red Hills* 52 Why not tell it? Dod blast it, they've separated. **1960** Mason *Memoir* 18 Mawwwwwwww, fetch me that old claw-hammer off the fire shelf, this dad-blasted ole steers busted up my plow and hits the only one I had. **1972** Hall *Sayings* 54 You mighty dag-gone right I would!; well, I'll be dag-gone. **1973** *Florence and Lawton* 199 Ever' dadblamed time I'd cut up, I'd get a whippin'. **1974** *No Sang* 17 Dad jim they [= moles] just love those roots like nobody's business. **1974–75** McCracken *Logging* 3:24 There were some big white pine, but there wasn't much of it and it wasn't too good. It was all dad burned old. **1976** Carter *Little Tree* 37 Anyhow it's another one of them dadblamed words [he always used "dadblamed" instead of "damn" in front of Granma] that we can do without. **1984** Woods *WV Was Good* 231 For more vehement expression of disgust or anger, one might exclaim, "Dadburnit, let me alone." *Doggone* it was equally adequate. *Dadshameit* was sometimes used. **1992** Morgan *Potato Branch* 87 We could even hear Anner's "Dad blast it, be still," to a milk cow. **2002** Myers *Best Yet Stories* 173 One of my half-brothers was once asked who was the best among the revenuers. He replied, "My Dad's, Dad-jimmed old mule!" **2012** Still *Hills Remember* 347 You dadjim right she can work, and she will work.

[DARE *dad* n² especially South, South Midland]

dad-blamed, dad-blast, dad-blasted, dad-burned, dad-busted, dad-drat, dad-drot See **dad-.**

daddy

A *noun*

1 A stallion. See also **daddy cow, gentleman cow, male brute.** **c1960** Wilson *Coll.*

2 Used as a respectful term of address for an older man upon meeting.

1948 Chase *Grandfather Tales* 68 "Howdy-do, daddy." "Good morning, sir."

B *verb*

1 To father (a child, especially an illegitimate one). See also **pappy B.**

1916 Combs *Old Early English* 291 "Who *daddied* that kid?"—([said] usually in the sense of an illegitimate child). **1952** Wilson *Folk Speech NC* 532 = to beget a child. "He's *daddied* more children than he can feed." **1988** Smith *Fair and Tender* 212 I hear that he has daddied him some babies here and there though. **1996** Montgomery *Coll* (known to Adams, Ledford, Oliver).

2 To resemble (one's father).

1916 Combs *Old Early English* 283 That kid *daddies* itself (resembles its father). **1982** Slone *How We Talked* 8 = to resemble one's father.

daddy cow *noun* Used as a euphemism for bull. See also **bull A1, daddy A1, gentleman cow, male brute.**

1966 *DARE Survey* (Cherokee NC) = bull.

[DARE *daddy* n 5 chiefly South, South Midland]

dad-gone, dadjim, dad-jimmed, dad-rabbited, dad-samped, dadswamped, dag-, daggone See **dad-.**

dairy (also *dairy house*) *noun* A small outbuilding in which dairy products and other food are kept cool and fresh, most often built over a spring. The more common term in the mountains generally is **springhouse.**

1936 (in **2009** Powell *Shenandoah Letters* 72) I am asking you if I can have any of my buildings. I have one old building 10 × 16 planed logs, one building 6 × 10 dairy house. **1973** Miller *English Unicoi Co* 75 *dairy* = (place where you actually keep your milk and butter) attested by 6 of 6 speakers. **1976** Garber *Mountain-ese* 20 *dairy* = milk cooling house. "Put milk in the dairy so it won't clabber afore supper." **1977** Pederson *Dugout* 88 A notable discovery in East Tennessee was the recurrence of the term *dairy* as a room dug into the ground or the side of a hill, where dairy products are stored in the summer and vegetables are stored in the winter. . . . This geographical area is remarkably coherent, bound on the northeast by Cross Mountain (the southern boundary of Shady Valley) and the Holsten [sic] Mountain (the eastern boundary of Sullivan County), on the south by the Great Smokies, and on the west by the Great Valley of East Tennessee. Although the concept was vigorously investigated in the southern mountains of East Tennessee, across the Great Valley and throughout the Cumberland region, not a single instance of the hillside dairy was reported. **1978** Reese *Speech NE Tenn* 32 *dairy* = attested by 6/12 (50%) speakers. **1986** Pederson et al. *LAGS*: *dairy* = attested by 14/60 interviewees (23.7%) from E TN; 14/41 of all LAGS interviewees (34%) attesting term were from E TN; *dairy house* = attested by 3/60 interviewees (5%) from E TN; 3/7 of all LAGS interviewees (34%) attesting term were from E TN. **1996–97** Montgomery *Coll*: *dairy* (known to Ellis); *dairy house* (known to Adams, Cardwell, Norris). **1997** *Dante OHP-14* We had a smoke house up over the dairy, had a dairy where we put our canned stuff and the lard and stuff like that . . . the dairy was right close to the house and the smoke house. **2006** *Encycl Appalachia* 433 Some apples and pears were stored in cool places such as cellars or outside "dairies," which were rock-walled buildings partly submerged into the hillside. **2009** Roberts *Outbuildings* 335 In parts of the southern mountains, "dairy" referred (and still refers) to a structure banked into a slope or hillside. . . . Here, families stored milk in a container on a dirt floor half-submerged in a stone trough of cold well or spring water.

[DARE *dairy house* n especially South, South Midland]

damage *verb* To suffer harm.

1957 Combs *Lg Sthn High: Word-List* 26 = become damaged. Ex.: "That corn'll damage ifn it don't come on rain soon."

damify *verb* To damage, injure; hence participial adjective *damified.*

1924 Raine *Saddlebags* 101 His mill war consid'able damified (damaged). **1957** Combs *Lg Sthn High: Word-List* 26 = damage, injure. It is a var[iant] of the sixteenth century damnify, with the same meaning. **1960** Westover *Highland Lg* 19 *damified* = damaged.

[cf OED3 *damnify* v "to cause injury, loss, or inconvenience to" (very common in 17th c.; now rare)]

damsel *noun*

1 The damson plum tree (*Prunus domestica*).

1985 Irwin *Alex Stewart* 205 We had a tree we called a damsel (damson). It was a kind of plum and we'd dry them and make prunes. It was a regular prune tree.

[folk etymology from *damson*]

2 See citation.

2007 Ball *Tub Mills* 9 The corn was gravity fed to the stones [of a **tub mill**] by a "shoe" under the hopper shaking against a "damsel" or "rattle staff" connected to the top of the millstone shaft.

dance in a/the hog trough (also *dance in a pig trough, dance in the pig trough*) *verb phrase* Usually of an older sister: to have a younger sister marry first and thus be compelled to show mock shame.

1863 *Bradshaw CW Letters* (Jan 29) frank has got a girl of his one

[= own] now tell Jones that pery will leave him to dance in the troft. **1937** Wilson *Folklore SE KY* 24 She left her older sister dancin' in the hog trough. (She married before her older sister [Bell Co KY].) **1956** Hall *Coll* (Gatlinburg TN) Fifty years ago if a younger sister married first, folks would say the older sister "had to dance in a hog trough." [**1971** *AOHP/ALC-137* When Lydia Ann got married, she was younger than Nancy. . . . Lydia Ann married before Nancy did. Nancy was older, and some of them went and packed the hog's trough in on the porch and made her dance in it.] **1972** Clarke *Dance in Trough* 68 One or more students in each class have expressed familiarity with the expression, usually as *You'll have to dance in a pig trough* as a teasing and humorous remark to an unmarried girl who is approaching the age when she will be considered an "old maid." Some were specific in applying it to a girl whose younger sister seemed likely to marry first. Two students professed to use the expression themselves to tease a young male who was in danger of losing his girl friend to a rival. More often students have attributed the expression to older members of their families, especially grandparents. **1972** Cooper *NC Mt Folklore* 90 *danced in the pig trough* = remained single after an older brother or sister had married. [**1982** Slone *How We Talked* 17 When a boy or girl got married, having older brothers or sisters at home still single, the older ones were supposed to dance in the hog trough at the wedding as punishment for letting the younger get married first.]

[DARE *dance in the hog trough* v phr chiefly Midland]

dancingest *adjective* Dancing the best, most proficient at dancing. See also **-est** and Grammar and Syntax §3.4.1.

1955 Parris *Roaming Mts* 146 He's got a great helper in this field in Sam Queen of Maggie, dancin'est man in all the land, who set 'em on their ear at New York's Waldorf-Astoria with his clogging.

dancy See **dauncy A.**

danger (also *dangers*) *adjective* Dangerous.

1862 *Shifflet CW Letters* (Dec 8) hit is mity dangers to dissert So I will Stay tell Spring I will keep trying to git a furlow and come home. **1863** *Bradshaw CW Letters* (Feb 27) I was sory to hear that the small pox was raging up thare Nancy I hope you will be cearful and not go in reach of them tha[y] are a dangers complaint. **1917** Kephart *Word-List* 410 = dangerous: "Thet's a powerful danger axe."

dangerous *adjective* Critically ill.

1862 *Carter CW Letters* (June 6) the rest of the neighbors boys are well except clint Good he was left behind sick I heard from him the other day he was not dangerous. **1863** *Kendrick CW Letters* (Aug 7) arthur is in the horse pittle at the junc tion he was not dangerous. **1921** Campbell *Sthn Highlander* 204 When his own knowledge and the offices of those near at hand fail, the Highlander goes for the doctor, if there be one within reach; but usually it is not until the patient is "dangerous."

[OED3 *dangerous* adj 4 "in danger, as from illness; dangerously ill," now dialect and U.S. colloquial]

dangerously *adverb* Extremely.

1863 *Leigh CW Letters* (July 12) there is several others sick in the companey but I dont think very dangerousley bad off.

dangers See **danger.**

dar See **dare.**

darb *noun* Something superlative, "just the thing."

1941 Stuart *Men of Mts* 80 S Get your hoe . . . It's the darb for cuttin sprouts and killin copperheads. **1968** Clarke *Stuart's Kentucky* 155 The big one-eyed hoe was the darb for cutting sprouts—the little sourwood sprouts, and the saw briars, which were toughest of all.

dare *verb* variant infinitive forms *dar, dast*, negative form *dassent*.

1913 Kephart *Our Sthn High* 288 When the mountain boy challenges his mate: "I dar ye—I ain't afeared!" his verb and participle are of the same ancient and sterling rank [as the time of Layamon]. **1928** (in **1952** Mathes *Tall Tales* 52) This is God A'mighty's house, an' ye dassent profane it with yer strife! **1952** Wilson *Folk Speech NC* 526 Don't you *dast* cheep what I just told you. **c1959** Weals *Hillbilly Dict* 3 Don't you dast drink no whisky in hyar. **1974** Fink *Bits Mt Speech* 6 They don't *dast* go. **1994** Montgomery *Coll* (known to Cardwell).

[DARE *dare* v A2 These forms probably represent primarily the archaic past *durst* influenced by the vowel of pres *dare*; back-formation from the negative *da(r)snt*, following the analogy of *durst/dursn't*, and the archaic 2nd sing *darst* may also have played a role]

daresome *adjective*

1 Afraid.

1969 *DARE Survey* (Louisa KY) I'm daresome to do it (= when you're afraid to do something).

2 Intrepid, daring.

1978 Hiser *Quare Do's* 149 A few of the more daresome young fellers in thare heared of it. **1989** *Matewan OHP-89* You was daresome to stick your head then [i.e. out the door during the gunbattle]. **dark corner** (also *dark cove*) *noun* A remote or secluded area that is difficult to police, as for the making of illegal liquor. Same as **booger holler.**

1862 *Neves CW Letters* (Jan 9) we have a companey up her that cauls them Selves the Dark corner mountainyears. **1913** Kephart *Our Sthn High* 193 There are some "dark corners" of the mountains, mostly on or near state boundary lines, where there are bands of desperadoes who defy the law. **1964** Reynolds *Born of Mts* 81 Dark Corners was another name, one that often indicated more of moonshine and a shady deal than it did a tree-shaded area so popularly supposed. **1983** *Dark Corner OHP-28A* Somebody asked him, says, "Well, what do you think of the place up there?" "Ah law," he says, "that's a dark corner," and it's had that name ever since. **1995** Montgomery *Coll*: *dark corner* (known to Adams); *dark cove* (known to Oliver). **2000** Morgan *Mts Remember* 5 The senator was building a turnpike from Charleston to the mountains, to open up the Dark Corner of the state for commerce he said.

dark moon See **dark of the moon**.

dark of the moon (also *dark moon*) *noun* The period in the lunar cycle when the moon is waning or decreasing. See also **light of the moon**, **new of the moon**, **old of the moon**, **shrink B**.

1907 Parker *Folk-Lore of NC* 243 To effectually kill the trunks, roots, and sprouts of trees, bushes, briars, etc., on land which is being cleared, they should be cut during the dark moon in August. Timber will last much longer if cut in the dark of the moon. **1926** Lunsford *Folk-Lore* 13 For instance, the writer has been vanquished time and again in this goodly land with argument to the effect that the earth has corners and a foundation and that the moon is placed in the heavens for signs and that therefore the "twelve signs of the zodiac" may be absolutely relied upon as a true guide to poultry and hog raising, laying of worm fences, and planting of various crops. It is established beyond all question in some of our communities that the bottom rail of a worm fence should be laid upon the light of the moon and that the top rail should be laid in the dark of the moon so that the fence will thereby curl together so securely that a Wilkes County ox couldn't push it down. **1955** Washburn *Country Doctor* 76 From Fonzo B. and others I learned that the moon exerts an "awful" influence on farming and on life in general. The rule to be followed is to plant root crops, such as potatoes and turnips, on the dark of the moon, while crops such as corn, peas, or beans, which bear fruit above the ground, should be planted on the light of the moon. **1977** McClelland *Wilson Douglas* 18 If you put them [= roof boards] on when the moon is light, they'll curl up; but you put them on in the dark moon, it'll lay flat till it seasons. And you plant corn in the dark moon it won't get as high as my hand, it won't do no good; plant it in the light moon, the fodder'll be ten foot high.... In a dark moon the brine won't raise on your cabbage to sour your kraut.

darksome *adjective* Tending to be dark. See also **-some 1**.

1957 Justus *Other Side* 10 "Better throw a pine knot on the hearth. It's getting darksome," said Mammy. **1958** Campbell *Tales* 44 Then a king's son came riding along and they made little Two Eyes go and hide in a darksome place under the stairs. **2009** Holbrook *Upheaval* 31 [The cigarette smoke] hangs a few feet above their heads in a darksome cloud.

dark-thirty *noun* See citation.

1997 Roe *Teaching Stories* 207 Dark-thirty ... is a specific time of day just before night falls. During that thirty minutes, it is neither day nor night and shadows begin to cast a [sic] eerie spell. **2013** Venable *How to Tawlk* 11 = well after sunset: "Slim never would come home from a'fishin' 'til dark-thirty."

darnful *adjective* See citation.

1944 Combs *Word-List Sthn High* 18 = gloomy, mournful, lugubrious.

darning needle (also *devil's darning needle*) *noun* A dragonfly.

1884 Smith *Arp Scrap Book* 73 He showed me the devil's darning needle which winds up the old fellow's stockins. **1934–47** *LAMSAS Appal*: *darning needle* = attested by 26/148 speakers (17.5%) from WV and 2/12 (16.7%) from GA; *devil's darning needle* = attested by 2/148 speakers (1.4%) from WV and 2/12 (16.7%) from GA. **1949** McDavid *Grist* 108 (Rabun Co GA) (also *devil's darning needle*) = dragonfly. **2015** *Blind Pig* (May 26) In Swain County [NC] where I grew up, we also called them darning needles and helicopters because of their ability to hover.

[Web3 *darning needle* n 2 dialect]

darter See **daughter**.

dassent, **dast** See **dare**.

datter See **daughter**.

daub *verb* To make (a chimney, house, etc.) snug by covering **chinks** or outside cracks with mud and clay, sometimes with lime added, and reinforced with sticks, wood, etc.; hence noun *daubing* = such material.

1835 *McLean Diary* (Oct 18) Dabd [= daubed] my house. **1881** Pierson *In the Brush* 51 The chimney, built upon the outside of the house, was made of split sticks, laid up in the proper form, and thoroughly "daubed" with mud, so as to prevent them from taking fire. **1914** Arthur *Western NC* 258 The walls of these log houses were "chinked and daubed." That is, the spaces between the logs were filled with blocks or scraps of wood and the interstices left were filled with plain, undisguised mud—lime being too expensive to be used for that purpose. **1937** Hall *Coll* (Mingus Creek NC) In the old days chimleys were made of wood and daubed with mud. **1957** Broaddus *Vocab Estill Co KY* 25 *daubing* = mud put around the chinking when building a log house. **1972** *AOHP/ALC-413* It [= a **double log house**] was chinked with slabs of wood and mud, hung in there, tucked in there at an angle shape, and cracked and then daubed it with blue mud ... most everybody had the chinked and daubing. **1975** Purkey *Madison Co* 6 The house on Lost Creek, in Madison County, was a typical mountain one, with its scalped logs and mud daubed "chimley." **1991** Haynes *Haywood Home* 38 The spaces between the logs were chinked and daubed.... On the outside the cracks were daubed with mud against the chinking until the mud was even with the hewn exterior of the logs. We used a blue clay mud for daubing since we had a small deposit at the Blue Mud Spring. Properly daubed, this clay would be almost as hard as concrete when it dried. We would have to repair the daubing about every two years.

daughter *noun* variant forms *darter*, *datter*, *dorter*.

1863 *Matthews CW Letters* (Dec 3) my children is all all [sic] in the war but a dorter and I am Left a Lone. **1867** Harris *Sut Lovingood* 61 He watched fur openins tu work off sum kind ove devilment, jist es clost es a ole 'oman what wer wunst onsanctified hersef, watches her darters when a suckus ur a camp meetin am in heat. **c1950** Adams *Grandpap* 55 When he'd got ready to start, he called up his oldest girl an' said, "I'm a-goin' to town today, Darter. What do you want me to bring you back?" **1961** Williams R *in Mt Speech* 6 Frequently r is inserted in other words: *bursh, pursh* ... *dorter* (but also *datter*).

dauncy

A variant forms *dancy, dauncey* [see **1987** in **B1**], *donsie* [see **1952** in **B1**].

1992 Jones and Miller *Sthn Mt Speech* 74 *dancy*.

B *adjective* [Editor's note: The senses below cannot always be differentiated; see **1976** in **B1**.]

1 Sickly, infirm, frail, dizzy.

1891 Primer *Studies in WV* 169 I feel rather dauncy, meaning I feel rather poorly. **1933** Carpenter *Sthn Mt Dialect* 25 In central and southern West Virginia and Kentucky dauncy is used for infirm or feeble. One hears "Ol' man Brown's gettin' dauncy; in fact he's gettin' so feeble he can't get 'round much." **1938** Hall Coll (Emerts Cove TN) Dauncy about eatin' = don't feel good, don't feel like eatin'. **1952** Justus *Children* 36 Herb tea is a mighty fine tonic when a body is feeling dauncy—and so is good company. *Ibid.* 105 She said he was looking dauncy and needed dosing up a bit, but the medicine that she gave him was mostly spicy sassafras tea liberally sweetened. **1952** Wilson *Folk Speech NC* 532 *donsie* = sick, sickly. **1967** Wilson *Folkways Mammoth Cave* 23 = dizzy or nauseated. **1976** Weals *Words Stay* [D]onsie or *dauncy* is another vanishing mountain word that appears to have meanings that differ when it is applied to self and when it applies to another person. "I feel donsie," might mean I feel dizzy, or slightly ill, or nauseated. When put on somebody else donsie can mean, at least in some localities, that the person is intoxicated, addled, silly, stupid, or, according to some local interpretations, quick-tempered, and even saucy and pert. **1982** Hurst *Appal Words* 99 "Dauncy" came to mean a sickly person or one afflicted with a queasy stomach. **1987** Carver *Regional Dialects* 180 One expression that was almost surely brought to America by the Scotch-Irish is *donsie* or *dauncey*, ultimately deriving from Scotch Gaelic *donas* (= evil, harm, bad luck).

2 Fastidious, squeamish, particular.

1913 Kephart *Our Sthn High* 289 A remarkable word, common in the Smokies, is dauncy, defined for me as "mincy about eating," which is to say fastidious, over-nice. **1927** Woofter *Dialect from WV* 352 *dauncy* = fastidious. "She is so dauncy about her work that no one can please her." **c1945** Haun *Hawk's Done* 324 He seed it took me back, so he was quick to say, "I just allowed she might hunt something to eat at night; but I reckon not—she seems so dauncy about her eating." **1952** Wilson *Folk Speech NC* 532 *donsie* = particular.

[OED3 *dauncy* adj "sickly; delicate" U.S. and dialect; CUD *donsie* adj "unfortunate; neat" < Irish Gaelic *don(a)saí* < *donas* "bad luck"; DARE *donsie* adj 1 Scots, nEngl dialect probably from Scottish Gaelic *donas* "evil, harm" perhaps with influ[ence] from obsolete *daunch* "fastidious, squeamish," *dunce*, and other words]

davenet (also *davenette*) *noun* See citations.

c1960 Wilson Coll = a small davenport; a very modern word. **1983** Broaddus *Estill Co KY Word List* 37 *davenet* = a short davenport.

[DARE *davenette* n chiefly South Midland]

day and time *noun phrase* A period of time (especially in phrases in *that day and time, in this day and time*).

1913 Kephart *Our Sthn High* 285 Pleonasms are abundant ... "In this day and time." **1939** Hall Coll (Hazel Creek NC) Now lately [you] don't find it in this day and time that way. *Ibid.* A honeymoon in that day and time was a-straddle of a rail. **1952** Wilson *Folk Speech NC* 532 *day and time, in this* = now, at this time. **1953** Hall Coll (Bryson City NC) There wasn't so many bear back at that day and time as they is now. **1971** *AOHP/ALC-147* People made moonshine that day and time more than they do now, 'cause now they don't have to. **1989** *Matewan OHP-18* It used to be people helped one another, this day and time, they don't do anything but it's for pay. **1997** *Dante OHP-53* Most of them was good church people, but this day and time they's not many people going to church. The older people are not teaching their children the values that I think they should have.

[DARE *day and time* n chiefly South, South Midland]

daybust (also *day dawn, dayrise*) *noun* Daybreak.

c1940 Aswell *Glossary TN Idiom* 6 *dayrise* = sunup. **1943** Justus *Jerry Jake* 41 Now that Jerry Jake was back in school he was busier than ever, with no idle time to spare from day-dawn to day's end. **1971** Dwyer *Dict for Yankees* 25 day bust = dawn. **1995–97** Montgomery Coll: *daybust* (known to Brown, but not to other consultants from the Smoky Mountains); *dayrise* (known to Oliver, but not to other consultants from the Smoky Mountains).

[Web3 *daydawn* n archaic]

day dawn See **daybust**.

daydown (also *daylight down*) *noun* The evening, sunset.

1939 *FWP Guide NC* 98 Late in the afternoon is "The pink of the evenin'" or "daydown." **1973** Davis *'Pon My Honor* 95 (also *daylight down*) = when the sun goes down. **1995–97** Montgomery Coll (known to Brown, but not to other consultants from the Smoky Mountains).

daylight *noun* Dawn (especially in phrase *break daylight*, often with stress on both *day* and *light*).

1937 Hall Coll (Smokemont NC) [By the] time we got the tree cut down, it was day, just breakin' daylight. **1939** Hall Coll (Cable Branch NC) We just stood there till it went to breaking daylight and got to snowin'. *Ibid.* (Hartford TN) I was a-going to the mill one morning before daylight. Moon was a-shining bright. **1973** Jones *Cades Cove TN* 73 = attested by 5/5 speakers in preference to *sunrise, sunup*. **1975** GSMNP-62:4 The first money I ever made in my life was twenty five cents a day, and [I] worked daylight to dark. **1991** Thomas *Sthn Appal* 171 We sailed out, dist at day-light.

daylight down See **daydown**.

dayrise See **daybust**.

dead

A *adjective* Unconscious. See also **dead as four o'clock**.

1904–20 Kephart *Notebooks* 2:475 He was knocked dead for a while. **1927** Mason *Lure of Smokies* 198 He lay thar two days, hand-runnin', dead—and dead drunk betwixt it. **1994–97** Montgomery *Coll* (known to Adams, Brewer, Brown, Cardwell, Oliver).

[cf OED3 *dead* adj 2 "benumbed, insensible"; EDD *dead* adj 3; DARE *dead* adj B1 South, South Midland]

B *adverb* Precisely, completely.

1863 *Copenhaver CW Letters* (July 9) Miss Mag wrote a leter & requsted me to mail it for her I told her I would do so Jack you have got her in hot water I told her you was ded in love with her. **1960** Burnett *My Valley* 20 Dead at the mouth of the cave was the mother wolf.

C (also *deaden*) *verb* To cut a strip of bark (or **dead ring**) from the girth of (a tree), preventing its sap from rising and thus causing it to die and eventually fall; to clear (an area of trees) using this method. Same as **collar**. See also **deadening, log rolling**.

1842 *McLean Diary* 77 Some Rain fell Deddened som Beach on the 8. **1921** Campbell *Sthn Highlander* 251 With pioneer and characteristically American disregard of the future, he girdled the trees to "deaden" them, thus furnishing sunlight for his crop. He planted the crop that fed him and his stock, namely corn, and when the virgin fertility of his clearing was impaired because of successions of the same crop, or, as was more often the case, because the humus and the underlying soil itself were washed away, he would "deaden" another field and plant corn again. Scores of such "deadenings" may be found in a short journey through the mountains, the stark trees still standing in abandoned and gully-furrowed fields as sad monuments of ignorance and neglect. **1984** *GSMNP-153* They had to be awful careful about deadening trees, if they were of a big nature. Going back and plowing . . . Maybe a windstorm would come and blow an old dead one. They's a few people that got killed like that. **1991** Thomas *Sthn Appal* 176 Generally, during the winter when there was little farm work to be done, a man would cut a ring all the way around a tree two or three feet above the ground to "deaden" it. He would cut the trees in next summer, then invite his neighbors to a "log-rolling" in the fall after the crops were harvested and stored. Those who came would help drag or carry the logs in teams and pile them into heaps, where they were set on fire and burned. **1996–97** Montgomery *Coll* (known to Bush, Hooper, Ledford).

dead as four o'clock (also *deader than four o'clock*) *adjective phrase* Unquestionably dead, unconscious, silent.

1940 Hall *Coll* (Gatlinburg TN) I plugged the bear through and stood by an old pine tree . . . the bear tuck up this tree crazy as a bed bug . . . then fell out dead as four o'clock in the morning. **1956** Hall *Coll* (Gatlinburg TN) I fainted as dead as four o'clock. **1981** Whitener *Folk-Ways* 41 The dark depressing time just before dawn [is] "dead as four o'clock." **1986** Pederson et al. *LAGS* (Sevier Co TN) [It] killed her deader than four o'clock. **1990** Bailey *Draw Up Chair* 14 Around four o'clock in the morning was a particularly bad time, and from it came the expression, "as dead as four o'clock," still used by people with a lingering touch of Old English in their speech. **1999** Brewer *Appal Lg* Somebody in West Virginia or East Tennessee might say, "Jed reached for his ax, but the sheriff shot him dead as four o'clock." **2000** Montgomery *Coll*: *deader than four o'clock* (known to Ellis). **2007** McMillon *Notes* = the stillest part of the night, when it is believed that those on the verge of death pass on.

[from the stillness of the 4 a.m. hour; DARE *four-o'clock* n 5 southern Appalachians]

deadbeat *verb* To waste time, pretend to work.

1967–70 *DARE Survey* (Rome GA) = pretend to be sick [often to get out of doing something]; (Gatlinburg TN) = to go about aimlessly, with nothing to do; (Jasper TN) = waste time by not working on the job.

[DARE *deadbeat* v especially South, South Midland]

dead devil *noun* See citations.

1968 *End of Moonshining* 100 *dead devils* = tiny beads in the proof vial which indicate that the whiskey has been proofed sufficiently. Stop adding water or backings at the moment shaking the proof vial produces dead devils. **1969** *DARE Survey* (Dillard GA) If it's too high proof, the beads will be very coarse or very large and as you bring the alcoholic content of it down, which is called the gauge of it or the proof of it, the beads will get finer, and when they get very fine, it's dead. And when these very fine beads and little fine specks come up, we call them dead devils, and when that happens you have killed it.

deaden See **dead C**.

deadening (also *deading*) *noun* The practice of killing a tree by cutting a circular strip of bark (or **dead ring**) around the trunk, eventually preventing the flow of water and nutrients and causing the tree to die and fall; hence an area of ground where trees have been killed by girdling and sometimes cleared in preparation of a **new ground** (see 1924, 1981 citations), also a place where trees are dead from natural causes (see c1979 citation).

1844 *McLean Diary* 87 [I] Chopt Some logs in the Dedning. **1864** Gilmore *Down in TN* 100 A poor white man, however, who could be trusted, had a small "dead'nin'" about a mile away. **1881** Pierson *In the Brush* 48–49 I came upon a large "dead'ning," where the underbrush had been cut out and burned off, the large trees had been girdled and had died, and a crop of corn had been raised among the dead forest-trees, before the new-comer in this wilderness had been able to completely clear a field around his newly-erected log-cabin. **1913** Morley *Carolina Mts* 24 These "deadenings" are made and abandoned one after another as the thin soil wears out, which on the poorer slopes happens in a year or two. **1924** Raine *Saddlebags* 30 In earlier days a settler would locate at the mouth of a creek. He would first clear the lower levels, then part of the hillsides, not by cutting the trees down, but by belling them. He would notch a six-inch band around the tree and remove the bark therein so that the sap could not go up to nourish the tree. In a few weeks the leaves would wither and the trees would die. A field of such trees is called a "deadening." This is the quickest way to make a cornfield. **1939** Hall *Coll* (Smokemont

NC) We decided we'd go on down the Sugar Orchard, and we went down to the deadenin'. **1973** GSMNP-5:27 They was an old woman and she moved in what they called the deading. It's two mile from Caldwell Fork right up the creek. **c1979** Chiles *Glossary* 2 = a place where the trees were dead either from natural causes or from girdling by man to kill them for cutting. **c1980** Campbell *Memories of Smoky* 68–69 A "deadening" is a new field, usually called "newground," in which the trees have been killed by girdling—the removal of about two or three feet of the bark all around the trees. **1981** Brewer *Wonderment* 117 "Deadening" refers to the old mountain practice of [killing] trees by girdling them with an axe in the spring of the year, preparatory to the clearing of "new ground" the following spring, at which time the previously deadened trees were cut down, piled up and burnt.

[DARE *deadening* n 1 chiefly South Midland]

deader than four o'clock See **dead as four o'clock**.

dead furrow *noun* See citation.

1997 Montgomery *Coll* = a furrow at the center of a field where the top soil is plowed to either side (Hooper).

dead hand *noun* See citation.

1964 Clarkson *Lumbering in WV* 360 = a sunken or partly sunken log.

dead head (also *dead sender*) *noun* See citation.

1998 Buchanan *Logging Terms*: *dead head*, *dead sender* = the man who pulls stuck logs out of a pond. Sometimes he would have to go under water to do this. He unjammed logs.

deading See **deadening**.

dead land *noun* See citations.

1988 Dunn *Cades Cove* 70 Ayers and Ashe pointed out in 1905 that there were spots in the cove of so-called "dead land," where the soil seems to contain some ingredients unfavorable to plant growth. **1997** Montgomery *Coll* = also land between two property boundaries not deeded to anyone [= no man's land] (Brown).

dead-level best *noun* (One's) utmost.

1963 Edwards *Gravel* 69 She did her dead-level best to unseat the rider, and he did his best to keep his seat. **1976** Garber *Mountain-ese* 21 = utmost. "I did my dead level best to git here on time but I jist couldn't make it."

dead man *noun*

1 See citations.

1974 Brewer *Your Community* 2 = a log you planted in the ground on angle to hook a tackle block on for a team to pull a log in an open field where there was no stump or tree to hang the block on. A team would just pull it deeper into the ground instead of pulling it up. This was for logs so large a team could not pull without a tackle and block. **1975** *Another Look* 136 You can make a dead man is what we called it. You take two poles and canvas or ropes and put on that like a stretcher. Man, you can truck it that way. When we first started out, that's what it was called: a dead man. **1982** Powers and Hannah *Cataloochee* 382 In Cataloochee, the "dead man" is not something scarifying, but merely a heavy post which is set in the ground to hold up cables for a footlog or bridge. **2015** Waters *Swinging Bridges* 20 The swinging bridge was not a difficult bridge to build. It was a suspension bridge with two steel cables supporting the wood deck. On each bank the two cables were anchored in the earth by what was called a "dead man." It was helpful when the bank was steep and high.

2 See citation.

c1975 *Miners' Jargon* 3 = a barrier erected behind wheeled equipment consisting of two timbers.

3 See citation.

1990 Clouse *Wilder* 65 Again and again he drilled until a line of holes covered the block. While John drilled, Barney prepared the charges. Black powder was fixed with fuses and shoved far back into the holes. Dead men, papers tightly rolled with dirt, were then tamped into the hole.

4 See **deadman still**.

dead man's pinch *noun* See citation.

1953 Davison *Word-List Appal* 10 = used to explain a black and blue spot on one's skin that one cannot account for.

deadman still *noun* A simple coffin-shaped **still**. Same as **coffin still**, **flat (still)**.

1972 *Foxfire I* 279 These diagrams illustrate perhaps the simplest still of them all—the "dead man" or "flat" . . . the still itself—a rectangular box. *Ibid.* 323 [The dead man still] is a purely modern variety with a tremendous yield. The beer, rather than being made in separate boxes, can be made right in the still. **2007** Alexander *Moonshiners Gone* 140 What appears to be a metal coffin forlornly sitting amidst the cold and snowy mountains of N.E. Georgia is in reality a "dead man" or "coffin" or "pan" still, well known to the law.

dead ring *noun* A circular strip of bark cut from the trunk of a tree, preventing the flow of water and nutrients and causing the tree to die and fall. See also **dead C**, **deadening**.

1925 Dargan *Highland Annals* 205 When one o' his fields got wore out he would pick out the richest piece on the place, where the big timber growed, an' cut a dead-ring around the oaks an' chestnuts an' poplars. **1996–97** Montgomery *Coll* (known to Adams, Brown, Cardwell, Ledford).

dead sender See **dead head**.

dead up the branch See **something dead up the branch**.

deadwood *noun* in phrases *get the deadwood on*, *have the deadwood on* = have an advantage over, have incriminating or compromising evidence on.

1926 Lunsford *Folk-Lore* 13 I got the deadwood on 'im. **1956** Hall *Coll* (Del Rio TN) *he had the deadwood on him* = he had the advantage over him; he had the upper hand. **1995** Montgomery *File* (known to 85-year-old man, Greenbrier TN).

[DARE *deadwood* n chiefly South Midland, West]

death bell *noun* A ringing or tinkling in the ear that is an omen of death.

1824 (in **1912** Doddridge *Notes on Settlement* 127) This science announces that a death bell is but a momentary morbid motion of the ear. **1931** Thomas *Ditties* 19 She'd even heard death bells a-ringin' in her ears. **1940** Haun *Hawk's Done* 105 Something was bound to take place that night. I recollected about hearing death bells in my ears before midday that day. That meant somebody was going to die before midnight. **1975** Montell *Ghosts Cumberland* 217 = tinkling sounds in one's ear before the death of a friend or relative. **1998** Montgomery *Coll* (known to Brown, Bush, Jones, Norris).

[DARE *death bell* n South Midland]

death crown *noun* See citations. Same as **crown**.

2000 Morgan *Mts Remember* 85 The way her head sunk into the towel on the pillow reminded me of the old story of the death crown. Oldtimers used to say that when a really good person, say a preacher that's saved lots of souls or a woman that's helped her neighbors and raised a lot of kids, is sick for a long time before they die, the feathers in the pillow will knit themselves into a crown that fits the person's head. The crown won't be found till after they are dead of course, but it's a certain sign of another crown in heaven, my Daddy used to say. I've never seen one myself but the oldtimers say they're woven so tight they never come apart and they shine like gold even though they're so light they might just as well be a ring of light. **2012** Milnes *Signs Cures Witchery* They called it a death crown. If anybody had them on their deathbed when they'd had to die, and their head was laying on this pillow, why these feathers in there would knot up great big, big as your fist, and just seemed like just growed together where they'd been picked off of the chicken, and they'd open them feather ticks after the funeral was over and take that ball out of there, and you couldn't pull it apart. . . . They said it was a death . . . crown, and they wouldn't put it back in the pillow . . . and when that was formed in somebody's pillow, they were to die. . . . If that was there, they could [be] pretty sure they went to heaven.

death watch *noun* See citation.

2006 *Encycl Appalachia* 855 When the physical condition of a mountaineer was considered life threatening, neighbors and friends performed what was called the "death watch." Someone would sit with the ailing person until he or she either recovered or died. A gurgling sound caused by excessive respiratory secretions known as the "death rattle" was an important sign that death was imminent.

(the) decay *noun* Infantile malnutrition; rickets.

1933 Miller *Healing Gods* 471–72 Most of us who are familiar with the customs of rural West Virginia know that many an infant suffering from malnutrition or rickets, familiarly known as "the decay" or the "gobacks," must be measured by some old woman before he will get better, which is much more certain and less expensive than cod-liver oil and tomato juice.

de-church *verb* See also **church 1, 2.**

1977 Shackelford et al. *Our Appalachia* 49 Some called it "de-churched," or "You're excluded," and that was just terrible for anybody who belonged to the church to be excluded, unless he was just so mean that he didn't care anyhow.

decide on *verb phrase* To persuade, bring (someone) to a decision.

1957 Parris *My Mts* 32 Nobody ever has figured out whether it was the lemon-julep or the rocking chair, or both, that decided them on buying a piece of property in these parts and settling in. **1995–97** Montgomery *Coll* (known to Brown, Ellis, Oliver).

deck *noun* See citation.

1964 Clarkson *Lumbering in WV* 360 = a pile of logs in the woods at a landing.

decker *noun* See citation.

1964 Clarkson *Lumbering in WV* 360 = one who rolls logs onto a skidway or a log deck.

deck hand *noun* See citation.

1994 Farwell and Buchanan *Logging Terms* = a member of a logging crew who cleaned logs of rocks, dirt, or any other foreign material not removed by a pond man.

decorate *verb* See citation. See also **Decoration Day.**

2014 *WV Talk* = clean off the graveyard and place flowers and other decorations on the graves. This was a family occasion. The men mowed and the women decorated the graves and assembled a picnic lunch. The children played but were cautioned to never step on the graves.

decorating *verbal noun* See citation. See also **Decoration Day.**

1924 Raine *Saddlebags* 204 Another custom peculiar to the Mountain People is the "decorating" of burial grounds, a community celebration which has no apparent connection with the well-known memorial services for old soldiers.

Decoration Day (also *decoration*) *noun* An annual commemoration held by a family, present-day or former community, or church congregation at a stated time of the year during which descendants gather to clean and place flowers (now usually artificial ones) on graves; in many places a full Sunday of activities follows the cleaning, including a church service (indoor or outdoor), hymn-singing, testimonials about the departed, a **dinner on the ground(s)**, family reunions, and cemetery visits. While the commemoration has been moved to coincide with the national Memorial Day in some places, in Western North Carolina and East Tennessee it may be held from late spring to late summer. In recent years the term has sometimes been replaced by **Memorial Day** or **homecoming**. Also called **family decoration**.

1935 Sheppard *Cabins in Laurel* 214–15 Among the mountain people, the national Memorial Day passes unnoticed. In its place each of the country churches has its own "decoration," when the congregation holds a memorial service for the dead. These individual services, in a long procession from late spring to midsummer, are a timely chance for wide inter-churchly visiting. **1952** *Asheville Citizen-Times* (July 27) A long standing custom of the mountain people is the annual Decoration, held by many families in the Spring, at which family cemeteries are given annual cleanings. These decorations are much more than gatherings to place flowers on the graves of the departed. They are great reunions of entire families; often of a whole clan of the same name. Held always in the warmer months of the year, a decoration is usually an all-day affair on a Sunday. People gather early and stay most of the day. Religious services are conducted by as many as four or five ministers who have served the community. Conducted out-of-doors, unless interrupted by a summer shower, the settings of these decorations under the clear mountain skies and in surroundings of solid greenery have a peculiar atmosphere that is so easily sacred to all who take part in them. **1971** Fetterman *People Cumberland Gap* 617 Late in May, on Memorial Day weekend, the hollows are clogged with the automobiles of mountain natives who come home from Detroit, Chicago, Cincinnati, Dayton, and dozens of cities where they have found employment. The mountain people know this gathering as "Decoration Day," and it is a weekend of mass reunion across the mountains, a time to groom and decorate the graves of kinfolk, a time to pray, a time to feast—a time of reassurance that the mountain way of life still exists. **1993** *Smokies Guide* (Autumn) 10 As a way of remembering departed friends and relatives, many churches and communities held a yearly cemetery decoration day. Prior to the scheduled date, which was normally during the summer, men of the community would gather to clean the cemeteries and straighten headstones, while the women picked flowers or made artificial ones from paper. On decoration day, families would gather at various cemeteries for a memorial service and to decorate the graves with flowers. The tradition of decoration day is still observed by many churches and families today, including at some of the more than 200 cemeteries located within Great Smoky Mountains National Park. **2009** Jabbour *Decoration Day* 280 Decoration Day observances typically fall on different Sundays in the same community, permitting people to attend more than one decoration. The variable date bespeaks a fundamental connection to the decentralized Protestant (especially Baptist) worldview of the dispersed rural settlement of the Upland South.... Many special customs are associated with Decoration Day, such as the oft-cited rule that every grave in the cemetery must be decorated—a powerful statement of communal responsibility. In the old Upland South, decorations were also associated with the custom of remounding each grave annually with a mound of earth running the length of the grave. Remounding, which in effect reburies the loved one symbolically each year, supports the argument that such decorations are ceremonies of family piety. **2010** Jabbour *North Shore Assn* 25–26 The annual schedule for North Shore [NC] decorations is widely distributed throughout the region, and decorations are attended both by immediate family members and by friends, well-wishers, and others from the region and beyond.... The tradition of cemetery decoration is diffused across a wide swath of the Upland South, but the tradition seems to be practiced more widely, more conservatively, and with greater devotion in the areas of western North Carolina just east of Great Smoky Mountains National Park. **2010** Jabbour and Jabbour *Decoration Day* ix Decoration Day is a widespread cultural tradition in a swath of the American South extending from east of the Appalachians to west and southwest of the Ozarks. In the fullest form of the tradition, people visit a cemetery where family members are buried to provide an annual or periodic cleaning. Then they decorate the graves with flowers and other symbols of affection. Finally, they gather as a family or community in a religious service in the cemetery reaffirming their connections with each other and with the community beneath the ground. The service may involve preaching, prayers, hymn singing, and a ritual meal known as "dinner on the ground." Decoration Day—its practitioners often call the event simply a "decoration"—is a powerful ritual of piety. At the practical level, it provides a cultural motivation for cleaning and repairing a cemetery, which, if not properly maintained, can be reclaimed by the forest of the Upland South with astonishing speed. At the social level, it serves as a focal point for gathering a community, and it has long provided an occasion for community members from afar to return to their homeplace. At the deepest spiritual level, a decoration is an act of respect for the dead that reaffirms one's bonds with those who have gone before.

deed and double *adverb phrase* Certainly, to be sure.

1910 Cooke *Power and Glory* 17 Deed and double you couldn't live without her, now could ye? **1944** Wentworth *ADD* (eWV) (Common).

deedie *noun* A baby chicken. See also **biddy**, **dibbler**, **diddle**[2] **A.**

1885 Murfree *Down Ravine* 98 Rufus Dicey, had sent to him from the "valley kentry" a present of a pair of game chickens, and ... this deedie was from the first egg hatched in the game hen's brood. **1994–97** Montgomery *Coll* (known to Brown, Shields).

[DARE *deedie* n South, South Midland]

deef *adjective* variant of *deaf*.

1895 Dromgoole *Humble Advocate* 323 Hev ye gone spang deef that ye can't hear noways, when I call ter yer? **1934–47** *LAMSAS Appal* (Madison Co NC, Swain Co NC). **1942** Hall *Phonetics Smoky Mts* 21. **1967** Wilson *Folkways Mammoth Cave* 25 = formerly almost universal. **1973** *GSMNP-86:43* One of the girls was deef and dumb. **1994** Montgomery *Coll* (known to Shields).

deep *adjective* High—used as an informal measurement in compounds such as **hub deep**, **shoe mouth deep**, **straddle deep**.

1917 Kephart *Word-List* 417 The fog is friz *shoe mouth* deep on the mountains. **1927** Woofter *Dialect from WV* 364 *shoe-mouth deep* = deep as the mouth of a shoe. "The snow was shoe-mouth deep this morning." **1941** Hall *Coll* (Del Rio TN) We had an awful rain the other day. I waded water straddle deep in the highway. **1956**

Hall Coll (Townsend TN) I've seed this road down here when they'd wagon over it hub deep.

deep study *noun* See citation.

1990 Cavender *Folk Medical Lex* 21 = a vacuous state of mind characterized by staring off into space. **1994** Montgomery *Coll* (known to Cardwell, Ogle).

deep-water Baptist *noun* A member of a Baptist church that practices baptism by total immersion.

1923 (in **1952** Mathes *Tall Tales* 9) These here deep-water Babtists [are] a-puttin' their trust in goin' under the water instid o' gittin' under the blood! **1994–97** Montgomery *Coll* (known to Bush, Jones, Shields).

[DARE *deep-water Baptist* n chiefly South, South Midland]

deer *noun* Construed as a count noun; hence plural form *deers*.

1939 Hall *Coll* [There] was deers and bears and all kinds of wild animals, I reckon. *Ibid.* (Smokemont NC) My father said they was lots of deers. **1973** GSMNP-76:30 They used to be plenty of deers, but they claim the black tongue got among the deers and killed them all. **1984** GSMNP-153 Deer Lick Branch . . . is where they'd salt deers, you know, and they'd come down and lick the salt.

deerberry *noun* A blueberry (*Vaccinium stamineum*) that bears small, edible berries said to be a favorite food of deer. Same as **gooseberry, squawberry.**

1964 Stupka *Trees Shrubs Vines* 128 The deerberry, locally called "gooseberry," has numerous clusters of white bell-shaped flowers which make it a conspicuous shrub when in bloom. **1977** Shields *Cades Cove* 35 Berry stemmings occurred in late August or early September when the "gooseberries," sometimes called deerberries and related to the blueberries, were harvested.

deer drive *verb phrase* To hunt deer with **drivers** and dogs that force deer past a **deer stand** occupied by **standers.** See also **bear drive.**

1939 Hall *Coll* (Deep Creek NC) The next mornin' we went a-deer drivin'. We didn't start ary deer. *Ibid.* (Hazel Creek NC) When we was a-deer drivin'.

deer-eyed daisy (also *deer eye*) *noun* Same as **yellow daisy.**

1964 Reynolds *Born of Mts* 18 The blackeyed Susan they called "deer eye," and rock lichens were called "pot scrapings." **1975** Hamel and Chiltoskey *Cherokee Plants* 30 Coneflower, Black-eyed Susan, Deer-eyed daisy . . . *Rudbeckia fulgida.*

deer lick *noun* See citation. See also **lick B3.**

1973 AOHP/LJC-350 They had deer licks here. Deers would come and lick the saltpeter that was in the rocks, you know. They'd come and lick all the salt of it off.

deer meat *noun* Venison. See **meat A** for similar compounds.

1939 Burnett *Gap o' Mountains* 10 "Have some of the deer meat," the host would say. **1939** Hall *Coll* (Wears Cove TN) Me and brother Baus could just get out there and kill a deer anytime we took a notion to, and kept deer meat and bear meat and coon meat and turkey all the time.

deer rifle *noun* See citation.

1941 Kendall *Rifle-Making* 22 The calibre of the mountain rifles deserves a word of mention. Strictly speaking, these rifles had no calibre in the ordinary sense of the word. Usually, however, four kinds of rifles were made: one of about .35 calibre (0.35 inch) which was called a squirrel gun; one about .40 calibre (0.40 inch) called a turkey rifle; one about .45 calibre (0.45 inch) called a deer rifle; and one of approximately .50 calibre (0.50 inch) called a bear gun.

deer stand *noun* See citation. See also **drive B2, deer drive, stand B1, stander.**

1949 Hall *Coll* (Del Rio TN) A deer stand is a certain place where deer run through the mountains or cross a river. You can hide in them places and kill him as he comes through these stands. Hunters go and stand there and wait for the deer to run through those places.

deer-tongue (also *buck tongue*) *noun* A vanilla plant (*Carphephorus odoratissimus*).

[**1901** Lounsberry *Sthn Wild Flowers* 501 = although again and again assured of its likeness by the natives, it was rather a strain on my imagination to see that . . . its thick leaves resembled the tongue of either a deer or a hound.] **1970** *Hunting Stories* 35 I had a leaf then, buck tongue or deer tongue. When it first grows up it makes a real leaf t'call [turkeys] with.

[DARE *deer-tongue* n 1 Southeast]

deestric, deestrict, de-strick See **district.**

de'il See **devil.**

delcymore See **dulcimer A.**

demijohn *noun*

A variant forms *jimmie john* [see **1890** in **B**], *jimmy-john* [see **1889** in **B**].

B A liquor jug.

1889 Murfree *Broomsedge Cove* 200 Jes' ketch a-holt o' the handle o' that thar jimmy-john in the corner. **1890** Fruit *KY Words* 65 *jimmie john* = a demijohn. **1964** Reynolds *High Lands* 9 One can also get lost in the Smoky Mountain Park of North Carolina where fog lingers on the top of the mountains and sometimes lowers quickly, thus on Deep Creek two skeletons were found who may have died happily, for they had a demijohn between them. **1997** Montgomery *Coll* (known to eight consultants from the Smoky Mountains).

[DARE *jimmy-john* n 1 chiefly South, South Midland]

den *verb* See also **denning place.**

1 (also *den up*) Of a bear or other animal: to go to its den, especially for the winter.

1913 Kephart *Our Sthn High* 79 That's whar the bears den. **1927** Woofter *Dialect from WV* 352 = to seek winter quarters. "The groundhogs denned there last year." **1937** Thornburgh *Great Smoky Mts* 39 In these parts, Mr. Bear generally begins to den about the last of November. **c1960** Wilson Coll: *den up* = common for hibernate. **1967** Miller *Pigeon's Roost* (July 20) But the gray fox can't be chased so long before it dens up or gives up to the pack of hounds.

[DARE *den* v especially South, South Midland]

2 To inhabit, make a den.

1973 GSMNP-80:3 He said they'd been a-denning in there so long they had all the moss wore off, you know, just had the trail a-going in there and out.

denning place *noun* A hole, recess, or other place where bears, snakes, or other animals stay.

1953 Hall Coll (Plott Creek NC) When I got those dogs out to the edge of the orchard where the bear had left to go up to his denning place, or up to his lying place up in the [laurel thicket], Mr. Parker told me that he was ready to turn the dogs loose. **1994** Montgomery Coll It's the worst denning place in the whole ridge for snakes (Shields).

denounce *verb* See citation.

1957 Combs *Lg Sthn High: Word-List* 28 = weep, bewail. Ex.: "Old Aunt Florence kept on denouncin' all day."

den up See **den 1**.

deserve *verb* To be owed to or due to.

1982 DeArmond *So High* 65 "Ye jest have to take what's deservin ye," said Isaac as he pulled off his black, wet coat.

desk *noun*

1 variant form *dest*.

1984 Burns *Cold Sassy* 143 Pretty soon he come back to the hotel dest.

2 variant plural form of two syllables: *desk-es*, *desk-ies*.

1973 Foster *Walker Valley* 9:52 We had deskes, and I remember I'd lay down and go to sleep. **1975** *AOHP/ALC*-930 We had benches, and we had deskes in [the schoolroom] on the backs of the chairs, on the backs of the seats and for the books. **1983** Pederson *East TN Folk Speech* 96 (Cocke Co TN) *deskes*. **1998** *Dante OHP*-71 The county took a lot of stuff out of the school, you know, deskes and stuff, and left the building. **2008** Salsi *Ray Hicks* 72 We set in iron leg deskies facin' forward with the teacher in the front of the room by the blackboard. I set on one with another boy. It was two boys settin' together and two girls.

deskes, **deskies** See **desk 2**.

desperate *adverb* Extremely, gravely.

1863 *Kiracofe CW Letters* (Aug 9) I have not been well since returned from Pennsylvania that was a desperate hard trip the hardest trip we have had and a very hard fight. **1967** *DARE Survey* (Gatlinburg TN) *desperate ill* = when a sick person is past hope of recovery.

despise (+ *infinitive*) *verb phrase* To scorn, dislike intensely.

1878 Guild *Old Times TN* 50 We had no visiting cards in those days. You never heard a lady say, "I must make," or "I must return a call." I despise to hear it now. I have commanded my pretty daughters never to use the term, but they wont obey their "daddy." **1942** Hall *Phonetics Smoky Mts* 51 I despise to see a fence growed up like that. **1963** Watkins and Watkins *Yesterday* 42 I shore did despise to eat meals with some of our neighbors. **1987** (in **2015** Yarrow *Voices* 26) I despise to drill water. **1995** Mullins *Road Back* 69 "Be sure to cut all the weeds you see," he ordered. "I despise to strip the blades of corn to make fodder when the balks are full of Spanish needles, cockleburrs, and ragweeds. Be sure that you don't miss any Spanish needles."

[OED3 *despise* v 1b obsolete →1621; DARE *despise* v South, South Midland]

despite of *phrasal preposition* Despite.

1975 *AOHP/ALC*-1128 People did venture out despite of all these edicts, and they come these very mountains passages where nobody's been. **1988** Smith *Fair and Tender* 89 Momma is still as thin and as flat as a bord despite of Genevas cooking. **1998** *Dante OHP*-45 [I] just had the ambition to go and despite of all the hardships that I had to go through with the cold.

dest See **desk 1**.

destroy *verb*

1 To kill (a person).

1975 Fink *Backpacking* 47 I heered you'd gone to the war, and I was afeered you'd been destroyed. **1996** Montgomery *Coll* (known to Brown, Cardwell).

2 To defile.

1933 Thomas *Traipsin' Woman* 144 She said despairingly, "Didn't know I wuz destroyed?" Her fingers twitched convulsively. "She'd be a year old come next spring—if—she'd lived."

3 To be injured severely or killed.

1919 Combs *Word-List South* 33 = to become, or get destroyed. "If hit don't stop rainin', them taters'll *destroy*." Knott Co [KY].

destroyment *noun* An instance of destruction.

1925 Dargan *Highland Annals* 272 It wuz awful the way she made a destroyment of things in the house. **1997** Montgomery *Coll* (known to Brown); The wind came through and made a destroyment of the field (Andrews).

destructious (also *destructuous*) *adjective* Of an animal or child: destructive.

1924 Raine *Saddlebags* 102 Bears air destructious, they kill hogs. **1942** Thomas *Blue Ridge* 289 "Dynamite is powerful destructious!" one tells the other. *Ibid.* 313 "If all this had been on top of the earth," my mountaineer guide declared, "[a] destructuous man would have laid it waste long ago." **1970** Roberts and Roberts *Time Stood Still* 31 "So when you see one of them signs up here about a landslide," says Mr. Wright, "remember they kin be destructious." **1994–97** Montgomery *Coll*: *destructious* (known to Adams, Brown, Jones, Oliver, Shields).

destructuous See **destructious.**

devil

A variant forms *de'il*, *devel* [see **1862** in **B**], *divil*.

1924 Abernethy *Moonshine* 113 How the divil did that thing ever get past me? **1980** Still *Run for Elbertas* 88 "Hit's the De'il," someone breathed, and the primer children huddled together.

B *verb* To tease, torment, provoke. See also **devilment B.**

1861 Lance *CW Letters* (April 28) you no a man can bee deviled out of his life by a foole. **1862** Shifflet *CW Letters* (Nov 19) I think I can git a furlow at that time I intend to hav one or I will devel them all the time tell I git one. **1895** Edson and Fairchild *TN Mts* 371 Johnny, quit *devilin'* the cat. **1937** Hall *Coll* (Cades Cove TN) I don't want to be deviled with it. **1939** Hall *Coll* (Cades Cove TN) We was small both of us [and] they got to deviling us about sparking. **1940** Haun *Hawk's Done* 156 All the boys come by after him and they deviled him till he give in. **1962** Dykeman *Tall Woman* 157 While I'm working around, when the children aren't deviling me with questions, I get to studying about it. **1979** *Preacher Cook* 199 They caught a rattlesnake and deviled it all week just to make it ill. **1982** Maples *Memories* 27 I guess it would be called "teasing" nowadays, but mountain people would say "deviling." **1986** Ogle *Lucinda* 62 Crockett said he kept bothering him until he told him my name, and now Crockett said I must answer his letter or he would devil him to death. **2005** Williams *Gratitude* 489 To tease, or "aggervate" somebody in a playful way is to "devil 'em." One favorite way men had of devilin' one another was to tell tales or lies on each other—so outlandish that nobody in their right mind could believe them.

[DARE *devil* v 1 chiefly South, Midland]

devil and Tom Walker *noun* The devil (used in exclamations and as an intensifier).

1936 Carpenter *WV Expletives* 346 Some of our expressions do smack of a desire to be humorous . . . the devil and Tom Walker. **1958** Stuart *Plowshare* 145 What in the devil and Tom Walker's got into you here lately? **1969** GSMNP-37:2:13 I laid down and got me a drink and got up. I looked around, I says "Why the devil and Tom Walker," I says. **1972** Hall *Sayings* 56 As bad as the devil and Tom Walker.

[from title of a short story by Washington Irving; DARE *devil and Tom Walker, the* n chiefly Northeast, South Midland]

devil around the bush See **beat the devil around the bush.**

devil box (also *devil's box*, *devil's riding horse*) A fiddle.

1933 Hooker *Religion in Highlands* 150 Many refer to [church] organs as "new-fangled divil boxes." **1977** Wolfe *TN Strings* 17 Many of the strict pioneer religious frowned on the fiddle or instrumental music of any sort; the fiddle became known in some communities as "the devil's box," and stories were told of finding fiddles walled up in old cabins, put there when their owners "got religion" and stopped fiddling, yet could not bring themselves to destroy their beloved instruments. **2007** Milnes *Signs Cures Witches* 153 The conservative religious belief is that fiddle playing is sinful. The instrument has been called the devil's box, the devil's riding horse, and similar terms.

devil-dancer *noun* A small, momentary whirlwind that blows leaves and other objects around, often presaging a rainstorm.

1957 Parris *My Mts* 169 You've seen them whirligusts. Some folks call 'em devil-dancers and little whirlwinds. **1970** Clark *NC Beliefs* 55 When whirligusts, called devil dancers and little whirlwinds, are seen along roads, it is a sure sign of rain. **1995–97** Montgomery *Coll* (known to Brown, Shields), = a small whirlwind that blows leaves around in a circle, sometimes lifting them up in into a tiny tornado-like funnel (Oliver).

devil door *noun* See citation.

2007 Milnes *Signs Cures Witches* 55 German motifs were carved into furniture and painted on chests and barns and the like, including many painted and decorated "Pennsylvania" or German-Swiss "bank barns." The most common are ones painted red with decorative white bordering, and some have "devil doors" (painted arches over the doors) and white stars painted on the doors.

devil in a jar *noun phrase* See citation.

2007 Alexander *Moonshiners Gone* vi All kinds of names were given homemade alcohol. These included Mountain Dew, Hooch, White Lightning, Devil in a Jar, Liquid Dynamite, Juicy Lightning, Rot Gut, Hill and Hollow Soup, Bootleg, Mule Kick, Corn Squeezings, Stump Water, Hog Jaw, Stump Likker, White Liquor, Scatterbrain, Sugar Liquor, Rye Whiskey, and on and on.

devil is beating/whipping his wife *phrase* It is raining although the sun is shining.

1889 Mooney *Folk Carolina Mts* 100 A sun shower is caused by the devil whipping his wife, the raindrops presumably being her tears. **1919** Combs *Word-List South* 36 *devil a-whuppin' his wife* = a sign that it is raining, and the rain drops are the tears falling from the eyes of the devil's wife! **1941** Hall *Coll* (Allens Creek NC) The devil's whuppin' his wife, and all her feathers are comin' out. **1952** Brown *NC Folklore* 393 *devil is beating his wife* = [said] when rain and sunshine come together. **1995** Adams *Come Go Home* 47 I also knew that rainbows could be seen only when "the devil was a beatin' his wife."

[DARE *devil* n B4 chiefly South, South Midland]

devilish *adjective* Tormenting, annoying, infernal.

1939 Hall *Coll* (Eagle Creek NC) Those tarnal devilish things! (said of panthers). *Ibid.* (Hazel Creek NC) We'd watch for 'em and kill them devilish, infernal panters, ever' one we know, where the dogs would run 'em.

[DARE *devilish* adj chiefly South, South Midland]

devilment *noun*

A variant form with secondary stress on the last syllable. For similar forms, see **-ment A.**

1942 Hall *Phonetics Smoky Mts* 71 The suffixes *-dent* and *-ment* (except in *independent*) in most instances have secondary stress: *accident, confident, devilment, instrument, monument, payment, settlement, testament*, etc.

B Teasing, mischief; meanness, villainy. See also **devil B.**

1864 Chapman *CW Letters* (Jan 24) thare is a heap of steeling & Robing houses in the country & it is supposed the scatering soldiers is doing the develment. **1873** Smith *Arp Peace Papers* 121 [I wish] we boys had knowed they was a goin to keep up this devilment so long. **1904** Johnson *Highways South* 132 "They was up to all sorts of devilment," Mr. Gliddon affirmed, "an' the people on their own side here didn't like 'em much better than the Yankees did." **1929** (in **1952** Mathes *Tall Tales* 148) "Mister," he said, when the laughter had abated somewhat, "you must excuse me an' Amos fer havin' our devilmint." **1975** Brewer *Valley So Wild* 221 On the river in that day without radio, television or any public place to go, young folks thought up their own "devilment." **1983** *Dark Corner OHP-5A* He was just full of it, pretty full of devilment like that, and he wanted to do things. **1994** Parton *Dolly* 15 There is still a certain kind of devilment that is going to enter that kid's mind. **2005** Williams *Gratitude* 490 = something done out of pure low-down meanness to hurt somebody, different from just aggervatin' 'em or devilin' 'em for fun.

[DARE *devilment* n chiefly South, South Midland]

C *verb* To act in a mean way.

1891 Moffat *Mtneers Middle TN* 319 I hate powerful to be disobleegin', but ef he comes devilmentin' areound me again hit seems like I've jes' natchully got him to kill.

devil's-apple *noun* Same as **mayapple.**

1964 Reynolds *Born of Mts* 84 For the Mandrake, or Devils Apple, there is a Womandrake, although the latter is not mentioned in the Bible, and for that matter even our mandrake is thought to be different from the Biblical one.

devil's box See **devil box.**

devil's brew (also *devil's juice*) *noun* Homemade whiskey.

1927 Furman *Lonesome Road* 126 I hain't touched the devil's brew sence, onless in actual need. **1943** Justus *Bluebird* 80 "Yes, I heard tell o'that," Grandy said, "and I heard tell how it happened—drunk on the devil's brew, he was, out of a moonshine still." **1990** Merriman *Moonshine Rendezvous* 102 Jim sold moonshine whiskey from 1933 to 1940 around the Buffalo Valley area in Putnam County, and Luke hauled the crystal clear devil's juice to him and others around Middle Tennessee. **1997** Montgomery Coll (known to Brown).

devil's corner *noun* The rear rows or rear corner of a church, where latecomers to a service and those wishing to avoid attention sit.

1994 McCarthy *Jack Two Worlds* 5 = an area in the back of the church where no lantern shone, where the unregenerate could come just to hear the preaching without ever stepping forward into the light of judgment. **1996** Isbell *Last Chivaree* 116–17 Normally the young men would look for a seat on the back rows. But Ray had learned at churches over on the Watauga River to sit down front. Tonight, however, he was late; he slipped quietly into the meeting and seated himself beside his male friends. It was a section the preacher called "the devil's corner." ... The preacher droned on, and in the devil's corner Ray's friends fidgeted and whispered. **2008** Salsi *Ray Hicks* 82 Castin' them devils out taken a lot of energy. [The preacher would] put hisself into the job till he was exhausted. The whole time, he'd keep an eye on the back of the church that was called the devil's corner, the place the tardy people 'ud snuck to.

devil's darning needle See **darning needle.**

devil's ditty *noun* A secular song, usually a traditional ballad. See also **ballad B1**, **love ballad**, **mountain song**, **song-ballad B1.**

1933 Thomas *Traipsin' Woman* 136 Woman, do you reckon it's harm for a body to sing them song ballets you wuz singin'? ... I al'lus had a favorance for that song you wuz singin' about the lady fair and beauty bright. I tried to sign it oncet, but Alamander put a stop to it. Says he, "Emmaline! I'll have no such singin' of Devil's ditties under this rooft!" **1959** Roberts *Up Cutshin* 44 The ballads had been fading out of tradition for a generation or two. They had come to be called "love ballets" or "devil's ditties," and had begun to die on the lips of the folk, even before the phonograph and the radio inundated them.

devil's dung *noun* Same as **asafetida.**

2007 Myers *Smoky Mt Remedies* 136 Some in our area actually used the very old remedy, asafetida, also known as "Devil's Dung." **2011** Richmond *Appal Folklore* 18 Asafetida ... had the unsavory folk name of "devil's dung." It was thought to be a cure for colds, fevers, and the flu.

devil's eye-water *noun* See citation.

1977 Pederson *Randy Sons* 115 = [homemade] whiskey.

devil's footprint *noun*

1 Same as **bald B.**

2012 Jourdan *Medicine Men* 161 Scientists disagree about why the flora of the balds is so utterly different from that of the rest of the mountains. The locals believe they know why. They call the areas *Devil's footprints*.

2 See citation.

2009 Fields *Growing Up* 328 = a heavy summer rain.

devil's footstool *noun* A large, poisonous mushroom.

1995 Montgomery Coll (known to Shields).

[DARE *devil's footstool* n chiefly South, South Midland]

devil's footwasher *noun* A severe rainstorm.

1991 Still *Wolfpen Notebooks* 92 The hard rain we had the other day that done so much damage to the crops was one of the Devil's footwashers.

devil shoestring See **devil's shoestring 2**.

devil's juice See **devil's brew**.

devil's kitchen *noun* A shed housing a **still** for making illegal whiskey; more generally, a place where illegal or immoral activity takes place.

1937 Hall *Coll* (Bradley Fork NC) A still house [is] a house for the still and to keep beer warm and from freezin'. My mother called it "the devil's kitchen." **1976** Dwyer *Southern Sayin's* 6 = reference by women to a man's still-house. **1999** Carver *Branch Water Tales* 1 A licker still ain't nothing but the Devil's kitchen.

devil's pack peddler *noun* See citation.

1939 Farr *TN Mt Regions* 90 = a gossiper: "She's a devil's pack peddler."

devil's riding horse *noun*

1 See **devil box**.

2 A praying mantis.

1992 Brooks *Sthn Stuff* 39 devil's riding horse, n. A praying mantis.

[DARE (at *devil's horse* n 1) chiefly South, South Midland, TX]

devil's rope *noun* See citation.

2009 Sutton *Me and Likker II* 215 A lot of people don't know what the Devil's Rope is but it is damn barb wire.

devil's shoestring *noun*

1 A low-growing, densely branching plant (*Viburnum alnifolium*). Same as **hobblebush**.

1860 Curtis *Plants NC* 91 Hobble-Bush ... (V. lantanoides.) ... The branches spread upon the ground ... form well secured loops for tripping the feet of ... wayfarers; a habit ... revenged ... by the unlucky, in the names ... American Way-fairer's [sic] Tree and the Devil's Shoe-strings. **1901** Lounsberry *Sthn Wild Flowers* 478 Its branches sprawl often, or lie over on the ground forming great loops which root readily from their ends. By this means it trips up many that seek to pass through its meshes, and the natives have therefore deemed "Devil's shoestrings" a not inappropriate designation.

[DARE *devil's shoestring* n 2 chiefly NC]

2 (also *devil shoestring*) The goat's rue (*Tephrosia* spp).

1884 Smith *Arp Scrap Book* 73 Then there's some flowers he wears in his button-hole called the devil's shoestring and devil in the bush. **1938** Stuart *Dark Hills* 89 The devil shoestring vines ran over the loamy overflowed land.

[DARE *devil's shoestring* n 1 chiefly South, South Midland]

devil's snuff (also *devil's snuff box*) *noun* The puffball plant (*Lycoperdon* spp), which has powdery spores used in traditional mountain medicine to stanch bleeding by placing them on a wound.

1884 Smith *Arp Scrap Book* 73 One day he showed me the devil's snuffbox which explodes when you mash it, and one ounce of the stuff inside will kill a sound mule before he can lay down. **1940** Haun *Hawk's Done* 116 She watched the blood gush out of his upper lip. She got some devil's snuff and some spider web to doctor it. **c1945** Haun *Hawk's Done* 233 Said she died from a big boil that ... wouldn't ever stop bleeding—no matter how much spiderweb and devil's snuff they dusted on it. **1994** Parton *Dolly* 11 I would find a patch of dandelions on one hill, on another a devil's snuffbox, as we called them. These were little mounds that grew low to the ground. I believe they're related to mushrooms. In the summer they get dried out so that the outside is like a piece of dark brown paper and the inside is filled with powder that puffs out like a dragon's breath when you stomp it. **1995** Montgomery *Coll*: *devil's snuffbox* (known to Cardwell, Shields).

[DARE *devil's snuffbox* n 1 chiefly South, South Midland]

devil's walkingstick *noun* A small, prickly tree (*Aralia spinosa*) with showy flowers; its berries and bark have medicinal uses. Also called **Hercules'-club**.

1937 Thornburgh *Great Smoky Mts* 24 A shrub about which many visitors inquire is the showy Hercules club, or devil's walking stick. You will recognize it in the summer by its mass of white blossoms at the top and by the cluster of blue-black berries in the fall. **1970** Campbell et al. *Smoky Mt Wildflowers* 104 Another common name [of the Hercules club] is devil's walking-stick. [**2006** Howell *Medicinal Plants* 66 The Cherokee used the berries and bark to relieve rheumatic pain. Roasted, pounded roots were used in a decoction to make a very strong emetic.]

(the) dew *noun* Homemade whiskey. See also **mountain dew**.

1885 Baine *Among Moonshiners* 15 The still has remained undisturbed for six years, during which it has turned out nearly or quite 22,000 gallons of the "dew." **1892** Dromgoole *War of Roses* 482 [T]o say nothing of the visions of pumpkin pies, pumpkin bread, apple butter and apple cider, barbecued pig, and the *dew*.

dewberry *noun* A trailing vine (*Rubus* spp) that produces a sweet berry and is closely related to the blackberry.

1883 Jones *Highlands N Carol* 379 Mountain-trout and wild game are brought to our door by grizzled men who have been fishing in the cold streams or hunting in the forest, barefooted boys present themselves with buckets of blackberries or dewberries or huckleberries, which they offer for five cents a quart. **c1960** Wilson *Coll* = a trailing species of blackberry, with very luscious fruit; never as common as the tall species (*Rubus flugellaris*). **1974** Cate et al. *Sthn Appal Heritage* 85 Ripening early were dewberries, their large-leafed vines trailing across the ground. Many a housewife complained of backache for days after wandering through old, uncultivated fields and bending to gather this fruit. The berries were large, but so were the seeds and cores. Consequently a gallon of berries produced disappointingly small returns. But many people endured the discomfort and scant reward because of the delightful flavor of dewberry jelly. **1985** Irwin *Alex Stewart* 188 Dewberries grow flat on the ground on a vine. I've picked many a gallon of dewberries. They've got the best flavor of any berry you ever eat when they're good and ripe. They make the best jelly.

[DARE *dewberry* n 1 chiefly South, Midland]

dew cut *noun* See citation. See also **dew poison**.

2003 Carter *Mt Home* 5 In the very early mornin's when the dew was still on the grassy fields, I often got cuts on my toes by walkin' in the wet grass of the fields. Mama called it a "dew cut."

dew poison (also *dew poisoning*) *noun* A bacterial or fungal skin rash, especially through a cut on the feet, once attributed to the toxic effect of walking barefooted on the grass especially in the late summer (and therefore associated with the **dog days**). See also **dew cut**, **fall sore**, **ground itch**, **mud poison**, **toe-itch**.

1913 Kephart *Our Sthn High* 229 Some of the ailments common in the mountains were new to me. For instance, "dew pizen," presumably the poison of some weed, which, dissolved in dew, enters the blood through a scratch or abrasion. As a woman described it, "Dew pizen comes like a risin', and laws-a-marcy, how it does hurt. My leg swelled up black clar to the knee . . . I lay on a pallet on the floor for over a month. My leg like to kill me. I've seed persons jes' a lot of sores all over, big as my hand, from dew pizen." **1955** Washburn *Country Doctor* 12 A complaint with many children as well as adults was "dew p'izen," characterized by slow-healing sores on the feet and legs and often on the hands and arms. At the time I did not recognize "dew poison" as the preliminary stage of hookworm disease nor did I associate it with the stunted anemic condition of the mountain children. The absence of privies at the homes made the disease very prevalent. **1960** Hall *Smoky Mt Folks* 50 St. John's weeds wet with dew . . . will cause sores and "risin's" (dew poisoning) on the skin. **1968** Wilson *Folklore Mammoth Cave* 36 = an infection of the toes, now known to be connected with hookworm; also called *toe (-eetch)*. [**1997** King *Mt Folks* 103 They got sores (the dew was poison in dog days); so they boiled blackberry brier leaves, mixed it with lard to stay on, and put it on the sores.] **2017** *Blind Pig* (Aug 30) If Granny has a cut or scratch on her hands or arms, she bandages it up tight before going out into the wet dewy garden for fear of getting dew poisoning.

[DARE *dew poison* n chiefly South Midland, especially southern Appalachians]

diamond *noun* variant forms *diamont*, *dimunt*.

1923 Greer-Petrie *Angeline Doin' Society* 19 She had dimunts on her fingers. **1944** Combs *Word-List Sthn High* 18 Diamont ['daɪmənt].

diamont See **diamond**.

dib *noun* A small quantity or portion.

1922 Kephart *Our Sthn High* 200 A tablespoonful, in company, was his limit . . . Just "a little dib [of liquor]," you know, now and then to tone [the stomach] up. **1966** Dykeman *Far Family* 114 I can tell you one thing: I'm no dirt farmer, raising a dib of this and a dust of that. **1994–97** Montgomery *Coll* (known to Adams, Brown, Cardwell, Jones, Norris, Oliver, Weaver).

[cf DARE *dib* n[1] 1 "probably from EDD *dib* sb[3] 2, 3 'a sheep's knucklebone or pebble used in the game of *dibs*'"]

dibbler (also *dibby*) *noun* A baby chicken. See also **biddy**, **deedie**, **diddle[2] A**.

1978 Montgomery *White Pine Coll* III-2 The old hens would seal their nests up and lay and hatch little dibblers. **1996–97** Montgomery *Coll*: *dibby* (known to Ledford, Oliver). **1997** Nelson *Country Folklore* 62 In the spring when the garden was planted, our job would be to keep the hens and her baby chicks (dibbies) from scratching up the seeds.

dibby See **dibbler**.

did[1] See **do A4**.

did[2] See **diddle[2] A**.

didapper *noun* (with stress on initial syllable) The pied-billed grebe (*Podilymbus podiceps*); by extension = a person lacking consistency or purpose.

1967 *DARE Survey* (Maryville TN) = small, dull-colored duck commonly found around ponds and lakes. **1968** Wilson *Folklore Mammoth Cave* 17 = the pied-billed grebe (*Podilymbus podiceps*). **1997** Montgomery *Coll* = a person who does not accomplish much and who does not stay in one place long (Cardwell).

[DARE *didapper* n 1 chiefly South, South Midland]

diddie See **diddle[2] A**.

diddle[1] *verb*

1 See 1981 citation.

1940 Still *River of Earth* 144 I diddled in my mind. Sunlight sifted through the leaves, slowly, wavering. **1981** Whitener *Folk-Ways* 61 *Diddle* as a verb in mountain speech means to "fool around; waste time; pretend to be busy at accomplishing a task." It suggests *cheating* or *pretending*. **1984** Woods *WV Was Good* 221 = to move about jerkily or in undertain manner, or to waste time foolishly. (He diddled around over there for a month.) To us this word did not refer to the sex act as it does in some other parts of the country.

2 See citations.

1957 Combs *Lg Sthn High: Word List* 29 = copulate. **c1960** Wilson *Coll* = to copulate, especially illegally.

diddle[2] (also *did*, *diddler*, *diddly*, *diddy*, *doodle*, *doodling*)

A *noun* A baby chicken or a duckling. See also **biddy**, **deedie**, **dibbler**.

1925 Dargan *Highland Annals* 196 For the diddlies, we carried strips from an old sawmill and made coops which we could set about in sunny places. **1948** Still *Nest* 21 She saw herself yesterday hiding in the brood house playing with newly hatched diddles . . . and the newly hatched diddles moist from egg scrambling to her lap, walking under her spread palms. **1949** Arnow *Hunter's Horn* 5 They's a old hen—that old dominecker, th one th hawk pulled her tail feathers out—she hid her nest out an has hatched eleven diddles right here, nearly September. **c1950** Adams *Grandpap* 165 The Johnnycake Boy just kept a-runnin' an' a-runnin'. Come to a fox a-sneakin' up on an old hen an' her little dids. **1950** Justus *Luck for Lihu* 43 I can always tell whenever a young'un's puny, going around like a diddler with the limberneck. **1952** Wilson *Folk Speech NC* 533 *diddy* = a little chicken. **1976** Garber *Mountain-ese* 22 *diddle* = baby chicken or duck. **1978** Slone *Common Folks* 230 That old flag has kept many a gang of doodles from getting wet when it rains, warm when it's cold, and a shade when it's hot. **1982** Slone *How We Talked* 26 *diddlies* = baby chickens. **c1982** Young *Colloquial Appal* 7 *doodling* = very young chicken. **1996–97** Montgomery *Coll*: *diddle* (known to eight consultants from the Smoky Mountains); *diddler* It's time to feed them diddlers (Andrews); *diddly* (known to Brown, Jones); *diddy* (known to Bush, Cypher). **2008** Salsi *Ray Hicks* 114 Daddy 'ud bring home a rooster and baby diddles in a box and set 'em in the yard. **2017** Kinsler *Take Girl* 42 Sometimes, grandma put several eggs in her incubator in order to hatch doodles (baby chickens).

[cf EDD *diddle* sb[6] "duckling"; DARE *diddle* n[2] chiefly southern Appalachians]

B *interjection* Come! (used as a call to young chickens or ducklings to come for food); often repeated, as *diddy! diddy!*

1997 Montgomery *Coll*: *diddy!* (known to Bush, Cardwell, Jones, Ledford, Oliver, Weaver).

diddy See **diddle[2] A.**

didn't See **do A5.**

didn't go to See **go to 3.**

didn't make no never mind See **never no mind.**

didn't say dog See **never say dog.**

dido *noun*

1 In phrases *cut a dido, do a dido* = to do a prank, cut a caper; to throw a fit.

1944 Williams *Word-List Mts* 28 = to have a fit of anger or drunkenness, or to show any uncommon behavior. "Your pa'll *cut a dido* when he finds out about this." **1987** Davenport *Pine Grove* 16 At practically all fords, there were cable suspension foot bridges, commonly called swinging bridges. They also went the way of the abandoned fords. Kids would do all sorts of didos on those bridges. Bouncing up and down and swinging sideways rhythmically would set it in motion to produce a thrilling experience. **1994** Montgomery *Coll*: *cut a dido* (known to Shields).

[DARE *dido* n 1 especially New England, South, South Midland]

2 In phrases *cut a dido, do a dido* = to execute a dance step gracefully, do a dance, especially in **buck dancing**. See also **pigeon('s) wing.**

1983 Matthews *Cutting a Dido*. **2005** Williams *Gratitude* 490 *cut a dido, do a dido* = do a little dance; dance a jig. . . . "She *cut a dido* when she found that $50 bill."

[OED3 *dido* n[2] "a prank, caper; a disturbance" dialect and U.S.; HT n "antic, caper (usually only in plural)"]

3 See citation.

2007 McMillon *Notes* = an object unnamed.

[origin unknown]

didy *noun* A diaper.

1957 Broaddus *Vocab Estill Co KY* 22 *didies* = diapers. **a1975** Lunsford *It Used to Be* 174 "Didies" and "Hippins" are expressions used for diapers. **1979** Slone *My Heart* 52 We used old bed sheets—after they became so thin you could sun bees through them—for diapers or "diddies" as we called them. **2003** Carter *Mt Home* 2 She changed Lou-Anns didys and set and held her a lot.

die away, die off See **die out.**

die on See **on A1.**

die out (also *die away, die off*) *verb phrase* Of a person: to die. See also **pass 1.**

1913 Bruce *Terms from TN* 58 My old woman *died out* last Monday. **1928** Thornburgh *Americans Forgot* 42 That gal's fust man died out on her. **1937** Hall *Coll* (Cades Cove TN) Old Bill Oliver, he died out. **1960** Campbell *Birth* 60 Asked later about the health of "Mrs. Henry Ford [= Wiley Oakley's daughter]," Wiley sadly announced, "She died out on me." **1966** Dykeman *Far Family* 105 He just died off last year. **1975** Chalmers *Better* 25 Lord Ha' mercy, Miss Marjorie, I thought you had died out. **1978** Montgomery *White Pine Coll* IV-2 Most of my people lived to be up in years, but I had some to die off a-young, too. **1983** *Dark Corner OHP*-3A What ain't moved away, died away. **1983** Page and Wigginton *Aunt Arie* 166 Van died out, didn't she?

diffabitterance (also *diff of bitterance*) *noun* A bit of difference.

1921 Combs *KY Items* 119 *diff of bitterance* = bit of difference. **c1960** Wilson *Coll*: *diffabitterance* = a humourous transposition of *bit of difference*, usually said to indicate one's utter lack of interest in what is being discussed.

[DARE *diffabitterance* n chiefly South Midland]

differ

A *verb* To matter, make a difference.

1917 Kephart *Word-List* 410 It didn't *differ* what that cow [weighed]. **1962** Clark *Folk Speech NC* 313 *it don't differ* = it doesn't matter. **1964** Glassie *Mt Jack Tales* 96 It's a 'chanted harp to play any song you think of. [It] don't differ what it is. **1989** *Matewan OHP*-9 You can run anything in the ground. [It] don't differ what it is. **1997** Montgomery *Coll* Hit don't differ to me (Brown).

[DARE *differ* v South, South Midland]

B *noun* A difference (of view, opinion, etc.).

1859 (in **1974** Harris *High Times* 244) He dident tell yer that our habits had a bigger differ nor our tastes, an in our plannin this mustn't be forgot. **1884** Murfree *In TN Mts* 141 He'll see a mighty differ nex' time. **1913** Kephart *Our Sthn High* 94 They mean nigh about the same thing, only there's a differ. **1929** (in **1952** Mathes *Tall Tales* 134) That settles it! If he wants it that bad, I give in, no differ what Paw says. **1962** Dykeman *Tall Woman* 218 "Makes no differ to me," he mumbled, but he went to fetch another bucket of water. **2003** Gibson *Sthn Mt Dialect* Hit don't make no differ.

[OED3 *differ* n Scot and dialect, shortening of *difference*, influenced by *differ* v; CUD *differ* n 1 "difference"; DARE *differ* n chiefly South, South Midland]

differents *noun plural* Two or more items not alike.

1932 Creal *Quaint Speech* Differents is frequently heard, meaning different ones.

difficulty *noun* variant form with primary stress on the second syllable: *di-FI-culty*.

1895 Edson and Fairchild *TN Mts* 375. **1942** Hall *Phonetics Smoky Mts* 66–67. **1997** Montgomery *Coll* (known to Brown, Bush).

dig *verb* variant past-tense and past-participle form *digged*.

1934 Carpenter *Archaic English in WV* 77 Rambling about the central and southern counties of [WV] I have found a couple of dozen words generally assumed to be local mutations which are in truth handed down from past generations. Among these are . . . *gaumed up*, *crope* for *crept*, *boughten* and *digged*, to mention only a few. **1977** McGreevy *Breathitt KY Grammar* 93 = attested by 1 speaker. **1978** Reese *Speech NE Tenn* 173 = attested by 1/12 (8.3%) speakers.

dike out *verb phrase* To dress up in fine clothes.

1927 Woofter *Dialect from WV* 352 He was all diked out for the party. **1942** Campbell *Cloud-Walking* 10 Ain't you got new shoes to dike out in? **c1960** Wilson *Coll*: *diked out* = dressed up, sometimes obviously so; probably *dight*.

[DARE *dike* v chiefly South, South Midland]

dilatory

A *adjective* variant forms *dilitary*, *dilleterry*.

1913 Kephart *Our Sthn High* 287 She's so dilitary! **1931** Combs *Lg Sthn High* 1304 That gal of Zeke's is shorely dilitary. **1976** Garber *Mountain-ese* 22 He's so dilleterry he won't never git his homework done.

[DARE *dilatory* adj South Midland]

B *verb* To waste time.

2001 Montgomery *Coll* (known to Cardwell).

dilitary, dilleterry See **dilatory**.

dilley weed *noun* The dillweed plant (*Anthemis cotula*), used for spicing food and as a medicine. Same as **dog fennel**.

1940 Caton *Wildflowers of Smokies* 59. **1996** Houk *Foods & Recipes* 60 A bit of "dilley weed" makes [pickled beans] pretty good. **1997** Montgomery *Coll* = local term for dill (Cardwell).

dimunt See **diamond**.

ding dong *verb phrase* See citations.

1944 Williams *Word-List Mts* 29 = to annoy: "He just ding-dongs his pa till he gets whatever he wants out of him." **c1960** Wilson *Coll* = to annoy by repeating a scolding or an order.

dinged *adjective* Used as a euphemism for *damned*.

1873 Smith *Arp Peace Papers* 94 Three of the dinged things stung me afore I could rise.

dingus *noun* A small item whose name is momentarily not recalled.

1944 Laughlin *Word-List Buncombe Co* 25 = a small article. **1952** Wilson *Folk Speech NC* 533 = a thing (Swain Co). **1997** Montgomery *Coll* (known to Brown).

dinner *noun* The midday meal, traditionally the main meal of the day.

1861 (in **1992** Heller and Heller *Confederacy* 82) we put up our tents and got every thing reaglated by dinner. at 2 o'clock hit commenced raining and the wind a blowing and heavy thunder. **1924** Spring *Lydia Whaley* 1 Pap let the county build a school house free on his land which was nigh enuf for 'em to go home to dinner. And he was "powerful to send us to school." **1940** Oakley *Roamin'/Restin'* 128 Its dinner in the mountains at 12 noon and supper at night. **1959** Pearsall *Little Smoky* 91 "Let's get us some dinner" may be said any time from 11:00 A.M. to 2:00 P.M. **1972** Cooper *NC Mt Folklore* 159 I want to go back where they eat three meals a day—breakfast, dinner and supper, where the word *lunch* will never be heard again. **1996** Houk *Foods & Recipes* 7 Before noon, women headed home to fix "dinner," the main meal of the day, consisting of hot cornbread, beans, pork in some form, and possibly a dessert. Duly fortified, they went back out to the cornfield for the afternoon. What appeared on the table for supper often closely resembled what was left over from dinner. **2016** Netherland *Appal Cooking* 9 There would always be a table full of food. But it was difficult to go back to the field after a meal of that magnitude. The noon meal was called "dinner," while the evening meal was "supper." Most times, supper was leftovers from dinner.

dinner bucket (also *dinner pail*) *noun* A metal container carrying the midday meal, carried to school or work; traditionally it was most often a lard bucket, but more recently a lunch box.

1913 Morley *Carolina Mts* 222 Even at the school-house far from the road, and hidden so well that it is cause for wonder that the children ever find it, one has seen them come darting out of the forest like rabbits, barefooted and sunbonneted, carrying such books as they had, and swinging their "dinner buckets"—lard pails most of them. **1927** Justus *Peter Pocket* 30 He hurried away so fast that he forgot his dinner pail and had to scurry back to get it. **1940** Still *River of Earth* 82 Two bats flew around the eaves, disappearing with the dull squeaks, and then we heard the dinner buckets of the scholars cracking together upcreek and down. **1991** Thomas *Sthn Appal* 55 When I'z jist a boy, about ten ur twelve year old, I'd carry a dinner-bucket to school. Mother'd putt jist whatever we had for breakfast. Yeah, it'ud be ribs or backbone pork.

We had some of them, in th' late fall, an' biscuits. Or sausage, boiled eggs. Ennything like that, that we eat on th' table, we'd have it put in th' dinner-pail, take it fer dinner. **1991** Weals *Last Train* 47 A working man's lunch box at that time was called a dinner pail or a dinner bucket, and those of the two dead men were found in the wreckage. [**1998** *Dante OHP-45* Everybody brought their dinner in a bucket, in a lard bucket, and most of the time it was milk and bread, milk and bread, cornbread and milk.] **2013** Venable *How to Tawlk* 11 = lunchbox: "By any chance you gotta spair samich in yore dinner bucket?" **2016** *Blind Pig* (Aug 30) According to my late father, children literally carried buckets to school with their humble fare (often cornbread or biscuits with some sopping syrup (molasses) in the bottom of the bucket). *Ibid.* The "dinner bucket" originated with the bucket for "dinner" such as the coal miners used. The bottom held drinking water. Then an upper insert that was dry held the food.

dinner hole *noun* A recess in a coal mine where miners gather to eat a meal.

c1986 (in **2015** Yarrow *Voices* 70) When I go to the dinner hole every day I tell my people, "You keep your curtain up." **1987** (in **2015** Yarrow *Voices* 21) One day I was cleaning the dinner hole and this big timber was in my way . . . so I just picked up one end and slung it out of the way.

dinner on the ground(s) *noun phrase*

1 A midday meal in connection with a church **meeting**, revival, **association**, **singing convention**, **Decoration Day**, **homecoming**, or other event when families bring prepared food, eat on tablecloths spread on the ground, and enjoy leisurely fellowship. Also called **basket dinner**, **big dinner**.

1890 Fruit *KY Words* 65 A "basket-meetin'" is a two or three days' meetin', when they have "dinner on the ground." **1945** Wilson *Passing Institutions* 76 Be it said frankly, the dinner on the ground was the great thing; the sermon was only sauce to the appetite. **1968** Clarke *Stuart's Kentucky* 79 A more frequent and popular church social was the basket dinner, or dinner on the grounds. When an all-day service made it practical, the women of the church prepared abundant food on Saturday for dinner on the church grounds preceding the evening preaching services. **1976** Braden *Grandma Was Girl* 77 Once in a while the Clinton Baptist Association met at our church. That was a great occurrence for the community. At this meeting were visiting ministers and delegates from all the member churches of the Association. It lasted for two or three days. Meals were served as "dinners on the ground." We would spread tablecloths on the ground, and put all kinds of dishes of food on the cloths. Everybody was welcome to come and eat. **1978** Petersen and Phillips *New Harp of Columbia* xxv It is almost as though the morning sing points the way to dinner on the ground. There is nearly audible relief when, as noonday approaches, a break is suggested so the tables can be unfolded and loaded with the covered dishes. Dinner is outdoors in good weather, up the center aisle in bad. It is a time not only for nourishment but for fellowship, for renewing acquaintances with those not seen for as long as a year, or meeting visitors and singers who have come to the sing from places far from Wear's Valley. **1996** Parton *Mt Memories* 172 Church singings, with "dinner on the ground," are a tradition that has survived the test of time. Each family brings dishes of food to the church, and after the worship service, tables are put up outside. Sometimes the tables are nothing more than rough planks on sawhorses, covered with tablecloths. The women arrange the food on the table, with meat dishes placed together, the vegetables, desserts, and so on. If you've never attended a Sevier County dinner on the ground, you've missed out on some of the greatest food in the world. [**2009** Roebuck *Dinner on Grounds* 283 The practice developed among congregations whose churches had no space for indoor dining; when church-goers wanted to share a meal—on special occasions such as homecomings, decoration days, graveyard association days, family reunions, and all-day singings—they moved outside to the church grounds.] **2010** Jabbour and Jabbour *Decoration Day* 8 They returned and began spreading tablecloths and arranging an amazingly varied offering of food on the tables. This was the portion of the decoration ritual known as "dinner on the ground." The term is consistently used for the cemetery meal on Decoration Day throughout the Upland South, from the Appalachians to the Ozarks. It is also used for the after-church outdoor meals of southern congregations. Dinner on the ground was originally a picnic-like meal, spread on blankets on the ground in the cemetery. . . . Whatever the actual circumstances of the meal, people cling affectionately to the term "dinner on the ground" for the time-honored communal experience it conjures up.

[DARE *dinner on the ground(s)* n chiefly South, South Midland]

2 Formerly, a festive meal held by the Eastern Band of the Cherokee. See citation.

1989 Woodside *Hungry for Dance* 24 The Green Corn Dance . . . took place on a now overgrown corn field by the Raven's Fork River in August, to celebrate a good harvest. Women folks cooked the corn, beans, taters, whatever they had, they cooked it, took it down to the ball field, and they called it Dinner on the Grounds.

dinner pail See **dinner bucket**.

dinner poke *noun* A small bag for carrying one's lunch to school.

1978 Parris *Mt Cooking* 182 When I was going to school, I always carried a fried pie in my dinner poke.

dint See **do A5a**.

dippy *noun* Gravy.

c1960 Wilson *Coll* = old name for gravy. **1974** Dwyer and Dwyer *Mt Cookin'* 31 = gravy: "She kin marry enny feller she wants 'cause of her dippy!" **2009** Sohn *Appal Home Cooking* 301 "Soppy" and "dippy" are colloquial terms for milk gravy, squirrel gravy, and sausage gravy. Mountain cooks make these gravies with milk, flour, and pan drippings, and they serve them over biscuits.

dip stick *noun* See citation. Same as **toothbrush**.

1941 Harper *Way We Said* 130 = a twig, broken from a tree and shredded at one end, used to apply snuff to the gums.

[DARE (at *dipping stick* n 1) chiefly South, South Midland]

directly *adverb*

A variant forms *dreck'ley* [see **1982** in **B2**], *dreckly*, *d'reck'ly*, *terectly*, *terrectly*, *thereckly* [see **1957** in **B2**], *tirectly* [see **1933** in **B2**], *tor(r)eckly*.

1913 Kephart *Our Sthn High* 277 No one can write [dialect] without using the apostrophe more than he likes to; for our highland speech is excessively clipped. "I'm comin' d'reck'ly" has a quaintness that should not be lost. **1921** Greer-Petrie *Angeline at Seelbach* 7 Terectly he would git out and projick around the back premises. **1956** Hall *Coll* (Cosby TN) "If you don't speak to me," [the ghost] said, "I'll shoot you dreckly." **1988** Dickey and Bake *Wayfarer* 49 You know, there's goin' to be a point to the [story] toreckly, but we ain't in no hurry, usually, to get to it.

[DARE *dreckly*, *toreckly* (at *directly* adv A) all forms chiefly South, South Midland]

B *adverb* [Editor's note: The interpretation between the senses below is sometimes variable and thus not always distinct, meaning that a user may exploit the term's ambiguity to delay an action or response. See **1996–97** in **B2**.]

1 Immediately, right away.

1956 Hall *Coll* (Cosby TN) "If you don't speak to me," [the ghost] said, "I'll shoot you dreckly." **1965** *Dict Queen's English* 17 = immediately. "I'll do that *to-reckly*."

[DARE *directly* adv B1 chiefly South, South Midland]

2 In a little while, before long, as soon as may be convenient

1933 Thomas *Traipsin' Woman* 33 I wuz a-clearin' some brush on my place, and tirectly I heared a couple shots and I seen Little Doc there. **1939** Hall *Coll* (Deep Creek NC) "They're not a-going let him cross the Smoky," I said, "He'll turn back down directly." **1956** McAtee *Some Dial NC* 13 *dreckly* = soon or at a convenient time, but not immediately. **1957** Combs *Lg Sthn High: Word List* 101 *thereckly* = directly. Frequently used for soon, in a short time: "It will rain thereckly." **1969** GSMNP-25:2:8 I could show you directly, but it's hard to tell you because I did have pillars laid up till I could tell you. **1970** *Hunting* 75 When you call to [the turkey] and he gobbles, put'cher call in yer pocket, never say another word, an' directly he'll come slippin' up. Might be an hour, mebbe quicker, mebbe longer. **1982** Slone *How We Talked* 29 *dreck'ley* = after a while; soon, but not just now. **1996** Isbell *Last Chivaree* 27 I introduce myself, but she does not invite me to sit. She says that Ray will be out "directly." **1996–97** Montgomery *Coll* consultants from the Smoky Mountains concur that the usual sense is "in a little while, soon," indicating a definite intention or purpose, but sometimes the term conveys "after a while" if a person wishes to procrastinate; one consultant from the Smoky Mountains states that, depending on context, it may mean "at once, immediately." **2005** Williams *Gratitude* 490 *dreckly* = in a little while, or soon, as "I'll be there *dreckly*." **2007** McMillon *Notes* = in a little while, but not immediately. **2009** Benfield *Mt Born* 123 *be there directly* = you are making a casual promise to be somewhere in the future. It does not mean straightaway as it implies, but in a while, as soon as the speaker gets around to it, which could be minutes, hours, or weeks. A man is not to be hurried.

dirt daub *verb phrase* To kill time.

1997 Montgomery *Coll* (known to Brown).

dirt eater *noun* The runt of a litter.

1996 Montgomery *Coll* (known to Adams).

dis' See **just**.

disabled (+ *infinitive*) *adjective* Made unable, as a result of illness, age, etc.

1978 Reese *Speech NE Tenn* 41 He got disabled to doctor.

disablest *adjective* Most disabled, least able.

1863 *Vance Papers* (July 13) this is to inform you Dear Sir how the Surgent Doctor acted when the militia was cald oup to forty five he Discharged the Men Seems like that was his friends and the Disablest Bodyed Men that wasent he Dident. **1917** Kephart *Word-List* 410 = antonym of ablest. "We're all strong enough to work, except Johnson; he's the *disablest* one of the family." **1943** Hannum *Mt People* 148 Jim's the disablest one of the family. **1957** Combs *Lg Sthn High: Word List* 29 = superlative form of *most disabled*. Ex.: "Little Sam is the disablest of the whole set." **1994–97** Montgomery *Coll* (known to Brown, Norris, Oliver).

discipline *noun*, *verb* variant form with primary stress on the second syllable: *dis-CIP-line*.

1942 Hall *Phonetics Smoky Mts* 66. **1967** Wilson *Folkways Mammoth Cave* 53 Discipline /dis-CIP-line/ was likely to be severe, but so was discipline at home. **1996** Montgomery *Coll* Churches used to have a discipline committee; they used to discipline their members (Cardwell). **2007** McMillon *Notes*: dis-CIP-line.

[DARE *discipline* n, v chiefly South Midland]

discomfit *verb*

A variant form with primary stress on final syllable: *dis-com-FIT*.

1998 Montgomery *Coll* (known to Bush, Cardwell, Weaver).

B To inconvenience (someone).

1917 Kephart *Word-List* 410 = to inconvenience. "I hope it has not *disconfit* [sic] you very bad." **1939** Hall *Coll* (Big Bend NC) I wouldn't want to discomfit you. **1974** Fink *Bits Mt Speech* 6 Ef I don't *discomfit* ye none. **1994–95** Montgomery *Coll* (known to Shields); I'd like to buy some corn from you if it won't discomfit you (Cardwell).

[EDD *discomfit* v Scot; DOST *discomfit* v 1375→; CUD *discomfit* v "put to inconvenience"; DARE *discomfit* v chiefly southern Appalachians]

disease and cure *noun* A children's game. See citation.

1941 Hall *Party Games* 69 In "Disease and Cure" two lines, one of boys and the other of girls, were formed facing each other.... A boy, a self-elected leader, went down the boys' line, whispering to each a disease and a cure. The cure was applicable not to his own but to his partner's ailment. Meanwhile, an assistant, a girl, went down the girls' line doing the same thing. Then all was in readiness to begin. Each girl asked her partner in the opposite line to name his disease and, upon being told, stated the cure previously indicated. Then the roles of "doctor" and "patient" were reversed.... The fun, of course, consisted in the mention of humorous afflictions and treatments, in the complete lack of connection between the two, and in the ridiculous situations which would thus occur.

disencourage *verb* To discourage.

1917 Kephart *Word-List* 410. **1922** TN *CW Ques* 1387 (Wilkes Co NC) Tha[t] was very much disincareged. **1925** Greer-Petrie *Angeline Hill Country* 97 They mustn't git disincurridged, fur they could soon larn. **1994–97** Montgomery *Coll* (known to Bush, Cardwell, Jones, Shields).

[DARE *disencourage* v chiefly South Midland]

disfellowship *verb* See citation. See also **fellowship 1**.

1995 McCauley *Mt Religion* 94 For the Regular Baptists—out of which developed most of the Old Time Baptists church traditions characteristic of Appalachia's mountain regions—the association could "disfellowship" or break relations with an individual church or another association with which it was "in correspondence" (that is, in receipt of letters during an association's annual meeting).

disfurnish *verb* To inconvenience (someone), deprive (oneself).

1863 Wesson *CW Letters* (March 12) tel pap to See mr renolds and git me a litle money and Send to me as Soon as he can do it I dont want yo to disfornesh yor Self of any thing to git money for me. **1864** Chapman *CW Letters* (May 14) I rote to you to buy me a watch but I dont want you to disfurnish yore self for you mite get sick and nead yore money be fore you could get to come home. **1917** Kephart *Word-List* 411 = to deprive (oneself). "Don't *disfurnish* yourself." **1924** Raine *Saddlebags* 103 If it don't disfurnish ye none, I'll pay ye later. **1979** Carpenter *Walton War* 178 Hit is good of you to divide with me, but I hate for you to disfurnish yourself. **1982** Slone *How We Talked* 30 = to sell or give away so much of what one has that one is in need oneself. **1995** Montgomery *Coll* Would you sell me some if it won't disfurnish you? (Cardwell).

[DARE *disfurnish* v 1 South Midland, South]

disgust *verb*

A variant third-singular form of three syllables: *dis-gust-es*. See also **-es**[2].

1996 GSMNPCOHP-1:4 It disgustes me now to drive down through this cove.

B To have an aversion or distaste for.

1913 Kephart *Our Sthn High* 282 In mountain vernacular many words that serve as verbs are only nouns of action, or adjectives, or even adverbs ... "I disgust bad liquor." **1988** Smith *Fair and Tender* 11 I disgust them and wish for wooden shoes and a lace cap like yourn and such pretty long white stockings. **1994–97** Montgomery *Coll* (known to Brown, Cardwell, Ledford, Shields).

[OED3 *disgust* v 1a obsolete; DARE *disgust* v South Midland, relic]

dish clout *noun* A rag or cloth used to dry dishes. See also **clout**.

1940 Haun *Hawk's Done* 57 She saw his neck was limber. Limber as a dish clout. **c1945** Haun *Hawk's Done* 311 Thinking's not the same as knowing—not ever the same—and I heard him say it one time about the bent sapling making a crooked tree and about Sade Hyangton's girl, that she was wore out like an old dish clout.

dish pan army *noun* See citation.

1990 Moore *Pittston Strike* 8 Mother Jones, the fiery labor organizer, led "dish pan armies" of miners' wives to confront mine guards and strikebreakers by banging pots and pans during the early 1900s.

dishrag gourd *noun* A cucumber-shaped gourd (*Luffa aegyptiaca*) whose fibers make it suitable as a sponge.

1998 Olson *Blue Ridge Folklife* 158 After a meal, people would clean pots and utensils with salt, rags, or homegrown luffa ("dishrag") gourds.

[DARE *dishrag gourd* n chiefly South Midland]

disinfect *noun* Disinfectant.

1941 (in **1944** Wentworth *ADD* 166) (eWV) = disinfectant. **1971** *Granny Women* 251 She said that she always washed her hands well with "disinfect."

dismals *noun plural* Low spirits, "the blues."

1939 *FWP Guide TN* 134 "I've got them weary dismals today," moans the hillman. **1952** Wilson *Folk Speech NC* 533 = the melancholies, low spirits. **1998** Montgomery *Coll* = a bad day, Monday blues (Brown); He has had the dismals for three days or more (Cardwell), = the blues, depression (Jones).

[DARE *dismals* n pl 1 especially TN]

disobliging *adjective* Inconveniencing, failing to accommodate.

1891 Moffat *Mtneers Middle TN* 319 I hate powerful to be disobleegin', but ef he comes devilmentin' areound me again hit seems like I've jes' natchully got to kill him.

[OED3 *disoblige* v 3 obsolete or dialect]

displeasure *verb* To displease. See also **pleasure**.

1940 Bowman *KY Mt Stories* 237 = displease.

[OED3 *displeasure* v 1a archaic]

disrecollect *verb* See citation. Same as **disremember**.

a1954 Adams *Word-List* = do not recollect.

disregardless *adverb* Regardless.

1917 (in **1944** Wentworth *ADD* 166) (sWV) = regardless. **1974** Fink *Bits Mt Speech* 6. **1996–97** Montgomery *Coll* (known to Adams, Brown, Jones, Oliver).

[redundant form; DARE *disregardless* adj, adv chiefly southern Appalachians]

disremember *verb* To forget, not recall (something or someone). Same as **disrecollect**. See also **misremember**.

1895 Edson and Fairchild *TN Mts* 371 I *disremember* to have heard anyone call. **1913** Kephart *Our Sthn High* 78 I mind about that time, Doc; but I disremember which buryin'-ground they-all buried ye in. **1922** *TN CW Ques* 404 (Washington Co TN) I inlisted in sixty two I disremember the month and date. **1953** Hall *Coll* (Bryson City NC) We had Doctor Stuart Robison here at Hazelwood and three or four doctors from down in the eastern part of the state. I disremember their names right now. **1962** Williams *Verbs Mt Speech* 18 The "biddies" and goslings around the kitchen door might' nigh drive her crazy with their "infernal and everlastin' whoodling" because she has "disremembered" to feed them. **1973** Foster *Walker Valley* 9:83 I disremember who told me that, but it ain't been long ago. **1973** GSMNP-5:32 I disremember what preacher it was. **2015** Dykeman *Family of Earth* 2 This moment came for me after my father's death. There was a funeral, which I disremember.

[OED3 *disremember* v chiefly dialect; DOST *disremember* v 1584→; CUD *disremember* v "forget, especially when one is unwilling to answer a question"; DARE *disremember* v probably originally Scots]

dist See **just**.

distance *noun* A duration of time.

1939 Farr *TN Mt Regions* 92 I've knowed him fur some distance.

distill See **still**.

distiller's beer *noun* Same as **beer**.

1985 Dabney *More Mt Spirits* 38 Moonshiners, particularly, have been noted for drinking the "distiller's beer" from mash boxes.

district *noun* variant forms *deestric(k)*, *deestrict*, *de-stric*.

1864 Gilmore *Down in TN* 93 Them fellers wull raise the deestrict, Leftenant. **1881** Atkinson *After Moonshiners* 36 As we passed the line of civilization, going further and still further into this gloomy and most uninviting "deestrick," I was more than ever impressed with the poetry of Allison's "Night along the Hills." **1913** Kephart *Our Sthn High* 394 She's got, I reckon, about the toughest deestric in the ceounty, which is saying a good deal. **1939** Hall *Coll* (Tobes Creek NC) Politics has gone too far. . . . We've got two squires to every deestrict. One's a-plenty. **1942** Hall *Phonetics Smoky Mts* 15 *District* was ['distrɪc(t)] in all instances noted, but this pronunciation is probably limited to old-timers. **1969** Medford *Finis* 117 By then I had shed my "gal's" dress, just before entering school, at the "de-strick" log school house. **1975** AOHP/ALC-961 In this area right here has mostly always been Democrats, is a strong Democrat deestrict.

disturbament See **disturbment**.

disturbment (also *disturbament*, *disturbmint*) *noun* A disturbance.

1942 (in **1987** Perdue *Outwitting Devil* 72) Then the little black devils got mad. They started a disturbment. **1957** Combs *Lg Sthn High: Word List* 30 *disturbment*, *disturbament*, *disturbmint* = disturbance.

disturbmint See **disturbment**.

ditch line *noun* A ditch alongside a graded road.

1965 *DARE Survey* (Adams KY, Clayhole KY, Hazard KY, Brasstown NC, Gatlinburg TN). **2009** Holbrook *Upheaval* 68 He pitches the rind of his sandwich toward the ditch line and takes a drink of water to rinse his mouth out. **2017** Williams *Murmuration* 14 His name was painted white on a painted-gray brick wall, across from the old hospital on the other side of a ditch line.

[DARE *ditch line* n chiefly southern Appalachians].

ditney tea See **dittany**.

ditn't See **do A5**.

dittany (also *ditney*) *noun* A small, fragrant plant (*Cunila origanoides*) of the mint family; for its medicinal uses in a tea, see 1975 citation.

1937 Hyatt *Kiverlid* 80 "I ain't no fool about sassafac," Calhoun said, "I'd ruther have ditney tea." **1971** AOHP/ALC-4 They'd make them tea. They'd make them dittany tea. You'd go to the woods and gather dittany, and they would make tea and give [children] that, and that would break them out. **1975** Hamel and Chiltoskey *Cherokee Plants* 32 = [used as] tea for colds, headaches; fevers; to increase perspiration; tonic; stimulant; snake-bite; strong tea to increase labor pains and facilitate childbirth. **2003** Onchuck *Mud Pie Memories* 100 Dittany—once proclaimed as curing "anything," now is all but forgotten as an herbal remedy.

div See **dive**.

dive *verb* variant past-tense and past-participle form *div*.

1913 Kephart *Our Sthn High* 101 The bear div down into the sink-hole with the dogs a-top o' him. **1917** Kephart *Word-List* 411 I div right out and hired me a cook. **1952** Wilson *Folk Speech NC* 532 *div* = past and past participle of *dive*. **1952–57** (in **1986** McDavid and McDavid *KY Verb Forms* 285) *div* [as past-tense form] = attested by 13 of 14 (93%) of E KY speakers for the Linguistic Atlas of the North Central States. **1953** Atwood *Verbs East US* 9 The form *div* /dɪv/ shows the typical distribution of an archaism, being most common in n.e. N. Engl. and the coastal and mountain areas of the South and South Midland. **1994–97** Montgomery *Coll* (known to Adams, Brown, Cardwell, Jones, Oliver).

[DARE *dive* v 1, 2 occasionally South, South Midland]

divide *noun* A mountain, ridge, or hills separating two watersheds, such as the **Smoky Mountain**, forming the border between North Carolina and Tennessee; also used in place-names, as in *Noland Divide* (NC) and *Cataloochee Divide* (NC).

1925 Davis *KY Mts* 42 The region is covered with a network of rivers, creeks, and forks which head against one another on opposite sides of the ridges, which constitute the divides between the drainage basins. **1926** Morgan *Smoky Mts* 461 The range consists mainly of a main ridge which forms the divide between Tennessee and North Carolina. Oft times the spurs and peaks leading away from the main line of "Big Smokies" . . . attain a greater height than the main ridge. **1956** Fink *That's Why* 4 Ridges, particularly those running down from a high peak or standing out like buttresses from the main divide, have various designations. Ridge is the most common, but there are others in frequent use, like Rocky Spur and Long, Crooked or Bent Arm. **1999** Coggins *Place Names Smokies* 164 = the ridges or regions of high ground that separate stream valleys.

divil See **devil**.

djuke See **jook**.

do

A *verb, auxiliary verb*

1 *do* = if (to introduce a conditional clause). [Editor's note: This usage does not occur in ATASC and may reflect a literary convention.]

1962 Dykeman *Tall Woman* 80 Do we reach the house-place before dark, we'd better get back onto our path. *Ibid.* 190 Mark has taken a little sang. I'm saving for the children's sub-scriptions, do we get our school started up again. **1991** Still *Wolfpen Notebooks* 83 These dog-peter gnats, do you get one in your eye, hit'll burn like a coal.

2 *don't*.

a in third-person singular present tense.

1774 *Dunmore's War* 245 If Ammunition don't come soon, I will have no Argument that will have any force that will detain them. **c1844** Beckner *Shane Interview* 227 They may make as much fun of me as they please, it don't hurt me. **1861** *Chapman CW Letters* (Feb 2) you must not think hard of me if he dont com and see you. **1864** *Reese CW Letters* (April 3) my leg dont seem to mend vary fast the joint is vary stif. **1895** Murfree *Phantoms* 92 He don't take his wrath out on folkses' wallets; he grips thar throats, or teches the trigger o' his rifle. **1939** Hall *Coll* (Hazel Creek NC) It don't cost you much, about twelve dollars and a half. **1969** GSMNP-25 A sheep killer is usually a stray dog that don't have no home, so he grows up by hisself. **1977** Shackelford et al. *Our Appalachia* 287 A preacher gets in the stand and he don't make up what to preach, he don't think about what to preach. **1989** *Matewan OHP*-9 He don't know nothing about God. He might think he does, but he don't. **1998** *Dante OHP*-45 he's been out there all this time, about thirty-five years, and don't own anything. **2004** Fisher *Kettle Bottom* 50 That's got to mean something, don't it? **2011** *Massey Report* 17 Stanley replied, "It don't, does it?"

b as an auxiliary inverted with the subject in a negative statement or clause.

1927 Camak *June of Hills* 198 Don't nobody but them furren gals wear breeches. **1930** Armstrong *This Day and Time* 31 Don't none of 'em like to be stopped. **1939** Hall *Coll* (Deep Creek NC) There's an old house up here, but don't nobody live in it. **1961** Murry *Salt* 24 He's a ole feller an' has been stillin' for ten years I know of, an' there don't never nobody bother his still. **1972** *AOHP/LJC*-203 They don't need any help now. Don't nobody need nothing now. **1978** Montgomery *White Pine Coll* IV-4 I guess don't anybody do them anymore. **1984** Page and Wigginton *Foxfire Cookery* 168 Don't many people fry squash just one layer at a time in a pan and brown it on each side. **1988** Dickey and Bake *Wayfarer* 3 After I seen you walkin' down here, goin' the wrong way, on toward where don't nobody lives, I thought I'd just make a turn on the switch-back and meet up with you. **1990** Clouse *Wilder* 36 Don't nobody want a strike. That hurts us as much as it does the company. **1999** Morgan *Gap Creek* 65 Don't nobody give her orders but me.

c contracted to *n't* and attached to an interrogative form.

1883 Murfree *Old Sledge* 548 Ef yer air in sech a hurry, why'n't yer cut them thar kyerds for deal? **1941** Still *Troublesome Creek* 31 "Why'n't you kiver him?" he asked crossly. "He might a-been seen." **1955** Ritchie *Singing Family* 168 Jewel said whyn't we all sing a very long song and race to see if we could get done with the dishes before we got done with the song. **2000** Morgan *Mts Remember* 149 Whyn't you get the law after him in the first place?

3 *does*

a variant negative form *dudn*.

1984 Burns *Cold Sassy* 104 You need to understand that in Cold Sassy . . . [w]e . . . say . . . *dudn'* for *doesn't*.

b Contracted to *'s* and attached to an interrogative form.

1971 *AOHP/ALC*-377 Where's your sister live? **1973** Davis *'Pon My Honor* 77 What's he look like? **2014** Williams *Coll* What's he plan on doing—kegging out all summer?

4 *did*.

a as an auxiliary verb in a statement, often to express certainty about the following clause. [Editor's note: When occurring in a verb complement after a main clause with a negated verb, this usage may express a degree of uncertainty and can often be paraphrased with "exactly"; thus, I don't know now what they did use = I don't know now exactly what they used.]

1813 Hartsell *Memora* 123 ther was nine or ten Companeys thare, the Cane was so thick that we cold not Stand till the men Did cut it Down. **1862** *Roddie CW Letter* (April 7) [He] ses thay ar the best fixed people that ever did go on the field to fight. **1939** Hall *Coll* (Cherokee NC) That's about the best place ever I did live until I lived on Indian Creek. *Ibid.* (Cable Branch NC) I don't know how long we did stay there. **1942** (in **1987** Perdue *Outwitting Devil* 39) He had one brother an' he'd married an' moved way off summers. He didn't know jes 'zactly where he did live. **1971** *AOHP/ALC*-277 I don't know how many acres we did have, but we just had plenty of cows, mules, horses to plow. **1973** *AOHP/LJC*-296 I don't remember just how much we did get now, cut half the time. **1973** GSMNP-79:26 I could go over and over and tell so many things that did happen in the mountains. **1975** *AOHP/LJC*-384 Finally they went back, and I never did see nor hear tell of those men no more. They had some kind of secret ballot. I don't know how they did have it fixed. **1979** *Big South Fork OHP*-1 I couldn't tell you how hit did stay [in business]. **1985** Irwin *Alex Stewart* 124

I commenced making plows and I don't know how many I did make. **1991** Thomas *Sthn Appal* 87 They killed that bear, an' they didn't even have a gun. I don't know now what they did use. **1997** Andrews *Mountain Vittles* 40 That's how my folks always did save their seed to plant the next year. **2013** Shedlarz *Rosa Hicks* 3 We did have some special foods at Christmas time you didn't have at any other time.

b as variant past-participle form.

1862 *Councill CW Letters* (April 27) I halled out tweentey [= soldiers who have died of sickness] last weak an has did three in too dayes. **1873** Smith *Arp Peace Papers* 23 The thing could not be did in that brief interval. **1968** *Faith Healing* 62 [It's] close to fourty [sic] years I've did it. **1972** *AOHP/ALC-241* Have you ever did anything like that? **1980** Miles *Verbs in Haywood Co* 152 They might have did but I don't even know. **1983** *Dark Corner OHP-10A* They hadn't did that back [during the Depression by the CCC]. **1993** Burton *Take Up Serpents* 86 He's never did it no more. **2008** *Rosie Hicks* 4 Hit must have did after.

[DARE *do* v B6 past pple especially South, South Midland]

c inverted with the subject without *if* to introduce an adverbial clause expressing a conditional or contrary-to-fact reality (thus *did I get* = if I got). See also **can[1] B3**. [Editor's note: This usage does not occur in ATASC.]

1919 Combs *Word-List South* 293 Did I tell him, would he believe me? **1962** Dykeman *Tall Woman* 118 Did they know who the renegades were, they'd never tell me. **1966** Dykeman *Far Family* 262 Did some men know all they think they do, they'd be driving teams of their own instead of ground-hogging it around from one job to the next. **1978** Hiser *Quare Do's* 132 My cyores wouldn't work did I take pay, she said. **1980** Still *Run for Elbertas* 86 He'll pull a trick did it cost him his ears, and nobody on earth can stop him laughing. **1991** Still *Wolfpen Notebooks* 65 Back yonder when he got married and the preacher asked him did he take the woman for his lawful wedded wife, he said, "I do, I reckon."

5 *didn't.*

a variant past-tense forms *dint, ditn't.*

1940 Adams *Coll* 2315 [She] felt she was plain, old fashioned and had on her work dress, so she hid and dint come from the kitchen to meet him. **2005** Williams *Gratitude* 480 *I'll be blest* if she ditn't take ever last dime I had.

b as an auxiliary verb inverted with the subject of a clause.

1923 Montague *Today Tomorrow* 163 Every feller seen his own past, but couldn't see the t'other feller's; so didn't nobody know what it was ole Brother Mutters seen. **1953** Wharton *Dr Woman Cumberlands* 65 She cooked on it a day or two, but didn't nothin' taste like hit orter. **1969** *GSMNP-37:1:5* Didn't anybody have enough sense to teach us up here. **1981** *GSMNP-122:16* Didn't nobody up in there in Greenbrier know nothin' 'bout it till they run up on it. **1984** Smith *Oral History* 36 Didn't nobody know how he got that gal. **1991** Thomas *Sthn Appal* 181 Course everybody'd try to go to them works, if they could. Cause didn't nobody know whuther he'd haff to look to th' neighbors fer help, jist enny time. **1998** *Dante OHP-71* Didn't none of them didn't want to live on the farm.

6 *done.*

a (also *doed, doned, dun*) as a past-tense form.

1803 *Paw Paw Hollow Church Minutes* 9 The church met at Br. Ominets and after worship done no business. **1840** *McLean Diary* 67 The ice Done a Greadeal of mischhief. **1861** *Chapman CW Letters* (March 2) I will now tell you what i dun this morning. **1863** *Ibid.* (Dec 10) The rebel flag bearer planted his Collours on top of our Breast works but the minit he done that he fell lifeless to the ground. **1913** Kephart *Our Sthn High* 161 You say Washington done that? **1922** *TN CW Ques* 9 (Jefferson Co TN) Mother done all kinds house work including cooking spinning, sewing washing & mending. **1939** Hall *Coll* (Emerts Cove TN) Yeah, I think they done wrong running the boys out of here. **1953** Hall *Coll* (Bryson City NC) I lived at Proctor on Hazel Creek and done the most of my hunting out from that. **1969** *GSMNP-37:2:12–13* That's what we done and went on down there and stayed all night. **1977** McClelland *Wilson Douglas* 20 I've sacrificed a lot to play music. But it done me a lot of good. **1979** *Big South Fork OHP-4* I had a few that doed me thataway. **1984** *GSMNP-153* she done a lot of her canning on the wood stove. **1989** Landry *Smoky Mt Interviews* 194 Atter we got our wheat sowed and everything in the cove is when we done our bear hunting. **1998** *Dante OHP-61* We doned it [= the bathing] in the house through the winter. **2003** LaLone et al. *Farming Life* 318 He jumped out of a barn and done something to his heel.

b (also *dun*) as an auxiliary verb or adverb = completely, thoroughly; already. See also Grammar and Syntax §7.2.

(1) in phrase *done been* = have already been.

1957 Combs *Lg Sthn High: Word List* 31 = an elliptical expression much used. Ex.: "Won't you come in and eat a bite?" "No'm (No, Madam), I've done been (to supper)."

(2) followed by the past-tense form of a verb.

1975–76 Wolfram/Christian *WV Coll* 22 They let her up the second day [after giving birth], and when she come home the next day, she done had the fever. That's what you call the childbed fever, and that'll kill you. **1990** Clouse *Wilder* 118 It was me she loved, son. She done told me. **2004** Larimore *Bryson Seasons* 23 "I told you!" the deputy exclaimed. "I done told you! I ain't never seen nothin' like this here. Never!"

(3) followed by the past-participle form of a verb.

1824 Knight *Letter from KY* 106–7 Some words are used, even by genteel people, from their imperfect education, in a new sense; and others, by the lower classes in society, pronounced very uncouthly . . . did done do it, done done did it. **1858** (in **1974** Harris *High Times* 142) I'd a dun been outen the city while he wer still in reach ove a pound-rock. **1864** *Chapman CW Letters* (April 11) last year we was dun planted by the fiftenth of the month. **1864** *Warrick CW Letters* (April 8) I can tell you that they have Dun Stoped furlowing. **1873** Harney *Strange Land* 431 The use . . . of "done" and "gwine" as auxiliaries, is peculiar to the mountains. **1883** Murfree *Old Sledge* 552 "I done tole yer, Budd," turning again to Wray, "I'll put up the house an' land agin the truck." **1900** Harben *N GA Sketches* 50 I've done sold 'em an' used the money. **1910** Essary *TN Mtneers* 18 "Oh, I see," said the justice, "he's done been tried and sent to the pen for twenty years." **1929** (in **1952** Mathes *Tall Tales* 112) His paw an' maw has done give him up. **1939** Hall *Coll* (Copeland Creek TN) I never did say anything about this at all till after the White Caps was done put out. The Blue Bills cut them out. **1953** Wharton *Dr Woman Cumberlands* 64 Uncle Pink's done broke his laig. **1968** *Faith Healing* 67 They all said that he'd never live while they's a'totin' him out a'there. That he'd done bled all the blood there were in him out. **1972** GSMNP-86:28 I was done supposed to been there. **1973** GSMNP-87:2:11 My daddy bought the place, but the mill was done been washed away and the pieces was still there. **1979** *Big South Fork OHP*-10 Hit'd done already run into a couple of cars up here at Oneida Cross. **1983** *Dark Corner OHP*-4A I was done married then, but I just turned that little calf out and let him go. **1985** Irwin *Alex Stewart* 70 All the help I had has done gone and left us. **1991** Thomas *Sthn Appal* 255 I've done been over to th' sawmill and made arrangements for me some lumber. **2009** Burton *Beech Mt Man* 52 Before I got out in the yard, he done got to his car. **2012** Jourdan *Medicine Men* 114 Boy, you have done took the cake with this'n.

[DARE *do* v C5 chiefly South, South Midland]

(4) followed by an adjective or similar structure.

1890 Fruit *KY Words* 67 He is done gone. **1937** Hall Coll (Cades Cove TN) There weren't a sprig of fire in his place. The fire were done out. **1953** Hall Coll (Bryson City NC) We'd go out and holler for and see if we could hear 'em [= hunters] coming in anywhere. It was done dark then. **1961** *Coe Ridge OHP*-339B her husband was done dead as far as I can remember. She was always a widow as far as I can remember. **1969** GSMNP-25:2:10 The older ones was done through school and married. **1971** *Boogers* 36 One of'em had th'jug done full and th'other had it 'bout nearly full. **1980** Miles *Verbs in Haywood Co* 117 The others was done knee high when he planted them. **1983** Page and Wigginton *Aunt Arie* 6 I'd done eat and was done in th'bed and was just about ready t'go t'sleep. **2002** Rash *Foot in Eden* 89 It's done over and finished between us.

(5) followed by *and* + past participle.

1939 Hall Coll I done and eat [i.e. I ate]. *Ibid.* (White Oak NC) They shut the plant down until the crops is done and made. **1955** Ritchie *Singing Family* 54 I was about to bust out crying then, and I hollered, "I've done and seen him!" **1962** Rouse *Colorful Tint* In these parts, if you've done and done something, you haven't done it twice, it means you've already done it. **1969** GSMNP-46:11 He said "She's done and brought her second calf." **1974** Dabney *Mt Spirits* 129 You're done and gone, you see, before these other officers that is hid around up on the other hill can get down there.... You're done out of sight and gone. **1979** Slone *My Heart* 19 Cindy done and went off and fergit her baby.

[DARE *do* v C6 especially South Midland]

(6) followed by a present participle.

1813 Hartsell *Memora* 129 When we war done mustering, I went to whare Colonel Lillard and the General was standing. **1862** McFee *CW Letters* (Oct 10) the troops is don cuming hear now. **1863** Wilson *Confederate Private* 20 (May 30) when he was dun preachen then thay stept up an was married. **1864** *Forgotten Ancestors* (Jefferson Co) 1 tel Johnny to be a good boy and when I get dun feting rebs I will come home again. **1939** Hall Coll (Wears Cove TN) Before they got done buying, they felt pretty bad about it. **1973** GSMNP-70:1:12 When the Little River people got done logging up there. ... [Uncle Levi Trentham] bought all that territory in there, and his boys built and settled up. **1979** *Big South Fork OHP*-10 This place up here was done washing out but they got over it. **1983** Pyle *CCC 50th Anniv* B:3:3 When you got done smoking, you didn't throw that old cigarette out like that. **1993** Burton *Take Up Serpents* 14 [They] said that she was done getting stiff, and that she was cold, she wasn't breathing, no heartbeat, no pulse.

(7) See citation.

1911 Shearin *E KY Word-List* 538 *done* = used idiomatically in the expression, "I wasn't done it." = "I was not the one who did it."

B *verb* Senses.

1 See **doing.**

2 (also *do mean, do to*) To (mis)treat, behave unfairly or maliciously toward (someone); to swindle, cheat.

1901 Harben *Westerfelt* 2 John Westerfelt has done you exactly as he has many a other gal. **1910** Weeks *Barbourville Word List*: *do* = to treat badly: "It wasn't fair for you to do me like that." **1935** Sheppard *Cabins in Laurel* 62 Doc Hoppas, the son of a Union soldier, says, "It makes me mad to even think of the Home Guard for the way they done my daddy and my grandmammy." **1940** Haun *Hawk's Done* 10 He done Tiny the same way. **1973** GSMNP-83:18 I've got two little girls buried there, and we ain't been there in six or seven years [because] they wouldn't let you park there. They done so dirty. **1976** *Bear Hunting* 260 He learned me all I know. And that's the way I did that boy of mine. **1977** Moore *Jenks* 30 Well, that's just the way we did, you see. **1979** *Big South Fork OHP*-10 That's the way he done him. **1983** Page and Wigginton *Aunt Arie* 168 I don't know what makes'em do me that way. **1991** Thomas *Sthn Appal* 115 That's th' way I did when they come in. **1993** Page and Smith *Foxfire Toys and Games* 114 Momma didn't do us that way. **1993** *Stories 'neath Roan* 19 He done a lot more people that way after he would spend the night with them. **1996–97** Montgomery Coll: *do dirty* = to cheat on a spouse or lover (Ledford). **2004** Fisher *Kettle Bottom* 18 No telling how they'll do you. **2008** *Rosie Hicks* 4 I didn't know you done Daddy that bad. *Ibid.* Never do me like that no more.

[DARE *do* v D2 South, South Midland]

3 To suffice, be sufficient for.

1863 *Warrick CW Letters* (Aug 9) we could get along very well if we got enough to eat. But we dont get half enough to do. **1863** Wilson *Confederate Private* 32 (Nov 14) if pap has eny pork for sale you must by it or enough to do you and the children. **1931** Goodrich *Mt Homespun* 40 Ever since my old man died, I've made enough corn to do me, and sweetening too. **c1950** Adams *Grandpap* 84 He was awful nearsighted, Will was. Couldn't see anything, to do any good, more than six inches from the end of his nose. **1964** Roberts *Hell-Fer-Sartin* 153 [He] sold the hide for four dollars, and had possum meat enough till he dried it and it done him all summer. **1975** GSMNP-59:18 Everybody made a good cane patch, and they had put up enough syrup to do, they figured. **1984** Page and Wigginton *Foxfire Cookery* 191 That makes fourteen biscuits, and that does us all day. **1993** *Stories 'neath Roan* 24 My dad would haul in enough wood in the fall to do for several months.

4 To go about one's accustomed activities.

1956 McAtee *Some Dial NC* 12 = perform housework: "She helped me to do." **1971** *Granny Women* 253 [Doctors will] have'em up again and goin' and doin' and th'next day send'em home.

5 To prepare (a meal).

1944 Justus *Billy and Bones* 45 Aunt Mary came to the kitchen door to say that supper was done.

C *noun* See **do one's do.**

do about (also *do around*) *verb phrase* To busy (oneself), bustle about.

1910 Cooke *Power and Glory* 7 I wisht I could git up from here and do about. **1956** McAtee *Some Dial NC* 12 = engage in earnestly; keep busy. **1998** Montgomery *Coll*: *do around* (known to Adams, Brown, Bush, Cardwell, Oliver, Weaver), = can also be used to describe busying oneself with tasks in a slow, methodical manner as well as a bustling manner (Ledford); She was doing around the kitchen all day (Norris).

[DARE *do around* v phr South, South Midland]

do a dido See **dido 1, 2.**

do a gee-haw *verb phrase* To get along well with one another. Same as **gee.**

1967 Fetterman *Stinking Creek* 80 We lived together forty-five years, but we just couldn't do a gee-haw. We even got a divorce.

do around See **do about.**

dob *noun* See citations.

2005 Williams *Gratitude* 490 = a medium amount, more than a *dab*. A *dob* is a wad or amount you just reach and get in, or with, your hand—like put a *dob* of lard in the flour for biscuits. **2013** Venable *How to Tawlk* 12 Hit don't take but a little dob of Preparation H to cam yore asteroids.

[alteration of *dab*]

dobbly *adjective* Frail, unsteady on one's feet.

1969–70 Stubbs *Mountain-Wise* (Dec–Jan) 16 One day we met a man named Bruce on the street and inquired about the health of his elderly mother. He replied: "My Maw is a-gittin' a little *dobbly*."

dobie *noun* See citation.

1976 Dillon *They Died* 71 In early days of coal mining, the workman had to shoot his own coal, i.e., he had to drill or bore a hole into the solid coal six feet or more [and] place in dynamite or black powder charge to the farthest depths. He inserted a fuse from the explosive to extend to the outside of the hole, then he tamped the shot or "dobied" the hole.

dock *noun* An edible, perennial wild green (*Rumex* spp) with medicinal uses. See also **narrow dock, speckled dick, yellow dock.**

1943 Hannum *Mt People* 113 A poultice of dock leaves could draw the soreness out of boils. [**1971** Krochmal et al. *Medicinal Plants Appal* 218 In Appalachia the root is placed in vinegar and the wash is used to treat ringworm; the leaves are used in a poultice to treat hives. The Indians used the root for a yellow dye.] **1975** Riedl *House Customs* 49 [At a house raising] there were chicken and dumplings, beans, "hanover" (rutabaga), corn, rhubarb, greens such as poke salet and dock, pumpkin pie, milk, and jellies.

doctor *verb* See also **doctoring, doctor out.**

1 (also *doctor on, doctor up*) To render (a person, animal, or ailment) medical treatment; to serve as a doctor.

1863 Lister *CW Letters* (Dec 14) I wod Wate a while and ef it wasent mending I wood Get Mr lands to doctter it. **1863** *Vance Papers* (Aug 16) I want you to let me stay at home awhile and be doctord up and without being interupted if you pleas. **1910** Cooke *Power and Glory* 115 If we fell sick they'd doctor us for little or nothin'. **1937** Hall *Coll* (Catons Grove TN) For fever we generally had a doctor, [but mostly] people doctored their own selfs. **1940** Haun *Hawk's Done* 7 If it got so I couldn't doctor folks I might not ever see anybody. **1949** Arnow *Hunter's Horn* 111 She's been wanting some good safe whisky spirits to doctor Deb's croup. **1961** *Coe Ridge OHP*-335B She'd doctor all these women when they give birth. **1969** GSMNP-38:107 [He] just went and got some whiskey, you know, and doctored them himself. **1973** GSMNP-78:8 He had to decide whether to take Jasper back home and doctor him up and try to cure him and save his life or whether to knock him in the head with a pine knot and kill him. **1977** *Shenandoah OHC* 136 When we lived back there, they'd always doctor on their own self. **1985** Irwin *Alex Stewart* 139 She put her hand on the girl and said a few words and directly she had her doctored. **1997** GSMNPCOHP-3:13 They didn't have nothing to doctor that kind of flu. **2012** Milnes *Signs Cures Witchery* You have to doctor the baby. *Ibid.* Dovie doctors for witches, meaning she uses methods she sees as being sanctioned by the Bible to remove and reverse spells she feels are put on her and her family by other people. **2013** Shedlarz *Rosa Hicks* 23 She doctored on the horse's sores.

[DARE *doctor* v 2 chiefly South Midland]

2 In phrase *doctor with* = to treat with, apply as a remedy to.

1939 Hall *Coll* (Emerts Cove TN) Why, she'd doctor with boneset tea. **1969** GSMNP-44:14 Back them days doctors didn't have much to doctor with, and old John doctored old man Conner and he just looked like he was going to die. **1973** GSMNP-76:35 They was lots of old medicine they had to doctor with. **1989** *Matewan OHP*-9 Us older ones doctored with whiskey. Well we still do, if I take the flu of a wintertime, I get me two lemons and boil them, and ginger to put in it and put a little whiskey in it. **1996** GSMNPCOHP-1:4 About the only thing that we had in here to doctor with was whiskey.

3 To take medicine, receive medical treatment or care.

1865 *Joyce CW Letters* (March 12) I have got the old Each the wost sort tell thim they must bring Down me a pot full of poke root for I think I Shal haft to be gin to Docter fort it. **1976** Garber *Mountain-ese* 23 I've been doctorin' fer a cold almost all winter. **1996–97** Montgomery *Coll* (known to Brown, Cardwell, Jones, Ledford, Norris, Oliver).

[DARE *doctor* v 1 chiefly South, South Midland, New England]

doctor book *noun* A medical textbook.

1958 Sanderson *County Scott* 178 According to "Granny's" advice, there are plenty of cures for sickness that are not in the "doctor books."

doctor cow *verb phrase* To serve as a veterinarian.

1973 GSMNP-76:32 I had him doctor cow for me, and Mack Whaley did up there [too].

doctor dentist *noun* A dentist. See also **tooth dentist**, **tooth jumper**.

1978 *Smokies Heritage* 135 She had to wait until her baby was born and a month old, then we made the long trip to the doctor-dentist. **1996–97** Montgomery *Coll* (known to Brown).

doctoring *noun* The practice of medicine, treatment with medicine. See also **doctor 1**, **doctor 2**, **witch doctor**.

1929 (in **1952** Mathes *Tall Tales* 100) Doctorin's a gift, I say, which them that's got it don't need no schoolin', an' them that ain't, schoolin' wouldn't do 'em no good nohow! **1939** Hall *Coll* (Catons Grove TN) Back in my young days we couldn't get no doctors them days hardly ever, and we had to do our own doctoring and we learnt up on these herbs. **1956** Hall *Coll* (Big Bend NC) We didn't have no doctorin' there in the Big Bend. **1973** *AOHP/ASU*-233 You did most of your own doctoring, and when they died you just kept them at home and fixed them theirselves. **1977** Madden and Jones *Mt Home* 6 Margaret Jane, no doubt, learned her "doctoring" from her mother who was a midwife and "herb doctor."

doctor man *noun* A physician.

1908 Smith *Reminiscences* 421 Even in the dialect of the people one is often reminded of Homeric speech. For example, the mountaineer says not simply "doctor" or "widow," but "doctor-man," "widow-woman," "cow-brute," "apple-fruit," just as the Homeric man three thousand years ago spoke of a "healer-man," a "widow-woman," a "lady-mistress," a "master-lord." **1937** Wilson *Folklore SE KY* 32. **1940** Haun *Hawk's Done* 7 Of course, there is that town doctor man that lives in Del Rio. Folks say he don't know much. **1943** Justus *Bluebird* 80 I don't need and I don't want a doctor man!

doctor medicine (also *doctor stuff*) *noun* Medicinal remedies employed by a licensed physician, as opposed to home remedies or herb treatments such as those provided by an **herb doctor**.

1889 Murfree *Broomsedge Cove* 223 The rest of 'em in the Cove better not git sick soon; no mo' doctor-stuff whar that kem from. **1910** Thompson *Highlanders* 22 Many herbs of medicinal properties grow in abundance in these regons—even to this day the "yarb doctor" is not so uncommon ... herbs the essence of which are often used as simple remedies by these people, and frequently with more effect than "doctor stuff," as the people sometimes derisively refer to the medicine given by practicing physicians. **1917** Kephart *Word-List* 411 *doctor medicine* = differentiated from home remedies. **c1940** Simms *Coll* One good laugh is better than ten dose of doctor medicine. **1952** Wilson *Folk Speech NC* 533 *doctor medicine* = medicine prescribed or given by a doctor. **1973** GSMNP-86:40 I didn't never use no doctor medicine till after, here for the last late years. **1981** Brewer *Wonderment* 197 I never took a dose of doctor medicine till I was fifty-five years old. **2003** Cooper *Gathering Memories* 44 "Doctor medicine" might have its place, but home remedies were considered more reliable and available.

[DARE *doctor medicine* n southern Appalachians]

doctor on See **doctor 1**.

doctor out *verb phrase* To dispense (medicine).

2011 Shearer *Moonshine Trade* 160 Doctor Elijah was doctoring out medicine in his young days.

doctor stuff See **doctor medicine**.

doctor up See **doctor 1**.

doctor with See **doctor 2**.

doctor woman *noun* Traditionally, a midwife or **herb doctor**; occasionally, a female physician.

1953 Wharton *Dr Woman Cumberlands* 50 Jess, you take my jenny and carry the doctor woman back to Pleasant Hill when she's done seen yore paw. **1972** Cooper *NC Mt Folklore* 91 = a midwife or female herb doctor. **1982** Powers and Hannah *Cataloochee* 245 Grannywoman, a term often used in the mountains, was not used by Fannie Hannah, who preferred to be known as a doctor-woman. **1997** Montgomery *Coll* = term has both meanings (Brown).

[DARE *doctor woman* n 2 "midwife" South, South Midland]

dod- See **dad-**.

doddle *verb*

1 To toddle, move slowly about; hence adjective *doddling*. See also **dobbly**, **doddly**.

1952 Giles *40 Acres* 202 He swings his arms high and his head doddles on his neck. **1957** Combs *Lg Sthn High: Word-List* 30 *doddlin'* = tolerably well, in answer to a greeting.

[Web3 *doddle* v 1 now dialect]

2 To nod or shake (one's head).

1940 Stuart *Trees of Heaven* 216 Anse doddles his head as the lightning flashes. **1943** Stuart *Private Tussie* 114 Grandpa and Grandma went around all day a-doddlin' their heads. They were so sleepy they couldn't stay awake.

[Web3 *doddle* v 2 chiefly Midland]

doddly *adjective* Especially of a person: unsteady, shaky. See also **doddle**.

c1960 Wilson *Coll* = shaky, unsteady. **1983** Broaddus *Estill Co KY Word List* 37 = shaky, unsteady. **1994–96** Montgomery *Coll* (known to Adams, Cardwell, Jones, Ledford, Norris, Oliver, Shields).

[DARE *doddly* adj South Midland]

dodge

A (also *dodge about, dodge out*) *verb, verb phrase* To avoid, especially to elude capture or conscription during the Civil War by living crudely in remote country.

1863 *Reese CW Letters* (Feb 26) I will Cum home any how if you think we can meck out By my do[d]ging A Baut to ceep out of the way. **1863** *Wiseman CW Letters* (March 16) I inqurd of thes mens authority when I was in Knox ville the other day and they are not known By the goverment they are conscripts from East Tenn that are trading Back wards and fort[h] to dodg. **1915** Hall *Autobiog Claib Jones* 14 I took to the brush and began dodging for my life. **1969** GSMNP-46:24 They dodged out till after the war was over, and they come in and give up. **1973** GSMNP-2:7 These two people that was killed was kind of dodgin' out.

B *noun* in phrase *on the dodge* = avoiding or hiding out from the authorities.

1917 Kephart *Word-List* 411 *on the dodge* = given to dodging or evading, especially the police. "His boy was sorter *on the dodge*."

dodge about See **dodge A**.

dodge bread See **dodger**.

dodge out See **dodge**.

dodger (also *dodge bread, dogger*) *noun* Cornmeal hand-fashioned into a round cake to be fried in a pan or baked in an oven; such a cake. Also called **corn cake**, **corn dodger**, **corn patty**, **hobby**, **plain dodger**.

1853 Ramsey *Annals* 719 Mixed with cold water, [cornmeal] is, at once, ready for the cook . . . put in an oven, and covered over with a heated lid, it is called, if in a large mass, a pone or loaf, if in smaller quantities, dodgers. **1862** *Robinson CW Letters* (July 18) me & J. P. Freeman went out a wensday while we was at the River & baught 4 doggers of corn Bread for 5 cts. **1890** Fruit *KY Words* 64 We have what we call "plain dodger," in which the meal is made up with cold water into pones; then, "shortened dodger," in which the meal is made up with lard, or grease of some kind. Our "crackling bread" is a corn-dodger made up with cracklings. **1966** Dakin *Vocab Ohio River Valley* 316 The names *corn cake, hoe cake, corn (bread) dodger* (occasionally *dodge bread* in Kentucky), *johnny cake* (only in Ohio and eastern Indiana), and (very rarely) *hobby* are used above the river as well as in Kentucky. **1982** Slone *How We Talked* 36 *dodger* = a pancake of cornbread baked by placing it directly on the top of the stove. **1989** Smith *Flyin' Bullets* 54 The children's lunch basket, or pail, might consist of a "dodger" of cornbread, onion, cold sweet potato, and an apple, or maybe a piece of apple stack cake.

[DARE *dodger* n[1] probably Scots *dadge* "a bannock," perhaps influenced by Scots *dodge* "a pretty large cut of any kind of food" (DSL) or *dodgel* "a large piece or lump" (DSL)]

dodie See **doted**.

do dirty See **do B3**.

doed See **do A6a**.

does See **do A3**.

do for *verb phrase* To support, take care of, assist.

1910 Cooke *Power and Glory* 10–11 He has to have somebody to do for him. **1993** Cunningham *Sthn Talk* 41 You won't find no finer feller than Morris Gallion. He allus does for old folks an' widders an' won't take nothin' fer it. **2000** Morgan *Mts Remember* 63 It was the way his brothers had run over him, and the way Mother and Father had always expected him to do for them. **2002** Ogle *Remembrances* 52 Then he would wade the deep snow back up Oakley Branch where he lived to do for his own family.

dog[1] *noun* (also *dogged* adjective) Used to form a mild oath. See also **dog my cats**, **I'll be dog**.

1852 *Carson Letter* 147 Now dog bite you John, I want you to write to me and tell me all the news and a little more and I will do the same with you. **1927** Montague *Funny Bone* 333 You'd think it would be a powerful awesome sight, but dogged if it tuck them two fellers thataway. **1996** Woodring *Times Gone By* 17 While he uz gone a puff of wind come and got that dogged thing to turning and like to beat me to death.

dog[2]

A *noun*

1 See **dog iron(s)**, **iron dogs**, **never say dog**.

2 Any of various implements used in logging. See citations. See also **dog down**, **dogger**[2], **hammer dog**.

1964 Clarkson *Lumbering in WV* 360 = various pointed pieces of metal attached to rings or chains and used in constructing log rafts and booms; also = a hook on the carriage of a band sawmill used to hold logs; also = a short, heavy piece of steel, bent and pointed at one end and with an eye or ring at the other. **1994** Farwell and Buchanan *Logging Terms* = a spike on a frame that helped control a log for sawing; the spikes were arranged on a circular frame.

3 See citation.

1949 Maurer *Argot of Moonshiner* 9 Same as *bull dog*.

B *verb*

1 See **bulldog**.

2 To hunt or pursue (game) with dogs.

1937 Wilburn *Notes* (Big Creek NC) Neither my father, Joe Phillips, nor my grandfather, Tobe Phillips, would dog bears, but would always still-hunt.

3 To cheat (someone).

1972 *AOHP/LJC-259* They just dogged the old people out of all the, all of it [= land] and they got it.

do-gadget *noun* An object without a name.

1987 Young *Lost Cove* 84 Fonzer Hicks was listening while he whittled away on a do-gadget.

dog alley See **dogtrot**.

dogbit *adjective* Bitten by a dog. For similar forms, see **bite A2**.

1920 Ridley *Sthn Mtneer* 85 "Guess I know when I'm dog-bit," said the complainant, "an' yore dog done it." **1934–47** *LAMSAS Appal* (Madison Co NC, Swain Co NC). **1939** Hall *Coll* (Tobes Creek NC) He got dog-bit in Asheville. **1953** Atwood *Verbs East US* 6 An interesting geographical phenomenon is the combination *dogbit* ("he was dogbit," or "he got dogbit"), which covers the South Midland and adjoining parts of the South. . . . In W.Va. south of the Kanawha and in s.w. Va. it is practically universal. **1978** Slone *Common Folks* 208 Not even my father could have touched [the guarded quilt] without getting dog bit. **1985** Irwin *Alex Stewart* 241 Twice in my life I've borrowed a little money out of the bank. The first time was when I got mad dog bit.

dog branch *noun* See citation.

1968 *DARE Survey* (Brasstown NC) = an unpaved road.

dogbread *noun* Baked corn bread fed to dogs, variously made. See citation.

1994–97 Montgomery *Coll* = cornbread made from plain meal without salt, soda, milk, or baking powder (Adams), = made of old or weavel meal, meat scraps, and bran, and baked for dog or hog food only (Brown), = cornbread sometimes that was more gritty and had more lard than normal (Cardwell), = regular cornbread cooked in a pan to feed the hunting dogs (Norris). **2014** *Blind Pig* (Jan 2) Over the years I've made "dog bread" when I couldn't afford to buy or ran out of dog food and had to make do. They really liked that bread with gravy over the top.

[DARE *dogbread* n South, South Midland]

dog days *noun* The annual period of hot, sultry weather in July and August, with which various superstitions and ailments are traditionally associated. See 2007 citations. See also **dog-day sore**.

1832 *McLean Diary* (July 30) the dog days set in early this year. **1961** Miller *Pigeon's Roost* (July 13) The old-timey date for dog days to begin is July 3rd. There is two other dates which is July 4th and 14th, but the 3rd day date is the most adhered to and dog days is the only superstition sign notice that is yet given in several almanacs and calendars. One adage that goes along with many other old sayings about dog days is that if it rains the first four days of it we will have plenty of rain and if there be no rain it will be hot and dry weather. There is another saying that if chickens is hatched out during dog days they will not live. **2007** Farr *My Appalachia* 66 The dog days of summer runs from July until mid-August, when the Dog Star rises and sets with the sun. . . . It is a season of mold, mildew, and the pestilence of stagnant water. Mama and Granny Brock warned us about dog days. We children were not to wade in the creeks because the stagnant water would make "fall sores" on our legs. I remember how impossible it was to stay out of the creek during the torrid days of summer, when every bug bite and scratch turned into a sore. . . . We were told that dogs went mad during dog days, so we were terrified of any strange dog that happened to wander our way. **2007** Milnes *Signs Cures Witches* 35 One aspect of the astrological calendar year that is particularly observed by country people is the arrival of dog days. They "come in" about July 3, when the "dog star" (Sirius) appears to rise with the sun. It is the brightest star in the constellation, Canis Major. The weather on this day will foretell the weather for the growing season or the remaining period of dog days, which lasts forty days. If there is even the slightest rainfall on this day, it bodes well for the crops. Beyond this, it is believed that birds and snakes "go blind" during dog days, and that snakes are particularly venomous. At the same time, hawks whistle and the dog star "rules."

[from its association with the ascendancy of Sirius, the "dog star"]

dog-day sore *noun* See citation. See also **dog days**, **fall sore**.

1933 Miller *Healing Gods* 469 It is still common to hear impetigo contagiosa spoken of even by physicians as "dog-day sores" because of its prevalence during the forty days that the dog star Sirius is in the ascendancy.

dog down *verb phrase* See citation. See also **dog² A2**.

1998 Farwell *Logging Terms* = to hook chains to a log; fasten a dog hook to a chain on a log.

dog fennel *noun* The dillweed plant (*Anthemis cotula*) used to spice food and as a medicine. Also called **dilley weed**, **fennel weed**.

1866 Smith *So Called* 35 Flowers have bloomed sweetly . . . dog fennel has yallered the ground. **1937** Hall *Coll* (Cosby TN) Dog fennel for rheumatiz. **1942** Thomas *Blue Ridge* 107 A sure cure for stomach trouble is a tea made from dog fennel. **1968** Wilson *Local Plants* 323 = Anthemis cotula. Dogfennel tea was a cure-all for internal upsets. **1971** *AOHP/ALC-147* If we was cramping, she would take dog fennel and make tea from it and give it to us for cramps. **1987** Davenport *Pine Grove* 27 A cure for rheumatism is a tea made from dog fennel. **1998** Montgomery *Coll* = same as *fennel weed* (Cardwell).

[DARE *dog fennel* n 1 chiefly South Midland, South]

dog for *verb phrase* To serve (someone) servilely.

1940 Haun *Hawk's Done* 51 Her and Barshia made things together, and me and Amy got to rest from being bossed about and dogging for him.

dogged See **dog¹**.

dogger¹ See **dodger**.

dogger² *noun* See citation.

1994 Farwell and Buchanan *Logging Terms* = in logging, a man who uses spikes or *dogs* to fasten a log on a carriage carrying the log to the saw.

doggins *noun* See citation.

1949 Maurer *Argot of Moonshiner* 9 = liquor obtained from used barrels by the process of sweating.

dog head *noun* See citations.

1968 *End of Moonshining* 100 *dog heads* = when the beer is almost ready to run, it will boil up of its own accord in huge, convulsive bubbles which follow each other one at a time. **1974** Maurer and Pearl *KY Moonshine* 117 = a large viscous bubble that forms in the still just before the cap is sealed.

dog hobble *noun* A common evergreen shrub (*Leucothoe* spp) with dense, tangled limbs and branches; the leaves and flowers are sometimes gathered for sale as an ornamental decoration. Also called **bear hobble**, **drooping leucothoe**, **fetterbush 1**, **leucotha**, **shinhobble**, **switch ivy**.

[**1901** Lounsberry *Sthn Wild Flowers* 389 The shrub's interwoven, thick growth makes it impossible at times for a dog to pass through.] **1926** Hunnicutt *Twenty Years* 124 This gave the coon a minute start and it went into the dog hobble. . . . Dog hobble is an evergreen vine, and I began to think that she was not going to catch up with the coon at all. **1963** Lord *Blue Ridge* 22–23D The dog hobble is the exasperation of the bear hunter and his dogs. The bear can "brute" his way through the bramble of bushes, but dogs and hunters get all hobbled up. The leaves and blossoms of dog-hobble resemble those of fetterbush, but each plant groups its own way. Fetterbush is an upright shrub; dog-hobble is low and fern-like. [**1970** Campbell et al. *Smoky Mt Wildflowers* 64 The strongly scented white flowers hang in clusters and appear in May and June. . . . In pre-park days, when bear hunting was practiced, the heavy bears could escape pursuing dogs by forcing their way through dense thickets of these shrubs, whereas the dogs became "hobbled" by the tangled growth.] **2013** DeLozier and Jourdan *Back Seat* 20 The bad news was that we were nearly surrounded by an impenetrable thicket of leucothe shrubs. The locals called them *dog hobble* and *witch hobble*.

[DARE *dog hobble* n 1 chiefly southern Appalachians]

doghole *noun* A primitive coal mine with a small opening. Also called **house coal mine**, **scab hole**.

1943 Korson *Coal Dust* 4 Some farmers . . . operated small mines variously called "country banks," "wagon mines," "dog holes," "gopher holes," or "father-and-son" mines. **1973** Preston *Bituminous Term* 34 = a very small mine operated by a few men, usually taking coal which lies very near the surface. Also known as a *house coal mine* or a *punch mine*. **1974** Murray *Down to Earth* 108 They're called dog holes because you stay on all fours in low coal and they're only knee high to a dog. Hell, a dog wouldn't go in one. **2002** Armstead *Black Days* 243 = [a] small, privately owned mine in which the operator can choose to deny his employees UMW affiliation. **2006** Mooney *Lg Coal Mining* 1028 Many [coal-mining] terms make use of analogies to nature or to animals. . . . A "dog hole" is a small mine, generally unsafe and often non-union (thus sometimes called a "scab mine").

[from the appearance of such a mine, which has a hole so small only a dog could enter]

dog iron(s) (also *dogs*) *noun* A frame or stand, typically with two supports, for burning wood in a fireplace. According to 1983 Pederson *East TN Folk Speech*, *dog irons* is the most common term for the fireplace object in East Tennessee. Also called **fire dog(s)**, **iron dogs**, **log dogs**, **pig irons**.

1867 Harris *Sut Lovingood* 92 Clapshaw's ole mam wer es deaf es a dogiron. **1915** Dingus *Word-List VA* 182 *dog-arns* = fire irons. **1934–47** *LAMSAS Appal*: *dog irons* = attested by 50/148 speakers (33.7%) from WV, 15/20 (75%) from VA, 11/37 (29.7%) from NC, 5/14 (35.7%) from SC, and 1/12 (8.3%) from GA; *dogs* = attested by 19/148 speakers (12.8%) from WV, 1/20 (5%) from VA, 1/37 (2.7%) from NC, 1/14 (7.1%) from SC, and 1/12 (8.3%) from GA. **1938–46** Oliver *Fifty Years* 5 If the torch began to get dim, we would snub it on the dog irons to remove the burned coals, like snubbing the ashes from a cigarette. **1946** Nixon *Glossary VA Words* 20 *dog irons* = iron utensils used to support wood in a fireplace . . . common from the Blue Ridge westward. **1949** Kurath *Word Geog East US* 51 The andirons in the fireplace are generally known as *fire dogs*, *dogs* or *dog irons* in the greater part of the South, the South Midland, and in southwestern Pennsylvania. **1963** Edwards *Gravel* 92 He buried the potatoes in a deep bed of hot ashes between the dog irons, and we settled back to wait for them to bake. **1966** Dakin *Vocab Ohio River Valley* 34 The predominant *dog irons* of the South Midland is the most common term among those who do not usually say *andirons*, but *fire dogs* competes on about equal terms in Kentucky east of the Green-Barren River excluding the Bluegrass. **1968** Wilson *Folklore Mammoth Cave* 33 [*Andirons* is] always known, but the common term is *dogirons*, with *firedogs*, *fireirons*, and *dogs* sometimes heard. **1978** Reese *Speech NE Tenn* 29 *dog irons* = attested by 9/12 (75%) speakers. **1986** Pederson et al. *LAGS*: *dog irons* = attested by 39/60 interviewees (65%) from E TN and 7/35 (20%) from N GA; 46/283 of all LAGS interviewees (16.2%) attesting term were from Appalachia; *dogs* (Sullivan Co TN, Lumpkin Co GA). **1995** Montgomery *Coll*: *dog irons* = common term for andirons (Cardwell). **1997** *Dante OHP-14* Fire logs . . . was huge. You put one [log] way back in the back, you know, and you'd put the smaller ones in front on the dog irons.

[Web3 *dog iron* n 1 South and Midland; DARE *dog iron* n 1 chiefly South, South Midland]

dog-mean *adjective* Malicious, spiteful; hence noun *dog-meanness*.

1896 Fox *Vendetta* 122 "Y'ure mean, Jas Lewallen," she cried, hotly; "that's whut ye air, mean, dog-mean." **1914** Furman *Sight* 70 I just slid right down thar on my unworthy knees . . . and with bitter tears beseeched of her to forgive and forgit my hard-heartedness and stone-blindness and dog-meanness. **1927** Furman *Lonesome Road* 10 Hit was dog mean of me to let you. I won't let you no more.

dog my cats (also *dog my hide*) *interjection* Used as a mild oath expressing amazement, surprise, indignation, etc.

1941 Stuart *Men of Mts* 27 Dog my hide if it ain't old Dusty Boone. **1956** McAtee *Some Dial NC* 12 *dog my cats* = a mild imprecation. **1957** Combs *Lg Sthn High: Idioms* 14b Dog my cats if he didn't thrash me! **1998** Montgomery *Coll*: *dog my cats* (known to Brown, Cardwell); *dog my hide* (known to Ledford, Oliver, Weaver).

[DARE *dog my cats* interj chiefly South, South Midland]

dog of one's own trot *noun phrase* A person of independent mind or ways.

1956 Hall *Coll* (Gatlinburg TN) Sam is his own man. He is a dog of his own trot.

do good *verb phrase* To have success, be proficient.

1935 Sheppard *Cabins in Laurel* 139 They had lots of guns and ammunition, but they couldn't shoot to do any good. **1937** Hall *Coll* (Collins Creek NC) The fish ain't a-bitin' to do no good. **1939** Hall *Coll* (Deep Creek NC) [We] had a bear fight, but the dogs lit across the mountains an' went into Tennessee. [We] didn't do no good a-bear-huntin'. **c1950** Adams *Grandpap* 84 He was awful nearsighted, Will was. Couldn't see anything, to do any good, more than six inches from the end of his nose. **1978** Montgomery *White Pine Coll* X-2 I never could write to do no good. **1989** *Matewan OHP*-11 All at once it seemed like that Ackerman couldn't do no good with him.

dog pecker gnat *noun* An unspecified variety of gnat.

2009 Sutton *Me and Likker II* 207 When one of them Dog Pecker Gnats find[s] you tempering a run of likker they will go back and tell their Damn Buddies what they found and By-God there will come 5 hundred more. In the summer time I bet you I have seed 2 thousand damn gnats fly in a tub of likker.

dog pelter *noun* Used as a term of contempt for a public official or military officer. See 1944 citation.

1859 Taliaferro *Fisher's River* 232 Sich a onhuman man can't git my vote fur dog-pelter. **1862** *Reese CW Letters* (Oct 29) I dont like to taulk ABout my offficers But I hav hearn lots of our men say that the Colonel Cood not Be Elected fur dog Pilter. **1863** *Lister CW Letters* (Nov 8) ther isent a Officer in the redgment thats fit for a Dog pelter no how. **1944** Laughlin *Word-List Buncombe Co* 25 = a term of contempt; an officer of extremest inconsequence. My father used to say: "I wouldn't vote for a Democrat for a dog-pelter." **c1960** Wilson *Coll* = an imaginary worthless official; a fling at some self-important officer.

[DARE *dogpelter* n chiefly South Midland]

dog run See **dogtrot**.

dogs See **dog iron(s)**.

dog tick *noun* A castor bean.

1939 Still *Twelve Pears* 16 Hain't everybody breathes till their veins get blue as dog-tick stalks. **1940** Still *River of Earth* 18 You ought to plant a leetle dogtick around. Hit's the best mole-bane I ever heered tell of.

dogtrot (also *dog alley*, *dog run*) *noun* A roofed passageway between two enclosed parts of a cabin (the kitchen/living room and the sleeping quarters); by extension = a house with such a passageway. The construction does not always reflect an original design, as a second room (or **house**) is sometimes built and joined to a preexisting one, creating a wide shelter from the elements for both people and canines and a space to store firewood, tools, furniture, etc. Also called **hallway**, **through C3**, **turkey trot**. See also **double cabin**, **upper dogtrot**.

c1900 (in **1997** Stoddart *Quare Women* 253) This has been his home all his life, and in his early days it must have been a pretentious one, as there were two rooms and a "dog run" between. **1901** McClintock *KY Mts* 11 After the one-room cabin comes the two-room. It consists, sometimes, of two rooms under one roof, with an open space between, called a "dog-trot." **1937** Eaton *Handicrafts* 48 [In the early development of the log cabin] came the more adequate but still simple form of two rooms with a loft over each, the rooms separated by a covered passageway from three to eight feet wide called a "dog-trot." **1948** Dick *Dixie Frontier* 28 After a time, as his family increased, the squatter who stayed in the area and became prosperous built a second cabin and connected the two by a covered passage eight or ten feet wide. This, commonly known as the dogtrot, was a cool place for the family to eat in summer. **1961** Medford *History Haywood Co* 75 Another type sometimes seen was the "dog-trot house." This was really two houses, since the smaller one (the kitchen) was in line with the "big house," the end doors facing each other about four feet apart. This space was bridged by a broad slab or strong boards, so crossing from one house into the other was easy. The dogs would often lie on this connecting board-walk, would trot across it from one house to the other—hence, "dog-trot house." **1968** Glassie *Material Folk Cult* 89 At about . . . 1825, the dogtrot house, loved by writers of local color and travel literature, arose. This one-story house, composed of two equal units separated by a broad central hall and joined by a common roof, has been attributed to Scandinavian influence and pioneer ingenuity. **1991** Williams *Homeplace* 74 The "dogtrot" house is a clearly related building variant [of the saddlebag house type], although the presence of the open passage also makes it akin to the central passage I-house in spatial usage. While a few dogtrot houses do survive in southwestern North Carolina, most are early and all have been enclosed. **1995** Jones *Early Sevier Archit* 12 Noticeably absent from the county are log dog-trots, which are found throughout Tennessee and the South. These one- and two-story dwellings featured two equal-sized log pens that were separated by an open central breezeway. Although numerous log dwellings are thought to be half of an original log dog-trot, only one example survives in the county which retains both log pens—the Maples-Sharp House. **1995–97** Montgomery *Coll*: *dog alley* (known to Brown); *dog trot* (known to Cardwell). **1995** Trout *Historic Buildings* 16 The dog-trot could be built as such all at one time, or created later. It consisted of two identical cabins built side-by-side, about 8′–10′ apart, with an open breezeway or dog-trot between. All was covered by one continuous roof. This provided a room for cooking and eating on one side, and sleeping or living space on the other. The dog-trot offered sheltered space for working or socializing. Obviously, the dogs made good use of this space, which was cool in the summer and relatively warm in the winter.

[so called from a dog's access; DARE *dog run* n chiefly South Midland, occasionally South; *dog trot* chiefly South, South Midland]

dog up *verb phrase* To round up (cows) with the assistance of dogs.

1983 Montell *Don't Go Up* 41 We turn the cows out in the woods and we dog them up when it's time to milk them, and their bowels act while the dogs are running them. So we don't have this stuff to clean out!

dog won't hunt See **that dog won't hunt**.

dogwood season *noun* See citation.

1929 Duncan and Duncan *Sayings* 235 = wet spell while dogwoods are in bloom.

dogwood squall See **dogwood winter**.

dogwood winter (also *dogwood squall*) *noun* A frost or freezing spell in April or May when dogwoods are in bloom. For terms describing a similar phenomenon, see **blackberry winter**.

1907 *Dogwood Winter* 236 In May, when the dogwood tree is in bloom . . . there is cold, disagreeable, cloudy weather and often a touch of frost. Down our way it never fails, and we call it *dogwood winter.* **1940** Still *River of Earth* 127 "Even come spring," grandma said, "we've got a passel of chills to endure: dogwood winter, redbud, service, foxgrape, blackberry. . . . There must be seven winters, by count. A chilly snap for every time of bloom." **1962** Dykeman *Tall Woman* 14 After the cold spell, when dogwoods bloomed, there would be whippoorwill winter and blackberry winter. "Dogwood winter" happens in April, but it is soon followed by another spell of cold called "blackberry winter," which occurs in May when blackberry briars put out their delicate flowers. **1970** Vincent *More of Best* 64 Sometimes dogwood buds burst into full bloom up here, and the very next day top coats won't feel a bit too warm. This is what we in these parts call "Dogwood Winter." **1982** *Smokies Heritage* 123 In the warmth of Spring may come a sudden chill, with even a hint of snow. This is "dogwood winter," usually here when dogwood blossoms hang white upon the trees and wildflowers are beginning to appear. **1994–97** Montgomery *Coll* (known to Adams, Brown, Cardwell, Shields). **2014** *Blind Pig* (April 16) Spring ain't here yet. We still have Blackberry squall and Dogwood squall to go. **2016** *Blind Pig* (June 7) We are prsently having frost and freezing in the NE cornner of TN which is being attributed to "Dogwood Winter."

[DARE *dogwood winter* n chiefly South Midland]

dogwood winter bird *noun* The scarlet tanager (*Piranga olivacea*).

1951 McAtee *Bird Names* 277 (DARE) In the eastern Kentucky mountains, an unseasonable cold spell occurs often enough at the time when the flowering dogwood is blooming to have received the name dogwood winter. The scarlet tanager, migrating and thus being seen most frequently at about the same period, is accordingly termed dogwood-winter bird.

do how? *phrase* Used as a response asking a person to repeat a question. Same as **do what?**, **say what?**

1971 *AOHP/ALC-66* [Speaker A: What did you do for recreation when you was a child?] [Speaker B: Do how?] [Speaker A: What did you do for recreation, you know, how did you play, what games did you play and everything?]

doing

A See **be a-doing**.

B *noun* (usually plural) Social activities; a lively affair or function, especially a large or elaborate one. See also **to-do**.

1862 *Fuller CW Letters* (Nov 7) John you do not no that you have ether father or brother and no on to look to for pertecion but me and do you think I am or will put up with such doins. **1863** *Shifflet CW Letters* (Feb 13) She beg them to not take her things for her little Children wood Starve if tha[y] took her provishion but tha[y] went a head and took I hav saw a heepe such cases as that tell I am tired out of Such doings. **1892** Fruit *KY Words* 229 *doin's* = entertainment: "What kind o' doins are you goin' to have at your house?" **1931** Goodrich *Mt Homespun* 55 Aunt Lizzie was sitting in a low "rocky chair," that had been brought out onto the grass before the house that she might watch "the doin's." **1938** (in **2009** Powell *Shenandoah Letters* 139) This is doings that old people like us cant stand. and we need the help of the Government. **c1950** Haun *When the Wind* 13 Folks around talked of course about Bob sending Eula off, for nobody had ever heard tell of such doings. **c1959** Weals *Hillbilly Dict* 3 = affair, as in church doin's, school doin's. **1966** Dykeman *Far Family* 194 I tell you, Preacher, I leave the biggest part of the church doings to Martha. **1991** Thomas *Sthn Appal* 107 They had bigger doin's always at Johnson City—carnival an' big picnic, an' thangs like that. **1996–97** Montgomery *Coll* (known to Cardwell, Ledford, Oliver); We had a big doin's on Decoration Day (Brown). **2000** Miller *Looneyville* 45 = a local formal ceremony or elaborate social function that most of the local community was expected to attend: "Are you going to the Linden lodge doins Friday night?"

[DARE *doing* n 2 chiefly New England, South, South Midland]

doings See **doing B**.

dolesome *adjective* Of a person: depressed, doleful.

1941 Still *Troublesome Creek* 129 I knowed you'd get dolesome ere we reached Troublesome Creek.

do-less (also *do-little*) *adjective* Lazy, shiftless, lacking ambition or energy; hence noun = a person with such qualities.

1922 Cobb *KY Mt Rhymes* 40 Riders and their horses / Have a favorance, too; / Some are mean or do-less, / Some are sound right through. **1943** Justus *Bluebird* 133 The Tylers were everly doless folks. **1944** Justus *Billy and Bones* 55 Do-less folks, he had noticed, soon wear out their welcome. **1952** Wilson *Folk Speech NC* 534 *do-less* = a person who does little; a lazy, worn-out person. **1957** Broaddus *Vocab Estill Co KY* 25 *do-little* = shiftless. **1958** Wood *Words from TN* 10 *do-less* = lazy. **1974** Fink *Bits Mt Speech* 6 *do-less* = lazy or trifling. "I'm feeling plumb *do-less* this morning."

[OED3 *do-less* adj "inactive, inefficient" dialect and colloquial; SND *daeless* (at *dae* v) "lacking in energy, improvident"; CUD *doless* (at *do1*) "idle, shiftless"; DARE *do-less* adj chiefly South Midland]

do-little See **do-less.**

doll's eye(s) *noun* The white baneberry (*Actaea pachypoda*), a highly toxic herbacious plant from whose roots a medicinal tea is made.

1968 *Sang Signs* 47 Another sang-sign plant [i.e. a plant indicating the presence of ginseng] . . . is the white baneberry (Actaea), the "doll's-eyes" of the mountain healers. **1982** Stupka *Wildflowers* 34 From late July through September it bears glossy white, oval, berrylike fruits, accounting for its alternate names "doll's eyes" and "white beads." **1983** Patterson *Spring Wildflower* 18 Lucinda and her late husband Earnest [sic] hiked local trails, gathering specimens like "Tinker Bell," "Doll's Eye," "Dog Hobble," "Fairy Wand," and "Black-Eyed Trillium." **1996** White et al. *Wildflowers* 100 From July to August [white baneberry] is often called "doll's eyes" because of its large white berries. A dark central spot on these round berries remind[s] many of the porcelain eyes of old-time dolls. **2012** *White Baneberry* White Baneberry is also known as Doll's Eyes. . . . Native Americans used a root tea for various problems including pain, colds and coughs. The Cherokee use it to revive a patient near death.

dom See **dominicker.**

dome *noun* A high, somewhat rounded mountaintop. In the Smoky Mountains, this is applied only to Clingman's Dome on the TN/NC state line, the highest elevation in the park at 6,642 feet.

1943 Peattie *Indian Days* 40 Dome may describe a shape, but often indicates a barren rock summit.

do mean See **do B2.**

domestic *noun* Common cotton cloth.

1952 Giles *40 Acres* 134 Forty years ago the huckster made his weekly trip around the ridge in a covered wagon, peddling such things as country people buy . . . Thread, needles, pins, unbleached domestic, and cotton batting. **1990** Clouse *Wilder* 174 Grinning broadly, he reached under the domestic and pulled out the pistol.

[DARE *domestic* n 1 chiefly South, South Midland]

dominacker, dominecker See **dominicker.**

dominicker *noun*

A variant forms *dom* [see **1937** in **B**], *dominacker* [see **c1945** in **B**], *dominecker* [see **1962** in **B**], *dominicky* [see **1884** in **B**], *dommer* [see **1940** in **B**].

B A speckled or mottled fowl, especially a Plymouth Rock chicken.

1884 Murfree *In TN Mts* 41 A newly hatched brood . . . under the matronly guidance of a "Dominicky hen." **1930** (in **1952** Mathes *Tall Tales* 171) But if ye ain't keerful about settin' round an' dozin' atter dinner ye'll find the dominicker hen has laid egg in that thar nest, or ol' Puss has went an' had a litter of kittens in it! **1937** Hall *Coll* (Cosby Creek TN) I thought you-all would kill them doms. **1940** Still *River of Earth* 84 "We're reading *Henny Penny*," he said. "Look at that old dommer hen planting three grains of wheat." **c1945** Haun *Hawk's Done* 316 They sold the chickens and hogs—every lasted [sic] one of them—took off first the hogs and the chickens—a bunch every Saturday, till the last old dominacker hen was gone, and we were out. **1962** Dykeman *Tall Woman* 58 Had the war lasted a turn longer, I foresee you'd have had the old Dominecker rooster helping in the fields! **1998** Hyde *My Home* 80 That one big old Dominecker rooster . . . was a big scutter, and mean.

[< *Dominique, Dominica*, an island in the West Indies; DARE *dominicker* n 1 scattered, but chiefly South, South Midland]

dominicky, dommer See **dominicker.**

dona See **doney.**

done See **do A6.**

done been See **do A6b(1).**

doned See **do A6a.**

done for *adjective phrase* Exhausted, worn out.

1941 Stuart *Men of Mts* 282 They thought I's out'n my right mind and all done fer but I warn't. **c1960** Wilson *Coll* = worn out with old age.

done up *adjective phrase* See citations.

c1960 Wilson *Coll* = very tired, worn out. **c1982** Young *Colloquial Appal* 7 = exhausted.

doney

A (also *doney-gal, doney girl*) *noun* A sweetheart.

1913 Kephart *Our Sthn High* 289 A queer term used by Carolina mountaineers, without the faintest notion of its origin, is doney (long o) or doney-gal, meaning a sweetheart. **1917** Kephart *Word-List* 411 *doney* = sweetheart. Also *doney gal*. [Editor's note: **Sashiate** is Kephart's third term of "foreign origin"]. **1921** Combs *Slang Survivals* 116 Dona, a semi-slang word and term of endearment, meant in England a mother. . . . In the hills, *dona* means sweetheart, usually coupled with "gal," as in "dony-gal." **1952** Wilson *Folk Speech NC* 534 *doney (gal)* = a female sweetheart. **1955** Parris *Roaming Mts* 21 Doney-gal means sweetheart, an expression British sailors picked up in Spanish or Italian ports and preserved by backwoodsmen whose ancestors for two centuries never saw the tides.

[DARE *doney* n² probably variant of British slang < Spanish *doña* "a woman, sweetheart"; chiefly southern Appalachians]

B *adjective* Sweet-natured.

1994 Montgomery *Coll* She's a doney little girl (Cardwell).

donnick See **dornick.**

do no good See **do good**.

do nothing See **smoke grinder**.

donsie See **dauncy**.

don't See **do A2**.

don't make me never no mind See **never no mind**.

doodle[1] See **diddle**[2] **A**.

doodle[2]

A *noun*

1 A rounded pile of hay set in the field. Same as **hay doodle**.

1938 Stuart *Dark Hills* 33 He tore down a doodle of Mr. Wheeler's cane hay by running and tumbling over it. **1949** Kurath *Word Geog East US* 35 Among the local words we may mention *doodle* . . . for the haycock, which we encounter from the crest of the Alleghenies to the Ohio state line and again in a well-defined area on the lower course of the Kanawha in West Virginia. **1996** Spurlock *Glossary* 395 = a mounded pile of loose hay or straw (about 5′ × 5′), which may be picked up with a pitchfork and thrown into a wagon or sled.

2 Any pile or lump with such a shape.

1940 Stuart *Trees of Heaven* 125 He walks up to the stack of [dead] crows. "Gentlemen," he says, "the biggest doodle of crows I ever saw in one doodle." **1999** Montgomery *Coll* = anything rounded and small, "I'll bring a doodle of cornbread," also = any small portion, "I want you to bring more than a doodle of beans to the picnic" (Cardwell).

B *verb* See citation.

1944 Wentworth *ADD* 173–74 (neKY) We were doodlin' the hay up—"stackin'" I guess you say.

doodlebug *noun* The larva of an antlion (*Myrmeleon* or related genera) that digs a small funnel-shaped pit in the ground and lurks at the bottom to snare unwary insects that fall into it. The animal is the object of children's taunting for its tendency to emerge from the pit when its name is called. See also **doodlebugging**.

1911 Shearin *Superstitions Cumberland* 319–20 The "doodle-bug," a small insect that lives in moist, rotten wood, will come from its burrow if addressed by these words: "Doo-dle-bug, Doo-dle-bug, Doo—dle-bug! [sic] Your house is burning up!" **1917** Kephart *Word-List* 413 = the ant lion, so-called because it is said to emerge from its pit if one calls "*doodlebug, doodlebug*." **1964** Miller *Pigeon's Roost* (May 7) My three children had never seen a doodle bug's home and it was very interesting to them to see the doodle bug moving back the dirt as it crawled in the little round circle. But here was the most interesting thing to the children—that they too could call up the doodle bug by just keeping on hollering for it. You never can make it crawl by trying to find it with a stick, as you just have to call the doodle bug by its name to get it to crawl and as long as you call it, it will keep on crawling. **1990** Ogle *That's Why* 18 Children nowadays don't know what you are talking about when you ask, "Did you ever call a Doodlebug up from his home?"

[DARE *doodlebug* n 1 South, South Midland]

doodlebugging *verbal noun* Engaging in pointless activity (usually a children's term). See also **doodle bug**.

1997 Montgomery *Coll* (known to Andrews, Brown, Bush, Jones, Oliver).

doodley squat *noun* The slightest thing; something worth little or nothing.

1976 Garber *Mountain-ese* 24 = worthless thing. "He bought a new car but it haint worth doodley-squat." **1998** Montgomery *Coll* (known to eight consultants from the Smoky Mountains).

[DARE *doodl(e)y squat* n chiefly South, South Midland]

doodling See **diddle**[2] **A**.

doogaloo (also *dugaloo*) *noun* Same as **scrip**.

1974–75 McCracken *Logging* 2:8 They called it [= the currency] doogaloo. They just punch it like they would on a train or anything else. They just punch out the twenty-five cents or dollars or what not. *Ibid.* 5:79–80 Doogaloo, that was the scrip they issued at the store. It was aluminum money, and you go in and draw your five, ten, or twenty dollars, whatever you needed. **1977** *Foxfire IV* 311 Since they were only paid every thirty days, [logging camp] employees would make their purchases with what they called "doogaloo" credit vouchers against their forthcoming paychecks. **1981** Stokely and Johnson *Encycl E TN* 181 Small log houses sheltered other workers and their families, and this area in Embreeville became known as "Poletown." The company built a small track up to Peach Orchard to haul the ore, carry the men to and from the mines, and bring groceries up from the company store. At first, paper coupons called "scrip" were used as a means of exchange at the company store; later, a lightweight metal coin called "doogaloo" was used. **1984** Wilder *You All Spoken* 196 = credit vouchers against upcoming pay in the Champion Fibre lumbering operations in old days in western North Carolina. **n.d.** *Tremont Logging* 9 Very little cash changed hands, as employees used company scrip, nicknamed "dugaloo" or "doogaloo." When the purchases were made, the scrip, which was metal coinage, was exchanged for merchandise. **2006** Farwell *Logging Term* 1021 Men were paid in "scrip," or "dougaloo," and dropped "tokens," small company coins, into a pail before each meal. **2006** *Foxfire 40th Anniv* 311 Since they were only paid every thirty days, employees would make their purchases with what they called "doogaloo"—credit vouchers against their forthcoming paychecks. At the end of the month, they would draw the balance of what was left in their accounts in cash. Such a commissary might serve as many as twenty camps, the band mill, the general public, and the independent loggers, like Millard Buchanan, who cut boundaries of timber themselves, were paid by the thousand feet of timber they brought in, and could make purchases here on credit against what the company would owe them at the end of each month. **2009** Lloyd *Tremont*

32 Company scrip called "doogaloo," one-of-a-kind metal coins custom-made for Tremont employees, exchanged hands between store clerk and shopper far more often than cold hard cash. Today the coins are about as useless a currency as Confederate notes, though as a reminder of days gone by they're priceless.

doomawhichit *noun* An object whose name is momentarily not recalled.

1996 Montgomery *Coll* (known to Adams).

do one's do *verb phrase* See citations.

1917 Kephart *Word-List* 411 The fall of the year is when sweet-potatoes does their do. **1927** Woofter *Dialect from WV* 352 = to have done all that one can. "He did his do before the harvest was gathered." Or, "The crops will have to do their do before frost comes."

door knob *noun* See citation.

1980 Riggleman *WV Mtneer* 126–27 [Loggers] usually had nick-names for everybody and everything around the camp. Dough-nuts were "fried holes" or "door knobs."

door neighbor *noun* See citation.

1952 Giles *40 Acres* 57 Frony was almost, but not quite, a "door neighbor." A door neighbor, of course, lives right next. She is the one who can tell when your light goes on at three thirty in the morning. Who knows by your chimney smoke what time you're having dinner, who counts your trips you take to the outhouse. She is your nearest link in the ridge necklace, the immediate joint in the ridge grapevine.

doorstone *noun* A large, flat stone serving as a door step or thresh-old.

1935 Sheppard *Cabins in Laurel* 64 He had to hack him to pieces on the door stone to the house. **1943** Hannum *Mt People* 93 White chickens war a-scratchin' on the doorstone, and la, we didn't have a white chicken on the place! **1995** Montgomery *Coll* (known to Cardwell).

[EDD (at *door* (23)) Scot, nEngl]

dope *noun*.

1 An analgesic; more generally, any type of medicine.

1939 Hall *Coll* (Little Greenbrier TN) I took a backset after I got to knockin' about [after a case of "pneumony fever"]. We used strong, hot, creamy coffee for dope. **1995** Montgomery *Coll* = an-algesic (Brown, Cardwell), = general term for medicine (Bush, Cypher).

[probably by extension from *dope* "opium"]

2 (also *doper*) Any flavored carbonated drink (i.e., not neces-sarily a cola). Also called **big dope**, **soda dope**.

1918 Steadman *NC Word List* = coco-cola. **c1959** Weals *Hillbilly Dict* 3 = soft drink. "All I had was a dope and a moon pie." **1963** Watkins and Watkins *Yesterday* 160 Many people called Coca-Colas dopes and believed they contained some kind of narcotic. Some looked upon them as a habit-forming horror. Many a person who enjoyed frequent medicinal drinks of whisky believed that a per-son who occasionally drank a Coca-Cola was ruining his life with "them old dopes." **1967** *DARE Survey* (Maryville TN) = carbonated soft drink. **1981** Dumas *Appal Glossary* 17 I want a *brown doper* (Coca-Cola). An *orange doper* is an orange drink. **1992** Giardina *Unquiet Earth* 5–6 Rachel trades for a CoCola in a little green bottle, what some call a dope and others call a sodypop. **1995** Williams *Smoky Mts Folklife* 103 Inhabitants also resemble other southerners in their passion for soft drinks (still called "dope" or "sodey dope" by old-timers). **1996–97** Montgomery *Coll* (known to Jones, Led-ford, Norris); I want a yellow dope and a moon pie (Brown). **1997** Nelson *Country Folklore* 41 There was always someone hanging around drinking the drinks like Orange Crush, strawberry and grape Nehi or Cokes (all called dopes). **2005** Williams *Gratitude* 491 = any brand of soft drink.

[perhaps from the "tonic" effects early soft drinks were thought to have]

dope box *noun* See citation.

2014 Ellis *Coll* When I was a kid, every little country store had a "dope box," a fairly large metal, refrigerated cooler full of soft drinks [of many flavors].

dope down *verb phrase* To sedate or treat oneself with medicine.

2001 Lowry *Expressions* 7 When his chest hurts, he can't work until he has "doped down."

doper See **dope 2**.

dopey *adjective* Of wood: decayed from rot. See also **doted.**

1974–75 McCracken *Logging* 3:24 There were some big white pine, but there wasn't much of it and it wasn't too good. It was all dad burned old. It was dopey. If you had a big perfect white pine tree, you didn't expect to get much out of it because usually it was so old it had what we called a dry dope. The wood would be there, but when the tree fell it would break all to pieces.

[perhaps influenced by *doted* or *doty*]

dornick *noun* A rock or stone small enough to be thrown.

1927 Woofter *Dialect from WV* 353 = a stone. "They threw dor-nicks at us." **1967** Wilson *Folkways Mammoth Cave* 28 *donnick* = a throwing rock, remembered by only a few people as having been used by very old folks or in old songs. **1975** Gainer *Speech Mtneer* 9 = a stone small enough to be thrown. "He hit him with a dornick." **1997** Montgomery *Coll* = pronounced *donnick*, usually thrown at livestock to make them move (Hooper). **2016** *Blind Pig* (May 25) Daddy would call a particular rock a donnick. "Particu-lar" usually mean "big." But it could be anything outstanding about it. Like an odd shape or something. *Ibid.* I heard that word [= donnick] used regularly as a kid. . . . A typical usage would be something like: "If you don't leave me alone, I'm going to pick up the biggest donnick I can throw and chunk it at your head."

[< Irish Gaelic *dornóg*/Scottish Gaelic *doirneag* < *dorn* "fist"; cf SND *dornack* n]

dorter See **daughter**.

dose

A variant form *dost* [dost], variant plural form of two syllables: *dost-es*.

1867 Harris *Sut Lovingood* 97e [sic] Hit wer the biggest mixtry ove a dost ever tuck by man ur beaste, septin ove my soda. **1891** Brown *Dialect in TN* 172 In *oncet, twicet, acrost, dost,* and *clost,* we have a final t added. **1937** Hall *Coll* (Cosby TN) To cure yourself of the worms, take the seed off a Jerulem oak, bile it with molasses. The dost is a spoonful. **1942** Hall *Phonetics Smoky Mts* 92 Many speakers pronounce the following words with excrescent final t: *cliff, trough; close, dose, fence, once, twice, orphan, vermin.* **1971** *AOHP/ALC-193* They wouldn't give you a dost of medicine for nothing like that at all. **1974** Fink *Bits Mt Speech* 6 She taken two *dostes* o' medicine. **1997** Montgomery *Coll* That dost of medicine made her get easy (Brown). **2006** Ledford *Survivals* 1014 Other language peculiar to mountain speech appears in writings from the colonial period . . . *pizen* "poison" and *dost* "dose."

[DARE *dose* n A chiefly South, South Midland]

B *noun* A given measure or extent (i.e. of something other than medicine).

1975 Chalmers *Better* 44 Hit'll shore kill ye if'n ye take hit, but hit's a sight better than airy dost of the fever. **1997** Montgomery *Coll* Bill got a dost of head lice (Brown).

C (also *dose out, dose up*) *verb, verb phrase* To administer medicine to (someone); to prescribe (medicine); to take a portion of medicine; hence verbal noun *dosing up*. See also **dosing**.

1929 (in **1952** Mathes *Tall Tales* 100) I don't want no book doctor a-dosin' me ner mine. **1940** Bowman *KY Mt Stories* 237 *dost up on corn licker* = drink a lot of Moonshine. **1952** Justus *Children* 105 She said he was looking dauncy and needed dosing up a bit, but the medicine that she gave him was mostly spicy sassafras tea liberally sweetened. **1962** Dykeman *Tall Woman* 149 Heedless of protests, Aunt Tildy dosed everyone in the house, including herself, with sulphur and molasses. **1967** Wilson *Folkways Mammoth Cave* 8 The country doctor *dosed out* some of these medicines to chase away *agers*. **1982** *Smokies Heritage* 52 When a baby was born in pioneer times, he or she was usually dosed with herb teas by the midwife or granny-woman to make him break out in hives (tiny raised spots on the body).

dose out, dose up See **dose C**.

dosing *noun* One or more administrations of a measured quantity of medicine.

1943 Justus *Bluebird* 130 [The illness] lasted six weeks, day and night, in spite of all my dosing. **1982** *Smokies Heritage* 10 Some folks took malodorous tonics of sulfur and molasses, yeast and water, or vinegar and honey, but such "dosings" were awfully hard to swallow.

dosing up See **dose B**.

dost, dostes See **dose A**.

dote *noun* Decay or rot in wood or timber; wood affected by such decay. Also called **dry dote**. See also **doted**.

1917 Kephart *Word-List* 411 = wood partially decayed by a fungus. **1964** Clarkson *Lumbering in WV* 360 = the general term used by lumbermen to denote decay or rot in timber. **1994–97** Montgomery *Coll* (known to Adams), = *old-fashioned* (Cardwell).

doted (also *dodie, doty*) *adjective*

1 Of timber: rotting or rotten (and thus not useful to burn). See also **dopey, dote, foxfire**.

1834 Crockett *Narrative* 183 [I] had found that [the tree] was nothing but a shell on the outside, and all doted in the middle. **1917** Kephart *Word-List* 411 dotey. **1939** Hall *Notebooks* 13:2 (White Oak NC) The log was doty. **c1945** Haun *Hawk's Done* 221 He liked to set in the hollow of it and come out smelling of the doty wood and to hear Cathey brag on him for being a real woods man. **1962** Woosley *Water Witching* 141 *Doty* . . . was obsolete in neither my father's vocabulary or in mine. We always advised against splitting doty wood for firewood, which had to be hard and dry to keep the cooks happy and dinner on time. And I still speak of rotten wood or lumber that shows decayed patches as being too doty for use. **1975** Chalmers *Better* 43 She's got a doty tooth that's pure misery. **1994** Montgomery *Coll* This wood is doty (Shields).

[DARE *doty* adj 1 chiefly South, South Midland]

2 See citations.

1953 Davison *Word-List Appal* 10 *doty timber* = use[d] figuratively = to indicate that one has some bad traits. "Dan is jest doty timber. He'll never amount to nothing." **c1960** Wilson *Coll* [applied to] somebody who is becoming old and declining in strength and in mental power. **1974** Fink *Bits Mt Speech* 7 = aged or senile: "He's got plumb *dotey*."

do the pigeon wing See **pigeon('s) wing**.

do to See **do B2**.

doty See **doted**.

double (also *double and twist, double back, double distill, double foot, double still*) *verb, verb phrase* In distilling, to strengthen (whiskey) by adding the **singlings** of an earlier distillation **run** to the **mash** of the next distillation and then its vapors through using a copper **coil** or **condenser**, giving the whiskey higher proof and making it smoother; to make whiskey in this manner. See also **double corn whiskey, doubling**.

1939 Hall *Coll* (Cades Cove TN) That's when you double back to start up again [i.e. when you run the liquor through the still the second time]. **1956** Hall *Coll* (Waynesville NC) It was double stilled, you might call it, and you had to have your worm sit down in water to condense. You had to condense the steams to make liquor. In other words you had to condense the steam here and run it into alkyhol. . . . It had to be doubled, in other words boiled twice. It had to be boiled twice because you had to boil the steam. When it first come off, why it was alkyhol, and then hit would break and then run your backings as long as they was sweet, until they got sour, and in fact when they got sour, it would lose its strength. **1959** Hall *Coll* (Del Rio TN) You double it back and you run it again. Then you get your good whiskey, which the old people called "corn squeezin's." **1967** Hall *Coll* = to "double back" liquor being distilled, i.e. to redistill the first-run whiskey (singlings). "Twist" may possibly refer to condensation of the steam in the worm, or, tautologically, to the doubling back process (or there may perhaps be an allusion to twisting tobacco). **1968** *End of Moonshining* 100 In the stills, all the singlings were saved and then run through at the same time thus doubling their strength. Whiskey made in this fashion was called doubled and twisted. **1971** *AOHP/ALC*-137 One day I had to take him a keg up there, and I took him a keg up there and he was a-doubling. **1974** Maurer and Pearl *KY Moonshine* 117 *double, double foot* = to remash in the same place, in the same vats, using the slops from the preceding distillation as a part of the mash. "We doubled back and made a good run." **1978** Parris *Mt Cooking* 210 All the old master distillers double-distilled their whiskey. They called it "doublings." That meant running it through the still twice. But even in double distilling a feller could come up with a bad run of whiskey. If a second distillation wasn't carried far enough the whiskey would be rank, though weak. **1985** Dabney *More Mt Spirits* 76 "Double and Twisted" whiskey, a favorite of old North Georgia distillers, is also called "Singlin' and Doublin'" in some localities. It is simply the distilling of whiskey twice (without the use of a "thumper" or "doubler" keg between the distilling pot and the condenser). The "twist" merely refers to the kinky twist of the finished product.

[CUD *double* v 2 "put a second run of poteen through a still"; DARE *double* v 4a southern Appalachians; *double and twist* v phr southern Appalachians]

double and twist, **double back** See **double**.

double band mill See **band mill**.

double boxed See **boxed house**.

double cabin (also *double house, double log cabin, double log house, double pen, double-pen cabin, double-pen house, double-pen log cabin, double pen log house*) *noun* A log dwelling with two enclosed areas (or pens) that are essentially independent log structures connected by a roofed passageway that is sometimes enclosed. See also **dogtrot**, **log building**, **pen**[2], **saddlebag 1**, **single-pen cabin**.

1885 Murfree *Prophet* 74 The fitful glimmer of firelight from an open door . . . revealed the presence of a double log cabin. There was an unenclosed passage between the two rooms, and in this a tall gaunt woman was standing. **1914** Arthur *Western NC* 258 A single room was as much as could be built at first, then followed a shed, a spring house, a stable and a crib. Then would come the "double" log house. In some of these houses there might be as many as six rooms, including two garret or loft rooms above the two main rooms of the house, and two shed rooms or lean-tos. **1968** Glassie *Material Folk Cult* 78–79 Frequently the cabin has another added to one of its ends; if the addition is made onto the chimney end, the house is a saddlebag . . . if the addition is built onto the end opposite the chimney, a double-pen with end chimney house results . . . both types came to be commonly built in log or frame as one story houses composed of two equal units with two front doors and one chimney. **1987** Williams *Rethinking House* 176 The single-room plan is often described as a one-room house. A more accurate description, particularly as it pertains to log [construction] is that the single-room house was often a story and a half in height, creating an upstairs room. The bottom floor of a rectangular single-pen house was sometimes partitioned. Therefore two or three rooms were possible within the log unit. . . . Despite the possibility of two or three rooms within the plan, by modern standards single-pen houses were exceptionally small. Today it is often assumed that small log houses were built solely out of necessity, either by early pioneers who had no access to sawed lumber or skilled labor or by later mountaineers who were simply too poor or isolated to build anything else. . . . Older people who speak of a single-pen house often refer to it as a "big house" or (more frequently "big house and kitchen"). **1991** Williams *Homeplace* 74 In southwestern North Carolina the central chimney "saddle-bag" house is far more prevalent than the double pen plan with exterior end chimneys. **1995** Williams *Smoky Mts Folklife* 67 The most common of the double-pen log houses was the saddle-bag plan dwelling: two equal-sized rooms on either side of a chimney, known regionally as a "double house" or house with a "double chimney." **2002** Tate *Log Houses* 5 The double pen house is formed by placing an abutting second pen on the gable end opposite the chimney. . . . Other variations of the double pen include the saddle-bag or central chimney, and the dogtrot house.

[DARE *double cabin* n chiefly South, South Midland]

double chimney (also *double fireplace*) *noun* Same as **stack chimney 1**.

1991 Williams *Homeplace* 76 The saddlebag plan is usually described as a house with a "double fireplace," "double chimney," or "stacked chimney." **1995** Brewer *Cow Flats* We came to the tumbled-down stone chimney that had stood above a double fireplace that had warmed the living room and a bedroom of the Whaley home.

double corn whiskey *noun* Corn whiskey that has been distilled a second time to produce a higher proof of alcohol. See also **double**, **double-run**, **single corn whiskey**.

1953 Shelton *Autobiog* I 7 They gave us a nice warm supper after we had warmed a while, and some hot tea, probably boneset or catnip spiked a little with the old time single or double corn whisky to ward off a cold.

double cousin *noun* A person who is related to a cousin through both parents as a result of the marriages of two siblings from one family to two siblings of another family.

1989 *Matewan OHP*-23 I'm double cousins. I'm a double.

double crib barn (also *double-crib log barn*) *noun* A barn with two **cribs**. See citations.

1984 Morgan *Log Barns* 90 A great majority of the log barns of Blount County [TN] were built as double-pen or double-crib structures.... More than 90% of the double-crib barns have frame overlapping upper floors, supported by large timber beams, which are referred to as cantilevers. **2007** Milnes *Signs Cures Witches* 68 The farm has a large double-crib log barn, the most common older style in the area. Log structures are built in squares, called cribs, so the logs support each other. Two cribs placed near each other with a passage between form a "double-crib" structure. This main Pitsenbarger barn is on a slightly raised, well-drained area, and there are barns in all of the various meadows to store hay. Most of the oldest barns in the South Branch watershed are of this double-crib type.

double dulcimer *noun* See citation. Also called **courting dulcimer**.

2006 *Encycl Appalachia* 181 In some parts of the region, especially in eastern Kentucky, a young couple might be allowed to visit without parental supervision if they jointly played the "courting dulcimer," an Appalachian instrument possessing two fretboards. As long as the nearby parents could hear both sets of strings being strummed, they could leave the couple unobserved, knowing that the young man and woman were properly preoccupied.

double fireplace See **double chimney**.

double float *noun* See citation.

1983 Montell *Don't Go Up* 198 = double block of logs, one behind the other [forming a raft].

double foot See **double**.

double-foot plow (also *double-footed plow, double plow, double shovel, double shovel plow*) *noun* A type of **bull-tongue** plow with two metal shovels attached to a single heavy beam. See also **foot B1**, **single plow**.

1924 Raine *Saddlebags* 228 A makeshift, called a "hillside turner," is widely used, and the simple "bull-tongue" or shovel plow (occasionally the "double-shovel") does what plowing is possible. **c1960** Wilson *Coll*: *double shovel* = a plow with two bull-tongue points, esp. designed, it seems, to bust the middles when corn is laid by. **1963** Edwards *Gravel* 68 Many a boy at Speedwell in those primitive days when I was growing up was following a horse tied to a double-shovel (that's a plow) by the time he was ten or eleven years old. **a1975** Lunsford *It Used to Be* 7 A double-foot would be possibly the fastest, but it is more commonly the single-foot or bull-tongue plow, going one row at a time plowing the fields. **1976** Garber *Mountain-ese* 24 *double-shovel* = two-point plow "We allers lay off our garden with a bull tongue and cultivate it with a double-shovel." **1983** Montell *Don't Go Up* 198 *double shovel* = a small, one-horse cultivating plow containing two legs with a small plow point on each. **1984** Smith *Enduring Memories* 17 Two of the most widely used plows on the farm were the double-shovel and gee-whiz. Each was pulled by a single horse or mule and were used from the initial breaking of the ground to laying by the corn. The double-shovel had only two plow arms while the gee-whiz had from five to seven plow arms. The double-shovel was used more for developing new ground and plowing crops that needed the soil plowed deeply, while the gee-whiz was used to scratch the soil on top and smooth the soil. The double-shovel was a difficult plow to handle as the plow arms would sink very deep in the ground if the person using it did not hold up on the handles, which meant that after plowing with it all day the user was a very tired person. **1986** Pederson et al. *LAGS*: *double-foot plow* (Sevier Co TN, Polk Co TN, Gilmer Co GA) 3/4 (75%) of all LAGS interviewees attesting term were from Appalachia; *double-footed plow* (Bradley Co TN); *double-shovel plow* = attested by 13/60 interviewees (21.7%) from E TN; 13/67 of all LAGS interviewees (19.4%) attesting term were from Appalachia. **1987** Carver *Regional Dialects* 167 Two types of plows he might use in setting his crop are a *double shovel plow*, which is simply a plow with two shovels or blades, and a *bull tongue plow*, which has a shovel shaped something like a tongue. Both terms have been in use since the early nineteenth century. **1987** Davenport *Pine Grove* 41 They came out with a double footed plow which would cut their work in half by running only twice between rows.

[DARE *double shovel plow, double shovel* chiefly South Midland]

double house, **double log cabin**, **double log house** See **double cabin**.

double marriage *noun* See citations. See also **double married**.

1996 Dorgan *Baptist Diversity* 10 Should divorce and then remarriage while the former spouse still lives (known as "double marriage") be permitted? **1997** Dorgan *Happy God* 9 = remarriage after divorce, while the original spouse still lives.

double married *adjective phrase* See citations. See also **double marriage**.

1982 Slone *How We Talked* 74 = a person having been divorced or married to someone that had been married before, as long as their former partners were living, are said to be "double married." Some churches will not accept them. Others will accept them, but will not let them preach. Churches that do let them [preach] cannot preach with those that do not. **1989** Dorgan *Regular Baptists* 52 The I Timothy rule that presents Old Regularism with perhaps the most trouble is the one concerning being "the husband of one wife." This is generally interpreted to mean that divorced and remarried men ("double married") may not become elders, even when the divorce in question was obtained on the grounds of adultery. Usually such a man will be required to wait until his first wife dies—if she goes prior to him—before he can be ordained.

double pen, **double-pen cabin**, **double-pen house**, **double-pen log cabin**, **double-pen log house** See **double cabin**.

double plow See **double-foot plow**.

doubler *noun* See citations. Same as **thump barrel**.

1949 Maurer *Argot of Moonshiner* 9 = a processing keg placed between the still and the flakestand, used to redistill the liquor by utilizing the heat of the vapor itself. This eliminates the necessity for distilling twice or using separate stills: "Listen to that old doubler chuckle." **1985** Dabney *More Mt Spirits* 147 If you do not wish to use the thumper keg, you can run the hot vapors from the pot directly into the condenser. Of course, what you have is "low wines"—or singlings. And you will have to take what you get from six or eight "runs" of the singlings and put it into the pot for a "doubling run." You avoid all this when you use a thump keg, which is called by many people a "doubler."

double-rider fence *noun* See citation.

1957 Broaddus *Vocab Estill Co KY* 25 = a modification of the stake and rider fence.

double-run *adjective* Of whiskey: having been put through a **still** for a second distillation. See also **double.**

1967 Williams *Moonshining* 13 This will produce one to one and a half gallons of double-run whiskey.

double shovel, double shovel plow See **double-foot plow.**

double singletree *noun* Same as **doubletree.**

1986 Pederson et al. *LAGS* = 2/8 of all LAGS interviewees (25%) were from Appalachia.

[DARE *double singletree* n scattered, but chiefly Central and South Atlantic]

double still See **double.**

doubletree *noun* A pivoting wooden crossbar on the front of a horse-drawn vehicle whose center is attached to the vehicle and each of whose ends is attached to a **singletree.** Also called **double singletree.**

1836 *McLean Diary* 45 [I] Got my Doubel trees Ironed. **1915** Dingus *Word-List VA* 190 = [used] for two horses. **1934–47** *LAMSAS Appal* (Madison Co NC, Swain Co NC). **1966–68** *DARE Survey* (Brasstown NC, Cherokee NC, Spruce Pine NC, Maryville TN, Gatlinburg TN) = longer piece to which bars are tied.

[probably by analogy with *singletree,* a folk etymology for *swingletree*]

doubling *noun*

1 The process of running **singlings** through a second distillation to strengthen the proof of the whiskey and remove impurities. See also **double, singling(s).**

1881 Atkinson *After Moonshiners* 20–21 This low wine is again boiled in the still, and run through the worm, a second time, which produces high wines, or whiskey. This process is called "doubling." Doubling day at a mountain distillery is almost as important in the mountain community as the coming of a circus is to the small boy in the towns and villages. **1946** O'Dell *Moonshine* 3 This "low wine" which emerged at the bottom of the "Flake-stand" was also called "singlings." This was then returned to the still and passed through a second time when it came out whiskey. This process was known as "doubling."

2 (usually plural; also *doubling liquor*) The whiskey produced as a result of a second distillation; redistilled whiskey. See also **singling(s).**

1859 (in **1974** Harris *High Times* 242) This yere trail goes to Fryer's still-house an I'm gwine thar. He made a dubblin yesterday, an hits outen corn at that. **1892** Doak *Wagonauts Abroad* 62 A hale, hearty, ruddy-faced, good-natured old man of about sixty shook hands heartily and drew out a tin cup of "doublins," holding his rifle in the hollow of his arm. **1914** Arthur *Western NC* 273 When a sufficient quantity has been produced, the mash is removed from the still, and it is washed out, after which the "singlings" are poured into the still and evaporated, passing through the worm a second time, thus becoming "doublings," or high proof whiskey. **1939** Hall *Coll* (Emerts Cove TN) They run [the liquor] up just through the worm, and then after they run out singlings, then they'd put it all back in the still and run up what they call doublings. **1955** Parris *Roaming Mts* 84 It [= a beer] must be redistilled at a lower temperature to rid it of water and rank oils. When it is run through a second time it becomes "doublings" or "double-footing." **1974** Dabney *Mt Spirits* xxi *doubling liquor* = whiskey run through a copper pot still twice, which produces a proof of well over 100. Sometimes known as high wines or "doubled and twisted whiskey." **1974** Fink *Bits Mt Speech* 7 = whiskey put through the still twice, to eliminate solid matter and other impurities; a process generally eliminated by the use of a thumping chest or keg. **1992** Gabbard *Thunder Road* 150 The first time they run the mash, it was pretty poor. They called it "singlin's," 50 or 60 proof, something like that. They'd pour it back in the mash or give it to young boys who worked the still because it was weak and they wouldn't get drunk as quick. When they ran it the second time, they was called "doublin's." That was the moonshine they sold.

[cf CUD *double* n "the second run of poteen through a still"; DARE *doublings* n a chiefly South Midland]

doubling liquor, doublings See **doubling 2.**

dough beater *noun* A wife.

1911 Shearin *E KY Word-List* 538 = wife. **1941** Stuart *Men of Mts* 288 I'd give everything that I own if I had a doughbeater pretty as Daisy who thought that much of me. **1967–68** *DARE Survey* (Adams KY, Cumberland Gap TN, Big Stone Gap VA) = joking name that a man may use to refer to his wife. **1991** Still *Wolfpen Notebooks* 70 Somebody asked him did he think he could find himself a dough beater at his age and he said, "Any good woman will do." **2000** Montgomery *Coll* (known to Cardwell).

[DARE *dough beater* n southern Appalachians]

dough roller *noun* See citations.

1968–69 *DARE Survey* (Brasstown NC, Dillard GA) the big [marble] that's used to knock others out of the ring. **2018** *Blind Pig* (Sept 14) = an oversized marble, roughly twice as big as standard ones, sometimes used as a shooter.

dough sop *noun* See citations. See also **sop A.**

1973 *Words & Expressions* 134 = bread soaked in gravy. **2008** McKinley *Bear Mt* 46 They used the more common mountain term for gravy which was "dough sop." Maybe it had been named because brown gravy was actually a form of thin dough that could be sopped with bread.

do up

A *verb phrase* To perform or complete (a household chore), straighten and make ready for use.

1908 Johnson *Life KY Mts* 182 As I went about doing up the little chores, feeding the hogs and chopping wood, I noticed that [his dog] was very restless, going from place to place and very ill at ease. **1940** Haun *Hawk's Done* 79 She aimed to go over there as soon as we got the work done up. **1941** Stuart *Men of Mts* 102 It will soon be dark and our men that are alive will be slippin back through the woods to their homes to do up their work. **1964** Roberts *Hell-Fer-Sartin* 110 So he went and done his work up and set down by the door and took his baby on his knee. **1973** *AOHP/ASU-92* Everybody went home in time to do up the evening work. They had their chores to do, and they had to go home and do them. **1985** Wear *Lost Communities* 12 Every morning we had to (as mother called it) "do up the work." **1997** Montgomery *Coll* (known to nine consultants from the Smoky Mountains); Make sure you do up your bed (Norris).

B *noun* A celebration, festive event.

1990 Wigginton *Foxfire Christmas* 31 They'd always have some kind of church business, and that's one thing we had to go to. They'd have singings and preachings. Everybody would come in and have a big do-up.

dourie *adjective* See 1952 citation.

1952 Wilson *Folk Speech NC* 534 = uneasy, worried. **1995** Montgomery *Coll* (known to Oliver, but not to other consultants from the Smoky Mountains).

[cf EDD *doury* adj "dismal, gloomy"]

do what? (also *do which?*) *phrase* Used as a response asking a person to repeat a question or statement. Same as **do how?, say what?**

1918 Steadman *NC Word List* 20 *do which* = "what did you say?" Used in asking for the repetition of a question. **1952** Wilson *Folk Speech NC* 533 *do what?* = used in asking one to repeat what he said = "What did you say?" **1976** GSMNP-114:10 [Didn't they use salt blocks to try to keep [the cattle] to the balds too?] Do what? **1979** *Big South Fork OHP-10* [Speaker A:] Why do you think they chose the route that they did then? [Speaker B:] Do what? [Speaker A:] Why do you think they chose this route with all the bridges? **1995–97** Montgomery *Coll*: *do what?* (known to Adams, Brown, Cardwell, Jones, Ledford, Norris, Oliver); *do which* (known to Cardwell). **2005** Williams *Gratitude* 490 *Do what?* = an answer meaning, "repeat that," given when the question is not understood or is beyond belief. Same as: "Huh?"; "Come agin!"; "What jew say?"; "Shot who?"; "Run that by me one more time."

down

A *preposition*

1 Used in phrasal prepositions. See **down about** and Grammar and Syntax §14.5.

2 At, in. See also **down the country.**

1975 *AOHP/ALC-1128* Many years down the commissary we never saw anything but mine script, the company money. **1997** *Dante OHP-53* They come from down Saint Paul to our house and talked to him all day trying to sell him a car for five hundred and twenty-seven dollar.

B *adjective*

1 Of a tree or limb: fallen, felled.

1935 (in **2009** Powell *Shenandoah Letters* 54) Will you please let me get two loads of down wood. **1943** Hannum *Mt People* 147 Shapes of phrases repeat themselves and the same sounds re-echo, giving, oddly enough, vividness rather than monotony—as in their use of double words: "down-log." **1974** Fink *Bits Mt Speech* 7 A heap of *down* timber. **1991** Thomas *Sthn Appal* 70 They'uz a big down white pine up there . . . down on th' ground. *Ibid.* 87 That deer had life enough left in it, that hit'ud dive in under them down-limbs, an' wuz a-layin' there.

[DARE *down* adj D2 chiefly Midland, West]

2 Of a plant: growing low to the ground.

1939 Hall *Coll* (Cataloochee NC) Down laurel [is] laurel on a mountain, right on the ground, like a jungle, and you can't get through it hardly. . . . Well sir, it was just so rough [that the bear] couldn't run. Hit was down laurel and he couldn't do nothin' but jump up and down. *Ibid.* (Deep Creek NC) Hit was so rough down laurel that I couldn't see without gettin' right up in strikin' distance. **1969** Hannum *Look Back* 172 Find yourself a downlog and set. **1987** Hall *Coll* (Del Rio TN) Down laurel will grow close to the ground with limbs growing low and then turning up.

3 (also *down sick*) Seriously ill, incapacitated, bedridden.

1826 *Whitten Letter* Betsey was down most of the time and some of the children. **1862** *Cunningham CW Letters* (June 22) I have not been down Sick nar a day Since I have left home But I have been Some what puny Several thimes. **1862** *Huntley CW Letters* (July 16) it seems to me that more than half the Regiment is down sick and they are all vary mutch Depressed in spirits and Out of hart. **1862** *Mangum CW Letters* (June 23) R A Marlow is down with the feavor. **1881** Atkinson *After Moonshiners* 152 One of the gals in the neighborhood was sick with the breast complaint, and another was down with the yaller janders. **1957** Combs *Lg Sthn High: Word List* 32 *down sick* = bedfast with sickness. **1971** *AOHP/ALC-160* They would bring baskets of food. They would see that they didn't want for anything while they were down sick. **1973** *Flu Epidemic* 108 [The flu] killed people, and people were down with it. **1982** Powers and Hannah *Cataloochee* 260 Father said, "I want you to go up and see about Uncle George and the family. They may ever' one of 'em be down up there." **1989** *Matewan OHP-9* [I remember] going with her up there to cook for them people that was all down with the flu.

4 Confined to bed due to pregnancy.

1930 Armstrong *This Day and Time* 25 I'll be down afore long.

C *adverb* Used to extend or intensify the action of a verb. See Grammar and Syntax §14.4.

1939 Hall *Coll* I shot the bear in the mouth and killed him down.

D *verb*

1 To vanquish, suppress, thrash.

1898 Elliott *Durket Sperret* 12 Aunt Warren . . . in her rage declared that Hannah should marry Si, if only "to down thet sassy hussy, Minervy." **1899** Crozier *White-Caps* 7 After two years of white-capism, another organization was formed to "down" the "White-caps," called "Blue Bills." **1941** Stuart *Men of Mts* 229 Now Shan Powderjay—remember if you ever tell anything, the rest of us will down you and cut your tongue out.

2 To insult, denigrate.

c1986 (in **2015** Yarrow *Voices* 43) If I went along to a meeting I'd probably get downed like I don't know what.

down about (also *down around across*, *down in on*, *down in under*, etc.) *phrasal preposition* Below, beneath. See also **up in**.

1861 *Hileman CW Letters* (Aug 24) I dont think the Battle will be near Manassas Junction I think it will be down about Fairfax Court House. **1863** *Woody CW Letter* (May 3) I can Say to you that creen went down about the holer popler and the malita went and kild tom baley and told hur to leev in too days. **1939** Hall *Coll* (Cataloochee NC) Old Uncle Steve Woody says "I'll go around down thisaway below him and you go down in on him." I went right down in on him and give him another shot. **1964** Williams *Prep Mt Speech* 54 It is with the clustering of prepositions that mountain folk often amaze outsiders. The prepositions the mountaineer finds particularly useful in indicating changes of reference. The angry mother scolding the stubborn child who has hidden under the table is exact in her command: "You git up out from down in under that thar table, er I'll whup ever' bit a hide offen (off from on) yer back." The switch is snatched "down from up over" where it "stays at." **1969** GSMNP-25:2:16 You've been through there I guess and saw, well, right in under from the bridge right down in under the bridge, sort of in that house. **1969** GSMNP-46: 16 Smith's home was down in under there. **1970** *Hunting Stories* 31 They run him down around across the country there, an' then he raised back up and went way down nearly t'th'settlement. **1974** Roberts *Sang Branch* 233 She went down in that place and they was a house down in under there. **1979** *Big South Fork OHP-11* You went away off down in under the railroad. **2012** Milnes *Signs Cures Witchery* We had one lived down over the hill.

down-and-out *adjective*

1 Mentally depressed, in low spirits.

1968 *DARE Survey* (Brasstown NC) = depressed and in a gloomy mood. **1994–97** Montgomery *Coll* = depressed, grieved, homesick (Adams); He's been down and out since he lost the election (Brown), = depressed, "He's been down and out since he got laid off" (Cardwell), = mentally depressed, often because of money or family problems or because of illness (Ellis), = depressed, having had bad luck (Ledford), = worried, anxious (Norris).

[DARE *down-and-out* adj 3 scattered, but especially South, South Midland]

2 In economic hardship.

1976 Garber *Mountain-ese* 24 = poverty stricken. "The Simonses used to be rich but now they're down and out." **1993** Ison and Ison *Whole Nother Lg* 17 = without material goods. **1997** Montgomery *Coll* = poverty-stricken (Oliver).

down around across See **down about**.

down at the heel *adjective phrase* See citation.

1927 Woofter *Dialect from WV* 353 = [in] poor condition physically. "I have felt down at the heel all spring."

down-country *adjective phrase* Pertaining to regions of lower elevation and their more cosmopolitan culture.

1931 Hannum *Thursday April* 18 His movements carried a directness and sureness which bespoke the tempering of down-country training.

down diddy *noun* See citation.

1960 Westover *Highland Lg* 19 = little chick.

down-face *verb* To discourage, dishearten; hence *down-faced* = dejected.

1973 Davis *'Pon My Honor* 37 She trembled like a dog in a wet sack, and I never did see in the course of a day or a dream at night anybody so down-faced. *Ibid.* 95 = discourage, contradict.

down-go, on the *adjective phrase* Declining in health; deteriorating in economic or physical circumstances. See also **go-down, on the**.

1917 Kephart *Word-List* 411 = decline in health. "I love strong coffee, but when I get *on the down-go*, I cain't hardly come it." **1931** Hannum *Thursday April* 228 Hit's jest scandulous the way them women of Penlin's let things peeter out. Hain't a thing about the house but what's on the down-go. **c1940** Simms *Coll* She ain't vi-grous no more; she's been on the down-go since last corn-choppin' time. **1952** Wilson *Folk Speech NC* 536 That family is surely on the *down-go*. **1961** Seeman *Arms of Mt* 94 That feller was on the down-go fer a week. **1974** Fink *Bits Mt Speech* 7 He's been on the *down-go* for some time. **1996–97** Montgomery *Coll* (both meanings known by Adams, Brown, Cardwell, Jones, Norris, Oliver).

[DARE *down-go* n 1 southern Appalachians]

down head *noun* A dandelion.

1972 *Foxfire I* 88 *Taraxacum officinale* . . . down-head.

downhill-of-life *noun* The creeping Jenny plant (*Lysimachia nummularia*).

1930 Armstrong *This Day and Time* 212 I 'ull be a-plantin' downhill-o'-life on the old man's grave.

down home *noun, adverb phrase* One's native or ancestral area; in or to one's native or ancestral area. See also **homeland, up home**.

1924 Greer-Petrie *Angeline Gits Eyeful* 1 Down home, when a passle of able-bodied men and wimmen have a getherin', they all jine in and skear up somethin' to do that's been a-needin' gittin' done, if 'tain't nothin' but a log rollin', or house raisin', or corn shuckin'. **2005** Hicks *Blood and Bone* 30 The first Sunday we didn't drive down home, / to the church. **2014** House *Talking About* I went down home last night for a funeral. I live less than an hour north of my home county in a wonderful town, but it's not down home. Down Home is where I'm from. Down Home is my people. Down Home is where my accent doesn't announce me as an outsider, where gas stations offer soup beans and corn bread for sale, where folks sit in a circle in plastic lawn chairs to watch the cool of the day roll in after a long day of work.

down house *noun* See citation.

1961 Niles *Ballad Book* xiv Some of these people lived in what we call "down houses"—that is, houses just this side of complete ruin.

down in (on) See **down about.**

down in one's back *adjective phrase* See citations.

1862 *Watters-Curtis CW Letters* (Aug 22) As to health But i am down in my Back But i think I will Be well in a few dayes. **1927** Woofter *Dialect from WV* 353 *down in yer back* = one who is crippled by a weak back: "Grandfather has been down in his back all week." **c1960** Wilson *Coll* = suffering from lumbago or any other back trouble.

[DARE (at *down* D5) chiefly South Midland]

down in under, down over See **down about.**

down sick See **down B3.**

downspout *noun* A heavy local rain.

1934–47 *LAMSAS Appal* = attested by 3/14 speakers (21.4%) from SC. **c1960** Wilson *Coll* = a sudden, heavy shower, a downpour. **1994** Montgomery *Coll* (known to Shields).

[DARE *downspout* n especially South Midland]

down the country *adverb phrase* In or into a rural area.

1864 (in **1976** Lawson *Hammontrees Fight* 121) (Nov 29) we was don the country severel miles forther at a ton by the naem of Pulaska & had to fall back & burn the ton up. **1969** GSMNP-38 [I] stayed here till we moved that big old hewn log house down the country here. **1985** *Schools and Pastimes* 42 I was taught by a friendly, good-looking young lady from "down the country," who offered a prize of a little penknife to the first grader who could be first to learn to sing the alphabet to the tune of "Baa, Baa, Black Sheep." **2009** Burton *Beech Mt Man* 56 It was at Dave's place, down the country.

down the mountain See **mountain C.**

down to a gnat's bristle *adverb phrase* See citation.

c1960 Wilson *Coll* = something done exactly and meticulously.

[DARE (at *gnat's bristle* n) chiefly South, South Midland, West]

dozen *verb* See citation.

1927 Woofter *Dialect from WV* 353 = to gether [sic] the bound sheaves by dozens. "The boys have dozened all the wheat on that side of the hill."

drab See **drib.**

drabble *verb*

1 To wet and soil, as by dragging through mud; hence *drabbled*, *drabble-tailed* = soaked in water and mire.

1929 Kephart *Smoky Mt Magic* 11 On rainy days I have to traipse out in the wet and go draggin' along in this long skirt like a drabble-tailed chicken. **1973** Davis *'Pon My Honor* 95 = very wet and muddy; made wet by dragging in mud. **1984** Woods *WV Was Good* 229 If a hen led her brood through wet morning grass, she was said to *drabble* them. **1996–97** Montgomery *Coll*: *drabbled* (known to Adams, Brown, Cardwell, Jones, Ledford, Norris, Oliver).

[EDD *drabble* v 1(1) Scot, nEngl; SND *drabble* v 1(1) "To dirty, to besmear"]

2 See citation. Same as **grabble.** See also **granny B2, scrabble 1, scratch² B.**

1953 Davison *Word-List Appal* 10 = to dig up: "I must go to the garden and drabble some potatoes."

drabble-tailed See **drabble.**

draft *noun*

1 A plan drawing the warp through the heddles of a loom to produce a certain pattern in weaving; the written pattern of the plan itself. See also **chart.**

1931 Goodrich *Mt Homespun* 6 For the "beaming" and "drawing through," a whole day's work is required; that is, for rolling the chain evenly onto the back or warp beam of the loom, passing it through the "rack" on the way, to divide it properly, and drawing each separate thread through the harness eye indicated for it in the "draft" or pattern and through the slits in the reed or "sley." *Ibid.* 8–9 In the "drawing in" and the actual weaving of a coverlet, a design or pattern was necessary and this was called a draft. The good offices of a preacher or lawyer were called upon to "draw off," that is, to copy, a draft. It was written on a narrow slip of paper, from four inches to half a yard long according to the length of one unit to the pattern and was fastened on the front of the loom in plain sight of the weaver. Old drafts are often written on the backs of letters or bills or law papers. The draft consists of lines and figures, or—if the weaver could not read figures—lines only, mystifying to the uninitiated. . . . When spread out [drafts] are seen to be marked with multitudinous pin pricks as one worker and another has put in a pin to keep place in the "drawing in." **1937** Eaton *Handicrafts* 107 They have collected throughout the mountains many old drafts and among their products are textiles in plain weaving, overshot, summer and winter, and double weaving. **1945** McNeer *Sthn Highlands* 25 The old woman works at her weaving as mountain women have done for a hundred years or more. She is ready with her thread chain spooled on corncobs, hollowed in the center where she has burned them out with a hot poker. The cob spools are arranged on the rack according to a "draft," which Granny has had in her family for a century. This is a plan for the design. **1960** Hall *Smoky Mt Folks* 48 Most of the elderly women liked to speak of their weaving . . . "My coverlid (bedspread) designs were the Irish Chain, the Double Rose and the Fan." Coverlids were made according to a "draft" or pattern. **1976** Bullard *Crafts TN Mts* 55–56 Old looms were found and reconditioned or rebuilt. Forgotten "drafts"—the strange looking patterns for coverlets—began to turn up on yellow and wrinkled paper, most of them tied with bits of thread and showing innumerable pin pricks where the weavers had marked their places on the patterns. **2001** Wilson *Textile Art* xii An overshot coverlet weaver began with a pattern draft that indicated how to thread the warp and needle the pattern. A long, narrow piece of paper, rolled tightly, was marked with shot lines indicating how to group warp threads in series of repetitions that formed the squares and circles for the final pattern. Weaving drafts were passed between family members, sent to distant relatives, and copied from friends. A weaver could adjust a draft to suit her vision or use color to change the appearance of the design. *Ibid.* 104 = the paper diagram that instructs a weaver how to thread a pattern through the heddles onto the loom shaft.

[DARE *draft* n B4 chiefly South Midland]

2 A small stream or a tributary of one.

1788 (in **1940** McJimsey *Topo Terms in VA* 173) To a spruce Pine and a Lynn standing on the South West branch of Mill Run a Draft of Pattisons Creek. **1944** Combs *Word-List Sthn High* 19 = a brook or small stream. **1995** Montgomery *Coll* (known to Cardwell).

[DARE *draft* n B1 chiefly Appalachians]

3 A ravine or gully through which water intermittently flows or once flowed.

1760 (in **1912** Chalkley *Augusta Co VA* 3.364) (DARE) 510 acres on head of east fork of Cook's Creek and a draft of Smith's Creek. **1886** Smith *Southernisms* 45 = valley of any stream smaller than a creek. **1894** Lanier *Wild Turkey* 883 Now you climb up and down a never-ending succession of ridges and "drafts," as the ravines are called. **1968** *DARE Survey* (Marlinton WV) = a very narrow valley. **1995** Montgomery *Coll* (known to Cardwell).

[DARE *draft* n[1] B2 chiefly Appalachians]

drag

A *verb* Principal parts.

1 variant past-tense form *drug*.

1861 (in **1974** Aiken *Offield CW Letters* 118) (Dec 16) I am informed that they drug you out as a molitia and I want you to let me kno how you like the opperations of a soldiers life. **1873** Smith *Arp Peace Papers* 111 [He] throwd mud on him, and drug him about and rubbed sand in his eyes. **1895** Dromgoole *Fiddling to Fame* 59 Then the boys bust in an' ordered me inter my clothes and drug me out fur a speech. **1913** Kephart *Our Sthn High* 284 Examples of a strong preterite with dialectical change of the vowel are bruk, brung, drap or drapped, drug. **1937** Thornburgh *Great Smoky Mts* 93 A party of hunters came up from Knoxville and kilt 'em a load o'bear an' drug 'em down to the head of the creek an' skinned 'em. **1953** Atwood *Verbs East US* 9–10 *Drug* . . . occurs in W.Va., and in almost all parts of the S[outh] A[tlantic] S[tates] to and including N.C. **1973** GSMNP-14:2 I drug along behind. **1978** Reese *Speech NE Tenn* 173 *drug* = attested by 9/12 (75%) speakers. **1985** Irwin *Alex Stewart* 251 They just drug her a little ways out from the house and buried her. **1991** Thomas *Sthn Appal* 180 He cut th' trees down an' hewed 'um. Then they drug 'um—he had a big yoke a' cattle—an' he drug th' logs in. **1998** *Dante OHP-61* That incline line run about, around a big sprocket wheel and drug the coal down.

2 variant past-participle form *drug*.

1862 *Poe Family Papers* (Sept 23) I am well as to helth but I am trubled in mind I have bin drug off from my family rends that was near an dear to mee. **1864** *Mangum CW Letters* (Sept 18) I want to sea you as bad as I can but it wold not be any pleasure to me to sea you drug a bout hear as some is. **1867** Harris *Sut Lovingood* 155 I left in a peart trot, an' soon got on ole Stuff's trail. It wur like a waggin hed been drug upside down by a par ove runaway muels. **1900** Harben *N GA Sketches* 265 He's too good a citizen to be hauled an' drug about like a dog with a rope round his neck. **1913** Kephart *Our Sthn High* 37 Sometimes no harrow was used at all, the plowed ground being "drug" with a big evergreen bough. **1953** Hall *Coll* (Bryson City NC) I heard one [dog] open, and I turned the rest loose, and they took after Bob where he had drug this bear. **1973** GSMNP-86:36 Well, something had slid down there, looked like a log had been drug down that little hollow. **1979** Carpenter *Walton War* 162 My younguns git so dirty every day they look like they had been drug up the chimbley.

B *verb*

1 To embarrass, tease (someone).

1915 Dingus *Word-List VA* 182 = to tease, twit. **1924** (in **1952** Mathes *Tall Tales* 25) He had not come by his sobriquet "Draggin' Ellick" by accident . . . And by the way, lest the plainsman reader find no light from his flat woods dictionary upon this word "draggin'," he is hereby apprised that in Appalachia, where we are content to keep the English language in the form that was good enough for Ben Jonson and Shakespeare, and Bunyan, "drag" still means, on occasion, to embarrass or silence by swift and telling repartee. **1928** (in **1952** Mathes *Tall Tales* 68) He good-naturedly replied to the banter of his mates, "All right, Uncle Nelse, ye drug me purty hard that time, didn't ye?"

[DARE *drag* v B2 chiefly South Midland]

2 To loaf, waste time.

1939 *FWP Guide KY* 271 The farmer tells his wife, "Court day hain't no fit'n time fo'r women folk to be draggin' roun' town nohow."

[DARE *drag* v B5 chiefly South, South Midland]

3 To cultivate (a field) with a rudimentary harrow.

2002 Morgan *Mt Born* 60 If Grandpa's disk harrow was not available, Paul would "drag" the recently plowed fields. A "drag" was a contraption made by nailing several heavy pieces of timber together. The whole contrivance should have been about seven feet wide by five feet long. Usually, rocks were piled on top of it for extra weight, or the driver or children could ride it for extra weight as needed.

C *noun*

1 A prank, jest.

1924 (in **1952** Mathes *Tall Tales* 25) "That's a plumb good idy, boys," he said. "I'll banter him to do hisself proud this time, an' then I've jest thought of a brand-new drag I'll git off on him."

2 A ravine.

1969 GSMNP-27:9 Here [the bear] come, right up that drag, just took on up that tree.

3 (also *drag harrow*) A rudimentary or makeshift harrow consisting of one or more planks or boards with nails driven into it, used to break clods of dirt after plowing. See also **plank drag**.

1938 Stuart *Dark Hills* 88 They're weak on pulling a little drag of wood into the yard. **1973** Miller *English Unicoi Co* 146 = a heavy board or log used for breaking up the clods in a freshly plowed field. **1986** Pederson et al. *LAGS*: *drag* = attested by 18/60 interviewees (30%) from E TN and 7/35 (20%) from N GA; 25/62 of all LAGS interviewees (40.3%) attesting term were from Appalachia; *drag harrow* = attested by 10/60 interviewees (50%) from E TN and 5/35 (14.3%) from N GA; 15/30 of all LAGS interviewees (50%) attesting term were from Appalachia. **1995** Alexander *Mt Fever* 99 After the plowed fields had been exposed to rain and wind for two to three weeks, dirt and turf settled fairly well around the seed pieces. Then a homemade drag—two-by-six boards five or six feet long, overlapped and nailed together—was dragged over the field. **2002** [see **B3**].

[DARE *drag* n 1 chiefly Inland North, Midland]

4 See citation. See also **scrip**.

1943 Korson *Coal Dust* 72 The same colloquial terms were used for scrip and store orders, such as "stickers," "clackers," "flickers," and "drag."

5 A load of wood, as on a sled.

1996 Spurlock *Glossary* 396 = a sled loaded with firewood.

drag harrow See **drag C3**.

dragon *noun* The devil. Same as **Old Scratch**.

1983 Broaddus *Estill Co KY Word List* 38 = the devil. **1996–97** Montgomery *Coll* (known to Adams, Brown, Bush, Cardwell).

[OED3 *dragon* n[1] 4a 1340–1707; DARE *dragon* n B1 especially South, South Midland]

drag out *verb phrase* To exhaust, wear out; hence adjective phrase *drug out* = exhausted.

1931 Owens *Speech Cumberlands* 93 I was plumb drug out by the time I got there. **1935** Sheppard *Cabins in Laurel* 51 Mammy couldn't stand it no more. She was plum drug out. **1952** Wilson *Folk Speech NC* 535 *drug-out* = tired out: "I'm allus so drug-out when dinner is over, I can't hardly git out of my cheer." **1986** Pederson et al. *LAGS* (Cocke Co, Hamilton Co TN). **1996–97** Montgomery *Coll*: *drug out* (known to nine consultants from the Smoky Mountains). **1999** Morgan *Gap Creek* 117 When we got back to the house I was so dragged out I dropped on the sofa.

drag sled *noun* Same as **land sled**.

1981 Williams *Storytelling* She fixed him a little budget of grub [to] last him about three days, I reckon, piled him some house plunder in a drag sled, and he started out.

drag up *verb phrase* To pull (especially a chair) close (usually expressed as an invitation). See also **draw up 3**.

1974 Russell *Hillbilly* 24 Some other expressions in our community included ... "Drag up a cheer and set a spell," "Shet the door," "How air ye?" and "Reckon I'm tolerable pwert [sic]." **1991** Still *Wolfpen Notebooks* 57 Come in and drag up a chair.

drain

A *noun, verb* variant forms *drean, dreen.*

1886 Smith *Sthn Dialect* 349 They all have the authority of old or dialect English, or many of them belong to all parts of the South, if not elsewhere ... dreen (drain). **c1926** Bird *Cullowhee Wordlist* He dreaned all the water out. **1985** Irwin *Alex Stewart* 106 All that blood will drop and dreen (drain) out before it closes up, and they do better, not to put nothing on them. **2001** Lowry *Expressions* 2 The sore on my leg "dreens" all of the time.

[DARE *drain* v, n[1] A chiefly South, South Midland, occasionally New England]

B *noun*

1 A small stream.

1804 *Jefferson Co Wills I* 46 I give and Bequeath unto son in law John Hill fifty Acres of Land off of the Tract I now live on. Beginning in the Bank French Broad River at Parmenas Taylors corner, and extending across the bottom along said Taylors line opposite to the mouth of the first drean thats next to John Hill, then up the Drean to the road. **1926** Hunnicutt *Twenty Years* 147 They crossed the creek and went up through the Flat Laurel on the other side and came to another little drain that came in on that side of the creek. **1939** Hall *Coll* (Cataloochee NC) So we was goin' to the trap, and we went to jump across a little swampy dreen and jumped right into the old bear's face. *Ibid.* (White Oak NC) = a small spring where there's very little water, on a mountain side or in a little hollow, not the same as a marsh or swamp. [Moonshiners] set up their still on a little dreen, a good place for a still because revenuers hunt up creeks and a dreen would be hard to find. The dreen is up so steep they could dam it up and pipe it up and pipe it to the barrel. [The word] is nearly always "dreen." **1974** Roberts *Sang Branch* 54–55 I clomb up on a little hickory pole that I had cut right at the mouth of the dreen, just sawed him down and never cut him plain off. **1997** Hufford *American Ginseng* 5 The hollows, deep dendritic fissures created over eons by water cutting through the ancient table land to form tributaries of the Coal River, receive water from lesser depressions that ripple the slopes. These depressions are distinguished in local parlance as "coves" (shallower, amphitheater-shaped depressions), "swags" (steeper depressions, "swagged" on both sides), and "drains" (natural channels through which water flows out of the swag or cove). **2016** *Blind Pig* (March 30) Where the creek comes out of the Walnut Cove and runs into that other little old bitty drain ain't nothing but a spring drain, you know, comes out there.

2 A ravine, small valley.

1915 Hall *Autobiog Claib Jones* 7 I traveled all that day in the woods, late in the evening I went up a drain, struck a fire and roasted my meat. **1941** Stuart *Men of Mts* 42 I rode up a little drain where the bright water dashed over the rocks. **1974** Roberts *Sang*

Branch 3 His house was propped on a hillside in a small drain. **1989** *Matewan OHP-23* It's not a hollow. It's just a drain where the water runs out where you go up to the radio station.

dram

A *noun* A (usually) small measure or portion of a liquid, especially whiskey.

1864 *Brown CW Letters* (Aug 15) the pilet and eight of us went to a Still house and got two Can teens of brandy witch made a dram round for the b[o]ys. **1864** *Chapman CW Letters* (June 11) his father Was at my house Last Evning Wanted mee To go down to ashes with him and drink a dram. **1913** Kephart *Our Sthn High* 286 I ginerally, usually take a dram o' mornin's (in a storm). **1937** Thornburgh *Great Smoky Mts* 32 I jist take a bottle an' suck a good dram outen it before my meals. **1939** Hall *Coll* (Proctor NC) Walt Proctor was an old timer, deacon of the church, and superintendent of the Sunday school. One day he got drunk, and he was called before the church. When they put a member out, they called a meeting of the whole church. At that time he said, "I took about thirty drams too many." They didn't church him when they give him the trial. **1953** Hall *Coll* (Deep Creek NC) I ain't drunk a drop of whiskey in forty-seven year. I ain't took a dram. I did dabble with whiskey away back, before I was married. I made some peach brandy but didn't sell it. **c1960** Wilson *Coll* = a good-sized drink, larger than a snort or a snifter. **a1975** Lunsford *It Used to Be* 156 "Sugar drip" is a name for illicit whiskey. And what you take is a "snort," that's a dram. Or, you say, "Let me have a shot of that" and "Give me a swig of that." If you use the term "swig" it has an idea that you feel what you're getting is a little better than just "bust head" or "white lightning."

[DARE *dram* n 1 chiefly South Midland]

B *verbal noun* Tippling, drinking liquor in small portions.

1924 Raine *Saddlebags* 134 The habit of tippling or dramming is not uncommon. But the men that drink heavily do so only on great occasions which they "celebrate" by drinking steadily until completely intoxicated. **1942** Campbell *Cloud-Walking* 121 Neither one wouldn't stand for no drinking and no dramming and going hog-wild with celebrating.

dram drinker *noun* One who drinks liquor in only small portions.

1939 Hall *Coll* (Jefferson City TN) A dram drinker makes a drunkard. **1976** Garber *Mountain-ese* 25 = a light social drinker. "Dwayne ain't no drunk; he's jist sort of a dram-drinker."

dram drinking *verbal noun* Imbibing alcoholic beverages in only small portions.

1856 *Zion Church Minutes* 42 The church met and after the common forms of worship, found all in fellowship but Brother Andrews Letterman who kept his seat—and his cause for so doing that he could not fellowship with the practice of members dram drinking any longer. **1973** *AOHP/ASU-111* A lot of the older people believed in dram drinking, and some of them would get too far along.

drank See **drink A2**.

drap See **drop A**.

drapped, drapt See **drop B**.

drasted *adjective* Used as a euphemism for *damned*.

1987 Young *Lost Cove* 193 The drasted dog snored so loud that the Saints who sat in the hallowed pews began to kick the others with hopes of keeping them awake.

drat *verb* To confound.

1969–70 Stubbs *Mountain-Wise* (Dec–Jan) 16 A lady friend of the victim and his family, on hearing this false report, said in good but archaic English: "I got downright *dratted*."

draw

A *verb* Principal parts.

1 variant past-tense forms *drawd, drawed*.

1813 Hartsell *Memora* 110 one of the others Striped him; another put a rope round his neck and drawed him Round the neck to the other two. **1834** Crockett *Narrative* 20 He hung onto the canoe, till he got it stop'd, and then draw'd it out of danger. **1861** *Estes CW Letter* (Sept 29) We Drawd [= were issued] our guns to Day. **1863** *Walker CW Letters* (Nov 17) I Will tell you What We hav to eight [= eat] heir hard tak Sow belley Coffey shuger Salt fish pikles Curcumbers Crout unions that is more than we ever drawd before. **1913** Kephart *Our Sthn High* 284 In many cases a weak preterite supplants the proper strong one: . . . drawed, growed, knowed, throwed. **1939** Hall *Coll* (Wears Cove TN) [The bear] drawed back with that dog and it throwed him about twenty feet right down the mountain. **1953** Atwood *Verbs East US* 10 In Pa. a little less than half the informants of [Type I] use [*drawed*]. To the southward it becomes more frequent, being used by nearly nine tenths of Type I informants [i.e. older speakers with little formal education] in N.C. **c1960** Wilson *Coll*: *drawed* [preterit], *drawed* [past participle]. Almost universal. **1974–75** McCracken *Logging* 2:8 The most of the people that worked for them, they hardly ever drawed any money. **1978** Reese *Speech NE Tenn* 173 = attested by 8/12 (66.7%) speakers. **1989** *Matewan OHP-102* He just made [the insurance payment] to her, and she drawed on that as long as she lived. **1998** *Dante OHP-45* She retired and drawed her Social Security, but she'd still work.

[DARE *draw* v B1 especially South, South Midland]

2 variant past-participle forms *drawd, drawed, drew*.

1805 *Globe Creek Church Minutes* 20 money [was] drawd from the Decon one half Dollar. **1813** Hartsell *Memora* 100 we have not drew aney foder and never since. **1836** *Sullivan Co Soldiers* We haven't drew on pay yet but we expect to draw the 7th of next month. **1863** *Sexton CW Letters* (Dec 20) I can in from you that we have drawed a Suiet of close all a round. **1864** *Poteet CW Letters* (Aug 21) I haint drew no money yet and I dont now when I will. **c1945** Haun *Hawk's Done* 228 It was drawed on something that looked like paper but wasn't. [See **c1960** in **A1**.] **1978** Reese *Speech NE Tenn* 173 *drawed* = attested by 7/12 (58.3%) speakers. **1980** Miles *Verbs in Haywood Co* 89 He's drawed me a picture. **1985** Irwin *Alex Stewart* 159 He'd been a soldier in World War I and he drawed a pension. **1998** *Dante OHP-*

57 His mouth was drawed around that way, and his eyelids was dropped down. **2004** Adams *Old True Love* 35 He was setting on the porch, long legs drawed up, head resting on his knees, and he never even looked up when I howdied the house.

[DARE *draw* v B2 especially South, South Midland]

B *verb* Senses.

1 To drain the fluid and swelling from.

1956 Hall *Coll* (Big Bend NC) One time Aunt Nancy had bone arsiplas. Old man Joe Packett started to get some red oak bark to make some ooze to draw her arm. . . . Slippery elm bark [is used] for drawin' boils.

2 To receive (a specific amount) of regular financial support; to accept financial support. See also **draw one's rocking chair**.

1967 Fetterman *Stinking Creek* 33 The words of Golden Slusher: "What don't work is drawin'." The majority are "drawin'." They draw welfare checks or commodities or both, and these are the basis of their economic security. **1985** Irwin *Alex Stewart* 52 I believe it was two dollars and a half a month that the teacher drawed.

3 (also *draw fire, draw fire out, draw out fire*) *verb, verb phrase* To treat a burned area on the skin by using home remedies or, more often, casting a spell. See also **blow fire**, **fire burn**, **talk fire out**.

1939 Hall *Coll* (Hazel Creek NC) To draw the fire out, take and blow over it three times. Say some kind of ceremony. **1962** Hunter *Folk Remedies* 101 The first and most important thing to do for a burn is to "draw the fire out." Baking soda works for some people, while others use vinegar, kerosene, black ink, and March snow water. **1968** *Faith Healing* 67 Stoppin' blood's just like drawin' out fire. It's the same identical thing. You do it with th'words and th'same verse and everything. *Ibid.* 64 If it's a pretty bad burn and I go to draw th'fire out of it, it hurts worse'n when it went in for a minute. . . . But in maybe thirty minutes time it's quit hurtin' and you've forgot all about it. **1972** *Foxfire I* 347 The healers with whom we spoke are sought after primarily for their skills in three areas. The first of these is burns. Their theory is that when a person has been burned, the fire continues to flame inside the wound until it has been "blown out" or "drawn." If this is not done, they claim, the fire continues to burn into the flesh until it reaches the bone. *Ibid.* 367 To draw fire pass your hand over the exposed burn, open and palm down, in a direction away from you and away from the patient. . . . Do this slowly three times, at the same time blowing gently on the burn. . . . Simultaneously, and each of the three times you do the above, repeat the secret healing verse silently. **1979** Smith *White Rock* 17 Burns were painful and little could be done to treat them, but Grandpa could remove the pain, or draw the fire from the burn. Grandpa would murmur a verse from the Bible, blow on the burn, and miraculously remove the pain. **1994** Montgomery *Coll* (known to Shields).

C *noun*

1 See citation.

1967 DARE *Survey* (Gatlinburg TN) = a stretch of still water going off to the side from a river or lake.

2 A gully or ravine or gully through which water intermittently flows or once flowed.

1927 Woofter *Dialect from WV* 353 = the head of a hollow which slopes gently. "I found the horses eating in the head of the draw." **1941** Still *Troublesome Creek* 37 I heard footsteps yon side the barn in a brushy draw, though I couldn't see for blackness till they'd topped the ridge. **1961** Douglas *My Wilderness* 160 In the valleys water is in good supply and it sparkles in every draw, sweet, fresh, and cold, with little mineral content. **1963** Edwards *Gravel* 106 The road to Tackett led up a long draw deeply and heavily wooded on either side, which narrowed to a bridle path near the top of a rough ridge. **1985** Edwards *Folksy Sketches* 87 Upon one occasion Theseus made a wonderful find of ginseng growing in a little fertile draw that he hoped no other person had spotted yet. **1994** Montgomery *Coll* (known to Adams, Brown, Bush, Cardwell, Jones, Ledford); Go right up that draw there (Shields).

3 A particular amount of regular financial support, especially public welfare.

1892 Edwards *Waste-Basket* 263 In Tennessee, at a stated time in the year, the school-teachers assemble for "the draw," the receiving of their salary, which is graduated to the number of scholars the teacher has. **1952** Giles *40 Acres* 161 We thought it mighty fancy of them to spend their draw [= welfare payment] on boloney, bubble gum, and soda pop instead of good, solid food.

drawbar *noun* A removable bar or pole in a fence, as for livestock. See also **gap 2**, **slip gap**.

1859 Taliaferro *Fisher's River* 119 At last we cum chug up to a fence that had no draw-bars nur gate. **1864** *Watkins CW Letters* (July 20) last fryday it raind so harde that the gulley at our draw bars Jest liked 3 bars a running over the top I Jest no I never Saw such a rain fall. **1917** Kephart *Word-List* 411 = a removable bar in a fence. **1937** Hyatt *Kiverlid* 30 Watching Marthy Lou come down the path from the draw-bars with her piggin and pail brimming with foaming milk. **c1960** Wilson *Coll* = poles or rails that can be drawn out of place to open a gate in a fence; also called *slip gap*.

[DARE *drawbar* n 1 formerly New England, now chiefly South Midland]

draw breath *verb phrase* To inhale. See also **blow breath**.

1937 Hall *Coll* (Wears Cove TN) = the old expression for "to inhale."

drawd, drawed See **draw A1**, **A2**.

drawed up See **draw up 2**.

draw fire, draw fire out See **draw B3**.

drawing in *noun* See citation. See also **draft 1**.

1931 Goodrich *Mt Homespun* 8–9 In the "drawing in" and the actual weaving of a coverlet, a design or pattern was necessary and this was called a draft. . . . When spread out [drafts] are seen to be marked with multitudinous pin pricks as one worker and another has put in a pin to keep place in the "drawing in."

draw off *verb phrase*

1 To copy by hand. See also **draft 1**.

1909 Bascom *Ballads and Songs* 242 [The song] is first given as it was sung by the author, then as it was "drawed off" for the author by the musician, a mountain girl of "considerable schoolin'." **1931** Goodrich *Mt Homespun* 8–9 The good offices of a preacher or lawyer were often called upon to "draw off," that is, to copy, a draft. *Ibid.* 58 "A preacher drawed that off for me nigh on to fifty year ago," said Hannah.

2 To produce (a **run** of **moonshine** whiskey).

1902 Hubbard *Moonshiner at Home* 234 [The arrest] must have come about the time Silas got his "still" goin', for he was drawin' off his first batch, and had his back to the door when he heard some one yell.

draw one's rocking chair *verb phrase* See citation. See also **draw B2**.

1969 *DARE Survey* (Sawyer KY) "drawing his rocking chair" = someone who's drawing welfare (most often), or a pension, or Social Security.

draw out *verb phrase*

1 See 1990 citation.

1990 Cavender *Folk Medical Lex* 21 = to induce an illness, such as a cold or fever. **1994** Montgomery *Coll* (known to Cardwell).

2 See citations. See also **draw B1**.

1956 GSMNP-22:4 She told me she drawed it [= poison from a snakebite] out with a bag of hot salt. **1990** Cavender *Folk Medical Lex* 21 = to treat a boil or other lesion by application of medicinal substances. **1994** Montgomery *Coll* (known to Ogle, Shields), = often done by means of a poultice (Cardwell).

draw out fire See **draw B3**.

draw slate *noun* Slate that falls from the mine roof as coal is removed. See also **kettle bottom**.

1971 *AOHP/ALC*-66 When I first went [to work in a coal mine], they had timbers, set timbers all the time, and then they put bolts in, you know, up in this draw slate, run the bolts up through that there draw slate into the solid.

draw up *verb phrase*

1 Of clothes: to shrink.

1974 Fink *Bits Mt Speech* 7 My jacket *drawed up* 'till [I] purt nigh couldn't get hit on. **1976** Garber *Mountain-ese* 25 = shrink, decrease. "You'd better buy yore overalls long; they'll draw up when they're washed." **1976** Thompson *Touching Home* 13 = to shrink. **992** Brooks *Sthn Stuff* 43 *draw up* = to shrink. "If this dress draws up even one fraction of an eench, I'll nevuh be able to get in it."

2 Of a person's physique: to shrivel, contract; hence participial adjective *drawed up*.

1973 GSMNP-57:10 He says he just drawed up. **1985** Irwin *Alex Stewart* 177 He'd died all humped up—drawed up. **1990** Cavender *Folk Medical Lex* 22 = a contraction of the arms, legs, hands due to cramping or injury. **1994** Montgomery *Coll* (known to Shields), You're all drawed up and about to blow away (Cardwell), = also due to arthritis (Ogle).

[DARE *draw* v C3 chiefly South, South Midland]

3 To pull (a chair) close; to pull close—usually expressed as an invitation. See also **drag up**.

c1959 Weals *Hillbilly Dict* 3 Draw up a cheer and set a spell. **c1960** Wilson *Coll*: *draw up a chair* = said to a guest before a fireplace or at table. **1975** Chalmers *Better* 37 Draw up an' warm. **1994–97** Montgomery *Coll* (known to Shields); Draw up a chair and set a while (Brown).

[DARE *draw* v C2 chiefly South, South Midland]

4 To arrive ultimately.

1940 Still *River of Earth* "Where air we expecting to draw up to?" **1996** Montgomery *Coll* (known to Cardwell, Jones, Ledford, Oliver).

5 To squeeze or crowd more closely together.

1996–97 Montgomery *Coll* (known to Adams, Cardwell, Jones, Ledford, Norris, Oliver); Draw up so I can take a picture of the whole family (Ellis).

draw up the idea *verb phrase* To suspect.

1923 Greer-Petrie *Angeline Doin' Society* 2 Somehow, he'd draw'd up the idy [= idea] the parson had stretched his blanket.

[DARE *draw* v C15 especially Ozarks]

dread *noun* A spell of loneliness or anxiety.

1982 Slone *How We Talked* 8 *I got a dread on me* = a lonesome feeling, a forewarning of a coming disaster. Many people believed they were warned of their death or the death of a loved one.

dreadless *adverb* Without doubt or fear of mistake.

1958 Combs *Archaic English in KY* 35 = no doubt: "She is dredless sick."

[OED3 *dreadless* adj B, →1535]

dream *verb*

1 variant past-tense forms *dreamp, dreampt, dreamt, dremp*.

1813 Hartsell *Memora* 102 on the same knight I dremp I met my mother and went in to the house with hur where I saw my wife making of corn bread. **1863** *W Robinson CW Letter* (Jan 6) I dremp last nite of Seeing her drest in black Silk. **1864** *Poteet CW Letters* (Dec 3) I Dremp last night that I saw you and I Dremp that I got wounded in the hip and in the sholder. **1901** Harben *Westerfelt* 13 It's about me 'n' yore pa—some'n' you never dreamt could 'a' happened. **1913** Kephart *Our Sthn High* 104 Last night I dremp me one that never was knowed to fail yet. **c1926** Bird *Cullowhee Wordlist*: *dreampt*. **1937** Thornburgh *Great Smoky Mts* 132 I never dreamt she'd believe it. **1939** Hall *Coll* (Smokemont NC) His brother was telling me of a dream he dremp one time. We weren't gone but two hours that morning when he got a bear. **c1945** Haun *Hawk's Done* 222 I thought about it in the daytime and at night time I dreampt about it. **1953** Atwood *Verbs East US* 10 This loss of the preterite affix [i.e. in *dremp*] is common everywhere, but particularly in the South and South Midland: e.g., in N.C. about four fifths who use the form *dreamt* drop the final /t/. **1974** Fink *Bits Mt Speech* 7 I *dremp* of rain last night. **1978** Reese *Speech NE Tenn* 174 *dreamp* = attested by 3/12 (25%) speakers; *dreampt* = attested by 1/12 (8.3%) speakers.

[DARE *dream* v 1 *dreamp* chiefly South, South Midland]

2 variant past-participle forms *dreampt, dremp.*

1863 *W Robinson CW Letter* (Jan 6) I have dremp of her twice heare of late. **1892** Dromgoole *Dan to Beersheba* 80 I hev dreampt it twic't.

dream-drunk *adjective* See citation.

c1940 Hall *Coll* = that's when you're sorty drunk; when you are so damn drunk you couldn't wake him up.

dreamp See **dream 1.**

dreampt See **dream 1, 2.**

drean See **drain A.**

dreck'ley, dreckly, d'reck'ly See **directly A.**

dreen See **drain A.**

dremp See **dream 1, 2.**

dress *verb* See citations.

1944 Wentworth *ADD* 180) (WV) Dress the table. **1975** Dwyer *Thangs* 19 = to set a table or make up a bed.

dress up *verb phrase* To skin and clean (the carcass of a killed animal), separate the edible parts, etc.

1939 Hall *Coll* (Smokemont NC) Then we made another round for home, come in, skinned our coons, dressed them up, dressed their hides, and went to bed and slept till next night.

drib *noun* A small portion or amount (especially in phrase *dribs and drabs* = little by little).

c1960 Wilson *Coll* = a small amount. **1996–97** Montgomery *Coll: dribs and drabs* (known to Adams, Brewer, Cardwell, Jones, Norris, Oliver); He just drank a drib of shine (Brown).

[cf OED3 *drib* n Scot and dialect "a drop, a petty or inconsiderable quantity"; EDD *drib* sb 2 Scot, Irel, nEngl; CUD *drib* (at *dribble* n) "a drop . . . small quantity of anything"; HT *drib* "a small amount (of liquid)"; DARE *drib* n probably back-formation from *dribble*, chiefly Midland]

drib out *verb phrase* To squeeze (drops) out.

2007 Milnes *Signs Cures Witches* 144 Mom had a cow over there. Now we went out and milked her that morning . . . suckled her calf, and milked her, and dribbed out what the calf didn't take. Mom always dribbed the last milk out and put it in her cream jar, she called it.

dribs and drabs See **drib.**

driddle *verb* To trickle, dribble.

1976 Still *Pattern of Man* 112 Although a fire burned under the pot, a steam wasn't yet up. The worm [of the still] hadn't begun to driddle.

[cf SND *driddle* v 2 (1) "to spill, dribble, trickle, drop in small quantities"]

drift *noun*

1 A mass of branches, trees, or other debris carried downstream by a **tide** of water, often collecting before the water recedes, caught in a stream or along a bank; a place in a stream where floating objects collect.

1923 (in **1952** Mathes *Tall Tales* 14) The narrow creek-bed was washed into a broad river-channel down which the drift scudded—countless logs, occasional bridges, haycocks, hen-coops and small out-buildings. **1939** Hall *Coll* (Deep Creek NC) They had came a water spout in time and drifted in a whole lot of . . . timber, spruce, and hemlock and stuff, and the bear was in under this drift, and the dogs was, was a-barking around the drift. **1994** Montgomery *Coll* = often forms in high water, then remains when water recedes (Shields).

2 (also *drift mine*) See citations. See also **drift mouth.**

1973 Preston *Bituminous Term* 34 *drift* = a coal mine, opened into the side of a hill or mountain, which has its opening at the same level as its passages and working places. **1982** Eller *Miners* 174 Most southern Appalachian mines were of the drift mine variety, which allowed for easy entry and minimized the need for expensive ventilation and transportation equipment. The coal seam of a drift mine was located on a hillside above the valley floor, and workers entered the mine laterally rather than the vertical shafts characteristic of other American coal fields. The drift mine not only drained well and was less gaseous, but because it required little machinery, operations could be undertaken with very little initial investment. **2006** Mooney *Lg Coal Mining* 1028 In a drift mine, the most common type in Appalachia, workers walked or now ride into an entryway that slopes gently upward, providing natural drainage. **2007** *Mining Terms* = a horizontal passage underground [in coal mining]. A drift follows the vein, as distinguished from a crosscut that intersects it, or a level or gallery, which may do either.

3 See citation.

1983 Montell *Don't Go Up* 198 = raft as large as three blocks of logs wide and three or more blocks deep.

drift mine See **drift 2.**

drift mouth *noun* See citations. See also **drift 2.**

1939 Still *Two Eyes* 12 They were setting in wait for me at the drift mouth this morning. **1973** Preston *Bituminous Term* 35 = the opening to the outside of a drift mine. **1977** Shackelford et al. *Our Appalachia* 276 It blowed railroad cars out of that driftmouth plumb across that river down here. **1989** *Matewan OHP-2* They put a board up across the mouth of the drift mouth and [if] a lump of coal raked off on that board, they docked you a half a ton. **2004** Fisher *Kettle Bottom* 45 That was when I heard the rush of rats to the drift mouth.

drindle (also *drindle down, drindle out*) *verb, verb phrase* To degenerate, shrink, decrease in vigor, health, or size; hence adjective *drindling* = sickly, wasting away. See also **dwindle down.**

1924 Raine *Saddlebags* 14 I've had my health for nigh onto sixty years, but now I'm foolish and kind o' drinlin'. **1942** Thomas *Blue Ridge* 289 When a body's old and drindlin'. **1944** Combs *Word-List Sthn High* 19 *drindlin* = puny, ailing. **1946** Dudley *KY Words* 271 The creeks has just kindly drinnled out. **1973** *GSMNP*-91:18 The school just kept drindlin' down, she said, and they's just two left. **1995** Montgomery *Coll*: *drindle down* (known to Cardwell).

[probably variant of *dwindle*, but cf EDD *drindle* v 3 "to trickle, run slowly"; DARE *drindle* v chiefly South Midland, especially southern Appalachians]

drink *verb*

A Principal parts.

1 variant past-tense forms *drink*, *drinked*, *drunk*.

1813 Hartsell *Memora* 101 the hole army whare we lay Shot and Drunck tell midnight for joy, which made much Noise. **1858** (in **1974** Harris *High Times* 152) Then I drunk a bowl ove coffee made outen an ole chopped wool hat. **1862** *Robinson CW Letters* (Sept 24) [We] found a litel stream that you wouldent drink out of thare & we thought it was the best water you ever drink. **1864** *Hancock CW Letters* (June 18) [There were] the most nises plases that I ever seen in aul of my lif an the Best water that I ever drunk. **1913** Kephart *Our Sthn High* 283 In mountain vernacular the Old English strong past tense still lives in begun, drunk. **1934–47** *LAMSAS Appal*: *drinked* = attested by 6/148 speakers (4.0%) from WV, 4/20 (20%) from VA, 3/37 (8.1%) from NC, 3/14 (21.4%) from SC, and 3/12 (25%) from GA. **1941** Stuart *Men of Mts* 267 Sall got my breakfast and I drinked a couple o' cups o' good hot black coffee. **1952–57** (in **1986** McDavid and McDavid *KY Verb Forms* 287) *drinked* [as past-tense form] = attested by 16 of 29 (55%) of E KY speakers interviewed by Linguistic Atlas of the North Central States. **1953** Atwood *Verbs East US* 11 In the Midland *drunk* is somewhat more frequent . . . showing some regularity of occurrence in s. c. Pa., W.Va., and the westward portions of Va., N.C., and S.C. **1953** Hall *Coll* (Bryson City NC) We all stayed out in that [camp] that night and told jokes and drunk strong coffee. **1973** *GSMNP*-5:14 Them little old young ones drink that the same as I was. **1978** Reese *Speech NE Tenn* 174 *drinked* = attested by 3/12 (25%) speakers; *drunk* = attested by 5/12 (41.7%) speakers. **1985** Irwin *Alex Stewart* 163 I drunk a pint or more of liquor every day for, I guess, 40 years. **1989** *Matewan OHP*-33 I chased around with the doctor [and] drinked with him a little bit. **1997** Montgomery *Coll*: *drinked* (known to Brown, Bush, Cardwell, Jones, Ledford, Oliver, Weaver). **2009** Burton *Beech Mt Man* 96 Ever'body I saw was drinkin', and I drunk ever'body's liquor.

2 variant past-participle forms *drank*, *drinked*, *drinken*.

1796 *Big Pigeon Church Minutes* 24 [The church] agread to Infirmation being made to the Church that James Wiseheart hath Drank to Exces the Church hath declared their none fellowship on that account. **1845** (in **1974** Harris *High Times* 49) We had danced, kissed and drank ourselves into a perfect thrashin-machine apetite. **1861** *Gilley CW Letters* (Nov 8) mony is scace her corn forty and fifty cents an whisky ten dollar per gallon & we hav not drank but one pint sinc we left home I want bill or bob to to hav a Jug full time. **1934–47** *LAMSAS Appal*: *drank* = attested by 23/148 speakers (15.5%) from WV, 9/20 (45%) from VA, 17/37 (43.2%) from NC, 7/14 (50%) from SC, and 1/12 (8.3%) from GA. **1939** Hall *Coll* (Cataloochee NC) I had drank the quart and spilled a part of it and had to go down get me some more liquor. **1975** *GSMNP*-59:15 Them that made whiskey had drank whiskey and red horsemint. **1978** Reese *Speech NE Tenn* 174 *drank* = attested by 5/12 (41.7%) speakers; *drinked* = attested by 1/12 (8.3%) speakers; *drinken* = attested by 1/12 (8.3%) speakers. **1989** *Matewan OHP*-33 [I] ain't drank a bottle of pop in ten year, I don't guess. **1991** Thomas *Sthn Appal* 243 I've never drinken one gill of soft drink out-side of lemonade, orange juice . . . an' coffee—hot water.

B To be suitable for drinking.

1864 *Chapman CW Letters* (May 10) they are some good springs in this country but it dont drink like the water in old east tennessee. **1917** Kephart *Word-List* 411 = to discharge the function of drink. "Wonder if that water'd *drink*?" **1997** Montgomery *Coll* (known to Adams, Bush), = only for liquor (Brown), = only for liquor (Ellis).

drinked See **drink A1**, **A2**.

drinken See **drink A2**.

drinking gourd *noun* A dried, hollowed gourd kept at a spring, well, or other source of water and used as a drinking vessel by one and all.

1938 Stuart *Dark Hills* 105 The gourds had long crooked necks and little round plump bodies. "These are to make drinking gourds out of."

drink of lonesome waters See **lonesome waters**.

drint *verb* To fade.

1915 Pollard *TN Mts* 242 The dress drinted a good deal. The drinted spots were mostly on the underside. [**1995** Montgomery *Coll* (unknown to consultants from the Smoky Mountains).]

[cf EDD *drent* sb "also in form *drint* . . . a stain or mark left on badly-washed linen . . . If where the water has dried back; they are then said to have drinted, or to be covered with drint"]

drip *noun* The edge of a roof, from which rainwater falls.

1967 *DARE Survey* (Maryville TN) [To remove a wart] tie a knot in a yard-string for each wart, put it in the drip of a house; when it rots, the warts will be gone. **1996** *GSMNPCOHP*-1:2 At home they had a water barrel, where the drip of the house poured in, you know?

[DARE *drip* n 2 chiefly South Midland]

dripping saint *noun* See citation.

1994 Dorgan *Liquid Graves* 10 New Christians have been immersed in outdoor "liquid graves" and ceremoniously raised again as "dripping saints" for many centuries. *Ibid.* 11 The waters of the "liquid grave" cover all, cleansing and purifying. From this symbolic descent, the "dripping saint" then arises, sputtering from the water, shaking from the cold, and probably crying from the emotional trauma.

driprock *noun* See citation.

1957 Broaddus *Vocab Estill Co KY* 26 = a dripstone, stalagmite.

driv See **drive A**.

drive *verb*

A Principal parts.

1 variant past-tense forms *driv, drived, druv*.

1863 *Walker CW Letters* (Sept 12) We Driv the rebels 25 Miles then Fel bak to Dedcater. **1873** Smith *Arp Peace Papers* 50 He driv out in the e[d]ge of the woods and got out of the waggin and laid down by a tree to sleep. **1895** Murfree *Phantoms* 196 I druv him out the house. **1913** Kephart *Our Sthn High* 284 In many cases a weak preterite supplants the proper strong one: div, driv, fit, gi'n or give, rid, rive, riz, writ. **1925** Carter *Mt White Tales* 346 Jack throwed them in and then he driv his sheep drove home and when I left there Jack was rich. **1937** Hall *Coll* (Little Greenbrier TN) He driv many a beef off on foot. **1956** Hall *Coll* (Gatlinburg TN) A witch doctor drawed a picture of the witch and nailed it back of the door, druv a nail in her heart, and then she died. **1957** GSMNP-23:11 They driv them through Cades Cove and took them down to the end of the mouth of Tuckaseegee and back in there. **1962** Williams *Verbs Mt Speech* 17 Verbs which retain either the strong preterites of Middle English or variant preterites of the English dialects [include] *drive* (present), *driv* (past). **1970** Broome *Earth Man* 62 Once we druv a cyar through a creek and wet its shassy and then came a big freeze and froze it to the ground. **1971** *AOHP/ALC*-137 He drived a mule. He'd take big kegs of whiskey over there to this old man, and he would sell it. **1979** *Big South Fork OHP*-1 They'd put this here and then put this cap board here and drived it like you was driving a wedge. **1999** GSMNPCOHP-1:5 I heared you when you driv up.

2 variant past-participle forms *driv, drove, druv*.

1774 *Dunmore's War* 247 I heartily wish you could have some of them drove to the Fort for the use of the Company. **1788** *French Broad Petitions* 213 [O]ur Horses and Cattle [were] drove from our Stations And often we not able to do more than Defend ourselves from our Walls, under these our distresses. **1861** Hedgecock *Diary* 104 The Rebels had drove off from West Liberty some 20 wagons of ammunition and flour the morning on which day our troops entered in the evening. **1862** *Reese CW Letters* (Dec 27) [T]he news was yester day that the yankeys has druv our troops Back seven mils. **1895** Dromgoole *Logan's Courtship* 140 He punched [the guinea hen] with a fence rail till he broke three eggs; but he got her druv off at last. **1929** (in **1952** Mathes *Tall Tales* 144) "Amos," he began, "here's a gent that's driv a right smart ways, an' he 'lows he might like a apple or somethin' to take the dust out o' his goozle." **1939** Hall *Coll* (Cades Cove TN) I've drove a yoke of cattle over the place, fixing ground to plant corn, you know, but we'd still work the horse stock making the farm. **c1940** Simms *Coll*: *druv*. **1941** Still *Troublesome Creek* 116 I'm aiming to get [the cow] bought and driv to the railroad siding at Jackson in four days. **1953** Atwood *Verbs East US* 11 *Driv* occurs elsewhere[,] principally of the coastal and mountain areas of the South and South Midland. [See **1962** in **A1**.] **1973** GSMNP-83:13 I've drove four yoke a many a day, put shoes on them. Their shoes just had two nails. **1978** Reese *Speech NE Tenn* 174 *drove* = attested by 5/12 (41.7%) speakers. **1980** Miles *Verbs in Haywood Co* 98 I have drove but I didn't have a license. **1989** *Matewan OHP*-28 I've drove twenty-five mile to tell you you etter pray. **2000** Morgan *Mts Remember* 20 Why friend, we've driv these cattle all the way from Tennessee.

B *verb* Senses.

1 To flush and pursue (usually game, with the aid of dogs) to a place where one animal can be shot. See also **driver 1**, **stand**, **stander**.

1970 *Hunting* 72 They'd deploy several men to either side of the top of a likely gap, set the dogs loose, and then waited for the dogs to drive the bear through the gap past their stands.

2 To scour an area; to comb (an area) for game.

1913 Kephart *Our Sthn High* 79 That's whar we're goin' to drive; but hit's no use if the bear don't come over. **1927** Mason *Lure of Smokies* 222 We was drivin' Shet-In thet mornin' for deer. **1939** Hall *Coll* (Deep Creek NC) So our drivers driv the west side of Deep Creek, the Easy Ridge and Pole Road with the bear hounds tied, and driv out to the Burnt Spruce Gap. **1953** Hall *Coll* (Bryson City NC) So then in this hunt, [hunters] went down the next day and drove the Bone Valley Creek and didn't get up anything.

[DARE *drive* v B2 now especially South, South Midland]

3 In phrases *cut drive, let drive* = to discharge a gun, throw or let loose (especially a rock). See also **cut down**.

1894 Wingfield *Big Buck* 400 So I took very careful aim along the barrel of my rifle, as I could not see the sights, and let drive at his neck. **1919** Combs *Word-List South* 35 Jep cut drive with a big rock an' scamped Dish. **1929** Kephart *Smoky Mt Magic* 21 Bupply rose on one knee, adjusted his knee, drew it to the head [of the arrow] and let drive. **1939** Hall *Coll* (Deep Creek NC) I let drive at him and broke both of his underjaws, cut them in two. **1941** Stuart *Men of Mts* 271 I took th' big ripe peach and I cut drive at that spider's eyes. **1960** Hall *Smoky Mt Folks* 12 He let drive at him [with his rifle], and the bear broke to run. **1996–97** Montgomery *Coll*: *cut drive* (known to Brown, Jones, Oliver).

4 To float logs downstream to a sawmill. See also **driver 2**.

1964 Clarkson *Lumbering in WV* 361 = to float logs from the forest to the mill. **2006** *WV Encycl* 431 The Greenbrier became the most famous of the driving rivers, its reputation mythologized in the popular novels of W. E. Blackhurst and the poetry of Louise McNeill.

C *noun* The process of floating logs downstream; the logs being floated. See also **main drive**.

1954 Blackhurst *Riders of Flood* 63 Sometimes in dreams he found himself above dashing waves or poised above muddy, sucking whirlpools. That others [= loggers] looked forward to the drives with eagerness mattered not at all. **1964** Clarkson *Lumbering in WV* 361 = [a] body of logs in the process of being floated from the forest to the mill.

drived See **drive**.

drive one's ducks to a bad market (also *drive one's ducks to a poor pond* and other variants) *verb phrase* To make a poor choice in marriage.

1937 Hyatt *Kiverlid* 48 "She is a smart an' likely girl, but jist betwixt you-an-me-an' the gatepost, Granny," whispered Nancy, "I'm afeared she is drivin' her 'ducks to a bad market.'" **1941** Stuart *Men of Mts* 288 [It] looks to me like she driv her ducks to a bad market by taking that thing. **1946** Stuart *Plum Grove Hills* 133 "He's driven his goose to a bad market," Pa said. **1976** Thompson *Touching Home* 18 *drive one's ducks to a dry pond* = to marry a worthless man: "I'm afraid she's driving her ducks to a dry pond." **1991** Still *Wolfpen Notebooks* 67 Gosh dog! Is she going to marry that fellow? She'll be taking her ducks to a poor market. **1995–96** Montgomery *Coll*: *drive one's ducks to a poor market* (known to Cardwell, Jones, Ledford). **2002** Myers *Best Yet Stories* 55 If a girl married beneath her social status, she had driven her ducks to a poor pond according to my mother.

[DARE *drive one's ducks to a poor market* v phr *market* figurative reference to marriage (cf EDD *market* sb 2 (4) (5) and SND *mercat* n 4), chiefly South Midland, South]

driver *noun*

1 A hunter (usually with dogs) who flushes and pursues game toward one or more other waiting hunter or **standers**.

1878 Coale *Wilburn Waters* 90 I had been hunting a long time, but always preferring the post of "driver," had never had the pleasure of killing a deer. **1883** Zeigler and Grosscup *Heart of Alleghanies* 48 It is a shelter only for the time being; no one expects to return to it, for by the following night the hounds may be 20 miles away, and the drivers and standers toasting bear steaks in their cabins, or encamping on some distant height preparatory to resuming on the morrow the chase of a bruin who had through one day eluded their pursuit. **1939** Hall *Coll* (Nine Mile TN) He says for us drivers to go to the Calhoun Ridge and start this bear. **1973** GSMNP-84:12 Doc Jones, he was usually the driver, and he would go down here in these roughs with his dogs, and he could trail a bear a day and night after he had passed along. **1976** *Bear Hunting* 281 The drivers, they were the men that led a dog through the woods to pick up the track. **2008** Plott *Hunting in Smokies* 54 The hunters with the strike dogs are "drivers," who hit a bear trail and run a bear toward the stander, who either makes a kill himself or releases more bear dogs to "pack" the trail.

2 A logger who helps float logs downriver. See also **drive B4**.

2006 Farwell *Logging Term* 1021 Where rivers could be used, the timber was "boomed," or "bound," into "cribs" and floated downstream by "drivers."

driving See **drive B4**.

droll *adjective*

1 Odd, unusual.

1931 Hannum *Thursday April* 129 Merrily she turned to Square and Phoebe to exclaim, "Yore pap's plumb droll turned." **1958** Campbell *Tales* 8 He 'lowed Big Nelt was mighty quare-turned and droll-natured but a right accommodating man.

[DARE *droll* adj 1 South, South Midland]

2 See citation.

c1982 Young *Colloquial Appal* 7 = backward, unmannerly.

drone (also *droning*) *noun* See citations.

1979 GSMNP-118:23 They had singin's up there, old harp singin's, and they had dronin's. I don't know if you know about a dronin' or not. Well, they'd be two stand and sing. And then they'd form a ring around them where they was standing, of the others that sing with them, and they'd sing maybe a verse or something anyway. They'd start, they called it dronin'. And these two in the middle they sung the song and these that went around, some sung bass, some tenor and some different, you know, and they'd just held a sound like they sung. [**1984** Garber *Old Harp* 31 Singers would "drone" the last hymn of former sings. Two sopranos at the front of the church would sing the hymn while the rest of the singers moved around the church droning, or humming, holding the pitch.] **1998** Olszewski *Old Harp* 13 Droning, initiated by T. J. Lawson in his singing schools in Cades Cove, is not dead.... Droning, as used by T. J. Lawson, was when he got the class to sound the starting chord of a song and march around in a circle holding that chord, while he listened to a quartet sing their parts in the center of the circle. This way he would keep order in the class by getting everyone focused on holding the sound for as long as possible, while also getting them up and moving around, usually to the rhythm of the music being sung. **2002** Myers *Best Yet Stories* 150 During the very early days someone might call for a "drone." This unusual procedure called for the entire group of singers to stand up and march around the room humming, after which they would sing as they continued to march. It is thought that the drone started shortly after the Civil War in Cades Cove when Thomas S. Lawson was leading a singing school.

drooped up *adjective phrase* Ailing; indisposed, depressed in spirit.

1972 Cooper *NC Mt Folklore* 91 = disappointed in love, ill or indisposed. **1996–97** Montgomery *Coll* (known to Adams, Cardwell), = more common meaning is "ailing" (Brown), = ailing (Bush).

drooping leucothoe *noun* Same as **dog hobble**.

2006 Ellison *Nature Journal* 36–37 Sometimes called drooping leucothoe, switch ivy or fetterbush, highland doghobble is one of the more common shrubs in the southern mountains, especially the Blue Ridge portions of North Carolina, Tennessee, South Carolina and Georgia. Several other closely related species, coastal doghobble (*L. axillaries*) and swamp doghobble. *L. racemosa*), are found mostly in lowland situations.... Its long arching branches often cover entire slopes, frequently in association with rosebay rhododendron and mountain laurel.... But it's the arching branches that are doghobble's primary claim to fame. These often rot at their tips, creating an extensive tangle that is almost impenetrable. A black bear fleeing hunting dogs will intuitively head for a doghobble tangle situated on a steep slope, which it can easily bound through going upgrade. Pursuing dogs and hunters are quickly left behind, "doghobbled" by the rooted branches and sharp leaves.

drop

A variant form *drap* [dræp].

1824 Knight *Letter from KY* 106–7 Some words are used, even by genteel people, from their imperfect education, in a new sense; and others, by the lower classes in society, pronounced very uncouthly . . . drap. **1858** (in **1974** Harris *High Times* 143) I'm told he won't tetch a drap ove sperits. **1904–20** Kephart *Notebooks* 4:859 I got the drap on him. **1924** (in **1952** Mathes *Tall Tales* 35) We're pore folks an' hain't got nothin' much, but if ye ever git out in them mountings yander we'd be real proud fer ye to drap in. **1942** Hall *Phonetics Smoky Mts* 28 [dræp]. **1974** Roberts *Sang Branch* 13 Another of my men goes up and helps push [the load] down along the lumberyard, and they drap off the stuff at the right stacks.

[OED3 *drap* (at *drop* n) Scottish dialect form; SND *drap* n, v; DARE *drop* n, v A chiefly South, South Midland]

B *verb*

1 variant past-tense forms *drapped, drapt*.

1895 Dromgoole *Fiddling to Fame* 53 When my oldest brother stepped up an' drapped in a vote fur me, I cl'ar furgot myself. **1923** Greer-Petrie *Angeline Doin' Society* 21 He could spar' him one of his knives and forks, fur someone had drapt sev'ral extry ones at his plate. **1939** Hall *Notebooks* 9:29 (Hartford TN) That bear run down the ridge about one hundred and fifty or two hundred yards and drapped dead. **1956** Hall *Coll* (Big Bend NC) He slipped up there and drapped that rock down in on her and just skinned the side of her face all over, and the witch come off of him then. **1973** *AOHP/ASU-53* [Revivals lasted] generally about ten or eleven days, sometimes two weeks, and everybody drapped work and went to meeting of a day. **1981** *GSMNP-122*:67 The bloom just drapped off.

2 variant past-participle form *drapped*.

1859 Taliaferro *Fisher's River* 56 I thought I'd a drapped in my tracks.

C *verb*

1 Of a cow: to give birth to (a calf); to give birth.

1966 Dakin *Vocab Ohio River Valley* 234 A third old expression *drop a calf* (also *drop her calf* and rarely in the absolute construction *drop*) has a somewhat different distribution. This old English expression is used by scattered speakers in Kentucky from the southern Pennyroyal to the Bluegrass and northern Mountains. **1996** Johnson *Lexical Change* 138 *drop a calf* = statistically more common in the mountains of South Carolina and Georgia than in the Piedmont and Coastal Plain c1990.

2 Of an unborn child: to change position just before birth.

1949 Arnow *Hunter's Horn* 273 She studied Milly's abdomen with a critical tilting of her head and declared she thought the child had dropped already.

3 See citations. See also **dropper**.

1944 Dingus *Tobacco Words* 66 = to distribute [tobacco] plants on the row in the proper places. **1967** Key *Tobacco Vocab* Before the mechanical transplanter . . . one person went ahead and "dropped" a seedling at regular intervals along the row. Another person followed behind and "set" the seedling, making a hole with a peg and pushing the dirt up around it.

[DARE *drop* v D1 chiefly South, South Midland]

drop dead *verb phrase* To faint. Same as **fall dead**.

1994–97 Montgomery *Coll*: *drop dead* (known to Brown, Cardwell, Oliver, Weaver).

drop edge of yonder *noun phrase* The brink of death.

1939 *FWP Guide TN* 134 Granny Tatum's standing on the drop-edge of Yonder, and we'll soon be laying her down in her silent grave. **1984** Wilder *You All Spoken* 207 *standin' on the drop edge of yonder* = about to peg out; about to hang it up.

[DARE *drop edge of yonder* n phr especially TN]

drop off (also *drop out*) *verb phrase* To die.

1913 Kephart *Our Sthn High* 224 Looks like he mought drap off, him bein' weak and rather narvish and sick with a head-swimmin'. **1928** Thornburgh *Americans Forgot* 28 When one of the old-timers drap out, I feel like a bright jewel was droppin' out of the risin' generation. **1936** Stuart *Head of Hollow* 168 We want it in paper with strangers so they won't be no trouble if me or your Pop would drop off. **1994–98** Montgomery *Coll*: *drop off* (known to Brown, Cardwell, Oliver, Weaver); *drop out* (known to Bush). **2007** McMillon *Notes*: *drop off* = to die.

[DARE *drop off* v phr 1 especially southern Appalachians]

dropper *noun* See citation. See also **drop C3**.

1969 Miller *Raising Tobacco* 29 Moving behind the *dropper*, the setter put the plant into the earth by taking the plant by the roots and, using the index and middle fingers, making a hole in the soil and slipping the plant into a standing position.

dropsy *noun*

1 Heart disease, especially edema around the heart; edema generally.

1862 *Warrick CW Letters* (Aug 17) you wanted to know something about Henry he was only sick two days his disease was Appoplexy, he had the Dropsy too I think. **1863** *Vance Papers* (Aug 16) I have got the Dropsy verry bad and one eye is entierly out and the other is not good, I believe it will be out in A month or two. **1967** Jones *Peculiarities Mtneers* 66 Sourwood bark tea thickened with flour and made into pills was used in the treatment of dropsy, a disease modern doctors call "edema." Another remedy for dropsy was made by steeping elder bark in vinegar in which rusty nails and bolts had been soaked. Tea made by boiling cowslip plants was another favorite dropsy remedy. **2006** Cavender *Medical Term* 1022 Health-care providers in contemporary Appalachia may still encounter antiquated medical terminology such as . . . *dropsy* "heart disease."

2 Lethargy, fatigue.

c1960 Wilson *Coll* = humorous reference to a person's habit of dropping into a chair too often and too easily; hence must have dropsy. **1967–69** *DARE Survey* (Moorefield WV) *dropsy and heart trouble* = that's when you drop down and ain't got the heart to get up.

[DARE *dropsy* n 1 especially South, South Midland]

drown *verb* Principal parts.

1 variant base form *drownd*. See also **stall**.

1865 *Misemer CW Letters* (April 30) I Jumped over board among countles numbers of drownding men and made my way to the bank after hard swiming of 8 or 9 miles. **1891** Brown *Dialect in TN* 172 In *drownded, stallded, attackted*, etc., there may be an error as to what is the present tense of the verb. **1927** Furman *Lonesome Road* 8 In song-ballats hit's allus young, beautiful ladies . . . that gets their hearts broke and drownds theirselves in swift-flowing waters. **1974** Roberts *Sang Branch* 224 He set a day to kill his girl by drownding her. **1989** *Matewan OHP*-18 She said, "I'm afraid he'll drownd," said, "would you pray with me?" **1996** Montgomery *Coll* (known to Ledford).

2 variant past-tense forms *drownded, drowndid*.

1861 *Chapman CW Letters* (Nov 2) tha[y] was scard so bad that Som of them roun [i.e., run] inn the River and Drounded. **1868** (in **1974** Harris *High Times* 306) He never drowndid, an' aint fish'd out yet. **1953** Atwood *Verbs East US* 12 Elsewhere in the Eastern States *drownded* is distinctly a Type I form [i.e. of older speakers with little formal education], varying in frequency from one third (e. N.Y.) to nine tenths (N.C.). In Type II [i.e. younger speakers with more formal education] *drownded* is used by less than one tenth in e. N.Y., about one fourth in Pa., Va., and N.C., and by slightly less than half in W.Va. **c1960** Wilson *Coll*: *drownded* = almost regular for past tense and past participle. **1976** *GSMNP*-109: 14 We had a cloudburst on Webbs Mountain on the Webbs Creek side which cascaded down the mountain and drownded four people in one family. **1978** Reese *Speech NE Tenn* 174 *drownded* = attested by 4/12 (33.3%) speakers.

3 variant past-participle form *drownded*.

1859 Taliaferro *Fisher's River* 21 It was "narrated" all through the country that "famus was drownded in a mash tub." **1923** (in **1952** Mathes *Tall Tales* 10) Well, I 'low the Lord A'mighty knows more about who'll git drownded when the floods come than some that holds theirselves up fer prophets. **1939** Walker *Mtneer Looks* 10–11 Sump'm tol' me that if I didn't move purty quick I'd be purt' nigh drownded. **1942** Hall *Phonetics Smoky Mts* 83. [See **1960** in **2**.] **1978** Reese *Speech NE Tenn* 174 *drownded* = attested by 8/12 (66.7%) speakers. **1999** Morgan *Gap Creek* 215 "We can't go out in a flood in the dark," I said. "We'd get drownded." **2013** DeLozier and Jourdan *Back Seat* 37 I should have drownded you when I had the chance.

drownd, drownded, drowndid See **drown**.

drug See **drag A1, A2**.

drug out See **drag out**.

drugs *noun* Dregs.

1891 Brown *Dialect in TN* 172 We hear also . . . *drugs* for *dregs*. **1895** Edson and Fairchild *TN Mts* 371 = *sequelae*, dregs. "The old woman has the rheumatiz; I reckon hit's the *drugs* of the fever." **1917** Kephart *Word-List* 411 = variant of *dregs*. **1985** Dabney *More Mt Spirits* 75 When [the liquor] comes out over hyar it would be clear as a crystal and no drugs or nothin' about it.

drumly *adjective* Muddy; of weather: gloomy.

1952 Wilson *Folk Speech NC* 535 = muddy. **1996–97** Montgomery *Coll* (known to Brown, Norris).

[OED3 *drumly* adj 2 "of the sky, the weather, etc.: gloomy, dark, cloudy"; SND *drumlie* adj 2 "of the weather: dark, gloomy, sullen"; DARE *drumly* adj, adv Scots and English dialect]

drummer (also *drummer fellow, drummer man*) *noun* A traveling salesman. See citations.

1931 Owens *Speech Cumberlands* 92 *drummer man* = a traveling salesman: "If you lose your store, you could be a drummer-man for the Big Sandy Fruit." **1966** West *Dialect Sthn Mts* 31 A drummer-feller (salesman), up from the lowlands, asks the old lady how she is. **1979** Slone *My Heart* 77 Every two weeks a salesman or a "drummer," as we then called them, would come from Paintsville, Kentucky. Verne Stumbo, a very good friend of mine who is now dead, was a drummer. All his life he came riding a mule and carrying large saddle bags filled with his sales books and samples. It took him all week to visit the stores up the many small hollows in his territory. **1983** Montell *Don't Go Up* 198 = salesperson who traveled in a horse-drawn vehicle filled with merchandise. **1987** Smalling *Watauga Co* (as of 1921) In order to sell everything, as one person put it, "from a shoe-button to a saw-mill," vendors sent traveling salesmen or "drummers" from such large wholesale houses as E. W. King Dry Goods, King Brothers Shoe Company, McClung Hardware and Summers Hardware, to name a few. The "drummer" would frequently stay the night with the Miller family before traveling on. **1989** *Bryson City Centennial* 21 On the first floor were the kitchen, large dining room, lobby, and an extra room called the "Sample room," in which drummers arranged their displays of merchandise. **1989** *Matewan OHP*-9 We had a little store, a country store, and they had what they called a drummer. He rode a horse back in here, and he'd take the orders from these little country stores and send the order in to where they made it.

[DARE *drummer* n 6 widespread, but chiefly South, South Midland]

drummer fellow, drummer man See **drummer**.

drummy *noun* See citation.

2002 Armstead *Black Days* 243 = [a] mine roof condition which sounds loose, hollow, or weak when tested by pounding with a tool [indicating] gaps above the cap rock and potential danger.

drunk *adjective* See citation.

1944 Wilson *Word-List* 42 *drunk* = said of cake, bread, potatoes, etc., which "fall" or become heavy when cooked.

drunkard *noun* A fruit fly.

1975 *Cucumber Doll* 376 The [cucumber] doll wouldn't last more than a day or two, because drunkards (fruit flies) would get after it. **2007** McMillon *Notes* = a fly that slowly flies around grapes.

[DARE *drunkard* n 1 chiefly Mid Atlantic]

drunk as a boiled owl *adjective phrase* Extremely intoxicated.

1960 Hall *Smoky Mt Folks* 62 *as drunk as a biled owl*. **1979** Melton *'Pon My Honor* 64 When he started home that night, he was not only three sheets in the wind, he was drunk as a "biled owl."

druther *auxiliary verb* (Had or would) rather; hence noun (usually plural) = a preference, choice.

1863 *Robinson CW Letters* I would drother abin at home but I could not nor I don't know when I will. **1863** *Shifflet CW Letters* (Feb 13) hit dus me a heepe a good to her from you but I had a heepe drother see you all. **1925** Dargan *Highland Annals* 60 I felt 'most froze to the ground, an' I thought if Reenie was only livin' I'd let her do her own 'druthers the rest of her days. **1940** Haun *Hawk's Done* 77 It is just like I told the youngons when I come home—if I had my druthers, I would druther the Lord knowed about my sins than for Preacher Jarvin to. **1967–68** *DARE Survey* (Maryville TN) = as noun. "If I had my——, I'd take a dog." = as verb. "I'd druther" (Brasstown NC). **1985** Irwin *Alex Stewart* 192 I would have druther seen my coffin a coming, might near it, than to have seen another bucket of that sap. **2005** Williams *Gratitude* 491 = rather; would rather.

[contraction of *would rather* or *had rather*]

druv See **drive A1**, **A2**.

dry bone *noun* One opposed the drinking of alcoholic beverages who sought out and reported **moonshiners**.

1982 Absher *Wilkes County* 69 Most of the people in these neighborhoods, if not involved, were careful not to stumble onto a suspected stillsite, but this was not always the case. One woman who found a still stood guard while her husband went for the law. When three hapless stillhands showed up, she held them under citizen's arrest and the nose of the gun until the officers came. Another "dry bone," as moonshiners called them, made seeking out and reporting stills practically a full-time career.

dry-clothes man *noun* A revenue officer

1938 Stuart *Dark Hills* 135 (*DARE*) He thought I was a "dry-clothes" man snooping around to see if he was selling licker.

dry dote *noun* See citation. Same as **dote**.

1974–75 McCracken *Logging* 3:24 There were some big white pine but there wasn't much of it and it wasn't too good. It was all bad burned old, it was dopey. If you had a big perfect white pine tree, you didn't expect to get much out of it because usually it was so old it had what we called a dry dote. The wood would be there but when the tree fell it would break all to pieces.

dry drought *noun* A lengthy period of very dry weather.

1884 Smith *Arp Scrap Book* 176 Them snakes I've been killin' brought all this dry drouth in my land and ruined my crop.

[DARE *dry drought* n chiefly GA, SC, Gulf States]

dry fly *noun* A cicada. Same as **jar bug**.

1966 *DARE Survey* (Burnsville NC) = insect that sits in trees or bushes in hot weather and makes a sharp, buzzing sound.

[DARE *dry fly* n 1 chiefly South, South Midland]

dry grin(s) *noun* (usually in phrase *the dry grins*) An embarrassed or forced grin.

1892 Fruit *KY Words* 230 *have the dry grins* = the smiles of one teased. **1915** Dingus *Word-List VA* 182 = said of one sorely teased but striving to smile. **1956** McAtee *Some Dial NC* 14 = a forced or embarrassed grin. **1968** *Expressions* 25 Another told of a friend he knew who, when caught in a white lie or practical joke, would look sheepish and "take a bad case of the dry grins." **1998** Montgomery *Coll* (known to Brown), = grinning when you are not amused, as when someone has gotten your goat (Jones).

[DARE *dry grin* n chiefly South, South Midland]

dryhouse *noun* A shed for drying and storing fruits and vegetables.

1971 Costner *Song of Life* 45 They had a dryhouse, a house built around and over a furnace.

dry hull(y) *noun* A bean dried in its pod.

1975 Jackson *Unusual Words* 155 Dried beans had numerous names—*leather-britches*, *fodder beans*, *shuck beans*, and *dry hulls*. **1995–97** Montgomery *Coll*: *dry hully* (known to Shields).

dry kiln *noun* A furnace on which fruit is placed for drying out. See 1996 citation.

1937 Hall *Coll* (Ravensford NC) We had a dry kiln made out of rock. [There was] a shed over that, just like a molasses furnace. [We] dried peaches and fruit. **1964** Clarkson *Lumbering in WV* 360 = a building so constructed as to permit drying of lumber by steam or hot air. **1985** Irwin *Alex Stewart* 204 [Speaker A:] Pap made two dry kilns for Mama to use. Things would dry so much quicker in a kiln, and they weren't as tough. The sun makes them tough. [Speaker B:] What do you mean by a dry kiln? [Speaker A:] He'd build a furnace out of clay and rock about eight feet long and four feet wide. He'd put a big flat rock on top and cover it good with clay mud. He put a chimney at one end, just like you was going to make molasses. Build you a big fire under that and before long that rock would dry out and be just as hard as concrete. That would hold the heat for hours. **1996** Houk *Foods & Recipes* 74 Apples could be dried on a "dry kiln," which is like a sorghum furnace. Put a fire under it as you do to make molasses, heat rocks under scaffold, and place fruit on top to dry. This kiln would hold three to four bushels of fresh apples, which would dry down to about a bushel.

dry-land Baptist *noun* See citations.

1982 Slone *How We Talked* 77 = nickname for someone that has all the appearances and actions of a Christian, believing in the

Baptist church, yet has never been baptized. **1989** Dorgan *Regular Baptists* 74 The Old Regular [Baptist is] cautious about making judgments about the state of grace of other people, as is suggested by Bull Creek's tradition of reading the list of deceased individuals who regularly attended but were never baptized, individuals whom Elder Atlas Hall identifies, not disparagingly, as "dry land Baptists." **2014** Montgomery *Doctrine* 110 Dry land Baptist = those who seemingly enjoy church, who attend church services more than some members, and contribute financially to the church, yet never join and enter into the ordinance of baptism. No matter how many times they hear the message preached and rejoice in it, never act on it by way of public profession.

dryland cress (also *dryland crease*) *noun* An edible **cress** (*Barbarea verna*). See 1988 citation. See also **cress, land cress, watercreases, wintercress.**

1952 Giles *40 Acres* 116 The first spring we were here, one of my neighbors came by with a sack and her little paring knife one day. "Where are you going?" I yelled at her. "To hunt dry land creases. Come go along." [**1973** *Foxfire II* 78 This cress grows to two feet high in damp ground, along streams, and in old fields.] **1988** Lambert *Kinfolks* 21 Another sure sign of spring was going out to look for "dry land creases." This particular type of wild green, which I have subsequently identified as winter cress, grew in fields that had been cultivated the year before. The greens grew in a flat circle very low to the ground, and you wandered through the previous year's cornfield looking for the green leaves of creases among the brown of the field.

dry-land fish *noun* An edible mushroom, especially a morel (*Morchella* spp), which has a fish-like taste when fried. Also called **wildfish, woodfish.**

1952 Giles *40 Acres* 93 We also have *dry-land fish*. Mushrooms to you. But they are not the familiar mushrooms of the city market. They are a big, oval, porous plant, brown on top and pink underneat. Henry tells me their botanical name is the common morel. They spring up in shady, damp places in the woods, especially after a rain, and we gather them by the pecks. . . . They do have a slight fishy taste. I think it is more a fish texture than a taste. **1969** *DARE Survey* (Berea KY) = umbrella shaped, but honeycombed, shaped like Christmas tree bulb; (Hardshell KY, Hindman KY, Tompkinsville KY) = an edible mushroom, tall and cone-shaped, 2–6″ high; a cone-shaped mushroom, eatable, a spring delicacy. **1983** Montell *Don't Go Up* 178 Times was hard during the Depression. I know one time we was hunting dryland fish. We called it that—some type of mushroom. Only come up in the spring of the year when peach and apple trees are in full bloom. They only stay up for a week or ten days. They were a specialty because it was something different from the beans and potatoes you was used to. **1993** Ison and Ison *Whole Nother Lg* 18 = a large fried mushroom. **2001** Joslin *Appal Bounty* 11–12 Known by a variety of names, from simply "the mushroom" to the more exotic "dry land fish," the morel has been a favorite of mountain folks for generations. . . . The morel is an elusive quarry that requires well developed hunting skills. The hunter must be extremely observant and steeped in the lore of the morel. Just strolling into the forest hoping to chance upon these mushrooms will leave you almost always disappointed.

[DARE *dry-land fish* n 1 chiefly KY, TN]

dry-land sled *noun* Same as **land sled**. See also **half sled, lizard 1.**

1974 Fink *Bits Mt Speech* 7 = sled to be used in fields or dirt roads. **1982** Slone *How We Talked* 133 = a long, low, wide sled. **1996–97** Montgomery *Coll* = used to haul produce, wood, or manure (Cardwell), = made of sourwood logs that curved up in front, same as *land sled* (Jones).

dry out *verb phrase* See 1978 citation.

1978 *Smokies Heritage* 334 For ailments of the digestive system, such as dysentery, the astringent properties of blackberry and willow leaves were used in making teas, powerful teas which were capable of "drying out" the disease. **1997** Montgomery *Coll* (known to Bush), = also for cows in springtime to counter scours (Weaver).

dubby *adjective* See citation.

c1982 Young *Colloquial Appal* 7 = blunt or dull (hoe or ax).

dubious *adjective*

A variant forms *juberous* [see **1895**, **1974** in **B**], *jubers* [see **1937** in **B**], *jubus* [see **1859** in **B**].

[DARE *dubious* adj *juberous/jubers* chiefly South Midland, also New England, South, *jubus* South, South Midland]

B Hesitant, uncertain, afraid.

1859 Taliaferro *Fisher's River* 204 I felt mighty skittish and jubus of Davis, fur he was allers a-swaggerin', and cavortin', and boastin' about. **1895** Edson and Fairchild *TN Mts* 372 He was *juberous* about crossing the stream. **1921** Greer-Petrie *Angeline at Seelbach* 5 We was both a little jubus about enterin'. **1937** Hall *Coll* (Wears Cove TN) I was jubers of that. **1939** Hall *Coll* (Cataloochee NC) Uncle Steve said, "You go around [the bear]. I'm jubers and I'll go below him." **1942** Hall *Phonetics Smoky Mts* 70 The common pronunciation . . . of *dubious* "timid, bashful" as ['ʤubɚs]. **1972** Cooper *NC Mt Folklore* 93 *jubus, juberous*—dubious, frightened. **1974** Fink *Bits Mt Speech* 13 I was juberous of that all the time. **1989** *Matewan OHP-45* You can tell whenever people is afraid of you . . . and they was kindly juberous of me.

duck-bill *noun* A type of house design.

2006 *Encycl Appalachia* 744 Some residents gave these homes distinctive vernacular names; the "duck-bill" house, for instance, was a two-story, four-room house with prominent overhanging porches on the first story.

duck fit *noun* A tantrum, outburst of emotion, sometimes one greater than called for. See also **cat fit, take C5.**

1927 Woofter *Dialect from WV* 353 = showing ill temper without cause. "He took a duck-fit because I dropped the hammer on the ground." **1940** Haun *Hawk's Done* 116 Ad and Linus took a duck fit when they found out Meady had slipped off and got married. **1968** Wilson *Folklore Mammoth Cave* 41 Nervous fit[s], often suspected as hardly genuine . . . were *duck fits, conniption fits, jeeminy fits, the allovers,* and, very recently, the *heebie-jeebies,* or the *whitty-jiggers.* **1978** Parris *Mt Cooking* 115 Grandma, who was just about the best cornbread maker in the world, would have had a dying duck-fit if Grandpa had ever fetched home some of the meal that's put out nowadays. **1994–95** Montgomery *Coll* (known to Cardwell); Somebody will have a duck fit if they find out about this (Shields).

[DARE *duck fit* n chiefly South, Midland]

duckings *noun* See citation.

1940 Farr *More TN Expressions* 447 = overalls: "The boys wear duckings in the 'bacco patch."

duck nest *noun* See citation.

1985 Dabney *More Mt Spirits* 156 To prevent heat loss, the distillers built up a firebox of fieldstone chinked with mud around the sides, back and front, closing over the still at the cape. This is called a "stump furnace," a "duck nest," a "bedrock furnace," and sometimes an "eyebrow singer." "Any good 'shiner could put his overall jumper under a pot (over the bedrock), and it would never scorch," a state revenuer recalled. Through this method, distillers avoided scorching the beer. The copper pot still, also known as the "blockade," "buccaneer," or "turnip type" variety, ranged in capacity from 10 gallons to 100 gallons. Many of the "copper pot craftsmen" soldered connections with silver solder, although most stills were so tight-fitting, they did not require soldering, being put together with rivets and brads on crimped edges.

duck's nest *noun* See citation.

1957 Broaddus *Vocab Estill Co KY* 27 = a chuck hole.

dud oneself *verb phrase* To undress.

1927 Woofter *Dialect from WV* 353 *dud yourself* = to remove your clothes: "Let's see who can dud himself and be in the water first." **1975** Gainer *Witches Ghosts Signs* 9 You got your clothes all wet; you'd better dud yourself before the fire.

dugaloo See **doogaloo**

duke's mixture *noun* An assortment or hodgepodge; a person or animal of mixed lineage.

1997 Montgomery *Coll* (known to Adams, Brown, Cardwell, Jones, Ledford, Norris, Oliver), = a dog or other animal of mixed lineage (Cardwell), = a mixture of food or other items, as in a grabbag at the fair (Weaver). **2003** Blaustein *Thistle and Brier* 44 My father's side is a combination, as I say, a "Duke's Mixture," They are some Highland Scot, Lowland Scot which became Ulster Scot, English, Dutch, French Huguenot, that's it. A real mixture of things.

dulcimer (also *dulcimore*) *noun*

A variant forms *delcymore, dulcymore.*

1997 Smith *Dulcimer Traditions* 3 In its traditional world, the instrument's name was and is widely pronounced "dulcymore" or "delcymore."

B A musical instrument with three or four wire strings across a fretted soundbox and of two types unrelated except in name: the trapezoid-shaped hammered dulcimer (usually set on a stand before the musician, who uses two small hammers to strike the strings); and the **mountain dulcimer** or **Appalachian dulcimer** (held in the lap with strings plucked or strummed). [Editor's note: Consultants from the Smoky Mountains agree that the instrument was little known in the area, most of them first seeing one only later in life, usually in the 1960s.] See also **church dulcimer, double dulcimer, feather harp, hog fiddle, mountain dulcimer.**

1917 Campbell and Sharp *Engl Folk Songs* x In Kentucky . . . singers occasionally play an instrument called the dulcimer, a shallow, wooden box, with four sound-holes, in shape somewhat like a flat, elongated violin, over which are strung three (sometimes four) metal strings, the two (or three) lower of which are tonic-drones, the melody being played upon the remaining and uppermost string which is fretted. As the strings are plucked with the fingers and not struck with a hammer, the instrument would, I suppose, be more correctly called a psaltery. **1937** Eaton *Handicrafts* 198 In many instances the instruments were made by the singers themselves, the one most frequently used to accompany the singer being the dulcimer, or, as it is called, the "dulcimore," indigenous to and still made in many parts of the Highlands. **1944** Combs *Word-List Sthn High* 19 = a native harp of the highlands; it has nothing in common with the classic dulcimer, resembling rather an ancient, oriental psaltery. **1963** Ritchie *Dulcimer Book* 7 As long as I can remember, and as long as my father could remember, and as long as *his* father could remember, there have been dulcimers, or "dulcimores," played in our Kentucky mountains. *Ibid.* 14 Where then *did* the Appalachian plucked dulcimer come from? I believe it came from many places, just as our songs did . . . like the songs, folk instruments came remembered in the mind and heart. **1975** *Foxfire III* 188 There is no standard-sized or -shaped dulcimer. Every maker has the one he likes best. I use the same general pattern and vary the type of wood, or number of strings. Kentucky, Mountain, and Appalachian are all names for the plucked dulcimer, which may have any number of strings. Mountain people call them "dulcymores" or "delcymores." . . . [I] never saw nor heard of the dulcimer until the late 1940s. Some of the craftsmen of the Southern Highland Handicraft Guild began making them, using old ones for patterns. Their popularity has been growing ever since . . . with the revival of the folk music and handicrafts. **1979** Irwin *Musical Instruments* 64 As the dulcimer was developed in southern Appalachia, the fingerboard was almost always raised, and the instrument took on a variety of curvaceous shapes. They were seldom straight-sided and rectangular, as they seem to have been in the Pennsylvania area. And they became more crude, less refined and more diversified in style, decoration, and construction. Why the mountaineer changed the instrument into its present shape and form is still being studied by students of the subject. **1995** Williams *Smoky Mts Folklife* 48 The only instrument generally associated with the home-based ballad tradition is the Appalachian dulcimer. However, there is little evidence that the dulcimer actually existed in the Great Smoky Mountains region until the mid-twentieth century. **2008** Joyner *Dulcimer* 223 The plucked dulcimer, often called the Appalachian dulcimer, is a southern mountain folk instrument. Its sound is soft and restrained, with a gentle charm and a slight touch of melancholy. Its diatonic scales and heavy drones make it sound like a gentler version of the bagpipes. The most common shapes are the "tear-drop" and the "figure eight." Dulcimers usually have three or four strings (although they may have as many as eight) running over a fret board.... Mountain people have used them for generations to accompany the tragic English and Scots ballads, as well as to play spritely instrumental pieces. **2009** Miller *Nigh Gone* 127 Of the many legends that thread through the fabric of the history of mountain music, the most persistent and least founded is that of the dulcimer (or "dulcimore" in Appalachian English) as a traditional musical instrument of the southern highlands. The truth of the matter, as reported by Rosenbaum, is that "less than 10 percent of mountain people had heard of one until recent years." The myth about the universality of the instrument stems undoubtedly from the performances of Jean Ritchie, the youngest of fourteen children in a family from the eastern Kentucky village of Viper. She took her dulcimer to New York City in 1945 and became the rage of the Big Apple with her traditional folk singing. In the wake of her phenomenal success and the tremendous interest generated in her instrument, dulcimer makers sprang up everywhere, and the instrument became a staple of the inventory of every mountain crafts shop inside and outside Appalachia.

[< Middle English *dowcemere* < Old Italian *dulcimelo* < Latin *dulcis* "sweet"; DARE *dulcimer* n formerly Appalachians, now widely recognized]

dulcymore See **dulcimer A.**

dull as a froe *adjective phrase* Very dull.

1952 Callahan *Smoky Mt Country* 10 [The froe] was a blunt, scythe-like instrument with a thick edge, from which the expression "as dull as a frow" originated. **1967** Hall *Coll* (Del Rio TN) That pocket knife is dull as a froe. A froe was kept dull so as not to splinter the logs in making shingles.

[DARE (at *dull* adj 3B) chiefly South, South Midland]

dullsome *adjective* Tedious, tiresome.

1949 Arnow *Hunter's Horn* 185 Maude was carrying a colt and the children were too young to be fully broken to dullsome work.

dumb bull *noun* See citations.

1933 Thomas *Traipsin' Woman* 226–27 "Laban's been goin' to bellin' ever since I can memorize. He takes delight in it." ... He showed us how the hollowed log gave forth such a sound. Two feet long, it was, and over one end a tanned piece of coon-hide was tightly stretched like a drumhead; through a hole in its center a string was run. It was carried by a leather handle. "Now take the piece of rosin in your hand," he said, handing the lump of rosin to me ... "Now reach your hand up inside the log and pull on the string; hold fast the rosin." I did so. The raucous sound filled the kitchen. It was enough to startle anyone, even with the connivance there before your very eyes. **1970** *Hunting* 10 You ever seed a dumbull? Piece a'board about that long [= about six inches—right thin]—y'cut'em off sort'a in the shape of a old fashioned coffin—diamond shaped. He'd made'im one once, and I heered it, an' I thought it'uz somethin' in th'river at th'start. I thought it'uz a dog takin' a fit. **1993** Page and Smith *Foxfire Toys and Games* 156 Bill Lamb, my uncle, was bad to make things. He'd make what they called the "Dumb Bull." It was made in a way that when you whizzed it around, it would make an awful racket! He'd take a plank and whittle it down thin [about ten inches long and three inches wide] and sharpen the edges in some way [similar to airplane wings], and bore a hole in one end. You'd attach a string to it [about five feet] and whirl it around and it'd make the awfullest racket you ever heard!

[DARE *dumb bull* n 1 especially South Midland]

dumb supper *noun* Formerly, a mock meal prepared, set out, and conducted in silence, in which girls seek to meet and identify their future mates.

1936 McDowell *Background* 4 A strange custom brought down from the remote past by tradition was the "Dumb Supper." As practiced in my neighborhood the person setting the dumb supper would on a certain night set the table without saying or hearing a word. Every person present must be perfectly quiet and every action must be performed backward. On these two points hinged the success of the charm. If everything was correctly performed, the end of the ceremonial supper would be marked by the appearance of a visible ghost, whose person and actions would plainly foretell the fate of the one who set the supper. Usually it was undertaken by an unmarried woman, who expected her future husband to appear. In one instance, often told to our horror stricken ears, a coffin appeared and the poor girl died within the year. **1943** Bandy *Witchcraft* 12–13 If a young girl wants to know her future husband, she sets out a "dumb supper." True to name, not a word must be spoken while the supper is being prepared or else the charm will be broken. The first thing the participants do is to cut their finger-nails and toe-nails. The parings are then tied up together in a little bag. The girls then go about preparing a supper for their future husbands. All the walking around must be done backwards; all food must be prepared with the hands behind the back. When the supper is ready the chairs are placed—one for each girl taking part. The girls then sit down by the fire and pitch the little bags of nail parings into the fire. In a short while the wind begins to blow, the dogs to howl, the doors will fly open, and in will walk the future husband of each girl and sit down in the chair prepared for him. If one of the girls is to be an old maid, no man comes in to occupy her chair, but two men carrying a coffin will place it on the chair of the girl destined never to be married. **1993** Burleson *Aunt Keziah* 2 We wuz the self-same ones that set Dumb Suppers and all that stuff to try to tell our fortunes, who we'd marry etc. Now the way abody sets a Dumb Supper, you git a bunch of single gals and git supper, but you do hit all backards, even to setting the table. When you git hit on the table, whoever you aim to marry was sposed to come in and set down.

dummern *noun* A woman.

1907 Dugger *Balsam Groves* 158 I'll be bound ever'thing has to be packed on a pour ol' dummern. **1913** Kephart *Our Sthn High* 279 in Mi[t]chell County, North Carolina, we hear the extraordinary forms ummern and dummern ("La! Look at them dummernses a-comin'!"). **1952** Brown *NC Folklore* 401 Hits a poor dummern that can't daddy her youngun by hits favor. **1997** Montgomery *Coll* (known to Ellis).

[alteration of *womern* "woman" perhaps influenced by *dumb'un* "a dumb one"]

dumper *noun* See citation.

1911 Shearin *E KY Word-List* 538 = a tobacco grower who refuses to pool his crop, but sells as soon as the "pool" has forced the price up, thus enjoying an advantage which he did not aid in bringing about.

dun See **do A6a**.

dusk dark (also *dusky dark, dust dark, dusty dark*) *noun* The time of day when and shortly after the sun goes down; partial darkness, in contrast to complete darkness (**black dark**). Also called **gray dark**.

1938 (in **2005** Ballard and Chung *Arnow Stories* 101) Nights when she was a cookin supper about th time a dusty dark she'd stand in th kitchen door an listen up th holler. **1939** Hall *Coll* (Hazel Creek NC) It was just about dusky dark. It was snowin' like water pourin' out of a bucket. **1941** Still *Troublesome Creek* 158 A shade hung the window and it was dust dark. **1955** Ritchie *Singing Family* 93 We'd sit on the porch until abut dusty-dark and then we'd get up and go in by the fire. **1969** Roberts *Greasybeard* 156 He borreyed a horse and buggy from a neighbor and propped [the dead woman] up in the front seat and drove down in town about dust dark. **1972** *AOHP/ALC-226* We struck out running down that holler, and it was . . . dusty dark, just before dusty dark. **1976** Carter *Little Tree* 2 She picked out our bus, right on the nose, just as dusk dark was settin in. **1976** Tyler *Man's Work* 28 You could be under [the trees] in the middle of the day and the sun shining bright, and it looked like dusty dark it was so thick and heavy overhead. **1986** Ogle *Lucinda* 61 I was sitting on top the rail fence, and it was getting dusky dark when I saw something moving toward us out of the Rhododendron thicket. **1986** Pederson et al. *LAGS* (Greene Co TN) *dusky dark* = just before dark, after [the] sun is down. **1997** Montgomery *Coll* (two consultants from the Smoky Mountains know *dusk dark*, nine know *dusky dark*). **2008** *Rosie Hicks* 1 I was scared 'cause it [was] getting dusty dark.

[cf EDD *dusk o' dark* is a folk etymology for *dusky dark*; DARE *dusk dark* n chiefly South]

dusky See **come down dusky**.

dusky dark See **dusk dark**.

dust (also *dusting*) *noun* Usually of a granular substance: a small but indefinite amount. See also **grain A**.

1913 Kephart *Our Sthn High* 33 Marg walked five miles to the store with a skinny old chicken, last of the flock, and offered to barter it for "a dustin' o' salt." **1937** Hall *Coll* (Hartford TN) They had muzzle-loading guns but not a dust of powder. **1939** Farr *TN Mt Regions* 90 = a small amount: "I had to borrow a dust of meal to make pony bread for supper." **1941** Still *Troublesome Creek* 171 We could do with a dust o' honesty. **1952** Wilson *Folk Speech NC* 535 I'd like to buy a *dust* of flour till I can go to the mill. **1966** Dykeman *Far Family* 114 I can tell you one thing: I'm no dirt farmer, raising a dib of this and a dust of that. **1981** Williams *Storytelling* They looked in the meal barrel and they wasn't a dusting of meal in there. **1994–97** Montgomery *Coll*: *dusting* = used for anything powdery (Brown), = applies to snow, cheese, etc. (Cardwell), = applies to "a little bit of anything" (Norris).

[DARE *dust* n[1] 2 chiefly South, South Midland]

dust dark, dusty dark See **dusk dark**.

dust devil *noun* See citation.

2017 *Blind Pig* (Oct 20) = when the wind moves in a tight circular motion across the ground.

dusting See **dust**.

dust one's pants *verb phrase* To spank one.

1996 Montgomery *Coll* If you don't stop doing that, I'll dust your pants (Norris).

Dutch *adjective* German, of German ancestry; hence noun = a person of German ancestry. See also **Black Dutch**.

1937 Hall *Coll* (Copeland Creek TN) He talked like he might be a Dutch. *Ibid.* (Wears Cove TN) [There are] two Dutch centers—Byrds Chapel and Fox schoolhouse. **1939** Hall *Coll* (Cable Branch NC) My grandfather could read and count Dutch.

[folk etymology for German *Deutsch* "German"; OED3 *Dutch* adj 1 obsolete except as a historical archaism, and in some parts of U.S.]

Dutch cheese *noun* Cottage cheese.

1934–47 *LAMSAS Appal* = attested by 14/148 speakers (9.4%) from WV and 2/20 (10%) from VA.

Dutchman's breeches (also *Dutchman's britches*) *noun* The bleeding heart, a wildflower (*Dicentra cucullaria*). Also called **little boy plant**, **staggerweed 1**.

1940 Caton *Wildflowers of Smokies* 7 This picturesque little bloomer undoubtedly is the most attractive of the smaller plants of the whole Park, its forked flower bearing such a striking resemblance to the odd little trousers that the mythical Dutchman is so prone to wear. **1981** Brewer *Wonderment* 22 What we call various plants depends somewhat on our point of view of those doing the calling. For instance, there's Dutchman's-breeches. At least, that's the name that most wildflower fans use for the beautiful little plant whose blooms look remotely like a pair of britches. **2006** Ellison *Nature Journal* 45 Pollination of Dutchman's-breeches (the dainty little plant with blossom spurs that make it look for all the world like pantaloons hung out to dry) and the closely related squirrel corn can only be accomplished when a bumblebee forces apart the partially fused petal tips to sip nectar with their long tongues. **2012** *Smokies Guide* (Spring) 2 Unless the spread of garlic mustard is halted, wildflower lovers won't be seeing as many trilliums, hepatica, toothworts, spring beauties, Dutchman's britches, and other vernal favorites.

[DARE *Dutchman's breeches* n 1 chiefly North, North Midland]

Dutchman's-pipe *noun* A perennial wildflower (*Aristolochia durior* or *A. macrophylla*) with brownish, pipe-shaped flowers and whose roots have medicinal uses.

1970 Campbell et al. *Smoky Mt Wildflowers* 20 This climbing vine gets its name from the similarity of the flower's shape to that of the traditional pipe of the Dutch. **1971** Hutchins *Hidden Valley* 45 Dutchman's-pipe flowers are unusual, but their pollination is certainly unique. [**1971** Krochmal et al. *Medicinal Plants Appal* 64 Preparations made from [the roots of] this herb have been used as aids in dyspepsia [and] as spasmodics.]

[from the shape of the flower]

Dutch oven *noun* A heavy, cast-iron pot with three legs and a close-fitting lid, set among coals at the front of a fireplace or having coals piled on top, sometimes hung over the coals on a hook and bail. The vessel was widely used, most often to bake corn bread, before the introduction of stoves. Also called **baker**, **oven**.

1793 *Jefferson Co Wills I* 39 An inventory of the estate . . . of Abijah Fowler decd. returned by Eleoner Fowler Administratrix. Five head of Horses. Four head of Cattle. 1 sheep. 17 head of Hoggs. 10 Piggs. 2 Potts. 2 Dutch Ovens. **1883** Zeigler and Grosscup *Heart of Alleghanies* 151 Corn-meal, water, and salt were soon stirred up for the dodger; the small, round skillet with cover (Dutch oven they call it) was set over a bed of coals; the tea-kettle was singing on the fire, and some chunks of venison boiling in the pot. **1889** Mooney *Folk Carolina Mts* 96 At meal time a hole is scooped out in the coals for the pot, and another by its side for the old-fashioned Dutch oven, a sort of pot, having a lid made with a high rim in order to hold the coals which are heaped upon it. **1931** Greve *Tradition Gatlinburg* 69 Cooking was done on the open fire in an iron pot suspended over the flame by a hook swung from an iron bar inside the chimney; or in a "spider," a spider-legged skillet, that stood in the coals; and bread was baked in the hot ashes in the "Dutch oven," a heavy iron vessel with a thick lid that was lifted, not by a handle, but by the three-pronged pot hooks that caught in three gadgets at the edge. **1971** *Cooking* 91–92 One of the most useful cooking utensils was the dutch oven. It is a heavy, round iron pot with a handle and an iron lid that has a half-inch lip all the way around the edge. One variation looks like a large frying-pan with four small legs. It is usually called an "old-timey oven," or an "old bread oven." The dutch oven was sometimes used out-of-doors, but usually it was used inside by the fireplace. It was placed on hot coals raked directly onto the hearth. The lid and oven were usually preheated before using, the oven being preheated on the coals themselves, and the lid directly on the fire. When the oven and lid were hot, whatever was to be baked was placed or poured inside, the lid set in place with a pair of tongs, and coals piled on top of the lid. . . . Dutch ovens were usually used for baking bread and biscuits, but they could also be used for baking Irish potatoes, sweet potatoes, roasting meats, and heating soups and stews. **1978** Montgomery *White Pine Coll* III-2 Cooking on the fire, she had what they called a Dutch oven, and she'd pull the coals out of the hearth and set this oven on that and heat it, and then make our cornmeal batter real thin and pour it in that oven where she'd greased it and . . . then you put the lid on that oven and then put the hot embers out of them hot ashes on top of that, and that just made the heat from the bottom and the top, and that'd be the prettiest brown bread you ever seen, and it tasted so good to us children. **1990** Oliver *Cooking Hazel Creek* 7 The ubiquitous Dutch oven was practically indispensable. It had three short legs, a lid & a bail, and was used mainly for baking bread. **1991** Haynes *Haywood Home* 79 She baked bread in a covered cast-iron Dutch oven with three legs. She'd put her dough in and set her oven into the hot coals at the front of the fireplace.

Dutch rub *noun* The vigorous rubbing of someone's scalp with the knuckles.

1938 Stuart *Dark Hills* 17 He reached out with the handle part of his cane and hooked me around the neck . . . drew me over to him and gave me what he called the "dutch-rub" . . . rubbing his fist over my head. **1968** *DARE Survey* (Milton WV) *Dutch rub* = vigorous rub with the fist on the head.

[DARE *Dutch rub* n chiefly North Midland]

dwarf rhododendron *noun* An evergreen rhododendron (*Rhododendron minus*).

1961 Douglas *My Wilderness* 175 Higher up, dwarf or Carolina rhododendron shows rose-pink flowers along the trail. At times this low shrub grows so thick it crowds the trail. **1964** Campbell *Great Smoky Wildflowers* 48 The dwarf rhododendron (R. minus) . . . is the only one of the three evergreen rhododendrons with short leaves (3 or 4 inches long).

dwelling house *noun* On a homestead, a building inhabited by people, as opposed to various buildings for animals, storage, etc., and to **church house**, **school house**.

1796 Dunlap *Will* To son Adam Dunlap—the plantation on which I now live agreeable to the lines already mentioned to the other boys and the dwelling house at his mother's death. **1863** *Hall CW Letters* (June 12) wee had Recovered our dwelling house and Smoke house and patched up the Rest of our buildings. **1937** (in **2009** Powell *Shenandoah Letters* 97) For the past ten years I have been living in the dwelling house on Major Rollers land located on the North Fork of Moormins River. **1950** Miller *Pigeon's Roost* (July 13) Roscoe Bennett had water put in his dwelling house last week. **1963** Edwards *Gravel* 90 Her voice seemed to be coming from somewhere near the kitchen, or perhaps beyond; maybe from as far away as the smokehouse, which was just outside the dwelling house, behind the kitchen. **1974** Roberts *Sang Branch* 35 There, as if hidden from the world, was a large white store, and to the left behind the stream was a white dwelling house. **1978** Reese *Speech NE Tenn* 34 = attested by 5/12 (41.7%) speakers. **1979** *Big South Fork OHP*-4 We bought an old parsonage over here and tore it down and built the dwelling house out of it. **1995** McCauley *Mt Religion* 60 Brother Cory Miser . . . was a coal miner and a laborer who built what he called "dwelling houses" (a common expression, serving to distinguish them from "church houses"). **1998** *Dante OHP*-24 [The church] originated from the other hollow over there out of a dwelling house that was converted to a church. **2004** Burton *In Memoriam* 140 Herbs is gone, and galax is gone, fer as makin' anything out of 'em. People live in dwelling houses where I used to gather herbs.

dwindle down *verb phrase* To decline in health and lose weight, waste away. See also **drindle**.

1922 Cobb *KY Mt Rhymes* 15 And now this body's dwndling down— / I'm aiming for to die. **1987** Young *Lost Cove* 208 Somewhere up in the pasture field a cowbell dins faintly as the day dwindles down. **1991** Thomas *Sthn Appal* 203 They've dwindled down till they—you kain't hardly git a bunch enny more. **1994–97** Montgomery *Coll* (known to Adams, Brown, Jones, Norris, Oliver, Weaver); She started dwindlin' down last spring and she never recovered (Cardwell).

dwindle out *verb phrase* To diminish.

1973 *AOHP/ASU*-160 Back before then now they had midwives, along the year that I was born back there, but then they kind of dwindled out.

dying *adjective* Damned.

1939 Hall *Coll* Now that's the dyin' truth.

dynymite *noun* Dynamite.

1942 Hall *Phonetics Smoky Mts* 60 A few words are generally sounded with [ɪ]: *alcohol, dynamite*.

E

each See **itch**.

each and every *pronoun phrase* Everyone, one and all.

1913 Kephart *Our Sthn High* 298 Phil's Ann give it out to each and every that Walt and Layunie'd orter wed. [**1992** Montgomery *Coll* (unknown to consultants from the Smoky Mountains).]

[DARE *each and every* pron South Midland]

each one *pronoun phrase* Used immediately following a coreferent noun or pronoun (thus *we each one* = each one of us).

1942 (in **1987** Perdue *Outwitting Devil* 67) They each one had half of the gold tied around his waist. **2009** Holbrook *Upheaval* 38 I only regret that I didn't throw them each one out a window.

each one of us *pronoun phrase* Coreferent with the subject of the clause but having syntactic position within the predicate.

1864 *Vance Papers* (April 17) we are veary ancious to get to our o[w]n State and to get in the Same Regment as we have Each one of us a Brother in that Regment.

ear *noun* variant forms *year, yeare*.

c1789 (in **1989** Fink *Jonesborough* 13) In said action he had just reasons to believe that said Massengill had his right year cut off by a Brittish Dragoon, and the same is ordered to be recorded. **1813** Hartsell *Memora* 103 I cold not git one yeare of corne. **1834** Crockett *Narrative* 141 There the people stood all the while, with their eyes, mouths, and years all open, to catch every word I would speak. **1861** Griffin *CW Letters* (Aug 3) Mat and Nancy I want to know if you got your year bobs and brest pin. **1863** *Tesh CW Letters* (Sept 9) sam fanny and bet was all sick last weake with colds and year ache. **1891** Brown *Dialect in TN* 175 Ear is called *year*, but *yeast* is called *east*. **1928** Justus *Betty Lou* 90 They have blinded their eyes and kivered their years and shet up the door of their hearts. **1942** Hall *Phonetics Smoky Mts* 16 [jɪɚ]. **1963** Edwards *Gravel* 131 I got to looking at them years and I shucked one out. **1974** Fink *Bits Mt Speech* 30 *year*. **1989** Landry *Smoky Mt Interviews* 181 If he was working, give him twelve years of corn.

[DARE *ear* n South Midland]

early candlelight (also *early candlelighting*) *noun phrase* Dusk. See also **candlelight 2**.

1899 Frost *Sthn Mts* 10 Another ride would bring us to our third school-house, where we would speak, take supper in the neighborhood, and preach at "early candlelight." **1920** Ridley *Sthn Mtneer* 69 The following night Ben was at the church at "early candle light" anxiously awaiting the arrival of the girl. **1923** (in **1952** Mathes *Tall Tales* 3) Accordingly it was "norated around" that there would be "preachin' ever' night at early candle-lightin', beginnin' with the new moon in May." **1961** Medford *History Haywood Co* 33 Then there was preaching . . . at eight and eleven A.M., at three P.M., and at "early candlelight." **1996–97** Montgomery *Coll* (known to Brown, Cardwell).

[DARE *early candlelight* n chiefly South Midland]

earmark *noun* Same as **mark A**.

1948 Dick *Dixie Frontier* 35–36 When first turned out, the hogs were marked with certain cuts in the ears, and these marks were registered. The following earmark recorded in the court records of Pulaski county, Kentucky, is typical: "On motion of Peter Kemey his ear mark (to wit) a half crop in the right ear and a swallow fork and undercut in the left ear is ordered to be recorded." **c1960** Wilson *Coll*: *earmarks* = slits, crops, etc., used in an animal's ear to denote ownership. **1991** Thomas *Sthn Appal* 35 For a few years, it seemed safe to turn the hogs loose in the woods, after they had been identified with "ear marks." **2003** *Smoky Mt News* (Jan) The hogs ranged the woods communally most of the time so that their owners had to pay them little or no mind. In order to recognize which hog was whose when rounded up, each farmer's animals were documented via distinctive ear marks; that is, various combinations of slits, notches, and holes cut into their ears while young.

[DARE *earmark* n now chiefly South, Midland, West]

earn *verb*

A variant form *yearn*.

1824 Knight *Letter from KY* 106–7 Some words are used, even by genteel people, from their imperfect education, in a new sense; and others, by the lower classes in society, pronounced very uncouthly . . . yearn for earn. **1913** Combs *KY Highlander* 16 Old English and words closely related to it . . . *yearn* (*earn*). **1924** Raine *Saddlebags* 105 They take the "y" from "yeast" but add it to "earn." **1966** Medford *Ol' Starlin* 80 "Spring an' this good sunshine—a season for plantin' our seed an' tendin' of crops—to give ever'body a chanst to yearn their meat an' bread," continued Eve, lapsing into her philosophical mood.

[DARE *earn* v chiefly South Midland]

B variant past-tense forms *earnt*, *yearnt*, *yernt*.

1862 Smith *CW Letters* [I]f bet shoes is give out I want you to get her a pare if you please for if She has wove as mutch Cloth as She says she has I think that she has yernt one pare [of shoes]. **1925** Furman *Glass Window* 114 Money I yearnt that way wouldn't never do me no good. **1940** Still *River of Earth* 179 The baby is buried here, and I've earnt a breathing spell.

earnt See **earn**.

earth *noun* variant forms *yarth*, *yearth*, *yeth*; hence adjective *yearthly*.

1824 Knight *Letter from KY* 106–7 Some words are used, even by genteel people, from their imperfect education, in a new sense; and others, by the lower classes in society, pronounced very uncouthly . . . yearth. **1847** (in **1974** Harris *High Times* 71) I seed his foot go plumb out of sight in the fork of your coat tail, and you rise from that yearth like shootin. **1859** Taliaferro *Fisher's River* 87 We looked, and the limbs uv my tree had riz from the yeth full four foot, and his'n three foot. **1860** Olmsted *Back Country* 262 The woman said that she could make "as good butter as any ever was made in the yarth, but she couldn't get anything for it." **1895** Murfree *Phantoms* 217 It's a mighty satisfyin' thing ter be well off in yearthly goods an' chattels. **1974** Fink *Bits Mt Speech* 30 *yearth*.

[DARE *earth* n chiefly South, South Midland]

ease *verb* (in phrases *ease around*, *ease in*, *ease off*, *ease over*) To slip about, move furtively or unobtrusively.

1940 Haun *Hawk's Done* 20 The Old Man and Ad kept easing off by the littles till they finally went on away. **1961** Seeman *Arms of Mt* 36 My mammy could tell when there was a witch easin' around—the baby 'ud get the dry colick, the butter jest wouldn't come, and old Brindle 'ud go to smolickin' around kickin' up her heels and actin' mighty quair. **1967–69** *DARE Survey* (Walker KY, Cumberland Gap TN) *easing around*, (Dillard GA) *easing in* (to the house) = to walk very quietly. **1995** Adams *Come Go Home* 68 He started to ease off, to the side, trying to get a car between him and the wildly gesticulating Chester. *Ibid.* 71 Chester started easing over to the table, talking kind of low and soothing-like.

[DARE *ease* v 3 chiefly South, South Midland]

ease in See **ease**.

easement *noun* Relief.

1914 Furman *Sight* 37 When my first little gal come along, I named it Evy, thinking to give her some easement or pleasure. **1957** Combs *Lg Sthn High: Word List* 33 = relief, ease; not a legal term here.

ease off, ease over See **ease**.

easing powder *noun* An opiate; more generally, any analgesic taken in powdered form, as for a headache (often construed as a count noun; hence plural form *easing powders*). Same as **resting powder**. For similar forms, see **powder 1**.

1913 Kephart *Our Sthn High* 224 Cain't you-uns give her some easin' powder for that hurtin' in her chist? **1974** Fink *Bits Mt Speech* 8 *easing powders* = a drug to ease pain. "They ought to give him some *easin' powders*." **1976** Dwyer *Southern Sayin's* 30 = medicine that allays pain. "I need some easin-powder." **1995–97** Montgomery *Coll*: *easing powder* (known to Brown), = aspirin and similar medicines, as "Have you got any easing powders? I've got a headache" (Cardwell).

[DARE *easing powder* n southern Appalachians]

east and west *noun* See citation.

1985 Irwin *Alex Stewart* 137 We first got the roots of hemp. He called it "east and west."

Easter bush (also *Easter flower*) *noun* The common forsythia plant (*Forsythia viridissima*).

1944 Hayes *Word-List NC* 33 *Easter bush* = forsythia. **1960** Stubbs *Mountain-Wise* (April–May) 6 It is readily seen from its blooming season how forsythia acquired the name "Easter flower." **1995** Montgomery *Coll*: *Easter bush* (known to Cardwell).

Easter flower *noun*

1 See **Easter bush**.

2 The trailing arbutus plant (*Epigaea repens*). Same as **gravelweed**.

1939 Jennison *Flora Great Smokies* 280 On dry hillsides in out-of-the-way places, the Trailing Arbutus, or "Easter Flower," as the mountain-man calls it, may be found.

[perhaps from the time of its blooming]

3 (also *Easter pretty*) A daffodil (*Narcissus* spp). Same as **buttercup**.

c1960 Wilson Coll: *Easter flower* = daffodils. Also called buttercups, cups and saucers, March flowers. **1982** Slone *How We Talked* 47 *Easter flower* = jonquil. **1995–2000** Montgomery Coll: *Easter flower*, *Easter pretty* (known to Cardwell).

[DARE *Easter flower* n 2 chiefly Midland]

Easter pretty See **Easter flower 3**.

Easter winter *noun* See citation. For terms describing a similar phenomenon, see **blackberry winter**.

1957 Broaddus *Vocab Estill Co KY* 27 = a period of cold weather at Easter time.

East Virginia *noun* See citation.

1992 Brooks *Sthn Stuff* 46 = what West Virginia used to call Virginia to keep it in its place.

easy

A *adjective*

1 Cautious, moving carefully.

1974 GSMNP-51:4 We was awful easy about leaving the house, because we didn't want to wake him up.

2 Bending or yielding easily.

1967 DARE *Survey* (Gatlinburg TN) That willow branch is very easy.

3 Likely, prone, having a tendency.

1937 Wilson *Folklore SE KY* 260 He's easy to fly off the handle. (He can't control his temper [Bell Co KY].) **1966** Dakin *Vocab Ohio River Valley* 468 *Easy to get mad* is attested several times in the southern Mountains. This expression also appears in the Indiana hills and in the Pocket. **1968–69** DARE *Survey* (Milton WV) *easy to take exception*, (Sawyer KY) *easy to get out of hand* = to lose patience easily. **1972** *AOHP/LJC-104* They was easy to take it [= influenza]. **1983** McDermitt *Boy Named Jack* 19 Unlucky Jack . . . was easy to lose out. **1984** Smith *Oral History* 28 He was always so easy to laugh. **2008** *Rosie Hicks* 1 It scared her to death because I was easy to faint.

[DARE *easy* adj 3 South, South Midland]

4 Comfortable, relieved of pain, discomfort, or anxiety. See also **easy-like**.

c1844 Beckner *Shane Interview* 226 [He] continued his hold until she would submit. "I've said all I want to say," or "I feel right easy." **1864** *Conley CW Letter* (June 28) He Seemed to Suffer for two days after which he appeared easy untill the 23 when he became worse until he died. **1873** Smith *Arp Peace Papers* 112 Maybe I've sed enuf. But I don't feel easy yet. **1933** Thomas *Traipsin' Woman* 189 I'll be there if this risin' in my side gets easy. **1955** Washburn *Country Doctor* 64 It's med'sin' Mandy needs—some'n ter ease 'er pains. If you'll furnish that an' get 'er easy so she won't throw-up so powerful bad, a pint o' sweet ile'll make them gallstones pass. **1985** Irwin *Alex Stewart* 151 Thirty minutes after I'd pulled it [= a tooth], I went to getting easy. **1997** Montgomery *Coll* I got easy from the dost of sang, that dost of medicine made her get easy (Brown). **2007** McMillon *Notes* = relaxed, comfortable, pain-free.

B *adverb*

1 Easily.

1863 *Bradshaw CW Letters* (Feb 27) tell Father to not let Frankling and John nor non of the rest go a near them fur tha[y] are easy Caut and dangerous. **1927** Montague *Hog's Eye* 194 He could easy see the young feller was mighty conscientious. **2009** Holbrook *Upheaval* 108 They think I'm easy controlled.

2 Agreeably, inclined to.

1984 GSMNP-153:2 Daddy asked her how much he owed her and she was a easy talking woman, and she said about two dollars.

easy as an old shoe See **old shoe**.

easy-like *adjective* Relaxed. See also **easy A4**.

1895 Dromgoole *Fiddling to Fame* 48 The old man in the cabin begin ter grow more easy-like and took ter readin' an' war not ill-pleased ter git the news. **1923** (in **1952** Mathes *Tall Tales* 8) I'd allus heared him preachin' in his big roarin' voice, but that day he was plumb gentle, and his voice was soft and easy-like. **2004** Fisher *Kettle Bottom* 10 I begin to feel easy-like, moving through the dark.

eat *verb*

A Principal parts.

1 variant base form *et*. [Editor's note: Joseph Hall did not observe *et* as either a base or inflected form in his nearly forty years of research in the Smoky Mountains, nor is it attested in ATASC, wherein *eat* is the universal past-tense and usual past-participle form. Citations of *et* below are mainly from written sources and may be misinterpretations of *eat*, making the status of *et* less certain. At best it is a rare form.]

1989 Landry *Smoky Mt Interviews* 191 When they went to the table to eat, they went to et. They said, "Let's go et."

2 variant past-tense forms *eat*, *et*.

1799 (in **2008** Ellison *High Vistas* 37) We all eat our breakfast & set out on the line, went 3/4 mile. **1822** (in **2007** Dunkerly *Kings Mt* 40) I shall begin the day before the battle where we eat our fresh beef in the morning without bread or salt. **1861** *Lance CW Letters* (Nov 10) we Stayed in charleston 2 night and et at the hotell. **1862** *Robinson CW Letters* (May 7) you Rote Something about baking me some bread but he never Sead eny about it so I exspect he eat it. **1922** *TN CW Ques* 867 We slept in the open, had no tents, eat when we had anything to eat. **1940** Haun *Hawk's Done* 11 I didn't ask Tiny if she eat breakfast before she left home. **1942** Hall *Phonetics Smoky Mts* 18 For *ate*, the historic [it] is universal (except as corrected to [et] in a few individual cases). **1953** Atwood *Verbs East US* 12–13 *Eat* covers a large area in c. Pa., part of e. W.Va., most of Va. except the

Tidewater area, and nearly all of N.C. In this entire area the frequency of *eat* is very great, particularly as one moves southward. In the N.C. area of *eat* nearly nine tenths of Type I informants [i.e. older speakers with little formal education] use it, as well as more than half of the Type II informants [i.e. younger speakers with more formal education]. **1961** *Coe Ridge OHP-333A* I've eat a many a times over there. *Ibid.* 340B They et with the Winchester across their laps, carried them in the courthouses when they started the court. **1973** GSMNP-4:2:3 Back when I was a kid they was a lot of families that eat corn bread three times a day. **1980** Miles *Verbs in Haywood Co* 98 She eat them Sunday and she eat them yesterday. **1989** *Matewan OHP-9* We raised what we eat, and we had as much to eat through the Depression as we had any other time. **1998** *Dante OHP-61* She eat a pretty fair breakfast, and she seemed to be pretty pert. **2007** (in **2012** McQuaid *Interface* 271) When I was a-growing up, you know, we raised everything we eat.

[DARE *eat* v A2 a, b chiefly South, South Midland, *et* scattered, but especially South, South Midland, North Atlantic]

3 variant past-participle forms *ate, eat, et.*

1774 *Dunmore's War* 142 I have been in the Greatest misery Ever any felow was in, Since Last Monday with a pain in my Jaw one of my Eyes Has been Shut up Ever Since and has hardly Either Eat or Slept. **1834** Crockett *Narrative* 175 We had just eat our breakfast, when a company of hunters came to our camp. **1862** *Martin CW Letters* (Jan 26) I have eat So Much Nasty beef that I am A Shamed to See A Cow & it almost Makes me Sick to See A Cow. **1862** *Robinson CW Letters* (Sept 7) phillopinner is not well at this time she hant et eny thing hardley sence i saw you. **1934** Carpenter *Archaic English in WV* 79 Quite often we hear *eat* in the past tense and past participle when *ate* and *eaten* are proper. This unchanged inflection of *eat* is also found in Shakespeare. In *Much Ado About Nothing* are the lines: "Time hath not yet dried this blood of mine, nor age so eat up my invention." **1934–47** LAMSAS *Appal: eat* (Madison Co NC, Swain Co NC). **1957** Parris *My Mts* 70 "I've eat many a pone of bread baked right there on that hearth," he said. **1969** GSMNP-38 An old bear'd got some cattle. I remember one time they killed one just about a quarter of a mile from the house up there, and it had eat a mess out of it. **1976** Lindsay *Grassy Balds* 177 I reckon the stock kept the weeds eat out. **1984** GSMNP-153:38 I thought that was the best stuff that I've ever eat. **1989** *Matewan OHP-28* She'd cook beans and then she'd take the beans after we'd eat from them, and she'd mash them up and make bean cakes out of them. **1994** Montgomery *Coll: et* (known to Shields). **1998** *Dante OHP-25* I had eat dinner . . . and got to started shoveling, and my knees got to shaking and I just sat down there on something, a lump of coal. **2008** *Rosie Hicks* 1 We had too many, you know. We could not get them eat.

[DARE *eat* v A3 a, b chiefly South, South Midland, *et* scattered, but especially South, South Midland, North Atlantic]

B Senses.

1 To have a certain taste when consumed, be suitable for consumption (especially in phrase *eat good* = to be tasty or appetizing).

1862 *Epperly CW Letters* (July 20) wee can get Blackberrys Somtimes to bake pies they eat verry well. **1864** *Hill CW Letters* (Nov 27) I Cookd amess of my peas to day I tell you thay Eat fine. **1895** Edson and Fairchild *TN Mts* 371 [A woodchuck] *eats* like bar [= bear]. **c1900** (in **1997** Stoddart *Quare Women* 61) I never heard of puttin' flowers on a eatin' table. I never thought of it before, but things do eat better when they look nice. **1913** Kephart *Our Sthn High* 282 In mountain vernacular many words that serve as verbs are only nouns of action, or adjectives, or even adverbs . . . "This poke salat eats good." **1939** Hall *Coll* (Hartford TN) He said, "I'll guarantee you in the morning, it'll eat just as good as it is now." **1973** GSMNP-88 They [= ramps] eat better than a onion. **1974** Fink *Bits Mt Speech* 8 Bear meat eats good. **1985** Irwin *Alex Stewart* 205 Didn't you ever eat dried blackberries? They eat good. **1994–97** Montgomery *Coll* (known to Brown, Shields). **2008** Terrell *Mt Lingo* If he wanted to pay the cook the highest compliment, he would say, "This eats right where you hold it."

[DARE *eat* v B3 chiefly South, South Midland]

2 To chew (tobacco).

1952 Callahan *Smoky Mt Country* 14 Most of them chewed tobacco—they often called it "eatin' terbaccer," supposedly because they swallowed some of the juice—, and a great number of the women either smoked a pipe or used snuff.

3 To furnish (a family) with food, feed.

1913 Morley *Carolina Mts* 180 The land is so good that two or three acres of it will "eat a family." **1997** Montgomery *Coll* (known to Bush, Cypher, Oliver).

[DARE *eat* v B2 especially South, South Midland]

4 See citation.

2000 Lowry *Folk Medical Term* = to take a pill or tablet. "I eat my medicine every night."

eatch See **itch**.

eat good See **eat B1**.

eatingest *adjective* Inclined to consume food frequently or in large quantities.

1979 Melton *'Pon My Honor* 16–17 Besides being the eatenest set, they was allers having somebody to fetch and carry fer 'em.

eating table *noun* A table for meals.

c1900 (in **1997** Stoddart *Quare Women* 61) I never heard of puttin' flowers on a eatin' table. I never thought of it before, but things do eat better when they look nice. **1938** Stuart *Dark Hills* 383 I got upon the eatin' table at home and put a toe under each corner and my hands on the other corners and stretched. **1982** Slone *How We Talked* 32 = diningroom table. **1987** Young *Lost Cove* 26 How in the Sam Hill Joe Lum and Jace kept food on their *eating table* was hard to tell. **1998** Montgomery *Coll* (known to Adams, Brown, Bush, Cardwell, Jones, Norris). **2007** Alexander *Moonshiners Gone* 57 Four or five cows supplied the large family with fresh milk and butter. There was always plenty of food on Silas Butts' eatin-table.

[DARE *eating table* n chiefly southern Appalachians]

eat up *verb phrase*

1 To bite badly, mangle, consume. See also **bite up**.

1878 Coale *Wilburn Waters* 79 Them darned dogs that's been frightened won't get as far from us as our shadows for fear the infernal varment will eat 'em up. **1939** Hall *Coll* (Deep Creek NC) It was one of our bear hounds, a black and tan hound, and he was just eat up, bloody all over [from a bear fight]. *Ibid.* (Hartford TN) He come up to a party had been a-fightin' a bear with dogs, an' it had eaten up their dogs in a laurel bed. **1953** Hall *Coll* (Bryson City NC) Part of my dogs were eat up and worn out, and I taken five [of them] and went over. **1977** Shackelford et al. *Our Appalachia* 23 They turned their roosters in there and my grandfather's roosters just eat them up real quick. **1985** Irwin *Alex Stewart* 253 When I got there a big dog had a hold of her and was just about to eat her up. **1999** Morgan *Gap Creek* 10 Sure enough, the dog set up a growl and a bark. He come running from the porch and stood behind the gate snarling. He would have eat up anybody that come through that gate. **2001** Lowry *Expressions* 5 My mother-in-law was operated on 3 weeks ago, and she was eat mortally up with cancer.

2 To render effusive affection or hospitality (toward), hug and kiss (someone).

1936 Stuart *Head of Hollow* 207 Tillie was took to death to see any of us over to her place. She was just fit to eat us up.

eavening, eavin See **evening A.**

-ed *suffix*

1 added to a verb to form a past-tense or past-participle form. See **blow A1**, **blow A2**, **born**, **catched**, **drawed**, **growed**, **knowed**, **teached**, **throwed.**

[DARE *-ed* suff 2 chiefly South, South Midland]

2 added excresently or pleonastically to a verb and pronounced as a separate syllable. See **attackted**, **drownded**, **galded**, **tosted**, **yelded.**

edzact *verb* To make precisely correct or exact; to figure or reason (a problem, issue) out.

1913 Kephart *Our Sthn High* 288–89 Our schoolmaster, composing a form of oath for the new mail-carrier, remarked, "Let me study this thing over; then I can edzact it"—a verb so rare and obsolete that we find it in no American dictionary, but only in Murray. **1952** Wilson *Folk Speech NC* 536 I'd better *edzact* that out for myself. **1972** Cooper *NC Mt Folklore* 91 = to reason out.

[DARE *edzact* v 1 southern Appalachians, Ozarks]

e'en See **evening A.**

e'er See **ever**, **ever a.**

eetch See **itch.**

ef See **if.**

effen, eff'n, efn See **iffen.**

egg *noun* variant forms *agg, aig.*

1867 Harris *Sut Lovingood* 219 Her eyes swelled tu the size an' looks ove hard-biled aigs, an' she ris hersef ofen the coffin a littil wif her hans. **1939** Burnett *Gap o' Mountains* 55 No, that pot houn ain't wuth nothin . . . haint got no affection for nobody, and is a natural born aig sucker. **1942** Hall *Phonetics Smoky Mts* 20 [eg, eɪg]. **1969** Roberts *Greasybeard* 105 He went after a goose agg in the nestes while Sally built a fire in the stove.

[DARE [æg] (at *egg* n A) chiefly South Midland]

egg bread *noun* Cornbread made with eggs, sometimes containing cracklings.

1886 Smith *History KY* 400 (DARE) A most delicious egg-bread . . . is made. The same cornmeal is the body; and to this is added buttermilk, soda, and salt, eggs, milk, and some lard. **1901** Harben *Westerfelt* 45 I can taste your slice-potato pie yet, and your egg-bread and biscuits. **1949** Kurath *Word Geog East US* 39 From the Chesapeake Bay to the western parts of Virginia and the Carolinas . . . *egg bread* for a special kind of corn bread is current. **1998** Montgomery *Coll* (known to Bush, Shields).

[DARE *egg bread* n 1 chiefly South, South Midland]

egg dye *noun* A tickseed plant (*Coreopsis major*).

1941 Walker *Story of Mt* 52 Starry coreopsis is one of the most abundant yellow flowers growing on . . . the mountain. . . . The mountain people know it by the name of "egg dye," because they use its green leaves for coloring eggs.

egg fighting *noun* See citation. Same as **picking eggs.**

1964 Smith et al. *Germans of Valley* 113 A popular Easter game among the young people was called "picking" eggs or egg "fighting." A person selected what he considered to be his strongest egg and challenged someone else to "pick" against him. The eggs were tapped against each other until one of the shells cracked, then the owner of the other egg claimed the cracked one as prize.

eggshell tree See **egg tree.**

egg-sucker *noun* See also **egg-sucking**, **suck-egg.**

1 A worthless animal, especially a dog.

1939 Burnett *Gap o' Mountains* 55 No, that pot houn ain't wuth nothin—won't ketch a hog, won't drive cattle, fights every dog he sees, lazy, haint got no affection for nobody, and is a natural born aig sucker. **1984** Burns *Cold Sassy* 13 "But first you gather the eggs like you been told to. You go'n let the rats get'm. Or that no-count egg-sucker dog of yours." **1994–97** Montgomery *Coll* (known to Brown, Cardwell, Ellis, Ledford, Shields).

[DARE *egg-sucker* n 1 South, South Midland]

2 A worthless person.

1976 Garber *Mountain-ese* 26 = a sneak-thief, rascal. "Jud ain't no good, he's allers been an egg sucker." **1994** Montgomery *Coll* (known to Shields).

egg-sucking *adjective* Worthless, contemptible. See also **egg-sucker**, **suck-egg.**

1901 Harben *Westerfelt* 108 I don't respect you as much as I do a decent egg-suckin dog. **1940** Haun *Hawk's Done* 121 No more use in arguing with him than with an egg-sucking dog, she said. He had his head set. **c1960** Wilson *Coll*: *egg-sucking dog* = also used to mean a sneak-thief. Sometimes suck-egg dog. **1995–96** Montgomery *Coll* (known to Norris, Oliver); He's as lowdown as an egg-sucking dog (Cardwell). **2014** *WV Talk* = creature, man or beast, that you don't want around. Useless, mean.

egg tree (also *eggshell tree*) *noun* A tree decorated with dyed, colored egg shells.

1933 Thomas *Traipsin' Woman* 21 Beside the kitchen door bloomed a tree! Blossoms in November. I could not believe my eyes. Blossoms of red and pink and blue and purple. I leaned forward the better to see the strange sight. Blossoms on a pine tree! "Yonder is Aunt Delinthe Buffum's eggshell tree," drawled Still Tongue, shifting his cud of tobacco from one cheek to the other. **1979** Slone *My Heart* 54 Even the eggshells were not wasted. They were browned and fed to the hens, or strung on the twigs of a tree in the yard to become an "egg tree."

egg turner *noun* See citation.

c1960 Wilson *Coll* = a spatula or pancake-turner.

[DARE *egg-turner* n chiefly South, South Midland]

egg up *verb phrase* To incite, provoke (unruly behavior).

1998 *Dante OHP*-61 They accused me of egging up strikes.

egg yellow *noun* Egg yolk.

1954 Roberts *Bought a Dog* 22 Tom threw down his egg and a great river of egg yellow came around her.

eh la (also *ah law, aih Lord, ay-la, eh law, ey law*) *interjection* See also **ay**, **la**, **they**[3].

A variant forms *ah law* [see **2016**], *aih Lord* [see **c1950** in **B**], *ay-la* [see **1952** in **B**], *ey law* [see **1930** in **B**].

B Used to form mild oaths to express resignation, surprise, or acknowledgment, especially in responding to another person's statement. See 1965, 2009 citations. See also **la**, **lawd a mercy**.

1930 Greer-Petrie *Angeline Outsmarts* 31 Ey law! I putt him in his place, and told him whar to head in! **c1950** Adams *Grandpap* 144 "Aih, Lord!" sighed Mammy. "I don't know what ort to be done with such people." **1952** Wilson *Folk Speech NC* 517 *ay-la* ... Exclamation of assent (yes), surprise, grief ... Old persons. Rare. **1965** *Dict Queen's English* 22–23 *eh la* = an interjection used in responding to a speaker. It can indicate agreement, puzzlement, encouragement to continue, or melancholy endorsement. For example, one person may say, "What do you think of the price of cotton?" The response may well be, "Eh law!" **1966** Dykeman *Far Family* 48 "Eh law, it's a satisfaction to bake these old bones," she said each night when they settled her in the chair just after supper. **1976** GSMNP-113:9 No, I don't think so, eh law. Oh lord have mercy. **1998** Montgomery *File* I've usually heard this used to fill in a pause or to trail off a sentence with this when you don't have anything else to say, used like "oh well" or "lawsy me." It's also used as a noncommittal remark when someone has made a statement that you don't care to comment on. (51-year-old woman, Jefferson Co TN). **2009** Benfield *Mt Born* 140 = an exclamation, at times in wonder, sometimes in resignation, tinged with sadness. "Eh la, what am I going to do now that Henry's gone?" **2016** *Blind Pig* (March 30) I use the term in exasperation ... as "eh law," I don't know how I'm going to get something done, or over something. *Ibid.* I most often hear the phrase used when there just ain't nothing that can be done about an unfortunate situation, and everybody in the conversation knows there ain't nothing that can be done. A sad resignation over something you just can't understand, explain, or justify. *Ibid.* I have not heard "Ah law" in awhile but am very familiar with it. Depending on the situation, it can convey about any emotion. But ... it tends to be most commonly used to mean a compound of regret, sadness and resignation.

[probably originally from French *hélas*, meaning "unfortunate," and the more common English *alas*.]

either

A (also *either one, either ... one*) *pronoun* One or the other (following two conjoined elements). See also **neither B**. See also Grammar and Syntax §18.1.

1928 Justus *Betty Lou* 141 He'll shoot the Doctor or Pappy either if he gets half a chance at them. **1938** Justus *No-End Hollow* 40 I guess I've got enough book learning. I can read and write—and that's more than Pap can do, or Grandpap either. **c1950** (in **2000** Oakley *Roamin' Man* 54) Well I dont have that turkey or chicken eather but I am still in hopes. **1969** GSMNP-46:2 It was just about as steep as a yoke cattle could go up or come down either one, and you had already got over rough ground. **1973** GSMNP-4:22 You never had any trouble out of them people, from Big Catalooch or Little Catalooch either. **1973** GSMNP-76:30 You didn't have no other way to ride without you ride a steer and either a horse one or go in by sled. **1975** Screven *John B Wright* 13 Man, that's the prettiest weed you ever did think in the world, buddy, when it's yellow or green either one. **1983** *Dark Corner OHP*-10A They claimed that [the fire] would kill the snakes out, but it didn't. It just drove them down to the low part of the country, so the snake's going to either go down in the ground or go in front of the fire, one. **1989** Landry *Smoky Mt Interviews* 181 She found out how to get moonshine without making it or buying it either one. **2001** Montgomery *File* The rosebud and the dogwood were not out either one. **2004** Fisher *Kettle Bottom* 53 They nailed the lid on Daddy's box afore me nor Mama either one got a chance to see him.

B (in phrase *or either*, preceding the second of two alternatives) *conjunctive phrase* Or.

1961 *Coe Ridge OHP*-333A He had his gun across his lap or either beside him. **1971** *AOHP/ALC*-33 They would go to one another's houses and help them to hoe their corns out or either come at sickness in the family, and then they would help out and do all the work and their washing and cooking and waiting on sick people. **1971** *AOHP/ALC*-147 If you liked it [= the meat of a freshly slaughtered hog] smoked, well you smoked it with hickory bark or either apple tree. **1971** *Granny Women* 249 Most all [midwives] I can remember walked, or either there would be somebody go get them in a buggy. **1997** *Dante OHP*-53 They'd turn all that stale air in on the people [in the mines] and kill them, or either water would come through and drown them. **1997** *Dante OHP-53* We'd a-walk through the tunnel or either have to walk across the mountain. *Ibid.* The family or people in the community [would] make a wooden casket and bury them, or either they would come over and buy the casket off the company.

either one, either . . . one See **either A.**

either one of them *pronoun phrase* variant position in the predicate.

2007 McMillon *Notes* That was more than they either one of them would do.

ekal *adjective, verb, noun* Equal.

1867 Harris *Sut Lovingood* 97b [sic] They aint human; theyse an ekal mixtry ove stud hoss, black snake, goose, peacock britches—an d—d raskil. **1888** Meriwether *Mt Life in TN* 458–59 Thar ain't many left as can ekal her in cookin' and keepin' house. **1898** Elliott *Durket Sperret* 146 Hannah hed done met up alonger her ekals. **1942** Hall *Phonetics Smoky Mts* 88.

[DARE *equal* n, v, adj chiefly South, South Midland]

elder *noun* A lay preacher, especially in a **Primitive Baptist** church.

1942 Thomas *Blue Ridge* 151 How happy the young couple were as they stood before the elder, the groom with his waiter at his side, and the bride with her waiter beside her. **1963** Edwards *Gravel* 75 Dallas couldn't understand the Elder's attitude. Why didn't he offer to go and lay on hands and pray? **1989** Dorgan *Regular Baptists* 60 It is not uncommon for an elder to become so absorbed with his own sermon (he would call this "inspiration" or possession by "the Spirit") that he will lose track of time. **1989** *Matewan OHP-9* Our preachers [i.e. in Primitive Baptist churches] goes by the name Elders. **1994** Montgomery *Coll* Baptists would usually call their preachers "Elder" since they were lay preachers, and anyone called "Elder" was liable to be called on to do a little preaching on occasion (Cardwell).

elder blow *noun* The blossoms of the elder tree (*Sambucus canadensis*), which can be dried and made into a medicinal tea.

1980 *Smokies Heritage* 208 Flat clusters of flowers bloom [on the common elderberry] in June and July, pale white against their leaf-green background. To those who cherish them, these flowers are known as "elder blow"; when dried, elder blow can be brewed into a wondrously curative tea for weak stomach. **1996** Houk *Foods & Recipes* 53 Around old homesites and fields in the lowlands of the Smokies are found tall elderberry bushes. In June and July the shrubs bear big clumps of white flowers the old timers called "elder blow." **1996–97** Montgomery *Coll* (known to Brown, Cardwell, Jones).

[*elder(berry)* + *blow* "bloom"]

elder tea *noun* A medicinal tea. See citation.

1957 Combs *Lg Sthn High: Word List* 33 = tea made from the bark of the elder. In accordance with an old superstition, if the bark is pulled upward on the shrub, the child drinking the tea from it will vomit; if downward, its bowels will move to excess. This folk conception of the efficacy of direction and method is noticeable in various superstitious practices, witchcraft, etc. in the Highlands.

electric *noun* Electrical service, electricity.

1942 Thomas *Blue Ridge* 263 That unseen juice, or 'lectric . . . "I'd druther have 'lectric than a new cookstove . . ." any mountain woman will tell you. **1954** Arnow *Dollmaker* 72 They's many a time Meg would ha traded her electric fer a week's grub ahead. **1971** *AOHP/ALC-4* We moved here in fifty-three, and they'd had electric here a few years when we moved here. . . . [The coal companies] made their own electric up there. They had a big generator. **1989** *Matewan OHP-33* [We] didn't have no electric them days. **1998** *Dante OHP-69* [The house] had a bathroom and electric. **2008** Salsi *Ray Hicks* 21 I was a growed-up adult afore we got electric. Up till then, we lived the ol' way by the sun. **2013** Venable *How to Tawlk* 29 TVA brung us the lectrick in 1943.

[Web3 *electric* n 4 dialect]

elem See **elm.**

elements *noun*

A variant pronunciation with secondary stress on the last syllable: EL-*e*-*ments* [see **1913** in **B**]. For similar forms, see **-ment A.**

B Weather, the sky, clouds.

1913 Kephart *Our Sthn High* 79 "I'll go see what the el-e-ments looks like." **1929** Kephart *Smoky Mt Magic* 94 Haven't you heard the mountaineers say "the el-e-ments looks like rain—hit's goin' to weather"? **1931** Combs *Lg Sthn High* 1304 The elements looks threatenin, (It may rain, or snow.) **c1960** Wilson *Coll* = the sky or weather. **1973** Davis *'Pon My Honor* 52 Then the elements opened up and hit rained cats and dogs. **1994** Montgomery *Coll* (known to Cardwell).

[DARE *element* n 1 chiefly South, South Midland]

Elijah room *noun* An enclosed room on the porch for an overnight guest or a traveler passing through. Same as **stranger room.**

1995 Trout *Historic Buildings* 37 Whether they charged for the service or not, mountaineers created little barriers between themselves and their overnight guests. Some Cades Cove residents framed in their porches for this purpose and called them "stranger rooms" or "Elijah rooms," for the Biblical character. A latch string in the front door of the home, pulled in, locked the family in and the stranger out. **1996** Montgomery *Coll* = in earlier days, this was usually reserved for a pastor, who traveled a circuit with a number of churches under his care and would stay only overnight when preaching in a community. Thus when the preacher arrived in a community, he might be told "Go on down to Joe's. He's got an Elijah room" (Cardwell).

elixir of life (also *water of life*) *noun* Homemade whiskey.

1995 Parce *Twice-Told* 34 Some people call the corn whiskey of the mountains the "elixir or water of life" while others call it "popskull." The "elixir" name probably came about when whiskey was considered a medicine in an era when doctors and pharmacies were few and far between. Besides herbs, or "yarbs," as the mountain people called them, there was a number of elixirs or patented medicines on the market between 1860 and 1940 that had as their base alcohol. Whiskey in any form was considered good for chills, spills, snakebite and general malaise. Alcohol was an important ingredient in the production of medicines in the "blockade" era. What made it better was the fact it could be made at home with material at hand. Do-it-yourself mountain medicine was a mountain way. Thus, whiskey played a role in the home. If an old-timer wanted to entertain a guest at his cabin or camp, he'd call upon a member of the family to "fetch the elixir." Corn liquor is what the head of the household asked for and received. It often was retrieved from under the floor of the corn crib, considered a safe place.

ell and yard (also *ellenyard*) *noun* See citations.

1952 Wilson *Folk Speech NC* 536 *Ell and yard* = the three stars in the belt of Orion. **c1960** Wilson *Coll*: *Ell and yard* or *Ellen Yard* = the three stars in Orion's girdle. This was common at Fidelity as far back as I can remember.

[DARE *ellenyard* n South, South Midland]

elleber *noun* A plant of the genus *Veratrum*. See citations.

1894 Bergen *Plant Names III* 102 (Banner Elk NC) = equivalent to branch hellebore, i.e., the hellebore which grows along the brooks or "branches." **1941** *FWP Guide WV* 357 Along the course of Red Lick Run and in other moist spots grows the deep-rooted, spiral inflorescence of the bright green American hellebore, which the natives call "elleber." **1952** Strausbaugh and Core *Flora WV* 226 (DARE) V[eratrum] viride . . . Called Elleber by mountain-folk, whence the names of topographical features such as Elleber Ridge and Elleber Run (Pocahontas County).

ellenyard See **ell and yard**.

ellum See **elm**.

elm *noun* variant forms *elem*, *ellum*.

1925 (in **1935** Edwards *NC Novels* 82) *ellum*. **a1954** Adams *Word-List*: *ellum*. **1962** Hunter *Folk Remedies* 102 One man I know would treat a sprain by making a poultice of slippery "ellum" bark. **1973** *AOHP/ASU-124* [She] used slippery elem bark. **1973** Miller *English Unicoi Co* 93 *ellum* attested by 5 of 6 speakers. **2007** Preece *Leavin' Sandlick* 49 John Henry 'erbed the hillsides in the summer ever'day looking fer sweet elem bark, ginsang, and yeller root. **2013** Venable *How to Tawlk* 13 = a large deciduous tree often found in cities: "I shore do like to park my truck under a shady elem on hot summer days."

[DARE *elm* n somewhat more frequent South, South Midland]

elseways (also *elsewise*) *adverb* Otherwise.

1895 Murfree *Phantoms* 201 Elsewise I wouldn't hev gin my cornsent ter hev lef the leetle lam', Lee-yander, in yer fold. **1955** Ritchie *Singing Family* 93 It's something to do, I don't move around much elseways.

[Web3 *elseways* adv dialect]

elsewheres *adverb* Elsewhere.

1976 Still *Pattern of Man* 65 My solid Salt Springs following, tacked onto the votes elsewheres, and laid alongside the Roaring Fork support, ought to raise a pile nobody can top. **1978** Reese *Speech NE Tenn* 162.

elsewise See **elseways**.

ember days (also *amber days*) *noun* According to folk tradition, days on which it is propitious to clear land but not to plant (apparently based on the Anglican or Catholic observance of three days set aside for prayer and fasting four times a year).

1960 Miller *Pigeon's Roost* (Sept 22) One farmer said that he noticed it to be a certain sign that if it rained on the 8th day of June which he said it rained on that day this year, that there would be no grapes that year. The farmer explained that was one of the first of the three ember days of the month and on the 8th day of the month was the day before the full moon. There was three other ember days before those in June of this year which were on the 9th, the 11th, and 12th of March. One of the old sayings is that you can kill a locust tree by peeling it during the ember days of June and it will rot out by the root, that is if you will strip up on the bark when you are peeling it. **1969** *Ibid* (June 5) Wednesday, Friday and Saturday of this week is ember days and what I can learn, there will be several farmers in this lower end of Mitchell County section who will not set out any plants on ember days, especially tobacco plants. It is proclaimed that plants set out on these three ember days will not grow. But it is said that you can peel locust trees on ember days and they will die out by the roots and soon turn up by the roots. Ember days has long been looked forward to by the farmers of this area. [**1982** Slone *How We Talked* 99 On these days if you chopped on a tree it would die.] **1983** Page and Wigginton *Aunt Arie* 92 Y'don't never plant nothin' when th'Amber Day is here. **1996** Montgomery *Coll* = a period of time in mid to late August when the sap runs in trees, this period being especially appropriate for cutting a ring of bark off a tree in order to kill it and move it to clear land (Brown).

-en[1] *suffix* added redundantly to prepositions and subordinate conjunctions. See **abouten**, **afteren**, **unlessen**, **withouten**.

-en[2] *suffix* alteration of *of*. See **inspiten of hell and high water**, **offen**, **outen**[1], **outen**[2].

-en[3] *suffix* added to adjectives to form verb past participles. See **hotten**.

-en[4] *suffix* added redundantly to past participles. See **blood-shotten**.

end off *verb phrase* To terminate, come to an end.

1931 Thomas *Ditties* 53 Such occasions [i.e. community work parties] always "ended off" with a frolic or a play party.

end of one's row (and variants) *noun phrase* The limit of what one can tolerate or endure.

1904 Harben *Georgians* 2 The old chap certainly is gittin' desperate.... It's my opinion he's at the end o' his row. **1967–69** *DARE Survey* (Berea KY) *end of my* (or *the*) *row*; (Rogersville TN) *end of my* (or *your*) *row*; (Spencer WV) *end of the bean row*. **1994** Montgomery *Coll* He reached the end of his row (Shields).

[probably influenced by *end of one's rope*; DARE *end of one's row* n chiefly South, South Midland, except Middle Atlantic]

endurable *adjective* Long-lasting, capable of enduring; hence *endurabler, endurablest*.

1886 Smith *Southernisms* 38 *Endurable* for "durable," may still be heard in some parts of Tennessee, and no doubt elsewhere (Ohio). I heard myself last summer a "foot-washing" Baptist preacher in Craddock's Great Smoky Mountains say, "Stone is the most *lastiest*, the most *endurablest*, material there is." **1924** Raine *Saddlebags* 102 Log houses are a heap endurabler. **1938** Stuart *Dark Hills* 141 Their dreams were being worked into steel and fashioned into short endurable things. **1995** Montgomery *Coll* I've got an endurable pair of shoes (Shields).

[blend of *endure* + *durable*; DARE *endurable* adj especially southern Appalachians]

enduring

A *adjective* Entire, livelong.

1834 Crockett *Narrative* 178 They had treed the bear about five miles off, near to a man's house, and had barked at it the whole enduring night. **1928** (in **1952** Mathes *Tall Tales* 60) Fer five year he's been in a endurin' tarmint. **1936** Justus *Honey Jane* 14 That old dominecker rooster has stood before the door and crowed the whole endurin' mornin'. **1967** Giles *40 Acres* 4 A thing which lasts is "enduring." Something very old lasts "forever and enduring." **1988** Dickey and Bake *Wayfarer* 70 He would hold a grudge on you; he was somebody that liked revenge better than anything you could think of in this endurin' life.

[DARE *enduring* adj chiefly South, South Midland]

B *preposition* During.

1908 Smith *Reminiscences* 409 As we lay that night on the ground of the stillness of the primeval forest, under cover of rude shelter of bark, they told their experience "endurin' the war." **1917** Kephart *Word-List* 419 I never did cry but wunst; I whinnled a little *endurin'* the war. **1943** Hannum *Mt People* 106 [Bears] don't eat endurin' that time, just lay suckin' thar front paw, so that when they're killed in the spring their guts is just as clean as the inside of yore hand. **1963** Edwards *Gravel* 122 It was endurin the time of the Civil War. **1974** Fink *Bits Mt Speech* 8 Did he stay *enduring* the night?

[OED3 *enduring* prep obsolete →1650; DARE *enduring* prep South, South Midland]

engern See **onion**.

enjoy *verb* To entertain (someone).

1913 Kephart *Our Sthn High* 198 "Well," he exclaimed, "mebbe we-uns can find ye a pallet [to sleep on]—I'll try to enjoy ye somehow." Which, being interpreted, means, "I'll entertain you as best I can." **1995–97** Montgomery *Coll* (known to Adams, Brown, Bush).

[Web3 *enjoy* vt 3 now dialect]

enough of *adjective phrase* Enough.

1861 *Click CW Letters* (June 3) I hope thay may never get up the Vally as far as harrison burge for I think thay have doen a nough of damage in the Vally all reddy. **1861** *Hileman CW Letters* (Sept 18) I reckon surely they will leave you all Enough of Horses for you all to do your seeding with. **1974** *AOHP/ASU-233* I wove, and I carded and spun enough of yarn to weave a blanket. **1979** *Big South Fork OHP-1* They brought enough of logs out of there up that incline to run the band mill. **1985** Dabney *More Mt Spirits* 45 Take a foot adz and *dig* a big enough of a trough to pour four or five bushels of apples in it. **1998** *Dante OHP-71* They didn't have enough of students to come to school and keep the school going.

entertain *verb* To be engaged or occupied with (something) foolishly.

1994 Montgomery *Coll* He's entertaining a poor do [= he's engaged in a project of little consequence or merit] (Cardwell).

entry *noun* An unenclosed hallway between rooms of a two-room house.

1913 Kephart *Our Sthn High* 76 A sagging clapboard roof covered its two rooms and the open space between them that we called our "entry." The State line between North Carolina and Tennessee ran through this uninclosed hallway.

epizootick(s) (also *epizoodicks, epizoomicks*) *noun*

1 In livestock, especially horses, a disease of indeterminate nature.

2012 Still *Hills Remember* 360 The word turned the agent again. "Epizoomicks?" He batted his eyelids. "Are you referring to an epizootic, an epidemic among animals?"

2 In humans, an undiagnosed, unspecified, or imaginary illness.

1957 Neel *Backwoodsman* 15 *epizootick* = an undiagnosed illness, or illness of an unspecified nature. **1966** *DARE Survey* (Spruce Pine NC) = joking name for an imaginary illness. **1992** Brooks *Sthn Stuff* 47 *epizootics* = any disease of indefinite nature. If an animal is off his feed, or ailing for no known reason, he has the epizootics. (Used humorously, also, in speaking of humans.) **2013** Venable *How to Tawlk* 13 *epizoodicks* = an unidentified and sometimes unmentioned disease: "When Hortense come down with the 'sociable epizooticks,' Doc Jenkins made a salve outta lard and camphor and rubbed it on her gentiles."

er See **ah**.

-er *suffix*

1 Added to form regular comparative forms. See **gooder**.

2 Added redundantly on comparative forms. See **worser**.

3 Used in double comparatives. See **more**.

e'r a, ery See **ary**.

-es[1] *suffix* Added to form the plural of a noun. See also **-s**[7].

1 As an additional syllable, as **beastes, postes, waspes**.

1960 Sutherland *Folk Speech* 13 The old syllabic plural is retained in many words, especially in words ending in st, as beastes, nestes, postes, lastes, fastes.

[DARE *-es* suff 1a chiefly southern Appalachians, Ozarks]

2 As an additional syllable after excrescent -t. See **class, dose**.

3 As a redundant double plural. See **folkses, gallus**. (See Grammar and Syntax §1.6).

[DARE *-es* suff 2 chiefly South, South Midland]

-es[2] *suffix* Added to a third-person singular verb to mark agreement with the subject. See **cost A1, B, taste, waste**.

1976 Brandes and Brewer *Dialect Clash* 287 *es* is retained in a small number of third person singular forms of present tense verbs, e.g. *costes, rustes, tastes,* and *wastes*, as in "He wastes his money."

[DARE *-es* suff 3a chiefly southern Appalachians, Ozarks]

-est *suffix* [Editor's note: Though always conveying "most," this form may also express "best."]

1 Added to an adjective of two or more syllables, especially *-ing* participles (as *aggravatingest, bear huntingest, beatingest, cheatingest, dancingest, fightingest*, etc.) to describe a person or thing that is extremely or most proficient at or inclined to a certain activity or to perform it in an extreme or outstanding manner or degree. See Grammar and Syntax §3.4.1 for the variable interpretation of such forms.

1826 *Whitten Letter* [It is] the beautifulest country I ever saw. **1865** (in **1974** Harris *High Times* 158) My eyes swelled es big es aigs at the bran new sights and sounds, and me just plum ready to ketch the runninest kine of skeer. **1895** Edson and Fairchild *TN Mts* 374 She is the *talkenest* woman I ever saw. **c1900** (in **1997** Stoddart *Quare Women* 19) The local people gave special names to each of the women, with Katherine Pettit the "up-and-comingest," May the "ladyest," Katherine Christian the "goodest-cooking," and Curry Breckingridge the "commenest." **1912** De Long *Troublesome* You can place dependence in 'em like you could in their paw,—the respectablest, orderliest-walkin' man on God's earth. **1916** Schockel *KY Mts* 129 Law me, Honey, I'm glad to be back from the plains. Wooded mountains make the restiness place to lay your eyes on. **1919** Combs *Word-List South* 32 *bread-eatin'est* = familiar example of the mountaineer's fondness for using the superlative suffix attached to the present participle. . . . Sometimes this suffix is attached to a past participle . . . "That's the torn-downdest ole shack of a house aroun' here." **1925** Dargan *Highland Annals* 190 By the end of the summer Serena would be as duckless as at its beginning, but she had had many a pleasant, shady jaunt in search of them "outdoin'est things." **1927** Bolton *Mt Girl Speaks* 4 A favorite method of securing a descriptive word is to make a present participle a superlative in degree, thus "She is the talkingest woman; he is the chair-flingingest boy; they are the money-makingest people; she is the knittingest woman in the community." A woman said to me once that "'Chattanoogay' was the businessest city in the state." **1931** Combs *Lg Sthn High* 1321 The comparative and superlative endings are freely added to words that do not permit them: "I feel resteder now." "It's (she's) the shootin'est gun in town." "It's the loudest-ringin'est bell in the valley." "That's the melodiousest fiddle in the party." **1939** Eastridge *Folklore Adair Co* 134 "That's the preachingest man I ever heard." = He's the best preacher I ever heard. **1939** Hall *Coll* (Bryson City NC) That's the cheatin'est place here at the [Cherokee Indian Fair]. **1939** Walker *Mtneer Looks* 2–3 There are few words so characteristic as *beatin'est* and *workin'est*, which in politer society would be *strangest* and *most industrious*. **1953** Wharton *Dr Woman Cumberlands* 166 Hit makes the pitifulest cryin' I ever hear. *Ibid.* 169 I thought of something Jennie had said of these mothers, bearing their pain with more than Indian stoicism, "Ain't they the endurinest?" **1957** Combs *Lg Sthn High: Word List* 9 Such irregular comparatives and superlatives, formed on the pres[ent] part[iciple], are common. Ex.: "He's the beatin'est hand at corn-shuckin' I ever seed, but I am a corn-hoeiner man than him." **1957** Parris *My Mts* 57 From the beginning, the Wilsons were destined to become the bear-huntin'est family in all the land. **1964** Roberts *Hell-Fer-Sartin* 138 Boy, you're the powerfulest little man I ever saw in my life. **1968** Vincent *Best Stories* 81 Little Sam was the highest-tempered, and the cussingest young fellow in the whole neighborhood, and his mammy and pappy felt awful about it. **1970** *Valuable Possession* 242 A cookstove would be really the importantest thing for a woman. **1973** *AOHP/ASU-106* He's got a farm, the workingest fellow you've ever saw hit the ground. **1975** Schrock *Exam of Dialect* 469 I heard and recorded a word having the *-est* suffix applied twice, along with the use of *most*, in the sentence, "he was the most moaningestfullest hound I ever did see. **1978** *Horsetrading* 47 Court then would run a week or two weeks. And that was the tradinest place you ever went into. **1985** Irwin *Alex Stewart* 218 The wood that man could cut. He never stopped, and he was the choppin'est man in this whole country. He cut, I guess, a thousand cords of wood for Lou. *Ibid.* 252 He had the successfulest dog I ever seed in my life. **1987** Young *Lost Cove* 60 A verb was made into an adjective by adding "est" to its tail end. "They are the fightingest folks that ever fotch a breath" or "Iffin he ain't the huntingest hound that ever tracked a rabbit" can be heard even today in the Lost Cove. **1989** *Matewan OHP-18* He was the shoutingest old man you ever seen when he finally got saved. **1991** Thomas *Sthn Appal* 158 That dog was th' ground-hoggin'est dog I ever saw. He treed two in one den in th' ground one time. I dug 'um out an' killed both of 'um. **1998** Montgomery *Coll* (consultants from the Smoky Mountains interpret this form in the following ways: eight as "works more than anyone else," five as "works better than anyone else," and eight as "enjoys working more than anyone else"). **2004** Fisher *Kettle Bottom* His uncle Joe . . . was the laughingest, sparkliest-eyed man you ever seen. **2007** McMillon *Notes* All my family thought that was the wonderfullest thing ever was. She was sure Earl Quillen was the lyingest preacher ever was.

2 Added redundantly to an adjective.

1961 *Coe Ridge OHP-334B* They made the bestest song about that ever you seen. **1967** Stubbs *Mountain-Wise* (June–July) 17 My

Maw . . . is the most superstitionest thing you ever seen. **1973** Foster *Walker Valley* 9:46 Doc was the most wealthiest man this part of the country for to buy at that time. **1986** Ogle *Lucinda* 44 What we called "Sweetbread" she could make the bestest in all the country we thought.

3 Added to an adjective or adverb not usually considered gradient.

1988 Smith *Fair and Tender* 14 I reckon that migt [sic] even of been the lastest time my Daddy ever lifted her up, or lifted ary thing else heavy. *Ibid.* 75 He said it was the leastest he could do for such good biskits. **1995** Montgomery Coll Who got there firstest? Who got there secondest? (Cardwell).

et See **eat A, B.**

eternal *adjective* Infernal

1939 Farr *TN Mt Regions* 92 He's an eternal worm eater.

eve-gloom See **gloam.**

even, even' See **evening A.**

even-gloom See **gloam.**

evening *noun*

A variant forms *eavening* [see **1862** in **B**], *eavin, e'en, e'ening, even, even', evning* [see **1813** in **B**].

1862 *Lockmiller CW Letters* (June 29) the companey has not cum to take our place yet . . . it will bee here this eavin or to morrow and then wee will leave here. **1864** *Brown CW Letters* (July 3) [the mail] comes from Knoxville of a mor[n]ing and from Nashville at two o'clock in the even. **1917** (in **1944** Wentworth ADD 197) (sWV) *good even'* = good evening. **1971** AOHP/ALC-107 They signed their name up down there and so that e'ening the man said . . . everybody come out in the morning. **1983** Broaddus *Estill Co KY Word List* 38 *e'en* = evening. **2007** Preece *Leavin' Sandlick* 17 She said a couple other ladies were goina hep her and they'd have it ready by this even.

B The latter half of the day, between the middle of the day (usually marked by **dinner**) and dusk.

1780 (in **2007** Dunkerly *Kings Mt* 27) We came up with him in Craven County, South Carolina, posted on a height called King's Mountain, about twelve miles north of the Cherokee ford of Broad River, about two o'clock in the evening of October the 7th instant. **1813** Hartsell *Memora* 124 about tow oclock in the Evning [we] Came to one small Indian Hous. **1862** *Martin CW Letters* (March 8) this is About three oclock P.M. Saterday eavening. **1886** Smith *Southernisms* 45 Common Southern expressions . . . *evening* (afternoon). **1910** Weeks *Barbourville Word List* 457 = afternoon. Used by everybody. **1931** Goodrich *Mt Homespun* 57 Early in the "evening" (a part of the day that begins at 12 p.m.), Martha prepared to start, for the days were shortening and she must be home by sundown. **1934–47** *LAMSAS Appal: evening* = attested by 87/148 speakers (58.7%) from WV, 17/20 (85%) from VA, 37/37 (100%) from NC, 14/14 (100%) from SC, and 8/12 (66.7%) from GA. **1943** Hannum *Mt People* 131 For southern mountain people "evening" begins at twelve o'clock noon. For them the morning and the evening are the day, as it is recounted in Genesis of a world still in the making. **1956** Chapman *Folk Retain* If you ask him, "Would you like to ride into town this evening?" he will expect you to go sometime between noon and sundown for to him those are the evening hours; after that, it is "night." The word "afternoon" is practically unknown in the mountain speech. **1966** Dakin *Vocab Ohio River Valley* 11 Almost every Kentucky informant, even those who usually say *afternoon*, is familiar with *evening* = from noon on." Most accept either term as a "natural" suggested alternative to whichever term they give first. The younger and better educated often characterize *evening* as older or more rural even though they themselves may use it in conversation. **1973** GSMNP-78:21 At twelve we would arrange our benches and have a spelling bee all Friday evening. **1984** Gibson *Remembering* 1 We were small so about three o'clock in the evening Mama would send us a snack to the field by one of the children that wasn't big enough to work much as yet. **2003** LaLone et al. *Farming Life* 363 You would keep adding apples to [the kettle] up until about three or four o'clock in the evening. And then it would keep cooking and steaming down.

[DARE *evening* n B chiefly South, South Midland]

evening calm of day See **calm daylight.**

evening-glom See **gloam.**

ever *adverb* See also **ary, every**[1], **every**[2].

A variant syntactic position preceding the subject of a dependent clause (usually follows a superlative or comparative form).

1813 Hartsell *Memora* 100 the loock out mountain Is the Longes[t] mountain and strates[t] mountain and the biges[t] fase of a mountain that ever I saw. **c1841** Shane (in **1998** Perkins *Border Life* 198) Things came on sooner that spring than ever I knew them. **1858** (in **1974** Harris *High Times* 126) A good, holesum par ove laigs is the best thing ever a man-body kerried. **1862** *Lister CW Letters* (June 11) I never herd guns fired before hit was wors than eney starm ever you herd. **1863** *Click CW Letters* (Aug 11) the Damest Raskal that ever I had enny thing to doo with in my life. **1895** Edson and Fairchild *TN Mts* 370 Well, I wish I may *never*, if you aint the *beatenest* boy ever I *see* (saw). **1913** Kephart *Our Sthn High* 72 A herdsman who was out at the time, and narrowly escaped a similar fate, assured me that "that was the beatenest snow-storm ever I seen." **1939** Hall Coll (Deep Creek NC) The last [deer] ever I saw in the woods, I killed it with a pocket knife. *Ibid.* (Cherokee NC) That's about the best place ever I did live until I lived on Indian Creek. **1955** Ritchie *Singing Family* 48 You know a throwed joint ought to be put back into place as soon as ever it can be. **1972** AOHP/LJC-104 I was thirteen years old ever before I eat any cheese. **1975** Screven *John B Wright* 12 I made the prettiest ship ever you saw, buddy, on that thing. **1980** GSMNP-115:50 Before ever that'un was built up yander I quit school. **1989** *Matewan OHP-102* I had had one or two [boyfriends], just, but not really. I mean of course I've talked with two or three before ever I met him. **1998** *Dante OHP-24* That was the first time ever I tried to preach.

[DARE *ever* adv B chiefly South, South Midland, occasionally New England]

B Always.

1861 *Cushwa CW Letters* (Nov 14) I have not any perticular news for him onely we are getting along as ever. **1864** *Poteet CW Letters* (Aug 19) we are all well at this time ever hoping this will Reach your kind hands and find you in good health. **1940** Haun *Hawk's Done* 145 Wilbur was ever wanting to read. And he said he was going to high school or he was going to bust a gut. **1942** Thomas *Blue Ridge* 50 Twistin' the end of her apron like she ever did when she was warried. **1997** Andrews *Mountain Vittles* 52 Thanksgiving pies I sell at the stand is still the favorite it ever was.

[OED3 *ever* adv 2 "always" archaic and northern dialect; DARE *ever* adv C1 chiefly South, South Midland]

ever a *adjective phrase*

A variant forms *air* [see **c1950** in **B**], *e'er a* [see **1940** in **B**]. See also **ary**, **nary**.

B Any, a single.

1940 Haun *Hawk's Done* 26 Old Man Brock and Sadie stood there like locust posts, not turning over a hand to do e'er a thing. **c1950** Adams *Grandpap* 66 I ain't got to sleep air night with him myself yet. **c1950** Haun *When the Wind* 3–4 [He] didn't say er'a nother word.

ever and See **evern**.

ever and when *conjunction* Whenever.

1997 Montgomery *Coll* (known to Brown, Bush, Oliver); Ever and when you get home, I want you to give me a call (Cardwell).

everbody *pronoun* Everbody.

1939 Hall *Coll* (Smokemont NC) Ask Will Elmore where he is. [He] knows everbody in that country. **1942** Hall *Phonetics Smoky Mts* 64 *Everybody*, *everything*, and *everywhere* are most often . . . ['ɛvə̣bɑdɪ], ['ɛvɚθɪŋ], ['ɛvɚhwæɚ]. **1971** *AOHP/ALC-177* Everbody is welcome in my house, one or the another as they are in this world. **1975** Purkey *Madison Co* 26 They're shut off from ever'thing and ever'body and no way to earn cash money. **1992** Gabbard *Thunder Road* 119 The night everbody got out of school from graduation, me and him went straight to the still place and fired up.

everhow

A *conjunction* However.

1978 Montgomery *White Pine Coll* XII It seems like they take them in or something, everhow you want to put it.

B *adverb* However.

1975–76 *Wolfram/Christian WV Coll* 30 We used to build down and back out, up in the hollow above the house, five or six of us boys, everhow many was in the, you know, lived close to us. **1989** *Matewan OHP-7* We'd just choose up and whether we had a whole full nine course or just ever how many we had but choose up there and play agin each other. *Ibid.* 23 You'd climb in those empty coal cars, and they'd haul you through under that hill, say a mile or a mile and a half, everhow far it was in there. **1997** Andrews *Mountain Vittles* 10 1 tater for ever how many folks you have. **2002** Rash *Foot in Eden* 26 I'd imagine a child at six or eight or ever how many years had passed since the miscarriage.

[reversed compound]

everlasting

A *adjective* Infernal; uninterrupted, without exception.

1873 Smith *Arp Peace Papers* 87 Ever sinse this everlastin war, I have been parshal to a forked dirt road. **1935** Sheppard *Cabins in Laurel* 168 They just hawked hell out of me with their everlasting talk. **c1960** Wilson *Coll* = a term of reproach, almost equivalent to *damned*. **1963** Stubbs *Mountain-Wise* (Feb–March) 8 There is a story of an old man who lived "under the hills," who, when talking, used the expression "everlastin'" in describing almost anything. An "everlastin'" cold snap caused a thin film of sleet over already frozen ground. Wood to make fires gave out. He started up the hill to get a "poke o' wood" and he "everlastin'" slipped back two steps every time he took one. **1994** Montgomery *Coll* (known to Shields).

B (also *everlastingly*) *adverb* Utterly, infernally.

1928 Justus *Betty Lou* 44 "Ye needn't be so everlastin' slow about it!" the voice rasped out again. "If ye was as nigh dried up as I be ye'd manage to git a leetle move on ye." **1940** Haun *Hawk's Done* 44 That was the reason he was so everlasting hateful and always poking fun at other folks. **c1950** Adams *Grandpap* 51 That just teetotally an' everlastin'ly scared the old man to death.

[DARE *everlasting* adj, adv B chiefly New England, South Midland]

C *noun* Any decorative evergreen, especially **galax**.

1995–97 Montgomery *Coll* (known to Brown, Bush, Cypher, Oliver); I put out everlastin' in my yard so I could enjoy them in the winter (Cardwell).

everlastingly See **everlasting B**.

everly *adverb* Always, continually.

1916 Combs *Old Early English* 288 It has everly been the custom. **1943** Justus *Bluebird* 127 "Fearsome news it everly is, fire on the mountain," Mammy said, turning anxious eyes every now and then to the murky mountaintop. **1952** Wilson *Folk Speech NC* 538 = always, continuously. **1995** Montgomery *Coll* He was everly going down to the store (Cardwell).

[EDD *everly* adv Scot, nEngl; cf CUD *always and everly* (at *ever* adj) "always"; DARE *everly* adv southern Appalachians, Ozarks]

evermore *adverb* See citation.

c1960 Wilson *Coll* = occasionally used for *ever*: "As soon as evermore I can, I will pay you."

evern (also *ever and*) *conjunction* Same as **everwhen**. See also **whenevern**.

1928 (in **1952** Mathes *Tall Tales* 60) Ever'n he sees pore sinners wrastlin' under conviction, why, here he comes a-rippin' an' a-tearin', a-pitchin' an a-rarin', to keep 'em from gittin' away! **1952**

Wilson *Folk Speech NC* 538 Yes, and I'll put the law on you *evern* you do that. **1979** Carpenter *Walton War* 147 Evern (ever when) he told me, it sort of swagged down my feelins. **1996** Montgomery *Coll* Evern you do that, you'll come home and find a cold supper (Cardwell). **2007** McMillon *Notes* Ever and I went to school, that's where I went. *Ibid.* = short for *ever and*, means both *ever when* and *if ever*.

[contraction of *ever* + *and* or *ever* + *when*]

ever one See **every one**.

everthang, everthing See **everything**.

ever whar See **everywhere**.

ever whars See **everywheres**.

everwhat

A *pronoun* Whatever.

1915 Dingus *Word-List VA* 179 Compound words are sometimes exchange places: . . . *everwho, everwhat, everwhich, everwhere*. **1939** Hall *Coll* (Sevierville TN) We'll do everwhat Jim wants to do. **1940** Haun *Hawk's Done* 53 He would hit us with everwhat he had in his hands when he got mad because we didn't do things to suit him. **1969** GSMNP-28:42 Everwhat it was, they was two wagon loads went out from there. **1971** *AOHP/ALC-33* They didn't have no dinner pails or nothing back then [to bring the lunch in]. You just [had] buckets, just everwhat you get to eat out of, and that's what they'd bring. **1975** *We Sing* 19 All the good that's in you and me come from Him—ever what and who He is, the Unseen. **1978** Montgomery *White Pine Coll* VI-4 I go to Knoxville two or three times a week to pick up flowers and everwhat my needs may be. **1984** Page and Wigginton *Foxfire Cookery* 300 I want a piece of it, ever what it is. **1991** Thomas *Sthn Appal* 177 They'd investigate whuther the corn need hoein', ur th' grain need cuttin', ur everwhat it may be done. *Ibid.* 143 You had to git on one side ur th' other, to fight. Yes, suh! Ever-what side ye fell on. **2009** Burton *Beech Mt Man* 97 I just go and break it up, save her from gettin' everwhat they goin' do to her.

B *adjective* Whatever.

1969 GSMNP-37 They just followed everwhat job that they could get. **1979** *Big South Fork OHP-18* We had them big tin, big sheet irons for to put in there as a sifter. It'd sift through there everwhat grade they wanted to sift it to.

[reversed compound; DARE *everwhat* pron chiefly southern Appalachians, Ozarks]

everwhen *conjunction* When, whenever, at whatever time or moment that, if ever. Also called **evern**. See also **whenever, whenevern**.

1924 Raine *Saddlebags* 77 They told him an old woman across the valley had died with a shriek, ever when the man shot the picture with his rifle-gun. **1929** (in **1952** Mathes *Tall Tales* 105) Everwhen ye git to dostin' up on them pizin pills this here young whippersnapper of a sawmill doctor gives, ye're like as not to wake up a-layin' in yer coffin! **1939** Hall *Coll* (Cataloochee NC) They run [the bear] off I guess for a half a mile before they got up with it and treed it. Everwhen we got there, Jack reached for his gun. **1957** Hall *Bear Stories* 71 We just put our dogs in atter one of the yearlin's. And they run hit and treed it. . . . Everwhen we got there, why, I back-ridged [= went back along the ridge], got Jack's gun. **1974** Roberts *Sang Branch* 39 Hit'd pleasure the chillern to death everwhen he come. **1976** Dumas *Smoky Mt Speech* 26 I'll name it everwhen you say. **1985** Irwin *Alex Stewart* 28 Right out from his house, about as far as from here to the woodshed (a distance of 30 feet) is where they'd go, just ever when the pain struck. **2015** *Blind Pig* (Sept 29) Everwhen you can, get this guitar so I can get my fiddle out.

[reversed compound; DARE *everwhen* conj, adv[1] southern Appalachians, Ozarks]

everwhere

A See **everywhere A**.

B *conjunction* Wherever, at whatever point or place, in whatever direction.

1915 Dingus *Word-List VA* 179 Compound words sometimes exchange places: . . . *everwhere*. **1939** Hall *Coll* (White Oak NC) [Where do we go from here (on a squirrel hunt)?]: Everwhere the dog trees. **1940** Haun *Hawk's Done* 133 They had to get their breakfasts, eat, and be in the field or everwhere they were working, by a way before daylight. **1994** Montgomery *Coll* They just squatted down everwhere they were (Shields).

[reversed compound; DARE *everwhere* conj especially southern Appalachians]

everwheres, ever'wheres See **everywheres**.

everwhich

A *adjective* Whichever. See also **every which**.

c1945 Haun *Hawk's Done* 330 Everwhich one come nigh always come down to the house and stayed full half the night. **1979** *Gamecock* 165 Ever which guy's weight compared closest with your weight was the guy that you fought. **1984** Burns *Cold Sassy* 298 Like I used to tell yore granny, everwhich side I'm on is the right side. **2002** McGowan *Beech Mt Tales* 95 I'll throw my old hat right up in the air, and ever-which road it falls in that's the way I'll go. **2009** Burton *Beech Mt Man* 32 They give me nine months, but said they'd put me on three-year probation, ever which one I wanted to take. **2013** Venable *How to Tawlk* 14 Everwitch [sic] way you want to go is fine by me.

B *pronoun* Whichever.

1915 Dingus *Word-List VA* 179 Compound words are sometimes exchange places: . . . *everwhich*. **1979** *Big South Fork OHP-18* You put up timbers, props, timbers, everwhich you want to call them.

[reversed compound; DARE *everwhich* adj, pron chiefly southern Appalachians, Ozarks]

ever which and that *pronoun phrase* All kinds of things. See also **every which**.

1987 Young *Lost Cove* 67 Wagon loads of *ever which and that* were piled clear to the ceiling.

everwhichaway, ever which a way See **every which away**.

everwho *pronoun* Whoever.

1915 Dingus *Word-List VA* 179 Compound words are sometimes exchange places: . . . *everwho*. **1919** Combs *Word-List South* 33 = transposition for *whoever*. "He give it to Cece er Mose, one, *ever who* I was with." Perry Co [KY]. **1939** Hall *Coll* (Cataloochee NC) Everwho hears that will be surprised. **1958** Wood *Words from TN* 9 = whoever. **1969** Roberts *Greasybeard* 95 He said ever who the shoe fit she would be his wife. **1978** Montgomery *White Pine Coll* I-1 Everwho's higher in seniority gets to keep his job. **1996** Montgomery *Coll* It's interchangeable, according to everwho was speaking (Cardwell). **1997** *GSMNPCOHP*-5:19 He would make those molasses for them. Everwho came first, what order they came in, that's the way he made the molasses. **2009** Burton *Beech Mt Man* 65 Ever who done it paid 'em off.

[reversed compound; cf HT *iver who* "whoever"; DARE *everwho* pron chiefly southern Appalachians, Ozarks]

everwhurs See **everywheres**.

everwhy *conjunction* Why.

2016 *Blind Pig* (Sept 21) I use everwhat all the time along with everwho, everhow, everwhy, everwhen and everwhere.

every[1] (also *evry*) *adverb* Ever.

1834 *McLean Diary* 26 Cool frosty Wether Every Since Aprile Came in. **1861** *Proffit CW Letters* (Sept 8) thay Look better than i evry saw them. **1863** *Watkins CW Letters* (March 4) I cold eat one of the bigest baits you evry saw. **1979** *Big South Fork OHP*-4 I pieced them, quilted all before I was every married. **1988** *Augusta Heritage* 153 I've knowed Jack Keith every since waking up to the world. **1998** *Dante OHP*-61 He was one of the best switchmans that every went in the mines.

every[2] *adjective* variant form *ever*, including in compounds *everbody*, *everone*, etc.

1845 Wyrick *Letter* 3 tha[y] is all well that is alive . . . but Hugh Wirick, he shakes ever day. **1864** *Misemer CW Letters* (April 21) I want you to write to me ever week if you can. **1864** *Warrick CW Letters* (May 21) I want you to rite to me ever chance you get and back them to Dalton Ga as you hav bin doing. **1895** Dromgoole *Fiddling to Fame* 47 She holped me ever way. **1929** (in **1952** Mathes *Tall Tales* 108) He says wearin' a lump of asafidity round yer neck an' takin' a little balsam ile ever-day will keep off might' nigh any sickness. **1939** Hall *Coll* (Bradley Fork NC) They said, "You've done more than ever man that's lived here. We've got a good civilized country and a good church." **1942** Hall *Phonetics Smoky Mts* 64 *Everybody*, *everything*, and *everywhere* are most often . . . ['ɛvə̣-bɑdɪ], ['ɛvɚ-θɪŋ], ['ɛvɚ-hwæɚ]. **1961** *Coe Ridge OHP*-339A He hunted ever night in the week. **1974–75** McCracken *Logging* 6:88 He could look at the side of that mountain over there [and] pick out ever piece of curly wood there was on it. **1982** Powers and Hannah *Cataloochee* 260 They may ever' one of 'em be down [= sick] up there. **1989** *Matewan OHP*-102 She made ever kind of a preserves that you could think of. **1997** *GSMNPCOHP*-3:13 Ever summer we go up and have a short service and singing there.

[DARE *ever* adj chiefly South, South Midland, especially TX]

every bit

A *noun phrase* A thing in its entirety (used as an apposition following it; thus, *it every bit* = all there is of it).

1942 (in **1987** Perdue *Outwitting Devil* 40) The Devil had a whole peck o' gold. An' they started playin' poker, an' they played for about an hour an' Willie won hit ever' bit. **1979** *Big South Fork OHP*-11 I'm going to spend it every bit for whiskey. **1979** *Daddy Oakley* 176 She carried that sack full of eggs over there and traded it every bit for candy. **1985** Irwin *Alex Stewart* 205 You could take him a wagon load and he'd buy it every bit.

B *adverb phrase* Completely, fully, just as.

1900 Harben *N GA Sketches* 220 I'd every bit as soon whip my mammy as a body feelin' like you do. **1975** *AOHP/LJC*-384 They all owned that. Now it's every bit gone.

every bit and grain

A *noun phrase* See citation.

1952 Wilson *Folk Speech NC* 538 *every bit and grain* = all there is of a thing. "I'll bet he's spent *ever' bit and grain* of his poor wife's savings."

B *adverb phrase* Fully, entirely.

1949 Hornsby *Lonesome Valley* 196 The clock was big as a wagon wheel, and the hands were every bit and grain as long as wagon spokes. **c1960** Wilson *Coll*: *every bit and grain*: "He's every bit and grain as old as Grandpap." **1995–97** Montgomery *Coll*: *every bit and grain* (known to Brown, Shields).

every one *pronoun phrase*

A variant form *ever one*.

B Syntax.

1 (also *every one of them*) Coreferent with the subject of the clause but having syntactic position within the predicate.

1924 Raine *Saddlebags* 91 Aunt Marthy . . . has twenty-four, fourteen boys and ten gals, and they're every one living, or was the last I knowed. **1939** Hall *Coll* (Little Cataloochee NC) They can every one sing. **1940** Haun *Hawk's Done* 128 They'll every one run if you shake a finger at them—just won't fight you at all. **1969** *GSMNP*-37:2:19 They'd get them girls to come and teach school over here. They's every blamed one teachers, school teachers, even the boy. **1973** *Flu Epidemic* 107 When I went back, they'uz ever'one dead. **1979** *Preacher Cook* 194 They'd everyone come to the revival meeting. **1982** Powers and Hannah *Cataloochee* 260 Father said, "I want you to go up and see about Uncle George and the family. They may ever' one of 'em be down [= sick] up there." **1985** Irwin *Alex Stewart* 190 After you gather them in, you can take and put them in water and them bugs will everyone float off. **1995** Adams *Come Go Home* 2 Granny clapped her hand over my mouth when she saw the thousand-legs, because if you show them your teeth, they'll every one rot out. **2005** Joslin *Handcrafters* 96 I just stuffed my pockets till they was everyone full.

2 (also *every one of them*) immediately following a coreferent noun or pronoun (thus *we every one* = every one of us).

1901 Harben *Westerfelt* 52 Ef you don't watch sharp he'll cut you every one out. **1930** Justus *Foot Windy Low* 12 He had shifted his crazy quilt bundle until he could see them every one. **1939** Hall Coll (Hartford TN) We every one had just about what we could tote of bear meat. **c1950** Adams *Grandpap* 80 I hope that you ever'one live up to what he expected of you! **1959** Roberts *Up Cutshin* 90 He stopped and saw old Mat right in the top of that hornbeam bush just a-wringing and twisting and a-tying them limbs in knots, and them dogs every one turning on the back track. **1960** McCaulley *Cades Cove* I knew them every one. **1972** *AOHP/ALC-226* About a minute before midnight, that light went to go out. We every one went to running. **1974** Roberts *Sang Branch* 10 We everyone, that is all seven of us at home, learnt to play that old banjer, even all the girls. *Ibid.* 293 When he tetched them all they every one of them turned into rocks. **1975** Carawan and Carawan *Voices from Mt* 52 They every one rallied. They jumped up and clapped their hands. **1976** *Bear Hunting* 295–96 He got six [pups], and he raised them every one. **1977** *Jake Waldroop* 168 Them cattle of yourn . . . they everyone was down there in Dismal. **1983** *Dark Corner OHP-24A* I guess it was up in the thirties. We every one like to died with that typhoid. **1985** Irwin *Alex Stewart* 141 She had a gang of children and they every one had the scald head. **1998** *Dante OHP-71* We met them every one right there in the Abingdon Hospital.

3 Having one or more intervening words following a preceding coreferential pronoun.

1863 *Chapman CW Letters* (Dec 10) I want you all to write to me ever one. **1940** Still *River of Earth* 125 They tuck oath on the Book. Tuck it everyone except Jolly, he being only twelve, and too young for swearing.

every one of them See **every one B1**, **B2**.

everything *pronoun variant forms everthin, everthang, everthing.*

1863 *Karnes CW Letters* (March 15) your leter has bin more consolation than ever thing else. **1867** Harris *Sut Lovingood* 169 Jis run over ur thru everthing yure durndest, till yu gits cumfort, that's hit. **1895** Dromgoole *Fiddling to Fame* 51 Jube war buckin' up the boys right peart, an' war about ter sweep off everthing. **1925** Dargan *Highland Annals* 161 It was the masterest sight, him goin' over ever'thing like he had wings in his insides. **1942** Hall *Phonetics Smoky Mts* 64 *Everybody*, *everything*, and *everywhere* are most often . . . ['ɛvə̜-bɑdɪ], ['ɛvə-θɪŋ], ['ɛvə-hwθæə]. **1975** Purkey *Madison Co* 26 They're shut off from ever'thing and ever'body and no way to earn cash money. **1985** Williams *Role of Folklore* 300 Ever'thin's fine. **1991** Thomas *Sthn Appal* 113 Everthang is sold yit on terms. **2013** Venable *How to Tawlk* 16 Sandy had his dawg so well-trained, it fotched everthang he shot, squirrels to quail.

everywhere

A *adverb, conjunction variant forms ever whar, everwhere, evry were* [see **1865** in **B**].

1862 *Shifflet CW Letters* (March 18) th[e] nuse is good ever whar on our side and I donte want to come home tell the war is over and I think that wont be long. **1974–75** McCracken *Logging* 5:53 Everwhere Eli lived, he had him a good-sized garden. **1997** *Dante OHP-14* About everwhere you go anymore it's like that.

B *conjunction* Wherever, at any point that.

1865 *Martin CW Letters* (Jan 21) we have to go evry were our officers sees proper to send us. **1960** McCaulley *Cades Cove* I've spent half of my life in Smoky Mountain, just laid out just everywhere night come on. **1985** Irwin *Alex Stewart* 79 Down below the house there was several outcropping of big limestone rock and everywhere you saw one of them, why you found a big, nice, black walnut tree.

everywheres *adverb*

A *variant forms ever whars* [see **1862** in **B**], *everwheres, ever'wheres* [see **2009** in **B**], *everwhurs* [see **c1940** in **B**].

1957 Broaddus *Vocab Estill Co KY* 28 *everwheres* = everywhere.

B Everywhere. See also **anywheres**, **nowheres**, **somewheres**.

1862 *Lockmiller CW Letters* (Sept 25) our fokes ar whopen thern ever whars and i hope that pas will be mad. **c1940** Padelford *Notes* Hit's selfishness ever'whurs. **1974** *AOHP/ASU-204* We had to walk over that mountain up there everwheres we went to school. **1982** Ginns *Snowbird Gravy* 8 You see, then people walked about everywheres they went to work. **1983** Page and Wigginton *Aunt Arie* 99 On a certain day they'd have a corn shuckin' and get all th'neighbors from everwheres t'come in here. **2003** Carter *Mt Home* 38 All the Daddys and Mamas around ever-wheres warned their youngens to stay away from mud puddles and water holes for they thought that was where the polio virus germs come from. **2009** Burton *Beech Mt Man* 24 I was a-slingin' corn ever'wheres. I was goin' crossways then.

[*everywhere* + -s adverb-forming suffix; cf **-s**[5]; Web3 *everywheres* adv chiefly dialect]

every which *adjective phrase* See also **every which away**.

1 Every single, each.

1955 Ritchie *Singing Family* 182 I was so bashful that whenever a boy looked at me sideways, my tongue would cleave to the roof of my mouth and my face would turn every which color.

2 Whichever.

1973 *AOHP/ALC-154* They were two sides, of course. One side in the community would be for a certain person and the other side would have their candidate, and every which side they knew how many people there were in the community and they knew who was related to so and so and how they could work this man in the community to get the most votes. **1977** Shackelford et al. *Our Appalachia* 52 They'd put the girls up on the stage [and] every which one they put the most money on would be the prettiest girl in the community.

every which away (also *everwhichaway, ever which a way, ever-which-way, every which-a-ways*). Every which way, in all directions. See also **a**[3], **any which way**, **everwhich**, **every which**, **whichaway**.

1938 Justus *No-End Hollow* 98 I'm plumb addled every which-a-ways. **a1954** Adams *Word-List*: *ever-which-way* = in all directions. **1974** Dabney *Mt Spirits* 13 The old man trimmed out little trails through the laurels, "just a forkin' ever which a way." **1983** *Dark*

Corner OHP-28A I guess they's just a-running every which away a-hiding their liquor. **992** Brooks *Sthn Stuff* 47 *everwhichaway* = in all directions; in a senseless, crazy, or confused way. "Whin he's drunk, he jumps in his ole Ford an' drives down the road everwhichaway but straight."

every which-a-ways See **every which away.**

every whipstitch *adverb phrase* See citation.

1957 Broaddus *Vocab Estill Co KY* 28 = very often.

every word *noun phrase* variant syntactic position in the predicate. See also **every one B1**.

1901 Harben *Westerfelt* 131 I reckon it wus every word the truth. **1979** Melton *'Pon My Honor* 41 Her father is Jim Davis, so I reckon this one is ever word so.

evning See **evening.**

evry See **ever.**

evry were See **everywhere.**

ewe *noun* variant forms *yo, yowe.*

1891 Primer *Studies in WV* 166 The word *ewe* (jiu) has frequently the pronunciation (joo). **1915** Dingus *Word-List VA* 193 *yo* = ewe (*ewe* is not heard). **1941** Stuart *Men of Mts* 187 I saw her Pappie out cutting stove-wood by the rose bush and he was tall like a bean-pole with a yowe neck and a little face that had a sharp pointed nose stuck on it. **1956** Hall *Coll* (Wears Cove TN) He killed that old yo. **c1960** Wilson *Coll*: *Yo* is almost universal; *ewe* would require explanation to many people. **1961** Kurath and McDavid *Pron Engl Atl Sts* 157 Four types of pronunciation are current in the eastern states.... The type of /jo/ is heard in all parts of the Eastern States. In the South and South Midland it has rather general currency, except among the cultured; in the North Midland it is common in rural areas. **1973** Miller *English Unicoi Co* 84 *yo* attested by 4 of 5 speakers. **1980** *Smokies Heritage* 233 The ewe (pronounced yo in the Smokies) grazed in the Flanagan field for a while, but dogs began bothering her, and she had to be sold.

[DARE *ewe* n chiefly South, Midland]

except *conjunction* Unless.

1862 Huntley *CW Letters* (May 4) I have some idea of going to Capt Eaves Company at Raleigh Except I get some Body to take my place. **1964** Roberts *Hell-Fer-Sartin* 55 Nothing can help me except you go to the end of the world and get me a bottle of water.

[at DARE *except(ing)* B South, South Midland]

exclude *verb* Of a church congregation: to dismiss (a person from membership) for violating a standard of conduct. See also **church 1, 2.**

1845 *Zion Church Minutes* 25 Church Conference found all in fellowship. Whereas the case of Lucy Law was taken up and she failed to give satisfaction and was excluded. **1860** *Toe Valley Church Minutes* 48 The cace of Brother Harvy Presnell tak[en] up and acted upon by the church and Brother Presnell [was] excluded. **1977** Shackelford et al. *Our Appalachia* 48 To show how strict they were, they tried a woman who had come to church while pregnant. That was an offense. She was excluded from their fellowship for not knowing any better than to come to church in that particular situation. *Ibid.* 49 Some called it "de-churched," or "You're excluded," and that was just terrible for anybody who belonged to the church to be excluded, unless he was just so mean that he didn't care anyhow. **1987** Dorgan *Glory to God* 18 One ceases to be a member of a local Primitive [Baptist] church by being dismissed by letter to another church, by dying, or by being "excluded." This exclusion, often referred to in the mountains as being "churched," is an act by which an errant member is literally expelled from membership. This may occur as a consequence of doctrinal errancy or a lack of attendance and involvement, but occasionally it may come in response to a lifestyle not acceptable to the membership. **2014** Montgomery *Doctrine* 117 = when a person loses their church membership through the action of the church.

exhorter *noun* A lay preacher.

1901 Harben *Westerfelt* 253 I got hugged by a whole string of exhorters. **1946** Stuart *Plum Grove Hills* 40 Harley Skaggs ... was a preacher; that was almost a preacher in them days. When the people shook with fear back in the churchhouse—when they heard the sermons of fire and damnation—the exhorter went back atter 'em and hepped 'em to the altar where they prayed fer forgiveness of their sins. **1971** Wood *Vocab Change* 38 = a part-time preacher whose professional training may lie only in what he has read from the Bible. **c1980** Roberts *Olden Times* 61 Apparently realizing that the people needed the Gospel long before they were able to erect church buildings, the Methodists sent to the frontier missionaries known as circuit riders whose objective was to find the people and to conduct religious services in their homes. They then organized "classes" of about 12 persons who were to meet weekly in their homes for prayer and to hear a simple sermon by the local leader or exhorter, and to pay tithes. **2014** Montgomery *Doctrine* 117 *exhorters* = men who are gifted in encouraging the church in a speaking way but are not necessarily called to the ministry.

expect *verb*

A variant forms *speck* [see **1867** in **B**], *spect* [see **1883** in **B**].

[DARE *expect* v A chiefly South, South Midland]

B To suppose, believe, surmise. See also **allow B1, reckon B.**

1862 *Martin CW Letters* (July 13) I have Seen Such heard times that I have fell of So if you had Seen Me Last winter & to Se Me now you would not no Me I expect. **1863** *Kinsland CW Letter* I expect I cold sell it all out by the quart at 5 dollars a quart write soon and tell me what yow think wold be best. **1867** Harris *Sut Lovingood* 42 I speck she thot the devil wer a-huggin her, an' she wer durnd near right. **1883** Zeigler and Grosscup *Heart of Alleghanies* 87 I spect he would ef I hadn't bought him out when I did. **1939** Hall *Coll* (Proctor NC) I guess it is about fifteen, I expect. *Ibid.* (Emerts Cove TN) I expect my daddy owned about as much as, not hardly as much as Fred Emert, but he was right at it.... I don't expect they'd approve of it very much. **1956** Hall *Coll* (Townsend TN) It was closer down there than I expect to Cades Cove. **1973** GSMNP-61:6 I spect they did. **1979** *Big South Fork OHP*-9 I expect he was about eleven or twelve, somewhere along there, when he started playing the guitar. **1983** *Dark Corner OHP*-13 I expect you remember Doctor Gibson at Inman. **1991** Thomas *Sthn Appal* 146 I've wondered what would a' happened to me if our family's got rich. I don't know what. I don't 'spect I'd a' lived this long.

expect for *verb phrase* To expect.

1961 *Coe Ridge OHP*-342B They was expecting for a lot of trouble and didn't have it.

experience meeting *noun* See 1996–97 citations.

1861 *Kiracofe CW Letters* (Aug 26) last Sunday morning we had an experience meeting & the Lord was with us our hearts ware made to leep for joy to know that though we ware far from home among Strangers that the Lord would Condecend to bless us. **1905** Miles *Spirit of Mts* 102 Although she has been a widow these twenty years and has lost three children, she invariably states at experience meeting that her soul is happy and that she has a heap to be thankful for, which is quite true. **1928** Justus *Betty Lou* 121 Uncle Dan'l prided himself on having read the whole Bible through six times. It was a fact he never missed giving in experience meeting or Sunday school if he had the least chance. **1987** Trent *Yesteryear* 91 There happened to be a local Methodist preacher who was also the presiding elder in the town. He called the people together and told them he was going to have an old-fashioned experience meeting. He wanted them to tell how they conducted the family worship at home. One by one, they went round the circle. **1996–97** Montgomery *Coll* = a church service where individuals are encouraged to stand and publicly confess their sins, joys, frustrations, thankfulness, or prayer requests (Brown), = a church service where people testify or stand up and make a statement about their blessings, etc. (Oliver).

extery See **extra**.

extra

A variant forms *extery, extrey, extry*.

1813 Hartsell *Memora* 98 I and my surboltens never drew aney extrey rations from the day we started up to this time. **1861** *Martin CW Letters* (Oct 6) every six months we get 21 dollars extry to by clothing withe. **1863** *Brown CW Letters* (Nov 4) [I] bin in the surves twelv month and i hant bin put on extery duty yet. **1923** Greer-Petrie *Angeline Doin' Society* 21 He could spar' him one of his knives and forks, fur someone had drapt sev'ral extry ones at his plate. **1940** Simms *Wiley Oakley* 16 I'll not charge anything extry for guidin' the valet. **1973** GSMNP-79:21 I thought the people down here just tried to work too hard and to make that extry money. **1979** *Big South Fork OHP*-4 They would take them maybe somewhere else and get a extry price for them thataway. **1989** *Matewan OHP*-7 He was a-trying to make a extry run [of whiskey]. **1998** *Dante OHP*-12 [In] this home, they had a big extry room, and that's where that I went to school.

B *adjective* Very good, excellent.

1939 Hall *Coll* (Cosby Creek TN) He was a extry hand to work. [DARE *extra* adj B chiefly South, South Midland]

C *adverb* Very.

1989 *Matewan OHP*-102 They was extry large rooms.

extrey, extry See **extra**.

ey See **ay**.

eye *noun* A removable circular lid on top of a wood-burning stove; the opening for this lid. Also called **cap A6**.

1939 Hall *Notebooks* = an opening in the top of a wood stove. **1971** *Cooking* 93, 94 [A woodstove] has six circular eyes. The eyes and their partitions are easily removable for cleaning. . . . The cooking surface of a wood stove usually has six "eyes" or "caps." Sometimes they are of the same size—sometimes they are of varying sizes. The one at the center at the back of the stove is the hottest, the two over the firebox are the next hottest, and the other three are the cooler ones. **1991** Thomas *Sthn Appal* 51 That'un had six eyes, I b'lieve it wuz—they wuz five eyes an' six eyes on differ'nt stoves.

[DARE *eye* n[1] 1 chiefly South, South Midland]

eyebright *noun*

1 A bluet (*Houstonia caerulea*). Same as **innocence**. See also **babytear, Quaker lady**.

1928 Chapman *Happy Mt* 311 = a mountain flower known also as bluet or "Innocence"; of the madder family (*Houstonia caerulia*). **1996** Montgomery *Coll* = bluet (Cardwell).

2 An annual wild plant (*Lobelia inflata*) with medicinal uses. Same as **Indian tobacco**.

1940 Caton *Wildflowers of Smokies* 87. [**1971** Krochmal et al. *Medicinal Plants Appal* 164 The herb yields lobeline sulfate, which is used in anti-tobacco therapy. It is also used as a stimulant, anti-asthmatic, and expectorant in cases of bronchitis.] **1997** Montgomery *Coll* (known to Brown), = used by women to dilate pupil for cosmetic purposes (Andrews).

eye(d) hoe *noun* A hoe whose blade has a hole in it for inserting a handle.

1960 Mason *Memoir* 16 The chief tools were the ax, saw, eyed-hoe, scooter plow, mowing blade and cradle. *Ibid.* 22 The eyed-hoe was made from a thin, flat five by six inch piece of iron or steel. **1982** Ginns *Snowbird Gravy* 64 We lived and made out. Dug our ground up with old eye-holes. Got one up in the shop now. Sort of like a mattock, you know, but we called 'em eye holes. And we'd dig up the ground with it.

eyewater (also *Thomson's eyewater*) *noun* See citations.

1940 Farr *More TN Expressions* 447 = liquor: "Eye water's more plentiful in Jackson County now than common." **1969** *DARE Survey* (Dillard GA) *Thomson's eyewater* = illegally made whiskey.

ey God, ey gonnies, ey law See **ay**.

F

face *noun*

1 See citations. See also **working 2.**

1973 Preston *Bituminous Term* 36 = the area of the coal seam, at right angle to the top and bottom of a passage or room, and usually at the farthest advance, from which the coal is removed by whatever method is employed. **c1975** *Miners' Jargon* 3 = in any tunnel, slope, chamber room, or entry [of a coal mine], the end at which work is progressing or was last done. Also called *working face.* **1977** Shackelford et al. *Our Appalachia* 236 A lot of places used mules to pull the coal from the face; some of the places used electric motors. **1989** Giardina *Storming Heaven* 23 This is called our place and that there is the face of the coal. We drill in there with our auger and then we tamp in the powder and dirt and the needle. **1990** Clouse *Wilder* 65 The older, more experienced miner usually worked the "face" while the younger loaded the coal into the cars. **2002** Armstead *Black Days* 243 = the exposed area of a coal seam where miners and/or machines extract the coal in a room, heading, or longwall operation. **2006** Mooney *Lg Coal Mining* 1028 The miners bore vertically into the coal seams, or the "face," manually with picks in the old "handloading" days or, in the contemporary era, with machines called "continuous miners," machines that use rotating drill bits to chew out coal. **2007** *Mining Terms* = the exposed area of a coal bed from which coal is being extracted.

2 Presence.

1931 Combs *Lg Sthn High* 1307 Git out o' my face, or I'll slap ye into the middle of next week.

face boss *noun* See citations.

1973 Preston *Bituminous Term* 36 = a worker in charge of the men at one working end of a face of coal usually concerned with cutting, shooting, loading gathering motors or belts, clean up, and timbering. **c1975** *Miners' Jargon* 3 = a supervisor of the unit located at the face of the coal.

face down *verb phrase* See citation.

1957 Combs *Lg Sthn High: Word List* 35 = to lie boldly, or dissemble to one's face. Ex.: "He faced me down he didn't steal the hog."

face out *verb phrase* To put (a schoolchild) in the corner as punishment for misbehavior.

1972 GSMNP-69:9 I used to . . . get faced out every once in a while for making pictures instead of studying my books.

face powder *noun* Women's facial powder (construed as a count noun; hence plural form *face powders*). For similar forms, see **powder 1.** See also **whitening.**

1930 Armstrong *This Day and Time* 7 That here is all the style this day an' time—paint an' face-powders.

face whitening See **whitening.**

fad die (also *fad-die-and-sink, had-(dy)-die*) *interjection* See 1957 citation. Same as **hope (to) my die, I.**

1911 Shearin *E KY Word-List* 538 = if I had to die, a phrase of asseveration, e.g., "Fad die, I'll do it." **1916** Combs *Old Early English* 297 Words and phrases of asseveration and "cuss"-words of Elizabethan England still survive. Among these we find . . . "Fad die," . . . (If I had to die). **1941** Still *Troublesome Creek* 21 "You'll spy and won't go." [But I replied,] "fad die." **1957** Combs *Lg Sthn High: Word List* 35 *fad-die-and-sink* = corruption of a phrase of asseveration, "If I had to die and sink (in hell)!" Other forms: *fad die, haddy die* (had to die); *had die; if I die.*

[DARE *fad die* exclam southern Appalachians]

fade *verb* See citation.

1940 Farr *More TN Expressions* 447 = to die: "Aunt Mittie faded last night."

fady *adjective* Faded.

1955 Ritchie *Singing Family* 51 It's his first one [= letter] he ever wrote to me. Handle it careful, it's old and crackly. Hard to read, too, yellow and fady, but you can tell what a pretty hand to write he was then.

failing disease *noun* Tuberculosis or a similar mortal illness.

1911 Shearin *E KY Word-List* 538 = consumption, tuberculosis. **1952** Wilson *Folk Speech NC* 538. **1957** Combs *Lg Sthn High: Word List* 35 = tuberculosis of the lungs. **1998–99** Montgomery *Coll* (known to Brown, Bush, Cardwell).

[cf OED3 *fail* v 3a "to lose power or strength"]

fail out *verb phrase* See citation.

1910 Weeks *Barbourville Word List* 456 = fail: "I failed out in three of my examinations."

faint bottle *noun* A small bottle with odoriferous contents kept on hand to revive one who has fainted.

1963 Watkins and Watkins *Yesterday* 120 A woman who fainted lay on the floor unconscious and pale and looking barely alive. Every family kept a "faint bottle" with whiskey and camphor in it. It smelled strong enough to wake the dead.

faintified (also *fainty*) *adjective* Feeling suddenly weak or faint, inclined to faint.

1952 Wilson *Folk Speech NC* 538 This hot, dry weather makes me feel sickly and *faintified.* **1967** *DARE Survey* (Gatlinburg TN, Maryville TN) *faintified* = having a sudden feeling of weakness, when sometimes the person loses consciousness. **1969** Doran *Folklore White Co* 112 *faintified* = on the verge of fainting. **1995** Montgomery *Coll* I'm a little fainty this morning (Cardwell). **2005** Williams *Gratitude* 55 Camphor was used as a rub, too, but they kep' some around to put a dab on a haincher for people to smell of and brang 'em around when they felt faintyfied. **2016** *Blind Pig* (July 22) I wish you had waited to have surgery when it was cold weather. This heat will make anyone "faintified," especially after having teeth pulled in this mountain oven.

[OED3 *fainty* adj 1 obsolete except dialect; DARE *faintified* adj chiefly South]

faint(s) *noun* See 1974 citations. See also **heads**, **middlings 2**, **tailings**.

1917 Kephart *Word-List* 411 *faint* = worthless residue in the "thumper" after distilling whiskey. **1968** *End of Moonshining* 100 *faints* = dead beer; or backings that steam has been run through in a thumper to strengthen a run. These are drained and replaced before each new run. **1974** Dabney *Mt Spirits* xxi *faints* = leftover liquid in a thumper keg after a run . . . These are withdrawn after a run and replaced with fresh beer or backings, to provide alcohol for the thumper's doubling effect. **1974** Maurer and Pearl *KY Moonshine* 117 = 1) low-proof distillate that comes through the condenser at the end of a run. Also called "tailings." Sometimes applied to weak *first shots*. 2) heated slops used for setting mash. **c1999** Sutton *Me and Likker* 104 = the left over liquid in the thump keg [that] must be turned out and washed, then replaced with fresh backins before the next run.

[from the low alcohol content; DARE *faint* n South Midland]

fainty See **faintified**.

fair

A *adjective* Open to view.

1965 *Dict Queen's English* 14 The money was lying there as fair as your hand. **1998** Montgomery *Coll* (known to Brown, Cardwell, Ellis, Jones, Oliver).

[Web3 *fair* adj 8 archaic]

B *noun* See citation.

1944 Wilson *Word-List* 42 = female sweetheart (Mitchell Co., N.C.)

C (also *fairly*) *adverb* Entirely, positively.

1940 Still *River of Earth* 14 "I figure they're fair ready for biling," he would say. "Time we had a mess." **1979** Melton *'Pon My Honor* 71 He took off down the road so fast that his shirt-tail fairly stood out in the wind behind him.

fairly See **fair C**.

fair off (also *fair up*) *verb phrase* Of the weather: to clear up, become bright and cloudless.

1886 Smith *Southernisms* 38 To *fair* off or *fair* up, for "clear off" or clear up . . . is very common . . . in the South, but was evidently imported from Scotland. **1891** Primer *Studies in WV* 170 In expressions of the weather I find the following in my note-book; to fair off, meaning to clear off. **1917** Kephart *Word-List* 411 It may *fair up* and be a pretty week. **1934–47** *LAMSAS Appal*: *fair off* = attested by 87/148 speakers from WV, 1/20 (5%) from VA, 1/37 (2.7%) from NC, 2/14 (14.3%) from SC, and 1/12 (8.3%) from GA. **1939** Hall *Coll* (Byrds Creek TN) I think hit'll fair up. **1950** Hall *Coll* (Del Rio TN) Now it is raining like sixty, and maybe in a few more months it will fair up. **1966–67** *DARE Survey* (Spruce Pine NC) *fair off* = when the clouds begin to decrease; (Gatlinburg TN) *fair up* = when the fog begins to go up in the air. **1979** GSMNP-112:6 I went back to school when it did fair up. **1996–97** Montgomery *Coll*: *fair off* (known to nine consultants from the Smoky Mountains); *fair up* (known to Adams, Cardwell, Brown, Jones, Ledford, Oliver).

[DARE *fair off* v phr chiefly South, South Midland]

fair to middling See **middling A**.

fair up See **fair off**.

fairy candles *noun* A bugbane (*Cimicifuga racemosa*), a perennial wild shrub whose roots and rhizomes have medicinal uses. Same as **black cohosh**.

1997 Montgomery *Coll* (known to Cardwell).

fairy cross (also *fairy stone*) *noun* A staurolite, a type of stone formed naturally with a cross formation.

1940 *FWP Guide VA* 610 Fairy Stone State Park [in Patrick Co VA] . . . was so named because of the small stauroline crystals, locally called fairystones, found in profusion in the area. **1970** Clark *NC Beliefs* 49 Fairy or lucky crosses (found in North Carolina and Virginia and thought to have been dropped from the skies and then formed into crosses) are said to have magic properties to protect owners from witchcraft, sickness, and disasters. **1976** Anderson *Fairy Crosses* 25 One mineral noted for its significance in the Copper Basin area is staurolite, better known as "fairy crosses." Rock hounds come from other areas to find this unusual looking rock formation. . . . There are two main legends of how staurolites formed. One says they are the tears of the Cherokee Indians who went on the "Trail of Tears" from the southern states to Oklahoma in the 1800's. Another says that when the fairies heard of the crufixion of Christ they were [sad] and their tears crystallized in the form of crosses. . . . The most prized [shape] is the Maltese Cross. However, it is difficult to find a perfectly even and well formed cross. A more common shape that is easier to find is the angled "St. Andrew's Cross." The most common formation is the "prismatic." Most staurolites are imperfect in shape and quality. **1988** Russell and Barnett *Ghost Stories* 64 For those who might be skeptical of the existence of the spirit people and fairies of western North Carolina, evidence has been left behind. Besides the mounds and the mysterious smoke rising from underground Nunnehi fireplaces, relics known as fairy crosses are sprinkled throughout the area. Found even to this day, fairy crosses are small crystals formed in the shape of a cross. Along with North Carolina gemstones, fairy crosses are polished to perfect symmetry and are valued additions to numerous gem and rock collections across the country. Found in the largest numbers in Cherokee and Clay counties, fairy crosses are believed by some to be the crystallized tears of the Nunnehi. Others insist that the Nunnehi were able to make themselves visible and invisible at will because they each possessed a fairy cross, which they wore on strings around their necks. Nunnehi who lost their fairy crosses also lost the ability to become visible, and were destined to live in the invisible world beneath the rocks and water forever.

fairy diddle See **ferrididdle**.

fairy stone See **fairy cross**.

fairy wand *noun* The blazing star (*Liatris* spp), a perennial wildflower with medicinal uses. See also **button snakeroot**, **rattlesnake master 2**, **rattlesnake root 1**.

1941 Walker *Story of Mt* 55 The staminate flowers of the fairy-wand is an exquisite floral creation blooming in April and May on the side of the mountain. **1971** Hutchins *Hidden Valley* 187 There must have been great need for tonics, since a wide variety of plant teas were used, including those made from maidenhair fern root [and] fairy wand.

[from the wandlike stem and raceme of white flowers]

faith *verb* To trust, respect.

1951 Craig *Singing Hills* 35 "No," she drawled. "I don't faith religion none." **1987** Young *Lost Cove* 57 Church-goers who forgot and blackguarded once in a while were not faithed much by members of the Amen Corner. *Ibid.* 213 *faith him* = respect him as a Christian.

[Web3 *faith*² v archaic]

faith doctor *noun* A folk healer considered to have a divine gift of healing who treated illness by faith or using biblical formulas rather than modern medical practices. See also **blood doctor**, **fever doctor**, **witch doctor**.

1901 Price *KY Folk-Lore* 32 To stop hemorrhages, this same "faith doctor" has a second person repeat, with the patient, the following text from Ezekiel: "And when I passed by thee, and saw thee polluted in thine own blood, I said unto thee, Live." **1963** Miller *Pigeon's Roost* (Aug 1) I recall of Joe Honeycutt, Mosie's son, one time of telling me that when he was a lad that he took down sick with dyspepsia and his dad took him to a man who was called a faith doctor that advised and treated patients without making any charge. **1977** Shackelford et al. *Our Appalachia* 54 My right leg was drawn up under my body. A faith doctor blew on my leg, and with the help of Daddy and Mother and with home remedies that Mother made out of the white of an egg and alum this drew the fire out. They straightened my leg. **1989** *Matewan OHP-56* Dad Henderson Huff was a faith doctor. . . . He traveled by horse all over the country, and he was a cancer doctor. He would take the cancers off of people, external cancer. Internal, external cancers, he could remove them. He had some kind of a potion. **1991** Still *Wolfpen Notebooks* 45 I know a fellow over in Floyd County who is a faith doctor, and I'll take you to him and he'll do something, and the knot [on your head] will disappear.

fall

A *verb*

1 variant past-tense form *felled*.

1998 *Dante OHP-71* Tom was picking up the trash and stuff that felled and everything and putting it in a basket and pushing it out of the way.

2 variant past-participle form *fell*.

1774 *Dunmore's War* 231 It has fell out extremely unlucky, that both them Gentlemens ranging Stations, was very thin when [the] Indians came. **1789** *French Broad Petitions* 219 Some of our Citizens have fell a sacrifice to Their Savage Cruelty. **c1844** Beckner *Shane Interview* 236 He had fell in with one Sprowl at Lexington, with whom he had had some acquaintance in Virginia. **1862** Hedgecock *Diary* 105 At 3 o'clock we halted to wait for those who had fell behind in order to make our march to Greenupsburg as imposing as possible. **1863** *Thompson CW Letters* (May 24) I think the yankes has fell back from raleigh at this time. **1913** Kephart *Our Sthn High* 225 She's fell down. **1940** Haun *Hawk's Done* 21 Ma will think I have fell into the spring. **1953** Hall *Coll* (Bryson City NC) Then [the bear will] go back and just step up . . . looking for chestnuts and beechnuts on the ground after they've fell out of the trees in the fall of the year. **1961** *Coe Ridge OHP-336B* If he'd have fell off there, he'd hit right in the water. **1973** GSMNP-84: 26 They had fell out with these Tiptons over a certain preacher. **1989** *Matewan OHP-1* I've fell on them steps a many and a many at a time. *Ibid.* 7 **1998** *Dante OHP-71* The whole fireplace had fell in but it didn't hurt the baby. **2009** Sutton *Me and Likker II* 217 I wonder how many people have fell off in that damn place.

B *verb* To cut down (a tree) using a **broad ax** or **felling ax** (especially in phrases *fall a tree*, *fall the timber*).

1927 Woofter *Dialect from WV* 354 = to cut a tree down. "Do not fall the tree on the fence." **1956** Hall *Coll* (Emerts Cove TN) I was fallin' a big chestnut tree, and it struck a dead locust which fell against me, and I had to lay out doin' anything for two or three weeks. **1960** Mason *Memoir* 110–11 It was the responsibility of the chipper to decide the most desirable direction in which to fall the tree. **1983** Pyle *CCC 50th Anniv* A:2:18 Somebody in the crew is supposed to know how to fall a tree.

[OED3 *fall* v 51c now dialect, U.S.]

C (also *falls*) *noun* A waterfall.

1883 Zeigler and Grosscup *Heart of Alleghanies* 150 Hit was the dry nest of a master old varmint under thet fall. **1926** Hunnicutt *Twenty Years* 51 Old Muse trailed up the creek to the falls and there she got bothered very badly. **1974–75** McCracken *Logging* 3:10 You hit that first river over there and go up it to where they's a fall up there.

fall a tree See **fall B**.

fall away (also *fall off*) *verb phrase* To lose weight or become thin, usually as a result of illness.

1863 *Robinson CW Letters* (Feb 11) I have fell away 26 lbs cence I came through Mobiel I am so weak that I can hardley walk. **1863** Wilson *Confederate Private* 29 (Aug 23) I had a rite smart atack of fevar I hav fel of so mutch that you wodent hardly [k]no[w] me. **c1900** (in **1997** Stoddart *Quare Women* 128) He fell away 18 pound. **1924** Greer-Petrie *Angeline Gits Eyeful* 12 She'd fell away and lost ten pounds the past month and wuz a-hopin' she'd lose as much ag'in the follerin' month. **c1945** Haun *Hawk's Done* 228 He fell off till he was slim as a rail almost and took to groaning in his sleep and singing love songs about hard-hearted girls. **1946** Matthias *Speech Pine Mt* 190 *fall off* = to become thin: "She's fell off somethin' turrible, last two-three months." **1967** *DARE Survey* (Gatlinburg TN) *fall off* = to lose weight as a result of illness. **1990** Cavender *Folk*

Medical Lex 22 She's fallen off quite a bit since she became sick. **1999** Morgan *Gap Creek* 26 He had fell off so much he didn't look like a grown man in the bed.

[DARE *fall off* v phr 1 chiefly South, South Midland]

fall back to *verb phrase* See citation.

1915 Pollard *TN Mts* 242 *fall back to* . . . To revert to (one) as an obligation. "All the things fell back to Papa to sell."

fall bean *noun* See citations. Same as **October bean**.

1941 Stuart *Men of Mts* 71 The wind smells of the bean vines that climb the corn stalks where Mom has planted her a patch of fall beans. **1957** Broaddus *Vocab Estill Co KY* 28 = a type of green beans that get ripe in the autumn. They are rather tough. **1968–69** *DARE Survey* (Adams) Fall bean—the hull is white with red streaks; (Berea KY) Fall beans are the same as cranberry beans; (Hazard KY) Fall beans are red beans with green hulls; (Hindman KY) Cream-colored fall beans [are] bunch beans; (Walker KY) *fall beans* = both bunch and pole varieties.

fall dead (also *fall out*) *verb phrase* To faint, collapse. Same as **drop dead**.

1861 *Mingus Letters* 29 (Oct 6) Jackson Beck had a little girl to fall out . . . the blade cut her throat, it lived 15 minutes. **1863** *Proffit CW Letters* (June 24) It was said that many marched until they fell dead on this march. **1957** Broaddus *Vocab Estill Co KY* 28 *fall dead* = to faint. **1973** Kahn *Hillbilly Women* 141 They just fall out, out maybe for fifteen minutes, just like they're dead. **1983** Wolfram/Christian *WV Coll* 212 She'd take on out a fit and fall out just like she was dead. **2008** Plott *Hunting in Smokies* 51 You don't reckon I faint do you? Women faint. I fell dead! You see, all the blood in me jumped over my heart into my head, and of course it finished me for a time.

[DARE *fall out* 2 chiefly South, South Midland]

fallen weather See **falling weather**.

faller *noun* A logger who cuts down trees.

1998 Farwell *Logging Terms*.

fall grape *noun* A wild grape. See also **fox grape**, **possum grape**.

1966–69 *DARE Survey* (Dillard GA) = the same as possum grapes; they make good jam and jelly; (Walker KY) = sweet and good; (Cherokee NC) = wild grapes. **1996** Montgomery *Coll* (known to Adams, Brown, Cardwell, Jones, Ledford, Norris, Oliver).

[DARE *fall grape* n chiefly southern Appalachians]

falling ax See **felling ax**.

falling weather (also *fallen weather*) *noun*

1 Rain or snow, a change in weather for the worse.

1864 *Chapman CW Letters* (Feb 5) to day it looks like we will have falling wether before long of some kind. **1927** Woofter *Dialect from WV* 353 = damp, rainy, or snowy weather. "The rheumatism always bothers me before a spell of falling weather." **1938** Justus *No-End Hollow* 227 By falling weather she meant rain or snow. **1939** Hall *Coll* (Sevierville TN) We're gonna have some fallin' weather. **1962** Drukker *Lg By-Ways* 51 Rain is "falling weather." **1976** *Carrying Mail* 101 When the roads were so bad and the weather wasn't fallin' weather (an expression used when it was raining or snowing), I would have to ride Bess.

2 Autumn weather.

1942 Thomas *Blue Ridge* 63 It was in the falling weather. These hills . . . were a blaze of glory.

[DARE *falling weather* n both senses chiefly Midland]

fall into *verb phrase* To begin. See Grammar and Syntax §7.3. See also **fall to**, **set in 1**, **start in**, **take to 1**.

1939 Hall *Coll* (Smokemont NC) I fell into work there. **1940** Oakley *Roamin'/Restin'* 117 Mr. Huff said to me Wiley fall into eating and eat plenty for you boys may hafto stay out all night and it may be you wont have any chance to eat untill sometime tomorrow so I eat and cramed it down. **1967** Hall *Coll* (Del Rio TN) Feather into, that means to fall into something and get right with it.

fall off See **fall away**.

fall out See **fall dead**.

fallover trousers *noun* See citation.

2004 Mays *Passion* 65 Charles and his younger brother, Rex, used to stand outside the shop door and peer around at the old man curiously. They were especially interested in his "fallover" trousers that buttoned from the side, rather than from the front.

fall rose *noun* A zinnia.

1925 Furman *Glass Window* 237 She carried in her hand a large bunch of zinnias. "Miss Christine sent you these fall roses," she said. **1979** Slone *My Heart* 45 She had a very large garden—row after row of vegetables, but the very best, with the richest soil, she used for her flowers: fall roses (zinnias), marigolds, bachelor's buttons, and touch-me-nots, and many others, too many to name.

falls See **fall C**.

fall sore *noun* A bright red skin lesion, usually impetigo. See 1996–97 Cardwell citation. See also **dew poison**, **ground itch**, **mud poison**, **toe-itch**.

1960 Westover *Highland Lg* 19 = impetiginous skin lesions. **1964** Wright *Mt Medicine* 9 There was a lot of impetigo. It went by such names as "Tomato Sores," and "Fall Sores," and "Weed Sores." **1996–97** Montgomery *Coll* (known to Brown, Jones, Ledford), = any sore that was aggravated by the heavy dews of autumn; mountain people often claimed the autumn dews to be poisonous (Cardwell). **2003** Cavender *Folk Medicine* 100 Also known as "dew poisoning" and "ground itch," fall sores are lesions on the feet, legs, and arms caused by scratches becoming infected by bacteria. In the past, they were most common in the fall, but they also appeared in the dog days of summer.

fall the timber See **fall B.**

fall to (+ *verbal noun or present participle*) *verb phrase* To begin. See also **fall into**, **set to**, **start in**, **take to 1**. See also Grammar and Syntax §7.3.

1892 Dromgoole *Dan to Beersheba* 82 He fell to eating hurriedly. **1928** Justus *Betty Lou* 47 This was so comical an idea that both Betty Lou and Milly fell to laughing. **1939** Hall *Coll* (Cataloochee NC) I fell to shootin' [the bear] and shot 'im ten times then before I killed him. **1940** Oakley *Roamin'/Restin'* 13 Soon the dogs struck the trail of some kind of animal and soon they fell to barking. **1957** Justus *Other Side* 14–15 As soon as the "Amen" was said, everyone fell to eating the corn pone, bacon, and gravy, which were placed in the middle of the table.

fall to staves *verb phrase* To collapse, fall apart.

1924 Raine *Saddlebags* 104 We had a cedar churn, but it fell to staves. **1940** Haun *Hawk's Done* 28 "Granny, you're nigh tired to death, ain't you?" And I did feel all at once like I was about to fall to staves. **1967** *DARE Survey* (Maryville TN) = collapse.

fall up *verb phrase* See citation.

2008 Williams *Dialect Scott Co TN* = become very ill.

false *noun* An untruth, lie.

1923 Greer-Petrie *Angeline Doin' Society* 2 If he [= a preacher] had told a false, Lum wanted to be able to tell . . . about hit when he got home.

fambly *noun* variant of *family*.

1896 Fox *Vendetta* 126 You'd ha' thought he hed been convicted, though none o' our fambly hev been much atter religion. **1913** Kephart *Our Sthn High* 121 Let ary thing go wrong in the fam'ly . . . and we can't git a doctor up hyar less'n three days. **1933** Carpenter *Sthn Mt Dialect* 24 Fambly for FAMILY is prevalent in the southern Appalachians and is sometimes heard in Kentucky. **1974** Roberts *Sang Branch* 6 Grandfather came back [from the Civil War] and raised a big fambly, and one of his boys was named Tom—he is my father.

family decoration *noun* See citation. Same as **Decoration Day**.

1944 Hayes *Word-List NC* 33 = the annual decoration of graves in the family burying plot. Each family has a different Sunday during the summer or fall for decoration. The ceremony consists of placing flowers on the graves, singing without accompaniment, and listening to sermons by three ministers. The service may last hours.

family mill *noun* A small gristmill owned and operated by a family to grind its own corn.

1961 Medford *History Haywood Co* 52 Some of these early mills, termed "family mills," were small and crudely built.

family pie *noun* A deep-dish fruit pie. Also called **cobbler pie**, **pot pie**.

1934–47 *LAMSAS Appal* = attested by 16/148 speakers (10.8%) from WV, 19/20 (95%) from VA, and 26/37 (70.3%) from NC. **1973** *GSMNP-4:2:2* Family pie we call it, blackberry, huckleberry, apple, peach. **1973** Medford *Long Hard Road* 15 [Apples] were made into apple butter, jelly, cider, as well as pies of all kinds (including the "family" (or deep-dish) pie . . .) and fried pies, made from dried apples. They were canned and baked, as well as stewed. **1984** Woods *WV Was Good* 24 For a light supper Mother often made a huge family pie, as we called it. (Cobbler to you.) **1986** Pederson et al. *LAGS* = attested by 13/60 interviewees (21.7%) from E TN; 13/18 of all LAGS interviewees (72.2%) attesting term were from Appalachia; (Johnson Co TN) = layers of fruit and pastry. **1996–97** Montgomery *Coll* (known to Bush, Ledford, Norris), = also a meat pie (Brown).

fancy-fine *adjective* Showy, impressive.

1943 Justus *Bluebird* 59 Then her books would be ready to go to school in their new clothes, each in a fancy fine dress. **1952** Justus *Children* 36 "Oh, Aunt Sally," Letty Ann cried, "what a fancy-fine notion!"

fan mill *noun* A hand-cranked machine with a fan to blow away and separate the chaff from wheat grains.

1945 O'Dell *Old Mills* 1 After the wheat was well threshed with the "frail" it was placed in a "fan mill." This was made of wood and operated by a double-geared crank. . . . The fan mill was screened, and thus the grain was retained while the chaff blew away.

far[1] see **fire**.

far[2]

A *adjective, adverb*

1 variant forms *fer*, *fur*.

1845 Wyrick *Letter* 4 all is well as fur as I no at this time. **1863** *Reese CW Letters* (Oct 27) I want you to git A nuf of wheat if you can to sow the ground on the fur Cide of the Branch. **1882** Winstadt *Letter* The rest of the connection is all well as fur as I no. **1922** Kephart *Our Sthn High* 95 Not fur from where we are now, he stepped into a bear trap that was hid in the leaves, like this one. **1939** Hall *Coll* On the fer side of the mountain. **1942** Hall *Phonetics Smoky Mts* 30 *Far* in untutored speech is always [fɚ]. **1963** Hooper *Unwanted Boy* 228 That covey of partridges "uses" in the "fur" field. **1974** *AOHP/ASU-204* We'd go and play with Mary Isaac's kids, and things like that, and hit was so fur. **1991** Thomas *Sthn Appal* 248 Somehow another, I didn't git that fer.

2 comparative forms *farrer*, *fudder*, *furder*, *furer*, *furrer*. See also **further 1, 2**.

1862 *Robinson CW Letters* (Sept 24) I am furder from home then I wanted to be. **1863** *Brown CW Letters* (Oct 4) you sayd you went to knoxville to se Cornel Pickns i shure you went furder to se a lyer then i wold. **1883** Zeigler and Grosscup *Heart of Alleghanies* 59 When they git it high nuff, they dig a tunnel from the furder side o' the log, an' then crawl through an' under the brashe. **1937** Haun *Cocke Co* 3 [Roads] make a trip to church seem furder than hit is.

1952 Wilson *Folk Speech NC* 539 *farrer, furrer.* **1970** *Hunting Stories* 31 M'dogs couldn't trail no fudder an' they just blowed out on it an' I had t'quit. **1974–75** McCracken *Logging* 10:20 Then they got up a little furder. They had Camp Nine. **1993** Cunningham *Sthn Talk* 56 *furer* = further, farther. **2002** Morgan *Mt Born* 163 *furder.*

[DARE (at *far* adv, adj B a, b) *farrer, furder, furrer* chiefly South, South Midland]

3 superlative forms *ferrest, furdest, furest, furrest.*

1922 Kephart *Our Sthn High* 23 Bushnell's the furdest ever I've been. **1957** Combs *Lg Sthn High: Word List* 37 *ferrest* = superlative of "fer." **1969** Roberts *Greasybeard* 123 He helt it till she quit bleeding and he goes back in the furest room to put the blood away. **1997** Montgomery *Coll: furest* (known to Cardwell).

[DARE (at *far* adv, adj C b) *ferrest, furrest* chiefly South Midland]

B *adjective*

1942 Justus *Step Along* 5 They had been down creek a far way with a turn of new corn for grinding at Uncle Eben's mill.

fare sumptious *verb phrase* To eat heartily.

2005 Bailey *Henderson County* 30 "I want ye to fare sumptious," said a host to the guests at his table. "We don' want to see no timid eaters." When a person has "fared sumptious" the appetite has done full justice to the meal, but a "timid eater" is too "choicy" to make the efforts of the cook worthwhile.

fare-thee-well (also *fare-you-well*) *noun* (in phrases *to a fare-thee-well, to a fare-ye-well, to a fare-you-well* = to a finish, to perfection or completely).

1929 (in **1952** Mathes *Tall Tales* 116) You an' the little lady has fit it out with Death an' ye've whupped him to a fare-ye-well! **1940** Still *River of Earth* 153 Mad though I was anyhow for the blame they brought, and I cussed all three to a fare-you-well. **1956** McAtee *Some Dial NC* 15 *to a fare-ye-well* = thoroughly. "Bob licked him to a fare-ye-well." **1957** Hall *Coll* (Mt Sterling NC) Jason Collins was lit up to a fare-you-well. **c1960** Wilson *Coll: fare-thee-well* = to perfection. **1963** Carson *History Bourbon* 111 Within three days the boy understood the biz thoroughly and could make "doublins" to fare-you-well.

farewell *noun* An aftertaste.

1917 Kephart *Word-List* 412 = after taste. "That ain't got no bad taste; it has a leetle *farewell* to it as though it had campfire in it." **1927** Woofter *Dialect from WV* 354 = aftertaste. "That liquor has a good farewell." **1997** Montgomery *Coll* (known to Brown).

[OED3 *farewell* n 3 obsolete; EDD *farewell* n "an ill aftertaste or twang"; DARE *farewell* n 1 Midland]

farewell-summer (also *farewell-to-autumn, farewell-to-summer*) *noun* Any of several asters (*Aster* spp, especially the blue aster), which bloom only weeks before frost. See also **goodbye-to-summer, summer-farewell.**

1943 Stuart *Private Tussie* 217 Aunt Vittie had a cluster of farewell-to-summer blossoms wreathed in her hair. **1951** Barnwell *Our Mt Speech* Often they call our snowy dogwood "bride of the woods," the lovely asters, so varied and abundant in the fall they call "farewell summer." **1996** Montgomery *Coll: farewell to autumn, farewell to summer* (known to Cardwell).

[DARE *farewell-summer* n chiefly central Appalachians]

fare-ye-well, fare-you-well See **fare-thee-well.**

farm in the woods *verb phrase* See citation.

1972 *Foxfire I* 305 The sheriff had gotten a report about one of his [= a friend's] stills, [so] he would . . . [say], "I hear you're farmin' in th' woods." The moonshiner would know that that was a warning for him to watch his step.

farm stuff *noun* Vegetables. See also **garden salad, stuff.**

1949 Arnow *Hunter's Horn* 316 Willie spoke the truth; times were good; all things were getting higher, even the little farm stuff a man had to sell.

far piece *noun phrase* A relatively great distance. See also **little piece, piece 1.**

1927 Shearin *Speech of Fathers* 6 It's a pretty fur piece over to that mill. **1940** Haun *Hawk's Done* 34 It seemed like it was a right far piece to the cave. **c1959** Weals *Hillbilly Dict* 4 *fur piece* = long distance. "It's a fur piece to town." **1962** Dykeman *Tall Woman* 140 What I hear, it's a far piece West and back. **1975** Chalmers *Better* 37 Hit's right cold out this mornin' atter th' rain an' hit's a fur piece up the hollow. *Ibid.* 65 A short road is a piece ways, or, if the road is longer, it may be a fur piece. **1975** Purkey *Madison Co* 81 Women were especially good at "hollerin'." Their shrill high-pitched voices carried a "fer piece." **1982** Slone *How We Talked* 26 *a fer piece* = a distance of many miles. **2007** Homan *Turkey Tracks* 86 Based upon the folks I talked to—an admittedly small and much older than average sample—I compiled five alternative measures of Appalachian distance. The smallest component was tater chunk, as in "you're real close, it's just another tater chunk down the road." Following tater chunk in progression were yonder, hoot and a holler, a piece, and a fer piece.

[DARE *far piece* n 1 scattered, but chiefly South, South Midland, North Central]

farr See **fire.**

farrer See **far**[2] **A2.**

fasola *noun* A method of singing using **shape notes** or **patent notes.** See 1977, 2008 citations.

1957 Parris *My Mts* 204 The heart-stirring voices of the fasola singers can still be heard here in the highlands where folks never have lost the feeling for Christian harmony. **1977** Wolfe *TN Strings* 12 Much of the early singing was congregational singing done from songbooks by shape notes: notes where pitch is indicated by shape rather than position on the staff. Such singing was called "fasola" singing for two reasons: The old singers usually started songs by singing note names instead of words, and, instead of the modern scale names (*do re mi fa sol la ti do*), the older singers knew only four names (*fa sol la* and an occasional *mi* thrown in). They sang the scale as: *fa sol la fa sol la mi fa*. **1995–97** Montgomery *Coll* (known to Brown, Cardwell, Ledford, Norris), = singing school teachers taught singing from shape-notes, which are easier to read than the traditional notes on the scale. To get the singers all "tuned," the teacher would have them sing fa so la in harmony (Oliver). **2008** Eskew *Sacred Harp* 129 In sacred harp singing it has become standard practice to sing through first using the fa-sol-la solmization syllables before singing the words, hence the designation "fasola" singing.

[*fa* + *sol* + *la* "names for tones of a diatonic scale"]

(as) fast as a martin to her gourd *phrase* Very fast.

(as) fast as Snyder's pup See **Snyder's hound/house cat/pup**.

fat *noun* See citation.

1923 Combs *Addenda KY* 242 = lard.

fatback (also *fat meat*) *noun* Fatty meat from the back of a hog, usually salted and often cooked with vegetables for seasoning, with more fat than **middling C**. See also **side meat**, **sow belly**, **streaked bacon**, **striped meat**.

1864 Hill *CW Letters* (March 16) it is corn choping the roughest Sort and fat mete a third of a pound to the man for a day. **1934–47** *LAMSAS Appal*: *fatback* = attested by 1/20 speakers (5%) from VA, 3/37 (8.1%) from NC, 14/14 (100%) from SC, and 7/12 (58.3%) from GA; *fat meat* = attested by 1/20 speakers (5%) from VA, 2/37 (5.4%) from NC, 1/14 (7.1%) from SC, and 2/12 (16.7%) from GA. **1949** Kurath *Word Geog East US* 70 Less common terms [for salt pork in the South and South Midland] are *fat-back* . . . and *fat-meat*. **1952** Giles *40 Acres* 104 In the winter, just after hogs are killed, fresh pork is plentiful. During the summer there is side meat, jowls, and what we call fat back. Fat back is the fat, white, salted meat that is usually used for cooking. **1977** Hamilton *Mt Memories* 103 Kate would fry strips of fat meat—we called it bacon—and make gravy by stirring flour into the drippings and adding milk. **1990** Oliver *Cooking Hazel Creek* 13 When a settler wanted a mess of [green beans] during the winter they were unstrung, broken up, washed & put to soak for awhile, and then cooked like fresh green beans with fatback or streaky lean for seasoning.

[DARE (at *fatback* n 1) *fatback* chiefly South, South Midland, also Northeast, *fat meat* chiefly Midland, also South]

father-and-son mine *noun* Same as **doghole**.

1943 Korson *Coal Dust* 4 Some farmers . . . operated small mines variously called "country banks," "wagon mines," "dog holes," "gopher holes," or "father-and-son" mines.

father cow *noun* Used as a euphemism for bull. See also **bull A1**.

1966 *DARE Survey* (Cherokee NC).

fatigue tea *noun* An **herb tea** designed to restore energy.

1975 *Foxfire III* 332 [In the summer] sometimes various plants are combined in special mixtures. For example, "fatigue tea" combines nettles, dandelions, and yarrow.

fat meat See **fatback**.

fat pine *noun* A knot or piece of wood from a particularly resinous pine tree used for kindling or as a torch or crude lamp. See also **light pine**, **lightwood torch**, **pine heart**.

1845 (in **1974** Harris *High Times* 48) Jim Clark has gone to the woods for fat pine, and Peggy Willet is along to take a lite for him—they've been gone a coon's age. **1849** Lanman *Alleghany Mts* 92 A couple of torches made of the fat pine. **1949** Kurath *Word Geog East US* 51 In the Southern area kindling is called *lightwood*. In the Midland, *pine*, *fat-pine*, *pitch-pine*, *rich pine*. **a1975** Lunsford *It Used to Be* 177 "Fat pine" means the pine knots and the old stumps that are full of resin and they're good to kindle fires with. **1982** Irwin *Baskets* 14 A piece of rich "fat" pine the size of one's finger would burn for minutes as if it had been soaked in gasoline. **1999** Spencer *Memory Lane* 25(4):5 She said that so often the candles didn't furnish the required light and often it was her job to hold a torch of fat pine.

[Web3 *fat pine* n 2 "kindling" chiefly Midland; DARE *fat pine* n 2 "knot" chiefly South, South Midland]

fattening day *noun* See citation.

1930 Pendleton *Wood-Hicks Speak* 87 = Saturday, or Saturday afternoon, spent in town, particularly after pay is received.

fat-to-my-jassum *interjection* Used as a mild oath.

1964 Roberts *Hell-Fer-Sartin* 118 "Well," he said, "fat-to-my-jassum, we're all here, le's go!"

fatty *noun*

1 A square on which a game of marbles is played. See also **rolly hole**.

1963 White *Marbles E KY* 61 (Carter Co) = the squared pattern on which marbles are played. *Ibid.* 62 (Floyd, Perry, Pike, Johnson, Knott, Carter, Breathitt, Rowan, Greenup, Boyd, Morgan Counties) = the name of the area inside the lines of a square.

2 (also *fatty hole*) The game of marbles played on such a square.

1940 Still *River of Earth* 82 The boys crouched on their knees to play fatty hole, the bright marbles spinning from rusty fists into the dirt pockets. **1968** *DARE Survey* (Logan WV) Fatty is played in a small square. A player knocks a marble out. If his stays in, he gets to shoot again. The one who shoots out the most marbles wins.

fatty bread (also *fatty dodger*) *noun* Same as **crackling bread**.

1937 Hyatt *Kiverlid* 68 "Alright, Granny," said the girl, "I'll make one fatty dodger." **1940** Still *River of Earth* 212 When the cushaws were boiling Mother got a bag of cracklings. She crisped a handful of rinds in the stove. "Six pones o' fatty bread I'm going to make," she said. **1984** Wilder *You All Spoken* 88 *fatty bread* = cracklin' bread, usually made with corn meal, sometimes with flour, and cracklin's, of course. **1997** Montgomery *Coll*: *fatty bread* (known to Brown, Bush, Hooper).

[DARE *fatty-bread* n 1 chiefly South Midland]

fatty dodger See **fatty bread**.

fatty hole See **fatty 2**.

faucet *noun* A cow's teat.

2002 Myers *Best Yet Stories* 140 It is funny today to think that people do not know how to milk a cow. That was an important task when I was young. Facing a cow, walk to your left—being the right side of the cow. Put your head into her flank to help prevent her from kicking when you get to work on the udders or "faucets."

fault *verb* To blame (someone).

1896 *Word-List* 416 = blame. "I didn't *fault* him for that." **1913** Kephart *Our Sthn High* 282 In mountain vernacular many words that serve as verbs are only nouns of action, or adjectives, or even adverbs . . . "Granny kept faultin' us all day." **1928** (in **1952** Mathes *Tall Tales* 65) They ain't no use faultin' the boy fer somethin' he ain't to blame fer. **1937** Hyatt *Kiverlid* 26 I ha'n't faultin' Jed's Maw none. **c1959** Weals *Hillbilly Dict* 4 = blame. "I don't fault you fer the cow gittin' out." **1962** Dykeman *Tall Woman* 166 "She's always faulting herself for her cooking," Paul teased. **1979** Carpenter *Walton War* 144 I hain't minded to fault him none. **2009** Holbrook *Upheaval* 37 I don't fault Mommy for leaving out.

[DARE *fault* v 1 chiefly South Midland]

faut See **fight 1**.

favor

A (also *flavor*) *verb* To resemble (especially a member of one's family) in looks, character, or disposition, or to inherit qualities from; to resemble one another. See also **favor B**.

1863 *Hall CW Letters* (Aug 3) Francis Sade She has bin to See you & States that you was well & that my baby favord her famley. **1863** *Hundley CW Letters* (Aug 21) John dont fever his self no more than if it wasant him. **1898** Elliott *Durket Sperret* 11 All the same, Mertildy, Hannah don't favor Si. **1946** Matthias *Speech Pine Mt* 190 (sometimes *flavor*) = to resemble each other in appearance: "Are you brothers? You don't favor"; "Joline and Arwillie's sisters, but they don't favor." *Favor* is in common colloquial use as a transitive verb ("He favors his father"). **1957** Broaddus *Vocab Estill Co KY* 29 = to resemble a person in looks. **1961** Miller *Pigeon's Roost* (Aug 24) One man that we talked to after the service said it favored the meetings like they had long ago when there was so much "shouting." **1974** Fink *Bits Mt Speech* 9 The boy *favors* his daddy. **1977** Shackelford et al. *Our Appalachia* 92 [Ginseng] turns a pretty yellow color and there ain't another weed in the hills that favors it. **2004** House *Coal Tattoo* 37 He did favor Elvis Presley a bit. **2014** Williams *Coll* You and him favor.

[DARE *favor* v C1 widespread, but chiefly South, South Midland]

B (also *favorance*) *noun* Family resemblance.

1910 Norman *English of Mtneers* 277 Those girls are of a favor. **1915** Dingus *Word-List VA* 182 *favorance* = resemblance (of features). **1937** Hall *Coll* (Smokemont NC) They say that Abraham Lincoln showed a favorance to the Enloes. **1939** Hall *Coll* (Cataloochee NC) She shows a favorance of his father. **1996–97** Montgomery *Coll*: *favor* (known to Brown, Bush, Cardwell, Cypher, Hooper). **2001** Lowry *Expressions* 13 I see a favorance.

[DARE *favor* n B1 South, South Midland; *favorance* n 1 South Midland]

favorance See **favor B**.

favorite

A variant form with stress on both first and last syllables: FA-vor-ITE.

1942 Hall *Phonetics Smoky Mts* 75 *Favorite*, usually with [-ɪt], but sometimes with [-aɪt]. **1952** Wilson *Folk Speech NC* 539. **1962** Wilson *Folkways Mammoth Cave* 9 The secondary accent is really a second primary accent, fully as strong as the supposedly main one. Mammoth Cave people spoke of *favorite* as /FA-vor-ITE/. **1991** Thomas *Sthn Appal* 8 He soon became a favor-ite among the college students, which added much to his growing circle of friends.

B *noun* A close friend.

1895 Edson and Fairchild *TN Mts* 371 Me an' Abernathy is great *favorites*. **1996–97** Montgomery *Coll* (known to eight consultants from the Smoky Mountains).

feared See **afeard**.

featherbed tick See **feather tick**.

feather crown *noun* See citation. Same as **crown**.

2007 Milnes *Signs Cures Witches* 51 Occult belief, oral tradition, folklore, and material culture collide within the presence of a "feather crown" or "death crown." The belief is that a person, who is about to die, is dying, or has died will cause a metaphysical effect within the pillow on which their head lays. A portion of the feathers inside the pillow will clump or form into a circle or "crown," which is seen as a token or sign in some way representing the death or its consequence to the pillow user.

feather dance *noun* See citations. Same as **buckdance**.

1983 Matthews *Cutting a Dido* 105 The "feather dance" [is] a local *sobriquet* [in Haywood Co NC] for old style buckdance: "A 'feather dance,' that's just a little toe dance. You just kind of move from your knees down, a little feather dance. The old-timers said that when you were a smooth dancer, a feather dancer, that you could dance with a bucket of water on your head and never spill it." . . . The "feather dance," a name which in itself evokes images of flight, is a light, soft subtle dance that satisfies the dance ideologies of freedom and spontaneity.

feathered out *adjective phrase* Dressed up, wearing fancy clothes.

1937 Hall *Coll* (Cades Cove TN) She was all feathered out. **1995** Montgomery *Coll* (known to Cardwell).

feathered tick See **feather tick.**

feather harp *noun*

1999 Milnes *Play of Fiddle* 136 Other names I have heard for dulcimers in central West Virginia are hog harp, hog fiddle, feather harp, or church dulcimer (which was used to describe a large, six-stringed dulcimer in Nicholas County).

feathering *noun* See citation. See also **snuff 2.**

2003 Smith *Orlean Puckett* 101 Aunt Orlean produced from her bag a goose feather. She stuck it into the fire and then placed the smoking feather beneath the mother's nose. The mother started coughing and sneezing and the baby was born immediately. That practice is called feathering.

feather into *verb phrase*

1 To attack (someone) furiously, shoot (someone).

1917 Kephart *Word-List* 412 = to attack, as with arrows piercing to the feather. "He *feathered into* him, feedin' him lead." **1931** Combs *Lg Sthn High* 1308 "Feather into one" means to attack him violently. **1952** Wilson *Folk Speech NC* 539 = to fight, to light into. **c1960** Wilson *Coll* = to attack vigorously, tear into.

[cf SND *feather* v 5 "fig. to beat, chastise"; DARE *feather* v 5 South Midland]

2 To begin vigorously to finish (work).

1937 Hall *Coll* The man feathered into his crop. **1939** Hall *Coll* He seed the work had to be done, and he just feathered into it. **1967** Hall *Coll* (Del Rio TN) Feather into, that means to fall into something and get right with it.

feather-legged *adjective* Cowardly.

1952 Wilson *Folk Speech NC* 539 = frightened, cowardly. "I get sorta *feather-legged* when I get around her." **1972** Cooper *NC Mt Folklore* 91 = cowardly. **1995–97** Montgomery *Coll* (known to Brown, Cardwell, Norris).

[DARE *feather-legged* adj South, South Midland]

feather tick (also *featherbed tick, feathered tick, feather tick pillow*) *noun* A bed **tick** or pillow filled with feathers, sometimes light enough to sleep under in winter. See also **flock tick, shuck bed, straw tick, tick.**

1941 Stuart *Men of Mts* 191 We put a featherbed tick on a set of springs in the bed and a couple of feather pillows and a sheet to go over Fern. **1975** Purkey *Madison Co* 40 Spring cleaning was another important event in our household. On a bright sunny day everything in the house was carried outside, and the straw ticks were emptied and refilled with fresh straw. The younger fry loved to play and turn sommersaults [sic] among the feather ticks as they lay sunning in the front yard. **1991** Haynes *Haywood Home* 41 Most everyone had cord beds in their homes. On top of the cord webbing, they put a straw tick, and on top of that, a feather tick. In spring, all the feather ticks would be taken outside to be sunned for several days. **1995** Andrews *Jes' Broguin'* 6 She went off into the back room to her feather tick bed to snuggle under the quilts. **2008** Salsi *Ray Hicks* 17 When a new baby come in our house, the other young'uns was told God had sent it down from heaven in a feather tick. I was always mad I hadn't stayed up late enough in the night to see it come down. **2008** West *Country Boy* 46 I would have felt much better at home bedded down in one of them feathered ticks.

feather tick pillow See **feather tick.**

fedded See **feed.**

(the) Federal *noun* The US Bureau of Alcohol, Firearms, and Tobacco, which is tasked with enforcing regulations on the distillation of liquor. Same as **revenue.**

1985 Dabney *More Mt Spirits* 100 Uncle Amos in the late 1800's had numerous run-ins with "the Federal," the hated revenooers.

feed *verb* variant past-tense and past-participle form *fedded.*

1957 Combs *Lg Sthn High: Word List* 37 *fedded* = past-tense and past participle of *feed.*

feed lead *verb phrase* To shoot (someone).

1917 Kephart *Word-List* 412 He feathered into him, feeding him lead. **1931** Combs *Lg Sthn High* 1308 Many terms for . . . killing abound. And so: to "feed one hot lead," to shoot.

fee grabber *noun* A law-enforcement officer paid on the basis of how many fines he or she assesses.

1967 *DARE Survey* (Maryville TN) = a policeman, sheriff, deputy sheriff, or constable. [**1968** *End of Moonshining* 40 Despite the fact that the sheriffs at that time [= early days of Prohibition] were paid on the "fee system," and thus their entire salary depended on the number of arrests they made, they did not go out looking for stills.] **1998** Montgomery *Coll* = a constable whose only pay was the fees he got for arrests, etc. (Brown), = a deputy or any law enforcement officer (Cardwell).

[DARE *fee grabber* n TN]

feel for to (also *feel to*) *verb phrase* To be inclined to.

1863 *Proffit CW Letters* (June 4) I feel to hope that you are stout and harty. **1864** *D Walker CW Letters* (Sept 17) I am in toleberl health I am giten purt nie well a gane and feeles to thank the Loard fore his murses [= mercies] tord me. **1925** Furman *Glass Window* 174 I allow you don't maybe feel to take me in with you a-Monday? **1931** Combs *Lg Sthn High* 1304 I feel to know that hit's true. **1974** Fink *Bits Mt Speech* 9 I didn't feel for to work. **1996–97** Montgomery *Coll: feel to* (known to Brown, Bush).

feel of *verb phrase* To touch (something), usually delicately. See also **of 3.**

1940 Haun *Hawk's Done* 35 It looked like a brown diamond, Bessie's hair did, it was so shiny and soft. I couldn't help going over and feeling of it. **c1950** Adams *Grandpap* 80 He took out his sword, right there in front of her, an' felt of the point. **1960** Hall *Coll* Feel of it now. **1972** *AOHP/ALC-226* [The doctor] told them what they needed, felt of my forehead and said, "Little girl, you got it [= whooping cough] too." **1977** Norman *Kinfolks* 90 I felt of his neck and found a pulse, and I seen him still bleeding. **1996–97** Montgomery *Coll* (known to Brown, Cardwell, Ellis, Ledford, Norris, Oliver).

[OED3 *feel of* (at *feel* v) now U.S.; DARE *feel of* v phr chiefly South Midland, South]

feel one's corn *verb phrase* See citation.

1890 Fruit *KY Words* 64 Of a frisky fat horse, we say, "He feels his corn."

feel one's keeping *verb phrase* See citation.

1927 Woofter *Dialect from WV* 354 = being in excellent physical condition. "If he is feeling his keeping so well, give him some more work to do."

[DARE *feel one's keeping* v phr chiefly South Midland]

feel to See **feel for to**.

feered See **afeard**.

feets See **foot A**.

feet washing *noun* Same as **foot washing**, but much less common.

1905 Miles *Spirit of Mts* 38 That Brother Absalom Darneys's gwine to hold a feet-washin' at the Blue Spring Church on a-Sunday and start a distracted meetin', and you can jist fix to stay with her while hit's continued on. **1995** McCauley *Mt Religion* 102 Footwashing is also sometimes referred to as "feetwashing," since both feet are carefully washed in the service. **1995** Montgomery *Coll* (known to Adams, Cardwell, Jones, Weaver). **1998** *Dante OHP-24* The Freewills believes in feet washing. **2014** Montgomery *Doctrine* 121 = a special service held during Communion, where the Saints wash each other's feet. As per the commandment in John 13:13–15, "Ye call me Master and Lord: and ye say well; for so I am. If I then, your Lord and Master, have washed your feet; ye also ought to wash one another's feet. For I have given you an example, that ye should do as I have done to you."

feints See **faint(s)**.

feist

A variant form *fice* [see **1886** in **B**].

B (also *feist dog, feisty dog*) *noun* A small dog, especially one of mixed or uncertain ancestry, as one kept for its loud bark, propensity to chase or catch rodents, or usefulness in driving livestock or hunting bears. See also **feisty A**, **mountain feist**, **treeing feist**.

1858 (in **1974** Harris *High Times* 147) [He] spread his fore laigs wide like ontu a bench laiged fice. **1886** Smith *Southernisms* 39 Fice ... is the name used everywhere in the South, and in some parts of the West, for a small, worthless cur. **1913** Kephart *Our Sthn High* 94 A feist is one o' them little bitty dogs that ginerally runs on three legs and pretends a whole lot. **1939** Hall *Coll* (Proctor NC) That little old feist, he got after it [= a raccoon] and run about as fer as that house out there, a hundred yards, and went to barking up a big spruce. **1949** Hall *Coll* (Del Rio TN) = a little dog that stays around the house and keeps the varmints—foxes, coons, and so on—run off. [It] barks more than anything else, just a "scare dog" you might call him, a shade bigger'n a terrier. ... He's not got no hound in him. ... He's a mixture with a cur. **c1951** Chapman *Speech Confusing* They would have a little bitty feist, and see he'd run in and take [bears], nip them by the heels and the bear can't stand that. **c1960** Wilson *Coll*: *feist* = a mongrel or nondescript small dog, especially one that is playful or nosey or always in the way. **1966** *DARE Survey* (Cherokee NC) = dog of mixed breed. **1976** *Bear Hunting* 282 Usually, you can take two little ol' feists, and if they'll fight, they'll do more with a big bear than a bunch of hound will because they're so little and so quick they can get out of the way where a big dog can't get away thataway. **1983** *Dark Corner OHP-11A* He said when he would turn in at that road, there was a little white feist dog that would appear and follow him till he got to a branch, and when he got there, the little dog would disappear. **2006** Davis *Homeplace Geography* 82 Although I was told a number of times that a feist is just a "little mixed-up dog," everyone interviewed in the study either had specific physical characteristics in mind or could pick out a feist from magazine photographs and therefore had definite ideas on what is or isn't a feist.

[shortening and alteration of obsolete *fisting* "breaking wind"; DARE *feist* n 1 chiefly South Midland]

C *verb* To draw attention to oneself, act in a saucy or provocative manner or as if one were on display.

1923 Furman *Mothering* 122 Jason he got to feisting around him ag'in, and he just grabbed him unexpected, and laid him out, and now he's choking the life out of him! **1931** Combs *Lg Sthn High* 1306 Quit feistin' aroun' me; I'll slap the taste outn ye mouth. **1940** Haun *Hawk's Done* 186 I recollect naming it to Enzor one day how Tiny was a-feisting around every man and boy she seed. **1968** *DARE Survey* (Brasstown NC) = to move around in a way to make people take notice.

[DARE *feist* v southern Appalachians]

feist dog See **feist B**.

feisty

A variant forms *ficety* [see **1886**, **1912** in **B1**], *ficy* [see **c1960** in **B2**], *fisty* [see **1895** in **B1**].

B *adjective*

1 Agitated, excited, impertinent. See also **feisty-britches**.

1886 Smith *Sthn Dialect* 350 There are still others [= terms] which have not, so far as I know, the authority of Old English: ... ficety ("bigity"). **1895** Edson and Fairchild *TN Mts* 371 = low, mean ... cross. "That cow is fisty." **1912** Perrow *Songs and Rhymes* 139 *Ficety* is an adjective applied to one who is "too big for his breeches." **1913** Kephart *Our Sthn High* 94 Feisty means when a feller's allers wigglin' about, wantin' ever'body to see him, like a kid when the preacher comes. **1943** Hannum *Mt People* 148 Out of Chaucer comes their term "feisty," meaning impertinent. **1974** Fink *Bits Mt Speech* 9 = pert, impudent.

[Web3 *feisty* adj 1 chiefly South and Midland; DARE *feisty* adj 1 chiefly South Midland]

2 Flirtatious, showing off, putting on airs.

c1960 Wilson *Coll* (or *ficy*) = showing off, prissy.

[Web3 *feisty* adj 2 South and Midland; DARE *feisty* adj 2 chiefly South Midland]

feisty-britches *noun* A child acting in an impudent or provocative way.

1955 Ritchie *Singing Family* 57 Hush, you scamp [= a young girl]. You don't have to holler so loud and act so crazy. Wait'll I catch up with you, little feisty-britches!

feisty dog See **feist B**.

fell See **fall A**.

fellar See **fellow**.

feller[1] *noun* A logger who cuts down trees.

1998 Farwell *Logging Terms*.

feller[2] See **fellow**.

feller said/says, as a See **fellow B1**.

felling ax *noun*

A variant form *falling ax* [see **1972** in **B**].

B Same as **pole ax(e)**. See also **broad ax**.

1972 *Foxfire I* 41 The tools needed [for hewing] are a broad-axe, a foot adze, a "falling" or pole axe, and a chalk box. Hewing is the skill needed in order to make support beams and wall logs. By hewing, the rounded sides of a log are made flat. **1989** *Smokies Guide* (Summer) 5 A variety of tools would be necessary for construction, including a felling axe, broad axe, adze, saws, froe, draw knife, and auger. **c1995** *Cades Cove* 6 The round logs were *scored* first along their entire length with a felling axe, then *hewn* with a broad axe.

fellow *noun*

A variant forms *fellar, feller*.

1863 *Zimmerman CW Letters* (Feb 10) he looked so bad in so short a time poor feller has gon as many will have to go before this ware ends. **1867** Harris *Sut Lovingood* 49 Lite, lite, ole feller, an' let that roan ove yourn blow a litil. **1886** Smith *Sthn Dialect* 348 Well, fellers, ef you'uns cross the mountains about dinner time, you'd better come by and git yer dinner. **1939** Hall *Coll* (Cosby Creek TN) Levi Jenkins was the crabbedest old feller ever I seed. **1941** Stuart *Men of Mts* 229 You fellars follow me tonight. *Ibid.* 275 Th' poor fellar wants a match. **1969** Roberts *Greasybeard* 114 "You sure have a lot of flies in your house, old feller." Said, "Last night they lit on me and just like to worried me to death." **1975** *AOHP/ALC-930* Elbert Owens, he was an old feller that taught school then. **1989** *Matewan OHP-2* he was a very well known feller in this country and mean as a snake. **1998** *Dante OHP-45* Him and a feller made good whiskey.

B Senses.

1 One, a person (especially in such adverb phrases as *as a/the feller says* = as they say).

1900 Harben *N GA Sketches* 103 I ort to be thankful, an' beggars mustn't be choosers, as the feller said; fer no other family in the county would take me in. **1913** Kephart *Our Sthn High* 286 These ridges is might' nigh straight up and down, and, as the feller said, perpendic'lar. **1939** Hall *Coll* (Hazel Creek NC) I was borned here, and as a feller says, I'm still here yit. **1957** Combs *Lg Sthn High: Word List* 37 *as the feller says* = frequently used for the indefinite pronoun one . . . Ex.: "As the feller says, he ain't no dam fool, that ferriner." "A feller wouldn't do a thing like that." **1961** Williams *Content Mt Speech* 10 Wal, now, if ye make yer bed yerself ye jist have to lay in it, as the feller says. **1963** Edwards *Gravel* 94 It was getting along on the shank of the evening as the feller says, sun maybe a hour high. **2007** Hardy *Remembering Avery Co* 16 That's just what I was leading up to. As a feller says, I heard you when you first drove up.

[DARE *as the feller says* adv phr chiefly New England, South Midland]

2 An individual person, regardless of age or gender. See citation.

1957 Combs *Lg Sthn High: Word List* 37 = used indiscriminately for men and women, boys and girls, as in: "You fellers (you all) come down and see us."

fellowship *verb* See also **disfellowship**.

1 Of the members of a church: to associate with one another in peace and harmony.

1856 *Zion Church Minutes* 42 The church . . . found all in fellowship but Brother Andrews Letterman who kept his seat—and his cause for so doing that he could not fellowship with the practice of members dram drinking any longer. **1946** Stuart *Plum Grove Hills* 146 Before we really begin this service for a departed Brother . . . we had better "fellowship." Now if any of you Brothers or Sisters know of any body that you have anything against . . . get up and tell us about it here.

2 To visit and commune with present or former members of a church congregation.

1968 Clarke *Stuart's Kentucky* 77 Baptists from one or more counties met to report on the year's work and make plans for the coming year; they fellowshiped together, listened to budget reports and long sermons, ate much fried chicken, and gloried in being Baptists. **1995** McCauley *Mt Religion* 69 Churches making up an association carefully schedule their local memorial meetings, homecomings, sacramental meetings (combining communion with foot-washing)—all annual events—because of the high value they put on "fellowshipping" for members traveling from their home church to worship at other churches.

felon *noun* An inflammation or infection that comes from underlying tissue, especially on the end of a finger or on a bone of the hand, a whitlow. Same as **bone felon**.

1861 *Neves CW Letters* (Jan 16) Emily has had a felon on her hand she hasent done any thing for over a week Dr Miles split hit and hit is a good deal better now. **1862** *Copenhaver CW Letters* (Nov 6) Noah St John is staying at mrs Ransbarger with a felon on his finger. **1924** Spring *Lydia Whaley* 2 Her recipe for taking care of a fellon [sic]: Take the long roots of the white sumac that sticks up. Wash roots. Take enough for poultice. Add old rusty bacon grease—the older the better. **1957** Broaddus *Vocab Estill Co KY* 29 = a hard, painful infection on the end of the finger. **1966–67** *DARE Survey* (Burnsville NC, Gatlinburg TN, Maryville TN) = the hard painful swelling, especially on a finger, that seems to come from deep under the skin. **1996–97** Montgomery *Coll* (known to nine consultants from the Smoky Mountains).

[< Middle English *feloun* "suppurative sore"; CUD *felon* n 2 "a boil, an inflammation," English dialect and southern Scots]

feltwort *noun* The common mullein, a tall biennial plant (*Verbascum thapsus*) from which a medicinal tea is made. Same as **flannel leaf, velvet-plant.**

[**1971** Krochmal et al. *Medicinal Plants Appal* 264 A tea made from the leaves is used in Appalachia for colds.] **1982** Stupka *Wildflowers* 102 Of its many local names, ones like "flannel-leaf," "velvet plant," and "feltwort" refer to its exceptionally dense wooliness.

[from the woolly texture of its leaves]

fence balk *noun* See citation.

1927 Woofter *Dialect from WV* 354 = uncultivated ground when the fence is removed: "That fence balk will have to be grubbed out."

fence law *noun* A regulation governing the erection and maintenance of fences, especially one requiring property owners to protect their crops from cattle, which were allowed free, open range. It was sometimes known as **no-fence law** (see 1956 citation). See also **no-fence law, open range, open stock law, stock law.**

1956 Hall *Coll* (Roaring Fork TN) At this time we had what we called a fence law, and people that herded cattle, owned cattle or sheep or hogs would run 'em in the woods. There was plenty of acorns and chestnuts. They were plentiful at that time, and if you raised any vegetable garden or any corn crop, you had to fence it in. They'd split rails and build rail fences to protect their crops, and the law was to build it five rails high, and if a cow brute broke over that and hit five rails high, the owner of the brute had to pay for the damage, but if it was under that, the damage was his loss. **1963** Watkins and Watkins *Yesterday* 79 The cow had to find her own living in the summer by eating whatever wild grasses happened to grow. Before the fence law, some [farms] had no fences, and the cow roamed over the countryside, hunting for a place to graze. She wore a cowbell so that the family could tell where she was. **a1975** Lunsford *It Used to Be* 60 They'd have to fence their crops or their cattle. In some places they would have the fence law, that is, the field would be fenced and the cattle would run outside. In other places they would have the Stock Law, and the cattle would be fenced and the field would be open.

fence scorpion *noun* See citation. See also **scorpion B.**

1999 Milnes *Play of Fiddle* 136 = a type of lizard or skink seen on rail fences.

fence worm See **worm 2.**

fennel weed *noun* Same as **dog fennel.**

1997 Montgomery *Coll* = local term for dill (Cardwell).

fer See **far**[2] **A1, for**[2] **A, furrow.**

fergit See **forget 1, 2.**

fergive See **forgive 1.**

fernenst, fernent, fernenth, ferninst, fernint See **fornent.**

fer piece See **far piece.**

ferrididdle (also *fairy diddle*) *noun* A diminutive red squirrel (*Tamiasciurus hudsonicus*). Same as **boomer 1.**

1893 Bolton *Waste-Basket* 143 = this is a common name in the mountains of Virginia. **1917** (in **1944** Wentworth *ADD* 212) (sWV) = a squirrel betw. gray & ground squirrel. **1936** McCutshan *VA Expressions* 372 Fairydiddle (or possibly ferrydiddle) . . . is used in and around Bath County, Virginia, to mean a certain kind of squirrel. The first instance I noted in which fairydiddle was used was when some one said, "He is as quick as a fairydiddle." . . . A man . . . said that it is not a flying squirrel, but a little ground squirrel, smaller than the common gray variety but larger than the chipmunk. It is striped, and "when he runs, his tail points straight up in the air, and they're quick all right!" **2006** *WV Encycl* 228 In West Virginia the term fairy diddle refers to a near-mythic creature, and may be used for various woodland rodents, including tree squirrels, flying squirrels, ground squirrels, and even baby groundhogs. Most observers agree, however, that whatever the fairy diddle is, it is fast, smaller than the average tree squirrel, and makes a lot of noise if disturbed. This accurately describes the American red squirrel, also called the pine squirrel or chickaree.

ferriner See **foreigner.**

ferro See **pharaoh.**

fertilize *noun* Fertilizer.

1937 Conner *Ms* 4 We never heard of Fertalizer's untill I was 13 or 14 year's old, yet we made plenty to live on, and to spair, and now it takes all our crops to pay our Fertalize bills. **1940** Still *River of Earth* 78 Stands to reason Aus is using a poison fertill'z. **1944** Wentworth *ADD* 213 (eWV) I bought 4 tons of fertilize. **1976** GSMNP-114:3 He'd have thirty-five or forty acres in corn. No sich a thing as fertilize then. **1983** *Dark Corner OHP-4A* Wait about two more weeks, go in there, and throw your soda and fertilize in that middle of the big old sweep, and just finish tearing it down, just lap it and make it pretty and smooth as that yard, lay it by. **1989**

Matewan OHP-102 The most of the fertilize they had was from the horses and cows, the manure. They kept that and put it . . . on the gardens, and that was all the fertilize we had. **1995** Montgomery *Coll* (known to Cardwell); He bought a bag of fertilize (Shields). **1999** Landry *Smoky Mt Interviews* We'd go get a wagon load of fertilize and fertilize the corn.

[by apocope]

fetch *verb*

A Principal parts.

1 variant infinitive/base form *fotch.*

1824 Knight *Letter from KY* 106–7 Some words are used, even by genteel people, from their imperfect education, in a new sense; and others, by the lower classes in society, pronounced very uncouthly . . . fotch. **1913** Kephart *Our Sthn High* 107 We gutted [the bear], and left him near the top, to fotch in the mornin'. **1937** Thornburgh *Great Smoky Mts* 155 I recall the mountain weaver who invited us to "come in the fire and set a while," calling her son to "fotch a pail of water." **1939** Hall *Coll* Fotch me that poker. **1940** Still *River of Earth* 63 Fotch the hone rock, a needle, and a waxed thread.

[DARE *fetch* v A1 especially South Midland]

2 variant past-tense forms *fotch, fotched.*

1862 *Watters-Curtis CW Letters* (April 18) [I] want you to Send that miniture that John potts fotch. **1895** Edson and Fairchild *TN Mts* 376 *fotch* for *fetched.* **1924** (in **1952** Mathes *Tall Tales* 31) "Yes, sir, we fotch hit," the older woman continued. "Virgie, give hit to the man." **1975** Chalmers *Better* 67 They fotched 'em home atter th' service, and that-a-way hit saved a sight o' time and shoe-leather. **1978** Burton *Ballad Folks* 21 They just fotched their horses, sometimes a yoke of oxes and a wagon. **1983** *Dark Corner OHP-22A* Lloyd fotch me about that much [homemade whiskey] up in one of them little Coca-Cola bottles. **1986** Ogle *Lucinda* 42 He "fotched" in all the wood he could "tote." **2013** Venable *How to Tawlk* 16 Sandy had his dawg so well-trained, it fotched everthang he shot, squirrels to quail.

[DARE *fetch* v A2 especially South Midland]

3 variant past-participle forms *fotch, fotched.*

1806 *Globe Creek Church Minutes* 21 the book was fotch forward the 8 day of february 1805 at night. **1963** Edwards *Gravel* 128 Napp aint fotch in his corn yet! **1979** Carpenter *Walton War* 149 Fiddles was fotched (fetched) in by our forebears, but banjers (banjos) and gittars (guitars) has about run 'em out now.

B Senses. [Editor's note: The senses below cannot always be differentiated.] See also **fetch to**, **fotch-on**.

1 (also *fetch in, fetch on*) To bring (forth, in, up, etc.).

[See **1806** in **A3**.] **1854** *Elijoy Church Minutes* 81 Church met . . . Took up a case of Asa Rogers & catherine Mcafee agreed to come forward next meeting & both partyes fetch on their evidence. **1861** *Shipman CW Letters* (June 28) I must fettch my leter to a close. **1862** *McFee CW Letters* (Oct 10) tha[y] hav bin fetching in prisners amost every day. **1900** Harben *N GA Sketches* 88 I was standin' in the edge o' the crowd when some neighbor fotch' 'er up in his wagon. **1943** Hannum *Mt People* 115 Others used very strong doses of hot pepper tea to "fetch on the child-thing" [i.e. expedite childbirth]. **1950** Stuart *Hie Hunters* 181 These hides will fetch ye some money. **1992** Offutt *KY Straight* 139 That woman fetched me into this world.

2 (also *fetch up*) To go or come after (someone or something) and bring back.

1863 *D B Walker CW Letters* (Nov 29) I Had reather you wold git Siles Morgan to bring you out and try to mak areangments with him to fetch you. **1864** *Stepp CW Letters* (June 12) [I] wood like to fetch them and see how they fit. **1937** Hall *Coll* (Cades Cove TN) [The dog] has been teached to fetch the cows. **1939** Hall *Coll* (Bradley Fork NC) I just left and went to Jackson County when the park came in. They asked me to come back. They fetched me back. *Ibid.* (Wears Cove TN) Fetch me the hammer. **1962** Dykeman *Tall Woman* 218 "Makes no differ to me," he mumbled, but he went to fetch another bucket of water. **1973** Wellman *Kingdom of Madison* 160 Some blockaders set up their stills near the Tennessee line and climbed trails on the far side to fetch back their raw materials, often in darkness. **1983** *Dark Corner OHP-24A* She fotch that book. She went home and got it. **1997** Montgomery *Coll* Fetch up a pail of water (Brown). **2006** Shelby *Appal Studies* 30 The job I liked best was of an evening to go up in the woods to fetch the cow.

3 To convey (someone), especially home.

1862 *Fitch CW Letters* (May 13) he was be[d]rided yesterdy . . . the cornel was not wilen for any of ous to fetch him home. **1862** *Revis CW Letters* (Nov 3) [They] have fetcht his horse home. **1862** *Robinson CW Letters* (March 25) I hant got mone[y] a nuff to fetch me home. **1939** Hall *Coll* (Proctor NC) We come in home, fetched them in home, and went back. **1956** Hall *Coll* (Hartford TN) I pitched and staved a heap of times. [My boss] fetched me home. **1969** *GSMNP-37* They fetched [the men] down across Deep Creek.

4 To move (something) forcibly.

1862 *Robinson CW Letters* (June 22) Our troups Cut our tents all to peaces & break all the Cook vessels & spiket long tom that tha[y] took at the Manases battel & fetch it dow[n] abluf whare tha[y] cant git it out.

5 (also *fetch up*) To give birth to (offspring); to rear (a child).

1927 Furman *Lonesome Road* 104 On my creek, Rakeshin, where I was fotched up, nobody never thought of being sober for twelve days [of the Christmas season]. **1937** Hyatt *Kiverlid* 31 The set o' them horns p'ints that she'll be a pow'ful fine milker when she fetches a calf. **1961** Seeman *Arms of Mt* 27 Over on Colt's Foot Branch, a neighbor's old mammy-cat has fetched a gang of kittens.

fetch fire See **come to borrow fire**.

fetch in, fetch on See **fetch B1**.

fetch-taked *adjective* Used as a mild oath. See also **plague take**.

1930 Greer-Petrie *Angeline Outsmarts* 6 He's so fetch-taked triflin', he'd be willin' to sakerfice a laig to get his ease. **1953** Davison *Word-List Appal* 10 = mild expletive used when speaking to dogs: "Begone, you *fetch-taked* dogs!"

fetch to *verb phrase* To revive.

1859 Taliaferro *Fisher's River* 90 The poor 'oman fainted away, and we liked to a nuver a fotched her to.

fetch up *verb phrase*

1 See **fetch B2, B5**.

2 To arrive, end up.

1883 Zeigler and Grosscup *Heart of Alleghanies* 297 "Only three mile further," said my companion, when he noticed how I was lagging in my pace, "and we'll fetch up at Ramear's cabin." **1996–97** Montgomery Coll (known to Brown, Bush, Ellis, Jones, Oliver).

3 To rear (a child).

1913 Kephart *Our Sthn High* 94 Good la! Whar was you fotch up? **1925** Furman *Glass Window* 136–37 Giles is hurted a sight wusser than Ronny, having fetched him up from a babe like he has. **1929** (in **1952** Mathes *Tall Tales* 133) The squire beamed upon her. "I'm proud ye've been fotched up proper, Miss Pennylope." **1967** DARE *Survey* (Maryville TN).

[DARE *fetch* v B12 "to rear" Scots, nEngl dialect]

4 See citation.

2007 McMillon *Notes* = to grow up.

fetterbush *noun*

1 Same as **dog hobble**.

1939 Jennison *Flora Great Smokies* 279–80 The Fetter-bush (*Leucothoe catesbaei*) of uncertain fragrance, but with showy, pointed, green leaves is quite deserving of the local name of "dog-hobble." **1964** Stupka *Trees Shrubs Vines* 121 The fetterbush is endemic in the Southern Appalachian Mountains.

2 A wild shrub (*Pieris floribunda*) that grows at higher elevations of the mountains.

1901 Lounsberry *Sthn Wild Flowers* 393 It is only through the mountainous parts of its restricted range that this most exquisite of the fetter bushes is found, and there it usually secludes well itself near the summits of the highest peaks. . . . Early in the spring it is most lovely when fairly loaded with innumerable pure, white flowers. Its charm at all times moreover is heightened by being an evergreen. **1963** Lord *Blue Ridge* 22D-23D The thick, matted branches of the fetterbush, or mountain pieris, have a way of fettering anyone who attempts to push through them. . . . The leaves and blossoms of dog-hobble resemble those of fetterbush, but each plant groups its own way. Fetterbush is an upright shrub; dog-hobble is low and fern-like.

fever (often *the fever* or in combination specifying its type) *noun* Any disease that causes an abnormally high body temperature, especially typhoid. See also **bilious fever**, **brain fever**, **childbed fever**, **lung fever**, **mountain fever**, **pneumonia fever**, **typhoid fever**.

1833 *McLean Diary* 21 [I] Viseted Mr. Caplinare and John Willmouth the Latter is Very poorley with the Nerves feever. **1862** Gilley *CW Letters* (Aug 3) he has bin sick for three days tho he can go about a little I think he is got the fever tho I think or inhops that he wont get bad off. **1921** Weeks *Speech of KY Mtneer* 11 Fevers are common, but we are never satisfied with one—at least we always have a fever in the plural. Not yet content with our possessions, we aggravate conditions by taking on another malady. "Jim has pneumony fevers" is no oncommon piece of news among us. **1937** Hall Coll (Cosby TN) Sometimes the type of fever is specified as e.g. "lung fever" (pneumonia, though one may also hear the expression "pneumonie"), brain fever, and bilious fever. "A sight of people died of the fever [= typhoid] on this branch twenty-five or thirty year ago. [It] began when loggin' started and the stumps soured." **1953** Davison *Word-List Appal* 10 = pneumonia. **1957** Combs *Lg Sthn High: Word List* 38 = always used after the names denoting the kinds of fever, as in: pneumonia fever, typhoid fever, etc. **1966** Frome *Strangers* 251 As nurse Helen Phyllis Higinbotham, of the Pi Beta Phi Settlement School at Gatlinburg during the early twenties, wrote, "I have had to get used to getting most of a woman's symptoms from her husband, and not having heart failure when a messenger comes with the news that so-and-so is 'bad off'—'about to die'—or 'got the fever.'" **1975** Chalmers *Better* 44 Hit'll shore kill ye if'n ye take hit, but hit's a sight better than airy dost of the fever. **1975** GSMNP-62 They give that butterfly root to break up the fever. **2001** Joslin *Appal Bounty* 136 The story of witherod tells of the days when the forest served as the people's pharmacy. Known as shonny haw, the plant's bark, when brewed into a tea, provided the settlers with a cure for fevers and the colic.

fever doctor *noun* A folk healer who purportedly has the skill to relieve fevers. See also **blood doctor**, **faith doctor**.

1983 DeLozier *Work and Play* 69 There was a "fever doctor" who was renowned in the area. He seldom made more than one or two visits to his patients, however, and if they died, he could not be found.

fevers See **fever**.

fever up *verb phrase* To develop a fever.

1937 Hyatt *Kiverlid* 38 I allus say when abody gits fevered up, hit takes a lot of tonnickin' on good yarb tea and sich, and aplenty of it, to bring 'em out. **2001** Lowry *Expressions* 8 She fevered up at 4 o'clock this morning.

feverweed *noun* A perennial wild plant (*Eryngium aquaticum*) from whose roots a tea is made to reduce fever.

1937 Hall Coll (Big Creek NC) Fever weed breaks the fever on a body. **1949** Arnow *Hunter's Horn* 373 She wanted to give all the others a round of molasses and wormseed and sulpher now, and then, just before they went to bed, some good strong tea made with life everlasting, sweet fennel, ratbane, and feverweed, for every last one of them was wormy as could be and full of cold.

fever worm *noun* A large, woolly-haired caterpillar, the larva of the Isabella moth (*Isia isabella*). Same as **wooly worm**.

1901 Price *KY Folk-Lore* 35 If you see a hairy caterpillar (called a "fever-worm" in some sections of the country), spit on it, and it will save you a spell of fever. **1929** Rainey *Animal Plant Lore* 10 I stopped to pick up the larva of the Isabella moth, known in my youthful days just as "Caterpillar." But the boy beside me said, "You should spit three times when you see a fever worm." I asked if that was a fever worm and he replied, "Sure. Where were you raised? Spit three times or you will have a fever."

[DARE *fever worm* n chiefly KY]

few

A *adjective*

1 In phrase *few ways* = a short distance.

1933 Carpenter *Sthn Mt Dialect* 23–24 In Virginia, Kentucky and southern West Virginia *few ways* for a SHORT DISTANCE is often heard, but I don't recall ever having heard it in central or northern West Virginia or the adjoining section of Virginia.

2 Some (modifying a mass noun).

1934 Carpenter *Archaic English in WV* 77 Almost every one who is familiar with the common speech in West Virginia has at some time heard the phrase "a few cheese" [= a small amount of cheese].

[DARE *few, a* adj phr South, South Midland]

B *noun* A degree or portion. See also **few bit.**

1936 Farrier *Few Of* 278–79 [In Giles Co VA] a mountaineer, for emphasis, would say: "The lake is a few of the pretty this morning," or "It's a few of the hot today, hain't it?"

few bit *adverb phrase* Somewhat, to some degree. See also **few B.**

1936 Farrier *Few Of* 278–79 [In Giles Co VA] one heard this variation: "That feller's a few bit the lazy," or "I'm a few bit tired tonight."

few ways See **few A1.**

fexatially (also *fexatiously*) *adverb* Completely, utterly, perversely.

1931 Combs *Lg Sthn High* 1306 Well, I'm fexatially (or fexatiously) whipped out. (That is, completely surprised, or astonished.)

fice See **feist B.**

ficety, ficy See **feisty.**

fiddle-box *noun* A fiddle.

1941 Still *Troublesome Creek* 156 Where you see 'Lihu, you see his fiddle-box, and him itching to play.

fiddle dust *noun* The powdery residue from resin that has been applied to the strings of a fiddle. See 1997 Ellis citation. See also **fine as fiddle dust, fizzle dust.**

c1945 Haun *Hawk's Done* 321 Some he had ground hisself, and Ma said it was fine as fiddle dust. **1997** Montgomery *Coll* (known to Adams, Brown, Bush, Cardwell, Jones), = very fine, powdery dust which adheres easily to the surface. Some old-timers liked to let this build up on the end of the fingerboard and on the top of the fiddle between the f-holes (for visual effect), although eventually it would react with the varnish and ruin the finish. It was called *rosin dust* or *fiddle dust*, particularly in the alliterative phrase *fine as . . .* (Ellis).

fiddle gourd *noun* A gourd that was suitable to be hollowed, dried, and fashioned into the frame of a musical instrument.

1943 Justus *Bluebird* 89 Uncle Jed Woody had promised Matt to help him make a fiddle if he would grow a fiddle gourd. **1997** Montgomery *Coll* (known to Brown, Bush).

fiddlehead *noun* The frond of any of several ferns when eaten in fresh greens.

1991 Still *Wolfpen Notebooks* 77 What I look forward to in the spring hain't garden sass. Hit's wild greens. They grow where God planted them. What you want to look for is . . . fiddle-heads. **2006** *Encycl Appalachia* 935 Other spring greens found in the region include chickweed, corn salad, dock, fiddleheads, purslane, ramps, shepherd's purse or St. James's wort, winter cress or creases, and mouse-ear. **2009** Sohn *Appal Home Cooking* 296 When ferns sprout in the spring, they send up coiled shoots or fiddleheads. . . . Mountain foragers know that any tender fiddlehead is good in a pot of greens or an herb salad.

fiddle worms *verb phrase* To send vibrations into the earth by drawing a saw, pole, or other metal implement across a stump or post with a metal arm; such vibrations cause earthworms to come to the surface, where they can be gathered for fishing bait.

1997 Landry *Smoky Mt Interviews* [In] fiddling worms, they ought to come out of where they're at.

fidget(s) *noun* Nervousness, uncontrolled uneasiness.

1953 Davison *Word-List Appal* 10 I got the fidgets all over. I wish Lem would come home before the snow gets deep. **1998** Montgomery *Coll* (known to ten consultants from the Smoky Mountains), = a temporary condition, such as in "I can't keep my legs still, I have the fidgets," a child who wouldn't keep still had the fidgets (Norris).

[DARE *fidget* n 1 chiefly South, Midland]

fidity See **asafetida.**

field *noun* A meadow in the higher reaches of the mountains. See citation.

1967 Campbell *Memories of Smoky* 128 Two of these "meadows in the sky" were not known as Balds but as "fields." These are Spence Field, just west of Thunderhead, and Russell Field, a few miles to the west. There is good evidence that both of these "fields" were cleared.

field a bond *verb phrase* See citation.

1974 Maurer and Pearl *KY Moonshine* 118 = to make, fill, or get bond when arrested. Origin of this idiom is obscure. "Bill could help us field a bond." "If I can't field a bond, I'll rot in this damned place."

field apricot *noun* Apparently the same as **maypop.**

1978 Parris *Mt Cooking* 23 Some of the Cherokee still make a drink out of the juice of 'possum grapes and another out of the juice of maypops or field apricots.

fieldball *noun* See citation. Same as **town ball.**

1993 Page and Smith *Foxfire Toys and Games* 6 Apparently every community played its own version of ball, sometimes using different names. Fieldball is a variant of Catball, sometimes under the same name—the most common being Townball. There are common elements: pitcher, catcher, batters, bases, and, of course, ball and bat. (We did find one variant, Bullpen, described by Ernest Rogers, that does not use a bat.) Most were played with homemade balls and homemade bats. Games usually ended when it got dark. Baseball and Softball, with their standardized rules, replaced Townball, Catball, and Fieldball, with their adjustable rules and local adaptations. Store-bought, manufactured balls and bats replaced homemade.

field pea *noun* See citation.

1997 Montgomery *Coll* = a black-eyed pea planted in rows of corn after the corn is near grown (Cardwell).

[DARE *field pea* n South, South Midland]

field soaker *noun* A heavy thunderstorm.

1980 Bledsoe *Just Folks* 204 She'd thought the men might come back after dinner, but a storm came instead. It brought sharp lightning and heavy black clouds that sent water gushing down gullies in the road, a "real field soaker," Luemer called it.

fiffle *adjective* See citation.

c1982 Young *Colloquial Appal* 8 = trite, worthless.

Fifth Sunday meeting *noun* A special church service held when a fifth Sunday occurs in a month.

1937 Hyatt *Kiverlid* 49 Lookit the time at Shady Grove at the Fifth Sunday Meetin', and hit wus the Footwashin' too, how she whiffeled right through the man's-door, brazen as gull, and took her seat on the man's side of the Meetin' House. [**1982** *Foxfire VII* 39 They agreed to [let us] have foot washings and be in the association. . . . We do it whenever there's a fifth Sunday in the month.] **2012** Still *Hills Remember* 169 I was stone-blind jealous of Harl Burke taking her to Fifth Sunday meetings.

figger See **figure B**.

fight verb

1 variant past-tense forms *faut, fit, fitted*.

1861 *Poteet CW Letters* (Aug 7) they fit one hole day they only kiled about 5 hundred of our men. **1863** *A B Walker CW Letters* (Jan 7) the Sothern [soldiers] fit like wild cats they stud up man to man all the time. **1867** Harris *Sut Lovingood* 152–53 He fit mitily fur the chance he had, but I soon seed he had a cross ove bar in 'im. **1901** Harben *Westerfelt* 250 Them that shouldered muskets an' fit an' lived on hard-tack don't want no more uv it. **1939** Hall *Notebooks* 13:6 (White Oak NC) *faut* = very common among people of more than middle age. **c1945** Haun *Hawk's Done* 218 He could tell them that was the way he got his wife—he fit for her. **1953** Atwood *Verbs East US* 14 Several instances [of *fit*] may be noted along the Upper Ohio and throughout n. W.Va. In the area south of the Kanawha, including s.w. Va. and w. N.C., this form is nearly universal in Type I [i.e. older speakers with little formal education] and has considerable currency in Type II [i.e. younger speakers with more formal education] as well; in most communities in w. N.C. *fit* is used by both older and younger informants. **1957** Broaddus *Vocab Estill Co KY* 29 *fitted* = past tense of fight. **1971** GSMNP-66:2 They drunk the whiskey and then they fit all night. **1973** Jones *Cades Cove TN* 71 *faut*. **1978** Reese *Speech NE Tenn* 174 *fit* = attested by 3/12 (25%) speakers. **1989** Landry *Smoky Mt Interviews* 194 Mister Oliver, he fit his case. That's the only one I know of a-fighting it. **2009** Burton *Beech Mt Man* 103 "Did you ever fight any of her people?" "No," [he] said, "I never fit a Hicks."

2 variant past-participle forms *fit, foughten*.

1862 *Lister CW Letters* (Dec 26) Jenerl Walker Ses he thinks the last fite is fit. **1867** Harris *Sut Lovingood* 35 I wudnt a fit es nasty a fite es that wer, in my fines' shut, wu'd yu, Bill? **1883** Zeigler and Grosscup *Heart of Alleghanies* 51 Why, I've fit bars from the Dark Ridge kentry to the headwaters of the French Broad. **1908** Smith *Reminiscences* 406 Such uncomplimentary nicknames are not uncommon in that region, especially among the numerous Walker family, whose great ancestor "had fit with Gin'ra Jackson at New Orleans." **1929** (in **1952** Mathes *Tall Tales* 116) You an' the little lady has fit it out with Death an' ye've whupped him to a fare-ye-well! **1939** Hall *Coll* (Sugarlands TN) He hadn't fit none of the time. **1972** *AOHP/ALC-342* They've fit one another ever since independence was signed. **1975** Gainer *Speech Mtneer* 10 It was a hard-foughten scrap.

fight a circle saw (also *fight a circle sawmill, fight a circular saw*) *verb phrase* To fight against great odds, be eager to fight and afraid of nothing.

1901 Harben *Westerfelt* 57 I hain't got much use for Toot, but he'll fight a circular saw bare-handed. **1931** Combs *Lg Sthn High* 1306 That MacDuff boy'd fight a circle saw! (He is not afraid.) **1939** Hall *Coll* (Gumstand TN) He said he made it in his mind to never surrender. He could a fit a circle saw mill. (Said apparently of General Morgan who fought at nearby Greeneville in the Civil War.) **1962** Williams *Metaphor Mt Speech I* 12 If she is "nervey," the kind "that'd fight a circle saw," the husband takes the offensive "the minute he enters the door," and starts "cuttin' the awfullest shine that ever was" with his "rippin' and stavin', his swearin' and swarpin' around." **1971** Hall *Coll* (Gatlinburg TN) That man would fight a circle saw and hit a-turnin'. **1984** Yeatts *Old Mayberry* 39 Mr. Duncan had a passel of boys who were not known for their pacifism. They'd "fight a circle saw," as the saying goes, and if no saw was available, they'd just fight each other. **1989** *Matewan OHP-94* Anybody that knew Bill Blizzard, Bill Blizzard would fight a circular saw.

fight fist and skull *verb phrase* To fight bare-handed. See also **fist and skull**.

c1926 Bird *Cullowhee Wordlist* = bare-handed. "They fought fist-and-skull." **1939** Hall *Coll* (Sugarlands TN) I got to looking at it . . . scared to look at a bear thinking a man of my age or size would jump on a bear to fight fist and skull without something to fight with.

fightingest *adjective* Fighting the most or most inclined to fight; fighting the best or most proficient at fighting. See also **-est 1** and Grammar and Syntax §3.4.1.

1922 Cobb *KY Mt Rhymes* 61 Grandsir' was the fightingest of all the Randall lot. **1960** Burnett *My Valley* 134 Daddy said he was the gamest and fightingest little rascal he ever hunted. **c1982** Young *Colloquial Appal* 8 = best fighter.

[DARE *fightingest* adj especially South Midland]

fight one's face *verb phrase* To eat voraciously.

1950 Stuart *Hie Hunters* 138 "I feel like I could fight my face, too," Peg said . . . "Give a body a hankerin' fer grub to walk up here."

fighty *adjective* Pugnacious.

1944 Wentworth *ADD* 215 (WV) = pugnacious. **1989** *Matewan OHP-94* He was sort of a fighty guy.

fightyfied *adjective* Inclined to fight. See also **-ified.**

1952 Wilson *Folk Speech NC* 540 = inclined to fight, easily angered. **1975** *GSMNP-62:3* We'd trim him and turn him loose, and he wouldn't be so fightyfied.

figlin See **metheglin.**

figure

A *noun* See **cut a big figure.**

B (also *figger*) *verb* To use or do arithmetic, calculate. See also **figures.**

1953 Hall *Coll* (Bryson City NC) He went a term or two to school . . . till he learned to read and write and figger some. **1971** *AOHP/ALC-137* He never went to school, but boy, he could figure like anything. He could beat you a-figuring with his brain. **1977** *Foxfire IV* 129 I never learnt to figger none. I didn't know a thing about arithmetic. But I've learnt someway. You can't figger [= cheat] me out of nothing. I can figger with any of'em. **1985** Irwin *Alex Stewart* 51 By that time we had us a little slate apiece that we'd figure and write on.

figured wood *noun* See citations.

1905 Ayres and Ashe *Appal Forests* 38 The hard, fine-grained wood [of the sugar maple] is sawed for flooring; the figured wood for furniture stock. **1991** Thomas *Sthn Appal* 151 I ewst to work in th' curly timber bizness. Some called it "figured wood." It's what ye call curly maple. An' it brought a high price.

figures *noun* Arithmetic. See also **figure B.**

1989 Still *Rusties and Riddles* [58] = arithmetic. Spelling and figures were the popular subjects.

fill up *verb phrase* Of the moon: to become full. Same as **full A.**

1991 Thomas *Sthn Appal* 247 I liked to kill my hogs when th' moon's a fillin' up . . . increasin'. An' I always thought my meat tasted fuller. Wouldn't shrink up s' bad.

filter

A *noun* See citation.

1949 Maurer *Argot of Moonshiner* 9 = a strainer, usually of felt, though sometimes of other material, used to remove foreign matter or cloudiness from liquor.

B *verb* See citation.

1949 Maurer *Argot of Moonshiner* 9 = to filter the distillate: "You filter what's in the catch-can . . ."; "Get that filter off that bush. This stuff's cloudy."

filter keg See **slobber keg.**

filth *noun* Weeds, underbrush. See also **filth land, foul.**

1924 Raine *Saddlebags* 103 As *wealth* is the collective noun made from weal, and *stealth* the thing one steals, and *spilth* what one spills, so *filth* in the mountains means the leaves and driftwood that fill up. **1957** Combs *Lg Sthn High: Word List* 38 = driftwood, weeds etc. that fill up holes and fence corners after a "tide," or high water in the mountain streams. **1975** Gainer *Speech Mtneer* 9 = brush and weeds growing in pasture land. "I cut filth all day yesterday." **1994** Montgomery *Coll* (known to Shields). **2007** Milnes *Signs Cures Witches* 34 People cut "filth" (brush) when the moon and signs are right so that it will not spring back to life. **2009** Wiles and Wiles *Location* 112 "Filth" was any plant growth that would, if left uncut, turn the unplanted ground and fencerows into a patch of wild briers and brush that would soon take over a farm.

[cf EDD *filth* sb[2] 4 "weeds"; DARE *filth* n southern Appalachians, especially WV]

filth land *noun* See citation. See also **filth.**

1930 Pendleton *Wood-Hicks Speak* 87 = land not tilled and grown over with weeds and underbrush. Farmers frequently speak of "cutting filth" when they mean scything the grass and weeds on the rough hillsides.

filthy *adjective* Having weeds, underbrush.

1963 Hooper *Unwanted Boy* 229 I must chop out that gyarden—hit's getting mighty "filthy." **1973** *AOHP/ASU-111* He had three acres in tobacco, and it got so filthy that they wouldn't take it no longer. **1996** Montgomery *Coll* (known to Jones).

finacious *adjective* Final, complete; hence adverbs *afinaciously, finaciously* = finally, completely. See also **finatially.**

1925 Furman *Glass Window* 169 I know jest the kind you'd want, and I warn you right now hit'll be your finacious ruination! **1963** Williams *Metaphor* 53 Fust thang he knows he'll wake up some o' these hyar mornin's and find hisself finaciously rurnt. **1978** Hiser *Quare Do's* 136 This here Joe took it into his head he'd play one on My Old Man at'd stop his hunting and trapping and fishing afinaciously and forever more.

[DARE *finatiou* adj chiefly eastern KY]

finaciously See **finacious.**

finally *adverb*

1 variant forms *finely*, *finly*.

1925 (in **1935** Edwards *NC Novels* 81) *fin'ly*. **1942** Hall *Phonetics Smoky Mts* 60 Omission of the [medial] vowel is frequent . . . Examples: . . . *finally*. **1954** Arnow *Dollmaker* 242 I fin'ly git home an the place is in a mess. **1963** Edwards *Gravel* 8 Finely, (that's the way we pronounce it in Speedwell), I crave to pass along a tale. **1984** Burns *Cold Sassy* 32 "Is she still hiccuppin'?" I whispered back. "No, it fine'ly stopped, thank the Lord." **2008** McKinley *Bear Mt* 48 When the Korean War began in 1950, Granny "shore hated to see'm have to fight a'gin so soon after World War II was fine'ly over."

2 As variant *a-finally*. See citations.

1957 Combs *Lg Sthn High: Word List* 38 = entirely, completely. Used intensively, as in: "I'll beat you a-finally to death!" **1981** Williams *Storytelling* She walked fast as she could, [an] hour or two, and a-finally she seed them way on down the road there ahead of her.

finatially *adverb* See citation. See also **finacious.**

1931 Combs *Lg Sthn High* 1308 I'm wore finatially to death!

find *verb*

A Forms.

1 variant past-tense form *fount*.

1962 Williams *Verbs Mt Speech* 17 The -d and -ed endings of past forms of verbs are frequently pronounced -t . . . A few such examples are found, fount. **1975–76** Wolfram/Christian *WV Coll* 1 We fount some money. **1995** South *What It Is* 11 He said he fount just the one [to help my wife clean house]. **2005** Williams *Gratitude* 148 When we fount it [= the nest], usually they'd be a big pile a eggs in it.

2 variant past-participle form *fount*.

1972 *AOHP/ALC-241* They never got no proof fount on nobody who done that.

B Especially of livestock: to give birth to (offspring).

1917 Kephart *Word-List* 412. **1927** Woofter *Dialect from WV* 354 = to give birth to. "The cow found a calf last night." **1939** Bond *Appal Dialect* 107 = to bear, as in "the sow's found pigs." **1956** McAtee *Some Dial NC* 15 Old Red's found a calf. **1966** Dakin *Vocab Ohio River Valley* 234 Another old expression *find a calf* (sometimes *find her calf* and rarely *find calf*) is fairly common in the Bluegrass and surrounding Knobs [of KY]—where it stands beside *bring a calf*. **1996** Johnson *Lexical Change* 138 *find a calf* = statistically more common in the mountains of South Carolina and Georgia than in the Piedmont and Coastal Plain c1990. **1996–97** Montgomery *Coll* (known to Brown, Bush, Ellis, Hooper, Ledford, Norris, Oliver). **2007** McMillon *Notes* She found her calf.

[DARE *find* v B2 chiefly South, South Midland]

fine[1] *adjective*

1 Of the voice: high-pitched.

1939 Hall *Coll* = high-pitched (of the voice). **1984** Wilder *You All Spoken* 170 He who sings coarse sings bass. . . . A tenor sings fine and a soprano sings shallow. **2003** Howell *Folklife Big South Fork* 148 Most fiddle tunes consist of two strains of equal length: a high-pitched part sometimes referred to as the "Fine" and a low part known as the "Coarse." Each part is usually repeated once, but this practice varies from one performer to another. Most tunes begin with the "Fine" and end on the "Coarse" and are played over and over for as long as the dance demands or until the musicians give out.

2 Affected, pretentious.

1939 Hall *Coll* = used in ironic and contemptuous sense of mountain people who "put on airs" or act like city folk: "People who talks proper around here are called fine people"; "To try to act fine."

fine[2] *verb* variant past-tense form *found*.

1962 Wilson *Folkways Mammoth Cave* 19 The jury found him ten dollars and costs.

(as) fine as fiddle dust (also *fine as frog hair* and other variants) *adjective phrase* Rare, delicate, thin, superlative.

1927 Woofter *Dialect from WV* 354 *finer than frog's hair* = too fine to be seen. "Those scratches are finer 'n frog hair." **c1945** Haun *Hawk's Done* 321 Some he had ground hisself, and Ma said it was fine as fiddle dust. **1960** Westover *Highland Lg* 19 *fine as frog's hair* = fine. **c1960** Wilson *Coll: fine as gnat's whiskers*. **1968** *Expressions* 24 *fine as frog hair*. **1996–97** Montgomery *Coll: fine as fiddle dust* (known to Ellis); *fine as frog hair* (known to Adams, Brown, Cardwell, Jones, Ledford, Norris, Oliver). **2005** Williams *Gratitude* 495 When something's as fine as it can be, it's said to be *as fine as frawg hair (split down the middle)*. **2007** McMillon *Notes: fine as frog's hair split four ways*. **2017** Kinsler *Take Girl* 71 *finer 'n frog hair* = things are going well.

[DARE (at *froghair* n 2b) chiefly South, South Midland]

finely See **finally 1.**

the finest kind *adverb phrase* Very much, in the greatest way. See also **(the) best kind.**

1940 Still *River of Earth* 28 "I'd like the finest kind to give you something for helping out," Clabe said.

finger fishing *noun* Same as **noodling.**

2003 Carter *Mt Home* 141 Daddy and the boys went down to the creek and done what Daddy called fanger fishin'.

finly See **finally 1.**

fire

A *noun, verb* variant forms *far*, *farr*, *foir*, *for*.

1917 Kephart *Word-List* 409 That's the most coggled up far I ever seed. **1923** Greer-Petrie *Angeline Steppin' Out* 29 They didn't have no forplace. **1931** Combs *Lg Sthn High* 1316 "Farr" (fire). **1933** Thomas *Jilson Setters* 28 To this day his folks cook at the open fire-place and cut pumpkin in rings and dry it on a stick suspended from the foir-board (the mantel). **1940** Still *River of Earth* 41 I bet

Aus won't be going before the grand jury saying I fired his barn. **1942** Hall *Phonetics Smoky Mts* 44 [fɑr]. **1976** GSMNP-113:3 I'd chop wood and sich as that. We cut wood, you know, with the axe, build us a far. **1991** Haynes *Haywood Home* 77 Jut would say far (fire).

[DARE *fire* n, v especially Midland]

B *verb*

1 To set (woods) ablaze, as to clear land or rid it of animals; to clear an area by fire.

1940 Oakley *Roamin'/Restin'* 64 We planed to have a apple orchid and other fruit trees and I started a grape vine in a small way and a number of trees. Someone fired the woods and the high winds rose and of all the forest fire we had one. **1954** GSMNP-19:8 Now this blue haze you see on the mountains, lot of people thought that it was the Indians a-firing the woods. *Ibid.* (Townsend TN) There was one herd of cattle at Gregory Bald and another herd at Thunderhead. The herders burnt off the brush on top of the mountain. If they hadn't fired, they couldn't have herded Smoky Mountain.

2 (also *fire up, fire up on*) To apply artificial heat to (tobacco).

1967 Key *Tobacco Vocab*: (NC) When they get the barn full, then they fire up on it; (TN) Some fire it up when it isn't curing right; (KY) Fire it.

fire and tow *noun phrase* in phrases *all fire and tow, all fire in tow* = excitable, quick-tempered.

1956 McAtee *Some Dial NC* 15 *fire and tow* = excitable, hot-tempered. **c1960** Wilson *Coll*: *fire in tow* = high-tempered, quick to explode. Said of [a] cow, person, or any other creature. Also *fire and tow*. **1975** Dial *Yesterday's Lg* 92 = said of a high-tempered person: "Man! She's *all fire and tow*!" **1984** Wilder *You All Spoken* 14 = ready to explode. **2007** McMillon *Notes* = fiery: "That woman is all fire and tow."

fireation *interjection* Used as a mild oath.

1991 Thomas *Sthn Appal* 68 Shucks, fire-ation an' Tom Walker! He raised lots of turkeys, an' drove 'um to market.

fire ball *noun* See citation.

1973 *Holidays* 332 Of th'night th'old people'ud make kerosene balls. Make a big ball of old cloth and yarn an' soak'em in kerosene an' light'em an' get out in the meadows an' play. "Fire ball," they called it.

fire-blossomed *adjective* See second citation. See also **country legs, pieded 2**.

1994 Montgomery *Coll* (known to Brown, Bush). **1994** Montgomery *File* = having red and white spots on one's legs from having sat close to a fire (82-year-old man, Gatlinburg TN).

fire blower *noun* Same as **blow doctor**.

1967 Wilson *Folkways Mammoth Cave* 43 A *fire-blower* merely blows his breath on a burned place to allay suffering.

fireboard (also *fire shelf*) *noun* The horizontal shelf or ledge over a fireplace; the framework around a fireplace.

1886 Smith *Sthn Dialect* 350 There are still others [= terms] which have not, so far as I know, the authority of Old English: . . . fire-board (mantelpiece). **1915** Dingus *Word-List VA* 183 *fire-board* = framework around a fire-place, usually a shelf. **1933** Thomas *Jilson Setters* 28 To this day his folks cook at the open fireplace and cut pumpkin in rings and dry it on a stick suspended from the foir-board (the mantel). **1934–47** *LAMSAS Appal*: *fireboard* = attested by 29/148 speakers (19.5%) from WV, 15/20 (75%) from VA, 35/37 (94.6%) from NC, 11/14 (78.5%) from SC, and 8/12 (66.7%) from GA. **1939** Hall *Coll* (Maggie Valley NC) She got a big pistol and laid it up on the fireboard, and she said, "You see this gun. If anything takes place here tonight," she says, "I'll use this gun on ye." **1949** Kurath *Word Geog East US* 36 We find *jacket* for a man's vest and *fireboard* for a mantel shelf not only in the Southern Appalachians . . . but also in the corridor between the Cape Fear and the Peedee. **1960** Mason *Memoir* 18 Mawwwwwww, fetch me that old claw-hammer off the fire shelf, this dad-blasted ole steers busted up my plow and hits the only one I had. **1966** Dakin *Vocab Ohio River Valley* 36–38 Throughout the Kentucky Mountains, the eastern and southern Knobs, and the eastern Pennyroyal corridor some older informants know only the distinctive South Midland *fire board*. Younger and more educated informants here know and use *mantel*, but it is almost invariably characterized as "new," "used only by the younger generation," etc. **1966–68** *DARE Survey* (Brasstown NC, Spruce Pine NC, Gatlinburg TN) *fireboard* = the shelf over the fireplace. **1976** Ledford *Folk Vocabulary* 279 *Living room, gutters, mantel* . . . have completely replaced *big house, eaves trough, fireboard* . . . throughout the area. **1986** Pederson et al. *LAGS*: *fireboard* = attested by 18/60 interviewees (30%) from E TN and 10/35 (28.6%) from N GA; 28/69 of all LAGS interviewees (40.5%) attesting term were from Appalachia. **1989** Oliver *Hazel Creek* 14 A log hewed flat formed the mantel, which was called the fireboard. **1995** Montgomery *Coll*: *fire shelf* (known to Cardwell, Shields). **2004** Purkey *Home Revisited* 7 The mantel, or fireboard, was like a museum, a catchall for odds and ends. Mama kept the castor oil and turpentine bottles there, out of the reach of younger children.

[CUD *fireboard* 2 (at *fire* n) "mantelpiece"; DARE *fireboard* n 1 chiefly South Midland]

fire boss *noun* See citations.

1971 *AOHP/ALC-66* A fire boss . . . goes in of a morning, about five o'clock, make[s] a run in all places, see[s] if there's any gas in there. They mark up ever man's place. **1973** Preston *Bituminous Term* 36 = a worker who carries a safety lamp throughout the mine, particularly to the working faces, before the day's work begins and shuts off all sections which are gassy. **c1975** *Miners' Jargon* 4 = a certified union worker who checks the faces, abandoned workings and seals [of a coal mine] to see if they meet safety standards. **a1987** (in **2015** Yarrow *Voices* 12) The fire boss on the belts checks to make sure all failsafe methods are in operation. You have sprays, and cut offs, and sequence switches.

[DARE *fire boss* n Appalachians, West]

firebox *noun* An ashpan.

1955 Parris *Roaming Mts* 2 Everybody had a firebox to fetch coals from a neighbor's when his fire went out. **1962** Dykeman *Tall Woman* 188 This-here's the firebox, and under it there's this ash catch to keep your floor from getting gaumed up when you clean out the ashes.

[DARE *firebox* n 1a especially South, South Midland]

firebug *noun* A firefly.

1974 Dabney *Mt Spirits* 21 We gave him a drink. It was over 100 proof. His tongue lit up like fire bugs.

fire burn *noun* A burned area on the skin or in the woods. See also **blow fire, draw B3**.

1939 Hall *Coll* (Proctor NC) You blow three times where the place is burnt and say [a verse] each time you blow. It cures just any kind of a fire burn. **1974–75** McCracken *Logging* 11:43 We were talking about that fire burn [in the woods]. **1996–97** Montgomery *Coll* = (both senses): "The scar on his face is a fire burn, that bare spot on the side of the mountain is caused by a fire burn" (Cardwell), = both senses (Norris), = refers only to a fire in the woods (Oliver). **2007** McMillon *Notes* = a burnt place in the woods or on the skin.

fire cherry (also *firescald cherry*) *noun* A small cherry tree, the pin cherry (*Prunus pennsylvanica*), which rapidly populates areas denuded by fire. Also called **Peruvian cherry**. See also **scald**.

1961 Douglas *My Wilderness* 176 The fire cherry is here too; and thick stands of it mark great windfalls and places once burned. This small tree has taken possession and will hold on until the spruce and balsam once more command the ridges. **1964** Stupka *Trees Shrubs Vines* 84 Pin Cherry, Fire Cherry, Prunus pensylvanica. At middle and high altitudes, in localities where fire or other disturbances have affected the climax forest in recent decades, the pin cherry is an abundant tree. **1974–75** McCracken *Logging* 6:115 [There] wasn't a thing in the world but ramps and firescald cherry and this old yellow vine. **1992** Toops *Great Smoky Mts* 32 Where trees fall, pin cherry colonizes. Also called "fire" cherry because it invades after fires, it produces clusters of bright red berries in August.

fire chunk (also *fire coal*) *noun* A hot coal in or from a fire, an ember. See also **chunk A2**.

1845 Carpenter *Diary I* 80 Franky Davis . . . fite wolves all nite at shogar camp to save her caff throde fire chunks to save caff. **1917** Kephart *Word-List* 412 *fire coal* = an ember. **1959** Hall *Coll* (Mt Sterling NC) I like the old way [of making liquor] best because there was more or less vorde greese [ver de gris] as we called it, and strain it through fire coals. **1969** *Own Log Cabin* 13 The small box contained either "fire coals" (crushed charcoal) or a mixture of pokeberry juice and lime [for marking logs].

[DARE *fire coal* n chiefly South Midland]

fire coal See **fire chunk**.

firecracker *noun* See citations.

1964 Clarkson *Lumbering in WV* 362 *firecrackers* = beans. **2006** Farwell *Logging Term* 1021 Provisions were "bait," beans "firecrackers," and biscuits "cat heads."

fire-cured *adjective* See citation.

1940 Fitzpatrick *Lg Tobacco Market* 134 = type of leaf cured by smoke and heat from smoldering open fires.

fire damp *noun* See citations.

1973 Preston *Bituminous Term* 37 = an explosive gas released from the coal, chiefly methane. **2007** *Mining Terms* = the combustible gas, methane, CH_4. Also, the explosive methane-air mixtures with between 5% and 15% methane. A combustible gas formed in mines by decomposition of coal or other carbonaceous matter, and that consists chiefly of methane.

fire doctor *noun* See citation. See also **burn doctor**, **take out a burn**.

2003 Cavender *Folk Medicine* 97 In almost every community there were individuals known as "fire" or "burn" doctors who possessed the ability to "talk the fire out of a burn." It is not difficult to find people in the region today who will gladly provide testimonials about the effectiveness of these folk healers. . . . Usually the doctor recited the [magical] charm in a murmur three times while moving his hand across and slightly above the burn, pushing the hand in a direction away from the victim, as though pushing the heat away, all the while blowing on the burn. According to tradition, one can teach only three other people how to "talk" or "blow" fire out of a burn.

fire dog(s) (also *fire irons*, *fire rock*, *fire rocks*) *noun* Same as **dog iron(s)**.

1793 (in **1956** Eliason *Tarheel Talk* 271) (Wilkes Co NC) *fire doggs*. **1931** Greve *Tradition Gatlinburg* 69 Stones were used for the andirons—"fire dogs" they were called—that supported the forestick of the wood fire. **1934–47** *LAMSAS Appal*: *fire dogs* = attested by 39/148 speakers (26.3%) from WV, 7/20 (35%) from VA, 24/37 (64.9%) from NC, 11/14 (7.1%) from SC, and 9/12 (75%) from GA; *fire irons* = attested by 2/148 speakers (1.4%) from WV, 1/20 (5%) from VA, 2/14 (14.3%) from SC, and 3/12 (25%) from GA; *fire rock* = attested by 1/148 speakers (0.7%) from WV and 1/37 (2.7%) from NC; *fire rocks* = attested by 7/148 speakers (4.7%) from WV and 6/37 (16.2%) from NC. **1937** Wilburn *Notes* 1 Firedogs were two small rocks used to hold the fore stick up. **1946** Nixon *Glossary VA Words* 21 *fire dogs* = iron utensils used to support wood in a fireplace . . . [a term used] in the southern part of the Blue Ridge and all of the Piedmont. **1949** Kurath *Word Geog East US* 51 *Fire dogs* [predominates] in South Carolina and the greater part of North Carolina. Scattered instances of *fire dogs* occur also in Eastern Pennsylvania, and the term is not unknown in New England. **c1950** Adams *Grandpap* 71 Granny, tapping the ashes from her pipe onto the end of the firerock next to her, cast Grandpap an underbrow look of disapproval. **1976** Ledford *Folk Vocabulary* 279 It seems obvious that the local term *fire dogs* has already begun to disappear and will eventually be replaced by *andirons*. **1978** Reese *Speech NE Tenn* 29 *fire dogs* = attested by 2/12 (16.7%) speakers. **1983**

Dark Corner OHP-5A They's a lot of people that over this country went around and picked up them [spent artillery] shells, you know, and then they'd sell them to people at Greenville. They'd make fire dogs out of them. **1986** Pederson et al. *LAGS*: *fire dogs* = attested by 3/60 interviewees (5%) from E TN and 18/35 (52.7%) from N GA; 21/210 of all LAGS interviewees (10%) attesting term were from Appalachia. **2002** Oliver *Cooking and Living* 7 The fireplace also had heavy iron andirons or "fire dogs" which held the logs off the floor of the fireplace and kept them from rolling out of the fireplace. None of them had firescreens, and none were very wide.

[DARE *firedog* n scattered, but especially frequent southern Appalachians, South Atlantic, Gulf States]

fire guard *noun* A person hired to keep watch for fire in the mountains, fire warden.

1981 Weals *Fire Towers* Russell Edward Whitehead was one of the first fire guards after Great Smoky Mountains National Park was created in the 1920s. . . . In Russell's working years a lookout spent six months of the year in the tower and nearby cabin. They were the drier months when the woods was most prone to fire.

fire hunt *verb phrase* To pursue game at night by using a torch. See 1841 citation. See also **fire-lighting**.

1859 Taliaferro *Fisher's River* 155 I don't 'clude I'll fire-hunt no more.

fire in the hole *interjection* Used as a warning cry: in **moonshining** that law officers are in the vicinity, or in coal mining that a controlled explosion to free coal from a wall is imminent. See citations.

1974 Maurer and Pearl *KY Moonshine* 118 = local warning cry, especially on Coe Ridge in Cumberland County, Kentucky, and elsewhere near the Tennessee line, heard immediately after word has spread that the "law's in." Called in a high-pitched, far-carrying yodel, it is necessary to know the words in order to understand them. Adapted from the coal mines, where it is used to indicate that the fuse has been lit and a powder charge is about to explode. **1986** (in **2012** Portelli *They Say* 140) He [= a coal miner] would then put charges of black powder [in], tamp them with paper cylinders filled with earth, move away, light the fuse, shout the warning cry of "fire in the hole," and wait for the explosion to shake the coal from the face. **1992** Brooks *Sthn Stuff* 49 far in the hole! [See **far**.] This was the traditional shout used by a moonshiner's lookout to give warning that the federal men were getting close; but if a human holler was going to be too risky, the watchman gave a brief bird call instead. "Whoo-ee! Whoo-ee! Whoo-ee!" **2006** Mooney *Lg Coal Mining* 1029 After kneeling or lying on his side and "undercutting" the seam (which had to be further supported with short timbers or "sprags"), the miner drilled blasting holes with a "breast auger," used a "tamping rod" to pack his black powder, inserted a "clay dummy" for proper repercussion of the explosion, lit the fuse, and yelled "Fire in the hole!" or perhaps "Shootin' coal!" to warn other miners of the impending blast.

fire in tow See **fire and tow**.

fire irons See **fire dog(s)**.

fire-lighting *verbal noun* Hunting animals at night by shining light in their eyes. See also **fire hunt**.

1849 Lanman *Alleghany Mts* 48 In killing wild animals he pursues but two methods, called "fire-lighting" and "still-hunting."

[DARE *fire-lighting* vbl n especially NC]

fireman *noun* See citation.

1994 Farwell and Buchanan *Logging Terms* = a member of a logging crew who fired a boiler that uses sawdust and chips for fuel.

fire new (also *firing new*) *adjective phrase* Completely new, freshly made. Same as **brand-fire(d) new**.

1925 Dargan *Highland Annals* 93 "Oh, my gun?" says he, a little set back, fer it was fire-new, as you can see. **1952** Wilson *Folk Speech NC* 540 *firing new* . . . Brand-new. **1996–97** Montgomery *Coll*: *fire new* (known to Brown, Cardwell, Ledford).

[OED3 *fire-new* adj now archaic and U.S. regional]

fire pink *noun* A perennial wildflower (*Silene* spp) with a star-shaped blossom and medicinal uses. Also called **catchfly**.

1943 Peattie *Wild Flowers* 196 Nature plunged boldly ahead with her efforts to mingle vermillion with lilac, by adding everywhere the shooting stars of the fire pink, which is about as "pink" as the dress uniforms at Buckingham Palace. [**1996** White et al. *Wildflowers* 120 One look and you'll ask "who called this brilliant red flower pink?" "Pink" refers not to the color of the petals, but to their shape. Each of the five petals is pinked or notched at its tip.]

fire rock(s) See **fire dog(s)**.

fire room *noun* The room in the house where the fireplace is located; the living room. See citations.

1972 Cooper *NC Mt Folklore* 31 Because the kitchen had formerly occupied a small separate building, the room occupied during most of the day by the family and [that] was larger than the other rooms was called the *big house* or *big room*. Later, it became the *front room*, although it occupied the end of the house, and eventually it became known as the *fire room*. **1986** Pederson et al. *LAGS* (Greene Co TN, Pickens Co GA). **1987** Young *Lost Cove* 33 A few others saved up and brought radios back from Johnson City. Their fire-rooms were crowded every night with neighbors who listened to WLW, KDKA and WSM. **1993** Burleson *Aunt Keziah* 1 [The house] had newspapers on the wall, and a farplace so big I could stand in hit. Everybody then called the living room the far room, cause that's where the far allus wuz. **1996–97** Montgomery *Coll* (known to Adams, Brown, Cardwell).

[SND (at *fire* n 7(24)) 1700→, now only historical]

fire scald *noun* An area made bare of vegetation by fire, then quickly covered with **fire cherry**; also used in place-names (see 1968 citation). See also **scald**.

1908 Smith *Reminiscences* 437 Husky was on watch for bear-signs, and presently when he came to a "fire-scald" (spot where the fire had once been burned) he stepped, raised his hand warningly, and peered intently into the blackberry thicket. **1913** Kephart *Our Sthn High* 99 It was above the Fire-scald, a brulé or burnt over space on the steep southern side of the ridge between Briar Knob and Laurel Top, overlooking the grisly slope of Killpeter. **1926** Hunnicutt *Twenty Years* 34 We would go up a [trail] that leads up the right hand prong of Deep Creek, and then from there to the fire-scald on Shot Beech Ridge. **1939** Hall *Coll* (Dellwood NC) A firescald is where you burn all the timber off. **1968** Powell *NC Gazetteer* 171 [There are a dozen places named Fire Scald in w NC, four of them representing ridges.] Firescald Ridge, in Swain Co in Great Smoky Mountains National Park, a spur of Welch Ridge.

firescald cherry See **fire cherry**.

fire set *verb phrase* To set fire to.

1939 Hall *Coll* (Roaring Fork TN) They fire set our fence.

fire shelf See **fireboard**.

fireside industries *noun* See citation.

1937 Eaton *Handicrafts* 54 It was in the mountain cabins that leaders met for the counsel and co-operation that enabled them to continue the old crafts and to lay the foundation for the new ones they were to develop, and it is fitting that this work which has been carried on largely within the mountain homes should come to be known as "fireside industries." **1983** Whisnant *Native & Fine* 62 Local men and women were encouraged to bring their handmade baskets, brooms, quilts, coverlets, chairs, and other items to the school [= Hindman Settlement School] for marketing by Fireside Industries, the school's production and marketing organization. **2006** *Encycl Appalachia* 802 For people in the Appalachian craft revival of the early twentieth century, the term *fireside industries* came to identify a type of cottage industry in which craft items were made at home for sale. Though other terms were used for these enterprises, *fireside industries* carried a romantic connotation that appealed to craftspeople and consumers alike. William Goodell Frost, the third president of Berea College in eastern Kentucky, is credited with coining the term for home-based crafts manufacture[d] in an 1898 article in *Outlook*, a weekly magazine. . . . Fireside industries provided jobs for women with few opportunities for paid employment, and working at home allowed them to continue gardening, rearing children, and doing other household chores. While some centers marketed baskets, wood carvings, or other small craft items, weaving dominated fireside industries as a whole.

fire stick *noun* A small stick of wood fashioned for starting a fire.

2008 *Rosie Hicks* 6 He's made these fire starters, fire sticks, and I've got some of them yet.

fire the woods See **fire B1**.

fire up See **fire B2**.

fire water *noun* See citation.

2003 Triplett *Mt Roots* 12 Moonshine whiskey had several different names among mountain folk, including . . . "fire water."

firing new See **fire new**.

first *adjective* See also **firstest**.

A variant form *fust*.

1867 Harris *Sut Lovingood* 38 The fust thing he did thar, wer to proffer tu tend the Capitol grouns in inyuns, an' beans, on the shears. **1901** Harben *Westerfelt* 135 Somebody told 'er some'n Liz said away back when you fust started to fly around 'er. **1913** Kephart *Our Sthn High* 281 Much oftener the r is dropped from dare, first, girl, horse, nurse, parcel, worth (dast, fust, gal, hoss, nuss, passel, wuth). **1938** Bowman *High Horizons* 46 As a rule the mountain girl or boy who attends school says, "first" and "worst," whereas their parents say "fust" and "wust." **1942** Hall *Phonetics Smoky Mts* 42, 89. **1961** Williams *R in Mt Speech* 6 In a few words, however, r is omitted: . . . *fust*, *hathrock* (hearthrock), and *onery* (ordinary).

B in phrase *the first* = a single, any, the most basic.

1858 Webb *Letter* 109 you have sent to the rong place for Money there is none in this county. I have not collected the first dollar. **1861** *J Love CW Letter* (Nov 10) I hav wrote you 6 letters and I hav never receivd the first one yet. **1861** *Martin CW Letters* (Dec 21) Chrismas is Most hear and I have Not Seen the first partical of frost yet. **1973** *GSMNP-83*:38 They didn't give it the first thought of it ever being [of] value of any kind. **1981** Irwin *Arnwine Cabin* 31 They didn't have the first cookin' pot. They jest lived on parched corn and Irish taters cooked in the ashes. **1993** Burton *Take Up Serpents* 67 The old rattler sang in our hands and did not strike the first time. **2000** Montgomery *File* I didn't understand the first thing he said.

first dark *noun* Twilight.

1952 Giles *40 Acres* 160 As first dark begins to settle down over us, a thrush lifts its song from the head of the hollow. **1984** Burns *Cold Sassy* 23 The men are rushin' to get'm through town before first dark.

[DARE *first dark* n chiefly South, especially South Atlantic]

firstest *adverb* See also **-est 3**.

A variant form *fustest*.

B First.

1974 Fink *Bits Mt Speech* 10 Who got there *fustest*? **1988** Smith *Fair and Tender* 50 When we come back to the house the firstest thing we saw was Danny and Johnny out in the muddy yard wearing nothing but ther drawers. **1995** Montgomery *Coll* Who got there firstest? (Cardwell).

first footer *noun* See citation.

2009 *DSAE File* The first time I heard of "first-footers" was in Big Ridge [Jackson Co NC]. I was told by some elderly Pruitts that Christmas [season] could be dangerous. This was especially true of the first visitors to your home on New Year's Day. The first person who set foot across your threshold would determine the kind of life you had for the rest of the year. Red-headed people (especially women) must be avoided at all cost since their visit would bring a year filled with discord and bad luck. However, dark-haired visitors would bring happiness and prosperity.

first shot(s) *noun* See 1949 citation. Same as **high shots**.

1911 Shearin *E KY Word-List* 538 *first shot* = the last and therefore strongest run of whiskey from the still. **1939** Hall *Coll* (Cades Cove TN) I was drinking first shot of singlings, you know, and it made me drunk. **1949** Maurer *Argot of Moonshiner* 10 = the high-proof alcohol which comes off when the stilling process is started: "This 'ere still [is] yet runnin' first shots." **1963** Carson *History Bourbon* 236–37 (or *foreshot*) *firstshot* = the first portion of spirit that vaporizes when the still begins to work. The term is applied to both the production of high wines and low wines.

[DARE *first shot* n B3b South, South Midland]

first table *noun* The initial seating of people for dinner, usually consisting of the men and the guests.

1940 Bowman *KY Mt Stories* 2 The food all tasted good on that snappy winter morning. The men and boys sat down at the "first table"; and I, as company, was seated with them. The mother and girls waited table.

fish bait (also *fishing bait*, *fishing worm*, *fish worm*) *noun* The common earthworm used as bait for fish.

1929 Rainey *Animal Plant Lore* 9 In books I see them called "angle worms." I never hear a real live flesh and blood boy so call them. They are mostly "fishin' worms." **1952–57** (in **1973** McDavid and McDavid *Vocab E KY* 151) *fish worm*. *Ibid*. 152 *fishing worm*. **c1960** Wilson *Coll*: *fishing worm* = the common earthworm. *Fish worm* is about equally common. **1966** Dakin *Vocab Ohio River Valley* 394 *Fish(ing) bait* is fairly common beside the usual *red-worm* in southern Kentucky. **1966–67** *DARE Survey* (Spruce Pine NC, Maryville TN) *fish worm*. **1968** Wilson *Folklore Mammoth Cave* 17 *fishing worm* = the commonest name for the creature. *Redworm* is fairly common, *earthworm* is rare, *angleworm* is literary. **1986** Pederson et al. *LAGS*: *fish-bait* = attested by 10/60 interviewees (16.7%) from E TN; 10/27 of all LAGS interviewees (34%) attesting term were from E TN. **1996** Johnson *Lexical Change* 138 *fishing worm* = statistically more common in the mountains of South Carolina and Georgia than in the Piedmont and Coastal Plain c1990.

fish hook *noun* A mark indicating a debit on a worker's paycheck at a logging camp. See citation.

1984 Wilson *Train Ride* 7 Some of the people here get carried away and spend all their money and have to buy groceries on credit. When they do this their next check (already spent) comes to them with a question mark on it. This question mark has become known as a "fish hook."

fishing bait, **fishing worm** See **fish bait**.

fish pole *noun* A lightweight pole serving as a fishing rod.

1939 Hall *Coll* (Mt Sterling NC) He jumped and broke to run, and the panther took after him, and he still had his fish pole in his hand. **1996** Montgomery *Coll* (known to Cardwell).

fish rain *noun* A rainstorm accompanied by spouts of wind that suck small fish from the water and shower them on nearby land. Same as **frog rain**.

1993 Parris *Folklore* 497 There's frog-rains and fish-rains, the kind of rain that rains frogs and little bitty fish and worms. Why, many's the time I've seen it rain frog and redworms and fish. Not all at the same time. They come in the summer. And when they do, the ground'll just be covered with little bitty frogs and not much bigger than a body's thumbnail. **1995–97** Montgomery *Coll* (known to Brown, Bush, Cypher).

fish worm See **fish bait**.

fist *noun* variant plural form of two syllables: *fist-es*.

1858 (in **1974** Harris *High Times* 140) I jist swung round one ove my fistes an' sent hit at him. **1919** Combs *Word-List South* 39 *fistes*. **1942** Hall *Phonetics Smoky Mts* 82. **1974** Fink *Bits Mt Speech* 9. **1978** Reese *Speech NE Tenn* 155 = attested by 3/12 (25%) speakers. **1998** *Dante OHP-61* I'd have a chunk [of ice] as big as your two fistes on Saturday. **2005** Williams *Gratitude* 21 He'd git mad and jerk off his gloves and go at him with his fistes.

[DARE *fist* n especially South Midland]

fist and skull (also *fist and skull battle*, *fist and skull fight*) *noun phrase* A bare-fisted fight. See also **fight fist and skull**.

1861 *Carden CW Letter* (Oct 6) they went at it after A long fist and skull fight he fetch him in and he is now at Richmond where we send All our prisners. **1935** Allen *Annals Haywood Co* 268 It was a great rendezvous for the people, where all the then sports of the day were engaged in, such games as pitching quoits, running foot races, shooting matches, wrestling, and, sometimes a good fist and skull fight. **1940** Oakley *Roamin'/Restin'* 72 Living on this little creek these 2 men had a fist and skull fight as it was so-called in the Old days. **1971** *AOHP/ALC-193* I guess now if a fellow wanted to just get out to find him a fist and a skull battle to fight, he could find him somebody that'd take him on. **1989** Landry *Smoky Mt Interviews* 181 I never did see what we call a fist and skull.

[DARE *fist and skull* adj phr chiefly South, South Midland]

fistes See **fist**.

fisty See **feisty**.

fit See **fight 1**.

fitiddy See **asafetida**.

fitified (also *fittified*) *adjective* See also **running fit**.

1 (also *fitty*) Of a person or animal: subject to fits of temper or epilepsy; paralyzed with fear.

1913 Kephart *Our Sthn High* 70 He arrested Tom Hayward, a chunk of a boy, that was scared most fitified and never resisted more'n a mouse. *Ibid.* 222 Mountaineers never send their "fitified folks" or "half-wits," or other unfortunates to any institution in the lowlands, so long as it is bearable to have them around. **1939** Hall Coll (White Oak NC) That cat's fitified. **1957** Combs *Lg Sthn High: Word List* 39 *fitty* = "fitified," epileptic. **1963** Edwards *Gravel* 23 "You wouldn't think he used to be fitified now, wouldje?" "No," said Ma. "He's completely outgrowed it." **1976** Garber *Mountain-ese* 30 *fittified* = subject to fits. "She's so fittified you have to handle her with kid gloves." **1990** Bailey *Draw Up Chair* 14 If a person working unusually hard is said to be "workified," logically one suffering from spells or fits is "fittified."

[DARE *fitified* adj 1 chiefly Midland, also South]

2 Of a spring: spasmodic, erratic (especially in reference to one on the side of Mt. LeConte on the TN side of the Smoky Mountains named *Fitified Spring*).

1937 Thornburgh *Great Smoky Mts* 104 Often during October and November [the spring] is irregular and is referred to as "the fittified spring" by the mountain people. **1981** Roth *Greenbrier Early Days* 7–8 This spring is called the fittified Spring. It will be running for about twenty minutes, and then suddenly it will stop and be almost dry for about the same amount of time. The old-timers said it was caused by an earthquake in 1915. This spring has been doing this ever since [as of 1940s].

[*fit* n + *-ified*]

fit of cold shudders *noun* Convulsions of fear.

1997 Montgomery Coll When I seed what that thar panter done to Bill's face, I had a fit of cold shudders (Brown).

fitted See **fight 1**.

fitten (also *fittin*, *fitting*, *fitty*) (+ *infinitive*) *adjective* Suitable, ready, prepared.

1863 Gilley *CW Letters* (Oct 5) you said you would like to be with me this is not no fiten place for a woman to be at. **1902** Harben *Abner Daniel* 140 She'd a-gone as shore as preachin' ef she'd a-had a dress fitten to take the trip on the train. **1922** Kephart *Our Sthn High* 214 A good name: it is fitten. *Ibid.* 229 The words that man used ain't fitty to tell. **1952** Wilson *Folk Speech NC* 541 *fitten* = fit, suitable. "He ain't *fitten* to be a officer." **1975** Chalmers *Better* 66 I taken you-uns potion, for I had a misery, but now I am fitten to circulate around again.

[alteration of *fitting*; DARE *fitten* adj 1 chiefly South, South Midland]

fittidy See **asafetida**.

fittified See **fitified**.

fitting See **fitten**.

fitty[1] See **fitified 1**.

fitty[2] See **fitten**.

five-dollar Indian *noun* A person of mixed Cherokee and white ancestry who can claim Cherokee identity and the accruing social or economic benefits by registering for a small fee with the county officially as an Indian (usually a term of contempt used by other Cherokee).

1991 Neely *Snowbird Cherokees* The term, "five-dollar Indian," is also used in the same derogatory way on the main reservation to refer to minimal-blood-degree Cherokees. *Ibid.* 103–4 In the past it was often better to identify as white and the census records' fluctuations in Cherokee County Indian population may represent the community's fluctuations in ethnic identity. Fullbloods' reference to white Indians, like those in Tomotla, as "five-dollar Indians" reflects the perceptions of white Indians as people who, at least symbolically, can buy their way into the Indian community when the occasion requires or sell out to the white world if there is more advantage in that.

five-gallon Baptist *noun* A member of the Baptist church who undergoes total immersion when baptized. See also **forty-gallon Baptist, half-pint Baptist**.

2002 Myers *Best Yet Stories* 44 "Half-pint Baptists" sprinkled only the head. If the body became thoroughly wet, members were called "Five-Gallon Baptists."

five-leaf *noun* A partially mature ginseng plant.

1997 Hufford *American Ginseng* 12 Other strategies for conserving ginseng include scattering seeds where ginseng is known to grow, snipping the tops off of "five-leaves" and "two-prongs" so that less scrupulous diggers won't find them until they are bigger in future years.

five-leaf poison vine *noun* A type of poison ivy.

1986 Pederson et al. LAGS = attested by 3/60 interviewees (5%) from E TN; 3/3 of all LAGS interviewees (100%) attesting term were from Appalachia.

five-ten *noun* A children's hiding game.

1955 Ritchie *Singing Family* 214 All right, we going to play five-ten. I'll count first and everybody hide, but not more'n a hundred feet away.

fix *verb*

1 Of a person, the weather, a meal, etc.: to become ready, get organized.

1834 Crockett *Narrative* 76 He was not then ready to start, but was to fix that evening, and overtake us at the fork road where I was to meet Major Gibson. **1859** Taliaferro *Fisher's River* 128 They fixed to shave tharselves 'cordin' to this rule when they got into the Topic of Capincorn. *Ibid.* 179 Hollin and his darter was a-fixin' away, sorter like they was glad. **1862** Epperly *CW Letters* (July 10) the yankeys is now in about 20 milds of Richmon they ar reinforsing and fixing for a nother fight. **1863** Sexton *CW Letters* (Nov 5) fix and Both come to gether if you please. **c1900** (in **1997** Stoddart *Quare*

Women 82) We asked why the funerals were so long delayed and they said they "could not fix to get ready any quicker." **1913** Kephart *Our Sthn High* 298 Well, come agin, and fix to stay a week. **1926** Hunnicutt *Twenty Years* 35 We fixed for the night and fed our dogs. *Ibid.* (Nine Mile Creek NC) They was fixed up to go back in to help pack out the bear, and they was eleven of them went back in. **1939** Hall *Coll* (Sugarlands TN) I fixed to stay a week to bear hunt. **a1975** Lunsford *It Used to Be* 46 When it is time to kill the hog (butcher it), they generally fix to let it out of the pen because it is liable to break a ham in the struggle. **1983** *Dark Corner OHP-3A* You can stay at home and fix to die. **1995** Montgomery *Coll* The weather was a-fixin' for a change (Cardwell). **2007** McMillon *Notes* You'uns stay, and we'll fix to eat in a bit.

2 (in phrase *fixing to*) To get ready to, be about to; to intend to.

1861 *Martin CW Letters* (Nov 15) there is great maney fixing to Leve this Eavnig & great more expcts to go Next week. **1863** *Hundley CW Letters* (Aug 6) Father is A fixing to start in the morning. **1874** Swearingen *Letters* 165 Mary is fixing to make her some cotton dresses. **1899** Crozier *White-Caps* 116 I grew uneasy and was fixing to leave as soon as pay day come, but its too late, now. **1924** (in **1952** Mathes *Tall Tales* 23) Lyin' Dave's fixin' to tell another'n! **1939** Hall *Coll* (Cataloochee NC) He looked around and he saw a large panther a-laying on a log fixing to jump on him. **1955** Parris *Roaming Mts* 243 It looks like it's fixin' to weather up. **1970** *Burton-Manning Coll-94A* He was fixing to drown her and she drowned him. **1978** Montgomery *White Pine Coll* VI-2 They may be fixing to get back like they once was. **1982** Powers and Hannah *Cataloochee* 281 It was a-fixin' to come a storm. **1989** *Matewan OHP-18* Mommy's just fixing to get well, and I walked to that bed and prayed for that woman. **1998** *Dante OHP-61* They's still renting the houses then, they was a-fixing to get ready to sell them. **2007** (in **2012** McQuaid *Interface* 283) The corn's just now fixing to come in. **2014** Williams *Coll* = often used in threats. "I'm fixing to jerk a knot on your head."

3 (as a quasi-passive).

1966 West *Dialect Sthn Mts* 32 While supper was a-fixin, he and my father would have rared back in split-bottomed cheers and jawed or chawed the fat about this year's craps.

4 In phrase *fix the bed* = to make the bed.

1982 Ginns *Snowbird Gravy* 189 The girl . . . fixed the bed and come back in there and smiled at me and said, "Ray, have a good night."

5 See citation.

1940 Bowman *KY Mt Stories* 241 *fix the fire* = to replenish the fire.

fixen (also *fixin*) *noun* A mischievous or devious person.

1924 Greer-Petrie *Angeline Gits Eyeful* 17 That child is . . . the antickest little fixin'. **1963** Edwards *Gravel* 19 Keep outen my pockets, you little fixen! **1969** Dial *Dialect Appal People* 464 That trifling old fixin ain't worth a haet!

[variant of *vixen*]

fixin See **fixen**.

fixing *noun*

1 An accessory.

1859 Taliaferro *Fisher's River* 129 I kep' in my pocket allers a tin water-tight fixin', which I toated my smokin' apperatus in. **1862** *Kiracofe CW Letters* (May 25) I have some little yankey fixins I will send you the first Chance I have I have writen this letter on yankey paper. **1903** Fox *Little Shepherd* 6 Aunt Jane wouldn't 'a' keered about these leetle fixin's, fer I have to have 'em. **1917** Kephart *Camping & Woodcraft* 1:110 An old campaigner is known by the simplicity and fitness of his equipment. He carries few "fixings," but every article has been well tested and it is the best that his purse can afford. **1919** Combs *Word-List from South* 39 *gun fixin's* = guns, pistols, etc. **1924** Raine *Saddlebags* 165 When she's "clean out o' baking powders, an' has broke her needle, and wants a new dress," the "woman" takes her baby and a basket of eggs to ride to the little store five miles away to barter for groceries and "fixin's."

2 (as plural) Food.

1990 Clouse *Wilder* 90 We best be getting over there. I told Ruby's ma I'd help with the fixins.

fixing to See **fix 2**.

fix the bed See **fix 4**.

fix the fire See **fix 5**.

fixy *adjective* Fussy, particular.

1900 Harben *N GA Sketches* 20 Bein' as they say he's so fixy, I'm a-goin' to fetch in the lookin'-glass. **1933** Thomas *Jilson Setters* 29 "She's not fixy like that young widder-woman over on Brushy." He leaned closer with scandalized expression . . . "That widder-woman wears pink sun-bonnets." **1952** Wilson *Folk Speech NC* 541 = well groomed, fastidious. A fixy girl is one who dressed with unusual care and "keeps her things nice." **c1960** Wilson *Coll* = dressy, particularly about one's face or complexion; sometimes about one's clothes.

[DARE *fixy* adj 1 chiefly South Midland]

2 Fancy.

1942 Thomas *Blue Ridge* 285 All these here fixy contrapshuns [= electrical appliances].

[DARE *fixy* adj 2 chiefly South Midland]

fizzle dust *noun* See citation. See also **fiddle dust**.

2005 Williams *Gratitude* 494 = description of something almost nonexistent, or as finely ground as possible, as: He ground that cornmeal into *fizzle dust*.

flag (also *flag lily*) *noun* An iris (*Iris prismatica*).

1884 Murfree *In TN Mts* 18 Among their roots flag-lilies . . . and devil-in-the-bush mingled in a floral mosaic. **1995–97** Montgomery *Coll*: *flag* (known to Ellis); *flag lily* (known to Adams, Brown, Cardwell, Norris, Oliver).

[DARE *flag lily* n chiefly South, South Midland]

flail

A *noun, verb* variant form *frail*.

1973 AOHP/ASU-97 We rented it [= a parcel of land] then, the rye and the wheat, and my daddy frailed out with a frail.

B (also *frailing pole, frail pole*) *noun* An implement for threshing grain or beating flax consisting of a wooden handle at the end of which is a short stick attached so that it swings freely. See 1945, 1982 citations.

1895 Edson and Fairchild TN Mts 375 *frail*. **1922** TN CW Ques 1386 (Wilkes Co NC) I worke on the farm plowing . . . thrashing with a frail braking [sic] flax. **1931–33** (in **1987** Oliver and Oliver *Sketches* 25) They would thresh out their wheat with flails, clubs and sticks and would clean it up by two men with a sheet making wind while a third one would hold it up and sieve it down for the other two to blow out the chaff. **1945** O'Dell Old Mills 1 First the wheat was cut by hand with a scythe and then spread out on the barn floor for threshing. This was done with a "frail"—a twisted pole of hickory wood one end of which had been beaten with an axe until it was very soft. **1957** Broaddus *Vocab Estill Co KY* 31 *frailing pole* = a flail. **1967** DARE Survey (Gatlinburg TN) *frail pole* = an instrument used for thrashing, to separate the wheat from the chaff. **1982** Powers and Hannah *Cataloochee* 319 A Cataloochee flail [was made from] a small even-sized young tree. Hickory is best—about 1.5 inches at the butt. [It] should be 10 feet in length. From the butt end it should measure 3 feet to the place to be twisted. Use a pole ax or hammer and beat on each side of the stick 12 inches until it can be twisted so the flail can turn in the user's hands. Twist it when not in use and burrow in water. **1995** Montgomery Coll: *frail* (known to Cardwell).

[DARE (at *frail* n 1) chiefly South Midland, Northeast]

C (also *frail out*) *verb, verb phrase* To thresh (as grain) or beat (as flax) by using such an implement; to beat, strike, or whip. See also **frail rocks**.

1904–20 Kephart *Notebooks* 4:868 He frailed him well. **1927** Woofter *Dialect from WV* 354 *frail out* = to beat out grain. "We frailed out thirty bushels of wheat yesterday." **1939** Hall Coll (Smokemont NC) I beat and frailed on the door. **c1940** Aswell *Glossary TN Idiom* 8 *frail* = thrash. "I'll take a switch and *frail* you to a frazzle." **1977** Shields *Cades Cove* 22 Thrashing the grain was done at first by flailing. This was done in a clean area and on a windy day, since the wind hastened removal of the chaff. **1995** Montgomery Coll I'll frail the daylight out of you (Cardwell). **1997** King *Mt Folks* 111 Osie Ownby began "frailing" a banjo when he was about five years old—more than eighty years ago.

[DARE (at *frail* v 1) chiefly South, South Midland]

flair See **flower**.

flaish See **flesh**.

flake stand *noun* In distilling, a container with cold, flowing water in which the **condenser** of a **still** is set. Also called **cooling stand**, **cooling tub**. See 1949 citation.

1949 Maurer *Argot of Moonshiner* 9–10 = the container, filled with cold water, in which the condenser is immersed, so that the alcohol vapor will condense. Usually a barrel or a drum. **1956** Hall Coll (Mt Sterling NC) The coils is set into what's called the flake stand, the cooling stand. **1967** Williams *Moonshining* 14 In higher altitudes, the worm is stretched like a coil spring and fixed rigidly in the open air, but in most of the mountain country the coil is immersed in a barrel of cold water (called the "flake" stand) and projected about three inches from the bottom of the barrel, which is placed on a platform high enough to permit vessels to be set with ease under the end of the worm. **1968** *End of Moonshining* 49 = the container through which water is constantly flowing for final condensation of the steam. Holds the worm, condenser, or radiator, depending on which apparatus is being used. **c1999** Sutton *Me and Likker* 104 = also called a cooling tub. That is what your worm or condenser sets in with cold water piped to the bottom to push the hot water off the top to keep it cool. **2007** Rowley *Moonshine!* 161 = a watertight container that holds a copper worm, the end of which emerges from the bottom of the container. It may be a keg, a large tin, an olive barrel, a pickle bucket, etc. In modern setups, cool water enters from the bottom and exits the top of the container through hoses. Flake stand water never comes in direct contact with the spirits.

[SND *flake* n[1] 2(4) "a wooden box containing water through which the worm passes"; DARE (at *flake* n2) southern Appalachians]

flambeau *noun* A torch or other makeshift lamp with an open flame (as a kerosene-soaked rag stuck in a bottle).

1940 Still *River of Earth* 91 Leth had a flambeau made of a rag stuffed in a bottle of coal oil. **1986** Pederson et al. LAGS (Hamilton Co TN).

[DARE *flambeau* n 2 chiefly South, South Midland]

flame See **phlegm**.

flame azalea *noun* A deciduous rhododendron. Same as **wild honeysuckle**.

1941 Walker *Story of Mt* 48 Flame azalea is also an exquisite creation in the acid soil area. **1985** Wiseman *Autobiography* 37 The next to come in [in the spring, after the mayapple] was the fruit that grows on the "honeysuckle" or flame azalea. It is juicy, crisp, and tender, but does not have much flavor. **1991** Walker *Great Smoky* 32 The Great Smoky Mountains National Park has two different types of balds, grassy balds and heath balds. . . . Heath balds are predominantly comprised of rhododendron, flame azalea, laurel, and sand myrtle, all of which are evergreen, except the flame azalea, and are spectacular when in bloom.

flander *verb* To splinter, shatter, spill. See also **flinders**.

1904–20 Kephart *Notebooks* 2:639.

flander around *verb phrase* To wander about, become distracted.

1994 Montgomery Coll (known to Norris, Oliver); Quit your flanderin' around; We flandered all over the mountain looking around for the still (Cardwell).

[perhaps a variant of *flounder*]

flang See **fling**.

flannel cake *noun* A pancake.

1895 *Word-Lists* 392 = pancake. **1946** Nixon *Glossary VA Words* 22 = a pancake . . . [a term used] mostly west of the Blue Ridge. **1949** Kurath *Word Geog East US* 34 *Flannel cake* for a griddle cake made of wheat flour is . . . in common use beyond the Alleghanies on the Youghiogheny in southwestern Pennsylvania, and scattered instances of it have been noted even farther west. **1995–97** Montgomery Coll (known to Brown, Cardwell, Oliver).

[cf EDD *flannel* sb 3 "a coarse oatcake"; cf SND *flannen bannock, flannen biscuit*; cf CUD *flannel-bread* (at *flannel* n) "bread made with maize meal"; DARE *flannel cake* n chiefly Appalachians]

flannel leaf *noun* The common mullein, a tall biennial wild plant (*Verbascum thapsus*) from which a medicinal tea is made. Same as **feltwort**.

[**1971** Krochmal et al. *Medicinal Plants Appal* 264 A tea made from the leaves is used in Appalachia for colds.] **1982** Stupka *Wildflowers* 102 Of its many local names, ones like "flannel-leaf," "velvet plant," and "feltwort" refer to its exceptionally dense wooliness.

flannel-mouthed *adjective* See citation.

1962 Drukker *Lg By-Ways* 51 A "flannel mouthed" man is one who has experienced considerable difficulty or tragedy during his lifetime but who, in spite of all his troubles, speaks "soft and gladsome" words.

flannen *noun* Flannel.

1806 (in **1956** Eliason *Tarheel Talk* 310) (Davie Co NC) *flanin*. **1861** Griffin *CW Letters* (Nov 24) we want some flanin shirts. **1863** *Reese CW Letters* (April 23) tena I will send my flanen shirt and drawers Back home the first good Chance I have. **1895** *Word-Lists* 388 = flannel (common in N.C. and Ky.). **1923** Greer-Petrie *Angeline Steppin' Out* 39 He wen't none too hot with a suit of red flannins on. **1987** Trent *Yesteryear* 5 Flannel cloth was referred to as flannen. **1996–97** Montgomery Coll (known to Brown, Ledford).

[< Middle English *flanyn*; SND *flannen* n; DARE *flannen* n chiefly South, South Midland]

flapjack *noun* See citation.

2005 Williams *Gratitude* 494 = cornmeal stirred up together with a little flour, salt, bakin' sodie, and enough water or milk to make a fairly thick batter, then fried like a pancake. When it gets brown on one side, it is flipped (flapped) over in the pan by holding onto the handle and tossing the *flapjack* into the air to turn it. Hot *flapjacks* is a real treat with butter and surp (syrup) on them. After I got grown, I heard people call them *hoecakes*.

flapper *noun* The wing of a fried chicken.

1987 Young *Lost Cove* 24 The children, who always ate at the second table when company was present, had to be content with the flappers, scratchers and backs [i.e. pieces of chicken].

flappy jawed *adjective* See citation.

2017 *Blind Pig* (April 28) Where I come from, people who like to talk too much are flappy jawed.

flare See **flour, flower**.

flash See **flesh**.

flash off *verb phrase* See citations.

2013 Pierce *Corn in Jar* 12 Experienced makers [of homemade whiskey] can judge proof with a quick shake of the vial and observing the "bead." The size of the bubbles which form—the bead—and the speed that they dissipate, or "flash off," indicates the degree of proof.

flash tide *noun* A flash flood. See also **fleshy, tide A**.

1999 Morgan *Gap Creek* 210 "We're already having a flash tide," Hank said. **2000** Morgan *Mts Remember* 12 On ground this steep it can come up a flash tide pretty quick.

flashy See **fleshy**.

flat (also *flats*) *noun* A relatively level stretch of land surrounded by slopes, often one that has a specified growth of plants, as in the place-name *Spruce Flats* (TN), or proximity to a site, as in the place-name *Cabin Flats* (NC). See also **buckeye flat, chestnut flat(s), flatwoods**.

1832 (in **2008** Ellison *High Vistas* 38) we crossed a high spur of the Roan Mn to a low gap therein where we encamped at a pleasant Beech flat & good spring. **1937** Hall Coll (Little Greenbrier TN) [I did some] bootleggin'. It used to be made in the slicks, made later in the flats. **1939** Hall Coll (Sugarlands TN) [The bear] rolled off down the mountain a piece, tore loose from the dogs, and run a way on down the flat and treed up another tree. **1949** McDavid *Grist* 108 (Fannin Co) *flat* = a level place, in hilly country. **1958** GSMNP-110:14 [They] logged all that big poplar timber out up from the bridge yon way up to that flat with a groundhog skidder. **1964** Reynolds *Born of Mts* 4 [They] live high up on some mountain plateau between upper and lower fogs. There perhaps, they found more acreage to cultivate than down on the flats, as the mountain men call anything that is 45 per cent or less in slope. **1966** *DARE Survey* (Cherokee NC) *flats* = a good-sized stretch of level land with practically no trees. **1971** *AOHP/ALC*-147 We would have to go up the hill down here at Old Uncle Will's place and around the flat to get up in the Inman Branch where we lived. **1973** GSMNP-5:10 They was right next to Caldwell Fork there, the Den Flats was. **1975** GSMNP-62:16 They had the bear down here at Cabin Flats. They had it killed and skinned when we got back down to them. **1998** *Dante OHP*-12 That's the only place that I've ever found them was over there at the flat. **1999** Morgan *Gap Creek* 148 I guess bottom land along the creek was too valuable to use for pasture on Gap Creek, for only a few acres of pasture was near the creek flats.

flat as a fritter (also *flat as a flitter, flatter than a fritter*) *adjective phrase* Extremely flat.

1957 Combs *Lg Sthn High: Idioms* 14b He upped and knocked me as flat as a flitter (fritter). **1997–2000** Montgomery *Coll: flat as a fritter* (known to Brewer); *flatter than a fritter* (known to Ellis).

1999 Brewer *Appal Lg* "Flat as a flitter" is the condition in which you don't want to find one of your tires on a cold morning when you're already late for work.

flat cake *noun* A large pancake made from flour, with less yeast than white bread.

1986 Pederson et al. *LAGS* (Sullivan Co TN, Chattooga Co GA).

flatfoot *verb* To dance with a sliding step; hence noun *flatfoot (dance)* = such a dance step, *flatfooting* performing such a dance step. See 1993–94 citation. See also **buckdance, clogging.**

1976 Garber *Mountain-ese* 30 = [to] dance solo. "When the fiddle played, all the old timers started to flat-foot." **1992** Seeger *Talking Feet* 23–25 I go from flatfoot to clog and just a little bit of "cutting the pigeon wing"—that's the first steps I do when I go into my dance . . . back in the earlier years, it was just the flatfoot dance. I'd say back in the years, back in the fifties, that the dance that we do in this day and time, that we recognize as clog and flatfoot dancing, wouldn't have been recognized at that time. Because your feet were supposed to be close to the floor, you weren't supposed to get your feet over three inches off the floor. . . . In some places now, they even judge in taps and they call it flatfoot, but it's not right. Flatfoot dancing is really just on the soles of your shoes. That's the way it always has been up until the later years. **1993–94** Jamison *Jubilant Spirit* 17, 51 In Flatfoot dance the feet stay close to the floor, and the steps tend to have more of a sliding nature rather than up on the toes. . . . Clogging steps . . . tend to have a stomping feel to them. . . . In both Buckdance and Flatfoot dance, the dancers seem to be sliding over the surface of the floor; in Buckdance up on the toes, and in Flatfoot, with more of a sliding appearance.

flat-footed

A *adjective* Firm, plain, unambiguous.

1927 Woofter *Dialect from WV* 354 = firm in the position assumed. "He stands flatfooted in that matter, and will not change his mind." **c1960** Wilson *Coll* adj. and adv. = plain, forthright; unequivocally. **1995** Montgomery *Coll* He's a flat-footed talker (Cardwell); He's a flat-footed liar (Shields).

B *adverb* Plainly.

[See **c1960** in **A.**] **1974** Dabney *Mt Spirits* 129 [I] just flat-footed outrun him and holler[ed], "Come on, come on, here I am!"

flatform *noun* An open platform.

1924 Greer-Petrie *Angeline Gits Eyeful* 23 A feller a-standin' on a little raised flatform in the back of the ball room turned a strong light on her to git a better look. **1986** Pederson et al. *LAGS* (Rockdale Co GA).

[DARE *flatform* n chiefly South, South Midland, New England]

flathead *noun* A member of the Catawba tribe (term reportedly attested by the Cherokee).

1957 *GSMNP*-23:1:11 The old Cherokee Indians holped gather up these Catawbas, Flatheads they called them.

[Web3 n "any of several Indian peoples . . . of North America that formerly practiced head-flattening"]

flatlander *noun* A person from the lowlands, especially one insensitive to or unaware of mountain ways. See also **foreigner, outlander, outsider.**

1976 Carter *Little Tree* 71 Flatlanders could never understand what it meant to bust up a mountain man's still. **1999** Montgomery *Coll* (known to Cardwell). **2004** Larimore *Bryson Seasons* 19 Most of the folks were natives, as were their parents and their parents' parents. Most all of the physicians, and the nurses for that matter, were in at least their third to fourth decade of practice. They had their way of doing things and didn't "hanker to outsiders"—whom they called "flatlanders" if they liked you, or "lowlanders" if they did not.

flat of *adverb phrase* Flat on.

1901 Harben *Westerfelt* 230 Luke happened to go 'long the Shader Rock road t'other day an' seed John lyin' flat o' his back in the woods. **1938** Stuart *Dark Hills* 224 He laid right there flat of his back. **1952** Wilson *Folk Speech NC* 570 = on, upon: "He put that fellow flat of his back." **1993** Page and Smith *Foxfire Toys and Games* 70 I just grabbed that ax and hacked that tree and down he come. He hit flat of his back and it knocked him out. **1997** Miller *Brier Poems* 66 You've had your head eat off, or else you're flat of your back looking up into the guts and gears of America.

[DARE *flat of* (at *of* prep C5) chiefly South, South Midland]

flat-out

A *adjective* Utter, plain, unambiguous.

2009 Williams *Maw Surry* Maw Surry's eyes told the flat out truth of youthful years lived at the mercy of pure meanness.

B *adverb* Utterly, plainly.

1973 Kahn *Hillbilly Women* 149 Some of the girls who worked there just flat out wouldn't sign union cards. **2004** House *Coal Tattoo* 45 You are flat-out beautiful. **2006** Sohn *Whistlin' and Crowin'* 122 She labeled herself as a "flat-out good student" when she had been in school.

[DARE *flat-out* adv chiefly South, Midland]

flatrail fence *noun* See citation.

1957 Broaddus *Vocab Estill Co KY* 30 = a post-and-railing fence.

flats See **flat.**

flat (still) See citation. Same as **deadman still.**

1972 *Foxfire I* 279 These diagrams illustrate perhaps the simplest still of them all—the "dead man" or "flat" . . . the still itself—a rectangular box.

flatter than a fritter See **flat as a fritter.**

flat-top box *noun* See citation.

1997 Montgomery *Coll* = jocular name for a guitar or banjo (Hooper).

flatwoods *noun*

1 A relatively low-lying, level area in the mountains covered with trees. See also **flat**.

1926 Hunnicutt *Twenty Years* 157 Finally [the fox] got in the flatwoods of Hammer Branch. **1939** Hall *Coll* (Deep Creek NC) [They] fought down into the flatwoods at the point of the ridge.

[DARE *flatwoods* n pl chiefly South, South Midland]

2 See citation.

c1930 Goff *Dialects Sthn Mtneers* 6 The North Georgians speak of the country outside the mountains as the "flatwoods." The wilder parts of the mountains are called the "sticks."

flatwoods folks *noun* See citation.

1967 *DARE Survey* (Maryville TN) = what the country people around Maryville call themselves. "Flatwoods folks are infinitely superior to mountaineers!"

flavor

A *noun* See 1979 citation.

1979 Carpenter *Walton War* 166 Smells will be cited as "flavors." **1995–97** Montgomery *Coll* (known to Brown, Cardwell, Cypher, Oliver).

B *verb* See **favor A**.

flavorable *adjective* Flavorful.

1994 Landry *Coll* It's more flavorable if you like corn bread.

flax *verb* To hurry, bustle.

a1954 Adams *Word-List* = to bestir oneself. **1955** Ritchie *Singing Family* 67 Then they finally all left out, and Katty flaxed about like the Devil was atter her, blowing out lights east and west to save waste. **1974** Fink *Bits Mt Speech* 9 I'll *flax* around and git dinner.

flaxbird *noun* A goldfinch (*Spinus tritis*).

1980 Still *Run for Elbertas* 76 She didn't eat enough to do a flaxbird.

flax brake (also *flax break*) *noun* A machine for separating the woody stem tissue of flax from its fibers. See also **hackle**, **linsey**.

1937 Hyatt *Kiverlid* 55 We allus gethered up the drappin's under the flax-break and 'round the scutchin' board, and 'ud take an' spin hit into coarse thread. **c1980** Roberts *Olden Times* 81 Some 80 years ago flax was grown in the region near Lost Mountain for home use. . . . The manufacturing of this flax consisted of a wooden machine called a flax break. This homemade machine was made up of a frame work of wooden blades set close together. Similar blades were placed in a framework that was hinged at one end and were so arranged that they were allowed to go between the lower blades. The operator would take a bunch of flax in his left hand and with his right hand raise the upper blades. He would lay the flax across the lower blades and would continue in a chopping motion. This broke up the inner part of the flax into short pieces called "shives." Then he would shake this out leaving the fiber. **1991** Thomas *Sthn Appal* 222 We had a flax brake; and when it got dry, we braked those flax stalks. An' mother spun it into thread, an' made it into cloth.

flax break See **flax brake**.

fleak

A (also *fleek*, *fleeker*, *fleke*) *noun* A flake, fleck, slice.

c1926 Bird *Cullowhee Wordlist* The snow fell in big flekes. **1933** Thomas *Jilson Setters* 29 The elder . . . cyarved me a fleek (slice) of ham-meat the size of my pam (palm). **1936** Stuart *Head of Hollow* 58 Who sewed up the duck's back that the hound pups tore the skin off in a three-cornered fleek? **1939** Hall *Coll* (Alexander NC) *fleek of snow* = the expression is common. **1964** Clarke *Stuart's Writings* 160 Several informants in Wayne County, W.Va., knew *fleekers* to mean "pieces, often pieces of flesh torn loose." **1973** Miller *English Unicoi Co* 146 *fleaks* = flakes, used with reference to the condition of molasses just ready to be removed from the heat.

[DARE *fleak* n[1] South Midland]

B *verb* To split away from; hence noun *fleaking (point)* = the final stage of boiling **molasses**.

1936 Morehouse *Rain on Just* 153 The molasses, so pretty with its fat brown breaking bubbles, boiled almost to the fleaking point. *Ibid.* 156 "They're fleaking proper," roared young Emmet, testing the syrup. Just so much and no further should a good run of molasses boil. Boil to the fleaking so that a ladle full held up drips off in shield shaped drops. **1939** Hall *Coll* He fleaked off from Democracy [i.e. the principles of the Democratic Party]. **1942** Hall *Phonetics Smoky Mts* 18 *Flake* was [flik] in the sentence, "They fleaked out and left the church."

[DARE *fleak* v South Midland]

fleech *verb* To flatter.

1952 Wilson *Folk Speech NC* 540 = to flatter. **1962** Rouse *Colorful Tint* = to flatter.

[cf OED3 *fleech* v "beguile, cajole, coax" Scot and north dialect; EDD *fleech* v 1 Scot, nEngl; SND *fleech* v[1] 1 "to coax, wheedle, flatter"]

fleek, fleke See **fleak**.

fleem See **phlegm**.

flesh *noun* variant forms *flash*.

1942 Hall *Phonetics Smoky Mts* 20 [æ] is common also in . . . *flesh*.

[DARE *flesh* n A South Midland]

flesh crawl, make one's *verb phrase* To cause one to shudder.

c1960 Wilson *Coll*

[DARE *flesh crawl, make one's* v phr chiefly South, South Midland]

fleshen up *verb phrase* To put on weight.

1952 Wilson *Folk Speech NC* 541 = to take on weight, to become fat. **c1960** Wilson *Coll* = to put on weight or "flesh"; to become fleshy. **1995–97** Montgomery *Coll* (known to Brown, Cardwell, Norris, Shields).

[EDD (at *fleshen* v) "to put on flesh, grow fat"; DARE *fleshen up* v phr South, South Midland]

fleshy *adjective*

1 Of a stream: at flood tide. See also **flash tide.**

1923 Combs *Addenda KY* 243 *get fleshy* = to rise: of water. **1983** Broaddus *Estill Co KY Word List* 39 (also *fleshy*) = swollen (a creek), flush.

2 (also *flashy*) Of a person: corpulent.

1863 *Bartlett CW Letters* (March 12) I am fleshyer at this time than I have ben sentse I was maried by five or ten pounds. **1864** *Reese CW Letters* (May 1) if I was at home I wood git vary fleshey. **1974** Fink *Bits Mt Speech* 9 She's a *fleshy* old woman. **1979** Carpenter *Walton War* 59 He was, according to Mother, a big "fleshy" man, red-faced and hearty. **2006** Cavender *Medical Term* 1022 One who is slightly overweight is "fleshy," but "stout" if excessively fat (or strong or robust). **2013** Venable *How to Tawlk* 16 *flashy* = obese: "Pearlie Mae has a sweet face, but she shore is flashy."

flickem *noun* See citation.

1940 Farr *More TN Expressions* 447 = biscuit: "Susie Jane cooks flickems of a morning."

flicker *noun* See citation. Same as **scrip.**

1943 Korson *Coal Dust* 72 The same colloquial terms were used for scrip and store orders, such as "stickers," "clackers," "flickers," and "drag." **1973** Preston *Bituminous Term* 37 = scrip.

[DARE *flicker* n^3 southern Appalachians]

flinderation (also *flinteration*) *noun* Fragments collectively; the condition of being rendered to fragments. See also **flinders.**

1927 Woofter *Dialect from WV* 354 The wind blew the roof of the barn to flinderation. **1957** Combs *Lg Sthn High Word List* 39 (also *flinteration*) = splinters, used idiomatically, as in: "Up come the storm and tore my hog-pen all to flinderation." **1981** Williams *Storytelling* He broke that there little old house all to flinterations. **2018** *Blind Pig* (Nov 23) I used to hear it as in, "He wrecked his car and tore it all to flinderation."

flindering *adverb* Extremely.

1859 Taliaferro *Fisher's River* 175 I was a-workin' fur 'Squire Freeman one flinderin hot day.

flinders (also *flinters*) *noun* Splinters, fragments, shards (especially in phrase *all to flinders*). See also **flander, flinderation.**

1873 Smith *Arp Peace Papers* 41 The ball went ded throu a house and tore a buro all to flinders. **1957** Combs *Lg Sthn High Word List* 39 *flinters* = splinters. **1963** Edwards *Gravel* 118 "I'll gi' you one more chanct to speak howdy," said Zeke, "and if you don't, I'll blow you into flinders wi' this shot gun." **1969** Dial *Dialect Appal People* 464 He dropped the dish and busted it all to flinders. **1995–96** Montgomery *Coll* (known to Cardwell, Ellis, Ledford, Norris, Oliver, Shields). **2000** Morgan *Mts Remember* 67 Like most new-marrieds we was afraid to disagree, afraid the world would bust up and go to flinders if we was to argue.

[DARE *flinders* n pl 1 chiefly New England, South Midland, South]

fling *verb*

A variant past-tense form *flang.*

1998 Montgomery *Coll* (known to Brown, Bush, Ellis, Jones); Leave her where Jesus flang her = [let it alone] (Oliver).

B (also *fling up*) To vomit.

1917 Kephart *Word-List* 412 *fling.* **1931** Hannum *Thursday April* 170 Pap . . . wouldn't swaller a drap of his licker efn hit was poured down him. He'd fling hit up first. **1939** Farr *TN Mt Regions* 90 "He's flinging up his supper." **1966** Dakin *Vocab Ohio River Valley* 484 Other neutral terms are attested only once or twice. These include . . . fling up.

[DARE *fling* v B1 chiefly South Midland]

fling up See **fling B.**

flinters See **flinders.**

flint rock *noun* Quartz.

1950 King and Stupka *Geology and Natural History* 33 In the stream beds or the soil of the mountains one frequently sees blocks of white, milky quartz, locally known as "flint rock." **1973** *Words & Expressions* 134 = quartz.

flip *noun*

1 (also *flip gun, flip-jack, flipper, flip-shot*) A homemade slingshot. See 1952 citation. Same as **bean flip.**

1940 Haun *Hawk's Done* 15 He made her flips and shotguns and things like that. **1952** Brown *NC Folklore* 1:234 *flippers* = these were made from strong, springy wood like hickory or oak. A small limb or the trunk of a small tree was used. They were left round on one end for a handle. The other end was shaped off much like the half of a bow. They were held with one hand, while the other hand was used to hold a small pebble to shoot out for a distance of forty to fifty yards. Small boys used to use them in war games. **1982** Ginns *Snowbird Gravy* 131 They showed me how to build a flip shot, a slingshot—some called 'em a flip shot—out of the old red inner tube that was in the Model T and the A Model Ford. **1985** Irwin *Alex Stewart* 54 We'd make what they called flippers. Take a small forked stick and tie a piece of leather to each end of the fork and you could shoot a gravel a long way. **1988** Dickey and Bake *Wayfarer* 35–36 A gravel shooter is like—well, it's a flip, you know. You use rubber from somebody's old inner tube, and you shoot rocks with it. I used to be pretty good with one myself. They'll shoot hard if you got long hands, shoot a rock out of sight, straight up. **1993** Page and Smith *Foxfire Toys and Games* 172 We'd make slingshots. We called 'em flip-jacks. I have to say we shot birds. **2018** *Blind Pig* (Sept 8) Dad and his brother used ball bearings ("steelies") as ammunition in their sling shots (we called them "flip guns").

[DARE *flip* n^1 1 Midland, South]

2 (also *flip-flop*) A somersault.

c1960 Wilson *Coll*: *flip* = a somersault. **1974** *Instrument Makers* 200 Here come a buck sheep and hit just turned him a flip-flop.

flip-flop See **flip 2.**

flip gun, flip-jack, flipper See **flip 1**.

flipperdinger *noun* A homemade toy. See 2005 citation.

1972 Cooper *NC Mt Folklore* 34 For many decades and until stores became plentiful, the children's Christmas toys and gifts were mainly homemade. There were dolls, yarn balls, whistles, geehaw whimmydiddles or ziggerboos, rattle traps, noisemakers or bull roars and flipperdingers. **2005** Joslin *Handcrafters* 42 Twigs from the elderberry bushes could be combined with acorn caps to produce the flipper dinger. The pith was pushed from the twig to form a hollow tube. A smaller hollow twig was inserted near the end, which was plugged. Then an acorn cap with a hole was set on the smaller twig. A raised wire ring, like a basketball hoop, was placed on the end. A light puff ball with small wire hooks was placed in the acorn cup, and the player blew through the tube to raise the ball where it could hook onto the basket. **2006** *Encycl Appalachia* 803 The names of these toy creations are a part of the folklore. Whimmydiddle, flipperdinger, bullroarer, limber jack, jumping jack, and penny pincher are just a few of the hundreds of imaginatively named toys.

flip shot See **flip 1**.

flit like a butterfly from flower to flower and land on a cow crap See **fly all around the pretty flowers and light on a chicken turd**.

flitter, flitter bread, flitter cake See **fritter B**.

flitter out *verb phrase* To fail, lose intensity or interest.

1939 Farr *TN Mt Regions* 90 He's flittered out at every job he's tried. **1995–97** Montgomery *Coll* (known to Brown, Cardwell, Norris, Oliver, Weaver).

flitting *noun* See citation.

1917 (in **1944** Wentworth *ADD* 223) (sWV) = a moving van of household goods.

floaterial (also *floterial*) *adjective* Pertaining to a legislative or convention district composed of more than one county.

1884 Milliken and Vertrees *Code of TN* 106 The governor, secretary of state, and attorney-general for the state [shall] be, and they are hereby, constituted a board of inspectors, whose duty it shall be to compare the vote for senators and joint representatives in the several senatorial and floaterial districts of the state, and declare the result. **1952** Mathews *Matters Lexicographical* 126 Another paragraph in the same letter mentions "Floterial Districts" and gives an 1869 example of its use. **1970** *DARE Survey* (TN) [He] is the floaterial representative from Knox County [TN].

float out *verb phrase* See citation.

c1975 *Miners' Jargon* 4 = [to] relieve an equipment operator [in a coal mine].

flock tick *noun* A bed **tick** filled with feathers. See also **feather tick, shuck bed, straw tick, tick.**

1942 Thomas *Blue Ridge* 151 While the bride was changing to her infare dress, older hands quickly took down the bedsteads, tied up the flock tick and shuck ticks in coverlids and quilts, shoved them back into the corners so as to make room for the frolic and dancing. **1996–97** Montgomery *Coll* (known to Brown, Bush).

floojins See **flugins**.

Flordy dude (also *Flordy people*) *noun* A native or natives of Florida who has moved to or lives seasonally in North Carolina. See also **Floridiot, Floron.**

2003 Onchuck *Mud Pie Memories* 9 We "tar heels" used to mock and scoff at the tourists for driving so slowly. We always referred to them as "Flordy people." Of course they, not being used to the curves and drop-offs, were more cautious than were the local folks. **2007** McMillon *Notes: Flordy dude*.

Floridiot *noun* A tourist or recent migrant (usually a seasonal one) to western North Carolina from Florida who is the butt of mountain humor because he or she knows little about mountain ways and has little interest in or regard for them. See also **Flordy dude, Floron.**

1995 Williams *Smoky Mts Folklife* 123 Much of the humor about Floridians has an edge to it. . . . Much of the tension exists because these outsiders do not respect the egalitarian ideals of the region and "look down" on local people. They want to enjoy the scenery of the mountains but do not respect the country ways of its people. "Floridiots," its permanent residents in turn mutter under their breath. **2006** *Encycl Appalachia* 229 More recent terms have been invented for specific groups of furriners and find usage in either joking or serious connotation. In western North Carolina, where furriners in increasing numbers retire, vacation, or construct summer houses, the terms *floridiot* and *half back* came into usage in the late twentieth century.

Floron *noun* See citation. See also **Flordy dude, Floridiot.**

2005 Starnes *Land of Sky* 182 Despite the economic power of tourism in the region, some residents were particularly derisive in their description of visitors. A common regional expression asks, "What do you get when you cross a Floridian and a moron?" The answer is "a Floron."

floterial See **floaterial**.

flounder *verb* To become sick from overeating, founder.

1982 Ginns *Snowbird Gravy* 173 We set down to the table, and I said, "Well, I don't want no 'lasses." And Daddy said, "Well, what's the matter?" I said, "Well, we got floundered on 'em. We just eat too many and got sick on 'em and don't want none." **1994** Montgomery *Coll* The old heifer got into my crib and floundered (Cardwell).

flour *noun* variant forms *flare*.

1942 Hall *Phonetics Smoky Mts* 46 [flæ:ɚ]. **c1959** Weals *Hillbilly*

Dict 4 *flare*. **1989** *Matewan OHP-102* She would make her own paste, just take flour, and you'd stir it up in water and boil it till it was thick enough.

flour bread *noun* Any bread made from wheat flour, especially biscuits. See also **light bread**, **loaf bread**, **wheat bread**.

1862 *Warrick CW Letters* (March 9) hear we get good fat hog and dumpling and good Flour Bread to eat com. **1864** *Chapman CW Letters* (May 15) I am tierd of eating flower bread I can buy musterd [greens] lettis and onions when ever I want them. **1958** Wood *Words from TN* 10 = a kind of bread made from wheat. "Biscuit dough rolled thin and cut in four or five inch squares is referred to as flour bread." **1960** Mason *Memoir* 95 We had lived on flour-bread, fat-back, and black-berries. **1996** Montgomery *Coll* (known to Adams, Cardwell, Jones).

[EDD (at *flour* sb) Scot; DARE *flour bread* n 1 now chiefly South, *flour bread* n 2 chiefly South, South Midland]

flour poke *noun* A sack made of woven cotton muslin, in which flour is sold. See also **poke**[1].

1956 GSMNP-22:7 We strained [the milk] through these flour pokes, didn't we? **1973** GSMNP-86:41 Well, they didn't none of us ever get snakebit, but their work animal did. Hit got snakebit and they got wild touch-me-not, put it in a flour poke and boiled it and got the strength out, and then they took a cloth or something and bathed its foot where it got snakebit. **1986** Pederson et al. *LAGS* (Sevier Co TN).

flower

A variant forms *flair*, *flare*.

1942 Hall *Phonetics Smoky Mts* 46 [flæ:ɚ]. **1986** Helton *Around Home* 378 *flare*. **1998** Giardina *No Scapin* 129 Theyd be lots of flairs, specially roses. **2013** Venable *How to Tawlk* 37 Miss Mary Ann grows the purtiest piney flares you ever seed.

B *verb* To flatter, compliment (someone).

1925 Dargan *Highland Annals* 106 I knew he was jest a-flowerin' me.

flowerdy (also *floweredy*) *adjective* Having a floral pattern or design, flowery.

1949 Arnow *Hunter's Horn* 7 Twelve-year-old Suse came skipping through the kitchen, folded lengths of the flowerdy goods floating from her shoulders. **1952** Justus *Children* 14 Yes, if I have enough berry money, I'll buy a floweredy dress. **1984** Burns *Cold Sassy* 255 Why shouldn't you . . . wear a flowerdy dress if it might lift your grief a little? **1997** Andrews *Mountain Vittles* 69 Her floweredy house dress and apron [were] wringin' wet. **2004** Fisher *Kettle Bottom* 7 Ted didn't want floweredy goods on his shirt.

[*flowered* adj + -*y* adj forming suffix]

flowerpot *noun* A bouquet.

1940 Bowman *KY Mt Stories* 238 = bouquet. **1953** Davison *Word-List Appal* 10 = bouquet. "You ought to see Aunt Bett's coffin; it looks like a flowerpot." **1960** Stubbs *Mountain-Wise* (April–May) 6 If you should stop to admire, you would probably be asked if you would like a "flower-pot" to carry home. If you expected to receive a vase or potted plant you would completely misinterpret the intention of the gardener. Instead you would receive a generous bouquet of flowers, fresh-cut from her garden. That, I had to learn, is a "flower-pot." **2000** Montgomery *Coll* (known to Cardwell).

[cf EDD (at *flower*); DARE *flowerpot* n 1 chiefly VA, NC]

flower pretty *noun* A small object with a floral design. See also **pretty D1**.

1955 Washburn *Country Doctor* 42 There is a striking use of double words in description, some of the more common being: cash money, sun ball, cow beast or cow brute (bull), church house, bare naked, fire hearth, play game, flower pretty, and rock boulder.

flowers of the Cross *noun* The columbine plant (*Aquilegia* spp).

1962 Stubbs *Mountain-Wise* (Aug–Sept) 8 Columbine has the local name of *flowers of the Cross*, for tradition has it that these flowers were laid at the foot of the cross when Jesus was crucified.

fluffed up *adjective phrase* See citation.

c1982 Young *Colloquial Appal* 9 = irritable, huffy.

flugence See **flugins**.

flugins (also *floojens*, *flugence*) *noun* Hell, "tarnation."

1859 Taliaferro *Fisher's River* 204 I was mad as flugence. **1895** *Word-Lists* 388 *flugins* (Winchester, Ky.) in phrase *cold as blue flugins*. **1983** Page and Wigginton *Aunt Arie* 24 It's hot as floojens.

[DARE *flugens* n chiefly South]

fluken *noun* See citation.

1895 *Word-Lists* 388 = a new slang word that has been spreading in certain portions of western N.C. since the fall of 1884. It is used in this sense: To put the *fluken* on one = to "do him up"; to get the advantage of him, etc. It originated, as a phrase, in this manner:—A very dramatic murder trial was held in Lenoir, Caldwell County, in 1884, of two men who blockaded a half-dozen mica miners in a mine shaft and killed three of them. Several of the witnesses described the bodies as having had "the fluken put on them." *Fluken* is the local name for the scaly, whitish soil dug from mica mines. Since then the phrase, meaning what I above state, has been in common use in the region.

flusterate (also *flustrate*) *verb* To frustrate.

1864 *Proffit CW Letters* (June 20) If you are a mind to bee flustrated a bout sutch a beeing as I am. **1867** Harris *Sut Lovingood* 260 He mus' a been sorter flustrated at me, fur the cabbidge leaves wer wilted wif sweat. **1921** Greer-Petrie *Angeline at Seelbach* 6 I was too flusterated to notice anything but them lights. **c1960** Wilson *Coll*: *flusterated* = frustrated, chagrined. **1984** Burns *Cold Sassy* 7 Mama was always fair, even when flustrated to distraction. **1984** *Six Hill 'n Holler* 5 *flustrated* = more than frustrated: "He couldn't fix it and got plumb flustrated."

flustery *adjective* Distracted, confused, upset.

1952 Justus *Children* 54 I feel too flustery to fix up any fancy-fine food. **1996–97** Montgomery *Coll* (known to Adams, Brown, Cardwell, Jones, Norris, Oliver).

flustrate See **flusterate.**

flustration *noun* Frustration.

1927 Mason *Lure of Smokies* 213 He plum' fergot about the hide in the flustration. **1984** Burns *Cold Sassy* 8 Tears of flustration wet her red face.

flutter mill *noun* A toy waterwheel.

1866 Smith *So Called* 85 The Choctaw children built their flutter mills. **1943** Justus *Bluebird* 19 No time to make a new whistle or whittle out a fluttermill or a whirligig. **1968** Wilson *Folklore Mammoth Cave* 42 = a home-made water wheel, with a joint of cornstalk for the hub of the wheel and paddles made from the outer hard coverings of the cornstalk. Placed in a small stream, it runs on and on, just like a mill-wheel. **1988** Russell *It Happened* 121 These wooden fluttermills were small turbines that provided some fun for play in the water. **1993** Page and Smith *Foxfire Toys and Games* 138 Another thing we made was a little mill—set it in the creek. We called it a Fluttermill. Take two pieces of wood and cross 'em, and then had to bore a hole in here [at the intersection] and put an axle on it. Then you set it somewhere [in a stream] between two forked sticks.

[DARE *fluttermill* n 2 chiefly South, South Midland]

(the) flux *noun* Severe diarrhea or dysentery. See also **bloody flux.**

1862 *Hitt CW Letter* (May) I have had the flux I was vary bad three days and nits that nothing but blud past thru mee but I am well of that now. **1864** *D Walker CW Letters* (Aug 18) thear is a good eal of Sickness in the Rigment at this time and the most of the Sickness that is her is the flux. **c1900** (in **1997** Stoddart *Quare Women* 25) Pettit made at least one visit to their branch and noted five cases of the flux and homes which she described as "wretched." **1937** Hall *Coll* (Upper Cosby Creek TN) To cure the flux, drink a tea of sweet gum bark or take some mutton taller melted. **1960** Hall *Smoky Mt Folks* 50 The "flux," that is, diarrhoea, might be relieved by a preparation compounded of sweet-gum bark and melted mutton tallow. **1967** *DARE Survey* (Gatlinburg TN) = dysentery. **1967** Jones *Peculiarities Mtneers* 69 Sliced cumphery roots, when soaked in cold water, was rated as a remedy for diarrhoea, a disorder known in the mountains as "flux" or "summer complaint." It was usually quite prevalent among small children. **1977** Hamilton *Mt Memories* 15 The woman was pretty old and knew a lot about sickness. She said Tim had a very high fever and he might have "flux" (dysentery). **1997** Johnson *Melungeon Heritage* 19 If you ate a lot of them [= apples from the tree], you could get an upset stomach or something called "the flux," after which you usually got a spanking.

[DARE *flux* n "diarrhea; dysentery" chiefly southern Appalachians, Lower Mississippi Valley]

fly

A *verb* variant past-participle forms *flew, flue.*

1861 *Griffin CW Letters* (n.d.) he had flue round enuf. **1862** *Robinson CW Letters* (April 2) if I hadent a flew tha [they] would a thought I was giting away. **1969** Roberts *Greasybeard* 126 When we got to where we could see out we realized that the bird had flew off and we were way up in the air. **2004** Adams *Old True Love* 17 Hackley had picked up the fiddle when he was five and had flew right into playing.

B *verb*

1 In phrases *fly hot, fly mad* = to become angry suddenly.

1917 Kephart *Word-List* 412 I don't know what the fraction was, but he flew mad about something. **1973** GSMNP-91:26 He was awful bad to fly mad, you know. He didn't control his temper. **1982** DeArmond *So High* 27 Seems he went and flew mad and killed a man last night. **2001** Lowry *Expressions* 15 I think I was sweating normal and then I flew hot. **2009** Burton *Beech Mt Man* 65 I think people kills people when they fly mad—adrenalin kicks in.

2 In phrases *fly off, fly up* = to indulge in an angry outburst.

1949 Arnow *Hunter's Horn* 84 Pop, he'd jist fly up an tell her to mind her own business.

3 In phrase *fly all over one* = to cause one to become angry.

[**1915** Pollard *TN Mts* 242 *fly one over* = to overcome with surprise: "It flew me all over in a minute."] **1940** Haun *Hawk's Done* 118 Meady said that it just seemed to fly all over him when he seed the babies. **1961** Seeman *Arms of Mt* 57 What flew all over me was that Tracy had sent word fer me to meet him—right thar among them same pines whar he kilt Clyde!

C *noun* See citation.

1973 Preston *Bituminous Term* 53 = [in underground coal mining] an entry cut off a main entry at more than a ninety degree angle.

fly all around the pretty flowers and light on a chicken turd (also *flit like a butterfly from flower to flower and land on a cow crap, fly all over a daisy field and settle on a cow pile, fly over a field of clover to land on a cow pile*) *verb phrase* To ignore better choices (especially of a mate) before picking a poor one.

1997 Montgomery *Coll* I 'lowed Susy would fly all over a daisy field and settle on a cow pile [in hunting a husband] (Brown). **2002** Myers *Best Yet Stories* 55 She told of the most beautiful girl among her childhood friends who apparently married beneath her social status. Mother described that situation by saying, "she flew all around the pretty flowers and lit on a chicken turd." **2009** Benfield *Mt Born* 143 *flit like a butterfly from flower to flower and land on a cow crap* = a fickle young person might date and discard many fine, respectable (dull) prospects, then settle on an outrageously unsuitable (exciting) ne'er-do-well. **2015** *Blind Pig* (May 8) I swear she would fly over a field of clover to land on a cow pile. In other words: some people seemingly pass by something really good to get to something really bad.

fly all over one See **fly B3.**

fly around

A *verb phrase*

1 To flirt, gallivant; to court (someone).

1861 *Hanes CW Letters* (Sept 19) write where the boys are flying a round at and how they are getin along with the girls. **1861** *Neves CW Letters* (Dec 25) I wood like to be up in Greenville to spend Christmass and have Some fun but I am not thare so you must fly round and have some fun for me. **1901** Harben *Westerfelt* 135 Somebody told 'er some'n Liz said away back when you fust started to fly around 'er.

2 To hustle about.

1863 *Huntley CW Letters* (May 20) I Waunt them tow marrow on review so fly round if You please I Waunt them all soon.

B *noun* A social engagement, party.

1861 *Dalton CW Letters* (Dec 16) christ mus is not fur off now I wish i was thair to go to Some fly rounds.

flybroom (also *flybrush*, *flybush*, *flyflap*, *flyflapper*, *fly minder*, *fly scare*, *fly shake*, *fly sweep*, *fly swing*) *noun* An implement of various constructions (as a leafy branch, a set of feathers, or a stick draped with strips of cloth or paper) waved over the meal table usually by children to ward off flies; occasionally it is driven by a pedal or by pulling a string. See also **swith**.

1924 Raine *Saddlebags* 13–14 Then the eldest girl, constantly swinging a "fly-bresh,"—a branch from a lilac bush,—kept passing the various dishes and urging us to "try to mek out a meal." **1937** Eaton *Handicrafts* 235 In addition to this type of fan, a "fly bush" of peacock feathers is made. A gorgeous object that was used before the days of mosquito netting and wire screens to shoo the flies away from the dining table. **1946** Maloney *Time Stood* 16 When we sat down to eat, a wide "fly sweep" made of thin strips of newspaper fastened to a stick above the table was kept gently swishing to keep flies away. **1952** Wilson *Folk Speech NC* 541 *fly flapper*. **1967** Campbell *Memories of Smoky* 146–48 There were no screens on the doors or windows, and it was necessary to use the "fly-brush" to keep the flies away from the table while the meal was being eaten. Most mountain families used a very simple fly brush, in some cases just a branch from a tree and in most cases a long, slender piece of newspaper tacked to a strip of wood with the paper cut into narrow strips. The branches were swung back and forth across the table throughout the entire meal. **1968** Wilson *Folklore Mammoth Cave* 36 *fly broom* = a straight stick with a fan-like appendage made by sewing some stiff paper around the stick and then cutting the paper into long narrow strips. Waved gently over the table, it sometimes scared away a few flies, the less bold ones. **1987** Young *Lost Cove* 47 There were no window screens to keep out the flies. An older girl was assigned the task of swishing them away with a flyshake. **1988** Russell *It Happened* 8 Still hanging on another wall was the summertime fly-minder made from a section of the Knoxville Journal by fastening it onto a round stick about a yard long and then cutting the paper in strips. **1992** Morgan *Potato Branch* 31 Grandmother Morgan had a straight sassafras stick with a thick row of brown paper ribbons cut from grocery bags fastened to the end. I waved the fly scare over the heads of the diners when I saw a fly dive for any dish on the table. **1995–97** Montgomery *Coll*: *fly brush* (known to Adams, Brown, Ledford, Norris), = hand-sized pieces of cheesecloth attached to a wire hanger (Jones); *fly flap* (known to Ledford, Norris, Oliver, Shields); *fly flapper* (known to Adams, Brown, Ledford), = split pages of a Sears Roebuck catalog that would swing over the meal table (Cardwell); *fly minder* (known to Cardwell); *fly sweep* (known to Adams, Cardwell), = same as *fly brush* (Jones), = paper folded over a limb or stick and cut in strips to make a fringe (Norris); *fly swing* (known to Cardwell). **2002** Myers *Best Yet Stories* 232 To stay cool in summer, doors and windows had to be open. Of course, flies gathered around the dinner table. A "fly-sweep" made of thin strips of newspaper fastened to a pole and mounted on a contraption that sat on the floor underneath the table was pedaled by foot, shooing the flies away. **2005** Houk *Walker Sisters* 29 The one thing that could detract from the pleasures of a fine meal was the presence of flies. The sisters' resourcefulness glimmered in a contraption employed to keep the pesky insects away from the table. As one guest described it, the "fly-brush" was a vertical piece of wood suspended from the ceiling, with a crosspiece extending the width of the table to which strips of newspaper were attached. A diner would pull a string to move the "brush" back and forth across the table, thus warding off flies while they ate. **2013** Patton *Go Back* 4 It might be said that a family rated according to the kind of fly brush it had. The very poor used a limb cut from a mulberry tree; the middle class had one cut out of newspaper; the upper rich had one of a peafowl's tail.

fly brush, **fly bush**, **fly flap**, **fly flapper** See **flybroom**.

fly gun (also *flykiller*) *noun* A children's toy.

1963 *Chr Sci Monitor* 26 Apr 6/6 (in *DARE File*) [In Boone NC] the flykiller, a combination of woods plus a metal screw, projects a wooden pellet missile with terrific force derived from pressure created by releasing a curved bow. **1980** Wigginton *Foxfire VI* 200 In Watauga County, North Carolina, numerous craft shops . . . market a toy called a fly gun. A white-oak split propels a projectile out of the end of the toy. We could find no contacts who remembered seeing this toy as children.

fly hot See **fly B1**.

fly in (also *fly loose*) *verb phrase* To begin working vigorously, throw oneself (into something).

1971 *Corn Shuckin's* 101 When somebody went t'build a house, ever'body flew in and helped'em. **1975** *Foxfire III* 267 I flew loose to digging that darn thing and it was the biggest root I ever got in my life over that small a top.

flying jenny (also *flying-jinny*, *fly-jinny*) *noun* A makeshift merry-go-round consisting of a plank or pole fixed atop a post or stump, on each end of which one or more children ride by pushing it round with their or an animal's feet.

1941 Still *Troublesome Creek* 86 I'm bound to ride the fly-jinny.

Ibid. 96 I studied the flying-jinny, noting its pattern in my head. I felt bound to have Father make one. A long hickory pole it was, pegged in the middle to a sourwood stump. I straddled the limber end of the pole, hungry to ride. **1956** McAtee *Some Dial NC* 16 *flying jenny* = play device consisting of a plank mounted at the middle in a pivot fixed at the top of a post about breast high; this was pushed around more and more rapidly to give the thrill of speed to those clinging to it, and to test their ability to hang on; sometimes it was provided with crosspieces to aid riders to stick. **1968** Wilson *Folklore Mammoth Cave* 42 *flying jenny* = a home-made merry-go-round, usually made from a long pole with an auger hole through it to fit a trimmed post, even the stump of the tree itself. **a1975** Lunsford *It Used to Be* 130 *Flying Jenny* You find a stump where possibly a tree had been cut off up to about three-and-a-half or four feet high. You'd get a large beam and put a hole through it and a pin down through it into this tree stump. Two boys were on one end of that beam and a big ram was on the other end—that is, he had that bar run through the circle of his horns. He was walking on his hind feet pushing that flying jenny around. **1976** Miller *Mts within Me* 42 Some permitted their children to build "flying jennies." These were made of boards with holes drilled in the centers and then placed on poles or tree stumps with metal stobs as pivots. One person would sit on each end, and someone would push them around and around—like a merry-go-round except much faster. "Jennies" were extremely dangerous and sometimes riders would get "slung" off or the whole contraption would fly off the axis. It is a miracle there were no more broken bones than there were. **1986** Lauterer *Runnin' on Rims* 205 Lucy remembered at recess they played with something called a Flying Jenny. She described it: "You take a stout sapling and cut if off about waist-high. Then you take a little sapling and split it and put it on the post. Then you can push it around and around and around."

[Web3 *flying jenny* n South and Midland; DARE *flying jenny* n 1a *jenny*, probably from its earliest form being a pole that was ridden astride, chiefly South, South Midland]

flying-jinny See **flying jenny.**

flyings *noun* See citations.

1940 Fitzpatrick *Lg Tobacco Market* 134 = the lowest leaves of a Burley plant. **1944** Dingus *Tobacco Words* 66 = the lowest leaves, poor in quality but generally marketable.

[DARE *flyings* n 2 chiefly Midland]

fly-jig *noun* Same as **gee-haw whimmy diddle.**

1940 Still *River of Earth* 228 [A]nd beginning to stroke the notched stick of a fly-jig.

fly-jinny See **flying jenny.**

flykiller See **fly gun.**

fly loose See **fly in.**

fly mad See **fly B1.**

fly minder *noun*

1 See **flybroom.**

2 The person designated to hold or wave a **flybroom** at a meal. **1996** Montgomery Coll (known to Cardwell).

fly off See **fly B2.**

fly over See **fly B3.**

fly over a field of clover to land on a cow pile See **fly all around the pretty flowers and light on a chicken turd.**

flyrocks *noun* Airborne rocks blasted from a site of strip mining for coal.

2012 Portelli *They Say* 349 Since blasting away mountain tops is less expensive than using earth removal machinery, explosions and "flyrocks" threaten nearby homes and villages.

fly scare, flyshake See **flybroom.**

fly-slapper See **flyswat.**

flyswat (also *fly-slapper*) *noun* A fly swatter.

1940 Stuart *Trees of Heaven* 257 She takes a fly swat and shoos away the fat flies. **1967** *DARE Survey* (Gatlinburg TN, Maryville TN) *flyswat.* **1991** Still *Wolfpen Notebooks* 87 I can trap a fly in my hand. All it takes is know-how. I've never wasted a dime on fly-slappers. **1995** Montgomery Coll: *flyswat* (known to Cardwell, Shields).

[DARE *flyswat* n chiefly South, South Midland]

fly sweep, fly swing See **flybroom.**

fly up *verb phrase*

1 See **fly B3.**

2 Of a person (by analogy with a chicken): to go to bed for the night.

1967 *DARE Survey* (Maryville TN) *fly up the roost.* **1980** Still *Run for Elbertas* 75 Let's fly up if I'm to rise early. **1985** Edwards *Folksy Sketches* 94 "Our bus to High Fork is slower than the slow train through Arkansas," Lance said. "A feller's going to have to fly up to roost before long." **1993** Ison and Ison *Whole Nother Lg* 22 = to go to bed at night. **1996** Montgomery Coll (known to Adams, Cardwell).

[DARE *fly up* v phr 2 chiefly South, South Midland]

fly-up-the-creek *noun* See citations.

1939 *FWP Guide TN* 135 A person who changes his mind often is called a "fly-up-the-creek" or a "whip-around." **1967** Wilson *Folkways Mammoth Cave* 29 = the green heron, also applied to some hare-brained or empty-headed person.

fodder

A (also *fodder and tops*) *noun* Coarse food (as hay, or corn stalks) for domestic animals. See also **blade fodder, fodder pulling time, pull fodder, roughness.**

1835 *McLean Diary* (Jan 30) [I] halled my foder and what Corn I have left. **1881** Pierson *In the Brush* 66–67 Our horses were put in the stable and bountifully fed with corn in the ear and fodder. "Fodder" in these regions has a limited signification, and is applied only to the leaves which are stripped from the corn-stalks, tied in small bundles, and generally stacked for preservation. The stalks are not cut, as in the North and East, but the leaves are stripped from them while standing. This is the usual feed for horses in the place of hay. **1939** Hall *Coll* (Smokemont NC) Teacher would commence maybe sometime up in August and for three or four weeks then and probably stop then about two weeks, for the people to take fodder and so on, and we would be out for a while. **c1960** Wilson *Coll* = blades of corn and sometimes the whole stalk above the ear, cut while still green, for stock food. **1967** Miller *Pigeon's Roost* (April 13) Farming in this hilly country during last 20 years has changed like daylight is from dark. Take for instance, one time every farmer pulled fodder—that is, pull green blades from corn stalks, tie the blades and corn tops in bundles and set five or six of them in a shock and let the fodder cure out, then put the bundles of fodder in a stack. It would take about 50 shocks to make a good stack. **1979** Slone *My Heart* 62–63 Fodder also had to be saved. All the blades from where the ear of corn grew down were stripped from the stalk, leaving the one on which the corn grew. Every few handfuls were placed between two stalks close to the ground; here they would cure out. After a few days, these would be tied into bundles, and stacked in a shock, or hauled to the barn. The remaining stalk was cut off just above the ear of corn, and tied into bundles and placed together in smaller shocks. These were called "tops" and were not as valuable as the blade fodder. The tops were usually fed to the cows, and the rest kept for the horses. **1986** Watts *Same Block* 75 The dictionary says fodder is any food for cattle, horse, sheep, etcetera, like cornstalks, hay, and straw; but around here fodder meant the blades only. These blades were put in what they called "hands" as they were pulled, and placed between the stalks above the ground.

[DARE *fodder* n 2 chiefly South, South Midland]

B *verb* See citation.

1944 Hayes *Word-List NC* 34 = to pull fodder: "When it gets through weathering, I'll finish foddering."

fodder and tops See **fodder A**.

fodder blade See **blade 1**.

fodder(ed) bean *noun* A green bean strung and dried in the pod to preserve it for winter consumption. Same as **leather britches**.

1930 Thomas *Death Knell* The mountaineer has invented many words to suit his meanings. Beans dried in the pod are variously called shuck-beans, fodder-beans, and leather-britches, to distinguish them from shelled beans, which he calls soup-beans. **1949** Arnow *Hunter's Horn* 170 He didn't like fodder beans much anyhow, and when he did eat them he wanted plenty of meat seasoning. **1972** Hall *Coll* (Emerts Cove TN) [In the Depression] we lived purty high on the hog, with potato dumplin's 'n sich, foddered beans, fried mush fried in the mornin' for breakfast with molasses, brown-eyed peas, pickled cucumbers. **1985** Wear *Lost Communities* 35 Fodder [beans], or shab beans, were prepared as for canning, except the pods were not broken up. **2003** Howell *Folklife Big South Fork* 62 Dried beans, locally called fodder beans (also known as shucky beans or leatherbreeches), were prepared by cutting the whole beans into bite-size lengths, then boiling them for a long time with a little fat meat for seasoning.

[DARE *fodder bean* n South Midland]

fodder pulling time (also *fodder pulling*, *fodder time*, *fodder weeks*) *noun* The period of one or two weeks in the early fall when blades and tops of corn plants are stripped for **fodder**; in former days school was dismissed and all members of the family might be put to work in the process. See 1975 citation. See also **blade fodder**, **cutting tops**.

1922 *TN CW Ques* 18 (Cocke Co TN) [School] amed to run 3 mos but stoped through fodder pulling and molasses making. **1937** Conner *Ms* 37 f. Now I am coming to some more of my short school term's, which lasted from eight to twelve week's [sic] ordinarily including fodder week's and other loss of time, so by the time we reviewed up on our studies we got the benefit of approximately about nine week's in which to advance our studies. **1956** Hall *Coll* (Cosby TN) The teachers would stop a couple of weeks for fodder pulling time. The people would pull fodder for feed. **1959** Hall *Coll* (Hartford TN) During fodder pullin' time, we worked till midnight putting it up. **1968–69** *DARE Survey* (Brasstown NC) *fodder time*; (Ball Ground GA) Possum hunting would be in what we called the fodder-pulling time. We would pull fodder during the day, wait for the dew to dampen that which had been pulled two days before, tie it in bundles, get home after dark. **1975** GSMNP-59:7 We'd go to school maybe a month, or five or six weeks possibly, but then . . . fodder pulling time come along and the school had to shut down. They shut down then for a week or two there for the kids to go in and help pull the fodder and take care of the feed.

[DARE *fodder pulling* vbl n chiefly South, South Midland, *fodder pulling time* n chiefly South Midland, *fodder time* chiefly South Midland]

fodder shock (also *fodder stack*) *noun* See c1960, 1996–97 citations.

1866 Smith *So Called* 54 The Governor . . . is constrained to get on a fodder-stack pole. **1941** Stuart *Men of Mts* 76 Look at the pumpkins to roll in the fodder shocks here this fall. **1948** Chase *Grandfather Tales* 187 [The bull] run around the fodder stack so hard he butted his own rump. **c1960** Wilson *Coll*: *fodder stack* = a stack of bundles of fodder, with the tips of the bundles turned in toward the stack pole. **1962** Wilson *Folkways Mammoth Cave* 12 Fodder, formerly saved, was also tied into bundles and then put into a *fodder stack*. **1978** Hiser *Quare Do's* 12 They got along the best, like two families of mice in the same fodder shock. **1993** Stuart *Daughter* 231 In the fall of the year corn stalks are cut and arranged vertically against a "horse," made by tying together four cut stalks. The stalks are secured by a stout string tied around the shock near the top, making the shock of stalks resemble a tepee. The ears of corn can be harvested from the stalks at a later date and the dried stalks (fodder) fed to livestock during the winter months. Inside the shock, ears of corn, pumpkins, turnips and green tomatoes may be stored. **1996–97** Montgomery *Coll*: *fodder stack* (known to Adams, Brown, Cardwell, Jones, Ledford, Norris), = a stack of whole stalks of corn, with leaves/blades still attached, arranged upright and tied together with some of the long leaves/blades (Oliver).

[DARE *fodder stack* n South, South Midland]

fodder time, **fodder week** See **fodder pulling time**.

foggy *adjective* See citation.

1982 Slone *How We Talked* 18 *foggy hair* = unbrushed or not combed. "Your hair is all foggy and your clothes don't fit you right."

fog horn *noun* See citation.

1964 Clarkson *Lumbering in WV* 362 = smoking pipe.

foler See **follow A**.

folk *noun* People in general. See also **folks C1**, **C2**.

1864 *Chapman CW Letters* (April 13) I would like to see them ther foalk is all well. **1921** Weeks *Speech of KY Mtneer* 3 My material has been gleaned largely from the everyday English of our students and from the interesting things they tell of the folk back home. **1962** (in **2014** McCarter *Memories of Boy* 22) There were the usual good-byes with folk crying, for we were really going out of this world, all the way to Oklahoma. **1973** Kahn *Hillbilly Women* 125 You never lose a thing in the world by being good to folk. **1986** Ogle *My Valley* 39 Here we mountain folk used to fish for the now rare native brook trout; hunting in the shallows for what we called stick bait. **1993** Burchill et al. *Ghosts and Haunts* 105 Surely it wasn't a night critter, a fox or an opossum; they were smart enough to stay away from folk.

folks *noun*

A variant plural form **folkses**.

1895 Edson and Fairchild *TN Mts* 371 = folks, people. **1924** (in **1952** Mathes *Tall Tales* 44) "Howdy Folkses!" came a neighborly greeting out of the dusk. **c1940** Simms *Coll* We'uns come from educated folkses. **c1960** Wilson *Coll*: *folkses* = folks, people (usually humorous).

[DARE *folk* n B2 South, South Midland]

B variant possessive form **folkses**.

1973 *Foxfire Interviews* A-73-86 [The land] was their folkses come down to Ron.

C Senses.

1 People in general. See also **folk**, **menfolk(s)**, **womenfolk(s)**.

1939 Hall *Coll* (Catons Grove TN) I guess you people would like to know about serenades and how young folks got along back seventy years ago and longer. **1940** Haun *Hawk's Done* 141 He said them two years seemed right long because the folks there weren't like the folks he had always knowed in Cocke County. **1978** Montgomery *White Pine Coll* VI-1 If they had a been anything said up there, at that time, anything would have got a bunch of folks killed.

2 (also *folk*) One's family, especially one's parents.

1863 *Mangum CW Letters* (April 8) I recievd your letter dated the 31 of march and was glad to hear from you and to hear that you and the rest of the folks was all well. **1863** Wilson *Confederate Private* 1 (Feb 1) Paps foakes is well except pap. **1901** Harben *Westerfelt* 33 The preacher promised me this mornin' he'd wait on me an' my folks. **1941** Justus *Kettle Creek* 122 "Of course," agreed Aunt Emmy, "you must get home before dusky dark lest your folks worry over you." **1974** Ogle *Memories* 44 Everytime it came up a big rain, my folks were afraid the river would come down and we couldn't get home. **1978** Montgomery *White Pine Coll* VI-1 There were a lot of folk that they wouldn't dream of letting their children play cards when we were growing up. **1997** Andrews *Mountain Vittles* 40 That's how my folks always did save their seed to plant the next year. **1999** Morgan *Gap Creek* 184 I felt so warm and at ease to have some of my folks around me, to have Lou with me. **2010** Owenby *Trula Ownby* 16 My folks took the Knoxville paper and they would read it during the day.

folkses See **folks A**, **B**.

foller See **follow A**.

follow *verb*

A variant forms *foler*, *foller*.

1862 *Shifflet CW Letters* (Feb 28) hit is Seventy miles to nashville I think that is as fur as well foller them. **1863** Wilson *Confederate Private* 33 (Dec 10) it is thot that we wil turn back to morrow for the yanks is folering us. **1961** *Coe Ridge OHP-336A* The second night after he got to Missouri, he stepped out in the yard, and the dog and this man was a-follering him. **1975** *AOHP/ALC-1128* When his son got big enough to work, he follered his father's footsteps taking him to the mines.

B To engage in (a pursuit, custom, profession, or trade) as a practice; to have (a habit, custom, or tendency for) (usually followed by a verbal noun).

1860 Olmsted *Back Country* 258 We don't foller takin' in people. **1862** *Vance Papers* (Nov 4) we have a cooper in the twenty sixth regiment that went as a conscript that we cant well do with out he was all the man that followed this Trade anywhere near in this neighborhood. **1864** *Chapman CW Letters* (Feb 13) let me no what you follow for past time. **1913** Combs *KY Highlander* 34 The Mountaineer "follers pickin'" [the dulcimer] by means of a quill, by which he strikes the three strings at the same time with his right hand over the right hand, over the gap at the larger end, at the same time using in his left hand a small reed with which he produces the air, or "single-string variations." **1917** Kephart *Word-List* 412 = to do as a practice or custom. "What do you'uns *foller* for a livin'?" **1922** *TN CW Ques* 1094 (Sullivan Co TN) I followed farming. **1935** Sheppard *Cabins in Laurel* 197 Abe says, "I don't follow drinkin' any more but I'll try some." **1940** Bowman *KY Mt Stories* 239 *follers the Law* = studies the law or is an officer. **1953** Hall *Coll* (Bryson City

NC) In his early married life he went into and made a preacher, Baptist preacher. And he followed that all the rest of his life. **1960** Hall *Smoky Mt Folks* 30 (Bradley Fork NC) I don't foller drinking, but I've made liquor. **1969** Roberts *Greasybeard* 87 He went in, set the girl down and said to her, "What do you foller when you are at home?" She said, "Washing and cooking." **1979** Carpenter *Walton War* 150 He is a smart-turned youngun but he follers havin' the croup. **1982** Ginns *Snowbird Gravy* 137 I followed cuttin' timber there for several years, foxhunting all the time. **1985** Irwin *Alex Stewart* 103 He lived on the river and followed fishing and he made his own boats. **1988** *Augusta Heritage* 153 Did he follow any kind of work? **2007** McMillon *Notes* = to have a habit, occupation, or hobby: "I follered sangin' [= singing] 'bout all my life."

[DARE *follow* v B1 chiefly South Midland]

follow talking *verb phrase* To say the blessing before a meal.

1957 Combs *Lg Sthn High: Word List* 40 *foller talkin'* = to say grace at the table. Ex: "Stranger, do ye foller talkin'?"

follow the signs *verb* In a Pentecostal worship service, to exemplify the "signs" of possession by the Holy Spirit identified in the Gospel of Mark 16:9–20, specifically the handling of poisonous snakes, drinking of deadly liquids, laying on of hands to heal, and so forth. See also **serpent handling**, **sign follower**, **take up a serpent**.

1993 Burton *Take Up Serpents* 1 The worship service was much like that witnessed in many churches throughout the area—preaching, singing, and praying. What made this service different was a practice that is referred to as "following the signs" as set forth in the sixteenth chapter of the Gospel according to Saint Mark, a practice that includes handling deadly serpents.

follow up *verb phrase* To trail. See also **up A1**.

1954 GSMNP-19:23b [I'd] go out and catch the bees off of the flowers and then watch which way they'd go, and then I'd follow them up and cut down my bee tree.

fool

A *noun* One who has lost restraint or has a fondness for (especially a certain dish of food). See also **foolish about**.

1913 Kephart *Our Sthn High* 293 If one is especially fond of a certain dish he declares that he is a fool about it. **1940** Still *River of Earth* 116 Boone allus was a fool for wild meat. "Hi now," he said, a-cracking bones betwixt his teeth, "I'd give a pretty for a pot-pie cooked out o' these birds." **1956** Hall *Coll* (Raccoon Creek NC) This man was also a coon hunter, and he was a terrible fool about sauerkraut. **1957** Parris *My Mts* 159 When it comes to bread, he'd druther bite into a pone of hot gritted bread baked in a greased skillet than to have buttermilk biscuits three times a day, seven days a week, and he's plumb fool about buttermilk biscuits. **1994–97** Montgomery *Coll* (known to Cardwell); He's a fool about sweet potatoes (Ellis).

B *adjective* Ridiculous, nonsensical (usually expressing the exasperation or disgust of a speaker).

1873 Smith *Arp Peace Papers* 47 What do you ax such a fool question fur? **1885** (in **1972** *Burial Customs* 8) he had some fool Dr. tending on him. **1908** Fox *Lonesome Pine* 17 I'll knock yo' fool head off the fust thing you know! **1939** Hall *Coll* (Hazel Creek NC) God, we had one more time with this fool bear, driving and everything. **1953** Hall *Coll* (Bryson City NC) We carried that fool horse up the mountain. **1955** Ritchie *Singing Family* 184 Never saw anyone study so hard as you do. Here, shut up that fool book and talk to me. **c1960** Wilson *Coll* Where is that fool boy? **1977** Hamilton *Mt Memories* 14 Aunt Lela caught me by the arm and led me outside and said, "Don't ask your Mama any more fool questions." **1978** Hiser *Quare Do's* 69 When I told her Demaris Rose, she exclaimed, that's the foolest name I ever heared tell of.

[DARE *fool* adj formerly widespread, now especially South, South Midland]

C *verb* To loiter, waste time.

1969 Burton-Manning *Coll*-93A They weren't fooling and making a lot of noise or cutting up a lot.

[DARE *fool* v 1b scattered, but chiefly South Midland, Gulf States, Central]

fool along *verb phrase* To dawdle, work slowly.

1866 Smith *So Called* 44 You get a government contract for a few thousand pounds, and you fool along with it, selling what you do make to these drug men at a bigger price.

fool away (also *fool out*) *verb phrase* To waste (time).

1937 Hyatt *Kiverlid* 15 We cain't fool the day out when we've got the puttin' in of a piece to do. **1939** Hall *Coll* (Deep Creek NC) I just fooled away all the evening after and then got into camp.

foolish *adjective* See citation. See also **foolish about**.

1924 Raine *Saddlebags* 14 I'm foolish and kind of drinlin' = frail.

foolish about (also *foolish over*) *adjective phrase* Fond of, infatuated with to the point of lacking judgment or control.

1925 Dargan *Highland Annals* 202 He's foolish about Ben. **1936** (in **2005** Ballard and Chung *Arnow Stories* 54) She's awful foolish over thet Zorie. **1956** Hall *Coll* (Gatlinburg TN) She is plumb foolish over him. **1989** Smith *Flyin' Bullets* 56 Reed was "full of jokes and awful foolish over th' young'uns." **1997** Montgomery *File* He's just naturally foolish about ramps (50-year-old woman, Jefferson Co TN). **2008** McKinley *Bear Mt* 181 *plumb foolish over* = very fond of. **2009** Benfield *Mt Born* 144 Foolish about = so in love as to lavish boundless affection and let the object of one's love rule one's life. "Daddy's plumb foolish about his dogs."

[DARE *foolish* adj 2 chiefly South, South Midland]

foolishment *noun* Foolishness.

1955 Ritchie *Singing Family* 147 I aim to go to bed. Come on, Mom, leave the young uns to their foolishment. **1979** Carpenter *Walton War* 187 Hit allus seemed a lot of foolishment to me how a woman will break her back growin' yard flowers that ain't fit fer nothin' but to be looked at. **1995–97** Montgomery *Coll* (known to Brown, Cardwell, Ledford, Shields).

[DARE *foolishment* n chiefly South, South Midland]

foolish over See **foolish about.**

fool off on *verb phrase* To ridicule, make fun of (something).

2009 Burton *Beech Mt Man* 12 He started foolin' off on my name—I don't know why he got so mad.

fool out See **fool away.**

fool up *verb phrase* To deceive, trick.

1983 *Dark Corner OHP-5A* You can't go up there and dig it [= a spent artillery shell] up in them mountains, come down, and fool these people up. **1983** McDermitt *Boy Named Jack* 11 It was Jack just fooled him up. **2008** Salsi *Ray Hicks* 74 Tootsie could figure how to get the boys in trouble any time she felt like it. All the while, she was actin' innocent and foolin' up the adults.

fool with *verb phrase* To spend or waste time (or to cause to spend or waste time) with (an activity, person, or concern considered to be of little consequence).

1863 Rector *CW Letters* (May 20) a man was fooling with his gun last night drunk the pin went off shot him through the body he died immediately after he was shot. **1956** Hall *Coll* (Byrds Creek NC) They wouldn't fool with you. . . . Me and ever'body else went to foolin' with [moonshining]. **1974** Dabney *Mt Spirits* 14 I fooled with whiskey from the age of sixteen till I was nineteen. Quit foolin' with it when I got another job. **1992** Joslin *Mt People II* 158 We fool with this here mill and raise some garden. We can still work pretty good.

foot *noun*

A variant plural form *foot* (following a numeral or other quantifier), *feets.*

1939 Hall *Coll* (Hartford TN) I saw something step in the branch, looked to be four or five foot long, way long something. **1975** Dwyer *Thangs* 33 Double plurals—quite common in mountain speech . . . "Please scrape off your feets." **1978** Reese *Speech NE Tenn* 165 *feets.* **1989** *Matewan OHP-11* The station I presume was about maybe a hundred and fifty foot from one end and the other. **1998** *Dante OHP-51* It was about a thirty-degree incline down, about four hundred foot underground, the dump where they dumped the coal.

B Senses.

1 The main cutting unit of a plow. See **double-foot plow, high foot plow, low foot plow, single foot, three-foot(ed) plow.**

1966 Guthrie *Corn* 87 The simplest plow was the *bull-tongue.* This was made either by the farmer himself or by a neighboring blacksmith. It had a wooden *beam* or *tongue,* wooden curved handles, and a wooden *foot* with a wide iron *point* attached. **1977** Shackelford et al. *Our Appalachia* 126 My daddy made his plow stock hisself. He'd go to the woods and stay gone all day till he'd find enough timber that would be crooked enough to make the handles of the plow. And then he'd find the beam for the plow and a piece to make the foot to put the plow on. **1996–97** Montgomery *Coll* (known to Adams, Brown, Cardwell, Jones, Ledford, Norris).

[DARE *foot* n C3 chiefly southern Appalachians]

2 The last quarter of the lunar cycle.

1981 GSMNP-122 There's the best time to plant, on the foot of the moon, when the sign's in the thighs. That's an awful good time.

foot adze *noun* A long-handled implement with a wide metal blade set at a right angle to the handle, used for chipping, shaping, and smoothing the surface of wood, especially in fashioning **puncheons**, floors, and benches.

1915 Dingus *Word-List VA* 183 = adze. **1937** Hall *Coll* (Emerts Cove TN) [A] foot adze or adze made puncheon floors, smooth[ed] puncheon floors until after the Civil War. **1953** Hall *Coll* (Bryson City NC) They crossed the river at that time in canoes, dugout canoes, cut out of trees. They'd cut down a poplar tree and dig it out with a foot adze and a axe and make a canoe out of it. **1995** Trout *Historic Buildings* 26 Puncheons were used where sawn lumber or nails were not yet available. The workman would split a short log, in the manner of a hot dog roll, and lay the halves from joist to joist, round side down. The roughly flat upper surfaces would then be dressed with a foot adze or ax until smooth enough to eliminate toe-catching edges and large splinters.

[perhaps from the motion of the instrument toward one's feet when being used, or from the shape of the instrument's head; DARE chiefly South Midland, West]

footback in phrase *on footback:* On foot. See also **go footback.**

1867 Harris *Sut Lovingood* 60 He wer a mighty mean Yankee rayshure grinder, what wunst cum tu Knoxville a footback, wif a mercheen strapt ontu his shoulders like ontu a patent cornsheller. **c1940** Aswell *Glossary TN Idiom* 8 = on foot. "I'm going to town on *footback.*" **1952** Wilson *Folk Speech NC* 542 *go on footback* = to walk. **1997** Montgomery *Coll* (known to Brown, Bush, Cypher).

[by facetious analogy with *on horseback;* DARE *footback* adv especially South Midland]

footbridge *noun* A log pedestrian bridge over a stream, **puncheons**, or other wooden components. See also **footlog.**

1904 Johnson *Highways South* 134 In mid-creek a log was lodged and served as a support for a plank extending to it from either shore. I went over to the dwelling by this plank footbridge. **1939** Hall *Coll* (Smokemont NC) They come a big rain and washed the old foot bridge plumb into the hallway between the barns. **1939** Wilburn *Notes* I built a foot bridge just above the old ford. **1973** Foster *Walker Valley* 9:94 We used the old footbridge, the old bridge down there till Little River got to wanting the cables for to take to skid with 'em somewhere. **1987** Davenport *Pine Grove* 16 At practically all fords, there were cable suspension foot bridges, commonly called swinging bridges. They also went the way of the abandoned fords. Kids would do all sorts of didos on those bridges. Bouncing up and down and swinging sideways rhythmically would set in motion to produce a thrilling experience.

footercooter *verb* To waste time, work lazily or ineffectually.

2000 Morgan *Mts Remember* 78 Then Myrt would find us and tell her to quit footercootering and bring the water on up to the house here [because] they was about to boil some corn.

[cf HT *footer* v "work or handle in an ineffectual, lazy or absent-minded way"]

foot in hand, take one's *verb phrase* To set out walking.

1859 Taliaferro *Fisher's River* 73 I tuck my foot in my hand and walked all the way back to Old Bucksmasher. **1952** Wilson *Folk Speech NC* 542 *foot, to take (one's)—in (one's) hand* = to depart, to set out walking. **1997** Montgomery *Coll* (known to Bush).

[SND (at *fit* n[1] 28); DARE (at *foot* C5a) South, South Midland]

foot it *verb* Of a person: to hasten on foot.

1863 (Feb 18) next morning we got out & footed it down to Hanover & took the Cars for Guinea Station. **1940** Haun *Hawk's Done* 46 Ad left Old Maud for her to ride when she got ready to come and he footed it on back. *Ibid.* 150 Wilbur didn't wait for school to be out that evening. He come a-footing it on in home.

footlog *noun* A simple hewn-log bridge over a stream. See also **footbridge.**

1883 Zeigler and Grosscup *Heart of Alleghanies* 292 Where the road comes down to its fords under the concealing chestnuts and oaks, long foot-logs reach from bank to bank. **1901** Harben *Westerfelt* 23 Sally fell off'n the foot-log into the creek this mornin' an' was drowned. **1956** Hall *Coll* (Gatlinburg TN) He was crossin' a foot log over a small creek. . . . [When something scared him] he said he gave a leap off of the foot log and started runnin'. **c1960** Wilson *Coll* = a log, hewn or not, across a stream to accommodate pedestrians. **1991** Thomas *Sthn Appal* 101 They had what they called little foot-logs. They'd walk that foot-log, across a creek ur branch. They didn't have no bridges ur nothin' like that then.

[Web3 *footlog* n chiefly Midland and West; DARE *footlog* n chiefly South, South Midland]

foot mile *noun* A mile traveled by foot.

1979 Carpenter *Walton War* 93 Living many weary foot-miles from his work, he was away from home from before dawn until after dark at his ten hour a day job—ofttimes was required to stay away overnight. **1995–97** Montgomery *Coll* (known to Brown, Bush, Cardwell).

foot washer *noun* A Primitive Baptist.

1997 Montgomery *Coll* (known to Ellis).

foot washing *noun* A ritual in which church members (especially Primitive Baptists) wash one another's feet as a sign of humility, in conformity with Jesus' washing of his disciples' feet on the evening before his arrest and crucifixion (John 13:14). Same as and more common than **feet washing.** See 1924 citation. See also **foot-washing meeting.**

1895 *Mt Baptist Sermon* 15 Wy, the Babtists over in Laurel thar aroun' me is gettin' too stuck up to wash one another's feet. They uster hev foot-washin' reg'lar. But now I hev to go over into Whitley to get my feet washed. **1924** Raine *Saddlebags* 201–2 The "good old Baptis'" churches still practice foot washing. If the ceremony is to take place in the church-house, the church-members are invited to come forward to the front benches. The Elder (as they usually call the ministers) takes the basin and towel and begins the ceremony by washing the feet of some of the men, they in turn washing others. The women wash each other's feet. Sometimes for this ordinance the congregation goes to the edge of a near-by creek and the rite is performed with less ceremony. **1968** Clarke *Stuart's Kentucky* 76 Not all mountain churches practiced footwashing, not even all Mountain Baptist churches; but among those who practiced it, the ceremonial was significant and private. **1979** *Preacher Cook* 199–200 We had some modern preachers that objected to a foot-washing church being taken into the Association. *Ibid.* 202 = a practice that is patterned after New Testament scripture. It is an expression of humility and love and usually is done in conjunction with the Lord's Supper. **1995** McCauley *Mt Religion* 102 Footwashing is today widely practiced in many traditions identified with the Appalachian region, although with varying schedules of frequency. **1995** Patterson *Sound of Dove* 6 For the foot washing that follows [Communion], they distribute small basins of water and long "towels" made of cotton cloth that can be tied around the waist, leaving the hands free. Men are paired with men, women with women. Without speaking, they take turns washing each other's feet in a simple act that symbolizes humility and expresses bonds of Christian love. **1995–97** Montgomery *Coll* (known to Brown), = nowadays held only by Primitive Baptists (Cardwell). **1997** GSMNPCOHP-3:13 On Sunday morning after the revival was to end they was going to have a foot washing. **1999** Schwartz *Holiness Believers* 24 He looks up at me and says, "Foot washing teaches us humility. Would you like to join us?"

[DARE *foot washing* n chiefly South Midland]

foot-washing Baptist *noun* Same as **Primitive Baptist.**

1886 Smith *Southernisms* 38 I heard . . . a "foot-washing" Baptist preacher . . . say, "Stone is the most lastiest . . . material there is." **1949** Marshall *Squire Jim* 59 [He] was a church man, a Foot-washing Baptist, and a man of deep convictions.

foot-washing meeting *noun* A church service at which **foot washing** is practiced.

1931 Burns *Coves Blount Co* 55 In the years prior to the Civil War there was nothing of an exciting or spectacular nature other than . . . the annual sacramental or footwashing meetings of the old Baptist church to which people came from as far away as Dumplin in Jefferson County. **1967** Hall *Coll* (Townsend TN) They have their sacrament meetin', their footwashin' meetin' there at the Baptist Church in Cades Cove. **1976** GSMNP-114:8 He'd come off and spent the weekend [at] some foot-washin' meetin' over there in Cades Cove.

for[1] See **fire.**

for[2] See also **for to.**

A *adverb, preposition variant forms fer, fur.*

1861 Shipman *CW Letters* (Sept 22) pay Jack five dolers fer me.

1864 *Apperson CW Letters* (Jan 6) I would rether bee at home with you then any person in this world fer I dont git nothen her[e] to eat. **1864** *Chapman CW Letters* (July 20) I have been wating on him fur better than two weak. **1942** Hall *Phonetics Smoky Mts* 34 For is almost always [fɝ] stressed, [fɚ] unstressed. **1969** GSMNP-37 I take water in there and sprinkle that ever day till it [= an ear of corn] sprouts, whenever it come through the sack about that fer. **1974** *AOHP/ASU-204* [The land] is in my granddaddy's name. Nobody's got a deed fer hit excepting him, and he's been dead for forty-seven years. **1981** GSMNP-117:25 They was all Primitive Baptist and Missionary Baptist, I mean as fer as religious matters was concerned. **1997** GSMNPCOHP He gave my daddy some pills, but I don't know what they were fer.

B *preposition* Senses.

1 Because of, on account of.

1939 Hall *Coll* I couldn't see across that log for the fog. *Ibid.* (Cades Cove TN) We'd eat bear meat until you couldn't dress for it.

2 In phrases *be for, be in for* = ready or eager for, in favor of.

1894 Wingfield *Big Buck* 400 I was in for going to camp and coming back in the morning after the game. **1939** Hall *Coll* (Deep Creek NC) He was in for going and I told him, I said "Doc, you'd better stay out of there." **1953** Hall *Coll* (Plott Creek NC) Now when [the dogs] begin to strike a hot trail, it seems that these [Plott hounds] get mad, and they're in for killing as soon as they can get there. **1990** Clouse *Wilder* 122 Let's be for climbing down from there now and leave the man be.

[CUD *for (doing something)* "intending, proposing (to do something)"]

3 Without.

1852 *Carson Letter* 146 Well John I had better try to tell you something about our trip out hear if I can do it for swearing.

for all *conjunctive phrase* Even though.

1951 Giles *Harbin's Ridge* 154 For all he hadn't liked the ridge school, [it] seemed like he realized what he'd be missing.

forbid *verb* variant past-tense and past-participle form *forbid*.

c1950 Adams *Grandpap* 78 She couldn't keep her mind off'n that room that he'd forbid her to go in. **2004** Fisher *Kettle Bottom* 60 Daddy forbid us to go in under there looking for her.

force put *noun* A necessity, an unavoidable action.

1976 Still *Pattern of Man* 61 If it comes to a force put, I'll forge a pair of shoes for her [= a mare] my own self.

[OED3 *forceput* n now dialect]

for certain (also *for sure*) *predicate adjective phrase* Certain, sure (usually in negative constructions).

1940 Hall *Coll* (White Oak NC) I ain't for sure. **c1950** Adams *Grandpap* 31 When she seed that he was for sure a-goin', she forgot all about a-bein' afraid of the strange men. **1973** GSMNP-2:8 I'm not for sure, but I think his brother's name was Andy. **1983** Pyle *CCC 50th Anniv* A:2:5 I ain't for sure, but I believe Herb Clabo was in the CCs. **1985** Irwin *Alex Stewart* 270 It seemed like they was horse leather, but I can't be for sure. **2001** House *Clay's Quilt* 201 I'm not for certain you're ready to settle down. **2015** Holbrook *Something* 166 She was not for sure how much he was awake yet.

forebay *noun* See citation.

1944 Hayes *Word-List NC* 34 = the end of the sluice where the water meets the mill wheel.

fore-handed (also *front-handed*) *adjective* Forthright, honest; prudent, foresightful.

1955 Washburn *Country Doctor* 42 To be forehanded—to be saving. **1979** Carpenter *Walton War* 175 He wuz a man that wuz always fore handed. **1995–97** Montgomery *Coll* = not beating around the bush, up front with the truth, not passing the buck (Brown), = honest, forthright (Bush), = forthright, honest, trustworthy (Cardwell), = straight-forward, saying what one thinks (Hooper), = wise, always thinking things through before acting (Norris). **2007** McMillon *Notes* (also *front-handed*) = open and straightforward, always with one's hands out in front where they can be seen.

[OED3 *fore-handed* adj 2a "prudent, thrifty" now only U.S.]

foreign *adjective*

A variant form *furrin*.

1867 Harris *Sut Lovingood* 63 Bake, instid ove duin better, got wus—sot intu readin in sum furrin tung, sorter like Cherokee, wif a sprinkil ove Irish. **1942** Hall *Phonetics Smoky Mts* 33.

[DARE *foreign* adj (pronc) especially southern Appalachians]

B Originating from outside the mountains or the local vicinity (i.e., not necessarily coming from another country) and unfamiliar and not necessarily sympathetic with mountain ways.

1908 Fox *Lonesome Pine* 292 She had shaken down her beautiful hair and drawn it low over her brows, and arranged it behind after the fashion of mountain women, and when she went up the steps of the porch she was outwardly to the eye one of them except for the leathern belt about her slenderly full waist, her black silk stockings and the little "furrin" shoes. **1960** Hall *Smoky Mt Folks* 32 In view of the usual meaning which "foreign" (usually pronounced "furrin") acquired in the mountains (that is, "distant," and not necessarily "over the ocean"), it was impossible to learn from him whether his father was an early immigrant to the United States or merely moved to Cades Cove from some other region like Virginia or South Carolina. **1966** Cox *Dialect Scott Co TN* 47 The Southern Mountain dialect speaker is slow to adopt words of furrin (foreign) origin, and by furrin he means anything alien to his mountain world. **1981** Alderman *Tilson Mill* 24 Too often the "foreign" preacher sent in from the urban center would try to bring to the mountaineers some new religious ideas that were foreign to their nature.

[EDD *foreign* adj 1 "not local, not from the immediate neighborhood" general dialect use in Scot, Irel, Engl; CUD *foreigner* (at *foreign* n 2) "a stranger . . . someone from a different district"]

foreigner *noun*

A variant forms *ferriner* [see **1957** in **B**], *foriner* [see **2009** Fields in **B**], *furriner* [see forms in **B**].

1915 Dingus *Word-List VA* 183 *furriner.*

B One native to or originating from beyond the mountains or the local vicinity (i.e., not necessarily from another country) and unfamiliar and not necessarily sympathetic with local mountain ways. See also **flatlander, Flordy dude, Floridiot, Floron, half back, outlander, outsider.**

1883 Zeigler and Grosscup *Heart of Alleghanies* 249 Wal, stranger—I reckon you's a furriner—I kin do hit, but I'm powerful tired: worked all day. **1895** Edson and Fairchild *TN Mts* 371 *furriner* = persons not living in the vicinity. **1904–20** Kephart *Notebooks* 4:763 In the same spirit, the man who rejects the appellation of "mountaineer," or something vaguely derogative that the "furriners" have invented, will call himself a "hill-billy" or a "mountain boomer." **1908** Fox *Lonesome Pine* 2 For many days now she had heard stories of the "furriners" who had come into those hills and were doing strange things down there, and so at last she had climbed up through the dewy morning from the cove on the other side to see the wonders for herself. **1908** Smith *Reminiscences* 427 "There's a power o' people coming in ev'y summer," said old Burt Chrisson, the hunter; "furriners from ev'ywher'. They come from as fur as Richmond, Virginia." **1913** Kephart *Our Sthn High* 16 The mountaineers of the South are marked off from all other folks by dialect, by customs, by character, by self-conscious isolation. So true is this that they call all outsiders "furriners." **1916** Schockel *KY Mts* 107 Between 1830 and 1850 the four interstate roads declined gradually to a wretched condition and state of non-use; for the Blue Grass and Ohio regions were finding other routes to market, by use of steamboats, etc. Therefore the mountain counties lost their market and received little outside help for roads. As a result, these peoples, who have never been able to travel freely among themselves within their mountains, have since about 1815 suffered the further handicap of being cut off from the outside world, and have lived in surprisingly complete isolation. Presently the civilization of the rest of the Americans changed, and they became "foreigners" to the mountain folk. Thus the mountaineers have lived isolated by topography and social antipathy. **1933** Thomas *Traipsin' Woman* 15 It would be a long and silent journey, I feared, to the countyseat twenty miles away. Silent, for not only was I a lone traveler, but I had been cautioned by those who knew that a "furriner from the level land" (as we from the valleys were sometimes called) was to ask no questions, show no surprise at the way things were said, and evidence no concern over the way things were done in the mountains of Kentucky. Once a newcomer proved himself worthy of confidence, mountain folk were friendly enough and they would talk, too, if they were so inclined. But the "furriner" had best keep quiet. **1937** Thornburgh *Great Smoky Mts* 13 The mountain people are proud, independent, yet sensitive and afraid that outsiders—"furriners"—will make fun of their ways. . . . Their seeming stolidity deceives many who make a brief stay in the mountains and return to their desks in the cities and write stupid things about them. **1957** Combs *Lg Sthn High: Word List* 20 *furriner* = an outsider. Used especially to differentiate a lowlander from a mountaineer. For example, one may be from Louisville, but to the Highlander he is not a citizen. However, a North Carolina Highlander is to the Kentucky Highlander a citizen. The resident of Louisville is termed a ferriner. **1965** *Dict Queen's English* 11 *furriner* = a foreigner or stranger. Used primarily in mountain regions to designate someone from outside the community. "He's a *furriner* from the lowlands." **1968** Wilson *Folklore Mammoth Cave* 39 Most of the preachers were local, but occasionally a "furriner," that is, a man from another part of the county or from a neighboring county, came in to preach and enjoy the hospitality of the brethren and sisters. **1975** *AOHP/ALC-1128A* They always want to go back to the country, because they'd been breathing, and they wanted to be free. They always had wanted to be a free people. Well, [when] people would come in and try to intrude on them too much, they'd call him "foreigner." [When] somebody come from the outside, even though it was another state, they'd say, "I don't want no truck with a foreigner, because he's not my kind of people." **1989** Landry *Smoky Mt Interviews* 191 If you didn't live no further away than Knoxville, you was a foreigner. **2004** Larimore *Bryson Seasons* 54 It could be the president of the garden club or a new developer in the area who was trying to attract foreigners—our name for rich folks from Florida who knew neither how to drive on mountain roads nor the true value of mountain property (as they always paid way over market value). They clogged our roads in the summer and ran up our property prices in the spring and fall. Then they abandoned us for the winter. **2006** *Encycl Appalachia* 229 In the Appalachian vernacular, the term *furriner* (for "foreigner") denotes not just a person from a foreign country, but also one from another state, county, or any place not local and well known. Even if a furriner arrives in a mountain area when young and stays a lifetime, his or her status as an outsider is never entirely forgotten, though it may become the subject of good-natured humor. . . . More recent terms have been invented for specific groups of furriners and find usage in either joking or serious connotation. In western North Carolina, where furriners in increasing numbers retire, vacation, or construct summer houses, the terms *floridiot* and *half back* came into usage in the late twentieth century. **2009** Fields *Growing Up* 36 Them foriner fellers up there in the north shore did make a lot of good guns. **2009** Miller *Nigh Gone* 150 His experience with the federal programs created to protect, preserve, and transform his cherished mountains have given him cause in his own mind to be wary of the "furriners." When Uncle Sam came in proposing to improve his life and habitat, it would always raise the mountaineer's unbridled, independent spirit. The native viewed these outsiders in terms of how they impacted his personal life, home, and property. Many were not concerned with how this activity could save the region's scenic and natural resources from exploitation and destruction.

[OED3 *foreigner* n "one of another county, parish, etc., a stranger, outsider, little-known person"]

foreman *noun* variant plural forms *foremans, foremens.*

1939 Hall *Coll: foremans.* **1975** *AOHP/ALC-961* They [= the miners] took an oath to run off one of the foremens of the name Bill Hicks. **1980** *GSMNP-115:50* A lot of the foremans that worked for the CC[C] stayed here with daddy. **1989** *Matewan OHP-18* They always needed foremans, and quick as they got a opening, why then I'd take that place. **1998** *Dante OHP-61* They went in there and them foremans tried to outdo the other man. Ever foreman tried to get more coal than the other one.

foremans, foremens See **foreman**.

foreparent *noun* An ancestor. See also **back parent, forepeople.**

1913 Kephart *Our Sthn High* 355 My foreparents war principally Scotch. **1937** Haun *Cocke Co* 2 My foreparents have lived, farmed, and sung these songs since the county was formed. **1957** GSMNP-23:2:16 My foreparents was in George Washington's day. **1994** Montgomery *Coll* = more common than *ancestors*, the latter being a book term (Cardwell). **1997** Miller *Brier Poems* 61 Our foreparents left us a home here in the mountains, but we try to live in somebody else's house. . . . Our foreparents left us a very fine inheritance, but we don't believe it. **2012** Milnes *Signs Cures Witchery* She learned it from old people, her ancestors, including her Swiss and German foreparents.

[DARE *foreparent* n chiefly South Midland]

fore part *noun phrase* The earlier, front, first (half). See also **after C.**

1862 Kiracofe *CW Letters* (May 6) we have been marching pretty mutch all the time since I wrote to you last which was sometime the fore part of last week. **1915** Dingus *Word-List VA* 183 *fore part* = the early part, as the forepart of the day. **1926** Hunnicutt *Twenty Years* 65 A fox always comes down in the fore part of the night. **1983** Broaddus *Estill Co KY Word List* 39 *fore part of the night* = from suppertime to bedtime or midnight. **1989** Landry *Smoky Mt Interviews* 181 Those big possums wouldn't come out in the fore part of the night. They'd come out in the after part. **1993** Ison and Ison *Whole Nother Lg* 23 = front, being first, or early, as in the "fore part" of the night.

forepeople *noun* Ancestors. See also **back parent, foreparent.**

1978 Hiser *Quare Do's* 66 All we knowed for sure about our fore-people was they come from Virginia into Buncombe County, North Carolina.

foreses See **forest.**

foreshortly *adverb* See citation.

1957 Combs *Lg Sthn High: Word List* 40 = immediately, at once.

foreshot *noun* See citation.

1972 Carr *Oldest Profession* 78 A veteran moonshiner can hear the creeping vapor as it starts through the still, and he waits for the first sign of passage through the worm, called the "foreshot." **1974** Dabney *Mt Spirits* xxi = the first whiskey to come out of a condenser at the beginning of a run. **2007** Rowley *Moonshine!* 161 = the first sputters of poisonous liquid that emerge from the condenser at the beginning of a run, high in fusel alcohol and undesirable congeners such as methanol. Must be discarded.

forest *noun* variant plural form as three syllables: *for-es-es.*

1994 Landry *Coll* We'd take axes and things and clear the foreses to make new ground to plant corn next year.

forestick *noun* A log put at the front of the fireplace, one smaller than the backlog and placed on the andirons if they were present. Also called **front stick.** See also **backstick.**

1848 (in **1870** Drake *Pioneer Life KY* 107) In the morning, a buckeye backlog and hickory forestick resting on stone and irons, with a Johnny-cake on a clean ash-board set before it to bake. **1927** Woofter *Dialect from WV* 354 *forestick* = a small log placed in the front of a wood fire. "Those foresticks were cut too long." **1931** Combs *Lg Sthn High* 1306 Ed, go out an' snake a back-log an' a fore-stick in. **1948** Chase *Grandfather Tales* 4 Tom took hold of the poker and pushed the forestick against the backlog. **a1975** Lunsford *It Used to Be* 6 I've been to places where they'd get up, rake the live coals in the old fireplace out a little closer to the front and put in a large backlog,—and I mean a large one. Then the forestick was put on, then some smaller kindling down between the forestick and the backstick. **1986** Pederson et al. *LAGS:* = attested by 9/60 interviewees (15%) from E TN; 9/14 of all LAGS interviewees (64.2%) attesting term were from Appalachia.

[OED3 *forestick* n 1 U.S.]

forethoughted *adjective* Foresighted, marked by forethought.

1961 Murry *Salt* 63 A forethoughted man.

foretop *noun* A forelock of a person or horse.

1927 Woofter *Dialect from WV* 354 = the hair between the ears of the horse. **c1960** Wilson *Coll* = a lock of hair on front of head.

forever *adverb* variant syntactic position within the predicate.

1860 *Week in Smokies* 125 I do declare I believe a body might larn a lawyer something, if he would only use his own eyes and sense, and not be forever gwine to his books to ax them everything. **1940** Haun *Hawk's Done* 29 I was forever telling Amy to take her out into the yard. **1974** *No Sang* 8 People are forever trying to fool them by mixing the two kinds of roots together. **1991** Haynes *Haywood Home* 36 Shoe buttons were forever catching in the hems of these skirts and causing all kinds of problems. **1997** Montgomery *Coll* He is forever talking about how sorry his young'uns are (Andrews). **1997** Nelson *Country Folklore* 92 We were forever stepping on glass and nails. **1998** Dante *OHP*-58 They was forever borrowing our hammer.

foreverlasting *adverb* Always, for all time.

1940 Haun *Hawk's Done* 45 He was foreverlasting fussing about us not keeping the house clean. **1994** Montgomery *Coll* (known to Shields).

fore-yard *noun* The front yard.

1945 Thomas *Mt Folk* 49 Pa, you don't need to look further than your fore-yard. **1995–97** Montgomery *Coll* (known to Brown, Cardwell, Oliver).

forgave See **forgive 2.**

forgenst (also *forginst*) *preposition* Against.

1919 Combs *Word-List South* 33 *forgenst* = against: "Over forgenst the mountain." **1972** Carson and Vick *Cookin* 2 13 Forginst the church graveyard was a grassy plot where women folks would spread their table cloths on the grass after the mornin preachin.

[cf DOST *forgane* prep "over against"; Web3 *forgainst* preposition, chiefly Scotland]

forget *verb*

1 variant base forms *fergit, forgit.*

1867 Harris *Sut Lovingood* 95 Now don't forgit that about that hos' thar wer a good time bein had ginerally. **1925** (in **1935** Edwards *NC Novels* 68) *fergit.* **c1940** Padelford *Notes* I don't reckon the larnin' hurts 'em none—they soon fergit it all.

2 variant past-participle forms *fergit, forgot.*

1774 *Dunmore's War* 205 I hope he has not forgot to inform you about them. **1791** (in **1941** Rothert *McDowell Letters* 176) If Billey had ever told me of it I had totaly forgot. **1835** Click *Departed Voice* we all are living and not forgot them and wants them to let us all know how all friends and acquaintances are doing. **1864** *Chapman CW Letters* (May 14) a few lines from William Evans he says he hant forgot you. **1896** Fox *Last Stetson* 205 I hain't fergot how ye kin handle a gun. **1939** Hall *Coll* (Hazel Creek NC) I ain't forgot that never. **1969** GSMNP-44:20 There was several from Tennessee. I've forgot their names. **1978** Montgomery *White Pine Coll* II-3 I've done forgot what they call theirself. **1979** Slone *My Heart* 18 He axed Vince did he recollect him, and he said yeah, he had never fergit him. **1983** Pyle *CCC 50th Anniv* B:6:42 I believe his last name was Hall. I've forgot his last name. **1994** Montgomery *File* Dolly [Parton] is one person that hasn't forgot her raisin' (65-year-old man, Gatlinburg TN). **1998** *Dante OHP*-58 I never have forgot it [in Hungarian], "how me to say, can I borrow your hammer?"

forginst See **forgenst**.

forgit See **forget 1**.

forgive *verb* Principal parts.

1 variant past-tense forms *fergive, forgive.*

1875 *Tuckaleechee Cove Church Minutes* 27 She made Confession of her fault and the Church forgive her. **1896** Fox *Last Stetson* 196 He fergive 'em while they was doin' it. Thet's whut got me. **2004** Adams *Old True Love* 268 He forgive him. Took him in his old arms and loved him.

2 variant past-participle forms *forgave, forgive.*

1874 *Tuckaleechee Cove Church Minutes* 23 Sisters Sarah Abbott & Margaret Franklin volentary confess their faults to the Church & were forgive. *Ibid.* 24 Sister Jane Myrs confessed her faults to the Church for some imprudent conduct of hers & was forgave. **1938** (in **2009** Powell *Shenandoah Letters* 144) Tell them to see that my boy is forgive for This Time for being in co with this other boy. **1972** GSMNP-73:48 The Lord's forgive me, and I think you folks ought to forgive me. **1989** Giardina *Storming Heaven* 42 What if I'd missed? I'd never have forgive myself. **1998** *Dante OHP*-25 He said, "I know I ain't lived right, but," he said, "the Lord's forgive me."

forgot See **forget 2**.

foriner See **foreigner**.

fork *noun*

1 One of two or more tributaries meeting to form a watercourse of varying size; also used in place-names, as in *Bradley Fork* (NC).

1939 Hall *Coll* (Deep Creek NC) The bear and dogs crossed to the other fork of the river . . . they went on up the left hand fork of the creek. . . . I heard the dogs a-barking right in at the head of the right hand fork of the left hand fork of Deep Creek. **1956** Fink *That's Why* 4 Fork and prong generally have added the name of the larger stream of which it is tributary, as West Prong of the Little Pigeon River, or Straight Fork of Oconaluftee River. **1963** Lord *Blue Ridge* 43D "Prong" and "fork" are descriptive names applied to many mountain streams. Their course is swift and straight, and they merge into each other at a sharp angle. Prongs are generally smaller streams and join into forks. **1974** GSMNP-50:2:5 One was on the left hand fork, one on the middle fork, one on the right hand fork. **1989** *Matewan OHP*-9 We lived up in the head of this creek, the left fork of Blackberry [Creek]. **1996** Linn *West Fork* 3 The West Fork of the Little Pigeon begins at the juncture of Walker Prong and Road Prong.

2 (usually *forks*, interpreted as singular) The point at which tributaries meet to form a stream or river; the immediate area around this point.

1797 *French Broad Church Minutes* 35 Agreed that our next Association be held at the forkes of little pigeon the Second friday in August 1798 and that Jon Mulkey open the same by Sermon in case of faillure Isaac barton. **1863** *Vance Papers* (Aug 18) I hope you will giv me somthing that I can Stand up to Do I Belong to your old companey I hope you will let me no Dy Rect to the forks of Pidgeon [River] Haywood co[unty]. **1912** De Long *Troublesome* The forks of the Troublesome [are] forty-five miles from the railroad, where neighbors often live "two whoops and a hollo" apart. **1939** Hall *Coll* (Deep Creek NC) I crossed the river and clim out on the opposite side, a half a mile I guess, and heared no dogs, [and] come back in to the forks of the river. *Ibid.* (Smokemont NC) We come to a forks, [and] we took the left-hand fork. **1973** GSMNP-69:30 Well, Old Isaac Trentham used to have a post office right by the forks of the river. That's where Fighting Creek comes into [the] Little Pigeon. **1981** Roth *Greenbrier Early Days* 9 At the forks of the river, there was a store, a grist mill and the old Schooich Lumber Mill. **1985** Reagan *Sugarlands* xiv There was a forks one crossed over the river (wood bridge) and went up the river on the West side through that part of the community.

[DARE *fork* n B1 chiefly South, South Midland]

3 The corner of the mouth.

1939 Hall *Coll* (Deep Creek NC) So pretty soon I seed just [the bear's] nose from about the forks of his mouth down.

forked-end *noun* The lower half of the body.

1985 Wiseman *Autobiography* 39 If someone asked her how she was feeling, she usually answered, "I've still got the fork-ed end down and am ready to go."

fork ridge *noun* A ridge between two forks of a stream.

1939 Hall Coll (Deep Creek NC) They turned right back down the Big Wooly Head Ridge, the fork ridge between the two forks of the left-hand fork of Deep Creek. **1969** GSMNP-37:2:13 I come back and hit the fork ridge and come in here.

forks See **fork 2**, **3**.

form thing *noun* The least thing, anything.

1952 Wilson *Folk Speech NC* 542 I don't owe him a form thing. **c1960** Wilson Coll She didn't do the first form thing to help Aunt Mary with the washing . . . Didn't do a form thing.

[DARE at *first form thing* n phr chiefly Midland]

fornent *preposition*

A variant forms *fernenst* [see **1964** in **B**], *fernent* [see **1886** in **B**], *fernenth* [see **a1975** in **B**], *ferninst* [see **1960** in **B**], *fernint* [see **1937** in **B**], *forninst* [see **1911** in **B**], *fornint* [see **1952** in **B**], *furninst* [see **1867** in **B**].

B Alongside, close to; in front of, up against, beneath, opposite (to).

1835 Crockett *Account* 123 I walked with them to a room nearly fornent the old state-house. **1867** Harris *Sut Lovingood* 58 As I started, a black bottil ove bald-face smashed agin a tree furninst me, arter missin the top ove my head 'bout a inch. **1886** Smith *Sthn Dialect* 349 They all have the authority of old or dialect English, or many of them belong to all parts of the South, if not elsewhere . . . fernent (opposite). **1904–20** Kephart *Notebooks* 4:749 Just afore it got quite fernent me, I shot. **1911** Shearin *E KY Word-List* 538 *forninst* = near to, adjoining. **1913** Kephart *Our Sthn High* 280 Since the Appalachian people have a marked Scotch-Irish strain, we would expect their speech to show a strong Scotch influence. So far as vocabulary is concerned, there is really little of it. A few words, caigy (cadgy), coggled, fernent, gin for if, needcessity, trollop, almost exhaust the list of distinct Scotticisms. **1937** Hall Coll (Hartford TN) I crawled down through the alders by the river till I got fernint [a bear], and then I laid off my linen and swum across the river. **1939** Hall Coll (Cosby TN) He lived over fernint the store. *Ibid.* The bear went up a tree ferninst us. **1952** Wilson *Folk Speech NC* 542 *fornent*, *fornint*, prep. and adv. = opposite, in front of. **1960** Hall *Smoky Mt Folks* 9 He "clim" the tree "ferninst" the place where the animal was clinging, and "onbeknownst" to the bear, prepared to shoot it. **1964** Williams *Prep Mt Speech* 54 A few rare prepositions may be heard occasionally . . . Fernenst means in front of and close by at the same time but not as close as against. **1966–69** *DARE Survey* (Pensacola NC, Gatlinburg TN, Jonesborough TN, Rogersville TN) *fernent* = opposite to; (Adams KY, London KY, Warm Springs VA) *ferninst* = opposite to; (Maryville TN) *fernint* = close to, only a short distance away from. **a1975** Lunsford *It Used to Be* 174 "Fernenth" means beyond and opposite, as "Look yonder fernenth that sassafras and find my mattock." **2015** Jones *Tintagel* 54 The castle ruin, a long way down / fornent the treacherous promontory / of the relentless, pulsing sea.

[ultimately < *fore* adv + *anent*; OED3 *fornent*, *fornenst* prep 1 "right opposite to, over against, facing" Scot and north; EDD *forenent* prep Scot, Irel, nEngl; CUD *forenent* (at *fore* adv) "opposite, in front of; over against"; HT *fornenst* "facing, directly opposite"; Web3 *fornent* prep "in front of; near to" chiefly dialect; DARE *fornent* prep 1 chiefly Midland]

forninst, **fornint** See **fornent**.

forrard, **forrid** See **forward(s)**.

for sure See **for certain**.

for to *infinitive phrase* See also Grammar and Syntax §10.1. See also **for**[2].

1 (+ *verb*, in an adverbial clause expressing purpose) In order to.

1774 *Dunmore's War* 204 It was some Bacon that was kept in reserve, for to carry out in case of a pursuit, and for the use of the Spys. **1785** *Bent Creek Church Minutes* 5 Tidence Lane was chosen by the church and desired some time for to consider on the call. **1815** (in **1920** DeWitt *Sevier Journal* 58) (June 29) It is said that the goods is since ordered to be given over to Genl. Jackson for to be distributed as presents. **1833** *Paw Paw Hollow Church Minutes* 67 The Baptist Church of Christ at Pappaw hollow met and after worship enquired for the peace and union of the Church and found all in peace then opened a door for to Recive members. **1834** Crockett *Narrative* 62 It was about two weeks after this that I was sent for to engage in a wolf hunt. **1861** Hedgecock *Diary* 107 Great preparations going on for to be ready to march when ordered. **1862** *Warrick CW Letters* (July 29) I seat my self down this eavning for to drop you a few lins to let you no that I am not well. **1866** *Elijoy Church Minutes* 110 Church met after sermon proseeded to business . . . Adopted resolutions for to unite with the postoar church. **1939** Hall Coll (Copeland Creek TN) I had to pick sang and pick up chestnuts for to buy what we had to wear. **1953** Atwood *Verbs East US* 34 *For to tell* occurs in all major portions of the M[iddle] A[tlantic] S[tates]. . . . [I]t is most frequent in W.Va., where it is used by a majority of Type I and Type II informants [i.e. both older speakers with little formal education and younger ones with more formal education]. In the S[outh] A[tlantic] S[tates] as far south as N.C. *for to tell* is used by a little over half of the Type I informants [i.e. older speakers with little formal education], and by a little less than one fourth of the Type II [i.e. younger speakers with more formal education]. **1963** Edwards *Gravel* 18 I didn't come for to eat your dad-blasted hen but if she's well b'ilt and they's plenty of dumplins cooked with her I might take a leetle taste just to see if I remember how chicken tastes. **1972** *AOHP/ALC-276* You had to save your innard from a hog that you didn't use for to make your soap. **1973** Foster *Walker Valley* 9:94 We used the old footbridge, the old bridge down there till Little River got to wanting the cables for to take to skid with 'em somewhere. **1998** *Dante OHP-69* The only time he comes is when he brings his clothes home for to be washed. **2008** *Rosie Hicks* 1 I'd rather for not to see Santa.

[OED3 (at *for* 11a) now archaic or vulgar; CUD *for to* (at *for* 2); cf HT *for till* (at *for*)]

2 To (with no implication of purpose). See also **feel for to**.

1862 Edmonston/Kelly *CW Letters* (Sept 16) it is the gratins pleasure amagionable for to write to you. **1864** Proffit *CW Letters* (June 20) I want for to see you and the children Just as Bad. **1897** *Incidents* 27 My frens, you all can't help ahavin' bad thoughts kum inter yer heads, but ye hain't got no necessity fer ter set 'em a cheer. **1916** Combs *Old Early English* 289 For to is widely used in the Southern Mountains, even when there is no motion implied, or emphasis . . . E.g. (With motion or emphasis implied), "I went for to tell him a piece of my mind!" E.g. (where no motion is implied) "I'm a-goin' for to explain to you," etc. **1991** Thomas *Sthn Appal* 178 Well, now, I've got a little work out here fer t' do. I'll jist hire you to work fer me a while.

3 with an intervening subject, especially following like.

1863 Lister *CW Letters* (Nov 18) you sed you wood like for me to Come home A few days so wood I. **1865** Hill *CW Letters* (Feb 22) we exspect for the yankeys to attact owr men. **1896** Swearingen *Letters* 167 I would like for you to write me again in a few days. **1927** Justus *Peter Pocket* 10 He would like for me to do that, wouldn't he? **1938** Stuart *Dark Hills* 70 I'd like for you to go ahead. **1966** Dykeman *Far Family* 195 I'd like for you to give me help here whenever your time allows. **1972** *AOHP/ALC-355* We'd like for you to do something with these hogs here. **1978** *Horsetrading* 43 Wayne begged for me to take it home with me. **1984** GSMNP-153:12 He told him, said "This fifty-acre tract of land up here is for sale, and I'd like for you to advise me if it's too much."

[DARE *for* prep B3 chiefly South, South Midland]

for true *adverb phrase* For sure.

1949 Arnow *Hunter's Horn* 5 She hid her nest out an has hatched eleven diddles right here, nearly September; frost'll git 'em fer true fore they feather out. **1964** Stubbs *Mountain-Wise* (Feb–March) 8 "Now, I don't know fer true," answered the man next to him, "but I do know one thing fer shore. If he's alive, he's agoin' to die. I don't know when, but when his time comes, he's agoin' to die."

[DARE (at *for* prep B4a(2)) South]

forty-five degrees *noun* See citation. See also **worm fence**.

1915 Dingus *Word-List VA* 183 = [a] galloping fence, a fence of rails set in the ground at about forty-five degrees, crossing each other at the opposite end. Such fences were formerly used on steep hills.

forty-gallon Baptist *noun* A Baptist who espouses the practice of baptism by immersion. See also **five-gallon Baptist**, **half-pint Baptist**.

1940 Stuart *Trees of Heaven* 292 He was kicked out'n the Forty-Gallon-Baptist Church.

forty-rod *noun* Potent homemade whiskey.

c1960 Wilson *Coll* = whiskey of unusual potency. **1991** Miller *Revenuers and Moonshiners* 33 Some of these descriptions fit a beverage called "mountain dew," but others are more appropriate to concoctions denominated "white-lightnin'," "bust-head," "pop-skull," "white-mule" (because of the kick), "red-eye," "forty-rod" (the distance the stuff makes one run before passing out).

forward(s) (also *forrard*, *forrid*) *adjective* Of a crop or growing season: advanced in development, producing early.

1865 *Chapman CW Letters* (May 5) Crops looks very well wheat in per tickler this is a very forwards Spring heare. **1895** Edson and Fairchild *TN Mts* 371 I've got some *forrard* peaches. **1921** Greer-Petrie *Angeline at Seelbach* 11 I had no idea the gyarden in Louisville was so forrid (forward). [**1995** Montgomery *Coll* (unknown to consultants from the Smoky Mountains).]

[OED3 *forward* adj 5b "of a plant, crop, or season: well-advanced, early"]

for why *adverb phrase* Why, for what reason. See also **what for A**, **why for**.

1913 Kephart *Our Sthn High* 297 The speech of the southern highlanders is alive with quaint idioms. "I swapped horses, and I'll tell you fer why." **1931** Combs *Lg Sthn High* 1305 If ye ax (ask) me on it I'll tell ye fer why. **1944** Laughlin *Word-List Buncombe Co* 25 He went downtown. I don't know for why. **1961** Seeman *Arms of Mt* 115 No fox is goin' to ketch this hen, I'll tell you fer why: she's so techious, if she was to hear the least little bit of a fuss, she'd up and sail fer a treetop—jest like a bird. **1974** Fink *Bits Mt Speech* 9 I don't rightly know *for why*.

[OED3 *for why* adv/conj A2 obsolete →1710; CUD *for why* interrog pron; HT; DARE *for why* adv chiefly South Midland]

fotch, **fotched** See **fetch A**.

fotched-on See **fotch-on**.

fotch-on (also *fotched-on*) *adjective* Of a thing: imported to the mountains, bought rather than made, and thus incongruent with mountain ways, impractical, or of inferior quality; hence outlandish. Of a person: coming from outside the mountains, usually with formal education, and thus not informed of or sensitive to mountain ways, "high-falutin'." See also **brought-on 1**, **2**, **store**, **store-bought**.

c1900 (in **1997** Stoddart *Quare Women* 19) The camp [at Cedar Grove KY] became a source of great curiosity and people traveled considerable distances to see the "quare women" or "fotch-on women," as they were often called by the mountaineers. **1911** Shearin *E KY Word-List* 538 *fotch-on*, *fotched-on* = same as *brung-on*. **1913** Kephart *Our Sthn High* 285 Peculiar adjectives are formed from verbs . . . "Damn this fotch-on kraut that comes in tin cans." **1922** Cobb *KY Mt Rhymes* 45 After the quare, fotched-on women came, / (That's how we called the College Ladies then,) / Thar was a sight of passing in and out. **1931** Owens *Speech Cumberlands* 93 *fotched-on* = an article of clothing or the material with which to make it, that has been bought in town: "Liza looks proud o' Jeems in his fotched-in suit o' clothes." **1943** Peattie *Great Smokies* 12 Though a "fotched-on" woman, one who came from the outside, there are few better qualified . . . to tell the tale of mountain ways. **1952** Wilson *Folk Speech NC* 542 *fotched on* = mainly of persons but sometimes of things: not of the community or section; educated; used in contempt. "He's one of them *fotched-on* school-teachers, and knows everything." **1957** Combs *Lg Sthn High: Word List* 41 *fotched-*

on = imported from the Lowlands; "brought-on"; not hand-made. Ex.: "fotched-on" clothes; "fotched-on" or "store" teeth; and even "fotched-on" preachers! A "fotched-on" woman, or lady. **1975** Chalmers *Better* 37 Carding, spinning and dyeing with home made vegetable dyes is not so common in these days when "fotched-on" or store-bought threads are so easy to obtain. **1984** Wilder *You All Spoken* 156 *fotched-on* = outlandish; said of something to be resented or distrusted. **1992** Brooks *Sthn Stuff* 53 *fotched-on* = put-on airs; newly richlike; brought in from another place. "Her an' them fotched-on airs of her'n!" **2006** *Encycl Appalachia* 230 When furrin women such as Katherine Pettit and May Stone from the Bluegrass area of Kentucky approached some areas of the southern Appalachian mountains, residents welcomed their offers to establish settlement schools. These women became known as "fotched-on" women, or women who were "fetched" from a distance to establish educational institutions.

[DARE *fotch-on* ppl adj 2 chiefly South Midland]

fotch up, fotched up See **fetch up 3**.

foughten See **fight 2**.

foul *adjective* Overgrown with weeds. See also **filth**.

1941 Stuart *Men of Mts* 50 Look how foul this corn has gone on me. **1996–98** Montgomery Coll (known to Brown, Bush, Jones), = filled with grass and weeds, needs hoeing (Weaver).

[EDD *foul* adj 3; DARE *foul* adj South Midland]

foulbruting *noun* See citation.

1979 Carpenter *Walton War* 129 "Foulbrutin'" was the job of untangling these log jams on the mountainside.

found See **fine**[2].

foundation(s) *noun* See citation.

1967–69 *DARE Survey* (Wytheville VA) *good foundation*; (Walker KY, Cumberland Gap TN) *big foundations* = a joking name for unusually big or clumsy feet.

founder *noun* A cold.

1861 *Patton CW Letters* (May 26) we have all ben enjoying very good health since we left home except the bowel complaint and a few founders.

[EDD *founder* sb 4 "A catarrh, cold; an illness"]

fount See **find A.**

four paws *noun* See citation.

1964 Clarkson *Lumbering in WV* 261 = two sets of couplers or grabs fastened together with a short chain. Used on exceptionally large logs.

fouter *noun* A despicable person.

1936 Coleman *Dial N GA* 25 "Fouter" means a despicable fellow. The word "foutra"—fig—is a word of contempt. Shakespeare says, "a foutra for the world and worldlings base [in *Henry IV*, Part 2]."

[SND *fouter* n "a hateful, objectionable person"; Web3 *fouter* n "an objectionable person; a worthless person"]

fox and dog(s) (also *fox and hound, fox and hound(s)*) *noun* A children's chasing game in which one child (the fox) usually has a head start and tries to elude the others (the dogs).

1938 Stuart *Dark Hills* 99 When we played Fox and Dog, Big Andy was always the Fox. He could outrun the rest of us over the big meadows on the uplands, through the woods and down the hollows. **1963** Watkins and Watkins *Yesterday* 9 Fox and dog races were the favorite sport. A good runner was picked as the fox, and all the others chased him. The fastest hound always threatened to catch the fox in a short race. Toughened by plowing and hoeing from sunup until sundown, the boys were good runners, and many a chase lasted several miles. The fox who was not caught was a hero. **1968** Clarke *Stuart's Kentucky* 19 Boys' games that usually were too fast or too rough for the girls were Fox and Dog and Buckeyes. The former was an imitation fox chase, with the fastest runner holding the honored title of Fox. The Hounds sometimes chased the Fox over meadows, through woods, and down hollows during the entire lunch hour on school days. **1979** Melton *'Pon My Honor* 7 At Windle school the boys always loved to play Fox and Hound. The boy that was the fastest runner usually got to be the fox, and the rest would be the hounds and chase him. But so as to give the fox a better start, the hounds would always hide their faces so they couldn't tell which way he went. Now running fast wasn't exactly all there was to it, for the fox had to outsmart the hounds, too. So sometimes he'd climb a tree, crawl in a holler log, swing across the gully on a grape vine, or do might nigh anything to throw the hounds off. **1980** Wigginton *Foxfire VI* 284 *fox and hounds* = a rough game usually played just by big boys . . . The fox would start running and try to find a small tree . . . and climb it. The dogs would be chasing him. When they caught up with him and treed him, the person with the ax would come along and chop down the tree. If the fox could get away without getting caught, he'd start running again and climb another tree. **1996** Isbell *Last Chivaree* 59 The game of fox and dogs had been played in Pickbritches long before Ray was born. Typically two or three boys would be foxes; the others would be dogs. The fox would find a tree, usually a sapling that bent just to the right tilt under a boy's weight. The one playing fox would climb up and out on such a hidden sapling. The others would search the woods; they would sniff, bark, and howl just as fox-hunting dogs might. Once they discovered their quarry, they would climb up after the fox, who might jump from tree to tree to avoid his pursuers. If he was trapped in a tree, he would go out as far as he could before turning to fight.

[DARE *fox and hounds* chiefly Midland]

fox and geese *noun* A board game with many geese and one fox, the object being either for the fox to capture geese by jumping them or for the geese to corner the fox.

1976 Braden *Grandma Was Girl* 83 The only game I remember playing in the house was "Fox and Geese." We had our board marked on the bottom of the half-bushel measure, and we played the game with grains of white corn for the geese, and red ones for the foxes. There were two foxes, and, as best I could remember, 14 geese placed on the board. I don't remember which could move first, but the fox could move in any direction, while the geese could only move forward. The aim of the fox was to jump all the geese. The aim of the geese was to corner the fox so he couldn't move. **1977** Stratton *Grassy Cove* 5 When a small boy I would ride a horse to the mill with what we called a "turn of corn" to be ground and while waiting for my turn to come, we boys would parch corn and play "fox and geese" with the red and white grains of corn, like playing checkers. **1980** Wigginton *Foxfire VI* 285 Fox and Geese [was] usually played at the mill while people were waiting to have their corn ground.... The miller was usually the fox and he was usually the winner because he got so much practice at it. **2003** Carter *Mt Home* 138 Daddy made a board game for us on a piece of cardboard called Fox and Geese.

fox and hound(s) See **fox and dog(s)**.

foxfire *noun* A luminescent fungus that grows on rotting wood, especially dogwood; the wood itself. See also **doted**.

1824 (in **1912** Doddridge *Notes on Settlement* 290) If they had seen any thing like fire, between that and the fort, it must have been fox fire. **1885** Murfree *Prophet* 65 A rotting log in the midst of the debris in the stream, in a wild tangle of underbrush and shelving rocks, showed fox-fire and glowed in the glooms. **1890** Fruit *KY Words* 64 = phosphorescent wood seen at night after continued rain. We have an expression, "That is all fox-fire," meaning, of no consequence. **1956** Hall *Coll* (Cosby TN) Fox fire—hit glows of a night, kind of rotten, doty wood. At night it will shine like fire. **1976** Garber *Mountain-ese* 31 What many think is ghosts is jist foxfire on a dotey tree stump. **1995** *Smokies Guide* (Fall) 9 Mountain folk call it foxfire, the fungal strands of certain mushrooms that glow in the dark. The root-like strands penetrate wood and give decaying logs a subtle, greenish light.

[DARE *foxfire* n 1a chiefly South, South Midland]

fox grape *noun* A woody vine (*Vitis labrusca*) that bears small, edible grapes that are green in color but later turn brown. See also **fall grape, possum grape**.

1867 Harris *Sut Lovingood* 208 His eyes wer es big es fox grapes, an' mos' all ove em outside ove his head. **1978** Reese *Speech NE Tenn* 35 = attested by 4/12 (33.3%) speakers. **1984** Smith *Enduring Memories* 41 The fox grapes were larger grapes and almost the size of the tame concord grapes. They too were very spicy but because of the size we ate all we could find. The fox grapes were not as plentiful and when a vine was found we would watch it carefully until the grapes ripened and try to beat the birds or animals to them. **1997** Nelson *Country Folklore* 49 After the frost, fox grapes that grew wild were gathered to make jelly.

foxgrape winter *noun* A period of cold weather in the spring. For terms describing a similar phenomenon, see **blackberry winter**.

1940 Still *River of Earth* 127 "Even come spring," grandma said, "we've got a passel of chills to endure: dogwood winter, redbud, service, foxgrape, blackberry.... There must be seven winters, by count. A chilly snap for every time of bloom." **1941** Still *Troublesome Creek* 37 We hovered to a smidgen of fire. We trembled in the night chill, for it was foxgrape winter.

fox horn *noun* See citations.

1939 Hall *Coll* = a steer's horn used by hunters, especially fox hunters, to call their dogs. **1946** Stuart *Plum Grove Hills* 113 The last spell I took was one night I's out with the men fox huntin'.... I cussed and laughed. I called my dogs. I tooted my fox horn. **1969** *DARE Survey* (Sawyer KY) We have what we call a fox horn, made outer a steer horn, and blow it, and ... most of 'em 'll come to you, that is if they've run any length of time. **2000** Venable *Mt Hands* 41 Mom got the fox horn down from the wall and blew it to call me in out of the woods.

[DARE *fox horn* n chiefly South Midland]

fox in the corner (also *fox in the morning*) *noun* A children's game in which players seek to run from base to base without being tagged by the "fox."

1946 Lassiter *Games Played* 18 Some of the mixed games required a good deal of running, as "Buzzard," "Base," and "Fox in the Morning, Goose in the Evening." **1952** Brewster *Games and Rhymes* 78 "Fox in the Corner" ... Fox: Fox in the corner. / Geese: Geese in the corner. / Fox: How many men you got? / Geese: More than you're able to catch. / The geese then try to get to the fox's home.... The fox catches as many as he can.

fox race *noun* Pursuit of a fox with dogs.

1894 Wingfield *Big Buck* 400 They had not gone 200yds on the fox race. **c1960** Hall *Coll* = pursuit of a fox with dogs, in a hunt. **2017** Corbin *Battle Branch* 28 The party of hunters would build a campfire on top of a high knoll where they could hear the hounds from more than a mile away. Then they would sit around the fire and tell stories, drink moonshine, and comment on the "fox race," as Dad called it.

[DARE *fox race* South Midland]

foxy *adjective* Moderately inebriated, but feeling good and acting playful.

1939 Hall *Coll* (Gatlinburg TN) You sure was foxy last night when we left you. **1962** Williams *Metaphor Mt Speech I* 11 The man who has drunk enough to glow, sing, and laugh freely but whose tongue might become twisted on a word now and then is "foxy." The "foxy" one has an "eetchin' heel" and likes to "find a little patch of the fun." **1994** Montgomery *Coll* (known to Shields).

fraction *noun* A disturbance, fight.

1917 Kephart *Word-List* 412 = ruction. "I don't know what the *fraction* was, but he flew mad about something." **c1950** Adams *Grandpap* 51 She seed one of the robbers a-slippin' back to see what the fraction was. **1952** Wilson *Folk Speech NC* 542 = a fight, disturbance, disagreement. **1975** Jackson *Unusual Words* 157 A *racket* implies more actual contact, whereas *ruckus* or *rookus*, *fraction*, and *fray* all mean a fist fight or gun fight.

[OED3 *fraction* n 3 "a breach of the peace, brawling" obsolete; DARE *fraction* n 1 South Midland]

fragrant mountain water *noun* Illegal homemade whiskey.

1996 Spurlock *Glossary* 398 = moonshine.

frail, frailing pole See **flail**.

frail out See **flail C**.

frail pole See **flail B**.

frail rocks *verb phrase* To break rocks; figuratively = to serve time in prison. See also **flail C**.

1939 Hall *Coll* (Gatlinburg TN) He's a-frailin' rocks.

fraish See **fresh**.

fram *verb* To beat, pound. See also **fram pole**.

1952 Wilson *Folk Speech NC* 548 = to whip, beat: "He *frammed* the old feller pretty good." **1962** Rouse *Colorful Tint* To fram a child means to spank him. **1996–97** Montgomery *Coll* (known to Brown, Ledford, Oliver).

[perhaps echoic; Web3 *fram* v South and Midland]

frampold *adjective* See citation.

1967 Jones *Peculiarities Mtneers* 32 A dish-faced, white eyed horse was sure to be foolish and vicious, maybe even "frampold." ("Frampold" is a perfectly good old English word, now obsolete, which means such an animal was a mean, vicious and dangerous killer.)

[origin unknown; OED3 *frampold* adj 2 "chiefly of a horse: fiery, spirited" now archaic and rare]

fram pole *noun* See 1952 citation. See also **fram**.

1952 Wilson *Folk Speech NC* 542–43 = a weapon; a stick or some other object with which to beat one. "Goin' a get me a *fram-pole* and beat you up." **1962** Rouse *Colorful Tint* A fram pole is a switch to spank [a child] with. **1996–97** Montgomery *Coll* He thrashed his oats with a fram pole (known to Brown, but not to other consultants from the Smoky Mountains).

France harp See **French harp**.

franzied See **franzy A**.

franzy

A (also *franzied*) *adjective* Delirious.

1885 (in **1972** *Burial Customs* 8) He was franzy at times but he could talk till the very last. **1896** *Word-List* 417 *franzy* = delirious. "The medicine made her *franzy*." **c1926** Bird *Cullowhee Wordlist*: *franzy* [is] used in the sense of *wild* or *out of (one's) head* due to sickness, a fever, etc. "He's been awful sick for several days and has been franzy most of the time." **1952** Wilson *Folk Speech NC* 543 *franzied* = crazy.

[DARE *franzy* adj 1 South, South Midland]

B *noun* An excited state.

1924 Raine *Saddlebags* 98 = an excited state. **1942** Campbell *Cloud-Walking* 19 [She] ought not get in a franzy fretting about a youngun being puny.

[variant of *frenzy*; DARE *franzy* n chiefly South, South Midland]

frash

A *adjective* See **fresh**.

B *verb* See citation.

1953 Davison *Word-List Appal* 10 = to upset or unnerve: "I was jest a-pranking. I didn't know it would frash her that way."

fray *noun* A fight or brawl, often with deadly weapons.

1913 Kephart *Our Sthn High* 294 If they quarrel, it is a ruction, a rippit, a jower, or an upscuddle—so be it there are no fatalities which would amount to a real fray. **1940** Haun *Hawk's Done* 62 I reckon they might nigh had a fray. **1956** Chapman *Folk Retain* The use of "fray" for a fight, especially one involving bloodshed, is right out of Shakespeare, one of whose characters inquires, "Who began this bloody fray?" **1975** Jackson *Unusual Words* 157 A *racket* implies more actual contact, whereas *ruckus* or *rookus*, *fraction*, and *fray* all mean a fist fight or gun fight.

[shortening of *affray*]

fray out *verb phrase* See 1975 citation.

1975 Jackson *Unusual Words* 152–53 To *fray out* grain suggests *wear by rubbing*. **1996** Montgomery *Coll* (known to Cardwell).

frazzle (also *frazzle out*) *verb*, *verb phrase* To become fatigued physically and emotionally.

1890 Fruit *KY Words* 64 *frazzle* = to fray: "This cloth frays, or frazzles." To frazzle out is to fray out. Also as a noun: "Look at the frazzles!" **1895** Edson and Fairchild *TN Mts* 371 *frazzled* = tired out. **1960** Cooper *Jularker Bussed* I was frazzled (very tired) yesterday, but today I feel middlin' peart (refreshed). **c1960** Wilson *Coll* (usually *frazzle out*) = [to be] fatigued, worn out, tired. **1994–97** Montgomery *Coll* (known to Adams, Brown, Jones, Ledford, Norris, Oliver, Weaver); I'd go with you but I'm frazzled out (Cardwell).

[< *frazzle* alteration of English dialect *fazle* "to tangle"; DARE *frazzle* v 1 chiefly South, South Midland]

frazzle-headed *adjective* Usually of a child: having tousled or unkempt hair.

1983 Broaddus *Estill Co KY Word List* 40 = having messed-up hair. **1996** Montgomery *Coll* (known to Adams, Ellis, Jones, Ledford, Norris, Oliver); He was a cute little frazzle-headed boy of about six (Cardwell).

frazzle out See **frazzle**.

frazzling *adjective* Trifling, worthless.

c1940 Aswell *Glossary TN Idiom* 9 Ain't got a frazzling thing to do. 1995–97 Montgomery *Coll* (known to Adams, Brown, Ledford, Oliver); He just runs around with a frazzling set of people. It's no wonder that he don't behave any better (Cardwell).

[DARE *frazzling* adj 1 South, South Midland]

freckledy *adjective* Freckled.

1984 Burns *Cold Sassy* 283 Her freckledy face was lit up with excitement all day, and seemed like Grandpa couldn't keep his eyes off of her.

freckle face *noun* The evening primrose (*Oenothera biennis*), the leaves of which are an edible green. Same as **sheep's tongue**.

1988 Dyer *Farmstead Yards* 25 In a recent interview, Inez Adams recalled the folk names of her mother's favorite wild greens (which, presumably, fall into Shields' "field cresses" category): "crowsfoot," "freckleface," "gravy leg," and "narrow dock."

free *adverb* Freely.

1939 Hall *Coll* They used to make it [= liquor] free. They used to make it purty free. People would come in here after it.

free for all *adjective phrase* Of a church service: open for all to attend, regardless of affiliation.

1940 Bowman *KY Mt Stories* 3 Only two preachers were present; five are usually required for a "big Meetin'" or a "Free-for-All Meetin'" or a "Buryin'." *Ibid.* 239 *free for all meeting* = a meeting open to all Faiths. *Ibid.* 239 *free for all preaching* = a meeting open to all preachers. 2014 Montgomery *Doctrine* 126 = a meeting where there are no invited speakers and most, if not all the ministers who come are used in a preaching way.

free-hearted *adjective* Generous. See also **open-hearted**.

1940 Haun *Hawk's Done* 125 The Drennons were free-hearted. 1941 Hall *Coll* (Mitchell Co NC) Windy Bill, you're too free-hearted with your money. 1958 Sanderson *County Scott* 177 Folklore in Scott County [TN] goes from the cradle to the grave. The "granny" woman psychoanalyzed the "youngun" at birth. If it was born with big ears and its hands open, it would be "freehearted." 1966 *DARE Survey* (Burnsville NC, Spruce Pine NC) = very generous.

[DARE *freehearted* adj 1 chiefly South, South Midland, Northeast]

free school *noun* A school operated at public expense for all children of a district, superseding the **subscription school** at different times in various parts of the mountains. In the early days of free public education the school term often ran for only three months in the fall and was supplemented by a **subscription school** in the winter.

1922 *TN CW Ques* 20 (Greene Co TN) I attended a Free school som time and sum time a subscription school. 1930 Pendleton *Wood-Hicks Speak* 87 Free school, public school, a term widely used in this vicinity. It originated evidently in the distinction drawn in the time within the recollection of men now living when there were . . . only pay- or subscription-schools. 1935 Allen *Annals Haywood Co* 212 In 1839, the system of public schools called the "free schools" began by a vote of the people on the basis of raising by taxation twenty dollars in each district in the county to be matched by forty dollars from the State fund. 1939 Hall *Coll* (Cataloochee NC) [We] didn't have grades then, went until we completed the free-school books. 1953 Hall *Coll* (Tuckaleechee Cove TN) [There used to be] a free school at Tuckaleechee and a kind of high school at Frogtown. 1967 *DARE Survey* (Maryville TN) He's in free school = [said] when grade school was tuition-free and high school was paid. 1973 GSMNP-88 They all got a good free school education.

freeseed peach (also *freestone peach*) *noun* A peach whose pulp comes easily off the seed. Same as **open peach**. See also **cling peach**.

1949 Kurath *Word Geog East US* 72 *Free-stone peach* is current in the greater part of the Midland and in the entire New England settlement area. It is the regular expression in West Virginia and the Shenandoah Valley and has survived to some extent in the westernmost parts of Virginia and the Carolinas. As an innovation, it appears now also in Tidewater Virginia and on the North Carolina coasts. 1966–67 *DARE Survey* (Burnsville NC, Spruce Pine NC, Gatlinburg TN) *free-stone* = a type of peach in which the center is loose. 1996–97 Montgomery *Coll*: *freeseed peach* (known to Adams, Brown, Cardwell, Ledford, Oliver).

[DARE *freeseed* n especially Appalachians]

freestone (also *freestone water*) *noun* Water with a soft texture and purer taste from its relative lack of minerals, in distinction to slate water, which is hard.

1862 *Edmonston/Kelly CW Letters* (Sept 1) Lime Stone water [is] just as good as the free Stone. 1862 *Robinson CW Letters* (May 12) we can get eny Sort of water heare that we want free Stone lime Stone Minrel & Sulfer. 1863 (in 1999 Davis *CW Letters* 92) it is mor Rough and Mountainous than in our Country. the water is pure & free Stone. 1905 Miles *Spirit of Mts* 19–20 The mountaineer takes the same pride in his water supply as the rich man in his wine cellar. . . . None but the purest and coldest of freestone will satisfy him. 1939 Hall *Coll* (Waldens Creek TN) = any clear water without mineral properties. *Ibid.* (Gumstand TN) Freestone water—hit's just pure water. Hit runs over the white rocks. 1982 *Smokies Heritage* 43 A "free-stone" spring brings forth soft water, fine for drinking and cooking, as it has no mineral taste.

[DARE *freestone water* n chiefly South Midland]

freestone peach See **freeseed peach**.

freestone water See **freestone**.

freeze *verb* Principal parts.

1 variant past-tense form *freezed*, *friz*, *fruz*.

1859 (in 1974 Harris *High Times* 251) The coon would eat isecrem, (they'se ove a cool nater eny how,) ontil the har ontu his tail friz together hard enuff tu shell corn ontu hit. 1864 Gilmore

Down in TN 87 He war so cool he fruz the whole grave-yard so tight they hed ter thaw it out with light'ood. **1913** Kephart *Our Sthn High* 78 You remember the big storm three year ago, come grass, when the cattle all huddled up a-top o' each other and friz in one pile, solid. *Ibid.* 284 Examples of a strong preterite with dialectical change of the vowel are bruk, brung . . . friz. **1957** Combs *Lg Sthn High: Word List* 42 *fruz* = past-tense and past participle of *freeze*. **1962** Williams *Verbs Mt Speech* 17 Verbs which retain either the strong preterites of Middle English or variant preterites of the English dialects [include] freeze (present), friz (past), friz (past participle). **1978** Reese *Speech NE Tenn* 175 *freezed* = attested by 2/12 (16.7%) speakers. **1986** Helton *Around Home* 379 *friz*. **1994** Montgomery *Coll*: *friz* (known to Cardwell).

[DARE *freeze* v A2 chiefly South, South Midland]

2 variant past-participle forms *frez*, *friz*, *frose*, *froze*, *frozed*.

1832 *McLean Diary* (Jan 24) the ice is from 12 to 15 inches thick all the Mill froze up. **1858** Webb *Letter* 110 we have some frost but the ground has never froze to hard to plow. **1864** *Dalton CW Letters* (Dec 15) the boys was out all Day and all nigh[t] tha[y] come back nerly frose. **1892** Dromgoole *Dan to Beersheba* 77 Old Marlow was right—the whole South was "frez up." **1901** Harben *Westerfelt* 136 I was mighty nigh friz, an' I reckon he soon got that away. **1923** Greer-Petrie *Angeline Doin' Society* 24 You'd better git in sev'ral buckets of water tonight, Betty, for I'm a-thinkin' everything will be frez up solid by mornin'. **1934–47** *LAMSAS Appal* (Madison Co NC, Swain Co NC) *friz*. **1939** Hall *Coll* (Maggie Valley NC) I told her I was starved and froze and give out. **1953** Hall *Coll* (Bryson City NC) It'd froze hard. **1973** Miller *English Unicoi Co* 132 *Froze* (as past participle) attested by 3 of 6 speakers. **1974** Fink *Bits Mt Speech* 9 The river was *friz* over solid. **1977** *Jake Waldroop* 149 It was the best tasting beef, a whole lot better than this froze beef. **1978** Reese *Speech NE Tenn* 184 The field was frozed. **1991** Thomas *Sthn Appal* 12 She said 'at they was so hungry . . . on their way back out a' th' [Civil] War . . . that they eat froze punkins. **2008** *Rosie Hicks* 1 [She] could reach in there and get the taters out when it was froze up and you couldn't get no other way.

[DARE *freeze* v *frez*, *friz* A3 chiefly South, South Midland]

freezed See **freeze 1**.

freeze on to *verb phrase* See citations.

1927 Woofter *Dialect from WV* 354 I froze onto the pair of shoes that I bought at the sale. **c1960** Wilson *Coll*: *freeze on* (or *onto*) = to cling to, sometimes very nervously. **1966** *DARE Survey* (Boone NC).

[DARE *freeze on to* v phr chiefly Northeast, South Midland]

freeze out (also *freeze up*) *verb phrase* To freeze completely.

1953 Hall *Coll* (Bryson City NC) The coons, they was hung up to where they froze up and was all right. **1973** GSMNP-80:8 We would get out in the snow and ride snow sleds and walk through the snow. If I was to do that now, I'd just freeze out.

French harp (also *France harp*) *noun* A harmonica. Also called **breath harp**, **harp**, **mouth harp**, **pocket harp**.

1909 Bascom *Ballads and Songs* 238 The mountaineer who cannot draw music from the violin, the banjo, or the "French harp," is probably non-existent, and not infrequently one may see a gaunt idler squatting by the roadside, picking the banjo, and at the same time working the "French harp," held in place by a wire around the player's neck. **1915** Dingus *Word-List VA* 183 = a harmonica. **1939** Hall *Coll* (Jefferson City TN) I'm going to play you a tune on this French harp. **1958** Miller *Pigeon's Roost* (Sept 25) The hill-billy talent instrument also included the French or France harp, now always called the harmonica. **1966–68** *DARE Survey* (Brasstown NC, Burnsville NC, Cherokee NC, Spruce Pine NC, Gatlinburg TN, Maryville TN) = harmonica. **1978** *Smoky Vistas* (July–Sept) 7 Harmonicas, often called French harp, and the Jew's harp, or "jaw harp," were available from the general stores. **1979** Irwin *Musical Instruments* 83 The Jews harp and the harmonica, most often called a French harp in this area, have been a part of the music of this region since the first settlers came in the 1700's. Remnants of these two instruments are often found in the ruins of the earliest military forts of this area. **1986** Pederson et al. *LAGS* = attested by 41/60 interviewees (68.3%) from E TN and 14/35 (40%) from N GA; 55/292 of all LAGS interviewees (18.8%) attesting term were from Appalachia. **2005** Williams *Gratitude* 495 = harmonica.

fresh *adjective*

A variant forms *fraish*, *frash* [see **2005** in **C1**], *frish* [see **1805** in **B1**], *frush*.

1904–20 Kephart *Notebooks* 4:749 The sign was spang fraish. **1939** Hall *Notebooks* 9:27 The tracks [of the bear] was frush across the trail. **1942** Hall *Phonetics Smoky Mts* 20 [fræʃ], [freɪʃ].

[DARE *fresh* adj especially South Midland]

B *noun*

1 A sudden surge of water in a stream, a flash flood, especially after springtime rain(s). See also **freshet**, **May fresh**, **spring fresh**, **tide A**.

1805 *Globe Creek Church Minutes* 21 No meeting upon the account of a very wet day and a very grait frish in the night. **1834** (in **1956** Eliason *Tarheel Talk* 272) (Burke Co NC) The letter miscarried at the time of the last fresh. **1863***Walker CW Letters* (April 10) thear was one har[d] trile we had her was a mity hy frush doun her in march and it rose over the prisen. **1875** Reid *Land of Sky* 59 You see the river, it's been awful high all summer, and they say the ford's dreadful washed out by the big fresh last spring. **1896** Fox *Last Stetson* 184 You'll ketch yer death o' cold swimmin' this way atter a fresh. **1937** Hall *Coll* (Cosby TN) [There] come a fresh an' knocked [a splash dam] out. **1985** Kiser *Life and Times* 59 Many times flash floods, or "freshes" as the old folk sometimes called them, would come on warm spring days. **1997** Montgomery *Coll* (known to Brewer, Bush).

[EDD *fresh* sb 12 Scot, nEngl; CUD *fresh*[2] n "flood, rise in the level of a river"; DARE *fresh* n 1 chiefly South, South Midland]

2 See citation.

2007 McMillon *Notes* = a freshwater spring that spouts out of the ground after a heavy downpour.

C *verb*

1 (also *be fresh*, *come (in) fresh*, *freshen*, *freshen up*) Of a cow: to resume giving milk after calving. See also **come in**.

1927 Woofter *Dialect from WV* 354 *freshen* = spoken of domestic animals whose period of pregnancy is nearly up. "The cow will freshen next month." **1930** Armstrong *This Day and Time* 177 More 'an apt Daisy won't never be fresh agin. **c1960** Wilson *Coll*: *come fresh* = to have a calf and, therefore, be giving milk again. **1966** Dakin *Vocab Ohio River Valley* 233 In Kentucky the two expressions [*freshen* and *be fresh*] stand side by side in about equal numbers . . . *Fresh* ("She *freshes*," "she's going to *fresh*") is used by a few older speakers in Kentucky. **1966–67** *DARE Survey* (Spruce Pine NC) *freshen* = to have a calf; (Gatlinburg TN) *fresh*. **1986** Pederson et al. *LAGS come in fresh* = attested by 3/60 interviewees (5%) from E TN and 1/35 (2.9%) from N GA; 4/11 of all LAGS interviewees (36.4%) attesting term were from Appalachia. **1991** Haynes *Haywood Home* 44 Often neighbors would loan a cow to other families to furnish them with milk and butter until their cow came fresh again. **1996** Johnson *Lexical Change* 138 *come in, come in fresh* = statistically more common in the mountains of South Carolina and Georgia than in the Piedmont and Coastal Plain c1990. **1996–97** Montgomery *Coll*: *come fresh* (known to Adams, Brown, Bush); *come in fresh* (known to Adams, Brown, Norris, Oliver) = a heifer quit giving much milk and we quit milking about five to six weeks before she come in fresh (Ledford), = because it is yellow and is full with lumps of colostrom, the cow's milk is not drinkable for a few days after giving birth; when the lumps disappear and the milk becomes white, the cow is said to have come fresh (Cardwell); *freshen* (known to Weaver); *freshen up* I'll be able to repay you when my cow freshens up (Cardwell). **2005** Williams *Gratitude* 143 They [= cows] was bred so they wouldn't come in frash (bring a calf) close to the same time. *Ibid*. 486 When a cow gave birth, or "come in," she was said to have *found a calf*, or *come in frash* (*fresh, frush*).

2 Of water in a stream: to surge suddenly after heavy rain.

1884 Smith *Arp Scrap Book* 139 It ain't done freshin' yet, for the frogs are croakin' and the camphor bottle is cloudy.

D *adjective* Of a cow: giving milk, especially but not necessarily after calving. See also **fresh C1**.

1939 Bond *Appal Dialect* 107 = lactating, used in reference to recent mothers as well as to cows.

freshen, freshen up See **fresh C1**.

freshet *noun* A surge of water in a stream, causing it to overflow, especially in the spring after heavy rain. See also **fresh B1, May fresh, spring fresh, tide A.**

1824 (in **1912** Doddridge *Notes on Settlement* 114) A freshet came and washed them [= the knots of wood to be carved] all away. Not one of them was ever found. **1861** Hedgecock *Diary* 101 23rd, great freshet in the river overflowing its banks. **1873** Smith *Arp Peace Papers* 182 They got washed away in a freshet, and had to take a new start. **1960** Stubbs *Mountain-Wise* (June–July) 7 I remember that freshet. It was on the 17th of April and what we had was seven inches of rain on top of thirteen inches of snow, and all this water is got to go somewhere. **1966** *DARE Survey* (Burnsville NC) = a sudden rush of water coming from a heavy rain. **1984** Smith *Oral History* 33 Little freshets of water is busting outen the rocks all around, the way they do in the spring of the year. **1994–97** Montgomery *Coll* (known to Brown, Bush, Cardwell, Jones, Oliver), = a rush of water from a sudden storm (Ogle). **1996** Cole *Forney's Creek* 20 Logs were built into rafts, and when freshets came they were floated down the Little Tennessee and other streams to sawmills.

fresh-like See **-like**.

fried backing *noun* See citation. See also **backing**.

1939 Hall *Coll* "Fried backin's" [was] a drink said to have been made by Sam Burchfield of notorious Tab Cat Creek by putting spices in the backin's. [Said also to have had enough strength "to elevate the spirits."]

fried bread *noun*

1 Same as **poor do 1**.

1990 Oliver *Cooking Hazel Creek* 10 What to do with left-over corn bread was solved by turning it into something called Poor Do or Fried Bread. To make this dish, take day-old, or older, cornbread, slice it and fry the cut sides in a little grease until brown. Then add enough milk to about half cover the bread and simmer for awhile. This dish lingered on & had a big revival in popularity during the Depression years when people all over the country sometimes made an entire meal from it. **1996–97** Montgomery *Coll* = a makeshift meal of ingredients, odds and ends (Andrews), = corn meal sliced and fried (Brown), = a cornmeal dumpling, sometimes cooked on turnip greens (Cardwell), = cornbread cut into pieces, then sliced and fried, with milk sometimes added to the pan when almost done, also called *fried bread* (Oliver).

2 See citation.

1986 Pederson et al. *LAGS* (Sevier Co TN) = corncake.

fried hole *noun* See citation.

1980 Riggleman *WV Mtneer* 126–27 [Loggers] usually had nicknames for everybody and everything around the camp. Doughnuts were "fried holes" or "door knobs."

fried meat *noun* Bacon.

1966 Dakin *Vocab Ohio River Valley* 334 Some Kentuckians say the name *bacon* applies only to side meat after it is fried—that is, frying makes it bacon, and as such the Mountain expression *fried meat* seems to be a synonym.

fried mush *noun* Cornmeal boiled, cooled, sliced, and then fried. See also **liver cheese, mush.**

c1960 Wilson *Coll* = ordinary corn-meal mush, allowed to cool, then sliced and fried. **1966** *DARE Survey* (Spruce Pine NC) = a type of fried cornmeal. **1972** Hall *Coll* (Emerts Cove TN) We entered the Depression with nothing and we come out of it with nothing, but we never remember bein' hungry. In fact, we lived perty high on the hog, with potato dumplin's 'n sich, foddered beans, fried mush fried in the mornin' for breakfast with molasses, brown-eyed peas, pickled cucumbers.

fried pie *noun* See 1978 citation. Also called **hand pie, moon pie, mule ear.**

1936 Morehouse *Rain on Just* 78 Granny Elvy settled back . . . a dish of fried pies in one hand, a pan of ash cakes close by. **1973** Medford *Long Hard Road* 15 [Apples] were made into apple butter, jelly, cider, as well . . . fried pies, made from dried apples. **1978** Slone *Common Folks* 309 Apples were used in fried pies, apples or apple butter folded into small thin sheets of dough and fried in deep fat. I have also heard these called half-moon pies or moccasin pies. **1995** Trout *Historic Buildings* 69 A special treat all winter long, sulphured apples could be used to make stack pie, cake, or fried pie. **2006** *Encycl Appalachia* 932 Culinary cousin of the baked fruit turnover, fried pies were a winter favorite among old-time mountain residents when fresh fruit was not available. **2014** *WV Talk* = a round of biscuit dough filled with apples, folded and baked in the oven with a lot of grease.

[DARE *fried pie* n 1 chiefly South, South Midland, Northeast]

friendly brier *noun* The Canadian blackberry, which grows at elevations above three thousand feet in the Smoky Mountains.

1974–75 McCracken *Logging* 15:11 Then blackberries came in there and we called 'em the friendly briars. They didn't have no stickers on 'em hardly, and they had a different taste from these old field blackberries too.

friendly-like *adjective* Friendly.

1955 Ritchie *Singing Family* 184 Don't look so all-fired mad, I ain't going to ask you to shoot yer granny. I just want to be friendly like.

friendship quilt *noun* A quilt stitched and donated by a group of friends, especially to a woman as a wedding gift.

1972 *Foxfire I* 149 The most captivating custom . . . was that of the Friendship Quilt. This was a quilt much like the others . . . with the added feature of a number of names embroidered on the squares themselves. . . . "The name of everyone that pieced a square was supposed to be put on the quilt." . . . Such quilts were made . . . whenever a young person . . . got married, when a neighbor lost his house by fire, for a newborn child in the neighborhood, or just for a keepsake. **1984** *Sevier Settler* 1:21 In the earlier days each woman brought a few scraps, and quilts were made for newly married couples in the community. These became known as friendship quilts and are still a tradition. In the years gone by mothers made their daughters quilts to keep until they were married.

fright *verb* To frighten (someone).

1989 Giardina *Storming Heaven* 35 How'd she fright you? **1992** Giardina *Unquiet Earth* 20 She told me there's something about him that frights her.

fright tale *noun* A scary story, as a **haunt tale** or **panther tale**.

1986 Lewelling *White Caps Sevier Co* 156 The White Cap era is a chapter of Sevier County history that many in that county would like to forget. . . . It has been a source of "fright tales" to some . . . and embarrassment to others.

Frigidaire *noun* A refrigerator of any brand.

c1960 Wilson *Coll* = a name for any electrical refrigerator. **1972** *AOHP/LJC-104* They had wells, didn't have frigidaires, didn't have any electric. **1992** Brooks *Sthn Stuff* 53 = any electric icebox. "Margie-Ann got herse'f a new Frigidaire." "Oh, she did? What kind?" "A Kelvinator." **2005** Williams *Gratitude* 495 What most folks call a refrigerator, probably because one of the first ones manufactured was Frigidaire brand.

[DARE *frigidaire* n widespread, but less frequent Inland North, PA, West]

fringe bush (also *fringe tree*) *noun* A small deciduous tree (*Chionanthus virginicus*) that has bushy, white flowers, dark, purplish berries, and bark with medicinal uses. Also called **granny gray beard**, **old man's beard**.

1941 Walker *Story of Mt* 61 Fringe-tree, or Old Man's Beard, which is more often a shrub than it is a tree, builds snowlike spots in many places on top of the mountain, especially along Little River. Its flowers are delicately fragrant, and it is worthy of a place on any man's lawn. **1943** Peattie *Great Smokies* 166 The sourwood, the fringe bush, and the mountain laurel, are understory trees. [**1971** Krochmal et al. *Medicinal Plants Appal* 92 The bark is used as a diuretic, tonic, and astringent; it is also used to reduce fever. In Appalachia, a liquid of boiled root bark is applied to skin irritations.] **1995** Montgomery *Coll* (known to Cardwell).

[DARE *fringe tree* n chiefly South, South Midland]

frish See **fresh**.

fritter

A variant form *flitter* [see **1968**, **2005** in **B**].

B (also *flitter(s)*, *flitter bread*, *flitter cake*, *fritter bread*) A fried pancake-like pastry made usually from cornmeal or occasionally from flour, usually cooked with fruit in the batter. See also **corn fritter**.

1862 *Lockmiller CW Letters* (April 18) easter is nere cume down and take breackfast with us and we will fill a egg and stick flitter knock a virgin pullet in the head stew sum Suthern coffey for breackfast. **1862** *Watkins CW Letters* (June 20) you must come and tak a bate of fliters with me and al come and see how good we can fri them. **1934–47** *LAMSAS Appal*: *flitter* = attested by 54/148 speakers (36.4%) from WV, 10/20 (50%) from VA, 27/37 (73.0%) from NC, 3/14 (21.4%) from SC, and 4/12 (33.3%) from GA; *flitter cakes* = by 4/148 speakers (2.7%) from WV, 5/20 (25%) from VA, and 3/37 (8.1%) from NC. **1960** Burnett *My Valley* 25 Corn fritters were good eating beside the campfires. **1966** Dakin *Vocab Ohio River Valley* 328–29 People in the Mountains and in southern Kentucky generally, sometimes in the Bluegrass, and along the river in southeastern Ohio remember but apparently seldom use the old name *fritter* or *flitter*—a thin griddle cake, not the dumpling-like cake fried in deep fat like a doughnut. Where it is preserved in Ohio, this term always seems to be *flitter*, as it also is in the Mountains. *Fritter* appears in the Bluegrass and in southwestern Kentucky. Comments [indicate] that the term is old—"real old people say this." **1968** Wilson *Folklore Mammoth Cave* 17 *flitter* = the commonest name for pancakes. Batter (or batty) cakes, flitters (or flitter cakes), fritters, griddle cakes, hot cakes are all known and occasionally used. **1986** Pederson et al. *LAGS*: *flitters* = attested by 13/60 interviewees (21.7%) from E TN and 2/35 (5.7%) from N GA; 15/73 of all LAGS interviewees (20.5%) attesting term were from Appalachia. **1989** Smith *Flyin' Bullets* 55 Corn bread might be eaten for breakfast with "saw mill gravy," a gravy made of corn meal. Or they might have "flitters," pancakes made of corn meal, with hot maple syrup, honey, or molasses poured over them. **1995–97** Montgomery *Coll*: *flitter* (known to Jones, Ledford, Norris), = a cornmeal pancake (Adams), = any bread fried on top of stove, may be mixed with meat, fruit, or berries (Brown), = often called corn fritter, sometimes topped with sorghum, served as a snack (Cardwell), = a pancake or a doughnut with fruit (Hooper), = cornmeal pancake (Oliver). **1997** Andrews *Mountain Vittles* 17 Some folks calls 'em fritter bread or corn dodgers. I always called 'em flitter bread I reckon because you sort a flip 'em over flitty like. **2005** Williams *Gratitude* 494 *Flitters* is made by stirring up flour, salt and bakin' sodie together with enough water or milk to make a batter, then fried like pancakes, only they're thicker. They're sometimes made in place of biscuits when you want some quick bread. *Flatter'n a flitter* is a term used to describe something as being very flat.

[OED3 *fritter* n[1] 1 "a portion of batter sometimes containing apples, meat, etc."; DARE cf English dialect *frit* "a kind of pancake" and *fritter* "a small pancake containing currants"; DARE *fritter* n 1 South, South Midland, Northeast]

fritter bread See **fritter B**.

fritter-minded *adjective* Scatter-brained, simple-minded.

1931 Hannum *Thursday April* 83 Thursday April persuaded Joe to buy him a fiddle. Joe fussed and fumed at such fritter-mindedness and said it was a sight of nonsense. **1939** Campbell *Play Party* 17 These "old-time gatherings where the fritter-minded song ballets belong to be sung" have not "plumb passed away."

[DARE *fritter-minded* adj South Midland]

friz See **freeze**.

froe (also *frow*) *noun* An implement with a broad, wedge-shaped metal blade set at a right angle to its handle, used to split wood into **boards** (shingles) from a block of wood with the aid of a mallet or **maul**. See 1960 citation. See also **dull as a froe**.

1824 (in **1912** Doddridge *Notes on Settlement* 107) The boards were split four feet long, with a large frow, and as wide as the timber would allow. They were used without planing or shaving. **1836** *McLean Diary* 44 [I] Lent Jobe Wees my frow. **1915** Dingus *Word-List VA* 183 *froe* = a wedge-shaped broad blade of iron for riving shingles. **1937** Eaton *Handicrafts* 60a This boy is riving boards or shingles with a froe and maul from white oak and hickory, as his ancestors have done for generations. **1960** Arnow *Seedtime* 264 Once the board log was bolted, heart and sap wood taken off, and the quarters split to size, eight to ten inches square, for roof boards, it was time for the froe. This was a short-handled, dull-bladed tool, designed for riving wood so as to get as much flat surface as possible, and so, driven in by a light wooden mallet, was used to make roof, door, and shutter boards as well as staves for barrels and setware such as churns. **1964** Clarkson *Lumbering in WV* 362 *froe* = a cleaving tool with handle at right angles to the blade. Used for splitting shingles and staves. **1982** Powers and Hannah *Cataloochee* 316 Shakes or "boards" for a roof were best rived with a froe out of Northern red oak. **2005** Williams *Gratitude* 495 *froe* = a tool used to split wood to make shingles. It was left dull on the edge so it would not cut the wood fibers, just separate them into shingles when the *froe* was struck on the top edge with a mallet. Hence the saying, "Dull as a froe."

frog

A *noun*

1 Used as an inclusive term for both frogs and toads.

1913 Kephart *Our Sthn High* 295 In the Smokies a toad is called a frog or a toad-frog, and a toadstool is a frog-stool. **1994–97** Montgomery *Coll* (known to ten consultants from the Smoky Mountains).

[DARE *frog* n B1 chiefly South, South Midland]

2 A section of a gristmill into which corn falls before being fed to the millstone for grinding.

1973 GSMNP-78:23 The object of the mill that we're looking at now, which is the hopper and also part called the frog, you first pour the corn into the hopper, which is made to hold about a bushel of corn, and it poured and it was made, well it run to a sharp point in the bottom, so the corn would pour down to that into that thing. I believe they call it frog or something like that anyway. **1980** *Smokies Heritage* 9 You poured the corn in [the hopper], and it fell into the frog underneath. Now there was a long eight-sided stick across from the frog—you lifted or lowered the stick to control how much corn fell from the frog into the millstones below. The more that fell, the coarser the meal would be.

3 The palm (of one's hand).

1938 Still *Bat Flight* 13 I held them in the frog of my hand. **1940** Still *River of Earth* 145 I spat into the frog of my hand, slapping the wet spot with a forefinger.

4 See citation.

1900 *Trestise Coal Mining* 53 A trip of empty [coal] cars is coming in at the siding. . . . Cars are lowered to the siding D and empty cars are taken up from the siding—while a trip of empty cars is coming into the siding. The frogs used in connection with the track are usually made from rails. The tongue of the frog is made of two short pieces of rail, cut and riveted together so as to form the required frog angle. The wing-rails are a part of the switch rails leading away from the frog, but are bent to suit the frog angle by means of a rail-bending machine.

B as verbal noun *frogging* (also *frog gigging*) Hunting for frogs with a **gig**.

1917 Kephart *Camping & Woodcraft* 2:415 When fishing is very poor, try frogging. It is not sport of a high order, though it may be called angling. **1944** Hall *Coll* (Del Rio TN) We went frogging and stayed all night, got in the next morning at ten o'clock. **1972** Hall *Coll* (Emerts Cove TN) I can never remember goin' in the smoke house and not findin' meat—hams, wild meat of the forest, snappin' turtle hard shelled, frog legs, possum meat rolled in flour and black pepper and salt. We'd go frog giggin'.

frog drowner (also *frog storm, frog strangler*) *noun* A sudden, hard, flooding rain. Same as **toad strangler**. See also **goose drownder**, **gullywasher**.

1974 Murray *Down to Earth* 62 It's going to come a real frog strangler the weather man says. **1981** Dumas *Appal Glossary* 17 *frog drowner, frog strangler* = a hard rain. **1995** Adams *Come Go Home* 87 It was raining harder than any of us had ever seen. Chuck Arnold said this must be what old folks back home called a "frog strangler." **1995–96** Montgomery *Coll*: *frog drowner* = any heavy storm (Cardwell); *frog storm* = any heavy storm (Cardwell); *frog strangler* (known to Adams, Cardwell, Norris).

[DARE *frog-strangler* n chiefly South, South Midland]

frog-eye *noun*

1 Same as **red-eye gravy**.

1940 Farr *More TN Expressions* 447 = red gravy: "Pass the frog-eye." **1995** Montgomery *Coll* (known to Cardwell, but not to other consultants from the Smoky Mountains).

[DARE *frog-eye gravy* n chiefly South Midland]

2 See citations.

1972 Carr *Oldest Profession* 79 The first bead to be evident from the singlin's he called "frog eyes" because of the larger than usual bubbles or beads. **1985** Dabney *More Mt Spirits* 178 The first shots of this "doubled" whiskey . . . will be about 160 proof alcohol, very "beady," or "frog-eyed."

frog gigging, frogging See **frog B**.

frog hair See **fine as fiddle dust**.

frog house *noun* See citation.

1904 (in **2002** Gibson *Gibson Remembers*) 16 Kids had fun in the summer in the dust. They'd find a spot with just a bit of moisture, not wet but just enough to stick together. They'd sit and make "frog houses." To make a frog house they'd cover their feet with a thick coat of dust then ease their foot out, leaving the foot-size hole of the front of the feet. Those were the "frog houses." After making several of the houses, they'd build a fence all around them, by patting and shaping with their hands and smoothing the fine, fine dust on the ground around their houses and fences.

frog in the middle *noun* A children's tag game played in a ring.

1940 Still *River of Earth* 198 We could hear bare feet whispering on the floor. They played frog-in-the-middle, making out there were a full dozen in the ring.

[DARE (at *frog in the meadow* n) chiefly South Midland]

frog one's sides *verb phrase* See citation.

1939 Farr *TN Mt Regions* 90 = eating [sic] heartily: "He's frogging his sides."

frog rain *noun* A rainstorm accompanied by spouts of wind that may pick up small frogs and shower them on nearby land; a very heavy rain. Same as **fish rain**. See also **rain bullfrogs**.

[**1929** Rainey *Animal Plant Lore* 13 The toads avoid sunlight as much as possible and take refuge under shrubs and grasses during the heated part of the day. Occasionally after a shower, they will emerge from their hiding place. This has given rise to the legend that little toads are rained down.] **1993** Parris *Folklore* 497 There's frog-rains and fish-rains, the kind of rain that rains frogs and little bitty fish and worms. Why, many's the time I've seen it rain frog and redworms and fish. Not all at the same time. They come in the summer. And when they do, the ground'll just be covered with little bitty frogs and not much bigger than a body's thumbnail. **1995–97** Montgomery *Coll* (known to Bush, Brown, Cardwell), = a rain heavy enough to bring frogs out of the ground and trees (Hooper).

frogskin *noun* A piece of paper currency, specifically a dollar bill. Same as **toadhide**.

1941 Still *Troublesome Creek* 165 I need me a new set o' teeth, but I've got no money. It takes many a frog skin. **c1960** Wilson *Coll* = any kind of bill: $1, $5, $10, $20. **1963** Edwards *Gravel* 33 "There's a frog skin," said Gabby, "but that ain't no money. Let me hear a bid." *Ibid.* 141 "Got to buy shells with this here frogskin," and he exhibited a new, crisp dollar bill. **1997** Montgomery *Coll* (known to Brown, Bush, Hooper).

[DARE *frogskin* n scattered, but especially South, South Midland]

frog spayer *noun* See citation.

1967 *DARE Survey* (Gatlinburg TN) = nickname for men's sharp-pointed shoes.

frogstick (also *frogsticker*) *noun* A pocketknife with a long blade. See also **sticker 1**.

1892 Fruit *KY Words* 230 *frog-sticker* = the old blunt-pointed Barlow pocket-knife bought for children. Schoolboys say, "Loan me your frog-sticker." **1927** Woofter *Dialect from WV* 354 *frog-sticker* = a penknife with a long blade. "It is against the law to carry such a frog-sticker." **1939** Hall *Coll* (Tobes Creek NC) *frogstick* **1952** Wilson *Folk Speech NC* 542 *frogsticker*. **1957** Broaddus *Vocab Estill Co KY* 32 *frog sticker* = a large pocket knife with 2 folding blades. **1995–97** Montgomery *Coll*: *frogsticker* (known to Cardwell, Hooper, Shields).

[DARE *frogsticker (knife)* n chiefly South, South Midland]

frog-stool *noun* A toadstool.

1895 Edson and Fairchild *TN Mts* 371 = toad-stool. **1913** Kephart *Our Sthn High* 295 In the Smokies a toad is called a frog or a toad-frog, and a toadstool is a frog-stool. **1934–47** *LAMSAS Appal* (Swain Co NC). **1986** Pederson et al. *LAGS* (Cocke Co TN, Jefferson Co TN). **1995** Montgomery *Coll* (known to Brown, Cardwell, Ellis, Norris, Oliver).

[DARE *frogstool* n chiefly South, South Midland]

frog storm, frog strangler See **frog drowner**.

frog trouncing *noun* See citations.

[**1946** Stuart *Plum Grove Hills* 253 The frog-trouncer was a heavy plank balanced on a wooden horse like a teeter-totter. On one end a toad frog was placed and and was tied there, so it couldn't jump, with a white thread. The man trouncin' the frog hit the other end of the trouncer with his mallet and it sent the frog toward the sky, and when the frog fell to the ground, it was dead as four o'clock. One had to hit the trouncer exactly right to send the frog straight into the air; if he didn't hit it right, the frog would go sidewise.] **1968** Clarke *Stuart's Kentucky* 220 Jesse Stuart's Kentucky, so rich in authentic detail—from highly localized peculiarities of speech to such a rare Elizabethan hangover as frog-trouncing—becomes a token of the world at large. [**1980** Wigginton *Foxfire VI* 286 Place a flat board on a block or stump or something of that nature (in a seesaw position). Place a frog on one end of the board, the end that is touching the ground. Take a mallet or sledgehammer and hit the end opposite that the frog is on. The object of the game is to see who can get the frog the highest.]

frolic

A *noun*

1 A lively party with music, dancing, games, and often drinking, usually held at a private home and sometimes in conjunction with a wedding, a **working** (as a **quilting frolic**), or contest (as a **rifle frolic**). See 1914, 1972 citations.

1814 Hartsell *Memora* 129 he said that he wold bee verey hapey to give us a crismass frolick. **1824** (in **1912** Doddridge *Notes on Settlement* 102) In the first years of the settlement of this country a wedding engaged the attention of a whole neighborhood; and the frolic was anticipated by old and young with eager expectation. **1834** Crockett *Narrative* 140 Before the regular frolic commenced, I mean the dancing, I was called on to make a speech as a candidate. **1838** *Elijoy Church Minutes* 35 The church on Elijoy met & 1st first the church Excludes Samuel Murrin for dancing at a frolic and threatening to leave the church. **1851** *Paw Paw Hollow Church Minutes* 117 Church met and after worship. excluds B[rothe]r Jesse Baly for having a frollick at his house and dancing. **1861** *Martin CW Letters* (Nov 15) Mr. B—had a cotting [= cotton] picking last week and corn shucking at night and a frolick after that. **1863** Hill *CW Letters* (Feb 20) Jinny sed that she was loking for a frolic ever day and night and I must come home and play the fiddle. **1901** (in **2014** Spalding *Appal Dance* 127) Petit and Stone learned that here, even Christmas (the "new" Christmas on December 25) was not a time when the religious ceremony and family celebration to which they were accustomed [was held]; instead, young people had "frolics," with "no giving of presents or any religious celebration, but drinking of moonshine, fighting, and a general carousing." **1913** Kephart *Our Sthn High* 266 Be that as it may, they [= church strictures] certainly have put a damper on frolics, so that in very many mountain settlements "goin' to meetin'" is recognized primarily as a social function and affords almost the only chance for recreation in which family can join family without restraint. **1914** Arthur *Western NC* 268 The country "frolics" or "hoedowns" . . . as a rule, the dancing had to take place on the uneven puncheon floors and in a very restricted space, often procured by the removal of the furniture. **1959** Pearsall *Little Smoky* 12 El freely admitted to being a terrible sinner in his youth, fiddling and attending "frolics." **1966** Dakin *Vocab Ohio River Valley* 509 *Frolic* as a common usage [for a party] is limited to the Mountains from the headwaters of the Licking and the Kentucky southward. It is also used by some older speakers in the eastern Knobs and the Bluegrass . . . *Frolic* has apparently never had much currency [in the Ohio Valley] except in eastern Kentucky. **1972** Cooper *NC Mt Folklore* 21 Dancing parties, often referred to as frolics or hoedowns, occurred in most neighborhoods, but not in many homes of the neighborhood. These were held only in homes that had a room sufficiently large, after the furniture had been removed, to accommodate the dancers and musicians. **1986** Pederson et al. *LAGS* = attested by 2/60 interviewees (3.3%) from E TN and 3/35 (8.6%) from N GA; 5/20 of all LAGS interviewees (25%) attesting term were from Appalachia. **1995** Williams *Smoky Mts Folklife* 54 Workings and other community events provided occasions for dances, or "frolics," as they were often known. **2007** McMillon *Notes* = an event usually with dancing, but gone [in the TN/NC mountains] by the mid-20th century. **2007** Milnes *Signs Cures Witches* 66 Most people who remember the frolics, or work parties, in the neighborhood, remember that banjos and fiddles were almost always present and that square dancing usually ensued. (This English word frolic, like the German cognate fröhlich, is common in eastern West Virginia as a term for these affairs.) *Ibid.* 71 The old double-crib log house was "built by frolic" in 1845. House raisings were a common reason for frolics, but log rollings and snitz stringing, among other events, were also popular. **2015** Jamison *Hoedowns* 202 = informal rural dance party.

[DARE *frolic* n 1 chiefly South Midland]

2 A gathering of people for the birth of a child. See also **granny frolic**.

1957 Combs *Lg Sthn High: Word List* 42 = widely used for square dance, "shindig"; sometimes, for a party. Also the occasion of a woman undergoing childbirth: "There was a frolic at Bill's house last night; it's a boy."

B *verb*

1 To dance, engage in merry making at a party; hence verbal noun *frolicking* = partying, dancing, as when following a **working**.

1848 *Paw Paw Hollow Church Minutes* 136 Church met and after worship. Excluded Martha Bales for dancing and frollicking. **1857** *Carson CW Letters* (Jan 13) they frolic and danc from hel to brekfust her[e] they dont Stope for Snow in this Cuntry. **1864** *Tesh CW Letters* (Jan 26) Branns has been a frolicing ever since Chrismas. **1924** Raine *Saddlebags* 83 Arter everybody eat, they began to frolic and dance. **1937** Hall *Coll* (Emerts Cove TN) A frolic [is] a party. Frolicking [is] dancing. **1939** Hall *Coll* (Cherokee NC) They never had no fellowship there. They didn't have frolicking up in there much. Sometimes they'd gather up a crowd of them and have a little play, [but] they never had time to have [a] frolic, had to work too hard. **1962** Dykeman *Tall Woman* 168 "It was lonesome, coming back from all that frolicking to find nobody here," she pouted to Paul. **1966** West *Dialect Sthn Mts* 34 She's purty as a picher and has sot her cap to frolic tell the cows come home.

2 To menstruate.

1929 Duncan and Duncan *Sayings* 235 Frolickin' (menstruating) women musn' make kraut ur can fruit.

frolic around *verb phrase* See citation.

1997 Johnson *Melungeon Heritage* 60 "Frolicking around" meant flipping around from one place to another. It also meant you felt pretty.

frolicking See **frolic B1**.

from *preposition*

1 From the time that one was.

1913 Kephart *Our Sthn High* 170 I've knowed him from a boy. **1994–97** Montgomery *Coll* (known to Adams, Brown, Ledford, Norris, Oliver, Weaver).

2 Used in phrasal prepositions.

1964 Williams *Prep Mt Speech* 54 It is with the clustering of prepositions that mountain folk often amaze outsiders. The prepositions the mountaineer finds particularly useful in indicating changes of reference. The angry mother scolding the stubborn child who has hidden under the table is exact in her command: "You git up out from down in under that thar table, er I'll whup ever' bit a hide offen (off from on) yer back." The switch is snatched "down from up over" where it "stays at." **1983** Page and Wigginton *Aunt Arie* 80 I run into th'house and got th'DDT and sprayed it all-l-l over t'run [the snake] out from in under there. **1985** Irwin *Alex Stewart* 273 It comes from back over on the second ridge from here.

from can to can't See **can see to can't see**.

from pillar to post *phrase* See citation.

2007 McMillon *Notes* = dashing around but accomplishing nothing.

front-handed See **fore-handed**.

front name *noun* A given or Christian name.

1950 Wood *Sure of Life* 52 We heerd tell yore front name's Robert. **c1960** Wilson *Coll* = one's Christian name or the first of two given names.

front stick *noun* Same as **forestick**.

1968 Wilson *Folklore Mammoth Cave* 33 [The backlog was] the large stick placed at the back of the fireplace. The smaller one, on the andirons, was the forestick or front stick. **1986** Pederson et al. *LAGS* (Claiborne Co TN).

frost *verb* variant third-singular form as two syllables: *frost-es*. See also **-es**[2].

1983 *Dark Corner OHP-4A* After it frostes, you can just hang a beef up right on your back porch, good cool air, and he'll keep.

frost-bit *adjective* Bitten by frost. For similar forms, see **bite A2**.

1864 *Brown CW Letters* (Jan 20) a great meny of the boyes has got their feat frost bit Mat has his frost bit. **1922** *TN CW Ques* 850 (Rhea Co TN) [I] was badly frost bit at Nashville. **2001** House *Clay's Quilt* 4 His little hands is plumb frostbit.

frostes See **frost**.

frousty *adjective* See citation.

1952 Wilson *Folk Speech NC* 542 = slouchy, disorderly. **1997** Montgomery *Coll* (known to Oliver).

[cf EDD *frowsty* sb 3 "ill-tempered"]

frow See **froe**.

frowzed *adjective* Of the hair: unkempt, rumpled, disheveled.

1945 Vincent *Here in TN* 9 After a bit the door to his place opened, and a frowsed head poked out.

froze, frozed See **freeze 2**.

froze fog (also *frozen fog*) *noun* Hoarfrost.

1961 Seeman *Arms of Mt* 217 We have only to look up to the top of the ridge to see, against the gray winter sky, the whole forest blooming white with "froze fog." **1967** Campbell *Memories of Smoky* 160 "Frozen fog," as hoarfrost is called by most of the mountain people, is formed when the clouds are down on the mountain and the temperature is below the freezing point. As the particles of moisture in the clouds touch a twig or other object it is transformed into tiny ice crystals. When there is little or no wind, as is usually the case in the deep forest, the ice crystals form on all sides of the twigs.

fruit *noun* Apples preserved, stewed, or made into sauce (see 1973 citation). See also **apple fruit**.

1917 (in **1944** Wentworth *ADD* 236) (sWV) *stewed fruit* = apple sauce. Not applied to other stewed fruits served at meals. **1926** Wilson *Cullowhee Wordlist* = apples. "We have lots of fruit this year, but no peaches." **1939** Hall *Coll* (White Oak NC) Will you have some of the fruit [passing the apple sauce]. **1973** *GSMNP-4:2:4* A lot of times we'd have applesauce. We called it fruit. **1973** Medford *Long Hard Road* 14 Apples, back in the old days, contributed a big part to the family living. It was just spoke of as "fruit." You didn't call it apple sauce. Apples fit into every meal, as well as to eat raw between meals—and at night, as we sat around the fire. They were dried, smoked, treated with sulphur or bleached. They were made into apple butter, jelly, cider, as well as pies of all kinds (including the "family" (or deep-dish) pie . . .) and fried pies, made from dried apples. They were canned and baked, as well as stewed. **1974** Fink *Bits Mt Speech* 10 = applies to apples only. "Have some *fruit*." **1984** Dykeman and Stokely *At Home* 55 Called simply "fruit" by the early settlers, apples such as the favorite Limbertwigs and Milams gave both variety and nutrition to the pioneer diet. **2005** Williams *Gratitude* 495 = cooked apples (what Yankees call "apple sauce"). Dried cooked apples is *dried fruit*.

[DARE *fruit* n 1 chiefly South Midland]

frush See **fresh A.**

fruss (also *fruster, frusterate*) *verb* To upset, fluster.

1925 Dargan *Highland Annals* 99 He got frustered then, an' said he'd come fer bear, an' he was goin' to have one if he had to go on by hissef. **1978** Montgomery *White Pine Coll* VI-2 They was some of them so frussed about it after they did it, but I didn't want it tuck off then. **1995–96** Montgomery *Coll*: *fruster* (known to Cardwell, Jones, Ledford, Oliver); *frusterate* (known to Ledford).

fruster, frusterate See **fruss.**

fruz See **freeze 1.**

frying size *noun* See citations.

1927 Woofter *Dialect from WV* 354 = young chickens large enough to kill. **1946** Wilson *Fidelity Folks* 80 You recall . . the old-fashioned country home, with its well-stocked smokehouse and with plenty of frying-sized chickens running around.

[DARE *frying size* adj 1 chiefly South, South Midland]

fry pan *noun* A frying pan.

1984 Page and Wigginton *Foxfire Cookery* 7 Then we had a great big old fry pan with a big long handle, and that's what she fried her meat in.

full

A (also *full up*) *verb, verb phrase* Especially of the moon: to fill, become full.

1913 Kephart *Our Sthn High* 252 Git the almanick and see when that feller'll full. **c1945** Haun *Hawk's Done* 210 My old woman always has to git the almanac to see when I'm going to full. **1953** Davison *Word-List Appal* 11 We will plant cucumbers when the moon fulls. **1961** *Coe Ridge OHP*-341B He just watched things like that, see, and kept up with it, and I mean he couldn't read and write. He didn't know his name up in front of his face, and he could tell you when the moon fulled or when it quartered, the hour and the day. **1981** GSMNP-122:66 If you want good kraut, you make it on the full of the moon. Don't never make it after it fulls. **1983** *Dark Corner OHP*-9A On the new of the moon most of the times you can cut a tree and it'll dry out and get right, and just after the moon fulls, if it fulls, you can cut one and cut it down right there and that thing will just [be] soft, the edges, just rotten. **1991** Still *Wolfpen Notebooks* 90 Look at that moon fulling up! If it gets any bigger it's liable to bust.

[DARE *full* v 1 chiefly South, South Midland]

B *adverb* Entirely, quite. See also **full dark.**

1924 Raine *Saddlebags* 199 Ye'll find a heap more that's full as good. **1965** Miller *Pigeon's Roost* (Dec 23) I full do remember that we would always hear the roar of shooting on Christmas day which shotguns was the firearms and the 12 gauge was the most common ones used. **1975** Fink *Backpacking* 222 A quarter of the way down we ran full into the marks of a terrific windstorm of some years before, a "blowdown" where trees by the hundreds had been blown up by the roots by the tornado and pitched around like jackstraws. **1999** Offutt *Out of Woods* 46 [It] still ain't full safe for me.

full dark *noun* Nighttime.

1928 Chapman *Happy Mt* 9 It was full dark now . . . [with] but one thin slice of day on the far edge of Big Gully Hill. **1949** Arnow *Hunter's Horn* 278 Now git on, so's you can git back before full dark. **1977** Arnow *Old Burnside* 77 Granma Simpson came one evening with Paps before full dark when the whippoorwills had started calling.

full-handed *adjective* Prosperous, well-supplied.

1917 Kephart *Word-List* 412 = well supplied, well to do. "He was a *full-handed* man, had a-plenty." **1927** Woofter *Dialect from WV* 354 I am full-handed now as far as help is concerned. **1962** Drukker *Lg By-Ways* 51 [A] "full-handed" person is one who is born to ample worldly possessions and who has all of this world's goods he needs. **1994–97** Montgomery *Coll* (known to Brown, Cardwell, Ledford, Shields).

[cf EDD *full-handed* (at *full* adj 7 (3)) "in good circumstances"; DARE *full-handed* adj South Midland]

full up See **full A.**

fun *verb* To kid, tease, joke (often in phrase *just funning*).

1888 Meriwether *Mt Life in TN* 460 Brother Harkins, you must be a funnin'. **1941** Stuart *Men of Mts* 23 I thought he was just a funning me a little. *Ibid.* 277 We's jist funnin' with you about th' match. **1962** Hall *Coll* (Del Rio TN) I didn't mean to scare you. I was just funnin' with you. **1986** Helton *Around Home* 379 = to joke, kid. **1991** Haynes *Haywood Home* 25 Everybody who knew Cora and Robert knew how they funned with each other. **2000** Carden *Mason Jars* 4 I figured she was "just funning," but I got the wood anyway.

[cf EDD *fun* sb/v 4 "indulge in fun"; DARE *fun* v 2 chiefly South, South Midland]

funeral *noun* A funeral, formerly often preached at a memorial service at a time after a person's death and burial. Also called **preaching funeral.** See also **funeralize, funeral meeting.**

1863 *Gilley CW Letters* (Jan 12) I would like to be thair when Johns funnal is preach if I could. **1864** *Watters-Curtis CW Letters* (July 18) I have got a leter from tempy curtis this morning and her and Dutch is going to have paps and Jims f[u]nerels preached the 16 of august and told me to Rite to you all and tell you all that they want us all to come. **1967** Combs *Folk-Songs* 8 [Grave sites] are seldom visited except at a burial, or at a "funeral," which is usually preached many years after the burial. **1987** Irwin *Museum Appalachia* 13 All the Big Valley people, it seemed to me, had said at one time or another: "I want Uncle John to preach my funeral." **1996–97** Montgomery *Coll* (known to Adams, Brown, Cardwell, Jones, Ledford, Norris).

[DARE *funeral* n B1 especially South Midland]

funeralize *verb* To hold a funeral service at a later, more convenient date for (i.e. after burying a person immediately); of a minister: to officiate and preach at such a service. In former times the service could come weeks or months afterward, in order to await better weather or allow extended family members to attend; hence noun *funeralizing* = a memorial service subsequent to a person's burial, often involving several preachers and lengthy testimonials; it was sometimes held annually for several years.

1895 Edson and Fairchild *TN Mts* 371 The bereaved parents, whom we are *funeralizing* to-day. **1921** Holton *Robber's Creek* 588 Peculiar to the Southern mountains is the custom of funeralizing. When a man dies, he is buried with no ceremony whatever, with not even much mourning on the part of the relatives. Ministers are few and scattered, there are no means of prompt communication with them and with interested friends at a distance, so only the demands of decency are complied with. After several members of the family have died, however, a pittance from the meager income is saved up for the purpose of hiring several ministers to conduct a funeral meeting, an elaborate event that more than atones for the apparent neglect. **1946** Stuart *Plum Grove Hills* 154 A memorial service for the dead ... is held at the graveside some time after the burial, sometimes several years later; in some instances the same person has been funeralized repeatedly. In some communities these services are called "Graveyard Meetings." The difficulty of getting a minister into the hills in bad weather surely accounted for many of these delayed funerals. "We wondered what Jason would think of the funeralizing, since he wasn't a Mountain Baptist." **1953** Davison *Word-List Appal* 11 *funeralize the dead* = to hold memorial services every year during the summer months, at which time several ministers preach sermons eulogizing those who have been dead many years. **1959** Roberts *Up Cutshin* 56 This gave rise to long protracted meetings ... and what came to be called funeralizings. Simply stated, this last custom was the preaching of the funerals in good weather of all those who had died during the long winters when ministers could not be called. **1975** Chalmers *Better* 17 Word reached us at breakfast that she had gone, and "please would the nurse come up and make her ready for the funeralizing." **1987** Young *Lost Cove* 45 Funeralizing the remains of the one who had been called took most of an afternoon and wore two or three preachers to a frazzle. **2006** *WV Encycl* 92 Because many preachers traveled extensive territories, "funeralizing" might be held only once a year, preferably on Memorial Day and often in the graveyard rather than the church.

[DARE *funeralize* v South, South Midland]

funeral meeting *noun* A memorial service, traditionally often for several people and with several preachers. Same as **memorial**. See also **funeral**.

1921 Holton *Robber's Creek* 588 After several members of the family have died, however, a pittance from the meager income is saved up for the purpose of hiring several ministers to conduct a funeral meeting, an elaborate event that more than atones for the apparent neglect. **c1950** Adams *Grandpap* 209 As food was as essential to a funeral-meeting as the preaching was, it may have influenced Mammy to do something about the memory of Grandpap Short. **1982** Slone *How We Talked* 75 = a yearly church service to celebrate the funerals of the people who died within the past year. **1995** Montgomery *Coll* = now called *memorial service*, which was often held during *protracted meeting* in May and across different denominations (Cardwell).

funeral pie *noun* See citation.

2006 *Encycl Appalachia* 933 The offering of food acts as a measure of the deceased's place within the community. For instance, those who only knew the deceased or his or her family in passing may offer one small dish such as a "funeral pie," a generic term encompassing many types of simple pies often given to bereaved families. Individuals who knew the deceased well are likely to offer more elaborate or homemade dishes—cakes, cooked hams, or chickens—or to bring more than one dish over several days. In this way, the amount of food brought in both before and after the funeral can serve as a gauge for the popularity of the deceased.

funk *noun* An offensive odor of something spoiled, rotten, or decaying, as from mold, tobacco, or mildew in meal barrels; hence adjective *funked* = having a rotten odor.

1892 Fruit *KY Words* 230 *funked* = rotten; used only of tobacco. **1917** Kephart *Word-List* 412 = an offensive smell. "Open the door and let the *funk* out." **1937** Hall *Coll* (Cades Cove TN) [It's necessary to smoke] barrels because they get funk. Meal makes funk. The barrels get slimy. Smoke kills the scent. **c1960** Wilson *Coll* = a bad odor from something spoiled, like funked tobacco. **1996–97** Montgomery *Coll* (known to Adams, Brown, Cardwell, Oliver, Weaver).

[OED3 *funk* n[2] 1 obsolete except U.S. dialect; DARE *funk* n 1 chiefly South Midland]

funky *adjective* Having an offensive odor from something spoiled, rotten, or decayed; musty.

1940 Hall *Coll* it smells funky as hell = of something starting to rot like old moldy grąss. **1957** Broaddus *Vocab Estill Co KY* 32 = [having] the smell of a damp, closed-up cellar. **1974** Dabney *Mt Spirits* 9 When that bead breaks, when you run them low wines in there, it gets down to a funky scent, leaves a bad odor in your connections. **1983** Davis *Multi-lingual Mule* 55 The fire hissed and crackled and soon drove out the spring chill and carried the funky air up the chimney. **1995** Montgomery *Coll* (known to Cardwell).

[DARE *funky* adj 1 chiefly South, South Midland]

funnel it down *verb phrase* See citation.

c1960 Wilson *Coll*: *funnel it down* = to drink a lot and too fast and hoggishly.

[DARE *funnel* v chiefly South, South Midland]

funny-turned *adjective* See citation.

2014 Williams *Coll* = odd. "He would go out to the barn anytime company came over. He was funny turned."

fur[1] See **furrow**.

fur[2] See **far**[2] **A1**.

furder See **far**[2] **A2**.

furderer See **further 1**.

furderest See **far**[2] **A3**.

furdest See **far**[2] **A3**, **further 2**.

furer See **far**[2] **A2**.

furest See **far**[2] **A3**.

furninst See **fornent**.

furnishment *noun* An implement, possession, piece of furniture.

1930 (in **1952** Mathes *Tall Tales* 164) They was a young captain up in Virginny—I disremember his name—that was broke up right atter the Civil War an' had to sell his furnishments. **1999** Montgomery *Coll*: *furnishments of a farm* = tools and implements (Cardwell).

fur piece See **far piece**.

furrer See **far**[2] **A2**.

furrest See **far**[2] **A3**.

furrin, **furriner** See **foreign**, **foreigner**.

furrow *noun* variant forms *fer*, *fur*.

1864 *Chapman CW Letters* (Feb 5) if I had bin at home I exspect I should run a fiew fers if the wether was as nice thare as it was hear. **1915** Dingus *Word-List VA* 183 *fur*. **1973** Miller *English Unicoi Co* 86 *Fur* used by 5 of 6 speakers. **1979** Melton *'Pon My Honor* 25 At the edge of the clearing he could see Billy going down the fur behind the old mule.

further *adverb* See also **far**[2].

1 variant comparative form *furderer*.

1957 Combs *Lg Sthn High: Word List* 36.

2 variant superlative forms *furderest*, *furdest*.

1913 Kephart *Our Sthn High* 23 Bushnell's the furdest ever I've been. **1925** Dargan *Highland Annals* 255 I reckon he wuz the furdest from the Amen row right then that he ever wuz in his life. **1940** Haun *Hawk's Done* 63 She was hid in the furderest corner that evening. **1997** Montgomery *Coll*: *furdest* (known to Oliver).

fuss

A variant forms *furs*, *furse*.

1911 Shearin *E KY Word-List* 538 = pronounced *furs*. **1927** Furman *Lonesome Road* 81 I never wanted no furse made over me. **1931** Combs *Lg Sthn High* 1316 *Fuss* often becomes "furse."

B *noun* A dispute, argument, commotion, display of excessive or unnecessary emotion.

1861 *Rogers CW Letters* (June 24) well william I would like to write you a interresing letter but I can not my mind is so torin up and so d—d much fuss here. **1864** *Copeland CW Letters* (March 27) my notion is that this Fuss will end by the first of next Septtember But the most of us may be kild by that time and it never will doo us aney good. **1867** Harris *Sut Lovingood* 126 I hearn a tarin big fuss on tuther side, squawkin, cussin, hollerin, an' a gineral soun ove things a-smashin. **1939** Hall *Coll* (Little Cataloochee NC) The bear sort of made a ugly fuss, and finally [Johnny] hollered pretty loud to try to scare the bear away. **1956** Hall *Coll* (Jones Cove TN) So this old woman come to this old man, Sam, and raised a fuss with him . . . and they got into a fight. **1972** GSMNP-92 They'd get into a fuss. They wouldn't fight with nothing but their fists. **1993** Parris *Folklore* 471 When the fire roars up the chimney like it wants to get out of the house, you can look out for a fuss in the family.

[DARE *fuss* n B3 chiefly South, South Midland]

C *verb* To dispute, argue, raise a commotion, display excessive or unnecessary emotion.

See also **fuss at**, **fuss out**.

1900 Harben *N GA Sketches* 84 Me an' Joe was eternally a-fussin', an' mother allays tuk his part. **1931** Combs *Lg Sthn High* 1308 As would be expected, many terms for fussing, fighting, and killing abound. **1963** Watkins and Watkins *Yesterday* 60 Rufe had to be fussed out of bed every morning. **1981** Alderman *Tilson Mill* 8 On one occasion he was marking a tree to be used in making peavey handles, he said, and boomer squirrels in the tree fussed and fussed at him all the while. Then he said, "I fussed right back at them." **1984** Burns *Cold Sassy* 67 I could still hear those two fussing after I passed the foundry. **1992** Davis *Jack Tales* 89 "We didn't do nothing!" both of them fussed right back at him. **1995–97** Montgomery *Coll*: *fussed* (known to Adams, Brown, Cardwell, Norris). **2005** Williams *Gratitude* 496 = what you do before you start fighting . . . you get in a big fuss, or git'n a big racket.

[DARE *fuss* v C3 chiefly South, South Midland]

fuss at *verb phrase* To scold (someone).

1940 Haun *Hawk's Done* 97 Then he let in to fussing at me because I let her go over there to spend two weeks with Amy. **c1945** Haun *Hawk's Done* 241 After that they fussed at her all the time and threatened to have her churched, claiming she wasn't good enough to be a member. **1976** Wolfram and Christian *Appal Speech* 97 She'll probably give me a whippin' or I'll get fussed at.

[DARE *fuss* v C4 chiefly South, South Midland]

fuss out *verb phrase* To berate or castigate (someone) severely. See also **fuss A**, **fuss at**.

1971 *Granny Women* 258 [Her words] kind'a didn't do no good, so she really got onto'im and fussed'im out.

fussyfied *adjective* Angry, "worked up."

1944 Justus *Lizzie* 42 Don't feel fussy-fied, Grampy.

fust, **fustest** See **first**, **firstest**.

G

gad *noun* See citation.

1957 Broaddus *Vocab Estill Co KY* 33 = a goad for oxen.

[OED3 *gad* n[1] 4a "a pointed rod or stick used for driving oxen" dialect]

gaddy around *verb phrase* To go or wander about idly or without serious aim.

1978 Montgomery *White Pine Coll* X-2 I haven't done anything except just gaddy around and build a few fences and help the tobacco and raise a garden and something like that.

gaev See **gaff**.

gaff *noun*

A Variant form *gaev* [see **1969** in **B1**].

B Senses.

1 A spur-like implement used in preparing tobacco. See also **stringer 1**.

1969 Miller *Raising Tobacco* 31–32 Three words for this implement were commonly used in western North Carolina: *stringer*, *needle*, and *gaev*. . . . The cutter then passed the stalk to the *stringer* who laid the stalk on the sharp point of the *gaev* about eight inches from the butt and pressed down. . . . There were stories and warning about men who had stumbled and fallen on a *gaev*, who had pierced an ear or lost an eye to a *gaev* as their head moved down when pushing a stalk to the bottom of a stick.

2 A similar implement used in cock-fighting.

1979 *Cockfighting II* 155 Before the cocks are put into the pit, gaffs are put on them. The standard length for the gaff is about two and three-quarters inches long. **2005** Williams *Gratitude* 496 *gaff* = a metal spur fastened to the leg of a rooster to be put into a cock fight.

[< French *gaffe*]

gaily *predicate adjective*

1 (also **gayly**) Of a person: in good health or spirits, lively.

1861 *Martin CW Letters* (Sept 20) father we are all as galey as you ever saw. **1862** *Lockmiller CW Letters* (Aug 14) the boyes is all well as common at this time and all galey. **1895** Dromgoole *Logan's Courtship* 150 She seemed mighty willin', bein' young an' gayly. **1913** Kephart *Our Sthn High* 285 An adverb may be used as an adjective: "I hope the folks with you is gaily" (well). **1939** Hall *Coll* (Bryson City NC) Do you feel gaily tonight? **1944** Combs *Word-List Sthn High* 23 I'm as gaily as a buck (Feeling in excellent spirits). **c1951** Chapman *Speech Confusing* A mountain woman asks, "Are you pert today?" meaning "Are you in good health?" She means the same thing when she inquires, "Is all (everybody) at your house stout?" or "All your folks feeling gaily?" **1972** Cooper *NC Mt Folklore* 92 = well; recovering from illness. **1975** Chalmers *Better* 66 "I feel gaily," said Aunt Charity, "stout with health and religion, but last week I wasn't much." **1992** Brooks *Sthn Stuff* 55 *gayly* = in good spirits; well (in health). "You're feeling mighty gayly today, I'm glad to see."

2 Of an animal, especially a horse: frisky, rambunctious.

c1970 Handlon *Ol' Smoky* 20 Also, the horses we were riding appeared to be a little "Gaily." Mountain people said that horses "get gaily" if they are not exercised enough.

[SND *geylies* adv; CUD *gaily* adv (at *gay* adj) "well; very"; DARE *gaily* adj both senses South Midland]

gaint See **gaunt A**.

galack See **galax C**.

galacking See **galax C**.

galak See **galax A**.

galax

A *noun* Construed as a plural count noun; hence singular *galak* through back-formation [see also **C** below].

2008 *Rosie Hicks* 1 Then he'd buy galak. **2009** Burton *Beech Mt Man* 118 One of 'em McGuires' wife was in the woods pulling these galax.

B *noun* A common evergreen plant (*Galax aphylla*) whose glossy, leathery leaves and branches are harvested and sold especially for ornamental greenery for the holiday season; it also has medicinal uses. Also called **beetleweed**, **coltsfoot**. See c1975 citation.

[**1901** Lounsberry *Sthn Wild Flowers* 402 To many that have never seen the blossoms, these leaves are familiar, for the mountain people pick them by the million and tie them into little bunches of a hundred each which later are sent to a florist in different parts of a country.] **1941** Walker *Story of Mt* 53–54 Galax . . . is one of the plants that is more prized for its round heart-shaped evergreen leaf than for its long spikelike raceme of white flowers. . . . The foliage of galax has been collected in the mountains of North Carolina, Tennessee, and Virginia so persistently that the plant is threatened with extinction in some localities. Galax's long leafstem adds much to the convenience in working into sprays and wreaths, and the bronzy hue that the foliage takes on in the latter part of the year contributes much to its popularity. This plant has the distinction of being the only species belonging to its genus. **c1975** Lunsford *It Used to Be* 69 When you go pretty far back in the coves there's a vocation that is peculiar to the high reaches of the Blue Ridge Mountains, and that's the gathering of an unusual plant called galax. There's a place up in Virginia close to the North Carolina line called Galax,—Galax, Virginia. Following the Blue Ridge clear on through Mt. Mitchell, on the higher elevations this plant is found. The old folk name for it would be "coltsfoot." The higher up you go into the Blue Ridge, the larger the leaves, and, in colder weather and in the spring, they turn bronze. They're used for decorations and so on in many places. In the Blue Ridge section especially they're gathered by mountaineers along with locothia, locothia spray or dog-hobble, and other evergreens, and shipped. Many people have made fortunes in the gathering of galax. **1982** Rives *Blue Ridge Parkway* 36 Growing in beds beneath tall trees, galax leaves are shaped like rounded, ruffled hearts with a shiny, leathery [leaf], and are deep green or red in color. When winter comes and all seems bare and brown, the galax adds its lovely color to the forest floor. These plants have played an important part in the lives of many mountain dwellers, as they were one of the "cash crops." In fall many families would go into the woods and gather galax leaves in burlap sacks. These gatherings could be sold to a local merchant, who would in turn ship them to florists all over the country. Galax leaves retain their vibrancy for a long time after being picked. In the days before refrigeration florists would use them in funeral wreaths and floral displays, a lasting bit of green to grace a winter grave. While not so common as it once was, the practice of gathering galax in the fall still exists in the mountains of North Carolina. **1982** *Smokies Heritage* 22 There remains forever the beauty of May's wildflowers: the white spires of galax rising from its glossy green leaves (galax is frequently called "colt's foot" because its leaves are shaped like a colt's hoof). **2008** *Rosie Hicks* 2 We'd go get a box of evergreens ... like galak, bridal wreath, silver pine.

C (also *galack*) *verb* To gather this plant or others as ornamental evergreens for sale during the holiday season; hence noun *galacking*, *galaxing* = the gathering of such plants (less commonly done in the Smokies than in the Blue Ridge Mountains of North Carolina and Virginia), *galack* verb = to gather this plant or other ornamental greens to sell to florists.

1941 *Words* 31 To a vast, scattered army of North Carolina galakers Christmas is in the air. Galaking is the business of collecting decorative greens, the term being derived from galax leaves. **1949** Sharpe *Lowgap Man* "I'd ruther," said a picker, "galack than evergreen. Galacking is slavish work, but it's plumb healthful." **1957** Parris *My Mts* 242 As an industry confined to our mountains, gallackin'—that's what mountain folks call gathering the leaves—is comparatively new ... Always Money in Galaxin'. *Ibid.* 243 Now some 45 years later, Haynes is one of the top gallackers in all the mountains, with a galax and evergreen "factory" here in Old Fort from which he ships out thousands of pounds of galax leaves and other evergreens week in and week out during the year. **1976** Garber *Mountain-ese* 32 *galack* = pick galax. "In the spring the wimmen get their baskets and go galacking together." **1995–97** Montgomery *Coll*: *galax* (known to Adams, Brown, Cardwell, Jones, Ledford); *galack* (known to Adams, Jones, Ledford, Norris); *galacking* (known to Cardwell, Ledford); *galaxing* (known to Brown, Cardwell, Ledford, Norris, Shields).

[*galack* back-formation from *galax*, interpreted as a plural noun; DARE *galak* v Appalachians]

gald (also *galld*) *verb* To chafe or irritate (as the skin of a person or hide of an animal) or cause blisters from chafing, irritation, or overwork; hence participial adjectives *galded*, *gallded*; by extension = to insult.

c1940 Aswell *Glossary TN Idiom* 9 = chafe. "This saddle has *gallded* my mule raw." **c1960** Wilson *Coll* The collar gallded the horse's neck. **1963** Watkins and Watkins *Yesterday* 123 A man who plowed in hot weather, sweated a lot, and used a cob for toilet tissue would get chafed, or "galded," he said. As a cure, he used elder leaves instead of cobs. Sometimes a man's crotch became so "galded" that he could hardly walk, and some used flour as a powder to help cure the "galding." **1979** Carpenter *Walton War* 179 "Gallded" was another expression used for completely worn out, irritated or blistered. **1995–97** Montgomery *Coll* He gallded me every time he preached (Brown), = usually associated with irritation in the groin (Ledford). **2003** Cavender *Folk Medicine* 203 = [having] heat rash or chafed skin, as in "My leg is so galded I can hardly walk." **2005** Williams *Gratitude* 484 *gall* = made sore by rubbing, as in riding a horse. *Galded* is a worse condition than *chafted*. **2006** Cavender *Medical Term* 1022 Chafed areas of skin, especially in the groin, are described as "galled" or "gallded."

[back-formation from *galded*, pleonastic past participle of *gall*; DARE *gald* v chiefly South, South Midland]

galded, galding, galld, gallded See **gald**.

gallant (also *glant*) *verb* To court or flirt; go about with members of the opposite sex.

1859 (in **1956** Eliason *Tarheel Talk* 273) (Alexander Co NC) I would like to know ... what girl you was gallanting. **1862** *Baggarly CW Letters* (Jan 29) we are a fraid that we will forget how to glant with the gentle men before they get back but i recon thay will not want to glant with us tho we nead not scear our selvs. **1863** *Rogers CW Letters* (March 24) tell lige to go up to old fort Payne and Glant them girls Round ther.

[cf DARE *gallant* v chiefly South, South Midland]

gallflower (also *gallweed*) *noun* A gentian wildflower (*Gentiana quinquefolia*), from which is made a tonic to treat a fever. Same as **agueweed 1**.

1901 Lounsberry *Sthn Wild Flowers* 428 The stiff gentian, a quaintly pretty one among them all, grows in either dry or moist soil and often ascends to a considerable height in the mountains. ... In these parts of the country the mountain people call it the gall-flower because its juices are so bitter, and ague-weed on account of the extract they make from its roots and employ in curing fever. **1982** Stupka *Wildflowers* 88 Of all the various gentians in the southern mountains this species is readily recognized by the small size of the individual flowers and by the profusion of blossoms on a single plant. ... Such local names as "ague-weed" and "gall-weed" relate to its former use as a tonic.

gallinipper *noun* Any of several insects, especially a large mosquito (*Psorophora elliata*).

1862 *Barkley CW Letters* (June 23) I Returnd from picket yesterday almost Eat up with the Musqueters & galnippas they are the worst I Ever saw they can nip you threw your coat & shirt. **1962** Wilson *Folkways Mammoth Cave* 21 The long-legged cranefly was a *gallinipper*. Its bite was supposed to be very poisonous, though there seem to be no recent records of its ever biting. **1964** Reynolds *Born of Mts* 9 Mosquitoes, called Swamp Angels or Gallinipers by the natives, cannot breed in running water of mountain streams, so there are few of them. **1967** *DARE Survey* (Maryville TN) = extra-large mosquito. [**1995** Montgomery *Coll* (unknown to consultants from the Smoky Mountains).] **2017** Heinmiller *Coll* That gallinipper was bigger'n a daddy long-legs!

[origin unknown; DARE *gallinipper* n 1a chiefly South, South Midland, especially South Atlantic]

gall of the earth *noun* A wild plant (*Prenanthes trifoliata/serpentaria*) from whose bitter root an antidote for rattlesnake venom is prepared. Also called **rattlesnake root 2**.

1982 Stupka *Wildflowers* 132 "Gall-of-the-earth," another name of this plant, refers to the intensely bitter roots. **1997** Montgomery *Coll* = no insect will eat this plant (Cardwell).

gallon *noun* Variant plural form without -*s* following a numeral.

1939 Hall *Coll* (Emerts Cove TN) That way you get about, well an average of five gallon [of] whiskey to that if it turns out right. **1974** *AOHP/ALC*-807 We stayed over there with them till we drink it all up, drunk the six gallon or gave it away. **1997** *Dante OHP*-45 We'd get out in the summertime and pick blackberries. We'd sell a hundred gallon of blackberries.

galloping consumption *noun* Virulent tuberculosis.

1914 Furman *Sight* 33 She died of the breast-complaint; some calls it the galloping consumpt'. **1955** Washburn *Country Doctor* 12 Other complaints were "pneumony fever," "side pleurisy," "joint rheumatism," "jumping toothache," the "bloody flux," and the "gallopin' consumption," to give the more descriptive designations of well-known diseases.

galloping dandruff *noun* Head lice.

1940 Farr *More TN Expressions* 447 = head lice: "The baby's head is full of galloping dandruff." **1968–69** *DARE Survey* (Dillard GA, Richwood WV) = a head louse, or body louse.

galloping fence *noun* A **rail fence** laid out in zigzag fashion. Same as **worm fence**.

1896 *Word-List* 417 *gallopin fence* = fence made of rails stuck in the ground criss-cross. **1952–57** (in **1973** McDavid and McDavid *Vocab E KY* 155) = rail fence laid as successive tripods, attested by 7/52 (13.4%) of E KY speakers for the Linguistic Atlas of the North Central States. **1957** Combs *Lg Sthn High: Word List* 43 = a fence of ordinary rails, whose ends are set in the ground at an angle, one opposite the other, and which cross near the top. Especially suitable for hillside terrain. **1986** Pederson et al. *LAGS* (Lumpkin Co GA). **1999** Montgomery *File* (known to 85-year-old man, Greenbrier TN).

gallus *noun* (usually used in plural) A suspender for men's trousers. Also called **strop**.

1862 *Reese CW Letters* (Sept 29) if you Can send mee an thing doo it I need A pair of gallisses and Socks. **1864** *Tesh CW Letters* (Jan 26) I sent you a pair of gallowes in that Box to wear with your new pants. **1867** Harris *Sut Lovingood* 154 His coat-tails wur blowed off tu his shoulders, the hine aind ove his galluses wus raped round his neck. **1883** Zeigler and Grosscup *Heart of Alleghanies* 249 An unbleached, linen shirt, crossed by "galluses," which held his homespun pantaloons in place, covered his body. **1934–47** *LAMSAS Appal* (Madison Co NC, Swain Co NC). **1961** *Coe Ridge OHP*-336B I'm going to shoot him right in the cross of the galluses. **1973** *GSMNP*-14:4 He didn't have a thing on but his galluses and his shoes. **1982** DeArmond *So High* 10 Mama bent to button the top button of Papa's one and only, best shirt, then fastened the galluses to the bib of his overalls. **1986** Pederson et al. *LAGS* (Blount Co TN, Cocke Co TN, Jefferson Co TN, Sevier Co TN). **1991** Haynes *Haywood Home* 35 I realize galluses are supposed to be called suspenders, but we called them galluses. **2002** Myers *Best Yet Stories* 49 When they shot at the Yankees, Rebel soldiers were to aim the shot "betwixt the gallowses."

[variant of *gallows* construed as a singular noun + -*s*; OED3 *gallows* n 6 now dialect, Scot, and U.S.; cf EDD *gallows* n 6; SED nEngl]

gallweed See **gallflower**.

galoot *noun* A man, usually an older, foolish, or unattractive one.

1883 Zeigler and Grosscup *Heart of Alleghanies* 146 "Ef yer hunters," said one, "we're only too glad to see ye; but at fust we didn't know whether ye war gentlemen or a sheriff's posse, the road-boss or revenue galoots." **1976** Garber *Mountain-ese* 33 = old fool. "The Salvation Army gave the old galoot food and a pallet to sleep on." **1998** Montgomery *Coll* (known to Bush, Jones, Norris, Oliver), He's as crazy as any old galoot (Cardwell), = general term of derision for an old man (Ledford).

[DARE *galoot* n perhaps *ga*- variant of *ker*- + *loot*, Scots variant of *lout*]

galvanize *noun* The nickel plating on an object made of steel. See also **gray cloud**, **silver cloud**.

1917 Kephart *Word-List* 412 = nickel plating. "The *galvanize* wore off my pistol." **1940** Stuart *Trees of Heaven* 315 There was a washpan layin there. Boliver grabbed it and seized it with his teeth. The galvanize flew off in tiny white flakes. **1972** Hall *Sayings* 126 Moonshine whiskey [can be] "clouded" by the "galvanize" corroded from a steel (rather than copper) still by the acid of the mash ("beer").

galvate *verb* See citation.

c1982 Young *Colloquial Appal* 10 = [to] wander, stray.

gambling stick, See **gambrel**.

gambrel (also *gambling stick, gambrel stick, gimble pole, gimbling stick, gimlet stick*) *noun* A bent piece of iron used to hang the carcass of an animal, especially a hog, by the hind legs when it is to be dressed after slaughtering. See c1975, 1997 citations.

1938 Stuart *Dark Hills* 212 The clean sweet-smelling hog bodies [hung] to a scaffold with a gambling-stick sharpened on both ends and run under the leaders of each hind leg and resting on top of the scaffold with the weight of the hog swinging below. **1952** Wilson *Folk Speech NC* 544 *gimbling-stick*. **1963** Watkins and Watkins *Yesterday* 96 After the hair was removed, the farmer stuck a hickory gimlet stick about two feet long under the leaders in the hog's hind legs. **1968** Clarke *Stuart's Kentucky* 164 The men cut the flesh around the leaders in the hogs' hind legs, and put the sharpened ends of the gambling stick (gambrel) behind each leader. **1970** *Dressing and Cooking* 18 Skinning and Dressing [the raccoon]: . . . skin out both hind legs, and make a small slice between bone and tendon and insert the gambling stick . . . Hang the coon up. **1972** *Foxfire I* 192 When the hide was scraped clean, the hamstring was exposed on both hind legs, and a gambling stick sharpened on both ends—or a singletree—was slipped behind the exposed tendons. The hog was then strung up on a strong pole. **c1975** Lunsford *It Used to Be* 46, 161 They have what they call a white oak split. They take that stick which is sharpened at each end—called a gamblin' stick—and put it between the two hind feet. A little strip of the skin has been cut between the tendon and the bone of the hind feet. The stick is placed in one hind foot, and several people together raise the hog above a pole. Then the loose end of the stick is placed in the other hind foot, and the hog is led down so it hangs from the pole. . . . That's a stick about two feet in length sharpened at each end to put between the tendons of the hind feet of a hog to hold him up on a pole while being butchered. That is one of the first things that is done at hog killing time after the hog has been scraped clean of hair. Then the butcher takes a knife and cuts a hole in the skin enough so that he can pull the tendon up, slip in the sharp end of the gamlin' stick on one side and then cut the other foot and slip it in on that side, then two or three men raise the hog up and slip that loose when they get it high enough to push one end of that gamblin' stick over the pole and skip it in under the tendon again. Then they let the hog down. That's the "gamlin' stick." **1997** Montgomery *Coll*: *gambrel* = stout wood stick inserted in a gimbling hole, then hoisted up for gutting (Brown), = also called a *gambling stick* or *gambrel stick* (Jones), = the gimble pole was used to hang the slaughtered hog by the tendons of its rear legs (Ledford). **1999** Morgan *Gap Creek* 21 he usually got another man to help him hoist the hog once it was scraped and slide the gambrel stick up a pole so it hung high enough to be gutted and dressed. **2005** Williams *Gratitude* 496 When a hog was slaughtered and they were ready to clean (gut) it and drain the blood from the carcass, they needed a means of hanging, or suspending it by the back legs. A short stout pole long enough to separate the legs and strong enough to support the weight of the hog was cut, then tapered and sharpened on each end. This was called a gamblin' stick. A slit was cut in the hog's hind legs, down next to the foot, between the main leader (tendon) and the bone. The sharpened end of the gamblin' stick was pushed through the slit in each leg. Then the hog could be raised and hung by pulling on the rope or chain attached to the center of the gamblin' stick.

[cf OED3 *gambrel* obsolete except dialect; DARE *gambling stick* n chiefly South, South Midland]

game *noun* Used as a euphemism for *dance*. Also called **play**.

1945 McNeer *Sthn Highlands* 21 The play-parties began to be called that because the church could not countenance dancing. And the dances were called "games."

game stew *noun* A stew boiled in a pot into which is put any variety of game killed and skinned by a party of hunters during the day.

1982 *Smokies Heritage* 96 The hired girl ladled out a trencher (bowl) from the pot bubbling over the fire—a game stew perhaps, made from rabbit or squirrel, and an ashy piece of johnny cake baked upon the hearth. **1995–97** Montgomery *Coll* (known to Adams, Brown, Cardwell, Jones, Norris).

gamling stick See **gambrel**.

gammick (also *gammock*) *verb* To romp about, frolic.

1918 Combs *Word-List South* 34 = to play, gambol (of children). **1976** Still *Pattern of Man* 91 Uncle Mize took his rebirth like a sheep to green ivy, gammicking over his farm, beating in a crop, cussing and bossing as in his younger days.

[OED3 *gammock* v < *gammock* n[2] 1 "a piece of fun . . . a jest" or 2 "fun; sport" chiefly English regional; EDD *gammock* v 2]

gander *verb* See citations.

1952 Wilson *Folk Speech NC* 544 = to remain near one's pregnant wife. **c1975** Lunsford *It Used to Be* 172 "Gandering" is a term describing a husband expecting his wife to bear him a baby and he has to stay around home a good deal. He says he is just gandering because the gander sets on the nest while the goose is away.

gander pull (also *gander pulling*) *noun* A competition in which mounted riders gallop past a rooster or turkey whose neck had been greased and that has been either hung upside down from a limb or buried in the ground to its neck. The rider able to snatch the head off the bird is [was] declared the winner and awarded the beheaded bird as the prize. See 1997 citation.

1818 Fearon *Sketches* 247 They have also another practice . . . called "gander pulling." This diversion consists in tying a live gander to a tree or pole, greasing its neck, riding past it at full gallop, and he who succeeds in pulling off the head of the victim, receives the laurel crown. **1885** Murfree *Prophet* 103 Rick knew that they were making ready for the gander-pulling, which unique sport had been selected by the long-headed mountain politicians as likely to ensure the largest assemblage possible from the surrounding region to hear the candidates prefer their claims. **1972** Carr *Oldest Profession* 64 "Gander Pulling" was a rather cruel sport of the mountains. A gander (male goose) was hung by the feet to a high tree limb and his neck greased. Ringmasters then lined up participating riders who would go in a gallop under the tree, all the while making a lunge at the greased neck of the gander. The gander's neck was hard to break at best, but thoroughly greased, it took repeated effort. At the expense of being called an amateur psychologist, this sport, though cruel by standards of today, did serve a purpose. It was one of the many ways a mean mountain man vented his hostility. **1974** Dabney *Mt Spirits* 97 Gander-pulling was one of the diversions Owens offered to his guests.

Cruel though it was, gander-pulling, which came from England, was one of the most popular diversions among mountain people in the 1800s. **1997** Montgomery *Coll*: *gander pull* = the gander turkey or rooster was buried in the ground with only his head showing, and mounted riders would race by snatching its head without leaving the saddle (Brown). **2007** McMillon *Notes* = [took place] only in former times.

[DARE *gander pulling* n chiefly South Midland, South]

gandydancer *noun* In logging, a member of a railroad crew who maintains the track and helps build railroads using a pick and shovel.

1964 Clarkson *Lumbering in WV* 362 = pick-and-shovel man who works on the railroad. Syn. section hand. **1974–75** McCracken *Logging* 20:41 The gandy dancer they called them, or their section hands were about the lowest pay.

gang *noun* A large number of people; a herd or flock of animals or birds of the same kind in company.

1834 Crockett *Narrative* 85 I took my rifle and cut out, but hadn't gone far, when I discovered a large gang of hogs. **1864** Stepp *CW Letters* (May 14) itel you my dear iam tired of Staying here and living the way wee doo i am tired of sleeping among a gang of men on the ground like hogs. **1864** Wilson *Confederate Private* 41 (March 30) one day there was three deer all in a gang come past here & I put Link after them. **1904–20** Kephart *Notebooks* 4:749 Let a bear take to a gang o' hogs an' he'll never quit 'em. **1913** Morley *Carolina Mts* 194 "We used to have great gangs of sheep," the people say, "but now we have to buy all our wool, and it don't pay to weave noway." **1924** Spring *Lydia Whaley* 2 At that time they had no money but gangs of hogs and lots of sides o' meat. **1937** Hall *Coll* (Cataloochee NC) They was ten big gobblers in the gang. *Ibid.* (Mingus Creek NC) They was a pretty smart gang of 'em [= Yankee soldiers passing through the Oconaluftee during the Civil War]. **1939** Hall *Coll* (Deep Creek NC) While we was up in there our dogs got atter a gang of coons an' run 'em in on the head of Reagans Creek. **1954** *GSMNP*-19:5 [If] I'd shoot right down the tree thinking I'd kill them, [it] might be just a gang of wolves or bears or something. **1956** *GSMNP*-22:16 I was afraid they'd bite my children. I had a gang of children up there. **1962** Hall *Coll* (Cataloochee NC) I had a big gang of children and had to school 'em. **1971** *AOHP/ALC*-137 They had lots of cows and horses and a big gang of sheep. **1983** *Dark Corner OHP*-5A I was a member of the Pig Club when I was a boy going to school. You know, they'd give you a pig, and you raise a gang for them, and you give another boy a pig. **1989** *Matewan OHP*-33 Them hogs could smell that [= a moonshine still] for a long ways, and they'd be gangs of them come there.

[OED3 *gang* n 10 U.S.; DARE *gang* n 1 now chiefly South Midland]

gant See **gaunt.**

gant lot See **gaunt lot.**

gant up See **gaunt C.**

gap *noun* See also **gape.**

1 A low place or pass along a mountain ridge or range; sometimes, the territory immediately on each side of it; also used in place-names, as in *Newfound Gap* (TN/NC) and *Low Gap* (TN/NC). See also **saddle A1**, **sag 1**, **swag B2**.

1741 (in **1940** McJimsey *Topo Terms in VA* 265) Thence . . . to a Walnut and an Ash at the lower end of an Island near the Gap in the North Mountain. **1821** (in **2018** *Davenport Survey* 19) If there ever is a wagon road through the Big Smokies it must go through this gap. **1862** *Kiracofe CW Letters* (April 18) the aleghanah army ware stationed Some say on the Shenandoah Mountain others say at Buffalow gap. **1939** Hall *Coll* (Proctor NC) [Bears] generally cross over the highest knob they is within reach of. They don't go th'u a gap like a deer. **1956** Fink *That's Why* 3 Here [in the Smokies] these lower places between peaks and along ridges are almost invariably known as gaps, with an occasional swag. **1972** *GSMNP*-69:11 Manning McCarter lived in the gap of the mountain up there. **1973** *GSMNP*-84:30 Well, I got up here at the gap of the ridge and I heared them down there whooping and hollering. **c1980** Campbell *Memories of Smoky* 199 Low places along the main crest of the Smokies also provide some little bit of confusion for visitors, especially those from the western mountains and from New England. Here those low places are designated as "gaps." In the west they are "passes" and in New England they are "notches." **1982** Rives *Blue Ridge* 21 These were the places the mountains could be crossed most easily; Indians, settlers, and the wild game all came through the gaps. **1986** Pederson et al. *LAGS* = attested by 33/60 interviewees (55%) in E TN and 10/35 (28.6%) in N GA; 43/125 of all LAGS interviewees (34.4%) attesting term were in Appalachia. **1991** Reeder and Reeder *Shenandoah Secrets* 3 When we speak of a gap today, we usually mean the "saddle" or low point between two peaks. Historically, though, a gap has meant the entire passage across the mountain, including the hollows on either side of the saddle.

[DARE *gap* n 1 widespread, but especially Appalachians]

2 One or more removable fence rails or poles forming a makeshift gate so that livestock, vehicles, etc. can pass through (as in phrases *lay a gap in the fence*, *let down the gap* = to take down fence rails to create an opening to permit one to walk or drive animals through the opening). See also **drawbar**, **mind the gap**, **put up the bar**, **slip gap**.

1867 Harris *Sut Lovingood* 23 When we cum tu the fence I let down the gap, an' hit made dad mad; he wanted tu jump hit on all fours hoss way. **1943** Chase *Jack Tales* 41 The old ox followed the fence to where the gap was at and Jack let the bars down and the old ox got out in front of Jack, and they went on down the public road. **1956** Hall *Coll* (Del Rio TN) Hoss, lay a gap in that fence, so we can get out. **1962** Hall *Coll* (Del Rio TN) Lay a gap in that fence, Joe. **1976** Ledford *Folk Vocabulary* 281 *let down the gap* = open the gate. **1976** Weals *Mountaineer* In rail-fence days in the mountains, well within the memory of many still living, the rails might be stacked in a certain section so they could be taken down easily, to let livestock in and out of the fence field. This makeshift gate was called a gap, and sometimes a country person will refer to a more modern, hinged gate as a gap. In rail fence days, after the rails had been laid down to let the cattle pass through, a child might be called on to "mind the gap" until the return trip. Thus he was to watch the gate until the rails could've been laid back in place. **1994** Montgomery *File*: *lay up the gap* = replace the fence rails so cattle cannot get out of the pasture (75-year-old man, Gatlinburg TN). **2013** Venable *How to Tawlk* 17 = the gate on a fence: "Be shore to close 'at gap adder you drive the tractor through."

[DARE *gap* n 2 now chiefly South Midland, South]

3 See citation.

1968 *DARE Survey* (Brasstown NC) = place in the road where animals regularly go across.

4 Same as **milk gap 1**.

1986 Pederson et al. *LAGS* = attested by 3/60 interviewees (5%) in E TN; 3/3 of all LAGS interviewees (100%) attesting term were in Appalachia.

gape

A Variant forms *gap* [see **1927** in **B1**], *gyap* [see **1963** in **B1**].

B *verb*

1 To yawn; stare with an open mouth.

1927 Montague *Hog's Eye* 196 "Hell is waiting for you, hell is gapping for you!" Brother Moses Mutters singsongs out at him. **1957** Broaddus *Vocab Estill Co KY* 33 *gap* = to gape, stare open-mouthed. **1958** Combs *Archaic English in KY* 37 *gape* = yawn: "He gaped because he was sleepy." **1963** Williams *Metaphor Mt Speech II* 53 He would "see her a-gyapin' in hell fust afore he'd ax her to go home with him fer dinner." **1982** Slone *How We Talked* 32 *gape* = to yawn.

2 To gasp, have difficulty breathing.

1863 *Robinson CW Letters* (Jan 2) while I would be loading my gun I would look Round & See Some one gaping for breth & Some Shot too dead to gape. **1940** Haun *Hawk's Done* 120 She kept on gaping for breath. **1966** *DARE Survey* (Burnsville NC). **1994–97** Montgomery *Coll* (known to Brown, Ledford, Shields, Weaver).

C *noun* A yawn.

1978 Hiser *Quare Do's* 109 That old hound give a couple of gapes and heaved up my moccasins.

gapes (also *gaps*) *noun* A disease (caused by the gapeworm) making young chickens yawn continuously. See also **gapy**.

1915 Dingus *Word-List VA* 183 *gaps* = a disease of young chickens. **1923** Greer-Petrie *Angeline Doin' Society* 24–25 Then I told them ladies if the gaps ever got amongst their brood, to get a hoss hair, and make a loop, and ram hit thoo a slit in the chicken's tongue. **c1982** Young *Colloquial Appal* 10 *gapes* = disease of young chickens.

[DARE *gape* n C2 chiefly Midland]

gaps See **gapes**.

gapy *adjective* Of a chicken: having **gapes**.

1941 Stuart *Men of Mts* 123 When I rech over and got a neck I pinched hit, Honey, like you would a gapy chicken's neck!

garb *noun*

A Variant form *gyarb* [see **1900** in **B**].

[DARE *garb* n, v South Midland, South]

B An article of clothing; also *garbs* = an outfit, set of clothes when worn.

1900 Harben *N GA Sketches* 260 Misfortune an' plague is boun' to foller them that winks at infidelity in any disguise ur gyarb. **1904–20** Kephart *Notebooks* (in **1993** Farwell and Nicholas *Smoky Mt Voices* 82) See the gyarb them children's in? **1938** Simms *Coll* Why, they'd a-lawed us as well as churched us, if we'd a gone about in such garbs (shorts, slacks, bathing suits, etc.) as they now shamelessly strut about Gatlinburg. **1939** Hall *Coll* (Jefferson City TN) He was dressed in an awful gyarb. **2005** Williams *Gratitude* 500 *gyarb* = the clothes a person is wearing, usually descriptive of mismatched, odd or outlandish clothes: "Are you aimin' to wear that *gyarb* to Sunday School?"

garbage bear *noun* Same as **beggar bear**.

1997 *Smokies Guide* (Summer) 1 Because people food is often higher in calories than wild foods, bears adandon their natural foraging habits and become "garbage bears." The demise of garbage bears is almost certain. Many are hit by cars, shot by poachers, or die from ingesting toxins and plastics.

garbroth *noun* Literally, a low-quality broth made from the garfish, used in comparisons to indicate something of poor or despicable quality.

1927 Woofter *Dialect from WV* 355 *meaner'n gar broth* = very mean. "That man treats his family meaner'n gar broth." **c1950** Adams *Grandpap* 138 He was called Wirebeard an' that he was as mean as gyarbrauth. **1956** McAtee *Some Dial NC* 18 [Used] in the simile: "Mean as garbroth." The gar fish is not regarded as edible.

garbs See **garb B**.

garden *noun, verb* Variant forms *gyarden, gyardin*.

1886 Murfree *In the Clouds* 257 Show 'em all the quilts ye have pieced, an' yer spun truck, an' yer gyardin. **1895** Edson and Fairchild *TN Mts* 372 They's the lastiest blossoms in the gyarden. **1913** Kephart *Our Sthn High* 277 The hillmen . . . [insert] sounds where they do not belong. Sometimes it is only an added consonant: gyarden, acrost, corkus (caucus); sometimes a syllable: loaferer, musicianer, suddenty. **1930** Thomas *Death Knell* Often syllables ending in an "r" sound have a "y" inserted in front of them, as cyar (car), gyarden, pyore (poor). **1939** Walker *Mtneer Looks* 5 Only a few mountaineers say *cyar* for *car* and *gyarden* for *garden*, but it would be an impossibility for most of them to pronounce *cow* any other way than *cyow*, or *care* any other way than *kyeer* or *kyer*. **1942** Hall *Phonetics Smoky Mts* 94 In the speech of older people this glide [j] is very common after [k] or [g] before [ɑ]; for example . . . *garden* ['gjɑɚdn]. **1963** Hooper *Unwanted Boy* 229 I must chop out that gyarden—hit's getting mighty "filthy." **1974** Roberts *Sang Branch* 271 [The farmer] made him a man out of tar and put him up in his gyarden to catch the rabbit. **1984** Woods *WV Was Good* 230 Many old people said . . . *gyarden* for *garden*. **2008** Salsi *Ray Hicks* 29

When I was ol' enough to walk and follow my parents and Lewis and Bessie, I was expected to help out in the gyarden and in the kitchen. **2014** *Blind Pig* (Aug 29) Many of the oldsters around here [= southwestern NC] pronounced garden as gyard'n.

[DARE *garden* n South, South Midland]

garden house *noun* Used as a euphemism for an outhouse. See also **johnny.**

1956 McAtee *Some Dial NC* 18 = a privy. **1975** Gainer *Speech Mtneer* 10 In wintertime it gets too cold to go to the garden house. **1986** Pederson et al. *LAGS* = attested by 3/60 interviewees (5%) in E TN; 3/4 of all LAGS interviewees (75%) attesting term were in Appalachia. **1996–97** Montgomery Coll (known to Brown, Bush).

[OED3 *garden-house* n 1b dialect and U.S.]

garden salad (also *garden sallet, garden sass, garden stuff, garden truck*) *noun* Homegrown vegetables. See also **farm stuff**, **salad B**, **sauce B2**, **stuff**, **truck 1**.

1867 Harris *Sut Lovingood* 126 Hit wer a market hous, whar they sells oncook'd vittils ove every kine, frum a rabbit to a cow's laig, an gardin truck tu kill. Hit wer plum full. **1885** Murfree *Prophet* 142 Air Old Mis' Cayce's gyardin-truck suff'rin' fur rain? **1923** Greer-Petrie *Angeline Doin' Society* 18 Betty wan't savin' nuther. She hadn't put up a can of fruit or gyarden sass. **1937** Hall Coll (Cosby Creek TN) *garden sass* = fresh vegetables in general. **1939** Hall Coll (Cataloochee NC) We have to buy our peaches and stuff that way, while we make our garden stuff we eat each year. *Ibid.* (Sugarlands TN) We'd just make a little crop of a summer, raised what potatoes and garden stuff we could get along with. **1957** Broaddus *Vocab Estill Co KY* 33 *garden sass, garden truck* = a general term for garden vegetables. **1957** Hall Coll (Gatlinburg TN) The expression "garden sass" was usually preferred to "garden sallet." **1966** Dakin *Vocab Ohio River Valley* 352 *Garden sass* (in the [KY] Mountains simply *sass*) is remembered as an old name or "heard from others" from the Scioto westward through Ohio, Indiana, and Illinois. *Ibid.* 353 In the southern Mountains and Knobs (beside *truck*), on the lower Kentucky in the Bluegrass . . . some people say *garden stuff*. **1972** Cooper *NC Mt Folklore* 124 Along with wild meat, honey, ramps and branch lettuce, it requires only a little garden sass and store-boughten food to satisfy nourishment for the body. **1983** *Dark Corner OHP*-10A People would trade lumber for feed for the cattle or for garden truck. **1989** *Matewan OHP*-102 We raised most of our own food, our garden stuff, and had our own cow and our own hogs. **1996** Montgomery Coll: *garden salad* (known to Adams, Cardwell, Ellis, Jones, Norris).

[OED3 *garden-truck* (at *garden* n C 2a) U.S.]

garden sass, **garden sallet**, **garden stuff**, **garden truck** See **garden salad.**

garner box *noun* See citation.

1973 Miller *English Unicoi Co* 147 = a large, long box with a heavy lid made of rough lumber, used for storing grain.

garree fly *noun* Same as **jar bug.**

1982 Slone *How We Talked* 45 = jarfly. We loved to hear them "sing" and wondered at their ability to know when you touched the tree on which they were, for they would stop suddenly.

gate post *interjection* I surrender! Same as **calf rope.**

1976 Still *Pattern of Man* 115 This was to be no fair fist scrape either, no mere knock-down, with the one who hollered "gate post" first the loser.

gathering *noun*

1 A community work activity to assist a family, such as a **house raising** or **log rolling** but especially to harvest crops, usually combined with socializing.

1881 Atkinson *After Moonshiners* 141 When building houses, or rolling [logs] into heaps to be burned, the neighbors are invited to assist in raising the houses or rolling the logs together. The timber is usually of such a size as to require a number of men to handle it; hence the necessity of these "gatherings," as they are familiarly called by the inhabitants. Besides, such occasions afford a jubilation and reunion of the mountaineers, which greatly add to their comfort and happiness. **1924** Greer-Petrie *Angeline Gits Eyeful* 1 Down home, when a passle of able-bodied men and wimmen have a getherin', they all jine in and skear up somethin' to do that's been a-needin' gittin' done, if 'tain't nothin' but a log rollin', or house raisin', or corn shuckin'. **2006** *WV Encycl* 271 Gathering, the harvesting of wild plant foods and herbs for domestic and commercial use, is practiced all over West Virginia.

2 See citation.

1927 Woofter *Dialect from WV* 355 = the amount collected each time. "We are boiling the last gathering of sugar water this morning."

gathering time *noun* Harvest season; the time for rounding up cattle to sell to buyers to take to market.

1962 Hall Coll (Cades Cove TN) = the first Monday in September, buyers would be [in Cades Cove]. Buyers would be there. **1975** GSMNP-59:24 [The cattle] stayed on the mountain then till the fifteenth of September, and fifteenth of September was what they called gathering time.

gather up *verb phrase* To assemble; to round (people) up, as before or after a hunt.

1939 Hall Coll (Nine Mile TN) A passel of us fellers gathered up here to bear hunt. . . . We all gathered up and we come down into what's called Cades Cove. *Ibid.* (Cataloochee NC) When we got the bear killed, we wanted to get our men all together. We fired our guns for signals to gather 'em up. **1954** GSMNP-19:9 A corn shucking . . . it's where people gathers up and shucks corn, in the fall when they get the corn gathered. **1960** Mason *Memoir* 75 On Christmas eve night, it was customary for a group of young men to gather up and go serenading. **1973** GSMNP-4:1:39 They would gather up on Sunday or something like that and sit and talk. **1995** Adams *Come Go Home* 23 The next day all the men gathered up and went back to see if they could find anything. **2005** Preece *I Grew* 33 Bean stringings took place then, up and down Backlog then at nearly every home on the front or back porches, but not much anymore, and gone are the old-timers gathering up to sing hymns or talk about Sunday's good meeting they had just returned from attending.

gaum See also **gaumy**.

A Variant forms *gawm* [see **1895** in **C1**], *gom* [see **1915** in **B**], *gome* [see **1963** in **B**], *gorm* [see **1913** in **C1**], *gum* [see **1974** in **C1**].

B *noun* A mess, state of disarray, usually one that is dirty, sticky, mucky, greasy, etc.

1904–20 Kephart *Notebooks* 2:438 I cain't leave everything in a gawm. **1915** Dingus *Word-List VA* 183 *gaum* = state of uncleanness from dirt, grease, etc. (applied to machinery as well as hands and face; also a verb): "See your hands, what a gom you're in!"; "Yes, I'm all gommed up." **1927** Mason *Lure of Smokies* 127 The pie is a conglomeration, a "mommick" or "gaum," to use mountain terms, of boiled dough and either apples or peaches with NO sugar! **c1950** Adams *Grandpap* 79 The floor was just a gaum of blood. **1963** Arnow *Flowering* 152 Gome, for example, did not mean [just] a sticky mass to us, but any kind of mess in need of cleaning up from the state of politics to milk spilled on the table. **1982** Slone *How We Talked* 21 *gom* = dirt; to make a mess. "You have made a messy gom of this house." "You have gom all over your face." **1995** Adams *Come Go Home* 42 He's been gone from this world a long time, and if'en we tried to move him, it'd just be a big gom, what with the coffin all rotted and him spillin' out the holes. **2005** Williams *Gratitude* 497 A youngen would make a *gom* a-tryin' to cook a meal.

[perhaps alteration of *gum*; Web3 *gaum* n "a greasy or sticky mess" dialect; DARE *gaum* n[1] 1 chiefly South, South Midland, but also New England]

C (also *gaum up*) *verb*

1 To disarrange or make (a room, one's clothing, etc.) messy, dirty, sticky, or greasy; to cover or strew with refuse or litter, create a mess; hence verb phrase *gaum around* and participial adjectives *gaumed*, *gawmed*, *gormed*; also used facetiously, as in Oliver 1996 citation. See also **gormy**.

1895 Edson and Fairchild *TN Mts* 371 *gawmed up* = covered with litter. **1913** Kephart *Our Sthn High* 392 If the house be in disorder it is said to be all gormed or gaumed up. **1921** Campbell *Sthn Highlander* 145 [I]f we recall provincial English, we understand the mother who apologizes for the smeared condition of the baby's face when she says it is "all gormed up." **c1945** Haun *Hawk's Done* 289 The porch is done gormed up. **1949** Arnow *Hunter's Horn* 182 He reminded himself to recollect to tell her that she must never leave a turn of corn untied; the rats had already been in it and spilled it and gomed it around. **1960** Cooper *Jularker Bussed* The drunkard gommed up (ruined) his family's life. **1967** *DARE Survey* (Gatlinburg TN) *gaum up* = to get something sticky or smeared up. **1969** GSMNP-27:16 She didn't want him to get his new shirt gaumed up with blood. **1974** Fink *Bits Mt Speech* 11 *gaum*, *gum* = to smear. **1996–97** Montgomery *Coll* Don't gom the place with those muddy boots (Ellis), = to cook, "I'll go in the kitchen and gaum up a little bit of supper" (Oliver). **2005** Williams *Gratitude* 497 *gom* = make an untidy or dirty mess; usually said as "messin' and gommin'." **2013** *Blind Pig* (Jan 10) My Granny always said "stop gauming around" or "you have gaumed it up now."

2 To cause (a mess), create (disarray).

1949 Arnow *Hunter's Horn* 334 She stooped with difficulty and took a bundle from the floor. "I'd better start putten this stuff away fore th youngens wake up—they'd be a messen an a gomen into everthing."

[perhaps alteration of *gum*; OED3 *gaum* v[2] "to smear with a sticky substance," cf *coom* n[1] 1 "soot"; EDD *gaum* v[3]; Web3 *gaum* v[2] "to smudge or smear (as with something sticky or greasy) dialect; DARE *gaum* v[1] 1 "to smear" formerly widespread, now chiefly Appalachians, v[1] 3 "to disarrange" chiefly South Midland, especially KY]

gaumed, gaum up See **gaum C**.

gaumy (also *gommy*) *adjective* Smeared or dirty with something sticky, muddy, dirty, or oily. See also **gaum**.

1954 Arnow *Dollmaker* 79 Cassie, you're the gommiest youngen; allus a spillen things. You're half pig. **c1960** Wilson *Coll* = messy, smeared, dirty. **1967** *DARE Survey* (Gatlinburg TN) I've got to wash my hands. They're all gaumy. **1984** Wilder *You All Spoken* 163 = in disorder; soiled; gummy, like a child eating peanut brittle. **1995–97** Montgomery *Coll* (known to eight consultants from the Smoky Mountains).

[EDD *gaumy* (at *gaum* v3); DARE *gaumy* adj[1] 1 scattered, but especially Appalachians]

gaunt

A Variant forms *gaint*, *gant* [see **1976** in **B**].

1891 Primer *Studies in WV* 163 Gaunt [is] pronounced [gænt]. **1988** Carden *Looking Out* 7 I had spent years trying to rid myself of . . . quaint expressions like "peaked" and "gaunt" (pronounced to rhyme with "saint"). **2003** Wolfram et al. *Mt Talk* My grandmother, she was always talking about people being stout or gaint. **2005** Williams *Gratitude* 496 *gaint*.

B *adjective* Of livestock: lean, deliberately underfed in order to have less fat and be driven more readily to market. See also **gaunt lot**.

1967 Hall *Coll* (Del Rio TN) [A gaunt lot is] made of rails to hold cattle until their owners came to pick them up. Not being free to range, they would lose weight and therefore be called "gant." **1976** Lindsay *Grassy Balds* 98 They usually held them there in the lot and while they were being held there they became fairly gant, that's why it's called a gant lot.

[cf EDD *gant* "slim, slender"]

C (also *gant up*) *verb, verb phrase* To make or become lean, as cattle by underfeeding.

1862 *Penland CW Letters* (Oct 12) We are getting tolerable plenty for ourselves and horses to eat but some of them are a ganting up. **1917** Kephart *Word-List* 412 *Gant* them cattle up; get the grass out of them so they can travel. **1927** Woofter *Dialect from WV* 355 = to give hard usage: "Gant those cattle up, so they won't be carrying so much grass." "He was riding a ganted horse." **1976** Lindsay *Grassy Balds* 164 Some of [cattle would] be in there two or three days without anything to eat, and they called that gantin' 'em. **1976** Weals *Plenty Water* Law our cattle's a-gantin' up awful bad in here but we'll put'm on good pasture when we get home.

2 To make (one) thin and shrill.

1951 Giles *Harbin's Ridge* 100 That's what eat into her an' ganted her up an' give her the sharp tongue she's got.

gaunt lot

A Variant form *gant lot* [see **1913** in **B**].

B *noun* A rail enclosure to keep cattle from grass so that they will lose fat before being sold. Penned after a summer of free ranging and no longer free to feed, they lose weight and can be driven more easily. They are enticed into the enclosure by the salt put there. See 1967 citation.

1913 Kephart *Our Sthn High* 93 [I] was surprised to see three of our men lugging across the "gant-lot" toward the cabin a small female bear. **1917** Kephart *Word-List* 412 *gant-lot* = an enclosure for cattle, to prevent their fattening on grass. **c1930** (in **2014** Oliver *Cades Cove* 34) The herding season ended on Labor Day. During the previous week the herders rounded up all the cattle and placed them in a corral of approximately 100 acres, fenced with chestnut logs. There was one spring in this enclosure. By the time a few hundred head of cattle remained here a few days and ate all the grass, they became somewhat gaunt or "gant" as some pronounced the word. Hence, this field or corral came to be called the Gant Lot. **1960** McCaulley *Cades Cove* [The herder would] drive [the cattle] off into the range that you wanted them to run in. Well, in the fall of the year, we'd gather these cattle and put them right back in that lot called a gant lot, [it] didn't have nothing to feed them, and they'd stay right there in that gant lot till the day's work was done and then they'd count out to the man all the cattle that he had. **1967** Hall Coll (Del Rio TN) = a pen made of rails to hold cattle until their owners came to pick them up. Not being free to range, they would lose weight and therefore be called "gant." **c1976** Cate *Cattle Herder* The day before a herd was driven down a trail, they were placed in a "gant lot"—or gaunt lot—actually an enclosure of rails, and were not allowed to eat fresh grass for several hours. Otherwise following them on the trail was too messy. **1976** Lindsay *Grassy Balds* 98 They usually held them there in the lot and while they were being held there they became fairly gant, that's why it's called a gant lot.

[DARE *gant lot* n chiefly Appalachians]

gaunt up See **gaunt C.**

gave See **give 3**.

gawm, gawmed See **gaum.**

gawp *verb* See also **gape.**

1 To yawn.

1955 Ritchie *Singing Family* 166 We were so sleepy we could hardly live, but we moaned and stretched and gawped and finally got awake enough to know what day it was.

2 To stare.

c1954 Adams *Word-List* = [to] gape, stare.

[cf Web3 *gaup* v "to stare, gape" dialect]

gayly See **gaily.**

gear

A *noun*

1 Belongings, property, equipment. See also **gear house.**

1922 Cobb *KY Mt Rhymes* 5 The ways of the mountains are passing—up Cyarr! / Moonshine stills and manhood, / Gear to weave and spin, / Good old Reg'lar Baptists / Preaching hell for sin. **1934–47** LAMSAS *Appal* (Madison Co NC). **1944** Wilson *Word-List* 43 = property, belongings. "And after the infare at her father's, they went to their li'l house, where there wa'n't much *gear*." **1965** Glassie *Old Barns* 22 The rectangular log construction unit still used in Europe as a granary was easily adapted to the storage of maize and became the corn crib found throughout the Southern Mountains. Frequently the corn crib has a shed for the storage of farm equipment—"gear" or "plunder."

2 (also *gearing, gears*) The harness and bridle of a horse or mule.

1838 *McLean Diary* 56 [I] Made Roape Geers and plow Lines. **1863** *Watters-Curtis CW Letters* (April 22) tell Engline that when Ever She gets old jimey Broke to the Gear She must rite to me and let me no it. **1867** Harris *Sut Lovingood* 22 Out we went tu the pawpaw thicket, an' peel'd a rite smart chance ove bark, an' mam an' me made geers fur dad, while he sot on the fence a-lookin at us, an' a studyin pow'rful. **1886** Smith *Sthn Dialect* 349 They all have the authority of old or dialect English, or many of them belong to all parts of the South, if not elsewhere ... gears (harness). **1915** Dingus *Word-List VA* 183 = harness. **1966** Dakin *Vocab Ohio River Valley* 290 The origin of *gear, gear up* used in the [Ohio] Valley is questionably the South Midland and the South. These verbal usages and *gears* (occasionally *gear* or *gearing*) used as a noun in the expression *put the gears on* are common everywhere in Kentucky. **1978** Reese *Speech NE Tenn* 34 *gears* = attested by 5/12 (41.7%) speakers. **1995–97** Montgomery *Coll*: *gear* (known to Adams, Norris, Oliver, Weaver); *gears* (known to Brown, Ellis, Jones). **2000** Robbins *Mt Museum* 9 A wagon loaded with ears of dried corn was driven under the shed of this structure and the corn was tossed over the log wall into the crib. The shed also provided covered storage for gear (harness) and other farm equipment.

[SED nEngl; DARE *gear* n 1 now chiefly South, South Midland]

B (also *gear up*) *verb, verb phrase* To catch and harness (a horse or mule).

1898 Elliott *Durket Sperret* 81 After dinner Hannah "geared up" old Bess and joined Dock in the fields. **1931–33** (in **1987** Oliver and Oliver *Sketches* 28) The way they used to gear their horses was large homemade hames with holes bored and ropes tied through the holes for traces. **1941** Stuart *Men of Mts* 91 I geared old Barnie up and took him over there. **1967** *DARE Survey* (Gatlinburg TN) *gear up* = to put harness and bridle on a horse. **1973** Miller *English Unicoi Co* 147 = to put harness on a horse for plowing. **1978** Reese *Speech NE Tenn* 34 = attested by 4/12 (33.3%) speakers. **1986** Pederson et al. *LAGS*: *gear* = attested by 8/60 interviewees (13.3%) in E TN and 5/35 (14.3%) in N GA; 13/37 of all LAGS interviewees (35.1%) attesting term were in Appalachia; *gear up* (Cocke Co TN, Sevier Co TN). **1995** Montgomery *Coll* Go gear up the horse (Cardwell).

[DARE *gear* v 1 chiefly South, South Midland]

gear house (also *gear room*) *noun* A room or building in which supplies and equipment are stored. See also **gear A1.**

1940 Haun *Hawk's Done* 137 He told them that after the boys emptied the feed out of the sacks into the tanks he went back over there and got the empty sacks out of the gear room. **1986** Pederson et al. *LAGS*: *gear house* (Cherokee Co GA); *gear room* (Sevier Co TN, Bradley Co TN). **1991** Bible *Bent Twigs* 169 For many years the payment was in kind, as old-timers remember, when they rode with their parents to the mill sitting on bags of wheat and corn in the back of the wagon. The miller's usual take was six pounds of flour for a bushel of wheat, which generally left the customer with 36 pounds of flour and twelve pounds of brans. (The bran was an important item in cattle diets.) It was usually kept in the "gear room" across from the stable in the barn, and woe betide the careless child who kept the gear room open. Cows had a way of straying in and getting foundered before somebody closed the open door.

gearing, gears See **gear A2.**

gear up See **gear B.**

gee (also *gee and haw, gee haw, gee together*) *verb, verb phrase* To get along well with one another. See also **do a gee-haw.**

1956 McAtee *Some Dial NC* 18 *gee* = to get on well together. "They don't seem to gee." **1957** Neel *Backwoodsman* 19 *gee* = to agree or get along well together. **1967** *DARE Survey* (Gatlinburg TN) *gee together*. **1993** Ison and Ison *Whole Nother Lg* 24 *gee haw* = to get along with others. **1999** Morgan *Gap Creek* 157 "Pappy and me didn't always gee-haw," Caroline said. "But it broke my heart to hear how he died." **2016** *Blind Pig* (April 19) "Don't gee and haw with each other" meaning . . . don't get along well enough to work together. Ibid. (Dec 15) I don't gee-haw with that outlook.

[DARE *gee* v² b chiefly South, Midland]

gee-haw whimmy diddle *noun*

1 A wooden toy consisting of two sticks; to the end of the stick held in the left hand a small propeller is loosely nailed and on its side several notches are cut, while a stick held in the right hand is rubbed vigorously across the notches, causing the propeller to spin; while saying "gee" (right) or "haw" (left) the holder can cause the propeller to change direction by shifting the position of the forefinger or thumb on the stationary left stick. Also called **fly-jig, idiot stick, jeep stick, lie detector, ziggerboo.**

1963 Corey *Folk Toys* Cherokee Indians knew the whimmy-diddle as a hoodoo stick. In Tennessee it's a ziggerboo, and Georgians know it as a gee-haw. . . . The gee-haw whimmydiddle is a notched stick with a whirligig on the end that "gees" or "haws" seemingly at command. Pressure of the finger or thumb on the top side of the notches does the trick. **1972** Cooper *NC Mt Folklore* 34 The children's Christmas toys and gifts were mainly homemade. There were dolls, yarn balls, whistles, geehaw whimmy-diddles or ziggerboos, rattle traps, noisemakers or bull roars and flipperdingers. **1980** Wigginton *Foxfire VI* 253 Some people call them "gee-haw whimmy diddles." [*Foxfire* Ed.: The "gee haw" part of the name that many people use comes from the fact that you can make the propeller go in either direction, just as the same commands make a mule or steer turn to the right or the left.] **1996–97** Montgomery *Coll* (known to Adams, Cardwell, Hooper, Ledford, Norris, Oliver), = also known as *lie detector*, because the user can control which direction it spins and can thus pretend it knows the truth from a lie (Jones).

[DARE *gee-haw whimm(e)y-diddle* n southern Appalachians, especially western NC]

2 See citation.

1989 Still *Rusties and Riddles* [59] = anything of little worth.

gee-o *interjection* Gee! Shucks!

1923 Furman *Mothering* 72 When I emerged, there was a chorus of pleased "gee-ohs" and a decided accession of friendliness, the boys trying who could be first in helping me over the frightful mudholes between the school and the village. **1940** Still *River of Earth* 128 Gee-o, I'm punishing to try walking agin myself.

geep *interjection* Come! (used as a call to pigs). Same as **ageep.** See also **pig-ee.**

1996 Montgomery *Coll* (known to Oliver).

gee together See **gee.**

gee whiz *noun* A harrow-like plow.

1984 Smith *Enduring Memories* 17 Two of the most widely used plows on the farm were the double-shovel and gee-whiz. Each was pulled by a single horse or mule and were used from the initial breaking of the ground to laying by the corn. The double-shovel had only two plow arms while the gee-whiz had from five to seven plow arms. The double-shovel was used more for developing new ground and plowing crops that needed the soil plowed deeply, while the gee-whiz was used to scratch the soil on top and smooth the soil. The double-shovel was a difficult plow to handle as the plow arms would sink very deep in the ground if the person using it did not hold up on the handles, which meant that after plowing with it all day the user was a very tired person. **1986** Pederson et al. *LAGS* (Jefferson Co TN, Sevier Co TN, Bradley Co TN, Forsyth Co GA).

general

A *adjective, noun* Variant forms *gineral, ginerl*.

1861 *Poteet CW Letters* (Aug 7) gineral Mcgrooder has tuck 10 thousand men down there And is agoing to attact newport news. **1863** *Lee CW Letters* (June 1) ginerl jhonson Division is all Advanceing to gether. **1881** Pierson *In the Brush* 258 The old feller, Saul, the gineral, he felt more chawed up and meaner than the sogers. **1914** Furman *Sight* 61–62 Fust thing is a new set of teeth,—you done gummed yourself into dyspepsy and gineral cantankerousness. **1969** Medford *Finis* 89 An' how about Covet-ishness?—that ol' gripin' skin-flint who passes fer re-spectability—in sheep's clothin', bowth in Church an' so-cietty in gineral.

B *adjective* Usual.

1940 Haun *Hawk's Done* 63 She drew her eyes to him, like general.

generally *adverb*

A Variant forms *ginerally, ginerly, ginly, gin'rally*.

1861 *Kendrick CW Letters* (Oct 30) Our company is ginerly well we only have one man sick and he is gitting better. **1867** Harris *Sut Lovingood* 95 Now don't forgit that about that hos' thar wer a good time bein had ginerally. **1884** Murfree *In TN Mts* 315 He jes' war constant in lettin' his friends, an' folks ginerally, off 'thout hevin' 'em fined. **1913** Kephart *Our Sthn High* 80 The older dog don't ginerally raise no ruction. **c1951** Chapman *Speech Confusing* You know a feist is one o' them little bitty ole dogs that ginerally runs up on three legs and does a heap of pretendin'. **2007** McMillon *Notes*: *ginly*.

B in combination with another temporal adverb (especially *always*).

1883 Bonner *Dialect Tales* 138 The boys most generally always paid Janey a good deal 'f attention. **1913** Kephart *Our Sthn High* 286 I ginerally, usually take a dram mornin's. **1928** Thornburgh *Americans Forgot* 28 Thar was most ginerally allers one big room with a lean-to in the rear and sometimes a loft above. **1931** Combs *Lg Sthn High* 1310 I gin'rally usually takes a dram o' mornin's. **1967** Hall *Coll* (Townsend TN) Over in the cove it generally always was a little cooler, you know, back then. **1973** GSMNP-74:25 We'd generally always have a pet ground squirrel or flying squirrel or groundhog or something. **1979** *Big South Fork OHP*-9 They'd generally always tried to mark when the sign would be in the legs and feet.

generated *adjective* Inborn, natural.

1939 Hall *Recording Speech* 8 It's not generated in me to steal.

generation *noun*

A Variant form *gineration* [see **1913** in **B**].

B An extended branch of a family. See also **push 1**, **set C1**.

1913 Kephart *Our Sthn High* 237–38 They married through and through till the whole gineration nigh run out. **1930** Armstrong *This Day and Time* 93 Hit runs in the Byrds' generation to kill. **1937** Hall *Coll* (Copeland Creek TN) The whole Morgan generation claimed to be half Indian, claimed also to be partly Black Dutch. *Ibid.* (Townsend TN) John Wear settled on Waldens Creek and fathered a generation of children. **1939** Hall *Coll* (Emerts Cove TN) I holped a party run [i.e. trace] his generation back not long ago. *Ibid.* (Waldens Creek TN) George Fox come to this country from England and started the Fox generation. **1943** Hannum *Mt People* 148 They use "generation" to mean a certain breed of people just as Moses did when he bemoaned the corrupt children of God as "a perverse and crooked generation." **1956** Hall *Coll* (Big Creek NC) The McMillans was a good generation of people. **1976** Weals *Funky Offends* "Generation," in a family sense, is another word that has slightly different meanings in mainstream English and in the vanishing language of the mountains. In the former a generation includes those born of the same set of brothers and sisters. But in the coves a generation includes all of a person's blood relatives, going back through father and mother and all grandparents and great-grandparents; and usually including at least first and second cousins. "They're of my generation" means, we all belong to the same family.

[DARE *generation* n chiefly Appalachians]

gentle (also *gentle down, gentle up*) *verb, verb phrase* To soothe or tame (usually livestock), make docile.

1862 *Gilley CW Letters* (July 13) puss I am [glad] that you can jentle my colt you must mind an not let hit hurt you. **1913** Kephart *Our Sthn High* 43 The backwoodsman does not want "critters that haffter be gentled and hand fed." **1917** Kephart *Word-List* 412 = to render tame. "He follers his hogs and corn feeds them, and *gentles* them up." **1927** Woofter *Dialect from WV* 355 = to tame: "He gentles animals well." **1969** GSMNP-46:1 I would get them a-gentled up and then I put the yoke on them. **1974** Fink *Bits Mt Speech* 11 See how he *gentles* the horse. **1984** Dykeman and Stokely *At Home* 92 Once every three weeks or so thereafter, they returned to salt and "gentle" [the cattle], thus keeping them familiar with their owners. **1987** Young *Lost Cove* 168 Just knowing that I was from the mountains of Tennessee gentled them down real soon.

[DARE *gentle* v especially South Midland]

gentle down See **gentle**.

gentleman *noun* A hunted animal, especially a bear; hence *gentleman bear*.

1937 Hall *Coll* (Wears Cove TN) Let me blaze that gentleman [= a bear] by the right of the ear. **1941** Hall *Coll* (Gatlinburg TN) Let me lay it in that gentleman. **1956** GSMNP-24:43 They were all gentlemen bears, were they?

gentleman cow *noun* Used as a euphemism for *bull*, especially one kept only for breeding. See also **bull A1**.

1969 Doran *Folklore White Co* 112 = bull. **1992** Bush *If Life* 62 He went with his female cow into Dr. Tittsworth's pasture where a one-eyed Jersey bull was angrily chewing his cud, and the ferocious "gentleman cow" at once showed his fight by butting Mr. King a very hard butt on the stomach. **1996–97** Montgomery *Coll* (known to Adams, Brown, Jones, Oliver).

gentle up See **gentle**.

genuine *adjective* Variant forms *genuwine, ginuwine*.

1936 (in **2005** Ballard and Chung *Arnow Stories* 51) I've wished we'd have a teacher that'ud risk givin' her a genuwine good spankin'. **1992** Brooks *Sthn Stuff* 57 *gin-u-wine*.

genuwine See **genuine**.

Georgia boy *noun* A marigold.

1971 Stubbs *Mountain-Wise* (May) 6 Marigolds are "Georgia boys."

Georgia buggy (also *Georgia wagon*) *noun* A wheelbarrow.

1985 Edwards *Folksy Sketches* 27 Maybe I can use you if you can roll a wheelbarrow. That limestone will get mighty heavy before sundown . . . now, grab that Georgia Buggy and start rolling. **1986** Pederson et al. *LAGS*: *Georgia wagon* (Cocke Co TN, Rhea Co TN); *Georgia wagon* (Cocke Co TN).

[DARE *Georgia buggy* n chiefly South, South Midland]

Georgia mule *noun* See citation.

1985 Sienkneckt *Rheumatic Diseases* 183 = a depressed or morose person: "You look like a bunch of Georgia mules eating mush."

Georgia wagon See **Georgia buggy**.

Georgia wiggler *noun* See citation.

1973 Miller *English Unicoi Co* 147 = very active, red, earth worm common to the area.

[DARE *Georgia wiggler* chiefly South Atlantic]

get *verb* See also **get to**, **get to be**, **git**, **got**.

A Variant form *git*.

1796 *Sinking Creek Church Minutes* II:5 Brother Bowers having heard that Brother William Matlock had been Several times at the Mason Lodge Labour'd for Satisfaction and did not Git Sadisfied. **1844** Willnotah *Ms* 15 he asked how he could git his children and his horses and cattle all there. **1861** (in **1992** Heller and Heller *Confederacy* 33) hit will be a day or two be fore we can git transportation owing to the many troops a leaving hear for west vergina. **1867** Harris *Sut Lovingood* 73 He's hot arter the rest ove em; sez he's in a hurry tu git thru, es he hes *yu* tu kill an' salt down afore day. **1917** Kephart *Word-List* 407 Every time I go to studyin' about it I git the all-overs. **1937** (in **2009** Powell *Shenandoah Letters* 101) It is not any apple around that one can git to use. **1956** Hall *Coll* (Big Bend NC) She'd get up soon in the mornin' and git out and work all day. **1972** *AOHP/ALC*-355 She'd just git on her horse, honey, and she'd go up onto the roadside path. **1979** Carpenter *Walton War* 166 He's a ridin' fer the town and a hopin' to git there afore dusky dark. **1983** *Dark Corner OHP* 5A They'd git them Irish taters.

B Principal parts.

1 Variant past-tense form *gotten*.

1884 Smith *Arp Scrap Book* 15 When he gotten over it he laughed sorter weakly. **1938** (in **2009** Powell *Shenandoah Letters* 149) I am Just writing you a few lines concerning the trouble that Ralph gotten into.

2 Variant past-participle form *got*.

1784 (in **1941** Rothert *McDowell Letters* 174) (Feb 12) We have now the Measles and Joseph has got over them. **1790** *Lenoir Papers* I have got over the Grammar once and are now a Reviseing it. **1815–18** (in **1881** Draper *Kings Mt* 552) When they had marched in that order about a mile, Col. Winston, by a steep hill, had got so far separated from the other columns as to be out of sight or hearing of them. **1836** (in **1998** Bueker *Head Letters* 15) Only Washing White and Juley An Sims has got married on the sixt. **1864** *Chapman CW Letters* (May 29) I dont now why you hant got wun of them. **1888** Cole *Letters* 72 I have riten to you three or four times but I have not got any answer from you yet. **1926** Hunnicutt *Twenty Years* 58 When I got back to camp they had all got in and my brother had killed a lot of squirrels. **1939** Hall *Coll* (Bradley Fork NC) The old fellow had got old. He couldn't do nothing. **1973** *GSMNP*-4:5 I've got up early in the morning and walked to the store and back by the time I went to school. **1978** Montgomery *White Pine Coll* VI-2 They used to just pick them, have no opposition, or I might not have got elected then. **1990** *Matewan OHP*-73 I'm telling you, it couldn't have got in no worse shape. **1998** *Dante OHP*-24 She was married to a Stansbury and she had got a divorce, so she had a stepson, Mike Stansbury. **2008** *Rosie Hicks* 1 It's got chopped up so fast. **2014** *Blind Pig* (Nov 21) If you've never got to visit the folk school-Morning Song is the start of the day for students taking classes.

C Senses.

1 To have (expressing an unintended result).

1957 *GSMNP*-23:1:17 I got it burnt up.

2 To kill (an animal); to shoot.

1937 Hall *Coll* First the panther came across, and later the bear. I got both of 'em. **1939** Hall *Coll* (Deep Creek NC) They got hit [= a small bear] right there at the tree. *Ibid.* (Cataloochee NC) The coon was smoked down, a-lyin' there, and I jerked him out on the ground an we got 'im. **1941** Stuart *Men of Mts* 93 I think I got that big green scorpion down there. **1985** Irwin *Alex Stewart* 265 When he [= the rattlesnake] done that, I got him in the head with a stick.

3 To become, reach the age of.

1970 Foster *Walker Valley* 24 Roseann and Uncle Mose lived till he got twenty-three and he died of what they called old consumption then, which would be TB today. **1971** *AOHP/ALC*-147 Of a morning, I had to get up and make the biscuits for my mother after I got twelve years old while she done the other breakfast, and we was cooking for fourteen. **1976** *GSMNP*-114:38 She'd . . . take cloth and make a bag about that big and stuff it full of sausage that long and hang it in the smokehouse where [when] it'd get wintertime it wouldn't freeze, bring that sausage out. **1977** McClelland *Wilson Douglas* 17 I used to think [my father] was too hard on us. Until I got a man, I saw he wasn't.

4 To be born.

1969 *GSMNP*-42:26 Abraham Lincoln was got right down there, old folks always told me.

5 (+ *verbal noun*) To start. See also **get to 1**, **go to**.

1969 *GSMNP*-38:93 He said them men got hollering at him and he give them a pumpkin. **1971** *AOHP/ALC*-129 I got talking with her. **1974** *No Sang* 18 I come on home and me and my wife got talking about it. **1974–75** McCracken *Logging* 1:16 James Thomas Walker had a big shoat [at the] same time that got missing. **1975** *AOHP/LJC*-384 One of them had waited till they got coming across that hill. **1990** Wigginton *Foxfire Christmas* 30 The next morning the man got looking for his wagon, and it was sitting astraddle on the corner of the barn, all put together and ready to go again. **2008** *Rosie Hicks* 6 We got digging dahlias and taking them down [to be sold].

6 To prepare, arrange (a meal).

1978 Slone *Common Folks* 209 Eva come out of the kitchen where she had been "getting" supper.

get about *verb phrase* To move around, be on one's feet.

1865 Hundley *CW Letters* (Feb 22) I am very unwell My Self & have Bin for Several Days I am hadley Able to get A Bout. **1865** *Revis CW Letters* (July 13) Davis he is not weell he has to get about with his crutches and you no that is sloe geting about. **1939** Hall Coll (Bradley Fork NC) I've reached the age of ninety-three, three month, a few days, and yet able to go on and get about. **1986** Pederson et al. LAGS (Habersham Co GA) able to get about.

[DARE *get about* v phr especially South, South Midland]

get age on See **age**.

get a hump on *verb phrase* To hurry, exert oneself more vigorously. See also **hump**.

1936–37 Still *Defeated Creek* 21 You'd better get a hump on. You're already late. **c1960** Wilson Coll = to try harder, exert oneself.

[DARE (at *hump* n 5) chiefly South Midland, South]

get (an) age on See **age**.

get a track *verb phrase* To find the trail or scent of a hunted animal.

1939 Hall Coll (Smokemont NC) We got a track, turned [the dogs] loose on it, and ... we never did see the bear.

get away with *verb phrase* To upset, embarrass, make uncomfortable.

1952 Wilson *Folk Speech NC* 544 = to embarrass. **1956** McAtee *Some Dial NC* 18 = embarrass. **1978** *Horsetrading* 49 Now he got away with me. **1996** Montgomery Coll (known to Jones, Ledford, Oliver).

[DARE *get away with* v phr 2 South Midland, South]

get down *verb phrase*

1 To give birth.

1994 Montgomery Coll (known to Adams, Norris); His wife is ready to get down (Cardwell).

2 To dismount, descend (usually as an imperative).

1931 Combs *Lg Sthn High* 1307 Git down and stay all night with us, stranger. **1941** Justus *Kettle Creek* 128 Get down—get down in a hurry, before I pull you offen that horse!

3 To become (infirm or incapacitated).

1862 *Bell CW Letters* (Jan 14) mike gray has bin complaining severl days and I am a fraid that he will get down. **1971** *AOHP/ALC-160* If the father of the family got down sick and laid up there, all the people that thought enough of them, they would come in. They would bring baskets of food. They would see that they didn't want for anything while they were down sick. **1974** Roberts *Sang Branch* 23 One summer we had a big crop, and my father got down with the sore-eye. **1983** *Dark Corner OHP-5A* She got down so poor, couldn't hardly eat nothing, couldn't hardly walk. **1998** *Dante OHP-45* Mommy at that time had had a stroke, and she got down and wasn't able to go anywhere or do anything.

4 See citation.

1974 Dwyer and Dwyer *Mt Cookin'* 18 = to plant: "I got the 'taters down!"

get easy *verb phrase* To gain relief (from medicine).

1933 Thomas *Traipsin' Woman* 189 I'll be there if this risin' in my side gets easy. **1997** Montgomery Coll That dost of medicine made her get easy (Brown).

get fair *verb phrase* Of weather: to clear up, become mild.

1996 Montgomery Coll (known to Cardwell).

[DARE *get fair* v phr especially South, South Midland]

get-go *noun* The beginning, the first step.

1984 Wilder *You All Spoken* 67 = the start; the beginning, as in "These are hard-core fans who've been with this band since the get-go." **2004** Adams *Old True Love* 1 I am older than God's dog and been in this world a long time and it seems to me that right from the git-go, Larkin Stanton had the longest and hardest row I've ever seen.

get gone *verb phrase* To leave, vanish; to take (oneself) away.

1925 Greer-Petrie *Angeline Hill Country* 98 After he got gone, we all peraded to the billiard room. **1938** Hall Coll (Emerts Cove TN) He got gone from here. **1963** Edwards *Gravel* 159 Davey must have been waiting for some time and he was ready to pay and get gone. **1971** *Granny Women* 257 The man got gone, and was nobody knowed where he was. **1973** GSMNP-70:1:2 I let him get gone now long enough to get in Wears Cove, three miles away from home. **1977** *Ben Chappell* 229 You're fixing to get yourself gone, are you? **2007** McMillon *Notes* I'll see you'uns before ye git gone.

[DARE *get gone* v phr chiefly South, South Midland]

get grown See **get up 5**.

get in a big way *verb phrase* To become worked up or excited.

c1950 Adams *Grandpap* 184 Little Preacher Wes and Daw and Pap, taking the stand in that order, all got in a big way. They whooped and hollered and stomped the floor, making the rafters ring. **1964** Roberts *Hell-Fer-Sartin* 144 He kept calling on the Lord until he got in a big way preaching, and the people got to shouting and stamping the floor. **2014** Montgomery *Doctrine* 136 = to get loud and fast with the voice and vocal delivery while preaching.

get into it *verb phrase* To quarrel, wrangle.

1985 Irwin *Alex Stewart* 260 Little George didn't like his uncle coming over into his territory selling liquor, and they got into it.

get killed with one's shoes on *verb phrase* To die a violent death.

1956 Hall Coll (Townsend TN) Jake Rose's boys, Eagle, Thee, and Pitt, they all got killed with their shoes on. They drunk and gambled and played cards.

get next to *verb phrase* See citation.

1986 Pederson et al. LAGS (Johnson Co TN) *I let it get next to me* = I let it bother me.

get obliged to *verb phrase* To have an obligation to. See also **have oblige(d)**.

1913 Bruce *Terms from TN* 58 I *got obliged* to go.

get on *verb phrase* See citations.

1974 Fink *Bits Mt Speech* 11 = accuse, berate: "She got on him about drinking." **1976** Garber *Mountain-ese* 33 = accuse, chide. "The boss is allers bad to git on the office boy fer ever bad job he does."

get oneself a cook *verb phrase* Of a man: to (seek to) get married.

c1960 Wilson *Coll* = to seek a mate, often with cookery as a major goal. **1995** Montgomery *Coll* (known to Cardwell, Shields).

[DARE *get oneself a cook* v phr scattered, but especially South, South Midland]

get one's nosed buttered *verb phrase* See citation.

2011 Montgomery *File* How many of you have ever heard of getting your nose buttered on your birthday? When I was growing up in the Floyd/Patrick/Carroll counties area of Virginia, it was traditional to attempt to sneak up on the birthday person and smear butter on their nose. Even our teachers in elementary school would get in on the action, going to the cafeteria and getting the butter.

get one's peas thrashed *verb phrase* To receive a thorough beating.

1937 Conner *Ms* 44 "O yes," I answered quietly, looking any minute to get my peas thrashed.

get religion *verb phrase* To profess religious belief, experience and exhibit religious conversion. See also **get through**.

1862 *Carter CW Letters* (June 16) I dont want you all to trouble about her condition for I believe she tried as hard to get Religion as ever any body did. **1862** *Cunningham CW Letters* (April 21) tell him that I want him to be a good boy and try and get religion. **1881** Pierson *In the Brush* 117 I determined to try and get religion at once, and be prepared for death. **1914** Crain *Life Story* 32–33 During this meeting I determined to get religion if there was any for me. **1927** Woofter *Dialect from WV* 355 I got religion when I was sixteen. **c1960** Wilson *Coll* = profess religon, join the church. **1979** *Preacher Cook* 198 One day they stopped their engine to pray before they turned over the mountain, and he got religion there. **1990** Clouse *Wilder* 108 Next thing you know, you'll be telling me you got religion.

[DARE *get religion* v phr chiefly South, South Midland]

get shed/shet/shut of, get shut on See **shut B**.

get the bugs in *verb phrase* See citation.

2007 Milnes *Signs Cures Witches* 67 The cider would "get the bugs in," meaning it got strong in alcoholic content.

get the deadwood on See **deadwood**.

get the punies (also *take the punies*) *verb phrase* To feel unwell. See also **puny**.

1937 Still *Brother to Methusalem* 48 Uncle Mize took the punies. **1995** Montgomery *Coll*: *get the punies* = not to be feeling well (Cardwell).

get the right scald on *verb phrase* See citation.

1927 Woofter *Dialect from WV* 355 = to do the matter under consideration exactly right.

get the wrong bull by the tail (also *get the wrong sow by the ear* and other variants) *verb phrase* See citations.

1901 Harben *Westerfelt* 223 You've got the wrong sow by the ear; a wagon went whizzin' by here a minute ago like it was shot out of a gun. **1927** Woofter *Dialect from WV* 355 *get the wrong bull by the tail* = to tell the wrong story, or to give an unsatisfactory explanation: "I got the wrong bull by the tail when I was explaining the matter to my friends." **c1960** Wilson *Coll*: *get the wrong bull* (*cow, bear, pig*, etc.) *by the tail* = tackle the wrong problem or person.

get through *verb phrase* To exhibit religious conversion. See also **get religion**.

1890 Fruit *KY Words* 65 At protracted meetings the "mourners" "git through" when they profess conversion.

getting

A Variant form *gitting* [see **1913** in **B**].

B *noun* A portion or helping of food; a load (as of wood).

1913 Kephart *Our Sthn High* 283 You can git ye one more gittin' o' wood up thar. **1940** Haun *Hawk's Done* 90 She could hear them teasing Murf, "We're having a getting of stovewood for you tomorrow, Murf." **1971** Dwyer *Dict for Yankees* 26 = a load, lot, a helping of food, i.e., "He et three gittin's of taters." **1995** Montgomery *Coll* (known to Cardwell).

get to *verb phrase*

1 (+ *verbal noun*) To begin to, reach the point of. See also **get C5**, **go to 1**.

1859 Taliaferro *Fisher's River* 79 I had got to turnin' up my nose whenuver Molly sot turkey on the table. **1861** *Shipman CW Letters* (Sept 24) at Sals Bury hall and Brown got to Drinking and hall kicked Brown and hurt him tolerabile Bad. **1864** *Chapman CW Letters* (March 4) thomas has got to elboen the girls rite smart. **1884** (in **1996** Edmondson *Crawford Memoirs* 130) On thinking over past events I got to thinking of my Fathers sickness and death. **1900** Harben *N GA Sketches* 153 When I seed 'im a-comin' towards me I jest gazed at 'im with all my might an' he got to lookin' at me. **1927** Justus *Peter Pocket* 51 He was afraid that, if he got to thinking about it, he would cry in spite of himself. **1939** Hall *Coll* (Cades Cove TN) We was small, both of us. They got to deviling us about sparking. **1940** Haun *Hawk's Done* 18 They got to hollering pretty loud and Miss Omie come out of the schoolhouse to see what was wrong. **1942** (in **1987** Perdue *Outwitting Devil* 11) So Jack got to starving nearly to death. **1956** Hall *Coll* (Roaring Fork TN) After the park took the Smoky Mountains a bear got to comin' out on our farm, killin' the stock around on the farm. **1957** *GSMNP-23:1:21* He went to going through there, and it got to snowing. **1960** Hall *Smoky Mt Folks* 52 They explained, "We put the woolen cloth (on the chest) when the fever got high or when she got to smotherin'." **1971** *Boogers* 39 The old man just hollered at it, but it didn't go very far before he heard it comin' back, so he hollered at it again. He got t'hollerin' at it and cussin' it. **1972** *AOHP/ALC-388* All of us was getting to taking a little hot toddy now and then if we could get ahold of it. **1973** *GSMNP-5:5* We was a-picking the banjo and playing the fiddle, and we got to picking "Down the Road." **1979** *Daddy Oakley* 175 He got away out in front of me and started running and I got to trying to keep up with him. **1983** *Dark Corner OHP-28A* He got to reporting them up. **1989** Landry *Smoky Mt Interviews* 195 Then I got to collecting the old stuff. **1998** *Dante OHP-25* They'd get to singing in church, and it's just beautiful.

2 To cause or prompt (one) to start.

c1950 Adams *Grandpap* 87 That got 'em to callin' her Catskin in place of Siniker. **1995** Adams *Come Go Home* 95 I reckoned that the best thing to do was to get her to dancing. **1999** Morgan *Gap Creek* 183 That got us to laughing again.

get to be (also *get up to be*) *verb phrase* To become, reach a state or position of.

1864 *Chapman CW Letters* (March 7) John Meador has got to be Squire. **1865** *Hill CW Letters* (Jan 19) I hav got to be tolerble Stout a gain. **1937** Conner *Ms* 25 Little Elmina Mingus, said to have been 8 year's old, got to be missing about the same time every, evening. **1979** *Daddy Oakley* 175 We were getting up to be pretty good-sized boys. **1991** Thomas *Sthn Appal* 184 We've got to be a nation that's so evil-minded. **1993** Parris *Folklore* 483 Her head got to be full of ballads and folk songs over the years. **1998** *Dante OHP-71* He got to be a chaplain of the union, Harry was a chaplain in the union, if the miner got killed, he went to that home to see what he could do, the union could do for the family.

get to beat *verb phrase* To win.

1913 Kephart *Our Sthn High* 297 Who got to beat? **1994–97** Montgomery *Coll* (known to Adams, Brown, Bush, Cardwell, Oliver).

get up *verb phrase*

1 To collect, acquire, organize (people, dogs, wood, food, crops, etc.); to assemble. See also **get up with**.

1873 Smith *Arp Peace Papers* 177 He said if they did git up a fite the old solgers wouldn't be into it much. **1875** Davis *Qualla* 578 It might be worth our while to ride up thar, provided Colonel Thomas, who was their chief, could git up a torchlight dance for us. **1889** Cole *Letters* 76 I want you to help father to get up money for me to Send my lawyers to Nashville for me. **1921** Campbell *Sthn Highlander* 128 A woman what ain't got sense enough to get her up an old man ain't got sense enough to vote. **1939** Hall *Coll* (Nine Mile TN) We let the bear get away, and then we all come in, all sad, you know, and had our wood to get up after dark. *Ibid.* (Cataloochee NC) I got up some fellers and we started out the next mornin'. **1953** Hall *Coll* (Plott Creek NC) So I got up the dogs and joined the parties. **1956** Hall *Coll* (Del Rio TN) We got our hay and tobacco up. Crops turned out pretty good so far. **1975** *Fiddle Making* 307 We'd git up enough wood t'last'em a month'r'two. **1975–76** *Wolfram/Christian WV Coll* 30 Mother would get you up some kind of sassafras tea. **1993** Parris *Folklore* 491 He used to tell how they had to get [the sheep] up and pen 'em up in the summer to keep the wolves from gettin 'em.

[DARE *get up* v phr 2 chiefly South, South Midland]

2 To roust or kill (game).

1953 Hall *Coll* (Bryson City NC) They ... drove the Bone Valley Creek and didn't get up anything. *Ibid.* (Plott Creek NC) They got up another bear that they run all day ... and we got on a real big bear just some little distance from the camp, and we got up two.

3 Of the wind: to rise.

1986 Pederson et al. *LAGS* = attested by 6/60 interviewees (10%) in E TN and 3/35 (8.6%) in N GA; 9/30 of all LAGS interviewees (30%) attesting term were in Appalachia.

4 To pay off (a debt).

1824 (in **1956** Eliason *Tarheel Talk* 273) (Haywood Co NC) To git up a note.

5 To become, reach (a particular stage or time).

1956 Hall *Coll* (Roaring Fork TN) After I got up grown, a man on my own, I prowled about quite a bit. **1969** Roberts *Greasybeard* 96 She went on along the road till it was getting up about dusty dark and here come a gang of wild shoats and old hogs with tushes a foot long. **1976** *GSMNP-113:4* After I got up grown I went to Noland Creek and stayed in there a long time. **1979** *Shenandoah OHC* 3 After we got up a little size, we would do the milking ourself.

get up and get *verb phrase* To leave in a hurry.

1903 Fox *Little Shepherd* 284 A voice bellowed from the rear ... "Git up and git, boys!" That was the order for the charge. **1952** Wilson *Folk Speech NC* 535 *get up and get*.

get up backwards *verb phrase* To be out of sorts or bad-tempered, have "gotten up on the wrong side of the bed." See also **backside outwards**.

1941 Hall *Coll* (Hot Springs NC) Me and Blondie got up backwards this morning.

get up to be See **get to be**.

get up with *verb phrase* To meet, gather (with a group). See also **get up 1**.

1978 Hiser *Quare Do's* 29 They got up with a old bunch of girls from the X that no local fellow would a been caught dead with. **1984** Wilder *You All Spoken* 103 = come upon, meet, assemble with.

get with *verb phrase* [with stress on both *get* and *with*] Especially of a bully: to fight with, come to blows with.

1939 Hall *Coll* (Proctor NC) He'll get with a feller.

ghost *noun* Variant plural forms of two syllables: *ghost-es*, *gost-es*, *gost-ies*.

1867 Harris *Sut Lovingood* 97j [sic] Ole Clapshaw believes in "witches, an warlocks, an long nebbed things" more than he does in Sicily an his "growin" skeer ov ghostes keeps him at home o' nights. **1922** Cobb *KY Mt Rhymes* 42 Honey, don't let pore dead ghostes / Hant us two. **1937** Haun *Cocke Co* 3 Ghostes are still seed. **1940** Haun *Hawk's Done* 13 You'd better watch out or the ghostes will get you—the ghostes will get you and take you too. **1961** *Coe Ridge OHP-335B* They used to see ghostes there. **1990** Whitener *Thrice-Told* 40 With the season of "goblins and gosties" well nigh upon us, it seems appropriate to pass on a McDowell County mystery tale which came our way through George Shade, a former Appalachian student. **2005** Williams *Gratitude* 496 *go-stes* = more than one ghost.

ghost bush *noun*

1968 Wilson *Folklore Mammoth Cave* 18 = Yucca filamentosa, sometimes also called beargrass. Ghost flower is rare.

ghostes See **ghost.**

ghostflower (also *ghost pipe*, *ghost plant*) *noun* Same as **corpse flower.**

[**1901** Lounsberry *Sthn Wild Flowers* 376 Its small nodding flowers are shaped like a pipe, and its look is ghost-like, the plant being entirely without the grains of chlorophyll, which produce the green colouring matter we are so accustomed to seeing in foliage.] **1937** Thornburgh *Great Smoky Mts* 23 Less conspicuous are . . . Indian pipe or ghostflower, with its fragile, leafless, pipe-shaped blossoms, from which it is said the Indians made a lotion for strengthening the eyes. **1978** *Smokies Heritage* 195 Their curious flowers crouch in darkness beneath deep forest pines, hidden from the glare of summer sunlight. Known as Indian-pipe, the flower is also called "ghost plant" by many local residents because of its startling paleness. **1982** Stupka *Wildflowers* 77 Indian pipe . . . is also called "ghost flower" and "corpse plant." **2016** Houk *Vampires* 63 Take one [parasitic plant] called Ghost pipe (*Monotropa uniflora*). Drained of color and devoid of chlorophyll, its fleshy stalks are translucent white. That sickly appearance also describes another common name, corpse plant. *Ibid.* 63 Ghost pipe 63 Ghost pipe is an example of one of the variations on the parasitic theme. It is a "mycotroph," a plant that gets carbon from a green plant via an intermediary fungus attached to the host's roots. Connected to the fungi, ghost pipe feeds indirectly off the tree in a three-way arrangement that complicates the picture even more.

[from its whiteness]

ghost pipe, ghost plant See **ghostflower.**

gig

A *noun* A small spear that is attached to a handle and has barbed prongs and is used to catch fish or frogs.

1952 Brown *NC Folklore* 1.234 Gigs made from dining forks and umbrellas ribs were used in catching fish and frogs in ditches and other shallow water. **1953** Hall *Coll* (Bryson City NC) Put a light up on the front end of a canoe . . . and take a gig and . . . gig fish of a night.

B *verb* To hunt (fish, bullfrogs) with such an implement. See also **frog B.**

1953 Hall *Coll* (Bryson City NC) Everybody that's lived right near the river pert' nearly had a canoe . . . and they used it for gigging fish. They'd gig fish in the wintertime. Put a light up on the front end of a canoe . . . and take a gig and . . . gig fish of a night. **1963** Watkins and Watkins *Yesterday* 55 Me and Rufe . . . gigged bullfrogs and et the legs. **1991** Thomas *Sthn Appal* 77 We liked to go giggin'. We used a three-prong gig. We had it made at the blacksmith shop. And a long, straight handle. Gener'ly, ye'd make th' gig handle out of a long pole. Or saw one out of a piece of lumber, and round it up. And ye'd have this gig sharp, an' beards on it. And when you gigged a fish, it wouldn't come off of there.

gill-flirted *adjective* See citation.

1968 Wilson *Folklore Mammoth Cave* 18 = a term applied to a mare that was ruptured in giving birth to a colt.

gillion *noun* See citation.

1973 Miller *English Unicoi Co* 147 = a castrated male horse.

[variant of *gelding*]

gilly balm (also *gilly tree*) *noun* Same as **balm of Gilead.**

1937 Still *Brother to Methusalem* 46 He'd loll in the shade of the gilly tree in the yard. **1941** Still *Troublesome Creek* 87 In a hollow stood the Burkhearts' great log house, and beyond under gilly trees was the sorghum gin. **1955** Dykeman *French Broad* 253 The balm of Gilead (or "gilly b'am"), ingredient of healing ointments, especially for earache, is left for winter.

gilt *noun* A young sow. See 1913 citation.

1913 Kephart *Our Sthn High* 295 A female shoat is called a gilt. **1957** Combs *Lg Sthn High: Word List* 44 = a young sow. **1994–97** Montgomery *Coll* (known to Brown, Bush, Cardwell, Hooper, Norris, Oliver).

[ultimately < Old Norse *gylt-r*]

gimble pole See **gambrel.**

gimbling hole *noun* See citation. See also **gambrel.**

1997 Montgomery *Coll* (known to Cardwell), = a hole in a hog's rear leg above the knee joint into which the gimbling stick is put in order to hang a hog that is being butchered, so that it can be cleaned (Brown), = the slit cut just behind the Achilles tendon above the hog's foot. The gimbling bar was inserted into the slits and used to raise the slaughtered hog into an upright position for dressing (Ledford).

gimbling stick, gimlet stick See **gambrel.**

gin[1] see **against.**

gin[2] see **give.**

gin[3] *conjunction* If.

1904–20 Kephart *Notebooks* 4:723 Ask the woman gin you can git a bite. **1913** Kephart *Our Sthn High* 280 Since the Appalachian people have a marked Scotch-Irish strain, we would expect their speech to show a strong Scotch influence. So far as vocabulary is concerned, there is really little of it. A few words, caigy (cadgy), coggled, fernent, gin for if, needcessity, trollop, almost exhaust the list of distinct Scotticisms. **1931** Combs *Lg Sthn High* 1303 = if. **1944** Wilson *Word-List* 43 = if. [**1992** Montgomery *Coll* (unknown to consultants from the Smoky Mountains).]

[OED3 *gin* conj of obscure origin, Scot and dialect; EDD *gin* prep/conj Scot, nEngl dialect; SND *gin* conj 2; CUD *gin*[1] "if"; DARE *gin* conj1 chiefly Appalachians]

gin[4] (also *gin around*) *verb, verb phrase* To do odd jobs or chores, go from one activity to another. See also **gin crew**, **gin hand**, **gin job**, **gin time**, **gin work**, **jim**, **jimhand**, **jinwhacker**.

1936 Stuart *Head of Hollow* 195 Reece wasn't able to work much. Just ginned here and there where he could get the ginning to do for fifty or seventy-five cents a day. **1940** Bowman *KY Mt Stories* 17 At first I could find no explanation for the word "gin" with a soft "g," used in this section of the foot-hill country instead of "chore," and the expression "ginnin' 'round" meaning "choring around." Then I discovered the word "gin" in the Bible, meaning "trap." No doubt, trapping or visiting traps was a very definite part of the chores in pioneering times; therefore, "ginning" came to be used for "trapping," and the word "gin" became established in their minds with chores and has been handed down by word of mouth ever since the earliest settlements in America. **1975** Jackson *Unusual Words* 151 *gin*. **1976** Dwyer *Southern Sayin's* 31 *ginning around* = fiddling, dabbling, moving about. **1976** Garber *Mountainese* 34 = do odd jobs. "Josh don't have no job atall, he jist likes to gin around the house." **1982** Slone *How We Talked* 20 *gin* (also *ginning around*) = doing odd jobs. Might be used as an expression to tell someone to hurry. "You better gin around and get this job done." **1996–97** Montgomery *Coll* (known to Brown, Oliver).

[from rapid circular motion, probably as in the action of a cotton gin]

gin crew (also *gin-works*) *noun* A work crew.

1941 Still *Troublesome Creek* 71 Be-dads, if the whole gin-works hain't got the punies. Even the mare tuck a spell today. **c1975** *Miners' Jargon* 4 *gin crew* = group of men responsible for any and all odd jobs [in a coal mine]. Similar to a construction crew.

gineral See **general.**

ginerally See **generally.**

gineration See **generation.**

ginerl See **general.**

ginerly See **generally.**

gin gang *noun* A crew of manual workers. See also **bull gang.**

1968 Clarke *Stuart's Kentucky* 177 In *Beyond Dark Hills* Stuart related his own experience at Armco Rolling Mills, where he began work on the gin gang or bull gang that did the odd jobs, such as cleaning out manholes, laying sewers for privies, unloading from the train coke and coal, picking up scraps of steel to be reworked.

ginger cake *noun* A cookie or small cake flavored with ginger.

1862 *Zimmerman CW Letters* (Sept 16) peaches is worth 25 cents a dozen you can tell from that how muney goes if we buy ginger cake 25 cents a pisce half as big as this paper. **1864** *Poteet CW Letters* (Feb 4) I sent you somthing to eat by Marion Higins five pies and five ginger Cakes one doz unions two custerds 1 ham of Meat and three twists of tobacco.

[DARE *ginger cake* n 1 especially South, South Midland]

ginger stew *noun* A mixture of ginger, whiskey, and other ingredients drunk as a tonic.

1973 GSMNP-4:1:29 People of a morning, the first thing when they would get out of bed, they would put it on the stove and boil it and put ginger and liquor and water and make what they called a "ginger stew." They would take liquor and weaken it down with water and make what they call "hot drink." And they would drink that. It would be the first thing they would drink of a morning when they got out of bed. **1975–76** Wolfram/Christian *WV Coll* 30 My dad would make a ginger stew with whiskey, give it to us kids if we got the flu or something like that. . . . Take the ginger and grind it up right fine, you know, and boil it in some water and put the whiskey in a little bit of water and drink it. That's the awfullest tasting stuff in the world, but it'll sweat you plumb to death. **1997** Montgomery *File* = a drink made from water heated on the stove, to which was added whiskey, ginger, red pepper, and sugar (70-year-old man, Maggie Valley NC).

[cf DARE (at *stew* n) especially Midland, South]

ginger tea *noun* A homemade medicinal drink, used to treat colds.

1956 Hall *Coll* (Sand Hill TN) If we tuck a hard cold, we drank ginger tea. **1994** Montgomery *Coll* (known to Shields).

gin hand *noun* See 1982 citation. See also **jim**, **jinwhacker.**

1982 Slone *How We Talked* 20 = a person who helps someone that has a more important job. **1997** Montgomery *Coll* (known to Brown). **2007** Baldridge *E KY Railway* 36 He began working for the Eastern Kentucky Railway in 1873 at the age of 15 as a gin hand. The Laurel stop was between Argillite and Hunnewell just on the north side of Sand Suck Creek.

gin job *noun* See citation.

1981 High *Coll* (DARE) = [an] odd job: "I got some gin jobs to do this evening. You want to help me cut the grass?"

ginly, **gin'rally** See **generally.**

ginseng

A Variant forms *sang* [see **1826** in **B**], *seng* [see **1926** in **B**], *sang root* [see **c1980** in **C**].

[DARE (at *sang* n) chiefly South Midland]

B *noun* A perennial wild plant (*Panax quinquefolium*) whose roots are harvested mainly for export to East Asia, where an extract is a reputed cure-all, used especially to treat fatigue, loss of memory, depression, and impotence. Most commonly known in the mountains as *sang*, the small, delicate plant has long been a source of income, and the lucrative hunting and harvesting of it in the wild has become regulated by both state and federal governments. Also called **new life root**. See also **blood medicine**, **little green men**.

1826 Royall *Sketches* 58 These counties, remote from commerce and civilized life, confined to their everlasting hills of freezing cold, all pursuing the same employments, which consist in farming, raising cattle, making whiskey, (and drinking it,) hunting and digging *sang*, as they say, present a distinct republic of their own. **1892** Allen *Cumberland Gap* 249–50 Formerly digging "sang," as they call ginseng, was a general occupation. For this China was a great market. It has nearly all been dug out except in the wildest parts of the country, where entire families may still be seen "out sangin'." They took it into the towns in bags, selling it at a dollar and ten cents—perhaps a dollar and a half—a pound. **1916** Schockel *KY Mts* 111 I came upon one old man and his wife, digging "sang" in the woods, who stopped to talk for an hour and wanted to know why it is that the Chinese can not live without the root, and what would happen to that people when the supply shortly would give out in America. **1926** Hunnicutt *Twenty Years* 211 Old man Henry said we have plenty of meat for tomorrow; let's hunt the Quill Rose ginseng patch.... On his way after the bear dogs he went through a patch of seng that looked to be a half of an acre or more. **1939** Hall *Coll* (Copeland Creek TN) I had to pick sang and pick up chestnuts for to buy what we had to wear. **1939** Jennison *Flora Great Smokies* 280 Ginseng is indigenous throughout the Appalachians, but except for cultivated patches, it is rare, and only the knowing "sang" hunters succeed in finding enough nowadays to make it worth going after. **1955** Dykeman *French Broad* 250 Ginseng in great quantities is shipped to China. The Chinese "doctrine of signatures" makes ginseng a supposed cure-all in that country. The name itself comes from the Chinese "jin-tsang," meaning "manlike," and by the doctrine of signatures any medicine brewed from a plant having the same shape as the afflicted limb or organ will be effective. Since many ginseng roots resemble the complete human figure, it, then, would be a general remedy for all ills. **1960** Price *Root Digging in Appal* 15 Ginseng is a sensitive herbaceous perennial that demands a rich mull soil and well-watered woodland shade. Through most of its range summer drought restricts it to north slopes and sheltered coves. **1971** Hutchins *Hidden Valley* 192 In Oriental lands ginseng root is chewed in the belief that it imparts strength, especially sexual vigor.... Considering this price, it is little wonder that the rangers of Great Smoky Mountain National Park must be continually on the watch for "sang" poachers. **1984** Dykeman and Stokely *At Home* 57 A chief medicinal herb was an unusual wild plant known as ginseng. Called "sang" in mountain vernacular, its value lay in the manlike shape of its dual-pronged roots. **1997** Hufford *American Ginseng* 5 Ginseng's etymology and economic value both come from China and neighboring countries, where the root has long been prized for conferring longevity and vigor of all sorts on its users. The term ginseng is an Americanization of the Chinese jin-chen, meaning "manlike." The Latin term Panax quinquefolia alludes to the five whorled leaves on each branch and the plant's function as a panacea. **2006** Howell *Medicinal Plants* 88 In North America, it was used extensively by eastern American Indians to relieve an array of symptoms including general fatigue, headache, palsy, fevers, thrush, rheumatism, breathing difficulties, and colic. It was also used as a good luck charm and was thought to prevent children from having bad dreams.

[< Chinese *jen2-shen1*]

C *verb* To search for in the wild and gather this plant, one of the few products sold for cash in many traditional mountain communities; hence verbal nouns *ginsenging*, *sanging* = searching for and gathering this plant on a regular basis.

1918 *Story* 19 One of the recreations is going "sanging." Sometimes whole families go out for a month at a time and camp in the woods, gathering ginseng, or "sang." They call this "going sanging." Sometimes they get a hundred dollars worth. **1939** Hall *Coll* (Cades Cove TN) Me and Tom [Gregory] was a-sangin'. **c1950** Adams *Grandpap* 192 While sanging was to Pap and Mammy the means of their most substantial income, it was also to them a sport. They'd race to see which one could find the most bunches. Every time that Pap found a bunch he'd whistle, once for each prong that it had. Mammy couldn't whistle, to do any good, but she'd say "Whoopee" every time she found a bunch. **1950** Woody *Cataloochee Homecoming* 14 The lazy man who wanted to take a day off or avoid a scolding wife could always go "sanging." **1959** Hall *Coll* (Roaring Fork TN) They were a-sangin' or cattle huntin' one. **1973** GSMNP-79:1:23 We used to like to get out in the mountain and fish and sang and hunt. **1975** GSMNP-62:13 We done a lot of ginsenging too. Ginseng was a dollar and a half a pound green and three dollars and a half dried.... I went plumb to the head of Balsam Branch and ginsenged, dug ladyslipper, all of them there. **1975** Screven *John B Wright* 14 I come up with them a-ginsenging; I learned it pretty quick. **c1980** Roberts *Olden Times* 104 Going "senging" has been a profitable side line for the people of this area for generations. In the olden days many families spent much of their time combing the mountains looking for ginseng. The practice was called "senging" and was the chief source of income for many families. In many cases the entire family spent days in a systematic search for the herb. In this community the custom of digging the seng roots wherever found has prevailed, and it is considered legal to trespass upon anyone's property to dig ginseng. In fact, many times the senging is done at night by use of lanterns. **1984** Dykeman and Stokely *At Home* 58 Sometimes several members of a family would wait until summer or early fall, then go out on extended "sanging" expeditions. **1988** Dunn *Cades Cove* 32 Although many [Cades] cove people engaged in "sangin'," or gathering ginseng roots to sell in Knoxville, there is no evidence that they ever used the herb in any home remedy or were even cognizant of its reputed properties. **1989** *Matewan OHP*-9 We'd seng, if you know what that is, in the mountains, go in the mountains and dig seng and dig herbs and roots and sell them and get what we could out of that. **1997** Hufford *American Ginseng* 5 A linchpin in the seasonal round of foraging, ginsenging is also essential to a way of life. "I'd rather ginseng than eat," said Dennis Dickens, eighty-five, of Peach Tree Creek. "Every spare minute I had was spent a-ginsenging." *Ibid.* 10 I'd say most of the people that ginseng are people that works. They just love to ginseng. I miss work to go ginsenging. **2006** Hufford *Ramp Suppers* 113 You'll come across a ramp patch when you're out ginsenging. Last week I dug more ramps than ginseng!

[DARE (at *sang* v 1) especially southern Appalachians]

ginsenging See **ginseng C.**

ginseng tale (also *sang tale*) *noun* An exaggerated account about the size or number of **ginseng** plants one has discovered.

1995 Peterson *Ginseng Hunter* 59 Zelotes says that sangers "would tell some of the awfullest sang tales," each one with a bigger, better find to tell about. **1997** Hufford *American Ginseng* 9 Ginseng money helped build the fortune of John Jacob Astor as well as the political career of an early senator from California, according to a "ginseng tale" told by Quentin Barrett. [**2009** Mould *Ginseng* 299 Men dominate the tradition [of hunting ginseng]. Most women rarely stay to chat with other hunters when selling their ginseng or compete with stories of the biggest root they ever found.]

gin time *noun* See citation. See also **gin**⁴.

1940 Bowman *KY Mt Stories* 239 = chore time.

ginuwine See **genuine.**

ginwhack See **jinwhacker.**

gin work

A *noun* Chores. See also **gin**⁴, **gin crew**, **gin hand.**

1938 Stuart *Dark Hills* 330 I work two days here a week and of a night when I come in off the railroad. I do my gin work on Sunday. **1939** Krumpelmann *WV Peculiarities* 156 In expression "gin-work"—odd jobs. A student applying for part-time work is asked: "What kind of work have you ever done?" or "What kind of work do you wish to do?" He answers: "Gin-work" (Cabell County). At first I thought he meant he had worked around a cotton gin, but later learned that 'gin-work' means any sort of odds and ends that a 'handy-man' generally does. . . . One member of the faculty who was born and bred in this region tells me there is a verbal colloquialism "to gin (or jim) around" which means "just to dabble around, to fool around, to fiddle around." "Well, what have you been doing during the holidays?" Answer: "Oh, just ginning (or jimming) around." **1941** Still *Proud Walkers* 114 "When a woman undertakes man's gin-work," he spoke, "their fingers all turn to thumbs." **1941** Stuart *Men of Mts* 61 Mr. Kirk, you stay here and get the weeds out'n your garden and get your ginwork done up. *Ibid.* 266 It's better 'n cuttin' timber fer fifty cents a thousand, or hoein' corn fer seventy-five cents a day or doin' gin work fer some farmer fer fifty cents a day.

B (also *gin-wrack around*) *verb phrase* See citation.

1960 Westover *Highland Lg* 19 *gin work* (also *gin-wrack around*) = do chores.

gin-works See **gin crew.**

gin-wrack around See **gin work B.**

girl *noun*

A Variant form *gyirl*. [Editor's note: The form *gal* is widespread in the US.]

1984 Woods *WV Was Good* 230 Many old people said *gyirl* for *girl*.

B A daughter.

1861 *Mingus Letters* 29 (Oct 6) Jackson Beck had a little girl to fall out . . . the blade cut her throat, it lived 15 minutes. **1940** Haun *Hawk's Done* 7 She is my oldest girl and it is right she should. **1963** Edwards *Gravel* 13 You're Mary McPheeters girl, all right; I can see that. **1971** *AOHP/ALC-277* Their girl was the best hand to play the banjo you ever seed. **1985** Irwin *Alex Stewart* 250 Uncle George Livesy had a girl that took the measles. **1989** *Matewan OHP-23* He married Dutch Hatfield's sister, a cousin of mine that was Gretchel Hatfield['s] girl. **1991** Thomas *Sthn Appal* 169 Her girl wonted t' go out an' work, an' make 'er a little money, t' buy 'er some clothes, an' thangs. **2005** Williams *Gratitude* 496 = daughter. "She's Uncle Joe's girl."

girl baby (also *girl chap*, *girl child*) *noun* A female baby or child. See also **chap.**

1941 Still *Troublesome Creek* 52 I bet them girl-chaps wear old flour-sack dresses, and you can read print front and back. **1962** Dykeman *Tall Woman* 16 I learned the costs of a new country to a woman—and to a girl-child. **1995–97** Montgomery *Coll*: *girl child* (known to Adams, Brown, Cardwell, Jones, Norris, Weaver). **2004** Fisher *Kettle Bottom* 22 A woman in a white dress [was] coming up behind that pony, carrying a girl-baby. **2018** *Blind Pig* (April 28) I was talking to my oldest girl the other day.

girlified *adjective* Especially of a boy: having feminine qualities or behaviors.

1940 Haun *Hawk's Done* 151 Everytime he got to feeling girlified and shamed because he had to cook supper, he made himself think about the books in the library. **c1945** Haun *Hawk's Done* 223 She made George set in the playhouse with her, and he would do it, no matter how much Pa teased him and called him girlified and threatened to make him wear dresses.

girt *noun* The leather strap buckled around a horse's girth to secure a saddle.

1957 Broaddus *Vocab Estill Co KY* 34 = a girth, a band put around a horse's middle to hold the saddle on. **1999** Montgomery *Coll* (known to Cardwell).

[OED3 *girt* n 1a obsolete except dialect; DARE *girt* n chiefly New England, South, South Midland]

git *verb* To leave hurriedly, "scram." See also **get A**.

1908 Fox *Lonesome Pine* 15 "Git" said the mountaineer, with a move of one huge hairy hand up the mountain. "An' git quick!" **1993** Cunningham *Sthn Talk* 58 I reckin we better git a-gittin'. **2007** Alexander *Moonshiners Gone* 25 When lunchtime comes, you "git" from here and you don't look back and don't ever come back. **2013** Salsi *Jack and Giants* 31 "Git out of here—don't come back." The giants gitted. They ran straight through the forest and knocked down every tree.

git box (also *git fiddle*) *noun* A guitar. See also **box 2**.

1974 Fink *Bits Mt Speech* 11 *git box, git fiddle*. **1976** Garber *Mountain-ese* 34 Hand me my git-box and I'll pick you a little tune I writ myself. **1994–97** Montgomery *Coll*: *git box* (known to Ellis, Ledford); *git fiddle* (known to Adams, Ellis, Jones, Norris, Oliver, Weaver), = not always facetious (Cardwell).

[blend of *guitar* + *box*, *fiddle*]

git fiddle See **git box**.

gitting See **getting**.

give *verb* Principal parts.

1 Variant infinitive/base forms *gave, gin*.

1863 *Epperly CW Letters* (May 12) I havent any nuse of any importance to write at preasent but I will write again in a fiew day and gave you all the nuse. **1863** *Hawn CW Letters* (May 19) I can not gin you an ancer today I will tell you more in mi next Letr.

2 Variant past-tense forms *gin, gi'n, giv, give, gived, given*.

1774 *Dunmore's War* 72 The consternation this appearance give the Traders was the foundation of the late report. **1794** *Big Pigeon Church Minutes* 18 The Breathren John Mathes and Frances McKelhaney made thear report to the Church that they did apply to David Melson.s [sic] formelley and giv them word to attend this Meeting but they failing to apear the Matter prospond til meeting in Corse. **1814** Hartsell *Memora* 138 ther was a doctor that Steped fored and toock the Sword out of his handes and give it to the General. **1832** *McLean Diary* 10 [I] Went to Cort Lifted Stouts Note and give my one. **1860** Olmsted *Back Country* 261 I gin this fellow $6 a month for six months. **1862** *Huntley CW Letters* (March 6) he given James Miller leaf to go home to make a company. **1864** *Sexton CW Letters* (March 18) i got your kind letter this mor[n]ing which giv me grate Satisfaction to her from all of you. **1871** *Tuckaleechee Cove Church Minutes* 9 the refference was called and read which set the ordination of Br J B J Brickey for the ministry of the gospel of Jesus Christ the Church received presbytery And give him up to the presbytery. **1873** Smith *Arp Peace Papers* 129 By double teamin they lickd us, and we gin it up. **1883** Zeigler and Grosscup *Heart of Alleghanies* 51 We,—thet is, Bill Massey who's awmost blind now, Bill Allen who gin up huntin' long ye'rs ago, my brother El, me, an' sev'ral others,—we started a bar on the Jackson county line nigh Scotts creek in the mornin'. **1913** Kephart *Our Sthn High* 284 In many cases a weak preterite supplants the proper strong one: div, driv, fit, gi'n or give, rid, riv, riz, writ. **1922** *TN CW Ques* 2160 (Wilkes Co NC) Three ladies in a dry goods store saw I was barefooted and give me a pair of womens shoes size 7. **1939** Hall *Coll* (Deep Creek NC) I went on out and give him [= the bear] a couple of more shots, and that finished him. **1953** Atwood *Verbs East US* 15 [South of New York] *give* is used by something like from two thirds (Pa.) to over nine tenths (Va. and N.C.) of Type I [i.e. older speakers with little formal education]. In Type II [i.e. younger speakers with more formal education] the frequency is considerably less, varying from about one fourth (Pa.) to about two fifths (W.Va.). **1969** GSMNP-25:1:4 One of these old hog rifle guns, now that's what he give for the place when he went there. **1977** McGreevy *Breathitt KY Grammar* 93 *gived* = attested by 3 speakers. **1978** Reese *Speech NE Tenn* 175 *give* = attested by 6/12 (50%) speakers. **1980** Miles *Verbs in Haywood Co* 101 He give my daddy a lot down there. **1983** *Dark Corner OHP-24A* We went and bought peppermint candy and put it in [the whiskey] and gived it to the children. **1998** *Dante OHP-25* He give a lot of them people up there houses, and he give us that building up there for a church. **2008** *Rosie Hicks* 3 It was too many for us, and I give them some.

3 Variant past-participle forms *gave, gin, give, gived*.

1794 *Big Pigeon Church Minutes* 14 Jesse Isbell has give his letter to the Church that he receivd it from and the church has considered the matter respecting of him and has brought it to excummunication. **1814** Hartsell *Memora* 133 ther was word gon on to the beoard of ware Conserning the Conduct of General Jackson about the usage that he head give his men. **1861** *Patton CW Letters* (June 8) we have gave Robert Vance thirty dollars to carey to you for we do not expect to need it. **1862** *Robinson CW Letters* (May 25) She doant get none but what is give to her. **1867** Harris *Sut Lovingood* 32 Frum the time I staid inside ove hit, I can't say that es a human shut I'd gin a durn for a dozin ove em. **1888** Meriwether *Mt Life in TN* 457 The old farmer refused to take payment for the breakfast, "'Lowing we'uns had gin him as much fun as the grub was worth." **1901** Harben *Westerfelt* 5 After all the advice I've give the foolish girl! **1939** Hall *Coll* (Hazel Creek NC) If I'd a knowed you fellows been a-coming and had studied up, why I could have give you fellows a whole lot of news. **1942** (in **1987** Perdue *Outwitting Devil* 64) There he met up with the old man that had gave him the golden goose. **1970** Foster *Walker Valley* 41 I'd a give ten dollars for one of them plank out of that house. **1978** Montgomery *White Pine Coll* XII People has always gave Cocke County a bad name. **1978** Reese *Speech NE Tenn* 175 *gave* = attested by 3/12 (25%) speakers; *give* = attested by 7/12 (58.3%) speakers. **1980** Miles *Verbs in Haywood Co* 101 I really hadn't give it much thought. *Ibid.* 102 She ain't gave me any yet. **1984** GSMNP-153:24 The park had give daddy twenty-four hundred dollars for what he had sold on Little Catalooch. **2001** House *Clay's Quilt* 87 It's something God has gived you. **2009** Ebel and Hicks *Jack Tales* 7 A big old sack of galax [was] on her back. You could see she was about gived out.

[DARE *give* (at *give* v A3) scattered, but especially South, South Midland]

gived See **give 2, 3**.

give down *verb phrase*

1 To admit, acquiesce, confess.

1917 Kephart *Word-List* 412 = to admit, confess. "He'll *give* it *down* at last." **1930** Armstrong *This Day and Time* 251 Give down to your misery, honey. **1961** *Coe Ridge OHP-336A* He couldn't talk. He just give down, broke down over it. **1995** Montgomery *Coll* (known to Oliver); He'll give down to any ailment to keep from going (Cardwell).

2 To become weary, wear out.

1922 *TN CW Ques* 2091 (Hamilton Co TN) I came to Nashville Tenn. and worked at box factory until my health give down on me. **1938** Stuart *Dark Hills* 125 I gave down on marching eight miles and carrying the pack.

3 Of a cow: to produce (milk).

1914 Combs *Magic in KY Mts* 328 If you kill a toad, the witches will cause your cows to "give down" bloody milk. . . . Cows are bewitched; and their owners complain that they are not "giving down" milk, whereas the cows belonging to witches are continually yielding a plentiful supply. **1982** Ginns *Snowbird Gravy* 127 If you talk ill to her or grumble or hit 'er or anything, she won't give 'er milk down. **2007** McMillon *Notes* = when a cow lets down her milk.

4 To pronounce (a word to be spelled in a spelling match). Same as **give out A3**.

1975–76 Wolfram/Christian *WV Coll* 153 Our school teacher got up and me and him was spelling and he give me down "wrapper."

give down the country (also *give down the road*) To berate, castigate, scold severely.

1924 (in **1952** Mathes *Tall Tales* 60) He's sure givin' the devil down-the-country tonight. **1936** Morehouse *Rain on Just* 150 Dolly had given Bilow down the road for chasing after her so. **1956** Hall *Coll* (Del Rio TN) Vernelle's givin' Paul down the country. **1956** McAtee *Some Dial NC* 13 *down the country* = blame, criticism. "They're allus givin me down the country." **1976** Garber *Mountain-ese* 34 Bett will shore give him down the road when she hears about this. **1982** Slone *How We Talked* 40 She gave him down the road (berated). **1996–97** Montgomery *Coll*: *give someone down the country* (known to eight consultants from the Smoky Mountains); *give someone down the road* (known to eight consultants from the Smoky Mountains). **2004** Adams *Old True Love* 130 Larkin had been stung by a hornet and Hackley was giving him down the road about it. **2009** Benfield *Mt Born* 202 *give someone down the road* = to tell someone off.

[DARE *down the country, give one* v phr probably *down the country* in ref[erence] to banishment, but sometimes reanalyzed as v + n phr, chiefly South, South Midland]

give howdy See **howdy B**.

give in *verb phrase*

1 To admit, announce.

1809 (in **1956** Eliason *Tarheel Talk* 273) (Davie Co NC) 7 bushels corn you gave in that you had taken. **1850** *Zion Church Church Minutes* 40 a door was opened when Margaret Deyton joined by experience. and Elizabeth McCracken and Nancy Letterman give in by recantation, all of which was received. **1925** Dargan *Highland Annals* 159 "Well, I ain't give in yit," Snead asserted, his yellow-brown eyes shimmering. **1939** Hall *Coll* (Wears Cove TN) The jury give it in that . . . he'd been killed by somebody.

2 To submit (an accounting, especially of one's property, in order that one's taxes may be assessed).

1863 *Vance Papers* (July 13) Some Men Could Give in the Best Surtificate of Diseases and woulddent Bee listened at. **1950** Woody *Cataloochee Homecoming* 11 Once a year it was necessary to "give in" one's taxes, and again there would be a period of two or three days when the able-bodied males were to "work the road." **1966** Medford *Ol' Starlin* 89 "Yes, that's what the Cor'nor give in," replied McDirk. **2007** Cave *Recollections* = to visit and declare each year at a county recording office the value of all personal property, including jewelry, furniture, dogs, livestock, etc., which was to be taxed the same way that real estate property would be.

give leg bail See **leg bail**.

give mouth (also *give tongue*) *verb phrase* Of a hunting dog on an animal's track: to bark excitedly. See also **mouth A2**.

c1939 (in **2005** Ballard and Chung *Arnow Stories* 191) Strung out along behind were the four Keith hounds, all giving tongue as if the fox were right under their noses. **1960** Burnett *My Valley* 137 On reaching the top of ridges, he would give mouth somewhat freely, as well as on down hill grades. **1960** Cooper *Jularker Bussed* Listen to them hound-dogs (hounds) a-givin' tongue (barking excitedly) up thar. **2002** Rash *Foot in Eden* 145 It wasn't long before I heard a bloodhound giving tongue over at Mrs. Winchester's.

[DARE (at *mouth* B1) chiefly South Midland]

give one's hand *verb phrase* See citation.

1982 Slone *How We Talked* 72 = asking for membership [in a church].

give out

A *verb phrase*

1 To fail, become fatigued or weak; to exhaust; hence participial adjective phrase *give out*.

1813 Hartsell *Memora* 121 a grate maney of ther Horses was likely to give out on their way to Roses for the lack of feed. **c1844** Beckner *Shane Interview* 235 He told Yeager he had given out. Yeager got down and let him have his horse. **1862** *Spainhourd CW Letters* (Sept 8) git me a pair of shous fo[r] my old ones ar ner[l]y give out. **1863** *Reese CW Letters* (Feb 27) [My eyes] giv out So Bad it taks mee two or three trials to Rite A letter. **1892** Dromgoole *War of Roses* 487 The kisses'll give plumb out afore my turn comes. **1924** (in **1952** Mathes *Tall Tales* 26) He was might'-nigh give out when he got to camp, but he said he'd foller us back as soon as he blowed a spell. **1939** Hall *Coll* (Deep Creek NC) He went on and he give out on them, fell in the creek and got wet all over and give out on them before they got in to the bear, and they had to carry him, pack him about the last two mile. *Ibid.* (Maggie Valley NC) I told her I was starved and froze and give out. **c1945** Haun *Hawk's Done* 303 Everything about the place seemed lonesome and give-out. **1954** Roberts *Bought a Dog* [22] My legs are give out and I dont have to run after you any more. **1966** Dakin *Vocab Ohio River Valley* 476 *Give out* is the southern Kentucky expression. It is also common in the Mountains and Knobs south of the upper Kentucky and Licking Rivers, but this term is not used in the Bluegrass and is attested by only one speaker north of the Green River. **1974–75** McCracken *Logging* 1:3 Agin I got up that twenty foot I was give out. **1978** Montgomery *White Pine Coll* III-2 No wonder the girls at these stands was give out teetotally. **1986** Ogle *Lucinda* 56 We went home that afternoon a different route or trail over the ridges and my legs give out. **1999** Offut *Out of Woods* 45 I got give out on it. **2009** Holbrook *Upheaval* 1 The stubbornness at least had give out.

2 To announce, state publicly.

1864 *C A Walker CW Letters* (April 3) There was one old Dunkard preached near here the other day and give out his text (12th) Chapter and 5th verse of the Revelations of St. John the Divine by God. **1913** Kephart *Our Sthn High* 298 Phil's Ann give it out to each and every that Walt and Layunie'd orter wed. **1937** Hall *Coll* (Cades Cove TN) They give it out that there would be some preachin'. **1974** Fink *Bits Mt Speech* 11 It was *give out* there was supposed to be a meeting last night. **1982** Slone *How We Talked* 73 *give out the next meeting* = announce the place and time of the next service. Many are "given out" at the close of each "gatherin'" for a different time and place. Lots of times folks have "church in their home," another carry-over from when we had few or no church houses.

[DARE *give out* v phr 1a chiefly South Midland, South]

3 To deliver, especially to pronounce (a word to be spelled in a spelling match or the words of a hymn to be sung). See also **give down 3**, **line out**.

1799 *Sinking Creek Church Minutes* III:4 this Church doth This day up to excommunication John Gillam for his Bad Condck in as much as he has Give out such Sinful Languag. **1901** Harben *Westerfelt* 266 The preacher gave out the hymn in a solemn, monotonous voice, and the congregation sang it. **1925** Furman *Glass Window* 91 Four boys got up and stood before him while he gave out the words. "Spell theory, the-*ater*, the-*sis*," he proceeded, pronouncing just one word of the ten correctly. **1956** McAtee *Some Dial NC* 18 = call the words in a spelling match. **1969** Foust *Kingdom of Wilkes* 62–63 It was the custom on Friday afternoons for the teacher to select the pupil who was supposed to be the best speller, and he was allowed to choose his opponent, and the two of them took "turns" choosing "sides" until all the students both great and small, were lined up in two rows extending the length of the room. Then the teacher, standing or sitting, between these two mighty heads started "giving out" easy words at the foot of the lines, gradually calling longer and more difficult words. The first to miss a word took his seat, and so on until all were "turned down" except the head of one of the lines, and he was declared the winner of the day's match. **1977** Moore *Jenks* 33 I believe it's much better where there's two a-singing it together, you see, because they can fill in with other words besides what just the lead man is giving out. **1982** Slone *How We Talked* 73 *giving out a song* = in some places it's called "lining a song." Long ago few people could read, few had song books, no one could read music. So, one person would read the song, two lines at a time. The congregation would sing those two lines and the one "giving out the song" would then read two more lines (in today's modern terminology of harmony, everyone sang lead) and so on until the song was finished. Some people can give out a song in such a way with such a beautiful rhythmical chant that it was more wonderful than the song itself. **1986** Tyson *Reflections* 29 We looked forward to Fridays. Most of the time we would get to have a cross bench spelling match. We put four benches together and the teacher would give out the word and if the one that sat by you misspelled the word and you could spell it you took their place and on that way 'til you got to the end of the bench. If you spelled the word, you crossed to the next bench and made one talley. **1997** *Dante OHP-14* I was in third grade, I believe, and it was in our spelling match where he give us out words and it was "appetite." **2006** *Encycl Appalachia* 1322 The term *lining* is not generally used by Old Baptists, who call what the leader does "giving out" the song.

[DARE *give out* v phr 1b chiefly South Midland, South]

4 To decide against, forgo, abandon (a plan, intention, etc.).

1836 (in **1956** Eliason *Tarheel Talk* 274) (Wilkes Co NC) Your father . . . had intended to go . . . To the burrow but give it out. **1862** *Robinson CW Letters* (July 13) I have give out going to the artilrey compney. **1864** *Edmonston/Kelly CW Letters* (July 24) I have give out the idie of coming to your Regt for awhile. **1975** Fink *Backpacking* 11 I'm about *give out* going.

[DARE *give out* v phr 3a chiefly South Midland, South]

5 To lose hope or expectation of (someone's arrival), despair of. See also **give up 2**.

1925 Furman *Glass Window* 46 Lowizy she's been keen for you to come, but has nigh give you out now. **1939** Bond *Appal Dialect* 107 = to decide that one is not coming. **1942** (in **1987** Perdue *Outwitting Devil* 32) The day was over half gone and he'd give her out a-comin' and he put his head in his hands and started cryin'. **1957** Broaddus *Vocab Estill Co KY* 34 = to give up looking for. **1984** Wilder *You All Spoken* 166 = give up on, as "Clara Della give out on seein' you ag'in, so she up an' lef' out of here with a fruit tree salesman." **1985** Irwin *Alex Stewart* 34 He finally give you out a little while ago.

[DARE *give out* v phr 3b chiefly South Midland, South]

B *noun*

1 An announcement.

1905 Miles *Spirit of Mts* 135 I don't know; there wasn't any give out at meetin' last Sunday. **1913** Kephart *Our Sthn High* 283 I didn't hear no give-out at meetin'. **1944** Combs *Word-List Sthn High* 19 = announcement. "I hyerd no *give-out* about it." **1994–97** Montgomery *Coll* (known to Brown), = old-fashioned (Cardwell).

[DARE *give-out* n especially southern Appalachians]

2 A handout, petty bribe.

1994 Montgomery *Coll* (known to Oliver, Weaver), I stood around all day for a give out [= a bribe for one's vote] (Cardwell).

giverment See **government**.

give tongue See **give mouth**.

give up *verb phrase*

1 To acknowledge or regard, be reputed.

1862 *Huntley CW Letters* (May 20) it is pretty mutch given up By all men about hear that the yankies Will take Richmond in a fiew days. **1923** Combs *Addenda KY* 242 *give up to be* = to admit, concede: "John Horseley's give up to be the knowin'est man, in these parts." **1936** Lyman *WV Idioms* 63 He was given up (cried up, reputed) to be a good writer. **1952** Wilson *Folk Speech NC* 545 *give up to be* = acknowledged to be, accepted as. **1956** Hall *Coll* (Roaring Fork TN) He was give up to be the best bear dog in the country. **1974** Fink *Bits Mt Speech* 11 He's *give up* to be the best doctor in town. **1985** Irwin *Alex Stewart* 13 Alex is give up to be the best hand around to make such as that. **1996–97** Montgomery *Coll* (known to Brown, Cardwell, Jones, Oliver).

[DARE *give up* v phr 1 chiefly South Midland]

2 To lose hope for or expectation for (someone's arrival), despair of (someone's) coming. See also **give out A5**.

1991 Thomas *Sthn Appal* 229 I'z jist about ready to give it up. **1995** Adams *Come Go Home* 74 "I had about give you up for comin'," she hollered, as I came up through the yard. **1998** Montgomery *Coll* (known to Adams, Brown, Bush, Cardwell, Ledford, Norris, Oliver).

givey *adjective* Unsteady, inclined to give way, not firm.

1895 Edson and Fairchild *TN Mts* 371 That table's *givey*. **1957** Combs *Lg Sthn High: Word List* 45 = moist, soft (of earth that easily gives underfoot). **1984** Wilder *You All Spoken* 17 = unsteady, as a just-dropped calf or a bar patron. **1998** Montgomery *Coll* = applies to buildings, fences, gates, etc. "Bob was givey on his feet" (Brown).

[OED3 *givey* adj dialect or colloquial]

glad *adjective* with ellipsis of following *if*.

1861 *Martin CW Letters* (Nov 10) you wrote somthing A bout sending me some provissons I would be glad you wood. **1863** *Carter CW Letters* (Jan 7) Now I would be glad you would come up here befor we move for fear we Should get further off.

glade *noun* An area of low, swampy land, also used in the place-name *the Glades*, an area between Gatlinburg and Emerts Cove (TN).

1999 Montgomery *Coll* = a low, swampy area (Cardwell). **2006** *WV Encycl* 275 Unique plants and animals occur in high altitude muskeg bogs called glades by local residents, left over from the Ice Age climate. These areas, the largest of which include Cranberry Glades, Canaan Valley, and Cranesville Swamp, contain numerous plant and animal species not found elsewhere this far south.

[DARE *glade* n 1 especially Mid and South Atlantic]

glad of *adjective phrase* Delighted with, grateful for.

1864 *Poteet CW Letters* (Feb 8) I was glad of the tobacco that you sent me.

gladsome *adjective* Producing gladness, cheery.

1938 Justus *No-End Hollow* 38 She had one gladsome thought, anyway Jeff and Jessie were off to school! **1996–97** Montgomery *Coll* (known to Brown, Cardwell, Norris, Oliver).

glaiket *adjective* Having poor judgment, stupid, careless; hence noun *glakedness*.

1928 (in **1952** Mathes *Tall Tales* 65) The bawling out continued: "This is a purty way to start on the big hunt tomorrer mornin'—gittin' the best young dawg in Big Smoky all skunked up the night before! I've a notion to bust ye open jes' fer yer glakedness!" **1952** Wilson *Folk Speech NC* 545 *glaiket* = lazy, careless, foolish. [**1995** Montgomery *Coll* (unknown to consultants from the Smoky Mountains).]

[cf SND *glaikit* adj "stupid, careless, foolish"; CUD *glaikit* (at *glaik* v) "foolish, stupid"; Web3 *glaikit* adj "showing a lack of common sense and good judgment" chiefly Scottish]

glant See **gallant**.

glarecoma *noun* See citation.

2000 Lowry *Folk Medical Term* = glaucoma.

glass *noun* See citation.

1895 *Word-Lists* 389 = mica (w. N.C.).

[shortening of *isinglass*]

glass snake *noun* A large, legless lizard of the genus *Ophisaurus*, which may be broken into fragments.

1939 *FWP Guide KY* 15 Less known are the several varieties of skinks and the fabulous glass or joint snake, which can shed its tail when attacked. **1995** Montgomery *Coll* (known to Cardwell).

[DARE *glass snake* n chiefly South, South Midland]

glib

A *adjective* Active for one's age, vigorous, brisk.

1934–47 *LAMSAS Appal* (Madison Co NC, Swain Co NC). **1956** Hall *Coll* (Indian Camp Creek NC) The old man was purty glib. *Ibid.* (Jones Cove TN) He told Gray John, "You are glibber than I am, so you go to the far pen." **1986** Pederson et al. *LAGS* = attested by 5/60 interviewees (8.3%) in E TN; 5/11 of all LAGS interviewees (45.5%) attesting term were in Appalachia.

[cf OED3 *glib* adj 1 "moving easily; unimpeded"; DARE *glib* adj chiefly South Midland]

B *adverb* See citation.

1946 Dudley *KY Words* 271 = briskly, quickly, vigorously: "I didn't think Gene would be walkin' along so glib."

glister *verb* To glisten.

1975 Gainer *Witches Ghosts Signs* 10 I saw a light glister a mile away.

gloam (also *glom, gloom*) *noun* (in compounds) Morning or evening twilight.

1944 Wilson *Word-List* 47 *morn-gloam* = the first light of morning. **1951** Craig *Singing Hills* 101 I sat by the spring . . . I watched eve-gloom come. *Ibid.* 130 That night Dale and I sat before Cap Dickey's house as even-gloom came. **1952** Wilson *Folk Speech NC* 537 *evening glom* = the melancholy close of day.

[Web3 *gloam* n "twilight, dusk" archaic]

glomb *verb* To poke.

1941 Stuart *Men of Mts* 122 I'll glomb them wax eyes from her pullet head. *Ibid.* 253 When he would say "Whoa back" he would glomb me in the eyes with his fingers like he was trying to stop a horse.

gloom See **gloam.**

(the) glooms *noun* Low spirits.

1978 Parris *Mt Cooking* 164 "A fill of wild strawberries," Grandpa said, "is the best thing in the world for a body when they're on the down-go or got the glooms."

glory *verb* To praise, celebrate, boast about (something of inflated or doubtful value).

1913 Kephart *Our Sthn High* 312 I'm a hillbilly, all right, and they needn't to glory their old flat lands to me. **1994–97** Montgomery *Coll* (known to Brown), Don't you glory yourself (Cardwell).

glory juice *noun* Homemade whiskey.

1970 Vincent *More of Best* 146 An old fellow who had got too much of "glory juice" was dozing, and when the choir boomed out "What Shall the Harvest Be?" he roused up, rubbed his eyes, and yelled: "Nubbins, by gosh!"

glow worm *noun* A type of worm used as fishing bait that has a luminescent substance on its skin.

1967 *DARE Survey* (Gatlinburg TN).

glut[1] *noun* A hardwood wedge for splitting blocks of wood or logs into boards.

1847 (in **1870** Drake *Pioneer Life KY* 70) When I got a tough log the wedges and "gluts" would fly out on being struck a hard blow. **1866** (in **1974** Harris *High Times* 284) The rale, pure puritan, yankee baby, has a naik like a gourd, a foot like a glut, an a belly like a mildew'd drum head. **1895** Edson and Fairchild *TN Mts* 371 = a wedge. **1960** Mason *Memoir* 21 If the saw kerf did happen to close on the saw, it was then necessary to drive large wooden gluts or wooden wedges between the nearest pole and the bottom of the bond tree. **1972** *Foxfire I* 38 Wooden wedges, or "gluts," were hewn out of eighteen-inch long, four- to six-inch thick sections of hardwood limbs. *Ibid.* 116 A second glut is driven into the crack still further down the trunk, and when the first falls out, it is driven into the crack beyond the second and so on, leapfrogging the gluts, until the trunk falls in half. **1973** *GSMNP-13*:11 They'd cut [the tree] down to a half, and they'd split logs with it and get gluts, locust gluts.

[OED3 *glut* n[6] 1 technical or dialect; DARE *glut* n[1] chiefly South, South Midland]

glut[2] *verb* To eat excessively, devour. See also **glutter.**

1992 Jones and Miller *Sthn Mt Speech* 83. **1994–97** Montgomery *Coll* (known to nine consultants from the Smoky Mountains).

[OED3 *glut* v[2] now rare; cf EDD *glut* sb[3] 4]

glutter *noun* See citation. See also **glut**[2].

1969 *DARE Survey* (Viper KY, Walker KY) = somebody [who] always eats a considerable amount of food.

glutton *noun* A greedy person, miser.

1996–97 Montgomery *Coll* (known to Brown, Cardwell, Jones, Ledford, Norris, Oliver).

[DARE *glutton* n 2 chiefly South, South Midland]

gnat ball *noun* See 1996 citation.

1957 Justus *Other Side* 38 She and Dovie made a playhouse in the woods behind the school, and into their favorite spot went all their wild wood treasures: . . . the gnat balls shaped like fairy balloons, the snail shells, and many other things. **1996** Montgomery *Coll* = ping-pong ball size delicate brown ball that falls off oak trees; gnats were supposed to hatch out of them (known to Oliver, but not to other consultants from the Smoky Mountains).

gnat hawk *noun* A dragonfly.

1934–47 *LAMSAS Appal* = attested by 2/27 speakers (7.4%) from VA.

gnat's bristle (also *gnat's eyebrow*, *gnat's heel*, and variants) *noun* used to indicate something small or precise.

1915 Dingus *Word-List VA* 183 *gnat's heel, to a* = precisely. **c1960** Wilson *Coll*: *gnat's eyebrow* = something done exactly and meticulously. **1968** Wilson *Folklore Mammoth Cave* 18 *gnat's bristle* (also *gnat's heel* or *gnat's hind leg*) = often used humorously to indicate small or insignificant. *Chigger's uncle* is similarly used. **1996–97** Montgomery *Coll*: *gnat's eyebrow* (known to eight consultants from the Smoky Mountains); *gnat's eyelash* (known to Brewer).

[DARE *gnat's eyebrow* n chiefly South, South Midland, West]

gnat smoke *noun* A smoldering fire built to ward off gnats. See also **smudge fire.**

1959 Roberts *Up Cutshin* 6 She would tell a story at the ends of corn rows . . . and of an evening around a gnat smoke in the yard. **1961** *Coe Ridge OHP-333A* [They'd] have a fire, make gnat smoke. They used to do that . . . gnat smoke out of chips and old rags and things, [to] run the gnats away. **1977** Adams *Remembering* 96 I remembered Grandma's gnat smoke in the yard late in the evenings. **1978** Hiser *Quare Do's* 76 He went out into the middle of the compound and built what we here in the mountains call a gnat-smoke, just a chunk of a fire, made to smoulder and send out a deal of smoke instead of burning out. **1983** Weals *Len Cogdill* They built a smoldering fire even on warm nights. They called it a "gnat smoke," and it was the only means they had of keeping the gnats away while they talked. **1991** Weals *Last Train* 83 You had to build gnat smokes to try to keep them away. **1994** Montgomery *Coll* = produced by rolled up rags that burned slowly and warded off gnats (Cardwell). **2004** Myers and Boyer *Walker Sisters* 31 When they sat outside in the yard, gnats were likely to bite them. A "gnat smoke" would have provided them with some protection. To make a gnat smoke, they placed cotton rags on top of coals in an open container. The rags smouldered, which provided smoke to drive away the gnats.

go *verb*

A Forms.

1 Variant present-participle form *gwine* [Editor's note: This form was not observed by Joseph Hall in the Smoky Mountains in the late 1930s.]

1860 Taliaferro *Ducktown* 341 Well, I must be a gwine. **1863** *Joyce CW Letters* (Feb 10) you must tell hear that I have quite [= quit] gwine to frolics and I have quite gitting drunk and have quit all such bad tricks. **1863** *Wright CW Letters* (March 31) I doe wish you cold See the mess that we ar Agwine to hav for din ner Some off the boyes hav gon out to hunte Some greeanes weades for Sallet for dinner I eate more at one time when i was at home than i eate hear All day. **1867** Harris *Sut Lovingood* 27 What wer agwine on at the cabin, this side the crick, when yu pass'd thar? **1886** Smith *Sthn Dialect* 348 He had hyeard ther might be a war 'twixt the Republicans and Dimercrats, but, as he hadn't hyeard any mo' about it, he reckined ther wan't gwine ter be none. **1889** Mooney *Folk Carolina Mts* 97 *Gwine* and *obleeged*, *tote* and *holp*, are universally used, and many words obsolete or almost unknown in other sections of the country are still retained here. **1913** Kephart *Our Sthn High* 201 Stranger—meanin' no harm—*whar* are ye gwine? *Ibid.* 284 There are many corrupt forms of the verb, such as gwine for gone or going, mought (mowt) for might. **1934–47** *LAMSAS Appal* (Swain Co NC). **1994** Montgomery *Coll* (known to Cardwell).

[DARE *go* v 4a chiefly South, South Midland]

2 Variant past-tense forms *goed*, *gone*.

1862 *Love CW Letters* (July 21) the yanks gone Back and in A few minets we went over to where they was. **1898** Elliott *Durket Sperret* 169 I tole him, an' they turned round and gone, lookin' like the dead. **1967** Fetterman *Stinking Creek* 135 Some men took a notion to go. They just up and gone. **1972** *AOHP/LJC-203* My granddaddy owned a farm up there and I goed there at nine years old. **1973** *Foxfire Interviews* A-73-87 It goed on here nearly all the time. **1984** Smith *Oral History* 22 It was the way she gone about everything, like she was too smart for this world. **2002** McGowan *Beech Mt Tales* 100 He took these old dirty clothes along with him too as he gone to see his mother and father.

3 Variant past-participle form *went*.

1800 (in **1920** DeWitt *Sevier Journal* 31) (Nov 15) Sproules and Love made their report on the land they had went to view & survey. **1814** Hartsell *Memora* 143 all of my men was present to answer to ther names but two, Moses Conk and James Vest, hoo had went own further than we got this nite. **1862** *Neves CW Letters* (Jan 16) we havent had any letters this week for the mail haint went sense saturdy. **1863** (in **1992** Heller and Heller *Confederacy* 104) I have went threw A heap of Narow esscapes since I have bine out her. **1868** (in **1974** Harris *High Times* 208) Then the cuss wudent a went, when his time had come. **1915** Hall *Autobiog Claib Jones* 16–17 The Rebels had placed themselves on all the roads and had captured every man that had went to camp. **1930** (in **1952** Mathes *Tall Tales* 171) But if ye ain't keerful about settin' round an' dozin' atter dinner ye'll find the dominicker hen has laid eggs in that thar nest, or ol' Puss has went an' had a litter of kittens in it! **1956** Hall *Coll* (Newport TN) She didn't know where he had went to. **1973** *GSMNP*-4:1:35 Now Big Creek has went down a lot. **1978** Montgomery *White Pine Coll* X-2 This nation would have been starved to death years ago if everybody had went by the signs. **1980** Miles *Verbs in Haywood Co* 110 His legs had went and he didn't know it. **1989** Landry *Smoky Mt Interviews* 194 I've went up over them rocks a many a time. **1998** *Dante OHP*-45 You might have went by there a while ago.

B Senses.

1 (also *go about*) To be active, on one's feet, or able to get about.

1862 *Gilley CW Letters* (Aug 3) I am sorry to inform you that bob is not well he has bin sick for three days tho he can go about a little I think he is got the fever tho I think or inhops that he wont get bad off. **1863** *Poteet CW Letters* (Nov 22) I hav bin so in my hips that I hardly could go. **1966** Hall *Coll* (Del Rio TN) So again let me say, hope everything is well with you and you are able to go. **1985** Irwin *Alex Stewart* 178 He hadn't been back home more than two or three days when he come down with it and he got to where he couldn't go at all.

[OED3 *go* v 1a obsolete; DARE *go* v C1 chiefly South, South Midland]

2 In phrase *go it* = to manage, maneuver, navigate. For the *it*, see also **bed B1**, **run it over**.

1863 (June 26) I want you to go it and do all you can & try to mak all you can to eat for your Mother and sisters & litel Brother & for me a gainst I come home. **1898** Elliott *Durket Sperret* 29–30 "Hit's a smart piece," Hannah went on, looking into the fire as if making calculations, "but you could go it on a nag." **1956** Hall *Coll* (Townsend TN) Roads got so bad you couldn't go it in a car. I've seed this road down here when they'd wagon over it hub deep where the wagon goes. **1973** *GSMNP*-88 This Cooper Road, you could go it with a wagon, but it was rough. **2015** Holbrook *Something* 156 She thinks she can go it on her own.

3 To attend.

1973 *AOHP/ALC-259* The first school I went was a little country school.

go across the branch *verb phrase* To go outdoors to relieve oneself, urinate.

1994 Montgomery *Coll* (known to Shields).

go and *verb phrase* To go (+ similarly inflected verb, used to convey that two actions are simultaneous or sequential and sometimes to reinforce the latter action). See also **send and**, **take and**.

1900 Harben *N GA Sketches* 15 I went an' seed Colonel Whitney fer you. **1928** (in **1952** Mathes *Tall Tales* 72) "That's the durn fool now," he muttered. "He thinks he's went an' done somethin' big!" **1944** Laughlin *Word-List Buncombe Co* 25 Let's go and coon some watermelons. **1964** Roberts *Hell-Fer-Sartin* 14 [The horse] heard 'em and it went and broke the stable door down and started down the road. **1973** GSMNP-5:7 They could pick and play the fiddle, and we would go and just have a time, running old country round up. **1978** Slone *Common Folks* 298 He went and bought him a gun, and knowing where Roy Land went across the hill to his W.P.A. job, he "lay waid" him with the intention of killing him. **1983** *Dark Corner OHP-28A* They went and went in his field and just pulled up his great big cotton that was setting. **1998** *Dante OHP-25* She went and put in her application. **2005** Williams *Gratitude* 535 *went and* = words added in between the person and what they did. "She *went and* told him. They *went'n* sold their place."

go around

A *verb phrase* See citation.

1949 Maurer *Argot of Moonshiner* 10 – to distill from all of one's fermenters in sequence. Thus if a moonshiner has three fermenters in operation he distills and remashes one of these each day. Hence, at the end of the third day he has "gone round" once. Bigtime operators consider it wise to run only a short time at one location and then move the still. The length of time is expressed, not in days, but in doublings or go rounds . . . "Hell, we went round six times at that old spring"; "Maybe we kin go round once more before we run out."

B *noun* See citation.

1949 Maurer *Argot of Moonshiner* 10 = one complete cycle of distillation from the fermenters.

go around the bend (also *go around the corner, go away, go on*) *verb phrase* To die.

1922 West *Songs of Mtneers* 24 In referring to death there are several terms used, all somewhat vague to one not thoroughly initiated in their quaint mode of expression. The more common terms are: "He went away. He left us. He has done gone on. He passed over." Cold and passionless these expressions seem when presented to the eye. There is a touch of pathos, a delicacy, a sacredness in the expression that makes them beautiful when they fall from the lips of a Mountaineer. **1936** Farr *Folk Speech Mid TN* 276 *go around the corner* = to die: "He nearly went around the corner." **1939** Farr *TN Mt Regions* 92 *go around the bend* = to die: "Jim Smith went around the bend this morning."

goat wobble *noun* See citation. See also **chicken wobble**.

1966 Dykeman *Far Family* 161 "What's a goat-wobble?" they were all screeching, and I told them it was just a hoedown where somebody provided all the roast goat and rotgut anybody could eat and drink—and got a little old vote in return.

go away See **go around the bend**.

gob

A *noun*

1 (usually plural) A large amount or number.

1859 Taliaferro *Fisher's River* 41 A heap uv groanin', gobs of shoutin' and cryin', goes a grate ways toads settin' off a meetin'. **1867** Harris *Sut Lovingood* 62 Bake dwelt long ontu the crop ove dimes tu be gethered frum that field; that he'd make more than thar wer spots ontu forty fawns in July, not tu speak ove the big gobs ove repertashun he'd tote away, a shinin all over his close, like litnin bugs ontu a dorg fennil top. **1966–68** *DARE Survey* (Spruce Pine NC, Gatlinburg TN) = a great deal of; (Brasstown NC) = all you need and more.

2 Especially in coal mining: loose waste rock; an old section of a mine filled with waste. See also **gob heap, gob mining**.

1941 Still *Proud Walkers* 111 Ruther to live on a gob heap than where no girls are. **c1975** *Miners' Jargon* 4 = applied to that part of the mine from which the coal has been removed and the space more or less filled up with waste. Also the loose waste in a mine. **1979** *Big South Fork OHP-19* [He] said don't delay the run. He wanted them to just throw him up in the gob. **2002** Armstead *Black Days* 243 = coal mine waste material consisting mainly of shale, slate, rock, and so forth. **2006** Mooney *Lg Coal Mining* 1029 The miner then cleaned his working room of waste rock, called "gob" or "bone" and eventually hauled outside and added to a massive "slag pile" and then headed home for the day.

B *verb* To become stuck by waste rock.

c1987 (in **2015** Yarrow *Voices* 12) You can get a belt on fire—say it will gob up under a tail-piece or start slipping in the head. It will burn a belt right in two.

gobacks *noun* See citation.

1933 Miller *Healing Gods* 471–72 Most of us who are familiar with the customs of rural West Virginia know that many an infant suffering from malnutrition or rickets, familiarly known as "the decay" or the "gobacks," must be measured by some old woman before he will get better, which is much more certain and less expensive than cod-liver oil and tomato juice.

gobbing *noun* See citation.

2002 Armstead *Black Days* 243 = [the] process of placing waste in mined-out areas to avoid the expense of transporting it to the surface.

gobble *noun* The sound made by a male turkey; hence verb = to make such a sound to lure it to where a hunter can shoot it. See also **gobbler**.

1939 Hall *Coll* (Deep Creek NC) So I got my place and I called a little, and he answered me. [I] gobbled three or four times there, he gobbled a gobble, and I wouldn't call no more.

gobbler *noun*

1 A male turkey. See also **turkey pen**.

1939 Hall *Coll* (Deep Creek NC) The birds begin to whistle, and we heard the gobbler gobbling across the far side of the right-hand fork of Indian Creek. **1959** Hall *Coll* (Newport TN) Turkey George [Palmer] made him a rail pen . . . [and caught] eleven hens and a big gobbler. **2011** *Blind Pig* (Nov 13) I still "take the shakes" after a long episode with a troublesome old gobbler.

2 A large drinking vessel, goblet.

1997 Montgomery *Coll* (known to Hooper).

gob heap (also *gob pile*) *noun* In coal mining, waste rock brought outside the mine and disposed of. Also called **bone pile**. See also **gob A2**.

1974 Murray *Down to Earth* 94 We're just getting filthy "gob piles," poison rivers, black lung, shacks to live in and half the people are on welfare. **1980** Still *Run for Elbertas* 100 Over the heads of the men I could see the whole of the camp, the shotgun houses in the flat, the smoke rising above the burning gob heaps. **1997** Miller *Brier Poems* 150 I was jerked up, hard, in a deep holler where smoke from the smoldering gob piles hung in air that smelled like carbide and warm dishwater. **2012** Portelli *They Say* 300 In coal fields with high sulfur content, as in much of eastern Kentucky, the "gob pile" of mining waste, containing sulfur, iron, and low-grade coal, can self-ignite and burn for years, causing further air pollution.

gob mining *verbal noun* See citation.

1961 Niles *Ballad Book* xx He was, in reality, a mine scavenger; he called it "gob-mining." This operation took him into abandoned or worked-out coal mines where, with a pick and wheelbarrow, he mined out the coal in the walls and its supporting pillars.

gob pile See **gob heap**.

gob rooster *noun* A coal miner subsidized by operators to be available to perform as a musician. See citation.

1943 Korson *Coal Dust* 17 Music was not discouraged by operators when it helped to keep their employees contented. Some even subsidized local bands and provided mining sinecures for bandsmen whom fellow workers called "gob roosters."

gobs See **gob A1**.

gob up *verb phrase* To pile (dirt separated from coal in a coal mine).

1973 *AOHP/EH-79* You put your dirt over there. They call that gobbing up your dirt. There wasn't a car to load up your dirt . . . They wouldn't let you gob it up on both sides over there.

go by shank's mare See **shank's horse**.

go deep *verb phrase* See citation.

2007 Plott *Story Plott Hound* 182 = refers to a dog that will go as far as necessary to find a game trail. Sometimes also described as "hunting wide."

go devil *noun*

1 A heavy axe-like implement for splitting or chopping logs, usually with a sledgehammer on one side of its head and a dull wedge on the other. See 1939, 1974–75 citations. For figurative use, see 1944 citation. Also called **grow devil**.

1930 Pendleton *Wood-Hicks Speak* 87 = a rather heavy splitting axe used especially in preparing wood for the chemical or pulp mills. **1939** Hall *Coll* (Proctor NC) = a hammer on one end and a kind of wedge on the other—to split logs with, a little sharper than a wedge, used like a wedge, only you strike with it. **1944** Wilson *Word-List* 43 = a heavy ax used to split logs. "You won't [stay at home], less'n it's raining *go-devils*." **1973** Brower *Split-Rail Fence* Webb examines the end of a log to be split to determine where to place his wedges. Then he drives the wedges into the log with a tool he said the old-timers called a "go-devil." Chestnut logs split cleanly. Locust logs splinter and must be coaxed with an ax. **1974–75** McCracken *Logging* 24:21 = a form of ax and hammer together.

2 A type of cultivator.

1986 Pederson et al. *LAGS* (Johnson Co TN, Washington Co TN, Blount Co TN).

godlings See **by**.

go-down, on the *adjective phrase* Declining in health. See also **down-go, on the**.

1965 *Dict Queen's English* 7 = sickly, not well. "She's been on the go-down ever since she caught a cold." **1998** Montgomery *Coll* (known to Brown, Ellis, Norris).

God's house See **rock house**.

God's plenty *noun* An abundance. See also **a-plenty**, **plenty A**.

1939 *FWP Guide NC* 98 A *smidgen* is a little, but a *slue* is a lot, and it might be a *lavish* or in some cases *a God's plenty*. **1941** Still *Troublesome Creek* 133 They get so much milk everybody has a God's plenty. **1949** Arnow *Hunter's Horn* 6 Lord, I've already got a God's plenty for supper with th possum an all. **1966** Dykeman *Far Family* 98 Old Tildy brought us and she didn't charge anything but board and room, although counting all the bellyaching and bossing she did that was a God's plenty. **1978** Hiser *Quare Do's* 34 When a little wild baby was to be born in the neighborhood (and they was a God's plenty, believe me) people'd get her for a midwife.

God's stone *noun* Same as **madstone**.

1978 Hiser *Quare Do's* 74 [He] was pottering about his homeplace (and quite vigorously, too, for an eighty-seven-year-old), and came across what he called "Preacher John B. Davis's God's stone," or what we in the mountains usually call a madstone. This stone, what in a human would be called a gallstone or a kidney stone, was found sometimes in the entrails of a deer, and was highly prized by our fore-fathers as a cure for a rattlesnake bite or the bite of a mad dog.

God's thing *noun* Used as a euphemism in phrase *not a God's thing* = nothing at all.

c1960 Wilson *Coll*: *not a Gawd's thing* = euphemism for *damned*. **1978** Hiser *Quare Do's* 15 [The doctors] tested and they progued and they listened. Not a God's thing could they find wrong with him.

God's truth *noun* The absolute truth.

1966 Dykeman *Far Family* 38 That trouble came out of a bottle. A bottle and old Hawk's meanness. And that's the God's truth.

goed See **go A2**.

go fetcher *noun* See citation.

1986 Pederson et al. *LAGS* (Rabun Co GA) = little notch in the throat.

go foolish *verb phrase* To seem strange; of a person: to behave strangely.

1967 Giles *40 Acres* 4 Anything different from the usual is "quare" or "goes foolish." **1979** Carpenter *Walton War* 171 When he axed (asked) me that question, it shore went foolish to me. **1995–97** Montgomery *Coll* (known to Brown, Bush, Ledford). **2004** Adams *Old True Love* 28 They went plumb foolish when he played. And Hackley loved the girls, any shape and any size. So he played a lot.

go footback *verb phrase* See citation. See also **footback**.

1967 *DARE Survey* (Maryville TN) = go on foot.

go good *verb phrase* To be tasty (along with another specified food or ingredient).

1913 Kephart *Our Sthn High* 33 There was not a bite in her house beyond potatoes, and "taters don't go good 'thout salt." **1994–97** Montgomery *Coll* (known to nine consultants from the Smoky Mountains).

go halvers *verb phrase* To share (a crop or investment) equally with another person.

1915 Dingus *Word-List VA* 183 = to share equally. **1936** Morehouse *Rain on Just* 117 Things might have been better if her mammy had gone havvers on saw milling with Garley Brock instead of blowing all she had so devil-may-care. **1985** Irwin *Alex Stewart* 71 I started raising corn, and wheat, and molasses, and we went halvers.

go home with us *phrase* See citations. See also **come and go home with me, stay all night, you'uns come.**

1955 Ritchie *Singing Family* 199 Some of the older folks had begun to stir around to go home; they gathered their buckets and their little children and lit their lanterns. They said, "Go home with us why don't you?" and "Can't tonight, I reckon. You'ns come," to each other, and pretty soon their lights were fading this way and that way through the hills. **1976** Weals *Two Minus* Although it is the cordial thing for parting guests to say, "Just go home with us," it is not necessarily good manners to accept the invitation.

go in *verb phrase* To join in working together.

1971 *AOHP/ALC-4* They all just went in and built the house, bought the lumber and built it.

go into *verb phrase* (+ *verbal noun*) To start. See also **go to.**

1939 Hall *Coll* (Hartford TN) We just broke to it as quick as we could, and all went into skinning that bear, skun it all out, took that hide offen it, and cut it into four quarter.

go in washing See **wash B.**

go it See **go B2.**

go kiting See **kite.**

goldarn(ed) *adjective* Used as a euphemism for *damn(ed)*.

1895 Dromgoole *Humble Advocate* 323–24 Gol darn ye, ef yer don't come in here an' fish out them victuals I'll fling the shovel at yer. **1984** Yeatts *Old Mayberry* 47 Now I'll be goldarned if I don't know that I've told you about that thing at least five times.

goldenseal *noun* A perennial shrub (*Hydrastis canadensis*) with petal-less flowers and inedible, raspberry-like berries; a medicinal tea is made from its dried rhizomes and roots. Also called **jaundice root, tonic root, yellowroot.**

1894 Bergen *Plant Names III* 102 Smilacina racemosa (Banner Elk NC). **1949** Arnow *Hunter's Horn* 377 She made another pot of tea strong with feverweed, black seneca, yellowroot, horse mint, golden seal, and life everlasting. **1960** Price *Root Digging in Appal* 18 Goldenseal or yellowroot (*Hydrastis canadensis*) is respected both for its curative properties and for the price it brings, long second only to that of ginseng. Unlike ginseng, which the collectors look upon as a Chinese whimsy, goldenseal is considered a sure cure for sores in the mouth and an aid for many stomach troubles, and it has also been used in the treatment of certain venereal diseases. Some Indians used if for a dyestuff (yellow puccoon), the Cherokees for a cancer cure, but American doctors were slow to recognize its value. [**1971** Krochmal et al. *Medicinal Plants Appal* 144 The pulverized rhizomes and roots have been used for a long time to treat mouth ulcers, and as a hemostatic. This preparation has also been used as a diuretic in catarrhal conditions and as an astringent for treating certain eye conditions. In Appalachia, a root tea is used as a tonic.] **c1984** Dennis *Smoky Mt Heritage* 7 [For] Blood Poisoning: Tea made from chick weed, plantain, and golden seal. **1985** Irwin *Alex Stewart* 145 The state of West Virginia published a most interesting magazine called *Goldenseal* on the folk culture and customs of the people of that state. According to this periodical, the plant goldenseal was commonly used by the Indians for treating skin diseases and sore eyes. It was subsequently used by the pioneers for the same purpose, and was later incorporated in manufactured medicines. It is sometimes used for these purposes even to the present day. In 1909, the magazine pointed out, goldenseal roots were selling for $1.50 per pound, and in 1975 the price was $50.00 a pound. **1989** *Matewan OHP-102* My daddy would go in the hills and mountains and dig yellow root. They call it goldenseal now, and we could boil it and hit was good for any kind of sore mouth or sore throat. **1991** Haynes *Haywood Home* 66 Goldenseal Root tea was a good heart tonic while Yellow Dock Root tea was good for circulation.

[*DARE goldenseal* n 1 ("refers to the 1/4 inch thick yellow underground stem with its seal-like scars where shoots of previous seasons emerged," according to a 1965 citation)]

golly washer See citation.

2017 Kinsler *Take Girl* 71 = heavy rain.

gollywhacker *adjective* Surprisingly large or extraordinary.

1973 Davis *'Pon My Honor* 31 All of a sudden, a gollywhacker hoop snake come out of the berry vines with hits mouth open and hits tail a flapping every which way.

gollywhopper *noun* Something surprisingly large or extraordinary of its kind.

1939 Farr *TN Mt Regions* 90 The fish which Sam caught was a golly-whopper. **1953** Stuart *Good Spirit* 119 Onct when I looked up, I saw a star leave the sky. It was a gollywhopper in size. **1959** Hall *Coll* (Hartford TN) They were a number of the neighbors would come in and asked her what she thought of the world beyond the mountain, and they asked her how big it was and she said "Lordy me," she said, "if the world's as big that way," pointing the opposite direction, "as it is that way," pointing toward out of Cosby, "my God, it's a golly whopper." **1999** Montgomery *Coll* She gave him a golly whopper [i.e. she hit him very hard] (Brown).

[DARE *golly-whopper* n chiefly South Midland]

gom, gome See **gaum**.

gommy See **gaumy**.

gon *noun* A railcar into which a coal miner places mined coal, to be sent to the mouth of the mine for weighing.

2000 Norman *Consciousness* 8 Around us all day, every working day, was the roar of the tipple as it processed the coal before dropping it into the great gons below, filling them one by one to make a train. **2006** Mooney *Lg Coal Mining* 1029 After the dust had settled the miner loaded the coal into a "gon," hung his "weigh tag" on a nail, and then pushed the gon out into the entryway for delivery outside the mine site, where the "checkweighman" credited it to the respective miner.

[shortening of *gondola*]

gonnies, ey See **ay, by**.

goober

A *noun*

1 (also *goober pea*) *noun* A peanut.

1858 (in **1974** Harris *High Times* 138) [The pole was] on t'uther, a bustin' out winders an' a sweepin' ove appils an' gouber-peas ofen the tables. **1861** *J Love CW Letter* (Oct 4) I have not seen any thing a growing here but goobers and yam potatoes. **1863** *Copeland CW Letters* (Feb 26) after the war is over then marry a rich widow [in] south Carelina Whar we Can mak Cotton and Seet patatoes and guber pees. **1863** *Tesh CW Letters* (June 15) we can By cake and cider and Goober peas and the way we make them get is a sight. **1889** Mooney *Folk Carolina Mts* 97 Ginseng is *sang*, the service tree is *sarvice* and peanuts are *goobers*. **1918** Combs *Word-List South* 36 *goober, goober pea* = peanut. **1934–47** *LAMSAS Appal* (Madison Co NC) *goober*; (Madison Co NC, Swain Co NC) *goober pea*. 1957 Broaddus *Vocab Estill Co KY* 41 *goober pea* = an "older" term for peanuts. **1966–68** *DARE Survey* (Maryville TN); *goober*; (Burnsville NC, Cherokee NC, Spruce Pine NC, Gatlinburg TN, Maryville TN); *goober pea*. **1986** Pederson et al. *LAGS*: *goober peas* = attested by 10/60 interviewees (16.7%) in E TN; 10/30 of all LAGS interviewees (33.3%) attesting term were in Appalachia. **1987** Carver *Regional Dialects* 168 Although *goober* is known throughout most of the South, the Upper South often uses the fuller form, *goober pea*, which first appeared in print in an 1833 Louisville, Kentucky, newspaper. **1987** Young *Lost Cove* 87 Old Doff was so busy eating goobers that he didn't pay any mind to big Clyde's doing. **1994–97** Montgomery *Coll*: *goober* (known to eight consultants from the Smoky Mountains); *goober pea* (known to eight consultants from the Smoky Mountains). **2009** Sohn *Appal Home Cooking* 297 *goober peas* = raw peanuts.

[DARE *goober pea* chiefly South Midland]

2 A countrified person.

2012 *Blind Pig* (Aug 12) Nana, Papaw, my aunt, and whatever "goober" friend Papaw brought would go out each Friday, and according to my aunt, Nana and Papaw would be "canoodling" while she and the goober friend sat there awkwardly.

B *adjective* Having rustic or crude qualities.

1937 Hall *Coll* = used in poking fun at the CCC boys who came from the "goober country," Georgia or Alabama.

goober grubber *noun* See citation.

1895 *Word-Lists* 389 = peanut digger (Tenn.).

goober pea See **goober A**.

good and always *adverb* See citation.

1892 Fruit *KY Words* 230 = forever.

goodbye-to-summer *noun* Any of several asters (*Aster* spp). See also **farewell-summer, summer-farewell**.

1996 Montgomery *Coll* (known to Cardwell).

good child to (also *good girl to, good man to, good woman to*) (+ *verb*) *noun phrase* One who is very capable of or expert in performing (a certain skill or task). For similar patterns with *to*, see Grammar and Syntax §10.2.

1877 Carpenter *Diary* I 148 Alex Wiseman ag 80 march 20 1877 war a good man to make brandy. **1941** Stuart *Men of Mts* 299 I saw her in the garden just a-digging away. She's a good girl to work. **1959** Pearsall *Little Smoky* 72 I had an awful good woman to work. **1972** *AOHP/LJC-259* He lived up in the holler. He was a good man to bottom chairs. **1978** Montgomery *White Pine Coll* III-2 They're awful good children to listen.

good dark *noun* Early nighttime.

c1950 Adams *Grandpap* 37 If you come back before gooddark, I'll whoop the hide off of you. **c1960** Wilson *Coll* = real darkness rather than twilight or dusky dark.

go odd with *verb phrase* To seem unusual (to one).

1979 Carpenter *Walton War* 178 Hit goes odd with me to hear his big fightin' tales. **1995–97** Montgomery *Coll* (known to Brown, Bush, Ledford).

gooder *adjective* Better.

1961 *Coe Ridge* OHP-333A He was one of the gooder fiddlers you ever heard. **1973** GSMNP-79:1:13 With your cornbread you could take [buttermilk], and nothin' [is] gooder than crumbled cornbread and milk.

[comparative of *good*]

goodest *adjective* Best.

1971 *Corn Shuckin's* 102 Thrash'em old peas out—have th'goodest old time y'ever seen.

[superlative of *good*]

good evening *interjection* Used as a greeting used at any time after the middle of the day.

1978 Head *Mt Moments* If the time was after the noonday meal, then the greeting was "good evening."

good fashion *adverb phrase* Thoroughly.

c1960 Wilson *Coll* = thoroughly.

[DARE *good fashion* adv chiefly South, South Midland]

good few *pronoun phrase* Quite a few, a fair number.

1895 Edson and Fairchild *TN Mts* 371 = many. **1974** Fink *Bits Mt Speech* 11 They's a *good few* apples this year.

[OED3 (at *few* adj 2d) dialect and colloquial]

good girl to See **good child to.**

good god *noun* A pileated woodpecker. For alternative terms, see 1945 citation. See also **lord god almighty.**

1945 McAtee *Nomina Arbitera* 46 (DARE) The most godified of our birds . . . is none other than the pileated woodpecker . . . this bird's roll of godly titles . . . is as follows: . . . good God, good God bird, good God woodpecker. . . . Various observers have said that the term Good God is in imitation of the bird's notes. Maybe it is, but to me the logcock repeats "cack, cack," or "puck, puck," with no touch of divinity about the performances. **1978** Hiser *Quare Do's* 10 Around one side a Good-God woodpecker was pecking a tattoo, and on the very jagged tip-top sat a bright redbird.

[DARE *good god* n 1 South, South Midland]

good hand See **hand A3.**

Good Husband Row *noun* See citation. See also **Quality Row.**

2006 Lalone *Coal Camps* 140 Each camp had a "Quality Row" or a "Good Husband Row" which contained the houses designated for the superintendent, store and medical personnel, and other company officials. While people acknowledge that the Quality Row families lived in somewhat better conditions, most people felt that among the working miners everyone lived much the same, and that no one family had it much better than any others.

good liver *noun* One who is prosperous; hence *best liver*. See also **hard liver.**

1881 Pierson *In the Brush* 18 We spent the night very comfortably with Brother H—, to whom I had been directed, who belonged to the class of farmers or planters known among these people as "not rich, but good livers." In other portions of the country he would have been spoken of as a man "in comfortable circumstances." **1962** Dykeman *Tall Woman* 14 "Ah, Hamilton's a well-turned boy, and the Nelsons are good livers," she had said when he brought Lydia home once from a sociable at the Burkes'. *Ibid.* 221 The Thurstons were fine people, "good livers," as folks said, with their busy sawmills and fat livestock and plentiful tables of food. **1972** *AOHP/LJC-203* I'm not boasting, but my daddy was counted one of the best livers, they called them. **1982** Powers and Hannah *Cataloochee* 338 She added that he had "right smart of money" and was a "good liver." **1986** Watts *Same Block* 141, 156 A man in the Valley who grew lots of corn was considered a "good liver." . . . The Ritchie family was spoken of as "good livers," because they planted big fields of corn and had many cattle. **1990** Wigginton *Foxfire Christmas* 82 After a while I guess I just had an idea because the best livers then that could afford them would get real nice things, you know, and us poor people never did get much. We called them the best livers.

[cf OED3 *good liver* n "a wealthy or well-to-do person" regional; CUD *good liver* 2 (at *good* adj) "someone who is well off"]

good man *noun* God, Jesus, the deity.

1862 *Carter CW Letters* (May 6) bee good children and mind your mother for them is the sort that the good man loves. **1917** Kephart *Word-List* 412 = God; child's term. **1928** Justus *Betty Lou* 66 I reckon the Good Man put it inter that head o'yourn. **1937** Hyatt *Kiverlid* 87 Some claimed them to be warnin's frum the Good Man. **1952** Wilson *Folk Speech NC* 546 = God; Jesus Christ. **1977** King *Her Story* 24 Some of my earliest recollections are of my mother telling me these birds were the Good Man's birds. **1982** Slone *How We Talked* 72 Our people thought of God as being too sacred to mention His name, calling Him, "The Good Man." **1995** Montgomery *Coll* (known to Cardwell), = Jesus (Oliver); I wonder what the Good Man thinks about that (Shields).

[EDD *the Good man* (at *goodman* sb 7) "a child's name for God"; DARE *good man* n Midland, especially South Midland]

good man to See **good child to.**

good'n See **good'un.**

good news bee *noun* See citation. See also **news bee 2.**

1993 Cunningham *Sthn Talk* 61 = a bee about the size and color of a yellow jacket which looks and hovers motionless like a tassel fly. "They say when the good news bee hovers near you, it is bringing good luck, and if it should light on you, that's very good luck."

good piece *noun phrase* A considerable distance. See also **far piece, piece 1.**

1863 *Chapman CW Letters* (Aug 12) it is not as far as some have been but i call it a good piece off. **1966** Dakin *Vocab Ohio River Valley* 297–99 Among those speakers who say *a little piece*, the expressions *a long piece*, *a good piece*, *quite a piece*, *a far piece*, and *a right smart* *piece*, are fairly common. It is quite evident, however, that many speakers who use *piece* in reference to a short distance restrict the word to that usage and say *way(s)* when speaking of a longer distance. **1986** Pederson et al. *LAGS* (Blount Co TN).

(the) good place *noun* Heaven.

1864 *Watkins CW Letters* (July 17) John I want you to doo right I want you to go to that good place where there is no wars Franky I am a going to try to doo right and I want you to doo the Same. **c1960** Wilson *Coll* = heaven; a child's word. **2000** Montgomery *Coll* Glenn, do all you can to get people to go to the good place. (Cardwell).

good to *adjective phrase* Good about, good for, tending to, capable of. For similar patterns with *to*, see the Grammar and Syntax §10.2. See also **awful to**, **bad to**, **great to**, **poor to**.

1926 Hunnicutt *Twenty Years* 62 I knew Old Trail was good to keep on the same track. **1939** Hall *Coll* Hit's [= catnip tea] good to cool ye down. **1940** Haun *Hawk's Done* 14 When Ad was sparking me he used to be pretty good to tell Joe stories about soldiers. **1940** Oakley *Roamin'/Restin'* 99 I always liked hound dog pups as I thot they was so good to smell up opsams coons and other wild animals. **1973** *GSMNP-61:4* The Queen family was all of them good to sing. **1974–75** McCracken *Logging* 24:15 [The motor] was awful good to start right off. **1978** Montgomery *White Pine Coll* IV-1 They're very good to keep up with me and my joys and sorrows. *Ibid.* IV-3 There was a doctor, Doctor Walker, that was mighty good to come anytime we'd call him. **1991** Thomas *Sthn Appal* 169 That horse 'uz awful good t' mind.

good'un (also *good'n*, *goodurn*) *noun* A fine specimen of something. See also **one 1**.

1934 Carter *Mt White Riddles* 76 The informants agreed that at the present time, while a riddle may be heard occasionally, they have lost their old importance and they "haven't heard a good'un in many years." **1939** Hall *Coll* (S. Woody, Cataloochee NC) He had one of these here hog rifles. Hit was a good'un too. **1941** Stuart *Men of Mts* 52 "Old hoe, you are a good'n," he says. **1967** Hall *Coll* (L. Myers, Townsend TN) Sherman could tell you some good'uns. He worked mostly on the loggin's works [where he picked up stories]. **1991** Thomas *Sthn Appal* 250 Jim wuz a fiddler from now on . . . he wuz a good'un when I can remember. **1997** *Dante OHP-14* I remember that. It was a good'un, too. **2013** Venable *How to Tawlk* 17 Bob's oldest son has shore turned out to be a goodurn.

goodurn See **good'un**.

good woman to See **good child to**.

goody *noun* The edible kernel of a nut, especially a walnut or hickory nut.

1859 Taliaferro *Fisher's River* 213 Sam Lundy always added a few items of his own to the above when he "sloped" to market; "wannit goody," "hick'ry-nut goody," and "hazel-nut goody." **1966–68** *DARE Survey* (Brasstown NC, Burnsville NC) = the edible part of a nut. **1998** Montgomery *Coll* (known to nine consultants from the Smoky Mountains, who agree term usually applies only to hard nuts, especially to walnuts and hickory nuts).

[DARE *goody* n 1 chiefly South, Midland]

gooee *interjection* Used as a call to pigs.

1962 Wilson *Folkways Mammoth Cave* 10 "Goo-e-e, goo-e-e" or "Hoo-e, pig" sounds inviting to pigs and hogs, just as "Soo-e" will drive all the hogs away.

go off to themselves (also *go out to themselves*) *verb phrase* Of a newlywed couple: to establish their own household.

1953 Davison *Word-List Appal* I said in speaking of a newly wedded couple who plan to live in their own home instead of living with the bride's parents, "No, Max and Louizy aim to go out to themselves, so they won't scrouge us." **1956** McAtee *Some Dial NC* 19 *go out to themselves* = said of newlyweds who start a new household. **c1960** Wilson *Coll*: *go off to themselves* = said of a young married couple who have moved to a house of their own rather than living with one set of parents. **1995** Montgomery *Coll*: *go out to themselves* (known to Cardwell).

[DARE *go out to themselves* v phr Appalachians]

google *noun* The throat, Adam's apple. See also **goozle**.

1859 Taliaferro *Fisher's River* 29 Two things he was particularly fond of, and upon which he flourished whenever he could get them—turnip greens and "hog's gullicks," the "Adam's apple" of a hog's haslet, or the "google," as it is commonly called. **1986** Pederson et al. *LAGS* (Sullivan Co TN) *google* = because it googles, makes a googling sound. **1997** Montgomery *Coll* (known to Brown, Bush, Oliver).

[DARE *google* n especially South, South Midland]

go on See **go around the bend**.

goop (also *woop*) *interjection* Come! (used as a call to pigs). Also called **ageep**, **geep**, **gooee**. See also **pig-ee**.

1949 Kurath *Word Geog East US* 44 The Carolinas have their own range of hog calls: *goop!*, *woop!*, and *piggoop!* . . . These calls are heard from the Neuse River southward and westward to the Blue Ridge. **1996** Johnson *Lexical Change* 138 = statistically more common in the mountains of South Carolina and Georgia than in the Piedmont and Coastal Plain c1990. **1996** Montgomery *Coll* = also pronounced *ageep*, *geep* (Oliver).

[DARE *goop* exclam especially South Midland, South]

goose *verb*

1 To weed, remove (plants) in the manner of a goose.

1958 Wood *Words from TN* 11 We are going to goose strawberries. **1996–97** Montgomery *Coll* (known to Brown, Bush, Cardwell).

2 To poke or prod, or to threaten to do so.

1952 Wilson *Folk Speech NC* 546 = to make a person jump or flinch by thrusting him in the side (or elsewhere) with the finger or thumb, or to make a pretense of doing so.

gooseberry *noun* A blueberry (*Vaccinium stamineum*) that bears small, edible berries. Same as **deerberry**, **squawberry**.

1925 Dargan *Highland Annals* 209 Here's these gooseberries got to be legged 'fore I can git supper, so's I can cook 'em while I'm bakin bread, an' save stove-wood. **1943** Hannum *Mt People* 140 There were the great puncheons to be hewn for the floor boards—leaving a few of them loose, so the wife-woman could store her preserves and pickles and jars of wild huckleberries and gooseberries underneath. **1964** Stupka *Trees Shrubs Vines* 128 The deerberry, locally called "gooseberry," has numerous clusters of white bell-shaped flowers which make it a conspicuous shrub when in bloom. **1977** Shields *Cades Cove* 35 Berry stemmings occurred in late August or early September when the "gooseberries," sometimes called deerberries and related to blueberries, were harvested. **1982** Stupka *Wildflowers* 84 A high-quality jam is made from the juicy sour berries. Locally this plant is called "squawberry" and "gooseberry."

gooseberry stemming *noun* Formerly, a neighborhood or family work activity to remove stems from gooseberries that have been picked.

[**1977** Shields *Cades Cove* 35 Berry stemmings occurred in late August or early September when the "gooseberries," sometimes called deerberries and related to the blueberries, were harvested.] **1996** GSMNPCOHP-1:2 Bean stringings, gooseberry stemmings, and all such stuff, they'd turn out, young people had somewhere to go, you know, have a big time.

goose drownder *noun* A sudden, hard, flooding rain, a downpour. See also **frog drowner**.

1939 Farr *TN Mt Regions* 90 The rain was a goose drownder.

goose eye *noun* A strong **bead** on distilled whiskey.

1968 *End of Moonshining* 101 = a good bead that holds a long time in the vial. **1974** Maurer and Pearl *KY Moonshine* 119 Goose eye . . . A perfect bead, indicating 100 proof.

goosefoot maple *noun* The striped maple (*Acer pennsylvanicum*), a small deciduous tree from whose bark are made a vermifuge, tonic, and treatment for eye trouble. Also called **moosewood**.

1901 Lounsberry *Sthn Wild Flowers* 323 Most often perhaps the mountaineers that "claim to know" all the trees, call it the goosefoot maple, because its leaves which broaden toward the summit and divide into three well cut lobes suggest to them that bird's foot. **1970** Campbell et al. *Smoky Mt Wildflowers* 22 Other common names [for the striped maple] include Pennsylvania maple, moosewood, and goosefoot maple. **1992** Toops *Great Smoky Mts* 32 Since its airborne seeds must land on the ground warmed by sunlight in order to grow, striped maple is an indicator of past disturbances to a site. . . . A local name for the tree is "goosefoot" maple, referring to the shape of its leaves.

[so called from the shape of its leaf]

goose hair *noun* See citation.

1940 Farr *More TN Expressions* 447 = [a] feather bed: "We'uns has slept on this goose hair fur twenty year."

goose knobs *noun* Gooseflesh.

2005 Williams *Gratitude* 498 = gooseflesh; chill bumps; cold chills.

gooseneck *noun*

1 A type of hoe with a curving metal stem.

1949 Hornsby *Lonesome Valley* 56 He got out two gooseneck hoes and sharpened them. **1976** Garber *Mountain-ese* 35 As soon as we could walk we wuz interduced to a gooseneck hoe.

[DARE *gooseneck hoe* n especially South Midland]

2 See citation.

1964 Clarkson *Lumbering in WV* 362 = a curved iron driven into the bottom of a slide to check the speed of descending logs, when approaching a turn or arriving at the delivery end of the slide.

goose nest *noun* A type of sinkhole.

1904 Johnson *Highways South* 148 The region about the cave [= Mammoth Cave] is hilly; but instead of watercourses and ravines, there are numerous rounded, basinlike hollows known as sink-holes. Often the sink-holes are acres in extent. . . . Their form and frequency has given the name of "Goose-nest land" to that part of Kentucky where they are most abundant. Some of these contain a pool of water, and these muddy ponds, though small, are frequently deep and many of them are never dry. **1939** *FWP Guide KY* 294 This is a cave region and sinkholes called "goose nests" by the natives, small caves, and sinking streams are prevalent.

goosey *adjective* Ticklish.

1939 Farr *TN Mt Regions* 90 = ticklish. **1939** Hall *Coll* = ticklish: "Are you goosy?"

[DARE *goosey* adj 1 scattered, but chiefly South, South Midland]

go out to themselves See **go off to themselves**.

goozle

A (also *goozlem*) *noun* The throat. See also **google**.

1915 Dingus *Word-List VA* 184 = variant of *guzzle*. **1917** Kephart *Word-List* 417. **c1960** Wilson *Coll* (or *goozlem*) = the neck or throat. **1976** *Bear Hunting* 292 We gutted [the bear]—took everything out plumb to his goozle—ears, lights, liver, and all. **1983** Montell *Don't Go Up* 64 Confederate raider Champ Ferguson, for example, was audacious enough to decapitate one man and stick a piece of tobacco stem down the dead man's "goozle." **1996** Montgomery *Coll* (known to Cardwell). **2002** Myers *Best Yet Stories* 78 = throat, [to] speak hoarsely.

[DARE *goozle* n chiefly South, South Midland]

B *verb* See citation.

1972 Cooper *NC Mt Folklore* 93 = to speak hoarsely; to swallow rapidly. **2002** Myers *Best Yet Stories* 78 = throat, [to] speak hoarsely.

goozle down *verb phrase* To guzzle, drink (liquor).

1994 Montgomery *Coll* They was always just a-goozling [alcohol] down (Ogle).

goozlem See **goozle A**.

goozler *noun*

1 See 1972 citation.

1972 Cooper *NC Mt Folklore* 93 = a boy whose voice is changing. **1996–97** Montgomery *Coll* (known to Bush, Cardwell).

2 See citation.

2007 McMillon *Notes* = big rain.

gopher hole *noun* Same as **doghole**.

1943 Korson *Coal Dust* 4 Some farmers . . . operated small mines variously called "country banks," "wagon mines," "dog holes," "gopher holes," or "father-and-son" mines.

gopherwood *noun* Same as **yellowwood**.

1937 Thornburgh *Great Smoky Mts* 28–29 "And this yellowwood," [the guide] adds, "is gopher wood. The old folks say that Noah's ark was made of it and I can't dispute it none." **1970** Campbell et al. *Smoky Mt Wildflowers* 40 Other common names [of the yellowwood] are chittum and gopherwood, which legend tells us was used by Noah in building his ark.

go-poke *noun* A traveling bag; a person always on the move. See also **go-way bag**.

1952 Wilson *Folk Speech NC* 547 = a traveling bag. **1977** Parris *Mt Idiom* = a traveling bag, suitcase, or a person forever on the go. **c1982** Young *Colloquial Appal* 10 = large paper bag. **1994** Montgomery *Coll* (known to Shields).

go queer *verb phrase* To seem strange, unusual. See also **go foolish**, **go odd with**, **go the queerest**.

1952 Giles *40 Acres* 67 Hit goes quare that any water could be so big.

gorge *noun* A deep, narrow passage cut between mountains by a river. See 1956 citation.

1956 Fink *That's Why* 3 Where a mountain range is cut through by a river, like the Delaware and Susquehanna Watergaps of the East, here [in the Smokies] the term is gorge. **1991** Thomas *Sthn Appal* 107 One time, they come up through the gorge there; they'uz five cars here, an' jist five coaches behind.

[DARE *gorge* n[1] scattered, but chiefly Northeast, Appalachians, Great Lakes, Southwest]

gorm, **gormed** See **gaum**.

gormy *adjective* See citation.

1992 Brooks *Sthn Stuff* 59 = sticky or smeary. "Who wants to pick up a youngun all gormy with butter and 'lasses?"

goslings *noun* See citation. See also **goozler 1**.

1957 Broaddus *Vocab Estill Co KY* 41 = the change of voice a boy experiences at puberty.

[DARE *gosling* n chiefly South Midland]

gospel bird (also *gospel fowl*) *noun* See citation.

1946 Woodard *Word-List VA/NC* 15 *gospel fowl* = a chicken. (So named probably because fried chicken is customarily fed to the preacher and taken to "protracted meetings.") **2014** Montgomery *Doctrine* 131 *gospel bird* = fried chicken.

gospel sing *noun* Same as **sing C**, **singing**.

2004 Rash *Saints at River* 39 People voted in this building, and occasionally a revival or gospel sing would be held.

goster *verb* To act in an overbearing or domineering way.

1937 Hyatt *Kiverlid* 37 Huh! . . . him just a-gosterin' about my old snags [= bad teeth], and tellin' 'em here to keep adostin' [= dosing] me on that bottle o' draps thar. **1952** Wilson *Folk Speech NC* 544 = to domineer.

[cf EDD (*gauster* v 1) "to bully . . . to brag"]

gosties See **ghost**.

got *verb* See also **get B2**. To have, possess.

1862 (in **1983** Walker *Tales Civil War* 15) Come if you Can for if yo dont I will haf to stay her longer and then bee sent to to the berix [= barracks] and stay thare maby 2 weeke and I dont got any blankits her. **1972** *AOHP/ALC-298* Do you got a lot of sisters? **1973** *Foxfire Interviews* A-73-86 They don't got no time for nothing else at all. **1989** *Matewan OHP-28* Why do I got any business putting you in? **1994** McCarthy *Jack Two Worlds* 54 What do I gotta do? **2008** *Rosie Hicks* 4 "Do you got food," he said. "I've got Ray Hicks and company."

[probably originally by elision from *has/have got*]

go the queerest *verb phrase* To seem the strangest or most unusual. See also **go queer**.

1979 Carpenter *Walton War* 177 Hit goes the quarest to see a youngun as little as hit is that can read. **1995–97** Montgomery *Coll* (known to Adams, Brown, Ledford).

go to *verb phrase*

1 (+ *verbal noun*) To begin, start, set about. See also **get C5**, **get to**, **get to be**, **go into**.

c1844 Beckner *Shane Interview* 237 They, of the station, just went back again to fiddling. **1860** *Week in Smokies* 125 Mister, the queen [bee] she goes to laying in February and lays on into spring. **1862** Robinson *CW Letters* (April 21) I told them to go to cooking & I went to sleep. **1864** Griffin *CW Letters* (Nov?) we will go to bilding next weake then we can injoy our Boxes when we git them. **1867** Harris *Sut Lovingood* 23 Dad wanted hit made kurb, es he hedn't work'd fur a good while, an' said he mout sorter fell his keepin, an' go tu ravin an' cavortin. **1884** Smith *Arp Scrap Book* 80 They ought to marry I reckon and go to raising fools for market. **1898** Elliott *Durket Sperret* 38 Don't you go to makin' her wuss mad 'an is needful. **1926** Hunnicutt *Twenty Years* 11 We turned the dogs loose and the dogs went to trailing at once and barking their best. *Ibid.* 38 We went to carrying in wood. **1937** Hall *Coll* (Cosby TN) He went to killing 'em [= bears] when he was twelve year old. **1940** Oakley *Roamin'/Restin'* 49 I went to chopping and sawing out wood things we had to have. **1957** GSMNP-23:1:21 He went to going through there, and it got to snowing. **1971** *Boogers* 47 When I go to milkin', there's a baby goes t'cryin' in that rock pile. **1974** GSMNP-50:2:7 Didn't we finally go to having preaching twice a month? **1977** Shackelford et al. *Our Appalachia* 252 When he slapped this woman, guns went to popping. **1991** Thomas *Sthn Appal* 60 When that tree starts t' thaw, an' poppin', it'ull go t' drippin' out there. **1997** *Dante OHP*-53 They went to making a little bit of wages, and they kind of controlled part of their life.

[DARE (at *go* v C2) scattered, but especially South, South Midland]

2 (also *go for to*) (+ *infinitive*) To intend (to), mean to (especially in phrase *didn't go to*).

1930 Armstrong *This Day and Time* 174 He didn't go to kill Godfrey, I don't reckon. **c1959** Weals *Hillbilly Dict* 3 *didn't go to* = didn't intend to. "I didn't go to hurt you." **1964** Williams *Prep Mt Speech* 54 A woman will sometimes confess that she "like to a simply a wore that youngin aout" when she really "didn't go for to do it." **1975** Jackson *Unusual Words* 153 *Intend* is the definition of *go* in the sentence "I didn't go to hit him." **1981** Dumas *Appal Glossary* 17 = intend to, mean to. "I didn't *go to* do it." **1994** Montgomery *Coll* I didn't go to do that (Shields). **1999** Morgan *Gap Creek* 219 "I didn't go to leave you," Hank shouted.

[DARE *go* v C6 chiefly South, Midland]

3 To have (as one's teacher).

1969 GSMNP-37:2:19 I went to school to about four or five of them [= teachers] over there at Galbraith's Creek. **1973** *AOHP/LJC*-350 I went to one teacher, Sol Noble, part of four year, and my children went to him, and my grandchildren went to him. **1985** Irwin *Alex Stewart* 51 The first teacher ever I went to was Mary Maxie. *Ibid.* 51 I think they was about eight of us in the school when I went there to Mary. **1989** *Matewan OHP*-1 I went to [that school] to Pauline Chancy and to Missus Phillips in the sixth grade, and then I graduated into the seventh and eighth, eighth to Missus Hoskins. **1991** Thomas *Sthn Appal* 199 I went to school to a Professor Finley.

go to grass *verb phrase*

1 Used as a euphemism for *go to hell* (usually as an imperative).

1890 Fruit *KY Words* 65 Go to grass, and eat mullein! **1915** Hall *Autobiog Claib Jones* 11 I then told him to keep his girl and the reward and to go to grass with them. **1927** Woofter *Dialect from WV* 355 = go no one cares where. "Let them go to grass." **1952** Wilson *Folk Speech NC* = a friendly imprecation. "Oh, you *go to grass*. I don't believe he said that." **1967** Wilson *Folkways Mammoth Cave* 37 Go to grass and eat mullein. Said of someone who has been impertinent. **1977** Hamilton *Mt Memories* 38 You can go to grass! **1998** Montgomery *Coll* (known to Bush).

2 See citation.

1939 Bond *Appal Dialect* 108 = to be in poor financial condition.

go to house *verb phrase* Of an animal: to go to its den.

1926 Hunnicutt *Twenty Years* 78 We believed the bear had gone to house.

go-to-meeting *adjective phrase* Of clothes: fancy, fine, suitable for wearing to a church service. See also **Sunday-go-to-meeting.**

1930 Justus *Pocket's Luck* 10 She would get out her gray go-to-meeting shawl, and lend it to Peter Pocket. **1943** Justus *Bluebird* 33 Pretty things like new books, or a go-to-meeting dress. *Ibid.* 109 Grandy, too, she saw at a glance, had honored the occasion by wearing his go-to-meeting coat and having his beard well trimmed. **2007** Preece *Leavin' Sandlick* 17 Wade only had a couple go to meetin' suits of clothes, and I allas kept them arned and ready fer him to wear.

go to straw *verb phrase* To be confined to bed in late pregnancy. See also **called to straw.**

1991 Still *Wolfpen Notebooks* 72 In the courthouse they didn't ask for ages [of people wanting to marry] for they saw she would soon be going to straw.

go to the bad *verb phrase* To deteriorate, decline.

1970 *Foxfire Interviews* A-70-75 My hot plate's gone to the bad. **1986** Lauterer *Runnin' on Rims* 127 Farming's gone to the bad even with tractors.

[DARE *go to the bad* v phr especially South]

gotted See **got.**

gotten See **get B2.**

gouge *verb* To stick (as with a needle).

c1960 Wilson *Coll* = [to] stick or hurt with a pin. **1968–69** *DARE Survey* (Rome GA) gouged a needle into; (Marlinton WV) gouged himself.

[DARE *gouge* v 1 especially South, South Midland]

go up (also *go up the spout*) *verb phrase* To become exhausted or defeated, deteriorate, disintegrate.

1864 Griffin *CW Letters* (March 22) thay Will all doo aney thing that Old Jeff Davis wants them to doo But I fear that the confedercy will go up the Spout this summer. **1864** *Mangum CW Letters* (April 15) our reinlisted furlows ar gon up for the presant.

gourd banjo *noun* A banjo whose bowl is made of a dried-out squash.

1980 Wigginton *Foxfire VI* 54 Since Mr. Hodges is a concert violinist and violin maker, we were surprised to learn that his first musical instrument was a gourd banjo made for him when he was a small boy in the mountains of North Carolina by his grandfather.

gourd bean *noun* A Guinea bean.

1978 *Gourd Bean* 226–27 Some people call them guinea bean, but we know them as gourd bean. I sure couldn't tell you if it was considered to be a gourd. The old people had the first'uns we ever heard tell of at Hiawassee, but I don't know [where they got them].... You have to have something for the gourd bean to run on. I usually have mine growing on the hog lot fence.... They taste different from squash—they've got a better taste, and the taste is not strong. **1984** Page and Wigginton *Foxfire Cookery* 152 I found out about the gourd bean about forty something years ago. We were working for a man hoeing corn, and [his wife] had some fixed for dinner. We ate them at that man's house there for dinner, and he give us seed of them, and we planted them, and I've been growing them ever since. Some people call them guinea beans, but we know them as gourd beans.

gourd egg *noun* A small gourd placed in a hen's nest to induce her to lay eggs. Same as **China egg**.

1986 Pederson et al. LAGS (Sevier Co, Sullivan Co TN).

gourd fiddle *noun* A stringed musical instrument made from a gourd, resembling a violin.

1843 (in **1974** Harris *High Times* 30) Thus on and on, till the night is gone—and the whisky, too, the dulcimer stops, and the gourd fiddle gives out, the hour for parting is come. [**1980** Wigginton *Foxfire VI* 54 His father and uncle had made such instruments . . . he remembered a photograph of them holding two such instruments, a fiddle and a banjo.]

gourd head See citation.

2005 Williams *Gratitude* 498 When somebody is inexperienced, they are said to be as green as a gourd. Somebody that ain't real smart is called a gourd head.

gourd tree *noun* A tree in which a dried, hollowed-out gourd is mounted to attract a purple martin to nest therein. See also **martin gourd**.

1942 Robertson *Red Hills* 59 There was a gourd tree for the purple martins, and beehives, and there was a well with an oak bucket.

gout *noun*

A A small piece of cloth.

1939 Farr *TN Mt Regions* 89 = piece of cloth cut out of a bolt of material. **1941** Justus *Kettle Creek* 45 Just a gout no longer than your finger. [**1995** Montgomery Coll (unknown to consultants from the Smoky Mountains).]

B (also *gout out*) *verb, verb phrase* Of a heavy rain: to create ruts and holes (in a road); hence participial adjective *gouted* (*out*).

1913 Morley *Carolina Mts* 249 These words from your driver bring your thoughts down to the road which, from recent rains and the passing of tanbark wagons, is, indeed, as he puts it, "terribly gouted out." **1940** Haun *Hawk's Done* 110 The roads were gouted out so bad he had to wait till spring. **1957** Combs *Lg Sthn High: Word List* 46 = to wash badly, as of rains on a road or highway. Ex.: "The heavy rain gouted the road." **1960** Westover *Highland Lg* 19 *gouted* = rutted.

gout out See **gout B**.

government *noun* Variant forms *giverment*, *gover(n)mint*, *gov'ment*, *gov'mint*, also with secondary stress on the last syllable: *GOV-er-mint*. For similar forms, see **-ment A**.

1883 Bonner *Dialect Tales* 135 Ain't it a pity, boys, to see sech a rifle as that throwed away on a damned Gov'ment officer? **1913** Kephart *Our Sthn High* 224 In mountain dialect such words as settlement, government, studyment (reverie) are accented on the last syllable, or drawled with equal stress throughout. **1927** Mason *Lure of Smokies* 171 We ain't got nothin' agin th' governmint, neither No'th nor South. **1940** Stuart *Trees of Heaven* 269 I'm gittin tired of all this petticoat gover-mint you got us under. **1942** Hall *Phonetics Smoky Mts* 41 [ˈgɪvə̝-mɛnt]. **1967** Fetterman *Stinking Creek* 48–50 Bartow keeps his ax sharp and his bull tongue free of rust so a livelihood can be wrung from the thin, steep soil of his farm. He scoffs at "governmint business." **1974** Dabney *Mt Spirits* 20 The Gov'mint says old silver cloud likker is poison. **1991** Thomas *Sthn Appal* 142 They had all kinds of gover'mint men there, takin' samples, an' testin'. **1994** Morgan *Hinterlands* 194 We didn't figure it was the giverments business, what we done with our corn and peaches and apples. The giverment was after the revenue.

government liquor (also *government whiskey*) *noun* Taxed, legally produced liquor.

1983 *Dark Corner OHP-5A* I don't want just government whiskey, don't like hit. **1984** High *Titan Rock* 49 At that time all legal liquor was called government liquor, because it was taxed. It was also called red liquor, because they colored it.

government still *noun* A legal distillery producing taxed liquor. See 1985 citation.

1985 Dabney *More Mt Spirits* 69 Verner remembers that his grandfather, George Fox, and his father operated a "government still" in the Stock Hill section. "A federal inspector would come ever so often and check it and take samples. They couldn't sell any of the still but they could give their friends a drink of it." **1985** Irwin *Alex Stewart* 205 Old Bill Green run a government still right up yonder, and he'd buy all the dried fruit you'd take him, to make brandy.

gover(n)mint See **government**.

governors *noun* See citation.

1957 Broaddus *Vocab Estill Co KY* 36 = testicles of livestock.

gov'mint See **government**.

go-way bag (also *go-way sack*) *noun* See citations. See also **go-poke**.

1917 Kephart *Word-List* 412 *go-'way sack* = satchel. Also *go-'way bag*. **1927** Woofter *Dialect from WV* 355 = suit case: "He was carrying a go-way bag in his hand."

go with *verb phrase* To become of, happen (to).

1859 Taliaferro *Fisher's River* 49 You'll see how it will go with us on that day, sartin. **1862** Epperly *CW Letters* (May 17) I dont no what would a went with them I am nearly out of money now. **1864** *Zimmerman CW Letters* (Jan 5) you wanted to know a bout James Clothing what he left in camp I cwooden [= couldn't] find out what wente with them. **1936** Coleman *Dial N GA* 16 "What has gone with it?" means "become of." **1941** Hall *Coll* (Waynesville NC) What went with the claw-hammer? **1956** Miller *Pigeon's Roost* (Jan 5) As we write this, we have not learned just who the sheep belonged to or what went with them. **c1960** Wilson *Coll* What's gone with him? **1976** *Bear Hunting* 312 I never did know what ever went with it, but that was the biggest [bear] that I've ever seed yet. **1979** Slone *My Heart* 127 I said, "No one knows what went with them," a mountain expression meaning that they were lost. When we don't know where something is, we say, "we don't know what went with it." **1983** *Dark Corner OHP-11A* I don't know what her other name was or what went with her.

grab[1] *noun* A heavy hook on a chain that is attached to a log or bear trap; the hook is designed to catch onto a tree, stump, or other fixed object and prevent further movement.

1930 Pendleton *Wood-Hicks Speak* 87 = a heavy iron hook to be driven into a log. **1937** Hall *Coll* (Cades Cove TN) *grab chains* = chains with hooks [= **grabs**] on a steel bear trap so as to prevent a bear from dragging away the trap in which he has been caught. The hooks would grab onto a tree or rhododendron, etc. and thus anchor the trap. **1939** Hall *Coll* (Cataloochee NC) Me and him, we decided to go to the trap one day, and it got a big bear in the trap and he'd come off down to the open woods.... The bear was hung on the laurel by the grabs. *Ibid.* (Little Greenbrier TN) Bears once caught in a trap can't go far dragging the trap with them because the grabs has 'em fouled. **1976** Tyler *Man's Work* 26 I guess I've done it all. Drove teams, drove grabs (device used to fasten a trail of logs together), swamped (cleared the ground of underbrush and fallen trees for road construction). **1998** *Dante OHP-12* Most of the time we just took the horse up into the mountain, cut the tree down, and we had what they call grabs that they drove into the side of the logs. **2006** *WV Encycl* 707 Moving the logs out of the woods was accomplished with a team of horses. When the day's work began the teamster curried and fed his team and drove them to the skidroad. Here the skidding crew prepared a train of logs, fastening a dozen or more together end-to-end with devices called grabs. A grab was a short piece of chain with a swivel in the middle and heavy pins at each end. The pins were driven into adjacent ends of the logs to fasten them together. The teamster then hooked the horse team to the front log with special grabs and the horses pulled the train of logs to a landing located either along a stream or along the logging railroads.

grab[2] *verb* Same as **grabble**.

1995 Montgomery *Coll*: *grab, grabble* = to grab a few potatoes without disturbing the plant (Cardwell).

grabble (also *gravel*) *verb*

1 To dig up (especially an early potato) with one's hands or a fork and then to replace the covering; to dig potatoes out of a hill; hence noun *grabbler*. Also called **drabble 2**, **grab**[2], **granny B2**, **scrabble 1**, **scratch**[2] **B**.

1864 Mangum *CW Letters* (Sept 9) we have a butiful rain this morning I think if I was thar I cold grabble a mess of potatoes. **1913** Kephart *Our Sthn High* 293–94 To "grabble 'taters" is to pick from a hill of new potatoes a few of the best, then smooth back the soil without disturbing the immature ones. **1941** Still *Troublesome Creek* 76 We went to grabble ratsbane, and the drummer chuckled all day. **1941** Stuart *Men of Mts* 17 You can gravel down there at them tater roots and you won't find taters bigger than a marble. **1957** Broaddus *Vocab Estill Co KY* 36 *grabble* = to dig more or less ripe potatoes out of the hill one at a time before the potatoes all get ripe. **c1960** Wilson *Coll* = to dig new potatoes out of the hill, usually with a table fork. *Gravel* seems to be more common [than *grabble*] for this idea. **1969** GSMNP-38:106 They'd plant a few rows of early potatoes to grabble out. **1977** Hamilton *Mt Memories* 33 Papa's big potato patch was outside the garden and we were not to "grabble" there, for he said it kept the plants from producing big potatoes. **1981** Brewer *Wonderment* 92 What Lucinda calls "grannying" is called "grabbling" in some quarters. **1982** Irwin *Baskets* 13 Each morning we would "gravel" enough Irish potatoes for dinner and supper, pick the tomatoes and okra, and gather enough roasting ears for the day. **1990** Oliver *Cooking Hazel Creek* 13 Everyone looked forward to new potatoes which, as soon as they had matured sufficiently, were "grabbled" out of the ground and then boiled in their jackets until tender; a gravy of flour & milk was then made in the water & the potatoes cooked & served in this. **1995** Montgomery *Coll*: *grabble* = to grab a few potatoes without disturbing the plant (Cardwell). **2002** Myers *Best Yet Stories* 103 When his mother said she was going to gravel potatoes, I sneaked along behind her watching to see what she did. Finding cracks in the ground around the new potato plants indicated a potato large enough to eat at that site. Scratching away the dirt, picking the potato, then covering the hole with dirt was what she called graveling. My family simply "dug" our potatoes. **2002** Oliver *Cooking and Living* 45 The first Irish potatoes to mature in the early summer were looked forward to with great anticipation. Not waiting for them to become fully grown, people "grabbled" with a spoon or fork among the roots of the hills, being careful not to destroy the plant or still-growing potatoes. These new, small, tender potatoes or "grabblies" had, as today, a delicious flavor and were cooked a variety of ways. **2003** Carter *Mt Home* 49 We moved the piece of tin covering the coal and started gravelin' the froze-together chunks of coal out of the pile and tossin' them in our buckets. **2005** Williams *Gratitude* 498 = to dig potatoes from the ground using just the hands or a small implement to rake them out without damaging the roots of the potato plant. Possibly derived from the word *grapple*. We had a big old handmade fork that we used for a "tater grabbler." **2008** *Rosie Hicks* 3 He always put him out a little patch of potatoes to gravel real early.

[OED3 *grabble* v 1 (frequentative of *grab*) "to feel or search with the hands, to grope about"; DARE *grabble* v 1 chiefly South, South Midland]

2 (also *gravel*) To fish with the bare hands, especially for spawning catfish as they lurk in underwater rock crevices. Same as **hand fishing, hand grabbing**. See also **noodling**.

c1960 Wilson *Coll*: *grabble* = to catch fish with bare hands in drifts actual or made to form a place of refuge for the fish. **1980** Brewer *Hit's Gettin'* In East Tennessee, a few people still "grabble" . . . for fish under rocks and stream banks. **1981** High *Coll* (DARE) = used in the Gorge as part of the phrase, grabbling for catfish, meaning to pull catfish by hand from under rocks and from holes while they're nesting in June, an illegal practice . . . "Grabbling for catfish is against the law, and I wouldn't do it myself, but I wouldn't turn people in for it." **1984** Wilder *You All Spoken* 38 *grabble* = find by working the fingers, as in . . . catching trout in mountain pools. **1991** Thomas *Sthn Appal* 75 I'd git down in th' creek an' gravel a big mess of 'um, maybe eight ur ten creek-suckers. **2014** *Blind Pig* (March 31) We used to go grabbling for catfish upinunder the rocks in the Little Tennessee.

[EDD *grabble* v 1; DARE *grabble* v 2 South, South Midland]

grabbler See **grabble 1**.

grabbly *noun* A small, tender potato dug up early in the season. See also **grabble 1**.

2002 Oliver *Cooking and Living* 45 The first Irish potatoes to mature in the early summer were looked forward to with great anticipation. Not waiting for them to become fully grown, people "grabbled" with a spoon or fork among the roots of the hills, being careful not to destroy the plant or still-growing potatoes. These new, small, tender potatoes or "grabblies" had, as today, a delicious flavor and were cooked a variety of ways.

grab chain See **grab**[1].

grab driver *noun* See citation.

1967 Parris *Mt Bred* 133 A Grab-driver is a fellow who attaches coupling grabs to a turn of logs and a grab-skipper is a short iron pry or hammer used to remove the skidding tongs from a log.

grabhook *verb* See citation.

1976 Garber *Mountain-ese* 36 = [to] snare fish: "We grabhooked a mess uv fish down at the crick."

grab jack *noun* See citations.

1994 Farwell and Buchanan *Logging Terms* = a member of a logging crew who hitched the teams to the logs by driving grabs into the logs and hitching the teams to grabs. **2006** *Foxfire 40th Anniv* 311 The list of employees required by a large operation was staggering, and would include . . . "grab jacks" (men who drove grabs into the logs so they could be pulled).

grab skip *noun* See citation.

1999 Hoyle *Handed Down* 23 The tools used in getting the logs out of the woods were called "jay-grabs" and "grab skips." The jay-grab was used on the lead log and the grab skip was used to drive the jay grab in.

grab skipper *noun* See citation. Same as **skip B1**.

1967 Parris *Mt Bred* 133 A Grab-driver is a fellow who attaches coupling grabs to a turn of logs and a grab-skipper is a short iron pry or hammer used to remove the skidding tongs from a log.

grade *verb*

1 To receive (a grade or mark, as on a school assignment or test).

1956 Hall *Coll* (Cosby TN) Your brother Tom graded ninety nine and a half in that examination.

2 To organize or arrange a school by grade levels. Traditionally there were no schools with grades in the mountains, only elementary schools in which one teacher in a single classroom taught all students.

1956 Hall *Coll* (Cosby Creek TN) They didn't grade back then like they do now.

grade out *verb phrase* To finish one's schooling.

1953 Hall *Coll* (Nine Mile TN) I went till I got to my second grade. I graded out then. I didn't go on because I had to mess around at home and maybe wouldn't get in till recess and got behind. **1995–97** Montgomery *Coll* (known to Cardwell, Weaver).

grader See **lumber grader**.

graf-phone (also *graphone*) *noun* A gramophone.

2005 Williams *Gratitude* 88 They played their dance music on a talkin' machine, or hand cranked "graphone," they called it, that played them big ol' heavy 78 rpm records. **2008** McKinley *Bear Mt* 60 Though it had once been a brand name, the term "gramophone" began to be used to describe any record player. Mountain folks further shortened it to "graf-phone," which was the word Granny and Grandpa always used.

graft widow See **grass widow 1**.

grain

A *noun* A bit, small amount, slight degree. See also **dust**.

1865 *Love CW Letters* (Feb 10) they nevr punished him one grain. **1900** Harben *N GA Sketches* 171 I'm a leetle grain older'n you, Mis' Gibbs, an' I've been about some. **1913** Kephart *Our Sthn High* 121 The only medicines we'uns has is yerbs, which customarily ain't no good 'thout a leetle grain o' whiskey. **1936** Ogden *Rescue Work* One mountaineer lamented, "She must be a leetle grain teched." **1937** Hall *Coll* (Cosby Creek TN) I reckon I'd better stay here and work a grain. **1937** Thornburgh *Great Smoky Mts* 98 Them fellers that said I didn't do nothin' but hunt was plum sorry they hadn't hunted a leetle grain more. **1939** Hall *Coll* (Cataloochee NC) Walk about a little grain; he stuttered a little grain. **1940** Still *River of Earth* 106 Now that I can't fotch and carry for them, they never give me a grain o' thought. **1955** Ritchie *Singing Family* 98 Shore, I could tell you're a Ritchie, fur as I could see you a-coming, but just which one was a puzzling me a little grain. **1969** Roberts *Greasybeard* 38 One of 'em dropped dead—with a bullet square through him—on the side of Pine Mountain a little grain above Nolan's Branch. **1974** Fink *Bits Mt Speech* 15 Give me a *little grain* of licker.

[DARE *grain* n 1 especially South Midland]

B *verb* To scratch, scrape.

1938 Stuart *Dark Hills* 101 The hard rocks that he had fallen on had grained and bruised the skin on his stomach.

grainery house *noun* A granary.

1981 GSMNP-118 The next one [= building] up there, they called that the grainery house, and why they called it that I suppose was . . . they had some great big garners [sic] they called them in there built, and they'd store their wheat, when they had their wheat thrashed.

grampus *noun* The larva of the dobson fly.

1917 Kephart *Camping & Woodcraft* 2:411 One of the best natural baits for bass, when the water is clear, is that fierce-looking creature called hellgrammite, dobson, or grampus. **1974** Russell *Hillbilly* 44 Hunting "grampuses" for fish bait was always fun. **1991** Thomas *Sthn Appal* 76 They was one of these thangs that growed under flat rocks in th' creeks, grampuses. **1994** Montgomery *Coll* (known to Shields).

gramy *verb* To vex, upset, anger.

1928 Chapman *Happy Mt* 312 = to vex. "It gramies me to have it get lost." **1971** Dwyer *Dict for Yankees* 26 = to vex, upset. "It gramys me to see naked pictures." **1992** Brooks *Sthn Stuff* 60 *gramy* = to annoy; to anger. "It gramies me whin he walks around with that silly grin on his face." **1996** Montgomery *Coll* (known to Cardwell, but not to other consultants from the Smoky Mountains).

[cf OED3 *grame* n 1 "anger, wrath" obsolete; SND (at *gram* v III) "to be in a passion"; Web3 *gramy* v now dialect]

grancer See **grandsir**.

grandboy *noun* A grandson. See also **boy**.

1939 *FWP Guide NC* 98 A common usage among older people is "gran'boy" for grandson. **1977** Norman *Kinfolks* 50 Did you whine and cry to your grandboy here like you do to everybody else? **1984** Burns *Cold Sassy* 296 This here used to be my sewin' room . . . But I fixed it up for my grandboys, Horace and Ulysses.

[DARE *grandboy* n chiefly South, South Midland]

grandchild *noun* Variant plural form *grandchilds*.

1989 *Matewan OHP-89* One of the grandchilds owns the flower shop now where the home ball field is.

granddaddy *noun*

1 A grandfather.

1859 Taliaferro *Fisher's River* 106 Sam J—was a little too hard for Dick in discussion, and Dick turned upon him with a "jodarter," and smote him thus "Sam, you's chock full of your granddaddy's blood!" **1862** *Shipman CW Letters* (Feb 6) Jackson Stapp sends his best Respects and he wants you to tell grandady and Grany howdy for mee and all the rest of his friends. **1957** GSMNP-23:1:9 That was my great granddaddy, the old ancestors away back yonder. **1970** Foster *Walker Valley* 21 Of course Granddaddy was an awfully lot like that too. **1983** *Dark Corner OHP-11A* His granddaddy came along and he happened to pick up one of Linda's violins that was in the room and he played what Will was playing. **1991** Williams *Homeplace* 78 Well, my granddaddy and them, they had two chimneys to their house. And kept a fire in both houses. **1998** *Dante OHP-14* Him and my granddaddy both built the Mount Zion Baptist Church.

[DARE *granddaddy* n 1 chiefly South, South Midland]

2 (also *granddaddy grey-beard*) The daddy long-legs spider.

1957 Combs *Lg Sthn High: Word List* 46 *granddaddy grey-beard, harvest-man* = an arachnid of the Phalangida family. If a boy, sent out into the woods to hunt the cow, gets down on his knees near this sage little creature and asks, "Gran'-daddy-grey-beard, which way has the cow gone?" it immediately lifts one of its elongated feelers and points in the direction of the cow. **1999** Montgomery *Coll: granddaddy* (known to Cardwell).

[DARE *granddaddy* n 2 chiefly South, South Midland]

3 Something of supreme size, as a **still** for making **moonshine**.

1977 Shackelford et al. *Our Appalachia* 37 It was the granddaddy still that I ever heard of in Knott County—we figured it would hold about 210 gallons—and it was hot.

granddaddy grey-beard See **granddaddy 2**.

grandma'am (also *grandmam*) *noun* A grandmother.

1930 Armstrong *This Day and Time* 26–27 Your daddy brung that 'ere spoon to your gran'mam, an' she sets a heap o' store by hit. **1999** Montgomery *Coll* We went up to visit grandsir and grandma'am once a year (Cardwell).

[DARE (at *grandma* n A6) chiefly Central Atlantic]

grandmam See **grandma'am**.

grandmammy *noun* A grandmother.

1935 Sheppard *Cabins in Laurel* 62 Doc Hoppas, the son of a Union soldier, says, "It makes me mad to even think of the Home Guard for the way they done my daddy and my grandmammy." **1951** Justus *Lucky Penny* 12 Grandmammy had most of her time taken up doctoring Grandpappy.

[DARE (at *grandma* n A10) chiefly South, South Midland]

grandmaw *noun* A grandmother.

1937 Hall *Coll* (Emerts Cove TN) My gran'maw was born in Old Virginia. **1950** Hall *Coll* They started runnin' and run on to their grandmaw's . . . where she was a-layin' a corpse. **1968** GSMNP-38 My grandmaw stayed there as long as she lived. **1973** GSMNP-79:9 We always had to go to Grandmaw's house to have a good chestnut bake. **1992** Offutt *KY Straight* 26 Grandmaw can outrun him and she's dead. **2013** *Blind Pig* (Sept 21) I think about my Great Grandma (though we said "Grandmaw").

[DARE (at *grandma* n A1) chiefly South, Midland, West]

grandmother rose *noun* An unspecified variety of rose.

2005 Houk *Walker Sisters* 20 Honeybees came out of their hollow log hives to buzz about the orchard and among the banquet of blossoms that adorned the Walker place—lilacs, hydrangeas, yucca (or Adam's needle), pink "grandmother roses," snowball bushes, rose of sharon, and bachelor buttons—more than 100 kinds of flowers by one person's count.

grandpap (also *grandpappy*) *noun* A grandfather (used both as a title and in third-person reference).

1864 Chapman *CW Letters* (April 10) I seen your Grandpap the other day. **1928** Ivey *Mt Whites* "My foreparents war principally Scotch," or "my great-grandpap he war Irish." **1930** Armstrong *This Day and Time* 22 You've growed a right smart since I saw you last, at the burying-ground, when they put your Grandpap Buckles away. **c1950** (in **2000** Oakley *Roamin' Man* 13) Some of the fondest memories of my childhood were of times spent with Grandpap Oakley while we lived at Scratch Britches Mountain. **1956** Hall *Coll* (Big Bend NC) Hit was a big rock mill. Granpap McGaha built it and owned it. **1962** Williams *Mtneers Mind Manners* 19 Thoroughly imbued by the principles of equality for which their grandpappies "fit" at King's Mountain, they consider themselves as good as anyone and often a heap better than "them low-down onery neighbors up the creek a ways." **1970** GSMNP-26:2 Now Jane was my grandpap's sister. **1971** Thornburgh *Great Smoky Mts* 154 Nor can I fish with bait for trout, nor kill a boomer, nor a bear on the land owned by my pap, and grandpap and his pap before him. **1986** Ogle *Lucinda* 46 How I remember Grandpap Oakley later was his long white beard and the clearest blue sparkling eyes. **1986** Pederson et al. *LAGS* = attested by 5/60 interviewees (8.3%) in E TN; 5/8 of all LAGS interviewees (62.5%) attesting term were in Appalachia.

[DARE (at *grandpa* n A4) scattered, but less frequent North Atlantic, Pacific]

grandpaw (also *granpaw*) *noun* A grandfather.

1937 Hall *Coll* (Cosby TN) My granpaw came to this country from across the waters about the time of the Old War [= the Revolution]. **1960** Hall *Smoky Mt Folks* 27 One of my grandpaws was part Black Dutch and part Irish. **1969** GSMNP-37:2:6 I believe that his daddy used to live on Coopers Creek, for becaze after my brother married, my oldest one, by God, he moved up there and they called it Grandpaw's place.

[DARE (at *grandpa* n A1) chiefly South, South Midland]

grandsir (also *grancer*) *noun* An older man, especially a grandfather.

1913 Kephart *Our Sthn High* 160 Hit was thataway in my Pa's time, and in Gran'sir's, too. *Ibid.* 290–91 We will hear an aged man referred to as "old Grandsir'" So-and-So. **1924** (in **1952** Mathes *Tall Tales* 43) Didn't I fashion it with yer grandsir's cold chisel an' carve the writin' on it with my own hand? **1975** Chalmers *Better* 35 On the fire-board, thick old slab of chestnut, smooth and silver with the years, stood an old weight clock, brought into the hills long since, when grandsir' brought his young bride to be his help mate and to mother his many children. **1999** Montgomery *Coll* We went up to visit grandsir and grandma'am once a year (Cardwell). **2014** *Blind Pig* (June 12) When Pap tells stories about days gone by, he often refers to someone who was elderly when he was a boy as grandsir. But I've never heard anyone else use the term. *Ibid.* Pearl Cable, the sweet young filly from way up on Pilkey Creek, referred to the patriarch of her family as "Grancer" Pilkington. . . . That's when it dawned upon me that Pearl's Grancer was a mountain version of Grand Sir. When Pearl heard it as a youngster, she'd understandably taken it to be his given name.

grandsire *noun* A male ancestor.

1996 Spurlock *Glossary* 398 *grandsires* = male ancestors.

grandy *noun* A grandfather; an older male relative who functions as a grandfather.

1943 Justus *Bluebird* 109 Grandy, too, she saw at a glance, had honored the occasion by wearing his go-to-meeting coat and having his beard well trimmed. **1997** Montgomery *Coll* = term for an older male relation who is like a grandfather to a child (Hooper).

grandyoungon See **grandyoungun**.

grandyoungun (also *grandyoungon*) *noun* A grandchild. See also **young one**.

1940 Haun *Hawk's Done* 98 Me and Ad had brought her up with our own youngons and she never did know she was just a grandyoungon. **1979** Carpenter *Walton War* 166 I want to see that grand youngun so bad I could taste it. **1986** Lauterer *Runnin' on Rims* 170 Joe's wife Demmie sat beneath a tree with a gaggle of "grandyoung'uns."

grannies See **granny C**.

granny

A *noun* [Editor's note: The sense "grandmother" is standard.]

1 Used as a quasi-honorific to express courtesy, familiarity, or respect for an older woman in the community not necessarily related to the speaker, often prefacing the woman's name, in third-person reference. See also **aunt B**, **dad**, **old aunt**, **old uncle**, **uncle**.

1952 Justus *Children* 149 She had no kin on the mountain, but everyone called her Granny out of love and respect. **1956** Hall *Coll* (Roaring Fork TN) Granny Shields lived in above us, and Granny Perryman lived right over in sight of us. Everybody called 'em granny. **1962** Williams *Mtneers Mind Manners* 21 Patriarchs are referred to as "old uncle" and aged women are called "granny" by everyone. **1998** Montgomery *Coll* (known to Brown, Bush, Cardwell, Jones, Ledford, Oliver, Weaver).

2 (also *granny midwife*, *granny woman*) A midwife; also used as a quasi-formal title. See also **granny doctor**.

1812 (in **1956** Eliason *Tarheel Talk* 274) (Haywood Co NC) Paid Granny Judy. **1868** Carpenter *Diary* I 149 Pegey Wise a 75 dide [= died] oc[t] 15 1868 she wars granny womin for contry. **1940** Haun *Hawk's Done* 46 That was before I started being Granny-woman so much. **1959** Pearsall *Little Smoky* 130 The only major differentiation of roles is between "man" and "woman," although some may in addition be "preacher," "grannywoman" (midwife), or "conjure doctor" by virtue of possessing more of folk knowledge than their fellows. **1966** Dakin *Vocab Ohio River Valley* 433 Older speakers above the river and almost all Kentuckians except those who live in the larger cities and towns use—or at least know—the old Midland-Southern folk term *granny woman* or the simplex *granny*. The latter is usual in the Bluegrass and northern Mountains and in western Kentucky. *Granny woman* is somewhat more common in the Mountains and in the southern and eastern Pennyroyal. **1971** *Granny Women* 247 In the state today there are about 85 granny midwives who are over 65 years of age, and there are only 196 total. They used to be up in the thousands. Rabun County dwindled down to absolutely nothing several years ago as far as granny midwife deliveries go. **1975** Chalmers *Better* 52 Etta Brown is the last of these "granny-women" trained by Miss Phyllis. **1986** Pederson et al. *LAGS*: *granny* = attested by 9/60 interviewees (15%) in E TN and 7/35 (20%) in N GA; 16/77 of all LAGS interviewees (20.7%) attesting term were in Appalachia; *granny woman* = attested by 9/60 interviewees (15%) in E TN and 7/35 (20%) in N GA; 16/77 of all LAGS interviewees (20.7%) were from Appalachia. **2002** Ogle *Remembrances* 6 That's what we were told when we asked where we had come from. "The Granny Woman brought you to us."

[OED3 *granny* n 2 U.S. local; CUD *granny* 1 (at *grand* adj); DARE *granny* n 3 chiefly South, South Midland]

3 See citation.

2000 Miller *Looneyville* 48 For some reason or another many of our ladies referred to the outside toilet (John) as a granny: "It is awful cold out there in the granny tonight."

4 See citation.

1957 Broaddus *Vocab Estill Co KY* 50 *granny* = first gear [of a truck or tractor].

B *verb*

1 To serve as midwife (for), assist in the delivery of (a child), assist at childbirth; hence verbal noun *grannying*.

1942 Campbell *Cloud-Walking* 15 Mostly grannying didn't misput Sary no great sight. **1956** Hall *Coll* (Big Bend NC) The old people done the doctorin', made their own teas. My mammy Nancy Hicks and Aunt Mary grannied me. **1978** Hall *Yarns and Tales* 3 Granny-Pop, returning late at night to Big Cataloochee after delivering ("grannying") a baby in Little Cataloochee, is said to have escaped from a panther by taking off and throwing down parts of her clothing, one piece at a time, so that the panther could claw and chew each piece and thus be delayed in its pursuit. **1978** Hiser *Quare Do's* 34 The thing I remember the best that she done was granny babies. **1995** Montgomery *Coll* When someone asked where our Grandma was, Grandpa would say, "Oh, she's off a-grannying" (Norris).

[DARE *granny* v 1 chiefly South, South Midland]

2 To gather potatoes or fish with the hands. See also **grabble 1, 2.**

1981 Brewer *Wonderment* 92 What Lucinda calls "grannying" [for potatoes] is called "grabbling" in some quarters. **1995** Montgomery *Coll* = to fish with the bare hands (Cardwell).

C (also *grannies*) *interjection* Used in phrases to form mild oaths. See also **ay**.

1952 Wilson *Folk Speech NC* 547 *Grannys alive*, *Granny sakes* = mild oaths. **1961** Medford *History Haywood Co* 186 I grannies—I can dance a jig, and me over a hundred. **1998** Montgomery *Coll*: *good granny* (known to Adams); *great granny* (known to Brown, Weaver).

granny doctor *noun* A woman who renders treatment in traditional medicine, especially a midwife. See also **granny A2**.

1917 Kephart *Word-List* 412 = any obstetrician. **1971** *Kenny Runnion* 131 Sometimes if y'got sick they'd have old granny doctors 'at'ud come see y[ou]. **1976** Still *Pattern of Man* 8 She questioned, "Was I the granny doctor who fotched you?" **1994–97** Montgomery *Coll* (known to Bush, Cardwell, Hooper, Norris). **2005** Williams *Gratitude* 11 We were born at home and delivered by a granny doctor (midwife) except for the last three, who were delivered by a doctor who came to our house.

granny frolic (also *granny racket*, *granny spree*) *noun* Formerly, a noisy party of women around a new mother and the assisting **granny woman** to celebrate the arrival of the newborn child. See 1978, 1979 citations. See also **frolic A2**.

1952 Law *Some Folklore* To provide help in childbirth, each community had one or more women who acted as nurse on such occasions. They got their rating by experience. They were called Granny Women and events of childbirth were called Granny Sprees. **1961** Williams *Content Mt Speech* 14 She's the best "baby snatcher" that ever attended a "granny racket" and "a great hand to set up with the dead." **1978** Slone *Common Folks* 258 In the old days, when a child was born, they had what they called a "granny frolic." The expectant mother prepared as if for a party, all the neighbor women were asked to come. After the baby was born, someone would ring the dinner bell, so everyone would know everything was alright. Then they would cook themselves a good dinner, no men allowed, it was a day for women only. For some reason I don't understand, they always cut up the Father's hat, if he did not have it hid where they could not find it. **1979** Slone *My Heart* 73–74 The birth of a new baby was another glad time for using the bell. What a time to have a party! That was one occasion when the women took over. No men were allowed; even the father must leave home after bringing the "granny" and letting the kinfolks know. This happy time was known as a "Granny Frolic," and the expecting mother prepared for it in advance by making piles of gingerbread and fattening some frying chickens. In some homes there would be a few pints of moonshine. Every married woman friend and relative was welcome; no young girls were permitted. Anyway they were needed at home to look after the small children and men folks. After the baby was born, bathed, and powdered with powder made from dry clay taken from between the rocks in the chimney, someone would remove the ax from under the bed. (It had been put there to cut the pains.) After ringing the dinner bell to let everyone know the baby was born and both mother and baby were alright, the party began. They always cut up the father's hat, if he had not hidden it. I don't know why—maybe it was supposed to bring good luck. **2003** Williams *Coming of Age*

183 Children in the home were sent to live with grandparents or other relatives until the birthing party, referred to humorously by menfolk as the "granny racket," was over.

granny gray beard *noun* See citation. Same as **fringe bush**.

2013 *BearPaw* (Spring–Summer) 4 Known more commonly as fringetree, *Chionanthus virginicus* may at first resemble privet with its simple opposite leaves that are smooth above and finely hairy below. . . . In Appalachia smoketree or fringetree is also known as Old Man's Beard and Granny Gray Beard. Native Americans dried its roots and barks for roots in treating skin inflammations, and in the 19th century physicians used its bark for a tincture for jaundice.

granny grease *noun* A home remedy of mixed ingredients applied to the chest to break up congestion.

2007 Milnes *Signs Cures Witches* 98 A plaster is a cloth soaked with a home remedy, often granny grease, that is placed on the chest to break up congestion and colds: "Granny grease, it was lamp oil and turpentine and camphor and hog lard and you mixed it all together you see and you get it good and hot and put it on you and put a flannel on him. Get it hot and rub with it."

granny hatchet *noun* A common gray lizard (*Sceloporus undulatus*).

1911 Shearin *E KY Word-List* 538 The gray lizard, *sceloporus undulatus*. **1930** Armstrong *This Day and Time* 81 You're pore as a weasel, Ivy, pore as a granny-hatchet. **1941** Still *Troublesome Creek* 134 They's a powerful mess o' fancy foolishness they teach a chap these days, a-pouring in till they got no more jedgment than a granny hatchet. **1957** Combs *Lg Sthn High: Word List* 46 = the common species of gray lizard, or the Sceloporus undulatus.

granny hole *noun*

1 A hole in the wall of a house functioning as a small window, usually found next to the fireplace, opening toward the road, and thus allowing someone inside to observe anyone approaching. It often has a covering of leather. See 1995 citation.

1965 Grossman *Jenkins Cabin* 6 One unusual feature which we do not remember observing in any other cabin in the Smokies is the absence of openings other than the doors; even the small shuttered opening next to the chimney, known locally as the "granny hole," is missing. (The favorite spot for most grannys (grandmothers) was close to the hearth and the small shuttered opening, usually not more than a foot square, permitted her to keep in touch with outside activities without getting too far from the warmth of the fire.) **1986** Scott and Scott *Beyond Beauty* 23 The only window in the cabin is the small "granny hole," which looks out on the corn crib. **1995** Trout *Historic Buildings* 26 Some log houses had a tiny, square window situated near the chimney. These were called "granny holes" because the grandmother of the household spent a lot of her time by the hearth. She would sit on a special low chair and sew or knit as she tended the cooking in the fireplace. The window gave her a little extra light to work by and let her keep track of the comings and goings outside of the house.

2 A river basin suitable for private swimming.

1975 Mull *Old Burke* 146 Upper Creek, which ran through Uncle Charlie's farm, was a fine place for little kids to go "skinny dipping," since the water was not very deep. The big "granny hole" on the John's River was the spot for the larger boys, and it was there, when I was older, that I first learned what a "streaker" was.

grannying See **granny B1**.

granny man *noun* A man who serves as a midwife, an occupation usually reserved for women (see Norris comment). See also **granny A2**, **granny woman A2**.

1994–97 Montgomery *Coll* (known to Weaver); He was the best granny man (Cardwell), = men were not allowed in the same room (Norris).

granny midwife See **granny A2**.

granny race *noun* See citations.

1982 Slone *How We Talked* 24 = the rush of a midwife to a home to deliver a baby. **1984** Wilder *You All Spoken* 36 = the hurryment of granny women—midwives—to help in childbirthing. Southern Appalachian granny women tried to outrace the baby and the doctor, if there was one on call, and have hot water on the stove and a chicken ready for frying after the main event. **1985** Jones *Growing Up* 116 He [= a doctor] was on another granny race. **1996–97** Montgomery *Coll* (known to Brown, Bush, Ledford, Norris).

[cf SND *race* n[1] 1 "a journey at speed, the act of running"; Web3 (at *race*) Scot "the act of rushing onward"]

granny racket See **granny frolic**.

granny scrape (also *granny trouble*) *noun* The birth of a child in one's house.

1940 Bowman *KY Mt Stories* 240 *granny scrape* = child birth. **1974** Fink *Bits Mt Speech* 11 He had *granny trouble* at his house last night. **1976** Garber *Mountain-ese* 36 = childbirth. "Ma is stayin' with Miz Brown, who is havin' granny trouble." **1996–97** Montgomery *Coll*: *granny scrape* = the sudden arrival of a child (Hooper); *granny trouble* (known to Brown, Jones, Ledford).

granny spree See **granny frolic**.

granny square *noun* See citations.

1986 Lauterer *Runnin' on Rims* 188 [Granny square] = a cutting of fabric used in piecing together a coverlet. *Ibid.* She was piecing together another Afghan coverlet for some lucky grandchild. The woolen blanket of highly colored "granny-squares" was for yet another generation.

granny trouble See **granny scrape**.

granny widow See **grass widow 1**.

granny witch See **herb granny B**.

granny woman

A *noun*

1 See **granny A2**.

2 A grandmother. See also **granny A1**.

1943 Hannum *Mt People* 142 There were the hoe handles to make, cutting each one to the proper size of each member of the family—for everyone took a row, from the "granny woman" down to the littlest "set-along child." **1975** Purkey *Madison Co* 55 Nice girls didn't smoke, but some of the old granny women did. That was a privilege granted very old women.

B *interjection* Used as an oath to express irritation.

1949 Arnow *Hunter's Horn* 54 He grabbed Ernest and scratched the match on his belt buckle, and it went out as he struck it. "That's bad luck," Ernest whispered, staring down at the glowing but flameless match. "Granny woman," Nunn said, and struck another match, and lighted his lamp and Ernest's.

granpaw See **grandpaw**.

grapevine telephone *noun* See citation.

1950 Stuart *Hie Hunters* 93 "All I haf to do is put the words yer pappy said about us on the grapevine telephone," Peg said, shaking his head and blowing a cloud of smoke. "It won't take long fer the news to git around."

graphone See **graf-phone**.

grass *noun* Early springtime (especially in phrase *come grass*).

1913 Kephart *Our Sthn High* 78 You remember the big storm three year ago, come grass, when the cattle all huddled up a-top o' each other and friz in one pile, solid. **1931** Combs *Lg Sthn High* 1305 I aim to foal that mare, come grass (in the spring).

grass, go to See **go to grass**.

grass bald (also *grassy bald*) *noun* A large, open, flat, meadow-like area at a high elevation, often above 5,000 feet in the Smoky Mountains. See 1979, 1988 citations. Same as **huckleberry bald**, **sods**. See also **bald B**, **heath bald**, **shrub bald**.

1960 Stupka *Great Smoky Mts* 18 There are treeless areas on some of the higher mountaintops and ridges. Owing to their lack of forest cover, such places are called balds. That designation, however, is a relative one since other plants form a dense carpet over the balds. If these plants are largely shrubs belonging to the heath family, such balds are known as heath balds; if grasses and sedges prevail, the balds are termed grass balds. **1962** Brewer *Hiking* 20 Gregory is classified as a grass bald because grass is its predominant cover. **1979** *Smoky Vistas* (Summer) 1 The Smokies is also famous for its treeless grassy balds. These open mountain meadows were used extensively for sheep and cattle grazing by the early settlers. Some of these are thought to have been cleared specifically for grazing. Released from disturbance in the 1930's, oaks, serviceberry and other woody species are fast invading the areas of mountain oat grass, and the grassy balds may disappear entirely in another 50 to 75 years. **1988** Dyer *Farmstead Yards* 15 In Appalachia, hogs, cattle, and sheep often grazed during summer months on "grassy balds" that occur on high mountainsides. Desirable features of "bald" grazing were generally high-elevation level lands, easy to maintain, covered with self-perpetuating native grasses, and far enough from croplands to eliminate competition among plants and animals. **1988** Houk *Exploring Smokies* 73 Grass balds, now predominantly mountain oat grass, appear to be closing in with trees. About twenty grass balds have been identified in Great Smoky Mountains National Park, at an average elevation of 5,100 feet. Some biologists predict that if natural succession continues, all will be gone in thirty to seventy years. **1991** Walker *Great Smoky* 32 The Great Smoky Mountains National Park has two different types of balds, grassy balds and heath balds. The grassy variety is predominantly grass-covered, while the heath balds, or laurel slicks as they are sometimes called, appear to be grassy from a distance but upon closer contact it is apparent that it is an extremely dense thicket of shrub. **2006** *Encycl Appalachia* 47 There are three main kinds of balds: grass or grassy balds, shrub balds, and heath balds. Grassy balds host diverse communities dominated by grasses, particularly mountain oat grass (*Danthonia compressa*), wildflowers, and other herbaceous plants. Shrubs such as blueberries and azaleas can also be prominent. Grassy balds tend to occur on broad upper slopes and summits.

grasshopper *noun* A type of **single plow**.

1986 Pederson et al. LAGS (Rhea Co TN) = plows with iron feet.

grass relation *noun* A person related to another through divorce and remarriage. See also **sod relation**.

1942 Robertson *Red Hills* 51–52 Our stepmother and our step-step-grandmother were sod relations of ours—not grass relations. We do not believe in divorce in South Carolina; it is against the law in South Carolina to seek divorce, so even until now we have never had a grass widower among our kinfolks—we have had men who have been left by their wives, but we do not count that.

grass sack *noun* Same as **tow sack**.

1966 Dakin *Vocab Ohio River Valley* 137 West of the *coffee sack* region of eastern Kentucky, but appearing side by side with this name in the southern Mountains and the southern and western Knobs and Bluegrass margins, are two terms common in the East. These are *grass sack* (never *sea-grass sack* in the Ohio Valley)—common around Chesapeake Bay and along the coast from Delaware to northern North Carolina—and *tow sack*—the North Carolina name. **1967** Wilson *Folkways Mammoth Cave* 29 = the big, coarsely-woven bag in which such things as fertilizer were shipped. **1989** *Matewan OHP-39* He had a grass sack on his back, and he had something in it, a-carrying it. **1997** *Dante OHP-53* I would draw powder for my dad and put it in a little grass sack.

[DARE *grass sack* n chiefly central Atlantic, Lower Mississippi Valley, Ohio Valley]

grass widow *noun*

1 (also *graft widow*, *granny widow*) A woman separated from her husband, by divorce or otherwise.

1927 Woofter *Dialect from WV* 356 *grass widow* = a woman, not divorced, who does not live with her husband. "There are three grass widows in this neighborhood." **1957** Broaddus *Vocab Estill Co KY* 36 *granny widow* = a woman whose husband has run off. **1967** *DARE Survey* (Brasstown NC, Maryville TN) *graft widow* = divorced woman. **1975** Gainer *Speech Mtneer* 10–11 = a woman separated from her husband but not divorced. "They tell me that young woman who has just come to town is a grass widow." **1977** Shackelford et al. *Our Appalachia* 84 Mother was very much opposed to divorce and we never had many divorced people in this country. Mother called them "grass widows." A grass widow seemed to be some kind of a mild stigma. **1978** Reese *Speech NE Tenn* 44 *grass widow* = a woman whose husband has left her. **1991** Still *Wolfpen Notebooks* 66 He's a grass widow. He's got a living ex-wife. If I married a widow-man, I'd want his other woman to be dead. **1994** Montgomery Coll: *grass widow* = general sense is that the husband is still alive, in contrast to other widows (Cardwell).

2 See citation.

c1982 Young *Colloquial Appal* 11 = widow looking for a husband.

grass widower (also *grass widow man*) *noun* A man living apart from his wife, by divorce or otherwise.

1930 Armstrong *This Day and Time* 155 I'm a widdy man, a grass-widdy man. **1942** Robertson *Red Hills* 51–52 It is against the law in South Carolina to seek divorce, so even until now we have never had a grass widower among our kinfolks.

grass widow man See **grass widower**.

grassy bald See **grass bald**.

grave *verb* To bury (someone).

1934 Simms Coll We just graved the old woman Sunday.

gravedigger's stew *noun* See citation.

2006 *Encycl Appalachia* 922 It was an Appalachian tradition for the families of the newly deceased to be comforted with platters of fried chicken, while gravediggers were fed gravedigger's stew made of boiled chicken and homegrown vegetables.

grave house (also *grave shed, grave shelter*) *noun* In the nineteenth and early twentieth centuries, a small shelter built over a grave, usually roofed to retard the elements and often enclosed to deter the body being disturbed by animals.

1923 Furman *Mothering* 113 Beneath spreading trees, were a dozen or more diminutive houses, with latticed sides and roofs of riven oak boards. Some were crumbling into decay, some new and substantial. The one to which Nucky led me was still yellow. "Here's where Maw lays," he said, almost in a whisper (I judge that one reason he finds it so hard to speak of her is his feeling that he, or rather, her desire for his education, was in a way the cause of her death), and I knew that this must be the family burying-ground, and these the grave-houses once so necessary for the protection of the dead from wild beasts, and still surviving here in the customs of the mountain country. *Ibid.* 153 We joined the crowd among the grave-houses. In front of the newest of these, saplings had been laid across logs to make seats; and the people who could not be accommodated here sat on the ground or walked quietly about. Even the numerous babies were quiet, as if knowing that a funeral occasion demanded it. **1942** Clark *Kentucky* 196 In earlier days when the body of a loved one . . . was consigned to the earthly bosom of the hill country, a grave house was erected over the mound. These little houses protected the grave from both the elements and that fiendish ghoul, the "grave robber." **1942** Thomas *Blue Ridge* 156 The grave house was a crude structure of rough planks supported by four short posts, erected at the time of the burial to shelter the dead from rain and snow and scorching wind. **1979** Slone *My Heart* 58 When my mother was buried there was a small house built to cover the grave. These are now a forgotten part of the past. The lower part of the house was latticework and the roofs were made of rough board shingles. The tombstone was of slate rock with the name and dates crudely chipped in with handmade tools. These houses protected the graves from the wild animals, and kept the rain from falling on a loved one's grave. **1984** Martin *Hollybush* 66 Ad and Tenia's graves are covered with a gravehouse, a once popular structure in [E KY] but rare today. Built ostensibly to keep weather off the graves, its other use was to prevent "graverobbers," small and mysterious animals believed to dig down through the freshly turned dirt, from feeding on the deceased. **1993** Montell *Cumberland Country* 117 Stone grave coverings include the rectangular "box grave," resembling an above-ground vault. Grave houses of this variety are often termed "peaked raves," "slab graves," "sandstone graves," "cattle rocks," "hog troughs," and "comb graves." Although they are sparsely located in certain parts of Alabama, Arkansas, and Texas, these traditional prismatic grave structures more than any other single cultural feature lend uniqueness to the folk cemeteries in the Upper Cumberland Valley. **2003** Jordan-Byshkov *Upland South* 76–78 The "graveshed" [is] a small, low, roofed structure with its sides either open or enclosed by pickets, lattices, boards, or wire. . . . Some of the oldest specimens are built of notched-log construction, with wide, open chinks between. . . . Clearly, it seems to me, the graveshed came to upland southern culture from the Indians by way of mixed-bloods, a diffusion paralleling that of the camp meeting grounds. Tennessee seems to have been the arena of cultural exchange. **2005** Ball *Gravehouse Origins* 26–27 Gravehouses represent neither more nor less than yet one additional variation on well-established and widespread functional themes—covering and protecting a grave—which originated in the British Isles and increasingly took root in the southeastern United States generally and Upper South specifically beginning about 1800. The inspiration for their construction appears to have been derived from stone-table and box-tomb coverings which gained a degree of popularity in England and Scotland in the eighteenth century and were subsequently introduced to America at least as early as 1765. The all-important perceived functions of the British prototype were rapidly modified into a wide array of regional expressions variously crafted in wood, brick and/or stone and reflective of taste, whim, cost, expediency, and the availability of preferred material(s). **2010** Jabbour and Jabbour *Decoration Day* 72 We found two regional examples of graveshelters, also known as gravehouses or grave sheds, which are shed-like rectangular structures with gabled roofs over the graves. Both are in the vicinity of Bryson City in Swain County. The example in Watkins Cemetery has a roof resting on five posts (four plus a reinforcing post) three to four feet above the ground and extending over the entire gravesite. It is open on all four sides, and the wood is painted red. . . . The example in Jenkins Cemetery, just off U.S. 19, west of town, has a more vertical design like a conventional shed, with lattice work on two of the four sides and the other two sides open. It is much taller than the Watkins Cemetery example and resembles more closely many graveshelters in other regions of the Upland South. . . . Within the graveshelters are the graves themselves with the customary headstones, footstones, and decorations. Graveshelters were once more common throughout the region, according to local historian William Crawford, and others told us of graveshelters, now vanished, that once graced various cemeteries . . . some existing grave borders may once have served as foundations or baseboards supporting graveshelters.

gravel

A *noun*

1 Construed as a count noun; hence plural form *gravels.*

1845 (in **1974** Harris *High Times* 52) Well, it is now sixteen days since that fite, and last nite Jule picked gravels out of my knees as big as squirell shot. **1939** Hall *Coll* (Cosby TN) These gravels are hard on your feet. **1940** Haun *Hawk's Done* 8 [The dogwood] sheds off its leaves in the fall and puts on little red seeds, round and hard as gravels. **1963** Edwards *Gravel* 22 We had been shooting gravels at fence posts with Wes's new sling shot which his pa had made for him. **1966** Dakin *Vocab Ohio River Valley* 216 Scattered speakers in Illinois [and Indiana] say a *pebble,* a term which seems to be the equivalent of a *gravel* used by scattered older informants in eastern Kentucky. **1969** Roberts *Greasybeard* 129 Jack took his pockets full of gravels and clumb up in the tree where they was eating. **1975** Woolley *We Be Here* 84 Don't drag them over all this highway and all these gravels. **1985** Irwin *Alex Stewart* 54 Take a small forked stick and tie a piece of leather to each end of the fork and you could shoot a gravel a long way. **1987** Perdue *Outwitting Devil* 44 The girl tol' him to git down off 'is hoss an' git a gravel an' put in her mule's year. **1998** *Dante OHP-24* He come up a-kicking them gravels, and I said "Hey, what are you doing, Abraham?" **2014** Graves *Basin Ghosts* 7 No one passed / But the mail, his blue jeep / kicking up gravels in the road.

[DARE *gravel* n especially South Midland]

2 A gallstone or kidney stone; the discomfort caused by a stone.

1967 Jones *Peculiarities Mtneers* 68 Tea made of sunflower seed, prickly pear and green coffee was rated as a cure for gravel. **1990** Cavender *Folk Medical Lex* 24 = gall or kidney stones. **1994** Montgomery *Coll* (known to Ogle, Shields). **2007** Myers *Smoky Mt Remedies* 10 *gravels* = gallstones.

3 See citation.

1982 Slone *How We Talked* 102 = cystetis, acute infection in the bladder or neck of the bladder. Cure: tea made from the "he plantain weed"; also, spignet plant, steeped (put in cup and covered with hot water). Pour off the water and drink.

B *verb*

1 See **grabble.**

2 See 1974 citation.

1974 Fink *Bits Mt Speech* 11 = annoy or embarrass. "That story always *gravelled* him." **1996–97** Montgomery *Coll* (known to Brown, Cardwell, Ledford, Norris).

[DARE *gravel* v chiefly South, South Midland]

gravelweed *noun* The trailing arbutus (*Epigaea repens*). Also called **Easter flower 2.**

1943 Stupka *Through the Year* 274 On making my way back to the valley, the unexpected discovery of the first trailing arbutus flowers of the year brought ample reward. For me these white and pinkish waxy blooms, as delightful in their fragrance as they are humble in their growth ("gravelweed," the mountain people call the plant), always serve to mark a significant period in the chronicle of the year.

grave robber *noun* A hypothetical animal thought to burrow into graves; preventing this was one motivation for building a **grave house.**

1982 Slone *How We Talked* 44 The "grave robber" was an animal that was feared because it was supposed to have dug into newly-dug graves and eat the bodies. I have not been able to prove nor disprove if there was such an animal. It was described to be the size of a fox, only larger around, black or dark brown, short legs, long pointed nose, long sharp teeth (could have been a wolverine). Our folks built small houses over their graves to protect them from these "grave robbers." They believed in them, feared and hated them even if they were true or mythical.

grave rock *noun* A gravestone. See also **tomb rock.**

1901 Harben *Westerfelt* 279 I'm goin' back to put a grave-rock over Jasper's remains. **1937** Hall *Coll* (Gatlinburg TN) = grave stone, memorial stone. **1960** Hall *Smoky Mt Folks* 35 A few "grave-rocks" lay round about, but they could not be distinguished from ordinary stones of the field.

[DARE *grave rock* n chiefly Appalachians]

grave shed, grave shelter See **grave house.**

grave vine (also *graveyard grass*) *noun* The common periwinkle (*Vinca minor*). Same as **cemetery vine.**

1930 Armstrong *This Day and Time* 71 I 'ud sooner be dead, 'way yonder, the grave-vine a-growin' on my grave. **1982** Stupka *Wildflowers* 89 Europe is the homeland of this hardy little evergreen vine that persists for decades around old homesites, gardens, and cemeteries. The latter habitat has given it another local name, "graveyard grass." **2003** Strutin *Hikes of Smokies* 113 The slope from campsite up to the knoll is covered with vinca, commonly called periwinkle. This non-native plant is sometimes called "graveyard grass," because it is planted as a decorative evergreen ground-cover in cemeteries.

graveyard cough *noun* See 1952 citation.

1952 Wilson *Folk Speech NC* 547 = a cough indicative of death; a tuberculous cough. **1969** Doran *Folklore White Co* 112 = cough caused by tuberculosis. **2002** Myers *Best Yet Stories* 78 = a tubercular cough.

graveyard dust *noun* See citation.

1980 Riggleman *WV Mtneer* 126–27 [Loggers] usually had nicknames for everybody and everything around the camp.... Snuff was "lung powder" or "graveyard dust."

graveyard grass See **grave vine.**

graveyard lily *noun* Same as **bear grass.**

1999 Montgomery *Coll* (known to Cardwell).

graveyard meeting *noun* Same as **memorial.**

1946 Stuart *Plum Grove Hills* 154 A memorial service for the dead ... is held at the graveside some time after the burial, sometimes several years later; in some instances the same person has been funeralized repeatedly. In some communities these services are called "Graveyard Meetings." The difficulty of getting a minister into the hills in bad weather surely accounted for many of these delayed funerals. "We wondered what Jason would think of the funeralizing, since he wasn't a Mountain Baptist."

gravy leg *noun* See citation.

1988 Dyer *Farmstead Yards* 25 In a recent interview, Inez Adams recalled the folk names of her mother's favorite wild greens (which, presumably, fall into Shields' "field cresses" category): "crowsfoot," "freckleface," "gravy leg," and "narrow dock."

grayback *noun*

1 A type of smooth, gray boulder often found in stream beds and on hillsides. See 1960, 1996 citations. Also called **mossback 1.**

1927 Mason *Lure of Smokies* 8 Giant "graybacks"—graywacke?—clutter up the ravines and block the mountain-sides where erosion and freezing and lightning have chipped them from the great blocks above. **1937** Thornburgh *Great Smoky Mts* 43 There is always the excitement of hopping the rocks, which the mountain people affectionately have named "greybacks" or "moss backs," according to their nature. **1950** King and Stupka *Geology and Natural History* 32 The great boulders, or "graybacks," are strewn over the mountainsides and choke each rushing torrent. **1960** Stupka *Great Smoky Mts* 5 The cold climate of that time left its mark upon the landscape in this area. The huge boulders, or "graybacks," lying on the slopes and in the valleys, were moved there by forces that are no longer evident. It appears that these rocks were broken off and removed from the mountaintops by frost action and they gradually accumulated as boulder fields on the slopes and in the valleys below. **1970** Broome *Earth Man* 7 Now we found it expedient and desirable to bend forward and use our hands to swing across some gap or to pull up over some smooth-surface "gray-back," as these monstrous, gray, rounded boulders are familiarly known to the mountain people. **1979** Cantu *Great Smoky Mts* 7 The boulders (called "graybacks" locally) are still continuing their imperceptible march down the mountainside, as they have with each succession of freezing and thawing since the first intense glaciation periods pushed them away from their faulted bedrock on a higher ridge. **1996** Linn *West Fork* 3 The huge boulders in the river and along its banks in the park area are classified by geologists as graywhake rocks. The colloquial term is "graybacks." The graywhake boulders are a conglomerate rock of sandstone, gneiss, feldspar, and perhaps others.

[DARE *grayback* n 5 east TN, western NC]

2 A body louse.

1864 *Brown CW Letters* (Jan 20) we did not fetch but one soot of close with us and the gray backs like to eat us up be fore we cold git to wash. **1955** Dykeman *French Broad* 111–12 His cavalry moved first, followed by the infantry still able to make jokes about "the graybacks," as they called the ever-present lice. **1964** Clarkson *Lumbering in WV* 363 *greybacks* = lice. **1980** Riggleman *WV Mtneer* 126–27 [Loggers] usually had nicknames for everybody and everything around the camp.... Lice were called "graybacks" or "sawdust with legs."

3 A Confederate soldier.

1864 *Chapman CW Letters* (March 6) one time more I Can worke with some plesure now the gray backs is goan. **1864** *Forgotten Ancestors* (Jefferson Co TN) 1 we are out on picket today awaiting for the old gray backs.

gray cloud *noun* Whiskey produced in a **pot still** made of galvanized steel, which sometimes corrodes, tainting and imparting a cloudy hue to the liquor and making it dangerous to drink. See also **galvanize, silver cloud.**

1956 Hall *Coll* (Roostertown TN) Give me some gray cloud. **1960** Hall *Smoky Mt Folks* 65 "Popskull" is the name for low-grade moonshine, a term now being replaced by . . . "gray cloud" . . . with reference to the "galvanize" (zinc) corroded from the steel still by the acid of the mash.

gray dark *noun* Same as **dusk dark.** See also **black dark.**

1955 Ritchie *Singing Family* 131 I reckon it was plum gray dark when we stacked up our hoes at the top and let out our yell.

graying *noun* See citation.

c1982 Young *Colloquial Appal* 11 = almost dawn.

graze *verb* See citation.

1961 Williams *R in Mt Speech* 6 In a few words *r* is substituted for *l* . . . glaze (graze, meaning to scrape).

grease *verb*

A Variant past-tense/past-participle form *grez.*

1923 Greer-Petrie *Angeline Doin' Society* 24 I told them I'd been a-givin' [the chickens] blue stone and puttin' coal ile in their drinkin' water and grez 'em good. **1952** Wilson *Folk Speech NC* 548 Grez [grɛz]: vb. Past tense and past participle of grease. **1960** Sutherland *Folk Speech* 13 *grez* = greased.

B To smear rendered animal grease over the skin of a child, as a purported medicinal treatment.

1964 Smith et al. *Germans of Valley* 139–40 Few were the individuals who reached maturity without having been greased from head to toe on several occasions. . . . A neighbor said, "We greased our children regular. We melted hog grease for them. . . . We greased them all over, even the bottom of the feet." Greasing the bottom of the feet was usually associated with fever. It was believed that the grease would draw the fever down.

grease-bitch lamp See **grease lamp**.

grease lamp (also *grease-bitch lamp, grease light*) *noun* See 1957, c1960 citations. Same as **slut**. See also **tallow dip**.

1937 Hyatt *Kiverlid* 76 They stink a sight wuss than a grease-bitch lamp or a taller slut. **1957** Broaddus *Vocab Estill Co KY* 36 *grease lamp* = a lamp made by putting a rag in a saucer of grease. **c1960** Wilson *Coll*: *grease lamp* = a primitive lamp with lard as fuel. Now only a memory among very old people. **1972** *AOHP/ALC-388* Sometimes they'd make a grease light, they would put a little grease in a little saucer or a little dish, what they call lard now, and then they'd cut a rag and lay it in there and light that rag and burn something like a candle. **c1975** *Miners' Jargon* 4 *grease light* = obsolete miner's light which used vegetable or animal oil.

grease light See **grease lamp**.

grease monkey *noun* See citation.

2006 Farwell *Logging Term* 1021 "Swampers" built [logging] roads maintained by "chickadees" and "grease monkeys," who kept them slick.

greasy

A *noun* See **greasy-back bean**.

B *adjective* Slick, slippery. See also **greasy door**.

1975 Broome *Out under Smokies* 100 The trail was "greasy" from the rain, where its surface had been planed and reworked two years ago.

greasy-back bean (also *greasy, greasy bean*) *noun* A green bean a large, crescent-shaped pod. Also called **creaseback**.

1984 Page and Wigginton *Foxfire Cookery* 148–49 The beans ain't near as good as they used to be. We had what we called greasy-back beans—I've not seen any of them in years. They were little white beans in a white pole bean. You can eat the greasy-back bean either green or dried. **1996** Houk *Foods & Recipes* 47 Smoky Mountain horticulture includes a lengthy litany of legumes—creaseback, cutshort, cornfield beans, bunch beans, pink or peanut beans, greasy beans, sulfur beans, and half runners. **1997** Montgomery *Coll*: *greasy back bean* (known to Andrews). **2006** *Encycl Appalachia* 421 Heirloom beans are described in terms of three general characteristics. Cut-shorts are beans packed so tightly in the hulls that the ends are squared off; that is, they cannot grow to full length inside the hull and are "cut short." Greasies do not have the fuzzy skins common to other beans but are shiny, or greasy, in appearance. One of the "three sisters" recognized by Native Americans, cornfield beans are climbing beans traditionally grown in corn along with pumpkins or squash, a technique that raises efficiency by fostering a symbiotic relationship among the plants. Beans can be any combination of these three types. For example, a particular bean might be described as a speckled long greasy cut-short cornfield bean. **2007** Farr *My Appalachia* 70 My mother . . . grew "greasy-back" beans, which we loved. They grew. six or more beans to a pod. Mama kept her own seed from year to year from the tender plants and never took a chance on store-bought seed. **2011** Best *Bean Terminology*: *greasy bean* = a name given to many heirloom bean varieties when the pods are slick and without the tight-knit fuzz of other beans. The slickness makes them appear to be greasy. . . . Most greasy bean varieties are found in Western North Carolina and Eastern Kentucky, but are spreading rapidly to other areas through farmers' markets and heirloom seed outlets.

greasy bean See **greasy-back bean**.

greasy door *noun* See citation.

1972 Cooper *NC Mt Folklore* 92 = doors [sic] of a family who have recently slaughtered hogs.

great *adverb* Very (especially in phrase *great long*). See also **great big old**.

1861 *Martin CW Letters* (Oct 6) my hair has growed out A gain and I have got A grat long thick set of whiscers. **1953** Hall *Coll* (Bryson City NC) So he set there and told a great long story about what he done trapping and how many bears he killed in one season. **1969** Hall *Coll* (Townsend TN) [The bear traps of the dead-fall type] was great wide, you know, had a hall door runnin' up to it, had a pen runnin' right through the back of it. **1973** GSMNP-82: 19 Doctor Saults, he had great long white whiskers come down to here. **1984** Page and Wigginton *Foxfire Cookery* 174 Cochan . . . has a forked leaf, and it's always great long. **1991** Thomas *Sthn Appal* 127 It'uz a great high fork, t' lay somethin' in, t' carry water. A spout. **1993** Page and Smith *Foxfire Toys and Games* 138 We'd get great, great old wide planks for paddles, and we'd get a sluice of water about as big as your arm and put a pipe in the branch out there. **2005** Bailey *Henderson County* 54 He had great long white horns that come out to the sides an' then turned back.

[DARE *great long* adj phr chiefly South Midland]

great big old *adjective phrase* Large (with *old* adding little other than perhaps a slight dramatic effect and a tone varying from familiarity to uncommonness to nostalgia). See also **big old**, **great**, **little old**.

1939 Hall *Coll* (Jefferson City TN) Poke sallet is made with poke weed. Poke weed has great big old heavy red-looking stalks. It grows by a new road or a new ground. **1973** GSMNP-70:2 Fill up a great big old straw mattress. **1973** GSMNP-84:21 These great big old horses, you know, do the logging. **1984** Page and Wigginton *Foxfire Cookery* 7 Then we had a great big old fry pan with a big long handle, and that's what she fried her meat in. **1989** *Matewan OHP*-22 My daddy had one these great big old cross-cut saws.

great day in the morning *interjection* Used as a mild oath to express disbelief or pleased surprise. See 1998 citation.

1926 Montague *Big Music* 425 "Great Day in the Morning!" Jimmy busts out, his eyes dancing, and him dancing with 'em. **1966** *DARE Survey* (Cherokee NC). **1972** Cooper *NC Mt Folklore* 91 Great day in the morning! **1998** Montgomery *Coll* according to consultants from the Smoky Mountains, the phrase expresses mainly pleased surprise, but sometimes exasperation or anger.

[in reference to Judgment Day; DARE *great day (in the morning)* exclam widespread, but chiefly South, Midland]

greater most (also *greater part*) *adjective phrase* Most, the majority. See also **bigger part** (at **big A5**).

1940 Oakley *Roamin'/Restin'* 102 I thot in the night I could feal somthing trying to climb up the tree where I was so I shot the grater most of my shells away. **1974–75** McCracken *Logging* 21:14 The greater part of that was logged from the start.

greater part See **greater most.**

great long See **great.**

great rhododendron *noun* Same as **rosebay rhododendron.**

2006 *WV Encycl* 616 The rhododendron maximum, more commonly called great rhododendron or big laurel, was designated the official state flower of West Virginia, January 29, 1903, after being recommended by the governor and voted on by students in the public schools.

Great Smoky *noun* The main chain or ridge of the Great Smoky Mountains, a single uninterrupted crest that runs the 54-mile length of Great Smoky Mountains National Park along the TN/NC state boundary. Same as **(the) Smoky.** See also **Big Smokies.**

1860 *Week in Smokies* 120 Who would have expected to find Harper at the foot of the Great Smoky?

great to *adjective phrase* Having a strong propensity or capacity to. See also **awful to, bad to, good to, poor to.**

1975 GSMNP-59:35 Kep and him, they was great to play set-back.

Great War *noun* The American Civil War. Same as **War between the States.**

1995 Adams *Come Go Home* 24 During the Great War, as it's called over home, there was a Rebel soldier who got set upon by some Yankees and was killed way back up in the Gudger Tract. **1997** Montgomery *Coll* (known to Brown).

great zonies *interjection* Used as a mild oath. See also **zonies alive.**

2000 Montgomery *Coll* Great zonies, you don't mean it! (Cardwell).

gredge *noun* A grudge.

1904–20 Kephart *Notebooks* 4:853 They had a gredge atwixt them.

greedy guts *noun* A glutton; a miser.

1996–97 Montgomery *Coll* = glutton (known to Adams, Brown, Cardwell, Jones, Norris, Oliver). **2007** McMillon *Notes* = glutton or miser.

[DARE *greedygut(s)* n 2 "a miser" especially South Midland]

green (also *green out*) *verb, verb phrase* To swindle, dupe (someone).

1904–20 Kephart *Notebooks* 2:459 I got a good one on him—greened him out bodaciously. **1913** Kephart *Our Sthn High* 294 To green out or sap is to outwit in trade. **1931** Combs *Lg Sthn High* 1305 Buck greened-out (outwitted) that Ashley feller in the trade. **1952** Wilson *Folk Speech NC* 547–48 = to outwit, make a fool of. "The merchants used to *green out* their customers quite a bit." **1957** Combs *Lg Sthn High: Word List* 46 = to out-trade, out-swap, swindle; to get the better of a bargain. Ex.: "Nord swapped him a grass-gutted calf fer a fat shote; he shore did green him out in that trade." **1996** Montgomery *Coll* (known to Brown, but not to other consultants from the Smoky Mountains).

[DARE *green, green out* (at *green* v 2) southern Appalachians]

green-apple high step (also *green apple trots*) See citations.

c1982 Young *Colloquial Appal* 10 = dysentery. **1985** Wiseman *Autobiography* 38 Sometimes we ate them too early and got the "green apple trots" as the result of our impatience.

green chain *noun* See citations.

1994 Schmidt and Hooks *Whistle* 21 Logs were hauled up the "green chain" from the pond, skinned, blocked in the saw carriage and passed back and forth through continuously running blades until the log was gone. *Ibid.* 157 = the mechanical conveyor system which raises logs from a log pond to the cutting floor of the mill.

green corn *noun* See citation.

2003 Strutin *Hikes of Smokies* 157 One of [Woody's] renters ran the mill, and it became known as a moonshine mill. Moonshine mash is made from sprouted corn, called "green corn." Most millers avoided grinding green corn because revenuers could easily spot its remnants on the mill stones. During Prohibition, a moonshiner could make a decent amount of money in the Smokies' cash-poor economy, so hidden mills dotted the slopes. Green-corn millers, too, made more money from the moonshine business than from grinding an equal load of cribbed corn.

green frog *noun* A dollar bill. Same as **toadhide.**

1997 Montgomery *Coll* (known to Cardwell).

green gold *noun* Ginseng.

2007 Joslin *Sang Season* 58 Many mountain men and women have followed the paths blazed by Boone and later by David Crockett in scouring the woods for "green gold."

green hat *noun* See citation.

c1975 *Miners' Jargon* 4 (or *orange hat*) = a newly hired [coal] miner.

greenie *noun* See citation.

1943 Korson *Coal Dust* 5 Full-time miners naturally resented them [= farmer-miners] and expressed their distrust by calling them "winter diggers," "wheats," "corncrackers," "hay johns," "pumpkin rollers," "clodhoppers," "greenies."

green liquor *noun* See citation.

1984 High *Titan Rock* 50 That green liquor—if people didn't know or didn't care what they was doing and used a bad rig—if that moonshine had a greenish cast, then you'd better not drink it.

green medicine *noun* Medicinal herbs collectively.

1982 *Smokies Heritage* 122 An abundance of medicinal herbs, often known as "green medicine," was found in the Smokies: some were worthless, but others contained drugs still used today by the medical profession. **1997** Montgomery *Coll* (known to Brown, Bush, Cardwell).

green molasses *noun* See citations.

1978 *Smokies Heritage* 315 Foamy skim [of boiling molasses] rises to the top and is quickly removed; otherwise, the molasses would be dark and bitter, a condition known as "green molasses." **1997** Montgomery *Coll* (known to Adams, Brown, Bush, Cardwell, Norris, Weaver), = molasses which have not been properly skimmed during the process of evaporation, as a result of which they are slightly green in color and taste bitter (Ledford).

green out See **green**.

green up (also *green-up time*) *noun* Springtime.

1976 Dwyer *Southern Sayin's* 23 *green up* = springtime. "It's comin' green up." **c1982** Young *Colloquial Appal* 11 *green up* = spring time. **1991** Haynes *Haywood Home* 56 Springtime, just at green-up time, was the time for making popguns and willow whistles.... It's the time when buds come on the willows and elders along the branches and creeks and their bark gets loose. **2017** *Blind Pig* (April 27) Every Spring I wish that I could put my finger on the exact moment green up magically occurs. I know it's not an instantaneous thing. Instead it happens in small increments until finally it arrives.

green up time See **green up**.

greist See **grist A**.

grew See **grow A2**.

grewed See **grow A1**.

grez See **grease**.

grice See **grist**.

griddle cake *noun* See 1976 citation.

1857 (in **1956** Eliason *Tarheel Talk* 275) (Haywood Co NC) At breakfast . . . your little Brothers snatch up all the Griddle Cakes they can reach. **1934–47** *LAMSAS Appal* = attested by 5/148 speakers (3.3%) from WV and 2/14 (14.3%) from SC. **1976** Ledford *Folk Vocabulary* 283 Griddle cakes were sometimes called corn dodger, and that term was frequently applied to corn bread baked in pones.

grind *verb* Variant past-tense forms *grinded, grined, grounded*.

1971 *AOHP/ALC-33* He had a big thrashing mill, and then he had one that grinded, and then he would grind it and make our flour bread. **2005** Williams *Gratitude* 499 = usually said as grined up, grinded up, or grounded up.

grinder *noun* Same as **cane mill**.

1957 Justus *Other Side* 52 A little way off they saw the cane mill, or, as some folks called it, the grinder, where the stalks of cane had been pressed dry to get the juice for boiling.

grinding horse *noun* A small stand on which a grindstone is mounted for use.

1957 Parris *My Mts* 14 The grindstone peddlar simply sold the stone and let the farmer make his own "grinding horse." **1995–97** Montgomery *Coll* (known to Adams, Brown, Cardwell, Ledford).

grinding rock (also *grind rock*) *noun* A large, oval stone for sharpening knives and other implements.

1895 Edson and Fairchild *TN Mts* 374 *grind rock* = grind-stone. **1913** Kephart *Our Sthn High* 297 He sharpens tools on a grindin'-rock or whet-rock. **1934–47** *LAMSAS Appal* (Swain Co NC) *grind rock*. **c1960** Wilson *Coll*: *grindrock* was formerly more common than *grindstone*. Also called *grinding rock*. **1974** Fink *Bits Mt Speech* 11 He sharpened his axe on the *grinding rock*. **1989** Still *Rusties and Riddles* [56] *grindrock* = a circular flint stone with projecting edges for grinding corn and wheat. **1994** Montgomery *Coll*: *grind rock* (known to Cardwell, Shields).

[DARE *grind rock* n chiefly South, South Midland]

grind rock See **grinding rock**.

grine See **groin**.

grine pone *noun* See citation. See also **pone A2**.

2013 Reed *Medical Notes* = lump on the groin.

grines See **groin**.

grippe *noun* See citations.

1971 *AOHP/ALC-193* When they got a bad, read bad cold, they'd call that grippe. **2006** Cavender *Medical Term* 1022 Health-care providers in contemporary Appalachia may still encounter antiquated medical terminology such as . . . *grippe* "flu."

grist *noun*

A Variant forms *greist, grice, gryste* (all with the diphthong [graɪst]).

1859 Taliaferro *Fisher's River* 141 He and I used to bake "johnny-cakes" to keep from starving while it was grinding my "grice." **1913** Kephart *Our Sthn High* 133 Red grains of corn being harder than white ones, it is a humorous saying in the mountains that "a red grain in the gryste will stop the mill." **1956** McAtee *Some Dial NC* 20 *greist*. **2007** Ball *Tub Mills* 21 He and I used to bake "johnny-cakes" to keep from starving while it was grinding my "grice."

B A load (especially of corn) taken to mill at one time. See also **armload, turn B2**.

1847 (in **1870** Drake *Pioneer Life KY* 59) My father never owned a hand-mill, but on those of his neighbors, when ten or twelve years of age, I have ground many a small grist. **1879** Jones *Backwoods Carolina* 752 Levi, in obedience to his father's orders to take a grist (long i) to mill, put a sack of corn on a horse, mounted bareback before it, and rode off whistling through a path in the woods to a mill miles away on the creek. **1946** Nixon *Glossary VA Words* 24 = the amount of corn taken to (or from) the mill at one time . . . [a term used] in the Shenandoah Valley. **1952–57** (in **1973** McDavid and McDavid *Vocab E KY* 154) *grist of corn* = attested by 2/52 (3.8%) of E KY speakers for the Linguistic Atlas of the North Central States. **1986** Pederson et al. *LAGS* = attested by 4/60 interviewees (6.7%) in E TN; 4/5 of all LAGS interviewees (80%) attesting term were in Appalachia.

[DARE *grist* n A especially Appalachians]

grit *verb* To grate (ripened, partially hardened ears of corn) against a roughly perforated tin sheet to make cornmeal to be baked into **gritted bread**. See also **grits, gritter**.

1897 Barton *Truth about Trouble* 15 (DARE) = to eat bread with a crust less hard and a texture less coarsely grained than gritted corn pone. **1948** Dick *Dixie Frontier* 289 When the kernels grew more mature and hard, the ears were rubbed over the rough side of a piece of tin studded with nail holes. This was called "gritting" (grating) and made the sweetest corn meal imaginable. **1952** Wilson *Folk Speech NC* 548 = to grate (corn on a gritter). **1971** Thornburgh *Great Smoky Mts* 160 The actors, mountain friends and neighbors, actually weave, card, spin, "grit" corn for corn-meal on an old-fashioned "gritter" or grater. **1973** GSMNP-70:2:1 When we gritted that bread, it was soft enough, you didn't have to put any water in it. Just season it was all you had to do, put salt and seasoning in it. Put it in that oven and that oven was just about airtight, put coals under it there, red hot coals, heat the oven first on the fireplace, and you always had a big meat skin to grease that with and then when they put the oven on the fire and heated it, the oven lid, and they'd heat it and set it on here, and hit was airtight, that no steam could get out of there, every bit of the flavor of that cornbread baked right in that thing.

[DARE *grit* v chiefly South Midland]

gritchel *noun* A piece of hand luggage.

1927 Woofter *Dialect from WV* 356 = a traveling bag: "Let me carry your gritchel for you." **1984** Wilder *You All Spoken* 28 = a valise.

[apparently a blend of *grip* + *satchel*; DARE *gritchel* n South, South Midland]

grit mill *noun* A grist mill for grinding corn and other grain. Same as **corn mill**. See also **hand mill, overshot, tub mill, undershot wheel**.

1939 Hall *Notebooks* 13:13 (White Oak NC) the old grit mill.

grits *noun* Grated kernels of corn with the hulls removed, made into a hot cereal. See also **big hominy, grit, lye hominy**.

1948 Dick *Dixie Frontier* 249 By means of a crude homemade sifter the coarse material, called grits, was separated from the fine and then boiled for hominy. **1978** Parris *Mt Cooking* 80 When I was growing up, we took grits left over from breakfast and sliced them and fried them for dinner. They were just the regular boiled grits in water. They're good, too, but not as good as fried grits that have been boiled in chicken stock. **1980** *Smokies Guide* (Summer) 7 A splashy creek, some carpentry skill and lumber were really all that was needed to erect a one family tub mill. These miniature mills practically lined the creek in some valleys and were capable of grinding about a bushel of corn per day. Corn was a staple for mountain people and with skill could be ground to different textures for bread, grits, mush, hominy or occasionally moonshine.

[DARE *grits* n pl 1b chiefly South, South Midland, especially South Atlantic, Gulf States]

gritted bread (also *gritting bread, gritty bread*) *noun* Bread made from semihardened kernels of corn grated into a coarse meal; the texture of this bread gives it an appealing taste. See 1892, 1975 citations. See also **grits, gritter**.

1892 Allen *Cumberland Gap* 252 A simpler way of preparing corn for bread than by even the hand-mill is used in the late summer and early autumn, while the grain is too hard for eating as roasting ears, and too soft to be ground in a mill. On a board is tacked a piece of tin through which holes have been punched from the under side, and over this tin the ears are rubbed, producing a coarse meal, of which "gritted bread" is made. Much pleasure and much health they get from their "gritted bread," which is sweet and wholesome for a hungry man. **1913** Kephart *Our Sthn High* 291 The ears are grated into a soft meal and baked into delectable pones called gritted bread. **1930** Thomas *Death Knell* When roasting-ears have passed the soft, milky stage, but are not yet hard enough to grind into meal they are grated and baked into a delectable pone called gritted bread. **1931** *Professor Learns* "Here, I brought you a turn of fresh water-ground meal," he said. "I've been up Buffalo fishing and got it at the Laytown mill. Bake you a hoe-cake out of it. It's so fresh it will taste like gritty-bread."

1957 Broaddus *Vocab Estill Co KY* 37 *gritting bread* = gritted bread. **1975** Purkey *Madison Co* 60 As soon as the first corn ripened, but before it was hard enough to shell, my father grated it on the big tin grater. He had made the corn grater by drilling nail holes in a piece of sheet iron, then fastening the tin in a half-circle to a large board, leaving the rough side exposed for grating. Hot gritted bread spread with freshly churned butter was a treat to remember. **1976** Braden *Grandma Was Girl* 29 Sometimes in the fall, we ran out of meal before the new crop of corn was hard enough to shell for the mill. Then we would grate some of the new ears to make "gritted bread." It was good bread. The grater we used to make this soft meal was a piece of tin full of nail holes, nailed on a board with the sharp points of the holes up. **1986** Pederson et al. *LAGS* (Scott Co TN) – scalded corn bread. **1990** Oliver *Cooking Hazel Creek* 9 One culinary pleasure in the late summer was gritted bread. It is made from corn that is too ripe or hard to be cut from the cob and fried or stewed, and yet not dry enough to be shelled. Moisture or milk still remains in the kernels, making them soft enough to be grated or gritted, as it was pronounced, from the cob. **1996** Houk *Foods & Recipes* 44–45 Past the roasting ear stage, the milky kernels were grated off the cob and baked into a mountain specialty, "gritted bread," or a cook might stir up a "run" of cornmeal mush. **2002** Myers *Best Yet Stories* 112 Corn, which had grown too hard for frying or creaming, was grated and baked into what was called gritted bread. The grater was a kitchen utensil made from wood and a piece of tin. Many nail holes were driven into the strip of tin. This strip was then fastened in a circular or rainbow fashion to a larger piece of wood. **2003** Howell *Folklife Big South Fork* 60 Gritted bread could be made late in the summer when the meal from last year's harvest might be running low. That recipe replaced meal with grated corn which was past the roasting ear stage, but still milky. **2009** Shelton *Gritty Bread* 28 No one in my family knows the exact origin of Gritty Bread, a recipe that made use of the bounty of the garden and the pasture field. Field corn, used to feed both animal and people, was the main ingredient. It was tougher than the sweet corns of today. Grating it for Gritty Bread made it more palatable and easier to cook.

gritter *noun* A grater, especially for corn, often a piece of tin perforated with jagged nail holes. See also **grit**, **gritted bread**.

1862 Hedgecock *Diary* Men carried their own gritters with them all day. **1863** *Levi CW Letters* (April 24) Wee made the Canteens into grittirs to grate our corn and wee Brild our meat on the Coals and travaid on to the ohio river. **1888** *Congress Record* (May 1) 3587 (DARE) The "gritter" is a piece of cast-away tin or sheet-iron, through which holes have been punched with a nail, so as to throw out the surface on one side and make it rough. In its use it is what we would call a grater. It is used by good Kentucky women . . . for rubbing the green corn from the cob in order to cook it for a family meal. **1952** Wilson *Folk Speech NC* 548 = a perforated piece of tin (about 8×24 inches) used to grate green corn on to make *gritted bread*. **1960** Hall *Smoky Mt Folks* 44 Bread trays or gritters are made by hand. Ears of fresh or dried corn rubbed on the gritters make good cereal grits or meal for gritted bread. **1981** Irwin *Arnwine Cabin* 20 Some of the most commonly found items in the old abandoned mountain homes of [Anderson County TN] were remnants of the corn gritter. After the corn had passed the roasting-ear stage and before it fully hardened, it could be grated, or gritted, into cornmeal by using this simple tool. The holes are made from the underside of the tin so as to cause a rough perforation around the edge sufficient to shave off portions of the corn kernel.

[DARE *gritter* n chiefly South Midland]

gritting bread, **gritty bread** See **gritted bread**.

grocer *noun* See citation.

1911 Shearin *E KY Word-List* 538 = a small hut where the "rat" . . . sells illicit whiskey.

grode See **grow A1**.

groin *noun* Variant forms *grine*, *grines*. See also **grine pone**.

1960 Westover *Highland Lg* 19 *grine*. **1997** Montgomery *Coll* My grines are a-painin' me something fierce (Brown). **2007** McMillon *Notes grines*.

ground clearing *noun* Same as **clearing**.

1985 Irwin *Alex Stewart* 167 I decided to have a ground clearing and log rolling, and I had 21 hands come to a working and I cleaned it up in one day.

ground frog *noun* A toad. See also **toad frog**.

1966 Dakin *Vocab Ohio River Valley* 391 *Ground frog* has some use in the Mountains but is attested nowhere else. **1986** Pederson et al. *LAGS* (Fannin Co GA). **1996–97** Montgomery *Coll* (known to Bush), = general term for a toad (Brown), = the American toad, also referred to as *toad frog* (Cardwell).

[DARE *ground frog* n especially South Midland]

groundhog

A *noun*

1 (also *ground puppy*) The woodchuck (*Marmota monax*). Also called **whistle pig**.

1859 Colton *Mt Scenery* 101 Then there is the ground-hog. As his name indicates, he burrows in the ground, and, like the prairie dog, builds a perfect city. He is about as large as a medium-sized opossum, and has similar hair. His color is a sort of dark gray. **1939** Hall *Coll* (Tow String Creek NC) Bishop told me to go ahead and kill the ground hog was eating up the country. **1940** Oakley *Roamin'/Restin'* 147 City people calls a ground hog a woodchuck but mountain people calls them whistle pigs or ground hogs. **1997** Montgomery *Coll* Jim chivvied the groundhog right out of that old hollow (Andrews). **2000** Miller *Looneyville* 48 = any of a group of common American burrowing and hibernating marmots with coarse brown fur. . . . It is a mystery how puppy wound up as part of the word in lieu of hawg: "Let's get the smoke poles and go get a mess of young groundpuppies."

[DARE *groundhog* n 1 perhaps calque from Dutch *aertoercken* archaic variant of *aardvarken* literally "earth pig"; widespread, but especially Midland]

2 See **groundhog skidder, groundhog still.**

B *verb*

1 In phrase *groundhog it* = to live on the barest income, be barely making a living.

1937 Hall *Coll* (Cosby TN) I'm just havin' to ground hog it. . . . A man that ground hogs it cain't help hisself. **1966** Dykeman *Far Family* 262 Did some men know all they think they do, they'd be driving teams of their own instead of ground-hogging it around from one job to the next. **1976** Dwyer *Southern Sayin's* 25 *ground-hog it* = [to be a] person or family who are forced to live in poor circumstances. **2002** Myers *Best Yet Stories* 113 To say someone was "Groundhoggin it" meant that he was barely getting by financially.

2 See citation.

c1999 Sutton *Me and Likker* 56 I have seen [boiling mash] literally jump 6″ above the barrel, like a artesian well, that is what they call "ground hogging." That's the term, the old moonshiners used.

3 See citation. See also **ground squirrel B.**

1939 Hall *Coll* = to pocket money during a poker game; i.e., to take money out of the game: "In a poker game a man will have so much money, maybe a dollar, and stick half a dollar in his pocket—that's what they call groun'-hoggin'." The speaker . . . explained the semantics of the term as follows: Ground referred to putting something in a hole; hog meant trying to get everything.

groundhog beater *noun* A banjo player.

1939 Farr *TN Mt Regions* 90 = a banjo player. "He's quite a ground hog beater." **1996–97** Montgomery *Coll* = the skin of a groundhog was sometimes used on the banjo (Brown), = banjo players were sometimes called this, for a groundhog skin, well tanned and stretched, makes a fine banjo head (Oliver).

groundhog case *noun* See citation.

1927 Woofter *Dialect from WV* 356 = something that has to be settled immediately. "But this is a ground hog case."

[DARE *groundhog case* n chiefly South, South Midland]

groundhog ear *noun* An edible wild green, so named because its leaf resembled the animal's ear.

1979 Slone *My Heart* 70 Then there were wild greens or "salet." There are many different kinds; sometimes the same plant was known by a different name by different people. "Plantin" [sic] is the one used most, a small thick-leafed green with a very distinct flavor, a little like cabbage. Then for cooking there was "sheep's leg," "groundhog ear," and "speckled dock."

groundhog grease (also *groundhog oil*) *noun* An oil rendered by cooking a groundhog. It is swallowed warm by the teaspoon or rubbed on the neck and chest to treat coughs and chest congestion.

1971 AOHP/ALC-147 Groundhog grease, that was good for the earache. **1973** GSMNP-4:1:28 Take anybody with the croup, take a kid choked up. Groundhog oil is the best thing in the world for that. **1982** Powers and Hannah *Cataloochee* 256 Groundhog grease [was] used on [the] chest for colds. **1989** *Matewan OHP*-56 They had what they called the groundhog grease they put around your neck or greased yourself in it. **1997** Nelson *Country Folklore* 40 For croup, groundhog oil. **2005** Williams *Gratitude* 499 *groundhog oil* = oil is rendered out of a groundhog, and is used for medicinal purposes. One use is to grease the chest with it to break up the croup.

groundhog hole *noun* See citation.

1955 Dykeman *French Broad* 269 A large part of this mining [for mica, feldspar, and kaolin] is done in small operations—"ground-hog holes," local people call them, [that] penetrate the sides of hill after hill . . . and the raw wound of many an abandoned digging gapes on the mountainsides, giving the country an appearance different from the rest of the French Broad.

groundhog it See **groundhog B1.**

groundhog liquor (also *groundhog whiskey*) *noun* Illegal whiskey made in a **groundhog still.** Same as **hog liquor.**

1883 Bonner *Dialect Tales* 157 I'd have as good shoes as you, Jane Oscar, 'f my man wuz in the ground-hog whiskey business. **1974** Dabney *Mt Spirits* 229 We decided we'd make some ground hog likker, and we had two big ground hogs. We paid so much a gallon for this feller to run it.

[DARE (at *groundhog* n 7) southern Appalachians]

groundhog oil See **groundhog grease.**

groundhog pot See **groundhog still.**

groundhog skidder (also *groundhog, ground skidder*) *noun* In logging, a mechanized **skidder** using a cable and sometimes runners to pull or push logs down a slope, often destroying vegetation in its path and carrying off soil and debris. See also **overhead skidder, skidder.**

1958 GSMNP-110:14 I never done no logging except for the skidder, the groundhog skidder. . . . [We] logged all that big poplar timber out up from the bridge yon way up to that flat with a groundhog skidder. **1970** Foster *Walker Valley* 38 *ground skidder* = a skidder on runners. It was a boiler on runners and he had two drums on him and you'd turn him around. **1974–75** McCracken *Logging* 2:2 They also had groundhog skidders in an area where it laid back for some distance flat, kind of flat, and where they didn't build a railroad into. *Ibid.* 23:7–8 They used what we call a groundhog. That just pulled the timber on the ground. That's what destroyed the timber and the soil and everything it drug off in them mountains. **1994** Schmidt and Hooks *Whistle* 157 = a machine for dragging logs along the ground by use of a cable and winch.

groundhog still *noun* See 1985 citation. See also **groundhog liquor, hog liquor, hog A3.**

1968 *End of Moonshining* 53 Diagram A illustrates an interesting variation on furnace design which was once fairly popular. Called the "groundhog" or "hog" still, it was unique in that the still sat directly on the ground, and the furnace of mud, clay and rocks was built up around it with the flue at the back. **1972** Carr *Oldest Profession* 187 Like the burrowing mammal from which the name is derived, the groundhog still ... sits snugly in a hole in the earth, with only the top exposed. The mash can be mixed and allowed to ferment in the still or mixed and allowed to ferment in barrels and boxes in another location and then emptied into the still. Designs utilizing a wooden bottom and wooden top have the heat for cooking applied to the metal sides of the still. **1985** Dabney *More Mt Spirits* 158 = this still—sometimes called a "hog"—is usually found dug into the side of a hill or bank (usually next to a stream). It is usually a huge metal cylinder with a wooden top and bottom. It is set up vertically in a bank with about two feet of space between its walls and the surrounding bank. Its wooden bottom is placed about a foot or two underneath the ground, to prevent it from being burned. The furnace for the groundhog is the air space around and outside the cylinder. The fire is placed next to the pot on the front. The flames wrap around it on either side, and exit at the top on the backside. This is sometimes called a "tail furnace." The heat chamber is covered all around on top with sheet metal, weighted with soil, almost level with the surrounding ground surface. A hole is cut right in the center of the wooden top, and onto this is placed the cap—sometimes a 50-gallon wooden keg, sometimes a metal drum and, on rare occasions, a hand-crafted copper cap. Developed in the 1930's, the groundhog still has a lot more capacity than most copper or metal pots, but its key difference is that, in addition to its greater capacity, it serves as both the fermenting pot as well as the distilling pot. Moreover, there is greater heat efficiency since more of the still's surface is in contact with the fire. A groundhog can be square, round, tall or long.

[DARE (at *groundhog* n 6) southern Appalachians]

groundhog Sunday *noun* See citation.

1980 Riggleman *WV Mtneer* 43 Sunday school was only held during the warm months and it was called "Groundhog Sunday School" because of this. As kiddies, we could not understand why it was thus called, but as we grew older we learned that it was because groundhogs only come out in the summertime.

groundhog thrasher *noun* A horse-powered threshing machine.

1949 McDavid *Grist* 109 (Fannin Co GA) = old-fashioned, horse-drawn threshing machine. **1968–69** *DARE Survey* (Dillard GA, Brasstown NC) = in an earlier day, an instrument used in threshing, to separate the wheat from the chaff. **1983** Montell *Don't Go Up* 199 = machine used for separating grain or seeds from straw, powered by four teams pulling a sweep in a circle.

[DARE *groundhog thrasher* n especially South Midland]

groundhog whiskey See **groundhog liquor**.

ground itch *noun* A fungal skin rash or bacterial infection, especially of the feet from having gone barefooted. See also **dew poison, fall sore, mud poison, toe-itch**.

1956 McAtee *Some Dial NC* 20. **c1960** Wilson *Coll.*

[DARE *ground itch* n chiefly South, South Midland]

ground ivy *noun* A creeping perennial vine (*Glechoma hederacea*) from whose leaves a medicinal tea is made, especially to treat babies for **hives**. Also called **jill all the ground**.

[**1904–20** Kephart *Notebooks* (in **1993** Farwell and Nicholas *Smoky Mt Voices* 81) *Glechoma hederacea*—"That'll break up the hives when nothing else won't."] **1939** Hall *Coll* (Catons Grove TN) Ground ivy is a good tea for hives for babies. **1965** Shelton *Pioneer Comforts* 5 Ground Ivy Tea [was used for] croup. **c1975** Lunsford *It Used to Be* 67 You'd take certain things like ground ivy, they called it. It's a little vine plant that has a little round leaf, ordinarily about the size of a quarter. It's green. You can take and make tea out of that. It causes sleep. It's very good tea for someone who can't sleep as well as they'd like to. **1984** Page and Wigginton *Foxfire Cookery* 47 Ground ivy does make a pleasant tea for anybody to drink, and old people was bad to give it to babies for colic. **1994** Montgomery *Coll* = made into tea to break the rash in a child (Ogle).

ground lug *noun* A grade of tobacco leaf.

1969 Miller *Raising Tobacco* 34 Raggedy lugs referred only to leaves pulled from the stalks at stripping time. There was a further grade called *ground lugs* which might be got by *priming* the patch before cutting time. Many farmers made no effort to save ground lugs.

ground nut *noun* A flowering vine (*Apios americana*) that grows along streams and in open fields and has a tuber that tastes somewhat like a peanut.

1934–47 *LAMSAS Appal* (Madison Co NC). **1996–97** Montgomery *Coll* (known to Adams, Cardwell, Jones), = a native, edible nut similar to a peanut, that grows in the Smokies (Oliver).

ground pine *noun* A ground clubmoss (*Lycopodium obscurum*) that resembles a miniature pine tree, sometimes used for holiday decoration. Same as **turkey's paw**.

1941 Walker *Story of Mt* 41 Beautiful lycopodiums, or ground pines, whose spores are so inflammable that they have been . . . used for making fireworks, especially in producing artificial lightning ... congregate under hemlocks. **1973** GSMNP-6:23 I was going to Bullhead to gather ground pine to make wreaths for Christmastime. **1999** Morgan *Gap Creek* 206 What I was looking for was turkey's paw, what some people call ground pine. It's [a] kind of club moss and grows in thickets, and on the north sides in damp shady places. It grows along a vine that runs under leaves and litter and lifts up yellow green leaves that look like turkey's feet. It's the perfect decoration for hanging along mantels and over doorways.

ground puppy See **groundhog A**.

ground robin *noun* The rufous-sided towhee (*Pipilo erythrophthalmus*).

1991 Alsop *Birds of Smokies* 123 The "rufous-sided" of the common name is in reference to the chestnut orange sides shared by both adult males and females and has led to a second, colloquial name, "ground robin." The species name, *erythrophthalmus*, comes from the Greek for "red-eyed" and if you are close enough for a good look you will see that this is descriptive as well.

ground scruffler *noun* An old-fashioned threshing machine.

1963 Medford *Mt People* 68 The first threshing machine the writer remembers was the old three-unit "ground scuffler," as they were called.

ground skidder See **groundhog skidder.**

ground squirrel

A *noun* Usually the Eastern chipmunk (*Tamias striatus*). [Editor's note: The term *chipmunk* is traditionally a book term.]

1867 (in **1974** Harris *High Times* 188) He jis' looked at me wild, half a moment—whined, an' axle-treed hisse'f intu the woods agin, like a injun arrer arter a groun' squirrill. **1934–47** LAMSAS *Appal* (Madison Co NC, Swain Co NC). **1949** Kurath *Word Geog East US* 15 *Ground squirrel* is shared by the Midland and the South as an old folk term, but *chipmunk* has largely replaced it in Eastern Pennsylvania and has spread to Maryland and the lower Shenandoah. **1971** Linzey and Linzey *Mammals of Smoky* 24 The Eastern Chipmunk, our only ground squirrel, is frequently seen in the Park. It has a striped face and five dark and four light body stripes that end at the reddish rump. . . . It is found at all elevations in the Park, but it is much less abundant in the spruce-fir forests than in the deciduous woodlands. It occupies such diverse habitats as rocky woodland, edges of grass balds and clearings, farm lands, and open woods. **1976** Ledford *Folk Vocabulary* 282 *Ground squirrel*, the old folk term in the South Midlands, has been almost completely replaced by *chipmunk*. **1982** Ginns *Snowbird Gravy* 51 The ground squirrels then would bury chestnuts. They call 'em chipmunks; we call 'em ground squirrels. **1986** Pederson et al. *LAGS* = attested by 39/60 interviewees (65%) in E TN and 17/35 (48.6%) in N GA; 56/241 of all LAGS interviewees (23.2%) attesting term were in Appalachia. **1995** Montgomery *Coll* (known to Shields).

[DARE *ground squirrel* n a chiefly Midland, South]

B *verb phrase* To conceal, hide (something) away. See also **groundhog B3**.

1939 Hall *Coll* (Madison Co NC) = slippin' money out of a pot you win and hidin' it; that is, takin' money out of the game. **1967** *DARE Survey* (Gatlinburg TN) = to hide something away for future use. **2005** Williams *Gratitude* 253 I didn't know how much money they got, and they won't nobody else never know neither, for they probably ground squirrel'd the biggest part of it.

ground worm *noun* Same as **worm 2**.

1911 Shearin *Superstitions Cumberland* 320 If one lay[s] the "ground-worm" of a rail fence during the new moon, it will soon sink into the ground and rot. **1952–57** (in **1973** McDavid and McDavid *Vocab E KY* 159) = attested by 2/52 (3.8%) of E KY speakers for the Linguistic Atlas of the North Central States.

grouser *noun* See citation.

1964 Clarkson *Lumbering in WV* 363 = a heavy chain wrapped around the leading log in a trail to help slow it down on a steep slope.

grove *noun* Combined with the name of the family owning the land to form place-names, as in Catons Grove (TN).

1937 Hall *Coll*: Catons Grove TN = place name for a small wooded area between Cosby and the French Broad River. **1939** Hall *Coll* (Gumstand TN) We built the road that goes up to Huskeys Grove. We was the first ones started that road there.

grove meeting *noun* Same as **camp meeting.**

1996 Isbell *Last Chivaree* 43 There, according to Ray, [the preacher] conducted a "grove" service. Such a meeting got its name, Ray says, because it was staged at a clearing in the woods. . . . Ray explained further: "They sawed off two chestnut saplings and nailed a board on them to make a pulpit. A place to hold his Bible, you know. Called it a grove meeting."

grove out *verb phrase* To clear (a piece of land of) briers, saplings, and other growth under trees.

1962 Stubbs *Mountain-Wise* (Aug–Sept) 8 We were bushwacking, clearing out undergrowth, "saw-briars," and saplings which were growing in the wrong places. A neighbor happened by and remarked: "I see that you are *groving it out*."

grow *verb*

A Principal parts.

1 Variant past-tense forms *grewed, grode, growed.*

1863 *Lister CW Letters* (Nov 10) I Cold sell ever apple that grode on That tree at home for 25 sents a peas if I had Them hear. **1867** Harris *Sut Lovingood* 243 The wool grow'd over his eyes, ontil hit wer fit tu shear, an' dam ef I warn't at the shearin. **1913** Kephart *Our Sthn High* 284 In many cases a weak preterite supplants the proper strong one: . . . drawed, growed, knowed, throwed. **1934–47** *LAMSAS Appal* (Madison Co NC, Swain Co NC). **1939** Hall *Coll* (Saunook NC) We had rail fence around it and that turnip, you know, it growed till it bursted that fence down. **1940** Haun *Hawk's Done* 5 She growed so big that when she died they couldn't get her out of the house to bury her. **1953** Atwood *Verbs East US* 15 *Growed* occurs in Type I speech [i.e. older speakers with little formal education] with a frequency varying from about one third (e. N.Y. and N.J.) to well over nine tenths (N.C.). **1973** GSMNP-76:28 We growed wheat way up to the hiking club. **1973** Miller *English Unicoi Co* 133 *growed* (as past tense) attested by 3 of 6 speakers. **1978** Reese *Speech NE Tenn* 175 *growed* = attested by 10/12 (83.3%) speakers. **1986** Pederson et al. *LAGS* (Jefferson Co TN, Sevier Co TN). **1998** *Dante OHP-61* She grewed up in Washington County before she left Washington County.

[OED3 *growed* (at *grow*) 17c→; DARE *grow* v 1 scattered, but chiefly South, South Midland]

2 Variant past-participle forms *grew, growed.*

1861 *Martin CW Letters* (Oct 6) my hair has growed out A gain and I have got A grat long thick set of whiscers. **1867** Harris *Sut Lovingood* 103 By golly, golly, he wer grow'd thar. **1905** Miles *Spirit of Mts* 16 He's always a growed-up man ag'in he wakes up in the morning. **1939** Hall Coll (Cades Cove TN) It's grew up. **1940** Oakley *Roamin'/Restin'* 91 Well I come to fiend out this tree had grew on an edge of a big clift as the tree leaned out over the edge of the clift. **1961** *Coe Ridge OHP-336B* You wasn't growed then. **1970** Madden and Jones *Ephraim Bales* 6 Being what I was, I reckon I'd have growed any place I was planted. **1971** *Boogers* 30 There'uz a boy that'd been murdered that's grew up with me was buried out there. **1973** GSMNP-70:2:7 He wanted someone to clean up a little part of his farm that had growed up in sassafras and bushes and one thing and another. **1978** Reese *Speech NE Tenn* 175 *growed* = attested by 6/12 (50%) speakers. **1985** Williams *Role of Folklore* 280 The first cousin, he'd grew taller than me. **1991** Thomas *Sthn Appal* 242 I always loved to work jist as hard as I could. I'd growed up that way, an' I loved it.

[OED3 *growed* (at *grow* v) 18c→; DARE *grow* v 2 scattered, but chiefly South, South Midland]

B Senses.

1 To raise (an animal for one's own consumption).

1937 Hall Coll (Cades Cove TN) We grow our own meat. **1996** GSMNPCOHP-1:2 Everybody growed his own meat for that matter.

2 Of the moon: to wax. Same as **increase A**. See also **light of the moon**.

1972 *Foxfire I* 218 Plant all things which yield above the ground on the increase or growing of the moon. **1975** Dwyer *Thangs* 26 Do not nail shingles, or boards, on the growing side of the moon or the ends will darken and curl and go crooked.

grow devil *noun* Same as **go devil 1**.

2005 Williams *Gratitude* 46 They driv them grabs down in the end of a log with a grow devil (go devil, a big old heavy hammer) [and] snaked the log by the chain.

grow down *verb phrase* Of a child's liver: to shrink, causing stunted growth.

1955 Washburn *Country Doctor* 56 The woman says [the child]'s allus been runty an' that she thinks its liver's growed down.

growed See **grow A1**, **A2**.

grown'un *noun* A grown person, adult. See also **little one**, **young one**.

1970 Foster *Walker Valley* 30 You know to do what the grown uns would do.

grow off *verb phrase* To grow rapidly, come to maturity.

1924 Raine *Saddlebags* 99 If you give your pigs a good start they'll grow off. **1939** Farr *TN Mt Regions* 90 = an expression meaning to grow up. "Your family has grown off fast." **1940** Haun *Hawk's Done* 47 Barshia growed off all right too, Dona said. **c1960** Wilson Coll = to grow well or rapidly. **1974** Ogle *Memories* 37 It wasn't long until he grew off and left me. **1996–97** Montgomery Coll (known to Brown, Cardwell, Jones, Ledford, Norris).

[DARE *grow off* v phr chiefly South, South Midland]

grow one's meat See **grow B1**.

grub *verb*

1 (also *grub off*, *grub out*, *grub up*) To dig up roots of trees, stumps, bushes, etc. from (a piece of land) in preparing a **new ground** for cultivation; hence noun *grubbing* = formerly, a community work activity to help a family clear a piece of land. See also **break B9**, **clean off**, **new ground**.

1842 *McLean Diary* 78 Commenst Grubing. **1931** Goodrich *Mt Homespun* 41 Her children made frequent visits, and she was called on as a matter of course to help whenever there was a "working"; whether "fodder pulling," "corn shucking," or "grubbing"; for no one else could superintend as she could the cooking of a big dinner. **1939** Hall Coll (Sugarlands TN) They'd bunch up if you was sick and come work your corn for you and make quiltings and roll logs and grubbings and one thing or another and help you when you was sick and disabled. **1940** Haun *Hawk's Done* 143 He was helping the Old Man Arwood grub off the persimmon sprouts in that field right above Burt's and Meady's house. **1956** Hall Coll (Cosby TN) Every man, he'd grub and clear up a piece of land, new ground, in the winter time. **1957** Justus *Other Side* 137 The sassafras roots which were grubbed up were saved for making tea. **c1973** Crabtree *Rememberin'* 30 The men used their mattocks and grubbed out the alder and sassafrass and other scrub trees that had taken over since children quit romping in the yard. **1980** GSMNP-115:53 They used to have grubbings. People would get together and go in and just have grubbing, grub up little new grounds, you know, for a man. **1986** Pederson et al. *LAGS*: *grub* = attested by 16/60 interviewees (26.7%) in E TN and 1/35 (2.9%) in N GA; 17/19 of all LAGS interviewees (89.4%) attesting term were in Appalachia; *grub out* (Cocke Co TN, Jefferson Co TN); *grub up* (Cocke Co TN). **2002** McGowan *Beech Mt Tales* 72 They had to get out and do all the farm work—the plowing, cleaning up the land, grubbing, you know, and piling up logs and chunks and stumps, grubbing briars and bushes. **2011** *Smoky Mt Times* (March 11) For a while during World War II—when the European wood traditionally used to make briar pipes was not available—burls on the roots of laurel and rhododendron in boggy places in the southern Appalachians were "grubbed up" as a substitute.

2 To dig young roots or root vegetables out of the ground.

1861 *J Love CW Letters* I want you to plant patoes plenty for I think I will be there in time to grubb them up. **1978** Slone *Common Folks* 303 Early in the spring, sometimes as early as January or February, we would begin "grubbin," digging the young sprouts that were beginning to grow around where the trees had grown. Mountaineers grub for poke, which means they dig for the roots from the ground with a heavy shovel or mattock when weeding the garden. They might also plant the roots in the basement and harvest the stems in the winter.

grubbing See **grub 1**.

grubbing hoe *noun* A type of heavy-duty hoe.

1938 Stuart *Dark Hills* 332 Get back in the old saw-briars and sassafras sprouts with a big one-eyed grubbing hoe. **1996** Spurlock *Glossary* 399 = a sturdy hoe with a 4″ × 7″-inch blade mounted on a wooden adz-head handle. **2017** *Blind Pig* (March

24) A grubbing hoe has a heavier blade and stouter handle than a garden hoe.

grub off, **grub out**, **grub up** See **grub 1**.

grudgment *noun* A grudge.

1940 Haun *Hawk's Done* 157 He was Wilbur's boss and it seemed like Wilbur had a grudgment against him from the first. *Ibid.* 168 I don't hold any grudgment against him for what he did.

grumble *verb* To cause (one) to grumble.

1943 Hannum *Mt People* 148 Hit grumbled the old woman, some.

(the) grunts *noun* Persistent grumbling or complaining.

1973 GSMNP-13:23–24 When your foot or your back would be hurtin', you had the grunts.

grunty *adjective* Grumbling, complaining.

1892 Smith *Farm and Fireside* 151 A man who ain't . . . gets on the piazza, tired and grunty.

gryste See **grist A.**

guard *noun, verb* Variant form *gyard*.

1917 Kephart *Camping & Woodcraft* 2 *gyard*. **1939** Burnett *Gap o' Mountains* 12 "I warn you," prophesied Old Joe, "that onless we git shet of sich a crime afore it gits a strangle holt on us; I warn you that onless we gyard the ballot in whuch our manhood and freedom air wropped—we will all be slaves." **1942** Hall *Phonetics Smoky Mts* 94 In the speech of older people this glide [j] is very common after [k] or [g] before [ɑ]; for example . . . *guard* [gjɑrd].

guitar *noun* Variant form with primary stress on first syllable.

1963 Arnow *Flowering* 138 There are questions, their answers not even partially revealed in writing [of settlers two centuries ago], of syllabication and stress. They undoubtedly stressed the syllables of many words differently than we do today. We smile, for example, at the hill boy who says "git-tarr," giving his instrument plenty of g, t, and r, but with more git than tar. There was no one by to smile at Samuel Pepys who must have pronounced the word in much the same fashion, as he sometimes spelled it guittar. **1991** Thomas *Sthn Appal* 96 I ordered me a guitar from Sears Roebuck. We lived at Green Cove an' it'uz about thirty miles to Marion, Virginia. An' th' guit-tar had to come by express. **1992** Brooks *Sthn Stuff* 56 *gee-tar, git-tar*.

[DARE *guitar* n (pronc) chiefly South, South Midland, especially Appalachians]

gullick *noun* The gullet.

1859 Taliaferro *Fisher's River* 47 I gulluped you down my gullick in whisky. **1952** Wilson *Folk Speech NC* 548 = gullet.

gully dirt *noun*

1 Exhausted land whose soil is of little or no worth.

1995 Montgomery *Coll* He's just got a gully dirt farm [i.e. used up, reduced to gullies] (Cardwell).

2 By extension = anything of little value and thus worthy of contempt.

1984 Wilder *You All Spoken* 9 [He] ain't worth gully dirt. **1995** Montgomery *Coll* He treated me like gully dirt (Cardwell).

[DARE *gully dirt* n South, South Midland]

gully jumper *noun* A rustic person.

1939 Farr *TN Mt Regions* 90 = farmer: "We're just poor gully jumpers." **1967** *DARE Survey* (Cumberland Gap TN) = nickname for a rustic or countrified person. **1992** Brooks *Sthn Stuff* 61 gulley jumper, n. A mountaineer; occasionally a farmer.

gullywasher (also *gully warsher*) *noun* A hard, flooding rain; the rush of water created by such a rain. See also **frog drowner**.

1934–47 *LAMSAS Appal* = attested by 7/20 (35%) from VA, 3/37 (8.1%) from NC, 13/14 (92.9%) from SC, and 3/12 (25%) from GA. **1958** Newton *Dialect Vocab* = common term in E TN mountains, attested by 17 of 36 speakers. **1966–67** *DARE Survey* (Spruce Pine NC, Gatlinburg TN) = a sudden rush of water coming from a heavy rain; (Maryville TN) = joking name for a heavy rain. **1967** Hall *Coll* (Townsend TN) When it comes a hard one, you know, and they're washing out of the bank, they call it a "gullywasher." **1986** Pederson et al. *LAGS* (Blount Co TN, Cocke Co TN). **1995** Montgomery *Coll* = any heavy storm (Cardwell).

gulver (also *gulver root*) *noun* Same as **Culver's root**.

1938 Hall *Coll* (Emerts Cove TN) Gulver, an old plant name. Dig the roots and make a tea. **1957** Hall *Coll* (Clyde NC) Gulver root. It was used as a tonic and laxative.

gum

A *noun*

1 A hollowed section of a **blackgum** or other log used as a barrel or other container to store foodstuffs. See also **meal bin**.

1917 Kephart *Word-List* 413 = 1. A hollow log; 2. A barrel. "I'm goin' to put my ashes into that *gum*." **1938** Maxwell *Valhalla* ix Feed for the stock was kept in "gums" or sections of hollowed out trees fitted with tops and bottoms. **1992** Montgomery *Coll* = the black gum tree had a tendency to be hollow was therefore used for making barrels, storing meat, etc. (Shields).

2 A section of a hollow tree, especially a **blackgum**, housing a colony of bees; hence a bee hive. Also called **bee gum 1**.

1891 Primer *Studies in WV* 168 Beegum was at first the body of the gum tree hollowed out and used for bees. A larger section, hollowed out in the same way, is used for a grain receptacle and is called a gum. **1895** Edson and Fairchild *TN Mts* 372 = bee-hive. "Folks is goin' into church to-day like bees into a *gum*." **1940** Oakley *Roamin'/Restin'* 50 Look the tree over and it is easy to find where the bees live then cut the tree and get their honey and put the bees in a gum or bee box with part of the honey and cone [sic]. **1955** Parris *Roaming Mts* 29 Why, I know the time when a feller was considered trifling if he didn't have a dozen or so gums. **1956** GSMNP-24:62 They came over here and robbed his bees, which were in some of these old log gums. **1966** Dakin *Vocab Ohio River Valley* 143–44 Many speakers in the Kentucky Mountains, and a few scattered older informants elsewhere, still say (or remember) *gum* or *bee gum* as a name for a cylindrical container made of a hollowed-out log. These containers were home-made substitutes for the product of the cooper's shop, but there seems to be no evidence that barrels constructed of staves are or were ever called *gum*. **1973** *Foxfire II* 32 In the early days of beekeeping, the hives were nothing more than twenty-four to thirty-inch long sections of hollow black gum trees—a fact that has caused even modern hives in the mountains today to be called "gums," "beegums," or "plank gums." **1978** Montgomery *White Pine Coll* III-2 My Dad's brother that lives up Del Rio in Cocke County, he had about twenty or twenty-five bee-stands. We called it, gums of bees. **1987** Trent *Yesteryear* 23 Every family had one or more hives out by the picket fence. Many of them were simply made from different length sections of hollow black gum trees. These trees were brought in from the woods, the inside rounded out smooth by using a long chisel. About the middle of the 24 to 30 inch section, four holes would be bored on all four sides. Sticks were put into the holes so the bees could hang their combs from these sticks. These "gum hives" were set on a bench like platform set up from off the ground level. The gums were slightly tilted so the bees could enter. **1996** GSMNPCOHP-1:2 John Oliver . . . had over a hundred gums, stands of bees.

[DARE *gum* n² 3b chiefly Appalachians]

3 A trap for small animals, especially rabbits.

1994–97 Montgomery *Coll* (known to Cypher, Hooper, Jones, Ledford), = made from the blackgum tree (Cardwell). **2006** Ellison *Nature Journal* 27 A small hollowed section of black gum could also be closed at one end, fitted with a triggered sliding door at the other end, baited and used as a rabbit trap. When I was a boy, an uncle of mine showed me how to make these traps, which he called "rabbit gums."

[DARE *gum* n² 3c especially southern Appalachians, Ozarks]

4 (also *gum spring*) A section of a hollow log used to enclose a spring. See also **well box**.

1901 Harben *Westerfelt* 13 She used to . . . set in the shady holler at the gum spring, whar yore pa went to water his hoss. **c1960** Wilson *Coll* = a hollow log used to enclose a spring.

[DARE (at *gum* n² 3d) especially Appalachians]

B *verb*

1 To catch (a rabbit or other small animal) using a trap fashioned from a hollowed section of a log. See also **gum A3**.

1997 Montgomery *Coll* He gummed a rabbit (Brown).

2 See citation.

1966 Parris *Time to Go* Come spring, when the sap was risin', we boys would get together on a Sunday and head for the pine ridge. We called it goin' gummin'. And we'd fetch pine resin. That was our chewin' gum. . . . Spring was the only time you could go gummin'. You got the gum when the sap was risin' in the pines or spruce or birch.

3 To chew and ingest food without the benefit of teeth.

1914 Furman *Sight* 61–62 Fust thing is a new set of teeth,—you done gummed yourself into dyspepsy and gineral cantankerousness.

gumbo-gobackum (also *gumbo-whackum*) *noun* See citation.

1968 Wilson *Folklore Mammoth Cave* 19 *gumbo-gobackum*, *gumbo-whackum*) = the local pronunciation of gum guaiacum, the resinous sap of two tropical trees—Guaiacum officinale and G. sanctum, formerly used by many people in cough syrups and still kept in stock by at least one drugstore in the region.

gumbo-whackum See **gumbo-gobackum**.

gum hive See **gum A2**.

gumption *noun* [Editor's note: The senses below cannot always be differentiated, but both appear to have been prevalent for several centuries.]

1 Common sense, good judgment, shrewdness, practical understanding.

1867 (in **1974** Harris *High Times* 181) I puts hit to you, as a man ove gumshun, if I orter add another word only to forewarn you not tu menshun marryin' tu me agin. **1895** Dromgoole *Humble Advocate* 330 Ye ain't got as much gumption as that thar chile thar this minute. **1937** Wilson *Folklore SE KY* 25 He ain't got no gumption. (= He's stupid [Bell Co KY].) **1940** Haun *Hawk's Done* 156 Wilbur didn't have any more gumption than to let Nick beg him into going. **1957** Justus *Other Side* 68–69 I was mightily afeared that book learning would spoil you, but you've still got a smidgen o' gumption. **1972** Cooper *NC Mt Folklore* 92 = judgment; good sense. **1987** Young *Lost Cove* 185 People said that he didn't have enough gumption to believe in ghosts. **1989** Landry *Smoky Mt Interviews* 191 They called that teaching you gumption, you know. Now they call it common sense. **1996–97** Montgomery *Coll* (known to Adam, Brown, Jones, Norris, Oliver); He had enough gumption to stay on the job he found (Cardwell), = especially in phrase *no more gumption than a Junebug* (Ellis).

[DARE *gumption* n 1 scattered, but especially South, South Midland]

2 Initiative, resourcefulness, resolute enterprise; audacity, bravery.

1974–75 McCracken *Logging* 11:81 If a fellow had enough gumption, why, it was worth something to him. **1994–96** Montgomery *Coll* (known to Adams, Brown, Jones, Norris, Oliver); He didn't have enough gumption to come in out of the rain (Cardwell). **2001** House *Clay's Quilt* 178 Sitting in water that was beginning to get cold, she wondered what had given her the strength, the gumption to actually walk out that last time, to leave and just think, *To hell with it all.* **2009** Fields *Growing Up* 328 = nerve; spunk; bravery. **2016** *Blind Pig* (Dec 15) Gumption can have a negative connotation, i.e. "She had the gumption to look me right in the face and call me a greedy-gut just because I eat the last blueberry muffin."

[OED3 *gumption* originally Scot (cf *rum-*, *rumble-gumption*) n 1 "common sense, mother wit, shrewdness, also initiative, enterprise"; EDD *gumption* sb 2 (both senses) in general dialect use; CUD *gumption* n 1 "common sense; shrewdness"; HT (at *rumgumption*) "common-sense, shrewdness"]

gum spring See **gum A4**.

gum swamp *noun* See 1998 citation.

1991 Alsop *Birds of Smokies* 38 Some of the best places in Cades Cove are the oxbow area of Abrams Creek about one-half mile upstream from the turnoff to the Abrams Falls parking area, and the "gum swamp" just east of the Cable Mill. **1998** Montgomery *Coll* = a level swampy area along slow-flowing streams, in which environment sweetgum trees grew profusely (Brown), = an area of collected water surrounded by sweetgum trees (Cardwell).

gun stick *noun* A ramrod for a muzzle-loading rifle. See 2014 citation.

1913 Kephart *Our Sthn High* 169 Yes, they are; plumb onery—lock, stock, barrel and gun-stick. **1915** Hall *Autobiog Claib Jones* 7 I then went up the road, set my gun stick against a tree, hung my shot pouch on my gun stick and threw myself into the mountains. **1943** Hannum *Mt People* 111 Hounddog, take that gun stick, boy, and rub a sulphur match on yore hindsights and yore foresights, and see can you get that top feller. **1950** Hall *Coll* = a ramrod. **2014** Ellis *Coll* A ramrod or gun stick (always made out of hickory) was sometimes used to clean out the barrel of a muzzleloading rifle, but its main purpose was to ram down the ball after a measured charge of black powder was poured down the barrel. After the powder was poured in, a greased "patch" made of coarse cotton or linen cloth was laid across the muzzle and the bullet pushed down until it was just inside the muzzle, then the excess cloth was trimmed off with a "patch cutter," usually a small fixed blade knife carried in the hunting pouch or in a little scabbard attached to the shoulder strap of the pouch.

gun thug *noun* An armed guard hired to police a coal camp, sometimes deputized by local authorities. Also called **thug**, **tin-bill**. See also **Baldwin thug**.

1973 Kahn *Hillbilly Women* 31 The miners was there to meet the gun thugs and killed seven of them. *Ibid.* 90 Some of the armed guards were deputized and given legal sanction to search houses of families on strike, to arrest any coal miner suspected of "insubordination" to the coal operators . . . one of these armed guards, commonly known as gun thugs, shot and wounded a coal miner. **1975** Woolley *We Be Here* 26 Like the thoroughbred scab, the gun thug usually is home-grown. He has lived in Harlan County, and perhaps on Clover Fork, for most of his life. Perhaps his father and grandfather lived there, too. If they were gun thugs before him, then he is a thoroughbred gun thug. **2016** Gipe *Gone to Water* 42–43 We grew up on tales of him shooting gun thugs from the woods above the road to mines on strike.

gurglymock See **Jerusalem oak**.

gut bell *noun* See citation.

2006 Farwell *Logging Term* 1021 A "gut bell" announced the meals, which the cook, called a "gut robber," had prepared with the help of "cookees."

gut bucket *noun* A makeshift string bass made from a single string or gut tied over a washtub. Also called **washtub bass**.

2005 Ebel *Orville Hicks* 115 When instruments were not available, folks on the mountain improvised. Orville shows his miniature version of the gut bucket, so named for the materials used to make it. "Folks couldn't afford a string bass," Orville says, "so they made these gut buckets, or washtub basses, as some people call them." Orville plucks the single string. In years past, the string would have been gut, or sinew.

gut hammer *noun* In logging, a dinner bell or triangular bar of steel struck vigorously by a metal stick to call loggers to eat or to rouse them in the morning.

1964 Clarkson *Lumbering in WV* 363 = a triangular piece of steel used for calling the men to meals. The gut-hammer was struck in a rotating fashion by another piece of steel. **1967** Parris *Mt Bred* 134 = dinner bell in a logging camp.

gut pearl *noun* See citation. See also **Tennessee pearl**.

1981 Henry *Alex Stewart* 55 Another thing that made musseling interesting were the pearls which were occasionally found in the mussel. Alex said they would occur in about one mussel in a hundred. The pearls were usually irregularly shaped. These were called "gut" pearls and were sold by the ounce. Round ones were rare and worth a lot more. Alex said the most he ever got for a single pearl was eight dollars.

gut robber *noun* A cook in a logging camp, especially an inferior one.

1967 Parris *Mt Bred* 134 = head cook. **1991** *Smokies Guide* (Winter) 14 Employees with a variety of skills worked for the companies. There were woodhicks (loggers), gut robbers (cooks), bullwhackers (oxen drivers), engineers, blacksmiths, doctors, and other specialists. **2006** Farwell *Logging Term* 1021 A "gut bell" announced the meals, which the cook, called a "gut robber," had prepared with the help of "cookees."

gut shoot *verb phrase* To scold (someone) in public.

1963 Williams *Metaphor Mt Speech II* 53 The offender may expect to be "gut-shot" at some public gathering place by a sharp-tongued matriarch whose sense of propriety compels her to take the offender "daown a peg or two fer a-tryin' to get beyanst her raisin'."

guttering *noun* Eaves troughs.

1823 (in **1956** Eliason *Tarheel Talk* 275) (Burke Co NC) thirty one feet of guttering. **1973** Miller *English Unicoi Co* 147 = gutters, eaves trough. **1986** Pederson et al. LAGS = attested by 7/60 interviewees (11.7%) were from E TN; 1/17 of all LAGS interviewees (41%) attesting term were from E TN.

[DARE *guttering* n chiefly South Midland]

guy[1] *verb* To tease, deride.

1892 Doak *Wagonauts Abroad* 82 This man's a guyin' of me; and ef he be, he's a dead man. **1939** Hall *Coll* (Tow String Creek NC)

These boys are always guyin' me about diggin' ground hogs. **1940** Hall Coll (Cataloochee NC) Quit guyin' me about it! **1944** Williams *Word-List Mts* 29 = to tease. **1992** Brooks *Sthn Stuff* 63 = to tease or to make fun of. "I just plain-out despise being guyed about my red hair."

[OED3 *guy* v³ 2 "to deride as if an effigy of Guy Fawkes"; DARE *guy* v scattered, but more frequent South, South Midland]

guy² (also *guy off*) *verb, verb phrase* To secure with cables a spar used in yarding logs.

1970 Foster *Walker Valley* 2 When you start to put your lines out, the first thing [is that] you guy your boom off. **1974–75** McCracken *Logging* 14:4 You'd take this big cable back and anchor it to a tree back there somewhere and guy the thing with a big inch and a quarter cable. **1976** GSMNP-114:25 You get a big tree there and guy it every way in the world.

guy off See **guy²**.

gwine See **go A1**.

gyarb See **garb**.

gyard See **guard**.

gyarden See **garden**.

gyirl See **girl A**.

gyp *noun* A female dog, bitch.

1946 Woodard *Word-List VA/NC* 16 = a female dog. **1974** Fink *Bits Mt Speech* 11 = a female dog. **1995** Montgomery File (known to 85-year-old man, Greenbrier TN). **2007** Plott *Story Plott Hound* 182 = term used to describe a female dog.

[OED3 *gyp* n² U.S.; DARE *gyp* n¹ chiefly South, South Midland]

H

ha *interjection* A high-pitched syllable articulated egressively at the end of a phrase or breath group or at the beginning of one, used especially as a preacher reaches an intensely emotional juncture of a spontaneous sermon or public prayer, adding a rapid, melodic, quasi-chant quality to the message. Same as **huh**. See also **ah**, **holy tone**, **huh**, **uh**.

1999 Schwartz *Holiness Believers* 18 You better get right with God—ha! because the JUDGMENT DAY IS NEAR—YES, IT IS.

hack *verb* To annoy, disconcert, embarrass (as by teasing).

1917 Kephart *Word-List* 413 = to annoy, nettle. "That joke *hacks* Steve to this day." **c1940** Aswell *Glossary TN Idiom* 10 = deflate, take down a peg. **1952** Wilson *Folk Speech NC* 548 = to embarrass, to tease . . . Somewhat rare. **1970** Vincent *More of Best* 41 Ben said that sort of hacked him. **1974** Fink *Bits Mt Speech* 12 = to annoy, embarrass. "That story sure did *hack* him." **2007** McMillon *Notes* = to nonplus someone, aggravate.

[OED3 *hack* v¹ 2c U.S. dialect; DARE probably < *hack* "chop," but cf EDD *hake* v 4 "to tease, worry, importune," also *hock* v 2 "to jeer"; DARE *hack* v¹ 2 chiefly South, South Midland]

hacking *noun* See citations.

1964 Clarkson *Lumbering in WV* 364 = [a] clearing made by girdling or hacking trees in order to kill them. Such trees were usually burned within a few years and the ground cleared. **1984** Woods *WV Was Good* 180 After a piece of land was cleared, it was called a "new-ground." But during the year or two that the clearing was in progress, the tract of land was called a "hacking," or a clearing. The brush and tree limbs were stacked into brush piles. Such brush piles were thick over the clearing, none being more than a few steps from its neighbors.

hackle

A Variant forms *hackerd* [see **1994** in **B**], *hatchel* [see **1976** in **B**], *heckle* [see **2001** in **B**], *hetchel* [see **2001** in **B**].

B *noun* A large comb with sharp metal teeth for dressing **flax** or hemp. See also **break B5**, **flax brake**.

1957 Hall Coll (Mt Sterling NC) The original hackle was a comb used for the rough part of hemp. It had many teeth in it. They talk about a dog's hackle too, that is, his bristles. **1976** Braden *Grandma Was Girl* 13–14 The flax hatchel, called hackle in this area [i.e. Anderson Co TN], was found in most all the homes of this region, indicating that flax was commonly grown for its fiber in the making of linen. After the flax stalks were broken on a flax break, or with a swinging-knife, they were combed through these hand-wrought tines, thereby removing all but the tiny hair-like fibers, which were used for spinning into thread. The hatchel was used in an "upside-down" position on a bench with two pegs extending through the holes on either end to secure it, and then a handful of flax would be pulled over the spikes until it was free of all the dead stalks, leaving only the usable flax. **1989** Oliver *Hazel Creek* 22 They [= stalks of the flax plant] had to be passed through a "hatchel" or iron comb similar to a card for carding wool, which further thinned the fibers to get them finally ready for the small, or flax, spinning wheel. **1994** McCarthy *Jack Two Worlds* 11–12 A hackerd is a thing that they used back at that time, that had steel points in it, sharp as a needle . . . What they called a hackerd was a brush, thing about that big around, had a handle on it, where it was in wood. **2001** Wilson *Textile Art* 104 (or *heckle, hetchel*) = a tool used for processing the flax fiber into linen thread.

had See **have C.**

had die, haddy die See **fad die.**

had ought to *verb phrase* Should. See also **may B2, ought B.**

1858 (in **1974** Harris *High Times* 138) You had orter seed that pole an them open umerellers clar the road. **1904–20** Kephart *Notebooks* 2:399 A feller'd orter have a good crowin' rooster. **1937** Hall *Coll* (Cades Cove TN) You'd orter see them. Law! **1939** Walker *Mtneer Looks* 1 I guess hit's a sin and I hadn't ort to do it, because they don't mean no harm. **1942** Hall *Phonetics Smoky Mts* 47 (Cades Cove TN) I reckon we'd orter be a-gittin home. The clouds are bilin' up there on them mountains. **1966** Dakin *Vocab Ohio River Valley* 2.384 [In KY] the only usage other than *ought not (oughtn't)* that is common enough on all social levels to be of significance is *hadn't ought to*. **1971** *AOHP/ALC*-66 I hadn't ought to tell it, but I started up in the road there one time, and I had a little drink of liquor. **1979** Carpenter *Walton War* 68 "Now you hadn't ought to talk like that, Ellie," the man said as the doctor went through the door. **1998** *Dante OHP*-71 I hadn't ought to say this on the tape. I won't say it on tape.

[EDD (at *ought* v II.1)]

haffen *noun* Half.

1884 Murfree *In TN Mts* 46 Let him treat haffen the country ez he done me, ef he wants ter. **1886** Smith *Southernisms* 39.

[DARE *haffen* adj, n *half* + *-en* (variant of *on* "of")]

haf'n See **have B6.**

haggedy *adjective* Haggard.

2005 Williams *Gratitude* 500 = looking rough, not up to snuff. "She was awful *haggedy* while she had the flu."

haggle (also *haggle up*) *verb, verb phrase* To cut or tear unevenly, give an uneven appearance to, mangle; hence participial adjective *haggled* = rough, uneven. See also **haggly.**

1975 Jackson *Unusual Words* 151 Material that is cut or torn unevenly is *haggled*. **1989** Landry *Smoky Mt Interviews* 195 They didn't want their fields haggled up with grass and weeds. **1991** Thomas *Sthn Appal* 75 If you haggle 'um [= fish being fileted] around, they'll jist be full a' bones. You never will git 'um all picked out. **1995** Montgomery *Coll*: *haggle* (known to Cardwell).

haggly *adjective* See citation. See also **haggle.**

1939 Hall *Coll* = rough, covered with rocks.

haint See **haunt A.**

hain't (also *hant*) *verb, auxiliary verb* See also **ain't.** See Grammar and Syntax §5.4, §6.4.

[DARE *hain't* v chiefly Northeast, South, South Midland, especially Appalachians]

A = negative forms of present-tense *be*.

1 = *am not, are not, is not*.

1862 *Shifflet CW Letters* (Jan) I think tha[y] hante no danger but I will git home. **1864** *Epperly CW Letters* (March 12) ther hant no plesure to be sean in this evel and distresin war. **1883** Zeigler and Grosscup *Heart of Alleghanies* 51 "What I don't know about these mountings," said he, directing his keen blue eyes upon one member of the group, "haint of enny profit to man or devil." **1901** Harben *Westerfelt* 142 I hain't in entire sympathy with Toot. **1937** Hall *Coll* (Tuckaleechee Cove TN) I hain't writin' you a list of rules. **1942** Hall *Phonetics Smoky Mts* 93 Inorganic [h] often occurs in *ain't* "am not," "is not," "are not," apparently by analogy with [hent], "has not," "have not." **c1945** Haun *Hawk's Done* 211 There hain't no commoner man living than old man Fuller. **1956** Hall *Coll* (Hurricane Creek NC) I thought, "Hain't no use to tell you anything about my sickness, Dr. Abels. I ain't got no money." **1969** *GSMNP*-46:2 They hain't a-going to do that. **1973** *GSMNP*-88:8 They hain't hardly a man that can get through there. **1983** *Dark Corner OHP*-9A Bees in May is worth a bale of hay, bees in June is worth a silver spoon, and bees in July hain't worth a fly. **1989** Landry *Smoky Mt Interviews* 194 They think they are, but they hain't. **1998** *Dante OHP*-61 "If your heart han't right whenever the breath leaves," I said, "You're just a hell-bound chicken." **2009** Fields *Growing Up* 36 This off-brand gun hant worth nothin a-tall.

2 Used in statements with inversion of the subject and verb.

1971 *AOHP/ALC*-32 Hain't nobody knows. **1972** *AOHP/ALC*-298 Hain't none of them married. **1974** Dabney *Mt Spirits* 118 I've made lots of it [= whiskey], a sight of it, that-a-way, but hain't nobody around this country that I know of that lives that knows of how to make a doubling liquor now. **1974** Roberts *Sang Branch* 20 I'll study some [songs] up and get that old banjer in order. Hain't no strings on it now.

B = negative forms of present-tense *have*.

1 = *has not, have not*.

1861 *Watters-Curtis CW Letters* (Dec 24) i know wat it is to bee Sick for if ihant exprionst it for the last to weaks nobo dy hant. **1862** *Enloe CW Letter* I hant any thing of much interest to right at this time. . . . I have wrote four letters to you and hant had no answer from you. **1862** *Watters-Curtis CW Letters* (April 12) I hant Not Mutch of importan[ce] To write to you. **1867** Harris *Sut Lovingood* 125 Sumtimes the boys gits ontu a "tare" ove nites, an' tries tu upset [the town] ontu hits side, but haint never got hit turn'd down. **1886** Smith *Sthn Dialect* 348 Well, fellers, ef you'uns cross the mountains about dinner time, you'd better come by and git yer dinner; you-uns hain't got the wuth of yer quarter yit. **1897** *Incidents* 27 An my frens, you all can't help ahavin' bad thoughts kum inter yer heads, but ye hain't got no necessity fer ter set 'em a cheer. **1913** Kephart *Our Sthn High* 130 Twa'n't (so and so) fer he hain't got no squar'-headed hobnails. *Ibid.* 119 Mister, we-uns hain't no call to be ashamed of ourselves, nor of ary thing that we do. **1939** Hall Coll (Cades Cove TN) They hain't found it yet. **1940** Haun *Hawk's Done* 127 Grandpa had a deed for it and we hain't never had it changed to our names. **1974** *AOHP/ALC-802* It's hard to understand if you hain't had the experience, and I've had plenty of it. **1983** *Dark Corner OHP-5A* Preacher Howard has told them some up yonder about these [people] getting killed up here at Romaine's, I guess, hain't he? **1986** Pederson et al. *LAGS* (Jefferson Co TN) It hain't been built but just a little while. **1989** *Matewan OHP-33* I hain't got no woman and don't want any. **1998** *Dante OHP-61* [The house is] right below that one that hain't got nobody living in it.

2 Used in statements with inversion of the subject and verb.

1953 Hall Coll (Bryson City NC) Hain't nobody never set it [= a bear trap] for any bears since. That's been thirty years ago.

hainted tale, **haint tale** See **haunt tale**.

hair *noun*

A Variant forms *har* [hɑr], *h'ar*, *ha'r*, *hawr*.

1859 Taliaferro *Fisher's River* 55 My har would stand on eend, stiff as hog's bristles, at the noise uv uvry lizzard that ran through the leaves. **1867** Harris *Sut Lovingood* 155 The idear now begin tu soak thru my har that owin to the fuss Stuff-gut an' me hed raised, that perhaps I'd better scoot, lest they mout want me. **1904** Johnson *Highways South* 141 Yo' hear that in the night an' hit'll raise the ha'r on yore head. **1913** Kephart *Our Sthn High* 107 He bit a hole under the foreleg, through hide and ha'r, clar to the holler. **1942** Hall *Phonetics Smoky Mts* 24 [hær]. **1967** Fetterman *Stinking Creek* 142 If you are a real good Christian you are not supposed to cut your hawr and wear this makeup. **1994** Montgomery Coll [hær] (known to Cardwell). **2006** Ledford *Survivals* 1014 The Appalachian tendency for r to modify the pronunciation of the preceding vowel (*tar* "tire," *har* "hair," and *arish potatoes* "Irish potatoes") is similar to phonetic spellings found in colonial writings.

B Forms.

1 Variant plural form without *-s*.

1940 Bowman *KY Mt Stories* 240 *hair* (no singular form used). **1996** Montgomery Coll I've got just a few gray hair (Adams).

2 Construed as a count noun in reference to the hair of the head; hence plural form *hairs*. See also **beard**, **moustache**.

1930 Armstrong *This Day and Time* 7 Ef she hadn't a'gone an' bobbed her hairs.

hair ball (also *hair ball*) *noun* A small wad of hair used either by a witch to cast a spell and inflict injury or by one seeking to counter a witch's action. Also called **conjure ball**. See also **witch ball**.

1914 Combs *Magic in KY Mts* 328 The picture of the victim crudely scrawled upon a tree . . . by a witch who wishes to work the black art, does not mean much unless the witch-ball or hair-ball is used. A small bunch of hair from a horse or cow is rolled between the two hands into a small round ball, and this ball is used as a bullet. In whatever part the ball hits the picture, in the corresponding part of the victim a wound is inflicted. **1957** Combs *Lg Sthn High: Word List* 47 = a dangerous ammunition used by witches and wizards. It is made by rolling between the hands a small bunch of hair from a horse or "cow-brute." If such a ball is shot from a gun at the crude image of the bewitched on a tree, etc., it will find its mark, and the bewitched person will die. But a silver bullet will kill a witch or wizard. **2007** Milnes *Signs Cures Witches* 167 Witch balls and/or hairballs are an unusual but fairly widely known supernatural phenomenon in the Appalachians. There are two very different classifications of a witch ball. The first kind, also called a hairball, is believed to be sent to people supernaturally as a curse. The second is made of glass and is commonly used for divination. **2012** Milnes *Signs Cures Witchery* Hair balls can just appear like a . . . tumbleweed for some reason . . . to see a hairball is like a curse.

[DARE *hair ball* n South Midland]

hairy tick *noun* See 1975 citation.

c1975 Lunsford *It Used to Be* 159 "Hairy tick" is an expression used for "heretic." Some person in church who has had an independent thought about something that's contrary to the idea of the person in authority of the predominating group would be pointed out as a "hairy tick." **1997** Montgomery Coll (known to Cardwell).

[folk etymology for *heretic*]

haith See **hearth**.

half-a-bushel gourd *noun* A gourd serving as a relatively large container when dried out.

1973 *Foxfire Interviews* A-73-43 They call them half-a-bushel gourds . . . they just grow up more like a pumpkin than anything else. People used to make them and they used them, old folks did, about putting things in, maybe keeping stuff in around the house.

half after *adjective phrase* Thirty minutes past (the hour).

1863 *Kiracofe CW Letters* (Feb 18) we took the Cars free of Charge & Came on to gordens till 12 oclock there being an Engine off the track we Could not get by we ware detained there till half after Four. **c1960** Wilson *Coll* = *half after ten: past* is about equally common. **1966** Dakin *Vocab Ohio River Valley* 16 Fairly common in the Mountains, and scattered throughout the rest of Kentucky, the expression *half after* is still used, most often in addition to the other expressions. North of the river *half after* is rare. **1986** Pederson et al. *LAGS* = attested by 10/60 interviewees (16.7%) from E TN; 10/31 of all LAGS interviewees (32.3%) attesting term were from E TN.

half back *noun* A northerner who retired or moved to Florida but more recently resettled to North Carolina because of not wanting to return to northern winters. See citation.

2006 *Encycl Appalachia* 229 More recent terms have been invented for specific groups of furriners and find usage in either joking or serious connotation. In western North Carolina, where furriners in increasing numbers retire, vacation, or construct summer houses, the terms *floridiot* and *half back* came into usage in the late twentieth century. *Half back* applies to New Yorkers or other northeasterners who moved to Florida before resettling to North Carolina, where they were "half back" to where they started.

half-brindle-to-buck *adjective phrase* Of cattle: having mixed or uncertain breeding.

1952 Wilson *Folk Speech NC* 549 = of uncertain pedigree or ancestry. "That bull is *half-brindle-to-buck*." **c1975** Lunsford *It Used to Be* 165 The term "half brinnel to buck" is speaking of a yearling or a calf, or a cow. You'd ask what stock it is and if it's kind of a mixed breed, they'd say "it's half brinnel to buck."

half do *noun phrase* Something poorly made or work only partially completed.

1957 Parris *Mt Mts* 69 Always had enough and then some on the table. She never made no half-dos. She didn't cook a lot of knick-knacks like womenfolks do nowadays. **1995–97** Montgomery *Coll* (known to Brown, Cardwell, Ledford, Oliver).

half man *noun* See citation.

1939 Farr *TN Mt Regions* 90 = a half pint of whiskey: "A half man laid him out."

[cf SND (at *half* n II I 14(b)) "a half bottle (of spirits)"]

half-moon pie *noun* A small fruit pie, usually with apples, eaten by hand. See also **fried pie**, **hand pie**, **moon pie**.

[**1967** Wilson *Folkways Mammoth Cave* 12 Though they were served in several ways throughout the winter, when fresh fruit was hard to get, fried pies, made in half-moon form, seemed the best liked use of all.] **1978** Parris *Mt Cooking* 114 Your great-grandma made apple pies that looked like a half moon or a new moon. She had a vessel that had a ridge in it. She'd bake part of the pie in one side and part in the other. Called 'em moon pies. **1983** Montell *Don't Go Up* 64 She cooked her apples and was gonna make these little half-moon pies, and it was customary to fry them. But she didn't have the lard to do it. **1992** Brooks *Sthn Stuff* 62 = a circle of rich dough that has been filled with stewed fruit, folded over, and fried. **2006** *Encycl Appalachia* 932 Fried pies are served hot or cold and are usually eaten not with a fork but out of hand. Also called half-moon pies because of their half-circle shape, they are formed from circles of biscuit or pastry dough, the size of the circle determining the size of the finished pie. One side of the circle is spread with fruit, the other side is then folded over and the edges sealed.

[DARE *half-moon pie* n especially South Midland]

half-pint Baptist *noun* See citation. See also **five-gallon Baptist**, **forty-gallon Baptist**.

2002 Myers *Best Yet Stories* 44 "Half-pint Baptists" sprinkled only the head. If the body became thoroughly wet, members were called "Five-Gallon Baptists." **2009** Skipper *Billy Bean* 141 When the third carload of necktied men and bright-bloused women passed on their way to the half-pint Baptist church two miles out the road, Lane spoke aloud to himself and realized he was really speaking to God.

half-runner (bean) *noun* A rambling legume. See 2011 citation.

1984 Head *Brogans* 108 He raised Kentucky Wonder green beans and some of the "half-runner" varieties, and they did well each year. **1986** Pederson et al. *LAGS* = attested by 20/60 interviewees (33.3%) in E TN and 2/35 (5.7%) in N GA; 22/32 of all LAGS interviewees (68.8%) attesting term were in Appalachia. **1996** Houk *Foods & Recipes* 47 Smoky Mountain horticulture includes a lengthy litany of legumes—creaseback, cutshort, cornfield beans, bunch beans, pink or peanut beans, greasy beans, sulfur beans, and half runners. **1996–97** Montgomery *Coll* (known to eight consultants from the Smoky Mountains), = most popular type of green bean in the area (Ellis). **2007** Farr *My Appalachia* 68 When the rows of corn were shoulder-high, Mama would stick in half-runner beans, which would grow up and twine around the cornstalk. This kept the beans off the ground and made picking them easier. The beans never hurt the corn. **2011** Best *Bean Terminology* = a term given to many varieties of beans where the runner is roughly from three to ten feet long. It might be more accurate to say that there are quarter runner beans, half-runner beans and full runner beans with full runner beans climbing to twenty feet or more. **2016** Netherland *Appal Cooking* 71 We also grew half runners—green beans with 2- to 3-feet runners.

[DARE *half-runner bean* n chiefly southern Appalachians]

half sense *noun* Ordinary intelligence, common sense. See also **bay horse sense**.

1937 Hall *Coll* (Copeland Creek TN) She didn't have more than half-sense nohow. **1956** McAtee *Some Dial NC* 21 If you had half-sense, you wouldn't do that.

half sled *noun* A sled of short length so as to be handled and turned more easily. See also **dry-land sled**, **lizard 1**.

1937 Wilburn *Notes* Also a half sled [was] used for snakeing [sic] wood. **1952** Wilson *Folk Speech NC* 549 = a sled for hauling logs. **1967** *DARE Survey* (Gatlinburg TN) = runners and sled, a low wooden platform used for bringing stones or heavy things out of the fields.

half-turnip *noun* A type of **still** for making whiskey.

1985 Dabney *More Mt Spirits* 154 The copper pot "mother still" is found in three configurations—the "turnip," round and fat; the "half turnip," and the upright copper pot, shaped like a metal drum and placed vertically in the furnace. It is also called the Buccaneer, the Blockade Still and the "mountain teapot." The American copper pot is very similar to the "poit du" (black pot) stills on display in the Highland Folk Museum in Scotland and the Poteen stills in Ireland.

hallo (also *hallo the house*, *hello*) *verb* To call or cry *hello* from a distance to announce one's presence, in order to ascertain if anyone is at home; to call to (presumed inhabitants); hence noun *hallo* = such a call. Same as **holler**[2] **A2**.

1860 *Week in Smokies* 121 I rightly concluded that I was at Mr. Huskey's—the greatest hunter of all that region. Halloing, I was answered by the fierce outcry of "both mongrel whelp and hound and cur of low degree." **1940** Bowman *KY Mt Stories* 240 *halloed* = called from a safe distance instead of knocking at the door. **1964** Roberts *Hell-Fer-Sartin* 4 If I had been alone I would have stood in the road and "halloed the house." **1977** Still *Wonder Beans* 28 When Jack tipped the ground he halloed to his mam, "Fetch the ax!" **1993** Cunningham *Sthn Talk* 70 *hello* = used instead of knocking on the door. **1996** Isbell *Last Chivaree* 125–26 He called his hallo from a comfortable distance, as mountain people are wont to do.

hall-tree *noun* See citation.

1957 Combs *Lg Sthn High: Word List* 48 = the hawthorn.

hallway *noun* An open passage between two buildings or two halves of a building, especially a barn. See 1956 citation. Same as **dogtrot**.

1939 Hall *Coll* (Smokemont NC) They come a big rain and washed the old foot-bridge plumb into the hallway between the barns. **1956** Hall *Coll* (Bryson City NC) In the old log houses the rooms were built separately (and detached), as the family needed more room, but were covered usually with a common roof. Often an open hallway (sometimes called a breezeway) separated two such linked log houses. **1963** Edwards *Gravel* 171 The black horse kicked a circle all around the hall-way, where he was tethered. **1967** *DARE Survey* (Cumberland Gap TN) = the part of a barn where horses are kept. **1986** Pederson et al. *LAGS* (Sullivan Co TN).

[DARE *hallway* n 1 especially TN]

halvers See **go halvers, on shares.**

ham bacon See **ham meat.**

hame *noun* A curved bar fitted into the harness and attached to the traces of a horse or mule; hence *hame string* = a short leather strap attached to the *hame* of a horse or mule. See also **bust a hame string.**

1967 *DARE Survey* (Gatlinburg TN) *hame strings*. **1990** Fisher *Preacher Stories* 57 When the preacher finished the row, sweating and dirty, he threw the lines over the hames, and walked back to where the farmer was still standing. **1995** Weber *Rugged Hills* 82 Then he'd set the grabs with a hammer or "skip." A skip had a steel mallet-like head on one end and a sharp point on the other. You used the hammer to set the grabs and the pointed end to pry them loose. The handle had a hole with a loop of rope threaded through it. That way you could just hang the skip from the hames on the horses' harness when you weren't using it. **2002** Hayler *Sound Wormy* 203 = curved pieces of harness that fit around the neck of a draft animal and to which the traces are attached.

hame string See **hame.**

ham meat (also *ham bacon, ham of meat*) *noun* Ham.

1863 *Copenhaver CW Letters* (Jan 12) I want you to send me a box of provision somthing that I can eat I have been about half Sick just for the want of something to eat that is good such as butter & appel butter or chickens or a ham of meat. **1864** *Poteet CW Letters* (Feb 4) I sent you somthing to eat by Marion Higins five pies and five ginger Cakes one doz unions two custerds 1 ham of Meat and three twists of tobacco. **1924** Raine *Saddlebags* 105 This desire for exactness has given such expressions as . . . ham-meat. *Ibid.* 211 Usually he slaughters a hog or two for his "meat." This, salted and sometimes smoked, provides the necessary supply of bacon, "ham-meat" and lard. **1937** Wilson *Folklore SE KY* 32 *ham bacon*. **1957** Combs *Lg Sthn High: Word List* 48 *ham of meat* = ham. **c1960** Wilson *Coll*: *ham-meat* = a tautology very common in this area. **1973** GSMNP-4:2:4 In might' near all homes you'd have biscuits and all the ham meat you wanted to eat. **1983** *Dark Corner OHP*-5A You'll have to go out yonder and get that last ham of meat we been saving. **1997** GSMNPCOHP-5:19 That was some of the best ham meat that I ever ate.

[DARE *ham-meat* n South Midland]

hammer dog *noun* See citation. See also **dog² 2.**

1994 Farwell and Buchanan *Logging Terms* = an implement that held the logs in place.

hammer-headed *adjective* See citation.

1927 Woofter *Dialect from WV* 356 = a horse with a head shaped like a hammer: "Pap came home with an old hammer-headed horse."

ham of meat See **ham meat.**

hamper *verb* See 1913 citation.

1913 Kephart *Our Sthn High* 295 Some highland usages that sound odd to us are really no more than the original and literal meanings, as . . . hampered for shackled or jailed. **1994–97** Montgomery *Coll* (known to Brown, Bush, Cardwell, Cypher, Oliver).

hancher (also *handkercher, hankcher, hankecher, hankercher, hankersher, hanksher*) *noun* A handkerchief.

1867 Harris *Sut Lovingood* 161 Pimple-face wall'd up his eyes, coff'd blow'd his nose in his hankecher, an' sorter looked behine the preacher, like he 'spected tu see a buzzard, or an' onbelever, or sich like, atween him an' the wall. **1927** Dingus *Appal Mt Words* 470 *hankersher*. **1931** Thomas *Ditties* 46 His magic fingers transformed his red bandana "hanksher" into something amazing. **1952** Wilson *Folk Speech NC* 549 *hancher* [ˈhæntʃɚ] = handkerchief. **1955** Ritchie *Singing Family* 83 He'd get that p'int expounded and then he'd take his hankcher and wipe off his face, and begin again. **c1975** Lunsford *It Used to Be* 174 "Hankercher" for handkerchief. "I always keep a little money tied in the corner of my hankercher." **1978** Burns *Our Sthn Mtneers* 12 He may speak of a "sight of flowers," "riving shingles," "handkerchers." **1995** Montgomery *Coll* Fay, I'm needing my handkercher (Cardwell). **2005** Williams *Gratitude* 37 *hancher*.

[OED3 (at *handkerchief*) formerly literary, still common dialect and vulgar]

hand

A *noun*

1 Handwriting, one's style of penmanship. Same as **handwrite**.

1939 Hall *Coll* (Hartford TN) I went to a writing school about a couple of days. I got some copy and I kept fooling with them copies till I could begin to write, and I got so I could write a pretty good hand. **1991** Thomas *Sthn Appal* 194 He took up writin'. An' he got so he could write a very good hand, to write.

2 A worker, hired person.

1939 Hall *Coll* (Cosby Creek TN) He'd jack up the best hand he had. **1978** *Smokies Heritage* 152 That man was a worker. About as good a hand as I ever seen to do just about anything.

[DARE *hand* n B1 scattered, but chiefly South, South Midland]

3 A person, with reference to an individual's skill, suitability, proficiency, or interest for a certain activity or task (especially with *at* or *to* in such phrases as *good hand at, no hand to*). For similar patterns with *to*, see the Grammar and Syntax §10.2.

1859 Taliaferro *Fisher's River* 111 Dick was a rough hand to joke people. **1877** Carpenter *Diary I* 112 Alek Wiseman . . . war good hand to mak brandy. **1900** Harben *N GA Sketches* 272 I hain't no hand to stir up strife in a community. I've tried to be law-abidin' an' honest. **1904** Johnson *Highways South* 124 The people are great han's for religion, and it's a common saying they got mo religion an' less morals than yo'll find anywhere else in the world. **1926** Hunnicutt *Twenty Years* 49 Andrew being a good hand to skin and dress coons, he proposed that he would skin and dress the coons. **1937** Hall *Coll* (Ravensford NC) She's an awful hand to fish [i.e. she's crazy about fishing]. **1939** Hall *Coll* (Cataloochee NC) Mont Hannah's a good hand on stories. *Ibid.* (Cosby Creek TN) I was a awful hand to coon hunt . . . He was a extry hand to work . . . I reckon I'm a poor hand to judge. *Ibid.* (Cades Cove TN) He was no hand to hunt. He made a few trips to bear hunt. He farmed mostly for a living. **1944** Wilson *Word-List* 46 He was a master hand at making chairs. **1955** Dykeman *French Broad* 237 He's the best hand in the country to pick a jury. **1973** GSMNP-85:1:21 I'm not a good hand to recollect back so much. **1974** Ogle *Memories* 4 Father was a great hand to sing, so in the winter especially, he'd call us kids and tell us to get our song books, that we were going to sing. **1981** Henry *Alex Stewart* 54 I's allus a pretty good hand to remember something once I'd learnt it. **1982** Powers and Hannah *Cataloochee* 232 He was no hand at loaferin' at all. **1984** Wilder *You All Spoken* 34 *good hand* = one adapted for, inclined to, fitted for jobs of work; a good tobacco hand sits at the first table. **1985** Irwin *Alex Stewart* 202 My Grandma Stewart was the best hand to garden, I guess, that they ever was in this country. **1997** Montgomery *File* He was a good hand to break a oxen (60-year-old man, Maggie Valley NC). **2004** House *Coal Tattoo* 138 You can make the corn bread—you're the best hand at making it. **2008** Salsi *Ray Hicks* 197 I wouldn't be such a good hand to tell the stories today.

4 A handful, usually tied, of leaves of tobacco or **blades** of corn. See citations.

1940 Fitzpatrick *Lg Tobacco Market* 134 (also *head*) = a number of leaves tied in a bunch. **1957** Broaddus *Vocab Estill Co KY* 38 = several leaves of cured tobacco tied into a bunch. **1968** Guthrie *Tobacco* 42 A *tobacco-stripper* usually picked up the plant with his left hand, removed the leaves of his grade with the thumb and first finger of the right, and held the stripped leaves between the fingers and palm of the right hand until their *butts* made a bundle the size of a half-dollar. The leaves were then tied into a hand by wrapping the butts with a good leaf of the same grade. **1984** Woods *WV Was Good* 22 When it [= tobacco] was dried, Dad took it down and packed it in what we called "hands"—bunches about the size of a large ham. **1985** Kiser *Life and Times* 58 The blades of the corn was all stripped off as much as the hands could hold. This "hand," as it was called, was placed between two stalks of corn. **1986** Watts *Same Block* 75 The dictionary says fodder is any food for cattle, horse, sheep, etcetera, like cornstalks, hay, and straw; but around here fodder meant the blades only. These blades were put in what they called "hands" as they were pulled, and placed between the stalks above the ground. Corn was grown with 2–3 stalks to the hill and if two stalks were close enough together the hands could be put between them and not touch the ground. If this was not the case, a blade was used to tie the hands to the stalk below the ears, but off the ground. **1995** Weber *Rugged Hills* 77 Years ago, farmers bunched their tobacco into "hands" of seven or so leaves, then bound them with a leaf on a flat oak basket for market—a job that took many hours in a cold dimly lit barn. **1996** Spurlock *Glossary* 399 = twenty to twenty-five leaves of moist, cured tobacco gathered together by the stem ends and bound ("tied") by a leaf tied tightly around these ends.

B *verb* To gather and tie (tobacco leaves) into small bundles.

1995 Weber *Rugged Hills* 77 In late autumn, shelling corn, getting in firewood and "handing" tobacco could leave fingers and toes more than a little cold. *Ibid.* 134 In the fall when barns are cold and dank, you can find the same families "handing" their tobacco—sorting it and getting it ready to bale.

hand at See **hand A3**.

hand-down *noun* An account or story passed on from a previous generation.

1983 *Dark Corner OHP-11A* Now this is a hand-down. It may not be a word of truth in it.

hand fishing *noun* Same as **noodling**.

2006 *Encycl Appalachia* 872 Native Americans caught spawning catfish with their hands, a practice that may be part of the origin of the sport of noodling. Also called hand grabbing, grabbling, hand fishing, or hogging, noodling is still a well-known activity in the larger rivers and reservoirs of Appalachia. Noodlers target most catfish species but their real prize is the flathead catfish, known in Appalachia as the mudcat. Noodling remains popular with some, but the method is only practical during the brief few weeks in which catfish spawn and noodlers can locate them in hollow logs and other cavities where they nest.

handful of minutes *noun phrase* See citation.

1953 Davison *Word-List Appal* 11 *Handful of minutes* . . . Denoting smallness: "She ain't no bigger than a handful of minutes, but she can whip us."

hand going *adverb phrase* In immediate succession, consecutively. See also **hand running**.

1862 Hitt *CW Letters* (May 27) [The dream] appeard plane to mee and Jest like wee talked to gether two nits hand going. **1890** Fruit *KY Words* 65 *hand running*. Hand running, *hand-going*. **1911** Shearin *E KY Word-List* 538 = in succession. **1944** Combs *Word-List Sthn High* 19 Mace's Jim sot up with (courted) Nance's Liz two nights hand-goin'. **c1945** Haun *Hawk's Done* 255 I sat on the mourner's bench three nights straight hand going with head bent down. **1969** Ferrell *Bear Tales* 27 "Last y'ar," Guy said with a zest undiminished by the passage of time, "I killed four b'ars in four days handgoing." **1994** Montgomery *Coll* (known to Shields).

[DARE *hand going* adv phr southern Appalachians]

hand grabbing *noun* Same as **noodling**.

2006 *Encycl Appalachia* 872 Native Americans caught spawning catfish with their hands, a practice that may be part of the origin of the sport of noodling. Also called hand grabbing, grabbling, hand fishing, or hogging, noodling is still a well-known activity in the larger rivers and reservoirs of Appalachia. Noodlers target most catfish species but their real prize is the flathead catfish, known in Appalachia as the mudcat. Noodling remains popular with some, but the method is only practical during the brief few weeks in which catfish spawn and noodlers can locate them in hollow logs and other cavities where they nest.

hand-holt *noun* The hole cut into the protruding stave of a **piggin** by which the vessel is carried.

1927 Mason *Lure of Smokies* 124 The "piggin" . . . was an odd pail, of red cedar usually, with the handle on one side made of an extended stave with a "hand holt" cut in it.

handily *adverb* Rightly, readily, reasonably. See also **handy B**.

1917 Kephart *Word-List* 413 = readily. "You couldn't *handily* blame him." **c1945** Haun *Hawk's Done* 310 I couldn't a-handily been blamed if I hadn't, I reckon, if I had stayed away and let the boys shift for theirselves. **1952** Wilson *Folk Speech NC* 549 = rightly, justly. "You can't *handily* get rid of her."

[Web3 *handily* adv 2 Midland; DARE *handily* adv southern Appalachians]

hand in one's checks See **check[2] 3**.

handirons See **andirons**.

handkercher See **hancher**.

handle *verb* To speak, use (a specified kind of language).

1976 Still *Pattern of Man* 80 Our soldier boys have come home telling a mixture of things. Most handle only the truth and if wonders they viewed grow big in their mouths I lay it to high spirits. **2001** House *Clay's Quilt* 2 Sides, you ought to be praying instead of handling bad language. **2005** Williams *Gratitude* 500 = to use a certain kind of speech, usually vulgar or profane. "You ortn't to be *a-handlin'* that kind of talk in front of women and childern."

handler *noun* See citation.

1936 Farr *Folk Speech Mid TN* 275 = name: "What is your handler?"

hand mill *noun* A small mill for grinding corn, operated manually. See also **hominy pounder**, **lazy Jim**, **pounding mill**, **quern**, **slow John**, **tri-weekly**.

1824 (in **1912** Doddridge *Notes on Settlement* 112) The hand mill was better than the mortar and grater. It was made of two circular stones, the lowest of which was called the bed stone, the upper one the runner. These were placed in a hoop, with a spout for discharging the meal. **1847** (in **1870** Drake *Pioneer Life KY* 59) My father never owned a hand-mill, but on those of his neighbors, when ten or twelve years of age, I have ground many a small grist. **1913** Kephart *Our Sthn High* 291 In some places to-day we still find the ancient quern or hand-mill, jocularly called an armstrong machine. **1948** Dick *Dixie Frontier* 250 Hand mills were sometimes used, succeeding hominy blocks. They consisted of two circular flat stones. The Corn was fed in through a hole in the runner. By means of a handle two people turned the runner, and the corn meal ran out of a spout on the side of the bed stone. In later times a small steel mill was used. **1956** Hall *Coll* (Big Bend NC) [How did people grind their meal when you were a boy?]: They'd have to grind their meal with a hand mill. There was a water mill at the mouth of Cold Spring [Creek].

handover See **hanover**.

hand pie *noun* A small fruit pie. See also **fried pie**, **half-moon pie**, **moon pie**.

1939 Still *Sugar in Gourd* 101 She handed us a plate of cold hand-pies, and a rag bag of a quilt. **1967** *DARE Survey* (Hardshell KY) = made of dried applies. **2016** Lundy and Autry *Victuals* 44 Half-moon-shaped hand pies are usually filled with a sweet dried apple or peach filling, but they were such a handy thing to pack inside a miner's lunch pail that some enterprising wives and mothers packed the pastries with meat.

hand running *adverb phrase* In immediate succession, continuously. See also **hand going**.

1814 Hartsell *Memora* 137 I have bin Caled to Set on Cort martial for four days hand runnin to try Delinquenerees. **1863** Robinson *CW Letters* (Feb 18) our Regt has bin on picket 5 nites han Runing. **1927** Mason *Lure of Smokies* 198 He lay thar two days, hand-runnin', dead—and dead drunk betwixt it. **1944** Wilson *Word-List* 43 = continuously. "I been setting up two nights *hand-running*." **1963** Edwards *Gravel* 108 They must have been a warning to me that you and Paw was not well, and I'm glad I did dream about you two nights hand running, or I might not have come. **1976** GSMNP-113:7 I raised six boys just hand runnin', then two girls, then the last'un was a boy. **1994** Montgomery *Coll* (known to Shields). **2008** McCaulley *Cove Childhood* 41 For thirteen years "hand runnin'," he said, "we had turkey breast with gravy for Easter dinner."

[OED3 *hand-running* adv phr English regional (north) and U.S. regional; EDD (at *hand* sb 1.79); CUD *hand running* (at *hand* n) "continuously"; HT *han-rinnin* (at *han*) "in succession, in a row"; DARE *hand running* adv phr 1 widespread, but more frequent South Midland]

handsome *adverb* Handsomely.

1913 Kephart *Our Sthn High* 121 The big fellers that makes lots of money out o' stillin', and lives in luxury, ought to pay handsome for it.

handspike (also *handstick*) *noun* See citations.

1946 Wilson *Fidelity Folks* 204 We could lift at the end of a handstick until our eyes bulged. **c1960** Wilson *Coll*: *handstick* = a strong stick, usually of hickory, used in lifting logs at a log-rolling. Called also *handspike*.

handstick See **handspike**.

hand to See **hand A3**.

handwrite *noun* One's handwriting, style of penmanship. Same as **hand A1**.

1863 *Robinson CW Letters* (Jan 6) I Recived your kind letter yesterday & was hapy to heare from you & to See Some of your hand rite. **1865** *Misemer CW Letters* (April 11) last night J W Maxwell got one [= a letter] from his mother and I suppoesed you was still alived as I recognised your hand write. **1922** *TN CW Ques* 1178 (Putnam Co TN) I will close as i am tierd hopeing you will excuse my bad hand write as I think you will after considering I am 80 yrs. old. **1940** Still *River of Earth* 77 "Jolly's name's signed," Mother said, "but it's not his handwrite." **1973** *GSMNP-83*:26 They was sixty words wrote, and they was two handwrites. **1985** Irwin *Alex Stewart* 37 He could write the purtiest handwrite ever I seed. **1995** Montgomery *Coll* He had a good handwrite [= cursive writing] (Cardwell). **2017** *Blind Pig* (Jan 12) Back then your handwrite was your photo ID. Like a fingerprint it could be used to identify you. People went to jail or were proven innocent by their handwrite.

[OED3 *handwrite* n originally and chiefly Scottish; cf SND *hand of write* (at *hand* n 8 (18)); CUD *handwrite* (at *hand* n) "handwriting"; DARE *handwrite* n chiefly South, South Midland]

handy

A *adjective* Of a person: adroit, dexterous.

1963 Edwards *Gravel* 82 It was common talk that the Preacher was handy among the women folks, often laughing . . . with the avowed intention of committing osculation. **1966** Dykeman *Far Family* 41 Just seems like you're so handy with criticizing others.

B *adverb* Easily, rightly, readily. Se also **handily**.

1861 *Hanes CW Letters* (Oct 7) tel Jim that I would A liked mity to a helpt him a shucked his corn but it was so I ouldent **handy** but that I will help harvest next sumer. **c1900** (in **1997** Stoddart *Quare Women* 127) I stade as long as I handy could. **1949** Arnow *Hunter's Horn* 14 They have to have a little ship stuff er I'd run out a corn, less'n I starved em, en a body cain't handy starve a lamben yoe. **1952** Wilson *Folk Speech NC* 549 = rightly, justly. "You just can't *handy* blame him for not telling you the truth."

handyover See **Antony-over**.

hang *verb* To persevere.

1913 Kephart *Our Sthn High* 80–81 A plumb cur, of course, cain't foller a cold track—he just runs by sight: and he won't hang—he quits. **1953** Hall *Coll* (Bryson City NC) So we just hung, went on, looked for our cattle. **1995–97** Montgomery *Coll* (known to Brown, Norris, Oliver).

hang fishing *noun* See citation.

1990 Davis *Homeplace* 18 Traditionally, those who fished with trotlines baited them with small frogs and/or "spring lizards" (salamanders) and set them just before dark. People on some parts of the Tennessee and Mississippi River valleys still practice this method of fishing today, and variations of it ("jug" or "hang" fishing).

hang the moon *verb phrase* See citations.

c1960 Wilson *Coll* = to be a VIP, especially to one's followers. **1992** Brooks *Sthn Stuff* 73 = [to be] greatly admired; well thought of. "Her mother wasn't silly about her, but her daddy—well, he thought she hung the moon."

[DARE *hang the moon* v phr chiefly South Midland]

hankcher, hankecher, hanksher See **hancher**.

hanker after *verb phrase* See citations.

1931 Owens *Speech Cumberlands* 90 = to hang around after: "You orter have more spunk than to hanker ater somebody who doesn't want you." **c1975** Lunsford *It Used to Be* 157 The word "hanker" means a person kind of has a desire for something: for friendship, or for some kind of chance in a trade, or, if he admires some young lady, they say, "He has a kind of hankerin' atter."

hankercher See **hancher**.

hankering *noun* A premonition, foreboding. [Editor's note: This term in the sense of "yearning" is widespread in the US.]

1940 Haun *Hawk's Done* 65 Enzor must have got a hankering some way, because when his horse come along Enzor wasn't on it.

hankersher See **hancher**.

Hannah sop *noun* Flour gravy. Same as **Betsy sop**. See also **sop A**.

1997 Montgomery *File* (70-year-old man, Maggie Valley NC).

hanover (also *handover*, *handover turnip*) *noun* A rutabaga.

1957 Broaddus *Vocab Estill Co KY* 38 *handover turnip* = rutabaga. **1968–70** *DARE Survey* (Laurel Fork VA, Marlinton WV, Milton WV, Richwood WV, Salem WV, Spencer WV) *hanover* = the large yellowish root vegetable, similar to a turnip, with a strong taste. **1975** Riedl *House Customs* 49 [At a house raising] there were chicken and dumplings, beans, "hanover" (rutabaga), corn, rhubarb, greens such as poke salet and dock, pumpkin pie, milk, and jellies. **2008** Salsi *Ray Hicks* 116 We called rutabagers "hand overs." Sometimes at the dinner table, we'd say "hand over" the "hand overs."

[DARE *hanover* n 1 especially WV, VA, MD]

hant See **haunt.**

hant bleach *noun* A pallor, facial appearance "as white as a ghost."

1940 Haun *Hawk's Done* 45 His skin, it was white as a strawberry blossom. Some folks said he looked like he had the hant bleach.

hanted See **haunt.**

hantle (also *hantle full*) *noun* An amount or number, interpreted variously in size. See citations.

1928 Chapman *Happy Mt* 63 The inside of the schoolhouse was scarcely to be seen for the hantle of people. **1936** Farr 275 *hantle full* = small crowd. "There was only a hantle full at the meeting." **1995** Montgomery *Coll* = a handful, small number (Bush), = a great plenty (Ellis).

[OED3 *hantle* n Scot and north dialect 1692→; EDD *hantle* sb 1 Scot, nEngl "handful"; SND *hantle* n 1 "a considerable quantity"; DARE *hantle* n chiefly southern Appalachians]

hantle full See **hantle.**

hant tale See **haunt tale.**

hap *adverb* Perhaps.

1921 Weeks *Speech of KY Mtneer* 19 Even after a feller has been to college he is liable to histe a winder an' put the chimley or chimbley on the coal oil lamp if hap be thar's a chimley or chimbley in the house. **1941** Still *Proud Walkers* 113 Then hap baby will go to sleep.

haper-scaper *adverb* In a disorderly pattern.

1979 Slone *My Heart* 52 To us a patch was not a bright colored swatch, placed "haper-scaper" on our jeans to make them look fancy. We patched our clothes to prolong their life and to keep the wind from whistling through a hole.

happen *conjunction* If it occurs that, would it occur that. See also **if happen.**

1953 Wharton *Dr Woman Cumberlands* 45 Happen you might look at them too? **1975** Chalmers *Better* 66 "It would pleasure me," Aunt Lou used to say, "for you to come and set a spell happen you pass."

[cf EDD *happen* v^1 2]

happen-so *noun* A chance occurrence.

1952 Wilson *Folk Speech NC* 549 = a coincidence, a thing that merely happened without pre-arrangement or intention. **1963** Edwards *Gravel* 146 That's how the Duffer happened to be along. The whole thing was a sort of happen-so. **1995** Montgomery *Coll* It was just one of those happen-so events (Cardwell).

[DARE *happen-so* n chiefly South, South Midland]

happen up *verb phrase* To occur, take place.

1970 *Burton-Manning Coll*-94A Hit might not all have happened up like that.

happy

A *adjective* Overcome with religious enthusiasm.

1901 Harben *Westerfelt* 286 I'd lost my senses, jest beca'se I cried when 'at ol' woman got so happy. **1952** Giles *40 Acres* 43 [The members of the congregation] want to be lifted out of their seats, made to feel guilty for their sins, made to sing and shout, made to repent and weep and wail. They want to "get happy" with their religion. **1963** Watkins and Watkins *Yesterday* 30 Once Mary Keith, a big fat woman, went to a baptizing wearing a brand new Sunday hat with red roses on top. As each one of the women rose from the watery grave, Mary became happier and happier. Finally she yelled, "I'm gonna shout or bust wide open." [**c1982** Young *Colloquial Appal* 10 = emotional state during worship.] **1998** *Dante OHP*-61 We all got happy and shouted, and she got saved. **2007** Farr *My Appalachia* 123 We took a notion to drop in and observe one of them snake-meetin's. They's already shoutin' all over the place time we got there. . . . One old man—he put me in mind of Old Man Andrew Brock—he got happy. Now it was wintertime and the heating stove was red-hot in places. That old man run up and just hugged that stove like it was his old woman. And he didn't even scorch a stitch of his clothes or burn a red place on his skin.

[DARE *happy* adj 1 chiefly South, South Midland]

B *noun* Pleasure.

1924 Raine *Saddlebags* 105 I want to buy a pretty for my baby-child. I told her she should have her happy.

happy juice (also *happy Sally*) *noun* An alcoholic drink, especially homemade whiskey.

1977 Shields *Cades Cove* 37 The church was not used for these events, perhaps because, in many instances, "happy juice" was passed around, and this could not be done at a church. **2009** Applegate and Miller *Lake Cumberland* 18 Other names for moonshine were corn liquor, skull cracker, sugar whiskey, rotgut, ruckus juice, happy Sally, hillbilly pop, and white lightning.

happy pappy *noun* A father of small children on federal assistance, often assigned to a make-work program.

1972 *AOHP/LJC*-104 What they call happy pappies, you see, they draw a check, and they don't even want to work. **1972** Walls and Stephenson *Appal in Sixties* 191 Sitting on the swaybacked porch of his shack in a hollow outside Hazard, Grover Chandler, father of seven and a Happy Pappy graduate said: About all I did in the vocation program was plant saplings. I don't want to lie about nothing. **1975** Carawan and Carawan *Voices from Mt* 90 On the "happy pappy" program we dug graves, cut weeds, fit fires, built bridges, did all kinds of things. It was officially called the "Work Experience and Training Program." We had to go to school one day a week. To be eligible you had to be unemployed and have one or more children. **1977** Shackelford et al. *Our Appalachia* 330 When the Happy Pappy program first started, to receive help they had to go out and do something for it, that's the reason he had some pride. **1982** Slone *How We Talked* 43 A "happy pappy" or "mushrat" were men working on a government program for unemployed fathers. **2001** Montgomery *Coll* (known to Cardwell). **2007** Preece *Leavin' Sandlick* 38 Some people made light of the program and called it the "Happy Pappy Gang," but them men went to work for poor people, fixin' ther homes up, and really did a lot o' good thangs fer people in these parts.

[DARE *happy pappy* n Appalachians]

happy Sally See **happy juice**.

har, ha'r See **hair**.

hard

A *adjective* Severe, rough, harsh. See also **hard feeling, hard fit, hard to.**

1915 Pollard *TN Mts* 242 *hard cold* = cold in the head. **1923** (in **1952** Mathes *Tall Tales* 18) You-uns has heared me say some mighty hard things about him an' his teachin's. **1956** Hall *Coll* (Big Creek NC) Farming was a hard go back when I was a boy. **1966** Dykeman *Far Family* 27 "That's a mighty hard knowledge to live with," Leck Gunter said.

B *adverb* Severely, roughly, harshly.

1913 Kephart *Our Sthn High* 253 I ain't that hard pushed yet. **1962** Hall *Coll* (Cades Cove TN) [Uncle Noah Burchfield] was one of the most highly honored men of this county because of his integrity, character. [He was] hard down on lawlessness.... He was ten year old when the Civil War came on.

hard ankle *noun* See citation.

1940 Farr *More TN Expressions* 447 = coal digger: "The hard ankles are on a strike."

hard-favored *adjective* Of a person: having coarse or repulsive features or a harsh, rough appearance.

1927 Woofter *Dialect from WV* 356 = presenting a poor appearance. "There were many hard-favored men at the first day of court." **1946** *Shore Sign* 4 I knowed when she got old and hard-favored, he'd start runnin' round with some young hussy. **1975** Gainer *Speech Mtneer* 11 He's a hard-favored man. **1995–97** Montgomery *Coll* (known to Cardwell, Weaver).

[OED3 *hard-favoured* adj now archaic; EDD (at *hard* adj 1 (17)) "stern-faced; coarse-featured"; CUD *hard-favoured* "stern-faced"; DARE *hard-favored* adj South, South Midland]

hard feeling *noun* Bitterness, animosity between people, either individuals or families. See also **hardness**.

1956 McAtee *Some Dial NC* 21 = ill feeling, enmity. **1999** Montgomery *Coll* There was real hard feeling between the Cardwell and Jones families (Cardwell).

hard fit *noun*

1 An epileptic fit.

1924 Spring *Lydia Whaley* 2 Aunt L[ydia] had hard fits when she was about 12 years old. **1941** Hall *Coll* (Alexander NC) = used of a dog that takes a fit and has a hell of a struggle gettin' over it. *Ibid.* (Dellwood NC) = used of anyone that's subject to fits. There are hard fits and light fits.

2 A spate of anger, tantrum.

1937 Hall *Coll* (Copeland Creek TN) He'd like to tuck a hard fit. **1984** Wilder *You All Spoken* 206 = a tantrum. **1992** Montgomery *Coll*: *have a hard fit* [= get angry] (Shields).

hard head *noun* A **Primitive Baptist**.

1967 *DARE Survey* (Gatlinburg TN).

hard liver *noun* One who is impoverished. See also **good liver**.

1970 Vincent *More of Best* 122 "They were very poor," the judge said. "Hard livers."

hard-luckest *adjective* Having the worst fortune.

1975 Chalmers *Better* 66 A man may be the hard-luckest man in the county, or if he has a violent temper he might be the chair-flingin'est one.

hardly *adverb* Used in constructions of multiple negation (i.e. with *not* or *never*).

1862 *West CW Letters* (June 25) We get Nothing to Eat here Hardley. **1863** *Lance CW Letters* (May 31) this is the worst place for water we cant hardly drink it. **1939** Hall *Coll* (Cataloochee NC) We didn't know hardly what to think. **1953** Hall *Coll* (Hartford TN) The snow never hardly got off the ground. **c1960** Wilson *Coll*: *hardly* is more often *not hardly*. **1974** GSMNP-50:1:10 I'm hoarse. I can't hardly sing, but that's the best I could do. **1976** Brandes and Brewer *Dialect Clash* 287–88 The Asheville, N.C. *Citizen-Times* on April 11, 1954, said: "Double negatives do not bother the mountain folk. They seem to regard added negatives as simply giving greater force to a statement and sometimes they employ triple, quadruple, even quintuple negatives." The example of the quintuple negative the *Citizen-Times* cited was: "Hit's so downright foggy today nobody can't hardly see nothing a-tall nohow." **1979** Slone *My Heart* 17 Ye won't have to water 'em none hardly a'tall. **1989** *Matewan OHP*-88 It didn't pay nothing hardly. **1998** *Dante OHP*-12 I was doing so much preaching, and I'd come in of the evening and I didn't hardly have time to wash the black off of me until I'd have to hit the road. **2008** *Rosie Hicks* 4 I just couldn't hardly say yes.

[DARE *hardly* adv chiefly South, South Midland]

hard mast *noun* See citations. See also **mast, soft mast.**

1997–98 *Smokies Guide* (Winter) 7 Wildlife biologist Bill Stiver has announced that the park's fall 1997 hard mast crop "is poor overall." Hard mast includes oak acorns, hickory nuts, beech nuts, and other nutritious tree seeds that deer, bear, Wild Turkey, squirrels, and other kinds of wildlife rely on. **2008** *Smokies Guide* (Autumn) 1 During fall, the success of bears in the Smoky Mountains depends almost entirely on what biologists call the "mast crop." They divide the mast into two groups, soft (blackberries, cherries, grapes, blueberries, etc.) and hard (acorns, hickory nuts, and beech nuts).

hardness *noun* Bitterness or animosity between people (used as both a count and an abstract noun). See also **hard feeling**.

1870 *Paw Paw Hollow Church Minutes* Church in cession moderator present the following business was done 1st appointed a committee of enquiry Viz J H Conner William Clifton J H Hickman Marion Petty and F M Putnam to enquire into a difficulty or hardness that seems to exist between Brethren R B Cate and J L Haggard. **1895** Edson and Fairchild *TN Mts* 372 There's a right smart of *hardness* between them two boys. **1917** Kephart *Word-List* 413 = ill feeling. "[It's] likely to get up right smart o' *hardness* between 'em." **1927** Woofter *Dialect from WV* 356 = ill feeling. "There has been a hardness between those families for a long time." **1931** Combs *Lg Sthn High* 1310 A "hardness" toward one is a dislike, or misunderstanding of one. **1940** Hall *Coll* (White Oak NC) They was some hardness between them. **1956** Chapman *Folk Retain* When mountain people dislike each other there is said to be a hardness between them. **1988** Smith *Fair and Tender* 11 There is her big father smiling holding her hand but now a hardness has come up between them.

[DARE *hardness* n chiefly Appalachians]

hard road (also *hard-surface road*) *noun* A paved road, as opposed to one with a dirt or gravel surface.

1946 Stuart *Plum Grove Hills* 62 Pa had been laid off the section, but he got a job pouring concrete in Greenup. They were putting in the first hard road in the country. **c1960** Wilson *Coll* = one paved by bituminous substance or cement. *Hard-surface road* is more common. **1997** Hufford *American Ginseng* 15 [The berries] rolled plumb down next to the hard road.

[DARE *hard road* n chiefly Midland, especially Illinois]

hard row of stumps *noun phrase* A very difficult situation.

1915 Dingus *Word-List VA* 184 *in a hard row of stumps* = in a bad way. **1927** Woofter *Dialect from WV* 356 = a job which presents many difficulties. "This contract has certainly been a hard row of stumps."

Hard Shell (also *Hard Shell Baptist*) *noun* A **Primitive Baptist**, a member of a loose grouping or **association** of church congregations viewed as strict and rigid in their beliefs and practice, opposing such "innovations" as a paid clergy, foreign missions, and the use of musical instruments in worship services. See also **Missionary Baptist**, **soft-shell Baptist**.

1867 Harris *Sut Lovingood* 49 Them hard shells over thar dus want me the wus kine, powerful bad. **1886** Smith *Sthn Dialect* 349 During a two days' stay in Cade's [sic] Cove, where the most original people were said to be, we attended a primitive Baptist footwashing service, which would draw together, we were told, all the ignorance of that part of the mountains, but we got little in the way of dialect, though we heard two sermons that surpassed any hard-shell sermon ever put into print. **1895** *Mt Baptist Sermon* 13 Now brethering, they haint no more harm in the doctorings of the ole Hardshell Babtist church-ah! than they is in thet ole stump. *Ibid.* 15 "Lemme jine the Babtist," sez I; "not the Missionary Babtist, nor the reg'lar Babtist, but the ole, Two Seed, Iron Jacket, Predestination, Hardshell Babtist." **1939** Hall *Coll* (Roaring Fork TN) My uncle was a Primitive Baptist or Hard Shell. **1957** Hall *Coll* (Mt Sterling NC) Old Baptists [are] Hard-shell or Primitive Baptists. **1975** Brewer *Valley So Wild* 283 Another name for the "old school" Baptists was "Primitive" and the new schoolers [sic] were called "Missionary." These terms still are retained by many local churches. Cades Cove, for instance, had both a Missionary and a Primitive Baptist church, still standing. The term "hardshell" (old) and "softshell" (new) also were used in some places. **1989** *Matewan OHP-1* She was a hardshell. She was the one that washed feet. I've seen her wash feet a many a times . . . they have a strict, you're either good or you're bad, there's no in between . . . you was a good person or you was a bad person. Now they didn't allow for nothing, and you was churched over nothing.

[DARE *hard-shell* adj 2 chiefly South, South Midland]

hard-surface road See **hard road**.

hardtail *noun* A mule; figuratively = a stubborn person.

1939 *FWP Guide TN* 275 It ain't nothing to see a man come in and trade in a tractor and a three-year-old Buick and $100 down on a span of hard-tails. **1967** *DARE Survey* (Gatlinburg TN) = joking name for a mule. **1983** *Dark Corner OHP-9A* [You] couldn't plow too many acres with [an] old hard-tail. **1995–97** Montgomery *Coll* (known to Adams, Bush, Jones, Norris, Shields). **2007** McMillon *Notes* = someone stubborn and hard to get along with.

[DARE *hard tail* n 4 chiefly South, South Midland, West]

hard to *adjective phrase* Unable to, having difficulty with or at (thus *hard to hear* = hard of hearing).

1973 *Words & Expressions* 134 I'm awful hard to remember names. **1984** *GSMNP-153*:61 One boy, he was a little bit hard to learn the shape of the letters. **2001** Montgomery *Coll* Speak up, I'm a little hard to hear (Cardwell). **2008** Salsi *Ray Hicks* 173 Mama was hard to let go of things. For some years the animals kept Mama happy and rememberin' the good ol' times.

hard-turned *adjective* Stubborn, having a difficult personality. See also **turn B1**.

1949 Arnow *Hunter's Horn* 137 He wondered if the doctor who lived in such a place wouldn't be a hard-turned man to deal with.

haricane See **hurricane A**.

harm *adjective* Unkind.

1990 Clouse *Wilder* 137 Have I ever done a harm thing to you?

harness *verb* Variant past-participle form of three syllables: *harnest-ed*.

1940 Oakley *Roamin'/Restin'* 75 Now heare you see a over shot wheel harnested to grind corn and to do other work you can buy corn meal watter ground.

harp *noun* A harmonica. Same as **French harp**. See also **harp sing**, **old harp**, **sacred harp**.

1942 Thomas *Blue Ridge* 320 He puts a harp in his mouth and plays it. **1973** *Holidays* 335 [For Christmas] we'd get a orange, an' a apple, an' three-four pieces of candy, an' maybe a harp. **1985** Edwards *Folksy Sketches* 49 Little Benny Shaw was sawing the fiddle, Sleepy Joe Ammons was thumping the banjo, and Silas Shipe was blowing the harp.

harp book *noun* A hymnal using **shape notes.**

[**1933** Jackson *White Spirituals* 94 B. F. White and E. J. King produced the first edition of the Sacred Harp in Hamilton, Harris County, Georgia, in 1844.... Its title was a favorite. The number of song books appearing in the first half of the nineteenth century with the word "Harp" in their titles is amazing, and there were several "Sacred Harps" among them.] **1986** Ogle *Lucinda* 56 I was little, but I tried to sing in [the] old Harp book way by shaped notes.

[< *Sacred Harp*, *Old Harp*, or a similar songbook employing *shape notes*; the books frequently had a harp on the cover]

harp sing (also *harp singing*) *noun* A community or church gathering, sometimes at a stated time of the year, in which a harp book or **shape note** songbook (such as *The Sacred Harp*) is used to sing hymns set out in **shape notes.** Formerly this event culminated a **singing school.** See also **singing school.** For further information, see George P. Jackson, *White Spirituals in the Southern Uplands*, especially chapter 23, "Old Harp Singers of Eastern Tennessee and Their Book." Also called **old harp singing.**

1926 Willy *Great Smoky Natl Park* 56 We spent an hour in the village church listening to the "harp singing," a service held here once a year and most impressive. The congregation consisted of about one hundred men typical of this mountain region.... When they sang it was with heart and soul; the right hand keeping tune, and the melody, mostly from the voices of men, such as only possible to those attuned to Nature. Each hymn had a separate leader. There was no musical instrument. The leader used the old-style tuning fork and hummed the tune before the hymn was sung.... The hymn book was entitled "The New Harp of Columbia; a new system of musical notation with a note for each sound and a shape for each note. Containing a variety of most excellent hymn tunes, odes and anthems; happily adapted to church service, singing schools and societies." **1937** Hall *Coll* (Emerts Cove TN) Harp-Singing was said to go on by the hour in mountain churches. **1956** Hall *Coll* (Townsend TN) In churches we had singin' schools [and] old harp singin's [i.e. from the old shape-note hymnals]. **1969** GSMNP-38:123 They had a many of an old harp singing right there in that old log schoolhouse. **1978** Petersen and Phillips *New Harp of Columbia* xviii Shape-note singing in East Tennessee predates *The New Harp of Columbia*, presently used in the traditional "harp sings" of the area. *Ibid.* xxiii Strong family ties were the rule, adding to the attraction of singing schools and their successors, "harp sings." **1991** Headrick *Headrick's Chapel* 207 The present Harp singing at Headrick's Chapel actually began at the Primitive Baptist Church of Townsend about 1920 when it was known as the Coker Hill Old Harp Singing. That singing migrated to Headrick's Chapel in 1968, when one group split off from the Townsend Primitive Baptist Church and came to the valley.

[< *Sacred Harp*, *Old Harp*, or a similar songbook employing *shape notes*; the books frequently had a harp on the cover]

harrican, harricane See **hurricane.**

harvest-man See **granddaddy 2.**

has See **have A.**

haslet(s) *noun* The edible viscera of a hog. See also **lights, liver and lights.**

1867 Harris *Sut Lovingood* 97a [sic] He orter have his durned haslet cut outen him, an I'll du hit fur him ef ever I ketches him, fur gittin me inter trubil, arter he did all the devilment, while I has to bar the blame. **1949** Kurath *Word Geog East US* 38 *Hasslet* is the usual Southern folk term for the edible inner organs of a pig. ... It has not entered the Shenandoah Valley but has been carried westward into the corridor that leads to the Cumberland Gap. **1952–57** (in **1973** McDavid and McDavid *Vocab E KY* 158) = attested by 2/52 (3.8%) of E KY speakers for the Linguistic Atlas of the North Central States.

hassle *verb* To breathe noisily, pant.

1939 Bond *Appal Dialect* 108 = to pant audibly. **1952** Wilson *Folk Speech NC* 549 = to pant, to be out of breath and breathe heavily.

[DARE *hassle* v chiefly Southeast]

hat ball *noun* See citation.

1946 Wilson *Fidelity Folks* 145 In Hat Ball we "nailed to the cross" the loser, that is, the one who got the most forfeits or "pigs." ... The boy, often a little fellow like me who could not throw well and had thus acquired many pigs, was stood against a sapling while all the boys took turns throwing a ball at him.

hatchel See **hackle.**

hatching jacket See **wear the hatching jacket.**

hate[1] (also *haet, hait*) *noun* A whit, the smallest thing.

1826 Royall *Sketches* 58 Their favorite word of all, is hate, by which they mean the word thing; for instance, nothing, "not a hate—not waun hate will ye's do." What did you buy at the store, ladies? "Not a hate—well you hav'nt a thing here to eat." **1895** *Word-Lists* 389 (Winchester KY) *didn't get a hate* = didn't get a thing. **1929** Carpenter *Evolution of Dialect* 9 = has been generally used as an equivalent for a thing.... It was once heard most in such expressions as I don't care a hate or I didn't have a hate to do. It was also used in such expressions as I couldn't turn a hate, meaning could not turn a wheel or make a move, and in I don't give a hate, an expression of indifference. **1933** Carpenter *Sthn Mt Dialect* 25 In parts of West Virginia hate is used to mean THING. One hears He didn't take a hate along, or He didn't get a hate while he was gone.

It is also used in couldn't turn a hate in the sense of COULDN'T TURN A WHEEL. **1969** Dial *Dialect Appal People* 464 "That trifling old fixin ain't worth a haet!" Haet means the smallest thing that can be conceived of, and comes from Deil hae't (Devil have it.) **1971** Dwyer *Dict for Yankees* 27 Hate, haet, hait—A bit, small amount. **1975** Gainer *Speech Mtneer* 11 "I don't give a hate" means "I don't care." "I don't give a hate what you do." **1995** Montgomery *Coll* (known to Brown, Cardwell).

[SND *haet* n 2; CUD (*the*) *deil haet* (at *have*) "lit. the devil have it = devil a bit, not a bit"; DARE *hate* n chiefly Appalachians, Ohio Valley]

hate[2] (also *hate it*) *verb, verb phrase* To regret, feel deeply sorry that.

c1815 (in **2007** Davis *Co Line Baptist* 111) I hated that a brother should lie under that Character & thought it not amiss to mention to one brother what nother was impeached with. **1861** Robinson *CW Letters* (Dec 8) I hated it when I found you was gone that I had not Stade til you started. **1864** Hill *CW Letters* (March 16) I hated the little sheep all dide. **1884** Bayless *Letters* 117 I hate it that I could not get up there before they all left. **1939** Hall *Coll* (Emerts Cove TN) You'll hate you said it. *Ibid.* (Waynesville NC) I hate you can't go with us. *Ibid.* (Wears Cove TN) He said he wouldn't hate to die if his daddy hadn't made him knock the man in the head with a pine knot. **1941** Hall *Coll* (Del Rio TN) I sure did hate that I didn't get to see you before you went back to New York. **c1959** Weals *Hillbilly Dict* 4 = regret. "I hate I cain't help ye." **1973** *Foxfire Interviews* A-73-87 I hate that it's in that book [that] he found out about everybody's relatives. **1985** Irwin *Alex Stewart* 271 My dog killed a big coon and when I examined it I saw that it was my pet. I always hated that. **1997** Nelson *Country Folklore* 24 We hated for the school to close in 1937 because we were all used to each other and everyone got along so good. **2005** Williams *Gratitude* 501 = regret, to be sorry. "I hate it that their house got burnt down." In the usual meaning of the word, when they hated something or somebody, they said "despised."

[DARE *hate* v KY, TN, Ozarks]

hateful

A *adjective* Variant superlative form *hatefullest* [see **1967** in **B**].

B *adjective* Troublesome, perverse, mean.

1939 Hall *Coll* Bear traps is hateful to set. **1940** Haun *Hawk's Done* 44 That was the reason he was so everlasting hateful and always poking fun at other folks. **1967** Fetterman *Stinking Creek* 78 "Knox is the hatefullest county there ever was," he said. "If it gets a chance to get a factory, they vote against it." **1969** Medford *Finis* 114 Now this little "Flat" field was one of the "hate-fullest" patches to cultivate on the farm—soured, often wet, cloddy and hard to work. **1972** *GSMNP-93* I took a young mare there [that had] never been shod before. She was right pretty hateful. **1983** Page and Wigginton *Aunt Arie* 100 If you'd been contrary or hateful. **1991** Thomas *Sthn Appal* 248 I was so hateful I wouldn't go to school—my dad died when I'z ten years old—and when I went, I wouldn't learn nothin'. **2013** Venable *How to Tawlk* 19 = a thing or a person that is obnoxious, irritating, ill-tempered, evil or mean: "'Em hateful skeeters are so bad this year, I done 'bout slapped my arms off."

[DARE *hateful* adj chiefly South, South Midland]

C *noun* An obnoxious or vexing creature.

1913 Kephart *Our Sthn High* 283 Them bugs—the little old hatefuls!

[DARE *hateful* n Ozarks, southern Appalachians]

hate it See **hate**[2].

hate out *verb phrase* Of a community: to ostracize and shun or drive out (one) who has violated its norms.

1824 (in **1912** Doddridge *Notes on Settlement* 158) The punishment for idleness, lying, dishonesty, and ill fame was generally that of "Hating out." **1941** *FWP Guide WV* 42 Violators of common rights were "hated out" of the neighborhood. **1948** Dick *Dixie Frontier* 263 So hot did public disapproval wax that he felt it more comfortable to leave the country. In such a case he was said to have been "hated out."

hath See **hearth**.

hathrock See **hearth rock**.

haul

A *verb* (in phrases *haul away, haul back, haul off*) (+ *and*) To ready oneself or set oneself in position (followed by a verb expressing consequent action).

1930 Greer-Petrie *Angeline Outsmarts* 31 I hauled away and kicked him on the chin! **1957** Combs *Lg Sthn High: Word List* 48 *haul back* = draw. Ex.: "He hauled back and knocked him down." **1972** *GSMNP-93:24* [The black snake] hild [the copperhead] out there a while and after a while he just hauled off . . . and swallowed it. **1973** *Florence and Lawton* 195 He just hauled off an' shot right up through there an' scared'em all out. **1974** Roberts *Sang Branch* 272 The tar man never did say anything, so he hauled back with his head and butted him and his head stuck. **c1982** Young *Colloquial Appal* 11 *haul off* = begin, proceed. **1989** *Matewan OHP-94* All [sic] kept calling me "Mister," figuring that I'd haul off and knock the hell out of him. **2007** Shelby *Molly Whuppie* 11 That made the other [giant] so mad he hauled off and hit that one over the head with the flat of a shovel and raised a big pump knot on his head.

B *noun* See citation.

1964 Clarkson *Lumbering in WV* 364 = the distance and route over which teams must go between two given points, as between the woods and a landing.

haul away, haul back, haul off See **haul A**.

haunt

A Variant forms *haint, hant*.

1867 Harris *Sut Lovingood* 117 Hit wer es black inter that durn'd ole hanted loft, es hit wud be tu a brine flea on a black catskin, onder the fur, an' hit onder forty bushil ove wet charcoal dust.

1890 Fruit *KY Words* 68 *hanted*. **1939** Hall *Coll* (Tobes Creek NC) The most of the people left Brown Valley after the war. They claimed it to be hanted. **c1940** Simms *Coll* A lanky man with ha'nting eyes. **1961** *Coe Ridge OHP*-342B Did you say you used to live in a house that was hainted? **1973** GSMNP-57:78–79 I've knowed lots of families lived in [the house], and the old saying was the place was hanted. **1985** Irwin *Alex Stewart* 117 Uncle Bert Goins, that was Grandpap's uncle, said that place was hainted (haunted) and him and Grandpap wouldn't come by there of a night because the haints had got after them.

[DARE *haunt* n, v A chiefly South, South Midland]

B *noun* A ghost or spirit usually one associated with a specific place and heard rather than seen.

1862 *Mangum CW Letters* (Dec 2) Mother I have saw hants since I saw you tho that small particule of faith has led me through safe and sound. **1895** Edson and Fairchild *TN Mts* 372 *hant* = ghost. "There is a *hant* in the mill." **1913** Kephart *Our Sthn High* 91 I'd believe [the bear is] a hant if 't wasn't for his tracks—they're the biggest I've ever seen. **1929** (in **1952** Mathes *Tall Tales* 136) For the love of God, Phrony, am I seein' a ha'nt? **1939** Hall *Coll* (Cataloochee NC) Lots believe in hants. You shouldn't go by a graveyard at night. **1956** Hall *Coll* (Cosby TN) They said if you crossed water, that got shet of the haint. **1973** Medford *Long Hard Road* 15 The elderly people, some of whom I knew but will not mention here, believed strictly in ha'nts and would talk of little else when they gathered together around the wood fires at night. **1975** Montell *Ghosts Cumberland* 218 *haint* = virtual synonym for ghost. Haints, generally, may be classified as that body of ghosts which are heard but not seen by the living. **1982** *Smokies Heritage* 128 My grandmother, being a brave woman, decided to spend one night upstairs to prove there were no "haints." **1994** Parton *Dolly* 35 I can remember some of the old folks talk about "haints" and tell some of the old tales that had been passed down through generations. **1997** King *Mt Folks* 45 The boy was later asked if he really did see a "haint."

[DARE *haunt* n B chiefly South, South Midland]

haunt tale (also *hainted tale, haint tale, hant tale*) *noun* A ghost story.

1938 Hall *Coll* (Emerts Cove TN) People's quit seein' hants and tellin hant tales. **1940** Haun *Hawk's Done* 174 Just some little old hant tales was all I knowed. **1955** Ritchie *Singing Family* 7 Now, hant tales scared me to death, but I could never keep from listening any more than the ones who had seen the hants could keep from telling them. We would always know when there was going to be hant talk among the old folks. Whenever Granny Katty was staying with us, she'd sit before the fire after supper, and by and by in would come Uncle Philip from down by the river, and after awhile here would be my second sister, Ollie, with her little ones from their house around the hill, and maybe Aunt Maggie would come over, and they all and Mom and Dad would draw up before the fireplace. Then all us young uns would shiver and grin at each other, for we'd know for a fact that the evening couldn't get by without hant tales. Oh, there'd be some weather and crop talk, too, and some singing around, but we waited for that sure quiet minute when someone'd say, "You hear bout that Wild Thing loose in the woods up behind Grandpa Hall's?" That's when we'd begin scrooching in close to the fire, elbowing silently for good safe places. **1963** Edwards *Gravel* 116 Uncle Bill, what about that haint tale you promised me? **1970** Hall *Witchlore* 2 As to ghostlore, some middle-aged and elderly people still enjoy the eerie excitement of relating encounters that they or others (almost always others) had with apparitions of various kinds. These narratives are locally called "hant" tales, but many people are convinced that the strange incidents they relate actually happened. **1983** McDermitt *Boy Named Jack* 4 The women didn't tell Jack tales . . . it was these other tales, hainted tales, ghost tales, the women told more, and Indian tales.

haunty (also *hanty*) *adjective* Frightening, haunted.

1955 Ritchie *Singing Family* 243 The noise she [= a train] made was enough to take the wits out of you, let alone the terrible looks of her. Put me in a mind of something alive, something big and black and—HANTY! Fire just a-working out of the insides of her, smoke just a-billern out of that big black funnel on her top. **1995** Montgomery *Coll* There was a hill over home, and it was a haunty place (Cardwell).

[DARE *haunty* adj South, South Midland]

have *verb, auxiliary verb* See also **hain't** and Grammar and Syntax §6.

A *has*.

1 With a third-person-plural subject that is a noun, conjoined personal pronouns, or any form other than a single adjacent personal pronoun. See also **be C1**, **-s³ 1**. See also Grammar and Syntax §4.1.

1774 *Dunmore's War* 58 The Cherokees has at length commenced hostilities. **1787** *Sinking Creek Church Minutes* I:2 Some of the Churches has Received the Same Princibels. **1826** (in **2003** *TN Petitions I* 119) the people living in the sd corner of Sevear has always paid taxes and done their duty in Jefferson. **1845** *McLean Diary* 91 Crops has improoved. **1863** *Brown CW Letters* (Nov 10) he told you i cold [resign], and him and me has had some short talk about it. **1885** Bayless *Letters* 118 Me and James Platt has been talking of a lot in Hampton. **1913** Kephart *Our Sthn High* 200 Stay on, stranger, pore folks has a pore way, but you're welcome to what we got. **1939** Hall *Coll* (Little Cataloochee NC) Most of them has left there and the young folks has left that place. It's a terrible bad place. **1954** GSMNP-19:1 He told me the other day that a cow rolled out of the pasture field and fell into the highway and I don't know how many has done that around here . . . one or two has broke their neck. **1973** GSMNP-78:16 They actually have folks here. Some of them has their grandmother and grandfather. **1978** Montgomery *White Pine Coll* XII People has always gave Cocke County a bad name. **1989** *Matewan OHP*-1 A man that raised nine girls has to be strict on them. **1998** *Dante OHP*-71 Me and him has traveled in Kentucky, West Virginia, Bluefield.

2 With a nonadjacent personal pronoun subject in the first or second person or in the third-person plural. See also **be C2**, **-s³ 2**. *Historical*.

1796 *Big Pigeon Church Minutes* 22 they Expressed a desire of

Comeing to this Meeting. but has not come. **1829** (in **2005** *Jefferson Co TN Petitions* 198) they were married and has continued to live together as husband & wife ever since. **1862** *Reese CW Letters* (Oct 29) I am un well and has Bin vary sick an yester day I was vary Bad. **1862** *Sutton CW Letters* (Nov 8) We have some sickness in camp of mumps and has had some of fever. **1959** Roberts *Up Cutshin* 7 They raised I think it was eight chillern and has taken in one or two to raise. **1993** Burton *Take Up Serpents* 19 You that's got the Holy Ghost has got it in you.

3 With an adjacent personal pronoun subject other than a third-person-singular one.

1858 (in **1974** Harris *High Times* 119) Theyse [= they has] all got a spite at me yet about that ar trubil. **1863** *Warrick CW Letters* (June 10) I has nothing of importanse to Rite to you at this tim times is verry dull hear. *Ibid.* (Aug 13) i doue pray for you all the tim that God my spar you to get home one time more for it has bin so longe sece we has seen you. **1922** *TN CW Ques* 1880 (McMinn Co TN) I was depty shurif six years sinc that time I has bin lame. **1938** (in **2009** Powell *Shenandoah Letters* 138) i have never had any help from them like they has helped other people. **1970** *Foxfire Interviews* A-70-75 Has you ever come up here in a truck? **1973** *AOHP/ASU-111* They has structure and things like that. **1975** *AOHP/ALC-930* They used to have some pretty rowdy bars down there. It seemed like the last few years they's got a little better. **1978** Reese *Speech NE Tenn* 191 They's heard.

4 Contracted to *'s* before *not*.

1961 *Coe Ridge OHP-336B* He's not done anything to you. **2009** Holbrook *Upheaval* 35 He's not been in uniform a full year.

B *have*.

1 Reduced to *a*. See **a**[2] **1**.

2 Omitted, especially after a modal verb or the infinitive marker *to*.

1774 *Dunmore's War* 105 I was in hopes there would been some flower fr[om] M. Thomsons for us before now. *Ibid.* 138 I was Expecting Orders to Gone Home to Seen Some What about my Affairs. **1797** *Big Pigeon Church Minutes* 31 this should been enterd in the month above. **1813** Hartsell *Memora* 104 I shold shot in aminit if he head not aspoock and shold kiled him without axsedent. **1861** *Griffin CW Letters* he thort he ought to got one to. **1862** *Cunningham CW Letters* (April 21) if I Cood had the pleaure to come home when my [time] is out and Stay thirty or forty days I wood bin better sadified. **1864** *Poteet CW Letters* (July 11) I would like to bin thare to eat with you but I could not. **1867** Harris *Sut Lovingood* 91 He fotch a deep loud rusty beller, mout been heard a mile, an' then and sot into an onended sistem ove backin. **1889** Cole *Letters* 79 I might have started and them devels killed me before I could got there. **1938** (in **2009** Powell *Shenandoah Letters* 154) Ef you want to you can Send Some Body to eastamate about what it would Been worth. **1954** *GSMNP-19*:18 All at once a rattlesnake cut loose to singing. You ought to seen us all a-jumping and running. **1961** *Coe Ridge OHP-339A* He wouldn't took a hundred dollar for his dog. **1966** Miller *Pigeon's Roost* (Jan 13) According to the weather predictions given by the wooly worm, which last fall had his biggest black markings in front, we was supposed to already had our worst weather. **1970** Foster *Walker Valley* 41 He must've died in the forties, must been forties whenever he died. (Arnold Thompson). **1972** *GSMNP-86*:28 I was done supposed to been there. **1978** Burton *Ballad Folks* 16 I don't believe the husband would took her back a'ter she done that, that was if he was a true lover and true love. **1981** *GSMNP-122*:32 You wouldn't ever thought about kids a-comin' out of them hollers and hills. **1998** *Dante OHP-65* Some woman was supposed to killed her husband there. **2008** *Rosie Hicks* 6 I thought they was some down yonder but it might died out. *Ibid.* 3 They shouldn't done them like that.

3 In the third-person singular in an existential clause.

1861 *Martin CW Letters* (Dec 25) they havent bin any Chrismast hear. **1864** *Chapman CW Letters* (April 12) they hav been a fear of that smal pox on the river. **1978** Montgomery *White Pine Coll* VI-2 They've been a big change, and I'd say not too much difference in White Pine and Morristown and any other town.

4 Contracted to *'ve* before *not*.

1937 *Hall Coll* (Cosby Creek TN) I've not tasted of it yet. **1941** *Hall Coll* (Mt Sterling NC) You've not met him, I don't guess. **1975** *AOHP/ALC-1128* Many a times I've not seen my father, even on Sunday. He had to work. **1977** Shackelford et al. *Our Appalachia* 249 No, you've not scared me. **1984** Page and Wigginton *Foxfire Cookery* 148–49 We had what we called greasy-back beans—I've not seen any of them in years. **1995** Montgomery *Coll* I've not hearn from him in twenty years (Cardwell).

5 Superfluous, especially after *had* in a conditional clause. Same as **a**[2] **2**.

1961 *Coe Ridge OHP-333A* If he hadn't have done that, he wouldn't have got a day [in prison]. **1972** *AOHP/LJC-104* I wish I had've kept all my old books. **1989** *Matewan OHP-22* I was old enough to remember it if I had have had it. **1997** *Dante OHP-14* If it had've come a storm or lightning or anything, buddy I'd a tore them [= cords used in medical tests] offen my head and come out. of there, I'm afraid of lightning, I dodge it every time.

6 Variant form *haf'n*.

1979 Slone *My Heart* 36 "A long trip to town and two dollars all went for nothin'," he laughed. "But less ways I won't haf'n to tell Maw after all."

C Syntax.

1 As an auxiliary verb with the past-participle form of the main verb following the direct object.

1926 Hunnicutt *Twenty Years* 160 After we had all our work done up and eaten a good camp supper, I told Mark let's organize for the hunt tomorrow.

2 In phrase *have . . . to* = to cause to.

1862 *Shipman CW Letters* (Feb 6) Paw pleas have Vandovar to make mee a good pare of boots no 8 and send them. **1864** *Kendrick CW Letters* (Sept 21) thay run up the norforlk her and has it to intersect with the sity point rode and then thay have run it round to the weldon rode. **1939** *Hall Coll* (Cades Cove TN) She'd have us to stay together all the time. *Ibid.* (Emerts Cove TN) They'd make sassafras tea, you know, and have us to drink it. **1961** *Coe Ridge OHP-333A* My grandfather had them to cut a ditch there. **1970** Foster *Walker Valley* 12 He'd just back him up, you know, and have him to back up, then have him to haul it out again. **1978** Slone *Common Folks* 215 As it was close to dinner time, Aunt Nance would have us to stay and eat with her. **1989** Smith *Flyin' Bullets* 61 He had Aunt Amy to get up and come in there so she could hear what he had to say. **1991** Haynes *Haywood Home* 37 Grandpa Hiram had the shoemaker to make him a white wool hat to wear to church. **1997** GSMNPCOHP-3:13 She had my grandmaw to get eighty five to a hundred cabbage plants to set out.

[DARE (at *to* prep 9a) chiefly South, South Midland]

3 In phrase *have . . . to* = to experience, have occur, have the result that.

1861 *Mingus Letters* 29 (Oct 6) Jackson Beck had a little girl to fall out . . . the blade cut her throat, it lived 15 minutes. **1864** *Kendrick CW Letters* (Sept 5) we have men to cock and bring it in to us of night. **1922** *TN CW Ques* 2234 (Hancock Co TN) I had my feet to freeze in stirrups many times. **1939** *Hall Coll* (Hazel Creek NC) I'd have my mustache to freeze [in the cold weather] till I could hardly get my breath. **1956** *Hall Coll* (Hartford TN) I had two uncles to die in the poor house. *Ibid.* (Jones Cove TN) I had an uncle to witch people. **1967** Miller *Pigeon's Roost* (April 13) McCoury also reported that he had a cow to die about a month ago when her calf was one day old. **1970** Hall *Witchlore* 4 I had a cousin to witch people. **1978** Montgomery *White Pine Coll* I-1 I had a sister to die several years before I was born. *Ibid.* III-1 I don't think I ever had one to come up to me and just outward tell me that they didn't want me to say anything to their kid about the way they talked. *Ibid.* III-2 Dad never would wean a calf when the sign was in the head. He said it'd bawl itself to death. . . . He never did have calves to bawl. **1997** *Dante OHP*-53 We had a lot of Hungarians and Polish people to come in here and different ethnic groups.

[DARE (at *to* prep 9b) chiefly South, South Midland]

4 As an auxiliary verb to indicate a one-time event in the past, especially with *ago*. See also **ago**.

1937 Conner *Ms* 19 some one, No doubt has made a souveneer out of it, long ago. **1939** *Hall Coll* (Bradley Fork NC) It's been twenty year ago they offered me a house and land. **1953** *Hall Coll* (Bryson City NC) Haint nobody never set [the trap] for any bears since. That's been thirty years ago. **1958** GSMNP-110:22 Lots of them big logs come out, washed out. That's been away back yonder. **1973** GSMNP-2:23 Yeah, that's been about forty years ago. **1974–75** McCracken *Logging* 14:18 It's been there three or four years ago. **1978** Montgomery *White Pine Coll* VIII-1 It's been a good while back, because I read it.

D *had.*

1 Contracted to *'d* in negative contexts.

c1950 Adams *Grandpap* 110 She wish she'd not made such a glutton of herself. **1983** McDermitt *Boy Named Jack* 9 I wouldn't have been livin, probably, if I'd not been Jack's friend. **1999** Morgan *Gap Creek* 170 I'd not been up there since we first come to Gap Creek. **2015** Holbrook *Something* 150 She'd not ever caught her in the act of drugging.

2 *hadn't* Used in statements with inversion of the subject and verb.

1999 Morgan *Gap Creek* I was going to say hadn't nobody else on the mountain had typhoid, but I didn't. **2016** Gipe *Gone to Water* 41 It was way far away from the Trail so hadn't none of us been out there much.

have a class to See **take a class to.**

have a travel *verb phrase* See citation.

1982 Slone *How We Talked* 73 *having a travel* = the journey from nature to Grace. The time between when you realize you are a lost sinner and when God forgives you of your sins and you become a Christian. Some believe it takes days, weeks, even years. Some believe it is instant.

have in head See **in head.**

have nothing for *verb phrase* See citation.

2014 Williams *Coll*: *have nothing for someone* = to not like someone.

have oblige(d) *verb phrase* To have an obligation, be obligated, ought. See also **get obliged to, oblige.**

1900 Harben *N GA Sketches* 53 The meadow-piece has obliged to be broke an' sowed in wheat. **1913** Kephart *Our Sthn High* 285 We have oblige to take care on him. **1929** Kephart *Smoky Mt Magic* 5 I've obleeged to be plumb keerful not to git damp in ary water dingier than trout-fish swim in. **1931** Goodrich *Mt Homespun* 79 "I'll be doggoned ef he ain't preached us a sarment I have obleeged to take to myself." said Jake, under his breath. **1974** Fink *Bits Mt Speech* 12 I *have obliged* to go. **1994** Montgomery *Coll* I have obliged and compelled to go (Cardwell).

have off *verb phrase* To remove (one's outer garment).

1937 Hyatt *Kiverlid* 14 Set down, Nancy, have off your shawl.

[DARE *have off* v phr[1] South, South Midland]

haverpoke *noun* A haversack.

1974 *No Sang* 14 I usually use a haverpoke. It's just a satchel with a strop goes across your shoulder.

have the big eye See **big eye.**

have the britches See **wear the britches.**

have the deadwood on See **deadwood.**

have to *noun phrase, adjective phrase* Something done only when forced to or an alternative is lacking; unavoidably necessary.

1962 Dykeman *Tall Woman* 18 I won't go to war unless it's a have to. **1978** Montgomery *White Pine Coll* XII I don't even get out unless it's a have-to case. **1995–97** Montgomery *Coll* (known to eight consultants from the Smoky Mountains). **2001** Lowry *Expressions* 6 I don't need medicine except in a have to case, and this is a have to case.

have . . . to See **have C2, C3.**

haw-eater *noun* See citation.

1944 Wentworth *ADD* 281 (WV) = a West Virginian, in ref[erence] to his eating the black haw.

hawk[1] (also *hock*) *verb* To cough to clear the throat of phlegm.

1929 Wolfe *Look Homeward* 175 (DARE) He passed on, hocking into the gutter a slimy gob of phlegm. **1984** Wilder *You All Spoken* 190 *hawk* = to clear one's throat with a harsh palatal sound.

[echoic; DARE *hawk* v[2] scattered, but especially Northeast, South Midland]

hawk[2] *verb* See 1952 citation.

1935 Sheppard *Cabins in Laurel* 168 They just hawked hell out of me with their everlasting talk. **1952** Wilson *Folk Speech NC* 549 = to annoy; to tease; to embarrass.

hawr See **hair.**

hay bean *noun* Same as **leather britches.**

2013 Beaver and Ballard *Voices* 295 You string up a thread with a needle and run through the beans and dry them. When you thread them, don't thread them through the bullet, thread'em on [the] side of it. People call them leather britches. I call them hay beans.

hayburner *noun*

1 A horse or mule.

1939 Farr *TN Mt Regions* 90 = a mule. **1997** Farwell *Logging* = a horse.

2 See citation.

1964 Clarkson *Lumbering in WV* 364 = a kerosene lantern.

haycock *noun* A small pile of hay in the field. Same as **cock**[2].

1934–47 *LAMSAS Appal* (Swain Co NC). **1946** Nixon *Glossary VA Words* 25 = a pile of hay in the field at haying time . . . [a term used] west of the Blue Ridge, on the Middle Neck, and on the Eastern Shore.

hay doodle *noun* Same as **doodle**[2] **1.**

1946 Nixon *Glossary VA Words* 25 = a pile of hay in the field at haying time . . . [a term used] in the Blue Ridge. **1952–57** (in **1973** McDavid and McDavid *Vocab E KY* 154) = attested by 2/52 (3.8%) of E KY speakers for the Linguistic Atlas of the North Central States. **1976** Still *Pattern of Man* 32 Everything they saw they remarked on: hay doodles in Alonzo Tate's pasture, a crazy chimney leaning away from a house, long johns on clotheslines.

hay farm *noun* See citation.

1957 Broaddus *Vocab Estill Co KY* 39 = a meadow.

hay frame *noun* A wagon frame used to haul hay; a hayrack.

c1960 Wilson *Coll* = a frame on a farm wagon arranged to hold a large load of hay. **1995** Montgomery *Coll* (known to Cardwell).

[DARE *hay frame* n chiefly South, South Midland]

hayjohn *noun* See citation.

1943 Korson *Coal Dust* 5 Full-time miners naturally resented them [= farmer-miners] and expressed their distrust by calling them "winter diggers," "wheats," "corncrackers," "hay johns."

hay mound (also *hay mow*, *hay mower*) *noun* A barn loft for storing hay.

1957 Broaddus *Vocab Estill Co KY* 39 *hay mound* = a place for storing hay in a barn. **1978** Reese *Speech NE Tenn* 35 *hay mower* = attested by 2/12 (16.7%) speakers. **2009** Wiles and Wiles *Location* 13 The barn stood about three hundred feet from the house. The original part of the building was constructed of poplar and chestnut, not chinked, for ventilation of the hay. This was called the hay mow.

hay mower See **hay mound.**

hay pile See **pile.**

hayrack *noun* See citation.

c1960 Wilson *Coll* = a place to put hay for one animal.

[DARE *hayrack* n chiefly South, South Midland]

hayshant See **hessian.**

Haystack *noun* A type of candy.

2011 *Blind Pig* (Nov 29) Granny has made Haystacks or Butterscotch Crunchies ever since I can remember.

hay thrashing *noun* Formerly, a work activity in which farmers bring their hay to a community location to be threshed to obtain grain or seed.

1956 Hall *Coll* (Townsend TN) Corn shuckin', hay thrashin', square dances [were among the good times in this cove before the Park era].

he *pronoun*

A Used redundantly for the subject of a clause.

1814 Hartsell *Memora* 138 General Robertes, the Commander of the two ridgementes of men, he told the men that ther times was out and they shold bee Discharged. **1916** Combs *Old Early English* 290 An anomaly that might be mentioned here is the redundant use of the pronoun as in the expression "John, he said so." **1939** Hall *Coll* (Proctor NC) Cope, he shot at [the bear] and never tetched it. It fell out in front of them dogs. **1950** Bray *Disappearing Dialect* 281 The double subject may likewise be defended [as formerly used in literary English]. "Brother, he come home," the highlander may say, or "That teacher, she says the outlandishest things." **1978** Montgomery *White Pine Coll* III-2 My dad's brother that lived up at Del Rio in Cocke County, why he had about twenty or twenty-five bee stands.

B *noun* Used as a euphemism for bull. See also **bull A1.**

1968 Wilson *Folklore Mammoth Cave* 14 [Buck is a] euphemism for the name of a male animal; some others are *brute*, *brute beast*, *daddy*, *he*, *male*, *old animal*, and *papa-cow*.

head

A *noun* See also **hand A4**, **old head.**

1 Variant plural form without *-s* to enumerate herd animals or persons (especially children).

1813 Hartsell *Memora* 108 In the Evning I went to the block house and counted Eighteen head of hoges that was kiled and brought to the house. **1863** (in **1983** *CW Harlan Co* 20) We also captured 11 head of horses, 8 saddle pockets, 8 sabres & a number of halters. **1863** Wilson *Confederate Private* 5 (Feb 15) she has some 35 hogs and 20 hed of cattle and one horse. **1939** Hall *Coll* (Emerts Cove TN) He'd keep as much as two hundred head of cattle there every summer. **1956** Hall *Coll* (Big Bend NC) I have five head of cattle. **1973** GSMNP-88:80 My daddy had sixteen oxens that we logged with and six head of mules that we logged and hauled lumber too with. **1976** GSMNP-114:5 My daddy always kept five or six head of horses and seventy-five or eighty head of cows. **1979** Carpenter *Walton War* 169 He's got seven head of younguns and don't turn a hair at havin' to feed and clothe 'em. **1983** Pyle *CCC 50th Anniv* B:2:12 We kept about forty head, on average about forty head [of hogs]. **1989** *Matewan OHP-9* We'd sell a few head of cattle. That's the way he got his money to pay his tax.

[OED3 *head* n 10b; DARE *head* n B3 chiefly South, South Midland]

2 A copperhead snake.

2001 Montgomery *Coll* My dog got bit by a old head (Cardwell).

B *verb* To surpass; hence participial adjective *headingest* = most surpassing, unusual.

1884 Murfree *In TN Mts* 3 This hyar Evander Price hev kom ter be the headin'est, no'count critter in the country. **1937** Hyatt *Kiverlid* 64 Hit ondoubtedly jist headed anything I ever seed! **1952** Wilson *Folk Speech NC* 549 *headingest* = most unusual or striking. **1995** Montgomery *Coll*: *head* (known to Brown); *headingest* (known to Brown, Bush).

C *adjective*

1 Most entertaining, remarkable, striking (as *head fellow* = a comic, very entertaining person).

1813 Hartsell *Memora* 135 this was the head time that I ever saw in my Life. **1892** Dromgoole *War of Roses* 496 Eb was himself the acknowledged "head fiddler o' that deestrict." **1895** Edson and Fairchild *TN Mts* 372 = best, chief. "That's the *head* trick I ever see." **1939** Hall *Coll* (Tobes Creek NC) He was the head feller that I ever saw. **1956** Hall *Coll* (Cosby TN) He's the head feller you've ever seed. **c1982** Young *Colloquial Appal* 11 *head sight of* = the most, a great amount. *Ibid.* 16 Clate Miller said that it was the head car that he ever laid eyes on. **1987** Young *Lost Cove* 113 I heard tell there was a head ruckus up your way yesterday. **2007** McMillon *Notes* He's the head fool ever I seed.

[cf EDD *head* II.18 "chief . . . best, most excelling"]

2 Oldest, first.

1956 McAtee *Some Dial NC* 21 He was the head brother in the family. **1973** GSMNP-76:14 They had this lower still set up on some posts. It was about as high as my head boy.

headache berry *noun* Same as **black cohosh**.

1957 Combs *Lg Sthn High: Word List* 49 = the black cohosh (Cimicifuga racemosa) berry.

headache medicine (also *headache whiskey*) *noun* Homemade whiskey. See also **cold medicine**, **snakebite medicine**.

1968 *End of Moonshining* 101 Names given moonshine include . . . headache whiskey. **1972** Hall *Sayings* 101 Common expressions about 1941 for whisky illegally manufactured were . . . "headache medicine" (with veiled meaning), "screw top," "snake juice," [and] "red eye."

headache piece *noun* See citation. Same as **thump barrel**.

1985 Dabney *More Mt Spirits* 113 = 2-gallon wooden keg. This is the "thump keg." One-inch holes must be bored on each side of the top of this, one for the insertion of the "thump post" and the other for insertion of the "headache piece." A ½-inch hole should be bored in the side of the bottom to draw the "feints" out, after a run.

headache stick *noun* See citations.

1968 *End of Moonshining* 49 = the long thump rod. **1974** Dabney *Mt Spirits* xxii = the long vapor line pipe that goes down into the thumper keg.

headache whiskey See **headache medicine**.

head cheese (also *head souse*) *noun* A dish prepared from scraps of meat from the head of a pig. Same as **souse B**.

1966 Dakin *Vocab Ohio River Valley* 339 Although no Kentuckian uses only *head cheese*, this term is scattered throughout the state and is clearly spreading as a newer name. In part at least the use of this term in Kentucky can be attributed to the use of *head cheese* as a trade word in recent years. **1982** Ginns *Snowbird Gravy* 36 They used all the parts of the hog—all of them. Out of the head they made head-souse, which was cooked, and you'd put vinegar over it and let it set for several days. **1996** Houk *Foods & Recipes* 16 Even the head of a pig, "rooter" and all, was cooked into something called souse, or head cheese. **2009** Miller *Nigh Gone* 78 The head, after the brains [of the hog] were removed [was served] with eggs at the next day's breakfast, and the feet were saved for use in making "souse meat" or "head cheese" after being boiled to release the gelatin that would hold it together when fashioned into a loaf.

[perhaps loan translation of Dutch *hoofdkaas*]

header *noun* See citation.

1930 Pendleton *Wood-Hicks Speak* 88 = the first log in a line of them to be dragged down a mountain side.

heading *noun*

1 A pillow; pillows collectively.

1943 Goerch *Down Home* 30 = pillows: "Have you enough heading?" **1982** Slone *How We Talked* 27 = anything used as a pillow. "Let me give you some heading for your bed." **1984** Wilder *You All Spoken* 28 = a pillow. **1997** Montgomery *Coll* (known to Bush).

[DARE *heading* n 1 South, South Midland]

2 The seedpod at the top of a stalk of sorghum.

1968 Birch et al. *Sorghum* 26 Before the cane could be cut, it first had to be "stripped." This meant walking through the field and stripping off all the leaves, or fodder, along with the "heading," or the seed pod at the top of the stalk. Sometimes these pods weighed as much as a pound each.

3 See citations.

1971 *AOHP/ALC-66* There's fellows shot down a heading of coal, and fire broke loose in it, and fire come back over top of us, just followed the roof down. **1973** *AOHP/EH-24* When I was driving that heading during the Depression, I was loading as high as ten cars [a day]. **2002** Armstead *Black Days* 243 = [a] coal mine tunnel where coal is, or has been, actively mined. **2004** *Early Mines* 27 (as of 1902) The headings were the places where coal was actually being dug. *Ibid.* 31 Usually two or three men worked in each heading. **2007** *Mining Terms* = a vein [of coal] above a drift. An interior level or airway driven in a mine. In longwall workings, a narrow passage driven upward from a gangway in starting a working in order to give a loose end.

4 See citation.

2007 *Mining Terms* = a passage leading from the gangway, commonly at right angles in a coal mine.

5 See citation.

1983 Montell *Don't Go Up* 199 = oak timber used to form the ends of whiskey barrels.

headingest See **head B.**

head knocker *noun* One in authority.

1997 Montgomery *Coll* = part of a [tree] limb with a swelling caused by abnormal growth; when cut down it makes a club known as a head knocker (Brown).

[DARE *head knocker* n South, South Midland]

headmark *noun* A mark of achievement for daily work done by a schoolchild, especially in spelling.

1968 Clarke *Stuart's Kentucky* 128 The more ambitious pupils, using outmoded and tattered books, tried to spell down their classmates and get the most headmarks. **1968** Wilson *Folklore Mammoth Cave* 43 = a merit mark given the child who stood, at the end of the class, at the head of the spelling line; then, the next day, he went to the foot of the class and worked his way back to the head by turning down the one above him who missed a word. **1994** Mullins *Coaley Creek* xi = bonus point earned while doing schoolwork. **1998** Hamby *Grassy Creek* 86 Headmarks were recorded by the teacher the entire school session and the one in each grade with the most headmarks the whole session received a prize from the teacher. **2008** Salsi *Ray Hicks* 72 Later on, Miss Trivette said, "Ray, you hain't got nairy a head mark on spellin'." She called out the word "churn" and it come to me afore the others could spell it. I was tickled and got excited and spelled it "c-h-u-r-n-u-r-n." She knowed I knowed it and give me the mark.

[DARE *headmark* n chiefly South, South Midland]

heads *noun* The impure early portion of a **run** of **moonshine.** See also **faint(s)**, **middlings**, **tailings.**

1963 Carson *History Bourbon* 104 The distiller was not overly concerned about cutting out the heads and tails [from his whiskey], and he was in no position to age his product. *Ibid.* 237 *heads and tails* = the condensate obtained at the beginning and end of a run, containing undesirable amounts of the congeneric substances.

heads and tails See **heads.**

head souse See **head cheese.**

head-swimming *noun* Dizziness.

1917 Kephart *Word-List* 413 = vertigo. **1927** Woofter *Dialect from WV* 356 = dizziness: "I have had head-swimming all week."

heal-all *noun* Self-heal, a perennial plant (*Prunella vulgaris*) with medicinal uses. Also called **carpenter's-herb**, **cure-all.**

1941 Justus *Kettle Creek* 95 [The herb pot] filled the kitchen room with a dozen different fragrances: the sharp scent of pennyroyal, the bitter smell of boneset, the honey sweet breath of dried elder flowers, and things more tangy than these: ragwort, May apple root, heal-all, wild ginger. **1971** Krochmal et al. *Medicinal Plants Appal* 100 = roots are used as a sedative and antispasmodic, diuretic, astringent, and tonic. [**1982** Stupka *Wildflowers* 97 This common and very widespread mint is thought to have been a native plant but has also been naturalized from Europe and Asia. In Europe, old-time herb doctors used [heal all] in the treatment of throat ailments and other afflictions, whereby it acquired its common name and other names as "self-heal" and "carpenter's herb."]

healing balsam *noun* The Fraser fir (*Abies fraseri*). Same as **balsam 1.**

1908 Britton *N Amer Trees* 76 (DARE) This southern fir, called . . . Healing balsam . . . occurs in the higher mountains of Virginia and West Virginia to North Carolina and Tennessee, where it sometimes forms forests, and reaches a maximum height of 25 meters.

heap

A *noun* Many, a great deal or number.

1824 Knight *Letter from KY* 107 Some words used, even by genteel people . . . in a new sense; and . . . pronounced very uncouthly, as . . . heap of times. **1859** Taliaferro *Fisher's River* 41 A heap uv groanin', gobs of shoutin' and cryin', goes a grate ways toads settin' off a meetin'. **1863** *Brown CW Letters* (May 31) We have had a heap of Sickness and i was Sick two Month. **1864** *Reese CW Letters* (May 31) we hav lost a heep of men and kild a heep of yankeys. **1895** Edson and Fairchild *TN Mts* 376 = many. **1913** Kephart *Our Sthn High* 288 Afore, atwixt, awar, heap o' folks, peart, up and done it, usen for used, all these everyday expressions of the backwoods were contemporary with the *Canterbury Tales*. **1924** Spring *Lydia Whaley* 3 I've seed a heap of ups and downs and had a world of trouble the whole world through and I hope I get to a better one some day. **1939** Hall *Coll* (Deep Creek NC) i caught a heap of fish in them mountain streams. **c1945** Haun *Hawk's Done* 223 George set a heap a store by Cathey. **1953** Hall *Coll* (Bryson City NC) So he sit there and told a great long story, how many bears he killed in one season. Mounted up to around fifty or something like that . . . And some set quiet for some time and finally this fellow Wilson raised up in the camp and says, "Boys, that was a heap of bears." **1957** Parris *My Mts* 7 Why, a heap of folks borrow trouble just because they don't read nature's signs and don't listen to their elders. **1962** Dykeman *Tall Woman* 50 There's been a heap of hard fighting over all these long months; the hospital was full and most were hurt worse than Paul. **1997** *Dante OHP*-14 He'd get whole barrels of flour at a time, a heap of big bags, and meal and whole sacks of brown and white sugar.

[DARE *heap* n 1 chiefly South, South Midland]

B (also *a heap*) *adverb*

1 Much, very, extremely, a great deal.

1862 Shipman *CW Letters* (May 1) [My horse] is a heap better and Mending every day he got very stiff and could hardly walk but is now well. **1864** *Epperly CW Letters* (March 25) I think wee all have stud it about as long as wee can unless our leading men dus a heap better than they ever have yet. **1881** Pierson *In the Brush* 261 [The armor was] all a heap too big, and he shucked 'em off d'rectly, and made for a dry branch down in the bottom. **1910** Cooke *Power and Glory* 113 I'd a heap ruther take care of my own child. **1939** Hall Coll (Wears Cove TN) I'd say nearer two hundred [bear] would come a heap closer. **1940** Oakley *Roamin'/Restin'* 16 Now I am writing these true storys as best as I know how and no dought this book will be different from any other book on the Smoky Mountains as the writer spent all my life among the heep big mountains, as the Indians sometimes say. **c1950** (in **2000** Oakley *Roamin' Man* 56) Well to my many friends who read my little story, I am on the road to gitting stroung and heap stought as the Indians say. **1972** GSMNP-93:2:7 [There] used to be a heap more snow. **1973** GSMNP-76:13 They built another one up in the field, a heap bigger one. **1973** GSMNP-85:1:18 I would heap rather see it back like it used to be. **2007** Shelby *Molly Whuppie* 31 The man decided he'd a heap rather eat cornbread than grub newground.

[DARE (at *heap* n 3a) chiefly South, South Midland]

2 In phrase (a) *heap sight* = a good deal, by far, extremely. See also **sight 2**, **sight in the world B**.

1895 Edson and Fairchild *TN Mts* 372 I'd a *heap sight* rather stay than go. **1904–20** Kephart *Notebooks* 4:749 I'd a heap-sight ruther hunt. **c1940** Simms Coll Why [the growth of flowers] kivers the mountains like cyarpets (carpets) and is a heap sight purty. **1957** Combs *Lg Sthn High: Word List* 90 = adverbially, in: "I'd a heap-sight druther have me a big pot o' shucky beans." **c1960** Wilson Coll = much: "I'd a heap sight rather go than stay here." **1978** Parris *Mt Cooking* 9 Back when I was just a shirttail of a boy, there was a heap sight of walnut trees. *Ibid.* 126 Pickling is a heap sight more than just preparing cucumbers. **2017** *Blind Pig* (Sept 10) To many a mountain woman who grew up at a time when the kitchen stove occupied most of her 16-hour-long day, pickling is a heap sight more than just preparing cucumbers.

hear *verb* See also **hear tell**.

1 Variant infinitive/base forms *hur, hyar, hyer*.

1978 Reese *Speech NE Tenn* 175 hur = attested by 7/12 (58.3%) speakers. **c1979** Chiles *Glossary* 3 *hyar, hyer*.

2 Variant past-tense forms *heared, hearn, heered, heyerd, hyaerd, hyeard, hyearn, hyerd*.

1813 Hartsell *Memora* 125 General Jackson fired three Canons off which was the first that I ever heared in my life. **1845** *Sevier Co Court* This cause comming on to be finally heared and determined before the Honorable Robert J. Anderson Judge. **c1850** (in **1931** Burns *Coves Blount Co* 52) In a deposition made by a witness in a case in chancery court in the 1850's the witness said he couldn't read but he "hearn" the document read by Reuben Allen or Jake Slaughter, he couldn't remember which. **1862** *Reese CW Letters* (Sept 29) O how glad was I and how I felt when I hearn houdey from my littel Children God Bless them. **1864** Wilson *Confederate Private* 50 (May 22) we heared the cannon plain but we have not heared what was done in the engagement. **1923** (in **1952** Mathes *Tall Tales* 6) Reckon ye heared they was a big-meetin' a-goin' on in the Babtis' church. **1939** Hall Coll (Hartford TN) It sprung right up, and I heared it hit the ground two or three times, and it run out of hearing. **1942** Hall *Phonetics Smoky Mts* 42 [hɪɚd]. **c1945** Haun *Hawk's Done* 264 I hyeard Elzie scolding them and telling them to shut up. **1952** Wilson *Folk Speech NC* 553 *hyearn* = past tense and past participle of hear. **1956** Hall Coll (Big Bend NC) I hearn the other day that he died hisself. **1973** GSMNP-84:30 I got up here at the gap of the ridge, and I heared them [= hunting dogs] down there, whooping and hollering, and of course it scared me. **1975** Jackson *Unusual Words* 150 The *y* sound inserted in words such as *hyar* or *hyer* (here) and *heyerd* (heard) suggest the lengthening of words that is characteristic of so much of the speech in northwestern North Carolina. **1980** Miles *Verbs in Haywood Co* 85 I'm going to tell him that I heared that. **1989** *Matewan OHP*-9 I heared my granddaddy talk about it. **2005** Williams *Gratitude* 136 *hyaerd; hyerd*. **2007** (in **2012** McQuaid *Interface* 272) I heared a baby a-screaming.

[DARE *hear* v A2b *hearn* chiefly South, South Midland]

3 Variant past-participle forms *heared, heered, hearn* [hwdn], *hern, hyeard*.

1849 Lanman *Alleghany Mts* 14 One of my neighbors killed about a hundred last year, and I've hearn tell that your land is very rich in snakes. **1859** Taliaferro *Fisher's River* 22 They fout for our liberties, and they must be hearn. **1861** *Martin CW Letters* (Dec 21) Father I have hern that you are al wel this week. **1862** *West CW Letters* (April 25) Edward West is pretty bad off I Reckon you have hearn hit. **1867** Harris *Sut Lovingood* 67 I'se allers hearn that hit tuck a mons'us wise brat tu know hits daddy, an' I thinks hit takes a wiser daddy tu know his own brats. **1886** Smith *Sthn Dialect* 348 When we offered pay, the men declined it, saying "he'd never tuck no pay fer nuthin' ter eat in his life, and he'd hyeard his father say he'd never tuck none, and he never 'spected to take none." **1891** Primer *Studies in WV* 165 The past participle of *hear* is pronounced either (Hiirn or Harn; or Hiird or Hard) according to the form used. **1896** *Word-List* 420 He was making the masterest noise ever I hearn. **1913** Kephart *Our Sthn High* 120 They've heered tell about the judges. **1928** Justus *Betty Lou* 77 I've hearn tell o' them good old days away back yander, yes, many be the time. **1939** Hall Coll (Cataloochee NC) He throwed that cat on that poor old horse's back, and then the row started. You've never heared no such a commotion in all the days of your life down there. [See **1952** in **2**.] **1972** GSMNP-68:6 I don't know anything about that. I've heared it spoke of, but I don't remember. **1980** Miles *Verbs in Haywood Co* 85 Have you ever heared of that? **1995** Montgomery Coll I've not hearn from him in twenty years (Cardwell).

[DARE *hyeard* as past-tense and past-participle (at *hear* v A2c) South, South Midland, especially Appalachians]

heared, hearn See **hear 2, 3, hear tell.**

hear on See **on B3.**

hear say, hear speak See **hear tell B, C.**

heart dropsy *noun* Congestive heart failure.

1973 *AOHP/ASU-111* [Speaker A: What did your mother die of?] Speaker B: Heart dropsy.

hear tell

A Variant past-tense and past-participle forms *heared tell* [see **1971** in **B**], *hearn tell* [see **1928** in **B**], *heern tell* [see **1913** in **B**].

B (also *hear say, hear speak*) *verb phrase* To be informed of, learn of by word of mouth, especially through gossip.

1843 (in **1974** Harris *High Times* 16) He is known a hundred miles round, as the owner of "Old Turkey Reacher," the best rifle you ever heard tell of! **1863** *Tesh CW Letters* (May 28) I knew that You would be oneasy a bout me as soon as You heard tell of the Fight. **1913** Kephart *Our Sthn High* 277 I heern tell you was one o' them 'sperts. **1928** Justus *Betty Lou* 77 I've hearn tell o' them good old days away back yander, yes, many be the time. **1939** Hall *Coll* (Tuckaleechee Cove TN) He never was heared tell of no more. **1954** Arnow *Dollmaker* 106 Clovis was a tellen me once he heared say or read they was mountains or rough wild country. **1956** Still *Burning of Waters* 58 I've heard speak of families of ginseng diggers roaming the hills, free as the birds. **1962** Dykeman *Tall Woman* 223 I heard tell you helped bring your sister-in-law's baby. **1971** *AOHP/ALC-277* You never heared tell of no other churches back then. **1973** *GSMNP-76:9* His brother left his daddy and mother, and they never heard tell of him from that day to this. **1974–75** McCracken *Logging* 3:17 They was hogs in them mountains 'fore that Smoky Mountain National Park was ever heard tell of. **1976** *Bear Hunting* 309 I've not heard no tell of him in a long time. **1981** Henry *Alex Stewart* 58 I never seed that lady before or since. And that merchant, he talks about it ever once in awhile. He said he never had seen or heard no tell of her. **1983** *Dark Corner OHP-3A* [They] used to call him Big Man Moses. You ever hear tell of that man? **1989** *Matewan OHP-89* I've heard say that she was a bootlegger. **1991** Thomas *Sthn Appal* 14 She never heerd no tell uv 'em ennymore.

C *noun phrase* Indirect information, a second-hand report, hearsay.

1940 Haun *Hawk's Done* 23 I don't know what all took place. I just have to go by hear-tell. **c1945** Haun *Hawk's Done* 319 I reckon, if a body can judge by hear-tell, they had nigh about everything sold before Granny was covered up in the grave.

hearth *noun* Variant forms *haith, hath.*

1867 Harris *Sut Lovingood* 97g [sic] I know'd that I hed planted a big skeer an that hit would bar fruit afore moon down, so I jist snatched up a chunk ove fire ofen the hath an toch off the powder onder the tail ove the ole hoss. **1942** Hall *Phonetics Smoky Mts* 30 [hæθ]. **1976** Ogle and Nixon *If Only* Go in "tother" house and set the churn on the "haith" (hearth) so the milk will turn clabber so's (so we) can have butter.

[DARE *hearth* n Ab especially South, South Midland]

hearth broom *noun* A short broom kept by the fireplace to sweep away ashes and embers, usually made of **broom cane** or **sedge grass** from which straws have been cut, bundled together, and tied with a strong cord to one end of a stick. See also **broom sedge.**

1996–97 Montgomery *Coll* (known to Cardwell, Ledford, Norris, Oliver), = a round broom made of stiff, dried broom corn tied to a short handle, usually with a hole in the handle for hanging (Brown). **2004** Snodgrass *Kitchen History* 323 In the Appalachian hills, home besom or broom makers collected twigs to dry for soaking, then bound or wired them to a stout ash, oak, or hickory stick. **2017** Blankenship *Songs of Whippoorwill* 37 "That way, it makes tougher brooms," he says, adding squarely: "Some people like a red-colored hearth broom. If the broomcorn isn't harvested, or cut, until after it is completely ripe, the straw will turn red."

[DARE *hearth broom* n chiefly South, South Midland]

hearth cake *noun*

c1940 Simms *Coll* = [corn]bread baked on [the] hearth.

hearth rock *noun*

A Variant form *hathrock.*

1961 Williams *R in Mt Speech* 6 In a few words, however, r is omitted: . . . *fust, hathrock* (hearthrock), and *onery* (ordinary).

B A hearthstone.

1925 Dargan *Highland Annals* 90 He'll lay on the hearth-rock thinkin' how he's goin' to git that fox. **c1950** Adams *Grandpap* 85 We shook our heads and tiptoed across the hearthrock to hunker down at his feet. **1971** *Boogers* 74 They killed him and buried him under th' hearth rock. **1995–97** Montgomery *Coll* (known to Adams, Brown, Cardwell, Jones, Ledford, Oliver).

[DARE *hearthrock* n chiefly Appalachians]

heart in one's mouth, have one's *verb phrase* To fear for one's life.

1939 Hall *Coll* (Nine Mile TN) I got to studyin' then how nigh that bear come a-gettin' me, and I just got scared so bad it just appeared like my heart was right up in my mouth just a-beatin'. **1994** Montgomery *Coll* (known to Shields).

heartleaf *noun*

1 The liverwort (*Hepatica acutiloba/americana*).

1889 Mooney *Folk Carolina Mts* 99 Liverwort is known by the appropriate name of "heart-leaf," and the peculiar shape of its leaves has suggested their use as a love philter. A girl may infallibly win the love of any sweetheart she may desire by secretly throwing over his clothing some of the powder made by rubbing together a few heart leaves which have been dried before the fire. She may, if she wish, have a score of lovers simply by carrying the leaves in her bosom. It is to be presumed that the recipe would be equally efficacious if used by one of the opposite sex.

2 (also *heart's leaf, heart leaves*) Wild ginger (*Asarum* spp). See also **monkey jug**.

1894 Bergen *Plant Names III* 97 *heart-leaves* = Asarum Virginicum (Banner Elk NC). **1940** Caton *Wildflowers of Smokies* 55 *heart's leaf* = ginger root, wild ginger. **1940** Haun *Hawk's Done* 6 On the east side of the house there's that little old haystacky-looking hill Ma always called Sals King Mountain. I have a time hunting heart leaves and ginseng on it. **1970** Vincent *More of Best* 41 He brews it from wild "yarbs" around there, yellowroot, sarsaparilla, rat's bane, heart leaf, burdock, poplar bark, wild cherry bark, scaly hickory bark and slippery elm. **1973** *GSMNP-76*:24 We got a leaf up there they call a heart's leaf. Now you can put two of them leaves together and they [are] just exactly like a woman's or a man's heart when they're grown. . . . That's what cured them was that heart leaf.

heart leaves See **heartleaf 2**.

hearts *noun* Kindling wood.

1986 Pederson et al. *LAGS* (Sevier Co TN).

hearts bustin' (also *heart a-bustin' with love, heart(s)-bustin'-with-love*) *noun* A burning bush (*Euonymus americanus*), a shrub that displays a brilliant orange-red seedpod in the early fall. Also called **cat's paw, jewel-box, swamp dogwood**. See also **arrowwood, Indian bitter, spindle bush, strawberry bush, wahoo 1**.

1928 Galyon *Plant Naturalist* 10 There is burning-bush, a wand-like shrub which glorifies the mountains in the fall with its cluster of peculiarly constructed cerise and coral fruits. The mountaineers so romantically call it "hearts bustin-with-love." **1937** Thornburgh *Great Smoky Mts* 25 The seeds of some shrubs are more spectacular than their flowers. This is true of one of the showiest shrubs in the Great Smokies, the euonymous, wahoo or spindlebush. It is especially lovely in October when its seed-pod bursts open, displaying orange-colored seeds in its glowing red heart. It has many descriptive local names—swamp willow, strawberry bush, catspaw, jewel-box, but most descriptive of all is the name given by a mountain man of, "Heart's-bustin'-with-love." This shrub has been adopted by the Smoky Mountains Hiking Club, whose greeting is, "Wahoo, wahoo!" and whose signature, "Heart's-bustin-with-love." **1941** Walker *Story of Mt* 59–60 A wild strawberry shrub with its greenish stems and foliage of the same color when young, becomes very ornamental in late summer and early autumn when its crimson red seed capsule bursts and shows a cluster of orange-scarlet seeds inside. This is a favorite shrub, and the sentimental people of the mountain refer to it as "heart a-bustin' with love." **1951** Pyle *Gatlinburg* 22 It is a local shrub, or hedge, or flower, or tree. I don't know what you call it. Anyway it looks like Christmas holly at first glance. But when you get up close, you see it has been a round pod, and then it has broken open and out have come four red berries, just like lights on a chandelier. . . . The real name of it is Wahoo, but around here it is always called "Hearts-a-Bustin'-with-Love." **1964** Stupka *Trees Shrubs Vines* 97 In this shrub the fruits are appreciably more showy than the flowers and account for the local name "hearts-a-bustin'-with-love" or "hearts-a-bustin'." The capsules begin to color early in August, and by late that month they are an attractive coral pink; in September these three- to five-lobed fruits split open exposing the bright glossy-red or orange seeds. **1970** Campbell et al. *Smoky Mt Wildflowers* 102 A beautiful shrub 5 to 10 feet tall, hearts-a-bustin' is found throughout the lower and intermediate elevations, usually near a stream. The early summer small flowers are inconspicuous, but the plant compels attention in early autumn when its wine-colored pods burst open, revealing brilliant, orange-red seeds. **1980** *Smokies Heritage* 153 [My father Wiley Oakley] named some wildflowers, too; he was the first to call one of our autumn bushes "Hearts a-bustin' with love," and it's a common name across the country now.

[DARE *hearts-a-bustin'-with-love* n chiefly southern Appalachians]

heartsease *noun* Any of several violets (*Viola* spp).

1941 Walker *Story of Mt* 46 There are some wild flowers which seem to have such good dispositions that they pay no attention to altitudes, and would as freely climb to a mountain's top as to remain and prosper in the valley. Among this class of flowers is heartsease, or field pansy, birdfoot violet, and harebell. **c1945** Haun *Hawk's Done* 263 He pointed to a plant. It was a small, tiny plant. About like heart's ease, save that it had sort of star-shaped leaves instead of heart-shaped ones, with red veins running through them.

heart's leaf See **heartleaf 2**.

heat

A *verb* See also **het up**.

1 Variant past-tense form *het*.

1913 Kephart *Our Sthn High* 284 There are many corrupt forms of the verb, such as gwine for gone or going, mought (mowt) for might, clim, het. **1956** *GSMNP-22*:18 [You] het hot water and poured it down through the cracks? **1959** Roberts *Up Cutshin* 132 I het them arns good and hot, and I slipped up to him, and I rammed about four of them right down that big eye. **1962** Williams *Verbs Mt Speech* 17 Verbs which retain either the strong preterites of Middle English or variant preterites of the English dialects [include] heat (present), het (past), het (past participle). **1974** Fink *Bits Mt Speech* 12 She *het up* the vittles. **1984** Page and Wigginton *Foxfire Cookery* 7 She always had a kettle that she "het" her water in—or she "heated" her water in. **2012** Milnes *Signs Cures Witchery* I het this stove so hot it was red all over.

2 Variant past-participle and participial adjective form *het*.

1939 Hall *Coll* (Haywood Co NC) This fish that was not het so much is better. **1979** *Big South Fork OHP-19* You paid so much for your water a-being het to wash. **2000** Miller *Looneyville* 50 = a colloquial expression for disturbed or disordered. To become quite upset about something: "Don't let something that simple get you all het."

B *verb* To disturb or distract.

[See **2000** in **A2**.]

C *noun* A heat rash.

1956 McAtee *Some Dial NC* 22 = prickly-heat, an inflammation of the skin in hot weather. **c1960** Wilson *Coll* (or *prickly heat*) = a rash, a "breaking out."

heater (also *heater box*) *noun* See citation.

1949 Maurer *Argot of Moonshiner* 10 *heater, heater-box* = a box into which beer is poured or pumped to be preheated. This process, found only on large stills, utilizes heat from the liquor vapor, and the heater serves double duty as both dephlegmator and pre-cooker: "Pump some beer in the heater-box, Joe."

heath bald *noun* A treeless area covered by shrubbery and thickets, usually on an upper reach of a mountain. See 1937, 1960, 1991 citations. Also called **shrub bald, wooly top**. See also **bald, grass bald**.

1937 Thornburgh *Great Smoky Mts* 26–27 It is an outstanding characteristic of the Smokies that its peaks are timbered to the top except on certain "balds." These "balds" and the reason for them has attracted the attention of scientists. Dr. Stanley Cain, until 1946 on the faculty of the University of Tennessee who spent several years studying the mountain top balds, draws a sharp distinction between the "grassy balds" and the "heath balds." "In the Great Smokies, areas of heath are to be found with a development of dry peat," he writes, "but a majority of heath balds have a remarkable development of moist, fibrous brown peat, frequently to the depth of one or two feet." **1943** Peattie *Great Smokies* 197 The "heath balds," as botanists call them . . . can only be compared to the *krummholz* of the Alps, or the "lashorn thickets" on dwarf spruce of the high mountains of Virginia, all of which are practically impenetrable growths of scrub. **1960** Stupka *Great Smoky Mts* 18 There are treeless areas on some of the higher mountaintops and ridges. Owing to their lack of forest cover, such places are called balds. That designation, however, is a relative one since other plants form a dense carpet over the balds. If these plants are largely shrubs belonging to the heath family, such balds are known as heath balds; if grasses and sedges prevail, the balds are termed grass balds. **1979** Cantu *Great Smoky Mts* 12 Heath balds (called locally "laurel slicks" or "hells," depending upon whether one is viewing them or hiking on them) are comprised almost entirely of rhododendron, laurel, sand myrtle, and azalea. **1979** *Smoky Vistas* (Summer) 1 Not all the peaks of the Smokies are covered by forest and some of the most interesting and scenic communities have no trees at all. Among these are the famous heath balds which are dominated by rhododendron, mountain laurel, and other evergreen shrubs. **1991** Walker *Great Smoky* 32 The Great Smoky Mountains National Park has two different types of balds, grassy balds and heath balds. The grassy variety is predominantly grass-covered, while the heath balds, or laurel slicks as they are sometimes called, appear to be grassy from a distance but upon closer contact it is apparent that it is an extremely dense thicket of shrub. Heath balds are predominantly comprised of rhododendron, flame azalea, laurel, and sand myrtle, all of which are evergreen, except the flame azalea, and are spectacular when in bloom. **2006** *Encycl Appalachia* 47 heath balds, also known as laurel slicks, are characterized by low-diversity evergreen shrub communities on convex upper-slope positions and narrow ridges. Although there have been no field experiments to directly test the mechanisms that may create or maintain heath balds, they are associated with sites that are steeply drained, exposed, and have acidic soils. Unlike grassy balds, heath balds are stable communities with little evidence of succession to forest. **2008** *Newfound Gap Road* 8 One of the interesting forest communities here is the heath bald, which you can see on the exposed, steep, high places [of road]. The soil there is too thin to support trees, and it's called a bald because all the plants—mountain laurel, blueberries, rhododendron, myrtle (the so-called heath)—grow to the same height and, from a distance, look smooth like a bald head. **2013** *BearPaw* (Spring–Summer) 10 Heath balds form on steep exposed mid-to-high elevation ridges with acidic bed rock such as Anakesta sandstone. Of the more than 400 heath balds in the Smokies, most are in Tennessee, and many, such as Brushy Mountain and Inspiration Point on Alum Cave, lie on the flanks of Mt. LeConte. Low evergreen broadleaved plants, mostly in the Heath family (*Ericaceae*) dominate heath balds, not only by crowding out potential tree seedlings, but also by maintaining the acidity of the soils and performing acts of chemical warfare.

heathen *noun*

A Variant forms *heathern, yeathen*.

1867 Harris *Sut Lovingood* 158 An' the nise—well, when I larns tu spell an' pernounce the flavor ove a ded hoss, play the shape ove a yeathen war-jug ontu a fiddil. **1942** Hall *Phonetics Smoky Mts* 70 [ˈhiðɚn]. **c1960** Wilson *Coll*: *heathen* is more often *heathern*. **1989** *Matewan OHP-9* [Missionary Baptists] wanted the Old Baptists to make up money to send preachers overseas to them heatherns when we had as many heatherns here as they had over there.

[DARE *heathen* n South Midland]

B An intractable or uncouth person, especially an unruly child; someone regarded as a stranger.

1954 Arnow *Dollmaker* 35 Make her behave, Mom, acten like a heathern. **2003** Carter *Mt Home* 24 I could tell how she acted, she thought we was a bunch of heatherns, anyhow. **2009** Benfield *Mt Born* 119 = behaving in a most uncivilized manner, rowdy manner, like savages. **2017** *Blind Pig* (Feb 28) Heathern was used when he/she moved out of the county. Glad he/she is gone, he/she was a "heathern."

heathern See **heathen**.

heave *verb*

A Forms.

1 Variant present-tense/infinitive form *hive*.

1971 *Boogers* 76 He got a'hold a'that rock and he begin t'hive and hive, and directly he pulled it up.

2 Variant past-tense form *hove*.

1910 Essary *TN Mtneers* 17–18 John Smith, attorney-at-law, hove in sight, hitched his "nag" to an apple tree, and then lugged his books into the yard.

3 Variant past-participle forms *hooved* [see **1980** in **B**], *hove* [see **1946** in **B**].

B (also *heave up*) Of the frost or a part of a person's body: to bulge, swell, expand.

1946 Matthias *Speech Pine Mt* 191 *hove out* = bulged, warped, swollen (used of wood work). **1969** Dial *Dialect Appal People* 463 When I first came to Lincoln County [WV] as a bride it used to seem to me that everything that did not pooch out, hooved up. **1980** Berry and Repass *Grandpa Says* 20 *hooved up* = expanded. **1994–97** Montgomery Coll (known to Jones, Ledford, Oliver, Weaver); The frost heaved up (Cardwell). **2000** Lowry *Folk Medical Term* My side hoved up three days ago.

heaven above *noun* Same as **peawood.**

1998 Montgomery Coll (known to Cardwell).

heavy *adjective* Adequate.

1986 Helton *Around Home* 379 = refers not only to weight but to adequacy. This wrench is heavy enough for the job. **1996–97** Montgomery Coll (known to Brown, Cardwell, Jones, Ledford, Oliver).

he-balsam (also *he-spruce*) *noun* An evergreen tree, either the red spruce (*Picea rubens*) or black spruce (*Picea mariana*). See also **balsam 1, she-balsam, yew pine.**

1860 Curtis *Plants NC* 27 Black Spruce . . . Called He Balsam. **1937** Thornburgh *Great Smoky Mts* 28 My mountain guide calls the red spruce "he-balsam" and the Fraser fir is a "she-balsam." **1943** Peattie *Indian Days* 161 In the trunks of the fir under the bark, there are often big rosin blisters filled with a clear liquid (the balsam of commerce) which the mountain folk have whimsically compared to milk. So they name this the "she-balsam." Thinking perhaps that [the she-balsam] needed a mate, and finding the spruce tree, which is devoid of "milk," commonly accompanying it, they named it the "he-balsam"! **1948** Baldwin *Big Trees* 174 These same mountain people, having called the balsam fir female, name the red spruce "he balsam" to keep her company. **1968** Connelly *Discover Appal* 165 Several northern evergreens are common in this atmosphere. The red spruce and the Fraser fir are the most common. With its dark, four-cornered needles and reddish cones, the red spruce is usually found growing side by side with the Fraser fir. To distinguish between the two species, mountaineers called the Fraser fir the "she balsam" because the large blisters of resin on its trunk resembled milk-filled breasts. The red spruce they called the "he balsam." **1974–75** McCracken *Logging* 21:5 While there was one named he-spruce and she-spruce; the balsam is the she-spruce. **1997** Montgomery Coll: *he spruce* (known to Bush, Cardwell, Ellis, Jones, Ledford, Oliver).

he-bear *noun* A male bear.

1927 Mason *Lure of Smokies* 218 A ole he-b'ar riz right up at me an' spit in my face!

he-brute *noun* Used as a euphemism for *bull*. See also **brute, bull A1, male brute.**

1973 Miller *English Unicoi Co* 148 = a male of the bovine family, a bull.

hecack See **heekack.**

heckle See **hackle.**

Heck was a pup See **since Hec(k) was a pup.**

heekack (also *hecack*) *noun* See citations.

1986 *DARE File* (neKY) = a noisy argument with everyone talking at the same time. Applied to both political and family disagreements: "I left because they got into a big heekack." Everyone in this part of the country has heard it and I've heard people use it for many, many years. **1992** Brooks *Sthn Stuff* 67 *hecack* = a big disturbance; a free-for-all altercation. **2008** *DARE File* = widely heard in the Ashland (KY)-Ironton (OH)-Huntington (WV) area . . . I would define [it] as a noisy quarrel or racket, as in "you never heard such a heekack," often used with the verbs "cause" or "raise," as in "it caused a heekack" or "he raised such a heekack." The word does connote a condition that would be very similar to "fit" used in the sense of "having or throwing a fit" or being seized in a fit of sneezing or hiccupping.

heel in *verb phrase* To store (a cabbage) for winter consumption by turning it upside down and burying it in the earth.

2003 LaLone et al. *Farming Life* 198 We grew [cabbage] the type that you could pull them up and turn them upside down. It was called "heeling them in."

heels over head *adverb phrase* Head over heels.

1939 Hall Coll (Mt Sterling NC) A dynamite explosion blowed out Sutherland for somethin' like a hundred yards, I suppose. Slapped him up agin the face of another cliff, heels over head.

[reversal of usual word order]

heel string *noun* The Achilles tendon.

1968 *Faith Healing* 22 He cut his heel string on this big broad axe . . . sharp on both sides.

heered See **hear 2, 3.**

heft *verb* To lift, hoist.

1939 Burnett *Gap o' Mountains* 101 The old man hefted the letter in his hand, read the address two or three times, turned it over and looked at the back of the envelope, held it between his eyes and the sun, then studied the post mark. **1967** *DARE Survey* (Maryville TN) That suitcase must be heavy. Just heft it. **1971** Costner *Song of Life* 69 Uncle Rog caught hold of a bush and hefted himself up on top of the wall. **1978** Hiser *Quare Do's* 88 She brushed the yellow jackets off the pile of peelings and cores off her ample apron, poured them into a bucket, took a basket of big apples into her hand, hefted it easily across me, and poured it into her lap to peel.

he-holly *noun* The male of the American holly tree (*Ilex opaca*), which bears no berries. See also **she-holly.**

1957 Parris *My Mts* 248 Guess you didn't know there was he-holly and she-holly. Well, there is. Only she-holly has berries.

1964 Reynolds *Born of Mts* 84 In North Carolina even the holly is given sex, there being a He Holly and a She Holly, for how else could the last-named have berries, the other having none. **1995** Montgomery *Coll* (known to Cardwell, Ledford, Norris, Oliver).

he-huckleberry *noun* A staggerbush (*Lyonia ligustrina*).

1968 *DARE Survey* (Brasstown NC) = grows on high bushes near the branches, small, dark, and polished in appearance.

heidi See **hidy**.

heifer *noun* A repulsive woman.

1867 Harris *Sut Lovingood* 96 Ove all the durn'd misfortinit weddins ever since ole Adam married that heifer, what wer so fon' ove talkin tu snaix, an' eatin appils. **1974** Fink *Bits Mt Speech* 12 That's the ol' *heifer* that lives up the holler. **1994** Walker *Life History* 137 He said he didn't want to see that "heifer" any more . . . he said he'd just about give [his property] away to get rid of his wife. **2003** Onchuck *Mud Pie Memories* 128 Daddy especially had different words for everything. He referred to foul language as "blackguard," and he called difficult women old "heifers" (a term used in the Bible by Samson to refer to his wife).

heighth *noun* Height.

1886 Smith *Sthn Dialect* 343 = height. **1961** *Coe Ridge OHP-343B* About how many people were over there at the heighth of the colony's growth? **1979** *Big South Fork OHP-18* They [= air channels] would be . . . I guess ten or twelve foot wide, aside the heighth of them. **1989** *Matewan OHP-7* That's what the heighth, what they referred to as the heighth of it [= the coal].

[according to OED3, the final consonant represents the older form]

heinious *adjective* Heinous.

1957 Wise *Mt Speech* 305 [I] is inserted before *ous*, as in *heinious* for *heinous*. **1975** Montgomery *File*: *heinious*.

heir

A *noun* A share of an inheritance.

1937 Hall *Coll* (Smokemont NC) We had an heir in the house, and we sold that to Bert Crisp.

B *verb* To inherit.

1927 Furman *Lonesome Road* 31 When he had fotched me into the good old house he had heired from his folks, I loved every log in it. **1937** Conner *Ms* 21 John Leonides Floyd heired his Grandfather Mingus'es fine home and property. **1937** Hall *Coll* (Emerts Cove TN) That old lady heired some land. **1970** Mull *Mt Yarns* 82 I heired the old farm thar from my ma. **1974** Fink *Bits Mt Speech* 23 My brother heired a large scope of land. **1984** GSMNP-153:12 To begin with, the Loves owned and heired all of this whole territory, and at one time they'd sell you a acre of land or a boundary of land for just anything that you would give them for it, so that they could write you out a deed for it.

[DARE *heir* v chiefly South Midland]

heist See **hoist A**.

helded See **hold B1**.

helicopter *noun* A dragonfly.

2015 *Blind Pig* (May 26) In Swain County [NC] where I grew up, we also called them darning needles and helicopters because of their ability to hover.

hell *noun* A dense, often extensive tract of **rhododendron**, **mountain laurel**, briers, etc.; also used in place-names, as in *Huggins Hell* (near Mt. LeConte TN) and *Jeffry's Hell* (TN, sw of the national park near Hangover Mountain). Same as **laurel bed**. See also **jungle**.

1883 Zeigler and Grosscup *Heart of Alleghanies* 139–40 Nature has . . . planted in vast tracts impenetrable tangles of the rhododendron and kalmia. These tangles are locally called "Hells," with a proper noun possessive in remembrance of poor unfortunates lost in their mazes. **1913** Kephart *Our Sthn High* 301 A "hell" or "slick" or "woolly-head" or "yaller patch" is a thicket of laurel or rhododendron, impassable save where the bears have bored out trails. **1937** Thornburgh *Great Smoky Mts* 27 The knife-like ridges are often covered with the Catawba rhododendron . . . and lower ridges with laurel and leucothoe, often so dense that they are locally called "Slicks" and "Hells." **1955** Parris *Roaming Mts* 53 There are rhododendron "hells"—a veritable maze of false paths and openings—in which men have been known to wander for days, and it was not uncommon a few years ago to see notices tacked up in the post office at Bryson City telling of someone lost in the jungle. **1967** Hall *Coll* (Townsend TN) I've been at the Hangover at the head of Jeffry's Hell. . . . Old Man Jefferson [sic] got lost in there, and he come out and they says, "What kind of a place was that?" and he says, "It's a hell of a place." And they named it that on that account. **1979** *Smoky Vistas* (Summer) 1 Even though they have magnificent flowering displays when they bloom in early June, the heath balds were called "hells" by the early settlers. As any old bear hunter knows, the stems of the heaths are so close together that it may be impossible to crawl, much less walk, through them. **1992** Toops *Great Smoky Mts* 41 I have never ventured more than twenty yards into a heath bald unless on a trail. To do so, you must crawl over and around the branches, often dropping to your knees and crawling. Settlers referred to these areas as laurel "hells."

[DARE in reference to its thorny, nearly impassable habit, but cf also OED2 *hele* n obsolete except dialect "A hiding place . . . cover"; cf also EDD *hell* sb 4 "A dark place in the woods" obsolete; DARE *hell* n 1 especially southern Appalachians]

hell a-hooting *phrase* See citation.

1972 Cooper *NC Mt Folklore* 93 = trouble starting; . . . serious quarrels or fights in progress.

hellbender *noun*

1 A large black salamander (*Cryptobrachus alleganiensis*) that grows up to two feet in length.

1943 Stupka *Through the Year* 284 The sluggish hellbender of our lower stream courses deposits her string of large creamy-white eggs in September. I have handled specimens of this huge salamander, the largest in America, measuring more than two feet in length. It is brownish or grayish-brown in color, with heavy depressed head, prominent lateral skin folds, and flattened tail. **1960** Stupka *Great Smoky Mts* 48 These mountain forests are the habitat for at least 27 kinds of salamanders, ranging from the pigmy salamander, less than 2 inches long when mature, to the big hellbender, which may grow to 29 inches. . . . The hellbender is entirely aquatic, living only in the warmer low-altitude streams. **1967** Huheey and Stupka *Amphibians and Reptiles* 11 The Hellbender is the largest salamander in the Great Smoky Mountains and the fifth largest in the world, being exceeded in size by two closely related species in China and Japan and by the greater Siren (*Siren lacertina*) and the Amphiuma (*Amphiuma means*) of the southeastern Coastal Plain. A female Hellbender measuring 29 1/8 in. in total length and a male measuring 26 in. are in the Park's collection of preserved amphibians; both record-sized specimens were taken in the West Prong of the Little Pigeon River, in Gatlinburg. The large size and the loose fleshy fold of skin along each side of the body make recognition of this salamander quite simple. **1997** *Smokies Guide* (Spring) 17 Hellbenders are the largest salamanders in the Smokies. They are common in low elevation streams where they prey upon fish, crayfish, and aquatic insects. When threatened, hellbenders can secrete toxins which kill fish in close proximity. **2004** Dodd *Amphibians Smoky Mts* 26 Two amphibians in the Great Smoky Mountains never leave the water, and instead carry out their entire life cycle in aquatic habitats. These salamanders are the Hellbenders and the Common Mudpuppy. Both are active more at night than during the day, when they hide under rocks and other bottom debris. . . . Larval Hellbenders likely bury down into the interstitial gravels of the larger streams, and have been found in Little River. Hellbenders are territorial during the mating season, but probably not at other times. *Ibid.* 111, 114 Eastern Hellbender Cryptobranchus alleganiensis Etymology Cryptobranchus: from the Greek kryptos, meaning hidden, and branchion, meaning gills. The scientific name refers to the lack of large external gills; alleganiensis: Latinized proper name in reference to the Allegheny Mountains, where it was first discovered. . . . Hellbenders are often mischaracterized as "ugly" or "poisonous," and therefore killed on sight. It is not unusual to see newspaper reports picturing one of these salamanders as being "never before seen" or "unknown to science." While it is true that some people might find them ugly, that they will bite to defend themselves, that they are slimy, and that they contain noxious skin secretions, they are still magnificent ancient inhabitants of the streams of the Southern Appalachians.

2 A drunken brawl or spree.

1976 Garber *Mountain-ese* 39 Uncle Cleve shore got on a hellbender last week-end. **1995** Montgomery *Coll* (known to Cardwell).

hell cat *noun* An irascible, spiteful person, especially a woman.

1927 Woofter *Dialect from WV* 357 = a trouble maker, usually used in reference to an elderly person. "That woman is a regular hell cat." **1956** McAtee *Some Dial NC* 22 = a trouble-making woman. **1976** Garber *Mountain-ese* 40 = a lewd person. "Llewellen sure married a hell-cat; they's no way on earth to handle her." **1998** Montgomery *Coll* = an evil person, drunkard (Adams), = also used for wildcat, panther (Brown), = a woman with a bad temper (Jones), = an oppressive, argumentative woman (Ledford), = a woman who is domineering, trouble making, or wild—drinking, cussing, and fighting—not accepted by the genteel women of the community (Norris), = bad-tempered (Oliver).

[DARE *hellcat* n 1 chiefly South, South Midland]

hell-fire(d) *adjective* Damned, confounded. See also **all-fired A**, **hen fire**.

1939 Hall *Coll* (Mt Sterling NC) These hell-fire drunkards! **1941** Hall *Coll* (Cosby TN) It was the hell-firedest wreck I've ever seen. **1982** Ginns *Snowbird Gravy* 191 "Well, I hunted in the hell-fired branch for three hell-fired rocks." (That was his by-word, hell-fired.) **2000** Morgan *Mts Remember* 165 When Mack [= a dog] runs out into the road my heart stops, for the way traffic goes today he wouldn't have a chance if one of these hell-fire drivers come along, and there are more of them now than ever.

hell-for-certain *noun* See citation.

c1960 Wilson *Coll* = a nickname for some out-of-the-way or run-down place . . . a seedy place.

hello the house See **hallo**.

hell-roaring *adjective* Undisciplined, rowdy.

1922 Kephart *Our Sthn High* 233 I asked a woods boss . . . why [the lumbermen] were treated . . . like convicts. He answered, "If you had to run a hell-roarin' bunch like mine, you'd kno-w why."

hell's banjer See **hell's banjo**.

hell's banjo (also *hell's banjer, hell's bells*) *interjection* Used as an oath.

1913 Kephart *Our Sthn High* 171 Hell's banjer! They don't go prodjectin' around looking for stills. They set at home . . . till some feller comes and informs. **1936** Carpenter *WV Expletives* 347 Law and Lordy may do duty for almost any emotion in this section of the country, as may also: I'll swan; Hell's banjer; Sakes o' mercy; and Sakes alive. **1966** Dykeman *Far Family* 154 "Well hell's bells," Clay muttered on the other side of the room, "I don't even belong to myself." **1976** Still *Pattern of Man* 5 He lifted his hands in defeat. "Hell's bangers!" he blurted. **1994–97** Montgomery *Coll*: *hell's banjo* (known to Brown, Cardwell).

[DARE *hell's banjer* interj southern Appalachians]

hell's bells See **hell's banjo**.

hell spot *noun* See 1996 citation.

1966 Medford *Ol' Starlin* 67 Some words like spider (for a small frying pan), straw-tick, tizicky, tintsey-bit, glut, hell-spot . . . and some others, are seldom heard any more. **1996** Montgomery *Coll* = a difficult place or a trying situation (Cardwell).

help

A *verb* Principal parts.

1 Variant infinitive/base forms *hep, holp* [holp, hop].

1863 *Whitaker CW Letters* (Aug 25) I fe[a]r I Shall be too far off to hep you as I would wish to do in your old age. **1917** Kephart *Word-List* 413 *holp* = to help. "I axed him to *holp* me out." **1962** Wilson *Folkways Mammoth Cave* 46 Holp . . . survived to our own time. Sometimes it was used in the present. **1971** *AOHP/ALC-193* I would be hired to work . . . on the farm hepping farmers do their work on their farm. **1980** Miles *Verbs in Haywood Co* 74 I looked to holp out with some of the classes. **2009** Burton *Beech Mt Man* 65 I'll just hep you kill yourself.

[DARE *hep, holp* (at *help* v A1a, b) both forms chiefly South, South Midland]

2 Variant past-tense forms *hept, holp* [holp, hop], *holped, holpen, holpt, hope.*

1862 *Councill CW Letters* (Feb 4) I coft all day an nite but I went to the docter an got some medisen an it hope me. **1862** *Watters-Curtis CW Letters* (Feb 4) i com too my camp the 2 day of this month and i think it hope Me. **1883** Smith *Southernisms* 49 Holp, the old past and past participle of help, is still used among the lower classes in many parts of the South, and from this they even form an infinitive holp (hope), instead of to help. **1889** Brown *Dialect Survivals in TN* 207 Holp as past and past participle of *help* is common in Shakespeare: "He holp the heavens to rain." ("Lear," iii, 7) . . . I have heard it frequently from old people in this state, and am informed that it is also used in Kentucky. **1913** Kephart *Our Sthn High* 283–84 In mountain vernacular the Old English strong past tense still lives in begun, drunk, holped, rung, shrunk, sprung, stunk, sung, sunk, swum. **1927** Woofter *Dialect from WV* 357 He holpen me over the creek. **c1945** Haun *Hawk's Done* 306 He always went and holp cut wood when somebody was sick. **1953** Atwood *Verbs East US* 16–17 To the west [of Roanoke] *holp* extends into s.w. Va. and a portion of s. W.Va. **1956** GSMNP-24:54 We chopped corn and holpt make molasses. **1957** GSMNP-23:1:11 My daddy holped old Samuel Wear drive them through this country, went up through Wears Cove. **1958** GSMNP-110:19 I holp set it up and holp log out that territory all around three forks there. **1962** Wilson *Folkways Mammoth Cave* 46 Holp . . . survived to our own time . . . Sometimes it also developed a new past—*holped*. **1968** *Raised Up* 9 I have hope my dad Shear Sheep a lot of times to get that wool. **1972** GSMNP-93:3:35 My daddy holp run 'em out of Gatlinburg. **1973** Jones *Cades Cove TN* 71 *holp*. **1976** GSMNP-113:10 The good Lord holped me that way, you know, had plenty of money and just went on. **1978** Reese *Speech NE Tenn* 176 *holp* = attested by 1/12 (8.3%) speakers; *holped* = attested by 2/12 (16.7%) speakers. **1980** Miles *Verbs in Haywood Co* 74 I holp out some with her over there. **1986** Pederson et al. *LAGS*: *hept* (Cocke Co TN); *holp* (Cocke Co TN, Sevier Co TN). **2007** Preece *Leavin' Sandlick* 18 Poor ole Wade worked so hard at loggin', I guess it hept to kill him.

[DARE *hept, holp, holped* (at *help* v A2a, b, d) all forms chiefly South, South Midland]

3 Variant past-participle forms *hepped, hept, holp* [holp, hop], *holped* [holpt, hopt], *holpen, hope.*

1861 *Carden CW Letter* (Oct 6) it is true it is harde that wives and husbands should be separated but it cannot be hope. **1862** *Griffin CW Letters* (July 31) I hate the name of secession for hit has cased so meny to see truble when hit cood ben hope if they had atride. [See **1883** in **2**.] **1925** Dargan *Highland Annals* 257 Callie wuz still alive, an' she seemed awfully hepped up about Nathe. **1937** Hall *Coll* (Big Creek NC) I've holped set fire and fight fire too. **1939** Hall *Coll* (Sugarlands TN) He'd had the axe to fight the bear with, and he'd laid it down and burnt the handle in two. He couldn't hardly find the axe, but he hadn't holp me a bit. **1955** Ritchie *Singing Family* 61 After I begged her awhile, she even let us drink a little bit of the elderberry wine that I had holpen her make, and she got to feeling better and better. **1971** *AOHP/ALC-260* Well, yeah, it's holped. It's holped plenty of people, that welfare has. **1972** *AOHP/ALC-355* Do you think they've hept Kentucky or what? **1973** Jones *Cades Cove TN* 71 *holpen*. **1975** Chalmers *Better* 33 The doctor-medicine had holp, a'ready, an' he'd be back next week, Lord willing. **1980** Miles *Verbs in Haywood Co* 75 I'd a-holp him straight on through. **1996** Montgomery *Coll* (known to Ledford), = *holpen* now rarely heard (Ledford). **2003** Gibson *Sthn Mt Dialect* In the early 1990s . . . one day a group of us were sitting outside having coffee during a break between classes. A lady made the statement that her mother had "holped" her with taking care of her children. A split second after saying the word "holped" she quickly said the word "helped." . . . She was embarrassed and very relieved when she realized no one had picked up on the word "holped." I had not heard this word used in many years. As a child in the 50s I heard this word used by an elderly couple in the West Robbins community. . . . I look back now and realized this couple used many words and phrases which is considered today as a Southern mountain dialect which can be traced back to the Elizabethan period.

[DARE *holp, holped, hope* (at *help* v A3a, b) both forms chiefly South, South Midland]

B *noun* Variant form *hep.*

1940 Stuart *Trees of Heaven* 56 No wonder Pa can't hire hep. **1984** Burns *Cold Sassy* 22 The day Camp walked into the store and asked for a job, Grandpa took one look and said he didn't need no hep right now.

help Andy *verb phrase* See citation.

1927 Woofter *Dialect from WV* 357 = to do nothing: "What are you doing today? Oh, I'm just helping Andy."

help my time *interjection* Used as an exclamation of surprise.

1924 Spring *Lydia Whaley* 2 Help my time. **1950** Wood *Sure of Life* 48 Help my time! Help my time! Lord have mercy! **1993** Ison and Ison *Whole Nother Lg* 29 = an expression used as a soft exclamation. **1996** Montgomery *Coll* (known to Cardwell). **2017** *Blind Pig* (June 10) I've heard variations, including "bless my time" and "save my time," although "help my time" is more common. *Ibid.* When I saw it, I said, "Help my time, wasn't that just yesterday? How did they grow up so dadjimmed fast?"

help up *verb phrase* To assist, encourage, benefit (a person).

1865 *Carson CW Letters* (April 2) I have bene graitley hope upe fur Severel dase tho I am doutful now that it is all in vane. **1914**

Furman *Sight* 60 It were the deed of a saint, and holp me up wonderful. **1925** Dargan *Highland Annals* 257 Callie wuz still alive, an' she seemed awfully hepped up about Nathe. **1942** Campbell *Cloud-Walking* 251 Nelt was mighty holp up to have Sary 'pear to be mending in health. **c1975** Lunsford *It Used to Be* 9 I'd plow the corn, and then, maybe, after I'd get through plowing, I'd get a hoe and help the others up. **1996–97** Montgomery *Coll* (known to eight consultants from the Smoky Mountains).

[DARE (at *help* B1) South, South Midland]

helt See **hold B1**, **B2**.

helve See **ax helve**.

hem (also *hem up*) *verb, verb phrase* To surround, corner (as an opponent or a hunted animal).

1862 Robinson *CW Letters* (Aug 29) we have got them hemd I think but I doant no how long tha[y] can live. **1913** Morley *Carolina Mts* 300 A bear ain't goin' to hurt a man noway unless he's hemmed, then he'll kill you. **1939** Hall *Notebooks* 9:8 (Cataloochee NC) One of the little dogs hemmed the bear and turned him away from Uncle Steve. **1954** Roberts *Bought a Dog* I looked over in a corner and saw my gun locks, stickin there on a rail, had that other goose hemmed. **1956** Hall *Coll* (Roaring Fork TN) [A bear scrape is] a fight with dogs to kill a "hemmed bear." **1976** Dwyer *Southern Sayin's* 6 *hem the bear* = to corner or put a person in a tight position. **1982** Ginns *Snowbird Gravy* 105 They say you can hem a jackrabbit, and a lot of them'll just fall dead. Half of 'em or more, right in the field where they was hemmed, fall down and go to kicking and dying because they was hemmed up. Heart failed 'em, they say. **1987** Trent *Yesteryear* 102 She lived her entire life of seventy-five years in her humble cabin hemmed in between two lofty peaks of the Clinch Mountains. **1988** Dickey and Bake *Wayfarer* 79 That third boy, Riley, will try to fool you, but you better not fool with him, or get him hemmed up.

[DARE *hem* v B1 chiefly South, South Midland]

hempine *noun* The eastern hemlock (*Tsuga canadensis*), the only native hemlock in the Great Smoky Mountains National Park. A medicinal tea is made from its bark. Same as **big spruce**, **spruce pine**.

1926 Hunnicutt *Twenty Years* 44 Old Trail turned the bear loose and ran out to the hempine tree and began to give the tree bark. **1967** Hall *Coll* (Townsend TN) They was plenty of hempine [in the Devil's Courthouse], big trees, three or four foot through. [**1971** Krochmal et al. *Medicinal Plants Appal* 258 The bark has been used primarily because of its tannist content, which makes it a strong astringent.] **1982** Powers and Hannah *Cataloochee* 440 The hemlock, known locally as the "hempine," covered 60% of the bottoms of Cataloochee in 1905. **1983** Pyle *CCC 50th Anniv* A:2:23 Some call 'em hem pines, an' some calls 'em spruce.

hem up See **hem**.

hen *noun* unmarked possessive form *hen*. See also **bird**, **hen apple**.

1881 Pierson *In the Brush* 261 He hunted five little rocks, smooth as a hen-egg [and] put 'em in a little bag where he carried his snack when he was a-tendin' the sheep. **1890** Fruit *KY Words* 68 *hen nest* = hen's nest. **1940** Haun *Hawk's Done* 16 Tiny Brock's hair looks like it has been fried in hen oil—nobody but a bastard would spark her. **1968** Wilson *Folklore Mammoth Cave* 19 *hen egg* = universal; *hen's egg* is unknown. **1973** *AOHP/ALC-586A* You'd eat duck eggs and goose eggs . . . just like a hen egg, only they're so much bigger. **1988** Russell *It Happened* 9 Nailed to one side of "The Old House" were two shingle-covered hen nests and on the opposite side was a grindstone set on a waist-high stand.

[DARE *hen* n[1] A2 chiefly South, South Midland]

hen a-pecking See **beat a hen a-pecking**.

hen apple (also *hen berry*, *hen fruit*) *noun* A hen's egg. Same as **cackleberry**.

1939 Farr *TN Mt Regions* 90 *hen apple*. **1969** Doran *Folklore White Co* 112 *hen fruit* = humorous term for egg. **1975** Jackson *Unusual Words* 156 Biscuits were often called *catheads*, and eggs were *hen fruit*. **1982** Slone *How We Talked* 36 *hen berry* = egg. **1995–97** Montgomery *Coll*: *hen apple* (known to Adams, Brown, Cardwell, Ellis, Jones, Weaver); *hen berry* (known to Brown, Cardwell, Jones, Oliver, Shields); *hen fruit* (known to Adams, Brown, Cardwell, Ellis, Jones, Oliver, Weaver).

hen a-rooting See **beat a hen a-pecking**.

hen berry See **hen apple**.

hen fire *interjection* Used as a euphemism for *hell fire* as a mild oath. See also **hell-fire(d)**.

1998 Brewer *Don't Scrouge* And Evelyn Kirby remembers children getting so furious they wanted to "cuss." They said, "Hen fire!" Was it a watered-down version of "hell fire?"

hen fooler *noun* A **gourd egg**, **China egg**, or similar object put in a hen's nest to induce her to lay.

1978 Slone *Common Folks* 226 A woman told how she had killed [a snake] that had swallowed a gourd egg, or "hen fooler," a small round gourd about the size of an egg.

hen fruit See **hen apple**.

hen nest See **hen**.

hen pop *noun* See citation.

1966 *DARE Survey* (Cherokee NC) = type of greens eaten cooked.

hen wallow *noun* A small area of dry dirt in which chickens and other fowl (including wild species such as ruffed grouse) wallow.

1999 Montgomery *Coll* (known to Cardwell).

hep See **help A1**, **B**.

hept See **help A2**.

her *pronoun* See also Grammar and Syntax §2.3.1.

1 Used reflexively as indirect object (the so-called personal dative) = (for) herself.

1874 Swearingen *Letters* 165 Mary is fixing to make her some cotton dresses. **1939** Hall *Coll* (Hazel Creek NC) She'd get her a wild leaf, flower or something or another and decorate the top of that, usually holly berries. **1956** Hall *Coll* (Big Bend NC) She went out to the apple orchard and picked her up a sack of apples. **1964** Roberts *Hell-Fer-Sartin* 49 She put her on a pot of water and put a little salt in it, and went out to pick her up a load of chips. **1978** Montgomery *White Pine Coll* III-2 [The hen would] steal her a place and lay her eggs and hatch 'em back in under these [piles of] hay and under different places about the barn. *Ibid.* IX-1 She went into the store to get her a pair of shoes. **1985** Irwin *Alex Stewart* 203 Any time during the winter that she wanted some parsnips to cook, she'd go pull her up two or three big ones. **1989** *Matewan OHP*-56 Then she would get her out her [sic] some chewing tobacco, and she'd set there and chew. **1998** *Dante OHP*-45 She'd take her a hoe or a stick and go kill it [= a snake]. **2012** Milnes *Signs Cures Witchery* She took some of that milk and went and dug her a hole in the ground, wrote her a ticket, and got her some kerosene, lamp oil.

2 As the simple subject of a clause. [Editor's note: This usage does not occur in ATASC.]

1916 Combs *Old Early English* 290 *Him* is often used for the nominative form *he*, and *her* for *she*. E.g. "Her was a mighty good woman." *Ibid.* 285 Her is the prettiest baby you ever see. **1939** Hall *Coll* Her got one yesterday. Her can sing good. They was her and her two daughters.

3 As part of the compound subject of a clause (thus *her and James* = she and James). See also **him 3**, **me 3**, **us**.

1836 *Sullivan Co Soldiers* I heard that her and James Worley was agoing to marry in a few days but if she please your eye cut ahead and don't back until the last hour. **1863** *Tesh CW Letters* (May 29) I must tell you that me and her Keep house while mother was gone. **1939** Hall *Coll* (Copeland Creek TN) Her and Rhoda Breeden come to my house. **c1945** Haun *Hawk's Done* 238 Her and Eli went right on over there to Noah's place in Hamblen County that Monday evening as soon as they got married. **1969** GSMNP-37:2:17 Her and her kids would walk from down there up here to this church every night. **1973** *Carpenter* 121 Pearl Watts, me an' her would try t'knit. **1973** GSMNP-5:3 Her and Jess and the girl is all buried there, on Caldwell Fork. **1974** GSMNP-51:13 She was a widow at the time her husband had died, and her and the girls was there. **1997** Andrews *Mountain Vittles* 62 Her and her folks are from the mountains of West Virginia. **1997** GSMNPCOHP-5:19 In later years her and my father married.

herb

A Variant forms *yairb* [see **1937** in **B**], *yarb*, *yearb* [see **1904** in **B**], *yerb*.

1884 Smith *Arp Scrap Book* 73 We have a plenty of peas and potatoes and other garden yerbs. **1911** Shearin *E KY Word-List* 540 *yerb*. **1952** Breckinridge *Neighborhoods* 170 Our older people speak of "yarbs"—which is correct. We have turned the "y" into an "h" and the "a" into an "e," so that we have a word the English call "herb" and we call "erb." Both of us have corrupted the true word, which is "yarb."

[DARE *herb* n, v A all forms chiefly South, South Midland]

B *noun* Any plant whose parts or ingredients (by extraction from its roots, leaves, bark, stalks, seeds, etc.) are used in traditional mountain medicine, especially as made into a tea. See also **herb doctor**, **herb tea**.

1867 Harris *Sut Lovingood* 105 The wimen fans 'im, fixes the bed close, an' biles yarbs fur 'im; an' the men iles his bruses, an' poltusis his body. **1904** Johnson *Highways South* 137 The sweet oil was an ingredient for one of these medicines, and he mentioned also using "mullein and evergreen biled together" and "a yearb called golden seal." **1913** Kephart *Our Sthn High* 121 The only medicines we-uns has is yerbs, which customarily ain't no good 'thout a leetle grain o' whiskey. **1924** Raine *Saddlebags* 130 The only medicines we-uns has is yerbs. **1937** Hall *Coll* (Big Creek NC) Whenever we'd get puny, mother would gather some barks or yairbs in the woods and make us a tea.... Yairbs, just bile 'em up and make teas out of 'em. **1939** Hall *Coll* (Catons Grove TN) Now back in my young days, we couldn't get no doctors hardly ever, and we had to do our own doctorin' and we learned up on these yarbs. **1939** Jennison *Flora Great Smokies* 280 Scores of other "yarbs," some of known value, like the bloodroot, the wild ginger-root, and the aconite are native to the Park. **1952** Wilson *Folk Speech NC* 609 *yarb*, *yerb*. **1960** Price *Root Digging in Appal* 3 A band of the faithful stick loyally to "natural" herb cures. None is more ardent than the old collector on an East Tennessee mountain who told me, "The good Lord has put these yerbs here for man to make hisself well with. They is a yerb, could we but find it, to cure every illness." **1965** Shelton *Pioneer Comforts* 8 Since "store medicine" was not easily located and midwives were not always near, every homemaker took pride in her own knowledge and collection of "yarbs." **1975** Chalmers *Better* 44 Many a kitchen garden had a little corner of "yarbs," and most houses had bunches of them hanging from the rafters to dry. **1981** Alderman *Tilson Mill* 16 Mountain folk called herbs, bark, roots, and various plants used in doctoring the sick "yarbs."

[cf EDD *herb* 3]

C *verb* To gather wild plants with medicinal uses; thus *herbing* = this activity, pursued by an individual or a group of people.

1964 Reynolds *Born of Mts* 19 Yarbing, as it was called, was the gathering by the mountain folk of certain roots and bark to send to drug dealers. **1992** Bush *Dorie* 104 More herbing was done on the North Carolina side than in Tennessee. **1999** Isbell *Keepers* 6 I could barely get through the woods, but herbing got into my blood. I'd dig and carry things for Dad. Could do galax pretty good, too. **2007** Preece *Leavin' Sandlick* 49 John Henry 'erbed the hillsides in the summer ever'day looking fer sweet elem bark, ginsang, and yeller root.

[EDD *herb* v 7 "to gather herbs"]

herb doctor *noun*

A Variant form *yarb doctor* [see **1901** in **B**].

B One (traditionally, a woman) who practices traditional medicine by using parts or ingredients from plants, especially prepared into teas. See also **conjure doctor**, **herb**, **herb granny**, **Indian doctor**, **wart conjurer**, **witch doctor**.

1901 Lounsberry *Sthn Wild Flowers* 498 From time almost immemorial, boneset has been utilised to make a strengthening tea. It is something that the "yarb doctor" never forgets. **1924** Raine *Saddlebags* 187 Now it happened that she was a "yarb-doctor." When the young teacher developed an eruption on his wrist, he went to her and asked whether she could give him some "yarb-tea" to cure it. **1967** Jones *Peculiarities Mtneers* 47 The "yarb" doctor was called in whenever any member of the family contracted any illness or distemper that failed to respon to the usual home treatments. . . . Most of the "yarb" doctors dispensed medicines that they had concocted themselves from leaves, roots, bark and herbs which they had personally gathered. **1972** Alderman *Big Bald* 37 Practically every settlement had its "Granny" or Male "Yarb Doctor." They were fetched when a member of the family had the Miss'rys. Their professional badge was the constant worn and used satchel. This traveling drug store usually contained Cherry Bark Bitter for spring tonics; Yellow Roots and Spice Wood for teas; Gold Seal for stomach disorders; Yellow Lady Slipper Roots for nervousness; Catnip and Dock Leaves for headache; Flax Seed and Honey for cough. For broken bones there was always a mixture made from Boneset to lower the fever and help bones knit back together. **1975** Chalmers *Better* 44 Undoubtedly many a "yarb-doctor's" mistake has been buried in the family burial plot. **c1984** Dennis *Smoky Mt Heritage* 7 There were individuals who spent a lifetime searching for the natural treatment and cure for various ailments. These folks were called "Yarb Doctors." The "Yarb Doctors" would search for sheep sorrel, or Indian turnips, ginseng, sassafras and many other plants that had medicinal properties. **1996** GSMNPCOHP-1:2 My old great granddaddy Sam Burchfield, now he was a herb doctor. He picked herbs hisself. People went to him for them herbs. **2003** Cavender *Folk Medicine* 147 Many communities had men or women known as "yarb doctors" or "herb doctors," who were recognized as being exceptionally well versed in the knowledge of medicinal plants. Women often served as both yarb doctors and granny midwives.

herb granny (also *herb woman*) *noun*

A Variant forms *hyarb woman* [see **2016** in **B**], *yarbwoman* [see **1982** in **B**].

B (also *granny witch*) An older woman possessing knowledge of herbs and their healing powers as well as skill in preparing them for medicinal use. See also **herb doctor**.

1964 Wright *Mt Medicine* 7 There also were the granny woman and the herb woman, who could and did treat anything that came along and did surprisingly well, going on the assumption that most common illnesses got well of their own accord, treatment or no treatment. **1982** Powers and Hannah *Cataloochee* 301 To look after their health, there had to be self-appointed doctors and dentists when the real thing couldn't make it in time. There had to be "yarbwomen" in lieu of pharmacists. **1995** Montgomery *Coll*: *herb woman* = a woman who doctored with herbs. We had one grandmother who was midwife and another who was herb woman (Norris). **1999** Morgan *Gap Creek* 102 I don't even know where there's an herb granny. **2016** Lundy and Autry *Victuals* 32 I think about my great-grandmother, who had been a "hyarb woman." When my mother was little, Ma Grinstead took her walking in the woods outside of Corbin, showing her the herbs and plants that she knew so well, teaching her their meaning and healing powers. **2016** Simmons *Legends & Lore* 122 Unlike most healers who are shrouded in mystery and secretiveness, grannies are usually quick to dispense the knowledge of how to "cure what ails ya." In more recent years, the term "granny witches" has come into vogue for describing these practitioners of mountain medicine. Many granny witches are able to cure thrash in an infant by blowing directly into a baby's mouth.

herbing See **herb C**.

herb tea *noun*

A Variant form *yarb tea* [see **1924** in **B**].

B A medicinal tea prepared from parts or ingredients of wild plants. See also **herb**.

1924 Raine *Saddlebags* 187 When the young teacher developed an eruption on his wrist, he went to her and asked whether she could give him some "yarb-tea" to cure it. **1952** Justus *Children* 36 Herb tea is a mighty fine tonic when a body is feeling dauncy—and so is good company. **1982** *Smokies Heritage* 52 When a baby was born in pioneer times, he or she was usually dosed with herb teas by the midwife or granny-woman to make him break out in hives (tiny raised spots on the body).

herb woman See **herb granny**.

Hercules'-club *noun* Same as **devil's walkingstick**.

1937 Thornburgh *Great Smoky Mts* 24 A shrub about which many visitors inquire is the showy Hercules club, or devil's walking stick. You will recognize it in summer by its mass of white blossoms at the top and by the cluster of blue-black berries in the fall. **1941** Walker *Story of Mt* 60–61 Hercules club appears in many localities from the north to the south end of the mountain. This shrub is covered with slightly curved spines which prick the hiker's hand when he grasps it for support in walking over beds of loose rocks.

herd sire *noun* Used as a euphemism for bull. See also **bull A1**.

c1930 (in **2014** Oliver *Cades Cove* 33) Uncle Hamp Myers bought him [= a sheep] for a herd sire, by then a fully grown buck. **1986** Pederson et al. *LAGS* (Cocke Co TN) Mother used phrase as [a] euphemism.

here *adverb*

A Variant forms *hur*, *hyar*, *hyer*, *hyere*, *hyur*, *yere*.

1858 (in **1974** Harris *High Times* 135) I kin tell you what becum ove me; I jist relyed on these yere laigs. **1863** Wilson *Confederate Private* 4 (Feb 14) I don't want eny close at this time only a pare of slips and I can get them hur for 75 cents a pare. **1867** Harris *Sut Lovingood* 171 Du yu see these yere laigs. **1905** Miles *Spirit of Mts* 178 Come hyer with a hick'ry, quick. **1907** Dugger *Balsam Groves* 140 You can jist axe the ol' man 'bout that; he's sangkoin' 'round hur somewhur. **1913** Kephart *Our Sthn High* 32 Thar's lots o' folks a-hurtin' around hyur for lard. *Ibid.* 122 From hyar to the railroad is seventeen miles. **1924** Raine *Saddlebags* 80 We couldn't ha' brung them in hyer, noway. *Ibid.* 130 We can't git a doctor up hyar less'n three days. **1939** Burnett *Gap o' Mountains* 11 In the shadder of these hyar hills we air as free as the eagle that nestes in yan furder mountain. **c1960** Wilson *Coll*: *here* is sometimes *hyar*. **1969** Hannum *Look Back* 85 Hyere's yore penny.

[DARE *hyar, hyer, hyur, yere* (at *here* adv, adj, exclam, pron A2, A3) all forms chiefly South, South Midland]

B in compounds. See **this here**.

[DARE *here* adv B1 chiefly South, South Midland]

hern (also *her'n*) *pronoun* Hers. For similar forms, see Grammar and Syntax §2.2.

1861 (in **1992** Heller and Heller *Confederacy* 27) I had jest rote and Seald one to send to Malinda when i got hern. **1862** *Joyce CW Letters* (Nov 8) you Rote to me that you had done broke one of you . . . teath and mary Eetter had fell dow[n] broke out some of hern. **1900** Harben *N GA Sketches* 92 Are you any kin o' hern? **1929** (in **1952** Mathes *Tall Tales* 107) She wouldn't let him doctor a sick hoss or a cow-brute of hern. **1934** Carpenter *Archaic English in WV* 79 The odd-sounding possessive *hern* for *hers* is an old English possessive form, as is *ourn* for *ours*. In one of the Wycliffe Bibles Mark XII, 7, reads: "The heritage schal be ourun." **1934–47** *LAMSAS Appal* (Madison Co NC, Swain Co NC). **c1945** Haun *Hawk's Done* 239 Then she asked Narcie where hern and Eli's room was. **1946** Cleaves *King's English* 35 "Ourn," "hern," "hisn," and "yourn" represent an attempt at uniformity. Since the forms "my" and "mine" developed from a common Teutonic source, a similar inflection was created to distinguish between the adjectival and substantive uses for the remaining personal pronouns. **1952** Wilson *Folk Speech NC* 570 That oldest youngon of *hern* is an outsider. **1973** GSMNP-85:2:18 I thought hern was prettier than mine. **1991** Haynes *Haywood Home* 77 Jut would say far (fire), tar (tire), yander (yonder), her'n (hers). **1997** Montgomery *Coll* The white mare is hern (Brown). **2009** Benfield *Mt Born* 154 = her own, a contraction of the two words.

[historically *her + n* by analogy with *my/mine*, now sometimes construed ahistorically as from *her + one* or *her + own*, thus producing the spelling *her'n*; EDD *hern* pron mEngl, sEngl, 1340→; DARE *hern* pron chiefly South, South Midland, New England]

herrycane See **hurricane**.

he-seng *noun*

1975 Screven *John B Wright* 13 It may be . . . he-seng (male plant), you know . . . That's just like sang, but it ain't got no berries. You can't sell it. But it's got a different leaf; it's got a round leaf on it more than ginseng has. I went up there and, boy, sure enough there stood them big four-prongs—big seeds a-hanging there, buddy, just as red as blood. **1997** Hufford *American Ginseng* Ginseng orders the landscape around itself, providing a basis for identifying related flora. Look-alike plants like sarsaparilla and cohosh have been given nicknames like "fool's seng," "he-seng," and "seng pointer." "The reason why they call it 'seng pointer,'" said Randy Halstead, "it's got three branches, one goes this way, one this way, and one goes straight out this way, and the old people would say that one would be pointing towards the ginseng plant. Of course it probably is somewhere within a hundred miles out in front of it, but that's how that got started. They like the same kind of a place to grow."

he-spruce See **he-balsam**.

hessian (also *hayshant*) *noun* A scamp, rascal (especially a child).

1930 Armstrong *This Day and Time* 26 You tech that 'ere spoon ag'in, you little Hessian, an' I'll wear ye out. **1944** Williams *Word-List Mts* 29 = a rascal, an annoying child: "Get out of the kitchen and leave them pies alone, you little hayshant." (Perhaps derived from Hessian, since most of the people of e. Ky. are descended from Revolutionary War soldiers who "settled" on land grants.) **1957** Combs *Lg Sthn High: Word List* 50 = term of reproach. The Highlanders have not forgotten the Revolution, in which their ancestors played an important role.

[Web3 *hessian* n 3a chiefly Midland; DARE *hessian* n chiefly South, South Midland]

het See **heat A**.

hetchel See **hackle**.

het up *adjective phrase* Animated, "worked up," upset.

1904–20 Kephart *Notebooks* 4:853 They was all het up. *Ibid.* 860 The boys was jist wrastlin', at fust, but they got het up. **1940** Stuart *Trees of Heaven* 229 Take a little along with you to keep you het-up after gettin hot at this dance. **1963** Medford *Mt People* 39 Thus daddy would narrate—around the crackling wood fires of winter, or at other times whenever he got all "het up" in his reminiscences. **1976** Carter *Little Tree* 15 He got so het up about it that Granma had to quiet him down. **1987** Trent *Yesteryear* 55 Don't let that get you all het up. **2013** Venable *How to Tawlk* 20 Laurie gits het up over the slightest thang.

[literally "heated up"]

hewing ax *noun* Same as **broad ax**.

1971 *AOHP/ALC-33* They'd take a log, great big log, and they would split it. See, they'd . . . had big mauls back then and things they split it with, and they would split it wide open in the middle, and then they would, had a big hewing ax they called it, broad ax.

hew out land *verb phrase* To clear trees from a piece of land in preparation for building a home and cultivating fields.

1939 Hall *Coll* (Wears Cove TN) Black Bill Walker was a short feller. He was a feller that went in there years and years ago and hewed him out some land.

hew to the line *verb phrase* See citation.

1984 Woods *WV Was Good* 15 The expression, "hew to the line," would have been equally explained by watching Bob Woods mark off a white oak tree he had just felled, using a tie-board, then hew to the line so beautifully that the resulting railroad cross-ties looked almost as if they had been cut by a sawmill. There was an extension of this saying when a man wanted to indicate a disregard for consequences—"Hew to the line, let the chips fall where they may."

hick *noun* A lumberjack; more generally, a rustic, person from the backwoods. See also **timberhick**, **woodhick 1**.

1964 Clarkson *Lumbering in WV* 364 = lumberjack; woodhick. **2006** *WV Encycl* 809 Loggers were looked upon as unsophisticated persons working in the woods, and since at least the 16th century the word "hick" has meant an ignorant country person. Perhaps it was for this reason West Virginia woodworkers were called woodhicks or timberhicks.

[< Hick, nickname for Richard]

hicker See **hickory**.

hickory *noun*

A Variant forms *hicker*, *hick'ry*.

1891 Brown *Dialect in TN* 175 The word *hickory* is pronounced *hick'ry*, and in connection with *nut* it becomes *hicker-nut*—sometimes pronounced almost as one syllable. **1949** Arnow *Hunter's Horn* 5 We found some hicker nuts.

B Senses.

1 (also *hickory flail*, *hickory whisk*, *hickory withe*) A long, limber twig or stick (not necessarily from a hickory tree) used as a switch to punish children, as a flail, or as an ox goad.

1824 (in **1912** Doddridge *Notes on Settlement* 79) On one occasion he took it into his head that he ought to be scourged; and actually prepared hickories, stripped himself, and made a mulatto man whip him until he said he had enough. **1862** *Ingram CW Letters* (Sept 29) they formed a line of all the men here in camp and ran them threw and every man had a hickory and had to hit each of them one lick. **1913** Kephart *Our Sthn High* 260 The oft-heard threat "I'll w'ar ye out with a hick'ry!" is seldom carried out. [She] went to Knoxville but likes it like a dog likes a hickory. **1949** Kurath *Word Geog East US* 37 In Western North Carolina . . . *hickory* is a common term for the ox goad. . . . [This expression is] not found elsewhere in the Eastern States. **1957** Broaddus *Vocab Estill Co KY* 40 *hickory withe* = a pointed stick of any kind of wood used as a goad for oxen. **1963** Watkins and Watkins *Yesterday* 16 She sent for a hickory, and the student returned with a hickory as long as the teacher. When Jim came to the front to receive his punishment, he looked like a giant standing beside a weak midget. **1966** Dakin *Vocab Ohio River Valley* 132 This Carolina Mountain term [i.e. *withe*] is sometimes given as *hickory withe*. It is common in the Mountains and is scattered to the west in Kentucky. . . . It is obvious, furthermore, that *hickory* has been extended in meaning and is in general use for any relatively lighter stick of varying length used to urge or guide horses—both when hitched to a vehicle or when used as pack or riding animals. Precisely the same situation seems true with respect to switch. This term is quite common in Kentucky east of the Green-Barren River, but is rare north of the Ohio. **1973** *AOHP/ASU-97* My daddly frailed out [the rye and wheat] with a hickory, hickory whisk. 1974 Fink *Bits Mt Speech* 12 If that young'un don't mind, I'll take a *hickory* to him. **1975** Purkey *Madison Co* 61 When the buckwheat was ripe, my father cut it with a cradle and thrashed it with a hickory flail. **1990** Bailey *Draw Up Chair* 14 "I jist got me a hick'ry out o' that apple tree yonder an' I whopped her," the woman said, using the familiar local connotation of the word "hick'ry." **1994–97** Montgomery Coll: *hickory* = for punishment (Cardwell, Ledford). **2000** Morgan *Mts Remember* 20 They was men behind popping their whips, and the boys with hickories run alongside hollering, "Aye, aye" when one of the animals slowed or started to turn aside. **2005** Morgan *Old Time Religion* 23 Husbands were the primary disciplinarians and meted out the severest discipline with a belt or a switch that was called a "hickory," pronounced "hickry." They believed literally the scriptural admonition to "spare the rod and spoil the child," and that "rod" was not a mere synonym for discipline. This mode of familial discipline was prominently displayed over the tops of doors in many homes for the edification of potential miscreants.

[DARE *hickory* n B2 chiefly South, South Midland]

2 (also *hickory stick tea*, *hickory tea*) A switching, whipping administered with a branch taken from a hickory tree. See also **birch tea**, **peach-tree-limb tea**, **willer tea**.

1939 Farr *TN Mt Regions* 90 *hickory* = a whipping. "The teacher feeds hickory to the bad boys." **1984** Head *Brogans* 77 The other day several friends and I were discussing some of the modern methods for disciplining children as compared to the old-fashioned ways. One person suggested that "hickory tea" was the most effective manner to get a child's attention, and it was a lesson he did not soon forget. **1992** Brooks *Sthn Stuff* 68 hick'ry stick tea, n. A switching. "If you don't straighten up and behave, you're going to get a big dose of hick'ry stick tea, young man." **1994** Montgomery Coll Quit your back sassing or you'll get some hickory tea (Shields). **2016** *Blind Pig* (June 2) Granny had to give me a dose of hickory tea for not minding or for sassing her.

3 See citation.

1915 Dingus *Word-List VA* 184 = a rapid gait.

[DARE *hickory* n B6 chiefly South Midland]

hickory chicken (also *hickory mushroom*) *noun* An edible mushroom, so called from its taste and tendency to grow under hickory trees. Same as **big-foot**, **merkel**.

1979 Brewer *Morels* When he was a young man . . . he called them "hickory chickens." This, she said, was because they grew under hickory trees in a damp area. **1997** Montgomery Coll: *hickory chicken* (known to Brewer, Brown, Bush), = fried in butter, eaten especially by the Cherokee (Andrews); *hickory mushroom* (known to Andrews, Cagle). **2007** Farr *My Appalachia* 107 One of the treats of springtime in the mountains was when Dad found hickory chickens and brought them home. I asked him once why he called them "hickory chickens." "I usually find them growing under hickory trees," he said, "and the way your mama fixes them they taste like chicken, only better." *Ibid.* 108 In Appalachia, besides being called "hickory chickens" as my dad did, they are known as "dry land fish," "markels" (Morchella esculent), and "big-foot."

[DARE *hickory chicken* n especially South Midland]

hickory flail See **hickory B1**.

hickory grubber *noun* See citation.

1957 Combs *Lg Sthn High: Word List* 50 = a "razorback" hog.

hickory hiding (also *switch hiding*) *noun* A children's game. See citation.

1985 Irwin *Alex Stewart* 53 We had a game that we called Hickory Hiding, or Switch Hiding. You'd get a great big long switch, and some of us would hide it. There'd be eight or ten out hunting and we'd be off a watching them. If they got way off from it, we'd say "cold, cold," and if they got close, we'd say "hot." They kept on till they found it and the one that found it, buddy, he'd whup the rest back to the line with that switch.

hickory mill *noun* A mill for cutting and fashioning objects from logs of hickory and other hardwoods.

1979 *Big South Fork OHP-1* They had a, what they called a hickory mill that they made different handles and stuff, used hickory and beech, hardwood.

hickory mushroom See **hickory chicken**.

hickory shirt *noun* A shirt with a checked or striped design, made from **hickory shirting**.

1900 Harben *N GA Sketches* 258–59 His blue lean trousers were carelessly stuck into the tops of his clay-stained boots, and he wore a sack-coat, a "hickory" shirt, and a leather belt. **1908** Johnson *Life KY Mts* 176 While the children of the "land owners" wore their nice new suits and their pretty caps and shoes, I had to wear my "jeans" pants, "hickory" shirt, bark hat and go barefooted, and this contrast would cause me a feeling of great shamefulness. **1927** Woofter *Dialect from WV* 357 = a homemade shirt of heavy cotton shirting. "There is no need to buy store shirts when I can make you good hickory ones at home." **1944** Laughlin *Word-List Buncombe Co* 27 = a calico or gingham (work) shirt. **1976** Garber *Mountain-ese* 40 Bascom wore his red and white hickory shirt to the square dance. **1995** Montgomery *Coll* (known to Cardwell).

hickory shirting *noun* A cotton fabric, usually checked or striped, used in making work clothes, especially shirts. See also **hickory shirt**.

1973 GSMNP-85:1:11 They got this hickory shirting and made them, you know. You ever see any hickory shirting, striped? **1977** Hamilton *Mt Memories* 57 He usually brought cloth Mama ordered, but this time he had money for only a few yards of "hickory shirting" as Mama called it.

hickory stick tea, **hickory tea** See **hickory B2**.

hickory whisk, **hickory withe** See **hickory B1**.

hick'ry See **hickory**.

hicky-my-funker See **ben-hicky-my-funker**.

hide and nasty *noun* A closet in which to store cleaning implements or materials that have an unpleasant or strong odor.

1992–97 Montgomery *Coll* (known to Brown, Bush, Shields).

hide and whoop *noun* The children's game hide and (go) seek. Same as **whoop and hide**.

1972 Cooper *NC Mt Folklore* 62 *Hide and whoop* was played wherever shrubs or other objects afforded a hiding place. The hunter tried to find the hidden players, one by one, then return to the home base without being caught by the found one. **1997** Montgomery *Coll* (known to Brown).

[cf EDD *hide* v² II.1 (9)]

hidey-hole *noun* See 2009 citation.

2009 Benfield *Mt Born* 154 = a good hiding place. Children sometime had a special spot, perhaps under a bank, where hurt feelings could be nursed away from the world. A hidey-hole also serves as a cache for private treasures. **2011** Powers *Haints Cave* 134 He followed his smelly friend up the rocky hillside. . . . He thought he knew the woods like Jake, but this was the second new hidey-hole he'd seen today. The opening seemed to fall away into blackness.

hidy *interjection* Hello! (used as a greeting).

1967 Fetterman *Stinking Creek* 137 He greeted the bereaved: "Hidy, Mrs. Sizemore." **1992** Offutt *KY Straight* 22 Hidy, by God. Think it'll rain?

[DARE *hidy* exclam chiefly South Midland, TX]

(as) high as *adjective phrase* (As) many as, (as) much as.

1892 Allen *Cumberland Gap* 240 I've cotched high as five 'coons out o' one tree. **1922** Cobb *KY Mt Rhymes* 39 Whar you look for me, / High as ninety riders / At a time you'll see. **1939** Hall *Coll* (Bradley Fork NC) I've saw as high as twenty drunk in the same day. **1952** Wilson *Folk Speech NC* 550 *as high as* = as many as. "I've killed *as high as* twenty squirrels a day." **1958** Miller *Pigeon's Roost* (Nov 13) Yes, there would be as high as six gangs of o'possum hunters in the woods in hearing distance of each other. **c1960** Wilson *Coll* = as many as or some good-sized number: "He's killed as high as ten squirrels in one morning." **1973** *Flu Epidemic* 104 A lot a'them folks had as high as twelve children. **1983** *Dark Corner OHP-27A* We have cut as high as forty-six distilleries in one month. **1989** *Matewan OHP-28* I seen his dogs run [after foxes] as high as three days and come in with such sore feet it'd take nearly a week before they could walk again. **1991** Thomas *Sthn Appal* 220 I've seen some women stand as high as ten [teeth] pulled, at a time. **1999** Montgomery *File* One policeman told me that they've arrested as high as twenty-one people a night over there (70-year-old woman, Gatlinburg TN).

highball (also *highball it*) *verb, verb phrase* To leave hurriedly.

1917 Kephart *Word-List* 413 *high-ball (it)* = to decamp: "I'll make him high-ball out o' here." **1968** *DARE Survey* (Buchanan VA) = to leave in a hurry.

(the) high blood *noun* Usually high blood pressure; for other senses, see 1990, 1992 citations. See also **low blood**, **thick blood**, **thin blood**.

1952 Giles *40 Acres* 163 He had the high blood, Mama Tooney said proudly. "When his blood gits up," she sighed, "he ain't good fer nothin'. Jist plumb gives out. He ortent to ever do a day's work in the sun." **1962** Hall *Coll* (Hartford TN) I worked at Waterville on a bittin' machine. I could have stayed there yit if I didn't have high blood. I pitched an' staved. He fetched me home. **1975** Chalmers *Better* 23 There were the regular preventive inoculations for all ages, and there were therapeutic inoculations ordered by various doctors for "low blood," "high blood," asthma, anemia, allergies and the like. **1990** Cavender *Folk Medical Lex* 25 = an excessive amount of blood in the body; high blood sugar; high blood count. **1992** Cavender *Folk Hematology* 24 Some informants, mainly those in the older group, defined high blood as having an abnormally high volume of blood. Symptoms of high blood defined in terms of volume included headache, dizziness ("feeling swimmy headed"), fainting or blackouts, rapid pulse, flushing of the face, and nausea. Viewed in terms of simple hydraulics, they attributed the illness of high blood to an increase in blood volume which, in turn, places pressure on the circulatory system, the heart, and the brain.... It appears that the biomedical concept of high blood pressure has been syncretized into the folk belief system as high blood pressure caused by having too much blood. **1993** Ison and Ison *Whole Nother Lg* 30 = hypertension. **2006** Cavender *Medical Term* 1022 In some cases, health-care providers and Appalachian patients may mistakenly think they are talking about the same thing.... Some Appalachian patients interpret a diagnosis of high blood pressure as "high blood," a folk illness caused by an abnormally high volume of blood in the body.

[DARE *high blood* n 1 chiefly South, South Midland]

high case (also *higher case*) *noun* See citations. See also **low case**.

1969 Miller *Raising Tobacco* 34 These *casing houses* were equipped with tierpoles so tobacco could be brought there in *low case* (moist enough to handle if you were careful, but not moist enough to work off) and brought into *higher case*.

high fly *noun* A state of inebriation.

1967 Williams *Moonshining* 15 The effects of this product are maddening, indeed, and those who suffer through a hangover from a "high fly" on this kind of moonshine whiskey refer to it as "rotgut." **1998** Montgomery *Coll* (known to Brown, Bush).

high foot plow *noun* See citation.

c1975 Lunsford *It Used to Be* 7 In those days, they had the two plows—the low-foot plow and the high-foot plow. The low-foot plow was homemade of wood. You'd put a bull-tongue plow on that foot. The tongue of wood at the back was morticed, the wooden foot put in, holes bored at the other end of the foot, and the bull-tongue plow put on by a heel screw. The handles were bolted to that foot, came back up, braced together and crooked over so you could hold the plow with the two hands. At the same time you'd have a line with a loop in it leading to the horse, and you'd put that loop around your wrist and drive your horse between the rows of corn. The high-foot was where the foot part was high enough to come up to about your waist and the tongue was morticed into that. Then the handles went down.

high grader *noun phrase* A student in an upper grade in school.

1973 GSMNP-5:25 [The teacher] would call the high graders up, you know, and get through with them and get the smaller ones. **1997** Montgomery *Coll* (known to Brown, Bush, Norris), = a high school student (Weaver).

high-headed *adjective* Confident, self-important.

1974 Roberts *Sang Branch* 250 Her girl was kindly high-headed. She met the bull and she spoke ill to it and it horned and hooked her and knocked her all around the road. **1995** Montgomery *Coll* = confident, having high self-esteem, "She is a high-headed gal" (Norris).

high kaflutin *adverb* Fancy, pretentious, overly formal.

1941 Stuart *Men of Mts* 39 I'm a man of mountain ways and I can't git high-kaflutin' and go back on what I was raised on. **1967** *DARE Survey* (Rogersville TN) [hɑkɑ'flutɪn].

[alteration of *high-falutin*]

high knob *noun* A mountain summit, high point on a mountain ridge. Same as **knob**. See also **big top**, **high top**, **top A1**.

1939 Hall *Coll* (Proctor NC) [Horace Kephart would] go out on them high knobs and look all about over them rough slicks. **1943** Peattie *Indian Days* 40 The word peak is found on our maps and might be understood in this region but it is really not native to it. The equivalent is top, or knob; high top and high knob indicate lofty peaks. **1989** Landry *Smoky Mt Interviews* 194 Thunderhead is a high knob up there. **1995–97** Montgomery *Coll* (known to Brown, Cardwell, Ellis, Norris, Oliver, Shields).

highlander *noun* One who lives in the mountains (a neutral term, one used mainly by outsiders and academics). See also **hillbetsy**, **hillbilly**, **hill william**, **mountain boomer 2**, **mountaineer**, **mountain hoosier B**, **mountain william**.

1921 Campbell *Sthn Highlander* 20 Perhaps enough has been said to suggest our difficulty in telling who the Southern Highlanders really are.... The people living within the boundaries of the Southern Highlands have too much that is worthy of conservation, both in the past and in the present, to allow themselves to ignore their solidarity or to apologize for it. **1984** Dykeman and Stokely *At Home* 73 The least offensive term [to mountain people for themselves] was "highlander," with its overtones of the misty Scottish landscape and fierce clan loyalties from which many of the Smokies' family lines were recently descended.

high life *noun* Homemade whiskey.

1963 Edwards *Gravel* 107 (as of 1920s) The horse shied, snorted, then jumped and broke into a wild run. The doctor was hard put to stay on his back. It was as if the horse had been shot full of "high-life," and he plunged forward down the entire length of the ridge road. **1998** Montgomery *Coll* (known to Cardwell, Jones, Oliver).

high lonesome *noun* See citations.

1915 Dingus *Word-List VA* 184 = a debauch, spree. **1961** Williams *Content Mt Speech* 16 If he did [plan to do it], he'd drag out his ol jug an' git on a high lonesome, jist like he allus does ary time he ever needs to git somepin done quick-like an' in a hurry.

high-minded *adjective* Proud, haughty.

1995 Montgomery *Coll* (known to Cardwell); He's a high-minded guy (Shields).

[DARE *high-minded* adj especially South, South Midland]

high power(ed) *noun* A rifle with a high power.

1927 Mason *Lure of Smokies* 226 Hit's the city fellers with their high-powers 'at's the ruination o' game. **1937** Hall *Coll* (Cades Cove TN) High power [is] a term for a gun. My daddy had one of those hog rifles. **1939** Hall *Coll* I'd like to shoot that crane with my high power. *Ibid.* (Deep Creek NC) I shot him with a twenty-two high power. **1956** Hall *Coll* (Byrds Creek NC) He may be gettin' his high power ready. **1973** Kahn *Hillbilly Women* 31 The thugs . . . would come to our house in four or five carloads and all had guns and belts around them filled with cartridges, and they had high powers. **1989** *Matewan OHP-89* Right over that mountain there, the high powereds were shooting.

high sheriff *noun* The chief elected or appointed law-enforcement officer of a county, in contrast to a deputy sheriff, constable, or other officer (sometimes used facetiously). See also **short sheriff**.

1928 Justus *Betty Lou* 210 I felt it my duty as a high sheriff o' this county to tell the truth. **1956** Hall *Coll* (Jones Cove TN) Grandfather come back up here to Jonesboro, Tennessee, and married in eighteen twenty-six. He was high sheriff there for a while. **1957** Broaddus *Vocab Estill Co KY* 43 = the elected sheriff, as opposed to a deputy sheriff. **1958** Wood *Words from TN* 11 Here . . . it is usual to refer to the duly elected sheriff as the *high sheriff*. Not only does this pay homage to his ascendancy, but it also distinguishes him from deputy sheriffs, constables, etc. **c1960** Wilson *Coll* = often used derogatorily. **1973** *GSMNP-4*:33 He was just a sheriff of that section over there. He wasn't high sheriff. **1978** Reese *Speech NE Tenn* 37 = attested by 5/12 (41.7%) speakers. **1989** *Matewan OHP-33* I knowed old Greenway Hatfield. He was the high sheriff of Mingo County. **2002** Rash *Foot in Eden* 7 When you are the high sheriff you spend a lot of time putting people at their ease. **2017** *Blind Pig* (Feb 22) I worked for 44 years as an active and auxiliary Deputy Sheriff. During that time I heard the term High Sheriff often. It referred to the elected Sheriff. High sheriff usage was pretty common in my neck of the woods. It was often used to emphasize deep trouble or a sarcastic reference to a local official.

[DARE *high sheriff* n chiefly South, South Midland]

high shot backings, high shot liquor See **high shots**.

high shots (also *high shot backings, high shot liquor*) *noun* See citations. Also called **first shot(s)**, **hot shots**.

1968 *Best Was Made* 106 After about seven runs, the net result will be seven to ten gallons of pure corn (unsugared) whiskey, for an average of about a gallon to a gallon and a half per bushel of corn. (With sugar, the result should be about six gallons to the barrel.) These are called the "high shots." They are about 200 proof and must be cut to be drinkable. **1968** *DARE Survey* (Dillard GA) It'll only take about a half a gallon of water to proof down what we call high shot liquor. . . . These backins that are barely dead, they are what we call the high shot backins, and the alcoholic content of 'em is very high. **1974** Dabney *Mt Spirits* 20 He was used to homemade corn of 120 proof and higher—and what he liked particularly were the "high shots" that even he admitted would "take your breath away." **1974** Maurer and Pearl *KY Moonshine* 119 = very high-proof liquor which must be cut with water or backings to 100 proof. **c1999** Sutton *Me and Likker* 6 I fired my pot up one morning and it got going real good. It had just started running high shots. That is what you call it when it first starts to come out. For so many jugs, then it turns to backins. *Ibid.* 104 = likker that first comes out of the worm, 180 proof. **2013** Pierce *Corn in Jar* 12–13 Another way of judging the proof is by watching the stream of alcohol coming out of the worm. At 160 proof, the stream becomes twisted and spirals into the catch container. This part of the run produces what distillers refer to as the "high shots."

high-tempered *adjective* Irritable, easily antagonized.

1925 Dargan *Highland Annals* 244 "She ain't so awful high-tempered," I says. **1937** Conner *Ms* 82–83 [The Collinses] are as a whole, very high tempered, only two has been Alledged with crime's. **1973** *GSMNP-5*:5 Old man Cal Parton was there and he was awful high tempered. **1981** Whitener *Folk-Ways* 69 Well, him and his boy Jim was right good hands at farming and keeping up their place in general, but Jake was so high tempered that a little thing would set him off.

[DARE *high-tempered* adj chiefly South, South Midland]

high tide *noun* An excessive flow of water in rivers and streams, as following spring or early summer rains, often required for floating logs downstream. Same as **tide A**.

1940 Bowman *KY Mt Stories* 9 "High Tides" . . . meant flood vacations and a chance to "get caught up" with work. **1960** Westover *Highland Lg* 20 = flood (of a stream).

high top *noun* A mountain summit, high point on a mountain ridge; also used in place-names, as in *Parsons High Top* (TN/NC). Same as **big top**, **top A1**.

1923 Williams *After Bruin* They were compelled to do this or starve, for there was nothing to eat on the high tops back toward the balsams. **1943** Peattie *Indian Days* 40 The word peak is found on our maps and might be understood in this region but it is really not native to it. The equivalent is top, or knob; high top and high knob indicate lofty peaks. **1960** Burnett *My Valley* 32 It was here the dogs went out of hearing some six miles from the standers who had made their way out to the high tops as darkness drew nearer. **1973** GSMNP-4:17 From the gap at Mount Sterling it's a mile to High Top. That's straight out the mountain from the gap at Mount Sterling. **1979** *Raising Dogs* 187 The way it worked was you'd go out on some high top where you'd hear them dogs.

highwall *noun* See citation.

2012 Portelli *They Say* 417 The "bench" and the "highwall" are the flat and the vertical cuts created by strip mining [of coal].

highwall mining *noun* Same as **contour mining**.

2006 Mooney *Lg Coal Mining* 1028 In "contour mining," also known as "bench mining" or "highwall mining," workers follow the contour or direction of a seam along a mountainside, cutting straight down to remove the overburden and expose the seam.

hike 'em *verb phrase* To leave, "get moving."

1923 Greer-Petrie *Angeline Steppin' Out* 42 He told Desdimony to "Hike 'em and be quick about hit, fur he couldn't promise how long his stren'th would hold out." **1930s** (in **1944** Wentworth *ADD* 292) (eWV) = to leave, get out: "Hikem out of there." Said to one or more persons.

hill *noun* A mound of earth or straw in which vegetables are stored for wintertime consumption. See also **potato hill 2**.

1990 Aiken *Stories* 97 Cabbage and potatoes were stored in "hills."

hillbetsy *noun* A female counterpart to a **hillbilly**.

1977 Shackelford et al. *Our Appalachia* 74 Her passion is correcting the misconceptions about "hillbillies" and "hillbetsies" spread by outsiders who have written books and produced television programs about eastern Kentuckians.

hillbilly (also *hillbillie, hill billie*) *noun* A native of the southern American mountains (i.e. the Appalachians or Ozarks), where traditionally the term has been little used, except jocularly, because of its widespread negative connotations; in the region today it is sometimes employed in self-reference (as in assertion, self-deprecation, or pride) or is applied to a mountain resident perceived to be of a lower class socially or from a remote area. For a sense of the intricacies of the term's use, see 1967, 1976 citations. See also **highlander, hillbetsy, hill william, hoosier B2, mountain boomer 2, mountaineer, mountain hoosier B, mountain william**. [Editor's note: This term reached mainstream currency originally in reference to early country music.]

1881 *Cincinnati Enquirer* (18 Oct. 2/1) Nicholasville, Kentucky . . . This has been Court-day, and a quiet one, until about dark, when ten or fifteen roughs, known locally as "Hill Billies," undertook to take the city. [**1900** *NY Journal* (April 23) In short, a Hill-Billie is a free and untrammelled white citizen of Alabama, who lives in the hills, has no means to speak of, dresses as he can, talks as he pleases, drinks whiskey when he gets it, and fires off his revolver as the fancy takes him.] **1904–20** Kephart *Notebooks* 4:763 In the same spirit, the man who rejects the appellation of "mountaineer," or something vaguely derogative that the "furriners" have invented, will call himself a "hill-billy" or a "mountain boomer." **1914** Wilson *Sthn Mtneers* 188 In the Tennessee legislature the "hill billy" legislators were the ones who really passed and enforced the prohibition law. **1917** Kephart *Word-List* 413 = a mountaineer: humorous or depreciative. **1927** Woofter *Dialect from WV* 357 = one who works in the woods or lumber camps. "I saw three hill billies going home to-day." **1941** Hall *Coll* (Mitchell Co NC) "Hillbilly" [is] not much used by mountain people because of its unfavorable effect. [It is] apparently used occasionally of mountain people of low class or uneducated types or by way of contrast with such types: for example, "She's no hillbilly," said of a person known for her fine qualities. *Ibid.* = people who live back in the hills; . . . "I've got an old hillbilly up here—got him to spend all his money on the piccolo [= nickelodeon]." **1955** Ritchie *Singing Family* 248 I guess if it hadn't been for radio, it's no telling how long it would have taken us to find out that we were supposed to be "hillbillies," or what kind of songs we were supposed to sing. **1957** GSMNP-23:2:7 I'm really not a hillbilly, but I'm a native, a mountaineer. I've been here all my life, and I'm proud of it, certainly am proud of it. They just got that name up there, the hillbilly there. They call lots of those folks hillbillies because they was raised up here. **1965** (in **2010** *Neal Bio*) When I had my strokes[, t]here were many who didn't think I would pull through. I had to have an operation that lasted seven hours, and I know very well my doctor thought I would conk out in the middle of it; but as I told him later, we Tennessee hillbillies don't conk that easy, so I stayed alive. **1967** Fetterman *Stinking Creek* 16 Actually, a hillbilly rarely lives upon a hill. He lives in a hollow. All hollows are basically the same: high mountain walls thrown up on either side by a whimsical nature millions of years ago; at the bottom of the fold in the land runs a stream that drains the watershed. The small hollows that begin high and near the tops of the mountain chains feed their streams into larger streams, which in turn flow along the floors of larger hollows. Along these streams, with the mountains soaring both behind and before him, the hillbilly dwells. In Appalachia there are thousands of such hollows, each with its own winding stream. All the hollows have two things in common: the streams become larger as they near their rendezvous with the larger streams they serve as tributaries, and the people at the mouths of these larger hollows and streams are more affluent. As you walk farther and farther up the hollow, both the size of the stream and the standard of living decline steadily. There are bathrooms in Appalachia—and television sets and radios and magazines and newspapers. But not many of these refinements find their way up to the heads of the hollows. So in judging a social, political, and financial status of a hillbilly, it is not enough to ask, "Are you a hillbilly?" One also must ask, "How far up in the hollow do you come from?" Or, as the hillbilly himself often asks, "Whose boy are you?" He knows that whether you reply Jones or Smith or Brown, he can pinpoint your distance up the hollow, and its corresponding degree of isolation from the main road to the county seat. The distance has as great a meaning to him as does the difference between Harlem and Park Avenue to the New Yorker. **1971** AOHP/ALC-193 I said, "if you'd talked to me in old hillbilly language like I was born and raised up in, instead of this medical terms," I said, "I could have understood what you was talking about, but" I said, "I didn't understand it, and all you done, you just explained to me by your medical terms or what they was going to do, and I didn't know nothing about it," I said, "if you'd have told me like that in my way of speaking, in my way of knowing things," I said, "I'd have told you right then I wouldn't go. If you'd have told me they were going to pump some fluid out of my back and put hit, put coloring in my back in the place of that fluid and then put a fluoroscope there, put me under a fluoroscope and see where that was a-pinching in my spinal back there," I said, "I told you then that I had already said that I wasn't going to take that." **1973** GSMNP-79:3 I have been borned just about as high in the mountains here as anyone, so I guess you can really tell I'm a hillbilly from my talk, or as some people says, we're mountaineers, said we're not hillbillies to start with. **1973** Kahn *Hillbilly Women* 97 It was sort of hard when I first moved here [= Cincinnati OH] because people was all the time calling me a hillbilly or throwing off on the way I talk. Buckeyes give hillbillies a hard time. They say "these dumb hillbillies don't know what they're doing." But I'd always tell them I was proud to be a hillbilly. **1976** Maloney *Appal Culture* 189 = this word has many connotations, including: 1) a derogatory meaning used to describe white southerners and all rural Americans; 2) it is used, along with other such terms as ridge-runner, briar-hopper, in either a friendly way or as a racial slur. Mountain people often apply these terms to each or to themselves in a friendly way; 3) it is sometimes used as a generic term to describe country and western or bluegrass music. **1977** Ross *Come Go* 139 Both the press and individuals often jeer at the "hillbilly" family that has been transplanted to the city. This makes for much unhappiness and, in many cases, has caused families to return to their homes in the hills. There they put up a defense mechanism and, by comparison, accept a lower standard of living. In defiance they are often heard to say, "I am a hillbilly and proud of it." The real meaning behind this statement is that they would never stoop to a level that would permit them to "poke fun" at anyone or belittle another person as they have been belittled. **1977** Shackelford et al. *Our Appalachia* 373 When you dropped your writing stick and called it a "pencil," or when you said "cheer" instead of "chair," that wasn't going to get you a good reaction at all. On the basis of that experience I've decided that what makes a hillbilly is language. **1977** Wolfe *TN Strings* 11 "The radio, which now operates in nearly every mountain home, has let loose a flood of 'hill-billy' and other popular music, and this is gradually submerging the traditional songs." [This] attitude of Maud Karpeless echoes that of many older folklorists: that "hillbilly" music was some culture from "outside" that was foisted on the people of the South, displacing somehow the more genuine folk songs. **1984** Dykeman and Stokely *At Home* 73 "Hillbilly" came to verge on insult, as it conjured up cartoons of lanky, subhuman creatures who were quick to feud, slow to work, and often indifferent to the "progress" by which helpful visitors would like to transform mountain lives and attitudes. **1985** Williams *Role of Folklore* 187 I got a sticker on the bumper of my truck that says "Hillbilly Power." And a lot of kids eight, ten, twelve years old their dads and mothers born and raised here, they say, "Hey, hey, I'm a hillbilly too." **1992** Offutt *KY Straight* 20 He'd heard that every hillbilly had one leg shorter than the other from years of walking "on the slant." **1993** Montell *Cumberland Country* xv Occupants of the Upper Cumberland recognize themselves to be the epitome of America's hillbillies and may even use the term in referring to themselves. Many fights have ensued, however, when that term, along with the equally derogatory "briar," has been cast at them by outsiders in northern and midwestern urban centers. **1993** (in **2000** Berry *Sthn Migrants* 172) If they called me a Hillbilly, I'd say, "there's two kinds of people in the world: one of them's a Hillbilly and the other one's a sonofabitch." [**2000** Norman *Consciousness* 9 We didn't think of ourselves as "mountain people," or "hillbillies" or "Appalachians" although I knew about hillbillies. Snuffy Smith and Lil' Abner and Ma and Pa Kettle, whose adventures we followed with great pleasure in the comic strips and movies, were hillbillies.] **2002** Ogle *Remembrances* 77 We were not hillbillies[,] we were mountaineers. When tourist[s] ask me the difference, I say "We work and live by the Ten Commandments. Not by religion denomination like Methodist, Baptist, etc. If everyone memorized them and lived by them today we would leave our doors unlocked and help each other out like the mountaineers use to as one big family." **2005** Preece *I Grew* 32 Appalachian people in general are strong, devoted and loving people to their families, friends, churches and communities, and it hurts to hear them referred to as Hillbillies in a derogatory way. I am proud to be a Hillbilly but my definition is a little different. I feel the people in the hills are the best people in the world. They are accommodating, respectful, God-fearing people who love to be good neighbors and friends. Only a few of the hill people would fit into the group of a stereotypical, Daisy Mae and Lil' Abner group. **2008** Terrell *Mt Lingo* These weren't hillbillies talking; they were mountaineers, rough as a cob and ready to cloud up instantly against anyone who called them "hillbillies." **2013** House *Own Country* 194 I have been taught that this word [= hillbilly] is acceptable only when another hillbilly is using it.

[origin obscure, attested only since late 19th century (for discussion, see **1965** Green *Hillbilly Music*); DARE *hillbilly* n 1 widespread, but especially frequent South Midland]

hillbilly highway *noun* A major roadway (such as US 23) along which residents of southern and central Appalachia migrated to the industrial Midwest in search of employment, especially in the 1950s and 1960s.

2006 Hufford *Headwaters* 27 Between 1951 and 1961 coal production declined dramatically. The roads leading out of Coal River to the factory towns in the north received a new name: Hillbilly Highways. "You had to learn the three r's," said Shorty Bongalis, "Reading, Writing, and Route 21. And if you couldn't swim, you better have help crossing the Ohio River." **2008** DSAE *Internet File* Dayton, Detroit, Columbus, Ashtabula. One thing they all have in common: they're at the end of the Hillbilly Highway.

hillbilly pop *noun* Homemade whiskey.

2009 Applegate and Miller *Lake Cumberland* 18 Other names for moonshine were corn liquor, skull cracker, sugar whiskey, rotgut, ruckus juice, happy Sally, hillbilly pop, and white lightning.

hill-rooter *noun* See citation.

c1960 Wilson *Coll*: *hill-rooter* = a lean long-nosed, bony hog, usually one half wild.

hillside navy (also *hillside tobacco*) *noun* Homegrown chewing tobacco.

1927 Woofter *Dialect from WV* 357 *hillside navy* = a twist of home-cured tobacco: "Can you chew hillside navy? No, it is too strong." **c1960** Wilson *Coll*: *hillside tobacco* = home-grown rather than store-bought chewing or smoking tobacco.

hillside plow *noun*

1 (also *hillside turner, hillside turning plow*) A **turner** plow with a reversible blade that is flipped over at the end of a row of crops. See 1996–97 citations. Same as **landside plow**.

1924 Raine *Saddlebags* 228 A makeshift [plow], called a "hillside turner," is widely used, and the simple "bull-tongue" or shovel plow (occasionally the "double-shovel") does what plowing is possible. **1949** Arnow *Hunter's Horn* 186 Maude pulled the heavy hillside turning plow less willingly, with less and less spring and eagerness to be done with the heavy tedious work than in the first day of plowing. **1969** Miller *Raising Tobacco* 30–31 The cultivator was distinguished from the *hill-turner*, used to break ground, and from the *single foot*, plow used to *run-up* ground. **1976** Garber *Mountain-ese* 41 *hillside plow* = mountain plow. "His land is so steep that he's obliged to use a hillside plow." **1983** Montell *Don't Go Up* 199 = plow that enables hill country farmers to plow horizontally along the sides of hills. The hillside plow had a moldboard and landside that could be flipped onto the opposite side of the plow at the end of each row. **1986** Pederson et al. *LAGS*: *hillside plow* attested by 8/60 interviewees (13.3%) in E TN and 1/35 (2.9%) in N GA; 9/15 of all LAGS interviewees (60%) attesting term were in Appalachia; (Rhea Co TN, Sevier Co TN, Rabun Co GA) *hillside turn*; (Rabun Co GA) *hillside turner*; (Sevier Co TN, Lumpkin Co GA) *hillside turning plow*. **1996–97** Montgomery *Coll*: *hillside plow* (known to Adams), = turning plow (Brown), = a plow with a wing so the plow could swing from one side to the other, a necessity for hillside plowing (Cardwell), = also known as *hillside turner* (Hooper), = a plow having a wing that could be flipped over so as to plow the other direction so that the turned earth always fell downhill (Jones).

[DARE *hillside plow* n chiefly Appalachians, southern OH]

2 See citation.

2014 Ellis *Coll* = has a small plowshare, same as *bull tongue plow* (Ellis).

hillside tobacco See **hillside navy**.

hillside turner, **hillside turning plow** See **hillside plow**.

hill up *verb phrase* To form a small mound around.

2002 Jones *Leicester Luminist* 22 [He remembered] his dead grandfather, and how they used to "hill up" potatoes, one on each side of the row.

hill william *noun* Same as **hillbilly**.

1981 Daugneaux *Separate Place* 32 In some papers in towns where an exceptionally good eating emporium is found, an ad even entices the hillwilliams in for ice cream!

hilt See **hold B1**, **B2**.

him *pronoun* See also Grammar and Syntax §3.1.

1 Used reflexively as indirect object (the so-called personal dative) = (for) himself.

1863 *Shipman CW Letters* (May 27) I expect poke will go down there to get him one. **1863** *Tesh CW Letters* (Feb 8) Father says you knee not by him any caps for he got him a box. **1915** Hall *Autobiog Claib Jones* 24 Jim Brown had worked him out a fine wether sheep. **1939** Hall *Coll* He put him a turnip hull on the end of his rifle gun so that he could see the darkness of the bear. . . . He wouldn't eat but two messes out of a big'un and then kill him another'n. *Ibid.* (Nine Mile TN) Directly he picked up him a little rock, and [the bear] took it right at the burr of the ear, and down he fetched it. *Ibid.* (Little Cataloochee NC) He got his water and set and come back out and thought he'd take him a smoke. **c1950** Adams *Grandpap* 38 Ever' time Jack got hungry, he'd just go an' screw his bull's horns off an' eat him a good bite. **1955** Ritchie *Singing Family* 49 That doctor like to had him a fit. He said, "Balis, who in God's green yearth done that to your arm?" **1956** Hall *Coll* (Newport TN) He put him in corn. **1970** Foster *Walker Valley* 71 George built him a house up there. **1971** *AOHP/ALC-32* He had him a farm over in Letcher County or something. **1979** *Big South Fork OHP-1* He'd took him a mattock and dug out these bushes and trees. **1983** *Dark Corner OHP-5A* One [cat] would go down in that sack and eat him a while, and he'd come out and the other one'd get up there and he'd go down. **1985** Irwin *Alex Stewart* 98 He had him an order to make six chairs, but he said, "Quick as I get this order filled, I'll make you one." **1989** *Matewan OHP-89* Harry got his ear cut off in a car wreck, and then he had him, you couldn't hardly tell it on, just a little different color, he got him one put back on. **1991** Still *Wolfpen Notebooks* 58 He raises everything he eats and here lately is putting him in a tobacco patch. **1998** *Dante OHP-51* He got him a little golf cart over at Clintwood to go to town, and the state police stopped him and gave him a ticket.

[DARE *him* pron B1 chiefly South, South Midland]

2 As the simple subject of a clause. [Editor's note: This usage does not occur in ATASC.]

1916 Combs *Old Early English* 290 *Him* is often used for the nominative form *he*, and *her* for *she*. E.g. "Her was a mighty good woman." **1939** Hall *Coll* (Mt Sterling NC) Him's got a ballet of it. *Ibid.* He said him didn't know.

3 As part of the compound subject of a clause (thus *him and me* = he and I).

1836 (in **2007** Davis *Co Line Baptist* 115) Him and his [family] is Dismiss when Ever he Joines any other Baptist Church. **1844** *Broyles Letter* Tell cousin Isaac that I would like to know how him and cousin Lizie are getting along. **1863** *Robinson CW Letters* (Jan 6) him & me has had Some long chats to gether. **1864** *Chapman CW Letters* (April 10) him and his wife and one child is dead and perhaps more. **1939** Hall Coll (Saunook NC) Him and some more boys was gone off that was going to help us make records. *Ibid.* (Sugarlands TN) Him and his brother-in-law one night, back years ago, about forty, went out a-bear hunting. **1940** Haun *Hawk's Done* 13 They like to fish and hunt, him and her did. **1969** GSMNP-46:3 Him and his buddy bought another yoke, and they was about as mean as I ever saw. **1973** GSMNP-5:1 Him and this Levi Shelton was a-laying out and dodging the Civil War. **1973** GSMNP-78:18 Him and his wife Nervie Reagan Bales raised a family of eight children here at the Ephraim Bales place. **1989** *Matewan OHP*-94 Him and his wife lived in back of that service station. **1997** GSMN-PCOHP-3:13 Him and dad and John Myers and Jim Taylor all lived close together in the cove there.

him and her schoolhouse *noun phrase* See citations.

1973 GSMNP-78:20 The next one they built was him and her with two doors, him and her schoolhouse. The boys sat on the right usually, [and] the girls sat on the left when we went to school. **1978** *Smokies Heritage* 256 The schoolhouse they built to replace it was what we called a "him and her" schoolhouse. The boys marched in one door and the girls another, both having their own entrance as well as separate sides of the room on which to sit.

hime See **hymn**.

hind-part-before *adverb* See citation.

c1960 Wilson Coll = with the rear part turned forward; hindforemost.

[DARE *hind-part-before* adv chiefly South, South Midland]

hindside first *adverb phrase* Backward.

1913 Kephart *Our Sthn High* 102 I wisht my legs growed hind-side-fust. **1944** Laughlin *Word-List Buncombe Co* = backwards. "You've put that neck-yoke hind-side first."

[cf SND *hin' side afore* (at *hint* adj 1(8)) "back to front"]

hine, hint See **behind**.

hip See **hippo A**.

hip and hurry *noun* A short period of time; hence adverb phrase *in a hip and hurry* = quickly.

1943 Justus *Bluebird* 166 Feeling ashamed of herself for being such a sleepyhead she hopped out in a hip-and-hurry. **1952** Justus *Children* 12 You pick in a hip-and-hurry—I don't mind taking pains to get only ripe ones.

[perhaps from Scots, nEngl dialect *hip* "to hop, skip"]

hippen (also *hipin, hippie, hippin, hippin'*) *noun* A baby's diaper.

1917 Kephart *Word-List* 413 *hippin'* = a diaper, breech clout. **c1940** Simms Coll: *hippen* = baby diaper. **c1945** Haun *Hawk's Done* 276 He tied the navel cord and carried out the afterbirth and washed Annie Lee and put her hipin and her nightgown on her and stood and stared at her so that Ma asked him what he wanted to call her, and he named her Annie Lee. **1968** DARE *Survey*: *hippen* = diaper (Brasstown NC). **1968** Wilson *Folklore Mammoth Cave* 37 *hippie* = occasionally heard for diapers or didies; also called hippies. **1975** Chalmers *Better* 40 She had a few left over from the last baby, but could use a gown or two and some more hippens. **c1975** Lunsford *It Used to Be* 174 "Didies" and "Hippins" are expressions used for diapers. **1999** Perry *Clinch River* On wash-day my job was to wash "Hippins," now called diapers, no disposables back then.

[OED3 n[1] variant of *hipping* Scot and north dialect; CUD *hippin* (at *hip*[1] n) "shoulder (of a hill)"; DARE *hippen* n chiefly South, South Midland]

hippie, hippin See **hippen**.

hippo

A (also *hip*) *noun* See citations.

1862 *Apperson CW Letters* (April 22) I like to no whether J. Jamerson has got wel ove the hippo yet. **1955** Washburn *Country Doctor* 79 Her ailments had been many and varied but I had been called to see her for some kind of digestive upset. My treatment not only failed to bring relief, but the symptoms became more complex and indefinite. On my last visit two days before I had decided that she was suffering from hysteria, pure and simple. This was also the opinion of many of the neighbors who called her sickness the "hippo," declaring that she was "hippoed." **1956** Settle *Beulah Land* 136 Ma's headaches is not coming so frequent. I would have wrote before, but she has had the Hip so bad I have not set down for a Moment. **1969** DARE *Survey* (Ball Ground GA) He's got a case of hippos.

[shortening of *hypochondria*; DARE (at *hypo* n 1) both senses chiefly South Midland]

B as past participial or adjective *hippoed* = inclined to hypochondria, afflicted by vague depression or unwellness, preoccupied with (a presumed, imaginary, exaggerated, or pretended ailment, especially to avoid work).

1862 *Bell CW Letters* (Feb 2) I wrote you by last fridays maile againe & now againe. I fear you are hipoed you ought to know me well enough to know that I would write you offtimes. **c1959** Weals *Hillbilly Dict* 10 *hippoed* = neurotic, marked by hypochondria. Obsessed with troubles and ailments. **1967–68** DARE *Survey* (Brasstown NC, Gatlinburg TN) *hippoed*. **1969** Dial *Dialect Appal People* 467 I'll just tell ye. Your man's hippoed. There's nothing ails him, but he spends more time using around the doctor's office than he does a-working. **1982** Slone *How We Talked* 103 = thinking you are sick, but you really are not. **1994** Montgomery Coll I reckon I'm just hippoed. **1994** Walker *Life History* 71 Dolly the trick horse got hippoed and couldn't get up (Cardwell). **2002** Myers *Best Yet Stories* 122 A very strange malady seemed to overtake a few mountain women. For whatever reason they spent most of their lives in bed. We spoke of them as being "Hippoed." This was probably a corruption of hypochondriac. The strange thing was they were not really sick. I recall a mother and daughter who were among those afflicted coming to our house. As they came through the front door, the mother said, "I'll take the bed and you can take the couch."

hip-poke *noun* A sack that rests on the hip, used to carry a large or heavy load.

1944 Justus *Lizzie* 48 Aunt Jody was well laden with a hip-poke and also a shoulder-patch.

hire *verb*

1 (also *hire out*) To sell one's labor, take a job for pay.

1862 *Love CW Letters* (Aug 9) they was A man shot at Drurys Bluff yesterday for Deserting he hi[r]ed as a Substitute and then ran off. **1898** Elliott *Durket Sperret* 119 The girl's face was white and set. "I'll hire out, or kill myself." **1915** Hall *Autobiog Claib Jones* 5 I hired to him to learn the trade. **1942** (in **1987** Perdue *Outwitting Devil* 35) He axed her how she would like to hire to him to do his work now that his wife and daughter had left him. **1974** GSMNP-50:1:23 I just hire out, you know, where they would need a girl. That was all the job I ever could get then. . . . We was poor folks and hired out [to] get enough money to buy cloth to make me a dress. They didn't have dresses made up in the stores then. **1974** Roberts *Sang Branch* 15 I went there and hired as a teamster to drive their mules, and they gave me a string of three mules, one behind the other. **1981** Alderman *Tilson Mill* 8 During our visit George Frank related a story of his young days, when he hired out to a man who had contracted to dig ditches to drain the ponds at Flag Pond.

2 To pay to have (something done).

1963 Edwards *Gravel* 79 (as of 1920s), He usually had to hire his plowing and hoeing done.

hire out See **hire 1**.

hisn (also *his'n, his'ne, his'un*) *pronoun* His. For similar forms, see Grammar and Syntax §2.2.

1859 Taliaferro *Fisher's River* 87 We looked, and the limbs uv my tree had riz from the yeth full four foot, and his'n three foot. **1862** Robinson *CW Letters* (June 7) Thomas O Wilson want him to take his letter to his father & george wants him to take hisn & leave it at his fathers. **1862** *West CW Letters* (April 25) I am a gowing to virginia When this fite is Over if I ant Kiled John Freussan is gowin to Take my place and I Take Hisun. **1892** Dromgoole *War of Roses* 492 I'll loan ye my fiddle ef Pete won't his'n. **1929** (in **1952** Mathes *Tall Tales* 138) You 'tend to yourn an' he'll look atter hisn. **1931** Combs *Lg Sthn High* 1320 It is unnecessary to comment on the well-known forms: "his'n" (his one, or own), "hern," "yourn." **1934–47** LAMSAS *Appal* (Madison Co NC, Swain Co NC). **1937** Thornburgh *Great Smoky Mts* 94 Thar was a barn o' his'n burnt up. **1940** Haun *Hawk's Done* 10 Joe reached over and took it out of her hand and give her hisn. **1946** Cleaves *King's English* 35 "Ourn," "hern," "hisn," and "yourn" represent an attempt at uniformity. Since the forms "my" and "mine" developed from a common Teutonic source, a similar inflection was created to distinguish between the adjectival and substantive uses for the remaining personal pronouns. **1956** Hall *Coll* (Bryson City NC) When they got through gettin' the revenue men swearin' about it, the lawyer pulled 'em out and made 'em swear almost positive. It couldn't be nobody else's, only hisn. **1964** Glassie *Mt Jack Tales* 94 He went over and he unlatched them lockets and he put 'em on his'n and his two brothers' necks. **1968** Ferrell *Bear Tales* 11 He didn't say a word but he just took the gun an' sort o' muffled it up in them whiskers o' his'n. **1969** GSMNP-37:2:3 My daddy hauled hisn [= apples] to Asheville. *Ibid.* 37:2:14 I don't know just how he made hisn [= whiskey]. **1973** GSMNP-78:26 If he was short of meal, possibly he would grind hisn and take it out then. **1991** Thomas *Sthn Appal* 236 He'ud be as fer as from here to th' road in front of some of th' fellers. He'd hoe his'un out, an' help them hoe theirs out. **1997** Montgomery *Coll* The bay horse is hisn (Brown). **2008** *Rosie Hicks* 1 He didn't give Papa a warning he was going to drop hisn. **2009** Benfield *Mt Born* 154 = his own, a contraction of the two words. **2013** Shedlarz *Rosa Hicks* 2 He didn't give Papa warnin he was goin' drop his'ne, and that fixed Papa's back.

[historically *his* + *n* by analogy with *my/mine*; now sometimes construed ahistorically as from *his* + *one* or *his* + *own*; EDD *hisn* pron mEngl, sEngl, 1450→?; DARE *hisn* pron chiefly South, South Midland, New England]

his'ne See **hisn**.

hiss *verb* To whistle at and motion to (a dog) so as to put it on the track of a hunted animal; to signal (a dog) to attack (game).

1926 Hunnicutt *Twenty Years* 93 When I got down to the creek where the bear had rolled I "hissed" the bulldog and he took hold of it. **1939** Hall *Coll* (Deep Creek NC) I patted him and muched him and hissed him, and he went right on back and commenced barkin' up the tree. . . . It was one of our bear hounds, a black and tan hound, and he was just eat up, bloody all over. Well, I hissed him, and he went back up to the tree and commenced to barkin'. **1940** Oakley *Roamin'/Restin'* 54 I hist the dog many times telling him to catch it waiting outside. **1970** *Hunting Stories* 81 He kep' lookin' on where th'bear had been, an' said directly he stuck his fingers down an' hissed his dog an' said, "Get 'im boy!"

[EDD (at *hish* v) "to make a hissing sound to hound on a dog; . . . to drive away an animal by making a hissing sound"; also SND *hish* v]

hisself *reflexive pronoun*

A Variant form *hissef* [see **1925** in **B**].

B Himself. For similar forms, see Grammar and Syntax §2.3.3.

1832 (in **2004** *TN Petitions III* 36) in December 1828 he Did obligate his self By Bond to mancipate and set free said Emley and her orkers if any. **1862** (in **1992** Heller and Heller *Confederacy* 51) his duty must be don for he owes it to his self his friends and cuntry. **1862** *Love CW Letters* (Aug 9) J W Hutcheson is well if he will take care of his self. **1900** Harben *N GA Sketches* 56 He'll work for hisse'f, but he won't budge fer me. **1913** Kephart *Our Sthn High* 81 Finally [the bear] gits so tired and het up that he trees to rest hisself. **1924** Spring *Lydia Whaley* 1 Had no edication hisself but wanted his chilurn to have it. He "professed religion and he possessed it." He teached his chilurn to read the Bible and do right. **1925** Dargan *Highland Annals* 99 He got frustered then, an' said he'd come fer bear, an' he was goin' to have one if he had to go on by hissef. **1934–47** *LAMSAS Appal* (Madison Co NC, Swain Co NC). **1939** Hall *Coll* (Mt Sterling NC) He went something near a mile back on into the spruce mountains and stayed by hisself all night. **1940** Haun *Hawk's Done* 41 Them things he made up hisself and sung, I thought were good. **1962** Dykeman *Tall Woman* 223 "Since Doc Hornsby killed hisself," Haddon whined, "there ain't nobody left to look after a woman on Thickety." **1973** *GSMNP-76*:31 He shot [the buck] and killed him. Well, he couldn't carry him in hisself. He was just up there by hisself. **1978** Montgomery *White Pine Coll* VIII-2 He was wanting somebody to take him over there so he could jump off the bridge and kill hisself one night. **1989** *Matewan OHP-102* He had to make caskets for these two young men and had to bury them hisself. **1998** *Dante OHP-51* I'm not going to let him go by hisself, so I went with him over there to tell Missus Noe. **2008** *Rosie Hicks* 1 He broke hisself up because he's just so good to kids.

[OED3 *hisself* pron 1389→; EDD *hisself* pron general dialect use in Scot, Irel, Engl; DARE *hisself* pron chiefly South, South Midland]

hissy (also *hissy fit*) *noun* An outburst of anger, a tantrum.

1976 Dwyer *Southern Sayin's* 8 = a fit of anger. "Don't you throw a hissy 'round here." **1976** Garber *Mountain-ese* 39 My wifemate will have a hissie iffen I don't git home in time for supper. **1990** Fisher *Preacher Stories* 31 My mother was "hopping mad," as they say in the mountains. She was "in a hissy." **1996–97** Montgomery *Coll*: *hissy* (known to Adams, Cardwell, Ellis, Ledford, Norris, Oliver); That woman is always in a hissy (Brown); *hissy fit* (Oliver). **2013** Venable *How to Tawlk* 20 Ellen was bad to throw a hissy if her boyfriend was late.

[perhaps influenced by *hysterical* or from echoic *hiss*, DARE chiefly South, South Midland]

hissy fit See **hissy**.

hist See **hoist**.

his'un See **hisn**.

hit[1] See **it A**.

hit[2] *verb*

1 Of a crop: to produce, bear fruit.

1895 Edson and Fairchild *TN Mts* = set fruit. "The peaches didn't hit this year."—a late frost destroying the fruit. **1981** High *Coll* (DARE) = for fruit to set, to have a large fine crop. This term is used commonly . . . throughout Appalachia . . . "The peaches hit this year, but they didn't last time." **1998** Montgomery *Coll* (known to Adams, Bush, Cardwell, Jones, Ledford, Weaver).

[EDD *hit* v II.7,13; DARE *hit* v 1 chiefly South, South Midland]

2 Of a dog: to find (an animal's track or scent). Same as **strike B1**.

1939 Hall *Coll* (Smokemont NC) We drove all day, never hit nary track. . . . Atter a while we hit a bear track. The dogs went to yellin'. We turned 'em loose.

3 (also *hit for*, *hit in*, *hit off*, *hit out*) To go, usually with speed, determination, or anticipation.

1915 Pollard *TN Mts* 242 *hit out* = to go (somewhere outdoors). "Somebody must hit out there and get chestnuts." **1939** Hall *Coll* (Nine Mile TN) We hit out down on what was called the Anthony Ridge. . . . We hit in that Devil's Courthouse atter it. . . . We hit in after [the bear] and it wandered around through them roughs, what we called the lettuce beds. *Ibid.* (Little Cataloochee NC) He hit down the road, down the hill, and jumped the fence and lost his shoe heel, run on to the house. **1942** (in **1987** Perdue *Outwitting Devil* 70) Soldier Jack he hit out, tryin' to make his way back home or to seek his fortune wherever he might find it. **c1950** Adams *Grandpap* 127 They slipped off from the old folks an' hit off down the road. **1963** Edwards *Gravel* 30 They paid Uncle Pete for the food and then strolled up the road toward the Jones farm, where they expected to eat supper before hitting out for the little schoolhouse. **1964** Roberts *Hell-Fer-Sartin* 19 He gave him all the meat he could eat. He hit out for home. **1991** Still *Wolfpen Notebooks* 56 You got to work back'ards with your young'uns. Something you want them to do, tell'em not to do it. Watch how fast they hit for it.

hit a lick (also *hit a tack*) *verb phrase* To make an effort, do any work.

1924 Greer-Petrie *Angeline Gits Eyeful* 2 They never hit a tap whilst they wuz thar. **1984** Wilder *You All Spoken* 170 Never turned a tap; never hit a lick: Never lifted a finger.

[DARE *hit a lick* v phr 1 chiefly South, South Midland, TX]

hit a tack See **hit a lick**.

hitch hiker *noun* See also **beggar('s) lice**.

2007 McMillon *Notes*.

hitchrack *noun* See citation.

c1960 Wilson *Coll*: *hitch rack* = a place where horses were tied up, as at the public square in town.

[DARE *hitchrack* n especially West, South Midland]

hitchrein *noun* See citation.

c1960 Wilson *Coll* = a bridle rein or rope by which a horse was tied to a post, tree, or rack.

[DARE *hitchrein* n especially South, South Midland]

hit for, hit in, hit off, hit out See **hit**[2] **3**.

hits *pronoun* Its. See also **it A**.

1867 Harris *Sut Lovingood* 67 I'se allers hearn that hit tuck a mons'us wise brat tu know hits daddy, an' I thinks hit takes a wiser daddy tu know his own brats. **1922** Cobb *KY Mt Rhymes* 19 The hand that creeps from graveyards off, / To charm a man, and kneels down by the bed, / With candle in hits hand. **1925** Greer-Petrie

Angeline Hill Country 87 [A] pianner that wuz damidged, fur one of hits laigs was missin'. **1931** Stuart *Yarb Doctor* 5 Kill a mole and cut hits foot off and tie around yer baby's neck and hits gums shore won't git sore. . . . Or ye can put a penny around yer baby's neck and hits gums won't git sore when it cuts teeth. **1944** Wilson *Word-List* 44 = its. "That dog done *hits* best to break loose." **1961** Williams *Content Mt Speech* 15 Pol tuck it home with 'er . . . hit's [sic] ma bein' so up-headed because her pap cussed the top of the house off when he larnt she was a-gittin' big. **1973** Davis *'Pon My Honor* 31 All of a sudden, a gollywhacker hoop snake come out of the berry vines with hits mouth open and hits tail a flapping every which way. **1974** *AOHP/ASU-204* That snake hit the ground right by the side of me, and hit went on hits way, and I went on the way I was a-going. **2009** Benfield *Mt Born* 155 = used in the possessive also.

hitself *reflexive pronoun* Itself.

1923 Greer-Petrie *Angeline Steppin' Out* 18 He 'lowd since a automobile don't eat nothin', hit would soon pay fur hitself. **1925** Greer-Petrie *Angeline Hill Country* 139 Hit would soon pay fur hitself. **1961** Williams *Rhythm and Melody* 9 Ye can see the lowdown thang [= a dog] a-layin' on the hathrock a-sappin' at its fleas and a-smoulin' over hitself.

hit the grit *verb phrase* To depart hurriedly.

1915 Hall *Autobiog Claib Jones* 28 He tried to bluff me, and I told him to hit the grit or there would be a dead coon left.

[DARE *hit the grit* v phr chiefly South, South Midland]

hit the lick *verb phrase* To expend an effort, apply oneself.

2014 *Blind Pig* (May 15) He helped me plant 7 rows of taters and I tell you what. When we finished, he was hitting the same lick he was when we started.

hit the tick *verb phrase* To go to bed, retire for the night.

1927 Woofter *Dialect from WV* 357 = to retire. "I am going to hit the tick now." **1937** Hall *Coll* (Emerts Cove TN) = reported, but "rarely heard now." **1961** Medford *History Haywood Co* 202 = go to bed. **1967** *DARE Survey* (Gatlinburg TN). **1997** Montgomery *Coll* (known to Brown).

[variant of *hit the hay*, *hit the sack*]

hive[1] See **heave A1**.

hive[2] *verb* To treat (a baby) for **hives**. See also **bold hives**.

1996 Cavender *Bold Hives* 19 I don't know what they do nowadays, but anyway, when a little young child was born the first thing was to hive it.

hives *noun* Same as **bold hives 1**. See also **hive**[2].

1939 Hall *Coll* (Catons Grove TN) Blacksnake root, that's one of the best remedies I ever saw used for hives. . . . Ground ivy is a good tea for hives for babies. **1971** *Granny Women* 252 Catnip tea, ground ivy, or red elder was supposed t'break'em out and make'em have th'hives—which th'doctors don't believe in now, and I don't either. **1975** Chalmers *Better* 45 This is a plant used for tea for small babies to break the hives out. **1982** Powers and Hannah *Cataloochee* 258 There was a vine she called "ground ivy" . . . she boiled it to make a tea to give small babies to break them out with the hives. **c1984** Dennis *Smoky Mt Heritage* 7 Brew a weak catnip tea and give to newborn babies to bring out the hives.

[EDD *hives* sb 1 Scot, nEngl "an eruption on the skin," 2 "an inward feeling of enlargement"; SND n 1 "any childish skin eruption" and n 2 "inflammation of the bowel"; CUD *hives* n pl 1 "a skin rash, especially red, itchy, spots on a child's skin"]

hoarse up *verb phrase* To become hoarse.

1904–20 Kephart *Notebooks* 2:475 I'm kinder hoarsed-up and cain't hardly talk. **1994–97** Montgomery *Coll* (known to Adams, Brown, Cardwell, Ledford, Weaver).

ho back *interjection, verb* Back up! (used as a call to a horse). Same as **whoa back**. See also **back C**.

1966 *DARE Survey* (Cherokee NC) = to make a horse go backwards.

hobblebush *noun* A low-growing, densely branching plant (*Viburnum* spp). Also called **devil's shoestring 1**, **tangle-legs**, **witch hobble**.

[**1901** Lounsberry *Sthn Wild Flowers* 478 Along the slopes of the high mountains in North Carolina, often where deep shadows fall, this viburnum is most conspicuous among the shrubbery. Its branches sprawl often, or lie over on the ground forming great loops which root regularly from their ends. By this means it trips up many seeking to pass through its meshes.] **1943** Stupka *Through the Year* 283 The hobblebush or witch hobble [is] an abundant high-mountain shrub whose large roundish leaves reach their color peak in September. The hiker will encounter this plant along all the trails which take him through forests of spruce and fir. Its orange-red fruit clusters are showy enough, yet these often go unnoticed against the richness and variety of leaf hues. **1997** *Smokies Guide* (Autumn) 1 At the higher elevations, where the climate is similar to New England's, displays start as early as mid-September with the turning of yellow birch, American beech, mountain maple, hobblebush, and pin cherry.

hobby (also *hobby bread*) *noun* A small, round cake of cornmeal. Same as **dodger**.

1907 Dugger *Balsam Groves* 138 How many hobbies uv bread would you want? **1949** Kurath *Word Geog East US* 36 Two sections of the South Midland, the Kanawha and Western North Carolina, have some interesting local expressons . . . *Hobbies* . . . for small hand-shaped corn cakes. *Ibid.* 68 In West Virginia south of the Kanawha the . . . term [corresponding to **corn dodger**] is hobby. **1952–57** (in **1973** McDavid and McDavid *Vocab E KY* 155) = attested by 19/52 (36.5%) of E KY speakers for the Linguistic Atlas of the North Central States. **1957** Broaddus *Vocab Estill Co KY* 41 *hobbies* = corn dodgers. **1966** Dakin *Vocab Ohio River Valley* 15 Several speakers in the Mountains appear to say *hobby bread* = pone or pone bread although *hobby* usually and much more commonly means a type of corn griddle cake.

[DARE *hobby* n 1 chiefly eastern KY, southeastern OH, southern WV]

hock See **hawk**[1].

hockey *noun* Feces.

1886 Smith *Southernisms* 37 *Hockie* is used in East Tennessee among little children, which may be connected with the original word "cacky," as also the exclamation of disgust used by an older person to a child that has befouled itself. **1998** Montgomery *Coll* (according to seven consultants from the Smoky Mountains, term is used by both children and adults, even in mixed company; according to two consultants from the Smoky Mountains, term is used by only children). **2007** McMillon *Notes* = usually a child's term, but not always. The statement "that's baby hockey" is used to stop a foolish query.

[DARE *hockey* n[2] chiefly South Midland]

hoe *noun* See citation.

1958 Wood *Words from TN* 11 = a frying pan . . . A spider (sometimes called hoe) is not the same, as it [= a hoe] has no sides—or practically none. It is a griddle for broiling, or for baking top-of-stove breads.

hoecake (also *hoe-johnny*) *noun* A small cake of corn bread the size of the hand or shaped by hand, originally baked on a hoe, on a board set in the coals of a fire, or in a **Dutch oven**. See also **ash-cake**, **corn dodger**, **dodger**, **jo cake**, **johnny bread**.

1853 Ramsey *Annals* 719 Mixed with cold water, [cornmeal] is, at once, ready for the cook . . . placed upon a piece of clapboard, and set near the coals, it forms the journey-cake; or managed in the same way, upon a helveless hoe, it forms the hoe-cake. **1862** Shifflet *CW Letters* (July 13) I went out in the Cuntry tother day and giv a quarter of a dollar for a little hoe cake of corn bread and hit was burnt on one side and had no Salt in hit but I eat hit all at once and thort hit was mity good. **1889** Mooney *Folk Carolina Mts* 95 Slavery was unprofitable, and the unfortunate owner of a narrow strip of bottom land, shut in on the one side by the mountain and continually washed away on the other by the river, found himself obliged to do his own work and keep his boys at home to help, while his girls stayed in the house to take turns with their mother at the spinning-wheel and the hoecake. **1937** Hall *Coll* (Emerts Cove TN) = corn bread baked in a hoe-cake baker over the coals, not in a stove. **1949** Kurath *Word Geog East US* 39 From the Chesapeake Bay to the western parts of Virginia and the Carolinas, *ash cake* and *hoe cake* are used or remembered as words for hand-shaped corn cakes baked before an open fire. **1956** Hall *Coll* (Cosby TN) We had to have corn bread, hoe cake, of a mornin'. **1960** Arnow *Seedtime* 394 The simplest form of bread was that made of meal, salt, and water, and known variously as corn pone, hoecake, or corn dodger. Hoecake is said to have been so named from the custom of the slaves in Virginia, who, given only meal, mixed it with water and baked it on their hoes. **1968** Wilson *Folklore Mammoth Cave* 19 = a pone of bread cooked on a griddle on top of the stove. Old people say that they have seen the bread actually cooked on a hoe held over the fire. **1970** Justus *Tales* 23 She might make hoe-cakes, which were round and flat. She might make corn dodgers, round and fat. She might make corn pone, round and even fatter. **1974** Cate et al. *Sthn Appal Heritage* 76 To eat with fish, many people preferred hoe cakes, which were cooked much as pancakes are made today. **1985** Jones *Growing Up* 3 After the stock had been watered, rubbed down, and fed, the aroma of frying side pork and hoe-johnny bread and strong black coffee smelled good. **1990** Oliver *Cooking Hazel Creek* 10 The name Hoe Cake supposedly came from the fact that the cakes were baked on the blade of a hoe in the field. Cakes of corn meal were, however, sometimes baked on a shovel if the cook didn't have a griddle. **1997** Montgomery *Coll* = cooked in iron pan with hot coals placed on top of lid (Norris). **1999** Nelson *Aroma and Memories* 9 Sometimes the men would clean and grease a hoe and hold it over the fire to make hoe cakes. **2016** Netherland *Appal Cooking* 33 Hoecakes are basically fried cornbread, with or without leavening. The story behind the term "hoecake" was that the mix was carried to the fields and the pone was cooked on the blade of a hoe over an open fire. Whle I have heard and read versions of this story many times, I can't recall anyone I know cooking hoecakes on the blade of a hoe.

[DARE *hoecake* n chiefly South, South Midland]

hoecake baker *noun* A pan with low edges; sometimes a topless **Dutch oven**.

1937 Hall *Coll* (Emerts Cove TN) = a cast iron pan set in the coals for baking hoe cakes. **1979** Melton *'Pon My Honor* 80 She put a hoecake baker on some coals to get hot while she made up some hoecakes. When the baker got good and hot, she greased it good with a meatskin and then she put a hoecake on to bake. **1986** Pederson et al. *LAGS* = attested by 5/60 interviewees (8.3%) in E TN; 5/12 of all LAGS interviewees (41.7%) attesting term were in Appalachia.

hoe down[1]

A *noun* A square dance party, usually with a string band supplying the music; also a dance step. [Editor's note: Joseph Hall participated in and recorded a number of these events, observing that they varied "from just good fun to hilarious occasions, providing excellent recreation and graceful creativity for both the musicians and the dancers."]

1883 Zeigler and Grosscup *Heart of Alleghanies* 90 The social ties between the young folks are kept warm principally by the old-fashioned "hoe-downs." **1915** Bradley *Hobnobbing* 101 The dancing became general. Couples faced each other for a "hoedown." The floor swayed, the house rocked, under the rhythmic assault of twenty pairs of stamping, shuffling feet. **1927** Woofter *Dialect from WV* 357 = a country dance. "I went to two hoe downs last week." **1953** Hall *Coll* (Bryson City NC) [There were] some hoe downs, regular square dances held in the school house at Proctor [on Hazel Creek NC]. **1959** Hall *Coll* (Hartford TN) We would have the apple peeling, the berry canning, the molasses making, and corn husking . . . these seasonal affairs that the older people would let the younger people gather and do the seasonal canning or processing of food and promise them that afterward they could have a little social life in the form of doing the buckwing or the hoedown. **1961** Medford *History Haywood Co* 93–94 So it was, that as the chill of late autumn nights grew on, the "parties" or "hoe-downs" were in order. These dance parties, generally alternating about in the homes where they were permitted, constituted the main social events of those days. They were of about the same order or pattern wherever they were held—and that was throughout this Southern Appalachian region. . . . Everything movable has been taken from the room where the dance is being held, to make room for maybe ten or twelve couples; even so, the onlookers must stand in the corners and doorways. **1968** Wilson *Folklore Mammoth Cave* 43 = a semi-disrespectful name for a square-dance party. **1972** Cooper *NC Mt Folklore* 21 Dancing parties, often referred to as frolics or hoedowns, occurred in most neighborhoods, but not in many homes of the neighborhood. These were held only in homes that had a room sufficiently large, after the furniture had been removed, to accommodate the dancers and musicians. **1977** Hamilton *Mt Memories* 129 There were no big parties, just a few family gatherings. Our parents never permitted us to attend the "hoe-downs," as the mountain dances were called. The boys would get drunk on moonshine and the parties usually ended in brawls. **1988** Kosier *Maggie* 26 Young and old alike participated in these "hoedowns," with a nip of corn liquor (white lightning) in the barn loft livening up the social event even more for the men. **1996** Montgomery *Coll* (known to Cardwell), = a party with music and dancing (Norris). **2007** McMillon *Notes* = only heard recently.

[probably from the fact that the dance takes place after a day's work in the fields and tools are put away]

B *verb* To perform **flatfoot** at such a dance.

1992 Seeger *Talking Feet* 28 My mother was 83 the last time she hoe-downed for us. . . . I'd get my banjo and I'd say, "Mom, hoe-down me once."

hoe down[2] *verb phrase* To run fast.

1956 Hall *Coll* (Cosby TN) [An apparent ghost] just come a-lopin'. He didn't know what it was that took after 'im. I guessed he hoed down. [**1995** Montgomery *Coll* (unknown to consultants from the Smoky Mountains).]

hoe-johnny See **hoecake**.

hoe pone *noun* See citation.

1967 *DARE Survey* (Gatlinburg TN) = biscuit dough not rolled out into biscuit, just placed in the pan.

hog

A *noun*

1 (also *hog meat, hog's meat*) Pork. See also **deer meat, meat A**.

1862 Lister *CW Letters* (Dec 19) we have a mong us yet a bout 75 pounds of hog meat that we brout from home. **1921** Weeks *Speech of KY Mtneer* 9 We don't often indulge in the luxury of eating pork in the mountains. After you have met on a Sunday afternoon ramble, a Kentucky porker ranging at large over the hills, or stumbled over him as he sleeps in the streets at night, you are convinced that hog meat is refined enough as a name for the marketable portions of the razorback. **1939** Hall *Coll* (Emerts Cove TN) [Squirrel] tastes similar to hog meat. **c1960** Wilson *Coll*: *hog meat* = pork rather than all other kinds of meat from hogs. **1975** Kroeger *WV Farm Life* 7 We raised our living mostly. We had our meat and our milk and our butter and our chickens and our eggs and our hog's meat. **1976** Garber *Mountain-ese* 42 *hog meat* = fresh pork. "Weuns had a big bait uv hog meat and fish-eye gravy for breakfast." **1981** GSMNP-121:51 We'd always look for a patch of ramps, and we'd have some hog meat with us, and we would make a fire and cook some bacon on a forked stick, have some of those ramps. **1982** Ginns *Snowbird Gravy* 16 We kept a hog, and [mother] fried the meat, the what-they-call pork; we called it "hog" all the time. Anymore, they call it "pork." **1997** Ownby *Big Greenbrier* I:20 She kept the fats from the hog meat, which she put with, for the lye, boiling it with the big iron kettle until it was thick enough for soap.

[DARE *hog* n B3a, *hog meat* both South, South Midland]

2 See citation.

c1960 Wilson *Coll*: *hog* = one of the numerous euphemisms for *boar*.

3 See citation. Same as **groundhog still**.

1974 Dabney *Mt Spirits* xxi This still, sometimes called a "hog," is usually found dug into the side of a hill or bank and is usually a huge metal cylinder with a wooden top and bottom.

4 See citation.

1974 Underwood *Madison Co* 45 The band saw used for cutting the logs into lumber was powered by a steam plant that burned chips. Slabs of wood were thrown into a machine called a "hog" and it ground them into chips.

5 A groundhog.

1995 Minick *Groundhogs* 15 We both disliked the "hogs," as we called them, because the ate our alfalfa, or if they were daring, they'd sneak into our garden and feast on our beans or cantaloupe or tomatoes.

B *verb* To scratch.

1917 Kephart *Word-List* 413. **1994** Montgomery *Coll* (known to Cardwell).

hog and hominy *noun phrase* See citation.

c1960 Wilson *Coll*: *hog and hominy* = food and plenty of it; originally probably literally hog-meat and hominy and nothing else.

hog apple (also *hog lemon*) *noun* Same as **mayapple**.

1966 *DARE Survey* (Pensacola NC) = mayapple. **1982** *Smokies Heritage* 22 In May, the Mayapple produces a single pale flower beneath its wide canopy of leaves, later followed by an edible "apple" which some folks know as the "hog lemon."

hogback *noun*

1 (also *hogback mountain, hogback ridge, hog ridge*) A mountain ridge that slopes sharply on each side and often has jutting rocks, resembling the high, narrow back of a wild hog.

1943 Peattie *Indian Days* 41 A hogback vividly if inelegantly describes a type of mountain so characteristic [of the Appalachian mountain range] that it might almost be called an appalachia. **1975** Brewer *Valley So Wild* 259 Now the dam water will cover all the bottoms and leave jest the hog ridges for farming. **1975** Fink *Backpacking* 47 Bracken's home ... stood where one first got a glimpse of the Chimney Tops, two spectacularly sharp peaks on a hogback ridge on the north flank of Sugarland Mountain. **1979** *Smokies Heritage* 199 After two days and one night of hard walking they finally established themselves on a little "hog back" ridge with a clear view of the gap of entry from Virginia (above Old Tarwell, southern end of Cumberland Gap). **2000** Miller *Looneyville* 49 *hogback* = a high steep point of ground that runs up and down a hillside. It had a land formation that resembled a hog's backbone structure: "That hawgback over there won't grow much bluegrass." **2003** *Smoky Mt News* (Jan) Hogback Gap, Hogback Holler, Hogback Knob, Hogback Ridge, Hogback Township, Hogback Mountain, and Hogback Valley. In addition there are six sites in Western North Carolina named Hogback Mountain. Proof enough, if anyone required it, that hogs are an essential part of the mountain landscape. **2007** Homan *Turkey Tracks* 85 Back in the depression, when I was about your age, I used to hunt squirrel and turkey along the hogback where you're going to walk.

2 An independent voter or candidate who casts a ballot against his or her traditional party allegiance; an independent ticket or candidate bolting from party affiliation; hence verb = to abandon one's political party.

1911 Shearin *E KY Word list* 538 = an independent voter, a bolter. Political slang arising in Breathitt County around 1905. *Ibid.* = to abandon: "He hog-backed his party." **1940** Still *River of Earth* 162 I get a vote any way can be got, buy or swap, hog-back or straddle-pole. **1977** Shackelford et al. *Our Appalachia* 33 When they saw that General was really going to get the nomination they had a brother of mine back in the room upstairs here wanting to run him on the Hog Back ticket. *Ibid.* 34 Candidates who were affiliated with neither the Republicans nor the Democrats were said to be running on the Hog Back ticket. Hog Back candidates either entered the campaign after the primary, or had competed in the primary under the rooster (Democrats) or log cabin (Republican) symbol and lost. In the November election they chose their own symbol—often a hen, plow, or mattock—for the ballot. The Hog Back practice was outlawed in the 1930's when the Kentucky legislature passed a statute requiring all candidates for public office to declare their party affiliation and participate in their party's primary in all races except nonpartisan judicial positions. **2009** Fields *Growing Up* 256 If the candidate was not running as a Republican or a Democrat, he was considered to be on the "Hogback ticket." The hogback ticket people could be anyone that considered themselves being independent.

[DARE *hogback* n 3 eastern KY]

hogback mountain, **hogback ridge** See **hogback 1**.

hog butchering See **hog killing time**.

hog calling *noun* A competition in which contestants produce original hog calls.

1938 Stuart *Dark Hills* 255 There is the nail-driving contest for women, the hog-calling contest, the cow-calling contest. **1986** Ogle *Lucinda* 66 The old folks and young would join in competing, such as string bands, single instruments, dancing, buck and wing, clog dancing, hog calling, husband calling, etc. **2003** *Smoky Mt News* (Jan) Rounding them up was part of the fun. Hog calling was a practical skill that some turned into an art form. Hog callings at Old Timers Day celebrations today are but a remnant of what once was a necessary skill.

hog claim *noun* Formerly, legal authority to hunt wild hogs on a specified tract of land.

1859 Taliaferro *Fisher's River* 52 I had a hog claim over beyant Moor's Fork. **2003** *Smoky Mt News* (Jan) Part of her incentive in purchasing a particular plot of land west of Bryson City was the additional value attached to it of a "wild hog claim." **2016** *Smoky Mt News* (Jan 27) A particular plot of land west of Bryson City was the additional value attached to it of a "wild hog claim."

[DARE *hog claim* n especially South Midland]

hog dollar *noun* A silver dollar.

1994 Mullins *Coaley Creek* xi = a silver dollar. **2005** Ebel *Orville Hicks* 3 A fellow with a "hog dollar" has a silver dollar, which was enough to buy a hog years ago.

hog down *verb phrase* See citations.

1957 Broaddus *Vocab Estill Co KY* 41 *hog it down* = to turn hogs into a field of corn after harvest to finish it off. **c1960** Wilson *Coll*: *hog down corn* = to allow hogs to eat corn in the fields rather than gather it.

[DARE *hog down* (at *hog* v C1) originally Midland, now also South]

hog fiddle (also *hog harp*) *noun* Same as **mountain dulcimer**.

1975 Dwyer *Thangs* 33 In various sections of the blue ridge country, the dulcimer is known by different names such as "hog fiddle"—"mountain zither" and "dulcimore." **1999** Milnes *Play of Fiddle* 136 Other names I have heard for dulcimers in central West Virginia are hog harp, hog fiddle, feather harp, or church dulcimer (which was used to describe a large, six-stringed dulcimer in Nicholas County). **2006** *Encycl Appalachia* 1145 Also known as the hog fiddle, music box, and harmony box, the fretted dulcimer is essentially a modified fretted zither approximately thirty-four inches in length and consisting of a narrow three- to six-stringed fretboard attached to a larger sound box.

hog fish (also *hog molly*, *hog sucker*) *noun* A scavenging fish, the log-perch (*Percina caprodes*). Also called **white sucker**.

1849 Lanman *Alleghany Mts* 65 I took the liberty of doubting the gentleman's word, and subsequently found out that the people of this section of country call the legitimate *pickerel* the "salmon," the *black bass* the "black trout," the *mullet* the "red horse," and a *deformed sucker* a "hog-fish." **1939** Hall *Coll* (Waldens Creek TN) The creek was full of fish—bass, white suckers, silversides, red horses, hog mollies in the creek. **1968** DARE *Survey* (Brasstown NC) *hog sucker* = freshwater fish not good to eat. **1976** Garber *Mountain-ese* 43 Sol is down at the crick tryin' to grab-hook hog suckers. **1995–97** Montgomery *Coll*: *hog fish* (known to Ledford), = a common brown sucker encountered in the larger creeks or in the rivers, often when fishing for trout. It was considered a "trash" fish not worth keeping (Ellis); *hog molly* = small catfish with a large head (Shields); *hog sucker* (known to Adams, Jones, Ledford, Shields), = a common scavenger fish in mountain streams (Cardwell), = fish with a flat head, big eyes, and a snout-like mouth (Hooper).

[DARE *hogfish* n b scattered, but especially South, South Midland]

hogging *noun* Same as **noodling**.

2006 *Encycl Appalachia* 872 Native Americans caught spawning catfish with their hands, a practice that may be part of the origin of the sport of noodling. Also called hand grabbing, grabbling, hand fishing, or hogging, noodling is still a well-known activity in the larger rivers and reservoirs of Appalachia. Noodlers target most catfish species but their real prize is the flathead catfish, known in Appalachia as the mudcat. Noodling remains popular with some, but the method is only practical during the brief few weeks in which catfish spawn and noodlers can locate them in hollow logs and other cavities where they nest.

hog ham (also *hoghip*) *noun* Meat from the upper part of a pig's leg.

c1982 Young *Colloquial Appal* 12 = ham. **2005** Ebel *Orville Hicks* 32 Later, Orville and his daddy took "hog ham" to the Mast Store in Valle Crucis.

hog harp See **hog fiddle**.

hoghead cheese (also *hog's head pudding, hogshead cheese*) *noun* A congealed preparation of edible scraps of hog meat (usually from the head and feet), pepper, and spices, pressed into the form of cheese, most often known as **souse meat** in the mountains. Same as **souse B**.

1968 *DARE Survey* (Big Stone Gap VA) *hog's head puddin'*. **1968** Wilson *Folklore Mammoth Cave* 20 (or *hogshead cheese*) *hoghead cheese* = souse. Pressed meat is occasionally used. **1996–97** Montgomery *Coll*: *hoghead cheese* (known to Brown, Bush, Cypher, Ledford).

[DARE *hog's head cheese* n chiefly South, South Midland, Northeast, especially South Atlantic, Gulf States]

hoghip See **hog ham**.

hog house *noun* A covered enclosure for swine.

1986 Pederson et al. *LAGS* = attested by 7/60 interviewees (11.7%) from E TN; 11/17 of all LAGS interviewees (64%) attesting term were from E TN. **1993** Page and Smith *Foxfire Toys and Games* 115 About the only playhouses we ever had that had the roof over it was after Daddy would kill the hogs. He wouldn't put any back in them till up in the spring. We'd go and clean the hog house out and that was a nice place to play.

hog-jawed *adjective* See citation. Same as **jimber-jawed**.

1957 Broaddus *Vocab Estill Co KY* 41 = with a projecting lower jaw.

hog killing time (also *hog-killing day*) *noun* Traditionally, an annual family or neighborhood work activity, usually taking place after the first hard frost of the fall, to slaughter, skin, section, and divide the remains of one or more hogs; the celebration thereafter or, figuratively, a very enjoyable time.

1957 Combs *Lg Sthn High: Word List* 51 *hog-killing time* = a very enjoyable or pleasant time. Ex.: "We had a hog-killin' time at the shindig last night." **1969** Hall *Coll* (Del Rio TN) *hog killing time* = when all the neighbors come in, when it's real cold. They're drinkin' some, wives cookin', makin' sausages. *Ibid.* "Hog-killing time" [was used sometimes] of a party or hoe down with a lot of fun. Everybody would get together and have music and dance. *Ibid.* That was a real hog killin' time! [**1977** Yeager *Mostly Work* 8 The big smokehouse . . . is where we kept the meat and lard from killing time to killing time. That's, I say, from the fall of the year when they kill until the next year, when they'd kill again.] **1990** Oliver *Cooking Hazel Creek* 17 Hog killing time began in the late fall when the weather turned cold and went on until the settler felt he had enough pork to last him till next fall. Four or five hogs were usually slaughtered and much of the meat was smoked or cured in the smokehouse so that it would keep for months. **2006** *Encycl Appalachia* 423 "Hog killing time," as it was commonly called in much of Appalachia, occurred during the months of November, December, January, and February, when the temperature was usually below thirty-two degrees Fahrenheit. This made it ideal to safely preserve freshly dressed pork. Hog killing time also provided opportunities for families and neighbors to get together and share in this activity and fellowship as a community. *Ibid.* 950 "Hog-killing day" could actually last several days, involving entire families and others who volunteered in return for fresh meat or for reciprocal help when their own day came around. This was cold-weather work, mostly outdoors, and it required strength, endurance, patience, and skill. A family might kill several hogs at once to produce their year's supply of meat for the smokehouse.

[DARE *hog-killing* n 1a chiefly South, South Midland]

hog lemon See **hog apple**.

hog liquor *noun* See citation. Also called **groundhog liquor**.

1985 Dabney *More Mt Spirits* 89, 90 "Hog Likker" is the kind you make in a groundhog still. In the groundhog still, the mash fermentation and distilling is done in the same container. . . . "For a five-hundred gallon still, you first have to put in a hundred pounds of malt sprouts and put a pound of sugar to each gallon of water—five hundred pounds. Then you cap it off with wheat bran. When it ferments, you boil it and it'll make, in that five-hundred gallon still, about seventy-five gallons of likker. That's hog likker. You don't 'slop it out.' After a run you just leave it in there. When you get through cooking, you still have four-hundred gallons of water in there. You just have to add on some water and the same amount of sugar—five hundred pounds—and fifty pounds of malt." **c1999** Sutton *Me and Likker* 82 Back years ago when wild hogs roamed the mountains, they did fall in [to boiling mash] and get drowned and the moonshiners was not about to throw out that beer. They pulled out the hog and throwed him down through the woods and run it anyway. Some of em did call it hawg likker.

hog lot *noun* An outdoor enclosure for swine. Same as **pig lot.** See also **lot A.**

1937 Hall *Coll* (Emerts Cove TN) = a floored pen for fattening hogs. **1950** Miller *Pigeon's Roost* (Nov 9) Miller went to his hog lot to feed a large fattening hog when he found it had rooted a hole in the ground and had crawled back under the floor of an old house where it became fastened. **c1960** Wilson *Coll* = an enclosure for hogs, bigger than a hogpen or pigpen. **1963** Edwards *Gravel* 18 Pa came back from the hog lot where he had gone to throw some weeds to the hogs and to give them the slop. **1967** *DARE Survey* (Maryville TN) = place outdoors where hogs are kept ("up to one acre"). **1986** Pederson et al. *LAGS: hog lot* (Sevier Co TN). **1987** Young *Lost Cove* 66 Strange odors worse than a hog lot caused a man's nose to run and his eyes to water. **2009** Wiles and Wiles *Location* 16 The hog house was located in the hog lot below the spring.

hog meat See **hog A1.**

hog molly See **hog fish.**

hogpen *noun* See citation. See also **hog lot.** [Editor's note: In reference to an enclosure for hogs, *hogpen* is standard.]

c1960 Wilson *Coll* = said of a very dirty room or premises.

hog pudding *noun* See citation. Same as **liver mush.**

1986 Pederson et al. *LAGS* (Scott Co TN) = liver sausage, cooked, sliced and fried.

hog ridge See **hogback 1.**

hog rifle [sometimes with stress on both of the first two syllables] *noun* A muzzle-loading, single-barreled hunting rifle of the type made in the mountains in the first half of the 19th century and which continued to be used into the 20th. Most were made by well-known rifle makers, such as various members of the Bean family of East Tennessee. Also called **pig-eye rifle.** See also **cap and ball gun, squirrel gun.**

1913 Kephart *Our Sthn High* 69 There is a class of woodsloafers, very common here, that ranges the forest at all seasons with single-barrel shotguns or "hog rifles," killing bearing females as well as legitimate game. **1917** Kephart *Word-List* 413 = a squirrel rifle. The stress falls on *rifle*. **1928** (in **1952** Mathes *Tall Tales* 72) He was brung up on the ol'-time hawg rifle, which it took a coon's age to load the blame thing, an' he jest had to git his b'ar the fust shot. **1939** *FWP Guide TN* 132 A unique sport . . . is the "turkey shoots" of the mountain people stemming from the rifle contests of pioneer times. Scorning modern breech loaders, the contestants use long-barreled cap and ball "hog" rifles, patterned after the famous guns of the frontiersmen. **1949** McDavid *Grist* 110 (Fannin Co GA) = a rifle with a comparatively short barrel, used for killing hogs. **1954** *Waynesville Mtneer* Aug 2 Ancient Muzzleloaders Cocked and Primed for Cataloochee Beef Shoot [headline] . . . immediate target a piece of charred wood, and their ultimate goal a quarter of beef. The shoot is open to "mountaineers" and "furriners" alike, but the "shooting-iron" must be a long-barrelled muzzleloader. . . . Many of the rifles are prized family heirlooms, some made in the Cataloochee area. Others are the famous "Lancasters" from Pennsylvania. Locally they are all called "hawg rifles." **1957** Combs *Lg Sthn High: Word List* 51 = the squirrel rifle commonly in use before the breech-loading rifle and shot gun. It is loaded from the barrel, and ignited by a percussion cap. **1957** Hall *Coll* (Del Rio TN) [The hog rifle] was used to kill any kind of game from squirrels to bears to deer. There is a few hog rifles scattered around this side of the mountains, but not used, just antiques. **1969** GSMNP-25:2:11 He was using what they call an old hog rifle, and you only shot them oncet till you took time to reload, which was a matter of, I'd say, five minutes. **1975** GSMNP-62:17 We used a hog rifle. You would load it and then shoot and then had to load it again, just one shot. That's what we used to, when I was a boy and a young man, kill bears with a hog rifle. **1995** Alexander *Mt Fever* 120–21 Mostly their armament would consist of .22-caliber rifles or single-shot shotguns, but sometimes one of the older men would be seen carrying an ancient muzzle-loading rifle, the long, graceful weapon of the type used by Daniel Boone and the frontier fighters of the American Revolution. These shoot homemade round lead balls, much larger than a .22 bullet, and possess greater killing power for dispatching large animals such as bear or deer. Compared to a modern high-powered rifle cartridge, the lead and black-powder ammunition costs almost nothing, so muzzle-loaders were frequently used to shoot pigs at hog-killing time and are still known throughout the mountains as "hog rifles." Most old families still had one or two, however rusted or in disrepair.

[DARE *hog rifle* n 1 southern Appalachians]

hogsback *noun* See citation.

2007 *Mining Terms* = a sharp rise in the floor of a seam [of coal].

hogshead cheese See **hoghead cheese.**

hog's meat See **hog A1.**

hog sucker See **hog fish.**

hog wallow *noun* A muddy area where swine wallow. See also **bear wallow, wallow.**

2005 Williams *Gratitude* 535 Where hogs waller in the mud is called a hog waller.

hogweed *noun* The ragweed (*Ambrosia artemisiifolia*), a common plant with yellow flowers that causes hay fever. Also called **bitterweed.**

1982 Stupka *Wildflowers* 124 Common ragweed, also called "Roman worm-wood," "hog-weed," and "bitter-weed," has deeply divided fernlike leaves and inconspicuous heads of green flowers. **1997** Montgomery *Coll* = so called because it grew quickly and was often fed to hogs (Cardwell).

hoist *verb*

A Variant forms *heist, hist.*

1867 Harris *Sut Lovingood* 98 Then he dug sum [dirt] outen a bank wif his ho'ns, an' smelt ove hit; then he tuck a twis' ur two intu his tail, an' histed hit, an' felt hissef then ready fur activ sarvice. **1884** Smith *Arp Scrap Book* 75 He had jest histed 'em all up about three inches. **1895** Dromgoole *Fiddling to Fame* 60 H'isted squar' on top uv all war a pole, a sign-board, with a flag a-flyin', an' on it my ole school-marm had writ a line:—"The plow-boy o' the Wataugy; Truth, the sledge hammer o' the mountaineer!" **1925** Furman *Glass Window* 182–83 If the other windows gives out, there's one h'isted up here I looked to have some day. **1939** Walker *Mtneer Looks* 6 The other vowel sound we can be reasonably sure of, the diphthong *oi*, is generally pronounced as in *p'inted, h'isted, j'ined* for *pointed, hoisted, joined.* **1960** Cooper *Jularker Bussed* He heisted (lifted) the poke (bag) of corn to his shoulder. **1975** *AOHP/ALC-961* The Secretary of the Interior, a Harold Engels I believe his name was at that time, put the mines open and heisted the American flag right in the middle of war.

B To set the musical key of (a song, especially a hymn) that others join in singing (used especially in phrases *hoist a hymn, hoist a tune*). Same as **raise B2**. See also **line B**.

c1940 Simms *Coll* = raise (a tune). **1948** Dick *Dixie Frontier* 189 The minister usually not only lined the hymn but "histed" it; that is, pitched it for the congregation. **1961** Medford *History Haywood Co* 184 Listen! They have now h'isted "How Firm a Foundation"—as more folks begin to crowd up the narrow steps leading to the attic. **1979** Carpenter *Walton War* 170 He can hist a song real good but he can't carry the tune. **1984** Wilder *You All Spoken* 180 *hist the tune* = the song leader pitches the tune of the song to be sung.

hoist a hymn, hoist a tune See **hoist B.**

hokey doh *interjection* All right! Okay!

1954 Roberts *Bought a Dog* 11 He said, "Hokey doh." Said, "I'll trade you the mill."

hold

A *noun* Variant form *holt.* See also **let all holds go.**

1865 *Smith CW Letters* 11 money is hard to get holt of and after a man gets it he cant by nothing with it, this ware canot last longer than till spring I Dont think. **1873** Smith *Arp Peace Papers* 93–94 My holt broak on one okkashun, a goin down a hill full of gullys. **1891** Brown *Dialect in TN* 172 We also say *all of a suddent, wisht* for the present tense of *wish, skift* for *skiff,* and *take holt of* for *take hold of,* etc. **1904–20** Kephart *Notebooks* 2:475 She had the trembles and drapped everything she tuk holt of. **1941** Stuart *Men of Mts* 300 I let my loving holts go on her and I says: "W'y, that's funny, a whippoorwill a-hollering this time o' year, in the middle o' the afternoon." **1964** Stokely *Harvest* 153 [I w]isht I could find some way to git a-holt of some money. **1977** Hamilton *Mt Memories* 86 They git holt o' that moonshine and hit peartens 'em up till they gotta show off.

[DARE *holt* (at *hold* n A1) chiefly New England, South, South Midland]

B *verb* Principal parts.

1 Variant past-tense forms *helded, helt, hilt, holded.*

1863 *Reese CW Letters* (April 23) I helt him By his Rite hand while he was Exchanging worlds. **1865** *Morrison CW Letters* 12 We helt our position till Monday eave when it was thought the yankeys was moving round to our right. **1892** Fruit *KY Words* 233 *hilt* or *helt*: for held: "He hilt 'im fast." **1922** *TN CW Ques* 21 (Greene Co TN) I helt that [job as storekeeper] for eleven years. **1939** Hall *Coll* (Cades Cove TN) The fireplace would be about five foot, you know. You just imagine . . . what a fire that helt. **1956** Hall *Coll* (Big Bend NC) Pete and Ham Hicks, the preachers, they was here the other day. They helt a prayer at the graveyard. **1962** Williams *Verbs Mt Speech* 17 Verbs which retain either the strong preterites of Middle English or variant preterites of the English dialects [include] hold (present), hilt (past), hilt (past participle). **1970** Roberts and Roberts *Time Stood Still* 31 He knowed he was on a slip and he grabbed aholt of a big sugar-tree and hilt on. **1971** *AOHP/ALC-193* I helt that revival there for four weeks. **1972** *AOHP/ALC-342* I believe he helded [the office] two terms. **1974** Fink *Bits Mt Speech* 12 They *helt* on tight. **1977** McGreevy *Breathitt KY Grammar* 93 *holded* = attested by 3 speakers. **1998** *Dante OHP-61* The pin helt the ring that was hooked on the cable that took the car back to the head house to the drum.

[DARE *helt, hilt* (at *hold* v A2a, c) both forms South, South Midland]

2 Variant past-participle forms *helt, hilt, holden.*

1829 *Providence Church Minutes* 5 the Church appoint brethren Samuel Pate and Thomas Atchely delegates to the assocation to be holden at Richland Meeting house. **1861** (in **1992** Heller and Heller *Confederacy* 31) Colnel Lee actain as general enspected our troops to day and we are still helt in readness. **1924** Raine *Saddlebags* 81 That iron kittle thar's helt many a bilin' o' soap, besides hog-water at butcherin' and clothes every Monday. **1952** Wilson *Folk Speech NC* 550 *hilt* = past . . . and past participle of *hold.* **1970** Foster *Walker Valley* 1:31 He was helt.

[DARE *helt, hilt* (*hold* v A3a) chiefly South, South Midland]

C *verb*

1 To adhere to.

1970 *GSMNP-26*:11 If he held any denomination at all, it would have been Primitive Baptist, but I have never saw Eph in the church house in my life.

2 To assert, maintain.

1979 Melton *'Pon My Honor* 94 I've been a-tryin' for quite a spell to get the old man to cut us out a winder. But you know he holds it's bad luck to cut out an opening atter the house is done built. **1988** Smith *Fair and Tender* 21 She tried to hold later that she was chasing after chickens but she was not.

hold back *verb phrase* To delay (the beginning of a school term) so that students who are completing a term elsewhere can attend.

1972 GSMNP-69:31 The school at Elkmont was held back. We call it holding it back. In other words they let all the other schools go through their season.

holded See **hold B1**, **hole**.

holden See **hold B2**.

hold oneself under *verb phrase* To restrain oneself, control one's emotions.

1979 Carpenter *Walton War* 150 Why, jest to hear that man preach, hit stirs my soul so I hain't hardly able to hold myself under. **1995–97** Montgomery Coll (known to Brown, Bush, Oliver).

hold one's hind leg *verb phrase* To be the best man at a wedding.

1849 (in **1956** Eliason *Tarheel Talk* 276) (Wilkes Co NC) I have just returned from a small wedding of one of my cousins.... I had the honor of holding his hind leg.

hold one's potato *verb phrase* To be patient, not be in such a hurry.

1936 Stuart *Head of Hollow* 39 Hold your tater, Symanthia, for mine's hot. **1969** DARE *Survey* (Walker KY). **1992** Brooks *Sthn Stuff* 70 *hold your tater* = just you wait a while!

[DARE (at *hold* v C1a) South, South Midland]

hold to *verb phrase* To adhere to (as a church affiliation or tradition); to endorse, maintain.

1904–20 Kephart *Notebooks* 4:775 She holds to the Babtis' and him to the Methodis'. **1978** Burton *Ballad Folks* 21 They have new songs and they're right pretty—some of 'em is—but I still hold to the old songs. **1984** Wilder *You All Spoken* 187 = advocate; endorse, as in "Sam Jones didn't hold to daylight savings time and income taxes." **1999** Carver *Branch Water Tales* 49 We had a lot of hunting dogs, but Dad didn't hold to one biting a body. **2000** Morgan *Mts Remember* 7 She'd didn't normally hold to such things, but I guess she was worried as I was.

hold up for *verb phrase* To support, take sides with.

1939 (in **2005** Ballard and Chung *Arnow Stories* 107) Law, Mother, I never meant it to sound like I was holdin up for him.

hold with *verb phrase* To endorse, agree with, approve of (a practice, point of view, etc.).

1922 Cobb *KY Mt Rhymes* 25 I never held with all these notions like / Curing the thrash with water from a shoe. **1937** Hall Coll (Copeland Creek TN) The White Caps got to be worse than the other side was. They whipped, they feathered the lewd women.... I didn't hold with no such whatever. **1939** Burnett *Gap o' Mountains* 14 "Pete was a good judge of a houn dog," Joe said, "and while I never exactly helt with him beatin' his wife, I know he had his good pints." **1971** Stevens *Mountain Craftsmen* 30 I don't hold with those who say you should never paint a woodcarving. **1978** Hiser *Quare Do's* 187 My mammy didn't hold with such doctrine. **1989** Giardina *Storming Heaven* 142 It was a cause of scandal to the Regular Baptists on Marrowbone Creek, whose preacher didn't hold with dancing. **1990** Aiken *Stories* 70 A lot of people "didn't hold with" distilling so sometimes the distiller was also a miller at least for his own purpose. **2000** Morgan *Mts Remember* 67 The Johnses are known for their crazy ways and goings-on and drinking, but they never held with no such foolishness as that. **2005** Williams *Gratitude* 502 = go along with or agree with some opinion; take sides with. **2009** Benfield *Mt Born* 156 = to be in agreement and great favor toward.

hole

A *noun* A deep coal mine.

1989 Millner *Letcher* 13 Bailey's folks were spread out over half the state, and Henry had worked in the holes with his relations.

B *verb* Variant past-tense form *holded*.

[See **1964** in **B.**] **1971** *AOHP/ALC-147* She canned it and put it away like that, holded up the taters and dried the apples.

C To drive (a game animal) into a hole.

1828 (in **1929** Summers *Annals SW VA* 1528) (DARE) Each claiming that his dog "holed" her [= a wolf]. **1950** Stuart *Hie Hunters* 30 If Shootin' Star [= a hunting dog] puts one in a hole, we'll have to dig it out. If he holes one in a hollow log, we can use the ax part of the mattock to chop him out. **1964** Roberts *Hell-Fer-Sartin* 158 We decided that was enough huntin' for one day and started back down the hill and all the dogs holded one in a huckleberry log about two foot through at the little end.

hole away See **hole up**.

hole in *verb phrase* Of a bear: to go to or remain in its den for the winter.

1976 Weals *It's Owin'* = stay indoors. "He'll hole in for the winter as soon as the first snow falls."

holer See **one holer**, **three holer**, **two holer**.

hole up (also *hole away*) *verb phrase* To store (as potatoes, other vegetables, or fruits) in the ground, especially for wintertime consumption.

1924 Raine *Saddlebags* 212 They may "hole up" in the garden a pyramid of potatoes, another of cabbage, and another of turnips, and dig them out when the larder runs low. **1974** Roberts *Sang Branch* 22 As for gyarden truck, we didn't have cans to can things back then. We would hole up nearly everything we raised, such as turnips, 'taters, cabbage, apples—even hole up our beets. Take our beets up when we needed 'em on the table and pickle 'em fresh. We would have enough fresh cabbage and stuff in them holes to last us till growing season next spring.

1976 Braden *Grandma Was Girl* 37 We "holed up" potatoes, cabbage, turnips, parsnips, carrots, and some kinds of apples. To do this, we made a large hole in the ground. We lined this hole with straw, put the vegetables in, covered them with straw, and then covered the whole thing heavily with earth. We put enough dirt over the straw so that the vegetables wouldn't freeze. When we needed any of the vegetables, we made a hole in the side of the heap, took out what we needed, and covered the hole back up again. **1979** Slone *My Heart* 63 The late apples could be "holed away" in the ground. Often the floor of the house was removed and the hole dug there. It was lined with straw, the apples were poured in, and more straw and dirt were mounded over the top. **1981** Irwin *Arnwine Cabin* 10 They'd dry all kinds of things—beans, pumpkins, apples, peaches—even blackberries and such as that. They'd bury their turnips, cabbage, taters, and dig out a few during the winter. And they'd be jest as fresh and crisp as when they were holed up. They called it "holding up" [sic] yer stuff. Everybody then would hold [sic] up things like that. **1985** Irwin *Alex Stewart* 208 Oh, everybody would hold [sic] up a lot of their stuff, if they had anything. I've helped my Grandma, and my mother too, bury cabbage. We'd pull them up by the roots and bury them upside down, with just a little bit of the root sticking out. That way you could find them and pull one up any time you wanted to cook a mess. They'd keep all winter and be just as pretty and white and crisp as they could be. The freezing made them tenderer. **1989** Oliver *Hazel Creek* 28 Some foods were kept over the winter by being "holed up," that is, buried in the earth in a straw-lined hole and then covered with straw and a thick layer of earth. **2006** *Encycl Appalachia* 433 Irish potatoes were dug in the fall and "holed up" for storage in a soil pit, from which they could then be taken up anytime during the winter as needed. **2007** Farr *My Appalachia* 84 Just before cold weather froze the ground, [Dad] would "hole them [= potatoes] up" for winter. First, he dug a big, round hole in the garden nearest the house. He would line the hole with straw and add enough potatoes to make a big mound above the ground. Then he put straw over the top of the mound, packing it carefully along all the edges. He covered the mound with a layer of dirt. Last of all he would put flat boards over the top, slanting them toward the ground at one end to drain off water. During the wintertime we would dig in the side of the mound and reach through the straw to take as many potatoes as were needed. Potatoes holed up this way kept sound and good most of the winter. . . . Dad holed up cabbage the same way when we had a good crop, and sometimes apples, too, although they did not keep as well as cabbage or potatoes.

[DARE (at *hole* v[1] 1) especially southern Appalachians]

Holiness *adjective* Pertaining to a religious group, often affiliated and meeting in small congregations, that emphasizes sanctification and the exercise of spiritual gifts (i.e. charisma) identified in 1 Corinthians 14; an individual or church following such practices, especially "speaking in tongues." See also **Holy Roller**.

1933 Hooker *Religion in Highlands* 188 A common reason for expulsion is lack of strict denominational loyalty, as in the case of the following entries on a church roll: "For going to Holiness meetings and speaking with tongues." **1960** Schwarz *Ordeal by Serpents* 406 The Holiness people see themselves as "the [true] children of God"; and the great threat of life, bodily death, is transposed into an eternal spiritual existence. **1973** Kahn *Hillbilly Women* 141 They was holiness people and they prayed for her and anointed her head with oil and laid hands on her. **1974** Murray *Down to Earth* 58 I call myself a Holiness, but it's having the spirit of Christ that will save you. **1976** Daugherty *Serpent-Handling* 238 Holiness church members live by a very strict personal code of morality. A large sign in the church at Jolo, W.Va., indicates that dresses must be worn below the knees, arms must be covered, no lipstick or jewelry is to be worn. No smoking, drinking, or other worldly pleasures are to be indulged in by "true believers." **1985** Kiser *Life and Times* 64 There was a church just across the river called Church of God, or many said Holiness Church. **1988** Brown *Beech Creek* 209 Holiness people does what the Bible tells 'em to do. **1995** McCauley *Mt Religion* 57 Holiness is the universal generic term for the presence of Holiness-Pentecostal movements in the mountains through independent nondenominational churches. The Holiness-Pentecostal movements in the mountains are represented only secondarily, but with a significant presence, by denominational identity, and national institutionalism defines them, rather than being defined primarily by their spiritual character or religious ethos like mountain religion's independent nondenominational churches. The Holiness and Pentecostal movements both have numerous denominations, church traditions, and submovements, as well as thousands of loosely affiliated or unaffiliated churches.

[DARE *holiness* adj, n chiefly South, Midland, Central]

holler[1] See **hollow A.**

holler[2]

A *verb*

1 Of a domestic or wild animal (as a mammal, bird, insect, etc.): to make its characteristic cry or scream.

1898 Elliott *Durket Sperret* 164 Granny couldn't sleep last night kase an owl come thar and hollered all night long. **1937** Haun *Cocke Co* 5 A dove sitting on top of the house hollering means that one member of the family will die within a year. **1939** Hall *Coll* (Proctor NC) About that time, just in a breath or two, why that feist went to hollerin' just like he was a-dyin'. *Ibid.* (Hartford TN) Me and a party were on Big Creek a-fishin', layin' out, campin' out in the woods, and we heard something a-hollerin'. . . . All of the men said that it was a panther a-hollerin'. *Ibid.* (Sugarlands TN) I knocked [the bear] in the head ever so many licks before I could get it to lay over and hush hollerin'. **1940** Haun *Hawk's Done* 7 It was just this morning I heard a screech owl hollering—in the daytime—giving warning that a death is nigh. **1941** Stuart *Men of Mts* 257 Whippor-wills hollered so lonely that they must have been in love with somebody they couldn't get. **1959** Hall *Coll* (Murphy NC) She heard her mother say that the panthers would sit on the comb of the house and holler. **1960** McCaulley *Cades Cove* We got to wanting to go to hunt wild game, you know, want to go to the mountain and camp out and hear the katydids holler right close up there. **1964** Roberts *Hell-Fer-Sartin* 45 Meanwhile, back home they's a little bird coming every evening to where her mother sewed, and it hollered. **1967** *DARE Survey* (Maryville TN) Frost will begin ninety days after [the katydids] begin to holler. **1973** Miller *Pigeon's Roost* (Sept 20) I only heard one hawk hollering during the 40 days of dog days time. **1976** *Bear Hunting* 277 You can hear the bear growling and popping his teeth and the dogs hollering. **1985** Irwin *Alex Stewart* 235 It's about time for katydids. They commence hollering about the time the sun goes down and they holler all night. **1995** Weber *Rugged Hills* 37 The two guinea hens that Smithy gave us hollered all day yesterday. Mama always told us that the weather was going to change when the guineas began to chant "pat-e-rack, pat-e-rack." **2007** Farr *My Appalachia* 69 Usually jarflies start their hollering around the summer, around the last days of June. It was a signal that plowing and hoeing of corn could be laid by. "There used to be lot more of them," Granny Brock said. "They hollered so loud people couldn't hear the cowbells."

[cf EDD *hollo* v 1 "of animals: to make a loud noise, to neigh, low, bark, &c"; DARE *holler* v B1 chiefly South, South Midland]

2 (also *holler hello, holler the house*) To call loudly upon approaching a house, as to apprise occupants of one's presence and ascertain if anyone is home; to call to (someone). Also called **hallo**.

c1950 Adams *Grandpap* 74 One evenin' they heard somebody a-hollerin' at the gate. **1967** Williams *Subtlety Mt Speech* 14 He walked up to the gate and hollered, "Hello!" **1979** Melton *'Pon My Honor* 96 When the Preacher hollered the house, the man come to the door and told him to get down and come on in. **1988** Russell and Barnett *Ghost Stories* 88–89 As a matter of both courtesy and self-protection, mountain settlers in western North Carolina developed the custom of hollering hello. A would-be visitor stood at the edge of a cabin's clearing and, putting both hands to his mouth, yelled to ask if anyone was home. Someone would step out onto the porch, and the visitor, if he was known, would be invited to approach. If there was no reply, the visitor simply made his call another day. In good weather, mountain residents were usually out working somewhere among the forested glens—tending cattle, feeding geese, keeping bees—so a visitor's holler was as likely to be answered from beyond the nearby trees as from the cabin itself. Approaching a home without announcing your presence was taken as an attempt to rob the cabin. **1999** Morgan *Gap Creek* 260 Hank and me was eating dinner on Saturday when we heard somebody holler from the road. **2004** Adams *Old True Love* 274 Late that summer Aunt Susan hollered me from the house and she had a grin on her face as big as a mile.

3 To yell loudly from a distance, as a form of communication.

1972 Alderman *Big Bald* 64 Neighbor's contact with neighbor across the valley was by hollerin'. This kind of communication was necessary and is centuries older than present civilization. . . . During early days a cove dweller would troll a message to a neighbor across the valley that all was well and there was peace in the valley. When help was needed, three quick whoops would bring assistance on the run. . . . Each holler had its own special meaning. Family calls would bring the young'uns home for food or chores. Certain calls warned of danger. Special shouts warned the blockader that strangers were in the hills. **1977** McClelland *Wilson Douglas* 16 Nowadays there's too much noise in the air—you can't holler and make anybody hear you. But once I could holler and you could hear me clear to that valley there. . . . And if our clocks stopped, well, we'd holler down here to these Ashleys [who] lived down here, holler down to see what time it was, to reset our clock, see. **1983** *Dark Corner OHP-27A* They could holler . . . louder than a gunshot. It was like they was calling a cow and all that, calling "Oooo."

4 See citation.

1968 *DARE Survey* (Logan WV) *hollered out loud*; (Milton WV) *hollered and laughed*; (Spencer WV) *hollered and laughed* = to suddenly break out laughing.

[DARE *holler* v B5 scattered, but chiefly South, South Midland]

B *noun*

1 See citation. See also **whoop and a holler**.

1937 (in **2002** Powell *Writing Geography* 87) When I was talking to LeRoy Nicholson about how near his nearest neighbor was, he said it was a couple of hollers away. I thought he meant it was two hollows in the mountains, two valleys away, but he meant that it was twice as far as you could holler or yell. Now that is a carry-over of what you read in Elizabethan language, "it's a far cry." You live a far cry from someone. That's as far as the human voice can carry. That had been altered in their expression, "it's a far holler."

2 A person's identifying yell; see citation.

1975 Gainer *Speech Mtneer* 11 *Holler* also means a combination of tones set to words or nonsense syllables, which a young man uses to identify himself, especially when he is approaching the home of his girl after dark. "There comes Jim, I know him by his holler."

holler hello *See* **holler**[2] **A2**.

holler horn *See* **hollow head**.

hollering school *noun* Same as **shouting school**. See also **blab school**.

1910 Cooke *Power and Glory* 16 Johnnie would have her time for every term of the "old field hollerin' school," where she learned to read and write.

holler out (also *holler up*) *verb phrase* To roust (someone), as from a house or bed, by calling out.

1955 Ritchie *Singing Family* 59 They all give their solemn promise not to do ary thing mean to us, and she stepped out on the porch and hollered us out. *Ibid.* 152 Edna and Kitty seemed like the ones who always saw that everybody got up and out for the caroling those cold mornings, so about three o'clock they hollered us all up. **1983** McDermitt *Boy Named Jack* 11 Directly it come daylight, an they hollered him up, an give him a little eatin. *Ibid.* 20 Next morning he hollered him out of bed. **2001** Montgomery *Coll* Holler me up before seven (Cardwell).

holler tail *See* **hollow tail**.

holler the house See **holler**[2] **A2**.

holler up See **holler out.**

hollow

A Variant form *holler* [see **1963**, **1984**, **2010**, etc. in **B1**].

[DARE *hollow* n, adj (pronc) chiefly South, South Midland, southern Appalachians, Ozarks]

B *noun*

1 A small, sheltered valley that usually but not necessarily has a watercourse; a community centered in such a valley; also used in place-names, especially informal ones, as in *Hell's Holler* (NC) and *Piedy Holler* (TN).

1736 (in **1940** McJimsey *Topo Terms in VA* 274) [T]o two Poplars and a Chesnut in the hollow of a Mountain. **1799** (in **2008** Ellison *High Vistas* 38) We turned back and camped at a very bad place, it being a steep Laurelly hollow. **1820** *Paw Paw Hollow Church Minutes* 39 The church met and after worship . . . Recived B[rothe]r Levi for Pasture and appoint him to write to the Arm of Dumplin at the Walnut hollow to ordain B[rother] Lockhart that he may be of service to us. **c1832** (in **2007** Dunkerly *Kings Mt* 85) We retreated across a little hollow and loaded[,] then advanced on them. **1861** (in **1980** Clark *Civil War Diary* 16) On the 10th we made our way across the rugged hills an hollows in the night. **1863** *Hundley CW Letters* (Oct 11) We have moved up hear in the mountains where there is nothing But hills & hollows though I think it is A very good nieghbor Hood. **1915** Hall *Autobiog Claib Jones* 8 I went up the hollow where I had left my gun, picked her up from against the tree, took my dog and went to the woods for my sport. **1939** Hall *Coll* (Saunook NC) He run me over a ridge and down the holler and over a ridge and down another holler to the river. **1943** Peattie *Indian Days* 41 A valley usually means a big valley; a small one is a hollow or a cove. **1956** Fink *That's Why* 3 Our hollow is very nearly the counterpart of the small canyon or arroyo of the West. **1957** *GSMNP-23:1:5* [I] carried the lumber on my back right up that hollow there. **1963** Hooper *Unwanted Boy* 217 They had grown up there in that holler, or on the foot of the mountain, and when he sold that place, he sold a lot more than real estate. **1973** *GSMNP-76:4* They was a big hollow run down here. They call it the Groundhog Hollow, and he went up it little piece and got down on Little Dry Ridge here. **1984** Head *Brogans* 31 Usually called "holler" by the local residents, a hollow has been and still is the home for thousands of people. The residents of a particular hollow develop a feeling of belonging and will defend each other if necessary. If a strange car enters the hollow, the local grapevine soon spreads the word, especially if the car sports out-of-state tags! **1989** *Matewan OHP-9* They went and got the three McCoys out and brought them around to this little holler. **1997** *Dante OHP-14* There used to be a sawmill around there in the hollow, I believe. **2010** Fugate *Found Me* 150 = a neighborhood or community. **2010** Jabbour and Jabbour *Decoration Day* 89 The rural coves comprise a different system, even if the residents relied on the larger towns as commercial centers. The word "cove" describes those narrower creek valleys that in other parts of the Appalachians, and often in western North Carolina, are called "hollows," or "hollers." Coves may contain arable bottomland, but usually less than in the larger river valleys. The coves are well suited for small subsistence farming augmented by modest cash crops, but less suitable for larger-scale commercial farming. The network of branches and creeks favors, or even dictates, a pattern of dispersed rural settlement. People of the coves did not cluster in tight villages; they spread out into small patches of arable land surrounded by woods. There they could combine subsistence gardening and farming with hunting and gathering from the surrounding woods and streams. That is the pattern of life that emerged in the nineteenth century.

2 A small stream that runs into such a valley; a branch of a larger watercourse.

1929 (in **1995** Williams *Become Teacher* 49) We planned our trip along the ridge between the school house branch, called locally Lear Hollow, and the next branch, called Wolf Hollow. **1982** Slone *How We Talked* 29 holler = hollow; the space between two hills. Also, could mean the small stream. **1995** Montgomery *Coll* (known to Cardwell).

[DARE *hollow* n B1a southern Appalachians, Ozarks]

3 The abdominal cavity.

1863 *Penland CW Letters* (March 2) I do not know if it [= a bullet] went to his hollow or not. **1895** Edson and Fairchild *TN Mts* 372 I 'low it struck the holler. **1913** Kephart *Our Sthn High* 107 He bit a hole under the foreleg, through hide and ha'r, clar to the holler, so t' you can stick your hand in and seize the bear's heart. **1939** Hall *Coll* (Hartford TN) [The bear] had the dogs down, and he run up and stobbed his knife into it, and cut a big long gash, plumb to the hollow of the bear. **1957** Combs *Lg Sthn High: Word List* 51 = the inside, or abdominal cavity. Ex: "That ferriner got hisself stobbed (stabbed) clean to the holler." **1968** *Faith Healing* 65 He had t'have a patch on his back 'cause he'uz burnt through t'th'holler. **1994** Montgomery *Coll* (known to Cardwell).

[DARE *hollow* n B4 southern Appalachians]

hollow head (also *holler horn, hollow horn*) *noun* A debilitating vitamin disease of cattle once mistakenly attributed to hollowness of the animal's horn. See also **hollow tail.**

1919 Combs *Word-List South* 34 *hollow-horn* = a mythical disease in cattle, which is supposed to make their horns hollow. A hole is bored in the horn with a gimlet. This custom gave rise to the epithet applied to people who have acted foolishly: "He ought to be bored for the hollow horn." **1945** Vincent *Here in TN* 40 "In that case," said Doctor Jim Thomas, "I can't do nothin' for her. All I know is holler horns, and worms in their tails. Your cow will die sure as heck." **1957** Combs *Lg Sthn High: Word List* 51 *holler-horn* = dullness, stupidity. Applied to any one who has committed an act of foolishness, as in: "That feller ought to be bored for the holler-horn." The figure derives from a mythical(?) disease of the same name, in cattle; the horns of a cow thus afflicted are bored into with a gimlet. **1968** Wilson *Folklore Mammoth Cave* 20 *hollow horn* = a condition in cattle caused by food deficiencies. The older remedy was to bore a hole into the horn or split the lower end of the tail and rub in salt and pepper. Modern cattle-raisers feed them plenty of vitamins and have not known any cases of this disease in years. **1973** *GSMNP-76:33* You put [turpentine] in a spoon, put it in cow's navel . . . Now, I've seen that done a cow or steer if they got the hollow head. **1975** Purkey *Madison Co* 72 If any of Miss Emmie's cattle got sick, she insisted that they had "Holler-horn." **1993** Weaver *Scotch-Irish Speech* 14 Cows that unexpectedly stopped milking were thought to have "hollow-tail" (Irish "worm in the tail"), "hollow-horn," or both, and were treated with turpentine or salt.

[DARE *hollow tail* chiefly South, South Midland]

hollow horn See **hollow head.**

hollowing tree *noun* A venue for selling **moonshine**. See also **blind tiger.**

1972 Carr *Oldest Profession* 59–60 Every hill and hollow in moonshining country had an outlet. The "hollowing tree" was always a well known spot. This retail outlet worked by a sign on a certain tree, saying, "Leave $2.00 and come back in 15 minutes." In fifteen minutes the two dollars would be gone, and the jug would be filled, with neither party speaking to the other.

hollow tail *noun* A debilitating vitamin disease of cattle once mistakenly attributed to hollowness of the animal's tail. See also **hollow head.**

1919 Combs *Word-List South* 34 *hollow-horn* = a mythical disease in cattle, which is supposed to make their horns hollow. A hole is bored in the horn with a gimlet. This custom gave rise to the epithet applied to people who have acted foolishly: "He ought to be bored for the hollow horn." **c1960** Wilson *Coll*: *hollow tail* = a disease of cattle, really a vitamin deficiency. Doctored, formerly, by splitting the end of the tail and rubbing [with] salt and pepper. **1968** Wilson *Folklore Mammoth Cave* 20 *hollow tail* = a condition in cattle caused by food deficiencies. The older remedy was to bore a hole into the horn or split the lower end of the tail and rub in salt and pepper. Modern cattle-raisers feed them plenty of vitamins and have not known any cases of this disease in years. **1972** Cooper *NC Mt Folklore* 26 Boys held the family cows while their fathers used a gimlet to bore for hollow horn or to make incisions for hollow tail. **1977** Brookman *Veterinary Diseases* 144 Hollow tail is a disease reported by some informants to be quite common in cattle, caused by a worm in the tail. It is treated by making a slit in the tail where the worm appears to be (shown by the tail being limp in that spot) and packing the opening with salt or salt and pepper or turpentine and wrapping it with a cloth. However, some informants and modern medical authority consider hollow tail to have no basis in fact. Some feel that it stems from undernourished or poorly nourished animals who seem unhealthy, and the old-time farmer, not knowing the cause, felt the animal must be treated for something, so he blamed it on "hollow tail." Those who believe in hollow tail defend it stoutly against non-believers. . . . Hollow tail is a very common fictional folk disease, with a great many believers. **2007** Myers *Smoky Mt Remedies* 128–29 When one of our cows ceased to chew her cud, it was called both "holler" horn or "holler" tail (hollow). A number of remedies were used. Dad held turpentine to their navel as a remedy. Others wrapped their horn in a flannel cloth soaked in turpentine for a few days. Some split their tails and inserted mixtures of things like salt, pepper, soot, and/or turpentine. Some bored holes in the horn and poured saltwater in the hole. **2012** Milnes *Signs Cures Witchery* Old man George Meadors had a cow down there that got sick, and they split her tail and put salt and pepper in it and that didn't pep her up. They called it the hollow tail that they had. Their tail would just hang limp like hanging a mop across the clothesline, and the only time there'd be any movement there would be when the wind would blow it along or something like that.

[DARE *hollow tail* chiefly South, South Midland]

holp, holped, holpen, holpt See **help.**

holt See **hold A.**

holy bean *noun* See citation.

2016 *Blind Pig* (Aug 2) [The beans] are far easier to get out of the hulls if they have been out in the sun (ideally on a tin roof or concrete) for several hours. This dries the hulls and makes them brittle. Then the step to make them "holy beans" . . . (you beat the hell out of them) works even better.

holy board *noun* See citation.

c1975 *Miners' Jargon* 4 = a board used in combination with a roof bolt to support the roof strata [in a coal mine].

Holy Roller *noun* A member of a **Holiness** (i.e. Pentecostal or charismatic) religious group that recognizes and exercises the spiritual gifts identified in 1 Corinthians 14, especially a person who engages in demonstrative exertions such as shouting or leaping during religious worship. The term is used mainly, if not exclusively, by nonmembers. Also called **bench walker**. See also **Holiness.**

1933 Hooker *Religion in Highlands* 192 Laymen and preachers alike were greatly exercised over the members lost from the churches to Holiness groups, the decline in interest in average services . . . and the general dearth of religious sentiment, which episodes of perfectionist excitement often leave behind. What to do about these so-called "Holy Roller" phenomena is one of the great unsettled questions of the churches and their preachers. **1963** Hooper *Unwanted Boy* 223 He very frankly answered, "I am loading up to argue with the damned Holy Rollers." *Ibid.* 228 Sal "jined" the "Holy Rollers" Sunday. **1971** *AOHP/ALC-137* He's a awful Holiness man. He was one of them Holy Rollers, and he give [the moonshiner] away to the law. **1976** Garber *Mountain-ese* 42 Mabel left the Baptists and jined up with the Holy-rollers. **1989** Giardina *Storming Heaven* 129 The only church on Grapevine or Scary when I was a child had been the Holiness church at the mouth of Bearwallow. Daddy didn't care for the Holy Rollers and all their noise. He wanted a church where he could sit quiet, but there had been no preachers raised up for that sort of thing in our vicinity. **1989** *Matewan OHP-28* They would mock and call us Holy Rollers before we built the front on our church over there. **1996–98** Montgomery *Coll* = only charismatics (Bush); She moved to Knoxville and joined a Holy Roller church (Cardwell), = Free Will Baptist, but also various charismatic or pentecostal sects (Ellis), = applies only to Pentecostals (Jones), = Church of God members who rolled on the floor and shouted when overcome, esp. women who would leap from bench to bench when overcome, also known as bench walkers (Oliver), = applies only to charismatics (Weaver). **2009** Callahan *Work and Faith* 130 Such spectacular physical behavior was frowned on by those in more emotionally constrained—both denominational and of mountain origin—and it earned Holiness believers the demeaning title of "Holy Rollers."

holy tone (also *holy whine*) *noun* A singsong, chant-like cadence used in spontaneous preaching, in which typically each phrase is punctuated by "ah!" See also **ah**, **huh**, **uh**.

1881 Pierson *In the Brush* 252 He had stentorian lungs, was wonderfully voluble, and his sing-song "holy tone" was most delightful to his audience. **1901** McClintock *KY Mts* 21 Good wind is certainly a necessary qualification for a successful mountain preacher, for he is expected to preach as long as the "speerit" lasts—generally hours. He throws in a little aspirate like er and ah, when he warms up, which produces the "holy tone." An old minister one day was exhorting his brethren to repentance. "Oh, brethren," said he, "repent ye, and repent ye of your sins, er; for if you don't, er, the Lord, er, he will grab yer by the seat of yer pants, er, and hold yer over hell fire." **1942** Posey *Frontier Baptist* 7 Often the preachers spoke with a twang called the "holy whine." ... This tone had much influence upon the emotions of the congregation, and it was often imitated for effectiveness.

homebrew *noun* Homemade whiskey.

1978 Hiser *Quare Do's* 145 Hit's done like that air homebrew we uset to make back yander; hit's done swole up and done busted. **1982** Maples *Memories* 72 As she got closer, she could see a barrel of what they call "homebrew." **1982** Slone *How We Talked* 69 = a kind of intoxicating drink made by using red malt.

homecoming (also *homecoming days*) *noun* An annual reunion of members of an extended family, former members of a church (whether or not the congregation still meets) who may have moved away, or descendants of a former church who gather for a reunion, including a special worship service, an outdoor meal (**dinner on the ground(s)**), often special singing, and a cleaning and decoration of cemetery graves (**decoration**, usually undertaken by a work crew before the main gathering). The term applies especially when participants identify with a community taken under federal jurisdiction, as for the Great Smoky Mountains National Park. In some parts of the TN mountains, but apparently not in NC, the term (but not the event) has been replaced by **memorial day**.

1969 GSMNP-46:25 They had a homecoming over here at Hyatt Chapel. **1973** GSMNP-61:3 I remember preacher Thad Watson and preacher Anthony and several more. I guess I could mention several of them that's been ministers there [= at Oconaluftee Baptist Church], but they was about the oldest ones I can remember. Mister Conner come from Tennessee there after we begin to have the homecoming days, and he was raised over here in this section too. **1987** Dorgan *Glory to God* 158–59 It is not unusual for people to drive hundreds of miles to attend a Southern Appalachian Baptist homecoming. The retired couple who sold their mountain farm and moved to Florida, the family who migrated to the Upper Midwest during World War II when labor was needed in war-related industries, folks who moved to another end of the county, preachers who once served the church, young people who got married in the church and now bring their own children to see "Grandma" and "Grandpa," and former members who moved their membership to follow a preacher or slid up a notch or two in the hierarchy of church affiliations—all of these individuals join with the current membership to celebrate the ongoing history of a particular church. Add to these the numerous visitors from neighboring fellowships, and a church whose regular congregation numbers only around a hundred may find its attendance swelling to three hundred or four hundred on this one day. **1988** Lambert *Kinfolks* 75 Summertime was also the time for the all-day dinner and singing on the grounds we talked about earlier. These "meetings" could take several forms. Perhaps the most usual—which I am happy to report is still alive in many rural churches—was the "homecoming," which was just what the name implies. It was a day set aside for all those folks who had gone off into the city—whether Knoxville or Detroit—to come back and partake of their heritage. There would be preaching, singing, and eating. There would be lots of visiting and gossiping and maybe some more singing and almost surely some more eating. All this could very easily last all day. **2005** Morgan *Old Time Religion* 105 Homecoming, a Sunday every summer that each church in the Nantahala community set aside to welcome all of their members who had moved away, as well as the local population, to spend the day meeting old friends and relatives was very much a part of old time mountain religion. The homecoming church provided all of the food, by longstanding tradition. People from outside the community were not expected to bring food, and they didn't. This function was not only important for provision of sustenance; it was an unspoken social affectation as well. For a church/community not to have provided enough food would have been anathema for their reputation! There was not any dearth of singers at these functions. People drove for miles to sing in quartets, trios, duets, and solos. Old folks shouted sometimes as often in these singings as in revival meetings!

home doctoring *noun* Medical treatment using herbal and other traditional practices.

1972 *AOHP/LJC-259* She always believed in your home doctoring. People had to. That was their only way.

home folks *noun* One's relatives, especially one's immediate family.

1863 *Dalton CW Letters* (June 10) my Deseas is not fit to Mension but as hit is Home folks hit makes now differns i have got the Dyrear verry bad. **1962** Dykeman *Tall Woman* 167 [It] peartens a feller up to see home folks. **1976** Garber *Mountain-ese* 42 = relatives. "John makes hisself ter home, just like he wuz homefolks."

[cf SND *hame-folk* (at *hame* III 9) "family, relatives"; DARE *home folks* n pl chiefly South, South Midland]

home guard *noun* A special military unit or a militia of local citizens detached during the Civil War (either the Confederacy or the Union, depending on local circumstances) and to protect local citizens against **bushwhackers** aligned with either side and patrol against Confederate draft evaders and deserters returning to the area.

1862 *Hynds CW Letters* (May 27) We have been. it seems to me, in every nook and corner in these mountains hunting up those interesting aids to Old Abes army styled "Home Guards" These pious and patriotic soldiers are composed of ignorant mountaineers who are too lazy to run and consequently unfit to serve Old Abe in the regular army but from their Knowledge of the mountains they are able to skulk about and murder our pickets and destroy the property of innocent persons under the coover of the Stars and Stripes. **1863** (in **1983** *CW Harlan Co* 19) On the same day a party of 40 men, 25 from Capt Powell's & 15 from Capt Morgan's companies, were detailed to go to the Salt well at mouth of Leatherwood Creek in Perry County Ky, to form a junction with some home guards who had stated that they wished to join our company. **1863** *Epperly CW Letters* (Aug 9) the home gards went to take [the deserters] up last tuesday and the deserters whiped them and taken six of them prisners and all thar guns. **1863** *Tesh CW Letters* (Dec 25) I want You to write when You think the Home Guard will have to go in camp a gain and if their is anny talk of takeing them out. **1864** *Copeland CW Letters* (March 27) I want you to rite to me what the inroleing officr have done with the home Gards as nus is Scare. **1864** *Epperly CW Letters* (March 5) I Beleave it will be mor credit for him to go in the Brush than to joine The suthern armey or home guardes. **1899** Temple *E TN Civil War* 186–87 Many [East Tennesseans who opposed secession] began to arm themselves as best they could. In some counties, notably in Roane and Blount, companies of "home guards" were organized and drilled. In Knox it was hard to restrain the infuriated Union men from acts of violence against the disunionists. More than once the leaders had to restrain them from marching into Knoxville in a body, and as they called it, "clearing out the secessionists in the town." *Ibid.* 210 [An act of the Tennessee state legislature] provided for raising by the county courts of the state "a home guard of minute men, consisting of companies of not less than ten for each civil district, whose duty it should be to 'procure a warrant from some justice of the peace, and arrest all suspected persons, and bring them before the civil authorities for trial, to prevent the assemblage of slaves in unusual numbers.'" **1904** Fox *Christmas Eve* 12 In the Kentucky mountains, there were more slaveholders than elsewhere in the mountains in the South. These, naturally, fought for their slaves, and the division thus made the war personal and terrible between the slaveholders who dared to stay at home, and the Union, "Home Guards" who organized to drive them away. **1939** Hall *Coll* (Bradley Fork NC) [I] lived right in this place when the [Civil] war started. Colonel Bill Thomas wanted me to stay here and sot my age back two years. I was here into the business of home guard under Joe Collins. [**1971** *AOHP/ALC-32* They ain't nothing I can tell you about them, only they'd just go, they'd just go about killing people and beating people up.... They's just like the Ku Klux was. If somebody'd do something that they didn't want them to do, why they'd kill them.] **1971** Lee *My Appalachia* 58–59 The McCoys, and their mountain neighbors, were pro-Union; and to protect their region against invasion by "Virginia Rebels," they organized a military company called the "Home Guards," There were occasional border clashes between the two forces, with casualties on both sides. The war ended only seventeen years before the feud began, and the bitterness still existed in the minds of the older generation. **1977** Shields *Cades Cove* 62 There were a few skirmishes between wandering Confederate units . . . and the Home Guard of Cades Cove and Tuckaleechee. Home Guard families placed their children at strategic spots . . . if strangers passed they would blow a hunting horn which could be heard throughout the cove. **2005** Fisher *CW in Smokies* 48 Many more Unionists [in E TN] who were not yet ready to leave home gathered into Home Guard units, militia-like companies that could mobilize quickly to confront Confederate troops and East Tennessee secessionists . . . in Blount County Unionists began drilling in early April [1861]. In Sevier County loyalists formed a mounted company the same day the referendum [for secession] was held, and formally organized their Home Guard in August. **2007** Ballard and Weinstein *Neighbor* 73 In the early years of the war the conscript law was not strictly enforced, but as the Confederate forces became depleted those who had been slackers, or "scouts" as they were called among themselves, were hunted down, relentlessly by the conscript officers and the Home Guard . . . In moving through Wilkes County in 1864, Union prison escapee William Burson was struck by how many of the Confederate home guard in the county were actually Unionist in sentiment. He asked one guard why he served in this capacity when it was against his principles; he replied that "it was merely to keep out of the army." Home guard duty was sometimes forced upon men suspected of Unionist sentiments and they later claimed to have taken advantage of that militia service by engaging in subversive activity or supporting fellow Unionists in their communities. Given regular troops' reluctance to confront this kind of opposition and their ineffectiveness when they did so, putting down guerilla activity often fell to home guard units. In June 1863 Governor Vance had authorized the establishment of such units in response to pleas from mountain residents for military protection. In all counties west of the Blue Ridge, men not subject to conscription were instructed to form companies that would serve only within their own counties. They would serve without pay but would be provided arms and ammunition by the state. Their purpose, according to Vance, would be "to repel invasion, break up and arrest gangs of deserters, preserve order and enforce the laws." All western counties quickly established home guard companies under these terms, but they remained relatively ineffective in achieving the aims Vance laid out. Much of their ineptness was due to a lack of will in their pursuit of their targets. By this point in the war, those available to fill home guard ranks were men who had to be forced into this localized military duty; thus, many found they had little stomach for waging war on their kinsmen or neighbors.

homeland *noun* The area where one grew up, one's native territory. See also **down home**.

1973 GSMNP-79:7 I guess if they got to set down and making a list out, they'd have one as long as your arm of all the good things and the nice things that they miss since they've left their mountain homelands. *Ibid.* 8 They wanted to be buried as close to their old homeland as they could when they passed away, so the children took them back, up on Roaring Fork. So that's their resting place. **1978** White *Champ Ferguson* 66 Some of these soldiers [from Pickett/Fentress County TN] would never again see their homeland, while others would return from war only to continue violent feuding with neighbors, family, and former friends. **1985** Gifford (in **1985** Williams *Better Man* 3) Perhaps more than any other American cultural group, Appalachian people have a great love for their family and their homeland. **1987** Obermiller *Labeling* 44 A most important ethnic signal for Appalachians is that of the homeland, the region back in the mountains where one still has family ties and returns for ceremonies, holidays, and vacations. **1995** Higgs et al. *Inside Out* 682 Appalachian literature conveys a strong sense of place. Appalachian writers and the characters they create frequently identify strongly with the mountain region as their homeland. **2000** Eller *Lost and Found* 129 Why had my father and his father before him had to leave their homeland in order to make a living for their families? **2000** Spencer *Memory Lane* III:7 She, too, loved the beauty of our homeland, and did much work in the yard. **2014** *Blind Pig* (Jan 15) To me my homeland is pretty much southern Appalachia but especially the Tails Creek area of Gilmer County Georgia. That is where my ancestors settled when coming from the Carolinas. They are all buried there and the old home place still stands. When I go there I am at peace and connected. **2014** House *Talking About* [A writer] in *The New York Times* . . . referred to Appalachia and the Deep South as "the smudge of the country." Well, I am that smudge. My people are that smudge. My homeland is that smudge. And we are much, much more than that. **2015** Jones *In Memoriam* 9 [Jean Ritchie] used her art and knowledge against the persistent problems and environmental degradation of her homeland.

homely *adjective* Reminiscent of home, staying at home.

1901 Harben *Westerfelt* 73 The veranda of the hotel was crowded with loungers, homely men in jeans, slouched hats, and coarse brogans. **1931** Hannum *Thursday April* 46 The sweet smell of the burning wood was homely, and she relaxed a little. **1967** Wilson *Folkways Mammoth Cave* 23 = stay-at-home rather than ugly.

[DARE *homely* adj B1 especially South Midland]

homemade cheese *noun* Cottage cheese.

1949 Kurath *Word Geog East US* 71 *Home-made cheese* . . . has considerable currency in western North Carolina and parts of the Appalachians. **1996–97** Montgomery *Coll* (known to Brown, Bush, Jones).

[DARE *homemade cheese* n especially South Midland]

homemade preacher *noun* A self-trained preacher lacking formal preparation.

1973 GSMNP-13:29 The old man Daniel Cook was a preacher, I mean just homemade preacher, yes.

homeplace *noun* The site of a residence established by an ancestor on which family descendants live or have lived for one or more generations. The term may include outbuildings and land, but most often it applies to the dwelling (or its remains) and its immediate surroundings. The term often suggests an extended family's psychological attachment to the place. See 1991 and 2006 citations. See also **house place**, **place**.

1931 Owens *Speech Cumberlands* 93 = the part of a farm on which the house and out-buildings are located: "Everybody expected Mattie's mother to leave her the home-place." **1961** *Coe Ridge OHP*-333A She left our old homeplace and went to Columbia. **1973** GSMNP-78:5 We're standing now in the old homeplace, where we moved to when we moved from Gatlinburg to the Spruce Flats, and we still see the sign of the foundation of the old home. **1973** GSMNP-78:10 We can see the image of the old homeplace enough till we recognize [it], although I could recognize it from the rocks and the other shrubbery around, but a lot of the people that don't have any idea as to where the homeplace was couldn't probably recognize the rocks and the other shrubbery. **1976** Carroll and Pulley *Little Cataloochee* 17 Although a number of the children eventually left the homeplace, the Hannahs played a vital role in the development of the Little Cataloochee community down to the establishment of the Great Smoky Mountains National Park. **1979** Slone *My Heart* 119 By the time I was about six years old, my father got a job making chairs for Mrs. Lloyd. About this time he "divided his land" and gave it to his children. My brother, Vince, got the "old home place." **1980** GSMNP-115 Uncle Calvin lived at the Huff place a little bit below there. **1985** Reagan *Sugarlands* xvi After 1930 they was forced to leave their home places for the Park and find other places to live. **1991** Williams *Homeplace* 117–18 In order to understand the meaning of old houses, one must first understand the use of the term "homeplace." In southwestern North Carolina, homeplace generally does not refer to the family's property. It is not the whole spread of land, Arvel Greene explained, just "the immediate area where the old house was, where they all lived and was brought up, they just called that the old homeplace." Although "homeplace" may include the area surrounding the house, it is seldom used as equivalent to "house and yard." The meaning is not a simple geographic designation. "Homeplace" under certain circumstances, however, may refer to the site of the house. Individuals may visit the "old homeplace" although the structure itself is gone. **1997** Miller *Brier Poems* 70 We've moved to the cities, moved to town and left our spirits in the mountains to live like half-wild dogs around the homeplace. **2000** *Smokies Guide* (Spring) 13 Their "homeplaces" often included several buildings: a smokehouse for meat, a springhouse to keep perishables cool, and a corncrib to store feed for livestock. **2004** Fisher *Kettle Bottom* 29 We buried our people up on top of Stepp Mountain, highest spot on the home place. **2006** *Encycl Appalachia* 219 Appalachians typically use and understand the term *homeplace* to mean the piece of property where an individual grew up or spent the most significant portion of his or her childhood. The term may also refer to the ancestral home of a particular family. In either case it is understood to mean the entire parcel of land and all its features, both natural and man-made, and not solely or even primarily the house in which the family lived. **2013** Dodson *Mt-Keeper* 6 He clung to 54 acres of land that had been in his family for over 200 years [and] spent the last three decades of his life resisting the advance of the coal industry that absolutely devastated the mountains all around his home place.

[DARE *homeplace* n 1 especially South, South Midland]

homeseat *noun* A site suitable for building a house.

1941 Still *Proud Walkers* 112 A fair homeseat we'll have once the crop's planted, and they's a spare minute. **1941** Still *Troublesome Creek* 114 Dark crept into Mayho by three roads, coming to sit among the sixteen homeseats crowding the creek or hanging off the hillsides.

hominy pounder *noun* Formerly, a primitive water-driven mill for grinding corn. See also **hand mill**, **lazy Jim**, **pounding mill**, **quern**, **slow John**, **tri-weekly**.

1948 Dick *Dixie Frontier* 249–50 When there was opportunity these sweep mortars were run by water power. It was so arranged that when a receptacle ran full of water, the sweep lifted the pestle. This poured the water out, allowing the pestle to fall down upon the corn. Then the receptacle began to fill and the process was repeated. It was called a hominy-pounder or "slow john."

hominy snow *noun* See citations.

c1910 (in **2014** Miles and Cox *I Had Wings* 26) A "little skift o' hominy snow" fell, and was blown into crevices and hollows. **c1960** Wilson *Coll* = small pellets of ice, snow or hail. **1976** Thompson *Touching Home* 14 = a granular snow that resembles hominy; when it falls, it is always a light snow: "Oh, it's just a little hominy snow." **1982** Slone *How We Talked* 99 The small, grainy snow was called "homney (hominy) snow." **1992** Brooks *Sthn Stuff* 70 = snow that's in fine grains, like hominy grits.

hone[1] *noun*

1 (also *hone rock*) A whetstone.

1940 Still *River of Earth* 63 Fotch the hone rock, a needle, and a waxed thread. **1986** Pederson et al. *LAGS*: *hone* (Cocke Co TN, Sevier Co TN).

2 See citation.

1973 Miller *English Unicoi Co* 148 = a piece of leather with which one sharpens a razor.

hone[2] *verb* To long, yearn (for), crave.

1867 Harris *Sut Lovingood* 184 He wer jis' a-honin arter that ball-face whisky; he'd a jis' kiss'd hit es sweet, an' es long, es ef hit hed been-a willin gal. **1892** Dromgoole *Dan to Beersheba* 81 I air not honin' ter keep warm on bresh whiskey. **1898** Dromgoole *Cinch* 22 You'd be honin' for the hills again in no time. **1917** Kephart *Word-List* 413 = to desire with craving. "He jes' *hones* atter it." **1937** Thornburgh *Great Smoky Mts* 152 I'd been out with paw and when I seed those bear tracks I honed to go atter that bear. **1939** Hall *Coll* (Saunook NC) She honed all evenin' to come over and set beside me. **1942** (in **1999** Williams *Come to Boone* 104) He had become a widower since I saw him last. Then 72, he was, as they say, "a-whettin' and a-honin' for him another womern." **1974** Fink *Bits Mt Speech* 12 He's *honing* for a mess of hawg meat. **2006** Awiakta *Abiding Appal* 38 With my head held high / I come / in the honing cry of the wind.

[< Old French *hoigner* "to grumble, murmur . . . repine"; OED3 *hone* v[2] 1 "to long, pine for; hanker after" dialect and U.S.; EDD *hone* v[2] 2 "to repine for want of; to long or pine for"; DARE *hone* v 1 chiefly South, South Midland]

hone down *verb phrase* To bear down, apply oneself.

1951 Giles *Harbin's Ridge* 120 Seemed like we all got creepy and jumpy. . . . Papa trying to keep up the work, and Faleecy John honing down trying to do his part.

hone rock See **hone**[1] **1**.

honey *noun* Used as a term of address to a male friend. [Editor's note: The usage of this word as a term of address for a woman is widespread in the US.]

1960 Schwarz *Ordeal by Serpents* 408 When the brethren and sisters arrive, they go among the congregation and onlookers to greet fellow members cordially. At times the saints, who are always male, hug and kiss each other with the greeting, "How are you, honey?" **1967** Fetterman *Stinking Creek* 90 When the boy finally fled, Henry turned and said: "Me and Fred got a hoss trade to make. You welcome to come along, honey." Honey. Don't smile. "Honey" is a word of friendship, like the western cowboy's "podner" or the soldier's "buddy." Big, powerful men, men who haul down logs and can fell a mule with a fist, use the word. Not an effeminate word, it is a term whose origin nobody seems to know. As visit after visit goes by, the word is used more and more. "Come to the hoss trade if you care to, honey." **1978** Reese *Speech NE Tenn* 47 = sometimes used between males. **1998** *Dante OHP-61* I've been in this thing about forty years or a little longer, honey, and I think I can help you.

honey dew *noun* See citation.

1939 Hall *Coll* (Cosby Creek TN) Bees don't do well unless there is honey dew, a dew which just wets the leaves of plants and makes them sticky.

honey dip *noun* See citation.

1991 Haynes *Haywood Home* 42 We made a kind of dip using honey mixed with cream. This honeydip was used on pies and cobblers like people use whipped cream nowadays.

honey drip *noun*

1 A type of sorghum cane.

1955 Parris *Roaming Mts* 160 I've been trying one called red-fox tail and it's might nigh as good as honey-drip.

2 A type of homemade whiskey. See also **sugar drip**.

1995–97 Montgomery *Coll* (known to Brown, Bush).

honey fuggle (also *honey fugle*, *honey snuggle*) *verb phrase* To "sweet talk," flatter insincerely, seek to ingratiate oneself or become cozy with.

1907 Dugger *Balsam Groves* 144 While you fellers honeyfugle with yer gals a little while, I'll look 'round and dig me a scrim-tic-le uv sang. **1914** Harben *New Clarion* 160 Nobody knows as well as I do how to honey-fuggle mountain men and women—especially women. I can just take one sweeping look at a farmer's wife or daughter and tell whether they are looking for hats, dresses, or cloaks, and I always put in a word that stirs their curiosity and makes them crazy to get to my Emporium of utility and fashion. **1957** Neel *Backwoodsman* 22 *honey fuggle* = to persuade by means of flattery. **1976** Dykeman *Additions* When Grandma's dog, named "Boy," or a child came to her for a hand-out, she would say, "Don't come honey-snugglin' me." **1997** Montgomery *Coll*: *honey fuggle* (known to Adams, Bush); *honey snuggle* (known to Brown), = to behave in a sly, flirtatious manner (Bush).

[DARE *honeyfuggle* v 2 perhaps variant of Engl dial *connyfogle* "to hoodwink, entice by flattery" influenced by *honey* n; see also EDD *gallyfuggle* v "to deceive, take in"]

honeymoon house *noun* A cabin serving as a temporary dwelling for a newly married couple, usually located on land of the husband's parents. See also **marriage house**, **weaner**.

1979 *Smokies Heritage* 308 When the oldest son (about eighteen years) decided to get married they built him a smaller log cabin and barn at the back of the Flats about half a mile away. This cabin was called the weaner cabin or Honeymoon house. **1995** Trout *Historic Buildings* 37 In Greenbrier, folks called these second homes honeymoon houses or "weaner" cabins. **2008** Cobb *Vacation Time* 15 The first house we came to on Grandpa's and Grandma's property was what was later dubbed "The Honeymoon House." It had been their first home. It was a two-room house with a kitchen and a bedroom. Later Grandpa and Grandma moved into the house that housed the grist mill. As each of their children married they too moved into the "Honeymoon House" and lived there until they moved into a more permanent home.

honey pond *noun* See citation.

1978 Hall *Yarns and Tales* 18 My father was lookin' for the honey pond in the flitter tree, my mother always said. (That is, looking for an easier way of life than in the hills of North Carolina.)

[cf DARE *honey pond and flitter tree* n chiefly South Midland]

honey pot *noun* A chamber pot.

c1982 Young *Colloquial Appal* 12.

honey snuggle See **honey fuggle**.

honeysuckle *noun* A wild azalea or pinkster bush (especially *Rhododendron periclymenoides*). Same as **wild honeysuckle**.

1937 Eaton *Handicrafts* 48 Mountain azaleas [are] called "honeysuckle" by the natives. **1937** Hall *Coll* (Cades Cove TN). **1964** Reynolds *Born of Mts* 18 The azalea the mountain folk call honeysuckle.

[DARE *honeysuckle* n 3 chiefly South Midland, South]

honey wagon *noun* See citation.

2006 *Encycl Appalachia* 184 Mill villages typically provided workers and their families with four-room houses, a store, a school, churches, organized activities, and dependable (if small) paychecks. While the store was a convenience to families, the company profited by circulating payroll outlays back to itself and by holding power over workers through credit. Paved streets and electric lights came slowly, but not as slowly as sewer systems, which were common in most other municipalities by 1916. Toilets drained into vaults, which had to be emptied by company conveyances known euphemistically as "honey wagons."

honggry, **hongry** See **hungry**.

hooder See **hudder**.

hoodger See **hoosier**.

hoof *noun*

A Variant form *huff*.

1867 Harris *Sut Lovingood* 263 We'd scasely got things fix'd an oursefs hid seperit when we hearn his ole hosses huffs soundin on the hard road. **1939** Hall *Notebooks* 13:23 (White Oak NC) *huff* = everybody around here says this, but the plural is *hooves*.

B Any hooved animal, especially a cow.

1967 Hall *Coll* (Townsend TN) [A: Do you have some cows?]: B: No, I ain't got a hoof.

hoof it *verb phrase* Of a person: to go on foot.

1974 Fink *Bits Mt Speech* 12 = walk. "Them as ain't got horses'll *hoof* it." **1995** Montgomery *Coll* (known to Cardwell).

hoogy, **hoojee**, **hoojer**, **hoojy** See **hoosier**.

hooker See **pinhooker**.

hook neck *noun* A long-stemmed violet used by children in a mock contest. See also **chicken fight**.

1991 Still *Wolfpen Notebooks* 96 The swamp violets growing along creek banks and in other wet places with stems a foot long we called "hook necks." Us young folks, when we were sparking, we'd hook the heads of the violets, and pull. The one whose bloom broke off first would be the first to marry. If they broke at the same time, we'd marry each other.

hooks *noun* See citation.

c1975 Lunsford *It Used to Be* 159 [There is a] natural wiper that's in the eye of the horse, that the horse uses to brush out some foreign matter that might get in the eye. When it comes up it has a kind of hook and they cut out the hook so that the horse will get well of the disease of the "hooks."

hoo owl *noun* A hoot owl.

1962 Wilson *Folkways Mammoth Cave* 10 Big owls of whatever species were *hoot*, or *hoo*, owls. **1996–97** Montgomery *Coll* (known to Adams, Andrews, Brown, Bush, Cardwell).

[echoic; DARE *hoo owl* n South, South Midland]

hoop hide See **whoop and hide.**

hoopie *noun* See citations.

1940 (in **1944** Wentworth *ADD*) (nWV) = a hillbilly. **1977** Maurer *Mt Heritage* 76 The West Virginian living below the Mason-Dixon line is sometimes referred to as "a hoopie," [and] this nick name came from his trade of barrel making. With an abundance of white oak, the most desired wood, barrels were made for home and farm use along with being the most important container for shipping merchandise. **2006** *WV Encycl* 348 "Hoopie" is a derogatory but usually good-natured name given to rural West Virginians (and sometimes Ohioans) who came north to work in the potteries of Chester and Newell, West Virginia, or East Liverpool, Ohio. The term is derived from the belief that many of these migrants or their ancestors had found employment making hoops in the cooper shops that supplied the potteries with barrels for packing chinaware. Today, it may refer to anyone from West Virginia and is used in a similar manner to "hillbilly" or "redneck." As with those names, hoopie is now sometimes appropriated by members of the target group, who refer to themselves as hoopies. "Hoopie" may also mean an area of West Virginia. For example, northern West Virginians may speak of going to "Hoopie," anywhere south of the Northern Panhandle, to visit relatives. The word "hoopie" seems to be largely limited to the upper Ohio Valley and the surrounding region.

hoopie hide See **whoop and hide.**

hoop snake *noun* A snake that purportedly has a poisonous spike on its tail, the capacity to roll itself into a hoop, and a tendency to chase humans; an identification has been proposed to be the blue racer (*Coluber constrictor foxi*) (see 1952 citation). Also called **stinger snake.**

1952 Beck *Herpetol Lore* 145 The problem of the hoop snake is more readily solved and extremely interesting. This creature has been the subject of folk tales and unnatural history since the days of the earliest writers about this continent. The solution of the problem was given by a man, Mr. Bumgarner in West Virginia, who pointed out that the blue racer, which is a reptile with a curiosity, will follow people. Instead of proceeding in normal fashion, it moves like an inch worm, hitching itself up in loops. To the eyes of the startled person glancing backward through his own dust, these loops might well be construed as hoops. Such a snake obviously would be believed to be dangerous. **1955** Washburn *Country Doctor* 77 According to Fonzy's account, when he was quite a small boy he accompanied his father to Andrews' mill, on Puzzle Creek, a few miles from his home. They both walked and were carrying bags of corn to be ground into meal. Along the way they stopped to rest under a large oak tree. Boy-like, Fonzy began to throw stones at a large rock which stood in the field below the road, and by chance a stone struck near where a hoop-snake was sleeping. The snake, being aroused, rose straight upon its tail and looked around; then, seeing the intruders, it took its tail in its mouth and began to roll up the hill toward them. Fortunately, they were on higher ground than the snake and this kept it from gathering speed as it rolled, thus giving Fonzy and his father time to dodge behind the big oak, which they did just as the snake reached them. By this time it was coming real fast and they jumped behind the oak so quickly that the snake rolled right into the trunk with such force that the sharp horn which grew out of the top of its head stuck into the bark and fastened it to the tree. **1968** Wilson *Folklore Mammoth Cave* 20 = a fabulous monster with a spiked tail attached to a poison sack. When irritated, the snake takes its tail into its mouth, forming a hoop, and rolls toward its enemy. It releases the poisonous spike and rarely misses its mark. Even trees in the range of that tail have been struck and killed instantly.

hoopy hide See **whoop and hide.**

hoorah's nest See **hurrah's nest.**

hoo-raw pole *noun* See 1998 citations.

1975 Carter *Gospel Truth* They persuaded a stubborn mule with a hoo-raw pole. **1998** Montgomery *Coll* = a hardwood pole 4′–5′ long applied from the front between the ears of a stubborn mule. When he revives, he will remember the hoo-raw pole forever (Brown), = *hoo raw* was used to describe agitated, violent activity or argument, as in "there was a real hoo-raw at the party last night when some likkered-up boys showed up and started some trouble," If you hit a mule with a pole, you probably got some violent, agitated activity from it, hence the term "hoo-raw pole" (Ledford).

hoosier *noun*

A Variant forms *hoodger* [hudʒɚ] [see **1941** Hall in **B1**], *hooger* [see **c1982** in **B1**], *hoogy* [see **1988** in **B1**], *hoojee* [see **1992** in **B1**], *hoojer* [see **1949** in **B1**], *hoojy* [see **1941** Wentworth in **B1**], *hootchee* [see **1977** in **B1**], *huger* [see **1924** in **B1**].

B Senses.

1 A person native to the hills or the backwoods, especially one considered less well mannered or unusually rustic. [Editor's note: In Joseph Hall's early research in the Smoky Mountains, mountain people often used this term to refer to themselves familiarly or jokingly.] See also **mountain hoosier.**

1843 (in **1974** Harris *High Times* 19) A right verdant Hoosier stepped up to me saying, "Stranger, won't they start afore long?" **1855** *Mitchell Letter* 3 The original hoosiers of these parts (as always happens in such cases) will infallibly retire further west, & people from the more eastern states will press in bringing with them all the improvements & elegancies of life, wherein you know this Yankee nation whips the airth. **1924** Bacheller *Happiest Person* 7 He weren't purty—just a big mount'in huger. But my! I did love him. **1934–47** *LAMSAS Appal* (Swain Co NC). **1938** Hall *Coll* (Emerts Cove TN) People don't like to be called hoosiers now. **1941** Hall *Coll* (Gatlinburg TN) Hoodgers, people speak of goddam hoodgers . . . a feller who don't know nothin' except what they've learned in the mountains. In town they speak of "country hoodger" or "mountain hoodger." Here in North Carolina they speak of "Tennessee Hoodgers." In Tennessee they speak of

"North Carolina Hoodger." **1941** (in **1944** Wentworth *ADD* 302) (WV) *mountain hoojy* [hudʒi], a hillbilly. **1948** Dick *Dixie Frontier* 24 The name "Hoosier" was often applied to these backwoodsmen even as far south as northern Louisiana and southern Arkansas. Everywhere the general characteristics of this tribe were the same, east to Georgia and from Mississippi and Alabama north to Illinois and Indiana. *Ibid.* 310 Before it was used to designate the citizens of Indiana, the term "Hoosier" was used in the South to describe a rough or uncouth person. **1949** McDavid *Grist* 111 (Rabun Co GA) *mountain hoojers* = mountain rustics. **1977** Maurer *Mt Heritage* 186 One recalls how even as late as the early twenties, [in WV] descendants of these early families were referred to as "old mountain hootchies." **c1982** Young *Colloquial Appal* 12 *hooger* = hillbilly, backward. **1992** Brooks *Sthn Stuff* 71 *hoojee* = [in Georgia] a hillbilly or a redneck.

[DARE *hoosier* n B1a chiefly South, South Midland]

2 See citation.

1939 Hall *Notebooks* 13:26 (White Oak NC) = a sharp-backed hog.

hoot *noun* A swig.

1938 Stuart *Dark Hills* 347 I'll do it if you'll give me a couple more big hoots of that old corn.

[cf EDD *hooter* sb[2] "a cone-shaped tin vessel used for measuring beer"]

hoot and a holler *noun* A short distance. Same as **whoop and a holler.**

2007 Homan *Turkey Tracks* 86 Based upon the folks I talked to—an admittedly small and much older than average sample—I compiled five alternative measures of Appalachian distance. The smallest component was tater chunk, as in "you're real close, it's just another tater chunk down the road." Following tater chunk in progression were yonder, hoot and a holler, a piece, and a fer piece.

hoot-and-hide See **whoop and hide.**

hootenaddy See **hootenanny A.**

hootenanny *noun*

A Variant forms *hootenaddy*, *hootnaddy* [see **1930s** in **B**].

1930s (in **1944** Wentworth *ADD* 302) (eWV) *hootenanny*.

B Usually an object whose name a speaker cannot recall. See citations. [Editor's note: This term referring to a gathering to sing folk songs was popularized and became widespread in the early 1960s.]

1930s (in **1944** Wentworth ADD 302) (eWV) *hootenanny* . . . *hootnaddy* . . . a dingus. Common. Also *hootenaddy*. **1964** Clarkson *Lumbering in WV* 364 *hootenanny* = a device used to hold a crosscut saw while sawing a log from the underside. *Ibid. hootenanny* = a nickname for almost any implement whose name is not known. **1992** Brooks *Sthn Stuff* 71 *hootenanny* = a thingamajig.

[Web3 *hootenanny* n 1 "a device or piece of mechanical equipment, used especially when the standard name is unknown" chiefly dialect]

hootenrankis *noun* See citation.

1944 Williams *Word-List Mts* 29 = a queer little fixture of some kind: "What's this little hootentrankis down on the steering wheel for?" . . . Rare.

hootie pole *noun* A phantom creature that lurked in chimneys, used as a figure in storytelling.

2008 Salsi *Ray Hicks* 26 Mama used to tell us about a rattler that stayed in the chimley at her house when she was a girl. She said nobody ever wanted to clumb [sic] up in there to get it out. That got me never wantin' to get too close to the fireplace. When I had to shovel out ashes, I'd think about what if an ol' "hootie pole" kind a snake thing 'ud come down on me.

hootnaddy See **hootenanny A.**

hoot owl *noun*

1 Homemade whiskey.

1952 McCall *Cherokees and Pioneers* 101 If you are invited to share a little something, whether it be called moonshine, corn juice, nubbin booze, Cain corn, white mule, stump juice, white lightning, Old Nick, hoot owl, O be joyful, or mountain dew, you should be warned that the thing meant is that powerful rank pizen what cheers the heart of even a man with a nagging wife.

2 (also *hoot owl shift*) Especially in coal mining, the late-night or overnight work shift.

1987 (in **2015** Yarrow *Voices* 27) You have three shifts, the day shift, the evening and the hoot owl. **1990** *Matewan OHP-73* Then they got the union. They had to put on three shifts, day shift and a hoot-owl shift and night shift. They had to make three shifts. **2007** Preece *Leavin' Sandlick* 42 I'll be working the hoot owl shift a while.

hoot-owl hide See **whoop and hide.**

hoot owl shift See **hoot owl 2.**

hooty owl *noun* Any of various owls that hoot, such as the great horned owl or the barred owl.

1937 Still *Brother to Methusalem* 48 Broadus and Kell were stretched behind a dead chestnut, a fruit jar between them, drunk as hooty owls.

hooved See **heave A3.**

hooving *noun* See citation. See also **heave B.**

1996 Spurlock *Glossary* 399 = [a] swelling.

hoozle *noun* A drink of liquor.

1918 Combs *Word-List South* 32 = a drink or swig of liquor. **1957** Combs *Lg Sthn High: Word List* 51 = a dram of whiskey. Cf. *Housel*, in the eucharist.

hope *verb* To wish.

1944 Hayes *Word-List NC* 34 *Hope, hope to luck out of (a venture)* . . .

I hope you luck out of (= from) it. **1959** Hall Coll (Newport TN) I hope you good luck. **1962** Clark *Folk Speech NC* 312 = to wish or desire. **c1999** Sutton *Me and Likker* 45 All he said was "I hope you the best" and he went on his way. **2017** *Blind Pig* (Jan 19) Hope to mean wish was definitely used in the Blue Ridge. I hope me die if it ain't so.

[DARE *hope* v South, South Midland]

hope how soon See **how soon**.

hope-ma-die See **hope (to) my die, I**.

hope (to) my die, I (also *hope-ma-die*) *interjection* Used to express intensity in making a vow. Same as **fad die**.

1923 Greer-Petrie *Angeline Doin' Society* 11 Hit looked like a great big red crawfeesh, and I hope to my die, if the thing didn't have laigs with claws on 'em, but law, hit never fazed Bob, and he gulped hit down like hit was nick nacks. **1924** Greer-Petrie *Angeline Gits Eyeful* 5 I hope to my die if even the wimmen wan't a-wa'rin' britches too! **1936** Carpenter *WV Expletives* 346–47 There is hardly an old man or woman that does not drop an expletive or two into almost every conversation. . . . Here are some of their favorites . . . Hope my die (Hope I may die). **1937** Wilson *Folklore SE KY* 22 = an expression of intensity (Bell Co KY). **1999** Milnes *Play of Fiddle* 94 Another common oral tradition in West Virginia is the byword. Most tale tellers mimic the actual speaking voices of the characters, including the identifying byword(s) interjected throughout the tale. . . . A common one is preceding a sentence with "I hope I may die," which comes out "hope-ma-die" and is shortened from "I hope I may die if this isn't the truth."

[DARE *hope to my die, I* exclam WV, KY]

hoppergrass *noun* A grasshopper.

1968 Wilson *Folklore Mammoth Cave* 20 = a humorous metathesis for grasshopper. **1986** Pederson et al. *LAGS* (Hamilton Co TN, Cherokee Co GA, Whitfield Co GA).

[DARE *hoppergrass* n 1 chiefly South, South Midland]

hopping bug *noun* A cricket.

1884 Smith *Arp Scrap Book* 90 The doors creeked welcum on their hinges [and] the hoppin bug chirruped on the hearth.

hoppy toad (also *hop toad*) *noun* A toad.

1966 West *Dialect Sthn Mts* 34 [He's] as happy as a hoppytoad in a fly factory. **1992** Brooks *Sthn Stuff* 72 *hoppytoad* = a toad-frog. **2014** *Blind Pig* (Nov 7) You young'uns be keerful, if you kill that hop toad, it will cause the cows to go dry.

horn *noun* A drink of liquor.

1911 Shearin *E KY Word-List* 538 = a dram of whiskey. **1940** Still *River of Earth* 193 "I hain't been well lately," he said. "A horn o' Indian Doctor tonic I'm taking after every meal."

horn blate *noun* The vessel sounded to imitate the cry of a sheep or to warn **moonshiners** of the presence of **revenuers**. See also **blate**.

1937 Hall Coll (Wears Cove TN) The horn blate attracted the bears. (In the past this would also be sounded to alert residents of the presence of revenuers in the community.)

hornus See **harness**.

hornyhead *noun* Same as **knotty**.

1960 Stupka *Great Smoky Mts* 53 Principal among the fishes found in the park is a minnow, the stoneroller or "hornyhead," which is abundant and widely distributed. Although small, rarely over 8 inches, it is favored as a table fish by many residents of this vicinity. **1986** Pederson et al. *LAGS* = attested by 8/60 interviewees (13.3%) from E TN; 8/12 of all LAGS interviewees (66.7%) attesting term were from E TN. [**1992** Brooks *Sthn Stuff* 72 = it is called this because during the breeding season, the male's head grows hornlike protuberances.)]

[from the tubercles on the fish's head]

horry See **howdy A**.

horse *noun*

A Variant form *hoss*. [Editor's note: This form was in common use in the Smoky Mountains in the late 1930s, especially by older and less-educated speakers.]

1862 Epperly *CW Letters* (May 1) Direct your letter to Williamsburgh In the Car if Captain Pelham Stuards hoss Artillary. **1863** Smith *Battle of Rome* xx Hosses hid in the cane brake. **1908** Fox *Lonesome Pine* 21 Hitch that 'ar post to yo' hoss and come right in. **1913** Kephart *Our Sthn High* 281 Much oftener the *r* is dropped from dare, first, girl, horse, nurse, parcel, worth (dast, fust, gal, hoss, nuss, passel, wuth). **1937** Hall Coll (Cades Cove TN) I yoked a hoss and a steer together. **1956** Hall Coll (Newport TN) She jumped on the hoss and rid down the mountain with him. **1961** Williams *R in Mt Speech* 6 In a few words, however, r is omitted: *cuss*, *futhuh*, *hoss*. **1997** GSMNPCOHP-1:4 All the tools they had back then was of course hoss-drawn.

B Senses.

1 In weaving, a fault in warping.

1937 Hyatt *Kiverlid* 19 I'm agoin' to make has'e all I can with the warpin' and you watch the bars keerful and see that I don't skip a peg and make a "horse" that would be a sight troublesome.

[EDD *horse* sb 14 "a fault in warping . . . when a pin is missed"]

2 See citation.

2007 Ball *Tub Mills* 9 The amount of corn fed to the stones [of a grist mill] could be regulated by lifting or lowering the shoe by means of a leather strap attached to a knob on the hopper stand (or "horse").

horse apple *noun*

1 A large, yellow apple often used in cooking.

1921 Campbell *Sthn Highlander* 200 The covered wagon with its load of crimson winesaps or big green "horse apples" is a familiar sight in many a mountain metropolis. **1949** Arnow *Hunter's Horn* 310 Wild-strawberry-picking time in June was hardly finished before . . . the first of the white horse apples were falling, begging to be canned or dried or made into vinegar. **c1960** Wilson *Coll* = a well-known old-fashioned apple with a tart and queer flavor: maybe a pippin. **1970** Vincent *More of Best* 103 Chestnuts and chinquapins are unknown to the present generation, and we doubt if any ever heard of a hoss apple. That was to us the best of all apples, and when it ripened about this time of year no nursery could ever reproduce its flavor. **1973** GSMNP-6:4 They had a big old what they called a hoss apple tree . . . and we'd get those big old whopper yellow apples. **1995** Montgomery *Coll* (known to Cardwell).

[DARE *horse apple* n 1 chiefly South Midland]

2 See citation.

1976 Still *Pattern of Man* 122 = horse dung.

horse-around *noun* Same as **cane mill**.

1978 Parris *Mt Cooking* 1–2 Grandpa made his own molasses too. Made them in a horse-around mill back of the house from sorghum he grew beyond the branch.

horseback (also *horse's back*) *noun* See citations.

c1975 *Miners' Jargon* 5 = a sharp rise in a coal seam, shaped like a horse's back, imbedded in the top. Especially dangerous because it can cause a fall without warning. Also called a *hogback*. **2006** Mooney *Lg Coal Mining* 1028 Many [coal-mining] terms make use of analogies to nature or to animals. A "horse's back" is the curved indentation left in a mine ceiling when a slab of rock or coal falls.

horse balm (also *horse weed*) *noun* The stoneroot, a perennial plant (*Collinsonia* spp) with strongly scented yellow flowers and roots that have medicinal uses. See also **richweed**.

1940 Caton *Wildflowers of Smokies* 104 *horse balm* = stoneroot. [**1971** Krochmal et al. *Medicinal Plants Appal* 100 Roots are used as a sedative, antispasmodic, diuretic, astringent, and tonic.] **1979** *Smokies Heritage* 220 We had an old smokehouse right beside the road; the lower side of which was surrounded by "horseweeds" higher than my head.

horse beast (also *horse creature, horse critter*) *noun* A horse. Same as **beast B1**.

1795 *Jefferson Co Wills I* 45 I give and bequeath to my Dear beloved wife during her widowhood her bed and beding, also her choice of one of my horse creatures. **1867** Harris *Sut Lovingood* 43 I wer jis' a-studyin how tu gin yu a sorter idear ove how things look'd arter them two hoss beastes mixed. **1898** Dromgoole *Cinch* 26 Thar ain't another horse critter in this country comes gallivantin' down the mount'n like Jerry Stampses. **1952** Wilson *Folk Speech NC* 552 *horse beast* = horse. **1996–97** Montgomery *Coll*: *horse beast* (known to Brown, Bush), = found only in old wills (Oliver).

[redundant form; cf EDD (at *horse* sb 1 (9))]

horse bird *noun* See citation.

1967 Wilson *Folkways Mammoth Cave* 30 = a local name for the brown-headed cowbird.

horse biscuit *noun* A patty of horse dung.

1984 Burns *Cold Sassy* 66 He and I had us a great manure war then, throwing dry cow cushions and sheep pills and horse biscuits at each other and dying laughing. **1992** Bush *If Life* 24 Good Lord, Bill, where did you take [the moonshine] and who'd drink it after a long journey covered with horse biscuits? **2007** McMillon *Notes* = a pile of horse dung.

horse blanket whiskey *noun* See citation.

1974 Maurer and Pearl *KY Moonshine* 119 = a crude form of liquor made by covering a boiling kettle of beer with a heavy, folded horse-blanket. When the blanket is heavy with condensed moisture, two men twist it to extrude the liquor. The process is then repeated. This technique is not approved by first-class moonshiners.

horse creature, **horse critter** See **horse beast**.

horse fiddle *noun* A noisemaker, especially one used at a **serenade** or **shivaree**.

1972 Alderman *Big Bald* 12 The new bride and groom would slip away to their own prepared cabin. After dark, the third night, the crowd would gather around the cabin of the new couple for the serenade. At a given signal a din of noise, that would scare the "hants" and everything else back into the never, never world, would break loose. Pans-a-poundin', guns-a-shootin', people-a-shoutin' and the big roarin' horse fiddle boomin' through the woods got the "shivaree" off to a thundering start. This final part of the celebration lasted all night. Sun-up would see the departin' couples drifting down their separate trails, homeward bound across the creeks and ridges, to the back of the beyond where they lived. **2009** Morgan *October Crossing* 25 To keep the squirrels from fields of corn, and crows also, those farmers made a kind of windmill out of rags and rusty parts. Old wires or bits of iron would scrape and scratch, screech out like owls or ghosts when a faint breeze would touch the rough contraption. A scarecrow for the ears, a thing they called a "horse fiddle" would cry out loud and shriek like fiddlers mad, or nails jerked on a blackboard.

horse logs *verb phrase* See citation.

1964 Clarkson *Lumbering in WV* 364 = in river driving, to guide stranded logs back to the stream by the use of peaveys.

horse lot *noun* An outdoor enclosure for livestock, usually around a barn. See also **lot A**.

1898 Dromgoole *Cinch* 36 Thar's the whole o' the roof-room fur yer, and, if that is too cramped, thar's the horse lot. **1968** Wilson *Folklore Mammoth Cave* 20 = the enclosure around a stock-barn. Called *barnlot*, *stablelot*, and, before strangers, *barnyard*. **1976** Braden *Grandma Was Girl* 10 Across the road from the house was a lot we called the "horse lot." In this lot were the small corn crib where the corn was stored, a log barn with stalls for cows and mules, and sheds for farm tools. Over the stalls was space for storing hay and fodder for the animals. Under the eaves, the pigeons nested.

[DARE *horse lot* n 1 chiefly Southeast, Lower Mississippi Valley, TX]

horse mill *noun* Formerly, a mill for grinding grain powered by a horse rather than by water or machinery.

1847 (in **1870** Drake *Pioneer Life KY* 59) Water and horse-mills had been built before I was old enough to perform the labors I have just noted; but they were for many years few and feeble. **1881** Pierson *In the Brush* 68 The wheat had been ground at a "horse mill" in the neighborhood, where they had no arrangements for separating the bran from the flour. **1975** Dwyer *Thangs* 3 Bring back them good ol' days! The wonderful days ... when you carried grain to the "hoss-mill" or "water-mill."

horsemint *noun* A perennial plant (*Pycnanthemum* spp) with medicinal use. See also **mountain mint**.

1937 Thornburgh *Great Smoky Mts* 29 Other herbs and roots used by the old folks in various ways are ... horse mint, butterfly root ... wild indigo, yellow fringed orchid or rattlesnake master. **1971** *AOHP/ALC*-147 If any of us had a high temperature, why she'd make ... tea from horsemint. She called it white horsemint, and it would take the temperature down. **1982** Stupka *Wildflowers* 100 Also called "horse-mint" and "basil," mountain-mint flowers on hillsides and in fields from July to October.

[DARE *horsemint* n 2 especially South]

horse mule *noun* A male mule.

1984 Burns *Cold Sassy* 62 [He] said he would lead the charge bareback on old Jack, his mouse-colored horse-mule.

horse pill *noun* See citation.

1996 Spurlock *Glossary* 396 *dry horse pill* = a clump of dry horse manure.

horsepitle, horsepittle See **hospital**.

horse-quart *noun* A quart container kept in one's saddlebags.

1941 Stuart *Men of Mts* 128 I pulled a horse-quart o' moonshine from my saddlebags.

horse's back See **horseback**.

horse sense *noun* Common sense, native wits. See also **bay horse sense**.

1898 Elliott *Durket Sperret* 96 Hannah Warren's got good horse sense, an' don't need no cawlidge.

horse's head *noun* See citation.

c1999 Sutton *Me and Likker* 103 = connects the arm on the cap to the thump post on a still.

horsetail *noun* Same as **mare's tail**.

1937 Still *Quare Day* 36 There were no clouds other than a scattering of horsetails.

horse-throwed *adjective phrase* Thrown by or off a horse. See also **-throwed**.

1904–20 Kephart *Notebooks* 2:475 He was horse-throwed, and lit on a stob, and hurt his shoulder. **1917** Kephart *Word-List* 413 Ever since I was *horse-throwed*. **1994–97** Montgomery Coll (known to Adams, Brown, Cardwell, Oliver, Weaver).

[DARE *horsethrowed* past ppl, ppl adj southern Appalachians, Ozarks]

horse up *verb phrase* To put (someone) on a horse.

1962 Hall Coll (Cades Cove TN) Rebel raiders came through [Cades Cove to] steal, plunder, and drive off cattle. Uncle Noah was his mother's only support. They hossed him up and rode him out. David ... told them to turn him loose.... They did.

horse weed See **horse balm**.

horsey *adjective* Bossy, self-important.

1999 Montgomery *File* She sure is acting horsey today (52-year-old woman, Jefferson Co TN).

horspittle See **hospital**.

hospital *noun* Variant forms *horsepital, horsepitle, horsepittle, horspittle*.

1862 Sexton *CW Letters* (July 12) he dide [= died] at the horse pitle at richmon. **1864** Councill *CW Letters* (March 29) they Said that they had Seed the wounded men a going to the horse pital. **1922** *TN CW Ques* 970 (Sullivan Co TN) On account of me having the mumps was in horsepittle at guntown twenty days. **1928** Justus *Betty Lou* 77 "Whoever heard of a horsepittle on a mountain?" cried somebody, and Uncle Dan'l Grigsby replied, "Whoever heard of a school—till it was put here?" **1939** Hall *Notebooks* 13:40 (White Oak NC) *horsepitle*. **1955** Washburn *Country Doctor* 65 We's all of us mighty scared of the horspittle, but Maw says she knows she cain't go through ernother 'tack erlive.

hoss See **horse A**.

hoss apple See **horse apple**.

hostle *verb* See citation.

1991 Weals *Last Train* 33 To "hostle" a locomotive was to work on it at night, empty the ash pans, clean the firebox of clinklers, refill the coal tender and water tender, load the sand reservoirs, oil several moving parts and sweep out the cab.

hot

A *adjective* See citation.

1969 Lee *Bloodletting* 48 This fall [of slate] caused the accumulation [to have] much more gas than usual. The mine officials and bosses knew that Parrel was a "hot" mine, and made inspections each shift before the men entered their working places. **2002** Armstead *Black Days* 244 = [having] high levels of methane and other explosive gases.

B (also *hot up*) *verb, verb phrase* To heat, warm (something or someone) up. Same as **hotten**.

1937 Campbell *KY Mt Community* 535 This old un was plenty good 'nough but Sally would be to [sic] have a stove what was purty and would git hotted up more quicker. **c1940** Simms *Coll* Warm weather "hots you." **1962** Dykeman *Tall Woman* 235 I'd better hot up the coffee for some of the folks in there. **1974** Fink *Bits Mt Speech* 12 Please *hot up* my coffee.

[DARE *hot* v 1 especially South, South Midland]

hot board *noun* See citation.

1979 Slone *My Heart* 51 A large smooth board was heated before the fire and carried along to supply a warm place for the feet. The board was taken back to the house to be used again next time. My stepmother told of using a "hot board" to stand on when they were washing clothes, or working at the loom [i.e. away from the fire].

hot drink *noun* A mixture of ginger and diluted whiskey, drunk as a morning tonic.

1973 GSMNP-4:1:29 People of a morning the first thing when they would get out of bed, they would put it on the stove and boil it and put ginger and liquor and water and make what they called a "ginger stew." They would take liquor and weaken it down with water and make what they call "hot drink." And they would drink that. It would be the first thing they would drink of a morning when they got out of bed.

hot-nosed *adjective* See citations. See also **cold-nosed**.

1937 Hall *Coll* = used of a dog that is better at following a hot trail. **2007** Plott *Story Plott Hound* 182 = another term used to describe the trailing abilities of a hound. The hot-nosed hound is better on a very "hot," very fresh or more recent game trail.

hot shots *noun* Same as **high shots**.

1969 *DARE Survey* (Dillard GA) When it [= doublings] comes out condensed at the end of your condenser or your worm, whichever you're using, then it is hot shots or high shots. **1972** Cooper *NC Mt Folklore* 93 = first whiskey that comes from the worm of a still.

hotten *verb* To heat (something or someone) up. Same as **hot B**.

1996–97 Montgomery *Coll* (known to Bush, Cardwell, Cypher, Oliver).

[*hot* adj + *-en* suffix (see *-en*[3]); DARE *hotten* v 1 South, South Midland]

hot up See **hot B**.

hot water tea *noun* See citations.

1971 Dwyer *Dict for Yankees* 28 = tea made of hot water, milk and sugar. **1997** Montgomery *Coll* = a drink of hot water, milk, and sugar, made especially for children because it is easily digested and settles the stomach (Andrews).

[DARE *hot-water tea* n South, South Midland]

hound dog *noun* A canine bred or trained to hunt bears, opossums, and other wild game. See also **bear dog**, **black and tan**, **blue tick**, **Plott**, **Walker**.

1901 Harben *Westerfelt* 203 I jest want some hound dog to come an' take my place on God's earth. **1913** Kephart *Our Sthn High* 344 [I'd] shoot enough meat off o' his bones to feed a hound-dog a week. **1940** Oakley *Roamin'/Restin'* 99 I always liked hound dog pups as I thot they was so good to smell up opsams coons and other wild animals. **1949** Hall *Coll* (Del Rio TN) A beagle is a hound dog. A hound dog is a good hunter, a tree dog. **1989** Landry *Smoky Mt Interviews* 191 They owned all this, plumb up to the gap, and he swapped a good section of this for a hound dog and a hog rifle.

[DARE *hound dog* n 1 chiefly South, South Midland]

house *noun* See also **big house**, **main house**, **new house**, **tother house**.

1 Any room of a dwelling, especially the largest one.

1895 Edson and Fairchild *TN Mts* 372 This grew up from the custom of having houses of one room, or two connected by a porch, each of which rooms was called a *house*. **1913** Combs *Kentucky Highlander* 18–19 If a house has an addition, or if it has more than one room, it is called "houses" and not "house." **1918** Combs *Word-List South* 32 = in a house of two or more rooms, the largest one is thus designated. House is synonymous with room, and a dwelling of more than one room is often called "houses." **1923** Furman *Mothering* 107 Supper at last being ready, Mr. Marrs, leaning feebly on his crutch, conducted me into "t'other house," the children took their stands and we our seats about the table. **1937** Eaton *Handicrafts* 48 The most elaborate cabin was that with new rooms or "new houses," as they are called by old inhabitants, built from time to time. **1938** Hall *Coll* = portion of the old-fashioned mountain house—two separate structures built of logs with an open space between and covered by one roof. "The hall between the houses." **1953** Hall *Coll* (Bryson City NC) We built the houses so as to build the chimley right on the state line, right in the middle of the house, one house at each end. **1991** Williams *Homeplace* 44 In late nineteenth- and early-twentieth-century rural western North Carolina, "house" could refer to any living room, but "big house" generally had a more specialized meaning. **1997** Nelson *Country Folklore* 11 Actually, the house was two houses joined together with a porch on one house and an opening between the two houses. The kitchen was the oldest house, and it was one big room, made with logs, with mud in between them.

[EDD *house* sb[1] 6; DARE *house* n B1a southern Appalachians, especially KY, TN]

2 The general living area of a dwelling, the living room. Same as **big house**.

[OED3 *house* n 1c now dialect; EDD *house* sb[1] 7; DARE *house* n B1b South, South Midland]

house coal mine *noun* Same as **doghole**.

1973 Preston *Bituminous Term* 34 *doghole* = a very small mine operated by a few men, usually taking coal which lies very near the surface. Also known as a *house coal mine* or a *punch mine*.

house covering *noun* Formerly, a community work activity to roof a family's new dwelling. See also **house raising**.

1972 *Kelly* 82 [They] got all their logs'n'ever'thing cut and they have what they call a house raisin'. Neighbors'ud come in an' help put the house up; and then when they got it up, well, they'd have a house coverin'. Crowd'ud come t'help.

household plunder See **house plunder 1, 2**.

house pattern *noun*

1 The cut lumber for a new house.

1924 Raine *Saddlebags* 104 We speak of a dress-pattern or a trousers-pattern, meaning not the shape, but the material out of which it is to be made. So we need not be surprised at—"He sawed him a house-pattern out of beech." **1931** Owens *Speech Cumberlands* 93 = the lumber needed in building a house: "Clevie got a house-pattern o' Jeems while the saw-mill was at his place." **1957** Combs *Lg Sthn High: Word List* 52 = lumber for a new house. Ex.: "I thought I'd send over in Clay County and git the saw mill to saw me out a house pattern."

2 See citation.

1967 Wilson *Folkways Mammoth Cave* 23 = a blueprint or drawing of a house.

house place (also *house seat*) *noun* The site of the main dwelling on a piece of property, whether the building remains or not.

1924 Raine *Saddlebags* 10 Where hills are somewhat rounded, a "house-seat" is often chosen upon one of the knobs. **1931** Owens *Speech Cumberlands* 93 *house seat* = site for a house: "That's a pretty house-seat. I'd like to give it to the oldest boy fer him 'n' Cindy." **1959** Roberts *Up Cutshin* 47 Jim pointed out the old big log house in a bend of the Clover Fork. We stopped and went toward the rustic houseseat, with its rived board roof, puncheoned floor, and beamed and raftered interior. **1973** GSMNP-88 His house set right down there in them big apple trees, and you can see the old house place right yonder, the cellar part, basement of it. **1996–97** Montgomery *Coll*: *house place* (known to Ledford); *house seat* (known to Brown, Cardwell, Jones, Ledford, Oliver). **1997** GSMNPCOHP-5:19 They's some old house places up on that creek. **2000** Morgan *Mts Remember* 54 "They say the house place is too far from the spring and I'd waste half my time carrying water," he said. "But I can pipe it down." **2005** Williams *Gratitude* 26 Then Dad and Mom decided to build a house, an they picked out their house place on the land that Pa Hicks was suppost to give them.

house plunder (also *household plunder*) *noun*

1 Furniture. See also **plunder 1**.

1934–47 *LAMSAS Appal* (Madison Co NC, Swain Co NC) *house plunder*. **1935** Sheppard *Cabins in Laurel* 180 Anyway, there is no hurry about getting house-plunder, because while they figure things out they can live with one family or the other. **1939** Farr *TN Mt Regions* 91 *household plunder* = household furniture. "Ella and Larry bought their household plunder from a mail order store." **1962** Dykeman *Tall Woman* 17 When your papa came from the Low Country, up into these mountains, and the load in the wagon had to be lightened, he threw out the household plunder and kept his box of books. **1972** *AOHP/ALC*-226 They had three wagons, had two wagon loads of corn and fodder, and one wagon load of house plunder, and I rode on one of the wagons. **1982** Powers and Hannah *Cataloochee* 91 The last trip out of there I drove a wagon with a team and had some chicken coops on it. And Daddy had hired a fellow with a truck to haul the household plunder. **1982** Slone *How We Talked* 5 Most often [newlyweds] lived with their parents for the first months, until they got together enough "house plunder." **1986** Pederson et al. *LAGS*: *house plunder* (Cocke Co TN). **1995** Montgomery *Coll* (known to Cardwell).

2 Odds and ends, miscellaneous goods. Same as **plunder 2**.

1931 Goodrich *Mt Homespun* 18 These rush baskets were made by the Indians as well as by white settlers, and were frequently in the shape of a squat jar, with a cover, very large and useful for storing "household plunder."

house proud *adjective* See citation.

2009 Benfield *Mt Born* 157 = an immaculate housekeeper, skilled in the domestic arts and in keeping the house in good order, making things all nice and comfy. "You're house proud, honey, and I'm a lucky man."

house raising *noun* Traditionally, a community work event to help a family construct a new dwelling. The event usually lasts for one day and is followed by an evening meal and social activity provided by the newly housed family. See 1971, c1975 citations. Also called **log raising**. See also **barn raising, house covering, log raising**.

1795 (in **1919** DeWitt *Sevier Journal* 178) (July 22) went to Jos. Seviers house Raising in Company with Mrs. Sevier & Betsy. **1824** (in **1912** Doddridge *Notes on Settlement* 88) The standard dish, for every log rolling, house raising and harvest day, is a pot pie, or what in other countries is called a sea pie. **1881** Atkinson *After Moonshiners* 141 Corn-husking, and house-raising, are very much the same as log-rolling, and are enjoyed fully as much. At night, following all these labors, comes the dance. **1913** Kephart *Our Sthn High* 308–9 There are today fewer log rollings and house raisings, fewer husking bees and quilting parties, than in former times. **1970** Mull *Mt Yarns* 19 Generally, when a community was established, they would have a "House Raising," where everyone would gather (after the logs had been cut, dove-tailed, and hewn) to help "raise" the house. **1971** *AOHP/ALC*-160 They still do it today, help them. They'd have house raisings and later have a grubbings, and they'd a have clearings and they'd have a corn hoeings. Everything along the same basis as the bean stringing and apple peeling . . . if anybody needs a house built. Usually they was a lot of them built out of logs. They'd go and cut the logs and bring them in. They'd have what they called a house raising. They'd lay these notched tree logs. Some of them was good with a ax, and they would notch these corners till they fit good and begin at the bottom, and they'd lay these logs as high as they wanted them laid, they'd be enough men gather around and do that in one day, and they got the good-sized house, and they'd always get together with food gathered. **c1975** Lunsford *It Used to Be* 21 The house-raising is usually for a house that is made of logs. There's a man in each corner. A corner man in a house-raising is a fellow who can notch those logs just right to fit together all the way down. The corner will be plumb after they get through. It isn't every man who can do that just right. Some men are more skilled than others. So if a man "takes up the corner," he's a skilled person. Sometimes they send for him a long ways. **1986** Ogle *Lucinda* 45 Such as when someone was sick, or after a fire, all people from miles around would come to a house raising a log rolling, etc. **1991** Haynes *Haywood Home* 44 Barn and house raisings, corn shuckings, quiltings, log rollings and such were not only community labor sharing projects, but were also social occasions. **1991** Thomas *Sthn Appal* 180 Th' men 'ud come fer miles to work at a house-raisin'. Course . . . they couldn't afford not to come. They might haff to have th' same thing donc fcr them. They'd put thur horse-feed in a sack, put it on their horses, an' ride in. Ride for miles.

[DARE *house-raising* n scattered, but especially frequent South, South Midland]

house seat See **house place**.

house snake *noun* The milk snake (*Lampropeltis triangulum*).

1991 Conant and Collins *Field Guide* 207 The house snake inhabits both wooded and open areas in the Great Smokies.

hove See **heave A2**, **A3**.

hover *noun* A small shelter for chickens.

c1960 Wilson *Coll*: *hover* = a small house for a chicken and her brood, a hovel. **1986** Pederson et al. *LAGS* (Hamilton Co TN).

[DARE *hover* n chiefly southern MD, northern VA, KY, TN]

how *adverb* Used to inquire when a listener has not understood (especially a speaker's name). See also **do how?**, **which C**.

1815 (in **1947** Read *Pickering Vocabulary* 283) (DARE) How? An interrogative very often used in Kentucky & North Carolina when a person does not distinctly hear or understand what is said to him, for "what do you say." **1915** Bradley *Hobnobbing* 100 You ask a Kentucky mountaineer a question he does not quite grasp, and he says "How?" A Tennessean, in like case, exclaims "Which?" **1919** Combs *Word-List South* 33 In inquiring after one's name: "How did ye say ye called yer name?"

how all *pronoun phrase* All the ways that. For other forms with *all*, see Grammar and Syntax §2.7.2.

1972 *AOHP/LJC-259* That was very interesting how all they did that.

how be you? *phrase* See citation.

1986 Pederson et al. *LAGS* (Sullivan Co TN) = expression used by grandmother.

how come *conjunctive phrase* [Editor's note: This phrase in the sense "why" when used alone or when followed by a subordinate clause with a present- or past-tense verb is widespread in American English (e.g. "That's how come one of his fingers is/was missing") and is not presented here. Many examples below can be paraphrased roughly as "in what manner it came about that," although the interpretation sometimes seems to be "by what cause it came about."]

1 + it = how it happened.

1973 *GSMNP-88*:120 He never would tell how come it. **1974** *AOHP/ALC-807* I don't know how come it, sure don't.

2 + (someone, something) + prepositional or adverb phrase = how it happened (or came about) that (NP/Pro) came to be. [Editor's note: When the subject of the tenseless clause is a personal pronoun, it appears in the objective case; hence *I don't know how come her that-a-way* = I don't know how come she was that-a-way.]

1930 Armstrong *This Day and Time* 250 I don't know how come her that-a-way. **1939** Hall *Coll* (Cades Cove TN) You see that cedar tree? One of my uncles brought that from Louisville [TN]. . . . That's how come that tree out there. **1967** Hall *Coll* (Townsend TN) Fonze was the driver. That's how come him in there. **1974** *No Sang* 22 That's how come that in Laney Cove there on Kelly's Creek. **1989** *Matewan OHP-2* We knew them people was in town and was looking for trouble. That's how come us in there.

3 + (someone, something) + infinitive phrase. [Editor's note: When the subject of the tenseless clause is a personal pronoun, it appears in the objective case; hence *That's how come us to leave* = That's how come we left.]

a In a nominal clause.

1862 *Robinson CW Letters* (May 7) [They] was out on picket & the yankes Cut off there Retreet is how Come them to git wounded. **1939** Hall *Coll* (Cades Cove TN) That's how come me to get back from the hospital. *Ibid.* (Hazel Creek NC) I don't know how come [Bone Valley] to get its name. **1956** Hall *Coll* (Raccoon Creek NC) So that's how come this particular branch here in Haywood County to be called Raccoon Creek. **1967** Hall *Coll* (Townsend TN) That's how come it to be called the Devil's Courthouse. **1970** *GSMNP-26*:8 I remember seeing it swim back up the mill race, and that is how come me to remember. **1975** *AOHP/ALC-903* How come me to quit, me and the motorman got into it, you see, out on the tram. **1975** *GSMNP-59*:16 That's how come him to move up there. **1976** *GSMNP-113*:9 That's how come us to leave there. **1985** *Irwin Alex Stewart* 72 That's how come me to own that place, cause of him liking that Jersey cow. *Ibid.* 158 He sent word for me to come up there one time and when I got there he wanted me to help him make a run, and that's how come us to get started together. **1989** *Matewan OHP-1* She ran a boarding house there with her girls for years, and that's how come her to be in Matewan. **1997** Ownby *Big Greenbrier* II:18 We never knew how come the fire to start. **1998** *Dante OHP-71* Harry would listen to the old ministers, and that's how come him to start out as a minister. **2005** Williams *Gratitude* 19 How come me to remember that, was that I was so amazed at that big long bridge before you git to town.

b In an interrogative sentence.

1927 Furman *Lonesome Road* 42 How come you to do so much for me? **1963** Edwards *Gravel* 147 How come him to run off and leave us? **1975** *AOHP/ALC-903* How come you to have your own house? **1989** *Matewan OHP-28* How come them to lose so many foremen? **1998** *Dante OHP-51* How come Frances to catch up with you? **1999** *Offut Out of Woods* 27 How come you to shoot him?

4 + *that* + noninverted word order = how did it happen that.

1971 *AOHP/ALC-32* How come that there was so much fights over the [county] elections? *Ibid.* How come that they come and got your grandfather? *Ibid.*-n.p. How come that two of them [= ancestors during the Civil War] decided to go with the North instead of the South?

how do *interjection* Hello! Same as **howdy A.**

1999 Morgan *Gap Creek* 33 "Howdy," he hollered to Mama, not paying much attention to me. "How do," Mama said, standing up. She had took to saying "How do" the way Papa used to.

how do ye come on? *interrogative phrase* = how are you?

1924 (in **1952** Mathes *Tall Tales* 21) [How d'ye come on?]: "Why, pardner, I come on my feet. How did ye reckon I come? Haw! Haw!" **1941** Justus *Kettle Creek* 67 Rider, moving around, took time to shake hands and to ask in kindly greeting, "How d'ye come on?" of everyone there. **1943** Justus *Bluebird* 117 "How d'ye come on?" Aunt Rhody asked them using the old-fashioned greeting, which means in the mountain way of speaking, "Are you well?"

howdy

A (also *horry, how d'y, howdye*) *interjection* Hello! Greetings! Same as **how do.**

1881 Pierson *In the Brush* 34 I met a countryman on his way to town, who greeted me with a pleasant "How d'y, sir?" and, as he scanned with a pleasant face my outfit, he added, "Traveling, sir?" **1903** Fox *Little Shepherd* 86 "How are you, John? Howdye, Dick?" Both men answered heartily. **1930** Armstrong *This Day and Time* 21 Her father had called down a low half-hostile "Howdy." **1938** Bowman *High Horizons* 31 "Howdy" is the usual greeting of the mountaineer in the Smokies, if one chances to encounter him on a side road or trail. **1962** Williams *Mtneers Mind Manners* 19 Mountain people speak one another when they meet, when they pass one another's houses, and when they assemble in groups. "Howdy?" "How'd do?" and "Horry?" are the usual salutations. **1978** Head *Mt Moments* If he met a friend in the morning, "good morning" or "howdy" was the greeting. **1988** Russell *It Happened* 37 The usual greeting that was used in the Smokies was the one word "Howdy."

[shortening of *how do you do?*]

B *noun in phrases give howdy, say howdy, send howdys, speak howdy, swap howdy, tell howdy, trade howdy* = to say hello.

1861 *Carden CW Letter* (Oct 6) I send howdy to Ant Nance and you allso. **1861** *Poteet CW Letters* (Aug 7) I want you to give John hemphill houdy for me. **1862** *Robinson CW Letters* (Dec 21) Susan ses howdy to you and fanny. **1865** *Epperly CW Letters* (March 4) Larah and Chriss sends houdy to you and sais they want to see you. **1865** Wilson *Confederate Private* 80 (Jan 18) tell houdy for grandma and give them a kiss. **1888** *Cole Letters* 72 Tell Johns father and all his folks hoddy for me and tell his father to pray for me. **1963** Edwards *Gravel* 123 The cap'm come over and spoke howdy to Pap and me thar at the shop. **1973** *GSMNP-70:8* Is these girls crazy? Every time they would pass a man have to speak howdy to him? **1984** Wilder *You All Spoken* 103 *swap howdy* = exchange greetings. **1993** Cunningham *Sthn Talk* 164 Them town folks ain't very sociable. When you try to trade howdies with them, they just look at you plumb quare. **1997** *Montgomery Coll*: *swap howdy* (known to Weaver); *trade howdy* (known to Bush, Jones, Norris, Weaver); Folks today have got too busy to trade howdies (Cardwell).

C (also *howdy with*) *verb, verb phrase* To express greetings with; to greet, pay a visit to (someone); to exchange greetings.

1892 Doak *Wagonauts Abroad* 156 Declining grog and breakfast, he said he'd only come to "howdy, ez he'd never seed sich gentlemen afore." **1931** Goodrich *Mt Homespun* 52 That was a day to remember; the leisurely ride through the autumn woods . . . the "howdying" between old friends that met seldom and were glad to meet; the making of new acquaintances. **c1940** *Simms Coll* Go howdy the lady; Come howdy with us; Howdy 'round a bit before the meetin'. **1950** Justus *Luck for Lihu* 31 When [the circuit rider] stopped to howdy the Linders, he heard of Little Lihu's troubles and right away offered to let the boy ride along with him. **1952** Justus *Children* 17 We'll howdy him and hurry on. **1975** Gainer *Speech Mtneer* 12 *howdy* = to greet one. "We've howdied, but we ain't shuck." This means, "We've spoken, but we haven't shaken hands." **1979** Melton *'Pon My Honor* 92 They hadn't got far when they met this man coming up the road. They stopped and howdied with him. **2004** Adams *Old True Love* 35 He was setting on the porch, long legs drawed up, head resting on his knees, and he never even looked up when I howdied the house.

[DARE *howdy* v 1 chiefly South, South Midland]

how d'y, howdye See **howdy A.**

howdy with See **howdy C.**

howsomever *adverb* However, nevertheless.

1859 Taliaferro *Fisher's River* 64 Howsomever, I blazed away at him, but he were goin' so fast around the Loaf, and the bullet goin' strait forrud, I missed him. **1873** Smith *Arp Peace Papers* 41 Howsomever, I spose Mr. Linkhorn will keep peggin away. **1901** Harben *Westerfelt* 276 Howsomever, she thought they wus from his tale an' his sad, mournful way o' talkin'. **1940** Bowman *KY Mt Stories* 241 = however. **1969** Medford *Finis* 94 Notis, I sed that we'de "kum down" to Streem-lined Religun; howsumever, Unkle Abe's not kwite shore 'bout that . . . hit mout be that we've gone UP in the skale uv religus developmint. **1984** Burns *Cold Sassy* 153 Howsome-ever, Miss Love needs something to take her mind off of Mr. Texas. **1998** *Montgomery Coll* (known to Brown, Bush, Cardwell, Ellis, Jones, Norris, Oliver).

[OED3 *howsomever* adv, now dialect; Web3 *howsomever* (alteration of *howsoever*) adv chiefly dialect; DARE *howsomever* adv 1 scattered, but chiefly South and Central Atlantic, South Midland]

how soon *conjunctive phrase* That soon, very (soon) (as in phrase *hope how soon*).

1862 *Crawford CW Letters* (April 29) we ar Looking out for heavy ingagement Evry hour and Wish how soon it may com and be over with. **1863** *Lance CW Letters* (April 6) it is a hard matter to get a long on the trains but I hope how soon he may come for I understand he has got some things for me and I am verry anxious to get them. **1923** Greer-Petrie *Angeline Doin' Society* 2 He hoped how soon Othello would choke the life out'n her. **1931** Hannum *Thursday April* 16 I hope how soon hit comes. **1936** Lyman *WV Idioms* 63 I hope how soon I'll see you = I hope I'll see you soon. **1946** Dudley *KY Words* 271 *hope how soon* = hope it may happen soon. **1952** Wilson *Folk Speech NC* 553 I hope *how soon* your mother will come back. **1969** Dial *Dialect Appal People* 464 "Law, I hope how soon we get some rain!" (How soon is supposed to be obsolete, but it enjoys excellent health in Lincoln County [WV].) **1981** Dumas *Appal Glossary* 17 = hope (that) soon. "*I hope how soon* the corn comes in" = "I hope the corn come in soon." **1994** Dumas *Hope How Soon* (Johnson Co TN) It was "check day," so [the general store] was busy. . . . There had been a bit of a dry spell, and one farmer was buying corn for his hogs and complaining about having to buy feed. At one point he looked skyward and sad, "I hope how soon it rains!" **1995–97** Montgomery Coll (known to Adams, Brown, Ellis, Jones, Ledford, Norris); I hope how soon he comes (Cardwell). **2000** Lyon *Growing Up* 85 I kept a journal too, where I set down things that interested me. One was a sentence I'd seen printed in crayon on a young child's paper at Pine Mountain Settlement Schoo: *I hope how soon Spring comes.* **2001** Lowry *Expressions* 6 I hope how soon I'll get better.

[DARE (at *how* conj) southern Appalachians]

how that, how . . . that *conjunctive phrase* How; for similar forms with *that*, see **that C** and Grammar and Syntax §15.4.

1863 *Carter CW Letters* (Nov 26) the boys will be to home in a few days they can tell you how that I am giting along. **1863** *Poteet CW Letters* (Nov 12) you dont now how bad that I want to see you and My littel Babes. **1956** Hall Coll (Waynesville NC) This is Taylor Sutton giving my version of how that the old-timers made whiskey. **1971** AOHP/ALC-32 I can't understand how that Martin Van Buren Bates was so big. **1973** GSMNP-4:15 They was a lot of tales about the Civil War over there, how that they came through that country and killed people and so on. **1984** GSMNP-153:27 My daughter was bragging about how nice that you people was in trying to help her find out and to get some of these pictures. *Ibid.* It was a little hard I suppose for the ranger to conceive or understand how that you could go on and not have any waste products at all. **1989** *Matewan OHP-9* Could you tell me how that you did that? **1997** *Dante OHP-53* They would tell him how much that they could spend. **2014** *Blind Pig* (Jan 10) When they pulled up, I was telling him how that I had been the one taking care of the place for the last several years.

hub deep *adjective phrase* Of mud or mire: reaching the hub of a wheel. See also **deep, shoe-mouth deep, straddle deep**.

1956 Hall Coll (Townsend TN) I've seed this road down here when they'd wagon over it hub deep.

huckleberry *noun* A blueberry (*Celtis* spp) that ripens in July, earlier than the common variety.

1862 *Lockmiller CW Letters* (July) i picted thim huckle bares that you spok ov and i will send thim to you if you will come down next Sunday and take dinner. **1954** GSMNP-19:30b These blueberries, some of them calls them huckleberries, same thing. **1983** *Dark Corner OHP-24A* Huckleberries don't get as big as the blueberries, you know. Blueberries get big old things. **1993** Ison and Ison *Whole Nother Lg* 32 = a small native blue berry that grows wild in the edge of wooded areas.

[probably variant of *hurtleberry*]

huckleberry bald (also *huckleberry scald*) *noun* Same as **grass bald**.

1892 Doak *Wagonauts Abroad* 85 Before us and to our right rises the long, whale-backed ridge of the Unaka Mountain—very like a whale and bare in patches, with what are called "huckleberry balds," which differ from the balds that lie above the timber line. **1958** Miller *Pigeon's Roost* (June 26) The huckleberry scalds on Unaka Mountain are visited by many people about this time of year.

huckleberry money *noun* Money saved from picking and selling huckleberries.

1943 Justus *Bluebird* 54 She had bought the new reader with her own huckleberry money.

huckleberry scald See **huckleberry bald**.

huckleberry shower *noun* A rainstorm around the time that huckleberries ripen in July.

1982 *Smokies Heritage* 123 These wet days are "huckleberry showers," coinciding with the growth of wild huckleberry bushes on hillsides in the Smokies valleys.

huckleberry timber *noun* Timber of negligible value.

1974–75 McCracken *Logging* 16:42 You had to get way up on a pine ridge to get any pine. Then they wasn't no bloomin' size; they wasn't worth going after. Call it huckleberry timber, just scrub pine and very little of it.

hudder *noun* The sheaf placed atop a **shock** of harvested grain, usually two bundles laid crosswise.

1968 *DARE Survey* (Buchanan VA, Lexington VA, Westover WV) *hudder* = the top bundle of a shock; (Sullivan Co TN) *hooder* = cap bundles; two bundles on top to shed water. **1997** Montgomery Coll (known to Brown).

[OED3 *hooder* n "hood-sheaf" local; EDD *hooder*; CUD *hudder* (at *hood* n) "a hood sheaf"; DARE *hudder* n especially southern Appalachians]

huff See **hoof A**.

hug

A *verb*

1 To shinny up (a tree). See also **bear hug**.

1969 *DARE Survey* (Hindman KY) = to climb the trunk of a tree by holding on with your legs while you pull yourself up with

your hands. **1996–97** Montgomery *Coll* (known to Adams, Bush, Cypher, Ledford).

[DARE *hug* v 1 chiefly South Midland]

2 To cling.

1937 Hall *Coll* The bear hugged round a big pine tree. **1996** Montgomery *Coll* (known to Adams).

B *noun* See citations.

1944 Wilson *Word-List* 44 = the enclosure made by the arms or the legs or both. "The dog was so scared he sat back in my *hug* and whined." [**1995** Montgomery *Coll* (unknown to consultants from the Smoky Mountains).]

hug-me-tight (also *hug-me-tight buggy*) *noun* A one-horse, two-wheeled, horse-drawn vehicle with tight seating.

1901 Harben *Westerfelt* 6 Westerfelt certainly is settin' square up to Ab's daughter lately. "I seed 'em takin' a ride in his new hug-me-tight buggy yesterday." **c1960** Wilson *Coll* = a very narrow-seated buggy . . . "Big enough for just one, but two sat in it."

[DARE *hug-me-tight* n 1 chiefly South, South Midland]

hug-me-tight buggy See **hug-me-tight**.

huh *interjection* Same as **ah**. See also **ha**, **holy tone**, **uh**.

1967 Fetterman *Stinking Creek* 54 Preacher Marsee forced each shouted sentence from his throat with an audible gasp of the last bit of breath remaining in his lungs. The gasps punctuated and emphasized them. And each one followed on the heels of the preceding sentence like a demon in pursuit of a soul. "Adam failed. Huh. He failed miserable. Huh. And Noah failed. Huh. Jacob failed. Huh. And Moses and Solomon. Huh. These were great men, but they went down under the blows of Satan, Huh. God's favored race has not produced one man who is a match for the Devil. Huh. Not one man or woman in this world is a match for the Devil. Huh." There was a rhythmic, hypnotic flow to Preacher Marsee's delivery, and his congregation sat transfixed. He leaned far out over the podium, pointed a slender forefinger toward the floor, and cried, "Even David, the great warrior. All these men went down. Huh." Briefly, there was silence, except for a faint spewing of the coal fire in the cast-iron stove that squats in front of the pulpit. But Preacher Marsee had not come to deal with the ancient past. He removed his coat, folded it, and laid it beneath the pulpit. Preacher Marsee had come to deal with the evil on Stinking Creek, and he turned eagerly to the business at hand. "Oh, my God, if an atomic bomb fell this morning, the only safe hiding place is in Jesus Christ. Huh. He would not fail, brother. Huh." In the congregation, a voice agreed, "Never." "I could call witness after witness. Huh. A woman touched His hem. He didn't fail. Huh. I could call the leper. Huh. I could call the blind man. Huh." Preacher Marsee began to precede an occasional sentence with a short, shrill cry of exultation. "Whooo! When He came out of the tomb, He came to man the lifeboat of salvation. Huh. And there is room in that boat for you, brother. God gave you a ticket. Huh. I'll preach what I'm preaching here anywhere. I'll preach it to kings and queens. You take that man on that hill with a bull-tongue plow. Huh. I'll preach it to him. Huh. I'll preach it in every cabin on that mountain. Huh. He said, 'I give eternal life and thou shalt never perish.' Huh."

hul gul See **hull gull**.

hull

A *noun*

1 A rifle cartridge.

1913 Kephart *Our Sthn High* 101 I went to shoot up at him, but my new hulls (cartridges) fit loose in this old chamber and this one drap out, so the gun stuck. **1952** Wilson *Folk Speech NC* 553 = a cartridge for a rifle, gun, etc. **1974** Fink *Bits Mt Speech* 12 I had just two *hulls* for my gun.

[DARE *hull* n B2c chiefly South Midland]

2 The pod of a pea or bean or the outer skin of an onion; hence verb = to remove (beans or peas) from the pod.

1957 Broaddus *Vocab Estill Co KY* 42 = the pod of a pea. **1966** Dakin *Vocab Ohio River Valley* 363 Many of the oldest generation . . . in north-central Kentucky say hull (sometimes hard hull or inside hull) and this term is common to speakers of all ages in the Mountains and the Purchase. **1967** *DARE Survey* (Gatlinburg TN) = as noun or as verb. **1972** *AOHP/ALC-413* We raised beans, corn, smoked our own apples, dried apples, pickled beans, stringing beans, dried beans, peeled our own hulls. **1977** Shackelford et al. *Our Appalachia* 76 Onion hulls made yeller dye. Walnut hulls made a brown.

[DARE *hull* n B2a(3 "pod of a bean or pea; shell of a peanut" chiefly South, Midland]

3 The outside covering of a walnut; hence verb = to remove (a nut) from its shell of a walnut.

1848 (in **1870** Drake *Pioneer Life KY* 101) The "hulls" of the black walnut gave us a rusty black [dye]. **1941** Stuart *Men of Mts* 297 Honey, it's never going to make you hull eighty bushels of walnuts. **1957** Broaddus *Vocab Estill Co KY* 42 = the thick, outside covering of a walnut. **2002** Davis *Step Back* 52 The cloth would be dyed with Indigo (blue) walnut hulls (brown) poke berries (rose) and various other plants were used for different colors.

[DARE *hull* n B2a(3) chiefly South, Midland]

B *verb* To remove the pod of (a pea or bean) or the shell of (a walnut).

1930 Armstrong *This Day and Time* 227 I won't hull no more nuts today. **1949** Kurath *Word Geog East US* 29 *To hull beans* . . . instead of *to shell beans* is a Midland expression that has lost much ground. it is still common on the lower Susquehanna and in the Ohio Valley, less so in the Alleghenies, in West Virginia, and in the Blue Ridge (as far south as North Carolina). **1978** Parris *Mt Cooking* 8–9 I figure I've got it all goin' down hill when I get six or seven bushels of walnuts hulled out.

[DARE *hull* v 1 chiefly Midland]

hull gull (also *hul gul*, *hully gull*, *hully gully*, *hully gully handful*) *noun* A children's guessing game involving nuts, parched corn, marbles, etc. See also **Jack in the bush**.

1905 Miles *Spirit of Mts* 7 Sometimes, instead of calling the primary arithmetic class, I set the little ones to playing "Hull-gull, hand-full, how many?" **c1945** Haun *Hawk's Done* 278 She brought acorns to play hull-gull with him and he set in the rocking chair with his leg stretched out in front of him whilst she told him about things she heard folks say, of how the war was going and where the men were hiding. **c1950** Adams *Grandpap* 54 Grandpap had a good fire going and we were sitting around playing hullygull with our chestnuts and cracking a few hickory nuts between calls. **1952** Brewster *Games and Rhymes* 39 This game is played with grains of corn or with chinquapins. Each child starts out with the same number. The first puts a small number in one hand, extends it toward the other, and says, "Hul Gul." The other responds, "Hand full." Then the first asks, "How many?" and the second must guess the number. If the guesser is correct, the guesser wins all that are in the hand. If wrong, he must give the other the number he guessed. The game is won by the player who has the most grains at the end of a certain time. **1963** Williams *Metaphor Mt Speech II* 51 So bowleggedy I'd be willin'—if I's a bettin' man—to bet ye a double handful o' hullgull chest'nits he couldn't hem a blind pig in a fence cyorner! **1972** Davis *Christmas* 52–53 One of the most entertaining fireside games, especially for boys, was called Hull Gull, or Jack in the Bush. This is really a game of chance, and its origin is unknown, but it is one of the oldest of these fireside games. It is played with, and while eating, parched corn, which was made by mixing corn kernels with a little lard and salt and setting a pan of it on red hot fire-side coals. It was kept stirred and parched to a golden brown. Then, while the company around the fire munched this delicacy, someone would start the game of Hull Gull, or Jack in the Box. One player would get some grains or parched corn in his or her hands and say "Hull Gull." The other player would say "Hand full." Then the first player would say "How many?" The second player would then try to guess how many grains or corn were in the hand of the first player. If he guessed too many, or too few, he had to give the other player as many grains of corn as the difference between his guess and the actual number in the first player's hand. If he guessed correctly (which he rarely did), he got all the corn in the other player's hand. The players took turns guessing until one of them was broke, or without any corn. **1980** Wigginton *Foxfire VI* 292 We would have some chestnuts in our hand and the first person would say "Hull gull." The second person would ask "How many?" Then the first person would say, "A handful." Then the second person was supposed to guess how many you had. For each one they missed the guesser had to give the holder however many it was. If they guessed it exactly, the holder had to give them all to the guesser. The object was to try to get all of the hulls. **1984** Smith *Enduring Memories* 29 Any number could play the game, however, it was primarily played by two persons. It could be played for fun or keeps. Each player would start with an even number of marbles, pennies, corn, rocks, etc., usually from five to twenty. One of the players would say, "Hully Gully," the other would say "Hands full," and the starter would say, "How many?" The person other than the one who started would have to guess how many (of what they were using) pieces were concealed in his hands. If you guessed the right number you would get the pieces. If you failed to guess the number you were required to make-up the difference between your guess and what he had in his hands. Example, if you guessed five and he had only one, then you were required to give him four pieces. You would alternate guessing until one person won all the pieces that you were playing with. You could redivide and play over and over. **1991** Haynes *Haywood Home* 50 Hull-gull was the most common game we played. It was a game in which we wagered the chestnuts we were roasting and the winner came out with most of the nuts.

[DARE *hull-gull* n cf EDD *hull* v² 1 "to conceal" + *gull-stones* (at *gull* sb⁶ 1) "a game played by boys, with rough stones for marbles"; South Midland, especially southern Appalachians, Ozarks]

hully gull, **hully gully** See **hull gull**.

humble *adjective* Variant form *umble*.

1942 Hall *Phonetics Smoky Mts Smoky Mts* 86 *humble* . . . occur[s] without [h].

humor *noun* Variant forms *umer, umor, yumor*.

1863 *Whitaker CW Letters* (April 18) I am more at lasier [= leisure] to day than comon & has had some half dozen calls Since I began to write these lines I do not git out of umer tho my patience is Some times tride. **1864** *Teague CW Letter* (March 8) i will get to combe home when the damd old South is Subegatede i guess i am not inn a very good umor this morning. **1934–47** *LAMSAS Appal* (Madison Co NC) *yumor*. **1942** Hall *Phonetics Smoky Mts* 86 *yumor*.

hump (*hump (to) it*) *verb, verb phrase* To exert oneself, move or work energetically. See also **get a hump on**.

1941 Stuart *Men of Mts* 84 You either hump to it, or I'll smear your baulk with weeds. *Ibid.* 266 It took me humpin' all day to do th' work that Lefty done. **1976** Still *Pattern of Man* 39 "Anybody spoiling to tussle," Godey challenged, "well, let'em come humping." **1990** Merriman *Moonshine Rendezvous* 62 You noticed I said "WE," because for once I humped like the rest of them. **2005** Bailey *Henderson County* 30 Someone in a hurry goes "a-humpin' it," exerting great effort according to definition.

hump banjo *noun* See citation.

1977 Shackelford et al. *Our Appalachia* 20 [My daddy] had an old homemade banjer, he made it himself. A "hump banjer" is what they call them. He'd kill a cat, tan the hide and make the [banjo] head.

hump (to) it See **hump**.

hump up *verb phrase* To balk, pout, become stubborn.

2005 Williams *Gratitude* 502 *humped up* = all pouted up about something. *Humped up* like a big frog. To stub up and not talk to nobody or have nuthin' to do with nobody.

hunard See **hundred**.

hunch *verb* To squeeze (a cow's udder).

1971 Costner *Song of Life* 129 Her udder was very full and he hunched her, she stood still but the big tears ran from her eyes.

hundred *noun* Variant forms *hunard, hundard, hunderd, hundret, hunered, hun'erd, hunnert.*

1861 *Mason CW Letter* 177 two hundered of our texis rangers maid a charge on six hunered of them and whip them. **1861** *Shipman CW Letters* (June 28) last evning we had a ragment Dress per rad with about 400 hunard. **1862** *Thompson CW Letters* (Jan 24) they killed a bout 500 hunderd of hour men. **1939** Hall *Coll* (Mt Sterling NC) Back in nineteen hunderd and six I was on the waters of Big Creek. **1954** Arnow *Dollmaker* 18 Th closest that ud take him with a disease like this is mebbe Lexington—an that's nigh a hunnert miles away. **1961** Murry *Salt* 4 I don't mean to be nowise oncivil, but that there cabin were built by Gran'fer an' his least boy nigh on to a hun'erd years ago an' ain't never had nary drap o' paint on h'it, an' I reckon h'it'll stand another hun'erd without no paint. **1967** Williams *Subtlety Mt Speech* 16 The two prongs [of the church] had jined back together agin atter a hundret yurs had gone by. **1969** Ferrell *Bear Tales* 27 Zeb tole me thet judgin' by them paws, thet b'ar maybe weighed so much as six hunnert pounds. **1992** Gabbard *Thunder Road* 65 Out of a 300-gallon still like this, you'd make approximately 13 or 14 gallons of high sugarhead, hundard [sic] proof. **2013** Venable *How to Tawlk* 21 = the number immediately following ninety-nine. "Hit must be a hunnert degrees today!"

[DARE *hundred* n A1 chiefly Atlantic, South, South Midland]

hungry

A *adjective, noun* Variant forms *honggry, hongry.*

1867 Harris *Sut Lovingood* 173 He gits him a long house, prints ontu the frunt ove hit sum ketchin name, tu tote in the hongry an' onwary, an' the dam fools ginerally, calls hissef the "Perpryiter." **1898** Elliott *Durket Sperret* 55 Pears like you ain't much honggry. **1942** Hall *Phonetics Smoky Mts* 40 ['hɔŋgri].

[DARE *hungry* adj, n especially South, South Midland]

B Thirsty. See also **starve.**

1937 Hall *Coll* (Wears Cove TN) The stock's hungry for water. We're hungry for water. **1939** Hall *Coll* (Waynesville NC) I'm hungry for a drink. **1995** Montgomery *Coll* (known to Cardwell); I'm hungry for water (Shields).

hunk *noun* An unsophisticated country person, rustic.

1890 Fruit *KY Words* 65 = a country fellow, as: "He is a country hunk." **1924** Greer-Petrie *Angeline Gits Eyeful* 21 If hit wuz the fashion fur rich wimmen to smoke seeg'rets, shorely and undoubtedly hit wuz all right fur us country hunks to . . . smoke our cob pipes, or chaw. **1986** Pederson et al. *LAGS* (Hamilton Co TN) *hunk;* (Jefferson Co TN) *absolute hunk.*

[DARE *hunk* n[1] 2 especially KY, TN]

hunker

A (also *hunkle*) *noun* The haunch or buttock.

1859 Taliaferro *Fisher's River* 152 He was ever busy . . . sitting on his "hunkers" cutting out millstones in the lonely mountains. **1913** Bruce *Terms from TN* 58 *hunkle* = haunch . . . "[He was] skrunched on his hunkles (haunches)." **1913** Kephart *Our Sthn High* 171 Hell's banjer. They don't go prodjectin' around looking for stills. They set at home on their hunkers till some fellers comes and informs. **1934–47** *LAMSAS Appal* (Swain Co NC) *hunkers.* **1939** Hall *Coll* (Cades Cove TN) We started along on our hunkers. **1974** Fink *Bits Mt Speech* 12 I sat back on my *hunkers.* **1986** Pederson et al. *LAGS* (Blount Co TN, Cocke Co TN, Jefferson Co TN).

[EDD (at *hunkers* sb) Scot, Irel, nEngl; DARE *hunker* n chiefly Midland, South]

B (also *hunker down, hunker up*) *verb, verb phrase* To crouch, squat down (as to rest one's weight on one's haunches); figuratively = to get down to work.

1868 (in **1974** Harris *High Times* 211) We wer all hunker'd round the hearth, sayin' nothin', an' waitin for the taters to roast. **1940** Stuart *Trees of Heaven* 60 Fronnie gets up from her hunkered position by the cane-mill. **1944** Wilson *Word-List* 44 *hunker up* = to squat on the haunches; to be humped up or bent over awkwardly. "It was so cold he *hunkered up* in the wagon." **1969** GSMNP-27: 12 You see he even seed us hunkered down at the house. **1975** Gainer *Speech Mtneer* 12 = to squat or to sit on haunches. "I hunkered down behind a bush and waited for him." **1984–85** *Sevier Settler* 3:7 I didn't know it at the time, but someone that worked there hunkered down behind the caskets, and when we were finished, he jumped out and scared the living daylights out of all of us. **1990** Bailey *Draw Up Chair* 12 He may have to "hunker down" and rest on one heel just as his Scottish ancestors did. **1996–97** Montgomery *Coll*: *hunker down* = always used figuratively in reference to work, as in "Let's hunker down and get this done" (Ellis); *hunker up* (known to Adams, Brown, Cardwell, Ledford, Oliver). **2007** McMillon *Notes*: *hunker up* = hunker down.

[SND *hunker* v 1; CUD *hunker* v 1 "crouch, squat so that the knees rest on the buttocks"; DARE *hunker* v 1a scattered, but especially South Midland]

hunker down, hunker up See **hunker B.**

hunkle See **hunker A.**

hunnert See **hundred.**

hunt *verb*

A Forms.

1 Variant past-tense form *hunt.*

1954 GSMNP-19:30b We hunt one night up on Scratch Britches Mountain and dark come along. **1957** GSMNP-23:1:11 Shields stay with my daddy and hunt my granddaddy. **1973** GSMNP-80:9 Thinking me a young woman, I hunt me another boy friend. **1973** GSMNP-87:2:7 I never hunt no bear much. I never could see good enough to kill bears.

2 Variant past-participle form *hunt.*

1975–76 Wolfram/Christian *WV Coll* 30 We've took and went and hunt for people before, and they'd be drunk crawling up in a hollow log somewhere or another.

B In compound verbs *bear hunt, chestnut hunt, coon hunt, possum hunt, rabbit hunt,* etc. = to hunt for bears, chestnuts, etc.

1939 Hall *Coll* (Nine Mile TN) A passel of us fellows gathered up here to bear hunt, and we appointed Doc Jones to lead the hunt. *Ibid.* (Hazel Creek NC) We went over there a-chestnut hunting and took our women with us. **1970** Foster *Walker Valley* 13 I've rabbit hunted some, but say, bear hunting and deer hunting and such as that, I never did go for it. **1975** GSMNP-62:2 We possum hunted and we coon hunted and we hog hunted and we done a little of this and a little of that out here, but the main joy part of it was hog hunting and coon hunting, you know, to have some fine races of coons and hogs, and we enjoyed that about the best of anything in the hunting line. *Ibid.* 13 We'd go way back there on the Enloe and Three Fork and fish, and we'd go there to ginseng hunt too. **1997** GSMNPCOHP-3:13 Dad never did do much bear hunting. Of course, he rabbit hunted and squirrel hunted and things like that.

huntingest *adjective* Hunting the most or with the greatest proficiency. See also **-est 1**. See also Grammar and Syntax §3.4.1.

1957 Parris *My Mts* 171 This was part of the story of Trim, the huntin'est coon dog in all the mountains—maybe in all the land—and of old Billy-B, the famous old hunter who put his dog above his son. **1991** Thomas *Sthn Appal* 158 When I wuz a boy, we had a little dog. We called 'im "Moss." He was th' huntin'est dog I ever saw in my life.

hunt up *verb phrase* To search for and find (something or someone).

1940 Oakley *Roamin'/Restin'* 114 We then pulled out these boards and carried them to the yard of the cabin where the ded man was and we hunted up hammer and hand saw. **1971** Thornburgh *Great Smoky Mts* 162 That writer-man hunted up the triflinest, the most no-countest family he could find to write up. **1983** McDermitt *Boy Named Jack* 19 He took out to hunt him up.

hur See **hear**, **here A**.

hurrah's nest *noun*

A Variant form *hoorah's nest* [see **1956** in **B**].

B A place or thing in complete disorder or confusion.

1940 Haun *Hawk's Done* 74 [She] said the house always looked like a perfect hurrah's nest—pet goats and everything. **1956** McAtee *Some Dial NC* 23 *hoo-rah's nest* = an untidy conglomeration.

hurricane *noun*

A Variant forms *harrican* [see **2007** in **B1**], *harricane* [see **1834** in **B2**], *herrycane* [see **1982** in **B1**].

1892 Fruit *KY Words* 233 *haricane*. **1923** Combs *Addenda KY* 242 *harricane*. **1942** Hall *Phonetics Smoky Mts* 42 ['hærɪkən].

[DARE *harricane* (at *hurricane* n A5) scattered, but chiefly South, South Midland]

B Senses.

1 A severe windstorm.

1834 Crockett *Narrative* 150 In the morning we concluded to go on with the boat to where a great harricane crossed the river, and blowed all the timber down into it. **1966** *DARE Survey* = a destructive wind that blows straight (Cherokee NC). **1969** GSMNP-38:135 A windstorm, we called it the young hurricane. **1982** Powers and Hannah *Cataloochee* 421 He said that he wished they'd come a herrycane and blow the cranberry bushes out of the ground. **1995** Montgomery *Coll* (known to Cardwell, Shields). **2007** McMillon *Notes*: *harrican* = a wind that blew over trees.

2 A growth of cane or other vegetation in an area where trees have apparently been leveled in the past by strong winds.

1834 Crockett *Narrative* 151 We cut out, and moved up to the harricane, where we stop'd for the night. **1918** Combs *Word-List South* 34 *hurricane* = a thicket of cane or other underbrush. **1960** McCaulley *Cades Cove* [He] carried that in to the hurricane, an old man. **1996** Montgomery *Coll*: *hurricane* (known to Adams, Cardwell, Ledford), = also refers to laurel thicket (Ellis).

[originally < Carib; DARE *hurricane* n B1c "land leveled by wind" especially South, South Midland]

hurt *verb*

1 Variant past-tense form *hurted*.

1913 Kephart *Our Sthn High* 284 There are many corrupt forms of the verb, such as gwine for gone or going . . . hurted, dremp. **1936** Coleman *Dial N GA* 26 "Hurted" [is used] for "hurt." **c1940** Simms *Coll*. **2000** Montgomery *Coll* (known to Cardwell).

2 Variant past-participle form *hurted*.

1925 Furman *Glass Window* 89 Their pride would be hurted if they didn't do theirselves full justice.

[DARE *hurt* v B chiefly South, South Midland, especially South Atlantic]

hurted See **hurt 1**, **2**.

hurt for *verb phrase*

1 To lack, be in desperate need of.

1913 Kephart *Our Sthn High* 32 Thar's lots o' folks a-hurtin' around hyur for lard. **1974** Fink *Bits Mt Speech* 13 = need. "This house is *hurting for* a coat of paint." **1976** Garber *Mountain-ese* 45 The corn crop is really hurtin' for water.

2 To deserve.

1975 Chalmers *Better* 66 One who is outspoken is said to speak with great liberty, and a brash child is a-hurtin' for a licking.

hurting *noun*

1 A pain, soreness, ache.

1862 Councill *CW Letters* (Feb 4) I stode gard nite beefore last an it give me a hurten in my brest an my head. **1862** *Watkins CW Letters* (June 8) William Briley has got the mesel So sargent Long ses and Tommson has got a hurting in his back. **1904–20** Kephart *Notebooks* 2:475 I've got a hurtin' in my chist. **1930** Armstrong *This Day and Time* 121 I taken a hurtin' to my side. **1957** Combs *Lg Sthn High: Word List* 52 = physical pain. Ex.: "She's got a hurtin' in her right breast." **c1960** Wilson *Coll* = a sort of indefinite ache or pain, like a hurting in the chest. **1967** *DARE Survey* (Maryville TN) = pain: "He's had a hurting in his side for a week." **1974** Fink *Bits Mt Speech* 13 I had a powerful *hurting* in my chest. **1985** Wear *Lost Communities* 18 Once when brother Jack was home on leave from the Navy he took a real bad hurting in his side.

[DARE *hurting* n 1 chiefly South, South Midland]

2 A fight that inflicts pain.

1867 Harris *Sut Lovingood* 97a [sic] No man an oman could ever get as clost as man and wife should, arter sich a h—l ove a fuss an hurtin as tuck place at ole Burns' that day.

husband call *noun* A woman's call for her husband's attention; hence *husband calling* = a competition in which women contestants display original calls for their husbands.

1937 Hall *Coll* (Gatlinburg TN) At the annual Old Timers' Day [in Gatlinburg], one woman won a prize for her husband call: "Corn pone? Come and eat it or leave it alone." **1978** Hall *Yarns and Tales* 1 Among other forms of entertainment like ballad and folk-song singing, music from mountain string bands, hog-calling, and husband-calling, the highlight was a contest of who could tell the "biggest" story. **1986** Ogle *Lucinda* 66 The old folks and young would join in competing, such as string bands, single instruments, dancing, buck and wing, clog dancing, hog calling, husband calling, etc.

husband-high *adjective* Of a young woman; fully grown and presumably old enough to marry.

1951 Craig *Singing Hills* 120 When she was husband-high she saw one man shoot at another.

[DARE *husband-high* adj especially Appalachians Ozarks]

hush-mouthed *adjective* See citation. See also **play hushmouth**.

1992 Brooks *Sthn Stuff* 74 = not revealing anything; keeping one's own counsel. "I swear, if he isn't the most hush-mouthed individual I ever met in my life!"

hushpuppy *noun* Ham gravy.

1939 Farr *TN Mt Regions* 91 = ham gravy: "I sop my bread with hush-puppy."

husk *noun* See citation.

2007 Ball *Tub Mills* 15 The husk [i.e. a heavy timber frame under the millstones; now commonly called a "Hurst" frame] was made of round logs built into the wall; the water or tub wheel was some three feet in diameter, and split boards driven into the sides of the shaft made the buckets.

hussif (also *huzzypocket, huzzypoke*) *noun* See 1975 citation.

1952 Wilson *Folk Speech NC* 553 *huzzy-pocket* = a pocket which is hung on the wall to put little things in. **1975** Gainer *Witches Ghosts Signs* 12 = a rectangular-shaped piece of cloth . . . with pockets sewed on it in which to keep needles, thread, and thimbles: "Aunt Sarry kept her hussif hangin' at the left of the fireplace." **1978** Hiser *Quare Do's* 140 Aunt Sibby Combs searched her huzzypoke [for a coin].

[variant of *housewife*]

hyanner See **yonder**.

hyar See **hear, here**.

hyarb woman See **herb granny B**.

hyear, hyeard See **hear**.

hyer See **hear, here**.

hyerd See **hear**.

hyere See **here**.

hyme See **hymn**.

hymn *noun* Variant forms *hime, hyme* [rhymes with *dime*].

1824 Knight *Letter from KY* 107 Some words are [pronounced] . . . by the lower classes in society . . . very uncouthly, as . . . hymn. **1881** Pierson *In the Brush* 116 "Such a thing as a hime" (hymn), continued the old man, "singin' himes or prayin', why, there wa'n't no such thing in all the neighborhood." **1890** Fruit *KY Words* 68 *hyme*. **1927** Furman *Lonesome Road* 54 He himself [was] always received as "Preacher Jared Stoll's boy," [and] the singing of the "hime tunes." **1974** Roberts *Sang Branch* 210 This boy's father took a notion he'd try to skeer Johnny with the corpse. He taken the corpse and set him up in a chear and placed a hime book in his hand, made him look right natural.

hymn lining *noun* See citation. See also **line B**.

1995 McCauley *Mt Religion* 107 The practice of hymnlining in Old Regular Baptist churches today has nothing to do with the absence of hymnals; rather, it has to do with melodies following no standard notation, having depended on the oral tradition for their continuation. The melodies are closely "modal" and are hard to follow using the standard notation of music.

hyonder See **yonder**.

hyur See **here**.

I

i See **ay**.

I be dod, I be dogged See **I'll be dog**.

I been (also *I've been, I've done been*) *phrase* See citations.

1939 Hall Coll [Come in and eat somethin' with us.] No, I been [i.e. I've already eaten]. **1975** Jackson *Unusual Words* 153 A man invited to dinner, [says] "I've been," a telescoping of the longer answer, "I've already been to the table." **1994–97** Montgomery *Coll: I've been* (known to Adams, Cardwell, Jones, Ledford, Norris, Oliver, Weaver), = more common form is *I've done been* (Ellis).

ice tide *noun* An excessive flow of water in rivers and streams, occurring in early spring and containing chunks of ice from higher elevations. See also **tide A**.

1972 *AOHP/LJC-104* About in March they'd be the awfullest ice tide that you ever saw. It would just turn over these big pieces a-grinding and a-going down through there.

icicle *noun* Variant forms *ishe-shicle, i-shickle*.

1925 Dargan *Highland Annals* 94 We's well up Smoky, an' the coldest wind ablowin' that ever made an i-shickle out of a man's gizzard. **1949** McDavid *Grist* 110 (Clarke Co GA) *ishe-shicles* = icicles. **1968** *DARE Survey* (Laurel Fork VA) = old-fashioned mountain pronunciation.

idea *noun* Variant forms *ideal, idear, idee, ider, idey, idy* (forms sometimes have stress on first syllable (['adi]).

1858 (in **1974** Harris *High Times* 154) The idear now seemed tu strike him fur the furst time that he could talk Dutch. **1862** Hitt *CW Letters* (May 21) you hant no idee how the Camp life is nor no body els but them how [= who] trise it thay ar All that nose. **1862** Reese *CW Letters* (Dec 27) I wanted to see you and my dear Children O how Bad you dont no you hav no idey. **1863** Hundley *CW Letters* (May 9) it has Bin So long Since I got ary letter from yo Before I got this I had given out the ider of getting eny more. **1866** Smith *So Called* 136 [W]ith nary idée that the winter will come again. **1891** Primer *Studies in WV* 167 *Idea* frequently has the accent on the first syllable (aídi, or aídië). **1900** Harben *N GA Sketches* 80 Do you have any idee what I cleared last year, not countin' bad debts an' expenses? **1936** (in **1952** Mathes *Tall Tales* 212) "Cole," the officer said quietly, "I guess you know what I've come for." "No idy at all," drawled Grannison. **1937** Wilson *Folklore SE KY* 30 *idear*. **c1940** Simms Coll A mountain man wanted to know, Who and what give the outlanders the idee (idea) that we'uns (the mountain people) air a lot ov hell-goin' trouble-raisers? **1967** Hall Coll (Townsend TN) I don't know what was their idy. **1975** Montgomery *File: ideal*. **1991** Thomas *Sthn Appal* 188 It's out to'ards Deep Gap. I have a idy.

ideal, idear, idee, ider, idey See **idea**.

idiot *noun* Variant forms *idjet, idjit*.

1892 Dromgoole *Dan to Beersheba* 79 [That's] what Joe ud say, ef he ain't a idjit born. **1954** Arnow *Dollmaker* 81 You're th biggest idjet. **1984** Burns *Cold Sassy* 163 I told her she sounded like a idjit.

idiot stick *noun* Same as **gee-haw whimmy diddle**.

1970 *DARE File* (seKY) = another name for a gee-haw whimmy-diddle—so called because only an idiot can make it work.

idjet, idjit See **idiot**.

idlesome *adjective* Shiftless, lazy.

1958 Campbell *Tales* 32 One of them was ugly as homemade sin and lazy and idlesome. Tother was pretty as a picture and helpsome and work brittle. **1997** Montgomery Coll (known to Brown, Cardwell).

[DARE *idlesome* adj especially South Midland]

I don't care (to) See **care B**.

idy See **idea**.

if *conjunction* Variant forms *ef, hif, ift*. See also **iffen**.

1843 (in **1956** Eliason *Tarheel Talk* 312) (Caldwell Co NC) *ef*. **1859** Taliaferro *Fisher's River* 117 [At l]ast I made out to ax Sally ef she'd have me. **1863** *Bartlett CW Letters* (April 4) ef I live I will get to go back to Tenn before long. **1863** *Shipman CW Letters* (July 20) Ef I hear eny thing Els about him I will let you no as Soon as I Can. **1886** Smith *Sthn Dialect* 348 Well, fellers, ef you'uns cross the mountains about dinner time, you'd better come by and git yer dinner; you-uns hain't got the wuth of yer quarter yit. **1895** Edson and Fairchild *TN Mts* 374 Ef the world's as big every way as she is that-a-way, she's a whopper. **1927** Mason *Lure of Smokies* 232 Ef them b'ar hadn't been sleepy an' doby, they would 'a' et him alive! **1930** Armstrong *This Day and Time* 7 Ef she hadn't a'gone an' bobbed her hairs. **1938** (in **2009** Powell *Shenandoah Letters* 154) Ef you want to you can Send Some Body to eastamate about what it would Been worth. **1963** Williams *Metaphor Mt Speech II* 51 El'zd better watch aout er he'll git hisself slished in two on that old brute—hif it don't fall daown with 'im ra't in the middle o' the big road and plumb sqush his soul-case. **1973** *Foxfire Interviews* A-73-86 I don't know ift anybody does it. **1974** Fink *Bits Mt Speech* 6 Ef I don't *discomfit* ye none.

[DARE *ef* (at *if* conj) chiefly South, South Midland]

iffen *conjunction* See also **if**.

A Variant forms *effen* [see **1974** in **B**], *eff'n* [see **1990** in **B**], *efn* [see **1957** in **B**], *ifn* [see **1995** in **B**], *if'n* [see **1984** in **B**].

B If.

1936 Skidmore *Lift Up Eyes* 11 Efn I didn't watch you, Blossom, you'd turn inter a cake o[f] sugar. **1939** Hall Coll (Cherokee NC) Iffen you folks now knows anything about when the Confederate War ended, why you can tell just how long I've been in Jackson and in Swain. **1942** Hall *Phonetics Smoky Mts* 93 Come into the fire iffen you-ones wants to. **1957** Combs *Lg Sthn High: Word List* 33 *efn* = evidently a contraction of *if* and *when*. Ex.: "Efn he comes,

I'll name (mention) it to him." **1962** Dykeman *Tall Woman* 249 "Iffen you've helped save Old Thunder, I'll be beholden to you," Morgan Bludsoe said. **1974** Fink *Bits Mt Speech* 8 I'll go *effen* you don't mind. *Ibid.* 13 I'll come *iffen* I can. **1975** Chalmers *Better* 5 As Preacher Pink used to say, "Folks, I've got a good discourse if-n the Lord'll jest give me the words to language hit out." **1984** *Six Hill 'n Holler* 7 = if: I'll go with you if'n hit's so's I kin. **1990** Aiken *Wiley Oakley* Don't complain. People ain't a-goin' to like you eff'n you are allus a grouching.... They like to do the grouchin themselves. **1995** South *What It Is* 42 Ifn I can kneel down, Charlie, I can touch it.

[DARE *iffen* conj perhaps pronunciation-spelling for *if* + *and* conj, chiefly South, South Midland]

if happen *conjunctive phrase* If it happens that. See also **happen**.

1943 Hannum *Mt People* 146 Their phrasing has a rhythm to it, such as ... "if happen you pass."

-ified *suffix* added to a noun, adjective, or verb to form an adjective. See also **-ify**.

c1945 Haun *Hawk's Done* 223 She made George set in the playhouse with her, and he would do it, no matter how much Pa teased him and called him girlified and threatened to make him wear dresses. **1957** Combs *Lg Sthn High: Syntax* 5–6 The suffix *-ified* is affixed to a large number of verbs and nouns, to form adjectives: "She went down on her bendified knees." "She's techified, don't touch her." "They say he's fittified." **1967** *DARE Survey* (Maryville TN) *faintified* = having a sudden feeling of weakness, when sometimes the person loses consciousness. **1975** GSMNP-62:3 We'd trim him and turn him loose, and he wouldn't be so fightyfied. **1981** Whitener *Folk-Ways* 54 Of course, modern long handles are a far cry from those of bygone days. They have been prettified, thermofied, and advertised until they have achieved social acceptance. **1990** Bailey *Draw Up Chair* 14 If a person working unusually hard is said to be "workified," logically one suffering from spells or fits is "fittified." **1997** Montgomery *Coll* I'll be blamified if I'll tell you (Cardwell). **1998** Montgomery *Coll* = mountaineers often make adjectives and adverbs from practically any noun or other part of speech by simply adding "fied,"—a person who is argumentative may be said to be "argufied," or a fish market might be said to smell "fishified," and it would not be uncommon for a person who exhibited characteristics of a town resident to be called "townified" (Ledford).

[DARE *-ified* suff chiefly South, South Midland]

ifn, if'n See **iffen**.

if so be *conjunctive phrase* If it happens that.

1931 Combs *Lg Sthn High* 1305 He'll name it (mention) to Jones, if so be he's there.

ift See **if**.

if that *conjunctive phrase* If; for similar forms with *that*, see **that C** and Grammar and Syntax §15.4.

1960 McCaulley *Cades Cove* I acted as undertaker. If that somebody died, they'd send for John McCaulley to come and dress this man and fix him up for burial.

if the world's as big *phrase* A favorite emphatic expression among older speakers in the Smoky Mountains in the late 1930s, as observed by Joseph Hall. See citations.

1895 Edson and Fairchild *TN Mts* 374 Ef the world's as big every way as she is that-a-way, she's a whopper. **1959** Hall *Coll* (Hartford TN) They were a number of the neighbors would come in and asked her what she thought of the world beyond the mountain, and they asked her how big it was and she said "Lordy me," she said, "if the world's as big that way," pointing the opposite direction, "as it is that way," pointing toward out of Cosby, "my God, it's a golly whopper."

-ify *suffix* added to a verb redundantly to form a verb or to a noun to form a verb. See also **-ified**.

1922 Cobb *KY Mt Rhymes* 25 Them fotched-on women, now, that runs the School, / And speechifies on Voting, and don't own / A man 'mongst them all. **c1945** Haun *Hawk's Done* 229 Abe and George took to argufying back and forth and fussing with one another and got dubious of one another and sullen.

[DARE *-ify* suff chiefly South, South Midland]

I God, I golly, I gonnies, I grannies, I growneys See **ay**.

I house *noun* See citation.

2002 Tate *Log Houses* 7 The I house is a traditional British folk form that was common in pre-railroad America ... and remained common throughout the Upland South until the turn of the century. The I house is a two story house that is two rooms wide and one room deep.

ilant See **island**.

ile See **oil**.

ill *adjective* Of a person or an animal: bad-tempered, irritable, vicious, harsh (as in phrase *ill as a hornet*).

1860 Olmsted *Back Country* 266 "Ill" is used for "vicious." "Is your horse ill?" **1862** *Lockmiller CW Letters* (June 22) the bees swarm Sonday after you left hare tha[y] wose So ill tha[y] tride to sting us all to dath wone stong me in the eye icod not see out of it for 2 or 3 days. **1886** Smith *Southernisms* 39 Ill, "vicious," is common in East Tennessee ... I heard a man in the Smoky Mountains say "Some rattlesnakes are iller'n others"; and another said that "black rattlesnakes are the illest." **1895** Edson and Fairchild *TN Mts* 372 The cow is ill when she is pestered. **1913** Kephart *Our Sthn High* 80 Hit's the younger [dog] that's ill. **1917** Kephart *Word-List* 413 = ill-natured, vicious. "That feller's ill as h[ell]." **1939** Hall *Coll* (Gatlinburg TN) He was a awful ill teacher. *Ibid.* (Tow String Creek NC) We understand your ill way of talking. *Ibid.* (White Oak NC) "He's as ill as a hornet" [said of a person who's been on a drunk or had a bad night of any kind]. **1941** Hall *Coll* (Alexander NC) That dog is as ill as a hornet. **c1960** Wilson *Coll* = angry, high-tempered; not [used] much for sick till lately. **1975** Chalmers *Better* 66 A cross person is as ill as a hornet. **1981** Brewer *Wonderment* 197 Oldtime beekeepers always claimed the bees "got a heep iller, would sting you quicker," when they were working on chestnut bloom. **1985** Irwin *Alex Stewart* 265 A rattlesnake ain't so ill as a copperhead. **1997** Montgomery *File* They're ill little fellows, them black jackets is (60-year-old man, Maggie Valley NC). **2003** Gibson *Sthn Mt Dialect* One personal story I will share with you concerning the words "ill" and "sick." We were living in Ft. Wayne, Indiana in the late 1950s. My brother and I were attending elementary school. It was during winter and I had a very bad cold and could not go to school one day. The teacher asked my brother about my absence. My brother Donny replied, "He is sick today." The teacher scolded him for using the word sick. She told him the proper word was ill. She also made a reference to our being from Tennessee and that we would have to learn to use good English. Needless to say this embarrassed my brother very much. Years later I was very happy to find out that the adjective "ill" was used since the 1300s to describe a person or animal as being "bad tempered" and not for being sick. Also that good English used the word "sick" to refer to bad health. The word sick was used long before people ever started saying "ill" to describe someone in bad health. **2017** *Blind Pig* (Nov 4) I can remember my gramma saying to me to not be so ill when I was pouting or acting up. *Ibid.* Ill means a person is in a bad mood. If someone is sick, I never say they are ill.

[OED3 (at *ill* 2a (of humans), 2b (of animals), the latter now dialect, but apparently Scots dial in reference to humans); cf SND *ill* adj I.4; CUD *ill* adv "sorely, badly"; HT *ill* adv "badly"; Web3 *ill* adj 5c "of an animal: dangerously fierce . . . of a person: cantankerous"; DARE *ill* adj chiefly South, South Midland]

ill-able (also *illy able*) *adjective phrase* Unable.

1823 (in **2003** *TN Petitions II* 206) at that time the friends to whose S[d] house whose duty it was to Secure the title to S[d] land from the State was Engaged in Saving their own lands and was very illy able to do anything more. **1922** *TN CW Ques* 1387 (Wilkes Co NC) But Ime now olde illabel to do enything looseing my reclection.

[SND *ill-able* adj "unable, unfit"]

ill as a hornet See **ill**.

I'll be bound See **bound B2**.

I'll be dog (also *I'll be dod, I'll be dogged*) *interjection phrase* Used as an exclamation or mild oath (often prefaced by *well* and with *will* elided to produce *I be*). See also **bedabs, b'gad, by, dad-, dog**[1].

1867 Harris *Sut Lovingood* 141 I be dod rabbited ef a man can't 'propriate happiness by the skinful ef he is in contack wif sumbody's widder, an' is smart. **1939** Hall *Coll* (Cades Cove TN) I'll be dogged if I know. **c1960** Wilson *Coll* I be dog. **1966** Dykeman *Far Family* 183 I *want* tenderloin and ambrosia, but I'll be dogged if I can find anything to fix it with. **1976** GSMNP-113:8 I'll be dogged if I know. We never fooled with medicine much. **1983** *Dark Corner OHP-5A* I seed they's a little hole in it. I thought, I said, "Well now, I'll be dogged if a rat hadn't got to [the smoked ham]." **1997** Montgomery *Coll*: *I'll be dogged* (known to nine consultants from the Smoky Mountains).

[euphemism for *I'll be damned*; DARE *dogged* (at *dog* v 6) chiefly South, South Midland, *I be* phr chiefly South, South Midland]

ill-convenient *adjective phrase* Inconvenient, unsuitable.

1826 (in **2003** *TN Petitions I* 119) We your petitioners living near the county lines of Knox and Jefferson Join with our Neighbours living in a corner of Sevear County North of bays mountain between the mountain and holstian River Consisting of only about four plantations which corner of sd County lies very il convenient to Sevierville or to the company muster ground. **1883** Murfree *Old Sledge* 552 It air a blessin' that I hev got it agin, for't would hev been might ill convenient round hyar 'thout it. **1917** Kephart *Word-List* 413 = inconvenient. **1965** *Dict Queen's English* 6 He got sick at an *ill-convenient* time. **1994–97** Montgomery *Coll* (known to Brown, Cardwell).

[SND (at *ill-* adv 1); CUD *ill-convenient* (at *ill* adv)]

illegal *adjective* Of a child: illegitimate.

1957 Broaddus *Vocab Estill Co KY* 44. **1997** Montgomery *Coll* (known to Adams, Brown, Bush).

[EDD *illegal* adj 2 "a bastard"; DARE *illegal* adj especially South, South Midland]

I'll swan See **swan**.

I'll tell you what's the truth *phrase* Used as an exclamation to emphasize the following assertion.

1937 Hall *Coll* (Smokemont NC).

ill-turned *adjective* Cross, quarrelsome, easily upset or provoked. See also **turn B1**.

1949 Arnow *Hunter's Horn* 331 Used to be Nunn and Milly never quarreled, but lately seemed like Nunn was so ill turned he quarreled at them all, even Milly.

I mean *interjection* I'll tell you!, I swear! (preceding or following a statement or in response to one, to express intensity, surprise, or certainty that what is said is true).

1953 Hall *Coll* (Bryson City NC) A yellow patch, that's where there's ivy, briars, hemlock, big trees, and I mean it's so rough nothing but a bear nor a good bear hunter goes, and a good pack of hounds. **1973** GSMNP-4:17 We didn't have them on Little Cataloochee. I mean we made a lot of music, but I mean we didn't have what we called shindigs, square dances. **1973** GSMNP-13:29 The old man Daniel Cook was a preacher, I mean just homemade preacher, yes. **1984** GSMNP-153 (Little Cataloochee NC) The little children, younguns was crying, you know, and hollerin' and takin' on and I mean that scared me up. **1998** *Dante OHP-12* They was stacking lumber sometimes high as them trees yonder, I mean acres of it.

imitate *verb* (usually in negative constructions) To compare with, match in quality.

1937 Hall *Coll* (Cosby Creek TN) These apples we have don't imitate those we had. **1973** *GSMNP*-79:9 We have chestnuts nowadays, but our chestnuts doesn't imitate the mountain chestnuts, so if you've never tasted the good sweet mountain chestnut, you've really missed a treat.

imitator salamander *noun* See citation.

2015 *Imitator Salamander* 4 Imitators are so-called because some of them sport red cheeks that make them look similar to Jordan's Red-cheeked Salamanders. It's wise to mimic Red-cheeked Salamanders because they are distasteful to many predators, including birds. The slick slime they produce also functions as a defense. So Imitators benefit from the predator avoidance without the need for the distastefulness. Virtually the entire range of Imitator Salamanders lies within the [Great Smoky Mountain National] park, as does the entire range of Red-cheeked Salamanders. A high degree of genetic diversity has been found to exist between populations of Imitators, and many individuals lack any cheek coloration. . . . Imitation is consistent with mimicry theory, wherein one species evolves to imitate another noxious species, though in the Imitator Salamander's case, it may not always be employed.

imp *verb* To imitate.

1911 Shearin *E KY Word-List* 538 = to imitate.

importantest *adjective* Most important.

1962 Dykeman *Tall Woman* 223 Remember, getting born will be one of the two importantest things that ever happens to a baby.

impress *verb* See citation.

1931 Combs *Lg Sthn High* 1303 Many formal words and terms are used glibly [by preachers], thus influencing everyday speech . . . My brethering, (or breethren), I feel impressed to tell ye the truth.

improve up *verb phrase* To mend in condition or health. See also **up A1**.

1939 Hall *Coll* (Emerts Cove TN) She's improved up a bit.

in

A *preposition*

1 (also *up in*, *upwards in*) Used to express one's age in decades (with the decade being singular).

1931 Goodrich *Mt Homespun* 39 When I first saw Aunt Liza she was "upwards in sixty," but still strong and active, with brisk step and bright eyes. *Ibid.* 71 Like she allays is, sorter poky, and on the backgrounds, but she 'peared to be mighty peart for the age she's gettin' to be. She must be upwards in sixty. **1937** Hall *Coll* (Cades Cove TN) Nathe Burchfield says he is in the eighty. **1938** Stuart *Dark Hills* 21 He must be up in eighty. **1958** Campbell *Tales* 181 Doc is way up in seventy, but he won't never own up to it. **1961** *Coe Ridge OHP*-333A I guess he's in seventy or maybe eighty. **1998** Montgomery *Coll* (known to Adams, Brown, Bush, Cardwell, Ledford, Norris).

2 Used as the initial element in phrasal prepositions (especially *in under*). See also Grammar and Syntax §14.5. See also **in under**.

1862 *Tesh CW Letters* (Dec 6) our hole army is Falling back to Take up Winter quarters Some Wher in a bout Culppeper Cort House or Gordonsville. **1939** Hall *Coll* (Cataloochee NC) Very near everybody made it. An uncle of mine and a cousin [were] making liquor in above my home. *Ibid.* (Deep Creek NC) He's laying right on the right in under the Smokies, the head of the left hand fork of Deep Creek. *Ibid.* (Proctor NC) They come on in down there then and skinned out and packed him [= a bear] out to the cabin that night. **1953** Hall *Coll* (Bryson City NC) Later on, in a few weeks or months after that, they found a dead pant'er in across at the river bluffs down to the end of the Smoky Mountain in there. **1960** McCaulley *Cades Cove* Let's go in down here on Monday morning and work that crop out. Well, we'd go out down there on Monday morning and work that crop out. **1969** *GSMNP*-46:20 Bradburn had a stack [of wheat] just in behind the schoolhouse out here at Shoal Creek, and they wouldn't go up there and thrash it. **1973** *Foxfire Interviews* A-73-86 We never did hardly ever go in down any further than the church. **1974** *AOHP/ASU*-204 My grandma and grandpap had three kids buried them away back out there in around the four creeks somewheres in a graveyard. **1974–75** McCracken *Logging* 5:49 About the first skidder I helped move after we left Elkmont set right about where we're at, right back in against the hill there. *Ibid.* 10:38 We had a big garden right down in under yonder. *Ibid.* 23:32 We started wooding there, along not far from Polls Gap and a-going back in on toward Heintoga, behind the timber cutting. **1974** Roberts *Sang Branch* 58–59 I remember they's a cornival in at Evarts in below Bailey's Creek one time. **1991** Thomas *Sthn Appal* 190 They'uz some loggin' people workin' in around there.

[SND *in* adv 1(9) before preps *in aboot* . . . *in at* . . . *in* has little more than intensive force]

3 Within, at a distance of.

c1841 Shane (in **1998** Perkins *Border Life* 196) Carr's Creek was in about 7 miles of us. **1861** *Griffin CW Letters* (Aug 3) the yankies is coming on they ar in twelve mils of our camp. **1863** *Revis CW Letters* (May 13) wee air in 8 miles of the cumberlan river. **1939** Hall *Coll* (Deep Creek NC) They was in three hundred yards of the top of Smoky fighting. **1991** Thomas *Sthn Appal* 104 He came jist in a hair of goin' right back over in th' waggin.

B *adverb*

1 Used to extend the action of a verb. See Grammar and Syntax §14.4.

1939 Hall *Coll* (Cataloochee NC) We dressed the bear and carried him in home. *Ibid.* (Cataloochee NC) He got up a big brush, whipped me all the way down the hollow in home. *Ibid.*

(Smokemont NC) The drivers . . . come on in down there then and skinned out and packed him [= the killed bear] out to the cabin that night. **1940** Haun *Hawk's Done* 150 He come a-footing it on in home.

2 In phrase *want in*. See **want[1] 2**.

in- *prefix* Un-; used with adjectives. See also **on-**, **un-**.

1916 Combs *Old Early English* 294 In, im, and un are often used interchangeably . . . *ingrateful*. **1983** *Dark Corner OHP-10A* I just found it ingracious that he'd do that. **1989** Landry *Smoky Mt Interviews* 181 I might have an inusual story how I got the three dollars to pay for the licen [i.e. a marriage license].

[OED3 *inusual* adj obsolete, rare]

in about See **in and about**.

in above See **in A2**.

in a common way *adverb phrase* Ordinarily, usually. See also **common**.

1917 Kephart *Word-List* 409 = ordinarily. "*In a common way* he's generally in here by the five of a mornin'." **1994–97** Montgomery *Coll* (known to Brown, Cardwell, Oliver).

in across at, **in against** See **in A2**.

in a manner See **manner, in a**.

in and about (also *in about*) *adverb phrase* More or less, approximately. See also **in A2**.

1834 Crockett *Narrative* 162–63 Looking on before my dogs, I saw in and about the biggest bear that ever was seen in America. **1861** *Click CW Letters* (Aug 19) thare are som whers in a bout a hunderd and thirty sick in our regiment. **1895** Dromgoole *Humble Advocate* 330 "Josephine Gary air in an' about deranged," said she. "She hev took ter vagrantin' roun' the mount'n till folks air talkin' mightily about her." **1927** Woofter *Dialect from WV* 358 = in the neighborhood of. "Here are certainly in and about ten bushels of potatoes." **1971** Dwyer *Dict for Yankees* 27 = approximately. "A gallon in and about." **1998** Montgomery *Coll*: *in and about* (known to Brown, Bush, Jones, Ledford, Oliver); We picked in and about ten bushels of corn (Cardwell). **2007** McMillon *Notes* In and about an hour we'll pull out for town.

[DARE (at *in about*) adv phr South, South Midland]

in a notion See **notion**.

in around See **in A2**.

in a strut See **strut B**.

in back of (also *in the back of*) *phrasal preposition* Of location or time: beyond, behind. Same as **back of 1**.

1966 Dakin *Vocab Ohio River Valley* 51 Scattered speakers elsewhere in . . . Kentucky east of the Green-Barren River also say only (*in*) *back of* [for "behind"]. **1981** *Smokies Heritage* 32:8 In the back of our house was a woodland. **1985** Dabney *More Mt Spirits* 112 That was the only way we had of making an honest dollar when we were growing up and the people in back of me. **1989** *Matewan OHP-11* [He was standing] right in behind him . . . right in the back of him.

in behind, **in below** See **in A2**.

inby *adverb* See citation.

c1975 *Miners' Jargon* 5 = in the direction of the working face [of a coal mine]. **2002** Armstead *Black Days* 244 = towards the active workings of a [coal] mine.

in case See **case 2**.

inch up *verb phrase* See citation.

1963 White *Marbles E KY* 65 = [in marbles, to try] to get [a] closer shot by placing the hand in a position nearer to the marble being shot at.

in course *adverb phrase*

1 Of course.

1867 Harris *Sut Lovingood* 21 Yas, ole Still-tub, that's jis the perporshun I bears in the famerly fur dam fool, leavin out Dad in course. **1961** Williams *Content Mt Speech* 16 Hit stands in course that they'd be a passel o' talk. **1997** Montgomery *Coll* (known to Brown, Bush).

[SND *in coorse* (at *in* B4.4(a)); CUD *in course* (at *in* prep) "of course"; DARE *in* prep B2 chiefly South, South Midland, somewhat old-fashioned]

2 See citation.

1977 Shackelford et al. *Our Appalachia* 47 Somebody would say they had a complaint to bring up against somebody not there a'tall. And then they'd appoint a committee to bring that person to the next meeting [of the church], "in course" they always said, in order to give an account of himself and to see what was going to happen.

increase

A *verb* Of the moon: to become larger, in the first half of the lunar cycle.

1991 Thomas *Sthn Appal* 247 That's one thing I always looked about when I'd go to kill hogs. I liked to kill my hogs when th' moon's a fillin' up . . . increasin'. An' I always thought my meat tasted fuller. Wouldn't shrink up s' bad.

B *noun* The first half of the lunar cycle, the waxing or **new** of the moon.

1927 Mason *Lure of Smokies* 115 Boards put up at the "increase" of the moon invariably cupped or warped. **1972** *Foxfire I* 218 Plant all things which yield above the ground on the increase or growing of the moon. **1975** Dwyer *Thangs* 26 Plant all things which yield above the ground on the increase or growing of the moon and all things which yield below ground (root crops) when the moon is decreasing or darkening.

[OED3 *increase* n I 1b obsolete →1665]

indeed and double *adverb phrase* Surely, absolutely (used to provide affirmative emphasis).

1926 (in **1944** Wentworth *ADD* 317) (WV) = indeed—emphatic.

independent rich *adjective phrase* Independently wealthy.

1938 Stuart *Dark Hills* 51 You ought to be independent rich.

Indian bead *noun* Same as **Job('s) tears**.

1973 Miller *Pigeon's Roost* (Oct 25) Mrs. Edith Miller growed a crop this year of Indian beads or some calls them Job's tears. She is being made busy these days stringing them into long strings.

Indian bean bread (also *Indian bread*) *noun* A heavy bread made from crushed, dried beans and cornmeal, originally made by the Cherokee. Same as **bean bread**.

1974 GSMNP-51:18 They'd put out a bog dinner there and we would have Indian bread and chestnut bread and oh there would be just the hill covered with people and wagons and buggies and horses. **1997** Andrews *Mountain Vittles* 63 Jeff made the gritted meal into bean bread or just plain bread. *Ibid.* 84 Most of his people just cook pinto beans and mash 'em up and add 'em to the corn meal now and make the famous Indian Bean Bread. **2016** Lundy and Autry *Victuals* 106 There are two kinds of bean bread, one with pintos baked into a cornmeal batter in a pan, the other more like a tamale, the beans speckled through a cornmeal mush wrapped in its husk and baked.

Indian bitter *noun*

1 A burning bush (*Euonymus atropurpureus*). Also called **wahoo 1**. See also **hearts bustin', spindle bush, strawberry bush**.

1859 Colton *Mt Scenery* 97 The wahoo, or Indian bitter, resembles both the cucumber and the linn. . . . The bark, steeped in liquor, is said to have miraculous effect in curing the chills and fevers.

2 A large deciduous tree (*Magnolia* spp). See also **cucumber tree, mountain magnolia, umbrella tree, wahoo 2, yellow linn**.

1968 Connelly *Discover Appal* 162 The cucumber tree is sometimes known as Indian-bitter. The distinguishing mark of this tree, a member of the magnolia family, is its unusual fruit. These "cucumbers," about three inches long, are rough, scaly, cone-shaped objects.

Indian bow *noun* See citation.

c1982 Young *Colloquial Appal* 13 = striped maple of the acer family.

Indian bread See **Indian bean bread**.

Indian cabbage *noun* The young growth of any yucca plant, eaten and used for poultices.

1984–85 *Sevier Settler* 3:19 Indian cabbage was cooked, eaten, and used for making poultices for boils. **1998** Montgomery *Coll* (known to Cardwell).

Indian cucumber *noun* A wild plant (*Medeola virginiana*) with an edible root that tastes similar to a cucumber.

1967 *Food Gathering* 23 Among those plants gathered in the spring and eaten fresh or boiled were . . . "Turkey Mustard" (Dentaria diphylla), Sachon, Heucheram, Shepherds Purse, Creases, ramps (Allium), "Beargrass" (Tradescantia virginiana), and Indian cucumber.

Indian devil *noun* The mountain lion.

2002 Myers *Best Yet Stories* 154 Also known as mountain screamers or Indian devils, [the panther] preys on deer, elk, mice and squirrels, even grasshoppers. It can see in the dark, swim, and climb trees. It can fall 50 feet and land on its feet unharmed. It can execute a 25 foot leap from a dead stop.

Indian doctor *noun* Traditionally, one who claims and applies special knowledge of herbal medicine acquired from Cherokee or other indigenous tribal lore. See also **conjure doctor, herb doctor, wart conjurer, witch doctor**.

1871 *DARE File* The celebrated Indian doctor, Congdon, who has been in our town for a week or so past, in his professional capacity, has been much encouraged by the large numbers of our citizens who have consulted him . . . that he has determined to remain a while longer in town. **1872** *DARE File* Wm. Norman, the Cherokee Indian Doctor, has located at John Mosier's near Johnson's Mill, Monroe county, Tenn., with a view of remaining one year or longer, to treat and cure all manner of Chronic, Insipient, Prevalent, Cutaneous, Eruptive or Private [diseases]. **1960** Mason *Memoir* 39 I remember an old Indian Doctor, Dr. John Honey, that rode a horse from settlement to settlement almost day and night. **1991** Neely *Snowbird Cherokees* 64 Occasionally, even the old Cherokee myths play a part in the lives of Snowbird people. During a sermon at Buffalo Baptist Church, an Indian minister referred favorably to the myth, "The Origin of Disease and Medicine." The myth, which explains the origin of conjuring, relates that human overpopulation became so intense that the animals in revenge for being crowded off their land sent diseases to afflict mankind. The plants, however, took pity on people, and each offered to be a cure for one disease. According to the myth, it is simply up to conjurors ("Indian doctors") to discover which plant is the cure for each disease. Instead of counterposing Cherokee mythology and Cherokee doctrine, the minister considered the two compatible. In the minister's reinterpretation of the myth, only Jesus can heal illness, accomplishing His purpose through physicians or "conjure men," whose duty it is to locate the plant or herb which will cure a particular disease. The same minister occasionally referred to himself jokingly as a "conjure man," "witch doctor," or "booger." **2003** Cavender *Folk Medicine* 172 This bit of family lore, whether true or not, no doubt suggested in some of his clients, just as it did the clients of white men referred to as

"Indian doctors" in the nineteenth century, that Gray possessed extraordinary knowledge of medicinal plants. **2006** *Encycl Appalachia* 868 Though family members, usually mothers, were well informed about medicinal plants, there were people known as "yarb" (herb) doctors who possessed extraordinary knowledge. Some of these herbalists were known as "Indian doctors" because they claimed, often falsely, to have acquired their knowledge of medicinal plants while living with Native Americans.

Indian grass *noun* A common wild grass (*Sorghastrum nutans*) native to the Smoky Mountains.

1941 Walker *Story of Mt* 49 Indian grass is a tall wild grass, quite ornamental, and grows in various places on the side of the mountain near the base. **1997** *Smokies Guide* (Autumn) 1 In Cades Cove this spring, Park Servicc fire crews intentionally burned nearly 100 acres of meadow to knock back non-native fescue grass and encourage the growth of such natives as sunflowers, asters, Indian grass, and big bluestem.

Indian head (also *Indian spike*) *noun* An arrowhead.

1981 Henry *Alex Stewart* 52 We're sitting there a' talking, and he's collecting. He'd get ever' good Indian head he could find. And he ask me if I had any Indian spikes. He called them Indian spikes and I called them arryheads.

Indian hen *noun* The pileated woodpecker (*Dryocopus pileatus*).

1963 Wilson *Regional Words* 82 = the big Pileated was an Indian hen, a woodcock, a woodhen, or, because of its piercing shriek, a good god. **1997** Montgomery *Coll* (known to Brown).

[DARE *Indian hen* n 3 chiefly South, South Midland]

Indian lemonade *noun* See citation.

2006 *WV Encycl* 568 The red fuzzy seeds of staghorn sumac were brewed into "Indian lemonade."

Indian meal *noun* Cornmeal.

1824 (in **1912** Doddridge *Notes on Settlement* 82) The Indian meal which he brought over the mountain was expended six weeks too soon, so that for that length of time we had to live without bread. **1879** Jones *Backwoods Carolina* 749 She made a johnny-cake of Indian meal and baked it on a board in front of the fire, and boiled coffee in a coffee-pot set on the coals.

Indian mustard *noun* Same as **crowsfoot**.

1978 Parris *Mt Cooking* 162 "Some folks," she said, "call crow's foot Indian mustard. But all the old folks referred to it as crow's-foot. If you'll examine the leaves, you'll see they look like crow's feet."

Indian nation *noun* The Qualla Indian Reservation in Swain County, North Carolina (officially called the Qualla Boundary).

1937 Hall *Coll* (Little Cataloochee NC) An Indian froze to death between the Indian nation and the Purchase years ago.

Indian old field *noun* Same as **old field**. See also **old field school**, **scald**.

1953 Hall *Coll* (Deep Creek NC) I worked at loggin' for eight year. [There was] a mill on Deep Creek on an Indian old field. **1988** Dyer *Farmstead Yards* 13 Indian old-fields may have been attractive to settlers who pressed into the Southern Appalachians, but, in spite of earlier land-clearing efforts, settlers were compelled to clear small fields for crops and occasional pasturing.

Indian peach *noun* A **clingstone** peach (*Prunus persica*) with red meat. Same as **plum peach**.

1962 Wilson *Folkways Mammoth Cave* 15 Red-skinned and red-meated peaches were called *Indian peaches*. **1966** Dakin *Vocab Ohio River Valley* 360 *Indian peach* is also used rarely in the Mountains south of the Kentucky headwaters, and one Mountain speaker says *sweet peach*. **1968** *DARE Survey* (Brasstown NC) = a red, clingstone peach. **1969** GSMNP-37:2:5 I can recollect . . . some big Indian peaches, might near as big as your fist, growed there on them trees that was around that hut. **1973** GSMNP-4:2:2 We used to have what we called Indian peaches . . . they was red, as red as a cherry all the way through. **1984** GSMNP-153:43 We had a what was called a Indian peach, and I'll try to describe it to you. You probably have seen one somewhere or 'nother. They didn't get very big. They wouldn't turn loose of the seed, but the inside of 'em was a real deep pinkish, and the juice of 'em was sweeter than some of 'em, and mother would can 'em whole. **1997** Montgomery *Coll* (known to Brewer, Brown).

[DARE *Indian peach* n 1 South, South Midland]

Indian physic *noun* Bowman's root (*Gillenia trifoliata*), the root of which has medicinal uses.

1824 (in **1912** Doddridge *Notes on Settlement* 116) Indian physic, or bowman root, a species of epicacuanha, was frequently used for a vomit, and sometimes the pocoon or blood root. **1893** Bergen *Plant Names II* 141 (Banner Elk NC). **1937** Hall *Coll* (Big Creek NC) Indian Physic Tea—Good to clean your stomach off. Good blood medicine. Lord, I've drunk a sight of it. **1982** Stupka *Wildflowers* 49 [Bowman's root] is also called "Indian-physic" and "false ipecac," as the bark of the root was once used medicinally.

Indian pink *noun* Same as **worm-grass**.

1941 Walker *Story of Mt* 52 Squawroot and Indian pink join a few other parasitic plants. [**1971** Krochmal et al. *Medicinal Plants Appal* 240 The root is used as a vermifuge, anthelmintic, and cathartic. In Appalachia, a tea made from the leaves is used to aid digestion.] **1982** Stupka *Wildflowers* 87 [Indian pink] is also called "pink-root," "star-bloom," and "worm-grass"—the last a reference to the use of the root by pioneers for expelling or destroying intestinal worms.

Indian pipe *noun* Same as **corpse flower**.

1937 Thornburgh *Great Smoky Mts* 23 Less conspicuous are . . . Indian pipe or ghostflower, with its fragile, leafless, pipe-shaped blossoms, from which it is said the Indians made a lotion for strengthening the eyes. **1982** Stupka *Wildflowers* As it is entirely lacking in chlorophyll, Indian pipe is white throughout—flower, stem, and leaves—and has a succulent waxlike appearance. **2006** Howell *Medicinal Plants* 96 This plant was well known to the Cherokee as a pain remedy of the highest order, comparable to morphine. They also used Indian pipe for petit mal seizures, Bell's palsy, nervous tics, and convulsions caused by fevers. Juice of the fresh plant, combined with saltwater, was used for inflammation of the eyes. **2016** Houk *Vampires* 62–63 Indian pipe is another well-known name for this plant, arising from a Cherokee legend. The Great Spirit witnessed leaders smoking a peace pipe before they had amicably concluded a disagreement. Deeming such behavior as selfish, the spirit turned the men into a plant called Indian pipe, and as a reminder, he had it grow in places where people quarreled.

Indian poke *noun* The white hellebore (*Veratrum viride*), a leafy perennial wild plant that is generally poisonous but, when properly prepared, has medicinal uses. Also called **itchweed.**

[**1971** Krochmal et al. *Medicinal Plants Appal* 262 The plant is very poisonous. The rhizomes and roots, when properly prepared, are a strong cardiac stimulant drug.] **1982** Stupka *Wildflowers* 4 "Indian poke" and "itchweed" are other names for [the white hellebore].

Indian pot *noun* See citation.

1968 *DARE Survey* (Brasstown NC) = a dish made with beans, peas, or corn.

Indian pumpkin *noun* See citation.

2006 *Encycl Appalachia* 927 All-white cushaws grow to twenty or thirty pounds and look like squat pumpkins. Indeed, some mountain people call them Indian pumpkins, but botanists are undecided about the relationship between the two.

Indian root *noun* Same as **spignet.**

1968 *Sang Signs* 49 = a "cure-all" . . . The roots were ground up with sowbugs and molasses for yellow jaundice, and also used in kidney ailments, female troubles, and for backaches.

Indian runner (also *India runner*) *noun* A type of mixed-breed duck.

1961 Seeman *Arms of Mt* 65 The ones that are part Mallard and part Peking—they call them "Indian runners" around here. **1997** Montgomery *Coll*: *India runner* (known to Ellis).

Indian spike See **Indian head.**

Indian story (also *Indian tale*) *noun* A story of an Indian attack in earlier times.

1973 GSMNP-79:28 I'd heared so many tales and stories. That was some of the pastime of the mountain people a telling scary stories and Indian stories and bear tales as they'd call them so. **1982** Ginns *Snowbird Gravy* 182 Gosh, I can remember them Indian tales! And wild boar tales! Now, I can remember a short Indian tale now. **1983** McDermitt *Boy Named Jack* 4 The women didn't tell Jack tales . . . it was these other tales, hainted tales, ghost tales, the women told more, and Indian tales.

Indian summer *noun* A period of unusually mild weather in the fall, especially after the first frost; hence figuratively = a time of harmony.

1955 Ritchie *Singing Family* 180 Lord, children, look what a pretty sight it is. I guess it's Indian Summer. My dad allus said you couldn't find anything so fair as an Indian Summer day. **1966–67** *DARE Survey* (Cherokee NC, Maryville TN) = a period of warm weather late in the fall. **1966** Dykeman *Far Family* 271 It was not a moment for books but for breathing in the heavy-laden air of Indian summer that would soon be gone. **1970** Lombard *Hills of Home* 100 The shelled corn was allowed to dry for a few days under the warm Indian summer sun, then was carried to an old water mill for grinding. **1972** Alderman *Big Bald* 50 Indian summer, what a pleasant sound. It was not so named by the Indians but is a relished period by mankind. When the first hard frost prances down from the hilltops, and nips the remaining green sprigs of the valley, you begin to get out your overcoat. Then a mild sun and clear skies are reflected on the autumn hazed mountains as this most wonderful period invades the hills and valleys. It gave the Indians and Pioneers time for the final harvest of crops and storage of winter meat. It is a season of reflection when man contemplates the events of the passing year. A peaceful season when man can be thankful. **1982** Slone *How We Talked* 98 = a few warm days in October when there is a haze over the sky. Folks said it was Indians burning off the prairies so new grass could grow for their buffalo herds. **1982** *Smokies Heritage* 123 Yet to come is "Indian Summer," which usually occurs from late October into November. The weather becomes suddenly warm; a smoky haze settles over valleys as though from the smoke of an Indian campfire.

Indian tale See **Indian story.**

Indian tobacco *noun* An annual wild plant (*Lobelia inflata*) with medicinal uses. Also called **eyebright 2.**

1892 Bergen *Plant Names I* 89 Not infrequently the "Indian" namesake of some well-known plant may be used as at least a nominal substitute for the latter, e.g. Indian tobacco, Antennaria plantaginifelia, is chewed by children. **1940** Caton *Wildflowers of Smokies* 87. [**1971** Krochmal et al. *Medicinal Plants Appal* 164 The herb yields lobeline sulfate, which is used in anti-tobacco therapy. It is also used as a stimulant, antiasthmatic, and expectorant in cases of bronchitis.] **1997** Montgomery *Coll* (known to Brown).

Indian turnip *noun* A perennial wildflower (*Arisaema triphyllum*) with various medicinal uses. Also called **Adam's apple, jack-in-the-box, jack-in-the-pulpit.** See also **Charley liniment.**

1803 (in **1920** DeWitt *Sevier Journal* 36) (Jan 5) To cure the pluricy & fluenzy when the pain and fever Begins you must take . . . half that much of Indian turnips and as much allum as the size of a large pen. **1967** *DARE Survey* (Maryville TN) = flower that comes up in the woods early in the spring, with three white petals that turn pink as the flower grows older. [**1971** Krochmal et al. *Medicinal Plants Appal* 62 The plant has been used as an expectorant, irritant, and diaphoretic.] **1977** Madden and Jones *Mt Home* 31–32 The mainstay of the Walker sisters' healing potions was "Charley linament," a "soothing balm" of secret ingredients concocted by Uncle Charley Walker. It was an herb mixture that used Indian Turnip and May apple root along with many others, and is remembered as being "hot as hell's hinges" and "mighty powerful." **1980** *Smokies Heritage* 61 Prominent in this herbal category is the jack-in-the-pulpit (Indian turnip), a perennial plant that was once called wakerobin by Smokies pioneers . . . jack roots, being of a starchy nature, also have value as an edible wild food, as the name Indian turnip would imply. Raw roots, washed and sliced thin like potato chips, are spread to dry in a warm room (such as an attic). . . . Dried root chips can be eaten as is, or ground into a fine flour for pancakes and breads. **1982** Stupka *Wildflowers* 1 A showy cluster of glossy red fruit replaces the familiar "Jack" by late summer or autumn. Known also as "Indian turnip," the plant's corm or bulblike root has a sharp taste until cooked. **c1984** Dennis *Smoky Mt Heritage* 7 There were individuals who spent a lifetime searching for the natural treatment and cure for various ailments. These folks were called "Yarb Doctors." The "Yarb Doctors" would search for sheep sorrel, or Indian turnips, ginseng, sassafras and many other plants that had medicinal properties. **2009** McNeely *Unlikely Flour* 14 After putting the plant's roots through a rather elaborate cooking process, Native Americans pounded them into powder to be used as a type of flour, hence Jack-in-the-Pulpit's other name is Indian Turnip. . . . This "Indian Turnip" is but one example of how Native Americans, often faced with lean times, learned to find nourishmenent in some of nature's most obscure places.

Indian up *verb phrase* To creep or sneak up on (someone or something).

1975 Fink *Backpacking* 27 I'd not yet learned how wary those fish were, how one had to "Injun up" on a pool and, hidden behind a rock, drop his line in beyond it.

Indian war *noun* US Army actions in the 1830s to remove all eastern indigenous tribes, especially the Cherokee, to the west of the Mississippi River (specifically, to Indian Territory [present-day Oklahoma]).

1957 GSMNP-23:1:10 My daddy was in the Indian War, but my granddaddy that was before his days, my old Billy Trentham, moved in here when the wild Indians were in this country. *Ibid.* 13 My mammy drawed a pension from the old Indian war.

in down See in A2.

in eighty See **in A1**.

inern See **onion**.

infair See **infare**.

infare (also *infair, infare supper*) *noun* Traditionally, the dinner or reception following a wedding, usually at the home of the groom's parents, with music, dancing, and other festivities, superseded in more recent times by the wedding reception hosted by the groom's parents. [Editor's note: This term was not encountered by Joseph Hall.] See also **infare days**.

1824 (in **1912** Doddridge *Notes on Settlement* 104) On returning for the infare, the order of procession and the race for black Betty was the same as before. The feasting and dancing often lasted several days, at the end of which the whole company was so exhausted with loss of sleep that several days' rest was requisite to fit them to return to their ordinary labors. **1824** Knight *Letter from KY* 92 On the day after the wedding, at the bridegroom's father's hall, is usually a sumptuous festival, called an inn-fare. **1834** Crockett *Narrative* 64 At our next meeting he set the day for our wedding; and I went to my father's, and made arrangements for an infair; and returned to ask her parents for her. **1848** (in **1870** Drake *Pioneer Life KY* 184) The "infare" of the following day presented on the winding road through the green woods a long and picturesque cavalcade, in which the cavalier and his lady-love were paired off with the groom and bride in the van. **1860** *Week in Smokies* 126 Mammy, is it true that when you come home with daddy to this cabin, you had nothing to eat at the infair but roasted taters? **1862** *Shipman CW Letters* (Feb 6) tell his friends that he is in the land of the living and would like to bee at one more infare and espeshly a frolic. **1915** Dingus *Word-List VA* 184 = a reception to bride and groom given by the groom's parents. **1939** Hall *Coll* (Emerts Cove TN) When one would start from where they was married to go to their husband's home, that was called the infare. **1955** Ritchie *Singing Family* 57 The old custom is to stay the first night at her father's house, have a party and the wedding breakfast and so on, then to go the next day to his father's house, for the infare. I remember we got up early that first morning of our married life, and we saddled the horses before the rooster crowed and were on the way to Clear Creek before the sun rose. **1957** Combs *Lg Sthn High: Word List* 53 = a dinner given the bride and groom by the groom's parents, after the festivities of the previous evening at the home of the bride. The word occurs frequently in British balladry in such forms as: infere, infeare, onfere, etc., meaning together, in company with. **1967** Jones *Peculiarities Mtneers* 63–64 Marriages in the mountains seventy years ago were usually followed by a season of merriment and feasting. Relatives and friends went to great lengths to entertain the bride and groom and their relatives. An almost universal custom was the "infair." On the day following the wedding, after the bride's parents served a bountiful wedding dinner, the parents of the groom were hosts to the wedding party, including the officiating minister and his wife, at the "infair." **1978** Parris *Mt Cooking* 148 When the preacher had spoken the word that made them one, the bride hurried into the house and changed her wedding frock for her infare dress. Then they all piled into their buggies and wagons and headed for the house of the groom's parents for the big infare supper and a night of music-making, singing, dancing, and games. **1981** Whitener *Folk-Ways* 72 For the uninitiated, the infare was a bit of frolicking at the home of the groom, usually in the afternoon after a morning wedding. At this occasion the groom furnished the whiskey, food, and sweets (usually candy for the ladies) for a proper celebration. The celebration itself usually included folk dancing, singing, games, and occasionally a certain amount of horseplay during which bride and groom were made to suffer certain indignities of a minor nature. **1986** Noonkesser *Crossing* 16–19 On December 31, 1879, there occurred the first recorded wedding in White Pine. . . . The next day there was a big dinner in the groom's home, known as an "infair." In those days an infair could not close without a big "to-do" at night. During the big "shindig" someone, just for fun, climbed on top of the cabin and poured a tub of water down the chimney into the fire. The folks seated around the fire were covered with soot and ashes, which ruined one of the lady's fine silk gowns. The prankster was forced to pay for the dress. **1991** Haynes *Haywood Home* 61–62 Infares were put on by the groom's parents and were wedding feasts (suppers). They started at least a week ahead to get everything ready. The best cooks on Fines Creek or Crabtree were invited to make sure everything was all right. After the couple was married in church, the wedding party went to the groom's parents house for the infare. . . . After supper, there'd be music and square dancing with local musicians playing. . . . Then about nine or ten p.m., all the guests would escort the bride and groom to their assigned sleeping quarters and inspect the room before they said goodnight.

[ultimately < Old English *infær* "an entrance" < in + *fær* "journey"; OED3 *infair/infare* n 2 "a feast or entertainment given on entering a new house, especially the reception of a bride in her new home" Scot, north dialect and U.S.; EDD *infar(e)* sb Scot, Irel, nEngl; SND *infare* n 2, CUD *infare* n 3 "the reception after a wedding"; Web3 *infare* n chiefly dialect; DARE *infare* n 1 chiefly South, South Midland, old-fashioned]

infare days *noun* See citation. See also **infare**.

1957 Broaddus *Vocab Estill Co KY* 43 = the honeymoon.

infare supper See **infare**.

in for See **for[2] B2**.

infoxicated *adjective* See citation.

1962 Williams *Metaphor Mt Speech I* 11 The man who has drunk enough to glow, sing, and laugh freely but whose tongue might become twisted on a word now and then is "foxy.". . . . If he continues to drink but responds to his condition with humor and gaiety, he might finally become "infoxicated," however.

in generally *adverb phrase* In general, usually.

1997 Montgomery *Coll* (known to Brown, Bush, Cardwell, Jones, Weaver).

[DARE *in generally* adv phr chiefly South, South Midland]

ingern, ingun See **onion**.

ingracious See **in-**.

in head *prepositional phrase* In mind.

1913 Kephart *Our Sthn High* 297 I had in head to plow to-day, but hit's come on to rain. **1995** Montgomery *Coll* (known to Adams, Brown, Oliver).

inkberry *noun* Same as **poke[2]**.

1970 Campbell et al. *Smoky Mt Wildflowers* 52 Another common name, ink-berry, was derived from the early settlers' common use of the fruit juice as ink.

in my knowing See **knowing A**.

innard (also *innards*) *noun* The gut, entrails.

1867 Harris *Sut Lovingood* 45 The tuther aind ove his inards wer tangled up amung the mar's hine laigs. **1972** *AOHP/ALC-276* You had to save your innard from a hog that you didn't use for to make your soap. **2009** Benfield *Mt Born* 161 = the intestines, or entrails, of a person or animal. **2016** Grimm *Moonville* 22 Laurette can't go in the water. It'd wreck her innards.

[variant form of *inward(s)*]

innocence *noun* A bluet (*Houstonia caerulea*). Same as **eyebright 1**. See also **babytear, Quaker lady**.

1901 Lounsberry *Sthn Wild Flowers* 475 [B]luets, innocence, Quaker ladies, or bonnets . . . grows erect, often many of the plants producing through moist, grassy places a most enchanting stretch of ethereal blue. **1992** Toops *Great Smoky Mts* 35 Bluets—four-petaled lavender flowers with bright yellow centers—are scarcely taller than the mosses. They grow in profusion around seeps and springs. Some settlers called them "innocence." **1994–97** Montgomery *Coll* (known to Cardwell, Shields).

[labeled "chiefly New England" by DARE *innocence* n 1, the occurrence of the flower/name in the Smoky Mountains illustrates the similarity of climatic zones of higher elevations to those of regions much farther north]

in on toward See **in A2**.

in reason *adverb phrase* In good estimation, with reasonable certainty, within reason.

1774 *Dunmore's War* 210 That number I realy believe Cannot be raised in Capt. Crocketts Company, unless Men were to Leave their wives and Children exposed to the Mercy of the Enemy, which we in reason Cannot Expect. **1889** Mooney *Folk Carolina Mts* 97 When one is strong and brave he is said to be "much of a man," and when he feels sure that he will dislike a new acquaintance he knows in reason that he cain't neighbor him. **1895** Dromgoole *Logan's Courtship* 135 It couldn't in reason be that thar frisky little Jinnie. **1913** Kephart *Our Sthn High* 297 I knowed in reason she'd have the mullygrubs over them doin's. **1931** Goodrich *Mt Homespun* 59 "I knew in reason she'd catch on to it," said Hannah, "but she's learnt the quickest ever." **1937** Hall *Coll* (Smokemont NC) I know in reason the house was built by Uncle Tom Bradley. **1952** Wilson *Folk Speech NC* 556 *know in reason* = to be certain or relatively certain. (Swain Co NC). **1961** *Coe Ridge OHP-339A* She paddled backerds plumb across the river and said in reason it looked just like a ghost. **1972** GSMNP-93:1:11 Well, I know in reason it was, 'cause my granddaddy, he was first. **1974** Fink *Bits Mt Speech* 13 I knowed *in reason* he'd go. **1985** Irwin *Alex Stewart* 227 Grandpap knowed in reason that it was old Adaline Jensey doing the witching. **1994** Montgomery Coll (known to Cardwell).

[DARE *in reason* adv phr southern Appalachians]

in seventy, **in sixty** See **in A1**.

in some wise *adverb phrase* To some degree.

1927 Mason *Lure of Smokies* 216 I was in some wise put out.

inspiten of hell and high water (also *in spite of creation*) *adverb phrase* Heedless to advice or restraint.

1927 Mason *Lure of Smokies* 40 Said "Uncle" Levi Trentham, in speaking of the tragedy, "We warned the old man not to go, but go he would in spite 'n o' hell an' high water!" **1996–97** Montgomery Coll (known to Brown, Bush, Ledford, Norris, Oliver). **1971** *Granny Women* 257 She'd climb that headboard and get up in spite of creation.

instanter *adverb* Right away, more quickly.

1913 Kephart *Our Sthn High* "No, my boy, that liquor goes down your own throat instanter." **1969** Medford *Finis* 113 Why, I would a-give them children up instanter and paid the Lord for takin' them off of my hands.

instead of *phrasal preposition* Variant forms *instid*, *in stid*, *stiddier* + *of* (and variants).

1865 *Walker CW Letters* (April 7) the time Will not be long till Wee can see each other an talk to gether in stid of Writing. **1867** Harris *Sut Lovingood* 63 Bake, instid ove duin better, got wus—sot intu readin in sum furrin tung, sorter like Cherokee, wif a sprinkil ove Irish. **1883** Murfree *Old Sledge* 554 He larned me hisself, an' ef I hed los' stiddier of him, he would be a-thinkin' now ez it's all right. **1899** Fox *Mt Europa* 42 Ye'd better bar out the gun [from the shooting competition] 'stid o' the gal. **1923** (in **1952** Mathes *Tall Tales* 9) These here deep-water Babtists [are] a-puttin' their trust in goin' under the water instid o' gittin' under the blood! **1934–47** LAMSAS *Appal* (Madison Co NC, Swain Co NC) *instid*. **c1979** Chiles *Glossary* 4 *instid*.

instermint See **instrument.**

instid, **in stid** See **instead of.**

instrument *noun* Variant forms *instermint* (especially with secondary stress on the last syllable: *IN-stru-mint*). For similar forms, see **-ment A.**

1929 (in **1952** Mathes *Tall Tales* 101) "I'll show 'im! Ey gonnies, I'll show 'im!" he muttered half aloud as he resumed the whetting of his "instermint." **1942** Hall *Phonetics Smoky Mts* 71 The suffixes *-dent* and *-ment* (except in *independent*) in most instances have secondary stress: *accident, confident, devilment, instrument, monument, payment, settlement, testament*, etc. **1994** Montgomery *File* (known to 82-year-old man, Gatlinburg TN).

intentioned *adjective* Having a certain aim, intending.

1937 Hall Coll (Mt Sterling NC) Hit was intentioned to bite me. I never heared a snake sing so vygrous. **1938** Bowman *High Horizons* 47 Besides illustrating the use of the strong old form "intentioned," the girl's speech indicates the stubborn way the mountaineer clings to the security of his hills.

[OED3 *intention* v obsolete, rare]

in that day and time See **day and time.**

in the back of See **in back of.**

in the bed See **bed A.**

in the eighty See **in A1.**

in the latter days See **latter days, in the.**

in the mud *adverb phrase* Not married.

1844 (in **1956** Eliason *Tarheel Talk* 284) (Buncombe Co NC) You . . . wanted to know whether she was still in the mud . . . she has got so far out of the mud as to get married.

in the notion See **notion.**

in the sixty See **in A1.**

in the world *adverb phrase* At all.

1968 *Faith Healing* 22 It was nine months he never walked a step in the world. **1970** *Aunt Airy* 88 It ain't a bit nasty in th' world.

in this day and time See **day and time.**

in time *adverb phrase* At one time, sometime ago.

1939 Hall Coll (Deep Creek NC) They'd been a water spout a cloudbust put there in time and run in, just a lot, awful lot of spruce and timber, spruce and hemlock and stuff. **1941** Stuart *Men of Mts* 311 Somebody had tapped 'em [= maple trees] in time. They have made maple syrup from them. **1973** GSMNP-86:36 The trail went around, well they had in time took a sled and wagon maybe around it. **1974** Fink *Bits Mt Speech* 13 = once. "A house stood there in time."

[DARE (at *time* n C3) southern Appalachians]

in town *adjective phrase* See citation. See also **town ball.**

1983 Broaddus *Estill Co KY Word List* 44 *in town* = at bat.

in under (also *nunder*) *phrasal preposition* Beneath, below, underneath; often used in combination with other prepositions; for such combinations, see **in A2.**

1927 Mason *Lure of Smokies* 222 That b'ar had been killin' three-year-old cattle an' draggin' them in under the cliffs to eat. **1939**

Hall Coll (Deep Creek NC) When I got out to the Bear Pen Gap, why, the dogs was a-fighting the bear right in under the top of Smoky, pretty close up to the top. **1954** Arnow *Dollmaker* 255 Pop got us right in under one [= a maple tree]. **1964** Williams *Prep Mt Speech* 54 Telescoped clusters of prepositions are discernible in offen (off from on), outen (out from in), nunder (in under), outnunder (out from in under), aponto or aponter (at upon to), alongst (alongside of) . . . No mother "fitten for to be called one" wants "outnunder her bounden duty." **1969** GSMNP-37:2:12 I told my brother, I says, "We'll have to go right around this, in under these big pines." **1972** *AOHP/ALC-342* He was in under old General Patton. **1977** Moore *Jenks* 32 The mines went right in under the road. **1985** Irwin *Alex Stewart* 266 We looked and saw a big black-snake crawling from in-under the floor into the yard. **1997** *Dante OHP-14* Peggy went up here in under the floor, and they liked to never got her out. **2003** Carter *Mt Home* 15 Fact of business, they was room nunder the house for a crawl space cellar to hold the many half gallon blue Mason Jars we filled for winters eatin'. **2005** Williams *Gratitude* 134 Mom never let us hang around th' kitchen inunder 'er feet.

[< Middle English *an* "on" or "in" + *under*; cf SND *anunder* prep 1 "under"; CUD *in under, inundher, inanunder* (at in prep) "under"; HT *in unther* "(emphatic form of) under"; DARE *in under* prep phr English dialect; probably variant of earlier *anunder*]

inusual See **in-**.

in yonder See **yonder D2**.

inyun See **onion**.

Irish cobbler *noun* A white potato. Same as **cobbler**.

1986 Pederson et al. *LAGS* = attested by 5/60 interviewees (8.3%) from E TN; 5/8 of all LAGS interviewees (62.5%) attesting term were from Appalachia.

Irish potato *noun*

A Variant forms *airish* [see **2016** in **B**], *arish* [see **1862** Huntley in **B**], *arsh potato* [see **1939** in **B**], *arsh tater* ['ɑrʃ 'tetɚ] [see **1991** in **B**], *ashtater* [see **c1954** in **B**], *orsh tater* [see **1924** in **B**].

[DARE (at *Irish* n, adj) especially South Midland]

B A common white potato (with *Irish* added to distinguish it from a sweet potato).

1862 Hitt *CW Letters* (May) ef you make aplenty of irish taters keeps sum tell I Come ef thay are red skins sort you no I lov them and milk and buter wold take vary well. **1862** Huntley *CW Letters* (July 16) I sufford a power for somthing to Eat While I Was in the horspital at Richmond I paid 50 cts a quart for some arish potatoes. **1924** Greer-Petrie *Angeline Gits Eyeful* 13 Fanchette would begin snatchin' the grub right out from under Mis' Clark's nose Orsh 'taters and cream and sugar. **1939** Hall Coll (Roaring Fork TN) This was a good country for arsh potatoes. . . . They'd take the potatoes to Knoxville, two hundred bushels from one acre. **1942** Hall *Phonetics Smoky Mts* 44 = the common white potato. **c1954** Adams *Word-List*: *ashtater*. **1991** Haynes *Haywood Home* 77 Jut would say . . . Arsh taters (Irish potatoes) and other idioms common to uneducated mountain people. **2006** Ledford *Survivals* 1014 The Appalachian tendency for r to modify the pronunciation of the preceding vowel (*tar* "tire," *har* "hair," and *arish potatoes* "Irish potatoes") is similar to phonetic spellings found in colonial writings. **2016** Lundy and Autry *Victuals* 50 My mama, like most mountain women I know, referred to potatoes as Irish (said more like "Air-ish") to differentiate them from the sweet potatoes we also loved.

[DARE *Irish potato* n scattered, but especially South Midland]

iron *noun* Variant form *arn*.

1915 Dingus *Word-List VA* 180 *arn*. **1942** Hall *Phonetics Smoky Mts* 44 In the speech of those who have been but little exposed to classroom influences, the sound is frequently [ɒ] or [ɔ] before r: *iron* [ɔɚn], *ironing* ['ɔɚnən], *Myers, wire*. **1952** Wilson *Folk Speech NC* 516 *arn*. **2005** Williams *Gratitude* 477 *arn*.

[DARE *iron* n chiefly South Midland]

iron blood (also *ironroot*) *noun* A **boneset** (*Eupatorium purpureum*) from which is made an iron-rich tea.

1940 Haun *Hawk's Done* 29 I thought maybe it was because Tiny had to do like she did, that maybe she hadn't give enough milk for Bessie. I give her bone-set tea and iron-root tea.

iron dogs *noun* Same as **dog iron(s)**.

1986 Pederson et al. *LAGS* (Scott Co TN, White Co GA) *iron dogs*. **1997** Montgomery Coll (known to Adams, Brown, Bush, Cardwell, Ledford, Weaver).

[DARE *iron dog* n 1 South, South Midland]

iron glass *noun* Mica.

1896 *Word-List* 419 = mica. **1998** Montgomery Coll (known to Brown, Bush).

ironroot See **iron blood**.

Ironside(s) *noun* Used as a nickname for a **Primitive Baptist**.

1891 Primer *Studies in WV* 168 One minister, a hard-shell Baptist, or Ironsides as they call this sect there, spoke of the texes [sic] from which he preached his sermon. **1926** Harris *WV Hand Book* 561 (as of 1861) (DARE) I concluded old Jack [= Stonewall Jackson] must be a fatalist sure enough when he put an Ironside Presbyterian parson as his chief of staff.

iron water *noun* Water containing iron salts.

1939 *FWP Guide TN* 311 [At] Galbraith Springs . . . It has been believed locally that the chalybeate water, commonly called "iron water," has medicinal properties.

ironwood *noun* The hop hornbeam (*Ostrya knowltonii/virginica*).

1940 Bandy *Folklore Macon Co TN* 57 A horn-beam is still "iron-wood."

is See **be C**.

I's See **be C3, E2.**

ishe-shicle, i-shickle See **icicle.**

island *noun* Variant forms *ilant* ['aɪlənt], *islant.*

1862 *Barkley Letters* (June 23) i wish you could git of that ilant i dont think any body can have ther helth there. **1862** *Mangum CW Letters* (June 23) I was on the islant at Bridg port Just a bove whar the bridg was burned a Sunday eavning. **1927** Woofter *Dialect from WV* 358 The creek is rising fast. It is almost over all the little islants. **1942** Hall *Phonetics Smoky Mts* 98. **c1960** Wilson *Coll*: *island* is very often *islant.*

[DARE *island* n chiefly South, South Midland]

ist See **just.**

I swan, I swanny See **swan.**

it *pronoun*

A Variant form *hit.* See also **hits, hitself,** and Grammar and Syntax §2.1.2.

1 General usage.

1910 Norman *English of Mtneers* 276 Richard Grant White told us that a hundred years ago "hit" was a form of that pronoun [i.e. *it*] often heard. Throughout Appalachian American, so far as I know it, the very pronoun is Shibboleth. The young mountaineer, returned from college in the low country, will carefully avoid the h, but in unguarded moments it comes to his lips. **1913** Kephart *Our Sthn High* 277 [The mountaineer's] pronoun *hit* antedates English itself, being the Anglo-Saxon neuter of he. **1935** Sheppard *Cabins in Laurel* 155 One peculiarity is perhaps worth the noting, namely the pronunciation of the impersonal pronoun with an aspirate—'hit'—a practice that seems to be universal. **1940** Bowman *KY Mt Stories* 16 Farther back from the viewpoint of time, another word that has persisted in preserving itself is the word "hit," used instead of and alternately with "it." "Hit" was perfectly good English in the time of Tyndale in the sixteenth Century as he used "hit" for "it" in his translation of the Bible. The people in the mountain region seem to use "hit" and "it" interchangeably as it suits their fancy—or perhaps whichever term is more easily pronounced. From my observation, they use "it" as an elision of "hit": for they pronounce "it" very distinctly. Most Americans usually elide "it" to "ut" or simply "'t." **1942** Hall *Phonetics Smoky Mts* 86 Even unstressed *hit* often occurs without initial loss [of h], as in the sentence . . . "I don't know how long hit's been." But unstressed *hit*, like *he, him, her,* etc. usually occurs without [h] . . . "I guess it's been ten or fifteen years ago." **2000** Miller *Ignorant People* 72 "Secondly," [the teacher] said, "we must work on the way that we speak so that we can be understood. No 'hits.' No 'hits.' No 'hits'!" Each time she said the word, she smacked Bob on the top of the head with her ruler.

2 Used as the subject of a clause.

1861 *Dalton CW Letters* (Dec 11) when this comes to hand i hope hit will find you all in joy the Same blesing. **1861** *Parlier CW Letters* (July 16) hit was 15 miles below here At aplace cald bethel Church. **1913** Kephart *Our Sthn High* 36 By that time the land will be so poor hit wouldn't raise a cuss-fight. **1939** Hall *Coll* (Little Cataloochee NC) Hit was several years before they had another school. **1953** Hall *Coll* (Bryson City NC) Hit [= a bear] went around the hill [and] clim up a birch tree. **1969** GSMNP-25:1:12 The kitchen, hit set out there that way. **1973** GSMNP-84:26 I know positive that hit wasn't all true. **1974** GSMNP-50:1:1 Hit must have been in the thirties, in the twenty-nine, because I was up there on that river about eighteen year. **1978** Montgomery *White Pine Coll* III-2 Hit's been handed down to him, you see, so he's the third or fourth generation. **1989** *Matewan OHP-1* she didn't get there in time and hit [= a train] passed her. **1998** *Dante OHP-12* Hit [= a train] didn't go plumb up to the mines.

3 Used as a direct object or object of a preposition.

1836 *Paw Paw Hollow Church Minutes* 78 The Church wish[es] Brother Lammon Jones to attend them twelve months longer & Br Jones agrees to hit. **1861** (in **1992** Heller and Heller *Confederacy* 27) I sent him a bundle of paper and envelops by express and ask him to write whether he got hit or not. **1863** *W Robinson CW Letter* I want you to try to have the wheat thrash and I dont want you to sell none of hit. **1939** Hall *Coll* (Little Cataloochee NC) They got him to go down and try to find out from them folks about hit. **1975** GSMNP-62:7 They might have just talked about building that room on hit. **1989** Landry *Smoky Mt Interviews* 194 I believe they called hit the Cable School.

[< Old English *hit*; *hit* was the usual Middle English form of the pronoun and prevailed generally into the 16th century, after which the form is found mainly in Scot, nEngl; EDD (at *hit* pron 1) Scot, nEngl; SND *hit* pron 1 (emphatic); CUD (at *it* prep) emphatic; DARE *it* pron A1 chiefly South, South Midland]

B That (with quasi-deictic force and usually contrastive stress).

1875 King *Great South* 788 Some of the mountaineers speak of "hit," instead of "it," and emphasize the word as in this case, "I meant to have brought my gun, but I forgot hit." **1895** Edson and Fairchild *TN Mts* 376 = sometimes used almost with the force of a demonstrative; e.g. a native, upon seeing a trolley car, points first to the car and then to the trolley, and asks, "Does *hit* run *hit*, or *hit* run *hit*?" **1960** McCaulley *Cades Cove* I couldn't write a book and put hit out, for I've never had enough of schooling to do that. You could sit down to a recorder right there and tell it on hit. **1973** *Foxfire Interviews* A-73-43 Every time they found the great big roots [of ginseng], they sell hit. *Ibid.* They's one more weed, but I don't know the name of hit. **1975** *AOHP/ALC-930* I don't remember of but one [= hanging of a man], and I never seen hit. **1979** *Big South Fork OHP-1* Then they took this fire clay they called it and ground hit up and put water and stuff with it. **1983** McDermitt *Boy Named Jack* 12 They said, "well, you brought in anothern." They paid him fer hit. **1985** Dabney *More Mt Spirits* 65 Now that crab-apple brandy, when we sold hit, it really had a good smell. **1998** *Dante OHP-61* Hit was for anybody that wanted to take it, electrical course that the government was giving. I've taken hit. *Ibid.* 71 He changed from this church to this church, Dickenson County Conference. He went into hit. **2008** *Rosie Hicks* 6 The yellow lady slipper, they use hit for nerves and headache. *Ibid.* 6 The catnip leaves, you gather hit. I think they give, make tea for the babies.

C Syntax.

1 Used to introduce an existential clause.

1863 *Vance Papers* (Jan 18) it is no nead of my saying any thing to you about the Fight at Newbern where I was taken for you was then Col of a reg in the same fight. **1931** Combs *Lg Sthn High* 1322 It also supplants *there*: "It ain't nary grain o' corn left." **1954** GSMNP-19:26 If you'd have seen what I made it with, it would be a lot of people would faint. **1956** Hall *Coll* (Sand Hill TN) When hit'd be a big snow on the ground, I had to get out and get the wood. **1972** *AOHP/ALC*-355 It wasn't nothing for people to do, chillens to do. **1973** GSMNP-1:30 Over yonder at Cove Creek it's a big sign there says something about the Asbury Trail. . . . It was two killed on Caldwell Fork. **1973** GSMNP-2:7 It wasn't many able bodied men in here. **1974** Ogle *Memories* 44 Everytime it came up a big rain, my folks were afraid the river would come down and we couldn't get home. **1979** *Big South Fork OHP*-1 It wasn't much corn raised around there. **1980** GSMNP-115:40 It come up a little shower of rain on 'em. **1983** *Dark Corner OHP*-10A It's very few people that get out of the wood business completely and stay out. **1989** Landry *Smoky Mt Interviews* 195 It was very little difference between the families. **1990** *Matewan OHP*-73 It's a lot of people went hungry, yes ma'am. **1991** Thomas *Sthn Appal* 205 It was too menny people would git involved in it. **1997** GSMNPCOHP-3:13 A big majority of the people went to church pretty regular. Of course it wasn't anything else to do. **2006** Childs *Texana* 16 It was several of them went to Allen [High School]. **2008** *Rosie Hicks* 4 Hit ain't no such a thing as a mule egg. **2012** McQuaid *Interface* 270) It was five guards quit, said it wasn't worth risking their life being taken to work there.

[OED3 it 2b Early Old English, now chiefly U.S. regional; SND it pers pron 4; DARE it pron C1 scattered, but chiefly South, South Midland]

2 Used in a tag question (corresponding to *there* in the main clause).

1969 GSMNP-25:12 There was one bedroom upstairs, wasn't it? **1989** *Matewan OHP*-11 There's a store there named Nenni's, isn't it?

3 Used reflexively as indirect object (the so-called personal dative = (for) itself).

c1950 Adams *Grandpap* 99 The little boar pig was a-cookin' it a pot of peas for supper.

4 Contracted to a preposition or adverb.

1883 Murfree *Old Sledge* 552 [It is] a blessin' that I hev got it agin, for't would hev been mighty ill convenient 'round hyur 'thout it. **1927** Mason *Lure of Smokies* 221 Hit wa'n't nothin' to brag on't. **1957** Combs *Lg Sthn High: Word List* 67 *nigh't* = clipped form of *nigh it*. Ex.: "She's might' nigh't dead." **1991** Thomas *Sthn Appal* 44 They're jist a reg'lar punkin—taste the same—but they're all meat, might-near't. *Ibid.* 171 They'd climb right straight up a hill, purt-near'it. *Ibid.* 239 Everbody you might-nigh't see, these days—they'll say, "I'm all right."

D *noun* A child, regardless of gender.

1861 *Mingus Letters* 29 (Oct 6) Jackson Beck had a little girl to fall out . . . the blade cut her throat, it lived 15 minutes. **1862** *Bradshaw CW Letters* (March 16) may god bless my little Peanutt Lodema Jane fur I never expect to see it a gain onley through the kind proverdence of kine heavin m[a]y God bless you all. **1864** *Poteet CW Letters* (Oct 4) I would love to kiss that littel one that I haint never seen you Rote that it had taken astart to grow and it was very purty and smart *Ibid.* (Nov 2) when it got so that it couldent talk it would point its little finger for what it wanted and the day before it died it would look at me and then point with its little finger towards the loft I think it saw the Angels that come to take it to heaven. **c1982** Young *Colloquial Appal* 13 = baby or child.

it ain't done it (also *tain't done it*) *phrase* It isn't so! I didn't do it! (usually a child's denial of misbehavior or a protest of innocence at being falsely accused).

1953 Davison *Word-List Appal* 10 When one is unjustly accused of wrong-doing, one may answer, "It ain't done it." **1957** Combs *Lg Sthn High: Word List* 99 = a negative expression among children, meaning, "It isn't true." Ex: "You went and stole my hat." "Tain't done it." **1997** Montgomery *Coll* (known to Adams, Brown, Bush, Ledford, Weaver). **1997** Montgomery *File* It ain't done it (40-year-old woman, Sevier Co TN).

[DARE *it ain't done it* phr chiefly South, South Midland]

itch *noun, verb* Variant forms *each, eatch, eetch*.

1863 *Reese CW Letters* (Oct 27) the Each and lice keeps mee Rite Bissey. **1865** *Hill CW Letters* (March 12) I am tolable well at this time all but the Each. **1867** Harris *Sut Lovingood* 116 Well, Lum an' George, thar, wer pow'fully exercised 'bout hit—wanted tu know the secret pow'ful bad—hit pester'd 'em ni ontu es bad es the eatch. **1917** Kephart *Word-List* 411 That's eetch-weed, good for the eetch. **c1960** Wilson *Coll* It's no disgrace to catch the eetch, but it's a disgrace to keep it. **1962** Williams *Metaphor Mt Speech I* 11 The "foxy" one has an "eetchin' heel" and likes to "find a little patch of the fun." **1969** Dial *Dialect Appal People* 486 You can hear many characteristic Scottish pronunciations . . . poosh, boosh, eetch, deesh (push, bush, itch, dish and fish). **1986** Helton *Around Home* 379.

[DARE *itch* n, v chiefly South, South Midland]

itchweed *noun* Same as **Indian poke**.

1917 Kephart *Word-List* 411 That's eetch-weed, good for the eetch. [**1971** Krochmal et al. *Medicinal Plants Appal* 262 The plant is very poisonous. The rhizomes and roots, when properly prepared, are a strong cardiac stimulant drug.] **1982** Stupka *Wildflowers* 4 "Indian poke" and "itchweed" are other names for [the white hellebore].

it's books See **books B**.

it wonders me See **wonder 2**.

I've been, I've done been See **I been**.

ivory See **poison ivory**.

ivy *noun*

1 (also *ivy bush, ivy tree*) The mountain laurel shrub (*Kalmia latifolia*). Also called **calico bush**, **mountain ivy**. See also **mountain laurel**.

1883 Zeigler and Grosscup *Heart of Alleghanies* 196 The arborescent kalmia and rhododendron, which grow along almost every mountain stream, have a practical use. The ivy and laurel, as they are locally called, attain, in some of the fertile coves, a diameter of three inches, and the roots are even larger. **1928** Galyon *Plant Naturalist* 7 Mountain laurel, known to the mountaineer as "ivy," reaches its maximum development in the Smokies. It is not unusual to find arborescent laurels one foot or more in diameter and many feet high. **1982** Stupka *Wildflowers* 80 Usually the attractive pink or white-saucered flowers are so abundant that the mountain laurel in full bloom is one of our most spectacular plants. It flowers in May and June, the later blossoms ordinarily occurring on plants growing in the higher altitudes. "Ivy" and "calico-bush" are among its other names. **1986** Pederson et al. *LAGS*: *ivy* = attested by 10/60 interviewees (16.7%) from E TN and 3/35 (8.6%) from N GA; 13/20 of all LAGS interviewees (65%) attesting term were from Appalachia. **1997–2001** Montgomery *Coll*: *ivy bush* (known to Cardwell); *ivy tree* (known to Brown).

[DARE *ivy* n 4 chiefly Appalachians, southern New England]

2 See citations.

1997 Brown *Listening* Any bush that was poisonous to man or beast was known to mountaineers as ivy. **2000** Montgomery *Coll* = called *ivy* because early settlers detected that its leaves were poisonous (Cardwell).

ivy bush See **ivy 1**.

ivy sickness *noun* The sickness that cows develop from eating the leaves of **ivy** or, as better known in the region, the mountain laurel (*Kalmia latifolia*).

1998 Montgomery *Coll* (known to Cardwell).

ivy slick See **slick A1**.

ivy tree See **ivy 1**.

I wonder me See **wonder 1**.

I wouldn't care to See **care B**.

izard *noun* The letter Z.

1914 Furman *Sight* 42 I were raised forty-five mile' from a school-house or church-house, and never had no chance to l'arn "a" from "izard."

J

jab See **job**.

jack[1] *noun* See also **cut up jack**, **stiff jack**, **tear up jack**, **tough jack**.

1 Used in compounds **jack oak**, **jack pine**, etc. to indicate inferior quality.

1913 Morley *Carolina Mts* 18 Of the numberless hardwood trees that flourish here, the oaks perhaps stand first because of their numbers and the many forms in which they appear, from the lordly white oak to the little ridiculous jack oak. **1946** Burnett *Shingle Making* 225 Latterly another tree has pushed its way to the front, not so much from obscurity as from disrepute and scorn. This is the pine known over the country as black pine, jack pine, old field pine, scrub pine, and bastard pine. It was not even esteemed for firewood, if anything else was available. In recent years, however, this renegade among the pines has attained a place in the economic world as pulpwood. Even in our small segment of the mountains it brought in a good many thousands of dollars during World War II.

2 (One's) fortune, money.

1807 (in **1956** Eliason *Tarheel Talk* 279) (Buncombe Co NC) She said . . . he'd make his Jack for a few years and then the mill would be done.

[DARE *jack* n[1] 16 especially South, South Midland]

3 A man or boy spoken of generically.

1946 Still *Pattern of Man* 100 Every man jack of us had to go to the bull-hole.

jack[2] (also *jackrock*) *noun* Waste rock, such as slate, associated with coal.

1940 Still *River of Earth* 66 Mothercoal Mine put fifty men to hauling fallen jackrock and setting new timbers. **1949** Arnow *Hunter's Horn* 48 A coal car had broken loose . . . and run backward; he had heard the man scream . . . and he'd gone with his miner's cap on his head and spotlighted the man's eyes— . . . and then they were not man's eyes, but only something glittering like glass or ice or a bit of jack. **1977** Shackelford et al. *Our Appalachia* 205 This coal was in two different veins and there was a streak of "jack rock" [between them]. Jack rock [is] just rock, something like flint rock. They couldn't sell that dirty coal, it just wasn't clean. It wouldn't burn, no account for anything. **1997** Miller *Brier Poems* 150 Their fists broke my teeth before I worked clinking shifts of hard coal seams and slabs, bolting the dripping roof of gray jack rock.

[cf EDD *jack* sb 30 "a portion of stone in the roof of a mine"; SND *jack* n[1] 3 "a large piece of rock in a coal seam"]

jackalantern See **jack-o'-lantern**.

jack bean *noun*

1 A horsebean, especially *Canavalia ensiformis*.

1885 Murfree *Prophet* 280 He sat upon the cabin porch beneath the yellow gourds and the purple blooms of the Jack-bean. **2008**

Rosie Hicks 1 She said, "This here is [a] big bean." She said that was a jack bean.

2 See citation.

1973 *Words & Expressions* 135 *jack beans* = lima beans.

jack bite *noun* A snack.

1949 Kurath *Word Geog East US* 36 On the Kanawha we find *check* and *jack-bite*... beside the Southern *snack* for a bite between meals. **1968** *DARE Survey* (Spencer WV).

jack bumps *noun* See citation.

1990 Cavender *Folk Medical Lex* 25 = acne.

jacker-mer-lantern See **jack-o'-lantern**.

jacket *noun*

1 A sleeveless garment worn over a shirt; also a poultice (see 2003 citation).

1934–47 *LAMSAS Appal* (Madison Co NC, Swain Co NC). **1946** Nixon *Glossary VA Words* 26 = a vest... [a term used] in the southern part of the Blue Ridge. **1949** Kurath *Word Geog East US* 42 The Midland *jacket*, which is still in common use in Western North Carolina and adjoining parts of Virginia, as well as the upper reaches of the Potomac, survives only in scattered relics in the [Shenandoah] Valley. **1966** Dakin *Vocab Ohio River Valley* 189 Above the Ohio River, *jacket* has the status of an old term only remembered and in some cases now regarded with amusement, but at least in the [KY] Mountains some say only *jacket*. **2003** Cavender *Folk Medicine* 85 The primary therapeutic locus for influenza, however, was fever. As for a cold, the central objective was to "burn" (sweat) the fever out of a body. This was done by administering a variety of hot teas, many of which were powerful diaphoretics like boneset, horsemint, and mustard seed, often in combination with other interventions such as onion poultices and "jackets" (poultices on the chest and back).

[DARE *jacket* n 1 chiefly Midland]

2 A yellow jacket wasp.

1969 *GSMNP-27:8* We would have to stop and wait on them. They would find an old jacket nest or bumblebee nest. **1998** Montgomery *Coll* (known to Brown, Bush, Cardwell, Jones, Weaver).

3 See citation.

1976 Miller *Mts within Me* 116 Because the still was sealed tight, the alcohol vapor could escape only through the "worm" which was placed in a container of cool water called a "jacket" or "cooler barrel" and set under a waterfall or placed in an adjacent stream where cold mountain water would pour over it. As the vapor passed through the cold coil it condensed into a watery whiskey which was drawn off by a petcock or run directly into a pail, keg or jug.

Jack Frost *noun* A heavy frost, especially the first one of the fall.

1934–47 *LAMSAS Appal* = attested by 2/148 speakers (1.4%) from WV, 1/20 (5%) from VA, and 2/14 (14.3%) from SC. **1986** Petersen et al. *LAGS* (Floyd Co GA, Pickens Co GA). **1983** Broaddus *Estill Co KY Word List* 45. **1997** Montgomery *Coll* (known to Adams, Bush, Cardwell, Jones, Oliver, Weaver).

[DARE *jack frost* n 2 chiefly South, South Midland]

jack house *noun* See citation. See also **johnny**.

1998 Montgomery *Coll* = an outhouse; also a small barn where the stud jack mule is housed (Bush).

[SND *jack* n² "a privy"]

jacking up See **jack up 1**.

jack-in-the-box (also *jack-in-the-pulpit*) *noun* A perennial wildflower (*Arisaema triphyllum*) with various medicinal uses. Same as **Indian turnip**.

1966 *DARE Survey* (Cherokee NC) *jack in the box*. **1980** *Smokies Heritage* 61 Prominent in this herbal category is the jack-in-the-pulpit (Indian turnip), a perennial plant that was once called wakerobin by Smokies pioneers (this name was dropped after a species of red trilium became known as the wakerobin).

Jack in the bush (also *Jacky in the bush*) *noun* A guessing game usually played with grains of corn, chinquapins, etc. See also **hull gull**.

1968 *DARE Survey* (Wytheville VA) Poppy used to play some chinquapin games.... We used to play "Jacky-in-the-bush, cut him down, how many lick." Well, I didn't know how many he had in his hand and of course I couldn't guess, so Poppy got all the chinquapins 'cause I couldn't guess it. **1972** Davis *Christmas* 52 Some people called this game Jack in the Bush. The first player would say "Jack in the Bush?" And the other player would reply "Hack him down." The first player then asked "How many strokes?" Then the second player guessed the number of licks required to knock him down, which would correspond with the number of grains in his hand. This game was often played with dry beans, parched corn, acorns, chestnuts, chinquapins, buttons or even pebbles. Of course, it was more fun to play with something that could be eaten. [**1980** Wigginton *Foxfire VI* 292 One person puts some marbles (or none) in his hand and says, "Jack up a bush." A second person says, "Cut it down." The first person says, "How many licks?" Then the second person guesses how many marbles the first person has. If he gets it right, he gets all of them, and if he doesn't, he has to give the first person the difference.] **1985** *Schools and Pastimes* 49 We had cute little games we played involving swapping handfuls of [nuts]. In one called "Jack-in-the-bush" the player held a number of nuts in his closed hand and said, "Jack-in-the-bush." The other player said, "Cut him down." The first answered, "How many licks?" If the other guessed the number of nuts in the hand, he won them for himself.

[DARE *Jack-in-the-bush* 2 chiefly Middle and South Atlantic]

jack-in-the-pulpit See **jack-in-the-box**.

jackleg (also *jacklegged, jake leg*) *adjective* Usually of a member of an occupational group: self- or poorly trained, lacking training or competence, often working part-time in a trade or profession, such as carpentry, law, medicine, auto mechanics, or preaching, and sometimes having a reputation for being unscrupulous as well as doing amateurish or shoddy work. See also **jakeleg 2**.

1901 Harben *Westerfelt* 259 I'm jest a plain Cohutta Mountain, jack-leg lawyer. **1915** Dingus *Word-List VA* 184 *jack-leg* = (one) poor in quality, as a jack-leg lawyer. **1934–47** *LAMSAS Appal* (Madison Co NC) *little old jackleg preacher*. **c1960** Wilson *Coll*: *jackleg* = a sorry or weak professional. **1966–68** *DARE Survey* (Spruce Pine NC) *jack-leg* = an unprofessional part-time lay preacher, also an uncomplimentary name for a lawyer; (Maryville TN) *jackleg lawyer* = uncomplimentary term for a lawyer; (Cherokee NC, Maryville TN) *jackleg preacher* = unprofessional, part-time lay preacher; (Brasstown NC) *jackleg* = a doctor who is not very capable or who does not have a very good reputation. **1973** Davis *'Pon My Honor* 68 "Looks like hit hain't no place for a jack-leg liar like me," and he lit out over the hill for the Tennessee Valley. **1976** Garber *Mountain-ese* 47 = untrained. "Lemuel is jist a jackleg carpenter but he can build a fair-to-middlin' house." **1977** Shackelford et al. *Our Appalachia* 203 There was one of them little jack-legged bosses standing there and [he] looked over at me, said, "You clean up?" **1986** Pederson et al. *LAGS*: *jackleg lawyer* = attested by 16/60 interviewees (26.7%) from E TN and 5/35 (14.3%) from N GA; 21/92 of all LAGS interviewees (22.8%) attesting term were from Appalachia; *jackleg plumber* = attested by 2/60 interviewees (3.3%) from E TN; 2/11 of all LAGS interviewees (18.2%) attesting term were from Appalachia; *jackleg preacher* = attested by 37/60 interviewees (61.7%) from E TN and 16/35 (45.7%) from N GA; 53/295 of all LAGS interviewees (17.9%) attesting term were from Appalachia; *jacklegged lawyer* (Sevier Co TN); *jacklegged preacher* (Cocke Co TN, Roane Co TN, Sevier Co TN); *jake-leg cobbler* (Lumpkin Co GA). **1988** Jones *Modesty* 84 If someone asked us to fix something, we'd say "Well, I'll see what I can do if you don't mind having a jack-leg mechanic tinkering with it." **1992** Brooks *Sthn Stuff* 77 = makeshift. "I'm so sick of this old jackleg furniture!" **1995–97** Montgomery *Coll*: *jackleg carpenter* (known to Cardwell, Norris); *jackleg preacher* (known to Bush). **2009** Benfield *Mt Born* 162 *jack-legged lawyer* = an worthless or crooked lawyer. **2012** Still *Hills Remember* 175 I bet this bluegrass woman never done a thing but set up in a courthouse and diddle jackleg lawyers.

[OED3 *jackleg* adj/n U.S. dialect and colloquial; DARE *jackleg* adj 1 chiefly South, South Midland]

jack loader *noun* In logging, the part of a **skidder** that picks up logs and loads them onto a flatcar or truck to be hauled away.

1974–75 McCracken *Logging* 20 There was a section of the Lidgerwood skidder that they called the "jack loader." The skidder that brought the logs in, that portion of it didn't load the logs. But on the same car, pulled from the same steam, was what they called the "jack loader" that did pick the logs up from the ground and place them on the dock. *Ibid.* 24 = a car that had a boom on it and it'd pick up the log, it'd turn halfway around and lay the log down on a flatcar. That saved the separate loader.

jack oak *noun* Any oak tree of little value or inferior quality, usually the **blackjack**.

1913 Morley *Carolina Mts* 18 Of the numberless hardwood trees that flourish here, the oaks perhaps stand first because of their numbers and the many forms in which they appear, from the lordly white oak to the little ridiculous jack oak. **1997** Montgomery *Coll* = an oak tree having stunted growth, not worth cutting (Cardwell).

jack-o'-lantern (also *jackalantern*, *jacker-mer-lantern*, *jacky-my-lantern*) *noun* A will-o'-the-wisp, light said to lead travelers astray at night.

1859 Taliaferro *Fisher's River* 155 [I] got lost—led out'n my way by a stinkin' jacker-mer-lantern. **1948** Chase *Grandfather Tales* 36 Some folks call it the Jacky-my-lantern, and some call it the will-o-the-wisp. **1967** *DARE Survey* (Maryville TN) = small light that seems to dance or flicker over a marsh or swamp at night. **1971** *Boogers* 34 They call them balls'a'fire jackalanterns. It's kind'a a round-lookin' thing, an' hit'll come and they'll play up—they'll go down low t'th'ground and high up. . . . They'd rise and they'd go up, and they're pretty good-sized lights, and they're playin' all over th'bottoms down there.

[DARE *jack-o'-lantern* n 1 chiefly South, Midland]

jack pine *noun* Any small pine of little value for lumber, especially *Pinus virginiana* or *Pinus rigida*.

1946 Burnett *Shingle Making* 225 Latterly another tree has pushed its way to the front, not so much from obscurity as from disrepute and scorn. This is the pine known over the country as black pine, jack pine, old field pine, scrub pine, and bastard pine. It was not even esteemed for firewood, if anything else was available. In recent years, however, this renegade among the pines has attained a place in the economic world as pulpwood. Even in our small segment of the mountains it brought in a good many thousands of dollars during World War II. **1958** GSMNP-110:25 I don't know whether there is any jack pine . . . what we call jack pine or yellow pine down in that hollow. **1960** Mason *Memoir* 98 One of my boys made the remark that Mr. Hoover was the only man that he knew of who could put jack-pine wood to peeling in the middle of the winter. **1968** *DARE Survey* (Brasstown NC).

jackpot

A *noun* An irregular pile of logs that have been pulled or pushed downhill.

1963 Lord *Blue Ridge Guide* 17D Shouting the warning "ball-hoot!," men dug their canthooks into the logs and sent them sliding and crashing into a "jack-pot" of logs in the hollow below. **1967** Parris *Mt Bred* 133 A jackpot is an irregular pile of logs and a katydid is a pair of wheels from 7 to 12 feet in diameter for transporting logs. **1973** Foster *Walker Valley* 9:9 They called that a jack-pot, where they team 'em down to and lower 'em off.

B *verb* To create such an irregular pile of logs.

1974–75 McCracken *Logging* 20:12 People would sell 'em logs, just people that logged it off and would haul, bunch 'em up, what they call jackpotting and scale 'em and buy 'em from them.

jackrock *noun*

1 See **jack**[2].

2 See citation.

1990 Moore *Pittston Strike* 12 Troopers discovered skunk scent in the vehicle and dead possums on the road spiked with "jack-rocks," nails spot-welded and twisted into an "X" to puncture tires [laid by striking miners].

jack rocks *noun* The children's game of jacks, played with rocks and a ball, with the object being to see who can first bounce or throw the ball and pick up all the rocks before the ball hits the ground or is caught.

1908 Johnson *Life KY Mts* 177 My happiest days were those spent at home in winter, after supper, before the fire on the old puncheon floor. Us boys and girls would gather around in a circle and play "Jack rocks" or "hull gull." For hours and hours this merry sport would continue until a gruff voice would command us to bed. [**1980** Wigginton *Foxfire VI* 292 You had five round rocks 'cause flat ones were much harder to pick up, and one rubber ball. You throw up the ball and reach down and get one rock while the ball is in the air, then catch the ball before it hits. Then you put the first rock back and throw up the ball again and this time pick up two rocks . . . and so on till you get all five.] **1997** King *Mt Folks* 33 Throughout the year, she and her three sisters played with paper dolls, played hopscotch, pushed a scotch wheel, and played jack rocks. Mama said she'd get so tired of hearing us say, "no slips, no slips." Campbell said they called out "no slips" if they dropped the ball or missed the jack rock so they would not have to give up their turn. **1998** *Dante OHP*-69 We'd get down in the floor and play checkers and stuff, you know, jack rocks and stuff like that. **2007** Rose *Games Mt Children* 15 Mama bought "Jack Rocks" for the girls. We loved this game. The rocks would be thrown on the floor, and the object was to pick up one, then two, increasing the number each time before the ball hit the floor. It was fun to see who could sweep up all ten jacks at one time.

jacks See **by**.

jack slip *noun* See 1976 citation.

1976 Clarkson *Logging in Appal* 120 When logs were brought to a mill, they were dumped into a pond. Here they were stored until they were taken up an incline trough called a *jack-slip* by a heavy endless chain with welded cleats called a *bull-chain*. **1989** Oliver *Hazel Creek* 67 The pond man, Preacher Thurmond Medford, who knew his logs, walked on a floating raft carrying a long pole with spikes in the end and would pull the logs one by one to the "jack slip" that hauled them up into the mill. **1994** Farwell and Buchanan *Logging Terms* = an opening for a log to go into the mill.

jacksnapper *noun* A click beetle.

1982 Slone *How We Talked* 45 = a long, black beetle that made a loud snapping sound when it snapped its head. We children loved to play with them and make them snap their heads.

[DARE *jacksnapper* n 1 especially South]

jack straws *noun* A children's game similar to pick-up-sticks.

1993 Page and Smith *Foxfire Toys and Games* 127 Bill's Jack Straws include a spoon, knife, sledge-hammer, soldering iron, stocking stretcher, churn dasher, birdhouse, laundry dolly, cracklin' press, garden hoe, tobacco knife, corn knife, bark spud, file, and saw. No two sets are the same, since his repertoire contains about 300 items. Each is approximately 6 inches long. Jack Straws is played just like Pick-Up Sticks, except that the eccentric shapes of the objects add more unpredictability to the behavior of the Straws.

jackum *noun* Anything at all, a single word.

1989 *Matewan OHP*-24 [They] never said jackum the first time.

jack up *verb phrase*

1 To scold, reprimand, berate; hence verbal noun *jacking up*.

1927 Woofter *Dialect from WV* 358 I got a good jacking-up when I went home. **1939** Hall *Coll* (Cosby Creek TN) He'd jack up the best hand he had. **1966** *DARE Survey* (Cherokee NC) = to put pressure on someone to do something that he ought to have done but hasn't. **1969** *Burton-Manning Coll*-89B She first wrote and jacked me up for not telling about [a] little marker or monument up there. **1971** *Kenny Runnion* 137 I never have [worked on Sunday]. I tried once and my brother jacked me up. **1976** Garber *Mountain-ese* 47 Old Lady Miller sure did jack up them young'uns for walkin' on her grass. **1985** Irwin *Alex Stewart* 164 He found out about it some way, and oh, he give me a jacking up. He said, "Now that's the worst habit you ever got into in your life. You better quit that." **1995** Montgomery *Coll* (Cardwell). **2008** Salsi *Ray Hicks* 150 He said, "Ray, I knowed ya didn't strip the cow. I've been payin' attention, and you do good work." Atter that, he give his daughters a good jackin' up. **2017** *Blind Pig* (April 28) I'm going to have to go down there and jack him up if he don't keep his long pointy nose outta my business. *Ibid.* I would get all jacked-up (angry, aggravated, frustrated) if someone kept tracking in mud on the floor.

2 To foul up, bungle.

2017 *Blind Pig* (April 28) When we use jacked up, we usually mean something messed up, like "he sure jacked up that table when he tried to fix it."

Jacky in the bush See **Jack in the bush**.

jacky-my-lantern See **jack-o'-lantern**.

Jacob's onion *noun* Apparently a variety of green onion.

1975 Purkey *Madison Co* 53–54 A variety of vegetables grew in long net rows: tender green onions (called Jacob's onions), peas, beets, carrots, radishes, lettuce, beans, parsnips, tomatoes, cucumbers, and sweet and Irish potatoes. *Ibid.* 106 I will never forget the endless bundles of crisp spring onions with their long white heads and slender green blades, which my mother prepared for market. Mama called them "Jacob's Onions." I don't know why unless it was because they were so prolific.

jag

A *noun* A small, often partial load of wood, corn, hay, etc.

1937 Hyatt *Kiverlid* 29 Tell Jason . . . to slip old Dorie's bridle and fling her a leetle jag o' roughness. **1949** Arnow *Hunter's Horn* 31 Th first day she got back she bought a little jag a beans an lard an meal on credit, an you know I don't hardly ever give credit; then pretty soon she was back an asken fer credit agin. **1949** Kurath *Word Geog East US* 31 A jag (of corn, wood) is North Midland and does not occur south of northern WV. **1957** Broaddus *Vocab Estill Co KY* 44 = a part of a wagon load. **1974** Fink *Bits Mt Speech* 13 = a small amount. "A *jag* o' corn." **1986** Pederson et al. *LAGS* (Johnson Co TN, Knox Co TN, Sevier Co TN). **1997** Montgomery *Coll* (known to Adams, Brown, Bush, Ellis, Jones, Ledford), = can refer to a small amount of anything, as "Give me a little jag of coffee" (Cardwell).

[cf OED3 *jag* n[2] "load . . . of hay, wood, etc." dialect and local; DARE *jag* n[2] 1c chiefly Midland, especially southern Appalachians]

B *verb* To stab, prick.

1862 *Neves CW Letters* (Jan 23) I am afraid you cant do much for the yankeys If tha[y] come. If you cant s[h]oot you must jage them tha[y] cant stand that. **2007** McMillon *Notes* Them brars is jaggedy. They'll jag ye.

[EDD *jag* v[1] B1 "Scots, Ir, nEngl dial"; CUD *jag* v 1 "prick"; Web3 *jag* vt 1 now dialect]

jaggedy *adjective* Of metal, wood, cloth, etc.: having a sharp, ragged, or frayed edge.

c1960 Wilson *Coll* = jagged, irregular. **1967** Williams *Subtlety Mt Speech* 16 He could see the jaggedy aidge of a great big rock poked aout away up high above him. **1997** Montgomery *Coll* (known to ten consultants from the Smoky Mountains), = refers only to metal (Ellis).

[CUD *jaggety* (at *jag* v) "rough or torn at the edge"; DARE *jaggedy* adj 1 South, South Midland]

jagger *noun* A spike on a barbed-wire fence.

1985 Irwin *Alex Stewart* 270 I thought them jaggers looked dangerous. People come from all over this country to look at that barb wire.

jag wire *noun* Barbed wire, used for fencing.

1968 *DARE Survey* (Big Stone Gap VA) = older term.

jailhouse *noun* A jail.

1930 Armstrong *This Day and Time* 80 Now he's a-spendin' his time in the jail-house. **1952** Wilson *Folk Speech NC* 554 = jail, the building. **1967** Fetterman *Stinking Creek* 88 I mind my business. I don't want no part of a town or a jailhouse. **1989** *Matewan OHP-11* That jailhouse must be at least over eighty years old. **1991** Thomas *Sthn Appal* 226 When I go to a new place for a meetin', I go into th' penitentiaries an' jail-houses, an' talk to th' people that're in there, an' I ask 'um why they're in there. **2002** Rash *Foot in Eden* 127 I ain't going to the jailhouse if I can help it.

[DARE *jailhouse* n scattered, but somewhat more frequent South, South Midland]

jair fly See **jar bug.**

jaisper See **jasper.**

jaist See **joist.**

jake

A *noun*

1 A rustic person, especially one considered uncouth or unsophisticated. Same as **country jake.** See also **jakey.**

1895 *Word-Lists* 389 = a rough, uncouth country fellow (N.C., Tenn.). **1901** Harben *Westerfelt* 243 Mrs. Floyd laughed slyly as she turned away. "You leave them two Jakes to me." **1941** Still *Stir-Off* 7 Tell that young jake to git his growth. **c1960** Wilson *Coll* (or *country jake*) = a corny, awkward, green fellow, no matter where he lives. **1992** Brooks *Sthn Stuff* 78 = a fellow; a guy (not complimentary). "I never see them two jaspers there that they ain't up to some kind of devilment." **1997** Montgomery *Coll* (known to Bush, Cardwell, Jones, Weaver).

[DARE *jake* n[1] 1 especially South Midland]

2 See citation. See also **jakeleg 2.**

1974 Dabney *Mt Spirits* 108 Just about the most horrible drink appearing during the Noble Experiment was "jake," an almost ninety per cent alcohol fluid extract of Jamaica ginger with wood alcohol added, which literally paralyzed its victims in the hands and feet. "Jake paralysis" victims walked with a goose step, their feet flopping around out of control.

3 A young turkey.

1997 Montgomery *Coll* (known to Brown).

4 See citation.

2007 McMillon *Notes* = used in query to what a person is doing: "Where ye gwine, Jake?"

B *verb* To loaf, shirk.

c1982 Young *Colloquial Appal* 13 *jaking* = shirking, pretending.

jakeleg *noun* See also **jackleg.**

1 Low-quality liquor.

1992 Gabbard *Thunder Road* 147 "Jakeleg" was the low-grade sugar liquor. **1997** Montgomery *Coll* (known to Cardwell, Ledford, Weaver).

2 (also *jakelegs, jake walk*) Paralysis or incapacitation of the legs caused by drinking low-quality (usually wood) alcohol. See 1981 citations.

1940 Stuart *Trees of Heaven* 182 The Lord ain't kind to moonshiners nohow. Look what happens to 'em. . . . I never saw so many men walkin on canes with the jakeleg. **c1960** Wilson *Coll*: *jakeleg* = a condition resulting from drinking bad liquor, a very modern word; give the *jakeleg* [i.e. poison with bad liquor]. **1967** *DARE Survey* (Gatlinburg TN) = delirium tremens. **1976** Garber *Mountain-ese* 47 = crippling limp. "Jeems kaint walk very fast since he's had the jake-leg." **1977** Wolfe *TN Strings* 50 Some Allen [Brothers] songs commented on topical events of the day: "Jake-Walk Blues" reflects the dangers of getting "jake-leg" from drinking Jamaican Ginger extract during Prohibition days. **1981** Dumas *Appal Glossary* 17 = paralysis of a lower extremity caused by drinking a certain variety of regionally available illegally manufactured whiskey. "He's got the *jake-leg.*" **1981** Whitener *Folk-Ways* 63 Then at about the turn of the 30's a new "cutting" solution for the jake was introduced: a compound known as TOCP (tri-ortho-cresyl phosphate). Soluble and tasteless, it appeared to serve its purpose well. Unfortunately, however, it also affected the cells of the spinal cord and often caused the user to develop what was known as "jake" or "jake leg" paralysis. *Ibid.* 64 If he recovered sufficiently to be able to walk, it was with a high-stepping gait somewhat akin to that of polio victims. It became known as the "jake leg" or "jake walk" and resulted from the inflexibility of the user's feet and ankles. **1987** Carver *Regional Dialects* 168 Drinking *any* adulterated liquor, particularly bad moonshine, or, according to some sources, drinking "sterno," will give one the jake-legs. **1990** Cavender *Folk Medical Lex* 25 = a disabled walk characterized by a loping gait when the feet fall hard or "slap" the ground; condition common in the 1920s and 1930s caused by drinking Jamaica Ginger, a ginger extract containing prophylene glycol. **1994–97** Montgomery *Coll* (known to Brown, Ellis, Jones, Ledford, Weaver), = a permanent crippled state resulting from consumption of poisoned liquor (Cardwell). **2003** Cavender *Folk Medicine* 204 = a neurological disorder caused by ingestion of adulterated Jamaican ginger ("jake"); symptoms included a spastic gait.

[DARE *jake leg* n[1] 1 "paralysis" chiefly South Midland, western Gulf States]

jakelegs, jake walk See **jakeleg 2**.

jakey *adjective* Acting like one who is uncouth or unsophisticated. See also **country jake, jake A1**.

1891 Brown *Dialect in TN* 173 If his clothes are tacky and he appears to be from the backwoods, he is called a country-jake, and is said to look jakey. **c1960** Wilson *Coll* = acting like a jake or a greenhorn. **2015** *Blind Pig* (July 8) She just looked so jakie when she tried to dress up.

jallus See **ay**.

jam *adverb* Completely.

1952 Wilson *Folk Speech NC* 554 He went *jam by* me and didn't see me. **c1960** Wilson *Coll* = completely, entirely. **1995–97** Montgomery *Coll* (known to Brown, Bush, Norris).

jamb-rock (also *jamm-rock, jamrock*) *noun* A stone forming one side of a fireplace.

1931 Thomas *Ditties* 2 [They were] scrouged up agin' the hot jam rock like a sick kitten. **1941** Stuart *Men of Mts* 95 She reached in her apron pocket and got a match. She struck it on the jamm-rock above the fireplace. **c1950** Adams *Grandpap* 122 He uncrossed his hands and made a motion towards the dogwood pokingstick, leaning against the jamrock on Grandpap's side of the hearth. **1992** Brooks *Sthn Stuff* 78 *jamrock* = one of the stones used in the facing of a fireplace. "Ever' jamrock in their fireplace she'd grubbed up from their own land." **1997** Montgomery *Coll* (known to Brown, Bush, Cardwell, Jones, Norris).

[cf EDD *jamb-stone* (at *jamb* 2 (3)) and SND *jam-stane* (at *jamb* 1 (2)); DARE *jamb-rock* n South Midland]

jam cake *noun* A spice cake flavored with jam. See also **stack cake**.

1949 Still *Master Time* 45 We sat to a feast of potatoes, hominy, cushaw, beans, fried and boiled pork, baked chicken, buttered dumplings, gravy, stacks of hand-pies, and jam cake. **1997** Montgomery *Coll* (known to eight consultants from the Smoky Mountains), = usually stacked with strawberry, blackberry, or other jam, while stack cake had layers of fruit, mostly dried apples (Adams), = a cake that has jam spread between two or three layers of filling (Oliver).

[DARE *jam cake* n chiefly South Midland, especially KY]

jamm-rock, jamrock See **jamb-rock**.

jam up

A *adjective phrase* See citation.

c1960 Wilson *Coll* = good, satisfactory, all that could be expected.

B *adverb phrase* Fully, completely, superlatively.

1866 Smith *So Called* 61 Linton played his part of the programme jam up. **1966** Medford *Ol' Starlin* 83 'Cordin' to the book, Washington was awful good gen'ral an' jam-up smart man. **1996** Montgomery *Coll* (known to Cardwell, Jones, Norris, Oliver). **2001** Montgomery *File* He's an all-around, jam-up good fellow (72-year-old woman, Bryson City NC).

[DARE *jam up* adv phr 1 chiefly South, South Midland]

jander *noun* Bread that has a yellow color due to an excess of baking soda.

1941 Still *Troublesome Creek* 63 A pone Father baked was a jander of soda.

janders *noun* Jaundice. Same as **yellow jaundice**. See also **yellow eye**.

1862 *Warrick CW Letters* (Aug 17) I hav got the Janders & A Bad Cold But I hope I will be strait agane soon. **1867** Harris *Sut Lovingood* 37 He wer eighteen an' a 'alf hans high, an' modeled like ontu a shingle maker's shavin hoss, an' were es yaller as a warter dorg wif the janders. **1940** Hall *Coll* (White Oak NC). **1973** Miller *English Unicoi Co* 105 = attested by 3 of 5 speakers.

[EDD *jaundice* sb; CUD *janders* n; DARE (at *jaundice* n) especially South, South Midland]

janes See **jeans**.

jangle ball hooker *noun* A member of a logging team that **skids** logs downhill.

2009 Lloyd *Tremont* 35 A skidder team included a bell boy, a fireman, a landing jack, two choker hookers, a jangle ball hooker, an engineer, and a foreman.

jant (also *ja'nt*) *verb, noun* To jaunt; a jaunt.

1891 Primer *Studies in WV* 163 [In] words like gaunt, haunt, jaunt . . . Sweet's low-front-wide [vowel] (= a in man) is commonly heard. **1901** Harben *Westerfelt* 166 He's got a-plenty [of horses], an' he won't need 'em atter our ja'nt. **1925** Dargan *High-*

land Annals (in 1935 Edwards *NC Novels* 67) *ja'nt*. **1952** Wilson *Folk Speech NC* 554 *jant*. **c1960** Wilson *Coll* Jaunt is sometimes /dʒænt/, now largely humorous.

jant up *verb phrase* To wear (an animal) out through overwork. See also **jaunt**.

1937 Hyatt *Kiverlid* 14 She ha'n't never been ja'nted up. Jeems don't put up with over-workin' and strainin' his horse-stock.

jape *verb* To copulate (with); to cohabit.

1917 Kephart *Word-List* 413 = to copulate. **1927** Woofter *Dialect from WV* 358 = to have sexual intercourse: "He said that he would jape that woman before another week." **1944** Combs *Word-List Sthn High* 19 = to cohabit, copulate. [**1992** Montgomery *Coll* (unknown to consultants from the Smoky Mountains).]

[OED3 *jape* v 2 obsolete; DARE *jape* v especially southern Appalachians]

jar[1] *noun* See citation.

1974 Dabney *Mt Spirits* xxii = a moonshiner term for whiskey containers, be they made of glass, tin, plastic, or ceramic.

jar[2] *verb*

1 To quarrel, bicker.

1949 Arnow *Hunter's Horn* 394 "Aw, you're all mixed up," Nunn said as he walked on; "if'n theys any truth to it atall, it's th Germans has bombed th Panama Canal—we own that an it begins with a P. They've all been a jarren an a fussen around a sight." **1962** Williams *Metaphor Mt Speech I* 12 If the stubborn wife persists in her "jarrin' and mouthin'," the irate husband is "like to commence a-foulin' one hock and a-rubbin' it on t'other" before he roars, "Shet up yer big mouth before I knock ye hell-western crookedy!" **1997** Montgomery *Coll* (known to Bush, Cardwell, Ledford, Oliver, Weaver).

[DARE *jar* v[1] B1 especially South Midland]

2 To cause to shake.

1970 *Hunting Stories* 34 God, [the turkey] gobbled an' just jarred th'ground.

jar bug (also *jar fly*) *noun* An annual cicada. Also called **dry fly**, **garree fly**.

1937 Wilson *Folklore SE KY* 14 [At the] first jar-fly = three months to frost (known to 10/31 speakers in Bell Co KY and 17/31 speakers in Blount Co TN). **1940** Haun *Hawk's Done* 85 The night jar flies and the crickets begun to sing. **1962** Wilson *Folkways Mammoth Cave* 18 The common summer cicada was a *jarfly*, so called because of its strident note. **1968** *DARE Survey* (Brasstown NC) *jar bug* = insect that sits in trees or bushes in hot weather and makes a sharp, buzzing sound. **1968** Wilson *Folklore Mammoth Cave* 20 *jarfly* = one of the summer cicadas (Cicadidae); not the seventeen-year locust (Magicicada septendecim). The name jarfly seems to have come from its jarring, rasping notes; also called dryfly because it sings in the dry summer months. **1976** Garber *Mountain-ese* 47 The jarfly in the tree made a most turrible noise. **1996** Parton *Mt Memories* 172 The faint sound of a barking dog, a mooing cow, or the loud "eeee-ar-eeee-ar" of a jar fly vied for the attention of the congregation. **1997** Montgomery *Coll*: *jar bug* (known to Brown, Cardwell); *jar fly* (known to ten consultants from the Smoky Mountains). **2007** McMillon *Notes*: *jairfly*.

[perhaps echoic or from the shape of the insect's body; DARE *jarfly* n 1 chiefly South Midland]

jar fly See **jar bug**.

jarhead *noun* A mule; by extension = a mulish person.

c1940 Aswell *Glossary TN Idiom* 11 = mule or mulish person. **1982** Powers and Hannah *Cataloochee* 383 A mule was sometimes called a "jarhead." Mark said it was because it was empty minded. **1997** Montgomery *Coll* (known to Brown, Bush, Cardwell, Jones, Ledford, Weaver).

jarsh *verb* See citation.

1994 Mullins *Coaley Creek* xi = to scrape a vegetable—usually a potato—to a mushy pulp.

jarve *verb* To quarrel, fuss.

1957 Combs *Lg Sthn High: Word List* 54 *jarving* = quarreling and fussing; jawing.

jasper (also *jaisper*) *noun* A fellow, stranger; a person who is unwanted or who behaves inappropriately.

1976 Still *Pattern of Man* 85 The jaspers deserved to swallow their tongues and swallow to death. **1991** Still *Wolfpen Notebooks* 55 That town-raised jasper moved up in the hollow and tried to farm. Naturally he starved out. He didn't even know what makes a pig's tail curl. **1992** Jones and Miller *Sthn Mt Speech* 89 I wouldn't associate with that jasper. **1996–97** Montgomery *Coll* (known to Brown, Bush, Hooper, Jones), = only an unworthy person (Norris). **2003** Wolfram et al. *Mt Talk* If it's somebody [my grandmother] didn't know, but he's probably all right. She didn't have any animosity for him. She would say he's a jasper: "there's this jasper come by here this morning, and he knocked on the door." But if it's a salesman, "it's just a peckerwood out there on the porch." **2005** Williams *Gratitude* 503 (also *jaisper*) = another name for feller (fellow). I've also heard a wasp (wasper) referred to as a jasper. **2014** Montgomery *File* = a stranger, untrustworthy person (40-year-old woman, Graham Co NC). **2015** *Blind Pig* (June 26) Old Wade Gass side-swarped that jasper in his 6th grade class up side the head with a dusty eraser.

jassack *noun* A jackass or mule.

1867 Harris *Sut Lovingood* 80 The 'saitful she torment [was] lookin es solemn es a jasack in a snow storm, when the fodder gin out. **c1960** Wilson *Coll* = humorous name for a mule.

[DARE *jassack* n scattered, but especially WV]

jaundice root *noun* Same as **goldenseal**.

1968 *Sang Signs* 15 Best known as sang-sign is the "little brother of the ginseng," the golden seal . . . Other names . . . include . . . jaundice-root. **1977** Coon *Useful Plants* 220 (DARE) = the roots are the parts used, either as a source for a yellow dye, or in reputable medical practice as an alterative and bitter tonic.

jaw back *verb phrase* To talk back (to someone) in a quarrelsome manner, argue. Same as **backjaw A**.

1923 Greer-Petrie *Angeline Steppin' Out* 42 She ought to a jaw'd him back. **1997** Montgomery Coll (known to eight consultants from the Smoky Mountains).

[DARE *jaw back* v phr especially South, South Midland]

jaw harp *noun* Same as **Jew's harp**.

1978 *Smoky Vistas* (July–Sept) 7 Harmonicas, often called French harp, and the Jew's harp, or "jaw harp," were available from the general stores. **1979** Irwin *Musical Instruments* 89 The Jews harp, probably correctly the jaw harp, has been played in Europe for hundreds of years, and in Appalachia since the first Whites entered the region. **1986** Pederson et al. LAGS (Rhea Co TN). **1997** Montgomery Coll (known to Jones).

[perhaps folk etymology for *Jew's harp*]

jay

A (also *jay off*) *verb, verb phrase* Of a teamster and a team of horses or cattle in logging, to step aside or away from a **skid road** into a **jay hole** to avoid oncoming logs being skidded down a slope under their own weight, thus allowing the logs to pass by; of a teamster: to direct (a team) to do so.

1932 Strong *Great Smokies* 31 Hit takes low gear to pull us up, an' low, high, *an'* reverse ter hold us back when we go a-jayin' down. **1964** Clarkson *Lumbering in WV* 365 *jay-off* = when a team steps aside to allow running logs to pass by. **1977** *Foxfire IV* 275 You jay your steers off and let the logs go on by theirselves. And whenever you go to jay, you just turn your spread hook over and put it in that grab and your spread hook turns loose and it just goes right on by. I've jayed off eighteen and twenty of them, and the cracker [= the last log in the string] would go past and he'd be a foot off the ground when he passed. *Ibid.* 276 It was a long time before they ever done that jaying with steers. . . . Then they got to learning steers to where they'd jay.

[perhaps from the shape of the *jay hole* "sidepath"; DARE *jay* v² Appalachians]

B *interjection* Look out! (used as a shout to get out of the way of oncoming logs being skidded down a mountain).

1973 GSMNP-87:2:14 Now [if] the logs got too fast and going to run over the horses, they'd holler "jay" at them and horses [were] trained to take off to that trail that went up the hill. **1995** Weber *Rugged Hills* 82–83 We always cut a trail where the team could turn out of the way. As the logs started to run, you hollered to your team, "Jay . . . jay . . . jay!" They knew the routine and scrambled up out of the way. We had one little marpoure that was kinda slow. She didn't "jay" fast enough and the bunch of logs caught up to her. They hit her in her back legs and pulled both her shoes off. It sprained her legs and she could hardly walk for about 2 weeks.

jaybird *noun* A blue jay, used in various similes.

1913 Kephart *Our Sthn High* 107 He's as antic as a jay bird when he takes the notion. **1952** Brown *NC Folklore* 1.431 As happy as a jaybird . . . As naked as a picked jaybird . . . As naked as a jaybird's ass . . . As saucy as a jaybird . . . Git along about as well as a jaybird does with a sparrer hawk . . . As spry as a jaybird in wild cherry time. **1956** Hall Coll (Del Rio TN) As naked as a jay bird. **1962** Dykeman *Tall Woman* 95 Mark's always speaking of her eyes, too; and the way she clings to him, the way she's so quick to walk, and talks already like a jaybird chattering—well, he thinks she's mighty nigh perfection itself.

[DARE *jaybird* n 1a chiefly South, South Midland]

jaybird legs *noun* See citation.

1997 Montgomery Coll = having crooked shanks or legs (Hooper).

jay grab (also *jay hook*, *J-grab*, *J-hook*) *noun* See citations.

1930 Pendleton *Wood-Hicks Speak* 88 *jay grab* = a hook used only on the header. **1964** Clarkson *Lumbering in WV* 365 *jay grab* = special type of grab or coupler used on steep slopes [that] permits the skidding team to step aside (jay off), become disengaged and stand while the logs continue down the slope. Syn J-hook. **1967** Parris *Mt Bred* 134 = [an instrument that] has a recurved head, to each end of which a grab is attached by a short chain. The J-hook is attached to the top of the forward log of a turn on a skipper road and serves as the point of attachment for the draft. If the logs start to run, the draft animals can be automatically freed by turning them at right angles to the road—into a J-hole. **1973** GSMNP-84:20 They had what they called jay grabs, and that jay grab was just like the headers that went around the log except it had one grab back here they drove down in the log, maybe two and one out here, with a grab cut off to about that much sticking up, and they had a great big hook and that jay grab stuck up like that and this header hooked in there like that. **1974–75** McCracken *Logging* 2:5 They called it a jay hook. It was a bar about that long and it had a thing welded up on top of it there. They hooked on it with, we called 'em spreads that the team hooked on. **1975** Brewer *Valley So Wild* 312 The "jay grabs" uncoupled automatically when the horses dodged into the "jay holes," allowing the logs to go skidding on their own momentum down the steep road. **1994** Schmidt and Hooks *Whistle* 157 = specially designed chain to link together logs on a slideway which allowed safer use of horses. **1995** Montieth *Tall Tales* 11 On steep grades the logs would sometimes go by horses; this was prevented with a "J-Grab," so as the log would go by, the teamsters would pull the horse to one side of a "J-Hole." **1995** Weber *Rugged Hills* 82 When the trailer was ready, you hooked your team to the first log with a "J-grab." It was called a J-grab because it kinda looked like the letter "J." It was made so that when the team pulled straight, the J-hook held.

[from the hook's resemblance to the letter J; DARE *jay grab* n Appalachians]

jayhawker *noun*

1 In the Civil War, a southerner who operated in an irregular cavalry unit serving ostensibly as Unionist **home guards** but often living in the hills and preying on civilians regardless of loyalty. See also **bushwhacker**, **tory**.

1862 (in **1974** Aiken *Offield CW Letters* 119) (April 17) On our last Trip, which was to a valley called Brimstone in Scott County Tenn near the Cumberland river, we had a fight with some Yankee homeguards as they call themselves, though we call them jayhawkers. **1862** *Hynds CW Letters* (May 27) A potion of our corps engaged a number of Jayhawkers about half way [on] our journey We killed one dead wounded another badly took 7 prisoners and captured a lot of guns ammunition and Camp equipag. **1904** Fox *Christmas Eve* 12 The "wild Jay-Hawkers of Kaintuck" were coming over into Virginia to get Flitter Bill's store, for they were mountain Unionists and Bill was a valley rebel and lawful prey.

2 See citation.

c1960 Wilson *Coll* = a rustic, with no reference to Kansas and earlier times.

jayho See **jay hole B**.

jay hole

A (*jay trail, J-hole, J-pit*) *noun* A level side path cut into a hillside along a **skid road** or **skidway**, into which a teamster and his team of animals can safely step to avoid logs being skidded down a mountainside behind them; a wider space on a road where two teams or vehicles may pass one another. See c1975 citation. See also **skid road**.

1932 Strong *Great Smokies* 164 About a hundred feet down, a jay-hole, a piece of level ground, was cut into the hillside, to one side of the jay-path. The horses stepped aside into this jay-hole and allowed the log to continue downhill. **1939** Hall *Coll* (Proctor NC) On a steep place on a skid road, you'd have a jay hole for your team to run into so as not to be injured by the logs. **1952** Wilson *Folk Speech NC* 554 *jay-hole* = space on a mountain road where a vehicle or team may pass another vehicle or team. **1964** Clarkson *Lumbering in WV* 365 *jay-hole* = space prepared along a skidway to permit a team to jay-off while logs run by. **1967** Parris *Mt Bred* 133–34 On steep skidding roads, a "Jay Hole" is a place of refuge for the team when the turn of logs has attained high speed and is so called because of the use of the J-hook . . . If the logs start to run, the draft animals can be automatically freed by turning them at right angles to the road—into a J-hole. **1973** GSMNP-87:2:14 They'd have trails built off for the horses to take up, you see. They take off up hill, just what they call a jay trail. Now [if] the logs got too fast and going to run over the horses, they'd holler "jay" at them and horses [were] trained to take off to that trail that went up the hill. **1975** Brewer *Valley So Wild* 312 Teamsters drove big horses—1600 to 2000 pounds—which could pull big logs and knew how to dodge back into a "jay hole" when a log started gaining on them in steep down-hill runs. "Jay holes," big enough to accommodate two-horse teams, were cut back into the banks of the logging roads at steep places. The "jay grabs" uncoupled automatically when the horses dodged into the "jay holes," allowing the logs to go skidding on their own momentum down the steep road. **c1975** Lunsford *It Used to Be* 165 "Jayhole" is a wide place, or a place that's trimmed out of the side of the mountain road, wide enough to hold a wagon and team or to hold a car or any vehicle that might be going along the road, in order to get the main traffic by. If it's a truck load of logs or if they are dragging some logs on a half-sled, or if a team is coming down with a wagon and there's no room to pass, one gets in a jayhole. They say, "look out boys!" **1977** *Foxfire IV* 276 If the ground's not level enough for a team to get out of the way when you jay off, you've got to dig that J-hole into the road bank for them to get into 'cause when those logs run, they've got to get in that so the logs can pass them up. **1983** Aiken *Mt Ways* 165 The horses got the log to going real fast, then to get out of the way the horses were trained to step aside into the "J" pit and the log released by the "J" hook went "ball hooting" down the mountain. **1995** Montieth *Tall Tales* 11 On steep grades the logs would sometimes go by horses; this was prevented with a "J-Grab," so as the log would go by, the teamsters would pull the horse to one side of a "J-Hole."

[DARE *jay hole* n Appalachians]

B (as form *jayho*) *interjection* Look out! (used as a warning by a logging teamster to those on the road below to indicate that logs are being released down the mountain).

1998 Farwell *Logging Terms*.

jay hook

A *noun* See **jay grab**.

B *verb phrase* To use a **jay grab**.

1973 GSMNP-84:19 They didn't jayhook them [= logs] with oxens.

jay off See **jay A**.

jay path *noun* A pathway down a mountain on which logs are pulled, usually by horses, and along which J-shaped side paths are built into which the horses can step if logs slip out of control. See also **jay hole**.

1932 Strong *Great Smokies* 164 When the log was in place at the top of the jay-path, the horses started downhill at a gallop, the log thundering after them. About a hundred feet down, a jay-hole, a piece of level ground, was cut in the hillside, to the side of the jay-path. The horses stepped aside into this jay-hole and allowed the log to continue downhill, gathering speed as it went.

jay trail See **jay hole**.

jeans (also *jeans cloth*) *noun*

A Variant form *janes* (reflecting an old-fashioned pronunciation in the late 1930s, according to **1942** Hall *Phonetics Smoky Mts* 13).

B Denim or other type of cotton fabric. [Editor's note: In former days (according to Joseph Hall's observation in the late 1930s), home-woven cloth of cotton and wool, made into quilts and such men's clothing as trousers and coats.]

1862 *Vance Papers* (Nov 6) I am Requested By our Col to ask you By Letter what to Give for Janes and Lincy cloth and socks & Blankets Janes has gone up in this part of the country to $5.00 pr yard. **1863** *Whitaker CW Letters* (June 28) I want you to make me a nice Soot of Janes cote & pants as Soon as you can. **1935** Sheppard *Cabins in Laurel* 47 He was also to teach the boy the art of farming. In the fall term of 1843 James Boon was allowed the apprentice service of Amos Boon until he should come of age in return for two years of schooling, one horse, saddle, and bridle, worth $80.00, and four suits of clothes, two of which should be good "janes" and two of everyday stuff, an axe, a good hat, and "a pare of shoes." **1937** Hall Coll (Catons Grove TN) Jeans is a cloth wove out of wool with three treadles and a twill in it. Hit's a men's cloth. *Ibid.* (Mingus Creek NC) Jeans—for men-folks. The chain was cotton and the fillin' was wool. *Ibid.* (Wears Cove TN) They pretty nearly used the jeans cloth. They called it the plain jeans. **1980** Riggleman *WV Mtneer* 18 We had no sewing machine—mother did all the sewing by hand. Mother got material called "jeans cloth" from a store or a peddler, for pants. It took fifteen cents of jeans cloth to make one pair of pants. **1995** Montgomery Coll: *jeans britches* (known to Cardwell).

je-daddled *past participle/adjective* See citation.

1939 Eastridge *Folklore Adair Co* 116 The little woman, who was about eighty years old, was shocked beyond words. She gasped and then said, "I'll be 'Je-daddled!'" Afterward she said she had never heard the expression before, but she had made it herself. That same expression is general now in that community, as it was taken up by the younger members of her family and then transferred to other people they know. Perhaps many of the expressions had their origin in similar ways; such as a very simple situation when no known word expressed the exact feeling of some one.

jedge See **judge**.

jedgmatically See **judgmatically A**.

jeeminy fit (also *jemyny fit*) *noun* An emotional outburst.

1865 *Brown CW Letters* (May 2) your Mother Sais to tell you she like to a took a jemyny fit when she heard it. **1968** Wilson *Folklore Mammoth Cave* 41 Nervous fit[s], often suspected as hardly genuine . . . were *duck fits*, *conniption fits*, *jeeminy fits*, *the allovers*, and, very recently, the *heebie-jeebies*, or the *whitty-jiggers*.

jeep stick *noun* Same as **gee-haw whimmy diddle**.

1980 Wigginton *Foxfire VI* 252–53 First one I ever saw was about twenty-five years ago. . . . When I first started making jeep sticks I told everybody I could tell their fortunes with them. The idea is to put your thumbnail up against the stick and it [= a propeller] will go one way. If you want it to go the other way, put your thumbnail under the stick. . . . I've always called them "jeep sticks," that's all I've ever call 'em. Some people call them "gee-haw whimmy diddles."

jellico weed *noun* The angelica plant (*Angelica atropurpurea/triquinata*).

1917 Kephart *Word-List* 413 = angelica. **1994** Montgomery Coll (known to Cardwell, but not to other consultants from the Smoky Mountains).

jenny[1] *noun* A makeshift merry-go-round, more often known as a **flying jenny**.

1997 Montgomery Coll (known to Brown, Bush, Cardwell).

[cf OED3 (at *jenny* n 4) short for *spinning jenny* "a spinning machine"; DARE *jenny* n 6 South, South Midland]

jenny[2] *noun* A female donkey.

1957 Broaddus *Vocab Estill Co KY* 44 = a female donkey. **1958** Miller *Pigeon's Roost* (Sept 11) Years ago, horses and the common mules as known today began to take much of the load from the jenny mules and oxen, but the oxen did prove to be about as much a favorite work animal among the farmers as any work animal ever did.

jenny barn (also *jennie barn*, *jimmy barn*) *noun* A roadhouse with **bootleg** liquor and women of ill repute.

1940 Bowman *KY Mt Stories* 8–9 One might wonder what would occur of interest when one was bottled up in a valley where there were no trains, highways for cars, stores as we "outlanders" know them, no place of amusement except the "Jimmy Barn" (road house), no telephones, and very few radios. **1990** (in **2012** Portelli *They Say* 111) A man would get him a little old house or a little old store along the side of the road, and he would put an electronic nickelodeon in there, and a slot machine, and one of these little machines where you make hot dogs on it, and that was his food that he was selling, and then he sold beer and liquor, and he had a room to the side, and he had a woman, or two women, or three women, depending on how popular that place was, that used the rooms on the side. And they called this a jenny barn. The jenny, you know, like the jenny, the cross between the horse and the mule. **1991** Still *Wolfpen Notebooks* 104 There have been two "jenny barns" I've visited in my life. Gone now. Long gone. Anything that was a sin or against the law you could get there—beer, whiskey, yeah, anything.

Jenny Lind house *noun* See citations.

1982 Eller *Miners* 184 The prevalent house style in the region was the "Jenny Lind," a one-story boxlike structure that rested on a foundation and contained three or four rooms. A pot-bellied stove, centrally located and fired with company coal, provided the building's heat. **2006** *WV Encycl* 382 A Jenny Lind house was built on a foundation of piers made from stone, block, brick, or wooden posts. The piers were aligned around the perimeter of the building, and across the center if the floor plan was large enough to require a central girder. Framing for the floor was formed by nailing together four planks set at right angles to each other, as if the builder were constructing the sides of a shallow box. This box sill sat on top of the piers and was supported by them. Floor joists spanned the inner space of the box, and plank flooring was nailed on top of the sill and joists. The construction of the walls is a defining feature of the Jenny Lind style. The walls had no studs or internal framing. The vertical planks were attached directly to the outside of the box sill at the bottom and nailed at the top to a horizontal two-by-four ribbon board running around the entire perimeter of the house.

jerkwater *noun* Very weak coffee.

1941 *FWP Guide WV* 403 Although changed in other respects, the West Virginia logger has retained his jargon . . . coffee is "jerkwater." **1964** Clarkson *Lumbering in WV* 365 = coffee.

jerp *noun* See citation.

1974 Dwyer and Dwyer *Mt Cookin'* 37 = a small quantity, most frequently said of sweets.

jerulem oak See **Jerusalem oak.**

Jerusalem oak *noun*

A Variant forms *gurglymock* [see **1939** *Ibid.* in **B**], *Jerulem oak* [see **1937** in **B**], *Jerusaly moke* [see **1982** in **B**], *Jerussely-moke* [see **1991** in **B**], *Jewsly moke* [see **1953** in **B**], *Jewsly mose* [see **1951** in **B**].

B An annual plant (*Chenopodium botrys/ambrosioides*) with large leaves resembling those of an oak; its seeds (often prepared with molasses) and an oil from the plant are given to children as an intestinal vermifuge. Also called **old Jerusalem, wormwood.** See also **worm syrup.**

1937 Hall *Coll* (Cosby TN) To cure yourself of the worms, take the seed off a Jerulem oak, bile it with molasses. The dost [i.e. dose] is a spoonful. **1939** Hall *Coll* (Catons Grove TN) Jerusalem oak's another good thing for worms in children. Take it and stew the seed in honey or molasses and give it to them a small teaspoonful 'fore bedtime. *Ibid.* (Chestnut Branch NC) They was a kind of weed that they call gurglymock seed. . . . Some of it grows here. **1951** McAtee *Names for Plants* 10 (DARE) *Chenopodium botrys . . .* Jewsly Mose, corruption of Jerusalem oak, Mitchell County, N.C. **1953** Davison *Word-List Appal* 12 *Jewsly moke.* **1968** *Remedies* 14 For worms . . . Mix Jerusalem Oak seeds with any kind of syrup to make a candy. Feed this to the afflicted person. **1968** Wilson *Local Plants* 323 = Artemisia santonica. A candy made from the roots and sorghum molasses was good for worms. **1982** Powers and Hannah *Cataloochee* 256 = worm medicine: Get seeds off Jerusaly-moke (Jerusalem oak) plant . . . put handful of seeds in pint of molasses on stove and bring to boil, when cool let child eat several spoonfull [sic] once or twice and the worms will be gotten rid of. **1991** Haynes *Haywood Home* 66 Jerussely-moke seed cooked in molassey candy would cure a child with worms. **1997** Nelson *Country Folklore* 40 Make a candy from Jerusalem Oak to get rid of worms.

Jerusaly moke, Jerussely-moke See **Jerusalem oak.**

jes See **just.**

jessie (also *jessy*) *noun* A hostile or painful time; hell.

1861 *Dalton CW Letters* (Feb 21) wee wod A giv them purfect jessy if tha[y] wod a come. **1944** Wentworth *ADD* (cwWV, as of 1890) "My arm is just givin' me Jessie" = paining greatly.

jest See **just.**

Jesus bug *noun* A water strider (family *Gerridae*).

1970 *DARE Survey* (Maryville TN). **1988** Kingsolver *Bean Trees* 2 (DARE) You could . . . watch the Jesus bugs walk on the water, their four [sic] little feet making dents in the surface but never falling through. **2004** House *Coal Tattoo* 92 His fingers danced across the strings as if barely touching them, like a Jesus bug walking across the river.

jewel-box *noun* A burning bush (*Euonymus americanus*). Same as **hearts bustin'.**

1937 Thornburgh *Great Smoky Mts* 25 The seeds of some shrubs are more spectacular than their flowers. This is true of one of the showiest shrubs in the Great Smokies, the euonymous, wahoo or spindlebush. It is especially lovely in October when its seed-pod bursts open, displaying orange-colored seeds in its glowing red heart. It has many descriptive local names—swamp willow, strawberry bush, catspaw, jewel-box, but most descriptive of all is the name given by a mountain man of, "Heart's-bustin'-with-love."

jewel flower (also *jewelweed*) *noun* A wildflower (*Impatiens* spp) that has medicinal uses, especially to treat the poison of snakebites. See also **snapweed, touch-me-not, water weed.**

1952 Beck *Herpetol Lore* 148 The first cure cited was snake weed, commonly known as jewel weed, which has a leaf shaped like a snake's head, grows to a height of about three feet and bears a yellow flower. Most efficacious in the cure of rattlesnake bite, the leaf is applied to the wound or taken internally, or both. **1975** Brewer *Valley So Wild* 336 Jewel weed stops poison ivy itching, says Leonard, a statement with which many agree. **1981** Whitener *Folk-Ways* 55 Thus if I felt I had been exposed to either ivy or oak, I simply broke some jewelweed stems and rubbed the juice over any exposed flesh. Perhaps water would have served the same purpose so soon after contact. But regardless of that possibility, I became a firm believer in jewelweed, or snapweed, as I occasionally hear it called in the Appalachians. **1991** Haynes *Haywood Home* 66 Jewel weed beaten to a pulp and applied as a poultice was good for stings and snake bites. **2006** Howell *Medicinal Plants* 99 The Cherokee used jewelweed juice to soothe poison ivy rash. The crushed leaves were rubbed on children's bellies to relieve a sour stomach. An infusion was used in a bath for women in the final stages of pregnancy. The plant was also used ceremonially.

jewelweed See **jewel flower.**

jewlark (also *jewlarker, jewlarkey, jewlarky, jularker*)

A *noun* See citations. See also **jusem-sweet.**

1892 *Fruit KY Words* 230 *jewlarky* = sweetheart: "I'm going to see my jewlarky." **1939** Farr *TN Mt Regions* 91 *jewlarker* = beau. "Susie's jewlarker bussed her." **1952** Wilson *Folk Speech NC* 555 *jularker* = a beau. (Avery Co. NC). **1968** Wilson *Folklore Mammoth Cave* 43 (*jewlark* or *jewlarky*) = one's sweetheart. **1972** Cooper *NC Mt Folklore* 25 In the long ago, a male sweetheart was a jularker and his sweetheart was a sweetie, darlin' or jusem sweet. **1997** Montgomery *Coll*: *jularker* (known to Brown).

[DARE *jewlarker* n cf *gill, jill* "a girl, sweetheart" + EDD *lark* v "to flirt," South, South Midland]

B *verb* See citation.

c1960 Wilson *Coll*: *jewlarking* = to go courtng.

Jew's harp (also *juice harp*) *noun* A small, sometimes homemade, lyre-shaped musical instrument held between the teeth and plucked by a metal tongue on its frame, using the jaws and the mouth as a resonance chamber. Also called **bow, jaw harp, mouth bow, song bow, tune bow.**

1919 Combs *Word-List South* 34 *juice harp*. **1927** Montague *Hog's Eye* 200 Tony fotched out his Jew's harp, and commenced picking out a mighty lively little tune, Plinketty-plink! Plunk! Plink! Plinketty-plunk! **1966–67** *DARE Survey* (Burnsville NC, Cherokee NC, Spruce Pine NC, Gatlinburg TN, Maryville TN) *Jew's harp* = small musical instrument that you hold between the teeth and pluck; (Brasstown NC) *juice harp* = plucked and held by the teeth. **1978** *Smoky Vistas* (July–Sept) 7 Harmonicas, often called French harp, and the Jew's harp, or "jaw harp," were available from the general stores. **1979** Irwin *Musical Instruments* 89 The Jews harp, probably correctly the jaw harp, has been played in Europe for hundreds of years, and in Appalachia since the first Whites entered the region. **1982** Powers and Hannah *Cataloochee* 369–70 Since he could play auto-harp, banjo, guitar, fiddle, harmonica and Jew's harp, we nearly always had one of each available to learn on. **1986** Pederson et al. *LAGS* = attested by 38/60 interviewees (63.3%) from E TN and 20/35 (57.1%) from N GA; 58/419 of all LAGS interviewees (13.8%) attesting term were from Appalachia. **1988** Stipe *Smokies Man* 17 There were seven musical instruments in the household, "if you count the jew's harp," he says, and it was just natural for people to "drop in for an evening of pickin' and singin'." **1997** Montgomery *Coll*: *Jew's harp* (known to eight consultants from the Smoky Mountains); *juice harp* (known to eight consultants from the Smoky Mountains). **2000** Miller *Looneyville* 52 *juice harp* = a musical instrument, held between one's teeth and played by striking the protruding free end of a piece of metal with a finger: "He can make 'Turkey in the Straw' sound beautiful with that juice harp." It is doubtful that any of the folks in Looneyville had any idea that the real name of the instrument was Jews harp.

[Web3 *jews harp* n perhaps from being purveyed by Jewish peddlers; DARE *Jew's harp* n, *juice harp* especially South, South Midland]

Jewsly moke, Jewsly mose See **Jerusalem oak.**

J-grab See **jay grab.**

J-hole See **jay hole.**

J-hook See **jay grab.**

jibbers *noun* See citations.

1963 Watkins and Watkins *Yesterday* 156 St. Vitus's dance, "the jibbers," was caused, the people believed, when a child was conceived while his father was drunk.

jibble *verb* See citation.

1957 Broaddus *Vocab Estill Co KY* 44 = to cut cloth, food, etc. into small pieces.

[cf EDD *gibbles* sb "odds and ends" Scotland]

jice See **joist.**

jiffling rod *noun* See citation.

2005 Williams *Gratitude* 503 = a pole or rod used for leverage.

jill all the ground *noun* A creeping perennial vine (*Glechoma hederacea*). Same as **ground ivy.**

1994 Montgomery *Coll* = ground ivy (known to Cardwell).

jill poke *noun* In logging, a steel beam tied to the bottom of a wagon and functioning as a brake if a load of logs being hauled gets out of control.

1974–75 McCracken *Logging* 6:108 In logging, [a jill poke] was a piece of railroad steel about eight or ten feet long cut off and tied right to the underside of the frame of whatever you were pulling. In case something broke, you had a scotch. It'd just run in the ground and hold it. . . . When you were hauling lumber and you were having to pull like across a mountain, you had a jill poke tied to the back axle of your wagon and just let it drag along on the ground. Well when you went to stop, your team rested. Then when they got ready to start, they just took off and this pole just drug along on the ground. Course when they got to the top, why they'd turn it around, slide it up into the wagon, tie it up. It's a safety catch is what it is, just something in case something goes wrong. It's just something to stop you right where you're at. . . . In case something broke . . . say this is your vehicle here, and on the back end here, right up against the trucks you took a piece of cable, run through the eye of this piece of steel and round something solid till it couldn't get loose, and when you was coming downhill, you had to take and tie the end of this jill poke up to keep it from hittin' the ground, but when you was goin' up, you untied these jill pokes and just let them drag along. *Ibid.* 16:3 They'd take a steel rail. They take a strand out of one of these big cables, just one strand, they'd roll it back in itself and they call it a Molly Hogan. This single strand would make a rope, as big as the original cable was. Then they'd take a steel rail, and lay it on the ground back here on this end. Then they'd pull this end up to the bottom of the Sarah Parker. Take one of them Molly Hogans and roll them in the eye in the hole in the rail, and then on the frame of the machine somewhere against the beams. And that was a safety in case a cable broke why this end going down, the jill poke would foul it, stop it.

jim (also *jin*) *verb* To do small chores, engage in part-time work or odd jobs. See also **gin**[4], **jimhand, jinwhacker.**

1927 Woofter *Dialect from WV* 358 *jim* = to work at odd jobs. "I jimmed after the ox team last week." **1939** Krumpelmann *WV Peculiarities* 156 One member of the faculty who was born and bred in this region tells me there is a verbal colloquialism "to gin (or jim) around" which means "just to dabble around, to fool around, to fiddle around." "Well, what have you been doing during the holidays?" Answer: "Oh, just ginning (or jimming) around." **1976** Garber *Mountain-ese* 48 We hired him as a part-time hand just to jin about the farm. **1997** Montgomery *Coll*: jin (known to Brown, Bush).

jimber-jawed (also *jimmer-jawed, jimmy-jawed, jip-jawed*) *adjective* Having a lower jaw that juts out or is crooked; nimble-jawed, being a good talker. See also **lantern-jawed, whopper-jawed**.

1885 Murfree *Prophet* 74 The youngest of the brothers, Solomon, was like him, except that his long chin, of the style familiarly denominated jimber-jawed, was still smooth and boyish. **c1960** Wilson *Coll*: *jimber-jawed, jimmer-jawed* = prognathous, lantern-jawed. **1971** Dwyer *Dict for Yankees* 28 *jimmy-jawed* = to have a projecting lower jaw. "She'd be real purty if she wern't jimmy-jawed." **c1975** Lunsford *It Used to Be* 166 "Jipjawed" is a term that has reference to an animal or mule whose upper jaw and lower jaw do not meet. **1996–97** Montgomery *Coll*: *jimber-jawed* (known to Jones, Ledford), = nimble-jawed, a good talker (Cardwell); *jimmy-jawed* (known to Ledford). **2007** McMillon *Notes* = having a projected lower jaw; also, a good talker.

[DARE *jimber-jawed* adj 1 *jimber-jawed* probably variant of *gimbal-jawed*, chiefly South, South Midland]

Jim Binder *noun* See citation.

1967 Parris *Mt Bred* 133 A Jim Binder is a springy pole used to tighten a binding chain on a load of logs.

jim-bob *adjective* Used as a mild oath.

1996 Huheey *Variant Names* 4 They was a jim-bob squirrel in that rattler.

jim dancer (also *jimmy dancer*) *noun* A homemade top fashioned from a spool.

1979 *DARE File* (eKY) The jimmy-dancer [is] a simple top made by whittling in two a wooden spool for sewing thread, driving a stick through the spool and whittling it to a point, leaving enough stem to flip the toy with the thumb and middle finger. **1990** Wigginton *Foxfire Christmas* 54 To make a top, or jim dancer as we called it, you start off by finding the center of your spool, and you score a ring around it. Then you taper the spool on each side of the ring until you get to the center. Then you break it in half, and you run a stick through each hole until it's good and tight. You can tell when you're getting to the center when both halves feel as though they are going to break apart. The last thing you have to do is trim the spool and stem together to a tapered point and cut your stem until it is how you like it. **2007** McMillon *Notes*: *jimmy dancer*.

jimhand *noun* One who performs odd jobs. See also **jim**.

1881 Atkinson *After Moonshiners* 154 When I'm at home I'm a kind of a jim-hand, and I tell you, judge, I've done nothen wrong. **1927** Woofter *Dialect from WV* 358 = one who works at all the odd jobs. "The jim-hand has to keep the camp clean."

jim jams *noun* Anxiety, restlessness.

1885 Murfree *Prophet* 153 Mirandy Jane hev fairly got the jim-jams. **1996–97** Montgomery *Coll* (Bush, Ellis, Oliver).

jimmer-jawed See **jimber-jawed**.

jimmie john See **demijohn**.

jimmies, have the *verb phrase* To be shaky or restless from fear or anxiety, sometimes due to the consumption of alcohol.

1997 Montgomery *Coll* (known to Adams, Brown, Bush, Cardwell, Oliver, Weaver). **2016** *Blind Pig* (Aug 5) I get the jimmies sometimes. It's like a restlessness that comes out of nowhere. Cleaning, whether it's the refrigerator or the house, makes very good use of the jimmies.

[DARE *jimmies* n pl[1] 1 especially South, South Midland, West]

jimmy *verb* To fit loosely, move from one position to another.

1940 Stuart *Trees of Heaven* 249–50 The pipestem jimmeys in Fronnie's mouth because several of her front teeth are out.

jimmy barn See **jenny barn**.

jimmy car (also *jimmy car house*) *noun* In logging, a small, portable dwelling that can be placed on a railroad car (or jimmy) and moved to a new site when a camp relocates. See also **rail house**.

1973 Foster *Walker Valley* 9:31 They were houses up through there, but that was just one portable built house all there was, the rest was jimmy car, I call 'em jimmy cars. **1974–75** McCracken *Logging* 11:48 Right back in that little hole right there [is] where his house set, one of those little old jimmy car houses. **2009** Lloyd *Tremont* 32 Unlike the car shacks at Tremont, his "jimmy cars" were constructed on site out of hemlock, or what lumbermen at the time called "spruce pine."

jimmy dancer See **jim dancer**.

jimmy jawed See **jimber-jawed**.

jimmy-john See **demijohn**.

jimmy up *verb phrase* To prop up, repair (something broken) in a makeshift fashion.

1998 Montgomery *Coll* (known to Cardwell); He just jimmied up the front steps rather than repair them (Norris).

jim-swing coat (also *jim swinger*) *noun* A long-tailed coat.

1972 Cooper *NC Mt Folklore* 93 *jimswinger* = a frock or long-tailed coat. **1984** Burns *Cold Sassy* 82 Hot as he was from running, he kept on the long black jim-swing coat till he saw me shivering, and then he put it around me. **1996–97** Montgomery *Coll*: *jim-swinger* (known to Brown, Bush).

[DARE *jimswinger* n 1 perhaps Jim given name common among Black men + *swinger* in ref[erence] to the motion of the coattails]

jimswinger See **jim-swing coat.**

jim-whack See **jinhack.**

jine See **join.**

jingle *noun* See citation. Same as **scrip.**

1973 Preston *Bituminous Term* 50–51 (TN) = tokens, bills, or other markers given to workers in place of money payment, which were good for full value at a company store but were discontinued [sic] as much as ten percent in other places.

jinhack (also *gin-whack, jim-whack*) *verb* To perform small or odd jobs, run errands. See also **gin**[1], **jim, jinwhacker.**

1936 Stuart *Head of Hollow* 121 I can make it all right with what little gin-whackin I do about the place here. **1957** Combs *Lg Sthn High: Word List* 44 *jinhack* = to run errands; to "piddle" about, working at odd jobs. Cf. The familiar *gin around.* **1975** Woolley *We Be Here* 47 You jim-whack around doing some other kind of work—setting timber, mucking track or other work—until he [= a mine inspector] gets gone. **1997** Montgomery *Coll: jinhack* (known to Brown).

jint See **joint.**

jinwhacker *noun* A handyman. See also **gin hand, jinhack.**

1976 Garber *Mountain-ese* 48 Mose ain't worth much money; he's just sort of a jinwhacker. **1997** Montgomery *Coll* (known to Brown, Bush).

jipjawed See **jimber-jawed.**

jis See **just.**

jise See **joist.**

jist See **just.**

job *verb* To strike, thrust, stab, pierce, or poke.

1884 Smith *Arp Scrap Book* 57 Is every man what can write a paragraph to consider us bears in a cage, and be always a-jobbin at us to hear us growl? **1904–20** Kephart *Notebooks* 2:429 Job that wood into the stove so it won't fall out on the floor. **1939** Hall *Coll* (Nine Mile TN) He run in there and jobbed his knife in him, and the old bear jumped. *Ibid.* (Deep Creek NC) I got up on the drift, got me a pole, and got up on the drift and laid down my gun and commenced jobbing down through the drift. **1942** Hall *Phonetics Smoky Mts* 26. **1960** McCaulley *Cades Cove* His daddy just grabbed him by the knuckles and there to the seat of the britches and just jobbed him up agin the ceiling four or five times and jumped out from under him and let him hit the floor. **1974** Fink *Bits Mt Speech* 13 He was *jobbed* with a knife. **1978** Slone *Common Folks* 211 [The gander] did not give up that easy, but kept running up and down, jobbing his head between the fine cracks [in the fence], squawking insults at me. **1984** GSMNP-153:29 [The stack pole] would job down in the hay, and that helt the hay, kept the wind from [blowing it away]. **1990** Cavender *Folk Medical Lex* 26 = used to refer to a sharp, stabbing pain. "The pain in my neck jobbed me all day." **2017** *Blind Pig* (April 28) He would tell us not to run with sticks because we might fall and job a hole in us or job an eye out.

[OED3 *job* v[1] 2a c1537→; DARE *job* v[2] 1 chiefly South, South Midland]

jobber (also *job-planter*) *noun* A small implement with which to plant (especially tobacco or corn) by poking a hole in the ground and releasing seeds or grains.

1947 Steed *KY Tobacco Patch* 88 (DARE) [In] the mountain country . . . most corn planting is done with a jobber. **1983** Montell *Don't Go Up* 47 The job-planters preceded by many years the mechanized one-row planters such as those made by Oliver and John Deere. Operated by hand, the job-planter was jabbed into the soil and then triggered so that one or two grains were released. This new device was not much faster than dropping seed by hand, but it was a back-saver and therefore highly prized. It was later used during replanting sessions, following the introduction of one-row planters. **1997** Montgomery *Coll: jobber* = a spade for digging holes for the seeds of corn and other crops (Adams, Brown, Bush, Cardwell, Ledford, Weaver). **2007** McMillon *Notes: jobber* = a pointy stick.

[cf EDD *job* v[2] 2; DARE *jobber* n chiefly South Midland]

Job('s) tears *noun* An Asiatic grass (*Coix lacryma-jobi*) whose hard seeds are fashioned into beads for homemade necklaces and other decorative objects. Also called **corn beads, Indian bead.**

1972 Miller *Pigeon's Roost* (May 11) Amanda Arrowood of Tipton Hill section planted her crop of Job tears or corn beads last week. Several folks in lower Mitchell County area grow Job tears to make homemade beads out of them. Some of the folks who grow Job tears sell them. *Ibid.* (Oct 25) Mrs. Edith Miller growed a crop this year of Indian beads or some calls them Job's tears. She is being made busy these days stringing them into long strings. **1979** Slone *My Heart* 51 Mountain people grew "corn beads" or "Job's tears." The seeds are very pretty, with a hole through the center, and can be strung like beads. They decorated beautiful "comb cases" and picture frames for the walls of their homes with these beads.

Job's turkey See **(as) poor as Job's turkey.**

jo cake *noun* See 1956 citation. See also **ashcake, hoecake.**

1956 Hall *Coll* (Sand Hill TN) Ma called it a jo cake. She took some lard and put it in the middle of some dough, then put the dough in the ashes, and laid the fire over it. **1997** Montgomery *Coll* (known to Bush, Cardwell).

jock *noun* Used as a euphemism for bull. See also **bull A1.**

1949 Kurath *Word Geog East US* 62 [Expressions for bull:] West Virginia . . . contributes *Durham, jock,* and *major.* **1984** Woods *WV*

Was Good 221 = polite word for bull. **2000** Miller *Looneyville* 52 = a polite word you used for bull when the females were present: "The jock is over in that field if you wish to turn your cow in with him."

[EDD *jock* sb[1] 4]

jockey *noun* See citations.

1939 Farr *TN Mt Regions* 91 = a horse or mule trader. **c1960** Wilson *Coll* = horse trader, usually a word that is hardly complimentary.

jodarter See **joe darter**.

joe boat (also *john boat, johnny boat*) *noun* A small rowboat, usually with squared ends.

1874 Collins *Hist Sketches KY* 1.238 (DARE) 5 persons, while crossing the Big Sandy river in Floyd co, in a joe boat, caught in the ice and drowned. **1938** Stuart *Dark Hills* 93 His big hands hit the water like john-boat oars. **c1960** Wilson *Coll: joe boat, john boat, johnny boat* = a small rowboat or fishing boat. **1966** Dakin *Vocab Ohio River Valley* 185 Several speakers along the Kentucky River also say *John boat*. *Joe boat* is the Kentucky name east of the Green River and this name also appears several times along the Ohio side of the river. **1993** Montell *Cumberland Country* 50 With their father, Hack and John made skiffs, johnboats, and other craft for their neighbors and the various crosstie companies that operated along the [Cumberland] river.

[DARE *joeboat* n chiefly Ohio Valley, especially KY, *johnboat* n Mississippi-Ohio Valleys]

joe darter *noun* Someone or something that is unsurpassed.

1859 Taliaferro *Fisher's River* 106 Sam J— was a little too hard for Dick in discussion, and Dick turned upon him with a "jo-darter," and smote him thus "Sam, you's chock full of your granddaddy's blood!" **c1960** Wilson *Coll* = an excellent thing of its kind, humdinger. **1976** Dwyer *Southern Sayin's* 30 = an unsurpassed person or thing. **1998** Montgomery *Coll* (known to Cardwell, but not to other consultants from the Smoky Mountains).

Joe-Pye weed *noun* A **boneset**.

1971 Hutchins *Hidden Valley* 187 There must have been great need for tonics, since a wide variety of plant teas were used, including those made from maidenhair fern root, fairy wand, spotted wintergreen, Joe-Pye weed, white ash bark, hydrangea, senica-snakeroot [sic], Solomon's-seal, willow bark, foamflower, prickly ash bark, and black cohosh. **1980** *Smokies Heritage* 295 Blooming with pink or purple flowers from July through late September, queen of the meadow is today known (less romantically, of course) as Joe Pye Weed. It is a flower of moist soils and mountain fields, occurring up to 3000 feet elevation and towering over the rest of the wildflowers—its height may reach from 12–15 feet. **1982** Stupka *Wildflowers* 118 Joe Pye is said to have been an herb doctor who lived in New England in colonial times, when the colonists made a tonic of these roots to treat diarrhea. The plant named for him is hardly a "weed" in the ordinary sense as it is one of our most stately and handsome herbs. **1999** McNeil *Purchase Knob* 69 Named for Joe Pye, an Indian witch doctor who practiced his trade in the time of the Pilgrims, old Joe cured people of typhoid fever by making concoctions from Joe-Pye-Weed's roots and florets. The herb was used for other ailments too. Joe-Pye's efficacy covered everything from improving the complexion to kidney disorders. A tonic made from the leaves could soothe nerves. [**2006** Howell *Medicinal Plants* 103 There are several legends about the origin of the common name. One asserts that Joe Pye was a so-called "Indian theme promoter," who marketed an extract of the plant as a cure for typhoid fever. Another source claims that the name derives from "jopi," the word for typhoid fever in an American Indian language. The Cherokee used the hollow tubes of the plant's stem through which to "bubble" or blow air into herbal medicines to activate them and increase their potency. The stems were also used to blow herbal remedies on and around the person to be healed.]

joggle *verb*

1 See citation.

1944 Combs *Word-List Sthn High* 19 = to walk along slowly and aimlessly. Variant of *jog*.

2 To bounce up and down on a makeshift seesaw.

2007 Rose *Games Mt Children* 15 Another activity we did was based on the same principle as the "see-saw," except the board was placed across a lower object. Once again one had to determine the balance of the weight. Each person would jump into the air, landing in place to send the person on the other end flying into the air. We called this "to joggle." Of course mama said we were going to kill each other if we didn't stop jumping so high.

john boat See **joe boat**.

John Constant *noun* Corn bread.

1968 Wilson *Folklore Mammoth Cave* 18 One very old man said that, in his youth, cornbread was called John Constant; biscuits were called Bill Seldom.

John corn *noun* Whiskey.

1941 Still *Stir-Off* 5 Air you been dranking john corn?

johnny (also *johnny house*) *noun* An outhouse, a small shed housing a toilet at a distance from the dwelling house. See also **back house**, **garden house**, **jack house**, **one holer**, **out building**, **shit house**, **two holer**.

1946 Woodard *Word-List VA/NC* 18 *johnny house* = a privy. **1952** Wilson *Folk Speech NC* 555 *johnny house* = a privy. **1961** Murry *Salt* 21 O' course the singletrees caught on them two johnnies, an' they was drug to the edge o' them big woods, where them horses was obliged to stop. **1986** Pederson et al. *LAGS: johnny* = attested by 2/60 interviewees (3.3%) from E TN and 4/35 (11.4%) from N GA; 6/51 of all LAGS interviewees (11.7%) attesting term were from Appalachia; *johnny house* = attested by 6/60 interviewees

(10%) from E TN and 2/35 (5.7%) from N GA; 8/22 of all LAGS interviewees (36.4%) attesting term were from Appalachia. **1994** Montgomery Coll: *johnny house* (known to Shields).

[DARE *johnny house* n chiefly South, South Midland, especially Middle and South Atlantic]

johnny board *noun* A board on which to prepare **johnny bread**.

1926 Thomas *Hills and Mts of KY* 154 The dough was prepared by sufficient kneading, working in plenty of grease, salt, soda, etc., after which it was placed on the johnny-board sufficiently close to the fire to admit slow baking; when one side was sufficiently done it was reversed and the other side prepared in the same way, after which the johnny-cake was ready to eat.

johnny boat See **joe boat**.

johnny bread (also *johnny cake*) *noun* A flat cake of corn bread baked on a board before the fire, in a **Dutch oven** set in the coals, or otherwise. Also called **journey bread**. See also **ashcake**, **corn cake**, **corn pone**, **johnny board**.

1799 (in **2008** Ellison *High Vistas* 37) Drank a cup of coffee, eat some broiled bacon and Johnny cake, then set out on the line with the prospect of a fine day. **1824** (in **1912** Doddridge *Notes on Settlement* 82) What a jubilee when we were permitted to pull the young corn for roasting ears. Still more so when it had acquired sufficient hardness to be made into johnny cakes by the aid of a tin grater. *Ibid.* 88 Johnny cake and pone were at the outset of the settlements of the country the only forms of bread in use for breakfast and dinner. **1847** (in **1870** Drake *Pioneer Life KY* 13) Father purchased a piece of "johnny-cake," as large as his two hands, for which he paid one and sixpence, or twenty-five cents. **1859** Taliaferro *Fisher's River* 141 He and I used to bake "johnny-cakes" to keep from starving while it was grinding my "grice." **1879** Jones *Backwoods Carolina* 749 She made a johnny-cake of Indian meal and baked it on a board in front of the fire, and boiled coffee in a coffee-pot set on the coals. **1926** Thomas *Hills and Mts of KY* 154 Another way of baking was the famous johnny-cake, which was as follows: A board was dressed very smoothly, and soaked thoroughly with lard or grease. The dough [sic] was prepared by sufficient kneading, working in plenty of grease, salt, soda, etc., after which it was placed on the johnnyboard sufficiently close to the fire to admit slow baking; when one side was sufficiently done then it was reversed and the other side prepared in the same way, after which the johnny-cake was ready to serve. **1939** Hall Coll (Tuckaleechee Cove TN) Your johnny cake's bakin' too brown (Jack Johnson in the song "When you go a-courtin'"). **1955** Parris *Roaming Mts* 171 I didn't realize there would be no more cider or johnny-cakes cooked on the hearth. **1958** Wood *Words from TN* 12 Johnny cake is corn pone baked on a plank before an open fire. Johnny cake . . . is the same as Southern hoe cake. **1966** Dakin *Vocab Ohio River Valley* 315 *Johnny cake* = "corn griddle cake" is . . . rare outside of Kentucky [in the Ohio Valley]. **1982** *Smokies Heritage* 37 At sundown there would be a hot dinner just waiting for a hefty appetite, and maybe a johnny cake baked on a board before the fire. **1984** Wilder *You All Spoken* 88 *johnny cake* = journey cake: Cornmeal cake baked crusty and brown on an open fire; it is made by pouring a mixture of meal and water—no baking soda, salt, buttermilk, or shortening—over hot coals and covering with more coals. Indians in southern regions baked such cakes to sustain them on long journeys. **2002** Morgan *Mt Born* 20 Sometimes [my mother] would make us "Johnny cakes." Scooping a large dollop of the cornbread mix from her mixing bowl, she would spread it out on the hot surface of the cook stove. When it had baked (blackened!) on the bottom, she would flip it over and bake it on the other side. It was fun watching it cook, and it would tide us over until dinner or supper was ready.

[perhaps alteration of *journey cake*; cf note in DA]

johnny house See **johnny**.

johnny humpback *noun* An earthworm.

1940 Still *River of Earth* 59 "Looks like a johnny-humpback," he said. It did look like a worm. *Ibid.* 172 There was no getting away from Fletch. We fished dirt holes for johnny-humpbacks. If I caught one first, he spat down the hole for spite.

johnny trots *noun* See citation.

1990 Cavender *Folk Medical Lex* 26 = diarrhea.

johnny walkers *noun* Makeshift stilts fashioned by children from branches, small trees, or poles. Same as **tom walkers**.

1948 Still *Nest* 54 Long wooden poles (often fashioned from small trees or branches) with a footpiece that children walk around on to make them tall; stilts. "She retraced her steps, walking stiffly as upon johnny-walkers, holding her hands before her." **1968–69** *DARE Survey* (Hardshell KY, Brasstown NC) = long wooden poles with a footpiece that children walk around on to make them tall. **1997** Montgomery Coll (known to Adams, Bush, Cardwell, Jones, Norris, Oliver).

[DARE *johnny walkers* n pl South Midland, especially TN]

join *verb*

A Variant form *jine*.

1852 (in **1956** Eliason *Tarheel Talk* 303) (Caldwell Co NC) *jine*. **1861** (in **1992** Heller and Heller *Confederacy* 39) he is well an lucks well. he sese that when his time is out that he will Jine Captain Baugs comane. **1883** Zeigler and Grosscup *Heart of Alleghanies* 362 I listened and "j'ined" in at intervals, and this I learned. **1913** Kephart *Our Sthn High* 106 He grabbed a laurel to swing hisself down by, but the stem bruk, and down he come suddent, to jine the music. **1939** Hall *Recording Speech* 6 One elderly woman of the Oconaluftee area declined the microphone, however, and informed the investigators: "I don't fancy no sich as that and I won't jine up with ye!" **1939** Walker *Mtneer Looks* 6 The other vowel sound we can be reasonably sure of, the diphthong oi, is generally pronounced as in *p'inted, h'isted, j'ined* for *pointed, hoisted, joined*. **1942** Hall *Phonetics Smoky Mts* 46. **c1945** Haun *Hawk's Done* 241 Eli told Cora to jine. **1961** *Coe Ridge OHP-342B* It's enough for a car to go around there . . . just enough to get around there and then into the next little section down in there. That's jining Coe Ridge. **1963** Hooper *Unwanted Boy* 228 Sal "jined" the "Holy Rollers" Sunday. **1980** GSMNP-115:28 If you don't jine a church and be baptized this time, I'll not never get to see you baptized.

B Of property: to be contiguous with, adjoin.

c1796 *Jefferson Co Wills II* 234 It is my will that my sons James and Jesse Ballinger is to have the remainder of a hundred and fifty acre tract, and a fifty acre of Land that is Joined the said hundred and fifty acres. **1823** (in **2003** *TN Petitions II* 206) We pray you therefore in your wisdom to . . . and convey Specially to the trustees of the methodist meeting house pine chappel . . . Eight acres of land Joining S^{d} two acres lying and being in the county of Jefferson. **1855** *Mitchell Letter* I have a clame of another [acre] joining my place. **1867** Harris *Sut Lovingood* 160 I planted my ball ho'nets colonys onder the bainches amung the straw onder the big shed what jined the chu'ch. **1931** Burns *Coves Blount Co* 58 This tract is described as joining the lands of William Crowson and James Smith (a brother of John Smith). **1938** (in **2009** Powell *Shenandoah Letters* 147) I purchased land which joins the park land. **1955** Ritchie *Singing Family* 141 They must have broken through the fence rails somewhere. Finally, I found the break. It was a corner where Uncle Lee Brashear's pasture joined ours and the rails were down in such a way that the stock in both pastures could have got out through the same hole. **1969** GSMNP-25:1:5 Down the stream it joined the old man Floyd's place. **1997** Montgomery *Coll* (known to ten consultants from the Smoky Mountains).

[DARE *join* v B1 chiefly South, South Midland]

joint *noun* Variant form *jint* [rhymes with *pint*].

1867 Harris *Sut Lovingood* 227 I kin feel the knobs ove her jints a-rattlin a-pas' my ribs yet. **1913** Kephart *Our Sthn High* 94 John Cable's sulkin' around with his nose out o' jint. **1928** Thornburgh *Americans Forgot* 28 Pap . . . made all the furniture we had, made it out of cherry and walnut and maple and pine, and he made fifes out of cane jints. **1937** Haun *Cocke Co* 3 Turkle doves build their nestes between two jints of a limb. **1942** Hall *Phonetics Smoky Mts* 46 [dʒaɪnt].

[DARE *joint* n especially South, South Midland]

joint snake *noun* The glass lizard (*Ophisaurus attenuatus*).

1967 Huheey and Stupka *Amphibians and Reptiles* 53 Farmers living just outside the western limits of the Park are familiar with the "Joint Snake," which they occasionally turn up with their plows. **1968** Wilson *Folklore Mammoth Cave* 21 = actually a legless lizard, the glass snake (Ophisaurus ventralis), which, like other lizards, can lose part of its tail and survive. But the folk belief is that it comes to pieces when attacked and then reassembles its pieces when danger is over.

joist *noun* Variant forms *jaist, jeist, jice, jise*, all [®aws(t)]]; variant plural forms *jeist-es, joist-es*.

1867 Harris *Sut Lovingood* 118 When they got thar, Lum he hapen'd tu step jis' a littil too short, an' he lit ontu the doated ceilin insted ove the jise. **1915** Dingus *Word-List VA* 184 *jice*. **1969** GSMNP-25:1:3 You know what people done? They went in there, and that overhead was put in there on top of them joistes. **1973** McKamey *Park VIP* Wiley Oakley mentions "joistes"—another Elizabethan term for 2 × 4's laid to form floors—without nails. Wiley says, "You know, we didn't have nails in those days." **c1975** Lunsford *It Used to Be* 162 "Jaist" is the word "joist," as "I kicked him twice as high as the jaist."

[DARE *joist* n 1 especially South, South Midland]

joke *verb* To tease, poke fun at, play a joke on (someone).

1859 Taliaferro *Fisher's River* 111 Dick was a rough hand to joke people. **1941** Still *Troublesome Creek* 101 U Z joked us, "Dive in, boys, and you kin stand yore breeches in a corner tonight." **c1950** Adams *Grandpap* 106 I'm not a-jokin' you! **1978** Montgomery *White Pine Coll* III-2 I don't think she approved a bit of that, them a-joking her about, you know, about going barefooted in Tennessee. **1979** Melton *'Pon My Honor* 54 Grandpa was full of fun, and he'd joke the preacher just as soon as his next-door neighbor. **1982** Slone *How We Talked* 6 Our folks did not mind being joked about their looks. **1998** Montgomery *Coll* (known to Brown, Ellis, Jones, Ledford).

jokey *adjective* Of a person: inclined to humor, especially of a simple-minded kind.

1955 Ritchie *Singing Family* 155 He's allus a right jokey kind of feller. Going across the Duane Mountain he got to showing off what a good rider he was. **1969** Doran *Folklore White Co* 144 My grandad was the awfullest jokey feller ever was. **1986** Pederson et al. *LAGS* (Claiborne Co TN) a jokey old fellow. **1997** Montgomery *Coll* (known to Brown, Bush, Cardwell, Jones, Norris, Oliver, Weaver).

[DARE *jokey* adj especially South, South Midland]

jollification *noun* See citation.

c1982 Young *Colloquial Appal* 13 = social gathering.

jolt seat *noun* The front seat of a **jolt wagon**.

1941 Still *Troublesome Creek* 64 A spring wagon rattled the stony creek-bed, pulled by a nag so small I could hardly believe it, and a man and a woman rode the jolt seat.

jolt wagon *noun* A springless wagon used in farm work and hauling produce but uncomfortable for travel, affording its passengers a bumpy ride. See 1993 citation.

1925 Combs *Folk-Songs* 6 During the winter months [the roads] are almost impassable. Rough "jolt-wagons" carry merchandise, and often passengers, in this "far country." **1931** Hannum *Thursday April* 79 The wheels of Joe's jolt wagon would not sink much over their hubs in mud. **1941** Stuart *Men of Mts* 230 We are getting our breaths like spans of mules pulling a jolt-wagon load of crossties out of W-Hollow. **c1950** Henderson *Ebenezer Mission* 2 These were the days of jolt wagons and horseback, when the mail carrier who served the Ebenezer Mission was compelled to ford the Big Creek forty times in his twenty-five mile round. **1950** Wood *Sure of Life* 38 A jolt-wagon is a contraption of the devil, devilishly attracted to every hole or boulder in the mountain roads. It's a wooden wagon with board seats on either side of the inner rim, pulled by a couple of horses. Hoops form an arch over the wagon and in rainy weather a canvas can be stretched over these hoops. **1963** Edwards *Gravel* 168 What some people refer to as the horse-and-buggy days but Speedwellians call the jolt-wagon days. **c1980** Campbell *Memories of Smoky* 3 The few roads were of such poor quality that they hardly deserved the name of roads. Most of those who went beyond Pigeon Forge or Townsend either went by horseback or rode jolt wagons. **1993** Ison and Ison *Whole Nother Lg* 35 = a four wheel wood and steel spoked wagon with a large box for carrying cargo, usually pulled by horses or mules. **1996** Spurlock *Glossary* 400 = the work wagon of a farm; a sturdily built mule- or horse-drawn wagon with a bed approximately 10½′ by 3½′, used to haul the harvest. The bed is mounted directly on the chassis and can support loads of up to three and one-half tons.

[DARE *jolt wagon* n South Midland, especially KY]

jolty *adjective* Of a wagon: causing a bumpy ride.

1962 Dykeman *Tall Woman* 21 Sarah Moore had held the clock, wrapped in blue and white catalpa-flower coverlet, in her lap while the family rode in the jolty wagon as far as they could. *Ibid.* 105 The trip down from the mountain was long, but they rode in the jolty farm wagon, pulled by Black Deuce.

[*jolt* n + *-y* adj forming suffix]

jonah

A Variant forms *joner* [see **1995–97** in **B1**], *jonie* [see **2007** in **B1**].

B *noun*

1 A troublemaker, one who brings bad luck (so called after the Old Testament character Jonah).

1895 Dromgoole *Fiddling to Fame* 57 The nex' day the papers named me fur a Jonah, an' said ez I wur showin' uv the East Tennessee streak ter my bacon. **1904–20** Kephart *Notebooks* 2:603. **1978** Ball *Speech Knox Co* 139 = a trouble causing object, synonymous with "lemon," "jinx": "That [television] set's been a Jonah to him." **1995–97** Montgomery *Coll* (known to Brown, Ledford, Oliver); You better watch him—he's a joner (Cardwell). **2007** McMillon *Notes*: *jonie* = a jinx.

2 An escape, evasion of responsibility.

1995 Montgomery *Coll* He pulled a joner [i.e. he ran away] (Cardwell).

C *verb* To bring misfortune (to).

1956 McAtee *Some Dial NC* 24 = to bring ill luck. **1995** Montgomery *Coll* He jonered me! (Ledford).

joner, jonie See **jonah**.

jook (also *djuke*) *verb* To duck, dodge, swerve, turn (the body) quickly.

1944 Williams *Word-List Mts* 29 *djuke* = to incline or duck: "He djuked his head and looked right at the ground." **1989** Landry *Smoky Mt Interviews* 181 [The panther] just jooked down like a cat about to leap on something.

[OED3 *jouk/jook* v² 1 of uncertain origin, Scot and north; EDD *jouk* sb 1 Scot, Irel, nEngl; SND *jouk* v I.1(1); HT "dodge, duck"]

joree (**bird**) (also *joreeper, jorigger*) *noun* The towhee (*Pipilo erythrophthalmus*).

1913 Kephart *Our Sthn High* 90 I could hear the *t-wee, t-wee* of "joree birds" (towhees) which winter in the valleys. **1919** Pearson et al. *Birds NC* 251 The towhee . . . most commonly known in this state as "Joree," "Joreeper," or "Jorigger," is found throughout the mountain region. **1927** Mason *Lure of Smokies* 23 Perhaps on a hazy summer afternoon the sojourner may hear in the far distance the clear cry of a towhee—"joree" the mountaineer terms the bird. **1944** Combs *Word-List Sthn High* 19 *joree* = the chewink, of the towhee or sparrow family. **1997** Montgomery *Coll*: *joree* (known to Cardwell). **1998** Hyde *My Home* 87 We hadn't quite reached the curve and had slowed down when I heard a Jo Ree start his chirping in the laurels across the meadow, "Jo Ree! Jo Ree! Jo Ree!" **2014** *Blind Pig* (Jan 10) I call the Towhee a joree. My Dad and family called it a joree-bird, a little orange-breasted bird, black tail feathers, is a joeree, not a towhee.

[echoic; DARE *joree* n 1 chiefly South, South Midland]

B *verb* See citations.

1984 Wilder *You All Spoken* 78 *Jawin' an' joreein'* = exchanging harsh words such as "You make my ass want to chew tobacco." **1992** Brooks *Sthn Stuff* 80 = jest with or at. "They're always joreeing him about his girl."

josey See **josie**.

josh *verb* To bump.

1984 Burns *Cold Sassy* 88 Smiley kind of joshed my shoulder as they moved toward the dining room.

[cf EDD *joss* v 4 "to bump, jolt, shake"]

josie (also *josey, josy*) *noun* Any of several women's garments, usually a shirt.

1859 Taliaferro *Fisher's River* 19 I visited them in 1857 and found "sacks" and "joseys" in full fashion. **1865** Hill *CW Letters* (Jan 19) you can ware that coat in the plase of a Josy if you want it and if you want to ware it you may keep it or do with it what you plese. **1997** Montgomery *Coll*: *josie* (known to Andrews).

[DARE *josie* n 1 chiefly South, South Midland]

josy See **josie**.

jounce *verb*

1 To whip, hit.

1931 Combs *Lg Sthn High* 1307 Cicero cut slip and jounced (whipped) Ike. **1941** Still *Troublesome Creek* 101 My pap could jounce him with one arm tied. **1952** Wilson *Folk Speech NC* 555 = to whip, beat. **1957** Combs *Lg Sthn High: Word List* 55 = to hit, or knock down (of persons).

[EDD *jounce* v 2 "to use some violent action by which the shape of a thing is altered"]

2 To bounce (along).

1895 Dromgoole *Logan's Courtship* 139 He'd come a-jouncin' back to poke another book at her. **1937** Thornburgh *Great Smoky Mts* 14 Discovering the animal [= a groundhog] under his bed, the guide jounced around on the springs and scared it off. **1976** Still *Pattern of Man* 69 "I've never yearned to travel," Trulla said, snatching up the baby and jouncing it nervously.

jour See **jower**.

journey bread (also *journey cake*) *noun* Same as **johnny bread**.

1853 Ramsey *Annals* 719 Mixed with cold water, [cornmeal] is, at once, ready for the cook . . . placed upon a piece of clapboard, and set near the coals, it forms the journey-cake. **1934–47** *LAMSAS Appal* (Swain Co NC) *journey cake*. **1941** Justus *Kettle Creek* 39 It's a good makeshift for journey bread. **1943** Justus *Bluebird* 164 If you'll look in my saddelbags, you'll find what's left of my journey cake that Granny Metcalf made me.

journey jaunt *noun* A venture, trip.

1952 Justus *Children* 11 Twins where they had gone for a journey-jaunt after huckleberries. *Ibid.* 13 If he could save enough money till he had the round-trip fare—a dollar and a half—he'd treat himself to a journey-jaunt with Uncle Bildad Cooley and see all there was to see in Far Beyant.

[redundant form]

journey-proud *adjective*

1 Excited or distracted at the prospect of taking a trip. See also **proud 1**.

1960 Westover *Highland Lg* 20 = worked up about a future trip. **1997** Montgomery *Coll* (known to Brown, Bush). **2002** Myers *Best Yet Stories* 130 Travel in early days was very rough and time-consuming, so that many people found it very difficult to sleep the night before a major trip. Being unable to sleep was described as being "Journey Proud!"

[EDD at *journey* 6; DARE *journey-proud* adj 1 chiefly South, South Midland]

2 Boastful from having taken a trip.

1939 *FWP Guide NC* 98 *Journey-proud* applies to one who won't stop telling you about a trip. **1965** *Dict Queen's English* 13 = enthusiasm resulting from a trip. "She was so *journey proud* when she returned from the city she couldn't stop talking about her trip." **1997** Montgomery *Coll* I reckon he's got the bighead. He's journey proud. He's been off to New York City (Andrews).

[DARE *journey-proud* adj 2 chiefly South, South Midland]

jow *verb* See 1952 citation. See also **jower A**.

1883 Murfree *Old Sledge* 549 Yer two might jow tergether some other day, it 'pears like to me. **c1945** Haun *Hawk's Done* 209 There wasn't any sense to gals jowing and carrying on with every stinking boy that come along. **1952** Wilson *Folk Speech NC* 555 = to talk loud and angrily.

[cf EDD *jow* v^3 "to talk loud"]

jower

A *verb* To quarrel, argue, wrangle (especially for a period of time). See also **jow**.

1883 Smith *Southernisms* 50 Jower or jour [is] quite common in the South in the sense of persistent quarreling or scolding. **1892** Fruit *KY Words* 230 = to quarrel: "They jowered ever so long." **1900** Harben *N GA Sketches* 297 He's been jowerin' at his paw ever sence supper fer treatin' you so bad. **1913** Kephart *Our Sthn High* 312 Boys, I did hone fer my dog Fiddler, an' the times we'd have a-huntin', and the trout-fishin', and the smell o' the woods, and nobody bossin' and jowerin' at all. **1952** Wilson *Folk Speech NC* 555 = to quarrel, talk incessantly. **1974** Fink *Bits Mt Speech* 13 They'd been *jowering* for a long time. **1983** Davis *Multi-lingual Mule* 89 Even Lizzie to jower and banter at him would have been a relief. **1994** Montgomery *File* He just bowed up and jowered at me (Vic Weals, reported from Pete Monroe, c1948).

[OED3 *jower* v dialect and local U.S.; Web3 *jower* v perhaps of imitative origin; DARE *jower* v chiefly South, South Midland]

B *noun* A quarrel, noisy argument.

1891 Brown *Dialect in TN* 175 *Jower* is a word in common use for a quarrel in which noise plays the principal part. **1913** Kephart *Our Sthn High* 294 If they quarrel, it is a ruction, a rippit, a jower, or an upscuddle—so be it there are no fatalities which would amount to a real fray. **1943** Justus *Bluebird* 50 We had a jower for certain about it—I say we did! **1952** Wilson *Folk Speech NC* 555 = quarreling, incessant talking.

[DARE *jower* n South, South Midland]

joyful *noun* Homemade whiskey. See also **O be joyful**.

1910 Essary *TN Mtneers* 12 Happy was a regular attender on all of the courts of his county town, although he never had any special business except to meet the boys and get a few drinks of the joyful, which the more fortunate always had on such occasions.

joy juice *noun* Homemade whiskey.

1994 Montgomery *File* (known to 82-year-old man, Gatlinburg TN). **2014** Cardwell *Yule Log* 3 When asked if any "joy juice" was part of this custom, Mr. Ownby said, "Why, yes, in some people's homes where moonshine was made, they offered you a nip if you so desired."

J-pit See **jay hole**.

juberous, jubers, jubus See **dubious**.

jucks See **ay**.

Judas tree *noun* The redbud tree (*Cercis canadensis*).

1901 Lounsberry *Sthn Wild Flowers* 359 About our American plants, we find very frequently that it has been through their similarity to European ones that early settlers to this country bestowed on them certain names. So this beautiful plant is called Judas tree as is the European species . . . although it could never have been the traditionary one from which the Apostle is said to have hung himself. **1961** Douglas *My Wilderness* 191 The redbud . . . is sometimes called the Judas tree, from the legend that it is the tree on which Judas Iscariot hanged himself. Its flowers, once said to be white, turned red with blood; and they grow right out of the branches. **1965** Shelton *Pioneer Comforts* 13 Judas Tree [was made into a tea for] chills and fever. **1970** Vincent *More of Best* 62 Along closer to the roadside here [he] saw pretty red blooms on some bushes. They are redbud bushes. They are sometimes called Judas Trees.

judge *noun, verb* Variant form *jedge*.

1867 Harris *Sut Lovingood* 255 Es he went, he flung that mortul buck's hine laig at the jedge's head. **1932** Strong *Great Smokies* 27 Ye ain't no hill-billy, I jedge? **1942** Hall *Phonetics Smoky Mts* 41. **1952** Wilson *Folk Speech NC* 554. **1974** Roberts *Sang Branch* 41 The jedge of the competition come around and put a dollar and fifteen cents in my hand.

[DARE *judge* n, v especially South, South Midland]

judge man *noun* A judge.

1940 Haun *Hawk's Done* 138 Pharis said the judge man didn't look at him e'er time while he was reading it.

judgmatically *adverb*

A Variant form *jedgmatically* [see **1974** in **B**].

B In one's estimation or considered opinion.

1913 Kephart *Our Sthn High* 117 Jedgmatically, I don't know. **1924** (in **1952** Mathes *Tall Tales* 30) "Air you a linkster?" the woman repeated. "We've jist come from Lawyer Taylor's office down yander in town, an' he 'lowed jedgmatically ye was." **1974** Fink *Bits Mt Speech* 13 *Jedgmatically*, he'll come tomorrow.

[DARE *judgmatically* adv southern Appalachians]

jug fishing *noun* See citation.

1990 Davis *Homeplace* 18 Traditionally, those who fished with trotlines baited them with small frogs and/or "spring lizards" (salamanders) and set them just before dark. People on some parts of the Tennessee and Mississippi River valleys still practice this method of fishing today, and variations of it ("jug" or "hang" fishing).

juggle *noun* A large chip hewn or scored from a log, especially in making railroad crossties.

c1960 Wilson *Coll* = large chips and slabs from making crossties. **1987** *Hewing Crossties* 210 He [= a hewer of crossties] works his way down the length of the log knocking off the sections between the notches. These sections are called juggles. He remembers when his parents would send the smaller kids to pick these up for firewood.

[DARE *juggle* n 2 South Midland]

jughead *noun* A mule or horse with a large head, especially a slow or stupid animal; figuratively, a person who is slow-witted (also a nickname).

c1960 Wilson *Coll* = contemptuous name for a colt, ox, mule, or horse; sometimes applied to a stupid-looking boy. **1997** Montgomery *Coll* (known to eight consultants from the Smoky Mountains).

[DARE *jughead* n 1 chiefly South Midland, West]

jug stack *noun* A type of haystack.

1966 Dakin *Vocab Ohio River Valley* 74 *Jug-stack* (Allen Cty., Ky.—built around a pole and "shaped like a jug"—thus *jug-stack*).

juice *verb* To milk a cow.

c1960 Wilson *Coll*: *juicing* = humorous term for milking. **1976** GSMNP-114:39 When I got to likin' juicin' myself, I had to juice. **1997** Montgomery *Coll* (known to Brewer, Bush, Cardwell, Ledford, Weaver).

[DARE *juice* v chiefly South, South Midland, West]

juice harp See **Jew's harp**.

jularker See **jewlark**.

jularkey *noun*

1 See **jewlark**.

2 See citation.

1969 Doran *Folklore White Co* 112 = nonsense.

julie *noun* A wheelbarrow.

1963 Edwards *Gravel* 165 One Monday morning he was given the job of pushing a Julie (wheelbarrow). **1998** Montgomery *Coll* (known to Brown).

July fly *noun* A cicada, whose nightly buzzing peaks in midsummer.

1939 *FWP Guide TN* 135 The old weather signs have vital meaning in the lives of rural people and farmers watch them closely. . . . Frost will come as sure as judgement just six weeks after you hear the first July fly. **1956** McAtee *Some Dial NC* 24 = Cicada of the genus Tibicen.

[DARE *July fly* n 1 chiefly Southeast]

July hound *noun* A type of hunting dog.

1949 Arnow *Hunter's Horn* 42 Newt Taylor, from the other side of Bear Creek, with his two fine spotted July hounds. *Ibid.* 216 Pinkney . . . talked of his own four hounds—not such great hunters—two Trigs and two Julys—but they had the prettiest tongues.

jump *verb*

1 To cause (a hunted animal) to flush from its cover; to startle, attack (game).

1878 Coale *Wilburn Waters* 84 [The dogs] "opened" in lively and eager chorus, soon jumped a large four-pronged buck, in full view from where I was standing, which, from the direction he took, I was satisfied would attempt to cross the river at the stand occupied. **1937** Hall *Coll* (Cades Cove TN) Them dogs was good ones to jump bear. **1939** Hall *Coll* (Proctor NC) The dogs, they just stove off the road into a little laurel patch, and there they jumped another big one. *Ibid.* (Cataloochee NC) They jumped the bear, and the bear come to the stands. I give him two good shots. **1966** DARE *Survey* (Cherokee NC) = when a hunter or a dog finds a game animal and makes it start running. **1967** Fetterman *Stinking Creek*

133 I allowed my dogs'd already jumped at least a rabbit by now. **1970** *Hunting* 70 A good beagle was often used in rabbit hunting. He could jump the animal for the hunter and give him a quick shot. **1972** Hall *Sayings* 92 A dog jumped a bear, and the bear went right over Uncle Proctor. Uncle Dan said, "Uncle Proctor would never be any whiter when he was laid out than he was then." **1984** Smith *Enduring Memories* 49 In the winter time the rabbits would sit in sage brush fields and briar thickets. We would line up in a field, about ten steps apart and walk slowly through the field trying to jump a rabbit.

2 To use a hammer and a nail to extract (a sore tooth). See also **tooth jumper.**

1975 Dwyer *Thangs* 3 Bring back them good ol' days! The wonderful days when the tooth dentist "jumped" teeth outen your mouth with a hammer an' chisel.

3 Of an animal: to copulate with (another animal).

1967 Fetterman *Stinking Creek* 64 I brought a sow over to Carmes' house, he jumped her once, and they said, "Get that sow out. One time's good as a dozen."

4 To fuel (a fire).

1967 *Grandmother Cherokee* 75 I kept th'fire jumped up fer'her. Same as **chunk B1.**

jumper jacket See **jump jacket.**

jumping board *noun* A board nailed to a stump or block for children to jump on.

1986 Pederson et al. *LAGS* (Hamilton Co TN, Stephens Co GA).

jumping coulter *noun* A type of plow. See also **bull tongue.**

1966 Guthrie *Corn* 87 For the initial plowing (turning) of a newground full of roots, the bull-tongue was limited in usefulness because the foot would catch on the roots and either stop the plow or break it as it was dragged along by oxen or mules. The jumping coulter plow was devised to overcome this difficulty. This was made like the bull-tongue, but had a flat piece of iron fastened to the beam and pointing backward at an angle toward the point. This flat piece of iron was sharpened on the front edge and since it was set at an angle would cut the smaller roots. This was a coulter. When it struck a hidden stump or larger root, it caused the plow to jump over it; hence the name of the plow. **1983** Montell *Don't Go Up* 199 = a broad, full metal blade inserted verticaly through the tongue of a plow and extended toward the ground at an angle that causes the plow point to come out of the ground when large tree roots are encountered.

jumping toothache *noun* A throbbing toothache.

1955 Washburn *Country Doctor* 12 Other complaints were "pneumony fever," "side pleurisy," "joint rheumatism," "jumping toothache," the "bloody flux," and the "gallopin' consumption," to give the more descriptive designations of well-known diseases. [**c1960** Wilson *Coll*: *jumping* = throbbing, like a jumping toothache.]

jump jacket (also *jumper jacket*) *noun* A man's work jacket, usually made of denim.

1941 Still *Troublesome Creek* 30 [The rooster] snuggled against my jump jacket, pecking at the buttons. **c1960** Wilson *Coll* = short work coat for me, usually jumper jacket. **1967–68** *DARE Survey* (London KY, Big Stone Gap VA) = same as jumper or overall jacket; (Barbourville KY) = made of denim; (Berea KY) = denim, lined with flannel. **1974** Fink *Bits Mt Speech* 13 = overall jacket. **1996** GSMNPCOHP-1:4 He had an old sawed-off shotgun under a jump jacket. **1997** Montgomery *Coll* (known to Adams, Brown, Cardwell, Jones, Ledford, Oliver). **1999** Perry *Clinch River* Dad would be wearing buckle overshoes, creased, best overalls . . . his heavy blue denim jump jacket, all the many pockets filled with goodies for his children.

[DARE *jump jacket* n South Midland, especially KY]

jump the broom (also *jump over the broom(stick)*, *jump the broomstick*) *verb phrase* To get married without the benefit of clergy or to reenact this folk ceremony at a **serenade.** The expression has a long history in the American South, often signifying a mock marriage ceremony, as in part of the script of a **serenade** or **shivaree.** See also **broomstick marriage, broomstick shindig.**

1939 Hall *Coll* (Big Creek NC) They would tote a man on a rail. Meanwhile they made the bride jump the broom. [*Ibid.* (Catons Grove TN) They never made us jump no brooms, but they made us bring out the cakes and everything.] **1944** Laughlin *Word-List Buncombe Co* 25 *jump over the broom-stick* = to get married (in some sections: common-law marriage). **1960** Hall *Smoky Mt Folks* 65 *jump the broom* = to get married, referring to an old protection against witches, by which a bride who jumps over a broomstick as she enters her new home protects herself. **1961** *Coe Ridge OHP-340B* That's the reason they say they jump the broomstick now is when they go to get married. **1967** *DARE Survey* (Maryville TN) *jump the broom* = joking way of saying that people got married. **1995** Montgomery *Coll*: *jump the broomstick* = to elope and get married, often without the benefit of clergy. In Cades Cove there was no ceremony, formal or informal, of acting this out; the term was used only figuratively (Shields). **2002** Myers *Best Yet Stories* 239 While none of our folk ever used this ceremony, we nearly always used that expression. Rather than saying "getting married," we would say they are "jumping the broom."

[based on a folk tradition in several European cultures, especially Wales; cf CUD *jump over the besom* (at *jump*) "live together without being married"; DARE *jump the broom* v phr scattered, but chiefly South, South Midland, TX]

jump the buckeye log *verb phrase* See 1952 citation.

1952 Wilson *Folk Speech NC* 523 = to die. "Ol' Daisy [= a horse] has *jumped the buck-eye log*. First time I ever knowed her to do that" (Swain Co.). **1962** Rouse *Colorful Tint* To jump the buckeye log means to die.

jump the pasture bars *verb phrase* See citation.

c1954 Adams *Word-List* = said of a married woman: illegitimately pregnant.

jump-up-johnny *noun* A violet.

1963 Edwards *Gravel* 85 Children romped barefoot . . . close to the foot of Cumberland Mountain, picking bunches of jump-up-johnnies from along the bases of old rotten logs, where they were wont to grow in profusion.

june *verb* To hasten, bustle about.

1892 Fruit *KY Words* 230 = to run fast: "She came a-june-in'." An onomatopoetic word, from the humming noise made by what we call June-bugs. They are the bronze-coated beetles that children catch to tie long strings to their legs to hold them while they hum in their efforts to fly away. **1940** Still *River of Earth* 199 This time o' year the mining business ought to be juning. **c1960** Wilson Coll Children . . . would tie a thread to one of its legs [of a June bug] and let the insect "June" around. **1984** Burns *Cold Sassy* 154 I really juned around when I got home that evening. I needed to lay in a store of good feelings as well as stovewod before asking permission to go camping.

Juneberry *noun* Same as **service B**.

1984 *Asheville Citizen-Times* (April 5) There are many names for this common tree: serviceberry, berry, servicetree, shadbush, shadblow, sugarpear and Juneberry. **1997** Montgomery Coll (known to Brown, Bush, Cardwell, Oliver, Weaver).

[so called because its fruit matures in the early summer, before most others]

jungle *noun* Same as **laurel bed**.

1878 Coale *Wilburn Waters* 61 It was a sultry, drizzly day, and the "sign" appearing to be several days old, and having greatly fatigued himself by working his way up through tangled vines and laurel jungles, and climbing over and around steep precipices, he lay down to rest under a shelving rock and fell asleep. **1936** (in **1952** Mathes *Tall Tales* 202) As the four gassed and gossiped, Sevier Dugger ambled out of the laurel that fringed the jungle and joined the group. **1939** Hall Coll (Deep Creek NC) I started on up through the jungles and got up two or three hundred yards above [the bear]. **1955** Parris *Roaming Mts* 177 Few men and dogs can follow them into the rhododendron jungles which are so thick that you have to crawl through them.

jusem-sweet (also *juseum-sweet*) *noun* See also **jewlark**.

1952 Wilson *Folk Speech NC* 555 *juseum-sweet* = a beau (Avery Co. NC). **1972** Cooper *NC Mt Folklore* 25 In the long ago, a male sweetheart was a jularker and his sweetheart was a sweetie, darlin' or jusem sweet.

just *adverb* Variant forms *dis', dist, 'ist, jes, jest, jist*.

1863 *Owens CW Letters* (April 26) we had Jes as wel go back to the union for the yankes say that we shant have no confedersy. **1864** *Joyce CW Letters* (June 18) the trafling yankes Jest tars up evry thing whare thay go thay Destroy all the propety thay can find. **1867** Harris *Sut Lovingood* 222 He jis' mow'd hit all down es he fled frum es jest a ritribushun as ever follered eny durn'd raskil. **1895** Edson and Fairchild *TN Mts* 375 *jes*. **1913** Kephart *Our Sthn High* 279 The same man at different times may say jest and jes' and jist. **1917** (in **1944** Wentworth *ADD* 336) (sWV) I dist does as good as anybody. **1937–40** Hall Coll (Great Smoky Mts) Jist a leetle. **1942** Hall *Phonetics Smoky Mts* 41 [ɪ] often appears in *just, such*, and now rarely in *cover* and *discover*. **1963** Edwards *Gravel* 43 "This here stove is jist about ready for yer dough, Sara," Mark said, opening the oven door to feel the heat and then closing it hurriedly. **1969** Medford *Finis* 61 Now, seein' that I've got 'im back, I jist as live keep 'im as not. **1991** Thomas *Sthn Appal* 75 I dis' love fish, to eat. *Ibid.* 247 That man dist throwed his plow-lines down an' run dist as hard as he could fly, home. **2005** Williams *Gratitude* 490 *dis', dist, 'ist, jist*.

just about *adverb phrase* Nearly (placed after construction modified). See also **about, nearabout**.

1973 GSMNP-4:22 They were all kinfolks just about you see, the Suttons and Caldwells and Hannahs and Messers and Palmers. **1975** *AOHP/ALC-1128A* Every coal company just abouts had a movie house. You'd go see a movie. **1985** Irwin *Alex Stewart* 231 Everybody, just about, was that way. **1997** Andrews *Mountain Vittles* 84 I don't care if it does take a sledge hammer just about to bust it.

just as good (also *just as well* in constructions *had/would ___ to, had ___ better, would ___ do better, might ___, etc.*) *adverb phrase* or *auxiliary verb* Might as well.

1862 *Councill CW Letters* (April 27) I thought that I had just as well have it as any body Else. **1863** *Owens CW Letters* (April 26) we had Jes as wel go back to the union for the yankes say that we shant have no confedersy. **1927** Bird *Among Highlanders* 27 He had just as well not have done so. **1937** Campbell *KY Mt Community* 548 They just as well keep together. **1956** Hall Coll (Waynesville NC) [The informant imitating a sermon]: If only one man in the meetin' wants to go to Heaven, and he's from South Carolina, we'd just as well to quit [preachin']. **1971** *Boogers* 31 If you don't believe th'Bible, you just as well not believe nothin'. **1973** *Gardening* 237 I don't get onions out in March; I just as well not to plant. **1974** *No Sang* 18 I just as well go dig what I can find of that in my bed [of plants]. **1983** *Dark Corner OHP-9A* If you find them [= bees] in there [= the hive] in July, you just as well as forget them. They going to die out there. **1985** Irwin *Alex Stewart* 186 You just as well take the bees and throw them in the creek. **1997** Montgomery Coll: *just as well* (known to ten consultants from the Smoky Mountains); *just as good* (known to Adams, Cardwell, Oliver).

[DARE *just as well* adv phr especially South, South Midland]

just as leave, just as lief See **lief B**.

just like one thing See **like one thing**.

K

kaeron See **carrion.**

kag, kaig See **keg.**

kar-acter See **character.**

kare See **care A.**

kase See **because.**

kattycornered See **cater-corner.**

katydid *noun*

1 A cicada.

1968 *DARE Survey* (Brasstown NC) = insect that sits in trees or bushes in hot weather and makes a sharp, buzzing sound.

2 See citation.

1967 Parris *Mt Bred* 133 A jackpot is an irregular pile of logs and a katydid is a pair of wheels from 7 to 12 feet in diameter for transporting logs.

kaze See **because.**

keeler *noun* A broad, shallow wooden tub. See 1944 citation.

1879 Jones *Backwoods Carolina* 751 The dish-washing was not done on the table, but at the hearth, the women preferring to bend over with their heads to the fire while they washed the dishes in a "keeler." A keeler is a wooden vessel resembling a foot-tub. **1905** Miles *Spirit of Mts* 32 Odd-looking utensils, these: boat-like bowls of maple for the kneading of bread, piggins and keelers of cedar, a wooden spurtle for stirring the evening kettle of mush, and a huge "gritter" on which green corn is grated for the making of "roas'n'ear" bread. **1935** Sheppard *Cabins in Laurel* 262 Uncle Milt is an expert at making wooden keelers, piggins, and buckets, the distinction being that a keeler is a wooden measure of peck size or less without a handle; a piggin has a straight handle on one side only, so that as it balances on the hip, the handle lies in the angle of the elbow; and the bucket has a complete bail. **1944** Wilson *Word-List* 45 = a wooden tub-like vessel five or six inches deep and eighteen or twenty inches in diameter, used to put milk or other warm liquids into to cool.

[OED3 *keeler* n[2] 1 obsolete except dialect; CUD *keeler* n "a shallow tub with handles on each side, used to let milk settle before churning"]

keen[1] *verb* To wail, lament.

1935 Sheppard *Cabins in Laurel* 218 If the preacher harrows the sorrowing kinfolks with the promise of Judgement and Wrath-to-come until they break into wild keening that sends shivers through the listeners, it is only what might be expected in bereavement, and likely to bring some sinner to his senses. **1971** Dwyer *Dict for Yankees* 28 = to wail, cry. "His daughter went to keening at the funeral." **1989** Giardina *Storming Heaven* 65 Aunt Becka commenced to keening. "Orlando's gone. Oh, Jesus, he's gone, my poor little brother that I carried in my arms oncet. And all for a handful of silver." **2004** Adams *Old True Love* 158 I started shaking all over and could not stop and my mouth opened and the awfullest sound come out, and I began to keen for that little part of me and Zeke that had left from this world. **2005** Hicks *Blood and Bone* 70 Blind John leaned / into the music, pulled his heart's / grief through the keening strings.

[< Irish Gaelic *caoinin* "I lament"; cf DHE *keen* v "to lament, to wail shrilly over the dead"; CUD *keen*[1] "cry of lamentation over the body of a dead person"]

keen[2]

A (also *keeny*) *adjective* Of one's gaze: piercing; of a twig: sharp (as one used to switch a child).

1883 Zeigler and Grosscup *Heart of Alleghanies* 51 "What I don't know about these mountings," said he, directing his keen blue eyes upon one member of the group, "haint of enny profit to man or devil." **1952** Justus *Children* 13 He sighed as he gave a keeny glance at his half-filled basket of berries. **1972** *AOHP/LJC-104* He'd take him a little keen switch, and he'd whip them frogs till they'd cry just like babies. **2005** Bailey *Henderson County* 32 Don't be too sure that a "hick'ry" was a keen and limber twig from a hickory tree. **2016** *Blind Pig* (June 2) You knew you were in BIG trouble when my grandmother said "I'm gonna get me a keen hickory."

[ultimately < Old English *cene*; DARE *keen* adj 2 chiefly South, South Midland]

B *verb* Of one's gaze, the wind, etc.: to pierce, stab.

c1940 Simms *Coll* Feel that keening wind? Hit'll likely frost this night. **1941** Still *Troublesome Creek* 13 He keened his eyes at Mother. "You hain't said what you want. All's had their say except you." **1992** Brooks *Sthn Stuff* 82 That girl was mad as fire. She keened her eyes at me ever'time I opened my mouth.

keen as a brier See **brier 3.**

keeny See **keen[2] A.**

keep

A *verb* Variant past-tense form *keeped*.

1964 Roberts *Hell-Fer-Sartin* 169 He keeped working his hands till finally he got them loose. **1978** Reese *Speech NE Tenn* 176 = attested by 3/12 (25%) speakers.

B *verb* Senses.

1 See citation.

1946 Dudley *KY Words* 271 = to dwell, reside, live: "Is this where Dr. Nelson keeps?"

2 Of a school term or church revival: to continue in session.

1974 Fink *Bits Mt Speech* 14 = stay in session. "Will school *keep* next week?" **1976** Garber *Mountain-ese* 49 = to continue, hold. "The revival will keep another week."

3 To stay.

1864 *Joyce CW Letters* (Dec 20) tell little James that he must not keep so fat for when hot wether Comes he will be two lazy to walk. **1864** *Zimmerman CW Letters* (May 2) I have planted about twenty acres in corn and am not quite done yet It keeps so wet I cant plant the bottoms It rains every day or so.

C *noun* See citation.

1975 Gainer *Witches Ghosts Signs* 12 = caution, care: "Take keep you don't get hurt."

keep one's britches on (also *keep one's lather down*) *verb phrase* Not to become upset or impatient (usually in the imperative *keep your britches on!*).

1966–70 DARE *Survey* (Spruce Pine NC) *keep one's britches on* = a sharp statement spoken to someone to be patient; (Buckhannon WV, Charleston WV, Milton WV, Moorefield WV, Richwood WV, Salem WV) *keep one's lather down* – be patient!, settle down. **1996** Montgomery *Coll*: *keep one's britches on* (known to Brown, Cardwell, Ellis, Jones, Ledford, Norris, Oliver).

[DARE (at *britches* n pl 2c) chiefly South, South Midland]

keep one's eye(s) skinned See **skin B1**.

keer See **care**.

keg *noun* Variant forms *cag(g)*, *kag*, *kaig*.

1782 (in **1996** Gump *Amis Ledger* 2) Cagg. **1863** *Copeland CW Letters* (Oct 16) I want you to send me some cloths by him the coat that I wore of before and my boots and one par of pantaloons and some socks and a cag of Brandy. **1863** *Reese CW Letters* (Dec 6) as soon as I git my money I am Cuming home and I want my little Cag ful of Brandey to work the Cold out of mee. **1867** Harris *Sut Lovingood* 109 They met up wif me, an' pinted out two kaigs tied across a muel's back, and told me tu smell at the bunghole. **1913** Kephart *Our Sthn High* 288 Ax for ask and kag for keg were the primitive and legitimate forms, which we trace as far back as the time of Layamon. **1934–47** *LAMSAS Appal* (Madison Co NC, Swain Co NC) *kag*. **1942** Hall *Phonetics Smoky Mts* 20 [æ] is common also in ... *keg*. **1973** Jones *Cades Cove TN* 111 *kaig*. **1973** Miller *English Unicoi Co* 77 *Kag* attested by 3 of 6 speakers. **1994** Montgomery *Coll* (known to Cardwell).

[OED3 *keg* n 1632→; earlier form *cag* < ultimately Old Norse *kaggi* "keg, cask"]

Kentucky board fence *noun* A type of **rail fence**.

1986 Pederson et al. *LAGS* (Sullivan Co TN) = cross pieces stacked, zigzag.

Kentucky dulcimer *noun* Same as **mountain dulcimer**.

1999 Milnes *Play of Fiddle* 136 The fretted dulcimer is also known as the mountain, Kentucky, Appalachian, or lap dulcimer.

Kentucky oysters *noun* Chitterlings.

1939 *FWP Guide KY* 406 Commonly known in this State as Kentucky oysters, chitterlings (hog intestines) may be prepared in several different ways.

ker- *prefix*

A Variant forms *ca-* [see **1968** in **B**], *co-* [see **1861** in **B**], *cur-* [see **1973** in **B**].

B Added to a verb, adverb, or noun to suggest suddenness or an echoic quality to the action expressed (as *calarrup*, *kerbiff*, *kersplunge*, etc.; see citations below).

1861 (in **1974** Harris *High Times* 266) I sot in tu sleepin in yurnest, when I hearn "kerdiff, kerdiff"—an thar stood the old par ove Windin Blades. **1861** (in **1938** Taliaferro *Carolina Humor* 19) Lazy Ephraim will be throwed sky high off uv his back, *co-whallop*, ah! **1867** Harris *Sut Lovingood* 25 Kerslunge intu the krick. **1878** Guild *Old Times TN* 168 I wished to give him rope, so I could "calarip" him. **1901** Harben *Westerfelt* 57 They both fell kerflop in front of 'im. **1927** Woofter *Dialect from WV* 358 *kerbiff* = said of a sudden, unexpected blow. "John hit the man kerbiff." *Ibid.* 358 *kersouse* = said of falling into the water unexpectedly. "The man fell kersouse from the raft." **1940** Haun *Hawk's Done* 119 He give one big jump and leapt out of all them men's hands. And hit the ground kerwhallop. **1942** Justus *Step Along* 16 Jerry Jake was so frightened that he lost his own grip on the handle bar, and the pushcart overturned, splang-ker-splang, on the middle of the trail. **1963** Edwards *Gravel* 139 All at onct that float started bobbin up and down an this way an that and kerplunge! under the water hit went an then up again and under again—the master lot of splashin ye ever heerd tell of in your life. **1968** Clarke *Stuart's Kentucky* 97 Some were content to smear a rival in his best clothes by hitting him casouse with tomatoes, peaches, and the like. **1973** Davis *'Pon My Honor* 57 I histed my rifle-gun to my shoulder and cut loose CUR-BANG. **1975** Carter *Gospel Truth* They hit [the mule] a "ker-wallop" or a "ker-warp." A rock went "ker-splash" in the water. A hickory went "ker-swish." **c1975** Lunsford *It Used to Be* 166 "Kerflumoxed" is a home-made word to show what happened when something falls, "He went over the bank kerflumoxed." **1995** Harrison *Smoke Rings* 165 Some hillsmen have coined the word "kerlarrippin." If a person goes about with no definite end in view, he is "kerlarrippin" around. **2017** *Blind Pig* (May 18) *Kerploosh*, *kersploosh*, *kersplat*, *kersplatter*, *kerpop*, *kerplop*, *kerflop*, *kerplunk*, *kersmack*, *kerchunk*, and many more are variations of *kersplung*. It all depends on the sound you make when you hit.

kerbiff, kerchunk, kerdiff, kerflop, kerflummox, kerlarrip around See **ker- B**.

kernel *noun* A hard lump or swelling under the skin; also, an enlarged lymph gland found in groundhogs that must be removed before the animal is cooked.

1917 Kephart *Camping & Woodcraft* 1:314 [How do you cook them?] Cut the leetle red kernels out from under their [= groundhogs'] forelegs; then bile 'em, fust all the strong is left in the water. **1974** Fink *Bits Mt Speech* 14 *kernels* = small glands in neck, armpits, groin, etc. These in some game animals must be removed if the meat is to be edible. **1978** Parris *Mt Cooking* 130 Unless you know about a groundhog's glands and remove 'em, you'll throw it out when you cook it. If you leave 'em in, the meat tastes awful. So, after you've killed your groundhog and brought him in and cleaned him, you cut out these little brown lumps. There's one under each foreleg and two in the small of the back. **1990** Cavender *Folk Medical Lex* 26 *kernels* = swollen lymph nodes on the arms, in the neck or groin. **1997** Montgomery *Coll* (known to nine consultants from the Smoky Mountains). **2003** Cavender *Folk Medicine* 120 "Kernels" (swollen lymph glands) were treated by applying the blood of a freshly killed black chicken. . . . As with goiter, there were people who had the ability to cure scrofula by rubbing the "kernels" while reciting an undetermined charm. **2006** Cavender *Medical Term* 1022 = a swollen lymph node in an armpit, on the neck, or in the groin. **2013** Shedlarz *Rosa Hicks* 11 He said there was kernels under the back legs or front legs [of a groundhog]. **2017** *Blind Pig* (May 18) = a growth that comes up under the skin.

[OED3 *kernel* n[1] 4 now chiefly dialect; DARE *kernel* n 4 especially South, South Midland]

kerosene oil *noun* Same as **lamp oil.**

1934–47 *LAMSAS Appal* (Swain Co NC). **1937** Hall *Coll* (Cades Cove TN) [For a rattlesnake bite] use kerosene oil, also whiskey and turpentine. **1973** *GSMNP*-4:1:7 You could buy your matches and soda, kerosene oil and stuff like that. **1984** *GSMNP*-153:55 [We would] put kerosene oil on [a cut], and a doctor would frown pretty heavy on that today, but now I thought a lot about it. That kerosene oil offered as a disinfectant. It'd kill a germ and in all probability it killed an infectious germ, and so kerosene oil was used to go on a fresh wound. Pour it on there.

kerploosh, kerplop, kerplunge, kerplop, kerplunk, kerslunge, kersmack, kersouse, ker-splang, kersplash, kersplat, kersplatter, kerswish, kersplunge, kerwhallop, kerwarp See **ker- B.**

ketch, ketched See **catch.**

kettle *noun*

A Variant forms *kitele, kittel, kittil, kittle.*

1813 (in **1920** DeWitt *Sevier Journal* 52) (July 10) Then sit the jar into a kittle of water and then boil it gently until the vinegar is sufficiently impregnated. **1813** Hartsell *Memora* 111 he kicked Several kiteles off the fire, and Spilt the Vituales that was in the Same. **1823** (in **1956** Eliason *Tarheel Talk* 313) (Burke Co NC) *kittle.* **1842** McLean *Diary* 81 [I] Baught too Kittel of[f] him at 7 Dollrs a piece makeing $14 and Credeted it on his Note. **1867** Harris *Sut Lovingood* 258 He'll sizzil like a wet cat flung intu a kittil ove bilin fat. **1904–20** Kephart *Notebooks* 2:367 You cain't scald the bristles offen a live hog; we poured kittles-full through the cracks [in the floor]. **1924** Spring *Lydia Whaley* 2 [I was] settin' up and cutin' [sic] up fruit when I saw a little black thing movin' in the yard. Went out to it and give it a hard kick and it was my little, black kittle. **1934–47** *LAMSAS Appal* (Madison Co NC, Swain Co NC). **1942** Hall *Phonetics Smoky Mts* 19. **c1945** Haun *Hawk's Done* 223 She liked most of all to play with that old iron kittle—the one that had a crack nigh the top of it from the water freezing in it. **1969** *GSMNP*-38: 110 They had big wash kittles to make the soap. **1972** *AOHP/ALC*-388 They had this great big fireplace in there, and they had that hook over the top of it where they could hang this kittle. **1976** *GSMNP*-114:7 He took that old kittle out there and made some cornbread. **1986** (in **2000** Puckett *Seldom Ask* 151) Get you one of these kittles out here. **1989** *Matewan OHP*-9 We had a big kittle outside in a furnace, and we'd put [the sap from a sugar maple] in there and boil it and boil it and boil it and boil it down till it made sugar. **1997** *Dante OHP*-14 We had our kittle where we had water and everything down at the creek, way down below the house.

[OED3 cites forms with i from c1000→; DARE *kettle* n chiefly South Midland, also Northeast]

B Same as **copper pot.**

1968 *End of Moonshining* 49 [A] Still [is] the container into which the beer is placed for boiling. Also called the . . . Kettle.

kettleback See **kettle bottom.**

kettle bottom (also *kettleback, kettle head*) *noun* See citations. See also **draw slate.**

1973 Preston *Bituminous Term* 47 *kettle bottom* = a large, rounded dark rock, often pressed slate, which protrudes only slightly from the top, but can fall without any warning whatsoever. **1974** *AOHP/ALC*-802 A kittle head is a stone or slate. . . . They can be both, that sets in the roof. I seen them fall out, weigh a ton. I've seen them, they all sizes, just sticking up there loose. Now they just drop loose all at once. You don't know when they're going to fall. . . . Sometimes they're not visible, maybe a little skim of coal or slate or something between them and you, but you can't see them all the time. Sometimes you can see them. I've worked the mines where you could just sit down to eat your lunch or rest or something. You can hear the spatting all over the mines. Kittle bottom's falling, and you had to try to dodge all of them you could. **c1975** *Miners' Jargon* 5 *kettle bottom* = a piece of slate that drops out of a smooth cavity in the roof of a [coal] mine. It loosens and falls without warning. The term *kettleback* is also used for this condition. **2004** Fisher *Kettle Bottom* 8 "Kettle bottom" . . . is the petrified tree trunk buried in the mountain, two, three hundred pounds. Drops through the mine roof . . . kills a man, just like that. **2006** Hicks *Mt Legacy* 144 I was told there were not a lot of kettle-bottoms on this mine, and many were on this section. Kettle-bottoms are rare rock boulders on the mine roof that can fall on you suddenly without warning. Each has a small head of coal around their exposed edge and covers the whole unseen body.

kettle head See **kettle bottom.**

kettle tea *noun* A drink of hot water, milk, and sugar or molasses, made when regular tea is unavailable.

1956 McAtee *Some Dial NC* 25 = drink made from hot water, milk, and sugar. **1971** Dwyer *Dict for Yankees* 28 = tea made of hot water, milk and sugar; also called "hot water tea." **1997** Montgomery *Coll* (known to Andrews, Brown, Bush).

[DARE *kettle tea* n especially South Midland]

kettling *noun* See citation.

1978 Reese *Speech NE Tenn* 46 = a small "run" of apple butter or the like.

kewter *verb* See citation.

2005 Williams *Gratitude* 504 *kewter to* = "cater" to every whim, as to spoil a baby. "She *kewtered to* it, and grabbed it up ever' time it cried." If a man let a woman lead him around (tell him what to do), he was *kewterin' to* her.

keyar See **car A**.

key log *noun* See citation.

1984 High *Titan Rock* 32 Workers constructed splash dams by building pens on both sides of the tributary, filling in between with tree trunks, branches, stones, and mud. Water backed up into a pool, which would be filled with mud. Usually a crew waited until after a soaking rain or when a "tide" or flood rose in the river. Then they knocked out the "key log" or "trigger," which released the logs and carried them toward the river.

kick

A *verb*

1 To reject (a suitor) in courtship, jilt.

1845 (in **1956** Eliason *Tarheel Talk* 280) (Yadkin Co NC) I am fearful . . . that I would be fool enough to make a speech to [a girl], and if so I would get kicked so far I would hardly get back in a coons age. **c1881** Pierson *In the Brush* 8 When such a suit had been unsuccessful, they did not say the lady rejected or "mittened" her suitor, but, "She kicked him." **1886** Smith *Southernisms* 46 = to reject a suitor. **1934–47** *LAMSAS Appal* (Madison Co NC, Swain Co NC). **1939** Burnett *Gap o' Mountains* 21 Turning a man down this way was called kicking him, and custom required that the fellow so bruised tie a handkerchief aroung his ankle and limp painfully away. **1940** Oakley *Roamin'/Restin'* 36 I went home and stayed for some few weeks thinking I had better quit this corting business as I had got kicked by my girl and had a broken leg. **1952** Wilson *Folk Speech NC* 555 = to jilt. **1966** *DARE Survey* (Cherokee NC) = if a man loses interest in a girl and stops seeing her, you'd say he kicked her. **1966** Medford *Ol' Starlin* 66 If a girl refused a young man's company or to walk with him, it was said that she "kicked" him. **1972** Cooper *NC Mt Folklore* 23 Refusing his offer was called *kicking* him, and a few girls who were asked for the first time really kicked the young man's shin, but lightly. **1995** Montgomery *Coll* (known to Cardwell).

[DARE *kick* v B1 chiefly southern Appalachians, South Atlantic]

2 To complain, criticize, disparage.

1930 Armstrong *This Day and Time* 172 A man's got no cause to kick ef he gits his coffee an' biscuits of a mornin' an' his beans an' a piece o' cornbread of a night. **1974** Fink *Bits Mt Speech* 14 = disparage. "I ain't *kicking* his work none." **1981** GSMNP-117:6 Lee and this other boy would come to school with beer all over 'em and smellin', and the children got to kickin' about 'em a-smellin' beer on 'em so strong. **1995** Montgomery *Coll* He's always kicking about something (Shields).

B *noun*

1 A complaint.

1985 Irwin *Alex Stewart* 103 I never had no kick about a boat I'd made. **1989** *Matewan OHP-9* He kind of was in favor of the company, but he come in there, and course they finally, after so long a time they made him leave, but it was open enough till there wasn't no kick on him a-coming in [to work in the mines again].

2 See citation.

1964 Clarkson *Lumbering in WV* 365 *kicks* = coarse shoes or loggers' boots.

kilfliggin *adjective* See citation.

1895 *Word-Lists* 390 = lazy. Ky. mountains.

kill *verb* See also **kill dead**, **kill down**, **kill out**, **kill up**.

A Principal parts.

1 Variant past tense form *kilt*.

1923 Furman *Mothering* 104–5 Seeing how he felt about it, they never come again for quite a spell,—not till after he kilt Elhannon in April. **1937** Thornburgh *Great Smoky Mts* 93 A party of hunters came up from Knoxville and kilt 'em a load o'bear an' drug 'em down to the head of the creek an' skinned 'em. **1966** Medford *Ol' Starlin* 83 Cain kilt his brother, an' whole lot o' the ol' kings was mean as all git out, yes, siree! **1974** Fink *Bits Mt Speech* 14 Who kilt that dog? **1989** *Matewan OHP-23* It about kilt me.

[SND *kill* v I 1; CUD *kilt* (at *kill*) HT *kilt* "killed"; DARE *kill* v B South, South Midland]

2 Variant past-participle form *kilt*.

1862 Sutton *CW Letters* (Nov 8) the wase five thousand yankey kilt. **1940** Haun *Hawk's Done* 106 Mos, we'll be kilt dead before we get there. **1960** Hall *Smoky Mt Folks* 16 Mack Hannah, Mark's daddy, has kilt a sight of bear. **1971** *AOHP/ALC-33* He was working the mouth of Dry Creek whenever he got kilt. **1993** Burleson *Aunt Keziah* 11 "What's the matter, son, air ye kilt?" Pappy yelled.

B Sense. To pour boiling grease over (wild greens) in preparation for eating, with onions and pork often added to the greens. Also called **wilt**. See also **killed salad**.

1939 Hall *Coll* (Jefferson City TN) Take small lettuce leaves and small green onions with stems and mustard. Take a hot pan of grease and pour over. This is called "killing with grease." **1979** Slone *My Heart* 71 "Crow's foot," "shoestring," "chicken salet," and "creases" were eaten raw, cut up, sprinkled with salt, and then "killed" by pouring real hot grease over them. **1979** Smith *White Rock* 34 From the streams we picked watercress which Mama "killed" with hot grease and served with young tender onions. **1982** Slone *How We Talked* 62 Some of the greens we used were not cooked, but eaten raw. They were "looked" (checked for bugs and rotting spots), washed, sprinkled with salt and wilted or "killed" by pouring real hot grease over them. **1995** Williams *Smoky Mts Folklife* 96 Other plants such as sorrel and young dandelion took only one boiling and then were dressed (or "killed") with hot bacon drippings. **1997** Andrews *Mountain Vittles* 15 Pour the hot grease over the lettuce leaves to kill or wilt them.

kill dead *verb phrase* To kill (someone) with certainty. See also **kill up 1**.

1862 Rudasil *CW Letters* (June 17) we went in the field with A bout 65 men and we lost 28 killed and woounded 9 was killed ded on the field. **1864** *Love CW Letters* (April 2) there Was 10 in our regment killed dead and 61 Wounded. **1890** Fruit *KY Words* 68 He kilt him dead. **1940** Haun *Hawk's Done* 13 Somebody kilt him dead. **1987** Young *Lost Cove* 88 It was a wonder that he wasn't killed dead. **1991** Thomas *Sthn Appal* 257 I never missed a one. I didn't mind killin' 'um dead.

[common redundancy; DARE *kill* v C2 especially South, South Midland]

kill-dead twist *noun* See citation.

1939 Hall *Coll* (Saunook NC) Kill-dead twist [is] homemade chewin' tobacco locally grown and cured.

killdee *noun* See citations.

1967 *DARE Survey* (Gatlinburg TN) = a person with skinny legs. **1976** Garber *Mountain-ese* 50 = a skinny legged lass. "Nobody will date Phoebe because she's nothing but a killdee." **1997** Montgomery *Coll* (known to Adams, Bush).

kill down *verb phrase* To kill; to reduce (an animal population).

1939 Hall *Coll* I shot the bear in the mouth and killed him down. **1989** Landry *Smoky Mt Interviews* 194 They kept [the deer] killed down so they wouldn't accumulate. **1991** Still *Wolfpen Notebooks* 56 They aimed to draft my son into the army, and I didn't want them to, and he didn't want to go either and get himself killed down.

killed *participial adjective* Exhausted; dead.

1986 (in **2012** Portelli *They Say* 62) Come on, child, he's killed. **2004** House *Coal Tattoo* 145 We've been up all night. . . . These children are killed. **2009** Holbrook *Upheaval* 68 I don't believe he's killed. **2015** Holbrook *Something* 151 One of her sisters called to tell her about him wrecking. "He's killed."

killed lettuce See **killed salad.**

killed salad (also *killed lettuce, kilt salad*) *noun* Edible greens prepared by pouring boiling grease over them. Also called **wilted salad**. See also **kill B**, **wilt.**

1976 Braden *Grandma Was Girl* 45–46 "Killed lettuce" was a kind of salad. We cut up leaves of lettuce and green onions together. Just before serving it, we poured hot fried meat grease on it. Sometimes we added a bit of vinegar to the hot grease. **1982** Powers and Hannah *Cataloochee* 355 No more wild greens and "kilt salad." **1996** Montgomery *Coll*: *killed salad* (known to Andrews), = lettuce eaten with onion and pork added (Cardwell). **2006** Sauceman *Place Setting* 53 *killed lettuce* = fresh lettuce wilted with a blending of bacon grease and vinegar.

killikinick (also *killikinik, kinnikinnick*) *noun* A mixture of tobacco and other dried leaves or bark, for smoking.

1873 Smith *Arp Peace Papers* 67 Kalmly and koolly we smoked our killikinik. **1884** Smith *Arp Scrap Book* 37 Calmly and coolly we smoked our killikinick. **2006** *WV Encycl* 199 Indians chewed dogwood twigs and used the bristle tip as a toothbrush. They also smoked the bark of shrubby dogwoods in their pipes, as part of a smoking mixture called kinnikinnick.

killjackum *noun* See citation.

1944 Combs *Word-List Sthn High* 19 = slang for sorghum molasses.

kill-kit'n kaboodle See **kit and boiling**.

kill me quick *noun* Homemade whiskey.

1963 Watkins and Watkins *Yesterday* 20 He preached against making and drinking whisky and called over the different names that show how bad it is—booze, killmequick, white-lightning, rotgut, and popskull.

kill one to death *verb phrase* To hurt (one) severely.

1956 Hall *Coll* (Cosby TN) My legs seemed like they was killin' me to death.

kill out *verb phrase*

1 To destroy, exterminate (a population of a plant or an animal).

1927 Mason *Lure of Smokies* 227 Le's have a war and kill out a few! **1953** Hall *Coll* (Bryson City NC) The [bear] come to the settlement, come in, raiding the people's corn cribs and after the stock, and soon killed them all out. **1969** GSMNP-25:2:24 I don't know whether people killed them out or what happened to them, but . . . a bear was just as scarce. They just wasn't any till . . . the park bought the land. **1970** *Burton-Manning Coll*-103A horse couldn't stand the walk. . . . You could kill a horse out in two or three months. **1973** Mullins *Herbs KY Highlands* 41 When cows had eaten fallen buckeyes, they would become poisoned on them and die. The liquid from the white oak bark would be poured down a cow to "kill out" the poison. **1974–75** McCracken *Logging* 5:58–59 This was a kudzu patch just a few year ago, and the park service sprayed it and killed it out. **1983** *Dark Corner OHP*-10A People used to feel like that if they'd set a fire on the mountain, that it would kill the snakes out. **1986** Pederson et al. LAGS (Campbell Co TN).

2 See citations.

1970 *Burton-Manning Coll*-94A A horse couldn't stand the walk . . . you could kill a horse out in two or three months. **2014** Williams *Coll* = to become exhausted.

kill up *verb phrase*

1 To kill (a person) with certainty; wipe out or decimate (a population). See also **kill dead**.

1834 Crockett *Narrative* 52 His [battalion] and the one Russell was now appointed to command, composed a regiment, which [was] to kill up the Indians on the Scamby river. **1863** *Woody CW Letter* (Feb 15) it lucks like the men is all a going to Dye and Get killd up. **1866** Smith *So Called* 29 You will have all the scum of your population killed up. **1924** Raine *Saddlebags* 99 The mountain man uses *kill up* as Shakespeare does, and also *live up*, and *teach up*, as in teach up children to have good manners. **1939** Hall *Coll* (Smokemont NC) It was more fun to us than anybody would think because we was so interested in getting that brute [= a bear] that was a-killing our cattle up off. **1976** *Digging Well* 134 If [the well] caves, if they've got time they'll pull you up. If they don't, they just kill you up. **1978** Burns *Our Sthn Mtneers* 12 "Kill up," "grow off," "live up," are from the same source [i.e. Elizabethan].

[DARE (at *kill* v C1) chiefly South, South Midland]

2 To injure severely.

1864 *Hundley CW Letters* (April 16) I wish that tha[y] would come to some conclusion and let the poor killed up men stay at home with ther famelys.

kill ye or cure ye *noun* Same as **boneset** when made into a tea.

1995 Montgomery *Coll* (known to Andrews).

kilt See **kill A**.

kilt salad See **killed salad**.

kin[1] *noun* See also **akin**, **kinfolks**.

1 A blood relative.

1862 *Warrick CW Letters* (Sept 17) Tell all of our kin to write to me. **1863** *Shifflet CW Letters* (March 15) he dide [= died] to day he has bin Sick fore weeks I donte no what was the matter with him So if you see enny of his kin tell them. **1884** Smith *Arp Scrap Book* 72 Then there is . . . snakes, which are my eternal horror, and I shall always believe are sum kin to the devil himself. **1937** Hall *Coll* (Cades Cove TN) A kin of mine.

[OED3 *kin* n[1] 3c archaic; SND *kin* n 1 "a kinsman"; CUD *kin* n (used of a single person)]

2 A blood relationship.

1862 *Tesh CW Letters* (Oct 13) I havent got no body of my Kin in the army. **1864** *Poteet CW Letters* (Feb 18) Joseph Landis was Married last Saturday Night to Jeanna Coopper a daughter of Bill Coopper what kin is he to Susy Coopper. **1961** *Coe Ridge OHP*-334A He was a friend of the Taylors, don't you see, a little bit of kin. **1970** *Burton-Manning Coll*-92A We wasn't so close to kin, but I was a Bailey and married a Bailey. **1976** *GSMNP*-114:4 Thcy was some kin. **1989** Landry *Smoky Mt Interviews* 194 We're a little bit of kin, not much. **1991** Haynes *Haywood Home* 70 He was not really our uncle. He was no kin to us that I know of. But the young of my time were taught to address older people as uncle or aunt whether they were any kin or not. It was respectful. **2001** House *Clay's Quilt* 15 They did everything together, warm in the knowledge that kin was nearby.

kin[2] *verb* To love and understand (another person) deeply.

1976 Carter *Little Tree* 38 Granma's name was Bonnie Bee. I knew that when I heard him late at night say, "I kin ye, Bonnie Bee," he was saying, "I love ye," for the feeling was in the words. And when they would be talking and Granma would say, "Do ye kin me, Wales?" and he would answer, "I kin ye," it meant, "I understand ye." To them love and understanding was the same thing. Granma said you couldn't love something you didn't understand; nor could you love people, or God, if you didn't understand people or God. *Ibid.* 46 Mind ye've little to meet it [= the future] with . . . but the mountains'll not change on ye, and ye kin them; and we be honest men with our feelings. **1999** Montgomery *File* I kin you = "I love you" (27-year-old woman, Robbinsville NC).

[perhaps from Scots *ken*]

kin[3] See **can**[1] **A1**.

kind *noun* Variant plural form *kind*.

1916 Combs *Old Early English* 293 These kind of people. **1970** Miller *Pigeon's Roost* (Jan 1) There was in those days only about three kind of men here whose jobs stayed them in the saddle so long going here and there, that their shoes would freeze in the stirrups. Them men were the preachers, the mailmen and the doctors, but they were very scarce. **1973** *AOHP/ASU*-111 They was so much of this country through here in woods and all kind of herbs, different kinds. **1973** Carpenter *Mid-Appal* 34 "These kind of fellows," can be heard as a slip away from accepted grammar [but] Shakespeare was a user of this very construction in the line from King Lear, "Those kind of knaves I know." **1974** *No Sang* 20 He said them kind of plants was very few and far between. **1989** *Matewan OHP*-33 They was mobs of them kind of birds. **1997** *Dante OHP*-14 Them kind of snakes is big'uns anyway.

kinder, **kindly** See **kind of**.

kind of *adverb phrase* Variant forms *kinder*, *kindly*, *kindy*, *kinely*.

1904–20 Kephart *Notebooks* 4:847 He used to be bad to drink, but he's kinder tapered off. **1910** Weeks *Barbourville Word List* 456 = kind of. Very common. "He was kindly angry at me." **1931** Combs *Lg Sthn High* 1306 Kindly crazy-like; he ain't nothin' above his eyes. **1937** Hall *Coll* (Cataloochee NC) I feel kindly tough [= sick] today. **1939** Hall *Coll* (in describing how the speaker's brother eluded conscription by the Confederate Army) He kindly hid and got into some bushes. **c1950** (in **2000** Oakley *Roamin' Man* 38) If its kindly late at night I open the restaurant door and stand a bit, and soon Mrs. Wiley will say, "Why don't you come and sit down with me." **1963** Edwards *Gravel* 52 [I] kinder expected to git my belongings together today and write a letter to a man about a new job. **1967** Williams *Subtlety Mt Speech* 16 His little pinchin pay . . . warn't more'n a nough to kindy keep body and soul together. **1972** *AOHP/ALC*-342 They kindly got that squished down and run that wire fence. **1974** Roberts *Sang Branch* 7 We was all kindy skittish about strangers that way. **1975** Chalmers *Better* 37 How true is the old saying in the mountains that "Men and dogs has it kindly easy in these here parts, but wimmen and steers has it mighty hard." **1978** Montgomery *White Pine Coll* X-2 We'd kindly get our lessons out of a spelling book. **1985** Irwin *Alex Stewart* 156 Joe went to collect it, and Milt kinder stuttered and said, "W-w-w-well, by God, you'll have to wait till I shear my hogs f-f-f-fore I p-p-p-pay you." **1991** Thomas *Sthn Appal* 164 I got a pattern out of a pair 'at 'ad been made, here. An' I cut 'um out, kinely, by it. **1998** *Dante OHP*-25 I tell you, it was kindly strange.

[cf EDD *kindly* adv 9 "rather, somewhat"; DARE *kindly* adv chiefly South, South Midland, especially southern Appalachians]

kindy, **kinely** See **kind of**.

kinfolks *noun*

A Variant plural forms *kinfolk, kinfolkses.*

1939 Hall *Coll*: *kinfolkses.* **1970** Justus *Holidays* 5 All the fathers and mothers and kinfolk and neighbors would come to the schoolhouse to hear the children recite and sing.

B (also *kinnery, kinpeople*) Relatives. See also **folk, kin**[1] **2.**

1862 Councill *CW Letters* (April 27) you rote to me to no if I was not willin for you to go an see your kinfolks. **1862** *Reese CW Letters* (Oct) I Saw Sum of my kin folks two of Jackson Reese Boys **1937** Hall *Coll* (Cosby TN) I know they was kin-folk. **1952** Wilson *Folk Speech NC* 556 *kinnery.* **1997** Montgomery *Coll*: *kinnery* (known to Brown); *kinpeople* (known to Adams, Bush, Cardwell, Jones, Ledford, Norris, Weaver). **2000** Walker *Affrilachia* An almost heroic notion / of family / and kinfolk / makes us kinfolk / somehow. **2002** McGowan *Beech Mt Tales* 82 Yes, yes, there's a little bit of things from my kinfolk. **2007** McMillon *Notes*: *kinpeople.*

[DARE *kinnery, kinpeople* n both forms South, South Midland]

king cure all *noun* The evening primrose (*Oenothera biennis*), whose roots have medicinal uses. Same as **sheep's tongue.**

1957 Combs *Lg Sthn High: Word List* 56 = a wild, whitish plant used for making poultices. Children also gather it and smoke it in pipes. **1969** *DARE Survey* (Hazard KY).

kinnery See **kinfolks B.**

kinnikinnick See **killikinick.**

kinpeople See **kinfolks B.**

kin-see to kain't see See **can see to can't see.**

kipper *noun* A maggot. Same as **skipper 2.**

1990 Oliver *Cooking Hazel Creek* 17 Next year, when the weather turned warm, the hams that were left were buried in ashes to prevent them from getting "kippers."

kirtle *noun* A woman's garment.

1958 Campbell *Tales* 35 She walked a long time till she came to a little house and met up with an old woman in a green kirtle.

[OED3 *kirtle* n 2b "a skirt or outer petticoat" archaic]

kissie *noun* See citation.

1960 Stubbs *Mountain-Wise* (April–May) 6 A diminutive wild campion, or pink, has two fetching names—"kissie" and "pretty Polly."

kit *noun* A wooden tub or small barrel (as for fish, milk, butter, or water).

1941 Still *Troublesome Creek* 12 I'm a-mind to buy a whole wooden kit o' mackerel. **c1960** Wilson *Coll* = a small tub.

kit and boiling (also *kill-kit'n kaboodle, kit and boodle*) *noun phrase* The entire group or lot. See also **boiling.** [Editor's note: The construction *kit and caboodle* is widespread in the US.]

1890 Fruit *KY Words* 63 "I can whip the whole kit and bilin' of you," i.e. "the whole kit and boodle of you." **1917** Kephart *Word-List* 408 = crowd. "The hull [whole] kit an' bilin' of 'em." **1952** Brown *NC Folklore* 1.433 *kit and biling.* **c1960** Wilson *Coll*: *kit and bilin'.* **1963** Edwards *Gravel* 26 Come when you can, the whole kill-kit'n kaboodle of you. **c1975** Lunsford *It Used to Be* 178 "The kit and biling" means the whole of the thing. "The whole kit and biling" means the kettle and what goes in it. [**1992** Montgomery *Coll*: *kit and boiling* (unknown to consultants from the Smoky Mountains).]

[OED3 *kit* n[1] 3 "a number of things or persons viewed as a whole; a set, lot, collection"; DARE *kit* n 2c chiefly South, South Midland]

kitchen house *noun* A kitchen set off from the dwelling.

1933 Thomas *Traipsin' Woman* 112 [The] kitchen-house put in order, we once again returned to the stoop, and Sister Julie was once again jolting to and fro, smoking complacently on her pipe.

kitchen safe *noun* A freestanding, ventilated cabinet or cupboard, especially one to protect freshly baked foodstuffs. See also **bread safe, pie safe, safe B.**

1957 Broaddus *Vocab Estill Co KY* 45 = a cupboard. **1968** Wilson *Folklore Mammoth Cave* 37 = the storage place for the dishes and food, now superseded by the refrigerator, the kitchen cabinet, the freezer or locker. **1992** Brooks *Sthn Stuff* 132 = an old-fashioned cabinet with perforated tin, or wire-mesh doors, for ventilation. They were used in the kitchen for the safekeeping of cooked foods.

kite *verb* To go rapidly, move like a kite; hence verb phrase *go kiting.*

1891 Brown *Dialect in TN* 173 *go kitin'* . . . presumably means "to go like a kite," that is, "to go rapidly." **1892** Fruit *KY Words* 230 = to move rapidly: "To go a-kitin." **1993** Ison and Ison *Whole Nother Lg* 25 *goin' a-kitin'* = moving at a fast pace or quicker than usual. **1995** Montgomery *Coll* (known to Cardwell, but not to other consultants from the Smoky Mountains).

kiting See **kite.**

kittel, kittil, kittle See **kettle.**

kitty corner See **cater-corner.**

kitty wants a corner *noun* A children's game. See also **cat 1.**

1986 Pederson et al. *LAGS* (Cocke Co TN) = a game with 4 bases.

kiver See **cover.**

kiverlet, kiverlid, kiverlit, kivirlid See **coverlet.**

klediments See **clatterment 2.**

knee *noun* See citation.

1951 Hodges *Handicrafts* 6 The roof was of boards laid across the rafters, fastened at both ends by means of pegs, and kept from moving by braces called "knees," which were wooden strips with notches cut on one edge like bent human knees, that were pegged in place.

knee baby (also *knee child*) *noun* A child able to stand at a parent's knee and usually no longer the youngest in the family. See also **arm baby, lap baby, set-along child.**

1939 *FWP Guide NC* 98 The boy, or "chap," may be called a little "shirttail boy" to distinguish him from her "arm baby and her knee baby." **1952** Wilson *Folk Speech NC* 556 = a child just old enough to creep or walk, a second baby. "I got a *knee baby* and a arm baby [one in arms, younger than knee baby]." **1960** Cooper *Jularker Bussed* The littlest-un (least one) is an arm-baby (baby held in the arms), but they also have a lap-child (child held in the lap), a knee-child (child tall as one's knee) and a shirt-tail (wearing shirts) boy. **1970** Mull *Mt Yarns* 118–19 Babies were generally classified as "Breast Babies," "Lap Babies," or "Knee Babies." **1975** Jackson *Unusual Words* 154 There were *breast babies, lap babies, knee babies,* or *little set along young'uns,* as well as the *chaps,* and this *growin' up generation.* **c1975** Lunsford *It Used to Be* 179 The "knee baby" is one able to stand and lean up against the knee. **1980** Matthews *Appal Physician* 153 Babies stayed on the breast from the time they became the lap baby until they were the knee baby, and even then they got some "ninnie" until they were shamed of it. **1984** Wilder *You All Spoken* 36 *knee baby* = next to the youngest, old and strong enough to play at a mother's knee. **1987** Young *Lost Cove* 169 Children, from the time they were knee-babies until they were old enough to venture alone in the nocturnal gloom, were taught to be alert to the dins of the dark and the lurking dangers of the graveyard.

[cf SND *knee-bairn* (at *knee* n I.1) "a child that sits on the knee, as not yet able to walk"; cf EDD n *knee-bairn*; DARE *knee baby* n South, South Midland, especially NC]

knee deep (also *knee deep frog*) *noun*

1 A bull frog; also sometimes a **peeper**. See also **spring cheeper, squealer.**

1949 McDavid *Grist* 110 (Rabun Co GA) *knee-deep frogs* = small frogs in upland swamps. **1951** Ulmer and Beck *Cherokee Cooklore* 51 Du-S-Du: Catch early frogs—Called Knee-Deeps—scald and skin. Parboil and cook like other meats. **1955** Parris *Roaming Mts* 232 Then there are "knee-deeps," which are really only bull-frogs. **1995–97** Montgomery Coll (known to Brown), = a fully grown bull frog having a deep voice (Cardwell), = *peep frog* (Oliver), = bull frog (Shields). **2000** Miller *Looneyville* 58 Pokey River fresh water frogs are small, four legged, leaping animals with long, powerful hind legs, short forelegs, web feet and no tails. In Looneyville, peepers meant any of several species of frogs that may have a high pitched, throaty sound rather than the deep throaty croak of most larger species: "The peepers are noisy down there in the lower medder crick this evenin'." Some folks referred to them as knee-deeps.

[echoic]

2 See citation. See also **stack cake.**

1977 Farthing *Food Customs* 42 A favorite dessert called "knee deeps" consisted of a stack of big thin molasses cookies with homemade applesauce as filling.

knee high to a duck (and variants) *adjective phrase* Very short, young, immature, or insignificant.

1892 Fruit *KY Words* 230 *knee high to a duck* = very short. **1900** Harben *N GA Sketches* 260 Them two has been a-settin' up to each other ever sence they wuz knee-high to a duck. **1927** Woofter *Dialect from WV* 359 *knee high to a grasshopper* = of no value or importance. "He doesn't stand knee high to a grasshopper in his own county." **1937** Hall Coll (Emerts Cove TN) I've knowed him since I was knee high to a duck. **1937** Wilson *Folklore SE KY* 18 *since you were knee-high to a grasshopper* (known to 29/31 speakers in Bell Co KY and 27/31 speakers in Blount Co TN); *knee high to a toad* (known to 8/31 speakers in Bell Co KY and 23/31 speakers in Blount Co TN); *knee-high to a duck* (known to 26/31 speakers in Bell Co KY and 14/31 speakers in Blount Co TN); *knee-high to a fence-post* (known to 8/31 speakers in Bell Co KY); *knee-high to a jack rabbit* (known to 15/31 speakers in Bell Co KY). **1940** Haun *Hawk's Done* 74 Her and Pairlee had played together ever since they had been knee high to a tadpole. **1956** McAtee *Some Dial NC* 25 *knee high to a duck, or a grasshopper* = very short. **1971** Justus *Jumping Johnny* 15 He had been high jumping over all of them [= mountains] since he was knee-high to a bird. **1982** Slone *How We Talked* 41 *knee high to a grasshopper.* **1983** Page and Wigginton *Aunt Arie* 52 Ever since I've been knee high to a duck's egg, they've made liquor up on Coweeta. **1989** *Matewan OHP-56* I knew Molly and she knew me since I was just knee high to a duck, as the saying is. **1997** Montgomery Coll: *knee high to a duck* (known to eight consultants from the Smoky Mountains); *knee high to a duck's back* (known to Weaver); *knee high to a grasshopper* (known to nine consultants from the Smoky Mountains).

[DARE *knee high to a grasshopper* adj phr chiefly South, South Midland]

knee high to a duck's back, knee high to a duck's egg, knee high to a fence-post, knee high to a grasshopper, knee high to a tadpole, knee high to a toad See **knee high to a duck.**

knewed See **know A1.**

knickknack *noun* An item of snack food.

1967 Fetterman *Stinking Creek* 152 They won't buy good food, just knickknacks, pop, ice cream—such as that.

[DARE *knickknack* n 1 especially South, Mississippi Valley]

knife *noun* Variant plural form *knifes.*

2005 Williams *Gratitude* 484 We had *case knifes,* like you eat with, an'en we had cuttin' knifes, like a pocket knife, parin' knife, [and] butcher knife.

knit back *verb phrase* Of a woman's reproductive system, according to folk belief: to recover to normal after childbirth.

2007 Myers *Smoky Mt Remedies* 15 A new mother was kept perfectly quiet in bed for at least ten days after the birth of a baby. This process was supposed to allow the organs to "knit back."

knob *noun* A mountain summit, high point on a mountain ridge; also, a small mountain; also used in place-names, as in *Anakeesta Knob* (TN).

1777 (in **1940** McJimsey *Topo Terms in VA* 278) From the ford aforesaid to the westerly end of Morris's Knob, about three miles above the Maiden Spring on Clinch. **1799** (in **2008** Ellison *High Vistas* 37) 27th—A fine pleasant morning set out on the line at 7 o.c. and continued about 1 1/2 miles to the top of a high knob from which the mns appear in every direction high and craggy. **1819** (in **2003** *TN Petitions II* 205) There is a part of the road which leads from Newport to Sevierville that leads through a parcel of hills or knobs, which renders the road exceedingly hard to keep in repair and very often in winter is almost impassable for waggons. **1839** (in **2003** *TN Petitions I* 126) Your petitioners are required and oppressed as they have to march six or seven miles over a range of rough and high Knobs to get to the present muster ground of the company they are attached to. **1881** Pierson *In the Brush* 24 In the light of the torches thoughtfully provided for me, I climbed up the sides of the knob—the higher elevations of land in this region are called "knobs"—to the home of my host. **1892** Doak *Wagonauts Abroad* 160 We have now passed over the interesting geological series between Knoxville and the Great Smoky—over limestone, shale, slate, micaceous slates—over "grey knobs" and "red knobs"—not at all attractively "knobby" to tourists with a balky horse. **1913** Kephart *Our Sthn High* 297 To the east [was] Cold Spring Knob. **1926** Hunnicutt *Twenty Years* 117 I will go back to this knob and call him. **1939** Hall Coll (Proctor NC) [Bears] generally cross over the highest knob they is in reach of. They don't go through a gap like deer. **1943** Peattie *Indian Days* 40 The word peak is found on our maps and might be understood in this region but it is really not native to it. The equivalent is top, or knob; high top and high knob indicate lofty peaks. **1956** Fink *That's Why* 3 Peak seldom appears in a mountain's name. Knob is the most common term. **1981** GSMNP-122:28 That little knob right in yander you can see in between the LeConte Mountain and Tater Hill—that's old Brushy. **1986** Pederson et al. *LAGS* = attested by 35/60 interviewees (58.3%) from E TN and 3/35 (8.6%) from N GA; 38/131 of all LAGS interviewees (29.0%) attesting term were from Appalachia. **2000** Wilkinson *Blackberries* 1 I swam in creeks and roamed the knobs and hills. **2006** *WV Encycl* 273 Peaks of hard sandstone on the ridge tops are called knobs, such as Bald Knob (4,840 feet) and Panther Knob (4,508 feet).

[cf OED3 *knob* n 2 "a prominent isolated rounded mound or hill, a knoll" U.S. 1650→; DARE *knob* n 1 widespread, but more frequent North Central, Appalachians]

knock *verb*

1 To abort (a pregnancy).

1940 Haun *Hawk's Done* 23 Sadie Brock just told me afterward that she tried to get Tiny to take pennyroyal tea to knock the youngon.

2 To hit with the fists, box; hence noun *knocking* = boxing. See also **knocker**, **knock fight**.

1861 *Hanes CW Letters* (Aug 18) I knocked Ed turner a few the other day for givin me the dam ly. **1923** (in **1952** Mathes *Tall Tales* 8) Those who remembered Wesley Shelton as a young man told thrilling tales of his prowess in the arts that constitute the pentathlon of the mountain youth—running, lifting, wrestling, boxing ("knocking") and swimming.

3 To thwart, counter the malevolent influence of.

2007 Milnes *Signs Cures Witches* 152 Johnny said that Ben Moats was thought to be able to "knock witches." Knock is another verb that is used to indicate power over witches.

4 In phrase *knock it* = to play a banjo in a style that gives a percussive effect.

2003 Howell *Folklife Big South Fork* 150 In the 1970's, distinctive nineteenth-century methods of playing the banjo were quite different and have recently gained renewed interest among fans of old-time music. The old minstrel show "frailing" or "clawhammer" style called "knocking it" by Big South Fork musicians was probably derived from the Afro-American banjo tradition. In this style of playing, the right hand functions as one rigid unit, with the thumb and the index finger held in a claw position.

knock about (also *knock along*, *knock around*) *verb phrase* To go about, get around.

1863 *Matthews CW Letters* (Oct 25) men [th]at is able to Nock round gits beef & bread I git a nuff to eat my Self or i dont want mutch & i git Some licker ever Day nearley. **1863** *Misemer CW Letters* (June 5) he has something like the dropsey But is able to knock about. **1864** *Watkins CW Letters* (Aug 24) Posey Guest has got home on a thirty days furlow he is able to knock about. *Ibid.* (June 7) I want you to nock along with yore crop the best you can tel I come home. **1921** Greer-Petrie *Angeline at Seelbach* 9 We would want to knock around the city some after dark.

knock down *verb phrase* To introduce (someone); hence noun = an introduction.

1910 Cooke *Power and Glory* 69 I'll go straight up and give you a knockdown. **1925** Greer-Petrie *Angeline Hill Country* 84 Betty called him Tomkins, and furgot to giv' us a knock-down to him. **1967** *DARE Survey* (Gatlinburg TN). **1986** Pederson et al. *LAGS* (Johnson Co TN) *give you a knockdown* = introduce you; (Sevier Co TN) *he gave me a knockdown to* = so-and-so introduced.

[DARE *knock down* v phr 1 now chiefly South, South Midland]

knocked in the head *adjective phrase* See citation.

c1975 Lunsford *It Used to Be* 170 The expression "knocked in the head with a churn dasher" is used a good deal in speaking of a calf that has been weaned too early because the family needed the milk. . . . The calf never did grow.

knock-em-stiff *noun* Homemade whiskey.

1864 Gilmore *Down in TN* 87 I'll prime the guard with knock-em-stiff. *Ibid.* 185 They obtain plentiful supplies of a vile fluid, which is compounded of log-wood, strychnine, juniper berries, and alcohol, and "circulates" among them under the appropriate names of "Tangle-foot," "Blue-ruin," "Red-eye," "Bust-head," and "Knock-'em-stiff."

knocker *noun* One who hits with bare fists, a boxer.

1913 Kephart *Our Sthn High* 141 He was what a mountaineer described to me as "a practiced knocker." This phrase, far from meaning what it would on the Bowery, was interpreted to me as denoting "a master hand in a knock-fight." **1960** Mason *Memoir* 22 The best fighter in a given settlement would be given the name *bully* or *champion knocker*. **1994–97** Montgomery *Coll* (known to eight consultants from the Smoky Mountains).

knock fight *noun* A fistfight.

1904–20 Kephart *Notebooks* 4:860 They up and had a knock-fight. **1974** Fink *Bits Mt Speech* 14 Them boys had a big *knock-fight*. **1994–97** Montgomery *Coll* (known to Brown, Cardwell, Jones).

knock winding See **winding**.

knot bumper *noun* A member of a logging crew who chops knots and limbs off a felled tree before the log is sawed and sent to the sawmill. Also called **chopper**, **log knotter**. See also **bump**.

1964 Clarkson *Lumbering in WV* 365 = man who cuts limbs from a felled tree. This work is done with a double-bitted or a pole ax. **1976** Tyler *Man's Work* 28 They used two men they called knot-bumpers. They would trim all of the limbs off of them logs, and run 'em out until they came down to about four inches in diameter. **1983** Weals *Ball-Hooting* It was the duty of a *knot bumper* to trim the knots off a tree after it had fallen, before it was sawed into logs of uniform length.

knot locked See **locked**.

knotty (also *knotty head*, *notty*, *notty-head*) *noun* A small, edible, freshwater fish (*Campostoma anomalum*). See 1970 citation. Also called **hornyhead**, **stoneroller**.

1970 Vincent *More of Best* 108 They are called knotties because when spring comes small knots grow on their heads, and these knots make it easier for them to root in the gravel bottoms of clear mountain streams for places to lay their eggs. **1974** Russell *Hillbilly* 44 Each spring when the fish which we called "notty-heads" fluttered where Two Mile Branch empties into the river, we children thrilled to the fun of catching fifteen or twenty of them in an hour or so. **1988** Russell *It Happened* 122 We sometimes dammed up the branch where it flowed into the river and caught the "notties" by hand. **2002** Rash *Foot in Eden* 149 The buzzards closed back in on Sam like knottyheads on stickbait.

knotty head See **knotty**.

know *verb*

A Principal parts [Editor's note: In the Smoky Mountains in the late 1930s Joseph Hall observed *knowed* to be nearly universal among the older as well as the untutored middle-aged and younger speakers for both the past-tense and past-participle form. Even some rural high school graduates preferred it to the sophisticated *knew*.]

1 Variant past-tense forms *knewed*, *knowed*, *known*, *nod*, *node*.

1852 (in **1998** Bueker *Head Letters* 17) He Said not that he nod of. **1852** Carpenter *Diary* I 148 Charles McKinney ag 72 dide [= died] may 1852 ware a farmer lived in blew ridge . . . he mad brandy all his lif never had no foes got along fin with everyibody [who] nod him. **1863** *Epperly CW Letters* (Feb 27) if I just node that you would come then I would wait with patians. **1864** *Poteet CW Letters* (Nov 20) Mr. and Mrs Landis wanted to now whether I node any thing about John Landis are not. **1867** Harris *Sut Lovingood* 27 "Law sakes!" sez mam; "I know'd he cudent act hoss fur ten minutes wifout actin infunel fool, tu save his life." **1913** Kephart *Our Sthn High* 284 In many cases a weak preterite supplants the proper strong one: . . . drawed, growed, knowed, throwed. **1937** Hall *Coll* (Mingus Creek NC) I never knowed nothin' about cannin' fruits and vegetables when I was a girl. **1939** Hall *Coll* (Deep Creek NC) We learned to spell purty well, but that's all we knowed was just spellin'. *Ibid.* (Cataloochee NC) His brother-in-law—lived at what we known as the Hickory Butt next to Pigeon River. **1953** Atwood *Verbs East US* 17 From c. Pa. to the south and southwest *knowed* becomes more and more common, being used by more than nine tenths of the Type I informants [i.e. older speakers with little formal education] in Va. and N.C. **1968** Stubbs *Mountain-Wise* (June–July) 12 He come to me to help him out, fer he knewed I had a ketch-dog (Pit bull) an' some hounds. **1969** GSMNP-37:3:7 I knowed Old Man Aden ever since I knowed anybody. **1973** GSMNP-84:15 She disappeared, and nobody never knowed whatever become of her. **1980** Miles *Verbs in Haywood Co* 92 I never knowed him to work a day in his life. **1986** Pederson et al. *LAGS* (Cocke Co TN, Jefferson Co TN, Sevier Co TN) *knowed*. **1989** *Matewan OHP*-9 I just knowed they had it. **1998** *Dante OHP*-71 I knewed it'd come to me sooner or later.

[OED3 *knowed* (as past tense of *know*) 14c→, EDD *knowed* (at *know* v 1) nIrel, Engl; CUD *knowed*; HT *knowed* "knew"; DARE *knowed* (at *know* v B4 a) scattered, but chiefly South, South Midland]

2 Variant past-participle forms *knew*, *knowan*, *knowd*, *knowed*, *new*.

1837 *McLean Diary* (Sept 16) the watters is loar tha[n] they evar was knowan by the present inhabitants. **1861** *Poteet CW Letters* (Aug 7) I supose the like never was knowd in the world. **1864** *Chapman CW Letters* (March 13) I would a sent you more if I had a new you had a kneeded it. **1865** (in **1974** Harris *High Times* 161) That feller mus a knowd me pussonally. **1913** Kephart *Our Sthn High* 170 I've knowed him from a boy. **1939** Hall *Coll* (Hazel Creek NC) If I'd a knowed you fellows been a-coming and had studied up, why I could have give you fellows a whole lot of news. *Ibid.* (Catons Grove TN) I've never knowed it to fail to cure hives in a baby. **1971** Foster *Walker Valley* 3:6 I've knowed of people a-fainting. **1973** GSMNP-2 If a fellow'd knew what the outcome of this country would be here, he could've took notes on it, kept in a diary. **1973** GSMNP-83:21 I've knowed him as long as I've knowed anybody. **1978** Montgomery *White Pine Coll* XII I've always knowed them all my life. **1980** Miles *Verbs in Haywood Co* 92 I wouldn't have knowed no better. . . . She'd a probably knew that he'd been joking. **1986** Pederson et al. *LAGS*: *knowed* (Jefferson Co TN). **1997** *Dante OHP*-14 That's the only church I've knowed of to be here.

[OED3 *knowed* as past participle *know* 15c→; EDD *know* v 1 nIrel, Engl; CUD *knowed* (at *know* v)]

B As a progressive verb. See also **want**[1] **4**.

1929 Kephart *Smoky Mt Magic* 166 There's no gittin' around such as that, when you're knowin' to it bein' true. **1969** *Burton-Manning Coll*-93A I've been knowing him for twenty years. **1972** Cooper *NC Mt Folklore* 93 *I'm a knowing* = I know. **1996** Woodring *Times Gone By* 25 I ain't knowin why, but I won't be satisfied!

C Syntax.

1 Followed by an embedded yes/no question that maintains inversion of the subject and verb (thus *know can you* = know whether/if you can). See also **ask B1**, **know C1**, **see B1**, **wonder 3**.

1974 Roberts *Sang Branch* 20 He wants to know can you sing any songs with that banjer. **1978** *Horsetrading* 64 This old man come and wanted to buy him, wanted to know would he work. **1985** Irwin *Alex Stewart* 151 He come over here and wanted to know did I know anything that would do him any good—help ease the pain. **1989** *Matewan OHP*-89 Do you know were there ever any houses of prostitution in ———? *Ibid.* Do you know did Sid shoot Mayor Testerman in the shootout so that he could marry Jessie?

2 Followed by a *wh*-complement that maintains inversion of the subject and verb (thus *know when can you see him* = know when you can see him). See also **ask B2**, **see B2**, **wonder 4**.

1929 Rainey *Animal Plant Lore* 11 I have found very few school or college boys [in KY] who know what is a dragon fly. **1967** Hall *Coll* (Townsend TN) I don't know what was their idy. **1989** *Matewan OHP*-94 I want to know when can you see him.

D To meet, make acquaintance with (someone).

1930 Armstrong *This Day and Time* 23 Proud to know ye, Ivy. **1941** Stuart *Men of Mts* 38 "I'm glad to know you," I says. **1970** Madden and Jones *Ephraim Bales* 8 My brother, Edward, said when we moved up there, the first time he knowed Caleb, Caleb told him he'd catch him and swallow him. **1973** GSMNP-5:39 They were real good religious people, I mean whenever I'd know them. **1975** *AOHP/LJC*-384 We'd learn them. We'd know them. **1983** *Dark Corner OHP*-5A It wasn't about six months from the time I first knew him though till we married.

knowan See **know A2**.

knowance See **knowing A**.

know as See **as A2**.

know B from bull('s) foot See **B from a bull's bag, not to know**.

knowed See **know A1**, **A2**.

knowing See also **know B**.

A (also in plural *knowings*; hence *knowance*) *noun* Knowledge, awareness, experience (especially in phrases *in my knowing*, *to my knowing* = as far as I know, to my recollection).

1861 *Patton CW Letters* (Sept 14) I would rathe[r] be under him than any man in my knowing. **1864** *Chapman CW Letters* (April 1) they both belong to the 120 indaania ridgement they say there is twelve new ridgements maid up there in his knowing. **1929** Carpenter *Evolution of Dialect* 9 One [now] rarely hears knowance for knowledge of, punishing for suffering, discomfort for inconvenience, feared for afraid, and skun or skint for skinned. **1937** Hall *Coll* (Copeland Creek TN) That's all the houses they was in my knowing. **1941** Stuart *Men of Mts* 298 Not to my knowings. **1942** Thomas *Blue Ridge* 135 It's more satisfaction to let a body's knowing fall on fresh ears. **1961** Medford *History Haywood Co* 185 I guess I've seed the snows of more winters than anybody, to my knowin'. **1973** GSMNP-88:100 John lived here on up in my knowin'. **1989** *Matewan OHP*-45 Not to my knowings. I never would, never would stay too long. **1991** Still *Wolfpen Notebooks* 110 He lived to be ninety-nine. Claimed to be a hundred. Never worked a job in his life to anybody's knowance.

[DARE *knowing* n 1 chiefly southern Appalachians, Ozarks]

B Senses.

1 Knowledgeable, well-informed.

1867 Harris *Sut Lovingood* 54 Sum ove the wimmen fotch a painter yell, an' a young docter, wif ramrod laigs, lean'd toward me monstrus knowin like, an' sez he, "Clar case ove Delishus Tremenjus." **1931** Combs *Lg Sthn High* 1306 Teach him up jist right, an' he'll make a knowin' man. **1938** Justus *No-End Hollow* 18 After Granny Turner came to live with them, life ran more smoothly, for Granny was a knowing woman, and wise in many ways. **1957** Combs *Lg Sthn High: Word List* 56 = familiar, conversant with. Ex.: "Was he knowin to the sarcumstance?" = educated, well read, wise. Ex.: "Shorely, Preacher Joe's a mighty knowin' man." **1969** Hannum *Look Back* 181 You couldn't rightly call him a preacher, but he was a knowin' man. **1994–97** Montgomery *Coll* (known to Brown, Cardwell, Shields).

2 (in phrase *knowing to*) *adjective* Aware of, familiar with.

1863 *Rogers CW Letters* (Jan 17) they was sum more knowing to it [= the plan to desert] but did [not] attemped to leave consiquently they come clear and the others are in the guard hous yet. **1913** Kephart *Our Sthn High* 297 Reckon Pete was knowin' to the sarcumstance?

knowings See **knowing A**.

know in reason See **in reason**.

knowledge *noun* A fact, thought.

1966 Dykeman *Far Family* 27 "That's a mighty hard knowledge to live with," Leck Gunter said. **1998** Montgomery *Coll* (known to Brown, Bush, Cardwell, Jones).

knowledge box *noun* One's head.

1859 Taliaferro *Fisher's River* 134 After wavin', brandisherin', and gleameratin' thar tommyhocks over my knowledge-box for a long spell, and then thar butcher-knives in the same threatnin' aspex, they helt a council over my case.

know maul *noun* See citation.

c1982 Young *Colloquial Appal* 13 = wooden maul made from tree burl.

know of *verb phrase* To know. [Editor's note: This phrase in the sense "know about" is widespread in the US.]

1973 *Foxfire Interviews* A-73-86 Do you know of their names? **1979** *Big South Fork OHP*-10 I don't know of whether they ever had the fourth one out or not.

know on See **on B3**.

knuckle *noun* See citation.

2004 *Early Mines* 31 (As of 1902) The knuckle was the place in the tracks [of a coal mine] where the cars entered the tipple.

Kohee See **Cohee**.

kolyum See **column**.

koop, kope See **cope**.

kotch See **catch A2, A3**.

kotched See **catch A2**.

kraut

A *noun* Sauerkraut, traditionally made at home in the mountains, stored in barrels, and kept for winter consumption; it is the most significant German contribution to mountain cuisine and the term one of the very few from German in the mountain vocabulary. [Editor's note: The term *sauerkraut* occurs rarely in ATASC.]

1862 *Reese CW Letters* (April 2) he has Bin home on fur low and got Back the othe[r] day and brat with him a Barrell of Crout to sell it went off like hot cakes at fiftey Cents pur pound. **1863** *Tesh CW Letters* (Aug 2) if live I intend to make a fine tub of craut and I think shorly you will get to come some time this fall or winter then you can have some. **1913** Kephart *Our Sthn High* 289–90 In the vocabulary of the mountaineers I have detected only three words of directly foreign origin. Doney is one. Another is kraut, which is the sole contribution to highland speech of those numerous Germans (mostly Pennsylvania Dutch) who joined the first settlers in this region, and whose descendants, under wondrously anglicized names, form to-day a considerable element of the highland population [Editor's note: **Sashiate** is Kephart's third term of "foreign origin"]. **1936** Coleman *Dial N GA* 19 Two other original foreign words used by mountaineers are "krout," from Pennsylvania Dutch; and "sashiate" (from French "chasse") used in calling figures at the country dances. **1939** Walker *Mtneer Looks* 3 The German word *kraut* survived, for the obvious reason that there was no equivalent in the technical vocabulary of the Scotch-Irish housewife. **1960** Mason *Memoir* 15 The barrels were utilized as containers for the storage of such mountain comodities [sic] as saur kraut, pickled beans, bleached apples, and pumpkin butter. **1962** Hall *Coll* (Newport TN) A pregnant woman will spoil kraut or [the] mash for a run of liquor. . . . A woman, when her menstrual period is on, when she makes kraut, it'll rot. **1971** *AOHP/ALC*-147 They would smoke apples in a barrel. They'd pickle corn in barrels, and they'd pickle beans in barrels and make their kraut in barrels, and that's about the way they put up what they had. **1973** *GSMNP*-80:15 We would put a cloth over the kraut now and pickled beans, and we'd put this big plank and then we'd hunt and get us a big heavy rock, wash hit off right clean and put it on the plank, and that would mash it down in below kraut, and that's how we would have it . . . we would just go get us a handful, squeeze the juice out and just eat a handful. **1977** Madden and Jones *Mt Home* 27 Pickled beans and kraut were kept in large stone crocks in the springhouse. **1977** McClelland *Wilson Douglas* 18 In a dark moon the brine won't raise on your cabbage to sour your kraut.

[DARE *kraut* n 1 chiefly Midland]

B *verb* To make sauerkraut of (cabbage).

1917 Kephart *Word-List* 413 I don't do like old Mis' Posey, *kraut* my cabbage whole. [**1992** Montgomery *Coll* (unknown to consultants from the Smoky Mountains).]

kraut juice *noun* Juice from sauerkraut used as a flavoring for food and as a home remedy.

1955 Parris *Roaming Mts* 165 "Kraut juice," she said, "is the best cough remedy there ever was." **1995–97** Montgomery *Coll* (known to Cardwell, Ledford, Oliver, Shields); I have a great recipe to make pickled beans and corn using kraut juice (Adams), = a wintertime tonic, also used to flavor stewed meat (Brown).

Kris Kringle *noun* A Santa Claus–like figure in German holiday tradition; hence verbal noun *Kriskringling*. See citations. See also **Belsnickel, Santa Clausing**.

1964 Smith et al. *Germans of Valley* 122 In some sections [of the Shenandoah Valley], in which people of German heritage are less numerous, a similar custom [i.e. to Belsnickeling] was practiced which was referred to as *Kris Kringling*. [Residents] claimed that when they "dressed up clown-like during Christmas time and wore masks and visited, it was called going Kris Kringling." **1995** Suter *Shenandoah Folklife* 31 *Kriskringle* is a derivative of *Christkindel*, or Christ child. Santa Claus, *Belsnickel* and Kriskringle are thus essentially the forerunners of our present-day Christmas customs. *Ibid.* 34 Kris kringling was observed only in eastern Rockingham County [VA]. . . . The custom was essentially the same as belsnickeling.

ku-jack See **cope**.

kuop, kwope, kwopie, kwup See **cope**.

kyah, kyar See **car A**.

kyarn See **carrion**.

kyor See **cure**.

kyurosity See **curiosity**.

L

la (also *law*) *interjection* Used to express surprise, wonderment, exasperation, acknowledgment, or other emotion, in responding to a question or agreeing with a statement. [Editor's note: This was a common usage observed by Joseph Hall in the Smoky Mountains in the late 1930s, especially among women of all social classes.] See also **ay**, **eh la**, **lawd a mercy**.

1864 *Chapman CW Letters* (April 23) I would not like to go any futher South for it will be two hot down thare for us this Summer, but law we shall have To go whare ever we are orderd. **1900** Harben *N GA Sketches* 260 Law, I hardly know what she didn't say! **1913** Kephart *Our Sthn High* 36 La, no! *Ibid.* 85 Good La! **1916** Schockel *KY Mts* 129 There also comes to mind the following expression: "Law me, Honey, I'm glad to be back from the plains. Wooded mountains make the restinest place to lay your eyes on." **1936** Carpenter *WV Expletives* 347 Law and Lordy may do duty for almost any emotion in this section of the country, as may also: I'll swan; Hell's banjer; Sakes o' mercy; and Sakes alive. **1937** Hall *Coll* (Cades Cove TN) You'd orter see them. Law! *Ibid.* (Cosby Creek TN) Why law, yes! **1939** Hall *Coll* (Deep Creek NC) Law, yes, I've seed a many a bear and eat the meat of them, coon too. *Ibid.* (Emerts Cove TN) Oh, law, I couldn't guess. **1955** Dykeman *French Broad* 333 Law, child, I've had to be strong. I'm eighty-four years old now and I've catched babies ever since I was twenty. **1957** GSMNP-23:2:20 Oh law, yeah, I've been to Cades Cove back when I was a little boy, a young fellow. **1963** Edwards *Gravel* 91 "I tell ye," said Nath, "they aint no tellin when we may git the call like Charlie done"; and Mary said, "Law me, no. Well now, I declare!" **1971** *AOHP/ALC*-137 Law, they used to have the awfullest times they ever was. **1974** GSMNP-54:6 Yeah, law, I think I've got the ballad of that one too. **1978** Montgomery *White Pine Coll* III-2 Law, that'd be something. **1979** Carpenter *Walton War* 188 "Law Me" is a localization of "Lordy me." The expression ... was a gentler way ... a circumlocution the mountain people were fond of. **1985** Irwin *Alex Stewart* 198 Law, back when people was raising wheat and oats this valley used to be full of bobwhite. **1989** *Matewan OHP*-9 Back then they just, law, just died everywhere with it [= the flu]. **1997** Montgomery *Coll* Law, law, Bob got his leg broke (Brown). **2003** Onchuck *Mud Pie Memories* 29 I could see they were fancy folks because they had on fine store bought clothes. I called to Mama, to come see, and as she looked out all she said was "Well, law ... me."

[apparently coalescence of lo and *law* (the latter a variant of Lord); OED3 *la* interj and *law* interj now only dialect, vulgar, and archaic; DARE *law* n², interj now chiefly South, South Midland, formerly also Northeast]

labor with *verb phrase* Of a church elder: to counsel with (a wayward church member), attempt to achieve reconciliation and restore (someone) to good moral standing in the church.

1793 *French Broad Church Minutes* 17 Br Gentry & Bro Osborn fulfilled their appointment in labouring with Westley White & his wife and they still neglected to attend. **1842** *Elijoy Church Minutes* 45 church met ... took a charge against Malden Delosier for disorder & John Tipton & Vincent Rogers to labour with him against next meeting. **1874** *Tuckaleechee Cove Church Minutes* 21 the Church appointed Br Willia Brickey & Br Henry Franklin to go and labor with them and cite them to come to our next Church meeting.

lack *verb*

A Variant form *like*.

1862 (in **1992** Jackson *Surry Co Soldiers* 292) We made them leave and the[y] liked a heap of taking Richmond. **1864** *Watkins CW Letters* (July 20) last fryday it raind so harde that the gulley at our draw bars Jest liked 3 bars a running over the top.

[DARE *lack* v 1 especially South, South Midland]

B See citations.

1946 Matthias *Speech Pine Mt* 190 = to fall short of (lack commonly has this meaning, but is here used in peculiar contexts): "I just lack the hem of having my dress finished." **1982** Slone *How We Talked* 34 I like one having enough. **1984** Burns *Cold Sassy* 104 You need to understand that in Cold Sassy [we] say ... like for lack, as in "Do you like much of bein' th'ew?" **2014** Williams *Coll* How much does it say we like?

lackaday *interjection* Used to express surprise, pain, dismay, etc.

1859 Taliaferro *Fisher's River* 59 Nur did I—lack-a-day!—know what were to befall me that drefful, drefful day. **1968** *DARE Survey* (Hillsville VA) = exclamation caused by sudden pain—a blow on the thumb.

[OED3 *lackaday* interj obsolete or archaic]

ladies'-tobacco *noun* A wild plant (*Antennaria parlinii*) whose leaves are used in a tea or smoked to combat respiratory infections. Same as **pearly everlasting**, **pussy toes**.

1999 Montgomery *Coll* (known to Cardwell).

lady cow *noun* Used as a euphemism for a heifer. See also **gentleman cow**.

1977 Still *Wonder Beans* 7 Jack hung a sign betwixt the cow's horns: "Lady cow for sale anybody." **1992** Bush *If Life* 62 He went with his female cow into Dr. Tittsworth's pasture where a one-eyed Jersey bull was angrily chewing his cud, and the ferocious "gentleman cow" at once showed his fight by butting Mr. King a very hard butt on the stomach. . . . The "lady cow's" fate was not mentioned. But then, that was before women's rights were an issue. **1997** Montgomery *Coll* (known to Cardwell).

lady pea *noun* A black-eyed pea.

1997 Montgomery *Coll* (known to Brewer).

[DARE *lady pea* n chiefly South, South Midland]

lady('s) slipper *noun* An orchid (*Cypripedium calceolus*) with having a yellow blossom, broad leaves, and roots that have medicinal uses. See also **whippoorwill's shoes**.

1937 Hall *Coll* (Cades Cove TN) [Lady slipper] is good blood medicine. [**1971** Krochmal et al. *Medicinal Plants Appal* 106 The plant is used as a sedative and in treating neuralgia. In Appalachia, a root tea is used to treat nervous ailments and headaches.]

1982 Stupka *Wildflowers* 17 Small yellow lady's slipper and a closely related larger-flowered form are among our showiest orchids. **2008** *Rosie Hicks* 6 The yellow lady slipper, they use hit for nerves and headache.

lag See **bootleg C**, **leg B**.

laig See **leg B**.

lairs (also *lares*) *noun* Plenty.

1944 Williams *Word-List Mts* 30 *lairs* = plenty: "They wuz lairs of poplar timber in these here woods when I was a boy." **1992** Jones and Miller *Sthn Mt Speech* 91 There's lares of sarvices in the woods when I was young. **1997** Montgomery *Coll*: *lares* (known to Jones).

laissy See **molasses**.

lamb's quarter(s) *noun* A goosefoot (*Chenopodium album*), the leaves of which are often eaten as greens in the spring. Also called **wild spinach**.

1937 Campbell *KY Mt Community* 530 Off and on he'd git him a mess of wild sallet and git granny to cook hit good. Wild lettuce and dandelion and pepper grass and poke and lamb's quarter and dock and sich makes right good sallet. **1957** Combs *Lg Sthn High: Word List* 57 = a small plant used for green salad. **1983** Farr *More Moonshine* 53 We did not know of the existence of vitamin pills and supermarkets, but we gathered these new green leaves and stems which were rich in vitamins and minerals. Lamb's quarters, for example, is rich in iron and potassium, and watercress has an abundant supply of iron, and vitamins A, B, and C. **1985** Irwin *Alex Stewart* 191 We'd go to the woods and fields and hunt different things. We'd get lamb's quarters. That's the best stuff you ever had. **1986** Pederson et al. *LAGS* (Johnson Co TN) *lamb's quarters* = a weed, used as a green. **1991** Still *Wolfpen Notebooks* 77 What I look forward to in the spring hain't garden sass—is wild greens.... What you want to look for is plantain ... lamb's quarter ... and blue thistle. And don't spare the seasoning. **2006** *Encycl Appalachia* 935 The three most common wild greens found in Appalachia are lamb's-quarters (*Chenopodium album*), pokeweed (*Phytolacca americana*), and dandelion (*Taraxacum officinale*).

lamb('s) tongue *noun* A dogtooth violet (*Erythronium americanum*) eaten as a wild green and valued as a medicinal ingredient. See also **adder's tongue**, **trout lily**.

1973 *GSMNP*-88:12 He said that was lamb tongue and them sheeps would just eat that a sight in the world. **1981** Brewer *Wonderment* 22 Lamb's tongue, Randy said, is trout lily. **1991** Weals *Last Train* 15 The cattle relished the first greens of spring—the ramps, bear lettuce, turkey mustard, lamb's tongue, and crow's foot—after their winter diet of hay. **2013** Pierce *Corn in Jar* 16 The cure of colds and flu called for a double dose of corn liquor: "Whiskey and honey and lamb's tongue and whiskey."

lamp oil *noun* Kerosene, used formerly in lamps and also in home remedies. Also called **coal oil**, **kerosene oil**.

1937 Hall *Coll* (Mingus Creek NC) Never knowed nothin' about lamps or lamp oils till I was nearly grown. **1949** Kurath *Word Geog East US* 31 Since West Virginia was the source of this commodity for the Piedmont of Virginia, *lamp oil* has become established there too ... in Western North Carolina and adjoining parts of Virginia it competes with *kerosene*. **1952–57** (in **1973** McDavid and McDavid *Vocab E KY* 154) = attested by 3/52 (5.7%) of E KY speakers for the Linguistic Atlas of the North Central States. **1961** Seeman *Arms of Mt* 35 If a thumb is bitten off by the family mule, the stump is merely dipped in "lamp oil" and has a rag wrapped around it. **1966** Dakin *Vocab Ohio River Valley* 183 [*Coal oil*] is used everywhere, standing beside *lamp oil* in almost equal numbers even in eastern Ohio.... Only two Kentuckians do not use it. **1969** Madden and Jones *Walker Sisters* 29 For a remedy [for "pneumonia fever"] her sisters put "lamp oil" (kerosene) on a woolen cloth and placed the cloth on the chest, rubbing camphorated oil on the chest to keep the lamp oil from burning. **1986** Pederson et al. *LAGS* = attested by 9/60 interviewees (15%) from E TN and 4/35 (11.4%) from N GA; 13/31 of all LAGS interviewees (41.9%) attesting term were from Appalachia.

[DARE *lamp oil* n 1 scattered, but especially Appalachians]

land cress *noun* See citation. See also **cress**.

1983 Patterson *Cooking* 20 "Greens" enthusiasts will search dales as early as February hoping to find a "mess" of Winter Cress greens (also known as Land Cress and Cressy Greens).

land debts *noun* See citation.

1956 Hall *Coll* (Emerts Cove TN) They just run me out of this district collecting land debts, that is, taxes on the land. They can homestead it and hold it for a lifetime and then collect the debt from the heir.

landing jack *noun* A member of a logging team that **skids** logs downhill.

2009 Lloyd *Tremont* 35 A skidder team included a bell boy, a fireman, a landing jack, two choker hookers, a jangle ball hooker, an engineer, and a foreman.

landing man *noun* See citation.

1994 Farwell and Buchanan *Logging Terms* = a member of a logging crew who [was] in charge of placing logs brought to a landing so that they could be easily rehandled or loaded by tongs onto a truck or rail car (the landing might be next to a railway, road, or stream).

land plane *noun* See citation.

1980 Riggleman *WV Mtneer* 126–27 [Loggers] usually had nicknames for everybody and everything around the camp.... A mattock was called a "land plane."

landside plow *noun* A type of **hillside** or **turner** plow.

1986 Pederson et al. *LAGS* (Claiborne Co TN) = a turning plow. **1998** Montgomery *Coll* = hillside plow, having a lever that switched the plow blade and turned the soil both directions (Adams),

= more commonly called hillside turning plow or tripwing turning plow, allowing soil to be turned down hill (Brown), = hillside plow (Cardwell), = a plow whose coulter could be turned over at the end of a row, so one didn't have to plow in circles (Weaver).

land sled *noun* A wide sled, as of logs, for hauling heavy objects over terrain too rough for wheeled vehicles. Also called **drag sled**, **dry-land sled**. See also **half sled**, **lizard 1**.

1961 Seeman *Arms of Mt* 17 We lugged all we could but had to leave most of the baggage to be dragged up in a "land sled"—an unwieldy cart, pegged together on wooden runners.

language out *verb phrase* To put (a message) into words.

1975 Chalmers *Better* 5 As Preacher Pink used to say, "Folks, I've got a good discourse if-n the Lord'll jest give me the words to language hit out."

lantern-jawed *adjective phrase* Having a protruding lower jaw. See also **jimber-jawed**, **whopper-jawed 1**.

1966–67 *DARE Survey* (Spruce Pine NC, Maryville TN) = having a lower jaw that sticks out prominently. **1996** Montgomery *Coll* (known to Adams).

lap[1]

A *noun* The top and branches of a tree left in the woods after logging or that have fallen. Also called **tree lap**.

1913 Kephart *Our Sthn High* 295–96 A treetop left on the ground after logging is called the lap. **c1926** Cox *Cullowhee Wordlist* = that part of the tree after the fallen log has been taken off. **1939** Hall *Coll* (Proctor NC) My dogs, they wouldn't run into the lap of it [a tree being cut with a raccoon]. **1941** Hall *Coll* (Alexander NC) "Trim up the lap of that tree" [means] cut the branches off the trunk of the tree. I've heared my pap tell me that. **1951** Giles *Harbin's Ridge* 74 By the light we could tell we were in a blowdown, with tree laps all around us. **1968** *Sang Season* 76 Along the craggy hillsides where ginseng might grow in the rich mould behind fallen chestnut laps, or under grapevine shade. **1974** Fink *Bits Mt Speech* 15 = tree tops and limbs left on the ground after cutting.

[cf OED3 *lop* n³ 1 "the smaller branches and twigs of trees"; cf EDD *lap* sb³ 2 "the lopped-off branches of trees"; DARE *lap* n especially South Midland]

B *verb*

1 Especially of a bear: to reach out and pull in a tree limb with its paw to eat acorns or nuts before they ripen and fall; to tear down (a limb of a tree, bush, or vine) to eat its nuts or fruit.

1926 Hunnicutt *Twenty Years* In the top of a large chestnut tree I saw a bear breaking chestnut burrs. I watched the bear lap the chestnut tree. **1939** Hall *Coll* (Deep Creek NC) One of my first cousins found a coon a-lapping a chestnut tree. **1956** Hall *Coll* (Big Creek NC) A bear had been a-walkin', I thought, goin' over there and lappin' chestnuts, eatin' chestnuts. You know, they just climb up a tree and break the limbs, as many as they thought they could eat, just get down and whack them off and eat them. **1976** *Bear Hunting* 281 If the nuts hadn't started falling yet, you might be able to find places where bears had climbed up into oak trees and broken limbs trying to get to them. . . . "We call it 'lapping.' I reckon what give it that name is a bear will just reach out and lap'em in."

2 To gather (vegetables, fruit, nuts, etc.) in one's apron.

1972 GSMNP-93:17 Then we used to [do what] we called lappin' chestnuts. We couldn't wait till they got ripe and fell out of the tree, you know, out of the burrs.

[probably variant of lop v "to cut off the branches, twigs, etc."; cf EDD *lap* v⁴ "to lop off branches of trees"; DARE *lap* v² especially Southern Appalachians, TX]

lap[2] *verb* To whip (a child); hence verbal noun *lapping* = a whipping. See also **larrup B**.

1927 Woofter *Dialect from WV* 359 = to whip with a stick. "The teacher lapped four of the scholars yesterday." *Ibid.* 359 *lapping* = whipping. "That girl needs a good lapping." **1975** Gainer *Speech Mtneer* 12 The teacher gave Harry a lappin'. **1995** Montgomery *Coll* (known to Brown, Cardwell).

[cf EDD *lap* v³ 1 "to flog, beat"]

lap[3] *verb* To wrap.

1930s (in **1944** Wentworth *ADD* 346) (eWV) = to wrap: "Lap up the groceries."

lap baby (also *lap child*) *noun* A small child still held in the lap; by extension = a spoiled child. See also **arm baby**, **knee baby**, **setalong child**.

1952 Wilson *Folk Speech NC* 556 *lap child* = a child small enough to sit on one's lap; a spoilt child of any size; a child that likes to sit on one's lap. **1970** Mull *Mt Yarns* 118–19 Babies were generally classified as "Breast Babies," "Lap Babies," or "Knee Babies." **c1975** Lunsford *It Used to Be* 179 The "lap baby" is one that you have to put to sleep on the lap. **1980** Matthews *Appal Physician* 153 Babies stayed on the breast from the time they became the lap baby until they were the knee baby, and even then they got some "ninnie" until they were shamed of it. **1997** Montgomery *Coll* (known to Brown, Bush, Cardwell, Oliver, Weaver); She's big as a cow [i.e. pregnant] and still has a lap baby (Norris).

[OED3 *lap-child* (at *lap* n¹ C1) obsolete; DARE *lap child* n South, South Midland]

lap organ *noun* See citation.

1939 Farr *TN Mt Regions* 91 = a baby: "His lap organ's playing."

lapping See **lap**[2].

lares See **lairs**.

larker *noun* See citation.

1921 Combs *Slang Survivals* 116 A "larker" in the hills is a shrewd, mischievous fellow.

larn See **learn**.

larning See **learning**.

larnt See **learn B**.

larp See also **larrup**.

A *noun* Usually a semi-liquid food such as gravy or syrup.

1915 Pollard *TN Mts* 242 = gravy. **1995–98** Montgomery *Coll*: *larp* = syrup. "Come eat with us if you like larp and bread" (Cardwell), = anything thick and runny (Oliver). **1998** Dabney *Smokehouse Ham* 361–62 Some mountain people loved a blackberry dish called "larp". . . . "We'd have a half gallon jar of larp for breakfast, along with biscuits and fried meat and sawmill gravy. The way Mother made larp, she'd take one of those half-gallon jars of blackberries and put it in the dish, along with a bit of flour and a sprinkling of sugar."

B *verb* To slurp (gravy).

1998 Montgomery *Coll* He larped up his gravy (Adams); He larped up the gravy and went for seconds (Cardwell).

larpin, **larping** See **larruping**.

larrip See **larrup**.

larriping See **larruping**.

larrup See also **larruping**.

A Variant form *larrip* [see **1995** in **B**], *larrip* [see **1995** in **B**].

B *verb* To strike, beat, whip; hence noun *larripin* = a beating. Same as **calarrup**. See also **lap**[2].

1859 Taliaferro *Fisher's River* 47 Put him up, and in the mornin', ef he ain't up to his eyes in corn and fodder, I'll larrup you well. **1950** Stuart *Hie Hunters* 168 If ye take another step, I'll larrup ye with this ear of corn right betwixt the eyes. **1973** Davis *'Pon My Honor* 31 She snatched the basket away from that gal and started in to larrupin her something awful. **1995** Montgomery *Coll*: *larripin* = a beating (Jones).

[cf OED3 *larrup* v "to beat, flog, thrash" dialect and colloquial, perhaps ultimately < Du *larpen* "to whip"; EDD *larruping* (at *larrup* v 1); Web3 n perhaps imitative]

C *noun*

1 A switch.

1938 Stuart *Dark Hills* (in **1944** Wentworth *ADD* 346) She'd use the larrup on us—right around the bare legs too.

2 Syrup.

1978 Parris *Mt Cooking* 168–69 "One of the things I do with blackberries," she said, "is to make blackberry larrup. . . . What you do is put on your berries and cook them until they get done and then you mix in some sugar and a little flour or cornstarch in. I always use the plain flour in mine. You stir that in until it thickens. Then you eat it with butter and biscuits. I also make strawberry larrup the same way. And peach larrup. Now, where that word larrup comes from I don't know."

larruping (also *larpin, larriping*) *adjective* Tasty, delicious; hence adverb = exceedingly (tasty or delicious, especially in phrase *larruping good*). See also **larrup**.

1961 Williams *Rhythm and Melody* 9 [The beans] will be larrupin' good fer sartain shore agin ye can step on the head o' yer shadder. **1967** *DARE Survey* (Maryville TN) *larrupin good*. **1975** Gainer *Speech Mtneer* 13 This pie is larpin' good. **1976** Garber *Mountain-ese* 51 I miss Ma's apple pie because it sure is larrupin' good. **c1982** Young *Colloquial Appal* 14 *larriping* = [having a] very good taste. **1995** Montgomery *Coll*: *larpin* (known to Shields), = good, great, as "We had a larping good time" (Cardwell); The jelly was larpin good on hot biscuits (Norris). **2005** Williams *Gratitude* 117 That really changed the flavor, and it was larpin' (delicious). *Ibid.* 505 *larpin'* = tastes extra special good, as: "That nanner puddin' was larpin'."

[Web3 *larruping* adv or adj "of notable quality or size" dialect]

lashhorn *noun* The Fraser fir (*Abies fraseri*). Same as **balsam 1**.

1878 Coale *Wilburn Waters* 19 The field . . . is bordered by . . . a growth of timber in that region known by the name of Lashorn. It is a species of and very much resembles Norway Spruce. . . . The lashorn of White Top is peculiar to that locality, and of the thousands that have been transplanted, not one has ever been known to grow, though some have lived several years. **1908** Britton *N Amer Trees* 76 This southern fir, also called . . . Lashhorn, occurs in the higher mountains of Virginia and West Virginia to North Carolina and Tennessee, where it sometimes forms forests, and reaches its maximum height of 25 meters. **1943** Peattie *Great Smokies* 197 The "heath balds," as botanists call them . . . can only be compared to the *krummholz* of the Alps, or the "lashorn thickets" of dwarf spruce on the high mountains of Virginia, all of which are practically impenetrable growths of scrub. [**1995** Montgomery *Coll* (unknown to consultants from the Smoky Mountains).]

[DARE *lashhorn* n Appalachians]

lashing(s) *noun* An abundance, plenty.

1939 *FWP Guide TN* 458 "Lashings" or "slathers" (liberal quantities) of sorghum, served with yellow butter on brown biscuits, battercakes, or flapjacks, is the "best eatin' ever intended to man." **1984** Wilder *You All Spoken* 71 *lashin's an' lavin's* = an abundance; plenty and some to spare; more than you can shake a stick at in a whole week. **1997** Montgomery *Coll* (known to Norris, Weaver).

[cf EDD *lashin(g) and lavins* (at *lashing* n 1) Scot, Irel, Engl; DARE *lashings* n especially South, South Midland]

lassengers See **molasses**.

lasses boiling See **molasses boil**.

lasses licking See **molasses licking**.

lassey See **molasses B**.

lassey cane See **molasses A**.

lassie See **molasses B**.

lassie making See **molasses boil**.

last[1]

A *noun* Variant plural form of two syllables: *last-es.*

1960 Sutherland *Folk Speech* 13 The old syllabic plural is retained in many words, especially in words ending in st, as beastes, nestes, postes, lastes, fastes. **1979** *Big South Fork OHP-9* He made shoes for people. He had the lastes and things. He used to make shoes for everybody in the country.

last[2]

A *verb* Variant third-singular form of two syllables: *last-es.* See also **-es**[2].

1971 *AOHP/ALC-260* I said farming just lastes a little while and hit's over. **1978** Montgomery *White Pine Coll* XII [At the annual festival] the parade like starts at ten o'clock of a morning, and it usually lastes just until ten that night.

B *adjective* (in phrase *the last* = every single).

1862 *Couch CW Letters* (Aug 9) I heard to day that our men taken a bout 200 waggons from the Yankees to day. We could of captured the last one of them if our Colonel could of had his own way. **1862** *Neves CW Letters* (March 30) old Eavens is a fixing to give them a brushing or run them all off or take them prisners, I hope he may kill the last one of them. **1862** *Patton CW Letters* (Jan 6) I hope they may kill the last one of them before they quit them. *Ibid.* (March 1) he will go through with it or loose the last man he has. **1867** Harris *Sut Lovingood* 97d [sic] [I] shuck hit up good, an jist drenched the durned big dromedary hoss with the last spoonful. **1900** Harben *N GA Sketches* 269 "Run an' tell yore pa they are all heer,—the last one of 'em, an' fer him to hurry right on to the house." **1923** Furman *Mothering* 117 This morning at recess I seed him whup out five-at-a-time. Yes, sir, five was on him, and by Ned if he didn't lay out the last one. **1930** Armstrong *This Day and Time* 150 I reckon the last one o' ye is starved to death. **1970** *Foxfire Interviews* A-70-75 I picked about the last one of them. **1983** Page and Wigginton *Aunt Arie* 95 Rabbits'll eat up ever sweet tater vine that's put out if you don't spray th'last one of'em. *Ibid.* 143 [They] enjoyed th'last bit of it. **1985** Irwin *Alex Stewart* 189 I saw Jim Maxie set down once with his hat full of pawpaws and eat the last one of them. **1987** Young *Lost Cove* 154 Tuther day [the cat] up and snuck into the hen house and killed half of Mandy's doodlings, then ruck all the fresh eggs out of the nest and broke the last one of them. **2012** *Blind Pig* (Oct 4) Have you ever known someone who sneezes every time they bend over—I mean every last time?

last button on Gabe's coat *noun phrase* All there is, the last piece or bit.

1915 Dingus *Word-List VA* 184 = the last of anything. **1957** Combs *Lg Sthn High: Idioms* 10 It's the last button on Gabe's coat. (The last of anything.). **1982** Slone *How We Talked* 19 = all there is. I am sure that at some time there was a man named Gabe, and for some reason this phrase got to be used; the reason lost in the past, the saying still used.

lastest *adjective* Last. See also **-est 3**.

1988 Smith *Fair and Tender* 14 I reckon that migt [sic] even of been the lastest time my Daddy ever lifted her up, or lifted ary thing else heavy.

last go trade *noun* See citations. See also **trade last**.

1956 McAtee *Some Dial NC* 26 = a compliment which will be imparted in exchange for one for the speaker. **1966** *DARE Survey* (Cherokee NC, Spruce Pine NC) = when someone wants to pass along a compliment about you in exchange for one about himself, he says, "I have a—for you." **1998** Montgomery *Coll* (known to Brown, Norris).

[variant of *trade-last*]

lastingest *adjective* Enduring the longest, most durable or memorable. See also **-est 1** and Grammar and Syntax §3.4.1.

1931 Goodrich *Mt Homespun* 46 "There now," said she, "that's twict as strong as 'twas before; squirrel hide is the lastin'est thing there is for to make a body a string." **c1940** Simms *Coll* the lastingest job. **1974** Roberts *Sang Branch* 27 The lastenest thing I can remember at school was the teacher's thrashing and whupping us.

lastly *adverb* At last, finally.

1944 Wentworth *ADD* 347 (WV) [You hunt & hunt] & lastly you see it.

last run *noun* Whiskey of the best quality, produced at the end of the distillation cycle. See also **run B2**.

1949 Arnow *Hunter's Horn* 42 "It's goen to be a shindig, all right," Jaw Buster promised. "You'll hear some real runnen, an I'll bet you a drink a J. D. Duffey's last run that old King Devil comes out."

lasty *adjective* Long-lasting, constant, durable.

1886 Smith *Southernisms* 38 *Endurable* for "durable," may still be heard in some parts of Tennessee, and no doubt elsewhere (Ohio). I heard myself last summer a "foot-washing" Baptist preacher in Craddock's Great Smoky Mountains say, "Stone is the most *lastiest*, the most *endurablest*, material there is." **1895** Edson and Fairchild *TN Mts* 372 = enduring. "They's the lastiest blossoms in the gyarden." **1930** (in **1952** Mathes *Tall Tales* 159) Made of genuwine walnut, the solidest, lastiest wood they is! **1937** Haun *Cocke Co* 8 That store-bought cloth never was very lasty anyhow. **1941** Still *Troublesome Creek* 36 A house proper to raise chaps in, a cellar for laying by food, and lasty neighbors. Now, that hain't asking for the moon-ball. **1943** Justus *Bluebird* 19 There's good heat in red cedar, and it's mighty lasty, too. **1961** Seeman *Arms of Mt* 19 Though every small boy in the mountains knows which kind of wood will burn down to make "lasty" coals, we have none of this lore. **1974** Fink *Bits Mt Speech* 15 Them was *lasty* britches.

[*last* n + *-y* adj forming suffix; EDD *lasty* adj Scot, nEngl; SND *lesty* (at *lest* v, n I); DARE *lasty* adj chiefly Appalachians, South Midland]

latch *verb* See citation. See also **latch string**.

1982 *Smokies Heritage* 67 = to lock up (as in the latch string on the cabin door).

latch pin *noun*

1 A safety pin.

1946 Matthias *Speech Pine Mt* 190 = safety pin: "I lost the button off'n my coat. You got a latch-pin?" **1975** Chalmers *Better* 8 One or two of the little girls had to be provided with improvised "under-pin[n]ing" when the every day clothes were exchanged for cheese cloth robes, and many were the "latch-pins" used in the process. **1997** Montgomery *Coll* (known to nine consultants from the Smoky Mountains). **2005** Williams *Gratitude* 50 She was careful about them big latch pins. As she took it out of the diaper, she'd pin one through her dress and latch it, an'en pin the other'ns through that'n.

[DARE *latch pin* n chiefly South Midland, old-fashioned]

2 A pin or peg to secure the front door of a house against outside entry. See also **latch string**.

1984 Wilder *You All Spoken* 32 = the wooden pin or peg over a door latch to keep it secured. **1997** Montgomery *Coll* (known to Brown).

latch string *noun* A string or leather cord used to lift an inside door latch from the outside; it can be pulled to the inside to secure the door against unwanted entrance or left outside, so that a visitor can pull it and open the door without knocking. The term is especially used in the phrase *(the) latchstring is out* = you are welcome to come in and visit at any time. See 1969, 1972 citations. See also **string latch**.

1881 Pierson *In the Brush* 52 His latch-string, made of hemp or flax that he has raised, or from the skin of the deer which he has pursued and slain in the chase, which, as the old song has it—"Hangs outside the door," symbolizes the cordial welcome and abounding hospitality to be found within. **1957** Parris *My Mts* 66 The latch-string hung outside and folks managed their time for a sight of visiting. **1969** Weslager *Log Cabin in America* 16 The door [of the log cabin] swung on wood hinges or strips of animal skin, which hung outside the door, and was usually mounted on the inside with a wood latch and crossbar. Attached to the latch, and threaded through a hole whittled in the door, was a string of buckskin which hung outside the door.... At night the string was drawn in through a hole and the door securely barred on the inside. The latchstring hanging outside the door became a symbol of pioneer hospitality. **1972** Cooper *NC Mt Folklore* 120 The heavy doors were hung on wooden hinges and had latches of wood, instead of doorknobs. From the latches, through a small hole in the doors, strong cords or leather strips, called latchstrings, hung outside. No visitor knocked on the door for admittance, for everyone in the mountains was familiar with the old rule that says, "Just pull the latchstring that hangs outside the door." **1998** Montgomery *Coll*: *the latchstring is out* is still used, according to five consultants from the Smoky Mountains, in the sense of "Come visit us anytime"; "The latchstring is always up and the welcome mat is out" (Cardwell). **2002** Myers *Best Yet Stories* 133 Before metal door knobs were available, early settlers used a latch string with which to "lock" or fasten outside doors. This cord was fastened to a moveable board that "bolted" or fastened the door on the inside. The latch string then threaded through a hole cut in the door several inches above the slot which held the moveable board. Pulling on this cord from the outside raised this board, thereby "unlocking" the door. To "lock" it, one simply pulled the latch string or cord to the inside.

lath-open bread *noun* See 1913 citation.

1913 Kephart *Our Sthn High* 293 Lath-open bread is made from biscuit dough, with soda and buttermilk, in the usual way, except that the shortening is worked in last. It is then baked in flat cakes, and has the peculiar property of parting into thin flakes when broken edgewise. I suspect that... lath-open bread denotes that it breaks into lath-like strips, but etymology cannot be pushed recklessly in the mountains, and I offer these clews as a mere surmise. **1998** Montgomery *Coll* (known to Brown, but not to other consultants from the Smoky Mountains).

latter days/years, in the *adverb phrase* In more recent times, nowadays; later.

1973 GSMNP-84:18 In the latter days it was horses, but back when I was a boy everything was oxens. **1974** GSMNP-50:2:8 Now in the latter days, on up in the twenties or the late teens and early twenties, the church went to calling pastors full time. **1989** *Matewan OHP-33* Then in latter days [the conviction] just come and the good Lord got to working on me. *Ibid.* 33 In latter years, that [= a realization] all come to me.

laundry powder *noun* Laundry detergent in powdered form (construed as a count noun; hence plural form *laundry powders*). Same as **washing powder**. For similar forms, see **powder A**.

2007 McMillon *Notes*: *laundry powders*.

laurel (also *laurel bush*) *noun* The evergreen rhododendron (*Rhododendron maximum* and *R. catawbiense*), which grows profusely at elevations below 5,000 feet and covers extensive tracts in thicket. Also used in compounds (as **laurel bed**, **mountain laurel**) and in place-names. See also **great rhododendron**, **rhododendron**, **rosebay rhododendron**.

1883 Zeigler and Grosscup *Heart of Alleghanies* 196 The arborescent kalmia and rhododendron, which grow along almost every mountain stream, have a practical use. The ivy and laurel, as they are locally called, attain, in some of the fertile coves, a diameter of three inches, and the roots are even larger. **1890** Carpenter *Thunderhead Peak* 142–43 There for the first time we saw the tangle of rhododendron which is called "laurel," and forms a dense thicket along all the mountain streams. **1937** Hall *Coll* (Cades Cove TN) We have white laurels and red laurels here in the mountains. **1982** Ginns *Snowbird Gravy* 130 The laurel, the "rhododendron," now they call it, won't poison 'em, but it'll just starve 'em to death. It'll just cause 'em to vomit all their eating up all the time. But what we called "ivy," what they call "laurel" now, it'd kill 'em dead. There was no way to save 'em when they'd eat a mess of it. **2001** Montgomery *Coll*: *laurel bush* (known to Cardwell).

[DARE *laurel* n 3 chiefly southern Appalachians, especially NC]

laurel bed (also *laurel hell*, *laurel patch*, *laurel rough*, *laurel slick*, *laurel* *thicket*) *noun* A dense, often extensive and impenetrable growth of **laurel** (i.e. rhododendron), **ivy** (i.e. laurel), and other plants. See 1999 citation. Also called **hell**, **jungle**, **lettuce bed**, **rough**, **slick A1**, **wooly B**, **yellow patch**.

1910 Smith *Tramping in Mts* 1 10 I have been many times before in the mountains without a canteen and have sometimes suffered intensely for water, because it was often so hard to climb down through almost impenetrable "laurel roughs" to the ravine where water is always to be had. **1921** Fink *Week in Smoky Range* 141 On the slopes and in the ravines are many "laurel-slicks," or patches of rhododendron, often many acres in extent, grown so thickly as to be impenetrable. **1939** Hall *Coll* (Proctor NC) [Kephart would] go out on them high knobs and look all about over them rough slicks, you know. We call 'em slicks, but it was just roughs, just laurel beds and ivy growed up, nothing in it hardly, just a tree once in a while. . . . The dogs, they just stove off the road into a little laurel patch, and there they jumped another big one [= a bear]. *Ibid.* (Cataloochee NC) We was in a laurel thicket. *Ibid.* (Hartford TN) He come up to a party [that] had been a-fightin' a bear with dogs, an' it had eaten up their dogs in a laurel bed. **1950** King and Stupka *Geology and Natural History* 42 Considerably different are other open areas on the ridge crests, the "heath balds," locally known as "laurel slicks." **1977** Hamilton *Mt Memories* 48 Far back in the big mountains were the infamous "laurel hells" where our tall laurel grew so thick with twisted branches, that a man venturing in there might never find his way out. **c1980** Campbell *Memories of Smoky* 220 They soon learn, often with sore muscles as a lingering reminder, that the so-called "laurel slicks" of the Smokies are far from being "slick" and that "laurel hells" make a much more accurate or descriptive name for what the botanists know as "heath balds." **1994** Beeson *Spirit of Adventure* 58–60) Well, after eating dinner on Guyot we struck a bearing to bring us out on the head of Big Creek, and slid straight down the mountain 4000 feet lying flat so as to slide under the limbs of the "laurel hells" as the thickets are called. **1999** Coggins *Place Names Smokies* 165 *laurel hell* = an area of thick, tangled, and almost impenetrable vegetation, mostly mountain laurel, rhododendron, dog-hobble, or similar dense, shrubby growth. **2017** *Blind Pig* (Jan 19) Anyone who doesn't understand why it is call a laurel "hell" needs to get lost in one of them. You lose all sense of direction. At night it is even worse. You can't see anything, and the only sounds you hear is your own heartbeat and breathing. You have to crawl along on the ground half the time and the rest of the time you are off the ground in the tangle of trees. People have been known to disappear into one and never be found. I can imagine Satan's abode itself being much the same. *Ibid.* The laurel hell is not an exaggeration. If you ever made the mistake of straying into a pure stand of mountain laurel up on a steep mountainside, you would quickly appreciate that it was indeed hellish, and do your utmost to backtrack out of there.

laurel bush See **laurel**.

laurel hell See **laurel bed**.

laurel lick See **lick B4**.

laurel patch, **laurel rough**, **laurel slick**, **laurel thicket** See **laurel bed**.

laurely *adjective* Covered with **laurel** (i.e. rhododendron).

1799 (in **2008** Ellison *High Vistas* 38) We turned back and camped at a very bad place, it being a steep Laurelly hollow. **1913** Kephart *Our Sthn High* 79 You see, the Tennessee side of the mountain is powerful steep and laurely, so 't man nor dog cain't git over it in lots o' places; that's where the bears den. **c1940** Simms *Coll* = covered with laurel. **1953** Hall *Coll* (Bryson City NC) It was so awful rough and laurely and not much open woods on that side of the mountain.

lausyday See **lawd a mercy**.

lavish *noun* An abundance, profusion.

1917 Kephart *Word-List* 414 = plenty. "If anybody wanted a history of this country for fifty years, he'd get a *lavish* of it by reading that mine-suit testimony." **1939** *FWP Guide NC* 98 A *smidgen* is a little, but a *slue* is a lot, and it might be a *lavish* or in some cases *a God's plenty*. **1944** Wilson *Word-List* 45 We have a lavish of fruit this year. **1974** Fink *Bits Mt Speech* 14 They was a *lavish* o' berries there. **1997** Montgomery *Coll* (known to Bush, Cardwell, Jones, Oliver). **1999** Morgan *Gap Creek* 114 Everybody thinks he hid a lavish of pension money somewhere.

[OED3 *lavish* n obsolete →1597; DARE *lavish* n 1 chiefly South Midland]

law[1] See **la**.

law[2]

A *noun*

1 (often *the law*) Federal or state law-enforcement officers collectively. Federal officers of the Bureau of Alcohol, Firearms, and Tobacco are also known as the **revenue** or **revenuers**.

1937 Hall *Coll* (Cades Cove TN) The law never raided many times. The state officers were stricter than the revenue. *Ibid.* (Gatlinburg TN) Shoot! The law couldn't do nothin' with [moonshiners on Cosby]. **1942** Thomas *Blue Ridge* 256 The revenooer (mountain folk usually call him the law). **1961** *Coe Ridge OHP*-342B These law shot him and killed him. **1983** *Dark Corner OHP*-3A We had the law so bad here without hiding up in the barn and jumping out of the barn. *Ibid.* 20A Lots of the law out at Greenville would come up there. **2009** Holbrook *Upheaval* 31 I'd as soon eat dirt as to give these like satisfaction.

2 An individual law-enforcement officer; hence plural *laws*. See also **county law**, **law dog**, **patrol**.

1979 *Big South Fork OHP*-11 He said, "Tell that law that I'll answer them in the boxcar when they come. **1983** *Dark Corner OHP*-20A Lots of laws from Greenville would come, and they'd have dinner. **1989** *Matewan OHP*-88 He was . . . a city law down there. **1991** Still *Wolfpen Notebooks* 115 Everybody got drunk, and they wasn't any Laws around, and we all had the best time ever was. **1998** *Dante OHP*-71 The laws didn't bother them around here too much. **2005** Williams *Gratitude* 505 = any member of law enforcement, whether city police, sheriff or deputy is "the law." **2007** Alexander *Moonshiners Gone* 186 The first thing in the mornin' you'll be a-runnin' to the laws.

3 In sayings. See citations.

c1940 Padelford *Notes* Mountain woman's man is her law and world. **1943** Hannum *Mt People* 83 Every man—at the head of his own house, the law in his own hollow—lived his own life.

B *verb* To sue, take to court; to engage in legal action.

1859 Taliaferro *Fisher's River* 185 He lawed the people at the justice's courts. **1913** Kephart *Our Sthn High* 320 If he or a kinsman be involved in "lawin'" with a member of some rival tribe, he does not look for impartial treatment. **1937** Hall *Coll* (Cades Cove TN) John Oliver, he's the one they lawed so much. *Ibid.* (Cataloochee NC) Calhoun was lawed for killin' a bear breakin' into his chicken house. Judge Webb told him to protect what he had. **1938** Simms *Coll* Why, they'd a-lawed us as well as churched us, if we'd a gone about in such garbs (shorts, slacks, bathing suits, etc.) as they now shamelessly strut about Gatlinburg. **1973** GSMNP-76:29 They lawed it two or three times, but you couldn't prove nothing on them. **1974–75** McCracken *Logging* 1:7 They lawed him and disallowed him to get off of his possessions, only to go to the store and post office. **1974** Roberts *Sang Branch* 6 They was a land company here in Harlan town claimed all the land they could get a claim on and tried to go over patents and get a clearer title to it. ... They lawed for that piece of land. **1978** Montgomery *White Pine Coll* VI-2 They got him up there in a cemetery and tied him to a tombstone. They lawed them over that, and I think they had to pay a fine. **1985** Irwin *Alex Stewart* 240 I guess he told the truth or they would have lawed him. **2004** Myers and Boyer *Walker Sisters* 6 When an otherwise honest, law-abiding citizen, whose children were starving and barefoot, was caught and "lawed" [for moonshining], it was hard to find a jury who would convict a mountaineer because jurors understood the circumstances.

[DARE *law* v 1 scattered, but more frequent South, South Midland]

lawd a mercy (also *lausyday, laws a mercy, lawsy me, lord-a-mercy, lord have mercy*) *interjection* Used to express surprise, consternation, or dismay, especially by older speakers. See also **ay, eh la, la, they**[3].

1859 Taliaferro *Fisher's River* 167 Lausyday, Hardy! is that you? **1901** Harben *Westerfelt* 272 Lawsy me, haven't I got a lots to tell you. **1931** Goodrich *Mt Homespun* 63 "How many drafts is they?" in response to a question from the little teacher. "Laws a marcy, honey!" **1972** *AOHP/ALC-276* Lawd a mercy, yes, what a different life people was a-living. **1972** GSMNP-68:10 Oh, laws a mercy, no, she seemed to be a real good Christian woman. **1977** McClelland *Wilson Douglas* 16 Lord-a-mercy, a dime was bigger than a million dollars!

law dog *noun* Used as a nickname for an agent for the Federal Bureau of Alcohol, Tobacco and Firearms. See also **law**[2] **A2.**

1976 Carter *Little Tree* 69 Grandpa said the law was just like hound dogs and had noses fer smell that could pick up a mash scent miles away. Granpa said he reckined that this was where the name "law dogs" come from. **1999** Carver *Branch Water Tales* 9 Shoot, ain't that old Luke Tester the meanest, vilest law dog that's been around here in a time and a time?

laws a mercy, lawsy me See **lawd a mercy.**

laxed privates *noun* See citation.

1990 Cavender *Folk Medical Lex* 26 = a prolapsed uterus.

lay[1] *verb*

1 (also *lay for*) To lie in wait; to lie in ambush for, plan revenge against.

1895 Edson and Fairchild *TN Mts* 372 *layin'* = lying in ambuscade. "He's a layin' to kill him." **1939** Hall *Coll* (Mt Sterling NC) How long did you lay to kill him? **1948** Chase *Grandfather Tales* 100 Way in the night some men come along, thought it was a highway robber layin' for 'em. **1977** Shackelford et al. *Our Appalachia* 58 If they found too many different men going to a woman's house after night they would lay for them and whip the woman, and the man too if they weren't afraid that he might be a little too formidable for them. **1998** Montgomery *Coll*: *lay for* (known to ten consultants from the Smoky Mountains); He lay for a good opportunity and it finally came (Cardwell).

[Web3 *lay* v 11 obsolete; DARE *lay for* v phr especially South, South Midland]

2 Of the wind: to abate, slacken. Same as **lie.**

1919 Combs *Word-List South* 34 = to lie (of the wind). "Wait till the wind lays." Knott Co [KY].

[cf DARE *lie* v 1 especially South]

3 To attribute (especially the paternity of a child).

1936 (in **1952** Mathes *Tall Tales* 215) Didn't ye know hit was bein' norated ye'd been killed, an' they was layin' it to Grannison here? **1957** Combs *Lg Sthn High: Word List* 58 = to swear to, in court (as of an illegitimate child). The mother of the child goes before the court and swears as to the father of her child. Ex.: "She laid the child to that railroader." A Tennessee mountain woman laid a child to a certain timid mountaineer, who was called into court to explain. On his return home, his wife met him at the door and stormed, "Well, what did they do?" He replied, "Did you know, that nasty-stinkin'-thing went and laid that brat to us?" **1975** Woolley *We Be Here* 14 I lay all that stuff on old Tony Boyle. **1982** Slone *How We Talked* 6 "Laying a child to someone" meant to tell who the father was. This phrase had its beginning before our folks left the "old country." Many times a poor girl, pretty enough to catch the eye of a rich neighbor, found herself pregnant and deserted. When the girl's father learned of it, he would take the baby and leave it at the door of the rich man. The guilty man would raise the baby as his own, never telling anyone that it really was his; she was "laying the baby to him."

[cf DARE *lay* v 2a chiefly South, South Midland]

4 To bet, wager.

1892 Fruit *KY Words* 230 "I lay you'll catch it," [is the] same as "I 'low you'll catch it" and "I'll be bound you'll catch it." **1912** Perrow *Songs and Rhymes* 138–39 Many old words appear, such as lay (wager).

lay[2]

A *noun* A turning lathe. See also **pole lay**.

1937 Eaton *Handicrafts* 151 The majority of chairmakers use simple equipment, some having no lathe for turning the posts, but those who make a number of chairs usually have some form of lathe or "lay," as it is often called in the Highlands. **1979** Slone *My Heart* 50 Some made beautiful chairs and fern stands with a "handmade lay" turned by a foot-powered pedal. **1982** Slone *How We Talked* 7 In making a chair the post was formed on a turning lay. **1997** Montgomery *Coll* (known to Brown, Bush, Jones, Norris, Weaver).

[SND *lay* n[2] 2; DARE *lay* n[2] South Midland, somewhat old-fashioned]

B *verb* To fashion wood with a lathe.

1961 Medford *History Haywood Co* 27 How many farmers today have used a poll axe, also "layed" and tempered in the blacksmith shop; or a wooden maul and gluts?

lay a caution on *verb phrase* See citation.

1984 Woods *WV Was Good* 230 *Laid a caution on him* meant he was alerted or warned.

lay (a) corpse *verb phrase* To lie dead, especially in being prepared for burial.

1936 Stuart *Head of Hollow* 292 They don't come when he lays a corpse and help lay him out for burial. **1944** Williams *Word-List Mts* 30 = idiom used to describe the wake for the dead body: "All the fam'bly gathered in when he lay a corpse." **c1960** Wilson *Coll* = to be a corpse laid out: "When Grandma laid a corpse, she looked so peaceful and rested." **1999** Morgan *Gap Creek* 109 There we was, in somebody else's house down in South Carolina, and him laying a corpse in the front bedroom. **2005** Williams *Gratitude* 505 *lay corpse* = be prepared for burial and placed in a coffin. "He *lay corpse* for two days."

[DARE *lay a corpse* v phr South Midland]

lay a gap in the fence See **gap 2**.

lay away *verb phrase* To bury (a person). Same as **put away**.

1956 Medford *Big Bend* The majority had been "laid away" without any rites.

lay back *verb phrase* To store, reserve (especially food) for the wintertime.

1979 *Smokies Heritage* 259 Thus, in this lull before winter, mountain folk began to "lay back" stores for the certain winter ahead—meats smoked and slated in murky smokehouses, apples and potatoes buried underground in a straw-lined bed, and precious dried "yarbs" (herbs) and wildflowers to make medicines for the wintry illnesses to come. **1991** Thomas *Sthn Appal* 55 We never laid nothin' back; we eat it an' got some more.

lay by

A *verb phrase*

1 To leave (a crop, especially of corn) to mature for the season after hoeing it for a final time in midsummer. See also **lay-by time**. [Editor's note: This phrase in the sense "to put aside for later use" is widespread in the US.]

1834 Crockett *Narrative* 154 Having laid by my crap, I went home, which was a distance of about a hundred and fifty miles. **1843** *McLean Diary* 84 [I] Laid by my Corn Staked Riders my wheet filed [= field] meusur my wheet 50 Dose. **1864** *Chapman CW Letters* (May 27) I finished my corn the first working about two ours ago and has laid buy my Irish potatoes. **1864** *Houston CW Letter* (May 3) that is a hard matter to get horses now till crops is laid by. **1881** Pierson *In the Brush* 80 The corn, which furnishes the most of their bread, is raised with but little labor. After it is planted it is plowed or cultivated, and "laid by" without any hoeing at all. **1905** *Cole Letters* 80 Soon as crops is laid by if I live expecting to here from you soon I remain your son. **1915** Dingus *Word-List VA* 184 = to finish the cultivation of with plow, hoe, etc. **1921** Campbell *Sthn Highlander* 134 Making the crop is not all a spring festival, however. The whole must be gone over at least three times with the hoes, chopping out grass and weeds and hilling the earth up to the plants. It is delving hard work for women and children before the last plantings are "laid by" to grow without further cultivating in the intense heat of middle July. **1953** Hall *Coll* (Bryson City NC) He'd take care of that ontil he got through and got his crop laid by. He'd generally git done laying by corn in the latter part of July. **1955** Dykeman *French Broad* 322 The third or fourth week in August, when crops were "laid by" and "garden truck" was at its most plentiful, families within a radius of many miles put finishing touches on their arrangement to attend camp meetings. **1967** Wilson *Folkways Mammoth Cave* 30 = to give corn its last plowing, by throwing dirt toward the stalks. **1976** Carter *Little Tree* 90 "Laying-by" time was usually in August. That was the time of the year when farmers were done with plowing and hoeing weeds out of their crops four or five times, and the crops was big enough now that they "laid by," that is, no hoeing or plowing while the crops ripened and they waited to do the gathering. **1979** Smith *White Rock* 47 All cornfields were hoed at least three times; the last time was called "laying it by." **1995** Weber *Rugged Hills* 67 "Well," someone will say, "the corn is 'laid-by' for this year." What they mean is that there will be no more hoeing or cultivating. Crops are now tall enough so that they won't be crowded out by weeds. Any weeds growing in the rows will be left where they are. **2005** Williams *Gratitude* 504 After the corn had been hoed three times, it was said to be laid by (not hoed again).

[DARE *lay by* v phr chiefly South, South Midland]

2 To plan, intend, decide.

1928 Thornburgh *Americans Forgot* 42 They had all kinds o' ruckeses and she laid by to divorce him. **1972** Cooper *NC Mt Folklore* 93 *laid by* = had intended.

B *noun* The final hoeing before a cultivated crop is left to mature in midsummer.

1860 Olmsted *Back Country* 222 Rye is sown in July, broadcast, among the growing corn, and incidentally covered with the plow and hoes at the "lay by" cultivation of the corn.

lay-by time (also *laying-by time*) *noun* A slack period between the final hoeing of a crop and its harvest. See also **lay by**.

1957 Parris *My Mts* 209 That's when it's laying-by-time, when the days whisper of autumn, when folks look to harvest and there's a rising joy in their hearts. **1982** Eller *Miners* 21–23 During the late summer, before the crops were harvested, families spent much of their "lay-by" time collecting ginseng, yellowroot, witch-hazel, sassafras, galax, golden-seal, and bloodroot. Most merchants were willing to accept these plants in exchange for commodities. **1984** Wilder *You All Spoken* 63 *lay by time* = usually from the Fourth of July to Labor Day; crop cultivation has about run its course, the last furrows have been busted, and there is a little slack before it's time to pull corn and pick cotton; now is time for fishing and for protracted meetings with dinner on the grounds.

lay down *verb phrase*

1 To surrender, give (something) up.

1984 GSMNP-153:56 Little Cataloochee Now in the latter days Daddy laid all of his drinking down.

2 To go to bed for the night. Same as **lie down**.

1962 Williams *Mtneers Mind Manners* 23 Since they must all get up early he "guesses" they had "better lay down." **1997** Montgomery *Coll* (known to Ledford). **2007** McMillon *Notes* = to go to bed.

3 To perform (a piece of music) in a lively manner.

1984 Head *Brogans* 20 Pappy could really lay down a tune while keeping time with his feet.

4 To shoot dead.

1977 *Jake Waldroop* 145 When [the bear] would come by one of 'em, why, he'd lay 'im down.

lay for See **lay[1] 1**.

lay in (also *lay into*) *verb phrase* To strike; to begin. See also **let in, let out, light in**.

1957 Parris *My Mts* 153 Course, I knew my pa would lay into me with a hickory if I smoked. I never started smokin' until I was about fifteen. **1992** Offutt *KY Straight* 43 The preacher laid in preaching and he went on till the lightning bugs had come and gone.

laying-by-time See **lay-by time**.

laying-off plow (also *lay-off plow*) *noun* A plow with a single long blade used to make or **lay off** furrows, especially for planting corn. Same as **bull tongue**.

1966–68 *DARE Survey* (Highlands NC) layoff or single foot [plow]; (Big Stone Gap VA) = same as bull-tongue plow, made a furrow in which beans or corn was planted. **1967** Key *Tobacco Vocab* 178 (DARE) They used to lay the rows off with a mule . . . [using] a layoff plow. **1973** GSMNP-4:1:10 It wasn't a turning plow, you know. It's just a straight, [what] most people call layoff plow now. **1986** Pederson et al. *LAGS*: *lay(ing)-off plow* = attested by 7/60 interviewees (11.7%) from E TN and 1/35 (2.9%) from N GA; 8/10 of all LAGS (80%) interviewees attesting term were from Appalachia. **1997** Montgomery *Coll* (known to eight consultants from the Smoky Mountains).

laying-out board *noun* Also called **cooling board**. See also **lay out 2**.

1994 Crissman *Death and Dying* 29 The method most frequently employed in preparing a body was placing it on a "cooling board" (sometimes called a "laying out board"), which has been described as "a board covered with a sheet," "two boards put together," "a scaffold of boards with a sheet," "a big wide board," and "a wide board." **2006** *Encycl Appalachia* 856 The early mountaineers placed the body on what was called a "cooling board" or "laying out board." It was generally a door removed from the hinges for temporary use or a special piece of wood designed for the purpose of "laying out" the deceased.

lay in the shade *verb phrase* See citation.

1984 Woods *WV Was Good* 228 When it comes to scorin' and hewin' crossties, no man would lay him in the shade. (*Laid in the shade* means *being outdone by another person*.)

lay into See **lay in**.

lay off *verb phrase*

1 To plan, intend (to do something) at some indefinite time in the future; to procrastinate, put off till later, or pretend to have an intention. See also **lay out 8**.

1883 Murfree *Old Sledge* 549 Thar is a word ez we hev laid off ter ax yer. **1891** Brown *Dialect in TN* 174 To *lay off* to do a thing, means to intend to do it. **1913** Kephart *Our Sthn High* 297 I've laid off and laid off to fix that fence. **1915** Dingus *Word-List VA* 184 = to plan, intend: "I've been a layin' off all summer to come to see you." **1931** Combs *Lg Sthn High* 1310 Been a-layin' off to come, a good spell. **1962** Dykeman *Tall Woman* 272 We're laying off to go down and see Papa one day soon, and does it suit Mark, we'll stay on through the evening and come to the preaching. **1974** Fink *Bits Mt Speech* 15 I *laid off* to go a long time ago. **1975** Gainer *Witches Ghosts Signs* 13 = to procrastinate. "I've laid off goin' to town for a week." **1979** Carpenter *Walton War* 148 I've been layin' off to do that for days now. **1989** *Matewan OHP*-33 I've been laying off of going around to see him. **1997** Montgomery *Coll* I laid off and laid off to visit Aunt Phoebe, but never got around to it (Cardwell). **2009** Benfield *Mt Born* 165 = to procrastinate, with a reason. To do something is to have every intention of doing it. There is the understanding that whilst one has not yet accomplished the task, it is because one is planning just how to do it.

[DARE *lay off* v phr 3 chiefly South, South Midland]

2 To be absent from work because of illness, indolence, or other reason. See also **lay out 6, lie out A1**.

1939 Hall *Coll* (Deep Creek NC) He was on the sick-list, kinda layin' off.

[by extension from *lay off* "to take a break from work, be idle"]

3 To remove (an article of clothing).

1937 Hall *Coll* (Hartford TN) I crawled down through the alders by the river till I got fernent [the bear], and then I laid off my linen and swum across the river.

4 To lie down.

1940 Haun *Hawk's Done* 118 He let her lay off there in the kitchen, on the floor, and have the twins.

5 To mark (a field for planting, a burial plot, etc.) with a light plow; hence verbal noun *laying off*. See also **laying-off plow**.

1915 Dingus *Word-List VA* 184 = to make furrows for planting grain in. **1939** Hall *Coll* (White Oak NC) Lay off [is] runnin' the furrows before you plant. **1940** Hall *Coll* (Tobes Creek NC) = to make little rows through the field with a bull tongue [plow]. **1941** Hall *Coll* (Mitchell Co NC) Lay off to plant it so you can have straight rows to plow it by. **1963** Watkins and Watkins *Yesterday* 74 A well-trained horse or mule easily learned here [= north GA] the plowman wished him to walk, and he could even lay off rows in a field where there was nothing to go by except the distance from another row. If rows were laid off in a curved contour, the horse or the mule learned to follow the curve of the previous row. **1976** Ledford *Folk Vocabulary* 280 The one horse plow was used for "laying off" (preparing the rows for seeds). **1994** Crissman *Death and Dying* 54 Under the direction of an older or knowledgeable person, the site for the grave was selected and marked off with respect to length and width. This procedure was called "laying off the grave."

[DARE *lay off* v phr 2 South, South Midland]

6 To mark (a quilting pattern) so that the quilter(s) will consistently follow it.

1973 *AOHP/ASU-160* It's not been over two or three years since I helped quilt a quilt and put the lining in the frames and put the padding on it and put the top on and base the top around on the lining, and then you've got, you're ready to lay off whatever design you want on the quilt and sew it.

lay off on (also *lay onto*) *verb phrase* To blame (something) on (someone).

c1950 Adams *Grandpap* 234 The fox said it wudden his fault an' waked up the rabbit an' laid it off on it. **1973** *AOHP/ALC-259* They laid it [= the Depression] off on the Republican President. **1975** *AOHP/ALC-903* Every time a strike come, they lay it onto me.

lay-off plow See **laying-off plow**.

lay on *verb phrase* To require of, as a duty.

c1940 Padelford *Notes* Hit was laid on him to revenge his Paw.

lay onto See **lay off on**.

lay out *verb phrase*

1 To kill (game).

1939 Hall *Coll* (Smokemont NC) We looked all around the tree and atter while we found [a raccoon] with a flashlight, and we laid him out. **1976** *Bear Hunting* 261 [I've] got an old shotgun down there that's flat laid the bear out.

2 To prepare (a dead body) for the wake, traditionally done by neighbors of the family of the deceased. See also **cooling board**, **laying-out board**.

1962 Dykeman *Tall Woman* 138 They're washing her up and laying her out. . . . We've got your mama laid out neat and pretty in the white dress she was wedded in. **1972** Hall *Sayings* 92 A dog jumped a bear, and the bear went right over Uncle Proctor. Uncle Dan said, "Uncle Proctor would never be any whiter when he was laid out than he was then." **1993** Montell *Cumberland Country* 112 Many local people knew how to take charge of the body and prepare it for burial, a process known as "laying out the corpse." Depending on the gender of the dead person, two or more women or men of the community bathed the body, fixed the hair, and dressed the body for public viewing and interment. Family members seldom took part in these proceedings. After the bed linens had been changed, the room aired, and other household chores attended to, the body was placed on the bed to await the arrival of the casket, or coffin, as it was often called. **1997** Montgomery *Coll* He laid the body out while he made the coffin (Cardwell). **2002** Nelson *Turn Back* 154 After the preacher heard the news [of a death], my mother would get her camphor and strips of old sheets and go immediately to the home. Dad went too. What they did was called "laying them out." They dressed the corpse and then dad put a piece of metal about the size of a fifty-cent piece on the eyes. Mother would saturate the white cloth with the camphor and put on the face and hands. The camphor kept the flesh from turning blue and kept down the odor.

[DARE *lay out* v phr 1 chiefly Midland, South]

3 To camp (out), spend the night out of doors.

1862 *Click CW Letters* (Jan 16) we wold hafto lay out with out enny thing to sleep under and then we wold almost freas. **1864** *Dalton CW Letters* (Dec 15) you wrot that you had ben sick I was verry sorrow to hear that I expeck that night we Laid out was the cose of you being sick. **1915** Hall *Autobiog Claib Jones* 9 I lay out a week at a time by myself with my faithful dog as my companion. **1939** Hall *Coll* (Hartford TN) Me and a party were on Big Creek a-fishin', layin' out, campin' out in the woods, and we heard somethin' a-hollerin'. *Ibid.* (Mt Sterling NC) They had old flint rocks to strike fire out of when they lay out. **c1950** Adams *Grandpap* 128 They come to an old waste house that nobody'd lived in for a long time an' they decided to go in an' lay out in it. **1957** GSMNP-23:1:18 We'd go out there and lay out, just me and him ourself. **1960** McCaulley *Cades Cove* I've spent half of my life in Smoky Mountain, just laid out just everywhere night come on. **1964** Roberts *Hell-Fer-Sartin* 111 He just put up in an old wastehouse. He aimed to lay out in that house. **1977** Shackelford et al. *Our Appalachia* 203 They'd lay out in the hills and some of them could barely walk. **2005** Williams *Gratitude* 251 Sometimes on a Saturday night we'd load up and go over to Chogie and lay out (camp).

4 To hide, especially to avoid conscription authorities in Civil War times. Also called **lie out A2**.

1895 Edson and Fairchild *TN Mts* 375 "He lay out among the varmints"—of one hiding from recruiting officers during the war. **1930** Smith *Reminiscences* 8 [During the Civil War] there were many men laying out in the mountains to keep out of the army, and they often made a raid in the valley for provisions. **1931–34** Oliver *Sketches* 23 My father did not enlist in the Civil War. He would lay out and work in the fields of a day to make bread for his wife and children. **1939** Hall *Coll* (Hartford TN) We was layin' out in the mountains, what's known as the Bend of the River. **1973** GSMNP-5:1 Him and this Levi Shelton was a-laying out dodging the Civil

War. **1989** *Matewan OHP-9* I've heard granddaddy say his daddy laid out a many a nights [during the Civil War], yeah, on account of [being] afraid they'd kill him.

5 To interrupt (work, a school session, etc.); to cease. See also **lie out A1**.

1956 Hall *Coll* (Emerts Cove TN) I was falling a big chestnut tree, and it struck a dead locust which fell against me, and I had to lay out doing anything for two or three weeks. **1976** GSMNP-114:2 [School] lay out . . . two weeks to pull fodder, then another two weeks to pick peas.

6 To play truant (from school), especially by alleging illness. Same as **lie out A2**.

1949 Kurath *Word Geog East US* 79 Played truant . . . *lay out* (of school), *laid out* (of school) . . . in Western North Carolina and adjoining parts of Virginia and South Carolina lying between the Neuse and the Peedee. Scattering instances of *lay out* and *laid out* have also been noted on the James and the Rappahannock. **1952–57** (in **1973** McDavid and McDavid *Vocab E KY* 156) = attested by 25/52 (48.0%) of E KY speakers for the Linguistic Atlas of the North Central States. **1966** Dakin *Vocab Ohio River Valley* 512 In all of southern Kentucky, in the Mountains south of the upper Kentucky and Licking Rivers, and among older speakers in the southern Knobs the expression of the Carolinas and western Virginia *lay out* (of school) is usual. *Lay off* is occasional in the same areas. **1966** *DARE Survey* (Cherokee NC) = to stay away from school without an excuse. **1986** Pederson et al. *LAGS* = attested by 23/60 interviewees (38.3%) from E TN and 4/35 (11.4%) from N GA; 27/56 of all LAGS interviewees (48.2%) attesting term were from Appalachia. **1987** Carver *Regional Dialects* 177 To *lay out* of school (= to play truant or hooky), however, is an expression found almost exclusively in the southern Appalachians from western Virginia and eastern Kentucky to the piedmont of Georgia and South Carolina. **1998** Montgomery *Coll* He decided to lay out from school (Cardwell).

7 Of a garden plot: to lie fallow.

1961 Murry *Salt* 108 We let that lower end o' the garden lay out last summer. **1979** *Smokies Heritage* 85 It was common practice in those days to "rotate tending" of crops; that meant we let a field "lay out" without being tended. The weeds grew high and were then plowed under as a sort of natural fertilizer.

8 To intend, plan. See also **lay off 1**.

1891 Primer *Studies in WV* 169 "I had laid out to go to the Dunkards to-night" is a not infrequent expression. **c1960** Wilson *Coll* = to plan something that is to be done. **1997** Montgomery *Coll* (known to nine consultants from the Smoky Mountains).

[OED3 (at *lay* v[1] 38c) now dialect and U.S.; DARE *lay out* v phr 3 especially South Midland]

9 See citation.

c1960 Wilson *Coll* (or *lay out cold*) = to scold severely.

layout *noun* An organized group of people, crowd, an "outfit."

1864 Odell *CW Letters* (Nov 6) Tell tom that I want him to writ to mee An tell mee how he is gitting along with his Layout up at bristol. **1884** Murfree *In TN Mts* 143 He went thar one day when all them Peels, the whole lay-out, war gone down ter the Settlemint ter hear the rider preach. **1891** Brown *Dialect in TN* 175 *Lay-out*, a noun, seems to mean *crowd* in such expressions as, "he is big enough to whip the whole *lay-out*," that is, to whip the whole shebang, or whole number of them. **1957** Combs *Lg Sthn High: Word List* 58 = bunch, crowd, family. Ex.: "The whole Brown layout was there."

[DARE *layout* n 2 chiefly South, South Midland, West]

lay over

A *verb phrase* To delay consideration of (an issue).

1793 *French Broad Church Minutes* 18 Westly White is still absent his case is laid over till meeting in cource. **1804** *Paw Paw Hollow Church Minutes* 10 The church met at lions creek meeting house and after worship the case of Br Frank and his wife was laid over til the next meeting. **1832** *Providence Church Minutes* 23 then the case of Brs George W. Russell and Robert Gant to fill the office of a deacon Laid over till next Meting in Course. **1860** *Toe Valley Church Minutes* 48 Also the cace of Brother William Fox taking up and laid over untill our next meating.

B *noun* A deadfall trap. See **1952** Wilson *Folk Speech NC* 557–58 for extended discussion; used figuratively in phrase *layover(s) to catch meddlers* (and variants), as an evasive answer to a pointed question one does not wish to answer, equivalent to "mind your own business."

1886 Murfree *In the Clouds* 406 When asked what she was talking about she would only reply in [the] enigmatic phrase "Laros to ketch meddlers!" and shake her head unutterably. **1917** Kephart *Word-List* 414 = trap; dead-fall. "That's a *lay-over* to catch meddlers." **1927** Axley *Larrows* 408 When I was a small boy in the mountains of North Carolina, my own overinquisitiveness was sometimes met with an answer still a little different in phraseology from the ones mentioned. *Lay-overs to catch meddlers* is the style of the rebuke as I always heard it. **1978** Hiser *Quare Do's* 27 "What are you making, Uncle Bob?" I asked. I'd seen him melt lead and run out bullets for the hog rifle, but never silver ones. "A lay over to catch meddlers," he said, puffing on the fire with the bellows. **1994–97** Montgomery *Coll* (known to Adams, Brown, Cardwell).

[OED3 *layer-over* n dialect; EDD *lay-overs* Engl; DARE *layover(s) to catch meddlers* n chiefly South, South Midland]

layover(s) to catch meddlers See **lay over B**.

lays *noun* See citation.

1996 Montgomery *Coll* = gravy, "All they had for breakfast was lays and biscuits" (Cardwell).

lay the chunk *verb phrase* See citation.

1984 Woods *WV Was Good* 225 For a few days he worked for who laid the chunk.

[cf DARE (at *who laid the rail* phr 2) "very thoroughly, vigorously, or well; to an extreme degree" chiefly South, South Midland]

lay the worm *verb phrase* To set the outline of a **worm fence** and the bottom rail. See also **worm 2**.

1975 *Rail Fences* 124 First Millard put strings along the fence's path so we could stay on course. Then, using the string as a guide, he helped us lay the first zig-zag course which is called "laying the worm." Then we put a rock under the ends of each rail so that no rails would touch the ground and rot.

lay up *verb phrase*

1 To store, put in reserve, save.

1977 Shackelford et al. *Our Appalachia* 209 I lived in one camp a while and when they shut down a lot of these older heads would always lay up food. *Ibid.* 332 You had to spend that check each month and [were] not allowed to lay up any of it.

2 In phrase *lay (something) up against* = to hold (an action or offense) against (someone).

1913 Kephart *Our Sthn High* 123 Oh, we-uns don't lay that up agin the Government! **1994–97** Montgomery *Coll* (known to Brewer, Brown, Cardwell, Oliver, Weaver).

3 To construct (a house of logs, as by raising them into place).

1972 *AOHP/LJC*-104 There was a great big log house there, great big logs . . . poplar logs, and they'd hew them all out, you see, and they'd lay up a big house with a great big room.

layway *verb* To obstruct (a road or track) and lie in ambush; to ambush.

1896 Fox *Vendetta* 137 They bushwhacked us durin' the war, 'n' they've laywayed us 'n' shot us to pieces ever sence. **1913** Kephart *Our Sthn High* 339 He is regarded as a busybody or suspected as a spy, and is likely to be run out of the country or even "laywayed" and silenced forever. **1973** *AOHP/LJC*-350 If you did something to somebody, they'd do their very best to get even with you, and they'd layway you. **1973** *GSMNP*-88:76 They'd layway the road sometimes and ambush 'em and make 'em turn 'em loose. **1979** Slone *My Heart* 19 I lay waid him as he come back out of the holler. **1989** *Matewan OHP*-39 They was out there, the miners was, a-laywaying Number Three passenger train that come through Matewan at noon. **1994** Montgomery *Coll* (known to Cardwell).

[reversed compound; DARE *layway* v chiefly South Midland]

lazy gal (also *lazy wife*) *noun* See citation.

1944 Hayes *Word-List NC* 34 (*lazy gal, lazy wife*) = a bucket operated by ropes passing through pulleys, used to bring water from a distant spring.

lazy Jim (also *lazy John, lazy Tom*) *noun* See 1953 citation. See also **hand mill, hominy pounder, pounding mill, quern, slow John, tri-weekly.**

1952 Wilson *Folk Speech NC* 558 *lazy tom* = a water-run hominy beater. **1953** Wilburn *Pounding Mill* Fifteen years ago, when I first came into the Southern mountains, I heard at times of a mysterious machine whereby a pestle was worked up and down by waterpower. This was called a pounding-mill, or facetiously, a "lazy-John" or "tri-weekly." The descriptions given by old settlers were certainly genuine; and yet I could not get through my head how such a thing would work. Then, last summer, I found a real pounding-mill, within six miles of my residence, Bryson City. It is at the home of Telitha Bumgarner, on a branch of Deep Creek, and was made by her son, Jim. **2002** Oliver *Cooking and Living* 13 As soon as they got a cabin built and the farm started, the pioneers built a pounding or Lazy Jim Mill and let waterpower do the work for them. The most elemental of watermills, none are in existence today, but every pioneer farm had one for they were easy to build, and needed only a flowing stream to do the work. A bucket on one end of a long seesaw pole alternately filled with water and emptied itself as it became over-balanced. The pestle on the other end did the work through the up-&-down motion inherent in the system. These primitive mills made about 3 cycles per minute, producing about 3 gallons of cornmeal per day, with about one-half of the meal suitable for cornbread and the other half for chicken feed. The obvious value of the pounding mill was that it required no attention at all. The miller could pour corn into the mortar, turn water into the bucket, and go about his day's work elsewhere. Long ago, one old-timer said there were so many of these mills when he was a boy that they awakened him many mornings with their constant thumping. Obviously, every farm had a pounding mill. Seeing how easy they were to build, the Cherokees began to construct them, which greatly pleased the women whose duty it had been to laboriously grind corn by hand every day.

lazy John, lazy Tom See **lazy Jim.**

lazy wife See **lazy gal.**

lazy wife bean *noun* A legume planted next to the house so its beans can be picked with little effort.

1941 Still *Stir-Off* 1 He swept an arm toward gourds of lard, strings of lazy-wife beans. **c1975** Lunsford *It Used to Be* 36 They have what they call the "lazy wife" bean (that's the name of a bean), and I think that came from Kentucky. It's a bean that you plant on the side of the porch and it runs over the edge of the porch like a vine, an ornamental vine. The wife can go out on the porch and pick enough beans for the family just from the porch without having to go out in the fields. So we call those the "lazy wife" beans. **1998** Montgomery *Coll* = any pole bean, a bean that needs a pole to support its vines, could be planted along the porch to ward off sun. Three common pole beans were Kentucky Wonders, Blue Ribbons, and cornfield beans (Cardwell), = a pole bean, the longest of the greasy beans (Jones).

lead *noun* [rhymes with *bead*] A long ridge between two mountain summits or a flank extending to lower terrain from a main ridge; also used in place-names, as in *Campbell Lead* (TN). See 1956 citation.

1913 Kephart *Our Sthn High* 20 There are few "leads" rising gradually to their crests. Each and every one of these ridges is a Chinese wall magnified from altitudes of from a thousand to two thousand feet, and covered with thicket. **1929** *Fastnesses* The trail from Indian Gap to Clingman's Dome follows the State line, or "lead," as the natives call it, and winds through a magnificent balsam forest mixed liberally with birch, beech, and giant hemlock.

1937 Thornburgh *Great Smoky Mts* 91 Brushy in reality is a "lead" off from Le Conte, part of the same mountain formation. **1956** Fink *That's Why* 4 Lead is sometimes used for a long ridge or one connecting two prominent points, and generally bears the name of one of these, as Chapman Lead, on the north flank of Mt. Chapman, or the Pinnacle Lead, between the Greenbriar Pinnacle and Old Black. . . . You may hear a native refer to the mountains along the State line as "the main Smoky lead." **1967** Hall *Coll* (Townsend TN) On the other side of the Briar Ridge, they call this the Devil's Courthouse Lead . . . the next lead on the other side of the Devil's Courthouse. **1973** *GSMNP*-78:2 We was noticing the buildings that was being built back in the Mount Harris section coming in towards the Campbell Lead.

[DARE *lead* n 3 southern Appalachians]

leader *noun*

1 A tendon, ligament.

c1844 Beckner *Shane Interview* 241 [She] lived two or three days and would have survived [but] the leaders in the neck were cut [in the attack]. **1907** Dugger *Balsam Groves* 135 Clippersteel had Skipper cut a slot through one of the hams, between the bone and the leader, near the shank end, and hang it in front of the tents. **c1926** Bird *Cullowhee Wordlist* = tendon. "He cut one of the leaders on his wrist." **1938** Stuart *Dark Hills* 200 We went out behind the corn crib to skin the rabbits. . . . He cut the flesh through under the leader of the hind leg and hung it over the nail. **1990** Cavender *Folk Medical Lex* 26 *leaders* = tendons or ligaments, most frequently used in reference to the ligaments in the neck and ankle. **1994–97** Montgomery *Coll* (known to ten consultants from the Smoky Mountains).

[DARE *leader* n 1 South, South Midland]

2 See citation.

1883 Zeigler and Grosscup *Heart of Alleghanies* 50 The best hounds, known as the "leaders," were fastened to poles stuck in the ground at the corners of our lodge.

lead horse *noun* The member of a two-horse team, more often the left-side horse, that guides the direction of the other. See also **off horse**.

1949 Kurath *Word Geog East US* 31 The Midland has four different terms for the left-hand horse of a team, *lead-horse*, *near-horse*, *nigh-horse*, and *saddle-horse*. *Lead-horse* is the usual expression . . . in the southern Appalachians and Blue Ridge south of the Kanawha-James line. *Ibid.* 66 Another expression, *lead horse* (leader), is fully established in two large detached sections of the Midland: (1) in southwestern Pennsylvania, from the lower Susquehanna westward, and (2) in the Blue Ridge and the Appalachians south of the James and the Kanawha.

leafer See **lief**.

leaf fat See **leaf lard**.

leaf lard (also *leaf fat*) *noun* See citations.

c1950 Adams *Grandpap* 47 Then he made the old woman render out the leaf fat an' put it in a big crock an' he said to her, "Hit'll be good to grease our cabbage heads with." **1956** McAtee *Some Dial NC* 26 *leaf lard* = the masses of fat about the viscera of an animal carcass. **1957** Broaddus *Vocab Estill Co KY* 47 *leaf lard* = lard made from the big segment of fat round the intestines. **1996** Houk *Foods & Recipes* 18–19 The white, fluffy "leaf lard" from the entrails [of the hog] was considered the best for biscuits.

leaf peeper *noun* See citation.

2006 *Encycl Appalachia* 851 In autumn, the mountains attract droves of so-called "leaf peepers" (tourists who come to see the glorious fall colors). Residents of the region decorate more during this season than at any other time of the year. Homes and businesses are adorned with corn shocks, gourds of many colors, pumpkins, and commercially produced seasonal decorations.

leak of the house *noun phrase* The underedge of a roof where rainwater runs off; the runoff itself.

1942 Clark *Kentucky* 119 Rub a wart with the skin of a chicken gizzard, and bury the gizzard under a stone at "the leak of the house." **1946** Dudley *KY Words* 273 = the flow from a downspout or gutter (the gutter or spout itself?) ". . . a bucket under the leak of the house." **1982** Slone *How We Talked* 22 "Under the leak of a house"—Under the edge of the roof, where the rain ran off. Tubs or barrels were set here to catch rain water.

[DARE *leak* n especially KY]

lean *verb* Principal parts.

1 Variant past-tense forms *leant* [lɛnt], *lent*.

1939 Hall *Coll* [Bill Ramsey] leant down to get a mess of fish he left in the creek, when a panther darted out from a thicket and got him by the seat of the "britches." **1942** Hall *Phonetics Smoky Mts* [lɛnt]. **1962** Williams *Verbs Mt Speech* 17 The -d and -ed endings of past forms of verbs are frequently pronounced -t . . . *lean*, *lent*. **1978** Reese *Speech NE Tenn* 176 *leant* = attested by 4/12 (33.3%) speakers. **2009** Benfield *Mt Born* 150 The fellow looked all around, leant close to my father and muttered.

2 Variant past-participle forms *leant* [lent], *lent*.

[See **1962** in **1**.] **1983** Pyle *CCC 50th Anniv* A:2:19 If it was lent heavy either way . . . that's the way it would fall, but if the tree stood pretty straight, you looked for the hanging limbs on it.

[DARE *lean* v A both forms especially South, South Midland]

leaner *noun* One who has reservations about or wavers in making a religious commitment.

2008 Salsi *Ray Hicks* 83 There was no sneakin' off to hear another preacher. Somebody'd tell on ya if you went to check out another church. And the Prims didn't want no leaners either. Ya had to be clear whatcha believed with no question. If ya was a questionin' beliefs, ya was called a "leaner." The members, includin' your own kin, 'ud treat ya like you wasn't a good church-goer.

leap *verb* Variant past-tense and past-participle form *lope*.

1962 Williams *Verbs Mt Speech* 17 Verbs which retain either the strong preterites of Middle English or variant preterites of the

English dialects [including] Present—leap[,] Past—lope[,] Past Participle—lope.

learn *verb*

A Variant form *larn*. See also **book learning**.

1813 Hartsell *Memora* 114 On last Evning we Recived orders on the first Day of December to prerade Everey Company at nine oclock in the morning To larn the Deferent Steps and the Deferent fasings. **1862** *Lockmiller CW Letters* (Feb 1) i Was glad to hear from you but soraw to larn that you Was not Well. **1863** *Hawn CW Letters* (June 16) I got back to summerseet on Monday the 15 day and larnd you had started home on friday before. **1913** Kephart *Our Sthn High* 94 I've larned now whar they're crossin'. **1937** Thornburgh *Great Smoky Mts* 154 There'll be furriners larnin' my children a lot o' truck that won't do 'em a mite o' good. **1940** *Hall Coll* (White Oak NC) Eugene's gran'pap said "larn."

[DARE *learn* v especially South, South Midland]

B Principal parts.

1 Variant past-tense forms *larnt, learnt*.

1867 Harris *Sut Lovingood* 97d [sic] Well, arter I larnt what road they run thar line over, an all the pints ove the case, I went tu work tu gin both a skeer. **1883** Murfree *Old Sledge* 549 I larnt how ter play when I went down yander ter the Cross-Roads. **1925** Greer-Petrie *Angeline Hill Country* 135–36 We soon larnt to jump the minit we heerd 'em squawk. **1939** *Hall Coll* (Catons Grove TN) Back in my young days we couldn't get no doctors them days hardly ever, and we had to do our own doctoring and we learnt up. **1961** Williams *Content Mt Speech* 15 Her pap cussed the top of the house off when he larnt she was a-gittin' big. **1973** *GSMNP-79*:20 As a young child a-growing up I think all the mountain kids learnt to fish.

2 Variant past-participle and participial adjective forms *larnt, learnt*.

1863 *Vance Papers* (March 30) I have raised Robert Hall and learnt him his trade. **1881** Pierson *In the Brush* 251 He's a Scripter preacher. He's not a larnt man, but he's a real Scripter preacher. **1931** Goodrich *Mt Homespun* 59 "I knew in reason she'd catch on to it," said Hannah, "but she's learnt the quickest ever." **1937** *Hall Coll* (Big Creek NC) That's the way I was larnt to spin. **1982** Ginns *Snowbird Gravy* 153 All that there fancy—I call it fancy—but that's what they've learnt and what they know.

C Senses.

1 To teach (a skill, subject, etc.); to train, instruct.

1796 *Bent Creek Church Minutes* 18 query Wheather doth not god Require All persons to larne there Servents to Read the Scripture. **1860** *Week in Smokies* 125 I do declare I believe a body might larn a lawyer something, if he would only use his own eyes and sense. **1864** *Mangum CW Letters* (April 8) I will sind you a balled but I cannot send you the tune you can lern the song and I will lern you the tune when I sea you. **1864** *McGill CW Letters* (May 22) Sarah you and mother I want you to lern the children ther prares. **1900** Harben *N GA Sketches* 18 They l'arnt 'im to read an' always let 'im stan' dressed up in his long coat in the big front hall to invite quality folks in the house. **1913** Morley *Carolina Mts* 193 The girls of the mountains prefer machine-made cloth. "I can't learn her noway," the mother says of her daughter [who takes no interest in the loom]. **1937** *Hall Coll* (Cades Cove TN) The dog's been learned to fetch the cows. **1953** Atwood *Verbs East US* 17 In all areas [of the Atlantic states] *learnt* predominates markedly (being used by two thirds of the informants); in some sections (e.g. most of Va.) *learned* hardly occurs at all. **1978** Montgomery *White Pine Coll* X-2 [They'd] learn you to read a little and try to learn you to write just a little bit, learn you to spell. **1980** Miles *Verbs in Haywood Co* 87 I learned every one of my children to drive. **1989** *Matewan OHP-39* We was all learnt to run under the floor and get behind the chimleys [when the shooting started]. **2008** *Rosie Hicks* 1 That learned me a lesson.

[OED3 *learn* v 4 "to teach" 1382→]

2 To meet, become acquainted with (someone).

1939 *Hall Coll* (Little Cataloochee NC) Where did you learn him? **1982** Slone *How We Talked* 16 We don't say that we "met" someone, but that we "learned" them. "Have you learned the new girl at school? I learned her brother last year."

3 To tell, inform.

1863 *Shipman CW Letters* (May 27) I will Send you a few lines By Polk Which will Learn you that I am well.

learning *noun* Variant form *larning*.

1913 Kephart *Our Sthn High* 80 I reckon he'll pick up some larnin' in the next two or three days. **1934–47** *LAMSAS Appal* (Madison Co NC). **c1940** Padelford *Notes* I don't reckon the larnin' hurts 'em none—they soon fergit it all.

learn off *verb phrase* To learn quickly.

1924 Raine *Saddlebags* 99 Susie hain't been much to school, but she learned off. **1957** Combs *Lg Sthn High: Word List* 59 = to learn quickly, right off. **1997** *Montgomery Coll* (known to Brown, Bush).

learnt See **learn B**.

least *adjective*

1 Smallest. See also **least one B1**.

1863 *Robinson CW Letters* (Jan 2) I have got a ax for John & a littel paire of sizers for Susa & the least paire you ever saw fore Mary. **1863** Wilson *Confederate Private* 7 (Feb 19) I will let you now I have soal 8 of them shotes the 2 least ones at three dollars a pease. **1904–20** Kephart *Notebooks* 4:751 Them's the least hooks I ever seen. **1931** Goodrich *Mt Homespun* 59 They're the least hands ever I see, on a woman. **1943** Hannum *Mt People* 113 It was the mountain men, however, who decided that "yarbs hain't nary bit of use without jest a lease [sic] grain of whisky."

2 Especially of a child: youngest. See also **least one B2**.

1899 Frost *Sthn Mts* 10 [Our] children was all gals—all but the least one. **1956** *Hall Coll* (Roaring Fork TN) My least boy says, "one of them little bears is a-breathin' yet, Daddy." **1974** Fink *Bits Mt Speech* 15 He's their *least* boy. **1975** Purkey *Madison Co* 17 Each one, from the biggest to the least, was expected to shoulder his load.

[*least* is historically the superlative form of *less*; DARE *least* adj 1, 2 chiefly South Midland, especially southern Appalachians]

leastest

A *noun* The smallest amount.

1988 Smith *Fair and Tender* 75 He said it was the leastest he could do for such good biskits.

b *adjective* Smallest. See also **least 1**.

2009 Burton *Beech Mt Man* 3 Really, they was the two leastest guys in the world to whup. **2017** *Blind Pig* (June 30) That half feist has to be the leastest hunting dog I've ever seen.

least one *noun phrase*

A Variant form *least'un* [see **1962** in **B2**]. See also **one 1**.

B Senses.

1 A small child; the runt of a litter of animals. See also **least 1**.

1910 Weeks *Barbourville Word List* 456 Lincoln used to take the least ones on his knee. **1924** Raine *Saddlebags* 5 There's allus room for a few more, and the big 'uns can wait on the least ones. **1982** *Smokies Heritage* 157 The least ones were easily entertained with a taffy pull, though most of the glossy candy ended up in their hair rather than their mouths. **1990** Clouse *Wilder* 72 Sarah agreed to let us have the two least ones and the older girls 'til she gets settled up north. **1997** Montgomery *Coll* = runt of a litter (Ellis).

2 The youngest child of a family. See also **least 2**, **little one**, **young one**.

1937 Hall *Coll* (Maggie Valley NC) Their mother died when the least one was about two year old. **1943** Hannum *Mt People* 88 I had brought a present for the "least one," a little boy about four. **1962** Dykeman *Tall Woman* 68 She saw the figure of her least'un that had been buried years before during an awful siege of the bloody flux. **1975** Chalmers *Better* 10 The "least-un" was a chubby, brown-eyed girl of four.

least'un See **least one**.

leastways (also *less ways*) *adverb* At least, at any rate.

1888 Meriwether *Mt Life in TN* 460 It's me as orter have boot; leastways the swap orter be even. **1898** Elliott *Durket Sperret* 97 Leastways, she tuck Lizer Wilson 'long to do the peddlin' an' lead the nag. **1913** Kephart *Our Sthn High* 380 The Bible says they're human—leastways some says it does—so there'd orter be a place for them. **1931** Goodrich *Mt Homespun* 41 I can't stand it to live with any of 'em, leastways with my daughter-in-law. **1954** Arnow *Dollmaker* 27 She'll know, or leastways, Pop'll know it was a tale you told. **1963** Edwards *Gravel* 117 All up and down the river they has allus been moonshine stills, I reckon, leastways as fur back as I ever heerd tell. **1966** Dykeman *Far Family* 50 "Leastways I'm not heading up the United States Government with my ignorance," Aunt Tildy snorted. **1979** Slone *My Heart* 36 "A long trip to town and two dollars all went for nothin'," he laughed. "But less ways I won't haf'n to tell Maw after all." **1997** Montgomery *Coll*: *leastways* (known to ten consultants from the Smoky Mountains).

[OED3 *leastways* adv b dialect and vulgar; SND *leastways* (at *least* adv 2); EDD (at *least* adj 1(I)(a); CUD *leastways* (at *least* adj) "at any rate"; DARE *leastways* adv especially South, South Midland]

leather britches (also *leather breeches*, *leather britches beans*) *noun plural* Green beans threaded with a needle (as at a **bean stringing**) and hung to dry in the pod over a fireplace or elsewhere or by being laid on trays or scaffolds in the sun for later boiling, rehydrating, and consumption. See 1939, 1978, 1990 citations. Also called **hay bean**. See also **fodder(ed) bean**, **shab bean**, **shoestring bean**, **shuck bean**, **snap bean 2**.

1913 Kephart *Our Sthn High* 292 Beans dried in the pod, then boiled "hull and all," are called leather-breeches. **1939** Hall *Coll* (Hazel Creek NC) They'd dry their beans, yes. They'd dry leather britches beans they called it. I dry mine in the sun. My grandmother dried hers on a string, hung them up in the porch or around the fireplace and dried 'em. I still dry those leather britches beans. That's what they called 'em then. **1957** Parris *My Mts* 212 It's a flour sack filled with dried beans-in-the-hull which mountain folks call "leather-britches." **1963** Watkins and Watkins *Yesterday* 49 We took a big sewing needle and string bean pods on strings about a yard long and strung them on the porch until they was dry. "Then we pulled the beans, or leather breeches, off the strings and stored them in flour sacks. They was dry and brittle as shucks. Leather breeches had to soak for hours before they was cooked. Us children could smell the cooking leather britches as soon as we opened the front door when we come home from school, and we run for the big black pot and beans to eat between meals. Biled with a piece of sidemeat, the beans was good, but they always had a dry burned taste." **1975** Jackson *Unusual Words* 155 Dried beans had numerous names—*leather-britches*, *fodder beans*, *shuck beans*, and *dry hulls*. **1978** Montgomery *White Pine Coll* III-2 Our beans, we would dry them. They called them leather britches, and you'd string them on your string till you got something like a yard long, then you'd hang them in the smokehouse or somewhere when it was warm weather, and they'd dry out. Then all you'd have to do in the winter if you took a notion for green beans, why you could go get your leather britches and put them in the water and soak them overnight and you'd just have a livelier spell of green beans than you ever had when it come out of the garden. **1983** *Dark Corner OHP-4A* They dried beans thataway, string beans thataway. They called them leather britches, you know, just hang them up on a wall, and then you'd take and soak them in a little warm salty water before you get ready to cook them, salt them up, then throw in a pot, a big hunk of meat in there, best eatings you ever eat, called them leather britches. **1990** Oliver *Cooking Hazel Creek* 13 To preserve green beans through the winter they were sometimes strung on strong thread & hung up to dry to make leather-britches. When a settler wanted a mess of them during the winter they were unstrung, broken up, washed & put to soak for awhile, and then cooked like fresh green beans with fatback or streaky lean for seasoning. **1995** Williams *Smoky Mts Folklife* 99 Dried beans took two forms: "leather britches"—dried green beans—and "shucky beans"—dried beans that would later be shucked. **1997** Montgomery *Coll*: *leather britches* = also called *shelly beans* or *shucky beans* (Ellis). **1997** Nelson *Country Folklore* 48–49 The beans were canned. Beans were also strung on a thread and dried. These were called "leather britches" or "shucky beans." After they dried they were placed in flour sacks for winter use. **2002** Oliver *Cooking and Living* 44 To preserve green beans throughout the winter, they were sometimes strung on strong thread and hung up to dry to make leatherbritches. Some people hung them in the sun to dry, while others, saying sun drying gives them the wrong flavor, hung them inside the cabin or barn, up near the roof, where they wouldn't have to be brought in if it rained, for they must not get damp or wet after they have begun to dry. (The beans' strings had to be removed before they were strung.) When a settler wanted a mess of them, they were unstrung, broken up, washed very thoroughly, and put to soak for awhile for they are extremely hard and tough, like old leather. They were then cooked like fresh beans, only longer. Their flavor is decidedly different from that of fresh or canned beans, strong and smoky. In some areas of the Smokies they were called SHUCK or SHUCKIE BEANS, but never that along the [Little Tennessee] river [in NC]. **2006** *Encycl Appalachia* 954 The first method involved stringing whole, unbroken pods, like stringing popcorn for Christmas tree garlands. Using a big darning needle, the processor carefully inserted strong thread between the two middle beans in a pod. When the string of whole beans was three or four feet long, the thread was knotted and the string of beans hung to dry, traditionally in such places as the porch, from roof rafters, or on a wall behind a wood burning kitchen stove. The beans slowly dried, turned straw colored, and shriveled. **2011** Best *Bean Terminology*: *leather britches* = also called shucky beans, shuck beans, and in some areas, fodder beans, are made from full green beans which have been strung, broken into pieces, and then dried. Traditionally they are dried by running a needle and thread through each piece and hanging them up in long strings behind a wood cook stove to dry out as quickly as possible. They can also be dried by spreading them out in a green house on bed sheets, newspapers, or window screens. Still another way of drying them is putting them on window screens on a tin roof and bringing them in at night. . . . Once eaten almost every day during winter and spring, they are now served mostly on special days such as family reunions, weddings, anniversaries, Thanksgiving, Christmas, New Years and other holidays.

[so called because after hung up to dry they shrivel and resemble pants on a clothesline; DARE *leather breeches* n pl chiefly South Midland, especially southern Appalachians]

leave[1] See **lief**.

leave[2] *verb* To allow (to), permit (to) (used especially as an imperative).

1832 *McLean Diary* 12 Rigimantal Muster [I] Receved a How from James Corder and Left Whitman Westfall have the same price 1$. **1925** Furman *Glass Window* 6–7 If you do your work well-up all week, I may leave you go in of Saturdays to see 'em. **1927** Woofter *Dialect from WV* 359 *leave that rest a bit* = let the matter alone for a while. "Keep quiet, and leave that rest a bit." **1935** Sheppard *Cabins in Laurel* 213 He begs the sinners to "leave-go" their sins and come up and pray with the Saved. **1941** Stuart *Men of Mts* 217 I could see him take this mattock and cut the sprouts from the fence rows and leave the wild rose stems stand. **1952** Giles *40 Acres* 105 I says to myself if she fills [the glass] up agin they ain't nothin' I kin do but leave her think what she will. I cain't go no more of it! She filled it up, and I just left it stand. **c1959** Weals *Hillbilly Dict* 5 = let. "Leave me do that." **1989** Landry *Smoky Mt Interviews* 195 We just left him run loose. **1989** *Matewan OHP-28* To me it's necessary for women to leave their hair go. **1995** Adams *Come Go Home* 42 We're just going to leave him lay; he'll never know the difference.

[SND *leave* v[2] 1 "to give leave to, permit"; CUD *leave* v 2 "allow to, permit to"]

leave off *verb phrase* To relinquish, quit (a practice), stop (an activity); also *leave off of* = to disappear from.

c1938 (in **2005** Ballard and Chung *Arnow Stories* 110) Must be gettin near supper time. I think I'll leave off ironin'. **1976** Still *Pattern of Man* 1 I figure a small thrashing would make her leave off this foolish notion. **1976** Weals *It's Owin'* = quit. "If he'll leave off talking I'll try to explain it to him." **1979** Melton *'Pon My Honor* 100 He had told again how the letters G P C in the clouds had told him to leave off farming and go to preaching. **1982** *Foxfire VII* 205 The deacons talked with me and they said that if I'd leave that speaking in tongues off that I could stay with them. **1991** Thomas *Sthn Appal* 251 Well, th' spell left off a' that cow, an' she got all right, to milkin' good. **1997** Montgomery *Coll* (known to ten consultants from the Smoky Mountains).

[DARE *leave off* v phr 1 chiefly South, South Midland]

leave off of See **leave off**.

leave out *verb phrase* To depart, disappear; also *leave out of* = to depart from.

1917 (in **1944** Wentworth *ADD* 353) (sWV) = to leave (a place), go: "He left out yesterday." **1937** Hall *Coll* (Copeland Creek TN) They left out of here. **1939** Hall *Coll* (Nine Mile TN) He left out and went back around by the standers and then come back. **1955** Ritchie *Singing Family* 73 Then they finally all left out, and Katty flaxed about . . . blowing out lights . . . to save waste. **1968** Ferrell *Bear Tales* 38 If a man departs this life he is said to have "died out"; in case he merely changes his earthly residence, he is spoken of as having "left out." In other words, gone. **1973** *GSMNP-87:1:17* When the park come along Davis and them had to leave out. **1978** Montgomery *White Pine Coll* I-3 They go to the drugstore, and they discuss the world problems and leave out convincing themselves that they knew very little concerning the world problems, because everyone has a different idea. *Ibid.* V-3 Moonshining is just about left out. **1984** *GSMNP-153:17* They don't remember too much about leaving out from over there because they were still wearing their diapers when they left. **2009** Holbrook *Upheaval* 37 I don't fault Mommy for leaving out.

[DARE *leave out* v phr 1 South, South Midland]

leave out of See **leave out**.

leavings *noun* See citation.

2006 *Encycl Appalachia* 950 The pig as symbol and substance, as pet and provider, attained an exalted place among mountain dwellers, whites and blacks alike, whether they could afford to eat "high on the hog" (tenderloins, chops, hams) or only the "leavings" (intestines, jowls, feet).

lectric(k) See **electric.**

leetle See **little.**

left-hand plow *noun* A type of **turner** plow with the coulter fixed on the left side to enable one to plow in circles, usually from the outside to the inside of the field.

1986 Pederson et al. *LAGS* (Sevier Co TN).

leg

A See **bootleg.**

B *noun* Variant forms *lag, laig.*

1864 *Mangum CW Letters* (June 4) he had ben struck by two balls on the left sholder and lag tho did not disable him for duty. **1867** Harris *Sut Lovingood* 54 A young docter, wif ramrod laigs, lean'd toward me monstrus knowin like, an' sez he, "Clar case ove Delishus Tremenjus." **1940** Vincent *Us Mt Folks* 14 Now Lord, I ain't a-fearin' of this man, nor no man that walks on two laigs. **1942** Hall *Phonetics Smoky Mts* 20 [æ] is common also in . . . *leg.* **1972** Hall *Coll* (Avery Co NC) I'm so tard I feel like my laig strings is a-breakin'.

[DARE *laig* (at *leg* n) scattered, but more frequent South, South Midland]

C *verb* To pull the stem off a berry in picking and preparing it to be eaten.

1925 Dargan *Highland Annals* 209 Here's these gooseberries got to be legged 'fore I can git supper, so's I can cook 'em while I'm bakin bread, an' save stove-wood. **1997** Montgomery *Coll* (known to Brown, Bush).

legal *noun* Currency.

1996 Isbell *Last Chivaree* 41 They'd ride horses and mules from way off [to attend church]. Mama and them couldn't afford to pay the bishop in legal; they'd have to bring food. Called it a pounding.

leg bail *noun* in phrases *give leg bail, take leg bail* = to abscond, fail to appear in court.

1915 Hall *Autobiog Claib Jones* 21 The Captain's men returned our fire and then took leg-bail and fled to the woods. **1917** Kephart *Word-List* 414 = to abscond. "He *give* 'em *leg-bail* and lit out for home." **1996–97** Montgomery *Coll*: *give leg bail* (known to Brown, Bush).

legger See **bootlegger.**

legging See **bootleg C.**

len *noun* A lens. See citation.

1962 Wilson *Folkways Mammoth Cave* 47 Nouns ending in an *s* or an *s* sound in the singular were often regarded as plurals . . . sometimes one of these *s* nouns developed a new singular: *species, specie; lens, len.*

[back-formation from *lens*]

lengthways *adverb* Lengthwise.

1994 Montgomery *Coll* (known to Shields).

lent See **lean.**

lenth *noun* Length.

1864 Wilson *Confederate Private* 44 (March 31) if we stay hur eny lenth of time I wil try & get a pas & come hom if I can. **1891** Primer *Studies in WV* 166 The g disappears in words like *length, strength,* etc., which are pronounced (lenth, strenth, etc.). **1937–39** Hall *Coll* = used by all but educated speakers. **1952** Wilson *Folk Speech NC* 559.

leprechaun hat *noun* The tiny flower of the sourwood tree (*Oxydendrum arboreum*).

1996 Landry *Coll* They call them leprechaun hats. That's sourwood blooms.

less[1] See **unless.**

less[2] (also *lesser*) *adjective* Small(er), short(er).

1886 Smith *Sthn Dialect* 349 Less (not so tall). **1910** Weeks *Barbourville Word List* 456 = smaller: "Give me the less apple." **1940** Haun *Hawk's Done* 73 A Spirit is not any bigger nor any less than the body it comes from. **1940** Oakley *Roamin'/Restin'* 66 I said you Old Bull Fighter if I ever catch you again fighting a lesser ground hog than you are, I will kill you. **1997** Montgomery *Coll* (known to nine consultants from the Smoky Mountains). **2005** Williams *Gratitude* 27 The big long pieces a lumber was called planks, and the lesser'uns was boards.

[OED3 *less* adj 1a "with reference to material dimensions" obsolete; DARE *less* adj chiefly South Midland]

lessen (also *less'n, lessun*) *conjunction* Unless. See also **unlessen.**

1883 Bonner *Dialect Tales* 139–40 Lizy is different. Can't tell why, less'n 'tis that I went to camp-meetin' an' perfessed a while befo' she was born. **1896** *Word-List* 420 *lessen* = unless. "I'll send, *lessen* you want to go yourself." **1917** Kephart *Word-List* 414 *lessun* = unless. "Men don't do nothing for amusement, *lessun* they chew terbacky." **1936** (in **1952** Mathes *Tall Tales* 211) They can't convict no man of a killin' less'n they perduce the corpus delicti. **1955** Ritchie *Singing Family* 79 We didn't do nothing with him, less'n he told us to. **1975** Chalmers *Better* 66 Some of them were awful sully—wouldn't ever talk lessen there was need.

[DARE *lessen* conj1 chiefly South, South Midland]

lesser See **less**[2].

less'n See **lessen.**

lesson *noun* A turn in a **harp sing.** See citation.

1995 Williams *Smoky Mts Folklife* 44 Usually a single individual presides over the singing. This person is responsible for selecting the song leaders. Anyone is entitled to lead a "lesson." In the past, women did not usually take the role of song leader, but this is no longer true. Regulars often have their own favorite song, which they are expected to lead. Songs may also be dedicated to others (or the memories of others). Song leaders typically lead a couple of songs before sitting down again.

lessun See **lessen**.

less ways See **leastways**.

let *verb* To leave behind.

1863 *Click CW Letters* (Aug 11) if you take too much you wont let a bit for me.

let all holds go (also *let one's holds loose*) *verb phrase* To relinquish one's grip or restraint, let loose, put everything aside.

1859 Taliaferro *Fisher's River* 60 I jist let all holts go, and begun to jump right up and down. **1937** Hall *Coll* (Wears Cove TN) [The bear] let all holts loose, fell on a pine knot, and killed hissef. **1940** Hall *Coll* (Gatlinburg TN) So when the bear got in the right position, I pulled the trigger on it. It just let all holts go and fell over on two limbs there and just laid there, just as dead as it could be. **c1960** Wilson *Coll*: *let all holts loose* = be unhampered.

let down the gap See **gap 2**.

let drive See **drive B3**.

let go *adverb* See citation.

1895 Edson and Fairchild *TN Mts* 372 = say: "The road is back yander, let go abeout [sic] a mile."

let in (also *let in on, let in to*) *verb phrase* To make a start on, rush into; to assail, pounce on. See also **light in**.

1859 Taliaferro *Fisher's River* 217 Once, at a gathering, Long Jimmy let in on a large tray of hog's feet that was set on the table. **1904** Harben *Georgians* 143 He let in to cussin' wuss'n I ever heard anybody in my life. **1940** Haun *Hawk's Done* 97 Then he let in to fussing at me because I let her go over there to spend two weeks with Amy. **1979** *Big South Fork OHP-11* Did you kind of feel like letting into him for hitting you with the limb, or not? **1997** Montgomery *Coll*: *let in* (known to ten consultants from the Smoky Mountains).

[DARE *let in* v phr 1 especially South, South Midland]

let on *verb phrase*

1 To pretend, claim.

1826 Royall *Sketches* 58 When they would say pretense, they say lettinon, which is a word of very extensive use among them. It signifies a jest, and is used to express disapprobation and surprise; "you are just lettinon to rob them spoons—Polly is not mad, she is only lettinon." **c1844** Beckner *Shane Interview* 230 They told her they had killed her husband; but she knew better and only let on [that] she believed them. **1862** *Robinson CW Letters* (July 28) She lits on like She thinks a heep of me & when I told her that I was marred She took aharty cry about it. **1869** (in **1974** Harris *High Times* 216) The wimmen folks seems to think its something worth fightin for—so we must sorter "let on." **1966–67** *DARE Survey* (Brasstown NC, Spruce Pine NC, Maryville TN). **1969** GSMNP-37:2:29 They come there, both of them, and let on like they'd been out on a drunk. **1978** Montgomery *White Pine Coll* VIII-2 I don't think White Pine has grown near as much because of the interstate that this article let on like it had.

[OED3 *let on* (at *let* v[1]) originally dialect and U.S.; SND (at *lat* v B.2.11a); CUD *let on* (at *let*[1]) 2 "act in such a way as to suggest that something is the case"; HT *let on* "pretend"]

2 To divulge, disclose, betray.

c1844 Beckner *Shane Interview* 229 It was [the] Sabbath and I never let on or told a word of it. **1885** Murfree *Prophet* 65 I hed n't let on a word. **1886** Smith *Sthn Dialect* 349 They all have the authority of old or dialect English, or many of them belong to all parts of the South, if not elsewhere ... let on (as "I never let on"). **1901** Harben *Westerfelt* 11 I was afeerd, though I couldn't let on at the time. **1939** Hall *Coll* (Copeland Creek TN) I passed on up, and the last one I was aiming to trot on and not let on like I saw them. **1940** Haun *Hawk's Done* 120 Burt didn't let on like he heard. **1956** McAtee *Some Dial NC* 27 They were talking about me but I never let on that I heard them. **1976** Garber *Mountain-ese* 53 He's purty sick but he's too proud to let on. **1989** Giardina *Storming Heaven* 9 I got riled when he said that, though I never let on, I tried to tell myself that nothing was changed, except that my papaw was gone. **2012** Jourdan *Medicine Men* 148 I never let on to the kids that I was worried.

[OED3 *let on* (at *let* v[1]) "reveal, divulge" originally dialect and U.S.; SND (at *lat* v B.2.11b); CUD *let on* (at *let*[1]) 1 "show knowledge of, act in such a way as to reveal"; HT *let on* "disclose"]

let one's holds loose See **let all holds go**.

let out *verb phrase* To make a start. See also **let in**.

1955 Ritchie *Singing Family* 64 She let out to give her a piece of her mind then. **1970** *Hunting Stories* 79 We let out runnin' till we caught up t'where we could hear th'dogs barkin'. **1976** *Bear Hunting* 316 We let out and we carried [the bear] on out to the next ridge coming thisaway.

letter-mail *noun* See citation.

1944 Hayes *Word-List NC* 34 = a letter.

let the latch down in one's barn *verb phrase* To take advantage of, get the better of (someone) in a trade.

1939 Hall *Coll* "Well," he says, "I sure did fix up that old fellow that I traded with," said, "I let the latch down in his barn."

lettuce *noun* Construed as a count noun; hence *them lettuce* = those heads of lettuce.

1975 Schrock *Exam of Dialect* 470 Other singular nouns which are considered plural I have collected are *cheese* (*them cheese*) and *lettuce* (*them lettuce*).

lettuce bed *noun* Same as **laurel bed.**

1917 Kephart *Camping & Woodcraft* 2:24 Those great tracts of rhododendron . . . cover mile after mile of steep mountainside where few men have ever been. The natives call such wastes "laurel slicks," "woolly heads," "lettuce beds," "yaller patches," and "hells." **1939** Hall *Coll* (Nine Mile TN) We hit in after [the bear], and it wandered around through them roughs, what we called the lettuce beds. Dark catched us in there, [and] we let the bear get away.

lettuce saxifrage *noun* Same as **bear lettuce.**

1970 Campbell et al. *Smoky Mt Wildflowers* 56 Michaux's Saxifrage . . . Another common name is lettuce saxifrage. **1971** Hutchins *Hidden Valley* 48 Also growing along the stream is brook lettuce, known as "lettuce saxifrage" (*Micranthes micranthidifolia*), a very common plant that thrives in wet places.

[DARE *lettuce saxifrage* n chiefly Appalachians]

leucotha *noun*

A Variant form *leucothy* [see **1940** in **B**].

B (also *leucothy bush*) An evergreen shrub common in the mountains (*Leucothoe* spp). See also **dog hobble.**

1940 Oakley *Roamin'/Restin'* 78 Leucothy is a shrub sometime [sic] called dog hobble. **1975** Broome *Out under Smokies* 14 One of the mountain men replied, "'Leucothy,' that's what we calls it." **1997** Montgomery *Coll* = formerly known as *leucothy bush* (Cardwell).

leucothy (bush) See **leucotha.**

leve See **lief.**

level *noun* An area of flat land found in the mountains. See also **bench, flat.**

1924 Raine *Saddlebags* 10 As there is a little larger level where the branch runs into the creek, there we usually find the home, with a "picketin'" fence around all the level land.

level land *noun* Settled regions in the lowlands beyond the mountains. See also **flatlander**

c1900 (in **1997** Stoddart *Quare Women* 28) The die had already been cast for the young "quare women" from the "level land." They had made a decision to found a rural settlement and school. **1968** Clarke *Stuart's Kentucky* 195 Until the communication lines were fully open—although the traditional way of doing things was modified—the hill people made little conscious effort to imitate in their clothing or in any other phase of their living the ways of the people down in the level land.

lever *noun* See citation.

1895 Edson and Fairchild *TN Mts* 372 = the common expression at Roan Mountain [TN] for *hand-car.*

liars' bench *noun* Same as **loafers' bench.**

1994 Speer *Power to Create* 2 Throughout Appalachia there are countless "liar's benches" in front of country stores, front and back porches, and a host of other culturally appropriate places for "tellin' a good 'en." **2000** Carden *Mason Jars* 196 Stanley stared at the Liars' Bench guys who all nodded solemn as owls. **2006** *Encycl Appalachia* 166 In much of Appalachia, however, there remain more traditional gathering spots such as the country store, with traditional pot-bellied stoves inside and "liars' benches" outside on the porch for telling good stories.

libel (also *libill*) *noun* See citations.

1952 Wilson *Folk Speech NC* 559 *libel* = a paper signed by a man acknowledging that he has been guilty of making false statements against some person. **c1975** Lunsford *It Used to Be* 162 "Libill" is used for the term "libel," as a legal term. The expression would be used in this way, "I'll make him take the libill and his word will be no more account in court."

[DARE *libel* n B especially South Midland]

liberate (also *liberise, libertize*) *verb* Of a church congregation: to grant one the freedom to preach to it or at another local church when invited to do so.

1838 *Zion Church Minutes* 21 [The Church Conference] moved and seconded that Brother Elijah Laws is liberised by the church to exercise his gifts and to stop if the church thought proper. *Ibid.* 22 Brother James W. Ayers came forward and professed a public gift and is liberised by the church to exercise his gift an to stop if the church thought he was likely to do more harm than good. **1987** Dorgan *Glory to God* 84 [Many denominations of] Baptists have a formal status for such preachers-in-training. The Sardis Association of Old Regulars, for example, calls these men "liberated brethren." The names of individuals holding this title are published in the association's minutes, to let affiliate fellowships know that it is acceptable to call on these men to preach. Then when a local church ordains a "liberated brother," his name is moved to the "Ordained Ministers" list. **1989** Dorgan *Regular Baptists* 52 Thornton Union identifies these men in their association as "libertized ministers," meaning that they are at the liberty to preach when invited to do so by a local church. Sardis Association calls them "liberated brethren." In some cases they are apparently referred to as "licensed preachers"; however, they should not be compared to "licensed preachers" in the Methodist faith, for they have gone through no course of study and have been examined by no ecclesiastical body other than the membership of their local fellowship. The emphasis is upon that divine "call to preach." **2014** Montgomery *Doctrine* 144 = an official act of a church that grants permission to an unordained preacher to exercise his gift at other churches and meetings.

liberise, libertize See **liberate.**

libill See **libel.**

licen, licenger See **license.**

license *noun* Construed as a plural count noun; hence singular *licen* through back-formation; *licen* is also sometimes construed as plural (see 1989 citation), with the variant form *licenger* (see 1907 citation).

1867 Harris *Sut Lovingood* 42 Thinks I, ole feller, *if* you gain *this* suit, yu may ax Satun, when yu sees him, fur a par ove lisence tu practize at his cort. **1907** Dugger *Balsam Groves* 189 As he entered the tent, Skipper arose, and, extending his hand, said, "I got 'um, goody; her's yer licengers." **1941** (in **1944** Wentworth *ADD* 356) (eWV) *licen*. **1968** Vincent *Best Stories* 101 "Well," growled the Squire, "jis stick the license under the door, and consider yourselves man and wife. I'll pick them up in the morning." **1979** Slone *My Heart* 36 Lay them license there in the fire. **1989** Landry *Smoky Mt Interviews* 181 I reckon most of the deal in getting your licen is having the three dollars that it cost maybe to pay for 'em. . . . The fellow gives in the licen and the preacher signs 'em later, turns 'em back in to the county. **2007** Milnes *Signs Cures Witches* 158 Because the word molasses ends with an *s*, "they" (molasses) are regarded as plural. Used this way, people say of molasses, "They are good." . . . Similarly, because the word license ends with an *s* sound, in Appalachian dialect, "they" are needed for driving.

[DARE *license* n 1 chiefly South Midland]

lick

A *verb*

1 To deliver a sharp or heavy blow to, beat up (someone), defeat; hence noun *licking* = a beating, whipping. See also **lickenest**.

1873 Smith *Arp Peace Papers* 121 [The magazine] is krowin [sic] bigger than ever since we got licked. **1881** Pierson *In the Brush* 259 He told the boys if any of 'em would go down and lick that big feller he'd give him his gal, and a right smart chance of plunder. **1900** Harben *N GA Sketches* 204 To night exactly at eight oclock we are comin after you in full force to give you a sound lickin. **1956** McAtee *Some Dial NC* 15 Bob licked him to a fare-ye-well. **1975** Chalmers *Better* 66 A brash child is a-hurtin' for a licking. **1994** Rash *New Jesus* 101 All we got to do is start a trend. Then we got it licked. **2005** Williams *Gratitude* 136 Any body that knocked their milk over got a good lickin'.

2 In phrase *lick it* = to move, travel.

1884 Smith *Arp Scrap Book* 64 He rode seven miles and back as hard as he could lick it.

B *noun*

1 A blow or stroke, as with the hand or a sharp or heavy instrument.

1862 *Ingram CW Letters* (Sept 29) two of them was taken up and fetcht back this morning they formed a line of all the men here in camp and ran them threw and every man had a hickory and had to hit each of them one lick. **1939** Hall Coll (Proctor NC) "Just hack it down. It'll fall just in a minute. Just hack it," he says. I struck a few licks on it, and it was just a little birch. *Ibid.* (Sugarlands TN) I knocked [the bear] in the head ever so many licks before I could get it to roll over and hush hollerin'. **1985** Irwin *Alex Stewart* 89 I commenced driving and I hit that drill a hard lick and hit broke in two right above his hand just as smooth as if you'd took a saw and cut it off. **1994** Walker *Life History* 75 The first lick he throwed he hit that wildcat and knocked it out. **1998** *Dante OHP*-51 She give everybody else five licks, she was a hard teacher.

[DARE *lick* n 1 chiefly South, South Midland, TX, OK]

2 (usually in negative constructions) A small amount or portion.

1845 (in **1974** Harris *High Times* 46) The supper is made up by the fellers; every one fetches sumthin; sum a lick of meal. **1862** *Robinson CW Letters* (Sept 4) I told them that I would be damd if I would Stricke anuther lick. **1884** Murfree *In TN Mts* 83 He hain't struck a lick of work fur nigh on ter a month. **1900** Harben *N GA Sketches* 49 He never would work a lick. **1956** Hall Coll (Big Creek NC) He never worked a lick. **1972** *AOHP/LJC*-259 At the head of this hollow, they got every lick of the coal. **1976** Carter *Little Tree* 65 When he tasted of it, it didn't taste one lick damn different from all the other whiskey he made. **1994** Rash *New Jesus* 65 Dooley never could swim a lick. **2008** Terrell *Mt Lingo* You know exactly what a fellow means when he tells you that somebody "ain't got a lick a sense."

[DARE *lick* n 5 chiefly South, South Midland]

3 A low-lying spot with a saline spring where animals come to lick. See also **deer lick**, **suck 2**.

1878 Coale *Wilburn Waters* 42 He had gone out to a "lick" a little before night to look for deer. These licks, or low marshy places, where there are deposits of sulphur, salt, &c., and which deer love to frequent, are very numerous in all this mountain region. **1972** *AOHP/LJC*-205 What caused them to be named that, now Lick Branch over here was, they was a place over there [where] the water run over them rocks and the deer would go down and lick that water because it's sulfur and a salty taste. **1973** Ganier *Wildlife First Met* 70 Early history and land-grant deeds refer frequently to the presence of "Licks." These were usually spring-heads, to which the animals came to drink. In summer, the Buffalo after quenching their thirst, would then paw up the ground about the creekside to form a loblolly of mud in which to wallow. **2006** *WV Encycl* 483 Salt was a necessary and scarce commodity during frontier times and was recovered from various natural seeps known as "licks."

4 A supply of salt for ranging animals to lick as desired, often placed in a cavity cut into a log. See also **lick-log**.

1937 Hall Coll A laurel lick [is] where deer used to come [i.e. a salt lick placed in a laurel thicket]. **1995** Alexander *Mt Fever* 99 Our route took us out through his far fields known as Ned's Licks. "Licks" are spots where settlers call up their cattle—usually every Sunday—after scattering salt on logs and flat rocks. This ritual provides the animals vital salt and an opportunity for farmers to check on sick or injured animals and losses or additions to their herds.

5 A spring or small stream; also used in place-names.

1945 Stewart *Names on Land* 152 (DARE) Not all the springs were good for drinking; some had films of oil upon them, and some were brackish with salt. Near these last the clay was salt to the taste, and the buffalo and deer came there in hundreds to lick it. So these were the best hunting-grounds. They were called licks and that name survived upon many streams and towns. **1955** Zelinsky *Place-Name Generics* 331 (DARE) The use of lick as a full generic term for stream occurs in scattered localities in West Virginia and in the adjoining portions of Virginia, Kentucky, Ohio, and western Maryland—as well as in north-central Pennsylvania. **1966** Caudill *My Appalachia* 19 I took for granted the high mountains, the narrow, tight creek bottoms, which often were little more than ravines, and the clear licks and creeks, and supposed that all the world was that like I knew. *Ibid.* 24 Off we set, skirting Broomsedge Hill, and crossed the mountain to the schoolhouse that stood on the other side of Clover Lick Creek. **1992** Offutt *KY Straight* 78 Lower Lick fed into Clay Creek, and Wayne's brother lived on the fork.

[DARE *lick* n 8 chiefly Allegheny Mountains]

6 See citation.

1974 Fink *Bits Mt Speech* 15 = molasses. "Give him some *lick* for his dodger."

7 A talent, knack.

1884 Smith *Arp Scrap Book* 66 The furrows I left behind looked like the track of a crazy snake. I used to could plow, but it looks like I have lost the lick.

lick and a promise *noun phrase* Especially with reference to a household chore: slight and hasty work, a task done in a slipshod or perfunctory manner.

1943 Justus *Bluebird* 18 They've had no more than a lick-and-a promise with a broom for quite a spell. **1966** DARE Survey (Spruce Pine NC) *give something a lick and a promise* = to do a job without proper time or care. **1980** Brewer *Hit's Gettin'* A "lick and a promise" is what we do when we fix something temporarily. **1995** Montgomery *Coll* = a half-hearted effort (Cardwell).

lickenest *adjective* Of a schoolteacher: giving students the most corrective whippings. See also **lick A1**.

1916 Schockel *KY Mts* 124 In some districts it is still thought by the school trustee that "the lickenest [i.e. the one who administered the most whippings] teacher makes the knowinest younguns."

licker scrape *noun* A fight involving one or more intoxicated participants. Same as **whiskey scrape**. See also **scrape A**.

1864 *Matthews CW Letters* (March 1) the[y] corme in and tuck him to gale and when tha[y] got him ther tha[y] had that licker scrape a gin.

lick-log *noun* A log or post into which notches are cut or chopped to hold salt for ranging cattle; used in figurative phrases *stand up to the lick log, salt or no salt* = to stand firm; *up to the lick log* = at a moment of change or decision. See also **lick B4**.

1834 Crockett *Narrative* 170 From this place I returned home, leaving the people in a first-rate way; I was sure I would do a good business among them. At any rate, I was determined to stand up to my lick-log salt or no salt. **1939** Wilburn *Notes* Trip with Ranger Kirkland of 20-mile Creek. At Salt Gap made picture of 15-hole "lick-log." This was the center of grazing activities of several families on 20-mile creek and other[s] further down the Tennessee River. **1948** Dick *Dixie Frontier* 105 The other cattle and horses were allowed to run in the forest on the range. Small troughs were cut in the trunk of a fallen tree and occasionally salt was placed there, making what was known as a "lick log." This formed a sort of community center around which the stock ranged instead of scattering too far away. **c1960** Wilson *Coll* = a fallen tree with a place chopped out for salt for the cattle in the woods. **1962** Dykeman *Tall Woman* 290 "Why, you only pledged away your selfhood, son," Jesse Moore said, "your narrow little self for a larger manhood. And now you're up to the lick-log; you've been called to keep that pledge." **1996** GSMNPCOHP-1:2 They had what they called lick logs in down trees. They'd cut these places to put that salt. It'd last for several days.

[DARE *lick-log* n 1 and 2 chiefly South Midland]

lick one's calf over (also *lick that calf again*) *verb phrase* To redo a task that was done inadequately the first time.

1931 Combs *Lg Sthn High* 1307 Go back and lick your calf over (Do the job over). **1979** Smith *White Rock* 48 Occasionally one of us who did a shoddy job had to go back and lick his calf over. **1981** Whitener *Folk-Ways* 19 One member, a trifle confused as to the meaning of another's statement, asked for enlightenment in the following way: "You're going to have to lick that calf again." **1997** Montgomery *Coll lick one's calf over* (known to Adams, Brown, Bush, Cardwell, Ledford, Weaver). **2014** *WV Talk*: *lick your calf over* = have to re-do a piece of work. It refers to a cow licking its calf from top to bottom then over again.

[DARE *lick* v B4 South, South Midland]

licksplit *verb* To walk rapidly.

1931 Hannum *Thursday April* 11 You licksplit as fast as yore worthless legs'll tote you up to Penlin Graham's and carry Phoebus Woodley down hyere. **1972** Cooper *NC Mt Folklore* 94 *lick-splitting* = walking rapidly.

lick that calf again See **lick one's calf over**.

lick thumbs *verb phrase* See citations.

1958 Wood *Words from TN* 12 = to reach an agreement. "Let's lick thumbs and quit, [used] to settle accounts when the country doctor had an account against a farmer [who had brought] a ham or a load of hay or corn along, and neither had much records." **1997** Montgomery *Coll* (known to Brown, Bush).

lid *noun*

1 The cover of a book, especially the Bible.

1959 Pearsall *Little Smoky* The necessity of preaching the Bible "from lid to lid." **c1960** Wilson *Coll* You can't find that between the lids of the Bible. **1976** Still *Pattern of Man* 80 I'm a Bible worm. I've read it lid to lid. **1985** Irwin *Alex Stewart* 238 I've read the Bible from lid to lid several times, and they can't no preacher get up and take his text without me keeping up with him. **1997** Montgomery *Coll* (known to Adams, Brown, Bush, Cardwell, Jones, Ledford, Norris).

[DARE *lid* n B1 chiefly South Midland]

2 The large, heavy, flat top of a deadfall bear trap. See also **bear pen**.

1939 Hall *Coll* (Smokemont NC) They decided they'd build a pen. They went and cut 'em some logs, floored it, built one log high. Then they built a lid for it, took triggers, set that bear trap, baited it with a piece of beef . . . And he said he . . . had [the bear] mashed down flat till he couldn't get up on his feet to raise the lid up.

Lidgerwood skidder *noun* A type of large, powerful machine used in skidding and loading logs harvested from the forest. See 1979 citation.

1974–75 McCracken *Logging* 23:7–8 They come in there with Lidgerwoods and then [when] they come in there, they used what we call a groundhog. **1979** Parris *Logging by Cable* The Lidgerwood machine I worked on when I was with Suncrest had a 70-foot steel tower with a 12-foot base at the bottom that sat on the logging railroad track. It had an overhead cable that ran 5000 feet to where it passed around a tail tree at the height of 25 or 30 feet and then was carried to a stump or a tree in the rear to which it was made fast. The trolley which traveled back and forth on the main cable was operated by an out-haul rope and skidding line. The skidding line was carried to a log or logs which were attached to it by tongs or chokers. The Lidgerwood machine I worked on ran from one mountain to the top of another mountain, and it had a ridge to get over.

lie *verb* Of the wind: to abate, slacken. Same as **lay**[1] **2**.

1864 *Chapman CW Letters* (May 13) it is mity cold this evning [it] Will frost if it clears off and the wind Lies. **1986** Pederson et al. LAGS (Rabun Co GA, Bartow Co GA).

[DARE *lie* v 1 especially South]

liebill See **libel**.

lie detector *noun* Same as **gee-haw whimmy diddle**.

1997 Montgomery *Coll*: = so called because the user can control which direction it spins and can thus pretend it knows the truth from a lie (Jones).

lie down *verb phrase* To go to bed for the night. Same as **lay down 2**.

1886 Smith *Sthn Dialect* 343 Lie down (go to bed). **1931** Combs *Lg Sthn High* 1307 I b'leve I'll lie down (retire). **1997** Montgomery *Coll* (known to nine consultants from the Smoky Mountains).

[DARE *lie down* v phr 1 scattered, but chiefly South, South Midland]

lief (also *liefer*) *adverb*

A Variant forms *leafer* [see **1973** in **B**], *leave* [see **1962** in **B**], *leve* [see **1867** in **B**], *lieve, lif, live* [see **1863** in **B**].

1942 Hall *Phonetics Smoky Mts* 13 *Lief* [has] [lɪf] in the Great Smokies. **1969** Medford *Finis* 61 An' now, seein' that I've got 'im back, I jist as live keep 'im as not.

B Gladly, willingly, likely, rather (especially in phrases *as lief, just as leave* + verb, *just as lief*).

1863 *Owens CW Letters* (April 23) it seames like i never git to come home to see you and Wm I had as live be ded as to never git to see my famly. **1864** *C A Walker CW Letters* (April 25) I would just as leave been in there as any where the boys all behaved gallantly. **1867** Harris *Sut Lovingood* 164 He looked at me like he wer sorry fur me, an' wud es leve pray fur me es not, an' went an' dipt his hed in the branch. **1896** Fox *Vendetta* 122 I reckon he'd jes as lieve have me ride him as you, Jas. **1904–20** Kephart *Notebooks* 2:642 Liefer as not, that's not so. *Ibid.* 4:855 I'd about as lief jump into a pant'er den in my shirt-tail. **1937** Hall *Coll* (Emerts Cove TN) I'd just as leave do that. **1962** Clark *Folk Speech NC* 314 *leave to* = just as soon do. **1973** Carpenter *Mid-Appal* 28 Such terms as leafer for would rather . . . are not corruptions in actuality, much as some of them may sound so; they are survivals from the past. **1983** Smith *Recollections of Blue Ridge* 13 I hated that job, I'd as lief not do it because I was ashamed to ride a mule. **1994–96** Montgomery *Coll* I'd just as lief hear a sow rub her ass as to hear a pianner, I'd just as leave go to hell as come to Gatlinburg in June (Cardwell). **2002** Rash *Foot in Eden* 133 I'd as lief it be the same now but I couldn't chance that.

[originally *would lief/liefer* "would gladly" but the auxiliary verb has largely been lost; *lief* is now confused with *leave* "permission, liberty"; DARE *lief* adv chiefly Northeast, Midland]

liefer See **lief**.

lie out

A *verb phrase*

1 To refrain from (especially work) on the pretext of illness. See also **lay off 2**, **lay out 6**.

1998 Montgomery *Coll* (known to Brown, Bush, Ellis, Oliver, Weaver).

[DARE *lie out* v phr 2 South, South Midland, especially southern Appalachians, GA, SC]

2 Same as **lay out 4**.

1863 *Brown CW Letters* (May 18) I Am beter Satisfied here than iwold at home and ly out.

B *noun* In Civil War times, a draft evader or deserter.

1864 *Cooper CW Letter* (June 28) the woods is full of Lyouts, some Bush whacken going on, a few killed on Both sides.

lie tale *noun* A false account. See also **tale**.

1940 Still *River of Earth* 31 "It's a lie-tale you heered," I said. **1968** Justus *It Happened* 17–18 Old Ben Bailey jumped up and down. "That's a lie-tale you're telling," he shouted.

lieve See **lief**.

life *noun* Variant plural form *lifes*.

1972 *AOHP/ALC-355* They stayed here, lived their lifes out, and then they'd quit and leave and go home.

life everlasting *noun*

1 A wild plant whose leaves are made into a medicinal tea or smoked to combat respiratory infections, apparently the same as **pearly everlasting**.

1939 Hall *Coll* (Catons Grove TN) Life everlastin', that's another good remedy for all colds and fevers, flu, pneumonia, a good remedy for . . . rub the breast good with turpentine and give good laxatives. Life everlastin' tea and balm of Gilead buds fried in fresh butter or sheep's tallow, boiled down and strained. It's the best tea, the best salve I've ever used. **1949** Arnow *Hunter's Horn* 373 She wanted to give all the [children] a round of molasses and wormseed and sulphur now, and then . . . some good strong tea made with life everlasting, sweet fennel, ratbane, and feverweed, for every last one of them was wormy as could be. **1962** Hunter *Folk Remedies* 97 The common cold has a wide variety of treatments. About the first one I can remember that we used at home was life-ever-lasting tea. Many people also smoked cigarettes made from life-ever-lasting. **1968** Clarke *Stuart's Kentucky* 200 Other weeds also have interesting folk names . . . life-everlasting, with its gray leaves resembling rabbits' tails, getting its name perhaps from its medicinal uses.

[so called because it keeps its form and color when dry; DARE *life everlasting* n 1 chiefly South, South Midland]

2 Cornmeal or flour mixed with gravy. See also **life saver**.

1978 Parris *Mt Cooking* 78 "Folks around here in the old days," she said, "they used to call it 'Life Everlasting,' because, they said, it had saved so many people's lives. It was just about all they had to eat. They make a meal on it and biscuits." **1984** Wilder *You All Spoken* 87 = gravy made from country ham grease, milk or water, and flour. **1998** Dabney *Smokehouse Ham* 217 The cheap, easy-to-fix cornmeal gravy caught on. While "sawmill gravy" was the popular nickname, some called it "Logging Gravy." Others called it Poor Do or Life Everlasting, a reference to what many felt was its role in keeping them alive.

life saver *noun* Gravy or potatoes eaten as food in impoverished times. See also **life everlasting 2**.

1939 Farr *TN Mt Regions* 91 = Irish potatoes: "We made a big crop of life savers." **1966** *DARE Survey* (Cherokee NC) = joking name for gravy. **1982** Slone *How We Talked* 33 = gravy (eaten as a dish, not as an additive).

lift *verb*

1 See citations.

1927 Woofter *Dialect from WV* 359 *lifted* = prepared. "Supper is lifted." **1952** Wilson *Folk Speech NC* 560 = to take food from a stove or fireplace to be served on the table. "Janie, lift the beans while I go get some onions."

[cf SND v 4(1) "to take up and convey"; DARE *lift* v 1b(2) especially Midland]

2 To settle or pay off (a debt).

1801 (in **1956** Eliason *Tarheel Talk* 281) (Burke Co NC) Lifted this Deed . . . & gave him a Deed for 311 acres in room of it. **1834** Crockett *Narrative* 19 He informed me that he owed a man . . . the sum of thirty-six dollars, and that if I would set in and work out the note, so as to lift it for him, he would discharge me from his service. **1861** *Hileman CW Letters* (Nov 6) lift Maththew Sheltmans 30$ and pay it over to his Mother. **1862** *Lockmiller CW Letters* (Sept 6) yew can take the mair up to o[w]ens and have shoos put on her and pay him $250 cents that I ow him and lift the note.

[cf SND v 4(2) "to take up, accept and pay (a bill of exchange)"; DARE *lift* v 2 especially South Midland]

3 Of a church: to take up (a collection).

1881 Pierson *In the Brush* 17 My friend with a speech to make reluctantly resumed his seat. I resumed and concluded my sermon, and was, in the vernacular of the people, about to "lift a Frontier collection." **1948** Dick *Dixie Frontier* 189 To denote the receiving of the offering, it was announced that the collection would be "lifted."

[SND *lift* v 4(4) "to collect money"]

lift, on the *adjective phrase*

1 Convalescing.

1892 Fruit *KY Words* 230 = convalescent: "He is on the lift." **1957** Broaddus *Vocab Estill Co KY* 53 = getting better after an illness. **1967** *DARE Survey* (Gatlinburg TN) – getting better after having been very sick.

2 Especially of a cow: weak or frail from sickness or old age.

1915 Dingus *Word-List VA* 184 = sick or very weak: "Old Pide [name of cow; pied?] is about on the lift." **1952** Wilson *Folk Speech NC* 560 = mainly of an animal: to be sick or injured to the point that the animal is unable to stand and must be lifted. **1962** Wilson *Folkways Mammoth Cave* 19 Sometimes an old nag, lovingly kept after her usefulness, had to be helped up when she was down; she was said to be *on the lift*; this expression was easily transferred to some elderly person or some chronic complainer. **1997** *Montgomery Coll* (known to Brown).

[SND (at *lift* v I.1.8); DARE *lift, on the* adj phr 1 chiefly South, South Midland]

light[1] See **light of the moon.**

light[2] (also *light and blow, light and come in, light and hitch, light and rest, light and set, light down*) *verb, verb phrase* To halt and dismount, step down or off, and rest or come into the house (used as a conventional greeting to stop and pay a visit, whether the person addressed was riding or not). See 1976 Weals citation.

1860 *Week in Smokies* 121 Light, stranger, light! **1867** Harris *Sut Lovingood* 49 Lite, lite, ole feller an' let that roan ove yourn blow a litil, an' I'll 'splain this cussed misfortnit affar. **1895** Edson and Fairchild *TN Mts* 374 Won't you light an' hitch to the post-and-railin'? **1914** Arthur *Western NC* 266 We invite you to "light" if you are riding or driving. [**1929** (in **1952** Mathes *Tall Tales* 99) "Howdy, doc! How's all?" Brinkley called them from his seat under the wagon bow. "'Bout as common, Harrison, Light and blow yer hosses."] **1935** Sheppard *Cabins in Laurel* 156 He greets you with "'Light and hitch!" or "Come in and warm," or "Set down and cool off," and urges you to stay for dinner. **1939** Farr *TN Mt Regions* 91 Hello, friend, light and set. **1944** Laughlin *Word-List Buncombe Co* 25 *light down* = to alight. **1958** Combs *Archaic English in KY* 38 = stop: "Light and spend the day." **1963** Edwards *Gravel* 171 "Light, boys; light and rest yer nags," said Doc . . . "Light and blow awhile." **1976** Thompson *Touching Home* 14 *light and come in* = to get out and come in. **1976** Weals *Two Minus* An old-timey mountain greeting to a visitor is, "Light and come in." It dates from the time when many travelers rode horseback, and fully spoken the greeting would be "Alight and come in." It is, however, also spoken to visitors who have arrived by walking. **1995** Montgomery *Coll*: *light and set* (known to Cardwell).

[shortening of *alight*; DARE *light* v[2] 1 scattered, but chiefly South, South Midland]

light and blow, **light and come in**, **light and hitch**, **light and rest**, **light and set** See **light**[2].

light a rag (also *light a shuck*) *verb phrase* To rush off, leave hurriedly. See 1956 citation. See also **borrow fire 1**, **cut a shuck**.

1913 Kephart Our Sthn High 297 He lit a rag fer home. **1955** Parris *Roaming Mts* 22 A man who jumps and runs has "lit a shuck for home." **1956** Hall *Coll* (Gatlinburg TN) In the old days a person would borrow fire from his neighbor by lighting a shuck of corn and hurrying home before the fire went out. Hence, "he lit a shuck" means went fast. **1961** Seeman *Arms of Mt* 93 Pete lit a rag fer the cabin, yellin', "Elviry! Elviry! Bresh me off!" **1983** Davis *Multi-lingual Mule* 5 He got his feet together and lit a shuck as fast as his trembling legs would carry him. **1997** Montgomery *Coll*: *light a shuck* (known to Adams, Brown, Bush, Jones, Ledford, Norris, Weaver). **2005** Williams *Gratitude* 506 *light a shuck* = get a move on, or cause somebody else to get a move on. Example: "Granny's going to *light a shuck* 'nunder your tail if you don't shake a leg." *Lit a shuck* means to take off quick—as in: "took off like Lindbergh, took off like a bat out of hades, or, took off like Snyder's pup."

[DARE *light a shuck* v phr South, South Midland]

light a shuck See **light a rag**.

light bread *noun* Bread made from wheat flour leavened with yeast, distinguished from heavier bread such as biscuit and corn bread. See also **loaf bread**, **wheat bread**.

1833 (in **1956** Eliason *Tarheel Talk* 281) (Burke Co NC) Supper litebread and butter. **1861** Painter *CW Letters* (Aug 22) we air fareing very [well] we get lite bread & bacon & rice & dride apples coffee beef sugar. **1864** Chapman *CW Letters* (May 10) we draw flower. crackers light bread sugar and coffee soap candles beans vinegar bacon beef pickel pork pepper &c. **1915** Dingus *Word-List VA* 185 = ordinary bread made with yeast, distinguished from biscuit. **1949** Kurath *Word Geog East US* 66. *Ibid.* 39 In the South and the South Midland . . . *light-bread* is the usual designation [for bread made from wheat and yeast], and this compound word is encountered up to the Pennsylvania line. **1966** Dakin *Vocab Ohio River Valley* 310 Kentucky has *light-bread* everywhere, but in this state where corn bread was (and is) more commonly eaten. **1968** Wilson *Folklore Mammoth Cave* 21 = any yeast-raised bread, to distinguish it from biscuit. **1973** Miller *English Unicoi Co* 149 = the wheat bread purchased at the store. **1982** Weals *Cove Lumber* The flour milling did not prove profitable. Cornbread was the bread of that time and place, and there was not yet much demand for "lightbread." **1990** Fisher *Preacher Stories* 25 In the economy of the mountains, most people ate cornbread at least twice a day. "Wheatbread," as it was sometimes called, was usually reserved for breakfast and many times only for special occasions, especially if it had yeast in it, in which case it was called "light bread." **1995** Williams *Smoky Mts Folklife* 92 Breads made from white flour, either homemade biscuits or store-purchased "light bread," were more prestigious than cornbread. **2016** Netherland *Appal Cooking* 45 Folks didn't make yeast breads nearly as often as quick breads and cornbread. But when we did, they seemed special. Any baked yeast loaf bread was called "light bread." In fact, any loaf bread purchased at the local store or supermarket we called light bread.

[DARE *light bread* n chiefly South, South Midland, TX, OK]

light down See **light**[2].

light entry *noun* See citation.

1973 Preston *Bituminous Term* 40 (eKY) = [an] air course [in a coal mine].

lightern See **lightwood**.

light in *verb phrase*

1 See **light off**.

2 To make a vigorous rush or hasty start. See also **lay in**, **let in**, **let out**.

1915 Dingus *Word-List VA* 185 = to begin work vigorously: "Light in and help me peel these apples." **1952** Wilson *Folk Speech NC* 560 *light in* = to begin. **1960** Miller *Pigeon's Roost* (Feb 25) She would crawl through a fence and slip into the 'tater patch—dig 'taters as fast as she could, in seven or eight hills; then she would light in and try to eat ever last one of 'em. **1961** *Coe Ridge OHP-340B* These other two Johns lit in to shooting him. **1983** Irwin *Guns and Gun-making* 51 If a body came by and wanted a hog rifle, he'd light in and make it from scratch. **2007** Shelby *Molly Whuppie* 31 Teddy and Taddy lit in to quarreling.

[DARE *light in* (at *light* v[2] 2) scattered, but especially South Atlantic, southern Appalachians]

lighting bug *noun* A firefly, lightning bug.

1982 Slone *How We Talked* 45 "Lighten' bug[s]" = . . . We loved to catch them and play with them. Sometimes we would rub the bugs on our finger-nails to make them glow in the dark.

light moon See **light of the moon**.

lightning (also *lightning liquor*, *liquid lightning*, *mule lightning*) *noun* Homemade whiskey. Same as **white lightning**.

1942 Robertson *Red Hills* 180 Bill fed the mules, cut stovewood, played on a banjo, drank lightning liquor, hunted possums, talked about the world and everything on the broad piazza. **1968** *DARE Survey* (Westover WV) *lightning*; (Marlinton WV, Spencer WV) *mule lightning*. **2007** Alexander *Moonshiners Gone* 29 People all over the United States, who had never heard the words "Moonshine" or "Liquid Lightning" suddenly came to know the terms as well about as well as they knew the names of their children.

lightning liquor See **lightning**.

lightning wood *noun* Small pieces of resinous wood to start a fire.

1986 Pederson et al. *LAGS* (Jefferson Co TN).

light off (also *light in*, *light out*, *light up*) *verb phrase* To move quickly, depart.

1895 Edson and Fairchild *TN Mts* 374 They jes squandered and lit out. **1913** Kephart *Our Sthn High* 297 I tuk my foot in my hand and lit out. **1939** Hall *Coll* (Cataloochee NC) He lit out and he was gone about three days and nights, come back in. He had a big horse. **1954** GSMNP-19:6 I lit out home next morning. **1978** Hiser *Quare Do's* 47 They lit off a that wagon and it [was hard] to tell which one was picking 'em and putting 'em down faster. **1979** *Big South Fork OHP*-10 We lit right out walking then, and then they sent another motor car to come and get us. **1985** Irwin *Alex Stewart* 86 I lit out a walking and I got over here about two miles from Jonesville, Virginia, and hit got dark and went to kinda drizzling rain. **1994–98** Montgomery *Coll*: *light in* (known to eight consultants from the Smoky Mountains); *light up* (known to Brown, Cardwell, Ellis, Jones, Oliver, Weaver). **1999** Morgan *Gap Creek* 57 I thought of packing up my things in the cardboard box and lighting out for home.

light of the moon (also *light moon*) *noun* The part of the lunar cycle between the new moon and the full moon, said to govern planting, domestic activities, the weaning or killing of animals, etc.; hence adjective *light* = of the moon: in the first half of a cycle. See citations. See also **dark of the moon**, **grow B2**, **shrink B**.

1873 Harney *Strange Land* 431 Leguminous plants must be set out in the light of the moon—tuberous, including potatoes, in the dark of that satellite. **1893** Wells *Superstitions* 299 What a vast array there is of credulous moon-observers, who scrupulously conform to all the phases of the moon, as essential to all their affairs of business. They will not have a roof placed on a building, nor their pork salted down, nor corn, beans, fruit-trees, or anything which bears its produce above ground, planted in "the dark of the moon," nor have a fence put up, or potatoes planted, or anything which yields edibles beneath the soil in "the light of the moon." It would be labor lost in all such cases; for the roof would curl and crack open; the fence would sink into the ground; the pork would rise out of the brine, even if weighted down; the vines would refuse to climb the supports or yield fruits, but would heedlessly run straggling about among the weeds; the esculent roots would disdain to bulb, and become spindly and worthless; in short, disaster would ensue in all directions, by "taking the moon crosswise," through negligence or willfulness. **1907** Parker *Folk-Lore of NC* 242 The moon seems to exert a powerful influence on many agricultural and domestic affairs. All plants which produce fruit above ground must be planted in the light of a moon, not necessarily in a new moon; and all plants which produce fruit underground, potatoes and such, must be planted in the dark of the moon. **1926** Lunsford *Folk-Lore* 13 The writer has been vanquished time and again in this goodly land with argument to the effect that the earth has corners and a foundation and that the moon is placed in the heavens for signs and that therefore the "twelve signs of the zodiac" may be absolutely relied upon as a true guide to poultry and hog raising, laying of worm fences, and planting of various crops. It is established beyond all question in some of our communities that the bottom rail of a worm fence should be laid upon the light of the moon and that the top rail should be laid in the dark of the moon so that the fence will thereby curl together so securely that a Wilkes County ox couldn't push it down. This same principle also governs the time for killing hogs in some communities, and a little laxity in the enforcement of this rule may even affect the taste of the "shortenin' bread." **1937** Hyatt *Kiverlid* 41 Can't hardly git grease out'n cracklin's if you kill a hog on the light moon. **1952** Giles *40 Acres* 96 We plant . . . things that ripen on the vine above the earth, in the light of the moon. And we plant . . . things which mature beneath the earth, in the dark of the moon. The theory is that in the light of the moon the pull is up, so things that ripen above the earth must be planted in the light of the moon to do well. **1955** Washburn *Country Doctor* 76 From Fonzo B. and others I learned that the moon exerts an "awful" influence on farming and on life in general. The rule to be followed is to plant root crops, such as potatoes and turnips, on the dark of the moon, while crops such as corn, peas, or beans, which bear fruit above the ground, should be planted on the light of the moon. Peanuts are an exception and should be planted at full moon or the pods will not fill up. **1976** Wolfram and Christian *Appal Speech* 171 He said if you killed it [= a hog] in light moon that the meat, when you fried it, would turn up around the edges. **1977** McClelland *Wilson Douglas* 18 If you put them [= roof boards] on when the moon is light, they'll curl up. **1978** Parris *Mt Cooking* 219 The light of the moon is the time for planting things that bear fruit above ground. **2007** Milnes *Signs Cures Witches* 35 Healing is best advanced in a light moon.

light out See **light off**.

light pine *noun* A knot or split piece from a pine wood rich in resin. See also **fat pine**, **lightwood torch**, **pine heart**, **rich pine**.

1914 Wilson *Sthn Mtneers* 72 The illumination was provided by beeswax tapers, or tallow dips, or "light pine" torches.

lights *noun* The lungs of a hog or bear eaten as a dish of food. See also **haslet(s)**, **liver and lights**.

1864 *Leigh CW Letters* (April 8) I have saw 40 wagons in a Company hunting corn and finding none when it comes to killing frames [= emaciated livestock] of Cows Just to get the liver & lites to eat you may say it is hard times. **1900** Harben *N GA Sketches* 149 I laid aside the lights o' that littlest shote an' firmly intended to ax you to fry 'em fer me. **1976** *Bear Hunting* 292 We gutted [the bear]—took everything out plumb to his goozle—ears, lights, liver, and all. **1997** Montgomery *Coll* (known to nine consultants from the Smoky Mountains). **2007** McMillon *Notes* = edible portion of a hog's lungs, but can also include the guts.

[from their lack of weight as compared to other animal organs; DARE *lights* n pl 1 scattered, but chiefly South, South Midland]

light up See **light off.**

lightwood *noun* Variant forms *litered* ['laɪtə·d], *lightern, light'ood.*

1864 Gilmore *Down in TN* 87 He war so cool he fruz the whole grave-yard so tight they hed ter thaw it out with light'ood. **c1975** Lunsford *It Used to Be* 177 "Litered" is the "light wood" they used to burn as a torch to go 'possum hunting and so on. **1992** Brooks *Sthn Stuff* 89 *lightern wood* = lightwood; any resinous wood used for kindling.

lightwood torch *noun* A torch made of a knot or split piece of resinous wood, usually pine. See also **fat pine, light pine, lightwood, pine heart, rich pine.**

1937 Wilburn *Notes* (Bradley Fork NC) After hunting with Tom Huskey one day I came home and found that my wife, who was visiting in Tennessee, was sick. I lit a lightwood torch and crossed the Smokies. I was at her bedside the next morning.

like See also **liked to.**

A Variant form *lack.*

1861 *Martin CW Letters* (Sept 29) the water we are geting to lack it beter but you never give up Pickens for no cuntry for the water is so good. **1863** *Lister CW Letters* (June 11) our compy had Lack to got ine the fite. **1895** *Mt Baptist Sermon* 13 Now I wanter tell you. Them folks is jist lack a ole hoss.

B *verb* (+ *preposition* or *adverbial*) with ellipsis of the following infinitive.

1975–76 Wolfram/Christian *WV Coll* 36 It [= the cat] liked around people.

C *noun* (in phrases *the like, the like of that*) So large or equal a number, so many, such a thing (especially in phrase *never see the like* or *never hear the like*).

1861 *Poteet CW Letters* (Aug 7) I supose the like never was knowd in the world. **1864** *Sullivan Co in CW II* 33 Apples has played out here but I never have seen the like of sweet potatoes in my life. **1873** Smith *Arp Peace Papers* 11 Feelin an intrust in the like of that, I stopt and listened. **1901** Harben *Westerfelt* 13 I'd 'a' told you before this but I 'lowed you was too young to heer the like. **1913** Kephart *Our Sthn High* 226 By God, I was expectin' to hear the like o' that! **1937** Hall *Coll* (Tight Run Branch NC) I never saw the like of soldiers in my life. **1969** Justus *Eben and Rattlesnake* 16 You don't mean it! I never heard the like in all my life! **1982** Weals *Hog or Cow Brute* There were many people in the mountains that did the like of that. They'd make moonshine liquor for a living and some would steal anything they could get hold of—a hog or a cow brute or anything. **1996** Landry *Coll* I never seen the like, I swanny.

D (+ *infinitive*) *adjective phrase* On the verge, in danger (of doing something) or appearing to be.

1862 *Copenhaver CW Letters* (Nov 6) I have never got with my company yet on the account of my hors he is like to die I am afraid I will loos him yet with the distempter.

-like *suffix, adverb* Seemingly, resembling, somewhat, rather, more or less (added to or following nouns, adjectives, and adverbs). See also **such like.**

1839 *McLean Diary* 65 Cool Like wether. **1923** (in **1952** Mathes *Tall Tales* 8) I'd allus heared him preachin' in his big roarin' voice, but that day he was plumb gentle, and his voice was soft and easy-like. **1929** (in **1952** Mathes *Tall Tales* 102) He's been our doctor here ever sinst I was a gallike. **1938** Bowman *High Horizons* 24 He'd been "careless like" with his first shot and couldn't reload his flintlock fast enough to end the wounded bear's agony. **1939** Hall *Coll* (Proctor NC) We didn't have no stove. We just cooked in a baker like. *Ibid.* (Hazel Creek NC) [I'll] tell you how the weather used to be back when I was a boy like and a man getting, a man grown. **1940** Haun *Hawk's Done* 34 The moon changed everything—the sweet williams smelt sweeter and it seemed like the air smelt more fresh-like. **c1945** Haun *Hawk's Done* 269 He come back into the house and looked at Froney real quare like and Froney bust out to crying. **1954** Arnow *Dollmaker* 256 A little peaked cedar like grows by th creek on a limerstone [sic] ledge. **1955** Ritchie *Singing Family* 91 Marthe was singing a high part-like, just sweet and cler as a whittle-ding. **1957** Combs *Lg Sthn High: Word List* 59 = a suffix often taking the place of some other suffix, or preceding modifier. Ex.: sick-like; blue-like; funny-like, for "a little sick," "somewhat blue," "a bit funny." **1959** Cooper *Corpse Could Sleep* My old man jist shut his eye peaceful-like and passed out as his speerit leapt beyant the furder bank of Jordan. **1971** *AOHP/ALC-139* He was an elderly-like man and had belonged to the church for years. **1972** *AOHP/ALC-226* He slipped around and filled his pockets full of walnuts with the hulls on, of course, and the hulls was crumbly like. **1973** *Florence and Lawton* 193 Some of'em 'ud be kind of music-like. **1973** *GSMNP-5:11* He was going to school at Big Catalooch when he was a young man like. **1978** Montgomery *White Pine Coll* III-2 He was so jolly, but he went right sudden like. **1983** Davis *Multi-lingual Mule* 39 Maybe I ought to do up the night work quick like while you stir up a bite to eat. **1997** Andrews *Mountain Vittles* 7 I guess to help make it a little bit more moist and tender like. **1998** *Dante OHP-71* Number Two [mine] was over in another hollow like.

[OED3 *-like* suffix 2a, originally and frequently Scot, now colloquial; SND *-like* suffix 1]

like a dog trotting *adverb phrase* Naturally, with ease.

1966 Medford *Ol' Starlin* 118 "Oh, she can reed it jist like dawg a-trottin'," replide the surveyor. **1978** Montgomery *White Pine Coll* X-2 Some people can work out something just like a dog a-trotting.

like a hen a-pecking *adverb phrase* Very fast.

1994–97 Montgomery *Coll* (known to Adams, Brown, Norris, Oliver); She went down that row like a hen a-peckin' (Cardwell).

like a scalded dog (also *like a scalded pup*) *adverb phrase* Very rapidly.

1939 Hall *Coll* (White Oak NC) That cat runs like a scalded dog. **1956** Hall *Coll* (Byrds Creek NC) He just took off like a scalded dog. **1992** Offutt *KY Straight* 138 I ran like a scalded pup and never told nobody.

like a yellow dog *adverb phrase* With contempt.

1929 (in **1952** Mathes *Tall Tales* 107) This, in substance, was the burden of the jilted one's original lament, but by the time it was bruited about for a week it was being indignantly told that "this here uppity furrin' woman jes' p'intedly ordered Doc Link out o' the house like a yaller dawg an' said she wouldn't let him doctor a sick hoss or a cow-brute of hern."

like common *adverb phrase* As usual, all right (especially in phrase *about like common* in response to a question about one's well-being). See also **common 1**.

1862 Robinson *CW Letters* (June 28) we had to make his compney up to 50 & it took 14 of us to do it & we had the privelidge of volenteaing & I was like Common the first man out thare. **1940** Haun *Hawk's Done* 151 The next morning he woke up and went on and caught the bus to school just like common. **c1959** Weals *Hillbilly Dict* 10 If I ask, "How are you today?" and you reply, "Oh, 'bout like common," then there's no cause to worry about you. **1993** Ison and Ison *Whole Nother Lg* 7 = getting along as usual.

liked to (also *liken to, like to*) *adverb phrase* (Have) nearly, (have) almost, (have) come close to. See also **like D**.

1774 *Dunmore's War* 244 The Indians had like to done Andersons Job, having struck into the stockade a few Inches from his Head. **1824** (in **1912** Doddridge *Notes on Settlement* 23) An uncle of mine, of the name of Teter, had liked to have lost his life by one of them [= bears]. **1838** (in **1956** Eliason *Tarheel Talk* 282) (Surry Co NC) I had like to of have said ugly. **1852** *Carson Letter* 146 that night it had like to have washed us all to thunder and demockracy. **1859** Taliaferro *Fisher's River* 76 I like to a sunk in my tracks. **1860** *Love CW Letters* (Oct 2) I like to fur got to tell you A Bout the wedding. **1862** *Proffit CW Letters* (June 12) I had Like to halv forgoten to ask you if you got them postedg stamps. **1864** *D Walker CW Letters* (March 2) then I was taken down very Badly with the Soar throt and had liken to of died. **1864** *D Walker CW Letters* (April 22) I was Sick So long after I got Back I had a like to of a Spent my wages I had a like to a dide [= died] and lay a long time. **1867** Harris *Sut Lovingood* 155 He's kill'd an 'oman an' nine children, an' I speck a dog, an' like tu whipped anuther plum tu deth. **1886** Bayless *Letters* 120 It like to of killed half and what it didn't[, it] hurt very bad. **1904–20** Kephart *Notebooks* 4:853 Them two preachers like to had a ruction. **1913** Kephart *Our Sthn High* 229 My leg liked to killed me. **1922** *TN CW Ques* 1074 (Tazewell Co VA) we had a flood in 1911 that washed every thing a way we all liked to have been drowned. **1937** Hall *Coll* (Emerts Cove TN) I like to have bled to death. **1939** Hall *Coll* (Gatlinburg TN) He scared the bear nearly to death and like to scared him to death too. **1940** Haun *Hawk's Done* 46 Marthy like to have died when Barshia come. **1954** *GSMNP-19*:5 I stayed in the tree all night and liked to froze to death. **1955** Ritchie *Singing Family* 230 They were so pretty and sweet, yet so natural and good, my heart like to burst. **1960** Hall *Smoky Mt Folks* 52 Despite this expert care, the convalescing sister said, "I like to took a backset when I got to knockin' about," that is, when she got on her feet again. **1970** *GSMNP-26*:12 Eph had his knife ready for him, so he waded in on him, as they used to say, with that little old knife and liked to have killed him again. **1970** Madden and Jones *Ephraim Bales* 8 [He] took a switch blade knife . . . and cut him up till he liked to bled to death "agin" they could get him home. **1973** *AOHP/EH-24* [The furniture] was shipped over there to Middlesboro, and it was gone three or four months and they liked to never located it. **1976** *Bear Hunting* 314 When [the bear] come down and tore that rock loose, it like to have scared him to death. **1978** Montgomery *White Pine Coll* He was the mayor the year they like to went broke down there. **1981** Williams *Storytelling* The poor old widow woman took sick and was like to die. **1983** Pyle *CCC 50th Anniv* C:1:6 I like to not a got away from him. **1989** *Matewan OHP-45* I wasn't exactly Republican. and they got me turned over and run on a Republican ticket, and I run and I'd liked to won. I come a little bit of winning. **1993** *Stories 'neath Roan* 92 Lord, that liked to killed us, ever'one. **1997** Johnson *Melungeon Heritage* 13 I like to never have got his attention so I could tell him what I had done. **2009** Holbrook *Upheaval* 33 I'd like to smacked her. **2011** *Blind Pig* (June 22) He like to of quit after they talked to him that away. There are Appalachian "talk" synonyms for "like to" and they ain't nearly or almost. Instead, they are "purt near," "near about," and "near nuff." **2017** *Blind Pig* (Aug 26) David cut his head in the woods and Hoyt put pine-rosin on it. We liked to have never got that pine-rosin off of him.

[from *had like to have* or *was like to have*; with the first element of the phrase being contracted or lost and the final *have* also reduced or lost, after which *like* is followed by a past-participle form usually becoming indistinguishable from a past-tense form; DARE *like* E b chiefly South, South Midland]

like for See **for to 3**.

likely *adjective* Promising, fit, able-bodied, capable, fit. See also **likely favored**.

1813 Hartsell *Memora* 102 [We] pased several good houses whare was some half breed lived, and they had some likely farmes. **1863** *Wright CW Letters* (Dec 20) the hogs are doing very well what few we have we lost the best sows we had the spotted sow has 7 likely pigs they are a week old to night. **1864** *Watkins CW Letters* (Aug 24) we hav got a good Crop of Corn an think we have a verry likly potatoes Crop. **1879** Jones *Backwoods Carolina* 747 You've no need to bring a feller down here with you from the North. We've got plenty of likely ones here: I've got six boys myself. **1900** Harben *N GA Sketches* 62 You are married now, an' got three as likely children as ever come into the world. **1927** Woofter *Dialect from WV* 359 = able-bodied. "He is a likely hand." **1931** Goodrich *Mt Homespun* 72 Cinthy was a likely gal; her hair was all black and curly, like Shad's gal, Millie, and her eyes had a snap to 'em. **1975** Gainer *Speech Mtneer* 13 = capable. "The big fellow is the likely one to do the job."

likeness taker *noun* A photographer.

1974 Fink *Bits Mt Speech* 15 = photographer. "Be you the *likeness taker*?" **1996–97** Montgomery *Coll* (known to Brown, Cardwell).

[from *likeness*, an early term for a photograph]

liken to See **liked to**.

like of that See **like C.**

like one thing *adverb phrase* In an unusual or exceptional fashion, to an unusual or exceptional degree.

1939 Hall Coll He can mimic him just like one thing. . . . They're baking just like one thing. **1940** Hall Coll (Cataloochee NC) [On inspection day] the boys in the cookhouse are bakin' just like one thing. **c1950** (in **2000** Oakley *Roamin' Man* 80) They both have a big head and can bite like one thang. **1969** GSMNP-27:10 He was a-climbing that hill just like one thing. **1969** Hall Coll (Big Bend NC) We met my daddy a-comin', a-runnin'. He was a-climbin' that hill just like one thing. **1991** Haynes *Haywood Home* 21 He was an excellent story teller and the best dancer on Fines Creek. He could Buck-dance like one thing. **1994** Schmidt and Hooks *Whistle* 140 She took that pig out and hugged that pig and it just a-squealin' like one thing and she wanted to know if they had another'n that she could buy.

like sixty *adverb phrase* See 1956 citation.

1955 Hall Coll (Del Rio TN) Now it is raining like sixty, and maybe in a few more months it will fair up. **1956** McAtee *Some Dial NC* 27 = intensifier in such phrases as going, talking, working like sixty.

like somebody See **somebody D.**

like that *conjunctive phrase* Like, that (usually following *feel, seem*).

1811 *Globe Creek Church Minutes* 34 the Church seems like that she has nothing to do. **1862** *Carter CW Letters* (July 4) it does Seem to me like that I have Seen my Shere of trouble. **1864** *Love CW Letters* (Jan 8) I here the torys and yanks are near Asheville now . . . it looks like that we cant keep them Back at all places. **1978** Montgomery *White Pine Coll* I-1 You only remember the ones that you feel like that you were in the family with. *Ibid.* III-2 I felt like that we needed the power. *Ibid.* IX-2 It seems like that your best land is the most suitable land to build houses on. **1983** *Dark Corner OHP-10A* People used to feel like that if they'd set a fire on the mountain, that it would kill the snakes out. **2008** *Rosie Hicks* 1 [It] seemed like that her cooking was so good.

like the fellow said *phrase* As they say. See also **fellow B1.**

1961 Stubbs *Mountain-Wise* (April–May) 9 Sam looks better and has gained some weight, but he's in bad shape. Just like the feller said, "He'll never git out of this world alive."

like to See **liked to.**

lil See **little.**

lillun See **little one.**

limb *verb* To thrash, whip.

1949 Arnow *Hunter's Horn* 168 Shut up that trashy talk, youngens. . . . I'll limb you fer sassen your mom.

limber *adjective* Limp, weak.

1866 Smith *So Called* 97 In a short space of time she became affected with drowsiness. Her neck became as limber as a greasy rag. **1927** Woofter *Dialect from WV* 359 *limber as a dishrag* = without muscular strength. "He lies there limber as a dishrag." **1949** Arnow *Hunter's Horn* 129 He jerked the warm shirt from his bosom and went to work on the lamb, a little ewe, limber lifeless, with its ears frozen and its nose frosted. **1956** McAtee *Some Dial NC* 27 *limber as a dishrag*: simile, i.e. limp. **1997** Montgomery Coll (known to nine consultants from the Smoky Mountains).

[Web3 *limber* adj now dialect; DARE *limber* adj scattered, but more frequent South, South Midland]

limber jack *noun* A jumping-jack toy.

c1960 Wilson *Coll* = a toy, jumping-jack. **1993** Page and Smith *Foxfire Toys and Games* 190 To operate the limberjack, sit on one end of the paddle in a chair, lower the limberjack so the feet barely touch the paddle, and tap out the rhythm. Moving the handle will cause the arms and legs to go around and kick out. With a little practice, the limberjack can be made to perform most tapdancing and clog dancing routines.

[DARE *limber jack* n 3 especially South, South Midland]

limber jim *noun* A switch used to punish children.

1941 Still *Troublesome Creek* 161 Mother was set as a wedge against tobacco. She wouldn't spare the limber jim. **1982** Slone *How We Talked* 32 = a small switch used to whip children.

limpsey-like *adjective* Limp.

1943 Justus *Jerry Jake* 49 Bruise [the leaves] between your hands till they are limpsey-like and well wilted.

[OED3 *limpsey* adj "limp" dialect and U.S.]

line

A *noun* A series.

1937 Hall Coll (Cades Cove TN) [Jack Johnson] can tell a great line of stories.

B (also *line off, line out*) *verb, verb phrase* Of a minister or song leader: to lead, by calling out, chanting, or reading a hymn line by line or phrase by phrase, which a group of worshippers then sings in a call-and-response manner. See c1975 citation. See also **give out A3**. See also **hymn lining, lined singing.**

1915 Dingus *Word-List VA* 185 *line out* = to read (hymns) from the pulpit, one or two lines at a time. **1921** Campbell *Sthn Highlander* 185 There are, however, still sung in certain neighborhoods the traditional tunes of older hymns, the words alone being printed or "lined out," that is, said or recited from memory, line by line, by the preacher. **1948** Dick *Dixie Frontier* 189 The minister usually lined or "passeled out" the hymn' that is, he read the first two lines, after which they were sung; then the next two were read. In this manner—piece-meal—the song was sung. The minister usually not only lined the hymn but "histed" it; that is, pitched it for the congregation. **1960** Westover *Highland Lg* 20 *line a song* = to lead the singing without books. **1967** Combs *Folk-Songs* 93 At [Primitive Baptist] services printed song texts are rare, which necessitates that someone "line off" the words of the songs, that is, chant them line by line, after which the assembly sings them, and so on, till the entire song is sung. **1967** Wilson *Folkways Mammoth Cave* 13 Before everybody had their own song book, or the churches had their own supply, it was necessary for the preacher to read the hymn aloud from beginning to end; then he went back and read a line or two at a time; the congregation sang this bit of the hymn; then others were read and sung. Long after songbooks became available, it was the custom of some of the older preachers to line the hymn that was to be sung just before the sermon. **1973** GSMNP-86 [We sung this Amazing Grace, sing the notes first, then they sang the text. Everybody joins and sing the notes first, but I don't know the notes. I can't sing the notes.] **c1975** Lunsford *It Used to Be* 97 The minister would line out his song and they'd sing it as the minister would line it out. He'd line out half the stanza, and the audience would sing. Then he'd line it again, and they'd sing another half stanza. **1977** Shackelford et al. *Our Appalachia* 45 Usually they met of a morning: they'd have their service about ten o'clock, and it would start with singing. Some one person would "line" the song. That is, he would read one line. Everybody would sing that. **1982** Ginns *Snowbird Gravy* 92 Used to, when a minister opened a service, before the prayer, he'd line out one of those old hymns, and they would sing it.... But we've got away from lining the songs out. We got away from that a whole lot because the older ones has died out, and the younger ones can't do it. **1984** Allison *Character Notes* 86 Some of the Psalm singers who still preferred the "lining out" system (wherein the singers repeated a line said or sung by the leader) felt that singing the fa-sola symbols was blasphemous. **1984** Wilder *You All Spoken* 180 *line a song* = line out.... The song leader reads aloud the first two lines of the song to be sung, and the congregation sings them. The next two lines are read, then sung, and in this piecemeal fashion the whole song is sung. **1989** Giardina *Storming Heaven* 136 "We're floating down the stream of time, we have not long to stay," she called out in a practiced monotone, and we took up the tune, repeating her words after she lined them. **1997** Montgomery *Coll*: *line out* (known to Brown), = was done by Old Regular Baptists and some Primitive Baptists still line out hymns as a ritual of hymnody and not because of a shortage of books (Jones), = done only on special occasions (Ledford), = done in shaped-note singing (Oliver), = done only when not enough hymnbooks were available (Weaver). **2006** *Encycl Appalachia* 1322 In Appalachian practice, the song leader sings the very first line of text, and the congregation joins in when they recognize the song. After that the song proceeds line by line: the leader alone briefly chants a line, and then the group repeats the words to a tune that is much longer and more elaborate than the leader's chant of lining tune. Music scholars call this procedure "lining out" or "lining."

[DARE *line out* v phr 1 chiefly South, South Midland]

lined singing *noun* See citations. See also **line B**.

1989 Dorgan *Regular Baptists* 6 A number of traditional customs of worship have been preserved, some by such determination that the particular liturgical practice has become one of the absolutes in defining Old Regularism. Such is the case, for example, with lined singing, a hymnody method in which a song leader (one of the elders) chants the hymn one couplet at a time, with each chanting then being followed by the congregation's rendition of that couplet. This is a singing method that apparently dates back to the practices of the Westminster Assembly of Baptists in England in the 1600s and which became highly serviceable in eighteenth- and nineteenth-century frontier America, when congregations often could not read and had no songbooks when they could. **2009** Miller *Nigh Gone* 115 "Purt nigh gone" from the old-time religion today is the practice of "hymn lining" or "lined singing." Of Welsh descent, it was used often in the early days when there were no hymnals or songbooks. The song leader, deacon, or elder quickly chanted two lines of a hymn, called "giving out the song," and then the congregation sang it at a much slower pace unaccompanied. It was a mournful, wailing sound without rhythm. Sometimes when a preacher really "got to going" and/or some in the congregation began to shout, the "precentor" interrupted the sermon and began to line out a hymn, and the congregation joined in on these "old songs of Zion."

line fence *noun* A fence serving as a boundary between two properties.

1941 Stuart *Men of Mts* 94 I've had enough of that damn war over a line fence. **1967** *DARE Survey* (Rogersville TN) = between two properties. **1979** Cook *Mt Grown* 97 We had discovered the "best Teaberry patch" in all of Knott County, the location of which was along the "line fence" on the mountain.

line off See **line B**.

line out *verb phrase*

1 See **line B**.

2 See citation.

1927 Woofter *Dialect from WV* 359 = to punish. "Your father will line you out when he comes home."

3 To straighten out.

1938 Stuart *Dark Hills* 284 My mind was in a muddle. If ever I could get lined out just right, I'd show them I wasn't a fake.

linger on *verb phrase* See citations.

1917 Kephart *Word-List* 414 = to be ailing. "I 'low Mr. Brooks is takin' the fever. He's jes been a lingerin' on for two or three days." **1927** Woofter *Dialect from WV* 359 = to be ailing. "I don't know what is the matter with me. I've just been lingerin' on for several days."

linguister

A Variant forms *lin-gis-ter* [see **1913** in **B**], *linkister* [see **1913** in **B**], *linkster* [see **1924**, **1974** in **B**].

B *noun* A person skilled in languages, interpreter. In East Tennessee and the North Carolina mountains this usually referred to a person who acted as an interpreter for the Cherokee.

1849 Lanman *Alleghany Mts* 97 The first [Cherokee] preacher who addressed the meeting was a venerable man, *Big Charley*, and he took for his text the entire first chapter of John; but, before proceeding with his remarks, he turned to Mr. Thomas and wished to know if he should preach with the "*linguister*," or interpreter, for the benefit of the young stranger. **1913** Kephart *Our Sthn High* 290 In our county some Indians always appear at each term of court, and an interpreter must be engaged. He never goes by that name, but by the obsolete title linkister or link'ster, by some lin-gis-ter. **1924** (in **1952** Mathes *Tall Tales* 31) Why, Mister, a linkster's a feller that can read writin' er understand talkin' in a furrin tongue—say like Injun er Dutch er somethin' thataway. **1932** Creal *Quaint Speech* A linkister is an interpreter, corruption of linguist. This word is employed a great deal in Western North Carolina in referring to those who know enough Cherokee to interpret in court for the Indian. **1944** Wilson *Word-List* 46 = an interpreter. "My grandaddy used to be a *linkister* for the Indians." **1974** Fink *Bits Mt Speech* 15 *linkster* = interpreter.

[OED3 *linguister* n 1 chiefly U.S. regional, now chiefly archaic; DARE *linguister* n chiefly southern Appalachians]

C *verb* To translate from one language into another.

1896 *Word-List* 420 He's going to preach to the Injuns to-day, but who's going to *linkister* for him?

link-cat *noun* A lynx.

1944 Wentworth *ADD* 362 (WV) *link-cat*.

linkister, linkster See **linguister**.

linsey (also *linsey cloth, linsey woolen, linsey-woolsey*) *noun* A strong, coarse fabric. [Editor's note: At the time of Joseph Hall's research in the late 1930s, the warp of this fabric was linen (later cotton) and the web was woolen. The older term (*linsey-woolsey*) had apparently passed largely from use.] See especially 1931 Goodrich citation. See also **chain**, **web**.

1861 *Huntley CW Letters* (Nov 22) if you can git some thin Lincy Wolen cloth it Will do vary Well. **1862** *Lockmiller CW Letters* (Sept 25) I hav got you a lincy shirt an apar of Slips. **1913** Morley *Carolina Mts* 194 Even the coarse "jeans" for her men's clothing and the "linsey cloth" for her own are regarded by her with affectionate pride, for has she not created them out of nothing, you might say? **1931** Goodrich *Mt Homespun* 11 In winter no one need be cold, for there was linsey-woolsey (contracted now to linsey) originally woven, as its full name implies, of woolen thread on a linen warp. Long ago cotton was substituted for the linen. The weaving of this was what is called plain weaving, drawn in without need of a pattern, on two sets of harness and tramped with two treadles. If striped, the striping ran across the web, as the colors could readily be changed in the shuttles at the will of the weaver, while the chain must remain of one color throughout the web. In a plain but bright color the linsey was often made up into winter shirts or jerkins for the men, and either plain or striped it furnished petticoats and dresses for the women and girls. **1931** Greve *Tradition Gatlinburg* 71 She raised the flax, "broke" it, spun and wove that, as well as the wool she carded (and sometimes sheared), into the linen, jeans and linsey-woolseys she and her husband and children wore. **1937** Eaton *Handicrafts* 97 In the Highlands the warp for most of the early coverlets was linen thread made from the home-grown flax which thrives in many parts of the region. Flax was much used in house-hold fabrics, and combined with wool, made the well-known linsey-woolsey, a favorite old-time dress material. **1937** Hall *Coll* (Big Creek NC) *linsey* = a cloth for underwear, all wool but the chain, cotton thread put into the loom to weave with. *Ibid.* (Ravensford NC) Three heddles for jeans cloth . . . two for linsey. **1939** Hall *Coll* (Cosby Creek TN) The men-folks wore linsey britches [and] cotton shirts. They wove them. **1952** Callahan *Smoky Mt Country* 12 Linsey-woolsey, a fabric with a flax framework filled in with wool, was widely used by the poorer women. **1956** Hall *Coll* (Waynesville NC) You must remember that women in those days wore a great many long petticoats that swept the ground. They were home-made from what was called linsey cloth. **1969** Madden and Jones *Walker Sisters* 30 Their winter clothes was made from linsey woolsey woven from the wool of their sheep. They wove the cloth on a hand loom made by their father John N. Walker. **2006** *Encycl Appalachia* 801 Sometimes, two or more types of fibers were combined. A popular cloth called "linsey woolsey" was once thought to refer exclusively to a combination of linen and wool woven together. However, textile historians now maintain that cotton was often substituted for linen or combined with the linen and wool fibers. Linsey woolsey was particularly desirable for pants, shirts, and skirts, offering the durability and warmth of wool while retaining the lightness and aesthetic qualities of cotton and linen fabrics.

linsey cloth, linsey woolen, linsey woolsey See **linsey**.

linthead *noun* A worker in a cotton mill, usually a Caucasian.

1939 McIlwaine *Southern Poor-Whites* 102 Ever since William Cullen Bryant had pictured Georgia tackies in these [cotton] mills and William Gregg, "factory master of the Old South" had proclaimed that such textile plants as his splendid one erected at Graniteville, S.C., were the panacea for the South's rural poor, the North had been aware of the tackies (also the mountaineers) as a potential supply of lint-heads. **1973** Kahn *Hillbilly Women* 6 The textile industry followed the coal companies to the Southern mountains to avoid dealing with unions in the North. . . . The textile industry in the mountains employed whole families. Hillbilly men and women went to work carding, spinning, and weaving cotton in mills that were filled with dust and were poorly ventilated. "Lintheads," as their bosses scornfully called them, worked ten and twelve hours a day to the sound of roaring machinery. **1984** Burns *Cold Sassy* 84 No town boy or girl from a nice home would be caught dead with a linthead. *Ibid.* 106 The school board voted to close the mill school and let the lintheads come to ours.

lip *verb* To place (snuff) between the lip and the gums.

1951 Giles *Harbin's Ridge* 15 She just lipped her snuff and looked wise.

[DARE *lip* v 1 chiefly South, South Midland]

lipping full *adjective phrase* Full to capacity.

c1978 Trout and Watson *Piece of Smokies* 39 By November, the corn crib, apple house, and smokehouse were "lippin' full."

[cf SND *lip* v 3(2) "to be full to the brim, or overflowing"; CUD *lippin* (at *lip* n) "full to the brim"]

liquid grave *noun* See citation.

1994 Dorgan *Liquid Graves* 10 New Christians have been immersed in outdoor "liquid graves" and ceremoniously raised again as "dripping saints" for many centuries. *Ibid.* 11 The waters of the "liquid grave" cover all, cleansing and purifying. From this symbolic descent, the "dripping saint" then arises, sputtering from the water, shaking from the cold, and probably crying from the emotional trauma.

liquid lightning See **lightning**.

liquor *noun* The common term in the mountains for illegally made whiskey.

1939 Hall *Coll* (Cades Cove TN) They was a lot of liquor made here till the park come in. *Ibid.* (Cataloochee NC) At that time we made a lot of liquor in this country. Very near everybody made it. *Ibid.* (Cataloochee NC) One time way back when I was just a boy, me and my brother, we decided we'd make some liquor, way back in Smoky Mountains in a place called Hell's Half Acre. **1962** Williams *Metaphor Mt Speech I* 12 Women and men might differ considerably in the connotation of their figures for moonshine whiskey, denominated generically as "that old whuskey" by women and "liquor" by men. **1973** GSMNP-5:14 He first give us a drink of whiskey and took a drink hisself, and then from the baby up he gave the liquor. **1975** GSMNP-59:16–17 Old man Quill Rose, he made liquor all of his life and believed that it was his right. He said he made his corn and lived, and he thought he ought to have a right to make his liquor if he wanted as long as he made it out of his own corn. **1978** Montgomery *White Pine Coll* V-3 They said, "If you fellows are deer hunting up in there, now watch about shooting down on us because we'll be up there making liquor." They didn't care to tell it.

liquor out *verb phrase* To pass out from inebriation.

1994–97 Montgomery *Coll* (known to Adams, Brown, Cardwell, Oliver).

liquor pellagra *noun*

A Variant form *pellagry* [see **1937** in **B**].

B The disease pellagra, characterized by gastrointestinal disorders, dermatitis, and other disorders, due to a diet deficient in niacin and protein from excessive consumption of liquor.

1937 Hall *Coll* (Cosby Creek TN) *liquor pellagry* = said to be common among those addicted to liquor and to the excessive use of corn in cooking (e.g. corn bread).

liquor up *verb phrase* To become intoxicated.

1927 Woofter *Dialect from WV* 359 = to get drunk. "The boys liquor up every time they come to town." **1937** Hall *Coll* He was all liquored up. **1996** Hughes *Swain County* 14 Some of the boys would get liquored up and enjoy racing their horses across the bridge, making enough noise to scare the donkies [sic] for miles around.

listed *adjective* Of livestock: having a stripe or band around the body.

1913 Kephart *Our Sthn High* 295 A spotted animal is said to be pieded (pied), and a striped one is listed. **1957** Combs *Lg Sthn High: Word List* 60 = having a white stripe (of animals). **1976** Garber *Mountain-ese* 54 The listed hogs are the ones with the stripe around the shoulder. **1992** Jones and Miller *Sthn Mt Speech* 92 = animals with a white belt around them, such as Hampshire hogs and Galloway cattle. **1996** Montgomery *Coll* = *belted* (known to Jones, but the term is otherwise unknown to consultants from the Smoky Mountains).

[OED3 *list* n³ "a border, hem, bordering strip" obsolete + *-ed*; cf DARE *list* n 2 "a stripe" chiefly southern Appalachians]

listenable *adjective* Pleasant to listen to.

c1940 Simms *Coll* He's a listenable man; I'll harken to his prattle, but I don't confidence what he says.

listen at *verb phrase* To listen to.

1863 *Vance Papers* (July 13) Some Men Could Give in the Best Surtificate of Diseases and woulddent Bee listened at. **1863** *Warrick CW Letters* (May 18) if I could see you I could tell you a heap of things that would be interesting for you to lisen at. **1905** Miles *Spirit of Mts* 125 I'm well used to that; hit don't disturb me none, and won't disturb nobody else that really wants to listen at the gospel. **1937** Hall *Coll* (Emerts Cove TN) Listen at them rocks a-rollin' down the creek! [said during a heavy rainstorm]. **1939** Hall *Coll* (Deep Creek NC) Listen at that pack of hounds! Does that sound like a wild-cat to you? **1953** Hall *Coll* (Bryson City NC) Everybody was setting and listening at him. **1973** *Church of God* 9 Some a'his new members is a'listenin' at me. **1983** *Dark Corner OHP*-3A I read my Bible and listen at the preachers and all, but as far as going to church, I don't go to church. **1989** *Matewan OHP*-28 I don't think Christian people ought to listen at it. **1997** *Dante OHP*-14 I don't believe we had a radio, but we went places to listen at the radio.

[EDD (at *at* IV(3)); DARE *listen* v 1 chiefly South, South Midland]

literary (also *literary society*) *noun* See citations.

1967 Jones *Peculiarities Mtneers* 90–91 Almost every mountain community supported some kind of "literary society." Once a month meetings would be held at the community school house. The girls and young ladies would recite such literary masterpieces as "Curfew Shall Not Ring Tonight" or "Enoch Arden." The boys would declaim in a tremulous voice, with frequent stops until prompted, such gems as "The Boy Stood on the Burning Deck" or "Invictus." But the real feature of these meetings was always a debate. Such world shattering questions as "Resolved, There is more pleasure in anticipation than in realization?" or "Resolved, Love is more powerful than hate?" were argued enthusiastically as the crowd registered its partisanship for the debater of its choice by frequent applause. **1975** Gainer *Witches Ghosts Signs* 23 By the beginning of this century the country school had become a center for community activities. The event that brought many people to the school on one night each month was called the "Literary." It was a meeting of all the pupils of the school, their parents and friends, who came to participate in such activities as debates, dramatic skits, readings, recitations, and spelling contests. Sometimes a team of pupils would debate against a team of adults on some popular subject. Spelling contests were popular, with pupils and adults participating. Choral singing was also an important part of the literary. **1975** Kroeger *WV Farm Life* 7 They used to have literaries in schools, you know, a long time ago, and they would take up a subject and one would argue one way and one another, you know, and that was pretty interesting.

litered See **lightwood**.

litter *noun* Used as a euphemism for barnyard manure.

1967 Fetterman *Stinking Creek* 50 Bargo . . . loaded the sled with "barn litter" and began throwing the rotted manure and straw on his garden plot. **1968** *DARE Survey* (Brasstown NC). **1997** Montgomery *Coll* (known to nine consultants from the Smoky Mountains).

[DARE *litter* n 1 chiefly South Midland]

little *adjective, adverb*

A Variant forms *leetle, lil*.

1867 Harris *Sut Lovingood* 110 Now s'pose I happens tu put in a leetle too much powder, an' skeer him plum outen the United States—what then? **1903** Fox *Little Shepherd* 136 I foller pickin' the banjer a leetle. **1975** Chalmers *Better* 34 Hit's jest a lil ol' set-along chile—cain't walk yet.

B Senses.

1 (to modify a count noun) Few.

1939 Hall *Coll* (Cataloochee NC) That was a good man. He helped more people than a little. **1973** *GSMNP*-88 They's been very little changes in the road.

2 Younger, junior.

1915 Dingus *Word-List VA* 185 = Junior: "I saw little Pat yesterday." Pat weighs 250 pounds, and has six children. His father, under normal size, is called Big Pat. **1948** Chase *Grandfather Tales* 5 "Little" Robin (i.e., Robin Weaver, Jr.) proved as tall as Old Kel must have been before age struck him.

little boy plant *noun* The bleeding heart, a wildflower (*Dicentra cucullaria*). Same as **dutchman's breeches**.

1970 Campbell et al. *Smoky Mt Wildflowers* 28 This distinctly shaped nodding flower, with spurs on the top, is found from 900 to 5,000 feet in the Smokies, but is rather rare. Because of the extended "trouser legs," it is sometimes called little boy plant.

little girl plant *noun* A bleeding heart plant (*Dicentra canadensis*). Same as **squirrel corn**.

1970 Campbell et al. *Smoky Mt Wildflowers* 28 Because of the rounded or "bloomer-like" top of its flowers, it is occasionally called little girl plant.

little grain See **grain**.

little green man *noun* Used as a nickname for a patch of **ginseng** found in the wild.

1968 *Sang Season* 73 Sang [= ginseng] hunters . . . would keep their own finds a secret, referring to the plant by the name of a person such as Pete or Long John, or merely as "the little green man."

little hominy *noun* Grits. See also **big hominy, lye hominy**.

1918 Steadman *NC Word List* 18 Big hominy [is] lye hominy of whole corn, contrasted with little hominy, or grits.

little house (also *little house behind the big house*) *noun* An outhouse, privy. See also **johnny**.

1952 Wilson *Folk Speech NC* 560 *little house* = a privy. **1966** *DARE Survey* (Cherokee NC) *little house* = outside toilet. **1986** Pederson et al. *LAGS* (Johnson Co TN, Sullivan Co TN) *little house*. **1992** Bush *If Life* 140 Long before Sears Roebuck and Montgomery Ward catalogs came into the mountains to be used in the "little house" out back, Paw Paw tree leaves were the pioneer's favorite bathroom tissue. **2007** McMillon *Notes: little house behind the big house*.

little laurel *noun* See 1901 citation.

1901 Lounsberry *Sthn Wild Flowers* 381 R[*hododendron*] punctatem, little . . . laurel . . . is the smallest of our evergreen species. **1921** Campbell *Sthn Highlander* 123 Close by is the branch, slipping through growth of "big" and "little" laurel and set with "holly-bush" and groups of towering "spruce-pine."

little men *noun* Ginseng.

2007 Joslin *Sang Season* 57 The Cherokee referred to ginseng as "little men" and used it to alleviate stomach ailments, convulsions, and headaches.

little'n See **little one**.

little Noah *noun* A torrential rainstorm. Same as **young Noah**.

1975 Carter *Gospel Truth* A big rain was a "sod soaker" or a "gully washer" or a "little Noah."

little old *adjective phrase* Used to express slight affinity or endearment, but sometimes disparagement (usually with stress on *little*). See also **big old, great big old**.

1863 *Wright CW Letters* (Nov 15) you never saw children grow as fast as budy and Matty does baby is the same little old scrap but is harty as a pig. **1864** *Stepp CW Letters* (May 17) it is about all the Satisfaction i see to get letters to read from home and to rite to you them and my little old book is asatisfaction to mee. **1913** Kephart *Our Sthn High* 367 Them bugs—the little old hatefuls! **1921** Weeks *Speech of KY Mtneer* 17 The term, little old, varies in meaning from one of extreme disgust to one of real endearment. I have heard of a little old late train, a little old cook stove, a little old coal mine, and a little old baby! **1926** Hunnicutt *Twenty Years* 12 This happened in a little old open place in the laurel about thirty feet square. **1939** Hall *Coll* (Proctor NC) That little old feist, he got after it and run about far as to that house out there a hundred yards. **1950**

Justus *Luck for Lihu* 82 He'd go back home where he wouldn't have to be with a bunch of little old young'uns. **1956** Hall *Coll* (Cosby TN) The first school I went to was a little old log-built house up on Cosby. **1967** Hall *Coll* (Del Rio TN) This little old boy, I forget what his name was. **1969** GSMNP-25:1:16 In the little old hollow there, [there was a] big old chestnut tree that had fell, laying right across the hollow. **1969** GSMNP-27:7 Them bears was in a little old log crib there, and they had them chained to it, just a little old small chain. **1973** GSMNP-5:14 Them little old young ones just drink that [whiskey] the same as I was. **1985** Irwin *Alex Stewart* 219 Her children was just stringy headed little old things, never no shoes. **1991** Thomas *Sthn Appal* 229 I've got these three little ol' young'uns here, I sez, "at I've got t' look after."

[DARE *little old* adj phr chiefly South, South Midland]

little one *noun* See also **one 1**.

A Variant forms *lillun*, *little'n* [see **1971** in **B**], *little un* [see **1910** in **B**], *little'un*.

1939 Hall *Coll*: *little'un*. **1975** Jackson *Unusual Words* 150 An object may be a *lillun*, a *bad'n*, a *big'n*, or a *new'n*; or an individual may remark. "I ain't seen nair'n," or "I ain't got air'n."

B A child. See also **grown'un, young one**.

1910 Cooke *Power and Glory* 5 Biney Meal lent me enough for the little un that died. **1924** Bacheller *Happiest Person* 7 The sun would be hot on the little uns comin' back. **1971** *Boogers* 37 That little'n had walked right at my heels ever step up that mountain till we got t'th'branch. **1979** Slone *My Heart* 5 You know I told you how the ol' Hoot Owl was goin' to bring us another little'un. **1997** Montgomery *Coll* (known to ten consultants from the Smoky Mountains).

little piece (also *little ways*) *noun phrase* A relatively short distance. See also **far piece, piece 1**.

1910 Cooke *Power and Glory* 62 You have to leave the road and walk a little piece. **1934–47** *LAMSAS Appal*: *little piece* = attested by 63/148 speakers (42.5%) from WV, 8/20 (40%) from VA, 33/37 (89.2%) from NC, 2/14 (14.3%) from SC, and 5/12 (41.7%) from GA; *little ways* = attested by 73/148 speakers (49.3%) from WV, 20/20 (100%) from VA, 36/37 (97.3%) from NC, 11/14 (78.5%) from SC, and 5/12 (41.7%) from GA. *Ibid*. (Madison Co NC, Swain Co NC). **1939** Hall *Coll* (Little Cataloochee NC) So [the boy] broke to run, and he run a little piece. *Ibid*. (Smokemont NC) The dogs struck, went up the creek a little piece, and treed up a little hempine. **1949** Kurath *Word Geog East US* 29 Instead of a *little way* (e.g. a little way down the road), or by the side of it, the Midland has a *little piece*. *Ibid*. 66 The expression *a little piece* is especially common ... in Western North Carolina, whence it spread down to the coast between the Cape Fear and the Peedee. **1958** Newton *Dialect Vocab*: *little piece* = attested by 25 of 36 speakers from E TN mountains; *little ways* = attested by 2 of 36 speakers from E TN mountains. **1964** Roberts *Hell-Fer-Sartin* 109 These two ole witches—one lived up on the creek just a little piece above the other one and each night one would go to the other'n's house to make up what evil thing they'd do that night. **1966** Dakin *Vocab Ohio River Valley* 295 The Midland expression *a little piece* is commonly used everywhere and at all social levels in Kentucky. Among the younger, more educated speakers and those who live in towns and cities this expression is usually used in addition to *a little way(s)*, a short distance, etc., but among many older rural speakers it appears to be the only and regular expression of this idea. *Ibid*. 297–99 Especially in Kentucky, the reduced expression a *piece* (down the road) is fairly common. This is frequently used in addition to *a little piece*, but for some *a piece* seems to be regular. A number of Kentuckians indicate the use of *a short piece* and several speakers in the southern Mountains say *a piece o'ways*. ... Among those speakers who say *a little piece*, the expressions *a long piece*, *a good piece*, *quite a piece*, *a far piece*, and *a right smart piece*, are fairly common. It is quite evident, however, that many speakers who use *piece* in reference to a short distance restrict the word to that usage and say *way(s)* when speaking of a longer distance. **1986** Pederson et al. *LAGS* (Blount Co TN, Cocke Co TN). **1998** *Dante OHP-45* I just went out the road here just a little piece from here and cut across to Austin Gap.

little recess *noun* Formerly, a short, scheduled break taken by schoolchildren from classroom activity.

1903 Fox *Little Shepherd* 41 When the first morning recess came—"little recess," as it was called—the master kept Chad in and asked him his name; if he had ever been to school, and whether he knew his A B C's. **1992** Brooks *Sthn Stuff* 90 little recess, n. [Accent on the "re"] A short recreational break in a school routine, as distinguished from "big re-cess," which is the longer period when lunch is eaten.

little red devil *noun* See citation.

2002 Ogle *Remembrances* 53 We played Little Red Devil (like tag), Granny come to light her pipe (take children to her house) and another was thread the needle (this was sort of a tug of war).

littles See **by the littles**.

little shaver *noun* A youngster, especially an adolescent boy before he begins to shave.

1938 Bowman *High Horizons* 48 My paw tuck land 'round old Blanket Mountain yander when I'se jist a little shaver, back atter the Civil War, an' we've been rooted as the trees ever since. **1963** Edwards *Gravel* 108 I ain't seen this feller since he was just a little shaver, and now he's a *big man*—Granny's man, that's what he is. **1973** GSMNP-87:2:2 I was just a little shaver then. I was four years. **1975–76** Wolfram/Christian *WV Coll* 146 My uncle used to chew when I was a little shaver and he'd buy it by the cord, and I'd go over there in there and whack me off a little piece there when he wasn't looking. **1996** Montgomery *Coll* = 16–18 years of age (Cardwell).

little'un See **little one**.

little ways See **little piece**.

little weedly *noun* See citation.

1984 Woods *WV Was Good* 221 *little weedlies* = chickens newly hatched.

littlings *noun* The endearments and caresses of new lovers.

1963 Edwards *Gravel* 14 The oldsters went off to bed leaving the newlyweds to retire as soon as they cared to. The young couple stayed up late enjoying the wonderful littlings of love, but finally went to bed.

live See **lief.**

live out *verb phrase* To stop living in a place, live elsewhere.

1973 GSMNP-88:50 I've lived over there ever since nineteen and nine till I lived out. Him and my mother both died in there.

liver See **good liver, hard liver.**

liver and lights *noun* The edible internal organs (liver and lungs) of a hog. See also **haslet(s), lights.**

1864 *Leigh CW Letters* (April 8) I have saw 40 wagons in a Company hunting corn and finding none when it comes to killing frames [= emaciated livestock] of Cows Just to get the liver & lites to eat you may say it is hard times. **1942** (in **1987** Perdue *Outwitting Devil* 15) So the next day she told her old man that she was longin' fer that strange bull's liver an' lights an' he'd have to kill him an' git his liver an' lights fer her. **1949** Kurath *Word Geog East US* 64 *Liver and lights* is of common occurrence (1) in the Maryland counties adjoining Pennsylvania and on Delaware Bay, and (2) in Western North Carolina. **1966** Dakin *Vocab Ohio River Valley* 261 The Southern and South Midland *hasslet(s)* still has considerable currency in southern Kentucky generally, however, and *liver 'n lights* is common in the southern Mountains. In this region *liver 'n lights* undoubtedly comes from western North Carolina.

liver bound (also *liver growed, liver grown*) *adjective phrase, noun* Of a baby: supposedly having a condition involving the growth or adhesion of the liver to the internal cavity or having symptoms allegedly caused by this condition; such symptoms. For its treatment, see 1924 and 1981 citations. See also **liver shakes, measure the baby.**

1924 Raine *Saddlebags* 207 Then I thought maybe hit were livergrowed. You don't know what that is? Well, you take the right hand and the left heel, and make 'em touch behind. Then I took the left hand and the right heel and they wouldn't touch. So I just pulled. The child cried mightily, but I knowed hit had to be done. **1975** Purkey *Madison Co* 86 "It's good for babies to be bounced and juggled about," she declared, "keeps 'em from being liver bound." **1981** Whitener *Folk-Ways* 50 For babies that were liver grown, which happened, she said, from too little exercise, she run them through an open back chair—the homemade kind that had three slats across the back. She took them between the slats three times, then she turned them on their stomach and took the right hand and touched the left foot. After this she took them by the heels and turned them upside down three times. When the exercise was over she gave them three doses of calomel and castor oil that was supposed to start them on the road to good health. **1982** Slone *How We Talked* 104 *liver grown* = of children, listlessness, inactivity. **1990** Cavender *Folk Medical Lex* 26 *liver grown* = also known as "liver bound" . . . [having] a physical disorder . . . [in which an infant's] liver becomes attached to the spinal cord due to remaining flat on the back too long in the crib. **1994–97** Montgomery *Coll*: *liver bound* (known to Ogle); *liver grown* = the belief that the liver was the major organ of the body controlling mental and physical health (Bush), = it was believed that the liver would adhere to the intestines in an inertive child (Ledford). **1995** Adams *Come Go Home* 106 There was a time when we talked of babies—we all had one then. Granny would move around, weaving between stretched out legs, smiling, talking, offering advice like . . . "When a young'un is six days old you've got to turn 'em up by the heels and shake 'em good. It keeps 'em from getting liver growed." **2003** Cavender *Folk Medicine* 138 Mothers closely monitored their infants and children for symptoms of livergrown or being livergrowed, thought to be a debilitating and potentially lethal illness caused by the liver, causing a fibrous growth attachment to the spine or ribs. Primary symptoms of livergrown were irritability and sensitivity to touch. It was believed that an infant was likely to form a liver attachment if it remained in a supine position for too long. Infants were therefore periodically rolled over onto their stomachs. Livergrown was also prevented by exercises such as stretching an infant's right foot to its left shoulder and left foot to right shoulder and by what was called "turning the baby." Turning a baby involved holding an infant upside down by one leg and then grasping an arm and rotating the baby to an upright position and back to an upside down position. This rotation was performed several times a session. Should symptoms of liver attachment manifest, a more drastic measure known as the "liver shakes" was used. The infant was held in the air by its feet and shaken vigorously up and down, the intent being to dislodge the liver attachment. . . . Livergrown is a German contribution to Euro-American folk medicine. Derived from the German word lebertran, the term "livergrown" was defined by the Pennsylvania Germans as a child-specific illness caused by "the liver attaching itself through some morbid growth to the neighboring and outer parts [of the body]." **2007** McMillon *Notes*: *liver growed.* **2007** Milnes *Signs Cures Witches* 107 In Pendleton County, babies were passed through a horse collar to be cured of livergrown. As I understand it, livergrown (Awachse) is a supposed ailment whereby the liver attaches itself (or grows) to the ribs. It was thought to strike when young babies were taken in carriages over rough roads. As with sensing when measles go "back in" on people, this seems a case in which people have some sixth sense to discern internal abnormalities.

[DARE *liver grown* adj chiefly southern Appalachians, PA]

liver cheese See **liver mush.**

liver complaint *noun* A disease or disorder of the liver.

1861 *Odum CW Letter* (Oct 10) I have got the liver complaint and I sufer a grat deal with it. **1862** *Bell CW Letters* (Jan 14) Pat Rone is verry sick now he has the mumps and the liver complaint but not daingeroust i dont think he caint set up but what it makes him sick he is in my mess and i am detailed to wait on him.

liver growed, **liver grown** See **liver bound**.

liver hash See **liver mush**.

liver lights *noun* in phrase *you scared the liver lights out of me* = you scared me to death.

2001 Montgomery *File* (known to 54-year-old woman, Jefferson Co TN).

liver mush (also *liver cheese*, *liver hash*, *liver pudding*) Liver sausage, made from a hog's liver that is cooked, ground, seasoned, and mixed with cornmeal and sometimes other internal organs, then molded into a loaf and sliced. Also called **hog pudding**.

1918 Steadman *NC Word List* 18 *liver-mush* = liver pudding. **1939** Hall *Coll* (White Oak NC) = hog's liver mixed with corn meal and fried. **1952** Wilson *Folk Speech NC* 560 *liver mush* = liver pudding. **1957** Hall *Coll* (Gatlinburg TN) Liver puddin' (or mush) is made from hog's liver portions of lean and fat pork, usually the pig's head, and thinned with water, then thickened with corn meal, then red pepper and sage added. Very good! *Ibid.* (Waynesville NC) [To make] liver pudding, boil a hog's or cow's liver till tender, mash and thicken with corn meal, add salt and pepper, make into a mold and keep in a cool place. Slice and fry if wanted. **1982** Ginns *Snowbird Gravy* 36 We made livermush from the liver. You know, we buy it in the store now, and it isn't fitten to eat. Always, when I made it, I cooked the onions and everything with it, salt, pepper, and onions. And then we'd make it out in cakes so we could slice it. **1986** Pederson et al. *LAGS*: *liver mush* = attested by 4/60 interviewees (6.7%) from E TN and 10/35 (28.6%) from N GA; 14/17 of all LAGS interviewees (82.3%) attesting term were from Appalachia; *liver pudding* = attested by 13/60 interviewees (21.7%) from E TN and 5/35 (14.3%) from N GA; 18/102 of all LAGS interviewees (17.6%) attesting term from Appalachia. **1997** Andrews *Mountain Vittles* 79 *liver mush*: Wash yer liver and scald to seal. Cut it up in a pot of water with a little fat meat and cook till done. Take out of water and grind with red pepper, sage, salt, and black pepper. Set on stove and cook 5 to 10 minutes longer. Pour in a dish and cool. To serve slice and fry. **1997** Montgomery *Coll*: *liver cheese* (known to Brown, Bush); *liver hash* (known to Brown, Bush, Ledford); *liver mush* (known to Brown, Bush, Ledford, Norris, Oliver, Weaver). **1997** Nelson *Country Folklore* 48 When hog killing time came, several days were set aside to render the lard, make sausage, souse meat, livermush, cure hams, and can the shoulders. *Ibid.* 117 The liver was cooked and mashed, then mixed with red and black pepper, salt, and cornmeal to make livermush. **1988** Lambert *Kinfolks* 131 The backbone, ribs, and tenderloin were put aside to be eaten fresh. The head—perhaps the feet and tail—were to be made into souse meat and the liver into what was called "liver pudding" or "liver cheese." While hog killing meant a lot of work, it also meant having pork for the next year. **1998** Dabney *Smokehouse Ham* 183 Liver mush was one of the delicious by-products of a hog-killing. A mountain delicacy, it was worked on a day or so later when the primary jobs had been taken care of. Chef and author Mark Sohn of Pikeville, Kentucky, puts liver mush in the same category with liverell, liver pudding, scrapple, and sausage scrapple, most of which combine pork liver and/or lean pork and are then thickened with corn meal. **2003** Howell *Folklife Big South Fork* 60 Liver mush is a liver sausage made with meal and sausage seasonings. **2009** Benfield *Mt Born* 84 After the hog was cut up, the liver was taken, cooked in salted water, then cut up. To the liver was added a bit of broth, cornmeal was added until thickened, then salt, pepper, and a bit of sage. The livermush was placed into a mold and stored. We ate it sliced, dipped in flour, and fried in bacon grease.

[DARE *liver hash* n chiefly South, South Midland; *liver mush* n NC, SC, GA, TN]

liver pudding See **liver mush**.

liver shakes *noun* See citation. See also **liver bound**.

2003 Cavender *Folk Medicine* 138 It was believed that an infant was likely to form a liver attachment if it remained in a supine position for too long. Infants were therefore periodically rolled over onto their stomachs. Livergrown was also prevented by exercises such as stretching an infant's right foot to its left shoulder and left foot to right shoulder and by what was called "turning the baby." Turning a baby involved holding an infant upside down by one leg and then grasping an arm and rotating the baby to an upright position and back to an upside down position. This rotation was performed several times a session. Should symptoms of liver attachment manifest, a more drastic measure known as the "liver shakes" was used. The infant was held in the air by its feet and shaken vigorously up and down, the intent being to dislodge the liver attachment.

live water (also *living water*) *noun* Homemade whiskey.

1940 Farr *More TN Expressions* 447 = liquor: "The mash will make ten gallons of live water." **1971** Lee *My Appalachia* 10 They "bootlegged" their product, which they called "living water" among the thirsty coal mines in Raleigh, Wyoming, Mercer, and McDowell counties [in WV].

living water See **live water**.

living waters *noun plural* Streams, lakes, etc., when used for a baptism by immersion.

1995 McCauley *Mt Religion* 87 Mountain people today, almost universally, continue to place great importance on baptism by immersion "in living waters," an extremely common expression meaning out-of-doors in a natural setting; indeed, many cannot imagine any other form of baptism as acceptable. Baptism "in living [running] waters" is a tradition established in the Appalachian region in its first years of settlement by Anabaptist groups such as pietists such as the German Baptist Brethren (Dunkards).

lizard *noun*

1 A crude, sled-like contrivance for hauling heavy objects, especially over rough or steep terrain; its bed is usually formed by the fork or crotch of a branch or small tree, with branches serving as runners and on which a flat surface such as of planks is sometimes secured; it is usually dragged by a horse, but a smaller version in the form of a drag cloth can be tied around a person's neck for the same purpose. See also **dry-land sled, half sled, land sled.**

1917 Kephart *Camping & Woodcraft* 2:64 Where logging operations have already begun, then, wherever a stump stands, it will not be hard to determine the direction in which the logs were twitched to the nearby "lizard road," where they were loaded on lizards (forks of timber used as sleds), or on wagons, and dragged to the nearest saw-mill. **1956** Hall *Coll* (Mt Sterling NC) They laid the log up on a lizard. **1957** GSMNP-23:1:10 They moved in here on what they called a lizard them days. . . . A lizard is a forked tree, a forked tree with pieces nailed across it. **1966** Dakin *Vocab Ohio River Valley* 2.161 Scattered informants in all four of the [Ohio] Valley states mention a *lizard*, a crude drag vehicle consisting of a bed of planks, etc., constructed on a tree fork which serves as runners. **1967** Wilson *Folkways Mammoth Cave* 30 = a V-shaped slide used to hold up the end of a log being dragged out of wet woods. **1968** *DARE Survey* (Brasstown NC) = used for hauling tanbark. **1968** Wilson *Folklore Mammoth Cave* 21 = a sturdy sled made of the branched trunk of a tree and shaped like a V-harrow. Used to drag logs out of muddy woods. **1992** Montgomery *File* = a drag cloth for one's belongings, tied around a man's neck (30-year-old woman, Gatlinburg TN). **1999** Montgomery *Coll* = a homemade contraption to haul things over rough terrain, spec. a forked tree, with the forked part being the end to which you hooked up the gears on the mule or horse. The single part of the tree literally was the tail of the device used for hauling stuff and dragged the ground like a lizard tail. The forked part was stripped with slits from an oak tree like one would bottom a chair, to keep the things being hauled from falling through (Cardwell). **2005** Williams *Gratitude* 26 They moved the lumber up to the houseplace on a thang they made, called a lizard. They made some struddy (sturdy) sled runners, and nailed some thick boards acrost the top, and put a stout crosspiece on the front to hitch a horse to. Then they stacked one end of the lumber up on the lizard and tied it down, a-leaving the other end to drag on the ground. **2015** Robbins *Land Sled* 13 A forked sled was often called a lizard, a name derived from its use in logging. When used for logging, a crosspiece was attached to the top of the runners so that it spanned the open end of the "V." Two uprights, called standards, were placed in large holes drilled into the top of each runner near the end of each leg of the "V." To move a log with the forked sled, the butt, or bottom end of the log was placed on the crosspiece between the standards and secured in place with a rope. As the horse or mule pulled the forked sled, the log trailing behind it evidently reminded people of a lizard's tail, hence the name.

2 See citations.

2007 Montgomery *File* The "lizard" was the nickname of a machine specially designed to maneuver in low-ceilinged, so-called 30-inch coal mines. *Ibid.* The motor (a front car that pulls all the other cars of coal) and possibly all the cars, were referred to lovingly as a lizard. In this case it was all electric driven. **2007** *Music of Coal* 19 In the 1940s, a motorized machine was invented to haul coal from the mines. One type was fondly nicknamed the "lizard" by the miners because of its low profile manufactured especially for maneuvering in low coal.

load

A *noun* The amount of wood, corn, or other material one can carry at a time. Same as **armload.** See also **grist B, turn B2.**

1949 Kurath *Word Geog East US* 29 *Arm load* and *load* are distinctive Midland expressions for an armful of wood. *Arm load* predominates in the North Midland, *load* in the South Midland. The term *armful* stands by the side of *arm load* in the North Midland. **1966** *DARE Survey* (Cherokee NC) = amount. **1984** GSMNP-153 I thought she was going on to get a load of wood, you know, and try to get out.

B *verb* Variant past-participle forms *loaden, loadened.*

1862 Zimmerman *CW Letters* (Sept 27) some of our men saw heaps of melted lead where they burned wagons loden with it. **1978** Hiser *Quare Do's* 182 I shot wild, shot my loadened hawg rifle with that silver bullet, right in amongst them thirteen black cats.

loaden, loadened See **load B.**

loader *noun* In logging, any kind of a rig used to load logs.

1983 Aiken *Mt Ways* 165 The steam driven "loader" is in the act of swinging aboard the logs.

loaf bread *noun* White yeast bread, usually commercially produced and sliced, in contrast to **corn bread.** See also **flour bread, light bread, wheat bread.**

1862 *Warrick CW Letters* (Aug 11) The women gave us plenty of good things to eat such as water melons, grapes, figs, tomatoes, Butter milk, loaf bred and boiled ham. **1864** *Love CW Letters* (Dec 21) We get a pound of loaf bread and a half a pound of beef and to day their Was nun come. **1934–47** *LAMSAS Appal* = attested by 7/20 (35%) from VA, 19/37 (51.4%) from NC, and 3/12 (25%) from GA. **1952** Giles *40 Acres* 103 Bread is corn bread to ridge folks. Biscuits are biscuits, loaf bread from the store is light bread or boughten bread, but when you say bread, you mean corn bread. **1966** Dakin *Vocab Ohio River Valley* 312 In addition to the terms already mentioned, Kentucky has *flour bread* and *loaf bread* as well as the rare combinations of *flour light-bread, yeast light-bread,* and *wheat light-bread.* **1967** *DARE Survey* (Maryville TN) = bread made with wheat flour. **1997** Montgomery *Coll* (known to nine consultants from the Smoky Mountains).

[EDD (at *loaf* sb 1(1)) Scot, nEngl, mEngl; SND (at *loaf* n 1) "wheaten-flour bread" (in contrast to oatbread/oatcakes); CUD *loaf* "bread in the form of loaves, often shop-bought bread"; DARE *loaf bread* n chiefly South, South Midland]

loafer (also *loafer about, loafer abroad, loafer around*) *verb, verb phrase* To loiter, roam, go about aimlessly. See also **loaferer.**

1864 *Chapman CW Letters* (Jan 24) our country is full of Lofeering yankis that had better bee in the army. **1917** Kephart *Word-List* 414 *loafer about* = to loaf. "That dog's just *loaferin' about*, up an' down this road." **1931** Goodrich *Mt Homespun* 71 You say, what did he do?

He hunted some, but most days he just loafered round. **1937** Hall *Coll* [What are you doin'?]: Just a-loaferin' around. **1949** Hornsby *Lonesome Valley* 282 He's done shaved and cleaned up! Plans to go down and loafer with Crit Marcum! **1961** Murry *Salt* 100 It was an ideal day for "loafering" and lazily passing the time, and we were making the best of it. **1973** GSMNP-57:11 He said he went around that mountain, said he loafered around through there. **1979** Carpenter *Walton War* 188 Ma used to say hit wuz as big a sin to lay in bed ater daylight as hit wuz to be a lofferin' abroad ater dark. **1991** Joslin *Mt People I* 237 It's a little job, but it keeps a feller from loafering. **1995** Alexander *Mt Fever* 100 [Wild dogs] jest loafer around over the mountains huntin' somethin' to eat. **1995** Weber *Rugged Hills* 38 It wasn't as hard to figure out what Dayton meant when he said that whenever his dad saw him "loafering" near the house, he'd whistle from the field. Then Dayton would have to grab a hoe and start chopping weeds out of the tobacco or corn. **2005** Williams *Gratitude* 507 = to get out and go nowhere in particular. A dog that won't stay at home is a *loaferin'* dog. When a man just wants to get out away from the house, he goes *a-loaferin'*.

[DARE *loafer* v chiefly southern Appalachians]

loafer about, **loafer abroad**, **loafer around** See **loafer**.

loaferer *noun* One who loafs.

1913 Kephart *Our Sthn High* 277 the hillmen . . . [insert] sounds where they do not belong. Sometimes it is only an added consonant: gyarden, acrost, corkus (caucus); sometimes a syllable: loaferer, musicianer, suddenty. **1994–97** Montgomery *Coll* (known to Adams, Cardwell, Ledford, Norris, Oliver, Weaver).

loafers' bench (also *loafers glory, loafer's glory*) *noun* A bench or step at the post office, courthouse, a general store, or other public venue where men regularly congregate to exchange stories, opinions, and gossip. See citations. Also called **liars' bench**.

1976 Miller *Mts within Me* 76 As a barefoot boy growing up in the mountains of Young Harris before the time of television and without a male companion at home, I spent many, many hours hanging around what is known as the "loafers' bench" at the country store where every night a dozen or more men would gather after the day's work in the fields or woods to gossip, talk politics, tell tall tales and generally "chaw the fat." In the summer it was outside on a bench and on nail kegs; in the winter, inside around a pot-bellied stove. **1996** Casada *Gospel Hook* 26 Then too, more than once as a youngster I heard fellows gathered at the local "loafer's glory" comment that "Mark could almost outrun the dogs, and somehow he was always the first man on the scene when they barked treed." **2009** Benfield *Mt Born* 168 There is a place in Mitchell County [NC] called Loafers Glory, named for some of the men who love to pass the time of day sitting on the front porch of the local store.

loan *verb* Variant past-participle form *loant*.

1921 Greer-Petrie *Angeline at Seelbach* 19 Thar was a whole passel of velvet basks and coats a-hangin' round that the Jedge said was loant by Miss Marshall Fields.

lobber *verb* See citation.

1973 *Words & Expressions* 135 = to go wandering.

lobby *noun* See citation.

1964 Clarkson *Lumbering in WV* 366 *lobby* = room in a logging camp where the men congregated after meals, before bedtime, on Sundays, etc.

lobbyhog *noun* See citations. See also **shit slinger**.

1930 Pendleton *Wood-Hicks Speak* 88 = the caretaker of the [logging] bunkhouse; a roustabout who does everything from building fires to making beds. **1954** Blackhurst *Riders of Flood* 52 The "lobby hog," a name given to a general handy man about the [logging] camp, and the cookee had been in disagreement for some time. **1964** Clarkson *Lumbering in WV* 366 = man who carried coal, swept floors, built fires, lit lamps, and did a multitude of other chores. Usually an undesirable job. **1967** Parris *Mt Bred* 132 = [the man who] cleans the sleeping quarters and stable in a logging camp, cuts firewood, builds fires, and carries water. **1978** Weals *Loggers Wrote* = the handyman who did the chores around the logging camp bunkhouse and dining room and kitchen. Washed dishes, scrubbed pots and pans after each meal, carried out the garbage, swept out the buildings daily and made the beds, gathered and carried in firewood for the kitchen and heating stoves; looked after the cows and [would] milk them daily (where remote camps had cows); fed the pigs (when they were there). **1994** Farwell and Buchanan *Logging Terms* = a person who kept the camp area clean and the buildings clean and warm and was responsible for keeping order and policing the conduct of men in camp. **1995** Montieth *Tall Tales* 11 Usually one man and his wife looked after the logging camp. The wife cooked the meals. The husband sometimes called "lobbyhog," [did] most outside chores. He fed the animals, mended harnesses, repaired tools, filed saws. **2006** Farwell *Logging Term* 1021 Adjoining the mess hall was a "lobby" where the men could socialize, ruled over by the "lobby hog," usually a tough old lumberman who played both housekeeper and peacemaker.

loblo̍lly *noun* A muddy puddle, mudhole.

1943 Justus *Bluebird* 54 Here and there they came upon rain puddles left in the hollows and had a fine time splashing in them with their bare feet, making loblollies in the soft mud. **1957** Justus *Other Side* 33 Her bare brown toes felt delightfully cool as she made loblollies in the mud puddles. **1963** Edwards *Gravel* 86 They [= The horses] would be tired and muddy, no doubt, for it had been raining all day and the road was a loblolly of slush and mud. **c1975** *Miners' Jargon* 5 = huge mudhole in [a coal] mine. **1976** Garber *Mountain-ese* 54 = mire, mudhole. "After the rain the road wuz one big loblolly."

[DARE *loblolly* n 2 scattered, but especially frequent South, South Midland]

lock *noun* A joint of the body.

1917 Kephart *Word-List* 414 = joint. "The pain's way back in the lock o' my jaw." **1927** Woofter *Dialect from WV* 360 = joint. "He stuck the axe in the lock of his knee." **1995–97** Montgomery Coll (known to Brown, Bush, Oliver); I've got a swelling in the lock of my jaw (Cardwell). **2001** Lowry *Expressions* 3 The pain is moving down into the lock of my hip.

locked (also *locky*) *adjective* See 1992 citation.

1992 Jones and Miller *Sthn Mt Speech* 93 = interwoven grains in wood. "This is hard to split—it's locked." **1996–97** Montgomery Coll: *knot locked* (known to Brown); *locked* (known to Bush, Cardwell, Hooper), = wood hard to split due to knots (Cypher); *locked grain* (known to Jones); *locky* (known to Cardwell).

locked bowels *noun* Constipation, especially when severe.

1990 Cavender *Folk Medical Lex* 26 = impaction of the bowels ... intestinal obstruction. **1997** Montgomery Coll (known to nine consultants from the Smoky Mountains). **2000** Lowry *Folk Medical Term* = intestinal obstruction, most often severe constipation. **2013** Reed *Medical Notes* = intestinal obstruction or constipation.

[DARE *locked bowels* n pl 1 chiefly South, South Midland]

locked grain See **locked**.

locky See **locked**.

locust *noun* Variant plural form *locuses, locustes* (for the insect or the tree).

1939 Hall Coll: *locustes*. **1973** Miller *English Unicoi Co* 93 *locuses* = attested by 1 of 6 speakers. **1991** Thomas *Sthn Appal* 236 They'd cut an' peeled locuses—great-big locuses—bigger'n a man's thigh.

loft (also *loft room*) *noun* The second story of a building, especially the attic of a house used for storage or sleeping quarters. See also **barn loft**.

1864 *Poteet CW Letters* (Nov 2) before [the child] died it would look at me and then point with its little finger towards the loft I think it saw the Angels that come to take it to heaven. **1881** Pierson *In the Brush* 25 That night I slept in the loft of a log-cabin. It was entirely unceiled, and the roof was so low that I had to stoop to make my way to my bed; and when in it I could easily place my hands upon the roof-boards and rafters. The openings between the logs afforded abundant ventilation. **1904** Fox *Christmas Eve* 162 One fool feller stuck his head up into the loft and lit a match to see if my boys was up thar. **1915** Dingus *Word-List VA* 185 *loft* = the second story of a house, upstairs. **1934–47** *LAMSAS Appal*: *loft* = attested by 26/148 speakers (17.5%) from WV, 4/20 (20%) from VA, 17/37 (43.2%) from NC, 9/14 (64.3%) from SC, and 5/12 (41.7%) from GA. **1937** Hall Coll: *loft* = the attic or garret of a house, the space under a roof, sometimes used for sleeping. Called "upstairs" even [if] no stairs or "up in the loft." **1962** Justus *Smoky Sampler* 33 In summer he slept out here instead of in the loft-room bed because he said it was cooler. **1966** Dakin *Vocab Ohio River Valley* 47 The older Kentucky word, which predominates in the Mountains and is still used by many throughout the state in addition to the newer *attic*, is *loft*. **1970** GSMNP-26:6 As far as I know he kept his meat a-hanging in the loft, had him a hole to go up in the loft. **1976** Ledford *Folk Vocabulary* 279 *Living room, gutters, mantle* ... have completely replaced *big house, eaves trough, fireboard* ... throughout the area. **1991** Thomas *Sthn Appal* 180 He called th' men back then—so menny weeks—an' they raised th' house four rounds higher, so he'd have a loft in it. **2004** Myers and Boyer *Walker Sisters* 16 The living room served as the bedroom for the parents and all the girls. The boys slept in the attic or loft, where there were more beds, chairs, and chests with many items attached to the walls and ceiling. To reach the upper bedroom or loft, one had to climb a ladder attached to a wall.

[DARE *loft* n 2 scattered, but chiefly South Midland, South]

log berry *noun* See citations.

1941 *FWP Guide WV* 403 Although changed in other respects, the West Virginia logger has retained his jargon. Cooks are still "stomick robbers"; their helpers are "cookees"; coffee is "jerk-water"; prunes, "log berries"; biscuits, "cat-heads"; and milk is "cow." **1964** Clarkson *Lumbering in WV* 366 *log berries* = prunes.

log boom *noun* Same as **boom[1] A**.

1977 Arnow *Old Burnside* 64 I had seen a log boom from the lower hill in the lower town.

log building (also *log-built house, log cabin, log house*) *noun* A dwelling built of whole or hewn logs, usually of one room (but see **double cabin**). [Editor's note: These terms were rarely heard in the Smoky Mountains by the 1930s because frame construction had replaced log construction when lumber became widely available and the standard of living improved in the early 20th century. Although the cabin has been the best-known structure, other buildings were also made of logs, such as barns, smokehouses, and corn cribs. For the most thorough discussions of types and constructions of dwellings in the southern mountains, see Glassie 1965, Glassie 1968, and Morgan 1990. In mountain speech *log house* has been the most common term.] See also **double cabin**.

1881 Pierson *In the Brush* 66 On reaching his house, I found three buildings—log-house, log-kitchen, and log-stable. **1937** Hall Coll (Bradley Fork NC) It was a log house that I was borned in. **1939** Hall Coll (Deep Creek NC) I was borned in Jackson County [NC] in a little old log cabin. **1956** Hall Coll (Cosby TN) The first school I went to was a little old log-built house up on Cosby. **1969** GSMNP-38 [I] stayed here till we moved that big old hewn log house down the country here. **1978** Montgomery *White Pine Coll* IV-4 Shingles are about gone from this territory, unless it'd be on an old log house somewhere. **1990** Morgan *Log House E TN* 19 After the Civil War the log house remained an important landscape feature in East Tennessee. ... As with the larger Upland South region, it is difficult to be specific about the decline of log house construction in East Tennessee. In some areas log construction may have declined soon after the Civil War, but in other areas log house construction persisted into the present century. *Ibid.* 59 The persistence of log house construction in Blount County and East Tennessee until the late nineteenth-century reflects a cultural tradition of the area's residents. Most of the nineteenth-century log houses were not built as temporary structures to be replaced shortly after construction by more substantial frame or brick buildings. On the contrary, the houses were generally well-constructed permanent buildings. **1990** Williams *Pride and Prejudice* 223 While log houses now are clearly seen as a part of folk tradition, boxed houses seem hardly to qualify as adequate housing. **1995** Jones *Early Sevier Archit* 10 Initial frontier dwellings were often hastily, and poorly, constructed and were not meant to be permanent, therefore no original eighteenth and very few early nineteenth century log buildings survive in [Sevier] county. Most of the remaining log buildings were built of better quality construction methods employed in the second quarter of the nineteenth century.

log-built house, **log cabin** See **log building**.

log-cabin bonnet *noun* See citations.

1957 Parris *My Mts* 229 The headpiece was stitched and places was left so you could stick pieces of cardboard or pieces of oak splits in [the bonnet] to make it stand up. When you washed it you took out the splits. That's why they called it a log-cabin bonnet. **1995–97** Montgomery *Coll* (known to Brown).

log cock *noun* The pileated woodpecker (*Dryocopus pileatus*).

1926 Ganier *Summer Birds* 34 The pileated woodpecker was noted at several points, including Gatlinburg and from Jakes Creek (2,700 feet) to the top of Miry Ridge (4,700). A number of their excavations were to be seen along this ridge. The "Log-cock" is one of the most picturesque birds of these fine forests. **1929** Kephart *Smoky Mt Magic* 89 Out of a tall tree flew a log-cock, or pileated woodpecker, filling the forest with a shrill, sharp cry of whicker—whicker—whicker—that warned every creature within half a mile that an intruder had come.

log crib *noun* A small outbuilding constructed of logs, used for storage. See also **crib 1**, **shuck pen**.

1969 Hall *Coll* (Big Bend NC) Them bears was in a little old log crib there. They had them chained to it, just a little old small chain.

log dogs *noun* Andirons. Same as **dog iron(s)**.

1986 Pederson et al. *LAGS* (Campbell Co TN).

log dog trot See **dogtrot**.

logging gravy *noun* See citation. Same as **sawdust gravy**.

1998 Dabney *Smokehouse Ham* 217 The cheap, easy-to-fix cornmeal gravy caught on. While "sawmill gravy" was the popular nickname, some called it "Logging Gravy." Others called it Poor Do or Life Everlasting, a reference to what many felt was its role in keeping them alive.

logging works *noun* A logging camp, logging operation.

1956 Hall *Coll* (Townsend TN) Sherman Myers had been on loggin' works, and he'd catch them tales and tell 'em.

log gum *noun* Same as **gum A2**.

1956 GSMNP-24:62 They came over here and robbed his bees, which were in some of these old log gums.

loggy (also *logy*) *adjective* Of a person or animal: sluggish, lethargic.

1946 Stuart *Plum Grove Hills* 161 I passed the jug around to the people that felt loggy. **c1970** Handlon *Ol' Smoky* 90 Ola explained that wasps were loggy in the fall. **1995** Montgomery *Coll* (known to Brown, Cardwell, Oliver), = not feeling well, without much energy (Jones), = sluggish due to overeating, constipation, or whatever (Weaver).

[cf EDD *louggy*, *loogy* "tired . . . slow" (Cornish dialect) and *loggy* adj 2 "heavy, slow-moving, dragging" (Hampshire and Isle of Wight)]

log house See **log building**.

log knotter *noun* See citation. Same as **knot bumper**.

1930 Pendleton *Wood-Hicks Speak* 88 = a trimmer of branches.

log-pull (also *log-pulling contest*) *noun* A contest to see which horse or mule can pull a log the farthest.

2012 Still *Hills Remember* 346 The judge paying four dollars out of his pocket for a day's rent, as well as putting up five as a prize for the log-pulling contest. *Ibid.* 354 If the ranks of the traders thinned, there was a gain in onlookers from the town roosting above the commotion, apparently awaiting the log-pull, as nothing else promised.

log-pulling contest See **log-pull**.

log raising *noun* Same as **house raising**. See also **barn raising**, **house covering**.

1864 Gilmore *Down in TN* 43 In April, 1862, he and his band came upon a party of neighbors collected at a log raising in Fentress County. **1924** Abernethy *Moonshine* 133 At "log-raisin's" Phil could outlift a dozen common men. **1973** GSMNP-6:2 When he got his logs all hewed, then they had a what they called a log raising. . . . The men came to help him lift the logs up after he'd probably pulled 'em in there with oxen from out back in the flats. **1989** *Matewan OHP-18* My father and my brothers, we had what they called a log raising. He cut the logs and brought them in. Then a whole gang of the neighbors come in and help us put the logs up, and he finished the top and everything on it, and rive boards. We'd cut trees up, oak trees, and rive boards to put the top on the house.

log roll See **log rolling**.

log-roller *noun* See citations.

1963 White *Marbles E KY* 58 = large marbles [sic]. **1968** *DARE Survey* (Big Stone Gap VA) = the big [marble] that's used to knock others out of the ring.

log rolling (also *log roll*) *noun*

1 Formerly, a community work activity to assist a family clear land by felling and trimming trees and then rolling the logs away to be piled and burned or otherwise disposed of, permitting a house to be constructed and cultivation to be begun. The family often treated neighbors to a meal and dance after the work was completed. See also **new ground**.

1824 (in **1912** Doddridge *Notes on Settlement* 88) The standard dish, for every log rolling, house raising and harvest day, is a pot pie, or what in other countries is called a sea pie. **1843** (in **1974** Harris *High Times* 29) The news goes forth that on such a day there will be a "log-rolling" and "quilting" at Capt. Dillon's. The sun has scarcely risen on that day, when every strong yeoman and buxom lass in the neighborhood are up and stirring, preparing for the "merry meeting." Hugh Dillon is started with the well-worn keg for first proof "mountain dew"; his sisters are preparing a sumptuous breakfast; corn-meal, eggs, and a large brown ham, are called into requisition, all of which are fast assuming "other shapes." **1881** Atkinson *After Moonshiners* 141 Corn-husking, and house-raising, are very much the same as log-rolling, and are enjoyed fully as much. At night, following all these labors, comes the dance. **1889** Phelan *History of TN* 28 In some localities more thickly settled than others, neighbors render each other mutual assistance. In this case, the trunks of very large trees were cut down, chopped into logs, rolled together, and set on fire. Hence the phrase log-rolling in the vocabulary of our political commonplaces. **1913** Kephart *Our Sthn High* 308–9 There are today fewer log rollings and house raisings, fewer husking bees and quilting parties, than in former times. **1939** Hall *Coll* (Hazel Creek NC) I've heared her tell about having log rollings, you know, back in her day. When she started raising a family. They'd have these log rollings. They'd all go and enjoy themself. **1948** Dick *Dixie Frontier* 125 One of the first of these [activities]in a frontier area was log-rolling, which prevailed until the last vestiges of frontier life had disappeared—long after the necessity that first produced it had passed away. Despite the fact that it was the hardest work on the frontier, it was an occasion of mirth and festivity and kept alive feelings of sympathy and neighborliness. **1956** Hall *Coll* (Cosby TN) Every man, he'd grub and clear up a piece of land, new ground, in the winter time. They'd have log rollin's in the spring. Maybe twenty or thirty helped each other, they'd pile logs and burn 'em before they could plant corn. They'd have a big dinner—chicken, blackberry pie. *Ibid.* (Cades Cove TN) They used to have log rollin's. They'd gather up crowds.... They'd have new ground, roll the logs together, and burn 'em. People would help another out. But that's a thing of the past now. **1972** *Graham County* 50 The girdling process of clearing land was slow; therefore, many pioneers preferred to cut down the trees immediately. The trees were then trimmed and cut into convenient lengths for handling. When time for the piling of the logs arrived, a farmer announced a "log rolling." All the neighbors would arrive early with hand spikes to help pile the logs in great heaps for burning. The "log rolling" was a cooperative enterprise in which everyone participated ungrudgingly without charge. The occasion was not only helpful as a source of labor supply but also a time of great merriment for the entire community. **c1975** Lunsford *It Used to Be* 21 Now, people going to marry or have married and need to have a few more quilts and things of that kind, why, they'll make up a lot of quilt tops and give a quiltin'. Of course, that's a lot of fun, and often they give a quiltin' at the same time they have a log rollin' or something of that kind,—a working, a house-raising. **1991** Haynes *Haywood Home* 44 Barn and house raisings, corn shuckings, quiltings, log rollings and such were not only community labor sharing projects, but were also social occasions.

[DARE *logrolling* vbl n 1 chiefly South, South Midland]

2 See citation.

1973 Miller *English Unicoi Co* 149 *log roll* = a celebration at which the mountain people gathered for the men to demonstrate their skill at cutting [and] handling timber.

log slide *noun* See citations. Same as **slide B2**.

1892 Doak *Wagonauts Abroad* 249 All along [the river] we can see lodged sawlogs among the rocks, log slides on the opposite bank, and great piles of logs, got down too late for the last "tide." **1961** Lambert *Little River* 36 Log slides, one of which was two and one-half miles long, were constructed to bring logs from the higher elevations down to the railroad. Horses were used to bunch logs at the slides and the railroad and for clearing skid roads as well. **1964** Clarkson *Lumbering in WV* 366 = a V-shaped trough built down a slope for the purpose of sliding logs to a landing at the bottom. **1994** Lambert *Sawmills* 44 The logs were brought down to the tram road by skidding and ballhooting, some of the hollows had log slides that the logs would be rolled into and would go down the slide at a fast pace.

logway *noun* See citation.

1977 Hamilton *Mt Memories* 28 From one place, near the mill, we could see the dam with water running over it. A rough bridge, near the mill, called a "logway," was used to bring logs across the river from the other side.

logy See **loggy**.

lone (also *lone self*) *noun* in phrases *all my lone*, *by my lone*, *to his lone*, etc. = by oneself, (all) alone, without company or assistance.

1898 Elliott *Durket Sperret* 15 You'll leave ole John to his lone. **1917** (in **1944** Wentworth *ADD* 15) (sWV) I was here all my lone. **1927** Furman *Lonesome Road* 118 Hit hurts me bad to think of you there all by your lone. **1973** GSMNP-6:24 He knew where I had gone on top of Bullhead by my lone self. **1996–97** Montgomery *Coll*: *by his lone* (Brown); *by my lone* (known to Adams, Brown, Oliver, Weaver); I guess I'll have to do it by my lone (Cardwell); *by his lone self* He lived by his lone self for two years after his wife died (Cardwell); *by my lone self* (known to Bush); *by my lonesome* (known to Jones, Weaver); He went there on his lone. **2007** McMillon *Notes*: *by his lone* = by himself.

[cf OED3 (at *lone* adj 6b) Scot and north dialect 1375→; EDD (at *lone* sb² 6(1)) Scot, nEngl; cf SND *one's langsome* (at *lane* adj 2), *lang* adj 2 with possessive pronouns]

lonesome

A *adjective* Of an place or inanimate object: gloomy, desolate, melancholic. [Editor's note: This term referring to a person's feelings is widespread in the US.]

1861 *Lance CW Letters* (Nov 10) I thought of youns at home and me here on the lonesom Sea Side and did not know what minute the yankies mite come. **1873** Smith *Arp Peace Papers* 124 We looked at our desolatid land, our loansum chimni[es]. **1941** Hall *Coll* (Waynesville NC) [The Shepherd of the Hills] was the lonesomest picture I ever saw. **1977** Douglas and McClellan *Fiddler* 21 When he tuned that old five-string banjo up, he'd play that banjo—it was so doggone lonesome that it was pitiful and you could hear it all over the country. **1982** Powers and Hannah *Cataloochee* 363 Os Deaver, a master fiddler before the Civil War, improvised a hauntingly lovely tune. . . . A woman, half-drowsing on a cot, sat up to cry, "Oh, play that lonesome thing again!" His tune was called Lonesome Laurel thereafter. **1992** Gabbard *Thunder Road* 65 They chose a mountain laurel thicket at the base of a lonesome hillside far removed from prying eyes. **1993** Parris *Folklore* 473 There's nothin' as lonesome as an owl a-hootin' in the night. **2009** Benfield *Mt Born* 169 This word has a meaning that is unique and haunting. It is to have pangs of sadness in remembrance of times past. Places that have known tragedy, or life that is no more, are lonesome places. Things lonesome are a cow lowing at night, an abandoned house, or the sudden recollection of a old love. There is the term "high lonesome," which means a place high and remote in the mountains.

[DARE *lonesome* adj C chiefly South Midland]

B *noun*

1 See **lone**.

2 Melancholy.

1958 Campbell *Tales* 38 He went hunting to wear off his lonesome, and he found his brother hiding amongst some golden lilies.

[cf SND *one's lanesome* (at *lane* adj 1.(6))]

lonesome bird *noun* A dove.

1957 Justus *Other Side* 27 "I was named for a bird," Dovie told her. "Pappy got it out of the Bible. But Mammy says she named me for the bird that sings away up on the mountain. Some folks call it the lonesome bird. Maybe you have heard it." **1998** Montgomery *Coll* (known to Bush, Cardwell).

lonesome waters *noun* The water(s) of one's native area; *figuratively* home, of which one is reminded by the taste of water there.

1936 Stuart *Lonesome Waters* 32 I told them that I loved our lonesome waters / Our woodland fern with fancy top that stoops / To kiss Kentucky's lonesome mountain waters. **1938** Stuart *Dark Hills* 222 I couldn't forget the old Kentucky lonesome waters. **1950** Stuart *Hie Hunters* 247 "Once you git the taste of fragrant light burley, you'll always have the taste, so they say. It's the same as drinkin' lonesome water." **1963** White *Marbles E KY* 76 An ambivalent love-hate for his environment is implicit in the highlander's expression that if once you take a drink of lonesome waters, you'll come back some day, implying that nostalgia will draw the wanderer home to die. **1964** Clarke *Stuart's Writing* 179–80 The lonesome waters of Kentucky and other parts of the hill country are the creeks, branches, and small rivers of the region. To drink of lonesome waters is to develop a strong attachment for one's native hill community, an attachment that will survive through years of absence from the hills and lead the native home to die. **1965** Clarke *Proverbs of Stuart* 155 The usual implication is that nostalgia for one's native hills and streams will draw him homeward to die.

[DARE *lonesome water(s)* n especially KY]

'long See **along 1**.

long-faced *adjective* Balding.

1936 Farr *Folk Speech Mid TN* 275 He's a long-faced old man. **1995** Montgomery *Coll* (known to Cardwell, Shields).

long fire *noun phrase* See citation.

c1975 Lunsford *It Used to Be* 168 "Long fire" is used in speaking about a gun firing, and the time it takes the hammer [that] comes down on the little cap that's put just over the tube in the old squirrel rifle that carries the fire down to the powder till the gun is fired. When the powder is damp, the gun will take "long fire." The cap will fire and the powder will be a long time burning enough to explode the entire amount of powder so that we say it "took long fire."

longful *adjective* See citation.

c1954 Adams *Word-List* = long.

long green *noun* See citation. Same as **hillside navy**.

c1960 Wilson *Coll*: = home-grown rather than store-bought chewing or smoking tobacco.

long handles (also *long drawers, long handled drawers, long handle underwear*) *noun* Underwear with long legs and sleeves, worn especially by children. See also **unionalls 2**, **woolies**. [Editor's note: The term *long johns* is widespread in the US.]

1954 GSMNP-19:16 Yeah, he had on some long handles, underwear. **1966** *DARE Survey* (Brasstown NC, Burnsville NC, Spruce Pine NC, Gatlinburg TN) *long handles*. **1975** Mull *Old Burke* 151 On Easter Sunday, if the weather was warm and clear, I could take off my winter shoes, roll up my "long handles," and go barefoot. **1978** Slone *Common Folks* 221 An old man climbed up there and took the flag down, and used it to make himself a pair of long-handle underwear. **1981** Whitener *Folk-Ways* 53 Knitting mills and department stores indicate that their sales of long handled drawers are up 200 per cent or more over last year's sales, with demand exceeding supply in many parts of the country. *Ibid.* 54 Of course, modern long handles are a far cry from those of bygone days. They have been prettified, thermofied, and advertised until they have achieved social acceptance. **1997** Montgomery *Coll*: *long handles* (known to ten consultants from the Smoky Mountains). **2016** *Blind Pig* (Jan 21) *long drawers*.

[DARE *long handles* n pl chiefly South, South Midland, West]

long-headed *adjective*

1 (also *long-minded*) Discerning, shrewd.

1957 Combs *Lg Sthn High: Word List* 61 *long-headed* = shrewd in business or trading. *Ibid.* 61 *long-minded* = shrewd, smart, intelligent.

[EDD (at *long* adj 1.64); SND (at *lang* I.6(22))]

2 Determined, stubborn.

1938 Hall *Coll* (Emerts Cove TN) = stubborn; with one's head set on something; can't get it changed. **1939** Hall *Coll* (Big Creek NC) [In "catching" babies] I was long-headed, wasn't afraid of nothin'. I never lost a baby in the whole boundary of 'em. *Ibid.* (White Oak NC) You're so long-headed [I] can't tell you anything. **c1960** Wilson *Coll* = obstinate, usually foresighted. **1973** Davis *'Pon My Honor* 76 Grand pappy remarked confidently, "I knowed she wuz a long-headed woman, and would come up with a good scheme." **1994** Montgomery *Coll* (known to Shields).

[DARE *long-headed* adj 2 "stubborn, obstinate" South, South Midland]

long hog *noun* See citation. Same as **side meat.**

1964 Clarkson *Lumbering in WV* 366 = pork but not in referring to hams or shoulders. Syn. side meat, sow belly. **1980** Riggleman *WV Mtneer* 126–27 [Loggers] usually had nicknames for everybody and everything around the camp. . . . Meat was "sowbelly" or "long hog."

long johns *noun* See citation.

1968 *DARE Survey* (Brasstown NC) = a child's stilts.

long-minded See **long-headed 1.**

long of See **along of 1.**

'long of See **along of 2.**

long red *noun* A superior grade of tobacco leaf.

1944 Dingus *Tobacco Words* 67 = the (small) upper leaves of high marketable quality. **1949** Arnow *Hunter's Horn* 69 LeeRoy sat a long time . . . not far from the schoolhouse and took a chew of long red.

[DARE *long red* n especially South Midland]

long rooter *noun* See citation. Same as **pine rooter, rooter.**

1975 Dwyer *Thangs* 27 Razorback hogs, called "long rooters," are variously colored, long-snouted, long-tailed, long-bodied, long-legged, long-tusked, even long in the squeal. Shaped in front like a thin wedge, he can easily go through laurel thickets. He has a tough hide cushioned with bristles. He despises thorns, brambles, and rattlesnakes, alike. He can run like a deer and climb like a goat. His long snout can scent like a cat's, yet it can burrow, uproot, and overturn heavy objects. He lives a communal life and unites with others of his kind for purposes of defense. . . . Wild razorback boars were a constant problem for the mountain man as the razorback boars would mix with his tame sows and shoats, then lead them away. His tame pigs would then revert to the wild.

long sweetening *noun* Any heavy, syrupy sweetener, usually molasses or honey. See also **short sweetening.**

1892 Allen *Cumberland Gap* 258 Another beverage is "mountain tea," which is made from the sweet-scented golden-rod and from winter-green—the New England checkerberry. These decoctions they mollify with home-made sorghum molasses, which they call "long sweetening," or with sugar, which by contrast is known as "short sweetening." **1895** Edson and Fairchild *TN Mts* 372 Will you have some long sweetening from this jug? **1901** McClintock *KY Mts* 12 There is either "short sweetening"—a cheap, brown sugar—or "long sweetening"—home-made molasses. **1955** Parris *Roaming Mts* 153 An old timer is one who remembers . . . when long sweetening was honey and short sweetening was maple sugar. **1959** Roberts *Up Cutshin* 8 [We] made our molasses into long sweetening and tapped our sugar trees for short sweetening. **1976** Garber *Mountain-ese* 55 We hain't got no boughten sugar but we've got plenty uv long-sweetenin'. **c1995** *Pioneer Farmstead* 10 Sorghum cane was for the pioneer the source of molasses, sometimes called "long sweetening" because of its rope-like texture. It was eaten straight from the jar or used in cooking as a general substitute for sugar. **1999** Montgomery *Coll* = only molasses (Cardwell). **2007** McMillon *Notes* = usually molasses, though there are a number of sweeteners made from other things, like maple, birch, etc.

[DARE *long sweetening* n chiefly South, South Midland]

long tom *noun*

1 Used as a nickname for a field cannon.

1861 (in **1974** Aiken *Offield CW Letters* 118) (Aug 4) We also took 82 pieces of the best artillery in the North and took a long cannon which they called long Tom about 20 feet in length. **1862** *Love CW Letters* (Sept 28) we sent down to fort fisher and got old long tom and brough him up and give them three rounds and they run back out of our way. **1862** *Robinson CW Letters* (June 22) Our troups Cut our tents all to peaces & break all the Cook vessels & spiket long tom that tha[y] took at the Manases battel & fetch it dow[n] abluf whare tha[y] cant git it out.

2 A rifle or shotgun.

1939 Farr *TN Mt Regions* 91 = a shot gun. "He took his long tom to the woods." **1972** Hall *Sayings* 97 He had an old Long Tom hog rifle, called it "Rattlesnake." **1993** Cunningham *Sthn Talk* 93 Grandpa toted a 36-inch long tom 12-gauge that would knock a squirrel out of the tallest tree in the woods.

3 See citation.

1940 *FWP Guide GA* 383 Placer mining, known here as deposit mining, utilized crude apparatus and was an inefficient process; as two men worked together, one would shovel gravel into the "long tom" or trough.

long tongue *noun* See citation.

1957 Broaddus *Vocab Estill Co KY* 48 = the spleen of a hog.

longwall mining *noun* See citation.

2002 Armstead *Black Days* 244 = [a] mining method that revolutionized the industry in which long sections of coal, up to one thousand feet across, are mined at a time. [A] shearer cuts and deposits coal directly onto [a] conveyor system. Shields support the roof and advance the longwall. As [the] system moves on, the wall collapses behind the work area. [A] small crew of operators can extract more than two hundred tons in one hour.

look *verb*

1 To examine or inspect (especially fresh vegetables) for dirt, foreign objects, impurities, or insects; to sort thoroughly.

1982 Slone *How We Talked* 62 Some of the greens we used were not cooked, but eaten raw. They were "looked" (checked for bugs and rotting spots), washed, sprinkled with salt and wilted or "killed" by pouring real hot grease over them. **1990** Bailey *Draw Up Chair* 12 I told her, "Now you be sure to look the beans." **1991** Thomas *Sthn Appal* 58 Th' hardest bunch of bees that I ever tried to find was back over here. Folks had course[d] 'um th' year before. An' ever tree in th' woods there had been looked. **1993** Ison and Ison *Whole Nother Lg* 40 *look the beans* = to inspect dried beans or other food for foreign objects. **2005** Bailey *Henderson County* 31 I told her, "Now you be sure to look the beans." I don't ever cook my beans without I look 'em first. **2007** McMillon *Notes* = to examine in order to detect dirt or impurities: "She looked the cabbage before rinsin' it."

[OED3 *look* v 2a(a) now regional; EDD *look* v 4 "to examine, view, inspect"]

2 To have the features of (a certain family).

1992 Offutt *KY Straight* 37 You look a Boatman . . . Got them shitty eyes all of us got. **1999** Offut *Out of Woods* 53 You look a Goins.

look for (also *look out, look out for, look to*) *verb phrase* To expect, look forward to; to intend to.

1834 Crockett *Narrative* 130 This almost alarmed her, for she was looking every minute for me to die. **1862** *Parris CW Letters* (Feb 6) we have one in the hospitel and we are looking for him in Camp. **1863** *D B Walker CW Letters* (Aug 3) we think we will be mounted and ef we are you may look out for us for we will be sertain and come. **1863** *Lister CW Letters* (Nov 18) thay seem to be looking for a powerful fite hear now. **1885** Bayless *Letters* 118 They are looking for her to die. **1910** Cooke *Power and Glory* 10 I'm a widder, and I never look to wed again. **1937** Hall *Coll* (Emerts Cove TN) He's lookin' for to quit. **1973** *Foxfire Interviews* A-73-86 I look to go to church and things like that. **1974** GSMNP-51:18 We didn't pay much attention to the Fourth of July, as I remember of, but we did look out for Christmas. **1979** *God Put Herbs* 10 There's an old lady in there. They're looking for her to die. **1999** Carver *Branch Water Tales* 2 I looked for her to set her foot down and not let me go with Dad.

[DARE *look* v B4 chiefly South, South Midland]

look out *verb phrase*

1 See **look for.**

2 To find, discover.

1862 *Robinson CW Letters* (May 25) you had better look you out Some old man that is too old to fite fur we are all in fur the ware.

lookout *noun*

1 An outlook, point of view.

1895 *Mt Baptist Sermon* 12 Ef they's ary man in this aujience thet don't agree with me, thet's his lookout, an' not mine. **1901** Harben *Westerfelt* 80 That's yore lookout, not mine, d—n you! **1994–97** Montgomery *Coll* (known to Brown, Cardwell, Jones, Oliver, Weaver).

2 A person watching the roads for law-enforcement officers searching for illegal **stills.**

1974 Dabney *Mt Spirits* 134 Cosby moonshiners had a unique way of signalling the arrival of revenuers—dynamite blasts. The first blast, set off by a "lookout" on a road leading through Cosby into the hills, would be repeated by subsequent blasts further into the hills, giving the moonshiner plenty of time to "pull the copper."

look out for See **look for.**

look over *verb phrase* To excuse, disregard, forgive (poor behavior or performance).

1862 *Neves CW Letters* (Feb 9) William you must look over my bad writeing as I havent my spectakles and cant see the ruling. **1862** *Shipman CW Letters* (May 26) I fear you cannot read this letter it is don in a hurry pleas look over it this time. **1886** Smith *Southernisms* 45 = overlook. **1938** Stuart *Dark Hills* 398 We'll look over all these lies he makes up about us and bring him home. **1938** (in **2009** Powell *Shenandoah Letters* 144) If they can look over old men an Rich men they sertain can look over boys an poor boys at that. **c1960** Wilson *Coll* = to forgive, overlook. **1997** Montgomery *Coll* (known to nine consultants from the Smoky Mountains).

[DARE *look over* v phr chiefly South, South Midland]

look to See **look for.**

look to die *verb phrase* See 1944 citation. See also **look for.**

1944 Williams *Word-List Mts* 30 = to be dangerously ill, on the point of death. "We are a-goin' to set up with Aint Hanner she is *a-lookin' to die.*" **1957** Hall *Coll* (Newport TN) The man was in the hospital lookin' to die. **1996** Montgomery *Coll* (known to Brown, Cardwell, Jones, Norris, Oliver).

looky spooky *noun* See citation.

2007 McMillon *Notes* = hide and go seek.

loom house *noun* A shed or small addition to a dwelling in which a loom is kept and weaving is done.

1995 Williams *Smoky Mts Folklife* 20 If the family did own a loom, it was often accommodated by some sort of shed addition or separate "house." Some loom houses were converted to kitchens, since cookstoves and separate kitchens became popular about the same time as store-bought cloth. **2001** Wilson *Textile Art* xiii Appalachian looms were large, cumbersome pieces of equipment made from kinds of wood and set up in the home, under a shed, or in an outbuilding called the "loom house."

loose *adjective* In bulk.

1939 Hall Coll The loose calomel that you buy at the drug store. **1986** Pederson et al. *LAGS* (Sevier Co TN) *loose coffee* = bulk coffee.

[cf SND *loup/lowp* v 1]

loosen *verb* See citation.

2009 Sohn *Appal Home Cooking* 298 = to thin. Mountain cooks loosen mayonnaise and breakfast gravy with milk.

lopper-jawed *adjective* Lopsided, crooked, askew. Same as **whopper-jawed 2.**

1927 Woofter *Dialect from WV* 360 = crooked. "That picture hangs lopper-jawed." **1975** Gainer *Speech Mtneer* 13 Your hat's on lopper-jawed. **1995–97** Montgomery Coll (known to Adams, Bush, Cardwell, Oliver, Shields, Weaver).

lord god almighty (also *lord god bird*) *noun* A pileated woodpecker (*Dryocopus pileatus*). See also **good god.**

1967 *DARE Survey* (Maryville TN) *Lord God Almighty* = pileated woodpecker. **1997** Montgomery Coll: *Lord God Almighty* (known to Cardwell). **2007** McMillon *Notes*: *Lord God bird* = pileated woodpecker.

[DARE *lord god* n 1 chiefly Southeast, especially Gulf States]

Lord have mercy See **lawd a mercy.**

Lord's bread wagon (also *Lord's corn wagon*) *noun* Same as **bread wagon.**

1913 Bruce *Terms from TN* 58 *Lord's bread wagon* = thunder. **1998** Montgomery Coll: *Lord's bread wagon* = thunder and rain, so called because we must have rain to make the corn grow (Brown); *Lord's corn wagon* (known to Jones).

Lord's corn wagon See **Lord's bread wagon.**

lose *verb*

A Variant past-participle form *losted*.

1927 Furman *Lonesome Road* 83 I couldn't take no pleasure in heaven knowing you was losted.

B To cause (someone) to become lost.

1989 Landry *Smoky Mt Interviews* 194 You can't lose a mountain man [i.e. he isn't going to get lost.] **2013** Byers *Mt Mother Goose* 155 Those dogs didn't come because that creature had carried them deep into the big swamp and had lost them or killed them.

[cf EDD Scot, Irish, northern English dial *loss*, southwest English dial *lost*]

lose one's taffy *verb phrase* See citations.

1927 Woofter *Dialect from WV* 360 = to fail: "He lost his taffy on that deal." **1939** Farr *TN Mt Regions* 91 *lost his taffy* = defeated: "He lost his taffy."

lostest *adjective* Most out of place.

1955 Ritchie *Singing Family* 49 I was the lostest thing for about six weeks. Couldn't work in the fields, nor do much of anything with my arm tied up.

lot

A *noun* An outdoor enclosure for domestic animals, especially for livestock, a pen. The term forms part of such compounds as **barn lot, calf lot, cow lot, gaunt lot, hog lot, mule lot, pig lot.**

1949 Kurath *Word Geog East US* 55 The yard adjoining or surrounding the barn is regularly called *barnyard* north of the Potomac, *lot* (or *stable lot, barn lot, farm lot*) to the south of it. **1966** Dakin *Vocab Ohio River Valley* 88 In the areas where *lot* competes with *barn yard*, the full *barn lot* is more common. *The lot* is common in eastern Kentucky and the usual term in the west. **1968** *DARE Survey* (Brasstown NC) = space near the barn with a fence around it where the livestock are kept.

[DARE *lot* n 1a scattered, but chiefly South, South Midland, TX]

B *verb* To confine an animal in such an enclosure, fence in.

1962 Hall Coll (Bryson City NC) He keeps them [dogs] lotted all the time. He can't let them out.

lots (in phrase *a lots*) *noun, adverb phrase* A large quantity, great deal, very much.

1900 Harben *N GA Sketches* 175 I'm a-gittin' to be a lots o' trouble to other folks. **1961** *Coe Ridge OHP-334A* I've heard that a lots of times. **1979** *Big South Fork OHP-27* They was a lots of people that rode [the incline] whenever I was with a-running it. **1983** *Dark Corner OHP-13A* They've even remodeled it and took a lots of it away. It was a two-story house . . . they used to be a lots of wheat, my husband raised a lot of wheat on this land. . . . Mister Gosnell used to do a lots of fox hunting up on the mountains. **2008** *Rosie Hicks* 3 It takes a lots of soil.

[DARE *lot* 3 chiefly South]

loud *adjective* Of an odor: strong, offensive.

1940 Stuart *Trees of Heaven* 31 I love that loud sweet smell. **c1960** Wilson Coll = having a very bad or offensive odor. **1967** Key *Tobacco Vocab* The tobacco smells loud when the stem gets rotten. **1968** *Expressions* 25 If something has . . . a strong scent, some say, "it has a good, loud scent."

[DARE *loud* adj B chiefly South, South Midland]

louse around (also *louze around*) *verb phrase* To freeload, idle about, waste time.

1917 Kephart *Word-List* 414 = to play the parasite. **c1920** (in **1993** Farwell and Nicholas *Smoky Mt Voices* 107) I don't see no use in jist louzin' around. **1994–97** Montgomery Coll (known to Brown, Bush, Cardwell, Oliver).

[cf EDD *lowse* v[1] 1 "to let loose, set free" Scot, Irel, nEngl, also v[1] 3 "stop working"; cf SND *lowse* v 6 "to become loose or free"; DARE *louse around* v phr especially South Midland]

louze around See **louse around.**

love *verb* To like, prefer.

1913 Kephart *Our Sthn High* 293 Your hostess, proffering apple sauce, will ask, "Do you love sass?" It is well for a traveler to be forewarned that the word love is commonly used here in the sense of like or relish. **1938** Hall *Coll* (Emerts Cove TN) I'd love to see him. **1939** Hall *Coll* (Gatlinburg TN) = to like; used without the emotional tone commonly associated with the word elsewhere. "Won't you love the fan?" **c1960** Wilson *Coll* = standard in the area for like. **1983** Broaddus *Estill Co KY Word List* 47 = to like (food).

[DARE *love* v D1 chiefly South, South Midland]

love ballad (also *love ditty, love song*) *noun* Usually a traditional Child ballad, but occasionally a secular song of another type, as opposed to hymns. See especially 1995 Williams citation. See also **ballad B1**, **devil's ditty**, **mountain song**, **song-ballad B1**.

1824 (in **1912** Doddridge *Notes on Settlement* 125) Singing was another, but no very common, amusement among our first settlers. Their tunes were rude enough, to be sure. Robin Hood furnished a number of our songs, the balance were mostly tragical. These last were denominated "love songs about murder." **1907** Parker *Folk-Lore of NC* 246 I am constrained to think that religion's austere disapproval of the banjo, the violin, the wicked "love songs," and all such ungodliness, has practically destroyed minstrelsy, and the memory of most of the old ballads. **1932** Sharp *Folk Songs* xxvi Very often they misunderstood our requirements and would give us hymns instead of the secular songs and ballads which we wanted; but that was before we had learned to ask for "love-songs," which is their name for the ditties. **1935** Sheppard *Cabins in Laurel* 277 At this time the modern folk songs, especially those featuring yodelling, are most popular with the young people, but the love songs (the mountain name for ballads), never lose their popularity. **1939** Hall *Coll* (Emerts Cove TN) I've heard her sing religious songs, [but] I never did hear her sing any love songs. **1955** Washburn *Country Doctor* 9 Their dialect and superstitions were interesting, as was also the fact that there were a number of older women who sang "love ditties," as they called the current ballads of the hill country, although the singing of these was frowned upon by the church folks. **1974** Roberts *Sang Branch* 39 The ballads had been fading out of tradition for a generation or two. They had come to be called "love ballets" or "devil's ditties," and had begun to die on the lips of the folk, even before the phonograph and the radio inundated them. **1978** Burton *Ballad Folks* 1 Mrs. Rena kept a "ballit" box. It wasn't a fancy one, rather it was a lap-sized cardboard box she had whipstitched along one edge for a hinge. It was in this box that she kept the "ballits" or words written down of "the love-songs or mountain songs, old people's songs"—the songs she had learned through the years. *Ibid.* 22 Apparently she learned mostly spiritual songs from her father and the lovesongs—"that's what they went by"—from her husband. **1995** Adams *Come Go Home* 81 A little before seven o'clock, every chair would be occupied by an ancient (ancient to me then meant over forty) male or female; and before long the room would swell with the sounds of the old love songs as one after the other of these singers took their turn. I attended many a Round Robin. **1995** Williams *Smoky Mts Folklife* 39 The category "love songs" covered the whole spectrum of secular song.... While they included the Child ballads, these antiquated ballads hardly exhausted the category of love songs. **2013** Hicks *Perception* 211 When I inquired of my grandmother about ballads, she firmly told me that "those old love songs" were about people who "didn't know how to act." All I ever heard her sing were hymns and gospel music.

love bump *noun* A small, infected pimple, usually on the face.

1997 Montgomery *Coll* (known to Brown, Bush, Cardwell).

[DARE *love bump* n 1 especially South, South Midland]

love comes bustin' out *noun* See **hearts bustin'**.

love ditty See **love ballad**.

love-entangled moss See **love in a tangle**.

love in a tangle (also *love-entangled moss*) *noun* A wall pepper (*Cedum acre*).

1962 Stubbs *Mountain-Wise* (Aug–Sept) 8 One of the smallest and most attractive of the sedums, or stone-crops, we were told, bears the name of *love-entangled moss*. **1975** Hamel and Chiltoskey *Cherokee Plants* 32 Love-in-a-tangle ... Cuscuta gronovii—Poultice for bruises.

love lick (also *love tap*) *noun* A rough caress.

1953 Davison *Word-List Appal* 12 = rough caress. **c1960** Wilson *Coll* = a rough caress; also love-tap.

love melon *noun* Same as **mayapple**.

1986 Pederson et al. LAGS (Cherokee Co GA).

love song See **love ballad**.

love tap See **love lick**.

love-vine *noun* A yellowish, twine-like, parasitic, wild plant, dodder (*Cuscuta* spp), manipulated to divine one's mate.

1894 Bergen *Plant Names III* 95 *Cuscuta compacta* = probably because used in love divination (Banner Elk NC). **1963** Watkins and Watkins *Yesterday* 99 The love vine, a small yellow plant which grew on weeds, was a parasite without a root system of its own. Someone pinched off a piece of the vine, slung it over his head three times, named it after his girl friend, and tossed it on the weeds. If it lived she loved him; if it died, she belonged to somebody else. **1968** Wilson *Folklore Mammoth Cave* 21 = dodder (Cuscuta, sp.). Youngsters tried their fortunes by throwing a piece of the plant on some growing weed or flower; if the parasite grew, that meant that one's sweetheart was true. **1982** Stupka *Wildflowers* 92 The host plant [of this parasite] furnishes all the food needed by the threadlike twining parasite, and its roots and lower portion soon dry up. "Love-vine" and "strangle-weed" are other names applied to this leafless, leechlike plant.

[DARE *love vine* n 1 especially South, South Midland]

low[1] See **allow.**

low[2] *verb* Of cattle: to make a low-pitched, deep call.

1892 Dromgoole *Dan to Beersheba* 82 Melia sighed, and taking her splint bonnet and piggin, went out to milk old Jule, lowing plaintively at the bars. **1925** Furman *Glass Window* 118–19 That hain't right Christmas, and never was: and the way I know it, the night afore Old Christmas, at midnight, all the cattle gets down on their knees and lows and prays, and the elders puts out a head of blossom. **1943** Hannum *Mt People* 93 The cows come down out of the woods to the barn lot and lowed and lowed. **1952** Beck *Herpetol Lore* 146 Then he kept the cow in late one morning and she began to low like she had a calf down in the field. **1966** *DARE Survey* (Burnsville NC, Spruce Pine NC) = the sound a cow makes, calling for her calf. **1980** Still *Run for Elbertas* 110 The cows began to gather at the pasture gate. They waited without lowing. **1987** Wear *Sevierville* 49 I loved to hear the cowbells and lowing of the cows as they moved up the street.

[echoic; OED3 *low* v[1] 1a c1000→); DARE *low* v chiefly South]

low[3] *adjective*

1 Short of stature.

1886 Smith *Southernisms* 40 Low, "short," as "a low, chunky man," is still very common in the South. **1918** *Story* 20 A petite lady is called a "low lady." **1939** Hall *Coll* (Waldens Creek TN) The Foxes are low, not tall, [with] small, black features. **1993** Ison and Ison *Whole Nother Lg* 41 = short of stature.

[DARE *low* adj chiefly South, South Midland]

2 Seriously sick or weak. Same as **low sick.**

1861 *Martin CW Letters* (Nov 29) Elijah Dunlap is verry low . . . they think he is taking the Fever at this time. **1862** *Epperly CW Letters* (July 27) it is Sad noos to my ears to hear from hur and to hear that She was so verry lo. **1863** *Leigh CW Letters* (May 14) I am sorrey to tell you that Mont Ledford is lying very low I dont think he can live very long he is as low as aney body can to be alive. **1900** Harben *N GA Sketches* 244–45 It looks like a shame, for brother is powerful low, an' any noise mought do 'im lots o' harm. **1997** Montgomery *Coll* She is very low with pneumonia (Norris).

low blood *noun* Usually low blood pressure or anemia; also through folk medical diagnosis, an inadequate supply of blood, a diagnosis based on the theory of humoral pathology, about which see 1990, 1992 citations and the entry "Folk Medicine" (pp. 866–68) in the *Encyclopedia of Appalachia*. See also **(the) high blood, thick blood, thin blood.**

1965 Weller *Yesterday's People* 119 Other common complaints are a "beeled head," "low blood," and "nerves." **1975** Chalmers *Better* 23 There were the regular preventive inoculations for all ages, and there were therapeutic inoculations ordered by various doctors for "low blood," "high blood," asthma, anemia, allergies and the like. **1982** Slone *How We Talked* 113 Low blood—Cure: Yellow Dock; also, drink Sassafras tea (This was a good tasting tea and was often used just for the taste.) **1990** Cavender *Folk Medical Lex* 26 = a) low blood pressure; b) an anemic condition; c) an abnormally low quantity of blood; d) low blood count. **1992** Cavender *Folk Hematology* 26–27 The majority of our informants defined low blood as a condition that would correspond symptomatically with anemia. Some defined low blood as low blood pressure, a condition, as one informant expressed it, "as bad as high blood pressure." . . . The primary symptom of low blood is fatigue. Some frequently used fatigue descriptors in the folk medical lexicon are "puny," "draggy," "give out," "hippoed," "down and out," and "peaked." Other symptoms are pale complexion, dizziness, and feeling listless and weak. **1993** Mason *Feather Crowns* 276 (*DARE*) "You're thinning out," Alma said to her. "You don't want to lose that weight too fast, or you'll have low blood." **1994** Montgomery *Coll* = anemia (Brown, Bush, Jones, Norris, Ogle). **2000** Lowry *Folk Medical Term* = anemia.

[DARE *low blood* n chiefly South, South Midland]

low case *noun* See citations. See also **high case.**

1969 Miller *Raising Tobacco* 34 These *casing houses* were equipped with tierpoles so tobacco could be brought there in *low case* (moist enough to handle if you were careful, but not moist enough to work off) and brought into *higher case*.

low coal *noun* Coal to be mined from a passage that has a low ceiling.

1976 Durrance and Shamblin *Appal Ways* 62 I worked in low coal and high mud when I first started. **1989** *Matewan OHP-102* The company asked him to go in low coal, at twenty-eight inch high, and he couldn't do it.

low-down

A *adjective*

1 Lacking energy, depressed.

1968 *DARE Survey* (Carroll Co VA). **1997** Montgomery *Coll* (known to Adams, Bush, Jones, Ledford, Oliver, Weaver).

[DARE *low-down* adj 2 especially South, South Midland]

2 Worthless, mean, contemptible (superlative form *low-downest*).

1863 *Vance Papers* (May 7) there are wealthy people here that furnish corn to persons that are not responsible for any thing and they do the s[t]illing while the weathy man reaps the benefit. they also get lowdown females to Still for them. **1899** Fox *Mt Europa* 33 Keep an eye open fer old Bill. They say that he air mighty low down, 'n' kind o' sorry 'n' skeery. **1963** Edwards *Gravel* 17–18 Every time a man gets a good meal planned in comes some of his wife's low-down kin folks to take it rat out from under his nose. **1976** Carter *Little Tree* 15 He said that was the low-downest bunch he'd ever heard of, Brutus and all the others, the way they went slipping up on a feller, outnumbering him and stabbing him to death. **1985** Dabney *More Mt Spirits* 28 A reporter's the low-downdest white man that's ever drawed a breath.

B *adverb* In a mean, hurtful, or despicable manner.

c1945 Haun *Hawk's Done* 266 Of course they done me low-down. But Ad brung Elzie up to be that way. And poor Froney don't know any better.

low foot plow *noun* See citation.

c1975 Lunsford *It Used to Be* 7 In those days, they had the two plows—the low-foot plow and the high-foot plow. The low-foot plow was homemade of wood. You'd put a bull-tongue plow on that foot. The tongue of wood at the back was morticed, the wooden foot put in, holes bored at the other end of the foot, and the bull-tongue plow put on by a heel screw. The handles were bolted to that foot, came back up, braced together and crooked over so you could hold the plow with the two hands. At the same time you'd have a line with a loop in it leading to the horse, and you'd put that loop around your wrist and drive your horse between the rows of corn. The high-foot was where the foot part was high enough to come up to about your waist and the tongue was morticed into that. Then the handles went down.

lowlander *noun* See citation.

2004 Larimore *Bryson Seasons* 19 Most of the folks were natives, as were their parents and their parents' parents. Most all of the physicians, and the nurses for that matter, were in at least their third to fourth decade of practice. They had their way of doing things and didn't "hanker to outsiders"—whom they called "flatlanders" if they liked you, or "lowlanders" if they did not.

low-minded *adjective* See citation.

1940 Farr *More TN Expressions* 447 = feeble-minded: "Taking a baby downstairs before he is taken upstairs will cause him to be low-minded."

low rate *verb phrase* To belittle, criticize, disparage (a person).

1939 Hall *Coll* (Swain Co NC) I don't like it [= Kephart's book] because he lowrates the mountain people too much. **1941** Still *Troublesome Creek* 142 They low-rated him partly because he didn't belong to the church, and never pulled his face down long as a mule's collar on Sunday. **1962** Dykeman *Tall Woman* 45 She wasn't low-rating Aunt Tildy who was salt and savor of their lives just now, but she was hungry for male voices and laughter, male appetites at the table, solid male footfalls on the floor. **1976** Still *Pattern of Man* 85 The Standing Rock schoolteacher and his bunch are low-rating me among the people. **1984** Burns *Cold Sassy* 211 She was just too busy low-rating Miss Love to fool with me. **2005** Williams *Gratitude* 507 = belittle . . . "She *low-rated* him right there in front of ever'body."

low sick *adjective phrase* See 1990 citation.

1990 Cavender *Folk Medical Lex* 27 = feeling very ill and near death. **1997** Montgomery *Coll* (known to Andrews, Bush, Ledford).

[DARE *low sick* adj phr South, South Midland, especially Gulf States]

low wine(s) *noun* In making liquor, the low-proof liquor produced by an initial distillation **run**. Same as **backing**, **singling(s)**.

1963 Carson *History Bourbon* 237 = a spirit low in alcoholic content resulting from the first distillation of the still beer; the first run. Also known as singlings. **1972** Carr *Oldest Profession* 78 The liquid distillate that comes from the still is called "singlin's" or "low wines." **1973** Wellman *Kingdom of Madison* 158 [Beer] went into the still, which was closed tightly and heated by a fire beneath. The rising vapor, condensed in the worm, became the first distillation, "singlings" or "low wines." This must be redistilled, with considerable expert attention, into "doublings." Carelessness will bring it out weak and distasteful or as pure alcohol. But when it is good, it is very good indeed. **c1975** Lunsford *It Used to Be* 81 Low wine is another word, and that is what is left after the first is run off and after they've proofed it. They proof it with a proof vial, mostly a ludnum bottle. Bateman's ludnum bottles are about seven inches long, broad bottom—an inch and a quarter at the bottom—and tapered to the top the size of your thumb. You get some of that collected in the bottle, shake it and judge as best you can whether it's high proof whiskey or whether it's low wine.

[OED3 *low wine(s)* n "the first liquid that is collected in the course of a distillation or series of distillations, which is typically further distilled into whisky or similar strong liquor," 1526→; Scots *lowins* "the low-quality spirit which results from the first distillation"; DARE *low wine* n chiefly South, South Midland]

L-type log house *noun* A dwelling with an L-shaped addition built onto the back of the kitchen. See 1995 citation. See also **log building**.

1954 Medford *Waynesv* [The John Rogers house on Upper Crabtree] had a kitchen addition to the rear, making it the common L-type log house of that day. It also had a wide chimney built of rock, affording a fireplace some 5 feet wide. This would give room for a large cooking or rendering pot (hung on pot hooks), a smaller hot water kettle and also the baking oven in front of the fire. **1988** Russell *It Happened* 8 The built-on ell housed the kitchen where again I can envision the wood-burning cook stove with its warming closet for the left-over sausage and biscuits or cornbread from noon meals and the reservoir for hot water. **1995** Trout *Historic Buildings* 17 A kitchen addition changed the configuration of the house. It was normally a separate structure that stood a few feet away from the house, or perhaps up against it, but whose walls were not actually tied into it. It was normally added to the rear, giving the house an "L" or "T" shape. The kitchen almost doubled the downstairs living space of early houses, which was good because so much of life centered on food preservation, preparation, and serving.

lug *noun*

1 (usually plural) An inferior grade of tobacco.

1940 Fitzpatrick *Lg Tobacco Market* 134 *lugs* = the leaves just above the flyings on a tobacco plant. **2007** McMillon *Notes*: *lugs* = the scraps when tobacco is handed off.

[DARE *lug* n^2 1 chiefly KY, VA]

2 See citation.

1890 Fruit *KY Words* 65 = a chew of tobacco.

lumber[1]

A *verb* To make a rumbling sound.

1890 Fruit *KY Words* 65 "Listen how he lumbers," said of a deep-mouthed dog's barking when he has treed a 'coon or 'possum. **1957** Combs *Lg Sthn High: Word List* 61 = to make a loud, boisterous noise.

B (also *lumberment*) *noun* A loud, boisterous noise.

1915 Dingus *Word-List VA* 185 (also *lumberment*) = loud noise. **1992** Jones and Miller *Sthn Mt Speech* 93 = a noise or commotion: "There's a lumberment in the kitchen."

lumber[2] *noun* Construed as a count noun; hence plural form *lumbers*.

1956 Hall *Coll* (Big Bend NC) They'd take lumbers and make their own caskets.

lumber grader *noun* See citation.

1994 Farwell and Buchanan *Logging Terms* = in logging, a person who determined quality of lumber by typing and grading it.

lumber herder *noun* In logging, a worker who helps steer logs down a mountain slope.

1966 Frome *Strangers* 169 Crews of "lumber herders," wearing calked shoes and armed with pickaroons and peaveys, broke log jams and sometimes rode downhill balancing themselves with a long pole while ducking low branches.

lumberment See **lumber**[1] **B**.

lumber room *noun* A room for storing unused or discarded items, more often known as a **plunder room**.

1982 Powers and Hannah *Cataloochee* 316 Out in the "lumber" room, a general storage place, was a loom. **1997** Montgomery *Coll* (known to Adams, Bush, Ledford, Oliver, Weaver).

[DARE *lumber room* n scattered, but chiefly South, South Midland]

lumber stacker *noun* See citation.

1994 Farwell and Buchanan *Logging Terms* = in logging, a person who determined which stack the lumber should be placed on.

lumber tipper *noun* See citation.

1994 Farwell and Buchanan *Logging Terms* = a member of a logging crew who put lumber on the proper stack, working with a lumber stacker.

lung balm *noun* A tea made from the bark of the black cherry tree (*Prunus serotina*), efficacious especially in treating a cough. See also **wild cherry**.

1980 *Smokies Heritage* 118 Fruit is only the beginning of the wild cherry's virtues. Mountain people have always known it as the "lung balm" tree, a source of medicine for the cold of highland winters. A tea of its bark, sometimes mixed with honey or whiskey, was given many a sufferer to still his cough.

lung fever *noun* A lung disease, usually pneumonia. Same as **pneumonia fever**.

1845 *Wyrick Letter* 3 a great maney died with the fever last fall and now the pepel are dien with the long fever. they have a little chil and then the fever rises. **1862** *Copenhaver CW Letters* (Aug 13) pa Snap [= his horse] has the lung feaver & I am afraid she is going to die She is geting vary thin. **1937** Hall *Coll* (Wears Cove TN) Lung fever [was the older term for] pneumonia fever. **1959** Pearsall *Little Smoky* 154 They take cognizance of vaguely defined maladies like "hives" and "bold hives," "phthisic" and other "lung fevers," "dew poison," "fall sores," "swelling" and "bloat."

lung powder *noun* See citation.

1980 Riggleman *WV Mtneer* 126–27 [Loggers] usually had nicknames for everybody and everything around the camp. . . . Snuff was "lung powder" or "graveyard dust."

Lydia basket See **Aunt Lydia basket**.

lye hominy *noun* Whole kernels of corn soaked in lye to remove the hulls before cooking. Same as **big hominy**. See also **little hominy**.

1957 Parris *My Mts* 110 Grandma made her own hominy. Folks called it lye hominy. She boiled shelled hard corn in a solution of lye water from hickory ashes poured into the ash hopper back of the house. **1995–97** Montgomery *Coll* (known to Ledford, Oliver, Shields), = some people made lye hominy and others made hominy using soda to skin the corn (Adams), = the lye softened the husk of the grain of corn so that it could be washed away in water (Cardwell); "I'm going to make lye hominy tomorrow" (Brown). **1998** Dabney *Smokehouse Ham* 316 [Mountain people] called grits "small hominy" in contrast to what they had eaten down through the years—whole-grain "big hominy," "whole hominy," or, the really traditional name, "lye hominy." The latter came from the pioneers' practice of boiling the whole grains of corn in their washpots after leaching off the bran with lye.

[DARE *lye hominy* n chiefly South, South Midland]

M

ma (also *maw*) *noun* usually [mɑ] or [mɒ].

1 A mother, or one's mother, sometimes used as a form of address. See also **mammaw 1, mammy.**

1861 Griffin *CW Letters* (Aug 3) I want you and his pa an ma to rase him to fite for his country and all the rest of the grand children. **1862** Epperly *CW Letters* (Aug 8) Tell Maw and the Boys to write to me soon. **1890** Fruit *KY Words* 68 *ma* = mother. **1901** Harben *Westerfelt* 131 Marthy come as nigh as pease a-doin' of it, her maw said. **1929** (in **1952** Mathes *Tall Tales* 112) His paw an' maw has done give him up. **1931** Goodrich *Mt Homespun* 54 Maw wants you should go with her tomorrow to her aunts' in Tennessy. **1934–47** *LAMSAS Appal* (Swain Co NC) *maw*. **c1945** Haun *Hawk's Done* 226 Ma just said, "Cathey's bounden to a-learnt sech from her Ma." **1960** Mason *Memoir* 18 Mawwwwwww, fetch me that old claw-hammer off the fire shelf, this dad-blasted ole steers busted up my plow and hits the only one I had. **1963** Edwards *Gravel* 108 "Maw, you aint as young as you used to be," protested Maudie, trying on one of her mother's large checked aprons. **1977** Hamilton *Mt Memories* 38 She called her parents "Pa" and "Ma" as most of the mountain children did, and she said, "I didn't tell Ma because she is sick and it would worry her." **1989** *Matewan OHP*-11 I don't think that Ma ever raised any garden after Pa went off.

[Web3 *maw* n chiefly South and Midland]

2 A grandmother. See also **mam, mammaw 2, mee-ma.**

1967 *DARE Survey* (Maryville TN). **1997** Montgomery *Coll* (known to Brown, Bush, Cardwell, Ledford, Weaver). **2005** Williams *Gratitude* 13 I've written very little about Pa and Ma Hicks because I was never around them very much when I was growing up, although they lived less than a mile from us. **2009** Williams *Maw Surry* Mom paused from chewing her chicken and glared across the table at her, but Maw didn't seem to notice she was being looked at.

[DARE *ma* n B1 especially South, South Midland]

3 A wife.

2013 Venable *How to Tawlk* 1 I told Maw I'd fix the roof adder turkey season.

4 A matriarch (used especially with the woman's surname).

1987 Wear *Sevierville* 40 "Ma" Gibson would bring her wagon to the corner and sell her wood each week for many years.

maar See **marrow.**

mackly *adjective* See citation.

1975 Gainer *Witches Ghosts Signs* 13 = spotted or soiled. "Jenny got her dress all mackly."

[< *macle* "spot, stain" + *-y* adjective-forming suffix; cf EDD *mackled* "spotted"]

mad *noun* Irritation, a fit of temper.

1867 Harris *Sut Lovingood* 188 He stood a-top ove the meal baril . . . his har a-swayin about wif pure mad, like a patch ove ripe rye in a wind. **1941** Stuart *Men of Mts* 294 Oh, I was in the mad enough to a bit. **1976** Garber *Mountain-ese* 33 Ever time Jeb goes to town Maud gits a mad on.

mad dog-bit *adjective phrase* Bitten by a rabid dog. For similar forms, see **bite A.**

1991 Thomas *Sthn Appal* 218 I had a ha'f brother that got mad-dog bit.

made-down bed *noun* A makeshift bed or **pallet** arranged for temporary sleeping on the floor. See also **make down, shake-up bed.**

1934–47 *LAMSAS Appal* = attested by 1/14 speakers (7.1%) from SC and 1/12 (8.3%) from GA. **1957** Combs *Lg Sthn High: Word List* 72 = a bed made down on the floor, of blankets and quilts. **1966** Dakin *Vocab Ohio River Valley* 198 This term [i.e. *shake-down* is] used in old communities on Zane's Trace is quite possibly related to a *made-down bed* and a *bed-down*—expressions which are used in eastern Kentucky.

[DARE (at *make down* v phr 1) chiefly South, South Midland]

made over See **make over 3.**

made-up school *noun* See citation.

2002 Myers *Best Yet Stories* 180 In very early days anyone who could read, knew the blue-back speller, and could write a good hand could make an agreement with concerned parents to teach the children. This was called a subscription or "Made-Up School."

madstone *noun* A porous stone or stone-like object taken from the stomach of a deer or other animal and popularly thought capable of drawing out venom from the bite of a snake or the poison of a rabid animal by rubbing it over the wound. See 1964 and c1975 citations. Also called **God's stone.**

1883 Zeigler and Grosscup *Heart of Alleghanies* 158 Yes, the mad stone. People believe it will cure snakebite and hydrophobia. Here's one. It was found in the paunch of a white deer that I shot this fall was a year ago; and, mind you, the deer with a mad-stone in him is twice as hard to kill as one of the ordinary kind. **1948** Dick *Dixie Frontier* 217 Nearly everybody believed in the mad stone. One of these at Huntsville, Alabama, was described as about the size of a walnut and porous like a honeycomb. When a person was bit by a mad dog, he was immediately taken to the precious stone, which stuck fast when applied to the bite. When the pores became full of poison, so the belief ran, it dropped off. When washed in warm milk and water, the poison was leeched out and the stone would stick on the wound again until all the poison was extracted. Then it would drop off. **1964** Wright *Mt Medicine* 8 In spite of all the reports of madstones we heard while we were in the area, not a madstone did we ever lay eyes on. The descriptions vary. It was smooth and white like marble. It was light and porous like a sponge. It was this and it was that. The most credible report was that it was the calculus from the stomach of a deer and was found rarely and held sacred by the lucky fellow who had one. If you were bitten by a supposedly mad dog, you sent for the possessor of the MADSTONE, and he came and after dipping it into hot water, applied it to the bite. After application it was returned to the water and if it turned green, the dog was mad. (I wonder why poison is always green. Poisonous green, we say. Never blue or pink or yellow.) What you did after that remained a mystery. There is no record of treatment beyond that point, but everyone with whom we talked had complete faith in its reliability. So we inferred that it drew out the poison when placed on the bite, and the green water was the end result. **1968** Wilson *Folklore Mammoth Cave* 21 = a calcareous accretion sometimes found in the stomach of a deer or cow. It is reputed to have the power to draw the poison out of a dogbite or a snakebite. **1970** Adams *Appal Revisit* 43 "Madstones" were eagerly sought after by the early settlers. If a deer or sheep were killed, the stomach was eagerly searched to see if a madstone could be found. It was thought by rubbing this stone on the bite of a dog which had the rabies the person could be cured. **1970** Vincent *More of Best* 35 Would you have thought we'd be able to find a madstone, that "magic rock-like substance found only in the stomachs of albino deer," and with which folks back yonder used to treat mad dog bites? **1972** Cooper *NC Mt Folklore* 17 Madstone Doctors attempted to cure hydrophobia and remove venom from snakebites with a small porous stone called a madstone, said to have been taken from the gallbladder of a deer. **c1975** Lunsford *It Used to Be* 117 When they butcher a deer sometimes they find the "mad stone." This person who showed it to me said he had used it a number of times when a person had been bit by a mad dog. He would take it and turn that little place downward on the wound and let it rest firmly against the place where the person had been bitten. He said it would take hold and would remain there for some time and they wouldn't allow anybody to touch it until it had turned loose and rolled off. He said they'd take it and put it in a pan of water and the poison that it had absorbed would be soaked out and it would turn the water green.

[from counteracting the madness brought by hydrophobia; DARE *madstone* n chiefly South, South Midland]

magazine-book *noun* A magazine. See also **book**.

c1940 Simms Coll Well hit now looks as if we'uns air steppin' right into the pages ov history, with all that bein' a-written about us in the papers and magazine-books.

mahogany birch *noun* The sweet-birch tree (*Betula lenta*).

1913 Morley *Carolina Mts* 20. **2007** McMillon *Notes* = sweet birch.

mail carrier *noun* A wildcat that seems to make rounds regularly from place to place.

1970 *Hunting* 11 Sometimes they'd be one old big'un [= a wildcat]. He'd come an' kill a bunch a'pigs, an' then he'd go back t'another section a'th'country. That's th'ones they always called th' mail carriers, and they'd all lay fer'em.

maim up *verb phrase* To disable or disfigure by a mining accident.

1975 Woolley *We Be Here* 42 [Coal mining] kills many men, sometimes by the dozens, in explosions and cave-ins, regularly by twos and threes in machinery accidents and rock-falls. Hundreds more each year are "maimed up."

main

A *adjective* Extraordinary, exceptional.

1924 Raine *Saddlebags* 103 He's a main worker; he has breskit. **1930** Armstrong *This Day and Time* 231 Ivy pulled him toward the shed by main force. **1937** Hall *Coll* (Townsend TN) He was a main hunter. **1939** Hall *Coll* (Cataloochee NC) He took after [the turkey], had a main race down there till the turkey flopped up agin a big log and couldn't get over it, and there they caught it. **1991** Still *Wolfpen Notebooks* 85 Goose grease is the main-est thing for waterproofing shoes.

[cf OED3 *main* adj² 2a "of an action, emotion, etc.: manifesting or requiring great force or energy; powerful, mighty, strong," obsolete; DARE *main* adj chiefly South Midland]

B *adverb* Exceedingly, very (especially in phrase *main big*). See also **master B**.

1895 Edson and Fairchild *TN Mts* 372 Hit's the main biggest rabbit I ever see. **1908** Smith *Reminiscences* 437 Husky pointed out the spot where had once skinned a "main big bear," having caught him in a trapped and then "snaked" (dragged) [him] down the mountain. **1937** Hall *Coll* (Townsend TN) That's a main big horse. **1939** Hall *Coll* (Bradley Fork NC) I don't know where [the panther] went, but he was a main big'un. *Ibid.* (Indian Creek NC) It's a main big old house. **1955** Ritchie *Singing Family* 194 I know this ain't the last skimmin', I'll finish filling it whenever you skim her for the main last time. That's the best foam. *Ibid.* 198 That's the main best eating in the world! **1974** Fink *Bits Mt Speech* 16 A *main* high mountain. **1993** *Stories 'neath Roan* 37 There were some main big old maple trees close by. **1998** *Dante OHP-71* He cut that main big one [= a tree] up there on that top of that hill.

[OED3 *main* adv "very, exceedingly" now regional; HT *main* adv "especially, particularly"; DARE *main* adv chiefly southern Appalachians]

main big See **main B**.

main drive *noun* A mass of freshly cut logs being floated downstream to a sawmill. See also **drive C**.

2000 Lewis *Appal Countryside* 41 These logs were split in two with the flat sides open, facing each other, and angled outward at the top. . . . At the confluence with the main stream, the logs were caught and held by booms until the main drive began. **2006** *WV Encycl* 431 The main drive down the river began with the first sign of spring when the ice began to break up. The logs were then rolled into the swollen stream and carried along by the current, with the arks following behind. Log driving was demanding, dangerous work, much of it performed in icy water.

mainest *adjective* Chief, principal.

1975 Woolley *We Be Here* 46 I guess safety is the mainest thing this strike is about.

main house *noun* Formerly, the principal room of a dwelling, usually the living room. See also **big house**, **house**.

1927 Furman *Lonesome Road* 12 Across the front of the home were two large rooms, "main-house" and "tuther-house," with "kitchen-house" in their rear. **1933** Thomas *Traipsin' Woman* 171 "There's a heap more room in kitchen-house. We'll have it to ourselves. Always someone pokin' their head in main-house" (Granny's word for the dining-room and office combined at the front of the house). **1942** Campbell *Cloud-Walking* 193 The other women set back in the cook room and talked, there not being room for all the folks in the main house.

main line *noun* See citation.

2002 Armstead *Black Days* 244 = a [coal] mine's main large tunnel where miners and machines move in and out and coal is transported out by cage, belt, or conveyor system.

main stout *noun* Same as **main strength**.

1927 Furman *Lonesome Road* 62 Air you a main stout-hearted feller? **1968** Stubbs *Mountain-Wise* (April–May) 10 He used an old wooden plow stock. He worked that ox for weeks but he never got nothin' worth-while done, but he plowed that ox like Samson worked hisn' by main stout.

main strength (also *main strength and awkwardness*) *noun phrase* Brute force, often with difficulty, sheer determination. Same as **main stout**.

1920 Ridley *Sthn Mtneer* 15 He practiced medicine by main strength and awkwardness and by the sheer force of his knowledge of folks. **1922** TN *CW Ques* 1158 (Washington Co TN) [I] helped bild houses, barns, cradled, mowed . . . hay & all kind of farm work by main strength. **1928** (in **1952** Mathes *Tall Tales* 78) The five noncombatants improvised a rude stretcher by poles and blankets, and by main strength and prodigious awkwardness bore the unconscious victor down the rough ridge. **c1960** Wilson *Coll*: *by main strength and awkwardness* = with difficulty, often clumsily. **1973** *AOHP/ASU-69* The carpenter work has changed a whole lot from what it used to be, you know. Used to we just had to do it all by these here [indicates with his hands], you know, by just main strength, and now they got that machinery. **1997** Montgomery *Coll*: *main strength* (known to eight consultants from the Smoky Mountains); *main strength and awkwardness* (known to Brown, Bush, Cardwell, Jones, Ledford, Oliver).

[DARE *main strength and awkwardness* n especially South, South Midland]

major *noun* Used as a euphemism for bull. See also **bull A1**.

1949 Kurath *Word Geog East US* 62 [Expressions for bull] in West Virginia . . . contributes *Durham*, *jock*, and *major*.

make

A *transitive verb*

1 To study for and become, train to be (a practitioner of a certain profession).

1939 Hall *Coll* (Cataloochee NC) Only one of his grandsons made a preacher, the Reverend B. B. Caldwell. . . . Naturally grandfather was kind of proud of him, that he made a preacher. **1953** Hall *Coll* (Bryson City NC) In his early married life he went into and made a preacher, Baptist preacher, and he followed that all the rest of his life. **1969** Medford *Finis* 109 We named him after a school teacher; and I think I'd like to see him make a school teacher. **1973** *GSMNP-88*:104 He made a judge and went on to Maryville. **1978** Montgomery *White Pine Coll* I-1 He was born and raised here, and he made a doctor, and he came back to White Pine. **1998** *Dante OHP-24* He wasn't a preacher at that time, but he made a preacher [later]. **2012** Jourdan *Medicine Men* 20 Because of my experience in the war, I wondered if there was any way I could ever make a doctor.

[DARE *make* v[1] C12b especially South, South Midland]

2 Of a person or animal: to mature into, become.

1942 (in **1987** Perdue *Outwitting Devil* 10) But the old man liked Jack and he give Jack a calf and the calf growed up and made a big fine black bull. **1959** Pearsall *Little Smoky* 102 He now begins to "make a man," which means he forsakes the world of women to follow his father and older brothers everywhere they go. **1976** Lindsay *Grassy Balds* 123 I growed up by that time and made a young man.

3 To raise or produce (a crop, food), bring (a crop) to maturity.

1858 (in **1974** Harris *High Times* 96) He pulled fodder fur me last week, an wer a cussin an a cavortin round yesterday at the still house, arter makin a fust rate crap. **1861** Griffin *CW Letters* (Aug 3) I wod like to know how much wheat you maid. **1862** Shifflet *CW Letters* (July 13) the South cant stand hit much longer for tha[y] will all Starve to death Shore for tha[y] hante a maken nothing to eat. **1862** Tesh *CW Letters* (July 4) Tell John and Sam I want them to make all the corn They can so they can have a big corn shucking this Fall. **1937** Hall *Coll* (Cosby Creek TN) We didn't make any beans last year, hit was so dry. **1939** Hall *Coll* (Indian Creek NC) Sometimes we didn't make enough corn to do us. . . . We [did] make enough meat to do us. **1940** Hall *Coll* (White Oak NC) They shut the plant down until the crops is done and made. **1956** Hall *Coll* (Cosby TN) We had to buy coffee and salt, but we made everything else, plenty of taters, cabbage. **1958** Wood *Words from TN* 13 A man who is farming, especially a renter, is said to be making a crop. **1969** Miller *Raising Tobacco* 27 During his lifetime he *made* over sixty crops of burley tobacco and, as a boy, assisted in producing still others. **1973** *Gardening* 241 Chicken manure will really make okra. **1974** Fink *Bits Mt Speech* 16 I'll *make* a good crop of corn. **1975** *GSMNP-59*:18 Everybody that made a good cane patch . . . put up enough syrup of every kind to do them from one year till the next. **1999** *GSMNPCOHP-1*:5 We'd just dig between the rocks. The ground was rich and you could make all kinds of vegetables.

[DARE *make* v[1] C1 chiefly South, South Midland]

4 See citation.

1957 Combs *Lg Sthn High: Word List* 62 = to compose, write (of songs). Ex.: "Nance's gal made this song." A similar usage is found in Piers Plowman.

B *intransitive verb*

1 Of a crop, unborn child, etc.: to develop, grow, mature. [Editor's note: The transitive use of this verb, as in "the wheat will make a good crop," is standard.]

1940 Haun *Hawk's Done* 89 She said she was going to be careful while her baby was making. **1940** Still *River of Earth* 133 "Aye, God, this land'll make," he said. "It's rich as sin." **1956** McAtee

Some Dial NC 29 = develop. "The leaves were just makin'." **1973** *Gardening* 237 [Onions] do better to put them out in March and under a dark moon, for they make under the ground. *Ibid.* 242 We didn't ever thin [the pepper plants] because pepper'll make pretty good. **2002** Reid *Hall's Top* 23 By late summer Grandma had dill pickles, sulfured apples, pickled beans and beets, and sauerkraut "making" in barrels and stoneware crocks.

2 To distill liquor; hence verbal noun *making*.

1953 Hall Coll (Cocke Co TN) We'd made about sixteen months [when] we found that the revenuers were coming. We just run our beer all off. We left our flake stand settin' there. They knocked the flake stand down. Next day we went back and made for sixteen months longer. **1956** Hall Coll (Bryson City NC) [Quill Rose] had his still right close to the house. He'd been makin' there for some years, several years. *Ibid.* (Del Rio TN) He'd been making there quite a bit. He thought he was pretty safe. **1972** Carr *Oldest Profession* 63 The husband had been caught for makin' and sent to prison, and the investigators were convinced the woman was sincerely raising money the only way she knew how. **1974** Dabney *Mt Spirits* 118 I done most of my makin' from the time I was eighteen years old. **1989** Landry *Smoky Mt Interviews* 181 She headed up the mountain where they was a-makin'.

[DARE *make* v^1 C9 "distill liquor illegally" chiefly South Midland]

make a beginning *verb phrase* To say a prayer at the beginning of a meal.

1881 Pierson *In the Brush* 54–55 Being seated at the table, the host, turning to the preacher, says, "Will you make a beginning, sir?"—all at table reverently bowing their heads as he extends the invitation, and while the blessing is being asked. So, too, I have "made a beginning" at many a hospitable board in many different States.

make a branch *verb* To urinate.

1952 Wilson *Folk Speech NC* 522 *branch, to make a* = to urinate. **c1960** Wilson Coll = a small child's word. **1969** Doran *Folklore White Co* 111 = to urinate.

[DARE (at *make* v D3) chiefly South, South Midland]

make a little bother See **bother B**.

make a long arm *verb phrase* To reach for food at the meal table.

1962 Williams *Mtneers Mind Manners* 22 Make a long arm and help yourself

make at *verb phrase* To thrust (a weapon) at, attack.

2002 McGowan *Beech Mt Tales* 111 They flew mad and begin to make at him with a sword apiece.

make-do *noun* See citation.

1939 Bond *Appal Dialect* 109 = excitement, enthusiastic outburst.

make down *verb phrase* To fashion (a temporary bed or **pallet**) on the floor for sleeping. See also **made-down bed**.

1913 Combs *Kentucky Highlander* 18 [The mountaineer] will send one of his family to a neighbor's to sleep or "make down a bed" in order to give you room. **1921** Greer-Petrie *Angeline at Seelbach* 16 He even made down beds for 'em to sleep on. **c1960** Wilson Coll: *make a bed down* = to arrange for a temporary bed on the floor when the company is too great for regular beds. **1978** Slone *Common Folks* 242 Larcy would go and feed these extra [guests], washing the dishes, then "making beds down," by placing feather beds and quilts on the floor, she would make room for them.

[DARE *make down* v phr 1 chiefly South, South Midland]

make for *verb phrase*

1 To fashion or employ (something) as.

1973 GSMNP-79:17 You could play out in the hallway where they'd waxed it, you know. We'd make that for a slide. Take a run and go and just slide all the way down to the hall and then up again.

2 To aim or direct one's course toward.

1966 Caudill *My Appalachia* 24 When school was out, most of the boys and girls made for the bridge with a whoop. **c1982** Young *Colloquial Appal* 16 = go toward.

make in one's mind *verb phrase* To determine, decide.

1939 Hall Coll (Gumstand TN) He said he made it in his mind to never surrender (with reference to a Civil War soldier).

make it up See **make up 2**.

make like *verb phrase* To pretend, act as if. See also **make out A3**.

c1950 Adams *Grandpap* 132 The old man made like he was so weak that he couldn't hardly stand up. **1983** *Dark Corner OHP-5A* [They'd] get logs and tarpapers and put a top over it, and you know, put dirt around it, make like it was a place where the war boys stay. **1994** McCarthy *Jack Two Worlds* 38 Directly he went to sleep, or made like he was going to sleep—he wasn't really sleeping.

make mock of See **mock B**.

make never no mind See **never no mind**.

make on *verb phrase*

1 To work on.

1940 Haun *Hawk's Done* 175 Where was the [quilt] you were making on?

2 To fare, manage, get by.

1933 Thomas *Traipsin' Woman* 193 Pore little Ellen Vinton, how's she makin' on these days?

3 To pretend, act as if.

1933 Thomas *Traipsin' Woman* 121 The Revenuers had no call to make on like they were friends with Crosswise's folks, eat their vittals, take the night, and all the time fixing to undermine Old Bije and Young Bije.

make one dance joober *verb phrase* See citation.

1890 Fruit *KY Words* 65 "To make a child dance joober" is to whip him.

make one's acknowledgment(s) *verb* To admit wrong-doing and ask forgiveness before a church congregation.

1800 *Globe Creek Church Minutes* 8 bro[the]r Richard Green came forward and Made his Acknowledgement conserning What he Said at our last Meeting. **1973** *AOHP/ASU-69* [Was there any way to get back in the church after you got thrown out?]: Oh yes, [if] you go back there and make your acknowledgment to the church, why, they'd forgive you and take you back, because I guess if they hadn't have, then it wouldn't have been according to the Bible. **1976** Thompson *Touching Home* 18 = to ask forgiveness: "He should come to church and make his acknowledgments."

make one's brags *verb phrase* To boast, make claims.

1924 Greer-Petrie *Angeline Gits Eyeful* 12 I heer'd her makin' her brags bekase she'd ... lost ten pounds the past month. **1930** Armstrong *This Day and Time* 45 "I made my brags," she said, a trifle bitterly, "an' now I'm back agin." *Ibid.* 141 He's made his brags he's goin' to break up me an' Novy. **1954** Arnow *Dollmaker* 83 None a th youngens around cain't make their brags no more. **1978** Hiser *Quare Do's* 16 [He] told them what had happened, and about Mike a-making his brags that he'd give his nickel to his (Barry's) widow the next day, Saturday. **2005** Williams *Gratitude* 508 = to go around bragging about what all you're going to do (or think you can do).

make one's flesh crawl See **flesh crawl**, **make one's**.

make out

A *verb phrase*

1 Of a person: to manage, get by; to find a way for, work out.

1824 (in **1912** Doddridge *Notes on Settlement* 79) Although he had an excellent tract of land, he could hardly make out to live. **1834** Crockett *Narrative* 41 I, however, made out to get to [a house] at last. **1861** *Patton CW Letters* (Oct 5) we are making out very well yet. **1862** *Warrick CW Letters* (Aug 17) As soon as I draw money again I will send it to you; try and make out to live the best you can. **1878** Coale *Wilburn Waters* 62 [The bear cubs] were in an open place, and it was very difficult to get within range without being seen, heard, or winded, but he made out to "snake" to within forty yards of them. **1925** Furman *Glass Window* 26 It seemed like I couldn't make out to come in. **1977** Shackelford et al. *Our Appalachia* 184 Mothers were tired, the children were tired, the men were tired trying to make out a living on those steep hillsides, and the cattle looked tired because they weren't getting the proper food.

2 To plan, determine.

1859 Taliaferro *Fisher's River* 117 Last I made out to ax Sally ef she'd have me. **1999** Montgomery *Coll* I made out to go to the market but my wagon broke down (Cardwell).

3 (also *make out like*) To pretend, act as if. See also **make like**.

1862 *Zimmerman CW Letters* (Nov 2) they are trying to slip around and get to Richmond and make out like they are yet at Fredricksburg. **1873** Smith *Arp Peace Papers* 109 It is very paneful, I asshure you, to dry up all of a sudden, and make out like we wasn't there. **1923** Montague *Today Tomorrow* 166 He jest kep' a-standing up thar on his gray rock with his arms folded, and trying to make out like he didn't keer nuthing for nobody. **1943** Hannum *Mt People* 100 He made out to get the lantern lit—and then like to died. **1956** McAtee *Some Dial NC* 29 *make out like* = to pretend. **1961** Stubbs *Mountain-Wise* (Oct–Nov) 8 It wasn't long before he fell in love with an Indian girl—or made out he did. **1984** Wilder *You All Spoken* 166 = communicate, often to deceive, as in "He made out that he thought a sight of her." **1992** Oxford *Ray Hicks* 86 Now if you don't make out like you're starved to death, I'll kill ye. **1993** Page and Smith *Foxfire Toys and Games* 110 We'd lay [the dolls] on our bed and make out like they was sick and things like that and we'd have the doctor to come and see them. **1997** Montgomery *Coll*: *make out like* (known to Bush, Cardwell, Ellis, Jones, Ledford, Oliver, Weaver).

[DARE *make out* v phr 2 "pretend" chiefly South, South Midland]

4 To portray or characterize (a person) as.

1975–76 Wolfram/Christian *WV Coll* 83 They all made him out the liar, but I believe he was telling the truth.

5 To eat (a meal).

1979 Melton *'Pon My Honor* 22 "Make out your dinner, boy," he said, "for we've got some mighty hard work ahead of us this evening."

6 To assemble, collect.

1806 *Globe Creek Church Minutes* 25 the Church makes out some money for the assn [= Association].

7 To suffice for or supplement.

1987 Young *Lost Cove* 48 During this time of the year the branch lettuce, ramps and other esculent greens from the forest helped to make out a meal.

B *noun* See citation.

1946 Matthias *Speech Pine Mt* 190 = a pretense: "That ain't nothin' but a make-out."

make out like See **make out A3**.

make over *verb phrase*

1 To praise, compliment, pet, fuss (over), brag about (a person).

1923 Furman *Mothering* 143 Although tears of joy stood in her eyes, she did not hug or kiss or "make over" her boys,—such displays of feeling being permissible only in or over babies. **c1950** Adams *Grandpap* 61 They were all glad to see her. An' they made over the baby. **1956** McAtee *Some Dial NC* 29 = to give excessive attention or preferential treatment. "Fathers are inclined to make over their girl children." **c1960** Wilson *Coll* = to spoil, pet, pay a lot of attention to. **1974** Ogle *Memories* 36 He made over me like it was something and this was what I wanted. **1980** GSMNP-115:41 They just made over 'em a sight. **1997** Montgomery *Coll* (known to nine consultants from the Smoky Mountains); He made over her good looks for an hour (Oliver).

[DARE *make over* v phr chiefly South Midland; also West]

2 See citations.

1976 Thompson *Touching Home* 15 = to sign over to someone else as a deed could be done. **1995** Montgomery *Coll* (known to Cardwell).

3 In phrase *be (someone) made over* = to resemble (someone) strongly.

1967 *DARE Survey* (Maryville TN) Just his father made over. **1997** Montgomery *Coll* (known to nine consultants from the Smoky Mountains). **2009** Holbrook *Upheaval* 7 Mabel's mother had used to tell her she was Granny Sal made over.

[DARE *made over* participial adj phr chiefly South, South Midland, also West]

make polite *verb phrase* To act courteously to; to feign politeness to.

2002 McGowan *Beech Mt Tales* 101 Well, Jack, he got tired of making polite of them and then he went on down to the road where his wife and driver was.

make prayer *verb phrase* Of a household: to have regular prayer.

1991 Thomas *Sthn Appal* 107 If we kain't go whur they made prayer ever night, we don't go.

make to *verb phrase* (with interposed object) To cause (someone) to.

1940 Haun *Hawk's Done* 64 Enzor made her to understand that he was through with her. **1965** Miller *Pigeon's Roost* (Jan 7) I appreciate your Christmas cards more so than you will ever know as this makes me to know that at least there is over a hundred who read my column. **1978** Montgomery *White Pine Coll* XII It made us all to know how close we all are, me and my Mamma and brother and two sisters.

make up *verb phrase*

1 To gather (people), collect (a sum of money), produce (a foodstuff).

1862 *Huntley CW Letters* (March 6) I Waunt you to do Every thing you can against him in making up a company and try to git Ben Washburn to do all he can against him Fo he is nothing But a fop and a drunkard. **1862** *Watson CW Letters* (March 8) they are a making up a nother company in Jackson. **1875** Reid *Land of Sky* 59 I'll make up a fire—here, Matildy, you and Jake bring some wood—so you kin dry yourself. **1885** (in **1972** *Burial Customs* 8) I want us all to make up the money and pay the bill. **1965** Hall *Coll* (Cataloochee NC) They would make up money to pay the preacher. **1971** *AOHP/ALC*-277 He made molasses for people when it come time of the year to make up molasses until he got old. **1973** *GSMNP*-70:3 I went past the first house, and they was a-making up molasses the old fashioned way. **1974** Dabney *Mt Spirits* 77 Once when his house burn down, we all went in together and made up money, and we built him back a house. [**1979** *Big South Fork OHP*-4 They said they meant to make up around and get enough money to sort of pay us for what they destroyed.] **1989** Landry *Smoky Mt Interviews* 181 We never made up money in our church. . . . We made up money for sick people, but not for pastors.

2 (also *make it up*) To decide, plan, agree, arrange (to do something).

1892 Fruit *KY Words* 230 Referring to something planned, it is asked, "When did you all make that up?" **1941** Hall *Coll* (Saunook NC) He made it up not to work tomorrow. **c1950** Adams *Grandpap* 147 They'd no more'n got out a-sight till the girls were a-makin' up what they were a-goin' to do. **c1960** Wilson *Coll*: *make it up* = to plan something to be done. **1989** Smith *Flyin' Bullets* 30 "A bunch of 'em had it in fer Peter and they knowed that he'd be a'comin' by that way," said Delia Noland, "so they made it up with a woman to have her a'standin' there, a'waitin' on him to come by." **1997** Montgomery *Coll* (known to eight consultants from the Smoky Mountains). **1998** *Dante OHP*-24 We made it up to slip off then.

[OED3 *make up* (at *make* 11b) chiefly Brittish regional, esp. Scottish; DARE *make up* v phr 1 scattered, but especially South, South Midland]

male *noun* Used as a euphemism for a male farm animal, especially one not castrated; the term is a euphemism for *bull*, *boar*, or *buck* and often forms part of a compound such as **male brute**, **male cow**, **male hog**. See also **cow brute**, **steer**.

1931 Combs *Lg Sthn High* 1322 "Male" is used for "bull" and "boar," or "boar-hog." **1939** Hall *Coll* (Jefferson City TN) Women will refer to a bull as a male, a male cow, a steer. In referring to a bull calf, a woman may say, "I have a fine young male out there," although some use the expression bull calf. **1957** Combs *Lg Sthn High: Word List* 62 = general term for the male species of animals. Bull, boar, etc. are inelegant in Highland speech. In general male animals are referred to as "male brutes." Even "male cow" is sometimes heard for bull. Such usage does not necessarily descend from Victorian prudery. It began . . . early in the nineteenth century. **1966** Dakin *Vocab Ohio River Valley* 230 *Male* is usual in the [KY] Mountains; *male cow* common elsewhere. *Brute* and *cow brute*, which are doubtless related to *stock brute*, *male brute* of western North Carolina, are used in Kentucky, chiefly in the southern Mountains. *Ibid.* 240 The clearly Southern-South Midland term the *male* is the more common of the polite names in the Mountains and southern Kentucky generally, but the Bluegrass and northern Pennyroyal have only *male hog*. **1968** Wilson *Folklore Mammoth Cave* 14 [Buck is a] euphemism for the name of a male animal; some others are brute, brute beast, daddy, he, male, old animal, and papa-cow.

male brute (also *male cow*, *male ox*) *noun* Used as a euphemism for bull. See also **brute**, **bull A1**, **daddy A**, **daddy cow**, **gentleman cow**, **male**, **steer**.

1913 Kephart *Our Sthn High* 295 A bull or boar is not to be mentioned as such in mixed company, but male-brute and male-hog are used as euphemisms. **1934–47** *LAMSAS Appal* (Swain Co NC). **1949** Kurath *Word Geog East US* 62 *Stock brute*, *male brute* [are found] in westernmost North Carolina. **1949** McDavid *Grist* 111 (Oconee Co SC) *male ox* = bull. **1956** Hall *Coll* (Newport TN) He bought him a big old male brute or bull. **1966** *DARE Survey* (Burnsville NC) *male cow* = used by women in mixed company for a bull; (Spruce Pine NC) *male ox* = used by women in mixed company for a bull. **1966** Dykeman *Far Family* 125 It's not proper for young ladies to be looking over male brutes. **1994–95** Montgomery *Coll* (known to Cardwell, Shields).

male cow See **male brute.**

male hog (also *male pig*) *noun* Used as a euphemism for a boar hog. See also **boar B**, **male.**

1913 Kephart *Our Sthn High* 295 A bull or boar is not to be mentioned as such in mixed company, but male-brute and male-hog are used as euphemisms. **1956** Hall *Coll* (Big Bend NC) Her an' pap an' Aunt Nance . . . went over to Slick Rock Branch, and they catched a big wild male hog once. **1975** GSMNP-62:2 We'd go out here and we caught a male hog. We'd trim him and turn him loose. **1986** Pederson et al. *LAGS* (Sevier Co TN) *male hog* (Campbell Co TN, Claiborne Co TN, Cherokee Co GA) *male pig*. **1994** Montgomery *Coll* (known to Shields).

male horse *noun* Used as a euphemism for a stallion.

1986 Pederson et al. *LAGS* (Johnson Co TN, Knox Co TN, Murray Co GA).

male ox See **male brute.**

male pig See **male hog.**

malt *noun* In making homemade liquor, sprouted, dried, and ground grain (most often corn, but sometimes barley or rye) that is ground and added to other ingredients to produce **mash** (see **mash**[2]). See also **malt corn, malt corn grinder, sprouting tub.**

1938 Hall *Coll* (Emerts Cove TN) Malt [makes] unfermented mash into fermented beer. **1939** Hall *Coll* (Emerts Cove TN) [In] making sugar liquor, they'd take a bushel, about a bushel of corn to the sixty gallon barrel, and a half a bushel of malt. **1990** Aiken *Stories* 199 For many years the whiskey was made from pure corn and malt. Malt is sprouted corn or barley. The grain for malt was put in a barrel or other receptacle and wet. The barrel was covered with a "tow sack" and left for several days until the corn had sprouted. The sprouted corn was then dried and ground at a local grist mill. The malt was mixed with ground cornmeal and water, then cooked to become "mash."

malt corn (also *malted corn*) *noun* Sprouted corn that is ground and added to other ingredients to produce **mash** (see **mash**[2]). See also **malt, malt corn grinder, malt liquor.**

1949 Maurer *Argot of Moonshiner* 10 = sprouted corn or corn malt. Barley malt is generally used in large operations, but corn malt is universally used in the eastern Kentucky mountains. It is made by burying a sack of corn under damp leaves until the corn has sprouted, then grinding the sprouted grain. "Yeah, I got a gunny sack of malt corn sprouted." **1956** Hall *Coll* (Del Rio TN) A half bushel of malt corn [is] sprouted [for each tub of mash]. **1959** Roberts *Up Cutshin* 62 We'd sprout what was called malt corn. Take and put corn in a coffee sack in water until it sprouted good. **1969** GSMNP-37:2:22 Then I grind my malt corn, generally ground it [in] a sausage mill, and I'd go back and grind that up and I'd take that malt corn and some rye meal and go back and I'd put a cap on that, break all that up and get it broke up real good and fill my barrel up as far as I wanted with water. Then I'd put a cap on it out of that rye meal and malt and, so I stirred the malt in there and then put the cap on it with my rye meal. Then I'd go back. Whenever it's cleared off on top, I'd take my still and go back and set it in, and start running. **1974** Roberts *Sang Branch* 49 Then we'd take an old sausage mill to grind our malt corn. We'd sprout what was called malt corn. Take and put corn in a coffee sack in water till it sprouted good, until good long sprouts come on it. Then we'd take this mill and grind this malt corn up, about a kag. And then you take your hands like making dough, and you bust ever' lump in there. Stir just like you was making gravy, to get it all dissolved like milk.

[DARE *malt corn* n chiefly South Midland]

malt corn grinder *noun* A device to grind corn in the production of **malt.**

1956 Hall *Coll* (Wears Cove TN) First sprout the corn, dry it, and then they have to grind it. [It] sprouts about a inch long. They run it through the malt corn grinder. Malt gives the liquor the good flavor. **1959** Hall *Coll* (Wears Cove TN) Malt corn grinder [was used] to grind sprouted corn (malt corn) for fermenting still mash.

malt liquor *noun* A fermented mixture of **malt corn**, cornmeal, and other ingredients, from which **beer** is produced in the early stages of the distillation of homemade whiskey.

1973 GSMNP-4:18–19 Now to make malt corn it would take about six or eight days I think for it to sprout. See, you have to just put regular corn in a bag and pour warm water on it and cover it up, dig a hole in the ground and pour this warm water on it every morning, and in about six or eight days it will have a sprout on that corn, see. The corn will sprout and then you take and dry it and then grind it up and put it in your beer before you run it off and that's malt liquor.

mam *noun* [mæm]

1 A mother (also used as a term of address).

1862 Huntley *CW Letters* (April 13) I think that I can make a niser Biscuit than you Or mam Either if I Ever git home We Will try it at any rate. **1867** Harris *Sut Lovingood* 23 [Dad] allers wer a mos' complikated durned ole fool, an' mam sed so when he warnt about. **1890** Fruit *KY Words* 68 = mother. **1896** Fox *Vendetta* 94 I want ye to stay home 'n' take keer o' mam 'n' the cattle ef fightin' does come. **1935** Murray *Schoolhouse* 78 Mam, you go the long way to town, and I'll go the short way. **1961** *Coe Ridge OHP*-335B Let Mam go on over there at that poor woman. **1986** Tyson *Reflections* 23 Mam would make apple butter and pumpkin butter in a big brass kettle. It took a lot of stirring, but was good when we got it cooked. **1991** Still *Wolfpen Notebooks* 53 There were so many of us in our family that pap and mam just named us and turned us loose. **2007** Shelby *Molly Whuppie* 56 Pap tried his best to talk the boys out of going. But Mam said he was wasting his breath and started in baking journey cakes.

2 One's grandmother.

2014 Hicks *Driving* 41 When Pap started to roam, family legend goes, Mam—my mother's Momma—sawed nearly through the metal braces under his galluses, his shoestrings the same.

mamaw See **mammaw 2.**

mammaw *noun*

1 A mother, one's mother. See also **ma 1, mammy.**

1861 *Odum CW Letter* (Oct 18) my dear little baby has bin very sick his mammaw had 3 doctors with him 3 days but he is as well now or was the last letter I got from them.

2 (also *mamaw, mawmaw*) One's grandmother (in third-person reference and used as a form of address). Same as **ma 2, mee-ma.**

1942 *Hall Phonetics Smoky Mts* 77 A curious form is ['mæ̞mɔ:], which I heard a middle-aged man use in addressing his grandmother. **c1960** Wilson *Coll*: *mamaw* = becoming common for a small child's name for a grandmother. **1962** Dykeman *Tall Woman* 135 "What happened to Mamaw Moore?" Martha asked, as Lydia braided her hair. **1975** Jackson *Unusual Words* 154 Grandparents were usually designated by the terms mammaw and pappaw. **1984** Head *Brogans* 99 If I had not already fallen asleep, as I did occasionally, [my] grandfather would tell Mammaw it was time for bed. **1997** Montgomery *Coll*: *mamaw* (known in both uses to eight consultants from the Smoky Mountains); *mawmaw* (known to Adams, Bush, Cardwell, Ledford, Weaver). **2004** Fisher *Kettle Bottom* 64 "The Farmer's Curst Wife" . . . is an old song my Mamaw Webb used to sing. **2007** Preece *Leavin' Sandlick* 46 Lassie left Betty Sue with her mom and mamaw and did the same, kneeling right beside Cleve. **2007** Rogers *Carson-Newman* 5 In response to the first question, "What do you call your father's mother?," the three most common responses were Granny (2), Mawmaw (2), and Mamaw (2). Rachel McGinnis was one of the two interviewees who replied "Mamaw," but she qualified her response with the following statement, "I call her 'Mamaw' in person, but to other people I call her 'my grandma,' so that people won't think that I'm backwards." **2009** Sohn *Appal Home Cooking* 122 As is often the case, when mountaineers gather at the homeplace, their minds drift off to mamaw and papaw or to age-old homeplace traditions. **2016** *Legends & Lore* 122 Appalachian people also have a name for their non-traditional home remedy healers in Appalachia; they are usually called "granny," "mamaw," or "nana."

[DARE *mammaw* n chiefly South, South Midland]

mammock See **mommick.**

mammy *noun*

1 A mother (in third-person reference and used as a form of address). [Editor's note: This term was frequently observed by Joseph Hall in the Smoky Mountains in the late 1930s except among educated speakers.]

1860 *Week in Smokies* 126 Mammy, is it true that when you come home with daddy to this cabin, you had nothing to eat at the infair but roasted taters? **1861** *Hanes CW Letters* (June 22) tell your mamy and dady that I am well and that I would like to harvest for them. **1864** *Poteet CW Letters* (Nov 24) you all so wrote to your mamy to not let your children suffer. **1873** Smith *Arp Peace Papers* 202 They git many a spankin when their mammys are thinkin about them Yankees. **1924** (in **1952** Mathes *Tall Tales* 44) Ye're all the child Tommy had, an' yer mammy died the night ye was borned. **1937** Hall *Coll* (Newport TN) My kinfolks on mammy's side settled in Greene County [TN]. **c1950** Adams *Grandpap* 73 So, they got married an' she promised her pap an' mammy she'd sure write 'em a letter or send 'em a word. **1956** Hall *Coll* (Roaring Fork TN) Old mammy bear will come direckly. **1957** *GSMNP-23:1:13* My mammy drawed a pension from the old Indian War. **1966** Dakin *Vocab Ohio River Valley* 425–26 In the [KY] Mountains *mammy* is regular in the more isolated sections but is giving way to *mommy* in the more accessible northern and southwestern sections. The obviously less familiar *mama* is beginning to spread into the Mountains in these same sections. **1971** *Granny Women* 257 We was just a'sweatin'—me and m'mammy. **1978** Hiser *Quare Do's* 85 I can't leave my mammy and pappy. They are starved so weak at I have to do the gin work. **1983** *Dark Corner OHP-4A* My mammy'd have a big bunch of hogs. We'd feed some of that corn meal to the hogs. **2018** *Blind Pig* (Jan 9) My husband has a sock hat his "Mammy" gave him for Christmas 38 years ago.

[DARE *mammy* n[1] 1a chiefly South, South Midland]

2 A grandmother.

1988 Lambert *Kinfolks* 11 While I'm on names, I should also mention forms of address. In the families I knew, the most common form of address for a grandmother was either "Mammy" or "Granny." I knew only one "Big Mama." Grandfathers were called "Grandpa" or "Dad." I knew one "Big Daddy" (you will be comforted to know that he was married to "Big Mama"). It was not uncommon to use the full name, saying "Mammy Dossett" rather than just "Mammy." **2005** Williams *Gratitude* 13 Mom's parents were Memory Allen and Emer Lavada Stephens Taylor, known to other folks as "Uncle Mem and Aunt Emer." We called them "Paw and Mammy." **2007** McMillon *Notes* = usually refers to one's mother, but may also refer to one's grandmother.

mammy cow brute *noun* A female bovine. See also **cow brute, male brute.**

1957 Broaddus *Vocab Estill Co KY* 49 = a cow.

man

A *noun* A male spouse or companion (used often by a woman in reference to her own).

1864 *D Walker CW Letters* (April 28) I got a leter from mother She rits that Sister Cathrins man is dead and Morgan is line [= lying] in the hospittel at Carrow [= Cairo IL] Sick with winter fever. **1895** Edson and Fairchild *TN Mts* 374 I studied about her hair to my man when I got home. **1910** Norman *English of Mtneers* 278 In such a home, the wife is "my woman," the husband, his wife's "man." **c1940** Padelford *Notes* A mountain woman's man is her law and world. **1956** Hall *Coll* (Gatlinburg TN) I got married when I was twenty-three. I was married in eighteen eighty-six. My man was seventy-three year old when he died. **1986** Pederson et al. *LAGS* = attested by 4/60 interviewees (6.7%) from E TN and 1/35 (2.9%) from N GA; 5/25 of all LAGS interviewees (20%) attesting term were from Appalachia. **1988–90** *Matewan OHP-33* Carrie was a bootlegger, and her man that worked at the same mine I did, he was a fine little guy.

[OED3 *man* n[1] 8a "a husband," now chiefly English regional north, Scot . . . except in *man and wife* a1325→; DARE *man* n C1 "in U.S. probably reinforced by the parallel use of the cognates in other Germanic languages"]

B *verb* To subdue, handle, manage (something difficult). See also **man-power**.

1917 Kephart *Word-List* 414 = to master. "You can't hardly *man* that (tough steak), can you?" **1994–97** Montgomery *Coll* (known to Brown, Cardwell, Ledford, Norris, Oliver).

[OED3 *man* v 8 now British regional and U.S.]

man body See **man person**.

man caught (also *man feed*) *noun* In logging, a worker who puts lumber into a boxcar.

1998 Buchanan *Logging Terms*.

man critter *noun* A human being.

1952 Wilson *Folk Speech NC* 563 = a human being.

mandrake *noun* Same as **mayapple**.

1967 *DARE Survey* (Maryville TN) = may apple. **1971** Hutchins *Hidden Valley* 48 May apples (*Podophyllum peltatum*) are often known as "mandrakes" in these mountains, and both leaves and roots are poisonous. **1982** Stupka *Wildflowers* 35 "Mandrake" is one of its many local names.

man feed See **man caught**.

manful *adjective, adverb* See citation.

1895 Edson and Fairchild *TN Mts* 372 = vigorous(ly). "The engineer'd whistle manful ef he'd see us on the track."

mang *noun* See citation.

1883 Smith *Southernisms* 51 Mang means in West Virginia the "slush about a pig-sty."

man grown *noun phrase* A grown man.

1939 Hall *Coll* (Emerts Cove TN) There's one man living [in Gatlinburg] yet, though, that was a man grown when I was just a little boy. **1956** Hall *Coll* (Big Creek NC) His wife learnt him a right smart. What Mack knows he learnt it after he was a man grown. **1958** Campbell *Tales* 50 She wanted him to promise her not to marry till their boy was a man grown.

[OED3 *man-grown* (at *man* n[1] C1) now Irish English (north); cf CUD *man-big* (at *man*[1]) "of a boy: man-grown"; cf HT *man-big* "having reached manhood"]

manhole *noun* See citation.

2002 Armstead *Black Days* 244 = a hole cut in the side wall, or rib, of a narrow rail entry for miners to jump into in case of an emergency, for example, runaway rail cars.

mannerable *adjective* Well-mannered, polite.

1940 Haun *Hawk's Done* 15 He was always mannerable toward Tiny. I couldn't help but take note of it. **1971** Dwyer *Dict for Yankees* 29 I like him 'cause he's so mannerable.

[OED3 *mannerable* adj now regional (chiefly U.S.); DARE *mannerable* adj South, South Midland]

manner, in a *adverb phrase* After a fashion, nearly, pretty much.

1913 Kephart *Our Sthn High* 225 Ike Morgan Pringle's a-been horse-throwed down the clift and he's in a manner stone dead. **1925** Greer-Petrie *Angeline Hill Country* 135 Here they wuz, afore our very eyes, not only runnin', but in a manner, flyin'. **1952** Wilson *Folk Speech NC* 563 = almost, after a fashion, not quite satisfactorily. **c1960** Wilson *Coll* = nearly, almost: "I'm in a manner through stripping tobacco." **1963** Edwards *Gravel* 116 Well, in a manner, yes; in a manner. **1974** Fink *Bits Mt Speech* 13 – nearly. "He's *in a manner* blind." **1997** Montgomery *Coll* (known to Adams, Brown, Cardwell, Jones, Norris, Oliver, Weaver).

[DARE *manner* n 2 chiefly South Midland]

man person (also *man body*) *noun* A man, human being.

1862 *Rector CW Letters* (Oct 2) we all want you to go home fi [= if] you pleas thear is no man person to tend to the things thiswinter youre mother cant hire any body to work fer her the conscript wont take you and it dose Jessy and me. **1867** Harris *Sut Lovingood* 87 I'll jis' gin yu leave tu go tu the devil half hamon, ef I didn't make fewere tracks to the mile . . . than were ever made by any human man body. **1913** Kephart *Our Sthn High* 285–86 Pleonasms are abundant . . . Everywhere in the mountains we hear of biscuit-bread . . . man-person. **1924** Raine *Saddlebags* 105 [The] desire for exactness has given such expressions as . . . cow-brute, man-person. **1943** Hannum *Mt People* 147 Shapes of phrases repeat themselves and the same sounds re-echo, giving, oddly enough, vividness rather than monotony—as in their use of double words: "down-log; sulphur-match; man-person." **1952** Wilson *Folk Speech NC* 563 = a human being, a man. "Yes these are right good shoes; maybe some *man-person* could fix them up like new."

[redundant form; DARE *man-person* n chiefly South Midland]

man-power *verb* To move (a heavy object) by human force.

1913 Kephart *Our Sthn High* 32 Wagoning, by the way, was no sinecure. Often it meant to chop a fallen tree out of the road, and then, with handspikes, to "manpower it outen the way." **1952** Wilson *Folk Speech NC* 563 = to employ the force of man. "I don't know whether I can *man-power* this boat against that current or not." **1974** Fink *Bits Mt Speech* 16 = to move some heavy object by human effort. "We'll have to *manpower* them logs up."

[DARE *man-power* v especially southern Appalachians]

mantelboard (also *mantel shelf*) *noun* The horizontal shelf or ledge over a fireplace. See also **fireboard**.

1913 Kephart *Our Sthn High* 244 The narrow mantel-shelf holds pipes and snuff and various other articles of frequent use, among them a twig or two of sweet birch that has been chewed to shreds at one end and is clearly discolored with something brown (this is what the mountain woman calls her "tooth-brush," a snuffstick, understand). **1933** Thomas *Traipsin' Woman* 23 Over the mantel-shelf I could see a long-barreled gun resting in wooden forks. **1934–47** LAMSAS Appal: *mantelboard* = attested by 10/148 speakers (6.7%) from WV, 2/37 (5.4%) from NC, 1/14 (7.1%) from SC, and 1/12 (8.3%) from GA; *mantel shelf* = attested by 1/37 speakers (2.7%) from NC and 8/14 (57.1%) from SC. **1966** Dakin *Vocab Ohio River Valley* 38 *Mantel board*, which would appear to be a blend of old *fire board* (which is *fire board* even if of stone according to some informants) and newer *mantel*, appears a few times in southern Kentucky.

mantrip *noun* See citations. See also **trip**.

1973 Preston *Bituminous Term* 42 = a locomotive and cars specifically designated to carry workers to and from working places in the [coal] mine. **1974** *AOHP/ALC-802* A man-trip . . . is kind of like a passenger train, pulled by a motor with several cars to it, and a man rides in the mines. That's a man-trip, what they take the men inside the mines with. **1977** Shackelford et al. *Our Appalachia* 274 They had to run a man-trip [to] haul the men from the starting place to their working place and they had to have certain cars to haul them in, they couldn't just pile them up in any kind of an old car. **1989** *Matewan OHP-23* It's a motor with empty cars, coal cars, hooked to it, to the back of it, and you'd climb in those empty coal cars, and they'd haul you through under that hill, say a mile or a mile and a half, everhow far it was in there. That was a mantrip. *Ibid.* 28 We didn't walk. We rode what they call the mantrip. The motor took us into the mouth of the section, and you walked to your place. **2004** Johnson *Camp Memories* 24 = a motor pullin' a string of coal cars out of the mine. And the men would be in these cars instead of coal. It was like a big bus, or somethin', pullin' miners out of the mine, Sometimes the car would be somethin' like thirty or forty cars long. And each one of the coal cars would have ten or twelve men in 'em. And they wouldn't be bringin' coal out that particular trip. **2006** Mooney *Lg Coal Mining* 1028 In a slope mine workers walked (or now ride a "man-trip") down a sloping entryway that is not nearly as vertical as in a shaft mine but which still slopes downward.

many (in *a many, a many a, a many and many a, a many of a, many a* (+ plural noun), *many of a*) *adjective phrase* More than one. [Editor's note: The phrase *many a* (+ singular noun) is widespread in the US.]

1862 *Epperly CW Letters* (July 10) a maney por Soul has bin rushed into ther graves in the last 20 days. **1863** *Revis CW Letters* (April 7) I hav thout of my littel sweet a many a time sinc I hav bin sick and wanted to be with you. **1884** Murfree *In TN Mts* 251 Thar hev been sech a many folks killed on the T'other Mounting. **1937** Hall *Coll* (Big Creek NC) I've sawed a many a hard day with my brother. I've grubbed, split rails, built fence. **1939** Hall *Coll* (Wears Cove TN) I've catched a many a bear in the mountains. I've catched them a sight. **1961** *Coe Ridge OHP-333A* I've eat a many a times over there. **1967** Hall *Coll* (Townsend TN) He'd killed a many of the turkey. **1970** *Burton-Manning Coll-94A* They's been a many of a persons started out a-going to do something big. **1971** Foster *Walker Valley* 3:19 I've seen my mother spin many of a time. **1974–75** McCracken *Logging* 7:47–48 I moved a many a one of 'em. **1975** *AOHP/ALC-1128* Many a days I worried my mother by going and playing around old mine machines. **1977** *Shenandoah OHC* 136 Just a many and many a night we stayed up till one or two o'clock ironing. **1979** *Big South Fork OHP-2* I was hauling many of a poplar log that I couldn't stand on the bump and see over it. **1989** *Matewan OHP-33* I seen him many a times. *Ibid.* 33 I'd read over that a many a times. **1998** *Dante OHP-71* I've went to church with him many a many a time. **2008** *Rosie Hicks* 3 Ray plants quite a many potatoes in there.

[DARE *a many* adj phr chiefly South, South Midland]

many much *phrase* Very many.

1973 GSMNP-4:1:56 Now you don't find many much.

many of a See **many**.

many of them *pronoun phrase* Used immediately following a coreferent noun or pronoun.

1955 Ritchie *Singing Family* 89 Solomon and all the others sure were glad to see her, they many of them thought they'd never set eyes on her again.

many's the *phrase* Many are (followed by a singular noun; used to introduce statements). See also **be A1a**.

1913 Kephart *Our Sthn High* 35 Many's the hill o' corn I've propped up with a rock to keep it from fallin' down-hill. **1976** Carter *Little Tree* 29 Granpa said he had many's the time seen that same kind of thing, feelings taking over sense, make as big a fools out of people as it had ol' Rippitt. **1994** Montgomery *Coll* (known to Cardwell).

[contraction of *many is*]

maple molasses *noun* Maple syrup. Same as **tree molasses**.

1985 Irwin *Alex Stewart* 193 Tree molasses, or maple molasses, is just a little thicker than tree syrup. That's all. You just let them boil a little longer.

maple orchard *noun* A grove of sugar maple trees. Same as **sugar orchard**.

1999 Spencer *Memory Lane* II:2 This maple orchard was far from settlers.

mar, marr See **marrow**.

marble *noun* Variant forms *marvel, marvle*.

1862 *Robinson CW Letters* (June 1) I play marvel all the time you had better lern prety fast or I will beat you when I come home. **1916** Combs *Old Early English* 285 Games of marvles (marbles) provide many [Elizabethan words and usages]. **1974** Russell *Hillbilly* 26 Horseshoes and "marvels" (marbles) were also favorites with the boys.

[EDD *marble* sb/v; DARE *marvel* n[1] chiefly South Midland]

March flower *noun* Same as **buttercup**.

1937 Hyatt *Kiverlid* 12 Bed of March flowers, all solid yeller 'fore they faded down. **1944** Hayes *Word-List NC* 35 = the daffodil. **1968** Wilson *Folklore Mammoth Cave* 15 [The] daffodil (Narcissus pseudo-narcissus) [is] called also Easter flowers, jonquils, March flowers.

March man *noun* See citation.

1959–60 Stubbs *Mountain-Wise* (Dec–Jan) 6 The garrulous person, native or outsider, is viewed with a certain amount of suspicion, if not downright distrust. Thus, one prone to talkativeness is described as a "March man," or "windy," and this is no compliment.

marcy See **mercy.**

mare's carry *noun* An overlong pregnancy (in allusion to a mare's eleven-month gestation period).

2003 Cavender *Folk Medicine* 130 Mothers were instructed . . . to avoid passing under a mare's neck to prevent "mare's carry" (an extended term of eleven months).

mare's tail (also *mare tail*) *noun* A cloud with a long, streaky trail. Same as **horsetail.**

1931 Combs *Lg Sthn High* 1304 Judging from them mare's tails, hit looks like warm weather. **1941** Stuart *Men of Mts* 87 There is dirty streaks on Pa's face of dust and grime like little maretails rubbed on clear-as-mountain-water sky. **1966** *DARE Survey* (Spruce Pine NC) = long trailing clouds high in the sky. **1995–97** Montgomery *Coll* (known to eight consultants from the Smoky Mountains).

mare tail See **mare's tail.**

mark

A *noun* A notch cut into the edge of a domestic animal's ear, used to identify its owner, especially for an animal that has been on **open range.** Also called **earmark.** See also **overbit, smooth crop, split B1, swallowfork, underbit.**

1901 Harben *Westerfelt* 131 Me an' 'er mother come to words one day about a shoat pig she claimed had her mark on its yeer an' was penned up with mine. **1915** Dingus *Word-List VA* 185 = a cutting of the ear (of hogs, sheep, cattle) for identification,—of various kinds: (smooth) crop, the tip cut square off.

B *verb*

1 To cause (an unborn child) to have a defect (as a physical mark or a behavioral tendency) from an experience or occurrence to the mother during her pregnancy; hence noun *marking* = this experience or occurrence.

1929 Duncan and Duncan *Sayings* 234 A woman that's big musn't look at nothin' or she'll mark hit [= the child]. **1949** Arnow *Hunter's Horn* 194 She was craving greens bad, and if she didn't get some pretty soon, this child she carried would be marked with greens and would never in all its life get enough of them to eat. **1961** Williams *Content Mt Speech* 15 Pol never let on. She jist said she reckoned all them thar shines and rusties the old man had cut had marked Lil's baby. **1963** Watkins and Watkins *Yesterday* 148 Hill women were extremely careful about everything they did or even thought when they were pregnant, because any unusual or frightening event could mark the baby they were carrying. . . . Dave Hobgood was marked by his father, who got drunk when his mother was pregnant and misbehaved so much that he marked his child. **1978** Morton *Superstitions* 2 Marking was of major concern during prenatal care. Marking was a prenatal experience of the mother showing up as a physical characteristic of the baby. . . . This marking was done mainly through experiences in which the mother was frightened and touched a spot on her body, causing a birthmark symbolic of whatever frightened to appear on her baby. The other effect was for the marking to be in the form of a physical defect in a cognitive or motor skill of the baby. Unusual cravings may also cause marks symbolic of the things craved, usually a mark resembling food to appear on the baby at birth. **1989** Giardina *Storming Heaven* 3 They is many a way to mark a baby while it is still yet in the womb. A fright to its mother will render it nervous and fretful after it is birthed. If a copperhead strikes, a fiery red snake will be stamped on the baby's face or back. And a portentous event will violate a woman's entrails, grab a youngun by the ankle and wrench a life out of joint. **1990** Cavender *Folk Medical Lex* 27 *marking* = a birthmark, physical characteristic or behavior trait caused during pregnancy by the mother having a frightening/unfortunate experience or violating a taboo.

[DARE *mark* v 3 chiefly South, South Midland]

2 To castrate (a male animal).

1952 Wilson *Folk Speech NC* 563 = to castrate; probably a euphemism. **1969** Doran *Folklore White Co* 113 = to sterilize a male animal.

[DARE *mark* v 2 chiefly South, South Midland]

3 To cut a distinguishing notch into the edge of a domestic animal's ear to identify its owner. See also **earmark.**

1862 *Poe Family Papers* (June 2) i wont you to rit to me an rit how you ar gitin along an how our stock is doin and how mutch wheat you think you wil mak an ef the Sows fetch up thar pigs git Jim to mark them for you ef he wil.

markel See **merkel.**

mark out *verb phrase* To custom measure the wood for (a coffin).

1967 Miller *Pigeon's Roost* (March 16) I have recently been told that there still remains on Pigeon Roost only enough chestnut lumber to build only one more free coffin out of, but all the coffin makers is dead now and I doubt where there could be one man found in and around here for many miles who could even mark out a coffin in the old time style.

marriage house *noun* See citation. See also **honeymoon house, weaner.**

1995 Trout *Historic Buildings* 37 On Ellis Montieth's place in North Carolina, a frame house built behind the main house was called the marriage house: where young people lived until they had enough money to afford a home of their own.

marrow *noun*

A Variant forms *ma'ar, mar, marr* [see **1925** in **B**].

1913 Kephart *Our Sthn High* 228 I've burnt my holler teeth out with a red-hot wire.... It'd sear the mar so it wouldn't be so sensitive. **1942** Hall *Phonetics Smoky Mts Smoky Mts* 25 *Arrow, harrow, marrow, narrow, sparrow, wheelbarrow.* Usage of [ɑ] and [æ] appears to be about evenly divided in these words. [Footnote:] Local informants say, however, that [ɑ] is much more frequent than [æ]. **1974** Fink *Bits Mt Speech* 16 *ma'ar* . . . marrow. "A ma'ar bone." **1997** Montgomery Coll (known to Bush, Jones, Ledford, Weaver).

[DARE *marrow* n chiefly South, South Midland]

B (in plural) One's knees.

1925 Dargan *Highland Annals* 153 All she done wuz to git down on her marr's an' pray fer my soul.

ma'rr up See **mire up**.

marrying *noun* A wedding ceremony.

1865 *Larue CW Letters* (Jan 5) you and John ou[gh]t to bin at home a christmas for ther was a grait meny Marrings. **1937** Campbell *KY Mt Community* 549 Whenever you set a date fer the marrying, no kinder weather nor nothing ort to stop hit. **1941** Still *Troublesome Creek* 102 Only a funeral occasion or a marrying would draw such a swarm. **1962** Dykeman *Tall Woman* 159 Young'uns always have one thing or another ailing them, but a marrying don't come along but once in a coon's age.

marry off *verb phrase* Of a child: to get married and leave the parental home.

1908 Johnson *Life KY Mts* 177 Before I was grown [my sisters] had all married off. **1969** *Burton-Manning Coll*-89B My children all married off and just left me alone. **1972** *GSMNP*-86:28 She lived over here with her and her mother and father. They'd all married off but her. **1985** Dabney *More Mt Spirits* 21 [I] raised nine children. Two's dead and seven's living and they all married off.

marry up with *verb phrase* To get married to.

1976 Garber *Mountain-ese* 56 I reckon that Jed is gonna marry-up with that young McCoy girl. **1987** Young *Lost Cove* 109 He married up with Betty Honeycutt and the two settled down on Big Rock Creek. **1996** South *Never Killed* 63 I married my wife two times and would have married up with her the third time but I couldn't get along with her.

martifie See **mortify**.

martin gourd (also *martin house*) *noun* A dried, hollowed-out gourd placed in a tree, on a pole, etc. for a purple martin (*Progne subis*) to nest in. See also **gourd tree**.

1975 *Foxfire III* 208 People in years back put up martin houses to entice the martins to stay . . . during the summer to chase off chicken hawks.... The primary reason people erect purple martin gourds . . . now is to keep flying insects away from their gardens.

martin winter *noun* See citation. For terms describing a similar phenomenon, see **blackberry winter**.

1995 Montgomery Coll = a frost or freezing spell in early May at the time that martins return from the south (Cardwell).

mar up See **mire up**.

marvel, marvle See **marble**.

mash[1] *verb*

1 (also *mash up*) To flatten, quash, crush (as a finger).

1901 Harben *Westerfelt* 94 I felt like mashing the head of that sheriff for beating him like he did. **1939** Hall Coll (Smokemont NC) Old Man Tom went back [to his pen trap], had about a two-year-old bear, and he said he had him mashed down flat so he couldn't get up on his feet to raise the lid up. **1963** Watkins and Watkins *Yesterday* 48 It's a wonder why no child ever got mashed to death sleeping under eight or ten quilts. **1968** *DARE Survey* (Brasstown NC) = to squeeze or crush something, as a finger in a door. **1976** Still *Pattern of Man* 79 As His disciple, everyone who steps on His toes mashes Mine. **1977** Shackelford et al. *Our Appalachia* 300 I believe I would rather a rock mash me up and kill me instantly than to cut air off of me and make me smother. **2007** McMillon *Notes* Ever time I go to close the door, I mash my finger.

[DARE *mash* v 1 widespread, but chiefly South, Midland; also West]

2 (also *mash down*) To press down.

1946 Matthias *Speech Pine Mt* 190 *mash down* = to push down: "Mash down on that handle." **1973** *GSMNP*-78:18a They would lay a big rock on top of [a bucket] to mash it down in the spring. **1976** Dwyer *Southern Sayin's* 5 *mash the light button* = to push on or off. **1994** Rash *New Jesus* 82 I crank up the truck and spray gravel as I mash the accelerator to the floor.

[DARE *mash* v 2 chiefly South, South Midland]

mash[2]

A *noun* In making whiskey, a mixture of **malt**, water, and grain allowed to ferment prior to distillation, the next stage in the production of whiskey.

1914 Arthur *Western NC* 273 When a sufficient quantity has been produced, the mash is removed from the still, and it is washed out, after which the "singlings" are poured into the still and evaporated, passing through the worm a second time, thus becoming "doublings," or high proof whiskey. **1938** Hall Coll (Emerts Cove TN) Malt [makes] unfermented mash into fermented beer. **1939** Hall Coll To turn fermented mash into steam, which is condensed in a cooling tank into liquor. The first run is known as "singlin's": the second is "doublin's." The second run is by-passed by the use of the "thump tank." **1949** Maurer *Argot of Moonshiner* 10 = the fermenting mixture in the vats, previous to distillation. **1956** Hall Coll (Mt Sterling NC) This is Taylor Sutton giving my version of how that the old-timers made whiskey. They didn't have any sugar, and they used grain and grain only. They would use rye, wheat, and corn, and they made up a mash and cooked it, put it in barrels, barrels that they had homemade, and they'd let it ferment. After it fermented, they put it into a still, which was made of copper, and the still was set on a furnace, and they put the cap on the still and they got their mash in it, and then you started boiling this, cooking it, and running from the still over to the cooling vat. **1959** Hall Coll (Mt Sterling NC) = whiskey that has been made in a big process and . . . they're making it on zinc, on tin, on everything they can get in other words to hold their mash while they cook it . . . and it is very dangerous to drink. **1962** Hall Coll (Newport TN) A pregnant woman will spoil kraut or [the] mash for a run of liquor. **1968** *End of Moonshining* 101 = corn meal made from grinding unsprouted corn kernels. It is put in the barrels, mixed with water, allowed to work until it is a suitable base for the addition of the malt. **c1975** Lunsford *It Used to Be* 79 Mash is the meal that's been put to ferment in the tubs around the building. If it's on the outside, it's just in the opening under the trees. They stir up the meal, sprinkle some rye malt over that. In a few days, if it's warm weather, it will ferment more readily. When it gets ripe to distill, after it's worked up to the point where possibly that still beer is drinkable, they'll be ready then to mash in. **1977** Shields *Cades Cove* 79f It was sort of a custom to have a party after a "run off" of moonshine whiskey. Sometimes called backins parties, these featured a quantity of the mash "backins" or spent beer, heated with spices and served along with food. . . . The alcoholic content of the drink is not high, but enough of it can elevate the drinkers' spirits. **1990** Aiken *Stories* 199 The malt was mixed with ground cornmeal and water, then cooked to become "mash." The mash was allowed to ferment and produce a "beer." The beer was then distilled to become "moonshine." **1992** Gabbard *Thunder Road* 67 The barrels are what you'd ferment your mash in. It'd take about three days for the mash to work off and clear off on top. **c1999** Sutton *Me and Likker* 104 = may be made out of corn, barley, rye that is sprouted, dried, and ground which breaks down the carbohydrates in the grain and turns them in to sugar. Modern day moonshiners don't go to the extra work and expense. They throw the damn yeast to it.

B (also *mash in*) *verb, verb phrase* See citations.

1881 Atkinson *After Moonshiners* 21 From ten to twenty tubs, usually of the capacity of about one hundred gallons is necessary, to make the mash, and ferment the beer. The meal is first placed in the tubs and is cooked by the use of scalding water. This is called "mashing." **1949** Maurer *Argot of Moonshiner* 11 *mash in* = to begin the process of whisky-making . . . = to put the ingredients (meal, sugar, etc.) in the vats for fermentation.

mash barrel (also *mash box, mash tub*) *noun* A container used in fermenting **mash** (see **mash**[2]) for distilling into **beer**.

1949 Arnow *Hunter's Horn* 207 Nunn, honey, you ain't a goen to stand an let 'em take you—it'll go hard—whiskey, mash barrel, squeezens, cooker, an all. **1974** Dabney *Mt Spirits* xxiii In copper pot stills, this leftover is dipped out and "slopped back" into the mash barrels and mixed with subsequent batches. *Ibid.* 127 You first put you twenty bushels of meal in the mash box. Then we'd take a big old hose leading from the boiler and pipe and pumped that steam into the mash boxes. That scalded and cooked your mash. **c1975** Lunsford *It Used to Be* 79 A mash tub is the tub that holds the mash, and sometimes they make boxes to take the place of that. **2009** Webb et al. *Moonshining* 329 Before World War I, southern moonshiners used "turnip stills," a turnip-shaped setup whose main parts are wooden "mash boxes," in which the grain mash mixtures fermented before distilling.

mash box See **mash barrel.**

mash hound *noun* See citation.

2007 Rowley *Moonshine!* 162 = a derogatory term for a person who drinks beer from mash tubs, sometimes in preference to moonshine, often to excess.

mash in See **mash**[2] **B.**

mash stick *noun* See citations. Also called **break stick, scrape paddle, stir stick, swab.**

1914 Crain *Life Story* 10 I could break up more mash with my feet than most people with their mash stick.

mash tub See **mash barrel.**

mason wasp *noun* A dirt dauber, mud dauber wasp.

1967 *DARE Survey* (Maryville TN) = mud dauber. **1998** Montgomery Coll (known to Brown, Bush, Cardwell, Jones).

[DARE *mason wasp* n chiefly Mid Atlantic, southern Appalachians]

massacre *noun, verb* Variant form with final syllable pronounced *cree* [kri].

1942 *Hall Phonetics Smoky Mts* 79. **1957** Combs *Lg Sthn High: Word List* 63 *massacree.* **1989** *Matewan OHP-39* That was before the massacree ever happened.

[CUD *massacree* v; DARE *massacre* n chiefly South, South Midland, old-fashioned]

massy See **mercy.**

mast *noun* A season's accumulation of fruit of the forest forming the natural diet of bears, wild hogs, and other animals, sometimes classified as **hard mast** (nuts, acorns, seeds, etc.) or **soft mast** (berries, cherries, grapes, etc.). See also **beech mast, chestnut mast, hard mast, soft mast.**

1855 *Mitchell Letter* I have a plenty of roughness to winter my cattel pork fattend on the mast. **1863** *Averett Letters* (Oct) the[y] is not but lettle mast this year and I have bin kept aup my old sow moust ever since you left home. **1881** Pierson *In the Brush* 78–79 The hogs find their food in the woods the greater part of the year, and in the fall they fatten upon the nuts or "mast." The oak, hickory, beech, and other trees that abound in these extensive forests afford vast quantities of these nuts, which these people claim for their own hogs, whoever may own the land. **1913** Kephart *Our Sthn High* 79 The mast, sich as acorns and beech and hickory nuts, is mostly on the Car'lina side. **1915** Bohannon *Bear Hunt* 461–62 In all the creek bottoms there was no chestnut mast, but of beech there was plenty, both in feeding grounds which lay on the North Carolina side of the main ridge and the lying grounds which are on the Tennessee side. **1953** Hall Coll (Bryson City NC) Sometimes we'd have mast in the head of Bone Valley and we'd hunt back that way. . . . There's no mast on that side of the mountain except some beech mast. . . . Mast means all kind of things for animals to eat in the woods, such as acorns and chestnuts, and berries and grapes. . . . Choicest food for the bear was to get beechnuts. Beechnuts. . . . chestnuts is the two choicest foods. **1956** Hall *Coll* (Big Creek NC) People didn't have to fatten hogs in the old days. They'd turn 'em out and let 'em eat mast. [The mountains] was a wonderful chestnut country. Chestnuts was one of the best fatteners and made wonderful meat too. They have a world of strength to 'em. **1975** *Foxfire III* 112 Hogs roamed the mountains, where there's all kinds of mast-chestnuts. The hogs'd get just as fat on them as they could be . . . And you could bring'em in an' kill'em right off the mast. **2008** *Smokies Guide* (Autumn) 1 During fall, the success of bears in the Smoky Mountains depends almost entirely on what biologists call the "mast crop." They divide the mast into two groups, soft (blackberries, cherries, grapes, blueberries, etc.) and hard (acorns, hickory nuts, and beech nuts).

[OED2 *mast* n[2] 1a 825→; DARE *mast* n[1] chiefly South, South Midland]

master

A *adjective*

1 Tremendous, outstanding, powerful.

1859 Taliaferro *Fisher's River* 60 I'll soon hev my basket full uv these master fellers. **1862** *Neves CW Letters* (Aug 14) I have Just Eat the master bait of Rosten Ear soop that you hav saw. **1863** *Brown CW Letters* (Dec 21) [I] Saw the master fite last nite i ever Saw. **1889** Mooney *Folk Carolina Mts* 98 One informant positively asserted the truth of this belief [in the signs of Old Christmas], because in order to test the matter she had once gone down to the stable on this night, and sure enough she found the cows kneeling on the ground and making "just the masterest moanin'." **1896** *Word-List* 420 = most powerful. "He was making the *masterest* noise ever I hearn." **1904–20** Kephart *Notebooks* 4:749 He was a master brute. **1913** Kephart *Our Sthn High* 283 That Nantahala is a master shut-in, jest a plumb gorge. **1925** Greer-Petrie *Angeline Hill Country* 89 They had the masterest hogs! **1939** Hall *Coll* (Cataloochee NC) They'd come buyers in here. When the buyers come in and bought 'em [= cattle], before they left they was a master drove too. **c1940** Simms *Coll* = great, big. **1962** Dykeman *Tall Woman* 56 By the sound of him he's got a master set of lungs, too. **1982** Powers and Hannah *Cataloochee* 89 We had the masterest lawsuit you ever seen. **1993** Soesbee *Wordlist* That was the masterest hog we've ever killed.

2 Extraordinary, expert, superlative (as to indicate command of a skill or exceptional proficiency). See also **master hand**.

1863 *Robinson CW Letters* (July 18) I must tel you that we took the master March we was orderd to march at 6 oclock last tusday evning back to the Clinch River. **1886** Smith *Sthn Dialect* 349 They all have the authority of old or dialect English, or many of them belong to all parts of the South, if not elsewhere . . . master (excellent, or adv very). **1915** Dingus *Word-List VA* 185 *masterest* = greatest, "awfulest." **1917** Kephart *Word-List* 414 He was the *masterest* bear-fighter I ever did see. **1919** Combs *Word-List South* 36 *masterest* = most masterful: "Zeke 'lowed ez how he'd been called to give his dream at the meetin', a-tellin' 'em how he'd dremp of drappin' down on his bendified knees in the cornfield, and a-makin' the masterest moanin' you ever hear." **1925** Dargan *Highland Annals* 205 He'd et and tell the masterest tales. **1937** Hall *Coll* (Cades Cove TN) Devil Sam Walker's a master mountaineer. *Ibid.* (Cades Cove TN) Fonze is a master hunter. *Ibid.* (Hartford TN) The bear was batting its eyes when the master hunter found him. **1939** Hall *Coll* He told some of the masterest stories. A body couldn't hardly believe them. *Ibid.* (Saunook NC) He's a master story teller. **1955** Ritchie *Singing Family* 59 We hid in thar and boys, that was a master hiding place. **1955** Washburn *Country Doctor* 66 Hain't that a master washin' [of clothes hung out to dry]? I bet some of their folks is down sick. **c1999** Sutton *Me and Likker* 38 He was a master still maker. He could make one that looked like it come out of a factory.

[DARE *master* adj chiefly South Midland, also ME]

B *adverb* Exceptionally, tremendously, very. See also **main B**.

1886 [See **A2** above]. **1917** Kephart *Word-List* 414 = masterfully. "He laughed *master*." **1939** Hall *Coll* (White Oak NC) [The fox] had a master big track. **1953** Hall *Coll* (Bryson City NC) [A catamount] has got a master big head. **1955** Ritchie *Singing Family* 121 They said Long John played "Killy Kranky" on the jew's-harp, master well too. **1994** Montgomery *Coll* (known to Cardwell).

[EDD *master* adv 17; Web3 *master* adv chiefly dialect; DARE *master* adv chiefly ME, southern Appalachians]

master hand *noun* A skillful person, expert. See also **master A2**.

1944 Wilson *Word-List* 46 He was a master hand at making chairs. **1957** Parris *My Mts* 171 He was a master-hand with the dogs and he trained her well. **1995–97** Montgomery *Coll* (known to Adams, Brown, Ledford, Oliver); He was a master hand when it came to building a chimney (Cardwell).

[DARE *master hand* n *master* adj + *hand* n; perhaps a reanalysis of *master hand* "the hand of a master" (OED2 at *master* sb 29)]

master root *noun* Apparently a cow parsnip (*Heracleum lanatum*), with many medicinal uses.

2007 Milnes *Signs Cures Witches* 171 Other occult tales among some German people in Pendleton County show great respect for a plant known as master root. Some men would carry it in their hunting coats to stop spells from affecting their dogs. When I questioned Johnny Arvin about master root, he remembered it. Then, after he consulted with his sisters, he told me they determined that it is a plant listed as masterwort in some taxonomy books.

mater, matoe, matter[1] See **tomato**.

matter[2] *noun*

1 See **such a matter**.

2 Pus.

1985 Sienkneckt *Rheumatic Diseases* 183 = purulent running; that which is formed by suppuration. **1986** Pederson et al. *LAGS* = attested by 4/60 interviewees (6.7%) from E TN and 1/35 (2.9%) from N GA; 5/27 of all LAGS interviewees (18.5%) attesting term were from Appalachia.

matter-mind *noun phrase* Same as **no never mind.**

(the) matter of *noun phrase* The trouble with.

1944 Combs *Word-List Sthn High* 20 What's the matter of that child? **1956** McAtee *Some Dial NC* 31 What's the matter of that child? **1997** Montgomery Coll (known to Brewer, Brown, Bush, Cardwell).

mattock (also *mattocks*) *noun* A tool resembling a pick but having a heavy, adze-like blade for breaking up ground and digging out roots.

1957 Broaddus *Vocab Estill Co KY* 49 *mattocks.* **1968** *DARE Survey* (Brasstown NC) = a hand tool used for cutting underbrush and digging out roots. **c1975** Lunsford *It Used to Be* 174 Look yonder fernenth that sassafras and find my mattock.

[DARE *mattock* widespread, but more frequent Appalachians]

maul rails *verb phrase* To split fence rails from a log using a maul.

1864 *Wester CW Letters* (Jan 5) I would be very glad to se all of you Tel Charles and Ben to Be sure to take care of Bet until I come home [tell] lige [= Elijah] I had much rather [be] their with him Maling rales. **1881** Pierson *In the Brush* 21 Another [lane] led me where some rails had been "mauled" and recently hauled away. **1914** Furman *Sight* 70 I laid my plans for to set the farm on its feet ag'in, and clear new ground, and maul rails for the fence. **1982** Slone *How We Talked* 10 "I feel like I been mauling rails"—meaning I am really tired.

[DARE *maul rails* v phr 1 chiefly South, South Midland]

maw[1] See **ma.**

maw[2] *noun* The stomach.

1937 Haun *Cocke Co* 2 Folks still have the maw ache from eating too much sallet, and blacksnake root is the only thing that will cyore it.

mawmaw See **mammaw 2.**

may *auxiliary verb*

A Variant past-tense forms *mought/mout* [rhymes with *out*]. [Editor's note: These forms do not appear in ATASC. Joseph Hall heard *mought* in the Smoky Mountains only in 1937 and only from old people.]

1818 (in **1824** Knight *Letter from KY* 107) Some words are . . . by the lower classes in society, pronounced very uncouthly, as . . . mought. **1832** (in **2004** *TN Petitions III* 36) Your petesnor said Emley mout obtain her freedom. **1862** *Gilley CW Letters* (Oct 7) I killed one for I saw him fall an an mought killed more. **1862** *Zimmerman CW Letters* (Oct 10) you mout look for me thare if you get very bad and have to go to the hosptle. **1866** *Chapman CW Letters* (Jan 1) Father and Mother is tolerable well as well as mought bee expected after witnessing such a Rebellion. **1867** Harris *Sut Lovingood* 23 Dad wanted hit made kurb, es he hedn't work'd fur a good while, an' said he mout sorter feel his keepin, an' go tu ravin an' cavortin. **1895** Edson and Fairchild *TN Mts* 370 Ef you'd a ben thar you mout (might) a got a bussy. **1895** *Mt Baptist Sermon* 14 You mought as well make a church outer the devils in hell as o' thet sorter people. **1913** Kephart *Our Sthn High* 201 "What mought you-uns foller for a living?" *Ibid.* 284 There are many corrupt forms of the verb, such as gwine for gone or going, mought (mowt) for might. **1924** Raine *Saddlebags* 98–99 Perhaps no phrase is derided as more uncouth than *mought* for might, yet here again Spenser is our refuge: "So sound he slept that naught mought him awake." **1937** Hall Coll (Emerts Cove TN) That mought be what makes them so sour. *Ibid.* (Wears Cove TN) (A question said to have been asked of strangers in the past was) "What mought your name be?" **1953** Atwood *Verbs East US* 18 *Mought* is primarily a rustic form, being used by more than half the Type I informants [i.e. older speakers with little formal education] in Va. and N.C., but less than one sixth the Type II informants.

[OED3 (at *may* v[1]) "the Early Modern English form *mought* . . . had an extensive literary currency in the 16th and 17th century. . . . The form had a continued existence in English regional use and in Scots until the 19th century": DARE *may* v Aa chiefly South, South Midland]

B Combined with another modal auxiliary verb. For *could might*, see **can[1] B4.**

1 *may* in phrase *may can.*

1934–47 *LAMSAS Appal* (Swain Co NC) *may can.* **2001** Montgomery File I may can get it out tomorrow (54-year-old woman, Jefferson Co TN).

2 *might* in phrases *might can, might could, mighta coulda, might ought to, might should ought to, might would.* See also **had ought to.** See also Grammar and Syntax §8.1.

1934–47 *LAMSAS Appal* (Madison Co NC, Swain Co NC) *might could.* **1937** Hall Coll (Wears Cove TN) You might could ask somebody along the road. (from woman of whom Joseph Hall was asking directions). **c1940** Simms Coll [They] might could increase their hog raising. **c1945** Haun *Hawk's Done* 307 Pony might ought not to be held to account for running after them Jarnigan girls. **1953** Atwood *Verbs East US* 35 Type I informants [i.e. older speakers with little formal education] offer [*might could*] with hardly any exceptions, and it is also used by from two thirds (Va.) to practically all (N.C.) of Type II informants [i.e. younger speakers with more formal education] as well. . . . A good many informants in the S[outh] A[tlantic] S[tates] use the form *mought* rather than *might* in this phrase. **1953** Wharton *Dr Woman Cumberlands* 41 "Paw wants the doctor woman to come as quick as she can git thar," he said. "Mammy's about to wink out." "Is it the flue?" I asked. "Hit might could be the pneumony fever." **1957** Combs *Lg Sthn High: Word List* 64 *might could* = might, might be able. Ex: "I might could do it." **1968** *Faith Healing* 68 They had th'mule's foot tied up, pulled up, tied 'cause Doc's afraid it'd kick him—might would, I guess. **1969** *GSMNP-27:23* It might could've been. I wouldn't say. **1972** *AOHP/ALC-342* He couldn't do what he wanted to and what he might would have done. *Ibid.* I might oughtn't talk this, they eat me up anyhow sometimes, and if I tell anything, I want to tell the truth. **1973** Foster *Walker Valley* 9:62 One of them might could tell a man where her grave is at. **1974–75** McCracken *Logging* 16:44 They might could have boated, pulled it up there in a tugboat. *Logging* 38 It would be a sight to see all he lumber I have sawed. You couldn't see it. You might could walk around it in a day or two, but you couldn't see it all. **1975** *We Sing* 14 You can see there wasn't no theatres around here and no city to do a lot of things we might a-could a-done. **1978** Montgomery *White Pine Coll* VI-2 I might not could have got enough to have went along with me, but I believe I could. *Ibid.* XIII If you're in a hurry, you might could pick up something. **1982** Ginns *Snowbird Gravy* 105 If they'd just laid down, the snakebite might wouldn't have killed a lot of them, with nothin' done. **1983** Pyle *CCC 50th Anniv* B:6:9 If you give me thirty minutes, I mighta coulda thought of some names. **1986** Pederson et al. *LAGS* You might could tell (Cocke Co TN); You might could get up here and help me (Hawkins Co TN); Now I might can tell you something (Johnson Co TN); She might would tolerate one (Knox Co TN); If you don't cure bacon, the worms might could get in 'em (Sevier Co TN). **1986** (in **2000** Puckett *Seldom Ask* 102) I might ought to bring some little things of milk. **1988** Dickey and Bake *Wayfarer* 24 You might could sit up a little bit, if you feel like it. **1995** Montgomery *Coll* I might can go with you tomorrow (Cardwell). **1996** Harrell *Fetch It* 163 We might ought to try to do something about that. **1999** Dumas *Sthn Mt English* 74 The "rule" in the Southern Mountain region is that these combinations are quite ordinary and usual. Even triple combinations occur, particularly with *ought to* (pronounced *oughta*), as in "She *might should ought to* leave well enough alone." **2004** Adams *Old True Love* 110 Some things I might not ought to have heard right out in the open that way, but I must say I took my time and meandered along trying to determine who was in what wagon. **2008** *Rosie Hicks* 1 Grandpa might would do it, but he had an idea where he'd better come. **2013** *Blind Pig* (May 29) "Might could" is a modest way of offering advice to someone without coming off like you think you're the smartest person on Earth who holds all the answers. *Ibid.* "Might should," "might ought," etc. give advice without being too direct or making it sound like it is the only thing that makes any sense to a rational person.

[cf SND *can* v[1] III.2; CUD *might can*, etc. (at *might*[1] 3); HT *might could* "may/might be able to"; DARE *may* v B1 chiefly South, South Midland]

3 *mought* in combination with *could* = might be able to. *old-fashioned*

1936 (in **1952** Mathes *Tall Tales* 212) We mought could he'p Grannison out if hit comes to court.

mayapple *noun* A small perennial plant (*Podophyllum peltatum*) with a succulent fruit; its leaves and roots are poisonous but from them a medicinal tea can be made. Also called **devil's-apple**, **hog apple**, **love melon**, **mandrake**, **raccoon berry**, **umbrella plant**.

1892 Allen *Cumberland Gap* 250 Not long since, during a season of scarcity in corn, a local store-keeper told the people of a county to go out and gather all the mandrake or "May-apple" root they could find. At first only the women and children went to work, the men holding back with ridicule. By-and-by they also took part, and that year some fifteen tons were gathered, at three cents a pound, and the whole country thus got its seed-corn. **1937** Hall *Coll* (Cades Cove TN) = mandrake. **1960** Price *Root Digging in Appal* 18 Mayapple or mandrake (Podophyllum peltatum) is a common forest plant, whose root is used as a purgative and in the preparation of the resinous material podophyllin. Its discovery is credited to the Cherokees. **1962** Hall *Coll* (Gatlinburg TN) = one of the most powerful laxatives, round like an apple. Just eat the inside—real juicy like a tangerine, has a delicious flavor. **1965** Shelton *Pioneer Comforts* 9 May Apple [bark and roots were made into a tea for] Constipation. **1967** Hall *Coll* (Townsend TN) People used to dig them may apple roots and sell 'em for medicine. When the fruit is yellow, they're good eating. **1977** Madden and Jones *Mt Home* 31–32 The mainstay of the Walker sisters' healing potions was "Charley linament," a "soothing balm" of secret ingredients concocted by Uncle Charley Walker. It was an herb mixture that used Indian Turnip and May apple root along with many others, and is remembered as being "hot as hell's hinges" and "mighty powerful."

may can See **may B1**.

May fresh *noun* A flash flood in May. See also **fresh B1**, **freshet**, **spring fresh**, **tide A**.

1953 Miller *Pigeon's Roost* (Dec 24) There are still signs of the May flood of 1901. The old people called it the May fresh. There have not been raging waters like it since. **1975** Brewer *Valley So Wild* 228 Records are sparse on the 1840 flood, but when TVA engineers in the late 1930's started gathering flood history on the Little Tennessee, they found a few old residents whose parents had pointed out to them the high water marks of the "May fresh" of 1840.

May meeting *noun* An annual church service in the spring at which communion is served. See also **sacrament meeting**.

1997 King *Mt Folks* 15–16 She remembers sitting on the second seat behind her father, a deacon, at Pearl Valley Baptist Church and the once a year "May meeting," for communion.

maypop *noun* A tall vine (*Passiflora incarnata*) with large flesh-colored flowers, edible, yellow fruit, and medicinal uses. Also called **molly pop**, **passion flower**, **wild apricot**. See also **molly pop**.

1913 Morley *Carolina Mts* 68 If you look over those fields where, in spite of the efforts of the farmer, the great blue passion flower bloomed all summer, you will see leathery fruits as large as a goose egg lying about by the basketful. These are maypops. **1970** Campbell et al. *Smoky Mt Wildflowers* 66 Also known as wild apricot and maypop, [the passion flower] is a vine up to ten feet in length. [**1971** Krochmal et al. *Medicinal Plants Appal* This plant . . . has been used to reduce blood pressure and to increase the rate of respiration.] **1982** Stupka *Wildflowers* 69 The fruit is a many-seeded berry the shape of a lemon. When ripe it is yellow and edible. The fruit accounts for the alternate names "wild apricot" and "maypop."

me *pronoun* See also Grammar and Syntax §2.3.1.

1 Used reflexively as indirect object (the so-called personal dative) = (for) myself.

1834 Crockett *Narrative* 157 I then cut me a pole and crawled along on my sapling till I got to the one it was lodged against. **1862** *Martin CW Letters* (March 2) yester day we drawed Money So I went yester day & bought Me Som pens. **1862** *Watters-Curtis CW Letters* (July 29) I wait un till I can kill me a seasesh. **1864** *Warrick CW Letters* (April 1) I have put me and Gimmna oup A hous and we ar A faring fin. **c1900** (in **1997** Stoddart *Quare Women* 127) I've got me three children dead. **1915** Hall *Autobiog Claib Jones* 23 I had got me another woman to stay with my children by the name of Hanshew. **1939** Hall *Coll* (Proctor NC) I got me a pole and got up on this drift, laid down my gun, and commenced punching down through where the drift was hollow. **1952** Giles *40 Acres* 49 Them's the purtiest shoes. . . . I wisht I had me a pair. **1956** Hall *Coll* (Roaring Fork TN) I had got big enough to trade me in two or three pistols. **1973** *Church of God* 13 The next day I went out and ordered me up a lunch, and they brought me up a dessert bowl of brown beans. **c1975** Lunsford *It Used to Be* 69 Like the girl said, "I'm gonna galax me out a pair of shoes before Christmas." **1978** Montgomery *White Pine Coll* VIII-2 As soon as I get out of school, I'm going to get me a job, try to get me one as a mechanic. **1985** Irwin *Alex Stewart* 165 I'd hide me out two big kegs in the field, and cover it over right good. **1991** Thomas *Sthn Appal* 164 I've made a lot of maple pegs. [I'd s]aw off me a block, off of a maple. **1993** Page and Smith *Foxfire Toys and Games* 116 I had me a little chimney and I'd build me a little fire in there. **1999** Montgomery *File* I thought me a thought (85-year-old man, Gatlinburg TN). **2008** *Rosie Hicks* 4 I want me a pair of mules. *Ibid.* 4 All I cared for was get me a gizzard. *Ibid.* 6 I want me some good water.

[OED3 *me* pron 4 now archaic except in colloquial (chiefly U.S. regional) usage; DARE *me* pron 3 scattered, but especially South, South Midland]

2 As the simple subject of a clause. [Editor's note: This usage does not occur in ATASC.]

1939 Hall *Coll* Me puts in twenty-five pound of sugar and didn't git a drap.

3 As part of a compound subject (thus *me and him* = he and I). See also **her 1**, **him 1**.

1862 *Shipman CW Letters* (Feb 6) mee and Stepp has got 7 blankets and one old wagon sheet. **1885** Bayless *Letters* Me and James Platt has been talking of a lot in Hampton. **1939** Hall *Coll* (Cades Cove TN) Me and Tom [Gregory] was a-sangin'. *Ibid.* (Tuckaleechee Cove TN) Me and my brother-in-law one time left the White Oak . . . and went a-coon huntin' one night. *Ibid.* (Wears Cove TN) Me and brother Baus could just get out there and kill a deer anytime we took a notion to. **1940** Haun *Hawk's Done* 31 Me and Amy made plenty of cherry bark tea. That is the first time I ever seen it fail to cure the fever. **1941** Hall *Coll* (Hot Springs NC) Me and Blondie got up backwards this morning. **c1945** Haun *Hawk's Done* 325 Me and her had borrowed Howard's axe and had been cutting wood during the cold days. **1953** Hall *Coll* (Bryson City NC) We went out, me and my father-in-law, to Hall's cabin. **1957** GSMNP-23:1:18 We'd go out there and lay out, just me and him ourself. **1969** GSMNP-37 Me and my Dad was coming by there and catched him at work. **1971** *AOHP/ALC-177* They had banjo, always did have one, and when me and Walter and a bunch of us get together. **1983** *Dark Corner OHP-5A* They wasn't but one chestnut tree up around that hollow when me and the old lady married. **1989** *Matewan OHP-9* Me and you are going to be in the hole ourselves. **1998** *Dante OHP-12* Me and my brother got lost one time. **2002** Rash *Foot in Eden* 141 I knew me and him was just getting started.

meadow *noun* Variant form *medder*.

1864 *Chapman CW Letters* (April 23) me & Harvy & Wm Harlas went the other day & picked about one bushel of Greens the Same Kind that we use to pick thare in Kincaids medder. **1939** Hall *Coll* (Hazel Creek NC) [Was there any one point where you herded cattle mostly?] We kept 'em on what we called on top of the medders, right on top of the Smoky Mountain, mostly there where the tame grass was sowed. [What meadows was that?] That's what they call Siler Medders. **1942** Hall *Phonetics Smoky Mts* 80 A considerable amount of education or subjecting to modernizing influences is required before speakers regularly avoid ['mɛdɚ] for general American [o]. Examples: . . . *meadow*. **1963** Edwards *Gravel* 134 I turned that mare and colt into the medder and jest set back and watched them fill out. **1973** *Foxfire Interviews* A-73-46 We'd gather up in some big medder, you know, and a crowd of us and play town ball and baseball. **1976** Garber *Mountain-ese* 57 The cows got out uv the barn lot and are grazin' in the medder.

[DARE *meadow* n A (pronc) chiefly southern Appalachians, Ozarks, occasionally New England]

meadow muffin *noun* A small pile of cow dung.

1993 Cunningham *Sthn Talk* 100 Take care you don't "cut your foot" on a meadow muffin out thar in that pasture. **1997** Montgomery *Coll* (known to Bush, Ellis, Jones).

meadow piece *noun* A parcel of land that is in meadow.

1900 Harben *N GA Sketches* 53 The meadow-piece has obliged to be broke an' sowed in wheat.

meal beer *noun* Homemade beer from cornmeal.

2009 Burton *Beech Mt Man* 114 My brother-in-law made what's called meal beer. I watch' him make it, and I wrote the recipe down, but I never could make it. It tastes like beer, but you make it out of cornmeal.

meal bin (also *meal box, meal chest, meal gum, meal tub*) *noun* A large container, usually of wood, in which cornmeal and sometimes flour were stored.

1931 Greve *Tradition Gatlinburg* 70 A table and a corner cupboard to hold the few dishes usually completed the furnishings, but some other necessities were often seen: the "meal gums" in the corners, hollowed-out sections of logs, fitted with bottoms and lids, to hold the supplies of flour and meal. **1940–42** Adams *Tales* 92 She slipped out and got a little meal where she had it hid and told them she scraped it out of the bottom of the meal tub, and she baked a little bread and give everyone a piece. **1940** Haun *Hawk's Done* 30 When I was over at the meal box and needed a knife or something out of the three-cornered cupboard I would tell her to bring it to me and them little old brown eyes would glitter. **1973** GSMNP-74:19 Papa come home and he poured [his ground corn] in the meal box. He said, "They's something wrong," he said. "I took the same amount of corn I always took," but it didn't fill the meal box up at all like it had a been filling it up." **1973** Miller *English Unicoi Co* 149 *meal gum* = a large, metal container for storing flour or meal or both, either made as a barrel or a chest divided into two compartments. **1983** Page and Wigginton *Aunt Arie* 107 We had a meal chest up on a bench, and I'd get me a chair, put it beside th'chest and stand on it, and sift my meal like that in a ol' sifter. **1985** Wear *Lost Communities* 12 There was the "meal gum" which consisted of a large hand-made box in which we kept the flour and meal and a home-made tray. **1996** Houk *Foods & Recipes* 82 When flour had to be purchased, it was in fifty- or 100-pound bags brought home and stored in a "meal gum," a hollow log or wooden box that was a fixture in many mountain homes. **1999** Morgan *Gap Creek* 112 I wiped the soot off the top of the meal bin and scooped out some cornmeal.

meal poke (also *meal sack*) *noun* A coarse cloth sack in which cornmeal is carried, as to or from the mill.

1927 Furman *Lonesome Road* 68 I paid for 'em and lit out for home, packing the books two hundred mile on my nag in my saddlebags and a meal poke. **1956** Hall *Coll* (Del Rio TN) You take good corn and put it in a meal poke. **c1960** Wilson *Coll*: *meal sack* = a heavy cotton bag, holding two bushels of corn or ground meal. These sacks were often made into strong, wearever towels for farm families. **1966** Dakin *Vocab Ohio River Valley* 2.140 Several miscellaneous names are used for the coarse sack . . . *corn sack, bran ~, meal ~*. **1986** Pederson et al. *LAGS* (Cocke Co TN).

meal pone *noun* A large piece of corn bread. See also **pone A1**.

1925 Dargan *Highland Annals* 92 Next mornin' he got up an' et nine slices o'bacon an' a meal-pone I cooked on a rock. **1995** Montgomery *Coll* (known to Brown), = hoecake (Cardwell).

meal room *noun* A small room near the kitchen in which cornmeal, flour, meat, and other goods are stored.

1968 *DARE Survey* (Laurel Fork VA) = the small room next to the kitchen [in older houses] where dishes and sometimes foods are kept. **1986** Pederson et al. *LAGS* = attested by 6/60 interviewees (10%) from E TN; 6/6 of all LAGS interviewees (100%) attesting term were from Appalachia.

meal sack See **meal poke**.

mean

A *verb* See **I mean**.

B *adjective*

1 Of a child: unruly, mischievous. See also **mean as a striped snake**.

1940 Bowman *KY Mt Stories* 243 = mischievous (when applied to a child). **1947** Gamble *Heritage* 46 "He was the meanest boy in the whole country," went on Aunt Bet. I later learned that she meant mischievous by the word "meanest."

2 Of liquor: poor in quality, harmful in effect.

c1960 Wilson *Coll*: *mean whiskey* = poor quality, cheap, not made right, harmful. **1967** *DARE Survey* (Gatlinburg TN).

[DARE *mean* adj 1 chiefly South, South Midland]

3 Ashamed from being spiteful.

1978 Reese *Speech NE Tenn* 41 I felt mean over it.

C *adverb* in phrase *mean mad* = spitefully, very mad.

1957 Parris *My Mts* 173 Reckon they never had words but twice in all their lives. The first time neither one of 'em got mean-mad. **1995–97** Montgomery *Coll*: *mean mad* (known to Bush).

D *noun* Spite, hatefulness. See **meanness**.

1971 *Sunday with Arie* 84 He was full'a mean. He had that born and bred in th'bone, and it never got out'a th'flesh.

mean as a striped snake (also *mean as a striped-tail snake, mean as snakes, meaner than a striped snake*) *adjective phrase* Given to unpredictable, hateful, or spiteful behavior.

1940 Stuart *Trees of Heaven* 176 They was a triflin lot and mean as striped-tailed snakes. **1941** Hall *Coll* (Mitchell Co NC) They're mean as snakes. She's as mean as a black snake. *Ibid.* (Waynesville NC) He's as mean as a striped snake. **c1950** Adams *Grandpap* 199 While she let on to him like she was just one step below the angels, she was as mean as a striped snake. **1952** Taylor and Whiting *Proverbs and Sayings* 477 As mean as a snake. As mean as a striped snake. **1989** *Matewan OHP-2* He was a very well-known feller in this country and mean as a snake. **1993** Burleson *Aunt Keziah* 13 You know how young'uns air, specially twins. Meaner than striped snakes. **1993** Ison and Ison *Whole Nother Lg* 42 *mean as a striped snake* = very, very mean. **1997** Montgomery *Coll* Joe is meaner than a striped snake (Brown). **2017** *Blind Pig* (Aug 19) The phrase *mean as a striped snake* is one I've heard my whole life. In most instances the phrase is said in a teasing manner about a person who is mischievous but not truly evil spirited. *Ibid.* I've even been called mean as a striped snake, pronounced stripe ed. I've only heard it used in a loving and kidding way never derogatory.

[DARE (at *snake* n 1b) chiefly South, South Midland, especially southern Appalachians]

mean as garbroth See **garbroth**.

mean as striped-tail snake, mean as snakes, meaner than a striped snake See **mean as a striped snake**.

meaner than garbroth See **garbroth**.

mean mad See **mean C**.

mean-mouth *verb* See citations.

c1960 Wilson *Coll* = to bemean, scold. **1969** *DARE Survey* (London KY) = to say uncomplimentary things about somebody.

meanness *noun* Spite, hatefulness, illicit or unprincipled behavior; mischief; a spiteful or hateful act.

1863 Reese *CW Letters* (Oct 27) lying and stelling and all the mean ness that Can Be thout of is going on out hear. **1863** *Revis CW Letters* (June 17) I Pay for all the Letters I start it is Jest meanness of the Post Masters that you have to pay for the Letters I send to you. **1896** Fox *Vendetta* 107 Ef a Stetson ever done sech meanness as that I never heerd it. **1904–20** Kephart *Notebooks* 4:853 He done me a meanness. **1937** Hall *Coll* (Copeland Creek TN) The White Caps got to doin' all sorts of meanness. **1939** Hall *Coll* (Gatlinburg TN) Don't go with Vater. He'll get you into some meanness. **1953** Hall *Coll* (Tuckaleechee Cove TN) I sent all mv children to school. All can read or write except one who can't read or write. About all he learned was meanness. **1961** *Coe Ridge OHP-334A* What broke up all that meanness out there and got them to quit making the whiskey and killing and everything [is that] one of them got religion and come back, and she begin to enlighten some of the rest of them about a little religion. **1971** *AOHP/ALC-32* [As a Justice of the Peace] I tried men for meanness. **1976** Thompson *Touching Home* 15 = hatefulness, as in "low-down meanness." **1978** Montgomery *White Pine Coll* III-2 I guess that people from other counties went over in there and helped to create the meanness. **1981** GSMNP-121: 30 The rest of us would be in all kinds of meanness if we could get by with it. **2005** Williams *Gratitude* 508 *meanness* = 1) a character trait—plain ol' mean or bad-tempered, as: "He whupped his younguns out of pure lowdown *meanness*." Or: "That youngun's just full of *meanness*"; 2) = devil-ment. To do something to aggervate somebody is to do it for devil-ment or meanness; 3) = tastin' forbidden fruit, as when a boy and girl slips off together, they're liable to git into *meanness*.

meany *adjective* Spiteful.

1980 Still *Run for Elbertas* 25 Fern roused, meany for being awakened with a start. **1984** Burns *Cold Sassy* 103 She'd get mad and hit me if I crossed her or sassed her, and I'd do meany things to her, like tripping her up or putting sugar in her salt cellar.

measle *verb* See citation.

1917 Kephart *Word-List* 414 = to catch measles. "The old cow measled, and she died last spring."

measle drop *noun* Same as **sheep pill**.

1971 *AOHP/ALC-139* [I'd] take the measle drop. Why, they'd give me sheep pills. They said it was a sure thing.

measle fever *noun* Measles.

1995 Montgomery *Coll* (known to Cardwell).

measure the baby *verb phrase* To stretch a baby out to determine whether it is **liver bound** or **liver grown**.

1997 Montgomery *File* (known to 50-year-old woman, Jefferson Co TN).

measuring *noun* The process of treating a child's respiratory condition by cutting a sourwood stick the height of the child and then disposing of the stick.

2003 Cavender *Folk Medicine* 44 Asthma was cured by a technique known as "measuring." One common example was cutting a stick (usually from a sourwood tree) the length of a child and then placing the stick up the chimney or in the attic. Over time the child would outgrow the asthma as she outgrew the length of the stick. *Ibid.* 122 The magical asthma remedy of "measuring" the height of a child with a sourwood stick . . . was also used for whooping cough. **2006** *Encycl Appalachia* 868 Two variant techniques of the sympathetic principle were "measuring" and "passing." Childhood asthma, for example, was often treated by cutting a stick, usually of sourwood, the exact length of the child and then placing the stick up the chimney or in the attic. As the child outgrew the length of the stick, he outgrew his asthma. Colic was treated by passing a child from mother to father, usually three times, under a horse or mule, through a horse collar, around a table leg, under a bush, or through a split sapling. The underlying notion was that the child would pass from a state of sickness to wellness.

measuring worm *noun* An inchworm.

1941 Stuart *Men of Mts* 270 He jist bent double like a measurin' worm and tumbled down out'n th' tree. **1992** Brooks *Sthn Stuff* 96 measuring worm, n. When this tiny worm is found on clothing, because of the consistent way it inches itself along, it is said to be measuring the garment. "Look, there's a measuring worm on you, and if you don't knock it off, that means you'll get a new dress." **2007** McMillon *Notes* = inchworm.

[DARE *measuring worm* n widespread except New England, West]

meat

A *noun*

1 Used in compound nouns, sometimes to distinguish the cooked animal from one on the hoof: *deer meat* (rather than *venison*), *hog meat* (rather than *pork*), *sheep meat* (rather than *mutton*). See also **deer meat**, **hog A1**, **sheep meat**.

1939 Hall *Coll* (Wears Cove TN) Me and brother Baus could just get out there and kill a deer anytime we took a notion to, and kept deer meat and bear meat and coon meat and turkey all the time. *Ibid.* (Emerts Cove TN) [Squirrel] tastes similar to hog meat. **c1960** Wilson *Coll*: *hog meat* = pork rather than all other kinds of meat from hogs. **1973** GSMNP-80:12 Law, yeah, [we'd] fatten a sheep and kill it. We kept sheep meat all the time to eat.

2 Pork.

1924 Raine *Saddlebags* 211 "Bread" and "meat" are the staples of diet. This means corn and pork. **1939** *FWP Guide NC* 101 "Meat" still means pork to many people in the state. **1952** Giles *40 Acres* 104 Because everyone raises one or two "meat hawgs" a year, very little meat is bought, so naturally *meat* is pork. **2005** Williams *Gratitude* 142 Whenever anybody said meat, they allus meant hawg meat.

B *verb* To serve as (meat), supply with (meat).

1913 Kephart *Our Sthn High* 282 In mountain vernacular many words that serve as verbs are only nouns of action, or adjectives, or even adverbs . . . "That bear'll meat me a month." **1917** Kephart *Word-List* 414 = to serve as meat. "That bear'll *meat* his fam'ly all winter." **1919** Combs *Word-List South* 32 Uncle Roger's got corn enough to bread 'im, and hogs enough to meat 'im fer two year. **1963** Hooper *Unwanted Boy* 228 Why, fellers, Old Ring is the beatinest tree dog I ever seed. I can depend on that dog to *meat* me and my family this comin' winter. **1974** Fink *Bits Mt Speech* 16 One hog will *meat* us all winter. **1994** Montgomery *Coll* (known to Cardwell).

[DARE *meat* v 1 especially South Midland]

meat hog *noun* A hog raised for butchering and consumption rather than for sale.

1952 Giles *40 Acres* 104 Because everyone raises one or two "meat hawgs" a year, very little meat is bought, so naturally pork is meat.

meat house *noun* Same as **smokehouse**.

1863 *Vance Papers* (May 25) there are a number of deserters Lerking about in this County and the malitia are making no effort to arrest them and they are a doing agreat deal of mischief Robing meat houses and Breaking open Mills and Stealing meal and flower. **1983** *Dark Corner OHP-5A* It was on one Sunday morning, and I went out there to get it [= the ham] and went at the meat house. **2003** LaLone et al. *Farming Life* 193 The meat house, or the smoke house . . . it was a place to store meat. The pork that you'd butcher in the fall, you'd salt here, keep them in that house there. And that was close to your kitchen cause that was what you used to season your food.

[DARE *meat house* n 1 chiefly South Midland]

medder See **meadow.**

mee-ma (also *mee-maw, mee-mommy*) *noun* A grandmother. Same as **ma 2**, **mammaw 2**.

1997 Montgomery *Coll*: *mee maw* (known to Adams, Brown, Bush, Cardwell, Ellis, Weaver). **1999** Wilson and Haas *Memory Quilt* 1 Ryan, that's a lot older than your MeeMa and Pappaw! **2018** *Blind Pig* (May 9) My grandboys called my wife Nana and call their other grandmother Mee-Mommy.

[DARE *mee-maw* n chiefly South, South Midland]

mee-maw, mee-mommy See **mee-ma.**

meeting *noun* A gathering of people, sometimes an informal one, for worship or a series of services with preaching. See also **arbor meeting, basket meeting, big meeting, brush meeting, camp meeting, communion meeting, cottage meeting, contracted meeting, experience meeting, Fifth Sunday meeting, foot-washing meeting, funeral meeting, grove meeting, May meeting, memorial, protracted meeting, quarterly meeting, revival meeting, sacrament meeting, snake meeting, testimony meeting, union meeting.**

1789 *Big Pigeon Church Minutes* 3–4 if any Member shall Neglect theare attendance Two Church Meetings togeather shall be liable to the Churches Censher without rendering a reasonable satisfaction for the same. **1793** *French Broad Church Minutes* 18 Br Gentry & Br Osborn chosen to labor with Westley and his wife concerning neglecting to attend church meeting and cite them to meeting in cource. **1795** (in **1919** DeWitt *Sevier Journal* 183) (Dec 26) Mr. R. Campble his wife & Mary Ann went to Mr. Doakes meeting. **1832** *McLean Diary* (June 5) Went to Meeting. **c1841** Shane (in **1998** Perkins *Border Life* 196) The men carried their guns to meeting, as regular as the congregation met. **1856** *Elijoy Church Minutes* 89 the Church met at Elijoy meting house & after Sermont they put the sacrement of till the next meting and all other business on the account of Sickness. **1859** Taliaferro *Fisher's River* 118 I sparked her a little that night, and told her I was a-gwine wiz her to meetin' next Sunday. **1863** *Lister CW Letters* (Nov 28) we have had a veary good meating hear last weak and the first of this Peary hawkins was the Preacher. **1890** Fruit *KY Words* 65 = for church, preaching: "I am going to meetin'"; "Big-meetin'" is protracted meetin'. A "basket-meetin'" is a two or three days' meetin', when they have "dinner on the ground." **1913** Kephart *Our Sthn High* 239 She actually changed her eyes to jet black whenever she went to "meetin'" or other public gatherings. **1931–33** (in **1987** Oliver and Oliver *Sketches* 24) He was active in religion always attending his meetings. **1937** White *Highland Heritage* 42 The high point of the year is the revival. It is called a "big meeting" or just a "meeting," no matter how many sessions are held. **c1950** Adams *Grandpap* 71 "You know," she said, "we never heard tell of the man till that day he come a-ridin' up to meetin' down there at the mouth of Daniel." **1956** Hall *Coll* (Gatlinburg TN) Generally the fall of the year they'd have what they called revival meeting one, two, three, or four weeks sometimes. They had meeting morning and evening or morning and night one all the time. *Ibid.* (Raccoon Creek NC) He got a preacher from over in Tennessee to come up there and hold a meeting. **1973** Foster *Walker Valley* 9:28 You went to school there and you went to Sunday school, you went to meeting. **1973** GSMNP-90:8 Old people talk about what kind of meetings they had when Preacher Evans come around. **1979** *Preacher Cook* 194 [When] I pastored up at Tuckaseegee, we had a great meeting up there. We had a revival meeting that went on a month. **1982** *Foxfire VII* 199 They had just run a Methodist meeting down here at the Methodist Church and I got under conviction and I was saved. **1982** Ginns *Snowbird Gravy* 146 They would dress up to go to meeting. **1991** Thomas *Sthn Appal* 209 I'd clean up, an' warsh up. An' I'd go to that little meetin' over there. Advent meetin'. **1998** *Dante OHP-24* They started a meeting up here in the hollow, and I got to going to church and was converted. **2001** House *Clay's Quilt* 235 Lord have mercy, if any church people drive by, they'll throw me out of the meeting Sunday.

[in the British Isles originally applied to services of dissenters (as opposed to those of the established church); OED3 *meeting* vbl n 3b 1593→; CUD *meeting* 1 "a church service"; HT *meetin* "a church service"; DARE *meeting* n 1a chiefly Northeast, South Midland]

meeting day *noun* Formerly, a Sunday when a preaching service is held.

1881 Atkinson *After Moonshiners* 161 I assure you, kind reader, that "meeting day" is no common event with these sons of the forest. They rarely fail to flock by the hundred, and for miles, to hear a preacher of the Gospel. I have known of persons on such occasions, with man and wife, and frequently a small child, on a single horse to travel ten or fifteen miles to attend "meeting"; and often take with them canteens well filled with illicit "applejack" to wash down their frugal lunches which they usually carry along. **1920** Ridley *Sthn Mtneer* 23 It was no uncommon thing to see gathered as Bill's friends on a "meetin' day" lawyers, doctors, preachers and ploughmen; for they all loved him.

meeting folks *noun* Churchgoers.

1917 Kephart *Word-List* 415. **1931–33** (in **1987** Oliver and Oliver *Sketches* 34) All the Olivers I ever knew were meeting folks and Primitive Baptist in principle. **1959** Roberts *Up Cutshin* 33 That day then and this day now is different. That day then you could get a meal anywhere just by going home with a crowd of the meeting folks. **1994–97** Montgomery *Coll* (known to Brown, Cardwell, Norris, Shields).

meeting ground *noun* Formerly, an outdoor area for holding preaching services. See also **brush arbor**.

1867 Harris *Sut Lovingood* 55 Ni ontu fifteen shorten'd biskits, a boiled chicken, wif hits laigs crossed, a big dubbil-bladed knife, a hunk ove terbacker, a cob-pipe, sum copper ore, lots ove broken glass, a cork, a sprinkil ove whisky, a squirt, an' three lizzards flew permiskusly all over that meetin-groun', outen the upper aind ove them big flax britches. **1955** Dykeman *French Broad* 323 The heart of the meeting ground was the "arbor," an open-air structure with a roof supported by stout locust posts, and no sides at all.

meeting house *noun* A building in which religious services with preaching are held (a term used principally in the 18th and 19th centuries, especially by Baptists and Methodists, to name houses of worship and in general reference, the latter usage being current well into the 20th century in some places). Same as **church house**. See also **meeting**.

1794 *Big Pigeon Church Minutes* 16 the Members appointed to look out a place for a meeting house. **1804** *Paw Paw Hollow Church Minutes* 10 The church met at lions creek meeting house and after worship the case of Br Frank and his wife was laid over til the next meeting. **1829** *Providence Church Minutes* 5 the Church appoint brethren Samuel Pate and Thomas Atchely delegates to the assocation to be holden at Richland Meeting house. **1838** *Paw Paw Hollow Church Minutes* 84 the Church agrees to have a subscriptsion paper drawn for the purpose of building a new meeting house. *Ibid.* 131 a revelution was made that any Church member being gilty of talking around the meeting hous shall be delt with in the Church. **1856** *Elijoy Church Minutes* 89 the Church met at Elijoy meting house & after Sermont they put the sacrement of till the next meting and all other business on the account of Sickness. **1860** *Week in Smokies* 124 When I got to the "meeting house," a very inflammable sort of person was beating the drum ecclesiastic to a very brimstonish sort of tune, and from the way he held on, I should say it was *long measure*. **1864** Wilson *Confederate Private* 65 (Aug 21) Johns made 8 or 9 bushels there is a two days meting at the meating house. **1883** Zeigler and Grosscup *Heart of Alleghanies* 263 The fields and meadows were vacant; and the mountaineers, observant of the Sabbath, were all within their homely dwellings, or assembled at the meeting-house. **1938** Justus *No-End Hollow* 198 He would make a joke, I do believe, right in the Amen corner of the meeting house, if he had half a chance! **1956** Hall *Coll* (Big Bend NC) Once in a while a minister would come in, hold a little sermon. [We] had no meeting house, didn't have any doctors, no cars, and I cain't drive ary'un. **1970** Miller *Pigeon's Roost* (Jan 1) During the freezing weather in the old man's young days everything went on as scheduled. If a revival meeting was going on and it came a big snow, the revival went on just the same, as everybody walked afoot to the little meeting houses anyway. **1989** *Matewan OHP*-7 It [the church] all started out with a meeting house over here on the point. Then we built over here on the back alley. **1997** Nelson *Country Folklore* 89 It was up to Grandpa to get us to church. He would say, "It's time to go to the meeting house." **1999** Bishir et al. *Archit W NC* 428 = a place of worship or public gathering, often preferred by dissenting denominations and sects over the word "church" when describing a building. Meetinghouses were typically plain rather than elaborated. They were planned to focus on the word, with emphasis on the pulpit rather than the altar. In a meetinghouse plan, typically benches or pews were arranged around the pulpit, which was often on the long side (often the north) rather than in the gable end. In many cases the main entrance was on the long side opposite the pulpit, and secondary entrances opened on the two gable ends.

[OED3 *meeting house n* 1 1632→]

meet up together *verb phrase* To gather with one another.

1940 Haun *Hawk's Done* 118 Burt and Linus had met up together.

meet up with *verb phrase* To encounter, fall in with (someone, as by overtaking).

1864 *Epperly CW Letters* (Feb 28) our sharp s[h]ooters advanst a fieu hundred yards when they met up with the yankees and tha[y] opend a heavey fire all along the line. **1881** Pierson *In the Brush* 255 Once, in riding late in the evening, I overtook—or, in the vernacular of the region, "met up with"—a boy some twelve or fourteen years old, who was riding a mule. **1889** Mooney *Folk Carolina Mts* 98 On one occasion, while riding in company with a friend, we "met up with" a man who had just come from the railroad station a few miles away. **1940** Bowman *KY Mt Stories* 243 *met up with* = overtook. **1973** GSMNP-86:36 He met up with something in [the] trail that he couldn't get past and said hit just rared up. **1985** *Sevier Settler* 5:3 They met up with a fierce Smoky Bear, but only one lived to tell the story.

meller See **mellow**.

mellion See **melon**.

mellow

A Variant forms *meller*.

1925 (in **1935** Edwards *NC Novels* 88) *meller*. **c1950** (in **2000** Oakley *Roamin' Man* 44) Thar is no master yit has found entrancing pictures to behold with the green and brown and yellow all the red meller gold all the colors of the rainbow in the morning.

B *verb* To make (something, as a person's head) soft or tender by beating (it) to a pulp.

c1960 Wilson *Coll* = to beat, smash, whether an apple or a head. **1974** Fink *Bits Mt Speech* 16 = to beat. "I'll *meller* his head if he pesters me." **1998** Montgomery *Coll* (known to Adams, Brown, Bush, Cardwell), = to make mellow, as a mellow (soft) apple (Jones), = to meller a nose is to beat it until it is soft and squishy (Ledford). **2005** Williams *Gratitude* 509 There's also a threat, said as: "I'll *meller* yer head fer ye." *Mellerin' yer head* usually meant rubbin' it real hard with the knuckles, but could be a lot worse.

[DARE probably < EDD *mell* v[1] "to hammer . . . beat severely" + *-er* frequentative; hypercorrect form *mellow*; DARE *mellow* v especially South Midland]

melon *noun* Variant forms *mellion, million*. See also **watermelon**.

1952 Wilson *Folk Speech NC* 565 *million*. **1998** Montgomery *Coll*: *mellion* (known to Ellis); *million* (known to Adams).

[DARE *melon* n chiefly South, South Midland]

melt *noun*

A Variant form *milt* [see **1894** in **B**].

B The spleen or pancreas of a slaughtered animal, as a hog or deer, when prepared as food; figuratively = a portion of courage.

1867 Harris *Sut Lovingood* 182 Hit mus' take a man wif a onnatrally big melt, not tu be fear'd ove his wife, onless she's blind ur hes a sweethart. **1894** Wingfield *Big Buck* 400 That was not a pleasing thought, with no supper but milt or liver fried, with no cover to sleep on or put over us. **1913** Kephart *Our Sthn High* 106 Then came the four men, empty-handed, it seemed, until John slapped a bear's "melt" (spleen) upon the table. **1983** *Dark Corner OHP-4A* The liver and the kidneys and the lights and the milt, cut all that up and mix it together in a big old pot, big black pot, and cook it all day. **1988** Lambert *Kinfolks* 136 If you aren't thrilled with the idea of eating any of the internal organs of any animal, you probably don't want to know that I have since learned that the "melt" was the pancreas. It was trimmed and dropped into the cooking lard, fished out when it had cooked through, sliced crosswise and eaten with bread. It tasted like very mild liver and had about the same texture. **1991** Still *Wolfpen Notebooks* 77 At hog killing time what I like best to eat is the melt. I could eat it [even] if I was tolerably sick. **1994–97** Montgomery *Coll*: *melt* (known to Brown, Cardwell, Jones, Ledford); *milt* (known to Ledford).

[OED3 *melt* (variant of *milt* n 1a) "the spleen, especially (now) the spleen of an animal reared for food"; SND *melt* n 1; CUD *melt* n 2 "the spleen"; DARE *melt* n 1 chiefly South, South Midland]

melt up *verb phrase* To dissolve.

1971 *AOHP/ALC-147* If you're in coughing, why they always . . . would take a half a pint of whiskey, and they'd fill the bottle full of rock candy then and let it melt up and then just take a spoonful of that. **1980** GSMNP-115:42 She'd melt that up and pour over it.

Melungeon *noun*

1 A member of a racially mixed group of people (traditionally viewed as Amerindian, European, sub-Saharan, and Saharan) centered in northeastern Tennessee and southwestern Virginia. See also **ramp 2**.

1849 Anon *Melungeons* 618 This gorge and the tops and sides of the adjoining mountains are inhabited by a singular species of the human animal called Melungens. The legend of their history, which they carefully preserve, is this. A great many years ago, these mountains were settled by a society of Portuguese adventurers. . . . These intermixed with the Indians, and subsequently their descendants . . . with the negroes and the whites, thus forming the present race of Melungens. **1889** Burnett *Note Melungeons* 347 No one seemed to know positively that they or their ancestors had ever been in slavery, and they did not themselves claim to belong to any tribe of Indians in that part of the country. They resented the appellation Melungeon, given to them by common consent by the whites, and proudly called themselves Portuguese. The current belief was that they were a mixture of the white, Indian, and negro. **1915** Dingus *Word-List VA* 185 = one of a race of people in southwestern Virginia and eastern Kentucky and Tennessee said to have partly Indian blood. **1940** Haun *Hawk's Done* 124 Drusilla had just enough of Burt's Melungeon blood in her to make her pretty big black eyes and long black hair. **1963** Berry *Almost White* 16 Mothers control their naughty children by threatening "the Melungeons will get you if you don't behave." *Ibid.* 18 The truth seems to be that among the earliest settlers of that region were a people of mixed race ancestry, who came there from Virginia and North Carolina in the 1790's. Apparently they were classified at one time as "free persons of color" . . . and they were deprived of the franchise in 1834. . . . For a century and a half the prolific Melungeons have migrated in all directions from Newman's Ridge. There are fifteen hundred in Lee County, Virginia. **2006** Puckett *Melungeon* 1022 *Melungeon* and its variant spellings refer to individuals or families who are presumed to have mixed-race ancestries and whose ancestors settled in out-of-the-way areas of eastern and southeastern Tennessee, far southwest Virginia, northwestern North Carolina, and southeastern Kentucky. The dominant scholarly view is that these ancestries were combinations of Native American, African, and northern European, although a few scholars now include a southern European or Mediterranean component. Popular and folkloric accounts of Melungeon physical features often refer to combinations of white and non-white characteristics such as straight black hair and blue eyes. These presumed features often do not conform to members' actual physiques or to photographs of their ancestors and kin. Strong evidence exists that *Melungeon* has been used as a non-member/outsider's term and was highly derogatory from its beginning. Many descendants of Melungeons still living in areas where the term has been common refuse to use the word, at least as one referring to themselves. The etymology of *Melungeon* is disputed, and more than fifty origins have been cited in published sources. Most of these lack historical or linguistic support. Current historical research supports the commonly-asserted French origin from *melange* "mixture" or its plural *mélangeon*. A French origin is supported by the late-18th-century presence of French Huguenots and other French speakers in the region where *Melungeon* emerged as a commonly-used term. The first documented record of *Melungeon* is found in the minutes of the Stony Creek Primitive Baptist Church, Scott County, Virginia, in 1813. Various 20th-century accounts report that *Portegee* or *Portuguese* was a term used by members to designate themselves. These terms are not necessarily linked to the modern-day Portuguese (denoting a citizen of Portugal), as they could also have been ethnic identifiers that simply circumvented stigmatized terms for African or African-American ancestry.... [M]any members calling themselves *Portegee* did not define the word as meaning they had ancestors who came from Portugal or as having any meaning other than a term that referred to themselves. *Melungeon* had largely fallen into disuse by the mid-20th century, in part because of diffusion of Melungeon community members into white populations through marriage and through other strategies that enabled them to be treated as white. The term occurred primarily in occasional published literary or scholarly works or in restricted speaking contexts such as expressions or discussions of the genealogies of deceased residents. The outdoor drama, *Walk Towards the Sunset*, of the 1960s rejuvenated *Melungeon*, however. Furthermore, the 1990s Melungeon identity movement and the Melungeon Heritage Association arising from it have given *Melungeon* an international recognition and is redefining it as a positive, respected word referring to mixed-heritage people who have suffered an oppressive and discriminatory past. Consequently, the current meaning of *Melungeon* is fluid, reflecting its changing usage by the different groups using it.

2 Hence used as a figure to warn children and make them behave. See also **booger A1**.

1999 Offut *Out of Woods* 42–43 He stared through the window at the court house and remembered his fourth-grade teacher threatening a child who was already late for school. "If you don't get up in time," the teacher had said, "the Melungeons will get you." **2016** Winkler *About Melungeons* A few generations ago, children in Tennessee, Virginia and surrounding areas were told, "If you don't behave, the Melungeons will get you!" Many people grew up believing the Melungeons were simply an Appalachian version of the boogeyman—a fearsome and mysterious but mythical bit of folklore.

membraneous *adjective* Membranous.

1937 Thornburgh *Great Smoky Mts* 30 Now take lobelia ... Its [sic] mighty common, and it's mighty good for membraneous croup, too.

memorial (also *memorial meeting, memorial service*) *noun* A religious service to recall and honor members of a community or family who have died, sometimes many years earlier, and at which multiple ministers are traditionally called on to preach. Also called **funeral meeting**. See also **memorial day**, **memorialize**.

1977 Shackelford et al. *Our Appalachia* 47 About a year after the death they'd always have the Memorial Service. Of course, they'd have a service when the person died and it was usually a sermon. The preacher would use the occasion as a time to admonish the people by [the dead person's example and say] they ought to live the right kind of life, even though they had to live it through grace. Something would be said about the person who had died, maybe a short biography. **1982** Plowman *Out of Sight* 49 Funerals and Memorials were "Preached" at the gravesite during the summer Sundays after corn was "Laid by." Every preacher was invited to join in and every preacher was expected to be heard.... This was a social time, as well as remembering family patriarchs and ones who had died the past year. The family and neighbors where the memorial was held usually killed a shoat or a sheep to roast plus other food carried in. Horses and mules were traded and sometimes, out of sight of the crowd, moonshine was drunk. **1982** Slone *How We Talked* 75 *memorial meeting*. **1989** Dorgan *Regular Baptists* 90 Old Regular family memorials, held annually or at irregular intervals as called, serve not only as religious events but as family reunions. Sons and daughters, grandchildren, great-grandchildren, in-laws, aunts, uncles, cousins, nieces, nephews, and all manner of relatives gather to pay respect to deceased family members and just to socialize and catch up with the lives of each other. The event becomes a demonstration of family cohesiveness and shows deep regard for the reigning family matriarchs and patriarchs. These are happenings filled with a wonderful amalgam of worship, reminiscence, respect-paying, comparing notes on the progress of offspring, family problem solving, gossip, tale telling, consoling for losses, reestablishment of a sense of place, eating, laughter, bragging, tears, and general familial love. **1995** Montgomery *Coll*: *memorial* (known to Cardwell). **2007** Preece *Leavin' Sandlick* 41 You know the Debord memorial meeting is comin' up this weekend at the ole country church on the hill.

memorial day (also *memorial service*) *noun* A weekend observance to clean graves and honor the dead of a family, a church, or a former church. In some parts of Appalachia the term is equivalent to or has replaced **decorating** or **Decoration Day**, or the activities of that observance have shifted to the last Monday in May, congruent with the national observance, although some variation remains from community to community. Same as **homecoming**. See also **memorial**.

1975 GSMNP-61:12 We had memorial day. I can remember that as far back as I can remember. On memorial day we had our flower gardens, you know, and the graves was always decorated and cleaned off and fixed up. **1978** Slone *Common Folks* 232, 233 We have a Memorial Service for each graveyard every year, at different dates. Ours, the Summer Slone's, is the first Sunday after the first Saturday in June.... In the old days we would begin planning for Memorial (pronounce Morriel by us) early in the spring, when we planted our beans and potatoes. **1991** Thomas *Sthn Appal* 205 The homecoming was a regular affair in late spring or summer, and it was in the nature of a memorial for kin and friends buried in the local cemetery. It usually was called "Memorial Day." **1992** Morgan *Potato Branch* 108 Each August, Zion Hill Baptist Church held a memorial day, a homecoming time with a program of all-day singing and dinner on the ground. **1994** Crissman *Death and Dying* 153 Mountain people used several different terms when referring to the day set aside to care for the cemetery and honor the dead, including "Decoration Day," "Memorial Day," "Meeting Day," "May Meeting," "Memorial Meeting," "Memorial Service," "Homecoming," and "Graveyard Meeting." ... As in funeralizing, mountaineers picked their own convenient day for memorial services, usually a Sunday between late spring and early fall. **1995** Montgomery *Coll* = in some parts of the Tennessee mountains, the term has now replaced *decoration day* (Cardwell).

memorialize *verb* Same as **funeralize**. See also **memorial**.

1972 *AOHP/ALC-188* We have developed within the Baptist churches more than, say, in the Presbyterian, the idea of the memorializing of the dead. That didn't mean that you just preach a funeral for one that just died. . . . Some minister might come there and preach the funeral of somebody who had been dead two or three years, and he'd preached it before, because that was a memorializing too.

memorial meeting See **memorial**.

memorial service See **memorial**, **memorial day**.

memorize *verb* To remember (a person or event).

1883 Zeigler and Grosscup *Heart of Alleghanies* 60 I memorize one time thet I war in a tight box. **1939** *English in Mts* Memorize is often used for remember: "I ain't seen my sister for nigh on to 20 years. I can't hardly memorize her." **c1945** Haun *Hawk's Done* 205 I don't memorize seeing you nowhere. **1960** Westover *Highland Lg* 20 = to remember.

[DARE *memorize* v B especially South Midland]

memory quilt *noun* See citation.

1994 Crissman *Death and Dying* 139 Occasionally, mountain women would take remnants of clothes belonging to someone deceased and make a "memory quilt." My sources stated that these quilts did not follow a specific pattern but rather were fashioned by the makers.

mend

A *verb*

1 (also *mend up*) To improve in health, recover one's health after illness or injury, regain weight or vigor.

1834 Crockett *Narrative* 130 At the end of two weeks I began to mend without the help of a doctor, or of any doctor's means. **1862** *Reese CW Letters* (Dec 27) I am still mending and will [be] Redy for dewtey in A fue more days. **1863** *Tesh CW Letters* (Sept 9) I was in hops you was a mending by this time if you can eat harty I think you will mend up before long if you dont get sick. **c1960** Wilson *Coll*: *mend* = to gain weight or strength. **1974** Fink *Bits Mt Speech* 16 = improve physically. "He's *mending* slowly." **1997** Montgomery *Coll*: *mend* (known to ten consultants from the Smoky Mountains); *mend up* (known to Adams, Brown, Bush, Cardwell, Jones, Norris, Oliver). **2007** McMillon *Notes*: *mend* = to gain flesh, put on weight.

[shortening of *amend*; EDD *mend* v 8 "to grow stout"; DARE *mend* v 2 chiefly South Midland]

2 To tend or add fuel to (a fire).

1938 Justus *No-End Hollow* 161 First she redd up the kitchen, mended the fire, and hung on the crane a pot of shucky beans. **c1960** Wilson *Coll*: *mend the fire* = to add fuel to it, chunk it up. **1997** Montgomery *Coll* (known to ten consultants from the Smoky Mountains).

[DARE *mend* v 4 chiefly South, South Midland]

B *noun* in phrase *on the mend* = convalescing, improving in health.

1862 *Ingram CW Letters* (Oct 4) he has ben poly But he is on the mend now. **2017** *Blind Pig* (Sept 28) Granny is on the mend and I'm so thankful.

mend one's licks *verb phrase* See citation.

1892 Fruit *KY Words* 230 = to quicken one's steps: "When the dog got after me, I mended my licks."

mend up See **mend A1**.

menfolk(s) *noun* Men collectively, the male contingent of a family, group, or community.

1867 Harris *Sut Lovingood* 53 This wer the way they wer tu sarve men folks. **1913** Kephart *Our Sthn High* 120 They know thar's a president, 'cause the men-folks's voted for him, and the women-folks's seed his pictur. **1931** Goodrich *Mt Homespun* 45 "It takes a heap of wool to do us," said Mrs. Fox, "what with all the men-folks goes through in a year, and for blankets, and for us a coat apiece." **1939** Hall *Coll* (Cosby Creek TN) The menfolks wore linsey britches [and] cotton shirts. **1963** Hooper *Unwanted Boy* 208 Ran called to his assistance the men-folks of the mountain family who had been living on the place, and with new axes and cross-cut saws they soon had the chopping under good headway. **1981** Alderman *Tilson Mill* 9 It was not long before some of the county and town women were up in arms about all the menfolk getting the attention from the turning lathe.

[DARE *menfolk(s)* n pl chiefly South, South Midland]

-ment *suffix*

A Variant pronunciation with secondary stress in *devilment*, *government*, *judgment*, *settlement*, etc.

1913 Kephart *Our Sthn High* 224 In mountain dialect such words as settlement, government, studyment (reverie) are accented on the last syllable, or drawled with equal stress throughout. **1940** Stuart *Trees of Heaven* 291 Let's git our heads togither here and come to some settle-ment. **1942** *Hall Phonetics Smoky Mts* 71 The suffixes -dent and -ment (except in *independent*) in most instances have secondary stress: *accident*, *confident*, *devilment*, *instrument*, *monument*, *payment*, *settlement*, *testament*, etc. **1966** Boykin *Study of Harris* 51 The restressing of syllables is common in the speech of the Southern Highlanders; sometimes final syllables receive secondary stress, as in séttlemènt and júdgmènt. . . . [George Washington] Harris indicates secondary stress on the suffix -ment by respelling it -mint (settlemint and refreshmint). **1974** Fink *Bits Mt Speech* 16 = accented last syllable in words as settlement', government', treatment', etc. **2014** *Blind Pig* (Nov 21) I began to think of other ment words. The first one that came to mind settlement. Pap uses the word settlement often to describe a more populated area. I said the word aloud—and I heard myself say it as settle ment.

Again like 2 words. More words came to mind government, treatment, and even studyment. I heard them all as 2 words.

[DARE *-ment* suff A chiefly South, South Midland]

B Added to a verb or an adjective to form a noun in **botherment, destroyment, foolishment, scatterment.**

mercy *noun* Variant forms *marcy, massy.*

1904–20 Kephart *Notebooks* 2:475 It'd be a marcy if he was to die. **1942** Hall *Phonetics Smoky Mts* 42 ['mæsi]. **1994–97** Montgomery *Coll*: *massy* (known to eight consultants from the Smoky Mountains).

mercy seat *noun* Same as **mourners' bench.**

1956 Carter *Methodists in TN* 357 The mercy seat is made of wild cherry according to the specifications found in Exodus 25:17–22. **1979** *Preacher Cook* 199 The altar is not for sinners; it's for Christians. The mercy seat is for sinners. It's in the same place and sinners come there to the mercy seat. The Christians pray with them until they get right.

merkel (also *markel*) *noun* An edible mushroom (*Morchella* spp). See also **dry-land fish, hickory chicken.**

1973 *Foxfire II* 53 Morel (*Morchella esculenta, M. crassipes, M. angusticeps*) (sponge mushroom, markel, merkel). *Ibid.* 54 Merkel pie: cut in small pieces. Cover bottom of pie dish with thin bits of bacon. Add layer of merkels, salt and pepper; then layer of mashed potatoes. **1983** Smith *Recollections of Blue Ridge* 29 Indians and early settlers relied on berries plus other wild edibles such as lambs quarter, wild asparagus, poke weed and morels to supplement their diet. The local name for morels is "Merkels" a definitive formed by a combination of miracle and morel. They are an elusive mushroom that grows in the spring.

mess

A *noun* [Editor's note: Senses 1 and 2 cannot always be differentiated.]

1 A hearty amount or number; a sufficient portion of a food (as meat, greens).

c1830 (in **2007** Dunkerly *Kings Mt* 32) I have often thought, if a man would eat a mess of parched corn and s[w]allow two or three spoonfuls of honey, then take a good draught of cold water, he could pass longer without suffering than with any other diet he could use. **1862** *Epperly CW Letters* (July 20) wee can get Blackberrys Somtimes bake pies they eat verry well wee had a mess of pies last eavning. **1863** *Robinson CW Letters* (Feb 6) I would give 5 dollars if I had it fur a mess of chicken & dumplins & coffey. **1864** *Chapman CW Letters* (April 23) I must tell you about what fine messes of greens we have had. **1913** Kephart *Our Sthn High* 98 I 'low I done growed a bit, after that mess o' meat. **1927** Furman *Lonesome Road* 21 My maw's got a big mess of boys. **1937** Hall *Coll* (Cosby TN) The bear killed lots of stock. He wouldn't eat but two messes out of a big'un and then kill him another'n. **1940** Haun *Hawk's Done* 112 I started that day I sent her up yonder to Arwood's branch to pick a mess of wild sallet. **1956** Hall *Coll* (Hartford TN) I've seed my daddy with as many as four bears in the smokehouse at one time. He could get a mess of bear meat out of it anytime through the run of the year he wanted it. **1957** Parris *My Mts* 230 There's nothing quite like a mess of groun'-hawg meat when it comes to choice mountain vittles. **1963** Arnow *Flowering* 141 In out-of-the way regions two women can still go to the local store, each ask for a "mess of steak," and one will receive two pounds, the other four, for mess meant enough to give the household one meal. **1963** Watkins and Watkins *Yesterday* 89 After a farmer killed a hog, he sent a good "mess of meat" to every close neighbor. **1965** *Dict Queen's English* 13 = enough for a meal. "She cooked a mess of cabbage for dinner." **1973** GSMNP-2:29 You let a cow get a mess of ramps, and it'd be three or four days before you could use the milk. **1976** Lindsay *Grassy Balds* 54 [If you] killed a turkey in the spring of the year, you had to go get yourself a mess of ramps to eat before you could eat. **1989** *Matewan OHP*-9 They'd usually just kill what they wanted for a mess, but now a feller goes out in the mountains now, if he sees twenty squirrels, he'd kill twenty if he had that many shells. **2006** *WV Encycl* 271 The tradition of gathering poke and other greens continues to this day. It is no uncommon sight in the spring to see women walking along the roadside picking a "mess of greens." **2017** *Blind Pig* (Oct 27) = just enough for each person to have some. Usually refers to a single meal of a nuclear family unless a greater or lesser number of people are clear from the context. For example, "mess" would not work if speaking of taking food to a church dinner where the number of people cannot be known. Unless leftovers are wanted, having just enough for everyone to have some speaks volumes about the high level of skill of those who gathered the ingredients and prepared the meal. *Ibid.* A mess is the exact amount required. A whole mess is way more than enough. "They've got a whole mess of youngins running around over there. I tried to count 'em all one time but they won't stand still long enough."

[OED3 *mess* n 1c "a quantity sufficient to make a dish" now U.S. regional; DARE *mess* n 1a chiefly Northeast, South, South Midland]

2 A take or haul, as of fish or game.

1862 *Zimmerman CW Letters* (Sept 14) I had a fine mess of fish this morning I caut yestarday. **1883** Zeigler and Grosscup *Heart of Alleghanies* 125 Without moving from a line of smooth, deep-flowing pools, we secured a mess of forty trout before it became too dark to cast our lines. **1937** Hall *Coll* (Groundhog Creek TN) I caught a mess of trouts today. **1939** Bond *Appal Dialect* 109 = used in connection with wild game, as a "mess of squirrel." **1939** Hall *Coll* (Hazel Creek NC) If we want to kill us a mess of squirrels, why we get out an' kill 'em here on our own land. **1969** GSMNP-44:26 These little old mountain boomers, you know what they are. Now they was just as thick as they could be, and they decided to kill a mess of them. **1973** GSMNP-4:1:43 You could kill you a mess of meat anytime you wanted it. . . . Anytime you wanted a mess of fish, all you had to do was go catch them. **1976** GSMNP-114:38 I'd like to have a good mess of seasonin' with leather-britches. **1984** GSMNP-153:39 Maybe we would go two or three times a year and catch a mess of fish.

3 A mischievous or humorous person.

1952 Wilson *Folk Speech NC* 564 = a person regarded as more witty, lively, entertaining, etc. than most people, a show. "Now ain't Mr. Jim a *mess*!" **c1960** Wilson *Coll* = a mischievous or joking person. **1997** Montgomery *Coll* (known to Cardwell). **2007** (in **2012** McQuaid *Interface* 275) He was a mess, I'll tell you. He'd come in church a-singing. **2009** Benfield *Mt Born* 118 = a person who is mischievous and fun. "I declare that Lenny is a mess if I ever saw one, always going on about something.

[DARE *mess* n 3 chiefly South Midland]

B *verb* To fool around, waste time (usually with *around*).

1978 Montgomery *White Pine Coll* III-2 I get down there and mess around a little with it sometimes. **1979** *Big South Fork OHP*-1 I don't work no more, I just mess around here. **1997** Montgomery *Coll* (known to ten consultants from the Smoky Mountains).

[ultimately < Old French *mes* "dish"; DARE *mess* v 1 especially South, South Midland]

metheglin (also *figlin, methelin, thiglum*) *noun* A beverage made from fermented honey and other ingredients.

1927 Mason *Lure of Smokies* 226 I reckon the smell o' [the turkey being roasted], as well as some thiglum we'd mixed with water and wild honey we'd got out of a tree drawed [the bears] thar. **1957** Combs *Lg Sthn High: Word List* 64 *metheglin* = a mild Elizabethan liqueur, still made in the Highlands. "Metheglin, from the Latin word mulsum is a kind of drink made of herbs, honey, spice, etc." **1970** Clark *NC Beliefs* 10 Methelin wine, made from fermented honey, yeast, and water, was good tonic, especially after fermenting a few months. **1985** Irwin *Alex Stewart* 159 We called it figlin instead of wine. You take good honeycomb and put it in a jar and pour some water over it and let it set till it works off. It makes the best drink you ever drunk. It'll make you feel funny but it won't make you drunk. It's about like beer. **1986** Pederson et al. *LAGS* (Rhea Co TN) = drink made from honeycomb and water.

[< Welsh *meddyg* "medicinal" + *llyn* "liquor"; DARE *metheglin* chiefly North, Midland]

methelin See **metheglin**.

Methodist measure *noun* See citation.

1980 Berry and Repass *Grandpa Says* 19 = a little overflowing: "He always gives Methodist measure."

[perhaps based on Luke 6:38]

Methodist pallet *noun* See citation. See also **Baptist pallet**.

1992 Brooks *Sthn Stuff* 97 = a crude makeshift bed made on the floor.

Methusaleh's housecat See **old as Methusaleh's housecat**.

Michaux's lily *noun* The Carolina lily (*Lilium michauxii*), named after an early botanist visiting the region.

1982 Stupka *Wildflowers* 8 [The Carolina lily] is also known as "Michaux's lily." **2001** Joslin *Appal Bounty* 14 While hunters and entrepreneurs like Daniel Boone have received the bulk of attention as explorers of the Southern Appalachians, it was the work of botanists and other such gentle spirits that led to some of the most important discoveries in the region. Two men who have left an enduring legacy of exploration and discovery are Andre Michaux and Asa Gray. Michaux, a Frenchman who ranged the mountains in the late 1700's, and Gray, an American who led this country's botanical studies during the mid-1800s, are linked by a small flowering plant that became the most famous species in the Blue Ridge Mountains. The story begins in 1788 when Michaux stopped to stay at the cabin of some Cherokee Indians. As he wrote: "I ran off to make some investigations. I gathered a new low woody plant, with saw-toothed leaves, creeping on the mountains at a short distance from the river." He wrote in his journal "aux clair de la lune (by the moonlight)," giving explicit directions to the place in which he had found the plant. He took his discovery with him to Paris, along with a large number of such New World botanical wonders. The next chapter of the tale takes place in 1839, half a century later, when the young American botanist Asa Gray visited Paris to examine Michaux's collection. He came upon an unusual plant, labeled "hautes montagnes de Caroline (the high mountains of Carolina)." Gray wrote: "I have discovered a new genus, in Michaux's herbarium, at the end, among the plantae ignotae. It is from that great unknown region, the high mountains of North Carolina."

[named after the 18th-century French botanist and explorer of southern Appalachia]

Michaux's saxifrage *noun* An edible wild green (*Saxifraga michauxii*).

1934 Wilson *Bog Plants* Among dense mats of pale green sphagnum moss on huge boulders over which water is constantly dripping there may be found one of the daintiest of plants—Michaux's saxifrage—a decided contrast to the mighty cat-tail. Botanists place this plant only in the mountainous sections of North Carolina, Virginia, and Georgia, that territory studied so extensively by the botanist and scientist Andre Michaux for whom the plant is named. The persons who once identifies this lovely plant is not likely ever to confuse it with other plants nor is he likely to forget its beauty. The hairy, thick sharply toothed leaves are reddish green or dark green above crimson beneath. **1968** Grimm *Flowering Plants* 124 Also known as Mountain-lettuce, as the leaves are used as a green by many mountain people . . . (*Saxifraga michauxii*) Michaux's Saxifrage grows in crevices on the face of rocky cliffs and on sunny, wet rocks in the southern Appalachians.

[named after the 18th-century French botanist and explorer of southern Appalachia]

middle *noun* The strip or ridge of ground between rows of a crop.

1995 Montgomery *File* (known to 85-year-old man, Greenbrier TN).

[DARE *middle* n chiefly South, South Midland]

middling

A *adjective* Fairly good, average, satisfactory (as in the phrase *fair to middling*), used as a response to a query such as "how are you doing?" about one's health, the weather, one's work, etc.). The phrase has a range of connotations depending on the context.

1796 *Cunningham Letter* through the Mearcies of a good kind and Bountiful God what is remeaning of us is alive and in a medling State of health at present. **1917** Burelbach *After Bruin* 315 I called it steep. Wunder agreed with me, but Dave called it "only middlin'." **1957** Parris *My Mts* 100 He done a fair-to-middlin' job, not being a cradle-maker by trade. **1976** Garber *Mountain-ese* 47 Lemuel is jist a jackleg carpenter but he can build a fair-to-middlin' house. **1995–97** Montgomery *Coll* (known to Shields), = in relation to job performance, craftsmanship, skill, or ability at something (Ellis).

B *adverb* Rather, fairly, moderately.

1813 Hartsell *Memora* 127 We air now In Camped on the South Side of vercy pleasant hill midelin handcy to wood but vercy Unhandey to water. **1862** Councill *CW Letters* (June 17) I tell you offensers will fare but midlen well Poley. **1885** Murfree *Prophet* 133 The girl admitted that it was "middlin' warm." **1895** Murfree *Phantoms* 221 Ab 'lowed ye war middlin' quick at figgers, Lee-yander. **1952** Wilson *Folk Speech NC* 565 I'm feeling *middling peart* today. **1962** Drukker *Lg By-Ways* 50 If a body isn't up to par in the matter of health he grades his "miseries" as being "jest punying 'round," "barly takin' vittles," on up to "bein' far t'middlin' well," "right tol'able," or "I'm a'feelin' purty paert." **1995–97** Montgomery *Coll* (known to Adams, Brown, Cardwell).

C (also *middling meat, middlin meat, middlings*) *noun* The middle part of a side of meat from a hog (or bear) between the shoulder and the ham; a slab (of a hog or of bacon). See also **fatback, side meat, sow belly, streaked bacon.**

1834 Crockett *Narrative* 151 I got also a large middling of bacon, and killed a large deer, and left them for my young man and little boy. **1863** *Robinson CW Letters* (Feb 6) Some body Stold 9 midlings of meat & 7 Joints from John Pitmans wife. **1928** (in **1952** Mathes *Tall Tales* 68) Birdeye Collins was the first to sling across his snack of corn dodger, streaked middling and home-ground coffee, rolled in an old blanket tied at the ends with leather thongs. **1934–47** LAMSAS *Appal* (Madison Co NC, Swain Co NC). **1937** Hall *Coll* (Emerts Cove TN) [He] stole two middlin's of bacon. **1939** Hall *Coll* (Sugarlands TN) We cleaned [the bear] and cut it up and cut middlin's out of it just the same as we was cutting up a hog. **1941** Hall *Coll* (Mitchell Co NC) Middlin' of a hog. That's the side of a hog, that's where you get your bacon. **1945** McNeer *Sthn Highlands* 33 Coons are hunted at night, with a man carrying a lantern, or a lightwood knot set ablaze. . . . Food is simply a piece of salted fat bacon, called "middlinmeat," and a little poke of meal, both to be fried over the campfire. **1949** Hall *Coll* (Bryson City NC) He hung two middlin's of bear up in his house for seasoning. **1949** Kurath *Word Geog East US* 32 In contrast to Northern *salt pork* and Southern *middlin(s)* the North Midland has the expression side meat. . . . In the Valley of Virginia and on the Kanawha *side meat* stands beside *middlin(s)*, and this Southern term has also gained a foothold in northern West Virginia. **1956** Hall *Coll* (Gatlinburg TN) Green beans [go well] with white "side meat," the middlin' of the hog. **1966** Dakin *Vocab Ohio River Valley* 336 *Side meat* is common in Kentucky east of the Green-Barren River . . . but the Southern-South Midland *midlin(s)* or *middlinmeat* is more common everywhere in Kentucky. **1974** Russell *Hillbilly* 57 The sow belly or middlins were salted down and used to fry streaked meat for breakfast and to provide grease for making the gravy and frying the eggs. **1978** Montgomery *White Pine Coll* IV-4 Bacon was made out of the middling part. **1979** Slone *My Heart* 24 Go back home and git two of ye biggest middlins and a ham. Take them to him, or if ye don't, I will haunt ye all ye born days. **c1982** Young *Colloquial Appal* 15 *middlings* = slabs of side meat. **1990** Oliver *Cooking Hazel Creek* 18 Hams, middlins and shoulders were hung in the smokehouse and cured by being rubbed with salt and smoked over a smoky fire made with corn cobs and green hickory chips. **1997** Nelson *Country Folklore* 16 After the hogs are killed and cut into the right pieces, like ham, middling meat, and fat back, we store it here in the shelves and hang the hams in flour sacks to cure. **1998** Dabney *Smokehouse Ham* 189 It was in this dark, windowless building that we salted down our hams, shoulders, slabs of "middlin" meat (or bacon). **2016** Netherland *Appal Cooking* 126 The pork bellies we normally called "middlin' meat" because it came from the center of the hog. The middlin' meat became bacon, streak o' lean and other seasoning meat after it was cured.

[DARE *middling* n 1 chiefly South, South Midland]

middling meat See **middling C.**

middling peart See **middling B.**

middlings *noun*

1 See **middling C.**

2 The middle portion of a **run** of **moonshine**. See also **faint(s), heads, tailings.**

2009 Thompson *Driving with Devil* 21 Even with the second batch, Parks had to make sure to toss away the first few quarts (the "heads") and the last few (the "tails"), which were both toxic, and to bottle only the pure and perfect "middlings."

middlin meat See **middling C.**

mid-doctor (also *midmother, midwoman*) *noun* A midwife.

1967 Wilson *Folkways Mammoth Cave* 31 *midmother* = a very rare local name for mid-wife. **1968** Wilson *Folklore Mammoth Cave* 44 *midmother* = a neighborhood nurse who, alone or as a helper for the family doctor, was present when a child was born. **1973** Miller *English Unicoi Co* 149 *mid-doctor* = one who helps a woman during childbirth. **1986** Wear *Sugarlands* 25 Mary Whaley from Bullhead was the mid-woman, she stayed about a week and took care of mother and the baby. **1997** Montgomery *Coll*: *midmother* (known to Bush, Cardwell); *midwoman* (known to Brown).

[DARE *midmother* n especially South, South Midland]

midmother, midwoman See **mid-doctor.**

miffle *verb* To miff, offend.

1961 Williams *Content Mt Speech* 14 A "miffled" hostess gives her guests "cold coffee."

might[1] See **may B2**, **mighty.**

might[2] *noun* A considerable quantity or amount.

1911 Shearin *E KY Word-List* 539 = a large quantity; e.g., "He is selling a might of timber lately." **1957** Combs *Lg Sthn High: Word List* 64 = a large quantity, or lot. Ex.: "Man! that's a might o' corn!"

[OED3 *might* n[1] 6 regional (chiefly U.S.)]

mighta coulda, **might can**, **might could** See **may B2.**

mightily (also *mitely*, *mightly*) *adverb* To a great degree or extent, very much.

1826 *Whitten Letter* The children was mightly pleasd at the sight & motion of [the steam boats]. **c1841** Shane (in **1998** Perkins *Border Life* 197) [They] shot the cows mightily with bows and arrows. **1864** *Love CW Letters* (April 24) our Brigade has sufferd mitely they aint 6 feald officers in the Brigade. **1867** Harris *Sut Lovingood* 97e [sic] I thot I'd fust sneak up to the house an see what wer a gwine on, an what I saw altered my plans mitely. **1884** Murfree *In TN Mts* 254 Caleb war mightily worked up 'bout this hyar finin' business. **1900** Harben *N GA Sketches* 52 I've jest done a thing that I hated mightily to do. **1924** Raine *Saddlebags* 15 Miz Browning, I'm a dying woman, and I bin wantin' mightily to see ye. **1957** Justus *Other Side* 68–69 I was mightily afeared that book learning would spoil you, but you've still got a smidgen o' gumption.

[OED3 *mightily* adv 3 now chiefly colloquial]

mightly See **mightily.**

might near See **mighty C.**

might near it See **mighty near it.**

might nigh See **mighty C.**

might ought to, **might should ought to**, **might would** See **may B2.**

mighty

A Variant forms *might* [see **1937** in **C**], *mity* [see **1864** in **B**], *mought* [see **c1940** in **C**], *moughty*, *mouty*.

1888 Meriwether *Mt Life in TN* 459 Yes, it is a mouty pretty country. **1917** (in **1944** Wentworth *ADD* 399) (sWV) *mouty*. **1942** Thomas *Blue Ridge* 288 Johnny's captain has writ moughty pretty about our boy. **1973** Davis *'Pon My Honor* 68 Afore you could say jack rabbit that ant wuz a feeling moughty good.

B *adjective* Great, large.

1864 *Chapman CW Letters* (April 10) thare was a mity shooting heard But I hant heard the result from it yet. **1948** Dick *Dixie Frontier* 313 When a man wished to compliment another on his crop, he said: "You've a mighty heap this year."

[DARE *mighty* adj widespread, but more frequent South, South Midland, Northeast]

C *adverb* Very, exceedingly (as in phrases *might near*, *might nigh*, *mighty glad*, *mighty near*, *mighty nigh*). See also **mighty near it**, **mighty well.**

1834 Crockett *Narrative* 41 I found it a mighty ticklish business, I tell you. **1862** *Sexton CW Letters* (Oct 24) [I] want to see them mity bad. **1863** *Revis CW Letters* (March 31) I am trubled to deth miteny b[e]case I can not be at home at work. **1863** *Tesh CW Letters* (Dec 5) Father I cant get You no caps to save my life I have tried mighty nigh every wher but I will keep a trying. **1864** *C A Walker CW Letters* (April 13) There is mighty apt to be a big battle near Richmond. **1873** Smith *Arp Peace Papers* 30 I hearn you and him were mity thik and affekshunate. **1886** Smith *Sthn Dialect* 348 When we asked for dinner, the man said, "Well, boys, hit's mighty rough, but ef you-uns kin eat it you're mo'n welcome ter it." **c1900** (in **1997** Stoddart *Quare Women* 93) You all are the friendliest ladies I mighty nigh ever saw. **1913** Kephart *Our Sthn High* 394 I'm a-tellin' ye hit takes a moughty resolute gal. **1934–47** *LAMSAS Appal*: *mighty glad* = used in introductions, expressions of appreciation, as "I'm mighty glad to meet you" (Madison Co NC). **1937** *Hall Coll* (Cataloochee NC) I saw where a bear might nigh bit a dog in two. **1939** *Hall Coll* (Cosby TN) Newport's a mighty fine place for a young man to go. He can really have a good time. **1940** Haun *Hawk's Done* 62 I reckon they might nigh had a fray. **c1940** *Padelford Notes* Hit's gittin raily mought nigh plumb cold. **1942** Justus *Step Along* 62 Jerry Jake was mighty much pleased. **c1945** Haun *Hawk's Done* 266 I noticed that she was mighty slow about making answer. **1954** GSMNP-19:23b Well, that's a mighty few words to leave this girl up here in the mountain. **1955** Ritchie *Singing Family* 117 You'd go by and ask her how her man was, and she'd might near always say, "Well, he ain't a-doing no good 'pears like." **1963** Edwards *Gravel* 123 Might nigh ever hoss in that company was limpin. **1971** *Granny Women* 261 I was might'near froze t'death when I got there. **1973** GSMNP-4:2:4 In might near all homes you'd have biscuits and all the ham meat you wanted to eat. **1973** GSMNP-80:7 He come up and that scared Ailey, my sister, mighty nigh to death. **1983** Mull and Boger *Recollections* 57–58 By now it's might-nigh daylight. **1991** Thomas *Sthn Appal* 44 If you've got a basement whor it's dry, you can keep 'um might-nigh all year. **1997** Montgomery *Coll*: *moughty* (known to Brown, Bush, Cardwell, Ledford). **2005** Williams *Gratitude* 509 *might near*, *might nigh* = close to, approximately. "It was *might nigh* dark when he left here."

[OED3 *mighty* adv C1 now chiefly North American and British regional, a1400→; DARE *mighty* adv especially South, South Midland]

mighty glad, **mighty near**, **mighty nigh** See **mighty C.**

mighty near it (also *might near it*) *adverb phrase* Very close to that. See also **mighty C**, **nigh it.**

1985 Irwin *Alex Stewart* 131 Everybody just went on about how good them girls looked, and every woman, mighty near it, up and down that creek started coming to have me cut their hair. *Ibid.* 141 Hit'll cure any kind of sore, might near it. *Ibid.* 189 You could smell a big vine of muscadines a half mile, might near it, and that's the best way to find them. *Ibid.* 220 I've got so sorry for them I could die, might near it. **1990** Clouse *Wilder* 115 I have might near enough [fertilizer] to finish out this row.

mighty well *adverb phrase* Very much. See also **very well.**

1862 *Watters-Curtis CW Letters* (Jan 17) [I]woud like to see you all myty well but ther ant now chanc now. **1901** Harben *Westerfelt* 112 I like her mighty well an so does yore mother.

milch cow *noun* A milk cow.

1864 *C A Walker CW Letters* (April 16) I hear you have lost all your meat and some person has stole your milch Cows. **1960** Mason *Memoir* 76 That same morning, Jake went out to feed his mule and behold it appeared that his mule had took on the features of a milch cow. **1988** Russell *It Happened* 14 Most families kept at least one milch cow.

[< Middle English *milche*; OED3 *milch cow* n 1 1424→]

mild-turned *adjective* Having a gentle or pleasing disposition. See also **turn B1.**

1937 Hall *Coll* (Emerts Cove TN) She's a mild-turned girl.

mile *noun* Variant plural form without -*s* following a numeral; see Grammar and Syntax §1.1.

1863 *Revis CW Letters* (June 23) we was ordered to talehomey and started to go thair and got 30 mile below clinton and the orders was counter manded. **1864** *Brown CW Letters* (July 28) they Can get a fite any day by goen out ten Mile. **1867** Harris *Sut Lovingood* 182 Ef thar's a frolic enywhar in five mile, Bart is sure tu be thar, an' Peg, too. **1939** Hall *Coll* (Bradley Fork NC) I first located on the little east fork in Sevier County, five mile above Sevierville. *Ibid.* (Swain Co NC) We had a hard time to hoe corn and work out in the field, had to walk two mile to school. **1969** GSMNP-42: 15 Old man Will Woody was up three mile and a half from there. **1974** GSMNP-51:6 I went to Whittier a lot of times, from home up there ten mile to Whittier horseback to get a doctor, you see, no telephones or nothing. **1975** GSMNP-59:2 They moved . . . down this river here, what was known as Wayside at that time. That was twelve mile below Bushnell. **1989** *Matewan OHP-33* He lived about three mile from where I did. **1993** *Stories 'neath Roan* 93 When we went to school, us younguns had to walk two or three mile to school. **1998** *Dante OHP-12* [The train] came up Chaney Creek, and I'd say probably about six mile from the mill.

mile-a-minute vine *noun* Kudzu, a fast-growing climbing vine introduced to the American South from Japan for controlling erosion.

1999 Montgomery *Coll* (known to Cardwell).

milk and water *adjective phrase* Weak, submissive.

1931 Hannum *Thursday April* 55 "He treats his women scandulous mean." "Hit's the Gawd's truth. Why, Thursday April, I've seed Poppy myself hitched to a plow and him a-drivin' her! She was milk and water to stand for hit!"

milk box *noun* Same as **box 3, spring box.**

1979 *Shenandoah OHC* 5 The spring was right here, and then you had your milk box and all down in here, didn't get right in the direct spring. . . . You let the water run out at the spring a little bit to cool your milk box. **1986** Pederson et al. *LAGS* (Johnson Co TN) = placed in the spring.

milk cheese *noun* Cottage cheese.

1949 McDavid *Grist* 111 (Rabun Co GA) = cottage cheese. **1986** Pederson et al. *LAGS* (Claiborne Co TN, Greene Co TN).

milk fever *noun*

1 Same as **milk sick.**

1973 GSMNP-74:7 Sometimes when [the cow] would have a young calf, why they'd have, they call it milk fever, and they just get down and they just die in a little bit if they wasn't something done for them.

2 See citations.

1968 *DARE Survey* (Brasstown NC) = a sickness a cow gets in her udder if she hasn't been milked in too long. **1977** Brookman *Veterinary Diseases* 145 Lactating cows sometimes suffer from Milk Fever, in which the cow gets sickly and the teats collapse, the inner walls of the teats sticking to each other. This disease is currently thought to be caused by malnourishment, especially telling when the cow begins to lactate. The old-time remedy is to put hollow quills up the teats and pump the bag full of air, leaving them this way for fourteen hours.

milk gap (also *milking gap, milking lot, milk lot*) *noun* A small enclosure or opening, usually at a rail fence in a field or pasture, where cows come to be milked or to nurse their calves. Also called **cow gap, gap 4.**

1913 Morley *Carolina Mts* 172 In some places the people still go to the "milking gap" to milk the cows. **1931** Goodrich *Mt Homespun* 50 In the twilight of early fall she went with Martha to the "milk-gap," the pasture bars, where the cows gathered to be milked, and learned from her a new name for Orion: "the Milking Stars," as night after night the constellation rose in the southeast at milking time. **1949** Kurath *Word Geog East US* 36 One of the striking South Midland innovations is the term *milk gap, milking gap* for a rail enclosure where the cows are milked. We find it in Western North Carolina and Virginia (south of the James), and in all of West Virginia except in the upper reaches of the Potomac and the counties bordering on the Ohio north of the mouth of the Kanawha. Not a single instance of this expression has been recorded outside the area. *Ibid.* 55 One of the few expressions in the southern mountains that cannot be traced back to Pennsylvania or the Southern area . . . *cow lot* and *milk lot* turn up in scattered fashion in different parts of the South and South Midland. **1952** Wilson *Folk Speech NC* 565 *milk-gap* = the gap through which cows pass at milking time. **1952–57** (in **1973** McDavid and McDavid *Vocab E KY* 153) *milk gap* = attested by 25/52 (48.0%) of E KY speakers for the Linguistic Atlas of the North Central States. **1961** Murry *Salt* 34 One night when she went up to the milk gap to do her milkin', that leetle cow brute failed to come in with the balance of 'em. **1966** Dykeman *Far Family* 133 The next morning Ivy went to the milk-gap by herself. She went earlier than usual. It would take her a long time to fill both pails by herself. **c1975** Lunsford *It Used to Be* 165 "Milk-gap" is the place where the milkmaid goes to let down the fence. She lets down the bars of whatever gap it might be to let the little calves in to the cows, so they can get their part of the milk first before she milks. She lets them go in and stay until they get what milk they're allowed to have, which would be half in each case. Then they are turned back, the gap is closed up, and the milkmaid milks the cows. **c1976** Cate *Ginseng Digger* He heard his wife calling the cows to the milk gap with a rhythmic "Sook, sook" and heard them answer the blatant bawling of hungry calves. **1976** Ledford *Folk Vocabulary* 281 *milking gap*. **1982** Ginns *Snowbird Gravy* 171 You know, there aren't many people that know what a milk gap is. It's a kind of fenced in little place. Maybe the cows are all in the pasture, and you call 'em in to milk 'em. And you get 'em in this little corral and feed them and milk them. **1986** Pederson et al. *LAGS*: *milk gap* = attested by 9/60 speakers (15%) from E TN; 9/10 of all LAGS speakers (90%) attesting term were from E TN; *milking gap* = attested by 9/60 speakers (15%) were from E TN; 9/10 of all LAGS users (90%) from Appalachia; *milking lot* (Gwinnett Co GA); *milk lot* = attested by 4/60 interviewees (6.7%) from E TN; 4/10 of all LAGS interviewees (40%) attesting term were from Appalachia; *milk pen* = attested by 3/60 interviewees (5%) from E TN; 3/9 of all LAGS interviewees (33.3%) attesting term were from Appalachia. **1995–97** Montgomery *Coll*: *milking gap* (known to Cardwell). **1999** Morgan *Gap Creek* 147 At the milkgap I climbed up on the bars and jumped down on the other side.

[DARE *milk gap* n chiefly southern Appalachians; *milk lot* n chiefly South, South Midland]

milking gap, milking lot See **milk gap**.

milking parlor *noun* A room or building with one or more stalls for milking cows.

2003 LaLone et al. *Farming Life* 235 We didn't have a milking parlor like this[.] We milked all twenty of ours in the barn. **2016** Netherland *Appal Cooking* Occasionally, I would help my grandfather milk cows in the barn's milking parlor. He milked half a dozen cows morning and night.

[DARE (at *parlor* n B) scattered, but especially Central Atlantic, North Central, Northwest]

milk leg (also *milk-leg fever*) *noun* Phlebitis (for related senses, see 1990 citation). Also called **child fever**.

1980 Matthews *Appal Physician* 128 We had more phlebitis then than now. This was called "milk-leg fever" I guess because symptoms started about the time milk started coming down good. **1986** Ogle *Lucinda* 54 Soon as Granny saw Momie she said "She has got child fever." (Now called phlebitis, I think. Or it is called milk leg by some old folks.) **1990** Cavender *Folk Medical Lex* 27 milk leg—a. phlebitis acquired by women shortly after birth. b. an infection in the veins of the legs. c. weakening of the arms and legs.

milk lot, milk pen See **milk gap**.

milk sick (also *milk poison, milk sickness*) *noun* A disease that gives cattle "the trembles" and, when passed to humans by ingesting the milk or butter from afflicted cows, often gives violent stomach pains, tremors, coma, and death. From pioneer days its source prompted speculation and fear, until in 1928 its cause was shown to be ingestion of **white snakeroot** (*Eupatorium* spp); also used in place-names where the disease was presumably prevalent in the past, as in *Milk Sick Gap* (NC). Same as **milk fever 1**. See also **milk-sick pen**.

1861 *Mingus Letters* 30 (Oct 5) Also Mr Lawrence died day befor yesterday with the milk sick. **1885** Murfree *Prophet* 47 His folks never knowed she had grazed thar till they had milked an' churned fur butter when she lay down an' died o' the milk sick. **1913** Kephart *Our Sthn High* 229 A more mysterious disease is "milk-sick," which prevails in certain restricted districts, chiefly where the cattle graze in rich and deeply shaded coves.... It disappears from "milk-sick coves" when they are cleared of timber and sunlight let in.... The prevalent treatment is an emetic, followed by large doses of apple brandy and honey, then oil to open the bowels. **1913** Morley *Carolina Mts* 281 It was in this region that one first saw a "milk-sick pen," and heard of the curious sickness which, attacking cattle that eat grass or leaves in certain well-defined spots, through the milk poisons the people, sometimes fatally. **1964** Cooper *History Avery Co* 31 It was once believed that milk poison was caused by a poisonous gas, dew or fog settling upon vegetation, but slowly people were puzzled by the fact that land once productive of milk poison, when cleared and tilled, was no longer dangerous as grazing areas. They thought that the stirring of the soil had "aired out" the poisonous gases. But this was not the case. Purdue University, in Indiana, after years of experimentation, proved conclusively—as it has since been established in Avery County—that the affliction is caused by animals eating one variety of the white snake root plant, of which there are 10 varieties, all of them harmless except one. **1971** Hutchins *Hidden Valley* 180 Early settlers in the Smoky Mountains were often ravaged by epidemics of a fatal disease they called "milk sickness." **1972** Cooper *NC Mt Folklore* 13 The Honey and Brandy Doctors claimed to know the exact amount of honey and brandy to be mixed, the size and timing of the doses, and the length of treatment required to cure a case of milk sick or milk poison. **2003** Cavender *Folk Medicine* 91 The Pole Creek section of western North Carolina lost so many residents to milk sickness in the 1880s and 1890s that it became known locally as "Milk Sick Cove." Unsure of what caused it, but noting an association between illness and place, many people abandoned their farms. In the 1820s several farms in Boone and Campbell Counties in Kentucky were abandoned and remained unoccupied for years because of the area's association with the illness. **2006** Ellison *Nature Journal* 59 Milk Sick Cove, Milk Sick Holler, Milk Sick Ridge, Milk Sick Knob and similar place names are common throughout the Blue Ridge. They are so-named because of an association with a once mysterious and deadly disease known variously as milk sick, milk sickness, puke fever, "the slows" or "the trembles." White snakeroot

(L. Ageratina altissima or Eupatorium rogusum), a close relative of joe-pye weed and white boneset, grows in profusion in the middle and upper elevations of the southern mountains, especially the Blue Ridge, and westward into the Mississippi Valley. It was scientifically identified during the first half of the twentieth century—after more than one hundred years of speculation—as the cause of milk sickness, when it was officially recognized that drinking the milk from cows that had eaten the plant often resulted in human fatalities, especially when consumed by infants.

[DARE *milksick* n chiefly South Midland]

milk sickness See **milk sick.**

milk-sick pen *noun* Formerly, an enclosure to quarantine cattle believed to be suffering from **milk sick.**

1885 Murfree *Prophet* 47 Folks in Eskaqua Cove 'low [he] let down the bars of the milk-sick pen an' druv Jacob White's red cow in. **1913** Morley *Carolina Mts* 281 It was in this region that one first saw a "milk-sick pen," and heard of the curious sickness which, attacking cattle that eat grass or leaves in certain well-defined spots, through the milk poisons the people, sometimes fatally.

milk weed *noun* See citation. Same as **weed B.**

2007 Myers *Smoky Mt Remedies* 19 Women sometimes had what they called "milk weed" or the "weed" after giving birth. This was mastitis or inflammation of the breasts. Treatments included placing hot compresses on the affected breast or taking doses of propolis, echinacea, or poke.

mill day (also *milling day*) *noun* See citations.

1940 McNeil *Mt Folk* Many of the mountain mill owners have certain days in the week set aside for "mill days." On these days they remain at their mills, which may be a mile or more from their home. On these days, too, the mill becomes a social center for the hard-working men folk who have "toted" bushels of corn on their shoulders over miles of the rough hill country. Tales of hunting adventure are swapped, courtships are gossiped about, and pocket knives are traded. **2004** *Smokies Guide* (Autumn) 1 Milling day was usually Saturday, and one or several members of the family might travel to the mill to have their corn ground into meal or wheat into flour.

miller (also *miller fly*) *noun* A small moth with dusty wings, often attracted to light. Also called **candle fly 1.**

1883 Zeigler and Grosscup *Heart of Alleghanies* 115 Here, in the still waters under a bridging log, or in some hole amid the exposed water-sunk roots of the rhododendron, lie the king trout, during the middle of the day, on the watch for stray worms, or silly gnats, and millers which flit above, then drop in the waters, with as much wisdom and facility as they hover around and burn up in the candle flame. **c1950** (in **2000** Oakley *Roamin' Man* 74) I have a phebby bird that bilt its nest on the porch and my garden is near so the bird ketches all the bugs and millers that lay eggs on the garden stuff. **1986** Pederson et al. *LAGS*: *miller* = attested by 12/60 interviewees (20%) from E TN and 5/35 (14.3%) from N GA; 17/42 of all LAGS interviewees (40.4%) attesting term were from Appalachia; *miller fly* (Hamilton Co TN, Gwinnett Co GA, Stephens Co GA). **1998** Montgomery *Coll*: *miller* (known to eight consultants from the Smoky Mountains).

[so called from the resemblance of the powdery wing scales to the dust accumulating at a grist mill]

milling day See **mill day.**

million See **melon.**

mill over *verb phrase* To ponder, consider (a matter) before deciding.

2000 Montgomery *File* I'm going to mill that over (55-year-old woman, Jefferson County TN).

[apparently a variant of *mull over*]

millrock *noun* A millstone.

1901 Harben *Westerfelt* 283 You've been my mill-rock long enough, an' now I'm goin' to take a new an' a firmer stand in my treatment uv you. **1963** Williams *Metaphor Mt Speech II* 50 He might be credited with enough strength to "th'ow a barn over his left shoulder" or a millrock over Big Sandy River. **1997** Montgomery *Coll* (known to Adams, Brown, Bush, Jones, Ledford, Norris).

[DARE *millrock* n South, South Midland]

milon See **melon.**

milt See **melt.**

mimic

A *verb* To resemble in appearance, represent.

1913 Kephart *Our Sthn High* 296 Many common English words are used in peculiar senses by the mountain folk, as . . . mimic or mock for resemble. **1917** Kephart *Word-List* 415 = to represent. "That *mimics* him right smart." **1944** Combs *Word-List Sthn High* 19 = to resemble in appearance. "He *mimics* his cousin a sight." **1988** Smith *Fair and Tender* 11 I picture the fotched-on candy from Mrs. Browns book about France, candy which mimicks roses. **1994–97** Montgomery *Coll* (known to Adams, Brown, Cardwell, Jones, Norris, Oliver, Weaver).

B *noun* A likeness.

1917 Kephart *Word-List* 415 = likeness. "That [photograph]'s a fair *mimic* of him." **1994–97** Montgomery *Coll* (known to Brown, Bush, Cardwell, Norris, Oliver).

mince *verb* To eat slowly and sparingly.

1915 Dingus *Word-List VA* 185 = to eat slowly and daintily. **c1960** Wilson *Coll* = to eat daintily, too daintily.

[DARE *mince* v widespread, but more frequent South, Midland]

mincer *noun* See citation.

1983 Broaddus *Estill Co KY Word List* 47 = a person lacking in appetite.

mincy *adjective* Finicky, overly dainty, fastidious, especially about eating.

1913 Kephart *Our Sthn High* 289 A remarkable word, common in the Smokies, is dauncy, defined for me as "mincy about eating," which is to say fastidious, over-nice. **1927** Woofter *Dialect from WV* 360 = particular in eating. "She is too mincy to suit me." **1952** Wilson *Folk Speech NC* 565 = over particular, over exact, finicky. "You're mighty *mincy* about your breakfast today. Are you sick?" **c1960** Wilson *Coll* = dainty, said of an eater. **1972** Cooper *NC Mt Folklore* 94 = finicky. **1991** Beverley *Old Mt Idiom* 147 = fastidious or prim. **1997** Montgomery *Coll* (known to nine consultants from the Smoky Mountains); Quit being so mincy and eat up (Cardwell).

[DARE *mincy* adj especially South Midland]

mind

A *noun*

1 See **a-mind, put one in (the) mind of.**

2 Attention, heed (especially in phrase *pay no mind*). See also **never no mind.**

1958 Campbell *Tales* 90 [They] stayed with an old woman who shook hands with the two oldest brothers but kissed the youngest. They had no knowledge that this was a token, and they paid her kissing no mind. **c1960** Wilson *Coll* = attention: "Pay him no mind." **1962** Drukker *Lg By-Ways* 51 A disobedient child is one who "didn't give his Pappy no mind." **1963** Edwards *Gravel* 141 He paid Elmer no mind but dipped right into his tale. **1966** Dykeman *Far Family* 70 I didn't pay it close mind. **1974** Fink *Bits Mt Speech* 19 Don't *pay* them *no mind*. **1982** Ginns *Snowbird Gravy* 136 Nobody paid it no mind. **1989** *Matewan OHP-45* He didn't pay me no mind. He just kept driving. **2004** Adams *Old True Love* 98 "Don't pay me no never mind," I said to Larkin. "I am just some woman who is bigged."

[DARE *mind* n B2 chiefly South, South Midland]

B *verb*

1 To remember, recall (a time).

1860 *Week in Smokies* 122 I mind I was powerful sick then, and I do believe, Mister, I should 'a' died but for some truck the Gineral gave me, God bless him! **1867** Harris *Sut Lovingood* 35 Dus yu mine my racin dad, wif sum ho'nets, an' so forth, intu the krick? **1910** Cooke *Power and Glory* 43 I mind when you was born. **1923** (in **1952** Mathes *Tall Tales* 8) I mind it jest like hit was yisterday. **1933** Thomas *Traipsin' Woman* 58–59 "Do you mind the time," she included the attorney and the Judge with a sweep of her twinkling eyes, "when Amos Sizemore was tore plum to pieces by a catamount?" **1960** McCaulley *Cades Cove* I can mind in my time when each person died, that there wasn't a man that worked in the bottoms in Cades Cove until after that funeral was over with. **1974** Fink *Bits Mt Speech* 16 Don't you *mind* the day he came? **1976** Weals *Mountaineer* At least a few people mind the day when the word *remember* was seldom used.

[OED3 *mind* v 2a now regional, a1384→; SND *mind* v 1; CUD v 1 "remember, recollect"]

2 To remind, put (one) in the mind.

1895 Murfree *Phantoms* 259 That thar fiddle 'minds me o' how unexpected 'twar whenst I met up with Lee-yander hyar. **1942** *Hall Phonetics Smoky Mts* 53 He minds me of you. **1963** Edwards *Gravel* 122 I'm minded of the time when I was a strip of a boy and Pap was alive.

[OED3 *mind* v 4a now rare; SND *mind* v 4; Web3 *mind* v 1a chiefly dialect; DARE *mind* v C1 chiefly South, South Midland]

3 To pay careful attention to, keep close watch on, watch out for (something); be careful. See also **mind out, mind the gap.**

1862 *Gilley CW Letters* (July 13) you can jentle my colt you must mind an not let hit hurt you. **1864** *Dalton CW Letters* (July 25) I was sorrow to hear that you fell off of the wagon and like to got kill you muss mind how you Drive them. **1939** Hall *Coll* (Sugarlands TN) I heard him a-hollerin'. He called for me to come up there and mind the coons up the tree. . . . We minded [the bear] up there a good long while. Finally it come down from up there. We had us a big fire made up at the root of the tree. When it come down why we had a good fire light to fight it by. **1974** Roberts *Sang Branch* 285 There we was on top of that board pile and that old bulldog a-minding us up there. **1986** Pederson et al. *LAGS* Always, one of the women, a mother or one of the girls, would have to mind them—flies, during meal. **1997** Montgomery *Coll* (known to nine consultants from the Smoky Mountains). **2007** McMillon *Notes* Mind the deep hole if ye go swimming.

4 To like, care for; hence participial adjective *minded* = inclined.

1895 Edson and Fairchild *TN Mts* 391 Near Asheville N.C., I heard a mountaineer say, "I didn't mind it a bit," meaning that he was terrified at looking over a precipice. **1925** Furman *Glass Window* 107 I allow Sam won't be minded to start to work till he gets him a bait of that squirrel, neither. **1979** Carpenter *Walton War* 144 I hain't minded to fault him none.

5 See citation.

1946 Dudley *KY Words* 271 = to object, be unwilling or reluctant: "I don't believe he minds to spend if he can get his money's worth."

mind off *verb phrase* To keep (especially flies) away.

1864 *Carter CW Letters* (Aug 19) Nancy & Deller my Dear little Children I wish I was with you Sow you could mind the flys of[f] of paps Stump I am as well tended to here as a man can be. **1942** Campbell *Cloud-Walking* 73 Ishmael was left to mind off the flies because Fess had gone off with Viny. **1942** (in **1987** Perdue *Outwitting Devil* 23) She told the boys not to give Jack's bull a bite and to mind him off from where the other cattle was eating. **1963** Watkins and Watkins *Yesterday* 43 Nobody minded the flies off while they et. They just swarmed all over everything.

[DARE *mind off* (at *mind* v C6) chiefly South, South Midland]

mind one's bees *verb phrase* See citation. See also **bees swarm, watch one's bees.**

1939 Hall *Coll* (Saunook NC) "Minding his bees" or "watching his bees" is used of a man whose wife is expecting a baby. Sometimes he stays home for this reason.

mind out *verb phrase* To be attentive to, careful about, on the lookout for. See also **mind B3.**

1890 Fruit *KY Words* 65 = to take care, to look out: "Mind out what you are doing." **1918** Steadman *NC Word List* 20. **1940** Bowman *KY Mt Stories* 243 = to look after the baby; care for it. **1997** Montgomery *Coll* (known to Brown, Bush, Cardwell, Norris, Oliver, Weaver).

[DARE *mind out* v phr chiefly South, South Midland]

mind the gap *verb phrase* To monitor a place where fence rails have temporarily been taken down to permit cattle to pass into or out of pasture, usually for a short period of time. See also **gap 2**, **mind B3**.

1922 *TN CW Ques* 866 I worked at all kinds of farm work. Making rails, building fence, plowing, hoeing, fixing up land, harvesting, making hay, milking and minding the gap. **1976** Weals *Mountaineer* In rail-fence days in the mountains, well within the memory of many still living, the rails might be stacked in a certain section so they could be taken down easily, to let livestock in and out of the fence field. This makeshift gate was called a gap, and sometimes a country person will refer to a more modern, hinged gate as a gap. In rail fence days, after the rails had been laid down to let the cattle pass through, a child might be called on to "mind the gap" until the return trip. Thus he was to watch the gate until the rails could've been laid back in place.

miner's asthma *noun* Black lung disease (pneumoconiosis caused by long-term inhalation of coal dust particles).

1973 *AOHP/EH-73* We had a lot of men die that the doctors would cut them off and say they had miner's asthma. We didn't know the difference [from black lung]. **1973** Kahn *Hillbilly Women* 105 Sometimes the miner's asthma gets him to where he can't do nothing at all. **2006** *WV Encycl* 62 As coal mining expanded, more workers exhibited symptoms of "'miner's asthma," as the disease was originally called. The higher levels of coal dust produced by 20th-century mine mechanization increased the frequency of the disease. **2012** Portelli *They Say* 153 Black lung came to be redefined as "miner's asthma," an ordinary condition that need cause no worry.

miners' strawberry *noun* See citation.

1943 Korson *Coal Dust* 69 Beans and white gravy made a popular combination in hard times, the beans under the name of "miners' strawberries."

mines *noun* Construed as singular; hence *this mines*.

1959 Roberts *Up Cutshin* 16 I had a buddy in this mines to help me in my room. **1974** Roberts *Sang Branch* 14 The first coal I ever dug was in a little old wagon mines on Bull Creek in Perry County. **1975** *AOHP/ALC-66* I worked at a mines for thirty-seven years. It was two hundred and forty-seven feet straight down in a shaft mine. **1975** *AOHP/ALC-961* Some feller that never worked a hour in a coal mines will be a-representing you to the coal owner. **1983** Wolfram/Christian *WV Coll* 212 I worked twenty six year in that mines. **1989** *Matewan OHP-28* I don't know as I ever walked up to a mines in my life that I didn't get a job at. *Ibid.* I've worked in a coal mines and come in and just barely get ready and go to revival. **1997** *Dante OHP-53* They didn't have the ventilation, and that's why that they shut that [sic] mines down.

minister-man *noun* A preacher.

c1940 Simms *Coll* All you-uns who ain't done conversin' with each other please step outside, ef you-uns cain't shet up whilest the minister-man is a-deliverin' his discourse.

[redundant form]

mink kettle *noun* See citation.

1978 Slone *Common Folks* 237 [To wash our clothes] the water was either carried from the creek, or drawn from the well or spring. A wash tub or "mink" kettle was placed on two rocks, with a space between them where the fire was "builded."

mirate *verb* To marvel or wonder at, to exhibit admiration for.

c1960 Wilson *Coll* = to wonder at, to take on over. **1992** Brooks *Sthn Stuff* 98 = to show admiration. **1998** Montgomery *Coll* (known to Oliver).

[shortening of *admiration*; OED3 *mirate* v back-formation from *admiration*, U.S. colloquial and dialect, DARE *mirate* v chiefly South, South Midland]

miration *noun* A clamor.

1898 Elliott *Durket Sperret* 133 T'other night they hearn a great miration in the chicken house, an' they ketched two critters eatin' jest ever'thing.

[DARE *miration* n chiefly South, South Midland]

mire up

A Variant forms *ma'rr up* [see **1982** in **B**], *mar up* [see **1994** in **B**].

B *verb phrase* To sink into or become stuck in mud.

1961 Medford *History Haywood Co* 19 Whenever wagons became mired up, which was often the case, "prize-poles" were often kept along the road of such mirey places. **1967** Parris *Mt Bred* 310 You'd mire up above the hubs, and the oxen would have to pull you out. **1982** Slone *How We Talked* 35 *ma'rr up* = sink. "You might ma'rr up in a mud hole." **1994** Parton *Dolly* xii Then I'd get completely marred up in the mud, and that was the worst of times.

mirey *adjective* Muddy, full of mire.

1961 Medford *History Haywood Co* 19 Whenever wagons became mired up, which was often the case, "prize-poles" were often kept along the road of such mirey places.

mis See **Mrs.**

misdoubt *verb* To have doubt about, disbelieve.

1927 Furman *Lonesome Road* 49 I misdoubt you're not able to get back over the mountain. **1942** Campbell *Cloud-Walking* 10 I don't misdoubt them women will turn out right common and good after they get habited to the pioneering ways of mountain folks. **1958** Campbell *Tales* 53 He made promise, and I don't misdoubt he aimed at the time to do like he promised. **1972** Cooper *NC Mt Folklore* 94 = doubt. **1979** Carpenter *Walton War* 170 I misdoubt I could ever draw a free breath if I had to stay shut up in a town. *Ibid.* 172 I misdoubt he ever knowed who stole his stuff, but I've heered him tell that tale times without number. **1994–97**

Montgomery *Coll* (known to Brown); I misdoubt that she could do that (Shields). **2007** McMillon *Notes* = to doubt: "I don't misdoubt it."

[OED3 *misdoubt* v 1 now chiefly dialect or archaic; EDD *misdoubt* v 1 in general dialect use; SND *misdoubt* v 1 "to disbelieve"; CUD *misdoubt* v 1 "doubt," 2 "have no confidence in," 3 "suspect"; DARE *misdoubt* v especially South, South Midland]

mise (also *mize*) *verb* To behave in a miserly fashion, hoard.

1924 Buffum *Shakespearean Survivals* 16 A woman who claimed kinship to a miser recently murdered near Tazewell, Tenn., because of his supposed wealth said of him, "I've known him from the time he was a boy and he's allus mised and mised and mised." **1940** Still *Snail Pie* 212 How much money have you mized.

miseries See **misery 2**.

misery *noun*

1 A pain or ache, especially a vague one.

1863 *Watkins CW Letters* (Oct 16) I have a Caugh and Misery in my breast and head and Just weakly. **1864** *Owens CW Letters* (Nov 22) I am about well altoo misery in my brest and the hard [= heart] burn. **1895** Edson and Fairchild *TN Mts* 373 I've got a *misery* in my back. **1904–20** Kephart *Notebooks* 2:475 He's got a misery in his back. **1937** Hall *Coll* (Emerts Cove TN) I have a misery in my stomach. **1953** Wharton *Dr Woman Cumberlands* 175 She complained of a "misery in my stummick." **c1960** Wilson *Coll* = a pain or ache, somewhat indefinite in intensity and location. **1962** Drukker *Lg By-Ways* 50 If a body isn't up to par in the matter of health he grades his "miseries" as being "jest punying 'round," "barly takin' vittles," on up to "bein' far t'middlin' well," "right tol'able," or "I'm a'feelin' purty paert." **1975** Chalmers *Better* 37 I've felt a sight on this earth bad, and I tell you what's th' truth, Tuesday t'was a week ago, I had sech a misery that I got clean out o' heart. **c1975** Lunsford *It Used to Be* 175 "Misery" is a term used to express any disease as pain. "He's got a misery in his side."

[Web3 *misery* n 4 dialect; DARE *misery* n widespread, but more frequent South, South Midland]

2 In phrase *the miseries* = vague pain, a general feeling of illness; menstrual cramps.

1957 Parris *My Mts* 140 Once, before he took his bed with the miseries and couldn't get about, not even to chop wood, he took me across the ridge and showed me the gover'ment's whiskey-makin' still. **1990** Cavender *Folk Medical Lex* 27 a. menstrual period. b. a tired, aching feeling. **1995** Montgomery *Coll* (known to Cardwell, Ellis, Ledford, Oliver, Shields). **2013** Reed *Medical Notes* = menstrual cramps.

misery whip *noun* A crosscut saw. Also called **brier 2**.

1967 Parris *Mt Bred* 132 "That," said the woodhick, "is a misery whip or a brier." He pointed to a seven-foot crosscut saw hanging on the wall. "It was designed for sawin' the huge logs of the virgin forest." **1984** Wilder *You All Spoken* 153 = a crosscut saw. When a crosscut saw buckles while in use, it is said to fold, and when it folds, it whips violently as it regains its shape. **1995** Montieth *Tall Tales* 11 All cutting was done by axe or cross cut saw, which was often called "Misery Whip." **1996** Harrell *Fetch It* 158 A misery whip is a two-man, cross-cut saw, with a handle on each end. Each man took an end, and they alternately pulled the saw back and forth against the grain of the tree until the tree was cut down. "Misery" is a pretty apt adjective to describe that saw. **2006** Farwell *Logging Term* 1021 Sawyers with their crosscut saws, called "misery whip" or "briars," formed [logging] crews with "buckers," who sawed timber in lengths.

mislick (also *miss-lick*) *noun* An errant stroke with an ax, hammer, or other implement.

1904–20 Kephart *Notebooks* 2:475 She hit a miss-lick with the axe, an' cut her fut fur a-plenty. **c1926** Cox *Cullowhee Wordlist*: *mislick* = a false blow. **c1950** Adams *Grandpap* 40 I'll not let nobody hold me but the old woman. An' you make a mislick an' hit her instead of me. **1952** Wilson *Folk Speech NC* 565 I made a mislick and hit my thumb. **c1960** Wilson *Coll* (*mislick* or *miss-lick*) = a false stroke, one that failed to land where it should have. **1991** Thomas *Sthn Appal* 145 They's somebody jist made a mis-lick, somehow. **1994** Montgomery *Coll* (known to eight consultants from the Smoky Mountains).

[DARE *mislick* n chiefly South, South Midland]

mislike *verb* To dislike.

1979 Carpenter *Walton War* 173 I reckin' I'm quare (queer); some folks I like and others I mislike, and I can't help it. **1984** Smith *Oral History* 24 I mislike Hoot Owl Mountain myself and don't go up it lessen I have to. **1995–97** Montgomery *Coll* (known to Brown, Ledford, Oliver, Shields).

misput *verb*

1 To inconvenience, annoy.

1946 Dudley *KY Words* 271 = to inconvenience, put out. **1951** Giles *Harbin's Ridge* 93 Papa didn't look for Ben to be much account. He misput himself with Ben just to help Faleecy John. **1979** Carpenter *Walton War* 171 I would like to have a little help if it wouldn't misput you any. **1995–97** Montgomery *Coll* (known to Adams, Brown, Cardwell, Oliver).

[DARE *misput* v 2 especially KY]

2 To misplace.

1997 Montgomery *Coll* I know I misput that book somewhere (Norris).

misremember *verb* To forget; to remember imperfectly. See also **disremember**.

c1960 Wilson *Coll* = can't remember or else have forgotten. **1997** Montgomery *Coll* (known to Brown, Jones, Weaver).

[SND *misremember* v "to forget, to remember incorrectly"; CUD *misremember* "forget"; DARE *misremember* v especially South Midland]

misris, misruz See **Mrs.**

miss *verb* To avoid (someone).

1973 GSMNP-76:3 I seen Oliver Whaley that's missing me around here like he was a-going up that hollow.

Missionary Baptist *noun* A member of a Baptist church that supports missionary activity; a Baptist church or denomination that supports such activity. See also **Hard Shell**, **Primitive Baptist**.

1856 *Chapman CW Letters* (Aug 13) the missionary Baptist will hold an association at the Bethel meeting house commencing Friday before the third Sabbath in September 1856. **1869** *Carter CW Letters* (Feb 4) Martha Austin has left the presbyterian church and has joined the missionary Babtis her & Six others were baptised one Sunday the 31 of January. **1908** Smith *Reminiscences* 412 The primitive or "foot-washing" Baptists still have their churches in the mountain coves, where their shepherds feed their flocks on sound and fury and nonsense; but the missionary Baptist and the circuit-rider follow steadily in the wake of the schoolmaster, and the sect in ignorance is already doomed. **1974** GSMNP-50:2:9 The Primitive Baptists and the Missionary Baptists, they went together [to share a building]. Now I don't know how long ago that was before my time, but they had a split over their doctrine, you see, and they wasn't a-getting along too good, but in the meantime, it come a windstorm and blowed the church down. **1986** Noonkesser *Crossing* 95 By 1819 the question of slavery was being debated in all denominations. In the East Tennessee area, the Baptists became involved in the arguments concerning missions, Sunday school and other matters pertaining to doctrine. Many felt money contributed for missions was being misused to promote the abolition movement and that God would find a way to save those intended for salvation. The anti-mission group became known as the old school; those who favored missions were known as the new school. In later years the two groups would be known as Primitive Baptists and Missionary Baptists. **1994** Montgomery *Coll* Missionary Baptists didn't wash feet, unlike Primitive Baptists, but both groups would baptize in the river (Shields). **1995** McCauley *Mt Religion* 125 Today, the designation "Missionary Baptist" is, for the most part, a distinctly Appalachian phenomenon. Churches calling themselves Missionary Baptist, be they independent or belonging to the Southern Baptist Convention, are found in much larger numbers in the Appalachian region than anywhere else in the nation, because nowhere else did the Anti-Mission movement and Old Regular Baptists have as great a sociocultural impact on the life of a region. Missionary Baptist as a term of distinction is, therefore, more highly meaningful throughout Appalachia than anywhere else.

missionary settlement *noun* Formerly, a residence, usually accompanied by a school and sometimes a church, established and supported by the "home missions" agency of a religious denomination to provide a mountain community basic educational and other services.

c1917 (in **1968** Sharp and Karpeles *Songs Sthn Appal* 9) We traveled through the mountains, generally on foot, staying in the homes of the people or a missionary settlement and calling, usually without introduction, at any dwelling that lay on our way.

miss-lick See **mislick**.

misspend oneself *verb phrase* See citation.

1953 Davison *Word-List Appal* 12 = to overreach: "Ben will misspend himself if he hunts on posted land."

miss tress See **Mrs.**

mistake *verb* Variant past-participle forms *mistaken'd*, *mistook*.

1862 *Hamblen CW Letters* 64 she has not mistook my Mises for Miss. **1867** Harris *Sut Lovingood* 130 I hed mistaken'd the givin-in signs; he wer madder nor ever. **1942** Campbell *Cloud-Walking* 148 Right there you are mistook. **1974** Fink *Bits Mt Speech* 16 *mistook* = mistaken or confused. "I've been mistook about that lots of times." **1976** Carter *Little Tree* 39 If words has been mistook to cause ye discomfort, I here and now state the sorrow of every man present. **1979** Slone *My Heart* 5 Well, Caney, me or that ol' Hoot Owl, one or t'uther got mistook, fer he is bringin' that young'un now.

mister *noun* See citation.

1967 *DARE Survey* (Gatlinburg TN) = title for a jackleg preacher.

mistote *verb* To miscarry a child.

c1940 (in **1994** Montgomery *File* (as of 1940)) Missus Maples, I'm sorry you mistoted (40-year-old man, Gatlinburg TN). **1992** Brooks *Sthn Stuff* 99 = to miscarry a pregnancy.

mistress, **mistrus** See **Mrs.**

mite *noun* A bit, small amount.

1931 Goodrich *Mt Homespun* 72 She's not one mite like the foolish young things out where I live. **1962** Dykeman *Tall Woman* 133 Afore you get down to making the journey in fact you'd best turn off a mite of work at home. **1971** Thornburgh *Great Smoky Mts* 154 There'll be furriners larnin' my children a lot o' truck that won't do 'em a mite o' good.

mitely See **mightily**.

mitten bush *noun* The sassafras tree, so called from the shape of its leaf, which often consists of one large and one smaller lobe.

1996 Isbell *Last Chivaree* 137 Look at the leaves on a sassafras tree. See all those little mittens. They come one for one hand, one for the other—more for the right hand than the left. That's why they call a sassafras tree a mitten bush.

mixed-up dog *noun* A dog of mixed breed.

1976 *Bear Hunting* 282 Maybe they'd be another dog—sometimes they'll use a mixed-up dog—that doesn't bark much, but he fights hard and tends to stop the bear. **1986** Pederson et al. *LAGS* (Cocke Co TN, Jefferson Co TN).

mix one's wool *verb phrase* To whip thoroughly in a fight.

1937 Conner *Ms* 88 I realy was craving a job of mixing his wool. **1997** Montgomery *Coll* (known to Brown, Bush).

mixtry *noun* A mixture.

1867 Harris *Sut Lovingood* 31 I wonder hit didn't work 'im pow'ful es hit wer; fur Betts cooks up sum tarifyin mixtrys ove vittils, when she tries hersef. **1937** Hall *Coll* A mixtry of purple and white rhododendron. **1939** *FWP Guide TN* 458 The "mixtry" is eaten with a knife or sopped up with a biscuit. **1942** *Hall Phonetics Smoky Mts* 79.

[DARE *mixtry* n chiefly South, South Midland]

miz See **Mrs.**

mize See **mise.**

mizriz, mizrus, mizruz See **Mrs.**

mizzle

A (also *mizzling*) *noun* Fine, misty rain.

1976 Garber *Mountain-ese* 58 It ain't raining much, jist a mizzlin' uv fallin' weather. **1987** Young *Lost Cove* 84 I reckon that this here mizzle will get all the fish to stirring. **1997** Montgomery *Coll*: *mizzling* (known to Brewer, Bush, Oliver).

[OED3 *mizzle* n[1] now colloquial and regional; DARE *mizzle* n chiefly South, South Midland]

B *verb* To rain in fine, mist-like drops; hence participial adjective *mizzling* = misty, drizzling.

1952 Wilson *Folk Speech NC* 565–66 = to rain in fine or foglike drops. **1962** Wilson *Folkways Mammoth Cave* 13 If rain came in small drops, it was *misting* or *mizzling*. **1973** Davis *'Pon My Honor* 99 = drizzle, rain with small drops. **1974** Fink *Bits Mt Speech* 16 They was a *mizzling* sort of rain. **1996–97** Montgomery *Coll* (known to Brewer, Brown, Bush, Oliver).

[OED3 *mizzle* v[1] now colloquial and regional (British and North American); DARE *mizzle* v[1] chiefly South, South Midland]

mizzling See **mizzle A, B.**

moaners' bench See **mourners' bench.**

moccasin pie *noun* See citation. Same as **half-moon pie.**

1978 Slone *Common Folks* 309 Apples were used in fried pies, apples or apple butter folded into small thin sheets of dough and fried in deep fat. I have also heard these called half-moon pies or moccasin pies.

mock

A *verb* To resemble.

1913 Kephart *Our Sthn High* 296 Many common English words are used in peculiar senses by the mountain folk, as . . . mimic or mock for resemble. **1957** Combs *Lg Sthn High: Word List* 65 = resemble. Ex.: "That young shaver mocks its daddy." **1994–97** Montgomery *Coll* (known to Adams, Cardwell, Jones, Norris, Oliver, Weaver).

[DARE *mock* v B chiefly South, South Midland]

B *noun* An imitation considered as a source or object of scorn or ridicule (especially in phrase *make mock of*).

1942 Thomas *Blue Ridge* 192 Becaze he made mauck of Pol Gentry. **1953** Davison *Word-List Appal* 12 = butt of ridicule. "Homer made a *mock* of me right before the whole school." **1989** *Matewan OHP-28* If the Spirit don't move on you to speak in tongues, you're making a mock. You ain't a-talking in tongues. It's just mock.

mocky *noun* Gravy.

1939 Farr *TN Mt Regions* 91 = gravy. "My woman makes good mocky." **1997** Montgomery *Coll* (known to Cypher).

moderator *noun* The title for a pastor in certain small Baptist denominations.

2005 Preece *I Grew* 55 The title of moderator of a church is not common either as it used to be when most of the older churches were organized around here. Moderator was the name of the pastor of the church and elders were the preachers, sitting with the moderator, and when he went visiting to other churches, he then was referred to as elder, or just brother. Only churches such as Old Regular Baptist[s], United Baptists and a few others still use those terms describing the preaching brethren.

modern Christmas *noun* December 25. Same as **new Christmas.** See also **old Christmas.**

2008 McKinley *Bear Mt* 181 = December 25.

mog along *verb phrase* See citation.

c1954 Adams *Word-List* = [to] move slowly.

moggy *adjective* Characterized by mire or swamp.

1941 Still *Troublesome Creek* 45 The draw was a moggy place. Wahoos grew thick against a limerock wall, and a sprangle of water ran out.

[perhaps a blend of *muddy* and *boggy*]

moist *verb* To moisten.

1924 Raine *Saddlebags* 79 Then he'd moist it and rub it and grain it through a fine sieve.

molasses

A Variant forms *laissy* [see **1957** in **C**], *lasses, lassey, lassie, lassies, lassy, molassey*.

1917 (in **1944** Wentworth ADD) (sWV). **1938** Stuart *Dark Hills* 257 The cane can be left over until Tuesday . . . the "lassies" will be just as good. **1941** Still *Troublesome Creek* 85 He teased as he whittled a molassy spoon for me. **1958** Morgan *Gift from Hills* 23 "Lassy" time was another diverting season up in our country. They didn't say 'lasses for molasses, their word was lassy. **1991** Haynes *Haywood Home* 48 Apples were picked and stored in a bed of straw in the molassey furnace after molassey time. **1997** Andrews *Mountain Vittles* 72 'Lasses was right popular with the old timers for sweetenin'.

B (also *cane molasses, lassey cane*) *noun* A liquid sweetener usually made from **sorghum** (but see 1937 citation). The term is traditionally construed as plural count noun; hence singular *lassey, molassey*, etc. through back-formation. (For types of molasses, see 1937 citation.) See also **long sweetening, short sweetening.**

1860 Olmsted *Back Country* 271–72 Molasses they always used as if in the plural number (like oats), urging me to take "them molasses—but perhaps I wouldn't like them with my bacon." **c1863** (in **1957** Monaghan *CW Slang* 128) The language spoken by Southern hill people amused New Englanders. A volunteer in the Massachusetts 36th Infantry remembered that his hostess in a cabin apologized for the proffered fare. . . . When asked if she had any molasses, he remembered that she replied, "Well, we haven't many but we have a few." **1863** *Reese CW Letters* (March 26) we onely draw half pound of Bacan pur day and one pound of meal pur day or A pound of pickeld Beef pur day and A fue molasses and A little Rice. **1864** *Poteet CW Letters* (March 16) I would like for you to send me sum Molasses in A bottel if you think that you can send them with out braking the bottel. **1913** Kephart *Our Sthn High* 297 Tomato, cabbage, molasses and baking powder are always used as plural nouns . . . "Pass me them molasses." **1913** Morley *Carolina Mts* 74 Besides the cornfields there are those frequent fields of something that "imitates corn a right smart," as the people say, but which is only sorghum, from which in the fall the mountaineer extracts molasses for home consumption. **1930** Armstrong *This Day and Time* 215 There's plenty of us to make them molasses! I promise you we 'ull make 'em good and thick. **1934–47** *LAMSAS Appal* = attested by 9/20 speakers (45%) from VA, 5/37 (13.5%) from NC, 1/14 (7.1%) from SC, and 1/12 (8.3%) from GA. *Ibid.* (Swain Co NC) *molasses is.* **1937** Hall *Coll* (Catons Grove TN) According to Rhoda Caton, molasses may be of four kinds: cane, pumpkin, persimmon, maple. **1956** Hall *Coll* (Cataloochee NC) We used to make molasses and sell 'em. **c1960** Wilson *Coll* = often (maybe most often) used as a plural. **1975** GSMNP-59:18 [Syrup] was all made out of just regular molasses, lassey cane. **1975–76** Wolfram/Christian *WV Coll* 31 We made them and I used to love them things, the old cane molasses. **1986** Aiken *Mt Ways Two* 212 The mountain people used the "lasses" for sweeting [sic] in many ways, in their cooking as well as plain or with butter on their biscuits. **1991** Haynes *Haywood Home* 46 Berry time was picnic time and it was always a community social occasion. Mostly young folks gathered with their berry baskets loaded with sausage or ham biscuits and molassy cookies. **1999** Morgan *Gap Creek* 144 The molasses could be warmed up, and they had the right flavor. There was four jugs of them. **2006** *WV Encycl* 667 In West Virginia sorghum molasses has also been called molasses, lassies, and sorghums, but today, producers sometimes call their product 100 percent pure sweet sorghum syrup because of the fact that stores now sell "molasses" that are mixtures of corn syrup, flavorings, food coloring, and other additives.

[DARE *molasses* n C1 widespread, but less frequent Inland North, Pacific]

C *verb* See citation.

1957 Combs *Lg Sthn High: Word List* 58 *laissy* = to cover or spread with molasses. Ex.: "Laissy that child's bread.

molasses boil (also *molasses boiling, molasses making, molasses stir-off*) *noun* Traditionally, an annual, all-day neighborhood work activity in the fall, with festivities lasting into the night; the juice pressed from stalks of **sorghum** was laboriously poured, stirred and boiled, producing a thick syrup that served as a principal sweetener for the traditional mountain table. As part of the festivities, young couples often fashioned into candy by pulling stretches or "ropes" of it until they cooled and hardened into edible sticks. See also **boiling, candy breaking, molasses pull, sorghum making, stir off.**

1922 TN *CW Ques* 18 [School] amed to run 3 mos but stoped through fodder pulling and molasses making. **1939** Campbell *Play Party* 18 Clearings, log-rollings, house-raisings, corn-shuckings, bean stringings, apple peelings, 'lasses stir-offs, and quiltings, though said to be not as common as they once were, still survive. **1945** O'Dell *Old Mills* 4 Molasses makings were gala occasions. Neighbors often helped with the tedious task. After all was finished, the last run was allowed to boil until it was ready for candy. While it cooled, all hands were washed in the nearby stream, greased thoroughly, and then each Jack chose his Jill for the candy-pulling. **1966** Frome *Strangers* 240 He remembered how the farmers never hired hands for wheat threshing, but would help each other; how the boys and girls shucked corn together and had a time telling tales and singing, as they did at spelling bees and "'lasses boilings." **1975** Gainer *Witches Ghosts Signs* 20 One of the most enjoyable of the harvest time activities that combined work with social activity was the making of sorghum, called the "molasses bilin'," which was held in the latter part of September. Almost every farmer planted a good-sized patch of cane in the late spring at corn planting time. It was planted in rows about three feet apart, which allowed room for working between the rows. In late September the leaves were stripped from the green stalks before the stalks were cut. Some farmers cut the stalks before the leaves were stripped, leaving the job of stripping to the women and girls. One man went into the business of molasses making and purchased the equipment for the molasses bilin' for as many as a half dozen communities. It consisted of a mill with large rollers which pressed the juice from the stalks of cane, and an evaporating pan in which the juice was boiled down to a thick and sweet consistency, called molasses or sorghum. The man who owned the equipment was an expert at making molasses, who knew when the juice had been boiled to the correct consistency to make good molasses. A schedule was arranged among farmers so that the molasses maker could take his equipment from place to place for all the farmers in the community. Sometimes a farmer who did not have a large crop of cane would cut his crop and haul it in a wagon to another farmers's boiling, so that several farmers might have molasses boiled at the same location. The mill which pressed the juice from the cane was turned by a single horse hitched to the end of a pole, which turned the rollers of the mill as the horse walked around the mill in a circle. The raw juice which flowed from the mill was poured into the evaporating pan, which was heated by a wood-fire under it. From one end of the long pan the juice was moved to the other end as it cooked. The master-maker, who was in charge of the entire operation, with a long-handled wooden paddle moved the juice slowly through the sluices in the pan until it was ready to be taken off through a spigot in the bottom of the pan. It was caught in buckets and poured into stone jars and jugs. **1979** Slone *My Heart*

43 Another happy time was a "molassie stir-off." Every family had a crop of cane that had to be harvested just as soon as the seeds became ripe. If left standing any longer, the stalks began to dry. If cut too soon, the molasses would have a sour taste and would not keep. There was usually just one person in a community with a gin mill and a molasses pan. **1982** Maples *Memories* 12 I still got to see the "lassie making" though. We kids would be on our way from school, and Uncle Burt Ogle would be making molasses. We would see the old mule going round and round, grinding out the juice of the sugar cane, as one of the men would feed the mill. **1988** Lambert *Kinfolks* 100 The juice [from squeezing stalks of **sorghum**] ran out the bottom [of the **cane mill**] into a pan. From here, it was poured into the top pan of the cooker and brought to a low boil. As it continued to cook and thicken, it was poured from one pan to the next at the critical point. In the meantime, the green foam which rose to the top was skimmed off by folks who tended the pans. It was important that the juice be kept hot enough but never get too hot, so someone with considerable skill was needed to tend the wood fire. Wood had to be kept ready, utensils had to be kept clean, and the mule had to be kept going in circles. It was a long, slow process which required a lot of folks to share the work, tell stories, eat and generally have a good time. **1991** Thomas *Sthn Appal* 62 Molasses-making generally started about the fifteenth to twentieth of September and had to be completed before the first hard freeze, which could take place during the first half of October. **2008** Salsi *Ray Hicks* 125 My favorite social was molasses boils. If you helped get in the cane, grind it in the mill, and then go and help in the stirrin', ya might be given a little to take home. There wasn't much white sugar to be had unless you was rich or if you traded herbs to get a little bit from the store.

[DARE *molasses making* n southern Appalachians]

molasses bread (also *molassie bread*) *noun* Bread made from adding molasses to flour as a sweetener.

1949 Arnow *Hunter's Horn* 61 Lureenie sat by the eating table and drank the coffee gratefully, and after only a little urging took a second cup and more than once glanced at a pone of molasses bread Milly had left on the table as a late snack for Nunn. **1978** Slone *Common Folks* 313 Some folks added cushaw or pumpkin to their cornmeal dough, and baked it. "Molassie bread" was made this way, also.

molasses butter *noun* A sweet spread put on biscuits, fried corn bread, or pancakes.

1997 Andrews *Mountain Vittles* 72 Best way [to eat it is to] pour some in yer plate and mix in some butter[,] Molasses Butter we call it.

molasses candy *noun* Stick candy or taffy made by stretching hot molasses into "ropes" until it cools and hardens. Also called **pull candy, stiff jack, tough jack.** See also **candy breaking, molasses boil, molasses pull.**

1939 Hall *Coll* (Cataloochee NC) We made our cane and made molasses candy . . . After we took off our molasses, we boiled it till it got hard.

molasses corn *noun* See citation.

1990 Oliver *Cooking Hazel Creek* 12 = a special treat was [at] molasses making time when barely full ears were shucked & put in the kettle of boiling molasses & allowed to cook into a sweet confection.

molasses furnace *noun* A furnace that has an overhead receptacle and is used for boiling **sorghum cane** juice.

1956 Hall *Coll* (Cataloochee NC) We never did have molasses pullin's. You have to have a lot of help when you go to make molasses. You have to have a molasses furnace. You have to have a cane mill. We used to make molasses and sell 'em. **1991** Haynes *Haywood Home* 48 Apples were picked and stored in a bed of straw in the molassey furnace after molassey time.

molasses licking *noun* Traditionally, a social event at the end of a **molasses boil.** See also **molasses pull.**

1941 *FWP Guide WV* 416 Everybody is thinking of the gaiety to come when the last day's work [of making molasses from green cane] is done. The event is celebrated with a "'lasses lickin'," attracting neighbors from near and far. The assembled guests are given small wooden paddles to scrape the generous leaving in the boiling pan; games are played; there is group singing; mountain minstrels enliven the gathering. . . . [Y]oung folks wander off in couples, for, as everybody knows and expects, "they's a sight o' courtin'."

molasses making See **molasses boil.**

molasses mill *noun* Same as **cane mill.** See also **molasses boil.**

1949 Arnow *Hunter's Horn* 28 Lucy and Deb put the can heads into piles: Nunn came behind with Maude and the sled: he cut two rows at once, threw the stalks onto the sled, and hauled them away to the molasses mill, where Suse and Lee Roy helped Sue Annie and Blare Tiller feed and grind and cook and keep the blindfolded old mule borrowed from John going round and round. **1958** Wood *Words from TN* 13 = a machine for pressing the liquid out of the cane. **1995** Montgomery *Coll* (known to Cardwell).

molasses pull (also *molasses pulling*) *noun* Traditionally, an evening social event following the making of molasses. Same as **candy breaking.** See also **molasses boil.**

1955 Parris *Roaming Mts* 151 An old timer is one who remembers when the social calendar swirled around corn-shuckin's, sewing bees, quiltin' frolics, bean stringin's, apple butter stirrin's, and molasses pulls. **1975** Dwyer *Thangs* 9 In the mountains, candy pullin's, sometimes called "molasses pullin's," started with the molasses-making season and continued through the winter. These "pullins" provided the excuse for a social gathering at someone's house, particularly for young courting couples.

molasses shed *noun* A small outbuilding in which molasses-making equipment is stored.

1997 Nelson *Country Folklore* 18 Down below the house, close to where we have the cane patch, is the *molasses shed*. The molasses mill is kept covered over until time to make the molasses. On the wall are dippers and stirrers and other things we use when making molasses. In the fall of the year just before frost, we cut the cane, pull off the fodder, and stack the cane away from the frost until there's time to make the molasses.

molasses stir-off See **molasses boil.**

molasses time *noun* The time in the fall when **sorghum** is cut, its juice is pressed from its stalk, and **molasses** is made from it.

1991 Haynes *Haywood Home* 48 Apples were picked and stored in a bed of straw in the molassey furnace after molassey time.

molassey See **molasses.**

molassie bread See **molasses bread.**

molassy cane *noun* Same as **sorghum.**

1991 Haynes *Haywood Home* 48 In September and October, we harvested pumpkins, squash, shelly beans, potatoes, apples, molassy cane and corn.

moldwarp *noun* See citations.

1944 Wilson *Word-List* 46 = a senseless person. **1952** Wilson *Folk Speech NC* 566 = a stupid person, a dolt. "That fellow's always doing the wrong thing; he's such a *moldwarp* he hacks me to death." [**1995** Montgomery Coll (unknown to consultants from the Smoky Mountains).]

[OED3 *mouldwarp* n literally "mole"; now chiefly regional; DARE *moldwarp* n especially southern Appalachians]

mole bean *noun* The castor plant (*Racinis communis*), whose odor is said to repel moles.

1950 Justus *Luck for Lihu* 47 "Some folks call [castor beans] mole beans," said Grandmaw. "They say iffen you plant a row of these beans close to your garden-patch, the moles won't bother anywhere nighabout." **1968** Wilson *Folklore Mammoth Cave* 22 = the castor bean (Ricinus communis), believed to be a protection against moles if planted around the edges of the garden.

[DARE *mole bean* n 2 especially South Midland, South Atlantic]

molly cottontail *noun* A cottontail rabbit, especially a female.

c1960 Wilson Coll = the ordinary cotton-tail rabbit known to everybody. **1998** Montgomery Coll (known to Bush, Jones), = only a female (Brown).

[DARE *molly cottontail* n chiefly South, South Midland]

molly-crawl-bottom *noun* A minnow.

1988 Mashburn *Mt Summer* 43 Things moved at about their usual rhythm, with us catching a few minnows or Molly-crawl-bottoms at each dark pool as we moved along the creek. **2012** *Blind Pig* (Aug 1) High school kids now don't know the Molly Crawl Bottom." The small sculpin (*Cottus bairdi*) is the most common fish in the watershed, but kids don't know it by any name, including the folk-name their ancestors used.

mollygrubs See **mullygrubs.**

Molly Hogan *noun* In logging, a loop of cable wire functioning as a temporary link.

1974–75 McCracken *Logging* 16:3 They'd take a steel rail. They take a strand out of one of these big cables, just one strand. They'd roll it back in itself and they call it a Molly Hogan. This single strand would make a rope, as big as the original cable was. Then they'd take a steel rail, and lay it on the ground back here on this end, then they'd pull this end up to the bottom of the Sarah Parker. Take one of them Molly Hogans and roll them in the eye in the hole in the rail and then on the frame of the machine somewhere against the beams. And that was a safety in case a cable broke. Why, this end going down, the jillpoke would foul it, stop it.

molly moocher *noun* A morel (*Morchella esculenta*). Also called **hickory chicken, moodger, muggin.** See also **dry-land fish.**

2006 Hufford *Ramp Suppers* 110 You're going to have to plant you a patch of ramps and some molly moochers. **2006** *WV Encycl* 271 Each season brings its share of wild edibles: the morel mushrooms known in various parts of the mountains as "moodgers," "muggins," and "molly moochers." **2008** Reed et al. *Cornbread Nation IV* 184 The term "molly moocher" appears to be unique to central Appalachia. Perhaps "molly," the Irish nickname for Mary, is a play on the French *morilla*, which might have sounded like "Maria" to the ears of the Irish who came to the region in the 18th century.

molly pop *noun* The fruit of the **maypop** or **passion flower** plant.

2006 *Encycl Appalachia* 933 The most exotic of the Appalachian wild fruits is the maypop (or "molly pop") fruit of the passion-flower vine. A Cherokee favorite, the ripe lemon-colored maypop has a mellow taste suggestive of apricot and is sometimes called field, mountain, or wild apricot.

mom (also *mommy*) *noun* One's wife; also used as a term of address.

1962 (in **2014** McCarter *Memories of Boy* 24) Uncle P. J. and Elizabeth returned to Tennessee to live, because he wanted "Mom" as he called her, to be near her people in case anything happened to him. **1971** *AOHP/ALC-129* I called her mommy. That was my wife. **1989** *Matewan OHP-28* He stopped his car and told his wife. He called her "Mommy."

mommick

A Variant forms *mammock* [see **1932** in **C**], *mommix* [see **1895** in **C**], *momox* [see **1867** in **B**].

B *noun* A state of disarray or confusion.

1867 Harris *Sut Lovingood* 92 The nex tail fus' experdishun wer made aginst the caticorner'd cupboard, outen which he made a perfeck momox. **1913** Kephart *Our Sthn High* 294 If the house be in disorder it is said to be all gormed or gaumed up, or things are just in a mommick. **1927** Mason *Lure of Smokies* 127 The pie is a comglomeration, a "mommick" or "gaum," to use mountain terms, of boiled dough and either apples or peaches with NO sugar! **1952** Wilson *Folk Speech NC* 566 *mommick* = a foul, torn-up mess.

[cf OED3 *mammock* n 2 "a scrap, shred, broken or torn piece" now archaic and regional; EDD *mammock* 1 Scot, Engl; DARE *mammock* n 2 chiefly South Midland]

C (also *mommick up*) *verb, verb phrase* To mix or mess up, tear to pieces, mangle, ruin, spoil; hence noun *momoxing*, participial adjectives *mommicked, mommixed*.

1867 Harris *Sut Lovingood* 298 Mout a-lookt for a gineral durn'd momoxin' of things, tho', when dad tuck the job wif Squire Haney to help. **1895** *Word-Lists* 391 *mommixed* = mixed up, in confusion (Winchester, Ky.). **1917** Kephart *Word-List* 415 = to ruin by bungling. "That was a waste of time, Uncle Bill; they just *mommicked* it up." **1932** Creal *Quaint Speech*: *mommick* = a variant of mammock meaning to tear to pieces. **1962** Dykeman *Tall Woman* 175 When that was finished and he tried to cut up the meat, Aunt Tildy exclaimed, "I never saw such a mommicked-up job!" **1962** Williams *Verbs Mt Speech* 18 The farmer scolds the child for taking out more "grub" than he can eat and "a-smoulin' around over it and a-mommickin' it up till nobody else can stommick it." **1976** Dykeman *Time to Build* Closely allied to "gaum" is "mommick," another distinctly descriptive word. It means to bungle, spoil, and make a mess of. **2008** McCaulley *Cove Childhood* 74 [Her quilts] were strictly covers for warmth, made of whatever worn-out clothes or other scraps she had "momicked together," in her words.

[cf OED3 *mammock* v "to break, cut, tear into fragments" now regional; EDD *mammock* 5; DARE *mammock* v 1, 2 both senses chiefly South, South Midland]

mommick up See **mommick C**.

mommix, momox See **mommick**.

mommy See **mom**.

money stick *noun* See citation.

2013 Montgomery *File* (N GA) When Dad's hands were not wrapped in plow lines, he pulled the "money stick" at a sawmill. A "money stick" is a hand-operated lever attached to belt-driven shafts that move the log carriage into the huge saw blade.

monkey flower *noun* A wild snapdragon (*Mimulus ringens*).

1967 *DARE Survey* (Maryville TN) = a hiking club term; most of the club members are from Knoxville.

monkey jug *noun* Wild ginger (*Asarum* spp). See also **heartleaf 2**.

1943 Peattie *Wild Flowers* 172 Certainly there is no odder flower on any tropic isle than that of our wild gingers—"monkey jugs" some mountain folk call them—each with its little jug-shaped calyx half buried in the earth and hidden under its mottled leaf.

monkey roll *noun* See citation.

1900 *Trestise Coal Mining* 92 The broken-coal screen is a screen that is very rarely double-jacketed. It is from 4 feet to 6 feet in diameter, usually from 9 feet to 12 feet in length, with an inclination of J inch to the foot, and is run 10 to 13 revolutions per minute. The segments used on this screen are either cast iron, wire, or punched wrought iron. It is usually driven by the large periphery spur-gear and pinion, in preference to bevel-gears. It takes the coal as it comes from the prepared rolls, often called the monkey rolls.

monkey rum *noun* Liquor distilled from **sorghum**.

1976 Dwyer *Southern Sayin's* 24 = distilled syrup of sorghum cane. **1997** Montgomery *Coll* (known to Bush). **2017** Blankenship *Songs of Whippoorwill* 24 Moonshine made with molasses—in times when the price of sugar had risen enough to make the use of it unprofitable—was called "monkey rum."

[DARE *monkey rum* n especially South Midland]

monstrous *adverb* Very, exceedingly.

1843 (in **1974** Harris *High Times* 28) I have been so monstrous busy, riding about, making speeches, soliciting votes, cajoling the husbands, shaking hands with the wives, kissing the children, and giving them dimes and half dimes. **1859** Taliaferro *Fisher's River* 92 I got onpatient, and moseyed a little to'ads it, and got on a log where I could see a leetle, which the laurel and ivy was monstrous thick. **1963** Edwards *Gravel* 30 He was monstrous hungry about that time, but he wanted to bid off a few pies at the Bluff, and never did like to buy a girl's pie and not be able to help her eat it. **1997** Montgomery *Coll* (known to Brown, Bush, Cardwell, Jones, Norris, Weaver).

[DARE *monstrous* adv B chiefly South, South Midland]

month *noun*

1 Variant forms *mont, munt*.

1862 *Love CW Letters* (Aug 17) we may not leave here in a mont. **1862** *Shipman CW Letters* (Feb 6) their is nearly 6 monts [pay] dew us when wee ar in the survis 12 months. **1991** Thomas *Sthn Appal* 145 Now, they'll cut as much coal in—I'll say—a week, cut as much coal in a week today as they would back then in two, three munts.

2 Variant plural form without *-s* following a numeral.

1864 *Chapman CW Letters* (April) Noah sexton has bin sick about two month with his brest But is about well again. **1973** *AOHP/LJC-296* She had cancer for about six month. **1998** *Dante OHP-61* I got a job up there and worked about two month for him.

monument *noun* Variant form with secondary stress on the last syllable. For similar forms, see **-ment A**.

1942 Hall *Phonetics Smoky Mts* 71 The suffixes *-dent* and *-ment* (except in *independent*) in most instances have secondary stress: *accident, confident, devilment, instrument, monument, payment, settlement, testament*, etc.

monument stone *noun* A sophisticated grave marker, usually a purchased one (the usual mountain term is **tomb rock** or tombstone).

1928 (in **1952** Mathes *Tall Tales* 56) He said they'd told him what was writ on Tom's monument stone, an' them words kep a-risin' up betwixt him an' his Maker. **1998** Montgomery *Coll* (known to Adams, Bush, Cardwell, Weaver).

mooch *verb* To move slowly or idly.

1974 Betts and Walser *NC Folklore* 13 "One day," said the old fellow, "I was moochin' along a mountain road trail when these here telescope eyes of mine spotted a buck."

moodjer See **molly moocher**.

moon See **moonshine A**.

moonball *noun* The moon. See also **sunball**.

1936–37 Still *Defeated Creek* 21 He cocked his chin and sighted the moon-ball. **1941** Still *Troublesome Creek* 36 A house proper to raise chaps in, a cellar for laying by food, and lasty neighbors. Now, that hain't asking for the moon-ball. **1982** Slone *How We Talked* 29 = moon.

moon calf *noun* An imaginary beast; a bastard; simpleton. See citations.

1913 Kephart *Our Sthn High* 287 I had supposed that the words cuckold and moon-calf had none but literary use in America, but we often hear them in the mountains . . . moon-calf [being employed] in its baldly literal sense that would make Prospero's taunt to Caliban a superlative insult. **1917** Kephart *Word-List* 415 = in mountaineers' superstition, a shapeless thing, without life, that a steer causes in a cow by worrying her. **1944** Wilson *Word-List* 46 = an imagined misshaped animal, a bastard, a simpleton. **1997** Montgomery *Coll* = a bastard (known to Brown).

[cf OED3 *mooncalf* n 2c "a born fool . . . a simpleton" colloquial]

moon doctor *noun* A folk healer who treats patients according to the signs and phases of the zodiac.

2007 Milnes *Signs Cures Witches* 158 He got out his almanac and got to reading and called Doctor Pettycoat, [who] was a moon doctor, and talked to him about it, and he told him what to do for the cow.

moon eye *noun* Insomnia. See also **big eye**.

1994–97 Montgomery *Coll* (known to Adams, Cardwell).

moon-eyed *adjective*

1 Of an animal: partially blind, suffering from moon blindness.

1889 Murfree *Broomsedge Cove* 24 105 Do ye know ennything 'bout'n a horse's eyes? I be sort'n 'feared he's moon-eyed, or suthin'. **1952** Wilson *Folk Speech NC* 566 = of horses: blind during certain phases of the moon. **1978** *Horsetrading* 66 If he had a moon-eyed horse, or a windy horse, or a lame horse, he'd go look at that place first on a horse he was tradin' for. **1997** Montgomery *Coll* (known to Brewer, Brown).

[DARE *moon-eyed* adj 1 chiefly South Midland]

2 See citation.

1940 *FWP Guide GA* 326 A Cherokee myth about the "moon-eyed folk," a strange white people who could see only at night, is supported in part by the theory of one ethnologist that albinos lived here and built fortifications along the Tennessee River until they were conquered by the Indians.

moon-faced *adjective* Of an animal: having a condition that causes it to be looking into a distance.

1997 Montgomery *Coll* (known to Hooper).

moon-fixer *noun* See citation.

c1960 Wilson *Coll* = a nickname for a tall, unusually lanky person; the opposite of *shorty*.

[DARE *moon-fixer* n chiefly South, South Midland]

moonlight school *noun* See citations.

1916 Schockel *KY Mts* 123 "Moonlight" schools [opened] in the Kentucky mountains in 1911 for children, parents and grandparents. **1937** White *Highland Heritage* 71 The famous "moonlight schools" in Kentucky, county night school organizations in North Carolina, and other efforts to teach adults . . . have markedly reduced the illiteracy that used to be so much talked about. **1982** Slone *How We Talked* 80 = sometime just after the turn of the century the government promoted a system where a teacher came to the homes and taught the old and the handicapped people to read and write. It did not last long.

moon pie *noun* See citation. See also **half-moon pie**.

1982 Slone *How We Talked* 58 Dried apples . . . were used most for to make fried apple pies, also called "moon pies," "moccasin pies" or "flip overs."

moonshine

A (also *moon*, *moonshine whiskey*) Hard liquor made without a government license or the payment of taxes.

1785 [See **1974** citation below]. **1875** King *Great South* 518 He was sober, and producing from his pocket a flask of "moonshine whiskey," invited us to drink. **1883** Zeigler and Grosscup *Heart of Alleghanies* 116 There is nothing particularly startling in this latter statement, except to the trafficker in "moon-shine," and the love-lorn mountain lad. **1913** Morley *Carolina Mts* 66 For corn is not only the principal food of the mountaineer, but supplies as well that important beverage, variously known as "corn-juice," "moonshine," "mountain-dew," "blockade," "brush whiskey," and in the outer world, "corn-whiskey," which is extracted from the grain and surreptitiously distributed. **1954** GSMNP-19:30b He said, "Get ye about a half a gallon of moonshine and a half a gallon of this mountain honey." See, the bears are crazy about this mountain honey, and he said, "Mix it all up and take it out on a trail and stir it up," and he said the bear will come after night. **1963** Carson *History Bourbon* 237 = distilled spirits on which the tax has not been paid or federal regulations observed as to materials and sanitation. **1968** Vincent *Best Stories* 16–17 If he caught a member drinking moonshine, or dancing, or doing any other of a number of things that were taboo, he'd have this member "Churched." [**c1970** Handlon *Ol' Smoky* 8 You know, mountain people don't call liquor moonshine. They name it mountain dew or white mule.] **1972** Carr *Oldest Profession* 74 Moonshine has been made from grain—corn or rye (often a mixture)—and the moonshine brandies usually from apples, apple cider or peaches. **1974** Dabney *Mt Spirits* xiv-xv The term "moonshiner" derives from "moonlighter." it was used in England prior to the 1700s to describe the night-time smugglers of brandy from Holland and Frances onto the British coast. *A Classical Dictionary of the Vulgar Tongue*, published in 1785, declared: "The white brandy smuggled on the coasts of Kent and Sussex is called moonshine." When the term caught on in America is not clear, but it likely came with the imposition of the excise taxes (which became permanent in 1862), when many whiskey-makers went underground, figuratively and in some cases literally, carrying out their illicit "stilling" at night. **1977** Shields *Cades Cove* 79f It was sort of a custom to have a party after a "run off" of moonshine whiskey. Sometimes called backins parties, these featured a quantity of the mash "backins" or spent beer, heated with spices and served along with food. . . . The alcoholic content of the drink is not high, but enough of it can elevate the drinkers' spirits. **1978** Montgomery *White Pine Coll* V-3 Cosby was noted all over the world for the moonshine capital of the world. **1985** *Smokies Anniv Book* 58 To snake bite victims, a "snort" of moonshine was a dose that usually warded off poison from any critter's bite. **1985** Williams *Role of Folklore* 280 I'd grew up with him, made moon with him for a long time. **1994** Montgomery *Coll* This moonshine's going to be the ruination of my family (Cardwell). **2006** *Encycl Appalachia* 943 Although the word *moonshine* had been used in the 1600s to describe whiskey runners along the British coast who were evading English taxes, the terms *moonshiner* and *moonshine whiskey* were not in common use in America until the late 1860s, after the United States government imposed excise taxes on distilled spirits to pay Civil War expenses. **2007** Alexander *Moonshiners Gone* v "Moonshine" is the general term applied to most any kind of spirituous drink, including brandy, made illegally across the Southern Appalachians of the United States. The term originated from the fact that the alcohol was made secretively, often dark nights deep in mountain forests. The only light available might be the shining light of the silvery moon. So, the term "moonshine" came to be applied to the illegally made variety of all types, because it was all assumed to be made at night and by moonlight. **2007** Rowley *Moonshine!* 9 *Moonshine* refers to illicitly distilled liquor—illicit because the distillers are unregistered, contrary to the law, and the liquor untaxed, also contrary to the law. **2007** *Smokies Guide* (Autumn) 5 Moonshine was relatively easy to make, though the quality of the finished product varied widely depending on how much of a hurry a moonshiner was in. Choice white corn was the grain used in the mountains. Once sprouted, the corn was ground and mixed with cornmeal and honey, sugar, or molasses to make a sweet mash. Fermentation started, and once the mash turned sour, it was ready for cooking in the still. The liquid formed at this stage was called "corn beer." Some people couldn't resist a sip or two. But real moonshine required heating this liquid to 173 degrees Fahrenheit, the temperature at which alcohol vaporizes; the spirits of the fermented liquid separated from the water and rose up through the still's "arm" and into a long copper tube called the "worm." Surrounded by cold water, the vapor in the worm condensed and came out moonshine. **2009** *TN Encycl* = untaxed liquor, furtively produced quite often by the light of the moon, or at least out of the immediate reach and oversight of law enforcement . . . the typical moonshine is clear in color and potent, usually approaching 100 proof, or 50 percent alcohol by volume.

B *verb* To distill liquor illegally (i.e. in order to avoid government taxes on its production); hence noun *moonshining*, *shining* = the making of whiskey or brandy surreptitiously (and usually at night), whether for private consumption or for sale. See also **moonshiner**.

1883 Zeigler and Grosscup *Heart of Alleghanies* 141 Blockading, or "moonshining" as it is sometimes called, because the distiller works by the light of the moon, is not as prevalent in these mountains as is generally supposed; and, besides, it is growing less with every year. **1913** Kephart *Our Sthn High* 122 The main reason for moonshining, as you'uns calls it, is bad roads. **1914** Arthur *Western NC* 272 Moonshining is so called because it is supposed that it is only while the moon is shining that illicit stilling takes place, though that is erroneous, as much of it is done during the day. **1916** Schockel *KY Mts* 114 Illicit distilling increased greatly after the imposition of the liquor tax of the Civil War. In 1877 the government began to suppress "moonshining" in the region. By 1882 the supremacy of the law had been established. But in 1894 the liquor tax was increased from ninety cents to one dollar and ten cents, which resulted in increased "moonshining." **1939** Hall *Coll* (Waldens Creek TN) Back thirty to forty years ago they moonshined up and down th'u here. . . . Revenue officers [were] officers of the law. They were federal or government men. They'd take [a moonshiner] down to Sevierville and take him before a commission. **1967** Williams *Moonshining* 12 Those unwilling to pay taxes began to hide their stills in deep hollows, thickets, coves, caves, and obscure ravines in order to escape the revenue collector. Producing whiskey in this fashion was safest at night, and easiest on moonlight nights. Hence, it came to be referred to as "moonshining." **1978** Montgomery *White Pine Coll* V-3 Moonshining is just about left out. **1998** *Dante OHP*-69 They wouldn't pull but about two years [in prison] and would be back to moonshining the next day. **2009** Fields *Growing Up* 100 We laughed because we all knew Elmer Cantrell had just spent thirty days in the slammer for "shinin'."

[perhaps from the necessity of making the liquor at night]

moonshine mill *noun* A gristmill that grinds sprouted corn, the chief raw material for **corn juice**.

2003 Strutin *Hikes of Smokies* 157 One of [Woody's] renters ran the mill, and it became known as a moonshine mill. Moonshine mash is made from sprouted corn, called "green corn." Most millers avoided grinding green corn because revenuers could easily spot its remnants on the mill stones. During Prohibition, a moonshiner could make a decent amount of money in the Smokies' cash-poor economy, so hidden mills dotted the slopes. Green-corn millers, too, made more money from the moonshine business than from grinding an equal load of cribbed corn.

moonshiner *noun* A distiller of whiskey without government license or payment of taxes; more generally, anyone involved in the business of distilling illegal whiskey. See also **bootlegger**, **shiner**.

1881 Atkinson *After Moonshiners* 14 The word "Moonshiners" applies to that class of persons usually found in the Southern States, who make the living by manufacturing spirits by moonlight in the defiles of the mountains, for the purpose of evading the tax levied upon all spirituous liquors by the Government of the United States. **1895** Wiltse *Moonshiners* 7 Before having too much to say about the moonshiner, it may be well to state who he is. The word is not exclusively American in its use, but belongs also to provincial English, and its general significance is "one who pursues a dangerous or illegal occupation at night." The smuggler along the British-American borders, or elsewhere, is therefore as much a moonshiner as the man who unlawfully manufactures whisky or brandy in the mountains of the South. The man of whom this is written, however, is he who manufactures or assists in the manufacture of liquor in violation of law, as well as he who sells it without license. The term is commonly applied indiscriminately to all engaged in the illicit traffic—manufacturers, peddlers, workers in the stills, those who remove the liquor from the stills, and even those who furnish material for its manufacture. **1897** Pederson *Mtneers Madison Co* 825 Night after night the lanterns of the revenue officers may be seen darting back and forth on the mountain side, in their perilous search for "moonshiners." **1912** Mason *Raiding Moonshiners* 199 It is only in the event of a tragedy like that at Hillsville in March that the outside world gets an inkling of how truly bad the moonshiner bad man is. **1921** Campbell *Sthn Highlander* 104–5 The moonshiner, as he is called without the mountains, or blockader, as he is more commonly known within them, is one who engages in the illicit distilling of spirituous liquors. Secrecy is necessary for this practice, and he is called moonshiner because it is supposed that he engages in his illicit traffic on moonlight nights when there is enough light to make work easy and enough darkness to make him secure. To dispose of the product of his still, he or his confederates must run the blockade thrown about the sale of liquor by government officials. He is, therefore, regarded as a blockade runner, or "blockader." While he may ply his trade with the assistance of but one or two associates, he is often a member of a ring made up of men of different groups, all of whom have more or less to do with the making or retailing of illicit liquors. **1973** GSMNP-84:28 In Cades Cove over here, it was filled up with moonshiners then. **1989** Smith *Flyin' Bullets* 111 Bootleggers and moonshiners could be very rough people to deal with. Moonshiners invested a great deal of money in producing illegal whisky and they were often quick to protect that investment. . . . Bootleggers and moonshiners, working on a large scale, were organized, many working for someone with contacts. Large sums of money exchanged hands which is evidenced by that cars were easily replaced as they were confiscated by the law. **1998** *Dante OHP-25* They'll run us out of there. They won't let nobody preach up there. He said they was bootleggers and moonshiners.

moonshine tripper See **tripper**.

moonshine whiskey See **moonshine A**.

moonshining See **moonshine B**, **shine B2**.

moon-up *noun* Moonrise.

1938 Stuart *Dark Hills* 303 I had stayed from sundown until moon-up.

moonwinder *noun* A children's toy. See citation.

2005 Joslin *Handcrafters* 41 "My grandmother was born in 1880. She said that when she was a young girl she didn't have any store-bought play pretties, but they did have fun. She took time to talk with me and play with me a lot," says Brucie, reaching into a round basket to pull out a disc of wood with string running through the middle. "This moonwinder—it's made of wood. But my Grandmother used to keep big buttons at her house with quilting needles. She made them for me with them," she says, grasping the handles on either end of the looped string, twirling the disc to wind the string, then pulling her hands apart. The disc hums loudly as it spins in a blur.

moosewood *noun* The striped maple (*Acer pennsylvanicum/striatum*). Same as **goosefoot maple**.

1961 Douglas *My Wilderness* 172–73 We saw occasional striped maples, some thirty feet high. This tree, that the mountain folk call moosewood, showed the first touch of the golden color it would soon display. **1970** Campbell et al. *Smoky Mt Wildflowers* 22 Other common names [for the striped maple] include Pennsylvania maple, moosewood, and goosefoot maple.

moralize *verb* To instill good morals in.

1916 Schockel *KY Mts* 125 With these conditions in mind the founder hoped that by starting a good school he "would help moralize the country." **1924** Raine *Saddlebags* 103 Hit'll take a right spell to moralize John Will. **1957** Combs *Lg Sthn High: Word List* 65 = to teach good morals. Ex.: "He aims to moralize this country." **1960** Westover *Highland Lg* 20 = to teach good to.

more *adjective*, *adverb* Used to form a double comparative. See also Grammar and Syntax §3.3.

1862 *Click CW Letters* (Sept 1) the time seam[s] more longer then it wold if we wold get a nough to eat. **1862** *Patton CW Letters* (Aug 15) I am inhopes we are getting into a more healthyer climate than we have been. **1927** Bolton *Mt Girl Speaks* 4 We are always worser off, but 'taint no need of telling us sich 'cause we come more harder to it. **1939** Hall *Coll: more pleasanter*. **1940** Haun *Hawk's Done* 33 I propped her head up on the pillow and it seemed like she looked more stronger than she had for over a week. *Ibid.* 35 I was getting closer and more closer with every step I took. **1971** *AOHP/ALC*-139 I taught at Pine Creek and Cram Creek and Bottom Fork, but I taught more longer on Bottom Fork. **1973** *AOHP/ALC*-259 They [= politics]'ve gotten more rottener than they was back then. **1978** Montgomery *White Pine Coll* IV-2 I'd say I was more healthier back then than I am now. **1983** McDermitt *Boy Named Jack* 16 Another way now that they tell it . . . he give 'em a hundred guineas which was about fifteen or twenty dollars, was the way they told it, and I think that's more right. **1989** *Matewan OHP*-28 [Children are] more smarter in it right now than I was when I was eighteen years old.

morn-gloom See **gloam.**

mort *noun* A great deal, a large quantity or number.

1931 Hannum *Thursday April* 9 They say he got him a heap of doctor l'arnin' down country and can cure a mort of sickness. **1946** *Shore Sign* 5 Peers like it caused a mort o' trouble. **1952** Wilson *Folk Speech NC* 567 = a great quantity, much. **1978** Hiser *Quare Do's* 138 Several of the neighbor women had biled up pots of coffee and baked a mort of sweetbreads which they passed out to all newcomers. **1991** Still *Wolfpen Notebooks* 50 We've had a mort of deaths amongst the old folks the past winter. [**1997** Montgomery *Coll* (unknown to consultants from the Smoky Mountains).]

[OED3 *mort* n[6] regional; CUD *mort*[2] n "a large number or quantity"; DARE *mort* n chiefly southern Appalachians]

mortal

A *adjective* Extreme, deadly, living.

1940–41 Still *Moving* 18 Hit's mortal sin to make gypsies of a family. **1955** Ritchie *Singing Family* 58 When my eyes hit that light I commenced batting my eyelids, couldn't see a mortal thing.

B *adverb* Extremely, exceedingly. See also **mortally.**

1835 (in **1896** Radford *Block Houses* 297) Cows is mortal feared, as well as horses, of them parfect devils, the Indians. **1884** Murfree *In TN Mts* 278 He air mortal low with the fever. **1895** Dromgoole *Logan's Courtship* 146 She says she knows he's mortal tired after his thirsty ride. **1941** Still *Troublesome Creek* 37 She knelt by the hearth, frying a skillet of hominy, cooking it mortal slow. **1956** McAtee *Some Dial NC* 30 = very. "So mortal hot." **c1960** Wilson *Coll* He's mortal ugly. **1997** Montgomery *Coll* (known to Adams, Brown, Bush, Ellis, Jones, Oliver, Weaver).

[OED3 *mortal* adj/adv 7b "extremely great, huge, extreme, excessive" now archaic or regional; DARE *mortal* adv especially southern Appalachians, New England]

mortally *adverb* Extremely, exceedingly, intensely; at all. See also **mortal B.**

c1940 Simms *Coll* She wuz so mortally glad to see us. **1940** Still *Snail Pie* 214 Maw did mortally relish partridge. **1955** Ritchie *Singing Family* 48 I just couldn't mortally stand to sit still on that log bench and that tune snakin around so. **1997** Montgomery *Coll* (known to Norris); It's mortally hot today (Cardwell). **2001** Lowry *Expressions* 5 My mother-in-law was operated on 3 weeks ago, and she was eat mortally up with cancer.

mortas See **tomato.**

mortified to death *adjective phrase* See citation.

1969 Doran *Folklore White Co* 113 = greatly embarrassed.

mortify (also *martifie*) *verb* Of a wound or the flesh: to decay, become inflamed or infected.

1939 Hall *Coll* (Saunook NC) He skinned his knee, and in two weeks it was plumb mortified. **1982** Slone *How We Talked* 34 *martifie* = to decay. Used when describing human flesh or bodies of animals. **1995** Montgomery *Coll* (known to Cardwell).

[OED3 *mortify* v 1d now rare or historical]

mossback *noun*

1 Same as **grayback 1.**

1937 Thornburgh *Great Smoky Mts* 43 There is always the excitement of hopping the rocks, which the mountain people affectionately have named "greybacks" or "moss backs," according to their nature. **1995** Montgomery *Coll* = refers to only the part of rock not in water (Cardwell).

2 (also *mossback farmer*) A small farmer.

1900 Harben *N GA Sketches* 78 You have to get up before day to get the best o' these Georgia mossbacks. **1980** Riggleman *WV Mtneer* 120 Now and then a farmer would come in and work a month or two after crops were put out or before harvest time. Sometimes they were nicknamed "Mossback farmer" by the loggers, but no one paid attention to that.

most

A *pronoun* See **the 5.**

B *adjective* Greatest, most usual or regular. See also **most times.**

1915 Pollard *TN Mts* 242 Any kind Mummy likes; that's the most kind I get. **1961** Miller *Pigeon's Roost* (Oct 12) It is reported that the most kind of the one herb that has been collected here for the Botanical market this season that is now closing appears to be the beadwood (witch hazel) leaves. **1969** Hall *Coll* (Del Rio TN) [At hog-killing time] wives [were] cookin', makin' sausages. They'd take all the fat off, wash 'em good. That's the real chitlin's, fry 'em. The most use we made for 'em was in shortnin' bread. **1979** *Big South Fork OHP*-10 The most thing they got over that way [was] when the waters got so high over the bridge.

C *adverb*

1 Nearly (sometimes placed after the form modified). See also **most all.**

1814 Hartsell *Memora* 139 they most all fell in and marched with us round. **c1844** Beckner *Shane Interview* 226 Oh, Caty! Ain't you most done? **1860** Olmsted *Back Country* 264 Nine tenths of them would do 'most anything to be free. **1861** *Martin CW Letters* (Dec 21) Chrismas is Most hear and I have Not Seen the first partical of frost yet. **1863** *Walker CW Letters* (June 21) We have been Marching and fighting most all the time since we have been down here.

1873 Smith *Arp Peace Papers* It's most too far to hawl rocks. **1904** Fox *Christmas Eve* 122 That's what I said more'n two year ago, when Rosie Branham was a-layin' up thar at Dave Hall's, white an' mos' dead. **1926** Hunnicutt *Twenty Years* 63 I knew a bear from there most always went to Rock Creek. **1931** Stuart *Yarb Doctor* 4 "How-do-ye-do, young man, and who may ye be?" came the instant reply, and "Ain't ye most lost in these here parts?" **1958** GSMNP-110:18 They could handle most any kind of a log. **1960** McCaulley *Cades Cove* We had most everything to eat. **1963** Edwards *Gravel* 16 Pa killed a rattler most a mile long out on the mining camp road. **1965** Hall Coll (Cataloochee NC) Everybody most would drink in that day. **1969** GSMNP-42:30 Well, I can tell you, most all of us took a piece of cornbread and a piece of meat for dinner to school. **1973** GSMNP-74:6 I'd help him do everything most. *Ibid.* 42 I could learn anything I wanted to most. *Ibid.* 43 I carried all the water most. **1979** *Big South Fork OHP-1* He raised tomatoes and anything most you could raise in a garden. **1987** Wear *Sevierville* 101 Most all foods were grown at home and prepared for use. **1997** GSMNPCOHP-3:13 Most everybody farmed.

[shortened form of *almost*]

2 Used in double superlatives. See also **mostest**. See also Grammar and Syntax §3.4.

1864 *Hancock CW Letters* (Aug 9) on reachin her I found this to Bee won of the most nises plases that I ever seen in aul of my lif. **1916** Combs *Old Early English* 284 That Boatright woman is the most knittin'est person I've ever seen. **1939** Hall Coll (Emerts Cove TN) Newport, though, is one of the most liveliest towns that I know of. **1940** Haun *Hawk's Done* 41 That is the most coolest spot a body can find in the summertime. **1973** Foster *Walker Valley* 9:46 Doc was the most wealthiest man [in] this part of the country for to buy at that time. **1989** *Matewan OHP-18* The chestnut was . . . one of the most valuablest trees we had in the forest. *Ibid.* 45 Matewan was one of the, one of the most boomingest, you know, the most prosperous towns there was in the country whenever I was growing up.

most all (also *most all of it*) *adjective phrase* Coreferent with the subject of the clause but having syntactic position within the predicate.

1955 Ritchie *Singing Family* 194 The last skimmin'll be most all of it pure molasses. **2003** Carter *Mt Home* 183 'Course, we usually most all had cold 'tater biscuits in our dinner pokes.

mostest *adjective* Most. See also **most C2**.

1937 Wilson *Folklore SE KY* 32. **1974** Fink *Bits Mt Speech* 16 Who growed the mostest corn? **1988** Smith *Fair and Tender* 15 She takes after Daddy the mostest. **2017** *Blind Pig* (Oct 27) [I] don't hear "mostest" anymore . . . Only when the Grandchildren were little. "That is the 'mostest' presents I ever got for my birthday."

most generally *adverb phrase* Usually.

1834 Crockett *Narrative* 50 I most generally carried her with me wherever I went. **1957** Combs *Lg Sthn High: Word List* 65 = usually. Ex.: "I most gin'rally allers takes a dram o' mornin's." **c1975** Lunsford *It Used to Be* 38 Someone there, most generally a woman, with what they call a strainer, dips out the impurities that have boiled up [from the pot of molasses]. She skims that, and that's called "skimmings." It's put off on the side. First, it's very green, but she keeps doing that until, after a while, it's all golden color and sweet as honey.

mostly *adverb*

A Variant syntactic placement after the form or phrase modified.

1927 Furman *Lonesome Road* 29 [She] tended us day and night and the cooking and cleaning too, mostly. **1975** *AOHP/ALC-961* We went and started a contract. Everybody mostly got familiar with it unless it was some fellow that don't know how to read. **1978** Burton *Ballad Folks* 42 I don't have any plans or whatsoever for the future because I feel like it's all in the past mostly. **1983** *Dark Corner OHP-27A* They make them [= moonshine stills] out of anything mostly. **1996** GSMNPCOHP-1:2 They'd set fires every fall mostly.

B Senses.

1 Usually. See also **most times.**

1931–33 (in **1987** Oliver and Oliver *Sketches* 33) Pine knots was mostly the light to work by. **1969** GSMNP-37:2:1 Mostly McHans teached this school. **1989** *Matewan OHP-1* All of the shooting took place mostly right there. **1997** GSMNPCOHP-3:13 She was one who mostly [delivered the babies].

2 Nearly, almost.

1895 Dromgoole *Fiddling to Fame* 50 Sometimes he'd say which beat in argufyin', but he mostly allus went with Alf. **1973** Kahn *Hillbilly Women* 205 Mostly everybody in Glenco Hollow's related to each other. **1983** *Dark Corner OHP-13A* Mostly everything else we raised it ourselves. **2004** Johnson *Camp Memories* 24 Mostly all the miners had wives and kids.

[EDD *mostly* adv 3 "nearly" Scot, Irel; DARE *mostly* adv chiefly South, South Midland]

most times *adverb phrase* Usually, most often. See also **mostly B1.**

1955 Parris *Roaming Mts* 17 Most times after a gander-pull there was a box-supper. A feller who had won the gander-pull was fresh meat for the losers. They'd see to it that he had to bid way up to get his girl's box. **1973** Foster *Walker Valley* 9:12 Most times the skidder buck would run down there to see what happened. **1981** Roth *Greenbrier Early Days* 11 Most times, the mountaineer married very young, and most of them had very large families, 10 or 12 children. **2009** Ebel and Hicks *Jack Tales* 27 Most times when we wanted to have fun, we had to make do ourselves. **2013** Shedlarz *Rosa Hicks* 4 Most times she did try to have a stack cake.

[DARE *most time(s)* adv phr especially South, Midland]

mother *noun* See citation.

1958 Combs *Archaic English in KY* 40 = an old woman: "I'm pleased to meet you, Mother."

mother-baby *noun* See citation.

1944 Hayes *Word-List NC* 35 = a boy or a man who is unhappy away from home.

Mother Hubbard dress *noun* See 1967 citation.

1939 Hall *Coll* (Copeland Creek TN) [The White Caps] all had on masks and uniforms, you know, made out of black cloth, just like Mother Hubbard dresses. **1956** Hall *Coll* (Cosby TN) I went after the granny woman for his wife.... She had a old big Mother Hubbard dress. **1967** *DARE Survey* (Gatlinburg TN) = a loose full house dress that ties at the waist.

Mother in Israel *noun* An older, especially devout woman in a **Primitive Baptist** church.

1995 Patterson *Sound of Dove* 73–74 I'd rather have an old mother in Israel praying for me than anything else in this world, I'll tell you that, brother. **2014** Montgomery *Doctrine* 149 = a female member of the church that acts as a mother figure. She may not have biological children of her own but due to her wonderful personality, wisdom and giving of herself, she serves as a beloved example and nurturing figure in the lives of many.

mother wit *noun* Common sense.

1861 *Kendrick CW Letters* (Oct 31) your good mother wit teaches you that we must be supperated. **1977** *Jake Waldroop* 175 To make a wise man, first thing he's got to have, we always call it the mother wit. **1988** Lincoln *Avenue* 260 The coo-koo is not a bird of principle. He ain't got no mother wit.... He's just a low-down opportunist.

[DARE *mother wit* n chiefly South, South Midland]

mother woman *noun* A mother.

1943 Hannum *Mt People* 147 Shapes of phrases repeat themselves and the same sounds re-echo, giving, oddly enough, vividness rather than monotony—as in their use of double words: "down-log; sulphur-match; man-person; flower-thing; mother-woman; storm of rain; tooth-dentist; neighbor-people; ocean-sea; ham-meat; cookin'-pan; belly-empty; biscuit-bread; rifle-gun; ridin'-critter; cow-brute; preacher-man; granny-woman; we-uns; chanty-song."

[redundant form]

motor *noun* See citation.

2006 *WV Encycl* 151 Underground mechanization first centered on haulage and undercutting. By the early 1900s, trolley-operated locomotives (often called "motors" by miners) replaced animal power for main-line haulage.

mought See **may A**, **mighty**.

mought could See **may B3**.

moughty See **mighty**.

mountain *noun*

A Variant form *mounting*.

1855 (in **1956** Eliason *Tarheel Talk* 314) (Burke Co NC) *mounting*. **1860** Olmsted *Back Country* 257 I 'low that hoss was raised in the mountings. **1862** *Neves CW Letters* (Aug 6) I wish you was here this morning to hunt my sheep for they have all taken to the mountings. **1862** *Poe Family Papers* (July 27) i hav Sen meny thing Snce i lef mobile i rid thru a monting on the car hit wos So dark i cod not se mi hand bi fore me. **1873** Smith *Arp Peace Papers* 82 The mountng seenry in this romantik kountry was grand. **1883** Zeigler and Grosscup *Heart of Alleghanies* 51 "What I don't know about these mountings," said he, directing his keen blue eyes upon one member of the group, "haint of enny profit to man or devil." *Ibid.* 109 The quaint pronunciation of "mounting" for mountain might better be used, in this connection, to convey an exact but wider meaning. **1886** Smith *Sthn Dialect* 349 Furthermore, *mounting* is heard in North Carolina, but not in East Tennessee. **1924** (in **1952** Mathes *Tall Tales* 34) We're pore folks an' hain't got nothin' much, but if ye ever git out in them mountings yander we'd be real proud fer ye to drap in. **1942** Hall *Phonetics Smoky Mts* 49. **1998** Montgomery *Coll* (known to Ledford).

[DARE *mountain* n chiefly South, South Midland]

B The main ridge of the Smoky Mountains along the TN/NC state border. Same as **(the) Smoky**. See also **Big Smokies**.

1969 GSMNP-25:2:24 I don't know whether people killed them out or what happened to them but . . . a bear was just as scarce. They just wasn't any till maybe, we'll say four, five year before the park bought the land they begin to see . . . bear tracks back in the mountain.

C In phrases *down the mountain, on the mountain, up the mountain*, etc. See also **(the) Smoky**.

1859 Taliaferro *Fisher's River* 56 I jumped forty feet down the mountain, and dashed behind a big white oak five foot in diameter. **1939** Hall *Coll* (Deep Creek NC) I got on up the mountain, nearly out of hearing from him. *Ibid.* (Smokemont NC) We shot [the coon] off, come on about a half a mile or three quarter, and dogs struck [and] down the mountain they went. *Ibid.* (Sugarlands TN) I'm going to talk a little more about that bear hunt that I took on the mountain up there when I killed that bear.

mountain balsam *noun* The Fraser fir (*Abies fraseri*). Same as **balsam 1**.

1908 Britton *N Amer Trees* 76 (DARE) This southern fir, called . . . Mountain balsam . . . occurs in the higher mountains of Virginia and West Virginia to North Carolina and Tennessee, where it sometimes forms forests, and reaches a maximum height of 25 meters. **1937** Thornburgh *Great Smoky Mts* 132 "Us mountain people," he explained, "call the spruce the 'he-balsam' and the mountain balsam we call 'she-balsam.'"

[DARE *mountain balsam* n 2 southern Appalachians]

mountain banana *noun* The pawpaw tree (*Asimina* spp) or its fruit.

1978 Parris *Mt Cooking* 238 The first reference to this curious fruit [= the pawpaw], which some folks call "mountain banana," occurs in the chronicles of DeSoto's expedition in America. **1997** Brown *Listening* "The mountaineers broke up the twig of the bush to make tea," he says, pulling at the limb of a pawpaw tree. "It was called mountain banana because of its fruit, which looked much like a banana. Pawpaws were used to make bread and pudding."

mountain boomer *noun*

1 A small red squirrel (*Tamiasciurus hudsonicus*), known for its noisy chattering and loud call. See 1971 citation. Same as **boomer 1**.

1859 Colton *Mt Scenery* 100 There is upon all the mountains, a little squirrel, in size between the gray and the ground squirrel, called, by the inhabitants, "mountain boomer." . . . They are a pretty animal, of a light red color, the under portion of the body very white. **1883** Zeigler and Grosscup *Heart of Alleghanies* 255 The blue-jay screamed through the forest, and around the boles of the trees and along the branches, squirrels, known as mountain boomers, chased each other, halting in their scampers to look down on the disturber of the solitude. **1913** Kephart *Our Sthn High* 87 Out of a tree overhead hopped a mountain "boomer" (red squirrel), and down he came, eyed me, and stopped. **1913** Morley *Carolina Mts* 84 The shy little red squirrel who hides in the depths of the woods is known as the "mountain boomer," a name also derisively applied to the mountaineer by his low-country neighbors. **1924** Abernethy *Moonshine* 14 A small red squirrel—called "mountain boomer" by the natives—bit off a twig overhead and threw it, as if in challenge, at their feet. **1971** Linzey and Linzey *Mammals of Smoky* 28 The Red Squirrel may be regarded as common to abundant in the Park. Locally known as "mountain boomer," this species reaches the southern limit of its range in northern Georgia. These squirrels are uniformly reddish, being paler on the back in winter and having a black line along the side in the summer. **1986 Petersen et al.** *LAGS* (Cocke Co TN, Sevier Co TN). **1977** Hamilton *Mt Memories* 77 The "mountain boomer" was a reddish colored squirrel and not considered good to eat. It made a booming sort of call, different from the one of the gray squirrel. Papa took aim first and missed. The boomer jumped from limb to limb booming angrily. Mama waited till he settled for a moment and then she brought him down.

[DARE *mountain boomer* n 1 chiefly South Midland]

2 By extension = used as a pejorative term for a native or resident of mountain woods (used in both self-reference and other-reference). See also **boomer 2**, **mountain hoosier B**. [Editor's note: This usage was not observed by Joseph Hall in the Smoky Mountains, having apparently been replaced in the Smoky Mountains by the less derogatory **mountain hoosier** by the late 1930s.]

1859 Taliaferro *Fisher's River* 33 A mountain "boomer," dressed in a linsey hunting-shirt down to his knees, with a leather band round his waist, a tow and cotton shirt, buckskin pants, with a few other things of minor importance, made up the uniform, the surplice and gown, of the Rev. Mr. Bellow. **1892** Doak *Wagonauts Abroad* 145 At last a "mountain boomer," who lived nigh where we expected to camp, would sell us oats, but no corn. **1904–20** Kephart *Notebooks* 4:763 In the same spirit, the man who rejects the appellation of "mountaineer," or something vaguely derogative that the "furriners" have invented, will call himself a "hillbilly" or a "mountain boomer." **1913** Kephart *Our Sthn High* 206–7 They call themselves mountain people, or citizens; sometimes humorously "mountain boomers," the word boomer being their name for the common red squirrel which is found here only in the upper zones of the mountains [see **1913** in **1**]. **1934–47** *LAMSAS Appal* (Swain Co NC). **1952** Wilson *Folk Speech NC* 567 = a mountaineer. **1962** Dykeman *Tall Woman* 75 Don't take Lydia and the baby and yourself up there to become mountain boomers. **1986** Pederson et al. *LAGS* = attested by 7/60 interviewees (11.7%) from E TN; 7/7 of all LAGS interviewees (100%) attesting term were from Appalachia; (Sullivan Co TN) = a hermit.

[DARE *mountain boomer* n 5 chiefly southern Appalachians]

mountain bugbane *noun* A perennial wild shrub (*Cimicifuga americana/racemosa*) whose roots and rhizomes have medicinal uses. See also **black cohosh**.

1997 Montgomery *Coll* (known to Cardwell).

mountain bump *noun* A violent shifting of the wall, ceiling, or floor in a coal mine. Same as **bump B1**.

c1987 (in **2015** Yarrow *Voices* 17) [In coal mining] a mountain bump is rock breaking two or three hundred feet above you. **2006** Hicks *Mt Legacy* 145 The safety timbers were meant to hold the mine's top until the temporarily until the pillars could be extracted. Often there were sounds of an occasional explosion in a distance. I knew this sound was called a mountain bump, and it was coming from the skeletoned ribs of the honeycombed coal left behind in the mined-out pillars. These thin ribs of coal were exploding under the extreme pressure from the mountain above as gravity was pulling it down.

mountain corn *noun* Homemade corn whiskey.

1964 Stubbs *Mountain-Wise* (Aug–Sept) 8 We took a jug of mountain corn into one of these high coves. Then we started a-tellin' stories, one by one, and each feller was a bigger liar than the last one.

mountain cur *noun* See citation.

1996 Spurlock *Glossary* 395 = a hunting dog of mixed breed.

mountain dew *noun* Homemade whiskey.

1843 (in **1974** Harris *High Times* 20) The sport seldom stops at the close of a race at the Stock Creek Paths: and on this occasion the choice "mountain dew" circulated as free as water. **1881** Atkinson *After Moonshiners* 25 Taking with him the town marshal, as an assistant, [the sheriff] proceeded to the place where the Tennesseans were dealing out their "mountain dew," and informed them that he was a revenue officer and that he now attached their teams, wagons and liquors. **1901** McClintock *KY Mts* 8 A member of the Baker faction in Clay county [KY] is said to have declared that three drinks of "mountain dew" cause, on the average, one fight. **1913** Kephart *Our Sthn High* 135 The maker of "mountain dew" has no other instrument than a small vial, and his testing is done entirely by the "bead" of the liquor, the little iridescent bubbles that rise when the vial is tilted. **1913** Morley *Carolina Mts* 66 For corn is not only the principal food of the mountaineer, but supplies as well that important beverage, variously known as "corn-juice," "moonshine," "mountain-dew," "blockade," "brush whiskey," and in the outer world, "corn-whiskey," which is extracted from the grain and surreptitiously distributed. **1941** Hall *Coll* (Del Rio TN)

All the boys said to tell you hello for them, to think of them when you was drinking that good old mountain dew. **1962** Williams *Metaphor Mt Speech I* 12 "White mule" will make "a rabbit twist a rattlesnake's tail" and "a tomcat spit in a bulldog's eye," but good "mountain dew," the kind made by expert hands and aged in a charred white oak keg, will make "a preacher lay his Bible down," "a man wink at his mother-in-law," and "the lamb and the lion lay down together." **1966–67** *DARE Survey* (Spruce Pine NC, Gatlinburg TN) = any kind of liquor; (Gatlinburg TN) = illegally made whiskey. **c1970** Handlon *Ol' Smoky* 8 You know, mountain people don't call liquor moonshine. They name it mountain dew or white mule. **1982** Maples *Memories* 72 When the moonshiner heard the shotgun beller somewhere on a mountainside or in a holler, he knew it was time to get his running legs, or to try to hide some of his mountain dew or some of his still before the sheriff got there. **1986** Pederson et al. *LAGS* = attested by 1/60 interviewees (1.7%) from E TN and 5/35 (14.3%) from N GA; 6/21 of all LAGS interviewees (28.7%) were from Appalachia; (Rhea Co TN) = general term, (Bartow Co GA) = lower-quality concoction.

[*DARE* *mountain dew* n scattered, but more frequent South, South Midland]

mountain doctor *noun* See citation.

1999 Montgomery *Coll* = midwife (Brown).

mountain dulcimer (also *mountain zither*) *noun* A musical instrument with three or four wire strings across a fretted soundbox, held in the lap by the musician, who plucks or strums the strings. [Editor's note: Consultants from the Smoky Mountains agree that the instrument was not traditional in the area, with most of them first seeing one only in the 1960s.] Also called **Appalachian dulcimer**, **hog fiddle**, **Kentucky dulcimer**.

1975 Dwyer *Thangs* 33 In various sections of the blue ridge country, the dulcimer is known by different names such as "hog fiddle"—"mountain zither" and "dulcimore." **1975** *Foxfire III* 188 There is no standard-sized or -shaped dulcimer. Every maker has the one he likes best. I use the same general pattern and vary the type of wood, or number of strings. Kentucky, Mountain, and Appalachian are all names for the plucked dulcimer, which may have any number of strings. Mountain people call them "dulcymores" or "delcymores." **2006** *Encycl Appalachia* 1145 The fretted dulcimer has long been associated with southern and central Appalachia to the extent that it has variously been referred to as the mountain, Appalachian, or Kentucky dulcimer. The instrument has also been called the plucked dulcimer to distinguish it from the hammered dulcimer, a trapezoidal instrument with a greater number of strings.

mountain dynamite *noun* Homemade whiskey.

1990 Merriman *Moonshine Rendezvous* 50 Since I didn't have the refrigerator crate put back on the truck yet, I had to come up with some way to camouflage the "mountain dine-o-mite."

mountaineer *noun* A native of the mountains (usually a neutral term, often used by mountain people in self-reference). See 1984 citation. See also **highlander**, **hillbetsy**, **hillbilly**, **hill william**, **mountain boomer 2**, **mountain hoosier B**, **mountain william**.

1862 Hynds *CW Letters* (May 27) We have been, it seems to me, in every nook and corner in these mountains hunting up those interesting aids to Old Abes army styled "Home Guards" These pious and patriotic soldiers are composed of ignorant mountaineers who are too lazy to run and consequently unfit to serve Old Abe in the regular army. **1862** Neves *CW Letters* (Jan 9) we have a companey up her that cauls them Selves the Dark corner mountainyears. **1910** Cooke *Power and Glory* 98 The ineradicable dignity of the true mountaineer, who has always been as good as the best in his environment, preserved Johnnie from any embarrassment, any tendency to shrink or cringe. **1936** Maupin *Pittman Center* 4 Along these small streams in the narrow valleys and on the sides of the foothills live a number of families commonly called mountaineers, a people who, as a rule, are very poor, but sensitive and proud, and who find it almost impossible to earn a living outside their mountain homes. **1937** Conner *Ms* 8 those mountaineer's [sic] could feed, and bed a fellow nice, most any time. **1954** *Waynesville Mtneer* Aug 2 Ancient Muzzleloaders Cocked and Primed for Cataloochee Beef Shoot [headline] . . . immediate target a piece of charred wood, and their ultimate goal a quarter of beef. The shoot is open to "mountaineers" and "furriners" alike, but the "shooting-iron" must be a long-barrelled muzzleloader. **1957** GSMNP-23:2:7 I'm really not a hillbilly, but I'm a native, a mountaineer. I've been here all my life, and I'm proud of it, certainly am proud of it. They just got that name up there, the hillbilly there. They call lots of those folks hillbillies because they was raised up here. **1984** Dykeman and Stokely *At Home* 73 Used to denote the proud individualism that characterized many of the stalwart men and women whose roots held deep and fast in this isolated place, "mountaineer" was a strong, acceptable name. But turned into some catchword for some picturesque, inadequate character who divided his time between the homemade dulcimer and the home-run distillery, "mountaineer" was suspect [to denote a native of the mountains]. **1986** Pederson et al. *LAGS* = attested by 10/60 interviewees (16.7%) from E TN and 3/35 (8.6%) from N GA; 13/44 of all LAGS interviewees attesting term (29.5%) were from Appalachia. **1989** *Matewan OHP-1* Matewan was fortified, and those mountaineers didn't take it easy, they didn't take no for an answer. **1997** King *Mt Folks* 46 This is one woman who is proud of sharing her mountain heritage. She loves being called a mountaineer, but not a hillbilly. "Mountaineers work," she explains.

[*DARE* *mountaineer* n scattered, but chiefly southern Appalachians]

mountaineous See **mountainious**.

mountain feist *noun* A small, high-spirited dog, sometimes a bred one. See also **feist B**, **penny feist**, **treeing feist**.

2012 Jourdan *Medicine Men* 11 This feisty disposition is not just in humans either. The dog indigenous to the Southern Appalachians is called a Mountain Feist, a scrappy little cur considered ounce-for-ounce to be one of the most courageous dogs around.

mountain fever *noun* Same as **typhoid fever.**

1913 Morley *Carolina Mts* 163 Typhoid fever is another frequent visitant, though the "mountain fever," as it is here called, appears in a light form that seldom results fatally. **1940** Haun *Hawk's Done* 31 Right then I knowed what was wrong. "Hit is mountain fever," I said. Me and Amy made plenty of cherry bark tea. That is the first time I ever seen it fail to cure the fever.

mountain finger *noun* See citation.

1993 Stuart *Daughter* 233 *mountain fingers* = the separate subordinate ridges running up to the main ridge atop a mountain.

mountain grill *noun* A mountain rustic.

1929 Wolfe *Look Homeward* 49 (DARE) Would any of them give a starving beggar a crust of bread? By God, no! . . . 'Twas a bitter day for me when I first came into this accursed country . . . Mountain Grills! Mountain Grills! **c1950** (in **1987** Bruce *Wolfe Stories* 38) It was W. O. [i.e. Thomas Wolfe's father], after all, who originated the term "mountain grill" as a derogatory stereotype of his own creation. In later years, when Mrs. Wolfe was asked where her husband had obtained the phrase, she replied, "I guess he made it up . . . East Tennessee mountain grill . . . If he wanted to make anybody mad he would say, 'Nothing but a mountain grill.'" **1989** *DARE File* (wNC) A mountain grill was an uncouth, raw, ignorant, often ill-mannered boy or man. (I never heard it applied to girls or women.) I believe it was used only of people known as "poor whites."

mountain grouse (also *mountain pheasant*) *noun* The ruffed grouse (*Bonasa umbrellus*). Same as **pheasant.**

1967 *DARE Survey* (Jonesboro TN) = the same as a ruffed grouse. **1991** Thomas *Sthn Appal* 66 Another name for that pheasant was mount'n grouse. **1997** Montgomery *Coll* (known to Adams, Brown, Bush, Cardwell, Ledford, Weaver).

[DARE *mountain pheasant* n especially South, South Midland]

mountain hog *noun* Same as **razorback.**

1939 *FWP Guide TN* 502 The mountain, or razorback hog, that lives in the woods upon acorns and roots, becomes comparatively fat in the late fall, when it is hunted and shot by the owner. **1986** Pederson et al. *LAGS* (Banks Co GA).

mountain holly *noun* A deciduous holly bush (*Ilex montana*). Also called **mountain winterberry.**

1943 Peattie *Men Mt Trees* 161 The two dominant species [= Fraser fir and spruce] may occur in pure stands, but a few deciduous trees are frequently found with them. Such are fire cherry, yellow birch, and serviceberry, mountain holly, beech, rowanberry, striped maple, and mountain maple. **1997** Montgomery *Coll* (known to Cardwell).

mountain hoosier *noun* A native of the mountains, especially a rustic one. [Editor's note: In Joseph Hall's research in the Smoky Mountains in the late 1930s, mountain people often used this term to refer to themselves familiarly or jokingly. It apparently supplanted **mountain boomer 2.** See also **hoosier.** For variant forms of this term, see **hoosier A.**] See also **highlander, hillbetsy, hill william, mountain boomer 2, mountaineer, mountain william.**

1924 Bacheller *Happiest Person* 7 He weren't purty—just a big mount'in huger. But my! I did love him. **1934–47** *LAMSAS Appal* (Madison Co NC, Swain Co NC). **1937** Hall *Coll* (Wears Cove TN) Mountaineers were once called mountain hoosiers. **1949** McDavid *Grist* 111 (Rabun Co GA) *mountain hoojers* = mountain rustics. **1957** *GSMNP*-23:2:20 He was a great mountain hoosier. **1968** *DARE Survey* (Brasstown NC). **1978** Hall *Yarns and Tales* 19 No longer is Gatlinburg, Tennessee, a town of "wood hicks" and "mountain hoosiers." **1986** Pederson et al. *LAGS* = attested by 18/60 interviewees (30%) from E TN and 7/35 (20%) from N GA; 25/32 of all LAGS interviewees (78.1%) attesting term were from Appalachia. **1999** Morgan *Gap Creek* 189 "All boys act like mountain hoojers when they're young," I said and laughed. **2007** McMillon *Notes* = anyone from the mountains.

mountain huger See **mountain hoosier.**

mountainious (also *mountaineous*) *adjective* Mountainous.

1915 Dingus *Word-List VA* 185 *mountainious*. **1957** Wise *Mt Speech* 305 [i] is inserted before *ous*, as in . . . *mountaineous* for *mountainous*. **1975** Montgomery *File*.

mountain ivy *noun* Same as **ivy 1.** See also **mountain laurel.**

1894 Wingfield *Big Buck* 400 It was getting dark and I began to fear lest the deer would make a plunge into the thick mountain ivy and get away from me. **1949** Arnow *Hunter's Horn* 356 The ewes, fat as they were, wouldn't poison themselves eating mountain ivy bush for a day or two. **1961** Douglas *My Wilderness* 175 Mountain people call laurel (whose regional name is ivy) the calico bush or mountain ivy. **1964** Reynolds *Born of Mts* 18 Mooney wrote of laurel as in two varieties, large and small (Rhododendron and Kalmia, or ivy), so the natives seem to know whereof they speak, but such interchange of names is all very confusing to the nonresident who is familiar with rhododendron as such and easily distinguishes it from laurel, but doesn't know what Kalmia, or mountain ivy, is. **1984** Gibson *Remembering* 14 The younger calves would sometimes eat what now is called laurel, but we knew it as mountain ivy.

[DARE *mountain ivy* n chiefly southern Appalachians, especially VA]

mountain laurel *noun* *Kalmia latifolia*, a book term for the plant usually known as **ivy** or **mountain ivy** in the region. See also **ivy 1.**

1943 Erskine *Adventures* 242 On your right the high peaks of the Pisgah National Forest keep tempting you to turn aside to see the famous "pink beds" of mountain laurel. **1982** Stupka *Wildflowers* 80 Usually the attractive pink or white-saucered flowers are so abundant that the mountain laurel in full bloom is one of our most spectacular plants. It flowers in May and June, the later blossoms ordinarily occurring on plants growing in the higher altitudes. "Ivy" and "calico-bush" are among its other names. **1992** Toops *Great Smoky Mts* 41 Although most of the trail traversed boreal forest, one section dropped into a heath bald or laurel "slick." Whoever coined the latter term was obviously looking from a distance! These areas contain head-high mountain laurels and nightmarish tangles of contorted rhododendron shrubs.

mountain lettuce *noun* Same as **bear lettuce.**

1954 *DARE File* Up on top of [Mount Mitchell] you will find Minnie bush (sometimes called he-honeysuckle), balsam trees (sometimes called she-balsams), mountain lettuce, St. John's wort, and the grave of the Rev. Elisha Mitchell, D.D. **1995** Elliott *Wild Roots* 20 The leaves are called mountain lettuce in some parts of the Appalachians and are eaten either in a salad or cooked as a potherb. **1998** Montgomery *Coll* (known to Brown, Cardwell, Norris).

[DARE *mountain lettuce* n chiefly Appalachians]

mountain lope *noun* A striding gait.

1929 (in **1995** Williams *Become Teacher* 66) As soon as I was out of site of people at Blaine, I stopped, changed from the new shoes to the old ones in my grip, rolled up the legs of my pants so I would not get mud on them, and struck the "mountain lope" for Caines Creek. **1992** Farwell *Stonewall* 22 He had all that he could do to prove that he had "an improvable mind" to endure the hazing (called devilment) by upperclassmen during "beast barracks," and to sustain the endless drilling, in which he was taught to stand straight and in which his loose mountain lope was changed forever to a stiff military gait.

mountain magnolia *noun* A large deciduous tree (*Magnolia* spp). See also **cucumber tree, Indian bitter 2, umbrella tree, wahoo 2, yellow linn.**

1937 Thornburgh *Great Smoky Mts* 20 The fragrant blossoms of the honey locust, the mountain magnolia or cucumber tree. **2011** *Smoky Mt Times* (June 1) Fraser's magnolia is named for the Scottish plant hunter, John Fraser, who also discovered Fraser fir and purple rhododendron. It is an upland tree that rarely strays out of the highlands region and is therefore also called the "mountain magnolia." It produces fruit from late July into early September. Magnolia cones are attractive scarlet to rust-brown aggregates composed of numerous pod or pocket-like follicles, each containing one or two crimson seeds the color of nail polish. When the cones reach the stage whereby seeds are ejected from the fruit pockets, a curious scenario ensues.

mountain mineral water *noun* Illicit homemade whiskey.

1972 Carr *Oldest Profession* 60 Would ye like to take some mountain mineral water back home to yur ailin' grandpappy?

mountain mint (also *mountain mist mint*) *noun* A perennial plant (*Pycnanthemum* spp) used as a spice and as a home remedy. See also **horsemint.**

1963 Lord *Blue Ridge Guide* 8D August is also bloom time for the southern mountain mint and ox eye. **1982** Stupka *Wildflowers* 100 Also called "horse-mint" and "basil," mountain-mint flowers on hillsides and in fields from July to October. **1997** Brown *Listening* The mountain mist mint was used in a salve. Mints were called self-healers or cure-alls, Cardwell says. **2006** Howell *Medicinal Plants* 115 The Cherokee used infusions of mountain mint to treat colds, fevers, stomach upsets, and as a penis wash to relieve inflammation. A poultice of fresh leaves was applied to the head to relieve headaches. Mountain mint has a long history of use as a folk remedy. The infusion was used to relieve indigestion, fevers, and as an inhalation for chest colds. There is also some evidence that it was a common home remedy used to bring on delayed menses.

mountain mist mint See **mountain mint.**

mountain oak (also *mountain rock oak*) *noun* Any of various oaks (especially *Quercus montana*) that grow at higher elevations of the mountains.

1913 Kephart *Our Sthn High* 54 Ascending above the zone of 3,000 feet, white oak is replaced by the no less valuable "mountain oak." **1939** Hall *Coll* (Deep Creek NC) Finally [the turkey] got up in about a hundred yards of me and stretched up, stopped right about a big mountain oak tree. My ball went into this tree and I killed him. **c1975** Lunsford *It Used to Be* 68 During that period, in all this mountain country, many a mountain rock oak,—and possibly a Spanish oak, or anything that would furnish the odd bark for tanning purposes—was fallen, and, of course, at that time there was no way of getting anything special out of the old trees. **1994** Montgomery *Coll*: *mountain oak, mountain rock oak* (known to Cardwell).

mountain orange juice *noun* Homemade whiskey, presumably mixed with orange juice.

1974 Dabney *Mt Spirits* 23 A drink famous in Rabun County, Georgia, is called "mountain orange juice," whose recipe was concocted by a one-time top state politician.

mountain oyster *noun* The testicle of a bear, bull, hog, or ram prepared as food.

1944 Combs *Word-List Sthn High* 19 = testicles of the boar, the bull (or the sheep), whenever the highland gourmet partakes of these delicacies at the table. **1976** Garber *Mountain-ese* 59 Uncle Joe served a big bait uv his famous mountain oysters today. **1982** Slone *How We Talked* 119 When hogs were "trimmed," . . . crushed tomato leaves or elderberry tree leaves were used to keep flies away and to stop the bleeding. Some people ate this part that was cut from the hog. It was called "mountain oysters" or "hog's nuts." **1990** Whitener *Thrice-Told* 79 Try dropping the term in a mixed gathering sometime and you'll see what I mean. Womenfolk will usually drop their eyes as if they shouldn't be a part of the conversation and men will grin and attempt to appear knowledgeable when most of them wouldn't know a mountain oyster from a sweetbread. **1995** Montgomery *Coll* (known to Cardwell, Shields).

[DARE *mountain oyster* n chiefly South Midland, West]

mountain pheasant See **mountain grouse.**

mountain rock oak See **mountain oak.**

mountain rosebay *noun* The **rosebay rhododendron** (*Rhododendron catawbiense*).

1901 Lounsberry *Sthn Wild Flowers* 379 *Mountain rose bay* grows on the highest summits of the mountains throughout its range, following the ridges. [**1908** Britton *N Amer Trees* 753 This evergreen shrub, sometimes becomes a small tree, and is also called Catawba Rhododendron and Carolina Rhododendron. It occurs mostly on mountain sides and summits, from Virginia and West Virginia to Georgia and Alabama, attaining a maximum height of 6 meters.] **1941** Walker *Story of Mt* 48 The most beautiful, perhaps, is rhododendron, known as mountain rose bay.

mountain sallet *noun* Wild angelica.

1978 Parris *Mt Cooking* 110 Wild-growing angelica, sometimes referred to as "mountain sallet," is a favorite dish of the Cherokee Indians.... Parboiled and then fried in grease, it's good with bean bread or cornbread. *Ibid.* 111 She heads for Big Cove and the high hills of Gilmore Branch to search out "mountain sallet." "Most of what I gather goes into cans," she said. "... Now I'm putting up angelica for next winter. It's mighty good to eat when the weather gets cold and you get a taste for greens."

mountain screamer *noun* The cougar, a large wild cat with a tawny coat. See also **panther**.

2002 Myers *Best Yet Stories* 154 Also known as mountain screamers or Indian devils, [the panther] preys on deer, elk, mice and squirrels, even grasshoppers. It can see in the dark, swim, and climb trees. It can fall 50 feet and land on its feet unharmed. It can execute a 25 foot leap from a dead stop.

mountain shamrock (also *mountain sorrel*) *noun* The wood sorrel wildflower (*Oxalis montana*). See also **alleluia**, **sheep sorrel**, **wood shamrock**.

1962 Brewer *Hiking* 29 A low-growing flower you'll see under thick stands of spruce and fir is mountain sorrel (Oxalis montana). *Ibid.* 54 Moss, ferns and wood sorrel, sometimes called mountain shamrock, carpet the ground.

mountain song *noun* A traditional or Child ballad. See also **ballad B1**, **devil's ditty**, **love ballad**, **song-ballad**.

1969 *Burton-Manning Coll*-89B Love songs or mountain songs is what we always called them.

mountain sorrel See **mountain shamrock**.

mountain spurge *noun* See citation.

1941 Walker *Story of Mt* 52 Pachysandra, or mountain spurge blooms in March and April in the rich soil in Lookout Mountain woods. Its spike of white flowers springs from the base standing up from ovate leaves 2 to 4 inches long.

mountain sumach *noun* The mountain ash tree (*Sorbus americana*), whose berries have medicinal uses.

1860 Curtis *Plants NC* 70 Mountain Ash ... is not very rare on our higher Mountains ... where it is called ... Mountain Sumach. The foliage is more like that of a Sumach than of any other of our trees. **1971** Krochmal et al. *Medicinal Plants Appal* 238 Mountain sumach ... The berries have been used to treat scurvy and as a vermifuge.

mountain tea *noun* The teaberry, a low evergreen shrub (*Gaultheria procumbens*) that produces bright berries in the fall and winter; a beverage made from the shrub. Its oil is used as a beverage flavoring (as to reduce the bitterness of a medicinal tea) or as a medicine. Also called **checkerberry**, **wintergreen**.

1892 Allen *Cumberland Gap* 258 Another beverage is "mountain tea," which is made from the sweet-scented golden-rod and from winter-green—the New England checkerberry. These decoctions they mollify with home-made sorghum molasses ... or with sugar. **1962** Brewer *Hiking* 24 You usually will find wintergreen, sometimes called mountain tea, in this type of woodland. **1970** Campbell et al. *Smoky Mt Wildflowers* 80 Before the days of synthetics, this plant was the source of wintergreen (or teaberry) flavor. Other common names [of the teaberry] are checkerberry, wintergreen, and mountain tea. **1979** Slone *My Heart* 115 There was also a small, thick-leafed plant with red berries that grew close to the ground on the tops of hills, which we called "mountain tea." We gathered and chewed the leaves and ate the berries. **1982** Ginns *Snowbird Gravy* 113 He stealed this here teaberry, which we call mountain tea. **1985** Irwin *Alex Stewart* 199 Once in a while we'd make mountain tea, but it wasn't too good. It'll thin your blood. **2005** Ebel *Orville Hicks* Sometimes Mama would bring us young'uns something from the mountain—a turtle or a little rabbit. Sometimes she brought us mountain tea [i.e., teaberry or wintergreen] to chew on. **2008** *Rosie Hicks* 1 Dorsie would kindly, you know, watch us and everything till Mama come back from pulling, I guess, mountain tea.

mountain teapot *noun* A type of **still** for making illegal whiskey. Same as **copper pot**.

1972 Carr *Oldest Profession* 183 Such a small unit could be used on a kitchen stove or in the mountains. Small stills such as this one, when used in the mountains, are called "mountain teapots." They are normally used for the needs of one or just a few families.

mountain trots *noun* Overactive kidneys or bowels.

1997 Montgomery *Coll* (known to Brown, Cardwell), = diarrhea from eating spring herbs and ramps (Andrews).

[DARE *mountain trots* n pl especially TN]

mountain water *noun* Homemade whiskey.

1938 Stuart *Dark Hills* 364–65 Didn't Jason keep his barrel and dipper throughout the whiskey drouth for himself and his thirsty friends so that they might sip the fragrant mountain water unmolested by the Law?

mountain william *noun* A person from the mountains, used mockingly or pretentiously to contrast to **hillbilly**. See also **hillbilly**, **hill william**.

1994 Bluestein *Poplore* 159 Musicians often joke: "They used to call me hillbilly, but since I sold a million records, I'm known as Mountain William." **2000** Bailey *Price of Assimilation* 34 For 40 years, Carl and Phyllis Bailey accepted a definition of urban Appalachians that excluded them [after having migrated from West Virginia to Chicago]. . . . The Baileys carefully differentiated themselves while maintaining a defensive pride. . . . When called a hillbilly, Phyllis would respond, "If you want to call me that you better say I'm a Mountain William!" **2007** McMillon *Notes* = a high-class hillbilly.

mountain wind *noun* A loud, violent wind that works its way down from the main ridge of the Smoky Mountains and indicates a coming storm. Also called **Smoky mountain wind.**

1967 *DARE Survey* (Gatlinburg TN) = old timers say that the north and south wind sometimes fight, and if the north wind wins, it'd be called a mountain wind. **1999** Montgomery *Coll* = a wind that is furious, raging, and damaging, usually one preceding a rain that comes down a mountain (Cardwell).

mountain winterberry *noun* A deciduous holly bush (*Ilex montana*). Same as **mountain holly.**

1963 Lord *Blue Ridge Guide* 19D Clumps of blueberry, bush honeysuckle, Catawba rhododendron, mountain winterberry, mountain-laurel, and serviceberry spread among open areas of coarse grass, trailed here and there with ground pine and ground cedar.

mountain zither See **mountain dulcimer.**

mounting See **mountain A.**

mourn *verb*

1 To grieve over one's spiritual condition, as at a revival service.

1863 *Gilley CW Letters* (Aug 29) ever thing is low sprited an they is a great chan[ge] in the men they have gone to praying very hard we have meeting ever night an ever day they a heap morning an geting Religion.

2 See citation.

1957 Broaddus *Vocab Estill Co KY* 51 = to moo.

mourner *noun* A person who publicly grieves and repents at a religious service; one who seeks religious experience but has not yet **come through.** See also **mourners' bench.**

1860 *Week in Smokies* 124 After [one preacher at the revival] was through, another minister arose to "exhort" and "call up mourners." **1863** *Lister CW Letters* (Nov 28) we have had a veary good meating hear last weak and the first of this Peary hawkins was the Preacher I joind and was a bout 50 moners when the meating closd. **1863** *Tesh CW Letters* (Aug 24) there was several mounas beck gardone was a mornour tha[y] all joind the church. **1895** Edson and Fairchild *TN Mts* 371 Here's a mourner just come through, an' wants to give his experience before the church. **1901** Harben *Westerfelt* 267 The preacher ended his discourse, started a hymn, and commenced to "call up mourners." **1931** Goodrich *Mt Homespun* 56 When the mourners get to takin' on and the others go to shoutin', you can't hear nothin'. **1940** Haun *Hawk's Done* 96 She knelt down by the side of Linus and prayed. And the preacher called for mourners. "What is your sin," he said, "what is your sin?" **1969** GSMNP-37:2:18 They'd just call for mourners, and they'd go up there and confess and have baptizing. **1974** Bruce *Sang Hallelujah* 71 Mourners were those sinners who had become convicted and were "mourning" for the doom which appeared inevitable. They were also called "anxious" or "penitent," words which have about the same connotations.

[cf EDD *mourn* 1 "to moan, complain"; DARE *mourner* n chiefly South, South Midland]

mourners' bench (also *moaners' bench*) *noun* A bench, seat, or row of seats at the front of a religious service reserved for those who are concerned about their spiritual welfare or seeking repentance to sit or kneel, especially during a revival. Sometimes the seats face the congregation. Also called **anxious bench, mercy seat.** See also **come through.**

1891 Murfree *Stranger People* 207 Fee Guthrie who has failed to find salvation at the mourner's bench and who has promised his dying father to support his cruel stepmother. **1915** Dingus *Word-List VA* 186 = a bench near the altar where "mourners" may kneel. **1924** Abernethy *Moonshine* 121 Hardened sinners, trembling with terror, overran the rude "mourner's bench," and rolled on the floor. **c1945** Haun *Hawk's Done* 255 The preacher man showed me the mourner's bench and tried to push me down on it, but I didn't take the mourner's bench that night. **1963** Watkins and Watkins *Yesterday* 28 Finally the time came for the invitation hymn. The congregation sang "Just as I Am Without One Plea," and sinners were invited to come to the mourners' bench. Many came down the aisle, gave the preacher their hand, fell prostrate on the bench, and wept with loud cries of anguish. The singing continued, and Preacher Stephens pled with sinners between stanzas, sang the hymn, and chanted his pleas between phrases of the music. Brothers and Sisters fanned the mourners, patted them on the back, pled with them, and asked them to give up and to accept the Lord's forgiveness of their sins. After a time someone started singing, "Lord, I'm Coming Home." A mourner would jump to his feet and grab the Christian nearest to him. Sister Doss, Brother Mulkey, and old Aunt Marthy Scott shouted and praised the Lord; others moved through the congregation, pleading with the unsaved sinners to come to the bench. More sinners rose from the bench with beaming faces and loud praise for the Lord. The cries of the damned mingled with shouts of joy of the recently saved. **1970** Mull *Mt Yarns* 116 Each night Mary Anne would go to the mourners bench and pray for forgiveness to no avail, until finally she agreed to a public confession. **1975** Purkey *Madison Co* 47 Another memory that was to live forever in my mind was the sight of some of the old patriarchs of the settlement who came regularly to church and Sunday School carrying their well-worn Bibles with them. They sat in the "Amen" corner, near the pulpit, and close to the Mourner's Bench. They were the ones most often called upon to pray. And when they prayed, they got down on their knees beside the pine benches and prayed loud and long. **1982** *Smokies*

Heritage 31 Instead of altar call, the preacher would invite sinners up front to the "mourners bench" (usually two front benches reserved for that purpose). **1987** Davenport *Pine Grove* 39 Sinners seeking forgiveness for their sins and acceptance into the Christian brotherhood of the church had to present themselves to the mourners bench on the front pew. There the preacher and church members prayed, tugged and pleaded with them until the sinner confessed he had been converted. During this ordeal, stirring invitation hymns were being sung, and loud shouting frequently erupted when confessions were made. Today most churches recognize a shorter route to salvation which bypasses the mourners bench, while some still cling to the old ritual. **1999** Montgomery Coll: *moaners' bench* (known to Cardwell). **2005** Morgan *Old Time Religion* 36–37 The altar was also known as the "mourner's bench." Actually there were two mourner's benches. The girls used the front pew that faced the side of the pulpit in the front corner of the sanctuary, and the boys used the first bench at the front on one side. The people who went there sat on the seat, laid their arms and hands on the back of the bench, and placed their heads on their forearms. At other times, they knelt in front of the bench and positioned their arms and heads on the seat of the bench. At the momentous time when it seemed that all who wished to come to the altar had done so, one of the most beautiful scenarios in all Christendom unfolded. The old, gray-haired women of the church, with their long, silver tresses wound up in buns on the backs of their heads, who almost never said a word in the mixed, adult Sunday school classes and never said a word in business meetings, now rose from their seats and gathered in the area of the mourner's bench. Soon a few younger women joined them. Why had they gathered there? One by one these old saints of God who had traveled many long years with the Lord moved quietly from one person to another at the mourner's bench, leaning down over each one in turn, and in subdued tones, told them how to be saved, how to pray, and so forth. This was called "working in the altar," and it was beautiful to behold! Meanwhile all of the singers who wished to do so gathered at the front of the sanctuary on the pulpit and sang the old invitational hymns one after another while the preachers and the older women, younger women, and a few men counseled and prayed with the mourners.

[DARE (at *mourners' bench* n) *moaners' bench*, *mourners' bench* both forms chiefly South, South Midland]

mourning cloth *noun* See 1996 citation.

1966 Frome *Strangers* 258 The family prepared a fresh coffin of poplar, lined it with black calico, the "mourning cloth," and sent for Reverend Thomas to officiate at the "funeralizing." **1996** Montgomery Coll (known to Brown, Bush), = cloth used to line the coffin of a dead person, usually black in color but sometimes white for children (Cardwell).

moustache *noun* A whisker; hence plural *moustaches* = hairs above a man's upper lip. See also **beard**, **hair 2**.

1965 Davis *Summer Land* 61 Sometimes ... he would scrooch up his shoulders and blow through his moustaches. "By God, boys, my wounds hurt me today."

mouth

A *noun*

1 The point at which a watercourse, hollow, base of a cliff, etc. opens or widens into a larger area.

1939 Hall Coll (Smokemont NC) At the mouth of Upper Creek the dogs struck, took right out up the creek, went about a mile and a half, and treed. *Ibid.* (Tuckaleechee Cove TN) The dog started right at the mouth of the Big Holler and run up to what's called the Hornet Tree on Defeat Ridge. **1953** Hall Coll (Bryson City NC) So he got all three of them bear there at the mouth of this clift at one time.

2 An individual hunting dog's distinctive barking. See also **give mouth**, **sweet-mouthed**.

c1939 (in **2005** Ballard and Chung *Arnow Stories* 189) With them came Blare and Joe C. Keith, each with two worthless hounds, mostly mouth. **1952** Wilson *Folk Speech NC* 567 = the voice, especially of a hunting dog. "That young dog of mine's jest naturally got the best mouth I ever heard in a race." **1960** Burnett *My Valley* 31 Each of them had a pretty mouth, both in running and at the tree. *Ibid.* 137 His voice was familiar to them and they recognized his mouth.... On reaching the top of ridges, he would give mouth somewhat freely, as well as on down hill grades.... As he came nearer the divide between the Toe and Cane rivers and was making his way out the rugged and steep climb to the gap, he was giving practically no mouth. **c1975** Lunsford *It Used to Be* 164 His dog has a good mouth. This is speaking of a fox hound. You say, "My dog's got the finest mouth in the whole pack." That means he's got the best voice or he's got an unusual voice. **1982** Ginns *Snowbird Gravy* 137 I could tell every one of my dogs. I don't care how many dogs was in that bunch, I could tell my dog's mouth, voice different from any of 'em. **2017** *Blind Pig* (Oct 27) My friend can tell his dog when he trees from all the others by his mouth. Don't pay a big price for a hunting dog without a good mouth, for it's a waste of time and money.

[DARE *mouth* n B1 chiefly South Midland]

B *verb* To argue, speak in a contentious way; hence noun *mouthing*.

1957 Parris *My Mts* 174 This last time I was along when they got into it. And it all started over somethin' that had got 'em to mouthin' against each other the first time. **1962** Williams *Metaphor Mt Speech I* 11 The mildest sort of quarrel, terminating in nothing more serious than one of the antagonists "running out his jaw" at the other because of a "floutin'," is called a "mouthin'." *Ibid.* 12 If the stubborn wife persists in her "jarrin' and mouthin'," the irate husband is "like to commence a-foulin' one hock and a-rubbin' it on t'other" before he roars, "Shet up yer big mouth before I knock ye hell-western crookedy!" **1995–97** Montgomery Coll (known to Adams, Brown, Cardwell, Ledford, Oliver).

mouth bow *noun* See 1979 citation. See also **bow**, **Jew's harp**, **music bow**, **song bow**, **tune bow**.

1979 Irwin *Musical Instruments* 59 As a child, I remember sitting on the front porch of the home of our next door neighbor ... listening to him play the mouth bow. The instrument consisted of a simple bow not unlike one used as a hunting bow. It was made of red cedar and the "string" was a tiny wire which he unraveled from a piece of the door screen. He played it by placing one end of the bow against a firm lower lip and by plucking the string with a rigid finger. The rhythm was acquired by the plucking, and the variation of the pitch was obtained by increasing or decreasing the mouth cavity in much the same manner of the Jews Harp. **1980** Wigginton *Foxfire VI* 54 In addition to the gourd instrument, we have been aware of the musical bow, which is played by musicians scattered throughout the region. We have one musical bow (called "mouth bow," "tune bow," "song bow," and various other names) in our collection. *Ibid.* 92 In the area surrounding Hancock County, Tennessee, they make instruments out of red cedar or hickory and wire and refer to them as "music bows," "mouth bows," or "tuning bows." **1985** *Smokies Anniv Book* 56 The mouth bow is another instrument that has been played in the hills of East Tennessee for centuries.

mouth harp (also *mouth organ*) *noun*

1 A harmonica. Same as **French harp.**

1998 Montgomery *Coll*: *mouth harp* (known to Brown, Bush, Cardwell, Ellis, Jones, Oliver, Weaver); *mouth organ* (known to Adams, Brown, Jones, Ledford, Norris, Oliver, Weaver).

2 A lyre-shaped musical instrument held between the teeth and plucked. Same as **Jew's harp.**

1998 Montgomery *Coll*: *mouth harp* (known to Brown, Bush, Norris); *mouth organ* (known to Cardwell).

mouthing See **mouth B.**

mouth organ See **mouth harp.**

mouty See **mighty A.**

mow *noun* A loft of a barn, used mainly to store hay.

1836 *McLean Diary* 44 [I] fild my Mow with hay. **1847** (in **1870** Drake *Pioneer Life KY* 66) We had no barn or mow, and both wheat & hay were stacked out. **1986** Pederson et al. *LAGS* = attested by 6/60 interviewees (10%) from E TN; 6/7 of all LAGS interviewees (85.7%) attesting term were from Appalachia.

[DARE *mow* n[1] 2 chiefly North, North Midland, West]

mowing blade *noun* Usually a tool for cutting grain, grass, weeds, and other vegetation.

1867 Harris *Sut Lovingood* 120 Thar sot a littil tabil wif a lit candil ontu hit, an' thar stood, bolt up on aind, a grim, grey-haired man, wif a glitterin drawn swoard in his han, es big an' as long es a mowin blade. **1915** Dingus *Word-List VA* 186 = sythe. **1957** Broaddus *Vocab Estill Co KY* 51 = a horse-drawn mower. **1960** Mason *Memoir* 16 The chief tools were the ax, saw, eyed-hoe, scooter plow, mowing blade and cradle. **c1960** Wilson *Coll* = a briar-hook; a long handled scythe used to cut briars and small bushes. **1961** Medford *History Haywood Co* 120 There was as yet no mowing machine, so the old Dutch hand-scythe or mowing blade was still the implement for cutting clover and grass. **1968** *DARE Survey* (Brasstown NC) = a hand tool used for cutting weeds and grass. **1973** GSMNP-90:28 We just had a mowing blade. We didn't have no machines. **1978** Montgomery *White Pine Coll* X-2 We had to mow it with mowing blades. **1985** Irwin *Alex Stewart* 79 I'd put up two or three stacks of hay there with a mowing blade. Didn't have no mowing machine, wasn't able to buy it, so I'd cut it with a mowing blade and stack it. **1994** Montgomery *Coll* (known to Cardwell).

[DARE *mowing blade* n chiefly South Midland, especially southern Appalachians]

Mrs. *noun* Variant forms *mis, misris, misruz, miss tress, mistress, mistrus, miz, mizriz, mizrus, mizruz.* See 1996 citation.

1844 *McLean Diary* 90 [I] viseted miss tress Caplinge. **1886** Smith *Sthn Dialect* 343 Mistress (pronounced in full, as in Shakespeare's time, instead of missess). **1913** Kephart *Our Sthn High* 290 A married woman is not addressed as Missis by the mountaineers, but as Mistress when they speak formally, and as Mis' or Miz' for a contraction. **1917** Kephart *Word-List* 415 Now, *Mistress* Cook, get me a little hot water. **1927** Bolton *Mt Girl Speaks* 4 In our everyday life we say Miz Jones for Mrs. Jones. But when we want to talk properly it is Mistress Jones for Mrs. Jones and you will find us to be very "obleeging" people. **1939** Hall *Coll* (Catons Grove TN) My name is Mizriz McMillon, Rhoda McMillon, I was born and raised in Cocke County. **1939** Krumpelmann *WV Peculiarities* 156 Mrs., title for a married lady. Many students invariably asked, when directed to address a letter to a lady: "Is it Miss or Mistress?" They always write, however, MRS. **1952** Callahan *Smoky Mt Country* 224 "Misris Simms, I'm a-tellin' ye the truth," he replied. **1960** Westover *Highland Lg* 20 *Mizriz* = Mrs. **c1960** Wilson *Coll*: *mizriz* = fairly common in some groups. **1976** Garber *Mountain-ese* 36 All the bachelors are anxious to meet Mizrus Lewis, the new grass widder. **1979** Melton *'Pon My Honor* 21 On the days they worked the fields nighest Uncle Will's house, Miz. Hull would get dinner for them. **1994** Montgomery *Coll*: *Mizriz* = one pronunciation that school teachers always tried to break the habit of (Cardwell). **1996** Bailey *Mizriz* 154 It was fall term [1988], at Berea College, Kentucky, in a basic-composition course. I had put on the board an innocuous exercise for working with grammar, something like the possessive in "Mrs. Smith's hat," and was proceeding with the lesson when a raised hand called my attention to a student. "How," he wanted to know, "do you pronounce that?" "Pronounce what?" I replied, uncertain what was difficult or puzzling in what I had written. "That name. We were told in school to call it [Mrs.] Misruz ['mɪzrɪz]. And we were told the other one [Mr.] is M [/m/], the 'r' is silent." While I never did run into further information about the single phoneme for Mr., the information on Mrs. was productive. . . . Others in the class did know both forms the student cited. And some of them had been similarly instructed in public school[, so] a pronunciation that one might reasonably expect to have died out by now is apparently alive, still being taught, and in use by teen-age speakers. **2005** Williams *Gratitude* 509 Miz, Mizrus, Mistrus = Mrs.

[DARE *mizriz* (at Mrs n) especially South, South Midland]

mucckly *adjective* Free-spirited, heedless of others and of propriety.

1996–97 Montgomery *Coll* (known to Bush); He's the same old mucckly fellow he's always been; he's not a-goin' to change (Cardwell).

much

A *pronoun* Many.

1973 GSMNP-57:64 I've saw as much as twenty-five people settin' on our porch.

B *adjective*

1 In phrases *ain't much, not much* = unwell, incapacitated, in poor health; not keen or enthusiastic.

1904–20 Kephart *Notebooks* 2:475 Nan, she ain't much. **1913** Kephart *Our Sthn High* 224 John's Lize Ann she ain't much; cain't you-uns give her some easin' powder for that hurtin' in her chist? **1937** Hall *Coll* (Gatlinburg TN) [How are you today, Swede?] Not much. **1960** Westover *Highland Lg* 20 *not much* = not in very good health. **1969** Hall *Coll* (Mt Sterling NC) [Mister McGaha, how are you feeling?] Not much. Just been here, I guess, too long. **1971** Foster *Walker Valley* 3:8 I never was too much to crawl around in holes as I wasn't any size. **1973** Davis *'Pon My Honor* 81 Now Grandpappy warn't much to back out. **1975** GSMNP-59:35 He wasn't much to just get out and talk. **1985** Kiser *Life and Times* 74 He was not much to miss school, he just didn't care much for the confinement of studying. **1990** Fisher *Preacher Stories* 24 The mountaineer is "not much on talking." **1997** Montgomery *Coll* I never was much for revivals; I never was much on revivals; I never was much to go to revivals (Ellis). **2008** Salsi *Ray Hicks* 148 The ol' folks was gettin' really ol' and was not much to get out.

[DARE *much* adj 2 chiefly southern Appalachians]

2 Many.

1973 *AOHP/ASU-111* [When people were sick, there] wasn't much places for them to go then other than home. **1975** *Change in Lifestyle* 45 There wasn't much roads up here. **1989** *Matewan OHP-56* I really don't know of any that played much musical instruments. **1991** Thomas *Sthn Appal* 207 They ain't got much convictions. **1997** GSMNPCOHP-1:5 They wasn't much other businesses.

C *adverb*

1 Very. See also **any much**, **none much**.

1861 *Dalton CW Letters* (Sept 24) Amus is got the mesels he is not much Bad he is Broke out. **1862** *Barkley CW Letters* (Oct 31) I hant much a fraid of the small Pox but I had rother not be wheare the[y] are. **c1900** (in **1997** Stoddart *Quare Women* 96) Here's Miss Pettit's bag, but it ain't much pretty. **1913** Kephart *Our Sthn High* 297 Your name ain't much common. **1925** Dargan *Highland Annals* 78 Well, the whipper-will ain't a much smart bird. **1937** Hall *Coll* (Cades Cove TN) Is that road much steep? **1939** Hall *Coll* (Waldens Creek TN) The Foxes are low, not tall, [with] small, black features. The Foxes are known as the "Black Dutch," Pennsylvania [is] as far back as we can trace them. The old ones couldn't talk much plain. **1940** Haun *Hawk's Done* 37 I'm not much heavy, am I? **1950** Justus *Luck for Lihu* 41 I'm not sick—just don't feel much peart. **1955** Ritchie *Singing Family* 213 I don't know the road much well. **1970** GSMNP-26:12 They said he never was much stout after that. **1971** *AOHP/ALC-193* I'd think most of them wouldn't be much bad. **1975–76** Wolfram/Christian *WV Coll* 153 He wasn't much well, and we'd go give him castor oil. **1978** Reese *Speech NE Tenn* 165 That white lightning ain't much safe to drink. **1985** Wear *Lost Communities* 27 She didn't seem to think it was much funny. **1999** Landry *Smoky Mt Interviews* They didn't grow stuff much good. **2005** Williams *Gratitude* 145 Flashlight batteries . . . ditn't last much long out a-huntin' at night.

[DARE *much* adv chiefly South, South Midland]

2 Following the noun or pronoun modified.

1864 *Blair CW Letters* (April 10) we hav no deauty to do at this time mutch. **1937** Hall *Coll* (Cosby TN) She ain't bigger'n a cricket much. **1938** Hall *Coll* (Cosby Creek TN) It has just rained all summer until people can't get to do any work much. **1939** Hall *Coll* I hadn't studied anything much about it. *Ibid.* (Smokemont NC) They were poor chances then for us young fellows a-growing up to get any chance much of schooling. **1961** *Coe Ridge OHP-333A* If you paid your way back, you wouldn't have no money left much. **1962** Williams *Mtneers Mind Manners* 23 My old fingers're gittin' so stiff I cain't do no good much no more. **1968** *Faith Healing* 24 A doctor can't do anything about it too much. **1972** *AOHP/ALC-241* They didn't pay nothing then much in Clark County for teaching. **1973** GSMNP-86 Do you know anything about the Bible much? **1975** *Logging* 38 They was a woodpile there and it just so happened that they wasn't any wood in it much. **1976** *Wooden Sleds* 150 I don't want no earthly things much. **1977** *Blacksmithing* 200 There wasn't anybody else much around blacksmithing much except Morgan and me. **1979** *Daddy Oakley* 180 They grow vines and no potatoes much. **1979** GSMNP-118:14 Back then you didn't pay 'em nothing hardly, didn't have no money much. **1983** Page and Wigginton *Aunt Arie* 25 I don't care nothin' about money much. **1989** *Matewan OHP-1* They was no account much. **1991** Thomas *Sthn Appal* 34 I never did hollar no time, much. **1997** GSMNPCOHP-3:13 They weather never got any colder up there much than it did here. **1999** Landry *Smoky Mt Interviews* It didn't have no vitamins much to it.

D (also *much out, much up, munch up, mutch*) *verb, verb phrase* To make much over, pet, caress; to coax or call (especially a hunting dog) by making a sucking noise through the lips and teeth.

1905 Miles *Spirit of Mts* 177 A sycophant is "anybody's dog that'll much him." **1913** Kephart *Our Sthn High* 283 Much that dog and see if he won't go along. **c1926** Bird *Cullowhee Wordlist*: *much* = call with lip sounds. "I mutched to my dog to come to me"; "He mutched to his horses and they pulled the wagon out of the hole." **1938** Hall *Coll* (Emerts Cove TN) Petting a dog is muchin' him. **1939** Hall *Coll* (Deep Creek NC) I patted him and muched him and hissed him, and he went right on back and commenced barkin' up the tree. *Ibid.* (Sugarlands TN) I muched the dogs a little and he come up to me. **1940–42** Adams *Tales* 125 It come a-running back just a yelping and hollering like it was about to die and run under the floor and they couldn't much it out anymore. **1944** Wilson *Word-List* 47 *much (up)* = to make much of, show affection for. "I muched the dogs up, and they got so they would follow me." **1975** Jackson *Unusual Words* 153 To *munch up* or to *mush up* a dog is to pet him and humor him. **1984** Wilder *You All Spoken* 105 *much up* = praise; make a to-do over, as you much up a bird dog for a good point or a smart retrieve. **1996–97** Montgomery *Coll*: *munch up* (known to Bush, Cardwell, Jones), = to call a dog to you (Brown).

[EDD *much* v[1] 1 "to pet, fondle, caress"; DARE *much* v chiefly South, South Midland]

muchly *adverb* Much.

c1982 Young *Colloquial Appal* 15 = much.

much of a *noun phrase* A great or sterling example of.

1889 Mooney *Folk Carolina Mts* 97 When one is strong and brave he is said to be "much of a man." **1919** Combs *Word-List South* 36 *much of a man* = a "stout" or strong or large man. **1938** Hall *Coll* (Emerts Cove TN) *much of a dog* = good at hunting or driving stock. **1952** Wilson *Folk Speech NC* 568 *much of a* = strong, great, valuable, followed by a substantive, "much of a man, car," etc. **1965** Hall *Coll* (Cataloochee NC) They met the bully of Catalooch there, Tommy Caldwell, so they had much of a time. **1965** Hall *Coll* (Cataloochee NC) He was much of a man. If there was any fightin' to do, he'd do it. **1987** Young *Lost Cove* 82 It took a much of a man to handle a full cud of his making. **1997** *GSMNPCOHP*-3:13 He was much of a man. **1998** *Dante OHP*-12 When I went in the mines, I had the dream of being much of a man.

[DARE *much* n 1 chiefly South Midland]

much out, much up See **much D.**

muckeley-dun (also *muckle-dun, muckle-ledun*) *noun* See citations.

1927 Woofter *Dialect from WV* 361 *muckeley-dun* = a word of indefinite meaning, which is used to signify contempt, and which has no reference to color. "Look at that old muckeley-dun horse." **1944** Wilson *Word-List* 47 *muckle-dun* = muddy-brown. **2017** *Blind Pig* (Feb 16) My mother-in-law used "muckle-ledun" for mingled colors.

mud-fat *adjective* See citation.

1952 Wilson *Folk Speech NC* 568 = very fat, generally in reference to an animal.

[DARE *mud-fat* adj especially South Midland]

mud pike *noun* A dirt road on which a toll is charged.

1937 Conner *Ms* 52 As we had no Car's, and few buggie's, and only Mud-pike's, high-way'es was un-known in those day'es, those Elder's visited the churches quarterly and repoart the condition's of each church.

mud poison *noun* See citation. See also **dew poison, fall sore, ground itch, toe-itch.** See citation.

1957 Combs *Lg Sthn High: Word List* 66 *mud pizen* = dew poison. For example, dew gets in the cracks under a boy's toes and causes him much discomfort.

mud puppy *noun* A large, entirely aquatic salamander (*Necturus maculosus*) with external gills.

1967 Brewer *Park Creepers* The next biggest salamander in the park is the mud puppy, sometimes more than a foot long. **1996** Montgomery *Coll* (known to Cardwell). **2004** Dodd *Amphibians Smoky Mts* 26 Two amphibians in the Great Smoky Mountains never leave the water, and instead carry out their entire life cycle in aquatic habitats. These salamanders are the Hellbenders and the Common Mudpuppy. Both are active more at night than during the day, when they hide under rocks and other bottom debris. Little is known about the life histories of these species within the Great Smokies, but both lay eggs that hatch into larvae. The larvae are very difficult to find. [*Ibid.* 172 The name refers to the spotted dorsum of many adults. Identification Adults. This is a large, fully aquatic salamander with conspicuous dark red, bushy gills. The head is squarish, and the body is light to dark brown, with black spots or blotches on the dorsum and sides. The belly is grayish in color. Tails are paddle-shaped, and they are marked similarly to the rest of the body.]

mud splitters *noun* Unusually large feet or heavy shoes.

1939 Farr *TN Mt Regions* 91 = heavy shoes: "My mud splitters are wearing out." **1969** *DARE Survey* (Walker KY) = joking name for unusually big or clumsy feet mud splitters.

mud worm *noun* An earthworm.

c1960 Wilson *Coll*: = earthworm. Rare. **1996** Johnson *Lexical Change* 138 *mud worm* = statistically more common in the mountains of South Carolina and Georgia than in the Piedmont and Coastal Plain c1990.

muggin See **molly moocher.**

mulatto land *noun* See citations.

1952 Callahan *Smoky Mt Country* 76 The land which lay along the foot of the mountains was called "mulatto land," being a dark soil with a dry foundation. **1984** Wilder *You All Spoken* 134 = rich but rocky soil.

mule *noun* See citation.

1971 *AOHP/ALC*-193 [On a section of a coal mine you] tamped ties or anything you had to do to keep the railroad up, put in ties or tamp them up, jack the track up, put ballast rock in there and take a big old pick. We called it a mule all the time . . . great old big, looked like a old-fashioned dirt pick but one end of it was battered up till it had a knot on it almost like your fist.

mule down *verb phrase*

1 To distill (homemade whiskey).

1959 Stubbs *Mountain-Wise* (Aug–Sept) 6 A less familiar expression occurred when some city visitors were enthusiastic over the taste of some sweet corn raised by a mountain farmer and wanted more to take home with them. The patch was growing on a far hillside so the farmer told them: "I'll git you some if you'll wait till I can *mule it down*."

2 (also *mule up*) To stop, become stubborn.

1962 Williams *Mtneers Mind Manners* 19 He begin to pull back, and I says, "You want me to sqush [sic] your head with this here

.45? He just muled right down. I popped the handcuffs on 'im." **1966** Medford *Ol' Starlin* 66 Whenever a person pretended to be asleep or dead, they had just "possumed up"—and when they were extremely stubborn in a matter they had "muled up." **1966** Stubbs *Mountain-Wise* (June–July) 14 One day a young mountaineer was working for us. His power-saw was balky, and, to begin with, reluctant to start. Finally, when it did, he remarked "I was a-feared hit wuz agoin' to mule-up on us."

mule ear (also *mule ear pie*) *noun* See citations. Same as **fried pie**.

1949 McDavid *Grist* 111 (Pickens Co SC) *mule ears* = fried pies (usually apple or peach). **1983** *Dark Corner OHP-4A* [The crust was] just round like a plate, and you'd just lap it over and it looks like a half moon, you know . . . but it also looks like a mule's ear . . . filled with apple or peach, any dried fruit. . . . Mostly we just called it mule ear pie, you know, 'cause it looked like a mule's ear laying out on a table. **2006** *Encycl Appalachia* 932 Dried apples are the most common fried pie filling, but peaches, apricots, and prunes are also used. In *Smokehouse Ham, Spoon Bread, and Scuppernong Wine: The Folklore and Art of Southern Appalachian Cooking* (1998), Joseph E. Dabney notes that some Carolinians call fried peach pies "mule ears."

[from its shape]

mule-high *adjective* Of a rail fence: having the height of a mule, for security.

1884 Smith *Arp Scrap Book* 69 Fences are a big thing in these parts, and if a man aint careful it will take about half he makes on his farm to keep 'em mule high and bull strong and pig tight.

mule lightning See **lightning**.

mule lot *noun* An outdoor enclosure for mules. See also **lot A**.

1939 Hall *Coll* (Nine Mile TN) John Cable and Allen Crisp, they was to go to the mule lot.

mule pullers *noun* See citation.

1989 Still *Rusties and Riddles* [80] = a joke tool.

mule train *noun* See citation.

1989 *Matewan OHP-94* "[They are] all time sending me word they've got a mule train coming up here to get me" . . . that's what he called it. What he meant by that is, they's going to have a gang of men come up here and beat the hell out of him.

mule up See **mule down 2**.

muley (also *muley bull, muley cow, muley heifer, muley steer*) *noun* A bovine that is naturally hornless.

1858 (in **1974** Harris *High Times* 155) He hed bet a feller his trunk agin a barrel ove sourcrout that he could drink lager bier faster and longer nur a big muley cow could salted meal slop. **1892** Fruit *KY Words* 231 *muley cow* = cow without horns. **1927** Woofter *Dialect from WV* 361 *muley cow* = a cow which is naturally without horns. "Have you seen the red muley cow to-day?" **1960** McCaulley *Cades Cove* [At] one time a muley cow didn't bring nigh as much on the price as a cow with horns on it. **1962** Dykeman *Tall Woman* 48 Come on, Robert, let's get our little muley-cow to work again. **1967** *DARE Survey* (Maryville TN) = cow that has never had horns. **1968** Vincent *Best Stories* 44 This cow ain't got no horns. She's a muley. **1970** Justus *Tales* Missy, the muley cow, was a great pet of Mammy's. **1975** *Logging* 181 If you had one didn't have horns, he was a muley. . . . He was a muley cow or a muley steer. It was just a rare thing. People was glad to get ahold of one. . . . They'd get them natural muleys—and they was long and far between—but they'd keep them natural muley heifers and then whenever they had a muley bull, they'd mate 'em up. **1993** Weaver *Scotch-Irish Speech* 14 The clear land might be grazed by "muley" cows (Irish "moily," a breed with no horns) or those which had been dehorned.

[ultimately of Celtic origin (cf Irish Gaelic *maolaí* and Scottish Gaelic *maolag*); OED3 *moiley* adj 1 Scot and Irish English, *muley* now chiefly U.S.; cf EDD *moiley* Scot, Irel, nEngl, Cornwall; SND *moylie* n 2; DHE *moiley*; CUD *moiley* n 1 "a hornless cow, bullock or bull"; form *muley* is probably American folk etymology based on similarity of headshape to a mule]

muley bull, muley cow See **muley**.

muley-hawed *adjective* Stubborn.

1904–20 Kephart *Notebooks* 4:855 You needn't be so muley-hawed about it. **1905** Miles *Spirit of Mts* 176 When he speaks of some perverse spirit as being perpetually "muley-hawed," has he not expressed the extreme of contrariness? [**1995** Montgomery *Coll* (unknown to consultants from the Smoky Mountains).]

muley heifer, muley steer See **muley**.

mullein tea *noun* See citation.

1975 Brewer *Valley So Wild* 239 "Mullein tea" made from dried leaves of the downy plant and sassafras in the spring when the roots were nice and red were [sic] brews that soothed sick children.

mulligrubby See **mullygrubby**.

mulligrubs See **mullygrubs**.

mullygrub *verb* See citations. See also **mullygrubs**.

1944 Laughlin *Word-List Buncombe Co* 25 = to be slightly unwell or upset, to have the blues. **1995** Montgomery *Coll* = to complain for no good reason (Norris).

mullygrubby (also *mulligrubby*) *adjective* Despondent, sulky. See also **mullygrubs**.

1952 Justus *Children* 12 Sammy, hunched on the dogtrot floor, eyed his basket of berries in a mullygrubby manner. **1957** Justus *Other Side* 70 Grandy moped around the house with a mulligrubby face, muttering about ill luck.

mullygrubs

A Variant forms *mollygrubs* [see **1996** in **B1**], *mulligrubs* [see **1940** in **B2**].

B *noun*

1 (usually with *the*) A state of despondency, sulkiness, vague unwellness. See also **mullygrubby**.

1941 Still *Troublesome Creek* 37 She was heartsick with the mulligrubs. **1943** Justus *Bluebird* 91 It was no use, she knew, trying to reason with her brother when he was having a spell of the mullygrubs. **1944** Williams *Word-List Mts* 30 = despondency: "He's in the mullygrubs this morning." **1996** Montgomery *Coll*: *mollygrubs* (Jones).

2 A state of upset, bad temper, excitement.

1913 Kephart *Our Sthn High* 297 I knowed in reason she'd have the mullygrubs over them doin's. **c1940** Aswell *Glossary TN Idiom* 13 *mulligrubs* = spell of evil temper. **1941** Still *Troublesome Creek* 37 She was heartsick with the mulligrubs. **1957** Combs *Lg Sthn High: Word List* 66 *mulligrubs* = a state of great excitement, or anger. Ex.: "He'll have the mullygrubs when he hears that." **1996** Montgomery *Coll*: *mollygrubs* (Jones).

[EDD *mullygrubs* sb 1 a fit of ill-temper or of sulks]

3 See citation.

1990 Cavender *Folk Medical Lex* 27 = stomach growling, hunger pains.

[EDD *mullygrubs* sb 1 a stomach-ache]

munch up See **much D**.

munt See **month**.

murderation *interjection* Used as an exclamation of surprise, disgust, or other strong emotion.

1936 Carpenter *WV Expletives* 37 Vexation for many, many years has manifested itself in West Virginia in: Thunderation; Murderation; Shucks.

murder up *verb phrase* To murder.

1961 Seeman *Arms of Mt* 57 [He] murdered up a man fer four dollars!

mursh See **mush**.

muscle out *verb phrase* To lift to shoulder level.

c1960 Wilson *Coll* = to lift something to the level of the shoulders. **1997** Montgomery *Coll* (known to Brown, Bush, Cardwell).

muscle up *verb phrase* To move or lift (a heavy object).

1913 Kephart *Our Sthn High* 282 In mountain vernacular many words that serve as verbs are only nouns of action, or adjectives, or even adverbs . . . "We can muscle this log up." **1974** Fink *Bits Mt Speech* 17 = lift by bodily strengh. "Hit took four men to *muscle* that rock up." **1994–97** Montgomery *Coll* (known to eight consultants from the Smoky Mountains).

mush *noun*

A Variant form *mursh*.

1933 Carpenter *Sthn Mt Dialect* 25 In parts of the mountains in certain words "r" is added where it does not belong. Among these are WASH, HUSH, and MUSH, which became warsh, hursh, and mursh. These are particularly noticeable in southern West Virginia and eastern Kentucky.

B A heavy cornmeal porridge. See also **fried mush**, **pumpkin mush**.

1853 Ramsey *Annals* 719 The catalogue of the advantages of this [cornmeal] might be extended further. Boiled in water, it forms the frontier dish called mush which was eaten with milk, with honey, molasses, butter or gravy. **1864** *Chapman CW Letters* (May 15) I buy me a hen some times and some times by me some sweetemilk to eat with mush. **1864** *Watkins CW Letters* (June 20) I tell you hit was like eating milk and mush with Spoons. **1939** Hall *Coll* (Cades Cove TN) They'll make up their mush first, make up the mush and let it stand about two days, and then you make up the mash, put it in and stir it till it begins to boil. **1967** *DARE Survey* (Maryville TN) = boiled corn meal. **1973** GSMNP-70:2:2 Everybody used what they called milk and mush for supper. **1982** *Smokies Heritage* 36 Cornmeal became many things: johnny cake, mush, bread, and corn pone—all, however, made from the same basic recipe of meal, salt, and water. It was seldom that one saw a pioneer table without corn pone or mush.

musharoom, **musharoon** See **mushroom**.

mush ice *noun* See citation.

1957 Broaddus *Vocab Estill Co KY* 51 = the very thin layer of ice that forms when a pond first freezes over.

[DARE *mush ice* n scattered, but chiefly South Midland]

mushmelon, **mushmilion**, **mushmillion** See **muskmelon**.

mushrat *noun* A muskrat.

1930 Armstrong *This Day and Time* 152 Hain't no eatin' on earth 'ull tech young mush-rats. **1967** *DARE Survey* (Maryville TN). **1975** Jackson *Unusual Words* 155 A *brute* was a cow; a *catamount*, a panther . . . and *mushrats*, muskrats. **1978** Hiser *Quare Do's* 136 He cotch a right smart bit of stuff, a couple of mushrats and such little matters in the holler. **1995–97** Montgomery *Coll*: *mushrat* (known to Cardwell, Ellis, Jones, Ledford, Oliver, Weaver).

mushroom *noun* Variant forms *musharoom*, *musharoon*, *mushyroom*.

1917 Kephart *Word-List* 415 *mushyroom*. **1934–47** *LAMSAS Appal* (Madison Co NC, Swain Co NC) *mushyroom*. **1981** Daugneaux *Separate Place* 31 This same Bessie refused to keep our cocker spaniel in the basement when her feet were muddy without turning on the light for her: "You ain't no mush-a-roon, air ya, Kippi?" **1995** Montgomery *Coll*: *musharoom* (known to Cardwell, Ledford, Oliver, Shields).

mushyroom See **mushroom**.

music *noun*

1 Any musical instrument with strings.

1939 Hall *Coll* (Gatlinburg TN) He was an old-time fiddler.... He could play every kind of string music. **1940** Hall *Coll* (Alexander NC) = any kind of string instrument.

2 The collective barking of hounds on a hunt.

1979 *Raising Dogs* 188 When [the hunting dogs are] all running together, it's pretty music, if you like that. **1997** Miller *Brier Poems* 155 The hounds ranged far, or trailed down a deep cove between high hills, and the music of the chase became for him snatches of song on some far-off station. **2008** Plott *Hunting in Smokies* 52 Give me my old flintlock shooting iron and let a keen pack of lean hounds be hoppin' ahead. And of all the sports, the master sport is following their music over the mountains, and winding up with a bullet or a sticker in a varminous old bear!

music bow See **mouth bow**.

musicianer *noun* A musician.

1863 *Vance Papers* (March 31) you will oblige me by riting to me and Col jarett and having it arraing So I Can go back to the Company pleas rite in hast your ould musisioner Eliha Chambers of the ruf an redy guards. **1891** Primer *Studies in WV* 168 A band of music is called musicioners. **1913** Kephart *Our Sthn High* 277 The hillmen ... [insert] sounds where they do not belong. Sometimes it is only an added consonant: gyarden, acrost, corkus (caucus); sometimes a syllable: loaferer, musicianer, suddenty. **1934–47** *LAMSAS Appal* (Madison Co NC, Swain Co NC) musicianer. **1940** Simms *Wiley Oakley* 34 Wiley [Oakley] is extremely fond of music. He feels certain that he would have "been a real musicianer" if musical instruments to play upon had been available in his young days. **1958** Morgan *Gift from Hills* 23 When the musicianers had warmed up their strings to their satisfaction, we would line up and go into the Virginia Reel with everything that was in us. **1977** Hamilton *Mt Memories* 153 When he played "Cripple Creek," the man said, "Billy, you shore air goin' to be a good musician-er." **1979** *Big South Fork OHP-9* She could play the fiddle and play the banjo, oh, and dance, a sight in the world ... what a musicianer she was. **1997** *Dante OHP-14* They had a dance every Saturday night down there, had musicianers, you know, and everything.

[OED3 *musicianer* n now colloquial and regional (chiefly U.S., Scot, and Irish English) 1540→; DARE *musicianer* n chiefly South Midland, formerly also New England]

musicker *noun* A musician.

1961 Williams *Content Mt Speech* 16 Lil jist got her head turned because Abe had been off out yander to the ocean-see, er sommers, an' was a good musicker, and could sang song-ballets. **1995–97** Montgomery *Coll* (known to Bush, Cardwell).

[OED3 *musicker* n now chiefly U.S. colloquial]

music makings *noun* See citation.

1964 Greve *Story of Gatlinburg* 76 In the "music makin's," which have come to be a popular form of amusement with the mountain people, we have usually four men, with fiddle, banjo, and two guitars, who play accompaniments to old songs and ballads, singing either solo or as quartette.

musket weed (also *muskrat weed*, *musquatch weed*) *noun* The tall meadow rue (*Thalictrum polyganum/pubescens*).

1982 Stupka *Wildflowers* 29 This is the tallest growing of the several species of meadow-rue that are found in the Southern Appalachian region. It is also called "muskrat weed," "musquatch-weed," and "musket weed."

muskmelon *noun* Variant forms *mushmelon*, *mushmillion*, *must millon*.

1861 *Neves CW Letters* (Sept 16) tell Will he came threw his corn to day and found a big must millon thinking it would spoil before he [c]ome to eat it. he took it. **1864** *Love CW Letters* (Jan 8) I will send this By him and I will [send] you and Geroge [sic] some mush melon Seeds in [the letter]. **1936** Coleman *Dial N GA* 27 "Mushmillion" is used for "muskmelon." **1939** *FWP Guide NC* 98 *Mushmillion* for muskmelon. **1957** Broaddus *Vocab Estill Co KY* 51 *mushmillion* = an oblong cantaloupe. **1962** Wilson *Folkways Mammoth Cave* 15 *Muskmelons/mushmelons* included the whole family; cantaloupes were the round ones ... but the word was never commonly used by many people. **1969** Doran *Folklore White Co* 113 *mushmillion*. **1976** Still *Pattern of Man* 81 They declare the world is round as a mushmelon, while the Book says plainly it has four corners. **1986** Pederson et al. *LAGS*: *mushmillion* = attested by 40/60 interviewees (66.7%) from E TN and 16/35 (45.7%) from N GA; 56/340 of all LAGS interviewees (16.4%) attesting term were from Appalachia. **1999** Perry *Clinch River* After teasing, last he cut rich, golden cantaloupes and I had my fill of Wylie's "mush" melons. **2009** Holbrook *Upheaval* 11 She had a goiter on her neck the size of a mushmelon.

[forms with *mush-* are attested in OED3 from the 17th century; DARE *muskmelon* n widespread, but more frequent South, South Midland, North Atlantic]

muskrat gang *noun* See citation.

1967 Fetterman *Stinking Creek* 80 The "project work" is one of the many facets of the welfare program extended to the mountains.... Its stated purpose was to provide aid for unemployed fathers.... They are assigned to crews that clean up the creeks, cut weeds from the roads, and perform any other chores their assigned supervisors ... dream up. In the towns, the crews are called "muskrat gangs" or "happy pappies."

muskrat weed See **musket weed**.

musquash root *noun* A water hemlock (*Cicuta maculata*) plant that has medicinal uses but is poisonous eaten in substantial quantities.

1975 Hamel and Chiltoskey *Cherokee Plants* 31 Musquash root, poison hemlock, water hemlock ... Suicide to eat large quantities. Chew and swallow roots for four consecutive days to become sterile forever; old timers used this to find out how long they would live, if they got dizzy chewing the roots they would die soon, if not they would live a long time.

musquatch weed See **musket weed**.

mussel box *noun* See citation.

1981 Henry *Alex Stewart* 55 Always thinking, Alex invented his mussel box. This made it much easier to find the mussels. The mussel box is twenty-four inches long and six inches square. It has a window in one end; the other end is open. There are two handles on opposite sides about ten inches from the end with the window. The joints in the box are sealed with tar. To find the mussels all you had to do was hold the box by the handles, push the end with the window into the water eighteen inches or so, and look into the open end. If a mussel's down there, you'll spot him.

must *auxiliary verb*

1 In phrases *musta did* (= must have done), *must(a) didn't* (must not have done), *must have could*, etc.

1975–76 Wolfram/Christian *WV Coll* 27 He musta didn't hear me. **1983** McDermitt *Boy Named Jack* 19 You must didn't do no good in twelve months. **2004** Fisher *Kettle Bottom* 70 They must of [= have] could hear her screaming for Jesus all the way down to the road. **2012** Montgomery *File* In spite of myself, I musta did the final drive right, I put close to 2000 miles on her and zero problems.

2 See citation.

1895 Edson and Fairchild *TN Mts* 376 = shall (invariably used for questions).

must million, must millon See **muskmelon**.

mutch See **much D**.

mutton *noun* A sheep, referring to the animal on the hoof as well as on the dinner table (sometimes construed as a singular noun; hence form *muttons* = sheep.

c1950 Adams *Grandpap* 177 She went to her safe an' got out a big butcher knife an' started whettin' it. Said she was a-fixin' to kill a mutton. **1966** Medford *Ol' Starlin* 43 They killed beeves, muttons, and chickens; baked loaf and biscuit, gingerbread and cake, also brought out jars of preserves and canned goods a plenty!

mutton tallow *noun* The rendered fat of a sheep, applied as a medicinal salve.

c1950 Adams *Grandpap* 159 Grandpap was making a salve of mutton tallow and some other ingredients to rub on my throat.

mux *verb* To mess up.

1934 Carpenter *Archaic English in WV* 78 One may hear *muxed* in certain sections of West Virginia now in the exact sense in which John Ridd [in Blackmore's *Lorna Doone*] used it. It is a term synonymous to messed up, rather than a form of mixed, as it might appear.

my opinion *adverb phrase* In my estimation or view.

1936 Still *One Leg* 9 My opinion, he's tuk off like Snider's hound with Poppy's money. **1976** Still *Pattern of Man* 48 Young'uns don't climb much above their raising. He'll follow his pappy in the log works, my opinion. **1992** Offutt *KY Straight* 21 [It's] halfway up the hill, my opinion.

N

na'ar See **narrow.**

nabel *noun* The navel.

1913 Kephart *Our Sthn High* 278 Most hillsmen say nabel. **1942** Hall *Phonetics Smoky Mts* 69, 99 ['neɪbəl]. **1967** *DARE Survey* (Gatlinburg TN). **1994–97** Montgomery *Coll* (known to Adams, Brown, Cardwell, Jones, Ledford, Oliver, Weaver), = especially in reference to young children (Ellis).

[DARE (at *navel* n) chiefly South, South Midland]

naer See **nary.**

naern See **nary one.**

nairn See **nary one.**

nairy See **nary.**

nairy'n See **nary one.**

naked *adjective* Variant forms *necked, neckid, nekked, nekkid.*

1862 *Mangum CW Letters* (Dec 2) I recevd my Close and letters yestoday and I recon that I was the proudestt boy that you ever saw for I was necked and barfooted and it a snoing half the time. **1915** Dingus *Word-List VA* 186 *necked.* **1942** *Hall Phonetics Smoky Mts* 18 ['nɛkɪd]. **1952** Wilson *Folk Speech NC* 569 *necked.* **1974** Fink *Bits Mt Speech* 24 They went swimming *start-nekked.* **1991** Thomas *Sthn Appal* 15 Gran'ma's boys was nearly nekkid. **2003** Carter *Mt Home* 28 When we had biled 'taters, we peeled 'em all over neckid. **2013** Venable *How to Tawlk* 33 Uncle Fred saw Sonny and Barbara Jean nekkid down at the swimmin' hole.

name

A *noun*

1 A mention.

1940 Haun *Hawk's Done* 18 Of course he knowed Shorty Shipley put it in there but he didn't make any name of it. *Ibid.* 28 We didn't make any name of it to Old Man Brock or to Sadie.

2 A reputation.

1973 *AOHP/ALC-259* He didn't kill just because of the name of killing. They's always some cause. Somebody'd do something to him or something.

B *verb* To mention, tell, call.

1862 *Love CW Letters* (Jan 21) ther has Ben So Mutch talk of a fight ihav got tiard of hering it namd. **1862** *Robinson CW Letters* (June 28) the last letter had 50 cents in it & you never named it in the letter. **1895** Edson and Fairchild *TN Mts* 373 If you see him, *name* it to him. **1910** Weeks *Barbourville Word List* 456 = to tell, to mention: "I named that to him a week ago, but he didn't do it." **1915** Pollard *TN Mts* 242 I told her not to name it to me again. **1929** (in **1952** Mathes *Tall Tales* 129) Howsomever, I'd do nothin without axin' Paw. I'll name it to him the fust time he draps in. **1939** Hall *Coll* (Tow String Creek NC) [When the speaker was reminded of an unfortunate incident, he said] If you just name that to me again . . . you'll go just the same route the other man went. **1940** Haun *Hawk's Done* 143 Pharis didn't name it to her about his stealing. **1960** McCaulley *Cades Cove* I've had it named to me many times, "Mister McCaulley, now why don't you write a book of your life and put it out?" **1962** Dykeman *Tall Woman* 18 That's all I came to name to you. **1976** Durrance and Shamblin *Appal Ways* 34 When I was just a nit of a girl I used to go to the woods and my daddy always named me to be the best sang hunter he knew. **1985** Irwin *Alex Stewart* 136 Fer God's sake, don't never name it to nobody! **1997** Montgomery *Coll* He didn't name it to me (Brown).

[OED3 *name* v 7b now chiefly U.S. regional; DARE *name* v chiefly South Midland, especially southern Appalachians]

name after one another *verb phrase* See citation.

1979 Slone *My Heart* 25–26 Our mountain people love to "name after each other." It is a great honor to have the same name as an uncle, aunt, or grandfather. I even know several folks named for their own sister or brother. It did get kind of confusing to try and keep it straight, especially when we all lived so close together. So nicknames were a "must do," or necessity. Four of the first white people to live on Caney—Alice, Isom, Isaac, and Shady—have many namesakes. You will find these names in almost all the Slone families. At one time there were eleven Isom Slones on Caney: my father Kitteneye, Fat Isom, Big Isom, Pot Stick, Stiller, Hard's Isom, Andy's Isom, Jailor Isom, Preacher Isom, Crazy Isom, and Salty Ice. Sometimes the father's name was added on, so as to tell just which one you were referring to, like Hard's Isom and Andy's Isom. Often using the father and grandfather's name, for example, we said, Hard Billie's Pearce, though I could never understand why as he was the only man named Pearce that I ever knew. Of course the women had nicknames too, as they were also named after someone else. When a boy was named for his father, it would be Big Sam and Little Sam. This begins to get funny when Little Sam weighs over 200 pounds and is six feet tall. My husband is still called Little Willie by some folks, although his Uncle Willie has been dead for over fifty years.

name for *verb phrase* To label (someone) as.

1895 Dromgoole *Fiddling to Fame* 52 He named me fur a idiot an' a upstart.

nana *noun* One's grandmother.

2016 Simmons *Legends & Lore* 122 Appalachian people also have a name for their non-traditional home remedy healers in Appalachia; they are usually called "granny," "mamaw," or "nana." **2018** *Blind Pig* (May 9) My grandboys called my wife Nana and call their other grandmother Mee-Mommy.

nancy-over-the-ground *noun* A foam-flower (*Tiarella cordifolia/trifoliata*). See also **coolwort.**

1940 Bowman *KY Mt Stories* 243 = a fragile blossom as described in "High Tide."

nannie (also *nanny plum*) *noun* A pellet of sheep dung. See also **nannie tea, pill, sheep pill.**

c1960 Wilson *Coll*: *nanny plum* = pellet of sheep manure. **1968** Wilson *Folklore Mammoth Cave* 22 *nanny* (or *sheep-nanny*) = sheep manure made into a tea to break out measles.

nannie tea *noun* A medicinal tea drunk to treat measles, made by boiling sheep droppings in water. See also **nannie, sheepball tea.**

1929 Duncan and Duncan *Sayings* 234 Give nannie tea (liquid made from sheep excretion) fuh measles. **c1960** Wilson *Coll*: *nanny tea* = tea made out of sheep manure, supposed to be the best remedy to break out measles. **1982** Slone *How We Talked* 106 = cure for measles, made from sheep manure tied in a rag and boiled in water; a stew made from whiskey, sugar and ginger. **2003** Cavender *Folk Medicine* 119–20 Sweating was thought necessary to prevent measles from "turning" or "burning" inward, a situation believed to result in severe debilitation or death. The notion held by some that "any ol' hot tea will do" is illustrated by the use of sheep nannie tea (also called "sheep pearl," "sheep pill," "sheep shit," "sheep bullet," or "sheep dip" tea), which is documented in sources almost as much as botanical tea. A little honey was added to make it more palatable.

[< *nanny* "a female goat"]

nap *noun* The back of the neck.

1957 Broaddus *Vocab Estill Co KY* 52 = the nape. **c1960** Wilson *Coll* = always [næp].

[DARE *nape* n especially Northeast, South, South Midland]

nap of sleep *noun phrase* A nap.

1931 Combs *Lg Sthn High* 1310 He tuk a nap o' sleep. **1933** Thomas *Traipsin' Woman* 63 I jest pulled my kivvers up around my head and dozed off to take me a nap a' sleep. **1946** Stuart *Plum Grove Hills* 106 You waked me up. I was about to take a nap o' sleep. **1975** Dwyer *Thangs* 17 Words used in the mountains to name something that can be adequately named by one—probably used for emphasis and to be "sure an' certain of clarity" ... nap o' sleep.

[redundant form]

nare won, narn, nar'n See **nary one.**

narr See **nary.**

narrate *verb* To report or circulate (information), spread by word of mouth. See also **norate.**

1859 Taliaferro *Fisher's River* 21 It was "narrated" all through the country "that Famus was drownded in a mash tub." **1867** Harris *Sut Lovingood* 138 She had narrated hit thru the neighborhood that nex Saterday she'd gin a quiltin—three quilts an' one cumfurt tu tie. **1998** Montgomery *Coll* (known to Brown, Cardwell, Jones).

narrer, narrey See **narrow.**

narrow *adjective* Variant forms *na'ar, narr, narr', narrer, narrey* ['nɑrɪ], *narr'r, narry.*

1885 Murfree *Prophet* 256 It looked mighty narrer. **1925** (in **1935** Edwards *NC Novels* 89) *narr'.* **1942** Hall *Phonetics Smoky Mts* 81 ['nɑrɪ]. **1971** Foster *Walker Valley* 4:18 It was pretty narrey at the time and then they had that washout back in twenty. **1972** Cooper *NC Mt Folklore* 94 *narr.* **1974** Fink *Bits Mt Speech* 17 *na'ar* = narrow: "a na'ar bridge." **1991** Thomas *Sthn Appal* 84 It'uz jist a narr'r pen, built out uv purty good size logs. **2005** Williams *Gratitude* 27 After the widest boards was used for the walls, narr'er (narrower) strips was nailed over the cracks on the outside to keep out the cold air. **2013** Crawford *Mt Memories* 58 You don't look like none of my kinfolks.... Your eyes is too narry.

[DARE *narrer, narrey* (at *narrow* adj) chiefly South, South Midland]

narrow dock (also *narrow-leaved dock*) *noun* An edible wild green (*Rumex* spp) that also has medicinal uses. See also **dock, speckled dick, yellow dock.**

1963 Wilson *Regional Words* 80 *Wild sallet* represents a whole slice of botany, with polk, narrow-leaved dock, lamb's quarters, peppergrass, wild mustard, dandelions, and many other plants included. [**1971** Krochmal et al. *Medicinal Plants Appal* 218 In Appalachia the root is placed in vinegar and the wash is used to treat ringworm; the leaves are used in a poultice to treat hives. The Indians used the root for a yellow dye.] **1975** Dwyer *Thangs* 13 Narrow leaved dock [is] common in the fields and along roadsides, in the spring and early summer. Use young leaves under one foot long and cook until tender. **1988** Dyer *Farmstead Yards* 25 In a recent interview, Inez Adams recalled the folk names of her mother's favorite wild greens (which, presumably, fall into Shields' "field cresses" category): "crowsfoot," "freckleface," "gravy leg," and "narrow dock." **1999** Perry *Clinch River* Nobody in our family said greens or landcress, it was Sallet. I especially like the homey names of plants Granny taught me to recognize, Narrow dock, speckled Dick, woolly britches.

narr'r, narry See **narrow.**

narvious, narvish, narvous See **nervous.**

nary See also **ary, nary one.**

A Variant forms *naer* [see **1862** in **C**], *nairy* [see **1975** at **B**], *nare* [see **1883** at C], *narry* [see **1863** in **C**], *ne'er* [see **1972** in **B**].

B *pronoun* Not a one, none, any.

1895 Edson and Fairchild *TN Mts* 376 I never seen nary 'thout that wasn't one. **1972** *AOHP/ALC-298* Now I ain't heared nary, have you, about witches? **1972** *AOHP/ALC-355* [I] ne'er seed nor heared of nary [witch doctors], not around here, not around here, no one never. **1975** Chalmers *Better* 65 Airy and nairy, they say, for any and none.

C *adjective, adverb* (especially in phrase *nary a* and with another negative) Not a single, no, neither, never, not, not any. See also Grammar and Syntax §3.2.

1862 Carter *CW Letters* (July 27) Sary I haint re cieved naer letter from you Sense your unkle D. H. Simmons come Back from nasvill. **1863** *Lance CW Letters* (May 31) this is the poorist cuntry I ever saw I havent Saw narry good farm in Mississippi yet. **1883** Murfree *Old Sledge* 552 I ain't a-goin' ter deal ye nare 'nother kyerd. **1904–20** Kephart *Notebooks* 4:853 There ain't nary bitty sense in it. **1915** Dingus *Word-List VA* 186 *nairy* = not any, not the least: "He wouldn't help nairy bit." **1916** Combs *Old Early English* 288 The mountaineer even supplies another article, a, e.g. in "I won't go nary a step!" **1937** Hall *Coll* (Cosby Creek TN) I ain't seed nary another'n. . . . [The bee stings] got so they wouldn't swell him nary a grain. *Ibid.* (Emerts Cove TN) [Addressing one who is a novice at poker]: Got ary pair? Hain't got nary pair. **1938** Bowman *High Horizons* 2 I'd like to, mister, only she ain't got nary mule. **1939** Hall *Coll* (Deep Creek NC) I couldn't get nary another shot there, so [the bear] went on out two or three hundred yards. *Ibid.* (Hazel Creek NC) That was the last you ever seed of any wolf in this country, never seed nary other wolf in this country anymore. *Ibid.* (Smokemont NC) We hunted all night, till ten o'clock the next morning, never struck nary track. *Ibid.* (Tow String Creek NC) I says "I don't want to hear that nary another time, boys. I'm a-showing you how to work, and I mean for you to know how to work." **c1940** Padelford *Notes* Nary a thing to do but watch the sun-ball rise and set. **1954** Arnow *Dollmaker* 70 Lots a time I don't think you love me, nary a bit. **1971** *AOHP/ALC-4* Now they hain't a house on Big Caney [Creek], and it ten miles long and nary a house on it. It's all gone. **1973** GSMNP-76:9 I don't know nary Reagan now that lived there. **1978** Montgomery *White Pine Coll* IV-2 I never have seen one of them tell him not to put nary dollar in it. *Ibid.* X-2 I never was mistreated not nary a minute by nobody. **1979** GSMNP-111:8 I ain't got on hardly nary thing. **1989** *Matewan OHP-9* They ain't got nary an aunt or uncle on my daddy's side a-living. **1991** Thomas *Sthn Appal* 195 They wuzent nary true word in it. *Ibid.* 235 They was some grandsons wouldn't work a lick. Wouldn't hepp 'im nary lick.

[alteration of *ne'er a*; OED3 *nary* adj, adv chiefly U.S. (regional and colloquial), England regional (southwest), and Irish English; EDD (at *never a*, *never a one*) Engl, Irel, cf *ne'er* adj; DARE *nary* adj 1 chiefly South, South Midland]

nary one See also **ary**, **ary one**, **nary**.

A Variant forms *naern* [see **1952** in **B**], *nairn* [see **1952** in **B**], *nairy'n* [see **1927** in **B**], *nare won* [see **1863** in **B**], *narn* [see **1952** in **B**, *nar'n* [see **1976** in **B**], *nary a one* [see **c1960** in **B**], *nary'un* [see **1949** in **B**], *ne'er a one* [see **c1960** in **B**].

B *pronoun phrase* Not (a single) one, no one, none.

1863 Epperly *CW Letters* (May 12) I thought Every eavning I would get a leter from you but I havent got nare won yet. **1863** Wilson *Confederate Private* (Feb 1) they hant nary one of them able to do much. **1864** Chapman *CW Letters* (May 29) harvy you must look over mi bad wrighting and s[p]elling for i cant do nary won you no i dont expect you can read hit you must spell hit and pronanes hit what hit is amost like. **1873** Smith *Arp Peace Papers* 94 There was nary one but what had the dyspepsy, or swinny, or rumaticks, or the blind staggers. **1927** Mason *Lure of Smokies* 232 "Didn't ye bring nairy'n with ye?" said Levi. **1934–47** *LAMSAS Appal* (Madison Co NC) *nary'un*. **1937** Hall *Coll* (Cataloochee NC) I never seed a deer nor saw nary'un's tracks. **1949** Hall *Coll* (Del Rio TN) Jack is an old hand to coon-hunt, but he never catches nary'un. **1952** Wilson *Folk Speech NC* 568 *narn*, *nairn*; I don't own a dog, and I don't want *naern*. **1956** Hall *Coll* (Roaring Fork TN) I won't shoot nary one of them. **c1960** Wilson *Coll*: *ne'er a one* (or *nary a one*) = not one; nary . . . ne'er a. **1970** *Burton-Manning Coll-94A* I never had rid the train nor nothing, nary one of us had. **1972** GSMNP-93:1:23 Nary one of the family never got bit. **1976** Weals *Two Minus* [Speaker A:] Can I borrow your automobiles? [Speaker B:] I ain't got nar'n. **1985** Irwin *Alex Stewart* 161 Son, if you never got a vote till you get one from me, you'll never get nary a one. **1989** *Matewan OHP-33* [I've] been married twicet and ain't got nary'un [= wife] now. **1991** Thomas *Sthn Appal* 54 I ewst to see 'um hoppin' around. But I ain't seen nary'un in th' last two years, I don't reckin. **1997** *Dante OHP-14* I had all of mine [= babies] at home. I never had nary one in the hospital. **2009** Burton *Beech Mt Man* 127 Ever'one I run around with when I was a teenager nary one of 'em goofed up. They all got jobs and married—nary one of 'em ever been divorced.

C Coreferent with the subject of the clause but having syntactic position within the predicate. See also Grammar and Syntax §18.3.

1888 Brown *Peculiar People* 508 These hyur young uns haint, nary one of 'em, got ary bit o' sense. **1956** Hall *Coll* (Byrds Creek NC) They wouldn't nary one of 'em go.

[DARE English dial *narn*, *ne'ern*, *nern*, contractions of *ne'er (a) one* (see EDD *never a one*, which lists multiple variants); DARE *nary* adj 1 South, South Midland]

nastiness See **nasty A**.

nasty

A *adjective* Disgustingly filthy, putrid; hence noun *nastiness* = filth, foul or putrid matter.

1862 *Shockley CW Letters* (March 7) I had no bed but slept three nights on the floor and it as nasty as it well could be and full of lice to boot. **1863** *Robinson CW Letters* (Feb 18) the mud Round our cook places is Shoe mouth deep in mud it is the nastes place heare I ever Saw in my life. **c1950** Adams *Grandpap* 185 Mammy, how can you tell if a woman is clean or nasty 'bout her cookin'? **1983** Page and Wigginton *Aunt Arie* 19 There's so much nastiness [upstairs], I don't know whether you can get up there or not. **1985** Irwin *Alex Stewart* 194 They [= possums] ain't a bit nastier [to eat] than a chicken or a pig. **1999** Morgan *Gap Creek* 65 You can find somebody else to clean up your nastiness.

[DARE *nasty* adj scattered but especially South]

B *verb* To defecate; to make filthy, soil (as one's clothing, especially by defecating). See also **benasty**.

1867 Harris *Sut Lovingood* 235 Lookin at his spread fingers like they warn't his'n, ur they wer nastied wif sumfin. **1957** Combs *Lg Sthn High: Word List* 67 = to respond to a "call of nature." **c1960** Wilson *Coll* = to make filthy, to defecate in one's clothes or the bed: "The old fellow nastied his bed." **1969** Roberts *Greasybeard* 74 Git away from here, you'll nasty my goose. **1976** Still *Pattern of Man* 113 He peed into the beer, not that you could nasty it worse than it was.

[DARE *nasty* v especially South Midland]

nasty-nice *adjective* Excessively tidy.

1942 Campbell *Cloud-Walking* 3 The neighbors said Sary was nasty-nice. She always hung up her dish rag all straight outside the cook room door. **c1960** Wilson *Coll* = too particular about one's manners, too well-bred.

nater See **nature**.

nateral See **natural**.

naterally See **naturally**.

nation *noun*

1 A great many, large number or amount.

1958 Campbell *Tales* 180 Granny kept a nation of herbs on hand to mollify different ailments. **1997** Montgomery *Coll* (known to Brown, Bush, Cardwell, Jones, Norris, Weaver).

[DARE *nation* n[1] chiefly South, South Midland]

2 Used in phrases as a mild oath, especially *what in the nation*.

1931 Combs *Lg Sthn High* 1308 "What in the nation are you doing!" recalls a line in Beowulf. **1957** Combs *Lg Sthn High: Word List* 67 *nation, how, what, or where in the* = an oath. Ex.: "What in the nation are you doing?" **1974** Roberts Sang Branch 285 He never did know what in the nation caused us to be out here and he went in and got our pants and we sailed out home. **1998** Montgomery *Coll: what in the nation* (known to eight consultants from the Smoky Mountains). **2007** McMillon *Notes*.

nat'ral See **natural**.

natural *adjective*

A Variant forms *nateral, nat'ral*.

1864 Gilmore *Down in TN* 94 I allers does thet bizness the nat'ral way. **1867** Harris *Sut Lovingood* 97a [sic] Now aint hit hard that being a nateral born d—d fool es I *owns* I is, I has to bar the blame of the doins of a infunel stumpy hon'd, curly faced hole fool bull. **1896** Fox *Last Stetson* 201 Do you think I'm a idgit, Eli? Actin' mighty nateral now. **1925** (in **1935** Edwards *NC Novels* 48) *nateral*. **1978** Hiser *Quare Do's* 99 Bill was a nateral born bachelor man.

B Honest-to-goodness.

1955 Ritchie *Singing Family* 59 We couldn't see a natural blessed thing.

natural born *adjective phrase* Inveterate, incorrigible, confirmed.

1867 Harris *Sut Lovingood* 29 Didn't du hit in the name ove common sense; did hit in the name, an' wif the sperit, ove plum natral born durn fool. **1883** Zeigler and Grosscup *Heart of Alleghanies* 94 A unique character, who frequently mingles with the crowd, is the "nat'ral-born hoss-swopper." **1939** Burnett *Gap o' Mountains* 55 No, that pot houn ain't wuth nothin—won't ketch a hog, won't drive cattle, fights every dog he sees, lazy, haint got no affection for nobody, and is a natural born aig sucker. **1978** Hiser *Quare Do's* 99 Bill was a nateral born bachelor man. **1999** Montgomery *Coll* (known to Cardwell).

naturalized, get *verb phrase* To become accustomed to.

1924 Raine *Saddlebags* 102 Our folks got *naturalized* to the doctor, and like him. **1940** Haun *Hawk's Done* 156 It was hard for him to get naturalized to their ways. **1964** Thomas and Kob *Ballad Makin'* 7 In his sunset days, this mountain minstrel regained his eyesight, through the miracle of surgery, so long had he walked in darkness, he had "got naturalized" to do without "book learnin'."

[OED3 *naturalize* v 6a "to familiarize or accustom (one) in or to a thing" U.S. regional]

naturally *adverb*

A Variant form *naterally* [see **1931** in **B**].

B By nature, simply, actually.

1913 Kephart *Our Sthn High* 78 Thar come one turrible vy'grous blow that jest nacherally lifted the ground. I went up in the sky . . . and I went a-sailin' end-over-end. **1924** Vollmer *Sun-Up* 22 He wuz jest naturally born without any backbone. **1931** Goodrich *Mt Homespun* 75 "I do naterally love a scrop quilt," she said. **1996** Casada *Gospel Hook* 26 "Poley," he said in a plaintive voice, "I'm just naturally a leetle bit colder than I thought I was." **1997** Montgomery *Coll* (known to Adams, Brown, Bush, Ellis, Jones). **1997** Montgomery *File* He's just naturally foolish about ramps (50-year-old woman, Jefferson Co TN).

[DARE *naturally* adv B South, South Midland]

nature

A Variant forms *natur, natur'*.

1867 Harris *Sut Lovingood* 59 Then he totch ontu me; sed I wer a livin proof ove the hell-desarvin nater ove man. **1885** Murfree *Prophet* 32 Nuthin' in natur' could hev held him. **1942** Hall *Phonetics Smoky Mts* 96 The older mountain forms of *pasture* . . . *nature*, and others . . . do not show [t] by assimilation of [t] and [j]. **1969** Doran *Folklore White Co* 113 *natur*. **1969** Medford *Finis* 66 Jim, being of a "skeery natur" anyway, gave up his part of the moonshine contract, leaving the responsibility to his younger partner. **1982** Slone *How We Talked* 8 Natur (nature).

B *noun* Sexual potency or desire.

2000 Lowry *Folk Medical Term* = libido. "My nature ain't right." **2003** Cavender *Folk Medicine* 204 = sexual drive, as in "My nature is not what it used to be." **2004** Adams *Old True Love* 168 We had many years of strong nature between us and when it began to wane, we still had the memory of it and every once in a while it would flare between us and we would act like young'uns again, if only for a little while.

[cf OED3 *nature* n 4b now chiefly U.S.]

natured *adjective* Naturally inclined or disposed. See also **turn B1**.

1924 Raine *Saddlebags* 102 Sheep is natured like a deer; they use up high. **1973** *Serpents* 46 In th'wintertime, [snakes]'re gone t'where they are natured to. **1975** Chalmers *Better* 17 He's jest natured that-a-way. **1982** Slone *How We Talked* 8 Natur (nature) also means personality . . . "She is natured just like her mother." **1984** Wilder *You All Spoken* 135 = something come by naturally, as in "This river bottom is right natured for corn," and "Steers are sort of natured like horses—they work like horses," and "Snakes are natured that way, and that's why a snake is a damned snake." **2004** Burton *In Memoriam* 142 Kathy, who according to her [sister] Jean is "more natured" like her daddy [i.e. Ray Hicks] than the rest, is pretty outspoken about her dad.

[DARE *natured* adj South, South Midland]

nature's mistake *noun* The flowering dogwood (*Cornus florida*).

1960 Price *Root Digging in Appal* 9 Certain compound terms arouse one's curiosity: "nature's mistake" for the dogwood.

near *adverb* See also **nigh**.

A Comparative form *nearder*, superlative form *neardest*.

1975 Gainer *Speech Mtneer* 14 You're nearder to the door than I am. **1995–97** Montgomery *Coll*: *nearder* (known to Bush, Cardwell, Oliver); *neardest* (known to Bush, Cardwell, Oliver).

[DARE *near* adv B chiefly South, South Midland]

B Nearly. See also **nearabout**.

1815–18 (in **1881** Draper *Kings Mt* 553) There were not near so many of the enemy wounded as were of the Whigs. **1861** *Martin Letters* (Nov 29) I have had A verry bad cold but I am pretty near well. **1863** *Edmonston/Kelly CW Letters* I have very near for gotten all I new Since I came to this place. **1910** Cooke *Power and Glory* 80 I'm not as near lost on it as I am at a loom, down in the factory. **1938** (in **2009** Powell *Shenandoah Letters* 144) We Pd out what we had on us a litle home an yet hasent near got it. **1939** Hall *Coll* (Mt Sterling NC) He was near a mile away from the little boy at this time. He went somethin' near a mile back on into the Spruce Mountains. **1975** *AOHP/ALC-930* They wasn't near as many children as there are now. **2002** Rash *Foot in Eden* 64 I'd near killed a young one once.

nearabout (also *near around*) *adverb, adverb phrase* More or less, approximately (sometimes following the construction modified). See also **about, just about, nearly, nighabout**.

1863 Wilson *Confederate Private* 31 (Oct 31) I feel near a bout wel agane. **1864** *Walker CW Letters* (Aug 25) Ner A bot al the Way was open grond We formed our lines rased the yel and stirted. **1885** *Bayless Letters* 118 Our wheat is all kill(ed) near about. **1932** (in **1935** Edwards *NC Novels* 104) *nearabout*. **1971** *AOHP/ALC-160* I took me a little hitch in the Army and come back and was a coal miner then for near around fifty years. **1981** Whitener *Folk-Ways* 11 He was so scared at seeing me on the scaffold that he nearabout fainted. **1984** Smith *Oral History* 20 They would kill each other or get kilt theirselves before they was through, which is nearabout what they did. **1988** Dickey and Bake *Wayfarer* 21 You been sleepin' all day, near about and you done broke a sweat, and that's good for you. **1999** Morgan *Gap Creek* 153 The water was so hot the steam near about burned me. **2002** Rash *Foot in Eden* 89 That was near about all I didn't allow him.

[DARE *nearabout* (s) adv 2 chiefly South, South Midland]

near cut (also *near way*) *noun* A short cut. See also **cut C1, new cut, nigh cut**.

1892 Dromgoole *Dan to Beersheba* 83 Somebody must take the near cut from *Dan to Beersheba* and warn Joe. **1915** Dingus *Word-List VA* 186 *near cut* = a short by-way. Also nigh cut. **1956** Hall *Coll* (Murphy NC) [My grandfather] thought he'd take a near cut through this laurel thicket, and he didn't know what he was getting into. **1960** Burnett *My Valley* 76 Often she would take near cuts and reach the stand before the deer. **1960** Mason *Memoir* 73 Billy knew a place where he could take a "near way" and get to camp ahead of his buddies. **1961** Murry *Salt* 14 Aimin' to cut the journey some, an' git in home soonest, I decided to undertake a near cut I had never tried. **1973** GSMNP-4:1:5 Now a lot of times we would take what we called near cuts, you know, through the woods rather than walking all the way around the highway road. **1973** GSMNP-84:29 This near way down through that old field, now it had been throwed out, and a public road made through that field. **1977** Hamilton *Mt Memories* 130 I knew there was what they called a "near way" across the ridge. **1982** Powers and Hannah *Cataloochee* 248 My father built a near way from the old Indian trail that's on that map now . . . a near way coming off to the Grooms Boys Branch from the Asbury Trail. **1986** Pederson et al. *LAGS*: *near cut* (Sevier Co TN); *near way* (Carter Co TN, Fannin Co GA). **1996** Woodring *Times Gone By* 3 Back 'en they had the trails that went across the mountains, you know, like just to take off a near cut. **2008** *Rosie Hicks* 1 We could make it a little longer or we could make it a little shorter . . . near cuts or nigh cuts or whatever you want to call it.

[CUD *near cut* "a short cut"; DARE *near cut* n chiefly South Midland]

nearder, neardest See **near A**.

nearly *adverb* following the construction modified. See also **nearabout**.

1813 Hartsell *Memora* 122 the water Standes all over the In-Campment nareley. **1863** *Reese CW Letters* (March 1) the waters is All up for it Rains hear Everi day nearley. **1953** Hall *Coll* (Bryson City NC) I love to hunt turkeys, and there was lots of them on the mountains at that time. No trouble to go out and kill a turkey at any time nearly. **1969** GSMNP-25:1:6 He sold it to him for nothing, you know, nearly then. **1969** GSMNP-37:2:5 They'd all moved out nearly when I got big enough to recollect anything. **1972** *AOHP/ALC-226* We broke our necks a-getting home nearly. **1973** *Florence and Lawton* 193 I'd always nearly go out 'ere set down a while, an' I'd see some kind of wild game. **1973** GSMNP-79:19 Everybody nearly that lived in the mountains loved to eat their ramps. **1973** GSMNP-91:25 I'm always at home nearly. **1974** Dabney *Mt Spirits* 122 Everybody nearly that you met out anywheres had a bottle in his hip pocket. **1989** *Matewan OHP-33* Everybody nearly was into it [= moonshining]. **1994** Thomas *Come Go* 32 I've done all the work they was on a farm, nearly.

near onto *adverb phrase* Nearly, close to. See also **nigh of**.

1990 *Matewan OHP-73* It was about a year, I'd say, near onto a year before we married.

near way See **near cut**.

neb *noun* The nose.

1867 Harris *Sut Lovingood* 97j [sic] Ole Clapshaw believes in "witches, an warlocks, an long nebbed things" more than he does in Sicily. **1950** Dalton *Wordlist Sthn KY* 23 Keep your neb out of things that don't consarn you. **1996–97** Montgomery *Coll* (known to Bush, Cardwell).

[ultimately < Old English *nebb*; OED3 *neb* n 2 now chiefly north and Scot c1000→; EDD *neb* sb 1 Scot, nIrel, nEngl; SND n 1 "the beak or bill of a bird . . . the nose(tip) of a person"]

nebby *adjective* Inquisitive to the point of rudeness, meddlesome, snoopy.

1946 Woodard *Word-List VA/NC* 21 = inquisitive (used disparagingly).

[DARE *nebby* adj chiefly PA]

neck comfort *noun* A woolen scarf. Same as **comfort 2**.

1862 *Chapman CW Letters* [March?] tell mother taylor and all the family to wright to me tell her that I am thankful to her for the neck comefort.

necked, **neckid** See **naked**.

necktie *noun* See citation.

1939 Farr *TN Mt Regions* 91 = yoke to keep a cow from jumping fences: "We put a necktie on old Bossy."

necktie party *noun* A public hanging; also used in proverbial sayings.

1952 Wilson *Folk Speech NC* 569 = a hanging, a lynching; sometimes used facetiously. **c1960** Wilson *Coll* = a hanging or lynching. **1976** Garber *Mountain-ese* 60 My uncle was a hoss-thief, and lost his life at a necktie party. **1998** Montgomery *File* He looks like he's ready to go to a necktie party [= a jocular compliment] (85-year-old man, Greenbrier TN).

ned See **by Ned**, **old Ned**.

need *verb*

1 + past-participle form of a verb, with ellipsis of the infinitive *to be*.

1967 Hall *Coll* (Townsend TN) He'd bring that old jack that needed shoed, you know, and he was hard to shoe. **1976** Wolfram and Christian *Appal Speech* 96 In A[ppalachian] E[nglish], as in other regional varieties of English surrounding this general area, the *-ed* participial can occur without *be* . . . It needs remodeled all over it . . . I like my hair, except it needs trimmed right now . . . just about everything that needs done. **1977** Shackelford et al. *Our Appalachia* 126 If we needed anything done we did it, such as taking care of the stock, hoeing corn, plowing, and making a garden, raising everything we eat. **1978** Montgomery *White Pine Coll* IV-4 They started before sunup and worked to after sundown, if you had a job that needed finished. **1980** Ogle *Joy and Sorrow* 103 When the aide spoke of something needed done Mr. Shirley turned on her and told her he would take care of the business not to worry herself about it. **1986** Huskey *Sugarlands* 5 There were men and women living in the Sugarlands with talent and the ability to do most anything needed done in the community. **1991** Montgomery *File* What else needs done?; The bathroom needs worked on. **1994** Montgomery *Coll* This job needs finished. That thing needs washed (Shields). **2001** House *Clay's Quilt* 282 "Darry needed stomped over the way he's done Dreama," Alma said. **2004** Fisher *Kettle Bottom* 68 Whoever it was took a shot at Don Chafin needs took up the hill and the tar beat out of him. **2007** Rogers *Carson-Newman* 4–5 An interesting Appalachian grammatical structure noted by Rogers is the occasional absence of the infinitive. She observes, "Sometimes my stepmother, who is from Southeast Kentucky, will say things like 'the food needs cooked' or 'the dog needs out.' What she means, of course, is 'the food needs to be cooked' or 'the dog needs to go out.'" **2016** *Blind Pig* (July 21) The boy's tooth needs fixed or pulled, one.

[cf SND *need* v 4; DARE *need* v 2 chiefly Midland, especially PA]

2 In phrase *needn't to* + *verb*.

1861 *Hanes CW Letters* (June 16) if you havent writen to me yet you needent to untel I get to garyesburge. **1863** *Walker CW Letters* (July 31) the captain was a frade that i wouldent come back but he nedent to a bin for i dont intend to bea caaled a disserter. **1913** Kephart *Our Sthn High* 312 I'm a hillbilly, all right, and they needn't to glory their old flat lands to me. **1922** Wolfe *Buck Gavin* 43 Tell the boys hello an' good-by fer me, an' tell 'em I says—But you needn't t' mind. **1930** Armstrong *This Day and Time* 58 "You needn't to think," she added, "I'm a-goin' to take my ducks, as the saying is, to no sech market, nohow." **1931** Goodrich *Mt Homespun* 45 There's one thing I neen'ter worry about now; when he's in jail he can't be killed or crippled in a fight with them revenues. **2005** Williams *Gratitude* 510 You neenta deny it; I seen you do it.

[DARE *need* v 1 chiefly South Midland]

3 (+ *preposition* or *adverbial*) with ellipsis of the infinitive of a verb of motion. See also **want[1] 2**.

1976 Dumas *Smoky Mt Speech* 27 Some other syntactic constructions we may find characteristic of Smoky Mountain speech are such things as . . . verb-of-motion ellipsis, i.e. "I need outside" instead of "I need to go outside." **1986** Pederson et al. *LAGS* (Rabun Co GA) That cat needs out. [See **2007** in **1**.]

needcessity *noun* (A) necessity.

1862 *Kendrick CW Letters* (March 16) I know that I feel needsesity that compells me to be out. **1864** *Epperly CW Letters* (Jan 23) I hate to send for money but I em a most needsesity compeld to have som. **1867** Harris *Sut Lovingood* 80 Then hit wer that I'd a-cut ole Soul's froat wif a hansaw, an' never batted my eye, ef she'd a-hinted the needsesity. **1898** Elliott *Durket Sperret* 38 Thar's no use a-flyin' in Granny's face 'thout thar's a needcessity. **1913** Kephart *Our Sthn High* 280 Since the Appalachian people have a marked Scotch-Irish strain, we would expect their speech to show a strong Scotch influence. So far as vocabulary is concerned, there is really little of it. A few words, caigy (cadgy), coggled, fernent, gin for if, needcessity, trollop, almost exhaust the list of distinct Scotticisms [in mountain speech]. **1924** (in **1952** Mathes *Tall Tales* 32) They wouldn't be no needcessity of that, Mister. **1943** Erskine

Adventures 203 When they made up their stock they peddled it from door to door and traded what they could at the store for tobacco, snuff, salt, cloth, and other "needcessities." **c1960** Wilson *Coll* = usually humorous. **1972** Cooper *NC Mt Folklore* 124 "I don't intend to dig myself half to death, when man's needcessities are so few," he once told a neighbor. **1994** Montgomery *Coll* (known to Shields).

[folk etymology for *necessity*; SND *needcessity* n; CUD *needcessity* (at *need* 1) "(a) necessity"; DARE *needcessity* n chiefly South Midland]

needled *adjective* See citation.

1949 Maurer *Argot of Moonshiner* 11 = a type of quick aging for liquor by means of inserting an electric needle in the keg. "That ain't aged likker, it's needled."

needmore *noun* See citation.

c1960 Wilson *Coll* = nickname for a ratty little country store.

need no crutches *verb phrase* Of coffee: to be very strong.

1966 *DARE Survey* (Cherokee NC) = very strong coffee.

ne'er See **nary**.

ne'er a one See **nary one**.

neighbor (also *neighbor with*) *verb, verb phrase* To share (with) or express friendship toward (a nearby resident), as in exchanging greetings, visits, or assistance; to associate with in a friendly way.

1889 Mooney *Folk Carolina Mts* 97 When one is strong and brave he is said to be "much of a man," and when he feels sure that he will dislike a new acquaintance he knows in reason that he cain't neighbor him. **1919** Combs *Word-List South* 37 I know in reason I cain't neighbor that feller. **1941** Stuart *Men of Mts* 26 After you get out of here you won't be at a place where we can neighbor like we used to neighbor. **1944** Laughlin *Word-List Buncombe Co* 25 = to exchange labor with, as in harvest time. **1964** Stokely *Harvest* 157 They ain't over half-dozen families nigh 'nough fer her to neighbor with. **1973** *AOHP/ASU-111* They don't anybody have time to stop and talk or neighbor with you much. . . . Now back there they'd take their whole families and go and spend, they'd set up a little later at night when your neighbors come in, and the children, they'd go off in a room or if it wasn't dark. . . . They usually started neighboring before dark . . . and they'd bring their children, and they had bigger families than they have now, and the children all got out and romped and played. **1974** Fink *Bits Mt Speech* 17 They're fine folks to neighbor with. **1986** Pederson et al. *LAGS* (Rhea Co TN) We neighbored with each other. **1993** Weaver *Scotch-Irish Speech* 14 Eventually you "neighbor with" (i.e., help) one another.

neighborhood road *noun* A local country road, often maintained by its users.

1915 Dingus *Word-List VA* 186 = a by-way, distinguished from a public road.

neighbor lady *noun* A midwife.

1971 *Granny Women* 241 Midwives (also known as granny women or neighbor ladies) used to serve each section of the County.

neighbor people *noun* Neighbors.

1913 Kephart *Our Sthn High* 286 Pleonasms are abundant. . . . Everywhere in the mountains we hear of biscuit-bread . . . granny-woman and neighbor-people. **1943** Hannum *Mt People* 147 Shapes of phrases repeat themselves and the same sounds re-echo, giving, oddly enough, vividness rather than monotony—as in their use of double words: "down-log; sulphur-match; man-person; flower-thing; mother-woman; storm of rain; tooth-dentist; neighbor-people." **1972** *AOHP/LJC-205* They was some neighbor people come here, and they was talking about how long it'd been since they had enough grease to grease their bread pan. **1975** Dwyer *Thangs* 17 Words used in the mountains to name something that can be adequately named by one—probably used for emphasis and to be "sure an' certain of clarity" . . . neighbor-people.

[redundant form]

neither *conjunction*

A Variant forms *nether* [see **1863** in **B**], *nother*, *nuther*.

1861 *Dalton CW Letters* (Sept 23) if non you won[t] right you can just let hit alone cage wont right nother. **1895** Dromgoole *Humble Advocate* 323 I didn't come ter him em'ty-handed nuther. **1900** Harben *N GA Sketches* 20 Big Joe won't have to tech his bare feet to the floor while he's puttin' on his clothes, nuther. **1925** Dargan *Highland Annals* 251 I said she wouldn't have to go fur, nuther, to git somebody to take keer of her right. **1942** *Hall Phonetics Smoky Mts* [ˈnʌðɚ].

B (also *neither one*) Either one (following conjoined elements). See also **either**, **one 2**. See also Grammar and Syntax §18.1.

1862 *Martin CW Letters* (Jan 12) the people cant get thread nor cardes neither. **1862** *Neves CW Letters* (Feb 9) your little bird as you call her want [= weren't] at meeting today nor her cousin neither. **1863** *Joyce CW Letters* (March 24) I dont se no pece now a tall an I dont Recon you do nether. **1899** Fox *Mt Europa* 27 She don' seem to take atter her dad nur her mammy nother. **1935** (in **2009** Powell *Shenandoah Letters* 44) My husband or I nether one have been messing with the mess of buildings up there or the buildings either. **1940** Haun *Hawk's Done* 41 He wouldn't allow me nor Amy neither one to sing around the house. *Ibid.* 62 I didn't think about Eloyd nor Enzor neither one to be there. *Ibid.* 131 Erve nor Pharis neither one couldn't get a job. **1954** *GSMNP-19:5* They wasn't a thing nor the dog neither. **1961** Williams *Content Mt Speech* 16 He's got a good little piece of crappin' land there, but he won't corn it ner hay it nuther. **2004** Adams *Old True Love* 77 Granny said her nor Hattie neither one thought she'd live after that second day. **2017** *Blind Pig* (Oct 12) Mercer Scroggs, the "mayor" of unincorporated Brasstown, used to have a sign in his store that read, "We don't care how you used to do it up north . . . and Florida neither!"

neither one

A *conjunction* See **neither B.**

B (also *neither one of them, neither one of us*) *pronoun phrase*

1 As an appositive.

1990 Clouse *Wilder* 82 I know this happened pretty fast and we neither one expected it. **1991** Thomas *Sthn Appal* 16 They neither one shot. **2003** Carter *Mt Home* 190 Him or Mama neither one hadn't never seen a movie 'fore either. **2007** McMillon *Notes* They neither one 'em wouldn't go down there.

2 Coreferent with the subject of the clause but having syntactic position within the predicate.

1930 Armstrong *This Day and Time* 192 Old Mag an' Mis' hain't neither one of 'em never made Gid and Novy do a earthly thing. *Ibid.* 213 We hain't neither one of us brung a copper. **1939–42** Adams *Tales* 125 At last they said they would neither one of them ever eat a bite or drink a drop till she told them.

neither one of them, neither one of us See **neither one B.**

nekked, nekkid See **naked.**

ner See **nor.**

nerveous, nervious, nervish See **nervous.**

nervous *adjective* Variant forms *narvious, narvish, narvous, nerveous, nervious, nervish.*

1862 *Huntley CW Letters* (June 1) you must Excuse my Bad Writing for I am nervious. **1863** *Proffit CW Letters* (Oct 8) we have been cooking three days rations to day in order for a march but to what place I am unable to say as news is scarce & my hand is quite nervious. **1904–20** Kephart *Notebooks* 2:475 Of course, I'm weak yit and right nervish. **1913** Kephart *Our Sthn High* 224 Looks like he mought drap off, him bein' weak and rather narvish and sick with a head-swimmin'. **1925** Furman *Glass Window* 43 Likewise [we] put a handrail on the foot-log for you, so's you won't get narvious a-crossing. **1927** Mason *Lure of Smokies* 215 Right thar I got nerveous! I thought I'd come to a b'ar convention! **1969** Dial *Dialect Appal People* 468 Words with er were frequently pronounced as if the letters were ar: sarvice, sartin, narvous. **1995** Montgomery *Coll*: *nervish* (known to Cardwell, Norris, Oliver, Shields).

[EDD *nervish* 3 Scot, Irel, nEngl]

nest *noun, verb* variant noun plural forms *nestes, nesties*; variant third-person-singular form *nestes* (all of two syllables).

1867 Harris *Sut Lovingood* 158–59 I purvided about a dozen ho'nets' nestes, big soun' wuns, en' stopped em up full ove disapinted, bewild'red 'vengeful, savidge, oncircumsized ball ho'nets, sharpnin thar stings redy. **1895** Edson and Fairchild *TN Mts* 375 The most interesting thing . . . is the use of a vowel in plurals and the third singular of verbs, giving such forms as *costes, vestes, postes, nestes.* **1913** Kephart *Our Sthn High* 285 The ancient syllabic plural is preserved in beasties (horses), nesties, posties, trousies (these are not diminutives). **c1926** Cox *Cullowhee Wordlist* The hens make their nesties in the deep weeds. **1937** Haun *Cocke Co* 3 Turkle doves build their nestes between two jints of a limb. **1940** Oakley *Roamin'/Restin'* 79 This clift is where they build their nestes. **c1940** Simms *Coll* waspes [i.e. wasps'] nestes. **1942** *Hall Phonetics Smoky Mts* 82. **1969** Roberts *Greasybeard* 105 He went after a goose agg in the nestes while Sally built a fire in the stove. **1986** Ogle *Lucinda* 42 The birds have built nestes (nests) in the spring house. **2005** Williams *Gratitude* 510 *nestes* = nests. **2012** Milnes *Signs Cures Witchery* Did he look to see if there was any yellow jacket nestes around there?

[OED3 *nestes* (at *nest* n) U.S. regional (south); DARE *nest* n pl especially South, South Midland]

nest egg *noun* An artificial egg placed in a hen's nest to induce her to lay. See also **China egg, cymling B, gourd egg, nest egg, setting egg.**

1986 Pederson et al. *LAGS* (Blount Co TN, Cocke Co TN, Jefferson Co TN, Sevier Co TN). **1996** Montgomery *Coll* (known to Cardwell). **2005** Williams *Gratitude* 148 We kept a nest aig in their nestes [and would] leave it in there so the hen'd come back to her nest and lay some more. If you took all of 'em out, she'd leave her nest. *Ibid.* 510 = an artificial egg that is marked and left in the nest when the fresh eggs are gathered. Marking the eggs to be left in the nest ensures that you will not get a bad egg.

nestes, nesties See **nest.**

net *verb* variant past-tense form *net.*

1939 Hall *Coll* (Hartford TN) I guess the bear would have net three hundred pound anyway.

nether See **neither.**

neumony fever See **pneumonia fever.**

never *adverb*

A Variant forms *ne'er, nuver.* See also **nary.**

1859 Taliaferro *Fisher's River* 76 I nuver tuck time to ondress him [= a deer]. **1972** *AOHP/ALC-355* [I] ne'er seed nor heared of nary [witch doctors], not around here, not around here, no one never. **1973** *Foxfire Interviews* A-73–86 [They] ne'er asked for it.

B Syntax.

1 Didn't (used to negate a single event in the past, often emphatically). See also Grammar and Syntax §11.3.

1863 Wilson *Confederate Private* 23 (June 19) I never received your letter until today it laid at Dublin and I sent for it. **1937** Conner *Ms* 4–5 we never heard of Fertalizer's untill I was 13 or 14 year's [sic] old. **1939** Hall *Coll* (Proctor NC) We never seen it then. It run back down there again and was coming back in, and they catched it before it got back to us. **1939** Walker *Mtneer Looks* 6 *Never* is always used in the negative preterite (cf. "I never seed him" for "I didn't see him"). **1952** Mathes *Tall Tales* 36 "No, Mister, I never fotch nary apple this trip," he replied to my inquiry. **1956** Hall *Coll* (Big Creek NC) If [the groundhogs] saw their shadow, they'd go back in and never came out for a while. **1961** *Coe Ridge OHP-333A* I never heard of that man before. **1972** GSMNP-93:2:10

We never married till we was thirty-five years old. **1973** GSMNP-85:2:10 She never died then. She turned over against the wall and she says, "Lord, let me live." **c1975** Lunsford *It Used to Be* 33 While there I met the members of the family, but Redmon never moved from there for years. **1976** GSMNP-114:3 You never seen a hillside plowed, did you? **1996** GSMNPCOHP-1:4 In nineteen twenty five we had a drought in here and never made nothing.

[DARE *never* adv B1 chiefly South Midland]

2 In phrase *never did* = didn't ever. See also Grammar and Syntax §7.2.

1886 Smith *Sthn Dialect* 343 *Never* did it (Didn't do it). **1918** *Story* 20 The intensive form of the verb is commonly used: "I never did see her." **1937** Hall Coll (Cosby TN) We never did hear from them. **1976** GSMNP-113:3 I never did go hardly any. **1991** Haynes *Haywood Home* 9 I never did see Grandma do any work of any kind.

3 Used elliptically.

1883 Murfree *Old Sledge* 549 Josiah Tait, fretfully anticipating Wray, spoke in reply: "No, he never. I fotched this hyar coal o' fire myself." **1960** McCaulley *Cades Cove* They's nobody ever went to the poor house in that place, I'm telling you, they never. **1970** *Hunting Stories* 77 "D'ja get him?" I said, "Yeah!" "Aw, you never." **1973** *Flu Epidemic* 107 I thought they should have give us somethin', but they never. **1977** Norman *Kinfolks* 94 I wanted to run off from that place and just keep on going and going. But I never. **1983** *Dark Corner OHP-24A* I can remember mama was spinning and weaving, but I never. **2007** Shelby *Molly Whuppie* 67–68 They went on in and Jack told them, said, "Don't kiss me." And they never. **2009** Burton *Beech Mt Man* 39 "Well, if they ever want to come see me when they get bigger"—but they never.

never did See **never B2**.

never hear the like See **like C**.

never no mind *noun phrase* A concern or difference, used especially in verb phrases *not to be never no mind* = not to be of concern, *not to make one never no mind* = not to matter or cause concern to one. See also **no never mind**.

c1959 Weals *Hillbilly Dict* 2 *ain't never no mind* = don't worry about it; makes no difference; don't let it bother you. **1995–97** Montgomery Coll: *that don't make me never no mind* (known to Adams, Brown, Cardwell, Oliver); I ain't never no mind [i.e. I hadn't given any thought to it], That ain't never no mind [i.e. that's trivial; don't worry about it] (Cardwell). **2001** Lowry *Expressions* 4 It don't make me never no mind.

never say dog (also *didn't say dog, never say jackum, never say scat, never say turkey*) *verb phrase* To fail to say anything at all. See also **pea turkey**.

1895 Edson and Fairchild *TN Mts* 376 *never say dog* = never say anything. "Where's that boy? He went off and never said dog." **1936** Still *Horse Doctor* 26 He never said scat. **1941** Stuart *Men of Mts* 322 I never could understand why we grieve over the whole and never say "scat" about one of the parts. **1983** Page and Wigginton *Aunt Arie* 169 [They] went off and never said turkey. **1989** *Matewan OHP-24* [They] never said jackum the first time. **1997** Montgomery Coll: *never say dog* (known to Adams, Brown, Bush, Cardwell, Jones, Weaver). **2014** *WV Talk* "He left and didn't say dog to nobody" = the person left without saying goodbye or anything else for that matter.

never say jackum, never say scat, never say turkey See **never say dog**.

never see the like See **like C**.

new *verb* Of the moon: to enter the first half of its cycle, which signals whether planting and other activities will be propitious. See also **new of the moon**.

1961 *Coe Ridge OHP-340B* When a moon news, the sign runs in the legs and down to the feet. It's when we do our work, I mean, you know, trimming. **1973** *Gardening* 250 [The] last quarter before it news, there's three dark nights before the new moon. **1981** GSMNP-122 The moon newed Sunday. It ain't no good time to plant nothing this week for me. **1995** Harrison *Smoke Rings* 165 "The moon newed a-Saturday" is a hillbilly way of saying there was a new moon the previous Saturday.

new Christmas *noun* Christmas as celebrated according to the modern western or Gregorian calendar on December 25. Also called **modern Christmas**. See also **old Christmas**.

1923 Furman *Mothering* 186 I allus used to swill all I could hold, from New Christmas to Old Christmas. **1927** Furman *Lonesome Road* 103–4 Now the Christmas season drew on.... They had never heard of a Christmas gift or tree. On other creeks, New Christmas, the twenty-fifth of December, was the signal for the beginning of wild and lively doings by the young people,—to dances, drinking, too often shooting, all kinds of gayety,—which, however, always came to an abrupt close on the night of the fifth of January, Old Christmas Eve. In the belief of all the older people, Old Christmas, was real Christmas, and discipline was sternly enforced when it began. **1955** Ritchie *Singing Family* 163 I reckon the New Christmas and the ideas of presents and the tree Mom read about in a paper or book of some kind. **1992** Bush *Dorie* 56 Many highlanders disapproved of the "new" Christmas observed on December 25.

new cut (also *newer cut*) *noun* A path or road made to reduce the distance covered by an older one. See also **cut C1**, **near cut**, **nigh cut**.

1973 GSMNP-4:17 From the gap at Mount Sterling it's a mile to High Top. That's straight out the mountain from the gap at Mount Sterling, but there's a new cut I was telling you about, what we call newer cuts, that goes right by this Indian grave that I'm telling you about.

newer cut See **new cut**.

new ground *noun* [often with stress on *ground*] An area of virgin land newly prepared or intended to be prepared for cultivation through clearing vegetation by **grubbing**, **deadening**, **log rolling**, burning, etc. See 1961, c1995 citations. See also **break B9**.

1795 (in **1919** DeWitt *Sevier Journal* 179) (Aug 24) [I] began to pull blades in the New Ground. **1842** Crosby *Journal/Account Book* 101 Planted the Lower New Ground Corn the first week of April and Planted the Upper New Ground 2nd week in April. **1843** *McLean Diary* 83 [I] Commenst plowing my New Ground. **1862** *Lockmiller Letters* (March 30) [We] have got the old grond brok up and the new grond purteni cland of[f]. **1865** *Brown CW Letters* (May 2) My corn is not planted yet I thought last winter I would try to get more corn put in than my new ground pease. **1914** Arthur *Western NC* 254 Land was plentiful in those primitive times and as fast as a piece of "new ground" was worn out, another "patch" was cleared and cultivated until it, in its turn, was given over to weeds and pasturage. **1939** Hall *Coll* (Saunook NC) After breakin' new land, it's new ground and is not called such after two or three year. Sprouts of sassafras, locust, and running briers come up during that time and you have to keep 'em cut down. **1956** Hall *Coll* (Cosby TN) Every man, he'd grub and clear up a piece of land, new ground, in the winter time. They'd have log rollin's in the spring. **1961** Medford *History Haywood Co* 74 The log rollin's and burnin's in those days before the Civil War (and for a long time afterwards) came from clearing up "new grounds." Thousands upon thousands of big prime logs (that would today be worth from ten to fifteen dollars or more per log) were rolled off the new grounds and burned or left to lie and rot. **1971** Foster *Walker Valley* 3:4 The way that you got your fuel, you cleaned up, you called it new ground. Just go out in the woods and you cleaned up some every year was the way my father done it. **1979** Slone *My Heart* 61 I've always been thankful we owned a farm of our own, to grow corn, for example. A "new ground" (pronounced as one word) was best. This meant the ground had been cleared of all the trees and underbrush, and was now ready to be planted. If you were lucky enough to have a new ground you would be assured of a good crop but a lot more work. It had to be all done by hand, using only hoes. Although most of the larger roots and stumps were removed—either by burning or dynamite, or sometimes pulled out by oxen—there were still too many small roots and sprouts to make plowing possible. **1980** *GSMNP*-115:53 They used to have grubbings. People would get together and go in and just have grubbing, grub up little new grounds, you know, for a man. **1982** DeArmond *So High* 63 Long before the first bud appeared, Robert and two of his neighbors were busy clearing the "new ground." **1989** Oliver *Hazel Creek* 15 This process of clearing a field was referred to as making a new-ground, and it was slow and arduous. **1994** Landry *Coll* We'd take axes and things and clear the foreses to make new ground to plant corn next year. **c1995** *Cades Cove* 5 Huge trees were cleared by girdling them with an axe. The first crops were planted among the soon-dead timber. After a few years the standing trees were cut down, rolled into piles and burned. Orchards and permanent fields followed quickly on the "new ground." Common sense told farmers to reserve the flat land for corn, wheat, oats, and rye. **2005** Williams *Gratitude* 510 = land that has never been plowed before.

new house *noun* A room added onto an existing dwelling. See also **big house**, **house**.

c1995 *Roaring Fork* 12 At some time, probably after Reagan's fifth or sixth child, he raised the roof to create the attic bedrooms and added the kitchen wing at the rear. The "new house" deserved sawn board paneling and ceilings, slicked down with a hand plane.

new life root *noun* Same as **ginseng**.

1997 Montgomery *Coll* (known to Brown).

newlight *noun* The white crappie (*Pomoxys annularis*) fish. See also **Campbellite**.

1887 Goode *Amer Fishes* 71 (*DARE*) Pomoxys annularis is also known by such names as "Bachelor" in the Ohio Valley, "New Light" and "Campbellite" in Kentucky, Illinois and Indiana, names given to it by the irreverent during the great Campbellite movement in the West nearly half a century ago. **2005** Friend *Maysville Road* 340 "New Light" was the colloquial name given the pomoxis annularis Rafinesque, the crappie species of sunfish first identified in the early 1800s.

new of the moon *noun* The beginning of the lunar cycle, when the moon emerges as a slender crescent from the **dark of the moon**, which signals whether planting and other activities will be propitious or not. See also **dark of the moon**, **light of the moon**, **new**, **old of the moon**, **shrink B**.

1939 Hall *Coll* Corn planted on the new of the moon will grow tall. **1961** *Coe Ridge OHP*-340B On the new of the moon, I mean, when a moon news, the sign runs in the legs and down to the feet, it's when we do our work, I mean, you know, trimming. **1963** Watkins and Watkins *Yesterday* 139 Hogs killed at the new of the moon had more lard in them than hogs killed on the old of the moon. **1972** *Foxfire I* 190 If you kill a hog on th' new of th' moon, slice it and put it in a pan; it'll just blow you 'til you can't fry th' grease out of it hardly. *Ibid.* 221 Dig a hole on th' new of th' moon and you will have dirt to throw away. **1979** *Daddy Oakley* 180 If you plant corn on the new of the moon, it just grows a-way up there—high. On the new of the moon, the ear wants to turn up the stalk. **1983** *Dark Corner OHP*-5A You only cut wood on the new of the moon. It dries out and makes it light, for stove wood, you know, and dry it quicker. If you cut it on the old of the moon, it'll mold, turn all blue and sog. It won't never dry out. **1984** Page and Wigginton *Foxfire Cookery* 271 In the new of the moon when the signs are below the knees is the best time you'll ever make pickled beans or anything else that you work in vinegar with.

new patch *noun* See citation.

2009 Benfield *Mt Born* 41 *new patch* = land that is newly cleared and being prepared for farming. When a man cleared a new patch of land, he was most often getting ready to put in a crop.

news bee *noun*

1 See citation.

1967 *DARE Survey* (Brasstown NC) = meeting where there is a lot of talking.

2 (also *news carrier, news fly*) See citations. See also **good news bee, study bee.**

1914 Crain *Life Story* 16 Mountain people are somewhat superstitious.... They also have a notion that the black news-fly brings bad luck, but that the yellow one brings good luck. **1940** Haun *Hawk's Done* x A honeybee or newsbee flying around one's head means good luck. **1962** Miller *Pigeon's Roost* (May 10) I saw my first "steady bee" of this year last Sunday, but have not seen a news carrier yet. The news carrier is colored like a yellow jacket but much bigger and longer. It seems they all the time want to buzz around your ear. They said when they come around, they have got some kind of news that they want to tell and most of the time bad luck will happen someway to the one who the news carrier tries to tell them something. **1971** *Granny Women* 254 Nora Garland ... talked at length about the "news bees" that are so common around here: "Well, now, there's yeller ones—that's good news—and they's black ones, and that's bad news." **2007** McMillon *Notes*: *news carrier* = looks like a fat yellow jacket but does not sting.

news carrier, news fly See **news bee 2.**

New Year's Eve gift (also *New Year's gift*) *interjection* Happy New Year! (used as a greeting on New Year's Day, often in a ritual wherein a person attempts to say it before others). See also **Christmas Eve gift, Christmas gift.**

1934–47 *LAMSAS Appal* (Madison Co NC, Swain Co NC) *New Year's gift.* **1949** McDavid *Grist* 111 (Fannin Co GA) *New Year's Eve gift* = a salutation. **1956** McAtee *Some Dial NC* 31 *New Year's gift* = salutation on the pattern of "Christmas Gift!" **1957** Broaddus *Vocab Estill Co KY* 52 *New Year's gift* = the same as "Christmas Gift!," only said on New Year's Day. **1986** Pederson et al. *LAGS*: *New Year's gift* (Banks Co GA, Claiborne Co TN, Cumberland Co TN).

[DARE *New Year's gift* exclam South, South Midland]

(the) next thing to *noun phrase* The closest thing to, a specimen very similar to.

1981 Henry *Alex Stewart* 57 The flavor is pretty much like, not vanilla, but it's just the next thing to it.

next to See **get next to.**

nib and tuck *adverb phrase* Very close, "nip and tuck." See also **nickety tuck, nippity click, nippity cut.**

1966 *DARE Survey* (Cherokee NC) = just about equal, very close: "They were both fast runners, and it was——all the way."

nicker (also *nickle*) *verb* Of a horse, donkey, etc.: to neigh gently, especially at feeding time. See also **whicker, whimper.**

1813 Hartsell *Memora* 103 I fetched a verey large load of cane for the horses, and came throw the incampment and some horses lay there, and as I pased throw the horses nickered for my cane tell my hart aked for them. **1867** Harris *Sut Lovingood* 168 They [= live-stock] ... roll'd over, run away, bawl'd, beller'd, nicker'd, screem'd, an' bray'd till they farly shuck the leaves ontu the trees. **1924** (in **1952** Mathes *Tall Tales* 47) Sure enough in a few minutes four lank horsemen were dismounting at the gate amid much nickering of horses and yapping of hounds. **1934–47** *LAMSAS Appal* (Swain Co NC) *nicker.* **1941** Hall *Coll* (White Oak NC) Nicker, whimper—these are the common expressions around the White Oak. Some say neigh. **1949** Kurath *Word Geog East US* 42 From the Virginia Piedmont *nicker* has spread westward all the way to the Ohio Valley ... and southward in the Blue Ridge and the Appalachians to Georgia. *Nicker* now dominates this vast area; only relics of the Midland *whinny* and the coastal *whicker* are found here and there. *Ibid.* 43 There is at least one clear case of a Virginia Piedmont term that has spread through the Appalachians and well beyond into the Ohio Valley. That term is *nicker.* **1966** Dakin *Vocab Ohio River Valley* 252–54 The *nicker* area which extends westward from Chesapeake Bay and the Virginia Piedmont continues almost unchecked through the entire Ohio Valley. This term is common everywhere and holds full sway over extensive regions. The related *nickle* appears twice in the [KY] Mountains. **1967** *DARE Survey* (Gatlinburg TN) = sound a horse makes. **1986** Pederson et al. *LAGS* (Blount Co TN, Cocke Co TN, Jefferson Co TN, Sevier Co TN). **1998** Montgomery *Coll* (known to Cardwell, Jones, Norris, Oliver, Weaver).

[OED3 *nicker* v 1a originally Scot, c1617→; EDD Scot, Irel, nEngl; SND *nicher* v; CUD *nicker* v 1 "neigh, whinny"]

nickety tuck *adverb phrase* See citation. See also **nib and tuck, nippity click, nippity cut.**

1904–20 Kephart *Notebooks* (in **1993** Farwell and Nicholas *Smoky Mt Voices* 116) Nipety-tuck, nickety tuck ... living marginally.... "It's just nickety tuck with 'em."

nickle See **nicker.**

nick-tailed *adjective* Of a horse: having the tail cut on the underside, so that it is carried high.

1867 Harris *Sut Lovingood* 19 A nick tailed, bow necked, long, poor, pale sorrel horse.

[DARE *nick-tailed* adj especially South, South Midland]

nigh

A *adjective*

1 Having an affinity or closeness; intimate.

1982 Slone *How We Talked* 4 The words "Nigh to me," can mean "We are close kin," but it means a lot more than just that. If you hear someone say of another person, "He is nigh to me," it represents a closeness, a belonging to each other, that no one nor anything can come between, not understood by outsiders. Some man might jokingly say of his wife, "I have lived with her so long that she has begun to feel nigh to me."

2 See citation.

1997 Johnson *Melungeon Heritage* 60 If somebody said they went "nigh" across the hill to visit a friend, it meant they took the short cut.

B *adverb* Near, close, nearly. See also **a-nigh**, **nighabout**, **nigh as a pea**, **nigh of**, **nigh't**, **pretty nigh**.

1774 *Dunmore's War* 141 The Boys left After these Signs nighest Home. **1862** *Warrick CW Letters* (July 22) I think it is mity hard for you to come that nie home and I cant get to see you. **1863** *Poteet CW Letters* (Nov 3) I am about thirty five miles nigher tha[n] when I was at Weldon. **1901** Harben *Westerfelt* 136 He reckoned the nigher people got to the railroad the furder they wus from the cross [i.e., Christianity]. **1913** Kephart *Our Sthn High* 312 I went down into the valley, wunst, and I declar I nigh sultered! **1939** Hall *Coll* (Nine Mile TN) I got to studyin' then how nigh that bear come a-gettin' me, and I just got scared so bad it just appeared like my heart was right up in my mouth just a-beatin'. *Ibid.* (Jefferson City TN) I could might nigh put my foot where hit killed the sheep. **1953** Hall *Coll* (Bryson City NC) [How long did Jake work for the lumber companies?]: Well, 'long about eighteen and ninety two and nigh up till about nineteen and ten. **1956** Hall *Coll* (Roostertown TN) I asked him to tell me [a tale], and I've damn nigh paid him for it. **1971** Foster *Walker Valley* 3:37 I never was nigh as good. **1973** GSMNP-85:1:16 They come mighty nigh hanging old Bob Catlett, too. **1991** Thomas *Sthn Appal* 236 I'z little an' I couldn't nigh keep up with 'im.

[DARE *nigh* adv A chiefly South Midland]

C *preposition* Near.

1938 Bowman *High Horizons* 16 "As I 'ezact' it," Steve [Ownby] said, "hit wuz nigh 1840 when they come to stay." **1956** Hall *Coll* (Jones Cove TN) Mark Hopkins in California was my grandfather's brother. He was born over nigh the Chucky River.

nighabout

A *adverb phrase*

1 Nearby, close at hand.

1884 Murfree *In TN Mts* 249 It's the onluckiest place ennywhar nigh about.

[DARE *nigh about* adv 1 chiefly South, South Midland]

B *preposition* Almost, close to. See also **nearabout**, **nigh B**.

1913 Kephart *Our Sthn High* 94 They mean nigh about the same thing, only there's a differ. **1924** Raine *Saddlebags* 83 I reckon thar must ha' been forty or nigh about. **c1960** Wilson *Coll* = almost: "Nighabout eighty year old." **1998** Montgomery *Coll* (known to all consultants from the Smoky Mountains); It was nigh about ten a.m. when we got started (Cardwell).

nigh as a pea *adverb phrase* See citation. See also **come a little bit of**.

1968 *Expressions* 24 "Nigh as a pea" (meaning very close to).

[DARE at *pea* n^1 5 especially South Midland]

nigh cut (also *nigher cut*, *nigh way*) *noun* A shortcut, short(er) distance. See also **cut C1**, **near cut**, **new cut**.

1898 Dromgoole *Cinch* 13 If I ain't forgot more'n I think, I know a nigher cut to the house than the big road. **1937** Hall *Coll* (White Oak NC) "Nigh cut" is also used but not as much as "nigh way." **1939** Hall *Coll* (Maggie Valley NC) I give [the raccoons] to my brother and told him to come back the nigh way and I'd go up to Balsam Corner to see if I could locate some bear sign. **1953** Wharton *Dr Woman Cumberlands* 75 I kin take ye there a nigh way, cross country. **1982** Slone *How We Talked* 34 *nigh cut* = a shorter distance: "Take the nigh cut around the hill." **1986** Pederson et al. *LAGS* (Cocke Co TN). **1989** Hannah *Reflections* 60 He turned off too quick and missed Hobart's nighway. **1990** Bailey *Draw Up Chair* 13 There and back Will had some twelve miles to walk even though he'd take [the] "nigh way" that cut across the ridge.

[DARE *nigh cut* n chiefly South Midland]

nigher cut See **nigh cut**.

nigh it (also *nigh't*) *adverb* See 1957 citation. See also **it C4**.

1957 Combs *Lg Sthn High: Word List* 67 *nigh't* = clipped form of *nigh it*. Ex.: "She's might' nigh't dead." **1978** Hiser *Quare Do's* 26 Uncle Bob purt nigh it cried.

nigh of (also *nigh on*, *nigh onto*) *adverb phrase* Nearly, close to. See also **near onto**, **nigh B**.

1867 Harris *Sut Lovingood* 243 The road led ni ontu Wat's, ur the widder's. **1895** Edson and Fairchild *TN Mts* 374 Judge Jackson's son has been talkin' to my daughter nigh on a year. **1939** Hall *Coll* (Wears Cove TN) We'uns can say nigh of two hundred would come a heap closer. **1951** Barnwell *Our Mt Speech* I ain't seen my sister for nigh on to twenty years; I can't hardly memorize her. **1957** Combs *Lg Sthn High: Word List* 67 *nigh onto* = approximating. Ex.: "He's been dead nigh onto twenty year." **1963** Edwards *Gravel* 89 We stood thar an talked fer nigh onto a hour and him a tellin all about how it wuz. **1967** *DARE Survey* (Maryville TN) *nigh onto* = nearly. **1974** Fink *Bits Mt Speech* 17 Hit's *nigh onto* a mile.

[DARE *nigh onto* adv scattered, but more frequent South Midland]

nigh on, nigh onto See **nigh of**.

nigh-sighted *adjective* Near-sighted.

c1940 Simms *Coll* Old nigh-sighted Jane.

nigh't See **nigh it**.

night chamber See **night glass**.

night crawler *noun* A large earthworm.

1966–67 *DARE Survey* (Burnsville NC, Spruce Pine NC, Maryville TN) = a type of worm used as bait. **1986** Pederson et al. *LAGS* (Cocke Co TN, Jefferson Co TN). **1997** Montgomery *File* (known to 60-year-old man, Maggie Valley NC). **2007** McMillon *Notes* = now the most common term.

night dog *noun* See citation.

1994 Farwell and Buchanan *Logging Terms* = an implement that was used to help control a log; it slid up and down on a bar and a lever was used to loosen or fasten it.

night glass (also *night chamber*, *night jar*) *noun* A chamber pot.

c1960 Wilson Coll: *night jar* = a chamber pot. **1968** *DARE Survey* (Springwood VA) night chamber. **1997** Montgomery Coll (known to Adams, Bush).

[DARE *night glass* n chiefly South, South Midland]

night-growing hemlock *noun* See citation.

1974–75 McCracken *Logging* 8:154 [A night growing hemlock] is one that just got about two logs in it and that s.o.b., before you can get a saw buried in it, hit's a-bindin'. You can drive four wedges in it and hit'll bind all the way through. It's what we'd call a scrub tree, and I don't know what they is about them, but them old timber cutters, I don't know where they ever got the name of night growing hemlock, but that's what they called 'em, and every once in a while, you'd hit one, it'd take a half day to cut it in two.

night peeper *noun* Same as **peeper**, **spring cheeper**.

2004 House *Coal Tattoo* 62–63 She could hear everything separately . . . the squeals of the night peepers.

night school *noun* Formerly, a rural school whose session was held at night so those who farmed could attend.

1953 Hall Coll (Hartford TN) Everybody had to work during the day, [so we] had night school.

night stick *noun* Same as **backstick**.

1995 Weber *Rugged Hills* 40 When we get our felled trees home, we first cut the trunks into chunks about 18 inches long and 12 to 16 inches in diameter. These make good "night sticks"—logs that are put in the fire last to give heat all night long. In olden times, these large logs were placed way in the back of the fireplace at night and were called "back sticks."

night watch See **watch night**.

nigh way See **nigh cut**.

nine bark *noun* A hydrangea (*Hydrangea arborescens*) whose bark has medicinal uses.

1901 Lounsberry *Sthn Wild Flowers* 221 Downy or Snowy Hydrangea. . . . In the mountains of the Blue Ridge and westward. . . . The mountaineers call the plant, "nine bark." A name significant of the way its bark peels off in little layers. This they collect and steep for use in various medicinal ways. **1964** Miller *Pigeon's Roost* (Nov 5) Miller said he has several sacks of hydrangea roots (called here nine bark) as well as wild lettuce leaves that he will get 25 cents a pound for.

ninnie *noun* Breast milk.

1980 Matthews *Appal Physician* 153 Babies stayed on the breast from the time they became the lap baby until they were the knee baby, and even then they got some "ninnie" until they were shamed of it. **1996–97** Montgomery Coll (known to Adams, Brown, Bush, Cypher, Oliver).

[DARE *ninny* n² etymology uncertain; perhaps hypocoristic, but cf **1949** Turner *Africanisms* 199]

nip *noun* See citation.

c1975 *Miners' Jargon* 5 = the device at the end of the trailing cable of a mining machine used for connecting the trailing cable to the trolley wire and ground [in a coal mine]. Also called *cathead*.

nippity click *adverb phrase* At a fast pace. See also **nib and tuck**, **nickety tuck**, **nippity cut**.

1999 Spencer *Memory Lane* II:7 He was very small in stature, and he walked energetically—nippity click.

nippity cut (also *nipety-tuck*, *nippity tuck*) *adverb phrase* Nip and tuck, by a small margin, very close, at close quarters. See also **nib and tuck**, **nickety tuck**, **nippity click**.

1901 Harben *Westerfelt* 222 Toot drove nipitytuck down the street from the Hawkbill as fast as he could lick it, and them a-gallopin' after 'im. **1904–20** Kephart *Notebooks* (in **1993** Farwell and Nicholas *Smoky Mt Voices* 116) Nipety-tuck, nickety tuck . . . living marginally. . . . "It's just nickety tuck with 'em." **1917** Kephart *Word-List* 415 *nipety-tuck* = nip and tuck. **1937** Hyatt *Kiverlid* 64 An' thar they had it nippety-tuck. **1942** (in **1987** Perdue *Outwitting Devil* 10) They hadn't gone fer tell Fourteen heard a fight start an' seed the giant a comin' and the lion right after him nippity tuck. **1997** Montgomery Coll: *nippity tuck* (known to eight consultants from the Smoky Mountains); They went nippity tuck down the field [i.e. side by side or one right after the other] (Cardwell).

[*nippity tuck* = variant of *nip and tuck*, perhaps influenced by *lickety-split*; DARE *nippity-tuck* adv, adj chiefly South Midland]

'nm See **and them**.

no *adjective* used in constructions of multiple negation.

1862 *Martin CW Letters* (March 2) when we Came back to this Island Last week I had No pen Nor No Money till yester day. **1922** *TN CW Ques* 1317 (Sullivan Co) there was not no one close to me that owned slaves. **1939** Hall Coll (Little Cataloochee NC) They was ignorant, raised up in ignorance, no Sunday School, no church nor nothing, nor no one to lead them on right, in the right way. **1972** *AOHP/ALC-298* [During the Depression it was] hard to get a-hold of no money. **1989** *Matewan OHP-11* At that time there wasn't no supermarkets. **1998** *Dante OHP-12* It wasn't no road like these over here.

no blood *noun*

1 See citations.

1990 Cavender *Folk Medical Lex* 28 = anemia. **1994** Montgomery Coll (known to Ogle).

2 See citations.

1990 Cavender *Folk Medical Lex* 28 = easily chilled or cold natured constitution. **1994** Montgomery Coll (known to Ogle).

nobody *pronoun* variant syntactic position within the predicate. See also Grammar and Syntax §18.3. See also **do A2a**, **do A2b**, **somebody B**.

1971 *Boogers* 48 They didn't nobody ever know what become of that man's wife and baby. **1977** Norman *Kinfolks* 46 You'd have him so spoiled they wouldn't nobody know him. **2000** Montgomery *File* We don't nobody know how long we have (71-year-old woman, Walland TN).

no call for, no call to See **call B**.

no circumstance to See **circumstance B**.

no-count *adjective* Of low or trifling quality, of little value or use, good for nothing; hence noun = a person of such worth.

1861 *Martin CW Letters* (Dec 21) any person that will Mar[r]y thes times is No count on the face of the earthe. **1862** *Lockmiller CW Letters* (Aug 14) excuse bad riting for my pen is no count and I am in abad fix to rite. **1867** Harris *Sut Lovingood* 106 I'm no count, no how. **1895** Edson and Fairchild *TN Mts* 372 These 'ere make-dos are no 'count. **1939** Hall *Coll* (Bradley Fork NC) I never was in such a law-breaking country in my life. It was no count. **1962** Dykeman *Tall Woman* 298 "Why should I take that no 'count land?" he demanded. **1984** Burns *Cold Sassy* 165 His daddy was lazy, leaving all the work to field hands or sorry no-count tenants and croppers. **1990** Clouse *Wilder* 78 I ended up fallin' in love with one of them no-counts.

[DARE *no-count* adj scattered, but chiefly South, South Midland]

no-fence law *noun* See 1939 citation. Same as **open stock law**. See also **fence law, open range, stock law**.

1939 Hall *Notebooks* Originally all owners of cattle and other stock could allow their farm animals to run freely in the woods, but early in this century the big stock owners got a law passed to require small land owners to erect fences around their land to protect their crops and stock from the free-ranging stock of large stock owners. Called also the fence law, it was much resented by the small landowner and cattle raiser. To the small farmer it was a "fence law"; to the large stock raiser it was a "no fence law," that is, for them. **1959** Hall *Coll* (Cataloochee NC) We raised cattle, sheep, and hogs. We had open range when we first married, until the No Fence Law, when we had to put everything up [in fences].

[This law would seem to have been a misnomer, in that it was a boon to major cattle raisers, who were no longer required to fence in their stock; instead, the small farmers and cattle raisers now had to fence their property]

noggin *noun* See also **kit**.

1 A bucket or small tub.

1885 Murfree *Prophet* 175 Mirandy Jane, seated on an inverted noggin, listened tamely to the conversation.

2 A small wooden vessel for liquids.

1824 (in **1912** Doddridge *Notes on Settlement* 109 The furniture for the table ... consisted ... mostly of wooden bowls, trenchers and noggins.)

no hand at, no hand to See **hand A3**.

no-heller *noun* A member of the Primitive Baptist Universalist denomination.

1996 Leonard *Ministering* 14 Primitive Baptist Universalists such as Davis are "No-Hellers." They are convinced that God ultimately will draw all persons to salvation, giving them hell in this world so that they can escape it in the next. **1997** Dorgan *Happy God* 4 This unique subdivision of the Primitive Baptist faith expounds an inclusive theology of universal atonement, claiming that, at the close of the temporal world, all humankind (past and present) will be redeemed from "sin, punishment, and death"; restored to that purified state that existed prior to Adam's fall, and thus prepared for an eternal and joyous communion with God. Known in Central Appalachia as the "No-Hellers" ... this unusual subdenomination of Baptists practices an extremely celebratory form of worship. **1998** *Dante OHP-24* They call them No Hellers. They don't believe in eternal punishment. **2009** Miller *Nigh Gone* 106 There were the Presbyterians, the Methodists, and the Baptists early on, but it did not take these three groups of independent-minded people long before they began to splinter. As they say in the mountains, they split "ever which way." This was particularly true of the Baptists. Fairly quickly this group divided into the United Baptists. There were Missionary Baptists and Old Missionary Baptists, who supported missionaries. There were Free Will Baptists, Southern Baptists, and American Baptists, which were once the Northern Baptists. In all, there were fifty or more divisions including the Primitive (Hardshell) Baptists and the Primitive Baptist Universalists, who were sometimes called the "No-Hellers" because they believed in heaven for everyone.

nohow *adverb* (used in contexts with another negative) In any manner or case, anyway. See also **noway**.

1862 *Robinson CW Letters* (Aug 3) I will leave the Subject with you it ant worth more paper then it is Rote on no how. **1863** *Revis CW Letters* (May 17) I never was as tired of any things in my life as I am of this old war for thare is no jestus in this old war no how. **1867** Harris *Sut Lovingood* 106 I'm no count, no how. **1929** (in **1952** Mathes *Tall Tales* 100) Doctorin's a gift, I say, which them that's got it don't need no schoolin', an' them that ain't, schoolin' wouldn't do 'em no good nohow! **1937** Hall *Coll* (Copeland Creek TN) She didn't have more than half-sense nohow. **1941** Stuart *Men of Mts* 56 I'm petered out, nohow. **1976** Brandes and Brewer *Dialect Clash* 288 Hit's so downright foggy today nobody can't hardly see nothing a-tall nohow. **1989** *Matewan OHP-28* They couldn't sell this one 'cause it wasn't anything but an old schoolhouse nohow.

[DARE *nohow* adv 2 especially South Midland]

noise *verb*

1 Of a person: to make the distinctive sound of, imitate.

1917 Kephart *Word-List* 415 = to make the sound of. "Any kind of thing ever heered tell of, he can *noise* it."

2 To publicize, circulate.

c1926 Cox *Cullowhee Wordlist* = to tell abroad.

3 To make sounds so as to disturb or drive away.

c1970 Handlon *Ol' Smoky* 17 "We'll noise 'em away," answered one of the boys.

no more *adverb phrase* Again, after that. See also **anymore 2**.

1972 *AOHP/LJC-203* When she left here she went to South America, and I never did know what happened to her no more. **1979** *Big South Fork OHP-11* I never was back there no more. That was my last trip.

none

A *adverb* At all.

1970 Vincent *More of Best* 112 "We ain't starvin' none," he said. "Here, let me show you."

B (also *none of them, none of us, none of you*) *pronoun* Coreferent with the subject of the clause but having syntactic position within the predicate. See also Grammar and Syntax §18.3.

1864 Lister *CW Letters* (May 9) All I no is we was nun of our redgt hert. **1864** *Warrick CW Letters* (Jan 3) I trust in God that you will none of you be sick much. **1900** Harben *N GA Sketches* 218 We hain't none of us got nothin' ag'in yore wife. *Ibid.* 224 They hain't none of 'em got sense enough to see what a good, lovin' man you are at the bottom. **1930** Armstrong *This Day and Time* 73 They don't none o' them want to play alike. **1964** Miller *Pigeon's Roost* (Nov 26) I guess we none like to forget a good deed we ever done. **1973** *Ethel Corn* 263 They didn't none want t'go, and they was a'sayin' over there that they didn't want'em. **1979** Slone *My Heart* 27 Somehow we none felt like fun any more so we started home.

none much *pronoun phrase* Very much. See also **any much, much C1**.

1953 Hall Coll (Bryson City NC) He was an old stock man way back about Civil War times, and he never did hunt none much. **1983** Page and Wigginton *Aunt Arie* 62 That's th'reason I never got t'play none much at home.

none of them, none of us, none of you See **none B**.

no never mind (also *no matter-mind*) *noun phrase* A concern, difference, significance; attention, notice, used especially in phrases *make no never mind* = not to matter, and *pay no never mind* = not to give any attention to. See also **never no mind**.

1927 Camak *June of Hills* 16 Well, that don't make no never mind, Honey. If you wants it, you'll git it. **1982** Slone *How We Talked* 6 *pay that no never mind* = Don't let that bother you. **1995–97** Montgomery Coll: *no nevermind* (known to eight consultants from the Smoky Mountains). **1995** South *What It Is* 53 Hit don't make no nevermind, Charlie. **1999** Goodman and Burgin *Daughters* 44 Ever'body knew that Leo Sellers just about beat Lorraine to death, but that don't make no never mind. **2004** Adams *Old True Love* 117 It don't make no matter-mind to us. **2005** Williams *Gratitude* 57 Didn't make no nevermind to her, she was goin' to do dist ezackly what she was goin' to do.

non-poison *adjective* Nonpoisonous.

1967 Miller *Pigeon's Roost* (Aug 22) I have killed a number of non-poison snakes here this year.

noodling *verbal noun* See citation. Also called **finger fishing, hand fishing, hand grabbing, hogging**.

2006 *Encycl Appalachia* 872 Native Americans caught spawning catfish with their hands, a practice that may be part of the origin of the sport of noodling. Also called hand grabbing, grabbling, hand fishing, or hogging, noodling is still a well-known activity in the larger rivers and reservoirs of Appalachia. Noodlers target most catfish species but their real prize is the flathead catfish, known in Appalachia as the mudcat. Noodling remains popular with some, but the method is only practical during the brief few weeks in which catfish spawn and noodlers can locate them in hollow logs and other cavities where they nest.

nor *conjunction*

A Variant forms *ner, nur* [see **1859** in **B1**].

1904–20 Kephart *Notebooks* 4:753 Hardshell turtles' eggs can't be cooked done, boiling ner frying; I've done tried it. **1929** (in **1952** Mathes *Tall Tales* 100) I don't want no book doctor a-dosin' me ner mine. **1961** Williams *Content Mt Speech* 16 He's got a good little piece of crappin' land there, but he won't corn it ner hay it nuther.

B Senses.

1 Than (following a comparative adjective or adverb).

1859 Taliaferro *Fisher's River* 64 He dashed round the mounting faster nur a shootin' star ur lightnin'. **1867** Harris *Sut Lovingood* 130 I hed mistaken'd the givin-in signs; he wer madder nor ever. **1881** Atkinson *After Moonshiners* 151 There's my old woman, she's whiter-headed than you are, jedge, and she's ten year younger nor me. **1975** Gainer *Speech Mtneer* 14 He's a better fiddler nor me. **1992** Jones and Miller *Sthn Mt Speech* 96 No bigger round nor your arm. **1996** Montgomery Coll (known to Jones, Oliver). **2007** McMillon *Notes* This'un's better ner that'un.

[OED3 *nor* conj[2] in recent use chiefly Scot, Irish English, U.S. regional, and English regional. CUD *nor*[1] 2 "than"; HT "than"]

2 Or (used to join two nouns, pronouns, or verb phrases not preceded by *neither*).

1862 *Revis CW Letters* (Nov 3) toliver nor clinton nor nun of them hant gote mee astick of wood sense you left home. **1862** *Watters-Curtis CW Letters* (June 6) tell ol uncle jim white not to shoot him Self when he goes and gets his gun nor kill no dead people. **1873** Smith *Arp Peace Papers* 32 Matthy Matiks nor his daddy couldn't figger out how long it will take you to get through. **1886** Smith *Sthn Dialect* 348 He did confess that "the mountain was a bad place ter raise chillern; no school, nor Sunday-school, nor meetin', nor nothin', and the chillern jest as wild as they could be." **1898** Elliott *Durket Sperret* 67 You ner Granny can't skeer me. **1922** *TN CW Ques* 9 (Jefferson Co TN) I nor my parents owned slaves. **1925** Dargan *Highland Annals* 156 Bub nor Bugle won't take hold o' that thing. **1939** Hall Coll (Bradley Fork NC) I never looked back. Fencing wasn't in my way nor nothing. **1941** Stuart *Men of Mts* 93 The Devil nor books nor nothin else can stop you from it. **1954** Weals *Lost Gold Mine* But, as said above, Shultz' widow nor anybody else ever was able to find the cliff with the skinned balsam. **1955** Ritchie *Singing Family* 185 I raced through the woods like a deer, swinging on grapevines and tree limbs, and laughing and making speeches on top of high rocks, and cutting such a shine that I was ashamed of myself, but that nor nothing else could stop me. **1961** *Coe Ridge*

OHP-339A In olden times [they] didn't have no floor in the kitchen ner in the hallways. **1985** Irwin *Alex Stewart* 164 Pap never drunk, but he never bothered them—never give them no trouble nor nothing. **1993** Burleson *Aunt Keziah* 2 Wars, nor Death, nor Time nor distance can ever destroy or diminish [Christmas memories].

[Web3 *nor* conj[1] 2 archaic]

3 And (to join independent clauses).

1861 *Watters-Curtis CW Letters* (Dec 18) I Never told Mother to keep your things Nor I do not owe baily nothing. **1862** *Councill CW Letters* (April 27) I ant thare nor I dont no when I will bee if Ever. **1865** *Hill CW Letters* (Jan 6) I dont think you get all my letters nor I dont get all of yourn for tha[y] dont cear if we here from one a nother or not nor tha[y] dont pay us off nor I dont be lev thea ever will. **1901** Harben *Westerfelt* 3 For a wonder, she wasn't married, nur never had been. **c1950** Adams *Grandpap* 35 [He] didn't have a sign of kinfolks that would do anything for him. Nor he didn't have no home nor nothin' hardly. **1971** *AOHP/ALC-193* The community wasn't as it had been in the past, nor it's not been that way no more since. **1974** GSMNP-51:16 Vickie didn't want to do that nor I didn't either. **1975** *AOHP/LJC-384* I never forgot that song nor I never forgot him. **1987** Elingburg *Mt Breed* 53 She can just play around in the room. She won't bother me nor she won't bother anybody else. **1997** *Dante OHP-14* Now Bill never sees a stranger nor Mack never either, nor never seen nothing and didn't know what it was but what he didn't ask.

[Web3 *nor* conj[1] 4 chiefly dialect]

norate (also *norate around*) *verb, verb phrase* To announce, advertise, report, spread (news or information) by word of mouth; to gossip about. See also **narrate.**

1859 Taliaferro *Fisher's River* 64 Ev'ry day for a week, I went to that spot, allers jumped him up in ten steps uv the same place, would fire away, but allers missed him, as jist norated. **1884** Smith *Arp Scrap Book* 13 Along in the evenin it was norated around that Ike was goin to banter me for a rassel. **1895** Edson and Fairchild *TN Mts* 373 *norate* = advertise. "We will *norate* the preaching" (i.e. announce the service to be held). **c1900** (in **1997** Stoddart *Quare Women* 82) One Sunday morning we attended a "funeral occasion" that had been "norated" for many months. **1918** *Story* 18 The most serious fault was in the divorce of religion and ethics. The ministers would drink, shoot men whom they considered their enemies, and never touch upon ethical questions in their sermons, which are a hodge-podge of fragments of Bible verses and rambling remarks, given in a sing-song voice, or, as they call it, "norating." **1921** Campbell *Sthn Highlander* 145 A man wishing to hold a meeting in the mountains has it "norated"—that is, the announcement of it spread by report. **1936** (in **1952** Mathes *Tall Tales* 215) Didn't ye know hit was bein' norated ye'd been killed, an' they was layin' it to Grannison here? **c1940** Aswell *Glossary TN Idiom* 13 *norate* = to gossip. **1941** Stuart *Men of Mts* 209 "Son, get on the mule," says Pa, "and go over the deestrict and norate that Pap is dead." **1973** Davis *'Pon My Honor* 59 Grandpappy trained his young coon dog Sugar Bell, until it was norated around that it was the best coon dog ever seen in these hills. **1987** Young *Lost Cove* 86 The fish and everything else were forgotten now that the problem of the painter was being norated. **1998** Montgomery *Coll* (known to Jones, Oliver).

[variant of *narrate*, probably influenced by *orate*; but perhaps a back-formation from *noration*; cf OED3 *norate* v 2 U.S., Irish English, and English regional; DARE *norate* v chiefly South Midland, South]

noration *noun* A report, announcement.

1859 Taliaferro *Fisher's River* 235 You are on the right track, Brother Walker. Go on with your noration. **c1950** Adams *Grandpap* 90 Finally-at-last, he put out the noration that he'd marry the girl that that slipper would fit. **1987** Young *Lost Cove* 84 "I reckon that this here mizzle will get all the fish to stirring," he offered as a way to start a noration with his old friend.

[variant of *narration*, probably influenced by *oration*; DARE *noration* n chiefly South Midland, South]

nose

A *verb* To remove the bark from and round the end of (a log so that it will slide downhill more easily).

1964 Clarkson *Lumbering in WV* 367 = to round off the end of a log in order to make it drag more easily. **1983** Weals *Ball-Hooting* Logs sometimes were *ballhooted*, or sent plunging, down steep slopes, and a big log had to be *nosed* for that also. **1991** Weals *Last Train* 26 When a tree was cut on a very steep slope, they would peel the logs and nose them, round one end so that once a log was started sliding it would "ballhoot" to the foot of the slope by its own momentum. **1995** Weber *Rugged Hills* 82 I'd drive the mules and he'd "nose" the logs with an ax so they'd slide good.

B *noun* The end of a log from which bark is removed and which is further rounded so that it will slide downhill more easily.

2003 Strutin *Hikes of Smokies* 70 During the first half-mile [of the hike], look for "ball-hoot" gullies scoring the slopes. On the steepest slopes, loggers would fell trees, peel off the bark, and round the "nose" of the log. Then they would start the logs downhill. These huge missiles would pick up speed, "ball-hooting" their way to the bottom of the slope.

no sech See **no such.**

nose poker *noun* A children's game. See citation.

2002 Ogle *Remembrances* 70 The children and Burns children from our cabin were playing cards. The Inspector asked what kind of card game they were playing and the children chirped at once, "poker." Turned out after I was embarrassed to death I found out that it was nose poker where they poke the loser's nose.

no sich See **no such.**

no such *pronoun phrase*

A Variant forms *no sech* [see **1974** in **B**], *no sich* [see **1939** in **B**].

B Anything or nothing (like it).

1937 Hall *Coll* (Copeland Creek TN) The White Caps got to be worse than the other side was. They whipped, they feathered the lewd women. I didn't hold with no such whatever. **1939** Hall

Recording Speech 6 One elderly woman of the Oconaluftee area declined the microphone, however, and informed the investigators: "I don't fancy no sich as that and I won't jine up with ye!" **1974** Fink *Bits Mt Speech* 17 = not anything. "I never said *no sech.*" **1983** *Dark Corner OHP-24A* Maybe [she] did that, but I don't believe no such.

not *adverb*

1 Full form when an auxiliary verb or form of copula *be* is contracted to the subject of the clause (thus *he* + *is* + *not* => *he's not*). See also Grammar and Syntax §11.6.

1927 Justus *Peter Pocket* 40 I'll not spend the hundred cents for candy. **1937** Hall *Coll* (Cosby Creek TN) I've not tasted of it yet. **1939** Hall *Coll* (Deep Creek NC) I've not got very much yet. *Ibid.* (Deep Creek NC) That's not a bear. Hit's a wildcat. **1940** Simms *Wiley Oakley* 16 I'll not charge anything extry for guidin' the valet. **1941** Hall *Coll* (Mt Sterling NC) You've not met him, I don't guess. **c1950** Adams *Grandpap* 39 He knowed if they killed his bull that he'd not get anything more to eat an' that would soon be the end of him. **1959** Roberts *Up Cutshin* 19 I've not got into that corn up yander yit—don't expect to. **1962** (in **2014** McCarter *Memories of Boy* 22) If you were coming east that was it, and they'd not see you again. **1974–75** McCracken *Logging* 1:16 That's not a cow brute's skull. That's a human skull. **1978** Burton *Ballad Folks* 4 Nobody's not to step in betwixt them, not even his daddy 'n' mother. **1983** *Dark Corner OHP-24A* You've not ever been up here before? **1989** Landry *Smoky Mt Interviews* 181 You'll not find no John [Ogle] blood around Maryville. **1989** *Matewan OHP-22* He'll get me by letting things out when he's not home. **1999** Axtell *Moonshine Making* 18 I've not heard tell of poisonous liquor.

2 Used in multiple-negative constructions, often contracted. See also Grammar and Syntax §11.1, §11.2.

1937 Hall *Coll* (Collins Creek NC) The fish ain't a-bitin' to do no good. *Ibid.* (Cosby TN) He weren't no hunter nuther. **1939** Hall *Coll* (Smokemont NC) There's an old house up here but don't nobody live in it, not noway. **1972** *AOHP/ALC-355* Yeah, eggs was two cents a dozen, but nobody didn't have the two cents, did they? **1979** *GSMNP-118:24* None of us wasn't real singers nor nothin' like that.

3 Contracted to *better*: See **bettern**.

not a circumstance to See **circumstance B**.

not a God's thing See **God's thing**.

not a tater in the patch *phrase* See 1939 citation.

1939 Farr *TN Mt Regions* 91 = a refusal to grant a favor. "There's not a tater in the patch." **1996–97** Montgomery *Coll* (known to Brown, Bush, Cardwell).

notch up *verb phrase* To cut the ends of a log to form notches and then to set the logs in place in constructing (a log house or **log building**).

1972 *Foxfire I* 79 The ends of the inside partitioning walls are clearly visible in this house, located on Dog Mountain near Highlands, North Carolina. Harley Thomas helped "notch up" this house in 1926 for Colonel Sewell who died not long after the house was finished.

note *verb*

1 To render into musical notation.

1974 Fink *Bits Mt Speech* 17 = to write music for. "Can he *note* a song?" **1976** Garber *Mountain-ese* 62 She got a musicianer to note the song ballet for her.

[Web3 v 1a(3) archaic]

2 To finger (a musical instrument) in order to produce a desired tone.

1956 McAtee *Some Dial NC* 31 = to finger a musical instrument. "He had rheumatism so bad he couldn't note his fiddle." **1959** Roberts *Up Cutshin* 9 I'd just watch ... my daddy note the strings and his fingers strike the chords, and then I'd grab the old banjer. I first learnt to play tunes by picking the strings while he noted 'em for me. **1975** *Foxfire III* 205, 206 Pick the melody by noting the first string only. Strum the other three strings; they are the drone strings.... Mark off the frets exactly as they are here, or the dulcimer will not note properly.

[DARE *note* v 2 South Midland]

note book *noun* See citation.

1946 Dudley *KY Words* 271 = a song book with music (distinct from the *Sweet Songster*, a small vest pocket book in which words only are written).

noted *adjective phrase* Reputed.

1939 Hall *Coll* (Cataloochee NC) Turkey George Palmer was noted as a great hunter, bear hunter. **1997** Montgomery *Coll* (known to Ellis).

note up for *verb phrase* See citations.

1974 Fink *Bits Mt Speech* 17 = denote, indicate. "Them clouds don't *note up for* rain." **1976** Garber *Mountain-ese* 62 = indicate, forecast. "The signs just don't note up for a very mild winter this year."

not far from an age *adjective phrase* See citation.

c1940 Simms *Coll* = old-aged.

nother See **another**, **neither**.

nothing *pronoun* Variant form *nuffin*.

1867 Harris *Sut Lovingood* 108 Nuffin but a rattil-tail snake; he's got livin rattils.

notice *verb*

1 To watch over, look after (one's valuables).

1944 *Picturesque Speech* 10 He decided to take a stroll about the station, and asked his new friend if she would watch his possessions. "I'll be glad to notice them for you," she replied.

[DARE *notice* v 1 South, South Midland]

2 See citation.

1977 Shackelford et al. *Our Appalachia* 48 My great-grandfather was brought in for walking in an un-Christian way in his community [in 1810]. He'd been drinking some. One time he denied it and that case lingered on. Time after time they would "notice" him to come back to the next [meeting]. Finally, he withdrew his membership, and he was going to leave that church.

notify *verb* To announce, report occurrence of.

1977 Weals *Cove Folk* If a family got sick, and they had a crop out, and that crop needed work on Monday morning, that'd be notified a-Sunday, at Sunday school and at church.

notion *noun* A fancy, inclination, or mood (especially in phrases *be in a notion, have a notion, take a notion* = to be inclined or decide to undertake a certain thing).

1834 Crockett *Narrative* 194 I took a notion to hunt a little more, and in one month I killed forty-seven more [bears]. **1862** Huntley *CW Letters* (March 6) try to get the peopell in the notion of putting fops and drunkards out of power and put in men in all publick matters that Will discharge their duty and go for the interest of Our Country. **1913** Morley *Carolina Mts* 11 When a mountaineer unexpectedly completes a piece of work . . . he will probably tell you it was because he "tuck a notion." **1924** Spring *Lydia Whaley* 3 There were two brothers in the Burg—one loafered, tother one was in a notion of marryin'. **1940** Haun *Hawk's Done* 43 We had to let him do it when the notion struck him. **1953** Hall *Coll* (Gatlinburg TN) [Woman telling of her husband]: He used to read the paper some, used to read the Bible when he took a notion. **1969** GSMNP-25 When they took a notion to move, they moved out and come on up here.

[OED3 *notion* n 8b Brit. regional (chiefly Scot.) and U.S. regional; EDD *notion* sb 1 nEngl, Scot; cf SND *notion* n 1 "a liking or affection"]

notionate *adjective* See citation.

1915 Dingus *Word-List VA* 186 = notional, given to hobbies, impulses, or whims.

[DARE *notionate* adj chiefly South, South Midland]

not much See **much B1**.

not to give snow water to *verb phrase* To pay no attention to, treat with disdain.

1942 Campbell *Cloud-Walking* 152 Draxie and Mort were a sight to humor Lexie so they give in to be at the singing though they wouldn't give snow water to Shy Isaacs. *Ibid.* 234 They weren't nary girl amongst them I'd give snow water to, say nothing of setting up to spark 'em.

notty, notty-head See **knotty**.

not worth a pewter('s) button *adjective phrase* See citations.

1939 Farr *TN Mt Regions* 91 *Not worth a pewter's button* = worthless or good for nothing: "He's not worth a pewter's button." **1969** DARE *Survey* (Hazard KY, Hindman KY) *not worth a pewter button* = not worth much.

not worth stump water *adjective phrase* Worthless.

1984 Woods *WV Was Good* 15 Still another expression came from the fact that the darkish rainwater was useless for any purpose. Because neither birds nor animals would drink the brackish stuff, a man might say of another, "He's not worth stump water."

noway (also *noways*) *adverb* In any way or fashion, at all (only in contexts of multiple negation). See also **nohow**.

1862 Spainhourd *CW Letters* (Nov 10) I hant no wais on easy a tall. **1862** *Warrick CW Letters* (June 15) he is Giting well he ant No ways Bad off. **1895** Dromgoole *Logan's Courtship* 134 Loge allowed he had about made up his mind it wuz to be one o' the Sid Fletcher gals [he would marry], though he ain't no ways had made up his mind as to which un. **1900** Harben *N GA Sketches* 194 I ain't no ways shore what she will do about me. **1917** Kephart *Word-List* 409 This here brought-on meat ain't *noways* as good as home-made meat. **1939** Hall *Coll* (Indian Creek NC) We didn't have no use for it noway. *Ibid.* (Smokemont NC) There's an old house up here but don't nobody live in it, not noway. **1969** Roberts *Greasybeard* 149 That night they tried and tried but the soldiers was watching so close they couldn't get noways near the barn. **1972** GSMNP-93:3:24 They ain't tuck care of 'em noways. **1978** Montgomery *White Pine Coll* III-2 You never do hear her name mentioned noway.

[DARE *noway* adv chiefly South, South Midland]

noways See **noway**.

nowheres *adverb* Nowhere, anywhere. See also **anywheres, everywheres, somewheres**.

1925 Dargan (in **1935** Edwards *NC Novels* 48) *nowheres*. **1938** Bowman *High Horizons* 38 We know how to make a livin' on our land, but we wouldn't live nowheres else, I reckon. **1957** Parris *My Mts* 140 It was a heap bigger than pa's but he said the whiskey wasn't nowheres as good as his. Pa said they single-footed theirs. He always double-footed his. **1972** GSMNP-86:31 I get close around four hundred dollars a month, and it don't go nowheres. It just don't go nowheres. Back then you get three dollars a month and lived good. **1998** Dante *OHP-71* We went everywheres to get a house. You couldn't hardly get a house nowheres.

[*nowhere* + *-s* adverb-forming suffix (cf **-s5**); OED3 *nowheres* adv, regional and nonstandard; Web3 *nowheres* adv chiefly dialect]

nubbin

A *noun* An underdeveloped or immature ear of corn, often fed to livestock.

1976 Garber *Mountain-ese* 62 = scrub ear of corn. "The corn crop didn't make much this year, jist a few measly nubbins." **1982** Slone *How We Talked* 9 = an ear of corn that is very small, but that did mature. Usually fed to the cows or calves with the shuck or husk attached. Phrase: "This good weather is going to spile (spoil) my nubbin crop, it's making big ears out of them." **1984** GSMNP-153:34 Course he had some nubbins, you know, like you'd find in all corn fields. **2005** Williams *Gratitude* 511 = immature or small ear of corn. Used for cattle or hog feed.

[OED3 *nubbin* n 1 originally and chiefly U.S. < *nub1* apparently variant of *knub* n]

B *verb* To feed (livestock) underdeveloped ears of corn.

1923 Furman *Mothering* 146 Then the steers must be brought down and "nubbined."

nubbin booze *noun* Homemade whiskey.

1952 McCall *Cherokees and Pioneers* 101 If you are invited to share a little something, whether it be called moonshine, corn juice, nubbin booze, Cain corn, white mule, stump juice, white lightning, Old Nick, hoot owl, O be joyful, or mountain dew, you should be warned that the thing meant is that powerful rank pizen what cheers the heart of even a man with a nagging wife.

nubbin killer (also *nubbin strangler, nubbin stretcher*) *noun* A heavy rain that causes corn to develop rapidly.

1915 Dingus *Word-List VA* 186 *nubbin killer* = thunder—because the rain develops the nubbin into a full grown ear of corn. **1966** Dakin *Vocab Ohio River Valley* 21 *Nubbin stretcher; nubbin strangler* [occur] three times, [in the] Kentucky Mountains. **1991** Still *Wolfpen Notebooks* 92 Pretty good rain last night on the corn. What you would call a "nubbin-stretcher."

[DARE (at *nubbin* n 1) especially eastern KY]

nuffin See **nothing**.

nunder See **in under**.

nurse

A *noun, verb* Variant forms *nus, nuss*.

1913 Kephart *Our Sthn High* 281 Much oftener the r is dropped from dare, first, girl, horse, nurse, parcel, worth (dast, fust, gal, hoss, nuss, passel, wuth). **1942** Hall *Phonetics Smoky Mts* 42 [nʌs]. **1961** Williams *R in Mt Speech* 6 In a few words, however, r is omitted: *cuss, futhuh, hoss, nus* (a verb meaning to hold another in one's lap).

B *verb* To care for (a child), hold (a child) in one's arms or on one's lap; to cuddle, cradle.

1862 *Lockmiller Letters* (Sept 25) you sed that you wanted to be at home an rest your head on mi nee i am able to nus yore head 2 days an nites [i]f you will com home. **1939** Hall *Coll* (Jefferson City TN) = fondle a child; hold a child in one's lap. "I nussed your child." **c1950** Haun *When the Wind* 18 Listen:—Now don't you tell me the words—Up in a tree top—nuss me whilest I sing the rest of hit—will you, Granny. **1957** Combs *Lg Sthn High: Word List* 68 = to nurse; that is, to hold in the arms (of babies). [See **1961** in **A**.] **1965** *Dict Queen's English* 15 = hold. "Maybelle, you *nuss* the kid for awhile." **1998** Brewer *Don't Scrouge* "Nuss" means holding someone on one's lap. Although it probably derived from "nurse," in mountain usage it has no connection to feeding an infant. Men and children as well as women nussed the baby. Sometimes if seating was limited a fellow could nuss his girlfriend, which, by the way, never seemed to scrouge him in the least. **2000** Morgan *Mts Remember* 147 This is something I dreamed about as a kid, a warm creek pool here the current caresses and nusses you. **2002** Myers *Best Yet Stories* 148–49 As a young child, when your mother, grandmother or a favorite aunt asked you to come sit on her lap, she said, "Come, let me nuss you." **2015** *Blind Pig* (Jan 16) I was going to bring you some eggs this morning, but I remembered I had to ride with Randy to work. I thought "well I'll have to nuss them in my lap." *Ibid.* Young children were often asked to nuss the baby while their mother did her work.

[DARE *nurse* v chiefly South, South Midland]

nus, nuss See **nurse**.

nuther See **neither**.

nutting party *noun* See citation.

1978 Parris *Mt Cooking* 10 About the only ones back then that took any notice of walnuts was the children. We had what you call nuttin' parties, and in the fall of the year when the walnuts started droppin' and coverin' the ground, we'd go out and gather 'em.

nuver See **never**.

O

oak bread *noun* See citation.

1997 Montgomery *Coll* = bread made from the acorns of the white oak, which was the only species from which the acorn could be ground to make *oak bread* (Cardwell).

oath word *noun* See citation.

1976 Thompson *Touching Home* 15 = cuss word.

obedient plant *noun* The false dragonhead plant (*Physostegia virginiana*).

[**1901** Lounsberry *Sthn Wild Flowers* 452 A curious point about the delicate flowers is that they seem to be overpowered by lassitude. They have no elasticity. So when one is turned with the thumb and finger to another than original position in the spike, it makes no effort to rebound, but remains most obediently wherever it is put.] **1982** Stupka *Wildflowers* 98 The tendency for the funnel-like flower to remain in whatever position it is placed accounts for the name "obedient flower."

O be joyful (also *overjoyful*) *noun* Homemade whiskey. See also **joyful**.

1952 McCall *Cherokees and Pioneers* 101 If you are invited to share a little something, whether it be called moonshine, corn juice, nubbin booze, Cain corn, white mule, stump juice, white lightning, Old Nick, hoot owl, O be joyful, or mountain dew, you should be warned that the thing meant is that powerful rank pizen what cheers the heart of even a man with a nagging wife. **2011** Shearer *Moonshine Trade* 167 It was not in evidence at the time, but there was plenty of evidence that overjoyful was made there at one time.

obleege See **have oblige(d)**, **oblige A**.

oblige *verb* See also **have oblige(d)**.

A Variant form *obleege*.

1889 Mooney *Folk Carolina Mts* 97 *Gwine* and *obleeged*, *tote* and *holp*, are universally used, and many words obsolete or almost unknown in other sections of the country are still retained here. **1891** Brown *Dialect in TN* 175 *Obliged* in the mouths of old people frequently becomes *obleeged*.

[DARE *oblige* v chiefly South, South Midland]

B Past participle *obliged* = required, compelled, constrained.

1862 Barkley *CW Letter* (March 7) they killed one of ours or wounded him so he is oblige to die. **1862** *Love CW Letters* (Oct 5) they time is not fare distent that the north will be ablege to acnoledge our independence. **1905** Miles *Spirit of Mts* 114 If they had any business thar that they had got obleeged to tend to, they'd set out on the porch. **1939** Hall *Coll* (Proctor NC) "I'm obleeged to go home." Mostly old women use that word. You can hear it once in a while. **1966** Frome *Strangers* 267 I insisted that it was Shoof's to down, and he was "right obleeged." **1994** Montgomery *Coll* I'm just obleeged to go home (Ogle).

[DARE *oblige* v Until at least the 18th cent [ə'bliʤ] competed with [ə'blaɪʤ] as the standard English pronunciation]

Oconee bell *noun* A wildflower (*Shortia galacifolia*).

1953 Greene and Blomquist *Flowers South* 93 (DARE) Oconee-Bells. . . . Only 3 species of this interesting genus exist in the world, 2 in the Orient and one in the gorges of the s. Appalachian Mountains on both sides of the border between N.C. and S.C. **2004** Rash *Saints at River* 163 When they built Jocastee Reservoir, they destroyed two-thirds of the Oconee Bells in the world.

October See **October bean**.

October bean (also *October*) *noun* A late-planted pole bean with shells up to ten inches long that is left in the field to mature and dry before being picked; the shell is rarely eaten, and the shelled-out beans have dark red speckles. Also called **fall bean**, **peanut bean**, **shelly bean**. See also **runner 1**.

1939 Hall *Coll* (Cataloochee NC) October beans or Octobers [are] cornfield beans. *Ibid.* (Proctor NC) = late beans, shelled. **1968** *DARE Survey* (Brasstown NC) = small white beans with a black spot where they were joined to the pod. **1986** Pederson et al. *LAGS*: *October beans* = attested by 10/60 interviewees (16.7%) from E TN; 10/15 of all LAGS interviewees (66.7%). **2011** Best *Bean Terminology* = beans which are typically planted later than other cornfield beans and which mature near the time the first frost is scheduled. Typically they have large seeds and sometimes have stringless hulls. They are often somewhat tougher than other heirloom beans which typically remain tender all the way to the shelly stage and beyond.

[DARE *October bean* n chiefly southern Appalachians, IN]

oddling *noun* A person or animal that is abnormal or eccentric, but harmless.

1941 Stuart *Men of Mts* 85 That's why I said you was one of God's oddlings, son. You won't even drink the licker like your Pap drinks and your Grandpa drunk. **1961** Williams *Content Mt Speech* 15 Atter a while the little oddlin' begun to look plime blank like its grampappy [sic]. **1997** Montgomery *Coll* There is always an oddling in a hatch of chickens, ducks, geese, etc. and even in human families (Brown).

[Web3 *oddling* n "a mildly eccentric individual" chiefly dialect]

odd-turned *adjective* Of a person: having an eccentric personality.

c1950 Adams *Grandpap* 144 Sol Conaway was a yellow-headed, beardy-faced, odd-turned sort of a character. **2003** Carter *Mt Home* 19 Anyway, what-ever their background roots was, they was odd-turned quare people and I never did get close to them.

of *preposition*

1 In the course of, on (used to indicate a regular, typical, or frequent activity or event). See also Grammar and Syntax §14.7.

a (in phrase *of a/an* + singular noun, as *of a day*, *of an evening*, *of a night*) At, on, in the.

1862 Robinson *CW Letters* (May 20) it is Cold anuff hear of amorning for frost. **1863** *Warrick CW Letters* (Jan 30) I wannt you to knit me a cape to go over my head and ears for thay are a grate help to a man of a nite to ceep his head and ears warm. **1910** Cooke *Power and Glory* 66 Shade used to meet her of an evening when she would be coming from the hospital. **1939** Hall *Coll* (Cataloochee NC) We would gather our apples in of a day and peel our apples of a night and put them out on a scaffold. **1953** Hall *Coll* (Bryson City NC) He farmed of a summertime, growed a crop of vegetables, corn, potatoes [etc.]. **1956** GSMNP-24:42 We'd cook our squirrels of a night over a thing like that out there.... We cook them of a night. **1969** *Burton-Manning Coll*-93A He goes over there every morning and comes back of a night. **1973** GSMNP-70:2:9 We would have singing of a night and of a Sunday. **1974** Roberts *Sang Branch* 58 Bootlaggers'd come in there with a load, and I'd buy 'em out and peddle it out of a night while I worked of a day, or peddle of a day while I worked of a night. **1979** *Preacher Cook* 196 We had two services—one of a morning and one of a evening. **1983** *Dark Corner OHP*-5A She got to having chills and ... a little bit of everything of a night. **1989** *Matewan OHP*-9 If I take the flu of a wintertime, I get it just as hot as I can drink it, and go to bed and sweat it out. **1998** *Dante OHP*-24 He'd take us over there of a morning, and we'd catch a bus back of the evening. **2008** *Rosie Hicks* 1 You had to skin it [= the groundhog], and we'd let it soak in water of a night.

[DARE *of* prep C3 scattered, but chiefly South, South Midland]

b (in phrase *of the* + singular noun). At, in the.

1863 *Revis CW Letters* (July 13) she ses all Day long she is thincking of you and of the night she ses she is Dreaming about you. **1975** *Richard and Margaret* 6 I always had a few hogs to feed and I would do that of the morning and night. **1976** Lindsay *Grassy Balds* 200 I'd fish of the evening. **1978** Montgomery *White Pine Coll* IX-3 They don't have no one to rely on of the night. **1984** Page and Wigginton *Foxfire Cookery* 191 That's what it took to feed them of the morning—fifty biscuits. **1989** *Matewan OHP*-94 I'd pick him up, and then of the evening, when I dropped him off at home, I'd gave him the ten dollars. **1998** *Dante OHP*-45 I'd get up of the night, and I'd go by his bed, and I'd hear him barely snoring.

c (in *of* + plural noun) At, on, in the.

1862 *Martin CW Letters* (March 8) we Live to far Apart to Viset each other of Seaterday eavenings. **1863** *Proffit CW Letters* (Sept 1) we haft to ware our coats of mornings. **1884** Smith *Arp Scrap Book* 79 He kept 'em at home of nights, and he made good men of them. **1931–33** (in **1987** Oliver and Oliver *Sketches* 24) My grandfather was troubled of nights in his sleep with what was called nightmares. **1934** Cushman *Swing Mountain Gal* 100 They was a pulpit that they used of Sundays.

2 Used redundantly following a verb of mental activity. See **recall of, recollect of, remember of.**

[DARE *of* prep Bb especially Appalachians, Lower Mississippi Valley, Southwest]

3 Used redundantly following a verb of sensation. See **feel of, smell of, taste of.**

[DARE *of* prep Ba scattered, but especially South, South Midland]

4 Used redundantly following a verbal noun. [Editor's note: Such constructions represent verbal nouns in the process of becoming present participles.]

1811 *Globe Creek Church Minutes* 35 (Caldwell Co NC) bro[the]r. James gilbirt made objaction of the bretheren receiving of there letters, on account of a Destress betwen the three brethren. **1813** Hartsell *Memora* 102 on the same knight I dremp I met my mother and went in to the house with hur where I saw my wife making of corn bread. **1845** (in **1974** Harris *High Times* 50) Jim Smith sot down on the bed alongside of Bet Holden (the steeltrap gall,) and jist fell to huggin of her bar fashion. **1861** *Watters-Curtis CW Letters* (Dec 24) ihave bin tendind of him about t[w]o weak ithink that it is agoine to hwup him to get well it has all come frome exposure and Drinking of rot gut Whisky. **1863** *Gilley CW Letters* (Nov 22) Paper all out say the yankees is a whipping of us in the state of Va. **1881** Atkinson *After Moonshiners* 152 I am tellen of the truth, too. **1904** Johnson *Highways South* 133 Carleton climbed up a ladder an' grab[bed] Gowler by the leg an' begun a jerkin' of him. **1913** Combs *Kentucky Highlander* 23 Gentlemen! whenever you see a great big over-grown buck sitting at the mouth of some holler, or at the forks of some road—with a big slouch hat on, a blue collar, a celluloid, artificial rose on his coat lapel, and a banjo strung across his breast, and a-pickin' of Sourwood Mountain, fine that man, gentlemen, fine that man! **1915** Dingus *Word-List VA* 186 = used redundantly with verbs, especially present participles following *keep*: "He kept a runnin' of (botherin' of, a-callin' of, scoldin' of, etc.)." **1940** Vincent *Us Mt Folks* 14 Now Lord, I ain't a-fearin' of this man, nor no man that walks on two laigs. **1944** Combs *Word-List Sthn High* 20 = used redundantly with transitive verbs. "I will not go to old Jo Clark's / A-stealing of his rye." **1973** *AOHP/ASU*-90 The young'uns was a-hanging of the stockings. **1996** Woodring *Times Gone By* 6 He said he took his rifle, and took a drink of liquor, and went on a huntin of em.

[DARE *of* prep Be chiefly South, South Midland]

5 From, with respect to.

1856 *Chapman CW Letters* (Aug 13) The cars are now Running daily to Abingdon about 14 miles of where we live. **1863** *Epperly CW Letters* (Aug 1) wee ar now about 16 milds of Knoxville. **1939** Hall *Coll* (Tuckaleechee Cove TN) He heared something holler and thought it was a man, but in a few minutes it hollered about fifty yards of him.

6 See **flat of.**

off *adverb, noun* (Far) away, at a place away from home; a place away from home or outside the mountains.

1924 Raine *Saddlebags* 95 There is often a marked difference between the language of a grandmother and that of the grandchildren, who have been "off" for some time at school. **1946** Matthias *Speech Pine Mt* 190 = away, absent from home: "She works off." **1952** Giles *40 Acres* 5 To my chagrin I learned that allowances were made for me because I was "from off," I had not been properly "raised up" and I therefore could not be expected to know much. **1955** Ritchie *Singing Family* 249 Newspapers from off said it was the first settlement school ever built or even thought of, out in the country like that. **1963** Edwards *Gravel* 132 Bout that time up come a buyer from off an he said, "Lemme see that corn." **1983**

Dark Corner OHP-24A I was sixteen when we moved from up there, but my older sisters worked off then. **1989** *Matewan OHP-33* I was somewhere off when the talkies come in. **2008** Hunter *Porch Sit* 10 A few who come to our meetings are, like me, "from off." But most were born and raised and still live here. **2013** House *Own Country* 193 This substitute teacher does not want to be here. Plus, she is from Off. Off is anywhere but here, and we hear people talk about it all the time ("Oh, that preacher don't know what he's talking about . . . he's from Off," "She's moved Off and completely changed, thinks she's better than us now"). **2018** *Blind Pig* (Jan 26) I've heard it used in my neck of the woods as meaning not being at home. If you aren't in the holler or home, you are Off.

offals *noun* Meat scraps, especially the edible internal organs of a hog or calf.

1966 Dakin *Vocab Ohio River Valley* 2.262 = a related term, apparently of North Midland origin and not a comprehensive term for internal organs, is occasional and scattered from Pennsylvania to the Mississippi and also known on the lower Kentucky. Several variations occur: *off fall(ing)(s)*, *off all(s)*, and *offal(s)*. For some speakers this was a comprehensive term for the ribs, backbone, and trimmings—the edible scraps from the less desirable parts of the animal—and for others a term for the internal organs, both edible and inedible. **1971** Dwyer *Dict for Yankees* 30 = pieces of food fallen from the table.

off-bear *verb* To remove boards and stack boards as they come off the carriage of the saw at a sawmill; hence noun *off-bearer* = a worker with such a duty. See also **turn down man**.

1968 Clarke *Stuart's Kentucky* 167 Mom remembers that Pap took the hardest job at the sawmill—he offbore the slabs. **1977** Hamilton *Mt Memories* 28 The machiner [of the sawmill] was under a long shed and there was a carriage to carry the logs to the saw. The carriage ran on a track and when a saw cut through the log it was carried back to the man called an "off-bearer" who laid the piece of lumber to one side while the carriage took the log back to the saw. **1985** Irwin *Alex Stewart* 94 Oh, I've worked in a sawmill, on and off might near all my life. I worked at a sawmill for my uncle before I married. I worked as an off-bearer. That's where you carry them big green slabs away as fast as they fall off. **1989** *Matewan OHP-18* I helped pack the lumber off. They call it off-bearing. **1994** Farwell and Buchanan *Logging Terms* = a member of a logging crew who kept slabs moving away from the carriage and from the board being cut [to] transfer slabs to a chain drive. **2013** Venable *How to Tawlk* 33 *off-bare* = laborer at a sawmill who removes and stacks boards as they come off the carriage; i.e, "off-bearer": "Punkin got hisself hard as an off-bare at Big Ed's sawmill."

off down *phrasal preposition* (see Grammar and Syntax §14.5).

1939 Hall *Coll* I come off down into the open woods. **1973** *GSMNP-86:36* It was steep off down to the river. **1996** *GSMNPCOHP-1:4* The cows would go way off down in them creeks.

offen (also *off'n*) *preposition* Off (of), from.

1863 *Confederate Coll* (July 31) i would like to show that old s-gutted bich how to ride ten miles out on the mountain an pilot them to the vally to ste[a]l horses an rob houses an steell bacon ofen her neighbors. **1867** Harris *Sut Lovingood* 29 Lite ofen that ar hoss, an' take a ho'n. **1873** Smith *Arp Peace Papers* 25 She ripped her star from offen the striped rag. **1895** *Mt Baptist Sermon* 14 The limbs commenced ablowin' off'n the trees. **1904–20** Kephart *Notebooks* 2:367 You cain't scald the bristles offen a live hog. **1924** (in **1952** Mathes *Tall Tales* 21) Ye look like the buzzards had drug you till ye rubbed all the ha'r offen the back o' yer head! **1939** Hall *Coll* (Hartford TN) We just broke to it as quick as we could, and all went into skinning that bear, skun it all out, took that hide offen it, and cut it into four quarter. **1941** Justus *Kettle Creek* 128 Get down—get down in a hurry, before I pull you offen that horse! **1961** *Coe Ridge OHP-340B* When they got offen the boat . . . they probably didn't have anywhere to stay. **1971** *AOHP/ALC-260* I went in and got offen the horse. **1989** *Matewan OHP-39* You could find big slabs knocked offen them houses, where the machine guns struck them. **1995** Adams *Come Go Home* 45 They would just say "sic-em-and-kill" and them dawgs was so fierce they'd run and jump up on ye and rip your throat right offen your neck. **1998** *Dante OHP-12* He tied the company up some way to get a royalty offen the timber that was cut for the mines. **2007** Preece *Leavin' Sandlick* 16 Wade Jr.'s gone on out to the barn to do chores to hep keep his mine off'n everthang.

[< *off* + *on* "of"; OED3 *offen* prep chiefly U.S. regional, English regional, and Scot; EDD *off* prep 2.(14) Scot, nEngl; cf SND *affin* prep "off"]

offer *verb*

1 To attempt (to do something).

1937 Hall *Coll* (Emerts Cove) I didn't offer to kill it [= a rattlesnake]. **1969** Roberts *Greasybeard* 132 [The] giant didn't offer to hurt Tom until he found out how brave he was. **1973** *AOHP/ASU-111* My brothers listened to what my daddy and mother said until they was eighteen and twenty years old. They really never offered to go out on their own or anything till they was older and they all got away after jobs. **1993** Burton *Take Up Serpents* 70 As soon as [the snakes] were touched by those under the power they wilted and never offered to bite anyone.

2 To substitute, serve the same purpose.

1984 *GSMNP-153:63* That kerosene oil offered as a disinfectant.

off horse (also *off-side horse*) *noun* One of a team of work horses, usually the one on the right-hand side. See also **lead horse**, **off steer**.

1967 *DARE Survey* (Gatlinburg TN) *off horse* = the horse on the left side in plowing and hauling. **1997** Montgomery *Coll*: *off-side horse* (known to Brown, Bush, Ledford), *off horse* was on the right, horse on left was *lead horse* (Jones).

[DARE *offside horse* n scattered, but especially northern Appalachians]

offish *adjective* Unsociable, aloof, unapproachable in manner.

c1940 Aswell *Glossary TN Idiom* 13 = distant, hard to get acquainted with. **1952** Wilson *Folk Speech NC* 570 = shy, not sociable.

c1960 Wilson *Coll* = unsociable, shy, sometimes arrogant, self-important. **1962** Rouse *Colorful Tint* Offish means unsociable. **1996–97** Montgomery *Coll* (known to Adams, Brown, Cardwell, Jones, Ledford, Norris, Oliver).

[DARE *offish* adj 1 chiefly South Midland, New England]

off-kilter *adjective* See citation.

1930s (in **1944** Wentworth *ADD* 340) (eWV) = out of kilter, awry, askew.

offlike *adverb* Offhandedly, in a casual manner.

1949 Arnow *Hunter's Horn* 43 When you're as old as I am, man, an if'n you've still not give your heart to God, you won't be a talken so easy an offlike about hell an them that's dead an cain't hep theirselves.

off'n See **offen**.

off of *phrasal preposition* From, off.

1862 *Kiracofe CW Letters* (Dec 17) the report says that he fairly swept them off of the face of the Earth. **1862** *Shifflet CW Letters* (Oct 26) my cap box was shot off of my belt and fore bullet holes in my blouse and my gun barrel Shot off at the britch. **1954** GSMNP-19: 23b I'd use a little of it [= honey] and go out and catch the bees off of the flowers and then watch which way it'd go, and then I'd follow them up and cut down my bee tree. **1976** GSMNP-114:6 They'd come up off of that job up there and buy their whiskey on up this way and get a plenty of whiskey. **1989** *Matewan OHP-1* those boys really established the groundwork of a firm union and the people are living off of it today. **2003** LaLone et al. *Farming Life* 322–23 You'd have to go in and strip all the leaves off of [the cane stalk], then cut it.

[DARE (at *off* adv C1) widespread, but more frequent South, Midland]

off one's box See **box 4**.

off one's mind *adjective phrase* No longer in one's memory.

1957 GSMNP-23:1:4 I don't remember the dates. It's off my mind.

off out into *phrasal preposition* (see also Grammar and Syntax §14.5).

c1950 Haun *When the Wind* 10 Bob, he said he knew what Eula was doing—she was taking Song-Boy off out into the fields and singing to him when she had been told better and he thought of his religion and helt in from cussing till he was red in the face from holding.

off out yander See **yonder B3**.

offset *noun*

1 A rocky spur or ledge jutting from the side of a mountain.

1926 Hunnicutt *Twenty Years* 207 He turned and tried to go back up the crevice where he had come down, but when he got back to the offset of the rock he failed to climb it. **1994–97** Montgomery *Coll* (known to Adams, Bush, Cardwell, Hooper, Oliver, Shields), = face of a rock that juts out from a hillside or mountainside (Weaver).

2 A foil, positive contrast.

1923 Montague *Today Tomorrow* 159 That little feller's faith in him tickled Tony right much. It was a kind of a offset to ole Preacher Moses Mutters, what was allus a-hanging round camp, and sing-songing out, "You can't do it, Tony—it's ergin reason!"

off-sided *adjective* See citation.

c1982 Young *Colloquial Appal* 16 = left-handed.

off-side horse See **off horse**.

off steer *noun* In a team of work steers, the one on the right-hand side. See also **off horse**.

1969 GSMNP-46:1 I would take the line off of the right hand steer, what we called the off steer, and just keep the line on the lead steer then till I got them to where they would mind what I'd say to them.

off yander *adverb phrase, noun* See citation. See also **yonder B3**.

1982 Slone *How We Talked* 18 = could mean just a few yards, like "I am getting so that I can't see off yander," or a long distance—"He comes from off yander," meaning another state.

oh my country alive *interjection* Used to express surprise or disbelief.

1937 Hall *Coll* (Gatlinburg TN) [Have you fought any forest fires?]: Oh my country alive! I've fit fires all my life!

oil *noun, verb* Variant form **ile**.

1867 Harris *Sut Lovingood* 105 The wimen fans 'im, fixes the bed close, an' biles yarbs fur 'im; an' the men iles his bruses, an' poltusis his body. **1929** (in **1952** Mathes *Tall Tales* 108) He says wearin' a lump of asafidity round yer neck an' takin' a little balsam ile ever-day will keep off might' nigh any sickness. **1955** Washburn *Country Doctor* 64 If you'll furnish that an' get 'er easy so she won't throw-up so powerful bad, a pint o' sweet ile'll make them gallstones pass.

old *adjective* See also **old of the moon**.

1 To convey a sense of familiarity or attachment: see **old lady**, **old man**, **old uncle**.

2 Following another adjective in expressions in which *old* has little or no meaning except perhaps to convey a degree a familiarity with or tenderness toward the object referred to. See also **big old**, **great big old**, **little old**.

1921 Weeks *Speech of KY Mtneer* 17 The term, little old, varies in meaning from one of extreme disgust to one of real endearment. I have heard of a little old late train, a little old cook stove, a little old coal mine, and a little old baby! **1926** Hunnicutt *Twenty Years* 12 This happened in a little old open place in the laurel. **1939** Hall *Coll* (Proctor NC) This big old coon come down about fifteen steps from where we was at. **1969** GSMNP-25:1:16 In the little old hollow there, [there was a] big old chestnut tree that had fell, laying right across the hollow. **1997** Andrews *Mountain Vittles* 17 Serve with a big old spoon. **2007** Milnes *Signs Cures Witches* 67 One time he told Johnny that he had a cow that was "as old as the North Star!" He used the adjective "old" before almost any name or object, as in "that little old baby."

old animal *noun* Used as a euphemism for *bull*. See also **bull A1**.

1963 Wilson *Regional Words* 81 = a male of the cattle family was, only among men, a bull; elsewhere he was a yearling (regardless of his age), an old animal, a steer, or a male-cow (by very modest people).

Old Arthur *noun* See citation.

1990 Cavender *Folk Medical Lex* 28 = arthritis.

old as Methusaleh's housecat *phrase* Extremely old.

1956 McAtee *Some Dial NC* 32. **1963** Williams *Metaphor Mt Speech II* 51 That mangy old Boog hoss is as old as Methusaleh's housecat and as pore as Job's turkey.

old aunt *noun* Used as a quasi-honorific to express courtesy, familiarity, or respect for an older woman in the community not necessarily related to the speaker. See also **aunt B**, **dad**, **granny A1**, **old uncle**, **uncle**.

1963 Watkins and Watkins *Yesterday* 28 Old Aunt Marthy Scott shouted and praised the Lord; others moved through the congregation, pleading with the unsaved sinners to come to the bench. **2013** Lyon *Voiceplace* 186 I wrote down a story she told me of Old Aunt Martha Money who could cure the summer complaint.

Old Baptist *noun* See citation.

1957 Hall *Coll* (Mt Sterling NC) Old Baptists [are] Hard-shell or Primitive Baptists.

Old Baptist pallet See **Baptist pallet**.

Old Betsy *noun* See citation.

1939 Farr *TN Mt Regions* 91 = the sun: "Old Betsy didn't shine today."

Old Billy Devil, **Old Billy Hell** See **Billy Hell**.

old blade *noun* See citation.

1967 *DARE Survey* (Maryville TN) = joking name a man may use for his wife.

old busthead *noun* Homemade whiskey of an inferior quality, so named from the effect it often has on the head. See also **busthead 1**.

1940 Farr *More TN Expressions* 447 = poor quality liquor. **1978** Hiser *Quare Do's* 145 I told Buttermilk that last batch of old busthead he made weren't no good. Too, I didn't bottle it at the right time. **1996** Montgomery *Coll* (known to Adams, Cardwell, Jones, Ledford, Norris, Oliver).

Old Christmas *noun* An alternative observance of Christmas, celebrated usually on January 6 and reflecting the date of the holiday according to the Julian (or Old Style) calendar. The more precise Gregorian (New Style) calendar was adopted in continental Europe (especially in Catholic countries) in 1582, but not until 1752 in Great Britain, where the populace had continued to observe Christmas according to the older calendar and associated the day with such miraculous events as the kneeling of livestock at the stroke of midnight Christmas Eve and the sudden blooming of flowers. Settlers brought this observance to North America, and in some places in southern Appalachia the belief that the day was the true, sacred Christmas persisted well into the twentieth century. The observance has no connection with the traditional feast day of Twelfth Night or Epiphany. See also **New Christmas**, **Old Christmas Eve**.

1895 Edson and Fairchild *TN Mts* 373 = January 6th (The day is remembered by those who never heard of Twelfth Night or Epiphany). **1905** Miles *Spirit of Mts* 107 He and Arth do not disagree about certain weather signs their mother had taught them when they were "shirt-tail boys," signs about Groundhog Day, for example, and the Ruling Days, the twelve days from the twenty-fifth of December to Old Christmas, each of which rules the weather of a month of the coming year. **c1940** *Newport (TN) Plain Citizen* Don't carry ashes out between Christmas and Old Christmas. In recent times, as Old Christmas becomes only a historical curiosity, it is sometimes supposed to have been an observance of Epiphany, but this is quite erroneous. **1942** Thomas *Blue Ridge* 158–59 There are people who may never have heard of the Gregorian or Julian calendar, yet in keeping Old Christmas as they do on January 6th, they cling unwittingly to the Julian calendar of 46 B.C., introduced in this country in the earliest years. To them December 25th is New Christmas, according to the Gregorian calendar adopted in 1752. They celebrate the two occasions in a very different way. The old with prayer and carol-singing, the new with gaiety and feasting. **1957** Combs *Lg Sthn High: Word List* 69 = January 6. Still observed here and there, in spite of the change which took place with the introduction of the Gregorian calendar (1751). Children sometimes hang up their stockings on Old Christmas eve. On this eve, at midnight, the elder blossoms out, the cows kneel and pray, and the cock crows all night long; which is reminiscent of the "bird of dawning," in Hamlet. **c1960** Wilson *Coll* = January 6, still remembered by older people as told to them by their parents. My mother always reminded us of the day and said that her mother always regarded it as the real Christmas. **1970** Adams *Appal Revisit* 46 One of the most beautiful superstitions was in connection with the celebration of "Old Christmas" which occurs on January 6, the date on which Christmas occurred in early England before the calendar change in the 18th century to December 25. The folk believed that on the eve of Old Christmas, the elderberry bushes shot out their blossoms and that at midnight the cattle would kneel down in their stalls to pay homage to the Baby Jesus who had been born in a stable. **2019** *Blind Pig* (Jan 5) I heard the words "old Christmas" growing up but had no idea what they meant. I never knew of anyone having any observances of January 6.

[DARE *Old Christmas* n From its being reckoned by the "old style" or Julian calendar; chiefly Mid Atlantic, South Midland]

Old Christmas Eve *noun* According to the Old Style (or Julian) calendar, the day before Christmas is observed. See also **Old Christmas.**

1927 Furman *Lonesome Road* 104 Dances, drinking, too often shooting, all kinds of gayety . . . always came to an abrupt close on the night of the fifth of January, Old Christmas Eve. In the belief of all the older people, Old Christmas, was real Christmas, and discipline was sternly enforced when it began. **c1950** Adams *Grandpap* 226 "Tomor's Old Christmas," said Aunt Nance Ann. "Yes it is!" said Pap. "An' tonight's the night that the elder buds swell." "An' at midnight, tonight," added Mammy, "is when the cattle are said to kneel and pray." "I 'member the time," said Uncle Sam, "that Pap an' Mother were gone from home one Old Christmas Eve an' us children were right there alone by ourselves. Me an' Brother Green were great big boys an' Sister Peggy was a rightsmart girl herself." **1981** *Smokies Heritage* 32:4 On Old Christmas Eve, all signs of merriment disappeared—the occasion turned suddenly somber. **1988** Smith *Fair and Tender* 25 On December 25 they is not a thing happening as a rule but on Old Christmas Eve that is January 5 this is when Gaynelle and Virgie Cline comes over and tells storys all nigt with Daddy as they did it when Daddy was young, this is Christmas to us. So to anser your question, on December 25 they was not a thing happening up here on Sugar Fork nor even down at Home Creek but that folks drinks likker and shoots off ther guns.

old consumption *noun* Tuberculosis.

1970 Foster *Walker Valley* 1:24 Roseann and Uncle Mose lived till he got twenty-three and he died of what they called old consumption then, which would be TB today. **1995** Montgomery *Coll* (known to Cardwell).

old coon See **coon B.**

Old Dragon See **(the) Old Scratch.**

older head See **old head.**

old field *noun* An open area thought to have been cleared and cultivated by Cherokees or another indigenous tribe or by earlier whites but then considered infertile; also a field abandoned due to uninterrupted planting. Because such land was not otherwise used, churches and schools were sometimes built on it. Also called **Indian old field.** See also **old field school.**

1842 Crosby *Journal/Account Book* 102 Sowd 3 1/2 Bushels of the Ruffled Oats joining the Pear Tree and 7 1/2 Bushels of the Common Oats in the Bale . . . of the Old Field at Rawleigh last of March. **1863** *Poteet CW Letters* (Nov 3) Last night I Just lay out in the open Old field. **1883** Zeigler and Grosscup *Heart of Alleghanies* 68 We were informed by mountaineers that flint arrow heads and broken pieces of pottery have been found in this old field, showing almost conclusively that some of the Cherokees themselves, or the nation that built the many mounds, laid the buried stone walls and worked the ancient mica mines, occupied it as an abiding place for years. **1913** Morley *Carolina Mts* 186 The tall picturesque broom-corn that ornaments the landscape, however, is raised to sell, the universal sweeping instrument of the mountains being made from the "broom-straw," or wild sedge that so beautifully takes possession of every "old field" not yet grown up to bushes. **1943** Peattie *Indian Days* 24 In many places white settlers found that the land had long been cleared by the Indians. At the head of the New River, and on the fertile plains of Tellico, as well as in the Watauga, Hiwassee, and Little Tennessee basins, settlers encountered these openings. They called them "old fields." **1986** Pederson et al. *LAGS* (Fannin Co GA) = abandoned land. **2000** Morgan *Mts Remember* 31 The Old Field there had grown up in briars and hogweed, but you could still see a few rotten corn stalks where the Indian women had farmed it at one time.

[DARE *old field* n 1 chiefly South, South Midland]

old field balsam *noun* Same as **rabbit tobacco.**

1982 Stupka *Wildflowers* 124 It is sometimes called "poverty weed" and "old-field balsam," because it thrives in dry areas and waste places. Names such as "sweet balsam" and "sweet everlasting" refer to its fragrance. Other names are "rabbit tobacco" and "cudweed."

old field pine *noun* A pine tree that commonly grows in an **old field.**

1883 Zeigler and Grosscup *Heart of Alleghanies* 177 "It strikes me," says I, "as rather a strange fact, that those pines are all the same size. What species are they?" "Those," replied my friend, "are what we call old field pine." **1997** Montgomery *Coll* (known to eight consultants from the Smoky Mountains), = Virginia pine, yellow pine, or short-leaf pine (Cardwell).

[DARE *old-field pine* n chiefly South, South Midland]

old field school *noun* An early public school built on an **old field** because it was open or easy to clear and the ground had presumably been worn out or otherwise rendered useless for agriculture.

1834 Caruthers *Kentuckian in NY* 1.26 (DARE) He sold his horse and cart too, and then turned in to keepin a little old-field school. **c1890** Job *Diary* 5 What schools we had were of the most primitive order. At the "old field schools" as they were called we had no recess as it is now called. It was study from morning till noon, then an hour for our playtime, and study from 1 o'clock till turning out time. **1941** *FWP Guide WV* 116 West Virginia's free school system . . . evolved from log structures built by early settlers to serve as both schools and churches. . . . The buildings were usually situated on hard-scrabble or worn-out lands and were called "old field schools." **1977** Shields *Cades Cove* 45 An old field school was a simple log structure with a dirt floor and a fire pit in the center. **1984** Dykeman and Stokely *At Home* 84 John Preston Arthur left a vivid memoir of his experience in one of these so-called "old field" schools, which were located on land no longer under cultivation. **1994** *Smokies Guide* (Winter) 6 Other times "old field schools" were constructed. These were usually rough log structures that were built in an "old field" that was no longer being used for agriculture. These schools provided few luxuries and the teacher often had to buy the school supplies out of his salary.

[DARE *old-field school* n South, South Midland]

old field tobacco *noun* See citation.

2007 McMillon *Notes* = rabbit tobacco.

Old Forked Toes, Old Gouge See **(the) Old Scratch.**

old harp *noun*

1 A system of representing hymn music by **shape notes**, most often sung in four-part harmony in a "singing square" in which the tune is first chanted in the notes of the musical scale (compare **fasola**) and then using the words. Same as **sacred harp**. See also **old harp singing.**

1977 Wolfe *TN Strings* 14 The religious song tradition took a slightly different direction in East Tennessee. By 1832 songbooks using a system of seven shapes—the familiar names of today's scale—were in use in the North, and by 1848 there appeared the first southern seven-shape book, W. H. and M. L. Swan's *Harp of Columbia*, published in Knoxville. This book for years dominated East Tennessee sacred singing, and was second in influence only to the original Sacred Harp. Throughout East Tennessee groups of singers using this book called themselves (and still call themselves) "Harp Singers" or "Old Harp Singers." [**1990** Aiken *Stories* 124 This style of singing originated out of necessity. There were no musical instruments to carry the tune so the human voice had to be the instrument; thus "old harp" meant the human voice.] **1992** Bush *Dorie* 102 In old harp, each note is represented by a different-shaped note.

2 (also *old harp (song) book*) By extension = music (especially hymns) set out in **shape notes**; a collection of hymns set to be sung by **shape notes.**

1939 Hall *Coll* (Cosby Creek TN) We used the old harp. **1978** Dykeman and Stokely *Highland Homeland* 101 In ancient Ireland and Wales songsters had been accompanied on the harp. Settlers had brought the Old Harp song book of early hymns and anthems with them from the British Isles . . . and across the mountains into these remote byways. **1986** Ogle *Lucinda* 56 After dinner we all went back and they had singing school in old harp books.

[< *Sacred Harp*, title of songbook by B. F. White and E. J. King (1844), chiefly South]

old harp book See **old harp 2.**

old harp singing Same as **harp sing.**

1969 GSMNP-38:123 They had a many of an old harp singing right there in that old log schoolhouse. **1991** Headrick *Headrick's Chapel* 207 The present Harp singing at Headrick's Chapel actually began at the Primitive Baptist Church of Townsend about 1920 when it was known as the Coker Hill Old Harp Singing.

old harp song book See **old harp 2.**

Old Harry See **(the) Old Scratch.**

old head *noun* An older person, as someone considered to embody the customs, attitudes, or wisdom of the community.

1977 Shackelford et al. *Our Appalachia* 209 I lived in one camp a while and when they shut down a lot of these older heads would always lay up food. **1978** Montgomery *White Pine Coll* VI-2 There's a few [= people who think that] but not too many. Seems like a lot of the old heads are dead. **1997** Montgomery *Coll* (known to eight consultants from the Smoky Mountains).

[DARE *old head* n chiefly South, South Midland]

old hen *noun* See 1957 citation.

1930 Pendleton *Wood-Hicks Speak* 88 = corn mash fermented and fortified with fruit juice or birch candy. **1957** Combs *Lg Sthn High: Word List* 70 = a sort of illicit beverage made of corn meal, and flavored with cayenne pepper. It produces a bursting headache upon "convalescence." So called because the ingredients must sit in the sun for three weeks, a period of time also necessary for a hen to hatch her brood.

[DARE *old hen* n especially VA]

Old Horny See **(the) Old Scratch.**

old Jerusalem *noun* An annual plant (*Chenopodium botrys/ambrosioides*) from which a vermifuge is made. More commonly known as **Jerusalem oak.**

1972 Cooper *NC Mt Folklore* 13 [Worm] medicine was made from the seeds of the vermifuge (Old Jerusalem) plant, which had been introduced into the mountains by early settlers.

old John Law *noun* A law-enforcement officer, especially a highway patrolman.

1990 Merriman *Moonshine Rendezvous* 27 Back in those days ol' John Law harassed you if they couldn't catch you haulin' whiskey.

old lady *noun* A man's wife, at any age (often used as a term of respect). Same as **old woman**. See also **old man 1.** [Editor's note: The usage of this term for one's mother is widespread in the US.]

1862 Smith *CW Letters* (n.d.) you no how the old lady is a bout things that is concerning me I am placed in a bad fix and you know that I cant help my self &c. **1863** *Vance Papers* (July 2) I am Seventy four years of age and my wife is Seventy and all three of my sones are in the army and me and the old lady are left a lone and I am blind and has been for ten years. **1939** Hall *Coll* (Bradley Fork NC) Finally I lost the old lady seven year ago last January. **1967** *DARE Survey* (Maryville TN) = joking name a man may use for his wife. **1969** Medford *Finis* 125 He talked and I talked: farming, school, politics—while his "old lady" worked the house, darting here and there, as the "gals" did some outside chores. **1976** *Bear Hunting* 301 Champ's old lady was named Melviney. **1983** *Dark Corner OHP-5A* He married me and the old lady, and we were the last couple he married. I reckon we killed him. **2005** Williams *Gratitude* 511 = wife; his woman.

old maid *noun* A zinnia (*Zinnia elegans*).

1940 Still *River of Earth* 104 Before frost fell we went to Grandma's flower bed in a corner of the garden and picked the dry seeds. We broke off the brown heads of old maids and the smooth buttons of Job's tears hanging on withered stalks. **1986** Pederson et al. *LAGS* (Blount Co TN, Cherokee Co GA).

[DARE *old maid* n 1 chiefly South, South Midland]

old man *noun* [Editor's note: The usage of this term for one's father is widespread in the US.]

1 A woman's husband or mate, at any age (often used as a term of respect). See also **old woman**.

1817 (in **1969** Royall *Letters from AL* 81) Whenever my old man would go out, he would be a axin me how many neighbors I had, how many were in each family, and how far distant the country was inhabited around us. **1859** Taliaferro *Fisher's River* 250 You could see the ox-carts coming in, the "ole man" driving and the "ole 'omun" sitting on top of the one, two, or three bales, and the "childering" walking. **1860** *Week in Smokies* 123 She told me that her "old man," as she called her husband, once, when she was sick, had bought some "store sugar." **1862** *Hanes CW Letters* (Feb 1) tel her to not get mared untel the war is over for fear they coms a drafft and they take her old man. **1895** Edson and Fairchild *TN Mts* 373 = invariably and respectfully used for *husband*. "*My old man is plowing*." **1898** *Incidents* 31 It is customary for a mountain couple as soon as married to refer to each other as "my old man" or "my old woman." The phrase is a sort of apology for the affection they feel, and does not strike them as odd. **1913** Kephart *Our Sthn High* 345 A woman, learning that her unarmed husband was besieged by his foes, seized his rifle, filled her apron with cartridges, rushed past the firing-line, and stood by her "old man" until he beat his assailants off. **1931** Goodrich *Mt Homespun* 40 Ever since my old man died, I've made enough corn to do me, and sweetening too. **c1951** Chapman *Speech Confusing* A mountain wife, though still in her teens, is called "the old woman" by her youthful husband. She likewise calls him "my old man," regardless of his age. **1967** *DARE Survey* (Gatlinburg TN, Maryville TN) = joking name a woman may use for her husband. **1972** *Anna Howard* 55 I've not had too much of a happy life since my old man died.

2 An older man in the community (used attributively, as a term of respect, usually with a man's full name and sometimes prefaced by *the*). See also **the 8**.

1863 *Zimmerman CW Letters* (Jan 10) if you and the old mans folks would Send me and Jackson a box a piece it it would not take so powerfull long. **1915** Dingus *Word-List VA* 186 = used without sense of disrespect. **1939** Hall *Coll* (Smokemont NC) the old man Tom Huskey rared up with his rifle and plugged him [= a bear] by the hind shoulder. **1973** *GSMNP*-4:2 Old man Dude Hannah they called him. Dude and Ross Hannah lived in that section you are speaking about. . . . The old man Bud Messer lived right in close to where you are speaking about, in that section in there. **1974** *AOHP/ALC*-733 They's a big lot of people that was preachers . . . back when I was a child, I remember the old man John Akers and Lewis Bryant. **1989** *Matewan OHP*-56 Then there was the old man John Nenni. He had the ice cream parlor and the beer joint. **1997** *Dante OHP*-53 I would go up and get groceries there and walk from where we lived over there up there and get stuff for my mother, and the old man Con Buttrey run that store.

Old Man Dark *noun* Nightfall.

1943 Justus *Jerry Jake* 41 Just as soon as school was out he footed it up the mountain to do as much as he could before Old Man Dark caught him.

old man's beard *noun* Same as **fringe bush**.

1941 Walker *Story of Mt* 61 Fringe-tree, or Old Man's Beard, which is more often a shrub than it is a tree, builds snowlike spots in many places on top of the mountain, especially along Little River. Its flowers are delicately fragrant, and it is worthy of a place on any man's lawn. [**1971** Krochmal et al. *Medicinal Plants Appal* 92 The bark is used as a diuretic, tonic, and astringent; it is also used to reduce fever. In Appalachia, a liquid of boiled root bark is applied to skin irritations.] **1997** Montgomery *Coll* (known to Cardwell).

Old Master *noun*

1 God.

c1960 Wilson *Coll* = God, probably an echo from slavery times. **1997** Montgomery *Coll* (known to Brown).

[DARE *Old Master* n 1 chiefly South, South Midland]

2 The Devil. See **(the) Old Scratch**.

old mill *noun* A **play party** game.

1939 Hall *Coll* (Roaring Fork TN) = girls and boys swinging around together. "Hands on the hopper" were some of the words of this play-party song.

old Ned *noun*

1 Fat pork.

1862 *Councill CW Letters* (Dec 21) I have to gow to put on some of old Nead to cook to pursurve life. **1913** Kephart *Our Sthn High* 75 "Old Ned" is merely slang for fat pork. **1976** Dwyer *Southern Sayin's* 22 = fat pork, home-cured bacon. "Have some old Ned." **1997** Montgomery *Coll* (known to Brown, Bush).

[DARE *Old Ned* n 1 chiefly South, South Midland]

2 The devil. See **(the) Old Scratch**.

Old Nick *noun*

1 The devil. See **(the) Old Scratch**.

2 Homemade whiskey.

1952 McCall *Cherokees and Pioneers* 101 If you are invited to share a little something, whether it be called moonshine, corn juice, nubbin booze, Cain corn, white mule, stump juice, white lightning, Old Nick, hoot owl, O be joyful, or mountain dew, you should be warned that the thing meant is that powerful rank pizen what cheers the heart of even a man with a nagging wife.

old of the moon *noun phrase* The latter half of the lunar cycle, the waning moon, which signals whether planting or other activities will be propitious or not. See also **dark of the moon**, **light of the moon**, **new of the moon**, **shrink B.**

1904 Johnson *Highways South* 165 You boil meat killed in the old of the moon, and it will all shrivel up and there won't be none of it. **1929** Duncan and Duncan *Sayings* 235 Kill hogs in the ol' uv the moon an' it 'ull go to grease. **1956** Hall *Coll* (Gatlinburg TN) Make it in the old of the moon is what I always did. **1959** Roberts *Up Cutshin* 35 We would kill our hogs all the time on the old of the moon. **1969** *Own Log Cabin* 12 Timber was cut, for example, only on the "old of the moon" . . . when the sap was down so that it would cure correctly. **1973** *AOHP/ASU-111* Some claim that if you plant beans in the old of the moon you'll make a good crop of beans, but if you plant of the new moon, you'll have no beans hardly on your vine. **1983** *Dark Corner OHP-5A* You only cut wood on the new of the moon. It dries out and makes it light, for stove wood, you know, and dry it quicker. If you cut it on the old of the moon, it'll mold, turn all blue and sog, it won't never dry out. **2001** House *Clay's Quilt* 234 They have to be put up tonight. They'll keep longer if they're put up in the old of the moon.

[OED3 *old* n[1] 3 now U.S. regional]

old Pete *noun* Starvation, scarcity of food; destitution.

1957 Neel *Backwoodsman* 36 = a scarcity of food and general poverty: "This mornin' ol' Pete was a-grinnin' into the skillet at my house" (the family had little to eat for breakfast). **1960** Mason *Memoir* 96 We now knew that we could keep *old pete* away as long as we could get a market for our cross-ties. **2004** Burton *In Memoriam* 139–40 As the old people said, "Old Pete was on the table." And they said when he was under it, you'd better be a-doin' somethin'. That meant your eatin' was gone. The best thing is keep, if you can, with a willin' mind and say "I'm here, and I didn't put myself here, and it hain't nothin' I can do about it."

(the) Old Scratch (also *Old Dragon*, *Old Forked Toes*, *Old Gouge*, *Old Harry*, *Old Horny*, *Old Master*, *Old Ned*, *Old Nick*) *noun* The devil; figuratively, mischief, devilry. Also called **Billy Hell**, **dragon**, **Scratch**.

1862 Robinson *CW Letters* (Dec 9) I want to come home worse then I ever did it may be that I will be spaird to come home Some time but old master will have it to kirb my temper if I do. **1867** (in **1974** Harris *High Times* 290) While this were gwine on, Old Thad were a tryin to claim kin wif the devil, a comparing his foot along wif ole Nick's. **1900** Harben *N GA Sketches* 48 Henry has had Old Nick in 'im as big as a house ever since Mr. Pelham went off an' left Cobb in charge. **1901** Harben *Westerfelt* 250 She's had the very old scratch in 'er ever since Toot was run off. **1915** Hall *Autobiog Claib Jones* 5 Me and the Trader family had all sorts of Old Harry. **1944** Hayes *Word-List NC* 36 = the devil, the bogey man. **1952** Wilson *Folk Speech NC* 588 = the devil. "If you aren't a good boy, *Old Scratch* will get you." **1957** Combs *Lg Sthn High: Word List* 86 = satan; used to quiet children: "The old scratch will get you!" **1963** Edwards *Gravel* 99 Her hair stood up on her head and she didn't know what to think. Maybe the old Scratch was acomin to git her. **1966–67** *DARE Survey* (Spruce Pine NC) *old Scratch*; *Scratch* = talking about a very mean person, you might say, "He's meaner than Scratch"; (ceTN) *Old Forked Toes* = common term for the Devil. **1973** Davis *'Pon My Honor* 23 Hit 'peared like the Old Scratch had whispered in the ear of the weather asker and that they was in cahoots to make it so cold in them hills that folks would rather have a chimney corner down in Hell than a cabin in the hills. **1976** Still *Pattern of Man* 81 They preach, and Old Horny reaps the benefit. *Ibid.* 84 Who sent you? Old Scratch? Lucifer incarnate? Old Gouge? **1981** Whitener *Folk-Ways* 49 Frank Hodges doesn't expect his double dulcimer either to summon up Old Nick or send its players to a fiery abode. **1987** Trent *Yesteryear* 82 Her knees gave way under her, and she sunk to the floor, but jist as she was asenkin down, she turned and then she saw him. There was the Old Scratch hisself, reachin his long hairy arms to git her. And his long forked tail was aswingin back and forth, and his peaked ears reached above the top of his head, and his eyes was like flashed fire. **1995–97** Montgomery *Coll*: *Old Dragon* (known to Adams, Bush, Cardwell); *Old Master* (known to Bush); The youngun is just full of old Ned (Norris); *Old Scratch* (known to eight consultants from the Smoky Mountains). **2007** McMillon *Notes*: *Old Dragon*. **2009** Wiles and Wiles *Location* 149 Another warning came in the form of Ole Scratch—If you didn't go to church, Ole Scratch would get you. If you didn't clean your plate, Ole Scratch would get you. If you didn't wash your ears or committed any number of transgressions, Ole Scratch was sure to get you.

[OED3 *Old Scratch* (at *scratch* n[2]) 1740→; DARE *Old Scratch* n chiefly South, South Midland, also New England]

old-seed folks *noun* See citation.

c1954 Adams *Word-List* = ancestors.

old settler *noun* An original settler in an area.

1973 *AOHP/EH-24* Old man Callahan was one of the first old settlers in this Callahan Creek up there by Appalachia.

old shoe *noun* Used in similes for someone ordinary or unaffected or of something comfortable.

1927 Woofter *Dialect from WV* 353 *easy as an old shoe* = very comfortable. "This is as easy as an old shoe." **1940** Haun *Hawk's Done* 73 I went all day and stayed with his woman once. She was plain as an old shoe and just as common as anybody. **1993** Ison and Ison *Whole Nother Lg* 50 *plain as an old shoe* = a person is common, not stuck up, will converse with anyone and is not conceited.

old sledge *noun* A 19th-century American version of the popular English card game "all fours."

1883 Murfree *Old Sledge* 544 Them thar boys rides thar horses over hyar ter the Settlemint nigh on to every night in the week ter play kyerds—"Old Sledge," they calls it. **1895** Dromgoole *Fiddling to Fame* 60 Jube war tol'rable fond uv ol' Sledge now'n then.

Old Smoky *noun* The main chain or ridge of the Great Smoky Mountains along the TN/NC state border. Same as **(the) Smoky**. See also **Big Smokies**.

1927 Mason *Lure of Smokies* 225 I was comin' over ol' Smoky with my woman and Ben, our oldest boy. **1938** Bowman *High Horizons* 11–12 Often described as the wildest feature in the Southern Appalachians, this segment consists of a central ridge known as "Big" or "Old" Smoky and many lesser ridges on either side roughly connected by the mountain masses.

old sow cat *noun* See citation.

1967 *DARE Survey* (Maryville TN) = joking name a man may use for his wife.

old time *noun phrase* A time long ago.

1974–75 McCracken *Logging* 14:18 I don't think they use them anywhere anymore. This was an old time.

old timers' day *noun* See citation.

1937 *Hall Coll* (Gatlinburg TN) In the 1930s and possibly since, this town had an Old-Timers' Day every summer, where tales and tall tales were swapped, old ways of doing things described, and songs sung.

old-timey *adjective* Characteristic of a former period, old-fashioned.

1937 *Hall Coll* (Emerts Cove TN) Old-timey people called it a cast biler. **1967** Fetterman *Stinking Creek* 127 Daddy's old-timey. He said he didn't want boys coming around here. **1970** Montell *Coe Ridge* 31 Dr. Moore, he was an old-timey pilldoctor that lived in that old house up here at Black's Ferry. **1973** GSMNP-90:4 The old-timey road was right there. I've walked up and down that road. **1975** GSMNP-61:12 They usually sung two or three old-timey songs. **1997** *Dante OHP-14* We used Arbuckle's coffee, and you had to grind it in an old timey grinder, and I'd run up in the smoke house to keep the preacher from hearing me grind coffee, when he'd stay all night.

[DARE *old-timey* adj chiefly South, South Midland]

old uncle *noun* Used as a quasi-honorific to express courtesy, familiarity, or respect for an older man in the community not necessarily related to the speaker, often prefacing the man's name. See also **aunt B**, **dad**, **granny A1**, **old aunt**, **uncle**.

1899 Crozier *White-Caps* 176 "Old Uncle Andy," as he was familiarly known, lived in the Henderson Spring neighborhood and was one of the oldest and best citizens in Sevier county. **1939** *Hall Coll* (Cataloochee NC) William Stafford said old Uncle Steve Woody wouldn't be any happier when he entered the gates of heaven. **1998** *Montgomery Coll* (known to Brown, Cardwell, Ledford, Weaver). **2007** Shelby *Molly Whuppie* 57 "Sorry, old uncle," said Will. "We ain't got enough for our own selves."

old Virginia *noun* The present-day state of Virginia, especially the portion east of the Blue Ridge, in distinction to the state of West Virginia.

1937 *Hall Coll* (Emerts Cove TN) My gran'maw was born in Old Virginia. *Ibid.* (Emerts Cove TN) My grandmother Bohanon came from Old Virginia. **1995** *Montgomery Coll* (known to Cardwell).

Old War *noun*

1 The American Revolutionary War.

1960 Hall *Smoky Mt Folks* 50 [Veenie Ramsey of Upper Cosby Creek TN] was proud of the fact that her "gramp" came to this country from across the waters about the time of the "Old War." **1962** Dykeman *Tall Woman* 38 [They took up] some vague land grants from the days of the old war, the Revolution.

2 The American Civil War. Same as **War between the States**.

1937 *Hall Coll* (Tobes Creek NC) Most people moved to Texas from the Smokies after the Old War. **1969** GSMNP-37:2:5 He was born right there in that time of the old war way back yonder. He wasn't big enough to be in it but his brother was in it. Him and his brother, them there fellows that come through here, stealing horses and things.

old woman *noun* A man's wife, at any age (often used as a term of respect or a form of address). Same as **old lady**. See also **old man 1**. [Editor's note: The usage of this term for one's mother is widespread in the US.]

1859 Taliaferro *Fisher's River* 250 You could see the ox-carts coming in, the "ole man" driving and the "ole 'omun" sitting on top of the one, two, or three bales, and the "childering" walking. **1860** *Week in Smokies* 122 Mister, you will find our house mighty rough, but you may look at my old woman there to see if we starve up here in the mountains. **1863** *Ingram CW Letters* (March 8) well old woman you said that Mother saide she wished That I was thare to eate diner with her. **1883** Zeigler and Grosscup *Heart of Alleghanies* 101 On inquiring whether our wants could be satisfied, he directed us to his "old woman." **1898** *Incidents* 31 It is customary for a mountain couple as soon as married to refer to each other as "my old man" or "my old woman." The phrase is a sort of apology for the affection they feel, and does not strike them as odd. **1940** Haun *Hawk's Done* 9 Ad's boys by his first old woman, I put their names in too. **c1951** Chapman *Speech Confusing* A mountain wife, though still in her teens, is called "the old woman" by her youthful husband. She likewise calls him "my old man," regardless of his age. **1983** *Smokies Guide* (Fall) 2 He and his wife, Jane, have raised five children, and now live in Whittier, North Carolina, in a 200-year-old log house that he laughingly describes as "so far up in the hills that when me and my old woman fuss, can't nobody hear us."

old woman is picking her geese (also *old woman is losing her feathers*) *phrase* It is snowing, especially in large flakes.

1931 Combs *Lg Sthn High* 1307 The old woman's a-losin' her feathers (Snow is falling). The old woman's a-pickin' her geese (Snow is falling). **1952** Brown *NC Folklore* 1.499 The old woman is picking her geese (It is snowing). **1962** Wilson *Folkways Mammoth Cave* 13 When large flakes came down, the "old woman was picking her goose." **1997** *Montgomery Coll*: *old woman is picking her geese* (known to nine consultants from the Smoky Mountains).

[DARE *old woman is picking her geese*, the phr especially Appalachians]

oman, omern See **woman.**

on

A Variant form rhyming with *own*.

2016 McCarroll *On and On* 46–47 I actively tried to talk right and hide my accent. One lingering linguistic marker caused me the most panic when I slipped . . . I stumbled over the word "on." When my mom told me to put my *coat on*, those words rhymed. She told me to call her when I was *on the road*. Those words rhymed. To my Appalachian tongue, *own* and *on* were pronounced exactly the same way.

B *preposition*

1 Used after a verb to express an occurrence that is unfortunate, unexpected, or beyond one's control (especially in phrase *die on*).

1923 Greer-Petrie *Angeline Doin' Society* 17 He 'lowed he wouldn't put that much money in hit . . . fur what asshorance would he have that the thing wouldn't die on him? **1929** (in **1952** Mathes *Tall Tales* 111) He's been doctorin' him fer a week, but he's skeered the little feller's goin' to die on him. **1960** Campbell *Birth* 60 Asked later about the health of "Mrs. Henry Ford [= Wiley Oakley's daughter]," Wiley sadly announced, "She died out on me." **1967** Fetterman *Stinking Creek* 134 I had a gray squirrel last year, and he died on me. **1979** Carpenter *Walton War* 172 When my cow up and died on me, hit wuz a main blow. **1991** Still *Wolfpen Notebooks* 65 All my sweethearts have got married on me. **1999** Offut *Out of Woods* 26 "I come for Ory," Gerald said, "but he's died on me." **2008** *Rosie Hicks* 1 We had so much meat I had to do something with some of it, 'cause it's going to ruin on us.

[cf DHE *on* 1 "indicating loss or injury"; CUD *on* 5 "to your disadvantage"]

2 On the basis of.

1997 Montgomery *Coll* I don't understand it, but I believe it on the Bible (Cardwell).

3 Of, about (used especially after a verb of sensation or mental activity such as *hear, know, think*). See also **think on**.

1860 Olmsted *Back Country* 260 "The fact on 't is," he said at length, as I pressed the enquiry, "there ain't anybody that means to work any in this country, except just along in harvest." **1867** Harris *Sut Lovingood* 49 Hits true, I did sorter frustrate a few lizzards a littil, but they haint members, es I knows on. **1883** Zeigler and Grosscup *Heart of Alleghanies* 61 I never hed no objections ter meetin' a varmint in a squar, stan'up fight,—his nails agin my knife, ye know; so without wunct thinkin' on gittin' outer the way, I retched fer my sticker. **1895** Murfree *Phantoms* 242 I'd hev hearn tell on it, sure, ef thar hed been enny sech word goin' the rounds. **1927** Mason *Lure of Smokies* 166 Thar'd be thar, or tharabouts, over fifty on 'em. **1930** Armstrong *This Day and Time* 102 He never did no harm, none I never heered tell on. **1940** Haun *Hawk's Done* 5 Maybe it's because I've thought a heap on Letitia. *Ibid.* 6 It makes me feel peaceable as a full kitten just to set here and look at the Family Record page and think on all the names. **1974** Fink *Bits Mt Speech* 18 = about. "I'll think on it." **1976** Still *Pattern of Man* 33 "Knock and beat and battle is all you think on," she snorted. **1997** Montgomery *Coll* (known to Brown, Ellis, Oliver). **2005** Williams *Gratitude* 145 I remember Mom a-cookin' some snowbirds oncet, and makin' dumplin's on 'em.

4 In phrase *on yesterday*.

1800 (in **1920** DeWitt *Sevier Journal* 25) (March 16) Mr. Blount taken ill on yesterday. **1861** *Martin CW Letters* (Dec 27) on yestarday they was an ofel fireing Some wheres on the Coast. **1864** Wilson *Confederate Private* 51 (July 4) the yankes atacted our lines on yesterday 13 times & was repulsed at every point.

[DARE on B2c VA]

5 In phrasal prepositions. See **on down in**, **on in down**, and Grammar and Syntax §14.5.

C *adverb*

1 Used to extend or intensify the action of a verb. See also Grammar and Syntax §14.4.

1939 Hall *Coll* (Smokemont NC) Then we come on in home and dressed them up and laid down and took a nap. *Ibid.* Go with me on after the dogs. **1953** Hall *Coll* (Bryson City NC) A bear looked along a little on the side of the tree and took up the tree and down the other side and ran on off up the hill. **1976** *Bear Hunting* 293 We start at [the bear's] heels and skin plumb on out down to his head. **1979** *Big South Fork OHP*-10 That road finally went on up on out on top up there to, on Fate Cooper's place. **1992** Oxford *Ray Hicks* 90 They finally got him on in home. **2003** Smith *Orlean Puckett* 56 There used to be a shed come plumb out over the yard. It come plumb on out from the roof of the [cabin] out over the yard.

2 With ellipsis of a verb.

1972 *AOHP/ALC*-276 They brought him to grandfather's, and I was there at the time when they brought him, and his wife, she on and took to run up and hug him.

on- *prefix* See also **in-**, **un-**.

1 Un-; used especially with adjectives, but also with adverbs, verbs, and participial adjectives; see citations.

1845 (in **1974** Harris *High Times* 51) The licken he gave me made me sorter oneasey. **1858** (in **1974** Harris *High Times* 119) He's an ongrateful beast. **1862** *Copenhaver CW Letters* (Aug 13) we m[a]y get home this winter but vary onsertain thay get hearder on us every day. **1862** *Walker CW Letters* (March 16) I am yet in the land of the living but i am verry on well At this time. **1864** *McGill CW Letters* (n.d.) I was verr ry onesey till I Receveid your cind letter. **1867** Harris *Sut Lovingood* 100 Ole Sock wer hurried on in this onnaterel an' onmannerly manner over a fell pine tree. *Ibid.* 121 His orful nakid wepun . . . cut the flat crown outen his cap, smoof es yu cud onkiver a huckleberry pie wif a case-knife. **1885** Murfree *Prophet* 24 I ain't onwillin' ter own it. *Ibid.* 28 They air mighty onsartin in thar temper. *Ibid.* 183 I feel ez onlucky an' weighted ez ef I war a-lookin' over my lef' shoulder at the new moon on a November Friday. **1898** Elliott *Durket Sperret* 39 She's been worrited an' onsettled all day, mad 'bout Lizer a-goin. **1901** Harben *Westerfelt* 195 Me 'n' Luke wus the cause o' yore comin' to this oncivilized place anyway. **1911** Shearin *E KY Word-List* 539 = a separative or negative prefix, as in *ontie, ondo, onlucky*, etc. **1925** Furman *Glass Window* 132 If hit hain't oncivil to ax, 'pears like hit would pleasure me a sight to have one of them pretty chains to hang around my neck. **1928** (in **1952** Mathes *Tall Tales* 65) You told him to ontie Coley atter dinner to run that shote out of the yard. **1929** (in **1952** Mathes *Tall Tales* 132) I'm oneasy they'll git Davy's feet in the miry clay. **1930s** (in **1944** Wentworth *ADD* 671) (eWV) *onhitch, onhandy, ontie, onlock . . . oneasy*. **1957** Combs *Lg Sthn High: Word List* 70 As a negative or separative prefix it [= *on-*] is common: *ondo; onlucky; onsartain* (uncertain); *ontie*. **1957** Wise *Mt Speech* 306 This [on-] prefix may be accompanied by the suffix -less, producing the effect of a double negative, as in *ongodless*. **1966** Medford *Ol' Starlin* 85 They said that the man, Buchanan, the Democrat, had made a mess o' things and orter have been onseated. *Ibid.* 89 "Hit was a lucky streak, I reckon, I had—'course onsuspected," Silas said. **1973** Carpenter *Mid-Appal* 32 It is heard in onreal, onnatural, onpack, "I didn't think I'd get things onpacked ontil morning." Other examples are: onknown and onwrap. **1999** Spencer *Memory Lane* I:10 Grandma was amused at how upset and oncertain he got. **2007** McMillon *Notes* = alternate pronunciation of un-, as in oneasy, onequal.

2 In-; used with adjectives and nouns; see citations.

1859 Taliaferro *Fisher's River* 232 Sich a onhuman man can't git my vote fur dog-pelter. **1865** (in **1974** Harris *High Times* 163) Jis then two perlease grabbed me, flung a blankit roun me and hauld me tu the work'us, ontu a forkid tail coat, charged wif an ondecint showin ove my pussin. **1898** Elliott *Durket Sperret* 85 Mebbe I'm a-doin' Dave a onjustice. *Ibid.* 130 Thar is onjestice been done, an' trouble 'll come. **1969** Medford *Finis* 94 My 'pinyun is that God A'mitey will jist pick out what little good thar is in both—an' then reject all the ignerant, the onsincere, the proud and so foarth.

[CUD cf *undecent/ondacent*]

3 Im-; used with adjectives.

1813 Hartsell *Memora* 129 he Stated that it wold bee on posebele for beter meletials [= militias] to be maid then was haeve at this time. **1859** Taliaferro *Fisher's River* 89 I sha'n't try to describe her, for it is onpossible. *Ibid.* 92 I got onpatient, and moseyed a little to'ads [the turkey], and got on a log where I could see a leetle. **1873** Smith *Arp Peace Papers* 75 "Won't you let these boxes go as bagidge?" "No, madam, it's onpossible." **1942** Hall *Phonetics Smoky Mts* 55 *onpossible*. **1994** Montgomery *Coll* ([*onpossible*] known to Cardwell).

4 Ir-; used with adjectives.

1867 Harris *Sut Lovingood* 71 When I'se in trubbil, skeer, ur tormint, I dus but wun thing, an' that's onresistabil, onekeled, an' durn'd fas' runnin, an' I jis' keeps at hit till I gits cumfort.

onbeknowenst, onbeknownst, onbenowen See **unbeknownst.**

once *adverb* Variant forms *oncet, oncst, onct, onst, wonest, wunst* [wənst].

1791 *Richland Church Minutes* 99 a desant diping of the whole Body under water in the name of the Father & of the Son & of the Holy Ghost onst as the three is one. **1812** (in **1920** DeWitt *Sevier Journal* 45) (March 29) Use a fresh poultice nixt morning & oncst in the middle of the day. **1824** Knight *Letter from KY* 106 The Phraseology in this state is sometimes novel. . . . Many from habit, like the Virginians, tuck a t at the end of such words as onct, twict, skifft [sic]. **1862** *Reese CW Letters* (Oct 29) I want you to Rite to mee onst ar twist A week. **1862** *Watters-Curtis CW Letters* (April 12) [I] hope that wee will have the pleashure of getting home to our wifes and litle Babes wonest more. **1891** Brown *Dialect in TN* 172 In *oncet, twicet, acrost, dost,* and *clost*, we have a final t added. **1913** Kephart *Our Sthn High* 120 I've traveled about the country, been to Asheville wunst, and to Waynesville a heap o' times. **1925** Dargan *Highland Annals* 81 They come down from the bear-ground on Smoky oncet in a while. **1939** Walker *Mtneer Looks* 4 [A] final t is sometimes added to words ending in the sound of s—of *twicet, oncet*. **1942** Hall *Phonetics Smoky Mts* 92 Many speakers pronounce the following words with excrescent final t . . . *once, twice*. **1957** GSMNP-23:2:1 He [= Francis Asbury] rode a horseback all the time, and he figured it up one time to see how many times, how much he'd rode. So he figured up I think around the world onst and a half. **1961** Kurath and McDavid *Pron Engl Atl Sts* 179 An added /t/ occurs in *once* and *twice* throughout the Midland and the South . . . Though most common in folk speech, it is widely used by middle-class speakers, especially in the South Midland. **1973** GSMNP-57:57 I try now to read the Bible through oncet a year. **1978** Montgomery *White Pine Coll* III-2 I write for the Jefferson County [newspaper] oncct a week. **1989** *Matewan OHP*-9 We have association every year . . . We have that oncet a year. **1998** *Dante OHP*-51 Oncet the play-offs was between St. Paul and Dante. Neither would agree to play on the other's field for the play-offs.

[*once* + excrescent t; DARE *once* adv A chiefly South, South Midland]

once and occasionally (also *once in occasion*) *adverb phrase* Once in a while, now and then.

c1960 Wilson *Coll*: *once and occasionally* = now and then, at times. **1997** Montgomery *Coll*: *once and occasionally* (known to Adams, Brown, Bush, Cardwell); *once in occasion* (known to Brown, Bush, Cardwell).

[DARE *once and occasionally* adv phr South, South Midland]

once in occasion See **once and occasionally.**

oncertain See **on- 1.**

oncet See **once.**

oncivil, oncivilized See **on- 1.**

oncst, onct See **once.**

ondecent See **on- 2.**

onder *preposition* Under.

1862 *Spainhourd CW Letters* (Nov 10) we lie onder a bresh tent. **1867** Harris *Sut Lovingood* 131 I sot these yere laigs a-gwine onder three hunder' pound preshure ove pure skeer.

onderstand *verb* To understand.

1858 (in **1974** Harris *High Times* 98) "I don't onderstand," said Ollfat, "adzactly. Was hit Davy or the Doctor at Sall Epps's on the night of May 8th?" **1885** Murfree *Prophet* 52 He war n't drunk *then*, ye onderstan'. **1924** Raine *Saddlebags* 83 Everybody on the creek was thar, that is, the young folks, ye onderstand. **1942** Hall *Phonetics Smoky Mts* 58.

on down in *phrasal preposition* (see Grammar and Syntax §14.5).

1969 GSMNP-25:1:15 It was just down where that road comes around there I noticed, on down in below where that road comes around. **1973** *Foxfire Interviews* A-73-46 [We'd] pile [the wood] in the house on down in the floor.

one *pronoun*

1 Reduced to *-un/'un* or *-n/'n* and attached to an adjective or pronoun. See also **another'un**, **other'un**, **us'uns**, **we'uns**, **young one**, **you'uns**. For further discussion, see Grammar and Syntax §2.8.

1904–20 Kephart *Notebooks* 2:483 The gooder'ns's all gone now! **1939** Hall *Notebooks* 9:25 (Little Cataloochee NC) [The community] finally got so that the old'uns and bad'uns died out. **1953** Hall *Coll* (Bryson City NC) It [= a bear] was one of about the biggest'uns I ever saw in my life, and he packed it in with its feet hanging up over his shoulder and its head hanging down at his shoe heels. [That's] as long as he was, from his shoulders to his feet. **1967** Hall *Coll* (Townsend TN) This here'un is made out of metal. **1973** *AOHP/ALC*-259 I knowed a few pretty tough'uns [= local ruffians]. *Ibid.* 77:10 I always enjoy comin' back to our old home place, where I was borned and raised, and I guess lot of other'uns same way. **1975** Jackson *Unusual Words* 150 An object may be a *lillun*, a *bad'n*, a *big'n*, or a *new'n*; or an individual may remark, "I ain't seen nair'n," or "I ain't got air'n." **1976** GSMNP-113:7 I raised six boys just hand runnin', then two girls, then the last'un was a boy, you know . . . I don't know what this'un done. **1981** GSMNP-122:51 Now let's see if I've left ary'un out. **1989** *Matewan OHP*-9 They was twenty-four [children born by his two wives]. There was twelve of the first'uns, and twelve of the last'uns. **2005** Williams *Gratitude* 134 It had t' be a good sized'un fer us all to git around it. **2012** Jourdan *Medicine Men* 30 Did them green pills hep ye? No? Then try some of these red'ns.

[cf SND *yin* "one" pron/adj 3]

2 One or the other, either one (following two words, phrases, or clauses conjoined by *or*). See also **neither B**. See also Grammar and Syntax §18.1.

1861 *Martin CW Letters* (Oct 31) I dont thank that thear will be Mtch mrry untill times changes far the beter orr wors one. **1863** *Warrick CW Letters* (June 10) I am going to Rite the old man tod to pay you that money or wheat one. **1863** *Warrick CW Letters* (Dec 10) thay came to the tope of the hill and they drove us from our batry and takend several of our Company or kild them one. **1895** Edson and Fairchild *TN Mts* 373 I will see you or send word, *one*. **1917** Kephart *Word-List* 415 = short for *one or the other*. "He either went to Medlin or to Bradshaw's, *one*." **1919** Combs *Word-List South* 33 He give it to Cece er Mos, one, ever who I was with. **1926** Hunnicutt *Twenty Years* 54 I told the boys in the morning we would have a coon race or a bear race one. **1937** Hall *Coll* (Bradley Fork NC) [Boneset is] bitterer than quinine, and hit'll kill ye or cure ye, one. *Ibid.* (Emerts Cove TN) He was in Tennessee or Kentucky, one. **1939** Hall *Coll* (Copeland Creek TN) She says, "I'm going home [and] see Emerts Cove or hell one before daylight." Now, that's what she said. **1956** Hall *Coll* (Gatlinburg TN) They had [revival] meeting morning and evening or morning and night one all the time. **1959** Hall *Coll* (Roaring Fork TN) They were a-sangin' or cattle huntin' one. **1962** Dykeman *Tall Woman* 55 I'll bring back the doctor or his instruments, one. **1970** *Foxfire Interviews* A-70-5 You had to work or starve one. . . . *Ibid.* I planted five rows, I reckon, or six rows, one. **1973** GSMNP-1:22 The first settlers come in here in the eighteen thirties or the forties one. **1973** GSMNP-48:8 I was taught to respect elderly people, and we were to refer to them as aunt or uncle one, if they were old. **1973** Miller *Pigeon's Roost* (Aug 2) If they don't live directly on their land and they have to be contacted by a letter, in most cases you just don't get their correct address or they ignore your desires one, as he said very few, if any, are ever heard from. **1976** *Hartley III* 7 His mind must have went off, or his woman one. **1983** *Dark Corner OHP*-10A They claimed that [the fire] would kill the snakes out, but it didn't. It just drove them down to the low part of the country, so the snake's going to either go down in the ground or go in front of the fire, one. **1989** *Matewan OHP*-88 When they voted [to establish a labor union], why the company had to recognize it or sell out one. *Ibid.* 102 We heard about them a-hanging these men down here. Just not very far from Matewan is where they hung some of the Hatfields or the McCoys one. **1994** Montgomery *Coll* I was anemic or low blood sugar one (Ogle). **2009** Burton *Beech Mt Man* 119 You got to survive or die, one.

[DARE *one* pron B chiefly South, South Midland]

oneasey, **oneasy** See **on- 1**.

one-eyed cat See **cat 1**.

one holer *noun* An outhouse with one seat. See also **two holer**, **three holer**.

1994 Montgomery *Coll* (known to Cardwell, Jones, Shields).

one more *adjective phrase* Of an event or thing: extraordinary, exceptional, quite a (as in phrases *one more time*, *one more sight*).

1913 Kephart *Our Sthn High* 286 "We had one more time" means a rousing good time. **1939** Hall *Coll* We had one more time in this world a-bear huntin'. *Ibid.* (Hazel Creek NC) We had one more time with that devilish infernal thing . . . God, we had one more time with this fool bear, driving and everything. **1940** Hall *Coll* "Ain't that one more sight!" = Isn't that a remarkable sight? **1951** Barnwell *Our Mt Speech* For something or someone unusual a mountaineer will say, "He's one more man; that's one more tree." **1967** Hall *Coll* (Townsend TN) [Said of a humorous or comic character]: John [McCaulley], he was one more sight, he was. **1974** Roberts *Sang Branch* 281 We sat down and had us one more feast. **1986** Wear *Sugarlands* 68 December 15th Jeannette was born. I had worked so hard my muscles would not give, so I had one more time having her. **2007** Shelby *Molly Whuppie* 11 That's one more thing about a giant. They cannot stand to be laughed at. **2018** Blind

Pig (Jan 26) The folks around here look puzzled when I tell them my grandson is one more ball player.

[DARE *one more* adj phr southern Appalachians]

one more sight, **one more time** See **one more**.

onesey See **on- 1**.

one thing another See **another B**.

ongodless *adjective* Godless, ungodly.

1957 Wise *Mt Speech* 306 This [on-] prefix may be accompanied by the suffix -less, producing the effect of a double negative, as in *ongodless*.

ongrateful, **onhandy** See **on- 1**.

onhuman See **on- 2**.

on in down *phrasal preposition* (see Grammar and Syntax §14.5).

1953 Hall *Coll* (Bryson City NC) They had dogs [that] had took after a bear and run him on in down there and treed him up a big hemlock tree.

onion *noun* Variant forms *aingern*, *angern*, *aynion*, *engern*, *inern*, *ingern*, *ingun*, *inyun*, *unern*, *ungyern*.

1867 Harris *Sut Lovingood* 38 The fust think he did thar, wer to proffer tu tend the Capitol grouns in inyuns, an' beans, on the shears. **1892** Smith *Farm and Fireside* 10 How they got to using such twisted language as you'uns and we'uns and inguns and mout and gwine and all sich is not known, nor was such talk universal. **1929** (in **1952** Mathes *Tall Tales* 127) As Old Doc Wheeler, the unlettered Aesculapius of Chinquapin, declared, "The sassafras, wild ingerns, an' Tadlocks had plumb took Bumpass county." **1938** Bowman *High Horizons* 46 These antique words, such as "engern" for onion . . . though plentiful, do not form the whole fabric of the mountaineer's daily speech as some people seem to think. **1940** Bowman *KY Mt Stories* 248 *inerns*, *unerns* = onions. **1972** Cooper *NC Mt Folklore* 89 *aingern*. **1978** Hiser *Quare Do's* 135 The good catfish fried up right crisp to eat with brown slabs of cornbread and angerns. **2007** McMillon *Notes*: *ungyern*. **2008** Salsi *Ray Hicks* 13 He was askin' for onions. I tells him we don't have nairy a one. He was a damn fool, he should have asked for aynions and we'd a had to give him some.

[DARE *onion* n chiefly South, South Midland]

onion set *noun* A miniature green onion. See also **set C2**.

1986 Pederson et al. *LAGS* = attested by 5/60 interviewees (8.3%) from E TN; 5/18 of all LAGS interviewees (27%) attesting term were from E TN. **2009** Benfield *Mt Born* 40 When onions were put out in the spring, they were always referred to as "onion sets."

onion skin *noun* See citation.

1990 Cavender *Folk Medical Lex* 28 = amniotic sac.

onjestice, **onjustice** See **on- 2**.

onkiver See **on- 1**.

onless See **unless A**.

onliest *adjective* Only, single, solitary.

1892 Dromgoole *War of Roses* 488 "I'd ruther be the onliest one ter wear her hones' colors," she declared, "ez ter be the onliest one not brave enough ter stand by her principles." **1922** Cobb *KY Mt Rhymes* 41 There lies my onliest babe I bore. **1931** Goodrich *Mt Homespun* 63 She's the onliest one I ever did know that could do such as that. **1961** *Coe Ridge OHP-343A* He's the onliest child they've got living in this community. **1971** *AOHP/ALC-107* The carnival would come along, and that's the onliest recreation we had. **1974** Fink *Bits Mt Speech* 18 Hit's the *onliest* knife I've got. **1994** Montgomery *Coll* She treated it as if it was the onliest one she had (Cardwell).

[DARE *onliest* adj chiefly South, South Midland]

onlucky See **on- 1**.

only

A *adverb* Variant forms *ondly*, *onley* [see **1862** in **B**], *on'y*.

1824 (in **1998** Bueker *Head Letters* 14) Sense he has been in this Country ondly last fall he had a spel of the aguand but at this time is as fresh Couler and as harty as he ever was. **1936** Skidmore *Lift Up Eyes* 8 "I'm dressen her," the older sister explained, "on'y she keeps layen back down."

B *preposition* Except (usually in negative contexts).

1783 (in **1941** Rothert *McDowell Letters* 173) (Sept 25) I have nothing to write only to tell you we are well. **1862** *Epperly CW Letters* (Aug 9) Stuart wont reseive any mor Substituts onley in one way. **1863** *Warrick CW Letters* (Jan 13) Dear wife I lost all my close only what I had on. **1863** *Walker CW Letters* (April 17) I have nothen of in portints to rit onely we have mooved about 8 miles below Nashville. **1910** Cooke *Power and Glory* 40 She never spoke a word like it, only to say now and ag'in, as we all do, that it was hard. **1936** (in **2009** Powell *Shenandoah Letters* 72) The doctor Said He was Not coming no whar only whar He could get in His car. **1973** *AOHP/ASU-111* We didn't know anything else only when we went visiting. **1973** *GSMNP-88* I never knowed it called anything, only the Caleb Branch after he went up there. **1978** Reese *Speech NE Tenn* 203 My mother never did call us only by the ring of the bell. **1989** *Matewan OHP-102* They never did pay only every two weeks. **1997** *Dante OHP-14* They wasn't ary high school, only at Council. That one was miles away, over in Buchanan County.

[DARE *only* prep scattered, but especially South, South Midland]

C *conjunction*

1 Except that.

1984 High *Titan Rock* 33 We didn't have much to entertain us, only we were a joy to one another. **1989** *Matewan OHP-1* [We] did not see any of the actual stuff, only I saw the men running down this alley here.

2 Unless.

1797 *Globe Creek Church Minutes* 2 (Caldwell Co NC) We believe that no ministers have a right to the administration of the ordinances only [they] are regularly called and come under the imposition of hands by the prisbatary. **1975** *AOHP/LJC-384* We didn't have any mail, only we'd go about three miles from here.

onmannerly, onnaterel See **on- 1.**

on one's lone See **lone.**

onpatient, onpossible See **on- 3.**

onriddle *verb* To figure out, solve.

1895 Dromgoole *Fiddling to Fame* 49 She onriddled me at onc't. **1948** Chase *Grandfather Tales* 172 "Onriddle this, boys," said Old Rob, "and if you know it already don't tell."

onsartin, onseat, onsertain, onsettle See **on- 1.**

on shares (also *on the halvers, on the halves, on the shares*) *adverb phrase* In an arrangement similar to sharecropping whereby a farmer, weaver, or other producer of work or material contributes a share of the harvest or final product (usually half) with an owner or other contributors. See 1995 citations. See also **go halvers.**

1859 Taliaferro *Fisher's River* 204 Josh tanned a "kipskin" for Davis "on shares," and there was a difficulty in their settlement in some way. **1863** *Martin CW Letters* (Oct 27) [I] have bin thinking about letting some boddy sow wheat on the shears. **1915** Dingus *Word-List VA* 190 = applied to tenure of land by payment of a fixed share of profits. Sometimes *on the halves.* **1931** Goodrich *Mt Homespun* 4 A skillful weaver of coverlets took the wool as it came from the backs of sheep belonging to a well-to-do neighbor and worked it up "on shares," thus getting her own supply of linsey or blanket or coverlet, without exchange of money. **1957** Parris *My Mts* 3 Cider and molasses were made on the shares. **1995** Montgomery *Coll*: *on shares* = an arrangement worked out between a landowner and a man who worked the owner's land, for a portion of the harvest, usually one-fourth to one-half, going to the owner (Adams), = corn grown on the shares meant an agreed percentage amount (Cardwell), = refers to people sharing the work and the profits or result of the work. Cider- and molasses-making were often two- or three-family jobs in which everyone contributed apples and sugar cane and then shared the cider or molasses (Oliver). **1995** Trout *Historic Buildings* 39 Completely self-contained, these little "peckerwood" mills operated on a scale small enough to make it financially feasible for the owner/operator to saw the pattern (all the sizes and quantities) for one building at a time. Sometimes the job was done on shares. **2005** Williams *Gratitude* 12 Paw Taylor and him had made some apple cider brandy on the halvers.

onsincere See **on- 2.**

onst See **once.**

onsuspected See **on- 1.**

ontel, ontell See **until.**

ontelling See **untelling.**

on the carpet See **carpet B.**

on the dodge See **dodge B.**

on the halvers/halves See **on shares.**

on the lift See **lift, on the.**

on the mend See **mend B.**

on the mountain See **mountain C.**

on the shares See **on shares.**

on the waters of *prepositional phrase* Beside (a river or stream).

1939 Hall *Coll* (Mt Sterling NC) Back in nineteen hunderd and six I was on the waters of Big Creek, and I heared an awful explosion of dynamite. *Ibid.* (Smokemont NC) We . . . moved into this county, and that was here on the waters of Lufty River.

on the wrong side of the blanket *adverb phrase* See citation.

c1954 Adams *Word-List* = of [an] illegitimate child.

onthoughtedly See **unthoughtedly.**

ontie See **on- 1.**

ontil See **until.**

onwell See **on- 1.**

on'y See **only A.**

on yesterday See **on B4.**

oodlins *noun* A large quantity, occasionally a surfeit of objects not wanted.

1886 Smith *Sthn Dialect* 350 There are still others [= vocabulary] which have not, so far as I know, the authority of Old English: . . . oodlins or oodles (large quantity). **1895** *Word-Lists* 392 = abundance, a large quantity; "dead oodlins" = a very great quantity (Winchester, Ky.). **1900** Harben *N GA Sketches* 188 The kitchen was liter'ly filled with all manner o' stuff, beer, bad-smellin' cheese, and oodlin's an' oodlin's o' milk in bottles. **c1960** Wilson *Coll* = plenty, lots, many. **1967** *DARE Survey* (Gatlinburg TN, Maryville TN) *oodlins and oodlins* = as much as you need and more. **1999** Montgomery *File* Daddy left oodlins of books (40-year-old woman, Del Rio TN). **2007** Alexander *Moonshiners Gone* 75 A great part of his long and satisfying law enforcement career has involved finding and destroying "oodlings" of illegal moonshine operations.

[variant of *oodles*; DARE *oodlins* n pl South Midland, especially KY, TN]

ooze *noun* A salve or syrupy preparation rendered from bark or other plant substance for topical medicinal use or for dyeing. See also **blackgum ooze**.

1912 De Long *Troublesome* They can weave many different kinds of baskets out of our native willow, sometimes of twigs with the brown bark left on, sometimes of the peeled twigs, left white, or dyed gray in onion-skin "ooze." **1937** Hyatt *Kiverlid* 45 The best thing fer a snake bite is strong ooze biled from rattlesnake master. **1939** Hall *Coll* (Big Creek NC) We'd get copperas and dye it. Any kind of color we wanted, why that's the kind of color we'd get. Dye it, boil it up, make a ooze out of it, and color our thread. Then we'd weave it. **1956** Hall *Coll* (Big Bend NC) One time [Aunt Nancy] had bone arsiplas. Old man Joe Packett started to get some red oak bark to make some ooze to draw her arm. **1957** Broaddus *Vocab Estill Co KY* 54 = the syrup made by boiling down medicinal herbs. **1959** Roberts *Up Cutshin* 95 Now if one had the misfortune of catching something like the eetch, she would take this old pokeroot and make a ooze out of it and boil it and wash you with it and kill that eetch dead as a nit. **1966** Frome *Strangers* 241 She knew how to make "ooze" out of barks, roots, and weeds and could explain every step in the making of "county pins" (counterpanes, in the outside world). **1973** GSMNP-76:23 We'd dig the roots of a big bunch of [mayapple]. They'd beat it up and cook it down to a strong ooze. Well then, they'd put some sugar in it. After we got it down thick, like you boil molasses down till they get thick, you know, that's the way we do this. **1981** High *Coll* (DARE) = medicine made from red oak bark which has been chipped and boiled, and is used in the Gorge to cure sores, cuts, and snake bite.

open (also *open up*) *verb, verb phrase* Of a hound: to bark on discovering a scent or sensing quarry.

1843 (in **1974** Harris *High Times* 16) Thunderbolt opened with a confident and delightful strain, and broke off at a rapid pace, with Locksley at his heels playing second fiddle. **1878** Coale *Wilburn Waters* 84 I untethered my canine companions and started them out upon their mission. They had trailed off but a short distance, when they "opened" in lively and eager chorus, soon jumped a large four-pronged buck, in full view from where I was standing, which, from the direction he took, I was satisfied would attempt to cross the river at the stand occupied. **1939** Hall *Coll* (Deep Creek NC) We had some old trained bear hounds that turned off in the roughs, the laurel on the Bear Creek side, and picked up a cold trail and started out up to the Bear Creek a-trailing, opening along. **1953** Hall *Coll* (Bryson City NC) I heard one [dog] open and I turned the rest loose, and they took after Bob where he had drug this bear. **1957** Woodbridge *Hunting Terms* 156 *open* = used of hunting dogs that bark on the trail; *open up* = to bark. **1970** *Hunting Stories* 28 When dogs "open on a track," they find the scent they're looking for and charge ahead. **2007** Alexander *Moonshiners Gone* 203 [The revenuer] would invariably wander off in some completely different direction ... distant fox hunters were heard blowing their horns and dogs were "opening up" on fox somewhere.

open barn *noun* A barn open on its sides to provide shelter.

1986 Pederson et al. *LAGS* (Sullivan Co TN).

open-hearted *adjective* Generous. See also **free-hearted**.

1939 Hall *Coll* (Little Cataloochee NC) [The inhabitants of the notorious Big Bend] are open-hearted folks.

opening *noun* See citation.

1990 Clouse *Wilder* 64 If a man was lucky enough to work a vein that was high enough, he could walk without stooping all the way to his "opening," the space he had dug out for himself and claimed as his own.

open peach (also *open-rock peach, open-seed peach, open-stone peach*) *noun* A peach whose pulp comes easily off the seed. Also called **freeseed peach**. See also **cling peach**.

1949 Kurath *Word Geog East US* 72 *Open peach* is also found in a coastal belt extending from the lower James to the Peedee, as well as on the Yadkin in North Carolina. Curiously enough *open-stone peach* and *open-seed peach* turn up again in Western North Carolina. **1966** Dakin *Vocab Ohio River Valley* 360–62 In the eastern Knobs, the Mountains, the southern Pennyroyal and the Purchase several other names are common. *Open-stone peach* (occasionally *open-seed peach* and once *open-rock peach*) is common in the eastern Knobs and northern Mountains and predominates south of the upper Kentucky. Leslie, Letcher, and Harlan Counties have only this term. *Open-stone peach* is not used west of the Mountain Margin. The common use of this name throughout southeastern Kentucky—where it certainly came from western North Carolina—suggests that it is old in all of the southern Uplands and that at an earlier period must have been distributed quite commonly throughout the Great Valley from the Maryland Piedmont to North Carolina. **1968** *DARE Survey* (Brasstown NC) *open-stone peach* = a type of peach in which the center is loose. **1986** Pederson et al. *LAGS*: *open-stone peach* = attested by 18/60 interviewees (15%) from E TN; 18/29 of all LAGS interviewees (62%) attesting term were from E TN. **1997** Montgomery *Coll*: *open peach* (known to Brown, Bush, Cardwell, Weaver); *open-stone peach* (known to Andrews, Hooper).

[DARE *open peach* n chiefly southern Appalachians, Mid Atlantic]

open range *noun* The practice of letting livestock graze freely in the summer months, especially in remoter areas or higher elevations, where fences are not needed. See also **fence law**, **no-fence law**, **open stock law**, **stock law**.

1939 Hall *Coll* (Cataloochee NC) We raised cattle, sheep, and hogs. We had open range when we first married, until the No Fence Law, when we had to put everything up [in fences]. [Editor's note: The term "No Fence Law" would seem to be a misnomer. Actually it was a boon to big cattle raisers, who were no longer required to fence in their stock; instead the small farmers and cattle raisers now had to fence their property.] **1976** Padgett *Clay Co NC* 11 Every house-hold had a milk cow, fattened hogs for their meat supply, and maintained a flock of hens for their eggs and meat. Until about 1920, most of the county had "open range" for their cattle. By that is meant, farmers had to build fences around the fields on which they expected to raise cultivated crops and they turned their cattle, hogs and sheep loose on whatever other land was available, whether it was their land or some-one else's. Many large farmers and cattlemen would drive great herds of cattle, hogs and sheep to the mountains for the summer months, where they would grow and stay fat on wild vegetation.

open-rock peach, open-seed peach See **open peach.**

open stock law *noun* Same as **no-fence law**. See also **fence law, open range, stock law.**

1991 Thomas *Sthn Appal* 41 Throughout the nineteenth century, and into the twentieth, there existed the "open stock law." People allowed their livestock to run out in the woods, an' they had to build an' maintain fences around their own crops.

open-stone peach See **open peach.**

open the church door *verb phrase* Usually at the end of a worship service: to invite anyone to make a public declaration of repentance and express the desire to join the church.

1982 Slone *How We Talked* 74 = to ask "Is there anyone who feels that God has passed by and pardoned their sins and they want to join the church, do so." They usually say this just as they are winding up church, as they sing the last song.

open up See **open.**

or . . . anyway *phrase* Or . . . at least, or . . . in any case.

1942 Justus *Step Along* 16 Reckon I've broken a bone, or sprained [my ankle] anyway. **1950** Justus *Luck for Lihu* 47 Now I know he's well again—or nighabout, anyway. **1964** Roberts *Hell-Fer-Sartin* 98 Dirty Jack he just down and skinned his bull and—you know, cow hides is mighty good and bring a good price, or did then anyway.

orange doper *noun* See citation. See also **dope 2.**

1981 Dumas *Appal Glossary* 17 I want a *brown doper* (Coca-Cola). An *orange doper* is an orange drink.

orchard *noun* A grove of trees, not necessarily fruit-bearing ones. See also **chestnut orchard, maple orchard, sugar orchard.**

1842 Crosby *Journal/Account Book* 101 Sowd 3 Bushels of the Common Oats and 3 1/2 of the Ruffle Oats on the hill in the Pine Orchard in the third week in March. **1939** Jennison *Flora Great Smokies* 287 The "cherry orchard" in the valley of Ramsey Prong contains many exceptionally large specimens [of cucumber trees], some having trunks three to four feet in diameter. **1943** Peattie *Men Mt Trees* 163 At high altitudes certain of these trees—the beech, yellow birch, and buckeye, northern red oak, scarlet and white oaks, and the dotted haw—become curiously dwarfed in stature, with thick stems when old, and the wide crowns that trees may develop when they are spaced far apart. They resemble old apple trees in outline, and for this reason the mountain people call them "orchards." In general there are no shrubs or understory trees in these sub-alpine orchards; the flowery herbs and ferns, growing shoulder-high, fill up the "orchards" the way timothies and daisies do in a real orchard. **1963** Lord *Blue Ridge* 39D The forest cover is an "orchard" of northern red oak extending up the sides of Steestatchee Bald on the near right.

orchard grass *noun* A common grass (*Dactylis glomerata*).

1987 Carver *Regional Dialects* 167 *Orchard grass*, on the other hand, is more widely known, especially in the North, though the greatest concentration of informants are in Kentucky, eastern Tennessee, and in the western portions of North Carolina and Virginia.

[DARE *orchard grass* n chiefly North, Midland, especially South Midland]

or either See **either B.**

orphant *noun* Variant form of *orphan*.

1866 *Hall CW Letters* (July 29) they often Name ther Pappy John poor little Orphants they dont Recolect him. **1915** Dingus *Word-List VA* 186. **1942** Hall *Phonetics Smoky Mts* 92 Many speakers pronounce the following words with excrescent final *t*: . . . *orphan, vermin*. **1973** Jones *Cades Cove TN* 114. **1979** Carpenter *Walton War* 159 Sometimes I think I'd of been better off if I'd been born a orphant.

[*orphan* + excrescent *t*]

orsh tater See **Irish potato.**

ort, orta, ortent See **ought.**

orter[1] See **ought.**

orter[2] *noun* An otter.

1971 Linzey and Linzey *Mammals of Smoky* 67 Otters, or "orters" as they were known to the mountain hunters, have been recorded at Sugarlands, Big Creek, Greenbrier, Bryson Place, Cataloochee, Gregory Bald, and Mt. Sterling.

oswego tea *noun* A small wildflower (*Monarda didyma*) with medicinal uses, more often known as **beebalm.**

1939 Jennison *Flora Great Smokies* 273 One will find little coves filled to overflowing with the Mountain Golden Glow, sometimes in company with the big red-headed Beebalm, also known as Oswego Tea.

othern, otherne See **other'un.**

other'un (also *othern, otherne*) *pronoun* Other one. See also **an-other'un, one 1, tothern.**

1862 *Hamblen CW Letters* 63 James is a going to gether the othern next week. **1863** *Walker CW Letters* (April 10) I Sent 2 pocket Knives one for Joseph and the otherne for Leonides. **1960** Mason *Memoir* 80 There dammit, knock the othern out and I'll be blundern aroun here blind as hell. **1971** *AOHP/ALC-32* They called one side Republicans and the other'un Democrats. **1981** GSMNP-122: 55 Gin we'd get there the other'un [= a bell] would ring. **1983** McDermitt *Boy Named Jack* 17 Here they come just a pourin through worser than the otherns. **1989** *Matewan OHP-9* They notched this end [of the log] to fit down over this other'un. **1998** *Dante OHP-12* I used to be on two stations there in Bristol, WFHG, and I forget the other'un.

[contraction of *other* + *one*]

ought (also *ought to*) *auxiliary verb* See also **have C2**.

A Variant forms *ort, orta, orter*; variant negative forms *ortent, ortn't*.

1862 *Sexton CW Letters* (July 14) we ort to pray to god for the meny Blesing he has Be stod upon us. **1864** *Chapman CW Letters* (March 13) you ort to do your fighting in tennessee and the border states. **1913** Kephart *Our Sthn High* 85 You hadn't orter a-told. **1937** Hall *Coll* (Cades Cove TN) You'd orter see them. Law! **1940** Oakley *Roamin'/Restin'* 97 I started out the door an as I looked back she sorta smiled and said I guess you ort to give me a lock of yore hare fore ya leave me up here in these wild mts. **1952** Giles *40 Acres* 163 He ortent to ever do a day's work in the sun. **1953** Atwood *Verbs East US* 33 [In *oughtn't*] in the South Midland and throughout N.C. phonetic, and probably phonemic, /r/ generally appears in this form. **1957** Hall *Coll* (Del Rio TN) He talked when he ort to have been listening. **1972** *AOHP/ALC-342* The way I feel about that, by jeminy, the government ortn't have to step in. **1973** GSMNP-88 They orta come in and try to make friends. **2008** *Rosie Hicks* 6 You ort to know I did.

[DARE *ought* v chiefly South, South Midland]

B Syntax.

1 In combination with another auxiliary verb. See **had ought to, may B2**.

2 Negative form *ought not*, without the infinitive marker.

1991 Thomas *Sthn Appal* 106 You'd be goin' along there, with an experienced fireman, an' he'll put coal in when he ought not put it in.

[DARE *ought* v C2a widespread, but more frequent South, South Midland]

ourn (also *our'n*) *pronoun* Ours. For similar forms, see Grammar and Syntax §2.2. See also **ournses**.

1861 *Huntley CW Letters* (Dec 29) Thare is about four Regiments hear Within half a mile of each other and they are all Building their houses for Winter quarters But ourn. **1864** Wilson *Confederate Private* 59 (July 14) the wheate is not much a count here ourn is lite and sow is paps. **1873** Smith *Arp Peace Papers* 143 We will help you plant agin the seed whose leeves, flowers, and froots shall be yourn and ourn to enjoy. **1910** Cooke *Power and Glory* 114 It's for their profit, not for our'n. **1946** Cleaves *King's English* 35 "Ourn," "hern," "hisn," and "yourn" represent an attempt at uniformity. Since the forms "my" and "mine" developed from a common Teutonic source, a similar inflection was created to distinguish between the adjectival and substantive uses for the remaining personal pronouns. **1958** Morgan *Gift from Hills* 17 I done contracted with Steve Sparks fer another little ol' steer calf, en I aim to break our'n in. **1969** GSMNP-37:2:6 I forget just what we paid, got a pound for it, generally sold ourn to a man on Coopers Creek. **1974** Fink *Bits Mt Speech* 18 Them's ourn. **1983** *Dark Corner OHP-4A* Me and my brother Marshall kept ourn [= cows] till they got grown. **1991** Thomas *Sthn Appal* 73 We jist went to th' pit, putt 'um together, an' our'n whipped what's in there.

[historically *our* + *n* by analogy with *my/mine*; now sometimes construed ahistorically as from *our* + *one*, OED3 *ourn* pron c1382→; EDD *ourn* pron 1 mEngl, sEngl; DARE *ourn* pron chiefly South, South Midland, New England]

ournses *pronoun* Our. See also **ourn**.

1904–20 Kephart *Notebooks* 26:63 Pap made liquor jist up the branch back o' ournses house. **1929** Kephart *Smoky Mt Magic* 19 "Lots o' room in our'nses' yard," the boy assured him. **1994** Montgomery *Coll* (known to Shields).

our own self See **own B**.

ourself(s) *pronoun* Ourselves. For similar forms, see Grammar and Syntax §2.3.2.

1861 *Martin CW Letters* (Oct 6) we are still in the moultre hous and enjoying our selfs as good as ever. **1863** *Tesh CW Letters* (Sept 2) now if you was here we would by 1 and then we would help our selfs right. **1922** *TN CW Ques* 1950 (Sullivan Co) General told us that pease was made and for us to take care of our self. **1939** Hall *Coll* (Deep Creek NC) We went by ourselfs to the head of Forneys Creek and fished. **1954** GSMNP-19:16 He fell through, but [of] course we kept that all to ourself. **1973** GSMNP-74:37 We built another little barn ourself. **1989** *Matewan OHP-1* We wasn't allowed to go in the barber shop by ourself. *Ibid.* 23 We had to do that ourself. **1998** *Dante OHP-71* We went in groups. We didn't get off by ourselfs.

[OED3 *ourself* pron 4, a1325→]

out

A *preposition*

1 Used in phrasal prepositions. See **out back down, out down, out up**, and Grammar and Syntax §14.5.

2 Out of, out on, out to.

1939 Hall *Coll* (Nine Mile TN) We went a-fishing, was going to go fishing, and went out the mountain. *Ibid.* (Cades Cove TN) They come on in down there then and skinned [the bear] out and packed him out the cabin that night. **1941** Stuart *Men of Mts* 260 I heard Sol getting out the bed. **1984** Burns *Cold Sassy* 288 Thet washout th'owed my car clean out control.

B *verb* To cheat, vex; to reject.

1884 Murfree *In TN Mts* 67 He was powerful outed when he had ter kom back, arter ten months, from them works. **1937** Campbell *KY Mt Community* 540 Grandpap wouldn't be outed. He fixed and cut that air winder hisself. **1940** Oakley *Roamin'/Restin'* 37 Well

I desided I couldent be outed so I went and asked another girl if I could walk home with her. **1994** McCarthy *Jack Two Worlds* 23 "Just quit," [she] said, "you've done outed me."

C *noun* An attempt, effort, or outcome (especially in phrase *poor out*).

1863 *Matthews CW Letters* (April 27) he is sorow he went an left me i dont no what of a out i will make. **1904** Harben *Georgians* 176 Warren got down on his knees then and actually tried to pray; but he made a pore out. **1915** Dingus *Word-List VA* 187 *poor out* = a weak effort without success; *purty out* = blunder, matter of embarrassment or annoyance. **1923** Greer-Petrie *Angeline Steppin' Out* 14 It's a pore out when a married couple can't find something bigger to quorl about than a pocket handkercher. **1950** Bray *Disappearing Dialect* 283 "He made a sorry out" (a poor performance). **1957** Combs *Lg Sthn High: Word List* 71 = attempt, effort, trial. Used derisively, when one has signally failed at something: "That's a bad out you made there." **c1960** Wilson *Coll*: *poor out* = a poor effort, one not good enough. **1977** Norman *Kinfolks* 3 "Wilgus Collier's my name. I don't have a middle name." The fat man shook his head and sucked his teeth. "Well," he said. "Either way, it's a poor out for a name." **1979** Carpenter *Walton War* 179 It would be a poor out if a body couldn't sheer (share) his plenty with a neighbor. **1995–97** Montgomery *Coll* (known to Adams, Bush, Cardwell, Cypher). **2008** Salsi *Ray Hicks* 163 I got to sayin' to everybody, if ya marry 'em for looks you've made a bad out.

[OED3 *out* n 5 chiefly U.S. colloquial; cf DARE *out* F1 chiefly South, South Midland]

D *adverb*

1 Used to extend and intensify the action of a verb. See also **starve out.** See Grammar and Syntax §14.4.

1862 *Martin CW Letters* (June 24) we get plent[y] to eat but it is jest flourer bread & beacon Day after Day evry Sunday we get beef & Molases So we are geting perfectly tired out on it. **1863** *Reese CW Letters* (April 2) men is starved out an Bred and meet so Bad that tha[y] will giv aney price for aney kind of Case [= *sass* "vegetables"]. **1939** Hall *Coll* Study it out while you are bringing in the water.

2 In the country, away from town.

1847 (in **1870** Drake *Pioneer Life KY* 66) We had no barn or mow, and both wheat & hay were stacked out. **1997** *Dante OHP*-14 Claude's uncle, Lihue Kiser, he lived out.

out back down *phrasal preposition* Followed by a preposition; see Grammar and Syntax §14.5.

1953 Hall *Coll* (Bryson City NC) [I] carried two dogs part of the way out back down to where I could get to the truck to them.

out building (also *outdoor house*) *noun* An outhouse. See also **johnny.**

1986 Pederson et al. *LAGS*: *outdoor house* (Cocke Co TN). **1988** Russell *It Happened* 37 Years ago there wasn't even a little outbuilding with a half-moon.

outby *adverb* See citation.

c1975 *Miners' Jargon* 5 = nearer to the shaft, and hence farther from the working face. Toward the mine entrance. The opposite of inby. **2002** Armstead *Black Days* 244 = toward the shaft, main line, or drift opening of a mine.

outdoingest *adjective* Most unusual or remarkable. See also **-est 1** and Grammar and Syntax §3.4.1.

1925 Dargan *Highland Annals* 190 By the end of the summer Serena would be as duckless as at its beginning, but she had had many a pleasant, shady jaunt in search of them "outdoin'est things." **1958** Campbell *Tales* 88 The outdoinest thing Nelt done for learning was when he brought on a grist mill. **1997** Montgomery *Coll* (known to Adams, Brown, Bush, Cardwell, Norris).

[DARE *outdoingest* adj especially South Midland]

outdone *adjective* Exasperated, vexed.

1863 (in **1983** *CW Harlan Co* 21) So outdone were [the reb]els that they are afraid [of the bor]ders of this county ever since. **1884** Murfree *In TN Mts* 260 Tony air mightily outdone 'kose the grand jury let him off. **1927** Montague *Hog's Eye* 193 While they was all standing around mighty outdone and trying to figger out what was to do next,—Pough! They heered a gun crack. **1942** Campbell *Cloud-Walking* 49 Marthy borned two babies . . . and Sary was so outdone it took her mind clean away from studying. **1973** Davis *'Pon My Honor* 37 Now Granny was outdone, and she got as white as an egg shell and as nervous as a rattlesnake. **1979** *Big South Fork OHP*-4 We was outdone to think he'd played off on us thataway. **1997** Montgomery *Coll* (known to eight consultants from the Smoky Mountains); I'm just plain outdone that I can't find that hammer (Norris).

[DARE *outdone* adj chiefly South, South Midland]

outdoor house See **out building.**

out down *phrasal preposition* (+ preposition). See Grammar and Syntax §14.5.

1939 Hall *Coll* (Nine Mile TN) We hit out down on what was called the Antony Ridge. We struck a big bear there. **1976** *Bear Hunting* 293 We start at [the bear's] heels and skin plumb on out down to his head. **1979** *Big South Fork OHP*-11 [I] come right across the Bald Rock Mountain, right up Slickford and right across Dry Hollow and across and out down by Tifton Grove. **1983** *Dark Corner OHP*-4A The wheat'd come out down under that thing in a troft. **1984** GSMNP-153:14 He got up on the porch and could see out down through there.

outen[1] *verb* See 1972 citation.

1972 Cooper *NC Mt Folklore* 94 = to extinguish, put out. "Would you mind if I outen the light?" **1996–97** Montgomery *Coll* (known to Brown, Bush, Cardwell, Oliver).

[OED3 *outen* v 1 U.S. dialect; perhaps influenced by Pennsylvania German]

outen[2]

A *preposition*

1 (also *outn, out'n*) Out of, out on.

1859 Taliaferro *Fisher's River* 72 True as preachin', the peach-tree was growin' out'n an old buck, right behind his shoulders. **1862** *Zimmerman CW Letters* (Aug 5) I want you to make me Some Shirts outen tha[t] Calico what I got at germington. **1873** Smith *Arp Peace Papers* 38 Sum went forward to rekonnoiter as skouts—first in the road and then outen the road. **1901** Harben *Westerfelt* 142 It's made a wuss devil 'n ever out'n 'im. **1913** Kephart *Our Sthn High* 80 You, Coaly, you'll git some o' that meanness shuck outen you if you tackle an old she-bear to-morrow! **1931** Combs *Lg Sthn High* 1304 Steve ups and runs like a bat shot outn hell. **1937** Thornburgh *Great Smoky Mts* 133 Thar was a cabin not fur away, and I thought a feller put his head outen the window and called to me. **1939** Hall *Coll* (Smokemont NC) He frailed the hell outen him. **1952** Wilson *Folk Speech NC* 572 My wife kin throw more out'n the window than I can bring in at the door. **1972** Cooper *NC Mt Folklore* 160 I would like to call a few doodle bugs outen their holes. **1974** Fink *Bits Mt Speech* 18 Put that dog outen the house. **1997** Andrews *Mountain Vittles* 26 We just ate 'em just hot right outen the oven.

[out + -en; cf *-en*[2] suffix; OED3 *outen* prep 1b Scot, English regional (north), and U.S. regional; EDD *outen* prep 3 Scot, nEngl; DARE *outen* prep[1] chiefly South, Midland]

2 See citation.

1895 Edson and Fairchild *TN Mts* 373 = without: "I can't go outen my sunbunnit."

B *adverb* Out.

1895 Edson and Fairchild *TN Mts* 373 = out. "I can't get the sliver outen."

outfavor *verb* To be better looking than (someone else).

1912 Perrow *Songs and Rhymes* 138–39 Many old words appear, such as outfavor (to be better looking than). **1944** Wilson *Word-List* 47 = to be better looking than someone else. Remark to a newborn infant: "You do outfavor your daddy, don't you?"

[DARE *outfavor* v especially South Midland]

outfit *noun* See citation.

1939 Bond *Appal Dialect* 110 = common name for a whiskey still.

outland *noun* Territory outside the immediate area. See also **outlander**, **outlandish A**.

1995 Parce *Twice-Told* 23 "Freighting" in the 1870's in Western North Carolina was the way manufactured goods were brought into the region from the "outland" and farm goods moved from the Blue Ridge Highlands to the lowlands of South Carolina.

outlander *noun* One who comes from outside the mountains, a stranger. See also **flatlander**, **Floridiot**, **foreigner B**, **half back**, **outlandish**, **outsider**.

1913 Kephart *Our Sthn High* 17 Foreigner, outlander, it is all one; we are "different," we are "quar," to the mountaineer. **1937** Eaton *Handicrafts* 232 Some "outlanders" had begun by building a foundation which, when the concrete forms were taken off, on measurement was found to be from a foot to a foot and a half in error. **1940** Simms *Coll* A mountain man wanted to know, Who and what give the outlanders the idee (idea) that we'uns (the mountain people) air a lot ov hell-goin' trouble-raisers? **1952** Justus *Children* 69 An outlander stood at the gate. An outlander man, she was certain-sure, by his manner of speaking. **1957** Parris *My Mts* 196 The day's hunt was over and Wid was rustling up some grub for a couple outlanders bent on putting him in a book. **1966** Caudill *My Appalachia* 20 Stella also taught me to say *please* and *thank you*, words that no one in our part of Appalachia ever used. Perhaps these gracious words were considered uppity and imitative of outlanders. *Ibid.* 36 That he was an outlander was evident from the store-bought clothes he wore, from the fine language he spoke, from the fancy manners to which he seemed to be born. **1975** Jackson *Unusual Words* 154 Those who are not so fortunate are known as *furriners*, *outlanders*, *outsiders*, or *lowlanders*; and it is difficult to overcome the stigma attached to such terms. **2006** *Encycl Appalachia* 229 While *furriner* is contemporarily used with humor, it has been replaced in a more serious vein by terms such as *outlander* and *outsider*.

outlandish

A *adjective*, *noun* Of a person: from outside the mountains, belonging to a foreign country; such a person. See also **flatlander**, **foreigner B**, **outlander**.

1913 Kephart *Our Sthn High* 17 Them's the outlandish. **1976** Garber *Mountain-ese* 65 = flatlander. "He's an outlandish fellow, he don't live in these here parts." **1994–97** Montgomery *Coll* (known to Brown, Cardwell, Shields).

[OED3 *outlandish* adj 1 now archaic]

B *adverb* Outrageously.

1975 *AOHP/ALC-1128* They sold pretty good stuff, but it's outlandish high, real high.

outlier *noun* A person hiding out in mountain forests, especially one evading conscription or deserting Civil War service in territory of divided allegiance such as the TN/NC border and the Cumberland Plateau of KY/TN. Such an individual often relied on sympathizers for food and supplies and became a **bushwhacker**, pillaging local citizens. See 1955, 1984 citations. See also **bee hunter**, **bushwhacker**, **scout C**, **tory**.

1953 Hall *Coll* (Bryson City NC) [During the latter part of the Civil War] outliers and deserters were stealing all of the food and supplies my parents had. **1955** Dykeman *French Broad* 113 Lonely trails became traps of theft and death, and nothing in the mountains was safe—corn in the crib, a gold piece in the cupboard, or breath in the lungs. A name was given to these bands: "the Outliers." They were the men both parties to the war should have hated most, had they not already pledged their emotions as well as their lives and possessions to hating each other, for this was the ancient, everlasting enemy—greed. **1956** Hall *Coll* (Hurricane Creek NC) Harmon Teaster, a deserter in the Civil War, an outlier, hid under a big old rock clift on that mountain. **1963** Medford *Mt People* 29 Toward the close of the war the Confederacy was sorely in need of troops; so often troops, generally the Home Guard, were sent into such sections to round up the "out-liers" and bring them in by force of arms. **1979** Carpenter *Walton War* 38 History buffs might recognize the terms "Outliers" and "Bushwhackers."

If not, they are still fairly descriptive of the Civil War deserters and draft dodgers who literally turned outlaw in order to avoid service, or after deserting, lived in hiding while killing and stealing as the means for a bare existence. **1983** Walker *Tales Civil War* 5 Besides the Unions and the Confederates (Yankees and Rebels, if you wish), there was another group which preyed on all. These were known as the bushwhackers, the outliers, or the scouts. No family was immune from their ravages. If the family was Confederate in sympathy, this group represented themselves as Union and vice versa. They swooped down and assaulted, destroyed, and confiscated as they saw fit. **1984** Dykeman and Stokely *At Home* 79 The war's severest hardships followed in the wake of the outliers, or the bushwhackers. These scavengers favored no cause. As the war dragged on, they ambushed and raided, stealing meat from the smokehouse, corn from the crib, and farm animals from barn and pasture. **1988** Trotter *Bushwhackers!* 222 [Captain John Peck] dressed, armed himself, and went outside to investigate. He discovered the outliers breaking into the salt warehouse. **1997** Davis *Cataloochee Valley* 67 Captain Albert Teague of the Home Guards and his Scouts had been active in raids on the Union sympathizers, especially in the Big Bend section (Haywood Co.) where it was mostly prounion in sentiment in at least ten or twelve families. Several of these were known as outliers (same as draft dodgers). They had been hiding out, and Teague was having trouble rounding them up. *Ibid.* 69 When these outliers hid out in the wilderness of Cataloochee, they lived in the woods, in caves, or hollow logs. Sometimes after dark they would slip into a barn loft and sleep under some hay, leaving early in the morning before the family caught them. They stole eggs and sometimes milked a cow before leaving. Sometimes they would beg from the settlers if they thought it was safe. If not they lived on wild game and berries and chestnuts. **2000** Morgan *Mts Remember* 23 When these outliers we got coming around here got started out, they didn't mean to be outlaws I would say, most of them. *Ibid.* It was the bushwhackers and outliers that give us no rest. They lived in the mountains in bands and raided the rich people in Flat Rock and decent people everywhere. They was just trash, deserters and outlaws, using the war as an excuse to rob.

outline *verb* Same as **line B**.

1971 *AOHP/ALC-4* [When I was young] sometimes they would outline [the hymns], and then sometimes they wouldn't.

outn, out'n See **outen**[2] **A1**.

out of bank(s) *adjective phrase* Of a stream or river: overflowing its channel.

1835 *McLean Diary* 34 Rain the River is ou[t] of its Banks. **1961** *Coe Ridge OHP-336B* The river was just full of people diving and trying to find him, but they never did get him. That river was out of banks nearly. **1967–69** *DARE Survey* (Rabun Gap GA) River is out of banks; (Rogersville TN) Water's out of bank.

[DARE *out of banks* adj phr especially South Midland]

out of fix *adjective phrase* Out of order or sorts, not working properly.

1892 Fruit *KY Words* 230 = out of health, out of humor, out of almost any normal condition of body or mind. **1928** (in **1952** Mathes *Tall Tales* 59) "Let me alone, I tell ye!" snarled Mag. "I'm needin' to stir. My liver's out of fix." **1940** Bowman *KY Mt Stories* 244 = upset. **1956** McAtee *Some Dial NC* 32 = of people, out of sorts, upset; of things, out of repair, not in running order. **1999** *Montgomery Coll* = refers to a machine, bodily organ, etc. that is not working well or at all (Cardwell).

out of heart *adjective phrase* Down-hearted, disconsolate, depressed.

1862 *Ferguson CW Letter* You must not get out of heart at the hard times, but do the best you can. **1863** *Ingram CW Letters* (March 8) I am pritenere out of hart Evere Seeing pease maid any more though I Hope it will be Maid. **1925** Dargan *Highland Annals* 59 I thinks I'll stop an' see if her jaw's broke yit, an' I finds ol' Jim so out o' heart about her, I stays to help him put over a couple o' hours. **c1950** Adams *Grandpap* 61 Nobody hadn't seed him. An' she was a-gettin' out of heart. Plum discouraged. **c1960** *Wilson Coll* = downcast, discouraged. **1975** Chalmers *Better* 37 I've felt a sight on this earth bad, and I tell you what's th' truth, Tuesday t'was a week ago, I had sech a misery that I got clean out o' heart. **1990** Cavender *Folk Medical Lex* 28 = low in spirit or deep mental depression. **1994** *Montgomery Coll* I get so out of heart I can't do nothing (Ogle). **2007** Myers *Smoky Mt Remedies* 77 Many used the expression "out of heart" to describe the condition we call depression today.

[DARE *out of heart* adj phr especially South Midland]

out of the way *adjective phrase* Of behavior: inappropriate, vulgar, immoral.

1805 *Globe Creek Church Minutes* 21 (Caldwell Co NC) 21 Jonathan Boone Came forward & told the Church that he got out of the way by drinking of too much of Speritious Likker. **1912** Mason *Raiding Moonshiners* 199 "Don't reckon they'll be anything out o' the way," he said. **1972** Cooper *NC Mt Folklore* 91 *done nothing out of the way* = did nothing wrong or immoral. **1975** *Fiddle Making* 308 You didn't see no drunks, nothin' that went on out of th'way. **1989** *Matewan OHP-94* I'd stop and talk to him, and never say nothing out of the way to him. **2005** Williams *Gratitude* 512 = descriptive of vulgar language, as *talking out of the way* in front of women and children.

outsharp *verb* To outdo, outwit, get the better of (someone).

1913 Kephart *Our Sthn High* 106 That bear outsharped us and went around all o' you'uns. **1949** Still *Master Time* 45 He batted an eye at us, "We'll not be outsharped." **1994–97** *Montgomery Coll* (known to Brown, Cardwell, Jones, Oliver, Weaver).

outsider *noun*

1 An illegitimate child.

1913 Kephart *Our Sthn High* 294 A bastard is a woods-colt or an outsider. **1927** Woofter *Dialect from WV* 361 = an illegitimate child.

"He cannot help being an outsider." **1952** Wilson *Folk Speech NC* 570 = an illegitimate child. "That oldest youngon of hern is an *outsider.*" **1975** Jackson *Unusual Words* 154 A bastard was known as a *woods-colt*, an *out-sider*, or *base born*.

2 See 2006 citation. See also **flatlander**, **foreigner B**, **outlander**.

1971 Justus *Jumping Johnny* 29 From here Johnny could see all around—away down Far-Side and over the county line to where the outsiders lived. **2006** *Encycl Appalachia* 229 While *furriner* is contemporarily used with humor, it has been replaced in a more serious vein by terms such as *outlander* and *outsider.*

out up *phrasal preposition* (+ preposition). See citations. See Grammar and Syntax §14.5.

1939 Hall *Coll* (Smokemont NC) We turned them loose, down through the sugar orchard they went out up across over on Enloe, back around to the big branch, out across the head of hit over on three fork. **1973** *AOHP/ASU-69* This old railroad went around here where they got this timber on out up in here.

oven (also *oven and lid*) *noun* Same as **Dutch oven**.

1861 *Hileman CW Letters* (Sept 22) I wish you could come down here to Eat Beef stake that oven you sent me is the very thing to fry Beef stake in. **1862** *Robinson CW Letters* (n.d.) the old lady give me apeck of Beans fur that & I went back to the camp & got a big oven & cook them that evning. **1937** Hall *Coll* (Cosby Creek TN) = [it] had a cover and legs and was set among the hot coals. **1939** Hall *Coll* (Cataloochee NC) We had what we called ovens. We'd put them on and heat them, put some coals on the hearth, and put the oven on it, put the bread, the dough in it, and put the lid on it, put some coals on top of that and bake our bread. *Ibid.* (Hazel Creek NC) Ma was one of the best old-timey cooks. . . . She baked in a oven. She baked on the fire. [She'd] take out her coals and put her oven down on the fire. She'd take her cornbread in pones. She'd put her cake o' bread in one side an' her potatoes in the other. **1958** Wood *Words from TN* 13 = a covered iron vessel: "A cast iron oven about 14 inches in diameter, 3 inches deep with legs about 1½ inches long and ears for pothooks, and a cast lid with a turned up rim and [a] loop on top to lift by . . . Put the lid and cover it with live coals." Known to the older generation; oven bread = a kind of corn bread: "Oven bread [was in ca. 1890] corn bread baked in an iron vessel complete with lid and legs . . . in hot coals before open fireplaces." **1966** Dakin *Vocab Ohio River Valley* 121 *Baker* . . . more often seems to be the name for a somewhat deeper utensil with straight sides, short legs (usually), a lid, and no handle. In the Mountain counties . . . and scattered elsewhere throughout Kentucky, Illinois, and Indiana the same vessel seems to be called simply *oven*, or . . . rarely *oven and lid*. **1973** GSMNP-70:2:1 Well, when we gritted that bread, it was soft enough. You didn't have to put any water in it. Just season it was all you had to do. Put salt and seasoning in it, put it in that oven and that oven was just about airtight. Put coals under it there, red hot coals. Heat the oven first on the fireplace, and you always had a big meat skin to grease that with, and then when they put the oven on the fire and heated it, the oven lid, they'd heat it and set it on there and hit was airtight, that no steam could get out of there. Every bit of the flavor of that cornbread baked right in that thing. **1984** GSMNP-153:21 In the wintertime mama would bake this cornbread in a oven, in the fire place, and I can remember that so well.

[probably short for *Dutch oven*; DARE *oven* n 1 chiefly South, South Midland]

oven and lid See **oven**.

over *preposition* Over at (or in, on, to).

1969 GSMNP-25:2:16 She lives over what they call Corn Pone, Cascades, a-going toward Wears Cove. **1969** GSMNP-44:28 They would put them in that lot and stay there for the night, and the next night they would drive to the turnpike over the edge of Buncombe. **1972** *AOHP/ALC-298* I've been over Virginia twice. **1973** GSMNP-79:4 He and his brother Frank Newman built a little store over what they call the old road up to the Sugarlands school. **1995** Adams *Come Go Home* 24 During the Great War, as it's called over home, there was a Rebel soldier who got set upon by some Yankees and was killed way back up in the Gudger Tract. **2004** Adams *Old True Love* 103 He looked like he could walk right in the store over home and not draw attention to himself. **2009** Burton *Beech Mt Man* 15 They said, "Come over my house, you can stay all night."

overbit (also *overslope*) *noun* A type of **mark** cut into the top edge of a domestic animal's ear to identify its owner. See also **smooth crop**, **split B1**, **swallow fork**, **underbit**.

1894 (in **1975** *Foxfire III* 87) Personally appeared before the undersigned John W. Hollifield who being duly sworn says on oath that his stock mark is a swallow fork in the left ear and . . . an over-bit in the right ear. **1915** Dingus *Word-List VA* 185 Under-bit, a triangular cut from the lower side [of the ear of a hog, sheep or cow], Over-bit, the same from the upper side. **1972** *Raising Sheep* 92 She explained what an overbit looked like: "It's a notch on the top of the ear. If it's on the underside, it's an 'underbit.'" **1982** Ginns *Snowbird Gravy* 129 Ours [= a mark on the ears of livestock] was a swallow fork in the left and a overslope in the right.

[DARE (at *over* adj C) South, South Midland, West]

overburden *noun* See citations.

1973 Preston *Bituminous Term* 45 = the soil, rock, and other material between the coal seam and the surface, particularly in reference to its weight. **2006** Mooney *Lg Coal Mining* 1028 In "pit mines," also called "area mines," workers use explosives and bulldozers to remove the trees and plant life, as well as the top soil, or "overburden," from a coal seam lying more or less level with the earth's surface. **2007** *Mining Terms* = layers of soil and rock covering a coal seam. Overburden is removed prior to surface mining and replaced after the coal is taken from the seam.

overcast *noun* In coal mining, an enclosed airway that permits one air current to pass over another without being interrupted.

1971 *AOHP/ALC-66* The cage come back bottom side upwards, and a car of coal come down in the sump and tore out all of that overcast on the bottom.

over down *phrasal preposition* (+ preposition). See citations. See Grammar and Syntax §14.5.

1939 *Hall Coll* (Sugarlands TN) I took them dogs off over down in North Carolina a little piece, give them all the grub they'd eat, scolded them off and let them go home.

overhall britches See **overhalls**.

overhall jacket *noun* A jacket made from denim material, like overalls.

1974 *AOHP/ALC-802* Most of us wore overhalls and gum shoes, mining caps and lamps, overhall jackets.

overhall pants See **overhalls**.

overhalls (also *overhall britches, overhall pants, overhauls*) *noun* Overalls.

1799 (in **1920** DeWitt *Sevier Journal* 20) (Oct 30) Give Mrs. Nelson order on Humes store for Linen for shirt & overhauls. **1952** Callahan *Smoky Mt Country* 86 The garb of the husband ordinarily was "overhalls," comfortable, cheap, and easily washed garments. **1963** Watkins and Watkins *Yesterday* 17 After the first day of school in the summer boys wore three pieces of clothes: a wide-brimmed straw hat, knee-length breeches or "overhalls," and a checked shirt. **1973** *GSMNP-4:1:54* That's what most of us wore at that time, you know, just a plain pair of overhauls. **1982** Powers and Hannah *Cataloochee* 212–13 Uncle Steve Woody's son, Floyd, remembers that the Woody boys only wore new "overhauls" on Sunday, as opposed to workaday "overhauls," echoing the brash simplicity of their father. **1984** *GSMNP-153:35* For Christmas, I got a new pair of overhalls. **1986** Pederson et al. *LAGS* (Sevier Co TN). **2005** Williams *Gratitude* 36 Overalls was called "overhalls," denim pants was "overhall pants" or "overhall britches," and any kind of pants was called "britches."

[folk etymology for *overalls*]

overhauls See **overhalls**.

overhead skidder *noun* A steam-powered **skidder** that carries airborne logs by a wire cable to a lower elevation. Also called **cableway skidder**. See also **groundhog skidder**, **skidder**.

1974–75 McCracken *Logging* 17:10 They had what they call ground skidders and skidded 'em on the ground, and then they had the overhead skidders which skidded up, carried the logs up in the air. **1975** *GSMNP-59:29* See, horses, they used them, but the skidders, they used this what they call overhead skidders, they'd stretch a wire from, you know, maybe what it is from one top of that and they used that in later years, but the first five or six years there they used horses altogether. [**n.d.** *Tremont Logging* 6 While most skidders dragged logs along the ground, Little River Lumber Company had special machines designed because of the Smokies' unusually rough terrain. Clyde Iron Works came up with an "overhead" model to solve the problem, a system which hauled logs in the air something like a ski lift. Overhead cables ran from the skidder to a big tree or stump on the mountainside as far as a mile away.] **2009** Lloyd *Walker Valley* 38 Clyde "overhead" skidders used settle cables 3,500 feet in length to drag logs to waiting railcars. Skidder Number Five at Tremont used a cable a mile in length—longer than any other skidder operating in the Smokies.

overheat *verb* variant past-participle form *overhet*.

1913 Kephart *Our Sthn High* 143–44 By the time they corralled him they were "plumb overhet."

overhet See **overheat**.

over home *adverb phrase* At home. See 2013 citation. See also **down home**.

1961 *Coe Ridge OHP-336B* I was expecting company tonight over home. **2004** Adams *Old True Love* 103 He looked like he could walk right in the store over home and not draw attention to himself. **2013** Landry *Tellin' It* 38 An interesting thing about Sneedville is everyone refers to it as "over home." If you're from Sneedville and you leave—say to work in Morristown and you talk about Sneedville—that's what you say: over home. Everybody does. For example, some asks "Where you going?" Everyone knows what you mean when you say "over home." It's the only place I've ever heard referred to in that way. That's Sneedville, in Hancock County.

overjoyful See **O be joyful**.

overlook *verb* To supervise (arrangements).

1928 Justus *Betty Lou* 241 Miss Witherington did not try to help with the actual disposal of the various articles, but she suggested what she thought the best ways of arranging everything, and overlooked everything and everybody.

overs *noun* See citation.

2000 Lowry *Folk Medical Term* = ovaries.

oversee *verb* variant past-tense forms *overseed*.

1922 *TN CW Ques* 966 (Sullivan Co TN) Father overseed negroes. **1980** *GSMNP-115:47* They's 'bout four of 'em kinda overseed that, papa, my daddy and Uncle Lewis King 'n' Uncle Dock.

overshot *noun*

1 A gristmill propelled by water pouring from a flume from above, filling buckets that descend by gravity, and turning an **overshot waterwheel**.

1982 *Smokies Heritage* 69 A wet, mossy waterwheel powered the mill, turned by water that fell from a chute (mill race) above—this type of gristmill was called an overshot.

2 (also *overshot weave*) See citation.

1999 Montgomery *Coll*: *overshot weave* = the most commonly woven and culturally important style of weaving in the region ... the coverlets passed from generation to generation and are still highly regarded today. In [southern Appalachia], when someone uses the term "coverlet," "kiver," or "kiverlet," they mean overshot coverlet woven with a natural colored cotton warp and a colored wool and natural cotton weft. It is commonly believed that coverlets have linen warps, but that is only the very rare exception. Flax is too brittle to use for a large piece especially under the tension that overshot demands. Appalachian coverlets were woven with a cotton warp (Wilson).

overshot waterwheel (also *overshot wheel*) *noun* The wheel of an **overshot** gristmill, driven by water pouring across the top. See also **overshot 1**, **tub mill**, **undershot wheel**.

1940 McNeil *Mt Folk* These water powered corn mills, as found in the North Carolina mountains, are of two principal types—the undershot wheel and the overshot wheel—the overshot type being far more prevalent. This is no doubt due to its less costly construction, its furnishing of a constant source of power, and its ability to utilize the power from small mountain streams. **1953** Hall *Coll* (Smokemont NC) Away back me and my brother rented a mill on Adamses Creek. It had a overshot wheel, and we ground for the public there. We made quite a bit of toll corn. We'd get a gallon out of every bushel. We'd average about a hundred and fifty bushel of toll corn [a season]. **1956** Hall *Coll* (Big Bend NC) The water mill washed away. Hit was a big rock mill, an overshot wheel. Sage Sutton got the rock. **1977** Shields *Cades Cove* 25 Around 1831 Robert Shields and David Emmett built a mill with a large overshot wheel and installed equipment with separate rocks for grinding both corn and wheat. **1983** Montell *Don't Go Up* 199 = wheel that is powered counterclockwise by the weight of water passing across the top. **1995** Trout *Historic Buildings* 73 All of the mills here were powered by running water from nearby streams. However, there were several different types of water-driven devices used: vertical waterwheels, horizontal tub wheels, and manufactured, enclosed turbines. The number and variety of functions varied with each mill. The John Cable mill in Cades Cove was powered by an overshot waterwheel. It is what we visualize when we think of "old mills." It could grind corn and wheat, but could not separate wheat products into whole wheat flour, fine white flour, middlings, and bran. **2006** *Encycl Appalachia* 936 The overshot wheel was turned when water spilling from the end of a flume above it filled a bucket or trough at the top of the wheel's rotation and then spilled into the buckets below, slowly rotating the wheel.

overslope See **overbit**.

over to *phrasal preposition* Over at. See also **over**.

1892 Dromgoole *Dan to Beersheba* 78 "I were thinkin'," she said, "'uv goin' ter Joe, over ter Beersheby." **1972** *AOHP/ALC-355* He's buried over to town, back on a high hill back there. **1989** *Matewan OHP-2* I played on the radio over to Williamson and down to Logan, too, during them times. **1991** Still *Wolfpen Notebooks* 109 Once he was over to the county seat to take an examination for a teacher's certificate and when he saw the questions he had the gumption to know he'd never make it. **2008** *Rosie Hicks* 4 We's a-having meeting over to the other place.

owing to *phrasal preposition* Depending on, according to.

1863 *Hawn CW Letters* (Feb 22) I hav bin trying the best I could ouing to the condishon I am place in tho I have tride to live in a way that I can dye happy and get to that good world above. **1922** *TN CW Ques* 1403 (Grundy Co) It was hard seem like for some to make a start oning to [sic] the man like it is now. **1953** Hall *Coll* (Bryson City NC) Sometimes we'd hunt one end of the mountain, sometimes the other, owing to what end had the best feeding ground for the bears to feed on. **c1975** Lunsford *It Used to Be* 91 Some would use mostly the type we would call the white spirituals, owing to the congregation considered, and others would use the standard hymnals of the different denominations. **1976** Weals *It's Owin'* ["Which is best?"]: "Hit's owin' to what kind you like." **1991** Thomas *Sthn Appal* 156 How ye chip, it's owin' to th' size of th' tree. Owin' to th' size whur you're cuttin'. An' it's owin' to what kind of timber you're cuttin', too.

[DARE *owing to* prep phr scattered, but especially South, South Midland]

owlhead (also *owlhead pistol*) *noun* A short, heavy revolver with a finger hole. See 1996 citation.

c1975 Lunsford *It Used to Be* 172 "Owl head" is a cheap pistol. They used to have one with an owl head on it. **1976** Garber *Mountain-ese* 65 = a small, cheap pistol: "Slim never goes to town without takin' his ole owlhead along." **1982** Powers and Hannah *Cataloochee* 186 This Indian had what we call an owlhead pistol. I don't know why they call them that. **1989** *Matewan OHP-2* I had a little thirty-two owl head pistol. I just thought to myself, "Well, I don't know what they're doing, but I'll see what it is." **1996** Spurlock *Glossary* 404 = a pistol with the back of the breech (hammer area) shaped like the top of an owl's head.

[DARE *owlhead* n 2 especially South, South Midland]

own

A (also *own to*) *verb, verb phrase* To acknowledge, admit (an error, the truth, one's responsibility for, etc.).

1863 *Gilley CW Letters* (Aug 19) we ar cirtainley Whiped all that is likeing [is that] they big men wont one it. **1865** *Epperly CW Letters* (March 4) they have noan it for some time but was ashame to own it. **1867** Harris *Sut Lovingood* 97a [sic] Now aint hit hard that being a nateral born d——d fool es I *owns* I is, I has to bar the blame of the doins of a infunel stumpy hon'd, curly faced hole fool bull. **1901** Harben *Westerfelt* 30 I am not ashamed to own that I had my heart and soul set on being your wife and making you happy. **c1950** Haun *When the Wind* 4 Eula, she never owned it to anybody the way he done her; but folks passed there and seed and knowed, and talked, of course. **1961** *Coe Ridge OHP-336A* He owned to killing him, and they sent him and Little John, the one that I was telling you about while ago, Little John. They sent them both to the pen for killing him. **1971** *AOHP/ALC-137* They got that old man in court, and he never would give them, own to it. **1981** Whitener *Folk-Ways* 29 When he finally pushed back his plate with a sigh of satisfaction, he owned that "that was the best stew I've ever tasted in my life."

B *adjective* In a reflexive pronoun phrase, with a preceding possessive pronoun followed by *-self* or *-selves* (thus *my own self* = myself). See Grammar and Syntax §2.3.4.

1868 (in **1974** Harris *High Times* 192) I jis' hollered for mam, hopin' to make far weather fur my ownsef. **1895** Dromgoole *Old Hickory* 31 Skinny was a Low Taxer his own se'f. **1905** Miles *Spirit of Mts* 107 You may see for your own self when ye go through the woods that some logs lays on top o' the ground and others sinks in till they're might' near buried up. **1913** Kephart *Our Sthn High* 118 So's't they could prove you took a hand in it your own self. *Ibid.* 122 I gather the corn, and shuck hit and grind hit my own self. *Ibid.* 170 Most of them were blockaders their own selves. **1937** Hall *Coll* (Catons Grove TN) For fever we generally had a doctor, [but mostly] people doctored their own selfs. **1942** Thomas *Blue Ridge* 71 "He built this house his own self," Aunt Sallie quietly reiterated that evening as some of us lingered to comfort her. **1969** *GSMNP*-28:10 Everybody took care of their own self. **1972** *AOHP/LJC*-205 You can certainly blame the whole lot of that on your own self. **1974** *AOHP/ASU*-204 Me and him had to load that casket by our own only selves on the sled. **1977** Shackelford et al. *Our Appalachia* 238 Each individual has to determine within his own self what is necessary for the time being. **1986** Pederson et al. *LAGS* (Campbell Co TN) He hung his own self, (Cocke Co TN) Tell them to half their own self. **1989** Landry *Smoky Mt Interviews* 181 Now that was an experience I experienced my own self. **1997** Montgomery *File* He has a little kit to give his own self a shot (60-year-old man, Maggie Valley NC). **1998** *Dante OHP*-71 You didn't have nothing to flush. It just flushed its own self. **2009** Burton *Beech Mt Man* 121 If you're with a man, let him protect his ownself unless somebody's got him down and trying to kill him or som'in'.

[OED3 *ownself* pron now chiefly regional (especially U.S. (south) and Caribbean); DARE *own self* pron chiefly South, South Midland]

own-born *adjective* Related by blood.

1954 Arnow *Dollmaker* 51 Your own born brother dead in a foreign land, en never once do you come an comfort your poor mother. **1977** Shackelford et al. *Our Appalachia* 84 If we were cousins we were all same as brothers and sisters. I know Mother and all the old folks used to talk about "own-born cousins."

[DARE (at *own* adj 1) chiefly New England, South Midland]

own self, own selves See **own B.**

own to See **own A.**

ox *noun*

1 Variant singular forms *oxen, oxten* [see **1997** in **2**].

1824 Knight *Letter from KY* 106–7 Some words are used, even by genteel people, from their imperfect education, in a new sense; and others, by the lower classes in society, pronounced very uncouthly . . . an oxen. **1939** Hall *Coll* (Nine Mile TN) He had a big old oxen. He fixed him a pack saddle on him, and he'd drive him over here in the cove and get him a load of provisions and take back to Eagle Creek. **1973** *GSMNP*-84:22 They raised that oxen plumb up off of the ground. **1978** Reese *Speech NE Tenn* 166 a oxen shoe. **1997** Montgomery *File* He was a good hand to break a oxen (60-year-old man, Maggie Valley NC). **2001** Cooper and Cooper *New River* 147 My dad had an oxen and a cane press. As the oxen was led around and around, another person was shoving in the cane after the leaves had been stripped off.

[DARE *oxen* (at *ox* n A1) chiefly South, South Midland]

2 Variant plural forms *oxens, oxes, oxtens.*

1861 *Painter CW Letters* (n.d.) you wanted to know what I asked for my oxens. **1864** *Chapman CW Letters* (April 4) our chance to mak a crop is the old mair & two colts the oxens. **1868** (in **1974** Harris *High Times* 200) Ox carts, with the oxes tuck loose, an' hitch'd in the shade, [were] full ove har trunks an' kaigs, an' them full ove cider, an' ginger cakes. **1937** Hall *Coll* (Cades Cove TN) [I] used oxen myself when up agin it, had two yoke of oxens. Oxens [are] still used in North Carolina. **1964** Glassie *Mt Jack Tales* 94 He looks around and around and around, a-tryin' to get a chance to steal them oxens. **1973** *GSMNP*-113:6 We snaked 'em in there with oxens. **1997** Montgomery *File* They are still a few oxtens left (60-year-old man, Maggie Valley NC). **2000** Montgomery *File*: *oxes* (known to 50-year-old man, Oconaluftee NC).

[DARE *oxens, oxes* (at *ox* n A2a, b) chiefly South, South Midland]

oxen See **ox 1.**

oxens, oxes See **ox 2.**

ox-eye daisy (also *ox eye*) *noun* A common field daisy (*Chrysanthemum vulgare*). Also called bull's eye daisy (see **bull's eye 1**), **whiteweed.**

1940 Caton *Wildflowers of Smokies* 42 = the common field daisy. **1963** Lord *Blue Ridge* 8D August is also bloom time for the southern mountain mint and ox eye. . . . Ox eye are tall clumps of sunshine on a stem. **1966** *DARE Survey* (Burnsville NC) = a bright yellow daisy with a dark center that grows along roadsides in late summer.

[DARE *oxeye daisy* n 2 chiefly Northeast, North Central, southern Applachians]

oxten See **ox 1.**

oxtens See **ox 2.**

ox wagon *noun* A heavy wagon used to carry freight, drawn by oxen. See 1995 citations.

1957 Parris *My Mts* 191 Large quantities of corundum were shipped out of Macon during those two years, being hauled by ox-wagon to Dillsboro, some 25 miles distance, and put on train cars there. **1995** Montgomery *Coll* = a large wagon with shafts that hooked to yoke oxen (Adams), = a long-tongued wagon so that two yoke of oxen could be used as wheel oxen (Brown), = a large, heavy wagon that, when loaded, only a team of oxen could pull (Oliver).

P

pa (also *paw*) *noun* usually [pɑ] or [pɒ].

1 A father (used in third-person reference and as a form of address). [Editor's note: In Joseph Hall's work in the Smoky Mountains in the 1930s, this term was less common than its alternatives.] Same as **pap 1**, **pappy A1**.

1862 Bradshaw *CW Letters* (Oct 28) I will close this letter by saying kiss my sweet little babe fur its Paw. **1863** Proffit *CW Letters* (June 26) giv my respects to Pa & Ma and in a particular manner to Elizabeth. **1890** Fruit *KY Words* 68 *pa* = father. Also *pap* and *papa*. **1905** *Cole Letters* 79 I was sorry to hear of paws death but such is life we are all living to die. **1923** Furman *Mothering* 8 [He] gave me the information that he was Philip Sidney Floyd, that his "paw" got his name out of a book, that his "maw" was dead. **1971** *AOHP/ALC-33* Paw, you see, he had a mill all the time. **1971** Thornburgh *Great Smoky Mts* 152 I'd been out with paw and when I seed those bear tracks I honed to go atter that bear. **1977** Hamilton *Mt Memories* 38 She called her parents "Pa" and "Ma" as most of the mountain children did, and she said, "I didn't tell Ma because she is sick and it would worry her."

2 A grandfather (in third-person reference and as a form of address). Same as **pap 2**, **papaw**, **pappy A2**, **paw paw**.

1986 Pederson et al. *LAGS* (Sullivan Co TN). **1999** Montgomery *Coll* (known to Cardwell). **2005** Williams *Gratitude* 13 Mom's parents were Memory Allen and Emer Lavada Stephens Taylor, known to other folks as "Uncle Mem and Aunt Emer." We called them "Paw and Mammy."

[DARE *pa* n B1 chiefly South, South Midland]

3 A husband (in direct address).

1999 Montgomery *Coll* (known to Cardwell).

pack

A *noun*

1 A group of dogs kept to hunt game. See also **pack dog**.

1953 Hall *Coll* (Plott Creek NC) The other pack of dogs had brought [a bear] out, run him out, and bayed him on top of what's known as the Locust Knob. **1960** Burnett *My Valley* 149 A pack of seven fine dogs led by Sooner was ready and eager, and was on the fresh track by sun-up. **1976** *Bear Hunting* 282 You use a combination—a team—gathered in a pack of six to twelve to fifteen [hunting dogs]. **1986** Lauterer *Runnin' on Rims* 132 When the pack heads out at daylight—eight or ten dogs have give chase—why, it puts a thrill in you. **2006** *Encycl Appalachia* 1373 Dogs that make up a pack tend toward hound and hound-mixed breeds, with offspring bred specifically for the purpose of bear hunting. **2007** Plott *Story Plott Hound* 183 = several hounds kept together at one location or kennel. A mixed pack indicates that both males and females are in the pack.

2 See citation.

1976 Thompson *Touching Home* 15 = cupboard for quilts, linens, handmade items.

B *verb*

1 To lug, carry (a load or heavy object, as wild game) on one's back, shoulders, or hip; to convey something on the back of a horse, mule, or other animal. See also **carry 1**, **pack tales**, **tale packer**, **tote**.

1863 Wilson *Confederate Private* 2 (Feb 3) we have to pack wood about a mile. **1864** *Chapman CW Letters* (March 28) I think that David goins will fall heir to the twist of tobacco I think hee ought to have it for his troubble packing Letters for me. **1895** Edson and Fairchild *TN Mts* 373 I have to *pack* the corn to mill. **1913** Kephart *Our Sthn High* 123 Whar one o' our leetle sleds can't go, we haffter pack on mule-back or tussle it on our own wethers. **1933** Carpenter *Sthn Mt Dialect* 23 Pack for CARRY is used in southwestern Virginia, southern West Virginia and in Kentucky, but it is not often heard in northern West Virginia or the adjoining part of Virginia. **1937** Hall *Coll* (Cades Cove TN) Just any number of fellers packed grain back there [to secluded places in the mountains to make liquor]. **1939** Hall *Coll* (Deep Creek NC) They was eleven men went back in that night and packed the bear out the next day. **1953** Hall *Coll* (Bryson City NC) [What were conditions like when you were a boy?] No roads. People packed their possessions on their backs. The first road was put in in eighteen eighty-six. You could hardly call it a road, could barely get a wagon over it. **1976** *Bear Hunting* 268 We just packed it [= the bear] in right behind the rest of them [= hunters]. **1985** Irwin *Alex Stewart* 222 I've seen her pack the heaviest load of poke stalks out of that mountain many a time, on her hip. **1989** *Matewan OHP-28* I helped pack the lumber off. They call it off-bearing. **2001** House *Clay's Quilt* 118 I pack you [= a small child] there on my hip all the time and lean over so you can put your face to the flowers.

[DARE *pack* v 1 chiefly West, Mississippi Valley, southern Appalachians]

2 In hunting for wild game, to increase the dogs on the trail, in order to pressure an animal being pursued. See also **pack dog**.

2008 Plott *Hunting in Smokies* 54 The stander . . . either makes a kill himself or releases more bear dogs to "pack" the trail.

pack dog *noun* See citation.

2007 Plott *Story Plott Hound* 183 = a dog generally released after the strike dog establishes the trail. These dogs then "pack" the trail to increase pressure on the game and provide more "dog power" to the chase.

packhouse *noun* A small building or room in which tobacco is stored or processed for market.

1969 Miller *Raising Tobacco* 34 In an effort not to be so dependent on the vagaries of weather, farmers often dug *casing houses*, also called *pack houses* or simply basements.

pack off on (also *pack on*, *pack onto*) *verb phrase* To shift the blame to (another person). See also **put off on**.

1907 Dugger *Balsam Groves* 158 I'll be bound ever'thing has to be packed on a pour ol' dummern. **1915** Pollard *TN Mts* 242 *pack onto* = to lay the blame or responsibility for (something) upon (one). "He packed my getting sick onto my getting dinner." **1952** Wilson *Folk Speech NC* 573 *pack off on* = to blame another for something one is guilty of himself. "He tried to *pack* that stealing *off on*

Ed." **1967** *DARE Survey* (Gatlinburg TN) *pack it on someone else* = to try to shift responsibility for something to someone else. **1971** Miller *Pigeon's Roost* (June 3) There has not been much blame packed on the crows for the bad corn stand as the farmers could readily see that the corn had never come up for the crows to take up. **1974** Fink *Bits Mt Speech* 19 *pack on* = blame. "Hit was all *packed on* him." **1996–97** Montgomery *Coll*: *pack off on* (known to eight consultants from the Smoky Mountains). **2005** Williams *Gratitude* 512 *pack off on* = lay the blame on. "They packed it off on Tom a-bein' the baby's daddy."

[cf EDD (at *pack* v 11) "to force an offense upon another"; DARE (at *pack* v 2c) southern Appalachians]

pack on, **pack onto** See **pack off on**.

pack peddler *noun* Formerly, an itinerant peddler selling or trading small personal goods from a pack.

1945 Wilson *Passing Institutions* 70 [We] married and died in a small area, learning of the big outside world only through books and an occasional pack peddler or clock tinker who came in. **1967–69** *DARE Survey* (Walker KY) = old-fashioned, before the use of trucks; (Hazard KY) = [went from] house to house. **1969** Hannum *Look Back* 62 Along with ginseng, mountain women began gathering other roots and herbs whose medicinal qualities had been fireside conversation for generations, trading their yield for other goods brought in by pack peddlers, who in turn sold it to outside drug markets. **1977** Norman *Kinfolks* 89 We lived right in the very head of the holler, you see, and we never saw anybody up there much except a few old pack peddlers from time to time, and now and then some kind of candidate out lectioneering from house to house.

packsaddle (also *packsaddler*, *packsaddle worm*) *noun* A brightly colored caterpillar (*Acharia stimulea*) that is shaped like an inverted saddle and has spines that deliver a painful sting. Also called **burning worm**, **stinging worm**.

1884 Smith *Arp Scrap Book* 72 I wonder if Harris ever saw a pack saddle. Well, its as putty as a rainbow, just like most all of the devil's contrivances, and when you crowd one of em on a fodderblade you'd think that forty yaller jackets had stung you all in a bunch. **1925** Dargan *Highland Annals* 208 I must git another big mess 'fore the frost struck 'em heavy, an' that field was plum full o' pack-saddlers. One stung me ever' time I laid my hand on a roas'in' year. Hit hurts worse'n a hornet fer a minute, an' it's harder on a body's temper than a hornet is. **c1960** Wilson *Coll*: *Packsaddle worm* = the larva of an insect often found on corn blades with a very violent sting; the worm itself is quite pretty, actually suggesting the form of an old-fashioned pack saddle. **1967–69** *DARE Survey* (Rome GA, Hindman KY, Walker KY, Brasstown NC, Maryville TN, Abingdon VA, Big Stone Gap VA) = looks like a saddle and stays on corn; light green, with poisonous spines on its backs. **1982** Slone *How We Talked* 44 *pack saddler* = a worm that was found on the blades of corn. We were always afraid of them when we were pulling the fodder. It stung by projecting spines from its back. It had a ring of these hair-like spines along its back that resembled a saddle. **1985** Kiser *Life and Times* 58 All the blades of corn was stripped off by hand, row by row, and woe to those who got into a pack saddler, a worm-like creature, green with a yellow caved-in center, thus called "saddler," with four feelers, or antler-like things sticking out on all four sides. They could sting, and sting they did, and it hurt. **1999** Montgomery *Coll*: *packsaddle* (known to Cardwell).

[DARE *packsaddle worm* n especially southern Appalachians]

packsaddler, **packsaddle worm** See **packsaddle**.

pack tales *verb* To spread gossip. See also **tale bearing**.

1933 Thomas *Traipsin' Woman* 15 He never took sides in any troubles. Never packed tales.

paddle *noun* Formerly, a wooden tablet imprinted with the alphabet or other rudiments of learning, a horn book.

1953 Hall *Coll* (Bryson City NC) The first school I went to, my father hewed me out a paddle with his knife and pasted the letters on the paddle. The first day or two I went, I didn't think I could learn 'em. I wet my finger and rubbed the hard ones off. I went home and my father looked at it, and he used the paddle on me.

paddling bench See **battling bench**.

pag See **peg**.

painter See **panther**.

painter leg *noun* See citation.

1977 Howard *Fifty Years* 13 = twisted hickory grub used to tie up log rafts: "Throw the painter leg in the crotch of that tree."

pair *noun*

A Variant forms *par*, *pare*.

1867 Harris *Sut Lovingood* 42 Thinks I, ole feller, if yu gain this suit, yu may ax Satun, when yu sees him, fur a par ove lisence tu practize at his cort. **1942** Hall *Phonetics Smoky Mts* 24 [pær] *pare*. **1974** *AOHP/ALC-834A* If you wanted to, had to have work clothes or a par of shoes to work in, you had to go to the superintendent and get a order. **1996** Montgomery *File* [pær] (known to 30-year-old woman, Gatlinburg TN).

B In phrase *pair of beads* = a series or set of more than two beads.

1967 Wilson *Folkways Mammoth Cave* 23 = a series, as a *pair of stairs*, or a *pair of beads*, just like the rosary of Chaucer's Prioress. **1975** Dial *Yesterday's Lg* 92 = string of beads.

pairboil See **parboil**.

pair of beads See **pair B**.

pale

A *noun* See **paling 1**.

B *verb*

1 (also *pale in*) To fence (a yard or garden) with **palings A1**.

1935 Sheppard *Cabins in Laurel* 180 Then she will sweep the yard, put out a garden and "pale" a few flowers in "brash" [= brush] against the ravages of the dogs and chickens. **1937** Hall *Coll* (Emerts Cove TN) They paled in the garden. **1940** Hall *Coll* (Tobes Creek NC) *pale* = to put a little old picket fence around. **1969** GSMNP-25:2:17 The palings come up like it did, but it cut through this way and right down by the edge of the house, and they [had] a little paled-in garden there.

[DARE *pale* v 1 especially South, South Midland]

2 See citation.

1986 Pederson et al. LAGS (Union Co GA) *pale them* = sharpen them at the top.

paled fence See **paling 2**.

pale in See **pale B**.

palen fence See **paling 2**.

paling *noun*

1 (also *pale*) A stake or slat, sometimes sharpened to a point at the top, driven upright into the ground, set side by side with others, and secured by horizontal rails or wire to enclose a garden or other area.

1831 *McLean Diary* (May 31) [I] Split pailans for Graveyard and made a gate. **1867** Harris *Sut Lovingood* 143 I jis' tore off a palin frum the fence, an' tuck hit in bof hans. **1937** Hall *Coll* (Emerts Cove TN) A garden fence has palin's on it. **1941** Stuart *Men of Mts* 98 The palins were tall and the tops sharpened so a body couldn't climb over the fence. **1977** *Shenandoah OHC* 136 We had palings, you know, around some of it [= the garden], you know, rive the wood out and make palings. **1989** *Matewan OHP*-28 You saw these paling slats stick up with the sharp ends on them? We used to rive them out of trees here. **1989** Oliver *Hazel Creek* 15 Chickens and hogs, of course, could come through a rail fence and to keep them out of the garden it was enclosed with a fence made of palings, which were strips of wood split with a froe or broadaxe and set as close together as possible. **1997** King *Mt Folks* 74 Daddy put a pine paling fence all around the house. He split the pine palings with a froe and sharpened one end . . . to keep out the chickens and all the other critters. **2006** *Encycl Appalachia* 433 The "crooked rail" fence typical of Appalachia during that time was almost exclusively made from chestnut, as was the "paling," or picket fence used around yards and gardens to keep poultry out.

[OED3 *pale* n[1] 3b ultimately < Latin *pâlus*]

2 (also *paled fence, palen fence, paling fence*) A fence or palisade of such stakes, as one surrounding a garden to keep animals out; usually the same as **picket fence**, but see 1995 citation.

1895 Dromgoole *Humble Advocate* 322 She stood there with one small, knotted labour-marked hand clasping the paling, the elbow of the other arm resting upon it, her chin in her hand, and her bright, brown eyes fixed in melancholy musing upon the distant peaks of mountain rising above the valley. **1949** Kurath *Word Geog East US* 15 In the Midland and in the South *paling fence* or *paled fence* is in regular use among all classes, *picket fence* only among younger people and especially among city dwellers. **1966** Dakin *Vocab Ohio River Valley* 92–95 *Paling fence* is still fairly common in parts of this area, however, and predominates to the virtual exclusion of *picket fence* in the Kentucky Mountains. Elsewhere in Kentucky it is the more common term. In the Mountains and among older people the most common form is *palings*. **1966** DARE *Survey* (Spruce Pine NC) *paling fence* = a wooden fence built around a garden or a house. **1971** AOHP/ALC-147 You had to have a paling fence to keep the stock out of the corn then. **1973** *Gardening* 235–36 Chestnut trees . . . would split awful easy and [my father] would just split palings about six to eight feet long. **1978** Evans *Palen Fence* 93 Although usually neglected by researchers in the field, presumably because they were so common-place, the palen fence nevertheless continued in popularity throughout the rural areas of the Appalachians until recent years. . . . Mr. Buford made the following observations concerning the method of constructing a palen fence as it was done in northern Hamilton County about the period 1920–1930: "When ye made a palen fence, back then, what ye would do is take an' put up your posts, jist like for a regular fence. Ye put the posts in the ground about eight feet apart. Then ye would nail on pieces of wood longways (i.e. horizontally) one about a foot above the ground, an' one up close to the top, an' one in the middle. Ye nailed ye palens on to these strips of wood." **1986** Huskey *Sugarlands* 6 Usually the house and garden were closed in by a paling fence. **1995** *Smokies Guide* (Summer) 13 Paling fences are similar, if not identical, to picket fences. According to one historian, the difference lies in the characteristic vertical stakes with the pointed tops. On paling fences, the stakes (or pales) were hand split from a block of wood whereas pickets on picket fences are cut with a saw. Paling fences can be traced to England and were used by the Cherokee in Tennessee as early as 1779. One version, where the pales are woven in and out of the horizontal supports, can be built without nails. The most common purpose for a paling fence in the Smokies was to keep chickens out of the yard or garden. The pointed pales discouraged the birds from fluttering to the top of the fence where they could perch and then hop down to the inside. A fine example of a paling fence can be seen around the log house at the Oconaluftee Mountain Farm Museum. **2006** *Encycl Appalachia* 433 The "crooked rail" fence typical of Appalachia during that time was almost exclusively made from chestnut, as was the "paling," or picket fence used around yards and gardens to keep poultry out.

paling fence See **paling 2**.

pallet (also *pallet bed*) *noun* Makeshift or temporary bedding spread on the floor or ground, such as a blanket or quilt. Also called **Baptist pallet, Methodist pallet**.

1864 *Carson CW Letters* (Oct 16) I often think of you and them litel Childern when I of [= ought] to bee asleape on my pallet. **1913** Kephart *Our Sthn High* 239 I lay on a pallet on the floor for over a month. **1939** Hall *Coll* (Maggie Valley NC) I started to bed. She made four pallets. They was her and two daughters. She made four pallets, made a pallet in each corner of the room. **1949** Kurath *Word Geog East US* 40 *Pallet* (29) for an improvised bed is known and used from the western shore of Chesapeake Bay southward, and westward to the mouth of the Kanawha. **1957** Broaddus *Vocab Estill Co KY* 54 *pallet* = a makeshift bed prepared by folding a couple of quilts on the floor. **1957** Combs *Lg Sthn High: Word List* 72 *pallet bed* = made down bed. That is, a bed made down on the floor, of blankets and quilts. **c1959** Weals *Hillbilly Dict* 6 = makeshift sleeping place with bedding laid on floor. When company filled all the beds, the children slept on pallets, sometimes of straw in a tick. **1982** *Smokies Heritage* 67 *pallet* = a rough bed made on the floor. **2005** Williams *Gratitude* 512 *pallet* = a quilt or padding put on the floor to sleep on when all the beds is full.

pallet bed See **pallet.**

palm *noun* Variant form *pam* [pæm].

1942 Thomas *Blue Ridge* 53 I give Buck one good wollop across the rump with the pam of my hand. **1973** Jones *Cades Cove TN* 114 [pæm]. **1995** Montgomery *Coll* (known to Cardwell).

pam See **palm**.

panel entry *noun* See citation.

1973 Preston *Bituminous Term* 35 (eKY, sWV) = an entry cut at a right angle to the main entry from which rooms are necked off and [which] serves as a haulage road to the main haulage system.

pan still *noun* A type of **still** for making whiskey.

2007 Alexander *Moonshiners Gone* 140 What appears to be a metal coffin forlornly sitting amidst the cold and snowy mountains of N.E. Georgia is in reality a "dead man" or "coffin" or "pan" still, well known to the law.

panter See **panther**.

panther *noun*

A Variant forms *painter* ['paɪntɚ] [see **1883**, **1976** in **B**], panter ['pæntɚ] [see **1937** in **B**].

[DARE *painter* (at *panther* n A1 (pronc)) scattered, but more frequent Appalachians, Inland South, *panter* (at *panther* A2 (pronc)) chiefly South, South Midland]

B The common term in the mountains for the mountain lion or cougar, a large wildcat with a tawny coat. See also **mountain screamer**.

1824 Knight *Letter from KY* 106–7 Some words are used, even by genteel people, from their imperfect education, in a new sense; and others, by the lower classes in society, pronounced very uncouthly . . . painter for panther. **1834** Crockett *Narrative* 19 This alarmed me, and I screamed out like a young painter. **1860** *Week in Smokies* 125–26 Why don't you say you found the painter lying dead beside the sheep? **1883** Zeigler and Grosscup *Heart of Alleghanies* 303 We returned to the cabin, and my conclusions were confirmed by their immediate affirmations that, "nairy varmint but a painter hed made them tracks, an' they 'lowed the cabin mought not be hanted arter all." **1913** Kephart *Our Sthn High* 99 Wolves and panthers used to be common here, but it is a long time since either has been killed in this region, albeit impressionable people see wolf tracks or hear a "pant'er" scream every now and then. **1937** Hall *Coll* (Bradley Fork NC) When I was a boy, the woods was chuck full of deer, panter, and wolves. A plagued panter run me from the top into the field. I headed downhill and nothin' in the way. First I seed him, he was placin' his feet to jump on me. I've saw one or two since. Haven't saw a panter's track or deer's track in fifty year. When the deer went out, the panter and the wolf had to go. **1959** Hall *Coll* (Hartford TN) All of the mountain people called the panther a "painter." **1971** Linzey and Linzey *Mammals of Smoky* 68 The present status of the "panther" or "painter," as this large, long-tailed cat is sometimes called in the Southern Appalachian region, is uncertain. **1976** Lindsay *Grassy Balds* 82 My great-grandfather, I guess it was, had an encounter with a mountain lion, rather as he called it "painter," that raided his barn and tried to carry off a newborn calf. **2016** Ellison *Excursions* 108 Panthers are also called "cougars," "mountain lions," and "painters." Mature panthers range anywhere from 70 to 105 inches from tip of nose to the tip of its tail and weigh anywhere between 100 to 220 pounds.

[DARE *panther* n C1 widespread, but chiefly Northeast, South, South Midland]

panther piss (also *panther sweat*) *noun* Homemade whiskey of low quality.

1963 Carson *History Bourbon* 104–5 The still house [had] a rough bedstead with several quilts and blankets for the use of the man who slept at a still when a run was made. There was also a skillet and coffeepot, an axe for cutting firewood, a rifle in the corner to discourage unwanted visitors, and a little jug of panther sweat to keep off the seed ticks. **1978** Montgomery *File: panther piss* (known to 29-year-old man, White Pine TN). **1981** Morrell *Mirth* 29 No narrative of the Great Smokies would be complete without at least one story about "Moonshine" whiskey, also known as "Splo," "panther sweat." **1996** Houk *Foods & Recipes* 151 Scorpion juice, panther sweat, white lightning, corn squeezins, moonshine—this powerful alcoholic drink made from corn has had many names attached to it, along with equal parts of myth and truth.

panther tale *noun* An account of an encounter with a panther, especially an exaggerated or fantastic account. See also **bear tale**, **snake tale**, **wild hog tale**.

2002 Morgan *Mt Born* 21 What made us more jumpy than anything, especially us kids, were the "painter" tales that were always floating about the Nantahala community when blackberries started to ripen. "Painter" was the word mountaineers used for panther. Every summer, someone would start a tale about a varmint, sometimes a bear, or wildcat, but most often, a painter, having been seen in the area. In hindsight, this was just to frighten people so they wouldn't venture into the wild blackberry fields. Then, there would be more for the tale-tellers.

pap *noun*

1 A father (in third-person reference and as a form of address). [Editor's note: In Joseph Hall's work in the Smoky Mountains in the late 1930s, this term was more common than its alternatives.] Same as **pa 1**, **pappy A1**.

1861 *Carter CW Letters* (Dec 5) I want you to hug and kiss Nancy and deller for me tell them that pap is still a live. **1863** *Shipman CW Letters* (May 1) Pap if you and Elyzabeth goes to git maried you must Let me no it in time to giv you an ansuer. **1924** Spring *Lydia Whaley* 1 Pap let the county build a school house free on his land which was nigh enuf for 'em to go home to dinner. And he was "powerful to send us to school." **1934–47** *LAMSAS Appal* (Swain Co NC). **1937** Hall *Coll* (Catons Grove TN) Pap was born here in the mountains, but Mother was born in Georgia. **1941** Stuart *Men of Mts* 235 Now we must all get home and help our Mas and Paps. **1956** Hall *Coll* (Big Bend NC) Her an' pap an' Aunt Nance ... went over to Slick Rock Branch, and they catched a big wild male hog once. **1966** Dakin *Vocab Ohio River Valley* 423 *Pap* and *pappy* are clearly "more Mountain," but are by no means limited to this section. Older and middle-aged speakers throughout Kentucky use these affectionate terms and they are also used north of the Ohio. **1967** Hall *Coll* (Townsend TN) Labe and Pap was the ones that killed the bear. **1983** *Dark Corner OHP-5A* I'll tell Pap and a bunch of them around there, get the word out over around here. **1986** Pederson et al. *LAGS* = attested by 8/60 interviewees (13.3%) from E TN and 8/12 of all LAGS interviewees (66.7%) attesting term were from Appalachia. **1989** Landry *Smoky Mt Interviews* 181 I called my father pap and [my mother] mammy. **1996** *GSMNPCOHP-1:4* When I was growing up Pap would always say stay away from the upper end [of Cades Cove]. **2005** Hicks *Blood and Bone* 23 Pap's last words written / in my journal mock me / here along with my guitar.

[shortened form of *papa*; DARE *pap* n 1 chiefly Midland, South Atlantic]

2 A grandfather. Same as **pa 2**, **papaw**, **pappy A2**, **paw paw**.

2014 Hicks *Driving* 41 When Pap started to roam, family legend goes, Mam—my mother's Momma—sawed nearly through the metal braces under his galluses, his shoestrings the same.

papa cow *noun* Used as a euphemism for bull. See also **bull A1**.

1968 Wilson *Folklore Mammoth Cave* 14 [Buck is a] euphemism for the name of a male animal; some others are *brute, brute beast, daddy, he, male, old animal,* and *papa-cow*.

papaw (also *pappaw*) *noun* A grandfather (in third-person reference and as a form of address). Same as **pa 2**, **pap 2**, **pappy A2**, **paw paw**.

1942 Hall *Phonetics Smoky Mts* 77 A curious form ... ['pæ̞pɔ:] for *grandfather* is also said to be current. **c1960** Wilson *Coll* (DARE) *papaw* is becoming common for grandpa. **1969** *DARE Survey* (Adams KY) *pa-paw*. **1975** Jackson *Unusual Words* 154 Grandparents were usually designated by the terms mammaw and pappaw. **1980** *GSMNP-115:47* They's 'bout four of 'em kinda overseed that, papa, my daddy, and Uncle Lewis King 'n' Uncle Dock. **1984** Head *Brogans* 62 My wife, Joyce, tells about her Pappaw Earls who lived next door to her when she was growing up. **1987** Wear *Sevierville* 95 Papaw says that he would work from dawn to dark for fifty cents a day or a bushel of corn. **1989** Giardina *Storming Heaven* 5 Papaw had the naming of me because my daddy died of the pneumonia before I was borned, and the childbirth took my mother away right after. **1997** Montgomery *Coll*: *papaw* (known to nine consultants from the Smoky Mountains). **2009** Sohn *Appal Home Cooking* 122 As is often the case, when mountaineers gather at the homeplace, their minds drift off to mamaw and papaw or to age-old homeplace traditions. **2014** Graves *Basin Ghosts* 31 [He was] retracing forever the afternoons his Papaw's / Old Ford rumbled them through town, / Their hands still locked together in time.

[DARE *pa-paw* n scattered, but chiefly South, South Midland]

paper poke *noun* A small paper bag or sack. See also **poke**[1], **penny poke**.

1934–47 *LAMSAS Appal* (Madison Co NC). **1957** Parris *My Mts* 65 Well, that sun had got so hot it had got that pan hot right through that coffee and that paper poke and had started parchin' that coffee. **1963** Edwards *Gravel* 21 He had picked me up on one arm and was digging into his pocket to bring out the paper poke that held the two sticks of candy. **1966–67** *DARE Survey* (Spruce Pine NC, Maryville TN) = a smaller paper container for bringing home groceries from the store. **1974** Russell *Hillbilly* 25 A few students living within a mile of the school went home for lunch, but the majority carried a lunch in a lard bucket or paper poke. **1979** *Big South Fork OHP-11* They'd set [the lunches] in a paper poke on a little table, and everybody just went by and picked his little poke up and took it. **1986** Pederson et al. *LAGS* = attested by 15/60 interviewees (25%) from E TN and 3/35 (8.6%) from N GA; 18/33 of all LAGS interviewees (54.5%) attesting term were from Appalachia.

papoose root *noun* A perennial wildflower (*Caulophyllum giganteum*) whose root has medicinal uses. Same as **blue cohosh**.

1970 Campbell et al. *Smoky Mt Wildflowers* 18 Other common names [for the blue cohosh] are electric light bulb plant and papoose-root. **1971** Krochmal et al. *Medicinal Plants Appal* 78 This herb has been called papoose root or squaw root because of its use by American Indians to facilitate childbirth.

pappaw See **papaw**.

pappie See **pappy B**.

pappy

A *noun*

1 A father (used in third-person reference and as a form of address, often to express fondness or endearment). Same as **pa 2**, **pap**.

1862 *Carter CW Letters* (May 9) your Pappy is yet alive and he hopes to live to get home to live with you all again. **1863** (in **1992** Jackson *Surry Co Soldiers* 301) (Jan 8) [The baby] is as pretty as its pappy and it can walk and it ain't been named yet. **1883** Bonner

Dialect Tales 167 He's going to marry me, pappy, when—when the baby comes. **1915** Dingus *Word-List VA* 187 = father. **1924** (in **1952** Mathes *Tall Tales* 43) Pappy's dead an' gone, an' John Cutshaw's been in the pen fer five years now. **1937–41** Hall *Coll* (various locations in TN, NC) "Shoot him, pappy, he's a revenuer—he's got shoes on" (a popular saying). **1941** Stuart *Men of Mts* 250 She laughed at him when he used to hoe corn for her pappie for twenty-five cents a day. **1956** Hall *Coll* (JG, in telling a local tale) My pappy is swelled powerfully. **1970** Justus *Tales* 16 He saw Mammy's bonnet away up front and Pappy in the Amen corner, and there was Uncle Tobe from Yon-Side sitting beside him. **1975** *AOHP/LJC-384* Pappy used to raft.

[DARE *pappy* n 1 chiefly South Midland]

2 A grandfather (in third-person reference and as a form of address). Same as **pa 2**, **pap 2**, **papaw**, **paw paw**.

1984 Head *Brogans* 20 As a child I spent a lot of time at my grandfather's house because he seemed to enjoy my company and I know I enjoyed his. Pappy was a talented country musician. **1986** Pederson et al. *LAGS*: *pappy* = attested by 3/60 interviewees (5%) from E TN; 3/10 of all LAGS interviewees (30%) attesting term were from Appalachia.

[*papa* + *-y* diminutive suffix; Web3 *pappy* n chiefly South and Midland]

B *verb* (as *pappie*) To father (a child).

1940 Stuart *Trees of Heaven* 169 Funny how a man that ugly could pappie a gal purty as Subrinea.

par See **pair**.

paralysis of the heart *noun* A heart attack.

1975 Fink *Backpacking* 75 People who died suddenly were frequently victims of "paralysis of the heart," etc. **1997** Montgomery *Coll* (known to Cardwell).

paralyzed *adjective* Firm, solid.

1924 Greer-Petrie *Angeline Gits Eyeful* 12 I'll take a poralized oath ev'ry word I a-tellin' you is the Gospel truth.

parbile See **parboil**.

parboil *verb* Variant forms *pairboil*, *parbile*, *pearbile*, *power boil*.

1904 Johnson *Highways South* 141 "You take 'em that time of year," explained the doctor, "and parbile 'em, and pour off the water, and then salt and pepper 'em and bile 'em agin, and after that bake 'em and they're all right. I love a parbiled groundhog." **1942** Hall *Phonetics Smoky Mts* 30 [ˈpæɚ̯baɪl] [ˈpæɚ̯bɔɪl]. **1981** Whitener *Folk-Ways* 32 Gather spice wood when the sap first comes up, store away to dry. It makes good tea, but if you have any kind of wild meats, just break up some of the spice wood and wash clean, power boil [= parboil] with your wild meat. **1991** Thomas *Sthn Appal* 52 You take a squirrel and dress 'im up good, an' nice. An' fry 'im—I didn't pair-bile 'im—an' fry in grease. **2008** *Rosie Hicks* 6 We always did pairboil it and then fry it.

parcel *noun*

A Variant form *passel*.

1913 Kephart *Our Sthn High* 281 Much oftener the r is dropped from dare, first, girl, horse, nurse, parcel, worth (dast, fust, gal, hoss, nuss, passel, wuth). **1915** Dingus *Word-List VA* 187 *passel*. **1942** Hall *Phonetics Smoky Mts* 30.

B Senses.

1 A tract or portion of land, especially a large one.

1937 Hall *Coll* (Emerts Cove TN) He passel of land. **1939** Hall *Coll* (Hazel Creek NC) They's passels of land that's back of that ridge right there, and there's a hundred acres on this side.

2 A large number (of people, animals, or things), quite a few.

1774 *Dunmore's War* 179 I am this minet Return'd from Greasey Creek after a parcel of Fellows that Engaged with Tomy Ingles Some time Agoe. **c1841** Shane (in **1998** Perkins *Border Life* 198) A parcel of children were out at the time; some here, some there. **1859** Taliaferro *Fisher's River* 126 I seen a passel ov men com trucklin' to me, rockin' along, see-saw one side, then see-saw t'other side. **1862** *Warrick CW Letters* (Oct 6) I expect that there will be a parcel of us go to Chattanooga before many days. **1864** *Poteet CW Letters* (April 7) there aint any thing to come for but a parcel of half perished women and children. **1889** Murfree *Broomsedge Cove* 251 I hev got a whole passel of guineas. **1937** Hall *Coll* (Cosby TN) He put a passel of corn on a old mule. **1939** Hall *Coll* (Nine Mile TN) [A] passel of us fellows gathered up here to bear hunt. **c1945** Haun *Hawk's Done* 328 A whole passel of men had gathered themselves together and followed them, just to let them know they didn't have any use for their ways. **1962** Dykeman *Tall Woman* 139 You're a kindly passel of folks to share like this, but Lydia's got to have a chance to collect herself. **1989** Giardina *Storming Heaven* 177 To them we're just a passel of ignorant hillbillies. Anything we do will be done our own selves.

[OED3 *parcel* n 6a "company of people" now English regional and U.S. colloquial]

parcel out See **line B**.

parch *verb* To toast, roast (as peanuts, dried grains of corn, etc.).

1797 Imlay *Western Terr* 237 (DARE) Parched meal . . . is a very nourishing food, and is an excellent provision for travellers. **1862** *Fuller CW Letters* (Nov 24) I have not got 1 grane of salt sence you left I am aliving upun parch meal coffee and bread with out salt. **1862** *Martin CW Letters* (June 22) I have heard A Many A Soldier Say that he had March three Days on eating parch Corn. **1956** McAtee *Some Dial NC* 32 *parched peanuts*. . . . A more general term is roasted peanuts. **1982** Slone *How We Talked* 90 *parch corn* = the regular white corn used for feed or bread. Brown in a hot skillet, to which has been added a little salt and grease. Stir until it becomes brown and "crunchie" or "bricklie." Eat as popcorn.

[DARE *parch* v chiefly South, South Midland]

pare See **pair**.

pareboil See **parboil**.

parfeckly See **perfectly**.

parson *noun* A clergyman. See 1997 citation.

1875 King *Great South* 519 We were presently invited to remain at the cabin all night, as "the parson never refuses nobody." **1939** Hall *Coll* (Jefferson City TN) = a black preacher (the usual term for a white man is **preacher**). **1997** Montgomery *Coll* (consultants from the Smoky Mountains agree this is a general term for a minister, regardless of denomination, but far less common than *preacher*), = often referred to a clergyman from outside the community, such as a circuit rider or one visiting to preach at revival services (Hooper).

particular

A *adjective* Of work: cautious, requiring or receiving special care in execution.

1937 Hall *Coll* (Ravensford NC) [Weaving and making clothes] was a purty particular job. **1952** Wilson *Folk Speech NC* 573 = careful, cautious: "Be particular when you cross the street." **1983** *Dark Corner OHP*-28A They was particular about their sheriffs. **2008** McKinley *Bear Mt* 182 *purty partic'lar* = highly skilled, intricate.

[DARE *particular* adj B1 especially South, South Midland]

B *adverb* Especially.

1983 *Dark Corner OHP*-9A I never have particular watched it.

[DARE *particular* adv D especially South, South Midland]

particulars *noun*

1 See citations.

1917 Kephart *Word-List* 415 = perishable foodstuffs. **1996** Montgomery *Coll* (known to Bush); When you're going to dinner on the ground, you better be careful about your particulars (Cardwell).

2 (usually plural) The testicles of a slaughtered hog.

1976 Still *Pattern of Man* 11 "[Do you w]ant the lights saved?" "Yes, s'r," Ulysses replied. "Heart-lump?" "Yip." "The particulars?" "Nay-o."

partridge *noun* Variant forms *paterage, paterdge, pateridge, patridge, patteridge* (all usually with /æ/ in the first syllable).

1841 Donaldson (in **1934** Smith *Tennessean's Pronunciation* 263) *patridge*. **1853** (in **1956** Eliason *Tarheel Talk* 315) (Surry Co NC) *paterage*. **1942** Hall *Phonetics Smoky Mts* 30 ['pætrɪʤ] ['pɑtɚʤ]. **1954** Roberts *Bought a Dog* I fell on a whole flock of pateridges and killed 'em. **1963** Edwards *Gravel* 44 Ye can't hear a thing but the bark of a squirrel or the flutter of a paterdge. **1975** Gainer *Witches Ghosts Signs* 14 He shot a patteridge with his new gun.

[cf DARE *paterage* (at *partridge* n A3) chiefly South, South Midland]

party game See **play**.

pass *verb*

1 (also *pass out*) To die. See also **die away**. [Editor's note: *Pass on* is widespread in the US.]

1939 Hall *Coll* (Bradley Fork NC) I stayed with [Horace Kephart] until he passed out. **1973** GSMNP-5:16 He got sick and passed out. **1982** Powers and Hannah *Cataloochee* 271 The doctor arrived during the night but could not save the patient. He passed in the next twenty-four hours. **1984** Burns *Cold Sassy* 304 She said, "If'n I pass, I hope . . . Well, find you another wife and I'll take it as a compli-ment." **1986** Pederson et al. *LAGS*: *pass out* = attested by 2/60 interviewees (3.3%) from E TN and 3/35 (8.6%) from N GA; 5/24 of all LAGS interviewees (20.8%) attesting term were from Appalachia. **2017** *Blind Pig* (May 18) My great aunt passed Easter weekend and her funeral was the following Thursday.

[OED3 *pass* v 6b "to die" now chiefly North American; DARE *pass* v 1a chiefly South, South Midland]

2 To treat a child for illness by handling the child in one of various ways.

2003 Cavender *Folk Medicine* 44 Another sympathetic, passive technique, "passing," was used to treat a variety of childhood maladies. Colic, for example, was treated by passing a child from mother to father, usually three times, under a horse, mule, or bush, through a horse collar or a split sapling, or around a table leg. . . . The underlying assumption was that the child would pass from a state of sickness to wellness. *Ibid.* 122 The magical technique of "passing" was also used to cure whooping cough. Two people stood on opposite sides of a mule and passed a child under the mule's stomach and over his back three times. **2006** *Encycl Appalachia* 868 Two variant techniques of the sympathetic principle were "measuring" and "passing." Childhood asthma, for example, was often treated by cutting a stick, usually of sourwood, the exact length of the child and then placing the stick up the chimney or in the attic. As the child outgrew the length of the stick, he outgrew his asthma. Colic was treated by passing a child from mother to father, usually three times, under a horse or mule, through a horse collar, around a table leg, under a bush, or through a split sapling. The underlying notion was that the child would pass from a state of sickness to wellness. **2007** Milnes *Signs Cures Witches* 107 In Pendleton County, babies were passed through a horse collar to be cured of livergrown. . . . In many documented cures in German folk culture a child is passed through some unusual object to effect the cure. The object could be a horse collar or a hole in a tree, as mentioned, or even a hole under a berry vine that had bent down and taken root. It is thought that when a natural object grows or is shaped so as to make a hollow passage in an unnatural way, this passage will magically affect those passed through it (usually three or three times three times).

pass and repass *verb phrase* To meet casually and then part, pass (someone) repeatedly, acknowledging him or her slightly or not at all; hence, barely to get along with someone, especially a neighbor, or to speak only when passing.

1937 Hall *Coll* (Collins Creek NC) I pass and repass him without speakin'. **1941** Stuart *Men of Mts* 114 Jist pass and repass with them and let that be all. **1979** Melton *'Pon My Honor* 9 Being good neighbors, folks still passed and re-passed with the Walkers, but nobody wanted to get too thick with them. **1984** Wilder *You All Spoken* 103 = speak when they meet but not on good terms. **1992**

Brooks *Sthn Stuff* 109 = to exchange only the amenities with someone. "We don't really know each other that well. Just pass and repass when we meet." **1997** Montgomery *Coll* (known to Bush, Oliver, Weaver), = to barely get along with someone, especially a neighbor (Brown), = to acknowledge another's presence but not enter into conversation with other than hello or howdy do (Cardwell), = to not get along, to pass one's neighbors frequently, but without speaking (Hooper).

passel See **parcel.**

passenger *noun* A traveler, passerby.

1862 *Huntley CW Letters* (Aug 15) We are about 80 miles from Richmond in Orrange County close to gordons ville I still hear from pasengers that you are Coming to see us.

[OED3 *passenger* n 3a "a person who passes by or through a place; a traveller, especially a traveller on foot" obsolete, →1675]

passion flower (also *passion plant, passion vine*) *noun* A tall vine (*Passiflora incarnata*) with large, flesh-colored flowers, edible yellow fruit, and medicinal uses. Same as **maypop**, **molly pop**, **wild apricot**.

1937 Thornburgh *Great Smoky Mts* 22–23 The strange, symbolic purple passion flower, the former state flower of Tennessee, grows in profusion and its fruit is prized by the mountain children who call it wild apricot. [**1970** Campbell et al. *Smoky Mt Wildflowers* 66 According to legend, the parts of the flower resemble the instruments of Christ's crucifixion—the corona representing the crown of thorn, the stamen and pistils, the nails of the cross; the petals and sepals, the faithful apostles.] [**1971** Krochmal et al. *Medicinal Plants Appal* This plant . . . has been used to reduce blood pressure and to increase the rate of respiration.] **1982** Stupka *Wildflowers* 69 Along roadsides, in open rocky places, and in old fields where dry conditions prevail, passion flower is a fairly common tendril-bearing vine that may climb to a height of 10 or 20 feet. **1994** Garza *Matchbox Mt* 6 From "passion plants" that grew alongside Grassy Creek Road, we collected all of its fruit that we could find (which we called "lollipops") and made all sizes of pigs for our hog pens. The legs were made of tiny sticks, and curly red tendrils from wild grapevines made colorful tails.

pass out See **pass 1.**

passover *noun* An impending rainstorm that fails to materialize.

1975 Jackson *Unusual Words* 158 A heavy rainfall is a gully-washer, and rain clouds that seem to be bringing rain may, after all, be only a passover.

pass words *verb phrase* To exchange hostile words; to converse briefly.

1992 Brooks *Sthn Stuff* 110 Verbally expressed hostility between people. "Ah'm mad as I can be at Mary Lee, but Ah'm not about to lower myself by passing words with her." **2002** Rash *Foot in Eden* 73 I'd passed words with Mrs. Winchester a few times but never a word with Holland.

[DARE *pass words* v phr 1 especially South, South Midland]

past common See **common 1.**

paster See **pasture.**

past of See **a-past.**

pastor See **pasture.**

pasture *noun, verb* Variant forms *paster, pastor.*

1861 *Hileman CW Letters* (Aug 24) we are kept in Just like you all keep Horses in pastors. **1863** *Click CW Letters* (July 17) won of Capton Bostons men got back to the plase where we have got the horses in paster. **1935** (in **2009** Powell *Shenandoah Letters* 55) Do you thank that Charlie magoon had a write to paster cattle on the park land? **1998** *Dante OHP-29* He leased a large spot because he made a paster. **2013** Venable *How to Tawlk* 37 *pastor* = a field for livestock: "They's aplenty of hay fer the cows in the back pastor."

pasture field *noun* A field.

1941 Stuart *Men of Mts* 94 Can't you hear the guns a-boomin at the fur-end of the pasture field? **1954** *GSMNP-19:25* Sometimes [the cattle] fall out of the pasture field because it was too steep. Once in a while they kill theirself. **1967** Stuart *New Wine* 24 They don't know either that over in some pasture field where boneset is growing, this strange plant (without a name) might be directly responsible for their being here, for its brew may have saved an ancestor from chills and fevers. **1986** Pederson et al. *LAGS* = attested by 12/60 interviewees (20%) from E TN; 12/14 of all LAGS interviewees (85.7%) attesting term were from Appalachia.

pat *verb* To tap or slap one's thigh or stamp one's foot in time with music.

1982 Powers and Hannah *Cataloochee* 171 They'us playin' the ole Virginia Reel, and she was a-pattin' . . . for that dance!

[DARE *pat* v 2 chiefly South]

patch

A *noun*

1 A plot of ground distinct from surrounding land by the crop, plant, or other growth that dominates it. Most often it is a cultivated plot of land detached from the main area of gardening or farming. See also **laurel bed**, **patch farm**, **truck patch**, **wooly B.**

1864 *Chapman CW Letters* (March 31) if you Can manage to plant A patch of Corne doo so. **1864** *Tesh CW Letters* (Feb 28) Mother I want You to plant the largest onion Patch You ever did so when I come Homes You will have a plenty. **1914** Arthur *Western NC* 254 Land was plentiful in those primitive times and as fast as a piece of "new ground" was worn out, another "patch" was cleared and cultivated until it, in its turn, was given over to weeds and pasturage. **1926** Hunnicutt *Twenty Years* 211 Old man Henry said we have plenty of meat for tomorrow; let's hunt the Quill Rose ginseng patch. **1937** Hall *Coll* (Hartford TN) I had a patch of land in corn, and the bears got to comin' into that cornfield. **1939** Hall *Coll* (Proctor NC) The dogs just stove off the road into a little laurel patch, and there they jumped another big one [= a bear]. *Ibid.*

(Cataloochee NC) [A bear] was usin' in a chestnut patch. *Ibid.* (Hazel Creek NC) We own this patch of land at the back of that ridge right there. **1956** Fink *That's Why* 4 [Tangles] of low rhododendron or kalmia . . . are also called woolies or woolly patches. **1962** Wilson *Folkways Mammoth Cave* 11 A small area cultivated was a patch, except where tobacco was grown; that was always a *tobacco* /tobacker/ patch, regardless of its acreage. **1973** *Foxfire Interviews* A-73-86 They'd all go in together and clean that patch up. **1982** Powers and Hannah *Cataloochee* 220 I found Uncle Steve and the fellow sitting on top of the bear in a rhododendron patch. **1995** Montgomery *Coll* He bows up when he catches kids in his watermelon patch (Shields). **1997** Nelson *Country Folklore* 128 Mark and his wife, Beenie, who we all called aunt and uncle, lived past a patch of woods in a clearing above the pea patch.

2 (also *patching*) Something comparable or equal (usually in negative constructions).

1915 Dingus *Word-List VA* 187 *not a patchin'* = by no means equal or comparable (to): "Slick Jim's coon dog's not a patchin' to mine." **1924** Greer-Petrie *Angeline Gits Eyeful* 16 Now you talk about them men a-bein' tryflin', they wan't a patchin' to them young married wimmen! **1957** Combs *Lg Sthn High: Word List* 72 (*patch* or *patching*) = a term either of approval or disapproval. Ex.: "You're not a patchin' to him!" That is, all your manners placed on his would make only a little patch. **1993** Ison and Ison *Whole Nother Lg* 48 *patching* = doesn't measure up. "She ain't a patchin of that other girl." **1997** Montgomery *Coll: patch* (known to Ellis); She ain't a patch on her sister when it comes to hard work (Weaver).

B *verb* To plant and tend (a crop or piece of land).

1940 Still *River of Earth* 101 Though Grandma was seventy-eight, she had patched two acres of corn. **1968** Clarke *Stuart's Kentucky* 130 He, too, preferred to marry a hill girl who would be a woman fer a livin' and go on with the corn and terbacker patchin'.

patch farm *noun* A piece of land planted only in sections; hence noun *patch farming*.

1939 *FWP Guide TN* 22 Thousands of tiny "patch-farms" are scattered through the uplands. **1972** *Graham County* 50 With the first stages of early clearing, the farmer did "patch" farming near the cabin. Many farmers today still speak of a "patch" of corn or other crops. The farmer gradually and systematically extended the patches into wider fields by each year extending his farming into a new area known as a "new ground."

patching See **patch 2**.

patent note *noun* Same as **shape note**. See also **old harp**.

1957 Parris *My Mts* 204 They are a unique coterie, practitioners of "do-ray-me" or "fa-so-la" singing, who apply Elizabethan names to the notes of songs made in pre-Revolutionary America and sing them with the help of the 155-year-old "patent notes." **1978** Horn *New Harp of Columbia* viii The first of these changes was shaped notes (sometimes called character notes, buckwheat notes, or patent notes), one shape for each syllable of the solmization used.

paterge See **partridge**.

patient *verb* See citation.

1895 Edson and Fairchild *TN Mts* 373 *patien'* (v.) = content. "I never could patien' myself to keep pets."

patridge See **partridge**.

patrol *noun* A Highway Patrol officer. See also **law**[2] **A2**.

1973 Kahn *Hillbilly Women* 43 It took three of them highway patrols to put him in the car.

patterdge, patteridge See **partridge**.

pattern *noun* See citation.

1957 Combs *Lg Sthn High: Word List* 72 = lumber for building a house.

paunch *noun* The stomach of an animal, especially as used for food.

1963 Watkins and Watkins *Yesterday* 48 Ma fried them [= the entrails] and the rest of the chitlins and the stomach, or punch. *Ibid.* 92 A mad stone taken from the stomach or "punch" of a deer was supposed to prevent and cure rabies. **1972** *Foxfire I* 206 Stomach [of a hog] (also called the "paunch" or "punch")—Cut the stomach free of intestines, split, and wash out well. Scrape it down and soak in salt water for three days. Then rinse, cut up, and cook like chitlins. **1982** Slone *How We Talked* 37 *ponch* = hog's stomach.

[DARE *paunch* n B South, South Midland]

paw See **pa**.

paw paw *noun* A grandfather. Same as **pa 2**, **pap 2**, **papaw**, **pappy A2**.

1968 *DARE Survey* (Brasstown NC) *paw paw* = a grandfather. **1976** *Bear Hunting* 306 Paw paw, I didn't shake when I was a'shooting at him. **2017** *Blind Pig* (March 31) I caught my grandkids sniggering at their Pawpaw.

payday *noun* A paycheck.

1963 Edwards *Gravel* 30 He works at the mines, and he'd spend his whole pay day before he'd let one of us knife into that chunk of sweetin. **1975** *AOHP/ALC-903* I went up to headquarters to ask them at the office. I told them to give me my payday. *Ibid.* When they's going to cut you [i.e. your wages], you wouldn't know it until you got your payday. You didn't have nothing to say about it. *Ibid.* I was off a week, and I went up to get my payday, and the motorman got to begging me, begging me to come back [to work]. **1989** *Matewan OHP-9* They always asked for a raise well before they got their first payday. The groceries had done went up more than their raise was. *Ibid.* 33 They [= prison guards] went there and shot their [= miners'] winders out, buddy, and shot some of them and shot from a shotgun, hit them in their feet in the bed, you know, and took their little paydays out, what little they'd just drawed. **2005** Williams *Gratitude* 513 = wages. "I got my payday today and it's already spent."

payment *noun* Variant form with secondary stress on the second syllable. For similar forms, see **-ment A.**

1942 Hall *Phonetics Smoky Mts* 71 The suffixes *-dent* and *-ment* (except in *independent*) in most instances have secondary stress: *accident, confident, devilment, instrument, monument, payment, settlement, testament, etc.*

pay mind, pay no mind See **mind A2.**

pay out *verb phrase* To pay a debt in full, settle up.

1939 Bond *Appal Dialect* 110 = to pay out of debt; avoid some difficulty by spending money. **1942** Thomas *Blue Ridge* 280 Calte was company-owned! If he lived to be a hundred he'd never be paid out. **1997** Montgomery *Coll* (known to Adams, Bush, Cardwell, Jones, Oliver, Weaver).

[DARE *pay out* v phr especially South Midland]

peaceable *adjective* See citation.

1958 Combs *Archaic English in KY* 41 = calm: "The weather was peaceable."

peach butter *noun* A thick, spicy spread for bread made from peaches. See also **persimmon butter, pumpkin butter, sweet potato butter.** See also **peach leather.**

[**1980** *Smokies Heritage* 101 *butters* = not simply butter churned from milk, but the spiced, sweet fruit spread made from apples, peaches, pumpkin, and persimmons during jelly-making season and autumn (for the last two).] **1991** Thomas *Sthn Appal* 54 When I'z a-growin' up, we made our jam an' apple butter an' peach butter—all kinds of butters that way—with molasses.

peach leather *noun* See 1978 citation.

1915 Dingus *Word-List VA* 187 = peaches crushed, spread out, and dried. **1936** Justus *Honey Jane* 91 I believe I'll take the best of these and make some peach leather. **1978** Parris *Mt Cooking* 47 The way we made peach leather was to take a peck or so of ripe peaches and press 'em through a coarse sieve. The riper the peaches the better. Then you mixed in some brown sugar and cooked 'em. When they was cooked, you took the sauce and spread it on plates and put the plates out in the sun to dry. Took two or three days in the sun to get it good dried. When it got properly dried, you could roll it up like leather. **1997** Montgomery *Coll* (known to Brewer), = peach butter spread out thinly and dried (Oliver).

peach-tree-limb tea (also *peach-tree tea*) *noun* A whipping. See also **hickory B2, willer tea.**

1915 Dingus *Word-List VA* 189 *peach-tree tea* = punishment with a peach tree switch. **1957** Combs *Lg Sthn High: Word List* 72 When a boy is whipped with a switch from a peach tree, he is said to be receiving peach tree tea. **2003** Cavender *Folk Medicine* 204 *peachtree limb tea* = a whipping with a switch, administered to a child.

peach tree rose *noun* The flowering almond (*Prunus triloba*).

1944 Hayes *Word-List NC* 35 = flowering almond. The leaves are like those of a peach tree, and the flowers are like tiny roses.

peach-tree tea See **peach-tree-limb tea.**

peacify *verb* See citations.

1930s (in **1944** Wentworth *ADD* 446) (eWV) = to pacify. **1952** Wilson *Folk Speech NC* 574 *peacified* = peaceable.

pea hulling (also *pea shelling*) *noun* Formerly, a neighborhood work activity to help a family shell its crop of peas, after which food and entertainment are often provided. See also **corn shucking, pea thrashing, working.**

1912 Perrow *Songs and Rhymes* 143 At "Square" Murray's, near the head of Wildcat, there is pretty sure to be, before many weeks pass, a "quiltin'," a "house-raisin'," a "workin'," a "watermelon-cuttin'," a "candy-pullin'," or a "pea-hullin'." **1937** Haun *Cocke Co* 15–16 All types of song are sung at corn huskings and pea hullings. . . . Everybody that finds a red ear of corn gets to kiss his girl. Or if he finds a pod with thirteen peas in it, he gets to kiss her. **1978** Montgomery *White Pine Coll* III-2 We didn't have anything like the children do nowadays to entertain ourselves, just being at home and going to a corn shucking or a pea hulling or something like that. **1986** Pederson et al. *LAGS* (Cocke Co TN) *pea hulling.* **1997** Nelson *Country Folklore* 10 The families in the entire community gathered for corn shuckings and pea shellings, hog killings, molasses making, and Sunday afternoon ball games.

[DARE *pea hulling* n southern Appalachians]

peaked *adjective* [pronounced as two syllables: *peak-id*]. [Editor's note: The senses below cannot always be differentiated.]

1 (also *peakedy*) Of a person: pale, sickly looking.

c1959 Weals *Hillbilly Dict* 6 = thin, pale. **1964** Reynolds *Born of Mts* 74 They just stay healthy, few are peaked, and many are rather good looking. **1986** Pederson et al. *LAGS*: *peakedy* (Stephenson Co GA). **1988** Kosier *Maggie* 113 He had gradually become more weak and "peaked." **1990** Cavender *Folk Medical Lex* 28 = having a pale appearance, indicating poor health. **1992** Bush *Dorie* 32 He said we'd grown a foot since we'd been gone, but Luther looked a "mite peaked." **1994** Montgomery *Coll* (known to Cardwell), = also indicates having lost weight, as "You're looking a little peaked. You need to eat more" (Ogle). **2000** Miller *Looneyville* 58 (pek'id) = sick looking person. Normally about someone who looked thin and drawn: "He's looking mighty peaked since he had the measles."

2 Languid.

1990 Cavender *Folk Medical Lex* 28 = feeling languid. **1994** Montgomery *Coll* (known to Cardwell, Ogle).

[< past participle of OED3 *peak* v[1] 3 "to become sickly or emaciated"; SND *peakit* (at *peak* v 4) "having a thin, drawn appearance"]

peakedy See **peaked 1.**

peanut bean *noun* See citation. Same as **October bean**.

1999 Montgomery *Coll* = a bunch bean that is ready to eat when its shell is striped red. It tastes like a dried or foddered peanut (Cardwell).

peanut social *noun* A community party at which peanuts are the snack food.

1941 *FWP Guide WV* 347 Whole families walk five or six miles to enjoy a few hours of entertainment at pie suppers, peanut socials, square dances, and bingo parties.

peanut store *noun* Used as a nickname for a small, local enterprise.

1967 Fetterman *Stinking Creek* 40 I just shop around these little places I call them peanut stores.

pear *verb* To seem.

1885 Murfree *Prophet* 177 It always 'peared ter me ez he war a mighty cur'ous man. **1890** Fruit *KY Words* 65 *pears* = appears. **1895** *Mt Baptist Sermon* 14 I got out on the mounting . . . an' 'peared lack I couldn't go home. **1921** Campbell *Sthn Highlander* 204 "'Pears like hit's bound to go plumb through a family," said a mountain girl wistfully when approached as to treatment for tuberculosis, from which five of her brothers and sisters had died. **1927** Woofter *Dialect from WV* 361 It 'pears to me that I have seen you before. **1941** Stuart *Men of Mts* 96 Pears like the fightin is the hardest in February and March when the ground is froze and we can't plow. **1958** Campbell *Tales* 148–49 She never 'peared to feel no shame about who she was marrying. **1984** Woods *WV Was Good* 230 *Appear* unfailingly was shortened to *peer.* (Hit peers like he ain't well.)

[shortening of *appear*; DARE *pear* v chiefly South Midland]

pearbile See **parboil**.

pearly everlasting *noun* A wild plant (*Antennaria parlinii*) whose leaves can be made into a tea or smoked to combat respiratory infections or problems. Also called **ladies'-tobacco, life everlasting, pussy toes**.

1975 Hamel and Chiltoskey *Cherokee Plants* 48 = make cold tea, pour over hot rock and breathe fumes. **1999** Montgomery *Coll* (known to Cardwell).

peart *adjective, adverb*

A Variant forms *peert* [see **1937** Hall in **B2**]; *pyeart* [see **1937** Haun in **B1**], *pyeert* [see **1923** in **B1**], *pyert* [see **1940** in **B1**].

1942 Hall *Phonetics Smoky Mts* 42 [pɪɚt].

B *adjective*

1 Lively, spirited(ly), full of vitality, especially after having recovered from an illness. See also **pearten**.

c1845 *Coffee Co TN Letters* Sath is as bad as ever, the little one is as peart as a Cricket. **1862** Lockmiller *CW Letters* (Feb 1) mary is as pert as a cricket and can say most any thing she tries to. **1895** Dromgoole *Fiddling to Fame* 64 The boys began ter pat [at the music]; soft at first, then a bit more peart. **1923** Furman *Mothering* 34 Before leaving, Mr. Wyatt said that Jason was right pyeert about learning, and, he added candidly, about meanness too, and he hoped I would not spar' the rod. **1930** Armstrong *This Day and Time* 98 He's the peertest old man to his age ever I seen. **1937** Hall *Coll* (Nine Mile TN) My daddy was feelin' peert the last time he was in the cove, but he's right puny now. **1937** Haun *Cocke Co* 2 [Men] have to ride mighty pyeart in order to have any time to waste in town. **1940** Haun *Hawk's Done* 31 The twenty-first morning she seemed pyert as a pup. **1966** Dakin *Vocab Ohio River Valley* 463 *Peart* is common in the Mountains from the headwaters of the Kentucky southward. This term is unknown in southern Kentucky west of the Mountains but has some rare use in the Bluegrass. **1984** Wilder *You All Spoken* 200 *peart* = in good health and spirits and couldn't be better. Peart conveys the impression of numerous qualities—full of life, of a joyous and happy nature, sprightly, fresh, sassy, impudent, alert, intelligent. **1986** Pederson et al. *LAGS* = attested by 15/60 interviewees (25%) from E TN and 4/35 (11.4%) from N GA; 19/43 of all LAGS interviewees (44.1%) attesting term were from Appalachia. **2008** McKinley *Bear Mt* 182 = feeling quite well under the circumstances of advanced age and/or poor health.

[DARE *peart* adj/adv chiefly South, South Midland]

2 Saucy, impudent, cheeky.

1937 Hall *Coll* (Copeland Creek TN) That little peert thing! (used in indignant reference to a National Park ranger who refused her request to cultivate a larger plot of land). [See **1984** in **B1**.]

(as) peart as Snyder's pup See **(as/like) Snyder's hound/house cat/pup**.

pearten (also *pearten up, pert up*) *verb, verb phrase* To enliven; to become lively.

1917 Kephart *Word-List* 415 *pearten* = to become lively or cheerful. **1952** Wilson *Folk Speech NC* 574 *pearten (up)* = to enliven, to cheer up; to become lively, cheerful: "That fellow certainly peartens a body up with his lively jokes." "I hear that Mary's baby is peartening up some." **1957** Justus *Other Side* 118 "For there's nothing like strong tea," Mammy said, "to pearten up a puny child." **1962** Dykeman *Tall Woman* 167 "You're looking peart," Paul said. "Peartens a feller up to see home folks." **1977** Hamilton *Mt Memories* 86 They git holt o' that moonshine and hit peartens 'em up till they gotta show off. **1986** Pederson et al. *LAGS* (Jefferson Co TN) [The toad] pertens up when the sun shines. **2008** McKinley *Bear Mt* 68 Granny dug the roots of the sassafras tree, pelled the bark, and boiled it with fresh spring water. She always declared it'd "peart-en a'body right up."

[OED3 *pearten* v dialect; Web3 *pearten* v chiefly dialect; DARE *pearten* v chiefly South, South Midland]

peartening juice (also *pearting juice*) *noun* Homemade whiskey.

1957 Parris *My Mts* 101 Your Grandma always said it was just imagination fed by the peartenin' juice my cousin sipped. **1966** Dykeman *Far Family* 30 We'll try a little peartenin' juice, toss around an idea or two about this new industrial park the county is thinking of developing. **1972** Cooper *NC Mt Folklore* 15 When neuralgia struck, peartenin' juice was sipped until one could not walk a crack in the floor. **1995** Montgomery *Coll*: *pearting juice* (known to Oliver). **2002** Oliver *Cooking and Living* 15 Close to the Chestnut Flats section of Cades Cove where there was a ready market for his "peartenin juice," Quill was caught and tried several times, and once a judge asked him if he didn't think likker was better when aged. To this Quill replied that he once tried keeping some for a week and found it no better than when new and fresh.

peartening powder *noun* A tonic medication taken in powdered form (construed as a count noun; hence plural form *peartening powders*). For similar forms, see **powder A.**

1974 Fink *Bits Mt Speech* 19 = tonic, vitamins. "Doc, John wants some more of those *peartenin' powders* that done him so good." **1998** Montgomery *Coll* (known to Cardwell), = strong laxative in powder form (Brown).

pearting juice See **peartening juice.**

pea shelling See **pea hulling.**

pea thrashing (also *pea threshing*) *noun* A social gathering at which peas are shelled by piling the pods on a large sheet and then beating them with sticks or poles. See 1971 citation. See also **pea hulling.**

1937 Still *Egg Tree* 103 This Little Angus hollow is dusty as a pea threshin'. **1971** *Corn Shuckin's* 101 Pea thrashin's . . . They'd go and pick'em and carry'em and pile'em in great big ol' piles. Put'em on big sheets, y'know. Then we all cut us a pole t'beat with and you'd just beat, then you'd stir up a while, and you'd beat again. The hulls'ud pile up on top. Then you'd stir t'get some more up that hadn't been hit, y'know. Then you'd beat'em again. **1973** *Florence and Lawton* 204 Th'only thing we ever went to would be a corn-shuckin', or a pea-thrashin', or a singin', or a candy-pullin'. **2003** Smith *Orlean Puckett* 10 Neighborhood corn shuckings, pea threshings, house raisings, and wood gettings may have meant hard work, but they were a way of socializing in many mountain neighborhoods.

pea threshing See **pea thrashing.**

pea turkey (also *p-turkey*) *noun* (in negative constructions, especially *never said pea turkey*) Anything at all. See also **never say dog.**

1976 Dwyer *Southern Sayin's* 9 *never said pea turkey* = never gave an invitation or offered information. **1984** Burns *Cold Sassy* 16 If she don't write them and don't hear from them and don't ever say pea-turkey about them to anybody, something's wrong. **1984** Wilder *You All Spoken* 152 *never said pea turkey* = failed to give information, or to invite one to some function, as "She lef' heah, I tell you, an' nevah said pea turkey." **1992** Brooks *Sthn Stuff* 118 *p-turkey* = practically nothing. "I near talked myself to death tryin' to entertain that woman, and she has yet to even say p-turkey to me." **1997** Montgomery *Coll* He got up and left without saying pea turkey (Ledford). **2009** Benfield *Mt Born* 180 = an expression indicating nothing has been said or done. . . . The pea turkey is the female turkey who, unlike the noisy male, is ever so quiet. "That stuck-up Gladys walked right by me and never said pea turkey." **2017** *Blind Pig* (Nov 14) My mother—whose family hailed from Vonore, TN . . . said "pea turkey" but not by itself. She used it as "he didn't know pea turkey from izzard!" *Ibid.* He stood there and let me make a fool out of myself and didn't say pea turkey. *Ibid.* It didn't mean that somebody didn't have anything to say. It meant that nothing they said related to anything important. Usually it was followed by "what" they didn't say "Peaturkey" about. "He didn't say pea turkey about when he would come back to fix the porch," meaning, he didn't bring up the subject, and neither did I. *Ibid.* My Granny & Grandad used the phrase a lot with the addition of one word . . . didn't say "pea turkey squat."

[DARE *pea-turkey* n 1 chiefly South, South Midland]

peavey (also *peevy*) *noun* In logging, a lever with a long spike on one end and a pivoting hook on the side, used to maneuver a log on a **skidway** or in water. See 1964 citation. See also **cant dog.**

1939 Hall *Coll* (Proctor NC) = it's got a spike on the end and a hook to turn or berl a log with. **1958** GSMNP-110:18 They took seven men on the ballhooting gang, and those seven men would run peaveys there. They could handle most any kind of a log. **1964** Clarkson *Lumbering in WV* 368 = a stout wooden lever, from 5 to 7 feet long, fitted at the larger end with a metal socket, a pike, and a curved steel hook which works on a bolt; used in handling logs, in river driving and in rolling logs on a landing. **1986** Tyson *Reflections* 8 The boys carried a tool they called a peevy. It had a hook on the end of the handle. When the log would get hung up, they would hook it over the log and loosen it. **1994** Schmidt and Hooks *Whistle* 157 = a heavy wooden handle with a pointed metal tip and a hinged hook near the end, used by lumbermen in handling logs. **1995** Weber *Rugged Hills* 84 We'd go down to the pile and knock the grabs loose with the skip. Then with "peaveys" and "cant hooks," we'd make a neat new pile. Later the logs were loaded and hauled to the railroad. **2006** Farwell *Logging Term* 1021 A Maine blacksmith, Joe Peavey, improved on the cant hook by adding a spike on the end, and the "peavey" can still be used to "muscle" logs.

peavine railroad (also *peavine train*) *noun* A short, winding, narrow-gauge railroad line for logging, especially the one that formerly followed the Pigeon River from Newport TN to the Big Creek logging camp near Mt. Sterling NC, used especially for hauling logs but also featuring an open-air car for passengers.

1910 Guerrant *Galax Gatherers* 115 At Newport, Tennessee, I took the little "Pea-Vine" railroad up the Pigeon River. **1948** Chase *Grandfather Tales* 186 He turned [the horse] loose in a peavine cove to die when he got too hard to work. **1957** Hall *Coll* (Mt Sterling NC) The Pea-Vine Railroad was called that because of the wild pea vines growing along the river. **1973** Van Noppen *Western NC* 266 Pea Vine was the popular name for a railroad connecting Clay and Cherokee counties NC for hauling lumber and pulpwood. **1984** Wilder *You All Spoken* 187 = one with a rambling route—no beeline here—as in a mountain lumbering operation. **2005** Williams *Gratitude* 24 They was a railroad in Hayesville called the "Pea Vine," with a nar (narrow) gauge railroad that branched off and went up Farses' (Fires') Creek.

peawood *noun* A common deciduous tree (*Halesia carolina*) in the region. Also called **bellwood, heaven above, rattlebox 1, silver bell, tisswood.**

1943 Peattie *Men Mt Trees* 162 Here and there the silverbell, called "peawood" by the mountain folk, shoulders its way up eighty or a hundred feet, to wave its flowers as high in the forest crown as any. **1967** *DARE Survey* (Gatlinburg TN) = same as bluebell—blue, looks like a peablossom, gets plumb full of little bells, real pretty. **1971** Hutchins *Hidden Valley* 31 One of the most attractive of all the large trees of the valley, especially from the standpoint of its flowers, is the mountain silverbell, called "peawood" by the settlers, a tree of the Styrax family, most of whose members grow in tropical regions, especially in South America.

[DARE *peawood* n western NC, east TN]

peck[1] *noun* A tool for sharpening the furrows on a millstone; hence as verb = to dress a millstone.

1952 Wilson *Folk Speech NC* 575 = to dress a millstone. **1982** Ginns *Snowbird Gravy* 85 When I'd sharpen it, I'd take a mill peck. That's a rock, and you just peck furrows in it, in the millstone. The stone was about forty inches across. I had to peck those furrows in it so it would grind.

[variant of *pick*]

peck[2] *verb* To tap, knock (as on a door).

1982 Ginns *Snowbird Gravy* 176 Got tired, wanted some water, and stopped at a house and pecked at the door.

[DARE *peck* v[1] 1 chiefly South, South Midland]

peck at (also *peck on*) *verb phrase* To nag (at). See also **pick A4.**

1952 Wilson *Folk Speech NC* 575 *peck at (on)* = to nag at, to find fault with. **c1960** Wilson *Coll*: *peck at* = to nag, pick at.

[DARE (at *peck* v[1] 2) scattered, but chiefly South, South Midland]

peckerwood *noun*

1 A woodpecker. See also **chuckwood, sapsucker, woodchuck.**

1866 (in **1974** Harris *High Times* 166) She had no sort ove fancy for Misses JARROLD's fool ways, an' valued Mister GRIPES about as she would any other peckerwood or pole cat. **1915** Dingus *Word-List VA* 179 Compound words sometimes exchange places: *peckerwood ... everwho ... everwhere.* **1941** Stuart *Men of Mts* 117 It is old and the peckerwoods fly in and out of the holes they have bored in the gable-end white-pine logs. **1949** Kurath *Word Geog East US* 43 *Peckerwood* for the woodpecker is common in the folk speech of the Virginia Piedmont and the adjoining parts of North Carolina. It appears again in the westernmost parts of Virginia and North Carolina, i.e., within the belt of the Virginia influence on the Appalachians. **1966** Dakin *Vocab Ohio River Valley* 395 In Kentucky, however, *peckerwood* [for a woodpecker] is common among older speakers everywhere and is regular in the southwest. In the Mountains and the eastern Knobs older speakers commonly say *woodchuck* (once *chuckwood* in Johnson County). **1966–68** *DARE Survey* (Burnsville NC, Cherokee NC, Spruce Pine NC, Gatlinburg TN, Maryville TN) = a woodpecker; (Brasstown NC) = joking name for a woodpecker. **2013** Venable *How to Tawlk* 37 = birds that cling to tree trunks and feed behind the bark: "They was a red-headed peckerwood in my hickories last week."

2 By extension = a rural white person, originally with little reference to social status; more recently, one who is poor and backward or is of scurrilous or contemptible character. [Editor's note: This term is now usually somewhat derogatory, but perhaps not as much in Appalachia as in the Deep South. Joseph Hall observed that in the Smoky Mountains in the late 1930s, it was applied frequently to enrollees in the Civilian Conservation Corps, the federal agency that created jobs building the roads, trails, campgrounds, and other facilities of Great Smoky Mountains National Park; the agency was called the *Peckerwood Army* or the *Peckerwoods* because men shifted from one camp to another of roughly two dozen in the newly developing park.] **1940** Hall *Coll* (Cataloochee NC) I'm still in the Peckerwoods [= Civilian Conservation Corps]. **1974** Dabney *Mt Spirits* 78–79 I was lucky to get off with six months in a CCC Camp—what I called the Peckerwood Army. **1976** Lindsay *Grassy Balds* 39 [Nineteen] thirty-six, when North Carolina and Tennessee was full of them peckerwoods. Peckerwood army [was the] CCC's. **1989** Nicholson *Field Guide* 61 = smart aleck human. "If that peckerwood says 'I told you so' one more time he can just get this tree off the tent his own self." **1994** Montgomery *Coll* He's just a peckerwood [i.e. he's a character, with no reference to social status] (Cardwell). **1994** Montgomery *File*: *peckerwood army* (known to 85-year-old man, Greenbrier TN). **2003** Wolfram et al. *Mt Talk* If it's somebody [my grandmother] didn't know, but he's probably all right, she didn't have any animosity for him. She would say he's a jasper: "There's this jasper come by here this morning, and he knocked on the door." But if it's a salesman, "It's just a peckerwood out there on the porch." **2013** Venable *How to Tawlk* 37 = a slightly derogatory term: "George is such a peckerwood!"

[inversion of elements; cf *backswitch*; DARE *peckerwood* n both senses chiefly South, South Midland]

peckerwood about *verb phrase* To move from place to place, causing destruction.

1994 Montgomery *Coll* (known to Cardwell, but not to other consultants from the Smoky Mountains).

Peckerwood Army See **peckerwood 2.**

peckerwood mill (also *peckerwood sawmill*) *noun* A small, portable sawmill, often of inferior construction and operation. See 1995 citation.

1966 Frome *Strangers* 165 At the outbreak of World War I North Carolina had the most [saw] mills, over 1200, though many were small "peckerwoods" or "coffeepot mills." **1980** Weals *Dunn Early* Charlie was of bigger than average size as a boy, and among his first jobs in the foothills hollows around home were [ones] at "peckerwood sawmills," so called because a "woodpecker could cut wood faster than that." **1995** Trout *Historic Buildings* 39 Small portable steam engines began to appear in the mountains in the 1890s. They were wheelmounted, horsedrawn units that could be taken into the woods and fired with slabs and scrap from the very logs that they sawed. Completely self-contained, these little "peckerwood" mills operated on a scale small enough to make it financially feasible for the owner/operator to saw the pattern (all the sizes and quantities) for one building at a time. Sometimes the job was done on shares. The landowner would give the sawyer half of the total number of logs in order to get enough timber for his own needs. The sawyer would then sell his half for cash. Many a church, school, store, barn, or house in the Smokies was "sawed out" in this way.

[DARE *peckerwood* n 3 "in logging: used attributively in reference to a small-scale or transient logging and milling operation" chiefly South, South Midland]

peckish *adjective* See citation.

1895 *Word-Lists* 392 = easily offended (s.w. Va.).

pee-dab (also *pee-dookie*) *noun* A small marble.

1969–70 *DARE Survey* (Jasper TN) *pee-dabs* = small marbles or marbles in general; (Rome GA) *pee-dookies* = small marbles or marbles in general.

peepaw *noun* A grandfather, one's grandfather.

2016 *DSAE Internet File* I think of Peepaw and Meemaw as Appalachian, not Southern generally. I grew up calling one of my two Appalachian granddads Peepaw. *Ibid.* My mother, age 82, called her beloved grandfather Peepaw. She grew up on the Ohio/Kentucky border.

peep-by-night *noun* Same as **pretty-by-night**.

1944 Wilson *Word-List* 47 = a flower that opens at night, the four o'clock.

peeper (also *peep frog*, *pete frog*) *noun* A small tree frog (especially *Hyla crucifer*) that chirps in spring in a loud, high-pitched voice. Also called **knee deep 1**, **night peeper**, **spring cheeper**, **squealer**.

1966–68 *DARE Survey* (Brasstown NC, Burnsville NC, Spruce Pine NC) *peep frog* = a small frog that sings or chirps loudly in spring. **1967** Miller *Pigeon's Roost* (March 23) The pete frogs is hollering everwhere in this section now which is certainly very early in the season for these kind of frogs to go to hollering. **1986** Pederson et al. *LAGS* (Carter Co TN, Rabun Co GA). **1989** Giardina *Storming Heaven* 133 The night was unusually warm for April and we sat on the front porch. A chorus of peepers cried from the creek. **1998** Montgomery *Coll*: *peeper* (known to Norris); *spring peeper* (known to Brown, Bush, Cardwell, Jones, Ledford, Weaver). **2000** Miller *Looneyville* 58 Pokey River fresh water frogs are small, four legged, leaping animals with long, powerful hind legs, short forelegs, web feet and no tails. In Looneyville, peepers meant any of several species of frogs that may have a high pitched, throaty sound rather than the deep throaty croak of most larger species: "The peepers are noisy down there in the lower medder crick this evenin'." Some folks referred to them as knee-deeps. **2007** McMillon *Notes*: *peep frog* = the first frog to holler (in February or March) from swamps or wet, boggy places.

peep frog See **peeper**.

peer See **pear**.

peerch See **perch**.

peert See **peart**.

peevy See **peavey**.

peewee See **pewee**.

peg *noun*, *verb* Variant form *pag*.

1942 Hall *Phonetics Smoky Mts* 20 [pæg]. **1959** Roberts *Up Cutshin* 25 He sawed off big solid cuts offen that blackgum, about twenty inches in diameter, with big auger holes in the center for his axles, and pagged on. Never had a nail then, and weren't a nail in the whole wagon.

pellagra, **pellagry** See **liquor pellagra**.

pellet *noun* The hide of a fox.

1989 *Matewan OHP-7* In the later years lot of people hunted [foxes] just to hear their dogs run, but now back in the earlier part of the century, why, they hunted them for their pellets. A good fox pellet'd bring you five or six dollars.

Pelsnickel, **Pelznickel** See **Belsnickel**.

pen[1] *noun*

1 An enclosure built of logs or rails, used to trap bears, turkeys, or other game. The **bear pen** is baited with meat and is of the deadfall type; the **turkey pen** is baited with corn and is a constructed enclosure, into which a turkey is lured by grains of corn scattered on the ground leading into it.

1937 Hall *Coll* (Cataloochee NC) I had a patch of land in corn. The wild turkeys was about to eat it up, so I built a pen to try to catch 'em. The pen was ten feet each way, and I covered over the top. Then I dug a ditch so as to draw the turkeys into the pen. Next morning there was nine big gobvblers in the pen and one outside. **1939** Hall *Coll* (Cataloochee NC) Turkey George . . . he couldn't kill the turkey with his gun. He'd missed so many he decided to build a pen and baited this pen with corn. He went up one morning and had, oh I don't know how many, but as the story goes it must have been a half a dozen of the turkeys in the pen, and Uncle George undertook catching them and bringing them home. *Ibid.* (Smokemont NC) Then they decided they'd build a pen. They went and cut them some logs, floored it, built one log high, then they built a lid for it, took triggers, set that bear trap, baited it with a piece of beef, and the bear come, throwed the trap. They never caught him.

2 Same as **bull pen 3**.

1964 Banks *Back to Mts* 22 A group of boys was herded into a marked off area. One outside the "pen" threw a ball with all his might straight at the group. Those inside the area dodged the ball or caught it. The one brave enough or skilful enough to catch that stinging ball was privileged to leave the pen and exchange places with the one who had just thrown it.

pen² *noun* A rectangular or square structural unit of horizontal log construction, as a section of a barn to hold livestock or fodder, built of rails or logs or a one-room dwelling of four walls with logs interlocked at the ends. When a second room (or **house**) was built next to the latter, often separated by an unfloored passage several feet wide, the two units were covered with the same roof and known as a double-pen log cabin (see **double cabin**). By the mid-20th century the term was rarely heard in the region, as sawmills had made frame construction prevalent and farm livings had improved.

1913 Kephart *Our Sthn High* 240 The mountain home of to-day is the log cabin of the American pioneer . . . a pen that can be erected by four "corner-men" in one day and is finished by the owner at his leisure. **1941** Stuart *Men of Mts* 171 The men lifted the big logs and skidded them up poles onto the square pen of pine, popular, oak and chestnut logs. **1965** Glassie *Old Barns* 21 From this ancient rectangular structural unit, usually in the mountains called a "crib" or a "pen," developed, partially in Europe and partially in America, most if not all of the traditional barn types today found in the Southern Mountains. **1970** Jones *Oliver Barn* 5 The barn is a two-part gable-roof structure with a one-pen lean-to addition . . . the three pens were originally fitted with doors. Only one is now in place. All three pens have earth floors. **1973** GSMNP-70:5 He got a job hewing them logs with a broad ax to make the tow boards and pen logs. **1999** Bishir et al. *Archit W NC* 429 = a rectangular or square structural unit. The term is usually used in referring to log buildings and specifies a structure enclosed by log walls. Most single-pen log houses had only one room in the space enclosed by logs, but within one pen there may be partitions dividing a space into smaller rooms, such as a hall parlor plans. Many dwellings in N.C. were single-pen structures. Often these were expanded into two-room houses, including the double-pen, saddlebag, or dogtrot plans. **2003** Jordan-Byshkov *Upland South* 31 Scholars discovered two basic plans: "single pen" and "double pen," using the folk word "pen" to mean a basic unit of four log walls notched together. These could be a single story in height, or instead elevated to one-and-a-half or two stories.

[cf SND (at *pend* n¹ 1 "an arch, vault"); DARE *pen* n B3 chiefly South, South Midland]

pencheon See **puncheon**.

pencil tail See **pestle-tail**.

penhook See **pinhook**.

penhooker See **pinhooker**.

penitentiary *verb*

A Variant forms *penitentiar* [see **1924** in **B**], *penitenture* [see **1963** in **B**].

B To send (someone) to prison.

1915 Bradley *Hobnobbing* 94 Although at his trial he had "come clear," he had been detained through one delay or another just as long as he'd been "penitentiaried." **1924** Raine *Saddlebags* 135 I wish I was on the jury, I'd penetentiar 'em every time. **1963** Williams *Metaphor Mt Speech II* 52 His pap, afore he was penitentured daown in Georgy, didn't hardly uver work none to speak of. **1974** Fink *Bits Mt Speech* 19 = send to prison. "They *penitentiaried* him for making licker." **1974–75** McCracken *Logging* 1:8 If it hadn't been for an old lawyer up there, Jim Wright, they'd a penitentiaried him. **1997** Montgomery *Coll* (known to Bush, Cardwell, Jones).

[DARE *penitentiary* v southern Appalachians]

penitent's pen *noun* See citation.

1948 Dick *Dixie Frontier* 199–200 As a frontier institution the camp-meeting developed a standard pattern during the first few years of the nineteenth century. A forest area was selected near a sparkling stream with plenty of shade and grass for hundreds of horses. A large square clearing was made and over this was constructed an immense brush arbor or, as a camp-ground became permanent, a long shed covered with clapboards. The logs were laid end to end in rows lengthwise, and rough slabs, split from other logs with wedges, were laid across these in tiers the full length of the arbor. At one end was a high platform, known as "the pulpit-stand," made of poles or poles and slabs. At the foot of the stand was a straw-floored enclosure about thirty feet square, known as "the altar" or "penitent's pen."

penitenture See **penitentiary**.

pen money *noun* Money from selling chickens or their eggs.

1967 Miller *Pigeon's Roost* (Jan 26) All the country stores bought chickens and eggs, but give you store goods for them. If you wanted to sell them to the buyer yourself and get the money for them, you could do so. About all the residents back in those days made a little money raising chickens to sell as well as selling eggs. Many people called it pen money.

penniwinkle (also *periwinkle*) *noun* A small water snail.

1957 Broaddus *Vocab Estill Co KY* 55 *periwinkle* = a water snail. **c1960** Wilson *Coll*: *penniwinkle* = a small water snail, a periwinkle.

[DARE *pennywinkle* n 2 especially South, South Midland]

Pennsylvania salve *noun* See citation.

1980 Riggleman *WV Mtneer* 126–27 [Loggers] usually had nicknames for everybody and everything around the camp. . . . Apple butter was "Pennsylvania salve."

penny feist (also *penny fice*) *noun* A small, yapping, mixed-breed dog, so called because it was considered of little value. See also **feist B**, **mountain feist**, **treeing feist**.

1975 Gainer *Witches Ghosts Signs* 9 To call one a penny-fice means that he is one who makes much noise that amounts to little. "The politician is nothing but a penny-fice." **1997** Montgomery *Coll* (known to Adams, Cardwell).

penny fice See **penny feist**.

penny pencil *noun* An inexpensive pencil without an eraser.

1978 Slone *Common Folks* 218 I already knew all the pictures in [the schoolbook]. I also had a big red back tablet, and a penny pencil. **1996** Isbell *Last Chivaree* 72 Early that year [in school] Ray "beat" in spelling and arithmetic. His reward was a penny pencil and a writing tablet.

[DARE *penny pencil* n chiefly South, South Midland]

penny poke *noun* A small paper container in which mixed candy is purchased. See also **paper poke**, **poke**[1].

1990 Clouse *Wilder* 99 I reckon I got enough draw left to buy a penny poke of candy. **2014** Hicks *Driving* 29 A candy case [was] filled with Baby Ruths, Snickers, Mars bars, loose candy to fill our "penny pokes," our parting treat.

pennyrile See **penny royal**.

penny royal *noun*

A Variant forms *pennyrile* [see **1937** in **B**].

B A branching annual mint (*Hedeoma pulegioides*) with many medicinal uses, especially to treat pneumonia and colds and as an abortifacient.

[**1901** Lounsberry *Sthn Wild Flowers* 455–56 The heavy oil distilled from the plant has various qualities among which not the least known is its obnoxiousness to mosquitos. Children pull and carry about bunches of it to protect them from these insects.] **1937** Thornburgh *Great Smoky Mts* 32 Take pennyrile—that little green weedy thing with teeny weeny leaves that grows in the field—hit makes good tea for colds, an' so does mullein. **1940** Haun *Hawk's Done* 103 "Three months?" I knew Pennyroyal tea won't do any good after a woman is that far gone. **1943** Hannum *Mt People* 113 If the cold went beyond the simple reach of sage, and developed into "pneumonia fever," then pennyroyal was called into use. **1960** Price *Root Digging in Appal* 10 Pennyroyal is thought to derive from the Latin pulegium, though the phonic connection is hardly evident. **1971** *AOHP/ALC-137* Whenever that any of us would get sick that way of a cold, why she would always make a tea of old field pennyrile and catnip together and mullein. [**1971** Krochmal et al. *Medicinal Plants Appal* 138 This herb is used as an antispasmodic, rubificient, and stimulant. In Appalachia, a tea is used for treating pneumonia.] **1994** Montgomery *Coll* = used to ward off fleas and chiggers (Ogle). **1999** Morgan *Gap Creek* 3 Everybody knows what you take for the colic is pennyroyal tea, and Mama boiled some as soon as the stove was hot, even before she cooked any breakfast.

peony *noun* Variant forms *peony rose*, *piano rose*, *piney*, *piney flare*, *piney rose* (some forms apparently to avoid pronunciation sounding like *pee*).

1930 Armstrong *This Day and Time* 6 Your cheeks was pink as pineys. **1937** Hyatt *Kiverlid* 6 The old fashioned "piney-rose" (peony) which is seen in the door yard of the feudist's cabin in Kentucky is still the "piney-rose" growing along the garden paths in the Smoky Mountains of Tennessee, and "piney-rose" to the hill people in the Blue Ridge of North Carolina. **1944** Hayes *Word-List NC* 35 *piney rose* = the peony. One mountaineer explained the name thus: "They smell like pines and look like roses." **1960** Stubbs *Mountain-Wise* (April–May) 6 If it looks and smells like a rose why not call it some sort of rose after all? Thus we have either "piano rose," "piney-rose," or "peony rose" as common names for the peony. **1966–67** *DARE Survey* (Maryville TN) *piney*; (Spruce Pine NC) *piney rose*. **1978** Reese *Speech NE Tenn* 36 *piney rose* = attested by 5/12 (41.7%) speakers. **2013** Venable *How to Tawlk* 37 Miss Mary Ann grows the purtiest piney flares you ever seed. **2015** *Blind Pig* (July 31) When she was a young girl they weren't allowed to say peony. Because it sounded like "pee." So they always called them "pineys."

peony rose See **peony**.

people *noun*

A Variant plural form *peoples*.

1970 *Burton-Manning Coll-94A* They's just old fools, peoples like I am here. **1983** *Dark Corner OHP-4A* We never did dry none [= apple slices], but a few peoples do it. **1985** Williams *Role of Folklore* 185 I think the fact it was all black peoples, they [= news media] jumped on it. **2009** Burton *Beech Mt Man* 117 Then peoples believes me, and they won't fight me.

B The members of a family, an extended group of kin collectively.

1861 *Poteet CW Letters* (July 16) I Was happy to receive your kind letter today for it dose me somutch good to here from eny of my People in this troublesum place. **1866** *Chapman CW Letters* (Jan 1) [I] would like very much to hear from you and have corrispondence wite you and all of my people. **1892** Dromgoole *War of Roses* 482 Mrs. Stiles promptly declared for the Democratic nominee, her people having always supported that ticket. But Pete's people had been stubbornly loyal to the other side. **1935** (in **2009** Powell *Shenandoah Letters* 57) All of his wife's people live here. **1941** Stuart *Men of Mts* 100 You know we aint on good terms with your people. **1957** *GSMNP-23:1:8* I don't talk about my people. If I can't say something good about them, I don't want to say nothing bad about them. **1961** *Coe Ridge OHP-333A* I know who he married and all, but who was he and who were his people? **1973** *GSMNP-70:2:6* My father's people was all raised up in Madison County, North Carolina. **1978** Montgomery *White Pine Coll VI-1* My husband's people were a very close-knit family. **1998** *Dante OHP-71*

They wouldn't come back since their daddy died. They don't have no people here or nothing like that. **2004** Fisher *Kettle Bottom* 29 We buried our people up on top of Stepp Mountain, highest spot on the home place.

[DARE *people* n B2 chiefly South, South Midland]

pepper grass *noun* See 1998 citation. See also **chicken mustard.**

1937 Campbell *KY Mt Community* 530 Off and on he'd git him a mess of wild sallet and git granny to cook hit good. Wild lettuce and dandelion and pepper grass and poke and lamb's quarter and dock and sich makes right good sallet. **1998** Montgomery *Coll* Chicken mustard is so called because it often grows around the chicken house and chickens frequently nibble at it when it comes up in the spring, also called pepper grass, because it produces pods of tiny seeds (Cardwell).

perch *noun*

A Variant forms *peerch* [see **1937** in **B**], *pyeerch* [see **1922** in **B**], *pyerch* [see **1904** in **B**].

B Usually a small-mouth black bass.

1904 Fox *Christmas Eve* 164 They made fun of our rods, and laughed at the idea of getting out a big "green pyerch"—as the mountaineers call bass—with "them switches." **1922** Cobb *KY Mt Rhymes* 26 Red-eyes we'd catch, an' suckers too, an' pyeerches by the score. **1937** Hall *Coll* (Cosby Creek TN) Them's not peerch. Them's bass. **1942** Hall *Phonetics Smoky Mts* 42 [pɪɚč]. **1991** Thomas *Sthn Appal* 76 I wouldn't eat suckers, an' th' sun peerches. Now, peer-ches, they're jist full of bones.

perfectly *adverb* Variant form *parfeckly*.

1937 Hall *Coll* (Emerts Cove TN) You're parfeckly welcome. **1942** Hall *Phonetics Smoky Mts* 42 = *old-fashioned*.

perish *verb*

1 (also *perish out*) To cause (someone) to die; to kill or starve (someone).

1863 *CW Soldiers' Letters* (Sept 10) we will sun peres[h] them out if tha[y] come hear without tha[y] bring ple[n]ty to eat with them. **1985** Dabney *More Mt Spirits* 23 Old Hoover liked to perished everybody to death.

[Web3 *perish* vt 1 chiefly dialect]

2 (also *perish away*) To deteriorate, decay, slowly die.

1862 *Fuller CW Letters* (Dec 28) i maid no crop of a count and wee wood have perished all to gether but now i hav maid a hansum sum of monney. **1862** *Martin CW Letters* (June 24) A great Many of our Citisen[s] perish as well as our Souldiers who are Dying So fast from Various Diseases, & A great Many perishes to Death ... for the want of attention. **1862** *Zimmerman CW Letters* (Sept 27) I allways can get as much meat and bread as we have had we will not perish. **1958** Campbell *Tales* 74 The youngest boy was well-hoped that he could find the golden bird, though, and save the king's apples so the king wouldn't perish away and die. **1978** *Horsetrading* 42 That [muscle] would perish away. **1983** *Dark Corner OHP-5A* People had to do that, you know, or perish to death back then.

[Web3 *perish* vi 3 chiefly dialect]

perish away See **perish 2.**

perish out See **perish 1.**

periwinkle See **penniwinkle.**

permillion (also *water permillion*) *noun* A melon.

1963 Edwards *Gravel* 175, 176 Who cut up the water permillions? ... Them's the same identical fellers that cut up the permillions!

permit *noun* Variant form with primary stress on the second syllable.

1973 GSMNP-117:27 They's a big bunch of us got permits, and we'd go up there ever'day after dinner.

pernext *preposition* Next to, in front of.

1992 Montgomery *Coll* (known to Cardwell, Oliver, Weaver). **1992** Montgomery *File* (known to 30-year-old woman, Gatlinburg TN).

[perhaps influenced by *fornent*]

persackly, persactly See **presactly.**

persimmon *noun* Variant form *simmon*.

1932 (in **1935** Edwards *NC Novels* 80) *simmon*. **1963** Edwards *Gravel* 18 You can smell a hen abiling furder'n a possum can smell ripe 'simmons, and I bet my hat on it. **1976** Garber *Mountain-ese* 82 Pa picked up a bushel uv simmons to make simmon brandy. **1983** *Dark Corner OHP-5A* They'd go out and pick little old huckleberries, and, and they picked 'simmons and make 'simmon pie and take them up there and sell them.

persimmon beer *noun* A homemade beverage made from fermented persimmons.

1955 Parris *Roaming Mts* 25 Somebody then mentioned persimmon beer and persimmon pudding and persimmon cakes. **1972** Alderman *Big Bald* 67 An age old custom has been the fall barrel of "Simmon Beer." One of the empty molasses barrels had been washed and cleaned in readiness for the annual ritual. Canes from the creek bank or oak strips have been stored to fill the bottom about half foot deep. Broom sage is cut, cleaned and spread over the strips. At least a good large bushel of best Persimmons has been picked, trashed and poured over the straw. To this is added a measure of sweet potatoes. Brewers in some sections add corn meal; others put in locust pods. Barrel is filled with water and the lid clamped on. Near the end of the third week the Master of the house draws a sample from the wood spigot placed in the bottom bung hole. It is his privilege to proclaim when the beverage has reached that just right taste. **1974** Dwyer and Dwyer *Mt Cookin'* 5 When the mountain family cow went dry, the neighbor usually provided milk until the cow "freshened" or, if there were no neighbors nearby (like about 5 miles), the mountain wife made up batches of various kinds of beers for her family to drink during the milkless period. Persimmon beer, made from apple cores, peelings, and persimmons was a real favorite: others were spruce beer, spice beer, and tomato beer.

persimmon butter *noun* A thick, spicy spread for bread made from persimmons. See also **peach butter**, **pumpkin butter**, **sweet potato butter**.

[1980 *Smokies Heritage* 101 *butters* = not simply butter churned from milk, but the spiced, sweet fruit spread made from apples, peaches, pumpkins, and persimmons during jelly-making season and autumn (for the last two).]

persimmon cake *noun* A homemade cake made from persimmons.

1955 Parris *Roaming Mts* 25 Somebody then mentioned persimmon beer and persimmon pudding and persimmon cakes.

persimmon pudding *noun* A homemade dessert made from persimmons.

1955 Parris *Roaming Mts* 25 Somebody then mentioned persimmon beer and persimmon pudding and persimmon cakes.

persuade *verb* To plead with, urge.

1931 Hannum *Thursday April* 83 Thursday April persuaded Joe to buy him a fiddle. Joe fussed and fumed at such fritter-mindedness and said it was a sight of nonsense, but in the end he traded a man from Turkey Cove a lean pig for a fair instrument.

[DARE *persuade* v especially South Midland]

pert near See **pretty near(ly)**.

pert nigh See **pretty nigh**.

pert up See **pearten**.

perty See **pretty**.

peruse (also *peruse about, peruse around, pruse*) *verb, verb phrase* To wander about, especially to snoop or prowl.

1884 Smith *Arp Scrap Book* 41 [In the piney woods] no unfriendly soldier was perusing around and asking for papers. **1940** Haun *Hawk's Done* 102 [How are you all getting along?] We are perusing about. **1984** Six *Hill 'n Holler* 10 *prusin* = to snoop: "It's comin up Christmas, don't you youngins be prusin none in the press." **1997** Montgomery *Coll* (known to Bush, Cardwell).

[SND *peruse* v "prowl around, stroll about"]

peruse about, peruse around See **peruse**.

Peruvian cherry (also *Peruvian tree*) *noun* An American cherry tree, the pin cherry (*Prunus mexicana*). Same as **fire cherry**.

1883 Zeigler and Grosscup *Heart of Alleghanies* 58 The most ornamental of the trees of the fir forests is the Peruvian, with its smooth, slender trunk, and great branches of brilliant red berries. **1913** Kephart *Our Sthn High* 54 Beech, birch, buckeye, and chestnut persist to 5,000 feet. Then . . . there begins a subarctic zone of black spruce, balsam, striped maple, aspen and the "Peruvian" or red cherry. **1953** Hall *Coll* (Bryson City NC) When I got down about fifty, seventy-five yards, Bob had clum a little Peruvian tree with a little bear. . . . That's the little tree that has the berry on it. Peruvian tree that Boone went up with the bear. That's a small tree that has a red berry on it. The bears like to eat them. **1974–75** McCracken *Logging* 23:26 Well, the first thing that begun to come back was that Peruvian cherry.

[DARE *Peruvian* n (probably from its medicinal use of its bark as a substitute for the *Peruvian bark* (Cinchona) bark, the source of quinine)]

Peruvian tree See **Peruvian cherry**.

perzackly See **presactly**.

pestle-tail (also *pencil tail*) *noun* A mule (with reference to its relatively hairless tail).

1918 Steadman *NC Word List* 19 *pestle tail* = mule. **1952** Wilson *Folk Speech NC* 575 *pestle tail* = a mule; perhaps because the tail of the mule is trimmed to the shape of a wooden pestle, or small maul. **1982** Powers and Hannah *Cataloochee* 383 A mule was also called a "pencil tail."

[DARE *pestle-tail* n especially NC]

pet *noun* A boil, mole, wart, pimple, or other blemish of the skin.

c1960 Wilson *Coll* = a humorous reference to a sore or boil. **1976** Dwyer *Southern Sayin's* 6 = boil, sore, wart. "I'm carryin' a pet on my nose." **1997** Montgomery *Coll* = any skin blemish that is unsightly or a nuisance (Adams), = any skin blemish (Bush).

[DARE *pet* n 1 chiefly South, South Midland]

Pete See **old Pete**.

pete frog See **peeper**.

pewee *noun* A phoebe bird (*Sayornis* spp).

1961 Miller *Pigeon's Roost* (Sept 28) We always call the chimney swift birds the chimney sweepers. The towhees, jorees; phoebee, pewees. **1986** Still *Wolfpen Poems* 71 I will long recall / . . . The fields and draws and coves where quails and peewees call. **1997** Miller *Brier Poems* 157 When he heard good bluegrass, or a peewee's call, he didn't want to pass from illusion's forest.

pewter('s) button See **not worth a pewter('s) button**.

pharaoh (also *ferro*) *noun* A locust or its distinctive cry (presumably based on reference to the plague of locusts visited on Egypt after the Pharaoh refused to free the Israelites; see Exodus 10:12–15). Also called **Bible bug**.

1913 Kephart *Our Sthn High* 295 In some places . . . the locust insect is known as a ferro (Pharaoh?). **1941** Still *Troublesome Creek* 61 It was the [summer] seventeen year locusts cried "Pharaoh" upon the hills, and branches of oak and hickory perished where their waxy pins of eggs were laid. [**1944** Combs *Word-List Sthn High*

19 = the locust.] **1975** Jackson *Unusual Words* 155 The most unusual word of all is *Pharaohs* for locusts. The explanation is that if one listens very carefully he will hear the locust say, "Pharaoh, Pharaoh, let my people go, let my people go." The term *Pharaohs* is simply a shortening of the longer, more precise term *Pharaoh's plagues*. **1994** Montgomery *Coll* (known to Cardwell).

[DARE *pharaoh* n chiefly southern Appalachians]

pheasant *noun* The ruffed grouse (*Bonasa umbrellus*). Same as **mountain grouse.**

1913 Morley *Carolina Mts* 293 The ruffed grouse, "pheasant," the people call it, is native to these woods and an encounter with one is always a surprise, and nearly always pleasant, though you once got a shock from a grouse that must pretty nearly have balanced the bird's own distress of mind. **1982** Powers and Hannah *Cataloochee* 475 Grouse, known locally as pheasant, are also uncommonly good to eat. **1997** Andrews *Mountain Vittles* 89 My pa loved to hunt what the old timers called pheasant. They are really the ruffed grouse and they are good stewed down with flour dumplings. **1997** Montgomery *Coll* (known to Ledford), = also called *mountain pheasant* (Cardwell).

[DARE *pheasant* n 1a chiefly Midland, especially PA, southern Appalachians]

phlegm *noun* Variant forms *flame, fleem, phleem.*

1942 Hall *Phonetics Smoky Mts* 21 Phlegm [flim] (usually; but in one area [flem] was said to be more common). **1969** Doran *Folklore White Co* 113 *phleem.* **1983** *Dark Corner OHP-24A* Everyone had that bad whooping cough hit on us at one time, and that was all we could get to cut that flame out of our throats. **2000** Miller *Looneyville* 47 = common corruption for phlegm, and probably derived from Middle English and Old French fleume: "Excuse me. I have fleem in my throat."

[DARE *phlegm* n especially South, South Midland]

phosphate gland *noun* See citation.

2000 Lowry *Folk Medical Term* = prostate gland.

phthisic *noun*

A Variant forms *tissic* [see **2000** in **B**], *tizik* [see **1956** in **B**], *tizzick* [see **1835** in **B**], *tizzy* [see **2006** in **B**].

B (often *the tizik/tizzick*) Difficulty of breath, caused by a range of pulmonary conditions from tuberculosis to a bad cold.

1835 Crockett *Account* 15 We all got seated, and moved slowly off; the engine wheezing as if she had the tizzick. **1937** Hall *Coll* (Cosby TN) To cure the croup and the phthisic, straighten a sourwood stick behind the back and head, cut it off even with the top of the head, and hide it where it'll never be found. **1939** Hall *Coll* (Dellwood NC) = it's more like asthma. You can't hardly get your breath. **1956** Hall *Coll* (Newport TN) She'd go get a sourwood switch she'd call it, and she would measure her children to cure the croup and the tizik. **2000** Lowry *Folk Medical Term*, *tissic* = a bad cold. **2005** Williams *Gratitude* 532 *tissic, tizik* = a catch-all name for various disorders, as I heard it given as a diagnosis of people's sickness from fussy babies to grandpa's stomach ache. **2006** Cavender *Medical Term* 1022 Health-care providers in contemporary Appalachia may still encounter antiquated medical terminology such as *phthisic* or *tizzy* "asthma."

[< Middle English *tisike*, ultimately < Greek; Web3 *phthisic* 2 obsolete]

physicker *noun* A physician.

1858 (in **1974** Harris *High Times* 99) Doctor Blank shell be my phisicker es long es he lives.

pianer, pianner See **piano.**

piano *noun* Variant forms *pianer, pianner.*

1895 Edson and Fairchild *TN Mts* 375 *pianer.* **1923** Greer-Petrie *Angeline Doin' Society* 25 A shaggy-ha'red feller play'd on a fiddle, while Betty play'd that pianner. **1942** Hall *Phonetics Smoky Mts* 55–56 *pianer* [pi'ænɚ], *py-aner* [paɪ'ænɚ].

piano rose See **peony.**

piazza (also *piazzer*) *noun* A wide front porch. [Editor's note: This term is more widely used in the Deep South.]

1879 Jones *Backwoods Carolina* 751 At the front of the house was a long porch—or "peazzer," as it was called—with a shelter and a railing. A continuation of its floor led to the kitchen, a few yards distant, but there was no protection against rain or snow. **1963** Watkins and Watkins *Yesterday* 38 He built a front piazzer where he could rest in the summer and pile his cotton in the early fall and his firewood in the winter. **1986** Pederson et al. *LAGS* = attested by 5/35 (14.3%) from N GA; 5/50 of all LAGS interviewees (10%) attesting term were from Appalachia.

[DARE *piazza* n chiefly Northeast, South Atlantic]

pick

A *verb*

1 To play or pluck (a guitar, banjo, etc.); to stroke a stringed instrument.

1861 *Huntley CW Letters* (Dec 3) thare is a Littell of a most every thing Carried on hear But more of Evil than any thing Eles We have Fidling Dancing Picking the Banjo Cursing plenty preaching praying Singing and other things that is as mean as any. **1939** Hall *Coll* (Proctor NC) Ike's girl Ethel picks and sings very well. **1942** Hall *Coll* (Waynesville NC) How long have you picked? **1959** Hall *Coll* (Hartford TN) Jim was settin' in the door pickin' a old banjer, with a jug of liquor settin' between his legs. He didn't stop pickin' [when the doctor came]. **1973** *GSMNP-5*:6 I could pick all night and never pick the same tune. *Ibid.* 7 They could pick and play the fiddle, and we would go and just have a time, running old country round up. That is the way we done. **1974** Roberts *Sang Branch* 28 They danced a lot, and they would get me to pick. I played for sets from the time I was twelve year old. If I didn't get to run many with 'em, I got a big kick outten playing the banjer for 'em. **1977** Nevell *Time to Dance* 167 "You should have seen this boy play," she said. "He would pick an hour and a half at a time for a square dance." **1989** *Matewan OHP-7* The younger sides of them could pick banjos and fiddles. *Ibid.* 102 At the bean stringings . . . somebody picked a banjo and they'd always be somebody that would dance.

[cf EDD Scot "to give a light stroke with any pointed instrument"]

2 To gather (wood, eggs, etc.).

1983 McDermitt *Boy Named Jack* 4 I helped to pick a lot of wood. **1997** Montgomery *Coll* = gather eggs (Adams, Bush, Ledford).

3 To pluck the feathers from (a goose or other fowl).

1841 *McLean Diary* 77 hot Drye wether picked Thare Gees. **c1950** Adams *Grandpap* 128 While Will killed an' picked the goose, Tom an' Jack got out an' rustled up some wood an' got a fire to goin'. **1958** Miller *Pigeon's Roost* (June 5) She used the gourd to put feathers in when she was picking ducks and geese. **1976** Bullard *Crafts TN Mts* 51 The women had to do all the cooking, washing, ironing, make the soap, raise and pick the geese (pick weekly, that is, for the down), set the hens and raise the chickens, milk the cows and churn the cream. **1977** Shackelford et al. *Our Appalachia* 128 I've picked a many of the geese [for feather pillows]. **1986** Helton *Around Home* 380 = pluck (a chicken). **1997** Nelson *Country Folklore* 61 Then we would try again and again until we would catch another duck. We proceeded to finish catching and plucking the feathers until every one had been "picked" as grandma would say.

4 (also *pick at, pick on*) To tease, nag (at). See also **peck**[2].

1956 Still *Burning of Waters* 58 He came in too weary to pick at us and he rarely saw the baby awake. **1957** Broaddus *Vocab Estill Co KY* 56 *pick at* = to nag. **1979** *Big South Fork OHP-11* They'd been a-picking me, all three of them had. **1998** *Dante OHP-69* He used to pick at Joyce Wolfe a lot. **2005** Williams *Gratitude* 513 *pick at, pick on* = to cruelly tease. **2016** Heinmiller *Coll* He's always picking at his little brother.

[DARE (at *pick* v 2a) chiefly South, South Midland]

5 (also *pick grass*) To graze. See also **picking**.

1971 *Granny Women* 252 You'll turn her [= a cow] out of her stall and she goes on a'pickin'. **1978** *Horsetrading* 52 [The horses] were pickin' in and around the strawberries. **1982** Slone *How We Talked* 28 *picking grass* = animals grazing, eating weeds and grass. **1983** McDermitt *Boy Named Jack* 18 [There] was a ranch on it, a horse ranch, sheep, cattle, an they was out there pickin. **2010** Owenby *Trula Ownby* 16 He went out and fed [the mule] a good supper and tied it out to pick.

B *noun* in phrase *have a pick on* = to feel ill will toward, hold a grudge against.

1930s (in **1944** Wentworth *ADD* 452) (eWV) *have a pick on someone* = pick on someone: "She's got a pick on me."

pickalilly (also *pickylilly*) *noun* See 1996 citation.

1925 Dargan *Highland Annals* 44 You don't eat pickle either—tomato-pickle, cabbage-pickle, beet-pickle, pickylilly, onion-pickle, pickle everything. **1996** Montgomery *Coll* (known to Cardwell, Norris), = a sweet relish with several vegetables in it, such as peppers, corn, and cucumbers (Jones), = a spicy relish (Oliver).

pickaroon *noun* A pike for handling lumber.

1966 Frome *Strangers* 169 Crews of "lumber herders," wearing calked shoes and armed with pickaroons and peaveys, broke log jams and sometimes rode downhill balancing themselves with a long pole while ducking low branches. **1967** Parris *Mt Born* 132 = used in handling lumber, poles, posts, and timber, is a recurved pike (a long pole having a metal point), or a pike and hook fitted to a handle from 36 to 38 inches long.

pick at See **pick A4**.

pick down *verb phrase* To become worse.

c1961 Cooper *Nairy a Word*: *picking down* = becoming worse.

picket *noun* A stake of split wood sharpened to a tip, driven upright into the ground, and set side by side with others to enclose a garden or other area, secured by horizontal rails or wire; hence *picket fence, picketing fence* (usually = **paling fence**, but see 1995 citation). For other types of fence, see also **brush fence**, **rail fence**, **worm fence**.

1966 Dakin *Vocab Ohio River Valley* 97 An interesting development among some older informants in the eastern Kentucky *palings, paling fence* area is the adoption of the newer name *picket fence* as *picketing fence*. **1967** *DARE Survey* (Maryville TN) *picket fence* = wooden fence built around a garden or near a house. **1967** Hall *Coll* (Townsend TN) I had a corn patch there, and that bear got to breakin' the pickets and comin' in there. **1978** Dykeman and Stokely *Highland Homeland* 22 The Allisons of Cataloochee had a wooden picket fence around their garden, while Mary Birchfield of Cades Cove had an unusual picket fence with wire wound around rather crude pickets. **1995** *Smokies Guide* (Summer) 13 Paling fences are similar, if not identical, to picket fences. According to one historian, the difference lies in the characteristic vertical stakes with the pointed tops. On paling fences, the stakes (or pales) were hand split from a block of wood whereas pickets on picket fences are cut with a saw. Paling fences can be traced to England and were used by the Cherokee in Tennessee as early as 1779. One version, where the pales are woven in and out of the horizontal supports, can be built without nails. The most common purpose for a paling fence in the Smokies was to keep chickens out of the yard or garden. The pointed pales discouraged the birds from fluttering to the top of the fence where they could perch and then hop down to the inside. A fine example of a paling fence can be seen around the log house at the Oconaluftee Mountain Farm Museum [in NC].

picket fence, **picketting fence** See **picket**.

pick grass See **pick A5**.

picking *noun* See citation. See also **pick A4**.

2007 McMillon *Notes* = edible grass and plants that animals eat from the pasture and woods.

picking eggs *noun* See citation. Same as **egg fighting**.

1964 Smith et al. *Germans of Valley* 113 A popular Easter game among the young people was called "picking" eggs or egg "fighting." A person selected what he considered to be his strongest egg and challenged someone else to "pick" against him. The eggs were tapped against each other until one of the shells cracked, then the owner of the other egg claimed the cracked one as prize.

pickle beans (also *pickled beans*) *noun* Beans of any variety that are salted, allowed to sour, and then canned or stored in barrels like sauerkraut. During fermentation, they create their own juice.

1960 Mason *Memoir* 15 The barrels were utilized as containers for the storage of such mountain commodities as saur kraut, pickled beans, bleached apples, and pumpkin butter. **1973** GSMNP-80:15 We would put a cloth over the kraut now and pickled beans, and we'd put this big plank and then we'd hunt and get us a big heavy rock, wash hit off right clean and put it on the plank and that would mash it down in below kraut, and that's how we would have it, you know, the kraut and pickled beans. **1986** Tyson *Reflections* 33 When we kids were growing up there wasn't much that we could do to pass the time. The only entertainment we had was when some of the neighbors would have a bean stringing. They would pick their greenbeans when they were ready to can and to put up for pickle beans. **2002** Oliver *Cooking and Living* 80 Pickled beans were made by washing & snapping the green beans; they were then blanched in hot water which was heated in a big black pot outdoors. They were then laid out on a table to drain. After that they were put in the barrel & salted, then weighted down till another picking. The same process was repeated until the barrel was full. The beans would then be weighted down, a cloth laid over the top, & the barrel of beans to cure or pickle for a few weeks before they were ready to use.

picklement *noun* A difficult or awkward situation.

1937 Still *Brother to Methusalem* 51 That brought-on woman has got us into a mess of trouble. A pure picklement.

pick on See **pick A4**.

pick sack *noun* See citation.

1961 Stubbs *Mountain-Wise* 11 Other double words are "poker-stick" for poker; "pick-sack" for use in picking apples; "churn-jar" for churn.

pick up *verb phrase* To gain weight.

1942 (in **1987** Perdue *Outwitting Devil* 15) An' he begin to pick right up fer he eat that way ever' day. **c1959** Weals *Hillbilly Dict* 6 I believe you've picked up some since I seed ye last. **1976** Thompson *Touching Home* 15 = to gain weight: "You've picked up a little bit, haven't you?" **1986** Helton *Around Home* 379 = gain in weight.

pickylilly See **pickalilly**.

picter, **pictur** See **picture**.

picture *noun* Variant forms *picter*, *pictur*, *pikter* (all [ˈpɪktɚ]), *pitcher*.

1863 *Revis CW Letters* (July 13) Sarepta is well and Jack is as prety as a picter. **1867** Harris *Sut Lovingood* 196 Thar he stood, the' mos' orful picter ove onregenerated rash, mortal man ever seed. **1873** Smith *Arp Peace Papers* 99 They are exhibitin on a pole the awful pikter of a Bear named *Habeas corpus*. **1913** Kephart *Our Sthn High* 120 The women folks's seed his pictur. **1938** Bowman *High Horizons* 43–44 Hit war showed me like a "pitcher" that the babe wuz asleep up in under a log. **1942** Hall *Phonetics Smoky Mts* 79. **1994** Montgomery *Coll* (known to Cardwell).

pictureman *noun* A professional photographer.

1997 Watkins *Photographers* 21 Out of relative obscurity emerged not only professional photographers such as Doris Ulmann and Bayard Wootten but also rudimentarily trained, indigenous "picturemen," such as Southwest Virginia's T. R. Phelps. *Ibid.* 22 The discovery of such images naturally led to a search for the photographers, the so-called "picturemen," who made them.

piddling

A *adjective* Trifling, trivial, paltry. See also **pindling 2**.

1998 Montgomery *Coll* (known to Adams, Bush, Jones, Ledford, Oliver, Weaver); I worked the whole summer but made only a piddling amount of money (Cardwell).

[< *piddle* "to deal or work in trifling or petty ways"; cf EDD *piddle* v[1] 1 "to perform work in a trifling, careless, or unskilful way"; cf DARE *piddle* v 1 "to dawdle, putter; to concern oneself with trifles" widespread, but less frequent North, infrequent Northeast]

B *noun* A small amount.

1997 Montgomery *Coll* (known to Bush, Cardwell, Norris, Oliver, Weaver); How can a body live on such piddlin's? (Brown).

piece *noun*

1 A distance, usually a short or indeterminate one (generally cannot be pluralized); hence *little piece* = a relatively short distance; *far piece* = a relatively great distance. See also **ways**.

c1841 Shane (in **1998** Perkins *Border Life* 199) The indians took him off a piece, but found he could not travel. **1862** *Councill CW Letters* (Feb 4) the water is bad an we have to tote it a good pese a bout a half mile. **1863** *Chapman CW Letters* (Aug 12) it is not as far as some have been but i call it a good piece off. **1910** Cooke *Power and Glory* 123 I wish't you'd walk a piece up the Gap road with me. **1934** Parke *Sthn Highlander* 8 The roadster groaned into motion as we wondered how many miles we could figure "a right smart piece" to be. A few miles and a few thousand jolts further a lone mountain man dressed in worn overalls and without shoes answered our inquiry by saying, "Around yon bend is the ho-ootel." **1939** Hall *Coll* (Hazel Creek NC) I run [a raccoon] a little piece and catched it. *Ibid.* (Smokemont NC) The dogs struck, went up the creek a little piece, and treed up a little hempine. **1973** GSMNP-76:3 He'd have went up the road a piece to get on the main road that went to Townsend. **1983** *Dark Corner OHP-3A* I used to live up there, about a little piece back up there. **1998** *Dante OHP-45* I just went out the road here just a little piece from here and cut across to Austin Gap. **2003** Onchuck *Mud Pie Memories* 13 We knew the distance of "right near" and "a right far piece" [but] explaining it was another thing. **2007** Homan *Turkey Tracks* 86, 87 Based upon the folks I talked to—an admittedly small and much older than average sample—I compiled five alternative measures of Appalachian distance. The smallest component was tater chunk, as in "you're real close, it's just another tater chunk down the road." Following tater chunk in progression were yonder, hoot and a holler, a piece, and a fer piece. . . . A piece and a fer piece expand and contract with the situation; they have fluid parameters, low and high ranges, an easy piece or a good piece. A walked piece is shorter than a driven one.

[OED3 *piece* n 10c "a distance, esp. a short one" now regional (chiefly N. Amer); EDD *piece* sb 6 Scot, nEngl; SND *piece* n[1] 3 "an indefinite distance"]

2 An indefinite, but usually short period of time.

1931 Hannum *Thursday April* 101 She studied about it for a good little piece. **1997** Montgomery *Coll* (known to Bush, Cardwell, Oliver, Weaver).

[EDD *piece* 7 nEngl]

3 A portion, section; a fragment or specimen. See also **piece-way**.

1863 *Tesh CW Letters* (June 15) now our Pickets are on the Banks of the Rhappohannock and we are a laying back in a Piece of wood[s] about a half a mile From the Breast work. **c1910** Frost *Success* 9 I am going to do the best piece of plowing that was ever done on the farm. I am going to make this field so smooth that we can cut the grain with a reaper. **1968** *DARE Survey* (Brasstown NC) *piece of a load* = part of a load; (Brasstown NC) *piece of an armful* = a partial load of wood. **1972** Hall *Sayings* 107 One day I asked Pettibone Gunter if he was sheriff of Cosby. He replied, "a piece of one," perhaps suggesting by this that he was the constable, not the sheriff. **c1975** Lunsford *It Used to Be* 12 I was spending the night with a fellow one time and he said, "I've got a very fine piece of corn right up there," pointing right up at an angle greater than forty-five degrees. **2014** *Blind Pig* (Aug 23) Piece was used as a noun—a small amount—I'll have just a piece of collards and biscuit.

[DARE *piece* n 2 "poor specimen" chiefly South, South Midland]

4 (also *piece meal*) A light meal.

1949 Kurath *Word Geog East US* 72 Scattered instances of *piece meal* . . . have been recorded in the Blue Ridge [in VA, NC] and on the Kanawha [in WV]. **c1960** Wilson *Coll* = a light lunch.

[DARE *piece* n 8 chiefly North Midland, West]

piece meal See **piece 4**.

piece of ways See **piece-way**.

piece-way (also *piece of ways*) *adverb* Part of the way.

1940 Still *River of Earth* 55 This chap can go piece-way home with me and fotch it back.

pieded *adjective*

1 (also *piedy*) Of the hide of an animal: mottled, with spots or blotches of different colors, also used in the place-name *Piedy Holler* on Rocky Top (TN), perhaps so named because of varicolored wildflowers there.

1895 Edson and Fairchild *TN Mts* 373 A sort of *piedy* cow. **1913** Kephart *Our Sthn High* 295 A spotted animal is said to be pieded (pied). **1924** Raine *Saddlebags* 98 Caliban's pied ninny, as also Milton's "meadows trip with daisies pied," come to mind when we hear a boy praise his pieded (or piedy) cow. **1940** Hall *Coll* (Pigeon River NC) *piedy* (said of a fish). **1952** Wilson *Folk Speech NC* 576 *pieded, piedy* = spotted, streaked, but not in a well-defined manner. "That's a right pretty *pieded* calf." (Swain Co NC). **1982** Hurst *Appal Words* 99 "Pied" (often pronounced as pieded) described certain creatures with spots, particularly cows, goats, and snakes.

2 (also *piedidy, piedied*) Of a person's skin: splotched or discolored, especially from exposure to a fire; hence noun *pieded legs*. See also **country legs, fire-blossomed**.

1867 Harris *Sut Lovingood* 252 Wirt wer bilin hot; nobody tu gainsay him, [the court testimony] hed made him piedied all over; he wer plum pizen. **1963** Watkins and Watkins *Yesterday* 39 The hot fire baked the blood in the front of the girls' legs, and they looked blood-shotten or piedidy. My older sisters wore thick cotton stockings and kept their dresses pulled down low for protection from the fire, but every woman had piedidy legs until the middle of summer. **1990** Cavender *Folk Medical Lex* 28 *pieded legs* = skin or wound having a variegated, blotchy appearance. **1994–97** Montgomery *Coll*: *pieded legs* = coloration on the legs coming from sitting close to the fire (Cardwell); Your legs are pieded from standing too close to the far (Norris). **2006** Cavender *Medical Term* 1022 The term *pieded* is used to describe variegated skin color, as in "My legs are pieded, and they hurt something awful."

[Web3 *pieded* adj dialect, *piedy* chiefly Midland]

pieded legs, piedidy, piedied See **pieded 2**.

piedy See **pieded 1**.

pieplant *noun* The rhubarb plant (*Rheum rhabarbarum*).

1962 Dykeman *Tall Woman* 181 This was the first year she had planted the roots Robert had brought her from town that she had had enough rhubarb, or pieplant, to make a decent dish. **1966–67** *DARE Survey* (Cherokee NC, Gatlinburg TN, Maryville TN) = rhubarb. **1977** Hamilton *Mt Memories* 51 There were some gooseberry bushes by the fence and a few clumps of pie plant (rhubarb). It was so good with hot buttered biscuits.

pie safe *noun* A ventilated, free-standing cabinet, usually in the kitchen, in which fresh-baked pie is kept. See also **bread safe, kitchen safe, safe B**.

1988 Kosier *Maggie* 109 Against the wall stood a wooden "pie-safe" with perforated, tin panels. **1990** Wigginton *Foxfire Christmas* 106 Now we didn't have what they called a pie safe, but most everybody did. My aunt had one. It had nailhead designs on a metal door. Mother just put her pies in the cupboard. **2008** Cobb *Vacation Time* 21 On a wall beside the stove hung her cooking utensils. On another wall was the pie safe, which was used for cooling pies, cakes and cookies. She had jellies and honey in the safe also. (A pie safe was a ventilated cupboard with tin doors that were perforated to let the air pass through.)

pie supper *noun* Formerly, a community event to raise money for a school, church, or other worthy cause, involving the auctioning of pies one at a time. Each successful bidder enjoys the privilege of eating the pie with the girl or woman who baked it. See also **box supper**, **poke supper**.

1974 Moore *Dr. Mac* 23 Pie and box suppers with cakewalks were fun. The girls and the women worked hard at the cooking and trying to make their box the prettiest one there. Often the bidding was fast and furious, the fellows wanting to be sure they got their best girl's box or the girls wanting their best beaux to have the pie or box. **1982** Slone *How We Talked* 79 = held when they needed to raise money for something extra for the school or Christmas presents for the students. **1983** Broaddus *Estill Co KY Word List* 50 = a party to which the ladies bring pies they have baked. The men bid on the individual pies, and the highest bidder gets to eat the pie with the lady, sometimes at a secluded spot. **1984** *Sevier Settler* 1:16 The pie supper was almost a deeply religious experience in Boogertown. All the young ladies would bake pies for this social gathering on Saturday night and hope that their best young man would make the highest bid so they could be together and eat her pie. **1994** Parton *Dolly* 30 I remember once going to a pie supper. That was where each girl baked a pie (my mother baked mine) and brought it to a social, where it would be auctioned off to the boy who bid the most for it. The boy who bought your pie had the right to sit with you while the two of you shared it. It was a sweet old country custom, and I guess it was a way of getting around shyness. It was a lot easier for a boy to act like he really wanted a pie than it was for him to admit he was interested in the girl who came with it.

pig *noun* The little brown jug plant (*Hexastylis arifolia*), whose clustered flowers resemble a litter of piglets waiting to feed.

1964 Campbell *Great Smoky Wildflowers* 36 Often hidden by the leaves, the interesting jugs occur at ground level. . . . Other names include *pigs*, *wild ginger*, and *heart-leaf*. **1979** *Smokies Heritage* 60 The jugs (known as a calyx) grow to roughly to an inch in length, and, clustered together, they look like piglets with open mouths waiting for supper. Little Brown Jugs were thus quite often called "pigs" by the local people.

[DARE *pig* n[1] B15 especially Southern Appalachians]

pig-ee (also *piggoop*, *piggy*, *pig-oh*, *pig-oo*, *pigooee*, *pigooey*, *pig-oo-(w)e*, *pig-oo(w)ie*, *pi-go-(w)ie*, *pi-gwoo-(w)ie*, *piuggy*) *interjection* Come! (used as a call to pigs at feeding time; the call is often repeated, with or without variation). See also **gooee**, **goop**, **sooey**.

1934–47 *LAMSAS Appal* (Madison Co NC, Swain Co NC) *pigooey*. **1949** Kurath *Word Geog East US* 44 The Carolinas have their own range of hog calls: *goop!*, *woop!*, and *piggoop!* **1963** Arnow *Flowering* 129 The calling of the chickens, like plowing with a team, demanded words—sounds only they would now be to most of us—and the words varied from neighborhood to neighborhood. We, for example, said sooee-sooee to drive the hogs away and called with a loud and ringing pigooee-pig-pig-pig, but I knew a family who called with a sooee, and no two families called their dogs in the same way, though most, even foxhounds, would come to the sound of the dinner conch shell. **1963** Medford *Mt People* 75 The calls "Pig-ee!—pig-oh!" and "Co'!" were made to resound in the valley. **1966** Dakin *Vocab Ohio River Valley* 282 Some residents of the Mountain region also use the call which occurs most frequently as *pig-oo-(w)e!* (also *pi-goo(w)ie!*, pi-gwoo-(w)ie!, pi-go-(w)ie!, pi-goo!, pig-oo!). This call, which unquestionably was brought into Kentucky from the southeast and carried northwest into Indiana and Illinois, would seem to be derived from the pig-goop! of the Carolinas although this eastern form is not used in the Ohio Valley. **1966–67** *DARE Survey* (Spruce Pine NC) *piggy piggy piggy* = call to get pigs in to feed; (Gatlinburg TN, Maryville TN) *pig-oh, pig-oh* = call to get pigs in to feed (2nd syllable minor 3rd higher than first). **1978** Head *Mt Moments* My grandfather Morgan called his animals this way: "Sook cow" for his milker; "chick, chick, chickie" for poultry, and "piuggy" for hogs. **1983** *Dark Corner OHP-24A* I'd call them "pig, piggy, piggy." **1996** Johnson *Lexical Change* 138 *pi-goo(p)* = statistically more common in the mountains of South Carolina and Georgia than in the Piedmont and Coastal Plain c1990.

pigeonberry *noun* Same as **poke**[2].

1981 *Smokies Heritage* 26:33 Pokeweed bears another, more plaintive, name, "pigeonberry." Even now, bird droppings formed from a pokeberry diet are recognizable from their rather lovely purple magenta color, rivaled only by fire cherry. **1997** Montgomery *Coll* (known to Cardwell).

pigeon-bird *noun* A pigeon. See also **-bird**.

1940 Still *River of Earth* 117 Pigeon-birds kept a-flying round in my head, thundering their wings. I tuck the big eye and never slept a wink that night.

pigeon('s) wing *noun* A step in traditional mountain buck dancing (see **buckdance**) in which the arms are held at one's side and one jumps and strikes the heels or legs together (especially in phrases *cut the pigeon wing*, *do the pigeon wing*).

1843 (in **1974** Harris *High Times* 30) The mirth becomes uproarious, the men jump high, "cut the pigeon wing," and crack their heels together. **1892** Doak *Wagonauts Abroad* 63 Our guide says you can dance. You don't look old, but I wouldn't expect you to cut the pigeon wing. **1903** Fox *Little Shepherd* 50 Then was there a dance indeed . . . neat shuffling forward and back, with every note of the music beat; floor-thumping "cuttings of the pigeon's wing," and jolly jigs, two by two, and a great "swinging of corners," and "caging the bird," and "fust lady to the right cheat an' swing." **1927** Woofter *Dialect from WV* 352 *cut the pigeon's wing* = to execute a series of intricate dance steps. "He cut the pigeon's wing for us several times last night." **1972** Cooper *NC Mt Folklore* 43 A young lady sang *Black Jack Davis* and *Barbara Allen*, a young man played the banjo which he had brought along, while an elderly man cut the pigeon wing. **1994–97** Montgomery *Coll*: *cut the pigeon wing* (known to Brown, Cardwell, Norris, Oliver); *do the pigeon wing* (known to Jones).

pig-eye rifle *noun* Same as **hog rifle**.

1989 Landry *Smoky Mt Interviews* 181 He was hunting with an old hog rifle. Some people called it a pig-eye rifle.

piggan, piggen See **piggin.**

piggin (also *piggan, piggen*) *noun* A bucket-shaped, wooden vessel with one stave extended upward; a hole is cut into this stave so that it can serve as a handle. See 1935 citation.

1791 (in **1956** Eliason *Tarheel Talk* 288) (Davie Co NC) 1 pail & 1 piggan. **1843** (in **1974** Harris *High Times* 28) The judges decided it a draw race, and that each party should keep his corn—as "crops is good, and no prospect of scarcity"—and treat: a quart of the good, just then being doubled by old Jo Cristy, to each of the judges, and a piggen full to the crowd. **1895** Edson and Fairchild *TN Mts* 373 = a wooden tub with a stave projecting above the rest. "The piggin is full of water." **1927** Mason *Lure of Smokies* 124 The "piggin," as old as Chaucer himself, was an odd pail, of red cedar usually, with the handle on one side made of an extended stave with a "hand holt" cut in it. **1935** Sheppard *Cabins in Laurel* 262 Uncle Milt is an expert at making wooden keelers, piggins, and buckets, the distinction being that a keeler is a wooden measure of peck size or less without a handle; a piggin has a straight handle on one side only, so that as it balances on the hip, the handle lies in the angle of the elbow; and the bucket has a complete bail. A pail is a measure over peck size with a handle like a bucket. **1937** Hall *Coll* (Emerts Cove TN) Piggins [were] wooden vessels used in the old days, cedar buckets. Coopers [made] the vessels. Piggins were a half-gallon and one gallon, the outside white and the inside red. **1957** Combs *Lg Sthn High: Word List* 74 = a pail or bucket without a bail. A stave on each side extends five or six inches higher than the others, which two staves are shaped for handles. Usually made of cedar, with hickory bands. The large piggin is used as a water bucket, the small one (sometimes without handles) for milk, butter, etc. **1964** Greve *Story of Gatlinburg* 49 A table and a corner cupboard to hold the dishes completed the list of the main furnishings, but they were clever at contriving many other small necessities . . . the "piggin," for milking, a bucket or half-barrel with one stave higher than the rest with a hole cut in the upper end for a handle. **1986** Pederson et al. *LAGS* = attested by 3/60 interviewees (5%) from E TN; 3/4 of all LAGS interviewees (75%) attesting term were from Appalachia.

[origin uncertain; EDD *piggin* sb 1 in general dialect; SND *piggin* n; CUD *piggin* n; Web3 *piggin* n chiefly dialect; DARE *piggin* n 1 chiefly New England, South, South Midland]

piggoop, piggy See **pig-ee.**

pig irons *noun* Andirons. See also **dog iron(s).**

1957 Broaddus *Vocab Estill Co KY* 56 = two pieces of cast iron used instead of dogirons. Perhaps these were pigs of iron from the blast furnace which operated in Estill County early in the 19th century.

pig lot *noun* An outdoor enclosure for swine. Same as **hog lot.** See also **lot A.**

1966–68 *DARE Survey* (Brasstown NC, Burnsville NC) = place outdoors where pigs are kept. **1996** Johnson *Lexical Change* 138 = statistically more common in the mountains of South Carolina and Georgia than in the Piedmont and Coastal Plain c1990.

pig meat *noun* Pork.

2002 Nelson *Turn Back* 47 Mid wives might have been paid a small amount of money [or] maybe they got paid, like a lot of the doctors did, in produce, chicken or pig meat, or they might have done this service for no pay.

pig-oh, pig-oo, pigooee, pigooey, pig-oo-(w)e, pig-oo(w)ie, pi-go-(w)ie See **pig-ee.**

pig oyster (also *pig's chestnut*) *noun* The testicle of a pig, eaten as food.

1991 Still *Wolfpen Notebooks* 77 At hog killing time what I like best to eat is the melt. I could eat it if I was tolerably sick. Some like the pig's chestnuts. *Ibid.* 78 When I was a shirttail boy my Pap used to kill us a mess of snowbirds in the winter time. A bite to a bird. Tasty as pig oysters.

pig salve *noun* See citation.

1936 Farr *Folk Speech Mid TN* 276 = lard: "How much is pig salve worth?"

pig's chestnut See **pig oyster.**

pigs-ear *noun* See citation.

1964 Clarkson *Lumbering in WV* 368 = a saloon, especially one where "home-brew" was sold.

pig shorts *noun* By-products from milling grain.

1976 Still *Pattern of Man* 114 It [= moonshine] had a whang of coal oil and lye, and the pig shorts in the mash didn't recommend it.

pig sticker *noun* A pocketknife with a long blade. See also **frog-stick, sticker 1.**

1997 Montgomery *Coll* (known to Cardwell). **1999** Carver *Branch Water Tales* 6 Smitty's hand rested on the handle of the pig sticker he carried in his front pocket.

pig-tight *adjective* Of a fence (usually a rail one): constructed strong enough to prevent pigs from getting through.

1942 Robertson *Red Hills* 209 "Boys," he shouted, "you got to keep your fences horse-high, bull-strong, and pig-tight."

pi-gwoo-(w)ie See **pig-ee.**

pike

A (also *pike road*) *noun* Originally, a road with a gate, toll-bar, turnstile (hence **turnpike**), or station at which a toll was collected from vehicles, drovers, and other traffic; more recently, usually any public through road (as Indian Gap Pike running from Bryson City NC to Gatlinburg TN) or later a highway (as Rutledge Pike from Knoxville TN to Rutledge TN). See also **turnpike.**

1861 Hedgecock *Diary* 110 Went on a pike leading a little south of west a distance of about 16 miles. **1863** Brown *CW Letters* (Aug 4) you may talk about rough Cuntry but here is the wirst rods to git of the pikes i ever Saw. **1881** Pierson *In the Brush* 27 My appointments for the week being all fulfilled, I took the turnpike and started for the county-seat. I was never so grateful for a good road, and never so willing and glad to pay toll. At various points along the "pike," as it was universally called, I saw tracks leading off into the woods, and was told that they were known as "shunpikes," and that some people in traveling would take these and go through the woods around the toll-gates, in order to avoid paying toll. **1937** Hall *Coll* (Emerts Cove TN) = a "rocked" country road, not a highway. *Ibid.* (Smokemont NC) Harvey Cameron has a store at the left. Go down the main pike until the road goes to the right. **c1960** Wilson *Coll*: *pike* = any prominent road, not necessarily one piked or paved. **1966** Dakin *Vocab Ohio River Valley* 214 The old name *turnpike*, most frequently used as the simplex pike and occasionally *pike road*, is quite common in Ohio and Kentucky—and some speakers say only pike for any kind of improved or paved road. **1967** *DARE Survey* (Maryville TN) *pike* = any paved road. **1976** Garber *Mountain-ese* 68 *pike* = public road. "You kaint miss us, the big pike runs right by our house." **1977** Norman *Kinfolks* 104 When they left the county pike and headed up the unpaved road that ran beside Bonnet Creek, they fell silent for awhile. **1977** Ross *Come Go* 18 Around 1804, one of the first toll roads was built west of the Wilderness Trail and known as the Old Jacksboro Pike. It extended from what is now Jacksboro, Tennessee, through Pine Knot, crossing the Cumberland River at Smith Shoals, a short distance above where Burnside came to be. The primary purpose of the road was for hauling some of the iron made at Jacksboro, to Lexington and other places where iron could be sold. **1986** Pederson et al. *LAGS pike* (Blount Co RN, Knox Co TN); *pike road* = attested by 4/60 interviewees (6.7%) from E TN and 1/35 (2.9%) from N GA; 5/5 of all LAGS interviewees (100%) attesting term were from Appalachia. **1991** Bible *Bent Twigs* 47 Before the pike road to Dandridge was built, the roads were not even gravelled, just narrow dirt ones called wagon roads, usually too narrow for wagons to pass in places.

[DARE *pike* n[2] scattered, but especially OH, PA, KY]

B (also *pike off, pike out*) *verb, verb phrase* To hasten, depart.

1859 Taliaferro *Fisher's River* 75 I tuck off his jacket quick, hung it up, and piked on furder. **1864** Gilmore *Down in TN* 87 When ye gits thar, pike off like lightnin' chasin' a whirlygust (hurricane). **1910** Cooke *Power and Glory* 15 Why in the world you'll pike out and go to work in a cotton mill is more than I can cipher.

pike off, pike out See **pike B.**

pike pole *noun* See citations.

1964 Clarkson *Lumbering in WV* 368 = a pole from 12 to 20 feet long, with a straight or curved spike on the end. Used in river driving and at the log pond at the mill. **1973** Schulman *Logging Terms* 36 = a long wooden pole fitted with a spiked iron hook on one end and used to move logs in the water. Also known as spike pole. **1983** Montell *Don't Go Up* 200 = pole with an iron hook on one end used to move logs.

pike road See **pike A.**

pile (also *hay pile*) *noun* See citation.

1966 Dakin *Vocab Ohio River Valley* 78 (Hay) pile, fairly common in eastern Pennsylvania and the Coastal South all the way to Georgia, is used quite commonly in the Bluegrass and the Mountains [of KY], frequently by informants who have no other word.

pile up *verb phrase* To collapse in a heap.

1945 Vincent *Here in TN* 17 It was near midnight, and the way back was so rough he just piled up and waited for daylight.

pilfer (also *pilfer about, pilfer around*) *verb, verb phrase* To loiter or roam, especially to disturb or rummage through objects, not necessarily with an intent to steal.

1919 Combs *Word-List South* 34 = to loaf, loiter [Knott Co KY]. **c1960** Wilson *Coll*: *pilfer around* = to disturb something that belongs to another, maybe break or steal it. **1974** Fink *Bits Mt Speech* 19 *pilfering around* = idly wandering, not necessarily to steal. "Them boys were just *pilfering around*." **c1982** Young *Colloquial Appal* 16 *pilfer* = loiter. **1992** Montgomery *Coll*: *pilfer about* = to mess around (Cardwell). **2007** McMillon *Notes* = to rummage around looking through goods, often done by children.

[DARE *pilfer* v South Midland]

pill *noun* A pellet of animal dung. See also **horse pill, nannie, sheep pill.**

1938 Stuart *Dark Hills* 342 I heard he hit a teacher in the face with a dry horse pill. **1948** Still *Nest* 54 She discovered a rabbit's bed in a tuft of grass, a handful of pills steaming beside it. **1963** Watkins and Watkins *Yesterday* 119 The best remedy for the measles was sheep manure tea, but some families argued that rabbit pills were as good as sheep pills. Most mothers gave their children two tablespoons of tea four times a day without telling them what the ingredients were. **1984** Burns *Cold Sassy* 66 He and I had us a great manure war then, throwing dry cow cushions and sheep pills and horse biscuits at each other and dying laughing.

[DARE *pill* n 2 especially South, South Midland]

pillar See **pillow.**

pillar robbing *noun* See citation.

1991 Shifflett *Coal Towns* 86 The few pillars that were left were not mined until the headings had reached the limits of the coal seam. Then began the process of "pillar robbing," whereby miners engaged in the more dangerous phase of taking out the pillars themselves, literally laying the roof on the floor.

pill doctor *noun* A practitioner of modern scientific medicine who relies on pharmaceuticals.

1970 Montell *Coe Ridge* 31 Dr. Moore, he was an old-timey pill-doctor that lived in that old house up here at Black's Ferry.

piller See **pillow.**

pillow *noun* forms pillar, piller.

1863 Fuller *CW Letters* (Feb 24) I never go to bed but I think and pitty you being on the cold ground and not a pillar to put under your pour old head. **1864** *Carter CW Letters* (July 14) I was glad to think that you had a bed to ly on and a pillar under your Sweet head. **1925** (in **1935** Edwards *NC Novels* 88) *piller*. **1991** Thomas *Sthn Appal* 68 We picked th' goose-feathers t' put in feather-beds an' make pillars out uv. **2006** Ledford *Survivals* 1014 In present-day Appalachia there are still survivals from colonial pronunciation. A final r in such mountain terms as *winder* "window" and *piller* "pillow" have their counterparts in colonial writings. **2012** Milnes *Signs Cures Witchery* Their head was laying on this piller.

pilot black snake *noun* The black rat snake (*Elaphe obsoleta*).

1967 Huheey and Stupka *Amphibians and Reptiles* 64 This large reptile, formerly called the "Pilot Black Snake," is common in the Great Smoky Mountains. [**1991** Conant and Collins *Field Guide* 197 So-called because it some times hibernates with Rattlesnakes and was thought "to pilot" the latter to the den sites.]

pime blank, pime plank See **point blank.**

pinch *verb* To invite (someone) to take a drink of liquor.

1939 Hall *Coll* (Hartford TN) If you want to ask for an invitation for a drink, you ask a person if he wants to pinch it. *Ibid.* (Hartford TN) "Pinchin'" [someone] was an invitation to come out behind the house somewhere to take a drink of liquor.

pinchy *adjective* Of the weather: chilly.

1984 Wilder *You All Spoken* 140 = biting cold. **1986** Pederson et al. LAGS (Hamilton Co TN).

pindle along *verb phrase* To waste away. See also **pindling 1.**

1931 Owens *Speech Cumberlands* 92 Poor Cora pindled along for a year after Jim was took with the breast-complaint afore she died.

[back-formation from *pindling*]

pindling *adjective*

1 (also *pindly*) Frail, delicate, ailing. See also **pindle along.**

1923 Furman *Mothering* 181 I hope I may die if he haint the worst handicapped for warfare ever I seed, with a family to feed, and a whole passel of young uns to be paw and maw to, and the babe pindling all the time. **1940** Still *River of Earth* 131 My chaps won't come when I'm sick and pindly; they hain't use in coming to see me lay a corpse. **1944** Combs *Word-List Sthn High* 20 *pindling* = ailing, weak; said of children. **1997** Montgomery *Coll*: *pindling* (known to Brown, Jones, Norris).

[OED3 dialect and U.S.]

2 Small, trifling. See also **piddling A.**

1914 Furman *Sight* 42 These few pindling present-day district-schools scattered here and yan they only spiles the young uns for work. **1936** Morehouse *Rain on Just* 13 Dolly was a smart young un ... for all her pindling size, her puny ways. **1942** Campbell *Cloud-Walking* 246 I told her they's a pindling chance it might do some good. **1997** Montgomery *Coll*: *pindling* (known to Ledford).

[OED3 *pindling* adj 1 U.S. regional; DARE *pindling* adj chiefly New England, South Midland; Web3 *pindling* adj perhaps alteration of *spindling*]

pindly See **pindling 1.**

pine blank See **point blank.**

pine heart See **pine knot.**

pine knot (also *pine heart, pine knot light, pine knot torch, pine light, pine lighter, pine torch*) *noun* A knot or split piece of pine wood rich in resin that burns easily and slowly, to serve as a rudimentary lantern lighting a room or carried by nighttime travelers or hunters. See also **fat pine, light pine, lightwood torch, rich pine.**

1799 (in **2008** Ellison *High Vistas* 38) [Painted Rock NC] bears few traces of its having formerly been painted, owing to its having been soked from pine knots and other wood from a place near its base where travelers have frequently camped. **1834** Crockett *Narrative* 79 They had bows and arrows, and I turned in to shooting with their boys by a pine light. **1881** Pierson *In the Brush* 16 I rode to a very plain house to which I had been directed, and received a most warm and cordial welcome. Large pine-knots were soon blazing and roaring in the ample fireplace to relieve me of the most wretchedly disagreeable of all sensations of cold—those of a damp, clammy, chilly winter day. **1883** Zeigler and Grosscup *Heart of Alleghanies* 91 Pitch some pine knots on the fire, and face hit an' the wall while wife an' me gits our duds on. **1905** Miles *Spirit of Mts* 102 We sit by the light of a small lamp, instead of a pine torch, but the effect is not seriously marred. **1926** Thomas *Hills and Mts of KY* 159 The question of lighting a house was very simple. No such thing as a lamp, gas or electricity was known ... another and very cheap way was by securing very rich or oily pine knots, splitting to the desired size and using them as needed by igniting one end and thrusting it into a crack or crevice of the building with no regard for soot or fumes produced by it. **1931–33** (in **1987** Oliver and Oliver *Sketches* 30) Old folks would attend carrying pine torches for lights as they had no other way to give light to walk by. *Ibid.* 33 Pine knots was mostly the light to work by. **1939** Hall *Coll* (Little Greenbrier TN) By a good warm fire / And a pine-knot light / She used to spin many yards / Of thread at night (From poem of one of Walker sisters on sale to tourists). **1939** Hall *Coll* (Gatlinburg TN) I've seen right there in the Sugarlands people usin' pine lights. That was over fifty years ago, sixty years ago. Cut pine sticks, the rich part of the pine tree from around a half to two feet long. Lay them on the fire, or [people] would hold them for lights. Also pine knots [were used] ... pine torches. **1955** Justus *Peter Pocket* 3 The cabin door had been shut tight for the night and a pine knot burned on the hearth to light the room. **1956** Hall *Coll* (Bryson City NC) They'd gig fish in the wintertime, put a light up on the front end of a canoe ... and put a pine torch on it and take and go out and gig fish of a night. You can see 'em in the bottom of the river. **1966–68** *DARE Survey* (Brasstown NC) *pine lighter* = a joint of pine wood that burns easily and makes good fuel; (Cherokee NC, Spruce Pine NC, Gatlinburg TN) *pine knot*. **1969** GSMNP-28:5

Back in the old days, before my time, they used pine torches instead of lamps. **1972** AOHP/ALC-388 She had the pine hearts. Now they didn't have candles, nor they didn't have oil lamps. They used pine hearts. You just go out in the hills and cut these pines and get them hearts, and they'd light that and stick it up in the house and pine hearts is what they had for a light. **1985** Irwin *Alex Stewart* 31 The main light way back then was a pine torch. Take the heart of a rich pine and split you out a great bunch of long splinters, and tie them together. *Ibid.* 125 When I's a very small boy I'd set and hold a pine torch for her to knit till late at night. **1990** Oliver *Cooking Hazel Creek* 7 Lighting was mainly supplied by pine knots that flamed brightly but smokily for only late in the century did oil lamps appear on the creek. **1991** Haynes *Haywood Home* 67 Most people on Fines Creek had lanterns for being out at night. But often, my brothers and others carried pine-knot torches when we went to church or socials at night.

pine light, **pine lighter**, **pine light torch** See **pine knot**.

pinely See **pointedly A**.

pine rooter (also *pine rooter hog*) *noun* A long-nosed hog allowed to run freely. Same as **razorback**.

1937 Wilburn *Notes* 2 [There were] plenty of long nosed or pine rooter hogs running in mast which furnished plenty of meat & lard for [the] family. **1956** McAtee *Some Dial NC* 33 = a hog turned out to get its living in the woods; a razorback. **1965** GSMNP 49:2 The hogs got fat and everybody had hogs there, and we called them pine rooters. They were long nosed.

pine torch See **pine knot**.

piney, **piney flare**, **piney rose** See **peony**.

pinhook (also *penhook*) *verb* To buy or sell (especially tobacco) directly rather than at auction; hence verbal noun *pinhooking* = buying or selling (tobacco) without going to auction.

1944 Dingus *Tobacco Words* 68 = to buy privately, usually small crops and at bargain prices, tobacco in the barn or at the warehouse. **1976** Garber *Mountain-ese* 68 Lonnie decided to pin-hook his tobacco crop for a sure amount. **1983** Broaddus *Estill Co KY Word List* 50 = to sell a tobacco crop directly to a buyer rather than auctioning it. **1983** Montell *Don't Go Up* 46 Today, some area residents . . . earn comfortable livings farming part-time and "penhooking" the rest of the time. They roam from farm to farm and from community to community, hoping to buy one or more head of livestock in order to turn a quick dollar. They may haul the stock to market and take their chances of prices there, or they may sell to another jobber without ever loading up the animals in their own trucks. In classic form, the pen-hooker hangs around the regional livestock market . . . he jumps onto trucks loaded with hogs or cattle and offers the owner "top dollar" for his cargo before he has the chance to yard the animals. **1994** Montgomery *Coll* (known to Shields).

[back-formation from *pinhooker*; DARE *pinhook* v 2 chiefly South Midland]

pinhooker (also *hooker*, *penhooker*) *noun* A local speculator who purchases or seeks to purchase (especially tobacco) directly from a farmer for a pre-auction price.

1936 Farr *Folk Speech Mid TN* 276 = dishonest tobacco buyer: "He is a pin-hooker." **1939** *FWP Guide KY* 352 At the old tobacco house in Pinhook, an early settlement in Robertson County, originated the term "pinhooker," which is applied to the tobacco brokers who refuse to buy until the prices are low and the farmers are at their mercy, then resell to the warehouse for a higher price. **1949** Arnow *Hunter's Horn* 79 Nunn said nothing. He never could make up his mind to deal with penhookers like these or sell it in the auction ring. Everybody said that either way a man was liable to get cheated out of his eyeteeth. John dealt with the hookers, but Preacher Samuel never would. *Ibid.* 94 "Name your price, boy," grinned one hooker, big bellied, big jowled, "an I'll pay it. I got it an I'll let it go. I don't mind." **1969** Miller *Raising Tobacco* 35 These baskets were then loaded and hauled to the tobacco warehouse where they were sold at auction, unless a farmer ran into a *pinhooker* (an independent entrepreneur) before unloading, who might *make him a price* for the crop, the pinhooker being dependent for his livelihood on reselling at a profit. **1993** Montell *Cumberland Country* 144 Many local livestock markets had their beginnings here. By the 1930s it was common practice to organize and charter livestock commission companies. On a set day each week these companies held livestock sales during which farm animals were auctioned off to the highest bidder. The commission company retained a modest fee for care and handling. Local "penhookers" were constant competitors to the livestock commissions, as they remained outside the livestock market building ready to jump onto each truck that pulled up with a cargo of livestock. They attempted to offer owners attractive prices for their animals, while allowing enough margin for a profit when the creatures were run through the sales ring or taken to a larger market miles away and sold there.

[DARE *pinhooker* n South Midland]

pinhooking See **pinhook**.

pink *noun* Late afternoon, early evening. See also **pink in**.

1939 *FWP Guide NC* 98 Late afternoon is "the pink of the evenin'" or "daydown." **1999** Montgomery *Coll* (known to Cardwell).

[cf SND n² 1 "anything very small"; Web3 *pink* n chiefly Scottish "a small gleam of light"]

pink bed *noun* An evergreen rhododendron (*Rhododendron maximum*), better known as **rosebay rhododendron**.

1883 Zeigler and Grosscup *Heart of Alleghanies* 187 What is locally known as the Pink [rhododendron] Beds, in the northwestern part of Transylvania [Co NC], a dense forest plateau, is an absolute wilderness in which a lost traveler might wander for days. **1943** Erskine *Adventures* 242 On your right the high peaks of the Pisgah National Forest keep tempting you to turn aside to see the famous "pink beds" of mountain laurel.

pink in *verb phrase* Of the daylight: to wane in the late afternoon. See also **pink.**

1939 *FWP Guide NC* 98 The speech of the countryman is full of imaginative phrases. . . . Late afternoon is "the pink of the evenin'" or "day down," or the time when "evenin' is a-pinkin' in." **1972** Cooper *NC Mt Folklore* 95 *pinked in* = late afternoon came.

pink-root *noun* Same as **worm-grass.**

1941 Walker *Story of Mt* 54 One of the handsomest wild flowers growing in the mountain's rich woods and in bloom in May and June, is pink-root whose long red tubular flower with a yellow throat grows in terminal one-sided spikes. Root-diggers once sought this plant so persistently that its numbers were greatly reduced. [**1971** Krochmal et al. *Medicinal Plants Appal* 240 The root is used as a vermifuge, anthelmintic, and cathartic. In Appalachia, a tea made from the leaves is used to aid digestion.] **1982** Stupka *Wildflowers* 87 [Indian pink] is also called "pink-root," "star-bloom," and "worm-grass"—the last a reference to the use of the root by pioneers for expelling or destroying intestinal worms. **2002** Oliver *Cooking and Living* 13 He also did a heavy trade in medicinal herbs such as snakeroot, pinkroot and ginseng. In 1834 he sent a wagonload of pinkroot to Augusta, Georgia, where it was processed into medicine, called Vermifuge, for intestinal worms.

pint See **point.**

pint blank, p'int-blank See **point blank.**

pintedly, pintly See **pointedly A.**

pipe-guts *noun* See citation.

1917 Kephart *Word-List* 412 = the dottle of a pipe.

piroot *verb* To dash about.

1866 Smith *So Called* 116 For four years the Confederate Horse-Stealing Cavalry have been pirooting around, preparing themselves for the frightful struggle that is to come.

[DARE *piroot* v chiefly South, Southwest]

pismire See **pissant.**

pissant (also *pismire*) *noun* A small black ant.

1867 Harris *Sut Lovingood* 32 I felt like I'd crowded intu a ole bee-gum, an' hit all full ove pissants. **c1960** Wilson *Coll*: *piss ant* = an ant of any kind: men's language; women and children say *ant*. **1973** Kahn *Hillbilly Women* 100 The teachers always told me not to use the word "ain't." They said there's no such word as "ain't." I says there are such a word as "ain't." I says there's piss ain't and there's your ain't. So they didn't bother me too much then. **1984** Woods *WV Was Good* 222 = nearly always used except in the presence of ladies and girls, to designate the ordinary ant. The term is said to have been derived from an earlier day use of ants for a remedial tea that induced excessive urination. **1996** Montgomery *Coll*: *pissant* (known to Cardwell, Oliver); *pismire* (known to Ledford). **2000** Miller *Looneyville* 59 *piss ant* = nearly always used by men except in the presence of the females to designate an ordinary ant. Some of my ancestors believe it was derived from an earlier day use of ants for remedial tea that induced excessive urination: "Watch out there, Joe. You are about to walk into a hill of pissants in your bare feet."

[SND *piss-ant* (at *pish* III(2)) "from the smell of the ant-heap"; CUD *pismire* (at *pish* v "urinate"); Web3 *piss* + *ant*; chiefly dialect; Web3 *piss* + *mire* "ant" (of Scandinavian origin)]

piss-wood See **peawood, tisswood.**

pistol gun *noun* See citation.

1974 Fink *Bits Mt Speech* 19 = pistol.

pitch *verb*

1 (also *pitch off, pitch out*) To thrust, move with vigor.

1860 (in **1938** Taliaferro *Carolina Humor* 8) They could make no money at home, and they "pitched" vigorously into this new operation, especially the Duck Townsmen. **1864** *Joyce CW Letters* (Aug 19) the yankeys was about to slip up on us we had to Drop every thing and pitch oute after them we whip them Back over the River. **1896** Fox *Last Stetson* 186 He pitched right into the feud, as he [= the preacher] calls hit, 'n' the sin o' sheddin' human blood. **1958** Campbell *Tales* 101 He met a giant and pitched into fight. **1975** Gainer *Speech Mtneer* 14 *Pitched off* (v.), left hurriedly. "When it began to rain, he pitched off for home."

2 To stagger, fall (as in phrase *pitch and stave*).

1962 Hall *Coll* (Hartford TN) I worked at Waterville on a bittin' machine. I could have stayed there yit if I didn't have high blood. I pitched an' staved. He fetched me home. **1971** *Granny Women* 255 Th'horses would break through th'ice and th'mudholes and just nearly pitch on their heads. **1976** Thompson *Touching Home* 15 = to fall: "I felt funny and started pitching." **1989** Landry *Smoky Mt Interviews* 194 I got out there in the creek, and I went to slipping and a-falling and a-pitching. **1997** Montgomery *Coll* = to have dizziness, stagger (Brown). **1999** Morgan *Gap Creek* 78 He was helping me to churn and just pitched forward into the yard.

3 Of a bird: to alight, perch. See citation.

c1975 Lunsford *It Used to Be* 162 "Pitch" means to light or perch, as "that hawk pitched in a dead chestnut." That is, he flew to a dead chestnut tree and was there on its perch.

4 In phrase *pitch a crop.*

1944 Wilson *Word-List* 48 = to plant a crop.

[DARE *pitch* v 1 South, South Midland]

5 To engage in (a form of unrestrained behavior).

1966 *DARE Survey* (Brasstown NC) *pitch a fit*; (Highlands NC) *pitch a drunk*. **1972** Cooper *NC Mt Folklore* 95 *pitch a fit* = to fuss or rave in anger.

[DARE *pitch* v 4 chiefly South, South Midland]

pitch a crop See **pitch 4.**

pitch and stave See **pitch 2**.

pitch off, pitch out See **pitch 1**.

pitch saw *noun* A two-man saw, apparently so called because one of the two sawyers worked from below, usually in a pit.

1956 Hall *Coll* (Jones Cove TN) Before we built the mill we had a whip saw, a pitch saw we called it, to saw lumber.

[folk etymology and modification of *pit* + *saw*]

pitiful *adjective* variant comparative form *pitifulest*.

1864 Poteet *CW Letters* (Nov 2) it was the pitifullest looking little Mortal you ever saw. **1953** Wharton *Dr Woman Cumberlands* 166 Hit makes the pitifulest cryin' I ever hear. **1991** Thomas *Sthn Appal* 198 That'uz the pitifulest man I ever seen in my life.

pit mouth *noun* See citations.

1973 Preston *Bituminous Term* 46 = the ground-level opening to a shaft or slope [coal] mine. **2002** Armstead *Black Days* 245 = a walk-out opening from a coal mine to the outside. Can be located at a manmade pit or at the base of a hill or mountain.

pity sake *noun* Pity, mercy (in phrase *take (a) pity sake on* = "take mercy on").

1952 Wilson *Folk Speech NC* 574 He took *pity-sake* on me and give me some work. **1961** Seeman *Arms of Mt* 55 He wouldn't take a pitysake on nobody.

piuggy See **pig-ee**.

pizen See **poison**.

pizen vine See **poison vine**.

place *noun* A homestead, house, farm, or site, especially one on ancestral property, often known by the name of a resident family or used in compounds such as **homeplace**. See also **(the) bad place**, **(the) good place**.

1935 (in **2009** Powell *Shenandoah Letters* 43) I have moved to the George Herring place. **1939** Hall *Coll* (Proctor NC) I thought we'd go up and stay two or three nights, you know, go up above the old Hall place up on Bone Valley. **1956** Hall *Coll* (Townsend TN) My daddy [= Dan Myers] used to herd at the Lawson Place. . . . We'd stay weeks at a time at the Spence Place [on top of Smoky]. **1969** GSMNP-25 His place joined the Bales place on above there. **1970** *Foxfire Interviews* A-70-5 They wasn't raised here on this place. **1973** *Foxfire Interviews* A-73-86 He lives up there on Mister Happ's place. **1973** GSMNP-3 [The stream] still goes by the McGee place there yet, and that branch is called the McGee Branch. **1986** Huskey *Sugarlands* 8 The main road went on up the river to the old schoolhouse at the Isaac Huskey place. **1999** Morgan *Gap Creek* 8–9 I heard a dog bark somewhere off in the woods near the Jeter place. **2007** McMillon *Notes* = a house, whether lived in or not; also a house or property where a house once stood: "Have you been to the old Carter place?"

plag See **plague**.

plague *verb*

A Variant forms *plag* [plæg], *plaguer* [see **1972** in **B1**], *pleage* [see **1862** in **B1**], *pleg*.

1891 Brown *Dialect in TN* 175 *Plague* is generally given with the short *e*-sound, *pleg*. **1942** Hall *Phonetics Smoky Mts* 18 *Ancient, plague, plait* v. ("weave") were heard only with [æ].

[DARE *pleg* (at *plague* n, v A) scattered, but especially frequent South Midland]

B *verb* [Editor's note: The senses below cannot always be differentiated.]

1 (also *plaguer*) To tease, embarrass.

1848 (in **1870** Drake *Pioneer Life KY* 184–85) Toward evening the young men would assemble, and amuse themselves by athletic exercises without, or talking to and "plaguing the gaals" [sic] within, the cabin. **1862** *Neves CW Letters* (Feb 13) she just wrote that to try to pleage me becaus I pleage her about fawl ing off so much. **1914** Arthur *Western NC* 266 [We] also say "plague" for tease, and when we are willing, we say we are "consentable." **1931** Combs *Lg Sthn High* 1310 "Plague" (*a* like *ai* in "air") means to embarrass. **1940** Haun *Hawk's Done* 13 Joe would be plagued but I could tell it did him good for Tiny to brag on him. **1972** Alderman *Big Bald* 12 The women would cook, quilt, and gossip. The men would drink, raise logs and swap ideas. The younger boys would spend a lot of time "plaguering the gals." **2007** McMillon *Notes* = to tease.

[DARE *plague-taked* ppl adj chiefly South, South Midland]

2 To irritate, torment, trouble, vex. See also **plagued**.

1813 Hartsell *Memora* 135 by this time the men had gathered from all the Companeyes round him, and plagued him tell he cried. **1940** Still *River of Earth* 126 It plagued her to lie abed, helpless. **c1945** Haun *Hawk's Done* 282 He asked her when her name was going to be writ on the marriage side, and it plagued her. **1955** Ritchie *Singing Family* 85 Honey, it's been a-plaguing me all the long night and day. **1985** Irwin *Alex Stewart* 272 It sorta plagued me when I found out what she wanted. **1996** Montgomery *Coll* She plagued me to death with her gossip. I'm too plagued to repeat it (Brown); She was plagued to death when she dropped the pie (Norris).

plagued *adjective* See also **plague B2**.

A Variant form of two syllables: *plague-ed* ['plægəd].

1942 Hall *Phonetics Smoky Mts* 83.

B (also *plaguey, plaguy*) Irritating, troublesome, annoying.

1859 Taliaferro *Fisher's River* 30 He had, moreover, a fund of sharp, provoking wit running into satire when necessary, which Johnson maintained "were worth more than all yer college lingo, a plaguy sight." **1863** *Lee CW Letters* (June 17) the pleged yankeys has got our Communication Cut of from three States. **1904** Fox *Christmas Eve* 130 Mace Day shot Daws Dillon's brother, as I rickollect—somep'n's al'ays a-startin' up that plaguey war. **1939** Hall *Coll* (Bradley Fork NC) A plagued panther run me into the field.

[EDD *plagued* ppl adj Scot and Amer; Web3 *plagued* adj dialect, *plaguey* adj chiefly dialect]

plaguer See **plague B1**.

plague take *verb phrase* To confound, damn (used to express abuse, impatience, or annoyance); hence participial adjective *plague-taked* = cursed, damned, *plague take it!* = confound it! See also **fetch-taked**.

1924 Greer-Petrie *Angeline Gits Eyeful* 3 I be consarn my skin if them men wan't too plague-taked lazy to tote them canvas bags theirse'ves. **1939** Burnett *Gap o' Mountains* 38 "Joe," he said; "plague take your pesky hide; I've stood your monkey shines long enough and now I'm agoin' to give you the best blamed lickin' you ever had in all your borned days." **1952** Giles *40 Acres* 70 "This dad-ratted dress," she fumed, "I'd ort to know hit was sleazy! . . . Crept up two, three inches at a time. I says to myself the plague-taked thing is goin' plumb to my knees!" **1963** Edwards *Gravel* 20 Now since you're so plague-taked interested in that candy you wouldn't mind paying a little for it wouldje? **1969** Doran *Folklore White Co* 108–9 Several mild expletives let off verbal steam respectably. People, unless they avoid "slangy words," use such expressions as these: "Land's sakes"; "For gosh sakes"; "Land's smuffin"; "Land-o-Goshins"; "Gosh darn it"; "Confound it"; "By Doggies"; "By grab"; "By cracky"; "By gum"; "Dad gum it"; "I'll be goll-durned"; "Good golliwogs"; "Plag on it"; "Plag take it"; "Geewhillikin"; "That son-of-a-billy goat"; and "Shoot fire and save matches." **1998** Montgomery *Coll* Plague take it!; I be plague taked. I can't seem to do anything right this morning (Cardwell), = expresses mild disappointment (Ledford), = expresses puzzlement or embarrassment, as "I'll be plague-taked if I can find that hammer" (Norris).

plaguey, plaguy See **plagued B**.

plain dodger *noun* See citation. Same as **dodger**.

1890 Fruit *KY Words* 64 We have what we call "plain dodger," in which the meal is made up with cold water into pones; then, "shortened dodger," in which the meal is made up with lard, or grease of some kind. Our "crackling bread" is a corn-dodger made up with cracklings.

plaisure See **pleasure**.

plank drag *noun* A rudimentary harrow. See also **drag C3**.

1967 *DARE Survey* (Maryville TN) = instrument used in a field after it has been plowed to break up the lumps. **1999** Montgomery *Coll* = usually homemade of wood, drawn behind a horse, having weights to press the ground (Cardwell).

plank gum *noun* See citation. Same as **gum A2**.

1971 *Beekeeping* 161 In the early days of beekeeping, the hives were nothing more than twenty-four to thirty-inch long sections of hollow black gum trees—a fact that has caused even modern hives in the mountains today to be called "gums," "beegums," or "plank gums."

plank house *noun* A dwelling constructed of vertical boards. See citations. See also **board 2**.

1831 *McLean Diary* 4 [I] fixt the plank House and put the staves to dry. **1972** *AOHP/LJC-259* We had owned a big home down there that burned up, a plank house. **1990** Williams *Pride and Prejudice* 221 Occasionally "log" houses were built with narrowly hewn or sawn timbers, such as the "whup sawn" log house one woman described, but the term *plank* in western North Carolina always refers to the vertical-plank house.

plank road *noun* A road built of a series planks laid crosswise on longitudinal timbers. See also **corduroy road, pole road**.

c1960 Wilson *Coll* = a corduroy or log road, formerly common in logging in wet times or places.

plant *verb* To bury (someone).

1913 Kephart *Our Sthn High* 78 I mind about that time, Doc; but I disremember which buryin'-ground they-all planted ye in.

plantain *noun* An edible wild green (*Plantago* spp) that also has medicinal uses.

1937 Thornburgh *Great Smoky Mts* 29 Spignot [sic] was used as a remedy for felons; plantains for bee stings. **1938** Still *Mole-Bane* 373 Before the garden was ready, Mother and Euly gathered a mess of plantain and speckled jack. **1991** Still *Wolfpen Notebooks* 77 What I look forward to in the spring hain't garden sass—is wild greens. . . . What you want to look for is plantain . . . lamb's quarter . . . and blue thistle. And don't spare the seasoning. **c1995** *Pioneer Farmstead* 11 After the pigs were fattened in pens, children might be set to work pulling weeds, particularly "plantains" and "pusley." These weeds, in addition to corn, were used to "harden" the fat. The pioneer put the wilderness and its own brands of food to good use; this way, he didn't have to waste any corn.

plantation dog *noun* See citation.

1970 *Hunting Stories* 13 Traditionally the mountain people kept several different kinds of dogs around their homes. Many had at least one "plantation dog" whose whole job was to keep the hogs and cows out of the corn.

plant the corn before building the fence (and variants) *verb phrase* Of a woman: to become pregnant during courtship. See citations.

1935 Sheppard *Cabins in Laurel* 172 He is a demanding and passionate lover. . . . Perhaps he overpersuades her and they "plant their corn before they build their fence"; if he fails to marry her, the child she bears out of wedlock will be a "woods-colt." **1982** Slone *How We Talked* 9 *planting the crop before building the fence* = getting pregnant before getting married, yet getting married before the baby is born. **1983** Mull and Boger *Recollections* 75 Sometimes during the courtship, "the corn is planted before the fence is built." **1987** Young *Lost Cove* 57 Most of the courting couples got married before they had time to plant their corn with no fence around the field. **1996** Montgomery *Coll*: *plant the corn before building the fence* = to get a woman pregnant before marriage (Ledford).

[DARE *plant one's corn before one builds the fence* v phr South, South Midland]

plasure See **pleasure**.

plat *adjective* See citation.

1958 Combs *Archaic English in KY* 41 = plain: "That is the plat truth."

play (also *playing game, play party, play-party game*) *noun* Formerly, a social gathering, especially of courting couples, to sing, chant, clap, tap feet, march, skip, and act out verses (as with calls and responses) with musical accompaniment in a lively manner with no bodily contact, such activities mimicking dances, which were often discouraged by church strictures; *play* was apparently an earlier term for a single round of a game at such a gathering or a single evening's activities. Also called **game**. See also **civil party**, **twistification**.

1841 *Elijoy Church Minutes* 43 The church passed an act against all kinds of plays that is against the word of God. **1858** *Elijoy Church Minutes* 94 The Church at Ellijoy met after sermont proceded to business 1st Took up the case of James Jeffres Received the Report of brother John Tipton he said Brother Jeffres said he did not know any thing of the play until they was playing and he did not want to drive them of and the Church unanimous forgave him. **1862** *Neves CW Letters* (Jan 28) we had a play though hit dident seem right to be aplaying and not see you. **1863** *Proffit CW Letters* (Sept 21) I want to come home about christmas if I live I want you to tell Davy that she must have a fine quilt as I shall expect her to have a fine quilting a play & a heap of fun &c. **1908** Johnson *Life KY Mts* 179 She knew more "calls" and could dance more "steps" than could any one else, and was always the life of the crowd and favorite at all of the dances and "plays." **1912** Perrow *Songs and Rhymes* 143 The parents of many of these young people allow them to come to this merry-making only on condition that they do not dance. But these young church members are ingenious. They propose a game of "Skip-to-my-loo," "Weavilly-Wheat," "Shoot-the-Buffalo," or some other equally innocent form of moving to the time of music. Here, of course, the fiddle is left out, and the "players" sing for an accompaniment to their "play." This, as everybody knows, is not dancing, this is "Skip-to-my-loo"; and yet by this name it seems as sweet to these thoughtless ones as the forbidden pleasure itself, while they have the added assurance that it leaves neither soil nor cautel to besmirch the virtue of their church records. **1913** Kephart *Our Sthn High* 264 In homes where dancing is not permitted, and often in others, "play parties" are held, at which social games are practiced with childlike abandon. **1917** Campbell and Sharp *Engl Folk Songs* xv I have no doubt that religious scruples have also been a contributory cause [of the decadence of dancing]—I noticed that in reply to my enquiries on this subject the euphemism "playing games" was always substituted for "dancing" by my informants. **1936** McDowell *Background* 7 In a few more years I began to attend the "Play Parties" given in the homes of the young people in the neighborhood. There we played the more interesting games that called for a more active choosing of partners, involving dance steps, holding hands, and even, in many cases, of kissing one's partner. The girls, who willingly entered the game with full knowledge of what it called for, always objected with native coyness to the kissing, which now [was] quite harmless by comparison with some modern practices. Some of the elders, however, frowned upon the kissing and dancing, and would not permit their daughters to attend the parties. Some of the games I remember best were "Weevily Wheat," "The Miller," "Skip, to my Lou," "Betsy Lina," "Mr. Boatlander," etc. Each of them had its own distinctive tune, which, like the words and the action involved, were traditional. I was only in my early teens when the changes taking place in the social and industrial life overwhelmed the "play parties," along with many other traditional customs. I have not for thirty years heard of a "play party." **1944** Laughlin *Word-List Buncombe Co* 25 = a party where dancing games are played to the singing of the participants. This is to get around the church's ban on dancing. The devil was seemingly in the fiddle. **1945** McNeer *Sthn Highlands* 21 The play-parties began to be called that because the church could not countenance dancing. And the dances were called "games." **c1960** Wilson *Coll*: *play party* = a dance without musical instruments; games played to music sung by dancers. **1967** Justus *Growing Up* 16 The play-party song such as "Fiddlers' Fair," "I'm as Free a Little Bird as I Can Be," [and the] "No-End Song," remind me of the fun that was allowed in the strict society prescribed among Church people who frowned upon dancing as the Devil's shenanigans. **1974** Roberts *Sang Branch* 85 When the beans were to be strung, the apples to be peeled, or the corn to be husked, the folk assembled on these lighter tasks as a pretext for a playparty for the remainder of the night. **1975** Gainer *Witches Ghosts Signs* 30 A social gathering at which singing games were the chief activity was called a "play party." The games were traditional and singing was without any accompaniment. Popular among the games were "Old Dusty Miller," "Red Bird Through the Window," "Three in a Boat," and "Virginia Reel." "Kissing games," in which the prize was the privilege of kissing the person of your choice, such as "Post Office," "Spin the Bottle," "Guess Who," and many others, were part of the activities. Refreshments were always served, such as pie, cider, cake, candied popcorn, and taffy. "Taffy-pulling" was often a part of the activities. In most homes square dancing was not permitted, for it was considered to be an activity suitable for the dance hall or for a barn-dance. There was usually singing at the play-party, the whole group singing together, and sometimes quartets and solos. The spirit of the play-party was one of informality, and many romances had their beginning at these parties. Invitations were not given to these parties, but word was passed around that there would be a party at a certain home and everyone was welcome to come. **1982** *Smokies Heritage* 157 The younger folk might have gone down the snowbound valley to a community barn dance, or if their elders didn't approve of such foolishness, perhaps to a "play party," where hands were clapped and feet were tapped in rhythm to the music. **1989** Friedland *Old Time Dancing* 4 Throughout the region the dance tradition has had to contend with objections from certain religious groups to both dance and instrumental music. Appalachians have come up with a variety of strategies over the years to try to resolve this tension between dance and religious beliefs. In many communities, individual dance figures were often transformed into play-party games. Though play-party movement patterns were similar to or, in some cases, identical to dance figures, they were not considered offensive because performers would sing their own accompaniment. **1991** Thomas *Sthn Appal* 92 Many families in early days in Appalachia—in some communities as many as half of them—disapproved of dancing, commonly the churchgoing families. Many of the parents' objections appeared to be related to the word "dancing," and some objected to fiddle music. Consequently, there evolved an alternate form of group recreation called "parties" or "play parties." At those play parties, routine folk dances were performed to group singing. To appease the parents, the dances were called "party games." The names of some of those "games" were "Shooting the Buffalo," "Skip to My Lou," and "Jump Josie." In some communities, those parties were called "Jump Josie parties." Participation in the play party games commonly was restricted to what the folks called the "good families," usually meaning the churchgoing families. **2015** Jamison *Hoedowns* 203 = dance games accompanied by singing rather than instrumental music.

[OED3 *play-party* (at *play* n C1) U.S. regional]

play-diddle *noun* A piece of playground equipment.

1991 Still *Wolfpen Notebooks* 47 The trouble with the schools nowadays is they got all them play-diddles in the yard. Young'uns can't think about their text books for wanting to get to the swings and ridey-horses.

play hob *verb phrase* See citation.

1939 Farr *TN Mt Regions* 92 = to act foolish: "You're playing hob."

play hushmouth (also *play shutmouth*) *verb phrase* To keep silent. See also **hush-mouthed**.

1976 Thompson *Touching Home* 16 *play shutmouth* = to be quiet. **1988** Brown *Beech Creek* 78 He just played shut-mouth and let Nancy Ann wear the breeches. **1994** Montgomery *File*: *play hushmouth* = to refuse to talk or divulge information (82-year-old man, Gatlinburg TN).

playing game See **play**.

play off on *verb phrase* To trick, mislead (someone).

1939 Hall *Coll* (Deep Creek NC) Me and Mark Cathey, we played off on 'em. We let 'em go, and we took up Nettle Creek.

play party See **play**.

play pretty *noun* A toy, plaything (often homemade). See also **pretty D1**.

1913 Kephart *Our Sthn High* 259 The children have few toys other than rag dolls, broken bits of crockery for "play purties" and such. **1939** Hall *Coll* (Waynesville NC) What kind of a play purty have you got there? (referring to my recorder when I was recording the square dance music at Masonic Hall in a big gathering on New Year's Eve). **1957** Broaddus *Vocab Estill Co KY* 57 = a plaything. **1962** Dykeman *Tall Woman* 64 The girls, Kate and Annie Marie and Elizabeth, had often wished to have the baby more to themselves, to fondle as a play-pretty. **1966–68** *DARE Survey* (Brasstown NC, Spruce Pine NC, Maryville TN) = a child's toy. **1975** Chalmers *Better* 8 Each child received a "play-pretty"—a new term to me, but so much more expressive than "toy." **1986** Pederson et al. *LAGS* = attested by 39/60 interviewees (65%) from E TN and 7/35 (20%) from N GA; 46/340 of all LAGS interviewees (13.5%) attesting term were from Appalachia. **2005** Williams *Gratitude* 160 We ditn't ever call 'em "toys," we called 'em play purties. **2008** McKinley *Bear Mt* 131 Every year I looked forward to spending mine [= dollar] for a coloring book and a big box of crayons. The little boxes I usually had didn't include my favorite color, pink. Being able to buy the big fifty-nine-cent box at Woolworth's was a real treat! Granny said they were "real nice 'play purties' for a little girl to have at Christmas."

[DARE *play-pretty* n chiefly South, South Midland, TX, OK]

play shutmouth See **play hushmouth**.

play smash (also *play smash with*) *verb phrase* To make a blunder, cause confusion; to wreak havoc with.

1884 Smith *Arp Scrap Book* 31 Durn the staff and Joe Brown, too. He played smash amazingly, writing pages against conscription. **1900** Harben *N GA Sketches* I had hardly got started out thar before [he] has played smash with all my plans. **1915** Dingus *Word-List VA* 187 = to make a great blunder, do something wholly wrong: "Well, now you've played smash." **c1960** Wilson *Coll*: *play smash with* = tear up, disrupt.

[DARE (at *smash* n 1) scattered, but especially South Midland]

pleage See **plague**.

please and displease (also *pleased or displeased*) *noun phrase* A children's parlor game.

1974 Roberts *Sang Branch* 30 Now in Pleased or Displeased they would all set down in a line, and they took it in rotation. Commence with the first one and say, "Pleased or Displeased?" "Displeased." "What would it take to please you better?" You could make any wish you wanted to to the crowd, you see. Maybe it would be for one to go bark up the chimley, or kneel down and pray, or whatever you put on him to do he had to do it. Make a drink, go wade the water, bring in a load o' wood for the far, bring you a drink, stand on their head. But most of the time it was hugging and kissing. Say it would please you to see some boy hug a purty girl, or some girl kiss a purty boy, you know, getting all the fun outten it you could. Sometimes some smart boy would want you to go pick up a rock and pack it a piece and lay it down, or go rub farcoals on your face and make your face black. Anything to get a good un on somebody. **1982** Slone *How We Talked* 95 They also played kissing games: "Please and Displease"—one person passed a hat or basket and each player dropped into it some personal item as a forfeit. . . . Another person sat in a chair while someone else held over his head one of the forfeits one at a time saying, "heavy, heavy, over your head." The one sitting in the chair asked, "Fine or superfine?" ("fine" meant the object belonged to a boy, "superfine" meant it was a girl.) "Pleased or displeased?" he was asked. If he said "Pleased." he was asked what it would take to please him any better, and he would say the person to whom the forfeit belonged must do something.

pleasure *verb* To gratify, give enjoyment (to). See also **displeasure**.

1913 Kephart *Our Sthn High* 282 In mountain vernacular many words that serve as verbs are only nouns of action, or adjectives, or even adverbs. . . . "I wouldn't pleasure them enough to say it." **1941** Justus *Kettle Creek* 131 "Thank you kindly, Glory. It'll pleasure me to have it," he told her. **c1945** Haun *Hawk's Done* 224 George, he would look at her and seem pleasured at her ways. **1957** GSMNP-23:1:18 [It] wasn't worth anything, only just to pleasure, look at. **1975** Chalmers *Better* 66 "It would pleasure me," Aunt Lou used to say, "for you to come and set a spell happen you pass."

[DARE *pleasure* v B1 chiefly South, South Midland]

pleasure after *verb phrase* To yearn for, crave.

1987 Young *Lost Cove* 26 Uncle Rack Wilson didn't pleasure after field work worth a hoot.

pleg See **plague**.

plenty *noun*

1 In phrase *a plenty* = an abundance, a sufficiency, enough. See also **a-plenty**.

1815–18 (in **1881** Draper *Kings Mt* 553) About sunset we met the footmen who they had left at Green river, who provided a plenty of rations, &c. **1862** *Mangum CW Letters* (May 18) we have as good fre stone water hear as I ever Saw and aplenty of it we have a plenty to eat. **1910** Cooke *Power and Glory* 5 He 'lowed he'd be home with a plenty before the baby come. **1939** Hall Coll (Tobes Creek NC) Politics has gone too far. . . . We've got two squires to every deestrict. One's a plenty. **c1945** Haun *Hawk's Done* 210 Me? I wouldn't care for any more—I've had a-plenty. **1962** Dykeman *Tall Woman* 34 "Well, that's a-plenty of tears," she said. **1976** GSMNP-114:6 They'd come up off of that job up there and buy their whiskey on up this way and get a plenty of whiskey. **1989** *Matewan OHP*-22 We always had a plenty [of food] now, as far as what it was, yeah, might not have been the best of all, but we had a plenty of it.

[OED3 *plenty* n 1c (with indefinite article) "an abundance, a large amount or quantity (of something)" now rare (chiefly U.S. regional in later use)]

2 With ellipsis of following *of*.

1939 Adams *Coll* 2324 We won't be gone long and there's plenty food on the table for you to eat if you are hungry. **1939** Hall Coll (Hazel Creek NC) The best I figured [is] that the bear had plenty other stuff to eat without catching the cattle. **1940** Oakley *Roamin'/Restin'* 61 We had plenty bear meat and we would sell the fur skin to some fur dealer or ship fur to some company.

pleurisy root *noun* The butterfly milkweed (*Asclepias tuberosa*), a perennial wild plant whose leaves have medicinal uses, as to treat respiratory ailments. Also called **butterfly root**, **chiggerweed**.

1940 Caton *Wildflowers of Smokies* 53. [**1971** Krochmal et al. *Medicinal Plants Appal* 70 Indians of Appalachia made a tea of the leaves to induce vomiting.] **2006** Howell *Medicinal Plants* 127 Pleurisy root has been an important remedy in American Indian and folk medicine for the treatment of respiratory and pulmonary problems. It was considered a specific remedy for chest complaints, coughing, congestion, and breathing difficulties and was used in combination with other herbs in the treatment of bronchitis, pleurisy, and pneumonia. Pleurisy root was also used for pulmonary edema to move fluids out of the chest in order to improve heart function.

pliam blank, **plime blank** See **point blank**.

Plott (also *Plott bear dog*, *Plott cur*, *Plott dog*, *Plott hound*) *noun* A large, fierce, mixed-breed hound, believed to have been imported from Germany in the eighteenth century and refined by the Plott family of Haywood Co NC.

1913 Kephart *Our Sthn High* 80 I've been told that the Plott hounds are the best bear dogs in the country. . . . The Plott curs are the best—that is, half hound, half cur. **1914** Arthur *Western NC* 254 To [hunt game] dogs were necessary, the long bodied, long legged, deep mouthed hound being used for deer, and a sort of mongrel, composed of cur, bull, and terrier was bred for bear. The Plott dog, called after the famous hunter, Enos Plott, of the Balsam mountains of Haywood county, was said to be the finest bear dogs in the State. **1953** Hall Coll (Bryson City NC) [We used] Plott hounds as near full-blooded as we could [get]. More vicious, bred especially for bear-huntin', a cross of the English hound and the blood hound, about half and half a cross between English black and tan or fox hound and a blood hound . . . we raised them specially to hunt bear with, and hunt anything else with, but they was more vicious and bred specially for bear-hunting dogs. *Ibid.* (Plott Creek NC) When my great grandfather came home, he brought about six dogs, of what is known now as our Plott bear dog . . . the Plott hound will fight anything, from a woods mouse to a grizzly bear. **1966** Medford *Ol' Starlin* 53 The Plott hounds are the most famous bear dogs in all the land. Their familiar cry—a spine-tingling, bugle-like call—has been ringing through these old hills for over 175 years. For downright courage and persistence, they have been the pick of mountain bear hunters since Henry Plott developed the breed back in 1780. Their exploits are legion and the years have shaped them into a legend. A thousand tales testify to their talents which, naturally, have led those who never have trailed a pack of Plott hounds to argue they are a myth. Actually, the Plott hounds trace their ancestry back to the Old World back to a breed that must have been just about the best hunting dog that ever lived. . . . That story begins in Germany when, in 1750, two young brothers decided to pull up stakes and settle in America. They took with them their cash earnings, a few possessions, and three large brindle dogs. Nobody knows what kind of dogs they were, but the brothers thought they would be useful in hunting bear, deer and buffalo on the frontier. . . . Eventually [one brother] settled in a valley in the promised land where the trees were bunched in squads on the ridges and where there was grass a plenty. His name was Jonathan Plott [and] his descendants still live in the Plott Valley, in the shadow of Balsam, a 6,000-foot peak near Waynesville, and on Jonathan's Creek. **2009** Plott *Legendary Hunters* 13 Family patriarch George (Johannes) Plott is generally thought to have brought the breed to America in 1750. However, recent research indicates that may have actually been as early as 1741. **2009** Prewitt *Coon Hounds* 273 Nowadays, the black and tan, the redbone, the bluetick, the English, the treeing Walker, and the Plott are among the standard breeds that hunters say can potentially make good coon hounds.

[DARE *Plott hound* n Southern Appalachians]

Plott bear dog, Plott cur, Plott dog, Plott hound See **Plott.**

plout *verb* To plunge.

1867 Harris *Sut Lovingood* 258 Wouldn't you like to be in a safe place to see him when he plouts in, wif a "whish" intu that ar orful strong smellin, melted mixtry ove seleck damnashun.

[cf SND *plowt* v 1 "to plunge or thrust (a thing) into a (liquid)"]

plow (also *plow out*) *verb, verb phrase* To drive (an animal) in plowing a field.

1939 Hall *Coll* (Deep Creek NC) I plowed a steer there for seven year until I got able to get a horse. **1940** Stuart *Trees of Heaven* 226 Anse walks behind the young mules. He plows Dick and Murt on the old ground slopes. **1971** *Dowdle* 18 My daddy plowed th'steers, and when th'ground got too wet t'plow, used t'go fishin'. **1980** Riggleman *WV Mtneer* 11 You could plow [oxen] without a line on them after you had them broke a year or two—"Gee" and "Haw"—just the same as you could horses. **c1988** (in **2012** Portelli *They Say* 39) Mommy used to plow out a horse, have a garden, load coal, do whatever come handy.

[DARE *plow* v B2 South, South Midland]

plowed flesh, plowed fresh See **proud flesh.**

plowlines *noun* See citations.

1935 Murray *Schoolhouse* 58 We had a pretty definite idea as to who had taken it, and was now using it for plow-lines. **c1960** Wilson *Coll* = ropes used to guide a horse or mule that is being used to draw a plow. **1993** Stuart *Daughter* 235 = two long ropes used to guide a horse or mule. The ropes are threaded through rings on either side of the breeching, the trace, [and] the hame and attached to either side of the bit. The opposite ends are tied together and rest over the shoulder of the plowman. A tug on either rope will signal the animal to move in that direction.

[DARE *plowline* n 1 South Midland]

plow out See **plow.**

pluck *noun* The internal organs of a slaughtered hog eaten as food.

1958 Wood *Words from TN* 14 At hog killing time, we had pluck for dinner, made of the liver, lights, and melts, and sometimes sweetbreads. **1997** Montgomery *Coll* (known to Andrews, Bush).

[< Middle English *plucken*; SND n[1] 5 "the viscera of an animal"]

pluck-me (also *pluck me store*) *noun* In a coal camp, a company store.

1943 Korson *Coal Dust* 72 [Miners'] grocery and supply bills were checked off their earnings even before they received their pay, and trading was compulsory. It hurt the miner's pride to know that he was being robbed in the "pluck-me," his term for the company store. **2006** Mooney *Lg Coal Mining* 1029 Every two weeks or month the miner collected his pay, often in the form of company money called "scrip" or "clacker" that had to be spent in the company store or "pluck me store" as miners called it because of inflated prices.

plug stick *noun* See citation.

1968 *End of Moonshining* 49 = a hickory or white oak stick with a bundle of rags fastened to one end. The rags jam into the slop arm thus sealing the bottom of the still.

plumb

A *adjective* Entire, excellent, perfect, absolute.

1895 Edson and Fairchild *TN Mts* 373 = excellent. "If I hed your gun, I'd hev plum fun." **1904–20** Kephart *Notebooks* 2:367 Them hogs are plumb pets. **1936** (in **1952** Mathes *Tall Tales* 213) Up in the plumb middle of Hell. **1940** Perry *Pronoun Hit* 47 That was just a plumb swamp, but I ditched it. **1979** Carpenter *Walton War* 151 Hit's a plumb sight how a thunderstorm jest gives her the hysterics. **1985** Edwards *Folksy Sketches* 22 "Harrel," said Marsh, "you're the only fellow I've ever traded with that told me the plumb truth about a nag trade."

B *adverb*

1 Directly, exactly, immediately.

1859 Taliaferro *Fisher's River* 55 I cum right plum upon one uv the curiousest snakes I uver seen in all my borned days. **1867** Harris *Sut Lovingood* 63 Up in the lof by a trap door, an' plum over the feller's hed, sot Joe Jacksin, a-holdin ontu a half barril full ove warter outen a puddil. **1989** *Matewan OHP-9* They had ice nails in their horseshoe nails or mules' nails, and they'd come plumb across that ice. **2012** Milnes *Signs Cures Witchery* Milk went all over this place, [and] I got plumb back out.

2 Completely, utterly; all the way. See also **clean B.**

1864 *Warrick CW Letters* (Aug 30) I am So proud that the yenkees has left here I wount them to Ceep on till they Git plum out of this Country. **1895** Edson and Fairchild *TN Mts* 373 = wholly. "I'm plum done out." **1927** Furman *Lonesome Road* 97 I won't go plumb home with you, but I'll put you off nigh it. **1931** Goodrich *Mt Homespun* 55 "They plumb give her up," said Serinthy, "but Doc Burns come by and he fotched her out of it." **1939** Hall *Coll* (Hartford TN) He run up and stobbed his knife into it and cut a big long gash plumb to the hollow of the bear. **c1940** Padelford *Notes* Hit's gittin raily moughty nigh plumb cold. **1957** Combs *Lg Sthn High: Word List* 75 = entirely, quite. Ex.: "He's plum deaf." **1961** *Coe Ridge OHP-334A* He come up with a double barrel shotgun and got down and kicked him from Old Town plumb up to New Town. **1963** Edwards *Gravel* 104 Somehow what Gabe said plumb took it out of my mind. **1969** GSMNP-37:2:10 I've hunted plumb to the Smokies back through here on Deep Creek and Indian Creek. **1971** *AOHP/ALC-33* Naman graduated. He went plumb through school. **1973** *AOHP/LJC-317* Might near all the people around here got their mail over there to keep from going plumb to Haddix. **1973** GSMNP-57:17 They was plumb sour. **1978** Montgomery *White Pine Coll* X-2 They run me way back, plumb back to the bottom.... You didn't get no rest. [You were] just wore teetotally plumb out. **1979** *Big South Fork OHP*-10 I never did plumb leave [that job] for a long time because I was the extra fireman and extra brakeman and extra night watchman. **1980** GSMNP-115:21 Oh law, he owned that, all this plumb back up yander to where the Bohannon's line come to going up and down a long ridge there. **1994** McCarthy *Jack Two Worlds* 52 I'm just wore about plumb out. **1998** *Dante OHP*-69 We went away over there sometime and sometimes go plumb on down to Marbone below Elkhorn.

[cf French *à plomb* "straight down" < *plomb* n "lead"; OED3 *plumb* adv 2a "as an intensifier," now chiefly North American colloquial; DARE *plumb* adv 1 "all the way, directly, right" scattered, but chiefly South, South Midland]

plum(b) blank See **point blank.**

plum granny *noun* A pomegranate.

1944 Combs *Word-List Sthn High* 20 = pomegranate. **c1960** Wilson *Coll* = the pomegranate, a small melon-like vegetable, often raised in old-fashioned gardens and made into excellent preserves; it also smells good when ripe. **1982** Slone *How We Talked* 26 = to us, a small melon, nice smell, edible but not tasty. **1985** Irwin *Alex Stewart* 267 You can smell a snake when he gets mad. Smells just like a plum granny. **1991** Still *Wolfpen Notebooks* 69 In my school days anybody who had a plum granny in his pocket would have the girls after him. A ripe plum granny smell [is] so famous you want to eat it but you can't. Tastes like a rotten cucumber. **1997** Montgomery *Coll* (known to Andrews).

plumie *noun* The petunia plant (*Petunia atkinsiana*).

1937 Hall *Coll* (Cades Cove TN).

plum peach (also *plumstone peach*) *noun* A small **clingstone** peach (*Prunus persica*) with red meat. Same as **Indian peach.**

1859 Taliaferro *Fisher's River* 84 These is the oncommonest biggest plum peaches I uver seen sense my peepers looked on daylight. **1949** Kurath *Word Geog East US* 43 *Plum peach* . . . for the *clingstone peach* is in common use in a broad belt extending in a southwesterly direction from the Rappahannock to Georgia. *Ibid.* 72 *Plum peach* is the Virginia Piedmont term which has spread in a southwesterly direction into southwestern Virginia, southern West Virginia, and the western parts of the Carolinas, where it is in competition with the Midland word *cling-(stone) peach*. **1952–57** (in **1973** McDavid and McDavid *Vocab E KY* 158) *plum(stone) peach* = attested by 26/52 (50%) of E KY speakers for the Linguistic Atlas of the North Central States. **1962** Wilson *Folkways Mammoth Cave* 15 Red-skinned and red-meated peaches were called *Indian peaches*. **1967** *DARE Survey* (Gatlinburg TN) = a type of peach in which the hard center is tight to the flesh. **1986** Pederson et al. *LAGS* = attested by 10/60 interviewees (16.7%) from E TN and 7/35 (20%) from N GA; 17/90 of all LAGS interviewees (18.8%) attesting term were from Appalachia. **1998** Montgomery *Coll* = a small clingstone peach, also known as Indian peach (Brown), = a peach the size of a plum (Cardwell).

[DARE *plum peach* n chiefly South, South Midland]

plunder

A *noun* [Editor's note: The senses below cannot always be differentiated.]

1 Assorted household belongings, furniture or personal goods; farm equipment and implements. See also **house plunder 1.**

1824 Knight *Letter from KY* 106 The Phraseology in this state is sometimes novel. When you arrive at a house, the first inquiry is, where is your plunder, as if you were a bandit . . . i.e. your trunk or valise. **1834** Crockett *Narrative* 155 [I] took my family and what little plunder I had, and moved to where I had built my cabin, and made my crap. **1870** *Hall CW Letters* (June 12) wee had tolerable good luck in getting our little property and plunder moved up. **1878** Coale *Wilburn Waters* 50 On Friday evening I made up my mind to go [to the camp meeting], fixed up my plunder, greased my boots, and started in that direction very early on Saturday morning. **1910** Cooke *Power and Glory* 113 When a fire starts in a row of 'em hit cleans up the Company's property same as it does the plunder of the folks that lives in 'em. **c1950** Adams *Grandpap* 20 Pap had sledded our plunder right up to the door. **1965** Glassie *Old Barns* 22 The rectangular log construction unit still used in Europe as a granary was easily adapted to the storage of maize and became the corn crib found throughout the Southern Mountains. Frequently the corn crib has a shed for the storage of farm equipment—"gear" or "plunder." **1977** Shackelford et al. *Our Appalachia* 191 We got up out of the bed and we packed our plunder and we came home. **1978** Reese *Speech NE Tenn* 33 = attested by 5/12 (41.7%) speakers. **1982** Slone *How We Talked* 33 = household goods; household furnishing. **1985** *Smokies Anniv Book* 30 Homemade tables, chairs, beds, stools and cupboards had to share space with trunks of quilts, blankets, spinning wheels, oil lamps, candles, cooking utensils, and all the other "plunder" that had no place to live but right out in the open. **2005** Williams *Gratitude* 514 = household items, goods or furniture.

[OED3 *plunder* n 3 chiefly U.S. regional; DARE *plunder* n 2a chiefly South, South Midland]

2 Odds and ends, miscellaneous items often of little value, discarded objects, junk. Also called **house plunder 2.**

1931 Goodrich *Mt Homespun* 41 It's got six rooms in it and some other little rooms where she keeps her plunder; calls 'em closets. **1934–47** *LAMSAS Appal* (Swain Co NC) = junk. **1940** Haun *Hawk's Done* 184 We didn't have anything at all up in the loft, and we never did use that little back room for anything save plunder. **1960** Westover *Highland Lg* 20 = odds and ends. **1986** Pederson et al. *LAGS* = attested by 9/60 interviewees (15%) from E TN and 2/35 (5.7%) from N GA; 11/57 of all LAGS interviewees (19.2%)

attesting term were from Appalachia. **1995** Trout *Historic Buildings* 70 Thus, the crib became a central core between "plunder" sheds, "plunder" being an old term for miscellaneous stuff. **1998** Montgomery *Coll* = contains items one doesn't use but doesn't want to throw away (Cardwell).

[DARE *plunder* n 3 chiefly South, South Midland, especially SC]

B *verb*

1 To rummage.

1948 Chase *Grandfather Tales* 202 Hit's a heifer plunderin' around out there. **1982** Slone *How We Talked* 33 = [to] ramble or look through: "I plundered through that old trunk." **2015** *Blind Pig* (June 26) Right now he's plundering around the Bryson City Cemetery trying to set local newspaper folks straight on some matters of town history and responsibility for that neglected graveyard.

[DARE *plunder* v[2] 1 chiefly South Midland]

2 In phrase *plunder up* = See citation.

1969 *DARE Survey* (Rome GA) *plundered it up* = [performed] a clumsy or hurried job of repairing something.

plunder house (also *plunder room, plunder shed*) *noun* A small building or room in which miscellaneous equipment and other items are stored. See also **lumber room, plunder A1.**

1949 Kurath *Word Geog East US* 42 For a storeroom . . . in the Carolinas *plunder room* predominates, a term that has also a degree of currency in Virginia. **1961** Seeman *Arms of Mt* 28 Hansel, Nelvie, and Denton herded me into the "plunder house," where a box of tiny kittens lay among broken crocks, old cow-chains, and rusty farm implements that would never stand another dragging over the stony ground. **1969** Medford *Finis* 81 Up in the attic, in some old "plunder-room," shed, or maybe in an antique shop, one may occasionally find some thing that to most of the young generation today would be a curiosity. **c1995** *Cades Cove* 16 Some, but not all, cribs had "plunder sheds" to protect tools and vehicles from the weather. **1995** Trout *Historic Buildings* 70 Thus, the crib became a central core between "plunder" sheds, "plunder" being an old term for miscellaneous stuff. **1998** Montgomery *Coll* Her house is just a plunder house [i.e. she is a poor housekeeper] (Cardwell).

[Web3 *plunder room* n chiefly Midland]

plunder room, plunder shed See **plunder house.**

plunder up See **plunder B2.**

pneumonia fever *noun*

A Variant form *neumony fever.*

1942 Hall *Phonetics Smoky Mts* 76.

[DARE *pneumonia* n chiefly South Midland, South]

B Pneumonia, for which various teas, poultices, and salves have been used as treatments in traditional mountain medicine. Also called **lung fever.**

1862 *Patton CW Letters* (March 1) he was very sick had the pneumonia fever. **1865** (in **1992** Jackson *Surry Co Soldiers* 258) (Jan 13) I like to fainted three times before I got here I had the neumony fever. **1915** Pollard *TN Mts* 242 pneumonia. **1921** Weeks *Speech of KY Mtneer* 11 Fevers are common, but we are never satisfied with one—at least we always have a fever in the plural. Not yet content with our possessions, we aggravate conditions by taking on another malady. "Jim has pneumonie fevers" is no oncommon piece of news among us. **1937** Hall *Coll* (Catons Grove TN) For pneumony fever, make a poultice of peach tree bark and peach tree leaves or of mustard. **1939** Hall *Coll* (Little Greenbrier TN) For pneumony fever, put lamp oil on a woolen cloth. Put camphorated oil on the chest to keep the lamp oil from burning. We used boneset and catnip tea. **1955** Washburn *Country Doctor* 12 Other complaints were "pneumony fever," "side pleurisy," "joint rheumatism," "jumping toothache," the "bloody flux," and the "gallopin' consumption," to give the more descriptive designations of well-known diseases. **1960** Hall *Smoky Mt Folks* 46 If one was attacked by "pneumonie fever," a strong tea made of black snake root and bone set would "break it up." **1973** *AOHP/ASU-124* She used mustard [poultice] and such as that for fever and pneumony fever. **2017** *Blind Pig* (Dec 30) He warned us not to get too close to him, cause he was just getting over pneumony fever.

[DARE *pneumonia fever* n South Midland]

pneumonia salve *noun* See 1939 citation.

1939 Hall *Coll* (Big Creek NC) We'd make poultices with fried onions and grease with pneumonia salve and loosen it up thataway. **1957** Parris *My Mts* 42 His wife, America, said maybe he ought to grease his throat with a bit of pneumonia salve. **1999** Morgan *Gap Creek* 59 The room smelled of pneumony salve and camphor.

pock *noun* Syphilis.

c1920 (in **1993** Farwell and Nicholas *Smoky Mt Voices* 125) He had the pock.

[back-formation from *pox*]

pocket bootlegger *noun* See citation.

1990 Merriman *Moonshine Rendezvous* 108 He was also a "pocket bootlegger"; that's one that carried a pint or two in his pocket, when he's around people.

pocket harp *noun* A harmonica. Same as **French harp.**

1940 Simms *Wiley Oakley* 34 As it is, he has made many a merry evening, around campfires, with his mouth-organ or "pocket-harp," which he always carries with him. **1997** Montgomery *Coll* (known to Bush, Cardwell, Weaver).

point *noun, verb* Variant form *pint* [paɪnt].

1797 (in **1956** Eliason *Tarheel Talk* 316) (Burke Co NC) *pint.* **1862** *Huntley CW Letters* (May 4) some times I Become vary mutch depressed in spirits then again hope Revives me up and pints me to something Bright in the future. **1867** Harris *Sut Lovingood* 109 We camp't jist tuther side that high pint yu see yander. **1895** Murfree *Phantoms* 208 That's jes what p'inted out my jewty plain afore my eyes. **1913** Kephart *Our Sthn High* 102 You'll find most o' the dead faces pintin' to the sky. **1939** Walker *Mtneer Looks* 6 The other vowel sound we can be reasonably sure of, the diphthong *oi*, is generally pronounced as in *p'inted, h'isted, j'ined* for *pointed, hoisted, joined.* **1941** Stuart *Men of Mts* 68 We'd go side by side up that pint where you can still see that dip in the ground. **1942** Hall *Phonetics Smoky Mts* 46 [paɪnt]. **1985** Irwin *Alex Stewart* 260 We put him on that sled to take and bury him back here on top of this pint (point).

[DARE *point* n, v chiefly South, South Midland, formerly also New England]

point blank

A Variant forms *pimeblank* [see **1963** in **B**], *pime plank* [see **1982** in **C**], *pine blank* [see **1961** in **C**], *pint blank* [see **1974** in **C**], *p'int-blank* [see **1901** in **C**], *pliam-blank* [see **1940** in **C**], *plime blank* [see **1977** in **C**], *plum(b) blank* [see **1998** in **C**].

[DARE (at *point-blank* adv, adj) A3 *pime blank* chiefly southern Appalachians, especially eastern KY; *pine blank* A2 chiefly South Midland, especially southern Appalachians; A1 *pint blank* chiefly South Midland; A4 *plime blank* chiefly southern Appalachians, especially eastern KY]

B *adjective* Exact, plain, absolute, direct, outright.

1898 Elliott *Durket Sperret* 138 This is the last chence I'm a-goin' to give her, an' thet's p'int-blank. **1937** Hall *Coll* (Cades Cove TN) Pint blank proof [of whiskey making] was necessary for an arrest. **1963** Edwards *Gravel* 134 Among them wuz a little sorrel mare with white feet and a white spot on her forred, and follerin her wuz a colt that wuz the pimeblank image of its maw. **2002** Myers *Best Yet Stories* 164 = [this] expression we used to emphasize a point as being exactly on target. We'd say it was a "point-blank" lie. This meant absolutely, positively! **2017** Kinsler *Take Girl* 71 That's a plum blank lie.

[DARE *point-blank* adj C South Midland]

C *adverb* Exactly, precisely, absolutely, directly, bluntly.

1867 (in **1974** Harris *High Times* 290) He ranged a big bom mortar, where we were in the boat, point blank at the hatch hole. **1901** Harben *Westerfelt* 242 They are every one p'int-blank alike. **1911** Shearin *E KY Word-List* 539 I say pime-blank that I'm right. **1913** Kephart *Our Sthn High* 286 "P'int-blank" is a superlative or an epithet: "We jist p'int-blank got it to do." **1924** Raine *Saddle-bags* 207 I'm pint-blank drug out, but I shan't keer nary grain if Sally Ann's baby lives. **1937** Wilson *Folklore SE KY* 22 *I swear pime blank* = an expression of intensity (Bell Co KY). **1940** Stuart *Trees of Heaven* 188 Son, you act pliam-blank like a spring redbird buildin' a nest. **1961** Medford *History Haywood Co* 34 I can hit a squirrel pine blank in the head on the highest limb with this-here gun, yes-siree! **1974** Fink *Bits Mt Speech* 19 I told 'em no—*pint blank.* **1977** Shackelford et al. *Our Appalachia* 287 If ye didn't know a letter in the world, [or] in the Book, and God blesses ye to preach, you'd preach plime blank what he wants ye to. **1978** Montgomery *White Pine Coll* II-3 Things get twisted around, if you're not point-blank open and explain. **1982** Slone *How We Talked* 28 *pime plank* = true or exactly; "That's just pime plank how it looked." **1993** Soesbee *Wordlist* He looked pime blank like Billy. **1998** Brewer *Don't Scrouge* "Plime blank" in our neck of the woods was "pint-blank." It means "exactly" or "right on target" (in other words, "point blank"). "That boy's pint blank like his daddy" or "that rock hit him pint blank on the nose," for example ... When we started with "plime blank" a month or two ago, I had no notion there were so many variations of it scattered from one holler to the next in Southern Appalachia. We've had "plime blank," "plum blank," "plumb blank," and "pint blank."

[DARE *point-blank* adv B South Midland, especially Southern Appalachians]

pointedly *adverb* See also **appointedly.**

A Variant forms *pinely, pintedly* [see **1927, 1961** in **B**], *pintly* [see **1941** in **B**].

1986 Pederson et al. *LAGS* (Johnson Co TN) *pinely.*

B Absolutely, without a doubt, thoroughly, exactly.

1834 Crockett *Narrative* 99 I know that all the world couldn't make him acknowledge that he was pointedly whip'd. **1896** Fox *Vendetta* 105 This shootin' from the bresh, hit's p'int'ly a sin 'n' shame! **1927** Woofter *Dialect from WV* 361 I pintedly believed that he did it. **1931** Combs *Lg Sthn High* 1305 Old Towser can pointedly get up and fly. **1941** Stuart *Men of Mts* 93 I would a cut it when I built this house, but it's pintly bad luck to burn it and I didn't want it a-layin around the place here in the way. **1961** Williams *Content Mt Speech* 15 Lil pintedly 'lowed she'd not leave that child thar to grow up an' swink an' tote fer the rest of 'em. **1974** Fink *Bits Mt Speech* 19 *pintedly* = thoroughly. "The big dog most *pintedly* whopped the other'ns." **1975** Gainer *Speech Mtneer* 14 He pintedly believes it.

[EDD *pointedly* ppl adv Scot; DARE *pointedly* adv chiefly South Midland]

point row *noun* See citations.

1927 Woofter *Dialect from WV* 362 = short row furrowed to straighten the rows in the corn field: "You are hoeing a point row." **1957** Combs *Lg Sthn High: Word List* 75 = an extra, short row in a cornfield, laid off to keep the long rows straight. Furrowed or laid off before the corn is planted, of course.

[cf SND *point* n I.5 "the tapering part of a field which is not completely rectangular; the furrows or drills which are shortened thereby"]

poison

A *noun, verb, adjective* Variant forms *pison, pizen* ['paɪzən], *pizin.*

1869 (in **1974** Harris *High Times* 214) She pizened a widder's spring. **1890** Fruit *KY Words* 69 *pizin:* for poison. In all words with an "oi" in them the "oi" was formerly pronounced ai. **1913** Kephart *Our Sthn High* 122 We-uns must travel back and forth at a heap of expense, or pay express rates on pizened liquor. **1937** Hall *Coll* (Cosby TN) For blood pizen, make a poultice of catnip and bead-wood bark boiled together. **c1940** Padelford *Notes* He's a-treated her mean as pizen. **1942** Hall *Phonetics Smoky Mts* 46. **1963** Hooper *Unwanted Boy* 221 No, the bees did not often sting him, but they would have stung me until I was all swelled up like a "pizened" poodle. **2006** Ledford *Survivals* 1014 Other language peculiar to mountain speech appears in writings from the colonial period ... *pizen* "poison" and *dost* "dose."

[DARE *poison* n, v, adj, adv chiefly South, South Midland, occasionally Northeast]

B *adjective* Poisonous.

c1900 (in **1997** Stoddart *Quare Women* 126) Rattle snakes is a heap pizener than copper heads. **1924** Raine *Saddlebags* 135 Possibly a majority of the women of his own age in that district might take a drink, but . . . he himself was known to be "mighty pizen agin whiskey." **1959** Miller *Pigeon's Roost* (Aug 31) He turned the rock over and killed eight of the poison snakes, three large ones and five young ones. **1970** *Snake Lore* 170 All these snakes ain't poison, but now they'll hurt y'just th'same as anything else bitin' blood out of y'will. **1978** Reese *Speech NE Tenn* 164 They're both a deadly poison snake. **1985** Irwin *Alex Stewart* 264 Said he'd seen two or three, and that they was as poison as a rattlesnake.

C *adverb* Extremely, viciously, deadly.

1958 Campbell *Tales* 51 She acted loving and gentle, though she was poison mean in her heart. **1968** *End of Moonshining* 111 "Who's been messing around my still?" he cries, poison mad.

[DARE *poison* adv D especially South Midland]

poison ivory *noun* Poison ivy (*Toxicodendron radicans*). Same as **poison vine**.

1966 Dakin *Vocab Ohio River Valley* 409 *Poison ivory* is fairly common among older, less educated speakers in Kentucky and is also used in southern Indiana and Ohio. **1986** Pederson et al. *LAGS* (Cocke Co TN, Jefferson Co TN). **1997** Montgomery *Coll* (known to Brown, Bush, Ellis), = also known as *ivory* (Cardwell).

poison vine *noun*

A Variant form *pizen vine* [see **1867** in **B**].

B Poison ivy (*Toxicodendron radicans*). Also called **poison ivory**.

1867 Harris *Sut Lovingood* 76 Ef her hate fell ontu yu, yu'd feel like yu'd been whipp'd wif a pizen vine, ur a broom made outen nettils when yer breeches an' shut wer bof in the wash-tub. **1917** Kephart *Word-List* 415 *poison vine*. **1934–47** *LAMSAS Appal* (Madison Co NC, Swain Co NC) *poison vine*. **1967** *DARE Survey* (Gatlinburg TN, Maryville TN) = more common than *poison ivy*. **1975** Chalmers *Better* 34 Splinters and briars, a "risin" to incise for drainage, a "creeled foot" strapped to relieve strained muscles, and "pizen-vine" rash. **1978** Reese *Speech NE Tenn* 39 = attested by 8/12 (66.7%) speakers. **1986** Pederson et al. *LAGS* = attested by 16/60 interviewees (26.7%) from E TN and 3/35 (8.6%) from N GA; 19/28 of all LAGS interviewees (67.8%) attesting term were from Appalachia. **1997** Montgomery *Coll* (known to Adams, Ledford); The berry patch is full of old poison vine (Cardwell).

[DARE *poison vine* n 1 chiefly Midland]

poke[1] *noun* A bag or sack. See also **Christmas poke**, **paper poke**, **penny poke**.

1860 (in **1938** Taliaferro *Carolina Humor* 10) He has a "poke" on his back, full of dried beef and venison, and corn bread. **1861** Painter *CW Letters* (Dec 11) Brother george had sent me a poke of chestnuts and a pair socks. **1863** Phillips *CW Letters* (March 22) I want you to write if you get the poke of things and dozen eggs I sent. **1883** Jones *Highlands N Carol* 379 Mountain-women in sunbonnets and short-waisted dresses of calico or domestic gingham bring "pokes," as small bags are called, full of apples, peaches, roasting-ears, cabbage. **1895** Edson and Fairchild *TN Mts* 373 He had a *poke* of peanuts. **1913** Kephart *Our Sthn High* 199 Her husband returned, bearing a little "poke" of cornmeal. **1937** Hall *Coll* (Catons Grove TN) Put meat in a poke and bury it [to cure pork]. **1949** Kurath *Word Geog East US* 56 *Poke* is current, often by the side of *bag* or *sack*, in a large area extending from central Pennsylvania westward, and southward to the Carolinas. In Virginia the Blue Ridge forms the eastern boundary of the *poke* area, in North Carolina the Yadkin. **1958** Newton *Dialect Vocab* = attested by 8 of 36 speakers from E TN mountains, the more common terms being *bag* and *sack*. **1966** Dakin *Vocab Ohio River Valley* 136 The name *poke* = (paper) bag is used by virtually every speaker in the Kentucky Mountains and is quite common in the Knobs between the Bluegrass and the Mountains. Poke is uncommon in Kentucky west of this region, however. **1966–67** *DARE Survey* (Cherokee NC, Gatlinburg TN, Maryville TN) = a smaller paper container for bringing groceries home from the store. **1973** *GSMNP*-5:18 Go and get that poke of yellowroot and show these boys. **1984** Woods *WV Was Good* 222 = a standard word with us for a bag or even a larger sack. We said, "a paper poke," or just as likely, "a poke of meal." **1986** Ogle *Lucinda* 56 [At Christmas] pokes were filled with one apple, orange, maybe a banana and two sticks of candy and some grocer mixed kind of candy. **1986** Pederson et al. *LAGS* = attested by 32/60 interviewees (53.3%) from E TN and 7/35 (20%) from N GA; 39/81 of all LAGS interviewees (48.1%) attesting term were from Appalachia. **1997** *Dante OHP*-12 We'd take eggs and go to the store to buy stuff. Mommy'd put in about two or three for us to get candy with, you know, but you could get a big poke of candy for one egg. **2007** Ball *Tub Mills* 37 It was well on in the night when her husband returned, bearing a little "poke" of cornmeal.

[< Middle English *poke* probably < Norman French *poke*, *poque*, of Germanic origin, akin to Old English *pokka* "bag, pocket"; OED3 *poke* n[1] 1 "a bag, now esp. a paper bag, a small sack" now chiefly regional; EDD *poke* sb[1] in general dialect use in Scot, Irel, Engl; CUD *poke*[1] n 1 "a bag, a sack"; HT "a pouch; a small bundle; an improvised, cone-shaped bag for sweets"; Web3 *poke* n 1a chiefly South and Midland; DARE *poke* n[1] 1a chiefly Midland, especially Appalachians]

poke[2] (also *poke root*, *pokeweed*) *noun* A perennial plant (*Phytolacca americana*) whose edible leaves are made into **poke salad** but are toxic unless boiled; the root is used to make a tonic and to treat skin rash, infections, and other ailments. Also called **Cherokee sallet**, **inkberry**, **pigeonberry**. See also **pokeberry**, **poke salad**, **poke stalk**.

1863 Hampton *CW Letters* (April 16) you wrote that Aris and Ephraim [had] Eaten polk and hit Cam very nigh Killing them. **1865** Joyce *CW Letters* (March 12) I am tolable well at this time all but the Each tell Davy and Josy that I have got the old Each the wost sort tell thim they must bring Down me a pot full of poke root for I think I Shal haft to be gin to Docter fort it. **1939** Hall *Coll* (Big Creek NC) Poke bark they'd make hit for tea, for a bowel complaint. **1959** Roberts *Up Cutshin* 95 Now if one had the misfortune of catching something like the eetch, she would take this old pokeroot and make a ooze out of it and boil it and wash you with it and kill that eetch dead as a nit. **1968** Wilson *Folklore Mammoth Cave* 23 *poke* = a very common plant (Phytolacca americana) that grows in rich soil and is used extensively in wild greens and was formerly a source of many folk remedies. Many people in the region now fill their frozen-food lockers with a winter's supply or else can it. **1968** Wilson *Local Plants* 323 Phytolacca americana. The leaves, eaten as sallet, immunized against chills and fever in summer; pokeberry juice, alone or with whiskey, was a standard remedy for rheumatism. **1972** Cooper *NC Mt Folklore* 12 Yellow dock, mandrake, poke root, blood root and black cohosh were used as alternatives to tone up the system and establish a healthy condition. **1975** Dwyer *Thangs* 9 Mention poke sallet to native mountain people and they immediately start drooling—and for good reason. Poke's asparagus-like stalks, rich in Vitamin C, iron and other minerals, besides being delicious, are eaten more than any other wild plant. Poke is undoubtedly the "king" of mountain greens.

[modification of *puccoon*; DARE *poke* n³ 1 chiefly Midland]

pokeberry *noun* The fruit of **poke²**, which can be made into wine, a dye, or ink, and has various medicinal uses.

1937 Eaton *Handicrafts* 139 Among other natural dye colors were . . . pinks and lavenders from pokeberries. **1940** Haun *Hawk's Done* 6 The pokeberry ink is faded till it looks like the name is writ with catnip tea. **1968** Wilson *Local Plants* 323 Phytolacca americana. The leaves, eaten as sallet, immunized against chills and fever in summer; pokeberry juice, alone or with whiskey, was a standard remedy for rheumatism. **1971** Krochmal et al. *Medicinal Plants Appal* 190 In Appalachia, pokeberry wine is thought to help alleviate rheumatism; and in some areas dried fruits are used as a poultice on sores. **1977** Hurst and Lewis *Roaring Fork* 23 "We didn't have pens or ink," Herb recalled. "But sometimes we'd crush the seeds out of pokeberries or blackberries and then we'd write with berry juice." **1997** Andrews *Mountain Vittles* 16 The old timers of course ever' year made some poke berry wine.

[DARE *pokeberry* n chiefly Midland, especially South Midland]

pokeberry corn *noun* A type of corn (*Zea mays* var *rugosa*) with deep red kernels; an ear of this corn.

1971 *Corn Shuckin's* 98 Sometimes th'first one that got a red ear'ud get a ten-dollar prize. That's what they called pokeberry corn. Looked like poke come in it. And ever' once in a while you'd get a plumb red ear. And th'girl that got th'red ear, she chose her partner t'dance with later. **1983** Montell *Don't Go Up* 49 Some farmers grew . . . pokeberry corn, which grew especially large in the river bottoms.

poke-easy *adjective* Moving slowly or lazily; hence noun = one who moves in such a manner.

c1975 Lunsford *It Used to Be* 179 "Poke easy" is some person that moves around slowly. "All right, step on it," we'd say, "Now step on it, step on it, poke easy." **1976** Dwyer *Southern Sayin's* 16 = lazy, slow person. "Like a poke-easy mule." **1984** Woods *WV Was Good* 230 = somebody whose slow body movements betrayed laziness. **1997** Montgomery *Coll* (known to Bush, Cardwell, Weaver). **2000** Miller *Looneyville* 61 = a lazy or slow moving person fond of comfort and idleness with no interest in work or employment: "A pokeasy like him ought to be flayed with a hickory wythe."

[DARE *poke-easy* n, adj chiefly South Midland]

poke root See **poke²**.

poker stick (also *poking stick*) *noun* A fire poker.

1954 Roberts *Bought a Dog* 17 They was a big bunch of arn a-layin around there, like pokin sticks for his far. **c1960** Wilson *Coll*: *poking stick* = an iron rod used to stir a fire; a poker. **1962** Stubbs *Mountain-Wise* (April–May) 11 Other double words are "poker-stick" for poker; "pick-sack" for use in picking apples; "churn-jar" for churn. **1972** Hall *Sayings* 107 = a poker for the fire: "[He's] stiffer than a pokin' stick," said of a corpse.

[DARE *poking stick* n Southern Appalachians]

poke salad *noun* See also **poke²**.

A Variant forms *poke salat* [see **1913** in **B**], *poke sallet* [see **1939**, **1940**, **1978** in **B**], *polk salad* [see **1989** Smith in **B**].

B The young stalks or leaves of **poke** boiled and eaten as greens. See also **poke²**.

1913 Kephart *Our Sthn High* 282 This poke salat eats good. **1939** Hall *Coll* (Jefferson City TN) Poke sallet is made with poke weed. Poke weed has great big old heavy red-looking stalks. It grows by a new road or a new ground. **1940** Haun *Hawk's Done* 111 We stopped down there in the hollow and I picked my dress tail full of poke sallet for supper. **1978** Parris *Mt Cooking* 161 Poke sallet is a favorite dish of mountain folks whose tastes run to natural food. Of all the wild greens, it's the best known and the most sought after. . . . Mountain women begin picking poke as soon as the young sprouts start shooting out of the ground and they keep right on picking it and serving it until the sprouts grow old and tough. **1982** *Smokies Heritage* 109 *poke salad* = a dish of early spring greens from the pokeberry plants, young leaves only, picked before the plant is eight inches tall. Boiled in at least three changes of water, poke was one of the potent spring tonics used by Smokies residents because of its vitamins. **1989** Nicholson *Field Guide* 36 *poke salat* = green, leafy vegetable found throughout the South. **1989** Smith *Flyin' Bullets* 55 Polk salad was made from the huge green leaves of the polk stalk, which grew wild in abundance. **1997** Montgomery *Coll* = made from the tender, early spring growth of wild pokeweed, boiled until tender, squeezed and fried in sowbelly (bacon) with scrambled eggs, and served with corn pone (Brown). **2005** Ellison *Mt Passages* 52 Poke sallet (Phytolacca americana) is also called poke, pokeweed, poke greens, pocan, pigeonberry, and inkberry. It can be found in abundance in open fields and along roadsides. . . . Young shoots no more than eight inches long can be prepared in a number of ways: like asparagus; cut and fried in a cornmeal batter like okra; and fried whole or cut up with scrambled eggs. Young leaves are prepared as a potherb green. **2006** *Encycl Appalachia* 935 Poke can be parboiled, dipped in cornmeal, and fried; it is also boiled, chopped, and fried with eggs to make poke sallet. **2008** McKinley *Bear Mt* 155 Poke salat was a seasonal food that only came once a year. It was gathered in the spring while the poke weed was only inches high. **2009** Miller *Nigh Gone* 82 "Poke sallet" is the young leaves of the pokeberry and is similar to turnip greens. The young stems can be fried like okra. The gatherers of it quickly learned that they must pick only the newest and tenderest of the shoots because the mature leaves and little grape-like berries were poisonous. . . . Preparation of "poke sallet" necessitated boiling the leaves all day and then frying or sautéing them in a skillet with bacon or ham drippings. It was often seasoned with peppers, and sometimes, when they were available, eggs were stirred into the "mess" as it cooked. It was served with potlikker into which hot cornpone was crumbled.

[DARE *poke salad* chiefly South, South Midland]

poke salat, poke sallet See **poke salad.**

poke stalk *noun* A rifle or shotgun.

1936 Farr *Folk Speech* 276 = shot gun. "He took his polk stalk to the woods." **1967–68** *DARE Survey* (Brasstown NC) = legs as straight as a poke stalk; (Westminster SC) = long-barreled single shot [rifle]; (Gatlinburg TN) = [a person who is very thin] Looks like a poke stalk.

[DARE *poke stalk* n 1 South Midland]

poke-stalk religion *noun* Religious conviction that wanes quickly.

1931 Goodrich *Mt Homespun* 57 "This poke-stalk religion ain't worth much, to my way of thinkin'," said Elvira, and seeing the puzzled look on Lois' face, she added, "Laws, child, ain't you seen pokeweed a growin' up in the summertime, and then in the winter nothing left of it but a gray rag you couldn't kinnle a fire with?"

poke supper *noun* Formerly, a social event at which unmarked bags with homemade desserts and other foods were auctioned off to raise money for a school, church, or other worthy cause. See also **box supper, pie supper.**

1913 Kephart *Our Sthn High* 264 A substitute for the church fair is the "poke-supper," at which dainty pokes (bags) of cake and other home-made delicacies are auctioned off to the highest bidder. Whoever bids-in a poke is entitled to eat with the girl who prepared it, and escort her home. The rivalry excited among the mountain swains by such artful lures may be judged from the fact that, in a neighborhood where a man's work brings only a dollar a day, a pretty girl's poke may be bid up to ten, twenty, or even fifty dollars. **1937** Haun *Cocke Co* 21–22 The boys in the Hoot Owl Section have a particular grudge against a "Silver City Gang" in Hamblen County, and if there is to be a poke supper anywhere in the Hoot Owl section the boys are always prepared for the crowd from Silver City. Poke suppers are usually given by schools or churches to raise money for bells, Bibles, and such things. Every young girl, for miles around, brings a poke (paper bag), filled with pie, cake, candy and pickles. Each poke is auctioned off to the highest bidder. The boy who buys it, takes it to the girl whose name is on the inside of the poke. She opens it and they eat what is in it. Of course every girl has her poke marked with a certain kind of ribbon or flower, and her beau always knows which one to bid on. The Hamblen boys enjoy running up the bids on the pokes. They usually either get to eat with the girl or make the Cocke County boy pay dearly for his poke.

[DARE *poke supper* n South Midland]

pokeweed See **poke**[2].

poking stick See **poker stick.**

pole

A *noun* A slender, unhewn log used in constructing a crude building or for other purposes. See also **pole cabin, pole road, prize log.**

1927 Mason *Lure of Smokies* 225 I didn't have nairy a gun, so I just tuk up a pole an' driv' him off. **1939** Hall *Coll* (Smokemont NC) I got up on the drift, got me a pole and got up on the drift and laid down my gun and commenced jobbing down through the drift. **1940** Oakley *Roamin'/Restin'* 23 The old man was chopping up poles as I call them. The man had cut down trees out at the edge of [the] yard or near by the woods and drag[ged] these poles into the house.

B (also *pole along, pole in, pole off*) *verb* To walk, go on foot slowly or aimlessly.

1930 Greer-Petrie *Angeline Outsmarts* 7 He'd come pollin' [sic] in, leadin' a purty girl to her seat. **c1960** Wilson *Coll*: *pole along* = to slouch, go slowly or aimlessly. **c1975** Lunsford *It Used to Be* 176 "To pole" means to walk. "I had to just pole it up through there." **1997** Montgomery *Coll*: *pole* = to walk cautiously with a cane or pole, also *pole along* (Bush). **2009** Benfield *Mt Born* 182 *pole off* = to go outside for a purpose, to embark upon one's business, always on foot.

[DARE *pole* v 1 chiefly South Midland]

pole along See **pole B.**

pole ax(e) *noun* A single-bitted, long-handled ax with a sharp blade on one side of its head and a flat square surface on the other side, used to fell trees, hew logs, and drive wedges.

1939 Hall *Coll* (Little Cataloochee NC) We heard some dogs a-comin', and we looked out and we saw a deer . . . and the dogs jerked him back, an' my grandmother, she grabbed the ax, the pole ax, and she went, hit it one lick. **1940** Oakley *Roamin'/Restin'* 22 We had an ax to chop down trees in case the dogs treed anything up a tree. This ax was called a pole ax in the mountains. **1963** Medford *Mt People* 34 The common pole axe was used not only in felling trees [and] cutting up the meat; it was also used for splitting rails, driving stakes, shaping handles, "barking" trees, and killing hogs—also to an extent in cutting up the meat, as a branding iron, and the handle as a two foot-measure. **1964** Clarkson *Lumbering in WV* 368 = an ax with a sharp blade on one side and square on the other side . . . Same as a single-bitted ax. **1973** Schulman *Logging Terms* 36 = an ax with a flat surface on one side of the head. The pole ax was used on a raft because it could be used for driving in raft pins as well as for chopping. **c1975** Lunsford *It Used to Be* 48 The only thing left to do was take a pole axe (that's an axe with the square part in the back) and knock the hog in the head.

pole bean *noun* A green bean grown on an upright pole or stick, in contrast to a **bunch bean**. See 2011 citation. Also called **runner 1**, **stick bean**. See also **bunch bean**.

c1960 Wilson *Coll* = general name for a bean with long vines necessitating supports. **1993** Ison and Ison *Whole Nother Lg* 51 = large green beans that vine up a pole, lattice, or corn stalk. **2006** *Encycl Appalachia* 935 Pole beans, which grow upward to a height of ten feet or more, require external support. Often trained up trellises or cornstalks, they will also wind around sunflowers. **2011** Best *Bean Terminology* – same as cornfield beans. When some gardeners stopped growing corn in their gardens, poles often substituted for corn stalks. They are often used in teepee style to give stability. More recently poles have given way to trellises which give more room and more sunshine to the bean vines. **2016** Netherland *Appal Cooking* 71 We planted beans beside the corn and allowed them to "run" up the cornstalks. These beans were called pole beans, or cornfield beans. Kentucky Wonder beans were the common pole beans, growing six to eight feet tall. **2018** Heinmiller *Coll* Make sure you have tall stakes for your pole beans. They'll take over your garden.

pole cabin (also *pole house, pole log house, pole shack*) *noun* A small, windowless dwelling of unhewn logs rounded at the end and joined with simple notches.

1924 Bacheller *Happiest Person* 7 John hired some land and built a pole cabin. **1937** Conner *Ms* 3 I've seen rough poal hous'es built without a nail, or rafter. **1966** Kniffen and Glassie *Building in Wood* 53 In this southern Appalachian region, corresponding roughly to the early settlement areas of Watauga, Holston, and Nolichucky, half dovetailing came to prevail on houses and on carefully made barns and outbuildings, and saddle notching—usually with the notching only on the bottom, occasionally with the notch on top—became dominant on contemporary cabins, or "pole shacks," and less carefully made barns and outbuildings. **1991** Williams *Homeplace* 31 The building of log dwellings diminished considerably after the turn of the century. Individuals who continued to use log construction frequently built "pole" houses of small, unhewn logs. [Ibid. 167 In southwestern North Carolina the term "pole" is commonly used for any house built of unhewn logs.] **2007** McMillon *Notes: pole log house*.

polecat grease (also *polecat oil*) *noun* See citations. Same as **skunk grease**.

1930 Armstrong *This Day and Time* 117 Law, yes, polecat oil, hits fine fer the whoopin' cough—hit an' chestnut tea. **c1930** (in **2003** Williams *Coming of Age* 39) Skunk oil ("polecat grease") was administered when we developed croup. Perhaps the worst medicine I ever took for an illness was rancid polecat grease. I was forcefully held and required to gargle with it when I developed croup one winter. **1977** Ginns *Rough Weather* 14 She'd come running with her polecat-grease bottle in her hand. And she'd grease him on his chest, between his shoulders, under his arms, the palms of his hands, and the bottoms of his feet. She'd just about grease him all over. **1985** Irwin *Alex Stewart* 217 [Polecat oil is] the best thing ever you put on leather. If you put it on a burn before it has time to blister, it'll never blister. It'll draw the fire right out. And it's good for croup. The kids used to be awful bad back then to take the croup, and they would be stopped up till they couldn't get their breath. You could take a teaspoon of that skunk grease and let them swaller it and in a few minutes it was all over with.

polecat oil See **polecat grease**.

pole house See **pole cabin**.

pole in See **pole B**.

pole lay *noun* See citation. See also **lay**[1].

1993 *Foxfire X* 396 Sometimes I will call it "lay" and then "lathe." The old-timers call it simply a "pole lay." That's what my dad called it. Where the tool gets its name is the pole, which plays an important part—it does half the work. You always keep the tension on it.

pole log house See **pole cabin**.

pole off See **pole B**.

pole road *noun* A crude road over rough or swampy terrain, consisting of a series of short logs laid like railroad ties transversely to the direction of travel, used by wagons or by horses to draw logs or lumber. Also called **corduroy road**. See also **plank road**, **pole A**.

1939 Hall *Coll* (Deep Creek NC) That's the dividing ridge between the pole road and Bear Creek. **1974–75** McCracken *Logging* 3:3 You take and throw a log down. Then you'd cut logs, short logs, and lay then across it. If one of them was a little bit high, you just took your axe and hewed it down so you get two or three loads of logs over it. Logs wear it down anyhow. Then they'd take and cut a long log. Then start spiking it around the side and they called that a fender, to keep the logs from running off of the outside. In a lot of places they get the logs on those slides and they'd run. They'd just sound like thunder a-coming off of that mountain. **n.d.** *Tremont Logging* 5 To make it easier for the horses, pole roads were constructed by partially burying small logs across the road every few feet. **1979** *Big South Fork OHP-10* They had a pole road that they hauled the lumber into Stockton till they got the railroad out there. . . . There used to be a pole road come from down here on the railroad where there's a big mill. They brought the lumber up on top of the hill . . . and that pole road come through here and was right out through there and to Rugby Road. **1983** Montell *Don't Go Up* 93 Some logging operations were large enough to merit construction of tram roads or pole roads from the river or railhead to the logging camps. **2003** Howell *Folklife Big*

South Fork 75 Pole roads were tracks of parallel peeled saplings, eight to ten inches in diameter, joined at the ends like sections of log pipe. Heavy flatbed wagons were pulled over these tracks by mules or horses.

pole shack See **pole cabin**.

police *noun* A police officer (sometimes with stress on initial syllable).

1961 *Coe Ridge OHP-343A* He killed two polices in Indianapolis and come back here and was a-hiding out on Coe Ridge in a cave. **1975** Woolley *We Be Here* 14 They was all against us. We had all the state polices, and they was against us. *Ibid.* 19 Them state polices was sent in here to break the strike. **1985** Dabney *More Mt Spirits* 180 A police was there and he says, "It [= sugar] goes out dry and comes back shakin'." **1989** *Matewan OHP-1* They met each other there, face to face, and killed each other . . . two local polices, two Matewan policemen. *Ibid.* 18 [I] never did see a police. **1998** *Dante OHP-12* I had a police that followed me one night from Abingdon to Hansonville. *Ibid.* 69 He used to be a state police, but he was a drunk, too. **2012** Montgomery *Coll* I carry my wallet so the polices can identify me.

[cf SND *police* n "a policeman, a police officer"; DARE *police* n B1 chiefly South, South Midland]

police foot *noun* See citation.

1963 Watkins and Watkins *Yesterday* 131 Athlete's foot, which for some reason the farmer called police foot, was treated with a poultice of cow manure.

policeman variant plural form *policemans*.

1989 *Matewan OHP-39* Somebody had cut down on them offen the mountain there, and he shot one of these state policemans in the thigh.

political speaking *noun* Same as **speaking 1**.

1926 Lunsford *Folk-Lore* 13 When a boy I remember hearing him "call the house to order" at a political speaking in Buncombe where the late Governor Craig and the Honorable Virgil S. Lusk were to measure swords in a political debate. He began by saying, "All right gentlemen, get quiet as soon as possible for we are soon going to start up the 'chin music.'"

politicianer *noun* A politician.

1859 Taliaferro *Fisher's River* 109 Speaking of politics reminds me of one more anecdote connected therewith. It was customary for "candidates" in olden times to treat with liquor; but after a while the temperance reformation reached Fisher's River . . . and "polititioners" in treating had to change their "tacktucks" a little.

[DARE *politicianer* n especially South Midland]

polk salad See **poke salad**.

polk stalk See **poke stalk**.

polluted *adjective* See citation.

1981 *High Coll (DARE)* = used in the Gorge with positive connotations, meaning to be thoroughly furnished with; "Them grapes used to be anywhere you went. The bushes were polluted with them and their vines just camouflaged the rocks."

pollyfox *verb* hence *verbal noun pollyfoxing*.

1 To delay, waste time. See also **bollyfox**.

1944 Laughlin *Word-List Buncombe Co* 25 = to dilly-dally, to waste time. **1976** Dwyer *Southern Sayin's* 21 = to dilly-dally, delay and discuss. "Get going and stop your polly foxing."

[DARE *polly-fox* v 1 chiefly Midland]

2 See citation.

1981 Daugneaux *Separate Place* 63 Polyfoxing [sic] is the art of making homemade medicine and was practiced in West Virginia (and other mountain states) during the period of pioneer settlements. The origin of the term is not found in any standard or medical dictionary. It may have been brought to the Appalachian Highlands by the Scots and English.

[origin uncertain]

pollyfoxing See **pollyfox**.

pollyrich *noun* The oven bird (*Seiurus aurocapillus*).

1932 Creal *Quaint Speech* A towhee is a joree and an oven bird is a pollyrich.

poly See **poorly**.

pomace *noun*

A Variant forms *pummies* [see **1974** Cate in **B**], sometimes construed as a plural count noun; hence singular *pummy* through back-formation [see **2003** in **B**].

[DARE *pomace* n 2b (used as a count noun) chiefly Midland, especially South Midland].

B The pulp left after crushing stalks of sorghum cane (to make molasses), apples (to make cider), or other fruit to extract juice from them.

1958 Wood *Words from TN* 14–15 = the crushed residue left after making cider (or in some areas molasses). "The crushed apples from the cider mill were referred to only as *pummies*." **1973** *GSMNP-57:85* They made a beer out of cane pummies. **1974** Cate et al. *Sthn Appal Heritage* 91 Vinegar was also made from the apple pulp, or "pummies," left after the juice had been extracted for cider. **1974** Fink *Bits Mt Speech* 20 = pomace, ground apples, peaches, etc. from which the juice has been pressed. "After they made cider, they threw the *pummies* on the ground." **1976** Braden *Grandma Was Girl* 39 Sometimes we made cider from the apples. We used the same grater to grate the apples that we used to grate corn for the gritted-bread. We then strained the juice out of the grated apples through a thin cloth. Some of this cider we let sour into vinegar, which we used for making pickles. We called the grated apples "pummies." This word, I suppose, is a corruption of the word "pomace," meaning crushed fruit, which is perhaps derived from the French word "pomate" (apple), and came into our vocabulary from my great grandmother, who was of French descent. **1992** Austin *Vanishing Art* 103 The flattened, dry [sorghum] cane, called "pummies," is then discarded, or used as fodder or garden mulch. **1996** Houk *Foods & Recipes* 150 To do this, they ground up whole apples in a cider mill; the ground apples, called "pummies," were put into the tub and pressed into fresh, sweet cider with just the slightest tang. **2003** Cooper *Gathering Memories* 45 Put apple pummy on a sprain.

pomper (also *pomper up, pomp up*) *verb, verb phrase* To spoil (a child or pet).

1885 Murfree *Prophet* 71 I never see a critter so pompered ez Jacob; he ain't got no medjure o' respec'. **1886** Smith *Southernisms* 41 Pomped, for pampered, I heard from a herder in the Great Smoky Mountains last summer, who spoke of a certain cow as "pomped up." **1922** Cobb *KY Mt Rhymes* 6 Where a pompered boy could lie, / Gee-oh, hit's long-ago days that cling! **1961** Seeman *Arms of Mt* 97 Brownie is the most "pompered up" ground hog in the county. **1974** Fink *Bits Mt Speech* 20 Them young'uns is plumb *pompered*.

[DARE *pomper* chiefly South Midland]

ponch See **paunch**.

pond man *noun* See citation.

1994 Farwell and Buchanan *Logging Terms* = a logger who washed logs.

pond monkey *noun* See citations.

1997 Farwell *Logging* = a man who works with a loader, getting the clean logs from the pond into the mill. **2004** *BearPaw* 5 The photos show the transformation from tree to board feet—men cut massive trees with crosscut saws ("misery whips" or "wood harps"), moved the logs with skidders, overhead cables, mules, or greased chutes (some a mile long), loaded them on train cars, dumped them in mill ponds (where "pond monkeys" with spiked boots rolled them around), and fed them into sawmills.

pone

A *noun*

1 (also *ponebread, pone of bread, pony*) A baked patty or cake of bread, especially of cornmeal (used frequently in compounds such as **corn pone**).

1824 (in **1912** Doddridge *Notes on Settlement* 88) Johnny cake and pone were at the outset of the settlements of the country the only forms of bread in use for breakfast and dinner. **1861** *Martin CW Letters* (Nov 10) send me A pone of loaf coarn bread & one of wheat bread. **1863** *Joyce CW Letters* (March 12) tell Mary Etter that I got up this mor[n]ing a bout two ours be fore day and backed me a grate big pon of bread. **1863** *Zimmerman CW Letters* (Jan 10) I wish you could send me a box with something if it was only a pone of corn bread. **1890** Carpenter *Thunderhead Peak* 144 At the second spring we stopped for lunch. A fire was started, and the pone put to bake on a wide chip. Pone is the common food of the mountaineers. Corn meal is stirred up with water and a little salt, and the solid mass is put to bake, or rather to dry, on a board by the fire. When done, it is the most solid food imaginable. Sometimes to make it more palatable and digestible, it is baked in the fat after the bacon is fried. Sad experience teaches the necessity of becoming "acclimated" to the food before starting on a mountain trip to the south. **1903** Fox *Little Shepherd* 59 Meanwhile, the mother had cooked a great pone of corn-bread, three feet in diameter, and had ground coffee and got sides of bacon ready. **1925** Dargan *Highland Annals* 26 We didn't have a dust o' flour, an' I couldn't set him down to ponebread an' him come all the way from Madison to see us. **1937** Hall *Coll* (Emerts Cove TN) *pone of bread* = term common only among old people, with *cake of bread* being more usual. **1939** Farr *TN Mt Regions* 91 *pony* = pone of bread: "She's cooking pony for supper." **1939** Hall *Coll* (Hazel Creek NC) She done her bakin' in a [Dutch] oven. She baked her cornbread in pones. **1949** Justus *Toby Has Dog* 11 He picked some extra fine stove-wood for Mother to use in cooking the chicken, two different kinds of pie, and the pone of gingerbread. **1966** Dakin *Vocab Ohio River Valley* 312 The use of *pone* = "loaf" (a pone of light-bread) is fairly common among older and rural speakers in Kentucky. *Ibid.* 313–15 The old terms *corn pone, pone bread,* and *pone* for large cakes or "loaves" of corn bread are commonly remembered or used everywhere in the [Ohio] Valley. . . . In Kentucky *corn pone, pone* and *pone bread* are about equally common. **1982** Slone *How We Talked* 31 *pone of bread* = a pan of bread (a whole pone; all of something). **1984** Page and Wigginton *Foxfire Cookery* 179 There was about ten in our family altogether, and it took a pretty good pone of bread to fill them up with just 'taters, butter, corn bread, meat, and milk. **1986** Pederson et al. *LAGS* (Jefferson Co TN) *pone bread* = light bread. **1996** Johnson *Lexical Change* 138 *pone, pone bread, pone of bread, pone of cornbread* = statistically more common in the mountains of South Carolina and Georgia than in the Piedmont and Coastal Plain c1990. **2008** McKinley *Bear Mt* 76 Now she was ready to bake a "pone" of cornbread in a heavy iron skillet and fry thick slices of streaked fatback bacon. **2016** Netherland *Appal Cooking* 34 The word "pone" can mean different things: some meanings are regional, others are family usage. My grandfather used the term to mean any cake, loaf, or piece of corn bread, and that usage was the most pervasive in our community. Others used the term to refer to a specific shape (usually oval) for baking unleavened corn bread.

[DARE *pone* n 1a chiefly South, South Midland, *pone bread* South, South Midland]

2 A lump, growth, or swelling on the body. See also **grine pone**.

1895 Edson and Fairchild *TN Mts* 373 = hard swelling. "He's got a *pone* in his side. I reckon ef it busts inside, he'll die right now." **1917** Kephart *Word-List* 415 = lump, swelling. "A *pone* came up on her side." **1929** (in **1952** Mathes *Tall Tales* 98) The "doctor" was putting the last touches of preparedness to his favorite and only surgical "instermint," with which he had lanced many a "bile, pone, or risin'." **c1960** Wilson *Coll* = a swelling from an injured or diseased part of the body. **1976** Garber *Mountain-ese* 70 = swelling or abscess. "He had to see the doctor about a pone on his right arm." **1990** Cavender *Folk Medical Lex* 29 = a painful lump on the body. "I've got a pone on my leg from when I accidentally hit myself with a hammer." **1994–97** Montgomery *Coll* (known to Adams, Brown, Cardwell, Jones, Ledford, Norris, Oliver). **2000** Lowry *Folk Medical Term* = a raised swelling in the form of a pone of cornbread.

[DARE *pone* n 3a chiefly Southern Appalachians]

B (*pone out*, *pone up*) *verb phrase* To swell, become puffed.

1962 Krutch *More Lives* 7 Probably few still living inhabitants of Knoxville now remember the odd terminology which was once taken for granted, but in the hills not far away so many Seventeenth Century words still linger that a local physician repeated only a few years ago the reply given by a patient who was asked the origin of a badly swollen ankle: "Well, Doc, I just hunkered down, it creeled, and then it poned up 'til I thought hit was agoin' to beal." All but one of the strange words, I believe, to be found in large dictionaries. Translation: "I squatted on my heel, it twisted, and swelled up so much I thought it might ulcerate." **1986** Pederson et al. *LAGS* (Johnson Co, Sullivan Co TN). **1990** Cavender *Folk Medical Lex* 29 *pone out* = used in the phrase "poned out" in reference to a swollen part of the body.

[of Algonquian origin, akin to Delaware *apan*]

ponebread, **pone of bread** See **pone A1**.

pone out, **pone up** See **pone B**.

ponhaws (also *pon hosh*) *noun* See citations. See also **poor do 1**, **scrapple**.

1946 Woodard *Word-List VA/NC* 24 *pon hosh* = grease from hog-killing mixed with corn meal, fried, and sliced. "Scrapple." "Solidified liquid leavings from liver pudding, etc., cooked (fried) with corn meal." Rural region of Salem [VA], 1940, 1946. **1949** Kurath *Word Geog East US* 32 *Ponhaws* . . . has survived also on the upper reaches of the Potomac in Maryland and West Virginia.

[< Pennsylvanian German *pannhas* "dish of leftovers" < German dialect *panne* "pan" + *has* "hare"; Web3 *panhaws* n Midland; DARE (at *panhas* n) scattered, but chiefly North Midland, especially PA]

pon hosh See **ponhaws**.

pon my honor, **pon my word** See **upon my honor**.

pony See **pone A1**.

pony saw mill *noun* See citation.

1939 Hall *Coll* (Cosby Creek TN) Pony saw mills [are] small mills which could be pulled [from place to place] by four horses or oxen.

pooch *noun* See citation.

1990 Cavender *Folk Medical Lex* 29 = hernia.

[DARE *pooch* n[1] chiefly South, South Midland]

pooch out

A *verb phrase* Especially of a part of the body: to protrude abnormally, bulge, swell.

1960 Cooper *Jularker Bussed* He just sets with his mouth pooched out (stuck out) since he discivered (discovered) he built the walls antigodlin (not plumb). **1969** Dial *Dialect Appal People* 463 When I first came to Lincoln County [WV] as a bride it used to seem to me that everything that did not pooch out, hooved up. Pooch is a Scottish variant of the word pouch and was in use in the 1600's. Numerous objects can pooch out, including pregnant women and gentlemen with "bay windows." **1973** Miller *English Unicoi Co* 81 If he puts too many things in the pockets, they pooch out. **1997** Montgomery *Coll* (known to Adams, Bush, Cardwell, Ellis, Ledford, Norris, Oliver). **2002** Rash *Foot in Eden* 100 Ella pressed her hand on my pooched-out belly. **2016** Heinmiller *Coll* [That baby's] belly just pooched out over his diaper.

[DARE *pooch* v chiefly South, South Midland]

B *noun phrase* An area of ground that protrudes or bulges.

1997 Montgomery *Coll* After the flood the hill had a big pooch out (Cardwell).

[ultimately related to *pouch* < Middle English *pouche* "pouch"]

poor *adjective*

A Variant forms *pore*, *pyore*.

1862 *Bradshaw CW Letters* (Oct 28) many a pore sistor is deprived of this blessing. **1905** Miles *Spirit of Mts* 18 They call us pore mountaineers! We git more out o' life than anybody. **1930** Thomas *Death Knell* Often syllables ending in an "r" sound have a "y" inserted in front of them, as cyar (car), gyarden, pyore (poor).

B Senses.

1 Thin, malnourished, scrawny (especially in phrase *poor as a snake*).

1863 *Revis CW Letters* (April 7) I am not fat b[u]t as pore as asnake. **1863** *Tesh CW Letters* (Aug 2) I am afraid that your health is not good as it has ben by your being so poor but your having to take such long hard marches I recon is the reason you have got so poor. **1939** Eastridge *Folklore Adair Co* 117 A person who is very lean, perhaps from a long illness, is described as being "as thin as a rail." In the same connection, "as poor as Job's turkey" is used. **1942** (in **1987** Perdue *Outwitting Devil* 23) Jack's bull was getting poor as a snake. **1963** Williams *Metaphor Mt Speech II* 53 If she is unusually thin, she is not only "as pore as a snake" but "has to stand twicet to make her shadder." **1977** Shackelford et al. *Our Appalachia* 241 I've seen [horses] so poor you can just about hang your hat on their hipbones. **1983** *Dark Corner OHP*-5A She got awful poor, and they carried her back to the hospital. . . . She got down so poor, couldn't hardly eat nothing, couldn't hardly walk. **1985** Irwin *Alex Stewart* 251 We drove her in the barn and caught her, and she was so poor she couldn't hardly walk. **2000** Morgan *Mts Remember* 64 When he took off his shirt I could see how poor he really was from starving in the prison camp.

[DARE *poor* adj Bb scattered, but especially South, South Midland]

2 See citation.

2018 *Blind Pig* (Aug 31) On Tennessee's Cumberland Plateau ... I continue to be amazed by the words and phrases I take for granted as just regular English when in fact they are part of our dialect! I recently used the term "poor" for someone having too much of something—like "shoe-poor" for having way too many shoes.

poor as a snake See **poor B**.

(as) **poor as Job's turkey** *adjective phrase* Indigent, impoverished.

1927 Woofter *Dialect from WV* 362 = very poor. "The people who live on that run are all poor as Job's turkey." **1965** *Dict Queen's English* = indicates extreme poverty. "The family was as poor as Job's turkey." **1978** Ball *Speech Knox Co* 138 = used to emphasize a point; term has at least two meanings: (1) poor, as "poor as Job's turkey," and (2) large, as "it's as big as Job's turkey." **1999** Montgomery *Coll* (known to Cardwell).

poor do *noun*

1 A makeshift or make-do meal, as one fashioned from left-over corn bread or other basic ingredients. See 1990 citation. See also **poor sole**.

1913 Kephart *Our Sthn High* 292 The old Germans taught their Scotch and English neighbors the merits of scrapple, but here it is known as poor-do. **1982** Slone *How We Talked* 33 = water gravy (gravy made from water in place of milk, when no milk is available). **c1982** Young *Colloquial Appal* 17 = a food of hot grease and bread. **1984** Wilder *You All Spoken* 84 = dumplin's of bread scraps dampened with water and baked; a concoction made by stirring corn meal and grease in a skillet, frying until it smokes, then adding water or milk. **1986** Pederson et al. *LAGS* (Cocke Co TN, Jefferson Co TN) = type of cornbread. **1990** Oliver *Cooking Hazel Creek* 10 What to do with left-over corn bread was solved by turning it into something called Poor Do or Fried Bread. To make this dish, take day-old, or older, cornbread, slice it and fry the cut sides in a little grease until brown. Then add enough milk to about half cover the bread and simmer for awhile. This dish lingered on & had a big revival in popularity during the Depression years when people all over the country sometimes made an entire meal from it. **1996–97** Montgomery *Coll* = a makeshift meal of ingredients, odds and ends (Andrews), = corn meal sliced and fried (Brown), = a cornmeal dumpling, sometimes cooked on turnip greens (Cardwell), = cornbread cut into pieces, then sliced and fried, with milk sometimes added to the pan when almost done, also called *fried bread* (Oliver). **1998** Dabney *Smokehouse Ham* 217 The cheap, easy-to-fix cornmeal gravy caught on. While "sawmill gravy" was the popular nickname, some called it "Logging Gravy." Others called it Poor Do or Life Everlasting, a reference to what many felt was its role in keeping them alive. **2007** McMillon *Notes* = not scrapple, but water, grease, cornbread, and any scraps from other meals thrown together and cooked to feed the family in hard times.

2 A person or situation of little account or worth.

1954 Arnow *Dollmaker* 71 Fer all my fixen and coal haulen, it's been a poor do. **1994–97** Montgomery *Coll* = of lodging: having only the bare necessities (Andrews); He's entertaining a poor do [i.e. he's engaged in a project of little consequence or merit], He married a poor do [= a ne'er do well person] (Cardwell).

[DARE *poor do* n 1, 2 both senses chiefly South, South Midland]

3 See citation.

1986 Pederson et al. *LAGS* (Jefferson Co TN) = like hushpuppies.

poor john *noun* Milk becoming sour.

1937 Wilson *Folklore SE KY* 8 If [the milk] is turning sour, it is "blinky" or "pore John."

poorly

A Variant forms *poly* [see **1862** in **B1**] *porely* [see **1863** in **B1**].

[DARE *poorly* adj chiefly South, South Midland]

B *adjective*

1 In poor health or condition, unwell, sickly in appearance.

1831 *McLean Diary* 2 [I] went to see old father Chenoweth[,] found him poorly. **1862** *Ingram CW Letters* (Oct 4) he has ben poly But he is on the mend now. **1863** Wilson *Confederate Private* 5 (Feb 15) he has had the fever He was rite porely the last I heard of him. **1910** Cooke *Power and Glory* 39 Pap's poorly again, and I'm obliged to put the late supper on the table. **1937** Hall *Coll* (Nine Mile TN) [How is your father?] He's poorly. **1959** Pearsall *Little Smoky* 88 He must provide for his family, but on days he feels "too poorly" to work no one is likely to press him. **1974** Fink *Bits Mt Speech* 20 I'm feeling purty *poorly*. **2009** Benfield *Mt Born* 183 = appear[ing] sickly and in ill health. This word invariably referred to physical looks.

2 Destitute.

1861 *Shifflet CW Letters* (Nov 10) we march thrugh a poly part of Country yesterday. **1931–33** (in **1987** Oliver and Oliver *Sketches* 30) Church houses was poorly in those days and very often they would hold their meetings at the home of the church members.

C *adverb* See citation.

1958 Combs *Archaic English in KY* 41 = in poverty: "They live poorly."

poor man's pie *noun* See citation.

1982 Slone *How We Talked* 65 = sweet-milk pie, made with left-over biscuits.

poor-mouth *noun* in phrases *put up a poor mouth, talk poor mouth* = to complain in an excessive or unjustified manner about one's fortunes or circumstances.

1892 Fruit *KY Words* 231 "to put up a po' mouth" = to plead poverty. **1952** Wilson *Folk Speech NC* 578 *talk poor mouth* = to plead poverty. **2007** McMillon *Notes* = to plead poverty when in reality the poverty is lacking.

[OED3 *poor mouth* n originally and chiefly U.S.; DARE *poor mouth* n chiefly Midland, South]

poor out See **out C**.

poor sole *noun* See citations. See also **poor do 1**.

1958 Wood *Words from TN* 14 = another name for *poor do*. **1986** Pederson et al. *LAGS* (Hawkins Co TN) = cornmeal dumpling. **1987** Trent *Yesteryear* 10 Way back in the mountains, or down south, "poor people" often found themselves with only a ham-hock and corn bread. They most generally had a bunch of hound dogs to feed. They made what they referred to as "poor soles" in the broth after the ham-hock had been cooked. After enjoying a hearty fill, they'd go to the door and toss out the remaining corn dumplings as they yelled, "Oh, you'n pore soles." The name pore soles is a colloquialism for "Poor Souls."

[DARE (at *poor soul*) TN]

poor to *adjective phrase* Ill-equipped to, barely able to (do something). See also **awful to, bad to, good to**.

1956 Hall *Coll* (Murphy NC) [Sometimes] you eat so much it makes you poor to carry it.

poor woman *noun* A woman carrying an illegitimate child.

1939 Hall *Coll* (Proctor NC) = a woman that's bigged, in a family way, in other words pregnant. I've heard it used a few times. Just old timers used it. **1954** Hall *Coll* (Smokemont NC) = a woman, generally unmarried or beyond marriageable age, who "has to get her children however she can."

pop[1] *noun* A grandmother.

1937 Wilburn *Notes* 29 An old woman they called "Pop Caldwell" was the mother of all the Caldwells in Cataloochee. [**1998** Montgomery *Coll* = there was also a woman called Granny Pop on Copeland Creek [in TN] (Cardwell).]

pop[2] *verb* Of a bear: to gnash or snap (its teeth).

1904–20 Kephart *Notebooks* 4:749 I heered the old she [bear] poppin' her teeth. **1913** Kephart *Our Sthn High* 81 They'll run right in on the varmint [= a bear], snappin' and chawin' and worryin' him till he gits so mad you can hear his tushes pop half a mile. **1939** Hall *Coll* (Hartford TN) He could feel [the bear] a-biting him nearly. He could hear it popping its teeth. **1970** *Hunting Stories* 79 They had th'big boar bayed. . . . He'uz standin' there chompin' his teeth, poppin' his teeth.

popcracker *noun* A firecracker.

1917 Kephart *Word-List* 415.

[DARE *popcracker* n VA, NC]

poppee doll See **poppie 1**.

poppet *noun*

1 (also *poppet doll*) A doll, especially a homemade one. See also **poppie 1**.

1918 Hartt *Lost Tribes* 401 It takes brains to make hempen-haired "poppet-dolls" of whittled wood. **1942** Thomas *Blue Ridge* 160 The children's play-pretties—the poppet, a make-believe corn-shuck doll—the banjo, and fiddle are put aside. **1968** Connelly *Discover Appal* 131 Toy making is another old mountain home industry which has been revived in recent years. In some mountain areas today, descendants of early whittlers still carve mountain dolls or "poppets" from cedar or buckeye. **1974** Fink *Bits Mt Speech* 20 The least one was playing with hit's [sic] *poppet*.

[< Middle English *popet, -ette*, agreeing in sense with French *poupette* "doll"; EDD *poppet* sb 1 mEngl "a doll, puppet"; Web3 *poppet* n 2a Midland; DARE *poppet* n 2 chiefly South Midland]

2 A small person, child.

1958 Combs *Archaic English in KY* 41 = little person: "She's a pretty poppet." **1997** Montgomery *Coll* (known to Cardwell), = also a young girl (Oliver), = also a mama's pet (Weaver).

poppet doll See **poppet 1**.

poppie (also *poppy*) *noun*

1 (also *poppee doll, poppy doll*) A rag doll, especially a homemade one, but sometimes one purchased from a store. See also **poppet**.

c1900 (in **1997** Stoddart *Quare Women* 128) = what children call store dolls because they have red cheeks like poppies. **1905** Miles *Spirit of Mts* 100 You little dawtie, little poppee-doll! Bless hits little angel-lookin' time! **1944** Combs *Word-List Sthn High* 20 *poppy doll* = a homemade rag doll. **1955** Ritchie *Singing Family* 174 Granny's voice sounded like she was talking to herself. "I thought it was a purty poppy-doll—hush and don't cry." **1997** Montgomery *Coll*: *poppie* (known to Oliver, Weaver), = a male doll (Brown).

[DARE (at *poppet* n 2) chiefly South Midland]

2 A father or grandfather; also used as a term of address.

1925 Dargan *Highland Annals* 192 The boys don't take after their poppie. **1941** Still *Troublesome Creek* 115 My poppy'd be scared, me not coming straight home. **1967** Campbell *Memories of Smoky* 143 Anybody and everybody should know "Mommy," he seemed to imply. A few weeks later I got to wondering why "Poppy" didn't also live there. **1973** *Ethel Corn* 262 Poppy always had his own cows, y'know. **1983** Page and Wigginton *Aunt Arie* 64 [The railroad] was a lot a'help t'us because Poppy worked on it. **1986** Pederson et al. *LAGS* (Sullivan Co TN, Forsyth Co GA). **1989** *Matewan OHP-1* Poppy wasn't in it. . . . I don't think he would have [been] picked up. **1995** Montgomery *Coll* (known to Adams, Bush, Cardwell, Jones, Ledford, Oliver, Weaver). **2000** Higgs *Two Pappies* 55 Whenever I look at the influences that helped to lead me to my profession I think of my two grandfathers, both called "Pappy" in the language of the day. **2007** Shelby *Molly Whuppie* 56 Jack was living up at the head of the holler with his mommy and poppy and his brothers Will and Jack.

poppie cap *noun* See citation.

1982 Slone *How We Talked* 33 *poppie caps* = popcorn; also called "cap corn."

poppie doll See **poppie 1**.

popple *noun* The poplar tree.

1937 Eaton *Handicrafts* 185 He likes to whittle out of chunks of "popple" (poplar) and other soft woods that grow around his cabin.

[OED3 *popple* n[1] now regional (chiefly N. Amer.)]

pop pop *noun* One's grandfather.

1999 DeRozier *Creeker* 26 Pop Pop went around to see Old Man Fannin to talk about it, and the brothers about beat him to death.

poppy See **poppie 1**, **2**.

poppycock *noun* See citation.

1973 *Words & Expressions* 135 = an "unnecessary" gathering, as a dance or a party.

poppy doll See **poppie 1**.

pop shot *noun* See citation.

c1975 *Miners' Jargon* 6 = an unconfined explosion or small blasts used to break down overhanging ribs of coal.

popskull *noun* Poor-grade, homemade whiskey (used as a term of derision referring to the effects of its consumption, especially a violent headache). Same as **busthead**, **old busthead**. See also **rotgut**.

1867 Harris *Sut Lovingood* 222–23 He jis' grabbed a bottil, an' tuck hissef a buckload ove popskull, an' slip't the bottil intu his pocket. **1913** Kephart *Our Sthn High* 137 As for purity, all of the moonshine whiskey used to be pure, and much of it still is; but every blockader knows how to adulterate, and when one of them does stoop to such tricks he will stop at no halfway measures. . . . Such decoctions are known in the mountains by the expressive terms "pop-skull," "bust-head," "bumblings" ("they make a bumbly noise in a feller's head"). **1939** Hall *Coll* (Sevierville TN) This is the worst pop skull ever I tasted. **1968** *End of Moonshining* 101 "Busthead" and "Popskull" are names applied to whiskey which produces violent headaches due to various elements which have not been removed during the stilling process. **1986** Pederson et al. *LAGS* = attested by 2/60 interviewees (3.3%) from E TN and 6/35 (17.4%) from N GA; 8/16 of all LAGS interviewees (50%) attesting term were from Appalachia.

[DARE *popskull* n chiefly Southern Appalachians]

pop snow *verb phrase* Of a fire: to crackle sharply, portending a snowfall.

2008 Salsi *Ray Hicks* 119 Ray, the fire's a poppin' snow. Be quiet and ya can hear a fluppin' of the blaze.

porch baby (also *porch child*) *noun* See citations.

1953 Davison *Word-List Appal* 12 *porch baby* = a baby that is able to walk but is not allowed in the yard without someone to take care of him. A gate is often put up to keep the child from getting off the porch. **1984** Wilder *You All Spoken* 36 *porch child* = one sufficiently advanced to play unattended on a porch with protective devices, such as railings. **1992** Brooks *Sthn Stuff* 117 *porch baby* = one who's not yet old enough to be allowed in the yard alone.

porch child See **porch baby**.

pore See **poor**.

porely See **poorly**.

possessed to *adjective phrase* Having a compulsion to.

1979 Carpenter *Walton War* 142 He allus was possessed to run after something new. **1995–97** Montgomery *Coll* (known to Adams, Cardwell, Ledford, Oliver).

possible *noun* See citations.

1985 Sienkneckt *Rheumatic Diseases* 183 = the perineum. **1990** Cavender *Folk Medical Lex* 29 = the genitalia or perineum.

possum *verb*

1 To pretend to be asleep or dead, feign, "play possum."

1956 Hall *Coll* (Roaring Fork TN) [While the neighborhood women were telling witch tales] I was a-possumin', that's right, and they start that hant tale.

2 See citation.

1944 Combs *Word-List Sthn High* 20 = to pout, sulk; from the sulking of the opossum.

[shortening of *opossum*]

possum apple (also *possum fruit*) *noun* A persimmon.

1968 *DARE Survey* (Buchanan VA) *possum fruit* = same as persimmons. **2003** Howell *Folklife Big South Fork* 254 *Diospyros virginiana* persimmon = possum apple . . . Fruit edible usually only after frost; Indians may have taught settlers to make persimmon bread.

possum baby *noun* See citations.

1980 Still *Run for Elbertas* 107 Rein, the youngest of eleven, the most cherished, was the "'possum baby," as the saying went. **1989** Still *Rusties and Riddles* [22] = a term of affection for an infant. **1991** Still *Wolfpen Notebooks* 62 He had a bunch of children, and the youngest was always his 'possum baby.

possum bush *noun* A willow.

1977 Shackelford et al. *Our Appalachia* 79 They used this pussywillow bark, they called it "possum bush," to cure the headache. And there's the same thing in it that's in aspirin. **1982** Slone *How We Talked* 106 Tea [was] made from possum bush bark (pussy willow).

possum fruit See **possum apple**.

possum grape *noun* A woody vine (*Vitis* spp) bearing small grapes made into jelly; it is green in color but later turning brown. See also **fall grape**, **fox grape**.

1966 *DARE Survey* (Cherokee NC) = a wild grape. **1981** High *Coll* = Vitis cordifolia, a type of small wild grape used in the [Red River KY] Gorge for jelly (mixed with other fruit) and for wine. Informants distinguish between this grape and the summer grape, or fall grape as it is sometimes called, which is slightly larger and used in jellies and pies. Neither variety fully ripens or sweetens until after the first frost. **1983** Farr *More Moonshine* 147 There were two varieties [of grapes] to be found: fall and possum grapes. The former were the size of English peas and the latter like small grains of popcorn. The smoky purple fall grapes were the pretties, and I liked to hunt them; they were also sweeter than the purple-black possum grapes which tended to be sour to the taste. **1997** Montgomery *Coll* = small, sweet wild grape, used for wine and jelly (Cardwell). **2013** Shedlarz *Rosa Hicks* 12 I use wild grapes for jelly—the small ones are called 'possum grapes and the larger ones, fox grapes. **2018** *Blind Pig* (Sept 24) What I call possum grapes are smaller than peas and grow in tight clusters on vines whose leaves look like muscadine leaves only smaller.

[DARE *possum grape* n 1 chiefly South Midland]

possum grease (also *possum oil*) *noun* A medicinal oil derived from the fat of an opossum, used to treat respiratory congestion (as by rubbing on the chest); also used facetiously.

1997 Montgomery *Coll*: *possum grease* (known to Adams, Bush, Cardwell, Norris), *possum oil* = a teaspoon was ingested to cure the croup; it was also rubbed on the throat and chest for the same reason (Andrews).

possum hunt See **hunt B**.

possum-huntingest *adjective* Best or most proficient at hunting opossums. See also **-est 1** and Grammar and Syntax §3.4.1.

1955 Parris *Roaming Mts* 25 "That's the possum-huntin'est dog you ever saw," Realus said.

possum oil See **possum grease**.

possum piss *noun* See citation.

2006 Mooney *Lg Coal Mining* 1028 Many [coal-mining] terms make use of analogies to nature or to animals.... "Possum piss" is the oil used underground to keep the machine parts from rusting. Sometimes surface or strip miners apply the term to the hydraulic fluid poured into their bulldozers and front-end loaders.

possum time *noun* Presumably the fall, after farmwork is done for the season.

1861 Shipman *CW Letters* (Oct 5) tell gorge Baley that I think I Will Return Shortly A Bout posom time.

post *noun* variant plural forms of two syllables: *post-es, post-ies*.

1867 Harris *Sut Lovingood* 129 Sez I, "Hes these postez got deep roots?" **1895** Edson and Fairchild *TN Mts* 375 The most interesting thing ... is the use of a vowel in plurals and the third singular of verbs, giving such forms as *costes, vestes, postes, nestes*. **1913** Kephart *Our Sthn High* 285 The ancient syllabic plural is preserved in beasties (horses), nesties, posties, trousies (these are not diminutives). **1937** Hall *Coll* (Cosby Creek TN) I wonder what they aims to do with these pine postes. **1940** Oakley *Roamin'/Restin'* 74 Look over on the side of the mountains you will see a little house on stilts or postes. **1942** Hall *Phonetics Smoky Mts* 82. **1970** GSMNP-28 It was just a little shed made up out of four postes ground in the ground. **1971** *AOHP/ALC-260* He had postes there and horseshoes to hitch the horses to, nailed on them posts. **1989** *Matewan OHP-28* He made these own chairs, and he'd make the back out of a sugar tree, and postes, he'd make them out of hickory.

[DARE *post* n 2a chiefly South, South Midland]

post and rail (also *post and rail fence, post and railing, post and railing fence, post and rider fence*) A straight **rail fence** made of horizontal wooden rails with vertical posts to connect them.

1895 Edson and Fairchild *TN Mts* 373 *post and railing* = a kind of fence. "Won't you light an' hitch to the post-an-railin'?" **1957** Broaddus *Vocab Estill Co KY* 54 *post and railing fence* = a wooden fence made by securing two or more rails horizontally between the posts. **1978** Dykeman and Stokely *Highland Homeland* 21 Sherman Myers ... leans against a sturdier post and rider fence near Primitive Baptist Church [in Cades Cove]. **1991** Haynes *Haywood Home* 45 Stock laws were passed only after barbed-wire came into more general use. Until then, the only way people had to fence was using rail fences. Rail fences were hard to build and people only built enough to fence their fields. First, they built crooked-rail fences, then they built post and rail (straight rail) fences. Even after barbed-wire was available, it was still expensive and landowners had more trees than dollars, so they continued to build rail fences even after they could get barbed-wire.

post and railing, post and rider fence See **post and rail**.

postes, posties See **post**.

post oak *noun* An oak (especially *Quercus stellata*) whose wood is suitable for fence posts.

1967 *DARE Survey* (Gatlinburg TN).

post pot *noun* See citation.

1957 Broaddus *Vocab Estill Co KY* 59 = a vase.

pot *noun* A cooking vessel used in making homemade whiskey. Same as **still pot**.

1949 Maurer *Argot of Moonshiner* 11 (or *still pot*) = the metal body of the still in which the beer is put to cook: "... old still pot's about burnt up." **1974** Maurer and Pearl *KY Moonshine* 30 A properly made pot still departs somewhat from the cylinder form in that it has its maximum diameter in the middle with a smaller diameter at each end. *Ibid.* 121 = variant of *still-pot*. **c1999** Sutton *Me and Likker* 6 I fired my pot up one morning and it got going real good.

potato *noun* Variant forms *tater, tatoe, tator*.

1845 (in **1974** Harris *High Times* 46) The supper is made up by the fellers; every one fetches sumthin; sum a lick of meal, sum a middlin of bacon, sum a hen, sum a possum, sum a punkin, sum a grab of taters, or a pocket full of peas. **1860** *Week in Smokies* 126 Mammy, is it true that when you come home with daddy to this cabin, you had nothing to eat at the infair but roasted taters? **1861** Hanes *CW Letters* (Oct 7) if you could hav seen or eat som of the slice tator pyes that I made the other day you would give me the praise. **1864** *Warrick CW Letters* (May 11) I wannt you to send me word if your Erish taters com up or not and how they look if they did com up. **1913** Kephart *Our Sthn High* 33 There was not a bite in her house beyond potatoes, and "'taters don't go good 'thout salt." **1937** Thornburgh *Great Smoky Mts* 132 Hit war cold that night and to keep 'em from freezin' I planted the taters under a balsam tree. **1953** Hall *Coll* (Bryson City NC) [I] did some farming all the time [while running a store], raised my own corn, taters, meat, a cow, chickens. **1970** *Burton-Manning Coll*-94A She just planted 'ta-toes. **1975** GSMNP-75 We made corn and raised corn and taters and things like that. **2004** Adams *Old True Love* 130 I fixed a big pot of stewed taters to take to the setting up and by the time I got over there the house was standing full. **2008** *Rosie Hicks* 1 Mama'd make a little, left a little hole when [she] buried the taters so she could reach in there and get the taters out.

potato bin *noun* See citation.

2005 Ebel *Orville Hicks* 23 The "tater bin" was a little room built off the kitchen. Mama kept some potatoes, a jug of water, and a crock of pickled beans there. On cold days, she could go to the potato bin without walking out to the cellar to get food.

potato bug *noun* A short, broad mandolin with a deep, teardrop-shaped bowl.

1979 Irwin *Musical Instruments* 91 The well-known European type mandolin [is] known in this region as a "tater bug" because of the striped, rounded back resembling the Colorado potato beetle, commonly called the potato or "tater" bug.

potato hill *noun*

1 See citation. See also **potato hole, turnip hole.**

1997 Montgomery *Coll* = a large hole dug when harvested potatoes are put aside for winter use (Cardwell), = potatoes were stored in the winter in a huge mound of straw and dirt called a potato hill (Norris). **1998** Hyde *My Home* 25 We had stored our Irish potatoes by digging a shallow hole in the garden, lining it with straw, piling in bushels of potatoes and then covering them with a layer of straw and then covering that with dirt. That was called a "tater" hill. When we needed potatoes we dug away some dirt, removed some straw, took the potatoes we needed and then restored the straw and dirt.

[DARE *potato hill* n 2 especially South Midland]

2 See citation. See also **hill.**

1997 Montgomery *Coll* (known to Adams, Bush, Jones), = a raised or mounded row of potato plants. As the plants were hoed, dirt was mounded around them (Ellis).

potato hole (also *potato tunnel, tater hole*) *noun* A cellar-like hole either outside a dwelling or underneath the floorboards near the hearth, in which vegetables (especially potatoes) are buried, often under straw or earth, for winter consumption. See 1977, 1995 citations. See also **potato hill 1, turnip hole.**

1977 *Smoky Vistas* (Winter) 6 Somewhere out in the garden area was the "tater" hole. Here were stored the potatoes, cabbage, carrots, parsnips and turnips. By digging a hole in well-drained soil and lining it with straw, a "tater hole" was ready to be filled with vegetables. It was then covered with straw and soil, and a few planks to keep the rain out. **1986** Pederson et al. LAGS = attested by 3/60 interviewees (5%) from E TN; 3/4 of all LAGS interviewees (75%) attesting term were from E TN. **1991** *Smokies Guide* (Autumn) 5 Many cabins even had "tater" holes for storing these foods. "Tater" holes were 2–3 foot deep holes conveniently located underneath the home's floor, usually near the hearth. Most people gained access to them by lifting a floor board or two. Park ranger Glenn Cardwell, who grew up in the Greenbrier area, recalls their "tater" hole was "big enough for five or six kids to hide in." **1991** Thomas *Sthn Appal* 20 Another item, hardly a real structure, was the "tater tunnel" or "tater hole," a hole in the ground near the house where "winter apples," cabbage, Irish potatoes, rutabagas and turnips were stored. [**1994** Huskey *County Squire* 13 Once we moved into the second house, we built a "wind house" to save the potatoes. There was no way to keep Irish potatoes from freezing except to bury them back in the ground. . . . We dug a hole in the ground, lined the hole with crab grass, poured in the potatoes and covered them with about six inches of dirt—about 10 bushels to a hole.] **1995** Trout *Historic Buildings* 58 The vast majority of people here simply did not build separate root cellars. Instead, they used the "tater hole," a depression dug in front of the hearth, under the floor of the cabin. In this sheltered location, it did not have to be dug so deep, was not subject to flooding, and was much more convenient than a separate building. The hole was covered with a hinged hatch in the floor. Potatoes there could be retrieved easily, and baked in the ashes in the adjacent fireplace.

potato house *noun* A small outbuilding in which vegetables, especially potatoes, are stored for winter consumption.

1967 *DARE Survey* (Maryville TN) = place for keeping carrots, turnips, potatoes, and so on over the winter.

potato slip See **sweet potato slip.**

potato tunnel See **potato hole.**

pot cheese *noun* Cottage cheese.

1964 Reynolds *Born of Mts* 70 Nowhere, however, did the writer observe a woman's drawers hanging up to strain the pot cheese, as has also been said. **1997** Montgomery *Coll* (known to Bush, Cardwell).

poterack See **potrack.**

pot licker *noun* A nondescript dog, one of little worth.

1926 Hunnicutt *Twenty Years* 105 I had just finished saying this when old Drum went on one of the "pot-lickers," and then the bear hounds each picked out a dog and we had a fight between the bear dogs and the "pot-lickers." **1949** Arnow *Hunter's Horn* 34 Them damned Tiller potlickers they'll be the ones to git King

Devil if he's ever got. **1960** Burnett *My Valley* 146 Pot Lickers, Blue Ticks, Black and Tans, sometimes, just any old shabby-looking breed or cross-breed meet the requirements and mixed breeds of old-fashioned cur and hound often make outstanding bear dogs. **1979** *Raising Dogs* 184 [They] had some old dogs—called them pot lickers.... That was the nickname for them. That was from licking pots ... you rolled the pot off down the hill and sent him after it to get him away from you. **1996** Montgomery *Coll* (known to Adams, Cardwell, Jones, Ledford).

pot likker See **pot liquor.**

pot liquor (also *pot likker*) *noun* The tasty, vitamin-rich juice left by vegetables (especially greens) and sometimes meat boiled in a pot, often used as a dip for cornbread. See 1996 citation.

1863 *CW Soldiers' Letters* (Oct) sis tell mar I wold like be at home to eat potlicker I am tiard of meat an bread for I cant cook it well. **1955** Washburn *Country Doctor* 15 I especially denounced the practice of feeding a new-born baby on "pot-licker," the local name for the water in which vegetables had been boiled, during the first four days of life or until it was possible for the mother to nurse it. **c1960** Wilson *Coll* = the water in which vegetables have been cooked, esp. greens. **1996** Houk *Foods & Recipes* 50 When turnip greens, cabbage, or the like were cooked, the liquid that remained was called "pot likker," a rich substance never discarded but always savored for cornbread dipping. **1997** Montgomery *Coll* = the broth from cooking greens, meat, etc. (Brown). **2006** *Encycl Appalachia* 936 If greens are boiled and not fried, they are seasoned with country ham, smoked ham hocks, smoked hog jowls, salt pork, or fatback. The cooking water becomes a valued broth that is called pot likker. The likker is used to moisten corn bread or cook dumplings. **2009** Miller *Nigh Gone* 86 While nutritional purists contend such cooking removes all the nutrients and vitamins from the vegetables, they reckon without the fact that the mountain palate prizes the juices produced by the cooking even more than the items cooked. Those juices or broth are what is known as "potlikker." It is prized beyond measure as a delicacy of mountain fare and often is eaten with crumbled (not sliced) cornpone as the principal entree of the main mountain meal of the day. Of all the various potlikkers, the most prized is that made from cabbage or turnip greens.

pot pie *noun* Same as **family pie.**

1986 Pederson et al. *LAGS* (Claiborne Co TN, Johnson Co TN, Sullivan Co TN, Union Co GA) = deep-dish pie.

potrack (also *poterack, potter-rack*) *noun* The cry of a guinea fowl; hence verb = to make this cry, often in alarm; by extension = the bird itself.

1940 Still *River of Earth* 33 Says she tuck a notion to get rid of these last two. Can't sleep nights for all their potter-racking. **1972** Carson and Vick *Hillbilly Cookin* 59 *poteracks* = guinea fowls: "You want any poterack eggs t'day?" **2002** Oliver *Cooking and Living* 57 Guinea hens, which had come from Africa, were rarely eaten for the settlers didn't care for their meat. These handsome but noisy birds were kept as "watch dogs" for when they saw a stranger or were disturbed they made a frightful noise. Because of their sound, they were usually called "pot-racks," which pretty well describes the noise they make.

[DARE *potrack* n chiefly South, South Midland]

pot still (also *pot-type distillery*) *noun* See citations. See also **copper pot.**

1963 Carson *History Bourbon* 237 *pot still* = a vessel shaped like a kettle, with a tapering neck connected to a condensing coil in which the alcohol has been liquefied and collected. **1972** Carr *Oldest Profession* 183 The pot still is the oldest of all the designs and is the mother Still of moonshining. It is occasionally called the "turnip bottom" still if it is made in the shape of a turnip (rounded bottom with tapering neck). The pot still is not always made in a pot shape and can be box shaped in design and still be within the pot-still family. **1985** Dabney *More Mt Spirits* 153, 154 Virtually all of the illicit stills operating in recent years in the South are classified by the ATF as pot-type distilleries.... The pot type distillery consists of a metal and/or wood still "in the form of a pot, kettle, box, drum or barrel." These pot stills produce whiskey when fire is applied directly to a surface of the still, with the exception of the steamer type where the mash is vaporized by steam fed into the pot by pipes. Some pot stills are used only for distillation of mash that is fermented in separate mash containers. These are primarily the copper and metal pots. In another type—primarily the Alabama Pot Type (sometimes known as Black Pots), and Groundhog—the mash is fermented and distilled in the same container.

pot-tail(s) *noun* The residue of **mash** (see **mash**[2]) left in a **still** after the first distillation of whiskey. See also **slops 1**, **still mash**, **sugar slop**, **swill.**

1917 Kephart *Word-List* 415 = the residue in a moonshine still after the backings are run off. **1956** Hall *Coll* (Mt Sterling NC) [When using the] thump keg, cook sugar in the pot-tails and realize more out of [the run of liquor]. *Ibid.* (Waynesville NC) It had to be doubled, in other words boiled twice. It had to be boiled twice because you had to boil the steam. When it first come off, why it was alkyhol, and then hit would break and then run your backings as long as they was sweet, until they got sour, and in fact when they got sour, it would lose its strength. It wouldn't have any more strength, and then you had to pour it up, as I say, had to clean your still, had to clean it all out, and they called it the pot tails.... Pot tails, that was just like for instance making mash, and it was good for nothing else because all the strength was gone. They wasn't any more strength in it. **1959** Hall *Coll* (Mt Sterling NC) [The liquor] wouldn't have any more strength, and then you had to pour up and clean your still, clean it all out, what they called the pot tails. **1968** *End of Moonshining* 91 At the end of each run, the plug stick ... is pushed in thus releasing the slop or "pot-tail" which flows through the tilted slop arm ... and trough into a bucket. **1974** Dabney *Mt Spirits* xxiii = the mash left after a distillation. In copper pot stills, this leftover is dipped out and "slopped back" into the mash barrels and mixed with subsequent batches to be fermented. The result is sour mash whiskey.

[DARE *pot-tail* n Southern Appalachians]

potterack See **potrack.**

pot-walloper *noun* See citation.

1927 Woofter *Dialect from WV* 362 = cook in a lumber camp: "Do you know where we can hire a good pot-walloper?"

pound

A *noun* variant plural form without -*s* following a numeral or other quantifier; see Grammar and Syntax §1.1.

1837 McLean Diary 48 [I] made 8 pound of Sugar makeing in all 366 3/4. **1863** *Fuller CW Letters* (Feb 24) I bought one 100 and 45 pound of porke from joseph ables at 25 senc pur pound. **1864** *Chapman CW Letters* (April 10) I Bought ten pound of cotten of hur and is to go after it nex sunday if it dont Rain. **1913** Kephart *Our Sthn High* 287 I can make a hundred pound o' pork outen that hog. **1934–47** *LAMSAS Appal* = attested by 22/148 speakers (14.8%) from WV, 6/20 (30%) from VA, 9/37 (24.3%) from NC, 9/14 (64.3%) from SC, and 2/12 (16.7%) from GA. **1939** Hall *Coll* (Cataloochee NC) We carried the bear in, took him to the scales and weighed him. He weighed four hundred and seventy-five pound. **1973** GSMNP-76:13a We'd go to town, take a little truck and buy a hundred pound [of sugar] and bring it and put in there. It would do us a week. **1989** *Matewan OHP-56* I used to be able to take a hundred pound of feed on each shoulder and take up off the mountain, where people bought feed for their cattle and their cows and things. **2013** Venable *How to Tawlk* 38 I bet 'at big rock 'll go a good 250 pound. **2017** Williams *Murmuration* 14 I bet I've lost a good thirty pound or better.

B *verb*

1 Traditionally, to compensate (usually a church pastor, but sometimes newlyweds) in small amounts of provisions in lieu of salary or as a gift, to ensure that recipients and their family were well stocked with food and supplies; to hold a welcoming party for or bring small gifts of produce, supplies, and other items to a newly arrived couple or family in the community; hence verb phrase *pound the preacher*, noun *pounding*, noun *pound party* = this method of welcoming and compensating a regular minister by supplying provisions in lieu of a salary.

1921 Combs *KY Items* 118 A pound party is a party in which the people voluntarily give the minister a surprise, by carrying in something like groceries, vegetables, etc.: "Last night they pounded the new preacher." **1946** Woodard *Word-List VA/NC* 24 *pound* = to victual an (incoming) parson. **1956** McAtee *Some Dial NC* 34 *pounding* = donation or pound party; originally from bringing a pound of something as a gift. "We gave the bride and groom a pounding." **1958** Wood *Words from TN* 14 To "pound" the preacher meant that the members of a congregation bring a pound of food to the new preacher. . . . Last year a young Methodist preacher's wife told me that they had been *pounded* the night before. **1962** Hall *Coll* (Del Rio TN) You never hear of poundings any more. [They] usually had it for a minister when he first moved in a parsonage. **1967** Jones *Peculiarities Mtneers* 90 Once in a while a Baptist or Methodist pastor, who usually served four different churches with once a month Saturday and Sunday services at each church, would elect to live in our community. When he moved in with his family, always a large one, they were invariably given a "pounding." Everyone for miles around would come swooping down on the pastor's home without notice bearing all kinds of food and household necessities. As a rule there would be enough food to last the family several weeks. **1968** Wilson *Folklore Mammoth Cave* 44 *pound party* or *pounding* = party to which each invited guest brings a pound of some food. Often given for a newly-married couple or a new preacher who had moved into the community. Sometimes it took the form of a donation party for the preacher and included household gadgets as well as food. **1977** Shackelford et al. *Our Appalachia* 50 One custom they had about dead now once a year when a new preacher would come into a Methodist community they would give him a "pounding." It started out with the idea that the members, or anybody else in the community that wanted to do so, would take a pound of groceries to his house at a certain time. That eventually spread into taking various things, whatever people might want. **1978** Cohn *Courtship and Marriage* 42 In East Tennessee, neighbors helped a couple set up housekeeping by giving them a pounding; articles of food and furniture were brought in a few days after the ceremony to help the couple begin housekeeping. **1979** Smith *White Rock* 15 Our preacher traveled by horseback many miles to minister to his churches. . . . Often he rode away on Sunday afternoon carrying his monthly income of chicken, eggs, pork, or garden produce. On special occasions, he received "poundings." On these occasions, he was presented shab beans, dried apples, coffee, sugar, and may[be] even a cured country ham. **1989** Landry *Smoky Mt Interviews* 181 Sometimes they'd give the preacher a pounding. . . . Anything that they had, they had canned stuff or whatever they had to eat, members of the church would bring it in and give it to the preacher, pastor of the church . . . any kind of canned stuff they had. It didn't make any difference what it was for the Banks family on a certain date. **1995** McCauley *Mt Religion* 61 Mountain preachers have always labored like everyone else to support themselves, offering as preachers and pastors their time and resources without charge or any expectation of recompense. The best-known exception from this norm is the early pioneer tradition of "a pounding," where periodically people would get together and bring for the preacher and his family a pound of coffee or butter or flour or sugar or whatever else was at hand. **2014** Montgomery *Doctrine* 162 = an occasion where church members give the pastor and his family gift offerings for Christmas. Usually the gifts consist of dry goods . . . also done for wedding showers. **2017** *Blind Pig* (Feb 17) The shivaree reminded me of another custom for newlyweds as they set up housekeeping. A pounding would often be included in the shivaree. Pounds of food, including canned goods, would be brought to the couple and given to them. Sometimes people took the labels off the cans so the bride would not know what was in the can til it was opened. Our church gives poundings to new ministers when they move into the parsonage. They did it last summer when our new pastor and his wife arrived. One was given to us when my husband came here in 1989. It is much more organized and scheduled than an old-style pounding. People arrived throughout the day.

[Web3 *pounding* "from the custom of giving a pound of sugar or some other edible commodity" South and Midland; DARE *pound* v chiefly South Midland, *pounding* n 1 chiefly South, South Midland, TX]

2 To donate provisions to neighbors in need; hence noun *pounding* = the provision of foodstuffs to a community family in need.

1997 Andrews *Mountain Vittles* 87 Now, nobody thought much about being in need and having to be helped 'cause ever'body reckoned it could happen as well to their families. Sometimes it would take several poundings to help a family back on their feet. **1997** Montgomery *Coll* Bill's been pounding them for years (Brown). **1998** Hamby *Grassy Creek* 77 There was an empty house in the Sussex community and it was made available to this family. They had with them only a few household items so word was spread around that there would be a pounding held for the Banks family on a certain date.

pounding See **pound B1, B2**.

pounding bench *noun* Traditionally, a bench put in the rear of a church on which members left food and provisions instead of paying the pastor in money. See also **pound B1**.

2008 Salsi *Ray Hicks* 88 Till after the World War II, there was no money involved in payin' him. There was no offerin' plate. There was a poundin' bench put in the church and people bring food and knitted clothes to leave on the bench each Sunday. That's the way preachers got most of the eatin' for their family.

pounding mill (also *pound mill*) *noun* A primitive water-driven mill for grinding corn, in which a pounding weight is attached to one end of a beam and a bucket to the other; as a stream of water fills the bucket, the weight is raised until the bucket overturns and spills the water, releasing the weight to fall on dried corn on a stump or other surface. See also **hand mill**, **hominy pounder**, **lazy Jim**, **quern**, **slow John**, **tri-weekly**. See 1975 citation.

1913 Kephart *Our Sthn High* 291 Someone who was irked from turning [the hand-mill] invented the extraordinary improvement that goes by the name of pounding-mill. **c1926** Cox *Cullowhee Wordlist*: *pound mill* = a water mill to pound meal from corn, by means of a box on a long beam which pounds when it fills with water. **1937** Thornburgh *Great Smoky Mts* 144 Almost all known types of mills have been found, from a primitive pounding mill on Deep Creek, to "tub" mills, overshot mills, and steel turbine mills. **1939** *FWP Guide TN* 302 Near the spring is a rock with a depression in which early settlers ground corn into meal with the aid of a heavy pestle attached to a beam propelled by the current of the stream. The operation of this device, called a "pounding mill," was slow, but it could be carried on without attention. **1953** Wilburn *Pounding Mill* Fifteen years ago, when I first came into the Southern mountains, I heard at times of a mysterious machine whereby a pestle was worked up and down by waterpower. This was called a pounding-mill, or facetiously, a "lazy-John" or "tri-weekly." The descriptions given by old settlers were certainly genuine; and yet I could not get through my head how such a thing would work. Then, last summer, I found a real pounding-mill, within six miles of my residence, Bryson City. It is at the home of Telitha Bumgarner, on a branch of Deep Creek, and was made by her son, Jim.... Jim's mill is now only used to pound up stock feed, and so requires no attention until the job is done. To make meal fit for bread, some one would have to go there every now and then to remove the pounded grain, sift out the finer particles, and return the coarser ones. Of course the process is slow; but time is no asset in the backwoods. The inventor and the place where the Pounding-mill was first used have so far evaded research. That it was in common use in earlier days, both in the park and in adjacent areas, is evidenced by the fact that there are in Swain County three or more "pounding-mill branches" and equally as many in Haywood County. **1963** Lord *Blue Ridge* 14–15D "K'splash, K'splash," the sound directs your eyes to a long wooden beam pounding down, "K'thud," into a sturdy wooden box. It's a pounding mill, an old-timey contraption of the mountaineer for grinding his corn the lazy way. Water power operates a see-saw beam that pounds the corn. One end of the beam has a water bucket. The stream pours into the upraised bucket, "K'splash." The now heavier hammer end of the beam whams down into the corn box, "K'thud!" **1975** Brewer *Valley So Wild* 107–8 The Payne "pounding mill" was on the principle of the Indian "kanonah" (mortar and pestle), except it was powered by water instead of woman. The mill consisted of (1) a hollowed-out stump in which corn was placed and (2) a see-saw with a heavy wood pounder on one end and a water bucket on the other. Water from a little stream poured into the bucket, causing it to drop to its low point and raising the pounder on the other end. The bucket tipped and the water spilled out at the low point, letting the pounder on the other end drop onto the corn in the stump. This was a slow way to make corn meal, and, a grandson remembers, someone had to stay at the mill to keep "varmints" from stealing the corn. **2002** Oliver *Cooking and Living* 13 As soon as they got a cabin built and the farm started, the pioneers built a pounding or Lazy Jim Mill and let waterpower do the work for them. The most elemental of watermills, none are in existence today, but every pioneer farm had one for they were easy to build, and needed only a flowing stream to do the work. A bucket on one end of a long seesaw pole alternately filled with water and emptied itself as it became over-balanced. The pestle on the other end did the work through the up-&-down motion inherent in the system. These primitive mills made about 3 cycles per minute, producing about 3 gallons of cornmeal per day, with about one-half of the meal suitable for cornbread and the other half for chicken feed. The obvious value of the pounding mill was that it required no attention at all. The miller could pour corn into the mortar, turn water into the bucket, and go about his day's work elsewhere. Long ago, one old-timer said there were so many of these mills when he was a boy that they awakened him many mornings with their constant thumping. Obviously, every farm had a pounding mill. Seeing how easy they were to build, the Cherokees began to construct them, which greatly pleased the women whose duty it had been to laboriously grind corn by hand every day.

[DARE *pounding mill* n b chiefly Southern Appalachians]

pound mill See **pounding mill.**

pound party, pound the preacher See **pound B1.**

pour *verb* variant past-tense form *pourt.*

1975–76 Wolfram/Christian *WV Coll* 31 He held me and Curtis Green pourt snow down my neck.

pourdown *noun* A downpour or sudden, heavy rain.

1934–47 *LAMSAS Appal* = attested by 10/148 speakers (6.7%) from WV, 3/20 (15%) from VA, 1/37 (2.7%) from NC, and 3/14 (21.4%) from SC. **1961** *Coe Ridge OHP-341B* They's a little cloud boil up, you see, and it come flying over. Well it just come a pourdown. **1986** Pederson et al. *LAGS* (Cocke Co TN, Johnson Co TN, Loudon Co TN, Sequatchie Co TN, Gordon Co GA).

pour the rain *verb phrase* To rain heavily.

1956 Hall *Coll* (Big Bend NC) If it poured the rain, she might shelter a little while till the ground settled. **1961** *Coe Ridge OHP-339A* It's about to pour the rain, it looks like. **1983** Page and Wigginton *Aunt Arie* 165 Yeah, it just poured th'rain. **1983** Pyle *CCC 50th Anniv* B:6:51 First night that we was in there, it poured the rain. **1987** Young *Lost Cove* 185 It poured the rain the following night and only a few came.

pour up *verb phrase* See citation.

1974 Maurer and Pearl *KY Moonshine* 121 = to distribute moonshine (after it has been temped to 100 proof) into containers for distribution.

poverty-poor *adjective* See citation.

1976 Garber *Mountain-ese* 71 = destitute: "We gave our used clothes to the poverty-poor families."

poverty weed *noun* Same as **rabbit tobacco.**

1982 Stupka *Wildflowers* 124 = sometimes called "poverty weed" and "old-field balsam," because it thrives in dry areas and waste places. Names such as "sweet balsam" and "sweet everlasting" refer to its fragrance. Other names are "rabbit tobacco" and "cudweed." **1997** Montgomery *Coll* = so called because it grows on depleted soil (Cardwell).

powder *noun*

A Construed as a count noun; hence plural form *powders.* See also **baby powder, baking powder, easing powder, face powder, laundry powder, peartening powder, talcum powder, washing powder.**

1861 Huntley *CW Letters* (Dec 29) I would like to have some Black powders & some Lobelia seeds if you can git any chance to send them. **1862** *Robinson CW Letters* (March 25) I have bin taken powders and pills from him ever cence I have bin hear but it dos me no good. **1921** Weeks *Speech of KY Mtneer* 11 Powder of any kind, from Royal Baking to Djer-Kiss talcum, is designated as "powders." **1930** Armstrong *This Day and Time* 7 That here is all the style this day an' time—paint an' face-powders. *Ibid.* 90 I'ull jest take a nickel's worth o' washin'-powders an' the balance that's comin' to me in snuff. **1968** *Faith Healing* 63 I just draw the fire out of [the wound] and take common old baby powders—talcum powders they used t'call 'em—baby powders that they used t'put on a baby. **1974** Fink *Bits Mt Speech* 8 *easing powders* = a drug to ease pain. "They ought to give him some *easin' powders.*" *Ibid.* 19 = tonic, vitamins. "Doc, John wants some more of those *peartenin' powders* that done him so good." **1981** Dumas *Appal Glossary* 16 *baking powders.* **2007** McMillon *Notes: laundry powders.*

B (also *black powder*) Dynamite, as that formerly used in small quantities to remove coal from the **face** of a seam being worked.

1973 *AOHP/EH-24* You had to make your own shots. You had to put 2 1/2 to 3 or 3 1/2 ft. powder in a hole to shoot. It took a lot of powder to pull a hole. Whenever they used machine coal, they shot it with this black powder. The company had a little house for every man to keep his powder in to dry. **1976** Dillon *They Died* 71 In early days of coal mining, the workman had to shoot his own coal, i.e., he had to drill or bore a hole into the solid coal six feet or more [and] place in dynamite or black powder charge to the farthest depths. **1982** Eller *Miners* 177 After taking two or three hours to make the undercut, the miner then drilled holes in the undercut, loaded the holes with black powder, and fired them, bringing down the undercut coal. **2006** Hicks *Mt Legacy* 47 Powder was the nickname he used for dynamite. He slipped a noose knot with the powder down about half way of the powder and pushed it into the drill hole. **2006** Mooney *Lg Coal Mining* 1029 The miner drilled blasting holes with a "breast auger," used a "tamping rod" to pack his black powder, inserted a "clay dummy" for proper repercussion of the explosion, lit the fuse, and yelled "Fire in the hole!"

powdering *noun* Facial powder.

1895 Edson and Fairchild *TN Mts* 373 She's got powdering all over her face. **1997** Montgomery *Coll* (known to Adams, Bush, Cardwell, Weaver).

powder-monkey *noun* See citation.

1964 Clarkson *Lumbering in WV* 369 = man who is especially skilled in using dynamite.

power *noun* A great deal, large quantity or number.

1860 *Week in Smokies* 123 I clarified some of [the sugar] and you can't think what a power of nastiness I got out of it. **1863** *Leigh CW Letters* (April 18) there is a power of sickness in the Regt. and 5 or 6 has died since I come here. **1863** *Reese CW Letters* (Jan 10) I saw a power of negras going thair yesterday to bild Brest works. **1873** Smith *Arp Peace Papers* 91 Atter the misery is past there's a power of kumfort of talkin it over and fixin up as big a tale as enybody. **1913** Kephart *Our Sthn High* 286 Many common English words are used in peculiar senses by the mountain folk, as ... a power or a sight for much. **c1959** Weals *Hillbilly Dict* 7 I ruck up a power of muck.

[OED3 *power* n[1] 10 now chiefly England regional, Irish English, and U.S. regional, except in a *power of good* (colloquial); DARE *power* n 1 chiefly South, South Midland]

power boil See **parboil.**

power doctor *noun* Same as **witch doctor.**

1955 Rogers *Switching* 109 There are some who connect "water-witching" with "power doctors," and yet the greater majority do not try to explain it at all—they just go ahead using their knowledge or skill in helping a neighbor locate a spot to dig his well where a sufficient supply of water may be found.

powerful

A *adjective* Extreme, great.

1831 *McLean Diary* (March 27) a powerfull Runn of Shoogar. **1863** *Reese CW Letters* (May 17) this is A good Country hear grate land and the powrfulst plac I Ever saw for pasture. **1866** *Chapman CW Letters* (Jan 1) the gals in this country was powerful Rebs but now they are all good union gals. **1933** Carpenter *Sthn Mt Dialect* 23 Powerful for QUITE A QUANTITY or BIG is heard in northern and central West Virginia, while in the southern West Virginia and farther south the expression is most often right smart. **c1950** (in **2000** Oakley *Roamin' Man* 13) My Daddy would git a powerful thrill out of shooting a bear. **1952** Wilson *Folk Speech NC* 596 He's in a powerful studyment to figure out how to get the money. **1957** Parris *My Mts* 43 Reckon I've made a powerful lot of chairs. **1974** Fink *Bits Mt Speech* 13 I had a powerful *hurting* in my chest.

[OED3 *powerful* adj 6 "great in number, quantity, or degree" chiefly Irish English and U.S.]

B *adverb* Extremely, greatly, thoroughly.

1862 *Martin CW Letters* (Jan 15) you wrote that you was all well whitch I was powerful Glad to hear of. **1863** *Reese CW Letters* (Oct 27) I was powerful glad to hear from you But was sory to hear that things was as tha[y] air in old BunComb. **1881** Pierson *In the Brush* 260 When the old gineral seed he was so plucky, and religious too, he know'd them's the kind that fit powerful. **1913** Morley *Carolina Mts* 11 "We're powerful poor around here, but we don't mean no harm by it," is the cheery greeting you get when you visit an ancient native of the forest who you know does not think himself poor at all. **1937** Thornburgh *Great Smoky Mts* 94 Gatlin didn't stay here so powerfull long. **1939** Hall *Coll* (Bradley Fork NC) I began stone-cutting at a powerful early age. **1986** Ogle *Lucinda* 61 City folks would ask Dad, "Wiley, have you ever been lost in these mountains?" and he would say, "No," wait a few seconds and say, "I have been powerful bothered for several days though."

[OED3 *powerful* adv "to a great degree, very, exceedingly" originally and chiefly U.S. regional (south); Web3 *powerful* adv chiefly dialect; DARE *powerful* adv C1 scattered, but more frequent South, South Midland]

powerfully *adverb* Very much, extremely.

1863 *Proffit CW Letters* (June 26) I would like powerfully to see her and the Children. **1867** Harris *Sut Lovingood* 116 Well, Lum an' George, thar, wer pow'fully exercised 'bout hit—wanted tu know the secret pow'ful bad. **1900** Harben *N GA Sketches* 15 Pete Gill, I'm powerfully afeerd you are in fer it. **1952** Wilson *Folk Speech NC* 578 He's powerfully pushed for something to eat. **1956** Hall *Coll* (Roostertown TN) My pappy is swelled powerfully.

powerful to *adverb phrase* Determined to, having a strong mind or inclination to.

1924 Spring *Lydia Whaley* 1 Pap let the county build a school house free on his land which was nigh enuf for 'em to go home to dinner. And he was "powerful to send us to school."

power monkey *noun* See citation.

c1975 *Miners' Jargon* 6 = shot fireman [in coal mining].

pow-wow *noun* In folk medicine, the use of incantations, charms, or other conjuring practices in healing. [Editor's note: While such practices originated in and were followed mainly by German communities in Pennsylvania, they have also been documented in German-settlement areas of eastern West Virginia.]

1964 Smith et al. *Germans of Valley* 153 The pow-wow booklet was discovered in a neighborhood in Pendleton County, West Virginia, where the dialect is still spoken by many residents. *Ibid.* 158 In almost every neighborhood of the Valley there was someone who was believed able to pow-wow for goiter. **1995** Suter *Shenandoah Folklife* 63 [The term] *powwowwing* ... apparently entered into the language [i.e. German from] Algonquin in the seventeenth century.... Many of the incantations used in powwowing incorporate biblical verses and invoke the help of holy personages and saints in warding off illness. **2011** Richmond *Appal Folklore* 7 Pow Wow incorporates a combination of herbs, chants, and dream divination for worship and healing services.

practice (also *practize, practyse*) *verb* Variant form with primary stress on both syllables: PRAC-TIZE.

1867 Harris *Sut Lovingood* 42 Thinks I, ole feller, if yu gain this suit, yu may ax Satun, when yu sees him, fur a par ove lisence tu practize at his cort. **1925** Greer-Petrie *Angeline Hill Country* 97 They could soon larn the lick hit's done with fur hit's all in the practyse. **1930** (in **1952** Mathes *Tall Tales* 180) I'll prac-tize up some new tunes an' I'll git off some new jokes fer 'em. **1999** Montgomery *Coll* (known to Cardwell).

practize, practyse See **practice.**

praise up *verb phrase* To compliment, flatter.

1884 Smith *Arp Scrap Book* 80 I praised 'em up lots.

prank (also *prank around*) *verb, verb phrase* To play or joke; to meddle or tinker.

1924 Raine *Saddlebags* 100 The children love to prank with the dog. **1927** Shearin *Speech of Fathers* 7 He was prankin' with the cat when it bit him. **1946** Matthias *Speech Pine Mt* 190 = to play: "The doctor pranked around in my eye." **1957** Combs *Lg Sthn High*:

Idioms 13 He got to prankin' around me, and I sunned his moccasins (killed him). **1971** Dwyer *Dict for Yankees* 30 = to experiment, manipulate. "He's a-prankin' with a motor." **1977** Norman *Kinfolks* 114 You can't see television because of this sarcastic neighbor Mr. Ortiz who pranks with the electricity. **1982** Slone *How We Talked* 30 "Prank" with someone = bother or tease. **1997** Montgomery *Coll* (known to Adams, Bush, Cardwell, Jones).

[SND *prank* v 1 "to play pranks, meddle or interfere"; DARE *prank* v[1] 1 chiefly South Midland]

prank around See **prank.**

prayer *noun* A prayer service.

1956 Hall *Coll* (Big Bend NC) Pete and Ham Hicks, the preachers, they was here the other day. They helt a prayer at the graveyard. **1997** Montgomery *Coll* (known to Cardwell).

prayer bones *noun* The knees.

1927 Woofter *Dialect from WV* 362 = knees. "Every one get down on his prayer bones."

pray through *verb phrase* To reach a state of religious conversion or spiritual euphoria through prayer; to assist (one) to reach such a state through prayer. See also **break through, come through, pull through, through C1.**

1938 Stuart *Dark Hills* 242 If you'd been there when I prayed through, / I would not be denied; / You'd been a-praying and a-shouting too, / I would not be denied. **1993** Burleson *Aunt Keziah* 3–4 The next thing we knowed they had one of them moonshine drinkers at the mourners bench. They prayed and prayed but he stayed down there akneeling, never got up. Finally the preacher said, we'll stay here all night, ifen hit takes hit, to git this brother prayed through.

[DARE *pray through* v phr especially South, South Midland]

preacher *noun* The common term in traditional mountain society for a clergyman (in preference to *pastor* or *reverend*, perhaps because the man was often an unsalaried farmer or other working member of the community who officiated at funerals and baptisms but had few other pastoral duties). The term is used as a title (with either or both the first name and surname), in direct address, or in quasi-honorific reference. See also **elder, parson, preacher man, preacher woman.**

1881 Pierson *In the Brush* 44 They got her out, preacher, and run her . . . and, preacher, she beat, she did. **1939** Hall *Coll* (Waldens Creek TN) He was the awfullest [i.e. best] singer ever I heared, Preacher Jim Lawson was. **1940** Mathes *Jeff Howell* 20 Ninety year of age, stone-blind, and all but bedfast with palsy, he was seldom seen in the valley any more, but when there was trouble, when the shadow of fear fell over the dark mountain slopes, they always sent for Preacher Pleas. **1963** Miller *Pigeon's Roost* (Nov 21) Preacher Arwood, as he was affectionately called on Pigeon Roost, lived here practically all his life until about ten years ago when he moved to Spruce Pine where his son Robert lived. Preacher Arwood had been an ordained minister of the Freewill Baptist church denomination for over 60 years and pastored churches until poor health prevented him from doing so some several years ago. **1964** Greve *Story of Gatlinburg* 33 Some of them were preachers—as their clergymen were always called—so there was no lack of the ministry of the "Word." **1973** *AOHP/EH-31* Preacher asked that question over the radio this morning. **1973** GSMNP-86:34 The old man Preacher John Stinnett, he's dead and gone now, but my, did he have the power. **1974** GSMNP-50:2:6 Well, when I first remember, we had church every Sunday, and Wednesday night, but we only had preaching once a month, and Preacher Newt Clabo was the pastor the first time I remember of anybody preaching up there. **1974** GSMNP-51:8–9 They didn't have no salary set whatever for a preacher. If he sometimes got in trouble, they would go and work out his crop, or got sick or come down, you would give him a sack of flour or ham or something, you know, for him to live on, and that's the way they paid the preachers. **1983** *Dark Corner OHP-5A* Preacher Howard has told them some up yonder about these [people] getting killed up here. **1989** *Matewan OHP-56* Preacher Joe Hatfield, now he might have married my mother and dad. **1998** *Dante OHP-24* How are you getting along in your work, preacher?

preacher man *noun* A clergyman (not used in direct address and sometimes slightly sarcastic). See also **preacher, preacher woman.**

1913 Kephart *Our Sthn High* 285–86 Pleonasms are abundant. . . . Everywhere in the mountains we hear of biscuit-bread . . . preacher-man. **1940** Haun *Hawk's Done* 61 One time he bolted in the church house and made her get up and go out because the preacher man spoke to her. **1972** Cooper *NC Mt Folklore* 95 *preacher-man* = preacher. **1981** *Smokies Heritage* 32:9 My daddy was an old time preacher man.

[redundant form; DARE *preacher-man* n chiefly South, South Midland]

preacher meat *noun* Fried chicken.

1978 *Smokies Heritage* 302 In fact some people referred to chickens as "preacher meat" as a chicken was almost always killed when the preacher came to dinner. **1997** Montgomery *Coll* (known to Andrews, Bush, Cardwell).

preacher woman *noun* A clergywoman. See also **preacher, preacher man.**

c1997 Jones *Why They Talk* 4 I met Glennie and we got married. A preacher woman married us.

preaching *noun* A religious service that includes a sermon. For many rural congregations in former times, such a service was held monthly. See 1974 citation.

1852 Carpenter *Diary* I 83 the raz 42 children belong to him all wen to prechin together. **1863** *Poteet CW Letters* (Nov 22) My Dear Wife I cant tell how mutch I would give to be at home this morning to go With you to Preachin and stay With you as long as I live. **1863** Wilson *Confederate Private* 25 (July 5) I must close and go to preching. **1923** (in **1952** Mathes *Tall Tales* 6) "The Lord willin', I aim to do it. I reckon some of you-uns'll be out to the preachin'," replied Brother Wes, turning Magdalene's head up the road. **1962** Dykeman *Tall Woman* 154 "We'll have the ceremony the next preaching Brother Gudger holds," Kate said. **1967** Fetterman *Stinking Creek* 47 He won't let them go in that store during preachin'. People go into preachin' and don't leave until it breaks. **1974** GSMNP-50:2:6 Well, when I first remember, we had church every Sunday, and Wednesday night, but we only had preaching once a month, and Preacher Newt Clabo was the pastor the first time I remember of anybody preaching up there. . . . He would come one Sunday out of the month and preach. That was the only preaching we had . . . but on Sunday morning when we didn't have preaching, we would meet and sing about an hour, had about an hour singing, and then we would have Sunday school, and after Sunday school a lot of the times we would sing for thirty minutes. **1974** GSMNP-51:12 We had Sunday school and we had preaching once a month on every third Saturday and Sunday. We'd have it two days there, you see, Saturday and Sunday, had business meeting on Saturday, they called it, and our daddy would say, "boys, get that work done and we'll go to church at eleven o'clock on Saturday," and we'd just have to do what he said. **2000** Spencer *Memory Lane* III:7 I would toddle along with John and Elzora to Sunday school or to both that and preaching. **2005** Williams *Gratitude* 515 = the part of the church service following Sunday School. Modern terminology is "Worship Service."

[EDD *preaching* sb Scot, Irel, Amer; SND *preachin* "a sermon"]

preaching day *noun* Traditionally, a Sunday on which a worship service including a sermon is held. In former times this took place once a month for many smaller churches.

1913 Morley *Carolina Mts* 90 The road leads to an unpainted church on the top of the mountain where on "preaching-day" the women assemble in their best black sunbonnets and the men in their Sunday clothes. *Ibid.* 218 If it is "preaching-day" the people are found all moving towards one point, the settlement church, which, like the school-house, generally stands "at a point equally inconvenient for everybody." **1973** GSMNP-2 They called it preachin' day back in the olden days, and they'd always gather before service and that's when they'd do most of their visitin', before regular church hours.

preaching funeral *noun* Same as **funeral**.

1924 Raine *Saddlebags* 202 One very obvious reason why so much of the preaching deals with death is the Mountain custom of "preaching funerals." The burial, of course, takes place immediately after death, but the funeral is "preached" in the early Autumn, when the weather is good, the cultivation of the crops is finished, the water in the creeks is at the lowest, and the kinsfolk and friends can gather for a fitting memorial. The chosen preacher takes the text selected by the departed, or, in the case of sudden death, a text chosen by the family. The choir, perhaps organized for this one occasion, sings the favorite hymns and perhaps one specially chosen on the deathbed. **1953** Davison *Word-List Appal* 13 = a memorial service in the summer for those who die during the year. . . . When a visiting minister came later during good weather the "funeral was preached." **1984** Wilder *You All Spoken* 208 = if bad weather or other adverse conditions prevailed when the burial was held, the preachin' funeral came later. Often in autumn when crops had been laid by, creeks were low, and relatives and friends had ample and proper time for last rights.

preaching point *noun* Formerly, a rural station along the route of a **circuit rider** at which he would stop on regular rotation and preach.

1984 *History of Beth-Car* 7 Beth-Car was one of the preaching points on the Greene Circuit and in all probability Pine Chapel was also.

preaching stand *noun* Same as **stand B4**.

1881 Pierson *In the Brush* 69 Having all dined, we returned to the preaching "stand," and the congregation reassembled. I preached to them at 4 P.M., and all the services were conducted to the close in a manner not essentially different from preaching services elsewhere.

preach it *interjection* Used as a shout during a sermon to encourage and urge on the preacher.

1987 Young *Lost Cove* 99 Members of the Amen Corner were lending a hand with the "hallelujahs" and "preach-its" when the preacher paused for breath and to recharge his vocal chords.

preachment *noun* A tedious or wearisome talk or discourse.

1913 Morley *Carolina Mts* 13 She began going to church and profiting according to her light on the "preachment." **1942** Campbell *Cloud-Walking* 135 That's too pretty and calm-like to make a loud preachment about. **1966** Medford *Ol' Starlin* 99 Silas went on to say that Eve, in her "preachments," always said that since the good Lord created the land there 'round Ol' Starlin—same as elsewhere, it must a been His will for folks to live on it, and enjoy life if they could, same as elsewhere. **1997** Montgomery *Coll* (known to Cardwell).

preach one's funeral *verb phrase* See citation.

c1960 Wilson *Coll* = to criticize bitterly.

preach up a storm *verb phrase* Of a preacher: to preach in a spirited, commanding fashion.

1997 Johnson *Melungeon Heritage* 45 When a preacher "got to going good" the congregation would say he was "preaching up a storm."

presactly *adverb*

A Variant forms *persackly* [see **1974** in **B**], *persactly* [see **1972** in **B**], *perzackly* [see **2007** in **B**], *prezackly* [see **1931** in **B**].

B Exactly.

1931 Combs *Lg Sthn High* 1318 *prezackly*. **1960** Burnett *My Valley* 111 His answer was, "I don't know presactly." **1972** Cooper *NC Mt Folklore* 94 *persactly* = exactly. **1974** Fink *Bits Mt Speech* 19 She done *persackly* right. **c1982** Young *Colloquial Appal* 16 *persackly* = exactly. **2007** McMillon *Notes* I don't know perzackly, but along about the middle of the night it commenced snowing.

[perhaps blending of *precisely* and *exactly*]

prescription school *noun* Apparently, a type of **subscription school** in which the county would pay the tuition for those unable to afford it.

1972 *AOHP/ALC-241* Most of them went to what they call a prescription school when they were kids back when I was young. Somebody would hire a man to teach the school. The county or other people put in enough money to hire another one [for a] hundred students, and they would teach them.

press *noun*

1 See **cane mill**, **cider mill**, **sorghum gin**.

2 A large, shelved cabinet or cupboard for the kitchen.

1977 Hamilton *Mt Memories* 9 Sometimes I would stand for a long while in front of the "press," whose upper shelves held lovely old plates, pitchers, etc. The press was handmade from choice cherry wood and I loved the elegant doors, with the panes of glass so expertly and intricately placed.

[EDD *press* sb 5 Scot; SND *press* n 2]

3 A movable closet for clothes. See also **chifforobe**, **clothes press**.

1960 Arnow *Seedtime* 379 The cabinet-maker able to build a press could, by varying the design, produce a wide assortment of furniture. He could leave out the upper shelves, set in pegs or put a pole across the top, and the housewife could use it for storing clothes instead of folded linens. He could lengthen the top, do away with the bottom entirely and have what we in my childhood still called a wardrobe, a variety of clothespress; walnut, dark and high, like a double coffin stood on end. **c1960** Wilson *Coll* = a movable or separate place to hang clothes . . . a wardrobe. **1975** Dial *Yesterday's Lg* 92 = a clothes closet or wardrobe: "Hang my clothes in the press."

4 A pressured condition or situation.

1967 Fetterman *Stinking Creek* 51 So much one season, so much another season; it keeps me in a press.

pressed hog's head See **press(ed) meat**.

press(ed) meat (also *pressed hog's head*) *noun* Same as **souse B**.

1968 Wilson *Folklore Mammoth Cave* 20 *press meat* (or *pressed meat* or *hogshead cheeses*) = souse. **1971** Wood *Vocab Change* 350 Pressed meat is found almost entirely [to the exclusion of other terms] in north Georgia. **1983** *Dark Corner OHP-4A* You take the head and the feet [of the hog] and cook them. Just put them in a big pot and boil them till they come all to pieces, and take that and just mash it up in a big old pan of a thing. They just cook together, you know, and press it down. They call it pressed meat. Just mash it down good and put a little vinegar on that and just put it in a big old platter or something or pan or crock and pack it down and set it back and just go slice some of that off. They call it pressed meat. That's something. **1984** Page and Wigginton *Foxfire Cookery* 118 Hog's head is also called "souse," "souse meat," "head cheese," or "pressed hog's head." Prepare the raw hog's head as follows: Trim, scrape, or singe off any hairs or bristles that are left. If you intend to use the ears, brain, snout, tongue or jowls for any purpose other than souse, remove them and set them aside to soak. Otherwise leave them on the head to be ground up. **1986** Pederson et al. *LAGS*: *press(ed) meat* = attested by 1/60 interviewees (1.7%) from E TN and 17/35 (48.6%) from N GA; 18/66 of all LAGS interviewees (27.3%) attesting term were from Appalachia.

press meat See **press(ed) meat**.

pretni See **pretty nigh**.

prettify *verb* To make pretty in an artificial way; hence participial adjective *prettified*.

1940 Bowman *KY Mt Stories* 245 = to decorate. **1981** Whitener *Folk-Ways* 54 Of course, modern long handles are a far cry from those of bygone days. They have been prettified, thermofied, and advertised until they have achieved social acceptance. **1999** Morgan *Gap Creek* 21 I'd never had the time to prettify myself and primp, and to study how to be at the right place to get a man's notice.

pretty

A Variant forms *perty*, *purt* [see **pretty near(ly)**, **pretty nigh**], *purty*.

B *adjective* Considerable, plentiful.

1977 *Jake Waldroop* 166 There'd be a pretty plenty of jobs [that year].

C *adverb* Fairly, rather, considerably (often in phrase *pretty plenty*).

1863 *Hogg CW Letters* (July 2) goods is scers and money prety plenty. **1958** *GSMNP-110:38* [There was] pretty plenty of spruce, and [we were] getting in the edges of it when I worked there. **1960** McCaulley *Cades Cove* We had pretty plenty of deer that they'd use back in the mountains back there. **c1960** Wilson *Coll*: *pretty plenty* = a good deal, ample, a whole. **1972** *AOHP/LJC-104* The women then made a lot of money too, because they'd wash and iron for people and made pretty much money. **2008** *Rosie Hicks* 3 Ray always put out pretty many potatoes. *Ibid.* 4 We still had pretty many pumpkins yet.

D *noun*

1 A small object of showy color or design, such as a plaything, flower, etc. See also **flower pretty**, **play pretty**, **spring pretty**.

1865 *Hill CW Letters* (Feb 25) here is a little pretty for little Jane that I fixt when I was Sick be Shore and giv it to her and tel her her pap Sent it to here. **1865** *Smith Letter* 11 Tell Frony and Nancy to be good girls and I will bring them a perty when I come home. **1913** Morley *Carolina Mts* 38 The "pretties," as the children here call all flowers, will linger day after day, week after week. **1915** Dingus *Word-List VA* 187 = any little thing of value, esp. a toy: "I wouldn't take a pretty for that." **1924** Raine *Saddlebags* 105 I want to buy a pretty for my baby-child. **1931** Hannum *Thursday April* 42 She would spend the rest of her days seeing that these last least ones got the life she had always wanted—the loving and pretties. **1959** Pearsall *Little Smoky* 86 The coffee tin of old nails and screws and the snuff jar with penknives and pencils stand on the mantel beside the lamp, the unused alarm clock, a few family photographs, perhaps some souvenirs of Holston or White City, and whatever small "pretties" the family possesses. **1962** Dykeman *Tall Woman* 37 Sometimes at night at home, when she and Kate and Annie Marie had had to sleep three in a bed and she had felt she would smother from the closeness and the heaviness of their sleep (she had paid Kate and Annie Marie a trunkful of pretties over the years to take the middle and let her sleep on the outside), she would ease out of bed and go to the window and look out at the night. **1967** *DARE Survey* (Maryville TN) = toy. **1973** GSMNP-85:2:3 We [would] just get leaves and pin them up and make all kinds of pretties. **1985** Irwin *Alex Stewart* 120 He picked it up and said, "Hebbins, I'll make you a purty out of that." **1997** King *Mt Folks* 54 For enjoyment, she had her garden and her "purties" or flowers. **2008** McKinley *Bear Mt* 82 The tall, ornately-carved organ in the corner of the living room . . . had big mirrors and lots of pretty shelves to display Granny's collection of "what-nots" (a mountain name for small, decorative ornaments. Another common name was simply "pur-ties").

[DARE *pretty* n C1a chiefly South, South Midland, especially Southern Appalachians]

2 An item of value.

1901 Harben *Westerfelt* 279–80 I'd give a purty to be thar when she comes, fer they won't know she's converted. **1952** Wilson *Folk Speech NC* 579 *bet (give) a pretty* = a form of light verbal wager: "I bet a pretty he never told her where he'd been." **1974** Fink *Bits Mt Speech* 20 = something of value. "I'd give a *pretty* to know."

pretty as a speckled pup See **speckled pup(py), as cute/pretty as a.**

pretty-by-night *noun* A nightshade plant (*Mirabilis jalapa*), which blooms late in the day. Also called **peep-by-night.**

1942 Thomas *Blue Ridge* 56 There was pretty-by-night, too, though their snow-white blossoms were closed tight in the bud for it was not yet sundown; only in the twilight and by night did the buds bloom out. **1943** Justus *Bluebird* 59 The scent of pretty-by-nights was sweet as it drifted through the window. **1967** *DARE Survey* (Maryville TN) = four o'clock.

prettyful *adjective* Beautiful.

1998 Montgomery *Coll* She's the most prettyful girl in the whole county (Brown).

pretty girls station *noun* See citation.

2005 Preece *I Grew* 76 The girls had a prissy little game called Pretty Girls Station. It went like this: teams of girls divide up in two rows. The first group walks forward (really prissy) to the other group and says, "Here we come." The second group asks, "Where are you from?" First group replies "Pretty Girl Station" and it continues in this manner, "What's your occupation," "Just about anything." "Well get to work and show us something." Then we would proceed to do a kind of charades game like pretending to iron clothes or wash clothes, be a secretary, or nurse or doctor. Just whatever we decided on. The other group talked their answer over and if they didn't guess right then we got to go again until they got it right.

pretty near(ly) (also *pretty near it*) *adverb phrase* See also **pretty nigh.**

A Variant forms *peart near* [see **2003** in **B**], *pert-near* [see **1982** in **B**], *prin nearly* [see **1975** in **B**], *pritenere* [see **1863** in **B**], *purt near* [see **1973** in **B**], *purt' near't* [see **1957** in **B**], *put near* [see **1862** in **B**].

B Almost, practically, almost entirely.

1862 *Councill CW Letters* (Oct 23) I have quit Swearing put near. **1863** *Ingram CW Letters* (March 8) I am pritenere out of hart Evere Seeing pease maid any more though I Hope it will be Maid. **1953** Hall *Coll* (Bryson City NC) Everybody that's lived right near the river pert' nearly had a canoe . . . and they used it for gigging fish. **1957** Combs *Lg Sthn High: Word List* 78 *purt' near't* = pretty near it; always a preceding modifier. Ex.: "He fell outn the cornfield and purt' near't broke his neck." **1973** *AOHP/LJC-317* They owned purt near all of Breathitt County, the biggest part of Breathitt County. **1975** Gainer *Witches Ghosts Signs* 15 *prin nearly* = almost. "He choked her prin nearly to death." **1982** Powers and Hannah *Cataloochee* 380 I pert-near got my eyes beat out last night. **1985** Irwin *Alex Stewart* 176 Everybody, pert near it, would come if they knowed about it [= a person's death], and help dig a person's grave when they died. **1991** Thomas *Sthn Appal* 138 They had them Shea engines, that'ud go purt-near't enny kind of a grade, ye know. *Ibid.* 171 They'd climb right straight up a hill, purt-near'it. **2003** Carter *Mt Home* 215 Aunt Ellen whispered, "She's peart near gone."

pretty nigh *adverb phrase* See also **nigh it, pretty near(ly).**

A Variant forms *pretni* [see **1863** in **B**], *purteni* [see **1862** in **B**], *purt nie* [see **1864** in **B**], *purt nigh* [see **1924**, **1974** citations in **B**].

B Very nearly, almost (entirely).

1862 *Lockmiller CW Letters* (March 30) [We] have got the old grond brok up and the new grond purteni cl[e]and of. **1863** *Revis CW Letters* (April 25) I am distrest to deth pretni about it but you and clint and elen must do the best you can. **1864** *Walker CW Letters* (June 19) I am giten purt nie S[t]out and harty agane. **1924** Spring *Lydia Whaley* 2 Put in the bigness purt nigh of a pullet egg. **1974** Fink *Bits Mt Speech* 20 *purt nigh* = almost, very close. "I *purt' nigh* fell in." **1982** DeArmond *So High* 23 "Course that thar boy pert nigh died, he wuz so shuck up," said old Jim, as he spit tobacco juice into the fire.

pretty plenty See **pretty C.**

pretty Polly *noun* See citation.

1960 Stubbs *Mountain-Wise* (April–May) 6 A diminutive wild campion, or pink, has two fetching names—"kissie" and "pretty Polly."

pretty smart *adjective* Same as **right smart B.**

1862 *Huntley CW Letters* (Jan 5) me and him and tolliver had a pretty smart singing Last night. **1865** *Martin CW Letters* (Jan 21) Ill Say to you that their was pretty Smart Battel near the pount yesterday between our own forse through mistake. **1939** *Hall Coll* They was a pretty smart gang of 'em.

prezackly See **presactly.**

prickly ash *noun* An ash tree (*Zanthoxylum* spp), from whose bark a medicinal tea is made. Also called **toothache tree.**

2006 *WV Encycl* 568 People chewed the inner bark of the prickly ash or toothache tree to numb aching teeth, and willow bark, which contains salicin (from which aspirin was later derived), to cure aches and pains.

pride *noun* An instance of being proud.

c1975 Lunsford *It Used to Be* 52 They said this man Sissom would go in there with a butcher knife, right into the den where there's several bears, and he just took a pride in going in and fighting with them.

prideful *adjective* Proud, haughty.

1958 Campbell *Tales* 25 The last time I saw Aunt Lizbeth she told me she always wore the gold beads inside her dress, "not to seem prideful with wearing golden jewels." **1997** Montgomery *Coll* (known to Bush, Cardwell, Jones, Ledford, Norris, Oliver, Weaver).

[OED3 *prideful* adj chiefly Scot and North American; EDD *prideful* adj Scot and Amer; SND *prideful* (at *pride* n[1] 1); CUD *prideful* "full of pride"]

pridy *adjective* Proud, haughty.

1961 *DARE File* "I wish you could have knowed him before he got like this. La, he was a pridey man!" That word pridey was a favorite of Mama's . . . If a thing is pridey, you can take great pride in it. *Ibid.* 31 La, black walnut's a pridey wood! That dado will be a grand sight.

[cf EDD *pridy* adj 1]

Prim See **Primitive Baptist.**

prime *verb* To pick the lower leaves off a growing tobacco plant; hence nouns *primer, primings*, verbal noun *priming*.

1944 Dingus *Tobacco Words* 69 = to pluck the lower dead or worthless leaves. (In Va., N.C.: also to pluck the good leaves for curing. Same as to pull. Current.) *primer* = one who primes tobacco. *primings* = the lower leaves, formerly waste, now one of the grades on the market. **1969** Miller *Raising Tobacco* There was a further grade called ground lugs which might be got by priming the patch before cutting time. **2015** Robbins *Land Sled* 15 As the tobacco leaves were harvested, or "primed" as it was called, they were placed in the sled, which, when full, delivered the leaves to the tobacco barn for curing.

primer, priming, primings See **prime.**

Primitive Baptist (also **Prim**) *noun* A sect of Baptists known for its legalistic strictures, adherence to predestination, practice of **foot washing**, and opposition to infant baptism and missions. See 1926, 1970 citations. Also called **foot-washing Baptist, Hard Shell.**

1856 (in **1956** Eliason *Tarheel Talk* 288) (Caldwell Co NC) Was recived by examinytion on the primitive baptis faith. **1908** Smith *Reminiscences* 412 The primitive or "foot-washing" Baptists still have their churches in the mountain coves, where their shepherds feed their flocks on sound and fury and nonsense; but the missionary Baptist and the circuit-rider follow steadily in the wake of the schoolmaster, and the sect in ignorance is already doomed. **1926** Thomas *Hills and Mts of KY* 97 There is no doubt but that the Primitive, or Regular Baptist Church had its origin in North Carolina shortly after the middle of the eighteenth century, and began to organize itself into "associations" in most of the Southern States in the first quarter of the nineteenth century. The doctrine and polity of the Primitive Baptists are unique. Their ostensible reason for springing up, their *raison d'être*, was to combat everything that seemed modern and progressive in the other communities; to fight Sunday schools, missionary movements, all sorts of church societies, and centralization in church circles. **1939** *Hall Coll* (Tobes Creek NC) The Primitive Baptists believe in absolute predestination, and they are opposed to foreign missions. **1965** Shields *Cades Cove* 8 Churches were organized early [in Cades Cove]. The Primitive Baptist sect, being the dominant one of the mountains, was the first to organize in 1876. The Olivers and Gregorys were very prominent in this church. **1970** Mead *Handbook Denominations* 45 The Primitive Baptists have the reputation of being the most strictly orthodox and exclusive of all Baptists. Unique in that they have never been organized as a denomination and have no administrative bodies, they represent a protest against "money-based" missions and benevolent societies and against "assessing" the churches to support missions, missionaries, and Sunday Schools . . . there was objection to the centralization of authority in [missionary] societies. Sunday schools also were unauthorized by Scripture. **1974** *GSMNP-50:2:9* The Primitive Baptists and the Missionary Baptists . . . now I don't know how long ago that was before my time, but they had a split over their doctrine, you see, and they wasn't a-getting along too good. **1982** Ginns *Snowbird Gravy* 96 Now, that 'sociation was when all the Prims met up. . . . They come in over here and got started. **1986** Noonkesser *Crossing* 95 By 1819 the question of slavery was being debated in all denominations. In the East Tennessee area, the Baptists became involved in the arguments concerning missions, Sunday school and other matters pertaining to doctrine. Many felt money contributed for missions was being misused to promote the abolition movement and that God would find a way to save those intended for salvation. The anti-mission group became known as the old school; those who favored missions were known as the new school. In later years the two groups would be known as Primitive Baptists and Missionary Baptists. **2013** Pierce

Corn in Jar 52 Primitive Baptists—common in the Smokies—seemed particularly tolerant towards the moonshiners in their midst. Primitives have never stopped using wine in communion and as historian Charles Thompson puts it, "Teetotal prohibition was never a stated Primitive Baptist goal." **2015** Kidd and Hankins *Baptists in Amer* 114 The antimission Baptists went by many names: "Black Rock Baptists," "Old School," "Old Fashioned," "Predestination," "Particular," and, more dismissively, "Square-Toed," "Hard Rined [sic]," "Broad-Brimmed," "Ironsides," and "Hard-Shell." Most commonly, they called themselves "Primitive Baptists," which to them meant biblical Baptists.

prink *verb* To primp, preen.

1934 Carpenter *Archaic English in WV* 77 A couple of years ago I heard a man in southern West Virginia who was somewhat witty, mention something about women prinking up so much.... Upon investigation I found that prink goes back at least nine hundred years.... One may find the word in the little volume Ballads and Ballad Poetry which is used in our public schools. It is in The Young Tamlane, one of our oldest recorded ballads. **1958** Combs *Archaic English in KY* 42 = primp: "Don't prink all day."

[OED3 *prink* v² 2b 1591→]

prin nearly See **pretty near(ly)**.

printh *noun* Prints.

1937 Hall *Coll* (Emerts Cove TN) We seed the printh of the bear in the mud. **1939** Hall *Coll* (White Oak NC) Many young and old say "printh" around White Oak. **1942** Hall *Phonetics Smoky Mts* 96.

priss *verb* See citations.

1968–69 *DARE Survey* (Big Stone Gap VA) = to move around in a way to make people take notice of you; (Ball Ground GA) = to "go out" a great deal, not to stay at home much. **1984** Burns *Cold Sassy* 201 "I don't need your permission," I told her, and I just prissed over and got them. **1988** Kingsolver *Bean Trees* 4 (DARE) Candy Stripers, town girls with money for the pink-and-white uniforms and prissing around the bedpans on Saturdays like it was the holiest substance on God's green earth they'd been trusted to carry.

[DARE *priss* v 1 chiefly South, South Midland, TX]

privy (also *privy bush*) *noun* The privet (*Ligustrum sempervirens*), a dense shrub that forms hedges.

1917 (in **1944** Wentworth *ADD* 476) (sWV) = privet: "sweep your yard with a privy broom." **c1960** Wilson *Coll* Privet (or privet bush) *privy* = a hedge shrub, often called *privy-bush*. **1982** Slone *How We Talked* 29 *privy bush* = a hedge bush.

[DARE *privy* n 1 especially Midland]

privy bush See **privy**.

prize (also *prize off, prize open, prize up*) *verb, verb phrase*

1 To pry, use a bar, the hands, or other instrument to move, raise or open (a heavy or shut object) with or as with a lever.

1824 Knight *Letter from KY* 107 Some words are used, even by genteel people, from their imperfect educations, in a new sense ... to prize for to raise by lever. **1861** *Painter CW Letters* (Sept 16) I seen men prising a yankey out of his grave the[y] took his teeth out and berried him a gain. **1895** Edson and Fairchild *TN Mts* 376 *prize*. **1937** Hall *Coll* (Emerts Cove TN) I prized open the door. *Ibid.* (Emerts Cove TN) Let's prize the car up. *Ibid.* (Emerts Cove TN) I prized up the side of the house. *Ibid.* (Jonathans Creek NC) One of the Plott boys went up and prized the panther's mouth open. **1959** Roberts *Up Cutshin* 16 I went out looking for a bar to prize with, and when I come back, he was lying there—killed. **1979** *Big South Fork OHP*-11 The carting wheel would hang on the tree, on each tree, and you'd have to prize it off. **2001** Lowry *Expressions* 14 My mouth is so dry I wake up at night and have to take my hands and prize my mouth open.

[DARE *prize* v² 1 chiefly South Midland, also South]

2 See 1944 citation.

1864 *Watkins CW Letters* (July 20) you sed for us to send you some tobacco thomas has got some prised to send to you. **1944** Dingus *Tobacco Words* 69 = to put [tobacco] in hogsheads for aging and press down hard with machinery.

[DARE *prize* v² 2 chiefly South Midland]

prize log (also *prize pole, pry pole*) *noun* A log, rail, or other long, sturdy object used to lever or move a heavy object. See also **pole**.

1953 Hall *Coll* (Plott Creek NC) When the boys got the pry pole on the lid of the [bear pen], it was a pen, a log pen.... I had the dogs standing in front of the pen. **1956** Hall *Coll* (Townsend TN) I reckon Aunt Becky Cable was the strongest woman in the Cove. She was a great big one. She'd plow. She'd be out with a prize pole and an axe pullin' them stumps out. **1961** Medford *History Haywood Co* 19 Whenever wagons became mired up, which was often the case, "prize-poles" were often kept along the road of such mirey places. **1973** GSMNP-70:2:5 These men down here was on that big dam with a big crowbar, raising them splash boards like that, you know, over a prize log. **1997** Davis *Cataloochee Valley* 139 Men used the pick, shovel, sledge hammer, prize poles, and employed rawhiding, and mainly strength and awkwardness in road building.

[SND *prise* n; DARE *prize log, prize pole* (at *prize* n 1b) chiefly South, South Midland]

prize pole See **prize log**.

prize up See **prize**.

prodjekt, prodjick See **project**.

professor *noun*

A Variant forms *fessor, perfesser* [see **1912** in **B1**], *perfessor*.

1932 (in **1935** Edwards *NC Novels* 84) *perfessor*. **1967–70** *DARE Survey* (Greenville SC, Dayton TN) *fessor*.

B Senses.

1 A schoolteacher, principal of a school; more generally, an instructor of any type.

1910 Thompson *Highlanders* 49 To get to teach a public school in a mountain district often places one high up among his fellows and usually bestows upon him the title of "Professor"! **1912** Perrow *Songs and Rhymes* 142 This teacher, called the "perfesser" (a title given in the South to all male teachers), teaches ten days for ten dollars, and "boards around" with his "scholars." **1962** Wilson *Folkways Mammoth Cave* 52–53 From the earliest times in the region the teacher occupied a prominent position. Even the most inexperienced boy, teaching his first school, was always "Professor" . . . and the teacher is still "Professor" to most of the people in the region. **1963** Edwards *Gravel* 164 There was the time at Wilson's school, for instance, when Professor Owenby was the teacher. **1967** Wilson *Folkways Mammoth Cave* 19 Usually each singing school master—often called a *Professor*—had a songbook to sell. But he never lacked for enthusiastic supporters, who bought his books and attended his schools. **1973** *AOHP/ASU-246* My father sent [my brother] over there to that high school. A Professor Factum was the teacher. **1983** Helsly *Country Doctor* 3 As we listened from our vantage point from the corner of our yard nearest to the school we could hear the students reciting their lessons. One was especially unusual. We could hear the powerful voice of the principal, Professor John Jenkins, as he taught mental arithmetic. **1998** Lambert *Kinfolks* 14 Just then, who should be coming up the hall but Mr. H. G. Loy, the principal of the school. As was often the case in small, rural schools, "Professor Loy" knew me and my family.

2 One who espouses religious convictions openly and ardently.

1864 *Bartlett CW Letters* (Oct 15) I was rejoiced to hear him say he was a professor of religion and a member of the Baptist Church. **1864** *Misemer CW Letters* (May 2) when they see a professer swareing blackguarding or cutting up in any way unbecoming a christian they bore him to the hollow. **1924** (in **1952** Mathes *Tall Tales* 49) Dilsie aims to go reg'lar to the pertracted meetin', an' I'd be proud if you-uns would come. I'd like to see all of ye perfessers afore I'm called. **1931–33** (in **1987** Oliver and Oliver *Sketches* 23) It has been said heretofore that neither of them were professors of religion.

proffer *verb* To offer (followed by an infinitive).

1931 Combs *Lg Sthn High* 1304 He proffered to go to mill fer me. **1952** Wilson *Folk Speech NC* 579 = to offer as a gift: to tender one's assistance: "He proffered to help me build the boat."

[DARE *proffer* especially Southern Appalachians]

project (also *prodject, prodjick, projeck, project around*) *verb, verb phrase* To walk or wander about; to pry into, meddle with.

1892 Smith *Farm and Fireside* 318 Who has been here projecting with my pens and letter pads, and turned over my inkstand and messed up my papers? **1913** Kephart *Our Sthn High* 171 They don't go prodjectin' around looking for stills. **1925** Greer-Petrie *Angeline Hill Country* 140 After prodjickin' with a little orn [= iron] rod that worked back'erds and forrids, he tuk a-holt of thatar stem. **c1926** Cox *Cullowhee Wordlist* = to tamper with. **1952** Wilson *Folk Speech NC* 579 = to wander about, walk about aimlessly, pry. **c1960** Wilson *Coll* (also *project around*) = to tinker or even meddle. **1974** Fink *Bits Mt Speech* 20 I've just been *projectin'* around. **1992** Brooks *Sthn Stuff* 118 *projeck* = to mess around with; to bother a thing. "Listen, you're not to projeck with my personal propitty, you hear me?" **1994** Montgomery *Coll* (known to Cardwell).

[DARE *project* v 1 chiefly South, South Midland]

prong *noun*

1 A tributary of a stream or river; also used in place-names, as for the three tributaries of the Little River, as in *Middle Prong of the Little River* (TN). See 1956 citation. See also **branch, fork.**

1779 (in **1940** McJimsey *Topo Terms in VA* 299) To the ridge dividing the waters of Tygers Valley and Buchanan prongs of the Monongalia [sic]. **1862** *Mangum CW Letters* (June 23) we crost the ner prong of the river and went to the other prong and thar was yankes aplenty in a swiming. **1863** *Reese CW Letters* (May 17) we air at fair feeld in 4 miles of war trace in 18 or 20 of murfrees Boro on one prong of duck River. **1883** Zeigler and Grosscup *Heart of Alleghanies* 58 On other slopes, like those descending to the west prongs of the Pigeon, it reaches downward for miles from the summit of the mountains, forming the wildest of wooded landscapes. **1895** Edson and Fairchild *TN Mts* 373 I come down the other *prong* of the creek. **1913** Kephart *Our Sthn High* 91 [The deer] tuk right down the bed o' Desolation, up the left prong of Roaring Fork. **1926** Hunnicutt *Twenty Years* 36 The dogs . . . went to the left of his stand, which put it above me on the creek at the main Smoky Gap prong at the head of the creek. **1942** Hall *Phonetics Smoky Mts* 32 *Prong* [is] much used in the sense of "a tributary stream," or "a large branch of a tree." **1956** Fink *That's Why* 4 Fork and prong generally have added the name of the larger stream of which it is tributary, as West Prong of the Little Pigeon River, or Straight Fork of Oconaluftee River. **1963** Lord *Blue Ridge* 43D "Prong" and "fork" are descriptive names applied to many mountain streams. Their course is swift and straight, and they merge into each other at a sharp angle. Prongs are generally smaller streams and join into forks. **1973** *GSMNP-84:6* I thought the world of Horace Kephart, and over here on Oconaluftee they named a prong of that river for him, Kephart Prong. **1974** *GSMNP-50:2:17* The left-hand prong, a middle prong, and a right-hand prong. That's the way they said it, you know, back at that time. **1996** Linn *West Fork* 3 The West Fork of the Little Pigeon begins at the juncture of Walker Prong and Road Prong.

[Web3 *prong* n 3c South and Midland; DARE *prong* n 1 chiefly South, South Midland]

2 The stalk of a ginseng plant.

1997 Hufford *American Ginseng* 10 The older the root, the more stalks, or "prongs," it sends up.

proof *verb* To gauge (the strength of alcohol in) distilled spirits.

[**1913** Kephart *Our Sthn High* 135 The maker of "mountain dew" has no other instrument than a small vial, and his testing is done entirely by the "bead" of the liquor, the little iridescent bubbles that rise when the vial is tilted.] **1967** Williams *Moonshining* 14 The doubling completed, the moonshiner then "proofs" the whiskey. **c1975** Lunsford *It Used to Be* 81 Low wine is another word, and that is what is left after the first is run off and after they've proofed it. They proof it with a proof vial, mostly a ludnum bottle. Bateman's ludnum bottles are about seven inches long, broad bottom—an inch and a quarter at the bottom—and tapered to the top the size of your thumb. You get some of that collected in the bottle, shake it and judge as best you can whether it's high proof whiskey or whether it's low wine.

proof down *verb phrase* To dilute (the alcoholic content in) a quantity of liquor.

1992 Gabbard *Thunder Road* 114 It was probably around 120 proof, but you could proof it down to any way you wanted it.

proof vial *noun* See citations.

1968 *End of Moonshining* 49 Proof Vial = a glass tube used to check the bead of the whiskey. A Bateman Drop bottle was the most popular as it held exactly one ounce, and was just the right shape. Others used now are bottles that rye flavoring comes in, or a government gauge. **1974** Dabney *Mt Spirits* xxiv = a small glass tube used to test the whiskey bead. The operator would shake the vial of whiskey and hold it horizontally to check the bead. Some distillers added drops of water to determine the proof and the volume of water needed for the "blending tub."

property *noun* Livestock.

1867 *Chapman CW Letters* (Nov 3) the Rebels done me a grate deal of harm they taken off too of my sons Israel and Theophilus and they taken my property and grain. **1870** *Hall CW Letters* (June 12) wee moved the last of our stock up here the week after Christmas wee had tolerable good luck in getting our little property and plunder moved up. **1914** Furman *Sight* 45 I am sot down here in the midst of rack and ruin, with . . . the fence rotten and the hogs in the corn, the property eatin' their heads off. **1952** Giles *40 Acres* 4 Here there is a pocket of pure Appalachianism and our older people still speak the tongue. . . . Livestock is called "property."

protract *verb*

1 To conduct (a **protracted meeting**).

1843 *Paw Paw Hollow Church Minutes* 117 Church ordered that Elders I Kimbrough Layman Tipton Langford and Hodges be invited to our communion meeting to be protracted in October.

2 To continue (perhaps through influence of **protracted meeting**).

1939 Hall *Coll* (Deep Creek NC) When I was a boy we had fiddlin' and dancin' between Christmas and New Year's. We just protracted the part from one house to another.

protracted meeting (also *protractive meeting, protract meeting*) *noun* Originally, an annual series of religious services held in the late summer or early fall, often running daily for a week or longer and usually featuring a guest preacher. In the mountains this term was replaced by *revival, revival services*, and similar alternatives after World War II, after churches generally acquired full-time pastors, and was held on a stated three- or five-day basis. See also **big meeting, camp meeting, contracted meeting, revival meeting**.

1841 *Paw Paw Hollow Church Minutes* 100 The Church met to hold a protracted meeting and communion at which the church was found in peace. **1858** *Elijoy Church Minutes* 94 The Church met at Elijoy and held aprotracd meeting which held 11 days. **1860** *Week in Smokies* 124 Having lent a helping hand for a while, I concluded to walk on down to a Baptist "protracted meeting" then going on some two miles further down the mountain. **1862** *Warrick CW Letters* (Sept 10) The Methodists round about here, have got a protracted meeting a going on, about three hundred yard from the hospital. **1863** *Proffit CW Letters* (Aug 23) ther hase binn aprotack meatin every sens I Came hare I am glade to tell you of the nuse thar hase binn some some [sic] Eighty soles Con[verted]. **1870** *Paw Paw Hollow Church Minutes* Protracted meeting continued 16 days during which time we received by Baptism and the right hand of fellowship Cora Petty. **1923** (in **1952** Mathes *Tall Tales* 3) Preacher Ike, as an ever-watchful laborer in the Lord's vineyard, discerned the signs of the time as auspicious for "protracted meetin'." **1973** GSMNP-14:12 He had protractive meeting. That's revival once a year. **c1975** Lunsford *It Used to Be* 91 At least once a year, and sometimes several, each church would be supposed to conduct a protracted meeting with the pastor leading. He'd generally get some visiting minister to help him. That was at a time when everybody in the community would be invited to come, and all the good people, even from any of the denominations, were considered welcome to come and take part in the meeting. When the Baptists got through theirs, the Methodists would be the next to have a meeting, or visa versa. **1998** Montgomery *File*, *protract meeting* (known to 85-year-old man, Greenbrier TN).

[DARE *protracted meeting* n chiefly South, South Midland]

protractive meeting, protract meeting See **protracted meeting.**

proud *adjective*

1 Pleased, delighted, honored. See also **journey-proud**.

1861 *Martin CW Letters* (Nov 6) I was proud to receive A letter from you to think that you thought enough of me to write to me. **1864** *Chapman CW Letters* (April 10) I Received your letter By the hand of Wiley Smith and was proud to hear from you. **1895** Edson and Fairchild *TN Mts* 373 She will be proud to have her tooth stop aching. **1917** Kephart *Word-List* 416 = pleased. "I was proud to hear from you." **1928** Justus *Betty Lou* 85 "Shore enough! Well, I'm proud to have ye," was the kindly welcome. "Come on in and rest a spell." **1937** Hall *Coll* "I'm proud to see you" = a common greeting. **1939** Hall *Coll* (Bradley Fork NC) I'm proud that the sun, moon, and stars are where they are at. Else man would try to change 'em and mess 'em up. *Ibid.* (Copeland Creek TN) When one's gone, the t'other's proud of it [speaking of her twin boys]. **1953** Wharton *Dr Woman Cumberlands* 94 We'd all be proud to he'p you with your movin'. **1970** Hall *Witchlore* 1 The mountain man, now safely away, answered "I'm mighty damn proud (glad) of it." **1999** Hodges *Tough Customers* 115 You know it'd cost me to get somebody to come up here and tote them off, and I'd sure be proud to get rid of them. **2007** Milnes *Signs Cures Witches* 77 It was about three weeks later that we visited again. Dovie was "proud" to have the company. **2014** *Blind Pig* (Jan 30) I'm proud to hear Pap is out of the hospital.

[OED3 *proud* adj 3 "gratified, pleased, glad" now regional; Web3 *proud* 1c chiefly Midland; DARE *proud* adj 1a chiefly South, South Midland]

2 Of a female animal: sexually excited.

1919 Combs *Word-List South* 34 = applied to a "hot" female dog, "bitch," or "slut." Knott Co [KY]. **1997** Montgomery *Coll* (known to Adams, Bush, Cardwell, Ledford, Oliver).

[OED3 *proud* 7a "of a female animal, esp. a bitch . . . in heat" now regional; DARE *proud* adj 2 South, South Midland]

proud flesh (also *proud fresh*) *noun* Granulation tissue that grows in a wound as it heals.

1966–68 DARE *Survey* (Brasstown NC, Burnsville NC, Cherokee NC, Spruce Pine NC, Gatlinburg TN) = red flesh that grows in a wound and keeps [it] from healing right. **1976** Garber *Mountain-ese* 71 = shriveled tissue. "The doctor trimmed away the proud-flesh around the wound." **1986** Pederson et al. *LAGS*: *proud fresh* = attested by 3/60 interviewees (5%) from E TN and 1/35 (2.9%) from N GA; 4/23 of all LAGS interviewees (17.5%) attesting term were from Appalachia. **1990** Cavender *Folk Medical Lex* 29 = granulation tissue. **2004** Larimore *Bryson Seasons* 86 One of Doc John's recipes had dramatically reduced the size of the eschar and begun to promote "proud flesh" formation more successfully than any other treatment.

proud fresh See **proud flesh**.

proudful *adjective* Full of pride.

1941 Justus *Kettle Creek* 61 She had never felt more proudful over anything.

[OED3 *proudful* adj now chiefly U.S. regional, south and south midland]

prove out *verb phrase* To confirm or be confirmed as.

1939 Hall *Coll* (Cades Cove TN) It'd already been tested, you know, proved out to be good. **1960** Miller *Pigeon's Roost* (March 24) With another old saying about "March coming in roaring like a lion and going out as meekly as a little lamb" may prove out this season. **1973** GSMNP-57:53 All of 'em has always proved out good workers, good neighbors. **1973** GSMNP-79:2:28 We haven't proved that out yet.

pruse See **peruse**.

pry pole See **prize log**.

psalm *noun* Variant form *sam* [sæm] or [sam].

1957 Wise *Mt Speech* 306 *sam*. **1962** Wilson *Folkways Mammoth Cave* 9 A few very old people may have called *Psalms* /sams/, but most church-goers knew better, even though they kept cool by using their *palm-leaf* /pam/ fans. **1996** Montgomery *Coll* (known to Cardwell, Weaver).

p-turkey See **pea turkey**.

public job See **public work**.

public road *noun* A through road, one not on private property.

1898 Elliott *Durket Sperret* 61 She passed quickly through the gate that Si held open, and turned into the public road going down the Cove. **1929** Kephart *Smoky Mt Magic* 160 Down where Degataga's lane joins the public road, and off a little way in the woods, a mule had been tethered. **1973** Medford *Long Hard Road* 15 The wagon roads (that is, the public roads) were found in more thickly settled communities and could scarcely be called *roads* at all today; for example, the road which was made to Cataloochee and finally on to Big Creek.

public work (also *public job*, *public works*) *noun* Employment providing a cash income from outside one's home or farm, whether at a commercial enterprise (as from logging or a factory) or at a government project (as road construction and repair).

1921 Campbell *Sthn Highlander* 211 Men, too, are accustomed to walk many miles under all sorts of conditions, to and fro from the "public works," as railroad, logging, and similar operations are called. **1924** Raine *Saddlebags* 9 Men take out logs, go to the monthly Court at the county seat, drive cattle, and occasionally go to earn some "cash money" at "public works" (by which is meant any enterprise employing a number of men, such as building a courthouse or a bit of railway, work at a sawmill or at a coal mine). **1956** Hall *Coll* (Byrds Creek NC) I didn't work at farmin' so awfully much. I worked at public works for twenty-five years. I started at the age of fourteen. *Ibid.* (Del Rio TN) *public work* = logging, working on a railroad, anything besides farming. **1967** Giles *40 Acres* 25 He had not done enough to provide for his family that year, so he had to go out and do "public work." **1975** *Logging* 40 I used to work for Genette [Lumber Company]. . . . That was the first public works I ever done. **1981** High *Coll* (DARE) *public job* or *public work* = any job done off the home place, and for which a person gets paid. I've heard both of these expressions used in the Gorge, and they seem to be a generalization of public works or official work done for public use. . . . "My first public work was teaming over at the oil fields." **1982** Eller *Miners* 121 The promise of a steady employment and a cash income pulled others into the mines and mills, into what mountain people called "public work." **2002** Oliver *Cooking and Living* 73 Working for a company was called "public work" by most people, and was resisted by many for it showed, in a sense, that their traditional farm work was not enough to provide for a family. **2003** LaLone et al. *Farming Life* 311 I had to farm for three years when I had to go to public work. **2009** Benfield *Mt Born* 183 If a man had a job off the farm, it was referred to as a public job. This did not mean one of the trades such as carpentry, but work at a mill or factory.

[DARE *public work* n chiefly Southern Appalachians]

puccoon (also *puccoon root*) Same as **bloodroot**.

1824 (in **1912** Doddridge *Notes on Settlement* 116) Indian physic, or bowman root, a species of epicacuanha, was frequently used for a vomit, and sometimes the pocoon or blood root. **1937** Eaton *Handicrafts* 153 [One chairmaker's] favorite color is orange made from "coon root," an abbreviation of puccoon, the Indian name for bloodroot. **1937** Hyatt *Kiverlid* 99 In them days most persons got poke berry juice fer writin' with, or sometimes they'd use puccoon root—blood root they called hit—but hit would soon fade down. **1960** Price *Root Digging in Appal* 9 Indian names are surprisingly few considering the Indians' use of plants; they include wahoo, from the Dakota for "arrowwood"; pipsissewa, Algonquian for "it breaks it into small pieces"; puccoon, a term for dye-yielding plants in Virginia; cohosh, Algonquian for "it is rough." **1982** Stupka *Wildflowers* 39 Among its other names are "puccoon-root" and "red Indian paint." **1991** Thomas *Sthn Appal* 116 Back then, he bought a few herbs, such as what we ewst to call puck-coon, or 'coon-root, an' mayapple, and ginseng, stuff like that.

puke *verb* Of a **still**: to boil over and mix ingredients, ruining the whiskey; to cause or allow this to happen. See also **puker**.

1949 Maurer *Argot of Moonshiner* 11 = to allow the still to boil over into the connections. It often necessitates dismantling the still and cleaning out the connections, the thumper, and the condenser: "Don't throw no more wood on that fire, you'll puke the still." **1974** Dabney *Mt Spirits* 126 Did you ever strain your whiskey? "No, because it bein' made with steam thataway, it never did puke. That's what you called it when it got that white [solid matter, meal, etc.] in it. That way you had to strain it." **1982** Slone *How We Talked* 70 Sometimes, if the fire got too hot under the still, it caused the mash to get mixed with the whiskey, ruining it. Then it was said that the still had "puked."

puker *noun* See citation. See also **puke**.

1974 Maurer and Pearl *KY Moonshine* 122 = a primitive dephlegmator between the still and the thump-keg that returns any boiled-over mash to the still, thereby preventing it from contaminating the distillate.

pull *verb*

A Variant past-tense form pult.

1923 Furman *Mothering* 198 He pult his Christmas knife out of his pocket and jobbed it in Hiram's wrist.

B To pick, gather, harvest (e.g. **galax** leaves and branches for sale). See also **pull fodder**.

1982 Ginns *Snowbird Gravy* 203 Mother said, "The last bread flour is gone. You better take Ray and go to Stone Mountain and pull some evergreen galax." **2008** *Rosie Hicks* 1 She didn't like to go into the woods, pull galax or get anything like that.

[DARE *pull* v 1a chiefly South, South Midland]

pull a joner See **jonah B2**.

pull bone See **pully bone**.

pull candy *noun phrase* Hard molasses candy, made by stretching warm molasses that hardened as it cooled. See also **candy breaking**.

1941 Still *Stir-Off* 3 I choose pull-candy to sirup. **1976** Still *Pattern of Man* 19 Apples were roasted on the hearth, potatoes baked in ashes, popcorn capped, and pull-candy made.

pulley bone See **pully bone**.

pull fodder *verb phrase* To strip the mature leaves from cornstalks for use as animal feed, usually done toward the end of summer.

1861 *Neves CW Letters* (Sept 27) I hav nothing new to write we are almost done puling foder wee hav about 1500 bundles tuck up. **1939** Hall *Coll* Saunook NC = one man goes between two rows, takin' two rows at a time. Get the fodder or blades in a small bundle and hang it on the stalk after the tops have been cut. Hang one bundle of fodder on stalks about fifteen feet apart. [After hauling the fodder from the field], put the roughness in one stack and the fodder in another, each around a pole in stacks about eighteen or twenty feet apart. **1948** Dick *Dixie Frontier* 100 Just before the blades began to turn yellow, the hands went down the rows stripping off the green leaves from the ears down. These were gathered in bunches and placed in a crotch between two stalks to dry. This was known as pulling fodder. **1956** Hall *Coll* (Gatlinburg TN) They stopped [the school] two or three weeks to pull fodder in the fall.... They reach to the top blade of the fodder and run one hand on each side of the stalk, pull the fodder off, then they'd tie it in bunches of the night when it was moist. They couldn't do the work in the hot time of day. **1966** Guthrie *Corn* 90 Others pulled fodder. They pulled the leaves (blades) from the plants and left them between the rows to be tied up when dampness made them pliable.... It was usually considered a sign of poor farming to have to cut tops or pull fodder for feed. **1988** Brown *Beech Creek* 41 Most Beech Creek families "pulled fodder." That is, they pulled the blades off, leaving the stalk with ears of corn still standing. **1996** Houk *Foods & Recipes* 46 After the tops dried, they were fed to the milk cows during the winter. Farmers also "pulled fodder," that is, removed the leaves from the stalks and fed them to the cows, horses, and sheep.

pullikins *noun* See citation.

1967 Wilson *Folkways Mammoth Cave* 23 = a dentist's forceps.

[DARE *pullikins* n chiefly South, South Midland]

pullingest *adjective* Most capable at pulling a heavy weight. See also **-est 1** and Grammar and Syntax §3.4.1.

1924 (in **1952** Mathes *Tall Tales* 23) And Dave would have the floor, with one of his homely romances, whether of the tallest hemlock, the biggest band-mill, the pullin'est team of hosses, the cussin'est boss, or the luckiest hand of cards that ever was on land or sea.

pull on out See **pull out**.

pull out (also *pull on out*) *verb phrase* To get up and leave, move out.

1943 Chase *Jack Tales* 3 Jack decided one time he'd pull out from there and try his luck in some other section of the country. **1970** *Hunting Stories* 30 They come before dark, an' we pulled out an' went over th'head'a that creek where Billy Long lives. **1984** GSMNP-153 On Monday morning he'd pull out across the mountain into Hartford, Tennessee. **1985** Irwin *Alex Stewart* 244 He was a worker and he just kept working at it till he saved up a little money, and he pulled out and went to Oklahoma. **2003** Carter *Mt Home* 81 We got Mama's list filled and pulled on out for home.

pull the copper *verb phrase* To remove or hide all or part of an illegal **still** in order to prevent its discovery by law enforcement officers.

1974 Dabney *Mt Spirits* 134 Cosby moonshiners had a unique way of signalling the arrival of revenuers—dynamite blasts. The first blast, set off by a "lookout" on a road leading through Cosby into the hills, would be repeated by subsequent blasts further into the hills, giving the moonshiner plenty of time to "pull the copper."

pull through *verb phrase* To experience religious conversion. See also **break through**, **come through**, **pray through**, **through C1**.

1968 Clarke *Stuart's Kentucky* 74 Sometimes the church bell rang out across the fields and hills in the early-morning hours to let the people know that the sinners had all pulled through.

pully bone (also *pull bone*, *pulley bone*) *noun* The wishbone of a chicken when cooked, the ends of which are pulled apart by two people seeking to divine the future.

1934–47 LAMSAS *Appal* (Madison Co NC, Swain Co NC). **c1950** (in **2000** Oakley *Roamin' Man* 38) I noticed when I eat all the meat off it wus the pulley bone so I no it was the chicken brest. **1958** Newton *Dialect Vocab* = attested by 21 of 36 speakers from E TN mountains. **1966** Dakin *Vocab Ohio River Valley* 260 In Kentucky *wishbone* is well established in the Bluegrass—especially around Lexington, Maysville, and in Louisville—and is spreading to the northern Pennyroyal and the Knobs. Older speakers still say *pully-bone*, however, and elsewhere in Kentucky *wishbone* is unused. **1966–68** DARE *Survey* (Brasstown NC, Spruce Pine NC, Gatlinburg TN, Maryville TN). **1968** Wilson *Folklore Mammoth Cave* 23 = the wish-bone, or furcula, of a chicken, often pulled after a meal, to determine who is to get married first. The holder of the shorter piece of bone sometimes places it over the door; the first person of the opposite sex to enter that door is the destined mate. **1976** Garber *Mountain-ese* 71 The kids pull the pully-bone to see who gets the short side for luck. **1986** Pederson et al. *LAGS*: *pull bone* = attested by 3/35 interviewees (8.6%) from N GA; 3/3 of all LAGS interviewees (100%) attesting term were from Appalachia; *pully bone* = attested by 43/60 interviewees (71.7%) from E TN and 21/35 (60%) from N GA; 63/463 of all LAGS interviewees (13.6%) attesting term were from Appalachia. **2000** Miller *Looneyville* 62 = the forked bone in front of the breast bone of a chicken. It came from a custom whereby two persons made a wish and then pulled the bone apart. The one holding the longest piece was holding a token of fulfillment of the holder's wish. The word wishbone never seemed to enter Looneyville people's conversation: "Grandma, whose turn is it to get the pullbone this Sunday?" **2005** Williams *Gratitude* 515 = the wishbone from the breast of a fowl. The *pulley bone* is prized for foretelling luck. A person catches hold of a prong on one side of the pulley bone, and another person holds onto the other prong, and they pull until one prong breaks off (probably where it got its name). The person who gets the short piece will have bad luck, the other, good luck. The whole bone is carried for good luck.

[cf EDD *pulling-bone* sb 1 "the merrythought of a fowl" and SED *pulling bone* Shropshire; DARE *pully bone* n chiefly South, South Midland, TX, OK, IL, IN]

pulpit *noun* Variant form with stress on both syllables: PUL-PIT.

1942 Hall *Phonetics Smoky Mts* 75. **1997** Montgomery *Coll* Thank you for opening the pulpit today (Cardwell).

[DARE *pulpit* n especially South, South Midland]

pulpit-stand *noun* See citation. Same as **stand B4**. See also **camp meeting.**

1948 Dick *Dixie Frontier* 199–200 As a frontier institution the camp-meeting developed a standard pattern during the first few years of the nineteenth century. A forest area was selected near a sparkling stream with plenty of shade and grass for hundreds of horses. A large square clearing was made and over this was constructed an immense brush arbor or, as a camp-ground became permanent, a long shed covered with clapboards. The logs were laid end to end in rows lengthwise, and rough slabs, split from other logs with wedges, were laid across these in tiers the full length of the arbor. At one end was a high platform, known as "the pulpit-stand," made of poles or poles and slabs.

pulse *noun* See citation.

1985 Sienkneckt *Rheumatic Diseases* 183 = purulent material.

[variant of *pus*]

pummies See **pomace**.

pumpkin *noun* Variant forms *puncan*, *punkin*.

1845 (in **1974** Harris *High Times* 46) The supper is made up by the fellers; every one fetches sumthin; sum a lick of meal, sum a middlin of bacon, sum a hen, sum a possum, sum a punkin, sum a grab of taters, or a pocket full of peas. **1862** *Warrick CW Letters* (June 13) they are sunburnt as yellow as a punkin and you may know they look Some bad. **1863** *Jones CW Letters* (Feb 18) tell him to rase mee a puncan too out of these seed. **1937** Hall *Coll* (Big Creek NC) [My pig] could eat the guts out of a punkin through a hole in the fence, its nose is so long. **1960** Hall *Smoky Mt Folks* 46 Punkin butter was made by cooking the pumpkin, adding cane syrup, and then boiling it down. **1982** Powers and Hannah *Cataloochee* 381 [The gun's] all shackley, must be a punkin' ball loose in your gun or your gun part's loose. **2008** Salsi *Ray Hicks* 113 We was a workin' our fingers to the bone tryin' to stay alive on what we growed. It was mostly 'taters, cabbage, squash, punkin, corn, apples, and thrash beans we dried for leather britches.

pumpkin bread *noun* See 1957 citation.

1907 Dugger *Balsam Groves* 207 This punkin bread's good enough fur me. **1957** Combs *Lg Sthn High: Word List* 77 = bread made of corn meal, mixed with small bits of dried pumpkin.

pumpkin bush *noun* Same as **catawba rhododendron**.

1960 Stubbs *Mountain-Wise* (April–May) 6 They do use the term rhododendron, but only in reference to that showy and astoundingly beautiful variety, the purple rhododendron. It is the earliest of the native rhododendrons to bloom and can be found only on high mountain-tops in the most inaccessible places. The books describe it as magenta-pink in color and label it rhododendron catawbiense. This, then, is what the natives mean when they say "rhododendron," unless, as many do, they call it "punkin-bush," a name so at variance with its beauty that it defies explanation.

pumpkin butter *noun* A thick, spicy spread for bread made by adding cane syrup to a baking pumpkin and then boiling this mixture down while stirring it. See also **peach butter**, **persimmon butter**, **sweet potato butter**.

1960 Hall *Smoky Mt Folks* 46 Fruit and beans were dried for use during the winter. Apple butter, "punkin" butter, and sweet "tater" butter were favorites. Punkin butter was made by cooking the pumpkin, adding cane syrup, and then boiling it down. **1960** Mason *Memoir* 15 The barrels were utilized as containers for the storage of such mountain commodities as saur kraut, pickled beans, bleached apples, and pumpkin butter. [**1980** *Smokies Heritage* 101 *butters* = not simply butter churned from milk, but the spiced, sweet fruit spread made from apples, peaches, pumpkin, and persimmons during jelly-making season and autumn (for the last two).] **1986** Tyson *Reflections* 23 Mam would make apple butter and pumpkin butter in a big brass kettle. It took a lot of stirring, but was good when we got it cooked. **1999** Spencer *Memory Lane* II:4 Hogs were on the hillsides, and would come in for corn; kegs of molasses were made, and lots of pumpkins were grown. Pumpkin butter was made, using the molasses for sweetening it.

pumpkin mush *noun* A heavy porridge made from pumpkins. See also **mush**.

2008 Salsi *Ray Hicks* 116 Havin' punkin mush and milk was a good treat.

pumpkin roller *noun* Used as a derogatory term for a country person.

1936 Farr *Folk Speech Mid TN* 276 = a farmer: "He is a poor pumpkin roller." **1943** Korson *Coal Dust* 5 Full-time miners naturally resented them [= farmer-miners] and expressed their distrust by calling them "winter diggers," "wheats," "corncrackers," "hay johns," "pumpkin rollers." **1990** Clouse *Wilder* 141 She had busted a woman square in the face for calling her a "punkin roller."

pumpknot (also *pump knock*, *punkknot*) *noun* A swelling usually on the head, as from a blow.

1944 Dennis *Word-List* 11 *pump-knot* = a swelling, such as that produced—"pumped up"—by a bump or blow, or the sting of a bee or wasp. **1952** Wilson *Folk Speech NC* 580 *pump knot* = a knot on the head produced by a blow. **1955** Ritchie *Singing Family* 189 Look out, biggety-britches, you going to fall and make a pump-knot on your noggin. **1967–68** *DARE Survey* (Big Stone Gap VA) *pump-knock*; (Brasstown NC, Gatlinburg TN, Maryville TN) *pump knot*; (Rogersville TN, Marlinton WV, Spencer WV) *punkknot*. **1978** Ball *Speech Knox Co* 140 *punk knots* = lumps on the head: "Ever since he was a kid he's always had punk-knots on the head." **1981** *GSMNP-117:7* In a little bit they's a big pump knot, I mean a big ridge swelled up across her forehead there big as your, nearly big as a pencil. **1990** Cavender *Folk Medical Lex* 29 *pump knot* = a swelling produced by a blow to the body or a sting from an insect. **1994** Montgomery *Coll* I'll put a pump knot on your head (Shields).

[Web3 *pumpknot* n Midland; DARE *pumpknot* n South Midland]

puncan See **pumpkin**.

punch See **paunch**.

puncheon *noun*

A Variant forms *pencheon* [see **1826** in **B**], *punchin* [see **1915** in **B**].

B A split log or rough timber with one face dressed by an adze, used for flooring, benching, siding of log buildings, etc. See 1995 citation.

1824 (in **1912** Doddridge *Notes on Settlement* 107) Another division [of men] was employed in getting puncheons for the floor of the cabin; this was done by splitting trees about eighteen inches in diameter, and hewing the faces of them with a broad axe. **1826** *Whitten Letter* [We cook] out of doors no time to get pencheons to lay the floor. **1863** *Gilliland CW Letters* (May 17) i want you to git Some of the boys [to] put them big puncheons over the well in the place of that oald plank for fear it brakes & lets some of you fall in. **1915** Pollard *TN Mts* 243 They keep the potatoes in the punchins [i.e. beneath the floorboards]. **1931** Greve *Tradition Gatlinburg* 69 Their floors were made of puncheons, huge poplar logs, two feet or more in width, hewn smooth on the upper side, but left rounded and with bark on beneath. **1956** Hall *Coll* (Hartford TN) I was raised on a puncheon floor split out and hewed with a broad axe or a fallin' axe. **1960** Arnow *Seedtime* 267 The cabin floor was usually made of puncheons; for these a ten-foot length of log was split, then each side hewed down to some manageable thickness, commonly about two inches; the great plank thus formed not only required a deal of work, but it was much as a man could do to lift one. **1974** Foster *Walker Valley* 8:4 Now the puncheon benches were hand hewn from our tulip tree just as our logs for our schoolhouse were hewn, with the broadax. **1995** Trout *Historic Buildings* 26 Puncheons were used where sawn lumber or nails were not yet available. The workman would split a short log, in the manner of a hot dog roll, and lay the halves from joist to joist, round side down. The roughly flat upper surfaces would then be dressed with a foot adze or ax until smooth enough to eliminate toe-catching edges and large splinters. **1999** Bishir et al. *Archit W NC* 430 = a slab of wood used for flooring; often, half of a split log, with the upper side smoothed flat and the lower side left round. Puncheon floors were used frequently in log houses, but relatively few examples are known to survive. They were often replaced when sawmills became numerous and convenient.

[OED3 *puncheon* n[1] 5 North America]

puncheon camp *noun* A lean-to shelter made from small hewn logs.

1960 Burnett *My Valley* 26 The lean-to or puncheon camp was his only shelter. **1997** Davis *Cataloochee Valley* 17 In the "Land Entry Book 1809–1842" for Haywood County (p. 63) No. 131, Henry Colwell enters 100 acres of land in Haywood County on Cataloochee Creek beginning on a large maple tree on the north side of said creek running down the creek including a "punchin" camp of Thomas Coldwell for complement entered January 20, 1814. **1997** Montgomery *Coll* (known to Brewer, Bush, Oliver).

punching stick *noun* An implement used to stir clothes in boiling water to wash them.

1997 Johnson *Melungeon Heritage* 22 We had a big black kettle, as big as a tub, which was fixed upon some rocks. We always started a fire under it to heat the water, and boiled the clothes first. A "punching stick" was used to move the clothes about in the hot water, and the soap we used was either lye soap or store-bought washing powder.

punch mine *noun* Same as **doghole**.

1973 Preston *Bituminous Term* 34 = a very small mine operated by a few men, usually taking coal which lies very near the surface. Also known as a *house coal mine* or a *punch mine*.

pune around (also *puny around*) *verb phrase* To ail, languish. See also **puny B**.

c1960 Wilson *Coll*: *puny around* = to act puny or ailing, esp. when the sufferer seemed to enjoy being puny. **1974** Fink *Bits Mt Speech* 20 I've been *punying* around quite a spell. **1976** Dwyer *Southern Sayin's* 10 *pune around* = to act sick, dull. "Pa's takin' to punin' around." **1982** Slone *How We Talked* 103 *puning around* = not real sick, yet not quite well. **2001** Lowry *Expressions* 6 I was punyin' around for two weeks.

[DARE *puny* v 1 chiefly South Midland]

punies See **get the punies**.

punish (also *punish out*) *verb, verb phrase* To suffer, endure punishment, fall on hard times.

1892 Fruit *KY Words* 231 = to suffer: "I punished so in my new shoes." **1931** Goodrich *Mt Homespun* 42 I'm right sharply decayed since you saw me. . . . I can't do much work and that frets me, but I ain't a punishing any; a body ought to be thankful for that. **1960** Westover *Highland Lg* 20 *punishing* = feeling sick. **1971** *AOHP/ALC*-193 They wouldn't give you a dose of medicine for nothing like that at all, so I had to punish that out. **1972** *AOHP/ALC*-342 Now people that didn't have stuff like that, they really punished. **1982** Ginns *Snowbird Gravy* 102 Just go on and give it to somebody that's a-punishin'. **1985** Irwin *Alex Stewart* 237 The reason I'm a setting here suffering today and a punishing is because I haven't done what the Lord wanted me to do. **1993** Ison and Ison *Whole Nother Lg* 52 *punishin* = sick or hurting in some way. "His wife left him and he's punishin something awful." **1997** Montgomery *Coll* (known to Adams, Cardwell, Jones, Oliver).

[cf HT *punish through* (at *punish*) "endure painfully, suffer through"; DARE *punish* v chiefly South Midland]

punk *noun*

1 Rotten or decaying wood, especially as used for tinder. Also called **spunk**.

1952 Huffman *Mt Memories* 36 Matches were scarce and hard to obtain, so we kept some punk, which really was decayed dry wood, in the wood box. We would start a fire by rubbing Indian darts together over the punk until a fire started. **1964** Clarkson *Lumbering in WV* 369 = rotten wood. **1977** *Foxfire IV* 128 Had to kindle a fire with a flint. Take one of these flints, and they was a maple that has what you call the "punk" in it. You take that flint and your knife and lay this punk down and you [strike the back of the closed knife blade against the flint] till it'll spark, you know. And that punk'll catch the spark and then you blow it and keep ablowin' it till it flames, and then you add shavings and build you a fire. **1981** GSMNP-121:36 We had a dry piece of wood that we called punk, come out of locust, usually dry locust. It looked like a piece of sponge, and if you keep that good and dry and take a flint rock, then take a knife and strike it thataway, a spark would fall out, then you set that under there and you would catch that punk.

[Web3 *punk* n[2] perhaps alteration of *spunk*, influenced by Delaware *punk* "fine ashes, powder"]

2 See citation.

1980 Riggleman *WV Mtneer* 126–27 [Loggers] usually had nicknames for everybody and everything around the camp. . . . Lightbread was "punk."

punkie *noun* A small, black, biting gnat.

1964 Clarkson *Lumbering in WV* 369 *punkies* = gnats. **1975** Fink *Backpacking* 99 One great pest of the mountains is the tiny black gnats, the "punkies" or "no-see-ums" that breed in countless legions by the margins of the streams and in marshy places. **c1980** Campbell *Memories of Smoky* 27–28 It was our worst encounter of the trip with "punkies" or "no-see-ums" or tiny black gnats. By whatever name you call them, their bite is just as irritating.

punkin See **pumpkin**.

punk knot See **pumpknot**.

puny

A *adjective* Lacking size, weight, or strength; in poor health, having a sickly appearance, ailing. See also **puny-turned**.

1864 *Chapman CW Letters* (May 3) wee are all well and Enjoying common health with the exception of myself I am Som what puny & has bin for several days. **1864** *Warrick CW Letters* (Aug 16) the boys all seem to be puny from lying in the ditches so much. **1915** Dingus *Word-List VA* 188 = not in good health, —antonym of peart.

1934–47 LAMSAS *Appal* (Madison Co NC, Swain Co NC). **1937** Hall *Coll* (Big Creek NC) Whenever we'd get puny, Mother would go to the woods, gather bark and yerbs, and make us some tea. **c1959** Weals *Hillbilly Dict* 10 = thin, poor. "She's so puny she had to stand in the same place twice't t'throw a shadder." **1966** *DARE Survey* (Cherokee NC) = doesn't look well/hasn't been well for some time. **1976** Thompson *Touching Home* 15 = small or sickly. **1986** Pederson et al. *LAGS* = attested by 18/60 interviewees (30%) from E TN and 7/35 (20%) from N GA; 25/95 of all LAGS interviewees (27.4%) attesting term were from Appalachia. **1996** Montgomery *Coll* (known to Cardwell). **2009** Benfield *Mt Born* 183 = pale, sickly looking, and maybe in need of a doctor.

[OED3 *puny* adj 2c "in poor health, ailing, sickly" < Middle French *puisné*; DARE *puny* adj 1 widespread, but especially South, South Midland]

B *verb* To ail, be sickly. See also **pune around, puny away**.

1933 Thomas *Traipsin' Woman* 146 If one were puneyin', the other blood-kin helped out.

puny around See **pune around**.

puny away *verb phrase* To grow thin and weak, waste away. See also **puny B**.

1966 Medford *Ol' Starlin* 99 Silas, her husband, would tell folks "She's bed fast jist about all the time—keeps punyin' away; an' thars nothin' much we can do for her, me an' Nancy."

puny-turned *adjective* See 1952 citation. See also **puny, turn A**.

1952 Wilson *Folk Speech NC* 580 = delicate, sickly. "All of his wives have been *puny-turned*." **1979** Carpenter *Walton War* 150 That girl is allright, but she allus was puny turned.

puore See **pure**.

pure

A Variant forms *puore, pyore*.

1924 Raine *Saddlebags* 211 Hit bubbles right out'n the ground, hit's bound to be puore. **1927** Dingus *Appal Mt Words* 470 *pyore*. **1941** Still *Troublesome Creek* 46 I can't dig a cellar through puore rock. **1942** Hall *Phonetics Smoky Mts* 37 [pjoɚ]. **1955** Ritchie *Singing Family* 81 That man's a pyore fool.

B *adjective* Real, genuine, simple, absolute. See also **pure out**.

c1940 Padelford *Notes* Hit's a pure sight. I'm speakin' the pure truth. **c1960** Wilson *Coll* = veritable, real: "It's a pure sin to do that." **1999** Morgan *Gap Creek* 134 You are a pure fool, I said to myself.

[DARE *pure* adj B South, South Midland]

C (also *purely*) *adverb* Really, absolutely, simply.

1923 Furman *Mothering* 238 It was allus purely silly about Blant, allowing he's its maw. **1939** Hall *Coll* (Oconaluftee NC) I thought I'd pure die [of fright]. **1956** McAtee *Some Dial NC* 35 = very: "It is purely warm today." **1958** Combs *Archaic English in KY* 42 = very: "She is pure lucky." **1972** Cooper *NC Mt Folklore* 95 *purely likes to eat* = really likes to eat. **1984** Burns *Cold Sassy* 151 Old Jack'd pure die from embarrassment. **1992** Davis *Jack Tales* 33 I left home to seek my fortune, and this job is purely holding me up. *Ibid.* 115 He was so pure tired after this day that all he could do was take a bath and eat supper before he was just falling off to sleep. **1999** Offut *Out of Woods* 126 It's pure built to hunt.

[DARE *pure* adv C South, South Midland]

pure-D, pure-god See **pure-T**.

purely See **pure C**.

pure of *adjective phrase* Uncontaminated by.

1944 Wilson *Word-List* 49 I was as pure of that blockading as the jest of God.

pure out *adjective phrase* Absolute. See also **pure C**.

1993 Sobol *Growing Up with Jack* 90 They were hunting stories, and pure out fool stories and that—the kind of stories that a kid in high school would be more interested in. **1998** Montgomery *Coll* (known to Brown, Bush, Norris, Oliver).

pure-T (also *pure-D, pure-god*) *adjective, adverb* Real(ly), genuine(ly), absolute(ly).

1972 *AOHP/ALC-388* All the neighbors [had] time to get the whiskey in the clear before the revenuers got to their house, and I remember this one particular time when we got the ring pure-T, I had whiskey in the kitchen a-tempering then. **1977** Norman *Kinfolks* 8 "He's a pure-god wildcat, this'un is," the fat man said as he clambered out of the truck to shake Glen's hand. **1996** Harrell *Fetch It* 4 I've seen bootleggers, I've seen Canadian wolves, I've seen revenue offices, I've seen pure-T outlaws. **2000** Norman *Consciousness* 9 As far as I was concerned, I and the people around me were pure-D Americans and damned patriotic, too, especially during the war years, with my father in the Army Air Corps in Texas and all four of my mother's brothers in danger in the combat zones of Europe and the Pacific.

[DARE *pure-T* (at *puredee* adj, adv) South, South Midland]

purple gill *noun* See citation.

1968 *DARE Survey* (Brasstown NC) = mushroom that grows the size of a globe.

purtenie See **pretty nigh**.

purt' near't See **pretty near(ly)**.

purtnie, purt nigh See **pretty nigh**.

purty See **pretty**.

puscle See **pussle**.

push *noun*

1 (often in phrase *whole push*) A crowd or gang of people, especially an extended family. See also **generation B, set C1**.

1921 Combs *Slang Survivals* 117 = a crowd, the "whole lay-out."

1976 Still *Pattern of Man* 5 "Hurry and get ready," he ordered, "the whole push of you." **1984** Wilder *You All Spoken* 189 *whole push* = all in a group, crowd, as in "the whole push got after him to join the church." **1992** Jones and Miller *Sthn Mt Speech* 101 = group, tribe. "I'm just sick of the whole push of them." **1996–97** Montgomery *Coll* (known to Brewer, Bush, Cardwell), = a ne'er do well family, a *set* (Jones).

2 In logging, a camp foreman or **woods boss**.

1994 Farwell and Buchanan *Logging Terms* = a member of a logging crew supervising a given part of the logging operation, such as measuring timber; he might serve as the lead cutter.

push boat *noun* See citation.

2006 *WV Encycl* 58 When the water was too low, poled wooden flats called "pushboats" took over and went as far upstream as Williamson, on the Tug Fork.

pushed *adjective* Under pressure, in difficult straits with money, health, the law, etc.

1913 Kephart *Our Sthn High* 253 I ain't that hard pushed yet. **1952** Wilson *Folk Speech NC* 578 *pushed for* = in need of. "He's powerfully *pushed for* something to eat." **c1960** Wilson *Coll* = in need of, often dire need: "I'm pushed for grub." **1994–97** Montgomery *Coll* (known to Adams, Brown, Cardwell, Jones, Norris, Oliver, Weaver).

[cf EDD *hard pushed* (at *hard* adj 1 45)]

pushency *noun* An emergency, urgent necessity.

1912 Perrow *Songs and Rhymes* 139 Suffixes are still alive: we hear such formations as pushency, botherment, and even footback.

[DARE *pushency* n chiefly South, South Midland]

push water *noun* Gasoline.

1940 Farr *More TN Expressions* 447 = gasoline. "I want five gallons of push water." **1969** *DARE Survey* (Dillard GA) = cheap gasoline.

pussle (also *puscle*) *verb* To bulge; hence noun *puscle-gut*, adjective *pussle-gutted*. See citations. See also **pooch out**.

1974 Dabney *Mt Spirits* 129 You know they always send up the holler two revenue men . . . great big fat, pussle-gutted. **1984** Woods *WV Was Good* 222 *puscle* = to bulge out or extend, as applied to the waistline from extended with fat. Hence, the term *puscle gut*, meaning an overly fat person.

pussle-gutted See **pussle**.

pussy toes *noun* Same as **pearly everlasting**.

1996 Montgomery *Coll* (known to Cardwell).

put *verb* Variant form putt.

1924 Buffum *Shakespearean Survivals* 17 Just as Ben Johnson [sic] pronounced "put" to rhyme with "cut," so do the mountain people. **1991** Thomas *Sthn Appal* 17 He said they putt log chains in them old cannons. **2007** McMillon *Notes*.

put a pack off on See **put off on**.

put a quietus on See **quietus**.

put at *verb phrase*

1 To badger, press (someone).

1940 Vincent *Us Mt Folks* 59 One time when Nancy's mother had the rheumatism, Nancy put at Bill to kill some crows so's she could render the lard, and rub it on her mother's joints. **c1960** Wilson *Coll* = to beg, importune: "They put at me to visit her next summer." **1984** Woods *WV Was Good* 226 Bill put at me to go berryin' with him that morning.

[SND (at *pit* v B2(8)); DARE *put at* v phr especially South Midland]

2 To charge (something) against (someone).

1984 Woods *WV Was Good* 227 Right there before everybody John put it at him (John charged him with something or accused him).

put away *verb phrase* To bury (a person). Same as **lay away**.

1863 *Proffit CW Letters* (March 11) we went and Saw him deseantly put a way we had him washed and dressed in white . . . his officers has a good coffin made for him and put him a way with thare own hands. **1864** *Chapman CW Letters* (July 21) he was as deacently put away as the nature of the case would admit of. **1936** Stuart *Head of Hollow* 91 He must be put away nice—not in a home-made coffin, but in one bought with a pretty linin'. **1956** Hall *Coll* (Big Bend NC) Back years ago when they died they made their own caskets and put 'em away, take their lumber and make their own caskets and dig their graves and put 'em away. **1959** Hall *Coll* (Newport TN) So they let him have the suit and everything to put [his father] away nice. **1972** *AOHP/ALC-298* My woman was put away the way she was [i.e. without being embalmed]. **1975** Gainer *Witches Ghosts Signs* 15 = to bury the dead. "They tuk Pa through that door when they put him away." **1985** Irwin *Alex Stewart* 177 They died, sometimes, might near faster than they could put them away. I've seed people put away without any coffins.

[EDD (at *put* II.2.7(b)); DARE *put away* v phr especially South, South Midland]

put back *verb phrase* To save (money) for later use.

1976 *Hartley III* 6 They were so hard up for a little money that they would even save the pennies. Put them back in a certain place to pay taxes with.

put down *verb phrase* To rain hard.

1946 Woodard *Word-List VA/NC* 25 = rain hard. **1958** Wood *Words from TN* 15 *puttng down* = raining: "It's just a-puttin' down out there."

[DARE *put down* v phr 3 especially South Midland]

put for *verb phrase* To head rapidly toward.

1864 Gilmore *Down in TN* 87 When I shouts "Glory, glory," twice, as ef the raal camp-meetin' power war on me, ye put fur the bushes on yer han's an' feet. **1924** Vollmer *Sun-Up* 45 I reckon he wuz a puttin' fer the woods back yonder. **c1960** Wilson *Coll* = to hurry away or go toward.

put in

A *verb phrase*

1 To propose, seek, request.

1925 Dargan *Highland Annals* 59 She'd put in to go to her pap's, an' I thought I'd git up a nice lot o' wood, make me a big fire, an' have my Christmas at home. **1985** Irwin *Alex Stewart* 131 Well, I'd been trimming the edges of his hair once in a while, and he put in for me to cut it the new way, and finally I did. **1997** Montgomery *Coll* (known to ten consultants from the Smoky Mountains).

2 To embark, start, go.

1834 Crockett *Narrative* 156 I put in, and waded on till I come to the channel, where I crossed that on a high log. **1926** Hunnicutt *Twenty Years* 35 About that time Old Boney put in with her on the same track. **1935** Stuart *KY Mt People* 258 They vote what is called the "straight ticket." Some say, "We'll put in under the Rooster and let him do the scratching." **1939** Hall *Coll* (Nine Mile TN) The dogs put in after him [= a bear] again, bayed him around there. **1941** Still *Troublesome Creek* 44 I put in to dig. Got three foot down and struck bottom. **1985** Irwin *Alex Stewart* 98 I put in and made me another one, and that's how I got started in the cooper trade. *Ibid.* 168 I told him what kind of timber to cut, and how big to get it, and he put right in and cut it and snaked it down close to the house seat.

[DARE *put in* v phr 2 chiefly South, South Midland]

3 To plant (a crop).

1949 Arnow *Hunter's Horn* 125 In good weather he would clear the brush from the sandfield and put it in corn next year—it ought to make good corn. **1988** Smith *Fair and Tender* 51 He has got our garden put in now, and they think so highly of him over ther.

B *noun* Intervention, intrusion.

1937 Hyatt *Kiverlid* 15 They ain't no body axin' fer your put in.

put near See **pretty near(ly)**.

put no store by *verb phrase* To place no stock in.

1957 Parris *My Mts* 64 I don't put no store by them newfangled percolators and things run by electricity. **1995–97** Montgomery *Coll* (known to Adams, Brown, Ellis, Ledford).

put off *verb phrase* To depart, set out.

1927 Mason *Lure of Smokies* 218 All three o' them b'ar put off together. *Ibid.* 224 I cocked my gun, but [the bar] heerd it an' put off toward the roughs.

put off on (also *put a pack off on, put pack on*) *verb phrase* To shift the blame to, speak disparagingly of (another). See also **pack off on**.

1911 Shearin *E KY Word-List* 539 *put pack on* = to blame; e.g., "He packed it off on me." = He held me to account for it. **1952** Wilson *Folk Speech NC* 580 *put off on* = to speak disparagingly of one. **1954** GSMNP-19:7 I'm like the movie star. I like to have two names. If something happens, why I put it off on the other fellow. **1989** Smith *Flyin' Bullets* 33 "A bunch of them made it up with that woman to put a pack off on him," she went on seriously, "because they had it in fer him and was a'tryin' to frame him!"

[cf EDD *put off* (at *put* 16c) "to ill-treat, impose upon"]

put on *verb phrase*

1 To assign (a task) to someone. See also **put to 2**.

1939 Hall *Coll* (Deep Creek NC) They put it on me to place the standers, so our drivers driv the Easy Ridge and pole road. *Ibid.* (Tuckaleechee Cove TN) They put it on me to serve up the beef. **1946** Matthias *Speech Pine Mt* 192 "Edna's been puny, so I don't put nothin' on her" (i.e., I don't make her work). **1959** Roberts *Up Cutshin* 33 Maybe the [choice in the group guessing game Pleased or Displeased] would be for one to go bark up the chimbly, or kneel down and pray, or whatever you put on him to do he had to do it. **1972** *AOHP/ALC-276* They put it on him to climb [the tree] to get the chicken. **1977** Shackelford et al. *Our Appalachia* 262 Whatever the boss puts on them they take it and they won't open their mouth.

2 To blame.

1903 Fox *Little Shepherd* 165 If the Dillons' dawg killed that sheep and they could put it on Jack—they'd do it.

put one in (the) mind of *verb phrase* To remind one of.

1862 *Shifflet CW Letters* (March 11) it puts me in mind of home. **1864** *Brown CW Letters* (July 26) it put me in mind of the time i had to leave home or be Conscript. **1940** Haun *Hawk's Done* 5 Puts me in mind of Letitia Edes Mountain, this page of names in the Family Bible does. **1957** Combs *Lg Sthn High: Idioms* 14 He puts me in the mind of his pappy (Reminds me of him). **1976** Weals *Mountaineer* And there is an expression, "puts me in the mind of," meaning, reminds me. "When he laughs, he puts me in the mind of his daddy." **1997** Montgomery *Coll* (known to ten consultants from the Smoky Mountains).

put out *verb phrase*

1 Of leaves or flowers: to come out, blossom.

1862 *Epperly CW Letters* (April 27) the timber is begining to put out right smart. **1941** Stuart *Men of Mts* 184 The Doctor said if he could pull him through the spring till the leaves quit putting out, then he would be all right till the leaves started to fall again. **1952** McCall *Cherokees and Pioneers* 100 The pinch comes in late winter when "leather breeches" (green beans strung on thread to dry), dried fruit, and holed-up potatoes begin to give out, and when poke, dandelions, "wooley breeches," and other "greens" have not yet "put out." **1997** Montgomery *Coll* (known to ten consultants from the Smoky Mountains); In the mountains, dogwood doesn't start putting out until late April (Cardwell).

2 To embark, depart.

1834 Crockett *Narrative* 62 I staid with her until Monday morning, and then I put out for home. **1861** (in **1974** Harris *High Times* 262) I put out tu meet him an tell ove the imedjut rath tu cum. **1864** *Cooper CW Letters* (May 21) the down train came on and we got on it and put out for Knoxville. **1920** Ridley *Sthn Mtneer* 104 I got skeered, so I put out atter him las' night, an' we got back 'bout breakfast time this mornin'. **1948** Chase *Grandfather Tales* 18

She throwed the bonnet on her head and put out. **1969** Roberts *Greasybeard* 159 Soon as Snack went on he turned and put out for the river. **1997** Montgomery *Coll* (known to Cardwell).

3 To claim.

1997 Montgomery *Coll* (known to Cardwell); Rattlesnakes ain't half as bad as they're put out to be (Weaver). **2008** Salsi *Ray Hicks* 151 They'd put it out that they'd do all kinds of things, and they didn't do nothin'.

4 Of a church congregation: to try (a member) for violating a standard of conduct. See also **church 1**.

1939 Hall *Coll* (Proctor NC) Walt Proctor was an old timer, deacon of the church, and superintendent of the Sunday school. One day he got drunk, and he was called before the church. When they put a member out, they called a meeting of the whole church.

put out to See **put to 2**.

put over *verb phrase* To pass (time).

1925 Dargan *Highland Annals* 59 I finds ol' Jim so out o' heart about her, I stays to help him put over a couple o' hours.

put pack on See **put off on**.

putt See **put**.

put the big pot in the little one (and variants) *verb phrase* To make hurried arrangements to feed unexpected or a large number of guests.

1892 Smith *Farm and Fireside* 81 Then the big pot ought to be put in the little pot, and everybody rejoice. **1927** Woofter *Dialect from WV* 362 *Put on the big pot and the little one* = to prepare to cook for a large number of people: "We will have to put on the bit [sic] pot and the little one, for there will be a lot of raftsmen here tonight." **1946** Woodard *Word-List VA/NC* 41 swVA We'll put the little pot in the big pot and stew the dishrag (We'll do our best to provide a meal for unexpected company).

[DARE (at *pot* n 11) chiefly South, South Midland]

put the law on *verb phrase* To have (someone) arrested.

1937 Wilson *Folklore SE KY* 24 I'll put the law on you (I'll have you arrested [Bell Co KY]).

put the quietus on See **quietus**.

put the shuck on *verb phrase* To evade.

1997 Montgomery *Coll* (known to Ellis).

put to *verb phrase*

1 To start, cause (one) to start.

1939 Hall *Coll* (Cades Cove TN) Then you put it to boiling. Boy, she gets to roar when she's boiling. **1960** Mason *Memoir* 98 One of my boys made the remark that Mr. Hoover was the only man that he knew of who could put jack-pine wood to peeling in the middle of the winter. **1985** Irwin *Alex Stewart* 227 He said that put him to thinking.

2 (also *put out to*) (+ *verbal noun*) To assign (one) to. See also **put on 1**.

1861 *Robinson CW Letters* (Dec 8) I exspected to come back when I went off that morning but Fulcher put me to filling and Pinning a Carridge Wheell. **1862** *Parris CW Letters* (Feb 6) you Can put him to Sprouting and Cleaning up grond tel time to plow. **1931** Goodrich *Mt Homespun* 71 Her boys was all gals and the whole passel of 'em was put to making the crop as soon as they was big enough to hannel a hoe. **1940** Still *River of Earth* 66 Mothercoal Mine put fifty men to hauling fallen jackrock and setting new timbers. **c1950** Adams *Grandpap* 81 She put the maid to watchin' the window. **1969** GSMNP-44:16 He said, "The only thing I know to do for him is to put him to using tobacco." **1975** *Used to Farm* 31 He just put me on [the harrow] and put me to draggin' the horse. **1993** *Stories 'neath Roan* 59 I guess I was about five years old when she put me out to pulling peppermint, out of the spring greens. To assign a task and start (one) on it. **2004** Adams *Old True Love* 275 I could hear Roxy out in front singing where we'd put her to silking and washing.

put-togethers, in all my *adverb phrase* In all of my experience.

1955 Wiley *Put-Togethers* 154 WV I never saw anything like that in all my put-togethers.

put up *verb phrase* To put away, store.

1969 *DARE FW Addit* (KY) = to store, put away, or put in storage as in a closet; (cwNC) *put it up* = put it away.

[DARE *put up* v phr 1 chiefly South, South Midland]

put up a poor mouth See **poor-mouth**.

put up the bar *verb phrase* See citation. See also **mind the gap**.

1981 Weals *Rocky Top* Owners of land through which the hikers passed warned them to "put up the bars." "That meant to replace the split chestnut rails which we let down to go through the pasture fences," Herbert says.

pyaner See **piano**.

pyeart See **peart B1**.

pyeerch, pyerch See **perch**.

pyeert, pyert See **peart B1**.

pyore See **poor, pure**.

Q

quail-bird See **-bird**.

quair See **queer**.

Quaker lady (also *Quaker maid, quaking lady*) *noun* A bluet (*Houstonia* spp). See also **babytear, eyebright 1, innocence**.

1901 Lounsberry *Sthn Wild Flowers* 475 Bluets, innocence, Quaker ladies, or bonnets. . . . [The flower] grows erect, often many of the plants producing through moist, grassy places a most enchanting stretch of ethereal blue. **1970** Campbell et al. *Smoky Mt Wildflowers* 74 Other common names [of the prostrate bluet] are innocence and quaker maids. **1994** Montgomery *Coll*: *quaking lady* = bluet (Shields).

quality folk(s) *noun* The social or economic elite of a community.

1845 (in **1870** Drake *Pioneer Life KY* 241) I was a great home-body; had never been out of the family more than a day or a night "at a time"; felt timid about going among strangers in a town, and mingling with "the quality." **1859** Taliaferro *Fisher's River* 105 The best of company, even the "quality," visited his house. **1900** Harben *N GA Sketches* 18 They l'arnt 'im to read an' always let 'im stan' dressed up in his long coat in the big front hall to invite quality folks in the house. **1915** Dingus *Word-List VA* 188 *quality folks* = people of high social status. **1984** Wilder *You All Spoken* 105 *quality folk* = people with class and pedigree. **1989** Giardina *Storming Heaven* 72 "Git him among quality folks," Isom mocked. "Like them coal operators."

[DARE *quality* n chiefly South, South Midland]

Quality Row *noun* See citation. See also **Good Husband Row**.

2006 Lalone *Coal Camps* 140 Each camp had a "Quality Row" or a "Good Husband Row" which contained the houses designated for the superintendent, store and medical personnel, and other company officials. While people acknowledge that the Quality Row families lived in somewhat better conditions, most people felt that among the working miners everyone lived much the same, and that no one family had it much better than any others.

quar, quare See **queer**.

quare-turned See **queer-turned**.

quarrel at *verb phrase* To scold, find fault with (someone).

1922 Cobb *KY Mt Rhymes* 12 I don't quarrel at the sorry contraptions / Maids wear nowadays. **1949** Arnow *Hunter's Horn* 331 Used to be Nunn and Milly never quarreled, but lately, seemed like Nunn was so ill turned he quarreled at them all, even Milly. **c1959** Weals *Hillbilly Dict* 4 = scold. "Mama quarreled at me for not eating my breakfast." **1973** GSMNP-80:5 I remember Etter quarreling at you and Ray, you know, for running through the house and making such a fuss. **1994** Montgomery *Coll* She quarreled at her husband so much that he left her (Cardwell). **2007** Preece *Leavin' Sandlick* 25 Git-up now, Bonnie; don't make me quarrel at ye.

[cf SND *quarrel* v² 2 "to find fault with . . . reprove"]

quarry *noun* Variant forms *querry, qurry*.

1971 *AOHP/ALC*-101 I first started working at a, a marble qurry. **1942** Hall *Phonetics Smoky Mts* 33 *Quarry* is always either ['kwɛrɪ] or ['kwɜrɪ]. **1973** GSMNP-87:2:23 Up here right here where the park headquarters is right across, you notice there's been a querry right over here, rock querry. **2005** Williams *Gratitude* 22 *querry*.

quarter

A *noun* variant plural form without -*s* following a numeral.

1939 Hall *Coll* (Hartford TN) We took that hide offen it [= a bear] and cut it into four quarter, the four of us, and we every one had just about what we could tote of bear meat.

B *verb*

1 To move diagonally; hence verbal noun *quartering* = diagonaling. See also **quartering B**.

1957 Broaddus *Vocab Estill Co KY* 61 *quartering across* = crossing a street at an angle. **1976** Garber *Mountain-ese* 73 = diagonaling: "This hoss ain't so fast but he is shore good at quartering."

[DARE *quarter* v 1 scattered, but especially South, South Midland]

2 Of the moon: to reach the halfway point between dark and full or vice versa.

1961 *Coe Ridge OHP*-341B He just watched things like that, see, and kept up with it, and I mean he couldn't read and write. He didn't know his name up in front of his face, and he could tell you when the moon fulled or when it quartered, the hour and the day.

quartering

A *verbal noun* See **quarter B1**.

B *adverb* Diagonally, obliquely. See also **quarter B1**.

1862 Gatlin *Immortal Hero* 6–7 I did not, however, put [the pistol] against him, but I put it very near him, and I shot him in the right breast, as he was in a position quartering to me. **1974** Fink *Bits Mt Speech* 21 He walked *quartering* across the field. **1997** Montgomery *Coll* (known to Bush, Cardwell, Ellis, Jones, Ledford, Weaver).

quartering time *noun* The midmorning break taken in the workday.

c1975 Lunsford *It Used to Be* 23 There used to be an old fellow working at a sawmill. He'd work on up till dinner time. He wouldn't even have what they call quartering time. Quartering time is the half-way point between the time they start to work, which would be early in the morning, and 12 o'clock noon which would be closing time for dinner. So half-way would be quartering time.

quarterly meeting *noun* A denominational gathering held every three months, most often by Methodists, of pastors and congregational delegates to conduct church business and hear one or more guest preachers.

1973 GSMNP-13:7 The biggest day that we'd have there then was the quarterly meeting. **1982** Powers and Hannah *Cataloochee* 160 Originally begun with another purpose in mind, as a religious event, the Quarterly Meeting seems to live in the minds of its participants as The Big Picnic, enlivened by rousing rhetoric from visiting preachers.

quarter time *noun* Traditionally, the holding of preaching services one weekend a month, often on both Saturday and Sunday, a schedule followed by smaller congregations without their own preacher, whose members often had great distances to travel. The church would often be served by a **circuit rider**. See citation.

1978 *Smoky Vistas* (Winter) 3 [M]any rural churches held services on what was often referred to as "quarter time," that is, only one Sunday a month. Part of this was due to the small size of many of the rural congregations, and also partly due to the distances that many families had to travel to attend church. Often times these monthly gatherings included a Saturday church business meeting as well as the Sunday worship service.

quates *noun* variant of *quoits*.

1966 Dakin *Vocab Ohio River Valley* 238 *Quates* in Kentucky clearly came from the south and east, and at an early period in the settlement of this state. The distribution suggests a Midland term carried down the Great Valley into the Carolina and Tennessee uplands and thence into southeastern Kentucky.

queel over See **quile[2] B.**

queen-of-the-meadow *noun* A **boneset.**

1937 Thornburgh *Great Smoky Mts* 23 In late summer or early fall one sees the tall-growing flowers, such as . . . the purple ironweed and lavender Joe-pye-weed or Queen-of-the-meadow. **1971** Stubbs *Mountain-Wise* (May) 6 Joe Pye weed may be either "Queen of the meadow," "gentleman's walking stick," or "bugle plant." "Fer," as explained to us, "hit has a holler stem and you can blow hit like a bugle." **1972** *Foxfire I* 242 Kidney Trouble . . . Take one root from a queen-of-the-meadow plant. Boil it in one pint of water until it makes a dark tea. Strain and drink a cup a day until you are well. **1980** *Smokies Heritage* 295 Blooming with pink or purple flowers from July through late September, queen of the meadow is today known (less romantically, of course) as Joe Pye Weed. It is a flower of moist soils and mountain fields, occurring up to 3000 feet elevation and towering over the rest of the wildflowers—its height may reach from 12–15 feet. **1981** High *Coll* Queen-of-meadow: . . . name used in the Gorge for Eupatorium fistulosum, a plant more commonly known as Hollow Joe-Pye Weed. This purple flower grows to a height of seven feet. Its hollow stem, according to one informant, was used to raid and sip whiskey hidden in the fields during the time moonshining flourished in the area earlier this century. **1982** Stupka *Wildflowers* 118 A more fitting name, "queen-of-the-meadow," is applied to [Joe-pye weed] in the southern mountains.

queer *adjective*

A Variant forms *quair*; *quar*, rhyming with *bar*; *quare* [kwær], rhyming with *rare*.

1863 *Dalton CW Letters* (May 5) hit makes me feel quair to Hear the boom ing can non & the Rat ling musketry. **1867** Harris *Sut Lovingood* 78 I felt quar in my in'ards, sorter ha'f cumfurt, wif a littil glad an' rite smart ove sorry mix'd wif hit. **1899** Fox *Mt Europa* 27 Bill allus had a quar streak in 'im, and was the wust man I ever seed when he was disguised by licker. **1913** Kephart *Our Sthn High* 17 Foreigner, outlander, it is all one; we are "different," we are "quar," to the mountaineer. **1933** Carpenter *Sthn Mt Dialect* 23 *Quare* for QUEER seems pretty well confined to the Kentucky and Tennessee mountain sections. **1940** Haun *Hawk's Done* 183 He got just plumb quare-looking. **1979** Carpenter *Walton War* 173 I reckln' I'm quare (queer); some folks I like and others I mislike, and I can't help it.

B Senses.

1 Mentally unbalanced or deficient, senile; defective. See also **queer-turned.**

1931 Combs *Lg Sthn High* 1310 As in slang, many words have taken on new meanings, several of which are the exact antitheses to each other . . . "Quair" (queer) means both "demented," or "unbalanced," as in "here lately she acts 'quair,'" and "large," or "unusual," as in "My feller! that's a 'quair' piece of horseflesh!" **1938** Justus *No-End Hollow* 25 Yes, uncle Zeb was a plumb quare man—but how he could make a fiddle play! **1939** Hall *Coll* (Gatlinburg TN) She's quar now and don't have good recollection. **1952** Chase *Hindman Pageant* 19 We sat absorbed in the wonderful story of the [Hindman] Settlement School: watching fifty years unfold, living old-time again, taken into a world of the hopes, disappointments, ambitions, and dreams of the two "quare" women, seeing the final fulfillment of their faith that "our people may grow better." **1952** Giles *40 Acres* 57 I was labeled and tagged "quare" from the beginning of course. On account of my furniture, on account of the way I talked, on account of my city ways and city clothes. **1978** Burns *Our Sthn Mtneers* 10 The mountaineer . . . believes that the animal is bewitched especially if it is a cow that gives "quar" milk or if the butter won't come. **1993** Howze *Schoolhouse* 32 He didn't learn well, being slightly retarded. His mother said he was "quare."

2 Excellent.

1927 Furman *Lonesome Road* 74 I'm all quare and swimmy in my head. **1931** Combs *Lg Sthn High* 1304 That's a quare (queer) knife (A very good one).

queer proper *adjective phrase* Of speech: unnecessarily formal or proper in the eyes of those who don't use it.

1963 Edwards *Gravel* 181 Any use of language not commonly heard in Speedwell environs is called "quare proper," and of course anyone who uses "quare proper" language is listened to with silence, but when he is gone his "quare proper" language is parroted with considerable laughing and derision.

queer-turned *adjective phrase* Having an unbalanced personality or disposition. See also **queer B**, **turn B.**

1931 Goodrich *Mt Homespun* 41 "Reckon I'm quare-turned and ill," she said, turning to me with a mischievous gleam in her eye, "but I can't stand it to live with any of 'em, leastways with my daughters-in-law; they're good women, too, but folks has their ways." **1937** Hall *Coll* (Emerts Cove TN) He was very contrary and quare-turned.

querl See **coil**.

quern *noun* A primitive, hand-operated mill for grinding grain, consisting of two circular stones, the upper one rotated against the lower one by hand or animal power, rather than by water. See c1950 citation. See also **hand mill**, **hominy pounder**, **lazy Jim**, **pounding mill**, **slow John**, **tri-weekly**.

1913 Kephart *Our Sthn High* 291 In some places to-day we still find the ancient quern or hand-mill, jocularly called an armstrong machine. **c1950** Wilburn *Quern* Another photograph in our series shows a Kentucky mountaineer grinding corn with a quern or handmill such as was used in ancient Britain. The nether stone is set in a hollow log similar to a bee-gum. The upper one has a hole through the center, where the grain is fed by hand, and is turned round and round by a driving-stick, the upper end of which is held in position by a right-angled arm.... It cannot be said that querns were in actual use in the Great Smoky Mountains National Park in 1926–1930. However, several of the old settlers were familiar with them and had seen them in use in earlier times. While "exploring" in a very secluded, and almost inaccessible area, some six miles down the Tuckasegee River from Bryson City, there was found a pair of very crude quern stones. It was well known in local tradition that a number of Cherokee Indian families had "hid-out" in this area during the removal period in 1838 and following; and that they eked out a most perilous existence for several months in the period in which Tsali and others were being hunted by United States soldiers. The stones (querns) in question were collected for possible museum display. Only one family lived in the area at the time. The name has been forgotten, but it is in the museum records. The man had, a good many years previously, used the querns as capstones on high wooden pillows under his barn. I helped him prise up the barn and replace the querns with other stones. As previously stated, these were of the crudest sort of querns. There was no sign of furrowing; the working faces were smooth and showed signs of abrasion by much use. They were about sixteen inches in diameter, three inches thick; roughly circular in shape, only the angular corners having been "pecked off" with a hammer, or most likely, with another stone. **1975** Dwyer *Thangs* 23 Before the gristmills were built and [when] the pioneer was practically alone in vast areas, the quern came into family operation.... The quern's bottom stone was set in a hollowed log. The upper stone had a hole through the center where the grain was fed by hand, and turned round and round by a driving stick, the upper end of which was held in position by a right-angled arm. Grinding corn with a quern was hard, tiresome work and, as soon as water-powered gristmills were built, the mountain folks took their grain to the gristmill and abandoned the quern along with their simple mortar and pestle grinders. **2002** Oliver *Cooking and Living* 14 According to very scanty information, at least one settler had a quern to grind his corn. One of the oldest and most primitive mills known, the quern consists of a bottom, fixed stone, and a top stone that is revolved by hand or animal power, rather than waterpower to grind the grain.

[OED3 *quern* n[1] < Old English *cweorn*; EDD *quern* sb 1 obsolete or obsolescent]

querril See **coil**.

querry See **quarry**.

quick (also *quicken*) *verb* To prick the hoof of (a horse) in improper shoeing, thereby crippling the animal. See 1997 citation.

1915 Dingus *Word-List VA* 188 *quick* = horse shoeing. To drive a nail into the quick. **1937** Hall *Coll* The nails in his feet quicked [the horse]. **1939** Hall *Coll* You quicken the heel when you stick a tack in it. **1997** Montgomery *Coll*: *quick* = to pare the hoof to the quick or drive a nail into the hoof (Jones), = done by inept shoeing (Weaver).

[DARE *quick* v chiefly South Midland]

quick as Snyder's pup See **(as/like) Snyder's hound/house cat/pup**.

quicken See **quick**.

quickie *noun* See citation.

1990 Cavender *Folk Medical Lex* 30 = a sore area on the body that has a normal appearance but is sensitive to the touch.

quick-like See **like 1**.

quieten (also *quieten down*) *verb, verb phrase* To become quiet and calm; to make quiet.

1937 Hall *Coll* (Cades Cove TN) You cain't come nigh a bear jest atter he's been caught in a trap. You have to let him quieten down fust. **1939** Hall *Coll* Quieten down a little! (Reproof to noisy children). **1976** *Bear Hunting* 296 [The mother bear]'d raise up and slap [the cubs] a little, and they'd quieten down and that was the last of it till daylight. **1976** Garber *Mountain-ese* 73 Jed, go outside and see iffen you can quieten them dogs from barkin'. **1982** *Foxfire VII* 205 Everything quietened down after a while and my nerves did too, a little bit! **1985** Irwin *Alex Stewart* 261 There was never a thing done about it, and them Thompsons quietened down after that. **1990** *Matewan OHP-73* Instead of state police, they was called Baldwin thugs, and they was sent in here ... to try to stop the fighting, you know what I mean, trying to quieten everything down.

[DARE *quieten* v chiefly South, South Midland]

quietus *noun* A hush or state of calm (as in the early morning or after a rain); something that brings calm or death to (someone or something) or that causes action to cease (as in phrases *put a quietus on*, *put the quietus on*).

1931 *Professor Learns* Of course he says reckon, and right smart, and you all and quietus, and pizen, and yon-side. **1939** *FWP Guide NC* 98 = the calm that comes to some living thing after death, used in pity by an old woman about a wild animal killed by the dogs. **1998** Montgomery *Coll* Jim put the quietus on that loud mouth (Brown); He put a quietus on the congregation when he come in, you kids better quieten down or I'll put a quietus on you (Cardwell); He sure put the quietus on him in a hurry (Jones), = a calmness with no time restrictions and not always associated with rain, I know the term in expressions such as "Although the boys had been arguing all day, their father put a quietus on them when he came home from work" (Ledford), = used by a parent to threaten a spanking, "I'll put the quietus on you if you don't settle down" (Norris), – to put a stop to, as in "He put a quietus to that lawsuit" (Oliver). **2005** Williams *Gratitude* 517 To put the quietus on it means to tone down or stop something. A teacher coming into a disruptive room full of kids would put the quietus on them.

[OED3 < Medieval Latin *quietus est* "he is gone" or "he has left" 1427→]

quile[1] See **coil**.

quile[2] *verb*

A Variant form *queel* [see **1970** in **B**].

B (also *queel over, quile down, quile up*) To make or become calm or quiet, settle down.

1824 Knight *Letter from KY* 106–7 Some words are used, even by genteel people, from their imperfect education, in a new sense; and others, by the lower classes in society, pronounced very uncouthly; as . . . to quile for to quiet. **1933** Thomas *Traipsin' Woman* 34 We'll get you sprung [from prison] in six months if you'll jest quile down. **c1945** Haun *Hawk's Done* 335 Tom told Hubert he would just have to quile down a bit, that they had to have the money. **1970** *Snake Lore* 176 Directly he sort'a queeled over on his side, an' in a few minutes he'uz dead. **1997** Montgomery *Coll* (known to Adams, Jones, Ledford, Oliver); Just quile down and behave yourself (Cardwell). **2007** Preece *Leavin' Sandlick* 20 Margot Jean, you go get on the other end and quile up a little and go to sleep, too.

[probably variant of *quail*; DARE *quile* chiefly South Midland]

quile over, quile up See **quile**[2] **B**.

quill

A *noun*

1 A straw.

1949 Maurer *Argot of Moonshiner* 11 = a straw used to sample beer in the vats. Still beer is considered at its best for drinking just before distillation. However, it is drunk at almost every stage after it has begun to ferment. Passersby often slip in to sample it, though this practice is discouraged. "Hand me that quill. I'm fixing to drink some beer out of this barrel." **1974** Dabney *Mt Spirits* xxiv = a straw used to sample still beer.

2 See citation.

1968 *Sang Season* 73 The conservative sanger only dug roots in the fall of the year and carefully replanted the seeds, or a rhizome extension called a "quill," or "bud."

B *verb* See citation.

2006 *Encycl Appalachia* 850 A traditional practice of "quilling," blowing red pepper or gunpowder through a quill into the mother's nose, also hastened delivery by causing sneezing and contraction of the diaphragm.

quillaree *noun* A wood thrush (*Hylocichla muestelina*).

1919 Pearson et al. *Birds NC* The Wood Thrush, "Wood Robin," "Swamp Robin," or "Quillaree," arrives in North Carolina in the forepart of April and has been observed as late as the middle of October. It breeds in May and June, building its nest chiefly of weed stems and leaves and plastering it inside with mud. The nest, as a rule, is placed in a small tree at a height of from three to twelve feet from the ground, and in it are laid four greenish-blue, unspotted eggs, which average about 1.00 × .7. This bird is a very melodious singer, the loud and liquid notes sounding particularly sweet in the early morning, and doubtless the mountain name "Quillaree" is a supposed imitation of its song. Pearson has called attention to the fact that among the large trees on the campus of the State University at Chapel Hill these birds greatly outnumber the robins, while on the campus at Guilford College, where apparently about the same natural conditions prevail, the reverse is the case. **1929** Kephart *Smoky Mt Magic* 8 Out of the deep forest at the back of the house came a low, dove-like twitter from a "quillaree," as the mountain folk call the wood thrush. **2002** *Smoky Mt News* (Aug 28) Quillaree Branch in the Great Smoky Mountains National Park is named for the Cherokee and early settler's term for the wood thrush.

quilting (also *quilting bee, quilting party*) *noun* Traditionally, a gathering of women to help a neighbor sew quilts and to socialize, sometimes in conjunction with a **working**; hence verb *quilt* = to sew rows of stitches to join the top fabric to the batting.

1843 (in **1974** Harris *High Times* 29) The news goes forth that on such a day there will be a "log-rolling" and "quilting" at Capt. Dillon's. The sun has scarcely risen on that day, when every strong yeoman and buxom lass in the neighborhood are up and stirring, preparing for the "merry meeting." Hugh Dillon is started with the well-worn keg for first proof "mountain dew;" his sisters are preparing a sumptuous breakfast; corn-meal, eggs, and a large brown ham, are called into requisition, all of which are fast assuming "other shapes"; the fire's crackling, the fat or sop, as it is better known by that name in the Coves) is hissing, ham frying, hoe-cake baking, and everything in a complete bustle, when the neighbors begin to arrive. **1861** Odell *CW Letters* (Oct 11) tell Adline & marget shiply that wee wood like to be to the quilten. **1915** Dingus *Word-List VA* 188 *quilting party* = quilting bee. **1924** Abernethy *Moonshine* 132 They never went anywhere; that is to say, the women went wherever there was a "quiltin'" or birth in the neighborhood; the men went to "corn-shuckin's," "log-rollin's," and, on every fifth Sunday, to the meetin'-house. **1948** Dick *Dixie Frontier* 131 The feminine accompaniment of practically all bees was the quilting. The hostess had her quilt blocks pieced and set together ready for the coming of the neighborhood women. The quilt was fastened to four frames of wood and hung from the pole rafters by means of four ropes. The women then sat around the quilt on all four sides and the ropes were adjusted until the quilt hung breast-high. As the flying needles finished one arm-length along one side, that portion of the quilt was rolled up and a new arm-length begun. Just as some men were more skillful than others at a house-raising and were chosen to notch the corners, so some women were clever at finishing the quilt corners. It was a hard day's work for ten women to quilt one quilt. If the quilt was not completed, it was drawn up overhead by the ropes. **1957** Hall *Coll* (Gatlinburg TN) *quilting* = up to 50 yrs. ago [the term] was used to describe a gathering of ladies to make a quilt, a new bed cover. [It's] never heard now as far as I know. **c1975** Lunsford *It Used to Be* 21 Now, people going to marry or have married and need to have a few more quilts and things of that kind, why, they'll make up a lot of quilt tops and give a quiltin'. Of course, that's a lot of fun, and often they give a quiltin' at the same time they have a log rollin' or something of that kind,—a working, a house-raising. *Ibid.* 40 The quilting party was a party in which the people of the house would have laid aside their quilt scraps,—that is, various scraps of cloth that from time to time had been left over from making dresses of various kinds. Sometimes they were pretty costly dresses, still that would go into a quilt. And then the children's dresses of the calicos and the ginghams and things of that kind would be saved. The older and more inactive women of the household would take time out to sew those scraps together (first with the fingers and then after a while with the sewing machines) until they'd made a quilt top. When one was finished, they'd begin another. They would make these quilt pieces or quilt squares into certain patterns, and it is a science in itself. When they'd get ready to make the quilts, they'd get the wool or the batting,—the cotton batting, or whatever it was,—and have all that ready. If they didn't have the quiltin' frames, they'd go and borrow them. *Ibid.* 41 The interesting thing about the old-time quiltin' was that after the work had been done and they were ready to take the quilt out, they would manage to induce some young fellow about the place into the room or out in the hall under some false pretext. The young man might be someone at the log-rolling, a member of the family, or some young man who'd been courting and getting along pretty well and it had been prophesied that he was going to get married pretty soon. They'd have some of the younger members of the party to do that,—one or two single ones and maybe the older ones that knew what was coming. **1984** *Sevier Settler* 1:20–21 Many times in the old days women gathered together to work on quilts. My mother and grandmother seem to remember these gatherings well. They were called quilting bees. Mother can recall playing with the neighboring children under the quilts, as the women worked on them. In the earlier days each woman brought a few scraps, and quilts were made for newly married couples in the community. **1991** Thomas *Sthn Appal* 225 It was not uncommon for a woman to invite neighbors to come and help her "quilt" the quilt, that is, sew rows of stitches across it; this constituted what was called a "quiltin'," a kind of women's social.

quilting bee See **quilting.**

quiltingest *adjective* Most devoted to or energetic at making quilts. See also **-est 1** and Grammar and Syntax §3.4.1.

1955 Parris *Roaming Mts* 163 "I reckon I'm the quiltin'est woman in all the land," she said.

quilting party See **quilting.**

quilt mat *noun* See citation.

1996 Isbell *Last Chivaree* 75 [To start a fire] he would need a "quilt mat" of spunk, called "dodie wood" in the mountains, and flint rocks for catching the sparks. He searched for dodie wood: the best comes from an old sugar tree—rotten dodie wood, where the tree's hollowed out and the wood inside is fine as wheat flour.

quilt pack *noun* See citation.

2005 Williams *Gratitude* 517 = the place in the house where folded quilts are stacked and stored.

quinsy *noun* Inflammation of the throat (of a person or animal), sometimes accompanied by wheezing; hence adjective = vaguely unwell.

1990 Cavender *Folk Medical Lex* 30 = inflammation of the tonsils and throat. **1994** Montgomery *Coll* (known to Ogle); I'm a little quinsey today (Cardwell).

[< Middle English *quinsie, quinesie* "inflammation of the throat" < Medieval Latin]

quirl *verb* To curl. See also **coil.**

1975 Chalmers *Better* 66 They will come a-tippin' in on their toes and quirl down on a little ol' settin' chair and linger up by the fire when the air is a'stirrin' cool.

[DARE *quirl* (at *curl* n, v) especially South, South Midland]

quirt *verb* See citation.

c1982 Young *Colloquial Appal* 18 = squirt.

quit *verb*

A Variant past-tense form *quitted.*

c1982 Young *Colloquial Appal* 18 = quit.

B Senses.

1 To depart from (a place), abandon (a person).

1862 *Councill CW Letters* (Feb 4) I quit they boys that I had bin a sleepin with an went to bill taners tent. **1939** Hall *Coll* (Deep Creek NC) He quit me there, said he was a-goin' to camp. *Ibid.* (Deep Creek NC) That bull was so dangerous everybody had to quit the mountain. **1964** Stubbs *Mountain-Wise* (Feb–March) 8 She just quit him and left out of here. **1972** *AOHP/ALC-226* When Dad always wanted me to quit a boy, he didn't have to do very much. **1994** Thomas *Come Go* 29 Mother put up with that as long as she could stand it. And then she quit him.

[DARE *quit* v 1 widespread, but less frequent Northeast, West]

2 In phrase *won't quit.* Used to describe something excellent or plentiful.

1956 Hall Coll (Hurricane Creek NC) I've got some apples that won't quit.

quit of *adjective phrase* Rid of.

1958 Combs *Archaic English in KY* 42 = rid of: "We are quit of that trouble."

quit off (also *quit out, quit out of*) *verb phrase* To stop, cease.

1927 Woofter *Dialect from WV* 362 = to stop. "I have quit off chewing tobacco." **1930** Armstrong *This Day and Time* 24 He had "quit off loggin'." **1973** *Flu Epidemic* 101 [The flu] went on there for several months like that, an' it just quit out. **1974–75** McCracken *Logging* 12:39 I had to quit out and go to school. **1989** *Matewan OHP-86* It was thirty-six, and I quit out of school right then.

quituate *verb* To leave school before graduating.

c1960 Wilson *Coll* = contemptuous reference to someone's leaving school without graduating. **1976** Garber *Mountain-ese* 73 Johnny couldn't pass his courses so he decided to quituate school. **1995–97** Montgomery *Coll* (known to Brewer, Oliver); John quituated after the ninth grade (Cardwell), = as in "Have you graduated from high school?" or "No, I quituated in the eleventh grade and went to work" (Ledford), = always humorous (Weaver).

[blend of *quit* and *graduate*]

quituation *noun* Withdrawal from school.

1937 (in **1952** Mathes *Tall Tales* 218) Shortly after Ike's "quituation" from Noah Dilrod's school, he was left an orphan with the farm and the bunch of yearlings on the pasturage. **1998** Montgomery *Coll* (known to Adams, Cardwell, Ledford).

[blend of *quit* and *graduation*]

quoby, quope, quopy See **cope**.

quorl[1] See **coil**.

quorl[2] *noun* See citation.

1927 Woofter *Dialect from WV* 362 = cluster. "There is a quorl of snake root."

quote *verb* To sound, make a noise.

1952 Wilson *Folk Speech NC* 581 = to sound, to make a noise: "I heard a gun quote over in the woods." **1972** Carson and Vick *Hillbilly Cookin* 59 = make a noise: "[I] heared a gobbler quotin on the ridge." **2001** Montgomery *Coll* (known to Cardwell).

quouk *verb* Of a bird: to squawk.

1937 Hyatt *Kiverlid* 27 I seed two of the hens makin' fer the big woods a-quoukin' purt nigh ever' mornin' about day-break.

quowa, quup See **cope**.

qurry See **quarry**.

R

rabbit fever *noun* Tularemia. See 1997 citation.

1992 Bush *Dorie* 17 People were dying from something called rabbit fever. **1997** Montgomery *Coll* = an infection carried by the larva of a fly that burrows inside the skin of a rabbit, meaning that the animal should not be eaten from April to September, during the life cycle of the larva (Cardwell).

rabbit gum See **gum A3**.

rabbit hunt See **hunt B**.

rabbit tobacco *noun* The catfoot plant (*Pseudognaphalium* spp, usually *P. obtusifolium*), which has medicinal uses and is sometimes smoked by children to imitate adults smoking tobacco. Also called **cudweed, old field balsam, poverty weed, sweet balsam, sweet everlasting, tobacco weed.**

1982 Stupka *Wildflowers* 124 It is sometimes called "poverty weed" and "old-field balsam," because it thrives in dry areas and waste places. Names such as "sweet balsam" and "sweet everlasting" refer to its fragrance. Other names are "rabbit tobacco" and "cudweed." **1992** Bush *Dorie* 104 My cousins smoked "rabbit tobacco," a green-gray plant that grew around the barn. **1996** Parton *Mt Memories* 10 We often copied Mother and Papa in their tobacco habits. We would smoke "rabbit tobacco" (a wild herb) because we'd learned that the real tobacco made us deathly sick. **2006** Howell *Medicinal Plants* 129–30 Rabbit tobacco has a long history as a remedy for both physical and psychological imbalances. American Indians relied on rabbit tobacco for general pain relief and as a muscle relaxant. It was used extensively for respiratory problems including coughs and colds, lung pain, and sore throats. The dried herb was smoked to relieve asthmatic symptoms and as a sedative.

rabbit wood *noun* The oilnut (*Pyrularia pubera*), a parasitic shrub from which an oil is derived for use in small lamps and fashioned for primitive candles. Same as **tallow nut**.

1901 Lounsberry *Sthn Wild Flowers* 148 By the mountaineers the plant seems to be wholly known as the "rabbit-wood," for these animals gnaw its bark to such an extent that it is unusual to find one which has not been more or less peeled. **1926** Shaver *Flowers of Smokies* 18 The mountaineers call the Oil-Nut "rabbitwood," because the rabbits in winter gnaw its bark, almost completely peeling it in some cases.

raccoon berry *noun* Same as **mayapple**.

2012 *Smokies Guide* (Spring) 12 This common wildflower's name relates to its fruit ripening in May. Another name for the plant is "raccoon berry," because raccoons like to eat the berries.

race[1] *noun* A small bar or piece, especially of ginger.

1905 Miles *Spirit of Mts* 174–75 When Gran'ma sends over to borrow a "race o'brimstone" it recalls a passage in *Twelfth Night* [sic for *The Winter's Tale*] about "a race or two of ginger." **1913** Kephart *Our Sthn High* 291 Can I borry a race of ginger? **1944** Combs *Word-List Sthn High* 20 = (From O. Fr. rais, "root.") A small quantity, or root (of ginger) . . . It is heard now only in race-ginger, that is, ginger in the root, not ground. **1982** Slone *How We Talked* 61 Boil a few "races" (the unground roots of the ginger plant) in water.

[DARE *race* n² now chiefly South Midland]

race² *noun* See also **granny race.**

1 The rush after a hunted animal, especially a fox, with dogs. See also **fox race.**

1939 Hall *Coll* (Cataloochee NC) He took after it, had a main race down there till the turkey flopped up agin a big log and couldn't get over it, and there they caught it. **1949** Arnow *Hunter's Horn* 31 Rans, he's big, but he's still a baby; he ain't through growen: he'll mebbe be bigger'n Zing. I don't think I'd let him run atall with other hounds in a race—mebbe not fore spring—treat him good, buy him some dog feed, an you'll have a rare good hound. **1970** *Hunting Stories* 31 Some wanted to cut th'tree, y'know, an' have another race and catch [the raccoon]. **1976** *Bear Hunting* 277 That day we got after a big bear, and we had a good race. **1977** *Jake Waldroop* 153 We'd turn the dog loose an' have a cat race and kill a wild cat. **1982** Powers and Hannah *Cataloochee* 165 Mark Hanah and Eldridge Caldwell related that Thanksgiving was the time for the traditional bear hunt and also the wild hog race . . . a "race" was the same as a hunt. They would race the small hogs or "ridgerooters," four or five year olds, each weighing two or three hundred pounds, way back in the mountains.

2 A hard rush to elude a pursuer, a chase.

1949 Maurer *Argot of Moonshiner* 11 = the chase to escape officers. It may be either by car or on foot. Such a chase is quite common, since Federal officers seldom shoot first at violators of the liquor law. "Me and the law had a race"; "I shore give the law a race yesterday."

race saw *noun* A saw driven by a millrace.

1973 *AOHP/LJC-296* They had a band saw and a race saw, and I don't know just how many saws they had in that mill.

rack *verb* in phrases *rack on, rack out, rack over, rack up* = to go energetically, set out. See also **rake out.**

1896 Fox *Last Stetson* 194 Ef ye air honin' fer Rome, why don't ye rack out 'n' go to him? **1904** Fox *Christmas Eve* 116 Jeb 'lowed he'd rack right over on Cutshin an' set up with Polly Ann Sturgill. **1927** Mason *Lure of Smokies* 217 [He would] rack up a tree nerveous jest like thet leetle cub was a-doin'. **1978** *Horsetrading* 43 [I] got on the old poor thing and we just went rackin' on up through there.

[DARE *rack* v² (from *rack* a gait of a horse) chiefly South Midland]

racket *noun* A noisy quarrel, altercation.

1859 Taliaferro *Fisher's River* 122 When they 'vited the mourners I went up, and you may s'pose there was some racket jist then. They all tuck on mightily. **c1950** (in **2000** Oakley *Roamin' Man* 73) I am a Scotsman when I hafto spend money on a bird that likes to have a racket with me ever day. **1962** Williams *Metaphor Mt Speech I* 11 If the "flouter" responds to the thrust of the jaw with a flood of invective that leads to threats of violence frustrated by bystanders who "hold 'em apart," the affair is characterized as a "racket." **1975** Jackson *Unusual Words* 157 A *racket* implies more actual contact, whereas *ruckus* or *rookus, fraction,* and *fray* all mean a fist fight or gun fight. **1975–76** Wolfram/Christian *WV Coll* 153 He had a right smart temper, but he never got mad at me. We got along all right. We never had no rackets. **1977** Norman *Kinfolks* 48 Get Jenny and her mother together, you're sure going to have a racket. **1979** Slone *My Heart* 123 He and Barbara must have had a big quarrel, or racket as we say, for she moved out and they stayed separated for over six months, but they got back together after a while. **1983** *Dark Corner OHP-9A* [They'd] take their shotgun or rifle to church with them. . . . They didn't carry it to have a racket or shoot somebody or something. They'd just carried it and get game. **1997** Montgomery *Coll* (known to ten consultants from the Smoky Mountains). **2005** Williams *Gratitude* 136 I study about Mom and Dad a-gittin' into a big racket at th' table one time.

[DARE *racket* n² chiefly South, South Midland]

racket store *noun* A variety store.

1910 Essary *TN Mtneers* 30 A big sign swayed in the breezes announcing the arrival of the proverbial "Racket Store." **1921** Greer-Petrie *Angeline at Seelbach* 22 I'd always thought the Rackit [sic] Store up at the county seat was a powerful high building, but I wish you might see some of them thar Chicago houses! **2007** Barksdale *Radford* 43 Max Rupe opened the New Racket Store in the west end of town about 1910. During this period, the term racket store was used to describe a variety store that sold common household items.

rack on, rack out, rack over, rack up See **rack.**

rael, r'al, rale See **real.**

raffle See **rifle.**

raft *noun* An abundance or collection, as of children.

1926 Wilson *Cullowhee Wordlist* = abundance. "There was a raft of children at play." **1997** Montgomery *Coll* (known to Brewer, Bush, Ellis, Jones, Ledford, Norris, Oliver); They had a raft of problems (Cardwell).

[OED3 *raft* n² originally North American]

raft tide *noun* The surge of a river or stream sufficient for loggers to float rafts of logs downstream to market. See also **tide A.**

1915 Dingus *Word-List VA* 188 = tide sufficient to float rafts. **1957** Garred *History of Garreds* 281 That old Big Sandy is a tough one, when at raft tide, swift and treacherous. Upon approaching a sharp bend, of which there are many, the "headman" or pilot has to know just how to head in, to keep from wrecking. **1976** Garber *Mountain-ese* 73 The loggers are waitin' for a raft-tide to market their logs. **2000** Ellis *KY River* 71 Not only logs, but railroad ties, barrel staves, and shingles were floated to market on the Kentucky River tides. "They had two tides," Homer Allen of Oneida recalled. "One was a raft tide and one was a tie tide." The first was higher and the latter was not as swift.

raggeddy See **raggedy**.

raggedy (also *raggeddy*) *adjective* Especially of clothing or appearance: frayed, untidy, unkempt.

1915 Dingus *Word-List VA* 188 *raggedy* = ragged. **1923** Furman *Mothering* 251 [He] had heared Dilsey tell Philip at recess she couldn't abide raggeddy boys. **c1950** Adams *Grandpap* 140 He was all raggedy an' he had an old, dirty cap on his head. **1969** Miller *Raising Tobacco* 34 Raggedy lugs, the bottommost leaves, thinner in texture and less gummy, were so-called because of their ragged appearance; since the leaves began ripening in the field at the bottom up. **1997** Montgomery Coll (known to ten consultants from the Smoky Mountains). **1997** Nelson *Country Folklore* 150 When we got there we were raggedy and dirty from riding in box cars. **2012** Milnes *Signs Cures Witchery* [They'd] dress up in their false faces and the raggedy old ugly clothes.

[OED3 *raggedy* adj 1a, 1b chiefly U.S. regional, British regional, and Irish English; SND *raggety* (at *raggit* adj)]

ragler, raglur See **regular**.

ragweed milk *noun* See citation. See also **bitterweed milk, weedy, wild onion milk**.

1967 *DARE Survey* (Gatlinburg TN) = milk that has a taste of something [specifically ragweed] the cow ate in the pasture.

raid (also *raid around*) *verb, verb phrase* Of law-enforcement officers: to search for (an illegal **still**) in order to destroy it and apprehend its operators; to go around searching for such stills.

1915 Bradley *Hobnobbing* 95 In places where the "revenuers" are "raidin' around right smart," even men known personally to the "stillers" are not allowed to visit the "stills." **1962** Hall Coll (Hartford TN) Joe Ray, deputy sheriff for Boyce Hardwood Company, [was] raidin' someone makin' liquor over on Hurricane Creek. **1973** GSMNP-83:17 I've raided more stills in them old mountains there and in Sevier County; I cut every old bootleg around there, on Fighting Creek, everywhere.

raider *noun* Same as **still raider**.

1885 Murfree *Prophet* 150 Him an' me run a sour mash still on the top of the mounting in the light o' day up'ards o' twenty year, an' never hearn o' no raider.

rail[1] See **real**.

rail[2] *noun* A slender, rough piece of wood split from a log, triangular in cross-section with the bark side somewhat concave, used in making fences, pens, etc.

A *noun Rail fence* = a fence made of such pieces of wood overlapped horizontally (in which case it is also known as a **snake fence, worm fence**, or **zigzag fence**), but also may be straight, with vertical posts to join the rails (known as a **post and rail** or **post and rider** fence).

1904–20 Kephart *Notebooks* 2:365 That pig o' Newt Wilson would cross hell on a rotten rail to git into a 'tater patch. **1949** Kurath *Word Geog East US* 55 [*Rail fence*] is also widely current in West Virginia and is in regular use in the mountains farther south. **1953** Hall Coll (Bryson City NC) The place was fenced with black walnut rails. **1956** Hall Coll (Roaring Fork TN) At that time we had what we called a fence law.... They'd split rails and build rail fences to protect their crops. The law was to build it five rails high, and if the cow brute broke over that . . . the owner of the brute had to pay the damage. **1991** Haynes *Haywood Home* 45 Stock laws were passed only after barbed-wire came into more general use. Until then, the only way people had to fence was using rail fences. Rail fences were hard to build and people only built enough to fence their fields. First, they built crooked-rail fences, then they built post and rail (straight rail) fences. Even after barbed-wire was available, it was still expensive and landowners had more trees than dollars, so they continued to build rail fences even after they could get barbed-wire.

B *verb* To construct (a fence) of such pieces of wood.

1953 Hall Coll (Deep Creek NC) I had a fight with a Jersey bull once. I thought he'd stay up there with the cattle. I built up the fence. It was old, railed. He run his horns under that [and got out].

rail fence See **rail**[2] **A**.

rail house *noun* A small house for loggers, transportable by rail from one encampment to another. See also **jimmy car**.

1989 Oliver *Hazel Creek* 62 This was done with small buildings, painted red and called "rail houses," that could be transported on logging cars to each site.

railly See **really**.

railroad *verb* To work on (something) quickly.

1938 Stuart *Dark Hills* 55 "You will have to miss school long enough to cut that knob piece of corn." "I'll cut it all on Saturday," I said. That Saturday . . . I "railroaded" the corn from daylight until four o'clock that afternoon.... My father would not believe that I had cut fifty-four shocks until he counted them.

railroad time *noun* Precise clock time. See also **sun time**.

1946 Wilson *Fidelity Folks* 42 He said that Fidelity kept sun time rather than railroad time because it was nearer the sun. **1956** McAtee *Some Dial NC* 36 = correct time. **c1960** Wilson Coll = standard time as opposed to "sun time."

raily See **really**.

rain bird See **rain crow 1**.

rain bullfrogs *verb phrase* To rain very hard.

1967 *DARE Survey* (Maryville TN). **1994–97** Montgomery *Coll* (known to Adams, Brown, Cardwell, Jones, Shields, Weaver).

[DARE (at *bullfrogs, rain*) v phr chiefly South, South Midland]

rain crow *noun*

1 (also *rain bird, rain raven*) The yellow-billed cuckoo (*Coccyzus americanuus*), so called because of the cry it often makes in lowering weather, thus thought to presage the onset of rain.

1939 Hall *Coll* (White Oak NC) Rain crows, when you hear 'em holler, it's going to rain. **1966–68** *DARE Survey* (Brasstown NC, Spruce Pine NC) *rain bird* = cuckoo; *rain crow, rain raven* (Cherokee NC) = a water bird that makes a booming sound before rain and often stands with its beak almost straight up. **1980** Brewer *Hit's Gettin'* A yellow-billed cuckoo is a "rain crow" both [in east TN] and [the Ozarks]. **1991** Alsop *Birds of Smokies* 51 The cuckoo arrives in late April and is usually gone by the middle of October. Most of the guttural song is heard from mid-June well into August. The locals know it as the "rain crow" because the singing is thought to signal coming showers. **1995** Montgomery *Coll*: *rain bird, rain crow* (known to Cardwell). **2011** *Smoky Mt News* (June 1) Rural residents know the yellow-billed cuckoo as the "rain crow" or "storm crow" because its guttural "ka-ka-kow-kow-kowlp-kowlp-kowlp" seems to be sounded just prior to a late evening thunderstorm. (The distinctive "kowlp-kowlp-kowlp" portion of the call sounds something like a small dog barking.)

[DARE *rainbird* n 1c chiefly Midland, especially Appalachians]

2 The mourning dove.

1981 High *Coll* (*DARE*) = mourning dove, whose call is supposed to indicate approaching rain: "When the rain crows start to holler, it's going to rain." **1993** Mason *Feather Crowns* 173 Christie fell in and out of sleep, reaching for the babies, confusing their cries with rain crows calling out for rain.

rain raven See **rain crow 1**.

rain toad *noun* A tree frog.

2001 Tilley and Huheey *Reptiles & Amphibians* 128 The voice [of Cope's gray treefrog] is a rapid, resonant trill which is also sometimes heard on rainy nights throughout summer and early fall, leading this species to be known among some locals [in the Smoky mountains] as the "rain toad."

[DARE (at *rainfrog* n) chiefly South]

raise

A *intransitive verb*

1 (also *raise up*) To grow up; hence *raising, raising up* = one's upbringing, early training in manners (thus *acting* (or *getting*) *above one's raising, go back on your raising* = being pretentious, "stuck up," acting as though the people and things of one's childhood have become inferior). See also **rear B1**.

1915 Dingus *Word-List VA* 188 = rearing: "bringing up." **1924** Raine *Saddlebags* 103 We didn't have no fotch-on clothes when I was a-raisin'. **1924** Spring *Lydia Whaley* 2 Never heard anyone swear except off in my raisin'. **1927** Woofter *Dialect from WV* 362 Have you children forgotten your raising? **1937** Hall *Coll* (Mingus Creek NC) In my raisin' up two or three beside your own [family] would set up with sick people. **1940** Haun *Hawk's Done* 61 Eloyd had just had too good a raising to act like it might have been best to act. **1955** Ritchie *Singing Family* 28 If you should start to talk about the other things, the things inside you, folks might think you were getting above your raising. **1956** Hall *Coll* (Newport TN) Mister Barnes lived in North Carolina and raised up there. **c1960** Wilson *Coll*: *raising* = one's native culture, manners, general attitude: "Show your raisin'." **1976** Dwyer *Southern Sayin's* 9 = rearing, manners, breeding. "He's got the raisin' of a hog." **1976** Still *Pattern of Man* 48 Young'uns don't climb much above their raising. He'll follow his pappy in the log works, my opinion. **1982** Slone *How We Talked* 13 Hill people saw no wrong in a person wanting to make something out of themselves, make money, improve their way of living, as long as they did not become ashamed of their parents and how they grew up. This was "getting above your raising." **1992** Brooks *Sthn Stuff* 17 *go back on your raisin'* = when you forget your humble beginnings, put on airs, an' get all biggety [q.v.]. "To go back on yore raisin' is a pretty serious charge if you're a Suthunuh." **1994** Montgomery *Coll* When I raised up, we didn't do that (Cardwell). **1995** Montgomery *File* Dolly [Parton] is one person that hasn't forgot her raisin' (60-year-old man, Gatlinburg TN). **2003** Gibson *Sthn Mt Dialect* I have found through research many people that move back to the place they were born will fall back into the local way of speaking to become part of the community again. If not then some will be accused by a few of the local people as "getting above their raising." **2007** Preece *Leavin' Sandlick* 39 Just don't forget ye raisin', Son, and get too big fer ye britches. **2009** Benfield *Mt Born* 145 *getting above one's raising* = living high and grand, forgetting the way he was raised. Most often used as a rebuke, but sometimes in jest.

[DARE *raise* v C2b especially Southeast, *raising* n 1 chiefly South Midland]

2 To rise.

1939 Hall *Coll* (Hazel Creek NC) They had a spout run up that way and poured this dough right around this lid, and hit would raise to the top with a hole in the middle. **1940** Haun *Hawk's Done* 5 Always in the summertime when I'm out on the porch I can see that mountain. It raises up above Hancock County, head and shoulders above any hill here in Cocke County. *Ibid.* 110 Cordia may have her back turned away from the Lord when she raises up to meet him. **1964** Miller *Pigeon's Roost* (June 11) It was like this—the voters met at the designated voting precincts and the voters who were for certain candidates raised from their seats and stood on their feet for the one they were in favor of. **1973** *Gathered Together* 30 She just raised t'her feet. **1977** McClelland *Wilson Douglas* 18 In a dark moon the brine won't raise on your cabbage to sour your kraut. **c1982** Young *Colloquial Appal* 29 I'll be there if the creek don't raise. **1989** *Matewan OHP-1* I knew I needed more education. I wanted to raise above my level that I was used to. **1990** *Ibid.* 73

They was just tickled to death getting them a charter, forming them a union, you know, and having union meetings, and wages begin to raise. **2008** *Rosie Hicks* 1 My bread don't look right. It ain't a-raising.

3 Of the wind: to increase.

1966 Dakin *Vocab Ohio River Valley* 22 Throughout the Ohio Valley *rising* and *raising* appear most commonly in this expression. In the Kentucky Mountains (especially Whitley, Bell, Harlan, and Letcher Counties) and the eastern Knobs.

B *transitive verb*

1 In phrase *raise up* = to rear and educate (a person or family). See also **rear B1**.

1939 Hall *Coll* (Little Cataloochee NC) They was ignorant, raised up in ignorance, no Sunday school, no church, nor nothing, nor no one to lead them on right in the right way. **1960** McCaulley *Cades Cove* I was raised up in that cove. **1973** GSMNP-70:2:6 My father's people was all raised up in Madison County, North Carolina. **1978** Montgomery *White Pine Coll* X-2 You're just what you're raised up to be. *Ibid.* He has a little farm there and raised them up, very, very common boys. **1989** Smith *Flyin' Bullets* 376 I was raised up where moonshine was made, but I never touched another still, it was the best lesson I could have ever had. **2001** House *Clay's Quilt* 49 We was raised up together. **2009** Burton *Beech Mt Man* 15 They was a-raisin' me up, and once I got grown—I don't think nobody should give you ulcers.

[DARE *raise* v B3b chiefly South, South Midland]

2 To set the musical key of (a song, especially a hymn and lead the singing (especially of a hymn); more generally, to begin the song impromptu, with others joining in. Same as **hoist B**. See also **line B**.

1905 Miles *Spirit of Mts* 122 Some of the amen-corner members raise a hymn. . . . They sing without books, for these hymns have never been printed. **1984** Wilder *You All Spoken* 180 *raise the tune* = the song leader pitches the tune of the song to be sung. **1995** McCauley *Mt Religion* 82 Services today for many churches are still regularly convened by those gathering inside "raising up a hymn," especially in traditions such as the Old Regular Baptists. **1997** Montgomery *Coll* (known to Bush); They accepted the invitation and came forward to raise a song, one enjoyed by all present (Cardwell), = to get the proper pitch and lead a song (Jones), = a song leader would start a song and the congregation joined in. He, supposedly, knew the key, same as *heist a tune* (Norris). **2007** McMillon *Notes*: *raise a song* = for one or more persons to begin singing, usually a hymn.

3 To rouse.

1915 Dingus *Word-List VA* 188 = to arouse so as to hold communication with: "I called loud at the house but I couldn't raise anybody."

4 Of a team of livestock: to climb (a hill).

1927 Woofter *Dialect from WV* 362 = to go up the hill. "We saw the team raise the hill more than an hour ago."

5 See citation.

1940 Bowman *KY Mt Stories* 245 *raise coal* = to mine coal.

C *noun*

1 A rise, ground that inclines upward.

1973 GSMNP-88 What they call the upper school set right up there on that little raise, above that bush. **1975** *AOHP/LJC-384* Our house was up on that raise kind of.

2 A surge of water caused by spring rains. See also **tide A**.

1989 *Matewan OHP-7* All the big raises we had would be along in March. It's different to what it is [now].

raise a rucket, raise a ruckus See **ruckus**.

raise a song See **raise B2**.

raise coal See **raise B5**.

raised in a barn *adjective phrase* Uncouth, lacking manners or social training, applied especially to one who comes in and leaves an outside door open. See 1998 citation.

1966 *DARE Survey* (Burnsville NC) = having unpleasant behavior or no manners. **1998** Montgomery *Coll* (consultants from the Smoky Mountains agree that general sense of the term is having no manners), = tracking in mud, dirty, selfish, animal-like (Brown), = used by adults to correct children for lack of manners, especially for forgetting to close a door or letting a screen door slam (Ellis), = implies that a person is careless about common household manners, does not close doors, tracks mud into the house, throws trash on the floor, etc., in general treats the home with disrespect (Ledford), = when a person went outside and left the door open, especially in the winter, he was asked "Were you raised in a barn?" Closing the door was important when you were heating with a fireplace (Norris). **1999** Brewer *Appal Lg* Were you "raised in a barn?" That's what you ask the fellow who bursts into the front room on a cold, snowy day and leaves the door open.

raise one's meat *verb phrase* To raise animals, usually hogs, for one's own consumption.

1956 Hall *Coll* (Big Bend NC) I buy my meal. All I have to buy [is] coffee and sody. I raise my meat, my berries and corn, hay.

raise up See **raise A1, B1**.

raising *noun*

1 See **raise A1**.

2 A rise, area of higher ground.

1953 Hall *Coll* (Bryson City NC) They came right down in a hundred yards of me and crossed and went out of hearing into a little raisin' up a creek.

3 An inflamed or swollen area of the skin. Same as **rising A**.

1998 Montgomery *Coll* (known to Bush, Ellis, Ledford, Oliver).

rake *verb*

A Principal parts.

1 Variant past-tense forms *roke, rook, ruck, rucked, ruke, ruked*.

1913 Kephart *Our Sthn High* 284 Examples of a strong preterite with dialectical change of the vowel are bruk, brung, drap or drapped, drug, friz, roke or ruck (rucked). **c1940** Simms *Coll*: *rucked*. **c1950** Adams *Grandpap* 24 He just ruck him up some leaves an' got him some old dry chunks an' built him a fire. **1962** Williams *Verbs Mt Speech* 17 Verbs which retain either the strong preterites of Middle English or variant preterites of the English dialects [include] rake (present), ruck (past), ruck (past participle). **1974** *Instrument Makers* 199 While he was gone, I took and rook up leaves and rook it up right in here on [the steers'] hind ends and took a match and lit it. **1978** Reese *Speech NE Tenn* 177 *ruke* = attested by 1/12 (8.3%) speakers; *ruked* = attested by 1/12 (8.3%) speakers. **1982** Ginns *Snowbird Gravy* 204 In ten or fifteen minutes, he ruck her out a 'tater. **2008** Salsi *Ray Hicks* 108 We sized up a place to bed down and ruck up some dry straw and leaves to form a place up under our quilts to make a comfortable place to sleep.

2 Variant past-participle forms *ruck, ruke, ruked*.

1936 (in **1952** Mathes *Tall Tales* 214) We've ruck over Huggins's Hell fer yer carcass, an' here ye turn up as lively an' as ornery as ye ever was! **1939** Hall *Notebooks* 13:5 (White Oak NC) It was ruck. [See **1962** in **A1**.] **1978** Reese *Speech NE Tenn* 177 *ruke* = attested by 1/12 (8.3%) speakers; *ruked* = attested by 1/12 (8.3%) speakers.

B Senses.

1 (also *rake him up one side and down the other, rake (one) over the coals*) To scold severely.

1927 Woofter *Dialect from WV* 362 *rake him up one side and down the other* = to reprimand severely. "The teacher raked the boys up one side and down the other for throwing snowballs." **c1960** Wilson *Coll* (DARE) (or *rake over the coals*) = scold very severely. **1963** Edwards *Gravel* 19 While Uncle Jeems was raking my pa I was going through his pockets to find the candy which I knew he had somewhere.

[DARE *rake* B1a chiefly South Midland]

2 Of a bear or a turkey: to sweep leaves off the ground in searching for acorns, chestnuts, and other foodstuffs; to sweep (leaves).

1939 Hall *Coll* (Proctor NC) [How do you begin looking for the bear?] We'd just go and look where they been a-feedin'. They rake just like turkeys, struttin'. **1953** Hall *Coll* (Bryson City NC) When [the bear] goes to feed on the ground, he'll rake around the hillside, rakin' the leaves just like you take a garden rake, and he'll rake a row clear around in a circle.... Then he'll go back and just step up a row like a man layin' off corn rows ... lookin' for chestnuts and beechnuts on the ground after they've fell out of the trees in the fall of the year.

rake him up one side and down the other, rake (one) over the coals See **rake B1**.

rake out *verb phrase* To depart energetically and with purpose. See also **rack**.

1939 Hall *Coll* (Proctor NC) We'd just go over [to the Hall Cabin on top of Smoky] and stay like we was stayin' at home ... And we'd rake out next morning after them bear. **1997** Montgomery *Coll* (known to Andrews).

[EDD (at *rake* 13) "to rouse, bestir oneself"]

ramick (*rammick*) *verb* To rush about, romp.

1922 Cobb *KY Mt Rhymes* 63 British Lady's my favorite [bird]— / If I was aiming to cast my vote— / Ramicking round so proud and free, / And preening his gayly scarlet coat. **1986** Still *Wolfpen Poems* 66 In your time, Bad Jack, / You rammicked, you cut, you shot.

[cf OED3 *rammuck* (probably an alteration of *rummage* v, after *ransack* v) v 2 "to rush about furiously," regional (chiefly British)]

ramic *noun* See citation.

1936 Farr *Folk Speech Mid TN* 276 = young calf: "The ramie is in the pasture."

rammick See **ramick**.

ramp *noun*

1 A wild leek (*Allium tricoccum*) whose bulbous root eaten raw or cooked has a pungent, sweetish flavor but gives the eater a strong, lingering, often offensive odor. Considered a delicacy by some, the plant is harvested each spring and celebrated at the Cosby (TN) Ramp Festival, the National Ramp Association's Ramp Fest in Richwood WV, and many other locales. It grows at higher elevations and is sometimes consumed as a **spring tonic**.

1894 Bergen *Plant Names III* 101 Allium, sp[ecies], ramps, Banner Elk, N.C. **1913** Morley *Carolina Mts* 259 Although the Nantahalas abound in beautiful flowers, they also have a reputation for the production of "ramps," as the people call the wild onions that are abundant enough in some regions to be a nuisance to the farmer. **1917** Kephart *Word-List* 416 = rampion; the wild garlic of the mountains. **1939** Jennison *Flora Great Smokies* 280 Species of wild onions are all too common to suit most farmers, and they are really difficult to eradicate, but one kind is much sought after by the mountain folk, who call it "ramps," and gather and eat its bulb with great relish. **1956** Hall *Coll* (Newport TN) Ramp Festival program: For generations people in the mountains have considered raw ramps, ramps parboiled and fried in grease, scrambled with eggs, or served up in various ways to possess wondrous medicinal properties, to be, in fact a necessary Spring tonic.... Some have called it the "vilest smelling and the sweetest tasting vegetable that grows." **1968** Comstock *Hillbilly* 105 Richwood [WV] is the home of the National Ramp Association, founded some three decades ago. In years past many from out of town and out of state flocked to town once yearly to indulge in a ramp feed, during which a huge mess of ramps was prepared in any of a number of ways. Ramps can be eaten raw, cooked, boiled, fried, or fixed in any manner commonly used in preparing vegetables. [**1970** Campbell et al. *Smoky Mt Wildflowers* 60 An annual festival is held near the Smokies to celebrate this "sweetest tasting, and foulest smelling, plant that grows." In early spring its tubers have a pleasant taste of sweet spring onions, but an obnoxious garlic-like odor persists for two or three days afterward. The broad leaves, resembling those of lily of the valley, appear in April on moist, wooded slopes at elevations of 1,500 to 4,000 feet.] **1995** Williams *Smoky Mts Folklife* 96–97 While the consumption of wild greens has been common throughout much of the southern United States, the most quintessentially "mountain" of the items gathered from the wild is the ramps, which only grow at elevations of three thousand feet or more. A wild leek, ramps are gathered in late April or early May in moist, dark coves. . . . They were also consumed as a spring tonic and were traditionally served with sassafras tea. Ramps are still eaten raw or are parboiled and fried in grease, frequently with scrambled eggs. **1996** White et al. *Wildflowers* 102 Traditionally ramps were dug for food during the Zodiac sign Aries. The symbol of Aries is the ram and this plant was called "ramson." This was shortened over the years to "ramps," always plural. **2001** Joslin *Appal Bounty* 4 Ramp aficionados extol both the flavor and the health-providing benefits of the wild leek. They eat it raw, fried, baked, boiled, and roasted over an open fire. It appears in stews, scrambled eggs, fried potatoes, spaghetti sauces, and soups. Even the foreign delicacy, vichyssoise, a creamy potato and leek soup, is excellent when made from ramps. Ramp feasts range from the lone mountaineer who takes a loaf of bread and a tub of butter into the hills to eat with the raw ramps beside a cold stream, to community-wide festivals that draw participants from hundreds of miles away.

[back-formation from *ramps*, taken as a plural < Middle English *ramson(s)* < Old English *hramsan*, popular etymology sometimes erroneously associates appearance of the plant in spring with the zodiac sign of Aries, the ram]

2 See citation. See also **Melungeon.**

1963 Berry *Almost White* 18–19 A thousand [Melungeons] are found in Wise Co. [VA], where they are known as "Ramps," and they have appropriated the steep slopes for their cabins and a cornfield. *Ibid.* 35 In Wise County, Virginia, a common name for its hybrid population is "Ramps." Its origin is debatable, but the local explanation is that it comes from "rampion," a wild, onion-like plant which these people gather and eat.

rampacious *adjective* High-spirited.

1900 Harben *N GA Sketches* 100 It serves 'im right for bein' so rampacious.

ramp and rave *verb phrase* To rant and rave.

1991 Still *Wolfpen Notebooks* 122 He wants to ramp and rave and cuss everybody all to pieces, and to do everything in five minutes.

rampshion See **rimption(s)**.

rampy *adjective* See citation. See also **bitterweed milk, ragweed milk.**

1976 Dumas *Smoky Mt Speech* 26 The adjective *rampy*, meaning "strong in odor" [is] applied generally to milk or butter that tastes of garlic or wild onions.

ramrod *verb* See citation.

1952 Wilson *Folk Speech NC* 582 = to force, deceive, or overpersuade one into doing something: "The politicians have ramrodded the people into voting for this measure."

ramsack (also *ramshack, ranshack*) *verb* To ransack, search through roughly and surreptitiously, leaving items in disorder or a wreck.

c1940 Aswell *Glossary TN Idiom* 14 *ramshack* = ransack. **1966** *DARE Survey* (Spruce Pine NC) *ramsack* = to look in every possible place for something misplaced. **1975** Jackson *Unusual Words* 151 If one has *ramshacked* a place, he has left it in a complete mess; *mommicked* is a close synonym. **1995–97** Montgomery *Coll*: *ramshack* (known to Adams, Bush, Cardwell, Norris, Oliver, Weaver); *ranshack* (known to Jones).

[*ramsack* probably variant of *ransack*; DARE *ramsack* v scattered, but chiefly South, Midland]

ramshack See **ramsack.**

ramshackledy See **ramshacklety.**

ramshacklety (also *ramshackledy*) *adjective* Rickety, in bad repair.

c1960 Wilson *Coll*: *ramshacklety* = shaky, in bad repair. **1997** Montgomery *Coll*: *ramshacklety* (known to ten consultants from the Smoky Mountains). **2010** Whisnant and Whisnant *Parkway Came* [7] The house wasn't big, and the barn was sort of ramshackledy, but every time we came up the road home, we thought it was the most beautiful place anybody could ever live. **2019** *Blind Pig* (March 19) Shackledy is a perfectly good word that perfectly describes those old and no longer occupied houses back in the mountains.

[EDD *ramshackle* adj 1 "rickety, dilapidated"; Web3 *ramshackled*, past part of *ramshackle*, alteration of *ranshackle*, frequentative of *ransack*; DARE *ramshacklety* adj chiefly South, South Midland, *ramshackly* especially South, South Midland]

ramstudious *adjective* Quarrelsome, having a chip on one's shoulder.

1939 Hall *Coll* (Gatlinburg TN). [**1995** Montgomery *Coll* (unknown to consultants from the Smoky Mountains).]

[EDD *ramstugious, ramstougar* Scot "quarrelsome, heedless"; cf SND *ramstougar* adj "rough, with the implication of strength"]

ran See **run A2.**

ranch See **rinse.**

ranshack See **ramsack.**

rantankerous *adjective, adverb* Extreme(ly).

1859 Taliaferro *Fisher's River* 89 It makes me rantankerous mad to hear sich little stuff, it does. *Ibid.* 134 This scrape had made a rantankerous impression on me. **1864** Gilmore *Down in TN* 95 I'd loike ter guv them ar rantankerous rebels a leetle h—ll fust.

[Web3 *rantankerous* adj alteration of *cantankerous*]

rare[1] See **rear.**

rare[2] *verb* To rage, throw a fit; to rage at. See also **rare and pitch.**

1922 Kephart *Our Sthn High* 138 Why, if there's liquor around, and she don't git none, she jist raars! **1910** Cooke *Power and Glory* 136 I r'ared out on her for buyin' [the clothes]. **1930** Armstrong

This Day and Time 109 You ain't a-stoppin' jest to rare on me, are ye, jest to bless me out? **1931** Goodrich Mt Homespun 50 She'll be a rarin' and a ragin'. **1940** Haun Hawk's Done 42 Every time anybody set down he would rare about them killing time. Ibid. 149 Ad cussed and rared a little bit. **c1960** Wilson Coll = to get into a rage (variant of rear). **1970** Hunting Stories 34 I yelped a time or two like a hen turkey, an' he was just a'rarin' a'gobblin'. **1981** GSMNP-117:19 Well, they cussed and rared around. That boy cussed. **1990** Wigginton Foxfire Christmas 39 He got up and he was just raring that we tied his shoestrings in knots. We got him good! **1995** Montgomery Coll He rared at me all night (Cardwell). **2018** Blind Pig (May 29) I don't care who he is! I'm gonna go down there and rare him out. There ain't nobody going to do my youngun like that!

[cf OED3 rear v[1] 16c "to make (the voice) heard" obsolete; cf EDD rear v 2 6 "to behave violently or excitedly"; SND rair v 6 "to weep, cry loudly"; cf HT rair[2] n "a roar"; DARE rare v 5a chiefly South, South Midland]

rare and pitch *verb phrase* See 1969 citation.

1898 Elliott Durket Sperret 58 Granny will r'ar an' pitch if he riles her 'bout the peddlin'. **1969** Doran Folklore White Co 114 = to rant, be extremely disagreeable.

rash *noun* Especially of foodstuffs: a spate, sudden or ample supply.

1975 Jackson Unusual Words 156 A rash of meat or bacon refers usually to a large quantity. **1997** Montgomery Coll (known to Bush, Cardwell, Jones, Ledford, Norris, Weaver).

[OED3 rash n[1] 3 Scot, obsolete; EDD rash sb[2] 1 Scot, York "a row, a number of anything"]

rassel, rassell See **wrestle**.

rastus plow (also *restus plow*) *noun* A cultivating plow with three or more shovels.

1957 Broaddus Vocab Estill Co KY 62 = three-shoveled plow. **1969** DARE Survey (Sawyer KY) restus plow = a three-footed plow for cultivating; (Yates Center KY, London KY) restus (plow) = implement used to clean out weeds and loosen the earth between rows of corn.

[DARE rastus plow especially KY]

rat *noun* See citations. See also **rat house**.

1911 Shearin E KY Word-List 539 = one who peddles, or otherwise retails "moonshine" whiskey "on the sly." **1957** Combs Lg Sthn High: Word List 11 A "blind tiger" is a small, windowless log hut where whiskey is sold illegitimately. The "rat" dispenses it by means of a drawer, which one pulls out, and into which the money for the whiskey is placed. The "rat" pulls in the drawer, takes the money therefrom, puts the whiskey into the drawer, then pushes it out to the thirsty customer. Ibid. 79 = a dispenser of illicit, moonshine whiskey; bootlegger.

ratbane (also *ratsbane, rat's bane, rat's vein, rat's wing*) *noun* A tall-growing, perennial evergreen plant (*Chimaphila maculata/umbellata*) whose leaves have medicinal uses, especially as a tonic and a vermifuge.

1892 Bergen Plant Names I 100 Chimaphila maculata, ratsbane; wild arsenic. Blue Ridge, Va. **1949** Arnow Hunter's Horn 373 She wanted to give all the [children] a round of molasses and wormseed and sulphur now, and then ... some good strong tea made with life everlasting, sweet fennel, ratbane, and feverweed, for every last one of them was wormy as could be. **1970** Vincent More of Best 41 He brews it from wild "yarbs" around there, yellowroot, sarsaparilla, rat's bane, heart leaf, burdock, poplar bark, wild cherry bark, scaly hickory bark and slippery elm. [**1971** Krochmal et al. Medicinal Plants Appal 88 According to at least two authorities, this plant is used as a diuretic, tonic, and astringent.] **1975** Hamel and Chiltoskey Cherokee Plants 62 rats bane = [make] tea of leaves for colds and fever; tea for milksick; tea to make baby vomit; use to kill rats. **1979** Big South Fork OHP-9 We'd get out and we'd gather different herbs [JS: Yeah], and we'd get a lot of this here, well we always called it rat's wing. **1983** Dark Corner OHP-5A They'd take whiskey and get all kinds of herbs and roots and barks, you know, and chinaberries and the wild cherries and all that and put it in the whiskey, and rat's vein and make the medicine. **2006** Howell Medicinal Plants 124 Folk usage of pipsissewa includes combining it with mullein leaf (Verbascum thapsus) to keep children from wetting the bed, and as a spring tonic and a general energy booster. Pipsissewa root was an ingredient in traditional root beer. According to Southern folklore, pipsissewa will repel or kill rats, hence the common name "rat's bane."

[DARE ratsbane n 1 chiefly South Midland]

rat cheese *noun* Cheddar cheese.

1956 McAtee Some Dial NC 36 = cheddar cheese, [used to] bait rattraps. **c1960** Wilson Coll = facetious reference to common hoop cheese. **1976** Miller Mts within Me 77 Mr. Jack would buy himself an "RC Dope" and a "hunk o' rat cheese" from the hoop of cheddar cheese which was a staple in every country store and always occupied a prominent place on a round cutting board with a cleaver-like knife on the main counter.

rather

A *adverb*

1 Variant form ruther. See also **druther**.

1863 Woody CW Letter (Feb 15) I understand by your leter to father that you are ruther Grumbling at me for not riting. **1883** Bonner Dialect Tales 135 I ruther think I know how t' use a shotgun. **1901** Harben Westerfelt 214 I'd ruther sleep in a hay-stack ur in a barn-loft. **1922** TN CW Ques 243 (Fentress Co TN) We hav a borde that wood ruther pension a man worth 20 thousand then a pore man. **1929** (in **1952** Mathes Tall Tales 145) I'd ruther ye'd make me a offer. I'm confident ye're a squar man. **1942** Hall Phonetics Smoky Mts 26. **1970** Burton-Manning Coll-94B I'd ruther be a old time Christian than anything I know. **1972** GSMNP-92 I'd ruther have the linn gum [to make a beehive]. They're hollow a lot of the times.

2 With an overt infinitive marker to or for ... to.

1941 Still Troublesome Creek 63 I'd ruther to have a colt than a basketful o' baby chaps. **1975** Woolley *We Be Here* 41 I'd rather for him to stay out than to go in there without safety. **2008** *Rosie Hicks* 1 I'd rather for not to see Santa.

B *noun* A preference (apparently an artificial variant of **druther**, learned in the classroom).

1913 Kephart *Our Sthn High* 283 "But," she added, "a person has a rather about where he'd be put." **1997** Montgomery Coll: *rather* (known to Adams, Cardwell, Ledford, Norris).

rat house *noun* See citations. See also **blind tiger**, **rat**.

1974 Dabney *Mt Spirits* 149 Before and after the turn of the century, "rat houses" had been part of the frontier scenery—small log cabins seven or eight feet square with tiny openings next to the road. The buyer [of illegal whiskey] would pass his jug into the hole, along with his money. From the inner darkness would emerge the filled jug, with only the hand of the seller to be seen. **1982** Slone *How We Talked* 69 = a small house with a little window that had a small wooden shutter with a hole through it, through which the transaction of selling whiskey was done without the buyer seeing or hearing anyone. Sometimes a hollow tree was used for the same purpose. You left your money in the tree, went around the bend in the road, waited for a little while, came back, and looked in the hole in the tree. Your money was gone and your whiskey was there. What kept them from just keeping your money? Mountain honesty.

rations *noun* An amount of food one allots for a hunting trip or other journey.

1939 Hall *Coll* (Deep Creek NC) We'd all just fix us up a sack of rations, you know, and every fellow would take his rations up there. *Ibid.* (Deep Creek NC) I was going up to my cabin with a pack of rations on my back. **1970** *Foxfire Interviews* A-70-5 I have to build a fire every time I have anything, and I can't eat cold rations.

ratsbane, **rat's bane**, **rat's vein**, **rat's wing** See **ratbane**.

rattlebox *noun*

1 Same as **peawood**.

1927 Mason *Lure of Smokies* 28 [P]lumed peawood [is] termed "rattlebox" by the mountaineer. **1998** Montgomery *Coll* = so called because its seeds rattle on the tree before falling off (Cardwell).

2 See citation.

1991 Weals *Last Train* 88 The men who worked around the noisy, steam-powered crusher called the machine a "rattlebox," and the creek branch that tumbles into Little River there is still called Rattlebox Branch.

3 See citation.

1997 Montgomery *Coll* = a box or gourd containing rocks that could be shaken to summon a boat or ferry from the other side of the water (Oliver).

4 A nagging, loquacious woman.

1996 *BearPaw* (Fall 8) Or was [Rattlebox Creek] named for a nagging and talkative old woman (called a "rattlebox" by old timers) who lived in the area? **1997** Montgomery *Coll* (known to Adams, Bush, Cardwell, Jones, Ledford).

rattlebug *noun* Apparently a rattlesnake.

1799 (in **2008** Ellison *High Vistas* 37) Seen a very large rattlebug; attempted to kill it, but it was too souple in the heels for us.

rattlesnake-bit *past participle, adjective* Bitten by a rattlesnake. For similar forms, see **bite 2**.

1985 Irwin *Alex Stewart* 265 As luck would have it, he didn't bite through my overalls, but I'll tell you, I come might near getting rattlesnake bit.

rattlesnake master *noun*

1 (also *rattlesnake orchid*, *rattlesnake plantain*, *rattlesnake's master*) A wild orchid (*Goodyera pubescens/repens*) that produces an antidote for snakebite.

1895 Dromgoole *Humble Advocate* 328 She jest doctored herse'f on corn whiskey whiles't she ware waitin' on the rattlesnake's-master, that thar time she got herse'f bit. **1937** Thornburgh *Great Smoky Mts* 29 Other herbs and roots used by the old folks in various ways are . . . horse mint, butterfly root . . . wild indigo, yellow fringed orchid or rattlesnake master. **1973** GSMNP-6:16 There wasn't nothing but a big patch of what we call rattlesnake orchids. **1992** Toops *Great Smoky Mts* 32 Nearby are rosettes of blue-green leaves netted with white veins. The overall pattern looks much like that of a coiled timbler rattler, and for that resemblance, the downy rattlesnake plantain was named.

2 (also *rattlesnake's master*) The blazing star (*Liatris* spp), a perennial wildflower that produces an antidote for snakebite. See also **button snakeroot**, **fairy wand**, **rattlesnake root 1**.

1937 Thornburgh *Great Smoky Mts* 29–30 Another plant, blazing star or button snakeroot, *lacinaria squarrosa*, is also called rattlesnake master by the mountain people, whose knowledge of medicinal herbs has come from their ancestors and from the Cherokee Indians. **1964** Reynolds *Born of Mts* 54 One should also carry about the person a root of the plant called "rattlesnake's master," whose magic makes the rattlesnake flee in terror. **1982** Stupka *Wildflowers* 119 Other names include "devil's bit," "gayfeather," and "rattlesnake-master."

rattlesnake medicine *noun* Homemade whiskey.

1983 Pyle *CCC 50th Anniv* A:3:16 = moonshine.

rattlesnake orchid See **rattlesnake master 1**, **2**.

rattlesnake pilot *noun* The copperhead snake (*Agkistrodon contortrix*).

c1960 Wilson *Coll* = a snake that is supposed to accompany a rattlesnake. **1963** Watkins and Watkins *Yesterday* 66 Most of the snakes was copperheads, what we called rattlesnake pilots.

rattlesnake plantain See **rattlesnake master 1**.

rattlesnake root *noun*

1 The blazing star (*Liatris* spp), a perennial wildflower that produces an antidote for snakebite. See also **button snakeroot**, **fairy wand**, **rattlesnake master 2**.

1970 Campbell et al. *Smoky Mt Wildflowers* 50 The plant is also known as rattlesnake root and devil's-bit.

2 Same as **gall of the earth.**

1940 Caton *Wildflowers of Smokies* 104. **1941** Walker *Story of Mt* 49 The old man reached his bony fingers into his trouser pocket and drew out a small rattlesnake-root about an inch long, with the request that it be eaten.

3 The erect trillium (*Trillium erectum*). Same as **wake robin.**

1971 Krochmal et al. *Medicinal Plants Appal* 256 *Trillium erectum* . . . Rattlesnake root . . . The Indians of Appalachia cooked pieces of the root in food as an aphrodisiac.

4 Same as **rattletop.**

1971 Krochmal et al. *Medicinal Plants Appal* 96 Rattlesnake root . . . In Appalachia, a tea made from the root is used to treat sore throat.

rattlesnake's master See **rattlesnake master 1, 2.**

rattle staff *noun* See citation.

2007 Ball *Tub Mills* 9 The corn was gravity fed to the stones by a "shoe" under the hopper shaking against a "damsel" or "rattle staff" connected to the top of the millstone shaft.

rattletail snake *noun* A rattlesnake.

1867 Harris *Sut Lovingood* 108 Nuffin but a rattil-tail snake; he's got livin rattils. **1998** Montgomery *Coll* (known to Adams, Brown).

rattletongue *noun* A gossiper.

1949 Arnow *Hunter's Horn* 177 Before God he wouldn't show it, no more than he would show he was afraid; not before Sue Annie, and have the old rattle-tongue tell . . . that he'd been scared.

rattletop *noun* A perennial wild shrub (*Cimicifuga racemosa*) whose roots and rhizomes have medicinal uses. Same as **black cohosh.**

1970 Campbell et al. *Smoky Mt Wildflowers* 82 Other common names [for the black cohosh] include black snakeroot, rattletop, and mountain bugbane. **1971** Krochmal et al. *Medicinal Plants Appal* 96 Rattle-top . . . In Appalachia, a tea made from the root is used to treat sore throat.

rattle trap *noun* A device whose vibrations create raucous noise when swung in the air, often used by pranksters, as at a **serenade** (for its construction, see c1975 citation).

1939 Hall *Coll* (Catons Grove TN) I guess you people would like to know about serenades and how young folks got along back seventy years ago and longer. We had serenades. They'd make old big rattle traps they'd call 'em . . . My, My! How they'd rattle and bang around. **1972** Cooper *NC Mt Folklore* 34 For many decades and until stores became plentiful, the children's Christmas toys and gifts were mainly homemade. There were dolls, yarn balls, whistles, geehaw whimmydiddles or ziggerboos, rattle traps, noisemakers or bull roars and flipperdingers. **c1975** Lunsford *It Used to Be* 128 A rattletrap is made by taking a piece of hard wood, first trimming it in such a way that you can hold it in the hand. And on the end you shape the wood into a cog that is longer on one face—rather in the form of a ratchet. One side of the tooth of the cog is trimmed long, the other short. Then on the end of that cog a piece is screwed down, just tight enough till it can revolve around as you swing it. You put in three pegs in that piece—that'd be, say, an inch and a half long. You take a tough, springy white-oak strip of wood so one end will rest on the cog. And as you swing it around it will make all the noise you want. That's what they call the rattletrap. **1982** Powers and Hannah *Cataloochee* 174 I was thinking of toys we had back in the hills. . . . We had a thing, I'm not sure what it was called, but I'll call it a ratchet, it was made of wood about so long, and at one end was a kind of sprocket arrangement with a handle, and you could make that thing go around and make a lot of noise . . . [Mark Hannah:] I've seen this one, too, I could also make one. I called it a Rattle Trap.

rattleweed *noun* The goat's beard plant (*Aruncus* spp).

1893 Bergen *Plant Names II* 136 (Banner Elk NC). **1939** Hall *Coll.* **1975** Hamel and Chiltoskey *Cherokee Plants* 30 = [mix] roots in alcoholic spirits for rheumatism.

raveling bee *noun* Formerly, a work activity, often serving as a courting occasion, at which old wool is unraveled, carded, and prepared for reuse.

1991 Haynes *Haywood Home* 59 Winter clothing was made of wool and we didn't waste anything. When clothing wore out beyond mending, we cut it into small squares to be unraveled, carded, and made into batting. Often, we would have "raveling bees." These ravelings (unravelings) would be courting occasions for the young. Groups of young people would gather at a community house to unravel and card old wool. Couples would sit facing each other and the boy would unravel wool squares into the girl's lap and she would card the old wool.

raven bird *noun* A raven. See also **-bird.**

c1950 (in **2000** Oakley *Roamin' Man* 38) And we saw one ravin bird and so meny little birds we couldent count them.

rawhead and bloodybones *noun* A hobgoblin used to warn children and make them behave; a figure in ghost stories.

1955 Ritchie *Singing Family* 13 We'd . . . raise such a ruckus that Mom would send in to tell us we better settle or Old Rawhead-and-Bloodybones would get us. **1984** Burns *Cold Sassy* 89 For a moment I swelled with importance, getting talked about like that. Then for no good reason I saw myself as Raw Head and Bloody Bones, spinning into nothing under giant [train] wheels and thunder.

[DARE *rawhead and bloodybones* n chiefly South, South Midland]

rawhide *verb*

1 To carry (a heavy load) on one's back, sometimes causing the skin to chafe one's shoulders; hence verbal noun *rawhiding.*

1917 Kephart *Word-List* 416 = to carry on one's back. "I *rawhided* that sack acrost the mountain." **1939** Hall *Coll* (Smokemont NC) Can I help you rawhide them suitcases over to the car? **1956** Hall *Coll* (Big Bend NC) [The new road to Mount Sterling store] saves me a lot of rawhiding. **1961** Seeman *Arms of Mt* 15 It was no drawback to Edwin that the bluff itself would have to be blasted out to obtain a "perch" for the cabins, or that the boards would have to be "raw-hided" up the steep bank, plank by plank. **1974** Dabney *Mt Spirits* 16 Many older mountain men with crooked backs can attest to their younger days of "rawhiding" sugar and meal into tough mountain terrain and then barrels of whiskey on the opposite trip out. **1979** *Smokies Heritage* 277 After the bark was peeled it was allowed to dry. It was then loaded in sacks and rawhided from the woods to the nearest wagon road. It was . . . called "rawhiding" for a simple reason. A heavy load of tanbark in a sack was guaranteed to wear all the hide off your shoulders in the course of a day.

2 To maneuver (logs) down a steep slope; hence verbal noun *rawhiding*.

1927 Woofter *Dialect from WV* 363 = to slip logs over steep places. "The men have raw-hided all the side of the hill." **1966** Stubbs *Mountain-Wise* (Feb–March) 13 "They's four ways of gittin' big logs out of the woods. . . . A fourth way," he continued, "is rawhidin', or totin' 'em out on your shoulder if they's not too heavy. But when a feller gits through with that, his hide is raw, fer he ain't got no skin left on his shoulders."

[DARE *rawhide* v 6 Southern Appalachians]

rawhider *noun* See citation.

2006 Farwell *Logging Term* 1021 Bark crews had "spudders" and "rawhiders," who removed and stacked bark from felled trees.

rawhiding See **rawhide 1**, **2**.

razorback (also *razorback hog*, *razorback mountain hog*) *noun* A wild or semiwild hog with a long nose, protruding lower tusks, long legs, a slender body, a tough hide, and a sharp, arched back. The term formerly referred to a domestic hog allowed to range freely in the mountains in the summer months before being rounded up in the fall to be sold or butchered. More recently it has been used only for wild hogs that are a menace to other wildlife and the environment. Also called **hickory grubber**, **long rooter**, **mountain hog**, **pine rooter**, **sand digger**, **windsplitter**. See also **ridge rooter**, **Russian wild hog**.

1889 *Hogs* I forgot you'uns don't [know] nothin' of Timberlake's razorbacks . . . he bought about a dozen half-wild, long-nosed hogs we call razorbacks or sanddiggers. They are death on snakes, them hogs is, and no snake in creation kin git away from them. They've got a nose 'bout one-quarter their length; they're long-legged, wide-bodied, and thin. They kin scoot through a canebrake and git out'n sight quicker'n a rabbit, but their princip'l virtu' is in killin' snakes. **1910** Thompson *Highlanders* 31 His meat or bacon he raises himself, seldom butchering anything but a "razorback," a term suggested by the thinness of the animal and also by the length of its nose. Needless to say that this species of swine is of mixed blood. **1913** Kephart *Our Sthn High* 45–46 The mainstay of every farmer, aside from his cornfield, was his litter of razorback hogs . . . the razorback differs even more from a domestic hog than a wild goose does from a tame one. Shaped in front like a thin wedge, he can go through laurel thickets like a bear. Armored with tough hide he despises thorns, brambles, and rattlesnakes alike. In courage and sagacity, he outranks all other beasts. The razorback has a mind of his own; not instinct, but mind. He thinks. **1982** Powers and Hannah *Cataloochee* 283 They're just old razorback mountain hogs, that's all. **1986** Pederson et al. *LAGS: razorback* (Blount Co TN) *razorback*. **1989** Oliver *Hazel Creek* 24 Since they were the major source of meat, hogs (razor-back or ridge-rooters) were raised first, and allowed to run wild around the farms, fattening on acorn and chestnut mast.

razorback hog, **razorback mountain hog** See **razorback**.

razorback ridge *noun* A sharp, narrow ridge at a higher elevation of the mountains.

1922 Kephart *Our Sthn High* 231 For Sugarland Mountain is, in fact, a "razor-back" ridge, rising 1,500 feet above its corresponding valley, and running for about eight miles down the Smoky divide, without a single gap along its crest. **1986** Still *Wolfpen Poems* 32 The hills muffle the long crying, then suddenly clear / Over razor-back ridges comes a wild freshet of barking. **1995** Trout *Historic Buildings* 8 Although old and worn compared to some other mountains, the terrain is steep and rocky at the higher elevations. Razorback ridges are divided by sharp ravines, where "the sun rises at ten and sets at two."

reach *verb*

A Principal parts.

1 Variant infinitive/base form *retch*.

1930 Armstrong *This Day and Time* 153 Retch me that spoon o' yourn. **1957** Combs *Lg Sthn High: Word List* 81 = present and imperative of reach (to hand). **1974** Fink *Bits Mt Speech* 22 I tol' him to *retch* me the shovel. **c1975** Lunsford *It Used to Be* 167 "Retch" is used for "reach." "Say, Tom, retch me that there pitchfork."

2 Variant past-tense forms *re'ched*, *retch*, *retched*.

1865 (in **2000** Tipton *CW in Greasy Cove* 15 (Jan 3) We started from Tennesee fryday morning about 9 o'clock and recht here on Saturday making a distance of 56 miles in less than (2) days. **1883** Zeigler and Grosscup *Heart of Alleghanies* 61 I never hed no objections ter meetin' a varmint in a squar, stan'up fight,—his nails agin my knife, ye know; so without wunct thinkin' on gittin' outer the way, I retched fer my sticker. **1901** Harben *Westerfelt* 100 You'd better thank yore stars we re'ched you when we did. **1939** Hall *Coll* (Smokemont NC) The bear retch around and snapped the drawin' chain in two. **c1950** (in **2000** Oakley *Roamin' Man* 42) Before we retched the cabin, we saw where a large snake had crawled acrost the road near the home of the Walker Sisters. **1959** Hall *Coll* (Newport TN) I retch over and got a limb and swung down. **1969** *GSMNP-28:12* She retched down, jerked off three or four of them sassafras sprouts. **1971** *AOHP/ALC-66* I could have retched out and laid my hand on him. **1978** Reese *Speech NE Tenn* 177 *retch* = attested by 8/12 (66.7%) speakers. **1996** Landry *Coll* He retch out and wove at me.

3 Variant past-participle form *retched*.

1957 Combs *Lg Sthn High: Word List* 81 *retched* = past-tense and past-participle form. **1989** *Matewan OHP-33* I could have retched out and touched that.

[DARE *reach* v A2a, b *retch* (all three Principal parts) chiefly South, South Midland]

B To hand, stretch, pass (something) to or toward (someone).

1939 Hall *Coll* (Sugarlands TN) My father said, "Reach me the gun," so I reached him the gun and some cartridges. **1958** Campbell *Tales* 22 Now would you reach this baby down offen the nag for me and let it run to its mammy? **1969** Roberts *Greasybeard* 164 I told my wife to reach me out a sack, so she reached me out a sack. **1974** GSMNP-51:15 I reached him the ticket, and he said it'll be back in a couple of days. **1982** Slone *How We Talked* 27 *retch* = pass something. **1985** Irwin *Alex Stewart* 53 I had a half pone of cornbread, and I retched (reached) it over to him, and he retched me back two biscuits.

[DARE *reach* v B1 chiefly South, South Midland]

read *verb* To state.

c1865 *Walker CW Letters* the papers reds a grate dell a bout pese and I hope that tha[y] is Some truth in hit. **1941** Still *Troublesome Creek* 22 Hit reads in a magazine where a feller kin sell garden seeds and make a profit.

read after *verb phrase*

1 To read (a book, etc.).

1824 Knight *Letter from KY* 106–7 Some words are used, even by genteel people, from their imperfect education, in a new sense; and others, by the lower classes in society, pronounced very uncouthly . . . best book I ever read after. **1881** Pierson *In the Brush* 261 My breethrin, that's the best story of a fight I ever read after. **1917** Kephart *Word-List* 416 = to read. "You write the nicest English I ever *read after*." **1921** Campbell *Sthn Highlander* 177 For one so little versed in reading [the mountaineer] has a remarkable knowledge of the Scriptures. He loves to "read after" them, and to "study on" them. **1951** Barnwell *Our Mt Speech* Of a speaker they say, "He's the best I ever listened at" and of a writer, "He's the best I read after." **1969** Doran *Folklore White Co* 114 = to read the works of an author. **1981** Alderman *Tilson Mill* 24 The mountaineer had a special way to interpret the Scriptures. He "loved" to "read after" them and to "study on" them.

2 To read about (something).

1937 Hall *Coll* (Emerts Cove TN) I've read after them. **1939** Hall *Coll* (Emerts Cove TN) I read after it last week. **1957** Combs *Lg Sthn High: Word List* 80 = read about, concerning. Ex.: "Little Math is a mighty knowin' man, and he's a-readin atter the war."

read one's plate *verb phrase* See citation.

1940 Farr *More TN Expressions* 447 *read your plate* = an expression used to indicate the returning of thanks at the table: "Will you read your plate, Miss Mary?"

ready *adjective* See citation.

1939 Hall *Coll* (Wallands Creek TN) A ripe and meller apple they'd call ready: "This apple is ready!"

ready-roll *noun* A factory-made cigarette.

1952 Callahan *Smoky Mt Country* 170 [Footnote:] Its [= cheap tobacco's] quality was not the highest but it was the best a lot of the boys could afford, and they rolled their cigarettes from it whereas formerly they had reveled in "ready rolls." **1982** Slone *How We Talked* 26 = cigarette. **2013** Venable *How to Tawlk* 41 = commercially produced cigarette, often considered lavish among grow-it-yourself mountaineers: "Nuthin' I hate more'n hearin' a man complain about bein' broke when he's a'standin' thar a'smokin' a ready-roll."

[DARE *ready-roll* n especially South, South Midland]

real *adjective* Variant forms *rael*, *rail*, *r'al*, *rale*.

1849 Lanman *Alleghany Mts* 89 I reckon it was a little to the left—where the water poured out in a rale catarock. **1867** Harris *Sut Lovingood* 19 You never seed a rale hoss till I rid up. **1901** Harben *Westerfelt* 190 I'm glad they did no rail harm. **1923** Greer-Petrie *Angeline Doin' Society* 3–4 Lum 'lowed if Mis' Seelback had just a-thought to leave the front door onlatched . . . we could tiptoe in r'al easy. **1925** Furman *Glass Window* 153 Books is her rael poppets. **1934–47** *LAMSAS Appal* (Swain Co NC). **1937** Hall *Coll* (Mingus Creek NC) Doctor Mingus was a rale good doctor. **1942** Hall *Phonetics Smoky Mts* 14 In the language of older people, *real* and *really* are often ['reəl] and ['relɪ]. **1963** Medford *Mt People* 173 Charlotte is some 200 miles from Teaster's mountain home, and a "rale big city" to him.

[cf SND *rael*; DARE *real* adj chiefly New England, South, South Midland]

really

A *adverb* Variant forms *railly*, *raily*.

1901 Harben *Westerfelt* 9 I railly would try to have a little more pride. **c1940** Padelford *Notes* Hit's gittin raily mought nigh plumb cold. **1942** Hall *Phonetics Smoky Mts* 14 In the language of older people, *real* and *really* are often ['reəl] and ['relɪ].

B *adjective* Actual, genuine.

1976 Still *Pattern of Man* 89 I've heard you brought a gill of water from the river called Jordan. Not the really Jordan, of course. **2008** *Rosie Hicks* 3 You have to get the right kind of soil for about anything you're growing, and I guess we just didn't have that really soil to make it.

reap hook (also *reaping hook*) A curved blade with a short handle, used especially for harvesting grain or cutting grass, a sickle.

1931 Hannum *Thursday April* 63 Thursday April stood . . . still gazing at the path in the grass which Joe's reaping-hook had left. **1967** *DARE Survey* (Maryville TN) *reap hook* = tool used for cutting grain. **1986** Pederson et al. *LAGS* (Johnson Co TN) = for harvesting wheat.

[DARE *reap hook* n chiefly South, South Midland]

rear

A Variant form *rare*.

1915 Dingus *Word-List VA* 188 *rare*. **1942** Hall *Phonetics Smoky Mts* 16.

B Senses.

1 In phrase *rear up* = to grow up. See also **raise A1**.

1939 Hall Coll (Smokemont NC) I've been here in these mountains ever since I reared up, just come up.

2 In phrase *rear up* = to bring up (a child). See also **raise B1**.

1940 Oakley *Roamin'/Restin'* 15 As I was the youngest of 8 and was reared up without any mother my oldest brothers wife said she had to take the place of my mother for a few years.

3 To lift or tip up or back.

1917 (in **1944** Wentworth *ADD* 494) (sWV) He rared the hog trough up and sot it on its end. **1997** Johnson *Melungeon Heritage* 7 Most chair backs were made of a beautifully cut piece of wood fitted into grooves cut into the wooden frames. Chairs made like this were unusually strong; people would often sit on the porch, "rared back" against the wall, whittling and looking out at the road.

rear up See **rear B1**, **B2**.

reasonable *adverb* Reasonably.

1939 Hall Coll They was pleased reasonable well when they started in, but they got till they didn't like it.

recall of *verb phrase* To remember. See also **recollect of**, **remember of**.

1961 *Coe Ridge OHP-334A* The last killing that I remember or recall of is about twenty-five years ago I guess. **1963** Miller *Pigeon's Roost* (Aug 1) I recall with my dad of meeting him once on a lonely mountain road far back in the reaches of Pate Creek area on Pigeon Roost.

receipt (also *receet*) *noun* A recipe.

1968 Wilson *Folklore Mammoth Cave* 38 *receipt* = the regular word for recipe, still heard quite often. **1979** Melton *'Pon My Honor* 9 They swapped receets, remedies and quilt patterns, and then the talk finally got around to vittles. **1981** Whitener *Folk-Ways* 42 A Washday. "Receet" and Some Tales. **1997** Montgomery *Coll*: *receipt* (known to Adams, Bush, Cardwell, Ellis, Oliver, Weaver).

the recipe *noun* Homemade whiskey.

2003 Triplett *Mt Roots* 12 Moonshine whiskey had several different names among mountain folk, including . . . "the recipe."

recitation bench *noun* Formerly, a bench at the front of a schoolroom to which a teacher calls students to examine them orally.

1949 Arnow *Hunter's Horn* 139 Lee Roy, you an Ruby git up to this here recitation bench; bring your arithmetic an tablets an pencils. Now, Ruby, soon's th door opens you stand up an start sayen th fives.

recken See **reckon**.

reckon *verb*

A Variant forms *raig'n*, *recken* [see **1863** in **B**], *recon* [see **1862** in **B**], *recond*.

1862 *Martin CW Letters* (June 10) this is the best wheat Country I Recond you ever Saw. **1984** Burns *Cold Sassy* 104 You need to understand that in Cold Sassy [we] . . . say . . . raig'n for reckon.

B To suppose, wonder (whether), imagine, think, assume, expect, be of the opinion (that), believe; to judge, figure, deduce; to admit or agree, with "I reckon" being an affirmative statement or reply ranging in sense from unqualified agreement to grudging acceptance to calculated ambiguity. [Editor's note: The many nuances of this term can cause difficulty for a hearer to interpret precisely. The expression *I reckon* occurs as both a response to a direct question and as a parenthetical to lend slight emphasis or add effect, as in storytelling. The interpretation of *I reckon* and of its frequent variant *I don't reckon* is highly sensitive to context, with the pragmatics ranging from mock agreement to admission to concurrence and assertion; see 1939 citation. *Reckon* may be used to begin a statement to convey "I suppose" or "I wonder" or questions to mean "Do you think?" or "Do you know?"] See also **allow B1**, **expect B**.

1862 *Councill CW Letters* (April 27) I dont recon that you want to go vary offen that they nead to bee a gromling at you. **1863** *Griffin CW Letters* (May 9) the Brigade male boy was rested and confined for braking open leters he is to be shot i recken. **1879** Jones *Backwoods Carolina* 747 Reckon she's got a chist of clothes to go. **1902** Hubbard *Moonshiner at Home* 238 The woman's out in the field, but she'll be back in a bit to fix the boy up [for the photograph]. Reckon you ain't in no hurry. *Ibid.* 239 "Reckon you've seen these rifles that shoot steel bullets?" asked Garret. "Well, I ain't got no use for them." **1913** Kephart *Our Sthn High* 225 Whut you reckon ails me? **1930** Armstrong *This Day and Time* 17 Reckon, Ivy, you don't never hear nothin' from Jim? *Ibid.* 128 I reckon, Mr. Dillard, you-all is well. **1939** Hall Coll (Big Bend NC) I reckon that's about all I know. *Ibid.* (Deep Creek NC) They found a bee tree one evening. Some boys wanted to cut it, and did cut it, I reckon, and I told them all I wanted out of it was a little bucket of honey. . . . I don't reckon he ever found out who cut the tree. *Ibid.* (Nine Mile TN) That's all, I reckon. **1949** Justus *Toby Has Dog* 15 Reckon we'd better leave that rowdy rascal at home. **1954** Arnow *Dollmaker* 86 I don't reckon you've heared enything about Clovis. **c1959** Weals *Hillbilly Dict* 7 = agree, somewhat reluctantly. **c1960** Wilson *Coll* = to wonder: "Reckon how long he'll be gone." **1967** Fetterman *Stinking Creek* 95 They asked with open concern, "Reckon how many the preacher will get to come forward?" **1970** Madden and Jones *Ephraim Bales* 6 Being what I was, I reckon I'd have growed any place I was planted. **1971** *AOHP/ALC-4* How did people court back then? There wasn't none of this running around, I don't reckon. **1971** *AOHP/ALC-129* Now the man who cured her, reckon what he give him, [the] man'd make the medicine that cured her. **1973** GSMNP-82:13 He's the only boy I reckon a-living. **1975** Woolley *We Be Here* 9 Reckon it's gonna be like that all over again? **1976** Dwyer *Southern Sayin's* 4 = [I] wonder. "Reckon what the old man wants?" = in questions [the word is also] equivalent to (Do you) know?—Reckon who he is?—Reckon what time it is?—Reckon how he does that?—Reckon where paw is at? Reckon what the old man wants? Now reckon what he ever did that fer? I reckon how many that car will hold? **1977** Shackelford et al. *Our Appa-*

lachia 287 Hit was [1973] May since I preached any I've been so bad off, but I ain't quit, I don't reckon. **1989** *Matewan OHP*-56 He never did do any, I don't reckon. **1999** Wilkinson *Being Country* 186 I would visit friends and cousins talking nonstop using as many "reckons" and drawing out my i's as I pleased. **2004** Rash *Saints at River* 25 I reckon you all will be at the meeting? **2007** Preece *Leavin' Sandlick* 9 Reckon how she snuck out of that thar house thout a one of them little rascals hangin' to her dress tail. **2008** Terrell *Mt Lingo* "Reckon" meant "believe" and could be used to ask a question. "Reckon it's gonna rain today" was an assertion that could be turned into a question simply by adding a questioning tone: "Reckon it's gonna rain today?"

reckon as how See **as how**.

recollect *verb* Variant forms *reecolect*, *reecollect*, *ricollict*, *rickollect*. See also **recollect of**.

1901 Harben *Westerfelt* 24–25 I reecolect that the young chap 'at stood up thar so spunky all by hisse'f last night in that moonlight an' sassed all of us to our teeth was Cap. **1903** Fox *Little Shepherd* 106 I've knowed him sence he was a chunk of a boy, but I don't rickollect ever hearin' his last name. **1917** (in **1944** Wentworth *ADD* 499) (sWV) *ricollict*. **1939** Hall *Notebooks* 13:38 (White Oak NC) both [i] and [w] in first syllable. **1942** Hall *Phonetics Smoky Mts* 21 [rɪk-]. **1957** Wise *Mt Speech* 311 rickollect, not ree-collect. **1961** *Coe Ridge OHP*-336A The first man that ever lived on that ridge was old man John Jeff Webb. I reecollect that now. My mother told me that, a white man.

recollection *noun*

A Variant form *reecollection* (with vowel [i]) [see **1939** in **B**].

B Memory; the period of time that one can remember (thus *in my recollection* = as far back as or fully as I can remember).

1937 Hall *Coll* (Emerts Cove TN) My recollection ain't so good as it used to be. **1939** Hall *Coll* (Gatlinburg TN) She's quare now and doesn't have good reecollection. *Ibid.* (Smokemont NC) Hit's been away before any of our reecollection, away back before the Sixty-Five War. *Ibid.* (Smokemont NC) My father said they was lots of deers. If my father killed ary 'un, hit was before my reecollection.

recollect of *verb phrase* To remember. See also **recall of**, **remember of**.

1915 Hall *Autobiog Claib Jones* 3 I can recollect as a boy of seeing deer and turkeys in long droves all over the woods.

recomember *verb*

A Variant forms *reecomember*, *riccomember*.

1957 Combs *Lg Sthn High: Word List* 80 *reecomember* (also *riccomember*) = remember, or recollect, from which two words [i.e. *recall* and *remember*] it is a scrambled but much used form.

B To remember.

1915 Dingus *Word-List VA* 188 *recomember* = combination of recollect and remember. **1976** Garber *Mountain-ese* 74 I can't recomember whether I shut the door or not. **1984** *Six Hill 'n Holler* 11 = recall, or remember: "I recommember [sic] the flood of '50." **1995–97** Montgomery *Coll* (known to Cardwell, Jones, Norris, Oliver).

[DARE *recomember* v chiefly South, South Midland]

recomembrance *noun* A remembrance, memory.

1984 *Six Hill 'n Holler* 1 If you have special recollections (recommembrances [sic]) of other such talk, please drop me a line and in some future edition I will try to include it.

recommend *verb*

A Variant form *reecommend*, *recommind* [see **1908** in **B**].

1942 Hall *Phonetics Smoky Mts* 21 [rik-].

B To report, consider.

1908 Smith *Reminiscences* 420 Rattlesnakes ain't half as bad as they're recomminded to be. **1997** Montgomery *Coll*: *reecommend* (known to Adams, Bush, Cardwell, Oliver, Weaver).

recommind See **recommend**.

recon, **recond** See **reckon**.

red See **redd**.

red back speller *noun* An elementary spelling book used in mountain schools in the early 20th century. See also **blue back(ed) speller**.

1973 *GSMNP*-78:21 The little class memorized the longest word I believe in the red back speller. We didn't study the blue back.

red bone (also *red bone hound*) *noun* A hunting dog with predominantly red markings, much used to tree raccoons and chase foxes.

1938 Hall *Coll* (Emerts Cove TN) = medium sized and red, about the color of a sorrel horse. **1949** Arnow *Hunter's Horn* 148 Hounds can git awful sick. I had one—an old red-bone, down for a week. **1949** Hall *Coll* (Del Rio TN) Mix a red bone and a feist, and he'll make a good tree dog. . . . A beagle hound is a hound dog. A hound dog is a good hunter, a tree dog. A red bone hound is a tree dog, runs foxes, but not like Walkers. **1957** Woodbridge *Hunting Terms* 156 *redbone hound* = strain of southern hound, now used almost exclusively for coon and possum hunting. A fine tree dog. **1975** *Foxfire III* 38 I had a good stock a'dogs—blue tick and redbone mix, and black and tan.

[DARE *red bone* n 2 chiefly South, South Midland]

redbud land *noun* An area where redbud trees abound, indicating that it is rich in limestone and thus has good soil.

1984 Wilder *You All Spoken* 134 = rich but rocky soil. **1986** Pederson et al. *LAGS* = attested by 4/60 interviewees (6.7%) from E TN; 4/4 of all LAGS interviewees (100%) attesting term were from Appalachia (Campbell Co TN, Greene Co TN, Sevier Co TN). [**1997** Montgomery *Coll* (unknown to consultants from the Smoky Mountains).]

redbud winter *noun* See 1982 citation. For terms describing a similar phenomenon, see **blackberry winter**.

1940 Still *River of Earth* 127 "Even come spring," grandma said, "we've got a passel of chills to endure: dogwood winter, redbud, service, foxgrape, blackberry. . . . There must be seven winters, by count. A chilly snap for every time of bloom." **1982** Slone *How We Talked* 98 = a few cold days in April when the redbuds bloom. **2005** Hicks *Blood and Bone* 68 April seeps into my coat, bites my fingers, stings my eyes / Redbud Winter falling hard.

redbug (also *red devil*) *noun* A reddish mite (*Trombicula* spp) that burrows under the skin, causing it to rise and itch. [Editor's note: This term predominates mainly in the Deep South, while its equivalent *chigger* is found mainly in the Upper South and Appalachia.]

1986 Pederson et al. *LAGS*: *redbug* (Blount Co TN, Cocke Co TN). **1992** Bush *Dorie* 25 The pinpoint-sized red devil—the chigger—was subdued by thick, brown tobacco juice, too. **1997** Montgomery *Coll*: *redbug* known to some consultants from the Smoky Mountains, but uniformly recognized as less common than *chigger*.

red coonroot *noun* Same as **bloodroot**.

1968 *Sang Signs* 50 Bloodroot . . . is the "red-coonroot" of the mountains.

redd (also *red, redden, redden up, redd up, reddy up, red off, red out, red up, ridden, rid up*) *verb, verb phrase* To clean, tidy, arrange, or straighten (a room, one's person, one's bed, etc.). See 1933, 1940 citations.

1886 Smith *Sthn Dialect* 349 They all have the authority of old or dialect English, or many of them belong to all parts of the South, if not elsewhere . . . red (to put in order—as, "red a room"). **1913** Kephart *Our Sthn High* 83 Then that tidal wave of air swept by. The roof settled again with only a few shingles missing. We went to "redding up." **1924** Raine *Saddlebags* 207 I hain't had time to redd my hair. **1930** (in **1952** Mathes *Tall Tales* 168) This bit of social and domestic philosophy brought no audible response from the busy wife, who was briskly "ridding up" the bed. **1933** Carpenter *Sthn Mt Dialect* 25 In central and northern West Virginia *rid* is used for ARRANGE or PUT IN ORDER. One hears We'd better rid up the house, Let's rid things up while we have a chance, and similar expressions. South of West Virginia the word is *red*. **c1940** Aswell *Glossary TN Idiom* 15 *red up* = tidy, clean. "She red up the house for the family reunion." **1943** Goerch *Down Home* 30 *red out* = to clean out or sort: "I'm going to red out this trunk." **1952** Wilson *Folk Speech NC* 583 *redd the hair* . . . To comb the hair. **c1959** Weals *Hillbilly Dict* 7 Red off the table right atter we eat. **1966** *DARE Survey* (Burnsville NC, Spruce Pine NC) *redd up* = to put a room in order. **1976** Braden *Grandma Was Girl* 110 *redden* = straighten or clean up a room or table. **1976** Garber *Mountain-ese* 74 *reddy-up* = tidy up, make neat: "Let's all get busy and reddy-up the kitchen dishes." **1979** Dressman *Redd Up* 142 [According to DARE, beyond the core area in western PA] a few users of *redd* are also found in western Virginia, central and southern West Virginia, western North Carolina, and eastern Tennessee. **1982** Slone *How We Talked* 20 *redden up the house* = making it ready for company. The daily chores; sweeping, dusting, making the beds. **1993** Stuart *Daughter* 236 *ridden the table* = to clear the eating table.

[*redd* < Middle English *redden*, probably < Middle Low German/Middle Dutch *reden*; OED3 *redd* v[2] 4a "to put in order, to make tidy" chiefly Scot, Irish English (north), English regional (north and midland), and U.S. regional (chiefly north Midland); SND *redd* v[1] 7(1) "of a room, building: to tidy (up), set in order" and *rid up* (at *rid* v 6); CUD *redd*[1] v 2 "clear, tidy up," *rid* 1 "set in order"; Web3 *redd* vt 2 chiefly dialect; DARE *redd* v 3a, b scattered, but chiefly North Midland, especially Pennsylvania, 3c especially Appalachians]

redden, redden up See **redd**.

reddening comb (also *redding comb, redding-out comb, reddying-comb*) *noun* A comb for removing tangles from one's hair. See also **tucking comb**.

1886 Smith *Southernisms* 42 Redding-comb, or reddying-comb, that is, the comb used to clear out the hair when tangled and long, as "Where's the reddin'-comb? I want to do up my hair." It is the opposite of tuck-comb. It is used in East Tennessee. **1923** Greer-Petrie *Angeline Steppin' Out* 5 He wanted me to git out me red'n comb and see if I couldn't fix my ha'r like them city wimmen was a-wearin' theirn. **1940** Bowman *KY Mt Stories* 245 *reddin'-out comb* = an ordinary comb. **1982** Slone *How We Talked* 21 A "reddin' comb" was of larger teeth or prongs. It was used to get the tangles from the hair, while the fine comb was used to get bugs from the hair. **1985** Kiser *Life and Times* 26 There were two combs, a "coarse" or "reddening" comb (for everyday combing), and a "fine" comb (for the unfortunates who picked up crawlers (head lice) in school).

[cf SND *red-kaim* (at *redd* v[1] 6(3)) "a comb for the hair"; cf Web3 *redd* vt 1b "unravel, disentangle"]

red devil See **redbug**.

red devil wasper *noun* See citation.

2015 *Blind Pig* (May 5) I have and my family has always called the red wasp the "red devil wasper."

redding comb, redding-out comb See **reddening comb**.

red dog *noun* See 1973, 2007 citations.

1973 Kahn *Hillbilly Women* 205 Now the hollow has no hard road. When they finished stripping in it they put "red dog" on it. That's the old slag that burns in the slate dumps. They covered the road with that. **1989** Giardina *Storming Heaven* 211 After singing, the women departed for the trains, blew on their gloved fingers as they stumbled over chunks of red dog in their heeled shoes, grimaced when they twisted their ankles. **2007** *Mining Terms* = a nonvolatile combustion product of the oxidation of coal or coal refuse. Most commonly applied to material resulting from in situ, uncontrolled burning of coal or coal refuse piles. It is similar to coal ash.

[DARE *red dog* n chiefly western PA, WV, OH]

redd up See **redd.**

reddying-comb See **reddening comb.**

reddy-up See **redd.**

redeye *noun* Low-quality whiskey, so named for its effect on the drinker.

1864 Gilmore *Down in TN* 185 They obtain plentiful supplies of a vile fluid, which is compounded of log-wood, strychnine, juniper berries, and alcohol, and "circulates" among them under the appropriate names of "Tangle-foot," "Blue-ruin," "Red-eye," "Bust-head," and "Knock-'em-stiff." **1952** Wilson *Folk Speech NC* 583 = very strong inferior whisky. **1970** Mull *Mt Yarns* 73 White lightning, "red eye," "stump water," or "sugar head," as blockade liquor is called locally, has never been considered a crime or illegal. **1972** Hall *Sayings* 101 Common expressions about 1941 for whisky illegally manufactured were . . . "headache medicine" (with veiled meaning), "screw top," "snake juice," [and] "red eye." **1973** Davis *'Pon My Honor* 100 = strong fiery liquor. **1986** Pederson et al. *LAGS* (Cocke Co TN, Sevier Co TN). **1995** Montgomery *Coll* (known to Shields).

red-eye gravy (also *red gravy*) *noun* Unthickened gravy made by adding coffee or water to the grease of ham fried in a cast-iron skillet. Also called **bay sop, frog-eye.**

1942 Robertson *Red Hills* 66 Hominy was such a good food, eaten with butter or with sliced tomatoes or with red gravy, and it was so cheap. **1957** Chiles and Trotter *Mt Makin's* Red eye gravy—when you fry ham, let it burn on the skillet a little; use a little water or coffee. **1978** Montgomery *White Pine Coll* IX-2 Red-eye gravy, they don't get that out of a fresh ham. **2005** Williams *Gratitude* 518 = When meat is fried, there are small browned bits stuck to the pan. While the pan is hot, some coffee is poured in, and the boiling loosens the bits, incorporating them into the liquid. This is *redeye gravy*. **2016** Netherland *Appal Cooking* 134 Red-eye gravy is made using water or coffee, add it it to the skillet after frying and browning the ham slices. Characteristic of this gravy is the red "eye" of the dark liquid and browned bits surrounded by lighter liquid. The red eye is more evident using water than coffee though many people prefer the taste of coffee in their red-eye gravy.

[DARE *red-eye gravy* n chiefly South, South Midland, *red gravy* n 1 chiefly South, South Midland]

red-fox tail *noun* A type of **sorghum cane.**

1955 Parris *Roaming Mts* 160 I've been trying one called red-fox tail and it's might nigh as good as honey-drip. **1995–97** Montgomery *Coll* = a type of milo, a low-growing feed grain with red seeds, its heads when ripe resembling fox tails (Brown).

red gravy See **red-eye gravy.**

red heart *noun* See 1997 citation.

1969 GSMNP-25:2:20 I believe pine was called red hearts. That was in next to the heart where it's doted. **1997** Montgomery *Coll* = fat rich pine, good for burning even if the remainder of the wood has rotted (Cardwell).

red hives See **bold hives 1.**

red horse *noun* An American sucker, a fish of the family *Catostomidae.*

1849 Lanman *Alleghany Mts* 65 On inquiring of a homespun angler what fish the river did produce, he replied: "Salmon, black trout, red horse, hog-fish, suckers, and cat-fish." **1939** Hall *Coll* (Waldens Creek TN) The creek was full of fish—bass, white suckers, silversides, red horses, hog mollies in the creek. **1966–68** *DARE Survey* (Brasstown NC, Cherokee NC) = fresh-water fish not good to eat. **2007** Milnes *Signs Cures Witches* 36 "Red horse," an edible kind of sucker or fish that are "gigged" for food, always "run" upstream in spring.

red Indian paint *noun* Same as **bloodroot.**

[**1971** Krochmal et al. *Medicinal Plants Appal* 226 [The juice] is an emetic, laxative, and emmenagogue; and because of its expectorant qualities, it has been used to treat chronic bronchitis. This plant is used both as a pain reliever and a sedative. When combined with oak bark, the roots give a red dye. In Appalachia, a piece of bloodroot is sometimes carried as a charm to ward off evil spirits.] **1982** Stupka *Wildflowers* 39 Among its other names [for bloodroot] are "puccoon-root" and "red Indian paint."

red in the comb *adjective phrase* Eager to marry.

[**1941** Stuart *Men of Mts* 293 W'y Lottie lost her man about two years ago. Her comb has been red ever since.] **1968–69** *DARE Survey* = (Adams KY, Cumberland Gap TN, Wytheville VA) = said of a man; (Adams KY) = said of a woman.

red laurel *noun* An evergreen rhododendron (*Rhododendron catawbiense*) that usually has purplish flowers. Same as **catawba rhododendron.** See also **laurel, rhododendron.**

1935 Sheppard *Cabins in Laurel* 215 Everyone wears his best clothes, and the woman and children carry flowers—"ivy" (mountain laurel) and "red laurel" (red rhododendron) just breaking the tight bud, lemon lilies, sweet peas, every flower in bloom at the season. **1937** Hall *Coll* (Cosby Creek TN) We have red laurels and white laurels here in the mountains. **1944** Hayes *Word-List NC* 35 Red laurel (when purple) . . . Rhododendron.

red light *noun* A traffic light.

1992 Brooks *Sthn Stuff* 126 = a traffic light, whether it's red, green, or yellow at the time mentioned. "Naow, you be caiful, Puddin', when you come to that red light up theah. Don't you dayuh cross till it's turned grain." **2005** Williams *Gratitude* 306 The town of Andrews had three red lights (traffic lights).

[DARE *red light* n 2 scattered, but chiefly South, South Midland, PA]

red liquor (also *red whiskey*) *noun* Legal whiskey with a reddish tint achieved by aging or additives.

1913 Kephart *Our Sthn High* 137 A slick-faced dude from Knoxville ... told me once that all good red-liquor was aged, and that if I'd aged my blockade it would bring a fancy price. Well sir, I tried it; I kept some for three months—and, by godlings, it ain't so. **1967** Fetterman *Stinking Creek* 152 Red whiskey costs $2 a half pint. **1984** High *Titan Rock* 49 At that time all legal liquor was called government liquor, because it was taxed. It was also called red liquor, because they colored it.

red men *noun* A secret vigilante group of citizens in West Virginia who ostensibly sought to enforce public order and morality by intimidating or punishing alleged offenders by rendering extrajudicial punishment; hence verb *red-man* = to render such judgment. See also **White Cap**.

[**1892** Cushing *Story of Post Office* (DARE) 354 There was ... an organization in West Virginia called "Red Men," who were banded together for certain purposes known only to themselves.] **1975** Gainer *Witches Ghosts Signs* 15 *red-man* = to punish without legal process, by vigilante organization: "They red-manned Si Tenner because he was allus beatin' his wife."

red nose *noun* See citations.

1911 Shearin *E KY Word-List* 539 = discouragement, the "blues," [from the verb meaning] to be downcast or discouraged. **1957** Combs *Lg Sthn High: Word List* 80 = the "blues."

red oak *noun* An oak (*Quercus rubra*) whose bark has medicinal uses.

1956 Hall *Coll* (Big Bend NC) One time [Aunt Nancy] had bone arsiplas. Old man Joe Packett started to get some red oak bark to make some ooze to draw her arm. **c1984** Dennis *Smoky Mt Heritage* 7 Strained Muscle: Use a poultice of red oak ooze.

red off, red up See **redd**.

red root *noun*

1 Same as **bloodroot**.

1971 *AOHP/ALC-4* It's a red root some people call it, but we always called it puccoon root.

2 New Jersey tea (*Ceanothus* spp), a common shrub that grows at lower and middle elevations of the mountains, from which are derived a medicinal tea and a dye.

1901 Lounsberry *Sthn Wild Flowers* 330 [I]n the autumn the dark red roots are collected, not only for the cinnamon coloured dye they yield, but also to be used as a curative for diseases of the spleen. Then in such enormous quantities do the mountaineers drink the decoction that by a native doctor I was told they often produce inflammation of that organ. **1941** Walker *Story of Mt* 59 The commonest shrub, perhaps, is New Jersey tea or red-root which grows profusely on the summit as well as on both sides of the mountain. Its creamy white flowers appear in May and June and are soft and fluffy. They are arranged on an umbrellalike cluster on the end of a long stem which grows from a leaf axil.

red snake See **snake A1**.

red-stemmed ivy *noun* See citation.

2017 *Blind Pig* (May 13) A local name in northeast GA for Piedmont (or Carolina) rhododendron is "red-stemmed ivy." On casual acquaintance it looks much like ivy.

red whiskey See **red liquor**.

red wiggler *noun* A type of earthworm.

1997 Montgomery *File* (known to 60-year-old man, Maggie Valley NC).

redworm *noun*

1 A common earthworm.

1934–47 *LAMSAS Appal* (Madison Co NC, Swain Co NC). **1938** Stuart *Dark Hills* 60 When the red worms came to the top of the ground around the hog pen it was time to go fishing. **1949** Kurath *Word Geog East US* 74–75 *Red worm* is the usual expression in the mountains of North Carolina and the adjoining parts of Virginia, West Virginia, and Kentucky, and relics of it occur in Pennsylvania, which may be the original home of this term. **1958** Newton *Dialect Vocab* = common term in E TN mountains for an earthworm. **1966** Dakin *Vocab Ohio River Valley* 393 *Red-worm* is common in all of Kentucky except the Bluegrass and is regular in the Mountains. **1971** *AOHP/ALC-4* Fishing worms they call them now, and they called them redworms. **1980** *Smokies Heritage* 171 Bait was whatever they could find. "Red worm, grasshoppers and black crickets," said Walter Cole. **2002** Rash *Foot in Eden* 188 It was strange how he said it, so calm and matter-of-fact, like we were going to go dig up some redworms for fishing.

[DARE *redworm* n 1 scattered, but chiefly South, South Midland]

2 An edible wild green.

c1950 Adams *Grandpap* 193 Sanging our way back home, in the cool of the afternoon, we'd gather Mammy's apron full of crowsfoot and redworms and Mammy would wilt them down in hot grease for supper. We never had any trouble with [identifying] the redworms as they are very distinctive plants.

reecolect, reecollect See **recollect**.

reecollection See **recollection**.

reecomember See **recomember**.

reecommend See **recommend**.

reelfoot *noun* A clubfoot or similar defect that causes a twisted gait.

1863 *Cathey CW Letter* (Jan 19) I am realfooted, James, Wm Cathys son. **1913** Kephart *Our Sthn High* 108 [The bear "Old Reelfoot"] got his name from the fact that he "reeled" or twisted his hind feet in walking, as some horses do, leaving a peculiar track.

reference *noun* See citation.

1977 Shackelford et al. *Our Appalachia* 47 In the [church] minute book you find that after the regular service was over, the moderator—every church had a moderator: he could be a preacher, or he could be just a regular member—would "open the doors," as they called it. There were two reasons to open the doors of the church: to find out whether there were any people being charged for misconduct in the community; or whether there was anybody who wanted to join the church. The parlance of the church was a "reference": "Are there any references?"

regular *adjective*

A Variant forms *ragler, raglur, reg'lar.*

1925 (in **1935** Edwards *NC Novels* 87) *reg'lar.* **1942** Hall *Phonetics Smoky Mts* 20 [æ] is common also in . . . *regular.* **1991** Thomas *Sthn Appal* 79 After he growed up, an' years later, he got t' be a rag-lur fisherman.

B *adverb* Regularly.

c1841 Shane (in **1998** Perkins *Border Life* 196) The men carried their guns to meeting, as regular as the congregation met. **1861** *Odum CW Letter* (Oct 18) I cant hear from my dear little children regular and it nearly kills me for I am sick. **1864** *Poteet CW Letters* (Jan 12) we dont get the mail regular. **1952** Giles *40 Acres* 59–60 Hit wouldn't be expected that you could play an' sing like them that follers it regular. **1973** GSMNP-88:26 I believe that the Indians kept this whole valley burned off regular. **c1986** (in **2015** Yarrow *Voices* 83) I go regular to union meetings.

relation *noun* One's relatives collectively.

1862 *Carter CW Letters* (July 27) Deare family are you are Any of My relatioun thinking of mee.

relative *noun* See citation.

1942 Hall *Phonetics Smoky Mts* 61 *Relatives* is sometimes (but not frequently) stressed [rɪ'leɪtɪvz].

relay arm *noun* See citation.

1974 Maurer and Pearl *KY Moonshine* 123 = the connection between the relay barrel and the still through which heated beer is piped.

relay barrel *noun* See citations.

1972 *Foxfire I* 315 = fifty gallon barrel with connections for the cap arm, relay arm, and long thump rod. Catches "puke" from the still during boiling and conveys it back into the still. **1974** Maurer and Pearl *KY Moonshine* 123 Relay barrel or keg . . . A large scale puker combined with a preheater arrangement for preheating beer and charging the still.

remember *verb* To remind.

1862 *Neves CW Letters* (May 1) I take the opportunity of writing you a few lines this evning to remember you of your old friends once more. **1941** Stuart *Men of Mts* 28 Now remember it to me when I get into office. **1952** Wilson *Folk Speech NC* 583 = to remind.

remember of *verb phrase* To recall, have memory of. See also **recall of, recollect of.**

1922 *TN CW Ques* 1098 I remember of one instance where town men ran for conty sherif and the non slaveholder beat the slave holder with a big majority. **1939** Hall *Coll* (Copeland Creek TN) I never can remember of having a pair of shoes till I was big enough to go to the Birds Branch. *Ibid.* (Emerts Cove TN) I can remember as far back as eighteen hundred and sixty-five. I can remember of seeing the soldiers at the close of the Civil War. **1956** Hall *Coll* (Gatlinburg TN) I can't remember of ever cooking [grits]. **1974** GSMNP-51:18 We didn't pay much attention to the Fourth of July, as I remember of, but we did look out for Christmas. **1978** Montgomery *White Pine Coll* VI-1 I don't remember of any of us that went on to college having any trouble when we got there. **1989** *Matewan OHP*-102 I can't remember of a doctor coming to our house but one time. **1997** GSMNPCOHP-3:13 Not any that I remember of. **2012** Milnes *Signs Cures Witchery* I remember of seeing that old lady just very dimly.

[OED3 (at *remember* v 7a) chiefly U.S. regional; SND (at *remember* v 1)]

remembrance *noun* (One's) memory.

1979 Carpenter *Walton War* 152 "The best I can find out, he has lost his remembrance." "Remembrance" here carried a lot more meaning than memory would have. This man meant his uncle had lost his mind.

rench See **rinse.**

renter *noun* A sharecropper who rents all or part of a farm, using his own equipment and livestock and paying an agreed portion of the crop as rent. See also **cropper.**

1939 Hall *Coll* (Cataloochee NC) Renters—they don't call 'em sharecroppers around here. **1942** Robertson *Red Hills* 164 In our state only a third of the farmers owned their own land. A third were renters, a third were croppers. **1956** Hall *Coll* (Waynesville NC) After receiving the report of the bear size, he got Jack Williamson, who was a renter on his farm. **1957** Broaddus *Vocab Estill Co KY* 63 = a sharecropper. **c1960** Wilson *Coll* = a tenant farmer who uses the implements and stock of his employer and gets a certain percentage of the crops for his own, the rest going as rent. Usually he is distinguished from the renter, who uses his own tools and stock. **1977** Shackelford et al. *Our Appalachia* 325 [The government] cut down on tobacco allotments on some of the farms and a lot of my relatives were renters so you only got a part of what you were growing anyway.

report (also *report on, report up*) *verb, verb phrase* See citations.

1949 Maurer *Argot of Moonshiner* 12 (or *report on*) = to inform the law as to a liquor violation: "He reported on me." **1983** *Dark Corner OHP*-28A He got to reporting them up, and . . . they got it in for him, and they just pulled up his cotton and his corn one night.

reporter *noun* One who informs authorities about the location of an illegal **still.**

1895 Wiltse *Moonshiners* 10 W. A. Roper was a "reporter"—or was suspected of being one—and as has been previously said, "reporter" is the name nearly always used by the moonshiners to designate people who inform the revenue officers of their performances and sometimes conduct them to the stills. **1974** Dabney *Mt Spirits* 77 Few dared to become a "reporter"—an informer—for fear of having his stock slaughtered and/or his barns and home burned. **1985** Dabney *More Mt Spirits* 28 A reporter's the low-downdest white man that's ever drawed a breath. **1997** Montgomery *Coll* = an informer, especially against a person making illegal whiskey (Andrews). **c1999** Sutton *Me and Likker* 105 = the most low down low life son of a bitch they are.

report on, report up See **report.**

rernt See **ruin A.**

resemble *verb* To recognize.

c1940 Simms *Coll* Look, you can resemble (recognize) Old Round Top in the distance. [**1995** Montgomery *Coll* (unknown to consultants from the Smoky Mountains).]

residenter *noun* An older inhabitant of the mountains, especially a native or an early settler in a given locality.

1788 *French Broad Petitions* 213 A land office shall be opened for that purpose of entering such lands, that is to each settler or residenter a survey of six Hundred and forty Acres att as low Rates as possible. **1788** *Greene Petition* 10 It is therefore the Earnest prayer of your petitioners that your Au[gu]st Body would take our distressed and local Situation under your Wise Consideration and grant us a Preference to our claims to land When a land office Shall be opened for the purpose of Entring Such lands, that is to Each Settler or Residenter a Survey of Six Hundred And forty Acres. **1938** Stuart *Dark Hills* 250 Some of them snakes was old residenters. They was so old they was scaly. **1939** Hall *Coll* (Nine Mile TN) This here's the old residenter and bear hunter. **1973** Foster *Walker Valley* 9:59 The old man John Huskey was the oldest residenter that I knew that lived up here. **1975** Dial *Yesterday's Lg* 93 = a resident, usually one who has resided in a locality for a long time. **1995** Mullins *Road Back* 56 That was the biggest rattlesnake that I ever saw. He was an old residenter timber rattler—the meanest kind of snake there is.

[OED3 *residenter* n 2 Scot, Irish English, U.S.; SND *residenter* (at *resident* v) "a resident, inhabitant, generally one of long standing"; CUD *residenter* n 1 "someone who has resided for a long time in a locality"; HT *resydenter* "resident"]

resolute around *verb phrase* See citation.

1917 Kephart *Word-List* 416 = to persevere: "To keep the hogs from resolutin' around."

rest *verb*

A Variant verb third-singular form of two syllables: *rest-es*. See also **-es**[2].

1973 GSMNP-79:1:18 Some of his relatives have put a little stone up there now and his name on it where we know our great grandfather restes on the hillside overlookin' his Sugarlands.

B In phrase *rest your hat* = take off your hat.

1895 Edson and Fairchild *TN Mts* 374 Won't you come in and rest your hat?

restes See **rest A.**

restes plow See **rastus plow.**

restingest *adjective* Most restful. See also **-est 1** and Grammar and Syntax §3.4.1.

1916 Schockel *KY Mts* 129 Law me, Honey, I'm glad to be back from the plains. Wooded mountains make the restinest place to lay your eyes on.

resting powder *noun* An opiate or analgesic. Same as **easing powder.**

1917 Kephart *Word-List* 416 = [same as] easin' powder. **1992** Jones and Miller *Sthn Mt Speech* 103 = a sedative. **1996–97** Montgomery *Coll* (known to Brown, Bush, Cardwell).

resty *adjective* Suitable for resting, restful, commodious.

c1940 Simms *Coll* This shore is a nice, resty place. **1997** Montgomery *Coll* (known to Adams, Bush, Cardwell, Jones).

[*rest* n + *-y* adj forming suffix]

rest your hat See **rest B.**

resume *verb* See c1926 citation.

c1926 Cox *Cullowhee Wordlist* = to bring in, as "Resume the breakfast into the dining room." **1997** Montgomery *Coll* (known to Brown, Bush).

retch, retched See **reach A.**

retreat mining *noun* See citation. Same as **robbing pillars.**

1990 (in **2012** Portelli *They Say* 141) The last job was the most dangerous, "robbing pillars" or "retreat mining." After an area is mined out, the pillars of coal that hold up the roof are pulled down, capturing the last fragments of usable coal and collapsing the roof as the men withdraw as fast as they can.

return thanks over the table (also *turn thanks over the table*) *verb phrase* To say the blessing at the beginning of a meal. See citation.

1953 Davison *Word-List Appal* 14 *'turn thanks over the table* = to say grace: "Miss Smith, will you 'turn thanks over the table?" Rock Creek, Mitchell Co., N.C. **2009** Whaley *Stoney Creek* 59 Now, honey, jist come right over here and be real quiet while the preacher turns thanks.

[DARE *return thanks* v chiefly South, South Midland]

revengement *noun* See citation.

1957 Combs *Lg Sthn High: Word List* 81 = revenge. "He'll breed revengement and a scourge for me."—I Henry IV, III, ii.

revenoo, revenooer See **(the) revenue.**

(the) revenue (also *revenoo, revenooer, revenoor, revenue law, revenue man, revenue officer, revenuer*) *noun* An agent from the US Bureau of Alcohol, Tobacco, and Firearms, the federal agency enforcing regulations on the distillation of liquor; such agents collectively. Also called **(the) Federal**. See also **still raider**.

1881 Atkinson *After Moonshiners* 33 If a strange personage is found by the moonshiners, or their friends, wandering around through the mountains, without any ostensible business, he is at once regarded as a "Revenue," and is at once informed that it is not at all safe for him to be prowling around alone; consequently, the best thing he can do is to leave for home, and at once, too. He may protest innocence as long and as loudly as he pleases, but he utterly fails to impress his auditors, in any other manner than that he is a Government spy.... Many an innocent party has been given but a very few minutes to get out of a neighborhood and assured that unless he obeyed, without delay, and if ever seen in that locality again, his body would be placed where even the vultures could not find it. **1892** Doak *Wagonauts Abroad* 56 He'll take you-uns fer the "revenues," but I reckon I kin keep him from shootin'. **1895** Wiltse *Moonshiners* 49 In moonshiner parlance, the revenue officers whose duties are to make seizures of property and arrests of persons are always, "The Revenues." They are marshals, deputy marshals, raiding deputy collectors, and posse men. **1902** Hubbard *Moonshiner at Home* 234 Dave had been "stillin'" over on the other side, but he'd decided to turn revenue and was expectin' his commission then. **1912** Mason *Raiding Moonshiners* 199 Our suspect, unaware of the presence of the "revenuers," was endeavoring to "pull" his outfit and get away before their arrival. **1913** Kephart *Our Sthn High* 170 You wunt find ary critter as has a good word to say for the revenue. *Ibid.* 171 He knows there'd be another revenue "murdered." **1935** Sheppard *Cabins in Laurel* 97 From his nine years as a "revenue" he had a good practical knowledge of every nook and cranny of the mountains from Virginia to Georgia. **1937** Hall *Coll* (Cades Cove TN) The state officers [in liquor control were] stricter than the revenue. **1937–41** Hall *Coll* (TN, NC) Shoot him, pappy, he's a revenuer—he's got shoes on. (a popular saying). **1939** Hall *Coll* (Cades Cove TN) I was about thirteen, fourteen years old and got word that the revenuers were coming, and so this uncle, he was scared, but decided to run the liquor anyway. *Ibid.* (Waldens Creek TN) Back thirty to forty years ago they moonshined up and down through here.... Revenue officers, officers of the law, they were federal or government men. They'd take [the moonshiner] down to Sevierville and take him before a commission. **1953** Hall *Coll* (Deep Creek NC) Patterson used to be a revenue officer ... I did dabble with whiskey away back before I was married. **1959** Roberts *Up Cutshin* 67 I peeped out in that old field, and there was one of them revenues, so close to me I could see him but his eyes. **1962** Hall *Coll* (Del Rio TN) Most revenuers are ex-moonshiners. **1963** Carson *History Bourbon* 110 All strangers were assumed to be with the "revenue," which often put a lumber buyer, mule dealer, or folklorist collecting ballads in a situation of potential danger. **1963** Hooper *Unwanted Boy* 225 In the background stood the wife, and I wondered if she was thinking that the "revenoos" were paying them a visit. **1969** Hall *Coll* (Mt Sterling NC) The revenue law is up there. **1973** GSMNP-90:26 My father, he was awful against liquor and things like that, and when the revenue man would come in and make a raid, they'd come to our house and sleep afterwards. **1978** Montgomery *White Pine Coll* V-3 The revenue has got so smart on that with technical things that they can't operate but a week or two. **1992** Gabbard *Thunder Road* 33 The "revenooers" would ride the roads and see if they could see paths off the road where you had stopped and toted stuff up a bank. Bootleggers were pretty sharp at how they handled their signs. We'd lay planks off the side of a truck and walk them planks to the top of a bank, then go into the woods and not leave a sign. The "revenooers" might smash up three or four stills at one time and wipe you out, so you'd have to start over again. **2007** Alexander *Moonshiners Gone* 20 Many moonshiners and probably even their "revenoor" [revenooer] counterparts saw indeed "thar was gold in them thar hills," in more ways than one.

[DARE *revenue* n, *revenuer* n chiefly South Midland]

revenue law, **revenue man**, **revenue officer**, **revenuer** See **(the) revenue**.

reverend (also *reverent*) *adjective*

A Variant forms *reverined* [see **1982** in **C**], *revernt, revrent.*

1832 *McLean Diary* (June 19) Meting held by the Revrent Brown. **1862** *Lister CW Letters* (Dec 19) we had preachin las thirsday nite by the revernt Willum farrow.

B *adjective* Usually of an alcoholic drink: undiluted, unadulterated, strong.

1886 Smith *Southernisms* 46 *reverent* = undiluted, of liquor. **1891** Primer *Studies in WV* 167 Reverent is used in the sense of genuine, thorough; as, a reverent scolding, that is a thorough scolding. **1971** Dwyer *Dict for Yankees* 31 *reverent* = strong, not diluted. "Do you want your whiskey reverend; or shall I mix coke in it?" **1998** Montgomery *Coll* (known to Bush).

C *verb* To revere, treat (family gravesites) reverently.

1982 Slone *How We Talked* 76 Each family had their own "plot." They "reverined" their dead to almost a worship.

[Web3 *reverend* 5 "strong, potent, undiluted" chiefly Midland; DARE *reverend* adj B2 chiefly South, South Midland]

reverined See **reverend**.

revival meeting *noun* An extended, sometimes open-ended, series of evangelistic services (earlier usually called a **big meeting** or **protracted meeting**) held by a church in the late summer or early fall, usually conducted by a guest preacher. See also **camp meeting**, **meeting**.

1956 Hall *Coll* (Gatlinburg TN) Generally the fall of the year they'd have what they called revival meeting one, two, three, or four weeks sometimes. They had meeting morning and evening or morning and night one all the time. **1973** GSMNP-84:24 One day I was a-walking through Wears Cove up here, and at the old church house where I used to go to church, they was a traveling preacher holding a revival meeting. **1975** GSMNP-59:31 In the fall of the year most of the time they'd run revival meetings. The other times people [were] working and, you know, having to make their crops and like that. They'd get all their corn and everything through and all the stuff took care of and then they'd generally along late fall of the year would have them revival meetings. **1989** *Matewan OHP-23* The Church of God would have revival meetings more so than any other church, more than the Methodist or the Baptist or anything.

Revolution War *noun* The American Civil War. Same as **War of the Revolution.**

1966 Dakin *Vocab Ohio River Valley* 516 Some older speakers in the Mountains [of KY]—and a few elsewhere—also seem to say *the War of the Revolution* or (more common) *The Revolution War*. **1967** Fetterman *Stinking Creek* He fought in the old Revolution War and didn't die 'til after I was married. **1983** Broaddus *Estill Co KY Word List* 53 = the War Between the States.

[DARE (at *Revolution*) South, South Midland]

revrent See **reverend.**

reward *verb* To offer a reward for the arrest of (someone); to be the subject of such an offer.

1915 Hall *Autobiog Claib Jones* 26 I was rewarded seven hundred dollars and one day at Salt Lick some of the Coburns tried to arrest me. **1924** Raine *Saddlebags* 103 "He rewarded Bill." This means no gift to Bill, but a reward offered for his apprehension.

rewmaticks, rheumatics See **(the) rheumatism.**

(the) rheumatism *noun* Variant forms *remedies, rewmaticke, rheumatics, rheumatiz, rheumaty, rhumatics, roomaticks, rumatis.*

1862 *Reese CW Letters* (Oct 29) I am afflic ted with Rumatis and cald. **1864** *D Walker CW Letters* (Sept 1) I have bin down with the rewmaticke painses now ever Sens the 4 day of July. **1867** Harris *Sut Lovingood* 33 I now thort I wer ded, an' hed died ove rhumatics ove the hurtines' kind. **1883** Zeigler and Grosscup *Heart of Alleghanies* 61 I'd git me a neat woman, an' go to the wildest kentry in creation, an' hunt from the day I was big nuff to tote a riflegun, ontil ole age an' roomaticks fastened on me. **1917** Kephart *Word-List* 407 He adopted a rheumatiz. **1934–47** *LAMSAS Appal* (Madison Co NC, Swain Co NC) *rheumatiz.* **1941** Stuart *Men of Mts* 228 Go out and lay around all night on the cold ground. That's the reason I'm so full of rheumatics today. **1968** Clarke *Stuart's Kentucky* 41 Other home remedies included Fronnie Bushman's use of groundhog grease for the rheumatics, and various treatments for snakebite. **1974** Fink *Bits Mt Speech* 22 He's got the *rheumatiz* bad. **1974** GSMNP-51:4 He had took rheumatics after then or something. **1975** Chalmers *Better* 33 The "shot o' rheumaty medicine" ordered by the city doctor was soon given, but there was news of the family to give and take. **1979** Slone *My Heart* 15 Jin was down with the "rumatis" again, and Frankie and the boys were thinking about having a "working," if it ever cleared up enough. **1995** Montgomery *Coll*: *roomaticks* (known to Oliver, Shields). [**2007** Myers *Smoky Mt Remedies* 23 The accent was on the first syllable with a quick "a-tis" following. It was pronounced a little like the word *remedies*.]

[cf SND *rheumatics*]

rheumatiz, rheumaty See **(the) rheumatism.**

rhododendron *noun*

A Variant forms *rhododendrum, rhododiniums.*

1976 GSMNP-109:9 [Fire] gets into and heats the leaves and the twigs up on these pines and laurel rhododendrum and hemlock. **1976** Lindsay *Grassy Balds* 203 A few of them there rhododiniums or what you call laurels—I call red laurel.

B A genus of plant with eight species (five deciduous, three evergreen) in the Smoky Mountains according to **1964** Stupka *Trees Shrubs Vines* 113–19. The most prevalent of these are **catawba rhododendron** (*Rhododendron catawbiense*) and **rosebay rhododendron** (*Rhododendron maximum*). See also **laurel.**

1883 Zeigler and Grosscup *Heart of Alleghanies* In vast tracts impenetrable tangles of the rhododendron and kalmia . . . locally called "Hells," with a proper noun possessive in remembrance of poor unfortunates lost in their mazes. **1913** Kephart *Our Sthn High* 295 The hemlock tree is named spruce-pine . . . balsam itself is she-balsam, laurel is ivy, and rhododendron is laurel. **1937** Thornburgh *Great Smoky Mts* 20–21 On the summits are two species of rose flower rhododendrons, the *rhododendron punctatum* and rosebay, a short shrub rarely waist high, with dense clusters of small rose-colored flowers which sometimes carpet an entire mountain slope, and the tall *rhododendron catawbiense*, which grows from eight to eighteen feet in height. **1943** Peattie *Indian Days* 40 Botanists speak of heath balds, meaning an area crowned with an intricate shrub tangle of the heath family, but mountain people call them slicks, and distinguish between laurel, rhododendron, and ivy (Kalmia or mountain laurel) slicks. **1960** Stubbs *Mountain-Wise* (April–May) 6 They do use the term rhododendron, but only in reference to that showy and astoundingly beautiful variety, the purple rhododendron. It is the earliest of the native rhododendrons to bloom and can be found only on high mountain-tops in the most inaccessible places. The books describe it as magenta-pink in color and label it rhododendron catawbiense. This, then, is what the natives mean when they say "rhododendron," unless, as many do, they call it "punkin-bush," a name so at variance with its beauty that it defies explanation. **1979** Cantu *Great Smoky Mts* 12 Heath balds (called locally "laurel slicks" or "hells," depending upon whether one is viewing them or hiking on them) are comprised almost entirely of rhododendron, laurel, sand myrtle, and azalea. **1982** Powers and Hannah *Cataloochee* 436 Cataloochans called rhododendron "laurel"—the purple variety being known as "blue l'arl." **1988** *Smokies Guide* (Summer) 5 The two main types of rhododendron in the Smokies are rosebay and catawba. Catawba rhododendron is the first to bloom and lives mostly in the Park's higher elevations. Its rose-colored flowers begin opening at the mid-elevations in early June and spread up the mountains until early July. Only in the southern Appalachians does the catawba occur. Rosebay rhododendron is more often found in the Park's lower elevations, especially along shaded streambanks and ravines. Its white to pink flowers start blooming in early June at the low elevations and creep up to the mid-elevations through July and into August. Both the catawba and rosebay are somewhat unusual for keeping their large green leaves through the winter.

rhododendrum, rhododinium See **rhododendron.**

rhumatics See **(the) rheumatism.**

rib *noun* See citations.

c1987 (in **2015** Yarrow *Voices* 17) = the walls of a mine tunnel. **2002** Armstead *Black Days* 245 = [a] side surface, or vertical side walls, of a mine heading, pillar, or room.

rib basket *noun* See citation. Same as **Appalachian basket.**

1995 Williams *Smoky Mts Folklife* 83 The rib basket, with its thin splits woven on a foundation of curved ribs, is the form most frequently associated with the region and is sometimes known as the "Appalachian basket." Frances Louisa Goodrich found this to be the most common form in the Laurel Country of Madison County, North Carolina.

ribble *noun* A miniature roll of dough put in soups.

2009 *Hard Life* 39–40 [The milk soup] was just blue john milk and what they called ribbles. A ribble was made out of flour. They put a little ball in it and made little balls. It was like what the lumps are in lumpy gravy.

[DARE (at *rivel* n) chiefly PA German area]

ribey *adjective* Skinny, scrawny.

1933 Carpenter *Sthn Mt Dialect* 25 Ribey looking is heard in Kentucky and sometimes to the north for what is commonly understood as SEEDY LOOKING. **1944** Wentworth *ADD* 509 (WV) = poor, skinny, a lean person or animal.

[DARE *ribey* adj southern Appalachians, especially WV]

riccolict See **recollect.**

riccomember See **recomember.**

rich pine *noun* A knot or split piece of pine that is rich in resin, burns easily and slowly, and can serve as a torch for indoor or outdoor lighting or as kindling for a fire. See also **fat pine, light pine, lightwood torch, pine heart.**

1883 Zeigler and Grosscup *Heart of Alleghanies* 149 Jake threw a rich pine knot on the fire; Kenswick ceased puffing his pipe for an instant; Sanford came from the door, and leaning against the chimney, stuck one of his feet toward the blaze. **1926** Hunnicutt *Twenty Years* 75 I got some rich pine and made a light for us to see by across Pull Back Mountain. **1934–47** *LAMSAS Appal* = attested by 2/148 speakers (1.7%) from WV, 1/20 (5%) from VA, 16/37 (43.2%) from NC, 1/14 (7.1%) from SC, and 3/12 (25%) from GA. **1938–46** Oliver *Fifty Years* 5 Some of the children would sometimes hold a rich pine torch light to give more light in the house. **1949** Kurath *Word Geog East US* 29 The Midland term for kindling wood is *pine, fat-pine, rich-pine.* **1958** Newton *Dialect Vocab* (Happy Valley, Miller's Cove TN). **1966–67** *DARE Survey* (Burnsville NC, Maryville TN). **1980** Weals *Strangers* "We'd blow the lamp out to save on coal oil. To make light we'd throw rich pine knots in the fireplace," Fred says. **1985** Irwin *Alex Stewart* 112 I went out in the woods the next day and got me some good rich pine knots, split them up in splinters and made two big torches. **1986** Pederson et al. *LAGS* = attested by 12/60 interviewees (20%) from E TN; 12/43 of all LAGS interviewees (27.9%) attesting term were from E TN. **2005** Williams *Gratitude* 518 = a portion of pine wood with a heavy accumulation of resin, usually close to a knot. It can be set on fire with a match, and, other than lamp oil, is the best thing available to start a fire.

[Web3 *rich pine* chiefly Midland; DARE *rich pine* n chiefly South, South Midland]

richweed *noun* The stoneroot plant (*Collinsonia canadensis*). See also **horse balm.**

1940 Caton *Wildflowers of Smokies* 104.

rick

A *noun* A stack of hay or wood in an elongated heap.

1949 Kurath *Word Geog East US* 54 Scattered instances of *rick* have been noted in West Virginia and in westernmost North Carolina. **1962** Wilson *Folkways Mammoth Cave* 12 A long, big pile of hay was known as a *rick*, or *hay-rick*. It lacked the center pole. **1985** Irwin *Alex Stewart* 210 He'd take and make him a rick of good hard wood and he'd cover that with good sized rocks. **1986** Pederson et al. *LAGS* = attested by 5/60 interviewees (8.3%) from E TN; 5/11 of all LAGS interviewees (45.5%) attesting term were from Appalachia.

B (also *rick up*) *verb, verb phrase* To stack or pile hay, straw, wood, rock, etc. in the field.

1941 Stuart *Men of Mts* 199 We cut the stove wood and ricked it for to season a few days before we hauled it to the woodshed. **1957** Broaddus *Vocab Estill Co KY* 63 *rick* = to put cut stovewood in a neat stack. **1996** Isbell *Last Chivaree* 83 Go up yander and beat that tree down and put it on the wood pile and beat it up into sticks and rick it up on the porch. **2005** Williams *Gratitude* 47 The sticks of wood would be a-layin' all over th' ground, and had to be gathered up, toted in, and ricked up (stacked).

rickollect See **recollect.**

rick rack fence *noun* A fence of solid logs laid out in a zigzag fashion.

1968 *DARE Survey* (Brasstown NC) = fence made of solid logs.

rick up See **rick B.**

rid[1] See **redd.**

rid[2] See **ride.**

riddie-bob See **ridy horse 2.**

riddle *noun* A coarse-meshed sieve.

1964 Roberts *Hell-Fer-Sartin* 47 She said if he would go to the spring and pack 'im some water in a riddle—bucket—that she'd bake it for 'im. Well, he went and he was at the spring and that riddle wouldn't hold water.

[OED3 *riddle* n² 1a "a coarse-meshed sieve, used to separate sand from gravel, ashes from cinders, etc."]

ride *verb*

A Principal parts.

1 Variant past-tense form *rid*.

1861 *Martin CW Letters* (Nov 29) I must Tell you first thing of my ride yesterday I rid Jenny from franks home. **1867** Harris *Sut Lovingood* 19 You never seed a rale hoss till I rid up. **1900** Harben *N GA Sketches* 16 Then Colonel Whitney got wind o' the matter an' rid over an' said, to accommodate me, he'd take the loan. **1913** Kephart *Our Sthn High* 284 In many cases a weak preterite supplants the proper strong one: div, driv, fit, gi'n or give, rid, riv, riz, writ. **1924** Abernethy *Moonshine* 118 I tuk my mule an' rid over to Lang Thomson's to git his kivvered buggy so as to go in some sorter style. **1934–47** *LAMSAS Appal* (Madison Co NC). **1937** *Hall Coll* (Cades Cove TN) Ye rid with him, didn't ye? **c1945** Haun *Hawk's Done* 254 We rid in the wagon with Thompkins. **1953** Atwood *Verbs East US* 19 The archaic *rid* . . . is extremely rare until one reaches the coastal and mountain areas of the South and South Midland. It has its greatest frequency in N.C., where it is used by about one third of the Type I [i.e. older speakers with little formal education] informants. **1956** *Hall Coll* (Newport TN) He said she jumped on the hoss and rid down the mountain with him. **1970** *Burton-Manning Coll*-94A I remember the first train I ever rid. **1979** *Big South Fork OHP*-11 He said, "I can carry you over there to Uncle John's," and he got on that horse and rid him up beside of the porch, and I slid off on him.

2 Variant past-participle forms *rid*, *rode*.

c1830 (in **2007** Dunkerly *Kings Mt* 120) He had principally rode this horse on the march. **1860** (in **1938** Taliaferro *Carolina Humor* 12) He's bin rode mighty hard ter day, I tell yer! **1900** Harben *N GA Sketches* 178 [The train] don't whiz nigh like some I've rid on out West. **1924** Raine *Saddlebags* 29 I reckon I have rid a bigger critter than ary one of you fellers ever seed. **c1940** *Padelford Notes* Clean to the cove I've rid today. **1963** Medford *Mt People* 115 Now, when Jerry had left home he had rid away on his white hoss—well, he was almost plumb white. **1969** Roberts *Greasybeard* 92 She went on to a horse, and the horse said, "Please ride me, little girl, I hain't been rode in several long years." **1970** *Burton-Manning Coll*-94A I never had rid the train nor nothing. Nary one of us had. **1976** Lindsay *Grassy Balds* 198 I've rode box cars out—on top of them—out of there when the railroad was up there. **1978** Reese *Speech NE Tenn* 177 *rid* = attested by 2/12 (16.7%) speakers; *rode* = attested by 8/12 (66.7%) speakers. **1980** Miles *Verbs in Haywood Co* 99 I've rode the wagon every year. **1989** Landry *Smoky Mt Interviews* 194 I ain't rode a lot. I've rid horses and mules.

B Senses.

1 To taunt, harass, ridicule (someone).

1956 *Hall Coll* (Emerts Cove TN) I was catty for a little feller. There was none of my size who could ride me. There was a big feller who says, "I'll whup you." I told him to pull away. I could ride him just as quick as he could ride me.

2 In children's play, to bounce up and down on a sapling and traverse ground quickly by leaping or springing from (one sapling or tree to another).

1925 Dargan *Highland Annals* 161 He jest rid the saplin's after them dogs. It was the masterest sight, him goin' over ever'thing like he had wings in his insides. . . . He was "riding the saplings" when we saw him. **1972** *AOHP/ALC*-355 [We'd] get out and bend us down some trees in the woods and ride them up and down. **1996** Isbell *Last Chivaree* 60 He would fling over into another tree, or hit the ground and climb another one. They'd ride a little tree down to the ground.

ride-a-horse See **ridy horse 1**.

ride a rail See **ride one on a (fence) rail**.

ride one on a (fence) rail (also *ride one on a pole*) *verb phrase* Of a wedding party: to perform the traditional ceremony of jostling a newlywed husband on a rail after arousing him from bed on his wedding night; hence verb phrase *ride a rail* = of a newlywed husband: to be subjected to this form of hazing. See also **serenade**, **shivaree**. See 1974 citation.

1939 *Hall Coll* (Catons Grove TN) [Did they ever make a bridegroom ride a rail?] They used to make the bridegroom ride a rail, they said, but they never treated me that dirty. **1974** GSMNP-51: 27 They'd ride him on a rail, you know. They'd get a real sharp rail . . . and put him on that [with] two men, one on each end, and put it on their shoulder, and they'd hold him on that rail, you know, where it's real sharp. And if it wasn't hurting him enough, why they'd jump up and down with him, trot with him. **1974** Russell *Hillbilly* 32 The community "serenade" often consisted of riding the groom on a fence rail and the bride in a big wash tub. **1982** Powers and Hannah *Cataloochee* 196 A bride and groom were apt to be greeted with a charivari which might include riding a groom on a rail . . . in his night clothes, and dumping him into a cold creek.

rider *noun* See citation.

1947 Stuart *Corn Cuttin'* 23 Then Pa counted six corn hills from the end of the field on the sixth row. And here he reached into the seventh row and bent over two stalks of corn and began wrapping their tops around the tops of the hills directly below until he had made them the shape of an oxbow. He wrapped them until he had made a substantial thing that looked like a tall spider with four strong legs. "This is what you call a rider," he said. "It's the underpinnin' of the corn shock. It must be made strong so it'll hold the corn shocks against the strong winds."

ride shank's mare See **shank's horse**.

ride the saw (also *ride the handle*) *verb phrase* See citations.

1921 Campbell *Sthn Highlander* 2 Pliny did not "ride the saw," but did his full share with his big brother Homer in cutting up the logs for firewood. **1984** Wilder *You All Spoken* 153 Ride the saw: Make somebody else do the hard work, the dirty work, while you pretend to bear your share of the load. The term comes from using a crosscut saw. **2005** Williams *Gratitude* 46 They'd git into it (argue), and one of 'em would accuse the other'n of ridin' the saw, or ridin' the handle.

ridey horse See **ridy horse 1**.

ridge *noun* A hill or promontory within a loop or horseshoe curve of a stream or river.

1939 Hall *Coll* (Proctor NC) The word ridge [is] used more than hill. Welch Ridge separates Hazel Creek and Forney Creek. [There is a lead] between Big Creek and Mount Sterling with ridges running up to the lead. **1961** *Coe Ridge OHP*-333A She never did live on the ridge.

ridge rooter (also *ridge runner*) *noun* A domestic hog allowed to range freely in the mountains until it becomes partially or wholly wild. See also **razorback**, **Russian wild hog**.

1937 Conner *Ms* 10 although our hogs were un-improved, they were mostly thorough bred ridge-rooter's. **1982** Powers and Hannah *Cataloochee* 165 They'd race small hogs or "ridge rooters," four or five year olds, each weighing two or three hundred pounds, way back in the mountains, sometimes to Hell's Half Acre or Piney Butt Mountain. *Ibid.* 282 When hogs went wild, they were known as ridge rooters. And it was quite a chase to round them up. **1989** Oliver *Hazel Creek* 24 Since they were the major source of meat, hogs (razor-back or ridge-rooters) were raised first, and allowed to run wild around the farms, fattening on acorn and chestnut mast. **1991** Haynes *Haywood Home* 45 Hogs go wild easier than any other livestock. And the hogs we had on Fines Creek were little ridge-runners that were close kin to true wild hogs.

ridge runner *noun*

1 See **ridge rooter**.

2 A person from the southern mountains, a rustic, sometimes without permanent employment. [Editor's note: This term is often, but not necessarily, deprecatory, and is apparently not used in self-reference.]

1930 Pendleton *Wood-Hicks Speak* 88 Ridge runner, a "hick" who has become discontented with his job, leaving it to find a new one, and going, of necessity, across the mountainous ridges of this section. Ridge running, the act of going across country in search of a new job. **1937** Leybourne *Urban Adjustments* 241 [Mountain people] are popularly called "hill-billies," "briers," and "ridge-runners." **1939** Hall *Coll* = a Tennessean. **1963** Edwards *Gravel* 7 Brother Lawrence Edwards has spent half a century soaking up the lore of his beloved Cumberland wonderland in East Tennessee. . . . He can't any more escape it than he can avoid saying "Thang" when he means "Thing." He is a ridge-runner and a cove-ite all kneaded into one, with gravel in his shoes. **1968** *DARE Survey* (Logan WV, Westover WV, Moorefield WV) = a rustic or countrified person. **1976** Maloney *Appal Culture* 189 Hillbilly . . . is used, along with other such terms as ridge-runner, briar-hopper, in either a friendly way or as a racial slur. Mountain people often apply these terms to each or to themselves in a friendly way. **1979** Slone *My Heart* 47 Of course, there were a few "mean" women or "ridge runners" who were free with their favors, and gave themselves to any man who asked. **1986** Pederson et al. *LAGS* = attested by 3/60 interviewees (5%) from E TN and 1/35 (2.9%) from N GA; 4/7 of all LAGS interviewees (57.1%) attesting term were from Appalachia. **1995–97** Montgomery *Coll* (known to Adams, Brewer, Bush, Oliver, Weaver), = person who lives in low mountain terrain (Cardwell), = any mountaineer or hillbilly (Jones), = a person from "back in the sticks" (Ledford), = a farmer who lives far back in the mountains (Shields). **2006** *Encycl Appalachia* 904 Dubbed "the invisible minority" by sociologists and the media, Appalachian migrants have been labeled as hillbillies and ridgerunners when their folk speech, lifestyles, and other identifiable cultural differences set them apart. Perceptions of the region and its lore preceded migrants' arrival in urban areas during the Great Migration in the 1940s, having been shaped by pervasive hillbilly stereotypes disseminated by the mass media and popular press. **2007** McMillon *Notes* = subsistence farmer (not derogatory).

[Web3 *ridge runner* n "a mountain farmer, hillbilly" chiefly Midland]

3 See citations.

1967 Parris *Mt Born* 132 A ridgerunner is a farmer who logs now and then. **2006** Farwell *Logging Term* 1021 Derogatory terms for loggers—such as *woodhicks* and *woodpeckers*—are no longer used, nor is *ridgerunner* applied to a farmer who logs part time.

4 See citation.

1947 Dunlap and Weslager *Tri-racial Groups* 82 = another name for Melungeons.

riding critter *noun* A horse for riding.

1943 Hannum *Mt People* 147 Shapes of phrases repeat themselves and the same sounds re-echo, giving, oddly enough, vividness rather than monotony—as in their use of double words: . . . ridin'-critter; cow-brute; preacher-man; granny-woman; we-uns; chanty-song. **1972** Cooper *NC Mt Folklore* 95 = a horse for riding; not a draft horse. **1997** Montgomery *Coll* (known to Cardwell, Jones).

riding horse See **ridy horse 2**.

rid up See **redd**.

ridy bob See **ridy horse**.

ridy horse *noun*

1 (also *ride-a-horse*, *ridey-horse*) A sapling that children bend down and bounce up and down on, especially in leaping from tree to tree. See also **ride B2**.

1946 Lassiter *Games Played* 17 Most every sapling around the school house was converted into a Ride-a-horse when this riding fever would break out. **c1975** Lunsford *It Used to Be* 130 A ridey-horse is a bush or tree down the road, or over on the hill, or wherever it may be, where they can bend it down and several can get on it. It's springy enough to let them ride up and down just like it was one end of a see-saw. **1976** Braden *Grandma Was Girl* 83 We made "ridey horses" by bending a sapling down, sitting on it, and making it go up and down. The ride was a sensation similar to what children get now on the artificial ponies at the grocery store.

[DARE *ridy-horse* n 1 chiefly Southern Appalachians]

2 (also *riddie-bob, riding horse, ridy-bob*) A seesaw.

1913 Kephart *Our Sthn High* 259 The children have few toys other than rag dolls . . . and such "ridy-hosses" and so forth as they make for themselves. **1949** Kurath *Word Geog East US* 59 The most widespread regional term [for a seesaw] is *ridy-horse* (riding horse). It occurs in Appalachia from central West Virginia southward. **1966** Dakin *Vocab Ohio River Valley* 171 The Southern *ridey-horse* (rarely, *riding horse*) predominates to the western Mountain margin [of KY] but is extremely rare beyond. **1966–69** *DARE Survey* (Hindman KY, Walker KY) *ridy-bob*; (Maryville TN) *ridy horse*. **1982** Slone *How We Talked* 94 *riddie-bob* = see-saw. A plank or pole was placed across a large log so as to balance each end. One or two children would sit on each end. With a slight push with their feet, they could make first one end go up and then the other. As one end went up, the other came down. **1986** Pederson et al. *LAGS*: *ridey horse* = attested by 4/60 interviewees (6.7%) from E TN and 3/35 (8.6%) from N GA; 7/29 of all LAGS interviewees (24.1%) attesting term were from Appalachia; *riding horse* (Carter Co TN, Sullivan Co TN). **1997** Montgomery *Coll* (known to Adams, Bush, Cardwell, Jones, Ledford, Weaver).

[DARE *ridy-bob* n especially KY, *ridy-horse* n 2 chiefly South, Southern Appalachians]

riffle *verb* See citation.

c1960 Wilson *Coll* = to accomplish something hard, like rowing a boat over a riffle.

rifle *verb* To raffle.

1915 Dingus *Word-List VA* 188 *rifle*. Variant of *raffle*. **1942** Hall *Phonetics Smoky Mts* 26 They're going to ['ræfcl] it off. **1976** Garber *Mountain-ese* 75 They're gonna rifle off a new car fer charity this year.

[DARE *rifle* v, n² Southern Appalachians]

rifle ball *noun* A bullet for an old-time muzzle-loading gun.

1967 Hall *Coll* (Del Rio TN) Those cast-iron kettles had potlegs on 'em. They'd break it off and make rifle balls.

rifle cracker *noun* A marksman.

1955 Parris *Roaming Mts* 201 Come next Wednesday the seventeenth annual Cataloochee Beef Shoot will draw mountain riflecrackers here to Tom Alexander's ranch atop mile-high Fie Top [sic] Mountain, reached by a three-mile gravel road connecting with U.S. 19 at Maggie. **1995–97** Montgomery *Coll* (known to Brown, Bush).

rifle frolic *noun* Formerly, a marksmanship competition held at a community party.

1955 Parris *Roaming Mts* 201 It is the traditional "shooting for the beef," commonly known as a shooting match, a custom that blossomed into a crackerjack sport because of such famed rifle-crackers as Daniel Boone and Davy Crockett. Only in those lean days it was called a "rifle frolic," and the shooting was for liquor, beef being scarce on the frontier. **1995–97** Montgomery *Coll* (known to Brown).

rifle gun *noun* A rifle, a long-barreled firearm whose bore has been grooved or rifled. See 1914 citation. See also **bear gun**, **hog rifle**.

1747 (in **1912** Chalkley *Augusta Co VA Chronicles* 1.529) (DARE) They were . . . robbed of . . . a rifle gun (double tricked). **1796** Dunlap *Will* To son Adam Dunlap—the plantation on which I now live agreeable to the lines already mentioned to the other boys and the dwelling house at his mother's death, a black mare, one cow and calf, the rifle gun he now has. **1862** *Spainhourd CW Letters* (Sept 8) we have drod [= drawed] rifel gones [that] will hold up from three to five hundreth yeards. **1867** Harris *Sut Lovingood* 77 Her ankils wer es roun', an' not much bigger nur the wrist ove a rifle-gun. **1883** Zeigler and Grosscup *Heart of Alleghanies* 150 Wal, I hed my rifle-gun an' the dogs fer company, countin' on gittin a crack at some varmint along the way. **1913** Kephart *Our Sthn High* 285–86 Pleonasms are abundant. . . . Everywhere in the mountains we hear of biscuit-bread, ham-meat, rifle-gun. **1914** Arthur *Western NC* 280 The word "rifle" is too generic a term for the average mountaineer; but he knows what a "rifle-gun" is. Some of the older [people] have seen them made—lock, stock and barrel. The process was simple: a bar of iron the length of the barrel desired was hammered to the thickness of about three-sixteenths of an inch and then rolled around a small iron rod of a diameter a little less than the caliber desired. **1939** Hall *Coll* (Mt Sterling NC) He put him a turnip hull on the end of his rifle gun, till he could see the darkness of the bear. *Ibid.* (Hartford TN) My father had a large rifle gun. It shot a good-size bore. **1991** Haynes *Haywood Home* 44 About the only thing I can remember that wasn't shared much or loaned out was a man's rifle-gun.

[probably from *rifled gun*; DARE *rifle gun* n now chiefly southern Appalachians, Ozarks]

rifle whiskey *noun* A bottle of whiskey won at a marksmanship competition. See also **rifle frolic**.

1955 Parris *Roaming Mts* 201 Only in those lean days [the shooting match] was called a "rifle frolic," and the shooting was for liquor, beef being scarce on the frontier. That's where the term "rifle whiskey" was born. **1995–97** Montgomery *Coll* (known to Brown, Bush).

rift *verb* To burp, belch.

1936 Morehouse *Rain on Just* 19 Probably old Sukey [= a cow] had bloated up, eating too much clover, and not rifting right. *Ibid.* 133 Women folks were pushing back and forth, in and out, toting nursing babies who were rifting more than need be.

rig *verb, noun* See citation.

1892 Fruit *KY Words* 231 = to tell a joke on: "He rigged him good." Also as a noun: "he got a rig on him."

right

A *adjective* Genuine, true, exact.

1927 Shearin *Speech of Fathers* 7 Boys, that's shore a right pocket knife. **1933** Thomas *Traipsin' Woman* 258 "He's a right scholar," said Louellen proudly as her boy had read the page from top to bottom without faltering. **1955** Ritchie *Singing Family* 132 Now it may be that I'm prejudiced; maybe I'm one of the low down ones. But then they have a right chance seems like a Ritchie will come out. **1975** *AOIIP/LJC*-384 She was a right Yankee.

B *adverb*

1 Precisely, entirely; just; in phrase *right today* = just now, even now. See also **right at.**

1941 Still *Troublesome Creek* 18 Right today I'll buy that kit o' fish. **c1950** Adams *Grandpap* 88 Siniker was left there right alone by herself. **1971** *Granny Women* 259 I was right about three years old. **1978** Burton *Ballad Folks* 18 I feel it's the same way right today, as it was then. **1989** Landry *Smoky Mt Interviews* 181 You find that right today. **1995** Adams *Come Go Home* 106–7 I'll have 'em figured out one way [and] then they've done right the opposite. **c1999** Sutton *Me and Likker* 66 I was drinking it like it was going out of style, still do right today.

[OED3 *right* adv 4a "precisely, exactly, just" now colloquial or regional, c900→]

2 Directly, immediately.

1953 Hall *Coll* (Plott Creek NC) He took pneumonia right following that and died in just a few days. **1961** *Coe Ridge OHP*-333A They would have right cleaned the ridge up that night. **1970** *Hunting Stories* 77 He'uz comin' right square t'me just as straight as he could be. **1972** *AOHP/LJC*-259 We own a big meadow right yonder. **1979** *Big South Fork OHP*-11 I come right around through Chestnut Grove. **1989** Landry *Smoky Mt Interviews* 194 The barn was right on out that road.

3 Very, considerably, rather. See also **proud, right smart C.**

1796 Cunningham *Letter* Jas. Cunningham is living on the Cataba River yet, and is maried to a mighty clever widow woman and is right full in the world. **1863** *Proffit CW Letters* (June 2) he was right sick but I hope not dangerous It was said that many marched until they fell dead on this march. **1863** Wilson *Confederate Private* 11 (March 15) I take my pen in hand to in form you that I am not rite wel yet. **1874** Swearingen *Letters* 164 We had a right funy runaway scrape in the neighborhood last Sunday. **1939** Hall *Coll* (Gatlinburg TN) A right old lady come in. **1965** Hall *Coll* (Cataloochee NC) I had a young horse that was right wild and foolish, and it was too fur for me to walk and carry [the lumber] on my back. **1978** Montgomery *White Pine Coll* III-2 I was right proud of it. It was right nice to do, and I appreciate it. **1991** Thomas *Sthn Appal* 224 Course, I didn't weave when I'z young, right young. **2003** LaLone et al. *Farming Life* 303 We raised right many food items in our garden.

[OED3 *right* adv 7 "very" nonstandard and regional, c1200→; DARE *right* adv B "very, quite" chiefly South, South Midland]

right at *phrasal preposition* Almost exactly, very near, close to.

1913 Kephart *Our Sthn High* 293 "That's right at a smidgen" = little more than a mite. **1937** Hall *Coll* (Big Creek NC) He lives right at Brown's house. **1957** Combs *Lg Sthn High: Word List* 81 = about, close to, very near. Ex.: "Hit's right at six mile to the gap on the mountain." **1993** Page and Smith *Foxfire Toys and Games* 127 I've sold right at a hundred sets of these things over the years. **1997** Montgomery *Coll* (known to nine consultants from the Smoky Mountains).

right hand of fellowship *noun phrase* See 2014 citation.

1870 *Paw Paw Hollow Church Minutes* Protracted meeting continued 16 days during which time we received by Baptism and the right hand of fellowship Cora Petty. **1999** Morgan *Gap Creek* 248 "Let's all come forward and give Sister Julie the right hand of fellowship," Preacher Gibbs said. **2014** Montgomery *Doctrine* 168 = [a handshake extended] after preaching to welcome new members to the church.

right-hand plow *noun* A type of **turner** plow with the coulter fixed on the right side to enable one to plow in a circle, usually from the outside to the inside of the field.

1986 Pederson et al. *LAGS* (Sevier Co TN).

rightify *verb* To correct, make right.

1957 Combs *Lg Sthn High: Word List* 81 = rectify, make right. **1991** Still *Wolfpen Notebooks* 120 I made a big mistake but I right-ified it with the man I done it to.

right natured for *adjective phrase* Suitable or natural for. See also **natured.**

1924 Raine *Saddlebags* 102 The land is right natured for corn. **1995–97** Montgomery *Coll* (known to Adams, Brown, Cardwell, Norris, Weaver).

right proud *adjective phrase* Very pleased (often used in expressing appreciation or in making an acquaintance, as *I'm right proud to meet you*). See also **proud, right B3.**

1934–47 *LAMSAS Appal* (Madison Co NC, Swain Co NC). **1981** Whitener *Folk-Ways* 82 An obliging native son seated at the end of the counter spoke up: "Excuse me, ma'am, but since you're in such a allfard hurry I'd be right proud to trade with you."

right smart

A *noun phrase*

1 Much, a large amount, quite a bit; hence adverb phrase *a right smart.*

1859 Taliaferro *Fisher's River* 76 I nuver tuck time to ondress him, which his skin would have been wuth a right smart uv ammernition. **1861** *Shipman CW Letters* (Oct 25) Wee hav A Right smart of Sick ness her. **1864** *Chapman CW Letters* (March 4) thare is rite smart to be maid in selling good now. **1895** Edson and Fairchild *TN Mts* 372 There's a right smart of hardness between them two boys. **1915** Pollard *TN Mts* 242 He raised a power and sold a heap and had a right smart left. **1921** Weeks *Speech of KY Mtneer* 15 "A right smart" is a common unit of measure in the mountains, applied to all commodities from a man's hillside acreage to his mental accumulations. **1937** Hall Coll (Ravensford NC) The soldiers destroyed and stole a right smart. **1939** Hall Coll (Waynesville NC) He has a right smart of an age on him. **1953** Hall Coll (Bryson City NC) A man had to be experienced and set traps to catch one of them [= a bear] because there is right smart of art in how to set it and where to set it and then what way to set it to get it to step in it, by burying it in the ground and covering it up. **1979** Slone *My Heart* 18 I see ye got a right smart of beans planted, got a sight of blooms on 'em. **1990** Clouse *Wilder* 11 It was a right smart of a climb. **2013** Venable *How to Tawlk* 42 = large amount: "He owns a right smart of land in Sevier County."

[Web3 *right smart* n chiefly South and Midland]

B *adjective phrase* Considerable, sizable, substantial, thoroughgoing. Same as **pretty smart**.

1863 *Click CW Letters* (Aug 11) you know that you have bin in the Army a wright smart while and if you go into it too strong at first you will be sure to inger your pretty little self. **1864** *Apperson CW Letters* (Jan 6) I would like if you can git any body to com over her to send me some thing rite smart to eate if you can for I neede it very bad surtin. **1867** Harris *Sut Lovingood* 22 Out we went tu the pawpaw thicket, an' peel'd a rite smart chance ove bark, an' mam an' me made geers fur dad, while he sot on the fence a-lookin at us, an' a studyin pow'rful. **1895** Edson and Fairchild *TN Mts* 374 I got a right smart little bit of roughness in for the beastis. **1939** Hall Coll (Cades Cove TN) His father lives a right smart piece from Bryson City. **c1950** Adams *Grandpap* 227 They were a-gettin' up to be right smart boys. Nearly young men. **1959** Pearsall *Little Smoky* 62 The War had a right smart effect around here. I've heard my mother talk about it. **1975** Kroeger *WV Farm Life* 39 I laid there a right smart little bit—thought I was killed. **1981** GSMNP-122:22 He's been dead a right smart bit. **1983** *Dark Corner OHP*-27A We had a right smart time catching him because he had a gun.... He was shooting back. **1987** Young *Lost Cove* 7 The first merchant whose name is known was Neally Campbell. According to oral history, he was also a right-smart carpenter. **2008** McKinley *Bear Mt* 25 Gradually, the only way to the Bear Mountain house became one of the mile-long foot trails. As Grandpa said, "It's a right smart piece," so after a few years they reluctantly sold their homestead.

[DARE *right smart* adj phr 1 chiefly South, South Midland]

C (also *right smartly*) *adverb phrase* To a considerable degree, quite a lot, a good deal.

1862 *Robinson CW Letters* (May 25) the big offerseres is flying Round Rite Smart. **1864** *Walker CW Letters* (Aug 18) I am on the mend I am abel to walk abowt rit Smartely tho in the hos pitel yet. **1884** Scott *Visit* 117 He said he could get a nice saddle-horse that would take me out "right smart." **1953** Hall Coll (Bryson City NC) We was out there one time on a hunt and old man Doctor Ables ... went down one of those trails and stepped into a [bear] trap.... It caught him in the leg ... the teeth went into his leg and hurt him a right smart. **1969** GSMNP-28:1 Sam, you're right smart older than I am. **1971** *AOHP/ALC*-66 I fished right smart. **1973** *AOHP/ASU*-124 I had to go into debt right smart. **1989** *Matewan OHP*-86 She's right smart, I think, older than I am.

[OED3 *right smart* adj/n/adv North American colloquial and regional; Web3 *right smart* adv South and Midland; DARE *right smart* adv phr chiefly South, South Midland]

right smartly See **right smart C**.

right today See **right B1**.

rimpshion See **rimption(s)**.

rimption(s) *noun*

A Variant forms *rampshion* [see **1995** in **B**], *rimpshion* [see **1917** in **B**], *rimtion* [see **1972** in **B**].

B An abundance, sizable amount.

1913 Kephart *Our Sthn High* 293 If the provender be scant the hostess may say, "That's right at a smidgen," meaning little more than a mite; but if plenteous, then there are rimptions. **1917** Kephart *Word-List* 416 *rimpshion* = abundance. "There's *rimpshions* of squirrels in the Hickory Cove." **1952** Wilson *Folk Speech NC* 585 *rimption* = a good deal. **1972** Cooper *NC Mt Folklore* 95 *rimtion* = a great deal. **c1982** Young *Colloquial Appal* 18 *rimption* = much. **1995** Montgomery Coll (known to Adams, Cardwell, Ledford, Oliver); I gave her a rampshion of meat (Norris).

[DARE *rimption* n chiefly Appalachians]

rimptious *adjective* Especially of a horse: lively, spirited.

1975 Jackson *Unusual Words* 159 A *skittish* or *boogerish* horse scares easily; to say a horse is *rimptious* or *foolish* means he is spirited; whereas, a rank horse is fast-gaited or spirited. **1997** Montgomery Coll (known to Brown, Ledford, Oliver), = refers to a person who has a lot of get up and go about them (Cardwell).

[cf EDD *rumptious* adj "riotous, unruly"]

rimreck (also *rimwreck*) *verb* To damage beyond repair, destroy; to behave riotously.

1940 Still *River of Earth* 120 Nary a son I had pleasured himself with shooting off guns, a-rim-recking at Hardin Town and in the camps. **1941** Still *Troublesome Creek* 118 "I wouldn't trust this pen more'n one night," Aaron said. "Hit's too small and rimwrecked." **1957** Broaddus *Vocab Estill Co KY* 64 *rimreck* = to tear down, destroy, ruin.

rinch See **rinse**.

ring *verb*

A Principal parts.

1 Variant past-tense form *rung*.

1913 Kephart *Our Sthn High* 283–84 In mountain vernacular the Old English strong past tense still lives in begun, drunk, holped, rung, shrunk, sprung, stunk, sung, sunk, swum. **1953** Hall Coll (Tuckaleechee Cove TN) When they rung the bell of a mornin' or took up books, they sung a song or two. **1972** *AOHP/ALC*-388 This one particular morning when the bell rung, I's in the kitchen a-tempering the whiskey. **1978** Reese *Speech NE Tenn* 178 = attested by 9/12 (75%) speakers. **1998** *Dante OHP-71* He went to answer the phone when the phone rung.

2 Variant past-participle form *rang*.

1983 Wolfram/Christian *WV Coll* 205 I hadn't been to my phone, or it hadn't rang, since I'd got back.

B Of a banjo: to have a good sound.

1975 *Foxfire III* 124 We found four major head styles [of banjos]: the all-wood head; the all-hide head; the wood head with the hide center; and the commercial head held on with brackets. Likewise, hoop styles and neck styles have great variety. In fact, there is so much variety in banjo construction that it would seem as though anything goes as long as it "rings." Stanley Hicks, for example, showed us a banjo his father made out of a cake box.

ringtail *noun* A raccoon.

1966–68 *DARE Survey* (Brasstown NC, Burnsville NC, Gatlinburg TN) = raccoon. **1995–97** Montgomery *Coll* (known to eight consultants from the Smoky Mountains).

ring-tail(ed) roarer (also *ring-tailed screamer, ring-tailed snorter, ring-tailed tooter, ring-tail rouser*) *noun* See citations.

c1960 Wilson *Coll*: *ring-tail roarer, ring-tailed screamer* = a loud-mouthed boaster; probably a left-over of actual pioneer boasting. Ring-tailed snorter (or roarer) . . . a mythical monster with which early pioneer bad men were always comparing themselves. [Also] ring-tailed tooter. **1963** Williams *Metaphor Mt Speech II* 51 Elz thanks he's a real rang-tail rouser, a-joggin' along thar on that old stove-up mare.

ring-tailed screamer, ring-tailed snorter, ring-tailed tooter See **ring-tail(ed) roarer.**

ringtail leader *noun* A "ring leader."

1989 *Matewan OHP-1* To arrest and take on [train number] sixteen to Bluefield, [they had warrants for] Sid Hatfield and Testerman and Ed Chambers all. . . . See they wanted to get the ringtail leaders out of Matewan so they could break the union.

ring-tail rouser See **ring-tail(ed) roarer.**

rinse *verb* Variant forms *ranch, rench, rinch.*

1886 Smith *Sthn Dialect* 349 They all have the authority of old or dialect English, or many of them belong to all parts of the South, if not elsewhere . . . rench (rinse). **1904–20** Kephart *Notebooks* 2:429 Rinch that out. **1915** Dingus *Word-List VA* 188 *rinch*. **1967** *DARE Survey* (Maryville TN) *rinch*. **1973** Miller *English Unicoi Co* 76 *rench* = attested by 4 of 5 speakers. **1974** Fink *Bits Mt Speech* 22 Be sure to *rench* the clothes good. **c1979** Chiles *Glossary* 5 *ranch*. **1989** Landry *Smoky Mt Interviews* 194 It was a good place to ranch your clothes. **1989** *Matewan OHP-102* Some of the times they would just take a stick and beat their clothes till they'd get them clean . . . and then they'd put them in this water to boil them, and then rinch them, and they was clean. **2008** McKinley *Bear Mt* 88 The process of hand-rinsing (called "ranching" or "renching") laundry in icy, mountain water could cause painful, chapped hands during the winter.

[DARE *rinch* (at *rinse* v 1) chiefly South, South Midland]

rip and stave (also *rip and tear*) *verb phrase* See citations. Same as **whoop and stave.**

1915 Dingus *Word-List VA* 188 *rip and stave* = to rage and scold about. **1952** Wilson *Folk Speech NC* 585 *rip and stave* = to curse, quarrel, to be noisily unpleasant. **1956** McAtee *Some Dial NC* 37 *rip and tear* = [to] curse, speak violently. **1957** Combs *Lg Sthn High: Word List* 82 = scold, fly into a rage. Ex.: "In popped Jude, a-rippin' and a-stavin'." **1972** Cooper *NC Mt Folklore* 95 *rip and tear* = to raise cain.

rippet (also *rippit*) *noun* A noisy quarrel, uproar, a disturbance or party.

1884 Smith *Arp Scrap Book* 97 They all put on their working aprons and went to beating eggs and stirring batter, and some more young ladies dropped in to help and I never heard such a rippet as they kept up all day. **1890** Fruit *KY Words* 66 = a great noise: "He made a great rippit." **1913** Kephart *Our Sthn High* 294 If they quarrel, it is a ruction, a rippit, a jower, or an upscuddle—so be it there are no fatalities which would amount to a real fray. **c1940** Simms *Coll* = quarrel, fuss. **1975** Jackson *Unusual Words* 157 The many words that mean fight attest to the prevalence of the activity. . . . A racket implies more actual contact, whereas ruckus or rookus, fraction, and fray all mean a fist fight or gun fight. Rippit is sometimes used in this connection, but it may also mean, as one man defined the term, "a cuttin' up sort of a night, a rousin' good time, drunk and dancin'." **1998** Montgomery *Coll* = can also refer to a loud party (Bush), = refers to any fuss (Jones).

[OED3 *rippet* (at *rippit*) perhaps of imitative origin, Scot and U.S. dialect; SND *rippet* n 1 "an uproar" and n 2 "a noisy quarrel"; CUD *rippet* n 1 "an uproar, a commotion"; DARE *rippet* n chiefly South Midland]

rippit See **rippet.**

riprap *noun* A rock pile or irregular, makeshift wall, as along a stream to prevent erosion.

1927 Woofter *Dialect from WV* 363 = a riffle that is full of rocks. "That creek has lots of rip-raps." **1973** Foster *Walker Valley* 9:39 Pull stuff out of your way, pull rock out of your way, build a rock riprap wall with it. **1997** Montgomery *Coll* (known to Brewer, Cardwell, Ledford), = large rocks placed along the banks of a stream to stop erosion (Oliver), = any makeshift structure, especially a wall (Weaver).

ripshack *noun* See citation.

1957 Combs *Lg Sthn High: Word List* 82 = an old sow; also a white striped lizard.

ripshin *noun* A brier or brierbush, as of blackberries, dewberries, etc.; formerly used in place-names in the Smoky Mountains, as in *Ripshin Mountain* (Sevier Co TN).

1927 Woofter *Dialect from WV* 363 = a running brier. "The hill field is full of ripshins." **1939** *FWP Guide TN* 430 Great boulders, left above the ground by erosion, are covered with moss and often lie in "ripshin" thickets of laurel, or rhododendron. **1944** Wentworth *ADD* 515 (WV) = dewberry bushes;—so named from the briars. **1971** Dwyer *Dict for Yankees* 31 = a briar, or a bush having briars. **1997** Montgomery *Coll* (known to Bush, Cardwell).

[DARE *ripshin* n Appalachians]

rise

A *verb* Principal parts.

1 Variant past-tense forms *rised, riz.*

1859 Taliaferro *Fisher's River* 84 Why, I hitched to the limb uv a big tree bent to the yeth with pigeons, you numskull, and when they riz the tree went up, and old Nip with it, fur sure. **1913** Kephart *Our Sthn High* 284 In many cases a weak preterite supplants the proper strong one: div, driv, fit, gi'n or give, rid, riv, riz, writ. **1934–47** *LAMSAS Appal: rised* = attested by 14/148 speakers (9.4%) from WV and 1/12 (8.3%) from GA; *riz* = attested by 6/148 speakers (4.0%) from WV, 8/20 (40%) from VA, 21/37 (66.8%) from NC, 10/14 (71.4%) from SC, and 5/12 (41.7%) from GA. *Ibid.* (Madison Co NC, Swain Co NC). **1940** Haun *Hawk's Done* 29 She thought the sun riz and set in Amy. **1953** Atwood *Verbs East US* 19 *Rised* occurs principally in W.Va. and adjoining parts of O[hio] and Va. **1961** *Coe Ridge OHP-341B* They was landed up and the river riz on them, and they was a-laying on a back tide. **1973** *GSMNP-76:4* It [= the still] was in the prettiest basin and spring that riz straight up from that place. **1979** Carpenter *Walton War* 181 When I riz this mornin', I seed there was a little skift of snow on the ground. **1986** Pederson et al. *LAGS* (Cocke Co TN, Jefferson Co TN).

2 Variant past-participle forms *ris, riz, rose.*

1859 Taliaferro *Fisher's River* All the limbs on his tree had riz from the yeth two foot. **1862** *Barkley CW Letter* (Feb 26) Rice has Ris [in price] sinse I lift to go home. **1937** Thornburgh *Great Smoky Mts* 135 When he explained it, my hair, which had riz straight up, begun to lay down again. **1961** *Coe Ridge OHP-334B* They run over a big old snag, and the river had rose and they didn't know where to drive the pilot. **1978** Reese *Speech NE Tenn* 178 *riz* = attested by 5/12 (41.7%) speakers; *rose* = attested by 2/12 (16.7%) speakers.

B *noun* (in phrase *the rise of*) Somewhat more than, in excess of (a specified distance, quantity, or period of time). See also **rising B.**

1863 *Neves CW Letters* (March 26) the yanks lost the Rise of 300 kild & grait many prisners. **1884** Smith *Arp Scrap Book* 31 It's now the rise of 42 years since I come into this cursed old world. **1915** Dingus *Word-List VA* 188 = slightly more than: "It's the rise of three miles to the mill." **1917** Kephart *Word-List* 416 = more than. "A leetle *the rise o'* six miles." **1924** Abernethy *Moonshine* 15 The mountain people have a way of saying it is the "rise" of so many miles to such a place; travelers have never been able to make out what "rise" means, unless it is that after one has gone the requisite number of miles he rises to "cuss" the fellow who directed him. **1925** (in **1967** Combs *Folk-Songs* 7) Jist ye foller right on up Carr's Fork till ye come to Arshman Creek, on the left-hand side, 'bout the rise o' four mile. **1939** Hall *Coll* (Hazel Creek NC) He axed me how long I'd lived here and I told him the rise of fifty year. **1974** Fink *Bits Mt Speech* 22 He had in the *rise* of twenty hogs.

[OED3 *the rise of* (at *rise* n P4) U.S., 1834→; DARE *rise* n 1 chiefly South, South Midland]

rise of See **rise B.**

rising

A *noun* A swelling, boil, abscess on the skin. Also called **raising 3.**

1808 (in **1920** DeWitt *Sevier Journal* 40) (July 9) The white flowered asmert is very fine for the Polleville in creatures or any rising or pains in a person. **1843** (in **1956** Eliason *Tarheel Talk* 290) (Wilkes Co NC) I . . . have suffered a great deal with a rising on my gum. **1862** *Lockmiller CW Letters* (July 18) mi risen has broke an has got beter. **1863** *Gilliland CW Letters* (Aug 30) [I] was Sory to here that Mother Webb had a nother one of them bad risings. **1904–20** Kephart *Notebooks* 2:475 I had a risin' on my side. **1913** Kephart *Our Sthn High* 296 Many common English words are used in peculiar senses by the mountain folk, as risin' for exceeding (also for inflammation). **1921** Campbell *Sthn Highlander* 202 That the Highlander is not immune to this diet, one may gather from the frequency of sallow complexions and the great prevalence of "risings"—a comprehensive term which may apply to anything, from a minute swelling to a carbuncle. **1937** Hall *Coll* (Cosby TN) Saint John weeds with dew on them makes sores, not biles and risin's. **1939** Hall *Coll* (Big Creek NC) You can put fat meat on a risin' or you can get tannin' bark. *Ibid.* Big Creek NC Catnip tea is the best thing in the world for a risin'. **1973** *AOHP/ASU-124* She used mustard [poultice] and such as that for fever and pneumonia fever and for the risings. **1975** Chalmers *Better* 34 Splinters and briars, a "risin'" to incise for drainage, a "creeled foot" strapped to relieve strained muscles, and "pizen-vine" rash.

[OED3 *rising* n 8a now U.S. regional; DARE *rising* n 1 chiefly South, South Midland, TX, OK]

B *adjective* Somewhat more than, exceeding. See also **rise B.**

1885 Murfree *Prophet* 9 She air risin' thirteen now. **1913** Kephart *Our Sthn High* 296 Many common English words are used in peculiar senses by the mountain folk, as risin' for exceeding. **1917** Kephart *Word-List* 416 He ain't but risin' sixteen. **1994–97** Montgomery *Coll* (known to Cardwell, Weaver).

[OED3 *rising* adj 6b U.S. 1775→; Web3 *rising* adj 3 chiefly Midland]

risk *verb* variant past-tense form *risk-ed.*

1989 *Matewan OHP-28* If you went over that picket line, you risk-ed your life 'cause them feller would hurt you.

risky *adjective* Willing to take risks, venturesome.

1943 Hannum *Mt People* 106 I was risky in them days. **1997** Montgomery *Coll* (known to Adams, Bush, Cardwell, Weaver).

rit, See **write 1, 2.**

riten See **write 1**.

riv See **rive A**.

rive *verb*

A Variant past-tense form *riv*.

1904–20 Kephart *Notebooks* 2:377 I riv some boards. **1991** Thomas *Sthn Appal* 249 I had a palin' up there that I had rivv out of white oak timber. **1994–97** Montgomery *Coll* (known to Brown, Cardwell, Jones, Oliver, Weaver).

B (also *rive out*) To split or cleave (shingles, boards, etc.) from a block of wood, as with a **froe** or similar implement.

1914 Arthur *Western NC* 258 [It was necessary] to rive out their shingles or "boards" for their roof covering and puncheons for their door and window "shutters" and their flooring. **1917** Kephart *Word-List* 408 *rived board* = a riven clapboard or shingle; others are called *sawed boards*. **1978** Burns *Our Sthn Mtneers* 12 He may speak of a "sight of flowers," "riving shingles," "handkerchers," and "soon starts," a traveler carries a "budget." **1986** Huskey *Sugarlands* 7 White oak could be split apart and [we could] rive splints for seating chairs, making baskets, and other things. **1989** *Matewan OHP-28* You saw these paling slats stick up with the sharp ends on them? We used to rive them out of trees here. **1993** Montell *Cumberland Country* 47 Long after roofs of tin and asphalt became common the technique once used to make board shingles—"riving" with a froe and mallet—remained the preferred method for producing high-quality hickory and oak tobacco sticks used in the harvesting of burley [tobacco].

rive out See **rive B**.

river boss *noun* See citation.

1964 Clarkson *Lumbering in WV* 369 = foreman in charge of a log drive.

river bottom(s) *noun* A low-lying, usually fertile area of land along a river. See also **bottom**.

1813 Hartsell *Memora* 130 ther was Some famous River botomes, verey large and leavile. **1861** (in **1980** Clark *Civil War Diary* 27) We campt two miles past Gainsborough in the bottom on the Cumberland River. **1862** *Mangum CW Letters* (June 16) it will be worse than any river bottom you ever saw. **1962** Dykeman *Tall Woman* 84 "River-bottom acres down next to Hawkins' new mill," Emma Caldwell answered promptly.

river hog *noun* See citation.

1964 Clarkson *Lumbering in WV* 369 = one who works on a river drive.

river man *noun* An imaginary figure said to live near a river and to threaten any who approach; a character used to warn children to behave themselves and to keep them from venturing near the water. See also **(the) bad man 1**, **booger A1**.

1996 Montgomery *Coll* = a fictitious person that parents employed to keep children away from the river, as in "You go down to that river alone and the riverman will grab you" (Cardwell).

river rat *noun* See citation.

1983 Montell *Don't Go Up* 200 = [a] person who lives on or near the water and obtains food from the river by fishing and trapping.

riving tree *noun* See citation.

1957 Broaddus *Vocab Estill Co KY* 64 = a straight-grained tree, good for riving into boards.

riz See **rise**.

riz bread *noun* Bread made from flour leavened with yeast.

1966 *DARE Survey* (Burnsville NC) = bread made with wheat flour. **1974** Fink *Bits Mt Speech* 22 = risen or yeast bread. **1995–97** Montgomery *Coll* (known to Adams, Brown, Bush); We had riz bread mostly on holidays (Cardwell).

roach

A *noun* A wave of hair combed or brushed sweeping up and back from the forehead. See 1952, 1993 citations.

[**1858** (in **1974** Harris *High Times* 136) The driver—a bald-faced, roach-maned, wall-eyed Irishman—cum down ofen the hary-cane deck an' cotch mister dandy by the collar an' the slack.] **1885** Murfree *Prophet* 17 His grizzled hair stood up in front after the manner denominated "a roach." **1952** Wilson *Folk Speech NC* 585 = a roll-back wave induced by combing or brushing the hair back. **c1960** Wilson *Coll* = a roll of hair or a method of brushing it to make it stand up from the forehead. (also verb). **1993** Ison and Ison *Whole Nother Lg* 56 = a lift to the front of a male's hair style, usually with the aid of hair creme.

[DARE *roach* n² chiefly South, South Midland]

B *verb* To comb or brush (one's hair) so that it sweeps up and back from the forehead.

1891 Moffat *Mtneers Middle TN* 317 The older girls wear theirs "roached" (combed back straight), and fastened in a loose knot at the back of the head with a "tucking comb"—a back comb without a top. **1919** Combs *Word-List South* 39 = to comb (the hair) straight back. **1939** Hall *Coll* (Indian Creek NC) She said she'd be out just as quick as she roached her hair back a little. *Ibid.* (Saunook NC) Give her the head-comb. She ain't even roached her hair back yet. **1952** Wilson *Folk Speech NC* 585 = a roll-back wave induced by combing or brushing the hair back; to comb or brush the hair in this manner. **c1960** Wilson *Coll* [see citation in **A**].

roach comb *noun* A comb for dressing one's hair in a **roach**.

1933 Thomas *Traipsin' Woman* 102 I'm satisfied that's for a half-round roach comb. I seen with my own eyes one of our fancy roach-combs on Florie Withers's head today.

road *noun* A way, path, route.

1826 Royall *Sketches* 58 For get out of the way, they say get out of the road: Road is universally used for way, "Put them cheers (chairs), out of the road." **1864** Reese *CW Letters* (April 3) this tena has giv mee more un Easness than any thing that has Cum my Rode senc I left home. **1941** Stuart *Men of Mts* 298 No children on the road are there? **1941** (in **1944** Wentworth *ADD* 517) Without [adjustable seats] tall people would have to drive with their knees in the road of their hands. **1943** (in **1944** Wentworth *ADD* 517) You can take some of these [= office chairs] out of the road. **1973** *AOHP/ALC*-97 You'd dig all the weeds out of the road, and then you just rake you some clean dirt around the corn. **1983** Page and Wigginton *Aunt Arie* 163 I miss goin' t'church, now, th'worst thing of anything that's come my road. **1985** Irwin *Alex Stewart* 265 A great big old rat had got down in my basement and was eating up my 'taters. I set me a steel trap in his road, where he went in and out. **1992** Offutt *KY Straight* 32 I'll just leave it lay and plow a new road around it.

[SND *road* n 5 (1) "direction, way, course, the route over which a person directs his journey"]

roadhouse *noun* See citations.

1986 Pederson et al. *LAGS* (Chattooga Co GA) = bar on the highway, place to dance. **2007** McMillon *Notes* = usually next to a county line, would usually have blockade [liquor] but sometimes also prostitution.

road monkey *noun* A logging worker who builds roads and keeps them free of debris, brush, and obstructions. Also called **chickadee**.

1930 Pendleton *Wood-Hicks Speak* 88 = a man building a logging road. **1964** Clarkson *Lumbering in WV* 369 = one whose duty is to keep a logging road in proper condition. **1974–75** McCracken *Logging* 5:76 Somehow or another he quit and went to West Virginia and when he come back he went to workin' on the incline as a road monkey, keepin' up roads and keepin' the roads piled with rock and first one thing and then another. **1989** Oliver *Hazel Creek* 65 The fellows responsible for keeping the logging road in proper condition were called "Chickadees" or "road monkeys." **2006** *Foxfire 40th Anniv* 311 Though most of the people in this photograph undoubtedly work for the company, only a few of them would be loggers. The list of employees required by a large operation was staggering, and would include . . . "road monkeys" (men who maintained the skid trails).

roasin ear, roas'n'ear, roasten ear See **roasting ear**.

roasting ear *noun* See also **roasting ear bread**.

A Variant forms *roas'n ear* [see **1977** in **B**], *roas'n year* [see **1915** in **B**], *roasten ears* [see **1884** in **B**], *roastnear* [see **1997** in **B**], *rosen yer* [see **1960** in **B**], *rosineer* [see **2006** in **B**], *rosten ear* [see **1862** in **B**], *rostnear*.

B An ear of corn sufficiently ripe to roast (traditionally in its husks in the ashes of a fire) to be eaten on the cob.

1824 (in **1912** Doddridge *Notes on Settlement* 82) What a jubilee when we were permitted to pull the young corn for roasting ears! **1847** (in **1870** Drake *Pioneer Life KY* 52–53) Now approached the daily feast of green corn—the era of "roasting ears," which began as soon as grains were half grown, and continued until no more milk would flow out to piercing the integument with the thumb nail. . . . My first business in the morning was to pull, and husk & silk enough for breakfast; and, eaten with new milk, what breakfast could be more delicious? **1861** (in **1980** Clark *Civil War Diary* 15) We left Adra campt at night at Large Branch on the right of the rode where the boys took the rostnears. **1861** Hedgecock *Diary* 102 Cut and hauled away a field of corn in roasting ears. **1862** *Neves CW Letters* (Aug 14) I have Just Eat the master bait of Rosten Ear soop that you hav saw latley we have had 2 baits off soop since we have bin heare. **1863** Wilson *Confederate Private* 29 (Aug 18) rosten years is from 50 cts to one 150 per doson. **1884** Smith *Arp Scrap Book* 402 We had roasten ears for supper and buttermilk and honey. **1915** Dingus *Word-List VA* 189 *roas'n years* = any dish made of green corn. **1921** Campbell *Sthn Highlander* 200 Young field corn is often eaten, "roasting ears" being considered a great delicacy. **1956** Hall *Coll* (Newport TN) A feller went in somebody's cornfield and got him some roastin' ears. **1960** Arnow *Seedtime* 390 When plump and filled with milk it was time for "rosen yers," beloved by most peoples who ever knew corn. Boiled, roasted, or cut off and fried, then seasoned with milk and butter, green corn served both as a vegetable and a substitute for bread. **1973** Foster *Walker Valley* 9:76 They didn't have nothing to eat there at the house, Aunt Clarinda didn't, but roasting ears and Irish potatoes. **1977** Hamilton *Mt Memories* 33 Papa planted corn in the garden for "roas'n ears" and we were not to go into the cornfield to gather corn from the main crop. We didn't have "roas'n ears" too often for Mama cut the corn from the cob and added milk and butter and thickening. **1997** Andrews *Mountain Vittles* 42 Momma sent me to the field a many of a time to pull an arm load 'a roastnears. **1997** Montgomery *Coll* = an ear of corn in the roasting stage, not hard (Cardwell). **2006** *Encycl Appalachia* 926 A more common, and arguably more flavorful, way of preparing fresh cob corn in the mountains is to roast it wrapped in shucks over the coals of a campfire, fireplace, or outdoor grill. So popular is this form of preparation that the term *roasting ear* (often elided and pronounced as one word: *rosineer*) is used throughout the middle and southern Appalachians to refer to any green corn for eating, even if the preparation method is to be boiling or frying. **2009** Sohn *Appal Home Cooking* 295 = young, not-filled-out, fresh sweet corn. **2016** Blind Pig (July 29) "Roast nears" are cooked in the oven. Sorta like parched corn, only you start with corn that is just starting to "come in."

roasting ear bread *noun* Corn bread made from grains of **roasting ears**.

1905 Miles *Spirit of Mts* 32 Odd-looking utensils, these: boat-like bowls of maple for the kneading of bread, piggins and keelers of cedar, a wooden spurtle for stirring the evening kettle of mush, and a huge "gritter" on which green corn is grated in late summer for the making of "roas'n'ear" bread. **1941** Justus *Kettle Creek* 35 "Let's have roas'n' ear bread!" The two girls brought back a sackful of tender green corn. . . . They all took turn and turn about grating the ears of corn. . . . Mammy put a pinch of salt in [the grated corn] and beat the batter with a spoon. Glory greased the griddle. . . . Mammy dropped a spoonful of grated corn on it, enough for a cake. **1964** Reynolds *Born of Mts* 10 Of the Katydid, the Cherokee say, "He has brought the roasting ear bread," because he is heard late in the season when corn is on the ear and doesn't say Katydid in their language. **1984** *GSMNP-153:49* They don't know what a roastin' ear is, but now . . . I mention havin' roastin' ear bread, and they're not acquainted with that. **1984** Page and Wigginton *Foxfire Cookery* 179 We used to dry the corn for roastin' ears. Then we shucked it and baked it in the oven. Then you could grate it off the cob, put you a little soda and salt and a little buttermilk in it and bake it. That's called "roastin' ear bread."

roasting ear pea *noun* See 1958, 1996–97 citations. Same as **cornfield pea**.

1931 *Professor Learns* "Do you like roas'near peas?" asked the man of the house cordially, before he served the visitor's plate. **1958** Wood *Words from TN* 15 = field peas or black eye peas that are turning yellow or are just ready to shell. **1996–97** Montgomery *Coll* (known to Brown, Bush, Jones), = field peas or black-eyed peas planted in rows of corn after the corn is nearly grown (Cardwell).

roastnear See **roasting ear**.

robbing pillars *verbal noun* See citation. Same as **retreat mining**.

2012 Portelli *They Say* 141 The last job was the most dangerous, "robbing pillars" or "retreat mining." After an area is mined out, the pillars of coal that hold up the roof are pulled down, capturing the last fragments of usable coal and collapsing the roof as the men withdraw as fast as they can.

robing *noun* Apparently a gown or robe.

1862 *Smith CW Letters* I will tell you what I have Drawd one pair of Drawers and one shirt and a Robin and a pare of pant they good yarn geans and a Cap and a pare of cotin socks. **1863** *Tesh CW Letters* (Nov 24) Tell John I said if he wants to he may take that Robin of mine and wair it out I dont care For it.

rock

A *noun*

1 Variant plural form without *-s*.

1939 Hall *Coll* (Gatlinburg TN) We had several rock on that trail and nothing to drill those rock with, only just steel and eight pound striking hammers, and I want you to know it was a very difficult job training those boys to drive steel with switch handles. **1972** *AOHP/ALC-388* They cooked on the fireplaces. They had great big iron kittles and a big, great big old fireplaces, and they's made out of huge rocks, you know, where they'd hewed them rock out and built. **1973** *GSMNP* 4:16 They call it the Indian Grave Ridge, you know, all these rock there. **1976** *GSMNP-114:22* The machine had blowed that out, all them buildings built there, hauled them rock off.

2 The pit of a peach.

1943 Chase *Jack Tales* 158 I couldn't find a thing but some peach seed where I been eatin' peaches and saved the pits to take home and plant. Jack . . . says, "Hand here one of them peach rock." **1969** *DARE Survey* (Hardscrabble KY, Walker KY).

3 Used in preference to *stone*.

1913 Kephart *Our Sthn High* 297 A mountaineer does not throw a stone, he "flings a rock." **1953** Hall *Coll* (Walland TN) I was born in a log cabin within a rock throw of where the hotel at Walland now sits.

4 In preference to *-stone* in compounds; see **grinding rock**, **sandrock**, **tomb rock**, **whetrock**.

B *verb*

1 To pelt (with rocks) in order to intimidate or to drive away or back, especially to ambush a rival in courtship on the latter's way home from seeing a girl (see 1987 citation); hence noun *rocking* = the action of pelting him with rocks on his way home from courting; *rock a house* = to warn or intimidate the inhabitants of a house by pelting it with rocks; *rock back home* = to drive cattle, chickens, or other animals home by casting rocks at them.

1910 Weeks *Barbourville Word List* 457 They rocked him on the way home from the party. **1913** Kephart *Our Sthn High* 259 A prime amusement of the small boys is "rocking" (throwing stones at marks or at each other), in which rather doubtful pastime they become singularly expert. **1921** Campbell *Sthn Highlander* 125 The boys "up the branch" or "down the creek" gather, especially on Sundays, for amusements which, if not vicious in themselves, are usually accompanied by more or less vicious features. It is such gangs that express their lawless independence and rural conservatism by "rocking" individuals and objects that meet with their disfavor, burning private and sometimes public property, robbing orchards, and similar offenses not peculiar to the mountain region. **1927** Bolton *Mt Girl Speaks* 5 A mountaineer does not throw a stone; he "flings a rock" or "rocks the chickens." **1939** Hall *Coll* (Nine Mile TN) He'd run a bear in on them, and they got to rocking it. **1953** Hall *Coll* (Deep Creek NC) [The bull] belonged to old man Collins. I told him if he tackled me I would have to shoot him. . . . I tried rockin' him to keep him off of me. **1964** Roberts *Hell-Fer-Sartin* 87 The next morning Tom arrived and he also rocked the little bird away when it came. **1970** Hall *Witchlore* 32 Incidentally, "rocking" (that is, throwing rocks at) was mentioned in two tales as the treatment for cows thought to be boogers or ghosts. **1986** *Sevier Settler* 8:25 "Rocking" people was a practice that was done on Halloween and throughout the year. If a fellow was walking his girl friend home from church, and if his friends knew which route he would be taking, the fellow's friends might hide in the bushes until the couple came along. Then someone would yell, "Pick 'em up," and his friends would throw a handful of rocks at the couple. The rocks were never meant to harm the couple, they were only meant as a teasing joke. **1987** Davenport *Pine Grove* 24 They called it a rocking but the object was just plain mayhem. The participants justified it by calling it a sport which was resorted to as a means of discouraging competition in courtship. This is the way the game is played. A boy, usually from outside the community, would attend some function such as a social, church service or pie supper where he would fall for one of the girls who was popular with community boys. Winning her attention, he would end up walking her home from the party. . . . In the meantime the boy who had been jilted by his girl was busy rounding up girls to help him teach that intruder a lesson on the evils of indiscretion. They would gather up all the rocks they could carry and from a vantage point alongside the road over which the intruder would return on the way home, they would ambush him. The sound of that flurry of rocks whizzing past him would motivate speed, the likes of which the fellow didn't know he had. They would pursue their prey until they ran out of rocks. Sometimes a rope or wire would be strung about knee-high across the road just beyond the point of attack, which was sure to give the victim a nasty fall just before he reached full speed. Only the foolhardy and those suffering from extreme love-sickness would take the second chance. **1997** King *Mt Folks* 52 "Ma" was married and living at Oldham's Creek in the days when people rocked houses. The White Caps (a band of hooded men who sought their own justice) threw rocks at houses as a warning of more severe punishment if the person living inside did not "mend their ways." **1997** Montgomery *Coll* = to drive animals toward home by throwing rocks at them (known to Adams, Bush, Cardwell, Jones, Ledford, Norris, Weaver).

[DARE *rock* v² 1 chiefly South, South Midland]

2 To cast (rocks) in a stream to cause fish to hide, thereby disturbing the water and preventing outsiders from encroaching on one's supply of fish.

1997 King *Mt Folks* 44 They'd rock a fishing hole, then send a runner upstream to warn someone else so they, too, could rock the hole and save the fish for the families along the creek.

rock along *verb phrase* See citation.

1972 Hall *Sayings* 115 *rockin' along* = going along as usual. "Everything is rockin' along just like when Lena was here."

[DARE *rock along* v phr chiefly South Midland]

rock back home See **rock B1**.

rock cliff *noun*

A Variant form *rock clift* [see **1913** in **B**]. See also **cliff**.

B A large overhang of rock that creates a shallow cave or sheltered area underneath. See also **rock house**.

1913 Kephart *Our Sthn High* 285–86 Pleonasms are abundant. . . . Everywhere in the mountains we hear of biscuit-bread, ham-meat, rifle-gun, rock-clift. **1934–47** *LAMSAS Appal* (Madison Co NC, Swain Co NC). **1939** Hall *Coll* (Bryson City NC) He come across a big rock clift and his dog got to barkin' into it. *Ibid.* (Nine Mile TN) We hit out down on what was called the Antony Ridge. We struck a big bear there, and we trailed him around, jumped him under some rock cliffs. **1957** Combs *Lg Sthn High: Word List* 82 *rock clift* = a large cliff, or "cliff house," with a small opening. Sometimes called "God's house." **1975** *GSMNP*-59:9 You just had to plant your corn and stuff sort of between the trees and the logs and rock cliffs and what have you. **1989** *Matewan OHP*-45 My daddy moved in onto that rock clift.

[DARE *rock cliff* n chiefly southern Appalachians]

rock dust *noun*

1 See citations.

1959 Roberts *Up Cutshin* 17 Safety crews install fans and test the air gas, and lay down rock dust to keep the bugdust from exploding. **c1975** *Miners' Jargon* 6 = limestone dust sprayed over roof, rib, and face, and throughout the mine to make exposed coal dust inert. **2002** Armstead *Black Days* 245 = white, powdered limestone sprayed in great quantities on mine roofs, bottoms, and ribs to eliminate the explosive qualities of coal dust. Mixes with coal dust particles to keep them apart. Critical to mine safety.

2 Pneumoconiosis incurred by long-term inhaling of such dust.

1975 Woolley *We Be Here* 92 I've got rock dust. I know that . . . When I lay down at night, my chest feels like somebody come along and set a big heavy plate of food on top of it. **1998** *Dante OHP*-53 If they [= miners] got rock dust and they got till they couldn't work, they didn't get anything out of it because it wasn't counted as a industry hazard.

rock fence (also *rock wall*) *noun* A fence constructed of stone or rock, usually without mortar. Same as **stone fence**. According to **1983** Pederson *East TN Folk Speech* 115, **rock fence** and **rock wall** were almost equally common in the Smoky Mountains and in East TN generally.

1862 Gilley *CW Letters* (Oct 7) they got me behind a rock fence wher my offercers put me an my company their. **1934–47** *LAMSAS Appal* (Madison Co NC, Swain Co NC) *rock fence*; (Swain Co NC) *rock wall*. **1949** Kurath *Word Geog East US* 40 *Rock fence* . . . is another Southern term that is fully established in the South Midland and the Shenandoah Valley. In West Virginia the Southern *rock fence* and the Midland *stone fence* occur side by side on the Monongahela and the upper reaches of the Potomac. **1958** Newton *Dialect Vocab*: *rock fence* = attested by 5 of 36 speakers from E TN mountains; *rock wall* = attested by 22 of 36 speakers from East TN mountains. **c1960** Wilson *Coll*: *rock fence* was the term used, but such fences were very rare, in the area. *Rock wall* was fairly common. **1966** Dakin *Vocab Ohio River Valley* 107 Regardless of the style of construction, these fences are usually known in Kentucky as *rock fences*. **1967–68** *DARE Survey* (Brasstown NC, Gatlinburg TN, Maryville TN) = a fence made of stone or rock without mortar. **1973** *GSMNP*-80:9 I can remember seeing her walk up the rock wall. You know, we had a great big rock wall where we carried rocks and built a rock wall. I couldn't see nothing but the top of her head a-coming. **1982** Maples *Memories* 79 There are many rock fences still standing throughout the Park. They marked boundary lines and kept the stock from straying. They were started when we plowed and tried to clear the garden. Every time you would hoe it seems like you would clang down on one of those rocks. **1986** Pederson et al. *LAGS*: *rock fence* = attested by 24/60 interviewees (40%) from E TN and 6/35 (17.4%) from N GA; 30/184 of all LAGS interviewees (16.3%) attesting term were from Appalachia; *rock wall* = attested by 18/60 interviewees (30%) from E TN and 7/35 (20%) from N GA; 25/121 of all LAGS interviewees (20.6%) attesting term were from Appalachia. **1987** Carver *Regional Dialects* 179 A much stronger fence, known in the Midland lexicon as a *rock fence*, is made from the stones removed from the fields by means of a *drag* or *sled*. **1991** Haynes *Haywood Home* 53–54 Daddy kept an ox-cart and sled for hauling rock out of fields. We built rock fences with most of the rock because we didn't have anything else to do with them and they had to come out of the fields.

rock house *noun* A precipice overhanging or sheltering a shallow space, especially providing refuge for hunters, travelers, or livestock, or as a temporary residence while a cabin is constructed; the cave itself. See 1860, 1964 citations. See also **rock cliff**.

1860 *Week in Smokies* 127 [Alum Cave] is not strictly a cave, it is what they call in the mountains a "rockhouse"—that is, a precipice so far over its base so as to shelter the space beneath from rain and snow. At Alums [sic] Cave the precipice is so great that it may well be called a cave. **1923** Furman *Mothering* 101 Trigger Branch is the most picturesque creek I have yet seen; along its sides cliffs and "rock-houses" alternate with rich hollows, small strips of bottom, and steep but flourishing cornfields. **1924** Raine *Saddlebags* 231 In many places they find shelter under the cliffs, in the shallow caves or "rock houses" that abound by natural formation. **1948** Dick *Dixie Frontier* 26 In the meantime the family had to be housed temporarily. Along the rivers in certain places the rocks projected out over the banks. Hunters and early settlers sometimes lived in the shelter of these for months. They were known as rock houses. It was in a shelter of this kind that Dr. Thomas Walker and his associates of the first American "land looking party," which came into Kentucky in 1750, lived for a time. **1952** Wilson *Folk Speech NC* 585 = a rock cave; an opening under a rock. **1957** Broaddus *Vocab Estill Co KY* 64 = a shallow cave, or a shelter underneath an overhanging cliff, used to house cattle. **1957** Combs *Lg Sthn High: Word List* 82 = a large cliff, or "cliff house," with a small opening. Sometimes called "God's house." **1964** Reynolds *High Lands* 14 A very small rock house put there by nature is passed on the way, one which has oft given shelter to hikers as a shower comes up. **1971** Fetterman *People Cumberland Gap* 594 The shop consists of a hand-cranked forge, an anvil, and a few tools, all of which John keeps in a shallow cave, or rock house, near his home south of Hyden (opposite). The term "rock house" is one of those handed-down phrases. Indians, early hunters from the Carolinas, and pioneer families lived in these rock houses while en route, while hunting, or while a cabin was being built. **1981** High *Coll* = a shallow cave under an overhanging rock or cliff. In the Gorge, these formations have been used for camping, keeping stock, or storing materials. Commonly found throughout the area. **1983** Broaddus *Estill Co KY Word List* 53 = a shallow cave, or a shelter underneath an overhanging cliff, used to house cattle.

[DARE *rock house* n 1 Appalachians, Ozarks]

rocking See **rock B1**.

rocking-chair (also *rocking-chair money*) *noun* Unemployment compensation.

1946 Hall *Coll*: *rocking chair money* = welfare payments: "Well, I haven't looked for a job yet, but I guess we could get one. I have been drawing rocking chair money." **1999** DeRozier *Creeker* 11 Whenever there was a lay-off or a shutdown at the mine, Daddy immediately found another job doing whatever kind of work he could scare up. One of the things he was proudest of was that he never took a day of "rocking chair" (unemployment compensation) in his life.

rockle *verb* To rock back and forth.

1943 Chase *Jack Tales* 18 He cloomb on up on the scaffle, rockled and reeled this-a-way and that-a-way. **1955** Ritchie *Singing Family* 133 He showed me the best rocks to step on, the ones that wouldn't rockle and make me lose my stand and fall into the branch.

rock-stone *noun* A tombstone.

1960 Stubbs *Mountain-Wise* (Aug–Sept) 9 He'd rather have "bachelor" wrote across his *rock-stone* than to marry a woman like —— (a woman of the community).

rock throw *noun* A short distance.

1953 Hall *Coll* I was born in a log cabin within a rock throw of where the hotel at Walland [TN] now sits.

rock wall See **rock fence**.

rocky chair *noun* A rocking chair.

1931 Goodrich *Mt Homespun* 55 Aunt Lizzie was sitting in a low "rocky chair," that had been brought out onto the grass before the house that she might watch "the doin's." **1997** Montgomery *Coll* (known to Adams, Bush, Cardwell, Weaver).

rocky horse *noun* A seesaw.

1986 Pederson et al. *LAGS* = attested by 3/60 interviewees (5%) from E TN; 3/3 of all LAGS interviewees (100%) attesting term were from Appalachia.

Rocky Mountain huckleberry *noun* See citation.

1980 Riggleman *WV Mtneer* 126–27 [Loggers] usually had nicknames for everybody and everything around the camp.... Prunes were "Rocky Mountain huckleberries."

rode See **ride A2**.

rogue

A *noun*

1 A thief; more generally, a scoundrel, an individual of unpredictable but treacherous or devious character.

1861 *Martin CW Letters* (Oct 13) wee have some Drunkards & liars & rogues but thay are few. **1863** *Gilley CW Letters* (Nov 22) I have got up my corn in the crib I think I have anuf to make out with if they government and rogus dont take it all away. **1939** Hall *Coll* (Saunook NC) When he found the rogue who stole those things, he didn't do nothin'. *Ibid.* (Tobes Creek NC) I think more of a rogue than of a man who'd lie. **1946** Hall *Coll* (Del Rio TN) It takes a rogue to catch a rogue.

[DARE *rogue* n 1 chiefly South, South Midland]

2 A domestic animal that displays wildness, as by breaking loose from its enclosure. See also **roguish 1**.

1957 Combs *Lg Sthn High: Word List* 82 = a domestic animal given to jumping over or breaking through fences, out of barns, etc. The Elizabethans knew the word with this meaning. It has a similar meaning in King Lear, III, vii.

B *verb*

1 To steal, swindle.

1896 *Word-List* 423 = to thieve. "The cat is *roguing* it some." **1939** Hall *Coll* (Saunook NC) He rogued me out of it. **1959** Hall *Coll* (Roostertown TN, from his ballad "Joe Dawson") He went to Big Creek to rogue and steal. **1992** Montgomery *Coll* = to engage in petty thievery or poaching (Cardwell).

[DARE *rogue* v 1 South, South Midland]

2 See citation.

1992 Montgomery *Coll* = to stray off course (Cardwell).

roguish *adjective*

1 Thieving, mean, ornery.

1864 Hill *CW Letters* (March 16) I hope the army will never hav to com thrugh wher you liv for tha[y] wuld Steal every thing you hav the Soldiers is the rogishist people that livs. **c1959** Weals *Hillbilly Dict* 7 = mean, ornery, devilish, mischievous. A girl might tell a boy, "Don't be so roguish!"

2 Of a domestic animal: displaying wildness, difficult to control, undisciplined, tending to break through fences. See also **rogue A2**.

1931 Combs *Lg Sthn High* 1304 That cow has turned roguish, and is up to meanness. (A "roguish" cow is one that jumps fences, etc.). **c1960** Wilson *Coll* = inclined to break fences and injure crops, as cows often do. **1974** Fink *Bits Mt Speech* 22 = descriptive of a cow inclined to jump the fence or stray from the pasture. **1986** Pederson et al. *LAGS* (Roane Co TN, Habersham Co GA). **1995** Montgomery *Coll* (known to Cardwell).

[DARE *roguish* adj 2 South, South Midland]

roke See **rake A1**.

roller bed *noun* See citation.

1994 Farwell and Buchanan *Logging Terms* = an arrangement of rollers used to get strips away from lumber being sawed; it had graduated strips on it to kick strips into chains that carried the strips to the slab saw.

roller hole See **rolly hole**.

roller mill *noun* See citation.

1983 Montell *Don't Go Up* 200 = mill designed to grind wheat into flour.

rolley-bat *noun* A children's ball game.

2013 *Blind Pig* (April 8) One of my very favorite ball games was "rolley-bat." What a hard time hitting the bat if the ground was bumpy with grass clumps.

rolley holie See **rolly hole**.

rollie holie See **rolly hole**.

rolling See **log rolling**.

rolling rear *noun* A logger tasked with keeping logs floating downstream. See citation.

1954 Blackhurst *Riders of Flood* 110 Duncan was "rolling rear." This man was given the task of rolling in beached logs or moving them over the shallows. Most of the men had this task assigned them. Some of the more skilled men were engaged in what was called "poling rear." These carried long pike poles, and most of their work lay on the water.

rolling roadblock *noun* See citation.

1990 Moore *Pittston Strike* 32 They [= striking coal miners] participated in "rolling roadblocks" of slow-moving vehicles that could force speeding coal trucks to drive the speed limit on the narrow roads.

rolling store *noun* Formerly, a small, makeshift emporium on wheels, usually operating on a barter system from the back of a truck, wagon, or a converted school bus that frequented mountain communities as late as the mid-20th century, but disappeared with the coming of grocery stores after World War II. By trading chickens, eggs, butter, and other products, customers could place an order for or receive such dry commodities as fabrics, brooms, matches, and gunpowder, such essentials as salt, coffee, kerosene, and baking powder, and other goods such as candy. It was operated by a parent store in town. Also called **store truck**.

1937 Hall *Coll* = a small store on wheels which came into mountain communities. **1975** Brewer *Valley So Wild* 255 Mountain families got staples from "rolling stores." These ran on a regular schedule out of Robbinsville or Bryson City. One week they picked up chickens, eggs, farm produce, and took orders for staples to be delivered the following trip. **1983** Montell *Don't Go Up* 200 = merchandise and produce vehicle traveling along established routes on a regular schedule. **1987** Wear *Sevierville* 100 Farm people who had eggs, chickens, and butter to sell would look for the weekly trip of the rolling store, a truck equipped with all the merchandise a family would need to buy. Some of the merchandise you could buy would be sugar, salt, coffee, oatmeal, kerosene, and sometimes candy for the children. **1996** Houk *Foods & Recipes* 19–20 Throughout the Smokies, an institution known as the "rolling store" developed after the community stores had closed in the Smoky Mountains in the 1920s and 1930s. A mobile merchant, complete with chicken coop atop his vehicle, made the rounds once every week or two, dispensing special delicacies such as coconut and candy in return for local butter, eggs, and vegetables. **1997** King *Mt Folks* 114 Driving a rolling store down the dusty roads of Sevier County in the late 1930s was a sight that Murrell Whaley said looked like "out our way." It was a '37 or '38 model pale blue Chevrolet truck with a black wooden store attached to the bed; on the side, the words "Butler's Rolling Store" were painted. There was a place on top of the store for cases of eggs, over the cab was a chicken coop, and at the back was a coal oil barrel with a spigot attached. **2002** *Cades Cove Preserv* 44, 45, 46 During the first half of the 20th Century, the folks living in Cades Cove and most other rural communities in America could see the dust cloud and hear the pots clanging before the rolling store ever came within view. But my, did it ever create a stir of excitement within the ranks of the barefoot kids and even among the grown-ups! The younger crowd were attracted by the promise of candy sticks and gum. The mature bunch were chasing worn-out chickens and gathering eggs for bartering ammunition. All were anticipating a glimpse, or more promisingly, acquisition of goods, seasonings and beverage makings like coffee and tea that could not be grown in the garden, hunted in the mountains, fattened in the pastures or obtained from nature's bounty. Now, the rolling store is as extinct as a doctor's house calls and is probably most closely approximated by our current pizza delivery vehicles. However the basic principle is pretty much the same, efficient curb service gratification of desired products not easily attainable otherwise.... Johnnie Bryant Sparks and Leon Sparks are among former Cades Cove residents who maintain childhood memories of the rolling store. Leon recalls those trucks rumbling over Rich and Cades Cove Mountains into Cades Cove until around 1936 when his family moved from the Cove. One was a flatbed truck with the stock protected by a tarpaulin cover. The other more closely resembled today's campers with a rectangular box constructed on the truck bed. A doorway was located at the rear where the storekeeper performed transactions on a 3 to 4 feet wide platform. A chicken coop was positioned on top and a kerosene tank at the rear.... The offerings of the rolling store included lamp globes, wicks, kerosene, needles, thread, flour, sugar, salt, soda, baking powder, coffee, tea, matches, pots, pans, chewing gum, bologna, salt pork (sow belly), livestock feed, candy, soap, pepper, socks, gloves, pencils, pens, ink, writing tablets, etc., etc. and gossip! The latter commodity was as important as any spice or house ware because electricity, radios and newspapers were only dreams for many and television was not even conceptualized for rural and Appalachian residents. The providers of staples distributed news and rumors from those on their service routes to very receptive and appreciative customers of the rolling store. **2002** Myers *Best Yet Stories* 195 Old school busses were converted into rolling stores. Shelves were built along each side after the seats were removed. The shelves were stocked with available canned goods. A chicken coop was fastened to the rear of the bus so that chickens could ... be traded in for groceries. Eggs, corn, and potatoes were also used as barter items. The rolling stores were very convenient when they stopped at the front door of those who lived in the country.

rolling store day *noun phrase* Formerly, a day of the week or month when a **rolling store** is regularly scheduled to visit a community.

2008 McCaulley *Cove Childhood* 40 On "rolling store days" I would search the yard for [the chickens'] hidden nests, gather as many of their little eggs as I could find, and take them to swap for sticks of hard candy.

roll the bed *verb phrase* See citations.

1935 Murray *Schoolhouse* 197 Night after night she "rolled the bed" which in Shady Grove means tossed about, was restless or sleepless. **1940** Bowman *KY Mt Stories* 246 = to toss about on the bed.

rolly hole (also *roller hole, rolley holey, rollie holie, roly-hole*) *noun* A game in which marbles must be rolled into a series of holes in sequence. See 1993 citation.

1892 Smith *Farm and Fireside* 267 What glorious sport in playing town-ball and bull-pen and cat and rolly-hole and knucks and sweepstakes. **1915** Dingus *Word-List VA* 189 *roly-hole* = knucks, a game of marbles. **1985** Irwin *Alex Stewart* 53 There was a marble game called Roller Hole. You'd find some smooth, hard ground and dig you out a good sized hole, and dig three smaller holes around it. And you'd get back off a ways and try to shoot a marble around them smaller holes and into the big one. That was called the Kingdom. We'd shoot to see who could get in the Kingdom first, and whoever did won the game. **1993** Montell *Cumberland Country* 148 Rolly hole was never played in all corners of the region; it has been historically centered in the counties of Clay, Jackson, Macon, and Overton in Tennessee, and Adair, Clinton, Cumberland, Metcalfe, Monroe, and Russell across the line in Kentucky. The two most prominent counties involved in rolly hole competition then and now are Clay and Monroe, separated only by the state line on which Dumas Walker's "beer joint" was located. Nor was the name "rolly hole" used to identify the game in all communities even where it was played. It appears that the term originated in the Jackson-Clay area with the likes of Hunter Reecer, Leslie Walker, and Millard Plumlee, all of whom were "old men" when Dumas Walker, who was born in 1915, was just a lad. Because of extensive television and newspaper coverage in recent years referring to the game as "rolly hole," that term eventually replaced the more typical label "marbles." As a child in northern Monroe County who actively participated in the sport, I knew it by the latter designation. "Let's play marbles" was the invitation to engage in this fascinating activity that often consumed an entire day. Most one-room schools in the area at one time had a marble yard, and many of these were still in operation until the advent of consolidated schools in the 1950s. Whether located on the school grounds or somewhere else in the community, such as in a blacksmith shop in Burristown, Jackson Country, or on the courthouse grounds in Celina, the marble yard used by youngsters was referred to as the "boy's yard," while the men's playground located nearby was known as the "big yard." ... Wherever it is played, the game of rolly hole marbles provides young fellows an opportunity to emulate their fathers and other older men. Too, the local form of marbles was and still is played in a social environment familiar to those who grew up with rural, agrarian lifestyles and who treasured periods of interaction with friends and neighbors. Rolly hole is a highly organized, fiercely competitive game of strategy involving two or more players, and has strict, unwritten rules for determining the winner. . . . Rolly hole is played with handmade stone marbles on a smooth, finely packed dirt court. While the marble yard's dimensions may vary slightly from community to community depending on the nature of the terrain, it is typically forty feet long and twenty-four feet wide. The edge of the yard is clearly marked either by the manner in which the surface is groomed or by wooden poles that contain the rectangular playing area. When a marble is knocked out of bounds, it must be shot from behind the line at the point where it went out. The yard contains three holes, each of which is the size of a typical marble. The holes are spaced ten feet apart in a straight line running lengthwise through the center of the yard. The game can be played by any number of individuals without partners, but the standard contest involves two teams with two players each. The object of the game is for both players on a team to shoot their marbles into all three holes as they move up and down the court three times. In other words, each hole has to "be made" three times by each player while he also assists his partner and keeps the opposing team from making the holes by hitting their marbles and knocking them away. **2009** Fulcher *Rolley Hole* 360 Rolley hole is a traditional marble game in which players roll flint marbles into a series of holes dug into a carefully leveled "marble yard." Though once common throughout the nation, the game is now thorougly known and passionately played in only one region of the South: Monroe and Clay Counties on the central Tennessee-Kentucky border. **2009** TN *Encycl* Rolley Hole, known as Three Holes, Poison, Granny Hole, or Rolley Holey, has also been widely played in Tennessee, but became especially identified with Clay County and Standing Stone State Park, which has hosted the National Rolley Hole Marbles Championship since 1983.

[DARE (at *rolly-holey* n) scattered, but chiefly South, South Midland]

roly-hole See **rolly hole**.

roof board (also *roof shake*) *noun* See citations. See also **board 1**, **shake B1**.

1960 Arnow *Seedtime* 263 These roof boards, still to be found on barns upriver and now and then a dwelling, were from four to six feet long, laid in overlapping rows, and held in place by long straight saplings known as butting poles. These were pegged at the ends, for a whole forted station could be built "without nail or screw." **1984** Roth *Reminiscences* The roofs of all cabins were made of handriven shingles [or] "roof boards." The shingles were split with the grain from white oak or hickory and all the cabins were built of handhewn logs. **1988** Smith *Fair and Tender* 28 We can see the house sticking up there outen the snow with smoke rising from the chimbly and snow on the roofshakes and isickles hanging down offen the roof. **1995** Trout *Historic Buildings* 22 True "roof boards" (as the old-timers call them) several feet long can be nailed from purlin to purlin, until the house is covered with only two or three courses of strong planks. This was an early form of roof construction, one that eliminated the need for sawn or split boards to close the gables, rows of lath on which to lay shorter shingles, and hundreds of nails.

roof shake See **roof board**.

roof tree *noun* The rafter set along the ridge of a house roof; figuratively = a roof over one's head, a place to reside.

1923 Furman *Mothering* 161 Yesterday, looking up from the garden, I was horrified to see him balancing on the roof-tree of the big house, with the slippery, frosty roof slanting steeply down on both sides. **1940–41** Still *Moving* 19 I say as long's a body has got a rooftree, let him roost under it. **1941** Still *Troublesome Creek* 13–14 Fifteen square acres we'd have to raise our chaps proper. Garden patches to grow victuals. Elbowroom a-plenty. Fair times and bad, we'd have a rooftree. **1986** Still *Wolfpen Poems* 35 O Do not wander far / From the rooftree and the hill-gathered earth. **1995–97** Montgomery *Coll* (known to Brown), = the long rafter that runs along, or supports, the ridge or top of the roof. The term came into use when the carpenter had to hew, from the length of the tree, a beam long enough to run the full length of the roof (Oliver).

roof working *noun* See citation.

2002 Armstead *Black Days* 245 = [a] thunderlike rumbling noise heard overhead as rock strata slip, slide, and settle to fill in mined-out areas. Common occurrence in underground mining. Can be a warning sign of a rock fall.

rook See **ruke**.

rookus See **ruckus**.

roomaticks See **(the) rheumatism**.

rooshian, **rooshin** See **Russian wild hog**.

rooster

A *noun*

1 A person outstanding as a joker or comic. See also **bird**, **captain**.

1917 Kephart *Word-List* 416 = captain. "He's a *rooster* of a feller." **1994–97** Montgomery *Coll* (known to eight consultants from the Smoky Mountains), = one who is always crowing about something, making a noise (Cardwell).

2 (also *rooster fight*) Any of several violets (*Viola* spp) used in a children's competition. See citations. Same as **chicken fight**. See also **rooster fight**.

1968 Wilson *Folklore Mammoth Cave* 23 (or *rooster fight*) = a violet of several species, often "fought" by children by hooking the heads together and jerking. **1978** *Smokies Heritage* 146 To mountain children the violet was known as "roosters." A favorite game resulted, "rooster fights," in which two violets were hooked together in the crooks of their stems and pulled; the winner pulled off the flower of the opposing violet. **1997** Montgomery *Coll* (known to Adams, Cardwell, Norris, Oliver, Weaver).

B *verb* Used as a euphemism for *cock*.

1913 Kephart *Our Sthn High* 101 Then the dad-burned gun wouldn't stand roostered (cocked); the feather-spring had jumped out o' place. **1952** Wilson *Folk Speech NC* 585 *rooster a gun* = to cock a gun; perhaps an example of verbal modesty or humor. **1957** Combs *Lg Sthn High: Word List* 82 = to cock (of a pistol, gun). A survival of the prudery and linguistic intolerance that began in the early years of the last century. Ex.: "This pistol won't stand roostered."

rooster fight See **chicken fight**, **rooster A2**

root-beer tree *noun* Same as **sassafras B.**

1973 *Foxfire II* 49 = [white] sassafras (Sassafras albidum).

root-cutter plow *noun* See citation. Same as **cutter** 3.

1968 Clarke *Stuart's Kentucky* 155 Walking between the handles of a mule-drawn or horse-drawn bull-tongue or root-cutter plow, the farmer broke up the root-filled rocky soil; he then harrowed it to break the larger clods before he *laid the ground off* in furrows.

rooter *noun* A hog with a long snout; the snout itself, sometimes cooked and eaten. See also **hill-rooter**, **long rooter**, **pine rooter**, **ridge rooter.**

c1960 Wilson *Coll* = a hog's snout. **1963** Watkins and Watkins *Yesterday* 87 Farmers who could not afford a Poland China pig bought razorbacks or pine rooters. They had long legs, a thin body, and a long slim nose or rooter. Neighbors laughed at a farmer for buying a hog that was "mixed with the possums." Or they said he fed his hog from a bottle and made its nose grow long and slender. **1967** *DARE Survey* (Gatlinburg TN) = a pig's nose. **1972** *Foxfire I* 205 Lot'a people throwed away that they called th' rooter. Oh I forbid that. I'd rather have that as any part a'th'hog. Oh that's good eatin'. **2004** *Smokies Guide* (Autumn) 10 Hogs used their rough snouts or "rooters" to dig up plant bulbs, roots, insects, and would also eat frogs, snakes, and lizards.

[DARE *rooter* n 3 chiefly South, South Midland]

root hog or die (also *root hog or die poor*) *verb phrase* To fend for oneself, work out one's own survival, be on one's own or caught between the need to work very hard and hunger or poverty.

1834 Crockett *Narrative* 117–18 It looked like it was to be starvation anyway, so we therefore determined to go on the old saying, root hog or die. [**1881** Pierson *In the Brush* 17 The swine were of the original "root-hog-or-die" variety, their long, well-developed snouts being their most prominent feature.] **1915** Dingus *Word-List VA* 189 = to look out for yourself or die. **c1950** (in **2000** Oakley *Roamin' Man* 91) But after a fue days the old folks would tell the young cupple to git busy and hunt a cabin or build one on the same place, and from then on it wus roat hawg or die. **1956** McAtee *Some Dial NC* 37 = work out one's own salvation. **c1982** Young *Colloquial Appal* 18 = work or starve. **1984** Woods *WV Was Good* 16 "Root hog or die" goes back to the colonial practice of turning hogs loose in the woods to make their own way. **1997** Montgomery *Coll* (known to Adams, Bush, Ledford, Norris); One has to root hog or die poor (Cardwell); It was a hard time. It was root hog or die poor (Jones), = settlers let their hogs loose to fend for themselves. They had to root or die. The proper form of the expression is "root, hog, or die" (Oliver).

root hog or die poor See **root hog or die.**

root tea *noun* A medicinal tea made from the roots of any of various plants such as **boneset.**

1991 Haynes *Haywood Home* 66 Root tea was good for hypertension.

rop See **wrap.**

rose See **rise A2.**

rosebay rhododendron *noun* An evergreen rhododendron shrub (*Rhododendron maximum/macrophylum*) that is the most abundant of all rhododendron species in the mountains, growing profusely at elevations up to 5,000 feet. Its flowers range from waxy white to pale rose-pink. In the southern mountains it is commonly known as **laurel.** Also called **big laurel**, **great rhododendron**, **pink bed**, **white laurel.** See also **catawba rhododendron**, **rhododendron.**

1941 Walker *Story of Mt* 48 Many members of the Heath family of plants are represented . . . the most beautiful, perhaps, is the rhododendron, known as mountain rose bay, which is in flower in the latter half of April and early May. **1977** Maurer *Mt Heritage* 12 It was a wise choice when the rosebay rhododendron was selected as West Virginia's state flower flower back in January 23, 1903, by a joint resolution of both houses of the legislature. **1988** *Smokies Guide* (Summer) 5 The two main types of rhododendron in the Smokies are rosebay and catawba. . . . Rosebay rhododendron is more often found in the Park's lower elevations, especially along shaded streambanks and ravines. Its white to pink flowers start blooming in early June at the low elevations and creep up to the mid-elevations through July and into August. Both the catawba and rosebay are somewhat unusual for keeping their large green leaves through the winter.

rosenyer See **roasting ear.**

rosin dust See **fiddle dust.**

rosineer, **rosten ear**, **rosten year**, **rostnear** See **roasting ear.**

rot, **rote** See **write 2.**

rotgut (also *rotgut liquor*, *rotgut whisky*) *noun* Poor-grade homemade whiskey (used as a term of derision referring to the physical effects of its consumption). See also **busthead**, **popskull.**

1859 Taliaferro *Fisher's River* 259 He had gone but a few minutes when "ole John" became very sick, and commenced throwing up his "rot-gut whisky." **1861** *Watters-Curtis CW Letters* (Dec 24) it is agoine to hwup him to get well it has all come frome exposure and Drinking of rot gut Whisky. **1864** *Chapman CW Letters* (May 3)

James Cooper has put [o]ut a grocery in his store hous sells rot gut at $3.00 per qt. **1901** Harben *Westerfelt* 146 We'll have to leave these barrels o' rot-gut with you. **1940** Haun *Hawk's Done* 156 He said all the while he was playing poker and drinking that old rot-gut liquor he thought about what a good time he could be having reading some book. **1966–67** *DARE Survey* (Cherokee NC, Maryville TN) = bad liquor. **1967** Williams *Moonshining* 15 The effects of this product are maddening, indeed, and those who suffer through a hangover from a "high fly" on this kind of moonshine whiskey refer to it as "rotgut." **1986** Pederson et al. *LAGS* (Blount Co TN, Cocke Co TN).

rotten *verb* To spoil, decay.

1937 Hyatt *Kiverlid* 68 I'll make one fatty dodger, but they ain't no use rottenin' Shad with spilin' in no sich a-way. **1957** Combs *Lg Sthn High: Word List* 83 = to rot. Ex.: "Then ingerns'll be a-rottenin' soon, if ye don't dig 'em." **1960** McCaulley *Cades Cove* I've made lots of caskets that's in them graveyards right there in Cades Cove now, a-laying there a-rottening. **1996** GSMNPCOHP I can show you poplar trees out there, five and six foot tree[s] a-laying on the ground a-rottening right now. **1997** Montgomery *Coll* (known to nine consultants from the Smoky Mountains).

[DARE *rotten* v scattered, but chiefly South, South Midland, Northeast]

rough (also *rough slick*) *noun* Same as **laurel bed**.

1908 Smith *Reminiscences* 438–39 Reader, did you ever crawl and climb through a laurel "rough"? If not, don't say you ever did anything difficult. **1915** Bohannon *Bear Hunt* 462 Lying grounds, you must know, are, in this country, always on the north or Tennessee side of the mountains, where are those laurel growths known variously as "woolly heads," "slicks," "roughs" and "yellow patches." **1937** Hall *Coll* (Cades Cove TN) Bears hide in the roughs and have trails through them. **1939** Hall *Coll* (Deep Creek NC) Those bears always fight up [i.e. not down a creek] into the roughs. **1953** Hall *Coll* (Bryson City NC) We would avoid huntin' on the Tennessee side as much as we could to keep from out of the roughs. It was so awful rough and laurely, and not much open woods on that side of the mountain. . . . The bear had left to go to his denning place in the rough. . . . Matt Hyde used to do some trapping back in there for bear, and they done that in back of the Smokies in those rough slicks, we call them.

[DARE *rough* n chiefly South Midland]

rough feed See **roughness**.

roughness (also *rough feed, rough stuff*) *noun* Roughage for livestock, including corn leaves, husks, and tops used as coarse fodder. See also **blade fodder**, **fodder**.

1813 Hartsell *Memora* 99 Did not draw aney rufness for our teeme. **1855** *Mitchell Letter* I have a plenty of roughness to winter my cattel pork fattend on the mast. **1863** Wilson *Confederate Private* 14 (March 27) everybody has fed out ther ruffiness but I think I can feed them. **1864** *Poteet CW Letters* (Oct 4) I would like to now how your Ruffiness held out for the Mare. **1870** *Hall CW Letters* (June 12) not Saveing Roughness I never was so hard run to keep my Stock alive. **1895** Edson and Fairchild *TN Mts* 374 = coarse fodder, hay, shucks, and the like, in contrast with grain. "The horses kin stay, but we've nothing but roughness fur 'em." **1913** Kephart *Our Sthn High* 38 Corn is topped for the blade fodder, the ears gathered from the stalk, and the main stalks afterwards used as "roughness" (roughage). *Ibid.* 112 She's in the field, up yan, gittin' roughness. . . . "Roughness," in mountain lingo, is any kind of fodder, especially corn fodder. **1939** Hall *Coll* (Alexander NC) Old people call feed "roughness." "Roughness" means corn-tops. Some folks call it "fodder." I'd call "fodder" mostly something like corn-blade feed. **1952** Wilson *Folk Speech NC* 586 *rough feed* = fodder, hay, and other heavy feed for cattle. **c1960** Wilson *Coll* (DARE) *roughness* = fodder, hay, straw—any stock feed besides grain. **1969** Doran *Folklore White Co* 114 *rough stuff* = such heavy animal feed as fodder and hay.

[DARE *roughness* n 1 South, South Midland, especially Appalachians]

rough slick See **rough**.

rough stuff See **roughness**.

round *noun* See citation.

1915 Dingus *Word-List VA* 189 *roun'* = rung (of a ladder).

[OED3 *round* n 13, c1450→]

round cat (also *round town, round-town ball*) *noun* A rudimentary form of baseball that involves fewer players. See also **blind cat**, **cat 1**, **town ball**.

1938 Stuart *Dark Hills* 237 The dead were now being buried on the ground where we used to play Fox and Dog, Jail, Among the Little White Daisies, London Bridge, and Round-town Ball with a twine ball. **1964** *DARE File* In the summer we played roundtown, or long cat or short cat, or drop-the-hat or hot pepper. **1979** Cook *Mt Grown* 9 Most of the kids . . . were busy on the sliding board, swings, see saw and running foot races. Others were trying to get together a game of stickball, referred to as roundtown. **1982** Slone *How We Talked* 94 A game we played which we called "round town" was very much like baseball, with a batter, pitcher, and first, second and third base, homeplate and striking out. **1989** *Matewan OHP-102* We'd play, they called it round town. That was kindly of a ball game . . . we played that at school. **2006** Shumate *Bridge Crew* 53–54 "Roundcat" was another game we enjoyed. It was similar to baseball except we used a soft rubber ball and a homemade bat. We could get a runner out by catching fly balls or first bouncers. We could get a runner out by throwing the ball between the runner and the base. Roundcat was fun but could be expensive. Our playing field was cramped between the creek and the schoolhouse and we collected more than our share of window panes. Each time that we hit a ball through a window, we had to cough up fifteen cents. As a result, we learned to pull the ball very early in our careers.

[DARE *round-town* n chiefly South Midland, especially KY]

rounders See **take roundance.**

round meat *noun* See citation.

1982 Slone *How We Talked* 43 = bologna.

round robin *noun* See citation.

1995 Adams *Come Go Home* 81 [Granny] would call up and order me to her house to haul the backwoods singers to some backwoods community center or the basement in some little church so far off the road that you had to drive as far as you could, then get out and walk a mile. These gatherings were called Round-Robins. The room would usually be empty except for a huge circle of chairs in the middle of the room.... A little before seven o'clock, every chair would be occupied by an ancient (ancient to me then meant over forty) male or female; and before long the room would swell with the sounds of the old love songs as one after the other of these singers took their turn. I attended many a Round Robin.

round town See **round cat.**

roust (also *roust up*) *verb, verb phrase* To rouse, drive (as one from bed or an animal from hiding).

1913 Kephart *Our Sthn High* 84 I knowed I couldn't roust ye no other way. **1928** (in **1952** Mathes *Tall Tales* 67) I dreamp me a dream last night, that we rousted up Ol' Lucky, that main big b'ar that killed them five dawgs last winter. **1994–97** Montgomery *Coll* (known to nine consultants from the Smoky Mountains).

[cf SND *rowst* v "to arouse, stir to action"; Web3 *roust* v "to rout out of bed" dialect; DARE *roust* v 2 chiefly South, South Midland]

rouster *noun* See citation.

1957 Neel *Backwoodsman* 39–40 = anything especially large or fine: "That coon I caught was a rouster."

roust up See **roust.**

route

A *noun* A rut or gouge in a road.

c1920 Kephart (in **1993** Farwell and Nicholas *Smoky Mt Voices* 138) That road has such bad routes in it. **1936** Coleman *Dial N GA* 25 The "rut" in a road is a "route." **1996** Montgomery *Coll* (known to Brown, Cardwell, Jones, Ledford, Norris, Oliver).

B *verb* See citation.

1996 Montgomery *Coll* The road was all routed out (Ledford).

rubbing doctor *noun* One who relieves or purports to relieve ills and pains by rubbing the part of the body affected.

1971 *Boogers* 36 We toted'em and ruffed 'em around [after they fainted]. Even got a rubbin' doctor from Pine Mountain when they came to.

rub board *noun* A washboard.

2002 Armstead *Black Days* 22 The next day she, or my older sisters, scrubbed them on rub boards, rinsed them, wrung them out by hand, and hung them outside to dry.

[DARE *rubboard* n 1 now chiefly South, South Midland]

ruck, rucked See **rake A.**

rucket See **ruckus.**

ruckus *noun*

A Variant forms *rookus, rucket.*

1942 Hall *Phonetics Smoky Mts* 41 *rookus* ['rukəs], *rucket* ['rʌkɪt].

[DARE (at *ruckus* n) especially South, South Midland]

B A disagreement, commotion, noisy disturbance; thus *raise a rucket, raise a ruckus* = to make a commotion or much noise; to have a boisterous time, as at a lively party.

1890 Fruit *KY Words* 66 *ruckus* = rumpus. **1939** Hall *Coll*: *raise a rucket, raise a ruckus.* **1957** Broaddus *Vocab Estill Co KY* 64 *ruckus* = a row, disturbance. **1966** *DARE Survey* (Spruce Pine NC) = a disagreement or quarrel. **1975** Jackson *Unusual Words* 157 A *racket* implies more actual contact, whereas *ruckus* or *rookus, fraction,* and *fray* all mean a fist fight or gun fight. **1983** *Dark Corner OHP-28A* He was a little better feller about raising a ruckus with you just for a fight than the Furman boys down here. **1993** Ison and Ison *Whole Nother Lg* 57 *ruckus* = a fight or argument that causes noise, etc.

[OED3 *ruckus* n origin uncertain; originally and chiefly U.S.; Web3 *ruckus* n probably blend of *ruction* + *rumpus*]

ruckus juice *noun* Homemade whiskey.

1968 *End of Moonshining* 101 Various names given moonshine include: ruckus juice (pronounced "rookus"). **1975** Carter *Gospel Truth* Whiskey was "ruckus juice" or "corn squeezins."

ruction (also *runction*) *noun* A loud, often violent quarrel or disagreement.

1904–20 Kephart *Notebooks* 4:853 Them two preachers like to had a ruction. **1913** Kephart *Our Sthn High* 284 If they quarrel, it is a ruction, a rippit, a jower, or an upscuddle—so be it there are no fatalities which would amount to a real fray. **1921** Combs *Slang Survivals* 117 *ruction* = a rough-and-tumble, free-for-all fight. **1957** Parris *My Mts* 179 There'd been a runction over on Hazel Creek. Some of the folks standing around were discussing it. "If a feller'd treated me the way Alf did," one said, "I'd get me a forty-some-odd and shoot enough meat off his bones to feed a hound-dog a week." **1974** Fink *Bits Mt Speech* 22 They was a turrible *ruction* at camp meeting. **1995–97** Montgomery *Coll*: *ruction* (known to Oliver); *runction* (known to Brown, Cardwell, Shields).

[OED3 *ruction* n apparently representing an Irish English pronunciation of a shortening of *insurrection* n. (earliest in form *'ruction*); DHE originally Irish alteration of *insurrection*]

rue back *verb phrase* To back out of a trade or agreement made in good faith; to regret and attempt to back out of one; hence verbal noun *ruing back* = backing out of a trade or agreement; noun phrase *rue back.*

1891 Brown *Dialect in TN* 174 To *rue back* is to *back out*, and is used in such examples as "he cheated me and I want to rue back." **1915** Dingus *Word-List VA* 189 = to "back down" from a bargain. **1952** Wilson *Folk Speech NC* 586 = to withdraw from a bargain. **1957** Combs *Lg Sthn High: Word List* 83 = to withdraw or be released from a trade or bargain. **1982** Slone *How We Talked* 5 Another well-known custom: if you asked a price for something, and someone offered to give you what you had asked, you must take this price, even if you had later changed your mind and did not want to sell at that price. It was counted very shameful if you did not, and was called "ruing back." *Ibid.* 39 = to back out of a trade, not accept an agreement already made. **1991** Still *Wolfpen Notebooks* 72 I know a man who swapped his wife for a mule, and it was as good a deal as ever made. All three were satisfied—the man who got the mule, the man who got the woman, and the woman who agreed to it. No rue back. **1996** Montgomery *Coll* (known to Brown, Cardwell, Jones, Norris, Oliver).

[SND *rue* v 2 "to break or withdraw from a bargain or contract"; Web3 *rue back* "to repent and try to withdraw from an agreement or bargain" South and Midland; DARE *rue* v chiefly South, South Midland]

ruffledy *adjective* Ruffled.

1984 Burns *Cold Sassy* 201 There were ruffledy yellow and brown checked curtains at the windows and the same cloth was on the ceiling, glued up there like wallpaper.

ruin *verb*

A Variant base form *rurn*, past-tense forms *ruint, rurned, ruirnt, rurnt*, past-participle forms *rernt, ruint, runt*; hence participial adjectives *runt, rurnt*.

1942 Hall *Phonetics Smoky Mts* 38 [rɝn]. **1961** Williams *R in Mt Speech* 6 Frequently r is inserted in other words . . . *breakferst, terbaccer, rurnt* (ruined). **1974** Fink *Bits Mt Speech* 22 They ruint me. **1982** Powers and Hannah *Cataloochee* 93 "Major" complained to Professor Hall about the new hunting rules imposed on him. "(The Park) has rernt this country. They have us hemmed in, 'n you cain't kill a thing." **1991** Thomas *Sthn Appal* 142 Hit's jist ruint that town, down there. **2001** Lowry *Expressions* 8 I've went through with so much, it's ruint my nerves. **2007** Preece *Leavin' Sandlick* 34 If'n it got wet it'd be ruirnt. **2013** Venable *How to Tawlk* 42 runt = destroyed: "Yeah, but she biled 'em 'taters 'til they's plum runt!" **2018** *Blind Pig* (May 29) Don't drink that milk, it's ruint! *Ibid.* I've also heard "rurned" instead of ruint but in the case of milk it would be spiled.

B Senses.

1 To injure, spoil, wreck, inflict serious but usually only partial or impermanent damage on.

1913 Kephart *Our Sthn High* 294 "I'm bodaciously ruint" (seriously injured). *Ibid.* 296 Many common English words are used in peculiar senses by the mountain folk, as . . . ruin for injure. **1925** Furman *Glass Window* 9 I'll gorrontee there hain't a one ruint. **1956** Hall *Coll* (Roaring Fork TN) I was taught not to use no bad language, and I bumped my toe, and I cut the nail off of it and I grabbed my foot up and I said, "God damn, I've ruint my foot." **1964** Roberts *Hell-Fer-Sartin* 158 He cut ole Shorty's long smooth tail off right behind his years. Just like to ruint my dog. **1974** *AOHP/ASU-204* Television ruint the country. **1985** Irwin *Alex Stewart* 150 I ruint my teeth cracking hickory nuts. **1994** Montgomery *Coll* (known to Cardwell). **2008** *Rosie Hicks* 1 Girls, you ruined my apples.

2 To seduce or rape (a woman), causing the lose her virginity.

1957 Combs *Lg Sthn High: Word List* 83 = to seduce (as of a virgin). **1988** Smith *Fair and Tender* 129 I think he likes me better since I am ruint! **2000** Morgan *Mts Remember* 26 When they ruint the MacDowell girl the Indians signed their doom in this valley.

ruinate *verb* To ruin, destroy (as one's reputation).

1867 Harris *Sut Lovingood* 49 Lite, lite, ole feller an' let that roan ove yourn blow a litil, an' I'll 'splain this cussed misfortnit affar: hit hes ruinated my karacter es a pius pusson in the s'ciety roun' yere, an' is a spreadin faster nur meazils. **1917** Kephart *Word-List* 416 = to ruin. **1927** Woofter *Dialect from WV* 363 = to ruin. "Jim ruinated a good game when he got that hand." **c1960** Wilson *Coll* = to ruin in any sense. **1994–97** Montgomery *Coll* (known to Brown, Cardwell, Oliver, Weaver).

[OED3 *ruinate* v 1 now frequently regional; EDD *ruinate* v in general dialect use; Web3 *ruinate* v 1 chiefly dialect]

ruination *noun* Ruin, destruction, or a cause of destruction (especially of one's morals).

1927 Woofter *Dialect from WV* 363 = cause of ruin. "That boy will be the ruination of his father yet." **1940** Haun *Hawk's Done* 47 Told her it was going to be the ruination of him. **1994** Montgomery *Coll* This moonshine's going to be the ruination of my family (Cardwell).

ruke, ruked See **rake A**.

rukshus *adjective* Disrupting, violent.

1955 Ritchie *Singing Family* 192 Mom said it [= shooting a gun to celebrate Christmas] just sounded plain rukshus to her, just blasphemous.

ruling days *noun* The twelve days beginning on December 25 or January 1, with each day said to govern the weather for one month of the ensuing new year.

[**1888** Brown *Peculiar People* 506 The weather during each of the first twelve days of the year is, consecutively, a fair sample of the weather that will prevail during each month of the year.] **1905** Miles *Spirit of Mts* 107 He and Arth do not disagree about certain weather signs their mother had taught them when they were "shirt-tail boys," signs about Groundhog Day, for example, and the Ruling Days, the twelve days from the twenty-fifth of December to Old Christmas, each of which rules the weather of a month of the coming year. [**1956** Freel *Cherokee Co* 48 One of the very oldest of the weather superstitions is that twelve days give a forecast of the twelve months of the year. This is the twelve days between

December 25, or Christmas, or Twelfth Night of Epiphany. What ever was happening for that day foretold the twelve months of the coming year. Other prognosticators of the twelve day theory took the first twelve days of January as the ruling theory or guide.] **1967** Jones *Peculiarities Mtneers* 81 January 1 to 12—These were "ruling days" for the entire year. The weather on each of the first twelve days of a new year determined the weather for the corresponding month. **1970** Clark *NC Beliefs* 51 Weather on each of the ruling days, January 1–12 was sign of same sort of corresponding month. [**1981** Alderman *Tilson Mill* 16 For a yearly forecast, he watched the twelve days after Christmas, for each day of the twelve indicated the weather for one month during the coming year.] **1995–97** Montgomery *Coll* (known to Adams, Bush, Cardwell, Jones, Ledford, Norris, Oliver). [**2005** Williams *Gratitude* 519 It is said that what the weather is like on each of the first 12 days of January rules, or foretells what the weather will be like for each of the 12 months of the coming year.]

rumatics See **(the) rheumatism.**

rumble *verb*

1 To pound, make a prolonged noise.

1925 Dargan *Highland Annals* 90 Then he goes to Len's an' rumbles on the door till Len gits up an' lets his dog out, an' Buck takes him off to hunt that fox. **1997** Montgomery *Coll* (known to Bush, Cardwell, Oliver, Weaver).

2 To be disconcerted, grumble.

1995 Montgomery *Coll* He kept rumblin' all day about that affair (Cardwell).

rumptafetida *noun* Same as **asafetida.**

1992 Jones and Miller *Sthn Mt Speech* 104. **1997** Montgomery *Coll* (known to Andrews, Bush, Jones).

[blend of *rump* + *asafetida*]

run

A *verb* Principal parts.

1 Variant past-tense forms *run, rund, runned.*

1795 (in **1919** DeWitt *Sevier Journal* 174) (Jan 25) Washington & John Fickee carried horses to Jonesbo[rough] That run away from Sevier & Ruthy. **1799** (in **2008** Ellison *High Vistas* 37) We run the line between the State of N.C. & T. on the extreme height of the Stone Mn to our camp at the upper Rye Patch. **1813** Hartsell *Memora* 122 they Run like lusty filowes. **1842** Carpenter *Diary I* 148 Abern Johnson ag 100.7 dide [= died] july 2 he war farmer and run forg to mak iron and drunk likker all his days. **1844** Willnotah *Ms* 15 His friends run out to see the site but could see nothing. **1861** *Carter CW Letters* (Dec 5) I never expect to forget the tears that run over my face the last night we stad to gather. **1864** *Hill CW Letters* (Oct 21) I run a bout 5 milse and tha[y] rund me through the river twise the river was about 50 yards wide and it was waist deep to me but tha[y] never got me. **1884** Smith *Arp Scrap Book* 78 At the first crack of the whip they . . . got loose and run away. **1922** *TN CW Ques* 1019 (Blount Co TN) My father was a shoemaker by trade and run his own shop. **1934–47** *LAMSAS Appal* (Swain Co NC). **1939** Hall *Coll* (Little Cataloochee NC) Johnny run to the fence and jumped the fence and never, never knocked a rail off, and it was about a eight-foot rail fence. **1953** Atwood *Verbs East US* 20 *Run* . . . is used by from two thirds (Pa.) to over nine tenths (W.Va.) of Type I informants [i.e. older speakers with little formal education] and by from one third (Pa.) to one half (W.Va. and Md.) of Type II [i.e. younger speakers with more formal education]. In Va. and N.C. *run* is used by nearly all the informants of both Type I [i.e. older speakers with little formal education] and Type II [i.e. younger speakers with more formal education]. **1969** *GSMNP-43:16* My father run a store there for years before he died. **1972** *AOHP/ALC-226* My brothers and sisters got out in his car while we was setting in the house and runned it over in a culvert. **1979** *Big South Fork OHP-27* We went from there down to the Beatty Well on Picklety Creek that run into the Big South Fork. **2001** Lowry *Expressions* 14 I runned a little fever last night. **2008** *Rosie Hicks* 1 I run around the house hunting for you and Papa and I couldn't find neither one of you'uns.

2 Variant past-participle forms *ran, runned.*

1862 Gatlin *Immortal Hero* 9 "Merciful God," exclaimed Mr. Elmore, "Keelan, have you went to sleep on the road, and has the train ran over you?" **1864** *Chapman CW Letters* (May 25) thay all believed he had ran away Sence news come that he had run a way. **1940** Haun *Hawk's Done* 189 I was still standing in the door, and if I hadn't dodged out of the way he would have runned right smack-dab over me. **1953** Wharton *Dr Woman Cumberlands* 66 You could buy whiskey for twenty-five cents a gallon from the still and hit had been runned through twicet. **1967** Hall *Coll* (Townsend TN) [The orchard] runned right down through the cove, you know, all the way through the cove. **1975** *AOHP/LJC-384* One fellow had ran away from him. **1978** Montgomery *White Pine Coll* V-2 He had took his car and ran into her house. **1989** *Matewan OHP-45* I'd used to trade with him. I'd runned a store.

B Senses.

1 Of a hunting dog: to drive or herd (especially cattle) to keep them from straying.

1937 Hall *Coll* (Cades Cove TN) Our dog has been teached to run the cattle. **1963** Watkins and Watkins *Yesterday* 79 Running a frolicky and stubborn cow was tiring, and the farmer despised the chase which took him away from more necessary work.

2 Of a hunter or hunting dog: to drive or chase (a game animal); of an army: to pursue (enemy troops).

1861 *Carden CW Letter* (Oct 6) [We] run them 14 miles east of here taken som provisins some of arms. **1927** Mason *Lure of Smokies* 231 Dogs ain't fit fer nothin' but runnin' deer an' killin' sheep. **1939** Hall *Coll* (Deep Creek NC) I've got some dogs in there that won't run nothin' much but a bear. *Ibid.* (Hartford TN) Older people told me that dogs wouldn't run a panther. *Ibid.* (Hazel Creek NC) They hain't one dog in a hundred that would run a panther [but] pretty near any of them will run a wolf. **1941** Stuart *Men of Mts* 190 Well I took old Satan out to the sweet clover and he runs a snake like a rabbit. *Ibid.* 228 I'm goin' out with Big Aaron Hargis to hear his hound pup run. **1956** Hall *Coll* (Raccoon Creek NC) The dogs begin running the coons. **1970** *Hunting* 14 When he got a new dog, he'd take him out, and whatever he ran, why, "that's what kind'a dog it'uz goin' to be." *Ibid.* 15 Your trouble is keepin' 'em from runnin' a deer. **1989** *Matewan OHP-9* Now in the later years lot of people hunted [dogs] just to hear their dogs run. **1996** Isbell *Last Chivaree* 12 That beagle'd run anything that makes a track—any kind of rabbit, groundhog, possum . . . he'd run another dog's track.

3 Of a hunted animal: to draw dogs on a chase.

1939 Hall Coll (Deep Creek NC) I could hear the bear run [the hunting dogs] and snap his teeth.

[SND *rin* v 7(2)]

4 Of a hunter: to release (dogs) to pursue a hunted animal.

1989 *Matewan OHP-28* He never killed [the foxes]. He just runned his dog. I seen his dogs run as high as three days and come in with such sore feet it'd take nearly a week before they could walk.

5 (also *run off, run out*) To distill (whiskey, brandy); make (sorghum molasses, syrup, etc.). See also **run C2**.

1939 Hall Coll (Newport TN) We used fifty pounds of sugar to a bushel of meal and ran it off a dozen times or so. *Ibid. Run off* = to turn fermented mash into steam, which is condensed in a cooling tank into liquor. The first run is known as "singlin's": the second is "doublin's." The second run is by-passed by the use of the "thump tank." **1949** Maurer *Argot of Moonshiner* 12 *run out* = to finish distillation of the beer on hand and cease operation, either temporarily or permanently: "We're gonna run out and quit"; "This set's hot, but we may have time to run it out"; "When we run out, we'll move up the creek." **1967** Williams *Moonshining* 14 The skilled moonshiner is most careful to "run his beer" at the time when alcoholic content is highest, for it begins to change to vinegar rapidly. **1974** Dabney *Mt Spirits* 15 Six days later, when that cap falls and the top gets clear, the mash became "beer" and it was ready to run off. **1976** Garber *Mountain-ese* 76 Come over tonight and help us run a stir of molasses. **1978** Montgomery *White Pine Coll* I-3 A lot of areas still have a lot [of moonshine] being passed between individuals who know someone who is still running a still and still running it off. **1985** Dabney *More Mt Spirits* 66 Old timers would beat apples up in November and December and just let 'em set thar and run 'em and make brandy in the Spring. **1989** Smith *Flyin' Bullets* 333 The "silver cloud" stills were big aluminum pots that held five or six hundred gallons. They just ran whiskey off on one worm. We would bring all the copper stills in but we cut down and destroy [sic] all the silver clouds. **2006** *WV Encycl* 496 The first step is to sprout the corn, then crush the sprouted grain and mix with water. This mixture, called mash, is fermented in open barrels. If moonshiners have yeast and use it, the fermentation takes up to four days; if they don't have yeast and if the weather is cool, fermentation takes longer, maybe two weeks. When fermentation is complete, the mildly alcoholic liquid, now called beer, is ready to distill or "run off."

6 To send (livestock) to forage or graze, especially on **open range**.

1937 (in **2009** Powell *Shenandoah Letters* 117) The man wanted me to let his cattle run up their when I lived their. **1939** Hall Coll (Cades Cove TN) We could run them [= cattle] on the mountain something like five months of the year. **1954** Blackhurst *Riders of Flood* 62 [He] always kept about two dozen razorbacks runnin' in the woods. **1979** *Raising Dogs* 184 Everybody run their cattle outside then and farms was all fenced.

C *noun*

1 A small, sometimes seasonal stream; a small valley (see 1973 citation) whose watercourse is that stream. [Editor's notes: These senses are difficult to distinguish because the two features normally co-occur on the landscape; the term has very limited currency in the NC/TN mountains (e.g. Bark Camp Run TN), but is progressively more common in VA and WV. When Joseph Hall began research in the Smokies in 1937, he was told that a well-known character of the Oconaluftee (NC) area lived on Tight Run Branch, a small, sluggish tributary of the Oconaluftee River. It was apparent that **run** and **branch** were redundant, arising from the likelihood that **run** carries like meaning in an area where branches and creeks and prongs and rivers are abundant. Thus, **branch** was apparently added to clarify the meaning of the place-name.]

1770 (in **1940** McJimsey *Topo Terms in VA* 386) For that Precinct on Mack's Run, a branch of New River. **1824** Knight *Letter from KY* 106 The Phraseology in this state is sometimes novel. . . . They here call a river, a run. **1833** *McLean Diary* (Oct 31) the Bridg Run Runs for the firs since July. **1927** Woofter *Dialect from WV* 362 The people who live on that run are all poor as Job's turkey. **1937** Hall Coll Tight Run Branch NC, tributary of Oconaluftee River, place name (where *run* seems to be fossilized in a redundant expression). **1949** Kurath *Word Geog East US* 32 Run appears in the names of many small streams throughout the North Midland, so that even those who no longer use *run* as a common noun have occasion to refer to a particular stream in the neighborhood as *the run*. **1952–57** (in **1973** McDavid and McDavid *Vocab E KY* 153) The North Midland *run* "small stream" is practically confined to the Ohio Valley, as is the pronunciation of *creek* . . . riming with *lick*. **1960** Hall *Smoky Mt Folks* 59 = a marshy place or small stream, as in Tight Run, near Ravensford. **1968** Powell *NC Gazetteer* 427 [Occasionally used for small watercourses]: Rough Run (Jackson Co, flowing into West Fork Tuckasegee River). **1973** GSMNP-76:4 They was a big hollow run down here. They call it the Groundhog Hollow, and he went up it a little piece and got down on Little Dry Ridge here. **1989** *Matewan OHP-39* I was borned at Coal Run, Kentucky, below Pikesville, Kentucky. **1994** Montgomery Coll = a stream, stream bed, or small hollow (Brown), = the smallest tributary of a stream, which may have four or five runs (Cardwell). **2007** Milnes *Signs Cures Witches* 65 The Annanias Pitsenbarger farm [was] just down the run and across the road from Johnny's farm.

[OED *run* n[1] II.9 "a small stream, brook, rivulet, or watercourse" chiefly U.S. and north(ern English) dialect; SND *rin* n 1]

2 (also *running, run off*) The production cycle of whiskey, brandy, molasses, etc.; the quantity produced in such a cycle. See also **run B5**.

1832 *McLean Diary* 10 Warm Wether Concidrabel of Run of sugar water hard Shower of Rain and thunder. **1863** *Vance Papers* (July 8) as to my stiling I sufferd the neighbours to make A fu runs but all that was stild was not Enought to Keep my hogs from suffering som died. **1881** Atkinson *After Moonshiners* 20 In one corner [of the still house] a rough bedstead is constructed, and on it are several quilts and blankets for the use of the person or parties who sleep at the distillery when a run is made at night. They also keep at the distillery a skillet, coffee pot, &c., with which they do their own cooking. **1922** Kephart *Our Sthn High* 220 No doubt he and his party were on the way to some still-house, where they would stay until the "run" was made. **1924** Abernethy *Moonshine* 95 He recently had disposed of a large "run" of apple brandy and was in possession of almost one hundred dollars, which in Jim's financial schooling simply represented so many meals. **1939** Hall *Coll* To turn fermented mash into steam, which is condensed in a cooling tank into liquor. The first run is known as "singlin's." The second is "doublin's." The second run is by-passed by the use of the "thump tank." **1962** Hall *Coll* (Newport TN) A pregnant woman will spoil kraut or [the] mash for a run of liquor. **1968** *End of Moonshining* 101 There's gonna be a runnin' tomorrow. **1974** Wood *Mt Memories* 7 I remember the old rock furnace where the boiler set, and also recall seeing some of the folks working by the light of the lanterns to finish the "run" of apple butter, as they would say. **1977** Shields *Cades Cove* 79f It was sort of a custom to have a party after a "run off" of moonshine whiskey. Sometimes called backins parties, these featured a quantity of the mash "backins" or spent beer, heated with spices and served along with food. **1984** Head *Brogans* 146 About 8 o'clock the mixture was ready! Four strong men lifted the vat [of boiling molasses] off the fire and carried it a few steps away. The molasses was then dipped out and strained through cheesecloth. This "run" was a little thick and the straining was a slow process. **c1999** Sutton *Me and Likker* 81–82 Your prime likker comes out of the second run. The third and fourth run is your best for quality. **2007** Farr *My Appalachia* 115 The first runoff was weak and impure and had to be redistilled to rid it of water and oils. The cooker was cleaned out in preparation for the second runoff. The first run was then put back in, some water was added, and the liquid was turned to steam, condensed, and collected again.

3 In phrase *the run of* = about, approximately.

1957 Combs *Lg Sthn High: Word List* 83 *run of* = about, near. Ex.: "The run o' six year or better."

4 See citation.

c1975 *Miners' Jargon* 6 = term given to an eight-hour working shift or location or a quantity of coal produced during a period.

run-ago, run-and-go, run-an'-go See **running go**.

run around *noun*

1 A place where a railroad engine can be turned around to reverse course.

1974 GSMNP-50:2:10 Just above Elkmont up there at the old run around they called it, where they turned the engines around.

2 A cul-de-sac.

1989 Landry *Smoky Mt Interviews* 181 [The spasmodic spring] is up at what they call the runaround up at the upper end [of Greenbrier].

3 A swelling or infection around a fingernail.

1863 *Love CW Letters* (Aug 26) the boys is all well except A W Smith and bob I heard from them yesterday they are a most well steve has three Sore fingers with runarounds.

run a set (also *run sets*) *verb phrase* To perform the figures of a square dance, using a caller but without music. See also **running set, set C4**.

1913 (in **2014** Spalding *Appal Dance* 124) Reports from Pine Mountain tell of boys and girls "running sets" at the school, the teachers offering occasions for dancing at which guns and alcohol were forbidden. **1914** (in **2015** Jamison *Hoedowns* 73) Friday night I ran sets for the first time . . . we "ran" for about an hour. My partner was Bird Turner, one of the best set-runners in the county. **1924** Raine *Saddlebags* 83 We sat by the fire whilst they ran a set or two, then Sally leaned over and said, "Ab, why cain't we run a set, too?" **1927** Furman *Lonesome Road* 105 The fiddle started in one of the large front rooms, a shuffling of feet began, and the floor was soon full of young folks "running a set." **1942** Campbell *Cloud-Walking* 123 The young folks run sets till daybreak and then the crowd broke up. **1962** Smith *Dancing and Singing* 272 Cecil Sharp, when he witnessed Appalachian square dancing in Kentucky, heard the expression "run a set." As a consequence, he later referred to the dance as "Running Set," a term that led to considerable confusion and misunderstanding. The "Running Set" is part of an Appalachian square dance.

run a stir *verb phrase* To make a batch of **sorghum molasses**. See also **stir-off**.

1976 Garber *Mountain-ese* 76 *run-a-stir* = make sorghum: "Come over tonight and help us run-a-stir."

runction See **ruction**.

rund See **run A1**.

rung See **ring**.

run it over *verb phrase* To treat (someone) unfairly. For the *it*, see also **bed it, go B2**.

1937 Hall *Coll* (Big Creek NC) They tried to run it over him.

runned See **run A1, A2**.

runner *noun*

1 (also *runner bean*) Same as **pole bean, stick bean**. See also **bunch bean, half-runner (bean)**.

1986 Pederson et al. *LAGS* (Cumberland Co TN, Lumpkin Co GA).

2 The top stone of a gristmill.

1937 Hall *Coll* [picture caption for an NPS photograph]: Site on Charlies Branch of Bradley Fork where "runner" now in service at Mingus Mill was quarried, No. XXIV.

3 One who hauls a load of **moonshine** to distributors, usually in high-powered cars. Same as **shine runner**.

2005 Good *Racing in Appalachia* 3 Tradition often proclaims that stock car racing owes its heritage to the bootleggers and whiskey runners (or trippers) in and around the southern Appalachian mountains . . . of them in southern Appalachia. Soon, the chase was on between the moonshine trippers and pursuing merit "revenuers."

runner bean See **runner 1**.

run 'n go See **running go**.

running See **run C2**.

running fit *noun* See citation. See also **fitified**.

1939 Hall *Coll* (White Oak NC) Dogs take a runnin' fit when they have worms. They also have jerkin' fits.

running go *noun* (also *run-ago, run-and-go, run-an'-go, run 'n go, runny go, run to go*) A running start, leap; an attack, energetic charge.

1915 Dingus *Word-List VA* 189 *run-an'-go* = a run before leaping. **1939** Hall *Coll* (Hartford TN) [The bear] wheeled back on the dogs. [The bear hunter] took a run-ago an' run his arm into that hole he cut into it, an' run it right up about his heart. **1955** Ritchie *Singing Family* 21 I snatched up an old broom handle lying in the yard and took a runago at the homemade screen door and rammed that stick plum through. **1956** Hall *Coll* (Del Rio TN) I took a run-ago at it and just frailed it. *Ibid.* (Newport TN) She took a runnin'-go at him. **1973** GSMNP-79:17 You could play out in the hallway where they'd waxed it, you know. We'd make that for a slide. Take a run and go and just slide all the way down to the hall and then up again. **1976** Thompson *Touching Home* 17 *take runny go* = to get a running start. **1978** *Bird Traps* 74 Let's take this umbrella, take a run to go, and jump out that lower door [of the barn]. **1991** Haynes *Haywood Home* 55 When it was really cold, ice skating on the branches and creeks was fun if we could get away with it. Of course we didn't have ice skates, so we'd take a running go and slide on our shoe soles. **1998** *Dante OHP*-51 The train had to go up and go way up here and get a run and go and come back. **2005** Williams *Gratitude* 519 *run 'n go* = to back up to get a good start and gain momentum as you run. For instance, if somebody was to try to jump over a fence or high bar, he'd back up and take a *run 'n go* at it. **2006** Shearer *Wilder Days* 21 In the wintertime our heat was the fireplace. Twenty foot to the bed. I'd get me one of these knitted 'boggins and I'd get it warm, just as warm as I could get it, and I'd take a runny-go and go jump in the bed and put that 'boggin with my feet down in it.

[perhaps influenced by *run and* + verb, as "run and tell your mother"; DARE *running go, run-an(d)-go, runago* n southern Appalachians]

running pine *noun* Same as **creeping cedar**.

1999 McNeil *Purchase Knob* 65–66 At eye level, in the brittle grass of an old road bank, I suddenly noticed a lush green ground cover spreading about under a mountain laurel. Its miniature, cedar-like fronds made springy green nests wherever they ran. The moss had the endearing quality of making you want to pet it. . . . "Creeping cedar" or "running pine" the mountain people call it, completely inaccurate but appealing "folk names." Lycopodium is not even vaguely related to pines or cedars.

running set *noun* A part of an Appalachian square dance, performed to a caller but without music. See also **run a set, set C4**. The dance, similar to a quadrille, was given this term by Cecil Sharp of the English Folk Dance Society, who witnessed it at Pine Mountain Settlement School (Harlan Co KY); and the term was quickly adopted by traditional dance circles in Appalachia. See 2015 citation. See also **run a set**.

1945 McNeer *Sthn Highlands* 21 The running set is a square dance of the highlanders, as a "caller" calls the figures, and the noise of clapping and tapping shakes the rafters. **1962** Smith *Dancing and Singing* 272 Cecil Sharp, when he witnessed Appalachian square dancing in Kentucky, heard the expression "run a set." As a consequence, he later referred to the dance as "Running Set," a term that led to considerable confusion and misunderstanding. The "Running Set" is part of an Appalachian square dance. **1996–97** Montgomery *Coll* (known to Brown, Cardwell, Oliver). [**2014** *Blind Pig* (April 16) Sharp was entranced by the dancing and took detailed notes that form the basis of his description in his *Country Dance Book*. He wrote in his diary (October 8, 1917), "This dance is as valuable a piece of work as anything I have done in the mountains."] **2015** Jamison *Hoedowns* 61 [Quoting Cecil Sharp c1917:] I came across a most wonderful dance the other day called "The Running Set." It is a form of circular country dance of a type about which I know nothing. There is certainly nothing of the kind in England at the present day and there is nothing that I know of in any of the old dance books. It is a very strenuous dance for six couples and extremely complicated. . . . This dance is as valuable a piece of work as anything I have done in the mountains.] *Ibid.* 72 For nearly a century, Sharp's name for the Kentucky dances, the "Running Set," has been associated with these southern Appalachian dances. Karpeles [= Sharp's assistant], however, admitted [in 1930] that Sharp had adopted [this term] "for the sake of convenience." The dancers in Kentucky did not use it: they referred to their dances as "frolics," "square dances," "dancing a set," or "set running." When they spoke of "running a set," however, the word "running" was used as it would be if one were "running a business." *Ibid.* 73 The term "running a set" originally referred to dancing a set of quadrilles, not a set of running dancers. As Bascom Lunsford pointed out in 1942, the name "Kentucky Running Set" comes from "an erroneous foundation" and it was not meant to "qualify the topic of the dance." *Ibid.* 74 The dances that Cecil Sharp called the "Running Set" were not, as he believed, an ancient, unadulterated form of English country dance but represented a more recent American hybrid that developed from diverse roots in the American South during the nineteenth century.

running side *noun* The smoother side of a log for more easily skidding it downhill.

1979 Carpenter *Walton War* 125 If a log's running side was not judged right and it rolled one way or another while being dragged, the grab chain and spikes could end up on the side or the bottom and it would either fail to "track" with the rest of the logs or catch the spike on the crosspoled road and make the whole thing too hard to pull.

runny go See **running go**.

run off

A *noun phrase* See **run C2**.

B *verb phrase*

1 See **run B5**.

2 To have diarrhea; hence *running off* = diarrhea.

1864 *Wright CW Letters* (Aug 2) I am well at this time as common only i am running off a little at my bowels. **1865** *Martin CW Letters* (Jan 29) my Bowls has bin runing off ever since but I am abel for duty. **1965** Weller *Yesterday's People* 118–19 My wife tells of an occasion when she sympathetically listened to a woman telling about her little boy, who had been "running off." My wife kept trying to find out what made the boy unhappy enough to do that. The dawn came when she discovered that "running off" is a term for diarrhea. If the boy had been running away from home, as my wife thought, the woman would have said he was "slipping off." **1979** *Preacher Cook* 200 My bowels were running off and [I was] vomiting—just as sick as a man could be. **1992** Brooks *Sthn Stuff* 130 *running off* = diarrhea.

run off at the mouth See **run one's tongue**.

run one's tongue (also *run off at the mouth*) See citations.

1952 Wilson *Folk Speech NC* 587 *run one's tongue* = to scold; to talk a great deal without saying anything. **1953** Davison *Word-List Appal* 13 *run (one's) tongue* = to be overly talkative. "Can she talk! You ought to hear her run her tongue." **1956** McAtee *Some Dial NC* 37 *run one's tongue* = be very talkative. **1982** Slone *How We Talked* 102 A person was said to be "runnin' off at the mouth" if a very talkative person.

run out *verb phrase*

1 See **run B5**.

2 Of a stream: to subside after a brief stage of high water.

1911 Shearin *E KY Word-List* 539 = applied to the subsidence of a stream after a freshet; e.g., "The creek run out yesterday."

run the benches *verb phrase* To rush from bench to bench in spiritual excitement at a revival service. See also **walk the aisle**.

1982 *Foxfire VII* 206 They'd dance and run the benches just like Pentecostals do now.

run together (also *run with*) *verb phrase* To regularly associate with; to spend time with one another.

1915 Dingus *Word-List VA* 189 *run with* = to associate habitually with. **1927** Furman *Lonesome Road* 7 "I'm lonesome, too," he insisted, "because I don't never have no boy to run with." **1937** (in **1961** *Coe Ridge OHP-336B* He did run with the Taylors. **1973** *AOHP/EH-73* Some old buddies that I run with were making better money than I was. **1978** Montgomery *White Pine Coll* Jerilyn and I run together a lot. **1989** *Matewan OHP-56* We three of us always run together. **1992** Brooks *Sthn Stuff* 131 *run with* = pal around with. "Is he still running with that same tacky bunch?" **1997** Montgomery *Coll* (known to nine consultants from the Smoky Mountains). **1998** *Dante OHP-24* A old man that lived right there, me and him run together and preached together.

run to go See **running go**.

run up on (also *run upon*) *verb phrase* To run across.

1927 Justus *Peter Pocket* 2 The brown rabbits made little nests and sat quietly until Peter and his dog happened to run up on them. **1966** Dakin *Vocab Ohio River Valley* 220 Kentucky has in contrast [to *run on to*] its own expression with run—run upon—which is not used north of the Ohio. This expression which is sometimes pronounced RUN up ON and sometimes *run UP on*, is used by some older speakers in the Bluegrass in addition to other expressions, and in the eastern Knobs and the northern Mountains as the only expression attested.

[DARE (at *run* v 9c) chiefly South, South Midland]

rupscud *noun* A quarrel, disagreement. Same as **upscuddle**.

1983 Pyle *CCC 50th Anniv* A:3:12 He and his mother-in-law had got in a rupscud and he's going back on Sunday afternoon.

rurn, rurnt See **ruin**.

Russian wild boar See **Russian wild hog**.

Russian wild hog (also *Russian wild boar*) *noun* Variant forms *Rooshian, Rooshin*. See also **razorback, ridge rooter**.

1939 *FWP Guide TN* 128 For Tennessee's newest big game animal—the Russian wild boar, locally called "Rooshian" wild hog—the ancient sport of boar hunting has been revived. . . . When jumped by the dogs, the "Rooshians" strike through brush-grown ravines and over laurel-covered mountain slopes. **1942** Hall *Phonetics Smoky Mts* 41 *Rooshian* ['ruʃən]. **1952** Callahan *Smoky Mt Country* 227 For thirty years there have been in certain parts of the Smoky Mountains ferocious wild boars known to many local folks as "Rooshian" wild hogs. **1966** Frome *Strangers* 273 Around the mountains between Robbinsville, North Carolina, and Tellico Plains, Tennessee, where they first arrived early in the twentieth century, they are known as "Rooshians," on the theory they came from Russia, if not Prussia. **1997** Axtell *Hog Wild* 3 The boars' geographic origin is something of a mystery, but Moore wrote the preserve's caretaker, Garland "Cotton" Maguire, that he bought the boars from an agent "who represented that they came from Russia," most likely the Ural Mountains. It's possible, though, that Moore's Berlin agent got the boars from Austria or the Black Forest in Germany. Regardless, locals referred to the boars as "Rooshins," indicating their faith in the animal's Slavic ancestry. **2005** Ellison *Mt Passages* 30 Area residents have long referred to the wild boar as the Russian or "Roossian" wildboar, but Jones speculated [in 1858] that the animals actually came from Germany. **2013** DeLozier and Jourdan *Back Seat* 25 These wild pigs are a cross between free-ranging domestic hogs and massive, wary Russian wild boars imported by a wealthy businessman for his private hunting lodge on Hoopers Bald, North Carolina in 1912. The beasts escaped, of course, and their hybridized descendants are amazing looking creatures with huge front shoulders and tiny back ends, called *Rooshins* by the locals.

rusty

A *adjective* Especially of the feet: discolored by dirt. See citations. See also **rusty-footed**.

1985 Irwin *Alex Stewart* 107 He was just a little old ragged thing, barefoot and his feet so sore, rusty and scaly he couldn't hardly go. **1998** Montgomery *Coll* = used to indicate that any part of the body is dirty. A mother might tell a child, "You can't put on you new shirt until you wash" or "Your neck is rusty" (Ledford), = dirty, a child could have rusty heels, elbows, or feet (Norris).

B *noun* See **cut a rusty**.

rusty-footed *adjective* Having feet dirtied from going barefoot; by extension = rustic, inexperienced. See also **rusty A**.

1969 Medford *Finis* 107 That was 73 years ago when I was a "rusty-footed" farm boy on my daddy's place down in Iron Duff township of Haywood County in Western North Carolina. **1998** Montgomery *Coll* = having dirty feet (Brown), = having rough feet from going barefooted (Jones), = dirty footed, = dirty feet, caused by wearing no shoes (Oliver).

ruther See **rather**.

S

-s[1] *suffix* As a contracted form of *was* with a subject other than a third-singular present tense one. See **be E3**.

-s[2] *suffix* On a verb to recount vicarious, narrative action in the past (especially with *says* or *thinks*), a usage sometimes known as the "historical present." See also Grammar and Syntax §7.4.

1939 Hall *Coll* (Copeland Creek TN) They comes back, and Scott says he was a-coming over to their house when Lester come back. *Ibid.* (Bradley Fork NC) I studied [sic] over one night, got up the next morning. I says, "Martha, I don't want to stay here till I have to go out." *Ibid.* (Nine Mile TN) One of my old dogs, he seen me, and he whupped off under the hill and went to hollering, I thinks to myself [that] I'll just slide down there and see if he'd make me holler. *Ibid.* (Hartford TN) I said to my father, I said, "Father," I says, "I'll have to quit eatin' this [bear] meat." He says, "Why is that?" I says, "I couldn't tote a quarter of this meat out in the mornin', if I can't eat no breakfast." He says, "Eat every bite you can eat." **c1950** Adams *Grandpap* 86 She said to herself, she says, "Now these people that live here are rich people!" **1961** Murry *Salt* 25 I didn' want to let h'it go, so that feller pulls out a quart bottle of white likker, and we takes us a dram. **1962** Williams *Verbs Mt Speech* 18 He begin to pull back, and I says, "You want me to sqush yer head wi' this hyar .45?" **1971** *AOHP/ALC-129* She asked me to pray for him. I says, "[I'll do] anything I can do." **1973** *Carpenter* 122 I thinks t'm'self, "She don't need t'read such junk." **1973** Davis *'Pon My Honor* 88 Bright and early next morning, I ups and hustled over to Gladesville Courthouse to talk with [the Sheriff]. **1973** GSMNP-86:42 I sit down there and I felt so queer and I thinks, well will I ever see my children any more that's in Knoxville. **1979** *Big South Fork OHP-4* One night at midnight I waked up, and I could hear glass a-breaking, and I thinks, "Well, I've overslept and somebody's bringing pop bottles and a-setting them down." **1983** *Dark Corner OHP-4A* When my uncle come out there one day, he says, "Why don't you sell?"

-s[3] *suffix* See also Grammar and Syntax §4.1.

1 On a verb with a third-person-plural subject, except if the subject is a single, adjacent personal pronoun. See also **be C1**, **have A1**.

1774 *Dunmore's War* 99 These men tells me they are fresh Signs of Indians Seen Every Morning about the plantation at Forbes. **1796** *French Broad Church Minutes* 32 if an offending member is excommunicated and comes and gives a repentance to the Church and all receives him except two or three is it agreeable to Gospel for them to be talking about their matter before any companion of people not in Church. **1799** (in **2003** *TN Petitions I* 114–15) We therefore Join the Request of our friend Richard Shields and prays Your honourable body will exempt him from paying Taxes. **c1815** (in **2007** Davis *Co Line Baptist* 111) the time has Roald around when those godlike virtures Seames to have fled from amongst us. **1840** *McLean Diary* 68 The woods Looks Green. **1864** *Walker CW Letters*

(April 17) pray for me for our Saver ses Blessed ar they that holds out fath[f]ull untell Death. **1867** Harris *Sut Lovingood* 37 The men invents rat-traps, man-traps, an' new fangled doctrins fur the aid ove the devil. **1913** Kephart *Our Sthn High* 79 I'll go see what the el-e-ments looks like. **1916** Combs *Old Early English* 292 The third person plural often ends in -s, the E[arly] E[nglish] northern ending. The Midland -en is rare, as a verb form. The former usage is common all through the Southern mountains, e.g. "Heavy rains hurts the vine-patches." **1939** Hall *Coll* (Tow String Creek NC) If you boys wants to be ill with me, why, I'm small but I'm hard to handle. **1954** GSMNP-19:9 It's where people gathers up and shucks corn, in the fall when they get the corn gathered. **1961** *Coe Ridge OHP*-343B They have two or three [children] that lives in Indianapolis. **1970** *Burton-Manning Coll*-92A Three men works on the ground and beside the derrick car foreman and the engineer and the fireman. **1973** GSMNP-88:67 That's the way cattle feeds. They feed together. **1989** Landry *Smoky Mt Interviews* 191 Things changes so much anymore. **1989** *Matewan OHP*-9 Our preachers goes by the name Elders. *Ibid.* 28 There's still some old people around knows what happened to them. **c1999** Sutton *Me and Likker* 45 Me and Tunney Moore and all the Moore Family goes back many years.

[< Scotland, northern Ireland, northern England; following a rule dating to medieval times and inherited through Ulster from Scotland]

2 Formerly, on a verb with a personal pronoun subject not adjacent to its verb in the first or second person or in the third-person plural; also, on a verb with an implied first-person singular subject, as in a letter's complimentary closing (see 1790, 1845 citations). See also **be C2**, **have A2**.

1790 *Lenoir Papers* No more at present but still Remains your most affectionate and humble servant. **1796** *Cunningham Letter* I am sixty four or five years of age and knows not the day of my death nor what is to befall me in my last days. **1799** (in **2003** *TN Petitions I* 114–15) We therefore Join the Request of our friend Richard Shields and prays Your honourable body will exempt him from paying Taxes. **1836** (in **1998** Bueker *Head Letters* 14) I am now Volenteard to gow to texcas against the mexicans and Expecks to start the last of September or the first of October. **1845** *Millsaps Letters* 2 So nothing more at presant but Remains yours untill Death. **1861** *Huntley CW Letters* (Nov 22) I stay at the head of our Row of tents and dines with the officers at a tabell. **1862** (in **1992** Heller and Heller *Confederacy* 51) we have got something to cook in an some straw in our tents an draws full rashons. **1863** *Bartlett CW Letters* (Feb 12) I mus close for the presant write soon and often but remains your afectonate Husban. **1864** *Forgotten Ancestors* (Jefferson Co TN) 1 Fare well for a little while so remains your husband until death.

-s[4] *suffix* As a syllabic marker to indicate agreement with a third-person-singular verb. See **-es**[2].

-s[5] *suffix* On an adverb indicating place or time. See **anywheres**, **beforehands**, **everywheres**, **nowheres**, **somewheres**.

-s[6] *suffix* On a noun as a redundant marker of plurality, as in **childrens**, **oxens**, **sheeps**. See also **-es**[1].

-s[7] *suffix* On a noun as a syllabic marker of plurality. See **nestes** (at **nest**), **postes** (at **post**), **waspes** (at **wasp 2**). See also **-es**[1] **1**.

-s[8] *suffix* As a possessive marker on a given name to specify a parent's child, as *John's Sara*.

1931 Combs *Lg Sthn High* 1306 Babe sot up (courted) till chicken-crow with ole Rance's Peggy. **1944** Combs *Word-List Sthn High* 19 Mace's Jim sot up with (courted) Nance's Liz two nights hand-goin'. **c1950** Adams *Grandpap* 20 Sissie married Uncle Will Sexton's John, but they didn't get along and she was back home in a week. *Ibid.* 213 Without any noticeable slackening of speed, he reached out a hand and nestled Uncle John's Dave against his knees. **1962** (in **2014** McCarter *Memories of Boy* 22) Joshua's Lizzie used to say to Mother, "After you get them through the gates at the [train] stations, they cant make you pay anything." **2007** McMillon *Notes* Bob's John and Jesse's John—a way to distinguish people with the same name.

-s[9] *suffix* On a noun as a possessive marker to indicate a family associated with an individual.

1863 Wilson *Confederate Private* 2 (Feb 3) I think you aor some of paps mite rite to me. *Ibid.* 67 (Aug 27) paps sent you 10 dolars more & sed thay had never heard whither you had got it or not. **1973** *Foxfire Interviews* A-73-86 Grandpa's had a house over there.

-s[10] *suffix* As a contracted form of *is* with a subject other than one that is third-singular present tense. See **be C3**.

sack *noun* A cow's udder.

1915 Dingus *Word-List VA* 180 = udder. **1949** Arnow *Hunter's Horn* 107 From the way their sacks were hardening up, it looked as if several would lamb anyway. **c1954** Adams *Word-List* = milk-cow's udder.

[DARE *sack* n 2a chiefly South Midland]

sacrament *noun* See citation.

1995 McCauley *Mt Religion* 102 Old Regular Baptists refer to communion as "sacrament" (pronounced "say-crament"), with no definite or indefinite article preceding the term.

sacrament meeting (also *sacramental meeting*) *noun* Formerly, a church service or **meeting** (i.e. sometimes lasting over the weekend) at which communion is taken. Depending on the denomination or congregation, this is traditionally held quarterly or annually at late-summer or fall revival services. Also called **communion meeting**. See also **meeting**.

1785 *Bent Creek Church Minutes* 5 the church appointed the second friday saturday and sunday for sacrament meeting. **1833** *McLean Diary* (April 20) Sacramental Meting comm[en]ced. **1851** *Paw Paw Hollow Church Minutes* 148 the Church also agrees to invite B[rothe]r Cowan, Burnet, Moris, Russle and B[rothe]r Tipton and Cate to atend our Sacrament meeting in October. **1877**

Elijoy *Church Minutes* 138 Church met after Sermon [and] Apointed our Sacramental Meeting to Commence on the fourth Saturday in May. **1931** Burns *Coves Blount Co* 55 In the years prior to the Civil War there was nothing of an exciting or spectacular nature other than an occasional visitor, or peddler; the quarterly meetings of the Methodist church; or the annual sacramental or footwashing meetings of the old Baptist church to which people came from as far away as Dumplin in Jefferson County. **1967** Hall *Coll* (Townsend TN) They have their sacrament meetin', their footwashin' meetin' there at the Baptist Church in Cades Cove. **1995** McCauley *Mt Religion* 87 The joining of communion with footwashing—which forms the annual "sacramental meeting" of Old-Time Baptist traditions such as the Primitive and Old Regular Baptists, and is sometimes held with greater frequency in traditions such as independent Holiness—complemented baptism by water to create the sacramental high points of mountain religious life. *Ibid.* 177 A sacramental meeting came to average, then, at least three to five days, extending to well before and after the actual serving of the communion elements.

sacred harp *noun* See citations. Also called **old harp 1**. See also **shape note.**

1992 Sabol *Sacred Harp* 1 Sacred Harp music is written in "shape notes," which resemble standard round notes in every respect except that the head of each note has one of the four shapes to indicate its interval from the key (tonic) pitch. This system was based on the practice originating in Elizabethan England of singing the seven notes of an octave with four-syllable solmization. The major scale is sung as *fa, sol, la, fa, sol, la, me, fa*, while the minor scale (1 1/2 whole notes down from the major scale) is sung as *la, me, fa, sol, la, fa, sol, la*. . . . The four-shape system (*fa* = triangle, *sol* = oval, *la* = square, and *me* = diamond) was invented around 1800 in the Northeastern U.S., and it enabled many untrained singers of the day to sight-read music without having to understand key signatures. Shape-note music immediately became popular, and it strongly stimulated the expansion of the singing-school movement, which had arisen in New England around 1720 and in which many Americans were taught to sing by itinerant singing masters. **2013** *Harp Singing* Sacred Harp singing is a non-denominational community musical event emphasizing participation, not performance. Singers sit facing inward in a hollow square. Each individual is invited to take a turn "leading," i.e. standing in the center, selecting a song, and beating time with the hand. The singing is not accompanied by harps or any other instrument. **2014** Montgomery *Doctrine* 176 = a type of singing that uses a four-note method as opposed to 7 notes. The name of the tradition comes from the title of the shape-note book from which the music is sung, "*The Sacred Harp*." The singers arranged themselves in a "hollow square," with rows of chairs or pews on each side assigned to the four parts: treble, alto, tenor, and bass. The treble and tenor sections usually are mixed, with men and women singing the notes an octave apart. There is no single leader or conductor; rather, the participants take turns in leading. . . . The music is printed in "patent notes," wherein the shape of the note head indicates the syllables.

[DARE *sacred harp* chiefly South, "the shape-note hymnals of this name in current use are descended from the *Sacred Harp* by B. F. White and E. J. King, first published in 1844"]

sad *adjective* Of a baked good: heavy from failure of the yeast to rise, somewhat tough or sodden.

1904–20 Kephart *Notebooks* 2:419 Biscuits [are] generally made with soda and buttermilk. . . . The dough is not rolled out and cut with a cutter, but moulded with the hands, hence biscuits are tough and "sad." **1991** Still *Wolfpen Notebooks* 86 Bread dough turns sad if it's left to sit too long. **1994–97** Montgomery *Coll* (known to Oliver, Weaver), = a baked good not made with enough shortening (Cardwell); A sad cake doesn't rise (Norris).

[OED3 *sad* adj 8f now chiefly regional; SND *sad* adj I.3; DARE *sad* adj chiefly South, Midland]

saddle

A *noun*

1 A low place or pass along a mountain ridge or range. See also **gap 1, sag 1, swag B2.**

1924 Raine *Saddlebags* 21 In Appalachia there are more than forty peaks over six thousand feet, besides forty miles of unnamed "saddles" or dividing ridges that attain that altitude. **1933** Fink *Early Explorers* 62 [William Davenport's] gap for a road was in the low saddle just under Myrtle Point, and he only discovered his mistake when he reached its heights. **1951** Still *Short Dog* 57 We mounted until we had gained the saddle of the gap. **1962** Brewer *Hiking* 11 Two miles and four peaks—with deep saddles between them—separate the Spence Field and Thunderhead markers. **1963** Lord *Blue Ridge* 8 = a saddle-like depression between two high points on a crestline.

2 See citation.

2003 LaLone et al. *Farming Life* 357 When the corn was cut we would put it in shocks, of, we would go from the edge of the corn field over about twelve rows and then row thirteen and fourteen you would pull four, four bunches of corn together and make what they call a saddle, tie that together. Then we'd carry the corn to that saddle and set the corn in this saddle until we got enough corn in it, enough stalks in it, to make a good sized shock.

B *verb* See citation.

1939 Farr *TN Mt Regions* 91 = to drink coffee with sugar: "Coffee's no good without it's saddled."

saddlebag

A *noun*

1 (also *saddlebag house*) A log dwelling with two rooms or **pens** (see **pen**[2]) built back to back, usually sharing a chimney in the center, a design sometimes reflecting an original one-room dwelling to which a second room has been added. See also **double cabin.**

1968 Glassie *Material Folk Cult* 78–79 Frequently the cabin has another added to one of its ends; if the addition is made onto the chimney end, the house is a saddlebag . . . if the addition is built onto the end opposite the chimney, a double-pen with end chimney house results . . . both types came to be commonly built in log or frame as one story houses composed of two equal units with two front doors and one chimney. **1987** Williams *Rethinking House* 178 Not all rural folk houses in southwestern North Carolina had single-pen plans. Somewhat larger houses could be created by the arrangement of two (more-or-less) equal size units. The most common variation of the double-pen plan is the central chimney saddle-bag plan, although double-pen houses with exterior end chimneys are found in western North Carolina. Double-pen houses could be built of log, frame, or boxed construction. In describing these houses, older western North Carolinians often say that they consist of "two houses." The saddlebag plan is further described as a house having a "double fireplace," "double chimney," or "stacked chimney": "Have two fireplaces in it, one room have one, you go into the other room and there'd be a big room in there with a fireplace . . . you could live on either side of the house if you wanted to." **1991** Williams *Homeplace* 27 Of the larger folk houses, the saddlebag plan with rooms of equal size on either side of a central chimney was the most prevalent . . . the saddlebag house often had an upstairs (usually the house was a story and a half, rather than a full two stories in height) and a separate kitchen. *Ibid.* 74 In southwestern North Carolina the central chimney "saddle-bag" house is far more prevalent than the double pen plan with exterior end chimneys. **1995** Trout *Historic Buildings* 16 The saddlebag house was sort of a reverse of the dogtrot. Instead of two units with a fireplace and a chimney at each end, the saddlebag consisted of two units so close together that they shared a common chimney. A fireplace in either side of the chimney heated each unit. From a distance this shape apparently reminded one of a pair of saddlebags hanging from the sides of a horse. **2003** Jordan-Byshkov *Upland South* 33 Featuring a massive masonry chimney placed between its two log pens that provides ventilation for fireplaces in each room, the saddlebag house provides a striking visual appeal and symmetry. Its name, derived from the vernacular speech of the Upper South, was prompted by its resemblance to the balanced double load borne by a pack horse. *Ibid.* 34 The saddlebag house belonged to the Watauga territory nucleus of the Upland South from the very first. . . . Its link to that hearth is revealed by the fact that the saddlebag achieved its greatest acceptance in central East Tennessee and adjacent southwestern North Carolina where it represents the most common double-house in multiple counties.

[DARE *saddlebag house* n South, South Midland]

2 Homemade whiskey. See also **bootleg B**.

1982 Powers and Hannah *Cataloochee* 76 Liquor that came out of Catalooch' was known as "saddlebag" because that's how they transported it.

B *verb* See citations.

1954 Blackhurst *Riders of Flood* 128 Holding near the shore, the big bunk ark had run aground on a flooded, low-lying island. With the flooded water entirely covering it, the steersmen had been unable to see the island, and now the big ark hung squarely over it and refused to budge. Loggers called this kind of lodging "saddlebagging." **1973** Schulman *Logging Terms* 36 = when a raft ran aground on a sand bar in the river, the raftsmen said it had saddlebagged the bar. The term indicated that the ends of the raft were hanging over a sand bar like saddlebags hanging over a horse.

saddlebag house See **saddlebag A1**.

saddle horse *noun* See citation. See also **lead horse**.

1949 Kurath *Word Geog East US* 31 The Midland has four different terms for the left-hand horse of a team, *lead-horse*, *near-horse*, *nigh-horse*, and *saddle-horse*. *Lead-horse* is the usual expression . . . in the southern Appalachians and Blue Ridge south of the Kanawha-James line.

saddle-pocket doctor *noun* See citation.

1981 High *Coll* = expression used for physicians who traveled through the mountains on horseback, often for great distances.

sad iron *noun* An old-fashioned, solid flat iron, pointed at both ends, for smoothing clothes after they have been washed.

1910 Cooke *Power and Glory* 3 I mighty nigh pounded my thumb off knockin' in nails with a rock an' a sad-iron last week. **1966** *DARE Survey* (Cherokee NC) = iron used for smoothing clothes after they're washed. **1985** Kiser *Life and Times* 21 "Hand irons" were known as "sad irons." **1997** Montgomery *Coll* (known to Bush, Cardwell, Norris).

[literally "heavy iron"; OED3 *sad iron* n now historical]

safe

A *adjective* Variant form *saft*.

1863 Warrick *CW Letters* (May 16) it is with pleasure that I tak my pen in hand to ancer your kind letter Which Come saft to hand. **1864** *Watkins CW Letters* (June 12) the boys got back to day saft.

B *noun* A freestanding cabinet or cupboard for storing food, dishes, bedding, etc. (such as one with glass doors and drawers or a perforated screen to protect freshly baked foods). See also **bedroom safe**, **bread safe**, **kitchen safe**, **pie safe**.

1863 Fuller *CW Letters* (Feb 24) caldonia wants to no if you will let her have that largest safe frome and whot you will charge. **1939** Hall *Coll* (Saunook NC) = a kitchen cabinet where food is kept: "You'll find some more milk in the safe." *Ibid.* (White Oak NC) = a pantry or cupboard, not built into the wall, but movable. **1959** Pearsall *Little Smoky* 85 There are no cupboards or closets except for the inevitable "safes" for storing dishes or bedding, and most possessions hang from nails. **1960** Arnow *Seedtime* 379 Another piece of furniture, primarily for kitchen use, was the safe, more often mentioned in early wills than the dresser. Designed primarily for the keeping of food, rather than cooking utensils, it was little more than a shelved box on legs with doors that had instead of wood for paneling, tin punched with holes, usually in some well known design such as six-pointed stars; other times the panels were of coarse linen affording the same protection from flies with circulation of air as did the punched tin. **1975** Purkey *Madison Co* 7 The tall cedar dish cupboard and the low wooden safe with its pierced tin doors had been made by my father who was handy with hammer and nails.

[DARE *safe* n 1 chiefly South, South Midland, TX]

saft See **safe A**, **soft**.

saft-sawder *noun* See citation.

1957 Combs *Lg Sthn High: Word List* 84 = nonsense, tommy-rot.

sag *noun*

1 A low place or pass along a mountain ridge or range. See also **gap 1**, **saddle A1**, **swag B2**.

1727 (in **1940** McJimsey *Topo Terms in VA* 387) Thence along the North Side of the Mountains . . . to a Corner Several Saplins by a Sagg. **1940** *FWP Guide GA* 476 South of Snake Mountain [in north-central GA] the crest of the Blue Ridge falls to a relatively low "sag," which in mountaineer dialect is known as the "Swag of the Blue Ridge." **1975** Fink *Backpacking* 81 Toward evening a deeper sag than usual on the ridge made us believe that we had reached Deep Gap. **1999** Coggins *Place Names Smokies* 166 = a low-lying area along a ridge or mountain top, not as pronounced as a gap.

2 An area of depressed ground with vegetation, found at any level of the mountains.

1927 Mason *Lure of Smokies* 22 Many of these "wallows" are scattered at intervals on high, isolated ridges and "sags" in the thick laurel.

3 An area of depressed ground, as in a field.

1941 Stuart *Men of Mts* 15 "That hill over there," says Pa, pointing to a sag of corn that fits into a lap between two hills, "w'y old Flem cleaned that up for me when you was just a boy." **1997** Montgomery *Coll* Stay away from that sag at the end of the field (Cardwell).

sage *noun* An aromatic, evergreen perennial plant (*Salvia* spp) with medicinal as well as culinary properties. The plant has wooly, gray-green leaves and violet-blue flowers.

1943 Hannum *Mt People* 113 Sage was the thing for common colds in those days. If the cold went beyond the simple reach of sage, and developed into "pneumonia fever," then pennyroyal was called into use. [**1971** Krochmal et al. *Medicinal Plants Appal* 224 In Appalachia, [sage] was thought to serve as a laxative and a gargle; and it was used to treat baldness, loose teeth, and gas . . . it has been used to achieve regularity of menstrual period. However, its major use is for culinary purposes.] **1972** Cooper *NC Mt Folklore* 12 Knowing some of the properties of medicine and that the action of a remedy upon the human system depends upon attributes peculiar to it, they used hot infusions of catnip, dog fennel, ginger, boneset, sage, butterfly weed and snakeroot as sudorifics for producing sweating in the treatment of measles, colds, grippe and pneumonia.

sage grass See **sedge grass**.

sage grass broom See **sedge broom**.

sager *noun* [rhymes with *wager*] Used as a derogatory term for a farmer or a rustic, a poor white.

1915 Hall *Autobiog Claib Jones* 28 We reached Beech mountain, stayed all night with an old sager. We laid in our bread and hired him and his horse to take us to the Beech mountain. **1943** Korson *Coal Dust* 5 Full-time miners naturally resented them [= farmer-miners] and expressed their distrust by calling them "winter diggers," "wheats," "corncrackers," "hay johns," "pumpkin rollers," "clodhoppers," "greenies," "scissorbills," and "sagers." **1986** Pederson et al. *LAGS* (Hamilton Co TN, Knox Co TN).

[DARE *sager* n South, South Midland]

sah See **saw**[2].

sail *verb* See citation.

1984 High *Titan Rock* 32–33 Elsewhere in Kentucky, workers threw together log rafts, which they would ride to get their logs to market. But in the [Red River] Gorge logs were not rafted but "sailed" or floated loose. . . . Depending on the current, it usually took a couple of days to sail the logs some twenty miles to Clay City.

saint *noun* A longtime, faithful, and revered member of a church congregation.

1960 Schwarz *Ordeal by Serpents* 405 "Saints" is a term used to denote those consecrated church members who have extraordinary faith and gifts. In some respects they may be considered to be "ministers." **1978** Hiser *Quare Do's* 68 He led me up front and we sat down among the preachers and saints. **c1982** Young *Colloquial Appal* 18 = honored member of the congregation. **1987** Young *Lost Cove* 49 Until 1940, the men sat on one side of the church aisle while the women sat on the other. The Saints, of course, sat in the Amen Corner. **2007** Farr *My Appalachia* 123 The people of the Holiness church call each other saints. They interpret Mark 16:17, 18 and Isaiah 43:2 literally. Some of them drink poison, some of them handle snakes and fire.

sainter See **saunter**.

salad *noun*

A Variant forms *salat* [see **1930** in **B**], *salet* [see **1979** in **B**], *salett*, *sallet*.

1859 Taliaferro *Fisher's River* 143 My sallet were meltin' away mighty fast. **1924** Raine *Saddlebags* 98 Shakespeare also calls a salad a *sallet*. **1934–37** *LAMSAS Appal* (Swain Co NC) *sallet*. **1971** Thornburgh *Great Smoky Mts* 162 Shakespeare used "salett" for salad, and "poke" for paper bag. **1983** Farr *More Moonshine* 84 I might say here that mountain people call salad greens "sallet greens."

[cf Scottish form *sallet*; DARE *salad* n A especially South, South Midland]

B (also *salad greens*) Edible greens, especially wild greens, eaten raw or cooked, as by pouring boiling grease over them. See also **garden salad**, **killed salad**, **poke salad**, **sauce B2**, **wild salad B**, **wilted salad**.

1864 *Chapman CW Letters* (May 10) I go out some times and git me a mess of Sallet I do have some fine messes. **1886** Smith *History KY* 157 (DARE) The indigenous salads and early berries came next, and finally the feast of garden vegetables. **1930** Thomas

Death Knell Greens of all kinds are called salat. **1941** Justus *Kettle Creek* 127 Then the creek bank and lower mountainside would furnish wild sallet greens for the pot. **1949** Kurath *Word Geog East US* 39 In the Valley of Virginia and in the western part of the Carolinas the Midland *greens* is still common by the side of Southern *salad. Ibid.* 73 The distinctive Virginia Piedmont term is *salad*, more commonly pronounced as *salat* in the speech of the folk. It is universal here and predominates over greens in adjoining parts of Maryland and North Carolina as well. In the greater part of the Carolinas *salad* and *greens* stand side by side, many persons using both terms. **1957** Hall *Coll* (Gatlinburg TN) Mustard, turnip, or wild greens were called "sallet." **c1959** Weals *Hillbilly Dict* 7 *sallet greens* = dish of spring greens: poke, dock, dandelion, cress, or any of several other greens edible in spring. **c1960** Wilson *Coll*: *sallet* = cooked greens, never applied to uncooked vegetables, like salads. **1963** Wilson *Regional Words* 80 *Greens* is distinctly a modern word; *sallet* is the standard word among older people, with such prefixes as *mustard, turnip,* or *wild. Wild sallet* represents a whole slice of botany, with polk, narrow-leaved dock, lamb's quarters, peppergrass, wild mustard, dandelions, and many other plants included. **1966** Dakin *Vocab Ohio River Valley* 373–74 Although it is evident that at least some speakers make a slight distinction in meaning between *greens* and *salad*, these terms stand side by side and essentially synonymous in the Mountains and in southern Kentucky generally as they do in the Carolinas. Both are unquestionably old. **1979** Smith *White Rock* 34 On land we found a wide variety of "salet" greens, crow's foot, yellow dock, tender plantain, tongue weed, lamb's tongue, brier leaves, and poke. **1991** Thomas *Sthn Appal* 199 A welcome addition to the spring diet is furnished by "sallets" of cress, poke, bear's lettuce, and various other young greens. **1993** Ison and Ison *Whole Nother Lg* 57 *sallet* = green leafy wild plants found early in the spring to cook as greens. **2008** *Rosie Hicks* 1 They called it sallet then . . . used to call it wild sallet. **2016** Lundy and Autry *Victuals* 55 A sallet of greens in the South is made by cooking particular fresh greens fairly quickly in a skillet of hot bacon grease. In the mountains, we make sallet with a variety of wild greens. The most famous of these is poke sallet, of course.

[DARE *salad* n B "edible greens" chiefly South, South Midland, TX]

salad greens See **salad B.**

salad pea *noun* A pea grown in the spring and eaten with wild or cultivated greens.

1960 Arnow *Seedtime* 411 Some families would have used a variety of pea, known as the salat pea, still a few years ago grown in the back. **1972** *GSMNP-93:3:26* Well, they call 'em salat peas, don't they? **1982** Powers and Hannah *Cataloochee* 352 I think sallet peas is one of the best vegetables in the world. We always grew some and made enough to can. . . . They're edible pods. Some think you have to pick 'em real early before their maturity.

[DARE *salad pea* n chiefly southern Appalachians]

salat See **salad.**

sales day (also *sales Monday*) *noun* Traditionally, a fixed day on the calendar for the buying, selling, and trading of goods.

1938 Stuart *Dark Hills* 305 It was so warm and pretty today and everybody stirring around in Greenup at the sales day. **1984** Wilder *You All Spoken* 75 Sales Monday . . . The first Monday in the month and time for trading livestock in sales usually near the county courthouse.

[DARE (at *sale day* n) especially South, South Midland]

salet, salett, sallet See **salad.**

salivate (also *salvate*) *verb* To punish, treat violently, make sick.

1940 Stuart *Trees of Heaven* 65 I'll git 'im before he ever has time to draw a gun on me if he's in my reach. I'll knock 'im cold as a cucumber. I'll salivate 'im. **1972** Carson and Vick *Cookin* 2 51 He tuk too much calomel and was salivated. **c1982** Young *Colloquial Appal* 18 = punish, whip.

sallet See **salad.**

Sally Lunn (also *Sally Lunn bread*) *noun* A sweet yeast bread.

1966–69 *DARE Survey* (Rogersville TN, Abingdon VA, Asheville NC) = risen, baked in a round tube pan, light and sweet; (Buchanan VA) = between a cake and a bread; used for Sunday night supper. **2013** Smith and Kraig *Food and Drink* 174 Sally Lunn is a delicate, fairly rich bread made with yeast, eggs, milk, wheat flour, butter, and a little sugar, much like the French brioche.

[DARE *Sally Lunn* n especially NC, VA]

salmon *noun* Variant plural form *salmons.*

1921 Campbell *Sthn Highlander* 203 An interesting side-light on diet in the mountains is furnished by the country store. Here one may purchase salt, vinegar, molasses, soda, coffee, sugar, white flour, and usually some kind of canned goods—"salmons," tomatoes, and peaches. **1921** Weeks *Speech of KY Mtneer* 10 "Do you like salmons?" is often heard during our evening meal. **1939** Hall *Coll.*

salt bacon *noun* See citation.

c1960 Wilson *Coll* = hog meat that has been preserved by salt.

[DARE *salt bacon* n chiefly South, South Midland]

salt bird *noun* The red crossbill (*Loxia curvirostra*).

1960 Stupka *Great Smoky Mts* 41 In years gone by when cattle ranged on the high mountain meadowlands, the herders knew [the red crossbill] as the "salt bird." Crossbills are exceptionally fond of salt, and since they were very approachable while feeding on the salt which had been distributed for the benefit of the cattle, the name they were known by was entirely appropriate. **1982** Powers and Hannah *Cataloochee* 478 The red crossbill . . . is known by the locals as the saltbird because of its habits of staying by the licklogs where salt was put out for cattle. **1995** Alexander *Mt Fever* 53 Our favorite pet at Three Forks was another bird, much tinier than the grouse and practically indifferent to humans. This was the red crossbill, which normally frequents the spruce woods of New England and Canada. From their avid love of salt, they are called "salt birds" by the mountain people. The early settlers became acquainted with them when they took salt to their free-ranging livestock in the mountains and saw the crossbills dart in to lick logs and rocks.

salt gourd *noun* The dried, hollowed shell of a squash in which salt is kept near at hand to add to food being cooked. See 1964 citation.

1927 Mason *Lure of Smokies* 122 Besides presiding over the salt-gourd, the "woman" of the household had other light diversions. **1953** Davison *Word-List Appal* 19 = a gourd kept near the stove where salt is kept. **1964** Greve *Story of Gatlinburg* 49 A table and a corner cupboard to hold the dishes completed the list of the main furnishings, but they were clever at contriving many other small necessities—the "meal gum" in the corner, a hollowed-out section of log, fitted with bottom and lid, to hold the family supply of meal or of flour; the "salt gourd," a long-necked gourd, with a semi-circular hole cut high on one side for the insertion of the hand, that hung near the fire where the cooking was done.

salt gum *noun* An open container made from a hollowed section of a tree, especially a **blackgum**, in which salt is stored for use in cooking. See also **gum A1**, **meal bin**.

2005 Houk *Walker Sisters* 17 All of these [implements and pieces of furniture] were in the sisters' cabin, along with six feather beds in a downstairs living room and a table, cupboard, flour bin, salt gum, and jelly box in the kitchen.

salt shake *noun* See citations.

1957 Broaddus *Vocab Estill Co KY* 65 = a salt shaker. **1987** Carver *Regional Dialects* 168 Although probably inherently salty, if one were to add more to it [= the gravy], one would use the *salt shake*. **2005** Williams *Gratitude* 519 = salt shaker.

[DARE *salt shake* n scattered, but especially South Midland]

salvate See **salivate**.

salvation cocktail *noun* A mixture of strychnine and other ingredients, drunk by certain groups of Pentecostal Christians who also handle snakes during worship services, both practices in adherence to a stricture found in the Gospel according to Mark 16:17.

1964 La Barre *Snake-Handling* 311 In late August, 1947, a thirty-four-year old farmer named Ernest Davis took several gulps of a "salvation cocktail" made with strychnine, in a meeting led by the Reverend Gordon Miller, and died from the effects four days later near Summerville, Georgia. **2003** Cavender *Folk Medicine* 45–46 Lamentably, journalists, novelists, and academics have given an inordinate amount of attention to the religiously grounded fatalistic outlook of the poor, and to some of the more ecstatic, but relatively rare, ritualistic behavior in certain sects and independent churches, such as handling poisonous snakes and drinking "salvation cocktails," of strychnine.

sam See **psalm**.

samkumsuly See **sanctum suly.**

sampson snakeroot See **Samson's snakeroot.**

Samson *noun* A prop put under a felled tree to suspend its trunk so that the first log could be sawed more easily and effectively.

1974–75 McCracken *Logging* 14:21 If the tree fell and bounced, the back end bounced up over something, you know. It was standing up four or five feet. He had to put what they called a leg under it, or a Samson. You'd take a piece of sapling the size of that and cut it off and he'd drive it under. He'd set one end down, he'd take his axe and drive that under and when they saw the first log off it, it wouldn't split the log.

Samson's snakeroot (also *Sampson's snakeroot*) *noun* A scurf pea (*Psoralea psoralioides*) from whose root a medicinal tea is made for use as a tonic and an antidote for snakebite.

1901 Lounsberry *Sthn Wild Flowers* 269 Although the common name of this rather unattractive plant seems undoubtedly to be Samson's snakeroot, it is the one which the mountaineers of the south reserve exclusively for the blue gentian; a plant especially well known to them for the purpose of making a powerful and invigorating tonic, which next to whiskey, coffee, and tobacco, holds a strong place in their affections. **1937** Hall *Coll* (Cosby TN) [For colic] use Samson's snake root. [It has] a little long blossom, blooms in September. [It has] a little pod and hit blue. **1941** Walker *Story of Mt* 48 Among the wild plants once employed as antidotes for the bites of poisonous reptiles, are rattlesnake-master, black snakeroot, rattlesnake-weed, Samson snakeroot or scurfy (whose tough fleshy root has long been used for tooth brushes), Virginia snakeroot, button snakeroot, and rattlesnake-root. **1967** Jones *Peculiarities Mtneers* 66 Sampson snakeroot tea was often used to treat colic, a disorder the old timers bluntly called "bellyache" in adults. [**1971** Krochmal et al. *Medicinal Plants Appal* 132 Because of its bitter flavor, probably the most useful application of this plant is as a tonic and astringent. In Appalachia, a root tea is drunk as a tonic, and a piece of the root is sometimes worn or carried to increase one's physical powers.]

sanco See **sango.**

sanctum suly (also *sankumsuly*) *noun* See citations.

1944 Williams *Word-List Mts* 30 = good whisky. Used by a Ky. moonshiner in describing his product. Perhaps derived from Latin. The mountaineer, however, was illiterate. **1962** Williams *Metaphor Mt Speech I* 12 If the vintage is raw and fiery it is said to be "as strong as akyfortis," but if it has mellowed in the moonlight it is sometimes referred to sweetly as "samkumsuly."

sand *noun* Courage, tenacity.

1867 Harris *Sut Lovingood* 102 I tell yu, he hes lots ove san' in his gizzard; he is the bes' pluck I ever seed. **1915** Dingus *Word-List VA* 183 *have sand in one's gizzard* = to have courage. **1930** Armstrong *This Day and Time* 44 Miz Phillips is allays so kind to a body . . . an' she's got plenty sand in her craw, too. **1956** McAtee *Some Dial NC* 38 = courage.

[DARE *sand* n 1 chiefly South, South Midland]

sand digger *noun* A **razorback** hog.

1889 *Hogs* He bought about a dozen half-wild, long-nosed hogs we call razorbacks or sanddiggers. They are death on snakes, them hogs is, and no snake in creation kin git away from them. They've got a nose 'bout one-quarter their length; they're long-legged, wide-bodied, and thin. They kin scoot through a cane-brake and git out'n sight quicker'n a rabbit, but their princip'l virtu' is in killin' snakes.

sand in one's gizzard, have *verb phrase* See citation.

1915 Dingus *Word-List VA* 183 *have sand in one's gizzard* = to have courage.

sandlapper *noun* The six-lined racerunner lizard (*Cnemidophorus sexlineatus*).

1967 Huheey and Stupka *Amphibians and Reptiles* 50 The Six-lined Racerunner, known locally as "Sandlapper," is abundant in the vicinity of Laurel Lake, a small impoundment in Tuckaleechee Cove within two miles of the Park line. **2001** Tilley and Huheey *Reptiles & Amphibians* 60 "Sandlappers," as they are known locally, are confined to only a few areas within the park boundaries, mostly in Tennessee. They may be quite common at the localities where they occur, such as along the Foothills Parkway near Look Rock. On warm, sunny days, racerunners are constantly on the move, foraging for insects and maintaining the highest body temperature of any reptile in the Smokies.

sandrock *noun* Sandstone; a piece of sandstone.

1935 (in **2005** Ballard and Chung *Arnow Stories* 44) Them hogs . . . are all in their holes under the sand rocks. **1941** Stuart *Men of Mts* 66 Pa's face is hard as a brown sand-rock. **1967** Williams *Subtlety Mt Speech* 15 He turned off to one side and clumb up a rough steep twardge a great big sandrock cliff that stuck right straight aout. **1969** Stubbs *Mountain-Wise* (April–May) 10 We spied a large, flat "sandrock," ideally suitable for a "stepping stone."

sand train *noun* See citation.

1980 Riggleman *WV Mtneer* 126–27 [Loggers] usually had nicknames for everybody and everything around the camp. . . . Sugar was "sand train."

sang See **ginseng**.

sang digger (also *sanger*) *noun* A person who searches out and collects wild **ginseng** for sale.

1962 Wilson *Folkways Mammoth Cave* 26 Gathering herbs was a seasonal way of picking up a little money . . . but a person who spent too much time in this sort of work was called a *sang-digger*. **1968** Wilson *Folklore Mammoth Cave* 23 *sang digger* = a low-class person who formerly dug ginseng and other herbs to make a living. He was often accused of being a thief. **c1975** Lunsford *It Used to Be* 65 There are people in the mountains known as "sang diggers." When you hear someone say he's a sang digger, don't think he's making light of anybody because the man might be a person who knows right where the sang root can be found, and he knows that if he gets a quantity of it, he'll really have some money when he comes back from the store, or from the Penney Company. **1995** Peterson *Ginseng Hunter* 57 Ginseng buyers in the United States take these circumstances into account when buying from sangers and cultivators and create market competition.

sanger See **sang digger**.

sang hoe (also *sanging hoe, seng hoe*) *noun* A small, short-handled, narrow-bladed implement for digging the roots of **ginseng** and other wild plants.

1888 *Congress Record* (1 May) 3587 (DARE) The "sang hoe" is a small hoe of domestic manufacture, with which the people dig ginseng root, which is the only agricultural staple of a portion of the mountain district in Southeastern Kentucky. **1957** Combs *Lg Sthn High: Word List* 84 *sangin' hoe* = the small, slender hoe used in digging the root. **1974** Fink *Bits Mt Speech* 23 *sanging hoe* = special implement for digging ginseng—narrow blade, short handle. **1975** Brewer *Valley So Wild* 114 A hunter sometimes carried a "sang hoe," a small tool to dig herbs, especially ginseng, called Pax quinquefolium by the botanist and "sang" by mountaineers. **1982** Slone *How We Talked* 133 *sang hoe* = a very short-handled hoe with a narrow, sharp blade, used to dig ginseng and other roots that were to be sold for medicine and dyes. **1997** Hufford *American Ginseng* 11 Slung over Williams's shoulder is a bag for carrying ginseng, and in his hand he carries a "seng hoe." Seng hoes are essentially double-bladed mattocks modified to serve as walking sticks. You cannot purchase one . . . seng hoes are produced by remodelling implements made for other purposes. **2006** Johannsen *Ginseng Dreams* 60 Ginsengers in Appalachia dig up the root using a sang hoe, a metal tool with a wooden handle. You won't find them in any store—they're often made from old miner's picks with the points cut off, or a broom handle with a piece of automobile spring attached. The long handle makes the tool useful as a walking stick, and also as a probe to check bushes for snakes, a common hazard along with bear and yellow jackets.

[DARE *sang hoe* n especially southern Appalachians]

sanging See **ginseng C**.

sanging hoe See **sang hoe**.

sangko around See **sango**.

sango (also *sanco around, sangko around, sango around, sanker, sanko around*) *verb, verb phrase*) To loiter, wander about; saunter. See also **saunter**.

1907 Dugger *Balsam Groves* 140 You can jist axe the ol' man 'bout that; he's sangkoin' 'round hur somewhur. **1949** Hornsby *Lonesome Valley* 18 His feet begged him to hurry, but he made them take their time. He sankoed out toward the gate. **1963** Williams *Metaphor Mt Speech II* 52 If 'twarn't fer a-hurtin' pore old Aint Sary's feelin's, I'd jis' sanker aout to that road and pull 'im offen thar and shake 'im till his toenails rattled. **1979** Carpenter *Walton War* 152 "I hain't been doin' nothin', jest sangoin around." "Sangoin" seems to be one of those words created by the mountaineer for his own purpose. It means loafing, sashaying; maybe "hanging" around. **1983** Broaddus *Estill Co KY Word List* 54 *sankoing around* = loafing, loitering. **1985** Irwin *Alex Stewart* 109 He was particular and didn't want kids hanging around there too much, but I'd go down there sometimes and just sanco around and look it over. **1995** Montgomery *Coll*: *sanko around* (known to Adams), = probably related to *saunter* (Oliver).

[cf DARE *sanko* v chiefly southern Appalachians, Ozarks]

sang rack *noun* See citation.

1983 Broaddus *Estill Co KY Word List* 54 = a rack for sawing wood. The legs are in the shape of two "X's" with the joining piece attached where the legs cross.

sang root See **ginseng**.

sang sign *noun* See citations. See also **sign 4**.

1968 *Sang Signs* 15 Certain plants that grow . . . in close association with the ginseng . . . are known as "sang-sign." They are indicators of where sang is found . . . Best known as sang-sign is the "little brother of the ginseng," the golden seal. *Ibid.* 47 True yellowroot (Xanthorhiza) . . . was also . . . a sang-sign plant. . . . Another sang-sign plant . . . is the white baneberry (Actaea), the "doll's-eyes" of the mountain healers. *Ibid.* 50 Bloodroot (Sanguinaria) is possibly the most common of the sang-sign plants. *Ibid.* 51 Two ferns [= Adiantum pedatum and Botrychium virginianum] mark the site of ginseng and are found in close association with the other sang-sign plants. The rattlesnake fern (Botrychium virginianum) is known as the "hope of ginseng."

sang tale See **ginseng tale**.

sanker, sanko See **sango**.

sanker pie See **sonker**.

sankumsuly See **sanctum suly**.

Santa Clausing *verbal noun* See citation. See also **Belsnickel, Kris Kringle**.

1975 Kroeger *WV Farm Life* 6 We've had Santas at our house clear from Lower Big Run, up there at home—Santa Clauses with their false faces on and old clothes try to make it look like Santa Claus. I went Santa Clausing with the (my) children a lot of times. I went with them and it was really funny. We had a good time fooling people, you know, and trying to guess who we were and everything like that. It was different from today. . . . Well, people would dress up, you know, with their false faces on and go Santa Clausing. We called it Santa Clausing. They would go to people's houses where they had little children, you know, and they would take them candy, and they never took toys, they just took candy then.

santer See **saunter**.

sap *verb*

1 See 1913 citation.

1913 Kephart *Our Sthn High* 294 To green out or sap is to outwit in trade. [**1992** Montgomery *Coll* (unknown to consultants from the Smoky Mountains).]

2 See citation. See also **sapping party**.

1981 High *Coll* = to peel off the bark of a sweet birch (Betula lenta) and scrape the sap to eat as a kind of natural candy, a treat to children in the Gorge: "We'd sap a birch, and it'd come out in strings and be a little chewy and real sweet, and had a teaberry flavor like teaberry gum."

sapping party *noun* A gathering to peel off the bark of a sweet birch tree.

1989 Still *Rusties and Riddles* [9] During the first full moon in June, when the signs of the zodiac were favorable, there were sapping parties. A black birch was felled, the inside bark was scraped off and mixed with sugar for chewing.

sapsuck *noun* See citation.

1972 Cooper *NC Mt Folklore* 95 = a half-wit.

sapsucker *noun* Usually a small woodpecker of the genus *Sphyrapticus*. See also **chuckwood, peckerwood 1, woodchuck**.

1957 Combs *Lg Sthn High: Word List* 84 = woodpecker. **1966** Dakin *Vocab Ohio River Valley* 395 In the southern Mountains [of KY] a number of speakers say *sap sucker* (for *woodpecker*). This name is recorded on scattered records throughout the Valley, but usually as the name for a specific bird, not as a general name for woodpeckers. *Ibid.* 397 Mountain speakers often say *sap sucker, woodchuck* = "any small woodpecker" and use *wood chicken, wood hen* = "big woodpecker." The latter terms are in fairly common use throughout the Mountains (but nowhere else in the Ohio Valley) and undoubtedly refer to the pileated woodpecker. The removal of the hardwood forests has greatly restricted the range of this large bird and it is probable that it is not common enough to be known and named anywhere in the Valley outside the Mountains.

Sarah Parker *noun* A small car that runs on a railroad track to pick up and load logs. It was used by the Little River Timber Company in Blount Co TN in the early 20th century. See 1974–75 citation.

1957 Weals *Sary Parker* The rig was called a "Sary Parker," says Jim. To get the Sary Parker up and across that incline bridge from the main railroad, the engineer, who was Lewis Rhea, would let the drum unwind while a crew of men took hold of the end of the big steel rope and dragged it up the bridge to a large stump on the top of the hill. **1958** GSMNP-110:23 Sarah Parker run on the incline road, and it [would] pick up the logs, pick them up and load them. **1974–75** McCracken *Logging* 15:14 The Sarah Parker car was on a standard gauge railroad just like the engine run here and just pulled its car back up with a rope. And let the load of logs out with that. No brakes on it.

Sara Jones *noun* A fruit jar with a small, pointed top.

1956 Hall *Coll* (Cosby TN).

sarch[1] See **search.**

sarch[2] *noun* A strainer, sift.

1933 Thomas *Traipsin' Woman* 213 Yander is the sarch in the flour barrel. **1945** O'Dell *Old Mills* 1 After the fanning process the wheat was washed and spread out to dry. Next it was ground on the "burr" or rock, after which it was sifted by hand through a sifter made of muslin stretched over a hoop. This was called a "sarch."

[OED3 at *searce* n obsolete; EDD (at *searce* sb 1) obsolete or obsolescent; SND *search* n[2]; Web3 (at *searce* n) archaic]

sarcumstance See **circumstance.**

sarmint, sarmon See **sermon.**

sarpent, sarpint, sarpunt See **serpent.**

sartain, sartin See **certain.**

sarve See **serve.**

sarvice See **service A, B1.**

sarviceberry See **service B1.**

sarvis See **service A.**

sarvisberry, sarviss, sarvissberry, sarviss tree See **service B1.**

sarvis winter See **service winter.**

sashay *verb* To glide, strut.

1974 Fink *Bits Mt Speech* 23 = saunter, strut. "He was *sashaying* around."

[< French *chassé*]

sashiate *verb* [pronounced *sash-i-ate*] To sashay (used in calling square dance figures).

1913 Kephart *Our Sthn High* 290 The third [word of foreign origin] is sashiate (French *chassé*), used in calling figures at the country dances. **1995** Montgomery *Coll* (known to Bush, Oliver, Shields).

[< French *chassé*]

sash mill (also *sash sawmill*) *noun* A small sawmill powered by a waterwheel. See citations.

1990 Aiken *Stories* 70 "Sash Mills" were also driven by the overshot wheels. These were mills in which saws were installed in a frame called a "sash." **1990** Morgan *Log House E TN* 63–64 Water-powered sawmills of Blount County used the sash saw (also called the "up-and-down saw"), which was "mounted vertically in a frame." The sawframe was connected to a water wheel by a series of belts, pulleys, and wooden gears. As the up-and-down saw "made its cut, the log was carried along on a carriage regulated by a hand-operated ratchet." After the "length of the log had been sawn," the carriage was returned to its original position, the log realigned, and the process repeated. The cutting capacity of sash sawmills was low and varied considerably with the amount of water flow. Early Appalachian sash mills had a capacity of approximately five hundred linear feet per day, no more than one-sixth the capacity of early steam-powered circular sawmills.

sash saw *noun* A thin, narrow saw held in a frame and powered by water. See also **sash mill.**

1945 O'Dell *Old Mills* 2 Occasionally there would be connected with the wheat and flour mill a "sash saw," which was something like a cross-cut saw but straight on the teeth side. This was fashioned in a sash or frame and propelled from a wheel below which sent the saw up and down. **1964** Clarkson *Lumbering in WV* 369 = water-powered saw wherein the saw is attached to a heavy sash that in turn is run by pitman attached to a water wheel.

sash sawmill See **sash mill.**

sass See **sassafras, sauce.**

sassafack, sassafact, sassafrac See **sassafras.**

sassafras *noun*

A Variant forms *sass* [see **1982** in **B**], *sassafack* [see **1930** in **B**], *sassafact* [see **1994** in **B**], *sassafrac* [see **1972** in **A**], *sassyfrac* [see **1994** in **B**], *sassyfras.*

1942 Hall *Phonetics Smoky Mts* 60 A few words are generally sounded with [ɪ]: . . . *sassafras, spectacles, sycamore.* **1972** Cooper *NC Mt Folklore* 95 *sassafrac.*

B A common deciduous tree (*Sassafras albidum*) that grows at lower and middle elevations. From its roots or bark *sassafras tea* (or *sass tea*) is made and drunk for kidney trouble, as a spring tonic, for refreshment, and to substitute for coffee. Same as **root-beer tree.**

1930 Thomas *Death Knell* Sassafras, an aromatic tree from which a delightful beverage is made, is sassafack. **1939** Hall *Coll* (Emerts Cove TN) When we'd get sick or anything, they'd make sassafras tea, you know, and have us to drink it. **1967** Jones *Pecu-*

liarities Mtneers 68 Sassafras tea was a very pleasant mild spring tonic, especially recommended for those who were recuperating from a serious illness. **1969** Doran *Folklore White Co* 143 To ensure better health by cooperating with nature in the spring, many families drank red sassafras root tea or ate sulphur and molasses to purify and thin the blood. **1975** GSMNP-59:19 If you didn't have coffee, you used sassafras tea or something like that. **1981** Irwin *Arnwine Cabin* 23 [Sassafras] was considered to have medicinal qualities. According to Elmer Sherwood, a 78-year-old mountain man who has worked at the Museum [of Appalachia] since its beginning, it was customary to start drinking sassafras tea in the spring, around the first of March, and continue to do so for at least a month. It, according to Elmer, would "clean and purify your blood." **1994** Montgomery *Coll* Nothing is better than cornbread, lasses, and sassafact tea (Cardwell); *sassyfrac* (known to Shields). **2001** Joslin *Appal Bounty* 111 The popularity of sassafras tea has dipped sharply in the past decade, as government warnings and regulations have frightened some from its consumption. Several years ago, the U.S. Food and Drug Administration banned sassafras tea for sale in interstate commerce for alleged carcinogenic properties. Safrole, part of the volatile oils of sassafras, was found to cause liver cancer in rats when it made up .5 to 1 percent of their total food. Some health food stores today sell safrole-free sassafras extracts for worried consumers. Homemade sassafras tea continues to appeal to mountain residents of all ages. **2006** Howell *Medicinal Plants* 139 Sassafras has a long history of use as a folk remedy in the southern Appalachians where it is still used as a traditional spring tonic to thin the blood after many months without fresh fruits and vegetables. The pith, or spongy, inner layer of the outermost branches, is dissolved in water to make a soothing wash for sore eyes. Hot sassafras root tea is drunk to relieve fevers from colds and influenza. Until recently, sassafras was used as a flavoring agent in commercial root beer.

[DARE *sass tea* n chiefly South, South Midland]

sassafras tea See **sassafras B**.

sass-box *noun* An impudent child.

1937 Hyatt *Kiverlid* 67 I'll let pappy take you down a few notches fer bein' a sass-box.

sassenger *noun* See citation.

1927 Woofter *Dialect from WV* 363 = sausage. "We had buckwheat and sassengers for breakfast."

sasser See **saucer**.

sasser and blow See **saucer B**.

sass hole *noun* A place to store **sauce**.

1917 (in **1944** Wentworth *ADD* 531) (sWV) Go to the sass hole & get some taters. **1958** Sanderson *County Scott* 179–80 There will be plenty of "grub" on the table and more in the "sass" holes. **1975** Jackson *Unusual Words* 155 Women would dry apple slices and beans and store them in the loft of the house or in the *sass hole*, also known as the *root cellar* or *can house* and they would be ready for use during the winter.

sass patch *noun* A vegetable garden. See also **sauce**, **truck patch**.

1977 Still *Wonder Beans* 6 They had to eat the corn seed held out to plant the sass patch in the spring.

sass root tea, **sassyfrac**, **sassyfras** See **sassafras**.

satchel stick *noun* In logging, a stick carried on the shoulder to support a bag containing a logger's personal belongings.

1998 Robbins *Logging Terms*.

satisfactionate *adjective* See citation.

1972 Cooper *NC Mt Folklore* 95 = satisfactory. **2008** Terrell *Mt Lingo* A lot of words were coined because of a lack of schooling. A fellow might be talking and come upon a word he wasn't sure of. Then he'd make up his own version, say it, and go right on. "Satisfactionate."

satisfactual *adjective* Satisfactory.

1891 Primer *Studies in WV* 167 *satisfactual*.

satisfied *adjective* Convinced, assured, having no doubt, persuaded by the evidence. See also **take one's satisfy**.

1863 *Warrick CW Letters* (Feb 12) I dont wannt to see them no more I am satsfide with them. **1864** *C A Walker CW Letters* (April 27) I felt that I was very well satisfied that I come out safe unhurt. **1931** Owens *Speech Cumberlands* 91 = quite sure: "Even John's mother feels satisfied he done the killin." **1937** Hall *Coll* (Cades Cove TN) I was satisfied he done it. **1955** Ritchie *Singing Family* 181 I'm satisfied that's the one allus bears the best of any around here. **1956** Hall *Coll* (Byrds Creek NC) That man has killed himself, I'm satisfied. **1971** *AOHP/ALC-193* I was very well satisfied that I wouldn't be able to do nothing else in coal mining. **1974–75** McCracken *Logging* 11:78 I'm satisfied they was cherry. **1979** *Big South Fork OHP-11* I'm satisfied he'll not even wind that clock up. **1989** Landry *Smoky Mt Interviews* 181 It would have lived if it'd been put in an incubator. I'm satisfied it would. **1995** Montgomery *Coll* I'm satisfied that she wrote it all down (Cardwell).

sauce

A Variant form *sass*.

1863 *Reese CW Letters* (April 2) men is starved out an Bred and meet so Bad that tha[y] will giv aney price for aney kind of Case [= sass]. **1942** Hall *Phonetics Smoky Mts* 33.

B *noun*

1 Apple sauce.

1913 Kephart *Our Sthn High* 293 Your hostess, proffering apple sauce, will ask, "Do you love sass?" **c1960** Wilson *Coll* apple sass. **1975** Jackson *Unusual Words* 155 [The word's] broadest meaning encompasses foods of all kind. The story of the hard times when women would come from far back in the hollows to the home of another woman whose husband was a good provider. Their comment was consistently the same, "Sass is sca'ce, hain't it?" The narrowest meaning is apple sauce, and a meaning between these two extremes is any kind of dried fruit or vegetables.

2 Vegetables (a term varying greatly in scope, from wild greens to all foods except meat, dairy products, and bread). See also **garden salad, salad B.**

1848 (in **1870** Drake *Pioneer Life KY* 107) Breakfast over, my function was to provide the "sauce" for dinner; in winter, to open the potato or turnip hole, and wash what I took out; in spring, to go into the fields and collect the greens; in summer and autumn, to explore the "truck-patch," or our little garden; and from among the weeds dig or pull whatever might be in season. **1862** *Hawn CW Letters* (May 24) we git aplenty of sugar . . . coffee and met and bred and rice and and some beenes we have no sass hear. **1863** *Epperly CW Letters* (Aug 1) you dont know how bad I want Som Sause to eat I get so tird on bread and meet and nothing else. **1915** Dingus *Word-List VA* 189 = vegetables for the table. **1937** Hyatt *Kiverlid* 79 I like this wild sass . . . better'n I do the gyarden sass. **c1960** Wilson *Coll* = garden vegetables; apple sauce. [See **1975** in **1**.] **c1975** Lunsford *It Used to Be* 158 The word for wild greens is called "sass." These are the greens that you pick in the spring of the year. Various kinds such as narrow-dock, lambs quarter, and poke are spoken of as "sass." **1982** Slone *How We Talked* 54 All food put away for winter use, except meat, milk and bread, was "sass"—all dried, canned and holed-away fruits, vegetables, berries and salt-pickled foods (kraut, corn, beans and cucumbers).

[DARE *sauce* n B1 chiefly New England, South, South Midland]

C *verb* To backtalk (to). See also **backjaw A.**

1905 Miles *Spirit of Mts* 115 There was a feller she'd called a cymblin'-headed fool that tried to act big-Ike and sass her back. **1955** Ritchie *Singing Family* 79 Mom hated most of all for us to sass her, and to sass Dad was just not done. I used to think that God would strike me with lightning if I sassed back to Dad. **1955** Washburn *Country Doctor* 46 This so riled 'er that she sassed the parson right out in public; an' then he withdrawed the hand of Christian fellowship from 'er. **1996** Montgomery *Coll* She backhanded her son for sassing her (Cardwell). **2004** Fisher *Kettle Bottom* 25 I was not raised in a barn, my mama has taught me DO NOT SASS.

saucer

A *noun, verb* Variant forms *sasser, saucy.*

1859 Taliaferro *Fisher's River* 55–56 There it lay on the side of a steep presserpis, at full length, ten feet long, its tail straight out, right up the presserpis, head as big as a sasser, right toards me. **1951** Craig *Singing Hills* 31 Saucy your coffee, boy! Ain't you got no manners? **1976** Ogle and Nixon *If Only* Get me a sasser (saucer) from the cupboard.

B *verb* In phrases *sasser and blow, saucer and blow* = to pour (especially hot coffee) into a saucer to cool.

1953 Davison *Word-List Appal* 13 Sister, we ain't given to waitin' on no one; jest sasser your coffee and make yourself to home. **1981** Whitener *Folk-Ways* 82 Excuse me, ma'am, but since you're in such a allfard hurry I'd be right proud to trade [cups of coffee] with you. Mine's already been sassered and blowed. **1994–95** Montgomery *Coll* (known to Ogle); He always sassers his coffee so it can be more comfortably drunk (Cardwell). **2017** *Blind Pig* (Feb 13) I remember my Great Aunt Pearl sitting at Granny Gazzie's kitchen table "saucer and blowing" her tea. And I've seen Granny saucer and blow her coffee over the years when it was too hot for her.

[Web3 *saucer* v dialect; DARE *saucer* v C especially Southern Appalachians]

saucy See **saucer.**

sauerkraut See **kraut.**

saugus cat *noun* An imaginary creature used to frighten and warn children. See also **catawampus**[1], **wampus B.**

1968 Vincent *Best Stories* 60 "That," sez I, "Were the Saugus Cat a-leavin' out." **1996–97** Montgomery *Coll* (known to Brown, Bush, Cardwell).

saunt See **send.**

saunter *verb* Variant forms *sainter, santer.*

1904–20 Kephart *Notebooks* 4:749 Le's santer around in the laurel and see if we find any bear signs. **1992** Brooks *Sthn Stuff* 132 *sainter.* **1994** Montgomery *Coll: santer* (known to Cardwell).

savagerous (also *servagerous, survigorous, survigrous* [sɚˈvaɪgrəs]) *adjective, adverb* Vigorous, fierce, vicious.

1866 Smith *So Called* 54 It is, perhaps, when suspended, the most savagerous beast that ever got after tories and traitors. **1913** Kephart *Our Sthn High* 294 Survigrous (ser-*vi*-grus) is a superlative of vigorous (here pronounced *vi*-grus, with long i); as "a survigrous baby," "a most survigrous cusser." **1927** Woofter *Dialect from WV* 363 *servagerous* = very active. "That is a servagerous coon dog." **1952** Wilson *Folk Speech NC* 596 *survig(o)rous* = fierce. **1957** Combs *Lg Sthn High: Word List* 98 *survygrous* [sɚˈvaɪgrəs] = fiery, prancing (of horses). **1974** Fink *Bits Mt Speech* 25 *survigorous* = vicious, exceedingly strong. "Hit was a powerful *survigorous* bear." **1975** Gainer *Speech Mtneer* 16 *servagerous* . . . very active. "That youngun is too servagerous to suit me. I can't keep up with him."

[perhaps alteration of *savagerous* by analogy with *vygrous* (variant of *vigorous*); cf CSD *savagiously* adv 1 "savagely"; cf Web3 < *sur-* + *vigorous*, chiefly South and Midland; DARE *savagerous* adj/adj especially South, South Midland, *servigrous* adj chiefly South, South Midland]

save *verb* To gather or harvest (a crop).

1862 *Huntley CW Letters* (June 1) When you Write tell me how your Wheat is I thought I Would git to come home at harvest and help Save the wheat But thare is no chance of it Save all you can of it. **1863** *Epperly CW Letters* (Aug 9) the people hear has all got along with thare work very well they hav got all thare grain savd. **1921** Combs *KY Items* 119 = to make or gather. "The whole family's a-savin' hay and punkins to-day." **1997** Montgomery *Coll* (known to Adams, Bush, Jones, Ledford, Norris, Weaver); We need to save the corn this week (Cardwell).

[DARE *save* v B1 South, South Midland]

save back *verb phrase* To put aside (especially food) for later consumption.

1923 Greer-Petrie *Angeline Doin' Society* 5 If the comp-ny has cleaned up the platter, or she's a-savin' her vittle back for tomorrow, I can make out fine with a glass of butter milk. **1973** *AOHP/ASU-160* When we had a field of potatoes, we didn't plant potatoes in the garden. We would save back potatoes to eat. **1996** Cavender *Bold Hives* 19 Well, we'd take a little of that [ground ivy], put some water on it, steep it a little while, and we'd try our best to save a little sugar back to sweeten that with.

save my time *interjection* Used as an exclamation of surprise. See also **help my time**.

2017 *Blind Pig* (June 10) I've heard variations, including "bless my time" and "save my time," although "help my time" is more common.

saving (also *saving and craving*) *adjective, adjective phrase* Frugal, thrifty.

1862 *Robinson CW Letters* (Dec 4) you must live as Saving as you can fur it is agoing to be hard times & the poore is oblige to Suffer. **1862** *Walker CW Letters* (March 16) Anna i want you an Susan to be good girls an work an try to make Corne an bee saveing of what Corne you have got. **1922** *TN CW Ques* 20 (Greene Co TN) When he was inclined to be saving the richer men helped him if hones[t]. **1973** *AOHP/ASU-89* We was saving with that money. We had to be or we'd have went naked. **1982** Slone *How We Talked* 24 It was very important for a girl to have learned to be "saving'" (thrifty) before becoming a wife and, if she had, she was thought to be a much better wife. Any woman that was wasteful was despised by her neighbors. **c1982** Young *Colloquial Appal* 19 *saving and craving* = frugal. **1983** Page and Wigginton *Aunt Arie* 89 They wadn't savin' about timber like they are now. **2005** Williams *Gratitude* 520 *saving with* = to be frugal with something, as: "We was *saving with* lamp oil."

saw[1] See **see A2**.

saw[2] (also *sah, so*) *interjection* Stand still! (used as a command to a cow at milking time). See also **soo calf**, **soo cow**, **sook**.

1900 Harben *N GA Sketches* 98 "So, so, Brin'!" she was saying softly. "Cayn't you stan' still a minute? That ain't no way to do. So, so!" **1934–37** *LAMSAS Appal* (Madison Co NC) *saw*. **1949** Kurath *Word Geog East US* 64 Calls to Cows during Milking . . . *saw!* . . . is current everywhere south of Pennsylvania. . . . In the greater part of this large area *so!* and *saw!* stand side by side. **1966** Dakin *Vocab Ohio River Valley* 272 [In the Ohio Valley] *so!* appears nowhere else west of the [KY] Mountains, *saw!* holding full sway. **1966–67** *DARE Survey* (Spruce Pine NC, Maryville TN) *saw*; (Gatlinburg TN) *saw heifer*. **1973** Miller *English Unicoi Co* 152 *saw* = a call to a cow to make her stand still for milking. **1978** Reese *Speech NE Tenn* 30 *sah* = attested by 9/12 (75%) speakers; 31 *saw, boss* = attested by 4/12 (33.3%) speakers. **1986** Pederson et al. *LAGS*: *saw* (Cocke Co TN, Jefferson Co TN, Sevier Co TN). **2002** McGowan *Beech Mt Tales* 106 The old farmer come along. "Sook, Buck, saw, Buck, let's get to town."

saw brier *noun* A greenbrier (*Smilax* spp) known for its sturdy vine. See also **bamboo brier**.

1859 Taliaferro *Fisher's River* 60 I felt suthin rakin' my feet wusser than sawbriers. **1937** Thornburgh *Great Smoky Mts* 23 A few of the more common vines you may encounter along almost any trail are . . . green brier, which is also called saw brier, cat brier, and bamboo brier. **1956** Hall *Coll* (Alexander NC) My father in his effort to hold the dogs he had on leash . . . tripped on a green saw brier, which is very strong. **1964** Stupka *Trees Shrubs Vines* 32 The saw brier has been noted at 3,000 altitude (trail to Greenbrier Pinnacle) and it probably occurs at somewhat higher elevations in the park. **1993** Stuart *Daughter* 236 = a brier with small but extremely sharp thorns. This brier can cause a long tear in one's clothing or skin (as though the skin had been sawed). **1996** Spurlock *Glossary* 407 = a briar with small but extremely sharp thorns which can cause a long tear in one's clothing or skin.

[DARE *saw brier* n chiefly South Midland]

sawbuck *noun*

1 (also *sawing horse, sawing rack, sawrack*) A sawhorse with X-shaped endpieces to hold firewood for sawing and a cross-bar attached where the legs meet.

1934–37 *LAMSAS Appal* (Madison Co NC, Swain Co NC) *sawrack*. **1949** Kurath *Word Geog East US* 35 *Saw buck* . . . is the usual word for the *saw horse* in Pennsylvania east of the Alleghenies (also on the upper Potomac and on the Yadkin in North Carolina). *Ibid.* 59 *Saw buck, wood buck*, sometimes simply *buck*, are characteristic of the entire German settlement area in Eastern Pennsylvania, western Maryland, the Shenandoah Valley, the upper reaches of the Potomac in West Virginia, and on the Yadkin in North Carolina. **1952–57** (in **1973** McDavid and McDavid *Vocab E KY* 159) *sawrack* = saw buck. **1957** Broaddus *Vocab Estill Co KY* 66 *saw rack* = a rack for sawing wood. The legs are in the shape of two "X's" with the joining piece attached where the legs cross. **1966–69** *DARE Survey* (Brasstown NC) *sawing horse*; (Sawyer KY, Maryville TN) *sawing rack*; (Spruce Pine NC) *sawrack*. **1998** Montgomery *Coll*: *sawbuck* (known to Brown); *sawing horse* (known to Cardwell); *sawrack* (known to Ledford).

[perhaps loan translation from Dutch *zaagbok* "a trestle, saw horse"; OED3 *sawbuck* n 1a U.S. 1855→; DARE *saw rack* n chiefly South, South Midland]

2 A ten-dollar bill.

1989 Still *Rusties and Riddles* [22] = a ten-dollar bill.

sawdust gravy (also *sawmill gravy*) *noun* A heavy gravy made with flour or sometimes cornmeal. Also called **logging gravy**.

1965 West *Time Was* 28 The gravy had been made by frying flour in pork grease for body, then stirring in milk while the gravy thickened.... She smiled ... "Anybody that's had as much practice doin a job as I've had makin sawmill gravy is bound to be a expert or crazy as a bedbug." **1966** Adams *Mt LeConte* 37 We ate well that night—fried squirrels, boiled potatoes, fresh green beans, "sawdust" gravy, bread and coffee. **1971** Hall *Coll* (Gatlinburg TN) *sawmill gravy* = white, thick gravy made with lard. **1977** *Foxfire IV* 315 She would make [the loggers] a big pan of sawmill gravy. She'd have a great big skillet and she'd put some meal or flour in it. You could make it out of corn meal or flour, but ... generally ... flour. She'd put that flour in that pan and she'd let it brown a little bit. Then she'd dump that milk in there—or water if she didn't have milk. So they'd have gravy. **1987** Hall *Coll* (Del Rio TN) Sawmill gravy was made with lard and flour. [With no milk?] No, because there was no way to get milk around the saw mills. **1989** Smith *Flyin' Bullets* 55 Corn bread might be eaten for breakfast with "saw mill gravy," a gravy made of corn meal. **1995** Montgomery *Coll*: *sawmill gravy* = always made out of cornmeal [rather than flour] (Cardwell). **1997** Andrews *Mountain Vittles* 19 That's exactly how this came to be called saw mill gravy. The cooks at the different loggin' camps that cooked fer the crowd of men folks in the loggin' crews, why those cooks used corn meal to make up a whole lot of gravy and I've heard that sometimes the men would laugh and accuse 'em of makin' up the gravy with the saw dust. **2005** Williams *Gratitude* 520 = meat is fried, leaving hot grease and browned bits in the pan. Flour is stirred into the fat, then water or milk is added until the *sawmill gravy* is the desired thickness.

[DARE *sawmill gravy* n chiefly southern Appalachians]

sawdust with legs *noun* See citation.

1980 Riggleman *WV Mtneer* 126–27 [Loggers] usually had nicknames for everybody and everything around the camp.... Lice were called "graybacks" or "sawdust with legs."

sawed *adjective* See citation.

1940 Farr *More TN Expressions* 447 = embarrassed: "Clyde was sawed."

saw gourds (also *saw on (one's) gourds*) *verb phrase* To snore loudly.

1890 Fruit *KY Words* 65 To "saw gourds" is to snore furiously. **1915** Dingus *Word-List VA* 189 *saw on (one's) gourds* = to snore. **c1960** Wilson *Coll*: *saw gourds* = to snore loudly.

[DARE (at *gourd* n 3) South, South Midland]

sawgrums See **sorghum**.

sawhorse *noun* A seesaw. [Editor's note: This term referring to a frame for sawing wood is widespread in the US; see **sawbuck**.]

1986 Pederson et al. *LAGS* (Washington Co TN, Hamilton Co TN, Lumpkin Co GA).

sawing horse, sawing rack See **sawbuck 1**.

saw log *noun* See citation.

1979 Slone *My Heart* 105 We did not get much candy, but each time my father went to the store he always brought back three large red and white peppermint sticks of candy, which were called "saw logs."

sawmill gravy See **sawdust gravy**.

saw on (one's) gourds See **saw gourds**.

sawrack See **sawbuck**.

say See **-s²**.

say howdy See **howdy B**.

say what? (also *say which?*) *phrase* Used as a response asking a person to repeat a question or statement. Same as **do how?**, **do what?**

1973 GSMNP-72 Say which? **1994–97** Montgomery *Coll*: *saw what?* (known to Adams, Brown, Cardwell, Jones, Oliver, Weaver).

scab hole *noun* See citation.

2002 Armstead *Black Days* 243 = dog hole.

scaffle See **scaffold**.

scaffold *noun*

A Variant form *scaffle*.

1942 Hall *Phonetics Smoky Mts* 91.

[DARE *scaffold* n especially South Midland]

B A plank, often forming a raised outdoor platform, on which sliced fruit is spread to dry; more generally, a shelf on which food is placed before being prepared for later consumption.

1939 Hall *Coll* (Cataloochee NC) We used to dry our fruit. We'd gather our apples in of a day and peel our apples of a night and put them out on a scaffold.... We'd fill our scaffold about every three days. When it got pretty dry, we'd take it off on a cloth and lay it out in the sun and fill our scaffold again. **1943** Chase *Jack Tales* 18 She started to climb up there on the scaffle, says, "You put your shoulder under it, Jack." **1974** Cate et al. *Sthn Appal Heritage* 63 Dolly would see that the chickens were fed, the eggs gathered, the cows milked, and the drying fruit put on the scaffold in the hot sun and brought in before the evening dew began to fall.

[DARE *scaffold* n B2 especially South Midland]

scairt See **scaredy**.

scald *noun* An area of ground that is infertile or worn out, having or supporting no vegetation, called a **fire scald** when denuded by fire. See also **old field**.

1883 Zeigler and Grosscup *Heart of Alleghanies* 68 There are other bare spots on these mountains known as scalds, and like this old field, situated in the heart of fir forests. **1939** Hall *Coll* (Alexander NC) = a bare place on a hill. *Ibid.* (Dellwood NC) = a place that's wore out. *Ibid.* (Saunook NC) Scald [is] a bare area from which the top soil is gone and no plant grows. *Ibid.* (White Oak NC) Scald on a hill [means that] nothin' grows on it, where they ain't no weeds nor nothin' on it, just a bare place.

scalded bread *noun* Corn bread made from cornmeal into which boiling water has been poured.

1982 Slone *How We Talked* 57 By using hot water to make cornbread we made what we called "scalded bread." It was very good to eat with milk. We sometimes added molasses to make molasses bread. Cooked cushaw or pumpkin was added also. **1995–97** Montgomery Coll (known to Bush, Cardwell), = cooked in the form of a pone and made from meal and hot water and cooked in a greased skillet (Weaver).

scalded dog See **like a scalded dog**.

scald head *noun* See citations.

2003 Cavender *Folk Medicine* 102 = a scalp infection . . . that caused partial or total hair loss. *Ibid.* 204 = favus [a fungus disease of the scalp]. **2007** Myers *Smoky Mt Remedies* 11 = scales or sores on one's head.

scald the walls *verb phrase* To clean and disinfect the interior walls of a dwelling with boiling water as part of spring cleaning.

1969 Madden and Jones *Walker Sisters* 33 Each spring [the Walker sisters] pitched in for the spring cleaning. One rather unique chore here was to "scald the walls".... Every inch of the interior was thoroughly scrubbed with boiling water. Newspapers and magazines were used to cover the walls, and of necessity were replaced after each scalding.

scalybark *noun* A variety of hickory (*Carya ovata/laciniosa*) distinguished by a thick, lightweight, gray bark that often curls back in large, loose plates and from which a medicinal tea is made; the nut of this tree, used in cooking.

1925 Furman *Glass Window* 21 I would dig out holes back in the clay with my hands, to hide my ill-got plunder in . . . chestnuts or scaly barks or warnuts which, in their season, I had robbed the barrels of. **1968** Wilson *Local Plants* 325 = Carya ovata. Tea made from the bark was used for indigestion and internal aches and pains.

[DARE *scaly bark* n chiefly Southeast, Lower Mississippi Valley]

scamp *verb* To graze, give a glancing blow to (someone).

1896 Fox *Last Stetson* 211 "Ef he was jus' scamped by a ball," said Steve, "you kin bet he tuk the boat." **1911** Shearin *E KY Word-List* 539 = to strike slightly, to graze; e.g., "The tree fell and just scamped my shoulder." **1919** Combs *Word-List South* 35 = to touch, or barely glance: "Jep cut drive with a big rock an' scamped Dish."

scandalization *noun* A scandal, scandalous act.

1981 GSMNP-117:22 That's the only two times that I knowed of any scandalization a-bein' done up there, just those two times.

scandalize *verb* To defame, bring (someone) into reproach; damage one's name.

1952 Wilson *Folk Speech NC* 587 = to cause a scandal to one. **1969** Doran *Folklore White Co* 114 = to damage someone's reputation. **1976** Garber *Mountain-ese* 78 Those rumors were just meant to scandalize my good name.

[OED3 *scandalize* v[1] 3 now somewhat rare →1865; Web3 *scandalize* v[1] 2 archaic; DARE *scandalize* v South, South Midland]

scandalous *adverb* Exceedingly, exorbitantly.

1922 Kephart *Our Sthn High* 121 We can't git a doctor up hyar less'n three days; and it costs scan'lous. **1923** Furman *Mothering* 26 I heared Blant was the quickest on the trigger of any boy ever lived, and laid out the Cheevers scandalous. **1974** Fink *Bits Mt Speech* 23 = very, exceedingly. "Clothes costes *scandalous* high these days." **1997** Montgomery Coll (known to eight consultants from the Smoky Mountains).

[DARE *scandalous* adv B especially southern Appalachians]

scantling *noun* A piece of lumber cut to a specific size for a carpenter's use.

1939 Hall Coll (White Oak NC) That's a two by four scantlin'. **1952** Justus *Children* 53 While you go atter them I'll take some strengthy scantlings and some twenty-penny nails and fix that broken fence. **1970** GSMNP-26:6 Most of them had good boards, you see, and some of it was split with more boards. It would be split. We call them scantlins sort of, which was some of them four foot long, paling type.

[OED3 *scantling* n from earlier *scantillon* "a builder's or carpenter's measuring-rod"; Web3 *scantling* n alteration of *scantillion* by influence of -*ling*]

scar *noun, verb* Variant forms *scyar, skyar*.

1904–20 Kephart *Notebooks* 2:475 You can see the scyar yit. **1939** Hall *Notebooks* 13:20 (White Oak NC) He's skyared all over. **1942** Hall *Phonetics Smoky Mts* 30 After [k] and [g], many elderly people and a few others use a palatal glide, as in . . . *scarred* [skjɑɚd]. **1994** Montgomery Coll (known to Cardwell).

scarafy See **scarify**[1] **1**.

scarce

A *adjective, adverb* Variant forms *scearse, skeerce, skyerce*.

1863 *Vance Papers* (April 27) Provesions is very scearse her at this tim. **1939** Hall *Notebooks* 13:16 (White Oak NC) *skeerce* = scarce. **2005** Williams *Gratitude* 40 *skyerce as hen's teeth*. **2008** McKinley *Bear Mt* 42 During Grandpa's early lifetime, leather shoes were "hard to come by." As he often said, "They was downright 'skeerce.'"

B *adjective* Sparing, parsimonious.

1989 *Matewan OHP-89* They were scarce about talking.

[OED3 *scarce* adj 2a obsolete]

C *adverb* Less.

1970 Madden and Jones *Ephraim Bales* 8 Eph told him there was going to be one man scarce lived on Roaring Fork some of these days. **1995–97** Montgomery Coll (known to Adams, Bush, Cardwell, Jones, Norris, Oliver, Weaver).

scare *verb*

1 Variant base forms *scear, scyure, skeer*.

1864 *Joyce CW Letters* (June 18) when we come thrugh the sitty the people was sceard vary bad thay give me as mutch meat and bread as I cold Eat. **1867** Harris *Sut Lovingood* 110 Now s'pose I happens tu put in a leetle too much powder, an' skeer him plum outen the United States—what then? **1895** *Mt Baptist Sermon* 15 I seed the lightnin' but hit didn't skeer me. **1974** Roberts *Sang Branch* 210 This boy's father took a notion he'd try to skeer Johnny with the corpse. **1993** Burleson *Aunt Keziah* 11 Mammy hyerd all the commotion and when she seed that blood hit scyured her so bad she wore Blesset and Lindy out.

2 Variant *past-participle, adjective* forms *scairt, scart, skeered, skeert.*

1923 (in **1952** Mathes *Tall Tales* 8) I was allus kind o' skeered of him till he came an' et at our house. **1935** Sheppard *Cabins in Laurel* 74 He did [stop], you bet, scart of his life, and he had been sent by Shay to say they was bringing the money fast as they could. **1937** Thornburgh *Great Smoky Mts* 135 I war plumb scairt. **1938** Hall *Coll* (Gatlinburg TN) . . . look like a skeered hant. **1942** Thomas *Blue Ridge* 53 That bull was riled plum to a franzy and that thin peddler was yeller as a punkin. Skeert out of his wits. **1971** Costner *Song of Life* 41 [M]aybe they were sca'rt because they'd slipped out from their pappy. **1976** Garber *Mountain-ese* 87 We got skeered when we hyard a big squinch owl in the tree. **2008** Salsi *Ray Hicks* 66 We called scairt dogs that are still a barkin' "booger barkin'."

[cf SND *skeer* v 1 "to frighten"]

scare booger *noun* A scarecrow. See also **booger**.

1973 *Gardening* 250 You could put up scare-boogers an' keep [the rabbits] out.

scaredy *adjective*

1 Afraid.

1955 Ritchie *Singing Family* 11 Law no, Mom, I couldn't stay, with all these four little uns—You with no lantern either, and them all scaredy. **1974** *AOHP/ASU-204* I don't think anybody's any scaredier of snakes than I was, black snakes, when I was a-little.

2 Frightening.

1989 Giardina *Storming Heaven* 35 She was telling you scairdy things about men, werent she?

scare out (also *scare up*) *verb phrase* To arouse or startle; to flush out (game).

1937 Hall *Coll* (Cades Cove TN) The storm scared us up. I told the preacher if he was goin' to ax a blessin', he had to do it while we was gittin' the grub out. **1939** Hall *Coll* (Cataloochee NC) We wanted to send some fellers to the stand and me and another feller, Jack Williamson, was a-goin' in there, gonna scare [the bear] out. *Ibid.* (Deep Creek NC) We didn't start ary deer, but they scared up some turkeys an' one of 'em came out by me an' I killed it. **1943** Hannum *Mt People* 101 I'll lay to hit that whoever killed that traveler got scared out and buried the money, and run. **1958** Hall *Coll* (Del Rio TN) That scared the officer up, and he decided it wouldn't be safe for that to be brought out. **1973** Davis *'Pon My Honor* 25 Pretty soon the dogs scared up a deer, and they skittered through them woods for a whet, singing out like a bell. **1983** *Dark Corner OHP-5A* Some fellow scared him up around Greenville. One of the deputy sheriffs or somebody got him. **1984** *GSMNP-153* The little children, younguns, was crying, you know, and hollerin', and takin' on, and I mean that scared me up. **1998** *Dante OHP-61* They got scared up and moved. **2008** *Rosie Hicks* 4 [The pumpkins] bust theirself open and scared up a rabbit.

scares See **scours**.

scare up *verb phrase*

1 See **scare out.**

2 To find or fashion by deliberate effort, prepare (especially a meal) quickly on short or no notice. Also called **whomp up.**

1940 Pyle *Roving Reporter* She just insisted that we get out and stay for lunch, and said she'd scare up a chicken somewhere and cook it for us. **1941** Stuart *Men of Mts* 27 I'm out to skeer me up a few votes. **1956** McAtee *Some Dial NC* 38 I'll see if I can scare up some supper. **c1960** Wilson *Coll* = to prepare dinner on short notice, rustle up; even used to get money for some needed purpose, public or private. **1997** Montgomery *Coll* (known to Cardwell). **2005** Williams *Gratitude* 520 = to forage around to find what you need to do something with. Examples: "I better go *scare up* some supper." Or, "I'll see if I can *scare up* enough boards to make some hen nests." **2008** McKinley *Bear Mt* 183 = prepare quickly without advance notice.

scarify[1] *verb* [first syllable pronounced as either *scar* or *scare*].

1 (also *scarafy*) To drain blood by making a narrow cut or scratch (on the temple) to relieve a headache.

1937 Hall *Coll* (Catons Grove TN) = [to make] a cut in the temple to relieve the pain of a headache. [We would] bleed for several things. **1937** Hyatt *Kiverlid* 7 I have seen a patient "scarafied" on the temple with a razor and blood drawn with a cupping glass for relief of neuralgia.

2 To make a similar cut (in the back of a baby) to relieve the **bold hives.**

1921 Combs *KY Items* 119 = to mark with a scar. Taken from a superstition among the hillsmen, that of "scarifying" infants for certain diseases. **1939** Hall *Coll* (White Oak NC) [To scarify], make a cut in the back of babies with a razor and suck the blood through the end of a gourd. They say it makes children grow. **1971** *AOHP/ALC-4* [They would take just the point of a razor and just between [a baby's] shoulders, they'd lay them across their lap, flat of their stomach, and they'd take a razor and just sort of clip the skin just a little, enough to get about three drops of blood, and they would put milk in that and give it to the baby and that would take care of it.] **1996** Cavender *Bold Hives* 20 = When a baby has the bold hives, its fingernails turn black. What you did was turn the baby on its stomach and make two or three small cuts with a razor in the area over the heart. You then took a cow's horn and put it on the slits and then suck the blood out, put the blood in a spoon and add breast milk to it and then feed it to the baby. **2003** Cavender *Folk Medicine* 204 *scarifying* = making incisions on the skin and then covering them with a hot cup, or performing suction on incisions by mouth with a cow horn to draw out blood; also known as "wet cupping."

scarify[2] *verb* To frighten, terrify.

1982 Powers and Hannah *Cataloochee* 382 In Cataloochee, the "dead man" is not something scarifying, but merely a heavy post which is set in to hold up cables for a footlog or bridge.

[*scare* + *-ify*; Web3 *scarify* v[2] dialect]

scarlet laurel *noun* Same as **catawba rhododendron.**

2007 McMillon *Notes.*

scar out *verb phrase* Of a heavy rain: to wash out (terrain).

1997 Montgomery *Coll* The cloud burst scarred out a new ravine (Cardwell).

scart See **scaredy.**

scary *adjective*

A Variant forms *skeary* [see **1862** in **B**], *skeery*.

1866 (in **1974** Harris *High Times* 167) I were bof sickly, an' skeery to look at, I swar I wer.

B Easily frightened, inclined to fright, skittish.

1862 Hitt *CW Letters* (April 23) I am not so skeary as you mite sopose I ant half so mutch so as I ust to bee. **1862** Tesh *CW Letters* (May 25) I tell you it made some of them Look mighty Skeery but it didant Frighten me a bit. **1869** (in **1974** Harris *High Times* 213) [Women] soon gits nervous and skeery, 'maginin vain things, an' givin' tharsefs up tu a fightin' virtue, an' a ghostly prudery. **1899** Fox *Mt Europa* 33 Keep an eye open fer old Bill. They say that he air mighty low down, 'n' kind o' sorry 'n' skeery. **1937** Haun *Cocke Co* 3 [Girls] mosey around over the hills like tarpins, are skeery of snakes when they see them quiled up, and they and lambs are supposed to be seely. **1956** Hall *Coll* (Roaring Fork TN) She was a big woman and awful scary appearantly. **1969** Medford *Finis* 66 Jim, being of a "skeery natur" anyway, gave up his part of the moonshine contract, leaving the responsibility to his younger partner. **1973** GSMNP-80:8 Now that was how scary Ailey was when she was a girl. **1980** Still *Run for Elbertas* 75 "You're taking it as seriously as the young'uns," Mother answered. "I believe to my heart you're scary." **1989** *Matewan OHP*-45 That made me that much scarier.

[OED3 *scary* adj 2 originally and chiefly North American, 1773→; DARE *scary* adj B scattered, but chiefly South, South Midland]

scary crow *noun* A scarecrow.

2001 Montgomery *Coll* (known to Cardwell).

scat (also *scat cat*, *scat there* and variants) *interjection* Bless you! (used as a response to another person's sneezing).

1983 Broaddus *Estill Co KY Word List* 54 *scat!* = said to a small child upon his sneezing. **1997** Montgomery *File* Some people just said, "Scat, cat!" whenever anyone sneezed. They also said "Scat there." I'm not sure if I'm right in this perception or not, but it seems that the "Scat, cat, get your tail out of my gravy!" was used more in familiar settings, as a mother to a child, etc. In my mind, men seemed to more often use the shorter version. I can still hear my grandfather saying, "Scat there!" when somebody sneezed.... I kind of associate the saying with the idea of a cat trying to get your food and rubbing his tail across your nose, making you sneeze (50-year-old woman, Jefferson Co TN). **2012** *Blind Pig* (Oct 4) From Sevier County Tennessee. My mama said "scat cat your tail's in the gravy" and others "scat cat your tail's on fire (far)." *Ibid.* I also heard just "scat Tom" sometimes too. *Ibid.* Family from Booneville KY always said "Scat there, Tom. Tail's in the butter!"

[DARE *scat* interjection South, South Midland, TX]

scatteration

A (also *scatterment*) *noun* A dispersion, state of being scattered.

1890 Fruit *KY Words* 66 = dispersion: "There was a great scatteration." **1942** Thomas *Blue Ridge* 53 The pack fell from his back and there was a scattermint of tinware from top to bottom of that hill. **c1960** Wilson *Coll* = dispersal, scattering. **1997** Montgomery *Coll*: *Scatteration* (known to Norris); There was a great scatteration of papers all over the floor (Cardwell); *scatterment* (known to Cardwell, Oliver).

B *interjection* Used as a mild oath.

1999 Montgomery *Coll* Scatteration! What are you up to now? (Cardwell).

scattering (also *scattern*) *adjective* Dispersed; sparse, broken up, occasional.

1931 Goodrich *Mt Homespun* 77 "Christians is mighty scatterin' around here," said Aunt Cinthy, "but there'll be several out to hear Elder Ryan." **1955** Ritchie *Singing Family* 262 No one set much store by the scattern tales spread about, that a railroad was coming through Perry County. **1975** Jackson *Unusual Words* 152 The corn is *scatterin'* this year if there are only a few years, or if most of it is only *nubbins*. **1978** Montgomery *White Pine Coll* IV-2 If they come from up north, maybe their speech is not exactly like ours. It's a little broken up, you know, maybe a little bit scattering or something like that. **1995** Montgomery *Coll* (known to Cardwell, Shields).

[DARE *scattering* adj formerly widespread, now chiefly South, South Midland]

scatterment See **scatteration A.**

scattern See **scattering.**

scatter off *verb phrase* To disperse, move off.

1991 Williams *Homeplace* 129 That's the old homeplace down there on Brush Creek. And we, after they all got scattered off, why at least for a year or two there, we had a regular family reunion.

scatter-wit *adjective* Scatter-brained.

1938 Justus *No-End Hollow* 38 Jeff was a scatter-wit person when it came to remembering mannerly ways, and he was apt to forget what she told him. [**1995** Montgomery *Coll* (unknown to consultants from the Smoky Mountains).]

scaver *verb* To hide out.

1989 Smith *Flyin' Bullets* 52 There was a cave down there below somewhere and he'd been stayin' in that cave. He said his name was Logan, Oklahoma and he'd got out of the pen and was scaverin'. He was hidin' from th' law. [**1995** Montgomery *Coll* (unknown to consultants from the Smoky Mountains).]

scear See **scare 1**.

scenery *noun* A spectacle, picturesque spot.

1896 *Word-List* 423 = picturesque spot. "This here's quite a scenery." **1922** TN *CW Ques* 1453 (Jefferson Co TN) A beautiful scenery all around a nice cemetary on the place & a Baptist Church in sight. [**1995** Montgomery *Coll* (unknown to consultants from the Smoky Mountains).]

[DARE *scenery* n B1 especially southern Appalachians]

scent hound *noun* See citation.

2007 Plott *Story Plott Hound* 184 = dog that runs courses or game by scent rather than sight. A sight hound is just the opposite and runs game by sight rather than scent.

schnitzing *noun* Traditionally, a family or neighborhood work event at which apples are peeled and sliced for drying. See also **apple cutting, snitz.**

1863 *Click CW Letters* (Aug 11) I wish that I cold have bin with you at the Snitcen I know that I cold injoyed my self with you and the girls.

scholar *noun*

A A schoolchild; more generally, any student.

1834 Crockett *Narrative* 29 I had an unfortunate falling out with one of the scholars,—a boy much larger and older than myself. **1848** (in **1870** Drake *Pioneer Life KY* 147) All the scholars brought their dinner, & it was generally a social meal. **1922** TN *CW Ques* 115 I attended subscription schools, my parent made $1 per months for each schoolar [sic]. **1931** Greve *Tradition Gatlinburg* 67 It is told of him that he once whipped a daughter of Daniel Wesley Reagan for spitting into the books of the other scholars. **1942** Thomas *Blue Ridge* 127 "Now, scholars," Whiffet brushed the black from his fingers, having replaced the charred stick in his pocket, "lend attention!" **1953** Hall *Coll* (Bryson City NC) Sometimes [the teacher] would board around amongst the scholars. **1956** Hall *Coll* (Cosby TN) [At a subscription school the] county would pay half and the scholars would pay the other half. **1973** GSMNP-74:41 [Daddy] just went to the third grade, but my mother was a pretty good scholar. **1975** Kroeger *WV Farm Life* 6 There would be about from 60 to 70 scholars and one teacher taught all of them. **1997** Nelson *Country Folklore* 29 After meeting the scholars, I realized there'd probably not be too much time for playing. I had some students in each grade.

[OED3 *scholar* n 1a "a boy or girl attending an elementary school" now somewhat archaic]

B *verb* To educate.

1860 Olmsted *Back Country* 259 He said he "wasn't scollar'd enough" to understand [the map], and I could not induce him to look at it. **1863** *Hundley CW Letters* (March 16) tell lisa that I recieved hur letter but I hant never got scoller a nuff to make it all out yet it was so badly rote. **1962** Williams *Verbs Mt Speech* 18 His preacher may not be scholarred [i.e. schooled] enough to read the Bible, but the hill farmer is "pleasured" to "listen at 'im" if he is a Scriptored preacher.

school *noun* A school session; formerly, an irregular session taught by a teacher on annual appointment.

1939 Hall *Coll* (Little Cataloochee NC) They was a woman went in there, and she taught two schools. **1956** Hall *Coll* (Cosby TN) The first school I went to was a little old log house up on Cosby [Creek]. That's up in the Park now. I just went a couple of schools. The schools were short, two or three weeks. Webster's Blue Back Speller and Sanders First Reader were about what we had. **1975** *AOHP/LJC-384* They taught about two schools there and then they built a school right at the mouth of Riley. **1985** Irwin *Alex Stewart* 52 I went to school right down here at Panther Creek, I believe it was the third school that I ever went to, and a man by the name of Haskew Fletcher was the teacher. **1989** *Matewan OHP-9* Anna Dotson, she taught one school, and Fred Hackney taught one school, so that's all I can remember of it.

school butter *interjection* Used as a schoolyard taunt by one daring to be caught by others.

1890 Fruit *KY Words* 66 = the direst insult to a country schoolboy. To cry out school-butter to a lot of boys is to invite a fight. **1915** Dingus *Word-List VA* 189 = used as a term of reproach to school children: "A man hollered out school butter to us and we grabbed him and giv' him a good duckin'." **1931** Combs *Lg Sthn High* 1306 Cass hollered out "School butter!" an' got ducked. (In the rural schools it has "everly" been the custom for the "scholars" to duck anybody who cries out "School butter," whether he be pupil or passerby.) **1972** Carson and Vick *Cookin* 2 4 2 In the old days, a feller who'd ride by a schoolhouse and yell "School butter," would bring teacher and boys a-running, ready to fight. **1975** *AOHP/LJC-384* He was coming around there one day and he hollered, "School butter." You know, that was an insult to the school. The teacher told the boys . . . He said, "Go, go get him, boys," and they jumped out and took after him. . . . He ran right up the hill as far as he could run, and they run him down and caught him. Whenever they caught him, they brought him back and there was a big hole, lot of water right along here above the schoolhouse. They ducked him in that hole of water. **c1975** Lunsford *It Used to Be* 176 "School butter" is an epithet of offense to a school group in rural western North Carolina. I know nothing about its origin. It has a tendency to provoke the school into taking the offender to a nearby branch and ducking him.

scimption See **scrimption**.

scissorbill *noun* See citation.

1943 Korson *Coal Dust* 5 Full-time miners naturally resented them [= farmer-miners] and expressed their distrust by calling them . . . "scissorbills," and "sagers."

scooch (also *scooch down, scooch up*) *verb, verb phrase* See c1960 citation. See also **scrooch**, **squidge 1**, **squinch**[1] **2**.

c1960 Wilson Coll: *scooch (down)* = to squeeze oneself into a small place. **2004** Adams *Old True Love* 132 I missed Zeke so bad that I finally scooched up next to Pearl and held on to what felt like all I had in this world left of him.

scooch down, **scooch up** See **scooch**.

scoot *noun* See citation.

1964 Clarkson *Lumbering in WV* 370 = lumber that is very defective and practically worthless.

scooter plow *noun* See citations. See also **bull tongue**.

1960 Mason *Memoir* 16 A scooter plow was a clumsy wooden contraption with two handles, a foot, and beam. A flat piece of painted steel was bolted to the foot of the plow and used to scratch up the ground, thereby, preparing a sort of seed bed in which we planted our small crops. **1981** Whitener *Folk-Ways* 26 The scooter plow was hard to keep in the ground under normal conditions but the stumps, rocks, and hidden roots of a steep hill-side new ground were a constant source of exasperation to the mountain farmer.

scootle *verb* To go in haste, depart.

1925 Dargan *Highland Annals* 57 [Y]ou scootle from here, Dan Goforth; don't you tech nary nuther tater in this patch! **1996–97** Montgomery Coll (known to Brown, Bush, Cardwell, Cypher).

scope *noun* An extent (of land, timber, etc.), especially a large one.

1784 *French Broad Petitions* 212 It leaves them in possession of a narrow scope of country, between the above mentiond river, and the mountains. **1864** *Chapman CW Letters* (April 23) we can walk out on those butiful hites and view at one Glance a vaste and butiful scope of ritch and furtile land. **1895** Edson and Fairchild *TN Mts* 374 My brother has a big *scope* of land. **1937** Hall Coll (Cades Cove TN) You go through a little scope of woodland. *Ibid.* (Emerts Cove TN) A good, big scope of country. **1960** Hall *Smoky Mt Folks* 21 (Cataloochee NC) There used to be a good big scope of seng on the mountain. **1974** Fink *Bits Mt Speech* 23 My brother heired a large *scope* of land. **1980** Still *Run for Elbertas* 80 "I'm the appointed caretaker of this scope of land," Father replied testily, "and I'll not leave till I get my ready on."

[OED3 *scope* n[2] 10 "a tract of land" Anglo-Irish; CUD *scope* n "an extent of land"; DARE *scope* n South, South Midland]

scorch *verb* See citation. See also **scorched whiskey**.

1949 Maurer *Argot of Moonshiner* 12 = to allow the meal which has settled to the bottom of the fermenter to burn before convection currents in the beer start agitation.

scorch cloth *noun* See citation.

1985 Sienkneckt *Rheumatic Diseases* 183 = a cloth that has been burnt to the point of charring and that is believed to be beneficial in drawing out corruption [i.e. pus].

scorched whiskey *noun* See citation. See also **scorch**.

1967 Wilson *Folkways Mammoth Cave* 31 = whiskey that is poured into a shallow pan or bowl, ignited, allowed to burn for a while, and then drunk hot as a medicine.

score out *verb phrase* To berate, scold severely.

1963 Medford *Mt People* 140 Others perhaps liked him best as a story-teller, and still others for his "scoring out" or bearing down on the cheat, the hypocrite, or tight-wad, maybe. [**1995** Montgomery Coll (unknown to consultants from the Smoky Mountains).]

scorpion *noun*

A Variant form *scorpon*.

1942 Hall *Phonetics Smoky Mts* 65.

[DARE *scorpion* n scattered South, South Midland, Southwest]

B A blue-tailed skink (*Eumeces* spp), mistakenly regarded as venomous. See also **fence scorpion**.

1913 Kephart *Our Sthn High* 70 The mountaineers have an absurd notion that the little lizard so common in the hills is rank "pizen." Oddly enough, they call it a "scorpion." **1937** Hall Coll = a blue-tailed skink or lizard. **1960** Stupka *Great Smoky Mts* 47 Of the eight kinds of lizards in the park, three belong to the group known as skinks, or blue-tailed lizards. Locally they are termed "scorpions" and, in spite of the fact that they are quite harmless, are considered dangerous. **1967** Huheey and Stupka *Amphibians and Reptiles* 51 Three species of skinks of the genus *Eumeces* occur in the Park. For the most part these lizards are quite similar in appearance, and close examination is usually necessary to distinguish one from another. All three have bright blue tails when young, and reddish-to copper-colored heads in the old males. They go by the name "Scorpion" and are regarded as venomous by some of the local people.

scorpion juice *noun* Homemade whiskey.

1974 Dabney *Mt Spirits* 25 The names go on: "scorpion juice." **1989** Oliver *Hazel Creek* 26 He made periodic visits to Hazel Creek and once told my grandmother, Sadie Farley, that some of his "scorpion juice" would be good for what ailed her. **1996** Houk *Foods & Recipes* 151 Whenever Quill Rose stopped in for a visit, he would offer Sadie some of his "scorpion juice" for what ailed her.

scorpon See **scorpion**.

scotch

A *noun* An object put under a wheel to prevent a vehicle from moving, a chock.

1974–75 McCracken *Logging* 6:108 In logging, [a jill poke] was a piece of railroad steel about eight or ten feet long cut off and tied right to the underside of the frame of whatever you were pulling. In case something broke, you had a scotch. It'd just run in the ground and hold it. **1991** Weals *Last Train* 69 Then he said to me, "Kick the scotches out." **2005** Williams *Gratitude* 521 = an object used to keep something from moving, as a rock placed behind a car wheel is used for a scotch to keep it from rolling.

[Web3 *scotch* n origin unknown; DARE *scotch* n chiefly South, South Midland]

B *verb* To prevent (especially a chair or the wheel of a vehicle) from movement; figuratively = to impede (someone's way).

1966 Dykeman *Far Family* 211 I thought it was the Bludsoes themselves scotching your way. **1978** Head *Mt Moments* To "scotch" a wheel meant to put a rock under it to keep it from rolling. **1991** Weals *Last Train* 69 Walter kicked away the rocks that were put in front of and behind both landing wheels to "scotch" them and keep the plane from rolling. **2005** Williams *Gratitude* 70 He'd lean backerds til the top of his chair was scotched back agin the wall with the front legs r'ared up off the porch and his whole weight on the two back chair legs.

[DARE *scotch* v¹ chiefly South, South Midland]

scotch wheel *noun* See citation.

1997 King *Mt Folks* 34 The Franklins used a stiff wire with a hook at the end (some used spools) for pushing a small wagon wheel rim called a scotch wheel.

scot loose *adverb* Completely loose, "scot free."

1989 *Matewan OHP-94* He was freed, turned scot loose. The trial lasted for about four weeks.

scours (also *scares*) *noun* Diarrhea, especially in livestock.

1927 Woofter *Dialect from WV* 363 = running off at the bowels. "The calves have the scours badly." **1966** *DARE Survey* (Burnsville NC). **1982** Slone *How We Talked* 118 = diarrhea in cattle, young calves, when they first began to eat grass and weeds. **1990** Cavender *Folk Medical Lex* 30 = commonly pronounced "scares." **1994** Montgomery *Coll* (known to Cardwell, Shields). **2000** Lowry *Folk Medical Term*. **2007** Myers *Smoky Mt Remedies* 11 = diarrhea: "He had the scours."

[derivative of *scour* v "to purge"]

scout

A Variant form *scyout*.

1942 Hall *Phonetics Smoky Mts* 46.

B (also *scout around, scout out*) *verb, verb phrase* To hide in or from; to be a renegade or fugitive, especially by hiding out or living in a wild or primitive state, most often applied during the Civil War to men evading conscription or deserting from active duty. See also **bushwhack A3**.

1913 Kephart *Our Sthn High* 296 Many common English words are used in peculiar senses by the mountain folk, as . . . scout for elude. **1922** *TN CW Ques* 2237 (Cocke Co TN) I scouted the mountains for about ten months from Big Creek Gap to Cumberland Gap and from there to Chicamaga fight. **1924** Spring *Lydia Whaley* 1 When [my] son was in the camp he got the measles, red and black. "He'd always scouted from the measles ter home." **1938** Bowman *High Horizons* 21 Many mountaineers avoided serving in the war by "scouting" in the mountains, as they called their method of hiding in the wildernesses of laurel and rhododendron that flourish in the highlands. **1957** Combs *Lg Sthn High: Word List* 86 = to be a fugitive from justice; escape, elude or dodge officers of the law. Ex.: "He's a-scoutin' aroun' since he stole that hog." **1973** *GSMNP-83*:18 He scouted out that Civil War four years there and lived there. **1974** Fink *Bits Mt Speech* 23 = [to hide] in woods or mountains to avoid capture by the law. **1976** Lindsay *Grassy Balds* 55 What few didn't go, they had to go scoutin' around, and bushwhackers [would] come over here from North Carolina and steal everything they had. **1994** Montgomery *File* He had to scout most of his life [i.e. to live by himself in a remote area in order to conduct moonshining activity without detection] (82-year-old man, Gatlinburg TN). **1996** Woodring *Times Gone By* 4 He said he stayed over air in Virginye a long time when he was scoutin' from the law.

[cf OED3 *scout* v¹ 1b "to lie hid . . . in concealment" obsolete except dialect; DARE *scout* v southern Appalachians]

C *noun* In Civil War times, a renegade, man who avoided conscription by hiding, fending for himself in the mountains and eluding patrols; an outlaw. See also **bee hunter**, **bushwhacker**, **outlier**.

1865 *Wax Letter* 40 We have now and then a Scout here but have to run out when Yankees get after them. **1927** Mason *Lure of Smokies* 173 Many of the rifle "experts" aforementioned were among the "scouts" and "bee-hunters" who roamed the woods to escape conscription in a war which they claimed was unjust and of no concern to them. **1939** Hall *Coll* (Waldens Creek TN) Ten or fifteen of these old citizens around here were Rebel scouts [looking for] corn, meat, and horses. **1983** Walker *Tales Civil War* 5 Besides the Unions and the Confederates (or Yankees and Rebels, if you wish), there was another group which preyed on all. These were known as the bushwhackers, the outliers, or the scouts. No family was immune from their ravages. If the family was Confederate in sympathy, this group represented themselves as Union and vice versa. They swooped down and assaulted, destroyed, and confiscated as they saw fit. **2007** Ballard and Weinstein *Neighbor* 73 In the early years of the war the conscript law was not strictly enforced, but as the Confederate forces became depleted those who had been slackers, or "scouts" as they were called among themselves, were hunted down, relentlessly by the conscript officers and the Home Guard.

scout around, scout out See **scout B**.

scrabble *verb*

1 To scratch or claw in the dirt, dig out (especially potatoes). See also **drabble 2**, **grabble**, **granny B2**, **scratch² B**.

1940 Still *River of Earth* 214 They scrabbled and they dug, and now they's only a foot o' rock betwixt. Any minute they'll dig through. **1997** Montgomery *Coll* = You would scrabble one or two potatoes from one side of the potato plant without disturbing the plant. The plant would continue growing and producing and you would have a mess of early new potatoes, as in "Go to the garden and scrabble us a mess of new potatoes" (Norris).

2 To eke out, maintain a bare existence.

1913 Kephart *Our Sthn High* 370 So, as the years passed, a larger and larger proportion of the highlanders was forced back along the creek branches and up along the steep hillsides to "scrabble" for a living. **1983** Aiken *Mt Ways* 83 Mountain people often had to "scrabble" for a living—and skinning the chestnut, oak and other trees for bark was one way to do it.

scraggeldy *adjective* Scraggly.

1949 Arnow *Hunter's Horn* 42 Nunn squatted a little apart from the others, with his back sheltered from the wind by a scraggeldy pine.

scrape

A *noun* A fight, violent encounter. See also **bear scrape, cutting scrape, granny scrape, licker scrape, shooting scrape, whiskey scrape.**

1859 Taliaferro *Fisher's River* 30 Invulnerable himself, in only one scrape was he "cotched." **1864** *Watkins CW Letters* (July 17) the 3 day of July we dug ditches [in] the 4 day in the eavning the yanks com and we had a powful scrape but me nor Press dident fire a gun. **1970** GSMNP-26:11 I have heard of different incidents where other people had got in sort of scrapes with him. **1989** Smith *Flyin' Bullets* 363 I believe they intended to rob him, but he put up quite a scrape, and apparently them became frightened and ran away.

B *verb* See citation.

1957 Combs *Lg Sthn High: Word List* 86 = to hoe corn, vegetables, etc. clean of weeds, especially in new ground. Ex.: "The field's scraped clean."

scrape-fire *noun* See citation.

1917 Kephart *Word-List* 416 = flintlock [firearm].

scrape paddle *noun* Same as **mash stick.**

1971 Gordon *Moonshining in GA* 58 You put a bushel of meal in it [= the still] and you stir it up good with your scrape paddle.

scrapple *noun* A dish of cornmeal mixed and cooked with chopped, spiced pork (usually scraps and the heart), then seasoned and pressed into a large cake, often served for breakfast. See also **poor do 1, souse B.**

1990 Oliver *Cooking Hazel Creek* 19 The meat is cooked from the bones, then chopped fine or ground, mixed with corn meal, allowed to congeal, and then sliced and fried. It was usually called souse meat, an English name, on Hazel Creek and in the Smokies, but scrapple, its German name, was often used in other parts of the country and is usually found in modern cookbooks. **1995** Montgomery Coll (known to Shields). **2002** Oliver *Cooking and Living* 72 SOUSE MEAT or SCRAPPLE was made from various parts of the pig such as liver, heart, head cheese and scraps on bones. The meat was cooked from the bones, then everything was chopped fine or ground, mixed with salt, pepper, sage and savory, then mixed with cornmeal, boiled for awhile, allowed to congeal, and then sliced and fried. Sometimes LIVER MUSH was made this way without the addition of other parts of the pig.

Scratch[1] See **(the) Old Scratch.**

scratch[2] *verb*

A Variant past-tense form *scrutch.*

1965 GSMNP-49:1:5 Then all that trainload of logs went off on Daddy Bryson, and just scrutch him into bug bites.

B (also *scratch out*) To dig up (potatoes). Same as **drabble 2, grabble.** See also **granny B2, scrabble 1.**

1997 Andrews *Mountain Vittles* 32 About the 4th of July Momma would send me out with a fork to scratch out a mess of taters. I would pick out a hill or two and scratch down very lightly uncovering the new taters growing there.

scratch-britches *adjective* Full of briers; also used in the place-name Scratch-Britches Mountain (TN).

1937 Thornburgh *Great Smoky Mts* 108 The down trail is what one mountain man described as "the worst scratch-breeches trail in the mountains." **1997** Montgomery Coll (known to Brewer).

scratch out See **scratch[2] B.**

screak *verb* To squeak, creak, squeal.

1925 Dargan *Highland Annals* 223 "Anybody," he said, "that would take pay from Viny fer the leetle mite she eats would be so stingy they'd screak." **1940** Oakley *Roamin'/Restin'* 30 The doors swung on wooden hinges and had to be greased to keep them from screaking and waring out too soon. **1973** GSMNP-57:80 All the doors in the house ... would screak.... That door just screaked and come open. **1982** Slone *How We Talked* 19 A stingy person was described as ... So tight he screaks when he walks. **1993** Mason *Feather Crowns* 236 All of the babies were sick. They were feverish and hot, with wrinkled, red faces and feeble, screaking cries. **2005** Williams *Gratitude* 521 *screak* = to squeak, or creak; the sound made by something that needs oiling, like a *screakin'* barn door.

[DARE *screak* v 2 chiefly South Midland]

screamer *noun* See citation.

1982 Slone *How We Talked* 35 *screamers* = nickname for the grains of popcorn that do not pop.

screaming owl See **screech owl.**

screech owl *noun* Variant forms *screaming owl, screet owl, scrinch owl, scrich owl, scritch owl, scrooch owl, squeech owl, squich owl, squinch owl.*

c1926 Bird *Cullowhee Wordlist: scritch owl.* **1939** Hall Coll (White Oak NC). **1949** Kurath *Word Geog East US* 73 *Scrich owl* and the less common variants *squich owl, squinch owl* are current in Virginia east of the Blue Ridge and in the adjoining parts of North Carolina; also in the westernmost parts of the Carolinas and Virginia and adjoining sections of Kentucky and West Virginia, probably as an importation from the Virginia Piedmont. **1952–57** (in **1973** McDavid and McDavid *Vocab E KY* 157) *scrich owl* = screech owl. **c1960** Wilson Coll: *scrooch owl,* because of his seeming to withdraw into as small a space as possible; *squeech owl,* because it makes a "squeeching" noise; *squinch owl,* [because] it squinches up its eyes in the light, or seems to, with its third eyelid. **1963** Wilson *Regional Words* 81 This is one bird that everybody knew, chiefly by his quivering call; he was a scrooch owl from his habit of sitting all scrooched up, a scritch owl from his voice, and a squinch owl because of his blinking in broad daylight. **1966** Dakin *Vocab Ohio River Valley* 386 *Scrich owl* is common in the Mountains and southern Kentucky generally . . . *Screet owl* [is attested one time] in Johnson County, Kentucky. **1967** *DARE Survey* (Maryville TN). **1972** Cooper *NC Mt Folklore* 127 "Scrooch owls or no scrooch owls," Zeke said, "I ain't selling that land. I've already ensured myself against scrooch owls by cutting down every bush and tree within two hundred feet of my house." **1973** *GSMNP-4:1:62* A lot of time what we call a screech owl get in the chicken house. **1976** Garber *Mountain-ese* 87 We got skeered when we hyard a big squinch owl in the tree. **1976** Ledford *Folk Vocabulary* 282 The [younger] informants made no distinction between *owl* and *screech owl*, although *screech owl* and *scrooch owl* are still common in the speech of the older generation in the area. **1981** Morrell *Mirth* 3 I've heard them before, the mountain people call it the screaming owl. **1986** Pederson et al. *LAGS*: *scrinch owl* (Cocke Co TN, Rockdale Co GA); *scrooch owl* = attested by 10/60 interviewees (16.7%) from E TN and 6/35 (17.4%) from N GA; 16/87 of all LAGS interviewees (18.3%) attesting term were from Appalachia. **1995–97** Montgomery *Coll*: *screaming owl*, *scritch owl* (known to Cardwell), = refers to the bird's squinting eyes in the sunlight (Weaver).

[DARE *screech owl* n 1 *scritch owl* chiefly South Midland, Central Atlantic, *scrooch owl* chiefly South, South Midland; *squinch owl* n chiefly South, South Midland]

screet owl See **screech owl**.

screw top *noun* Homemade whiskey.

1972 Hall *Sayings* 101 Common expressions about 1941 for whisky illegally manufactured were . . . "headache medicine" (with veiled meaning), "screw top," "snake juice," [and] "red eye." **1973** Davis *'Pon My Honor* 100 = strong fiery liquor.

scribe[1]

A *noun* A person adept in handling written language as a writer (as in penmanship) or reader.

1824 Knight *Letter from KY* 91 Others . . . can not read nor write; as one of wealthy exterior said to me, when I offered him a state-trial, that I was perusing—: "He was not scribe enough to read." **1939** Hall *Coll* (Saunook NC) You look the letter over because I'm not a very good scribe. *Ibid.* (White Oak NC) He's a pretty good scribe. He writes a nice hand. **1967** Hall *Coll* (Del Rio TN) Wesley Metcalf could read big print, could barely scribble his name, attended part of a three-month term of school. His father was a pretty good scribe. **1987** Young *Lost Cove* 27 For years on end he had been aiming to take the old writings from the bottom of the trunk to a scribe and find out what they said. **1991** Thomas *Sthn Appal* 194 Course, now, I don't b'lieve he'uz as good—much of a good—scribe hisself. He ordered his copies . . . he ordered th' copies fer his writin' school, he did.

[OED3 *scribe* n[1] 7a "a person who writes by hand; a penman"; DARE *scribe* n especially Appalachians, Ozarks]

B *verb* To write, copy.

1946 Dudley *KY Words* 271 = to write: "Sam, take your pencil and scribe down these measurements."

scribe[2] *verb* To mark and measure (as a piece of timber to be fitted into place in constructing a house). See citations. See also **scriber**.

1927 Mason *Lure of Smokies* 115 Every log of the frontier cabin was hewn with great care and precision and expertly "scribed" at the corners for the neatest fitting. *Ibid.* 124 The backwoodsman used a very ingenious instrument similar to a compass plane which "scribed" the edges of his wooden staves already pressed into position so that they fitted with airtight perfection.

[probably short for *describe*]

scriber *noun* A person skilled in marking, measuring, and fitting logs in constructing a log dwelling. See also **scribe**[2].

1927 Mason *Lure of Smokies* 115 It is a common occurrence to hear a mountaineer say of a certain expert cabin builder, "He was the best scriber I ever seed!"

scrich owl See **screech owl**.

scriffen, scriffin See **striffen**.

scrim around *verb phrase* To wander aimlessly.

1995 Montgomery *Coll* Quit your scrimming around and settle down (Cardwell).

scrimped *adjective* Crowded. See citation.

1957 Combs *Lg Sthn High: Word List* 86 = [be] crowded, by people or otherwise. Ex.: "Air ye scrimped fer a good view?" But *scrimp*, to crowd, is not heard.

scrimpshun See **scrimption**.

scrimption *noun*

A Variant forms *scimption* [see **1919** in **B**], *scrimpshun* [see **1867** in B], *skimption* [see **1984** in **B**].

B A very small amount or number, a scrap or piece; hence *scrimptions* = small pieces, fragments. Also called **scrimticle**.

1867 Harris *Sut Lovingood* 73 Pails hed lef' thar hoops, an' the delf war was in scrimpshuns. **1919** Combs *Word-List South* 40 *scimption* = a small thing. "That's a small scimption," equivalent to "I should worry." **c1940** Aswell *Glossary TN Idiom* 16 *scrimption* = small amount or number. **1952** Justus *Children* 45 Now all their food was gone, and there wasn't a penny to buy a scrimption of anything at Cross Roads Store. **1952** Wilson *Folk Speech NC* 591 *skimption* = a small amount; not enough to be concerned over. **1984** Wilder *You All Spoken* 73 *skimption* = a small amount; hardly enough to bother with. **1997** Montgomery *Coll*: *scrimption*, (known to Adams, Cardwell, Jones, Ledford, Norris, Weaver); *skimption* (known to Cardwell).

[OED3 *scrimp* "to cut short in amount, be sparing" + -*tion*; EDD *scrimption* sb "a very small piece, a miserable pittance"; DARE *scrimption* n chiefly South, South Midland]

scrimticle *noun* Same as **scrimption B**.

1907 Dugger *Balsam Groves* 144 "I'll look 'round and dig me a scrim-tic-le uv sang." A scrimticle meant a very small quantity, so he cut a stick about three feet long, cut one end as a substitute for a sang-hoe, and went prowling through the woods, gouging up and pocketing ginseng.

scrinch down See **scrooch.**

scrinch owl See **screech owl.**

scringe *verb* To cower, shrink in fear, flinch.

1895 Edson and Fairchild *TN Mts* 376. **1915** Dingus *Word-List VA* 189 = to cringe. **1944** Wilson *Word-List* 49 = to shrink from because of fear or dislike. **c1960** Wilson *Coll*: *cringe* is sometimes *scringe*. **1974** Fink *Bits Mt Speech* 23 I seen him *scringe* when he heared it. **1995–97** Montgomery *Coll* (known to Adams, Brown, Cardwell, Ledford, Norris, Oliver).

[OED3 *scringe* v[1] 2 "to flinch, cower" in later use English regional and U.S. regional; CUD *scringe3* v "strengthened form of *cringe*"; DARE *scringe* v 1 chiefly South, South Midland]

scrip (also *script*) *noun* A private currency, as of paper or metal disc, issued as wages to employees by a mining, logging, or textile company for temporary use, usually negotiable only at company stores. Also called **clacker, doogaloo, jingle, slicker, sticker 2.**

1863 *Watters-Curtis CW Letters* (Aug 11) I am going to Send Jimey William a Scrip Holder He must take good care of it & put His Scrip in it but not to put no Southern Scrip in it but union Scrip in it. **1966** Caudill *My Appalachia* 42 They found their shopping sprees made easy and painless through the use of scrip, metal discs and paper available in the same denominations as legal tender of twenty dollars and less. The scrip was issued by the coal company and was available from the company in any amount not greater than the wages due the miner on the date of asking. . . . The scrip was not acceptable at any store other than the commissary. **1973** Preston *Bituminous Term* 50–51 = tokens, bills, or other markers given to workers in place of money payment, which were good for full value at a company store but were discontinued [sic; discounted] as much as ten percent in other places. [Also known as *drag* in northern WV, *slicker* in southern WV, *sticker* in eastern KY, and *jingle* in TN]. **1975** *AOHP/ALC-1128A* Your name was on the script card. Every man had a number. That was before social security or anything was ever heard tell of. All you had to have was a script card and your name on the book as an employee of the company. **1977** Shackelford et al. *Our Appalachia* 194 Coal miners seldom saw much actual cash because the new industrial economy was based on scrip. Scrip was manufactured by individual coal companies and usually was a metallic or celluloid disk bearing the firm's name and a monetary value. On payday, which came once or twice a month, men received federally minted money. If employees wished to draw on their earnings between times—and by necessity most did—they received not cash, but scrip. Frequently families came to the coal camps with little or no money and began drawing scrip immediately after the man completed his first work shift, which meant there was rarely any cash on payday. Scrip had to be spent within the camp and was seldom accepted by private merchants or other coal companies if the employee moved elsewhere. In essence, scrip was a means of keeping miners at home and forcing them to patronize company-owned businesses, such as the commissary, movie house, and soda fountain. **1978** Slone *Common Folks* 274 All and all the miner began working already in debt to the company for sometimes his first payday. He could also "draw script" against future wages. Script (sometimes small tin discs) was used at the company store in place of money, and was issued by the company. **1994** Farwell and Buchanan *Logging Terms* = a paper certificate that could be used at the company store for cash. **2006** Mooney *Lg Coal Mining* 1029 Every two weeks or month the miner collected his pay, often in the form of company money called "scrip" or "clacker" that had to be spent in the company store or "pluck me store" as miners called it because of inflated prices.

script See **scrip.**

scripter See **scripture.**

script man *noun* See citation.

1994 Farwell and Buchanan *Logging Terms* = in logging, a man who worked at a company store who issued scrip to a logger or his family.

scriptur See **scripture.**

scripture *noun* Variant forms *scripter, scriptur*.

1881 Pierson *In the Brush* 251 He's a Scripter preacher. He's not a larnt man, but he's a real Scripter preacher. **1884** Smith *Arp Scrap Book* 73 This is what I call successful farmin—multiplying and replenishing according to Scripter. **1898** Elliott *Durket Sperret* 96 True as Scriptur! **1927** Furman *Lonesome Road* 34–35 His mind is so lifted up with seeing visions and studying Scripter he can't hardly bring it down to everyday life. **1960** Sutherland *Folk Speech* 13 *scriptur*.

scritch owl See **screech owl.**

scrivin See **striffen.**

scrooch (also *scrinch down, scrooch down, scrooch up, scroonch, scrootch up, scroudge, scrouge, scrouge around, scrouge down, scrouge over, scrouge up, scrounge, scrowdge, scrowge, scrunch, scrutch, skrunch*).

A *verb* To crowd, squeeze into a smaller space, move over to make room for others; to crouch, squat, huddle, snuggle. See also **scooch, squidge 1, squinch[1] 2.**

1845 (in **1974** Harris *High Times* 51) The little fiddler cum a scrougin past, holdin his fiddle up over his head to keep it in tune, for the fitin was getting tolerable brisk. **1862** *Gilley CW Letters* (May 15) I scrunched up under a branch bank an lay their till most night an some of them said the yankes was coming closter an I left their an come out of the road and lay their all night. **1862** (in **1992** Jackson *Surry Co Soldiers* 290) (June 9) Sometimes we have a tent brake to stretch over us and sometimes it is rainy and we all have to scrooch up under two or three of the brakes. **1895** Edson and Fairchild TN Mts 374 *scrouge* = crowd. "Oh, we *scrouge* 'em up." **1900** Harben N GA *Sketches* 235 Me an' grandpa scrouged down behind the chimney so as not to git struck an' watched the trap the bluecoats was a-layin' fer you-uns. **1913** Bruce *Terms from TN* 58 *skrunch* = to crouch: noted repeatedly in the vicinity of Knoxville. "Skrunched on his hunkles (haunches)." **1913** Kephart *Our Sthn High* 75 Git up, pup! You've scrouged right in hyur in front of the fire. **1915** Dingus *Word-List VA* 189 *scrutch* = to crouch. **1924** Raine *Saddlebags* 144 We hain't had much schoolin', and when judges and lawyers with heaps o' larnin' scrouges a pore ignorant jury, what can ye do? **1925** Dargan *Highland Annals* 161 "Scroonch up to that poplar," called Snead, "an' they'll pass us." **c1926** Bird *Cullowhee Wordlist*: *scroudge* = crowd. "Too many boys tried to scroudge in on one bench." **1934–37** *LAMSAS Appal* (Madison Co NC, Swain Co NC) *scrooch down*. **1942** Hall *Phonetics Smoky Mts* 92 *scrooch* [skruč], *scrowdge* [skræč]. **1944** Wilson *Word-List* 49 Scrooch, scrounge, scroonch, scrunch . . . To crouch, to crowd, to crowd oneself into. **1953** Hall *Coll* (Deep Creek NC) [In the early days] Indians had the upper end of Deep Creek. The whites kept scroungin' on 'em. **1955** Ritchie *Singing Family* 59 We scrooched the beds back against the wall and in no time atall we were all a-stepping Charlie. **1960** Cooper *Jularker Bussed* Scrouge up and give me settin' room (= sit closely and give me sufficient room.) **c1960** Wilson *Coll*: *scrooch down* = to get as far down as possible, hunker down. **1963** Watkins and Watkins *Yesterday* 15 Students straggled in from play, stood around the room, and scrooched up several to each desk. **1976** Braden *Grandma Was Girl* 110 *scrooching* = squatting down to make oneself small. **1979** Carpenter *Walton War* 164 The younguns was all scrootched up in the bedstid. **1982** *Smokies Heritage* 67 *scrutch* = to crouch down. **1986** Ogle *Lucinda* 60 So I scrouged around through the Rhododendron thicket and went on over the top to fill my sacks full of the pretty lacy ground pine. **1986** Pederson et al. *LAGS*: *scrinch down* (Gilmer Co GA), *scrooch down* = attested by 3/60 interviewees (5%) from E TN and 1/35 (2.9%) from N GA; 4/19 of all LAGS interviewees (21.0%) attesting term were from Appalachia; *scrunch down* (Washington Co TN, Hamilton Co TN). **1993** Cunningham *Sthn Talk* 135 *scrooch* = cuddle, snuggle. "Scrooch up here close to me an' I'll put my coat around you"; *scrowdge* = press, crowd. "Many's the time when they use to scrowdge six of us young-uns on a pallet, feet-to-feet." **1996** Montgomery *Coll* Scrooch up like you got a family. He scrooched up like he was freezing to death (Cardwell). **1998** Brewer *Don't Scrouge*: *Scrouge* is another [word that is dying away]. It describes the midway point between being crowded and squashed by another. As youngsters, we were forever yelling, "Mom, she's scrouging me" if a sister got a little too close. **1998** Montgomery *File* It's kind of scrowged in here (51-year-old woman, Jefferson Co TN). **2003** Carter *Mt Home* 167 That old neckid blue screech owl was scrooched up agin a hen, tryin' his best to push her off the roost. **2018** *Blind Pig* (Feb 14) They scrooched over so we could sit on our favorite pew. *Ibid.* If you'll scrooch those first two boxes a little closer to the wall I believe this third one will fit. *Ibid.* Tina scrunched up her little blankets and made a dog bed.

[OED3 *scrooch* v "to crouch or bend" dialect and colloquial, originally and chiefly U.S., *scrouge* alteration of *scruze* "to squeeze"; EDD *scrooch* v[1] "to crouch over, stoop down," *scrouge*[1] "to squeeze, press, crush"; SND *scrooch* v (variant of *crouch*) "to shrink, cower, cringe" and *scrounge* v "to squeeze, crush, press"; DARE *scrooch* v 2a chiefly South, South Midland, *scrouge* v (earliest in the U.S., but probably of Scots, nEngl dialect origin) chiefly South Midland; *scrowdge* v probably influenced by *crowd*]

B *noun* Room, space.

1994 Mullins *Coaley Creek* 5 Give me some scrouge.

scrooch owl See **screech owl**.

scroonch, scrootch up See **scrooch**.

scrop *noun* A scrap.

1923 Greer-Petrie *Angeline Steppin' Out* 31 The table scrops they was a-throwin' away. **1931** Goodrich *Mt Homespun* 75 "I do naterally love a scrop quilt," she said. **1973** Miller *English Unicoi Co* 112 *scrop* attested by 1 of 5 speakers. **1997** Montgomery *Coll* (known to Brown, Bush).

scrouge, scrouge around, scrouge down, scrouge over, scrouge up, scrounge, scrowdge, scrowge See **scrooch**.

scrub *noun*

1 (also *scrub calf, scrub pig*) The runt of a litter of animals; an undersized animal or child.

1966 *DARE Survey* (Spruce Pine NC) *scrub pig* = a pig that doesn't grow well and isn't worth keeping. **1979** *Big South Fork OHP-11* I want you to feed my calves for me, just little bitty scrub calves. **1993** Weaver *Scotch-Irish Speech* 15 If physically malnourished or stunted, [children] would be designated as "runts" or "scrubs," terms also usually reserved for animals. **1995–97** Montgomery *Coll* (known to nine consultants from the Smoky Mountains). **1999** Montgomery *File*: *scrub calf*. **2007** McMillon *Notes* The brindle cat was the scrub of the litter.

2 (also *scrub dog*) A dog of mixed breed.

1966 Dakin *Vocab Ohio River Valley* 224 *Scrub* is used by scattered speakers in Kentucky . . . *Feist, fice, fyce* (both pronunciations about equally common) have currency throughout Kentucky and Illinois. **1966** *DARE Survey* (Cherokee NC) *scrub dog* = dog of mixed breed.

[cf OED3 *scrub* n[1] 4a "an animal of inferior breed or pedigree; a beast of poor physique or performance" North American]

scrubber *noun* In distilling, an implement used to clean the inside of a barrel so another **run** of liquor can be made.

c1999 Sutton *Me and Likker* 81 I had an old broom and chopped it off 3″ from where the threads are and made me a scrubber out of the broom. Old folks used to take a hickory stick and lay it down on a stump and beat the Hell out of it to frazzle up the ends of it and that is what they made for a scrubber.

scrub board *noun* A washboard.

1993 Jacobs *Elbert Childress* 29 My mother left the washtub and scrub board, wiped the soapy water from her arms and wrote a letter on a piece of paper. **1997** King *Mt Folks* 76 She used the old time scrub board and boiled the white clothes, and she scrubbed the colored clothes and took her battling stick to loosen the dirt in them. Everybody had a battling stick and a battling board. It usually took the whole day to do the washing and a day to do the ironing.

[DARE *scrubboard* n 1 especially South]

scrub broom (also *scrubbing broom*) *noun* A short-handled broom usually made from a hickory sapling or limb, one end of which was sliced into **splits** (see **split 2**); the primary use of the implement was, along with sand and water, to scour wooden floors.

1937 Hyatt *Kiverlid* 46 I reckon you ha'n't got a rooster you'd keer to swap fer a good oak-split scrub broom? [**1948** Dick *Dixie Frontier* 302 A lighter broom for more genteel use was a short hand-broom known as a scrub. It was made exactly like the larger broom except that it was made from a smaller sapling and was shorter.] **1972** Cooper *NC Mt Folklore* 125 He scoured his bare floors with a scrub broom which he had made from a section of a hickory sapling. **1973** Miller *English Unicoi Co* 152 = a small, short-handled broom made of hickory which has been peeled back in thin curls to form a brush; used for scrubbing rough plank floors. **1974** Russell *Hillbilly* 19 The long handled "scrub broom" or scrub mop was made of strips of cornshucks. **1979** Slone *My Heart* 39 Split logs were smoothed on the flat side to make the floor, and were called "puncheons." To keep these floors clean, they were scrubbed with beat-up sand rocks and a scrub broom. **1992** Bush *Dorie* 24 Our scrubbing broom was made from a hickory limb about the size of a person's arm.

scrub calf See **scrub 1**.

scrub dog see **scrub 2**.

scrub pig See **scrub 1**.

scrum *verb* To skim (the green film that forms at the top of boiling **sorghum** cane) as it is cooked and made into **molasses**. See also **skimmings**.

1975 Brewer *Valley So Wild* 238 "You had to be careful to keep the sorghum scrummed while it was cooking," she remembered.

scrummish *verb* To wander.

1925 Dargan *Highland Annals* 99 I told him we'd scrummish around the mountain toward the sun, an' maybe I could shake off my chill. **1995** Montgomery *Coll* I knew he'd never settle down; he just scrummished around (Cardwell).

scrunch See **scrooch**.

scrush *verb* To crush, quash.

1974 Roberts *Sang Branch* 203 If he finds out you're here, he'll just scrush your bones.

scrutch See **scratch**[2] **A**, **scrooch**.

scuffling *verbal noun* See citation.

1979 Slone *My Heart* 137 It was not only in their work that mountain people competed. They ran foot races, pitched horseshoes, broad jumped, and had a form of wrestling, which they called "scufflin'."

scutch (also *skutch*) *noun* An implement for beating flax; hence verb = to beat flax with such an implement, give (someone) a whipping; hence noun *scutching* = a whipping.

1863 Wilson *Confederate Private* 1 (Feb 1) I han got eney of it cutck [i.e. scutched] yet. **1975** Dial *Yesterday's Lg* 93 *scutching* = [a] whipping: "He give me a proper skutching." **1989** Oliver *Hazel Creek* 22 After this [the stalks of flax were] "scutched" or beaten with a scutch or shaped board to separate the fibers.

scutter *noun* A mischievous or mean-spirited person (especially a child), rascal, scoundrel.

1952 Wilson *Folk Speech NC* 588 = a very mischievous person. **1968** *DARE Survey* (Brasstown NC) = nickname for a small child. "He's a healthy little scutter." **1985** Irwin *Alex Stewart* 257 He twisted it [= a handkerchief] up, tied a little switch on the end of it, put some medicine on the handkerchief, and pulled it clear through Uncle Bert. Pulled it out the other side, and the old scutter got well. **1998** Hyde *My Home* 80 That one big old Dominecker rooster . . . was a big scutter, and mean. **1998** Montgomery *Coll* (known to ten consultants from the Smoky Mountains as referring to a small child, to one consultant (Ledford) as applying to any worthless, dishonest, or undesirable person). **2005** Williams *Gratitude* 521 = rascal (man or beast).

[OED3 *scutter* n[2] U.S. dialect; Web3 *scutter* n 2 dialect "someone remarkable, as for rascality or excellence"]

scuttle hole *noun* See citations.

1967 *DARE Survey* (Gatlinburg TN) = the hole [in a barn] for throwing hay down below. **1987** Carver *Regional Dialects* 167 The hay chute in a barn is sometimes known as the *scuttle hole*, a landlubber extension of the nautical term for a covered hole or hatchway in the deck of a ship. The extended meaning, however, referring to any lidded hole in a roof or wall, is an early development (ca. 1700), but came to refer specifically to a hay chute only in the Upper South.

scyar See **scar**.

scyout See **scout**.

scyure See **scare**.

sealer *noun* See citation.

1994 Farwell and Buchanan *Logging Terms* = in logging, a man who puts a grade mark on a board showing its quality, working closely with a *grader*.

search *noun*, *verb* Variant form *sarch*.

1792 *Richland Church Minutes* 144 Tha[y] Requared for the time to consider and Sarch into the matter by the committee bringin their report condeming S. McGee. **1832** *McLean Diary* (April 1) Reverent Trnar preached from these words sarch the Scriptures for in them ye think ye have eternal life. **1859** Taliaferro *Fisher's River* 83 I mout as well a sarched fur a needle in a haystack. **1867** Harris *Sut Lovingood* 97d [sic] I tuck off the Doctor's squar bodied saddil bags an sarched em. **1901** Harben *Westerfelt* 179 S'arch them bags ... an' ef he makes anuther budge before it's done, or opens his mouth fer a whisper, drag 'im right down an' give 'im 'is deserts. **1937** Hall *Coll* (Mingus Creek NC) [Civil War soldiers] just went in and sarched all over the house. **1942** Hall *Phonetics Smoky Mts* 42 = *old-fashioned*. **c1975** Lunsford *It Used to Be* 158 The word "sarch" is for "search," like "Sarch me, I never heard."

season *noun* An opportune rainy spell for crops, especially tobacco.

1918 Steadman *NC Word List* 19 This cotton needs a good season. **1944** Dingus *Tobacco Words* 70 = proper amount of moisture in the air to put tobacco in condition to handle without crumbling. **1950** Stuart *Hie Hunters* 110 "We've got to work while we got a season," Peg said. "That's the reason we're workin' early and late hours to get this [= stripping tobacco] done." **1984** Wilder *You All Spoken* 140 = a long slow rain; a sizzle sozzle.

[DARE *season* n[1] 1 South, South Midland]

seben sleeper *noun* See citation.

1977 Shackelford et al. *Our Appalachia* 86 I've heard my wife talk about a family being a bunch of "seben sleepers" and they were considered trash—sorry people. A seben sleeper was somebody that laid in bed when they ought to be up and out working. Seben was a mispronunciation of "seven." You didn't want your boy or girl to marry into a family of seben sleepers.

sech See **such**.

Second Revolutionary War *noun* The American Civil War.

1986 Pederson et al. *LAGS* (Meigs Co TN).

seconds *noun plural* See citation.

1937 Hall *Coll* (Ravensford NC) The poorest grade of ground grain is the brans, which are fed to cows and hogs. Then come the shorts, which are used to make the best pancakes. Next best are the seconds, with which bread may be made, and finally comes the good flour.

second table *noun* A second (or subsequent) sitting of people for a meal, most often of children but sometimes of women and children after men have finished eating.

1949 Still *Master Time* 45 Why don't you eat with us women at the second table? **1963** Arnow *Flowering* 141 Many expressions such as "second table" used in connection with food and eating have all but disappeared. **1964** Roberts *Hell-Fer-Sartin* 6 Delbert gave directions in this vein as we passed the soup beans, scalloped potatoes, fried meat, and piping hot coffee. The mother fed the baby on a side table, but she did not eat a bite herself until we had left the table, a pioneer custom that persists in the hills to this day. The women serve strangers and visitors and wait for "the second table." Even if a courting young man is in the home, his sweetheart will wait the table while he eats with the men. **1967** Wilson *Folkways Mammoth Cave* 18 When there were enough grown folks to fill a table, the young folks had to wait for the second (sometimes the third or fourth) table. It was hard to endure the pangs of hunger, but, fortunately, there were no table manners insisted on when you finally got your chance at the big Sunday dinner. **1972** Carson and Vick *Cookin* 2 19 I do recollect having to wait at the second table when comp'ny was there for dinner. **1987** Young *Lost Cove* 24 The children, who always ate at the second table when company was present, had to be content with the flappers, scratchers and backs [i.e. pieces of chicken]. **1993** Cunningham *Sthn Talk* 135 Hit ain't no fair makin' us young-uns wait fer second table cause we don't ever hardly git no cake or pie.

secont *adjective, noun* Second.

1933 Carpenter *Sthn Mt Dialect* 24 In parts of southwestern Virginia, Kentucky and North Carolina certain words have [t] in place of [d]. SECOND is secont. **1991** Thomas *Sthn Appal* 9 They'uz three points in all speeches to make. First, was to state your subject. Secont was to discuss your subject. And the third was to quit. *Ibid.* 30 Well, ye'd gener'ly git a purty good crop th' first year; but it done better th' secont year.

section *noun* A neighborhood or district distinct economically, socially, or in some other fashion; also used in informal place-names.

1862 *Hundley CW Letters* (Aug 19) write how you a getting along and write all of the news in that section of Country. **1862** *Huntley CW Letters* (Feb 25) I can inform you that thare is a grate many peopell in this section that is in favor of appealing to england for help. **1937** Conner *Ms* 26 The section where he settled is now called "Mingus perairy." **1937** Haun *Cocke Co* 11 At Tumblebug store there has always been one man in the section who was present on cold snowy days to make music for the hunters that were likely to come in. **1956** Hall *Coll* (Big Bend NC) [I was born] in the Big Bend section. **1959** Hall *Coll* (Hartford TN) [We] just had one doctor to serve that entire section, didn't even have a horse doctor. [There were no roads], just cow trails. **1973** GSMNP-70:2:11 He was just from a bad section at that time. **1974** GSMNP-50:2:16 I don't remember of any more sugar orchards in the Greenbrier section.

sedge broom *noun* A broom made from cut stalks of **sedge grass** bound together.

1905 Miles *Spirit of Mts* 22 Sedge brooms are scrubbed to a stump every other week. **1982** DeArmond *So High* 55 Later, the hot soapy water and sedge brooms were used to scrub the pine floors until they were white clean.

sedge grass (also *sage grass*) *noun*

A Variant form *sage grass* [see **1973** in **B**].

[DARE *sage grass* (at *sedge grass* n 2) chiefly South, South Midland]

B A coarse grass (*Andropogon virginicus*) that often grows in open woods and abandoned fields and is used to make **sedge brooms**, baskets, and other items. Same as **broom sedge**.

1937 Eaton *Handicrafts* 176 [Basketmakers] sometimes employ a long-leaf pine combined with raffia, and also the native sedge grass which grows so abundantly in the Highlands, in combination also with raffia. **1940** Haun *Hawk's Done* 177 Ma was carried over the door sill and swept the walls down with a sage-grass broom. **1957** Justus *Other Side* 60 She swept the floor with a sage-grass broom, made a few days ago by Grandy. **1973** GSMNP-70:1:2 I had to go out and get tow sacks full of leaves and sage grass and one thing and another to lay on.

[DARE *sedge grass* n 2 chiefly South, South Midland, *sage-grass broom* (at *sage broom*) South, South Midland]

see *verb*

A Forms.

1 Variant past-tense forms *see, seed, seen, seened*.

1774 *Dunmore's War* 105 He Surely Seen the tracks of five or six Indans. *Ibid.* 140 They see the Indns sculping the Chldn. **1787** *Sinking Creek Church Minutes* I:2 they seed no need or Receiveing of them. **1799** (in **2008** Ellison *High Vistas* 37) [We] Seen a very large rattlebug; attempted to kill it, but it was too souple in the heels for us. **1813** (in **1920** DeWitt *Sevier Journal* 53) (Nov 4) I went to Knoxville & see Colo. Sparks & Lady. **c1830** Benson *Rev Pension Letter* The last time I seed him was at Fauquier court house and we drank som grog together for the last time I ever seed him in this world or ever shall again. **1833** *McLean Diary* 22 Every thing is Burnt up more than I ever see Before. **1862** *Watkins CW Letters* (June 20) I seen some of the compney that John was in but I dident see John he was gon in the mountens on a scout. **1863** *Poteet CW Letters* (Nov 23) I went over to Kinston and I seed sum Crackers and I give fifty cents for six about as big as a dollar. **1867** Harris *Sut Lovingood* 19 You never seed a rale hoss till I rid up. **1895** Edson and Fairchild *TN Mts* 370 Well, I wish I may *never*, if you aint the *beatenest* boy ever I *see* (saw). **1908** Fox *Lonesome Pine* 113 Up at the Pine now you said, "I seed you when I was a-layin' on the cliff"; now you ought to have said, "I *saw* you when I was *lyin'*—"I wasn't," she said sharply, "I don't tell lies—." **1922** *TN CW Ques* 393 (Rhea Co TN) I seen C. Harris, Andy Johnson and W. G. Brownlow and ... most of the politicians of the early sixty. **1931** Goodrich *Mt Homespun* 59 They're the least hands ever I see, on a woman. **1934–37** *LAMSAS Appal* (Madison Co NC, Swain Co NC) *seed*. **1939** Hall *Coll* (Proctor NC) We never seen [the bear] then. It run back down there again and was coming back in, and they catched it before it got back to us. *Ibid.* (Deep Creek NC) I went just on up to the top of the mountain, till I seed the dark was on me, and then I set down and stayed there all night. **1952–57** (in **1986** McDavid and McDavid *KY Verb Forms* 290) *seed* = attested by 17 of 21 (81%) of E KY speakers for Linguistic Atlas of the North Central States. **1953** Atwood *Verbs East US* 20 In the mountain areas south of the Kanawha [*seed*] becomes quite common, being used by most Type I informants [i.e. older speakers with little formal education] as well as by a few Type II [i.e. younger speakers with more formal education]. *Seed* extends more or less all across N.C., in some areas being the only preterite form in use other than *saw*.... *Seen* ... strongly predominates in the Midland area—including n. N.J., the southern three fourths of Pa., W.Va. (except a small southern portion), most of Del. and Md., part of n. and w. Va. [and] some portions of N.C. Throughout this territory *seen* is used by from two thirds of Pa. to nearly all (W.Va.) of the Type I informants [i.e. older speakers with little formal education], as well as by from half (Pa.) to two thirds (W.Va.) of the Type II [i.e. younger speakers with more formal education]. **1956** Hall *Coll* (Cosby TN) He looked and he seed something comin' across the air, just over the top of the timber. **1971** *AOHP/ALC-773* My daddy was the worst Democrat you ever seed in your life. **1973** GSMNP-70:2:7 They took up together, and wherever you seen one of them, you seen the other one. **1979** *Big South Fork OHP-1* That's the first instant coffee I ever seened. **1980** Miles *Verbs in Haywood Co* 107 He enjoyed hunting more than anybody you ever seed. *Ibid.* 108 That's the first time I ever seen it. **1989** *Matewan OHP-33* When they seen him come to town, buddy, everything got under cover. **1990** *Matewan OHP-73* He was one of them, so he seed what it was all about. **1998** *Dante OHP-61* I seened a radio down there. It was a radio and a record player combined.

[OED3 *seed* v 18c→]

2 Variant past-participle forms *saw, see, seed, seened, seent*.

1814 Hartsell *Memora* 146 this nite ther was more Snow fell then I have saw this winter. **1826** *Whitten Letter* I never have saw my family as hearty since I have had one. **1831** (in **2005** *Jefferson Co TN Petitions* 199) He has saw the said Sarah and the said James Davis beded together [but] further saith not. **1862** *Reese CW Letters* (Dec 27) my dear I thout I had saw you for the last time. **1862** *Warrick CW Letters* (June 15) I have heard a heap of talk about the Country But I have See as much of it as I wount to see. **1864** *Councill CW Letters* (March 29) they Said that they had Seed the wounded men a going to the horse pital. **1868** (in **1974** Harris *High Times* 199) I has seed wimmen in my time adzackly like Kate, both in looks an' manners, an' every one ove 'em wer oncommon people. **1901** Harben *Westerfelt* 69 You wus about the best-lookin' man she'd ever seed. **1913** Kephart *Our Sthn High* 120 They've seed the revenuers in flesh and blood. **1937** Thornburgh *Great Smoky Mts* 39 I've seed him out as early as January or February. **1939** Hall *Coll* (Deep Creek NC) I've saw all this place in wheat and corn on both sides of the river. *Ibid.* (Deep Creek NC) Law, yes, I've seed a many a bear and eat the meat of them, coon too. **1940** Haun *Hawk's Done* 32 Joe would have been proud to have seed me with her. **1961** *Coe Ridge OHP-343B* I'd liked to've stayed and seed some. **1969** *Burton-Manning Coll-93A* Nobody's ever saw nothing like that. **1972** *AOHP/ALC-355* I've seened a many a day hunting. I've seened a many a day for the guys left for the house, you know, to have meat. **1973** *AOHP/ASU-149* I've seent these old red Indian peaches. You may have seed them. They was red meat in them. **1973** GSMNP-76:34 There are [a] patch growed down here. One patch is all I've ever see, since I've been down here. **1980** Miles *Verbs in Haywood Co* 107 You've never seed as many operations as she's got. *Ibid.* 108 I hadn't saw him in five years. **1984** Burns *Cold Sassy* 111 I ain't never see sech a one for cleanin' house as Miss Love. **1986** Pederson et al. *LAGS*: *saw* (Cocke Co TN, Jefferson Co TN); *seed* (Cocke Co TN). **1989** *Matewan OHP-28* Have you saw these large water buckets?

B Syntax.

1 Followed by an embedded yes/no question that maintains inversion of the subject and verb (thus *see can you* = see whether/if you can). See also **ask B1**, **know C1**, **wonder 3**.

1910 Cooke *Power and Glory* 10 Reckon I better be steppin' over to Vander's and see can I borry their cow. **1927** Montague *Funny Bone* 329 "It ain't John Bunyan!" says Brother Mutters, feeling hisself all over to see was he fatally busted. **1943** Hannum *Mt People* 111 Hounddog, take that gun stick, boy, and rub a sulphur match on yore hindsights and yore foresights, and see can you get that top feller. **1948** Chase *Grandfather Tales* 158 Stand off there now, and let me see is it all right. **1976** Still *Pattern of Man* 32 Feed her a biscuit, and see will she mend. **1988** Smith *Fair and Tender* 138 Sometimes we will put our hands on the track and see can we feel it vibrate. **1998** Montgomery *Coll* (known to nine consultants from the Smoky Mountains).

2 Followed by an embedded *wh*-question that maintains inversion of the subject and verb (thus *see what was the problem* = see what the problem was). See also **ask B2**, **know C2**, **wonder 4**.

1948 Chase *Grandfather Tales* 196 [The mare] come on to the house and stood there to see what did the old man want. **1985** Irwin *Alex Stewart* 253 Just a little while after she left I heard her screaming and I run down there to see what was the matter.

seed[1] See **see A1**, **A2**.

seed[2] *noun*

1 A testicle.

1946 Dudley *KY Words* 271 I been injured; I've got one seed's big as your fist. **c1960** Wilson *Coll*: *seeds* = testicles. **1990** Cavender *Folk Medical Lex* 31 = testicles.

[DARE *seed* n 3 chiefly South, South Midland]

2 A remnant burning coal covered with ashes to preserve a fire overnight.

1931 Goodrich *Mt Homespun* 68 I keep the seed of my fire all night, so the corner here is warm a plenty for the pot.

seeker *noun* One who fervently seeks religious conviction or experience.

1859 Taliaferro *Fisher's River* 40 He joined . . . [a] church. . . . The great Goliath . . . was now a humble penitent and a devout "seeker." **1901** Harben *Westerfelt* 269 She laid her hand on his arm and looked up into his eyes. "Are you a seeker, John Westerfelt?" she asked. It is generally felt that this process of "praying one's way through to salvation" takes from seven to ten days. When salvation comes, the seeker sits erect on the mourner's bench, either crying from joy or smiling, thus announcing to others present what has happened.

[DARE *seeker* (at *seek* v) chiefly South, South Midland]

seely *adjective* Simple-minded, naive.

1937 Haun *Cocke Co* 3 [Girls] mosey around over the hills like tarpins, are skeery of snakes when they see them quiled up, and they and lambs are supposed to be seely. **1940** Haun *Hawk's Done* 58 Enzor was pure and seely.

[< Middle English *sely* < Old English *selig* "simple-minded"; akin to *silly*; Web3 *seely* adj archaic]

seem *verb* Variant third-singular form *seem* unmarked for subject-verb agreement.

1961 *Coe Ridge OHP-333A* It seem like I ought to know him, but I don't. **1973** *Gardening* 237 Seem like [the onions] just never would do no good. **1979** *Big South Fork OHP-10* [It] seem like he had a lot of lumber to come over up there. **1990** *Matewan OHP-73* It seem like it's right on the end of my tongue. **2008** *Rosie Hicks* 3 [It] seem like to me they weren't all that pink like I thought they would be.

seen See **see A1**.

seened, **seent** See **see A1**, **A2**.

seep *noun* A place where water oozes out, as from a sluggish spring or the roof of a coal mine, sometimes forming a very small stream.

1941 Stuart *Men of Mts* 268 "A lot o' seeps [are] comin' through here," says Lefty, "we must be under that damned sag." **c1960** Wilson *Coll* = a small spring or cozy place. **1986** Pederson et al. *LAGS* (Washington Co TN, Rabun Co GA) = smaller than a *branch*. **2000** Morgan *Mts Remember* 46 It wasn't much of a spring compared with Big Springs, or ours in the valley. It was really just a seep coming out of some rocks, and the basin was no bigger than a soup bowl. **2011** Hague *Spring* 7 It was a tiny seep rising from the twin trunk of a shagbark hickory far over the hill in the woods, right on the property line.

[DARE *seep* n chiefly South, South Midland, West]

see roses *verb phrase* To menstruate.

1990 Cavender *Folk Medical Lex* 31 *seeing roses* = menstruation.

seesaw-snake *noun* See citation.

1957 Combs *Lg Sthn High: Word List* 87 = a mythical, savory fish. Heard in the catch-question to children: "Which would you rather eat, a seesaw snake, or a sunburnt cake?" The child usually replies, "A sun-burnt cake," of course, not knowing that a "sun-burnt cake" is a pile of dry cow dung.

se-gogglin See **si-godlin**.

sell out *verb phrase*

1 To sell off (one's land), move (one's household); to leave with one's household.

1939 Hall *Coll* (Wears Cove TN) I had to move down here because the park bought us out up there, run us out. We sold out our land to the park up there. **1957** GSMNP-23:1:4 I sold it out, sold this out and bought up back on the Two Mile Branch. *Ibid.* 6 They lived on it till they sold out. They sold out to Uncle Ephraim Ogle. **1969** GSMNP-43:17 No, they had sold out, I think. Most of the people had sold out and left the creek. **1989** *Matewan OHP-2* I don't know what was in [the barrel]. I couldn't see . . . but I,

I sold out. *Ibid.* 9 Granddaddy's sister sold out above him, had a better house than him, and she was anxious to sell out, so he sold out the log house and we moved up to this one. **1998** *Dante OHP-45* I thought "well, I'll sell this place out." I was offered a hundred thousand dollars for it.

2 To move away, depart quickly.

1915 Hall *Autobiog Claib Jones* 30 I would have taken Bates' gun and sold out right then and there. **1938** Hall *Coll* (Emerts Cove TN) "He sold out from here" = he got gone from here. **1980** Weals *Strangers* He'd have me use the smoker, and when a bee'd get under my veil, I'd sell out, doctor. I'd get out of there a-flying. **1993** Cunningham *Sthn Talk* 136 Last time I see Luke he was in his old Ford headin' south on the hard road, sellin' out.

sell shadows *verb phrase* See citation.

1977 Howard *Fifty Years* 13 = bid on the shadow of a girl at a box supper.

sence See **since.**

send *verb*

1 Variant past-tense forms *saunt, sended, sont.*

1913 Kephart *Our Sthn High* 284 *saunt.* **1929** (in **1952** Mathes *Tall Tales* 104) "Hit's a good thing ye sont fer me," the old hillsman went on. **1957** Combs *Lg Sthn High: Word List* 93 *sont* = past-tense and past participle of send. **1973** *AOHP/ALC-505* I always sended Becky for it. She tried to get me to go. **1994–97** Montgomery *Coll*: *sont* (known to Brown, Cardwell, Weaver).

2 Variant past-participle forms *sont, sunt.*

1910 Cooke *Power and Glory* 6 I've done sont Bud an' Honey to Mandy Ann Foncher's. [See **1957** in **1.**] **1974** Roberts *Sang Branch* 27 [He] said if I didn't come back to school, he's aiming to have me sunt off.

send and *verb phrase* To send to (+ similarly inflected verb, used to convey that two actions are simultaneous or sequential and sometimes to reinforce the latter action). See also **go and, take and.**

1864 Lister *CW Letters* (Feb 27) I want you to take good cear of your self When you haf to go apon your crutches and if it takes eny back set send and get Mrs Bolews gall to stay with you. **1974** *GSMNP-51:22* They'd sent and got a witch doctor. He could take this spell off. **1977** Shackelford et al. *Our Appalachia* 129 I said, "Send and get a bottle and we'll make the nipple with a hole in it big enough that he can mash on it and mash him out a few drops."

[cf OED3 *and* conj[1] 10 now colloquial and regional]

send howdy See **howdy B.**

Seneca snakeroot *noun* A millwort (*Polygala senega*), a perennial plant with many medicinal uses.

1800 (in **1920** DeWitt *Sevier Journal* 28) (May 28) Senaca snake root powdered very good for worms in children. **1824** (in **1912** Doddridge *Notes on Settlement* 117) A plant with fibrous roots, resembling the seneka-snake root, of a black color and a strong, but not disagreeable smell, was considered and relied on for the Indian specific for the cure of a sting of a snake. **1956** Still *Burning of Waters* 59 A milkwort (Polygala senega) of eastern North America having racemes of small white flowers. **1967** Jones *Peculiarities Mtneers* 69 Seneca snake root tea was used as a remedy for hives, measles and all diseases that must be "brought out." It was also good for the whooping cough. [**1971** Krochmal et al. *Medicinal Plants Appal* 200 This plant is reportedly used as an emetic, purgative, diuretic, expectorant, and tonic.]

seng See **ginseng.**

seng hoe See **sang hoe.**

sense See **since.**

sensibly *adverb* Exactly.

1904–20 Kephart *Notebooks* 2:475 Right sensibly atween the shoulders I had a pain. **1994–97** Montgomery *Coll* (known to Brown, Bush, Ellis, Oliver); I can't right sensibly tell you where I'm hurting (Cardwell).

sensitive brier *noun* A mimosa (*Mimosa microphylla*). See also **shame brier.**

1941 Walker *Story of Mt* 58 Sensitive brier's runners cling to the ground and are tough and spiny. The leaflets fold quickly, following a sudden jar.

[DARE *sensitive brier* n South, South Midland]

sentiment *noun* See 1917 citation.

1917 Kephart *Word-List* 417 = sensation or feeling. **1995–97** Montgomery *Coll* (known to Brown, Cardwell, Jones).

[OED3 *sentiment* n 2 obsolete]

serenade (also *serenation*) *noun* A rowdy, prankish celebration late on the wedding night at the newlyweds' residence, to compel them to admit the revelers and to treat them with food or refreshment; it is characterized by the beating of pots and pans, ringing of cowbells, and various pranks (for which, see citations), but not music; a similar celebration going from house to house on Christmas Eve or other festive day; hence verb = to engage in such festivities and antics; verbal noun *serenading* = participating in such festivities and antics; noun *serenader* = one who participates in such festivities and antics. Also called **shivaree**, the latter being less common, especially in TN and KY. Also called **belling** in Central Appalachia. See also **rattle trap, ride one on a (fence) rail.**

1854 *Paw Paw Hollow Church Minutes* 156 the following resolutions where as the great evil of drm drinking & such as meeting in crowds about grogshops and shooting for sport and dealing in lotterys and sirnading. **1939** Hall *Coll* (Cades Cove TN) *serenadin'* = men would go from one house to another, makin' lots of noise, ringin' cowbells, shootin' guns. *Ibid.* (Catons Grove TN) I guess you people would like to know about serenades and how young folks got along back seventy years ago and longer. We had serenades. They'd make old big rattletraps they'd call them, and they'd have bells and plows and every old noise, and they'd run around the house, and they'd have awful times, and [if] they couldn't get in, why they'd just keep right on, and whenever they'd get in, they'd go through the house and my, how they'd rattle and bang around. **1949** Kurath *Word Geog East US* 78 *Serenade* [occurs in] the westernmost part of Virginia and the adjoining part of Kentucky. **1960** Mason *Memoir* 75 On Christmas eve night, it was customary for a group of young men to gather up and go serenading. We would take along all the old cowbells, muzzle loading shot-guns, horns, and any other noise making device which was available. There were always three or four banjoes and fiddles in the crowd. We would try to slip up to someone's house without being discovered. The serenade would usually begin with a long blast from a trumpet. The trumpets were usually made from rams horns. Then the firing of the shotguns combined with the ringing cowbells added to the commotion. If a family were somehow missed by the serenaders, they felt as if they had been slighted. **1960** Stubbs *Mountain-Wise* (Feb–March) 6 On his wedding night a bunch of folks decided to give Uncle Jim and his bride a "serenation." They went up to his house about ten o'clock, began to explode dynamite, ring cowbells and make all the noise they could. But when Uncle Jim came running out of the house in his "drawers-tail," he scared the girls half to death and put an end to the "serenation." **1966** Dakin *Vocab Ohio River Valley* 497 In eastern Kentucky *serenade* is still used by some of the oldest generation but the younger speakers say *chivaree* exclusively. **1972** Alderman *Big Bald* 12 Meanwhile the new bride and groom would slip away to their own prepared cabin. After dark, the third night, the crowd would gather around the cabin of the new couple for the serenade. At a given signal a din of noise, that would scare the "hants" and everything else back into the never, never world, would break loose. Pans-a-poundin', guns-a-shootin', people-a-shoutin' and the big roarin' horse fiddle boomin' through the woods got the "shivaree" off to a thundering start. This final part of the celebration lasted all night. Sun-up would see the departin' couples drifting down their separate trails, homeward bound across the creeks and ridges, to the back of the beyond where they lived. **1974** Russell *Hillbilly* 32 The community "serenade" often consisted of riding the groom on a fence rail and the bride in a big wash tub. **1975** Purkey *Madison Co* 63 Mama had a zest for living. She got us children up early on Christmas morning and we would steal out to our nearest neighbor's house and "serenade" them by banging pots and pans together and setting off firecrackers, which my oldest brothers somehow always contrived to get. Then we all yelled in unison, "Christmas Gift!" **1981** Brewer *Wonderment* 8 The young folks in the neighborhood gave them a shivaree, called a "serenade" in some communities. **1986** Pederson et al. *LAGS* = attested by 16/60 interviewees (26.7%) from E TN and 5/35 (14.3%) from N GA; 21/102 of all LAGS interviewees (20.5%) attesting term were from Appalachia. **1988** Russell *It Happened* 48 The serenade, or shivaree, would take place later at night, on after the supper and music making. **1990** Wigginton *Foxfire Christmas* 30 We thought if people ought to be serenaded, we'd give them a round. If anybody came in our settlement, they got serenaded whether they liked it or not. We have serenaded 'em till it made 'em so mad they'd die, nearly. **1993** Page and Smith *Foxfire Toys and Games* 74 The night before Christmas was always the big night back when I was a growing up. We'd get firecrackers and cowbells and shotguns and we'd just go from one house to another. We called it serenading. [Did you ever hear tell of that?] Yeah, we'd just go and slip up on a home. We'd wait till they went to bed, you see, before we started. And we'd slide up in the yard, because if they run out and beat you and hollered "Christmas gift" we had to have something to give them. But if we slid into the yard and went to shooting those firecrackers and ringing them cowbells—that big old bell that you could hear all over the mountains—and holler and whooping until they got up and then they brought us in and had to treat us with fruits and candies and stuff and maybe then some of them joined us and we'd go on to the next house and we'd be lucky if we got in just a little before daylight the next morning.

serenation See **serenade.**

serious *adverb* Seriously, acutely.

1973 *AOHP/ASU-111* When I was raised up, they was more consecrated Christians. It seemed like they took things serious. **1984** Wilder *You All Spoken* 45 *serious mad* = downright fire-eatin', ass-chewin' mad. **1999** Montgomery *Coll* (known to Cardwell).

sermon *noun*

A Variant forms *sarmint, sarmon, serment, sermond, sermont, surment.*

1803 (in **1956** Eliason *Tarheel Talk* 317) *serment.* **1827** (in *Ibid.* 317) sermont (Caldwell Co NC). **1856** *Elijoy Church Minutes* 89 the Church met at Elijoy meting house & after Sermont they put the sacrement of till the next meting and all other business on the account of Sickness. **1858** (in **1974** Harris *High Times* 121) When I got done with him his perporshuns wer changed—he wurnt over ten hans high, an es long es one ove ole Bullin's sarmints. **1861** *Carden CW Letter* (Oct 6) we had A good sermond to day deliverd by the Rev Wm Hicks for the first I have heard since I left home. **1862** *Lister CW Letters* (Dec 19) he preacht as able ar sur ment as I most ever herd. **1866** *Elijoy Church Minutes* 108 Church met & after sermond proseeded to business. **1913** Kephart *Our Sthn High* 238 Them leetle [boys]'d git 'em a crack and grin in at us all through the sarmon. **1927** Mason *Lure of Smokies* 199 I wisht many times some o' my men-folks c'd a' larnt thet sarmint. **1934–37** *LAMSAS Appal* (Madison Co NC, Swain Co NC) *sermont.* **1969** Medford *Finis* 78 Oh what "awful sermonts" he could preach—"awful" was the term usually used.

B A worship service.

1956 Hall *Coll* (Big Bend NC) Once in a while a minister would come in, hold a little sermon. [We] had no meetin' house, didn't have any doctors, no cars.

sermond, sermont See **sermon.**

serpenpines *noun* Used as a malapropism for *turpentine.*

1972 *AOHP/ALC-298* We got down to where I stayed at, put the oil of serpenpines on [the snakebite].

serpent *noun* Variant forms *sarpent, sarpint, sarpunt.*

1859 Taliaferro *Fisher's River* 50 The reader shall soon have abundant evidence of this admission in his numerous and rapid flights from "sarpunts." **1867** Harris *Sut Lovingood* 56 Brethren, brethren, take keer ove yerselves, the Hell-sarpints *hes got me!* **1939** Burnett *Gap o' Mountains* 11 Ary furrin' foe which mought pester us would larn that a pizen sarpent quiled in the bresh, is a plum innocent alongside a passel of tetchy mountain men who ain't afeard of nothin, and who cain't be druv, drug nor toled. **1998** Montgomery *Coll*: *sarpent* (known to Bush, Cardwell, Jones, Oliver). **2007** Ball *Tub Mills* 21 "Sarpunts" could move him to the speed of electricity.

serpent-bit *past participle* Bitten by a snake. For similar forms, see **bite A2.**

1993 Burton *Take Up Serpents* 58 Jean remembers once in Ooltewah when she was about twelve years old that her father was serpent bit.

serpent handler *noun* A member of a Pentecostal sect that practices the handling of poisonous "serpents" and the drinking of poisonous liquids in adherence to the Gospel according to Mark 16:17–18. Members of such groups usually refer to themselves as *serpent handlers* rather than *snake handlers* (following terminology in the King James Version of the Bible). See also **serpent handling, sign follower, snake handler, take up a serpent.**

1993 Burton *Take Up Serpents* 6 Contemporary adherents trace their beliefs of the words of Jesus to his disciples immediately prior to the ascension as recorded in Mark: "And these signs shall follow them that believe; in my name they shall cast out devils; they shall speak with new tongues. They shall take up serpents; and if they drink any deadly thing, it shall not hurt them; they shall lay hands on the sick, and they shall recover" (Mark 16: 17–18). Because of the initial words of this text, serpent handlers are often referred to as "sign followers." They consider themselves simply Christians who are following the will of God.

serpent handling *noun* See citations. Also called **snake handling.** See also **take up a serpent.**

1982 *Foxfire VII* 393 I believe in serpent handlin' a hun'erd percent. My wife never did believe in it. [*Ibid.* 481 The snake handlers read the verses located in the final portion of the Gospel of Mark [= 16:17–18 "In my name . . . they shall speak with new tongues; They shall take up serpents"] and insist that those words must be taken literally. Indeed they declare that if those prophecies are not true, none of the Bible is true.] **2006** Burton *Serpent Handling* 1350 Serpent handling as a modern Christian religious ritual emerged among southern Appalachian fundamentalists, principally Holiness-Pentecostal groups, within the first twelve years of the twentieth century. . . . Participants designate this practice as one of the five signs listed in Mark 16:17–18 that Jesus said would follow those who believe. Sign followers, often perceived as tempting God, instead see themselves as pursuing biblical precedent and "confirming the word" by taking up serpents, casting out devils, speaking in tongues, drinking deadly poisons, and healing the sick.

servagerous See **savagerous.**

serve *verb*

A Variant form *sarve.*

1867 Harris *Sut Lovingood* 53 This wer the way they wer tu sarve men folks. **1895** Dromgoole *Humble Advocate* 323 I hev sarved that thar man in thar ten year, good an' faithful. **1939** Hall *Coll* (White Oak NC) It sarves him right. **c1940** Padelford *Notes* Have a wing and drum-stick, Preacher. Let me sarve yer. **1942** Hall *Phonetics Smoky Mts* 42 = *old-fashioned.*

B To treat.

1939 Hall *Coll* (Cataloochee NC) Have you been well sarved since I saw you last? (reported use of old timers).

service *noun*

A Variant forms *sarvice, sarvis* [see **1939** in **B1**].

1867 Harris *Sut Lovingood* 98 Then he dug sum [dirt] outen a bank wif his ho'ns, an' smelt ove hit; then he tuck a twis' ur two intu his tail, an' histed hit, an' felt hissef then ready fur activ sarvice. **1895** Dromgoole *Humble Advocate* 343 I ain't lacked in my sarvice none nuther, as I can see. **1913** Kephart *Our Sthn High* 170 We know what they uster do afore they jined the sarvice, and why they did it. **1994** Montgomery *Coll* (known to Cardwell). **2007** Preece *Leavin' Sandlick* 15 I don't know who be in charge of sarvice that day.

B Senses.

1 (also *sarvice, sarviceberry, sarvicetree, sarvis, sarvisberry, sarvistree, sarviss, sarvissberry, sarvisstree, serviceberry, servicetree*) A common deciduous tree (*Amelanchier* spp) that grows at all elevations and is also known especially for its display of white flowers, which traditionally have been seen as the harbinger of spring. Also called **Allegheny servicetree** (see **service B1**), **Juneberry, shadblow.**

1883 Zeigler and Grosscup *Heart of Alleghanies* 58 Here also spring the service tree, with its red, eatable berry, ripe in August. **1889** Mooney *Folk Carolina Mts* 97 Ginseng is *sang*, the service tree is *sarvice* and peanuts are *goobers.* **1939** Hall *Coll* (Smokemont NC) They found [a bear] lappin' on sarvis. They went back [and] watched the sarvis trees two days. **1943** Stupka *Through the Year* 275 Ordinarily the "sarvice" tree becomes arrayed with heavy creamy white bloom by the first part of April. Known elsewhere by such names as "shadbush," "serviceberry," "Juneberry," and others, it occupies a greater altitudinal range (900–6,400 feet) than any other tree in the Smokies. **1972** Alderman *Big Bald* 21 Sarvice Tree, or Allegheny Serviceberry, is one of the some 140 species of trees in the vicinity of Big Bald Mountain [TN]. This early spring bloomer opens its flowers before the leaves appear. . . . Legend says that mountain women used the early blooming flowers to decorate churches for weddings, funerals and regular meeting services. This common usage is said to have started the name "Sarvicetree." **1974–75** McCracken *Logging* 3:18 They's some big sarvis right around those laurel slicks up there too, service berry or sarvis. **1998** Montgomery *Coll* (according to consultants from the Smoky Mountains, the most common terms for this plant are *sarvice, sarviceberry,* and *sarvicetree*). **2006** Ellison *Nature Journal* 31 The tree known as Allegheny serviceberry, Juneberry, shadbush, shadblow and sugarplum in other parts of the country is referred to throughout the Blue Ridge as sarvis or related forms such as sarviceberry, sarvisberry, sarvissberry, sarviss tree or sarviss. This supposedly colloquial pronunciation of "service" is often attributed to the fact that the tree's early blooms signaled the arrival of the traveling preacher, who would hold the year's first formal commemoration for those who had been unable to survive the winter. But tracking the precise origins of the designation sarvis and its related forms is actually more complicated than that.

2 The fruit of this tree.

1958 Wood *Words from TN* 15 *sarvises* = fruit of the sarvis-tree. **1982** *Smokies Heritage* 109 = an edible purple-red berry that grows upon the sarvis (service) tree, ripening in June. **1995** Montgomery *Coll* (known to Cardwell).

[< Middle English *serves* < Old English *syrve* ultimately < Latin *sorbus* "service tree"; the derivation from *service* "church meeting," on the basis that the tree's blooming signals weather permitting an itinerant preacher to visit rural communities is a folk etymology]

serviceberry See **service B1**.

service cow *noun* See citation.

1949 McDavid *Grist* 113 (Pickens Co SC) = bull.

servicetree See **service B1**.

service winter (also *sarvis winter*) *noun* A late cold spell around the time when the **service** tree is in bloom. For terms describing a similar phenomenon, see **blackberry winter**.

1940 Still *River of Earth* 127 "Even come spring," grandma said, "we've got a passel of chills to endure: dogwood winter, redbud, service, foxgrape, blackberry. . . . There must be seven winters, by count. A chilly snap for every time of bloom." **1983** Broaddus *Estill Co KY Word List* 54 *sarvis Winter* = a period of cold weather when sarvis is in bloom.

set See also **set in**, **sit**.

A *verb* Principal parts.

1 Variant infinitive/base forms *sit*, *sot*.

1971 *AOHP/ALC-147* You used the salt to put in that to sit the color and it made it fast colored then. **1989** Landry *Smoky Mt Interviews* 191 Things changes so much anymore. Now a lot of people don't know the word "sot" at all. If they do, it's applied to some fellow who's had a little too much to drink, you know. . . . Well, Miss Emily, here you're teaching us to say set and sit and sat. . . . At home we don't say nary one of 'em. Miss Emily, we just say sot. Hit don't matter if we're going to sot now or sot directly or sot an hour ago, still just sot. . . . Sot was the word they used. They used it all the time. They never did set or sit or sat. They just sot now, directly.

2 Variant past-tense form *sot*.

1864 *Love CW Letters* (March 16) the[y] Sot the house on fire and they Staid in till they Burnt up 5 of them. **1867** Harris *Sut Lovingood* 31 She imejuntly sot in, an' biled a big pot ove paste, ni ontu a peck ove hit, an' tole me I wer gwine tu hev "the gonest purty shut in that range." **1939** Hall *Coll* (Bradley Fork NC) Colonel Thomas sot my age back two years [so I could serve as a home guard in the Civil War].

3 Variant past-participle forms *sit*; hence participial adjective *sot*. See also **set in one's ways** *verb*.

1803 (in **1920** DeWitt *Sevier Journal* 37) (Dec 10) On the Fryday before New Years day he had sit out to the Great High Court. **1896** Fox *Vendetta* 123 Ye air so powerful sot on goin' to mill. **1969** Medford *Finis* 98 I notis in the news that them 3 Zog gals, sisters uv King Zog, will prob'ly inclood N.C. while on their American vizit; also that them ol' mades air ded sot on gitten 'em a hubby—uv sum de-skripshun.

B *verb*

1 To sit (used as present tense, past tense, and past participle).

1792 *Bent Creek Church Minutes* 12 the church met and delegated br[ethere]n Tidence Lane Isaac Barton & John Murphy members of conference to Set at Bent Creek meeting house the fourth saturday inst. **1831** *McLean Diary* 5 prisbetary set at the meeting house up at Sees. **1863** (in **2003** Watford *Civil War in NC* 98) O what a happy meeting it will be for mee to meet you and set down and talk with you. **1913** Kephart *Our Sthn High* 226 We'd set around and sing until he died. **1939** Hall *Coll* (Saunook NC) She honed all evenin' to come over and set beside me. **1953** Hall *Coll* (Bryson City NC) Everybody was setting and listening at him. . . . So he sit there and told a great long story, how many bears he killed in one season. Mounted up to around fifty or something like that . . . And some set quiet for some time and finally this fellow Wilson raised up in the camp and says, "Boys, that was a heap of bears." **1962** Wilson *Folkways Mammoth Cave* 46 Set did double duty for all of its uses and all of those of *sit*. . . . You *set* the table and then *set* down and rested till time to ring the dinner bell. **1971** Thornburgh *Great Smoky Mts* 155 I recall the mountain weaver who invited us to "come in and set a while," calling her son to "fotch a pail of water." **1973** GSMNP-87:2:4 I used to set and wish a log would fall. **1980** Miles *Verbs in Haywood Co* 112 When they get up there that big, they don't set down and play. . . . He said he'd set on the porch over there. **1985** Irwin *Alex Stewart* 16 I've set here and studied a heap about that. **1989** *Matewan OHP-9* They was a big store [that] set there about pretty close to where the bank is now. **1996** GSMNPCOHP-1:1 His barn set down in there.

2 To come, follow (a course).

1994 Montgomery *Coll* The wind's a-settin' from that direction (Ogle).

3 See citation.

1949 Maurer *Argot of Moonshiner* 12 (also *set in*, *set up*) = to prepare the equipment and place the mash in the vats for fermentation: "We got set in one Sunday, and run a month."

4 To put (a plant or crop) in the ground.

1968 Guthrie *Tobacco* 39 The father and older boys set the plants (the verb "plant" is not generally used for this operation even today).

5 To join together (the pieces of a quilt).

1999 Montgomery *Coll* (known to Cardwell).

C *noun*

1 A generation, part of a family (often accompanied by a surname); a group of people peculiar or distinct in some way. See also **generation B**, **push 1**.

1920 Ridley *Sthn Mtneer* 15 The whole damned set [of moonshiners] ought to be exposed. **1931** Combs *Lg Sthn High* 1308 A family that is disliked is referred to as a "set," as in "that Jones set." **1939** Hall *Coll* (Emerts Cove TN) [The Ogles] are a dark complected set of folks, and they have high cheek bones like the Cherokee. **1956** Hall *Coll* (Big Creek NC) The old set of Joneses has pretty good sense. **1973** GSMNP-84:10 Will Stinnett, he was [of] another set of Stinnetts, and I never knowed of them and this Little River Stinnetts being any related at all. **1977** Simpkins *Culture* 44–45 The clan still exists in Appalachia, they don't call it that but it's still here. . . . It determines what kinship system you marry into, what church you go to, who you swap work with, who you get drunk with, who you help in times of crisis, and so on. . . . They call it a set. They depend very heavily on kinsmen and neighbors. **1981** GSMNP-122:36 My dad and granny, my great-grandparents is what they call the new set of Whaley. **1986** Pederson et al. *LAGS* = attested by 10/60 interviewees (16.7%) from E TN; 10/15 of all LAGS interviewees (66.7%) attesting term were from Appalachia. **1988** Brown *Beech Creek* 95 There were, for example, many Andrews in this section of the county, and different groups of them were known as different "sets." There were the "Rabbit" set, the "Candy" set, the "Whistle" set, the "Red Aim" set, the "Poplar" set, the "Possum" set, and so on.

2 A young plant ready to put in the ground, specifically an onion. See also **onion set**.

1973 *Gardening* 237 The sets, they grow under th'ground—set out one big onion and little sets come out all around. **1986** Pederson et al. *LAGS* = attested by 5/60 speakers (8.3%) in E TN and 1/35 (2.9%) in N GA; 6/18 of all LAGS speakers (33.3%) are in Appalachia.

3 A period of sitting.

1939 Burnett *Gap o' Mountains* 21 Arrived at the girl's home, her escort might be told good night at once, he might rest at the gate for a few minutes unless her father called her in, (which he usually did) or he might, if he rated high, be permitted to enjoy "A Set."

4 See citations. See also **run a set**, **running set**.

1927 Furman *Lonesome Road* 105 Round dancing was absolutely unknown, but "sets"—a combination of quadrille and Virginia Reel—were enthusiastically danced. **1930** (in **2015** Jamison *Hoedowns* 72–73) It is very probable that the word "set" implies a "set of figures," in the way it is customary to speak of a "set of Quadrilles." **1993** Stuart *Daughter* 236 [In square dancing] four couples positioned in a square make a "set."

5 See citation.

1964 Clarkson *Lumbering in WV* 370 = the temporary station of a portable sawmill, a steam skidder, or a logging camp.

set across (also *set over*) *verb phrase* To ferry (someone) across a river.

1981 Irwin *Arnwine Cabin* 10 I used to set them across the river in a canoe when they wanted to go to the store . . . when they wanted to go, I set them across in my boat. **2007** McMillon *Notes*: *set over* = ferry across: "Uncle Tommy would set people over the river in his boat."

set a good table *verb phrase* See citation.

1980 Berry and Repass *Grandpa Says* 19 = be generous with food: "She sure did set a good table."

set-along child *noun* A small child able to sit up but not yet walk. Also called **sit-alone baby**. See also **arm baby**, **knee baby**, **lap baby**.

1913 Kephart *Our Sthn High* 285 Peculiar adjectives are formed from verbs . . . "When my youngest was a leetle set-along child" (interpreted as "settin' along the floor"). **1974** Fink *Bits Mt Speech* 23 = child big enough to sit on the floor but not walk. **1975** Jackson *Unusual Words* 154 There were *breast babies*, *lap babies*, *knee babies*, or *little set along young'uns*, as well as the *chaps*, and this *growin' up generation*.

set aside *verb* To consider (a church member) inactive until an issue of conduct is settled. See 1982 citation.

1843 (in **1956** Eliason *Tarheel Talk* 292–93) (Caldwell Co NC) The church Excludes him from there fellowship for giting drunk, for swering & for saying that he sworp a horse with Harriss & said Harriss was to give him said Coffey ten dollars when the Church could not find it true, so the Church sot him aside. **1982** Slone *How We Talked* 72 = not dismissed from membership [in a church], just to have their name put away for awhile, until something is settled about their guilt or non-guilt about something.

set a store by See **set store by**.

set back *verb phrase* To render (one) speechless or incapable of responding.

1927 Shearin *Speech of Fathers* 7 She was right put out about it, an' I wuz set back.

setback *noun* A game using playing cards.

1940 Haun *Hawk's Done* 134 Him and Carlous were going to play set-back. **1963** Edwards *Gravel* 113 We'll make coffee and have an all-night feed. We'll play Set-Back.

[DARE *setback* n 2 chiefly Southeast, Middle Atlantic, Appalachians, Connecticut]

set down *verb phrase*

To write down, write out (the words of a text).

1964 Thomas and Kob *Ballad Makin'* 9 Year after year in my travel through the mountains of Kentucky, on one mission or another, I "set down" all sorts of ballads and tunes, many of which the mountain minstrel, or his "own blood kin," claimed to have "made up right out of his head." **1995** Montgomery *Coll* I set that down on the calendar (Cardwell).

set in *verb phrase*

1 (also *set into*) (+ *verbal noun or present participle*) To begin. See also **fall into**, **start in**. See also Grammar and Syntax §7.3.

1867 Harris *Sut Lovingood* 95 Clapshaw crawled onder a straw pile in the barn, an' sot intu prayin—yu cud a-hearn him a mile—sumthin 'bout the plagues ove Yegipt, an' the pains ove the secon death. **1939** Hall *Coll* (Cataloochee NC) One of the little hounds come up. I just set into shootin' [the bear] as fast as I could shoot the little gun. **c1945** Haun *Hawk's Done* 231 He set into talking and told it. **1974** Fink *Bits Mt Speech* 23 Hit *set into* raining about dark. **1976** *Bear Hunting* 313 Every dog they had set in a'baying. **1995** Adams *Come Go Home* 63 Folks is a fixin' to set into showin' up fer the wake, and he does look plumb un-natural a-layin' there in the floor that a way. **1996** Dykeman *Memories* She set in to shouting and I caught hold of her dress-tail and we traveled all over that church. **2001** Lowry *Expressions* 13 She sets in a coughin' every night.

2 (+ *infinitive*) To begin.

1834 Crockett *Narrative* 40 I set in to work for a man by the name of James Caldwell. **1861** Hedgecock *Diary* 110 [It] set in at night to rain.

3 To begin a task or a session.

1925 Dargan *Highland Annals* 153 I set in then an' made her glad to git out. **1934–37** *LAMSAS Appal* (Swain Co NC) *set in*. **1974** Dabney *Mt Spirits* 121 The way we'd do, we'd set in of a morning, if we was a goin' to double it.

set in one's ways *adjective phrase* Variant form *sot in one's ways*.

1931 Hannum *Thursday April* 51 Joe had often made the remark that she was uncommon sot in her ways. **c1959** Weals *Hillbilly Dict* 7 *sot in his ways* = has his own ideas as to how things should be done and doesn't change his mind readily. **1986** Pederson et al. *LAGS* = attested by 12/60 interviewees (20%) from E TN and 6/35 (17.1%) from N GA; 18/120 of all LAGS interviewees (15%) attesting term were from Appalachia. **1994** Montgomery *Coll* (known to Cardwell).

set into See **set in 1**.

set-off house *noun* See citations. Same as **car shack**.

1991 Weals *Last Train* 56 The shanties were what Mary called "set-off houses," because they were brought to the site on railroad flatcars and "set-off" with a log crane. *Ibid.* 98 Most of the families lived in what were called "cars" or "set-off houses." . . . Several units could be joined end-to-end to accommodate more people, and they amounted to a primitive version of today's mobile home.

set one's cap for *verb phrase* To seek the attention or reward of, seek to attract (someone) for courtship; to seek such attention.

1924 Vollmer *Sun-Up* 4 I thought Emmy wuz a settin' her cap for Sheriff Weeks. **1959** Hall *Coll* (Gatlinburg TN) She set her cap for him. **1964** Smith et al. *Germans of Valley* 112 Young children expected a visit from the Easter Rabbit on Easter morn, so they "set their caps" or bonnets, in which they expected the rabbit would lay some eggs. The boys placed their caps, and the girls their bonnets, under the kitchen chair or table before they went to bed on Easter Eve. In the morning a cluster of hard-cooked, colored eggs would be found in the bonnets or caps. **1966** West *Dialect Sthn Mts* 34 She's purty as a picher and has sot her cap tell the cows come home. **1972** Hall *Sayings* 47. **1983** Broaddus *Estill Co KY Word List* 55 = said of a girl endeavoring to snare a man. **2008** McKinley *Bear Mt* 42 They knew if a young lady was so thoughtless about the cost of shoe leather, she would be a poor manager of a future household. Granny explained, "A boy wouldn't ever 'set his cap for' a girl like that."

set over See **set across.**

set running See **run a set.**

set store by (also *set a store by*) *verb phrase* To admire, esteem, think much of (someone or something).

1895 Dromgoole *Old Hickory* 32 He set a sight o' store by [the picture], Skinny did. **1931** Combs *Lg Sthn High* 1307 Jude sot a heap o' store by (thought much of) her. **1940** Haun *Hawk's Done* 10 He was tall, and I don't blame Tiny Brock for setting so much store by him. *Ibid.* 28 I told her all about Joe, how he looked and how much he set a store by her, and learned her to call him Daddy.

setter *noun* See citation.

1969 Miller *Raising Tobacco* 29 Yearling boys could carry big buckets of water up from the branch or from the sled or truck, placing them at stations in the patch where smaller boys and girls with smaller buckets could fill up and go behind the *setter*, pouring a dipper of water into the hole. . . . Moving behind the *dropper*, the setter put the plant into the earth by taking the plant by the roots and, using the index and middle fingers, making a hole in the soil and slipping the plant into a standing position.

setting *noun* A clutch (of eggs).

1930 Armstrong *This Day and Time* 76 You take you two settin's o' eggs when you go. **1975** Purkey *Madison Co* 34 They'll loan a body anything from a settin' o' eggs to the plow point. **1984** Gibson *Remembering* 27 Mama had sent me to a neighbor's home to get a setting of eggs. **2005** Williams *Gratitude* 72 You could pull up your apern tail, double it up and use it to pick up a hot pan [and] gether it up at the corners to carry a settin' of eggs.

[DARE *setting* n[1] especially South]

setting chair *noun* An ordinary chair, usually made without nails and especially one comfortable for long-term sitting.

1928 Thornburgh *Americans Forgot* 42 I can't make a rockin' chair in a day, but I can a settin' chair. I do everything but get the wood. **1937** Eaton *Handicrafts* 150–51 There are several kinds of mountain chairs: babies' high chairs and children's high chairs, old folks' rockers, and the type of chair that outnumbers all others, the well-known "settin' chair," made with a curved back for general use in a number of sizes and with slight variation in the pattern. **1975** Chalmers *Better* 15 Uncle Joe would sit topped back against the wall in his straight "settin' chair," and would smoke and listen while his wife talked, joining in, now and then, with reminiscences of his own. **1976** Bullard *Crafts TN Mts* 108 The old mountain "settin' cheer" which he sold by the dozen over a wide area was at the end as it was at the beginning, a nailless, screwless, glueless creation. **2003** Josheff *Craft Traditions* 12 The mule-ear, slat-back "setting" chair represented the simple and rustic nature of all Highland furniture. Chairmakers cut wood, often hickory, cherry, walnut or oak, which was partially seasoned, then worked with the axe, wedge, froe, and drawknife. The chair was assembled without glue or nails, but depended on the shrinkage of the wood for stability. The seat of the chair was woven from cornhusks, hickory bark, oak splits, or rush. **2016** Lundy and Autry *Victuals* 32 One of my favorites of the domestic crafts of the Appalachians—the cane-bottomed "setting" chair . . . is armless and sits lower to the ground than a conventional chair; the design allows someone to sit near the hearth to cook below the level of the smoke.

setting egg *noun* An artificial egg put in the nest of a hen to induce her to lay. See also **China egg**, **cymling B**, **nest egg**.

1986 Pederson et al. *LAGS* (Johnson Co TN, Loudon Co TN).

setting room *noun* The main room of a house, living room.

1934–37 *LAMSAS Appal* (Madison Co NC, Swain Co NC). **1991** Williams *Homeplace* 86 We just called it a room. . . . We used it as a setting room or we used it as a bedroom. We had to use it as a bedroom, and we kept it, you know, just as it is.

setting up (also *sitting up*) *noun* The occasion at which friends and relatives visit the home of a person who is gravely ill or a deceased person to provide steady comfort and help the family attend to that person or to prepare for burial. The gathering, which traditionally continues until the burial, may last from several hours to many days. See also **set up with 2**, **wake**.

1968 *DARE Survey* (Brasstown NC) *sitting up* = when friends and relatives gather together at the place where the body is, usually the night before a funeral. **1975** Gainer *Speech Mtneer* 16 When Uncle Isaac died, they had a big settin' up for him. **1977** Shields *Cades Cove* 42 Wakes, or "sitting up" with the dead as it was known in the cove, were not elaborate events, but solemn occasions. **1978** Hall *Yarns and Tales* 77 = a wake at which relatives and friends sit by or near the coffin, comforting the bereaved and each other, weeping, praying, reminiscing, etc. **1995–98** Montgomery *Coll* = a mountain tradition when the dead [person] was prepared for burial and was part of the funeral wake (Cardwell); (consultants from the Smoky Mountains identify *setting up* and *sitting up* as equally common, but *wake* as a formal term not often used in traditional mountain speech). **2007** McMillon *Notes settin' up* = used by white folks, but I always heard black folks call it a *wake*.

settle

A Variant form *sittle*.

1972 GSMNP-93:1:11 He sittled right here.

B *noun* A wooden bench with a high back, arms, and an enclosed space beneath.

1998 Montgomery *Coll* = a wooden bench with a back, used indoors, as in a church (Ellis).

settlement *noun*

A Variant forms with secondary stress on the last syllable. For similar forms, see **-ment A**.

1895 Edson and Fairchild *TN Mts* 375 *settlemént*. **1899** Fox *Mt Europa* 69 I 'lowed you folks from the settlemints thought hit was mighty scraggy down hyer. **1913** Kephart *Our Sthn High* 224 In mountain dialect such words as settlement, government, studyment (reverie) are accented on the last syllable, or drawled with equal stress throughout. **1931** Combs *Lg Sthn High* 1314 As to stress, or accent, a possible French influence survives in many words. A final syllable is frequently stressed, and we find: "settlement," or "settlemint," "cowardice," "easement," "judgement," or "judgemint," and many others. **1940** Stuart *Trees of Heaven* 291 Let's git our heads togither here and come to some settle-ment. **1942** Hall *Phonetics Smoky Mts* 71 The suffixes -*dent* and -*ment* (except in *independent*) in most instances have secondary stress: *accident*, *confident*, *devilment*, *instrument*, *monument*, *payment*, *settlement*, *testament*, etc. **1962** Wilson *Folkways Mammoth Cave* 9 The secondary accent is really a second primary accent, fully as strong as the supposedly main one. Mammoth Cave people spoke of *settlement* as /SET-tle-MINT/.

B Senses.

1 A small rural community of dispersed homesteads, sometimes informally named (as after an originating or prominent family or individual) and not on the map.

1800 *Globe Creek Church Minutes* 8 bro[the]r Wm Humphries had declared to some of the nabers of good credet that he had Seen a Negroe Man & a White woman together in the Globe settlement. **c1841** Shane (in **1998** Perkins *Border Life* 197) There were not but one or two familis that were not dutch and half-dutch, in tha[t] whole settlement. **1863** *Reese CW Letters* (March 1) I ust to lov to talk with you when I had Bin gon off any whair in the Settlment. **1864** *Chapman CW Letters* (Feb 13) rite me a letter your self and give me all the news and let me now all about what is agoin on in the settelment generaly. **1883** Zeigler and Grosscup *Heart of Alleghanies* 188 Across the Balsam range into Jackson and Swain counties we recognize newer settlements. **1890** Carpenter *Thunderhead Peak* 142 We passed the "Tuckaleech" settlement, consisting of a small store, a church, and two or three houses a half mile apart, and reached Freshour's at four o'clock in the afternoon. **1908** Smith *Reminiscences* 406 There, several miles from anywhere, you will find the cabin of "Black" Bill Walker. Rather we should call it a "settlement," for there are four cabins and a little corn-mill. **1915** Bradley *Hobnobbing* 97 Buckhorn, where we arrived that night, and were ferried across the river, in an old flat-boat, is not a county seat. It is merely a "settlement" that has grown up around a big Presbyterian school. **1931** Greve *Tradition Gatlinburg* 64 Descendants of the Whaleys live in great numbers in the valley, so many of them in the Greenbrier region that that place is often spoken of as the "Whaley Settlement." **1939** Hall *Coll* (Bradley Fork NC) I was there a few years and undertook to build a mill, eleven mile above on the head of Flat Creek, in Bird Settlement. *Ibid.* (Cataloochee NC) My grandfather, Jesse Palmer, was among the first to come to this place and start a settlement. **1950** Miller *Pigeon's Roost* (July 13) Miss Adean Byrd, daughter of Mr. and Mrs. Grove Byrd of Pigeon

Roost and Effel Lee Peterson, son of Mr. and Mrs. Maynaird Peterson of the Bailey settlement section near Poplar, were married on June 23. **1956** Hall *Coll* (Big Creek NC) Neil Phillips lived in the Brown Settlement, known to more people as Brown's Valley. **1957** GSMNP-23:2:10 They was several houses on up around up on Mill Creek and up in there and on up next to Fork of the River back up in there now where the old Carr Settlement [was]. I can tell you every man that entered land in this country. **1973** GSMNP-5:24 It was a good little school. We got along good, and our children and everybody in that settlement would go every Friday to hear them recite their little old speeches. **c1975** Lunsford *It Used to Be* 36 Some of the boys and girls would come together, and some of the boys from over the mountain on the other settlement would come over.

2 See citations.

1911 Shearin *E KY Word-List* 539 = an Eastern Kentucky expression used to designate the more populated district lying in the central part of the state. **2000** Morgan *Mts Remember* 42 It must be ten miles back down to the river valley and the settlements. **2014** *Blind Pig* (Nov 21) Pap uses the word settlement often to describe a more populated area.

settlement road *noun*

1866 Smith *So Called* 127 Leavin my wagin with a widder woman, I took it afoot across the country by a settlement road they called the "cut-off."

settle up *verb phrase* To populate.

1937 Conner *Ms* 128 many year's later the Nation's branch had been settled up. **1939** Hall *Coll* (Sugarlands TN) This country round here where I'm a-living now was just settled up thick. Lots of families lived around here.

set to

A *verb phrase*

1 (+ *verbal noun* or *present participle*) To begin; to cause (someone) to begin. See also **fall to**, **take to 1**.

c1815 (in **2007** Davis *Co Line Baptist* 112) our Charge was for holding generial redemption from hell for giting Drunk and for Seting his Son to fighting. **1904–20** Kephart *Notebooks* 4:856a Don't you set to cryin', honey. **1955** Dykeman *French Broad* 295 When he saw my father, he rode over to the field and they set to talking. **1970** *Burton-Manning Coll*-92 My children all married off and just left me alone, and I just set to writing them songs. **1989** Millner *Letcher* 11 It made me cold. Set my body to shaking. **2004** Adams *Old True Love* 45 "Well, he was a damn good coon dog," which set everybody to laughing including Hackley and Larkin.

2 (also *set up to*, *set up with*) To pay court to (a woman); to keep company.

1845 (in **1956** Eliason *Tarheel Talk* 293) (Yadkin Co NC) Mr Bogle . . . was setting up to Miss Charinten. **1881** Pierson *In the Brush* 8 They never said of a young man, or an old widower, that he was addressing or courting a lady, but, "He is setting to her," a figure of speech derived from bird-hunting with setter-dogs, as I suppose. **1900** Harben *N GA Sketches* 260 Them two has been a-settin' up to each other ever sence they wuz knee-high to a duck. **1911** Shearin *E KY Word-List* 539 *set up* = to call upon a woman in courtship; e.g., "He's a-setting up with Blue Joe's daughter." **1944** Combs *Word-List Sthn High* 19 Mace's Jim sot up with (courted) Nance's Liz two nights hand-goin'. **c1950** Adams *Grandpap* 72 He asked her to set up with him an' she said she would. An' they set up till nearly daylight. **1957** Combs *Lg Sthn High: Word List* 91 *set up* = to keep company with, call on, court. Ex.: "That new feller from over on Bristlebuck's a-settin' up with Cinthy." **1968** Wilson *Folklore Mammoth Cave* 44 = to be one's steady company. **1974** Fink *Bits Mt Speech* 23 Henry's setting up to widow Brown. **1998** Montgomery *Coll*: *set up with* (known to Brown).

B *noun* A confrontation, fight.

1999 Montgomery *Coll* They had a real set to at the barn dance last night (Cardwell).

set to one's feet *verb phrase* Of new shoes: to adjust to a comfortable shape.

1987 Young *Lost Cove* 31 Clacksaddle Smith's new shoes hadn't set to his feet and the agony kept him from caring one way or another.

set up

A *verb phrase* See **set to A2**.

B *adjective phrase* Conceited.

1938 Justus *No-End Hollow* 47 After she hears this, she won't be so set up over Abe's banjo playing.

[OED3 *set-up* (at *set* adj) dialect and colloquial]

set up to See **set to A2**.

set up with

1 See **set to A2**.

2 (usually *sit up with*) *verb phrase* To join (the family of a gravely ill or deceased person) to provide steady comfort and assistance, especially with burial preparations (as in phrases *set up with the dead*, *set up with the sick*). See also **setting up**.

1924 Raine *Saddlebags* 207 I been up the holler, sittin' up all night with Sally Ann's baby. **1937** Haun *Cocke Co* 13–14 When anyone in the district is much sick, a crowd gathers to "set up" with him, cut the wood, and take care of things that need doing around the house. If it is plowing time, they pitch in and do the plowing for him. It is thought necessary for some outsider to stay around and be ready to "carry the word" in case the sick person dies. The sick person, if he thinks he is going to die, from time to time asks those sitting up to sing. He usually calls for a spiritual or a religious song such as Huck's Farewell or Can the Circle be Unbroken? **1944** Williams *Word-List Mts* 30 *set up with* = to keep a wake for a corpse. **1956** Hall *Coll* (Townsend TN) They took care of one another back then. They'd set up all night with the sick. **1959** Hall *Coll* (Mt Sterling NC) Aunt Nancy Harrell lived on Big Creek [and] sat up with the sick, carried something for 'em to eat. **1970** Madden and Jones *Ephraim Bales* 6 I set up with him the night he was laid out. **1974** *Death and Burial* 59–60 Word of a death would spread rapidly in a neighborhood. Often it was not a surprise because it was customary for neighbors to visit and "set up" with the sick and provide help and relief for the immediate family at such times.... The custom of setting up with the corpse still persists, even though often in a modified form. Now the dead may be kept overnight in a country church or at the funeral parlor instead of at the home. Services may be held at either place. Formerly, neighbors and relatives gathered at the home of the dead person the night before burial somewhat in the manner of the Irish wake. Whatever its origin, the practice by this time was an expression of respect for the dead, sympathy for the bereaved, and neighborliness. It was customary to feed the crowd there, just as it was customary to prepare "feasts" for funeral meetings and welcome whoever cared to eat. **1977** Ross *Come Go* 109 When a death occurs in the community there is no duty too urgent to keep neighbors from going to the family and doing everything possible to ease the grief.... A respectable number of friends must be on hand at all times, day and night, to see to the digging of the grave, performing the chores, "setting up" with the dead, a kind of wake. Usually the discussions at the all night wake center around religion and all good points of the deceased. Each neighbor will tell of his dealings with the deceased. Any shortcomings are respectfully not mentioned. **1978** Montgomery *White Pine Coll* VI-4 I can recall that you set up with the deceased all night, if they took them home or at the funeral home either. **1978** Slone *Common Folks* 226 Two or three of the folks were going to stay all night. They would take turns "setting up" with Papa, while he took care of my sister. **1991** Thomas *Sthn Appal* 176 The custom of "sitting up with the sick" was well established. When there was within the community a person recovering from a lingering illness, such as typhoid fever, or terminally ill, as with cancer, neighbors would agree to sit up perhaps one night every week—even two nights a week—for months. In most instances, those volunteers possessed no special skills in looking after their disabled friends. They came to share the long nights with them, having only the light from an old-fashioned kerosene lamp, or the fireplace. **1993** Cunningham *Sthn Talk* 136 = a vigil, especially staying awake all night to minister to a person who is dangerously ill. **1993** Montell *Cumberland Country* 111 In earlier times, as death approached, two or three friends or relatives "set up" all night with the sick person, usually in an adjacent room. In some cases, this was done for the benefit of the sick; more typically, however, it was behavior meant simply to bind members of the community together. During these sessions, cards were played and tall tales and off-color jokes were told. Sometimes people still sit up with the very sick, even in hospitals where they may be compelled to confine their visiting to small lounge areas located near the terminally ill friend or relative. *Ibid.* 113 Once a casket was ready, the body was placed in it and set in the living room or front hall of the house with the lid left open so that everyone present could view the corpse and see what objects (jewelry, pictures, toys) had been placed in the casket for interment with the deceased. Many persons who came to pay their respects to the dead and make condolences to the survivors stayed throughout the afternoon and evening until the body had been interred. This custom was usually referred to as "setting up with the dead," and extended through the night so that family members could retire or console each other privately. Many present-day people consider this a somewhat gruesome practice that was best left to primitive ancestors. **1994** Crissman *Death and Dying* 16 It was nothing short of a crime for the neighbors not to "set up" with someone who was ill or dead. **2010** Heinmiller *Coll* I set up with her three nights before she passed.

several *noun*

A Variant plural form *severals*.

1774 *Dunmore's War* 139 There is Severals of them going on the Expedition.

[SND *several* adj/n; CUD *severals* n pl "several people or things"]

B A good many, quite a few. See also **some several**.

1892 Allen *Cumberland Gap* 241 "Are there many 'coons in this country?" "Several 'coons".... Here, among other discoveries, was a linguistic one—the use of "several" in the sense of a great many, probably an innumerable multitude, as in the case of the 'coons. **1911** Shearin *E KY Word-List* 539 = used only in reference to groups of about one hundred or more, even to thousands. **1913** Kephart *Our Sthn High* 77 "You'll spy, to-morrow, whar several trees has been wind-throwed and busted to kindlin'." I recalled that several in the South, means many—"a good many," as our own tongues phrase it. **1930** Armstrong *This Day and Time* 100 My cherries is a-gittin' ripe. There 'ull be several. The trees is loaded. *Ibid.* 157 I've got several, forty or fifty, I reckon. **1937** Hall *Coll* (Collins Creek NC) [Did you have many blackberries this year?] Yes, they was several of them. *Ibid.* (Sugarlands TN) Back several years ago, about forty or forty-five years ago, when I was married, the way people lived in this country, they had an awful hard time, couldn't hardly get any money. **1952** Wilson *Folk Speech NC* 588 = a great many: "I have several cherries this year." **1957** Combs *Lg Sthn High: Word List* 88 = an indefinite word that may mean hundreds, even thousands. Ex.: "It was a big meetin'; several were there." **1968** Ferrell *Bear Tales* 38 "Several" can mean anything at all, and so is completely confusing. Several may refer to a few, giving the word its ordinary meaning. Or a mountain man may say he has collected "several" lizards for fish bait, and the count total almost seven hundred by kerosene lantern some hours later. How do I know that "several" referred to over six hundred lizards? Because I was there when it happened and I helped Jesse to count them! **1971** *AOHP/ALC-4* You might remember Warren E. Bailey, a preacher. He went to college and made a teacher. He taught school a long time, several years. **1974** *GSMNP-62:8* It was several of them, you know ... I guess forty or fifty. **2003** LaLone et al. *Farming Life* 224 Then later on, we rented several acres of pasture—oh, I don't know, 200–300 I guess.

[OED3 *several* adj 4b "a good many" obsolete →1753; DARE *several* C especially Appalachians, Ozarks]

severe *adjective*

1 Considerable, vigorous.

1913 Kephart *Our Sthn High* 36 As one of my neighbors put it: "Thar, I've cl'ared me a patch and grubbed hit out—now I can raise me two or three severe craps!"

2 See citation.

1919 Combs *Word-List South* 35 = difficult, hard. "Hit's a severe walk up that 'ere creek." Letcher Co [KY].

3 Fierce.

1913 Kephart *Our Sthn High* 81 No hound'll raelly [sic] fight a bear—hit takes a big severe dog to [do that]. **1939** Hall *Coll* (Sugarlands TN) We had two pretty severe dogs, Plott hounds. **1974** Fink *Bits Mt Speech* 23 He's a terrible *severe* dog.

severely *adverb* Thoroughly.

1886 Smith *Sthn Dialect* 349 I was thankful to hear of her son speaking of an Indian burying ground that was "kivered *severely*" with stones, but from the old woman I got little in the way of dialect, and less of tradition—owing to her loss of memory.

shab bean *noun* See citations. See also **fodder(ed) bean, leather britches, shuck bean.**

1982 *Smokies Heritage* 134 Maybe a string of shab (leather britches) beans, ready to be hulled out in the pots. **1990** Aiken *Stories* 95 Fodder Beans, Shab Beans, Shuck Beans, Leather Britches: these were some of the names for dried beans. **2004** Myers and Boyer *Walker Sisters* 40 Dried beans were called "shab" or fodder beans. They were dried by the sun, put in a cloth sack, and hung on a wall inside the house.

shack *verb* To live by oneself, especially in a remote or primitive area.

1997 Montgomery *Coll* (known to Adams, Bush, Ledford, Norris, Oliver, Weaver); He was shacking way back up in the hills (Cardwell).

shackle along (also *shackle around*) *verb phrase* To shuffle, walk aimlessly.

1913 Kephart *Our Sthn High* 203 "Me? I'm jes' shacklin' around." . . . "shacklin' around" pictures a shackly, loose-jointed way of walking, expressive of the idle vagabond. **1917** Kephart *Word-List* 417 *shackle along* = to shuffle, as if shackled. "Just *shacklin'* along." **1994–97** Montgomery *Coll*: *shackle along* (known to Adams, Brown, Cardwell, Jones, Norris, Oliver).

shackledy (also *shackley, shackling, shackly*) *adjective* Shaky, rickety, in poor condition, uncertain; hence noun = a situation in such a state.

1863 (in **1938** Taliaferro *Carolina Humor* 74) I tried keepin' Bible laws a spell while I was in Passen Beller's church, and made a ding shacklin out of it, certin. **1913** Kephart *Our Sthn High* 29 Here is a land of lumber wagons, and saddle-bags, and shackly little sleds that are dragged over the bare ground by harnessed steers. **1915** Dingus *Word-List VA* 190 *shackelty* = loosely held together, run down: "Uncle Wesley's shackelty old mill." **1938** Justus *No-End Hollow* 113 The whole thing was getting shackly. **1939** Hall *Coll* (Gatlinburg TN) They never did get any more trace [of the person who did it]. Their proof was so shackledy. *Ibid.* (White Oak NC) Anything loose or tore up is shackly. **1961** Seeman *Arms of Mt* 122 I heard a scraping sound outside. . . . His old mare was dragging a shackly land sled. **1968–69** *DARE Survey* (London KY) *shacklety* = something that looks like it might collapse any minute; (Hillsville VA) *shacklety* = weak or unsteady. **1982** Powers and Hannah *Cataloochee* 381 = loose-sounding: "That's all shackley, must be a punkin' ball loose in your gun or your gun part's loose." **1989** Landry *Smoky Mt Interviews* 181 The mailbox was awful shackledy. **1994–95** Montgomery *Coll* (known to Adams, Bush, Jones, Ledford, Norris, Weaver); The weather is shackledy, it's going to be a shackledy day; That chair is too shackling to sit in (Cardwell). **2000** Morgan *Mts Remember* 4 I knocked most of it down with an ax, it was so shackly.

[OED3 *shackly* adj U.S. and dialect; Web3 *shackly* adj 1 "rickety, ramshackle; loose-jointed and shambling" probably from English dialect *shackle* "to shake, rattle" chiefly dialect]

shackley, shackling, shackly See **shackledy.**

shackling mad *adjective phrase* See citation.

1960 Westover *Highland Lg* 21 = [has one's] hackles raised.

shadblow (also *shadbush*) *noun* Same as **service B.**

1941 Walker *Story of Mt* 60 Among the early flowering shrubs which may attain the stature of a tree in some specimens, leading the early procession of wild flowers forth in their adventure in sunshine and cool spring nights, is serviceberry, sometimes called shadbush and Juneberry. **1984** *Asheville Citizen-Times* (April 5) There are many names for this common tree: serviceberry, sarvisberry, servicetree, shadbush, shadblow, sugarpear and Juneberry.

shadder *noun* A shadow.

1867 Harris *Sut Lovingood* 68 She out-run her shadder thuty yards in cumin half a mile. **1939** Burnett *Gap o' Mountains* 11 In the shadder of these hyar hills we air as free as the eagle that nestes in yan furder mountain. **1941** Stuart *Men of Mts* 76 The shadders are creepin' upon us, Shan. **1963** Williams *Metaphor* 53 If she is unusually thin, she is not only "as pore as a snake" but "has to stand twicet to make her shadder."

shader hat *noun* A hat with a broad rim to shade the head from sunlight.

1999 Montgomery *File* (known to 85-year-old man, Greenbrier TN).

shadow soup *noun* Soup with few ingredients but water. See citation.

1997 Montgomery *Coll* = soup with impoverished ingredients; literally, water over which a chicken's shadow has passed (Hooper).

shaft *noun* Variant plural forms *shaves, shavs.*

1963 Watkins and Watkins *Yesterday* 183 The shaves [of a buggy] came loose, and the lines wrapped around Henry's ankle. **1983** Broaddus *Estill Co KY Word List* 55 *shavs* = shafts.

[DARE *shaves* (at *shaft* n 2) chiefly South, South Midland]

shag *noun* See citation.

c1982 Young *Colloquial Appal* 19 = [a] sip, small amount.

shagnasty *noun*

1 An unkempt, disorderly, or disagreeable person.

c1940 Aswell *Glossary TN Idiom* 16 = a foul-mouthed fellow. **1972** Cooper *NC Mt Folklore* 95 = a low bred person. **c1982** Young *Colloquial Appal* 19 = rascal. **1996–97** Montgomery Coll (known to Brown, Bush), = an unkempt, disorderly person (Cardwell). **2002** Myers *Best Yet Stories* 80 = an ill bred person. [**2015** *Blind Pig* (June 10) You can put it any way you want, but that old fellow is just flat-out shagnasty ugly.]

2 A tantrum, fit of anger.

1997 Montgomery Coll = a fit of anger, as "She could throw a shagnasty" (Norris).

[perhaps blend of *shag(gy)* + *nasty*]

shake

A *verb* Principal parts.

1 Variant past-tense form *shuck*.

1867 Harris *Sut Lovingood* 97d [sic] [I] shuck hit up good, an jist drenched the durned big dromedary hoss with the last spoonful. **1942** Hall *Phonetics Smoky Mts* 37. **1964** Roberts *Hell-Fer-Sartin* 67 She clumb it and shuck the rotten pears off of it. **1973** GSMNP-87:1:11 Yeah, it shuck the whole house.

2 Variant past-participle form *shuck*.

1913 Kephart *Our Sthn High* 80 You'll get some of that meanness shuck outen you. **1982** Slone *How We Talked* 53 No man would ever break a promise after he had "shuck hands on it." **1984** GSMNP-153 The wind had blowed hard that night and had shuck the burrs out of the trees.

B *noun*

1 A tapered piece of split timber used to shingle a roof. See also **board 1**, **roof board**.

1881 Pierson *In the Brush* 51 The roof was made of "shakes"—pieces of timber rived out very much in the form of staves, but not shaved at all. These were laid upon the roof like shingles, except that they were not nailed on, but "weighted on"—kept in their places by small timbers laid across each row of "shakes" over the entire roof. These timbers were kept in their places by shorter ones placed between them. **1937** Eaton *Handicrafts* 41 In the spring of 1935 a short way off a modern highway in Tennessee settlers on subsistence homesteads were discovered riving boards by hand for long shingles or "shakes" as they are called . . . for the roofs of their houses just as had been done in the Highland country since the earliest settlers came. **1954** Arnow *Dollmaker* 115 If'n a maul ain't balanced just right it'll make splitten out chunks for them shakes twict as hard. **1963** Glassie *Appal Log Cabin* 9 The roof [of a log cabin] was generally lightly framed and covered with "shakes" which are long shingles split out of a short log. **1966** Frome *Strangers* 75 To split rails, shingles, and shakes when the moon was dark . . . prevented warping or cracking. **1995** Trout *Historic Buildings* 40 Sometimes, however, a farmer preferred "shakes," long tapered shingles usually made of oak.

[OED3 *shake* n[1] 10b chiefly U.S.]

2 See citation. See also **windshake**.

1964 Clarkson *Lumbering in WV* 370 = a crack in timber or lumber. Usually due to wind.

3 See citation.

1979 *Gamecock* 169 An old [gamecock] was called "a shake." If he weighed over five pound and a half, he was a shake.

shake a foot *verb phrase* To get up and move, as to dance. [Editor's note: The phrase *shake a leg* is widespread in the US.]

1924 Greer-Petrie *Angeline Gits Eyeful* 15 When the music started, she wuz the fust one on the floor to shake a foot.

shake-down *noun*

1 A makeshift, rudimentary dwelling.

1889 *Hogs* By this time we were close to Timberlake's shake-down, in fact almost in front of the primitive log shanty where he made his home.

2 See citation.

1957 Combs *Lg Sthn High: Word List* 88 = a rough, boxed-in shelf, or trough in which the children sleep when company is present, or when there are not enough "store beds" to go around.

shake rag *noun* See citation.

c1982 Young *Colloquial Appal* 19 = [a] dust cloth.

shake the cat See **cat shaking.**

shake the family tree *verb phrase* See citation.

2013 McMahan *Lem Ownby* 17 It has been said that when a couple planned to marry, their parents would start "shaking the family tree" to ensure the relationship was far enough removed so as to be of no consequence.

shake-up bed *noun* See citation. See also **made-down bed**, **shake-down 2.**

1924 Raine *Saddlebags* 74 They divide up the bedding and make shake-up beds upon the floor every night.

shaking palsy *noun* See citation.

1990 Cavender *Folk Medical Lex* 31 = Parkinson's disease.

shallow *adjective*

A Variant form *shaller*.

[See **1895** in **B.**] **1942** Hall *Phonetics Smoky Mts* 80. **2005** Williams *Gratitude* 18 Down in the woods b'low the house, he'd dug out a deep hole in the ground, squared off like a shaller grave.

B Of musical pitch: high.

1895 Edson and Fairchild *TN Mts* 374 "She's started it too shaller"—of a tune pitched too high. **1924** Raine *Saddlebags* 105 When a girl pitched a tune too high, an observer . . . remarked, "She started it too shallow."

shame brier *noun* The sensitive plant (*Mimosa* spp), a vine with a prickly stem and leaves that close when touched, as if in shame. See also **sensitive brier**.

1905 Miles *Spirit of Mts* 39 The little sensitive-plant caught at my skirt now and again and dropped its leaves instantly, bearing erect only its pretty blossoms—balls of rosy fluff dusted over with gold. This plant is here known as shame-brier or stingy-vine; both names are highly suggestive of its sudden drooping or closing and drawing back. **1917** Kephart *Word-List* 417 = sensitive plant. **1995** Montgomery *Coll* (known to Norris, but not to other consultants from the Smoky Mountains).

shamed See **ashamed**.

shammick (also *shammick off, shammock, shammuck along, shammuck around, shummick*) *verb, verb phrase* [accent sometimes on the second syllable] To amble about slowly, unsteadily, or indirectly; to lounge about, idle around.

1913 Kephart *Our Sthn High* 203 To "shummick" (also "shammick") is to shuffle about, idly nosing into things, as a bear does when there is nothing serious in view. **1917** Kephart *Word-List* 417 *shammick* = to lounge about idly. **1925** Dargan *Highland Annals* 76 I knowed that fox 'ud take him to Katter Knob, so I let him go on by hissef an' I shammucked along toward home. **1934–37** *LAMSAS Appal* (Swain Co NC) *shammuck around*. **1944** Wilson *Word-List* 49 *shammock* = to walk in a slouchy, unsteady manner. **1977** Howard *Fifty Years* 1 *shammick* = move slowly. "The man shammicked off down the road." **1994–95** Montgomery *Coll*: *shammuck* (known to Adams); I think I'll just go shammucking along (Cardwell).

[OED3 *shammock* v 1 "to walk with a shambling or unsteady gait" dialect; EDD *shammock* v mEngl, sEngl; Web3 *shammock* v chiefly dialect, perhaps alteration of *shamble*; DARE *shammock* v chiefly southern Appalachians]

shammick off, shammock, shammuck along, shammuck around See **shammick**.

shamp *verb* See 1913 citation.

1913 Kephart *Our Sthn High* 294 To shamp means to shingle or trim one's hair. [**1992** Montgomery *Coll* (unknown to consultants from the Smoky Mountains).]

Shanghai *noun* A now-extinct New Year's Day parading custom of uncertain antecedence in Virginia and West Virginia communities of German heritage; also verbal noun *Shanghai-ing*. See citations.

1936 Hench *Gleanings* 104 Hundreds of people from this and adjoining states attended the Shanghai parade here this afternoon. Shanghai is an old Lewisburg [WV] custom that was conceived by the pioneers of Greenbrier County in celebration of the New Year. . . . The grand prize went to Tom Reynolds, who drove an ox team attached to a pioneer wagon. Other entries winning prizes represented periods of local history. **1964** Smith et al. *Germans of Valley* 122 (DARE) In the past, there was a practice in several areas of the Valley called shanghai-ing, which was similar to belsnickeling. Although this custom is remembered by older residents in many towns and villages, it was actually engaged in by relatively few, but some can be found in Augusta and Highland Counties in Virginia and in Pendleton County, West Virginia, who actually took part in this activity. Shanghai-ing took place in the daylight hours during the same season when people went belsnickeling. Grown-up males dressed in clown-like disguises, with blackened or masked faces, and rode on horses or mules. Some rode in wagons in a group. They rode in single file, eight or more horses in a shanghai group. The merrymakers seldom visited at homes, instead they rode by as a parade, making noise by blowing a horn or shouting to attract attention. presented periods of local history. **1995** Suter *Shenandoah Folklife* 31 The words *belsnickel* and *kriskringle* are derived from German: *Belsnickel* contains the words *Pelz* (fur) as well as Saint Nicholaus (Santa Claus). . . . Santa Claus, *Belsnickel* and Kriskringle are thus essentially the forerunners of our present-day Christmas customs. **2006** *Encycl Appalachia* 851 In a few places in Appalachia, such as Lewisburg, West Virginia, communities still organize a Shanghai parade on New Year's Day, marching through town banging on pots and pans or using a variety of noisemakers and cross-dressing or wearing other masquerades in a traditional practice of inverting the normal social order. Although the origin of the name *Shanghai* is unclear, the traditions of noisemaking and guising harken back to the British Isles and Europe. **2012** Milnes *Signs Cures Witchery* We'd take some candy along and throw that on the floor, and the kids would be down grabbing that candy, and we had a switch, we would switch their fingers, and we'd go in daylight, and we'd call that Shanghai-ing.

shank it *verb phrase* To walk, go on foot. See also **shank's mare**.

1991 Still *Wolfpen Notebooks* 90 I had to shank it eight miles with the weather bumping zero.

shank of the afternoon/day/evening *noun phrase* The period late in or toward the close of the day.

1911 Shearin *E KY Word-List* 539 *shank of the afternoon* = latter part of the afternoon. **1940** Haun *Hawk's Done* 119 Along in the shank of the evening them little white sores broke out in her throat. **1952** Wilson *Folk Speech NC* 588 *shank of the evening* = late afternoon, early evening. **1995** Montgomery *Coll* It was along about the shank of the day when he left (Cardwell). **2007** McMillon *Notes*: *shank of the evening* = dusk. **2009** Benfield *Mt Born* 160–61 = Not the nighttime. This phrase is sometimes uttered as "on up in the shank of the evening," which meant just a tad on up the shank of time. The shank of a four-legged animal is the part from ankle to knee.

[OED3 *shank* n 9 "the latter end or part of anything" dialect and U.S.]

shank's horse See **shank's mare**.

shank's mare (also *shank's horse, shank's pony*) *noun* In phrases *go (by) shank's mare, ride shank's mare*, etc. = to walk, travel on one's own legs. See also **shank it**.

1927 Woofter *Dialect from WV* 364 *ride shank's horse* = to walk. "How are you going?" "Oh, I will ride shank's horse." **1952** Huffman *Mt Memories* 34 The only other way to get about was by what was called "shanks mare," which was by walking. [That] was often the safest because a journey often meant going uphill, downhill, and even over very steep mountains. **1954** Blackhurst *Riders of Flood* 16 There ain't no trains up the river. You ride shank's mare. **1967** *DARE Survey* (Maryville TN) *ride shank's mare* = go on foot. **1991** Still *Wolfpen Notebooks* 59 Them days, if you wanted to go somewhere and you had no horse, you went shank's-mare. **1992** Bush *Dorie* 154 Fred and Pa showed no interest in the car and still went by Shank's Mare (walking) or in the jolt wagon. **1994** Montgomery *Coll: go by shank's mare* (known to Shields). **2000** Miller *Looneyville* 66 *shanks pony* = going to or from some place on foot. "I tuk shanks pony to the meetin this mornin." **2005** Williams *Gratitude* 522 = when you walked somewhere, you *rode shank's mare*.

shank's pony See **shank's mare**.

shape note (also *shaped note*) *noun* A distinctive symbol for each of a four- or seven-noted musical scale, where the head of each note has the shape of a circle, square, diamond, etc. (rather than a position on the horizontal staff) to facilitate sight reading. Same as **buckwheat note**, **patent note**. See also **old harp**, **sacred harp**, **singing school**.

1931 Goodrich *Mt Homespun* 52 The singers had challenged the neighboring districts to bring along their shaped-note songbooks and sing them down if they could. **1942** Robertson *Red Hills* 291 We still sing from music books printed with shaped notes instead of round notes—with shaped diamonds, circles, squares, and triangles as William & Smith devised them at Philadelphia in 1798. **1952** Giles *40 Acres* 61 [Shape-note singing] must actually be very simple, because the least young'un on the ridge can read music. I have seen Hazel Gile's least one, who is barely four years old, pick up his father's hymnbook, clear his throat, sound off with a very treble "mi, mi, mi," and then, leading perfect time with his baton hand, launch into "Lead Me Home" with complete confidence. He can't read the words yet, but he sure can read the music. **1978** Horn *New Harp of Columbia* viii The first of these changes was shaped notes (sometimes called character notes, buckwheat notes, or patent notes), one shape for each syllable of the solminization used. **1992** Sabol *Sacred Harp* 1 Sacred Harp music is written in "shape notes," which resemble standard round notes in every respect except that the head of each note has one of the four shapes to indicate its interval from the key (tonic) pitch. This system was based on the practice originating in Elizabethan England of singing the seven notes of an octave with four-syllable solminization. The major scale is sung as *fa, sol, la, fa, sol, la, me, fa*, while the minor scale (1 1/2 whole notes down from the major scale) is sung as *la, me, fa, sol, la, fa, sol, la* . . . The four-shape system (*fa* = triangle, *sol* = oval, *la* = square, and *me* = diamond) was invented around 1800 in the Northeastern U.S., and it enabled many untrained singers of the day to sight-read music without having to understand key signatures. Shape-note music immediately became popular, and it strongly stimulated the expansion of the singing-school movement, which had arisen in New England around 1720 and in which many Americans were taught to sing by itinerant singing masters. **1995** Williams *Smoky Mts Folklife* 46 Singing schools that used the shaped-note books persisted into the twentieth century in many rural areas of the South, including the Great Smoky Mountains region. A singing master would make a circuit through rural communities during the summer. The singing schools in this region typically lasted two weeks, and frequently the singing master's circuit would culminate in an all-day singing in the early fall. . . . Shape-note singing also lives on in the memory of many older residents of the Great Smoky Mountains who do not participate in local singings. These people learned to read music in singing schools held periodically in their communities. It is not uncommon to find older people who will tell you that they can read shaped notes but not round ones. **2009** *TN Encycl* Shape-note singing, a predominantly rural, Protestant, Anglo-American music tradition, involves singing from hymnals or "tunebooks" having shaped notes (aka "character notes," "buckwheat notes," or "patent notes") as opposed to the standard "round notes." *Ibid.* The original four-shape-note and later seven-shape-note books which were developed for unsophisticated worshippers used a system of shapes for musical notation with a leader lining out the notation for a song and the participants singing the notation through before beginning the words. *Ibid.* In a further effort to help students learn to read "by note," a system of four shaped notes—Fa, Sol, La, and Mi—was invented in the early nineteenth century to be used with the four-syllable, "fasola" solminization system. **2014** Montgomery *Doctrine* 177–78 = a musical notation system where each note on the scale is printed by a specific shape. Usually the note "Do" is represented with a triangle, "Re" by a half-circle, "Mi" by a diamond, "Fa" by a half-triangle, "So" by a circle, "La" by a square, and "Ti" by an inverted triangle. Shape notes date from late 18th century America. . . . By the middle of the 19th century the "fa so la" system of four syllables had acquired a major rival, namely the seven-syllable "do ra mi" system.

shares See **on shares**.

sharp as a brier See **brier 3**.

sharpen one's hoe *verb phrase* See citation.

1957 Combs *Lg Sthn High: Word List* 88 = to whip, thrash. The origin of the figure is in the cornfield, where a boy sometimes lags behind as he hoes corn, complaining that he has a dull hoe. His father "sharpens the hoe" for him.

sharp time *adverb phrase* Punctually.

1885 Murfree *Prophet* 152 I waited fur Sol an' the corn right sharp time Wednesday morning.

sharp up *verb phrase* To sharpen (the blade of a tool).

1963 Medford *Mt People* 67 "Git out the cradles, boys, and sharp up the blades," he is telling Elihu and Rastus, between bites at the breakfast table. **1997** Montgomery *Coll* (known to Adams, Bush, Ellis, Ledford).

[cf SND *shairp* v "to sharpen"]

shave *verb* To cut down (a weed or brush).

1956 Hall *Coll* (White Oak NC) My father was a bush-cutter. If he found a weed growing anywhere on his farm, he'd shave it.

shaver See **little shaver.**

shaves, shavs See **shaft.**

Shawnee See **Shawnee haw, Shawnee lettuce.**

Shawnee haw (also *Shawnee*) *noun*

A Variant forms *shiney haw* [see **1970** in **B**], *shiny haw* [see **1976** in **B**], *shonny haw* [see **2001** in **B**], *sine* [see **1970** in **B**].

B A hawthorn tree (*Viburnum nudum/rufidulum*), from whose bark is made a medicinal tea.

1860 Curtis *Plants NC* 90 Possum haw . . . The fruit is a deep blue. In the Mountains I have heard this called Shawnee Haw. **1970** Stubbs *Mountain-Wise* (Feb–March) 8 A mild laxative can be made from boiling down the bark of a small mountain tree called "Sine," "Shiney haw," or "Southern black haw" (Viburnum rufidulum). **1976** Wigginton *Stanley Hicks* 356 We gathered shiny haw in the summer. These people that made medicine seed that. **1977** Hamilton *Mt Memories* 65 Sometimes, a number of us girls and boys would wade up Norman Creek looking for "Shiny haws" on bushes hanging over the creek. **1982** Ginns *Snowbird Gravy* 57 When students misbehaved back then they whipped 'em. Whipped 'em with what they called a "shonny haw." That was just a long switch with no limbs off of it or anything—just a long switch. **1985** *Schools and Pastimes* 44 [The schoolteacher] walked up Clear Creek and across Little Buck Hill, stopping to select and cut a half dozen hickory and shawnee haw switches about six feet in length on the way. **2001** Joslin *Appal Bounty* 136 The story of witherod tells of the days when the forest served as the people's pharmacy. Known as shonny haw, the plant's bark, when brewed into a tea, provided the settlers with a cure for fevers and the colic. Sold to herb houses, the plant gave the mountain folks a source of much-needed cash.

Shawnee lettuce (also *Shawnee, shonny*) *noun* See citation.

1937 Hyatt *Kiverlid* 79 We picked wild mustard an' Shawnee an' Injun collards, polk, blue-thistle . . . an' I don't know what all. **1983** Broaddus *Estill Co KY Word List* 55 *shonny* = a wild green. **1991** Still *Wolfpen Notebooks* 77 What I look forward to in the spring hain't garden sass. Hit's wild greens. They grow where God planted them. What you want to look for is plaintain [sic] . . . Shawnee [etc] . . . And don't spare the seasoning. **1997** Hufford *Stalking* In every season the forest supports the round, with spring greens (poke, dock, "crow's feet," "woolly britches," cresses, "Shawnee lettuce," dandelions, wild mustard and a number of others), berries ("sarvice" berries, wineberries, blackberries, raspberries, "sheep tits," huckleberries, and mulberries), and the nuts and fruits of fall (hazelnuts, acorns, chinquapins, beechnuts, butternut, walnut, persimmons, paw-paws, and bitternut, pignut, and mockernut hickory). There are mushrooms, the spring morels called "molly moochers," the red ones of autumn that Elsie Rich, of Jarrold's Valley, called "bull's tongue," and the "little white ones" that remind Mary Allen of choice seafood. "You cut them in two, they're kind of like a scallop," she said, "and roll them in flour and fry them, they're good."

she *noun* A female animal, especially a bear. See also **she-bear.**

1878 Coale *Wilburn Waters* 64 The sign having indicated to his unerring judgment, or rather instinct in such matters, that there were four bears in company—an "old she" and three half-grown cubs. **1927** Mason *Lure of Smokies* 220 I crawled inter a b'ar's trail onct an' shot an old she. **1939** Hall *Coll* (Cataloochee Creek NC) They was two old she's and three yearlin's [= bears].

sheaf cap See **cap A3.**

she-balsam *noun* The Fraser fir (*Abies fraseri*). Same as **balsam 1.**

1908 Britton *N Amer Trees* 76 (*DARE*) This southern fir, called She balsam fir . . . occurs in the higher mountains of Virginia and West Virginia to North Carolina and Tennessee, where it sometimes forms forests, and reaches a maximum height of 25 meters. **1937** Thornburgh *Great Smoky Mts* 28 My mountain guide calls the red spruce "he-balsam" and the Fraser fir is a "she-balsam." **1943** Peattie *Men Mt Trees* 161 In the trunks of the fir under the bark, there are often big rosin blisters filled with a clear liquid (the balsam of commerce) which the mountain folk have whimsically compared to milk. So they name this the "she-balsam." **1948** Baldwin *Big Trees* 173 This tree is called by the mountain people "she" balsam because they gather the "milk" or sap from the blisters found on the smooth trunks of these trees and use it for medicine or sell it commercially, it being the balsam of commerce. **1968** Connelly *Discover Appal* 165 Several northern evergreens are common in this atmosphere. The red spruce and the Fraser fir are the most common. With its dark, four-cornered needles and reddish cones, the red spruce is usually found growing side by side with the Fraser fir. To distinguish between the two species, mountaineers called the Fraser fir the "she balsam" because the large blisters of resin on its trunk resembled milk-filled breasts. The red spruce they called the "he balsam."

she-bear *noun* An adult female bear. See also **she.**

1913 Kephart *Our Sthn High* 80 You'll git some o' that meanness shuck outen you if you tackle an old she-bear to-morrow! **1956** Hall *Coll* (Jones Cove TN) Then he heared a cub bear go to bawlin'. Then he saw the old she bear come runnin' out of the laurel. And Styles throwed the gun down and the old she bear run after him.

she-boilers *noun* See citation.

1964 Clarkson *Lumbering in WV* 370 *she boilers* = women cooks.

shed log *noun* See citations.

1977 Adams *Remembering* 97 Two log pens were built and "shed" logs were placed on top of them. **1997** Montgomery *Coll* (known to Cardwell), = a roof log across both pens [of a house] to stabilize, connect, and be an anchor for the roof (Adams).

shed of, shet of See **shut B.**

sheep *noun* Variant plural form *sheeps*.

1831 McLean *Diary* 1 a Lamb [was] added to our flock of sheeps. **1964** Roberts *Hell-Fer-Sartin* 111 About an hour or two atter dark they come in cattle in that house and all around, and sheeps and cats. **1973** GSMNP-80:11 That big old bear had one of pap's little sheeps behind a big log, and it had eaten that little sheep, had it killed and was eating on it. *Ibid*. 12 He said that was lamb tongue and them sheeps would just eat that a sight in the world.

sheepball tea (also *sheep bullet tea, sheep dip, sheep dung tea, sheep nannie/nanny tea, sheep pearl tea, sheep shit tea, sheep tea*) *noun* A medicinal tea drunk to treat measles, made by boiling sheep dung in water. Same as **nannie tea**.

c1945 Haun *Hawk's Done* 310 I give Jamie sheepball tea to make the measles break out when he was two year old. **1957** Broaddus *Vocab Estill Co KY* 67 *sheep tea* = a medicine made by boiling sheep manure in water . . . to make measles break out when they otherwise won't. **1976** GSMNP-114:18 Dad said he wouldn't take that sheep tea either, but he did . . . He said that old aunt said them measles broke out. He just felt like a new man. **c1984** Dennis *Smoky Mt Heritage* 7 [For] Measles [take]: Whiskey and boiling water, or sheep dung tea. **1985** Irwin *Alex Stewart* 145 [Speaker A:] They was all kinds of sheep manure there and we would go there and dip that up and boil it and make a tea that was awful good to break out the measles. Sheep shit tea, they called it." [Speaker B:] Did you put anything else in it? [Speaker A:] No, that was all. Just boil them little sheep balls in water, strain it and drink it. Law, my mother poured, I guess, a pint down me one time." **1995** Montgomery *Coll*: *sheep bullet tea* (known to Cardwell); *sheep shit tea* (known to Shields). **1996** Cavender *Bold Hives* 20 "Sheep dip" or "sheep nannie" (dung) tea, also used in the Appalachian South to break out measles, was used in North Carolina . . . for hiving. **2003** Cavender *Folk Medicine* 119–20 Sweating was thought necessary to prevent measles from "turning" or "burning" inward, a situation believed to result in severe debilitation or death. The notion held by some that "any ol' hot tea will do" is illustrated by the use of sheep nannie tea (also called "sheep pearl," "sheep pill," "sheep shit," "sheep bullet," or "sheep dip" tea), which is documented in sources almost as much as botanical tea. A little honey was added to make it more palatable. **2007** Milnes *Signs Cures Witches* 97 The folk belief is that measles first break out on the inside of your body and "sheep nanny tea" will cause them to break out on the outside, the important first step toward recovery. . . . I had big measles. My mother was awful finicky about that stuff. Uncle Steve said—Pop had sheep—to go up and get some of those fresh sheep pills and make a tea out of it and give it to me. I was just a kid and had them big measles and they went back in on me.

sheep bullet tea, sheep dip, sheep dung tea See **sheepball tea**.

sheepie *interjection* Come! (used as a call to sheep). See also **co-sheep**.

1934–37 *LAMSAS Appal* (Madison Co NC, Swain Co NC). **1949** Kurath *Word Geog East US* 30 *Sheep!, sheepie!* . . . is the regular Midland call to sheep. In the Appalachians south of the Kanawha the Virginia Piedmont call *co-sheep!* now competes with the Midland call. **1986** Pederson et al. *LAGS* = attested by 9/60 interviewees (15%) from E TN; 9/17 of all LAGS interviewees (52.9%) attesting term were from E TN.

[DARE *sheepie* exclam scattered, but chiefly Midland]

sheep-i-nan *interjection* Come! (used as a call to sheep). See also **co-sheep**.

1921 Kirkland *Mt Music* When the sheep come scuttling and scurrying with sharp, hurried bleating across a pasture sown [sic] with boulders gray and shaggy as themselves, the cry that brings them to the salting is "sep-i-nan [sic], sheep-i-nan."

sheep-killing dog *noun* One who behaves in a shameful, reprehensible, or insensible manner.

1863 Wilson *Confederate Private* 3 (Feb 7) it is that that they war kild or took up with some sheep killing dog. **1904–20** Kephart *Notebooks* 4:785 Thar sot the old womern a-readin' Moody's books, and sayin', and tellin' Bob how he'd orter live. Bob sot thar pale as a corpse—it cut him to the gizzard—and soon he went upstairs lookin' like a sheep-killin' dog. **c1950** Haun *When the Wind* 4 [He] hung his head down like a sheep killing dog. **c1960** Wilson *Coll* = a person with low habits. **1989** Giardina *Storming Heaven* 138 I started to protest but Ben was up as well, he had their hats. They were both grinning like sheep-killing dogs.

sheep leg *noun* See citation.

1936 Farr *Folk Speech Mid TN* 276 = an old pistol: "He gave away his sheep leg."

[from its shape]

sheep meat *noun* Mutton.

1973 GSMNP-80:12 Law, yeah, [we'd] fatten a sheep and kill it. We kept sheep meat all the time to eat.

sheep mint *noun* A calamint.

1970 Clark *NC Beliefs* 27 Jimson weed and sheep mint, cooked with wax, was used as a remedy for hemorrhoids.

[DARE *sheep mint* n especially southern Appalachians]

sheep mustard *noun* See citation.

1983 Broaddus *Estill Co KY Word List* 55 = a wild green.

sheep nannie tea See **sheepball tea**.

sheep nanny See **nannie**.

sheep pearl tea See **sheepball tea**.

sheep pill *noun* A pellet of sheep dung. Also called **measle drop**. See also **nannie, pill, sheepball tea**.

1971 AOHP/ALC-139 [I'd] take the measle drop. Why they'd give me sheep pills. They said it was a sure thing. **1984** Burns *Cold Sassy* 66 He and I had us a great manure war then, throwing dried cow cushions and sheep pills and horse biscuits at each other and dying laughing.

sheep's eyes *noun* Apparently the bubbles that form on the surface of a liquid that are comparable in size to the eyes of a sheep and that indicate that the liquid is at a boil.

1941 Still *Stir-Off* 6 Stir till it 'gins making sheep's eyes, and mind not to over-bile.

sheep shit tea See **sheepball tea.**

sheep's leg *noun* An edible wild green.

1979 Slone *My Heart* 70 Then there were wild greens or "salet." There are many different kinds; sometimes the same plant was known by a different name by different people. "Plantin" is the one used most, a small thick-leafed green with a very distinct flavor, a little like cabbage. Then for cooking there was "sheep's leg," "groundhog ear," and "speckled dock."

sheep sorrel *noun* The wood sorrel (*Oxalis* spp), which has medicinal uses. See also **alleluia, mountain shamrock, wood shamrock.**

c1984 Dennis *Smoky Mt Heritage* 7 There were individuals who spent a lifetime searching for the natural treatment and cure for various ailments. These folks were called "Yarb Doctors." The "Yarb Doctors" would search for sheep sorrel, or Indian turnips, ginseng, sassafras and many other plants that had medicinal properties. **1985** Wear *Lost Communities* 17 Mother could make a salve out of a weed she called "sheep sorrell."

sheep's tongue *noun* The evening primrose plant (*Oenothera biennis*), the leaves of which are an edible green. Also called **freckle face, king cure all, tongue 1.**

1982 Maples *Memories* 74 The mountain people called [the flower] tongue or sheep's tongue. It was real bright yellow with spotted green leaves. [**1999** Montgomery *Coll* We would collect the leaves of this plant and mix them with our creasy greens and other spring plants and eat them while working on our garden greens each spring (Cardwell).]

sheep tail *noun* See citation.

1971 *AOHP/ALC*-33 We'd call [the carded wool] little sheep tails, rolled it out into rolls, and then we would spin it with that old spinning wheel.

sheep tea See **sheepball tea.**

she-gossip *noun* A woman in the community with a reputation for gossiping.

1956 Hall *Coll* (Del Rio TN) A feller in North Carolina took a girl up on the mountain, and they rassled around in a sinkhole, and the country's she-gossip come along and seen 'em. **1998** Montgomery *Coll* (known to Bush).

she-holly *noun* The female of the American holly bush (*Ilex opaca*). See also **he-holly.**

1957 Parris *My Mts* 248 Only she-holly has berries. You hear folks talk about years when there ain't no berries on the trees. **1964** Reynolds *Born of Mts* 84 In North Carolina even the holly is given sex, there being a He Holly and a She Holly, for how else could the last-named have berries, the other having none. **1995** Montgomery *Coll* (known to Cardwell, Ledford, Oliver).

shekel See **shuttle.**

shelly (also *shelly bean*) *noun* Any large, often speckled **bunch bean** that late in the season begins to dry in the **hull**, thus making it easily removed and cooked by itself.

1936 Farr *Folk Speech Mid TN* 92 = dried beans. "We eat shelly beans of a winter." **1958** Wood *Words from TN* 15 = type of legume that tends to shell itself during cooking. **1974** Roberts *Sang Branch* 23 We would dry a sight of beans by stringing them and then threading them up on strings to dry. I've knowed my mother to dry as many as eighteen bushel thrashed out for soup beans. I've beat 'em out a many a time that way, going atter 'em just like killing snakes, bust them hulls up, take them out on sheet or something, and sort the beans out of the hulls. We called these shelly beans. **1986** Pederson et al. *LAGS* = attested by 17/60 interviewees (28.3%) from E TN; 17/23 of all LAGS interviewees (73.9%) attesting term were from Appalachia. **1991** Haynes *Haywood Home* 48 In September and October, we harvested pumpkins, squash, shelly beans, potatoes, apples, molassy cane and corn. . . . Shelly beans were planted in corn fields or along fences so they would have something for the vines to run up on. We'd pick the beans and spread them on a wagon sheet (thick canvas) to dry in the sun. . . . After the beans on the wagon sheet dried, they were sacked in toesacks [sic] (burlap) and hung from a tree limb or rafter in a shed. Then we'd beat the day-lights out of them with a stick. Come the first good windy day, somebody would get up on a shed roof to wind-clean the shellies. **2009** Sohn *Appal Home Cooking* 293 Shelly beans or shellies are mature beans of any variety. They are picked when the seed has enlarged and the pod has started its decline. **2016** Netherland *Appal Cooking* 72 Sometimes the pole beans or confield beans were allowed to fill out and begin to dry on the vine. They were picked and shelled for the full bean inside, and, of course, they were called "shelly beans." Shelly beans were the only dried beans we cooked that we did not buy.

shelly bean See **shelly.**

Shelly car *noun* See citations.

1975 Woolley *We Be Here* 12 That was back when there wasn't no such thing as a continuous miner or a motor to pull coal with or a shell-y car or anything like that. *Ibid.* 48 = hauls the coal from the continuous miners [to the surface of a coal mine].

shelve *verb* To put aside indefinitely, suspend but not revoke the duties of (a church officer, deacon, Sunday School teacher, etc. who has failed to perform duties to standard). See also **set aside.**

1994 Montgomery *Coll* (known to Cardwell).

she-rain *noun* See citations.

1957 Parris *My Mts* 168 "Back when I was a boy," said the Old Man, "the Indians had a name for spring and summer rain. Called it she-rain because it made things grow." **1995–97** Montgomery *Coll* (known to Brown), = a soft, steady summer rain (Andrews).

sheriff *verb* See citations.

1917 Kephart *Word-List* 417 = to serve as sheriff. **1921** Campbell *Sthn Highlander* 102–3 The office of sheriff is perhaps the object of keenest competition—"sheriffing," as its pursuit is sometimes called.

she-root *noun* See citation.

1968 *Sang Signs* 50 Known as "[te]tterwort" or "sweet slumber" or "she-roots," the dried rootstocks were ground and used in an infusion.... As "she-roots," bloodroot was a remedy for female complaints.

shet See **shut**.

shettle, shickle See **shuttle**.

shifty *adjective* Resourceful, capable.

1915 Dingus *Word-List VA* 190 = industrious and successful. **1930** Armstrong *This Day and Time* 117 She's right shifty, she ain't no lazy bones. *Ibid.* 133 There's a heap a ways a feller kin do to make a livin', ef he's shifty an' got resolution. **1958** Wood *Words from TN* 15 = alert. "They use shifty in a complimentary sense. It doesn't mean sly but more as provident—the opposite of shiftless. **c1960** Wilson *Coll* = alert, able to take care of oneself. **1981** High *Coll* = handy, resourceful, said of a person who is a hard worker and can "make something out of nothing."

[DARE *shifty* adj chiefly South, South Midland]

shikepoke See **shitepoke 2**.

shindig (also *shindy*) *noun* A boisterous gathering or party with live music and dancing; a dance step.

1863 *Rogers CW Letters* (Jan 17) you say you and Jacob are having some verey amusing times I would like to of ben there at some of your shin digs. **1901** Harben *Westerfelt* 46 She's arranged to give you a shindig to introduce you to the young folks round about. **1926** Thomas *Hills and Mts of KY* 93 The night of the same day [of the wedding] is usually given over to the gay festivities of the quare [sic] dance, or the "shindig," and old games. **1927** Woofter *Dialect from WV* 364 = a square dance. "There was a big shindig at the camp last week"; *shindy* = a frolic. The boys had a regular shindy Saturday afternoon." **1961** Medford *History Haywood Co* 94 The old Virginia Reel (with its modified forms or figures) was danced to fast-time music, like the so-called "shin-digs" and buck dances. **1966** Dakin *Vocab Ohio River Valley* 508 *Shindig* is common in eastern Kentucky, Indiana, and Illinois, but rare in Ohio and unused south and west of the Bluegrass and Mountains in Kentucky. It does not mean only a dance. For some people *shindig* is a generic term for any social gathering, especially one inclined to be noisy and active. The term is frequently regarded with amusement, and it is quite clear from some comments that the "best people" did not attend shindigs. **1973** GSMNP-4:37 We didn't have them on Little Catalooch. I mean we made a lot of music, but I mean we didn't have what we called shindigs, square dances. On Big Creek we did have [them]. About every Saturday night we would have a square dance and chicken wobble. **2007** McMillon *Notes* = only heard recently.

[Web3 *shindig* n probably alteration of *shindy* (influenced by *shin* and *dig*) or *shinny*]

shine

A *verb* Principal parts.

1 Variant past-tense form *shun*.

1913 Kephart *Our Sthn High* 284 There are many corrupt forms of the verb, such as ... shun (shone). **1957** Combs *Lg Sthn High: Word List* 90 *shun* = past-tense and past participle of *shine*.

2 Variant past-participle form *shun*.

[See **1957** in **A1**.]

B *verb*

1 Of an animal's eyes at night: to reflect light.

1949 Hall *Coll* (Del Rio TN) The eyes of a cow, deer, dog, rabbit, possum, cat, whippoorwill shine at night.

2 To find (a hunted animal) at night by reflecting light into its eyes; to direct a light toward the eyes of (an animal); hence verbal noun *shining*.

1927 Woofter *Dialect from WV* 364 = to hunt bullfrogs at night by a bright light. "We shined the bullfrogs last night, and got a good mess." **1939** Hall *Coll* (Proctor NC) I says to Van, "Let's shine its eyes and shoot it [= a raccoon]." **1972** Carson and Vick *Cookin* 2 50 We'd gig 'em [= frogs] from a boat, shinin them with a bulls-eye lantern. **2009** Fields *Growing Up* 100 We laughed because we all knew Elmer Cantrell had just spent thirty days in the slammer for "shinin'."

C *noun*

1 A prank, caper.

1901 Harben *Westerfelt* 271 Don't cut up any o' yore shines with these Christian women who are tryin' to do good. **2000** Miller *Looneyville* 67 In Looneyville it meant causing a disturbance or commotion through a trick or prank at some of the gatherings such as dances and ball games: "Those fellers from Tater Run started some shines at the baseball game on Sunday."

2 The distance at which an animal's eyes reflect a light at night.

1939 Hall *Recording Speech* 8 Mention may be made of a quaint and picturesque use of the word *shine*, heard in the summer of 1937. An old hunter in Wears Valley said: "In just a thought or two the painter [= panther] came out and screamed. Hit wouldn't come up within shine of the fire."

3 Shortened form of **moonshine**. See also **shiner**.

1940 Hall *Coll* (Morristown TN) There is plenty of shine over here. Jerry is over here with me, and we drink our part of it. **1989** Landry *Smoky Mt Interviews* 181 Everybody'd meet up there, you know, and they'd drink shine till maybe nine or ten o'clock. **1993** Burchill et al. *Ghosts and Haunts* 40 Maybe it was the shine the boys had drunk, but the boys decided to fight a duel on the top of

Henderson Hill at midnight. **1994** Montgomery *File* Arlie made the shine and Hobe drunk it (82-year-old man, Gatlinburg TN). **2007** Alexander *Moonshiners Gone* 45 Famed NASCAR racing legend Junior Johnson learned racing skills while running "shine." **2013** Pierce *Corn in Jar* 72 The shine came out of the Great Smoky Mountains in souped-up cars, farm trucks, airplanes, and, late in the [Prohibition] period, tractor-trailers. **2014** Hicks *Driving* 41 After a nip of shine, Pap cut loose a buck and wing.

4 See citation.

1974 Maurer and Pearl *KY Moonshine* 124 = a moonshine still.

shiner *noun* Shortened form of **moonshiner**. See also **shine C3**.

1895 Wiltse *Moonshiners* 60 [The officer] proceeded to undo the great parcel under his arm and hold up that beastly looking pistol at an angle of about forty-five degrees—just the right angle, the "shiner" saw, to send the bullet precisely between his eyes, if the thing went off. **1961** Murry *Salt* 24 I ain't a'goin' to name the shiner, but don't care to tell you he lives in a wild-like place up on Long Hope. **1971** Lee *My Appalachia* 9–10 The region also became the scene of armed clashes between "shiners" and Prohibition officers, and brutal murders were almost commonplace. **1989** Smith *Flyin' Bullets* 202 These "Shiners" would have been even more wary of the local officers recently, if they'd have looked up in the air. **1990** Merriman *Moonshine Rendezvous* 25 My backer went halfers on each load, plus when the bootleggers were full and the shiners had run off a batch I would deliver it to his barn.

shine runner *noun* Same as **runner 3**. See also **tripper**.

1969 Lee *Bloodletting* 71 Mercer County [WV] officers arrested a McDowell County "shine runner" with fifty gallons of moonshine whiskey in his car. **1994** Martin *Stock Car Legends* 2 I remember Junior Johnson was one of the best shine runners ever was, and a good shine runner's first instinct is when your car wrecks, then you get out and take off running because more than likely the law was following you.

shine up to *verb phrase* To give special attention to (someone) in the hope of gaining favor.

c1970 Handlon *Ol' Smoky* 77 Leaf Evers told about his last slip from Grace, a shinin' up to another man's wife.

shiney haw See **Shawnee haw.**

shingle *verb* To cut (one's hair or moustache); hence noun = a haircut.

c1900 (in **1997** Stoddart *Quare Women* 127) Father has shingled his moustache and I hardly know him from another man. **1913** Kephart *Our Sthn High* 294 To shamp means to shingle or trim one's hair. **1956** McAtee *Some Dial NC* 39 = to cut the hair awkwardly, so that it has the appearance of shingles on a roof. **1994–97** Montgomery *Coll* (known to Adams, Brown, Cardwell, Jones, Oliver, Shields, Weaver); I still get my hair shingled [i.e. cut short in the back like a man's] (Norris). **2002** Myers *Best Yet Stories* 80 = hair cut.

shinhobble (also *shinhopple*) *noun* A common evergreen shrub (*Leucothoe fontansiana*) whose branches are gathered for sale as an ornamental green. See also **dog hobble**.

1964 Reynolds *Born of Mts* 99 From the many place names and expressions referring to shins, it may be seen that in the rough going of early years in the mountain country, our ancestors had to walk many shin miles among the shinhopple, a thick and viny, tangled undergrowth anciently called shinhobble, for it hobbled the shins and legs as one would hobble a horse.

shinhopple See **shinhobble.**

shining See **moonshine B**, **shine B2**.

shiny haw See **Shawnee haw.**

shirt-tail bird *noun* A pileated woodpecker.

1967 Stubbs *Mountain-Wise* (April–May) 9 In addition to the downy-headed woodpecker, we have the yellow-bellied sapsucker, the flicker, and, occasionally, the pileated woodpecker, called here "the shirt-tail bird."

[DARE *shirttail bird* (at *shirttail* n 2) Southeast]

shirt-tail boy (also *shirt-tail of a boy*) *noun* A small boy, originally one accustomed to wearing nothing but a long shirt.

1913 Kephart *Our Sthn High* 238 I may explain that it still is common in many districts of the mountain country for small boys to go about through the summer in a single abbreviated garment and that they are called "shirt-tail boys." **1939** *FWP Guide NC* 98 The boy, or "chap," may be called a little "shirttail boy" to distinguish him from her "arm baby and her knee baby." **1952** Wilson *Folk Speech NC* 589 = a small boy. Perhaps from the fact that some small boys in pre–Civil War days wore only a long shirt in warm weather. **1978** Parris *Mt Cooking* 9 Back when I was just a shirttail of a boy, there was a heap sight of walnut trees. **1991** Still *Wolfpen Notebooks* 78 When I was a shirttail boy my Pap used to kill us a mess of snowbirds for supper in the winter time.

shirt-tail of a boy See **shirt-tail boy.**

shitepoke (also *shikepoke*) *noun*

1 A green heron.

1939 *FWP Guide TN* 17 Numerous along all the State's water courses is the green heron, known variously as "shikepoke" and "fly-up-the-creek." **1967** *DARE Survey* (Maryville TN). **1980** Brewer *Hit's Gettin'* A "shitepoke" is a green heron. **1997** Montgomery *Coll* (known to Brown, Ellis). **1999** Milnes *Play of Fiddle* 92 A "shit-e-poke" is a green heron, which earned its descriptive appellation through its curious habit of defecating whenever taking to wing.

[OED3 *shitepoke*[1] n "heron" North American colloquial and regional]

2 By extension = a long-legged person or animal.

1976 Garber *Mountain-ese* 80 That shitepoke kid would make a good basketball player. **1977** Still *Wonder Beans* 7 [The cow] was all hide and bones. A walking shikepoke. **1996–97** Montgomery *Coll* (known to Adams, Brown, Cypher, Ellis).

3 A mean, uncouth, contemptible person.

1963 Williams *Metaphor Mt Speech II* 51 Who's that gimlet-ended shikepoke a-baouncin' up 'n' daown on that old rack o' bones jis' zackly and plime blank like a peckerwood on a rotten fence post?

shit house *noun* An outhouse, privy.

1994 Montgomery *Coll* (known to Cardwell, Shields).

shit slinger *noun* In a logging camp, the **lobbyhog** or other man assigned to serving food.

1998 Farwell *Logging Terms*.

shivaree

A Variant forms *charivari* [see **1982** in **B**], *chivalree* [see **1991** in **B**], *chivalry*, *chivaree* [see **1966** in **B**], *shivering*.

1986 Pederson et al. *LAGS* (Sullivan Co TN, Hawkins Co TN) *chivalry*. **1996** Montgomery *Coll* = also pronounced *shivering* (Norris).

B *noun* A raucous celebration after a wedding, usually held late at night at the newlyweds' residence and staged by friends and neighbors. It is characterized by noisemaking and pranks (for which, see citations). Same as **serenade**, but less common, especially in the TN mountains (see 1986 citations for the two forms).

1957 Combs *Lg Sthn High: Word List* 89 = (Pro[nounced] shiv-a-ree). Originally a serenade (mock) with discordant noises of horns, whistles, musical instruments, etc., to celebrate the nuptials of a wedding; young Highlanders now employ the custom as a means of obtaining a treat (usually of candy, or fruits) from the groom. The noise is continued till the groom comes out and treats the crowd. **1966** Dakin *Vocab Ohio River Valley* 497 In eastern Kentucky *serenade* is still used by some of the oldest generation but the younger speakers say *chivaree* exclusively. **1972** Alderman *Big Bald* 12 Meanwhile the new bride and groom would slip away to their own prepared cabin. After dark, the third night, the crowd would gather around the cabin of the new couple for the serenade. At a given signal a din of noise, that would scare the "hants" and everything else back into the never, never world, would break loose. Pans-a-poundin', guns-a-shootin', people-a-shoutin' and the big roarin' horse fiddle boomin' through the woods got the "shivaree" off to a thundering start. This final part of the celebration lasted all night. Sun-up would see the departin' couples drifting down their separate trails, homeward bound across the creeks and ridges, to the back of the beyond where they lived. **1972** Cooper *NC Mt Folklore* 22 When a couple was married, within a few nights it was serenaded or given a chivaree. The leader—every neighborhood had one—summoned his followers to meet him on a given night. The serenade consisted of dynamite and shotgun blasts, tootings of horns, the ringing of cowbells, beating of tin pans until the couple opened the door and invited everyone to come inside. **1982** Powers and Hannah *Cataloochee* 196 A bride and groom were apt to be greeted with a charivari which might include riding a groom on a rail . . . in his night clothes, and dumping him into a cold creek. **1986** Pederson et al. *LAGS* = attested by 16/60 interviewees (26.7%) from E TN and 2/35 (5.7%) from N GA; 18/181 of all LAGS interviewees (9.9%) attesting term were from Appalachia. **1991** Haynes *Haywood Home* 62 After the guests were gone, everything would be quiet for a while. Then bedlam would break loose outside the house as the Chivalree began. Wedding guests had returned with all kinds of noise makers imaginable. The couple was being serenaded in a special serenading and the racket went around and around the house. Then the men would go in and take the groom from his bed. The men would parade him on their shoulders around and around the house. If he was prepared, he had his clothes on. If not, they took him half-clothed. Around the house they'd go, laughing and joking at the groom's expense. Meanwhile, women would take gifts in the house and pile them on the bride's bed. After that, everyone went home for good and left the couple in peace.

C *verb* To give (a newly married couple) such a celebration.

1953 Boshears *Shivaree* 65–66 It was a custom in this area of East Tennessee to gather at the home of the newly-married couple to serenade or "shivaree" them . . . I was a very small child, about five years of age, when I had my first experience with "shivaree-ing." . . . I still remember that I carried a tin pie pan and beat on it with a stick, and also that they treated us with candy and fruit. **1957** Combs *Lg Sthn High: Word List* 89 They shivareed John and Masie last night. **1979** *Big South Fork OHP*-4 Nobody didn't know where we was at, and it was kind of died down, and they never shivareed us. **2003** Carter *Mt Home* 148 Daddy told the boys they would have to shivaree them so after the weddin', when Uncle Rafe and his new bride, Millie, come to Gran-pas to spend their first night together.

[alteration of French *charivari*]

shiver

A *noun* A splinter or fragment, as of bone or wood. See also **shiveration**, **sliveration**.

1904–20 Kephart *Notebooks* 2:475 A little shiver of bone come out. **1971** *AOHP/ALC*-147 For what they called consumption, they'd take in beech bark from the north side of the tree and hickory bark and a span of wild cherry tree bark, just what you could hold between your fingers . . . about eight little small shivers of bark, and you boiled that down, and then you take'd a quart of honey . . . you boiled that all down to one quart. You put it with your honey. Then you boiled it down in the honey until you just had the quart. **1995** Montgomery *Coll* (known to Brown, Cardwell, Ellis, Ledford, Norris, Oliver). **2007** Milnes *Signs Cures Witches* 145 I went out and got her a water bucket full of chips, you know, where Dad split wood . . . little shivers.

[cf SND *shiver* n² "a chip or splinter of stone"; CUD *shiver*³ n "a slice"]

B *verb* To reduce to fragments, crush.

1861 Hedgecock *Diary* 105 Today an accident occurred by the fall of a musket set up by a tree, resulting in shivering one man's leg so it had to be amputated.

shiveration *noun* Splinters or fragments collectively. See also **shiver A**, **sliveration**.

1928 (in **1952** Mathes *Tall Tales* 63) Yes, I tuck a hammer an' busted it all to shiveration! **1997** Montgomery *Coll* (known to Cardwell, Weaver).

shivering See **shivaree**.

shock

A (also *shock stack*) A small, usually round pile of hay, corn **fodder**, etc. left in the field, often in bundled sheaves set together around a **stack pole** and tied.

1845 *McLean Diary* 91 [I] Got my ots in Shock have 282 Dozen. **1863** *Lance CW Letters* (May 31) I saw corn in silk and Tasels and I saw lots of wheat cut and in shocks and som Stacked. **1949** Kurath *Word Geog East US* 39 The loose piles of hay in the meadows at haying time are called *shocks* . . . from Chesapeake Bay to South Carolina and also in the South Midland. **c1960** Wilson *Coll*: *shock* = a conical pile of hay in a field; also an arrangement of bundles of wheat, etc. **1966** Dakin *Vocab Ohio River Valley* 77 *Hay shock* (usually called simply *shock*) is the predominant term in Kentucky, and virtually the only one used west of the Mountains and the Bluegrass. **1966–68** *DARE Survey* (Brasstown NC, Spruce Pine NC, Gatlinburg TN) *shock* = a large pile of hay stored outdoors; (Gatlinburg TN, Maryville TN) *shock* = a small pile of hay standing in field; (Brasstown NC, Burnsville NC, Spruce Pine NC, Gatlinburg TN, Maryville TN) = sheaves of grain set together in a pile. **1973** *Corn Shocks* 325 Sometimes a barn can't hold all the corn from a field, so the farmer stacks the stalks in what is called a "shock." The shock is the stalks bundled together and capped around about a third of the way down from the top with twine. These shocks will stay out in the field and will stay good all winter unless they fall over. Then they will rot. . . . The corn shock is an efficient way of keeping feed for animals. . . . The ears can be taken off and the whole stalk and the shucks fed to horses, cows, and mules. **c1975** Lunsford *It Used to Be* 12 We went up to the mountains and put on a load of tops (that is, the tops of the corn stalks from the ear up which had been cut, put in bundles, put in shocks, and dried for feed). **1986** Pederson et al. *LAGS* = attested by 4/60 interviewees (6.7%) from E TN and 3/35 (8.6%) from N GA; 7/32 of all LAGS interviewees (21.8%) attesting term were from Appalachia. **2003** LaLone et al. *Farming Life* 312 After you got the hay mowed down and it cured out and raked up then you went along and put it in shocks. Then you would take the horses and drag all those shocks into one big haystack. **2007** McMillon *Notes*: *shock stack* = a stack of cornstalks tied in an upright bundle.

[DARE *shock* n[1] 1 chiefly Midland, South, West]

B (also *shock up*) *verb*, *verb phrase* To cut and tie (hay or fodder) into bundles in the field.

1863 (in **1992** Heller and Heller *Confederacy* 102) they stack ther wheat instead of shocking it. **1948** Chase *Grandfather Tales* 89 He cut the corn and shocked it in the orchard. **1975** *Used to Farm* 31 After the ear was harvested, the farmer stripped the corn blades, tied them in a small bundle and let them dry. After they were dry, they were stored in a barn for winter feed or "shocked" in the field. **1982** *Smokies Heritage* 137 Most people have shocked their corn into Indian tipees; others let the leaves fly free, to dance and dip in the wind like a rustic ballet. **1983** *Dark Corner OHP-4A* Sometime it'd set in and rain a solid week atter we'd cut our wheat and shock it up like that. **1991** Haynes *Haywood Home* 47 Winter grains like wheat, barley, rye and oats ripened by June. Men would cradle grain from dawn to dusk and women and children would follow them to tie and shock the sheaves. **1997** Nelson *Country Folklore* 146 The corn was cut and shocked and tied with grass strings. **2003** LaLone et al. *Farming Life* 322 We cut hay with a mower machine that the horses pulled and we raked it with a [horse-drawn] rake. Then you shocked it. You made little mounds that we would shock up into little balls with pitchforks. Then we had a pole that was hooked. You hook a horse to one end of it and you would run the pole under the shock and had a rope that went over the top and fastened on the other side of the pole to hold it down. And you pulled it into a pile called a haystack. **2004** *Foxfire XII* 59 We raised some feed on that hill—had to "shock it up." Have to take and cut the top of the corn and pull them blades and tie the tops and blades together and shock it up till it dries and then haul it in and stack it up in them stacks—big, high stacks. There is somebody up on the stacks, and they throw it up to them—bunch of men. **2007** McMillon *Notes*: *shock stack* = a stack of cornstalks tied in an upright bundle. **2009** *Hard Life* 42 The hills [for corn] were about 30 inches apart. When they cut the corn, they'd shock it, 16 hills square. They'd sell it out of the field in the shocks.

shock stack See **shock A**.

shock up See **shock B**.

shoe-around *noun* A country dance party.

1952 Wilson *Folk Speech NC* 589 = a country dance, a frolic, a party. **1966** Frome *Strangers* 304 He went around the hills, attending bean stringings, corn shuckings, shoe-arounds, and shindigs. **c1975** Lunsford *It Used to Be* 134 The shoe-around is just an old-time party, and they have been held under various circumstances. I remember one at the old Snowhill school, where they all went off in the daytime just as soon as dinner was announced, or they were dismissed for dinner. All the grown boys and girls and some of the smaller ones, of which I was one, went on down to an old log house there in the gap of the ridge, or mountain. Tom Boyd was there with the old banjo and he played, "Shout, Lullie," and the boys and girls started up: "Big ring, half way round, half back, break and swing your partner, promenade, and all go right," and so on, with the most fun in the world. **1997** Montgomery *Coll* (known to Cardwell, Jones).

shoemake See **sumac**.

shoe-mouth deep (also *shoe-top deep*) *adjective phrase* Of snow, mud, etc.: shallow, as high or deep as the top of a shoe. See also **hub deep**, **straddle deep**.

1861 *J Love CW Letter* (Oct 4) this is the darndest place I ever saw there is nothing here but Sand about Shoe mouth deep. **1863**

Robinson *CW Letters* (Feb 18) the mud Round our cook places is Shoe mouth deep in mud. **1917** Kephart *Word-List* 417 The fog is friz *shoe mouth* deep on the mountains. **1937** Conner Ms 9 (Oconaluftee NC) The snow was about shoe-top deep, and awfully cold. **1937** Hall Coll (Cades Cove TN) Snow is shoe-mouth deep in the cove when it's knee-deep on the mountain. **1938** Stuart *Dark Hills* 230 When the farmers dug them out of the mine, they had to wade in a puddle of blood shoe-mouth deep to get to Ennis. **1972** GSMNP-93:3:2 They call it the deer vine. They can get shoe-mouth deep in some places.

shoe soles *noun* See citation.

1930 Pendleton *Wood-Hicks Speak* 88 = a cook-shack term for fried beef.

shoestring bean *noun* Same as **leather britches**.

1973 AOHP/EH-31 I've dried beans. We call them shoestring beans, leather britches, different things, you know. Take green beans and string them on a thread and hang them behind the stove.

shoe-string farm *noun* See citation.

1916 Schockel *KY Mts* 118 Of necessity the people depend upon the lower slopes of the hills as much as upon the limited bottom lands, their "shoe-string farms" being found strung along little gullies as well as in broader valleys.

shoe-top deep See **shoe-mouth deep**.

shonny See **Shawnee haw**, **Shawnee lettuce**.

shonny haw See **Shawnee haw**.

shoo-fly *noun* See citation.

1998 Montgomery File = a large bowtie.

[DARE *shoofly* n 3 especially South Midland]

shoot

A *verb* To shatter (a wall of coal) by setting off a small plug of dynamite set into a hole drilled into the wall. See also **powder**, **undercut**.

1976 Dillon *They Died* 71 In early days of coal mining, the workman had to shoot his own coal, i.e., he had to drill or bore a hole into the solid coal six feet or more [and] place in dynamite or black powder charge to the farthest depths. He inserted a fuse from the explosive to extend to the outside of the hole, then he tamped the shot or "dobied" the hole. **1985** Irwin *Alex Stewart* 92 I've shot and loaded a heap of coal. **1989** *Matewan OHP-2* I shot coal for a while and then I cut coal for a while.

B *noun*

1 The discharge from a firearm.

1774 *Dunmore's War* 227 I think every Man have 1/2 doz shoots a piece. **1861** *Hampton CW Letters* (Sept 16) our company had to support the battle i shot 20 s[h]oots at them. **1862** *Neves CW Letters* (Aug 14) we have bin out on a scout tin partey 3 days & our boys got 5 shoots at the yankeys but kild narey one. **1891** Primer *Studies in WV* 167 *Shoot* is very common for *shot*; as, "he made a good shoot." **1913** Kephart *Our Sthn High* 91 I fired a shoot as she riz in the air. **1939** Hall Coll (Bradley Fork NC) I shot six shoots at the man. **1953** Hall Coll (Deep Creek NC) I tried rockin' [the angry bull] to keep him off of me. I shot him nine shoots . . . I never missed him ary shoot either. **1961** *Coe Ridge OHP-340B* Uncle John was shot two shoots.

[DARE *shoot* n 1 especially South Midland]

2 A load of powder or dynamite discharged at a one time.

1974 Fink *Bits Mt Speech* 23 *shoots* = charges or loads, as "two *shoots* of powder." **1976** Garber *Mountain-ese* 81 They set off three shoots of danny-mite in the rocks.

shooter *noun* One who indulges in the midwinter ritual and revelry of firing a shotgun into the air. See also **shoot in**, **shooting**.

2007 Milnes *Signs Cures Witches* 194 [In WV] some who participate in mumming events call themselves shooters. Shooting, another midwinter ritual with roots in Germany, to some may simply mean taking a shotgun out of doors and shooting up in the air on New Year's Eve at midnight (as my brothers and I did growing up). But shooting as a ritual practice had meaning and bearing on the fortune of local residents in West Virginia.

shoot in *verb phrase* Of a band of young people: to indulge in the boisterous midwinter custom of firing a shotgun into the air. See also **shooter**, **shooting**.

1964 Smith et al. *Germans of Valley* 101 Although the custom of "shooting in the New Year" is only a memory, some elderly residents remember shooters and others can describe their experiences as members of shooting parties. **1995** Milnes *Old Christmas* 29 In Pendleton [County WV], men would often go from house to house and "shoot in" the new year.

shooting *verbal noun* Formerly, indulging (by a band of young people) in the boisterous midwinter custom of firing a shotgun into the air. See also **shooter**, **shoot in**.

1964 Smith et al. *Germans of Valley* 103 As greeting cards came into popular use, "Belsnickeling" and New Year's Shooting gradually faded out of practice.

shooting match *noun*

1 A competition in marksmanship.

1899 Fox *Mt Europa* 28 When huntin's good 'n' thar's shootin'-matches round-about, she don't have to buy much meat. **1937** Hall Coll (Cades Cove TN) Shooting matches [were held] with cows as prizes.

2 A fight involving gunfire. See also **shooting scrape**.

1956 Hall Coll (Townsend TN) They had a shootin' match down there at Liddie ——'s. Liddie's boy shot Sam, burned a hole right th'u him. **1960** Schwarz *Ordeal by Serpents* 405 They had childhoods where one or both of their parents, siblings or other relatives died of disease, or in mining accidents or "shooting matches." **1989** *Matewan OHP-39* I saw him to have a shooting match with an old fellow that he was going with his girl.

shooting scrape *noun* A fight in which guns are used. See also **scrape A, shooting match 2.**

1977 Shackelford et al. *Our Appalachia* 257 About a year before my dad died he got into a shooting scrape here in Prestonsburg I remember very vividly.

shoot, or give up your gun *verb phrase* See citation.

1919 Combs *Word-List South* 35 = an expression often heard when some one keeps threatening to do something, and doesn't.

shore See **sure.**

shorely See **surely.**

short *conjunction* Unless.

1972 *AOHP/ALC-298* [We couldn't get much to eat], short it's canned.

short dog *noun*

1 A train or bus serving only a local route; a transport car in a coal mine.

1955 Ritchie *Singing Family* 266 Wouldn't a day pass . . . but what five or six big long trainloads of coal would rumble by. Then no time passed before they went to hauling out timber and livestock and such on the freight trains. Then they sent the short dog on the tracks, too, for people to travel on. **1963** Edwards *Gravel* 151 The little short-dog doesn't go any farther than Knoxville. Here you change to the Memphis Special . . . But I had learned something too: this was only a short-dog train. There were much better and faster trains. I would ride those someday. **1976** Dillon *They Died* 207 The coffins were not on hand immediately but soon arrived on the baggage coach of the "short dog" passenger train. **1991** Still *Wolfpen Notebooks* 163 Short dog bus: connecting line between Hindman and Vicco, Kentucky.

[DARE *short dog* n 2 especially southern Appalachians]

2 A homemade tractor.

1983 *Dark Corner OHP-9A* Short dog, that was a common name for the tractor which was homemade from an old truck. You cut it in two and you bring that differential, the back end of it, completely against the transmission, and no drive shaft and, made it real short and you stripped it all off, and then you could saw you out a wooden log and bore a hole through it, put a steel beam and you could make a lift. It would lift the logs off of the ground holding by hand.

shortened bread (also *shortened dodger, shortening bread*) *noun* See citations. Same as **crackling bread.**

1890 Fruit *KY Words* 64 We have what we call "plain dodger," in which the meal is made up with cold water into pones; then, "shortened dodger," in which the meal is made up with lard, or grease of some kind. Our "crackling bread" is a corn-dodger made up with cracklings. **c1920** (in **1993** Farwell and Nicholas *Smoky Mt Voices* 146) *shortened bread* = bread made with cooking fats: "My baby's sick; I believe it's [from] eatin' that shortened bread." **1966** Dakin *Vocab Ohio River Valley* 318 *shortening bread* (most often) or *fatty bread* (sometimes). These are names for corn bread baked with "lots of lard" shortening. **2003** Howell *Folklife Big South Fork* 60 White corn meal was used for bread. . . . The addition of cracklings, the crispy residue left from rendering lard or frying meat, made cracklin' bread or shortenin' bread.

[DARE (at *shortening bread* n) South, South Midland]

shorts *noun* See citation.

1976 Braden *Grandma Was Girl* 27–28 The unsacked grain was stored in the big barrel in the smokehouse to be used as our home supply of flour. Then we put it into sacks later, loaded it into the wagon, and took it to the mill to be made into flour. There were several grades of flour turned out by the mill that was run by a water wheel. The number one flour made the whitest cakes and biscuits. Number two flour had a little bran, but still made pretty good biscuits. The number three grade was called "shorts," and was almost like what we now call whole wheat flour. I didn't like the bread made from it, but the pancakes made with it were fine. The fourth grade was the bran for the cows.

short sheriff *noun* A local constable. See also **high sheriff.**

1967 *DARE Survey* (Gatlinburg TN) = constable. **1998** Montgomery *Coll* (known to Brown, Bush, Cardwell).

short sweetening *noun* Sugar in crystalline form, usually cane sugar, as distinguished from **long sweetening** (honey or molasses).

1873 Harney *Strange Land* 431 "Long sweet-'nin'" and "short sweet'nin'" are respectively syrup and sugar. **1901** McClintock *KY Mts* 12 There is either "short sweetening"—a cheap, brown sugar—or "long sweetening"—home-made molasses. **1911** Shearin *E KY Word-List* 540 = sugar. **1923** Greer-Petrie *Angeline Doin' Society* 11 If thar wan't no short sweetnin' (sugar) handy, long sweetnin' (molasses) would do. **1955** Parris *Roaming Mts* 153 An old timer is one who remembers when long sweetening was honey and short sweetening was maple sugar. **1974** Roberts *Sang Branch* 9 We raised beans and 'taters, cabbage, beets—everything that'd grow. Made our molasses into long sweetening and tapped the sugartrees for short sweetening. **1999** Montgomery *Coll* = grain sugar (Cardwell).

short talk *noun* Rude, quarrelsome talk; hence verb phrase = to quarrel with.

1952 Wilson *Folk Speech NC* 589 = to talk crossly. "It would shame Lige powerfully if you'd short-talk him in company." **1972** Cooper *NC Mt Folklore* 96 = quarrelsome talk.

shot foreman *noun* See citation. See also **shoot A.**

1977 Shackelford et al. *Our Appalachia* 205 Eventually, it got so tight that they put on what they call the "shot foreman." You'd drill your holes, have to furnish the powder, then this man would come and he'd shoot your coal for you so it wouldn't be shot too hard.

shotgun house *noun* A narrow, one-story, box-like dwelling with two or more rooms set one behind the other.

1968 Clarke *Stuart's Kentucky* 172 Nearby the rows of *shotgun houses* of three and four rooms strung behind one another like the barrel of a shotgun and the squat, boxlike structures of the railroad shacks offered little of natural or man-made beauty to the large families of the miners and railroad workers who lived in them. **1980** Still *Run for Elbertas* 100 Over the heads of the men I could see the whole of the camp, the shotgun houses in the flat, the smoke rising above the burning gob heaps. **1996** Spurlock *Glossary* 408 = a small, narrow house of two or three rooms, so named because if one opened the front and back doors, he could fire a shotgun straight through the two entranceways. **2004** House *Coal Tattoo* 225 She was meant to be in one of those shotgun houses that arrived preassembled on a railroad car.

[DARE *shotgun* n 1 chiefly South, South Midland]

shots *noun* In distilling, the high-proof whiskey produced at the beginning of a distillation cycle, usually mixed with **backings**. See also **third**.

1992 Gabbard *Thunder Road* 154 The first that was run, they called it "shots." It was strong. It would be twice as strong as it ought to be, and say if you run six gallon of shots, you'd have to run six gallon of backin's, put it all in a tub and mix it together to make your moonshine ever how strong you wanted to make it.

should *auxiliary verb* in verb phrases *should ought, shouldn't ought to*. See also **may B2**.

1967 Fetterman *Stinking Creek* 100 I reckon we shouldn't oughta throw that stuff in the creek. **1984** Smith *Oral History* 204 "You shouldn't ought've done that," said the Davenport girl. **1999** Offutt *Out of Woods* 143 [You] shouldn't ought to leave this laying around.

shouting school *noun* See citation. Also called **hollering school**. See also **blab school**.

1916 Schockel *KY Mts* 123 The day of the "shouting school" (in which the pupils indicate that they are studying by reading aloud) has passed in the mountains.

shoved *adjective* Hard-pressed.

1859 Taliaferro *Fisher's River* 196 [I would] git out'n the scrap ef possible, fur I were shoved fur the rent.

shovel Baptist *noun* See citation.

2014 Montgomery *Doctrine* 178 One who tends to sit close to the front and when the preacher begins to preach a really good "duty sermon," they set [sic] and shovel the sermon back over their shoulder. "Boy, I am glad the preacher is preaching this sermon, because the folks behind me really need it."

shovel plow *noun* A cultivator with one or more triangular-shaped shares. See also **bull tongue**. See also **double-foot plow**.

1847 (in **1870** Drake *Pioneer Life KY* 45) Deep plowing was not as necessary as in soils long cultivated, and if demanded would have been impracticable, for the ground was full of roots. After a first "breaking up" with the coultered plow, the shovel plow was in general use. In such rooty soils it was often difficult to hold the plow and drive the horse. **1948** Dick *Dixie Frontier* 99 [The crudest kind of homemade plow] was succeeded by the jumping shovel plow, which had an arched coulter that struck the roots and made the point jump them. **1961** Medford *History Haywood Co* 28 In those days when farmers gave little attention to crop rotation; plowed their land with a bull-tongue, shovel plow or boy Dixie (about 2½ inches deep); had no improved grasses to cover crops to keep his hillsides from washing away—just what could he do? **1972** GSMNP-93:39 Bull tongue, you know, that you put on your single foot. They was a shovel plow. In hard land you use that bull tongue and lay off your ground or loosen that to where it would be. A shovel plow they called it. **1981** Whitener *Folk-Ways* 11 I learned to plow with the big turning plow as well as the shovel plow, both pulled by mule.

show

A *verb* Variant past-tense forms *shone, shown*.

1861 Kendrick *CW Letters* (Oct 15) We stade there from Friday till sundy nig ht oclock and during all that time the people Shone us friend ship. *Ibid.* (March 19) I send my best respects to them for the kindness the[y] shown to you.

B (also *showing*) *noun* An opportunity, prospect, promise.

1925 Furman *Glass Window* 47 [He] allus had a craving for larning, though no show to git hit till he was nigh a man. **1956** Hall *Coll* (Hartford TN) I didn't stand no more show in the park than a one-legged man at a rump-kickin'. **c1960** Wilson *Coll* = chance, prospect, promise: "We've got a good show of taters." **1973** *AOHP/ASU-88* The young'uns has got a showing now, but they didn't have it back there.

shower of rain *noun* A rain shower.

1832 McLean *Diary* 10 Warm Wether Concidrabel of Run of sugar water hard Shower of Rain and thunder. **1941** Hall *Coll* = a passing shower. **1980** GSMNP-115:40 It come up a little shower of rain on 'em.

showing See **show B**.

shown See **show A**.

show out *verb phrase* To show off, make a spectacle of oneself.

1859 Taliaferro *Fisher's River* 176 He nuver said a word to me, but buckled up to the 'squire, like a little dog does to a big one when he wants to show out. **1944** Wilson *Word-List* 49 They was great folks for showing out. **1968** *DARE Survey* (Brasstown NC) = to move around in a way to make people take notice. **1969** GSMNP-28:53 If I give it to you over there, they'll think that I'm a-showing out. **1993** Ison and Ison *Whole Nother Lg* 60 = to make a scene and call attention to oneself. **2005** Williams *Gratitude* 523 = to misbehave in front of people, be a show-off. Usually, it's a loudmouth that *shows out*. **2007** McMillon *Notes* = to make a spectacle of oneself. **2009** Benfield *Mt Born* 190 = not showing off. If you are showing out, you are making a big, rousing display of yourself. Showing out is to misbehave. Children would be admonished thusly:

"Randall, you quit that showing out this minute or I'll give you a switching."

[DARE *show out* v phr chiefly South, South Midland]

shrieky *adjective* See citation.

1892 Fruit *KY Words* 231 = creaky.

shrink *verb*

A Variant past-tense forms *shrinkt*, *shrunk*.

1939 Hall *Coll* (Hartford TN) That bear shrunk down and bawled he said like a calf. **1957** McDavid *American Dialects* 521 *shrinkt*.

B Of the moon in its cycle: to wane; hence noun *shrinking* = this part of the moon's cycle. See also **dark of the moon**.

1970 *Slaughtering* 37 We kill hogs on th'full moon, or just after th'full moon. While th'moon was shrinkin', the meat'd shrink. There'd be a lot'a lard an' grease if it'uz on th'shrinkin' of th'moon. **1978** Parris *Mt Cooking* 219 "I always try," she said, "to plant my potatoes when there's dark nights in March. But this year it was too wet and I had to wait until a couple of days ago when the moon was shrinking." [**1992** *Smokies Guide* (Fall) 10 Butchering took place after the weather was cold enough to help preserve the meat. This often occurred around Thanksgiving, although many farmers waited until the signs were right, preferring to kill the animals at the time of a full moon. Many felt that if the animal was killed during a shrinking or waning moon, the meat would shrink when it was cooked.]

shrinking See **shrink B**.

shrub bald *noun* Same as **heath bald**, **wooly top**.

1979 Horton *Natural Heritage* 27 Shrub balds, also called wooly tops, laurel slicks, or laurel hells, usually contain many species of shrubs, but often the best represented family is the heath family which contains rhododendrons, azaleas, laurel or ivy, and many less well-known types of shrub. **1989** Oliver *Hazel Creek* 24 They are two types: shrub balds . . . and Grassy Balds or fields a little lower. **2006** *Encycl Appalachia* 47 Shrub balds represent a stage in this succession process. They were previously grassy balds, but their dominance has shifted to shrubs such as azaleas, blueberries, blackberries, and rhododendrons.

shrub off (also *shrub out*) *verb phrase* To clear a piece of land of brush.

1986 Pederson et al. LAGS (Greene Co TN, Sevier Co TN) *shrub out*; (Washington Co TN) *shrub out*.

shuck[1] See **shake A**.

shuck[2]

A *noun*

1 The leaf-like covering of an ear of corn, especially such coverings considered as a unit; these had many uses in traditional mountain society. See 1996–97 and 1997–98 citations. Also called **corn shuck**, **shucking 2**.

c1866 (in **2005** Fisher *CW in Smokies* 57) We were fed of bread made of meal in which the corn, cob and shuck had all been ground up together, and on rotten meat. **1866** Smith *So Called* 167 He never got any shucks from me. **1881** Atkinson *After Moonshiners* 115 "You know all about these illicit distillers," said Crowder, "and I believe you've got blockade liquor hidden under those shucks." **1949** Kurath *Word Geog East US* 40 In the South as well as the South Midland and the Shenandoah Valley the leaves on an ear of corn are called *shucks*. **1962** Dykeman *Tall Woman* 17 Her mother turned suddenly back to the crib and an armful of shucks. **1972** *AOHP/ALC-355* Corn shucking was a day, and [they] got the corn shucked and put it in the crib, and they took care of their shucks, put them in the cribs and saved them for, until the fall. **1996–97** *Smokies Guide* (Winter) 12 The tough, pliable shucks, or husks, were sometimes twisted and woven into chair seats, and could also be used to make hats, dolls, rugs, or mops, or used to stuff mattresses. **1997–98** *Smokies Guide* (Winter) 13 While a less frugal society might simply dispose of the green sheaths which protect corn ears, old-time farmers found over a dozen practical uses. All told, rural folks probably had more uses for shucks than the corn itself. Boiled corn shucks were stripped and stuffed into mattresses and pillows for a soft, sweet-smelling sleep many old-timers remember fondly. Farmers braided shucks into mule and horse collars as well as bridles and rope. Corn shuck mops and doormats were said to be functional and long-lived. Chair bottoms made from shucks are more comfortable than wood and sometimes outlast the chair. Any left-over shucks could be used as frost-resistant insulation for pumpkins, squash, and other food stuffs that were stored during winter. Craftspeople found even more uses for shucks. Hats made from shucks were worn by both men and women, especially during the Civil War when other materials were scarce. Corn shuck dolls with bonnets, dresses, and corn tassel hair are popular even today. Pressed shucks were the medium for lampshades, baskets, hand bags, pocket books, and hat bands.

[OED3 *shuck* n[2] 1a "a husk, pod, or shell" chiefly dialect and U.S. 1674→, origin unknown; EDD *shuck* sb[2] 1 "a husk, shell, pod" sEngl]

2 The outer covering or pod of a bean.

1946 Matthias *Speech Pine Mt* 191 = the pod of a green bean. **c1960** Wilson *Coll* = outside covering of beans or corn. **2016** Lundy and Autry *Victuals* 33 You will find several pictures of long sturdy threads strung with green beans in the "shucks," drying.

3 See **put the shuck on**.

B *verb*

1 (also *shuck out*, *shuck up*) To strip off (the outer covering of an ear of corn), as at the community or family work activity a **shucking**. See also **corn shucking**.

1861 *Martin CW Letters* (Oct 31) we have got hour corn haul in and shucked up. **1862** *Lockmiller CW Letters* (July 24) let him hall [the corn] to the crib and Shuck it and mesure it and let [the cow] stand good til he pays for her. **1892** Dromgoole *War of Roses* 481 All the squire intended, or thought of, was getting his corn shucked. **1935** (in **2009** Powell *Shenandoah Letters* 35) The people seem much upset. Many of them have been unable to shuck their corn because of the dry weather. **1963** Edwards *Gravel* 131 I got to looking at them years and I shucked one out. **1973** *Gardening* 237 When we shucked corn, we saved th'biggest an' prettiest [ears] for seed. **1977** Shackelford et al. *Our Appalachia* 20 They'd gather the corn all in and pile it up and they'd all gather plum around and shuck. **1982** Maples *Memories* 55 Shucking corn was a treat when we might run across a bright red Indian ear of corn. **1986** Pederson et al. *LAGS* = attested by 5/60 interviewees (8.3%) from E TN and 1/35 (2.9%) from N GA; 6/6 of all LAGS interviewees (100%) attesting term were from Appalachia. **1991** Thomas *Sthn Appal* 181 They'd shuck all that corn an' put it in th' crib. You'd put th' shucks in another bin . . . save 'um fer th' horses or cattle in winter-time. **2002** Oliver *Cooking and Living* 8 Some of the corn was eaten as it matured, and some was pickled, but most of it was allowed to dry on the stalks, gathered in the fall and placed in the crib to be shucked and then shelled for hominy, ground into meal for cornbread, and in some cases, made into corn likker.

2 To feed corn husks to (an animal).

1985 Dabney *More Mt Spirits* 36 Maud . . . worked as hard as the boys, "Plowing the mules many of a day on that mountain from sunup to sundown," growing corn, peas, beans and potatoes, "shucking" cows and feeding the mules and hogs every morning.

3 To remove the outer covering or pod from (beans); to take beans out of their pods.

1957 Broaddus *Vocab Estill Co KY* 69 = to remove dried beans from the pods. **1972** *AOHP/ALC-413* [We] raised peppers and red peppers, dried it, strung it on strings and dried it for seasoning, shuck your beans and put it in, made good seasoning.

4 (also *shuck off*) To remove (an article of one's clothing) quickly.

1881 Pierson *In the Brush* 261 The armor was too big, and he shucked 'em off d'rectly, and made for a dry branch down in the bottom. **1901** Harben *Westerfelt* 174 "Shuck off that coat an' shirt!" was his order. **1913** Kephart *Our Sthn High* 246 I "shucked off my clothes," tumbled in, turned my face to the wall, and immediately everybody else did the same. **1948** Chase *Grandfather Tales* 158 He shucked off his overalls and made like he was puttin' on the new britches. **1957** Combs *Lg Sthn High: Word List* 90 = to take off or remove quickly (of clothes). **1994–97** Montgomery *Coll* (known to eight consultants from the Smoky Mountains). **2010** Still *Bare-Bones* 23 Clebe shucked off his shoe and wiggled his toes in the water.

5 (also *shuck down*) To dupe, get (someone) to believe a false or far-fetched story. See also **put the shuck on**.

1982 Slone *How We Talked* 9 = to dupe, to get someone to believe a ridiculous story. **1996–97** Montgomery *Coll* (known to Brown, Cypher, Oliver); Everytime a politician come to the community, he'd try to shuck everyone down, and when he thought he had the job done, he'd move on (Cardwell); "Are you shucking me?" = are you kidding me/telling the truth? (Ellis).

shuck bean (also *shucky bean*) *noun* A green bean put on a string or thread (often at a **bean stringing**) and dried in the pod (or **shuck**) by hanging it on the porch, by the fireplace, in the rafters, or by placing it on a tray or **scaffold** in the sun. It is preserved for boiling in water and eaten in the winter, either in the pod or shelled. Same as **leather britches**.

1913 Kephart *Our Sthn High* 292 Green beans in the pods are called snaps; when shelled they are shuck-beans. **1917** (in **1944** Wentworth *ADD* 555) (sWV) *shuck-beans* = shelled string-beans. **1924** Raine *Saddlebags* 11 She dries apples and corn and shucky beans. The latter she strings with a needle and thread and hangs overhead. **1939** Hall *Coll* (Saunook NC) = beans strung on strings and dried in their shells, also called leather britches. **1946** Matthias *Speech Pine Mt* 191 Shucky beans, green beans dried in the pod . . . In eastern Kentucky, the green beans are threaded and hung to dry in long strings, usually from porch rafters in the sun. To prepare them for cooking, the housewife washes the pods and cuts them up as she would cut green string beans. **c1950** Adams *Grandpap* 115 Mammy and Granny busied themselves with hanging the bunches of onions and red peppers to nails in the joists and the pokes of dried pumpkin and shucky beans to pegs in the walls. **1976** Braden *Grandma Was Girl* 38 Drying was one way we preserved some foods. We would string green beans, then run long strings through them, and hang these strings of beans up to dry. They were called "shuck beans," and after they were dried we would cook them for hours with pork. They were good eating. **1995** Williams *Smoky Mts Folklife* 99 Many older women fondly remember "bean stringings." Dried beans took two forms: "leather britches"—dried green beans—and "shucky beans"—dried beans that would later be shucked. **2006** *Encycl Appalachia* 954 Unlike shelly beans, which are dried on the vine and then shelled, shuck beans include the entire dried pod and bean. Before the invention of preservation methods such as canning and freezing, drying was the only process for preserving beans. Among the favorite beans for drying were mountain white half-runners, striped cornfield beans, and Kentucky Wonders. **2016** Lundy and Autry *Victuals* 151 The commonly accepted folklore of the mountain South says that this was a tradition among the southeastern tribes, and contemporary Cherokee people continue to make shuck beans, as do contemporary Appalachians today. But it appears that the practice may have originated in Germany and been brought to the mountains by early settlers from the Palatinate, and then adopted by the rest of the people in the region. *Getrocknete Bohnen* is the term used in Germany to refer to any number of dried beans, including whole green beans strung on a thread and dried exactly as described here.

[DARE *shuck bean* n chiefly southern Appalachians]

shuck bed (also *shuck bed tick, shuck mattress, shuck tick*) *noun* A mattress or **tick** filled with shredded corn husks, usually replenished in the fall of the year. See also **featherbed tick**, **flock tick**, **straw tick**, **tick**.

1943 Stuart *Private Tussie* 190–91 After supper we slept on our shuck bed ticks on the schoolhouse floor. **1954** *GSMNP-19*:26 We had a shuck mattress. **c1960** Wilson *Coll*: *shuck bed* = tick or mattress made of shucks. **1999** Montgomery *Coll*: *shuck tick* = shucks were cut into slices etc. (Cardwell).

shuck bed tick See **shuck bed**.

shuck bin *noun* A covered, usually indoor compartment in which corn husks are dried or kept dry, for use to fill a **shuck bed**, make a **shuck mop**, etc.

1939 Hall *Coll* (Copeland Creek TN) They hid theirselves in a shuck bin.

shuck broom *noun* See citation.

1983 Broaddus *Estill Co KY Word List* 55 = a broom with the sweeping end made of corn husks.

[DARE (at *shuck* n[1] 1b(2)) South, South Midland]

shuck doll *noun* Same as **corn-shuck doll**.

1999 GSMNPCOHP-1:5 They'd make shuck dolls for the kids, the girls.

shuck down See **shuck[2] B5**.

shuck house *noun* A farm building in which **fodder** is stored.

1862 *Martin CW Letters* (June 30) their is enough of houses to hold it [= shucked corn] the old shuck house will do it I recon. **1963** Watkins and Watkins *Yesterday* 56 Old Lead slept in the shuck house and he barked and growled fierce enough to scare away prowlers.

shucking *noun*

1 Same as **corn shucking**.

1863 *Poteet CW Letters* (Nov 3) you Rote that if I could be at home to go with you to the shucking that you would be glad. **1864** *Blair CW Letters* (April 11) I wan you & luis make to make all the corn you can this sumer and ask mee to the shucking. **1892** Dromgoole *War of Roses* 481 Not a *husking*, mind you, but a *shucking*. Such as they have nowhere to such perfection as in Tennessee.

2 (usually *shuckings*) The leaf-like covering of an ear of corn. Same as **shuck[2] A1**.

1962 Clark *Folk Speech NC* 319 *shuckings* = corn shucks after shucking. **1996** Isbell *Last Chivaree* 70 He removed two ears [of corn], stripped them, and came back to Ray with the shuckings.

shucking bee *noun* Same as **corn shucking**.

1972 GSMNP-93:15 [If] the man had a big field of corn that he needed shucked, he'd just have a shucking bee. All the young people would come in, and it was a regular social gathering. **1991** Haynes *Haywood Home* 48 We'd sled the corn out of the fields, pile it in a huge heap next to the crib and wait for a "shucking bee" before we put it in the crib.

shuckins *interjection* Used as a mild oath to express annoyance, disbelief, etc.

1963 Edwards *Gravel* 23–24 Why shuckins no, I ain't aims to get married unless I might marry this here little curly-headed Hes. **1998** Montgomery *Coll* (known to Brown, Bush).

shuck mattress See **shuck bed**.

shuck mop *noun* A mop made from corn husks.

1940 Still *River of Earth* 178 The floors were scrubbed twice over with a shuck mop, and the smoky walls washed down.

[DARE (at *shuck* n[1] 1b(2)) South, South Midland]

shuck off See **shuck[2] B4**.

shuck out See **shuck[2] B1**.

shuck pen *noun* An enclosure or crib often attached to a barn for storing corn husks to be fed to cattle. See also **crib 1**, **shuck pen**.

1973 Miller *English Unicoi Co* 152 = a small enclosure in the farmyard where the shucks were piled and kept for later use. **c1975** Lunsford *It Used to Be* 35 When they'd finish up the corn and get ready to put up the shucks, they'd turn around, facing the shucks that had been thrown back of them, and they'd catch up each arm around the right and to the left in close contact circle. They'd take up the shucks, roll them into the shuck pen and tromp them down.

[DARE (at *pen* n B3) chiefly South, South Midland]

shuck pulling *noun* Same as **corn shucking**.

1975 Gainer *Witches Ghosts Signs* 16 There's goin' to be a shuck-pullin' at Hart's barn tonight.

shuck shredding (also *shuck tearing*) *noun* Formerly, a community work activity at which dried corn husks are separated and shredded for various uses (as to make a **shuck bed**). See citations.

1979 Smith *White Rock* 4–5 Grandma, as did her neighbors, invited friends in to help with the "shuck shredding." The harvested corn was put into cribs to dry. The hard outer corn shuck was fed to the livestock or put on the land to enrich it. The softer inner layers of the shucks were torn into tiny pieces and sticks into ticks or cases. Social life, like play, revolved around work, so "shuck shreddings" were made lively by singing, telling jokes, storytelling, and courting. **1985** Williams *Better Man* 17–18 He liked to hear accounts of 'possum hunting, ginsenging, berry picking, bean stringings, corn shellings, shuck tearings, and the like.

shuck (someone's) corn *verb phrase* To betray (a man) by having sexual intercourse with his wife; to be unfaithful in marriage. See also **shuck[2] B5**.

1982 Slone *How We Talked* 9 = to be unfaithful with another man's wife. **1996–97** Montgomery *Coll* (known to Adams, Brown, Cardwell, Ledford), = with reference to a woman, as "She'll shuck your corn" (Jones). **2004** Adams *Old True Love* 188 As bad as I hate to admit it, Larkin would have shucked Hackley's corn so quick it would've made your head spin, if only he'd knowed it could have been his for the shucking.

shuck the corn *verb phrase* See citation.

2014 Montgomery *Doctrine* 182 = to preach really, really well; to explain a scriptural subject in good form; to preach in a loud and fast fashion; to tell it like it is; to tell it like it should be;

to bear down on the doctrines of grace in a sermon with a little "Arminian Skinning" for good measure.

shuck tick See **shuck bed**.

shuck up See **shuck² B1**.

shucky bean See **shuck bean**.

shuffler *noun* See citation.

c1980 Roberts *Olden Times* 110 The threshing machines of earlier days, often called a "shuffler" or "chaff piler," were quite different from those of a generation or so ago. The earlier machines did not move from farm to farm, but instead were stationed at certain barns which had a "threshing floor"—loft floor without cracks upon which the threshed grain and the chaff could be spread. After the threshing was finished the grain and the chaff was then put through the windmill seed cleaners turned by hand. This blew the chaff from the heavier grain. Farmers from nearby brought their grain to the threshing floor to have it threshed and cleaned.

shumake See **sumac**.

shummick See **shammick**.

shun See **shine A**.

shunpike *noun* See citation.

1881 Pierson *In the Brush* 27 My appointments for the week being all fulfilled, I took the turnpike and started for the county-seat. I was never so grateful for a good road, and never so willing and glad to pay toll. At various points along the "pike," as it was universally called, I saw tracks leading off into the woods, and was told that they were known as "shunpikes," and that some people in traveling would take these and go through the woods around the toll-gates, in order to avoid paying toll.

shut

A Variant forms *shed* [see **1975** in **B**], *shet*.

1867 Harris *Sut Lovingood* 138 I'd 'bout es lief be shet up in a steam biler wif a three hundred pound bag ove lard, es tu make a bisiness ove sleeping wif that gal. **1913** Kephart *Our Sthn High* 257 He checks her with a curt "Shet up!" and the incident is closed. *Ibid.* 284 Examples of a strong preterite with dialectical change of the vowel are . . . shet. **c1959** Weals *Hillbilly Dict* 2 Shet the door. It feels sorta airish in here. **1973** Jones *Cades Cove TN* 117 *shet*. **1997** Montgomery *Coll* Shet the door, shet your big mouth (Brown).

B In phrases *be shet of*, *be shut of*, *get shed of*, *get shet of*, *get shut of*, *get shut on* = be or get rid of, be free from.

1859 Taliaferro *Fisher's River* 54 You see, I got shet uv my inimy, the sarpunt. **1863** *Brown CW Letters* (Sept 20) you wish i wold come home so you cold git shet of my thing. **1863** *Karnes CW Letters* (March 15) I tell you that I was hapy to git shet of the trip. **1895** Edson and Fairchild *TN Mts* 374 *get shet on* = get rid of: "I can't get shet on that dog." **1897** Pederson *Mtneers Madison Co* 830 He discoursed of the different varieties, and of how much this or that tree had borne, and of how he "got shet of" the borers and other pests. **1915** Pollard *TN Mts* 243 He just got shut of the horse. **1937** Hall *Coll* (Cades Cove TN) Law, we was glad to be shet of them mules. **1956** GSMNP-22:16 I always just got me a gun and killed them, got shed of them. **1956** Hall *Coll* (Cosby TN) They say if you crossed water, that got shet of the haint. **1975** GSMNP-59:24 They burnt that up [is] the first thing they done, to get shed of it. **1978** Montgomery *White Pine Coll* VI-2 I think we're shut of Baker. I doubt if we'll ever get shut of Jimmie Quillen, because he's another one of them that don't do nothing but politic. **1982** Abell *Better Felt* 49 The Bible says "No sin shall enter into heaven." We've got to get shed of these sins. **1983** *Dark Corner OHP-5A* I [had] seventy-five turkeys, big ones or little ones, and I had about fifty that I wanted to get shed of. **1985** Irwin *Alex Stewart* 202 Ashes is good to get shed of tater bugs. **1997** Montgomery *Coll* Get shet of the old hoss (Brown).

[OED3 *be shut of* (at *shut* v 11b) dialect]

shut-in *noun* A narrow, hard-to-access valley in the shape of a gorge; also used in place-names, as in *Shut-In Creek* (TN).

1913 Kephart *Our Sthn High* 283 That place Nantahala is a master shut-in, jest a plumb gorge. **1943** Hannum *Mt People* 88 For their mother, up in that wild shut-in, there was no such promise. **1968** Powell *NC Gazetteer* 454 Shut-in Creek [two sites, one each in Jackson and Madison Counties]. **1972** Cooper *NC Mt Folklore* 95 = gorge. **1995** Montgomery *Coll* (known to Cardwell).

[DARE *shut-in* n southern Appalachians, Ozarks]

shut-mouth (also *shut-mouthed*) *adjective* Reticent, reserved to the point of evasiveness. See also **play hushmouth**.

1929 Kephart *Smoky Mt Magic* 88 She can play shet-mouth good as ary man, when she wants to. **1937** Thornburgh *Great Smoky Mts* 94 Thar wuz lawin' about it, but my folks kept outen it by keeping shet mouth. And thar'd be a sight less trouble in the world, ef folks would mind their own business and keep shet mouth. **c1940** Simms *Coll*: *shetmouthed* = quiet, reserved. **c1945** Haun *Hawk's Done* 265 I thought he seemed mighty shutmouthed about something. **1997** Montgomery *Coll*: shut mouth (known to nine consultants from the Smoky Mountains); When we kids were being too noisy, my grandma would say, "Let's stay shutmouth a while" (Oliver).

shut of See **shut B**.

shuttle *noun* Variant forms *shekel*, *shettle*, *shickle*.

1917 Kephart *Word-List* 417 *shickle* = shuttle (of a loom). **1957** Combs *Lg Sthn High: Word List* 89 *shettle*, *shekel*. **1995–97** Montgomery *Coll*: *shickle* (known to Brown, Bush).

shy *verb*

1 To avoid, dodge in order to evade.

1937 Hall *Coll* (Mingus Creek NC) [Did you see many armies in the Civil War go through here?] No, we young'uns would shy 'em.

2 To become startled, take sudden fright.

1991 Haynes *Haywood Home* 25 Shiloh [= a horse] was bad to shy and run away at the drop of a hat.

shy off *verb phrase* To avoid contact because of bashfulness.

1973 GSMNP-70:9 She wasn't paying no attention to me. She shied off all the time.

si (also *s'i, si hell, sti*) *verb, verb phrase* Says I (used to recount one's own speech in live action to express what is known as the historical present). See also **-s²**.

1936 Coleman *Dial N GA* 17 "Si" is an abbreviation for "says I." "Sti" is also used, as "Sti, John, we can't go." **1961** *Coe Ridge OHP-334A* She used the word "si" . . . you ever hear the word used before, "si"? . . . it's "si, si" . . . I guess it meant "say," don't you? . . . Yeah, "si," "says you" or something . . . it's just a different way of the word "say." *Ibid.* 336A Old Catty bawled out at him to hurry up, and Tom didn't pay him any mind, and Catty reached down and got him a rock, said, "I said for you to trot," and Tom said, "Si, by God," he says, "I don't trot, I don't trot for myself nor nobody else." **1974** Fink *Bits Mt Speech* 31 *'s' I* = I said: "Your're [sic] crasy, 's' I." **2017** *Blind Pig* (Feb 18) Bud's habitual saying was "si hell." Pap said no matter what Bud was telling or talking about, he always started it with "si hell." Pap said one day Bud came around telling "Si hell, I killed a rattlesnake that was 5 foot long yesterday."

si-antigodlin See **si-godlin**.

sic (also *sic out, sic up*) *verb, verb phrase* To urge (dogs) to pursue and attack hunted game.

1925 Dargan *Highland Annals* 154 I'll take Bub an' Bugle, an' pap to carry the rope, an' when we find where he is, y'all stretch 'round above us, an' I'll go in an' sic up the dogs. **1948** Chase *Grandfather Tales* 54 They called the dog and sicked him out toward the gate. **1997–98** Montgomery Coll: *sic* (known to Brown, Bush, Cardwell, Jones, Ledford, Oliver, Weaver); *sic up* (known to Adams, Brown, Ledford, Oliver).

[Web3 *sic* vt alteration of *seek*]

sich See **such**.

sicha See **such C**.

sick *adjective* Cancerous.

1996 Montgomery *File* They took out six knots [from my arm]. Five of 'em was sick (45-year-old man, Gatlinburg TN).

sick bird winter *noun* A late-spring storm or cold spell. For terms describing a similar phenomenon, see **blackberry winter**.

1991 Still *Wolfpen Notebooks* 91 There are several winters: blackberry, redbud, and dogwood. After they're past, sometimes we have Sick Bird winter. Birds get wet and chilled, look pretty droopy. Come a Jackfrost, they die in piles.

sick headache *noun* See citation.

1977 Arnow *Old Burnside* 46 Mama suffered much from what we and neighbors called "sick headache," more commonly known as migraine.

sick to die *adjective phrase* Mortally ill. See also **take sick**.

1973 GSMNP-84:27 He remained out of the church till he got sick to die.

sic out, sic up See **sic**.

side-box kitchen *noun* A kitchen forming an extension to a house.

1971 *Boogers* 40 There was a side-box kitchen we called it, on th' far side.

side ford *noun* See citation.

1955 Dykeman *French Broad* 138 This French Broad road of the drovers was a triumph of scenic beauty, the despair of builders and an economic necessity, one of the few roads in the United States that required the ingenuity of side-fords. These were described, in the grave terms of an eyewitness, as, "places where, in the construction of the road down to the river bank, the builders encountered large precipices, usually ends of mountain spurs, whose bases the waters of the stream washed. In order to get around such precipices, the road was built at their bases into the water, usually for not more than an eighth of a mile around. These were called 'side-fords' and were impassable at times of floods in the river." To help in the upkeep of this road, tolls were charged by the various counties.

sidegodlin See **si-godlin**.

sideling (also *sidelin, sidely, sidlin*) *adjective* Of the ground: steep or sloping to one side.

1867 Harris *Sut Lovingood* 91 The hous' stood on sidelin groun, an' the back door wer even wif hit. **1930** Armstrong *This Day and Time* 68 [The land's] right sidlin', but the sun hits it so fair. **1974** Fink *Bits Mt Speech* 23 = slanting, as a hillside. "He planted his corn on *sideling* ground." **1982** Slone *How We Talked* 30 *sidelin'* = slanting; *sidelin' ground* = steep, at an angle. **1986** Pederson et al. *LAGS* (Washington Co TN) *sidely*. **1991** Thomas *Sthn Appal* 122 Whenever it tears that dish out of it, I don't care how much sidlin' th' land you go over [is]—break off that hub—bring it back! **1999** Milnes *Play of Fiddle* 93 A farmer on Birch River, whom I used to help put up hay, would say that the hill "went sidling" (got angled or precipitous) when it was too steep on which to drive a tractor. "Tipling" means the same thing. **2003** Carter *Mt Home* 60 I tripped on a loose clod of dirt and fell headlong over the sidlin' hill where we was a plantin' the garden.

[OED3 *sideling* adj A3 "of the ground: sloping, steep"]

side meat (also *side pork*) *noun* Meat from the side of a hog, bacon. See also **fatback**, **long hog**, **middling C**, **sow belly**, **streaked bacon**, **striped meat**.

1914 Wilson *Sthn Mtneers* 59 The field will provide corn for his "pone" bread, and a few razor-backed pigs grown, and fattened, on the mast in the woods will furnish his "side-meat." **1934–47** LAMSAS *Appal*: *side meat* = attested by 35/148 speakers (23.6%) from WV, 9/20 (45%) from VA, 5/14 (35.7%) from SC, and 3/12 (25%) from GA. **1946** Nixon *Glossary VA Words* 37 *side meat* = salt pork . . . [a term used] in the Blue Ridge and south of the lower James. **1984** Hall *Coll* (Del Rio TN) Side meat is what gives you your good bacon. **1986** Pederson et al. *LAGS*: *side meat* = attested by 11/60 interviewees (18.3%) from E TN and 7/35 (20%) from N GA; 18/85 of all LAGS interviewees (21.2%) attesting term were from Appalachia. **1996** Cole *Forney's Creek* 65–66 She fixed side-meat—what we would call now, bacon—or sausage; sometimes it was ham and biscuits and gravy. **1997** Montgomery *Coll*: *side pork* (known to Adams, Bush, Cardwell, Ledford, Norris, Weaver).

[Web3 *side meat* n chiefly South and Midland]

(the) side of *phrasal prepositional* Beside. See also **beside of**.

1939 Hall *Coll* (Wears Cove TN) We found him layin' in a sink-hole—just his bones there. Then his watch was layin' just the side of his bones. *Ibid.* (White Oak NC) Mountain people don't use the word "beside," they say "the side of."

side pleurisy *noun* Inflammation of the chest cavity, with fever; or an injury to the chest causing such inflammation. See citations.

1973 GSMNP-74:12 The sled got away from him and hurt him someway or another, and he took side pleurisy and died. **1973** GSMNP-82:19 [The doctor] told her that he could run [the pain] down in my side and told them I had side pleurisy, and I did. I had thirteen abscesses on that side when I was eighteen years old. It hurt me all them years. **1997** Montgomery *Coll* = inflammation of the inner chest cavity (Bush), = inflammation of the pleura (lining of the lungs) with fever (Jones), = an injury to the side which results in accumulation of fluid around the lungs (Ledford), = a complication from a severe chest cold, not an injury (Norris), = a swelling with excessive liquid inside (Weaver).

side pork See **side meat**.

side winder *noun* See citation.

1997 Farwell *Logging* = a tree knocked down unexpectedly by [the] felling of another tree.

sidlin See **sideling**.

sifflicated *adjective* Suffocated.

1904–20 Kephart *Notebooks* 2:475 I was that nigh sifflicated. **1994** Montgomery *Coll* (known to Cardwell, but not to other consultants from the Smoky Mountains).

sight *noun*

1 A large number, a great deal or amount. See also **heap B2**, **one more**, **sight in the world**.

1862 *Parris CW Letters* (July 3) our men has whipt them evry fite and has drove them Severl miles and has taken a Site of prisners with som six Jennerls. **1862** *Tesh CW Letters* (Jan 6) he was sent to a hors pitle the second day of April and died the 4 I tell you poly is in a sight of trouble about him. **1901** Harben *Westerfelt* 223 You've give me a sight of comfort. **1913** Kephart *Our Sthn High* 296 Many common English words are used in peculiar senses by the mountain folk, as . . . a power or a sight for much. **1937** Hall *Coll* (Big Creek NC) Indian physic tea is good to clean your stomach off. Good blood medicine. Lord, I've drunk a sight of it. *Ibid.* (Cosby TN) A sight of people died of the fever on this branch twenty-five or thirty year ago. **1939** Hall *Coll* (Cosby Creek TN) People in Elkmont had a sight of fruit [i.e. apples] to sell in the fall. **1985** Irwin *Alex Stewart* 75 He took sick one evening and he laid there and groaned right on up until he died. I've wondered a sight about that. **1997** Montgomery *Coll* Jim grew a sight of taters (Brown).

[Web3 *sight* n 3 "a great number or quantity; a great deal" chiefly dialect; DARE *sight* n 1 chiefly South, South Midland]

2 In adverbial phrase *a sight* = very much, a great deal.

1834 Crockett *Narrative* 31 My father told me, in a very angry manner, that he would whip me an eternal sight worse than the master, if I didn't start immediately to school. **1862** *Robinson CW Letters* (Aug 3) my littel girl thinks a durnd Site more of me then I do of her. **1864** *Tesh CW Letters* (April 3) just thought you could make a Little snack and bake me some cakes and send me some butter and it wouldant be much Trouble to him and would help me a sight. **c1900** (in **1997** Stoddart *Quare Women* 95) She's a sight good teacher. **1904–20** Kephart *Notebooks* 2:475 I'm a sight better. **1939** Hall *Coll* (Roaring Fork TN) We would play marbles a sight. We would shoot from fifty feet. That was the most interesting game when I was in school. **1956** Hall *Coll* (Big Bend NC) It's a-helpin' me a sight. **1973** GSMNP-80:10 I courted Alfred Reagan and Isham Bales both, but I liked Alf Reagan a sight the best. **1973** GSMNP-87:1:3 Fifteen years ago people could have told you a sight more than they can tell you now.

[DARE *sight* n 2 chiefly South, South Midland]

3 See citation.

1957 Combs *Lg Sthn High: Word List* 90 = a short distance. Ex.: "It's jist a sight down there."

4 An extreme or extraordinary thing.

1941 Stuart *Men of Mts* 292 It's a sight to hear Lottie go on about poor old Willie. **c1950** Adams *Grandpap* 41 They heard the awfulest bellowin' goin' on ahead of 'em. Oh, hit was a sight to hear. **1979** Melton *'Pon My Honor* 25 Uncle Dick was a sight for devilment, so as he went along through the woods where Billy was working, he kept thinking about what he could do to him. **1985** Irwin *Alex Stewart* 131 People laughed at him, and it was a sight to hear them talk. They said he was the funniest looking feller that they ever seed.

sight hound *noun* See citation.

2007 Plott *Story Plott Hound* 184 = dog that trails by sight rather than scent, generally a more hot-nosed dog.

sight in the world

A *noun phrase* An extraordinary or remarkable thing. See also **sight 4**.

1942 (in **1987** Perdue *Outwitting Devil* 9) He got up and went out to shet the gate and run over the skunk and when he come back he was a sight in the world to smell. **1957** Combs *Lg Sthn High: Word List* 90 = something unusual, remarkable, in the expression: "It's a sight in the world how that granny-hatchet can run." **1963** Edwards *Gravel* 94 It was a sight in the world to see them hongry hogs go for that slop, Johnny said.

B (also *sight on earth*) *adverb phrase* = very (much), a great deal. See also **sight 2**.

1938 Simms *Coll* The rats had "chawed [a sheep-skin] a sight in the world." **1953** Hall *Coll* (Gatlinburg TN) He loved to hunt a sight in this world. **1967** Hall *Coll* (Townsend TN) [The Appalachian Trail] is traveled a sight in the world. It's beat to death in the summer time. **1973** GSMNP-80:6 The wind blowed a sight in the world hard up there. *Ibid.* That there Bullhead wind, that used to blow a sight on earth, it don't blow like it used to. *Ibid.* 12 He said that was lamb tongue and them sheeps would just eat that a sight in the world. **1989** Smith *Flyin' Bullets* 242 He's helped me a sight on this earth. **2007** Myers *Smoky Mt Remedies* 11 I felt a sight on earth bad.

sight on earth See **sight in the world B**.

siglin See **si-godlin**.

sign *noun*

1 Used as a mass noun = evidence of the presence of an animal (such as a bear) in the form of tracks, excrement, refuse from feeding, markings on trees (by which a bear indicates its territory), etc. See also **bear sign**.

1878 Coale *Wilburn Waters* 61 Wilburn had found "sign" and had followed it up to a tall cliff near the summit of one of the highest and most inaccessible peaks in the range. **1886** Smith *Sthn Dialect* 350 There are still others [= terms] which have not, so far as I know, the authority of Old English: . . . sign (track of wild beast). **1913** Kephart *Our Sthn High* 97 John and the hunchback had found "sign" in the opposite direction. **1927** Mason *Lure of Smokies* 216 I follered th' bloody sign an' come to whar my b'ar was down agin a hollur tree. **1939** Hall *Coll* (Cataloochee NC) A bear was a-usin' in the chestnut patch, so we found his sign and found where he was a-layin'. *Ibid.* (Deep Creek NC) They was a little skiff of snow, and that was how come to see their sign. **1953** Hall *Coll* (Bryson City NC) They was an awful lot of sign where [the bear] had eaten the beech mast. **1970** *Hunting Stories* 16 A good place to find "sign" was around branches and the heads of springs where [raccoons] had been turning over rocks looking for crayfish and spring lizards . . . Sign could also be found around oaks and other trees where they'd been scratching for nuts. **1977** Shackelford et al. *Our Appalachia* 94 I could tell a red fox sign from a gray one: it was much bigger. Got a foot plime blank like a dog and them two front toenails are longer than the gray [fox's].

2 One of the twelve equal divisions of the Zodiac, each being distinguished by the name of a celestial constellation, each being associated with a given symbol, said to govern earthly affairs. See also **dark of the moon**, **light of the moon**, **new of the moon**, **old of the moon**.

1834 *McLean Diary* 27 [I] Sode my oats on the fortenth planted my corn on 15 and 16 Days the Sine in the hart hard frosts. **1864** *Chapman CW Letters* (April 10) I have fiften large hogs and 17 shotes & sent Billy Smith half bush[el] of sweat tater seed yesterday to com & spay them for mee when the sine gets right. **1926** Lunsford *Folk-Lore* 13 For instance, the writer has been vanquished time and again in this goodly land with argument to the effect that the earth has corners and a foundation and that the moon is placed in the heavens for signs and that therefore the "twelve signs of the zodiac" may be absolutely relied upon as a true guide to poultry and hog raising, laying of worm fences, and planting of various crops. It is established beyond all question in some of our communities that the bottom rail of a worm fence should be laid upon the light of the moon and that the top rail should be laid in the dark of the moon so that the fence will thereby curl together so securely that a Wilkes County ox couldn't push it down. This same principle also governs the time for killing hogs in some communities, and a little laxity in the enforcement of this rule may even affect the taste of the "shortenin' bread." **1963** Edwards *Gravel* 22 "Aw, they ain't nothing to them signs," deprecated Wes. "My pa says the best sign is the foot sign. When you see tracks then you know that somethin's been there." **1967** Jones *Peculiarities Mtneers* 22 In former times mountain farmers also paid much attention to the signs of the Zodiac. For instance, the time to kill weeds, prune an orchard, mow hay, plant a crop, paint a house, breed an animal, set a hen, wean a baby, pull a tooth, shear a sheep, start a journey, engage in romance or get married, go fishing—in face almost every activity was supposed by some mountaineers to be affected favorably or unfavorably by the current sign of the Zodiac or the phase of the moon. Such chores were never to be undertaken when "the sign" was not right. **1970** Adams *Appal Revisit* 41 The phases of the moon received considerable attention by mountain people fifty years ago. Almanacs were searched and the zodiac was carefully scrutinized to find out when the new and old phases of the moon occurred. If corn was planted on the new moon, it was sure to be all stalk and the ears of corn would not fill out properly. Farmers who covered their houses and barns with boards would not think of riving the boards on a certain phase of the moon. If the boards were riven on the new moon, they would curl up, thus permitting leaks in the roof. If paling slats were riven on the new moon, they would curl up permitting large cracks to occur. People killed their hogs when the signs in the moon were right. **1973** GSMNP-85:2:11 You plant beans when the sign is in the knees or arms, and you won't never fail. **1974** Roberts *Sang Branch* 31 My father used all the signs in his planting. He planted corn and beans when the sign's in the arms; 'taters when the sign was in the feet; sowed his cabbage and things like that growed heads when the sign was in the head; planted all his vines when the sign was in the secrets. We allas raised plenty of stuff and never did fail. They's three days of the year, called barren days, when he wouldn't plant anything. **1978** Montgomery *White Pine Coll* X-2 This nation would have been starved to death years ago if everybody had went by the signs. **1981** GSMNP-122:64 The first quarter sign's in the heart, [so] I never plant nothin' without it's beets. **1992** *Smokies Guide* (Fall) 10 Butchering took place after the weather was cold enough to help preserve the meat. This often occurred around Thanksgiving, although many farmers waited until the signs were right, preferring to kill the animals at the time of a full moon. Many felt that if the animal was killed during a shrinking or waning moon, the meat would shrink when it was cooked. **2007** Milnes *Signs Cures Witches* 31 Appalachian astrological beliefs are much simplified from the original, highly mathematical Greek formulas and today are limited to the "signs" and the phases of the sun and moon. While some still study the signs in great detail, without access to professional astrologers, most of today's practitioners, using an almanac or almanac calendar, are able to ascertain propitious days to go about common agricultural farm chores and domestic activities, with variations supplied by tradition. *Ibid.* 36 Old farmer Otis Rose told me that they never make kraut or pickle beans in the sign of the feet (Pisces), because "you know how your feet smell sometime." He believed the food took on that odor. . . . Cabbage and brussel sprouts do best if planted when the sign is in the head, as represented on the almanac Man. Kraut and pickles should be made in a light moon. Castration, dehorning, or any activity that could draw blood is best done when the signs are not close to the heart.

3 Evidence of an illegal distilling operation, especially tracks.

1974 Dabney *Mt Spirits* xxiv = the physical evidence leading to a distillery: tracks, broken undergrowth, spilled sugar, a trail. A favorite moonshiner expression was "put out the sign," i.e., sweep away the tracks. Revenue agents sought to "find the sign" or "cut off the sign." **1974** Maurer and Pearl *KY Moonshine* 124 = evidence of moonshine traffic. **1992** Gabbard *Thunder Road* 33 The "revenooers" would ride the roads and see if they could see paths off the road where you had stopped and toted stuff up a bank. Bootleggers were pretty sharp at how they handled their signs. We'd lay planks off the side of a truck and walk them planks to the top of a bank, then go into the woods and not leave a sign. The "revenooers" might smash up three or four stills at one time and wipe you out, so you'd have to start over again.

4 A formation of a plant taken pseudo-scientifically to signify the part of the anatomy on which its derived medicine has curative power.

1973 Mullins *Herbs KY Highlands* 36 An outgrowth of early medical science, a pseudo-science strangely mixed with theology, is the doctrine of the signature of plants. It is the belief that for every illness there is some herb with the power to cure it and that the herb bears the sign or mark by which it may be known against what particular disease or illness it may be used. This "sign" is often nothing more than a very superficial association suggested by the shape or color of the plant or even by its name.

sign follower *noun* An adherent to a Pentecostal sect that follows "signs" laid out in the Bible, specifically in the Gospel according to Mark, regarding the handling of snakes and drinking of deadly liquids. See also **serpent handler**, **take up a serpent**.

1993 Burton *Take Up Serpents* 6 Contemporary adherents trace their beliefs of the words of Jesus to his disciples immediately prior to the ascension as recorded in Mark: "And these signs shall follow them that believe; in my name they shall cast out devils; they shall speak with new tongues. They shall take up serpents; and if they drink any deadly thing, it shall not hurt them; they shall lay hands on the sick, and they shall recover" (Mark 16: 17–18). Because of the initial words of this text, serpent handlers are often referred to as "sign followers." They consider themselves simply Christians who are following the will of God.

si-godlin (also *se-gogglin, si-antigodlin, sidegodlin, siglin, si-gogglin, si-goggling, si-goglin, si-gogling, si-gonglin', si-waddlin, skigoglin, skygodlin, skygoglin*) *adjective, adverb* Askew, off-center, crooked, leaning to one side. See also **anti-godlin**, **cater-corner**, **catawampus**[2], **slanchways**, **slanti-godlin**.

1913 Kephart *Our Sthn High* 294 Slaunchways denotes slanting, and sigodlin or si-antigodlin is out of plumb or out of square. **1917** Kephart *Word-List* 417 *si-godlin* = slantindicular. "You sawed that log off a little *si-godlin'*." **1937** Wilson *Folklore SE KY* 7 It may have been "catawampus" or "si-waddlin," with many imperfections in architecture; but the mountain cabin held happiness and the opposite with a distinct way of expressing both. **1939** Eastridge *Folklore Adair Co* 115 "Si-waddlin'" or "catawampus" expresses the slant a thing may have, and it is made clear to the one who hears this explanation. Or if neither of these is used one may use "se-gogglin'" which is quite as expressive. **c1950** Haun *When the Wind* 11 Song-Boy turned his head up, that sigogling way, like he was trying to recollect it all with his mind and he said: "To the little white house." **1956** McAtee *Some Dial NC* 40 *skygodlin, skygoglin* = leaning, oblique, crooked. **c1960** Wilson *Coll: sidegodlin* = awry, out of balance. **1975** Jackson *Unusual Words* 159 Four terms suggest something out of line or out of plumb: *catty-cornered, catty-wampus, slaunchways,* or *sigodlin* (also pronounced *si-goglin*). **1976** Still *Pattern of Man* 80 A grandson of mine climbed a tower in Italy called Pisa, and to hear him tell it, it was out of whanker, leaning on air, against nature and the plan of the Almighty. Plumb si-goggling! **1986** Pederson et al. *LAGS* (Blount Co TN) *ski-goglin*. **1992** Brooks *Sthn Stuff* 139 *si-gonglin', si-antigodlin'* = leaning to one side; out of plumb; *si-gonglin'*. ". . . an old si-gonglin' barn." **1994–97** Montgomery *Coll: siglin* (known to Oliver); *si-godlin* (known to Adams, Cardwell, Ledford); *si-godlin* more common than alternatives (Brewer); *sigoglin* (known to Brown, Cardwell, Ledford), = crooked, used of an object hanging or sitting, something that needs to be lined up, "That picture looks a little si-gogglin" (50-year-old woman, Jefferson Co TN). **2005** Bailey *Henderson County* 30 Whatever may be its origin, the delightful word "si-godlin," meaning off-balance, is still heard occasionally through the mountains. "Set the baby up straight," a mother said. "She'll fall over if ye leave 'er a-settin' sigodlin."

[DARE *si-godlin* adj, adv especially Appalachians]

si-gogglin, **si-goggling**, **si-goglin**, **si-gogling** See **si-godlin**.

si hell Se **si**.

silent *verb* See citation.

1982 Slone *How We Talked* 74 To silent someone [is to] not allow them to preach.

silk *noun* One of many thin threads hanging in a tassel from an ear of corn. Same as **cornsilk**.

1986 Pederson et al. *LAGS* = attested by 28/60 interviewees (46.7%) from E TN and 19/35 (54.3%) from N GA; 47/256 of all LAGS interviewees (18.3%) attesting term were from Appalachia. **1993** Page and Smith *Foxfire Toys and Games* 86 We used to just gather some corncobs and we'd get us some dry silks and make the hair on them and then take a charcoal or a pencil or something and make the eyes in them.

silver bell *noun* A common deciduous tree (*Halesia carolina*) in the region. Same as **peawood**.

1963 Hooper *Unwanted Boy* 234 We timed this opening in April to coincide with the blooming of the dogwoods, red buds, and silver bells, as well as the numerous small wildflowers and many tame ones.

silver cloud *noun* In distilling, a large pot made of galvanized steel or other metal, used for making whiskey; as it corrodes, the metal taints and imparts a cloudy hue to the liquor, which is then dangerous to drink. See also **copper pot**, **galvanize**, **gray cloud**, **pot still**.

1955 Dykeman *French Broad* 244 Wood smoke has left the stills and so, for the most part, has copper. Big operators use the less expensive galvanized iron pots. They are subject to rust, but quality long ago yielded to quantity and a fast dollar. These galvanized drums are called "silver clouds." **1974** Dabney *Mt Spirits* xxiii A localized version of the metal pot still is the "silver cloud," common in East Tennessee, particularly around Cosby. They are cylindrical pots made of galvanized steel, with heat being applied by burners through single or twin flues through the lower third of the pot. Moonshine liquor, esp. that which is "clouded" by the "galvanize" corroded from a steel (rather than copper) still made by the acid of the mash ("beer"). **1985** Dabney *More Mt Spirits* 157 Silver Clouds [are] one of the unique, localized versions of the metal pot still. It is common in east Tennessee, centered in the area round Cosby in the shadow of the Great Smoky Mountain National Park. From a valley below, the "Cosby Silver Cloud" is said to resemble a cloud. They are cylindrical pots made of galvanized steel, with heat being applied by burners through single or twin flues through the lower third of the pot. Up to the 1950's, the Cosby moonshiners utilized copper for these stills, but this proved too expensive since they were losing so many to dynamiting by ATF agents. They resorted to the galvanized metal units, which they could buy, pre-cut, for around $40. These stills—which are used for fermenting mash as well as distilling it—are enormous in size—up to 1,000 gallons in capacity. **2013** Pierce *Corn in Jar* 59 The local moonshiners began making them [= stills] out of galvanized steel. With their huge size and shiny appearance, these stills became commonly known as the "Cosby Silver Cloud."

silverside *noun* The common minnow; any small fish with bright, silvery scales.

1939 Hall *Coll* (Waldens Creek TN) The creek was full of fish—bass, white suckers, silversides, red horses, hog mollies in the creek. **1984** High *Titan Rock* 31 [The Red River] and its tributaries also spawned great schools of fish, including white suckers, black suckers . . . and the little flashing silversides. **1998** Montgomery *Coll* = any streamlined 3″ to 6″ creek minnow (Brown), = a fish too small to eat but beautiful in appearance (Cardwell), = a minnow or small silvery fish (Jones), = the common minnow (Ledford), = a minnow or small fish like the snail darter (Weaver).

Silver War *noun* The American Civil War. Same as **War between the States**.

1976 Still *Pattern of Man* 82 Aye gonnies, the Silver War might have come out different did our side have them [weapons] then. **1992** Offutt *KY Straight* 74 He heard it off his daddy back before the Silver War. **2013** Montgomery *File* When I was growing up I didn't know the word "civil," so I called the conflict the Silver War (65-year-old man, Jefferson Co TN).

simblin, simlin See **cymling**.

simmon See **persimmon**.

since

A *conjunction, preposition* Variant forms *sence, sense, sinst*.

1862 *Neves CW Letters* (Jan 16) we havent had any letters this week for the mail haint went sense saturdy. **1864** *Chapman CW Letters* (March 25) Travis has Bin Laying in the brush ever sence the Vix Burg fight. **1883** Murfree *Old Sledge* 555 I hev been a-aimin' an' a-contrivin' ter tell yer ever sence ye war married ter Josiah Tait. **1913** Kephart *Our Sthn High* 170–71 Jim Cody ain't never showed his nose sence. **1929** (in **1952** Mathes *Tall Tales* 102) He's been our doctor here ever sinst I was a gallike.

B *preposition* From the time that one was.

1970 *Burton-Manning Coll*-94A I've knowed it since a little boy.

since Hec(k) was a pup (also *since Buck was a calf*) *phrase* Since a long time ago.

1915 Dingus *Word-List VA* 190 *since Hec was a pup* = for a long time. **1927** Woofter *Dialect from WV* 364 = a long time ago. "We have lived here since Heck was a purp." **1952** Taylor and Whiting *Proverbs and Sayings* 376 Haven't seen you since Buck was a calf. **1969** Doran *Folklore White Co* 98–99 He may not have seen them "in a coon's age" or "in a month of Sundays" or "in a blue moon" or "since Heck was a pup, and he's dead with old age now." **1982** Slone *How We Talked* 41 Ever since old Heck was a pup.

since the woods burnt over *phrase* Since a long time ago.

2002 Myers *Best Yet Stories* 111 I will never forget seeing two friends meet in the road one day. One exclaimed, "Why, I haven't seen you since the woods burnt over!"

sing

A *verb* Variant past-tense forms *singed, sung*.

1863 *Bell CW Letters* (Jan 11) I must confess that I am not as brave as I thought I was. I never wanted out of a place as bad in my life the balles hailed the shells sung & the grape rattled. **1895** *Mt Baptist Sermon* 15 I jist felt lack singin' an' I sung an' prayed an' shouted thar all night. **1913** Kephart *Our Sthn High* 106 Bill sung out, "Is it far down there?" **1939** Hall *Coll* (Bradley Fork NC) I'm going to sing a song that I sung when the old lady was on her death bed. She called me to sing her a song, and I moved up to her head, and I sung her this song, and the song is this. **1941** Stuart *Men of Mts* 197 The katydids sung down in the cornpatch and the beetles boomed all over the yard. **1969** *Burton-Manning Coll*-50A [She] got it in a different tune from what he sung it. **1970** *Hunting Stories* 34 Th'owls hooted and the robins singed, and different rackets took place. **1973** GSMNP-61:12 They usually sung two or three old-timey songs. **1978** Reese *Speech NE Tenn* 179 *singed* – attested by 2/12 (16.7%) speakers; *sung* = attested by 3/12 (25%) speakers. **1997** GSMNPCOHP We sung together I guess twenty-five year at church services.

B *verb* Of a rattlesnake: to shake its rattles noisily. See also **singer**.

1935 Sheppard *Cabins in Laurel* 89 You just had to take your chance of tromping on 'em and bear away from where you heard 'em sing. **1939** Hall *Coll* (Mt Sterling NC) Hit was intentioned to bite me. I never heared a snake sing so vygrous. **1956** GSMNP-22: 19 Rattling was what [the snakes] was a-doing . . . what we call singing . . . they sing a dry, rattling fuss. **1967** Fetterman *Stinking Creek* 119 Snakes is the worst at berrypicking time. They'll sit in the bushes, and sometimes you can't even hear a rattlesnake singing. **1985** Irwin *Alex Stewart* 265 When I started home for dinner I come down by there and I could hear that rattlesnake singing.

C *noun* Same as **gospel sing, singing**.

1936 Maupin *Pittman Center* 46 One of the main features of this and other mountain communities seemed to be the Sunday afternoon "sing," when everyone got together, with one or more leaders, and sang for two hours or more. . . . Young and old took part in these "sings," and once each month a trip was made to another community to visit and take part in their "sings." **1990** Aiken *Stories* 124 Reford Lamons and his wife Velma Ownby Lamons remember the "sings" of old and regularly participate in those of today.

sing down *verb phrase*

1 To outsing (someone) in an informal competition.

1931 Goodrich *Mt Homespun* 52 The singers had challenged the neighboring districts to bring along their shaped-note songbooks and sing them down if they could.

2 Of the congregation or choir of a church, especially in a **Primitive Baptist** church: to cause (a preacher) to curtail a sermon by beginning to sing; hence noun = such a method used.

1982 Slone *How We Talked* 73 *sing someone down* = If one of the preachers got "carried away" (became so involved in what he was preaching that he forgot the time) someone would start a song, reminding him to finish. **1987** Dorgan *Glory to God* 125 Usually the opening sermon [in Old Regular Baptist services] is the shortest of the morning, and it is always closed by a "sing down" as another elder lines a hymn and the congregation falls in behind. During this "sing down," all members and visitors rise and go through another round of handshaking and embracing. **1989** Dorgan *Regular Baptists* 60 In the past this "sing down" was a technique to force a preacher to close a sermon that had grown too long, and the procedure is still occasionally followed. Given the impromptu nature of Old Regular [Baptist] preaching, it is not uncommon for an elder to become so absorbed with his own sermon (he would call this "inspiration" or possession by "the Spirit") that he will lose track of time. **1991** Still *Wolfpen Notebooks* 127 We had a pretty meeting last Easter Sunday at Old Carr Churchhouse. Four preachers preached, and we had to sing down three of them. **1997** Dorgan *Happy God* 142 At the turn of the century and much later, the "sing down" was used to help the extemporizing preacher close out a sermon that had grown too long. **2014** Montgomery *Doctrine* 191 = an expression meaning that the preacher preached way too long and the congregation sang a song to hush him up and set him down. The "sit down" song is unusually [sic] started by a deacon.

singer *noun* The tail of a rattlesnake kept as an ornament. See also **sing B**.

c1950 (in **2000** Oakley *Roamin' Man* 42) Then on there porch we saw 4 rattle snake singers tide up on the porch.

singing *noun* A gathering, ranging in duration from an afternoon or evening affair to one of several days, for the singing of hymns and gospel songs; it varies in character from an informal event with group participation to a more formal one (traditionally using **shape notes** at the end of a **singing school**) to a competition between small groups of singers (as at a **singing convention**). Same as **gospel sing, sing C**. See also **all day singing, harp singing, old harp singing, singing convention.**

1862 *Huntley CW Letters* (Jan 5) you can tell Dobbins folks that Calloway is Well me and him and tolliver had a pretty smart singing Last night. **1868** *Kendrick CW Letters* (June 28) J. L. K. has a singing nearly every Sunday at Capurnum he has a large clas. **1912** Perrow *Songs and Rhymes* 142 If your visit to this country happened to be at the proper time of the week, you might be able some night to attend a "singin'." You would find the young folk gathered at the "meetin'-house," or still more probably at the home of one member of the "class." **1930** Schantz *Hill Dwellers* 3 The mountain people are deeply religious, and the principal expression of their religious sentiments is evidenced by the frequent "Singings." . . . The timing and harmony of the singers is perfect, and it is worth a journey to the mountains to attend one of these old services. **1937** Haun *Cocke Co* 17–18 The "Singings" held at churches or school houses are, of course, of a different nature from the Saturday night singings. They are all-day affairs with dinner on the ground. Crowds from all the surrounding counties come and join in. Hymns, both old and new, and the best known spirituals are sung at these gatherings. . . . The all-day singings are usually held early in the fall, following a singing master's summer circuit. The song leader sings over the notes of the song by himself, then the crowd sings them over with him, then they all join in and sing the songs. Only those known to be familiar to the whole crowd are sung. **1939** Hall *Coll* (Cades Cove TN) I never did live in a place like that where they was no meetings or no singings. **1973** Kahn *Hillbilly Women* 141 Every Saturday night we have a singing at some church or the other. **1977** Ross *Come Go* 103 Community singings are still rather common. The time and the place are announced in the county paper and at church. Sometimes the singing will be held at a church, sometimes at the county courthouse. More often, though, a smaller group consisting of two or three families will meet at one of the homes to sing several of the old-time hymns. **1984** Garber *Old Harp* 31 Today's "singings" incorporate the traditions of the singing school. . . . By calling on singers to lead some hymns the leader, or teacher, is testing different pupils. Yet the informality of earlier days persists. What matters is not the discipline but the enjoyment of the singing. **1991** Headrick *Headrick's Chapel* 207 The Headrick's Chapel singing is always on the fourth Sunday in September and is an all day affair, directed by Charlie Clabo. Singing begins at 11:00, with a break for lunch at noon, then a resumption of singing around 1:00. Most Old Harp singers agree that this is one of the best singings in the area. Everyone is invited to come and take part. **2014** Montgomery *Doctrine* 182 = a speciasl meeting where "Songs of Zion" are sung; a meeting where singing is done and there is no preaching. Singings are usually held tbrough Saturday with three singing sessions and some continue through Sunday morning. **2016** *Blind Pig* (April 12) At the end of the week, or sometimes two-week "singing school" course, we would have a "singing" and invite the whole community to come and hear the new songs we had learned.

singing convention *noun* A public gathering of duets, quartets, etc. to sing religious music, often in local or regional group competition in addition to performing. See also **singing**.

1958 Morgan *Gift from Hills* 38 It's a great pity that these all-day singings are gradually being discontinued, for nothing really takes the place of them. Radio and TV cannot compare, certainly not socially. They were tremendous occasions, eagerly looked forward to. People would plan and prepare for days ahead of time, baking and cooking. Sometimes a family would take a whole trunkful of food. Nobody ever attended a singing convention in our country without getting his fill of food as well as song. When the morning of the great day arrived, the choirs, the congregations and the visitors from hither and yon began to gather at the appointed church. The choirs were assigned their turns, the first choir would take its position and the all-day singing would be off to a melodious start. They began to have competitions and one choir would be voted best for the year, but after a time this competition detracted from the sheer joy of the singing and the fellowship, and it was discontinued. **1975** Fink *Foreword* ii Then there was the "singing school" in every community, followed by a big "singing convention," when classes from each school gathered to compete for honors. **1977** Wolfe *TN Strings* 11 Throughout the nineteenth century, "singing conventions" were held annually or quarterly in courthouse squares or churches throughout the South; people gathered to sing the old songs, visit, and enjoy "dinner on the ground." **2005** Morgan *Old Time Religion* 123 Singing was an important part not only of the spiritual life of the old time religion folk but also of their entertainment and recreational life. The greatest manifestation of the importance of singing was in the "singing conventions," which had all but died out by World War II. These affairs usually lasted three days and were held in the larger churches. Only one of these harmonious extravaganzas was held in Nantahala due to its small churches and its inaccessibility from the outside world. In these functions, quartets competed against each other. They took turns and were judged by a panel of fellow singers. There were certain factors that were looked for and judged accordingly: harmony, togetherness, and "sameness." Sameness meant that if a quartet sang a stanza and sang one note improperly, it was penalized for this error. If the quartet sang it differently, that is, correctly, in the next stanza, it was penalized again. These events were widely popular among the singers who would travel to the sites where the events were held. **2008** Malone *All-Day Singings* 162 Singing conventions are events that feature the performance of shape-note music, of both the four-shape and seven-shape varieties. . . . Although everyone in attendance is encouraged to sing, performances are also made by soloists, duets, and trios and often by visiting professional quartets. **2016** *Blind Pig* (April 12) The old courthouse at Blairsville . . . still sometimes hosts a day-long "singing" by shaped-note method. We called those gatherings a "Singing Convention" and they drew people from far and near—back in the day.

singing school *noun* Formerly, a one- or two-week session usually conducted on summer evenings at which an itinerant songmaster would teach the rudiments of sight-reading music (especially using **shape notes**). The school charged a small tuition, was open to one and all, and sometimes culminated in a competition or **singing convention**. See also **harp singing, old harp, singing, writing school**.

1862 *Fitch CW Letters* (May 13) you spoke of John Fitch taken up singing [s]cool I hope that you and the rest of folks will hav a good time. **1937** Haun *Cocke Co* 18 The singing teacher holds a two-week school usually, accepting as pay what corn, meat, and chickens the community can give him. He is glad to teach for nothing where he knows people do not have much to spare. He has with him books of all description, from the long and short measure books to the four noted books on up to the shaped-note versions in modern hymnals. And he makes use of all these in his teaching. [**1947** Gamble *Heritage* People in the community collected the money for the [singing] school teacher to come. When the school started everyone was welcome. . . . It started at eight in the morning and went to three in the afternoon. . . . The teacher had a blackboard with a staff. . . . The teacher sang through the song showing the rise and fall of the voice—the [wholes] and half note and quarter note and sixteenth note. The teacher was teaching the shaped notes, what they meant, at the same time teaching the correct pitch on the staff. The teacher sang over and over the hard places until everyone got it correctly. . . . He had a long pointer that beat out the time as they sang. The teacher had a tuning fork to get the proper pitch. After the song was learned, the teacher would choose someone to lead the song, and would teach him how to beat time. In this way he trained leaders to carry on after his departure. The teacher would also pick small groups to sing. All the men, women, and children of the community would come to the singing school whether they paid or not (John McCaulley).] **1959** Pearsall *Little Smoky* 135 Occasional "singing schools" where itinerant singing teachers taught part-singing by the shape note method seem to have been more popular and better attended than academic schools. **1982** *Foxfire VII* 280 Singing schools originated in eighteenth-century New England, being promoted by the clergy in an effort to teach their congregations to read music and thus restore some of the musical heritage that had perished with the first generation of settlers. *Ibid.* 283 The singing school taught that skill of reading the musical staff, reading rhythm, singing by syllables, and singing harmony parts. In addition, the singing school fostered the development of instructional materials, books containing music to be used as lessons for the above skills. *Ibid.* 294 Back then you'd pay fifty cents to go to singing school for ten days. That went for the teacher's salary. **1993** Montell *Cumberland Country* 98 The availability of these songbooks led to the creation of singing schools, another social and religious institution that was important during the late nineteenth century and the first fifty years of the twentieth century. Singing schools were typically sponsored by churches in the individual communities. A teacher versed in the rudiments of shape-note music and often representing such music companies as James D. Vaughan and Stamps-Baxter taught adults and children alike the fundamentals of sight reading music and singing the words to the tunes as indicated by the shapes of the notes. Such schools lasted from ten to fourteen nights, serving not only as a religious function but providing much-needed social diversion as well. **2009** *TN Encycl* Throughout the nineteenth century, shape-note singing schools were conducted all over the South, teaching a style of singing generally known as Sacred Harp singing, the name taken from the most famous tunebook—The Sacred Harp (1844). *Ibid.* In keeping with the tradition's foundations in the Singing School Movement, shape-note singing usually occurs in annual, one-to-three day "singings." These singings are not just musical, but social, pedagogical, and religious events. **2014** Montgomery *Doctrine* 182–83 = a time and place where people gather to receive musical instruction. These are usually bent toward the young people but all age groups are invited to attend and participate. The schools usually last a week and are held annually.

single corn whiskey *noun* Corn whiskey that has been run through the distillation process only once, resulting in lower proof than **double corn whiskey**. See also **singling(s)**.

1953 Shelton *Autobiog I* 7 They gave us a nice warm supper after we had warmed a while, and some hot tea, probably boneset or catnip spiked a little with the old time single or double corn whisky to ward off a cold.

single foot

A (also *single-foot(ed) plow, single plow, single shovel plow*) *noun* A type of **bull tongue** plow. See also **double-foot plow, foot B1**.

1969 GSMNP-46:12 They done their plowing just with a single foot and [would] just break it [= the ground] up and plant it. **1969** Miller *Raising Tobacco* 30–31 The cultivator was distinguished from the *hill-turner*, used to break ground, and from the *single foot* plow used to *run-up* ground. **1972** GSMNP-93:43 What they call a single foot plow . . . was made out of wood . . . they fixed a place down here at [the] foot of the plow, put the flare on, bore holes in there, a heel screw through there, tighten that screw up. **1973** *Gardening* 233 They call'em single-foots now, but back sixty years ago they called'em a bull-tongue, because most everybody plowed with steers. **1973** GSMNP-92:3 We just started plowing early in the spring with a horse and a single plow. The ground was so rough you couldn't use a turn plow, so we just used a single plow. **c1975** Lunsford *It Used to Be* 7 A double-foot would be possibly the fastest, but it is more commonly the single-foot or bull-tongue plow, going one row at a time plowing the fields. **1986** Pederson et al. *LAGS* (Sevier Co TN, Rhea Co TN). **1987** Davenport *Pine Grove* 41 He said they used a single footed plow which was called a bull-tongue, and ran four times between rows.

B *verb phrase* In making whiskey, to put (**mash**) through a single distillation or **run**. See also **singlings**.

1957 Parris *My Mts* 140 It was a heap bigger than pa's but he said the whiskey wasn't nowheres as good as his. Pa said they single-footed theirs. He always double-footed his, same as me.

single-foot(ed) plow See **single foot A**.

single-foot whiskey *noun* Same as **single corn whiskey**.

1985 Dabney *More Mt Spirits* 52 Moonshiners, generally, "temper" their brandy with a "single foot" whiskey.

single-pen cabin (also *single-pen house*) *noun* See citations. See also **pen**[2].

1991 Williams *Homeplace* 26 The common folk house types of rural southwestern North Carolina are typical of those generally found in the Upper South. The square, or more frequently rectangular, single pen house, with all its variants, was probably the most common folk house type in southwestern North Carolina during the nineteenth century. **1995** Trout *Historic Buildings* 15–16 The rectangular single pen was the most common configuration. It could be added onto in several ways as time and circumstances allowed. It was usually 1½ stories high, meaning that only two or three rounds of wall logs rose above the loft floor before the roof system began. This provided normal ceiling height downstairs, and enough headroom upstairs for the kids to sleep and move around. . . . The home had a fireplace with an exterior chimney at one end, a door centered in the front wall, and perhaps a back door aligned with the front one. Window openings were optional at the time of construction, because they could always be sawn out later. **2002** Tate *Log Houses* 8 Two types of single pen houses exist in the southern mountain regions of the United States: the rectangular and square pen house . . . reflecting several different ethnic origins of the colonists who settled in this area. . . . The ethnic groups responsible for the rectangular floor plan were largely the Germans and Scotch-Irish of the Middle Atlantic colonies.

single plow See **single foot A**.

single shovel plow *noun* Same as **single foot A.**

1986 Pederson et al. *LAGS* (Johnson Co TN, Roane Co TN). **1988** Moore *Emergence* 39 The double-shovel plow was made by attaching a second plowpoint on an outrigger to a shovel plow so that the staggered plowshares covered twice as much ground as did those on the narrow single-shovel plow.

singletree *noun* A whiffletree, the swinging horizontal bar to which the traces of the harness of a horse are fastened and by which a wagon, plow, or other conveyance is pulled. Also called **swingletree.** See also **doubletree.**

1892 Smith *Farm and Fireside* 52 [It] makes a good wagon tongue or a single-tree. **1915** Dingus *Word-List VA* 190 = whiffletree. **1949** Kurath *Word Geog East US* 58 In the South and the Southern Appalachians *singletree* and *swingletree* stand side by side, but *singletree*, a counter-term to *doubletree* (shortened from *double swingletree*), is gaining ground and already predominates decidedly in the Virginia Piedmont. **1966–68** *DARE Survey* (Brasstown NC, Burnsville NC, Cherokee NC, Spruce Pine NC, Gatlinburg TN, Maryville TN). **1990** Merriman *Moonshine Rendezvous* 61 The Gallatin bootlegger drew me a map to his home on Muddy Run on the "single tree" plow handle.

[U.S. alteration of *swingletree*, by analogy with *doubletree*]

singling(s) *noun* In distilling, the low-proof liquor produced by the initial distillation **run.** See also **backing, doubling 1, 2, low wine(s), single corn whiskey.**

1808 (in **1956** Eliason *Tarheel Talk* 294) (Wilkes Co NC) Beaten Allum put in the singling will make the whiskey good & clear. **1881** Atkinson *After Moonshiners* 20 In addition to the copper still, a copper or tin worm is necessary. It is submerged in cold water, which chills the steam as it passes from the still through the worm, and transposes it from a vapor into a liquid substance called "singlings" or low wines. **1913** Kephart *Our Sthn High* 135 The product of this first distillation (the "low wines" of the trade, the "singlings" of the blockader) is a weak and impure liquid, which must be distilled at a lower temperature to rid it of water and rank oils. **1914** Arthur *Western NC* 273 When a sufficient quantity has been produced, the mash is removed from the still, and it is washed out, after which the "singlings" are poured into the still and evaporated, passing through the worm a second time, thus becoming "doublings," or high proof whiskey. **1949** Maurer *Argot of Moonshiner* 12 = low-proof liquor which does not contain enough alcohol to be considered whisky. This liquor has been run through the still only once in cases where two stills or two distilling operations are used. Also applied to the condensate in the thump keg: "That ain't likker, that's jest singlin's." **1968** *End of Moonshining* 55 All the beer was run through, a stillful at a time; and the results of each run ("singlins") saved at the other end. When all the beer had been run through once, the still was thoroughly cleaned, and then all the "singlins" placed into the still at one time. Then the stillful of "singlins" was run through. The result was the "doublins," or good whiskey. **1992** Gabbard *Thunder Road* 150 The first time they run the mash, it was pretty poor. They called it "singlin's," 50 or 60 proof, something like that. They'd pour it back in the mash or give it to young boys who worked the still because it was weak and they wouldn't get drunk as quick. When they ran it the second time, they was called "doublin's." That was the moonshine they sold.

[*DARE singlings* n chiefly southern Appalachians]

singling keg *noun* In distilling, the container into which **singlings** are fed.

1968 Connelly *Discover Appal* 118 This worm rested in a cooling tub through which a stream of water constantly poured from a nearby branch or creek. This cooling process condensed the steam which fell into the "singling keg." For a higher-proofed whisky, the liquid was boiled again and passed through the copper tubing.

sing-songing *noun* See citation.

2014 Montgomery *Doctrine* 184–85 = a style of preaching where the delivery style sounds like a chant and each phrase is ended with the typical "uh!" or "ah!" The practice is not as ancient as some advocate; it began in the late 1800's in Appalachia and spread across the country.

sing up a fog *verb phrase* To sing with gusto and at great length, as though to create a change in atmosphere.

1939 Hall *Coll* (Smokemont NC) When I have a girl with me, I can sing up a fog. **1997** Montgomery *Coll* (known to Bush, Cypher).

[perhaps by analogy with *sing up a storm*]

sink

A *verb*

1 Variant past-tense forms *sinked, sunk.*

1862 *Sexton CW Letters* (March 11) thei fout four days and Sunk three yankys vesels. **1863** *Hall CW Letters* (Feb 29) another one of our boats got after it and sunk it. **c1950** Adams *Grandpap* 222 That was too much for Old Roany. Her back just broke right smack in two an' she just sunk down an' give up. **1961** *Coe Ridge OHP-336A* That old man just sunk down and he up and told, said he had killed that man and put him in that pond. **1978** Reese *Speech NE Tenn* 179 *sinked* = attested by 2/12 (16.7%) speakers; *sunk* = attested by 2/12 (16.7%) speakers.

2 Variant past-participle forms *sank, sinked.*

c1950 (in **2000** Oakley *Roamin' Man* 50) To make this story short we finly got off the mts. the sun had sinked below the mts. and the man got out a little packet book and out [s]ome silver and he said heare guide is all the money I have and I want to pay you before the sun is down. **1978** Reese *Speech NE Tenn* 179 *sank* = attested by 4/12 (33.3%) speakers; *sinked* = attested by 1/12 (8.3%) speakers.

B *noun* A low-lying area or basin with sunken ground; also used in place-names, as in *White Oak Sink* (TN). See also **sink hole.**

1927 Mason *Lure of Smokies* 224 They was on [the bear's] trail an' had him cornered in a sink. **1937** Hall *Coll* (Cades Cove TN) The White Oaks is now called the White Oak Sink. **1941** Stuart *Men of Mts* 69 You can find them [= old roads] on every ridge. You can find them running down the pints and across the hollows. You can see these great sinks in the land. They used to lead to houses. **c1960** Wilson Coll = a sinkhole. **1999** Montgomery Coll = a hole where a stump has rotted and left a depression (Cardwell).

sinked See sink **A1**, **A2**.

sinker *noun* See citations.

1952 Wilson *Folk Speech NC* 591 = dumpling cooked with chicken or some other meat. (Swain Co NC). **1997** Montgomery Coll = one of two very different types of dumplings (Ellis). **2006** *Encycl Appalachia* 956 In the central and southern mountains, dried salt pork, sometimes called a sinker, was added to soup beans.

sink hole *noun* Any area of ground with poor drainage. See also **sink B**.

1982 Slone *How We Talked* 31 = a dent place in the field or a mudhole in the road. **1995–97** Montgomery Coll (known to Adams, Cardwell, Ledford, Oliver, Weaver), = used more widely than in strict sense, but not for hole in the road (Ellis).

sinner *noun* (used attributively, as in *sinner man*, *sinner people*) See citations.

1967 Fetterman *Stinking Creek* 146 Sinner people don't understand prayin'. I tell you, I never did want to be a sinner person. **1995** McCauley *Mt Religion* 326 We have heard Brother Coy use the terms "backslider" and "sinner" or "sinner man" more than once. It is important to learn that these terms are not pejorative but descriptive and stem from the history of plain-folk camp-meeting religion.

[DARE *sinner* n especially South, South Midland]

sinner man, **sinner people** See **sinner**.

sinst See **since**.

sipher *verb* See citation.

2005 Williams *Gratitude* 524 = to siphon. "He siphered some gas out of his car."

siren *noun* Variant pronunciation with stress on both syllables: SI-REEN.

1985 Williams *Role of Folklore* 307 They was all runnin' just like rats, ya know. Boy them sireens and stuff was comin' around. **1992** Brooks *Sthn Stuff* 140 si-reen, n. Siren. "It makes you feel so bad when you hear one of those ole si-reens, 'cause you know an am-bulance is on its way." **1995** Cheek *Appal Scrapbook* 144 "Natalie called a 'sireen' a 'siren,'" Steve pointed out. "My cousin in Deetroit does that, too. And you both call corn shucks "corn husks."

sis *noun* See citations.

1915 Dingus *Word-List VA* 190 = used as a substitute for the Christian name: "We're a-goin' to see Aunt Sis Monday." **2010** House *Opening* 99 My aunt, Sis, was not fazed by the cold.

sister *noun*

A Variant plural forms *sisteren* [see **1886** in **B**], *sisterin*, *sistering*, *sistern* [see **1955** in **B**], *sistren*, *sistring*, by analogy with *brethren*.

1890 Fruit *KY Words* 67 I tell you, breetherin and sisterin. **1911** Shearin *E KY Word-List* 540 *sistren* = sisters, chiefly heard in the phrase, "brethren and sistren." **1952** Wilson *Folk Speech NC* 591 *sistren* = sisters. **1957** Combs *Lg Sthn High: Word List* 91 *sistren*, *sistering*, *sistring* = sisters (in the church). **2007** McMillon *Notes*: *sistring*.

B A female fellow church member, used to express solidarity and spiritual kinship, sometimes attributively as a title and as a form of address with a woman's given name or surname.

1791 *Bent Creek Church Minutes* 11 the church met and Sister Rebecca Dutton made application for a letter of dismission and it was granted. **1797** *Globe Creek Church Minutes* 3 No Member of the Church Shall Address another M[ember by] Any other term or Appelation but the title of brother or sister. **1859** Taliaferro *Fisher's River* 41 Brethering and sistering, one and all, I'll give you my 'pinion, though not axed fur it. **1860** *Toe Valley Church Minutes* 48 Whar as Sister Anny Laws and Sister Susannah Deyton joined another church not of our own faith and order, therefore, we say thes no mour of us. **1867** Harris *Sut Lovingood* 54 The hell desarvin ole raskil's speech now cum tu 'im, a'n sez he, "Pray fur me brethren an' sisteren, fur I is arastilin wif the great inimy rite now!" an' his voice wer the mos' pitiful, trimblin thing I ever hearn. **1874** *Tuckaleechee Cove Church Minutes* 23 Sisters Sarah Abbott & Margaret Franklin volentary confess their faults to the Church & were forgive. **1886** Smith *Sthn Dialect* 349 They all have the authority of old or dialect English, or many of them belong to all parts of the South, if not elsewhere . . . sisteren (sisters). **1928** (in **1952** Mathes *Tall Tales* 55) "Sister Tollett," he began, "if ever'body was a-ponderin' the Book thataway, they'd be souls a-bornin' ever' night." **1955** Ritchie *Singing Family* 82 The meetin' was long that day about four or five hours and about four preachers. This one was the last one and he kept a-saying, like most all of them do, "Now brethren and sistern I'm a-goin to quit. One more thing the Sperrit has give unto me to say unto you and then I'm shore a-goin to quit." **1997** Montgomery Coll (known to Brown, Bush, Cardwell, Oliver, Weaver). **2009** Callahan *Work and Faith* 44 Members of mountain churches referred to each other as "brother" and "sister" suggesting that church membership was considered an extension of membership and a form of fictive kinship, tying the church community to the home community and structures of authority. **2017** *Blind Pig* (Oct 12) He was a Deacon in a church where near everyone was called Brother or Sister, even the local postman or service station attendant.

sisteren, **sisterin**, **sistering**, **sistern** See **sister**.

sister to See **to 4**.

sistren, **sistring** See **sister**.

sit *verb* Principal parts. See also **set**.

1 Variant infinitive/base form *sot*.

1989 Landry *Smoky Mt Interviews* 191 Things changes so much anymore. Now a lot of people don't know the word "sot" at all. If they do, it's applied to some fellow who's had a little too much to drink, you know . . . Well, Miss Emily, here you're teaching us to say set and sit and sat . . . At home we don't say nary one of 'em. Miss Emily, we just say sot. Hit don't matter if we're going to sot now or sot directly or sot an hour ago, still just sot . . . Sot was the word they used. They used it all the time. They never did set or sit or sat. They just sot now, directly.

2 Variant past-tense forms *sit, sot.*

1795 (in **1919** DeWitt *Sevier Journal* 177) (June 27) [I] sit out in the morning in company with Col Hardin. **1859** Taliaferro *Fisher's River* 76 I looked up in a post-oak-tree right dab over me, and there sot the biggest painter that uver walked the Blue Ridge. **1861** *Mingus Letters* 29 (Oct 5) He sit up by the fire the night befor his death. **1864** *McGill CW Letters* (May 14) [I] sott in my Dog tent and Wrote this on my ne. **1900** Harben *N GA Sketches* 191 As soon as she got 'er things off, she jest sot down an' drooped. **1915** Hall *Autobiog Claib Jones* 30 Bates followed me in and sit down on the bed. **1937** Hall *Coll* I sot down there. **1956** Hall *Coll* (Hurricane Creek NC) We sit down to rest. **1972** *AOHP/ALC-276* He picked up his guitar and sit down and he played the Sweet By and By, the prettiest Daddy said he ever heard him make in there. **1973** *GSMNP-76*: 22 They all sot down. **1990** Merriman *Moonshine Rendezvous* 30 The policeman went flyin' by. For the next hour I sit there and drank. **1995** South *What It Is* 57 Dripping water was all I could hear as I sot thar. **2008** *Rosie Hicks* 1 He come in and sit to the arm of the bed.

3 Variant past-participle form *sit.*

1995 Williams *Smoky Mts Folklife* 87 I've sit and raveled on them rags for many of a night.

sit-alone baby (also *sit-alone child*) *noun* A small child able to sit by itself alone. Same as **set-along child.**

1957 Combs *Lg Sthn High: Word List* 87 = a "sit-alone" child. **1959** Roberts *Up Cutshin* 41 Its family broke up and scattered when it was just a sit-alone baby.

sitch See **such A.**

sitter *noun* A person attending a **setting up** or **wake.**

1977 Shields *Cades Cove* 42 If it was summer, the "sitters" would usually remain on the front porch or in the yard. Occasionally one of the group would take a look at the body, as if to be sure all was well. Most of the food during this time was brought in by neighbors to relieve the family of the responsibility.

sitting up See **setting up.**

sittle See **settle.**

sit up with See **set up with 2.**

si-waddlin See **si-godlin.**

sixty *noun*

1 See **like sixty.**

2 A children's game.

c1960 Wilson *Coll* = a child's game; I spy. **1968** *DARE Survey* (Laurel Fork VA, Wytheville VA) = hide-and-go-seek.

[DARE *sixty* n especially southern Appalachians]

Sixty-Five War (also *Sixty-One War*) *noun* The American Civil War. [Editor's note: In the Smoky Mountains in the late 1930s, Joseph Hall observed that these terms illustrate a local tendency to date events by the year in which they took place and also to avoid the term *Civil War.* However, the term *War between the States* was not often used, either. **Old War** referred to either the Civil War or the Revolutionary War, depending on the context. There are a few instances of *Civil War* in Hall's research, especially in TN, where sentiments were more often pro-Union than in NC.] Same as **War between the States.**

1939 Hall *Coll* (Little Cataloochee NC) The first families in Big Cataloochee come in before the Sixty-One War, about three year. *Ibid.* (Smokemont NC) Hit happened away back before the sixty-five war.

Sixty-One War See **Sixty-Five War.**

sizzle sozzle *noun* A gentle, steady rain.

1903 Fox *Little Shepherd* 59 Send us not a gentle sizzle-sozzle, but a sod-soaker, O Lord, a gully washer. **1940** Haun *Hawk's Done* 78 One cloudy night, after the thunder and lightning had quit and the rain had slacked to a mere sizzle-sozzle, I went out on the porch.

skeary See **scary.**

skeerce See **scarce.**

skeered, skeert See **scare 2.**

skeery See **scary.**

skeet *verb*

1 To slide on ice.

1927 Mason *Lure of Smokies* 26 You young uns quit skeetin' [= sliding on bare feet] on thet ice!

[DARE *skeet* v 3 South, South Midland]

2 See citations.

1948 Chase *Grandfather Tales* 49 [I] skeeted the rock across the water. **1967–69** *DARE Survey* (Elbert Co GA, Tompkinsville KY, Westminster SC) = to throw a flat stone over the surface of water so that it jumps several times.

[Web3 Probably alteration of *scoot*; DARE *skeet* v 3 South, South Midland]

skeeter *noun* A mosquito.

1867 Harris *Sut Lovingood* 250 My breff pizins skeeters, my yell breaks winders, an' my tromp gits yeathquakes. **1939** Hall *Coll* (Jefferson City TN) Lots of 'em call 'em skeeters. **1986** Pederson et al. *LAGS* (Murray Co GA). **1993** Cunningham *Sthn Talk* 109 Them dratted skeeters'll eat you alive. **2013** Venable *How to Tawlk* 44 I got a skeeter bite on my lag the size of a quarter.

skein *noun* [pronounced *skeen*] A metal thimble that protects the spindle of a wooden axle.

1939 Hall *Coll* (Gumstand TN) The axle-tree of tarpole wagons [was] made out of hickory [with] no skeins over it. **1942** Hall *Phonetics Smoky Mts* 18 *skeins* = the metal covering of the axle is apparently always [skinz].

skeller-eyed (also *skelter-eyed*) *adjective* See citation.

1944 Wentworth *ADD* (WV) *skelter-eyed*, or *skeller-eyed* ... cross-eyed.

[cf SND *skellie* adj "squinting, squint-eyed"; EDD *skelly-eyed* (at *skelly* adj 7.(2)) "having a squint, cross-eyed"]

skewbald *noun*

A Variant forms *sque-ball* [see **1982** in **B**], *stewball* [see **1977** in **B**].

B An ear of corn with grains of varied colors. [Editor's note: This term referring to a horse is standard.]

1923 Combs *Addenda KY* 242 = an ear of corn having fifteen or more red grains: "At corn huskings a speckled ear counts five, a red ear ten, and a skew-ball fifteen." **1977** Shackelford et al. *Our Appalachia* 20 Back then when they'd grow corn they had speckled ears [= red and white ones] and they'd have solid red ears. Then they'd have a "stewball"; if it had fifteen red grains in it, it was a stewball. It was a habit, an old saying, that the first one that got a red ear got to kiss the prettiest girl around the corn ring. And if you got a stewball you got to kiss her and hug her neck, too. **1982** Slone *How We Talked* 91 [At a corn shucking] finding a white ear [of corn] did not count anything. A red ear was twenty points, a blue fifty, and a speckled one fifteen. A "sque-ball" (one of many colors) was one hundred points.

[DARE *skewbald* adj chiefly South, South Midland]

skid

A *verb* In logging, to drag, slide, push, or haul a log from where a tree is cut to a **skidway** or **skid road**, in order to be moved down a slope, as to a landing to be rafted or loaded or to a mill to be sawed; hence verbal noun *skidding*. See also **skidder**, **skid road**.

1954 Blackhurst *Riders of Flood* 75 All the skidding had been done, and the last logs were now nearly tiered along the now worn slides. . . . With the skidding done, there was nothing for the men to work at when sliding weather failed. **1958** GSMNP-110:5 I done just about everything, till they got the skidder, and then I went to skidding. **1964** Clarkson *Lumbering in WV* 371 = to draw logs from the stump to the landing or mill. **1978** Dykeman and Stokely *Highland Homeland* 126 The most complex phase of the logging process was "skidding," or bringing the felled logs from inaccessible distances to the waiting cars. **1994** Lambert *Sawmills* 44 The logs were brought down to the tram road by skidding and ballhooting; some of the hollows had log slides that the logs would be rolled into and would go down the slide at a fast pace.

B *noun* See citation.

1964 Clarkson *Lumbering in WV* 371 = a log or pole, usually used in pairs, upon which logs are rolled or piled.

skidder *noun* A steam-powered machine used to convey logs off a slope, operating on either a surface rail or an overhead cable. See 1980 citation. See also **cableway skidder**, **groundhog skidder**, **overhead skidder**.

1958 GSMNP-110:5 I done just about everything, till they got the skidder, and then I went to skidding. **1966** Frome *Strangers* 169 There was the steam-powered Clyde skidder, dragging in huge logs by overhead cables extending nearly a mile in the woods . . . fires were started by sparks from wood-burning trains and skidders. **1980** Chiles *Logging Lingo* 21 = a steam powered machine that brought timber out of the woods and set it down at landings where steam powered cranes lifted it onto logging railroad flatcars. **n.d.** *Tremont Logging* 6 Skidders moved on rails and performed the vital link of dragging logs from the woods to the railroads. While most skidders dragged logs along the ground, Little River Lumber Company had special machines designed because of the Smokies' unusually rough terrain. Clyde Iron Works came up with an "overhead" model to solve the problem, a system which hauled logs in the air something like a ski lift. Overhead cables ran from the skidder to a big tree or stump on the mountainside as far as a mile away.

skidder buck *noun* In logging, the boss of a skidding crew.

1973 Foster *Walker Valley* 9:12 Most times the skidder buck would run down there to see what happened.

skidding road See **skid road**.

skid pole *noun* A pole inclined against a **log building** being constructed at a **log raising**, enabling workers to roll logs up the pole in building a side of the dwelling.

1971 *Corn Shuckin's* 101 When somebody went t'build a house . . . most of th'time they used what we called skid poles. They'd lay up poles against th'house, and four'r'five men'ud get ahold a'them logs and roll'em right up them poles on th'house.

skid road (also *skidding road*) *noun* A pathway along which logs are **skidded** to a **skidway**.

1954 Blackhurst *Riders of Flood* 71 At first only a thin trickle of logs had moved along the icy troughs of the slides, but with skid roads opened, more men moved into the hollows, and each slide was working at capacity. **1964** Clarkson *Lumbering in WV* 371 *skid road* = two skids laid parallel at right angles to a road or railroad. The skidway is usually uphill from the road and logs can be rolled from the skidway to a log car or a truck. **1966** Frome *Strangers* 168 At first, ox teams were used to drag logs to creeks and streams, and on the skid road to the yarding point or deck. **1973** Foster *Walker Valley* 9:6 Riggers, they would cut what we call a skidding road, you know, cut everything down. **2006** *WV Encycl* 707 Moving the logs out of the woods was accomplished with a team of horses. When the day's work began the teamster curried and fed his team and drove them to the skidroad. Here the skidding crew prepared a train of logs, fastening a dozen or more together end-to-end with devices called grabs. A grab was a short piece of chain with a swivel in the middle and heavy pins at each end. The pins were driven into adjacent ends of the logs to fasten them together. The teamster then hooked the horse team to the front log with special grabs and the horses pulled the train of logs to a landing located either along a stream or along the logging railroad.

skidway *noun* An inclined platform onto which logs are loaded in order to be rolled off into a vehicle.

1914 Bryant *Logging* 236 Logs are then snaked to a skidway at the head of the cleared strip, ready to be sent down by gravity. **1958** GSMNP-110:36 [They'd] roll them off a skidway, had a skidway built to the track, you know. They'd load them by hand, hand loaded, then rolled them on with peaveys. **1986** Smith and Eye *Hardwood Stands* 157 The feller operator could move off of the main corridors along the spur trails, cut the marked trees, back up to the main skidding corridor, and lay each cut tree along the skidway in a position ready for pick-up by the grapple skidder. **1991** Thomas *Sthn Appal* 152 We had skid-Ways, though—we put th' big logs on skid-Ways. Th' first'uns we had, th' skids would go right out about level with th' car we'uz gonna load it on.

skidway loader *noun* See citation.

2009 Wiles and Wiles *Location* 9 Back then there were no hydraulic log loaders [at the sawmill]. The driver [of the truck] and the skidway loader were responsible for the unloading. The first step was to insert the skid poles on the truck frame underneath the logs. When the log bunks were unlocked, these poles allowed the logs to roll off the truck and onto the skidway. The skidway was the means of rolling the logs to the carriage that pulled the log through the blade.

skiff *noun*

A Variant form *skift*.

1824 Knight *Letter from KY* 106 The Phraseology in this state is sometimes novel. . . . Many from habit, like the Virginians, tuck a t at the end of such words as onct, twict, skifft [sic]. **1891** Brown *Dialect in TN* 172 We also say *all of a suddent*, *wisht* for the present tense of *wish*, *skift* for *skiff*, and *take holt of* for *take hold of*, etc.

B A slight amount, thin layer, especially of snow.

1834 (in **1956** Eliason *Tarheel Talk* 294) (Haywood Co NC) last night we had a little skift of snow. **1862** *Barkley CW Letters* (March 9) on Last Friday we had a skiff of snow and it give the most of us a considerable coal. **1904–20** Kephart *Notebooks* 2:600 A thin skift of clouds. **1915** Dingus *Word-List VA* 190 *skift* = a thin layer of snow. **1939** Hall *Coll* (Cataloochee NC) They was a little skiff of snow, and that was how come to see their sign. **1953** Hall *Coll* (Plott Creek NC) When they first were back there, and they'd be snow or anything, a skift of snow around the pens, they'd be bears and wolf tracks all about there, trying to get the stock from the barn. **1966** *DARE Survey* (Burnsville NC) = the first thin ice that forms over the surface of a pond; (Spruce Pine NC) There's just a skiff of ice. **1972** *AOHP/ALC-241* There was a little skift of snow on the ground. He tracked the man and got him and then went back to the horse and got him. **2002** Rash *Foot in Eden* 83 The branches looked like there was a skiff of snow on them.

[OED3 *skiff* n² "a slight sketch, trace, touch, etc." chiefly Scot; cf CUD *skift* n "a light shower"; HT *skift* "a light shower"; DARE *skift* n² 1 widespread except Northeast, South, Southwest]

skifflin See **striffen**.

skift See **skiff**.

ski-goglin See **si-godlin**.

skim hole (also *skimming(s) hole*) *noun* A depression into which is shoveled the undesirable film that forms on top of sorghum juice as it is boiled to make **molasses**. Also called **slop hole**, **sorghum hole**.

1955 Ritchie *Singing Family* 207 Help yourselves to some good juicy cane stalks to suck on, then you can help dig the skimming hole. *Ibid.* 208 He dipped off as much as he could of the green jellyish skim which lay on the top, and the boys emptied it . . . into the skimming hole. **c1960** Wilson *Coll*: *skimhole* = the hole dug in the ground near the sorghum mills to receive the skimmings from the cooking molasses. Greenhorns were often lured into this hole, esp. when a group of young people would visit the sorghum-making. **1975** Gainer *Witches Ghosts Signs* 21 As the juice boiled and moved from one end of the pan to the other, a green scum rose to the top [of the molasses] and was skimmed off and thrown in a hole which had been dug in the ground near the pan. This was called the "skimmin' hole."

skimming hole See **skim hole**.

skimmings *noun* The thin green film that forms on the surface of **sorghum** cane as it is boiled and made into **molasses**; it contains impurities rendered by the boiling and must be scraped off during the cooking process. See also **scrum**.

c1975 Lunsford *It Used to Be* 38 Someone there, most generally a woman, with what they call a strainer, dips out the impurities that have boiled up. She skims that, and that's called "skimmings." It's put off on the side. First, it's very green, but she keeps doing that until, after a while, it's all golden color and sweet as honey.

skimmings hole See **skim hole**.

skimption See **scrimption**.

skin *verb*

A Principal parts.

1 Variant past-tense forms *skint*, *skun*, *skunt*.

1892 Fruit *KY Words* 234 *skint* or *skunt*: skinned: "He skunt his hand." **1925** Carter *Mt White Tales* 345 His brothers run out and shot some big fine horses and skun 'em. **1939** Hall *Coll* (Hartford TN) We just broke to it as quick as we could and all went into skinning that bear, skun it all out, took that hide offen it, and cut it into four quarter. *Ibid.* (White Oak NC) *skint.* **1942** (in **1987** Perdue *Outwitting Devil* 14) Jack got out his pocketknife and skun a piece of skin from the end of his bull's nose to the root of his tail. **1962** Williams *Verbs Mt Speech* 17 Verbs which retain either the strong preterites of Middle English or variant preterites of the English dialects [include] skin (present), skun (past), skun (past participle). **c1979** Chiles *Glossary* 6 *skun.* **1983** *Dark Corner OHP-4A* I want you to skin it for me. I never skint one in my life.

2 Variant past-participle forms *skin, skint, skun* [see **1962** in **A**], *skunt.*

1948 Gasque *Hunting Fishing* 160 Don't you want 'er skunt first, Pa? **1976** Carter *Little Tree* 35 He looked like he had been set upon by boar 'coons . . . he was that skint up. **1983** Belt *Chattooga Country* 465 It breaks my heart to see these mountains gettin' all skint up like this. **1989** Landry *Smoky Mt Interviews* 181 Yeah, I have skin a bear one time. **2003** Carter *Mt Home* 92 It seemed like if any of us got sick or skunt up, it was most usually him. **2005** Williams *Gratitude* 23 He was skint up some, but wutn't hurt bad.

B Senses.

1 In phrases *skin one's eyes, keep one's eye(s) skinned* = to be alert or vigilant.

1862 *Love CW Letters* (Aug 21) tel all of the girls to writ tel [name scratched out] to keep a Skind eye. **1862** *Watters-Curtis CW Letters* (April 12) we have to Ceapt our eyeskind hear wee have to gow on picket evry other Day. **1940** Still *River of Earth* 25 Skin your eyes and see the fishes. **c1960** Wilson *Coll*: *skin your eyes* = watch out, peel your eyes.

[DARE *skin* v B2 chiefly South, South Midland]

2 (also *skin up*) To climb up (especially a tree).

1939 Hall *Coll* (Hartford TN) Talk about a man a-skinnin' the saplin's. I skinned them saplin's. **1962** Dykeman *Tall Woman* 32 Skin up into . . . the loft, Robert, and make sure the meat's still there. **c1982** Young *Colloquial Appal* 20 *skin up* = climb.

skin one's eyes See **skin B1**.

skint See **skin A1, A2**.

skin up See **skin B2**.

skip

A *verb* See citation.

1937 Hall *Coll* = of a bullet: to graze: "I shot but just skipped him."

B *noun*

1 (also *skipper*) A logging implement. See 1995 Weber citation. Also called **grab skipper**.

1967 Parris *Mt Bred* 133 A skipper is a sledge hammer with pointed ends which is used to pry skidding tongs loose from logs. **1995–97** Montgomery *Coll* (known to Cardwell, Ledford, Shields), = usually called *grab skipper* (Brown). **1995** Weber *Rugged Hills* 82 Then he'd set the grabs with a hammer or "skip." A skip had a steel mallet-like head on one end and a sharp point on the other. You used the hammer to set the grabs and the pointed end to pry them loose. The handle had a hole with a loop of rope threaded through it. That way you could just hang the skip from the hames on the horses' harness when you weren't using it.

2 See citation.

2002 Armstead *Black Days* 246 = [the process of] moving a trainload of coal cars, one car at a time, to be loaded with coal, [including] the attending loud clang as rail-end couplings jolt apart and then together.

skipper *noun*

1 See **skip B**.

2 A maggot, especially one that infests meat. Also called **kipper**.

1917 Kephart *Camping & Woodcraft* 1:187 Smoked ham . . . is attractive to blow-flies, which quickly fill it with "skippers" if they can get at it. **1924** Spring *Lydia Whaley* 2 In speaking of the kettle of soap which she was making, [she] said skippers got in it. **1940** Still *River of Earth* 3 Skippers had got into a pork shoulder during the unnaturally warm December, and it had to be thrown away. **1972** *Foxfire I* 200 Cover the meat with a mixture of black pepper and borax to keep the "skipper" out. (Skippers are the larvae of the skipper fly.) The meat is then hung in the smokehouse. **1989** Oliver *Hazel Creek* 32 As warm weather approached, the left over smoked meat was buried in wood ashes to prevent it from being infested with "skippers." **1994** Montgomery *Coll* (known to Cardwell).

[OED3 *skipper* n^1 2d, dialect and U.S.; DARE *skipper* n 1 chiefly South, South Midland]

skirmish *noun* A thin layer of snow.

1961 Miller *Pigeon's Roost* (March 23) we have had another winter squall. It was really bad weather here in-the-neck-of-the-woods for four or five days. A skirmish of snow came along with the breezy wind storms.

skitter *verb*

1 See citation.

1973 Davis *'Pon My Honor* 101 = to move about often or aimlessly.

2 To scatter (objects).

1976 Still *Pattern of Man* 47 The wind answered, skittering the fallen leaves and making moan the trees.

skitters *noun* Diarrhea.

1973 Davis *'Pon My Honor* 101. **1996–97** Montgomery *Coll* (known to Ellis, Oliver).

[cf OED3 *skitter* v^1 "to void thin excrement" Scottish and dialect; SND *skitter* n 1 "thin excrement"; CUD (*the*) *skitters* n "diarrhoea"; DARE *skitters* n chiefly PA, MD, WV, OH]

skiver *noun* A small amount or portion of a substance.

1925 Dargan *Highland Annals* 196 Len sowed an acre of rye for green winter picking; also a "skiver of wheat" which was to be all Serena's, as a basis for "feed." **1996–97** Montgomery *Coll* (known to Bush, Cypher), = a small amount, as "We thought we were going to have one big storm, but we only got a skiver [of rain]" (Cardwell).

[cf SND *skiver* n "a splinter"]

skive up *verb phrase* To tear up, scar (the ground).

1936 Stuart *Head of Hollow* 234 He'd let the mule drag the plow along and skive up the grass and the saw briers. **1946** Stuart *Plum Grove Hills* 191 The sheriff took Willard to the scaffold. Willard scooted and skived-up the grass, cussed, hollered and prayed, and his wife and brothers followed him a screamin'.

skrutch See **scrooch.**

skullcap *noun* A perennial plant (*Scutellaria* spp) from which a medicinal tea is made, used to calm nerves.

1957 Broaddus *Vocab Estill Co KY* 70 = a medicinal herb "for nervous conditions." [**1971** Krochmal et al. *Medicinal Plants Appal* 232 It is reported to be a nervine, tonic, diuretic, and antispasmodic.] **1991** Haynes *Haywood Home* 62 Boneset or skull cap tea were given for a cold, headache or leg-ache. The taste of either one was a sure-cure, or at least you claimed that they worked. **2006** Howell *Medicinal Plants* 143 Throughout the region, skullcap was used as a folk remedy for mad dog bites and hydrophobia. It was also regarded as a potent restorative to treat symptoms of nervous exhaustion accompanied by insomnia, depression, anxiety, and muscle tremors or spasms.

skull cracker *noun* Homemade whiskey.

2009 Applegate and Miller *Lake Cumberland* 18 Other names for moonshine were corn liquor, skull cracker, sugar whiskey, rotgut, ruckus juice, happy Sally, hillbilly pop, and white lightning.

skull orchard *noun* A cemetery.

c1960 Wilson *Coll* = jocose name for a graveyard. **1970** *DARE Survey* (Dayton TN). **1997** Montgomery *Coll* (known to Hooper).

[DARE *skull orchard* n chiefly Appalachians, Southeast]

skulp *verb* To strike, smack.

1941 Still *Troublesome Creek* 75 My wife thinks more o' that nag than she does her victuals. She'd skulp me, was I to trade.

[cf SND *skelp* v[1] "to strike, hit, esp. with something flat, as the palm of the hand, etc., to slap, smack"]

skun See **skin A1, A2.**

skunk grease (also *skunk oil*) *noun* Fat rendered from the carcass of a skunk, used medicinally in a plaster or a tea. Same as **polecat grease.**

1964 Smith et al. *Germans of Valley* 139 The skunk is good for cures; its fat is rendered and it's good for greasing the chest. **1984** Smith *Enduring Memories* 59 There were many home medicine remedies that the farm families used, but the most bizarre one that I recall was the "skunk oil" that my grandfather gave me for the croup. He caught a skunk in his traps during the winter trapping season and after skinning and stretching the pelt, he picked pieces of the fat from the carcass and boiled the pieces for several minutes. After the mixture cooled enough to drink, he had me to drink a cup of it. I don't recall exactly what it tasted like but I remembered never to go around him when I had the croup again. **2007** Milnes *Signs Cures Witches* 98 Some people have used bear grease plasters for colds and croup. Another widely known ingredient used by itself or in a plaster is skunk grease—fat that is rendered from a skunk. Mary Cottrell said her mother would rub skunk grease on her nose to reduce stuffiness.

skunk up *verb phrase* To foul up, injure.

1928 (in **1952** Mathes *Tall Tales* 65) The bawling out continued: "This is a purty way to start on the big hunt tomorrer mornin'—gittin' the best young dawg in Big Smoky all skunked up the night before." **1998** Montgomery *Coll* (known to Cardwell).

skunt See **skin A1, A2.**

skutch See **scutch.**

skyar See **scar.**

skybugging *noun* See citation.

1982 Powers and Hannah *Cataloochee* 382 "Skybugging" has a certain charm. It means scanning the sky aimlessly as one's trusted old horse walks along a Cataloochee trail. Or, it can simply mean "not paying attention."

skyerce See **scarce.**

sky-godlin, sky-goglin See **si-godlin.**

slab-off *adjective* Fragmentary, split off.

1963 Watkins and Watkins *Yesterday* 34 The association of Baptist churches approved of the Scruggs baptisms, and some of the converts moved to other churches. In a sawmill metaphor the association branded Sharp Mountain [congregation] the "slab-off outfit."

slab of wax *noun* See citation. See also **wax.**

1939 Farr *TN Mt Regions* 92 = a piece of chewing gum: "Do you have a slab of wax in your pocket?"

slab-sided *adjective* Awkwardly or poorly proportioned.

1913 Kephart *Our Sthn High* 213 About two-thirds of them are brawny or sinewy fellows of grave endurance. The others generally are slab-sided. **1929** (in **1995** Williams *Become Teacher* 64) That restaurant . . . was operated by a hollow-eyed older man, his fat wife . . . and their slab-sided old maid daughter who served as the waitress. **c1960** Wilson *Coll* = poorly proportioned. **1961** Niles *Ballad Book* xiv A few were slab-sided lean-tos with pounded earth or puncheon floors, some were cabins, and a few were one- or two-storied houses with poplar weatherboarding. **1976** Dwyer *Southern Sayin's* 6 *you slab-sided galoot* = tall and lank, sometimes meaning fat.

slack dob *adverb phrase* Completely.

1999 Montgomery *Coll* (known to Cardwell).

slack-twist(ed) *adjective* Of fibers: not wound tightly, loose and tending to tangle when woven into thread; hence of a person: weak-minded, lacking discipline or character. See c1940, 1995 citations.

1895 Murfree *Witch-Face* 178 Dish up dinner, child, an' don't be so slow an' slack-twisted like yer dad. **1895** *Word-Lists* 394 = mentally weak, shiftless. (Ky., W.V.). **c1940** Simms *Coll* "Oh Lord, let us not be slack-twisted, may we straighten after sorrow, as a tree straightens after a storm" . . . the word "slack-twisted," so often found in mountain speech, comes from letting a warp (in weaving) have a slack and it twists back upon itself and is most difficult to untangle, or handle. **c1954** Adams *Word-List* = dawdling, slow, inefficient as housekeeper. **1957** Parris *My Mts* 61 As a girl she had heard the old ones say many a time that a slack-twisted person never could make a success as a weaver, especially of coverlets. **1984** Wilder *You All Spoken* 16 = lacking in courage; said of someone who makes false excuses for failures; one who feigns excuses to escape military duty. Comes from spinning and weaving in cottage operations; cloth from insufficiently twisted thread does not wear well. **1995** Montgomery *Coll* = when thread is spun on a spinning wheel the fibers must be held tight while the wheel spins or twists them into thread or yarn. If the spinner lets the fibers go slack, a poor quality thread is produced (Oliver).

[EDD (at slack adj.1 11.(15)) "an inactive, lazy, shiftless person"]

slade *noun* A sley, the movable comb-like instrument set in the batten of the loom and carrying the reed.

c1900 (in **1997** Stoddart *Quare Women* 61) We spoke to her and asked her what she had in her hand. She explained that it was a slade (sley) to use in her loom in weaving.

slag pile *noun* See citation.

2006 Mooney *Lg Coal Mining* 1029 The miner then cleaned his working room of waste rock, called "gob" or "bone" and eventually hauled outside and added to a massive "slag pile" and then headed home for the day.

slam (also *slap, slap-bang, slap-dab*) *adverb* Completely, absolutely, precisely, directly. See also **smack, square dab.**

1864 Gilmore *Down in TN* 108 I c'ud luck slap down over the side. **1921** Combs *Slang Survivals* 117 *slap bang* = exactly, precisely. **1944** Laughlin *Word-List Buncombe Co* 26 *slam* = directly and violently: "He hit slam against that tree." **1956** McAtee *Some Dial NC* 40 *slap* = abruptly: "I was cool but did a few chores and was slap hot again," = directly: "right slap on the nose." **1957** Combs *Lg Sthn High: Word List* 91 *slap bang* = suddenly. Ex.: "He run slap-bang into me." **1968** *Faith Healing* 22 He cut his heel string just slap in two. **1976** Carter *Little Tree* 15 He said, however, he had seen a doe deer one time, that was in heat and couldn't find a buck, go slap-dab mad, running into trees and finally drowning herself in the creek. **1976** *Digging Well* 134 You could reach the bottom with your hand! It had filled slap-dab up. **1993** Cunningham *Sthn Talk* 140 *slam* = totally, all the way. "It took eight gallons to fill the tank slam full." *Ibid.* I kain't bake no biscuits this mornin'; I'm slap out of flour. **1997–98** Montgomery *Coll: slam* (known to Andrews); *slap* (known to Adams, Bush, Ellis, Jones, Ledford, Norris, Oliver, Weaver); You'd walk slap out of your shoes (Andrews); We worked till slap dark (Cardwell); *slap dab* We worked till slap dab dark (Cardwell).

[DARE *slam* adv 1, 2 chiefly South, South Midland, especially Southeast, *slap* adv 2 "all the way, completely" chiefly South, South Midland; *slapdab* adv 1 "directly, abruptly, squarely" scattered, but more frequent South, South Midland; *slapdab* adv 2 "completely" especially South, South Midland]

slanchways (also *slanchwise, slaunchways, slaunchwise, slauntwise, slouchways*) *adverb* Slanting, oblique, crookedly, slanting(ly), diagonal(ly). See also **squanchways.**

1885 Murfree *Prophet* 207 An' if ye'll b'lieve me, Brother Jake Tobin, got up slanch-wise, and in sech a hurry the chair fell over ahint him. **1917** Kephart *Word-List* 417 slaunchways = slantingly. **1930s** (in **1944** Wentworth *ADD* 566) (eWV) *slanchways*. **c1950** Haun *When the Wind* 10 Once, the next time it was, he turned his head up slouchways and smiled with his eyes and said: "Away up onto Bay's Mountain." **1957** Combs *Lg Sthn High: Word List* 91 *slanchways* = slanting. **1974** Brewer *Your Community* 1 I always heard "slauntwise," instead of "slaunchwise," when somebody was talking about walking diagonally [or] obliquely. **2002** Myers *Best Yet Stories* 80 *slaunchways* = slanted.

[OED3 *slaunchways/slaunchwise* adv U.S. colloquial; Web3 *slaunchways/slaunchwise* adv alteration of *slantways/slantwise* adv and adj U.S. colloquial; DARE (at *slaunchwise* adj, adv) scattered, but chiefly West Midland, West]

slanchwise See **slanchways.**

slant *noun* See citation.

1973 Preston *Bituminous Term* 53 = [in underground coal mining] an entry cut off a main entry at more than a ninety degree angle.

slantendikular See **slantindicular.**

slanti-godlin *adverb* See citation. See also **si-godlin.**

1957 Combs *Lg Sthn High: Syntax* 12 "You drawed that line slanti-godlin." That is, crooked, cross-Ways, for "anti-godlin" or "anti-sigodlin."

slantindicular (also *slantendicular*) *adjective* Slanting, at an angle.

1873 Smith *Arp Peace Papers* 202 If we could have slid into it quietly and slantendikular, if slavery could have sorter tapered out and freedom sorter tapered in, everybody could have got used to it. **1892** Fruit *KY Words* 232 = slanting. **c1960** Wilson *Coll* = humorous for slanting.

[blend of *slant* and *perpendicular*]

slant-sided *adjective* Of land: sloping, at an angle.

2007 Homan *Turkey Tracks* 85 They salted their anecdotes with novel country sayings and language I liked, language straight from the "slant-sided" land.

slap, slap dab See **slam.**

slapjack *noun* A pancake.

1986 Pederson et al. *LAGS* (Rockdale Co GA, Union Co GA).

slash (also *slashing*) *noun* See citations.

1964 Clarkson *Lumbering in WV* 371 *slash, slashing* = the limbs and tops left after logging. **1997** Farwell *Logging*: *slash* = a cutover area; the aftermath of clearcutting.

slashways *adverb* At an angle. See also **slanchways.**

1986 Pederson et al. *LAGS* (Johnson Co TN).

slat *noun* A stick of chewing gum.

2001 Montgomery *Coll* (known to Cardwell).

slat bonnet *noun* Same as **split bonnet.**

1941 Stuart *Men of Mts* 73 She'll never dream of all of this when she comes and picks her apron full of beans—Mom with a slat bonnet on her head and drops of sweat standing like white blisters over her face and on her nose—Mom with her pipe in her mouth and blowing long streams of blue smoke to the wind.

[DARE *slat bonnet* n especially Middle Atlantic, South Midland]

slat fence (also *slatted fence, slatter-wire fence*) *noun* A fence of upright slats woven together by wire.

1966 Dakin *Vocab Ohio River Valley* 97 The name *slat(ted) fence*, scattered throughout Kentucky but rare north of the river, seems most often to be a synonym for *picket fence* = "woven in wire" in contrast to *paling fence* = "nailed." **1975** Montell *Ghosts Cumberland* 220 *slatter-wire fence* = colloquial for a fence constructed with wooden slats, pickets, or palings woven together by criss-crossed wire.

slather

A *verb* To spread lavishly or thickly (over).

1927 Mason *Lure of Smokies* 217 [The bear] skinned her lip back, an' slathered at the jaws, threatenin'. **1996** Houk *Foods & Recipes* 44 Slathered with country butter, fresh corn on the cob, toasted or boiled, was a true feast. **1997** Montgomery *Coll* = to spread thickly (known to Jones, Norris; Oliver). **2009** Benfield *Mt Born* 79 Biscuits are a many splendored thing . . . split and slathered with butter and jam, or molasses.

[cf OED3 *slather* v 2b "to spread or splash liberally on" chiefly dialect and U.S.]

B *noun plural* See citation.

1939 *FWP Guide TN* 458 "Lashings" or "slathers" (liberal quantities) of sorghum, served with yellow butter on brown biscuits, battercakes, or flapjacks, is the "best eatin' ever intended to man."

slatted fence, slatter-wire fence See **slat fence.**

slaunchways, slaunchwise, slauntwise See **slanchways.**

slay *verb* Variant past-tense form *slayed*.

1859 Taliaferro *Fisher's River* 120 We cum to another fence, and thar I slayed 'Gius. **1941** Stuart *Men of Mts* 307 It [= an ax] slayed the saplin fer me.

[DARE *slay* v 1 especially South, South Midland]

sled

A *noun* See **dry-land sled, half sled, land sled, lizard 1, sled drag, slide.**

B *verb* To convey (a heavy object) by dragging it on a sled (usually horse-drawn), made necessary by terrain too rough for a wheeled vehicle to do so.

c1950 Adams *Grandpap* 20 Pap had sledded our plunder right up to the door. **1974–75** McCracken *Logging* 11:70–71 The road that went to Blowdown [was a] sled road, something like a sled road. . . . They'd sled stuff out of here down to Blowdown, come out down here with sled. They didn't have no wagon. You couldn't wagon it.

sled drag *noun* A sledge for transporting heavy objects.

1981 Alderman *Tilson Mill* 14 Some customers arrived carrying a bag of corn on their shoulders; others came by ox, by horse, or on a sled drag (sometimes called a stone boat).

sled road *noun* A primitive road over rough terrain usually limiting passage to only a sled.

1936 Maupin *Pittman Center* 4 The only means of communication the people of Laurel valley have with Pittman is a narrow sled road following the stream. **1948** Still *Nest* 53 Beyond the gap would ascend the sledroad by which to hasten to Aust Clissa's, the chimney rising to view. **1970** Miller *Pigeon's Roost* (June 18) When this man reached the large rock cliff located at the top of a hill just below a sled road, he set up living quarters. **1972** GSMNP-71:42 We just had sled roads. You couldn't get over them with nothing but a sled or an old wagon, and it'd go up over them big rocks and bump. **1973** GSMNP-74:37 It was just a sled road, but it was all the way you could take anything up there. **1974–75** McCracken *Logging* 11:70–71 The road that went to Blowdown [was a] sled road, something like a sled road. . . . They'd sled stuff out of here down to Blowdown, come out down here with sled. They didn't have no wagon. You couldn't wagon it.

sleight *noun* A knack (at or in a particular task or activity).

1924 Raine *Saddlebags* 98 The mountain mother refers to her daughter's skill as "Sally's *sleight* at buttermaking," a use of the word found in Chaucer and identical with Spenser's "y-carved with curious sleights." **1931** Owens *Speech Cumberlands* 91 = a gift or knack for doing a specific thing: "Polly's sleight at biscuit-makin' made her the pattern helt up for the girls o' Coal Run." **1940** Haun *Hawk's Done* 21 Ma says I have a right smart sleight at it. **c1960** Wilson *Coll* = a knack at doing something: "He's got a sleight at setting tobacco." **1996** Montgomery *Coll* (known to Brown, Cardwell, Oliver). **2006** *WV Encycl* 235 There was art or what the natives called a "sleight" in this, as there was art in laying the worm for the fence—the first line of rails, each corner on a stone, upon which the structure of the fence was to be erected; after which it was finished with a stake and rider.

[OED3 *sleight* n[1] 3a now rare; EDD *sleight* sb/v/adj 2; CUD *sleight* n "the knack of doing something"; DARE *sleight* n chiefly southern Appalachians, Ozarks]

slew foot *noun* A foot that turns awkwardly outward; hence adjective *slew-footed* = having an awkward or clumsy gait.

1956 McAtee *Some Dial NC* 58 *slew-footed* . . . With the feet angling outward; the opposite of "pigeon-toed." **c1960** Wilson *Coll*: *slew feet* = clumsy [feet], turning out or having no spring about them.

[DARE (at *slue-footed* adj) chiefly South, South Midland]

slick

A *noun*

1 A dense thicket of laurel or rhododendron, known more formally as a **heath bald**. See also **hell**, **laurel bed**, **rough**, **wooly B**, **yellow patch**.

1913 Kephart *Our Sthn High* 301 A "hell" or "slick" or "woolly-head" or "yaller patch" is a thicket of laurel or rhododendron, impassable save where the bears have bored out trails. **1915** Bohannon *Bear Hunt* 462 They range in extent from a few acres to more than a thousand, and are laurel growths to the height of about twelve feet, without other trees or shrubs whatever, the tops being so even that at a distance they resemble smooth lawns of rich green grass, hence the name "slicks." **1937** Hall *Coll* (Little Greenbrier TN) They used to make liquor in the slicks. Later they made it in the flats. **1939** Hall *Coll* (Proctor NC) [Kephart would] go out on them high knobs and look all about over them rough slicks, you know. We call 'em slicks, but it was just roughs, just laurel beds and ivy growed up, nothing in it hardly, just a tree once in a while. **1943** Peattie *Indian Days* 40 Botanists speak of heath balds, meaning an area crowned with an intricate shrub tangle of the heath family, but mountain people called them slicks, and distinguish between laurel, rhododendron, and ivy (Kalmia or mountain laurel) slicks. **1953** Hall *Coll* (Bryson City NC) Matt Hyde used to do some trapping back in there for bear, and they done that back of the Smokies in those rough slicks, we call them, where they had trailways that they travel when they was going out and into them rough places. **1956** Fink *That's Why* 4 A slick is never a smooth rock ledge or a cliff. While from a distance it might appear to be a grassy slope, in reality it is a tangle of low rhododendron or kalmia, through which a bear can scarcely push. **1992** Toops *Great Smoky Mts* 41 Although most of the trail traversed boreal forest, one section dropped into a heath bald or laurel "slick." Whoever coined the latter term was obviously looking from a distance! These areas contain head-high mountain laurels and nightmarish tangles of contorted rhododendron shrubs. **2013** DeLozier and Jourdan *Back Seat* 139 I worried we'd encounter what the locals call a *slick*, an impenetrable thicket of a rhododendron or laurel, and have to hike a long way to get around it.

[DARE *slick* n 3 western NC, east TN]

2 (also *slick and go down*, *slick go down*) A large morel mushroom sliced and cooked; any food (as a greased dumpling) that is easy to swallow.

1955 Parris *Roaming Mts* 232 For a dish that belies its name, slick-go-downs is nothing more than mushrooms boiled and served with corn meal mush. **1988** Lambert *Kinfolks* 117 One of the common variations for dumplings was called "slicks." Simply prepare the dumplings as described above, but before cooking, spread the dumplings out on a clean dish towel and allow them to dry about an hour. Then proceed as above. This won't change the taste of the dumplings but will make a decided difference in their texture (as you can tell from their name). **1995–98** Montgomery *Coll* Dumplings were called slick and go down sometimes (Adams), = also called *slick* and *slick and go down* (Andrews), = Cherokee term for morel mushroom (Brewer); *slick go down* (known to Bush). **2006** Ellison *Nature Journal* 58 Armillariella mella is known to the Cherokees as "slicks" and to non-Indians as the honey mushroom. According to Cherokee native Amy Walker, an avid mushroom collector I spoke with some years ago, her people call them slicks because they "just slide right down your throat." This is true. Once the cap of a slick is heated, it becomes viscous and does indeed slide down your throat, one after the other, just like oysters.

[DARE *slick* n 8 western NC, east TN]

B *adverb* Completely, entirely.

1961 Seeman *Arms of Mt* 57 That was how the Law caught up with him—he slick forgot he'd left a picture of him and Rena Faye in the back of his billfold. **1999** Montgomery *Coll* (known to Cardwell).

slick and go down See **slick A2.**

slick down *verb phrase* To slide down.

1976 Still *Pattern of Man* 63 They'll pour the fried chicken to you, with a horn of something to drink beforehand to make it slick down easy.

slick dumpling *noun* See citation.

2009 Sohn *Appal Home Cooking* 300 Like a large flat noodle, these dumplings are usually unleavened. To make them, mountain cooks roll the dumplings out like a piecrust and then cut the dumplings. They boil slick dumplings in a sweet or savoury broth.

slicker *noun* Same as **scrip**.

1973 Preston *Bituminous Term* 50–51 (sWV) = tokens, bills, or other markers given to workers in place of money payment, which were good for full value at a company store but were discontinued [sic; discounted] as much as ten percent in other places.

slickery (also *slickry*) *adjective* Slippery, slick.

1859 Taliaferro *Fisher's River* 147 [The eels] was so slickery. **1892** Smith *Farm and Fireside* 13 Yes, I'll be dadburned if I wouldn't have got him, but the dinged thing was so allfired slickery. **1992** Brooks *Sthn Stuff* 141 *slickry* = slippery. "I'd like okra if it wasn't so slickry."

slickery elm See **slippery elm A**.

slick fat *adjective phrase* Of an animal: bulging from being well fed.

1972 AOHP/LJC-259 Emma [was] throwing that corn out and fattening those hogs and said they were slick fat. **1985** Jones *Growing Up* 44 I had fared pretty good through the winter. My team of big black mules were slick fat.

slick foot *noun* Insomnia.

1973 *Words & Expressions* 136 = to not be able to sleep at night: "I took a bad case of th'slick foot."

slick go down See **slick A2**.

slickry See **slickery**.

slicky *adjective* Slippery.

1957 Combs *Lg Sthn High: Word List* 92 = used literally only as a predicate: "The ice is slicky." But, as a preceding modifier, figuratively: "He's a slicky citizen." **2009** Burton *Beech Mt Man* 67 It was slicky, and we run off the road 'bout the time we run out of gas.

[DARE *slicky* adj especially South, South Midland]

slicky slide *noun* A playground slide.

1919 Wilson *Welfare* 23 Here on the giant stride, the swings, the slicky slide, the see saws, they develop their muscles while enjoying their play. **1930** *Charleston Daily Mail* (29 Sept) (DARE) A "slicky slide" for the playgrounds at Ward One school . . . has been ordered. **c1986** (in **2015** Yarrow *Voices* 30) March and April was my major depression, rejection after rejection after rejection. On the American Slicky-Slide.

[DARE *slicky slide* n chiefly South Midland, especially WV]

slidded See **slide A1**.

slide

A *verb* Principal parts.

1 Variant past-tense forms *slidded*, *slud*.

1952 Wilson *Folk Speech NC* 592 *slud* = past tense and past participle of slide. **1959** Roberts *Up Cutshin* 134 That old horse slidded up and fell. **1974** Roberts *Sang Branch* 228 [I] got over in the woods purty close to where my wild meat was at and that old horse slidded up and fell and hurt hisself, and he wasn't able to carry no bear in.

2 Variant past-participle form *slud*.

[See **1952** in **A1**.]

B *noun*

1 A wooden sled used to transport heavy objects.

1863 *Wright CW Letters* (Nov 15) the mule suits me finely for budy can hall wood with her and the slide. **1884** Murfree *In TN Mts* 156 Instead of a wagon, he had only a rude "slide." **1908** Smith *Reminiscences* 414 Walker . . . lived in a cove in the innermost recesses of the Smoky Mountains—a little valley occupied by only four families and accessible only on foot or horseback or with a wooden "slide." **1924** Raine *Saddlebags* 3 Some eight or ten grim-faced men were walking or riding beside a "slide" where on an armful of cornshucks lay the body, a gray blanket spread over it. **1972** Carson and Vick *Cookin* 2 52 Fall was the time folks shucked corn and brought it off hillsides in "slides."

[EDD *slide* sb 8; DARE *slide* n 1 chiefly South, South Midland, especially Gulf States, Lower Mississippi Valley, TX]

2 In logging, a trough down which logs are moved to a landing, there to be sawed or transported by vehicle or water to a sawmill. Also called **log slide**. See also **skid road**.

1954 Blackhurst *Riders of Flood* 71 At first only a thin trickle of logs had moved along the icy troughs of the slides, but with skid roads opened, more men moved into the hollows, and each slide was working at capacity. **1994** Schmidt and Hooks *Whistle* 42 In some of the hollows, slides or skid roads were used. These employed either gravity or, where the grade required it, horse power or oxen to move the logs down to the rail. Slides and skid roads were intended to avoid the problems encountered in "ballhooting" where cut logs were shoved or dragged over the edge of a slope to slide, sometimes not so freely, downward. To avoid the entanglement in other trees, stumps or brush, the slide was constructed of logs or cut lumber partly buried in the ground to form a V-shaped trough down the slope. Sometimes the slides were "blackstrapped" with crude oil, grease, or another lubricant to facilitate continuous movement to the landing at the bottom.

slide tender *noun* A logging worker who keeps **log slides** greased and watered.

1998 Robbins *Logging Terms*.

slide up *verb phrase* To lose one's footing.

2017 *Blind Pig* (Dec 10) I said it this morning as we trudged down the snowy driveway, "Be careful, girls, don't slide up!"

slighty *adjective* Insulting, disparaging.

1941 Justus *Kettle Creek* 148 He was always saying something slighty about girls thinking too much of clothes. **1963** Edwards *Gravel* 25 Now dust your greasy hide, Tom Barnhouse . . . just because I put on an apron to help fill yore big craw, don't think that calls for any slighty remarks.

[EDD *slighty* adj 2]

sling blade *noun* See 1968 citation.

1968 *DARE Survey* (Brasstown NC) = a hand tool used for cutting weeds and grass. **1998** Montgomery *Coll* (known to Cardwell).

[DARE *sling blade* n chiefly South, South Midland]

slip

A *verb* See citation.

1984 Page and Wigginton *Foxfire Cookery* 44 The spice bush (Lindera benzoin) grows along branch banks. It is best to gather the twigs in the early spring when the bark "slips," or peels off easily.

B *noun* See also **slips**.

1 A sprout or shoot of a plant cut for transplanting, especially a potato. See also **sweet potato slip**.

1968 Wilson *Folklore Mammoth Cave* 24 *slips* = a plant drawn from a hotbed or plantbed to be transplanted; these might include sweet potatoes, pepper, cabbage, tomatoes. **1973** *Gardening* 243 When [the seed potatoes] come up, you just slip one [sprout] off, an' another'll just come on. Tater'll just be covered up with slips. **1985** Irwin *Alex Stewart* 202 She'd make hills just like a haystack and put two slips (plants) in every hill. **1993** Bansemer *Mts in Mist* 176 In the early spring, when the [tobacco] plants are four to six weeks old, they become large enough to transplant. At this stage they are called "slips."

2 (also *slip in*) A landslide, cave-in. Also called landslip.

1924 Raine *Saddlebags* 29 One rainy spell I noticed a great raw area where a large landslide had evidently just occurred, and as I mentioned it at the house where I stopped for dinner, a man recalled with a chuckle a similar "slip." **1941** Stuart *Men of Mts* 279 They found th' entry you's in and it was caved in so they come outside and walked over th' hill and found th' slip. One crew o' men dug all night down through th' slip. **1957** Combs *Lg Sthn High: Word List* 92 *slip* = (land) slide. **1967–69** *DARE Survey* (Adams KY, Clayhole KY, Walker KY) *slip*; (Tompkinsville KY) *slip-in* = when a mass of earth and rock comes loose from a high place and rushes down.

[DARE *slip* n^3 1 especially KY, OH]

slip away (also *slip off*) *verb phrase* To elope.

1940 Haun *Hawk's Done* 116 Ad and Linus took a duck fit when they found out Meady had slipped off and got married. **1963** Edwards *Gravel* 19 I told Pa when Pat slipped off and married you that the only way she would ever get enough to eat would be to slip up when you was asleep and steal grub from her own cupboard. **1977** Shackelford et al. *Our Appalachia* 197 In case they did slip away and marry, this landlord would go and will the boy or girl out of his estate. **1991** Still *Wolfpen Notebooks* 68 "What did you say when you learned your son had slipped off and married that girl and her some kin to him?" "Hell shot a buck rabbit!" **1998** *Dante OHP-51* When you got married, did people know about it, or did you just slip off? **2001** Montgomery *File* (known to 28-year-old woman, Robbinsville NC).

slip-chuck See **slip-shuck**.

slipe *noun* A slice or a narrow, thin strip.

1890 Fruit *KY Words* 66 Cut me a slipe of that bacon. **1952** Wilson *Folk Speech NC* 591 = a small piece of land. **1997** Montgomery *Coll* (known to Bush, Weaver); She was just a slipe of a child (Cardwell).

[OED3 *slipe* n^2 "a slip or slice" now dialect (and U.S.); EDD *slipe* sb 20 "a long, narrow piece of something"; cf SND v^3 "to slip off, to peel"; CUD *slipe*^{2} v 1 "pare, slice"; DARE *slipe* n especially NC, VA]

slip gap *noun* One or more fence bars or rails easily removable to let livestock in and out of a pen or field. See also **drawbar**, **gap 2**.

1943 Justus *Bluebird* 50 I've fixed a slip gap in the fence so that you can turn her in without any trouble. **c1960** Wilson *Coll* = poles or rails that can be drawn out of place to open a gap in a fence; drawbars. **1982** Powers and Hannah *Cataloochee* 283 The side of the [pig] pen had a "slip gap" . . . two logs could be slid over and let hogs come outside. It was sometimes left open for months.

[DARE *slip gap* n South, South Midland]

slip in See **slip B2**.

slip off See **slip away**.

slippance *interjection* Used as a cry used by the shooter of a marble to signal that it accidentally slipped when being aimed.

1891 Brown *Dialect in TN* 173 He cries *slippance!* When his marble slips from his thumb, and this entitles him to another go.

[DARE *slippance* exclam South, South Midland]

slipperslide *noun* A shoehorn.

1939 *FWP Guide NC* 98 Common phrases of the household may be quaint and humorous . . . a shoehorn is a "slipper-slide." **1965** *Dict Queen's English* 16 = shoe horn. "The shoe was so tight he had to use a *slipperslide* to get it on." **1996** Montgomery *Coll* (known to Cardwell).

slippery elm *noun*

A Variant form *slickery elm*.

1967 *DARE Survey* (Jonesborough TN).

B A deciduous tree (*Ulmus rubra*) from whose bark is derived medicine to treat constipation and other conditions.

1847 (in **1870** Drake *Pioneer Life KY* 73) Of the whole forest the red or slippery elm was the best [for livestock fodder]. **1964** Reynolds *Born of Mts* 42 Slippery elm was also used by the Iroquois for easy childbirth, and in this connection Mooney wrote that the Cherokee used it during delayed delivery as boiled in water along with gunpowder. **1967** Jones *Peculiarities Mtneers* 70 Slippery elm bark when boiled down to a thick ooze was widely used to relieve various digestive troubles. It was also considered a valuable remedy for typhoid fever. This tea was also sometimes used as an emetic when anyone had swallowed poison. [**1971** Krochmal et al. *Medicinal Plants Appal* 260 In Appalachia, a tea made from the bark is used as a laxative.]

slips *noun* Men's underpants (a term especially common in western NC).

1813 (in **1920** DeWitt *Sevier Journal* 53) (Aug 13) Sent my letters into the post office—left with Mrs. Chambers 2 Irish linen new shirts & old cravit—1 silk velvet Jacket, & Johnsons dictionary (small) one pair cotton slips. **1862** *Reese CW Letters* (Dec 27) if I had A pair of yarn slips I wood be glad But I dont expect hee Can Bring mutch for you. **1862** *Robinson CW Letters* (Dec 4) the ladys of Wilks county gave me a nice Shirt & Slips & a paire of Socks & a nice bed quilt. **c1900** (in **1997** Stoddart *Quare Women* 128) = drawers.

slip-shuck (also *slip-chuck*) *verb phrase* To break the stem and remove the outer husks from (an ear of corn) in a single motion, leaving the other husks on the stalk; hence verb = to move quickly, escape, "pull a fast one"; to deceive, elude (someone).

1966 Guthrie *Corn* 89 The corn was slip-shucked as it was gathered, but the shucks nearest the ear were left on. . . . It was a sign of poor work not to slip-shuck and leave snouts on the corn. The corn was pulled from the stalks, slip-shucked, and thrown into a wagon-bed as the wagon was pulled through the field. **1979** Carpenter *Walton War* 173 We slip-shucked the crowd and he axed me to take the night with him. **1990** Merriman *Moonshine Rendezvous* 104 "How could Danny just disappear?" I told him, "You were slip chucked (given the slip)." **1995–97** Montgomery *Coll* (known to Bush, Cardwell, Cypher); We slip shucked (i.e., removed only the outer shuck) as we snapped the corn from the stalk (Brown), = literally, to break the stem and remove the outer shucks, usually done when gathering corn, leaving the outer shucks on the stalk (Hooper).

[DARE *slip-shuck* v 1 chiefly South, South Midland]

sliveration *noun* Splinters. See also **shiver A**, **shiveration**.

1997 Montgomery *Coll* (known to Adams).

slobber

A *noun plural* Profuse drops of saliva, as from an aroused animal.

1937 Hall *Coll* (Little Greenbrier TN) [The bear] made a big noise like an old sow [and] blowed slobbers in [his] face. [In a tale about how Black Bill Walker followed a bear into a cave and shot it; see **1960** Hall *Smoky Mt Folks* 17–19.] **c1950** Matthews *Smokey Hills* 30 With bristles standing out and slobbers pouring out from her mouth, she was ready for the charge. **2005** Williams *Gratitude* 524 = drool, salivate; saliva, slavers. "Don't let yer slobbers run back into the dipper when you're drankin' out of it."

B *verb* To cause (an animal) to salivate.

1937 Hall *Coll* (Big Creek NC) The horses eat a sight of clover and it slobbers 'em.

slobber keg *noun* See citation.

1985 Dabney *More Mt Spirits* 172 The alcoholic vapors from the still are piped to the bottom of the thumper keg. The heat from this causes a distillation from the surface of the mash, out a second pipe at the top of the keg. The vapors then travel to the condenser. Some stills have a series of these kegs—some of them dry—to serve as "cleaning barrels," or "filter kegs," or "slobber kegs," to pick up excess water or meal.

slop back *verb phrase* See citations.

1963 Carson *History Bourbon* 46 The sour mash method prevails today. It involves scalding the meal with the thin, spent beer left over from a run. The procedure is called, somewhat inelegantly, "slopping back." **1974** Dabney *Mt Spirits* xxv Slopping Back: Using hot pot-tails from a run to "start" a new batch of mash, yielding sour mash whiskey. *Ibid.* 128 We'd slop back—take the pot tail slop from the first run, and pumped it back into the mash box. That formed the grain base for the next run of whiskey, and it was already sour.

slop-dozzle *verb* See citation.

c1954 Adams *Word-List* = one who carelessly spills something is said to "slop-dozzle."

slope

A (also *slope mine*, *slope mines*) *noun* See citation.

1973 *AOHP/EH-31* He went over there and sunk a slope mines down for them, 165 feet. **2002** Armstead *Black Days* 246 *slope* = a tunnel or passageway that is carved out to get down to or up to a seam of coal. **2006** Hicks *Mt Legacy* 36 *slope mine* = one dug and blasted on an angle, to get to another coal seam below the valley.

B (also *slope off*) *verb*, *verb phrase* To slip away, abscond.

1859 Taliaferro *Fisher's River* 213 Sam Lundy always added a few items of his own . . . when he "sloped" to market. **1866** Smith *So Called* 19 I'm afraid I'll get in a tight place . . . and have to slope out of it. **1983** Broaddus *Estill Co KY Word List* 56 *slope off* = to slink off.

slop hole *noun* Same as **skim hole**.

1985 Jones *Growing Up* 3 After a while some of the men would ease away to their wagons and into their snoogins.

slops *noun*

1 See citation. See also **pot-tail(s)**, **still mash**, **sugar slop**, **swill**.

1982 Slone *How We Talked* 68 = the remaining residue left after the whiskey was made. Some was used to put back into the barrels of mash for the next "run" to help it to ferment quicker.

2 See citation.

1982 *Smokies Heritage* 37 Of course there was a pot of coffee and tea: these drinks were called "slops" by backwoodsmen who said they didn't stick to their ribs.

3 In plural form *slops* = kitchen refuse as feed for farm animals, especially hogs (used in proverbs).

1939 Hall *Coll* (Gatlinburg TN) The quiet hog gets the slops. **1967** Hall *Coll* (Del Rio TN) The still sow gets the slops.

slorate *verb* See 1917 citation.

1917 Kephart *Word-List* 417 = to slaughter. **1995–97** Montgomery *Coll* (known to Oliver, but not to other consultants from the Smoky Mountains).

slouch up *verb phrase* To perform (a task or a repair) carelessly.

1969 *DARE Survey* (Adams KY) *slouched it up*.

slouchways See **slanchways**.

slouchy *adjective* Slovenly, careless.

1969 *DARE Survey* (Berea KY) *slouchy work* = careless work.

(as) slow as Christmas *phrase* Of a moment in time, a person or animal's behavior, etc.: sluggish or slow-moving (used to spur a person to hurry, to describe one who is slow or tardy, to express exasperation, etc.).

1992 Offutt *KY Straight* 80 It's ready to jump, boy. You're slow as Christmas. **1998** Montgomery *Coll* = used to criticize slow or sluggish behavior or work, as "That mule is slow as Christmas but he's steady" (Brown); Don't give her the job, she's as slow as Christmas (Cardwell), = used especially by parents trying to hurry children, as in getting ready for church (Ellis), = used for any thing or person who is slow, as "He's as slow as Christmas" (Jones), = used with both children and adults as a general descriptive term, not just to get someone to hurry (Ledford). **2007** McMillon *Notes* = a long time a-comin'.

[DARE (at *Christmas* n 3) chiefly South, South Midland]

slow as Snyder's hound See **(as/like) Snyder's hound/house cat/pup**.

slowcome *noun* See citation.

1911 Shearin *E KY Word-List* 540 = a lazy, sluggish fellow.

slow Joe See **slow John**.

slow John (also *slow Joe*) *noun* A simple water-driven device for pounding dried corn into meal. See also **hand mill**, **hominy pounder**, **lazy Jim**, **pounding mill**, **quern**, **tri-weekly**.

1897 Skelton *Last Soldiers* 367 (DARE) Lieutenant Coleman had once seen a rude hydraulic contrivance called a Slow-John which was sort of a lazy man's mill. **1939** *FWP Guide TN* 286 The grist-mill, built in 1774, was one of the first water-powered mills in Tennessee and was an improvement over the hand-operated mill and the "hominy pounder" or "slow john," a crude but useful affair that operated by a process of hammering the corn with a wooden beam. **1948** Dick *Dixie Frontier* 249–50 When there was opportunity these sweep mortars were run by water power. It was so arranged that when a receptacle ran full of water, the sweep lifted the pestle. This poured the water out, allowing the pestle to fall down upon the corn. Then the receptacle began to fill and the process was repeated. It was called a hominy-pounder or "slow john." **1952** Wilson *Folk Speech NC* 599 *slow Joe* = a water-run hominy beater.

[DARE *slow John* n southern Appalachians]

slud See **slide A**.

slunk *verb* To slink.

1933 Thomas *Traipsin' Woman* 71 I ketched sight of young Johnnie Marbry slunkin' out of Lawyer Tabor's office a while back.

slut *noun* A crude candle, composed of a string or cloth dipped in lard or grease and set in a saucer. Also called **grease lamp**. See also **tallow dip**.

1913 Kephart *Our Sthn High* 245 The woman will pour hog's grease into a tin or saucer, twist up a bit of rag for the wick and so make a "slut" that, believe me, deserves the name. **1948** Dick *Dixie Frontier* 300 The cabin in the evening was ordinarily lighted by the flames of the fireplace, but in case of sickness or on other special occasions lamps were improvised. One such, called a "slut," consisted of a saucer or similar vessel filled with bear's oil or other fat. A strip of cotton cloth was then inserted, allowing one end to lie over the edge. This end of the wick was lighted. **1957** Combs *Lg Sthn High: Word List* 92 = a tallow light, made by putting a heavy piece of twine, or a narrow cloth wick in the tallow, in a saucer.

[CUD *slut* n "a home-made light made of tow dipped in oil, tallow or resin"; Web3 *slut* n 4 dialect]

slype See **slipe**.

smack (also *smack-dab*, *smack-jam*) *adverb* Completely, exactly, directly. See also **slam**, **square dab**.

1859 Taliaferro *Fisher's River* 43 I want some hog's gullicks and turnup greens right smack now. **1867** Harris *Sut Lovingood* 102 Jis' es soon es the sturn ove the Mills bull totch 'im, he went fur tail holt agin, an' by golly, he hilt hit this time ontil his shoes cum off, an' he fell smack atop ove Mills, face tu the tail. **1902** Harben *Abner Daniel* 14 It'll be started inside of the next yeer an' 'll run smack dab through my property. **1925** Dargan *Highland Annals* 53 "Swear to God," she repeated feebly, "unless, o' course, we're jest smack out o' stuff." **c1950** Adams *Grandpap* 99 It's a-cuttin' my tail smackdab off. **1967** Williams *Subtlety Mt Speech* 15 All of a suddent he come smack up to a big openin in the rock. **1995** Montgomery *Coll* Go smack and do it (Cardwell); He was smack dead, he was smack drunk (Ledford). **2007** McMillon *Notes* Hit was smack-jam by there. **2013** Venable *How to Tawlk* 44 = with great precision: "He fell 12 foot outta 'at elem tree but landed smack dab on his feet!"

[OED3 *smack-dab* adv "exactly, precisely": U.S. dialect and colloquial; DARE *smack* adv 2 "exactly, completely" especially South, South Midland; *smack-dab* adv 2 chiefly South, South Midland]

smack-dab, **smack-jam** See **smack**.

small hominy *noun* Grits.

1998 Dabney *Smokehouse Ham* 316 Mountain people gave [grits] short shrift in earlier days. They called grits "small hominy" in contrast to what they had eaten down through the years—whole grain "whole hominy," "big hominy," or, the really traditional name, "lye hominy."

small to *adjective phrase* Small for.

1937 Hall *Coll* (Emerts Cove TN) That bear was small to his age. **1978** Slone *Common Folks* 287 Vernon was small to his age (he only weighed sixty-eight pounds when he was eleven).

smart

A See **pretty smart**, **right smart**.

B *adjective* Of a person: industrious, energetic, capable; hence noun *smartness* = energy. See also **smartly**.

1859 Taliaferro *Fisher's River* 118 It was corn-gathering time, and, I tell you, I made things wake—wucked all day, wouldn't stop fur dinner—to show my smartness. **1862** Huntley *CW Letters* (Jan 5) you can tell Dobbins folks that Calloway is Well me and him and tolliver had a pretty smart singing Last night. **1863** *CW*

Soldiers' Letters (Feb 1) my Dear Son I want yo to bee a Smart boy while I am gon from yo an take car of yor hors. **1904** Johnson *Highways South* 134 Tige, yo' leave that pig alone—don't be so smart! **c1954** Adams *Word-List* = capable. **1968** *DARE Survey* (Walker KY) = feeling ambitious and eager to work.

[DARE *smart* adj 2 widespread, but chiefly South, South Midland]

(as) smart as Snyder's pup See **(as/like) Snyder's hound/house cat/pup**.

smart grass (also *smartweed*) *noun* A plant of the genus *Polygonum* with medicinal use.

1867 Harris *Sut Lovingood* 67 A hollyhock in a patch of smartweed. **1941** Stuart *Men of Mts* 174 There was the smelly smartweed that grew from the new-ground ash-heaps where the brush had burned. **1971** *AOHP/ALC-147* For our diarrhea, why she used this smartweed and boiled it down and give it to us. **1982** Slone *How We Talked* 47 = *smart grass* used to get rid of fleas, also put in a hole of water to make the fish come to the top of the water and could then be caught.

[DARE (at *smartweed* n) widespread, but chiefly Midland, North Central, Central]

smartly *adverb* Energetically, briskly. See also **smart B**.

1863 *Mangum CW Letters* (March 10) I think that I am fatning and that smartly too. **1923** (in **1952** Mathes *Tall Tales* 10) Grandad's stick rapped smartly on the stones as he turned toward his cottage nestling on a "bench" of the mountain, a hundred yards above the road.

smash See **play smash**.

smather (also *smatter, snatter*) *verb* To spread or pour (butter, gravy, syrup, or another substance) thickly on; to smear.

1996–97 Montgomery *Coll*: *smather* (known to Adams, Bush); I had my biscuits smathered with gravy this morning (Cardwell); *smatter* (known to Weaver); *snatter* (known to Weaver).

[DARE *smather* v chiefly South, South Midland]

smatter See **smather**.

smearcase (also *smearcheese*) *noun* Cottage cheese.

1930 Pendleton *Wood-Hicks Speak* 88 *smearcheese* = cottage cheese. **1934–47** *LAMSAS Appal*: *smearcheese* = attested by 50/148 speakers (33.7%) from WV, 9/20 (45%) from VA, 1/37 (2.7%) from NC, and 2/14 (14.3%) from SC. **1946** Woodard *Word-List VA/NC* 27 (swVA) *smearcase* = cottage cheese. **1958** Wood *Words from TN* 16 *smearcase* = cheese made of curd and sour milk. **1986** Pederson et al. *LAGS*: *smearcase* = attested by 3/60 interviewees (5%) from E TN; 3/4 of all LAGS interviewees (75%) attesting term were from Appalachia.

[< German "spread cheese"; DARE *smearcase* n chiefly North Midland, especially PA, OH, MD, WV]

smearcheese See **smearcase**.

smell of *verb phrase* To exercise or make use of the sense of smell on. See also **of 3**.

1883 Bonner *Dialect Tales* 179 "No, you don't, Jack Boddy," said a quiet voice. "Smell o' that." **1895** Wiltse *Moonshiners* 126 The attorney ventured to speak, and said he could tell [whiskey] by the smell of it. "You can, eh?" said the mountaineer, scornfully. "Well, you just smell of this, then, and tell us what it is," producing from his saddle-pockets a large bottle of corn whisky, well nigh as white and clear as distilled water. **1939** Hall *Coll* Smell of it (as an imperative). **1994** Walker *Life History* 133 She had a jar sitting on the back of the bathroom, and I got it, and smelled of it, and then I washed myself off real good, then I dried myself and used it.

[OED3 *smell* v 6a, now U.S.]

smell up *verb phrase* To find and follow the scent of (an animal).

1940 Oakley *Roamin'/Restin'* 99 I always liked hound dog pups as I thot they was so good to smell up opsams coons and other wild animals.

smidge See **smidgen**.

smidgen (also *smidge, smidgin, smitching*) *noun* An indefinite, small bit, portion, or amount, as of meal, powder, or grain.

1886 Smith *Southernisms* 43 Smidgen, "a small bit, a grain," as "a smidgen of meal" is common in East Tennessee. "He broke it all to smidgens" is a common expression. **1913** Kephart *Our Sthn High* 293 If the provender be scant the hostess may say, "That's right at a smidgen," meaning little more than a mite; but if plenteous, then there are rimptions. **1927** Furman *Lonesome Road* 97 I hain't got a smitching of doubt He [= God] tuck her in as willing dipped as ondipped! **1939** Hall *Coll* (White Oak NC) Go over an' borry a smidgen of salt. **1940** Haun *Hawk's Done* 28 The Old Man, he set right there without moving a smidgin. **1967** *DARE Survey* (Maryville TN) = small, indefinite amount, as of butter. **1974** Fink *Bits Mt Speech* 24 Jest a *smidgen* more sugar in my coffee. **2005** Williams *Gratitude* 524 *smidge* = just a teeny little bit, or a dab. Sometimes called a *smidge*.

[OED3 *smidgen* n "a tiny amount, a trace" originally and chiefly U.S.; cf SND *smitch* n "a very small amount"; Web3 *smidgen* n probably alteration of *smitch* "a small amount"]

smidgin See **smidgen**.

smiling mighty Jesus *noun* See citation.

2013 Reed *Medical Notes* = spinal meningitis.

smirr See **smur**.

smitching See **smidgen**.

smitherations *noun* Splinters collectively.

1997 Montgomery *Coll* (known to Cardwell).

smoke grinder *noun* A mechanical toy, in some cases an imaginary one. Also called **bull grinder**.

1980 Wigginton *Foxfire VI* 161 Of course, bull grinders are the only name it had. I've heard them called do nothings and smoke grinders. *Ibid.* 229 Another locally made toy Fred Potter stocks in his shop is the Smoke grinder. The point of the toy is set in a slight depression, and as the horizontal bar is pumped with two fingers, the influence of the string shifting around the shaft and the weight of the wooden disk make the toy spin back and forth in the depression. **2012** Still *Hills Remember* 352 Fes, old neighbor, I swear to my heart if I had a smoke-grinder for sale you'd be my first customer.

smokehouse *noun* A small outbuilding in which salt-cured or smoked preserved meat is stored, especially for winter consumption. Also called **meat house**.

1939 Hall Coll (Wears Cove TN) [We] kept deer meat and bear meat and coon meat and turkey all the time. We had a little black pine smoke house that we kept it hung in. We kept it full of bear meat and deer meat and turkeys all the time. **1961** Medford *History Haywood Co* 16 Soon thereafter the loom and spinning wheel were in place, and the "smoke house" with its meat troughs, bins, meat-hangers, etc. had been made. **1968** Clarke *Stuart's Kentucky* 187 Above the cellar, or in a separate structure nearby, was the smokehouse where cured hams (smoked with green hickory), middlings (middlin meat), sow-belly, jowl, dried fruits, and vegetables, some of the laundry and gardening equipment, and the rag bag were kept. **1971** *AOHP/ALC*-147 In the curing of the meat for the family, why when you killed the hogs, you cut them up and put them in the smokehouse. You salted it down, and you let it stay salted down for three days, and then you hung it up, and if you liked it smoked, well you smoked it with hickory bark or either apple tree. **1977** Yeager *Mostly Work* 8 We had the big smokehouse in the yard. They call it "big smokehouse" and we'd put out meat in there and then smoke it. That's where we kept the meat and lard from killing time to killing time. That's, I say, from the fall of the year when they kill until the next year, when they'd kill again. **1978** Montgomery *White Pine Coll* III-2 We'd sugarcure [the pork] with brown sugar and red pepper. Each piece was then bagged up and hung in the smokehouse, and there it hung till we got ready. **2003** LaLone et al. *Farming Life* 239 We never did actually smoke any meat, but they called it a smokehouse. But it was just a dry building, but there wasn't any heat or anything. It was open and you had screens and stuff and you salt cured in there. **2016** Netherland *Appal Cooking* 6 We did not smoke meat in the smokehouse, but it still carried that name from times when the meats curing there were hardwood smoked. Rather, it was an unheated and uninsulated building allowing the weather to help perform its function of curing the meats that were hung inside.

smoke like a two-dollar stove *verb phrase* See citation.

1968–70 *DARE Survey* (Buckhannon WV, Moorefield WV, Salem WV, Richwood WV) = to smoke a great deal.

smoke vine *noun* See citations.

[**c1960** Wilson *Coll*: *Bignonia capreolata*, a vine with a porous stem and with pith shaped like a cross; dried vines were smoked by boys.] **1982** Slone *How We Talked* 90 Smoked pieces of the smoke vine for pretend cigarettes.

(the) Smoky (also *the Smoky Mountain*) *noun* The main chain or ridge of the Great Smoky Mountains, a single uninterrupted ridge that runs the 54-mile length of Great Smoky Mountains National Park and forms the TN/NC state border. Also called **Great Smoky**, **mountain B**, **Old Smoky**, **top of Smoky**. See also **Big Smokies**.

1860 *Week in Smokies* 126 The rattlesnakes is sometimes powerful bad in the Smoky. **1921** Fink *Week in Smoky Range* 150 On the southwest [the Balsam Range] is joined by the main chain of Smoky, down which we had come, which continues a number of miles past Guyot to the gorge of the Big Pigeon River. **1926** Hunnicutt *Twenty Years* 57 The dogs are now fighting the bear on the other side of the Smoky Mountain. **1930** Fink *Trails* 68 Smoky is still a wilderness, and to wander out of the beaten way can—and generally does—involve one in difficulties which easily may turn to tragedy. **1939** Hall Coll (Deep Creek NC) The dogs was a-fightin' the bear right in under the top of Smoky. . . . They're not a-goin' to let 'im cross the Smoky. *Ibid.* (Wears Cove TN) We'd herd [cattle] along Smoky Mountain part of the time, and part of the time on what we call the Long Arm. . . . The dogs run up and jumped on the biggest bear I've ever saw in the Smoky Mountain. **1967** *Grandmother Cherokee* 79 He started to show him this silver mine, and got right close t'Luftee Gap in there on Smoky. **1976** GSMNP-114:5 I've been to Smoky Mountain in rounding up time. **1999** Spencer *Memory Lane* II:3 A few men were clearing a path up over old Smoky Mountain. **2002** Weals *Legends* 9 From Davenport Gap on the east to Deals Gap on the west they thought of it all as "the Smoky Mountain."

Smoky Mountain tea *noun* Homemade whiskey.

1990 Bush *Maize* 30 When the kernels became ripe and hard, it was made into hominy and corn meal and, yes, Smoky Mountain Tea (moonshine).

Smoky Mountain wind *noun* A loud, violent wind that works its way down from the main ridge of the Smoky Mountains and indicates a coming storm. Also called **mountain wind**.

1977 Adams *Remembering* 98 I remembered sounds of the wind, that special "Smoky Mountain" wind that would begin with an uneasy roar on the mountains before it swept into the valley.

smolick (also *smolick around*, *smommick*) *verb phrase* To act with abandon, cavort, engage in sexual play or activity.

1930s (in **1944** Wentworth *ADD* 572) (eWV) These young girls & their lipstick, smearin' an' smollickin' around. **1961** Seeman *Arms of Mt* 36 My mammy could tell when there was a witch easin' around: the baby 'ud git the dry colick, the butter jest wouldn't come, and old Brindle 'ud go to smolickin' around kickin' up her heels and actin' mighty quair. *Ibid.* 61 An old sweet'art of his—she was his double cousin—come up and smolicked around with him. **1997** Montgomery Coll = to carry on an illicit relationship with someone (Andrews), = to kiss and such (Jones), = to date, go out together (Oliver). **2007** McMillon *Notes* = to flirt, hang around. **2011** *Blind Pig* (Dec 11) When someone made a mess, my granny would say, "gom and Smollick, Smollick and Gom, that's all you're good for!" **2014** *WV Talk*: *smommick* = word describing the actions of honeymooners and others under the spell of love's first blush, before the "new" wears off. A public display of affection: kissing, fawning, hand-holding, moon-eyed looks. Also used derisively about someone who was goofing off with a friend having fun instead of getting his/her chores done: "Guess they're off smommickin' somewhere."

smommick See **smolick.**

smootch-eyed polecat (also *smotch-eyed polecat*) *noun* Used as a derogatory epithet to taunt or insult. See citations.

1923 Furman *Mothering* 38 Nucky kicked Killis on the shin; Killis called him a smotch-eyed polecat; the two grappled; Philip flew to Nucky's assistance. **1940** Bowman *KY Mt Stories* 247 *smootch-eyed polecat* = worst epithet possible.

smooth crop *noun* A type of **mark** cut into the edge of a domestic animal's ear to identify its owner. See also **overbit**, **split B1**, **swallowfork**, **underbit.**

1773 (in **1929** Summers *Annals SW VA* 209) (DARE) Ord[ered] that Uriah Humphries's ear mark be admitted to record, towit: two smooth crops and a slit in the left ear. **1915** Dingus *Word-List VA* 185 *mark* = a cutting of the ear (of hogs, sheep, cattle) for identification,—of various kinds: (smooth) crop, the tip cut square off.

smoothing iron *noun* An old-fashioned, nonelectric iron for pressing clothes, heated on a stove or before the fire.

1901 Harben *Westerfelt* 7 She stooped to put her smoothing-iron down on the hearth. **1976** Thompson *Touching Home* 16 = old-fashioned iron heated on the stove or before the fire. **1993** Montell *Cumberland Country* 33–34 [as of 1910] My mother used to put her smoothing irons on the fireplace in front of the coal grate and get them hot. She would then wrap them in a towel and take them into the attic and put them at the foot of the bed to have a warm place to place our feet when we went to bed. **2005** Williams *Gratitude* 38 We set the black cast iron "smoothin' arn" on top of the cookstove to git it het up (heated) enough to arn with.

[DARE *smoothing iron* n formerly widespread, now chiefly South, South Midland]

smotch-eyed polecat See **smootch-eyed polecat.**

smother *verb* To labor in breathing, experience shortness of breath; hence nouns *smothering fit*, *smothering spell* = a period of labored breathing. See also **smotheration**, **smotherly**, **smother out.**

1981 Whitener *Folk-Ways* 83 His nose was just flat on his face—just two holes for a nose and he breathed just like he was smothering something awful. **1987** Carver *Regional Dialects* 167 A momentary feeling of weakness accompanied by a rapid heart beat and difficulty in breathing is sometimes called a *smothering spell*. **1990** Cavender *Folk Medical Lex* 31 *smothering* = difficulty with breathing. **1994–97** Montgomery *Coll* (known to ten consultants from the Smoky Mountains); I couldn't sleep last night from smothering (Cardwell). **1999** McNeil *Purchase Knob* 29 Ernest told me one day when we were out in the woods that Leitha had had a "smothering fit" when they were up at the house checking on it that winter. **2005** Williams *Gratitude* 232 She took "smotherin' spells," and set out on the porch in her rockin' chair to get air. **2007** Preece *Leavin' Sandlick* 16 She smothered so bad at times ye could heer her all over the house tryin' to breathe, and Wade was gettin' the same way.

[DARE *smother* v 2 formerly widespread, now chiefly South, South Midland]

smotheration *noun* Shortness of breath, suffocation. See also **smother.**

1976 Garber *Mountain-ese* 84 = suffocation. "The room was so tight we almost died uv smotheration." **1996–97** Montgomery *Coll* (known to Brown, Cardwell, Oliver).

smothering fit, **smothering spell** See **smother.**

smotherly (also *smothery*) *adjective* Of air: very humid, close, hard to breathe; of weather: suffocating. See also **smother.**

1940 Haun *Hawk's Done* 63 I noticed that it was a smotherly evening. **1941** Stuart *Men of Mts* 65 It's gettin' hot and smothery to work in this corn now. *Ibid.* 270 Th' leaves on th' peach tree were thick and th' wind was smothery. **c1945** Haun *Hawk's Done* 304 The room smelt smothery. **1957** Broaddus *Vocab Estill Co KY* 71 *smothery* = a condition in which it is hard to breathe. **1968** DARE *Survey* (Brasstown NC) *smothery* = of air that is very still, moist, and warm.

smother out *verb phrase* To deprive of breathing room.

1973 GSMNP-6:32 Gatlinburg grew so fast that we wouldn't have been able to [breathe]. We'd just all been smothered out as the saying is.

smothery See **smotherly.**

smoul *verb* To slobber.

1961 Williams *Rhythm and Melody* 9 Ye can see the lowdown thang [= a dog] a-layin' on the hathrock a-sappin' at its fleas and a-smoulin' over hitself. **1962** Williams *Verbs Mt Speech* 18 The farmer scolds the child for taking out more "grub" than he can eat and "a-smoulin' around over it and a-mommickin' it up till nobody else can stommick it."

smudge fire *noun* A smoldering or smothered fire built, as on the windward side of a tent, to produce smoke and ward off such insects as mosquitoes and gnats. See also **gnat smoke.**

1969 Medford *Finis* 87 Looks like you fokes cud bild up some smudge fires, or sump'm.

[EDD *smudge* sb² 3 nEngl "a smoulder, a suffocating smoke or dust"; SND *smush* n[1] "a thick cloud of smoke or soot particles"; CUD *smudge*[2] v "smoulder"]

smur *noun* See citation.

1944 Wilson *Word-List* 49 = a fog almost as heavy as a rain.

[OED3 *smur* n 1 "fine rain; a drizzle of rain," dialect and Scottish; SND *smirr* n[1] "a fine rain, drizzle, occasionally also of sleet or snow"]

snab *verb* To nab.

1967 Williams *Subtlety Mt Speech* 14 He snuck up right easy and rech out and snabbed it [= a bumblebee] and popped it into a poke he had with 'im.

snaggeldy *adjective* Jagged.

1949 Arnow *Hunter's Horn* 283 He hadn't remembered it so small and thin and brown, with her front teeth showing brown and snaggeldy with rotten spots like those of an old woman.

snake

A *noun*

1 (also *red snake*) A curling line imprinted on a coal miner's pay statement indicating that he remains in debt to the coal company's store. See also **three pink kisses**.

1989 Giardina *Storming Heaven* 12 "Snake again," was all he would say, meaning he hadn't been able to mine enough coal to pay off the bills at the company store, that he still owed for food and doctoring and his work tools and blasting powder, that his paycheck had a single wavy line where the money figures should have been. **2006** *WV Encycl* 644 Miners often received pay envelopes marked with a curling line across them, a symbol miners called the "bobtail check" or the "snake." It meant no wages due.

B *verb*

1 (also *snake down*, *snake in*, *snake out*) To move (a heavy object, especially a log, as with a draft animal or a chain) forcibly downhill, often in a weaving path. See also **skid road**.

1903 Fox *Little Shepherd* 32 Tom was off to help a neighbor "snake" logs down the mountain and into Kingdom Come, where they would be "rafted" and floated on down the river to the capital. **1915** Hall *Autobiog Claib Jones* 10 We would . . . tie the bears to a single-tree by their heads and snake them in home. **1916** Schockel *KY Mts* 110 The mountaineer's way of lumbering is to cut a few choice trees and "snake" them down to the creek, where, as logs, rafts or railroad ties, they await the coming of the flood, or "tide," to be floated down stream. **1929** Carpenter *Evolution of Dialect* 28 Around logging camps, one finds examples of new words. Anyone who has frequented logging operations has heard snakin' and ball-hootin' logs. Snakin' means drawing a log along the ground endways by any form of power, and ball-hootin' means shooting logs down over a steep incline to a lower level. **1931** Goodrich *Mt Homespun* 39 It was a rough cart track, washed by rains and furrowed by the logs "snaked down" to the saw yard below. **1956** Hall *Coll* (Big Creek NC) They put a chain around [logs] and snaked them out. **1970** Madden and Jones *Ephraim Bales* 11 Normally he simply "snaked" entire trees to his front yard, and cut them into firewood as needed. Consequently, wood sheds were not common structures in these mountains. **1973** GSMNP-13:6 [We] had to snake [the cabins] out on a sled and then attach the sled to a truck. **1980** Matthews *Appal Physician* 69 He was too ill to be snaked down [on a sled]. **1982** Eller *Miners* 90 The farmer and his sons could "snake" the huge logs out of the mountains with a team of oxen and carry them to portable sawmills installed for that purpose, or he could drag the logs to the head of a creek and let the spring rains carry his product to market. **1999** Isbell *Keepers* 25 Max broke in a young ox to plow the fields; with the ox he "snaked in" firewood from nearby forests. **2006** Farwell *Logging Term* 1021 "Hayburners," or horses, their "teamsters," and oxen driven by "bullwhackers," all became outmoded, as did "crosspoling" logs across trails to make them sturdy and "swamping," or cutting, new trails to "snake" logs out of the forest.

2 To search (a cornfield) for snakes.

1941 Stuart *Men of Mts* 50 Pap used to tell us . . . that when weeds got knee high in a corn patch, we ought to go through with a stick and snake the weeds and run the vipers, copperheads, rattlesnakes, and blacksnakes out.

3 In phrases *snake the bed*, *snake the covers* = to search through or remove bed covers before retiring at night, in order to ensure that a snake has not crawled into them seeking warmth.

1935 Sheppard *Cabins in Laurel* 48 Aunt Polly can see the old times if not the new. Going barefoot to the long churchhouse, with rags wrapped around her legs for warmth; "snakin' the beds" before she would dare crawl in between the covers. **1953** Davison *Word-List Appal* 14 *snake the bed* = to search the bed before retiring to see if any snakes have crawled under the covers. Snakes often enter cabins that are not screened or [that] have a hole in the floor, and sometimes crawl into beds for warmth. **1970** Mull *Mt Yarns* 7 "Snaking the kivvers," that is removing all the bed clothes from beds before retiring and shaking them good, became essential. **1972** Cooper *NC Mt Folklore* 32 In early days, before the family retired for the night, the bedding was removed and shaken lest a snake had slithered into the house and was waiting to strike. This practice was called snaking the beds. **2018** *Blind Pig* (June 12) My Mom and Dad would always "snake the kivvers" when visiting their old homes, especially if we were to bed down in some of the rooms that hadn't been used in years.

snake-bit *past participle, adjective* Bitten by a snake; figuratively = jinxed. For similar forms, see **bite A2**.

1846 (in **1974** Harris *High Times* 56) Bed time came, and after reconnoitering his sleeping ground he proceeded to count his beads and the chances of being "snake-bit" before day. **1913** Morley *Carolina Mts* 288 Be mighty careful now, look where you step! I'd rather give a thousand dollars than get you snake-bit up here. **1973** GSMNP-4:1:67 There was very few people that I ever knew of getting snakebit, although they was plenty of snakes on Cataloochee and Big Creek. **1973** GSMNP-86:44 None of us ever [got] snakebit, but their work animal did. Hit got snakebit and they got wild touch-me-not, put it in a flour poke and boiled it and got the strength out, and then they took a cloth or something and bathed its foot where it got snakebit. **1976** Garber *Mountain-*

ese 84 = jinxed, unlucky. "Mark can't seem to win atall; he must be snake-bit." **1991** Haynes *Haywood Home* 40 One of the women finally saw me and screamed, "Oh Lordy! The child's been snake-bit!"

[DARE *snake-bit* adj 2 chiefly South]

snakebite medicine (also *snake medicine*) *noun* Homemade whiskey. See also **cold medicine, headache medicine.**

1968–69 DARE *Survey* (Wytheville VA) *snakebite medicine*; (Dillard GA) *snake medicine*. **1976** Garber *Mountain-ese* 84 I allers take along a bottle uv snake-bite medicine, jist in case. [**1985** *Smokies Anniv Book* 58 To snake bite victims, a "snort" of moonshine was a dose that usually warded off poison from any critter's bite.]

snake doctor (also *snake feeder, snake fly, snake master, snake skeeter, snake waiter*) *noun* A dragonfly.

1929 Rainey *Animal Plant Lore* 11 I have found very few school or college boys [in KY] who know what is a dragon fly. But, the Kentucky boy always responds to "snake doctor." And it is supposed to render professional services to snakes in the vicinity. . . . Kentucky superstitions state that if you kill a dragon fly (snake doctor) it will bring bad luck or that if one lights on your line when fishing, that the fish will not bite. **1934–47** *LAMSAS Appal*: *sake doctor* = attested by 72/148 speakers (48.6%) from WV, 12/20 (60%) from VA, 87/37 (21.3%) from NC, 24/14 (60.6%) from SC, and 6/12 (50%) from GA; *snake feeder* = attested by 114/148 speakers (57.2%) from WV, 17/20 (85%) from VA, 37/37 (21.3%) from NC, 20/14 (60.6%) from SC, and 8/12 (66.7%) from GA; *snake fly* = attested by 2/148 speakers (1.4%) from WV, 2/14 (14.3%) from SC, and 2/12 (16.7%) from GA; *snake master* = attested by 2/148 speakers (1.4%) from WV and 2/37 (5.4%) from NC; *snake skeeter* = attested by 2/37 speakers (5.4%) from NC; *snake waiter* = attested by 2/37 speakers (5.4%) from NC. **1937** Haun *Cocke Co* 5 If a snake feeder flies toward him, he will be killed by an animal within the next three months unless he kills the snake feeder. **1941** Dearden *Word Geog S Atl Sts* 11 *Snake feeder*, in general use in Pennsylvania, is the mountain term, now confined to the western part of Virginia and North Carolina. *Ibid.* 75 *Snake feeder* predominates also in the North Carolina mountains and in adjoining parts of Virginia and South Carolina. **1949** Kurath *Word Geog East US* 42 *Snake doctor* is also in regular use in the Shenandoah Valley and quite common in the southeastern half of West Virginia by the side of Midland *snake feeder*. Since *snake doctor* is indigenous to both Eastern Pennsylvania and the Virginia Piedmont, we must recognize a double source for it in the Valley and the Appalachians. **1952–57** (in **1973** McDavid and McDavid *Vocab E KY* 158) = attested by 21/52 (40.3%) of E KY speakers for the Linguistic Atlas of the North Central States. **1958** Newton *Dialect Vocab*: *snake feeder* = common term for a dragon fly in E TN mountains, attested by 27 of 36 speakers from E TN. **1966** Dakin *Vocab Ohio River Valley* 400–403 The dragonfly is known by many names in the Ohio Valley, but only *snake feeder* and *snake doctor* are distributed broadly enough to be called regional terms. Only in the eastern Knobs and the central Mountain counties (generally along the upper Kentucky area of easiest access from the Bluegrass) do these two terms commonly stand side by side. Elsewhere they are almost mutually exclusive. Even in the northern Mountain counties and in the south along the headwaters of the Cumberland, *snake feeder* is regular and *snake doctor* is rare. **1974** Russell *Hillbilly* 43 Across the deep hole from where I fished, there was a shaded moss-covered bank with scarlet flowers, and usually, snake feeders were flitting about them. **1986** Pederson et al. *LAGS*: *snake doctor* = attested by 4/60 speakers (6.7%) from E TN and 18/35 (52.7%) from N GA; 22/276 of all LAGS users (7.9%) were from Appalachia; *snake feeder* = attested by 41/60 interviewees (68.3%) from E TN and 4/35 (11.4%) from N GA; 45/55 of all LAGS interviewees (81.8%) attesting term were from Appalachia. **2015** *Blind Pig* (May 26) I grew up in E. KY. and always called them snake feeders. As a boy I thought they actually fed snakes. *Ibid.* I grew up in Southern West Virginia and always heard them called snake doctors. I had heard of dragonflies, mostly in books, but was an adult before I realized they were the same thing. *Ibid.* I don't think anyone in the East Tennessee I knew ever heard of dragon flies but everyone knew snake feeders. That's all I ever call them. *Ibid.* While growing up in the Northwestern part of N.C., I always heard dragonflies called "snake feeders." *Ibid.* The snake doctor term was used only for the smaller dragonflies that had the slender body. The larger ones with the thicker bodies were just called dragonflies.

[DARE *snake doctor* n 2 chiefly Midland, South, *snake feeder* n 1 chiefly Midland, Plains States]

snake dog *noun*

1 A dog trained to guard and protect children against snakes.

1993 Montell *Cumberland Country* 55 It was not uncommon for parents to take their babies and small children to the field, put them on a quilt brought along for the purpose, and place a trusted canine referred to as a "snakedog" close to the little ones to guard them. **1997** Montgomery *Coll* = a dog trained to catch and kill snakes (Brown).

2 See citation.

1973 Schulman *Logging Terms* 36 = a device made up of two iron spikes joined together by a chain of three or five links . . . used to snake logs in the woods.

snake down, snake in, snake off See **snake B.**

snake feeder See **snake doctor.**

snake fence *noun* Same as **worm fence.**

1995 *Smokies Guide* (Summer) 13 Although there were several types of rail fence used in the Smokies, the most common was the worm or "snake" fence. The zig-zag style of construction was among the most common and aesthetically pleasing in the mountains. One big advantage of the worm fence was that it was portable. Since there were usually no posts, they could be picked up and moved whenever a new field was created. Also, since there were no posts, no post holes had to be dug, an enormous consideration on rocky terrain.

snake fly See **snake doctor.**

snake handler *noun* See 1982 citation. See also **serpent handler, sign follower.**

1982 *Foxfire VII* 481 The snake handlers read the verses located in the final portion of the Gospel of Mark [= 16:17–18 "In my name . . . they shall speak with new tongues; They shall take up serpents"] and insist that those words must be taken literally. Indeed they declare that if those prophecies are not true, none of the Bible is true. **1999** House *Elements Appal Lit* 2 There are more snakehandlers in Appalachian literature than there are in Appalachia.

snake handling *noun* Same as **serpent handling.**

1982 *Foxfire VII* 393 I believe in serpent handlin' a hun'erd percent. My wife never did believe in it.

snake-handling meeting See **snake meeting.**

snake hunt *noun* An organized hunt to search for and kill poisonous snakes. See also **snake-killing party.**

1970 *Snake Lore* 168 Men go on "snake hunts" every fall, walking into the middle of rattlesnake dens with limber poles and killing twenty or thirty at a time.

snake in the woodpile *noun phrase* An untrustworthy, deceitful person, especially one who is seemingly harmless; an unexpected or uncertain situation.

1960 Mason *Memoir* 56 Ben and his two partners soon realized that there was a snake in the woodpile and then was planted the seed of hate which was soon to grow and blossom forth into murder. **1997** Montgomery *Coll* = there is some doubt, as "I don't believe everything is as they say, I think there's a snake in the woodpile somewhere" (Cardwell), = an unexpected event or happening (Jones).

snake juice *noun* Homemade whiskey.

1972 Hall *Sayings* 101 Common expressions about 1941 for whisky illegally manufactured were . . . "headache medicine" (with veiled meaning), "screw top," "snake juice," [and] "red eye." **1973** Davis *'Pon My Honor* 100 = strong fiery liquor. **1987** Young *Lost Cove* 176 "This stuff is real snake juice," he mumbled. "It ought to get me by that confounded graveyard."

snake-killing party (also *snake party*) *noun* A gathering of neighbors to hunt down and kill poisonous snakes. See also **snake hunt.**

1964 Cooper *History Avery Co* 11 After "snake parties" had destroyed most of the copper heads and rattlesnakes and hunters had killed off most of the wolves and bears, grazing became profitable. *Ibid.* 40 The bean-stringings, apple-peelings and molasses-boilings were held at night, with no refreshments being served, but at all others, except the snake-killing parties, the tables literally groaned with feasts of good food.

snake master See **snake doctor.**

snake medicine See **snakebite medicine.**

snake meeting (also *snake-handling meeting*) *noun* A Pentecostal religious service at which poisonous snakes are handled, in adherence to a stricture found in the Gospel according to Mark 16: 17. See also **serpent handling, snake handling.**

1997 Johnson *Melungeon Heritage* 38–39 I was once told that over forty years ago one of the first snake-handling meetings ever held in Hancock County was conducted unfer a big tree with copperheads and rattlesnakes. One of the preachers was bitten on the second event and almost died. Such gatherings were called "Snake Meetings" in Sneedville. **2007** Farr *My Appalachia* 124 They's having a snake meetin'—I believe Shilo Collins was the preacher.

snake party See **snake-killing party.**

snakeroot tea *noun* A medicinal drink made from **button snakeroot.**

1940 Haun *Hawk's Done* 33 It seemed like she looked more stronger than she had for over a week. Amy brought her some snake-root tea.

snake skeeter See **snake doctor.**

snake stick *noun* See citation.

1971 Fetterman *People Cumberland Gap* 600 Each hunter carried a "snake stick." Earl's was of metal; the rest were ingeniously fashioned from a stout hickory or oak stick and a piece of cord. The stick has two holes bored near one end, about three inches apart, and the string passes through them, forming a loop. When the loop is dropped over a snake's head, a quick tug on the string snares it, enabling the hunter to extract the snake from its hiding place.

snake tale *noun* An account of an encounter with a snake, especially an exaggerated or fantastic account. See also **bear tale, panther tale, wild hog tale.**

1953 Hall *Coll* (Del Rio TN) They got to tellin' snake tales. The rattlesnake got the black snake's tail, and the black snake got the rattlesnake's tail, and pretty soon there was just a spot of grease.

snake the bed, snake the covers See **snake B3.**

snake waiter See **snake doctor.**

snakey See **snaky.**

snaky (also *snakey*) *adjective* Of a place: infested with snakes or thought likely to be.

1937 Hall *Coll* Don't go in there. Hit looks like a snaky place to me. **1956** *GSMNP-22:15* "You always play on this old rock fence here," he said. "That's awful snaky." **1962** Miller *Pigeon's Roost* (July 19) This place has long been counted on as a snaky country 'cause there's been so many copperheads killed. **1970** *Snake Lore* 167 Time after time we have been on field trips with seasoned mountain people who refuse to enter an abandoned house or meadow or cave because it looks so "snaky." **1975** Screven *John B Wright* 14 Me and my mother-in-law and daddy (in-law) went up a big hollow and it was the awfulest snakiest place that ever was. **1984** High *Titan Rock* 36–37 Guidebooks downplay the presence of snakes, but local people think differently. They try to avoid any place that looks "snakey," which means virtually anywhere during this season, particularly in August when some believe snakes leave the ridgetops for cooler creeks and the river—closer to where people live. **1991** Haynes *Haywood Home* 46 There was greater danger in raspberry picking because they always grew best around rock piles, fences, fallen logs and other "snaky" places. **1995** Montgomery *Coll* That looks real snaky in there (Shields).

snap *noun*

1 A party game.

1945 Wilson *Passing Institutions* 192 Our liveliest game was Snap, a game that used to seem very exciting but now resembles Drop the Handkerchief.

[DARE *snap* n chiefly South, South Midland]

2 (also *snap bean*, usually plural *snaps*) Any green bean whose pod makes a sharp sound when broken.

1867 Harris *Sut Lovingood* 242 She'll back yu up in that ar statemint, ontil thar's enuf white fros' in hell tu kill snap-beans. **1913** Kephart *Our Sthn High* 292 Green beans in the pod are called snaps; when shelled they are shuck-beans. **1927** Woofter *Dialect from WV* 364 *snaps* = string beans. "We had our first mess of snaps Sunday." **1949** Kurath *Word Geog East US* 31 In Virginia and North Carolina the Southern *snap beans* is spreading westward. *Ibid.* 73 Three terms for string beans are current over large areas: *string beans* north of the Potomac, *snap beans* south of it, and *green-beans* in the West Midland. . . . *Snap beans* is the regular term in most of Virginia and in the adjoining parts of North Carolina east of the Blue Ridge. It competes with the Midland *green-beans* in westernmost Virginia and in western North Carolina and South Carolina, and with *string beans* on the Northern Neck of Virginia and on the Carolina coast. **1994** Montgomery *Coll* (known to Cardwell). **2000** Spencer *Memory Lane* III:4 Snap beans were grown by the bushels, and were canned or dried, or both, and pickled.

[DARE *snap bean* n scattered, but chiefly South, South Midland]

snap bean *noun*

1 See **snap 2**.

2 Same as **leather britches**.

1979 *Shenandoah OHC* 5 Most of them [= vegetables in wintertime] was dried. You take beans, you know, like you snap them now. Then you get [a] long thread and thread these things on cotton . . . just keep sticking the needle through and have strings of them that go clear across this room, and then when you get that on that good, drive nails and hang them clear across the room in every direction . . . until they dried good, and then you'd take them down and put them in sacks or cloth. [Q: Did you call them leather britches?] Snap beans.

snap coal *noun* See citation.

2002 Armstead *Black Days* 246 = [an] extremely dangerous mine-roof condition, caused by dense, compacted coal under pressure. Unpredictable "snaps" or cracks occur as small or large chunks of coal shoot down suddenly. Roof falls may occur as pressure shifts.

snapweed *noun* A wildflower (*Impatiens* spp), the juice from whose stem is used to treat poison ivy. Same as **jewel flower**, **touch-me-not**, **water weed**.

1981 Whitener *Folk-Ways* 55 Thus if I felt I had been exposed to either ivy or oak, I simply broke some jewelweed stems and rubbed the juice over any exposed flesh. Perhaps water would have served the same purpose so soon after contact. But regardless of that possibility, I became a firm believer in jewelweed, or snapweed, as I occasionally hear it called in the Appalachians.

snatch burr *noun* A weed whose seedpods cling to clothing.

1919 Combs *Word-List South* 35 = a bothersome, flat, triangular shaped little burr. Knott Co. [KY]. **1929** (in **1995** Williams *Become Teacher* 50) Before the afternoon was half over, we were all covered with burrs, Spanish needles, beggar lice, or snatchburs in little strings like beads, [and] cockleburs, which the children called "cuckleburs." **1940** Still *River of Earth* 43 "I put a handful of snatchburs behind the saddle," she said. **1957** Combs *Lg Sthn High: Word List* 92 = a small flat, triangular shaped burr that adheres to clothing like a leech.

[DARE *snatch burr* KY]

snatched *adjective* In a hurry, rushed.

1927 Woofter *Dialect from WV* 364 Don't get snatched. There's plenty of time. **1984** Woods *WV Was Good* 226 You hadn't oughta be so snatched. (You shouldn't get in a hurry.)

[DARE *snatched* adj especially South Midland]

snatter See **smather.**

snead (also *snede*, *sneed*) *noun* The curved handle or shaft of a scythe, a snath.

1917 Kephart *Word-List* 417 = the snath of a scythe. **1975** Gainer *Speech Mtneer* 16 = the handle of a scythe. "I like a scythe with a short snede." **c1975** Lunsford *It Used to Be* 14 When I grew older, I would go down and take part in that and cradle wheat or oats. The scythe-and-cradle has a scythe about three-and-a-half feet long on the side of the sneed, which was the handle that had two things to hold by.

[ultimately < Old English *snædan*; OED3 *snead/sneed* "the shaft or pole of a scythe" now dialect; cf CUD *sned*[2] n "the shaft of a scythe"; Web3 (at *sned*[1]) "the wooden handle of a scythe"; DARE *snead* n chiefly Midland]

snede, sneed See **snead.**

snew, snewed See **snow.**

Snider's hound, Snider's pup See **(as/like) Snyder's hound/house cat/pup.**

sniff

A *verb* See **snuff 2.**

B *noun* See citation.

c1960 Wilson *Coll* = a small dram; same as *snort.*

snipe *verb* See citation.

2005 Williams *Gratitude* 525 = [to] sneak around and steal something, sometimes with knowledge of the one stolen from. Different from downright stealing. Dad used to *snipe* a chicken from one or t'other of our neighbors when they were going to have a dance at our house. People planted extra corn so anybody who needed some could *snipe* a few ears all along.

sniper *noun* See citation.

1964 Clarkson *Lumbering in WV* 372 = one who noses logs in preparation for skidding.

sniptious *adjective* Superb; spruced-up.

1927 Woofter *Dialect from WV* 364 = fine. "That will be sniptious." **1957** Combs *Lg Sthn High: Word List* 92 = attractive, spruce, "catchy." **c1960** Wilson *Coll* = great, smart, spruced-up.

[DARE *sniptious* adj especially South, South Midland]

snirly See **snurly.**

snitz *noun* Slices of apples. See also **schnitzing, snitz stringing.**

1999 Milnes *Play of Fiddle* 90 I'm reminded of a story from rural Pocahantas County in which a teacher, trying to illustrate fractions to her class, cut an apple in half. She asked the class what she had. They responded "Halves." Then she cut it into quarters and received the correct "Quarters" response. She further cut the quarters into eighths, but in answer to her question as to what she now had, a boy answered, "Snitz," the German word for cut-up and dried apples.

snitz stringing *noun* Formerly, a community work activity to help a family string quartered apples for drying them for winter consumption. See also **schnitzing, snitz.**

2007 Milnes *Signs Cures Witches* 71 The old double-crib log house was "built by frolic" in 1845. House raisings were a common reason for frolics, but log rollings and snitz stringing, among other events, were also popular.

snooper *noun* See citation.

1971 Lee *My Appalachia* 22 Both the State and Federal Prohibition laws provided for the appointment of special enforcement officers, known as "Prohibition Agents." Among the bootleggers and moonshiners, however, they were known as "Snoopers," and it was always "open season" on them. Armed clashes between the groups were frequent.

snort *noun* A swig, swallow of liquor.

1935 Sheppard *Cabins in Laurel* 197 They didn't drink only just a little snort either, according to Bill, but that stuff sneaks up on you. **1941** Stuart *Men of Mts* 82 Finn, ain't it about time we have a little snort? **1967** *DARE Survey* (Maryville TN) = amount of liquor taken in one swallow. **1978** Montgomery *White Pine Coll* I-3 It wasn't unexpectable for people to come in and offer a taste of the final product, which we'd get in the back room and enjoy a snort of. **1985** *Smokies Anniv Book* 58 To snake bite victims, a "snort" of moonshine was a dose that usually warded off poison from any critter's bite. **1996** Casada *Gospel Hook* 26 At first Cathey staunchly refused, vowing he was done with Demon Rum. After several minutes of shivering before the fire and watching his comrades imbibe, though, he underwent a change of heart. "Poley," he said, "I believe I will have a little snort to fight off the chill." **2005** Williams *Gratitude* 21 When he'd just had a "snort" or two, he got mean and wanted to fight. **2008** Terrell *Mt Lingo* Now, let's go down to the barn and have a little snort.

snout *verb* See citation.

1978 Slone *Common Folks* 247 At first, everyone would "snout" the beans (pull the strings off).

snow *verb* Variant past-tense forms *snew, snewed.*

1915 Pollard *TN Mts* 243 It snewed yesterday. **1997** Montgomery *Coll: snew* (known to Bush).

snowball *noun* See citation.

1972 Carr *Oldest Profession* 76 The beginning of fermentation causes agitation within the worm, and such action is noted by bubbling and gaseous action in the mash barrels. Bubbles are called "snowballs" by some moonshiners.

snowbird *noun* The Carolina junco (*Junco hyemalis/carolinensis*).

1859 Taliaferro *Fisher's River* 95 Uncle Frost was up early, and went out, nervously awaiting Anderson's arrival, jumping about like a mountain snowbird, hitching up his "hipped britches," being an old-fashioned man he wouldn't wear "galluses," not he. **1861** *Griffin CW Letters* (Aug 3) we ar in the land whar the snow birds ar araising ther young. **1926** Ganier *Summer Birds* 35 Another bird of the higher altitudes which held my interest was the Carolina junco, commonly called "Snowbird." **1943** Stupka *Through the Year* The Carolina juncos ("Snowbirds") may be incubating eggs under a snow-covered canopy of rootlet and dried plant remains. **1966** *DARE Survey* (Burnsville NC) = comes in winter, stays on mountain in summer. **1982** Ginns *Snowbird Gravy* 22 We'd catch snowbirds. . . . Makes as nice a pot of gravy as you've ever seen if you get enough of 'em. **2002** Ogle *Remembrances* 3 The snowbird or Junco, moves up the mountain in summer, and down in winter.

snow cream *noun* See citations.

1956 McAtee *Some Dial NC* 41 = snow mixed with milk and sugar. **c1960** Wilson *Coll* Snow-cream. Sugar and milk added to snow, to form a back-country ice-cream. **2009** Holbrook *Upheaval*

19 He asked if anybody had ever eaten snow cream, "where you take snow and mix it in with sugar and whole cream and eat it while it's still froze."

snow tourist *noun* A winter tourist in the mountains, especially one who comes only to ski.

1997 Andrews *Mountain Vittles* 86 Of course in recent years with the ski resort and snow tourists and all we keep our roads passable all the time.

snow water See **not to give snow water to.**

snub *verb* To sob, whimper, snivel; hence noun *the snubs* = a fit of sobbing.

1915 Pollard *TN Mts* 243 She was crying and snubbing. **1938** (in **2005** Ballard and Chung *Arnow Stories* 100) Ain't ye ashamed, Son, a snubbin like a two year old? **1942** (in **1987** Perdue *Outwitting Devil* 33) Way long in the night Jack waked up and the girl was a-crying and a-snubbin'. **1955** Ritchie *Singing Family* 4 He wouldn't tell what was the matter for a long time, but finally he snubbed and said that he never would get to sleep with Mommie no more. **1957** Combs *Lg Sthn High: Word List* 92 *snob* = to sob, whimper. **1983** Broaddus *Estill Co KY Word List* 56 *snubbing* = sniveling. **2004** Adams *Old True Love* 2 Mommie was holding Emily who had cried so long she had the snubs.

[OED3 *snub* v² now dialect and U.S.; Web3 *snub* v² alteration of *snob*, chiefly Midland; DARE *snub* v² chiefly southern Appalachians]

snubs, the See **snub.**

snub up *verb phrase* See citation.

1957 Broaddus *Vocab Estill Co KY* 72 = to get stubborn.

snuff *verb*

1 To sniff.

1927 Mason *Lure of Smokies* 225 I heerd [the bear] snuffin' th' wind an' blowin'. **c1970** Handlon *Ol' Smoky* 72 That ol' b'ar snuffed and snuffed around her awhile, then went off.

2 (also *sniff*) To hasten labor in (a woman) by having her inhale tobacco snuff or other fine, powdery substance to provoke sneezing. See also **feathering.**

1970 Mull *Mt Yarns* 8 One custom that was quite prevalent was to "snuff" the wife at birthing time. **1972** Cooper *NC Mt Folklore* 14 To induce a quick delivery, she held powdered tobacco leaves or snuff under the patient's nose to produce sneezing. This was known as snuffing the patient. **2003** Cavender *Folk Medicine* 66 To induce labor, some granny midwives held a pallet of tobacco snuff or black or red pepper under the mother's nose that when sniffed caused her to sneeze. This was called "snuffing the baby." **2007** Myers *Smoky Mt Remedies* 15 A small amount of powdered snuff [tobacco] was placed on a plate. When it was nearly time for delivery, someone would say, "It's time to sniff her." At that time, someone blew the snuff into the expectant mother's face. Her reaction would be so violent as to bring forth the baby.

snuffbox See **devil's snuff.**

snuff eater *noun* See citation.

1968 *DARE Survey* (Brasstown NC) = person who makes a [tooth]brush of a blackgum twig and uses snuff as a tooth paste.

snuff egg *noun* See citation. See also **suck-egg.**

2009 Wiles and Wiles *Location* 142–43 Years ago when dogs were kept on the farm but not as pets, they were used for hunting, helping with the stock, as watchdogs or to keep the varmints under control. When you got a new dog, two things were a BIG CONCERN—Was he a sheep killer? Or an egg sucker? . . . Grandpa showed [Bill, his grandson] how to make a small hole in the egg shell with a nail and stir in some Scotch Snuff. Bill did that to several egg shells and placed them around where Smokey could find them. The dog grabbed one in his mouth, tipped back his head and crushed the egg, letting the insides roll down his throat. It didn't take many more snuff eggs to break him of the habit.

snuff mop (also *snuff stick*) *noun* A tender twig chewed into a fray at one end, used for applying snuff to the inside of the mouth or as a primitive toothbrush. See citations. Same as **toothbrush 1.**

1913 Kephart *Our Sthn High* 244 This is what the mountain woman calls her "tooth brush"—a snuff stick. **c1960** Wilson *Coll*: *snuff mop, snuff stick* = a toothbrush made of a blackgum twig, or hickory bark, or of sycamore stick. **1994–97** Montgomery *Coll*: *snuff stick* (known to Cardwell, Ellis, Jones, Norris, Weaver), = still used, the best ones being made by chewing the end of a three-to-four-inch young growth blackgum twig (Brown), = probably still in existence, such as a twig of sweet gum or birch, the end of which was chewed until frayed and brushy to make a little brush (Oliver).

[DARE *snuff stick* n chiefly South, South Midland, Southwest, TX]

snuff stick See **snuff mop.**

snuffy *adjective* See citation.

c1982 Young *Colloquial Appal* 20 = huffy, sulky.

snurl

A *noun* A knotty or twisted grain in wood, a gnarl. See also **snurly.**

c1926 Bird *Cullowhee Wordlist* = a knot or gnarl. **1941** Hall *Coll* (Gatlinburg TN) Snurl, a kind of knot in wood; snurly wood = woody with a wavy grain. **1946** Matthias *Speech Pine Mt* 191 = a gnarl: "I pulled up the plant to see if hit was a-growin', and thar was a big-old white snurl on the root." Snurl is in this sense akin to snarl, a tangle or knot, and to snare.

[EDD *snirl* sb² 6 "a gnarl or knot in wood"; DARE *snurl* n South Midland, especially southern Appalachians]

B *verb* To curl, turn up (the nose) in disdain or contempt.

1932 Poole *Nurses Horseback* 151 Many women nowadays send their wool to mills outside of the hills . . . But Nancy "snurled up her nose" at that. **1941** Hall Coll (Waynesville NC) She snurled her nose up when she passed me. **1946** Matthias *Speech Pine Mt* 191 = to wrinkle (the nose) in contempt: "He snurled up his nose." Here snurl is related to snarl, to growl with a display of teeth ("The dog snarled at me"), and to sneer, snore, and snort. **1960** Cooper *Jularker Bussed* She snurled her lips (sneered). **2005** Williams *Gratitude* 525 = snarl; wrinkle, as to "snurl up your nose," when you smelt something bad or snubbed somebody.

[OED3 *snurl* n 2 "a nostril" dialect, v 2 "to turn up (the nose) in disdain" dialect; EDD *snirl* v^2 1 "to twist, tangle, run into knots" Scot, nEngl; SND *snorl* n 1 "a knot, tangle, kink"; Web3 snirl alteration of *snarl*[2] chiefly Scot]

snurly (also *snirly*) *adjective* Of wood: knotty, gnarly, twisted. See also **snurl A.**

1925 Dargan *Highland Annals* 21 It had lost so many limbs when it was young and pushin' up, that it was jest the snirliest tree I ever saw. **1941** Hall Coll (Morristown TN) Snurl, a kind of knot in wood; snurly wood, woody with a wavy grain. *Ibid.* (Gatlinburg TN) I hit a snurly place in the wood [when sawing it]. **1952** Wilson *Folk Speech NC* 592 *snurly* = twisted, knotty.

[CUD (at *snarl* n) "a snarl, a knot, a twist"; HT *snurly* "gnarled or twisted"]

(as/like) Snyder's hound/house cat/pup (and variants) *phrase* Used in various comparisons.

1936 Still *One Leg* 9 My opinion, he's tuk off like Snider's hound with Poppy's money. **1937** Hall Coll (Emerts Cove TN) That plane went over here fast as Snyder's pup. **1937** Wilson *Folklore SE KY* 17 *run like Snider's pup* (known to 13/31 speakers in Bell Co KY). **1960** Hall *Smoky Mt Folks* 62 *as fast as Snyder's house cat; as fast as Snyder's pup.* **1977** Shackelford et al. *Our Appalachia* 33 He took off just like Snider's pup and we went to see [the merchant]. **1981** Whitener *Folk-Ways* 41 Grandma's peart as Snyder's pup. **1985** Edwards *Folksy Sketches* 2 When the ice pick struck the thigh of the black steer he bellowed and lunged forward what seemed to be twenty feet and really took off like Snyder's pup. **1990** Clouse *Wilder* 78 I married him and him sorrier than Duke Snyder's flop-eared hound. *Ibid.* 140 "We ain't gonna move. We ain't done nothin'. Now you clear outta here." And they took off like Snyder's pup. **1998** Montgomery Coll: *peart as Snyder's pup* (known to Brown, Oliver, Weaver); *quick as Snyder's pup* (known to Cardwell); *smart as Snyder's pup* (known to Jones). **2001** Montgomery File: *as fast as Snyder's hound* (known to 40-year-old woman, Bryson City NC). **2005** Williams *Gratitude* 149 When I throwed it [= a chicken] down, hit took off like Snyder's pup. **2009** Montgomery File My paternal grandmother and grandfather, born in Ansted, Fayette County, WV commonly said "slower than Snyder's Hound" instead of "faster than Snyder's Hound/Pup." I have no clue to the origin.

[DARE *Snyder's pup* n southern Appalachians]

soakie (also *soaky*) *noun* Sweetened coffee as a dip for biscuits; biscuits wetted and sweetened in this way.

1958 Wood *Words from TN* 16 = biscuit in sweetened coffee. **1996** Pardue *Recollections* 16 "Soakie" was biscuits broken up in a large coffee cup, wet down with coffee, and covered with a crust of sugar about an inch thick. **1997** Montgomery Coll (known to Andrews, Brown). **1998** Dabney *Smokehouse Ham* 126 "Soakie" was a dip—dunking biscuits into a cup of coffee. **2011** *Blind Pig* (March 28) I remember pouring coffee in a saucer, cooling it with my breath, then drinking it. Also I remember while I stayed with my grandparents on Buck Creek in McDowell County, we would pour sugar on a biscuit then pour cold coffee on it and eat it. We called it a "soaky."

soaking *noun* A simple meal of corn bread soaked in milk or coffee.

2013 Shedlarz *Rosa Hicks* 7 Lots of times, we just eat milk and bread—sometimes soakin's, where you use coffee on cornbread or biscuits. Most of the time it's cornbread.

soaky See **soakie.**

soap gourd *noun* See c1975 citation. See also **gourd banjo.**

1835 Crockett *Account* 192 I'd give my head for a soap-gourd, that Andrew Jackson never made the proposition for letters of marque and reprisal. **1884** Murfree *In TN Mts* 11 Ye ain't wantin' ter gin 'Vander the soap-gourd to drink out'n. **1939** *FWP Guide TN* 502 Large families often make a barrel of this soap, and at intervals the soapgourd is filled from the barrel. . . . Soap gourds are often handed down in families for several generations. **c1950** (in **2000** Oakley *Roamin' Man* 38) I eat so much I was about to pop open or bust wide open like a soap gord full of home made soap when you drop the soap gord on a rock. **c1975** Lunsford *It Used to Be* 43 Possibly, he had heard of a soap gourd, but I told him what it was. It was a gourd with all of the seeds taken out, dried, of course, and with a piece cut out about one-quarter of the way in,—a gap had been made and then cut down from the neck. That part of the shell had been taken out, and it left a hollow place. You could reach in with your hand and pour this liquid soap—kind of thick soap—into your hand and use it. You'd hang the gourd up by that crooked neck on a long nail that'd be driven into the wall.

[DARE *soap gourd* n South, South Midland]

soap grease *noun* See citation.

1915 Dingus *Word-List VA* 190 = entrails and other parts of a slaughtered animal used to make soap.

soap stick *noun* A paddle used in making lye soap.

1982 Slone *How We Talked* 66 [To make] homemade lye soap . . . Stir with a long-handled paddle or "soap stick."

soapwort *noun* The bouncing bet flower (*Saponaria officinalis*), from whose roots can be made a lather for washing clothes; the plant also has medicinal use.

1959 Chapman *Flower for Suds* There's a "weed" which the early settlers in the Blue Ridge sometimes used to make suds for washing clothes, for bathing, scouring, and other cleansing operations, especially when the cabin's supply of home-made lye soap was running low. Appropriately enough, some of its common names are soapwort, wash-weed, and scouring weed; but it has nearly 30 others. Probably no other weed or wild flower found in the Blue Ridge today has so many names. Usually from June to September this attractive plant has pink, or white clusters an inch or more in diameter, borne on stout stalks which grow one to two feet tall. During the day the odor of the blossoms is scarcely noticeable, but in late afternoon and at night the sweet, penetrating scent attracts the moths that cross-pollinate the species, which is known to scientists as Saponaria officinalis. One of its best known common names is bouncing Bet. It is also called pink Betty and sweet Betty. **1965** Shelton *Pioneer Comforts* 7 Soapwort tea of roots [was used for] rheumatism, gout. *Ibid.* 17 Wild Soapwort (Bouncing Bet) leaves and roots form a lather and was thought to be a good shampoo and washing aid. **1982** Stupka *Wildflowers* 27 "Soapwort," one of [bouncing bet's] many names, comes from a property the roots have of producing a soapy lather with water. This foamy solution was the pioneer's substitute for soap in cleaning silks and woolens.

so as, so as to See **so's**.

sob *verb* To become soaked or soggy; hence participial adjective *sobbing*. See also **sobbed**.

1917 Kephart *Word-List* 417 If you let a pine pole stay out and *sob*, the bark will rot off. **1952** Wilson *Folk Speech NC* 592 = to be thoroughly wet, soaked. "Your shoes are *sobbing*." **1994–97** Montgomery *Coll* (known to Adams, Brown, Cardwell, Jones, Ledford, Oliver, Weaver).

[OED3 *sob* v^2 now dialect and U.S.; EDD v^2 "to soak, saturate" mEngl, sEngl; DARE *sob* v chiefly South, South Midland]

sobbed (also *sobby*) *adjective* Soaked, soggy. See also **sob**.

1814 (in **1956** Eliason *Tarheel Talk* 296) (Haywood Co NC) she [was] kept too hot, especially while asleep, her skin looked water-sobbed and her flesh parboiled. **1883** Smith *Southernisms* 53 Sobbed or sobby, "soaked or wet," commonly applied to land, though also to other things, is the Southern word for soggy, which we seldom or never use, I think. **1913** Kephart *Our Sthn High* 296 Sobby wood means soggy or sodden, and the verb is to sob. **1939** Hall *Coll* (Cades Cove TN) That stove wood is sobby, and it don't burn good. **1967** *DARE Survey* (Maryville TN) *sobby* = heavy from being in water for a long time. **1975** Chalmers *Better* 66 A poor field is a sorry thing, and the earth may be too sobby and wet for working. **2005** Williams *Gratitude* 525 = soggy and heavy. Doughty wood gets sobby in rainy weather and won't burn.

[OED3 *sobby* adj now dialect and U.S.; DARE (at *sob* v chiefly South, South Midland)]

sobbing See **sob**.

sober down *verb phrase* To become sober, give up heavy drinking.

1939 Hall *Coll* (Bradley Fork NC) That country was all sobered down and seemed like a different country, and I left.

sochan (also *sochani*) *noun* An edible wild green (*Rudbeckia laciniata*). Same as **cochan**.

1966 *DARE Survey* (Cherokee NC) *sochan* = type of greens eaten cooked. **1975** Hamel and Chiltoskey *Cherokee Plants* 30 *sochani* = a wild green cooked and eaten in the spring. **1995** Williams *Smoky Mts Folklife* 100 Most of the wild plants commonly consumed by the North Carolina Cherokee today, such as ramps, sochan, poke, creases, and wild berries, are also eaten by non-Indians in the region. **2005** Ellison *Mt Passages* 52–53 Sochan (Rudbeckia laciniata), known as green-headed coneflower to non-American Indians, is one of the most prized spring greens the Cherokees gather. They sometimes call it so-cha-ni, with the accent on the last syllable. Their gardens often have semicultivated patches of the plant in damp, protected areas. Closely related to black-eyed Susan (Rudeckia hirta), sochan grows to ten feet tall in wet areas and along damp woodland borders. . . . The Cherokees recognize sochan as soon as it comes out of the ground in mid-spring by its distinctively lobed leaves and by its smell. They boil the young shoots and leaves with several changes of water. Prepared in this manner, sochan has a chewy texture and zesty flavor.

[DARE *sochan* n chiefly western NC]

soda *noun* Variant forms *sodey, sodie, sody*.

1862 Robinson *CW Letters* (July 28) milk & flower is worth 8 dollars per pound & Sody is worth 2 dollars per pound. **1864** Whitaker *CW Letters* (March 24) Provisions is very [s]carce in this country tho we git tolerable rations flower not bolted tho it dose very well neads no sodey the boys dos not grumble & seems content. **1925** (in **1935** Edwards *NC Novels* 85) *sody*. **1956** Hall *Coll* (Big Bend NC) I buy my meal. All I have to buy [is] coffee and sody. I raise my meat, my berries and corn, hay. **1969** Doran *Folklore White Co* 101 If the corn bread has took much soda, the husband is likely to ask the wife if he "doesn't need to go to the store and git some sodie," for she must be out, after using a box of it in the bread. **1972** *AOHP/ALC-342* It just tastes to me like a cake of sody. **1992** Giardina *Unquiet Earth* 5–6 Rachel trades for a CoCola in a little green bottle, what some call a dope and others call a sodypop. **2008** *Rosie Hicks* 1 I didn't put no salt and sody in the bread, and it ain't a-looking right.

[DARE *soda* n (pronc) chiefly South, South Midland, Northeast]

soda dope *noun* Variant form *sodey dope*. Same as **dope 2**.

1995 Adams *Come Go Home* 95 The lady of the house smiled and took us into the kitchen, where there must have been thirty men and women standing around eating southern fried chicken and drinking "sodey-dopes." **1995** Williams *Smoky Mts Folklife* 103 Inhabitants also resemble other southerners in their passion for soft drinks (still called "dope" or "sodey dope" by old-timers).

[DARE *soda dope* n especially NC]

soda pop moon *noun* Homemade whiskey. See also **moonshine**.

1963 Carson *History Bourbon* 104 The local baldface went into fruit jars, five-gallon tins and old soft drink bottles from which was derived a popular name for woods whiskey—Soda Pop.

sodey, sodie See **soda.**

sodey dope See **soda dope.**

sod relation *noun* A person related to another person as a result of remarriage of a widow or widower. See also **grass relation, sod widow.**

1942 Robertson *Red Hills* 51–52 Our stepmother and our step-step-grandmother were sod relations of ours—not grass relations. We do not believe in divorce in South Carolina; it is against the law in South Carolina to seek divorce, so even until now we have never had a grass widower among our kinfolks.

sods *noun* Same as **grass bald.**

1942 Thomas *Blue Ridge* 105 The bald is sometimes called the sods—where the trees can't grow because of high winds. **1969** *Sunday Gazette Mail* Elleber Knob is the summit of an area known as Elleber Sods, high-country pastureland in the Monongahela National Forest. The mountains around the sods are known for their good turkey hunting. **2003** *DARE File* (WV) Dolly Sods . . . In this part of the Appalachians, an open grassy area at high elevation is called a "sods." The name "Dolly" is a corruption of "Dahle," the name of the German immigrants who first owned this land.

[DARE *sods* n pl Appalachians]

sod soaker *noun* A heavy rainstorm.

1903 Fox *Little Shepherd* 59 Send us not a gentle sizzle-sozzle, but a sod-soaker, O Lord, a gully washer. **1940** Haun *Hawk's Done* 106 These here sod soakers make pine trees and cedars easy to blow up by the roots. **1967–69** *DARE Survey* (Clayhole KY, Wytheville VA) = joking name . . . for a very heavy rain. **1975** Carter *Gospel Truth* A big rain was a "sod soaker" or a "gully washer" or a "little Noah."

[DARE *sod-soaker* n chiefly South, South Midland]

sod widow *noun* A woman whose husband has died. See also **grass widow, sod relation.**

c1960 Wilson *Coll* = a widow whose husband is dead; not a grass widow.

sody See **soda.**

soft *adjective* Variant form *saft* [sæft].

1867 Harris *Sut Lovingood* 259 "What did yu say yer trade wer sir?" sed she, es saft an' sweet es a well-played flute. **1928** (in **1952** Mathes *Tall Tales* 79) He's allus makin' out like he's a turrible vyg-rous feller, but he ain't. Why, he's jes' as saft-hearted as a gal! **1942** Hall *Phonetics Smoky Mts* 33. **1961** Medford *History Haywood Co* 89 Then, when "saft soap" making time arrived (in the fall or spring), the ashes would be uncovered and water poured over them. **1995** Montgomery *Coll* (known to Cardwell).

[Scottish form of *soft*]

soft mast *noun* Berries, cherries, grapes, and similar fruit of the forest that forms the natural diet of bears, wild hogs, and other animals. See also **hard mast, mast.**

2008 *Smokies Guide* (Autumn) 1 During fall, the success of bears in the Smoky Mountains depends almost entirely on what biologists call the "mast crop." They divide the mast into two groups, soft (blackberries, cherries, grapes, blueberries, etc.) and hard (acorns, hickory nuts, and beech nuts).

soft peach *noun* A **freestone peach.**

1915 Dingus *Word-List VA* 190 = the freestone peach.

[DARE *soft peach* chiefly South Midland, especially southern Appalachians]

soft-shell Baptist *noun* A member of a group of Baptists (or the group collectively) other than **Primitive Baptists**, especially but not limited to **Missionary Baptists**. See also **Hard Shell.**

1957 Broaddus *Vocab Estill Co KY* 72 *Softshell Baptists* = all Baptists not Primitive Baptists. **1975** Brewer *Valley So Wild* 283 Another name for the "old school" Baptists was "Primitive" and the new schoolers were called "Missionary." These terms still are retained by many local churches. Cades Cove, for instance, had both a Missionary and a Primitive Baptist church, still standing. The term "hardshell" (old) and "softshell" (new) also were used in some places.

sog

A *noun* See citation.

1978 *American Chestnut* 243 [The wood] would eventually rot in a ditch where the air could not get in there. There's old sogs that you can dig out and they'll be just as sound as can be—logs that have been laying there for hundreds of years. Old sogs. That's an old tree that's fell and got burried [sic] up in the dirt an' sometimes covered with moss.

B *verb* To remain sodden.

1983 *Dark Corner OHP-5A* If you cut it [= wood] on the old of the moon, it'll mold, turn all blue and sog. It won't never dry out.

[DARE *sog* v 2 scattered, but especially South, South Midland]

soggrum See **sorghum.**

so help me, Hannah *interjection* See citation.

1998 Montgomery *File* = used to add emphasis or veracity to a statement, as equivalent to "I swear," "I declare," or "I swanney." "So help me, Hannah, if he didn't turn around and do it again!" (51-year-old woman, Jefferson Co TN).

solid *adverb* Absolutely, thoroughly, definitely.

1940 (in **1944** Wentworth *ADD* 577) (swWV) = surely, definitely: "He solid threw the ball, didn't he?"; "He solid whipped him, didn't he?" **1981** Whitener *Folk-Ways* 69 If you ain't back with it in a half hour I'll solid skin your hide and his'n too. **1992** Gabbard *Thunder Road* 39 I paid $600 for a brand-new Cadillac engine. That was in the '50s. They would solid fly. The law never caught one 'less somethin' happened. **1997** Montgomery *Coll* (known to Bush, Ledford, Norris, Weaver).

[cf EDD *solid* adv 13 "very, exceedingly, extremely"; DARE *solid* adv chiefly South Midland]

Solomonseal See **Solomon's seal.**

Solomon's seal (also *Solomonseal*) *noun* A perennial plant (*Polygonatum biflorum/pubescens*) with a showy blossom and edible young shoots that are harvested in the early spring, cleaned, and then parboiled or fried.

1937 Thornburgh *Great Smoky Mts* 19–20 In April, a wealth of spring flowers and flowering trees await you—trailing arbutus, violets of many kinds, Solomon's seal and Solomon's plume. **1971** Krochmal et al. *Medicinal Plants Appal* 202 *Polygonatum biflorum* = common names: Small solomonseal . . . dwarf solomon's seal, hairy solomon's seal . . . solomon's seal. **2006** Howell *Medicinal Plants* 145 Solomon's seal takes its name from the round stem scars on the rootstock that resemble a wax seal marked with an "S."

[from resemblance of the rhizome to a signet]

some (also *some of them*) *pronoun, pronoun phrase* Coreferent with the subject of the clause but having syntactic position within the predicate (especially in an existential clause). See also **somebody B**. See also Grammar and Syntax §18.3.

1939 Hall *Coll* (Proctor NC) They'd some go to the stands, you know, and generally two of us drove all the time. **1970** *Burton-Manning Coll*-94A They have some of them good meaning. **1972** *AOHP/ALC*-355 Right over here long that hillside they made some of them a cross. **1973** *GSMNP*-5:24 They [= pupils] was some of them higher than others, but it was a good little school. **1975** *GSMNP*-59:41 They was some of them downed him, and they took a rail and they got him down and held him down and tied him, got some ropes and tied him up and brought him here to Bryson City and put him in jail. **1978** Montgomery *White Pine Coll* VI-2 They was some of them so frussed about it after they did it, but I didn't want it tuck off then.

-some *suffix*

1 Added to an adjective to form an adjective: like, tending to be.

1938 Justus *No-End Hollow* 38 She had one gladsome thought, anyway Jeff and Jessie were off to school! **1957** Justus *Other Side* 10 "Better throw a pine knot on the hearth. It's getting darksome," said Mammy.

2 Added to a noun or verb to form an adjective: apt to, tending to.

c1945 Haun *Hawk's Done* 312 "Awkward," she would say, "and blundersome as a blind buzzard." **1946** Dudley *KY Words* 271 Kind of a smothersome day. **1957** Parris *My Mts* 141 Gettin' in here's kind of troublesome since there ain't nothin' but a trail. **1976** *Digging Well* 128 The best thing, boys, is to never look up . . . If you look up, it looks smothersome.

[DARE *-some* suff chiefly South, South Midland; also New England]

somebody *indefinite pronoun*

A Variant form with secondary stress on the first syllable and primary stress on the second syllables: some-BOD-y.

1913 Kephart *Our Sthn High* 275–76 Then, at a bound, [the girl] dodges into a thicket, doubles on her course and runs back as fast as her nimble bare legs can carry her to report that "Some-*body's* comin'!" **1997** Montgomery *Coll* (known to eight consultants from the Smoky Mountains).

B Variant syntactic position in an existential clause. See also **nobody**, **some**. See also Grammar and Syntax §18.3.

1978 Montgomery *White Pine Coll* IV-4 There'd somebody come around with a truck once in a while.

C A person of prestigious social position.

1929 Kephart *Smoky Mt Magic* 9 "Tom, now have some manners. She may be somebody," cautioned Sylvia, meaning someone of consequence. **2005** Williams *Gratitude* 525 *some by-dee* = a person who is respected in his/her own right and is of value.

D Someone; a human being (used in adverbial phrase *just like somebody* = as if it were human).

1940 Hall *Coll* (White Oak NC) That chicken slid down the [wet] bank just like somebody. **1941** Hall *Coll* (Alexander NC) "It was squallin' just like somebody" [was] sometimes said of a bob cat's cry.

some day another, somehow another See **another B.**

somehows *adverb* Somehow.

1885 Murfree *Prophet* 7 They hed crost him somehows, an' he war ailin' in his temper when I got home. **1931** Combs *Lg Sthn High* 1320 These forms are common: "somehows," "some'eres," "anywheres," "nowheres," "nohows," due to fondness for the *s*. **2007** McMillon *Notes* = used in phrase *somehows or another*.

some'n See **something.**

some of them See **some.**

some of these days (also *some of these times*) *adverb phrase* Someday, sometime, one day coming.

1863 Tesh *CW Letters* (Dec 5) I havent got anny thing to Give him now but I will have something some of these times. **1863** *Warrick CW Letters* (Oct 26) I am a fraid that we will have a fite here some of these dais beefore long the yankees is a try to go round us but I dont think that thay will quite mak the trip. **1883** Murfree *Old Sledge* 549 That thar tongue o' yourn will git cut out some o' these hyar days. **1903** Fox *Little Shepherd* 67 "Some o' these days," said the old Squire, "that fool Jake's a-goin' to pick up somethin' an' knock that mean Jerry's head off." **1955** Justus *Peter Pocket* 66 "Wait till she hears the first robin," said Mr. McGregory. "She will hear one some of these days. It won't be long till spring." **1973** *Foxfire Interviews* A-73-46 I decided I had to meet the Master some of these times. **1975** *Richard and Margaret* 8 They are makin' an easier way and they are going to run into a wall some of these days.

somepin, somep'n See **something.**

somers, some'r's See **somewheres.**

somerset *noun* A somersault. Also called **tumbleset.**

1849 Lanman *Alleghany Mts* 50–51 Vandever had obtained a fair hold of the buck's antlers, when the twain performed a somerset into the pool below. **1934–37** *LAMSAS Appal* (Madison Co NC, Swain Co NC). **1956** Hall Coll (Hurricane Creek NC) We rolled and turned somersets till we got to the bottom of the hill. **1967–68** *DARE Survey* (Brasstown NC, Maryville TN). **1969** GSMNP-46:3 If they start to turn the yoke on you . . . just let your leads turn a somerset if you can. **1997** Montgomery Coll (consultants from the Smoky Mountains agree that *somerset* was traditionally a more common term than *somersault*).

[OED3 *somerset* n[1] 1596→; Web3 *somerset* n alteration of *somersault* by influence of Somerset, the county in England; DARE *somerset* n chiefly South, South Midland]

some several *adjective phrase* A good number of, a few.

1895 Edson and Fairchild *TN Mts* 374 "Are there many squirrels this season?" "Yes, there's some several." **1963** Miller *Pigeon's Roost* (Nov 21) Preacher Arwood had been an ordained minister of the Freewill Baptist church denomination for over 60 years and pastored churches until poor health prevented him from doing so some several years ago. **1974** Fink *Bits Mt Speech* 24 = goodly number: "They was some several folks there."

something *pronoun* Variant forms *some'n, som'in', somepin, somep'n, sumpin, sump'm.*

1927 Mason *Lure of Smokies* 222 I had just arriv' when hit appears ter me I hears somep'n comin' the contrary way from the Sam's Creek side. **1939** Walker *Mtneer Looks* 10–11 Sump'm tol' me that if I didn't move purty quick I'd be purt' nigh drownded. **1953** Hall Coll (Plott Creek NC) That's a place where . . . nothin' but a bear or somep'n like 'at can go. **1955** Washburn *Country Doctor* 64 It's med'sin' Mandy needs—some'n ter ease 'er pains. **1961** Williams *Content Mt Speech* 16 If he did [plan to do it], he'd drag out his ol jug an' git on a high lonesome, jist like he allus does ary time he ever needs to git somepin done quick-like an' in a hurry. **1963** Williams *Metaphor Mt Speech II* 53 The mountain woman who, after moving to the county seat, achieves social standing and begins to "think she's sumpin on a stick," loses the respect of her country cousins for her "upheadyness." **2005** Williams *Gratitude* 138 Most of the time, we dist had milk and bread for supper, unless they was beans or sump'm like that left over. **2009** Burton *Beech Mt Man* 121 If you're with a man, let him protect his ownself unless somebody's got him down and trying to kill him or som'in'.

[DARE *something* n, adj, adv A3 chiefly South, South Midland]

something another See **another B.**

something dead up the branch *noun phrase* A situation or development that arouses suspicion.

1929 Kephart *Smoky Mt Magic* 86 "There's something dead up the branch," he averred, in the mountaineer's way of expressing suspicion.

[cf DARE *something dead up the creek* n South, South Midland]

something on a stick *noun phrase* Someone or something special; sometimes used sarcastically.

1939 *FWP Guide NC* 98 A mother speaks proudly of her boy . . . "he's something on a stick." **1940** Haun *Hawk's Done* 44 She told me how Barshia's ma had raised him up to think he was something on a stick, and how she had learnt him to think he was too pretty to work. **c1960** Wilson Coll = something special. **1963** Williams *Metaphor Mt Speech II* 53 The mountain woman who, after moving to the county seat, achieves social standing and begins to "think she's sumpin on a stick," loses the respect of her country cousins for her "upheadyness."

[DARE *something on a stick* n chiefly South Midland]

sometime *adverb* Sometimes, occasionally.

1940 Oakley *Roamin'/Restin'* 78 Leucothy is a shrub sometime called dog hobble. **1965** Miller *Pigeon's Roost* (Dec 23) Sometime there would be as many as 20 men shooting their guns. **1971** *AOHP/ALC-260* He said, "I don't see how you found that out," but now sometime people knows things to tell you. **1973** GSMNP-87:24 Sometime they'd let off three, four, five [sticks of dynamite] and later on got on top of the mountain up there . . . sometime would blow the whole mountain off at one time. **1996** *GSMNPCOHP-1:2* Sometime [a bear] would drift in. I don't know where he would come from, but he didn't last long.

[OED3 *sometime* adv 1a common in the 16th and 17th centuries, now rare or obsolete; Web3 *sometime* adv 2 archaic; DARE *sometime* adv chiefly South]

someway another See **another B.**

someways *adverb* In some manner, to some degree, somehow.

1936 Skidmore *Lift Up Eyes* 5–6 "We'uns can git along someways," she said after awhile. **1955** Ritchie *Singing Family* 121 Hit's a common-like little fooling tune, keeps dodging about in my head, but I'll get it out in a minute. Someways like this: [music].

somewhares, somewhars See **somewheres.**

somewhereabouts See **somewheres B.**

somewheres *adverb* Somewhere. See also **anywheres, everywheres, nowheres.**

A Variant forms *somers, sommers* [see **1964** in **B**], *some'r's, somewhares* [see **1921** in **B**], *somewhars, summers.*

1891 Brown *Dialect in TN* 175 [Somewheres] is usually heard as sume'r's, especially in the phrase some'r's else. **1895** *Mt Baptist Sermon* 12 My brethering, you'll fine my tex' somers in the Bible.

1910 Cooke *Power and Glory* 5 He's got a big scheme up for makin' his fortune somewhars else. **1963** Edwards *Gravel* 94 They was a driving along . . . somers away yander, somers near the Calinder line. **1984** Six *Hill 'n Holler* 12 *summers*: "Seems like I've seen you summers before."

B (also *somewhereabouts*) Somewhere, at some place or time, approximately.

1814 Hartsell *Memora* 145 ther was two Companeys of troopes Came Down in boates on thursday, the Day we Crossed Tennessee river, from somers about kingston. **1861** *Click CW Letters* (Aug 19) thare are som whers in a bout a hunderd and thirty sick in our regiment. **1861** *Martin CW Letters* (Dec 27) they was an ofel fireing Some wheres on the Coast we Suposed it to be A Batle though we havent heard yet whether it was or Not. **1921** Fink *Week in Smoky Range* 153 Disheveled, trail-worn and weary, we were happy, for as one of the mountaineers expressed it, we had "been somewhares an' seen somethin'." **1937** Hall *Coll* (Tight Run Branch NC) My daddy, som'ers in fifty [i.e. years of age], went with Colonel Thomas to the top of Smoky to keep the Yankees back. **1939** Hall *Coll* One-armed Jim is right feeble. I reckon a body'll find him dead somewheres. **1964** Roberts *Hell-Fer-Sartin* 193 She went on and maybe got some blackberries sommers else. **1968** *Faith Healing* 17 You can get that stoppin' blood out'a the *Bible*. It's in the Old Testament somewhereabouts. **1978** Montgomery *White Pine Coll* II-3 It would be somewheres in the twenties, and then of course he was raised up completely in White Pine. *Ibid*. IV-2 If you don't like the job, you can go somewheres else. **1989** *Matewan OHP-1* He always rent, he got a spot somewheres and raised a big garden. **2002** Rash *Foot in Eden* 7 He's probably just laying off drunk somewheres.

[Web3 *somewheres* adv chiefly dialect]

som'in' See **something**.

sommers See **somewheres**.

song-ballad *noun*

A Variant form *song ballet* [see **1915** in **B1**].

B Senses.

1 Any secular song (i.e. not only a traditional or Child ballad). See also **ballad B1**, **ballad box**, **ballet card**, **devil's ditty**, **love ballad**, **mountain song**.

1915 Dingus *Word-List VA* 190 *song ballet* = a song or ballad. **1931** Goodrich *Mt Homespun* 51 In the Chalmers home much of it [= the carding of wool] was done as the family sat around the hearth at night, when the talk and the old tales and the singing of "song-ballets" lessened the tedium and made the workers forget their fatigue. **1939** Campbell *Play Party* 17 These "old-time gatherings where the fritter-minded song ballets belong to be sung" have not "plumb passed away." **1982** Powers and Hannah *Cataloochee* 357 Hardly anyone living could remember these old "song-ballets" being sung in [Cataloochee] Valley, though everyone could remember hymns and more recent Grand Ole Opry music within this century.

2 A manuscript copy or the words of such a song.

1862 *Robinson CW Letters* (March 25) I Send you a Song balled it is Sung to a noted tune. **1863** *Mangum CW Letters* (May 6) I sent you a letter and two song balleds in it and then I sent you the picture of vicks burg and another song balled in it and I put 5 dollars in the one the balleds was in. **1931** Owens *Speech Cumberlands* 94 *song-ballet* = the long-hand copy of the words of a ballad: "Illa sent me a good song-ballad, 'Barbara ellen.'" **1939** Hall *Coll* (Smokemont NC) Her mother kept notebooks and had a collection of song ballets. **1967** Combs *Folk-Songs* 103–4 Here and there in the "archives" of some remote Highland home one finds a book of "song-ballets" in manuscript form. One of such books was given to me years ago, and contained a number of native American songs, but no Child songs. The songs thus preserved are usually those of the sentimental type, or those recounting some local incident, written by a local bard.

[DARE *song-ballad* n southern Appalachians, Ozarks]

song bow *noun* See citations. Same as **Jew's harp**, **mouth bow**, **tune bow**.

1980 Wigginton *Foxfire VI* 54 In Macon County, North Carolina, Babe Henson makes a "songbow" out of a sapling and cotton string. **1998** Olson *Blue Ridge Folklife* 150 Toys that served to help children develop their musical aptitude included . . . songbows (a green stick held in a bow-like shape by a single steel string, placed in a person's mouth, the string was plucked, and players changed the pitch of the resonating drone by alternating the size and shape of their mouths).

sonker (also *sanker pie*, *sonker pie*) *noun* A deep-dish fruit pie. See also **apple sanker**.

1934–47 *LAMSAS Appal*: *sanker pie* = attested by 1/20 speakers (5%) from VA and 4/37 (10.8%) from NC. **1936** Morehouse *Rain on Just* 261 Dolly had bribed Hector and Lector with fried pies and blackberry sonker. **1944** Williams *Word-List Mts* 30 *sonker* = a fruit cobbler. Perhaps related to an old Manx word meaning "heavy." **1984** Wilder *You All Spoken* 82 *sonker* = a deep-dish fruit pie sweetened with molasses. **1986** Pederson et al. *LAGS* (Johnson Co TN) *sonker* = thick bread with apples mixed in. **1992** Brooks *Sthn Stuff* 144 *sonker* = an extra-deep fruit cobbler—usually made with the most plentiful fruit of the season, or the one on hand at the moment. **2016** Lundy and Autry *Victuals* 237 Some sonkers are made with a cake-like batter while others come with a pie crust. Among the crusters there are schisms as to whether a sonker has a top crust, a bottom crust, or both. And then there are devoted outliers who make their sonkers with no crust at all, but with delectable dumplings floating on top of a sauce of sweetened fruit. All sonkers seem to have in common a sweetened milk "dip" that is poured on top and baked to a glaze.

[DARE *sonker* n especially Southern Appalachians]

sont See **send**.

soo calf (also *soo calfy*, *swoo calf*) *interjection* Come! (used as a call to a calf to come in from the pasture often spoken three times and drawn out, in falsetto voice. See also **saw**^{2}, **soo cow**, **sook**.

1934–37 LAMSAS Appal (Madison Co NC, Swain Co NC) *soo calf.* **1966** DARE Survey (Brasstown NC) *swoo calf;* **1976** Lindsay *Grassy Balds* 206 We'd call 'em like: Sooooo calf! Sooooo calf, like that. **1986** Pederson et al. LAGS (Cocke Co TN, Jefferson Co TN, Sevier Co TN) *soo calf.*

[*soo calf* perhaps alteration of *sook calf* (cf OED3 *sook* n³, interj "a call used to summon or drive away cattle (in Scot[land] generally calves)" Scot and U.S. dialect); DARE *sook* exclam chiefly Midland, South, TX]

soo calfy See **soo calf.**

soo cow (also *swoo cow*) *interjection* Come! (used as a call to a cow to come in from the pasture. See also **saw²**, **soo calf**, **sook.**

1966 Dakin *Vocab Ohio River Valley* 270 Call to cows . . . in pasture [include] *swookie!, swook!, swoo!, swoo cow!* [in KY Mountains]. **1966–68** DARE Survey (Brasstown NC) *swoo cow* = call to get the cows to come in from the pasture; (Spruce Pine NC, Gatlinburg TN) *soo cow* = call to get a cow to come in from the pasture.

soodlin *noun* A portion.

1997 Montgomery Coll Would you like a soodlin more gravy to sop that biscuit in? (Oliver).

sooee See **sooey.**

sooey (also *sooee, sooy, suboy*) *interjection* Move! (used as a call to pigs to come at feeding time or to shoo or drive them away); hence verb = to call pigs at feeding time. See also **pig-ee.**

1915 Dingus *Word-List VA* 190 *soo-y* = used in urging on hogs. Also *suboy.* **1955** Parris *Roaming Mts* 68 He caught the familiar cry "suboy! suboy! suboy!" Then a barefoot boy came into sight, scattering shelled corn. Behind came the first of a plodding, grunting drove of hogs. **1956** McAtee *Some Dial NC* 42 *sooey* = a command used in driving hogs, meaning "git along" or "git out o' here." **1963** Arnow *Flowering* 129 The calling of the chickens, like plowing with a team, demanded words—sounds only they would now be to most of us—and the words varied from neighborhood to neighborhood. We, for example, said sooee-sooee to drive the hogs away and called with a loud and ringing pigooee-pig-pig-pig, but I knew a family who called with a sooee, and no two families called their dogs in the same way, though most, even foxhounds, would come to the sound of the dinner conch shell. **1963** Edwards *Gravel* 96 Johnny said that Steve cut that twig off and used it to sooey the hogs with along the road that day.

[Web3 *sooey* probably alteration of *sow;* DARE *sooey* exclam chiefly South, South Midland, Central, TX]

soogan See **suggin.**

sook (also *sook boss, sook bossie, sook buck, sook calf, sook calfy, sook cow, sookee, sook heifer, sookie, sook sookee, soolk, suke, suke cow, swoo cow, swook, swookie*) *interjection* Come! (used as a call to cattle to come in from the pasture). See also **saw²**, **soo calf**, **soo cow.**

1886 Smith *Southernisms* 46 *suke* = call to cow. **1915** Dingus *Word-List VA* 190 *sook* = call to cattle at feeding time. Sometimes sook-calf(y), swook(y), swook-calf(y). **1940** Haun *Hawk's Done* 63 I got my bucket and called Old Heif. "Soolk, Heif, soolk, soolk." **1943** Chase *Jack Tales* 25 "Sook buck!" says the old lady. "Sook here! Sook buck! Stand still now!" **1949** Kurath *Word Geog East US* 38 The Midland call *sook!* has been carried rather farther into the piedmont of Virginia and North Carolina than most Midland expressions, perhaps as the result of the introduction of stock raising from the western parts of these states into the plantation country. **1958** Newton *Dialect Vocab: sook boss(ie)* = attested by 3 of 36 speakers from E TN mountains; *sook cow* = attested by 15 of 36 speakers from E TN mountains; *sookee* = attested by 8 of 36 speakers from E TN mountains. **1966** Dakin *Vocab Ohio River Valley* 266 Throughout the entire [Ohio] Valley, with the outstanding exception of the Marietta area, the Midland call *sook!, sookie cow!* predominate. These forms are the most common. *Sook!* and *sookie!* called with a great variety of stress and intonation patterns, usually with a number of repetitions, and sometimes in combination. Some speakers say that *sook!* is for cows and *sookie!* only for calves. **1966–68** DARE Survey (Burnsville NC, Maryville TN) *sook sookee* = call to get the cows to come in from the pasture; feeding time; (Spruce Pine NC) *sook calf, sook calf, sook calf* (call repeated twice); (Cherokee NC) *sook sookee* = call to a calf at feeding time; (Spruce Pine NC, Gatlinburg TN) *sook cow* = call to get a cow to come in from the pasture; (Gatlinburg TN, Maryville TN) *sook calfy.* **1977** Hamilton *Mt Memories* 60 I would look and look and call them, "Sook Jersey, Sook Bonnie" till old Jersey would shake her head at the flies, and the bell would tinkle. **1978** Reese *Speech NE Tenn* 30 *soo(k) cow* = attested by 7/12 (58.3%) speakers. **1986** Pederson et al. LAGS (Cocke Co TN) *sook calf.* **1993** Ison and Ison *Whole Nother Lg* 62 *sook heifer* = calling the cow to come in to be milked. **1994** Parton *Dolly* 13 I caught the first glimpse of the kerosene lantern Mama was holding as she called Bessie, "Sook, sook!" **1995** Montgomery Coll: *sookee* (known to Cardwell).

[OED3 *sook* n³, interj "a call used to summon or drive away cattle (in Scot[land] generally calves)" Scot and U.S. dialect; HT *sook! sook!* "feeding call to calves"; Web3 *sook* alteration of *suck; soo cow* perhaps alteration of *sook cow;* DARE *sook* exclam chiefly Midland, South, TX, *swoo* exclam scattered, but especially PA German area, southern Appalachians]

sook boss, sook bossie, sook buck, sook calf, sook calfy, sook cow, sookee, sook heifer, sookie, sook sookee See **sook.**

soon *adjective, adverb* Early.

1862 *Reese CW Letters* (Sept 18) I dont sleep mutch hear I am up lat at nite and up soon. **1895** Edson and Fairchild *TN Mts* 374 We'll have a *soon* supper. **1913** Kephart *Our Sthn High* 84 Rustle out, boys; we've got to get a soon start if you want bear brains and liver for supper. **1924** Raine *Saddlebags* 100 They "git up afore day to git a soon start." **1937** Hall Coll (Emerts Cove TN) We hadn't eat a bite since soon that morning. **1956** Hall Coll (Big Bend NC) She'd get up soon in the mornin' and git out and work all day. **1975** Chalmers *Better* 65 One should rise early and get a soon start if the way is long.

[DARE *soon* adv 1 chiefly South, South Midland; *soon* adj 1 South, South Midland]

sooner *noun*

1 A child born less than nine months after a couple marries. **2000** Montgomery *Coll* (known to Cardwell).

2 (also *sooner dog*) A mongrel.

1956 Hall *Coll* (Del Rio TN) I've got a sooner dog. He'd sooner lay in the house as out in the yard. **1971** Dwyer *Dict for Yankees* 31 *sooner* = mongrel. **1983** Broaddus *Estill Co KY Word List* 57 *sooner* = poor hunting dog: "Sooner lie down than hunt." **1997** Montgomery *Coll* (known to Bush, Ellis, Norris, Oliver).

[DARE *sooner* n² 2 scattered, but especially South, South Midland]

sooner dog See **sooner 2**.

soon's *conjunction* As soon as.

1913 Kephart *Our Sthn High* 101 Soon's I could shoot without hittin' a dog, I let [the bear] have it. **1938** Bowman *High Horizons* 41 I plants cucumbers afore sunup, so's the bugs won't eat 'em soon's they bust the dirt. **1962** Dykeman *Tall Woman* 193 "Soon's we get them all back up North where they belong," one man joked.

soon start See **soon**.

soorgan *noun* A deep-dish fruit pie.

1976 Braden *Grandma Was Girl* 46 The pan pies were made from the fruit in season—apple, blackberry, strawberry, gooseberry, peach and raspberry. We used biscuit dough for the crusts. For the cobblers (they were sometimes called "soorgans"; I don't know whether that is spelled correctly, or where the word came from), we used biscuit dough, too.

soot *noun* Variant form *sut* (rhymes with *cut*).

1891 Brown *Dialect in TN* 172 The word *soot* (or soot) is almost universally called *sut*. **1913** Kephart *Our Sthn High* 226 [I] tied [my foot] up in sut and a rag, and went to hoein' corn. **1915** Dingus *Word-List VA* 190 *sut*. **1934–37** *LAMSAS Appal* (Madison Co NC, Swain Co NC). **1942** Hall *Phonetics Smoky Mts* 38 *Soot* occurred only as [sʌt]. **1961** Kurath and McDavid *Pron Engl Atl Sts* 155 In the South and the South Midland *soot* has the vowel [ʌ] of *flood* quite regularly in the speech of the folk. **1963** Watkins and Watkins *Yesterday* 131 Smut or soot (the [latter] said "sut") mixed with sugar would stop the flow of blood. **1973** Jones *Cades Cove TN* 117. **1994** Parton *Dolly* 90 It was in the springtime, so the heater wasn't in use, but the black cloud of soot (we pronounced it "sut") that spewed from the old stovepipe got the boys' attention.

[DARE *soot* n (pronc) chiefly South, South Midland, less frequent Northeast]

soot tag *noun* See citation.

1986 Pederson et al. *LAGS* (Cocke Co TN) = dust web [that would] get the color of soot.

sop

A *noun* Grease, gravy (such as **red-eye gravy** or milk gravy), syrup, coffee, etc. in which food (especially corn bread or biscuits) is soaked or dipped before eaten. See also **bay sop**, **Betsy sop**, **dough sop**, **soppings**, **white sop**.

1843 (in **1974** Harris *High Times* 29) The fire's crackling, the fat (or sop, as it is better known by that name in the Coves) is hissing. **1895** Edson and Fairchild *TN Mts* 374 = gravy. "We ate light bread and *sop*." **1955** Ritchie *Singing Family* 98 Mom took up a long dish of bacon with plenty of sop to put on the lettuce, with salt. **1957** Broaddus *Vocab Estill Co KY* 73 = ham gravy flavored with coffee. **1979** Melton *'Pon My Honor* 80 She put a hoecake on to bake. Next she took up her meat and then poured up the big sop. She set the meat and the big sop on the hearth to keep warm. **1997** Montgomery *Coll* = red eye gravy. After frying bacon, ham, etc., remove meat, add water to pan and grease, and boil a few minutes. It would be watery. People sopped it up with biscuits (Adams); She made sop by browning flour in ham grease, then adding chicory (Brown), = usually milk gravy or other thin gravy (Ellis), = usually red-eye gravy or a gravy with more grease (Jones).

B *verb* To dip or swash (corn bread or a biscuit) in gravy, syrup, or coffee; to use gravy for such a purpose; hence noun *sopper* = one engaging in the practice of dipping effectively.

1941 Still *Troublesome Creek* 102 We've got more sirup now than can be sopped till Jedgment. **1957** Parris *My Mts* 135 Even if a feller was starving to death he wouldn't think of sitting down to a dish of potlikker without a pone or two of cornbread to crumble in or sop with. **1963** Watkins and Watkins *Yesterday* 46 Ma shore could make good gravy for us to sop our biscuits in—thickening gravy and hogeye or redeye or ham gravy. **1973** Cate *Molasses Making* Youngsters hurried home from school and quickly completed their chores so that they could go down and watch the "stir-off." Some chewed pieces of cane, others ate the foam skimmed from the thickening syrup or sopped up the molasses left in the cooking vat. **1976** Miller *Mts within Me* 94 In the mountains "sopping" involves a piece of bread and is most often done at breakfast. Highlanders dunk hot biscuits in steaming cups of coffee and call it "sopping" . . . it takes a deft hand to dunk the biscuit just far enough into the coffee and pop it in the mouth before it totally disintegrates in the coffee cup. It is recommended that beginning "soppers" dip the biscuit only half an inch or so—and do it very quickly—until they get the timing right. For the benefit of the devotees of Miss Post, it should be pointed out that the entire biscuit never is completely submerged and the fingers never touch the coffee. That would be uncouth! "Sopping" butter and syrup is another precise mountain technique. It is done by taking a helping of butter, covering it well with syrup and blending it with a fork to the consistency of thick cake batter. Then the biscuit is broken in half and dipped into the mixture. As with biscuits and coffee, it takes a delicate hand to "sop" syrup and butter right. . . . The master of this fine art always finishes his biscuit and syrup and butter simultaneously—with equal servings on each bite. **1997** Montgomery *Coll* Would you like a soodlin more gravy to sop that biscuit in? (Oliver). **2013** DeLozier and Jourdan *Back Seat*

32 He ate out of a plastic container, sopped Genevieve's yellow gravy with a dinner roll.

sopper See **sop B**.

soppings *noun* See citation. See also **sop A**.

1962 Clark *Folk Speech NC* 320 = gravy.

soppy *noun* See citations.

2009 Sohn *Appal Home Cooking* 301 "Soppy" and "dippy" are colloquial terms for milk gravy, squirrel gravy, and sausage gravy. Mountain cooks make these gravies with milk, flour, and pan drippings, and they serve them over biscuits. **2009** Wiles and Wiles *Location* 61 Breakfast might have been "soppy"—biscuit soaked in coffee and sprinkled with sugar.

soppy crumbs *noun* Same as **crumble in**.

2003 Carter *Mt Home* 45 Later in the day or evenin', the leftover cornbread was crumbled up and fried crispy brown in a lot of grease and made what we called "soppy crumbs."

sorghum *noun*

A Variant forms *sawgrums* [see **1956** in **B2**], *soggrum* [see **1991** in **B2**], *sorghums*, *sorgrums*. [Editor's note: Forms in -*s* refer to syrup, probably by analogy with *molasses*.]

1921 Weeks *Speech of KY Mtneer* 11 "Pears like to me them sorghums is bitter" might be heard on any little mountain farm in October when "sorghums air bein biled down an' stirred off." **1974** Fink *Bits Mt Speech* 24 *sorgrums*.

[DARE *sorghum* B chiefly South Midland]

B Senses.

1 (also *sorghum cane*) A plant growing 8 to 12 feet high, from whose stalk is squeezed a rich, sweet juice (usually at a **cane mill** or **sorghum gin**) that, after straining and other processing, is boiled into **molasses**, a common sweetener in traditional mountain cooking and into candy.

1977 *Smoky Vistas* (Fall) 3 Few mountain settlers could afford the cane mills necessary to squeeze the juice out of the cane. A man who owned one allowed his neighbors to use it. His land was alive with activity during sorghum season. **1997** *Smokies Guide* (Autumn) 13 Sorghum cane, which was introduced to this country from Africa in the 1700s, looks very similar to corn and is grown and cultivated much like corn as well. The crop was generally planted in late spring or early summer and was harvested in the fall. It was a fairly common crop in the Smokies, as well as in much of southern Appalachia.

2 (also *sorghum molasses*, *sorghum syrup*) A thick, sweet syrup made from the juice squeezed or beaten from the stalks of **sorghum** cane, to be strained, processed, and boiled. See also **molasses**.

[See **1921** in **A**.] **1939** Hall Coll (Tobes Creek NC) [How did they make sorghum in the old days?] Well, sir, they took a little pestle and beat out the juice and [boiled] it in water. [See **1942** in **A**.] **1956** Hall Coll (Cosby TN) [People would] make sorghum molasses by the barrel full. The cane patch had to be raised every year. They needed sweetnin' for bread. *Ibid*. (Waynesville NC) Now that's the way they made their sawgrums. [See **1974** in **A**.] **1991** Thomas *Sthn Appal* 238 We'd raise soggrum an' make m'lasses. **c1995** *Pioneer Farmstead* 10 Sorghum cane was for the pioneer the source of molasses, sometimes called "long sweetening" because of its rope-like texture. It was eaten straight from the jar or used in cooking as a general substitute for sugar. **1995** *Smokies Guide* (Autumn) 1 Sorghum was a common sweetener in the mountains and elsewhere prior to the widespread availability of sugar from sugar cane. Sorghum molasses was poured on cornbread and pancakes and used in recipes for everything from beans to cookies. **2006** Sauceman *Place Setting* 6–7 The terms sorghum and molasses are often used interchangeably, but Arland is quick to point out the difference. Molasses, he says, is a by-product of sugar-making and is often a by-product containing even as much as 20 percent Karo syrup. **2006** *WV Encycl* 667 In West Virginia sorghum molasses has also been called molasses, lassies, and sorghums, but today, producers sometimes call their product 100 percent pure sweet sorghum syrup because of the fact that stores now sell "molasses" that are mixtures of corn syrup, flavorings, food coloring, and other additives.

[DARE *sorghum* n B chiefly South Midland]

sorghum cane See **sorghum B1**.

sorghum gin (also *sorghum mill*, *sorghum press*) *noun* A small, box-like mill for pressing the stalks of sorghum for its juice, which is made into molasses. Same as **cane mill**.

1883 Zeigler and Grosscup *Heart of Alleghanies* 95 Tuk hit when they wuz drivin' im to Toe Eldredge's sorghum mill. **1941** Still *Troublesome Creek* 87 In a hollow stood the Burkhearts' great log house, and beyond under gilly trees was the sorghum gin. **1997** Montgomery Coll: *sorghum press* (known to Jones).

sorghum hole *noun* Same as **skim hole**.

1941 Still *Stir-Off* 6 Leander chunked the fire and U. Z. ladled green skimmings into the sorghum hole.

sorghum liquor *noun* Moonshine whiskey made from sorghum syrup.

1949 Arnow *Hunter's Horn* 60 He had drunk himself his own sorghum liquor, and now with his old feet full of undanced tunes and his heart soft with the love of his fellow man, he gave away the moonshine he should have sold.

sorghum making *noun* See citation. See also **molasses boil**, **stir-off**.

1987 Trent *Yesteryear* 19 "Sorghum makin'" was a sociable occasion in the life of the community. Relatives and friends would gather, particularly in the evenings, to drink fresh cane juice, chew cane, engage in pleasant conversation, and at the boiling off time, to sap up the syrup around the edge of the kettle with sticks of cane peel or wood paddles whittled from a sliver of wood off the fuel pile. It was a neighborly gesture for a farmer to invite family friends to the cane grinding but uninvited droppers-in were welcome too.

sorghum mill See **sorghum gin.**

sorghum molasses See **sorghum B2.**

sorghum press See **sorghum gin.**

sorghum syrup See **sorghum B2.**

sorgrums See **sorghum A.**

sorrow *adjective* Full of grief, regretful. See also **sorrow around.**

1863 *Hundley CW Letters* (March 2) I am sorrow to have to frank my letter but I Cant git stamps hear. **1864** *Walker CW Letters* (Aug 7) I receved your kind letter dated july the 27 and was sorrow to hear you was wounded but I hope you will be able to get home in a few days. **1910** Weeks *Barbourville Word List* 457 = this use is common among our students [at Union College in southeastern KY]: "Stevenson had the power to make a person feel very sorrow," "I am sorrow I haven't worked harder."

sorrow around *verb phrase* To wander about grieving.

1896 Fox *Vendetta* 171 Every day she went to the cabin, "moonin' 'n' sorrowin' aroun'," as old Gabe said; and she was much changed.

sorry *adjective* Of low or meager quality or worth, useless, wretched; mean, causing trouble; thoughtless. For nuances of the term, see 2006 citation.

1832 *McLean Diary* (Dec 31) Crops have bin sorry this year. **1862** *Spainhourd CW Letters* (June 25) it looks like we will soon perish if crops is as sorry evry whar els as they are down her. **1864** *Warrick CW Letters* (July 14) Crops is sorry what I have seen up hear and it is all gon to destruction. **1913** Kephart *Our Sthn High* 291 "Them sorry fellers" denotes scabby knaves, good-for-nothings. Sorry has no etymological connection with sorrow, but literally means sore-y, covered with sores, and the highlander sticks to its original import. **1926** Reinhardt *Speech and Balladry* 143 The Highlander employs the word sorry, not only to express grief or sympathy, but also . . . to voice contempt, "He is a sorry man." Shakespeare said, "This is a sorry sight." **1937** Hall *Coll* (Deep Creek NC, in complaining about the national park's restrictions) The worst, sorriest things they is, like bobcats, you cain't kill. *Ibid.* (Cataloochee NC) That's the sorriest sight in the world. **1975** *GSMNP-59:9* The saying was unless he's awful sorry, he'd have two or three cows, enough till they had milk and butter all the time. **1977** Shackelford et al. *Our Appalachia* 89 The sorriest man in the world is a vote seller. **1997** Montgomery *Coll* He is forever talking about how sorry his young'uns are (Andrews). **1999** DeRozier *Creeker* 31 My Grandma Emmie was "the finest old woman who ever wore shoe leather, but Lige Mollette was sorry as dirt." **2002** Rash *Foot in Eden* 169 He was a good football player at one time, but he was in sorry shape now. **2006** *Encycl Appalachia* 234–35 Sorriness is most associated with lack of desire to work, but the quality may also be ascribed to those who are considered troublemakers in the community or who lack common sense. The use of the term *sorriness* can be as much an expression of the region's dry, self-deprecating humor as of any reality. *Sorry* can be an affectionate term when applied to inlaws, hound dogs, and old drinking buddies, partly as a manifestation of regional humility. Sometimes people are called sorry with the unspoken understanding that they are wise not to compete or to work feverishly for futile goals. **2009** Callahan *Work and Faith* 47 For the man that doesn't provide for his family, the term "sorry" was the lowest term you could label him. **2015** Holbrook *Something* 152 The way she talked he was the sorriest thing on earth.

[< Middle English *sary* < Old English *sar* "sore' + -*y*"; DARE *sorry* adj B1 scattered, but especially Southeast, Lower Mississippi Valley, TX, OK]

sorter See **sort of.**

sort of *adverb phrase* Variant forms *sorter, sorty.*

1862 *Shifflet CW Letters* (Feb 28) I went to the River to day and wash a shirt or wash at it it want vary clean but it will sorter do. **1865** *Parlier CW Letters* (Jan 11) I can sorty rit that is all that I do. **1910** Cooke *Power and Glory* 49 Mr. Stoddard's got sorter brown eyes and hair. **1941** Stuart *Men of Mts* 182 I saw them lift the crazy-patched quilt off'n Fern's face—it sorty covered up part of her face. **1969** *GSMNP-27* He never did pastor any church. He was just sorty in the retired age, you might say sorty. **1973** *AOHP/ASU-106* I asked my son up here one day, he's sort of head of the church, sorter, in a way, I reckon. **1998** *Dante OHP-61* We went and [were] trying to get back reinstated into the [church] conference. One man sorty went agin us.

sorty See **sort of.**

so's *conjunction*

A Variant forms *sose* [see **1864** in **B**], *so's't* [see **1913** in **B**].

B So (that), in order (that).

1864 *Walker CW Letters* (Aug 18) live up to your duty and pray for me Sose that if we neve meet her on this trubelson eath no mor that we may be promited to meet in Heaven. **1864** *D Walker CW Letters* (Aug 23) I am mending I think very fast I have got Sose that I can walk about rit S[m]art. **1905** Miles *Spirit of Mts* 41 I'm glad hit's hot enough so'st I ain't needin any wood. **1913** Kephart *Our Sthn High* 102 So's't I wouldn't bark my shins. **1938** Bowman *High Horizons* 41 I plants cucumbers afore sunup, so's the bugs won't eat 'em soon's they bust the dirt. **1953** Hall *Coll* (Bryson City NC) His instruction was for everybody to kill something that day, get some game, so's we have camp rations at night. . . . He run his gun through a crack of the camp and killed one of them so's't they'd have them some turkey meat. **1967** Williams *Subtlety Mt Speech* 14 Atter while he came to a haouse [sic]. So's he walked up to the gate and hollered, "Hello!" **1978** Montgomery *White Pine Coll* III-2 I'm hoping and praying that it'd be, so's that we could get it in the future. **2007** Preece *Leavin' Sandlick* 26 I just want her to do her best and nothing more, so's she can live with hersef in the long run without being disappointed in what she did with her life.

[contraction of *so* + *as*]

so's't See **so's**.

sot See **set, sit**.

sound out *verb phrase* To challenge, investigate the character or authenticity of (someone).

1997 Montgomery *File* I believed he was a fake, so one day I sounded him out and found out he was not what he thought he was (85-year-old man, Greenbrier TN). **2007** McMillon *Notes* = to investigate the character of someone or check out an animal.

soup bean *noun* A dried bean, especially a pinto bean.

1930 Thomas *Death Knell* The mountaineer has invented many words to suit his meanings. Beans dried in the pod are variously called shuck-beans, fodder-beans, and leather-britches, to distinguish them from shelled beans, which he calls soup-beans. **1952** Giles *40 Acres* 113 Whatever else there is to eat, the soup bean is always present. In the city we call them pinto beans or brown beans, but any merchant in the small towns hereabouts knows what you mean when you say soup beans. . . . They are served floating in a big bowl of their own soup. The idea is to crumble a chunk of cornbread and pour the beans and soup over it. **2000** Wilkinson *Blackberries* 47 She was stirring the soup beans, beginning to wash the dishes, when it hit. **2003** Cavender *Folk Medicine* 11–12 Pinto beans, also known as "brown beans" and "soup beans," a mainstay of the diet, were not cultivated but purchased in general stores, as was white flour, salt, sugar, coffee, canned goods, soda crackers, and exotic fruits like bananas and oranges. **2005** Williams *Gratitude* 526 = dry beans, usually pinto beans. We cook 'em with enough water to make 'em good and soupy. **2016** Netherland *Appal Cooking* 73 When we cooked them [= pinto beans], we called them "soup beans." If you say "soup beans" to any native Southern Appalachian, he or she knew exactly what you meant. . . . Occasionally, my mother would drop some dumplings into the bean broth and we would eat bean dumplings. The beans were always seasoned with some cured pork meat, such as streaky lean, sidemeat, fatback or hog jowl, and occasionally some meaty ham hock.

sour gnat *noun* Usually a fruit fly; also, a type of gnat.

1936 Stuart *Head of Hollow* 29 I saw a knot hole upon the side and the sour gnats were comin out and goin in. **c1960** Wilson *Coll* = fruit flies. **1983** Broaddus *Estill Co KY Word List* 57 = a type of gnat that hurts worse than ordinary gnats when one gets in your eye.

sour mash *noun* In distilling, leftover **mash** from a previous **run** or distillation to which sugar is added to promote fermentation. See also **sweet mash**.

1963 Carson *History Bourbon* 237 = bourbon whiskey made by using in the fermentors part of the spent beer from a previous day's run, along with fresh yeast, to start a new batch of mash. **1974** Maurer and Pearl *KY Moonshine* 125 = mash made by scalding meal with hot slops, in contrast to sweet mash, which is made by scalding the meal with fresh water.

sour milk *noun* Buttermilk.

1886 Smith *Sthn Dialect* 349 = butter-milk. **1976** Garber *Mountain-ese* 86 = buttermilk: "We jist churned a whole batch uv sour milk and it's real good."

sourwood *noun* A small deciduous tree (*Oxydendrum arboreum*) that grows at lower and middle elevations of the mountains, the nectar of whose fragrant, white flowers is the source of a well-reputed honey, and whose bark is made into a medicinal tea; a folk belief attributes curative powers to a stem or limb cut from the tree. See also **sourwood sprout**.

1941 Walker *Story of Mt* 67 Sourwood is a favorite tree of both man and honey-bee. It grows throughout the length and breadth of the mountain. The strong acid content of its foliage gives it its common name. The flowers, which like the common elder open in June and the early part of July, are not killed by frosts. The nectar from the sour-wood thus assures the honeybees an ample supply of material out of which is made the clearest and best mountain honey. **1964** Stupka *Trees Shrubs Vines* 122–23 An abundant small tree at low and middle altitudes. . . . The attractive panicles of fragrant white flowers serve to decorate this tree from late June throughout July, at which time they attract large numbers of bees. These flowers are the source of an excellent honey. **1967** Jones *Peculiarities Mtneers* 66 Sourwood bark tea thickened with flour and made into pills was used in the treatment of dropsy, a disease modern doctors call "edema." **1970** Campbell et al. *Smoky Mt Wildflowers* 38 This small tree is conspicuous for its graceful sprays of white flowers from June to August and for the extreme brilliance of its leaves in autumn. The pale gray fruit, which remain through the summer, are often mistaken for flowers. It is our only member of the heath family that is truly a tree. The nectar from its flowers produces the choicest of all wild honey.

[DARE *sourwood* n 1 chiefly southern Appalachians]

sourwood sprout (also *sourwood stick, sourwood switch*) *noun* A stem or limb from a **sourwood** tree believed to have curative power, especially over childhood respiratory diseases.

1937 Hall *Coll* (Cosby TN) To cure the croup and the phthisic, straighten a sourwood stick behind the back and head, cut it off even with the top of the head, and hide it where it'll never be found. **1956** Hall *Coll* (Newport TN) She'd go get a sourwood switch she'd call it, and she would measure her children to cure the croup and the tizik. **1985** Irwin *Alex Stewart* 144 You take the child that's got the whooping cough and face him toward the south up against a tree, and mark his height. Then you go out and find a sourwood sprout and cut it the same length as the person is high. Hang that sprout up over the door where the child lives, and when it dries out the whooping cough will be gone.

sourwood stick, sourwood switch See **sourwood sprout**.

souse

A (also *souze*) *verb* To plunge, immerse, drench; to dash (a liquid).

1859 Taliaferro *Fisher's River* 197 He broke his holt as quick as when you souse a bucket uv cold water on two bulldogs a-fightin'. **1892** Fruit *KY Words* 232 = to plunge, to stick in: "Souse a pin into him." **1937** Haun *Cocke Co* 3 Setting hens are still soused down in water to break them. **c1945** Haun *Hawk's Done* 209 She's proud enough already—she tries to make her hair pretty by sousing it in sap from wild grape vines. **1973** GSMNP-75:3 He was the minister that baptized me when I was nine years old. They'd take ye out, roll ye up along, and then souse ye in under. **2005** Williams *Gratitude* 526 souse (*souze*) = to plunge something out of sight, like to souse it under water or liquid.

[DARE *souse* v[1] B2 "plunge" scattered, but especially frequent South, South Midland, *souse* v[1] B4 "immerse" especially South Midland]

B (also *souse meat*) *noun* A preparation of miscellaneous portions of a butchered hog, as from the head and internal organs, that is congealed, sliced, and often served cold. Also called **head cheese, hoghead cheese, press(ed) meat**. See also **scrapple**.

1934–37 LAMSAS *Appal* (Madison Co NC, Swain Co NC). **1966** Dakin *Vocab Ohio River Valley* 339 In Kentucky, where *meat* unless qualified frequently means "pork," the expression *souse meat* is common. **1966–68** *DARE Survey* (Brasstown NC) *souse* = made from parts of the head of a pig; (Burnsville NC, Spruce Pine NC, Maryville TN) *souse meat* = made from the head and inner organs of a pig. **1978** Montgomery *White Pine Coll* IV-4 People made what they called souse meat. They cut most of the head up, the jaws and then also the jowl. . . . Hog jowl came off of the bottom part of the head. They used all but the squeal, as they say. **1984** Page and Wigginton *Foxfire Cookery* 118 Hog's head is also called "souse," "souse meat," "head cheese," or "pressed hog's head." Prepare the raw hog's head as follows: Trim, scrape, or singe off any hairs or bristles that are left. If you intend to use the ears, brain, snout, tongue or jowls for any purpose other than souse, remove them and set them aside to soak. Otherwise leave them on the head to be ground up. **1984** Smith *Enduring Memories* 12 Souse was made by boiling the hog's head until all the meat could be stripped from the bone. We used only the solid meat and not any fat or cartilage. We would add salt, pepper, and sage to flavor to taste and then press the meat in something to get all the grease out. It would then be placed in pans or special bowls to chill and was ready to eat. **1986** Pederson et al. *LAGS*: *souse meat* = attested by 39/60 interviewees (65%) from E TN and 16/35 (45.7%) from N GA; 55/201 of all LAGS interviewees (27.3%) attesting term were from Appalachia. **1997** Nelson *Country Folklore* 117 After the hog's head was cooked, it was used to make souse meat. To make souse meat, you used salt, red pepper, corn meal, and vinegar. **2005** Williams *Gratitude* 526 = a gelatin-like meat dish made from the parts of a hog's head.

[DARE *souse, souse meat* n[1] C1b chiefly Midland, South, TX; *souse meat* n chiefly South, South Midland]

souse meat See **souse B**.

south end *noun* See citation.

1967 *DARE Survey* (Gatlinburg TN) = the rump of a cooked chicken.

souze See **souse A**.

sow *verb* Variant past-tense form *sown*.

1978 Reese *Speech NE Tenn* 179 = attested by 4/12 (33.3%) speakers.

sow belly (also *sow bosom, sow's belly, sow's bosom*) *noun* Meat from the side of a hog, bacon. See also **fatback, middling C, side meat, streaked bacon, striped meat.**

1862 *Shifflet CW Letters* (Dec 22) I will hav to take Sow belly and hard Crackers for my chrismas dinner I hav eat so menny hard crackers and fat Sow belly that my teeth is all wore out. **1913** Kephart *Our Sthn High* 219 On their arduous trips they find it burden enough to carry the salt for their cattle, with a frying pan, cup, corn pone, coffee, and "sow-belly," all in a grain sack tied to a man's back. **1936** Farr *Folk Speech Mid TN* 276 *sow's bosom* = bacon, variant of sowbelly or sow's belly: "I eat sow's bosom for breakfast." **1963** Wilson *Regional Words* 79 *sow belly* = bacon; this was a dignified word, but sow-belly was also common in the right company; hence some person who is trying to fly high is eating ham-meat on sow-belly wages. **1972** Carson and Vick *Cookin* 2 20 Here's a recipe that beats "sow bosom" and boiled cabbages. **1998** Joslin *Living Heritage* 24 I've known him to kill as many as eleven fat hogs in one season. They wanted that bacon—sow bosom I call it—and corn.

[DARE *sow bosom* n chiefly South, South Midland, Southwest]

sow bosom See **sow belly**.

sowbug *noun* A small crustacean (*Oniscus* spp) that lives off decaying matter such as rotting logs, sometimes collected and used to treat diseases such as jaundice.

1966 Frome *Strangers* 79 A combination of "sowbugs," found under the hearth rocks in the chimney, and 'lasses was prescribed for yellow jaundice, or "yaller janders." **1982** Slone *How We Talked* 45 = a small bug usually found under old, decaying logs. Used to cure diseases by tying them in a rag and wearing them around the neck. **1995** Montgomery *Coll* = nine sow bugs were swallowed to rid oneself of yellow jaundice (Cardwell).

sow cat *noun* See citations.

1915 Dingus *Word-List VA* 190 = a she cat. **1967** *DARE Survey* (Maryville TN) = joking name a man may use for a woman.

[DARE *sow cat* n especially South Midland]

sow coon *noun* See citation.

c1960 Wilson *Coll* = facetious name for a cyclone, which always means tornado.

[DARE *sow coon* n 2 especially South Midland]

sow's belly, sow's bosom See **sow belly**.

span cubes *noun* See citation.

1967 DARE *Survey* (Maryville TN) = joking name of an imaginary illness.

spang (also *spank*) *adverb* Directly, absolutely; entirely, completely.

1901 Harben *Westerfelt* 166 We've picked out a tree up thar that leans spank over a cliff five hundred feet from the bottom. **1913** Kephart *Our Sthn High* 282 Lacking other means of expression, there will come "spang" from his mouth a coinage of his own. **1917** Kephart *Word-List* 417 *spang* = exactly, directly. "He was right *spang* on the spot." **1927** Camak *June of Hills* 33 They'd starve spank to death before thar ever got to be that many ov 'em. **1943** Hannum *Mt People* 100 Though he was waiting for it, when it came, his hair rose straight up on his head, and his chin whiskers like to pulled spang out. **c1960** Wilson *Coll*: *spang* = directly, completely: "He jumped spang into the middle of the creek." **1974** Fink *Bits Mt Speech* 24 That dog jumped right *spang* into the creek.

[OED3 *spang* adv "with a sudden spring or impetus"; cf EDD *spang* v[1] 1 Scot, Irel, nEngl "to bound, spring, stride along"; cf SND *spang* n[2] "a long vigorous step, a bound"; CUD *spang* n 1 "a leap, a bound"; DARE *spang* adv 2 chiefly South, South Midland]

spangfired *adverb* See citation.

1974 Fink *Bits Mt Speech* 24 Spangfired new.

Spanish bayonet *noun* A yucca plant (*Yucca filamentatosa* or *Y. smalliana*). See also **Adam's needle**, **bear grass**.

1970 Campbell et al. *Smoky Mt Wildflowers* 34 Known as the Spanish bayonet because of its tough sword-shaped leaves, it is also one of several plants commonly called beargrass.

Spanish needle *noun* A prickly wild plant (*Bidens* spp). See also **beggar('s) lice**, **stickerweed**.

1847 (in **1870** Drake *Pioneer Life KY* 53) In the latter part of summer and in early autumn, after the corn was "laid by," various rank weeds, including Spanish needles and wild cucumber-vines, covered with an armature of bristles, would spring up among it. **1966–68** DARE *Survey* (Brasstown NC, Burnsville NC, Spruce Pine NC, Gatlinburg TN) = prickly seeds, small and flat, with two prongs at one end that cling to clothing. **1966** Dykeman *Far Family* 273 She walked on through the abandoned orchard, bedraggling her skirts with beggar-lice and Spanish needles and all sorts of weed dust. **1995** Mullins *Road Back* 69 "Be sure to cut all the weeds you see," he ordered. "I despise to strip the blades of corn to make fodder when the balks are full of Spanish needles, cockleburrs, and ragweeds."

[DARE *Spanish needle* n chiefly Midland, South]

spank See **spang**.

spanquitting *noun* See citation.

1957 Combs *Lg Sthn High: Word List* 93 = a mythical disease in horses. Heard in the expression: "He's got the spanquittin', he can't fart for shittin'."

spare See **sparrow**.

sparegrass, spargrass, spargus See **asparagus**.

spark

A *noun* A small bit.

1937 Hall *Coll* (Cosby Creek TN) [The lightning] didn't scare me a speck nor a spark. **1997** Montgomery *Coll* (known to Brewer, Bush, Cardwell); He didn't have a spark of sense (Weaver).

B (also *spark with*) *verb*, *verb phrase* Especially of a man: to woo, court (a woman); to engage in courtship; hence noun *sparking* = courting. See also **talk**.

1859 Taliaferro *Fisher's River* 118 I sparked her a little that night, and told her I was a-gwine wiz her to meetin' next Sunday. **1862** (in **1992** Jackson *Surry Co Soldiers* 289) (May 9) I have seed some of the pretys[t] ladies last Sunday I ever saw and I think if I should be so fortunate as to see this war ended I shall be bounded to spark them and give them a call anyway. **1892** Fruit *KY Words* 232 *sparking* = courting: "To go sparkin'"; "What girl were you sparkin' last Sunday?" **1935** Sheppard *Cabins in Laurel* 172 When he comes and takes her to the church-house and calls on her with presents of candy and Victrola records, they have advanced to the sparkin' stage. **1939** Hall *Coll* (Cades Cove TN) We was small, both of us. They got to deviling us about sparking, you know, and Will says, "Now, boys, that's got to be cut out, deviling them children. They don't know what sparking is." **1941** Stuart *Men of Mts* 110 She's sparked Sweet William goin' on four years now. **c1950** Adams *Grandpap* 77 He begged the old folks for three solid days an' sparked the girl for three solid nights. **1958** Newton *Dialect Vocab* (Happy Valley TN) *spark*; (Walland TN, Millers Cove TN) *spark with*. **1963** Medford *Mt People* 51 While the women never would encroach on the "men's" side, young men, when "sparking," would sometimes venture over to the "women's side" of the church or public meeting-place. **1982** Slone *How We Talked* 4 This word "sparkin'" got its beginning because the couple's only way to get to talk to each other was to sit side by side in two straight-backed chairs (homemade split bottoms) before the fire, after the family had gone to bed in the same room. Whispering to each other, sparks rising from the chimney told the neighbors that someone was up later than the usual bedtime. **1990** Merriman *Moonshine Rendezvous* 25 By May of '40 I was on the whiskey haulin' road day and night, it seemed. I was sparkin' (going out on dates) the second I unloaded, too. **2014** *Blind Pig* (Feb) I well remember that tree—I spent many an hour there . . . [I] would sit and spark a bit beneath that old beech tree.

[EDD *spark* v 4(4) "to court, woo"; CUD *spark with* (at *spark*[1] v 1) "court, flirt with"]

sparking, spark with See **spark B**.

sparr, sparr-bird See **sparrow**.

sparrow (also *spar*, *spar-bird*, *spare*, *sparr*, *sparr-bird*). See also **-bird**.

1915 Dingus *Word-List VA* 190 *spar* . . . clipped form of *sparrow*. **1931** Combs *Lg Sthn High* 1317 *Ow* final becomes *er*, or *y*, or else is dropped entirely . . . "sparr(ow)." **1940** Stuart *Trees of Heaven* 14 They won't nest on the ground like a ground spar. **1957** Broaddus *Vocab Estill Co KY* 73 *spar-bird* = a sparrow. **1957** Combs *Lg Sthn High: Idioms* 10 The sparr-birds is as thick as fiddlers in hell this year. **1992** Brooks *Sthn Stuff* 146 *spare* = sparrow, a very small and common bird.

[DARE *sparrow* South, South Midland]

sparrow-bird See **-bird**, **sparrow**.

sparrow grass See **asparagus**.

spat *noun* See citation.

1998 Buchanan *Logging Terms* = a motorized car, like a pump car, that runs up the railway tracks. It coughs and spits, hence the name.

speak *verb* Variant past-participle form *spoke*.

1864 *Brown CW Letters* (Aug 15) [I] have not spoke as plain as i think and if i dar do it i wold speak my sentiments i am for old abe lincon for preident. **1895** *Mt Baptist Sermon* 14 Ef a man's hed peace spoke to his never-dyin' soul, he kin mighty soon tell the time 'n' the place. **1969** GSMNP-46:15 I think I have heard him spoke of, and you have too, haven't you? **1973** GSMNP-78:24 [At] some of the other steam mills or some of the other big mills, the rock would run so fast that I've heared them spoke of as burning the meal up. **2002** Rash *Foot in Eden* 83 If I was to have my way about it, there'd not be a word spoke between us.

speak howdy See **howdy B**.

speaking *noun*

1 An occasion with one or more speeches at a public venue or ceremony, as by a political candidate or public official; a public speech or debate. Also called **political speaking**.

1862 *Watters-Curtis CW Letters* (June 1) Ther was abig picknet athursday and Speaking hear ther was agrate many people there. **1899** Frost *Sthn Mts* 10 Here, after the speakin', we would be invited to "come by" with a neighbor and take a "snack." **1924** Raine *Saddlebags* 212 A "meeting" is always a religious gathering; discussion of politics, good roads, or community betterment is a "speaking." **1926** Lunsford *Folk-Lore* 13 I remember hearing him "call the house to order" at a political speaking in Buncombe where the late Governor Craig and the Honorable Virgil S. Lusk were to measure swords in a political debate. **1942** Thomas *Blue Ridge* 155 Mountain folk love oratory. Men, especially, will travel miles to a public speaking—which may be a political gathering or one for the purpose of discussing road building. **1967** Wilson *Folkways Mammoth Cave* 8 In early days every candidate would speak on a given day in a community, and his partisans would follow him from one speaking to another. **1978** Burns *Our Sthn Mtneers* 11 They will travel miles to a speakin', religious or political, and [take] unusual delight in being swayed by oratory. **1983** *Dark Corner OHP-28A* They had a campaign speaking up there, and they was a bunch from Greenville come up here.

[DARE *speaking* n 1 South, South Midland]

2 A school event with public recitations or performances by students at the end of a week or a term. See also **speaking day**.

1946 Matthias *Speech Pine Mt* 192 Thar's a-goin' to be a speakin' at the school-house. **1957** Justus *Other Side* 108 In the afternoon came the speaking. . . . There were short speeches, long speeches, sad speeches, and funny speeches. **1965** Shields *Cades Cove* 8 At the schools there were "speakin's," spelling bees, and debates, participated in by pupils and parents alike.

speaking day (also *speaking time*) *noun* Formerly, a daylong school event with public recitations or performances by students.

1943 Justus *Bluebird* 102 Let's up and surprise Miss Judy on our next speaking day with some of these funny songs—the ones you are making the tunes for. **1944** Justus *Billy and Bones* 53 I want new shoes and a new dress for speaking time on Fridays.

speaking time See **speaking day**.

spec (also *speckle trout*) *noun* The speckled or brook trout (*Salvelinus fontinalis*), native to the Smoky Mountains. Same as **brookie**.

1979 Cantu *Great Smoky Mts* 20 There are three species of trout in the park, but only one of them is native, the Southern Appalachian brook trout, called affectionately "spec" or "brookie" by local folks. **1991** Walker *Great Smoky* 39 The southern Appalachian brook trout, sometimes called the "spec" or "brookie" by mountain residents, have lived in these mountain waters for several centuries. **1996** Huheey *Variant Names* 6 *speckle trout* = brook trout.

specie *noun* A species.

1939 Hall *Coll* A panter is more of a dog specie, a lot bigger and way longer than a wild cat. **1962** Wilson *Folkways Mammoth Cave* 47 Nouns ending in an *s* or an *s* sound in the singular were often regarded as plurals . . . sometimes one of these *s* nouns developed a new singular: *species*, *specie*; *lens*, *len*.

[back-formation from *species*]

speciment *noun* A specimen.

1892 Doak *Wagonauts Abroad* 189 At last he said he'd like to show us some "speciments" he'd gathered. **1944** Wilson *Word-List* 49 *speciment*.

speck See **expect A**.

speckled dick (also *speckled dock*, *speckled jack*) *noun* An edible wild green (*Rumex* spp). See also **dock**, **narrow dock**, **yellow dock**.

1938 Still *Mole-Bane* 373 Before the garden was ready, Mother and Euly gathered a mess of plantain and speckled jack. **1979** Slone *My Heart* 70 Then there were wild greens or "salet." There are many different kinds; sometimes the same plant was known by a different name by different people. "Plantin" is the one used most, a small thick-leafed green with a very distinct flavor, a little like cabbage. Then for cooking there was "sheep's leg," "groundhog ear," and "speckled dock." **1999** Perry *Clinch River* I especially like the homey names of plants Granny taught me to recognize,

Narrow dock, speckled Dick, woolly britches. **2002** DARE File (ceKY) Right about this time of year, I start remembering going "green picking" with mommy and friends. . . . Now I can tell you the difference in "sour dock" and "speckled dick" in a heartbeat.

speckled dock See **speckled dick.**

speckled gravy A light-colored gravy made with milk and pepper and thickened with flour or cornmeal. See also **red-eye gravy.**

1984 Wilder *You All Spoken* 87 = a gravy made of grease from fried country ham—add a couple of sloshes of black coffee and boiling water and stir.

[DARE *speckled gravy* n chiefly South Midland]

speckled jack See **speckled dick.**

speckled pup(py), as cute/pretty as a *adjective phrase* Naively or superficially attractive (sometimes used for veiled disparagement).

1915 Hall *Autobiog Claib Jones* 27 There was another girl by the name of Justus, as pretty as a speckled pup, and I also took her home with me. **1940** Haun *Hawk's Done* 45 Everybody said they thought he was right pretty. Pretty as a speckled pup. **c1950** Adams *Grandpap* 186 Another girl, purty as a speckled puppy an' all dressed up in fine clothes, come to the door an' asked him what he wanted. **1963** Williams *Metaphor Mt Speech II* 51 The middle-aged mountain man is likely to be harsh in his evaluation of the youth just rising to maturity and bent on proving his manliness to admiring maidens as "purty as a speckled pup/a peach," or "fairer'n finch-birds." **1972** Hall *Coll* She's as pretty as a speckled pup under a red wagon. **1976** Garber *Mountain-ese* 72 Their new baby is purty as a speckled pup. **1994** Parton *Dolly* 61 You could not have said that I was "as cute as a speckled pup" without expecting the speckled pup to piss on your leg out of resentment.

speckle trout See **spec.**

spect See **expect A.**

speechify *verb* To deliver a speech, whether the audience wishes one or not.

1922 Cobb *KY Mt Rhymes* 25 Them fotched-on women, now, that runs the School, / And speechifies on Voting, and don't own / A man 'mongst them all. **c1960** Wilson *Coll* = to make a speech, often not wanted.

speerit See **spirit.**

spell

A *noun*

1 An indefinite, but usually short period of time or weather. [Editor's note: This term referring to a period marked by an abnormal state or experience, especially of illness, indisposition, agitation, etc., is widespread in the US.]

1891 Swearingen *Letters* 166 We have been looking for a letter from you for quite a spell and haven't received one as yet. **1913** Kephart *Our Sthn High* 296 Spell is used in the sense of while ("a good spell atterward") and soon for early ("a soon start in the morning"). **1939** Hall *Coll* (Jefferson City TN) I went to Tempico School for a spell. **1966** Hall *Coll* (Del Rio TN) Maybe sometime you could come and spend a spell with us, as I am still at the old home place. **1978** Montgomery *White Pine Coll* IV-4 You'll have a warm spell when the moon's at different stages. **1984** Wilder *You All Spoken* 65 = an indefinite period—brief, extensive, or right square in between—depending on the situation. **1988** Russell *It Happened* 36 Other expressions that I remember are . . . "Come in and set a spell."

2 A short distance.

1997 Montgomery *Coll* (known to Bush, Cardwell, Ellis, Jones, Ledford, Oliver, Weaver). **1999** Hodges *Tough Customers* 78 It's just up the road here a spell.

B *verb* See citation.

1958 Combs *Archaic English in KY* 44 = tell: "I will spell you a story."

spell down

A *verb phrase* To win a classroom spelling match; to defeat (a competitor) in such a competition. See also **set down 2.**

1939 Burnett *Gap o' Mountains* 16 Occasionally when both sides had been spelt down, leaving only one of each group and the excitement was intense; one of the contenders, becoming nervous, might spell a word correctly but overlook the pronunciation of a syllable, and lose the match. **c1960** Wilson *Coll* = to win in a spelling match, over the one above you or over the whole school. **1998** *Dante OHP*-45 She was the best speller in the [school]. She even spelled her teacher down.

B *noun* Traditionally, a schoolroom spelling match involving two teams lined up against one another, spelling match. See also **cipher down.**

1957 Justus *Other Side* 107 In the morning came the "spell down." Two sides were chosen and these stood up and spelled against each other until only one lucky pupil was left. **1973** GSMNP-74:27 Then on the same Fridays we'd have spelldowns too, you know, have the row up and get [to] spell each other down, and then sometimes we'd have a little treat that you'd get for the one that won, the one that kept staying up there the longest.

spelling school *noun* Formerly, a short term of school in which a small fee was charged to teach rudiments of spelling.

1862 *Black CW Letters* (Feb 27) we had a fine spelling school last night there was a good many from the Vannati school up.

spend one's opinion (also *spend one's view*) *verb phrase* To state or express one's view.

1924 Raine *Saddlebags* 100 He carries a *budget* on his back, and *spends* his opinions as Othello did. **1937** Hall *Coll* (Gatlinburg TN) I would rather not spend my opinion (concerning a local death thought to be a murder). **c1960** Wilson *Coll*: *spend one's opinion* = to express an opinion, especially a pronounced one. **1970** *Burton-Manning Coll*-94A We can discuss these things and spend our views on them the best we know how. **1974** Fink *Bits Mt Speech* 24 I wouldn't want to *spend an opinion* on that.

[cf Shakespeare's *Othello* II.iii.212; DARE (at *spend* B2) southern Appalachians, Ozarks]

sperit, sperret, sperrit See **spirit**.

spew up *verb phrase* Of the ground: to heave up and form ice crystals.

1913 Kephart *Our Sthn High* 86 The ground, to use a mountaineer's expression, was "all spewed up with frost." **1957** Combs *Lg Sthn High: Word List* 94 *spewed up with* = covered with, as of frost. **1994–97** Montgomery *Coll* (known to Brown, Cardwell, Ledford, Shields), = loose soil will freeze and push up icicles, a grain of dirt on the end of each one (Norris). **1999** Morgan *Gap Creek* 241 The ground was spewed up in places with ice and crumbs of dirt stood on hairs of ice on the banks of the road. **2001** Joslin *Appal Bounty* 171 Then, sometime in the night, Harriet stopped talking. The frozen ground spewed up around them. **2007** McMillon *Notes* = the hoar frost would look like icetags growing in the wrong direction.

[DARE (at *spew* v 3) chiefly South, South Midland]

spice tree See **spicewood**.

spicewood (also *spice tree*) *noun* A deciduous tree (*Lindera* spp) whose sap is used in a bracing tea.

1962 Dykeman *Tall Woman* 4 The house was filled with a sweet aroma . . . there was a pot of spicewood twigs steeping in boiling water on the back of the hearth. **1967** Jones *Peculiarities Mtneers* 68 Spicewood tea was highly regarded as a spring beverage but no curative powers were attributed to it. **1975** GSMNP-62:14 We would get sassafras bark [and] roots and peel them, and make tea out of it to drink, and the spicewood, we done the same thing, just break up the limbs in short pieces and put them in water and boil them a little and then set them in a cold spring to have cold spicewood tea. **1981** Whitener *Folk-Ways* 32 Gather spice wood when the sap first comes up, store away to dry. It makes good tea, but if you have any kind of wild meats, just break up some of the spice wood and wash clean, power boil [parboil] with your wild meat. Take out the meat, eat as is with some salt and pepper or roll in flour and meal and fry. Every one says this is the best, most delicious meat they ever ate. **1982** Slone *How We Talked* 102 Another cure [for a cold] was . . . spicewood tea. **1997** Nelson *Country Folklore* 40 To help measles, use sassafras or spice tree tea.

[DARE *spicewood* n 1 now chiefly Appalachians]

spicket *noun* An indoor outlet for running water.

1949 Kurath *Word Geog East US* 56 The word *faucet* is known by that name only in the Northern area. The entire Midland and the South have *spicket* (occasionally *spigot*).

[OED3 *spicket* n now chiefly dialect and U.S.; EDD *spicket* sb 1 "spigot, wooden tap"; DARE *spicket* n B2 widespread, but especially Appalachians, Middle and Central Atlantic, eastern OH]

spider *noun* A shallow, heavy metal frying pan with a long handle and legs so that it can be set above hot coals.

1862 *Robinson CW Letters* (June 7) the wagoners broak my Spider a coming up hear & I went 5 miles to a furnes & baught me a littel oven to bake in. **1905** Miles *Spirit of Mts* 22 White sand is sometimes strewed on the kitchen floor and renewed from day to day; the iron cooking-pots and spiders are thoroughly burned to free them of rust and grease. **1957** Chiles and Trotter *Mt Makin's* 25 = an iron skillet on legs. **1958** Wood *Words from TN* 16 = not the same [as a skillet] as it has no sides or practically none. **1968** *DARE Survey* (Brasstown NC) = shallow heavy metal pan used to fry foods. **1982** Powers and Hannah *Cataloochee* 347 A spider is a long handled type of oven with legs. It can be covered or used open top. **1997** Montgomery *Coll* = small frying pan (Norris). **2007** McMillon *Notes* = an iron skillet with legs.

[DARE *spider* n 1 chiefly North, also Mid and South Atlantic]

spignet *noun* Spikenard, a perennial wild plant (*Aralia racemosa*) with a single long stalk, greenish-yellow flowers, and various medicinal uses. Also called **Indian root**.

1894 Bergen *Plant Names III* 90 (Banner Elk NC). **1917** Kephart *Word-List* 417 = wild spikenard. **1925** Dargan *Highland Annals* 46 There's shumake for a swelled throat, an' boneset for the ager, an' pokeweed for rheumatiz, an' spignet for consumption, an' a lot more I'll show you if you go home with me some time. **1937** Eaton *Handicrafts* 146 Another collector of herbs has a formula for carrying their benefit beyond the physical realm; "spignet," she is reported as saying, "is good for the back and balm fortifies the morals." **1937** Thornburgh *Great Smoky Mts* 29 Spignot [sic] was used as a remedy for felons. **1967** Hall *Coll* (Townsend TN) My mother used spignet a few times. She used spignet medicine for kidney trouble. [**1971** Krochmal et al. *Medicinal Plants Appal* 56 Roots and thizomes have been used to treat rheumatism, syphilis, coughs, and shortness of breath. In Appalachia, a tea made of roots is used for backache.] **1973** *Foxfire Interviews* A-73-43 I bet every one of you'uns here dig spignet [in] place of ginseng. [If you] see a big bunch of spignet, [you] say there's a bunch of ginseng and jump on it. **1982** Powers and Hannah *Cataloochee* 257 Spignet, like Indian turnips, said Mark, was good for the back.

[DARE *spignet* n scattered, but especially southern Appalachians]

spike *noun* An arrow; arrowhead.

1980 Still *Run for Elbertas* 88 "Did I have my bow and spike," Ard breathed, "they make the finest bull's-eye ever was." **1985** Irwin *Alex Stewart* 114 He got all right, but if it hadn't been for his clothes, that spike would have went two-thirds of the way through him. **2002** McGowan *Beech Mt Tales* 108 He give him a dodge like a rabbit and got him tangled with his britches under some thick laurel, the spikes in his britches, and him there a-pulling and hung up.

[DARE *spike* n 7 "arrow or arrowhead" chiefly South Midland]

spike pole See **pike pole**.

spike team *noun* A team of three oxen, two abreast and one in front.

1968 Stubbs *Mountain-Wise* (Aug–Sept) 12 "At times there'd be a 'spike team' used" . . . We interrupted him and asked what he meant by "spike team" . . . "Waal, hit wuz one drawn by three oxen," he replied. "One wuz up front and two wuz yoked behind clost to the waggin."

spile, spilt See **spoil**.

spilth *noun* That which is spilled.

1924 Raine *Saddlebags* 103 As wealth is the collective noun made from weal, and stealth the thing one steals, and spilth what one spills, so filth in the mountains means the leaves and driftwood that fill up, and blowth is the mass of blossoms that blow. **1960** Westover *Highland Lg* 21 = what one spills.

spin *verb* Variant past-tense form *spinned*.

1971 *AOHP/ALC-33* Yeah, we spinned our wheel.

spindle *verb* To weaken.

1979 Slone *My Heart* 17 They just spindled and died soon as they come up.

[OED3 *spindle* v 2b "to become spindly or weak"]

spindle bush *noun* A large bush (*Euonymous europaea*) with bright, showy flowers; it is sometimes confused with the **strawberry bush** (*Euonymus americanus*).

1937 Thornburgh *Great Smoky Mts* 25 One of the showiest shrubs in the Great Smokies [is] the evonymous [sic], wahoo or spindlebush. **1964** Campbell *Great Smoky Wildflowers* 78 Hearts-a-bustin' . . . Common names include strawberry bush, swamp dogwood, spindle bush [etc.].

spindling *adjective* Of a person: slender, thin; hence weakly developed, lacking vitality.

1941 Still *Troublesome Creek* 103 That spindling Branders stranger couldn't make a hum-bird a living. **1943** Hannum *Mt People* 147 She's a peart little thing, got plenty of sense, but the least spindlingest little old thing. **1997** Montgomery *Coll*: *spindling* (known to Adams, Bush, Cardwell, Jones, Ledford, Norris, Oliver).

spipin *noun* See citation.

1978 Reese *Speech NE Tenn* 43 = a small amount.

spire grass See **asparagus**.

spirit *noun* Variant forms *speerit, sperit, sperret, sperrit*.

1825 (in **1956** Eliason *Tarheel Talk* 318) (Stokes Co NC) *sperrit*. **1861** Neves *CW Letters* (July 6) Some of the Companey is Complaining but thay ar all in fine Sperits. **1863** Click *CW Letters* (Aug 11) your letter fond me injoying good helth and in fine sperits. **1867** Harris *Sut Lovingood* 58 Eny man who wud waste a quart ove even mean sperrits, fur the chance ove knockin a poor ornary devil like me down wif the bottil, is a bigger fool nor ole Squire Mackmullen. **1891** Primer *Studies in WV* 165 (Sperit) for spirit. **1898** Elliott *Durket Sperret* 50 All the Durkets hes sperret, an' Si ain't none o' your soft-walkin'—still-tongued folks like the Warrens. **1952** Wilson *Folk Speech NC* 593. **1955** Ritchie *Singing Family* 82 One more thing the Sperrit has give unto me to say unto you and then I'm shore a-goin to quit. **1959** Cooper *Corpse Could Sleep* My old man jist shut his eye peaceful-like and passed out as his speerit leapt beyant the furder bank of Jordan.

[DARE *spirit* n chiefly South, South Midland]

spit *noun* Exact likeness.

1886 Smith *Sthn Dialect* 350 = image, counterpart. **1919** Combs *Word-List South* 35 = exact likeness, replica. "That chap's the very spit of his daddy." **1927** Woofter *Dialect from WV* 365 = likeness.

spitting company *noun* See citation.

1991 Thomas *Sthn Appal* 105 In some of the nice-lookin' homes, maybe I couldn't sleep. They'd have what we called "spittin'-company" in th' bed—bed bugs.

splash board *noun* A plank forming the top of a **splash dam** to hold back water.

1973 *GSMNP-70:2:5* These men down here was on that big dam with a big crowbar, raising them splash boards like that, you know, over a prize log.

splash dam *noun* Formerly, a dam, as of upright boards or logs or of earth, built across a stream between high banks, backing up water and forming a reservoir below into which logs were dragged and massed before the dam was opened, releasing a head of water and propelling the logs downstream, producing a **splash flood**. See also **trigger A**.

1896 *NC State Board of Resources* 53 (DARE) Splash dams will be built on the creeks in Pisgah Forest, and the logs will be splashed into the French Broad river and carried on down to the mill. **1924** Raine *Saddlebags* 24 A creek is usually too shallow to float logs down to the river where they can be assembled into rafts. At some suitable place, between high banks, a splash dam is built. **1953** Hall *Coll* (Bryson City NC) Years later they built what they called splash dams and made splash floods to run these logs out that way and run 'em into the river, and then the natural tides took them down the river, and they'd raft 'em up down the river and pull 'em down into Chattanooga with a little old tugboat, down the Tennessee River. **1961** Lambert *Logging in Smokies* 352–53 In some areas on the upper tributaries temporary or "splash" dams were constructed to gather a supply of logs. When the splash boards were released, or dynamited, the impounded water bore the logs down to the main stream or to another dam. **1977** *Jake Waldroop* 146 They built a big splash dam out there. The way they built them back in them days mostly, why, they built 'em with logs an' rock . . . they'd build them big pens an' fill 'em with rock and sand an' dirt. They'd build them where they hold that water up. Then they had a gate, a splash gate to 'em, at the apron o' that dam where they could raise it or lower it. When they'd lower that, y'know, why, that shut the water off an' that dam would fill up. Well, you got a big batch o' water in the river why they'd let the splash dam off n' hit 'ud come on down an' pick 'em up an' carry 'em on down through Nantahala Gorge an' on in there at Nantahala station. **1982** Eller *Miners* 90 = an earthen dam built across a stream below the area being logged. A large gate made of straight poles was constructed in the middle of the dam, and after the logs were dumped into the creek below, the poles were pulled out, allowing the water to carry the logs out into the main waterway. **1984** Gray *Hazel Creek* 24 Before the serious cutting started, small amounts of high grade poplar and ash were removed and floated down to the Little Tennessee River by the use of splash dams. This method was used on Hazel Creek before 1900. A dam was constructed on a creek out of large hemlock logs, and the creek bed would be cleared of protruding rocks and trees. Ox teams would then skid logs to the growing reservoir, where loggers would wait for sufficient rains to break the dams. When the waters were released, the logs would be floated down the Little Tennessee to Chilhowee, where they were then towed to Chattanooga. Two such dams were built, one on Bone Valley Creek and the other on Hazel Creek just south of Walker Creek. Splash dams were probably the most destructive logging technique ever devised, and Hazel Creek still bears the scars on its banks.

splash flood *noun* A sudden, highly destructive release of water and logs impounded behind a **splash dam**.

1953 Hall *Coll* (Bryson City NC) Years later they built what they called splash dams and made splash floods to run these logs out that way and run 'em into the river, and then the natural tides took them down the river, and they'd raft 'em up down the river and pull 'em down into Chattanooga with a little old tugboat, down the Tennessee River.

splash out *verb phrase* To send (unguided logs) crashing downstream by releasing a head of water confined by a **splash dam**.

1924 Raine *Saddlebags* 24 As I travelled up one creek, a man told me he had "splashed out" thirteen thousand logs that season.

splatter bread *noun* See citation.

1997 Montgomery *Coll* (known to Bush, Cardwell), = bread dough mixed so thin that it splatters in a hot greased pan, baked the size of the pan (Brown).

splatterment *noun* A splatter, mess; commotion.

c1940 Simms *Coll* Ef [the sink] didn't have that drain pipe hit shore would create a awful splatterment under yer house. **1976** Thompson *Touching Home* 16 = a mess or fight, a quick emotional speech. **1992** Jones and Miller *Sthn Mt Speech* 109 = noisy dissension or mess. **1996–97** Montgomery *Coll* = a mess (Brown); = both meanings (Cardwell, Norris, Oliver).

splice *verb* To marry.

1900 Harben *N GA Sketches* 44 I soon got the papers in shape, an' Squire Ridley spliced 'em right on the sidewalk in front o' his office. **1923** Greer-Petrie *Angeline Doin' Society* 6 Our shack has been headquarters for good fun ever since we got spliced and settled down at Merry Oaks. **1988** Russell *It Happened* 47 Other expressions for it were "getting hitched," or "spliced," or "tying the knot."

splinder *noun* See citation.

1957 Combs *Lg Sthn High: Word List* 94 *splinders* = splinters. [OED3 *splinder* (at *splinter* n) chiefly Scottish; SND *splinder* n 1]

split

A *verb* See citation. See also **split brandy**.

1985 Dabney *More Mt Spirits* 51 Most "pure brandy" bought in the hills since the turn of the century has been "split"—that is, split between the fruit mash and grain mash. With a bit of sugar, honey or molasses thrown in to help it "work."

B *noun*

1 A type of **mark** cut into the edge of a domestic animal's ear to identify its owner. See also **overbit**, **smooth crop**, **swallowfork**, **underbit**.

1975 *Foxfire III* You'd know your hog by your mark. . . . Me and my daddy had the same mark—crop and split in the left ear, and a split in the right.

2 A ribbon of wood stripped from a white oak or hickory log and then interwoven with others to form an object (as a **split basket**, chair bottom, or **split broom**) or to reinforce an object (as a **split bonnet**). See also **white oak splint**.

1926 Thomas *Hills and Mts of KY* 155 Chairs were and are made by means of a shaving or drawing knife and small auger, bottomed with hickory bark or white oak splits. **1927** Mason *Lure of Smokies* 122–23 The heavy hickory split broom [was] made from [a] single piece of wood. The author has seen these made in the mountains and marvels at the patient craftsmanship required to split a great white log into thin ribbons, which were tied around the middle allowing them to spread much like a worn "toothbrush" of the mountain woman. White oak and hickory "splits" also made very excellent baskets and bottoms for chairs. **1937** Eaton *Handicrafts* 37 It has been interesting to trace the shaving horse, used by the mountain basket and chairmakers of North Carolina, Tennessee, Kentucky, and West Virginia to cut out their splints, or "splits," as they are commonly called in the Southern Highlands, and rungs, back to Shropshire County, England, where in its original form it is still used, or was until recently, to make "spelks" and "trugs" for local baskets. **1974** *Instrument Makers* 187 Many of the old banjos Mr. Worley remembered seeing had hoops made out of single strips of hickory. The hickory splits were either put in a form green and left thirty days to dry and cure, or the cured wood was steamed and then bent into shape. **1985** Irwin *Alex Stewart* 99 To make a nice basket you want to get your splits thin—as thin, might near it, as paper. If you work it when it's green, you can take and tie it in a knot it's so soft and strong. The width of your splits depends on the size of your basket. If you're making a small basket you need to have narrow splits; but if you're making a big basket you can use wider splits. **2006** *WV Encycl* 46 Split baskets have no such frame, but are constructed almost entirely from thin flat splits and include round, square, and rectangular shapes.

[cf SND *split* n 2 "a small piece of split reed or cane"]

split a frog hair down the middle *verb phrase* To cut apart a very fine object.

2005 Williams *Gratitude* 46 I can still sharp'm one [= a knife] so fine you could split a frawg (frog) hair down the middle with it.

split basket *noun* A basket made from **splits** (see **split 2**).

1949 Arnow *Hunter's Horn* 330 Milly came with Bill Dan on her hip and a half-bushel split basket swinging heavy on her free arm. **1961** Miller *Pigeon's Roost* (April 27) The old-timey kind, handmade split baskets, commonly made of white oak wood, is still used here in the hill country to carry eggs in to the country stores. **1973** GSMNP-48:1 That's the way we used to make our income in the wintertime would be by the split baskets. **1995** Williams *Smoky Mts Folklife* 83 While the rib basket was the most distinctive of the Appalachian baskets, the simpler split basket was more widespread. **2006** *WV Encycl* 46 Split baskets have no such frame, but are constructed almost entirely from thin flat splits and include round, square, and rectangular shapes.

[DARE *split basket* n especially South, South Midland]

split bonnet *noun* A woman's old-fashioned bonnet, especially one with a wide brim frame of slats, strips, or **splits** for protection against sunburn in the field; small slats of wood or cardboard are inserted into a wide brim to shade the face, and a capelike flap in back shades the neck. Also called **slat bonnet**.

1937 Hyatt *Kiverlid* She took the split bonnet from the toil-browned hands and hung it on the top shutter of the half-door. **1956** McAtee *Some Dial NC* 42 = a sun-bonnet, the hood of which was stiffened with thin slips of wood (splits); later, cardboard strips were substituted; and finally quilting or starch alone was used for stiffening. **c1960** Wilson *Coll* = a sunbonnet with pasteboard "splits" to make it stand out. **1967** *DARE Survey* (Maryville TN) = cloth bonnet worn by women for protection from the sun (used only at Hillbilly Homecoming).

[DARE *split bonnet* n chiefly South Midland, TX]

split brandy *noun* An alcoholic beverage made from apple **pomace** to which sugar is added to hasten fermentation. See also **split A**.

1985 Dabney *More Mt Spirits* 62 We made "split brandy" right along, with corn whiskey. Here's how we made it: Wash your fruit and put it in a 50-gallon barrel. Lots of people churn it up and down with a straightened out hoe. Let it set for 72 hours or so, souring. Then add about 20 pounds of sugar.

split broom *noun* A broom with a head of finely sliced strands of hickory or white oak.

1848 (in **1870** Drake *Pioneer Life KY* 94) We had always used a "split" broom, in the manufacture of which I have spent many a rainy day & winter night. A raw hickory sapling was the raw material. The "splits" were stripped up with a jack-knife and the right thumb, for 8 or 10 inches, bent back & held down with the right hand. When the "heart" was reached and the wood became too brittle to strip, it was split or sawed off, & the "splits" turned forward, and tied with a tow string made for the purpose on the spot. **1927** Mason *Lure of Smokies* 122–23 The heavy hickory split broom [was] made from [a] single piece of wood. The author has seen these made in the mountains and marvels at the patient craftsmanship required to split a great white log into thin ribbons, which were tied around the middle allowing them to spread much like a worn "toothbrush" of the mountain woman. **1927** Woofter *Dialect from WV* 365 = a broom made from shaving down a pole and wrapping the shavings. "I wish you would make me a new split broom the next rainy day."

split-log bench *noun phrase* A log split in half to serve as a crude bench, as in a schoolroom. See also **puncheon**.

1939 Hall *Coll* (Deep Creek NC) All the schooling we got in them days was in a little old log cabin, with a split-log bench, just a tree split open and legs bored in it. **1981** Whitener *Folk-Ways* 12 One teacher taught seven or eight grades and we all sat on split-log benches.

split the blanket (also *split the quilt*) *verb phrase* Of a married couple: to divorce, separate.

1944 Wilson *Word-List* 40 *split the blanket* = to separate, get a divorce. **1976** Dwyer *Southern Sayin's* 13 *split the quilt* = to separate, divorce. **1996–97** Montgomery *Coll*: *split the blanket* (known to Brown, Cardwell, Jones, Oliver).

[DARE *split the blanket(s)* v phr South, South Midland, West]

split the middles *verb phrase* See citation.

c1960 Wilson *Coll* = to plow out the space that has been left between rows of corn that has been laid by.

[DARE (at *split* v 1) especially South, South Midland]

splo *noun* Homemade whiskey, usually of a low grade.

1959 Forest *Jessie's* 14 Liquor (both the moonshine "splo" and bootlegged factory products) was more plentiful in Knoxville than in Chattanooga or Nashville, where it was legal. **1974** Maurer and Pearl *KY Moonshine* 125 = cheap low-grade whiskey. **1981** Morrell *Mirth* 29 No narrative of the Great Smokies would be complete without at least one story about "Moonshine" whiskey, also known as "Splo." **1986** Pederson et al. *LAGS* = attested by 6/60 interviewees (10%) from E TN; 6/10 of all LAGS interviewees (60%) attesting term were from Appalachia. **1994** Montgomery *File* (known to 82-year-old man, Gatlinburg TN).

[probably shortening of *explode*, from the drink's effect; DARE *splo* n South, South Midland, especially KY, TN]

splotchedy *adjective* Having splotches.

2017 *Blind Pig* (Feb 16) = how most people paint.

splunge

A *verb* To plunge (something) into water; to become immersed.

1923 (in **1952** Mathes *Tall Tales* 18) I seed that angel splunge right into the tide an' swim like no man on earth ever swum afore, till he throwed my baby squar' into her daddy's arms. **1937** Hall Coll (Ravensford NC) I never saw the like of soldiers in my life. Every man had two hosses. Hit tuck from ten in the morning till late in the evenin' for 'em all to get through. They hit that river a-splungin'. **c1945** Haun *Hawk's Done* 223 She would fill the kittel to the crack with muddy water and splunge chips and leaves down deep into it with her. **1975** Chalmers *Better* 65–66 He drug the ground and ruke the leaves, while his woman-person shuk the rug and rinsed the clothes by splunging them in the creek.

B *noun* A plunge.

1941 Hall Coll (Del Rio TN) Let's take a splunge from the divin' board.

[OED3 *splunge* v dialect and U.S.; cf SND *splunge* v "to splash about with the hands and feet in water"; DARE *splunge* v, n South, South Midland, especially southern Appalachians]

splut *noun* A fit, hurry.

1940 Haun *Hawk's Done* 187 I noticed how big a splut he was in every night to get ready. But I didn't think about who he was in such a hurry to see. **c1945** Haun *Hawk's Done* 247 That evening Cora said she had the quarest feeling when he left the house because he just looked like he was in such a splut to get away.

splutteration *noun* Motion full of starts and stops.

1859 Taliaferro *Fisher's River* 57 He kep' sich a movin' about and sich a splutteration that I couldn't git a bead at his head. **1998** Montgomery Coll (known to Adams, Brown).

[*splutter* "a hurry, bustle" + *-ation*]

splutterations *interjection* Used as an expression of disgust resulting from confusion, aggravation, etc.

1998 Montgomery Coll (known to Cardwell).

splutterment (also *spluttermint*) *noun* A commotion, disturbance.

1961 Williams *Content Mt Speech* 15 They's the biggest spluttermint in that house ever I hearn tell of, I reckon. **1996** Montgomery Coll (known to Adams, Brown, Cardwell, Jones, Norris, Oliver). **2007** Shelby *Molly Whuppie* 11 [If] any little disagreement comes up, they get in a splutterment over it.

[*splutter* "a hurry, bustle" + *-ment*]

spoil

A *verb*

1 Variant base form *spile*.

1860 *Week in Smokies* 125 Old man, why do you spile that story in that way? **1863** *Watkins CW Letters* (Oct 18) I want you to take good cear of my mare and don't spile heare. **1913** Kephart *Our Sthn High* 80 Fellers, you can talk as you please about a streak o' the cur spilin' the dog. **1959** Roberts *Up Cutshin* 26 We had to have a certain way to put [our corn] up to keep it from sp'iling. **1989** Landry *Smoky Mt Interviews* 191 If they ain't another day comin', they ain't no need a-spilin' this one. All you got is right now, and don't spile this day. **2007** Preece *Leavin' Sandlick* 10 Wouldn't want them to spile now would we?

[DARE *spoil* v A1 (pronc) chiefly South, South Midland; formerly also New England]

2 Variant past-tense forms *spiled*, *spilt*.

1867 Harris *Sut Lovingood* 265 The ole cuss wer pow'fly 'stonish'd hissef, and glad all over too, fur hit spilt Wat's title tu choke him tu deth. **1934–47** *LAMSAS Appal* = attested by 80/148 speakers (54.0%) from WV, 13/20 (65%) from VA, 28/37 (78.7%) from NC, 3/14 (21.4%) from SC, and 4/12 (33.3%) from GA. **1978** Reese *Speech NE Tenn* 180 = attested by 7/12 (58.3%) speakers. **2000** Montgomery Coll (known to Cardwell).

3 Variant past-participle form *spiled*.

1900 Harben *N GA Sketches* 17 The Whitneys has spiled 'im bad. **c1945** Haun *Hawk's Done* 310 Jamie I miss—the fiesty anticky little booger, spiled as a rotten apple.

B *noun* See citation.

2007 Kerns *Mountaintop Removal* 7 Any waste or debris (terms "spoil" or "overburden") is pushed into the valley below, which poisons or completely destroys the nearby streams with the arsenic, copper, cadmium, and other toxic metals that heretofore had been safely ensconced in the geographical timeline of the mountain itself, like rings in a tree.

spoke See **speak**.

spout pipe *noun* A vertical pipe on the side of a house to conduct water from the roof to the ground.

c1960 Wilson Coll = the pipe that takes water from the eaves to the ground, a downspout.

sprag

A *noun* See citations.

1979 *Big South Fork OHP-19* He's setting out there with a sprag in his hand. It's a wooden piece about that long. We spragged the cars. **2006** Mooney *Lg Coal Mining* 1029 After kneeling or lying on his side and "undercutting" the seam (which had to be further supported with short timbers or "sprags"), the [coal] miner drilled blasting holes with a "breast auger," used a "tamping rod" to pack his black powder, inserted a "clay dummy" for proper repercussion of the explosion, lit the fuse, and yelled "Fire in the hole!" or perhaps "Shootin' coal!" to warn other miners of the impending blast.

B *verb* See citations.

[See **1979** in **A**.] **1984** Woods *WV Was Good* 223 As with wheels, sprag meant to roughlock—that is, by thrusting a pole or spike between the spokes and securing it against wagon standards or otherwise . . . as applied to sleds, *sprag* meant breaking the speed of the sled, by means of stick brakes fastened to the sled runners.

sprangle (also *sprangle out*) *verb*, *verb phrase* Especially of a tree: to spread or branch out in different directions; hence adjectives *sprangled out*, *sprangling*, *springly* = spread out. See also **sprangly**.

1917 Kephart *Word-List* 417 *sprangle* = to spread out tortuously. "Little branches all *sprangle* out from Eagle Creek." **1929** Kephart *Smoky Mt Magic* 172 Laurel is of such sprangling growth that the dead tops mosly stand free from the ground, so they season snap-dry. **1936** Morehouse *Rain on Just* 239 [They] let their home place go clear to ground with fire . . . Only a chimney, mantel rock, and some springly cherry trees last time I was by. **1940** Hall Coll (White Oak NC) The tree limbs are sprangled out. **1974** Fink *Bits Mt Speech* 24 *sprangling* = spread out, like limbs of a tree. "Laurel is a *sprangling* sort of bush." **1984** Woods *WV Was Good* 223 *sprangle* = to branch out near the ground, as a bush or a large plant like the potato vine. It appears to have no relation to spangle. **2000** Miller *Looneyville* 72 *sprangle* = to branch out near the ground, as a bush or a large plant like the potato, but [the term] appeared to have no relation to any particular plant when folks used it on the head of the Pokey River . . . "My roses are all sprangled and not putting on any upper shoots for the bloom." **2001** Lowry *Expressions* 1 [I have a] spranglin' pain in my shoulders.

[OED3 *sprangle* v¹ 2 now dialect and U.S.; cf SND *springly* adj "twiggy, having many small shoots or branches"]

sprangled out, sprangling See **sprangle.**

sprangly *adjective* Of branches: spread out in different directions, sprawling. See also **sprangle.**

1917 Kephart *Word-List* 417 *Sprangly* bushes, like laurel. **1927** Woofter *Dialect from WV* 365 = spread out in all directions. "Look how sprangly those rose bushes are." **1937** Thornburgh *Great Smoky Mts* 32 Hit's tall, grows as high as my head, sort o' sprangly, with big spiked leaves. **1939** Hall Coll (Alexander NC) = said of a tree with a big bushy top. **1957** Combs *Lg Sthn High: Word List* 94 = spread[ing] thickly in all directions, as of the branches of shrubs and trees.

[OED3 *sprangly* adj "spreading, sprawling" U.S.]

spread *verb*

A Forms.

1 Variant past-tense form *spreaded*.

1977 McGreevy *Breathitt KY Grammar* 93 = attested by 1 speaker.

2 Variant past-participle form *spreaded*.

1984 Smith *Oral History* 25 Big old trees [were] all spreaded out, which lets the sun shine through.

B Senses.

1 (also *spread out, spread up*) To arrange the coverings on (a bad), make (a bed).

1951 Giles *Harbin's Ridge* 43 It troubled me a heap the way the woman had spread up her bed. Careless like. **1984** Wilder *You All Spoken* 28 = to arrange; make, as in "Spread the bed." **2015** *Blind Pig* (July 8) Mom spread the table and also spread the bed out.

[DARE *spread* v B1 chiefly South, South Midland]

2 To set (a table).

2013 *Blind Pig* (Sept 21) When she would call us in, we would "spread" the table.

[DARE *spread* v B2 especially South, South Midland]

spread adder (also *spreadhead, spreadheader, spreading adder*) *noun* A hognose snake (*Heterodon platirhinos*). Same as **blowing viper.**

1939 Hall *Notebooks* 13:13 (White Oak NC) *spreadhead, spreading adder* = common adder. **1940** Hall Coll (White Oak NC) *spread head* = a plain old adder. **1991** Conant and Collins *Field Guide* 177 As a result of their behavior, these harmless snakes have earned such dangerous sounding names as "hissing adder," "blow viper," "spreading adder," "hissing sand snake," and "puff adder." **2000** Montgomery Coll: *spread adder, spread head, spread header, spreading adder* (known to Cardwell).

[DARE *spreadhead* n chiefly South Midland, *spreading adder* n chiefly South, TX, Lower Mississippi Valley]

spreaded See **spread A2.**

spreader *noun* See citation.

1957 Broaddus *Vocab Estill Co KY* 74 = a doubletree.

spreadhead, spreadheader, spreading adder See **spread adder.**

spread out, spread up See **spread B.**

sprig *noun* A flame, fragment (especially of fire).

1937 Hall Coll (Cades Cove TN) Dad gone it, there weren't a sprig of fire in his place. The fire were done out. **1960** Allen *Land of Sky* 42 If it is in winter, he will be invited to share "a sprig o' fire." **1963** Edwards *Gravel* 18 A twist for a sprig of your sweet. **1974** Fink *Bits Mt Speech* 24 A tiny *sprig* of fire. **2002** Rash *Foot in Eden* 157 What sprigs of hair he had was blonde as corn silk.

[DARE *sprig* n 2 especially southern Appalachians]

spring

A *verb* Variant past-tense form *sprung*.

1813 (in **2007** Dunkerly *Kings Mt* 105) When Colonel Campbell came to the rising ground of the mountain he sprung off his horse and said dismount and tie your horses. **1831** (in **2004** *TN Petitions III* 34) The other prisoners having kept their seats in the back part of the dungeon with their hand cuffs off which your petitioner had not even suspected, sprung to the grate shutter and violently pulled it open swearing that he would be out or die in the attempt. **1913** Kephart *Our Sthn High* 283–84 In mountain vernacular the Old English strong past tense still lives in begun, drunk, holped, rung, shrunk, sprung, stunk, sung, sunk, swum. **1939** Hall Coll (Hartford TN) When I started my horse, [the animal] sprung right up, and I heared it hit the ground two or three times, and it run out of hearing, and if it wasn't one of them [panthers], I don't know what it could have been. **1965** Ferrell *Bear Tales* 14 Jest last fall Drucie Bartow was up thar huntin' with her husbin', an' a painter sprung right at her. **1975** *AOHP/ALC*-1128A The mines were opened up, and the mining camps sprung up. People did get to where they accepted the outsiders. **1978** Reese *Speech NE Tenn* 180 = attested by 7/12 (58.3%) speakers. **1989** Still *Rusties and Riddles* [10] They sprung riddles and pulled rusties. **2004** Larimore *Bryson Seasons* 125 This big ole bobcat sprung over a rock with his fangs and claws ready to grab him a big ole gobbler.

B *verb*

1 Especially of a cow: to show signs of calving. See also **springer.**

1982 Powers and Hannah *Cataloochee* 280 Aunt Polly raised cain with her menfolk for carrying her "springing" milk cow along with the others to the mountains. As a result, at the time of her calving, without attention, she died. **1988** Russell *It Happened* 37 One of my little brothers who helped around the barnyard said to the man teacher: "Charlie, you look like you're springing." **2002** Myers *Best Yet Stories* 193–94 When it became obvious that one of our cows was expecting a calf, my family would comment that "the cow is springing."

2 To sprain.

c1960 Wilson *Coll* = to sprain: "He sprung his ankle." **1969** Hannum *Look Back* 101 Young Jim Archer up the branch has fell out of a wagon bed and sprung his back. **2000** Lowry *Folk Medical Term* I sprung my ankle.

[DARE *spring* v B1 especially South, South Midland]

C *noun* A creek. See also **spring branch**.

1986 Pederson et al. *LAGS* (Cocke Co TN, Sevier Co TN).

spring box *noun* A small compartment set in running spring water for keeping milk and other perishable foods cool and fresh. Also called **box 3**, **milk box**. See also **dairy**, **springhouse**, **spring lot**, **spring run**.

1987 Young *Lost Cove* 27 The springbox kept the milk and butter so cold that it would make the teeth ache. [**1989** *Matewan OHP*-102 They was always a spring on ever farm, and [my father] built a little box and put it down in this spring ditch and fixed it so that the water . . . was higher up at the upper side and the water would run through that . . . and we'd set our milk in there and the water run continually all that time and it kept the milk cold.] [**1997** Ownby *Big Greenbrier* I:23 Someone had made a box and placed it in the spring branch. We kept our milk and butter in it to keep it cool.] **1998** *Dante OHP*-61 That there spring box would stay full all the time.

spring branch *noun* A small stream fed by one or more springs. See also **branch**, **head A2**, **spring C**.

1766 (in **1940** McJimsey *Topo Terms in VA* 396) Thence down the said spring branch to Russell's mill. **1867** Harris *Sut Lovingood* 201 He . . . sot intu flingin the bes' kine ove show actor summersets amung the roun rocks in the spring branch. **1873** Harney *Strange Land* 429 A spring branch oozes out of the rocky turf, and flows down to meet a shallow river fretting over shoals. **1913** Kephart *Our Sthn High* 233 I lay thar an' think o' the spring branch runnin over the root o' that thar poplar; an' I say, could I git me one drink o' that water I'd be content to lay me down and die. **1939** Wilburn *Notes* (Waynesville NC) = head stream. **1986** Pederson et al. *LAGS* = attested by 7/60 interviewees (11.7%) from E TN and 2/35 (5.7%) from N GA; 9/35 of all LAGS interviewees (25.7%) attesting term were from Appalachia. **1994** Montgomery *Coll* = a small branch originating at a spring (Shields).

[DARE *spring branch* n chiefly South, South Midland]

spring cheeper (also *spring peeper*) *noun* See citations. Same as **peeper**.

1967 *DARE Survey* (Maryville TN) *spring cheeper* = small frog that sings or chirps loudly in spring. **1998** Montgomery *Coll*: *spring peeper* (known to Brown, Bush, Cardwell, Jones, Ledford, Weaver). **2004** Dodd *Amphibians Smoky Mts* 229 Adult Spring Peepers are light tan to dark brown with a distinctive dark-colored X on the back. *Ibid.* 231 The familiar high-pitched "peep-peep" calls of this species are heard most frequently from late winter (e.g., 11 February 1998) through July, although singular calls are heard virtually throughout the year if cool, rainy conditions prevail. On cold, rainy spring nights, choruses of Spring Peepers occur in great numbers throughout Cades Cove. *Ibid.* 232 The Spring Peeper is familiar to millions of people in eastern North America as a harbinger of spring. Like many frogs, it has different types of calls depending on the situation, including mating calls (to attract females) and aggressive calls (to warn away rival males).

spring ditch *noun* A trough through which water from a spring flows and into which a **spring box** is built.

1989 *Matewan OHP*-102 They was always a spring on ever farm, and [my father] built a little box and put it down in this spring ditch and fixed it so that the water . . . was higher up at the upper side and the water would run through that . . . and we'd set our milk in there and the water run continually all that time and it kept the milk cold.

springer *noun* A cow that shows signs of calving. See also **spring B1**.

c1960 Wilson *Coll* = a cow that shows signs of being pregnant. **1976** Garber *Mountain-ese* 87 = pregnant cow. "We have three springers due in the spring." **1996** Montgomery *Coll* (known to Adams, Brown, Cardwell, Jones, Oliver).

spring fresh *noun* Waters from a sudden spring shower, resulting in a sudden rise in streams and rivers and sometimes a flood. See also **fresh B**, **freshet**, **tide A**.

c1960 Wilson *Coll* = a heavy spring rain. **1996–97** Montgomery *Coll* (known to Bush, Hooper, Oliver). **2007** McMillon *Notes* = a downpour big enough to make it flood.

springhouse *noun* A small room or outbuilding of log or stone construction above the waters of a spring, with a box or trough set in the water to keep milk, butter, and other perishable foods cool and fresh. Same as **dairy**. See also **spring box**, **spring lot**, **spring run**.

1961 Medford *History Haywood Co* 16 The spring-house with its milk trough, ash or lye-hopper and rendering kettle, "battling block," etc. also must be provided. **1966–67** *DARE Survey* (Spruce Pine NC, Gatlinburg TN) = a separate building where milk is kept cool. **1977** Hamilton *Mt Memories* 6 A small "spring house" would be erected beside the spring. The water from the spring ran through a sort of wooden trough in the house where the milk and butter were kept cool and fresh. **1977** Madden and Jones *Mt Home* 27 Pickled beans and kraut were kept in large stone crocks in the springhouse. **1986** Pederson et al. *LAGS* = attested by 21/60 interviewees (35%) from E TN; 21/67 of all LAGS interviewees (31%) attesting term were from E TN. **1987** Carver *Regional Dialects* 176 Spring houses were probably invented by the resourceful yeomen of the Blue Ridge mountains and valleys of western Virginia early in the eighteenth century. By building a small house over a spring or brook, perishable foods could be kept cool and safe from spoilage. **1989** Smith *Flyin' Bullets* 55 Milk and butter were kept in the spring-house, which was built over the branch of water that flowed by the house. Planks were laid over the branch with spaces to set the food between. Eggs and other items could be placed on the planks to keep them cool. **1991** *Smokies Guide* (Summer) 13 Another early use of water was in the spring house. The finding of a cold, clear, spring with a steady flow of water often determined the site of a home. A spring house was built over the spring to protect it from contamination by animals and to serve as a crude refrigerator. The cold spring water (around 40–45 degrees F.) and evaporation helped mountaineers preserve their vegetables, milk, and butter during the hot summer months. It was also a great place for hard working people to take a break from the sun and heat. **1999** Morgan *Gap Creek* 64 I took the water bucket to fill and rushed out to the springhouse. It was a low log building over the branch. The floor was water, except for a row of stepping stones from the door. And in the water set jars of milk and pitchers of cream, butter inside tin pails.

[DARE *springhouse* n formerly widespread, now chiefly Midland, South, especially Appalachians]

springling See **sprangle**.

spring lizard *noun* Any small salamander.

1892 Smith *Farm and Fireside* 323 The frog and the craw-fish and the spring-lizzard that used to excite her youthful fears, have departed this life intestate, they left children to inherit and enjoy. **1967** Brewer *Park Creepers* Most other salamanders are much smaller and are lumped together under the common name of "spring lizards." Most make good fish bait. **1981** *Smokies Heritage* 26:3 Overturn a wet rock with your toe, and a tiny orange salamander just might come skittering out . . . a creature which the Smokies folks have always called a "spring lizard" because of its resemblance to the fencepost variety lizard. **1996** Huheey *Variant Names* 5 = universal name for any small salamander. **2004** Dodd *Amphibians Smoky Mts* 4 In the South, the term "spring lizard," for example, is often used to refer to salamanders that are used as bait, regardless of the species involved, or whether the "lizard" is not a reptile at all, but an amphibian. **2006** *Encycl Appalachia* 89 Salamanders, including several species of genus Gyrinophilus, are so often found in Appalachian springs and their cool, clear mountain streams that they are commonly called "spring lizards" in the region.

[DARE *spring lizard* n chiefly South, South Midland]

spring lot *noun* A fenced-in area around a spring to protect food (especially dairy products) stored in a box or trough inside. See also **spring box**, **springhouse**, **spring run**.

1997 GSMNPCOHP-1:5 We had the spring lot we called it. The water run through it. There's where we kept our milk and different things like that.

spring needles *noun* See citation.

1982 Slone *How We Talked* 112 = whelps and bumps that came in the spring. Probably from an allergy to weeds.

spring onion *noun* See citation.

1975 Purkey *Madison Co* 106 I will never forget the endless bundles of crisp spring onions with their long white heads and slender green blades, which my mother prepared for market. Mama called them "Jacob's Onions."

[DARE *spring onion* n scattered, but chiefly South, South Midland]

spring peeper See **spring cheeper**.

spring pretty *noun* A showy spring flower. See also **pretty D1**.

1961 Niles *Ballad Book* xv The location of long-destroyed cabins may be rediscovered in the springtime by the blooming of perennial "spring-pretties" planted by long-dead hands.

spring race *noun* A trough or compartment built in a **springhouse** through which water from a spring is channeled.

1973 AOHP/ASU-160 Some people had spring houses and what we called a race of water ran in it, and anything you didn't want to sour, take it and sit it in the spring race . . . and that'd keep your butter and your milk, and anything you had cooked that you wanted to keep for another meal, why you'd take it and sit it in that water. That's all we had.

spring run *noun* A trough in a **springhouse** in which dairy products are kept cool. See also **spring box**, **springhouse**, **spring lot**, **spring race**.

1966 Dykeman *Far Family* 198 I'd like to have one thing: a drink of good fresh buttermilk right out of a crock in your spring-run, if you'd give it to me.

spring tonic *noun* A home medicine consumed in early spring that purportedly purges the system of impurities and thins the blood. It most often consists of sulfur and molasses, sometimes with whiskey or an herb added. See also **blood builder**, **sassafras B**, **strengthening tonic**, **sulfur and molasses**.

1982 Powers and Hannah *Cataloochee* 256 Spring tonic: One teacup of molasses, three tablespoons of sulphur. Stir and take some for spring tonic. **1992** Cavender *Folk Hematology* 28 During the spring a "spring tonic" was necessary to "thin" the blood and, more importantly, to cleanse or "purify" the blood of the impurities or poison accumulated during the winter. In fact, cleansing the blood of waste materials serves to "thin" the blood as well since the waste material is the thickening agent. **1997** Andrews *Mountain Vittles* 4 Early spring here in the Valley in ever' cabin we young uns could always count on our grandmas and mother to line us up and give us a spoonful of their own special remedy . . . spring tonic. **2002** Myers *Best Yet Stories* 193 Every spring we children were given sulfur mixed with molasses as a spring tonic to rev up our tired blood after the long cold winter months. **2003** Cavender *Folk Medicine* 124 In the spring the blood's invigorating properties were restored by taking a tonic, variously called a "blood builder," "blood restorer," "blood toner," or "spring tonic." The most popular tonic in Southern Appalachia was sulfur and molasses, which some thought was also good for cleaning the blood. **2007** Milnes *Signs Cures Witches* 94 We always have spring tonic of sassafras tea. The red is the best. It makes the best tea. It's the same thing but in different localities the roots are different because of the soil. . . . The old people always said that it (spring tonic) thins your blood after the wintertime you know. Cleared out the blood stream.

springy See **sprangle.**

sprout (also *sprout off*) *verb, verb phrase* To clear (land) of unwanted plant growth in preparation for plowing.

1862 Parris *CW Letters* (Feb 6) you Can put him to Sprouting and Cleaning up grond. **1864** *Chapman CW Letters* (March 6) we air farming a little we have got our l[o]gs rold and our Corn ground sprouted and stocks Cut we have ploud some. **1938** Stuart *Dark Hills* 342 We have to make the fences this month and get the pastures sprouted off in August. You can be sprouting the pastures while I paint the house and fix the roof. **c1960** Wilson *Coll* = to remove sprouts from a growing plant or to cut sprouts, such as the ubiquitous persimmon and sassafras sprouts of the area.

[DARE sprout v^1 2 Chiefly South Midland]

sprouted corn *noun* In distilling, an ear of corn made to produce sprouts, in order to induce the fermentation of **mash** in the absence of yeast. The process is sometimes hastened by covering with horse manure.

1956 Hall *Coll* (Del Rio TN).

sprouting hoe *noun* A heavy hoe. See also **sprout.**

1941 Stuart *Men of Mts* 65 Pa bends over and pecks with his sprouting hoe. He cuts the soft tender sprouts from the stumps. **1983** Broaddus *Estill Co KY Word List* 57 = a grubbing hoe.

[DARE *sprouting hoe* n chiefly South Midland, especially KY]

sprouting tub *noun* A tub for soaking corn until it develops sprouts, which are then ground into **malt.**

1972 *Foxfire I* 336 In winter, put this corn in a large barrel or tub, add warm water, and leave it for twenty-four hours. Then drain it and move it to the sprouting tub. Cover it with pretty warm water, leave it for fifteen minutes, then drain the water off. Put the tub close to a stove, and turn the cold side to the stove at least once a day. **1977** Arnow *Old Burnside* 8 Most farmers had from one to three stills, with accompanying sprouting and mash tubs.

sprout of a boy (also *sprout of a child*) *noun phrase* A youngster, especially a boy (consultants from the Smoky Mountains vary in understanding of the pertinent age range; see 1995–97 citation). See also **chunk A3, strip of a boy.**

1982 Slone *How We Talked* 8 "A sprout of a boy" or "a young sprout" also meant a young boy. From the word sprout (the young plants that came up from the roots when a tree was cut down). **1995–97** Montgomery *Coll*: *sprout of a boy* = under ten years old (Brown), = a thin, leggy child from 6 to 13 (Bush), = 6–10 years of age, as in "He was just a sprout of a child" (Cardwell), = a child under 10 (Cypher), = 12–14 years of age (Jones), = 10–12 years of age (Oliver).

sprout of a child See **sprout of a boy.**

sprout off See **sprout.**

sprout out *verb phrase* See citation.

1977 Howard *Fifty Years* 14 = for a young man to begin to court: "John has been sprouting out for three or four weeks."

spruce pine *noun* The eastern hemlock tree (*Tsuga canadensis*). Also called **big spruce, hempine.**

1892 Doak *Wagonauts Abroad* 74 Coming down at an angle of thirty degrees, [the trail] winds amongst great masses of granite and piles of drift logs, under a dense shade of giant hemlocks, or spruce pines, as they are called locally, in a deep, narrow gorge. **1913** Kephart *Our Sthn High* 295 The hemlock tree is named spruce-pine, while spruce is he-balsam. **1946** Burnett *Shingle Making* 226 What was almost universally called spruce, sometimes spruce pine, in our mountains, until the lumberman from up north came along and called it hemlock, is actually assigned by the botanists to the hemlock family, and the particular variety in our forests is termed by them *Tsuga canadensis.* Submissively we yielded to the name hemlock for the lumber, but that same tree, old or young, when it adorns the grounds of our dwelling places, we will call spruce until it shall be gnawed down by the tooth of time. **1983** Pyle *CCC 50th Anniv* A:2:23 Some call 'em hem pines, an' some calls 'em spruce. **1986** Huskey *Sugarlands* 7 Palings to fence around gardens and the homes were usually made from sprucepine trees (hemlock). **2004** Dodd *Amphibians Smoky Mts* 47 Two somewhat specialized forest communities are found in the Smokies. The hemlock community is dominated by Eastern Hemlocks (Tsuga canadensis), commonly called "spruce-pines" by natives of the southern mountains, and is common between 1,067 m (3,500 ft) and 1,524 m (5,000 ft) in elevation. Hemlocks descend to much lower elevations along the cold mountain stream valleys and overlap considerably with most hardwood forests and the spruce-fir forest of the higher elevations.

[DARE *spruce pine* n 1 chiefly South, South Midland]

sprung See **spring.**

sprung sore *noun*

2015 Dykeman *Family of Earth* 74 In the springtime [the children had] a mass of sores on their arms and legs. These were called "sprung sores," and were raw, bloody splotches of infected skin and flesh.

spud

A *noun*

1 A handheld implement with a flat, sharpened metal edge for chipping or peeling bark off a log, as to harvest it for **tanbark.** See also **bark spudder.**

1964 Clarkson *Lumbering in WV* 372 = a tool for removing bark. Used especially in barking hemlock for tan bark. **1982** *Smokies Heritage*14 The bark was then peeled off with the aid of a "spud."

2 Bark chipped or peeled from a felled tree.

1998 Farwell *Logging Terms* Spud usually came from tan bark. You would use the bark for tanning.... They would take the bark off to sell.

B *verb* To remove (the bark of a tree) using such an implement; hence verbal noun *spudding.*

[See **1964** in **A.**] **1976** Tyler *Man's Work* 27 You'd peel tanning bark in the summertime when the sap was up so it gets off the log, you know. I went there and he wanted to know if I could peel bark and I told him I could, I could spud or fit either one. **1997** Farwell *Logging* = to take the bark off a tree. "Some of those fellows were good at spudding. Especially in the spring of the year when they would really spud it off. They could spud the whole log that was four foot in diameter and keep [the bark] in one piece."

[< Middle English *spudde*, related to Old English *spædu* "spade"]

spud along (also *spud around*) *verb phrase* To loiter, amble or wander about.

1913 Kephart *Our Sthn High* 203 "No, I ain't workin' none—jest spuddin' around" ... "Spuddin' around" means toddling or jolting along. **1929** (in **1952** Mathes *Tall Tales* 149) Reckon I'll have to be spuddin' along if I'm goin' to sell the balance of this here white mule! **1936** Farr *Folk Speech Mid TN* 276 *spudding around* = loiter, do nothing worthwhile. "John's just spudding around."

[DARE *spud* v 1 chiefly southern Appalachians]

spud around See **spud along.**

spudder *noun* Same as **bark spudder.**

1976 Tyler *Man's Work* 28 The spudder's job is to come along with that spud (a chisel-like tool) and take the bark off of the log. And it'll come off in sheets four foot long, halfway around the log going each way, see. **2006** Farwell *Logging Term* 1021 Bark crews had "spudders" and "rawhiders," who removed and stacked bark from felled trees.

spudding See **spud.**

spunk *noun* Same as **punk 1.**

1892 Fruit *KY Words* 232 = punk.

[DARE *spunk* n scattered, but especially South Midland]

spunk water See citations. Same as **stump water 1.**

1967 Jones *Peculiarities Mtneers* 72 Tetter and eczema were treated by applying "spunk water" (rain water caught in a hollow stump). **2003** Cavender *Folk Medicine* 205 = healing water found in a stump or cavity of a tree. **2009** Wiles and Wiles *Location* 169 The cure for warts was to soak them in "punk water." Punk water is the water that collects in ole rotted tree stumps when it rains.

[DARE *spunk water* n South, South Midland]

spun-truck *noun* Yarn.

1892 Doak *Wagonauts Abroad* 41 Antique words, forms, and expressions, and the grammar and pronunciation of the illiterate may be found, but no dialect, scarcely even patois. "Spun-truck," for yarn or thread. **1895** Murfree *Phantoms* 331 The wife turned from the warping-bars with a vague stare of surprise, one hand poised uncertainly upon a peg of the frame, the other holding a hank of "spun truck."

squack *noun* A gray squirrel or the noise it makes.

1911 Shearin *E KY Word-List* 540 = the ordinary gray squirrel. **1957** Combs *Lg Sthn High: Word List* 95 = noise made by the squirrel; also, the squirrel, itself.

squaley See **squally.**

squall *verb* Of a wild animal: to cry or call loudly.

1926 Hunnicutt *Twenty Years* 69 For several years we could hear and see dogs fighting and coons squalling. **1939** Hall *Coll* (Smokemont NC) You could see two coons stick their nose out through the crack there, the dogs just a-biting them coons on the nose, them a-squalling. *Ibid.* (Wears Cove TN) Panthers "squalled" rather than "hollered." **1941** Stuart *Men of Mts* 93 Men come back to the waters o' the mountains, don't they, atter they've spent their boyhood days where they can drink them and hear them squall around like a panter at night.

[DARE *squall* 1 chiefly South Midland]

squalled *adjective* See citation.

1999 Milnes *Play of Fiddle* 93 Things might be "catawampers" or "squalled" (out of square).

squally (also *squaley*) *adjective* Uncertain, threatening.

1862 Thompson *CW Letters* (Feb 23) I cant tell whither I will ever See yew all or not times is Sqaley. **1862** *Wright CW Letters* (July 10) I have So much to do and it is such Squaley times that I cant write half as much I want to write at this time. **1863** *Woody CW Letters*(Feb 15) the times is also a geting very squally in this Cuntry there is a Strong talke of the hole Malishey a being ordered oute. **1944** Justus *Lizzie* 46 That roof hole must be thoroughly patched against squally weather.

[by analogy with weather]

squanchways *adjective* Crooked, diagonal. See also **slanchways.**

2000 Miller *Looneyville* 72 = something that was not on a direct straight line: "You have that in there squanchways. Please straighten it."

squander (also *squander around*) *verb, verb phrase* To wander, disperse; to cause to scatter or disperse.

1895 Edson and Fairchild *TN Mts* 374 They jes *squandered* and lit out. **1925** Furman *Glass Window* 22 Seems like to me, as I draw clost to threescore and ten, nigh all I used to set store by has squandered and gone. **1970** *Hunting Stories* 32–33 He says, "Turkeys won't gobble in th'fall of th'year." I says, "They will too, if 'ey get squanderin'." **1974** Fink *Bits Mt Speech* 24 = to scatter or wander idly. "Them little turkeys just *squandered* around every which way" or "I just *squandered* around all day." **1997** Montgomery *Coll* We heard the noise and the dogs squandered the chickens (Cardwell). **2007** McMillon *Notes* = to wander idly.

[DARE *squander* v 2 chiefly South Midland]

square around *verb phrase* See citations.

1956 McAtee *Some Dial NC* 42 = make room for another to sit. **c1960** Wilson *Coll* = to make room for another "cheer" around the fireplace.

[CUD *square yourselves round* "sit so as to widen the circle and make room for others"]

square dab *adverb phrase* Entirely, exactly. See also **slam**, **smack**.

1940 Haun *Hawk's Done* 65 He passed on by them, then stopped his horse as quick as he could and turned square dab across the road in front of them. **1998** Brewer *Words of Past* "The ball hit him square dab in the nose." It means the same as what some of us call "smack dab."

[DARE *square-dab* adv chiefly South, especially TX]

squawberry *noun* A blueberry (*Vaccinium stamineum*). Same as **deerberry**, **gooseberry**.

1982 Stupka *Wildflowers* 84 A high-quality jam is made from the juicy sour berries. Locally this plant is called "squawberry" and "gooseberry."

squaw corn (also *squaw flower*, *squaw root*) *noun* A small, leafless parasitic plant (*Conopholis americana*) that usually grows at the base of oak trees and has medicinal use. Same as **bear cabbage**.

1970 Campbell et al. *Smoky Mt Wildflowers* 12 = this parasite, growing on oak roots, is also known as cancer-root and squaw-corn. Ranging in height from 4 to 9 inches, the brown-colored plant, without chlorophyll, resembles a slender pine cone or a small ear of corn. **1971** Krochmal et al. *Medicinal Plants Appal* 256 *squaw flower*, *squaw root* = the Indians of Appalachia cooked pieces of the root in food as an aphrodisiac. **2011** *Blind Pig* (June 18) Like Indian Pipes/Ghost Flower, Squaw Root is a parasitic plant and is typically found in dry areas under oak trees where it feeds on their roots. Squaw Root grows up to 8 inches high. The common name, Squaw Root, comes from the use of the plant. Indian women used it to relieve pain from childbirth as well as from menstrual cramps.

squawed *adjective* See citation.

c1960 Wilson *Coll* = out of shape.

[perhaps a variant of *skewed*; DARE *squawed* adj especially South Midland]

squaw flower, **squaw root** See **squaw corn**.

squaw vine *noun* A creeping evergreen shrub (*Mitchella repens*) with medicinal applications.

1975 Hamel and Chiltoskey *Cherokee Plants* 47 = [used] to facilitate childbirth; . . . for baby before it takes the breast; for monthly period pains; for pregnant cat; for her kittens.

squaw-weed *noun* The ragwort plant (*Senecio aureus*), used medicinally. Same as **coughweed**.

1975 Hamel and Chiltoskey *Cherokee Plants* 52 *squaw weed* = *Senecio aureus*. Tea for heart trouble; tea to prevent pregnancy.

squealer *noun* A tree frog. See also **knee deep 1**, **peeper**, **spring cheeper**.

1967 *DARE Survey* (Gatlinburg TN) = a small frog that sings or chirps loudly in spring.

sque-ball See **skewbald**.

squeech owl See **screech owl**.

squeeze

A *verb* Variant past-tense forms *squez*, *squose*, *squoz*, *squoze*, *squozed*, *squz*.

1895 Edson and Fairchild *TN Mts* 376 *squez*. **c1940** Aswell *Glossary TN Idiom* 17 *squez*, *squoz*. **1940** Haun *Hawk's Done* 52 He took it in his hands and squez it. **1964** Roberts *Hell-Fer-Sartin* 138 He just helt it up and squez till the water just poured out of this piece of cheese. **1977** *Foxfire IV* 80 Th' big bear just wheeled around an' grabbed th'cub an' squz it t'death. **1997** Montgomery *Coll*: *squez* (known to Weaver); *squoz* (known to Bush, Cardwell, Ledford, Norris). **2001** Lowry *Expressions* 8 Oh! That hurt when you squez it. **2003** Carter *Mt Home* 123 She squose my hand so tight, all the blood was cut off to my fangers. **2005** Williams *Gratitude* 527 *squoze*, *squoz* = squeezed. **2007** McMillon *Notes*: *squozed*.

[DARE *squeeze* v Bb South, South Midland]

B *noun* See citation.

c1975 *Miners' Jargon* 7 = the settling, without breaking, of the roof and the gradual upheaval of the floor of a [coal] mine due to the weight of the overlying strata.

squeezings *noun* Dregs of a mash barrel after the completion of distillation of whiskey.

1949 Arnow *Hunter's Horn* 205 These squeezens now, we could feed'em right to Rosie and her pigs if they was handy.

squench (also *squince*, *squinch*) *verb* To quench, extinguish.

1948 Chase *Grandfather Tales* 46 Mutsmeg squinched the light-ball in the spring, and the old woman stumped her toe and fell and broke her neck. **1957** Combs *Lg Sthn High: Word List* 95 *squench* = quench. **1979** Carpenter *Walton War* 180 When I find my feelins air aimin' to burst forth, I jist grit my teeth and squinch 'em. **1982** Slone *How We Talked* 97 "Where is the fire?" "Water squinced it."

squenge *verb* To flinch, cringe.

1983 Page and Wigginton *Aunt Arie* 190 I can't walk in th'snow t'save my life. I just squenge. It squenges me all over.

squez See **squeeze**.

squidge *verb*

1 To squeeze. See also **scooch, scrooch, squinch**[1] **2, 3.**

1994–95 Montgomery *Coll* I squidged in a little more jam on your bread (Norris); We had to squidge in (Shields).

2 To shrink, subside.

1917 Kephart *Word-List* 417 *squidged* = subsided. "His hand was all swoll up, but now its all *squidged* down." **1994** Montgomery *Coll* (known to Brown, Cardwell, Oliver).

squince See **squench.**

squinch[1] *verb*

1 (also *squinch up*) To squint, contort or draw up one's face; hence adjective *squinch-eyed* = squint-eyed.

1892 Fruit *KY Words* 232 = "He squinches his eyes." **1941** Hall *Coll* (Del Rio TN) His eyes was squinched up. **c1960** Wilson *Coll*: *squinch-eyed* = squint eyed. **1968** *DARE Survey* (Brasstown NC) = to squint, close the eyes partway when looking at the sun. **1981** Williams *Storytelling* His ears just pointed right straight up like that, and his eyes was all squinched up in little squizzles of light. **1984** Woods *WV Was Good* 223 = to partly close the eyes, but in a firm manner. May be a corruption of squint. **1997** Montgomery *Coll*: *squinch-eyed* (known to eight consultants from the Smoky Mountains). **2000** Miller *Looneyville* 72 Partly closing the eyes in a firm or menacing manner . . . "Quit whispering. The school mom is squinchin."

[Web3 *squinch* v probably blend of *squint* and *pinch*; DARE *squinch* v 2 chiefly South, South Midland, TX]

2 To hunch, huddle next to. See also **scooch, scrooch, squidge 1.**

1944 Justus *Lizzie* 5 Lizzie Holloway squinched up her toes against the slippery pebbles covering the stretch of road to hotel grounds. **1971** Thornburgh *Great Smoky Mts* 162 Here's a little tree to squinch up by to shelter from a shower.

[DARE (at *squinch* v 4) scattered, but especially South, South Midland]

squinch[2] See **squench.**

squinch-eyed See **squinch**[1] **1.**

squinch owl See **screech owl.**

squinch up See **squinch**[1].

squire *noun* A justice of the peace, magistrate.

1862 *Fuller CW Letters* (Nov 7) Squire levet and the widow waggonner is marred. **1862** *Shifflet CW Letters* (March 18) I want you to go to Squire neff and see about your money for tha[y] ar a cheaten. **1867** Harris *Sut Lovingood* 97 [sic] Ef they don't fail, I may turn human sum day, that is sorter human, enuf tu be a Squire, ur school cummisiner. **1928** Busbee *Elizabethan Settlements* 21 A magistrate is the "squire." To his door a couple [planning to get married] drive up in an old buggy. **1939** Hall *Coll* (Tobes Creek NC) Politics has gone too far. . . . We've got two squires to every deestrict. One's a-plenty. **1963** Edwards *Gravel* 27 Dozens of his cronies would swear before squire or preacher that Genuwine Jones *never* had enough to eat. **1977** Shields *Cades Cove* 7 The voters of each district elected a constable and two justices of the peace, or squires. The latter from all the county districts made up the county court. The local constables and squires kept the peace and handled most of the legal business of the district . . . the justices of the peace advised in neighborly squabbles, wrote wills, helped in making deeds, performed weddings, and aided in all normal legal matters. **1986** Pederson et al. *LAGS* (Campbell Co TN) = member of quarterly county court.

squirrel *verb* To go hunting for squirrels; hence verbal noun *squirreling*.

1904–20 Kephart *Notebooks* 4:749 He's gone a-squirrelin'. **1913** Kephart *Our Sthn High* 282 In mountain vernacular many words that serve as verbs are only nouns of action, or adjectives, or even adverbs . . . "Are ye fixin' to go squirrelin'?" **1927** Shearin *Speech of Fathers* 7 Whur you goin', Bob? Out squirrelin'. **1994–97** Montgomery *Coll* (known to Adams, Brown, Cardwell, Norris, Oliver, Weaver).

[DARE *squirreling* vbl n 1 especially South Midland]

squirrel corn *noun* A bleeding heart plant (*Dicentra canadensis*) with medicinal use. Also called **little girl plant, turkey corn.**

1928 Galyon *Plant Naturalist* 7 Associated with dutchman's breeches, and a member of the same genus, is squirrel-corn. It is so named because of the yellow corn-like bulblets on the roots. **1967** Hall *Coll* (Del Rio TN) Squirrel corn purifies the blood. **1970** Campbell et al. *Smoky Mt Wildflowers* 28 Squirrel corn gets its name from a belief that squirrels enjoy its corn-like tubers.

squirrel gun (also *squirrel rifle*) *noun* A light, small-bore rifle suitable for hunting squirrels and other small game. See also **cap and ball gun, hog rifle.** See 1941 citation.

1900 Harben *N GA Sketches* 35 He sprang up and took down his long-barreled "squirrel gun" from its hooks on the wall. **1917** Kephart *Word-List* 413 = a squirrel rifle. The stress falls on *rifle*. **1941** Kendall *Rifle-Making* 22 The calibre of the mountain rifles deserves a word of mention. Strictly speaking, these rifles had no calibre in the ordinary sense of the word. Usually, however, four kinds of rifles were made: one of about .35 calibre (0.35 inch) which was called a squirrel gun; one about .40 calibre (0.40 inch) called a turkey rifle; one about .45 calibre (0.45 inch) called a deer rifle; and one of approximately .50 calibre (0.50 inch) called a bear gun. **1957** Combs *Lg Sthn High: Word List* 51 = the squirrel rifle commonly in use before the breech-loading rifle and shot gun. It is loaded from the barrel, and ignited by a percussion cap. **1992** Bush *If Life* 26 Thinking some kind of varmint had invaded [the chickens'] domicile, she took the squirrel gun and went to see what was wrong.

squirrel hawk *noun* See citation.

1914 Morton *Monroe Co WV* 14 Of those that nest here the birds of prey are the buzzard, the squirrel hawk, the blue chicken hawk, the striped chicken hawk, the bird hawk, the hoot owl, and the barn owl. **c1960** Wilson *Coll* = any large hawk, esp. the red-tailed.

[DARE *squirrel hawk* n 2 chiefly South Midland]

squirrel hunt *verb phrase* To go hunting for squirrels; for similar compound verbs, see **hunt B**.

1953 Hall *Coll* (Tuckaleechee Cove TN) I squirrel hunted, coon-hunted, possum-hunted as a boy. I never did fool any after the bear. I went deer-huntin' a time or two.

squirrel hunter *noun* A sentry for a **moonshining** operation who roams the woods nearby claiming to hunt squirrel.

1968 Connelly *Discover Appal* 119 In some areas, "squirrel hunters" are groups of armed mountaineers often seen by revenue agents in the vicinity of whisky-making operations. Of course, these men profess ignorance of the presence of a still in the vicinity.

squirreling See **squirrel**.

squirrel liquor *noun* Homemade whiskey.

1974 Dabney *Mt Spirits* 24 This is a hill country expression. After three or four drinks of "squirrel likker," imbibers would throw down their guns and climb the trees to get their squirrels.

squirrel out of *verb phrase* To evade, avoid (doing something).

1997 Montgomery *Coll* (known to Norris).

squirrel rifle See **squirrel gun**.

squirrel's ear *noun* An edible wild green (*Goodyera repens*).

1930 Armstrong *This Day and Time* 69 Nothin' kin beat a mess o' squirrel's ear, hit mixed with tongue-grass.

squirrel time *noun* See citation.

c1930 Goff *Dialects Sthn Mtneers* 6 "Squirrel Time" means what we call sun time.

(the) squirts *noun* Diarrhea.

1952 Wilson *Folk Speech NC* 594 = diarrhea. **1990** Cavender *Folk Medical Lex* 31 *the squirts* = diarrhea.

[DARE *squirts* n chiefly South, South Midland]

squose, squoz, squoze, squozed See **squeeze**.

sqush (also *squush*) *verb* To quash, crush, squash (as with one's hands or feet).

1915 Dingus *Word-List VA* 191 *squush* = to squash. **1940** Bandy *Folklore Macon Co TN* 52–53 If he can "sqush" a fight, that is as good as any other way of stopping it. **1957** Combs *Lg Sthn High: Word List* 95 *sqush* = quash. **1963** Watkins and Watkins *Yesterday* 2 Flies covered the sides of the churn, and she caught a handful, "squshed" them to death in her hand, and kept on churning. **1997** *Dante OHP-53* The whole mountain come down just like you would squush, take your foot and squush a tomato.

[DARE *squush* v 1 scattered, but especially South, South Midland, Northeast]

squz See **squeeze**.

stable horse *noun* A stallion, stud horse.

1915 Dingus *Word-List VA* 191 = a stallion. **c1954** Adams *Word-List: stable hoss* = stallion. **1983** Broaddus *Estill Co KY Word List* 57 = a stud horse. **1986** Pederson et al. *LAGS* (Greene Co TN, Sullivan Co TN).

[DARE *stable horse* n chiefly South, South Midland]

stable lot *noun* A barnyard. See also **lot A**.

1949 Kurath *Word Geog East US* 40 From the Rappahannock southward *lot, barn lot, stable lot* ... are the usual terms for the barnyard, and these expressions are current in all of the South Midland as well as in parts of northern West Virginia, but not in the Shenandoah Valley. In West Virginia north of the Kanawha.

[DARE *stable lot* n chiefly South, South Midland]

stack

A *noun* See citation.

1949 Maurer *Argot of Moonshiner* 12 = the rocks or bricks built around the still in pot operations, or the boiler in steam operations. "This still ain't been outa the stack for a month."

B *verb* See citations.

1949 Maurer *Argot of Moonshiner* 12 = to set the still or the boiler up in masonry so that a fire can be applied. *Ibid.* You stack the still while I get the ...

stack cake *noun* A heavy round cake of four or more layers or "stacks" of dough alternating with dried fruit, most often applesauce, apple butter, or dried apples. See 1974, 1997 citations. See also **jam cake, stack pie**.

1941 Justus *Kettle Creek* 137 The big stack-cake stood all by itself on a shelf in the corner cupboard ... ten layers high and as big around as a water bucket! **1955** Ritchie *Singing Family* 181 Edna ... mashed up dried apples and spiced them with cloves and sticks of cinnamon to go between the seven layers of Mom's gingerbread stack-cake. **1974** Cate et al. *Sthn Appal Heritage* 79 There [were] old-fashioned stack cakes, their thin layers interspersed with filling of spicy dried fruit. Sometimes called old-fashioned fruit cake. Make the dough the same as for gingerbread, but bake in a skillet or cake pan, each cake as large as the pan, and about one inch thick. "Smear" a plate with apple butter. Place one cake on the apple butter, put more apple butter on it, another cake, more apple butter, and so on. Make cake as high as you want, at least four or five [layers]. Cooked apples, applesauce, crushed peaches, and berries of any kind can be used in place of the apple butter. Cooked fried apples were also used. **1977** Arnow *Old Burnside* 69 [I] helped her make a stack cake of many thin layers, each cooked in an iron skillet on top of the stove, then put together and covered with a brown-sugar icing. **1980** *Smokies Heritage* 102 *stack cake* = a layered cake made of thin, sweet dough layers spread with spiced, dried apple filling. **1997** Montgomery *Coll: stack cake* =

made of six to eight thin, pancake-like layers, usually with apple butter between them. The layers are baked individually before the cake is assembled, and the cake is best when aged two or three days (Oliver). **2006** *Encycl Appalachia* 920 Lacking both the amenities of modern kitchens and the choices of leavenings and flavorings, the pioneer housewife seeking to create sweet treats for the end of a meal layered rounds of baked pastry with fresh or stewed fruit to create "stack" cake. This enduring favorite could have as many as sixteen layers. One of the most popular versions of this cake, especially during the winter months, was made with stewed dried apples. **2010** Jabbour and Jabbour *Decoration Day* 43 For dessert, several people mentioned not only ordinary pies and cakes but also "stack cake," a multi-layered molasses-and-spice cake resembling gingerbread. The filling between the layers is composed of cooked dried apples or peaches.

[DARE *stack cake* n chiefly South Midland, especially southern Appalachians]

stack chimney *noun*

1 (also *stacked chimney*) A double fireplace built in the center of a **saddlebag house**. Also called **double chimney**.

1953 Hall *Coll* (Bryson City NC) *stack chimley* = a big chimley built in the middle of the house with two fireplaces to it, and it was built up right through the center of the house and out the top of it. And by building it on the inside of the house and in the middle that way, the wind didn't affect it and it didn't smoke us and we had comfort out of it because smoke would go out the top and not come out in the house. **1991** Williams *Homeplace* 76 The saddlebag plan is usually described as a house with a "double fireplace," "double chimney," or "stacked chimney."

[DARE *stack chimney* n 1 especially South, South Midland, but also New England]

2 A chimney built of clay, mud, and sticks.

1941 *Land of Breathitt* 100 More elegantly built schoolhouses had "stack" chimneys of mud, sticks, and stones that vented both heat and light. **1986** Pederson et al. *LAGS*: *stack chimney* = attested by 1/60 interviewees (1.7%) from E TN, 3/35 interviewees (8.6%) from N GA; 4/10 of all LAGS interviewees (40%) attesting term were from Appalachia.

[DARE *stack chimney* n 2 chiefly South, South Midland]

stack of bones *noun* See citations.

c1960 Wilson *Coll* = a skinny old horse. **1968–69** *DARE Survey* (Ball Ground GA, Lexington VA) = a poor-looking cow.

[DARE *stack of bones* n phr chiefly South, South Midland]

stack pie *noun* A multilayered pie of dough alternating with fruit. See 1997 citation. See also **stack cake**.

1962 Dykeman *Tall Woman* 87 "Papa and Aunt Tildy are bringing up some of the victuals tomorrow," she told Jim Burke hastily, "and I'm making ready to fix corn pudding and bake a batch of stack pies." **1986** Pederson et al. *LAGS* = attested by 3/60 interviewees (5%) from E TN and 1/35 (2.9%) from N GA; 4/5 of all LAGS interviewees (80%) attesting term were from Appalachia. **1997** Montgomery *Coll* (known to Norris), = made from dried fruit baked into pies and stacked about 4–6 [layers] high (Cardwell).

[DARE *stack pie* n chiefly South Midland]

stack pole *noun* A sharpened pole driven into the ground to support a pile of hay, fodder, etc.

1964 Williams *Prep Mt Speech* 55 [The tree] wasn't about no biggerer a raound nor your arm; still yit, hit was a riht stout'n and rech up thar a right smart piece. 'Nother year and hit'll be 'baout big a nough for a stackpole, I reckon. **2002** Morgan *Mt Born* 67 He would cut two saplings, lop off the limbs, and drag them to the approximate center of the field. These were called "stack poles." Using the family ax, he sharpened the butt ends into long, tapering points. Then, he lifted one of these hefty poles upright and let it drop straight down to spike into the soft bottom soil. After three or four of these repeated drops, the pole would be deep enough and rigid enough to hold the tops and fodder that would soon be stacked around it. The other poles would be placed in like fashion, twelve or fifteen feet away.

stagger See **staggerweed**.

staggerweed *noun*

1 (also *stagger*) A bleeding heart wildflower (*Dicentra cucullaria*). Same as **Dutchman's breeches**.

1962 Miller *Pigeon's Roost* (May 10) He believed the cattle got poisoned by either eating wild parsnip or wild stagger, although he found some ivy shrubbery that something had been eating on. **1976** Lindsay *Grassy Balds* 74 Of course, the *Dicentra* never killed any cattle, but it would give them the staggers. A common name for it was staggerweed. **1981** Brewer *Wonderment* 22 What we call various plants depends somewhat on the point of view of those doing the calling. For instance, there's Dutchman's breeches. At least, that['s] the name that most wildflower fans use for the beautiful little plant whose blooms look remotely like a pair of britches. But a farmer or cattleman may call it stagger weed. For when a cow eats heartily of it, she gets sick and staggers.

2 The dwarf larkspur (*Delphinium tricorne*), which causes animals that eat it to lose coordination and become dazed.

1901 Lounsberry *Sthn Wild Flowers* 175 A plant of unusual and dignified aspect is the dwarf larkspur as it is seen growing through open, rocky woods, or cropping up along well-shaded roadsides. That it is generally called staggerweed is because it is poisonous to stock which in April eat of its young shoots. In wreaking this harm upon them, they, it would naturally be supposed, stagger about as though unconscious of their actions. **1971** Hutchins *Hidden Valley* 174 [The plants] are often called stagger weeds and, when eaten by cows, cause a staggering gait and loss of milk production. **1987** Young *Lost Cove* 28 The pieded cow and the heifer that was not yet with calf had wandered off in the woods the week before. It was a wonder they hadn't been poisoned on stagger.

[DARE *staggerweed* n 1 chiefly southern Appalachians, especially wVA]

3 Same as **white snakeroot**.

c1950 Adams *Grandpap* 193 We had to be careful not to get any staggerweed in with the crowsfoot when we were pulling it. The two plants are very much alike in leaf-form and manner of growth. But staggerweed is deadly poison, particularly so if you happen to get some of the root. **1996** Montgomery *Coll* (Cardwell).

staggle *verb* See citation.

1961 Williams *R in Mt Speech* 7 [In some words] l is substituted for r: . . . flitter (fritter), swaggle (swagger), staggle (stagger).

stairsteps *noun* A flight of stairs.

1921 Campbell *Sthn Highlander* 146 Redundancies such as "church house," "stair steps," and "tooth dentist" are frequent. **1956** McAtee *Some Dial NC* 43 = a flight of steps. **2007** Preece *Leavin' Sandlick* 12 Lucia and William had twelve children just like stair steps.

[DARE *stairsteps* n chiefly South, Midland]

stake and rider fence *noun* A stake fence topped by an additional rail to prevent animals from jumping over it. See c1975 citation.

[**1968** Clarke *Stuart's Kentucky* 187 The fields were once fenced with oak or chestnut rails, stake-and-ridered—some of them standing for several generations—but by Stuart's time a three- or four-strand barbed-wire fence tightly drawn and stapled to locust posts was the usual way of enclosing fields and marking boundary lines.] **1972** *AOHP/ALC-413* They had what they called a stake and rider fence, and they were big high fences . . . one rail on top of another'un between two postes, and nothing couldn't get through it, made out of good rail. **c1975** Lunsford *It Used to Be* 63 Then there's the stake-and-rider fence. For that you drive a stake down. Put another one in the ground diagonally, nail to that stake, and then you start it with a rider. One stake is driven in on the left side and let lean toward the right. Another is driven in on the right side and let lean toward the left. You put another rail in that fork and let it reach down horizontally, or parallel, to the first rail that's been put down, and then you drive your stakes again. And that is called a stake-and-rider fence, or a galloping fence. **1986** Pederson et al. *LAGS*: *stake and rider fence* = attested by 4/60 interviewees (6.7%) from E TN; 4/6 of all LAGS interviewees (66.7%) attesting term were from Appalachia; *stakes and riders* = attested by 5/60 interviewees (8.3%) from E TN; 5/14 of all LAGS interviewees (38.5%) attesting term were from Appalachia.

stalded See **stall.**

stalk *verb* In logging, to leave standing (the part of a tree that does not break cleanly at the stump) when the tree is felled.

1974–75 McCracken *Logging* 5:45 When I say stalking, when the chipper cuts the lead in a tree and they go to saw it down, if it doesn't break clean on the stump, is what they call stalking. If it runs up and leaves that lead on the stump, with a slab sticking up the side ten foot in the air, you've stalked a tree.

stall *verb* Variant past-tense forms *stalded, stallded*. See also **drown 2.**

1891 Brown *Dialect in TN* 172 In drownded, stallded, attackted, etc., there may be an error as to what is the present tense of the verb. **1919** Combs *Word-List South* 35 *stalded* = a survival of the inflection vowel . . . : "Our car stalded." **1921** Weeks *Speech of KY Mtneer* 19 Our car was stalded in a mud hole and it shore tuck two mule teams to haul us out. **1997** Montgomery *Coll* (known to Adams, Bush, Cardwell, Ledford, Oliver, Weaver).

[DARE *stall* v chiefly South, South Midland]

stand

A *verb* To take a position on an issue, take a side in a conflict.

1939 Hall *Coll* (Bradley Fork NC) All people through here stood on the Rebel side. . . . I've always made it a rule to stand up among men, stand up for your rights and for your country.

B *noun*

1 A fixed position at which a hunter awaits game such as a bear or deer, being driven within shooting range by **drivers** and their dogs. See also **drive, stander.**

1878 Coale *Wilburn Waters* 40 Next morning they were all on the ground at an early hour, and started the wolf within fifty yards of where the trap had been set. The men being stationed at various "stands" in the range, she found it difficult to get out, and doubled from point to point with the dogs on her trail. **1923** Williams *After Bruin* Breakfast over, the standers set out up the creek for the various stands. *Ibid.* 84 All except the drivers take stands. Deer, in warm weather, usually seek the highest, coolest and most inaccessible peaks in the mountains, and when started from their lairs run certain well-known routes, and make for the nearest stream, at certain points or crossings, which hunters call "stands." **1939** Hall *Coll* (Cataloochee NC) Me and Mister Steve Woody went on the stands. They jumped the bear, and the bear come to the stand where we was at, and I give him two good shots, and the bear run off down under the mountain. *Ibid.* (Cataloochee NC) We got to the top of the Shanty Mountain, but we wanted to send some fellers to the stand.

2 A hive of bees or a collection of hives. Also called **bee gum stand.**

c1960 Wilson *Coll* = a hive of bees. **1973** *GSMNP-74*:22 There was a bee shed where he had several stands of bees right out from the house. **1991** Thomas *Sthn Appal* 56 Generally, a "stand" or hive of bees was placed in the edge of the family's orchard, the better to have them ready to pollinate the fruit blossoms. **c1995** *Pioneer Farmstead* 8 A "stand" was a collection of hollow pieces of black gum logs. Black gum wood was best because it is tough and does not split easily. Each gum housed a colony of bees, usually captured as a wild colony from some bee tree.

[DARE *stand* n 3 South, South Midland]

3 An upright barrel, tub, or other wooden vessel used to store liquid or semi-liquid (food) products; the quantity of such products that is so stored.

1927 Dingus *Appal Mt Words* 470 A tub, churn or the like, filled with honey or beer. **1936** Coleman *Dial N GA* 23 There would be honey because almost every mountaineer keeps a "stand" of honey for "sweetenin'"—"stand" being simply a wooden churn. **1953** Davison *Word-List Appal* 14 = vessel for lard or molasses, etc. **1966** Dakin *Vocab Ohio River Valley* 144 A related term also commonly used by those who say *(bee)gum* is *stand*. This word—usually used in compounds a *stand of lard*, a *stand of honey*, etc., or *lard stand*, *fat stand*, *molasses stand*—is not a synonym for barrel or gum, but means "an upright open-end container for the storage of liquid or semi-liquid (food) products and the quantity of such product that is so stored." Comments indicate that a *lard stand* (for example) might be a barrel or a gum—but that in more recent years it might also be a five gallon tin container. This old substantive use of *stand*, which goes back to the Middle English period and which the OED says is "obsolete except in dialectical use," is attested [in the Ohio Valley] only in Kentucky and here only rarely except in the Mountains south of the headwaters of the Kentucky River.

[OED3 *stand* n² 1 obsolete except dialect; DARE *stand* n 1 South, South Midland]

4 A speaking platform or pulpit. Also called **preaching stand**, **pulpit-stand**.

1881 Pierson *In the Brush* 13 I preached in a log meeting-house, or at a "stand" erected in a grove at some cross-roads, or at a camp-meeting, or wherever else I should be able to meet and address the people. *Ibid.* 62–63 [At the basket meeting] the pulpit or "stand" for the preacher was originally and truly Gothic in construction. It was made by cutting horizontal notches immediately opposite to each other, in the sides of two oak-trees, standing about four feet apart, and inserting in these notches a board about a foot wide, that had been placed across a wagon and used for a seat by some of those present in coming to the meeting. The preacher placed his Bible and hymn-book upon this board, hung the indispensable saddle-bags in which he had brought them across one end of it, and so was ready for the services. **1948** Dick *Dixie Frontier* 199–200 A large square clearing was made and over this was constructed an immense brush arbor or, as a campground became permanent, a long shed covered with clapboards. . . . At one end was a high platform, known as "the pulpit-stand," made of poles or poles and slabs. At the foot of the stand was a straw-floored enclosure about thirty feet square, known as "the altar" or "penitent's pen." **1963** Edwards *Gravel* 79 He was capable of filling the stand (i.e., pulpit) when the pastor failed to appear at the regular monthly meeting. **1989** Dorgan *Regular Baptists* 54 Old Regular [Baptist] ministers never prepare sermons, at least not in any traditional way. Instead they "take the stand" and deliver wholly improvised messages, believing that written or outlined sermons allow only men to speak, but that improvisation subjects speakers to the divine inspiration of the moment and allows God to speak. **1995** McCauley *Mt Religion* 102 Church members sit apart from the congregation, on a raised platform with rows of benches arranged on a three-sided arrangement behind the preaching "stand," an open space on the raised platform in front of the benches with a pulpit in the middle.

[DARE *stand* n 4 especially South, South Midland]

5 A thick growth (of grass).

1891 Brown *Dialect in TN* 174 Every one speaks of a stand of grass, meaning that it is thick enough on the ground.

6 Formerly, a roadside stockade for feeding and quartering livestock as they were driven to market.

1982 Eller *Miners* 14 Not only did the farmers sell their surplus livestock to the passing drivers, but they commonly raised corn and produce to feed the animals and human travelers as they passed through. Along the road, merchants established stockades or "stands" where the animals could be fed and watered and where travelers could find overnight accommodation.

stand an examination *verb phrase* To take and pass a test.

1956 Hall *Coll* (Cosby TN) Anyone that stood that examination didn't have to stand nary another examination for five years. *Ibid.* (Cosby Creek TN) I stood the examination and got a first-grade certificate before I quit. I taught one school but didn't want another.

stand a show *verb phrase* To have a prospect or chance to demonstrate one's ability, talents, etc.

1956 Hall *Coll* (Hartford TN) I didn't stand no more show in the park than a one-legged man at a rump-kickin'. **c1960** Wilson *Coll* = to have a chance, esp. a remote one.

stander *noun* One of a group of hunters assigned to a fixed position or **stand** to await especially bear or deer being driven within shooting range by **drivers**. See also **stand B1**.

1883 Zeigler and Grosscup *Heart of Alleghanies* 48 It is a shelter only for the time being; no one expects to return to it, for by the following night the hounds may be 20 miles away, and the drivers and standers toasting bear steaks in their cabins, or encamping on some distant height. **1923** Williams *After Bruin* Breakfast over, the standers set out up the creek for the various stands. **1939** Hall *Coll* (Deep Creek NC) I placed the standers on the Bear Wallow Ridge beyond Bear Creek, and they turned the dogs loose to go back into camps. **1976** *Bear Hunting* 281 On the morning of the hunt, "standers" would be put out on ridges overlooking gaps that the bear would be likely to pass through once the dogs started chasing it. Once they were in place, the dogs would be put on the trail, and hopefully the bear would be located, and then either killed by one of the standers as it fled by, or, treed by the dogs and held in one place until the hunters could get there and kill it. **2008** Plott *Hunting in Smokies* 54 [He had] some of his hunting partners handle some of his start dogs as they struck a trail, while he would position himself strategically in nearby mountain gaps that he anticipated the bear would be driven to. In bear hunting terms, this is known as a "stander."

[DARE *stander* n formerly chiefly South, South Midland]

stand good for *verb phrase* To serve as security for (a debt or payment).

1936 Stuart *Head of Hollow* 67 The cows will stand good for the doctor's fee. **1941** Stuart *Men of Mts* 207 I'll stand good for your cost of the suit if you want the divorce. **1977** Shackelford et al. *Our Appalachia* 266 We can't do that unless your brother stands good for it. **1993** Cunningham *Sthn Talk* 147 I'll stand good for the boy to buy that car cause he kain't buy it without no credit. **1997** Montgomery *Coll* (known to nine consultants from the Smoky Mountains).

stand in with *verb phrase*

1 To side with, be on the good side of.

1904 Fox *Christmas Eve* 12 Of the "stay-at-homes," and the deserters roundabout, there were many, very many, who would "stand in" with any man who would keep their bellies full. **1975** *AOHP/ALC-903* I stood in with them [= company officials] pretty good.

[DARE *stand in with* v phr formerly more widespread, now chiefly South, South Midland]

2 See citation.

1957 Combs *Lg Sthn High: Word List* 95 = to stand up and fight with, or rather, against; to encourage one who is about to lose his nerve. Ex.: "Stand in with him, sonny!"

stand-table *noun* A table serving as a surface on which to keep objects.

1964 Roberts *Hell-Fer-Sartin* 194 Those two men which was there at his place had a big stand table out in the floor.

[DARE *stand-table* n chiefly South Midland]

stand up and down *verb phrase* See citation.

1892 Fruit *KY Words* 232 = to contend vehemently. "She stood me up and down that I was mistaken."

[DARE (at *stand down* v phr 2) South, South Midland]

stand up under *verb phrase* To endure, support.

1900 Harben *N GA Sketches* 84 I tol' 'em they was welcome to my intrust in the crap, an that I had had all I could stand up under.

star-bloom *noun* Same as **worm-grass**.

[**1971** Krochmal et al. *Medicinal Plants Appal* 240 The root is used as a vermifuge, anthelmintic, and cathartic. In Appalachia, a tea made from the leaves is used to aid digestion.] **1982** Stupka *Wildflowers* 87 [Indian pink] is also called "pink-root," "star-bloom," and "worm-grass"—the last a reference to the use of the root by pioneers for expelling or destroying intestinal worms.

star grass (also *star root*) *noun* A perennial wildflower (*Aletris farinosa*), from whose roots is made a tea to treat medical ailments.

1937 Thornburgh *Great Smoky Mts* 29 Other herbs or roots used by the old folks in various ways are . . . star root. *Ibid.* 30 Git ye some star root. Hit grows in the glades. **1970** Campbell et al. *Smoky Mt Wildflowers* 30. [**1971** Krochmal et al. *Medicinal Plants Appal* 40 In Appalachia a mixture of roots [from this plant] and brandy or whisky is drunk as a treatment for rheumatism.] **1975** Hamel and Chiltoskey *Cherokee Plants* 57 Stargrass, star-root (Aletris farinosa) . . . root prevents abortion. **1991** Thomas *Sthn Appal* 220 Since I've married, an' a-keepin' house, I've hunted sang roots an' star roots.

[DARE *star root* n 1 especially southern Appalachians]

start *verb*

1 To arouse (a game animal) for a hunt.

1878 Coale *Wilburn Waters* 40 Next morning they were all on the ground at an early hour, and started the wolf within fifty yards of where the trap had been set. **1926** Hunnicutt *Twenty Years* 160 I told the boys to turn their dogs loose for Old Muse had started a bear. **1939** Hall *Coll* (Nine Mile TN) He says for us drivers to go to the Calhoun Ridge and start this bear. **1941** Stuart *Men of Mts* 234 The dogs take to the hills to start the fox.

2 To send off by mail.

1861 *Neves CW Letters* (Dec 25) I had some letters wrote to send but he went off and forgot them but I started them by mail the next day. **1862** *Hawn CW Letters* (May 24) I have started you six letters and I have not got ary one from you as yet. **1864** *Councill CW Letters* (Nov 30) I started a letter to Carrie the 28 of this month but I dont [k]now whether She will git it or not. **1967** Giles *40 Acres* 4 A letter is not addressed, it is "backed." It is not mailed or posted, it is "started."

[DARE *start* v 3 chiefly southern Appalachians]

startation *noun* A beginning.

1966 Dykeman *Far Family* 274 We can make a startation before I bring you back this evening.

start in

1 (also *start in to*) (+ *verbal noun or present participle*) *verb phrase* To begin. See also **fall into**, **fall to**, **set in 1**, **start 2**, **take to 1**. See also Grammar and Syntax §7.2.

1896 Fox *Last Stetson* 185 He [= the preacher] put her 'n' the box on a big rock, 'n' started in a callin' 'em his bretherin' 'n' sisteren. **1940** Oakley *Roamin'/Restin'* 128 We started in to fishing near the Chimneys tops soon I heard a strange voice that said how are you getting along fishing. **c1950** Haun *When the Wind* 9 He started in to singing it himself: Rock a bye, Baby. **1972** *GSMNP-73* I started in working when I was eighteen year old for them, Dollar Zan Board. **1991** Joslin *Mt People I* 153 I started in helping my daddy when I was only this tall. **2000** Morgan *Mts Remember* 160 I expected him to start in telling me how Carlie had already drunk up half the price of the place, and smoked and borrowed the rest, like he always did. **2009** Holbrook *Upheaval* 113 She didn't start in crying, which was the next antic Shondra would have expected.

2 (+ *infinitive*) To begin; to cause (someone) to begin.

1910 Cooke *Power and Glory* 18 If you start in to pay off all the borryin's of the Passmore family since you was born, you'll ruin us. **1927** Mason *Lure of Smokies* 227 I might start ye to thinkin'. **1957** *GSMNP-23:1:17* I got so I could read it by heart, started in to read it by heart.

start in on *verb phrase* To begin scolding (someone).

2010 Owenby *Trula Ownby* 12 Coming in that afternoon Demaris started in on me. I told her if she didn't stop I would flail her over the head with that umbrella.

start in to See **start in 1**.

start-naked *adjective phrase* Completely naked.

1867 Harris *Sut Lovingood* 58 Passuns ginerly hev a pow'ful strong holt on wimen; but, hoss, I tell yu thar ain't meny ove em kin run start nakid over an' thru a crowd ove three hundred wimen an' not injure thar karacters *sum*. **1892** Fruit *KY Words* 234 He is a start-naked villain. **1939** Hall *Coll* (Jefferson City TN) *be stripped start naked*—It means plumb naked. **1962** Hall *Coll* (Cataloochee NC) The panther was so vygrous and mad, hit took each piece and tore it up. She tore all her clothes off and finally made it home start naked. **1974** Fink *Bits Mt Speech* 24 They went swimming *start-nekked*.

[this is the older, historical form, with *stark naked* being an alteration by reanalysis first recorded in 1530; OED3 *start-naked* adj, now chiefly U.S. regional; DARE *start-naked* adj phr South, South Midland]

start off to See **start to**.

start to (also *start off to*) (+ *verbal noun or present participle*) *verb phrase* To begin; to cause (someone) to begin.

1970 *Hunting Stories* 77 I didn't call n'more, an' he just started t'runnin'. **1974** *AOHP/ALC*-802 Do you remember when they first started to coming in here? **1974** GSMNP-51:20 They started off to hunting, so I don't remember whether he got a bear that time or not. **1978** Montgomery *White Pine Coll* VIII-1 They hollered [that] we was going to get a new school five years before they ever started drawing up the original plans or actually started the ball to rolling to get a new school.

starve *verb* To be very thirsty, especially in phrase *starve for water*; hence participial adjective phrase *starved for water*. See also **hungry B**.

1862 (in **1992** Jackson *Surry Co Soldiers* 300) (Sept 8) I am almost run to death and starved for water. **1937** Hall *Coll* (Wears Cove TN) I was starved to death for water. *Ibid.* (Wears Cove TN) The poor thing's a-starvin' for water. **1939** Hall *Coll* (Saunook NC) I was starvin' for water down there. **1980** Wigginton *Foxfire V* 486 See, what had happened, he was starving for water. **1995** Montgomery *Coll* (known to Cardwell, Shields).

starved out See **starve out**.

starve for water See **starve**.

starve out *verb phrase* To become destitute, famish from poor weather or poor farming; to die of starvation; hence participial adjective phrase *starved out*. See also **out A2**.

1863 *Reese CW Letters* (April 2) men is starved out on Bred and meet So Bad that tha[y] will giv aney price for aney kind of Case [= sass]. **1937** Hall *Coll* (Wears Cove TN) It's so dry that there'll be nothing made [for a crop], and we're bound to starve out next year. *Ibid.* (Cades Cove TN) We'll starve out, I reckon, before we git there. **1967** Fetterman *Stinking Creek* 65 Come on up to the porch, brother. You're welcome to stay with the Browns 'til you starve out. **1974** Fink *Bits Mt Speech* 24 That family's just about *starved out*. **2007** Hardy *Remembering Avery Co* 40 He would stay in that hole until he starved out.

staub See **stob B**.

stave *verb* See also **stove**.

1 To jab, jam or stub, thrust, plunge; to crush inward.

1904–20 Kephart *Notebooks* 2:475 I stove a nail into [my foot]. *Ibid.* 4:859 If you make a move, I'll stave your ribs in. **1913** Kephart *Our Sthn High* 296 Many common English words are used in peculiar senses by the mountain folk, as stove for jabbed. **1939** Hall *Coll* (Mt Sterling NC) Mister Sullivan picked up a piece of steel and stove down in on the dynamite and caused the explosion. **1957** Combs *Lg Sthn High: Word List* 96 = to stick or plunge (of a knife). Ex.: "He stove a knife in that rascal." **1960** Hall *Smoky Mt Folks* 12 He "stove" the [knife] into the animal's stomach and cut a hole five or six inches across. **1989** *Matewan OHP*-7 As long as John lived he always had that little ring there where that pistol, where he had stove that pistol into his cheek there and hard enough to make that ring in there. **2006** Cavender *Medical Term* 1022 I stove my finger when I caught the ball. **2009** Holbrook *Upheaval* 32 It's untelling which one would be worse off—her with her head stove in or him cut open.

[SND *stave* v 3 "to sprain, bruise or contuse a part of the body" Scot; CUD *stave*[1] v 1 "sprain, wrench (a finger, etc.)"; DARE *stave* v 4 chiefly Southeast]

2 To rush, hurry, storm about.

1925 Carter *Mt White Tales* 350 The old king stove out and ketched a rabbit right down in the thicket and he gave it to Jack. **1939** Hall *Coll* (Proctor NC) All the dogs was right with us. They just stove right out at it [= a raccoon].... The dogs, they just stove off... into a little laurel patch and there they jumped another big one. **1964** Glassie *Mt Jack Tales* 94–95 What you come a-stavin' in here this time of day fur without them oxens? **1967** Hall *Coll* (Mt Sterling NC) He come stavin' off the hill. The revenue law was in up there. **2005** Williams *Gratitude* 476 *A-stavin'* means that you come a-barrellin', but would be a-stompin' around like you was mad or something was bad wrong, as: "*a-stavin'* like a mad bull."

[DARE *stave* v 5 chiefly South, South Midland]

staving

A *adjective* Excellent, extraordinary.

1883 Bonner *Dialect Tales* 151 He had two blooded cows, and a stavin' young woman for a wife. **c1960** Wilson *Coll*: *staving time* = an unusually big time, an enjoyable time.

B *adverb* Very.

1892 Fruit *KY Words* 232 = very: "That is a stavin' fine horse."

stay *verb* To lodge, reside, make one's home; to stand.

1939 Hall *Coll* (Emerts Cove TN) There isn't anyone stays in Greenbrier Cove now except a few rangers and a few fire guards. There isn't any citizens that lives there at all now. *Ibid.* (Smokemont NC) Here on the waters of Luftee River, [I] stayed there from the time I were about fifteen years old, I think, on up till today. **1953** Hall *Coll* (Bryson City NC) I lived at the lower end of this county—was born and raised there—and stayed there up till nineteen forty-five. **1968** Miller *Pigeon's Roost* (March 7) The origin of the fire was not determined. Mrs. Pate, who stays alone, spent the night with her brother, Harris Street on Pigeon Roost. **1973** GSMNP-78:23 The old mill that stayed here first practically went into dirt before they got a chance to build it back. **1976** GSMNP-113:4 After I got up grown I went to Noland Creek and stayed in there a long time. **1999** Isbell *Keepers* 83 He'd tell audiences that to get to his place you'd have to ride as far as you could ride, run as far as you could run, walk as far as you could walk, crawl as far as you could crawl[, and] then you'd come to where he stayed. **2008** *Rosie Hicks* 1 They stayed down below us a little, not too far away.

[OED3 *stay* v[1] 8b Scottish, South African, India, and U.S.; EDD *stay* v 4 "to lodge, dwell, reside" obsolete; SND *stey* v "to dwell, reside, make one's home"; DARE *stay* v 1 chiefly South, South Midland]

stay all night *verb phrase* To spend the night (sometimes in an invitation or as an expression used at parting). See also **come and go home with me**, **go home with us**, **you'uns come**.

1795 (in **1919** DeWitt *Sevier Journal* 181) (Nov 15) rained all Night. Mr. Ward staid all night. **1836** (in **2004** *Bowman's Ms*) 54 From the ferry to Christiansburg 12 miles [I] turned off there and stayed all night. **1864** *Cooper CW Letter* (May 21) we got on our horses and rode down to William Liones and stayed their all night. **1864** *Hancock CW Letters* (July 30) we run them off and took possession of their camps and stayed all night there. **1924** Raine *Saddlebags* 4 The lad conducted me across the three fords and bade me good night, adding in response to my hearty thanks—for it would have been an insult to offer him money—"Well ye better go home with me and stay all night." **1939** Hall *Coll* (Smokemont NC) They got down to the creek. There they overhauled [the bear], killed him, taked him, dressed him up, took him up to the camp and stayed all night. **1940** Bowman *KY Mt Stories* 247 = expression used at parting instead of "Come again." **1954** GSMNP-19:15 Now you can't stay all night unless you're pretty well known, because [in] this here log cabin they all have to sleep together and sometimes the beds ain't two foot apart. **1973** *AOHP/ALC-259* Did you hear about all kind of teachers staying all night with the kids and their families back then? **1991** Thomas *Sthn Appal* 117 He stayed all night with some of his customers who usually were anxious to have visitors.

stay dog *noun* A foxhound with the endurance to remain in the chase after other dogs have tired.

1968 Clarke *Stuart's Kentucky* 120 The burn-out dogs began fast and tired the fox, but also tired quickly themselves; the cutter, or cuttin' dogs, cheated by taking the long circles around the mountain and along the ridges; stay-dogs had the endurance to remain long in the chase.

stay-place *noun*

1 A shelter for spending the night.

1917 Kephart *Word-List* 417 That shack was put up for a *stay-place* for them herders to pass the night in. **1967** Fetterman *Stinking Creek* 83 All a man needs is a stay place, and I'll take this as good as any. **1984** Wilder *You All Spoken* 74 = a temporary or overnight shelter, as for hikers on the Appalachian Trail. **1994–97** Montgomery *Coll* (known to Bush, Cardwell, Weaver).

[DARE *stay-place* n chiefly southern Appalachians]

2 A residence for an indefinite period (implying a long-term stay).

1970 Justus *Tales* 42 Of course, what he and Samson needed most was a home, a sure-enough stay-place where they could earn their board and keep. **1978** Hiser *Quare Do's* 65 I [go] to whatever place in Appalachia where I can find myself a little "Stay-place," as we natives denigrate an unprepossessing home.

steady *adjective, adverb, verb* Variant form *study*.

1860 *Chapman CW Letters* (April 29) i am working very study at my trade but i have stoped now to put in my crop. **1864** *Hill CW Letters* (May 6) we bin marcheing four days right Study. **c1926** Bird *Cullowhee Wordlist* He's a study boy. **1939** Hall *Coll* (Cataloochee NC) George studied hisself agin a saplin' and cut down and just busted that bear's head wide open. **1942** Hall *Phonetics Smoky Mts* 20. **1957** Broaddus *Vocab Estill Co KY* 75 *study* = steady. **1978** Head *Mt Moments* Other terms are "sorry" for disreputable; "study" for steady; "bad off" for sick; "stomp" for stamp; "play like" for pretend; and to "scotch" a wheel meant to put a rock under it to keep it from rolling. **2005** Williams *Gratitude* 22 Dad was an intelligent man who could do almost any kind of work and was a hard worker, but they wutn't no studdy (steady) work to be found.

[DARE *steady* adj, adv, v (pronc) chiefly South, South Midland]

steady bee See **study bee**.

steal *verb*

1 Variant past-tense forms *stold*, *stoled*.

1864 *Cooper CW Letter* (June 28) the robbers stold your Bacon all except seven peaces. **1967** *DARE Survey* (Gatlinburg TN) *stold* = past tense of steal. **1969** GSMNP-37 Them fellers . . . come through here stealing horses and things [during the Civil War]. They stoled his brother's horse. **1983** *Dark Corner OHP-5A* They got killed over whiskey . . . they just pointed to somebody's still or they stoled his whiskey or that he got the law or called the law and the law got his whiskey. **1989** *Matewan OHP-86* [It was] around here. Somebody stoled it. **1998** *Dante OHP-71* People went in and stoled things out of the house.

[DARE *stol(e)d* v B1b scattered, but most frequent South, South Midland, Southwest]

2 Variant past-participle forms *stold*, *stolden*, *stoldend*, *stole*, *stoled*.

1864 *C A Walker CW Letters* (April 13) I hear you have lost all your meat and some person has stole your milch Cows. **1864** *Poteet CW Letters* (Jan 7) he talked like you had stold the Blanket and gloves. **1939** Hall *Coll*: *stolden*. **1941** Hall *Ballads and Songs* 22 Then Scott and Mims asked for their stoldend shoes. **c1945** Haun *Hawk's Done* 230 For Abe took to claiming he believed George had stole part of the map out of his boot whiles he slept in the night. **1959** Roberts *Up Cutshin* 122 You caused me to kill my three girls, you drownded my old woman, and now you've stold my horse. **1973** GSMNP-79:24 Dad said he carried his still way up on Bullhead back in one of the hollers one time to set it up and said when he went back to it then, [he] said somebody had stold it. **1979** *Big South Fork OHP-4* [When] she went back the next morning to go to school, somebody'd stoled [the shoes].

[DARE *stol(e)d* (at *steal* v B2c) chiefly South, South Midland, Southwest]

steal out *verb phrase* See citation.

2009 Wiles and Wiles *Location* 138 There were always some hens that would not use the nests in the chicken house but instead would make a nest outside, called "stealing out" a nest.

steam barrel *noun* Same as **boiler B1**.

1937 Hall Coll (Cades Cove TN) The boiler of a still [is] the large metal tank in which the liquid of the mash is vaporized. Steam barrels were made locally, from sheet copper (unless a cheaper metal was used) obtained from the mail order houses.

steam donkey *noun* In logging, a large steam engine.

1996 Cole *Forney's Creek* 62 The motive force for the incline was provided by a large steam engine, commonly called a "steam donkey," that was operated at the top of the incline.

steam skidder *noun* See citation.

1964 Clarkson *Lumbering in WV* 372 = a steam engine, usually operated from a railroad track, which skids logs by means of cables.

steepy *adjective* Steep.

1957 Combs *Lg Sthn High: Word List* 95 = steep. The word has lost its poetical significance, and is generally used. Shakespeare speaks of the "steepy mount," in The Taming of the Shrew, I, I. **1991** Still *Wolfpen Notebooks* 75 His daddy left him a farm, pretty good land even if it was steepy.

steer *noun* An uncastrated male bovine (used as a euphemism for *bull*). [Editor's note: In the late 1930s Joseph Hall observed that in the Smoky Mountains *bull* was often somewhat taboo and was avoided in favor of *steer*.] See also **beast B2**, **bull A1**.

1963 Wilson *Regional Words* 81 = a male of the cattle family was, only among men, a bull; elsewhere he was a yearling (regardless of his age), an old animal, a steer, or a male-cow (by very modest people). **1966** Dakin *Vocab Ohio River Valley* 230 Steer [as a euphemism for *bull*] appears in the southern Mountains [of KY]. **1977** Hamilton *Mt Memories* 32 In one of the fields, we could see our heifers, the bull (Mama wouldn't let us say "bull." We called him a "steer"), and the two cows.

[DARE *steer* n (as euphemism) scattered, but somewhat more frequent South, South Midland]

steer squirrel *noun* See citation.

2006 *WV Encycl* 228 The red squirrel is omnivorous and will attack and eat other small mammals. This behavior may have given rise to the myth, common in West Virginia, that fairy diddles raid the nests of other squirrels and castrate their young, creating so-called steer squirrels.

step *verb* Variant past-tense form *stepted*.

1939 Hall Coll.

step off *verb phrase* To get married.

1930 Armstrong *This Day and Time* 82 When's you an' Uncle Abel a-steppin' off?

[DARE (at *step off the carpet* v phr) scattered but especially South]

step out (also *step out on*) *verb phrase* To be unfaithful to (one's spouse); to have an adulterous relationship.

1975–76 Wolfram/Christian *WV Coll* 30 She used to be so jealous of her husband. Oh, she was scared for him to step out. **1991** Still *Wolfpen Notebooks* 69 My husband knows a whole heap better than to step out on me. He knows I might catch him asleep and pour hot lead in his ear. **1992** Montgomery *Coll* = of a man: to cheat on his wife (known to Cardwell). **1993** Ison and Ison *Whole Nother Lg* 64 *step out on* = be unfaithful to a wife or husband, girlfriend or boyfriend, etc.

step rock *noun* A large stone laid at the door to a dwelling as a step.

1924 Raine *Saddlebags* 7 They's a big tide in old Greasy [Creek]. . . . Hit's over the step-rock. **1964** Thomas and Kob *Ballad Makin'* 90 A shingle warped and weather-beaten that had lain for many a day beside the step rock. **1995** Montgomery *Coll*: *step rock* (known to Cardwell).

step stove *noun* A woodburning stove that is set on legs and has a low cooking surface over the firebox and a raised oven behind.

c1960 Wilson *Coll* = a cooking stove with two levels on top. **1968** Wilson *Folklore Mammoth Cave* 38 = a two-level stove that came into use long ago, the first successor to cooking on the fire. **1973** Miller *English Unicoi Co* 154 = a small, wood or coal burning cook stove with two levels for cooking, the front being lower than the back. **1977** *Foxfire IV* 128 Mother's first stove was a number-six step stove. Then they come a number seven—a bigger one, you know. It's an iron stove up on four legs—a little flat feller. They's two caps [= eyes] down here, and then it raises up a little and they's two caps up here. They're a good cook stove. **1982** Ginns *Snowbird Gravy* 39 It was what we called a "step stove" in that day. Had two different tops on it, separated. Had two burners down here, and two up here.

[DARE *step stove* n originally widespread; later chiefly South, South Midland]

stepted See **step**.

stewball See **skewbald**.

stewed fruit *noun* Stewed apples. See also **fruit**.

1917 (in **1944** Wentworth *ADD* 236) (sWV) *stewed fruit* = apple sauce. Not applied to other stewed fruits served at meals.

sti See **si**.

stick

A *noun*

1 See citation.

1944 Dingus *Tobacco Words* 71 = a small (usually) flat piece of timber (four feet and four inches long) on which the freshly pulled or cut tobacco is hung before being cured (and packed away).

[DARE *stick* n 1 South Midland]

2 A log.

1954 Blackhurst *Riders of Flood* 76 Two men were often required to break loose sticks that one should have taken with one heave of a cant hook. **2018** *Blind Pig* (Dec 21) I always say I'm going to "throw another stick on" the fire.

3 (also *sticks*) A response used in a courtship ritual. See also **beeswax**.

1960 Hall *Smoky Mt Folks* 52 If a widower said "beeswax" to a widow whom he had been "sparkin'," he was proposing marriage. If she wished to marry him, she answered "sticks." **1996** Montgomery *Coll* (known to Cardwell); If a widower said "resin," he was proposing marriage. If a widow wished to marry him, she said "stick" (Cypher).

B *verb*

1 See citation.

2009 Wiles and Wiles *Location* 95 Garden crops like peas and beans needed support to keep them off the ground. Pea vines were "stuck" with twiggy bushes gathered from wooded areas. This gave the tendrils of the vine a place to take hold to keep them from running all over the ground.

2 See citation.

1944 Dingus *Tobacco Words* 71 = to arrange tobacco on . . . a stick; to punch a hole through the stalk horizontally before hanging.

[DARE *stick* v 2 especially South Midland]

stick-and-clay chimney (also *stick chimney*) *noun* A crude chimney fashioned of sticks **daubed** together. See also **cat-and-clay**.

1881 Pierson *In the Brush* 125 The fireplace, several feet long, filled with ashes, made an ample spittoon, and the large "stick" chimney, aided by the winds that circulated freely through the cabin, afforded what I have so often wished for—an ample funnel for the escape of the smoke and fumes of the tobacco. **1940–42** Adams *Tales* 121 The house was an old log house with a stick and clay chimney and an old woman came to the door and told him to come in. **1957** Broaddus *Vocab Estill Co KY* 75 = a chimney made of twigs and clay. **1982** Eller *Miners* 24 Most chimneys were built with native stone cemented with clay, but poorer cabins often had "stick chimneys" made of laths daubed with clay and tilted away from the cabin in case of fire.

[DARE *stick-and-clay chimney* n chiefly South, South Midland]

stick bait (also *stick-bait worm, stick worm*) *noun* The worm-like, aquatic larva of the caddis fly, which builds a stick-like case around itself. It is often used for bait in fishing, especially for catfish.

1883 Zeigler and Grosscup *Heart of Alleghanies* 110 The best fishing I ever saw done was a mountaineer, one day in early June, who used a green-winged, yellow-bodied, artificial fly with a stick-bait worm strung on the hook. **1890** Rush *Fishery* 376 About two weeks after my arrival at the fishing grounds, the stick worm became plentiful and then we gave up the red worm. . . . The stick worm is either white or light lemon-color; it is about three-fourths of an inch in length. **1917** Kephart *Camping & Woodcraft* 2:412 From early spring until June, or even July, it is easy to get "stick bait" (the larva of the caddis fly) in almost any trout stream. **1986** Ogle *My Valley* 39 Here we mountain folk used to fish for the now rare native brook trout; hunting in the shallows for what we called stick bait. (Now I've learned they are called caddis insects.) They make tiny cases of stick glued together almost like a cocoon, but lay under water until they hatch, making food for the fish, and an insect that flies, then they lay eggs so that the cycle starts all over again. **1996** Houk *Foods & Recipes* 21 In the side pools of the creek they gathered "stick bait," caddisfly larvae that built cases of sticks and pebbles around themselves.

[DARE *stick bait* n southern Appalachians]

stick-bait worm See **stick bait**.

stickball *noun* A ball game similar to lacrosse played by the Eastern Band of the Cherokee in North Carolina; after being banned by the US government around 1920 because of the traditional version's rough and no-holds-barred character, it has been modified and reintroduced.

1890 Mooney *Cherokee Ball Play* 109–10 The game, which of course has different names among the various tribes, [in the Cherokee language] is called anetsa. The ball season begins about the middle of summer and lasts until the weather is too cold to permit exposure of the naked body, for the players are always stripped for the game. The favorite time is in the fall. [*Ibid.* 131 It is a very exciting game as well as a very rough one, and in its general features is a combination of base ball, football, and the old-fashioned shinny. Almost everything short of murder is allowable in the game, and both parties sometimes go into the contest with the deliberate purpose of crippling or otherwise disabling the best players on the other side.] [**1937** Hall *Coll* (Ravensford NC) The Indians will conjure two or three days before a ball game. The night before a game they'll have a dance and conjure all night long.] **1998** Olson *Blue Ridge Folklife* 137 Another result of assimilation was the steady decline of stickball, which was played less often during the first half of the twentieth century, with less emphasis on its traditional rules and ceremonies. . . . After the U.S. government banned stickball around 1920 (reasons given being the game's roughness, the spectators' rowdiness, and the excessive wagering on the outcome of the game), the Cherokee introduced a revised version [and] this tamer version of the game was offered as an exhibition sport at subsequent Cherokee-sponsored events, such as the Cherokee Fall Festival.

stick bean *noun* Same as **pole bean**. See also **bunch bean**.

1967–69 *DARE Survey* (Berea KY, Hardshell KY, London KY, Sawyer KY, Rogersville TN). **1986** Pederson et al. *LAGS* = attested by 6/60 interviewees (10%) from E TN; 6/18 of all LAGS interviewees (33.3%) attesting term were from Appalachia.

[DARE *stick bean* n especially Inland South, Arkansas]

stick boy *noun* See citation.

1994 Farwell and Buchanan *Logging Terms* = in logging, a person who packed strips used to separate lumber in a stack so that they could be used and reused.

stick burr See **sticker**.

stick chimney See **stick-and-clay chimney**.

sticker *noun*

1 A long-bladed knife, as one to finish killing a hog. See also **frogstick**

1883 Zeigler and Grosscup *Heart of Alleghanies* 61 I never hed no objections ter meetin' a varmint in a squar, stan'up fight,—his nails agin my knife, ye know; so without wunct thinkin' on gittin' outer the way, I retched fer my sticker. **1995–97** Montgomery *Coll*: *sticker* = a long-bladed knife suitable to *stick*, i.e. reach the heart of a stunned hog (Brown), = a long-bladed knife used for cutting the jugular vein in the neck of the hog after it has been shot (Cardwell), = a small knife, sometimes called a frog-sticker (Oliver); *big sticker* (known to Bush, Cardwell, Shields, Weaver).

2 See citation. Same as **scrip**.

1943 Korson *Coal Dust* 72–73 [In coal camps] the same colloquial terms were used for scrip and store orders, such as "stickers," "clackers," "flickers," and "drags." **1973** Preston *Bituminous Term* 50–51 (eKY) = tokens, bills, or other markers given to workers in place of money payment, which were good for full value at a company store but were discontinued [sic; discounted] as much as ten percent in other places.

3 (also *stick burr*) The seedpod of a wild plant that latches onto clothing or hair, such as a **beggar's lice** or a **stick tight**.

1999 Russell and Barnett *Granny Curse* 110 He knew the old folks said witches rode horses and cattle at night when they found a horse or cow worn out in the morning in a sweat with stickers in its tail. **2009** Holbrook *Upheaval* 44 There's a ring of stick burrs in his hair.

stickerweed (also *stick tight, stickweed*) *noun* Usually the same as **beggar('s) lice** (*Bidens* spp); but more generally any of various plants whose burr-like seedpods attach easily to a passing object, as to a person's clothing or animal's fur; the seedpod itself. See also **Spanish needle**.

[**1901** Lounsberry *Sthn Wild Flowers* 527 Although they flare jaunty golden-heads, all the while they are preparing their flattened quadrangular or nearly terete seeds, with barbed and sharp-pointed awns. These, later, attach themselves to anything willing to carry them along and disperse them at a distance from the parent stem. . . . It would seem quite impossible to avoid them. And then so in harmony with their purpose is the instinct of humanity, that few people would be seen returning home while covered with their pods, but sit down by the edge of the woods or swamps to pick off the seeds and scatter them—usually in receptive soil.] **1982** Stupka *Wildflowers* 59 [The naked-flower tick-trefoil] is one of a number of "stick-tights" or "beggar-ticks" growing in the southern mountains. **1996–97** Montgomery *Coll*: *stickerweed, stickweed* = same as *beggar lice* (Brown); *stickweed* (known to Adams, Bush, Jones, Weaver), = fall-blooming purple aster (Cardwell), = an aster, tall in the form of a stick, having the texture of wood, used to start a fire (Brown).

[DARE *stickweed* n especially southern Appalachians]

sticking full *adjective phrase* Extremely full.

1955 Ritchie *Singing Family* 266 It was coal you know, that the trains come in after. These hills right sticking full of coal.

sticks See **stick A3**.

(the) sticks *noun* The backwoods, a rural or remote area thought to be little touched by "civilization." See also **flatwoods**.

1913 Kephart *Our Sthn High* 207 Among themselves the backwoods are called "the sticks." **1930** Armstrong *This Day and Time* 54 I see you're back in the sticks agin with us pore folks. **c1930** Goff *Dialects Sthn Mtneers* 6 The North Georgians speak of the country outside the mountains as the "flatwoods." The wilder parts of the mountains are called the "sticks." **c1950** (in **2000** Oakley *Roamin' Man* 44) I wus told the other day there wus some folks away back in the sticks of real mts. and these folks had never ben to school at all and dident see nuthing but a horse or a cow, pigs and chickens and sumthing of this nature. **1967** Miller *Pigeon's Roost* (July 20) One old timer here said, "Why anybody back here in the sticks couldn't raise nary chicken or keep one if these here fox hunters didn't sorter keep the foxes kindly scared by some fox hunter being in the woods at least three or four times a week." **1972** *AOHP/ALC-226* I lived up in the head of a holler and I guess the sticks, they called it. **1994** Montgomery *Coll*: *the sticks* = remote corner of Cades Cove (Shields). **1999** Montgomery *File* We just lived back in the sticks (40-year-old woman, Del Rio TN). **2004** Curry *The Sticks* 39 Other kids would question us about what it was like to live "in the sticks." We were rarely invited to the homes of our fellow classmates because, as one boy put it, "My mom doesn't want bus kids at our house." *Ibid*. 40 I am still and will always be a coal miner's daughter from "the sticks," and I will always be proud of it. **2006** Farwell *Logging Term* 1021 During the workday separate crews for each stage of the logging process fanned out in the forest, jokingly called the "sticks," where trees might be eight feet across.

stick tight, stickweed See **stickerweed**.

stick worm See **stick bait**.

sticky *noun* See citation.

1958 Wood *Words from TN* 16 *stickies* = cold biscuits split in two, buttered, molasses poured over them, then put in a hot oven.

[DARE *sticky* 1 especially South, South Midland]

stiddier See **instead of**.

stiff jack *noun* Same as **molasses candy**.

1982 Slone *How We Talked* 57 Stiff Jacks, or molasses candy.

still

A (also *still out*) *verb, verb phrase* To distill, make (usually but not necessarily whiskey; see 1976 citation); to produce an alcoholic liquor; hence verbal noun *stilling*.

1833 (in **2005** *Jefferson Co TN Petitions* 200) I have been a man [that] has laboured for my living and have for the few last years have made it principally by stilling. **1863** *Vance Papers* (Feb 15) thare is som men Stilling right a way and has not stoped at all sence tha[y] got done Stilling fruit tha[y] comenced on corn and is selling thare whiskey as fast as tha[y] can make hit. **1864** *Chapman CW Letters* (May 27) I think I hav better health than when I stilled So much and lay a bout in lazness. **1864** *Hill CW Letters* (Sept 1) I wold like to hear how Mr Lackey is is [sic] geting a long stilling the apples. **1902** Hubbard *Moonshiner at Home* 237 It is a mere matter of course that a man who "stills" will some time fall prey to the "revenues," and a conviction is merely a misfortune comparable to the capture of a soldier in wartime. **1913** Kephart *Our Sthn High* 121 The big fellers that makes lots of money out o' stillin', and lives in luxury, ought to pay handsome for it. **1961** Murry *Salt* 24 He's a ole feller an' has been stillin' for ten years I know of, an' there don't never nobody bother his still. **1969** *Hall Coll* (Del Rio TN) McCracken killed Joe Ray because Joe reported that McCracken was stilling. **1975** Fink *Backpacking* 146 They had no hesitancy in telling us of various incidents in "stillin' licker" and in offering to procure a supply for us. **1976** Wigginton *Stanley Hicks* 353–54 Another way we made a little money back then was stilling out our birch oil and mountain tea oil and sassafrak [= sassafras]. We'd still it [in much the same way people distilled moonshine] and sell it. We sold birch oil for twenty-five dollars a gallon. For sassfrak, we'd just use the roots, but birch, we'd use the bark. We could get the bark anytime, but in the wintertime you have to beat it off with an old poleax or a maul. In summer we could just peel it [with] a spud like peeling tanback. . . . And then we'd still pennyroyal out—pull up any herb and still it to get the oil out. That was for medicine. **1989** Landry *Smoky Mt Interviews* 181 Not too much stillin' was going on as far as I knowed.

[OED3 *still* v² 3a now rare or obsolete]

B *noun* In distilling, the pot or container (usually of copper or galvanized steel) into which **beer** is distilled; the entire set-up (i.e. everything needed to make whiskey). See also **cooker**.

1861 *Martin CW Letters* (Nov 29) their is petisions out to Tax the stiles untille war is over. **1900** (in **2009** Blackwell *Rough Place* 15) The laws against murder and manslaughter also are nullified by the moonshiner when deputy marshals become inquisitive, when neighbors turn informer and reveal to officers the hiding place of a "still," and occasionally even a stranger, whose business is not plainly evident and legitimate according to mountain ideas, ventures too far into the highlands. **1912** Mason *Raiding Moonshiners* 197 This man was to pilot us forty miles that night to two "moonshiner stills" in the "old tenth" district, one of the most notorious localities for illicit distilling in the foothills of the Smoky Mountains. **1939** *Hall Coll* (Cataloochee NC) We went over and put us up a still, and we was a-making some awful good [liquor]. It was so good you could taste the girl's feet in it that hoed the corn it was made out of. *Ibid.* (Emerts Cove TN) The steam comes from the cap of the still to the thump keg, and then goes to the bottom of the thump keg, goes in at the top of the thump keg into the bottom. **1949** Maurer *Argot of Moonshiner* 12 = the pot or container in which the beer is distilled to make whisky. In pot operations, a small copper container; in steam operations, a large vat, usually made of silo staves, but sometimes of metal: "We got us a fifty-gallon copper pot"; "That's a steamer. The still will hold 500 gallons of beer." **1956** *Hall Coll* (Bryson City NC) [Quill Rose] asked [the revenuers] to take a picture of him. He was sittin' up on the still house—on his still. **1973** *GSMNP-76*:4 They'd took the still away, but we got the worm and got some backing[s], poured them out. **1982** Slone *How We Talked* 68 = could mean the whole set-up, everything needed to make whiskey, or just the large copper drum used to cook or heat the mash.

[shortening of *distill*]

still and yet (also *still in all*) *adverb phrase* Nevertheless, but still. [Editor's note: The phrase *still and all* is widespread in the US.]

1977 Shackelford et al. *Our Appalachia* 197 A lot of times she'd just look straight at me and I knew that she was in the deepest sympathy with me. Still in all, we'd hear that wagon coming back from town, I doubt if you could have took enough rope to have tied me in there because I'd be getting away. **1987** Kytle *Voices* 162 Still and yet, we couldn't be sure, and anyhow, we liked for somebody to be there in case he roised up.

[DARE *still and yet* (at *still* adv 3) chiefly South, South Midland]

still beer *noun* Same as **beer**.

1881 Atkinson *After Moonshiners* 14 If . . . an illicit operator only produce one gallon per day, he could employ a farm hand to do his hard work while he himself could loaf around his still, drink "still beer" and "moonshine," and have forty cents of surplusage to lay by. **1972** Carr *Oldest Profession* 76 Emerging carbon dioxide gas and low-proof alcohol combine with other ingredients to produce what is called "distillers' beer"—or more commonly among moonshiners, simply "still beer." **c1975** Lunsford *It Used to Be* 80 First, it would be "hot shots," or almost pure alcohol. The next would be high-proof whiskey. Then there's still beer. Just before they get ready to "mash in," they get some of that beer, sometimes drink it.

[DARE *still beer* n chiefly southern Appalachians]

still cap *noun* See c1999 citation.

1940 Oakley *Roamin'/Restin'* 86 This was called a cap so I begain work on the still cap and Birdwell got buisy [sic] on the barrels, that hilt the mash or otherwise we had to make beer first called still mash . . . Birdwell wanted me to make a head for a still cap. **c1999** Sutton *Me and Likker* 103 = the cap [that] catches the alkihol vapors that come out of the still.

stiller *noun* A distiller.

1833 (in **2005** *Jefferson Co TN Petitions* 200) I do not hire stillers but make it all most all by my own labour &c. **1863** *Vance Papers* (Feb 15) you know when the stills is boling hit up that the stiller can aford to give all most Eny prise for corn. *Ibid.* (May 7) these persons that furnish this corn to stillers, willnot sell a grain to the poor for love or money. I want to know how a Justice will see that the law is put inforce, when the Stillers say that if a Justice issues a warrant they will burn their houses and barns. **1915** Bradley *Hobnobbing* 95 In places where the "revenues" are "raidin' around right smart," even men known personally to the "stillers" are not allowed to visit the "stills." **1922** *TN CW Ques* 53 (Sevier Co TN) He was a farmer wrote no books, but was an excelent stiller in his day. **1997** Ownby *Big Greenbrier* II:19 When a deputy and his helpers destroyed a still and the moonshine whiskey it would make the stillers angry.

still hog *noun* See citation.

1939 *Hall Coll* The mash after cooking is often fed to the hogs. A still hog is a hog that hangs around a still for the resultant mixture.

still house *noun* A shed or small building built over a **still** to protect it from the elements or detection.

1859 Taliaferro *Fisher's River* 21 Hamp Hudson was the only man in that whole country who kept a "still-house" running all the year. **1863** *Rector CW Letters* (May 20) another man went too the Still house and was bushwhack[ed] I havent hird whether he is dead or not. **1864** *Brown CW Letters* (Aug 15) eight of us went to a Still house and got two Can teens of brandy witch made a dram round for the b[o]ys. **1881** Atkinson *After Moonshiners* 20 The still house is usually a very rude structure, made of round logs. It rarely has more than one door, and has no windows or other openings. It is generally chinked and daubed to keep out the cold weather. In one corner a rough bedstead is constructed, and on it are several quilts and blankets for the use of the person or parties who sleep at the distillery when a run is made at night. They also keep at the distillery a skillet, coffee pot, &c., with which they do their own cooking. **1937** *Hall Coll* (Bradley Fork NC) = a house for the still and to keep the beer from freezin'. My mother called it "the Devil's kitchen." **1956** *Hall Coll* (Bryson City NC) [Quill Rose] asked [the revenuers] to take a picture of him. He was sitting up on the still house—on his still. **1976** Lindsay *Grassy Balds* 97 At the end of a runoff they would usually bring the backin's in out of the stillhouse to someone's house and have a backin's party. **2005** Williams *Gratitude* 15 They had to have water to run the still, so they usually hunted for a place for their stillhouse clost to the head of a branch.

stillhouse branch *noun* A stream next to which a distilling operation has been set up and from which it draws fresh water.

1976 Lindsay *Grassy Balds* 96 Stillhouse branches [were] all over the place.

still hunt *verb phrase* To hunt, especially for deer or squirrels, by using no dogs but waiting at a fixed location and shooting animals as they pass or come to drink or feed; to hunt (game) in such a fashion; hence nouns *still hunting*, *stilling*.

1849 Lanman *Alleghany Mts* 48 In killing wild animals he pursues but two methods, called "fire-lighting" and "still-hunting." **1867** Harris *Sut Lovingood* 59 The bes' thing they cud du fur the church, wer tu turn out, an' still hunt fur me ontil I wer shot. **1927** Mason *Lure of Smokies* 231 Still huntin' is the best way, and ef a man can't still hunt a b'ar, he ain't much hand to hunt. **1960** Burnett *My Valley* 23 Previous to their day, still-hunting was the method used, and one dog on the order of Tige was sufficient to bag the usual game. **1960** Hall *Smoky Mt Folks* 10 (Lewis Reagan) Another time a man was "still-hunting"—that is, hunting without dogs—up a creek above the camp when he caught sight of a bear through the underbrush. *Ibid.* 21 When ye still-hunt ye take a gun along but no dogs. **1972** *Foxfire I* 256 Most hunters "still hunted" (found a likely tree, sat down in a fairly concealed spot, and waited) for squirrel. The early morning or late evening, when they were cutting nuts in a hickory, oak, or chestnut, was a favorite time. **1989** *Matewan OHP-7* They still hunted, what we called still hunted. They'd take, in other words go out and just set and wait till a squirrel come along, you know, and rabbits. **1996** Houk *Foods & Recipes* 22 Early in the fall, Hubert Sullivan said he "still hunted" squirrels, that is he went into the woods without his dogs, while the leaves were still on the trees and the squirrels were "working on the hickory nuts." **1996–97** *Montgomery Coll*: *still hunting* = hunting in a blind (ducks) or a stand (deer) with no dogs, just set and be quiet (Adams), = hunting without a dog, in which the hunter sits in the woods and waits for game to come by (Brown), = hunting in a stationary position while waiting for game, especially deer, to arrive or pass, best done in a blind or camouflage (Cardwell), = a common method of hunting for squirrel or deer, involving having a likely spot picked out ahead of time, going there before daylight, and simply sitting still while waiting for the game to appear, usually called *stilling* (Ellis).

[probably back-formation from *still hunter*]

still in all See **still and yet**.

still man *noun* The owner or operator of an illegal **still**.

1992 Gabbard *Thunder Road* 73 The still men had to haul large quantities of corn, rye, sugar, apples, and peaches and the equipment to distill and handle their moonshine into hidden mountain recesses. It was back-breaking hard work, and once they got set up, makin' moonshine required more long hours at their stills. The ever-present fear of being discovered by the "revenooers" meant that they had to be careful not to leave signs of their work along roads and paths. Not only did the federal agents drive along back roads looking for evidence of moonshining, they also paid local people who reported suspected stills and still men.

still mash (also *still slop*) *noun* **Mash** from the **still** after distillation. See also **pot-tail(s)**, **slops 1**, **sugar slop**, **swill**.

1863 *Hogg CW Letters* (July 2) John Adams Randals sone fell in to a hot troft of Still Slop and burnt him so he dide [= died] in some three weaks after. **1913** Kephart *Our Sthn High* 129 Cattle, and especially hogs, are passionately fond of still-slop, and can scent it at a great distance. . . . [I]f there was the least taint of still-slop in the water, [the horse] would whisk his nose about and refuse to drink. The officer then had only to follow up the stream, and he would infallibly find a still. **1956** *Hall Coll* (Bryson City NC) When [the revenue officers] got to the house, he was feedin' his hogs some slop—took away from the still, fed his horse some mash after he'd took the liquor out of it. He said it was still mash.

still out See **still A**.

still place *noun* The site of an illegal distilling operation.

1970 Mull *Mt Yarns* 73 He remembered with a chuckle the time his pa got so mad at the local school master for ruining his "cooker" at the "still place." **1983** *Dark Corner OHP-10A* Back then if you had a still place, it cost you to set a place up. I mean it's not like somebody thinks you just go out and put you a few barrels up yonder. They have to make their boilers and their tubings and their pipes and everything, and somebody that couldn't afford it, he'd walk around and he'd find the still place and he'd just add him a few barrels on. **1992** Gabbard *Thunder Road* 119 The night everbody got out of school from graduation, me and him went straight to the still place and fired up.

still pot *noun* A cooking vessel used in making homemade whiskey. Same as **pot**.

1949 Maurer *Argot of Moonshiner* 4 Dead chestnut and ash, which make little smoke, are favorites [for fuel], and the heat is applied directly to a metal plate beneath the copper still pot, which is set securely in the rocks and mudded up with masonry so that a very effective draft is created.

still raider *noun* A law-enforcement agent who searches for stills, destroys them, and attempts to apprehend their operators. Same as **raider**. See also **(the) Federal**, **(the) revenue**.

1967 Hall *Coll* (Del Rio TN) = a revenue officer raidin' [stills], goin' in there and cuttin' 'em down.

still slop See **still mash**.

still-tongue(d) *adjective* Taciturn.

1898 Elliott *Durket Sperret* 50 All the Durkets hes sperret, an' Si ain't none o' your soft-walkin'—still-tongued folks like the Warrens. **1940** Farr *More TN Expressions* 447 *still tongue* = timid or untalkative: "Malissa is a still tongue woman."

[DARE *still-tongued* adj especially South Midland]

stinger snake *noun* Same as **hoop snake**.

1982 Ginns *Snowbird Gravy* 142 I don't know if you've ever heard of a stinger snake or not. A hoop snake. It rolls—a stinger on the end of its tail, and it's got a joint in it just like your finger. They call 'em "stinger snakes."

stinging worm (also *sting worm*) *noun* Same as **packsaddle**.

1967–69 *DARE Survey* (Rome GA, Walker KY, Brasstown NC, Westminster SC) *stinging worm*. **1999** Morgan *Gap Creek* 196 It must have been a jungle the summer before, full of snakes and spiders, hornet nests and sting worms.

stingy-vine *noun* See citation.

1905 Miles *Spirit of Mts* 39 The little sensitive-plant caught at my skirt now and again and dropped its leaves instantly, bearing erect only its pretty blossoms—balls of rosy fluff dusted over with gold. This plant is here known as shame-brier or stingy-vine; both names are highly suggestive of its sudden drooping or closing and drawing back.

stink *verb*

A Forms.

1 Variant past-tense forms *stinked*, *stunk*.

1978 Reese *Speech NE Tenn* 180 *stinked* = attested by 1/12 (8.3%) speakers; *stunk* = attested by 5/12 (41.7%) speakers.

2 Variant past-participle form *stank*.

1978 Reese *Speech NE Tenn* 180 = attested by 1/12 (8.3%) speakers.

B See citation.

1952 Wilson *Folk Speech NC* 594 = to omit a pleasant odor: "That pumgranny shore stinks good."

stink damp *noun* See citation.

c1975 *Miners' Jargon* 7 = hydrogen sulfide gas underground [in a coal mine].

stinking Willie *noun* The erect trillium (*Trillium erectum*). Same as **wake robin**.

1971 Hutchins *Hidden Valley* 55–57 Here beside the road I discover another trillium, this one a wake-robin (*Trillium erectum*). Its three petals are deep-purple red and the plant has a most unpleasant smell, which is the reason it is often known as "stinking Willie."

[DARE *stinking willie* n 2 especially southern Appalachians]

stint *verb* See citation.

1975 Gainer *Witches Ghosts Signs* 17 = to stop: "Don't stint till you've gone all the way home."

stir-off (also *stirring off*) *noun* Traditionally, the process of stirring and skimming **sorghum** cane as it is boiled and made into **molasses**; a neighborhood work and social activity at which this is done, usually followed by festivities. See also **molasses boil**, **run a stir**, **sorghum making**.

1923 Greer-Petrie *Angeline Doin' Society* 7 We have … log-rollin's, and quiltin's, and in the fall of the year, stir-offs. **1953** Davison *Word-List Appal* 14 *stir-off* = a neighborhood social event after molasses is made and the time has come to take it off. **1955** Ritchie *Singing Family* 119 At this minute Sarah came and fetched us for a dinner laid out on the kitchen table, fried chicken with gravy and dumplings on the side, new beans and corn bread, garden greens and thick, sweet molasses from last fall's stir-off. **c1960** Wilson *Coll*: *stir-off* = the run-off or finishing of a making of sorghum. **1973** Cate *Molasses Making* Youngsters hurried home from school and quickly completed their chores so that they could go down and watch the "stir-off." Some chewed pieces of cane, others ate the foam skimmed from the thickening syrup or sopped up the molasses left in the cooking vat. **1974** Roberts *Sang Branch* 29 We'd raise cane and have molasses all the time. Everybody raised cane. We would have a stir-off every night when we got to making 'lasses. Get the cane in to the mill and grind it into juice of a day, and then it would take us till sometimes two o'clock in the night to get it stirred off. Then we would carry the molasses in and get everything cleaned up for the next night. We would have some of the same games we had at the other get-together. Run sets, play Pleased or Displeased, or old Doc Jones or London Bridge. **1976** Braden *Grandma Was Girl* 31 The last day of molasses making, we would have a "stirring-off." It was usually at night. The neighbors came in. Some of the molasses was cooked into candy, and everyone had a good time. The boys enjoyed putting molasses in the girls' hair.

[DARE *stir-off* n chiefly southern Appalachians, especially KY]

stir stick See **swab**.

stob

A *noun* A sharp or jagged stake, stump, post, protruding branch or root, etc.

1883 Smith *Southernisms* 53 Stob, "a small post or stake or stump of a shrub," [is] commonly so used in many, if not all, parts of the South. **1891** Brown *Dialect in TN* 175 A *stob* is a stake driven in the ground, or the tall stump of a tree. **1913** Kephart *Our Sthn High* 91 I knocked her (the bear) over with a birch stob. **1939** Hall *Coll* (Proctor NC) We just went to cutting that old stob, you know, to start us a fire with. **1962** Dykeman *Tall Woman* 182 He had stepped on the sharp stob of a sassafras bush. **1964** Wright *Mt Medicine* 8 One whom John consulted on a very peculiar case which he had been called in to see (consisting of a particularly dangerous home-abortion attempt) said to him, "Dr. Wright, I have been in this country for twenty years, and I don't ask questions. If the patient tells you she fell on a stob, so far as I am concerned, SHE FELL ON A STOB." **1976** Thompson *Touching Home* 16 = a little stump or root sticking up.

[OED3 *stob* n¹ now only Scot and dialect; SND *stob* n 7; CUD *stob* n 1 "a stake, a post"; DARE *stob* n chiefly South, South Midland]

B (also *staub*) *verb* To stab, jab, stick.

1883 Zeigler and Grosscup *Heart of Alleghanies* 52 I drew back a step, an' as he [= a bear] brashed by me, I bent over him, grabbin' the ha'r o' his neck with one hand, an' staubed him deep in the side with the knife in the other. **1913** Kephart *Our Sthn High* 126 I'll bet he's stobbed somebody and is runnin' from the sheriff! **1927** Mason *Lure of Smokies* 201 We both tho'ght they was fussin' 'bout which was goin' ter git to stob us fust while we was asleep. **1939** Hall *Coll* (Hartford TN) [The bear] had the dogs down, and [my father] run up and stobbed his knife into it and cut a big long gash, plumb to the hollow of the bear. **1961** *Coe Ridge OHP-340B* He got up and stobbed him in the back. **1973** GSMNP-83:9 He was cutting the life out of him, stobbing him everywhere he could. **1985** Irwin *Alex Stewart* 253 I tried to get my knife out to stob (stab) him [= a dog] through his heart, but I couldn't do it.

[OED3 *stob* v¹ dialect; DARE *stob* v South, South Midland]

stock *noun* A log used in chimney construction.

1939 *FWP Guide KY* 127 Above the throat of the fireplace the chimney was constructed of "stocks" or logs carefully chinked, at first with clay but later with mortar. In time the "stock" chimneys, always in danger of burning, were replaced with stone.

stock barn *noun* See citation.

c1960 Wilson *Coll* = a building where stock, usually horses, are kept. **2013** Loop *Shadow of Appal* 70 The hay would be hauled to the stock barn and pitched into the hayloft to be fed to the horses and cows through the winter months.

[DARE *stock barn* scattered, but especially Midland]

stock brute *noun* Used as a euphemism for bull. See also **brute**, **bull A1**.

1926 Hunnicutt *Twenty Years* 110 I saw Old Riley throw a big stock brute the other day. **1949** Kurath *Word Geog East US* 62 *Stock brute*, *male brute* [are found] in westernmost North Carolina. **1973** Miller *English Unicoi Co* 154 = a male of the bovine species, a bull.

stock law *noun* An arrangement whereby livestock are fenced away from open fields of crops. See also **fence law**, **no-fence law**, **open range**, **open stock law**.

c1975 Lunsford *It Used to Be* 60 They'd have to fence their crops or their cattle. In some places they would have the fence law, that is, the field would be fenced and the cattle would run outside. In other places they would have the Stock Law, and the cattle would be fenced and the field would be open. **1975** *Richard and Margaret* 9 When they put the refuge in, they just said "You're gonna have t'fence up your place now, an' take your cattle an' hogs out of the mountains, or sell 'em." 'Cause of the stock law came into effect. **1993** *Stories 'neath Roan* 5 There wasn't no stock law and they would just turn their hogs loose back then. *Ibid.* 58 Where they run out and got wild, hogs killed a lot of the little timber out. They didn't have no stock law then, but they have got a stock law now. They marked all their hogs in the ear. **1997** Davis *Cataloochee Valley* 20 Turning on the range was taking the cattle out on the grassy balds to pasture for the summer. The stock range law was in effect for about 125 years. In many sections of our county, it was voted out in favor of the "stock laws" in the early 1890s.

stock pea *noun* A black-eyed pea. See citation.

c1960 Wilson *Coll* Peas (that is, cow peas or stock peas) [were] grown on most farms of other times. Some used for hay.

[DARE *stock pea* n 1 especially South Midland]

stog (also *stog off*, *stug*) *verb*, *verb phrase* To plod or trudge, move about in a heavy or clumsy manner.

1925 Dargan *Highland Annals* 247 They's all skeered to marry Nathe, an' no wonder when he kept stuggin' round the country lookin' like the hind wheels o' destruction. **1940** (in **2004** West *Lonesome Road* 41) He stogged off down a cotton row. **1967–69** DARE *Survey* (Sawyer KY) *stog* = to walk heavily, making a lot of noise. (Gatlinburg TN) *stog* = to move around in a way that makes people take notice of you. **1997** Montgomery *Coll*: *stog* (known to Oliver).

[OED3 *stog* v² 2 "to walk clumsily or heavily; to plod on" Scottish; EDD *stog* v³ "to walk heavily or awkwardly, to plod"; cf SND *stodge* v 1 "to walk with a long, slow, heavy, or deliberate step"; CUD *stog* v "walk heavily or awkwardly"; Web3 *stog* v Scottish, perhaps alteration of *stodge* "to trudge through, or as if through muck and mire"; DARE *stog* v southern Appalachians]

stog off See **stog.**

stoke *verb* To distribute (game meat, etc.) into roughly equal portions among hunters, often assigning one portion to each by a method of chance in which all hunters but one go out of sight and the remaining hunter calls out "Whose piece is this?" as names are successively called.

1913 Kephart *Our Sthn High* 102 The mountaineers have an odd way of sharing the spoils of the chase. They call it "stoking the meat," a use of the word stoke that I have never heard elsewhere. The hide is sold, and the proceeds divided equally among the hunters, but the meat is cut up into as many pieces as there are partners in the chase; then one man goes indoors or behind a tree, and somebody at the carcass, laying his hand on a portion, calls out: "Whose piece is this?" "Granville Calhoun's," cries the hidden man . . . And so on down the line. Everybody gets what chance determines for him, and there can be no charges of unfairness. **1984** Wilder *You All Spoken* 105 = shar[e] the spoils of a hunt. [**1992** Montgomery *Coll* (unknown to consultants from the Smoky Mountains).]

stold, stolden, stoldend, stole, stoled See **steal.**

stomach robber *noun* See citation.

1941 *FWP Guide WV* 403 Although changed in other respects, the West Virginia logger has retained his jargon. Cooks are still "stomick robbers" . . . and milk is "cow." **1964** Clarkson *Lumbering in WV* 373 = cook.

stomp

A *verb* To stamp; to crush or squash; to strike the foot heavily downward.

1867 Harris *Sut Lovingood* 54 Then he'd fetch a vigrus ruff rub whar a hosses tail sprouts; then he'd stomp one foot, then tuther, then bof at onst. **1942** Hall *Phonetics Smoky Mts* 26 [stɑmp], [stɒmp], [stɔmp]. **1964** Roberts *Hell-Fer-Sartin* 125 If you don't talk to me I'm going to stomp you. **1968** *Faith Healing* 64 [If] you tell it, I'll stomp you in th'ground. **1989** Smith *Flyin' Bullets* 278 A sharp anger went through T. J. as he stomped towards the passenger's door of the stopped car. **1999** Morgan *Gap Creek* 152 I stomped hard to make dints in the soft ground under the leaves, digging my heels into the steep side of the mountain, making steps. **2004** Fisher *Kettle Bottom* 13 It is good when Daddy don't stomp and Mama smiles.

B *noun* A clearing with little or no grass, especially one where livestock have worn it off. See also **cow stomp**. See also **stomping ground(s)**.

1974 Fink *Bits Mt Speech* 25 = clearing with grass trodden of[f] by cattle or horses. "They's a big *stomp* on top of the mountain." **1997** Montgomery *Coll* (known to Bush, Cardwell, Ledford, Weaver).

[DARE *stomp* n 1 South, South Midland]

stomp dance *noun* A traditional dance practiced by the Eastern Band of the Cherokee of North Carolina.

1990 Kline *Cherokee Songs and Ceremonies* 26 Friends and admirers from the western band of the Cherokee in Oklahoma have initiated an informal exchange with Walker [Calhoun] and his family. Twice an Oklahoma contingent has traveled to Big Cove [NC] to encourage the Calhoun family in reviving the stomp dance religion. **1999** Green and Fernandez *Native N America* 152 Southeastern Indian women (Cherokee, Choctaw, Seminole and Creek) make the rhythm for the stomp dance with the turtle shells they wear on their legs. Cherokees call the women "shell shakers."

stomping ground(s) *noun* A place much frequented, a habitual gathering place. See also **stomp B.**

1864 *Rogers CW Letters* (March 2) the yank has ben in three miles Dolton We drove them back to thair old stomping ground We skirmush with them most ever day. **1963** Medford *Mt People* 51 There were the "stompin' grounds"—so called, or loafing-places in every community. **1969** Medford *Finis* 100 When asked the whereabouts of someone in the family, the reply might be: "He's probably at the Stampin' Ground." That was a gathering or loitering place, one or two of which could be found in every community; a store front, blacksmith shop or even a cross roads might serve as such. **1976** Garber *Mountain-ese* 88 = habitat, haunt. "They came right back to their old stomping ground."

stone blind *adjective phrase* Completely blind, "blind as a stone."

1940 Mathes *Jeff Howell* 20 Ninety years of age, stone-blind, and all but bedfast with palsy, he was seldom seen in the valley any more, but when there was trouble, when the shadow of fear fell over the dark mountain slopes, they always sent for Preacher Pleas.

stone bruise *noun* A bruise on the sole of the foot, especially the heel, from going barefoot and stepping on a stone or other hard object; an abscess resulting from such a bruise.

1915 Dingus *Word-List VA* 191 = any bruise on the sole of the foot. **1933** Miller *Healing Gods* 475 The familiar "stone bruise" of barefoot days is relieved by binding on it a live toad with the abdomen split open. **1957** Combs *Lg Sthn High: Word List* 96 = a serious bruise on the sole of the foot, usually the heel. A barefoot boy sometimes acquires this inconvenience by jumping. **c1960** Wilson *Coll* = a sore on the underside of a foot, said to be from bruising (mashing) it on a rock. **1982** Slone *How We Talked* 101 = a kind of boil that came on the bottom of the foot, usually on the heel, caused by going barefoot and bruising the foot on the sharp stones. Cure: Stick the heel in a warm cow pile (fresh cow manure); a mixture of salt and meal scalded with hot water, or any other cure used for a boil. The skin of the foot was made more tough by going barefoot, causing the infection to be more difficult to get to break and drain. A stone bruise was very painful, and could cause one to have to stay in for a long time and not be able to walk for months. **1990** Cavender *Folk Medical Lex* 31–32 = an absessed sore on the heel of the foot caused by a severe bruise; common among children who go without shoes in the summer. **1997** Nelson *Country Folklore* 92 The very worst thing we had from going barefooted was stone bruises. There was lots of pain from these. The bottoms of our feet became tough and thick. So when we had a stone bruise they had to be opened with a razor blade. We dreaded it, but this was the only way we could get relief from the pain.

stone fence (also *stone wall*) *noun* A fence made of stone or rock, usually without mortar. See 1995 citation. Same as **rock fence**.

1862 *Kiracofe CW Letters* (May 25) they got up there . . . with their infantry & got the advantage of a stone fence. **1958** Newton *Dialect Vocab*: *stone fence* = attested by 2 of 36 speakers from E TN mountains; *stone wall* = attested by 7 of 36 speakers from E TN mountains, the most common term being *rock wall*. **1966** Dakin *Vocab Ohio River Valley* 108 *Stone fence* also has some currency in Kentucky, chiefly in the western Bluegrass and northeastern Pennyroyal. In this state, the relatively uncommon *stone fence* frequently appears as an alternative to *rock fence* in the speech of the same younger Type II [i.e. those with more formal education] informants, but it does not appear to be spreading very rapidly. There are indications that some of the speakers may in fact be distinguishing between *rock fence* = "a fence constructed of pieces of rock in its 'natural' form" and *stone fence* = "constructed of cut or split stone, secured by mortar; a more ornamental wall around a cemetery, etc., rather than a fence between fields." **1986** Pederson et al. *LAGS*: *stone fence* = attested by 5/60 interviewees (8.3%) from E TN and 3/35 (8.6%) from N GA; 8/71 of all LAGS interviewees (11.2%) attesting term were from Appalachia; *stone wall* = attested by 11/60 interviewees (18.3%) from E TN and 5/35 (14.3%) from N GA; 16/98 of all LAGS interviewees (16.3%) attesting term were from Appalachia. **1995** *Smokies Guide* (Summer) 13 Even sixty years after the establishment of the national park, stone fences remain on lands once used for agriculture. These painstakingly built and enduring structures served multiple purposes. For one, they were a place to put unwanted stones removed from a crop field or pasture. They also marked boundaries and kept pigs, cows, mules, and horses out of fields. In some cases, stone walls were even built as part of elaborate terracing systems to help level a mountainside field. The chief advantages of stone fences over wood were that the materials were plentiful, free, ready to use, and never rotted. The major disadvantage was that the materials weren't light-weight.

stoneroller *noun* Same as **knotty**.

1996 Houk *Foods & Recipes* 21 In March and April, fish called stonerollers were among the delectables found on mountain tables. **1997** Montgomery *Coll* (known to Cardwell).

stone wall See **stone fence**.

stool *noun* An invitation.

1891 Brown *Dialect in TN* 175 Stool is an old-fashioned word for an invitation; as, a stool to a party or a wedding. **1940** Farr *More TN Expressions* 448 = invitation: "I have a stool to the wedding supper."

[DARE *stool* n 1 southern Appalachians]

stop blood *verb phrase* To cause bleeding from a wound to cease (usually by reciting a Bible verse [e.g. Ezekiel 16:6] or using a charm). See also **blood doctor**, **charm doctor**.

[**1894** Porter *Folklore Mt Whites* 111 Hæmorrhage is arrested by thrice repeating the passage in Ezekiel beginning, "As I passed by thee," etc.] **1939** Hall *Coll* (Proctor NC) Old timers could stop blood by saying a verse over in the Bible to themselves. *Ibid.* (Proctor NC) A woman has to tell three men how to stop blood. **1954** Hall *Coll* (Del Rio TN) My mother quoted Scripture to stop blood, but said you must believe that the Lord would stop it. [**1956** Hall *Coll* (Roaring Fork TN) The old mountain people believed that there was a charm doctor in every community. Wes Rayfield's boy was cuttin' wood and cut an artery. She charmed it, but it just bled on. She got excited and missed a word. When she got in the house off to herself, she thought of the word and said the rhyme over and the blood stopped.] [**1974** Roberts *Sang Branch* 80 I asked him about the mystery of the charm, if it took faith, if he said words, or if he just thought of something. All he would say is that it cannot be divulged without losing it.] **2007** Milnes *Signs Cures Witches* 59 People dehorned cattle so they would not be dangerous to work around. One time, Johnny Arvin recalls, a cow was dehorned but was bleeding profusely. An old woman in the community, known as one who could "stop blood," was contacted. Through her actions, the blood was stopped. Johnny Arvin noted the common rule that governs transmission of this seemingly miraculous ability: a woman can tell a man how to do it, or vice-versa, but the knowledge can not be passed between members of the same sex. *Ibid.* 102 Of all the cures that fit into the vein of magical belief, stopping blood is the most common in West Virginia.

stopping *noun* See citation.

1973 Preston *Bituminous Term* 28 = erected walls of stone, rock, wood, or other permanent material that helps control the flow of air in a [coal] mine.

store

A *noun* Compounded with another noun to refer to an item manufactured and purchased commercially rather than one homemade or homegrown, as **store cloth**, **store medicine**, **store tea**, etc. See also **brought-on 1**, **fotch-on**, **store-bought**.

B *verb* To shop or **trade**.

1974 Fink *Bits Mt Speech* 25 = to trade in a store. "I've got a lot of *storing* to do." **1995** Montgomery *Coll* (known to Adams, Bush, Cardwell).

[DARE *store* v especially central Atlantic, southern Appalachians]

store back *verb phrase* To put (money) in reserve, conserve for later use.

1975–76 Wolfram/Christian *WV Coll* 83 Maybe he stored [my wages] back, cause I never went nowheres or nothing.

store-bought (also *store-boughten*) *adjective phrase* Purchased at a store, made, ordered, or brought from outside the community, as distinct from homemade or homegrown. See also **brought-on 1**, **fotch-on**, **store A**.

1883 Zeigler and Grosscup *Heart of Alleghanies* 91 The characters of most interest to all present were two good-natured-looking young men dressed in "biled" shirts, green neckties, "store-boughten" coats, and homespun pantaloons. **1938** Bowman *High Horizons* 55 A thrifty people, they have kept the skill with their hands which their ancestors acquired through necessity, because "store-boughten" articles were rare until comparatively recent times. **1950** Woody *Cataloochee Homecoming* 12 Every man had to be something of a carpenter and blacksmith; everything possible was fashioned by hand rather than "store bought." **1969** Madden and Jones *Walker Sisters* 25 Cloth for summer clothing was all "store bought," but the garments were all hand made. **1973** GSMNP-4:27 About the only thing they would ever order would be shoes . . . or maybe a hat or something like that . . . as far as dresses, I never saw a woman I guess with a store-bought dress on in that country until I was fifteen years old. They all made their clothes. **1974** GSMNP-50:2:15 This is a store-bought cake. You may not like it. I was too tired to make one. **1986** Pederson et al. *LAGS*: *store-bought* = attested by 5/60 interviewees (8.3%) from E TN; 5/20 of all LAGS interviewees (25%) attesting term were from Appalachia. **1987** Young *Lost Cove* 29 More and more they had been turning to the outside for a little folding money and spare change to buy store-boughten things.

[DARE *store-bought* adj phr 1 (of teeth) chiefly South, South Midland, Southwest]

store-bought bread (also *store-boughten bread*, *store bread*) *noun* Bread that is not homemade, usually wheat bread.

1966 Dakin *Vocab Ohio River Valley* 319–21 *Store bread* is . . . quite common in Kentucky in the Bluegrass and the Mountains (one of the rare terms which have this distribution and certainly a newer expression which has spread eastward from the Bluegrass). In Kentucky this expression is frequently *store bought(en) bread*. **1986** Pederson et al. *LAGS*: *store-bought bread* = attested by 5/60 speakers (8.3%) from E TN; 5/20 of all LAGS users (25%) attesting term were from Appalachia. **2018** *Blind Pig* (April 2) Biscuits and cornbread were everyday staples. We used to have light bread too, homemade white flour yeast bread. Then at times we had white "store bread."

store bread See **store-bought bread**.

store building *noun* A building that serves as a commercial establishment. See also **store house**.

1987 Young *Lost Cove* 6 A little log store-building was thrown up at the forks of the road to supply the forty or so families with the few goods they couldn't produce on their farms. **2010** Owenby *Trula Ownby* 14 Our first house was the old store building grandpa Reagan had. The store building was about twelve feet wide and forty feet long.

store cloth *noun* Cloth purchased rather than being spun and woven at home.

1916 (in **1991** Alvic *Weavers of Highlands* 2) After the war, "store cloth" was cheap, so that one woman after another put the old loom aside. **1975** Purkey *Madison Co* 66 My mother knew how to spin and weave, though she seldom did any of it now, as "store cloth" had become plentiful.

store clothes *noun* Clothing purchased at a store.

1869 (in **1974** Harris *High Times* 216) These store clothes folks has some mighty curious ways, any how. **1910** Thompson *Highlanders* 27 "Store clothes" may have come to many of these people, but the real mountain man prefers his "double Dutch breeches" and his brogan shoes tied with ground-hog hide. **1913** Kephart *Our Sthn High* 308 Homespun jeans and linsey used to be the universal garb of the mountain people. Nowadays you will seldom find them, except in far-back places. Shoddy "store clothes" are cheaper and easier to get. **1943** Bewley *Picturesque Speech* 4 In an earlier day only professional people, such as doctors, lawyers and preachers, wore "store clothes" in the hill country. **1989** *Matewan OHP*-102 Then we could get clothes already made, you know, we called them store clothes.

store credit *noun* See Cardwell citation.

1994–97 Montgomery *Coll* (known to Adams), = credit extended until the crops are sold in the fall (Brown), = credit extended by local storekeepers in the community. Purchases were recorded and identified by name and price in a ledger, and when the customer paid, the portion or amount was recorded in the credit column of the ledger. All mountain storekeepers kept ledgers and operated on a barter system. Customers usually paid in eggs, furs or hides, herbs, and the like (Cardwell).

store house *noun* A dwelling serving also as a small commercial establishment. See also **church house**, **store building**.

1915 Dingus *Word-List VA* 191 = a house where merchandise is sold. **1941** Still *Troublesome Creek* 118 For supper and breakfast we ate little fishes out of flat cans Aaron got at a storehouse. **1974** GSMNP-51:7 Him and Leery built a little store there on the side of the road, a little store house. **1979** *Big South Fork OHP*-10 They's about five houses there . . . besides the store house, the commissary, whatever you call it. **1998** *Dante OHP*-61 He had a store there then, and they had meetings there at his store house at that time.

store loafer *noun* A man who habitually loiters in a country store to gossip and stay out of his house.

1963 Edwards *Gravel* 125 Too much work involved in building a rock fence for our store loafers.

store medicine *noun* Commercially purchased medicine, as opposed to home remedies.

1965 Shelton *Pioneer Comforts* 8 Since "store medicine" was not easily located and midwives were not always near, every homemaker took pride in her own knowledge and collection of "yarbs."

store tea *noun* Ordinary tea, purchased at a store.

1913 Kephart *Our Sthn High* 98 It was the first time that Little John ever saw "store tea."

store teeth *noun* False teeth.

1957 Combs *Lg Sthn High: Word List* 96 = false teeth. **2008** Goan *Nursing Service* 156 Emergency gifts of seed, fodder, shoes, eyeglasses, and "store teeth" were common.

store tobacco *noun* Commercially processed and purchased tobacco.

1984 Yeatts *Old Mayberry* 54 Sometimes there was a little [money] left over for "store tobacco," which she carefully blended with the crumbling of long-leaf bright from Mt. Airy to be stowed away in bright tin boxes.

store towel *noun* A commercially manufactured towel of superior quality to a homemade one.

2013 Patton *Go Back* 4 I want to go back where all of the common, everyday towels were made of salt sacks, and where they was only one "store" towel which was put out only when the preacher came.

store truck *noun* Same as **rolling store**.

2005 Williams *Gratitude* 35 Mom sent him to the store truck (rolling store) one day to get a jug of bleach.

story *verb* To lie, tell a falsehood.

1921 Weeks *Speech of KY Mtneer* 19 We whup our children; we even wear them out when they story to us. **1952** Wilson *Folk Speech NC* 594 = to tell a falsehood. Generally euphemistic: "You storied to me about going to that dance." **c1986** (in **2015** Yarrow *Voices* 48) I said, "No, sir." He said, "Don't you story to me."

[DARE *story* v chiefly South, South Midland]

stout

A *adjective*

1 Vigorous, robust, full of energy; in good health (especially after recovering from an illness).

1834 *Seal Letter* My wife is very stout of her age and wants to see you and so does Zeally too and so does the children all. **1862** *Edmonston/Kelly CW Letters* I had the tooth ache too days but I had it taken out Since that I have ben Stout. **1864** *Chapman CW Letters* (April 23) I can inform you That I am Well and tolerbel stout at presant. **1908** Smith *Reminiscences* 407 "Mose, are you stout?" saluted "Devil" Sam. **1956** Hall *Coll* (Sand Hill TN) I thought it was too tough at home. Daddy wasn't stout, and when hit'd be a big snow on the ground, I had to get out and get the wood. **1970** GSMNP-26:11 He got into a cutting scrape with a fellow and cut him up till the other fellow didn't die, but he was never stout after it. . . . They said he never was much stout after that. **1994** Montgomery *Coll* Reckon you're stout? [= Are you in good health?] (Ogle).

[OED3 *stout* adj 6b "in robust health" obsolete except Scot; DARE *stout* adj 2 chiefly South Midland]

2 Powerful, strong in body.

1962 Hall *Coll* (Cades Cove TN) Becky Cable was a very stout woman. She did man's work. She lived to be ninety-six years old. **1971** AOHP/ALC-66 I wasn't but about twenty-four years old, stout as a mule.

B *adverb* Robustly, boldly.

1939 Hall *Coll* (Tuckaleechee Cove TN) We'd hear 'em talk big and stout, how they'd he'p carry the old bear out. [In "To the Bearhunters of Yesterday"; for this poem, see **1978** Hall *Yarns and Tales* 38–39.] **1975** Chalmers *Better* 66 Good shoes will wear stout even for this trifling generation.

stove (also *stove up*) *verb, verb phrase* To cripple, bruise, make stiff or sore in one or more joints from overwork or injury and sore to a degree that it is difficult to get around; hence participial adjectives *stove(d) up*. See also **stave**.

1915 Dingus *Word-List VA* 191 *stove up* = stiff from overwork: "That horse is mighty bad stove up." **1957** Combs *Lg Sthn High: Word List* 96 *stove up* = applied to a horse that has been worked so hard that he is stiff and unable to work longer. **1973** GSMNP-87:2:24 He lost a eye, and he was kind of what I'd call stove up all over. **1975** Gainer *Speech Mtneer* 17 That horse got stoved from being rid down hill too fast. **1976** Weals *It's Owin'* She was in a car wreck and got all stove up. **1979** Carpenter *Walton War* 178 He come home so stove up he couldn't hardly git in the bed. **c1982** Young *Colloquial Appal* 21 = sprained, jammed finger or toe. **1990** Cavender *Folk Medical Lex* 32 = to jam or stub a finger or toe. **1993** Cunningham *Sthn Talk* 149 *stove up* = injured or crippled to such a degree that it is difficult or impossible to get around. **1996** Spurlock *Glossary* 411 = to dislocate a joint. **2006** Cavender *Medical Term* 1022 She's been stoved up now for a week with the flu. **2016** *Blind Pig* (July 9) I've stove my fingers up many times when I played basketball and football. *Ibid.* (Sept 2) I know from a car wreck what it's like to be all stoved up.

[originally past participle of *stave*; cf SND *stave* v 3 "to sprain, bruise, or contuse a joint of the body"; DARE *stove* v² 4 especially wPA, OH, WV; DARE *stove up* adj phr 1 chiefly South, South Midland]

stove catch *noun* See citations. Same as **catch C2**.

1957 Combs *Lg Sthn High: Word List* 96 *stove ketch* = lifter for removing caps from a kitchen range. **1968–69** *DARE Survey* (Viper KY, Big Stone Gap VA) = the thing you use to remove the lids . . . from a wood-burning stove when it is hot.

[DARE *stove catch* n especially South Midland]

stoved up See **stove**.

stove room *noun* A separate room that contains the cooking stove, sometimes removed from the rest of the house.

1912 Perrow *Songs and Rhymes* 139 We hear stove-room (for kitchen), widder-man, home-house, and engineer-man. **1986** Pederson et al. *LAGS* (Elbert Co GA, Rockdale Co GA).

stove up See **stove**.

straddle *noun* The crotch; also used as a euphemism for the genitals.

1917 Kephart *Word-List* 418 = crotch. "Wet up to the *straddle.*" **1939** Hall Coll (Copeland Creek TN) They poured tar between her straddle. *Ibid.* I can see your straddle through them pants.

[DARE *straddle* n especially South Midland]

straddle deep *adjective phrase* Of water: up to the top of the leg in depth. See also **hub deep, shoe-mouth deep**.

1941 Hall Coll (Del Rio TN) We had an awful rain the other day. I waded water straddle deep in the highway. **1982** Slone *How We Talked* 99 The depth of the snow was described as: a skiff of snow; ankle-deep; knee-deep; straddle-deep; over your head.

straggeldy (also *straggly-headed, stratty-headed*) *adjective, adjective phrase* Having unkempt hair.

1954 Arnow *Dollmaker* 29 You ain't looked in a looken glass lately; you've got mud splashes all over and yer hair's all straggeldy. **1957** Broaddus *Vocab Estill Co KY* 76 *straggly-headed, stratty-headed* = with mussed up, straggly hair.

straggly-headed See **straggeldy.**

straight corn *noun* See citations. Same as **corn juice.**

1939 Hall Coll (Emerts Cove TN) They made straight corn. They didn't make no sugar liquor. **1949** Maurer *Argot of Moonshiner* 4 So-called "corn whisky" is still made, although the pure corn or straight corn of older days is now practically nonexistent. *Ibid.* 12 = liquor made from corn only, with no sugar. Rare in fact, but not so rare in claim. "Is this straight corn?" "Is this corn likker?"; "Shore it's pure corn likker"; "This is straight corn likker. No sugar."

straight out *verb phrase* To straighten out.

1966 Dykeman *Far Family* 118 "I've got it all straighted out, Martha girl," he said happily.

straight town *noun* See citation. See also **round town** (at **round cat**).

1915 Dingus *Word-List VA* 192 = of two kinds—straight-town and round-town—according to the position of the bases.

strainth See **strength.**

stranger man (also *stranger people, stranger woman*) *noun* One or more persons not from the immediate vicinity and thus unrecognized.

1891 Murfree *Stranger People* 7 He 'peared toler'ble disapp'inted till he hearn 'bout the Stranger People's buryin'-groun'. **1954** Arnow *Dollmaker* 135 I don't wonder . . . that a stranger woman like you is afeard of me. **1978** Hiser *Quare Do's* 81 We rushed out into the yard. Hit's Ance York's stave mill broke loose and flyin thu the air, some old stranger man said. Hit'll kill us all. Get the women and younguns under shelter where they'll be safe. I looked and seen some stranger people, and some bystander said what it was.

stranger people See **stranger man.**

stranger room *noun* An enclosed room on the porch for an overnight guest or a traveler passing through. See citations. Same as **Elijah room.**

1995 Trout *Historic Buildings* 37 Whether they charged for the service or not, mountaineers created little barriers between themselves and their overnight guests. Some Cades Cove residents framed in their porches for this purpose and called them "stranger rooms" or "Elijah rooms," for the Biblical character. A latch string in the front door of the home, pulled in, locked the family in and the stranger out. **2002** Myers *Best Yet Stories* 195–96 An enclosed room on the front porch of the George Tipton's home in Cades Cove was widely known as the "Stranger Room." The room had a private entrance and contained only a bed, a table, a chair, and an old oil lamp. It was free to people who were passing by to spend the night. It was often used by cattle drivers passing to and fro.

stranger woman See **stranger man.**

stratty-headed See **straggeldy.**

straw bed tick See **straw tick.**

strawberry bush *noun* A burning bush (*Euonymus americanus* or *E. atropurpureus*). Also called **arrowwood.** See also **hearts bustin', spindle bush, wahoo 1.**

1937 Thornburgh *Great Smoky Mts* 25 The seeds of some shrubs are more spectacular than their flowers. This is true of one of the showiest shrubs in the Great Smokies, the euonymous, wahoo or spindlebush. It is especially lovely in October when its seedpod bursts open, displaying orange-colored seeds in its glowing red heart. It has many descriptive local names—swamp willow, strawberry bush, catspaw, jewel-box, but most descriptive of all is the name given by a mountain man of, "Heart's-bustin'-with-love." **1970** Campbell et al. *Smoky Mt Wildflowers* 102 Common names include strawberry bush, swamp dogwood, spindle bush, arrowwood, wahoo, and a dozen others.

straw boss *noun* An assistant or foreman in a logging camp or one who supervises a small crew when the regular foreman is absent.

1964 Clarkson *Lumbering in WV* 372 = a sub-foreman in a logging camp. **1966–67** *DARE Survey* (Spruce Pine NC, Maryville TN) = assistant to the person in charge of a group of workmen, foreman. **1978** *Smokies Heritage* 113 The success of the above breakfast menu depends on how well coordinated the "hired hands" and the "straw bosses" are and how well everything is timed. **2013** Crawford *Mt Memories* 114 Foreman Frank's busy out there buckling down that first truck we loaded. So, I'm the "straw boss" and he told me to get word to you.

straw tick (also *straw bed tick*) *noun* A bed **tick** filled with straw, usually emptied and replenished in the spring of each year. See also **featherbed tick, flock tick, shuck bed, tick.**

1862 *Martin CW Letters* (Feb 10) if you pleas Send Me an old Straw tick to Make Me A bed. **c1945** Haun *Hawk's Done* 327 Said she smelt sulphur a-burning and that her straw tick was on fire. **1956** Hall Coll (Roaring Fork TN) I took a bale of straw and made a straw tick out of it. **1963** Watkins and Watkins *Yesterday* 41 A straw tick made a good mattress. When we first stuffed wheat or oat straw into a new tick, it was three feet high. Going to bed was like climbing a haystack. The little fellers had to have a chair to crawl up on the beds. **1975** Purkey *Madison Co* 40 Spring cleaning was another important event in our household. On a bright sunny day everything in the house was carried outside, and the straw ticks were emptied and refilled with fresh straw. **1991** Haynes *Haywood Home* 41 Most everyone had cord beds in their homes. On top of the cord webbing, they put a straw tick, and on top of that, a feather tick. In spring, all the feather ticks would be taken outside to be sunned for several days. The straw ticks would be emptied, the ticking washed, dried and restuffed with fresh wheat straw from the strawstack. **2003** Carter *Mt Home* 37 I tell you, them ol' straw bed ticks we slept on shore slept hard. **2008** McCaulley *Cove Childhood* 23 Those with suitable land also grew wheat, not only for the grain but because the straw was used for stuffing mattresses—"straw ticks." These would be filled with fresh straw each year at threshing time. People who had neither straw nor feathers stuffed their ticks with corn shucks.

streach *verb* To stretch.

1917 (in **1944** Wentworth *ADD* 603) (sWV) *streach*. **1942** Hall *Phonetics Smoky Mts* 21 An Emerts Cove family told, with some amusement, that a neighbor pronounced *stretch* as *streach* [strič]; an aged informant of Wears Valley said that this was once the usual pronunciation.

[DARE *stretch* n, v (pronc) especially Appalachians]

streaked *adjective* Variant form of two syllables: *streak-id*. See also **streaked bacon**.

1867 Harris *Sut Lovingood* 61 Thar wer durn'd littil weevil in his wheat, mity small chance ove warter in his whisky, an' not a drap ove streakid blood in his veins.

streaked bacon (also *streaked meat*, *streaked middling*, *streaking bacon*, *streak of lean*, *streaky lean*, *streaky meat*)

A Variant form of two syllables: *streak-ed* [see **1989** Smith in **B**].

B Meat from the side of a hog, bacon, usually with less fat than **fatback**. Also called **middling C**, **side meat**, **sow belly**, **striped meat**.

1900 Harben *N GA Sketches* 87 Sometimes I fry a slice o' streak-o'-lean- streak-o'-fat, ur a few cracked eggs, but it hain't half livin'. **1928** (in **1952** Mathes *Tall Tales* 68) Birdeye Collins was the first to sling across his shoulders his snack of corn dodger, streaked middling and home-ground coffee, rolled in an old blanket tied at the ends with leather thongs. **1940** Farr *More TN Expressions* 448 *streaked meat* = bacon. "City folks eat streaked meat." **1960** Burnett *My Valley* 26 As a precaution, a slab of streaked bacon was added. **1970** *Slaughtering* 43 Streak'a'lean is the same lean middlin' meat as the bacon, but it is only salt cured—not smoked. **1986** Pederson et al. *LAGS*: *streaked bacon* (Campbell Co TN, Habersham Co GA); *streaked meat* = attested by 6/60 interviewees (10%) from E TN and 2/35 (5.7%) from N GA; 8/18 of all LAGS interviewees (44.4%) attesting term were from Appalachia. **1989** *Matewan OHP-102* [They] would put at least a inch of salt over these middlings, and they would separate them. They was one side that was real fat, and the other side was like just streaking bacon, so they'd separate them and the ones that had the streaking bacon, they would try to cure that. **1989** Smith *Flyin' Bullets* 234 "All there was in it," said Delozier, "was a piece of streak-ed meat and a butcher knife!" **1990** Oliver *Cooking Hazel Creek* 13 When a settler wanted a mess of [green beans] during the winter they were unstrung, broken up, washed & put to soak for awhile, and then cooked like fresh green beans with fatback or streaky lean for seasoning. **2005** Houk *Walker Sisters* 23 "Everything was flavored with a streak of lean," said Robin Goddard, who spent many hours with the sisters when she was growing up. **2008** *Rosie Hicks* 4 I put my streaky meat fried real, real brown in between two raw potatoes.

[DARE *streaked meat* n chiefly South, South Midland, especially southern Appalachians]

streakedy *adjective* Having streaks.

1949 Marshall *Squire Jim* 285 Annie was examining the gray streaks in her hair before the little bit of a mirror. "Wont [= wasn't] his maw streakedy in the hair, too?" **2009** Miller *Nigh Gone* 97 = some sunshine, some rain.

[DARE *streakedy* adj South, South Midland]

streaking lean, **streak of lean**, **streaky lean**, **streaky meat** See **streaked bacon**.

streal See **streel**.

streel (also *streal*) *verb* To drag, strew, make a trail of.

1943 Stuart *Private Tussie* 65 Grandma came strealin' up the turnpike from town. **1997** Montgomery Coll (known to Cardwell).

[< Irish Gaelic *sraoilledhe*; OED3 *streel* v 1 chiefly Anglo-Irish; cf SND *strule* n "a stream or steady trickle"; CUD *streel*[1] v 2 "drag, trail along the ground"]

strength *noun* Variant forms *strainth*, *strenth*.

1796 *Cunningham Letter* my strenth is decaid. **1845** *Millsaps Letters* 2 I am a going to move from here this fall if it please god and to give me and my famley helth and strenth. **1863** *Woody CW Letters* (May 3) I am Blessed with helth and Strenth. **1864** *Walker CW Letters* (Aug 1) I doo feel thankefull to the Lord for Blessing me with even that much Strenth if no more. **1865** (in **1974** Harris *High Times* 159) I tuk me a double ho'n the fust thing on the strainth ov finding a safe spot. **1891** Primer *Studies in WV* 166 The *g* disappears in words like *length*, *strength*, etc., which are pronounced (lenth, strenth, etc.). **1907** Dugger *Balsam Groves* 29 Ef you had no more stren'th to manage that steer than he's got you'd mosy, too. **1932** (in **1935** Edwards *NC Novels* 53) *strenth*.

strength and awkwardness See **main strength**.

strengthening tonic *noun* A fortifying tea made from wild mints. See also **blood builder**, **sassafras B**, **spring tonic**, **sulfur and molasses**.

1982 *Smokies Heritage* 122 Then came the fragrant wild mints which grow on the banks of shady streams. Their dried leaves were used for teas as a "strengthening tonic."

strengthy *adjective* Strong; fortifying.

1928 (in **1952** Mathes *Tall Tales* 60) They's worse things than killin' a man's body, even the fine, strengthy body of a young man! **1944** Justus *Lizzie* 8 For drink there would be sassafras tea brewed till it was strengthy. **1952** Justus *Children* 18 It's tasty and it's strengthy. *Ibid.* 53 While you go atter them I'll take some strengthy scantlings and some twenty-penny nails and fix that broken fence.

[OED3 *strengthy* adj 1a "of a person: mighty, powerful" chiefly Scot and north; EDD *strengthy* adj "forcible, strong" nEngl; Web3 *strengthy* adj Scottish and dialect English]

strenth See **strength**.

strenthen *verb* Variant of *strengthen*.

1866 (in **1974** Harris *High Times* 171) He wer obliged to strenthen his purchase against the pullin at his tail some how.

stretch hives *noun* Same as **bold hives 1**.

2003 Cavender *Folk Medicine* 203 = an infant-specific and potentially fatal illness caused by hives remaining inside the body; also known as "stretch hives" and "red hives."

stretching leather *noun* See citation.

1982 Slone *How We Talked* 36 = rubber.

stretch the blanket *verb phrase* To exaggerate, embellish the facts of a story.

1923 Greer-Petrie *Angeline Doin' Society* 2 He'd draw'd up the idy the parson had stretched his blankit and if he had told a false, Lum wanted to be able to tell the fellers. **1927** Woofter *Dialect from WV* 348 = to exaggerate. "That man stretched the blanket when he told about Florida." **c1960** Wilson *Coll* = to lie, but usually not viciously. **1997** Montgomery *Coll* (known to eight consultants from the Smoky Mountains). **2007** McMillon *Notes* = to tell a big tale, exaggerate, or lie.

[DARE *stretch the blanket* v phr especially South Midland]

striffen (also *striffin*) *noun*

A Variant forms *scriffen* [see **1927** in **B**], *scriffin* [see **2003** in **B**], *scrivin* [see **1963** in **B**], *skifflin* [see **2007** in **B**].

B A membrane, especially of the entrails or the inside surface of an eggshell.

1917 Kephart *Word-List* 418 = the peritoneum of an animal. **c1926** Bird *Cullowhee Wordlist*: *striffin* = membrane. "He cut away the striffin from the man's insides so as to be able to see what was wrong with him." **1927** Woofter *Dialect from WV* 363 *scriffen* = membrane lining the abdominal cavity. "To relieve bloat in cattle, stick the point of a sharp knife through the scriffen." **1963** Watkins and Watkins *Yesterday* 123 Some broke an egg and used the membrane (which they called "scrivin" or "scriffen") just inside the shell as a medicine for risings. **1984** Woods *WV Was Good* 223 *striffen* = a bare covering of connection, such as the fibrous outside layer on skinned beef. It can mean a bare part, just a little bit of connecting tissue or flesh of any creature, such as, "Only a striffen of the crippled squirrel's foot held it to the leg." **1986** Pederson et al. *LAGS* (Scott Co TN) *striffen* = part next to shell. **1996–97** Montgomery *Coll* (known to Adams, Brown), *scriffin* = same as *striffin* (Ledford). **2003** Cavender *Folk Medicine* 95 For the boil [on the skin] itself, the most frequently reported remedy was applying a thin slice of fatback or side meat to it. Other topical applications included a biscuit soaked in sweet milk, "striffin" or "scriffin" (the membrane lining the shell of a chicken egg). **2007** McMillon *Notes*: *skifflin*.

[probably < Scottish Gaelic *streafon* "fringe"; EDD *striffin* sb 1 "a thin, membranous film; a thin skin or membrane" Scot, Irel, Amer; *scriffen*, *scrivin* perhaps influenced by Scots *scruif* (cf SND n 4 "a thin layer on the skin of anything, a film"); CUD *striffin* n "thin skin or membrane, such as that inside an egg-shell"; DARE *striffen* n chiefly South Midland]

striggle *verb* See citation.

1930s (in **1944** Wentworth *ADD* 604) (eWV) = to strew, spread, scatter: "You have striggled the milk all over your clothes."

strike *verb*

A Principal parts.

1 Variant past-tense form *strook*.

1939 Hall *Coll* (Hartford TN) We strook out, and we got to the old man just about sundown. **1978** Reese *Speech NE Tenn* 180 = attested by 3/12 (25%) speakers.

2 Variant past-participle form *strook*.

1937 Hall *Coll* (Cades Cove TN) Most every tree up there has been strook by lightning. **1939** Hall *Coll* (Wears Cove TN) His left leg was strook right below the knee.

B Senses.

1 Of a dog: to discover (an animal's track or scent). Also called **hit[2] 2**. See also **strike off**.

1926 Hunnicutt *Twenty Years* 51 We had not gone up Bear Creek very far until Old Muse struck a coon's track. **1939** Hall *Coll* (Proctor NC) That old dog we had with us, an old hound, he struck something's track, and he trailed on up that creek till I guess he trailed two mile, every bit of it. *Ibid.* (Smokemont NC) [We] hunted all night till ten o'clock the next mornin', never struck nary track. . . . We took right up the creek and dogs struck right out upper branch, over a ridge, treed. We went over there, and they's two coons up the tree. We shot them out. Then we went on around on the Chestnut Springs Branch. Dogs struck right over on the Chestnut Springs Branch and down hit about a mile. **1970** *Hunting Stories* 16 [A hunter would] then follow his dogs as best he could when they "struck." **1973** Joines *Twister Tales* 5 I set up on the ridge that night, and [my dog] just kept strikin' a coon, and he'd run it, and it'd make a big circle around over the mountain. **1982**

Ginns *Snowbird Gravy* 137 When they "strike" is when they hit the track, when they scent the fox.

2 To meet with, especially by chance.

1890 Fruit *KY Words* 66 = to meet, or to find: "I struck him at Jim Bell's."

3 To cut (a furrow) preparatory to planting.

1940 Still *River of Earth* 39 Not one furrow struck on his land.

strike a lick *verb phrase* To engage in work, make any effort (usually expressed in the negative).

1883 Murfree *Old Sledge* 545 He hain't struck a lick of work fur nigh on ter a month. **1953** Davison *Word-List Appal* 14 *strike a lick* = used in connection with work. "He's plum lazy. He didn't strike a lick of work." **2005** Williams *Gratitude* 527 A person who was too lazy to work at anything *woutn't strike a lick at nuthin'*.

[DARE *strike a lick* v phr chiefly South, South Midland]

strike dog *noun* See citations.

1976 *Bear Hunting* 282 The older, more experienced dog is your strike dog. He generally has a better nose and can smell a colder track. He's maybe a little smarter. Won't get excited and get off the track and lose it. **2006** *Encycl Appalachia* 1373 Dogs are also bred and trained for specific tasks in the hunt. Hounds with good scent ability are called "strike dogs." They must be able to detect and follow a scent trail and initiate the pursuit of a bear. A good strike dog is sometimes expected to find and follow an old scent track, or "cold trail." **2007** Plott *Story Plott Hound* 184 = a more cold-nosed hound with superior trailing skills used to strike (or establish) a definite game trail for the rest of the pack to follow.

strike in *verb phrase* To start off, as a school day.

1983 *Dark Corner OHP-28A* The next morning they come over there about the time school struck in.

strike off (also *strike out, strike up*) *verb phrase* To go with vigor and purpose in a certain direction or for a destination. See also **strike B1**.

1925 (in **1967** Combs *Folk-Songs* 7) Foller [the cow path] to the other side, and strike down Perkins Branch, till ye come to the main road, on Troublesome Creek. **1939** Hall *Coll* (Hartford TN) We strook out, and we got to the old man just about sundown. **c1950** Adams *Grandpap* 77 Then she got up behind him an' they struck off down the road. *Ibid.* 234 He knowed by that that Will was in trouble so he struck out, the way that Will had went, just as hard as he could go. **1964** Roberts *Hell-Fer-Sartin* 34 They got ready to leave, and they struck out. **1972** *AOHP/ALC-226* That was enough to scare us, and then we struck out running down that holler. **1972** Ensor *Tales of Supernatural* 64 I struck out down that branch, and I went down to Jack Bennett's almost. **1981** Henry *Alex Stewart* 53 I struck out and brought her up to my Pap's. **1985** Irwin *Alex Stewart* 105 I called to him and he struck right out and hauled that load to the house. **1995** Montieth *Tall Tales* 10 As I struck out across the mountain, I got to the top and heard a turkey way down in the hollow. **2002** McGowan *Beech Mt Tales* 106 Jack, just as quick as he got out of sight, untied and got the steer and struck up to the robbers', and was back with it in about two or three hours. **2005** Williams *Gratitude* 528 Dad *struck out* for the mountains to see about his still.

strike out, strike up See **strike B1**, **strike off**.

strike up with *verb phrase* To meet, run across (someone).

1969 Doran *Folklore White Co* 114 = to meet.

[DARE *strike up with* v phr South, South Midland]

string

A *noun* A series or number (of people, etc.). See also **string town**.

1939 Hall *Coll* (Cosby Creek TN) They was a string of fellows workin' along the river. **1966** *DARE Survey* (Cherokee NC) She has a whole string of cousins.

B *verb* To put (beans in the pod) on strings or threads for drying in the sun or by the fireplace, to be then hung away for storage and later cooked and eaten. See also **leather britches.**

1978 Montgomery *White Pine Coll* III-2 Our beans, we would dry them. They called them leather britches, and you'd string them on your string till you got something like a yard long. Then you'd hang them in the smokehouse or somewhere when it was warm weather, and they'd dry out.

string ball *noun* See citation.

1997 Montgomery *Coll* = a version of baseball using a makeshift ball fashioned from bits of cloth and string (Andrews).

string bow *noun* See citation.

c1975 Lunsford *It Used to Be* 172–73 "String bow" is a musical instrument. You take a bow of wood, stretch a cord across it, or a wire, from one end to the other in front of the bow. At one end the wood is turned down flat so the cord will lie close to it. You put that in your mouth and you govern the pitch by it, like playing a Jew's harp. It's one of the oldest musical instruments known.

stringer *noun*

1 Same as **gaff B1**.

1969 Miller *Raising Tobacco* 31 Three words for this implement were commonly used in western North Carolina: *stringer*, *needle*, and *gaev*.

2 See citation.

1993 Bansemer *Mts in Mist* 177 Inside, [the barn] will contain row after row of racks called "stringers" where the tobacco is hung to cure.

string latch *noun* See citation. See also **latch string**.

2005 Williams *Gratitude* 61 Another way to fasten the door was to make a string latch. You need one piece of board about ten inches long, two inches wide and about a half an inch thick for a bar. Hold it on the inside of the door so it sticks out past the door edge about three inches, then drive one nail through the far end into the door, loose-like, so the bar can swivel up and down. Take another piece to make the latch so the bar can come down and fit in behind it. You nail this piece up and down on the inside of the door frame, with the notch up, so the end of the bar can come down in the notch to latch the door. Then bore a hole over a little ways from the edge of the door, about five inches above the bar, jist big enough so your string will work through it easy, and poke the end of a leather strang [sic] through the hole from the outside. Then fasten the inside end to the bar. When the leather string is pulled from the outside, it pulls the bar up and unlatches the door.

string town *noun* A line of houses along a highway, railroad, etc.

1967 Stuart *New Wine* 20 Today if you travel in the hill country, you will find houses along the highways and byways. In some areas there are so many of them they're called String Towns on the Pike. **1974** Roberts *Sang Branch* 3 Putney, a stringtown along the winding Cumberland River, grew around the old seat of one of the largest sawmills in Eastern Kentucky. **1994** Schmidt and Hooks *Whistle* 90 Most camps, especially in steeply sloping terrain, were arranged in a line or string along the railway and were commonly known as "stringtowns." *Ibid.* 158 = a lumber camp with camp houses lined up in a row, usually along a railway and usually because the terrain is too steep to allow any other arrangement. **1997** King *Mt Folks* 53 While there, they also lived at Elkmont, Jakes Creek, Wildcat, String Town (named for the "string" of houses along both sides of the railroad track), Blow Down (named for the trees that had blown down during an earlier "cyclone"). **2009** Lloyd *Walker Valley* 37 Loggers, railworkers, and their families made their homes in four or five camps, each known as Stringtown, that lined the railroad.

strip *noun* A vertical board used to frame a **boxed house**.

1989 *Matewan OHP-9* It's a regular box house stripped with strips and ceiled in the inside, of course, had the old-time ceiling.

stripe

A *noun* A strip, slender piece.

1997 Andrews *Mountain Vittles* 7 Momma would roll out her pastry she called 'em dumplin's and cut 'em into stripes and drop 'em into the rollin' broth. *Ibid.* 25 Momma liked to perty it up and she always took a knife and cut the dough into stripes about 1 inch wide. **1997** Montgomery *Coll* (known to Weaver).

B *verb* To thrash, whip.

2014 *Blind Pig* (Nov 7) I can hear her now telling me, "Go to the woods and get me a switch to stripe your butt with for telling the world this."

striped *adjective* Variant forms of two syllables: *stripe-ed, stripe-id.*

1867 Harris *Sut Lovingood* 46 [I] pass'd a cabin whar a ole 'oman dress'd in a pipe an' a stripid aprun wer a-standin on the ash-hopper lookin up the road like she wer 'spectin tu see sumthin soon. **1962** Wilson *Folkways Mammoth Cave* 7 What is so funny, then, about *strip-ed* as two syllables and *posts* pronounced as *post-es*? **1989** *Matewan OHP-28* She would make us shirts out of them feed sacks. They was spotted and so on, stripe-ed and made pretty little shirts. My mom could really sew. **1997** Montgomery *Coll* (known to nine consultants from the Smoky Mountains). **2007** McMillon *Notes*: *strip-ed.*

striped meat *noun* [with *striped* pronounced as two syllables] Bacon. Same as **streaked bacon.**

1966 *DARE Survey* (Cherokee NC) = bacon. **1988** Moore *Mt Voices* 102 (DARE) She'd cook a great hunk of lean striped meat, good fresh pork, and then she'd soak that pumpkin and then cook it in that.

stripedy *adjective* Of a snake, etc.: having stripes.

1997 Montgomery *Coll* (known to Bush, Cardwell, Jones, Norris, Weaver). **2007** McMillon *Notes* = striped. **2014** *Blind Pig* (Nov 14) One of the biggest fears of my childhood was running across a "stipedy" snake.

strip of a boy (also *strip of a girl*) *noun phrase* A child. See also **chunk A3, sprout of a boy.**

1939 Hall *Coll* (Proctor NC) Strip of a girl, about twelve or thirteen . . . He had a strip of a girl there they sent to borry the handsaw. **1963** Edwards *Gravel* 122 I'm minded of the time when I was a strip of a boy and Pap was alive.

[cf SND *strip* n^1 4]

stripper *noun* See 1995 citation.

c1960 Wilson *Coll* = a cow in the second year of her milking period. **1995** Montgomery *Coll* = a cow not giving much milk, about to go dry (Cardwell).

[EDD *stripper* sb 3; perhaps influenced by Irish English, cf DHE; DARE *stripper* n 1 scattered, but more frequent Midland]

strive *verb* Variant past-participle form *strove.*

1831 (in **2004** *TN Petitions III* 32) Thomas K Ramsey has for a long time by a course of dissipation and profligacy kept her and her children in a state of want and dependence on the charities of others from which miserable condition she has strove by her own industry and economy to be released. **1976** Still *Pattern of Man* 85 I've strove earnestly with you. I've written you letters you never answered.

stroke *verb* To have a stroke.

2001 Lowry *Expressions* 6 I got so hot I thought I was going to stroke.

strollop

A *noun* See 1952 citation.

1940 Stuart *Trees of Heaven* 206 God knows the only way for a man to get it is from a old strollop. Just what Symanthia has got to be—a vidaciously, gallivantin, gadabout, Simpsonville strollop. **1952** Wilson *Folk Speech NC* 595 = a woman of loose or disreputable character. **c1960** Wilson *Coll* = an immoral woman, probably a corruption of trollop. **1997** Montgomery *Coll* = loose woman (Adams).

[apparently alteration of *trollop*; cf EDD *strollog* sb 1 "a slovenly, untidy woman or girl"; DARE *strollop* n especially South Midland]

B (also *strollop around*) *verb, verb phrase* To traipse, wander or go about in an unkempt, slovenly manner; to have a tendency for loose living; hence noun *strolloper*, verbal noun *strolloping*. See 1969 citation.

1925 Dargan *Highland Annals* 58 She's at the gate wantin' me to talk to her Lizy's girl who's fixin' to leave an' strollop over the country. **1939** Farr *TN Mt Regions* 92 *strollop around* = to travel about the community for a low or immoral purpose. "He's been strolloping around for a long time." **1969** *DARE Survey* (Rome GA) *strolloper* = a person who loiters about with nothing to do; (Rome GA); *strollop around* = to "go out" a great deal, not to stay at home much. **1995–97** Montgomery *Coll*: *strollop* (known to Adams, Brown, Norris); She'd be a good mother if she'd forget her strollopin' (Cardwell), = to walk aimlessly, as "Here she comes, a-strollopin' down the road" (Oliver). **2005** Williams *Gratitude* 528 = to git out and loafer around.

[EDD *strollop* v 4 "to go about in a slovenly, untidy manner"; DARE *strollop* v especially South Midland]

strollop around, **strolloper**, **strolloping** See **strollop B**.

strong

A *adjective* Of butter, bacon, etc.: rancid, having a disagreeable smell or taste from being no longer fresh.

1862 *Alexander CW Letters* (July 8) We have for breckfast loafbread and small piece of bacon that is very strong and fat. **1863** *Tesh CW Letters* (Dec 5) I eat the Last of my butter the 28th of last month but it was a geting sorta strong. **1986** Pederson et al. *LAGS* = attested by 19/60 interviewees (31.7%) from E TN and 2/35 (5.7%) from N GA; 21/78 of all LAGS interviewees (26.9%) attesting term were from Appalachia.

B *verb*

1 Of food: to cause (one who eats it or that person's breath) to have a foul odor.

1913 Kephart *Our Sthn High* 283 Baby, that onion'll strong ye! **c1940** Simms *Coll* Onion will strong you. **1961** Seeman *Arms of Mt* 189 Tino has grown to be the largest goat. His odor . . . is strong and rank as sea kelp—a sort of goat kelp. This odor resists hot water and soap. A lank old hunter drawled, "That thar smell will strong ye—hit jest burns my nose!"

[DARE *strong* v C1 southern Appalachians]

2 See citation.

1957 Combs *Lg Sthn High: Word List* 97 = to strengthen. Ex.: "That Indian turnip'll strong ye."

strook See **strike A1**, **A2**.

strop

A *noun*

1 A strap.

1812 (in **1920** DeWitt *Sevier Journal* 45) (April 12) Bought in the store of a German, one pair white silk stockings at 4 dollars & 25 cents—a par of razors & strops at three dollars. **1866** (in **1974** Harris *High Times* 284) He believes in schools an' colleges, as a barber dus in strops, an hones, as bein good tools to sharpen razors on. **1934–37** *LAMSAS Appal* (Madison Co NC, Swain Co NC). **1953** Hall *Coll* (Bryson City NC) So I just put my [rifle] strop around my back and slid down the stringer—about forty feet to the creek. **1974–75** McCracken *Logging* 3:30 You take and put a strop around that tree right up there. **1975** *AOHP/ALC-1128* They'd make good boys of them, put them over a barrel and whip them with a good strop. **1997** Montgomery *Coll* (known to eight consultants from the Smoky Mountains).

[DARE at *strop* n, v chiefly South, South Midland]

2 (as plural *strops*) Suspenders for a man's trousers. Same as **galluses**.

1986 Pederson et al. *LAGS* (Franklin Co GA).

B *verb* To sharpen (a razor) using a leather strap or belt.

1984 Yeatts *Old Mayberry* 12 He shaved with a straight razor, which he "stropped" with deliberate strokes, making a slapping sound which always reminded me of the times he punished me with the razor strap. **1997** Montgomery *Coll* (known to nine consultants from the Smoky Mountains).

strow *verb* To scatter, disperse (objects, pieces, etc.).

1937 Hall *Coll* (Cosby Creek TN) I saw where you strowed books on the floor. **1940** Bowman *KY Mt Stories* 247 *strowed all over* = scattered all around. **1940** Still *River of Earth* 243 Ma cut Aus's fences, burnt his barns, and strowed salt over his land. **1990** Wigginton *Foxfire Christmas* 156 He had that candy strowed everywhere. We went back down the road and picked up the sticks of candy where he split it—them long, hard sticks of peppermint.

[DARE *strow* v chiefly South, South Midland]

struck on *adjective phrase* Strongly attracted to, enamored or charmed by.

1940–42 Adams *Tales* 119 Here was a chance for their boy to get struck on one of the rich girls and marry. **1954** Roberts *Bought a Dog* 34 They were getting struck on one another by this time and she invited him to their party. **1969** Roberts *Greasybeard* 102 They talked and talked that night and the man got struck on the youngest looking girl there. **1991** Thomas *Sthn Appal* 95 I got struck on her. **2000** Morgan *Mts Remember* 82 One boy, Otho Jarvis, was struck on her more than the rest.

[DARE *struck on* adj phr chiefly South Midland]

strut

A (also *strut out*) *verb, verb phrase* To swell, bulge; hence participial adjective (phrase) *strutted*, *strutted out* = swollen.

1974 Fink *Bits Mt Speech* 25 My finger was all strutted out. **1990** Cavender *Folk Medical Lex* 32 *strutted* = filled to capacity, swollen to maximum extent. "He dropped a heavy box on his foot yesterday and now it's strutted." **1994–97** Montgomery *Coll* (known to Adams, Bush, Cardwell, Ogle, Oliver, Weaver). **2003** Cavender *Folk Medicine* 204 *strutted* = swollen, as in "My ankle is strutted and sore."

[OED3 *strut* v[1] 2a "to bulge, swell" obsolete; DARE *strut* v chiefly South, South Midland]

B *noun*

1 See citation.

c1960 Wilson *Coll* = a swelled condition: "My cut finger is in a strut."

[DARE *strut* n 1 South, South Midland]

2 In phrase *in a strut* = in a difficult strait, "in a bind," in strife or in a wrangle.

1921 Greer-Petrie *Angeline at Seelbach* 15 We et and et till we wuz in a lum strut. **1935** Murray *Schoolhouse* 14 One hears another man, this one in financial difficulty, speak of himself as "in a strut," which sounds odd until we remember the struts of a bridge, and how they stand braced and straining against heavy pulls from various direction. **1994–97** Montgomery *Coll* = in a bind (Jones, Shields).

[DARE *strut* n 2 chiefly South, South Midland]

strut-fart *noun* See citation.

1944 Combs *Word-List Sthn High* 21 = one who struts around, highly conscious of his own importance.

strut out, strutted, strutted out See **strut A**.

stub *verb*

1 (also *stub up*) To balk, pout, sulk; hence participial adjectives *stubbed, stubbed up*.

1940 Still *River of Earth* 134 The mule started, skin shivers quivering his flanks. "It's like that every time I stop," Uncle Jolly said. "A horse-mule stubs pine-blank like a man." **1941** Still *Troublesome Creek* 63 It was Lark and I who stubbed at meals. **1946** Dudley *KY Words* 271 *stub up* = to balk, become obstinate; also to shut up, become silent: "All the way we were talking along, but just as soon as we got near home she stubbed up and never said a word." **1975** Chalmers *Better* 66 Should you contrary him, he may sull or stub up. **c1982** Young *Colloquial Appal* 21 *stubbed up* = balky, stubborn. **1999** Montgomery *File*: *all stubbed up* = become stubborn, uncooperative (52-year-old woman, Jefferson Co TN). **2002** Myers *Best Yet Stories* 80 = [to] pout or sulk. **2005** Williams *Gratitude* 528 *stub up* = to balk; be stubborn; pout. Example: "We got ready, an'en he *stubbed up* and woutn't go." Or, "to *stub up* like a mule a-starin' at a new gate." **2017** *Blind Pig* (March 10) The sullen person, often a child or a childish adult, was described as "all stubbed up." To turn sullen was to "get stubbed up." Being stubbed up just got us kids in trouble at our house so we didn't get to indulge it very far or very often. **2018** *Blind Pig* (Aug 14) Remember what happened when you encountered soft ground? You kept walking but your Walkers [= stilts] stubbed up and wouldn't move.

[DARE *stub up* v phr southern Appalachians]

2 (also *stub along, stub off*) See c1960 citation.

c1960 Wilson *Coll*: *stub along* = to go along heedlessly or awkwardly. **1963** Edwards *Gravel* 46 Then into the room came blue-eyed, tousled-headed Tommy, stubbing along in his night gown, rubbing his nose with a short fat fist. **1987** Young *Lost Cove* 37 In a minute he got up and stubbed off up the Big Road.

stub along See **stub 2**.

stubbed, stubbed up See **stub 1**.

stubborn *adjective* Of a material object: stiff, tough.

1991 Still *Wolfpen Notebooks* 85 Corn meal that's not dried out proper makes stubborn bread.

[DARE *stubborn* adj 1 especially South, South Midland]

stubborndy *adjective* Stubborn.

1964 Williams *Prep Mt Speech* 54 A body mightenigh as well whup a gin pole . . . withouten he wants . . . to cut the blood outen the poor little stubborndy, loggeredy headed mule.

stub-headed *adjective* Stubborn, obstinate. See also **stub 1**.

1940 Still *River of Earth* 120 My boys were a mite stubheaded, as growing ones air.

stub off See **stub 2**.

stub up See **stub 1**.

study[1] See **steady**.

study[2]

A *verb*

1 To meditate, consider.

1862 *Warrick CW Letters* (April 30) I waunt you to try to be as easy as you can I no that it is hard to be a way from you but I try to ceep from studying. **1970** *Burton-Manning Coll-94A* Let me study just a minute. **1989** *Matewan OHP-9* Let me study a minute.

[OED3 *study* v 8a, obsolete; DARE *study* v[1] 1 chiefly South, South Midland, TX]

2 (also *study about, study on, study over*) To ponder, focus thought on before concluding.

1862 *Warrick CW Letters* (April 30) you are all that I study about in this world I think of you till I go to sleep and as soon as I wake up in the morning you are all that I study a bout. **1863** *Brown CW Letters* (Sept 20) you must not study about me so mutch i think you study two mutch. **1904–20** Kephart *Notebooks* 2:476 Everytime I go to studyin' about it I get the all-overs. **1916** Schockel *KY Mts* 125 That there was much whiskey and wickedness in the community where his grandchildren must be reared "was a serious thing for him to study about." **1921** Campbell *Sthn Highlander* 177 For one so little versed in reading [the mountaineer] has a remarkable knowledge of the Scriptures. He loves to "read after" them, and to "study on" them. **1923** Montague *Today Tomorrow* 160 When you come to study it over, you'll see thar was some sense in what he said. **1937** Hall *Coll* (Cosby TN) [After the dynamite explosion on Big Creek] they jes' come in, drapped down in chairs, and never said a word. I studied what was the matter. **1938** (in **2009** Powell *Shenandoah Letters* 142) I hope that you will study over it and say yes. **1939** Hall *Coll* (Nine Mile TN) I got to studyin' how near that bear come a-gettin' me. **1956** Hall *Coll* (Sand Hill TN) Whenever I get to studyin' about [those hard times], it just raises the hair on my head. **1985** Irwin *Alex Stewart* 97 I've studied about that a lot, and I've decided that he was just about right. **1991** Williams *Homeplace* 20 As many people say, they "study on" their past experiences, and they preserve these experiences by telling them over and over again.

[OED3 *study* v 5a, now English regional, U.S. regional, and Caribbean; DARE *study* v^1 2 chiefly South, South Midland, TX]

3 (also *study out*, *study up*) To devise, formulate.

1867 Harris *Sut Lovingood* 45 An' he look'd sorter like he'd been studyin a deep plan tu cheat sumbody, an' hed miss'd. **1939** Hall *Coll* (Mt Sterling NC) I just decided I'd study up some way to get them turkeys. **1948** Chase *Grandfather Tales* 101 [He] went to studyin' up some way to get shet of him. **1961** *Coe Ridge OHP*-340B I'd have to study them up. **2000** Morgan *Mts Remember* 12 It looks like there ain't nothing a man can't do if he just takes time to study it out.

[DARE *study* v^1 3 especially southern Appalachians]

4 See citation.

1895 Edson and Fairchild *TN Mts* 374 = talk, discuss: "I *studied* about her hair to my man when I got home."

B *noun* Meditation, pondering.

1863 *Bartlett CW Letters* (Jan 4) my hole Studdy is about you and my little chaps. **1870** (in **2016** *Blind Pig*) (Jan 30) Susan['s] hole study is on the friends that is left behind it is true I would like to see you all but my mane study is to do the best I can for my self and family.

study about See **study^2 A2**.

study after *verb phrase* To apprentice oneself to or study under (someone).

1995 Montgomery *Coll* He never went to college. He just studied after Dr. Massey (Cardwell).

study bee (also *steady bee*, *study john*) *noun* A small, hovering fly or bee. See also **news bee 2**.

1936 Morehouse *Rain on Just* 18 Dolly stopped for a moment to hunt for a "steady bee," one of the white-faced fellows whose big fat bodies buzzed ever so, but boasted never a sting to lean on. **1962** Miller *Pigeon's Roost* (May 10) Who has seen a "steady bee" this year? Or at least that is what us mountain folks call them. The "steady bee" is black like a bumble bee, but can't sting. I have heard it said they are the drone of the bumble bees. I saw my first "steady bee" of this year last Sunday, but have not seen a news carrier yet. The news carrier is colored like a yellow jacket but much bigger and longer. **1964** Reynolds *Born of Mts* 6 The natives call it "The Study Bee," or "Study John" from its habit of hovering before [a flower] in hummingbird fashion as if it were studying out the situation. **1968** *DARE Survey* (Brasstown NC) = a very small fly that doesn't sting but that is often seen hovering in large groups outdoors in summer. **1997** Montgomery *Coll*: *study bee* (known to Bush, Cardwell, Oliver); There's a yellow study bee. I'll have good luck today (Hooper), = called thus because it could hang steady in the air like a helicopter (Jones), *study john* (known to Cardwell).

[DARE (at *steady bee* n especially Appalachians]

study john See **study bee**.

studyment *noun*

A Variant form with secondary stress on the last syllable. For similar forms, see **-ment A**.

1913 Kephart *Our Sthn High* 224 In mountain dialect such words as settlement, government, studyment (reverie) are accented on the last syllable, or drawled with equal stress throughout.

B Reverie, contemplation.

1917 Kephart *Word-List* 418 He set thar all in a *studyment*; Nancy, honey, what's your *studyments* tonight? **c1926** Cox *Cullowhee Word-list* = dreaming. **1952** Wilson *Folk Speech NC* 596 = consideration, study, reverie. "He's in a powerful *studyment* to figure out how to get the money." **1994** Montgomery *Coll* (known to Cardwell).

[DARE *studyment* n 1 southern Appalachians]

study on See **study^2 A2**.

study out See **study^2 A3**.

study up See **study^2 A3**.

stuff *noun* Food, crops, garden produce, provisions. See also **farm stuff**, **garden salad**, **salad B**, **sauce B2**, **truck 1**.

1862 *Ingram CW Letters* (Oct 4) I want you to keep all the corn and stuf you rase. **1959** Hall *Coll* (Cataloochee NC) [We] dried apples and canned our stuff. We made what we eat. **1975** GSMNP-59:9 [The log] was too large to move, and so you just had to plant your corn and stuff sort of between the trees and the logs and rock cliffs and what have you. **1975–76** Wolfram/Christian *WV Coll* 22 It used to be the tenth of May when they thought all dangers of frost, but now sometimes it's in June before you can put a lot of your stuff out.

[OED3 *stuff* n^1 1e; EDD *stuff* sb^1 4 "corn, grain, produce"]

stug off See **stog**.

stump

A *noun* Early childhood or youth. See citation.

1967 *DARE Survey* (Maryville TN) = speaking of someone who has always been the same way, "He's been hot tempered from stump up."

B *verb*

1 To stub (one's toe or foot).

1956 McAtee *Some Dial NC* 44 = to strike the foot against an obstacle. **1965** West *Time Was* 7 He did not have to find everything out after a bloody nose or stumped toe.

[DARE *stump* v 2a chiefly South, South Midland]

2 See citation.

1994 Farwell and Buchanan *Logging Terms* = to remove stumps or splinters protruding from the stump after the tree has fallen.

stump-hole *noun* Homemade whiskey.

1968 *End of Moonshining* 111 I slurped up another sample or two of the stump-hole while I was about it.

[cf DARE *stump-hole liquor* n South, South Midland, especially NC]

stump juice *noun* Homemade whiskey. Also called **stump water 2.**

1952 McCall *Cherokees and Pioneers* 101 If you are invited to share a little something, whether it be called moonshine, corn juice, nubbin booze, Cain corn, white mule, stump juice . . . you should be warned that the thing meant is that powerful rank pizen what cheers the heart of even a man with a nagging wife.

[DARE *stump juice* n chiefly South, South Midland]

stump jumper *noun* A rustic.

1997 Montgomery *Coll* (known to Adams, Bush, Cardwell, Jones, Ledford, Oliver, Weaver).

[DARE *stump-jumper* n 1 scattered, but chiefly South, South Midland]

stump knocker *noun* A torrential rainstorm.

2008 Salsi *Ray Hicks* 57 Lord, you misunderstood me. I forgot to tell ya that I didn't mean for you to send a stump knocker. I just meant to have you send a two-week drizzle.

stump puller *noun* Homemade whiskey.

1974 Dabney *Mt Spirits* 25 The names [for corn whiskey] go on . . . "stump puller."

stump riser *noun* A torrential rainstorm.

2017 Lufkart *Comfort Zone* 81 A clearing shower is the little wind and rain you get before a "stump riser" hits, so smart people find shelter quickly when a clearing shower comes.

stump shot *noun* See citation.

1994 Farwell and Buchanan *Logging Terms* = the ridge left on the end of a board sawed by a simple upright saw, where the board is split off from its neighbors; also, large splinters left in a tree stump or in a log when a tree falls before it has been cut all the way through.

stump sucker *noun* An animal, especially a horse, that habitually sucks or gnaws on wood (posts, stumps, rails, etc.). See 1977 citation. Also called **wind-sucker.**

[**1901** Harben *Westerfelt* 23 I've been walkin' so blamed fast I've mighty nigh lost my breath. I'm blowin' like a stump-suckin' hoss.] **1968** *DARE Survey* (Brasstown NC) = [one with] large front teeth that stick out of the front of the mouth. **1977** Shackelford et al. *Our Appalachia* 24 Daddy'd have his [horse] tied up and if one was heaving or a stumpsucker. . . . If he was a stumpsucker he wouldn't tie him to a post because he'd just grab that post and rare back and say, "Roooooooooop!" and everybody'd know he was a stumpsucker and just didn't have no wind. . . . A "stump-sucker" is a horse that sets its teeth against a solid object, pulls back, arches its neck, and swallows air. Horsemen consider the vice a serious one because it is usually incurable and causes the animal to be a poor worker. **1998** Montgomery *Coll* = applies especially to children (Cardwell).

[DARE *stump sucker* n 1 especially South, South Midland]

stump water *noun*

1 Undrinkable, stale, acrid rainwater collected from a hollow stump or tree purported to have curative powers, especially to remove warts; hence an imaginary cure; figuratively = a worthless object or person. Also called **spunk water.**

1966 *DARE Survey* (Spruce Pine NC) = a magical cure for corns or warts. **1967** Miller *Pigeon's Roost* (April 20) Take stump water and put on a wart to get rid of a wart. You may wonder what stump water is like—well, it is water that has collected in a hollow stump and is as red as ash lye. **1968** Wilson *Folklore Mammoth Cave* 25 = the strongly-acid water found in hollow stumps, formerly used as a specific for freckles and other facial blemishes. **1984** Woods *WV Was Good* 15 Still another expression came from the fact that the darkish rainwater was useless for any purpose. Because neither birds nor animals would drink the brackish stuff, a man might say of another, "He's not worth stump water." **2002** Rash *Foot in Eden* 119 The air laid on the night still and stale as stump water. **2007** Farr *My Appalachia* 47 Aunt Mossie said that if I could find a tree stump with a hollow in the top where rainwater had collected, and bathe my face in the stump water, my freckles would disappear.

[DARE *stump water* n 1a chiefly South, South Midland]

2 Homemade whiskey. Same as **stump juice.**

1970 Mull *Mt Yarns* 73 White lightning, "red eye," "stump water," or "sugar head," as blockade liquor is called locally, has never been considered a crime or illegal. **1994** Montgomery *Coll* (known to Cardwell).

[DARE *stump water* n 2 chiefly South, South Midland]

3 In phrase *weak as stump water* = of homemade liquor: weak or unpalatable.

2005 Williams *Gratitude* 528 *stumpwater* = poor quality moonshine liquor is said to be as weak as stump water.

[DARE *stump water* 1b chiefly Inland South, Southern Appalachians]

stung by a trouser worm *verb phrase* See citation.

2002 Myers *Best Yet Stories* 224 If a group of men were out somewhere together, and a pregnant woman walked by, rather than say she was pregnant, they would say that she had been stung by a "trouser worm."

stupendious *adjective* Stupendous.

1957 Wise *Mt Speech* 305 [ɪ] is inserted before *ous*, as in . . . *stupendious* for *stupendous*. **2010** Montgomery *Coll* (known to Cardwell).

styles block *noun* A block of stone serving as part of a fence assisting one to cross or to mount a horse.

1923 Greer-Petrie *Angeline Doin' Society* 4 Any stranger that 'ud so much as set foot on our styles-block atter dark.

[DARE (at *stile block* n) chiefly South, South Midland]

submarine (also *submarine still*) *noun* See 1972 citation. Same as **black pot.**

1972 Carr *Oldest Profession* 185 The submarine still has replaced many of the small pot stills of earlier years. The name is derived from the elongated shape of the unit, which is really more like an army tank minus the tracks. The unit is simpler to build than the true copper pot still and less costly. The sides are wood, preferably with a wraparound sheet of copper but often of nothing more than galvanized sheet metal. **1985** Dabney *More Mt Spirits* 178 This is a "submarine" type distillery, found mostly in North Carolina and Southwest Virginia. **2002** Mitchell *Popcorn Sutton* further mused that the language of moonshiners is for the most part universal, but that there are a few local variations. "What we call a 'still' in North Carolina is a 'pot' in Tennessee. And here they call it a 'submarine' or 'black pot' or a 'black pot submarine.'" **2009** Webb et al. *Moonshining* 330 [After World War I] most moonshiners switched from the turnip still to the "submarine still," a large, flat-sided pot capable of holding several hundred gallons of mash in one firing.

suboy, **su-boy** See **sooey**.

sub-sawyer *noun* See citation.

1994 Farwell and Buchanan *Logging Terms* = a logger who ran the band saw from time to time.

subscription *noun* Tuition paid for a child's education. See also **subscription school**.

1962 Dykeman *Tall Woman* 190 Mark has taken a little sang. I'm saving for the children's sub-scriptions, do we get our school started up again. **1986** Scott and Scott *Beyond Beauty* 17 The school term varied, but normally it ran from November through January. If sufficient funds could be collected, that is "subscriptions," it continued through February and March.

subscription school *noun* Formerly, a school session funded by either parents of children enrolled or partly by the county (superseded by the public or **free school**); also, a school that offered instruction for a period (usually in the wintertime) that followed the end of the public school term (see 1979 citation) and was available only to children whose parents paid the tuition; also, a short session charging tuition to teach rudiments of singing or writing. See also **free school**, **singing school**, **writing school**.

1922 *TN CW Ques* 115 I attended subscription schools, my parent made $1 per months for each schoolar [sic]. **1931** Greve *Tradition Gatlinburg* 67 Men now living tell of their grandmothers having attended these early subscription schools more than ninety years ago. **1956** Hall *Coll* (Cosby TN) [In a subscription school, teachers would say] "We'll teach this school and you can pay me so much." The county would pay half and the scholars would pay the other half. **1959** Pearsall *Little Smoky* 135 In other places neighborhoods provided "subscription" schools when they could afford to and when some literate person desired to teach. **1979** *Big South Fork OHP-4* He'd teach about three months in the fall, and then he'd make up what they called a subscription school and taught through the winter months. He'd teach two a year. In the subscription school you'd pay so much, maybe a dollar or a dollar and a half a month for a child to go, and he'd get enough to make his wages thataway, and then he'd teach in the wintertime. **1994** *Smokies Guide* (Winter) 6 The educational needs of many early communities were filled by what were sometimes called "subscription schools." These were often organized by a local resident who would serve as the teacher. If the teacher was from outside the community, he or she would normally board with one of the families.

successfulest See **-est 1**.

such

A *adjective, pronoun, adverb* Variant forms *sech, sich, sitch*.

1860 *Week in Smokies* 129 [The panther] made sich powerful nice soap that my old man has made me keep some of it ever since for him to shave with. **1863** *CW Soldiers' Letters* (Sept 3) the oldes man livin know [= now] noes nuthing about camp life sech as we have know onley thoes that have ben in this weaked war. **1863** Wilson *Confederate Private* 23 (June 19) We dont get any sich meet. **1883** Bonner *Dialect Tales* 135 Ain't it a pity, boys, to see sech a rifle as that throwed away on a damned Gov'ment officer? **1904–20** Kephart *Notebooks* 4:773 I never seed sich takin's-on. **1954** Arnow *Dollmaker* 252 I've lived a long time without sich. **1963** Medford *Mt People* 116 Some folks don't b'lieve in sperits, ghosts, an' sitch like. **1984** *GSMNP-153* She cooked for all of his work hands. There was no sich a thing as me carrying my lunch basket or anything.

[DARE *sich* (at *such* adj, adv, pron A1) scattered, but chiefly South, South Midland; *sech* (at *such* A2) scattered, but chiefly South, South Midland]

B *pronoun* Anything like that. See also **no such**.

1939 Hall *Recording Speech* 6 One elderly woman of the Oconaluftee area declined the microphone . . . and informed the investigators: "I don't fancy no sich as that, and I won't jine up with ye!" **1974** Fink *Bits Mt Speech* 23 I never said no *sech*. **1997** Montgomery *Coll*: *any such* (known to nine consultants from the Smoky Mountains).

[DARE *such* pron B1 southern Appalachians]

C In phrases *sech a, sicha, such a n) adjective phrase* = the kind of.

1938 Stuart *Dark Hills* 47 That's what's a-matter with our country today—just sicha fellers as him. **1941** Stuart *Men of Mts* 39 He used sicha big words today I couldn't understand what he was talkin' about. *Ibid.* 110 "Dad-burned my cats, Ma," says Bill Dingus, "if I ever seed sicha hands on a man in my life." **1961** *Coe Ridge OHP-340B* You never seen such a hands.

such a matter *adverb phrase* Thereabouts.

1863 *Click CW Letters* (July 17) I got in to the fight a half a hour or such a matter before the boys was taken. **1915** Dingus *Word-List VA* 191 = thereabout: "Bill was here an hour ago, or such a matter." **1931** Combs *Lg Sthn High* 1305 It wuz about a week ago, er sich a matter. **c1960** Wilson *Coll* = about, nearly: "I've been crippled with the rheumatiz for ten years or such a matter."

such like *pronoun phrase* Things of a similar or the same kind.

1849 Lanman *Alleghany Mts* 89 The way the thing happened was this, and I reckon you never heard sich like afore. **1863** *Reese CW Letters* (June 28) he has Bin on detail the most of his time to work on Bri[d]ges and Sutch like. **1863** Smith *Battle of Rome* xx [They] begun to inter there money, and spoons and 4 pronged forks, and sich like. **1939** Hall *Coll* (Hazel Creek NC) I could tell ye something about the weather, such like as that. **1955** Washburn *Country Doctor* 54 As I promised I kep' my eye on the ole gent an' went over there ter buy eggs and sech like at all times o' day. **1963** Medford *Mt People* 116 Some folks don't b'lieve in sperits, ghosts, an' sitch like.

suck *noun*

1 (also *suckhole*) A whirlpool.

1780 Donelson *Journal* (March 8) We were now arrived at the place called the Whirl or Suck, where the river is compressed within less than half its common width above, by the Cumberland mountain, which juts in on both sides. **1939** *FWP Guide TN* 253 When the Cherokee and Creek besieged Fort Loudoun in 1761, the French in New Orleans sent a supply boat up the Tennessee to aid the Indians. The boat could not navigate the "Suck" of the Tennessee, however, and the goods were sold to the Indians near present-day Chattanooga. **c1960** Wilson *Coll*: *suckhole* = a whirlpool.

[DARE *suck* n 1 chiefly South Midland, *suckhole* n 1 chiefly South, South Midland]

2 A low-lying place to which animals are drawn to suck natural deposits of mineral salts. See also **lick B3**.

1832 Rafinesque *Atlantic Journal* 74 (DARE) They were called *licks* by the first settlers, because they noticed that buffaloes, elk and deer went *to lick* the saline ground, and *sucks* when they went to suck or drink the saline springs or pools. *Ibid.* 76 Licks became Sucks sometimes in the Winter or Spring, in rainy weather; and many Sucks became Licks in the dry season.

[DARE *suck* 2 especially VA, KY]

suck-egg *adjective* Especially of a dog: having a tendency to sneak into the henhouse and suck the contents of unhatched eggs; hence figuratively = base, mean, lazy, worthless, mean, contemptible. See also **egg-sucker**, **egg-sucking**.

1892 Fruit *KY Words* 232 A suck-egg dog is a superlatively mean dog: "He is as mean as a suck-egg dog." **1941** Stuart *Men of Mts* 92 "Well—I'm a suck-egg mule," says Finn, "I didn't believe a brute of any kind liked terbacker." *Ibid.* 141 I've bought her a twenty-gauge gun to kill suck-egg dogs with that come here when I am in the fields plowin'. **1966** *DARE Survey* (Spruce Pine NC) *suck egg dog* = uncomplimentary term for a dog. **1997** Montgomery *Coll* He's a real suck-egg dog (Ellis).

[DARE *suck-egg* adj chiefly South, Midland]

suckhole See **suck 1**.

sudden-quick *adverb phrase*

1916 Combs *Old Early English* 288 Two adjectives are freely combined together, e.g., "Rab jumped out'n the bushes sudden-quick."

[redundant form]

suddent *adjective, adverb* Sudden.

1891 Brown *Dialect in TN* 172 We also say *all of a suddent*, *wisht* for the present tense of *wish*, *skift* for *skiff*, and *take holt of* for *take hold of*, etc. **1940** Mathes *Jeff Howell* 21 A nice young man he was, Sir, an' we're sorry he had to go so suddent. **1967** Williams *Subtlety Mt Speech* 15 All of a suddent he come smack up to a big openin in the rock. **1997** Montgomery *Coll* (known to Bush, Oliver).

[Scottish form of *sudden*]

suddently (also *sudding*, *suddintly*) *adverb* Suddenly.

1915 Dingus *Word-List VA* 191 *suddently*. **1936** Coleman *Dial N GA* 20 "Suddintly," also "sudding" are used for "suddenly," as "He died suddintly."

suddenty *noun* Suddenness.

1913 Kephart *Our Sthn High* 277 The hillmen . . . [insert] sounds where they do not belong. Sometimes it is only an added consonant: gyarden, acrost, corkus (caucus); sometimes a syllable: loaferer, musicianer, suddenty. **1994** Montgomery *Coll* (known to Shields).

[OED3 *suddenty* n 1 chiefly Scot, obsolete except dialect, →1633]

sudding, **suddintly** See **suddently**.

sufferate *verb* See citation.

1995 Montgomery *Coll* = to endure calamities or hard times (Cardwell).

sufferation *noun* Someone or something that causes trouble or suffering.

1995 Montgomery *Coll* She's nothing but trials and sufferation (Cardwell).

sugar *noun*

1 A kiss, visibly demonstrated affection, especially given by a child to an older relative.

1862 *Neves CW Letters* (March 21) I have not saw youre shug since I saw you. **1986** (in **2000** Puckett *Seldom Ask* 173) Give papaw some sugar, and he'll fix your bike. **1990** Merriman *Moonshine Rendezvous* 64 I can see myself gettin' a lot of sugar from the cute blond as we rounded the curves too fast, on the way to spend the night at Shanks Hotel in Cookeville. **2001** House *Clay's Quilt* 288 "Give Auntie some sugar," he told the baby.

[DARE *sugar* n 3 especially South, South Midland]

2 (also *sugar diabetes*, *the sugar*) Diabetes.

1991 Still *Wolfpen Notebooks* 70 I've got the sugar. Can't eat sweet stuff. The doctor told me I couldn't even kiss my wife. **1999** Hodges *Tough Customers* 67 I know it's just going to be like this from now on, one thing happening after another, now you got the sugar and all. *Ibid.* 61 I've got sugar diabetes, and I don't heal too good—something else my daddy left me. **2005** Williams *Gratitude* 528 = the word "diabetes" was never used alone, it was *sugar diabetes*. **2017** Williams *Murmuration* 14 Sugar took her leg.

[DARE *sugar* n 2 chiefly east of Mississippi River]

sugar-booger (also *sugar-bugger*) *noun* A sweetheart; also, a term of endearment.

1976 Garber *Mountain-ese* 88 = sweetheart: "Jamie took his little sugar-bugger and went to the movin' pitcher show." **1994** Mullins *Echoes Appal* 75 "I had my mind, and eyes, on a pretty little sweet tater," Jake said, grinning. "You should have seen what a beautiful little syrup-soppin' sugar-booger she was."

sugar bread *noun* Same as **sweet bread 1**.

1926 Roberts *Time of Man* 167 They sat by the fire during the evening eating the sugar bread that Nellie had baked. **1997** Montgomery Coll (known to Bush, Jones).

[DARE *sugar bread* n especially South Midland]

sugar-bugger See **sugar-booger**.

sugar camp *noun* A camp operating beside a grove of sugar maple trees to draw sap and boil it down into syrup or process it into maple sugar; the grove of trees itself. See also **sugar grove**, **sugar orchard**.

1832 *McLean Diary* 10 fine Wether [we] opened our suger Camp on the 3 famley. **1864** *Kiracofe CW Letters* (April 3) David told sis this evening that she should go down to Mrs Jetts and see if we could get Thomas Sulivan and he would go up to the sugar camp and see Mr Croushorn. **1878** Guild *Old Times TN* 16 We had our sugar camps in what were called sugar orchards—groves of the sugar-maple—and in winter made our sugar and molasses, which were far superior to what we called New Orleans sugar and molasses. **1915** Dingus *Word-List VA* 191 = an orchard of sugar maples. **1949** Kurath *Word Geog East US* 36 Expressions that occur in western Pennsylvania, northern West Virginia, and in adjoining parts of Ohio are: *sugar camp* . . . for the sugar maple grove, in western Pennsylvania and all of northern West Virginia; *sugar grove* . . . for the sugar maple grove, from the Allegheny River to the Kanawha. **1952–57** (in **1966** Dakin *Vocab Ohio River Valley* 415 In Kentucky *sugar camp* is the most common usage between the Mountains and the Green-Barren River and is occasional in the Mountains. **1973** McDavid and McDavid *Vocab E KY* 160) = attested by 18/52 (34.6%) of E KY speakers for the Linguistic Atlas of the North Central States. **1982** Powers and Hannah *Cataloochee* 318 Neil Sutton had made wooden piggins to catch maple sap out of his sugar camp in Little Cataloochee. **1991** Thomas *Sthn Appal* 60 I know of a sugar camp they had over there at Silverthorne, up in there. An' they had it s' much wy [sic]—at that time, they didn't have no metal pipes like we've got fer t' run ennythang through now—an' these people over there cut down those little poplar trees, an' made a troft out uv 'um. An' laid 'um down there, an' run that sap water from th' trees plum over yonder to whur they'z a-boilin' it. Because that holler wuz full uv vessels an' tubs full uv that sap. An' they'd go up there ever evenin'. An' they had a big wooden tub down there, that'ud hold about five ur six hunderd gallons.

[DARE *sugar camp* n chiefly North Central, WV, western PA]

sugar cove *noun* A small valley abounding in sugar maple trees; also used in place-names, as in *Tipton Sugar Cove* (TN).

c1930 (in **2014** Oliver *Cades Cove* 99) Another area where the sap of the sugar maple trees was used to make maple syrup and sugar is known as the Tipton Sugar Cove. **1953** Hall Coll (Walland TN) I worked at loggin' for several years, mostly in this county . . . I worked on Smoky some, in the foothills. Some of the finest timber was in Aunt Becky Cable's Sugar Cove. [**1968** Powell *NC Gazetteer* 479–80 lists 9 NC place-names: 4 Sugar Cove, 1 Sugar Cove Branch, 2 Sugar Cove Creek, 2 Sugar Cove Gap beside many names of the type Sugar Creek, Fork, etc.] **1977** Shields *Cades Cove* 58 Steam-powered sawmills, such as the one in Lawson's Sugar Cove [c1908], changed house structures from log to sawed lumber.

sugar diabetes See **sugar 2**.

sugar drip (also *sugar drip liquor*, *sugar head*, *sugar head liquor*, *sugar juice*, *sugar liquor*, *sugartop*, *sugartop whiskey*, *sugar whiskey*) *noun* Homemade whiskey made by adding sugar to the **mash**. See also **honey drip 2**, **sugar jack**.

1939 Hall Coll (Emerts Cove TN) [In] making sugar liquor, they'd take about a bushel of corn to the sixty gallon barrel and a half a bushel of malt. *Ibid.* (Gatlinburg TN) *sugar drip liquor* = whiskey made by the process of adding sugar to the mash, the "newer" way of making liquor. **1959** Roberts *Up Cutshin* 65 Get you a sixty-gallon barrel and make her full up of meal and water like we done before, but instid of putting malt in it, you put in fifty pounds of sugar and stir that up good and let it set. And when you run it, you can get about eight gallons of sugartop whisky. **1970** Mull *Mt Yarns* 73 White lightning, "red eye," "stump water," or "sugar head," as blockade liquor is called locally, has never been considered a crime or illegal. **1974** Dabney *Mt Spirits* 24 While most modern-day corn whiskey is really mostly a sugar product called "sugartop," the mountain whiskey of frontier days was water clear, made wholly from corn and corn malt (sprouted and ground) which was often converted into meal in hand mills in the home or nearby tub mills. *Ibid.* 136–37 Just up the valley a piece from Cocke County is Greene County, which claims to have been the place where sugar whiskey was introduced around 1913 by a copper pot craftsman who grew a handlebar mustache. The story goes that the old man and his colleagues carried out a daring experiment by adding fifty pounds of sugar to a bushel of meal in a fermenting barrel. When that ran off, they found that it had made about a case of whiskey—six gallons! without the sugar they had been producing only about two and a half gallons on a bushel and a half of meal. **1982** Absher *Wilkes County* 69 Someone discovered that by cooking the distilled mash, which they called slop, from a run of corn whisky, putting it back in the fermenting box with sugar, water, yeast and some rye meal, a much larger amount of cheap secondary whisky could be made. They called it sugarhead, or, sometimes, white lightning; and it revolutionized a moderately profitable enterprise into a very lucrative and commercially attractive business. **1992** Gabbard *Thunder Road* 67 Out of a 300-gallon still like this, you'd make approximately 13 or 14 gallons of high sugarhead, hundard [sic] proof, then you'd catch about three cans of backin's behind it. You'd catch as many cans of backin's as you did sugarhead. **1999** Axtell *Moonshine Making* 18 Most of the illicit whiskey being made today in North Carolina's mountains is "sugar head liquor," consisting of sugar and a mixture of corn, oats, and rye. **2007** Alexander *Moonshiners Gone* 147 Better economic conditions so far as there being more jobs available now than in years past are thought to be some of the primary reasons for the demise of making "corn or sugar juice" by the light of the silvery moon. **2009** Webb et al. *Moonshining* 330 Once the still had been run, rather than replace the mash, moonshiners added large amounts of sugar to the leftover mash in the pot and used the same mash several times to make increasingly harsh "sugar liquor." **2013** Pierce *Corn in Jar* 57 According to local legend, a moonshiner in Greene County, Tennessee first started to produce what became known as "sugar liquor" at his Paint Creek still in 1913.

[DARE *sugar whiskey* n chiefly southern Appalachians]

(the) sugar foot *noun* Incapacity due to the effects of diabetes on circulation in one's feet.

2000 Montgomery Coll (Putnam Co TN) One of the men in his [roofing] crew, an older man in his late 50s, had missed several days of work. He was told by another worker that the man had the "sugar foot" and would be out of work for a few weeks.

sugar grove *noun* A grove of sugar maple trees. Same as **sugar orchard**. See also **sugar camp**.

1930 Armstrong *This Day and Time* 6 I rickolict the day you-all married in the sugar grove. **1952–57** (in **1973** McDavid and McDavid *Vocab E KY* 160) = attested by 22/52 (42.3%) of E KY speakers for the Linguistic Atlas of the North Central States. **1966** Dakin *Vocab Ohio River Valley* 415 Although it cannot be called common, *sugar grove* is known in all sections of Kentucky. **1986** Pederson et al. *LAGS* (Johnson Co TN, Sullivan Co TN).

sugar jack *noun* See citation. See also **sugar drip**.

1974 Maurer and Pearl *KY Moonshine* 126 = one hundred proof whiskey made from sugar without the addition of corn, except for a small amount to start and maintain fermentation.

sugar juice See **sugar drip**.

sugar knabs *noun* The white wake robin wildflower (*Trillium* spp).

1939 Jennison *Flora Great Smokies* 292 The White Wake-robin ... is truly grand! Its range is smaller than that of other white-flowered forms named (viz., *T. erectum* var. *album* and *T. undulatum*). Its large white flowers, which become pale-pink with age, make one estimate it to be among the handsomest of the lot. Some of the mountain folk call it "Sugar knabs."

sugar liquor See **sugar drip**.

sugar off *verb phrase* As verbal noun phrase *sugaring off* = pouring hot syrup into snow; hence noun *sugar off* = the candy that results from the process.

1982 *Smokies Heritage* 125 They boiled the colorless maple sap in a heavy kettle over a woodfire, taking particular care not to let it bubble over or scorch. When the sap boiled to 219 F it became syrup and was ready to pour off. (At this stage syrup makers often indulged in "sugaring-off"; that is, pouring hot syrup into snow still covering the ground. This "sugar off" cooled rapidly into a stringy maple candy.)

sugar orchard *noun* A grove of sugar maple trees. Also known as **maple orchard**, **sugar grove**. See also **sugar camp**, **sugar tree**.

1864 *Chapman CW Letters* (May 10) I have seen a great many sugar orchards but we are campt in the pretyest orcherd that I ever saw in my life. **1939** Hall Coll (Smokemont NC) Then the next day we decided we'd go back into the sugar orchard to see if ary'un would come in there. **1949** Kurath *Word Geog East US* 76 *Sugar orchard* is the characteristic expression in the Southern Appalachians from the northern watershed of the Kanawha to the Carolinas. **1966** Dakin *Vocab Ohio River Valley* 417 The fourth commonly used term is *sugar orchard*. This southern Appalachian term is regular throughout the Mountains and is scattered but not common elsewhere in Kentucky. **1974** GSMNP-50:2:16 I only knew two sugar orchards up there, and I guess they were more. I don't remember of any more sugar orchards in the Greenbrier Section.

[DARE *sugar orchard* n chiefly northern New England, southern Appalachians]

sugar party *noun* See citation. See also **molasses boil**, **stir-off**.

1969 Hannum *Look Back* 47 Sugar parties . . . were an early spring affair, when a family invited the countryside in to help boil down into liquid the sweet water they'd collected from maple trees—but not all of it. When the syrup reached the taffy stage, the big-eyed children were each given a little dish of it to roll into candy balls.

sugar slop *noun* The **mash** left in a **still** after a distillation **run** to which sugar has been added. See also **pot-tail(s)**, **slops 1**, **still mash**, **swill**.

1937 Hall Coll (Cades Cove TN).

sugar teat See **sugar tit**.

sugar tit (also *sugar teat*) *noun* A cloth into which sugar has been tied and which is dipped in water for a child to suck on.

1892 Fruit *KY Words* 232 = sugar-teat. Sugar tied up in a piece of cotton cloth for the fretful child to suck. **c1960** Wilson Coll = a rag tied around a mass of sugar and butter and used as a pacifier for a small baby. **1978** Morton *Superstitions* 18 Babies are given a "sugar tit" to pacify them. This is made by putting sugar in a cloth, tying it up and letting them suck on it. And sometimes a piece of cloth is tied into a knot and dipped into sweetened water for the baby to suck on. [**2002** Myers *Best Yet Stories* 197 If a newborn baby cried for food before the mother's milk became available, a lump of sugar was tied into a clean white cloth. The cloth was then dipped into water and given to the infant.] **2007** McMillon *Notes* = a cloth moistened with water and sprinkled with sugar for a baby to suck on.

[DARE *sugar tit* n scattered, but especially South, South Midland]

sugartop, sugartop whiskey See **sugar drip**.

sugar tree *noun* The sugar maple tree (*Acer saccharum*), which yields a sap from which maple sugar and maple syrup are made.

1799 (in **2008** Ellison *High Vistas* 37) The timber [is] generally sugar tree [sugar maple, Acer saccharum] & buckeye. **1843** *McLean Diary* 82 [I] opened part of my Shooger Trees. **1913** Morley *Carolina Mts* 19 The sugar-maple,—"sugar-tree" the native here calls it,—abundant in some regions, sweetens the corn-pone of the mountaineer as agreeably as in the cold North it embellishes the buckwheat cakes of winter's morning. **1934–37** *LAMSAS Appal* (Madison Co NC, Swain Co NC). **1949** Kurath *Word Geog East US* 31 From Western Pennsylvania to the Blue Ridge in North Carolina the sugar maple is called a *sugar tree*. In West Virginia and the southwestern corner of Pennsylvania this is the regular term; elsewhere in the West Midland *sugar maple* is equally common now and is clearly gaining ground. **1964** Stupka *Trees Shrubs Vines* 101 = a common forest tree in rich soils at low and middle altitudes . . . it is a dominant species in cove hardwoods, and in hemlock forests. . . . The Sugarlands . . . gets its name from the large sugar maples that grew there in pre-park days. These trees were usually tapped for their sweet sap in late winter. **1966** Dakin *Vocab Ohio River Valley* 411–12 Kentuckians in the Mountains and the Pennyroyal regularly say *sugar tree*, the name commonly used by older people everywhere south of the Ohio. **1986** Pederson et al. *LAGS* = attested by 8/60 interviewees (13.3%) from E TN; 8/22 of all LAGS interviewees (36.4%) attesting term were from Appalachia.

[DARE *sugar tree* n chiefly Midland]

sugar water *noun* The clear maple sap that rises in spring and that is tapped to make maple syrup.

1832 *McLean Diary* 10 Warm Wether Concidrabel of Run of sugar water hard Shower of Rain and thunder. **1864** *Copenhaver CW Letters* (March 24) We have made one hundred pounds of Shugar and the Shugar Water still Runing as Big as Indian Creek if it was in one Strem. **1925** Dargan *Highland Annals* 258 I found everything running like sugar-water in sap-time. **1941** Stuart *Men of Mts* 305 Each spring I tapped the maples and got sugar water.

[DARE *sugar water* n chiefly southern Appalachians, IN, OH, PA]

sugar whiskey See **sugar drip**.

suggin (also *snoogan, soogan, sujjit*) *noun* A pouch, carryall; also a bedroll.

1904–20 Kephart *Notebooks* 4:749 Better put a ration in your suggin, Bob. **1913** Kephart *Our Sthn High* 75 "Suggin" or "sujjit" (the u pronounced like the *oo* in *look*) is true mountain dialect for a pouch, valise, or carryall, its etymology being something to puzzle over. **1952** Wilson *Folk Speech NC* 596 *suggin* = a bag, wallet; probably same word as *soogan*. **1985** Jones *Growing Up* 3 After a while some of the men would ease away to their wagons and into their snoogins. **1997** Montgomery *Coll* (known to Oliver).

[< Irish Gaelic *súgán* "twisted rope of straw or heather"; cf CUD *suggan* n 2 "a straw horse-collar"; DARE (at *sugan* n 3) chiefly southern Appalachians]

suit *noun*

A head (of hair).

1886 Smith *Southernisms* 46 *Suit of hair* = head of hair. **c1960** Wilson *Coll* = a growth (or head) of hair: "a heavy suit of black hair."

suke, suke cow See **sook**.

sulfur (also *sulphur*) *verb* To dry fruit, especially apples, by exposing them to the smoke of burning sulfur, which killed bacteria while preserving the fruit for later consumption; hence verbal noun *sulphuring*. See 1974, 1995 citations. See also **sulfur bean**, **sulfured apple**.

1974 Cate *Winter Food Supply* A widely used method of preserving apples was sulphuring. After peeling and quartering a supply of fruit, the housewife placed a layer of it under a wooden barrel. She pushed the fruit from the center, hollowing a spot big enough for a teacup with a small amount of sulphur in it. Then the sulphur was set afire and a heavy cover, often an old quilt, was placed over the barrel. As soon as the cup's contents burned away, the housewife added a new layer of apples. This process was repeated until the barrel was full. **1985** Irwin *Alex Stewart* 207 We would take them apples, after they was sulphured, and put them in another barrel to store them in. We would just sulphur one run a day and it took nearly all summer, it seemed like, to get one big barrel of sulphured apples. **1995** Trout *Historic Buildings* 69 More common than a drying rock was "sulphuring" to preserve apples. The cook peeled and sliced pans of fruit, set the pans in a barrel, and laid a pan of sulphur on top. Igniting the sulphur and quickly covering the barrel with a cloth, she bleached the apples white. A special treat all winter long, sulphured apples could be used to make stack pie, cake, or fried pie. **1996–97** *Smokies Guide* (Winter) 12 Some families also "sulfured" apples to preserve them by exposing slices of the fruit to sulfur smoke to kill the bacteria.

sulfur and molasses *noun* A concoction used as a tonic in spring and thought to purify the blood and reinvigorate bodily systems, given especially to children. See also **blood builder**, **sassafras B**, **spring tonic**, **strengthening tonic**.

1970 Lombard *Hills of Home* 39 Maybe what I need for [spring fever] is some sulphur and molasses, like our mothers used to dose us with. I don't really know now why we took it, seems like we always felt fine back then, but it seemed like a good idea at the time and tasted so much better than the horrible castor oil. **1978** Montgomery *White Pine Coll* III-2 She'd give all of us kids a dose of calama in the spring and sulfur and molasses. Now that's another thing. She would mix half a teaspoon of sulfur and something like a tablespoon of molasses. She said there's nothing as good. **1982** *Smokies Heritage* 10 Some folks took malodorous tonics of sulfur and molasses, yeast and water, or vinegar and honey, but such "dosings" were awfully hard to swallow. **1991** Haynes *Haywood Home* 66 Sulphur mixed with molasses was a spring dosage to reinvigorate the blood. And if you took a dose of sulphur and molasses for three straight days before going to pick blackberries or huckleberries, chiggers wouldn't get on you.

sulfur bean *noun* A green bean dried and preserved by exposing it to the smoke of burning sulfur.

1996 Houk *Foods & Recipes* 47 Smoky Mountain horticulture includes a lengthy litany of legumes—creaseback, cutshort, cornfield beans, bunch beans, pink or peanut beans, greasy beans, sulfur beans, and half runners.

sulfured apple *noun* An apple cut into slices that are dried and preserved by exposing them to the smoke of burning sulfur.

1972 Hall *Coll* (Emerts Cove TN) We entered the depression with nothing and we come out of it with nothin', but we never remember bein' hungry. In fact, we lived purty high on the hog, with potato dumplin's 'n sich, foddered beans, [liver] mush fried in the mornin' for breakfast with molasses, brown-eyed peas, pickled cucumbers. [We had] a couple of barrels of sulfured apples, barrels of pickled beans and kraut. **2002** Reid *Hall's Top* 23 By late summer Grandma had dill pickles, sulfured apples, pickled beans and beets, and sauerkraut "making" in barrels and stoneware crocks.

sull (also *sull up*) *verb, verb phrase* To sulk, pout, act or become sullen, stubborn, or listless; hence to "play possum," pretend to be asleep or dead; hence participial adjective *sulled up*. See also **possum**.

1923 Furman *Mothering* 247 For two days he sulled, and never come anigh her mornings, and mended the back fence. **1944** Hayes *Word-List NC* 36 *sull up* = to "play possum," pretend to be asleep or dead. Applied to persons and opossums. **1956** Hall *Coll* (Mt Sterling NC) So mad you're foamin' at the mouth like an old bull when he is sulled up. **1962** Dykeman *Tall Woman* 150 Since his brother left, seems like he's just sulled up like a possum. **1964** Williams *Prep Mt Speech* 55 [By the time] I clomb down, that possum had sulled and was a layin like as if he were dead. **1974** Fink *Bits Mt Speech* 25 A 'possum'll *sull* when a dog ketches it. **1975** Chalmers *Better* 66 Should you contrary him, he may sull or stub up. **1995** Montgomery *Coll* He was sulled up all the time I was there (Cardwell). **2009** Benfield *Mt Born* 196 *sulled up* = in a pout, holding a grudge, or not speaking.

[DARE *sull* v chiefly South, South Midland, TX]

sull up See **sull**.

sully *adjective* Reticent, sulking, sullen.

1951 Giles *Harbin's Ridge* 64 He did take to drinking mighty heavy, and he got to acting sully and scowly. **1975** Chalmers *Better* 66 Some of them were awful sully—wouldn't ever talk lessen there was need. But others were right thoughty about the ways of the country.

sulphur, sulphuring See **sulfur**.

sulter See **swelter**.

sumac *noun*

A Variant forms *shoemake, shumake* [see **1925** in **B**].

1946 Stuart *Plum Grove Hills* 42 Clumps of shoemakes stood here.

[DARE *sumac* n especially South, South Midland]

B A bush (*Rhus glabra*) whose bark is made into a preparation to treat burns and whose blossoms and fruit are used for a tea drunk as medicine or refreshment and called **sumacade**.

1796 (in **1919** DeWitt *Sevier Journal* 192) (Dec 11) Take a single handfull of the white shoemake root bark, boil it in water till it is strong. **1808** (in **1920** DeWitt *Sevier Journal* 40) (May 13) [For botts, apply] a handful of white shoemake roots. **1925** Dargan *Highland Annals* 46 There's shumake for a swelled throat, an' boneset for the ager. **1927** Thornburgh *Tramping* 466 He also told me that the mountain people call hemlock "spruce pine," the black spruce "he-balsam," the Fraser balsam "she-balsam," the sumac "shumake," the butternut "white walnut," while cucumber is humorously called "cowcumber." **1941** Stuart *Men of Mts* 194 The shoemakes looked so pretty in the sun. **1966–68** *DARE Survey* (Brasstown NC, Burnsville NC, Cherokee NC, Spruce Pine NC) = causes itching and swelling. **1967** Jones *Peculiarities Mtneers* 71 Tea made of sumac leaves was given as a remedy for asthma and hay fever. Some dried the leaves and smoked them in a pipe. [**1971** Krochmal et al. *Medicinal Plants Appal* 214 The dried ripe fruit of sumac is valuable as a source of tannic acid. Preparations of these fruits are effective as astringents, antidiuretics, and tonics. In Appalachia, leaves are smoked to treat asthma.] **2006** *WV Encycl* 568 The tannin of chestnut oak, hemlock, and sumac barks was used to tan leather; sumac is still called "shoemake" by many country people.

sumacade (also *sumac lemonade*) *noun* See 1971 citation. See also **sumac**.

1955 Parris *Roaming Mts* 232 Sumacade is an appetizing pink colored drink, which contrary to popular belief is not poison. **1971** Chapman *Uses for Sumac* The berry clusters may be put into a large container, then covered with water, stirred briskly and pounded for perhaps 10 minutes with a potato masher. The son of one family in this area, after gathering a bushel of sumac heads, dumped them into the washing machine and, after covering them with water, ran the washer for 10 minutes, then caught the "sumac-ade" in a big kettle as the washer pumped it out. In any case the juice should be strained through several thicknesses of cloth to remove the fine hairs which form the outer coating of each berry. The berries contain sufficient acid to make a satisfactory emergency substitute for lemon juice. The settlers used sumac for a wide variety of medicinal purposes. One use was to gargle with an infusion of the berries, to relieve throat irritations. Sumac "lemonade" was used to reduce fevers. A decoction of the berries has been used for treating a number of ailments; and, because it is styptic, has been used in poultices for treating skin disorders. **1978** Parris *Mt Cooking* 23 [Sumacade] is made from the berries of red sumac. You pick them and shell them and rub them gently between the palms of the hands, being careful not to crush the berries but only the spines, then drop them into water, strain and sweeten to taste, cool and serve. **1982** *Smokies Heritage* 109 *sumacade* = a drink made by crushing and immersing the red berries of the staghorn sumac in water. This mixture, allowed to sit for a while, turned into a tangy, lemon-tasting drink considered quite refreshing on a hot summer day. **1998** Dabney *Smokehouse Ham* 165 While lemons were seldom seen throughout the Appalachian country in the 1800s, ingenious mountain people came up with a wonderful substitute, sumac. . . . Sumac lemonade not only had a delicious taste—with a tangy, lemon flavor—it was said to reduce fever and lessen fatigue. As for other herb drinks, you crush the sumac berries, put them in boiling water and steep them until they reach a strong color. The juice is strained through a cloth, sweetened with honey or sugar, and served cold.

sumac lemonade See **sumacade.**

summer *attributive noun* Of a lowlander: escaping to the mountains to avoid heat and enjoy recreation.

1921 Spalding *Hills o' Ca'liny* 143 The majority of the summer people are neither religious nor philanthropic. They have come here for rest, recreation, and pleasure. Their influence upon the mountaineer is by no means highly beneficial. **1962** Stubbs *Mountain-Wise* (April–May) 10 One day a visitor—a "summer" man—asked a Highlands boy how the people up there made a living. He answered promptly and tersely: "They live off of 'taters in the winter and tourists in the summer." **1963** Stubbs *Mountain-Wise* (Aug–Sept) 7 He drove a carriage and took paying passengers when room was available in his vehicle. The story is told that one day he was hauling some "summer ladies" up [to Highlands NC]. **1973** *Foxfire Interviews* A-73-86 Do you think a lot more summer people's going to be moving in up here? **2009** Sanders *Breakfast* 46 A plate warmer was a bit too much fuss for her taste, but it had been a gift from the Florida "summer neighbors" up the road, and she thought Harry might expect such niceties.

summer-and-winter weave *noun* See 1937 citation.

1937 Eaton *Handicrafts* 113 The three types of mountain coverlets . . . are the simple overshot weave, the summer-and-winter weave, and the double weave. . . . The summer-and-winter weave, the origin of which is attributed to America and that some authorities say is not found at all in Europe, is one in which, instead of making the long skips as in the usual overshot type, the pattern thread is closely interwoven with the base. **2001** Montgomery *Coll* (known to Wilson).

summer complaint *noun* Diarrhea, especially in children.

1914 Furman *Sight* 46 Seven sons of my body have I laid in the grave, three in infancy of summer-complaint. **1957** Combs *Lg Sthn High: Word List* 97 = diarrhea (especially of children), so-called because it is commoner in the summertime than in any other season. **1967** Jones *Peculiarities Mtneers* 69 Sliced cumphery roots, when soaked in cold water, was rated as a remedy for diarrhoea, a disorder known in the mountains as "flux" or "summer complaint." It was usually quite prevalent among small children. **2013** Lyon *Voiceplace* 186 I wrote down a story she told me of Old Aunt Martha Money who could cure the summer complaint.

summer-farewell *noun* Any of several asters (*Aster* spp). See also **farewell-summer, goodbye-to-summer.**

1930 Armstrong *This Day and Time* 135 The summer farewell's [are] all a-bloomin', an' everythin' [is] a-lookin' pretty.

summers See **somewheres.**

summer sores *noun* See citation.

1983 Broaddus *Estill Co KY Word List* 58 = impetigo.

[DARE *summer sores* n especially South Midland]

summons *verb* To serve (one) with a legal document; to order one to appear in court.

1895 Edson and Fairchild *TN Mts* 375 = summoned to court. **1941** Still *Troublesome Creek* 91 [The magistrate]'ll plague the stir-off. Fellers will think he's come a-summonsing. **c1960** Wilson *Coll* Uncle Ed has been summonsed to serve on the jury. **c1975** Lunsford *It Used to Be* 23 They would begin above here and they would summons their hands to work for two days starting at what they call Mark Culberson's big gate. **1989** *Matewan OHP-11* Then he was summons[ed] up to Welch, and that's when he, when he got killed. **1997** Montgomery *Coll* (known to nine consultants from the Smoky Mountains).

[DARE *summons* v chiefly Northeast, South, South Midland, Southwest]

sumpin, sump'm See **something.**

sunball *noun* The sun. See also **moonball.**

c1900 (in **1997** Stoddart *Quare Women* 95) Most of them would stay till the "sun ball went down behind the mountain." **1916** Combs *Old Early English* 294 = the sun. **1918** Hartt *Lost Tribes* 396 Let us consider the mountaineers a race apart and dwell lovingly upon such idiosyncrasies as "sun-ball," "church-house," "rifle-gun," and "man-pusson." **c1940** Padelford *Notes* Nary a thing to do but watch the sun-ball rise and set. **1941** Still *Troublesome Creek* 133 The sun ball dropped behind the beech woods on the ridge. **1997** Montgomery *Coll* (known to Adams, Brown, Bush, Cardwell).

[DARE *sunball* n chiefly southern Appalachians, Ozarks]

suncake *noun* Cow dung whose surface has been baked and hardened by the sun.

1983 Davis *Lucky Day* 71 What he was looking for was a good ripe suncake! He didn't want a fresh one you would cut your foot in, or an old hard one that was full of June bugs. No, he wanted one that had been put there by a cow about two days ago, so that it had a little dry crust on top, but was still fresh in the middle.

Sunday flour *noun* See citation.

2006 Sauceman *Place Setting* 31 Some cooks still refer to White Lily as "Sunday flour" since it was often saved for the most special meal of the week.

Sunday-go-to-meeting (clothes, hat) *noun* One's best clothes, suitable for wearing to a church service. See also **go-to-meeting.**

1859 Taliaferro *Fisher's River* 171 His "Sunday go to meetin'" hat is an old-fashioned, smooth, bell-crowned fur hat. **1962** Wilson *Folkways Mammoth Cave* 20 You were all fixed up in your Sunday-go-to-meeting clothes. **1967** *DARE Survey* (Maryville TN) = joking reference to one's best clothes. **1995** South *What It Is* 11 There 'uz Geraldine, fixed up in her Sunday go to meetin', in a short, low-cut dress.

Sunday quilt *noun* See citation.

1969 *Something Human* 6 Especially fine quilts were used to cover the bed on Sunday ("Sunday quilts") and when company came.

sundown *noun* (sometimes with stress on *down*) Sunset.

1861 (in **1980** Clark *Civil War Diary* 26) It is now nearly sundown and it is a raining. **1864** *Poteet CW Letters* (Oct 6) she died the 29 of oct last saturday a little while before sundown. **1924** Raine *Saddlebags* 76–77 He drew a picture of a witch-woman and told the man to set it up agin a stump and shoot it jest at sundown. **1934–47** *LAMSAS Appal* = attested by 87/148 speakers (58.7%) from WV, 17/20 (85%) from VA, 36/37 (97.3%) from NC, 13/14 (92.9%) from SC, and 9/12 (75%) from GA. **1956** Hall Coll (Indian Camp Creek NC) I've worked a many a day for twenty-five cents, worked from sunup to sundown. **1962** Drukker *Lg By-Ways* 50 There is no sunrise or sunset; it is sun-up or sun-down, probably the most acceptable description scientifically at that. **1967** *DARE Survey* (Maryville TN) = time of day when the sun goes out of sight. **1989** *Matewan OHP-22* We was in the field at daylight, good, and picked till sundown every night.

[DARE *sundown* n widespread, but more frequent South, South Midland, Southwest]

sung See **sing A.**

sun grins *noun* See citation.

1957 Combs *Lg Sthn High: Word List* 98 = grins caused by the glare of the sun. The sing[ular] is not heard.

sunmark *noun* A cut into a floorboard or other surface by which daytime hours are reckoned. See also **sunplank.**

1957 Combs *Lg Sthn High: Word List* 98 = a mark on the floor in the doorway, facing the rising sun, and indicating approximately the arrival of the noon hour. **1967** Miller *Pigeon's Roost* (March 30) People back in those days had sun marks on mountains, rocks or trees to go by to tell what time it was and when the sun was straight up over the area where you was. If you could see in any distance away at all, it was 12 o'clock.

sunpain *noun* A morning headache that improves as the day goes on.

1921 Combs *KY Items* 119 = a pain in the head . . . at sunrise. Neuralgia. **1982** Slone *How We Talked* 106 [Headaches] were called "a sun pain." Cure: get out of the sun.

[DARE *sun-pain* n chiefly South, South Midland]

sunplank *noun* A floorboard into which a cut is made by which daylight time is reckoned. See also **sunmark.**

1938 Justus *No-End Hollow* 135 The sky was clouded, and they couldn't tell time by the sun plank in the kitchen—a worriment they often had through the winter. **1942** Justus *Step Along* 57 Jerry Jake saw by the sunplank in the floor that it was time for dinner, and he asked the preacher man to stay to share the big corn-pone on the hearth and the stirabout in the kettle swinging on the chimney hook.

sun time *noun* Local time. See citation. See also **railroad time.**

1946 Wilson *Fidelity Folks* 42 He said that Fidelity kept sun time rather than railroad time because it was nearer the sun.

sunup *noun* (sometimes with stress on the second syllable) Sunrise.

1934–47 *LAMSAS Appal* = attested by 83/148 speakers (56.0%) from WV, 16/20 (80%) from VA, 34/37 (91.9%) from NC, 12/14 (85.7%) from SC, and 9/12 (75%) from GA. **1962** Drukker *Lg By-Ways* 50 There is no sunrise or sunset; it is sun-up or sun-down, probably the most acceptable description scientifically at that. **1966** Dakin *Vocab Ohio River Valley* 14 Among informants who commonly use only one of these terms, *sunup* is the more usual. It occurs 2 to 1 in . . . Kentucky (37 to 17). **1967** *DARE Survey* (Maryville TN) = time when the sun first comes into sight. **1978** Montgomery *White Pine Coll* IV-4 They started before sunup and worked to after sundown, if you had a job that needed finished.

sup *verb, noun* To sip; a sip.

1939 Bond *Appal Dialect* 111 *sup* = sip. **1949** Hornsby *Lonesome Valley* 112 She took a chicken wing and gnawed on it and supped her coffee. *Ibid.* 321 Uncle Lihugh was walking toward the spring for a sup of water. **1977** *Ben Chappell* 230 We took a few sups of it. It sure is good stuff. **1985** Dabney *More Mt Spirits* 39 Donald never drank more than a "sup," he said. **1998** Montgomery File Can I have a sup of your drink? (51-year-old woman, Jefferson Co TN). **2008** *Rosie Hicks* 6 You bite your bread and then sup your milk. **2016** *Blind Pig* (March 25) You can have a sup, but drink off the other side of the cup. . . . A sup is a sip taken from a common vessel.

[DARE *sup* n now especially South, South Midland]

sure *adjective, adverb* Variant form *shore*.

1862 *Love CW Letters* (July 21) this war will not last always that is shore. **1864** *Chapman CW Letters* (May 3) if you liv to get this leter I want you to bee shore to Righ back a mediately To mee. **1885** (in

1972 *Burial Customs* 8) They will suffer shore. **1902** Harben *Abner Daniel* 140 She'd a-gone as shore as preachin. **1913** Kephart *Our Sthn High* 83 Fellers, you want to mark what you dream about tonight: hit'll shore come true to-morrow. **1936** (in **2009** Powell *Shenandoah Letters* 71) He was shore you could give me the necessary information of them. **1942** Hall *Phonetics Smoky Mts* 37. **1973** GSMNP-88 I shore would. **1991** Thomas *Sthn Appal* 59 I can tell ye one thang: if I hadn't got them bees out of them overhalls, I'd a' shore a' run out a' them.

[DARE *sure* adj, adv 2 (pronc) chiefly South, South Midland]

sure-enough

A *adjective* Thorough, honest-to-goodness, genuine.

1863 (in **1938** Taliaferro *Carolina Humor* 77) It was a "sure-enough" Grocery, but Sam made it somethin else. **1886** Smith *Southernisms* 46 = genuine. **1913** Kephart *Our Sthn High* 94 We'll know by to-morrow whether he's a shore-enough bear dog. **1928** (in **1952** Mathes *Tall Tales* 66) Ain't ye 'shamed to run off that-away when I'm fixin' to take ye on a shore-'nuff hunt in the mornin'? **1941** Justus *Kettle Creek* 41 Let's get out pine knots in a hurry and then have some sure enough fun. **c1960** Wilson Coll: *sure-enough* = real, genuine (adj and adv).

[DARE *sure-enough* adj chiefly South, South Midland]

B *adverb* Surely, certainly; really, without fail.

1862 *Huntley CW Letters* (June 3) We expected to be Ordered to the Fight evry minit and sure enough We got Orders a Sunday Eaving to march to the Field of action. **1864** *Warrick CW Letters* (April 1) I think that tha[y] will hav fitin to Doo shor A nof for I think th[e] yankes will Giv us A fit be fore minnie Days. **1895** Edson and Fairchild *TN Mts* 374 = certainly, without fail. "Are you going, *shore nuff?*" **1939** Hall Coll (Tow String Creek NC) All you got to do is show us how, and we will sure enough put it [= a fire] out. **1963** Edwards *Gravel* 99 That's what scared her shore nuff. **1974** Dabney *Mt Spirits* 26 My daddy said they went to givin' corn likker to me when I was sure enough young, just a toddler. **1997** Montgomery Coll (known to nine consultants from the Smoky Mountains).

surely *adverb* Variant form *shorely*.

1901 Harben *Westerfelt* 18 Shorely he'll do a little some'n' in a case like this un. **1931** Combs *Lg Sthn High* 1304 That gal of Zeke's is shorely dilitary. **1954** Arnow *Dollmaker* 88 I'll shorely hear in this evenin's mail. **1974** Fink *Bits Mt Speech* 1 I'd shorely admire to see him agin.

surment See **sermon**.

surround *verb* To travel around, step or go wide of, bypass (an obstacle).

1910 Smith *Tramping in Mts* 2 10–11 Devil Sam Walker's excellent term, "sarround" (a peak or a swamp) will always do duty for me. **1921** Campbell *Sthn Highlander* 145 The injunction to "surround the hole at the ford" is easily understood in its archaic sense of "go around." **1937** Hall Coll (Cosby TN) I would rather surround a snake than kill it. **1963** Edwards *Gravel* 87 "Had to surround the pond," said Lowe simply. "Went way round by the Brice place on the back road an back on the main road at Willie Smith's. Dangerous to try that pond on a night like this." **1975** Fink *Backpacking* 28 This trail, as he phrased it, "surrounded the top," saving considerable climbing and rough going.

[OED3 *surround* v 4 obsolete "to go or travel around, make the circuit of" →1825; Web3 *surround* vt 5 chiefly Midland; DARE *surround* v chiefly southern Appalachians]

surtin See **certain**.

survigorous, survigrous See **savagerous**.

suspicion *verb* To suspect, view with suspicion.

1824 Knight *Letter from KY* 106–7 Some words are used, even by genteel people, from their imperfect education, in a new sense; and others, by the lower classes in society, pronounced very uncouthly . . . to suspicion one. **1839** *Elijoy Church Minutes* 39 James A. Davis made application to the church & presbytery to be Released from the office of a deacon thinking (he said) that he was not fit & that he was a suspicioned Character. **1867** Harris *Sut Lovingood* 67 I sorter suspishiond hit, but still hed hopes. **1900** Harben *N GA Sketches* 229 The blasted fellers have had reinforcements sence the sun went down. I know it, an' our colonel is beginnin' to suspicion it. **1935** Sheppard *Cabins in Laurel* 63 This here militia knowed grandpap was with the Union but they suspicioned he was home layin' out. **1937** Hall Coll (Mt Sterling NC) They suspicion a stranger. **1979** Melton *'Pon My Honor* 26 The very minute Billy laid eyes on Uncle Dick, he suspicioned something for Uncle Dick had pulled too many things on him before. **1982** Powers and Hannah *Cataloochee* 183 Johnny asked all or anyone to go with him. We suspicioned that he was scared of bears.

[OED3 *suspicion* v a dialect and colloquial, originally U.S.; DARE *suspicion* v scattered, but especially South, South Midland]

sut See **soot**.

swab (also *stir stick, swab stick*) *noun* See citations. Same as **mash stick.**

1968 *End of Moonshining* 50 Swab Stick or Toothbrush—a hickory stick half as thick as your arm and long enough to reach from the top to the bottom of the still. One end is beaten up well so that it frazzles and makes a fibrous swab. This is used to stir the beer in the still while waiting for it to come to a boil, thus preventing it from sticking to the sides of the still, or settling to the bottom and burning. **1974** Dabney *Mt Spirits* xxv *swab stick* = a hickory stick with the end beat up like an old toothbrush. Used by operators to scrub out the still and to keep the mash from sticking to the still wall before reaching a boil. Sometimes called a stir stick. **1985** Dabney *More Mt Spirits* 177 Man at right holds a handmade "mash stick," sometimes called a "stir stick." It is a hardwood pole about six feet long, with pegs inserted in the end to enable the distiller to stir and comb the lumps out of the mash. **2007** Rowley *Moonshine!* 163 *swab stick* = a wooden stick with one end splayed out into fine ends like a brush. Used to stir heating mash and to scrub the interior walls of a large still to keep mash from sticking before it boils.

swag

A *verb* To sag, sink or bulge downward, as from weight. See also **swag down**.

1889 Murfree *Broomsedge Cove* 42 The gate swags off'n the hinges. **1915** Dingus *Word-List VA* 191 = to sag. **1952** Wilson *Folk Speech NC* 596 = to sink down, to *sag*. **1974–75** McCracken *Logging* 20:35 [The skidder line] would be anchored over yonder, and the more logs you got on it, the more it would swag. [**1997** See **B2**]. **1998** *Dante OHP-71* The logs had rotted out. The church had swagged a little bit. **2004** Adams *Old True Love* 47 The men had knocked together a bunch of tables and they were already swagging with food by the time we got there to add our load.

[SND *swag* v^1 1 "to sway from side to side ... hang down heavily and lopsidedly, to sag"; DARE *swag* v 2 chiefly South, South Midland]

B *noun*

1 A low, often wet place in a field where land has settled; a piece of land with such a depression.

1905 Miles *Spirit of Mts* 91 At another time a hunter followed his dogs over a fill in the Suck regions, down across a "swag," and over the breaks of stream, before finally overtaking his quarry. **1941** Stuart *Men of Mts* 273 This peach tree is th' big tree that allus bore so many peaches. It's th' one in th' low swag by th' old rotted white oak stump. **1949** Arnow *Hunter's Horn* 301 He had crossed the graveyard field and was hurrying through the low rocky wooded swag between his place and where Lureenie had lived, not looking about for sheep. **1957** Broaddus *Vocab Estill Co KY* 77 = a piece of land often wet and soggy. **1986** Helton *Around Home* 379 = low spot.

[DARE *swag* n 1 chiefly South, South Midland]

2 A pass or low place on a mountain ridge (as in *Big Swag* on Round Mountain Ridge). See also **gap 1**, **saddle**, **sag 1**.

1927 Furman *Lonesome Road* 3 The Stoll household were hoeing corn high up on a bench or "swag" of mountain facing the home. **1937** Hall Coll (L. Myers, Cades Cove TN) = a level place on a ridge. **1939** Hall Coll (Mt Sterling NC) There's a bear waller in a swag under Spruce Mountain Tower where [the bears] use. **1956** Fink *That's Why* 3 Here these lower places between peaks and along ridges are almost invariably known as gaps, with an occasional swag. **1960** Hall *Smoky Mt Folks* 19 Finally he managed to grab hold of [the turkey's] legs, but as he did so, the turkey "riz" up into the air and carried him across a "swag" (gap) to the next mountain and courteously dropped him. **1970** Broome *Earth Man* 24 We dropped our packs in the low swag and began ascending the steep sides of the "puzzle" mountain. **1970** *Hunting* 71 Sometimes men would get on either side of a gap or swag, set the dogs loose, and let the dogs drive the deer through between them. **1997** Hufford *American Ginseng* 5 The hollows, deep dendritic fissures created over eons by water cutting through the ancient table land to form tributaries of the Coal River, receive water from lesser depressions that ripple the slopes. These depressions are distinguished in local parlance as "coves" (shallower, amphitheater-shaped depressions), "swags" (steeper depressions, "swagged" on both sides), and "drains" (natural channels through which water flows out of the swag or cove). **1999** Coggins *Place Names Smokies* 166 = a gap or depression along a ridge or mountain top, a swag.

[DARE *swag* n 2 chiefly South, South Midland]

3 A depression in a floor or road.

1952 Wilson *Folk Speech NC* 596 = a depression, a sag. "This floor has a big *swag* in the center." **2019** *Blind Pig* (Jan 15) A swag was a low place in the terrain, road, [or] animal's back.

swag down (also *swage down*, *swedge down*) *verb phrase* Of a swollen part of the body: to decrease in size, lessen in severity; figuratively = to cause to become assuaged.

1931 Goodrich *Mt Homespun* 56 "Poor sister ain't fit to go anywheres till that neck of hers gets swaged down, but I'm aimin' to go and see for myself, come Sunday," said Hannah. **1979** Carpenter *Walton War* 147 Evern (even when) he told me, it sort of swagged down my feelins. **1984** Wilder *You All Spoken* 206 *swaged down* = reduced in size, as with a boil. **1995–97** Montgomery Coll: *swag down* = to shrink (Adams); *swedge down* = to return to normal, as "My swollen ankle has swedged down since I used Epson Salts on it" (Norris).

[shortened forms of *assuage*; DARE *swage* v 2 chiefly South, South Midland]

swage down See **swag down**.

swaggle *verb* To swagger.

1961 Williams *R in Mt Speech* 7 In a few words ... *l* is substituted for *r*: fluster(at)ed, (frustrated), flitter (fritter), swaggle (swagger).

swaller See **swallow**.

swallop See **swollop**.

swallow

A *noun* Variant form *swaller* [see **1867** in **B**]; also *verb*.

1930 Armstrong *This Day and Time* 247 Try an' see if ye cain't swaller a few bites. **1939** Walker *Mtneer Looks* 1 It gits so I just make up a lot of stuff and tell it to ["them northern fellers"] like it was gospel truth, and they swaller it, hook, line, and sinker. **1954** Blackhurst *Riders of Flood* 64 When you go by the big rock at Spice Run you'll swaller enough spray to float you. **1973** Kahn *Hillbilly Women* 197 A good old mountain person has got too much damn pride to swaller that. **1985** Irwin *Alex Stewart* 144 You can have stomach burn and take you a goldenseal root and chew and swaller it and hit's all over with.

[DARE *swallow* v A especially South, South Midland]

B (also *swallower*) The throat.

1867 Harris *Sut Lovingood* 206 Jis' then I . . . cotch him by the har, an' pull'd up his head tu straiten his swaller. **1917** Kephart

Word-List 418 *swallower* = the throat. **1927** Woofter *Dialect from WV* 365 *swallerer* = throat: "That child has something stuck in his swallerer." **1983** Broaddus *Estill Co KY Word List* 58 = throat.

swallower See **swallow B.**

swallowfork *noun* A V-shaped notch cut into the edge of a domestic animal's ear, serving as an **earmark** to identify its owner. See also **overbit**, **smooth crop**, **split B1**, **underbit**.

1894 (in **1975** *Foxfire III* 87) Personally appeared before the undersigned John W. Hollifield who being duly sworn says on oath that his stock mark is a swallow fork in the left ear and . . . an over bit in the right ear. **1964** Wilson *Plants and Animals* 16 = two slits run together to form a W or an M. **1972** *Raising Sheep* 91 Lots of times they would split their ears—what they'd call a "swallow fork." They'd split the ear, either the right or the left one, and then cut off the end of the ears and call it a "swallow fork with a clip." **1977** *Foxfire IV* 129 I had thirty to forty head of hogs in the woods after I married. My mark was a swallow fork in each ear and an underbit in the right. **1982** Ginns *Snowbird Gravy* 129 Ours [= mark in the ears of livestock] was a swallow fork in the left and a overslope in the right.

[DARE *swallow fork* n chiefly South, South Midland]

swamp

A *noun* A relatively level area of poor drainage, often with thick vegetation, found at all elevations of the TN/NC mountains, even on some **balds**. Same as **bog**. See 1926 citation.

1926 Ganier *Summer Birds* 32–33 Large areas of laurel "swamp" are to be found at all altitudes, even the tops of some of the mountains being frequently an almost impenetrable jungle of "laurel" (rhododendron) and ivy. . . . The summits of other mountains, such as Mt. LeConte and Clingmans Dome, are "swamps" of small closely grown balsam spruce and the dead prostrate trunks and densely shaded ground are covered with a thick mat of damp, green moss. **1996** GSMNPCOHP-1:2 Now they was what we called swamps that had mostly bushes we called alders. . . . They'd get pretty big size. They wouldn't be trees, you know, along that creek. **1997** Montgomery *Coll* (known to Brown, Bush, Cardwell).

B *verb*

1 (also *swamp out*) To clear (land) of brush and trees; to clear the brush from a place.

1961 Seeman *Arms of Mt* 38 This very morning we have had two boys swamp out the saplings growing between the bend of the creek and the trail, for our prospective vegetable patch. **1984** Wilder *You All Spoken* 134 = clear off underbrush, as in "We swamped that ditch in no time a-tall."

2 To create a path or trail for loggers to have access to stands of trees; to clear brush from (a road). See also **buck swamper**, **swamper**.

1954 Blackhurst *Riders of Flood* 27 [There's] nothing to it [= swamping] but clearing out underbrush and limbs so teams can get to the logs. . . . If anyone asks, just tell him you've swamped roads ever since you was big enough to lift a hatchet. **1976** Tyler *Man's Work* 26 I guess I've done it all. Drove teams, drove grabs (device used to fasten a trail of logs together), swamped (cleared the ground of underbrush and fallen trees for road construction). **1980** Chiles *Logging Lingo* 22 = to slash a path through the trees and rhododendron for the building of skid roads. **1997** Montgomery *Coll* = to cut underbrush or growth for a logging road (Hooper). **2006** Farwell *Logging Term* 1021 "Hayburners," or horses, their "teamsters," and oxen driven by their "bullwhackers," all became outmoded, as did "crosspoling" logs across trails to make them sturdy and "swamping," or cutting, new trails to "snake" logs out of the forest.

swamp angel *noun* A type of mosquito.

1964 Reynolds *Born of Mts* 9 Mosquitos, called Swamp Angels or Gallinipers by the natives, cannot breed in running water of mountain streams, so there are few of them. **1997** Montgomery *Coll* (known to Bush).

[DARE *swamp angel* n 3 especially South, South Midland]

swamp dogwood (also *swamp willow*) *noun* A burning bush (*Euonymus americanus*). Same as **hearts bustin'.**

1937 Thornburgh *Great Smoky Mts* 25 The seeds of some shrubs are more spectacular than their flowers. This is true of one of the showiest shrubs in the Great Smokies, the euonymous, wahoo or spindlebush. It is especially lovely in October when its seedpod bursts open, displaying orange-colored seeds in its glowing red heart. It has many descriptive local names—swamp willow, strawberry bush, catspaw, jewel-box, but most descriptive of all is the name given by a mountain man of, "Heart's-bustin'-with-love." **1970** Campbell et al. *Smoky Mt Wildflowers* 102 Common names include strawberry bush, swamp dogwood, spindle bush, arrowwood, wahoo, and a dozen others.

swamper *noun*

1 A logging crewman who clears a path or road so that the rest of the operation can have access to stands of trees. See also **buck swamper**, **swamp B2**.

1927 Woofter *Dialect from WV* 365 = one who cuts road for hauling logs. "The swampers are not having to work hard this week." **1989** Oliver *Hazel Creek* 65 The first ones into the woods on a logging operation were the swampers, fellows who cleared the right-of-way, cut out the underbrush, for the skidding trails and the railroads. **1994** Farwell and Buchanan *Logging Terms* = in logging, a person who cleared land. **2006** Farwell *Logging Term* 1021 "Swampers" built [logging] roads maintained by "chickadees" and "grease monkeys," who kept them slick. **2006** *Foxfire 40th Anniv* 311 Though most of the people in this photograph undoubtedly work for the company, only a few of them would be loggers. The list of employees required by a large operation was staggering, and would include . . . "swampers" (the men who made the skid trails the horses and oxen used to drag the logs to a loading area).

[DARE *swamper* n 1 chiefly South, South Midland]

2 See citation.

2003 Triplett *Mt Roots* 13–14 Some of the Arbogasts may have been members of the Northern Home Guard or "Swampers" that fatally wounded Oliver Triplett and severely wounded Jasper at the Sinks of Gandy.

swamp out See **swamp B1**.

swamp willow See **swamp dogwood**.

swan (also *swanny*) *verb* To swear, declare (in phrases *I/I'll swan/ swanny*) to express surprise, indignation, or confoundment. According to consultants from the Smoky Mountains, **swan** is the more common form.

1888 Meriwether *Mt Life in TN* 457 "Well, I swan, but you're in bad luck!" said the tramp, striking a match and surveying my bedraggled duster and almost disintegrated straw hat. **1936** Carpenter *WV Expletives* 347 Law and Lordy may do duty for almost any emotion in this section of the country, as may also: I'll swan; Hell's banjer; Sakes o' mercy; and Sakes alive. **c1940** Aswell *Glossary TN Idiom* 11 *I swanny*. **1966–67** *DARE Survey* (Cherokee NC) *I swanny*; (Gatlinburg TN) *I swan*. **1973** Davis *'Pon My Honor* 53 I swanny, if there wasn't the prettiest big live catfish, must have weighed ten pounds or more. *Ibid.* 97 *I'll swan* = exclamation to back a vow. **1979** Carpenter *Walton War* 155 I Swan, I never saw the like. **1984** Burns *Cold Sassy* 159 I swanny to God, these modrun women are something else. **1989** Giardina *Storming Heaven* 10 "You should see their prices, Vernie. Twenty-five cent for a pound of coffee." "I swan!" said Vernie. **1996** Landry *Coll* I never seen the like, I swanny. **2000** Carden *Mason Jars* 187 I swan. I want you to listen! This woman lives in Sego, Nebraska, and she has sent me twelve Love Lies Bleeding seeds. Now, ain't that something? **2002** Myers *Best Yet Stories* 81 *I'll swan* = expression of surprise. **2009** Benfield *Mt Born* 158 An exclamation, quietly spoken, in wonder and astonishment. Often used as "Well, I swan" and as a complete remark on a situation, no further explanation needed. **2013** Venable *How to Tawlk* 23 *I-swan* = to lightly swear in polite company: "I-swan if a bire [i.e. a bear] didn't jest run acrost the trail up ahead!"

[probably < Scots/northern English *I'se warrant ye* "I'll guarantee you, I'll be bound," later taken as a euphemism for *swear* and adopted by Americans to avoid that word, following the Scriptural injunction in Matthew 5:34; DARE *swan* v South, South Midland; *swanny* v chiefly South, South Midland, formerly also New England]

swaney See **sweeny**.

swanny See **swan**.

swap *verb*

A Variant forms *swoop, swop*.

1940 Haun *Hawk's Done* 164 The very next day Miss Robinson would send a wagon up here with two brought-on bedsteads, pretty ones, she said, to swop for my two wild-cherry ones. **1940** Oakley *Roamin'/Restin'* 52 A man came around and wanted to buy this bob cat and I sold it for a razor or otherwise I swooped the skin for the razor and at the same time I dident have a beard or whiskers on my face.

B To hit, strike. See also **swarp B1**.

1969 GSMNP-46:4 I was swapping him right over the nose and the head, and I made him think I was going to kill him.

[OED3 *swap/swop* v 1a "to strike, hit"; SND *swap/swop* v^1 1 "to strike, hit, smite"]

swap ends *verb phrase* See citation.

2005 Williams *Gratitude* 529 *swappin' ends* = turning somersets, end over end; head over heels.

swap howdy See **howdy B**.

swap labor (also *swap work*) *verb phrase* To trade one kind or turn of work with a neighbor for another.

1859 Taliaferro *Fisher's River* 218 One neighbor would help another harvest his grain. . . . Corn-shuckings were conducted in the same way. . . . They "swopped work." **1967** Wilson *Folkways Mammoth Cave* 20 In early times it became customary to swap work with the neighbors, for some types of work were impossible without several helpers. Some of these were log-rollings, house-raisings, wheat threshings, wood-cuttings, tobacco-harvestings. **1973** AOHP/ASU-111 You never hired anybody on the farm. The people would go and swap work, they'd call it, and help each other. **1983** Montell *Don't Go Up* 201 *swapping labor* = two or more neighbors teaming up to help each other.

[DARE *swap work* v phr chiefly South, South Midland, TX, OK]

swapping *verbal noun* See citation.

1943 Gilbert *Eastern Cherokees* 211 "Swapping" of lands is a common practice. Persons are constantly moving from one town to another or from lowland to highland. Cherokees of the more conservative type are perpetually trying to locate further away from the trails which lead to the white man's world.

swap work See **swap labor**.

swar, sware See **swear**.

swarp

A Variant form *sworp* [see **1993** in **B3**].

B *verb*

1 To strike, lash, or push with a swinging or sweeping motion. See also **swap B, swipe, warp 1**.

1946 Matthias *Speech Pine Mt* 192 = to swing, strike, especially with a swinging or whipping motion: "His mother swarped the belt at him through the open door" . . . *swarp* = to wipe or "swipe": "I like a little [molasses] on my biscuits now and then. Then I like to pour a little on my plate and swarp a hot biscuit through them." **1968** Clarke *Stuart's Kentucky* 167 He watched carefully to avoid having the trace chains come loose and swarp the mules. **1982** Maples *Memories* 29 We would take an old cane pole, swarp [a bat] down, hold him by the wings, and see his little snapping teeth. **1989** Oliver *Hazel Creek* 31 He cut a large pole and when they would get too close to him he would lash out at them ("swarp" the ground) with the pole to drive them away. **1991** Still *Wolfpen Notebooks* 59 He grabbed off his belt and he swarped me, and he swarped me with the wrong end of it. **2005** Williams *Gratitude* 529 = to swat at. **2015** *Blind Pig* (June 26) You can swarp someone with a belt or other item, and you can also be swarped by a cow tail, a limb, or other item.

[cf SND *swap* v¹ 1 "to strike, hit, smite, deliver a sudden blow upon"]

2 To move with a dragging, sweeping, or brushing motion.

1946 Dudley *KY Words* 271 I like a little [molasses] on my bisquits [sic] now and then. Then I like to pour some on my plate and swarp a hot bisquit [sic] through them. **1961** Williams *Rhythm and Melody* 9 Hit won't be five minutes till that bag o' fleas [= a dog]'ll be right back in hyar a-swarpin' an' a-swarvin' around. **1961** Williams *R in Mt Speech* 6 = swipe, or possibly swipe + warp. **1976** *Bear Hunting* 284 The way [bears] wind around and swarp through them roughs and maybe make three or four trips around one knob, why, you may travel a long way. **2005** Williams *Gratitude* 529 = to brush harshly against something, as, "The limbs *swarped* ag'in the ground when the tree fell." Or tell a youngun: "I'll *swarp* your hind end."

3 (also *swarp along*) To move or behave in an erratic, unsteady, or awkward fashion.

1983 Page and Wigginton *Aunt Arie* 139 She goes up and down th'road a lot, swarpin' along. **1993** Ison and Ison *Whole Nother Lg* 66 *sworp* = move about unsteadily, from one side to another. **2015** *Blind Pig* (June 26) It is used to describe actions of an obnoxious, clutzy behavior. For instance, "He came swarping through the house like he owned the place."

4 (also *swarp around*) To enjoy the company of friends and acquaintances (as at a low-key, sometimes-impromptu get-together, often to drink and "let loose"); to behave with abandon, especially under the influence of alcohol.

1946 Dudley *KY Words* 271 = in the pple. form *swarping* only, the word has some currency in a sense roughly definable as wenching, hell-raising; or more mildly as skylarking, cavorting, playing: "The boys was out swarpin' (or 'swarpin' around') last night." The occurrence of the opprobrious sense appears to be spotty; the word is used in the other senses freely and without embarrassment by native speakers who are distinctly modest. **1999** DeRozier *Creeker* 44 I never heard anyone back home speak of someone drinking; they always said the person was "drinking and sworping." . . . It means wildly running around, cussing and hollering, and in general acting in ways no good, sane, sober person would ever behave. **2007** Preece *Leavin' Sandlick* 40 He wuz so bad to drank and come in jest a swarpin, trying to fight on Lassie Jo. **2014** *WV Talk* When my friend's mother Mrs. Brown saw us all dressed up, car keys in hand, she said we were "going sworping." Out to have a good time. Fanning around. **2017** Montgomery *File* The campfire swarp you refer to takes place during the Southern Appalachian Writers Cooperative (SAWC) Annual Fall Gathering. It is little more than a swarp around a campfire. . . . In modern terms, at least as we practice swarp, it no longer solely the domain of men. Everyone is welcome, but the spirit of light frivolity that does not get out of hand and does not (really) offend anyone (swarpers, loved ones or bystanders) remains central. If someone is swarping, they are not catting around and not causing trouble.

[DARE *swarp* v (all senses) chiefly southern Appalachians]

C *noun*

1 A cut, blow, or step, especially one made with a swinging motion; a dragging or swinging motion.

1940 Stuart *Trees of Heaven* 168 You can take six rows at a swarp around a newground slope. It'll shore look purty to see where you slice down six rows of weeds. **1945** Still *Mrs Razor* 55 One day he gets too sorry to bend and lace his shoes, and it's a swarp, swarp, every step. **1946** Dudley *KY Words* 272 Besides a cutting stroke this word as a noun sometimes means a swishing or swinging motion. **1963** Edwards *Gravel* 72 He kept saying "Whoa," and every time he said it, he gave her another sworp with the withe. **1982** Maples *Memories* 32 Dad said that he and a friend were riding one day, and the friend, acting smart, reached over and gave Dad's mule a swarp across the back. **2015** *Blind Pig* (June 26) He was out there mowing the grass and accidentally made one good swarp through his mama's flowers.

[cf SND *swap* n 1 "a blow, stroke, whack"; DARE *swarp* n southern Appalachians]

2 A low-key, sometimes-impromptu get-together of friends and acquaintances to enjoy one another's company.

2018 Montgomery *Coll* (34-year-old woman, Letcher Co KY).

swarp around See **swarp B4**.

swarpy *adjective* See citation.

1946 Dudley *KY Words* 272 = full, swinging: "A little old woman in a long swarpy dress."

swarth *noun* A row of grass cut for hay.

1984 GSMNP-153:28 [The mowing blade] had handles on it, and what he'd do is go to the upperside of the field. They called it swarth. When he struck, he would, you know, bring out the hay that he cut down with. It'd be in kind of a windrow up and down the hill. **1998** Montgomery *Coll* (known to Brown, Bush, Jones, Ledford, Weaver), = also referred to a row of wheat or grass cut by a hand tool (Cardwell).

[OED3 *swarth* n 1a alteration of *swath*, now dialect; Web3 *swarth* n dialect alteration (influenced by *swarth*¹) of *swath*]

swarthy *adjective* Sickly.

1986 Pederson et al. *LAGS* (Cherokee Co GA).

swear *verb*

1 Variant base/present-tense forms *swar*, *sware*.

1905 Miles *Spirit of Mts* 106 "I'll swar to Joshua, Joe," he says, "you're as superstitious as some ol' woman that smokes a pipe and don't know the war's over!" **1942** Hall *Phonetics Smoky Mts* 42 *sware* [swær].

2 Variant past-participle form *swore*.

c1950 Haun *When the Wind* 6 The draft board called him back to town and told him he had swore his ma in as his dependent and they were going to send him to the war straight off if he didn't take her back home. **1969** GSMNP-37:2:29 By God, they have swore a god-damned lie. **1977** Shackelford et al. *Our Appalachia* 268 The trouble [is], if you ain't careful, they mistreat you after they've held up their hand and swore they wouldn't. **1992** Gabbard *Thunder Road* 39 I wondered how the law had swore it was him.

swear off on (also *swear on*) *verb phrase* To attribute under oath (a deed, a child's paternity, etc.) to another person.

1972 *AOHP/ALC-276* Then him and Bob Mullins both sware it off on Ev, you see, and they hung Ev Hobson for the killing of that old man, you know, when he didn't do it. **2007** McMillon *Notes* She never swore her baby on anyone.

swear to *verb phrase* Of a woman: to claim, especially under oath, the paternity of (an illegitimate child) to a (certain man).

1975 Gainer *Speech Mtneer* 17 = to name the father of an illegitimate baby. "She never swore her baby to anyone." **1982** Powers and Hannah *Cataloochee* 202 You know that (an) old gal [is] going to swear a young'un to us? **1996–97** Montgomery *Coll* (known to Brown, Cardwell, Jones, Ledford).

[DARE (at *swear* C1) chiefly southern Appalachians]

swede fence *noun* A type of **stake and rider fence**.

1952–57 (in **1973** McDavid and McDavid *Vocab E KY* 160) = attested by 2/52 (3.8%) of E KY speakers for the Linguistic Atlas of the North Central States. **1966** Dakin *Vocab Ohio River Valley* 104 The three point contact with the ground of each section of this fence would clearly give it greater stability with steep hillsides in this area. The usual name for such fence is *galloping fence* . . . A Leslie County informant also unquestionably calls this fence a *Swede fence* . . . an Owsley County informant also seems to say *Swede fence* for this same type. **2004** Rehder *Appal Folkways* 104 A very rare fence in Appalachia is called the buck, reindeer, Irish, Shanghai, or Swede fence. Pairs of crossed rails form the vertical support of this fence, while diagonal rails form its linear axis.

[DARE *Swede fence* n especially southeastern PA]

swedge down See **swag down**.

sweeny *noun*

A Variant form *swaney* [see **1894** in **B**], *swinney* [see **1978** in **B**], *swinny* [see **1873** in **B**].

B Atrophy of the shoulder or hip muscles of a horse.

1873 Smith *Arp Peace Papers* 94 There was nary one but what had the dyspepsy, or swinny, or rumaticks, or the blind staggers. **1883** Zeigler and Grosscup *Heart of Alleghanies* 95 Bill, thet hoss looks ez tho' he hed the sweeney, wunct? **1894** Porter *Folklore Mt Whites* 112 "Swaney" in a horse's shoulder yields at once to the corresponding limb of a toad amputated at the same joint, and placed in a bag at the seat of disease. The mutilated animal is allowed to escape. **1940** Vincent *Us Mt Folks* 21 Sweeney, as you may know, is a very painful ailment that gets into the shoulders of animals. It hurts so that they sometimes nearly get down and crawl from pure misery. **1942** Hall *Phonetics Smoky Mts* 13 *sweeny* (lameness of the shoulder in animals) in its two occurrences was ['swɪnɪ]. **1977** Brookman *Veterinary Diseases* 146 A horse develops Sweeny by being worked unevenly or having the yoke pulled unevenly. As Mr. Elmer puts it, "One shoulder perishes and the horse takes to hopping." A poke root or penny is put into a slit made into the weak shoulder, left until the wound festers, and then cleaned out. Or the shoulder can be pumped up with air or simply massaged. **1978** *Horsetrading* 42 Then some horses had the swinney—that muscle where his leg starts across from the bottom, he's got a muscle there. That will just perish away. That muscle will go away and he'll be as slick as a board and he'll limp when he starts taking swinney. There's nothing you can do about it. **2007** Milnes *Signs Cures Witches* 105 Several people told me they can cure sweeny, a word not found in most dictionaries. The Oxford English Dictionary associates the word with German dialect and gives its meaning as "emaciation" or "atrophy." I have heard it used most often in reference to an affliction of horses, but Dovie knew a cure for people.

[Web3 < Penn German *schwinne* "to waste away, vanish"]

sweep *noun*

1 A cultivator blade.

1983 *Dark Corner OHP-4A* Wait about a week, two weeks, go back with a little bigger sweep, cut off a little more of that, you know, and hoe it in there. Wait about two more weeks, go in there, and throw your soda and fertilize in that middle of the big old sweep, and just finish tearing it down, just lap it and make it pretty and smooth as that yard, lay it by.

[DARE *sweep* n 1 chiefly South]

2 The lever arm of a rotating machine, such as a **sorghum gin**, powered by a horse hitched to it.

1975 *Foxfire III* 424 Years ago, the rollers of the mill were turned by a horse or mule. The animal was hitched to the end of a long rein pole or "sweep." A rod mounted horizontally in, and at right angles to, the butt end of the sweep was tied to a line that went to the horse's halter so that as the horse pulled the lead end of the sweep forward, the line connected to the butt end would keep him pulling himself around in a never-ending circle. **1995** Weber *Rugged Hills* 120 The cane is cut in the field, piled on a wagon and hauled to the barn. There the stalks are stripped and crushed in a mill. The mill has two heavy steel rollers that squeeze out the sweet juice. The rollers are turned by a horse that circles monotonously round and round, pulling a long pole called a "sweep."

sweet balsam *noun* Same as **rabbit tobacco**.

1982 Stupka *Wildflowers* 124 It is sometimes called "poverty weed" and "old-field balsam," because it thrives in dry areas and waste places. Names such as "sweet balsam" and "sweet everlasting" refer to its fragrance. Other names are "rabbit tobacco" and "cudweed." **1999** Montgomery *Coll* = children often chewed this in imitation of their parents chewing tobacco (Cardwell).

sweet Betty *noun* Same as **sweet bubby**.

1889 Murfree *Broomsedge Cove* 464 At the other window a series of straight wands rose up above the sill, and betokened the withered estate of the "sweet Betty" bushes.

[DARE *sweet Betty* n NC, TN]

sweet bread *noun*

1 A baked good (cake, gingerbread, cookies, etc.) that is sweetened, often with molasses. Also called **sugar bread**.

1864 *Chapman CW Letters* (March 13) hear is a ten dollar bill I will send for fear you hant drawed none yet it will do to buy your milk and Butter & pies and sweebred and apples. **1956** Hall *Coll* (Cosby TN) The cane patch had to be raised every year. They needed sweetnin' for sweet bread. **1957** Combs *Lg Sthn High: Word List* 98 = gingerbread, or sweet cakes of any sort. **1973** GSMNP-6:8 We'd make some sweetbread we called it, or gingerbread. **1982** *Smokies Heritage* 109 = the term used for cake or sweet cookies, particularly gingerbread. My paternal grandmother never says cake: she always asks for a piece of sweetbread for dessert. **1991** Thomas *Sthn Appal* 55 Ginger bread; we jist called it sweet bread then.

[DARE *sweet bread* n 2 South, South Midland]

2 The cooked pancreas of a hog or calf, usually sweetened with molasses.

1949 Still *Master Time* 44 We put by the sweetbreads. **1994–97** Montgomery *Coll* (known to Brown, Cardwell, Jones, Oliver, Shields).

sweet bubby (also *sweet shrub*) *noun* A sweet shrub (*Calycanthus floridus*), whose aromatic leaves are used as a perfume. Also called **Carolina allspice, sweet Betty**. See also **bubby**.

1913 Morley *Carolina Mts* 47 Another shrub that belongs to us and eastern Asia and that tempts one to nibble is what the people here call "sweet bubbies." [**1964** Campbell *Great Smoky Wildflowers* 50 Shrubs up to 6 or 8 feet tall bear a profusion of deep maroon or brownish flowers. . . . This shrub usually has a spicy fragrance. . . . It generally grows on stream banks and moist, wooded slopes at elevations below 3,500 feet. Other names are bubby-bush and Carolina allspice.] **1984–85** *Sevier Settler* 3:19 Girls used to pick sweet shrub and stick it in their bra so they would smell good.

sweet cake *noun* A cookie.

1984 Woods *WV Was Good* 10 In each stocking . . . was sweetcakes—we didn't know the word *cookie*—suspiciously like those Mother baked. **1998** Hamby *Grassy Creek* 73 We walked a distance of a mile and a half or more for Sunday School each week and for preaching when the pastor came. When there was to be preaching, my mother always had in her "satchel" (pocketbook) a "sweet cake" (sugar cookie) or a slice of lemon flavored pound cake for me, as the service was apt to be long.

sweetening *noun*

1 (also *sweeting*) An ingredient used to sweeten food or drink. See also **long sweetening, molasses, short sweetening, sorghum B2**.

1895 Edson and Fairchild *TN Mts* 374 = sugar. "Will you have some *sweetening* in your tea?" **1956** Hall *Coll* (Cosby TN) The cane patch had to be raised every year. They needed sweetnin' for sweet bread. **1986** Aiken *Mt Ways Two* 212 The mountain people used the "lasses" for sweeting in many ways, in their cooking as well as plain or with butter on their biscuits. **1991** Thomas *Sthn Appal* 56 We had plenty of honey an' maple-syrup an' molasses, like that. We never had to eat [apples] sour—we had plenty of sweetin'.

[DARE *sweetening* n 1 chiefly South, South Midland]

2 See citations.

2005 Williams *Gratitude* 529 *sweetnin'* = anything sweet, such as cake or candy. **2017** Kinsler *Take Girl* 71 = dessert.

sweet everlasting *noun* Same as **rabbit tobacco**.

1982 Stupka *Wildflowers* 124 It is sometimes called "poverty weed" and "old-field balsam," because it thrives in dry areas and waste places. Names such as "sweet balsam" and "sweet everlasting" refer to its fragrance. Other names are "rabbit tobacco" and "cudweed."

sweet flag (also *sweetroot*) *noun* Calamus, a perennial wildflower (*Acorus calamus*) that grows near water and has medicinal uses.

1934 Wilson *Bog Plants* Among the bog plants found in the Smokies, sweet flag or calamus with its stiff, sword-like leaves, its inconspicuous flowers, and its pleasant odor has, perhaps, been held in highest esteem by various peoples. **1939** Hall *Coll* (Catons Grove TN) Yes, sweet flag's good for stomach and for your gums. **1965** Shelton *Pioneer Comforts* 18 Calamus (also known as Sweet Root and Sweet Flag) was chewed to clear the voice. [**1971** Krochmal et al. *Medicinal Plants Appal* 32 In Appalachia the root is chewed to clear the throat and to cure stomach gas; and the powdered or ground plant is used in sachets.]

sweet gum *noun* A deciduous tree (*Liquidambar styraciflua*) of medium height whose bark is made into a medicinal tea and a gum chewed by children; the chewing gum itself.

1864 *Leigh CW Letters* (April 8) we are stationed on Nuce River it is a pine & sweet gum country. **1937** Hall *Coll* (Cosby TN) For flux [use] sweet gum bark and mutton taller melted. **1941** Walker *Story of Mt* 67 The sweetgum is one of the most beautiful trees on the mountain. Its foliage, which turns to a bronzy hue in autumn, gives a delicate touch to the rich colors of fall foliage. Its resinous sap has long been used by mountain children as their choicest chewing-gum. **1957** Broaddus *Vocab Estill Co KY* 77 = chewing gum. [**1971** Krochmal et al. *Medicinal Plants Appal* 162 Water- or brandy-soaked twigs are chewed to clean the teeth in some areas of Appalachia.]

sweethearting *verbal noun* See citation.

1972 Cooper *NC Mt Folklore* 95 *sweethearting* = dating or courting a sweetheart.

[cf DARE *sweetheart* v chiefly South, South Midland]

sweeting See **sweetening 1**.

sweet liniment *noun* See 1997 citation.

1969 GSMNP-28:64 After sugar got plentiful, they could get sugar. Then they'd sweeten it. They'd call it sweet liniment. **1997**

Montgomery *Coll* = any liniment that could be swallowed; pour one teaspoon to a glass, add one teaspoon of sugar, and fill with hot water (Cardwell).

sweet mash *noun* The product of a first **run** of whiskey, in which only fresh water (and not the **slops** from a previous run) has been added to the meal. See also **sour mash**.

1913 Kephart *Our Sthn High* 134 The sprouted corn is then dried and ground into meal. This sweet meal is then made into a mush with boiling water, and is let stand two or three days. The "sweet mash" thus made is then broken up, and a little rye malt, similarly prepared in the meantime, is added to it, if rye is procurable. **1959** Hall *Coll* The sour mash would always produce more whiskey than the first, which is called sweet mash. **1973** Wellman *Kingdom of Madison* 157 The sprouted corn was spread out to dry, and afterwards was ground to meal. Boiling water was added and the whole stirred into mush, which stood again to become firm. More liquid and meal, and another waiting process. The "sweet mash," so called, was fermented until, to use the phrase of the knowledgeable, "it could stand on its own legs." It produced a liquid mixture of alcohol and carbon dioxide, called "wash" by professional distillers, "beer" by mountaineers—a brew that would intoxicate, but with a forbiddingly sour taste.

sweetmeat *noun* See citation.

1982 Slone *How We Talked* 64 = the muscle near the back bone [of a slaughtered hog].

sweet milk *noun* Fresh, whole milk (in contrast to *buttermilk*).

1862 *Huntley CW Letters* (March 17) I Went out yesterdi evning and Baught me a quart of Sweat milk it hope me vary mutch I think if I could git milk and Butter that I Would git fat. **1864** *Chapman CW Letters* (May 15) I buy me a hen some times and some times by me some sweetemilk to eat with mush. **1921** Campbell *Sthn Highlander* 202 Buttermilk is a favorite beverage, referred to usually as "milk." If the guest wishes "sweet milk" he must so designate it. **1939** Hall *Coll* (Big Creek NC) Take the roots and beat it up, put sweet milk in it, and put it on it and it'll draw it white, and cure it up. **1972** Cooper *NC Mt Folklore* 26 Every country home had its springhouse, where buttermilk, sweet milk and butter were kept cold. **1981** Whitener *Folk-Ways* 62 When I was growing up there were but two kinds: sweet milk (whole raw milk) and buttermilk, though we did recognize the fact that sweet milk could be divided into cream and skim milk. Or perhaps I should say that the sweet milk simply divided itself by allowing the cream to rise and the skim milk to stay put. **1983** Helsly *Country Doctor* 19 Mama sat at the opposite end with her plate surrounded by a coffee pot on her right and on the left two pitchers of milk—buttermilk and sweet milk. **1998** Montgomery *Coll* = the common term for ordinary milk throughout the southern mountains (Ledford). **2003** Cavender *Folk Medicine* 12 Buttermilk was a favorite beverage and much preferred over "sweet milk."

[DARE *sweet milk* n especially South, South Midland]

sweet-mouthed *adjective* Of a hunting dog: having a pleasant-sounding bark.

1949 Arnow *Hunter's Horn* xx Oh, some might hunt for fun, and a sweetmouthed hound was a pretty thing to hear, but lots of times he got sick and tired of the business.

sweet pea *noun* See citation.

c1960 Wilson *Coll* = English peas . . . Garden peas as distinguished from field peas, cowpeas, stock peas, black-eyed peas.

[DARE *sweet pea* 1 chiefly South, South Midland]

sweet potato butter *noun* A thick spread, usually spiced and sweetened, made by stewing sweet potatoes. See also **peach butter, persimmon butter, pumpkin butter.**

1960 Hall *Smoky Mt Folks* 46 Fruit and beans were dried for use during the winter. Apple butter, "punkin" butter, and sweet "tater" butter were favorites. **1973** GSMNP-74:40 Some folks would make sweet potato butter. [**1980** *Smokies Heritage* 101 *butters* = not simply butter churned from milk, but the spiced, sweet fruit spread made from apples, peaches, pumpkin, and persimmons during jelly-making season and autumn (for the last two).] **1997** Ownby *Big Greenbrier* I:19 Mother made apple butter, sweet potato butter, pumpkin butter, jellies, gathered berries of all kinds, all kinds of fruits and canned them.

sweet potato pumpkin *noun* See citation.

1962 Wilson *Folkways Mammoth Cave* 15 Winter squashes were unknown, but their place was taken by the *cushaw*, or *crookneck*, often called a *sweet potato punkin*.

sweet potato slip *noun* A sprout or shoot taken from a sweet potato plant and replanted in a separate bed. Same as **tater slip**. See also **slip B1**.

1923 (in **1952** Mathes *Tall Tales* 3) With corn in the ground, tobacco planted, and "sweet-'tater slips" bedded this early, the farmers in the cove had more than their wonted leisure in the early summer. **c1960** Wilson *Coll* = a sweet potato plant, drawn from a potato bed. **1997** Montgomery *Coll* (known to Adams, Bush, Cardwell, Jones, Oliver, Weaver).

sweetroot See **sweet flag.**

sweet shrub See **sweet bubby.**

swell *verb*

A Principal parts.

1 Variant past-tense forms *swelt, swole, swolt*.

1895 Edson and Fairchild *TN Mts* 376 *swole*. **1959** Hall *Coll* (Hartford TN) He suffered several days [from a snakebite] and his body swole beyond recognition, but he kept drinking that liquor and he survived without any other medical aid. **1975–76** Wolfram/Christian *WV Coll* 153 His arm swelt. **1992** *Smokies Guide* (Fall) 10 One farmer in Cades Cove liked to say that he fattened his hogs "till their eyes swole shut." **2003** *Smoky Mt News* (Jan)

One Cades Cove farmer . . . claimed to have "fattened his hogs till their eyes swole shut and they couldn't stand up." **2009** Miller *Nigh Gone* 94 This [process of modifying verb endings] also applies in the form of changing the standard "d" or "ed" to a "t" in the past tense: e.g., "dast" for dared, "helt" for held, "het" for heated, "kilt" for killed, "ruint" for ruined, "swolt" for swelled, and "turnt" for turned.

2 Variant past-participle forms *swellen, swole, swoll, swolt.* [Editor's note: The form *swelled* is considered standard by the *Dictionary of American Regional English.*]

1862 Robinson *CW Letters* (Dec 21) [I was] sorry to here that his face was sweled so only one side of it is sweld and he ses that it is as big again as it augh to be. **1864** Wilson *Confederate Private* 71 (Oct 8) I am wel except my legs is sweln rite smart yet & is rite panful at times. **1895** Edson and Fairchild *TN Mts* 376 *swole.* **1917** Kephart *Word-List* 417 His hand was all swoll up, but now its all *squidged* down. **1949** McDavid *Grist* 114 (Fannin Co GA) *swellen* = swollen. **1974** Fink *Bits Mt Speech* 25 His face was all *swole* up. **1976** Garber *Mountain-ese* 90 The colt's laig was swolt to twice it's [sic] regular size.

[DARE *swold, swole, swolt* v 3b especially South, South Midland]

B *verb* To cause (one) to swell.

1937 Hall *Coll* (Cosby Creek TN) [Bee stings] got so they wouldn't swell him nary a grain.

swellen See **swell A2.**

swelt See **swell A1.**

swelter *verb* Variant forms *sulter, swulter.*

1913 Kephart *Our Sthn High* 312 I went down into the valley, wunst, and I declar I nigh sultered! **1994–97** Montgomery *Coll: sulter* (Brown, Bush, Cardwell, Cypher, Oliver); *swulter* (Oliver); *swulter, swultry* (Oliver). **2007** McMillon *Notes: swulter.*

[cf DARE *sulter* v chiefly southern Appalachians, Ozarks]

sweltersome See **sweltery B.**

sweltery *adjective*

A Variant forms *swoltry, swultry.*

1837 McLean *Diary* 51 Vary warm and Swoltry. **1983** Broaddus *Estill Co KY Word List* 58 *swultry.* **1996** Montgomery *Coll: swultry* (Oliver).

[cf DARE *swult(e)ry* (at *swulter* v) chiefly South Midland]

B (also *sweltersome*) Extremely hot, sweltering.

1895 Edson and Fairchild *TN Mts* 374 *sweltersome* = sweltering.

swifty *adjective* Of a stream current: rapid, swift.

1937 Hall *Coll* (Emerts Cove TN) Did you swim out to that swifty place?

swill *noun* The liquid of **still mash** after distillation, used for hog feed. See also **pot-tail(s), slops 1, still mash, sugar slop.**

1939 Wilburn *Notes* (Sylva NC) I also remember this old mill before the present mill [on Mingus Creek] was built. Yes, I used to suck "swill" through a quill at the Floyd still house. (Alice Enloe Dills).

swim *verb* Variant past-tense forms *swimmed, swum.*

1864 Leigh *CW Letters* (May 14) this batle was at Plymoth N.C. we faned the yanks out there we killed and captured all that was at the place only a few that swimed the River and got away. **1867** (in **1974** Harris *High Times* 290) He jist hopped overboard, an' swum over thar, an' tryin' his durndest *to turn hit tother way.* **1913** Kephart *Our Sthn High* 283–84 In mountain vernacular the Old English strong past tense still lives in begun, drunk, holped, rung, shrunk, sprung, stunk, sung, sunk, swum. **1941** Stuart *Men of Mts* 194 A big old sunfish swum out from under the bank and swallowed the grasshopper and went back. **1953** Atwood *Verbs East US* 23 In the M[iddle] A[tlantic] S[tates] *swum* predominates in Type I [= older speakers with little formal education] speech, its frequency varying from slightly over half (Pa.) to nearly nine tenths (N.C.). In Type II [i.e. younger speakers with more formal education] its occurrence is much more limited, varying from less than one sixth (Pa.) to nearly half (W.Va. and N.C.). **1954** Roberts *Bought a Dog* I swimmed, I kicked, and I paddled and when I finally got to the bank and got out I had 3000 pounds of fish in my hip boots. **1973** GSMNP-88:98 [That's] where he swum his horses across the river when he was carrying the mail. **1977** McGreevy *Breathitt KY Grammar* 93 *swimmed* = attested by 2 speakers. **1978** Reese *Speech NE Tenn* 180 *swum* = attested by 3/12 (25%) speakers. **2005** Williams *Gratitude* 529 He *swum*, or he *swimmed* (all the same).

[DARE *swimmed* (at *swim* v A1b) chiefly South, South Midland; *swum* (at *swim* v A1c) widespread, but especially South, South Midland, OK, TX]

swim-headed (also *swimmy-headed*) *adjective* Dizzy, giddy; hence noun *the swim head* = dizziness.

1956 McAtee *Some Dial NC* 45 *swim-headed* = giddy. **1973** *Flu Epidemic* 107 I had th'swim head with [the flu], and I'uz so sick I couldn't live. **1990** Cavender *Folk Medical Lex* 32 *swimmy-headed* = dizzy.

[DARE *swimmy-headed* adj South, South Midland]

swimmed See **swim.**

swimmy-headed See **swim-headed.**

swimp up *verb phrase* To shrink, shrivel.

1937 Hall *Coll* (Catons Grove TN) Dried apples swimp up.

swindiggle *verb* To swindle.

1973 GSMNP-6:32 Somebody'd swindiggled us out of everything we had.

[perhaps alteration of *swindle*]

swing *noun* A sling, a cloth or bandage for suspending an arm after an injury, etc.

1956 Hall Coll (Newport TN) Her [sore] arm, she had to carry it in a swing.

swinge *verb* To cook, burn.

1867 Harris *Sut Lovingood* 195 Es I went, I cud feel the fokis ove them specks a-burnin intu the back ove my head, an' I smelt my har swingin. **1924** Raine *Saddlebags* 99 When a mother asks her daughter to "swinge this chicken," she does not know that [Spenser] wrote: "The scorching flame sore swinged all his face." **1937** Hall *Coll* (Cades Cove TN) The fire swinged the limbs of the pine. . . . [We] swinge the hairs off a chicken. **1954** Arnow *Dollmaker* 153 You look so funny. Your hair's all swinged. **1995** Montgomery *Coll* He killed the chicken, plucked it free of feathers, and swinged it by holding it over a fire (Cardwell). **2003** Carter *Mt Home* 206 His hair was swinge'd and fried around the edges.

[OED3 *swinge* v² "to singe, scorch" now dialect and U.S., perhaps influenced by *sweal* v "to burn slowly"; DARE *swinge* v chiefly South, South Midland]

swingletree *noun* Same as **singletree**.

1793 *Jefferson Co Wills* I 39 An inventory of the estate . . . of Abijah Fowler decd. returned by Eleoner Fowler Administratrix . . . 1 pair of swingle trees. **1799** (in **1920** DeWitt *Sevier Journal* 21) (Nov 25) Bought of Charles Whitson 2 pr. Of fore Gears 1 Collar a stretcher 2 Bridles & 2 fore swingle trees at 2 dollars. **1863** *Vance Papers* (July 13) Soldiers wives and widows work is done with neatness and Sent home, whether paid for or not as they must live and be Seen to, he make plows, and plowstocks, Swingletrees, Stocks Sythes for mowing and Cradling purposes, mends waggons & Carts, or any thing belonging to farms, or kitchens, at low prices. **1949** Kurath *Word Geog East US* 58 In the South and the Southern Appalachians *singletree* and *swingletree* stand side by side, but *singletree*, a counter-term to *doubletree* (shortened from *double swingletree*), is gaining ground and already predominates decidedly in the Virginia Piedmont. **1969** Medford *Finis* 91 Sevril men rite here in Haywood have stood like a workhoss an' let collar, lines an' all be put on 'em—an' they no better than to kick over the swingle tree, too. **1983** *Dark Corner OHP-4A* We hung [the slaughtered hog] up out there in that old tree in my back yard and got a swingletree and put them hind legs and a piece of rope and tied him up and swung him up. **1986** Pederson et al. *LAGS* = attested by 15/60 interviewees (25%) from E TN and by 1/35 interviewees (2.9%) from N GA; 16/55 of all LAGS interviewees (29.1%) attesting term were from Appalachia.

[*swingle* + *tree*; DARE *swingletree* n chiefly Central and South Atlantic, Appalachians]

swink *verb* See citations.

1958 Combs *Archaic English in KY* 44 = work hard: "I swink all day long." **1961** Williams *Content Mt Speech* 15 Lil pintedly 'lowwed she'd not leave that child thar to grow up an' swink an' tote fer the rest of 'em.

swinney See **sweeny**.

swipe (also *swipe off*, *swipe out*) *verb*, *verb phrase* To wipe, brush or strike with a sweeping motion. See also **swarp B1**.

1943 Hannum *Mt People* 137 Pretty soon [God's] creatures got so derned ornery on His hands, He had to swipe 'em all out and start over again with Noah, who followed the trade of the sea. **1964** Roberts *Hell-Fer-Sartin* 46 They run in the house and just as she started in the house he swiped her dresstail off with his sword. **1973** *AOHP/ASU-111* [My daddy] sawed out croquet balls. He'd take glass [sic] and swipe them till they were as slick as glass. **1988** Landry *Coll* We were secure in the cove. You didn't have to fear if some calamity would swipe you off. **1996** Montgomery *Coll* Get out of here or I'll swipe you out (Cardwell). **2004** Adams *Old True Love* 236 The tears was just pouring down his face and he did not even try to swipe them and make like he was crying for all the world to see.

swipe off, swipe out See **swipe**.

switch *verb* To dowse (for water). Same as **water witch B**.

1955 Rogers *Switching* 108, 110 It is perhaps as axiomatic to say that there is a "water-witch" in every family as to say that any animal born with its eyes closed may go mad. The literal meaning of this may account for the frequency with which the peach tree switch is used in seeking for the hidden, underground stream as well as in the correction of the truant child. The practice of "switching" for water is a rather frequent skill with a believing number of individuals. . . . A Mr. Smith of Cookeville, Putnam County, reports that he switches with one hand by gripping the small end of the switch between the thumb and forefinger, letting the end of the switch rest against the palm. The switch is extended in a horizontal position and forward as he starts walking. When water is found, the loose end of the switch will start vibrating vertically. This will continue for a longer or shorter time depending on the strength of the stream. Horizontal vibrations indicate depth.

switch hiding See **hickory hiding**.

switch ivy *noun* Same as **dog hobble**.

2006 Ellison *Nature Journal* 36–37 Sometimes called drooping leucothoe, switch ivy or fetterbush, highland doghobble is one of the more common shrubs in the southern mountains, especially the Blue Ridge portions of North Carolina, Tennessee, South Carolina and Georgia. Several other closely related species, coastal doghobble (*L. axillaries*) and swamp doghobble. *L. racemosa*), are found mostly in lowland situations. . . . Its long arching branches often cover entire slopes, frequently in association with rosebay rhododendron and mountain laurel . . . But it's the arching branches that are doghobble's primary claim to fame. These often rot at their tips, creating an extensive tangle that is almost impenetrable. A black bear fleeing hunting dogs will intuitively head for a doghobble tangle situated on a steep slope, which it can easily bound through going upgrade. Pursuing dogs and hunters are quickly left behind, "doghobbled" by the rooted branches and sharp leaves.

swith

A *noun* The distance one can reach with a hoe or other implement; hence verb = to stretch such a distance. See also **flybroom**.

1979 Slone *My Heart* 61 Then we took hoes and shaved off the weeds. Each one working would take a "swith" and distance themselves as long as they could reach with a hoe, one above the other, each one just a little ahead of the one above. **1995** Montgomery *Coll* = the width one could reach with a hoe while cutting wheat or hay (Cardwell).

B *verb* See citation.

1979 Slone *My Heart* 40 If it was summertime, someone's job was to keep the flies from getting on the table. This was accomplished by waving a small branch or twig broken from a tree, backwards and forwards, over the food, while everyone was eating. Someone else took her place with the "swithin'" while she ate.

[perhaps a variant of *swath*]

swival See **swivel**.

swivel (also *swival*) *verb* To shrivel.

1939 *FWP Guide TN* 503 Kill hogs in the dark of the moon and the meat will "swivel" away and make more lard. **1942** Hall *Phonetics Smoky Mts* 99. **1963** Watkins and Watkins *Yesterday* 52 When she sucked on the pipe, her mouth looked like the blossom end of a swiveled cucumber. **1983** Page and Wigginton *Aunt Arie* 35–36 Dig your taters and sun'em till they gets th' least bit swivaled, I call it, and put'em in pasteboard boxes and cover'em up. **1995** Montgomery *Coll* He threw the taters away 'cause they were swiveled up (Cardwell). **2005** Williams *Gratitude* 529 *swivel*.

swively *adjective* Shriveled, withered, shrunken.

1956 Hall *Coll* (Newport TN) My berries is swively this year.

swivet (also *swivvet, swivvit*) *noun* A rush, state of agitation or nervous haste.

1917 Kephart *Word-List* 418 = hurry. "He's always in a *swivvit*." **1927** Mason *Lure of Smokies* 171 Old Dan Headrick he got all in a swivet and he fired to kill, while we was only aimin' to skeer 'em. **1937** Hyatt *Kiverlid* 90 He drug on in a turrible swivvet to git away. **c1960** Wilson *Coll*: *in a swivet* = in a state of agitation, or in a hurry, too obviously so. **1965** *Dict Queen's English* 17 = hurry, rush. "He was in a terrible *swivet* when he passed."

[OED3 *swivet* n dialect (chiefly U.S.); DARE *swivet* n chiefly South, South Midland]

swivvet, swivvit See **swivet**.

swoft *adjective*

2002 Myers *Best Yet Stories* 91 [To make a] fly catcher[,] homemade, mountain style, place raw fish in a canning jar and cover with water. Punch holes in the lid large enough to allow flies to crawl in. Once they get in, they cannot find their way out. When the jar is full or smells too "swoft," replace.

swol See **swell A2**.

swole See **swell A1, A2**.

swollop (also *swallop*) *verb* To slap, deliver a swinging blow; hence participial adjective *swolloping* = vigorous, verbal noun *swalloping* = a beating.

1867 Harris *Sut Lovingood* 119 He snatched a long strip ove the broken ceilin plank, es broad es a canew paddil at wun aind, in bof hans, an' jis busted hit intu seventeen an' a 'alf pieces at wun swollopin lick ontu the part ove Lum, what fits a saddil. **1999** Montgomery *Coll* = to slap, as a teacher punishing a pupil with a razor strap or belt, as in "Is that all the swalloping you're going to give me?" (Cardwell).

swolt See **swell A1, A2**.

swoltry See **sweltery**.

swoo calf See **soo calf**.

swoo cow See **soo cow**.

swoo heifer, swook(ie) See **sook**.

swoop, swop See **swap**.

swore See **swear 2**.

sworp See **swarp**.

swulter See **swelter**.

swultry See **sweltery**.

sycamore *noun* Variant forms *sic-ky-more, sykymore*.

1942 Hall *Phonetics Smoky Mts* 60 A few words are generally sounded with [ɪ]: . . . *sassafras, spectacles, sycamore*. **1973** Miller *English Unicoi Co* 94 Sykymore used by 2 of 6 speakers. **2014** Ellis *Coll*: *sick-y-more*.

[DARE *sycamore* n (pronc) chiefly South Midland]

sycle-rock *noun* A grindstone.

1978 Reese *Speech NE Tenn* 33 = attested by 4/12 (33.3%) speakers.

sykymore See **sycamore**.

T

table *noun* The meals regularly served at a particular place.

c1863 (in **1992** Jackson *Surry Co Soldiers* 251) We have table plenty at this place but it dont agree with me. **1901** Harben *Westerfelt* 75 I've heard a lot of good things about your mother's table. **1944** Justus *Billy and Bones* 47 I'm in the habit of earning my table room and board.

table-muscle *noun* See citation.

1944 Hayes *Word-List NC* 36 = a large girth, "pot belly."

tack *noun* See citation.

c1982 Young *Colloquial Appal* 22 = [a] small sack or pouch.

tackey (also *tacky*)

A *noun* An uncultured rural person, a poor white or a person viewed as dressing shoddily.

1836 (in **1956** Eliason *Tarheel Talk* 298) (Wilkes Co NC) I tell them I don know any better for I'm a mountain tackey sartin. **1891** *American Missionary* 45:415 (in **1892–2008** *DARE File*) In the foothills of the Cumberland Mountains in northwestern Alabama are a people called "Poor Whites" or "tackeys." **1958** Wood *Words from TN* 17 *Tacky, tackies* = unfashionable, shabby in dress, a person so characterized: "If hicks lived in town, they would be town tackies." **1992** Brooks *Sthn Stuff* 155 = a poor-white person.

[Web3 *tacky* n[2] South; DARE *tacky* n 2 South, South Midland]

B *adjective* Especially of dress: shabby, cheap-looking, in poor taste, dowdy.

1886 Smith *Sthn Dialect* 343 *tackey* = shoddy. **1891** Brown *Dialect in TN* 173 If his clothes are tacky and he appears to be from the backwoods, he is called a country-jake, and is said to look jakey. [See **1958** in **A.**] **1982** Slone *How We Talked* 30 *tackey* = ugly or cheap-looking. **1985** Irwin *Alex Stewart* 252 That was the tackiest looking man that you ever saw, but he was worth more than airy man in this county.

[OED3 originally and chiefly U.S.; DARE *tacky* adj[1] 2 scattered, but chiefly South, South Midland]

tacky See **tackey.**

tacky party *noun* A costume party to which guests come in shabby attire.

1897 Murfree *Juggler* 244 Their out-of-door attire of knickerbockers and flannel shirts ought to be deemed . . . shabby enough to appease the "tacky" requirements . . . for they were pleased to call their burlesque masquerade a "tacky party." **1976** Garber *Mountain-ese* 96 = costume party: They're havin' a tacky-party at school to celebrate Halloween.

[DARE *tacky party* n chiefly South, South Midland]

tad (also *tadpole, tadwhacker*) *noun* A small child, especially a boy.

1944 Justus *Billy and Bones* 42 My mammy used to sing me that old ballad when I was a little tad. **c1950** Adams *Grandpap* 86 "Well," he said, taking a fresh chew of tobacco, "my pap an' mammy used to tell it to me when I was just a little tad, back there on Jellico." **1963** Watkins and Watkins *Yesterday* 1 There's Jim. When he was a little tad a plowstock fell on his head, and he never has had good sense. **1980** Still *Run for Elbertas* 29 They's another thing we've got for sartin, and that's a name for this little tadwhacker. He's to be named for a feller proud as ever walked. **1991** Still *Wolfpen Notebooks* 62 He ran my daddy off this place when I was a tad and later he run my oldest brother off. **1997** Montgomery *Coll*: *tad* = small child (known to Adams, Bush, Cardwell, Ellis, Jones, Weaver). **2007** McMillon *Notes*: *tadpole* = a small child.

[Web3 *tad* n probably from English dialect *toad* < Middle English *tade, tadde*]

taddick, taddle See **toddick.**

tadpole, tadwhacker See **tad.**

taffy pull (also *taffy pulling*) *noun* Same as **candy breaking, molasses pull.**

1942 Thomas *Blue Ridge Country* 143 There was rarely a gathering . . . especially during the winter, that did not end with a taffy pull. That too afforded courting couples the means to pair off and pursue their romance. *Ibid.* 144 When the taffy had cooled so that it could be lifted up in the hands the fun of pulling it began. The girls buttered or greased their hands so that it would not stick, and the boys, of their choice, did likewise. Pulling taffy to see who could get theirs the whitest was an occasion for greatest merriment. **1968** *DARE Survey* (Big Stone Gap VA) *taffy pull*, (Romney VA) *taffy pulling*. **1975** Kroeger *WV Farm Life* 8 [We'd] meet at a certain place on Sunday and play games of all kinds, and tell tales, popped popcorn, cracked hickory nuts, had taffy pulls, and things like that. We always had molasses to make popcorn balls and make taffy.

taffy pulling See **taffy pull.**

tail end of misery *noun phrase* Someone experiencing great distress, suffering, or hard luck.

1999 Montgomery *Coll* I feel like the tail end of misery (known to Cardwell).

tailings (also *tails*) *noun* Inferior, low-proof whiskey at the end of a **run.** See also **faint(s), heads, middlings 2.**

1963 Carson *History Bourbon* 104 The distiller was not overly concerned about cutting out the heads and tails [from his whiskey], and he was in no position to age his product. *Ibid.* 237 *heads and tails* = the condensate obtained at the beginning and end of a run, containing undesirable amounts of the congeneric substances. **1972** Carr *Oldest Profession* 78 The last of the run is called "backin's," "tailin's," or "faints." **1974** Maurer and Pearl *KY Moonshine* 126 *tailings* = faints.

tails See **tailings.**

tail tree *noun* A tree at the periphery of an area being logged that supports an overhead cable system for moving logs.

1964 Clarkson *Lumbering in WV* 373 = in steam skidding, the tree at the end of the skid-road, to which the rigging used in skidding logs is attached. **1974–75** McCracken *Logging* 1:1 They had a buggy that run that rope plumb back to the tail tree, from the skidder to the tail tree.

tail twister *noun* See citations.

1968 *DARE Survey* (Brasstown NC) = someone who follows along behind others, especially a younger brother or sister. **1998** Montgomery *Coll* (known to Ledford).

taint *verb* Of milk or meat: to spoil.

1934 Carpenter *Archaic English in WV* 77 Among these [= words found in central or southern WV] are . . . taint for tainted (as used with milk) [etc]. **1986** Pederson et al. *LAGS* (Johnson Co TN) = of meat.

[cf Web3 *taint* vi "to rot" archaic]

'tain't *phrase* It is not.

1860 Olmsted *Back Country* 251 'Tain't so here; people's more friendly. **1929** Kephart *Smoky Mt Magic* 1 'Tain't no use keepin' a dog and doin' your own barkin'. **1974** Fink *Bits Mt Speech* 26 = it isn't: "Tain't what I wanted."

tain't done it See **it ain't done it**.

take *verb*

A Principal parts.

1 Variant past-tense forms *taked*, *taken*, *takened*, *tooken*, *tuck*, *tuk*.

1860 *Zion Church Minutes* 47 A door was opened for the reception of members and following came forrard and joined by letter: Joseph Bartlett and James Bartlett and his wife and both was gladaly recd and tuck the reit hand of fellowship. **1861** *Poteet CW Letters* (Aug 7) he dyde here and they tuck him home. **1863** (in **1999** *Davis CW Letters* 90) our boys Taken him up had him trid before a justice condemned him To hang and they hung him up. **1863** *Warrick CW Letters* (Dec 10) the yankees drove us from our ditches and takend them from us tho it was a very hard fight for som time. **1895** Dromgoole *Fiddling to Fame* 49 I tuk my fiddle down. **1904–20** Kephart *Notebooks* 2:475 She had the trembles and drapped everything she tuk holt of. **1914** Arthur *Western NC* 266 It is certain that we sometimes say "hit" for it and "taken" for took. **1939** Hall *Coll* (Smokemont NC) But we finally got our horses and taken part of [the bear meat] on one of 'em . . . and packed him in home. *Ibid.* (Smokemont NC) They got down to the creek. There they overhauled [the bear], killed him, taked him, dressed him up, took him up to the camp, and stayed all night. **1952–57** (in **1986** McDavid and McDavid *KY Verb Forms* 291) *tuck* = attested by 19 of 28 (68%) of E KY speakers for the Linguistic Atlas of the North Central States. **1953** Atwood *Verbs East US* 23–24 [In] nearly all of N.C. [*tuck*] becomes fairly common (being used by more than half of Type I [i.e. older speakers with little formal education] in N.C.) It also occurs with some regularity in s.w. Va. and throughout W.Va. . . . The preterite *taken* is also confined to the South and the South Midland, where it occurs rather commonly in Md. and W.Va., less commonly in Va., N.C., and S.C. **1961** *Coe Ridge OHP-335B* He run to him, tooken his head, and throwed it back. **1962** Williams *Verbs Mt Speech* 17 The past and past participle of . . . *take* [become] *takened*. **1971** *AOHP/ALC-160* Hit took jobs from the men when they brought the machinery in. That taken jobs from the men. **1974** *AOHP/ASU-265* They use these power saws, and one can cut the timber all right now, but it taked three hands at that time. **1976** Lindsay *Grassy Balds* 186 He come out about forty-six, I guess, when the TVA taken all the property over. **1982** Ginns *Snowbird Gravy* 22 She canned the apples, and then she taken the peelings and canned those. **1989** *Matewan OHP-39* There's another incidence that taken place just a while after that strike was going on. **1997** *GSMNPCOHP-5:19* It tuck us a day to go from Cades Cove to Maryville. **2007** McMillon *Notes*: *taked*.

[DARE *taken* (at *take* v A2c) chiefly South, South Midland; *tuck* (at *take* v A2a) chiefly South, South Midland]

2 Variant past-participle forms *takened*, *toock*, *took*, *tooken*, *tuck*, *tuk*.

1804 *Globe Creek Church Minutes* 18 the Church considered that she has took gospel steps for what she has done. **1813** Hartsell *Memora* 107 [I] Came to the Generals tent to know what to dow with the Indians that he and his men had toock prisoner. **1861** (in **1980** Clark *Civil War Diary* 25) We have now took up camps for the night and will remain here tomorrow to draw rations for the march across the mountain. **1861** *Poteet CW Letters* (Aug 7) gineral Mcgrooder has tuck 10 thousand men down there And is agoing to attact newport news. **1886** Smith *Sthn Dialect* 348 When we offered pay, the men declined it, saying "he'd never tuck no pay fer nuthin' ter eat in his life, and he'd hyeard his father say he'd never tuck none, and he never 'spected to take none." **1910** Cooke *Power and Glory* 122 I bet they got that stuff when I was took. **1913** Kephart *Our Sthn High* 200 I ain't never tuk money from company. **1937** Hall *Coll* (Bradley Fork NC) I allowed [the deer] might a tuck the black tongue and died, just like it tuck the cattle. **c1945** Haun *Hawk's Done* 266 "Is that all that has took place?" I ast her. **1960** McCaulley *Cades Cove* If it was a widow woman, she was took care of. **1962** Williams *Verbs Mt Speech* 17 The past and past participle of . . . *take* [become] *takened*. **1972** *GSMNP-93:3:24* Then they ain't tuck care of 'em noways. **1974** Fink *Bits Mt Speech* 27 The ham was *tooken* out of my smokehouse. **1975** Chalmers *Better* 58 Tim's wife is took right bad. **1977** Still *Wonder Beans* 9 Hit looked like Jack was being tooken. **1978** Reese *Speech NE Tenn* 181 *took* = attested by 6/12 (50%) speakers. **1980** Miles *Verbs in Haywood Co* 100 They was took better care of than when I was growing up. **1998** *Dante OHP-25* I just handed him my statements where they had took my dues out. **2008** *Rosie Hicks* 1 After she'd took over, I said, "Well, I'll help her some."

[DARE *tooken* (at *take* A3d) chiefly South, tu(c)k (at *take* v A3b) chiefly South, South Midland]

B (+ *verbal noun*) To go. See also **take to 1**.

1970 *GSMNP-26:10* He made a dive at my brother Richard, and he took running off.

C Senses.

1 To rush, go immediately with haste and energy (in combination with an adverb or preposition of direction such as *after, around, back, behind, down, off, on, out, under, up*).

c1832 (in **2007** Dunkerly *Kings Mt* 92) Ben Hollingsworth and I took right up the side of the mountain, and fought our way, from tree to tree, up to the summit. **1834** Crockett *Narrative* 188 I backed and went down a creek some distance till I came to a hollow, and then took up that. **1913** Kephart *Our Sthn High* 91 [The deer] tuk right down the bed o' Desolation, up the left prong of Roaring Fork, right through the Devil's Race-Path. **1915** Hall *Autobiog Claib Jones* 11 When I saw him coming, I took under the bank. **1924** Raine *Saddlebags* 25–26 You "take up" a stream for a mile or two, now on one bank, now on the other, sometimes in the bed of the stream itself, until you come upon its source, a spring near the top of the mountain. **1939** Hall *Coll* (Dccp Creek NC) So I went up and took around the mountainside and went across two or three spruce ridges. . . . All at once [the bear] came out and the dogs run out of the way and he took after me. *Ibid.* (Deep Creek NC) We let them go and we took up Nettle Creek. *Ibid.* (Little Cataloochee NC) [The deer] took back for the creek, made for the creek again. *Ibid.* (Mt Sterling NC) We heard a dynamite blast go off, and just in about a second another one went off. We took behind some trees. Rock flew all over us. *Ibid.* (Smokemont NC) Then we decided we'd go a-bear hunting. We took our dogs, took out to the top. *Ibid.* (Sugarlands TN) They just took on after the bear. **1941** Stuart *Men of Mts* 57 He takes back up the hill like a squirrel. *Ibid.* 258 He takes right out in front of me and runs up that ladder like a tom and pops in at the winder. **1942** (in **1987** Perdue *Outwitting Devil* 31) She seed Jack a'comin' and she tossed up her tail, throwed up her head, snorted and whinnied and took down the hill and across the valley with Jack right after her. **1952** Wilson *Folk Speech NC* 597 *take out* = to set out; to go. Generally indicates hurry. "He took out to town." **1958** *GSMNP*-110:16 It was fine timber up Jakes Creek, but those citizens had a whole lot of it and took out and sold it. **1964** Roberts *Hell-Fer-Sartin* 95 The daughter took out with Jack on her heels. **1970** *Hunting Stories* 78 He took right up th'mountain toward me. **1973** *GSMNP*-70:1:3 I just went up to the gap of the mountain up a little hollow and took up a long straight mountain. **1973** *GSMNP*-83:9 He just tore loose from him and took down the road. **1975** *GSMNP*-59:39 It made Grandpa mad. Grandpa grabbed a pitchfork and took after him with it. **1995** Montieth *Tall Tales* 10 I took off down the mountain. **2009** Burton *Beech Mt Man* 5 They said that guy took from that room ninety mile' an hour.

2 See citation.

1957 Combs *Lg Sthn High: Word List* 99 = to take to (in school). Ex.: "That boy takes larnin' easy."

3 To pass (a period of time, especially a night) as a guest.

1919 Combs *Word-List South* 35 *take a night* = to spend, or pass a night with. **1933** Thomas *Traipsin' Woman* 121 The Revenuers had no call to make on like they were friends with Crosswise's folks, eat their vittals, take the night, and all the time fixing to undermine Old Bije and Young Bije. **1940** Farr *More TN Expressions* 448 *take a night* = an invitation to spend the night: "Git off your horse and take a night with us." **1952** Giles *40 Acres* 21 Appalachian families visit much together. "Taking the day" with each other, and the church meeting, are the only social affairs. **1955** Ritchie *Singing Family* 10 Why Ollie, I thought you'd come to take the night. **1979** Carpenter *Walton War* 173 We slip-shucked the crowd and he axed me to take the night with him.

[DARE *take* v B5 chiefly Appalachians, especially KY]

4 To become afflicted with (a disease or ailment). See also **take with.**

1972 *AOHP/LJC*-104 He had two operations, and he took a brain hemorrhaging. *Ibid.* She got herself all wet in the weeds and everything and took TB. **1973** *GSMNP*-5:4 I took rheumatism in my hand, and I went to Doctor Bob Medford for a good bit, and he told me that death cured it and that is about right. **1974** *GSMNP*-51:4 He had took rheumatics after then or something. **1985** Irwin *Alex Stewart* 250 Uncle George Livesy had a girl that took the measles.

[DARE *take* v B1a chiefly South, South Midland, MO, OK, TX]

5 To have an attack of anger, throw a tantrum; to have a seizure. See also **duck fit.**

1915 Pollard *TN Mts* 243 *take a fit* = to have (i.e. undergo) a fit. **1927** Woofter *Dialect from WV* 353 He took a duck-fit because I dropped the hammer on the ground. **1937** Hall *Coll* (Copeland Creek TN) He liked to tuck a hard fit (referring to a ranger whom she verbally chastised because of park restrictions). **1957** *GSMNP*-23:2:21 Elder Ogle, he took a spasm about them catching that coon out of season. **1994–98** Montgomery *Coll* I'm going to take a fit if I don't get to go (Cardwell). **2005** Williams *Gratitude* 529 (1) have a seizure (2) bawl and squall and carry on about something (3) take a mad fit, or have a hissy (temper tantrum).

take account of *verb phrase* See citation.

1940 Bowman *KY Mt Stories* 248 = notice.

take a class to (also *have a class to*) *verb phrase* To take a class with, have as an teacher (a certain individual).

1935 Kenny *To in WV* 314 *to* = under or with (an instructor). Thus: "I had a class in German to Professor C." **1996–97** Montgomery *Coll* (known to Adams, Brown, Jones); I'm going to take a class to Miss Jones, or I'm not going to take one at all (Cardwell).

[DARE (at *to* prep B6 chiefly WV]

take after *verb phrase*

1 To go hurriedly after. See **take C1.**

2 In phrase *take back after* = to inherit qualities from or to follow (a parent, relative, etc.) in a pursuit, habit, or occupation. See also **favor B.**

1912 De Long *Troublesome* Folks takes back after their generations. **2007** McMillon *Notes: take back after* = to favor an ancestor.

take and *verb phrase* To start, go to work and (+ similarly inflected verb, used to convey that two actions or events are simultaneous or sequential and sometimes to reinforce the latter action). See also **go and, send and.**

1788 (in **1853** Ramsey *Annals* 415) Those that have arms, etc., and do not comply, take and give to those that will serve. **1924** Abernethy *Moonshine* 116 It were in the fall after the army that Bets tuk an' died. **1939** Hall Coll (Catons Grove TN) Take and pour in fresh butter or sheep's tallow, and then make some life everlasting tea, about a half a teacupful, and put in with it, and boil it down and strain it, and it's the best salve that I ever used. *Ibid.* (Deep Creek NC) They had to take and cut wood, build a big fire for him, and take off all their mackinaws and duck backs and wrop him up, keep him from freezing to death. **c1950** Adams *Grandpap* 42 When he does, you take an' skin a strip of my hide from the end of my nose to the tip of my tail an' take it up on the hill an' hit it across a hollow log an' make a wish an' it'll come to pass. **1956** Hall Coll (Del Rio TN) You take and dry the corn out real good and dry. **c1960** Wilson Coll: *take and (do something)* = to accept a responsibility and go to work on it. **1971** *AOHP/ALC-33* We'd put one [dress] on on Monday, and we would take and wear hit till Thursday, and then we'd have the other one cleaned to wear a-Friday. **1974** *No Sang* 18 I took and sowed sang all in there. **1977** Shackelford et al. *Our Appalachia* 201 He just about had to take and scrape bottom to make it through. **1989** Landry *Smoky Mt Interviews* 194 They's an old house up there, and they tuck and made a schoolhouse out of it. **1998** *Dante OHP-69* He sprouted that corn, and when it was sprouting he would take and chop it up and grind it up.

[cf OED3 *and* conj[1] 10 now colloquial and regional]

take and rake *verb phrase* See citation.

1936 Farr *Folk Speech Mid TN* 276 = invitation to commence eating: "Everybody take and rake."

take a notion (also *take the notion*) *verb phrase* To decide on a whim (to take a course of action). See also **notion**.

1863 *Proffit CW Letters* (June 26) if you take the notion to write me a letter please put in a good Knidle [= needle] and as much thread as you can. **1939** Hall Coll (Cataloochee NC) About nineteen years ago, me and William Stafford from Tennessee took a notion we'd go out and look for some bear sign. *Ibid.* (Wears Cove TN) Me and brother Baus could just get out there and kill a deer anytime we took a notion to. **1973** *AOHP/ASU-149* I took a notion to sell it and bought down here and built. **1981** GSMNP-117:7 When he took a notion to whup a boy, he'd bring 'im up there, and talk about the dust a-flyin'.

take around See **take C1**.

take a roundance on See **take roundance 2**.

take a shine to *verb phrase* To develop a liking or fancy for.

1899 Fox *Mt Europa* 110 I hev tuk sech a shine to ye. I kind o' think I'll miss ye more'n Easter. **1923** Greer-Petrie *Angeline Steppin' Out* 21 Some newspaper chaps tuck a great shine to me and Lum, and whilst they 'peared to be right nice sort of fellers, they shore had a lot of curossity, and was awful ill-mannered about axin' questions. **1954** Blackhurst *Riders of Flood* 34 Bill Brake took a shine to him and sent him up here, hopin' he'd make good. **1975** Jackson *Unusual Words* 153 *Take* also appears in such idioms as *take a fit over, take a shine to, take a likin' to, take a notion to,* and *take a turn to.* **1995** Montgomery Coll (known to Cardwell).

take back See **take C1**.

take back after See **take after 2**.

take backwater *verb phrase* See citations. Same as **backwater**.

1939 Farr *TN Mt Regions* 92 = to retract what has been said: "He took back water on what he said about the preacher." **c1960** Wilson Coll = to hedge, back away from a situation or statement.

take bad (also *take bad off, take bad sick*) *verb phrase* To become seriously ill or confined to bed. See also **take down 2**, **take sick**.

1863 *Penland CW Letters* (Aug 16) When I rote to you I thought I was Getting Better but was taken worse the same day. **1973** *AOHP/EH-31* He took bad sick, and he said nobody was going to get his money. **1975** Chalmers *Better* 59 Pink's wife's been took bad, and Doc wants you should come and he'p him. **1978** Hiser *Quare Do's* 4 Aunt Nance, my mammy is took just awful bad off. **1986** Ogle *Lucinda* 58 The cow had not been milked since Dad took bad, so she was calling so pitiful.

take bad off, take bad sick See **take bad**.

take behind See **take C1**.

taked See **take A1**.

take down *verb phrase*

1 To go down hurriedly. See **take C1**.

2 (also *take down sick*) To make or become gravely ill or confined to bed. See also **take bad**, **take sick**.

1864 *Hanes CW Letters* (Aug 8) I am sory to say but will hav to say I hav seen one of our company deposited in the grav it was Henry Hall he was taken down with the tifoid feaver a few weeks a go and died the sixt of this month. **1864** *Walker CW Letters* (March 2) then I was taken down very Badly with the Soar throt and had liken to of died. **1936** Skidmore *Lift Up Eyes* 33 I was to her place the last time she was took down with pleurisy. **c1950** Adams *Grandpap* 35 His pap an' mammy had took down sick an' died. **1973** GSMNP-85:2:9 They was six of them took down with the fever. They was all down sick, and we went over there and washed for them, me and my mother, and I stayed over there several nights to help Vishey, and then she took down and she died and her mother died. **1982** Slone *How We Talked* 112 Took down sick—became ill. **1993** Burchill et al. *Ghosts and Haunts* It's just a pity that your sister Mary got took down with the tuberculosis.

[DARE *take down* v phr b (in active constructions) scattered, but chiefly South, South Midland]

3 To depress.

1925 Dargan *Highland Annals* 282 Seemed like he wuz tuk down about it, an' never got back his spirit. **1995** Montgomery Coll My grandparents were so took down that they never could get over it (Cardwell).

take down sick See **take down 2**.

take fellowship with *verb phrase* To join or become associated with (a church congregation).

1989 *Matewan OHP-28* That's what I got to praying in, and I took fellowship with them.

take hold *verb phrase* To assume responsibility, take charge.

1939 Hall *Coll* (Cades Cove TN) [My grandfather] died, and father, he took hold at thirteen year old, and stayed on the place, not being away from home over two weeks at a time at work. He still lived on the place till he was eighty-six year old and died. **1941** Stuart *Men of Mts* 266 Warn't no standin' back and shirkin' when Lefty took holt o' a thing. **1958** Campbell *Tales* 242 You done the best you could; now I'll take hold and help you out.

take in *verb phrase* Of a church service, an assembly, or a school term: to begin, be held. See also **take up 4**.

1965 Stubbs *Mountain-Wise* (Feb–March) 10 There wuzn't no Saturdays fer them in those days neither. School took in six days a week. **1971** Dwyer *Dict for Yankees* 32 = to begin, as school classes or church services. "School takes in early." **1997** Andrews *Mountain Vittles* 53 Of course by September school at the old rock school house had taken in.

[DARE *take in* v phr chiefly South, South Midland]

take it tedious *verb phrase* To go to the trouble; to belabor.

1904–20 Kephart *Notebooks* 2:642 You needn't take it so tejus as to axe ary man you meet on Stecoah what his name is. Jist say, "Hello, Mr Crisp." **1994–97** Montgomery *Coll* (known to Brown, Cardwell).

take leg bail See **leg bail.**

take loose *verb phrase* To set out suddenly or hastily (to do something). See also **cut loose.**

1972 *AOHP/LJC-104* [The mule]'d take a-loose from the plow and take the singletrees from it. **1999** Landry *Smoky Mt Interviews* We tuck loose and let the cattle in.

taken See **take A1**.

takened See **take A1, A2**.

take off *verb phrase*

1 To go off hurriedly. See **take C1**.

2 To help oneself.

1913 Kephart *Our Sthn High* 296 Many common English words are used in peculiar senses by the mountain folk, as . . . take off for help yourself. **1995–97** Montgomery *Coll* (known to Brown, Bush, Cardwell).

take on *verb phrase* [Editor's note: Senses 2 and 3 cannot always be differentiated.]

1 To go on hurriedly. See **take C1**.

2 To make a noisy, protracted show of emotion about something, as in wailing, sulking, grieving, raving, cursing, or complaining.

1859 Taliaferro *Fisher's River* 122 When they 'vited the mourners I went up, and you may s'pose there was some racket jist then. They all tuck on mightily. **1863** *Gilliland CW Letters* (June 26) you statid in your leter that the children was all taking on a bout me I dont want them to do that at all for there is no use in that. **1864** *Watkins CW Letters* (Aug 24) Ant Sally Watkins said she wants to se you very bad she taks on mitly I can tell you. **1874** Swearingen *Letters* 164 They all cried and took on as bad as if she had died. **1895** Dromgoole *Fiddling to Fame* 49–50 When the mail war opened—Laud! how they swore an' tuk on. **c1926** Bird *Cullowhee Wordlist* His father died last spring and he took on awful. **1931** Goodrich *Mt Homespun* 56 When the mourners get to takin' on and the others go to shoutin', you can't hear nothin'. **1940** Haun *Hawk's Done* 19 She hollered and bawled and took on like a dying calf. **c1960** Wilson *Coll* = to make a great ado, or emotion, good or bad. **1963** Watkins and Watkins *Yesterday* 32 The family's love was measured by the noise of the weeping, by the "taking on," as the mourning was called. When a child returned home from a funeral, his brothers and sisters who had not gone asked him, "Did they take on a whole lot?" Then he tried to describe the hollering and fainting. **1983** Pyle *CCC 50th Anniv* A:3:27 He got sick one night, and he was just a-takin' on a sight on earth. **1994–95** Montgomery *Coll* Don't take on so (Cardwell); He was taking on something awful with the toothache (Oliver).

[DARE *take on* v phr "to display strong emotion" chiefly South; also South Midland, Northeast]

3 To exult or rave, express wonder or excitement about, be overly dramatic about.

1864 *McGill CW Letters* (July 25) doe not take on a bout me I am a going to take cear of nomber one. **c1926** Bird *Cullowhee Wordlist* The child just kept takin' on about its new dress. *Ibid.* He never did see an elephant till he went to that circus, and he ain't never quit takin' on about how big it was. **1995** Montgomery *Coll* (known to Brown, Cardwell, Ellis, Jones, Ledford, Norris, Shields). **2007** McMillon *Notes* = to express wonder and go on and on about it.

4 To imbibe.

1960 Mason *Memoir* 59 This struck a tender spot and Carl and Dan agreed to let Ernest take on a pretty good snort provided he promised that he would control himself.

take one's foot in hand See **foot in hand, take one's.**

take one's satisfy *verb phrase* See citation.

1977 Howard *Fifty Years* 13 = [to] get entire satisfaction: "I took my satisfy on him."

take one through *verb phrase* Of Jesus, God: to carry one to a state of religious euphoria and conviction. See also **through C1.**

2008 Salsi *Ray Hicks* 86 When I turned sixteen, Jesus took me through, right there in that little church I helped to build. Now, that was a feelin'.

take out

A *verb phrase*

1 To go out hurriedly. See **take C1**.

2 To pause, have a break (especially for a meal).

1958 Wood *Words from TN* 17 Whenever you take out for dinner, stop by here. **1962** Wilson *Folkways Mammoth Cave* 13 When the sun reached a certain plant, it was time to ring the farm bell for the hands to *take out* and come to dinner. **c1975** Lunsford *It Used to Be* 10 They'd drive the mule out to the end of the row, take out, and go to the house to get dinner. **1995** Montgomery *Coll* Maw, you just take out and rest (Cardwell).

3 To unhitch a horse or mule.

1943 Goerch *Down Home* 31 = to unhitch horses or mules. **c1960** Wilson *Coll* = to unhitch an animal from a plow or wagon; stop for dinner. **1969** Doran *Folklore White Co* 115 = to unhitch an animal.

[DARE *take out* v phr 3a especially South Midland]

4 See 1915 citation.

1915 Dingus *Word-List VA* 191 = used as a request at a table to help oneself to food in a dish. **c1960** Wilson *Coll*: *take out and help yourself* = an invitation to dinner. **1990** Fisher *Preacher Stories* 24 Now, Preacher, we don't make company out of nobody here. Just take out and eat your supper.

B *noun* A deduction from a paycheck.

1937 White *Highland Heritage* 51 For years men received better wages at mining than they could anything else, though a large proportion went back to the companies as "take-outs"—rent, light bill, doctor's fee, school tax in some places, shop rent for keeping tools sharp, charges for compressed air, various charges for insurance.

take out a burn (also *take out fire*) *verb phrase* To treat a burn through folk healing.

1901 Price *KY Folk-Lore* 32 To "take out fire" (cure burns) [a healer] wets his forefinger with spittle, and gently rubbed over the burned places, repeating some "ceremony." **2007** Milnes *Signs Cures Witches* 102 Of all the cures that fit into the vein of magical belief, stopping blood is the most common in West Virginia. Emogene Nichols hints that belief or faith is an important ingredient in any cure. Besides stopping blood, she also mentioned belief-oriented cures for "taking out burns." . . . The power is attributed to God. Some German American curers claimed they could "blow" the fires out of burns while invoking Scripture.

take out a rafter *verb phrase* To have a boisterous, spirited time.

1969 Doran *Folklore White Co* 99 They haven't been there in so long that he'll offer "to take out a rafter" to celebrate.

take out fire See **take out a burn**.

take out in trade *verb phrase* See citation.

c1960 Wilson *Coll* = to barter butter, eggs, and other farm products for sugar, coffee, and other store things.

take over See **take C1**.

take roundance *verb phrase*

1 (also *take roundance of*) To go around (an obstacle), avoid (a problem) by circumventing it; to avoid an obstacle or problem by going around it.

1892 Smith *Farm and Fireside* 246 Uncle Tom was advised to take roundance and never tackle the crossroads. **1940** Vincent *Us Mt Folks* 13 A member of Ol' Sledge's congregation advised him to take roundance of Devil Bill Jones' cross roads.

2 In phrases *take (a) roundance on, take rounders on* = to ascend a slope by winding around or back and forth rather than by going directly up.

1955 Dykeman *French Broad* 330 You cannot know this river simply by sitting on the level banks of its lower body or by striking out on any straight road up its course; you must judge the "lay of the land" and follow a wandering path that will take "rounders" on its sources high in the mountains. **1956** Hall *Coll* (Waynesville NC) *take roundance on* = to climb a hill or mountain by making switchbacks. Old timers watched cattle wind around in climbing a hill . . . [one might say]: Let's go this way, let's take a roundance on it.

[DARE (at *roundance* n 2) chiefly South, South Midland]

take roundance of See **take roundance 1**.

take roundance on, take rounders on See **take roundance 2**.

take roundins *verb phrase* See citation.

1915 Dingus *Word-List VA* 191 = in marbles, to change positions with reference to the ring or another taw.

take sick (also *take sick to die*) *verb phrase* To develop a life-threatening illness or condition. See also **take bad, take down 2**.

1835 *McLean Diary* 33 Babar preach in town Susan taken Sick. **1862** *Robinson CW Letters* (July 13) thare is Rite Smart Sickness in our Regt & men that has never bin sick when tha[y] take Sick tha[y] hardley ever git well. **1864** *Whitaker CW Letters* (Aug 5) Dear Father I write you a few lines tho I am in a bad fix to write I took sick some 2 weeks ago. **1953** Shelton *Autobiog* I 16 Father finally began to grow old . . . and he taken sick to die with pellagra . . . and he died over there. **1972** *AOHP/LJC-104* A whole lot of the hogs would take sick and die.

take sick to die See **take sick**.

take the notion See **take a notion**.

take the rag off of the bush *verb phrase* To be extraordinary or astonishing.

1859 Taliaferro *Fisher's River* 86 That takes the rag off uv the bush. **1923** Greer-Petrie *Angeline Steppin' Out* 34 We could have a dance that would simply taken the rag offen the bush.

take time about See **time about.**

take to *verb phrase*

1 (+ *verbal noun*) To begin. See also Grammar and Syntax §7.2. See also **take B.**

1864 *Chapman CW Letters* (March 28) I have a bout quit smokeing and tuck to chewing. **1904–20** Kephart *Notebooks* 4:855 He tuk to faultin' her. **c1945** Haun *Hawk's Done* 228 He fell off till he was slim as a rail almost and took to groaning in his sleep and singing love songs about hard-hearted girls. **1965** Miller *Pigeon's Roost* (June 17) The tobacco crops was set out real early—much earlier than most of the past years and the recent rains helped the freshly set tobacco to take right off to growing. **1984** Woods *WV Was Good* 224 That dog took to runnin' around. **1997** Andrews *Mountain Vittles* 36 You wanted to save the girls the pullets 'cause they took to layin' eggs and you didn't want too many roosters. **2004** Adams *Old True Love* 46 That was the first time that I heard how Hackley and Larkin had took to fighting back to back.

2 To tolerate, accept, take a favorable view of. See also **take with.**

1979 *Smokies Heritage* 167 Then, as now, people of this area just didn't take to favoritism, even in school. **1999** Russell and Barnett *Granny Curse* 27 He and Mavis fell into an awful argument about what church to go to on Christmas. She was Primitive Baptist, and Basil didn't take to the preacher there.

take to the hoe *verb phrase* Of a child: to begin sharing the hoeing of crops.

1930 Armstrong *This Day and Time* 39 They hain't hardly took to the hoe yit.

take tree *verb phrase* To hide, find a secure place behind a tree.

1963 Arnow *Flowering* 138 The Draper correspondents and othions such as "the men treed" or "I took tree," always meaning not to climb, but to get behind a tree.

take two rows at a time *verb phrase* To go hurriedly; figuratively = to sleep soundly.

1939 Hall *Coll* (Dellwood NC) I was taking two rows at a time when the breakfast bell rang this morning. **c1960** Wilson *Coll* = to go hurriedly or too actively.

take under See **take C1.**

take up *verb phrase*

1 To go up hurriedly. See **take C1.**

2 Of a civil or military official: to arrest, apprehend (someone).

1862 *Ingram CW Letters* (Sept 29) two of them [= deserters] was taken up and fetcht back this morning. **1863** *Epperly CW Letters* (Aug 9) the home gards went to take [the deserters] up last tuesday and the deserters whiped them and taken six of them. prisners and all thar guns. **1907** Dugger *Balsam Groves* 162 He looked so sneakin' and tol' so many different tales that I thought he stole the hoss an' ort to be took up. **1939** Hall *Coll* (Wears Cove TN) The law took him up, and they couldn't prove it direct on him, and they just turned him loose. **1974** Fink *Bits Mt Speech* 27 = arrest. "John was *took up* fer stealing corn."

3 To occupy and settle (land), claim title of by occupancy.

1824 (in **1912** Doddridge *Notes on Settlement* 81) Land was the object which invited the greater number of these people to cross the mountain, for as the saying then was, "it was to be land here for taking up"; that is, building a cabin and raising a crop of grain, however small, of any kind, entitled the occupant to four hundred acres of land, and a pre-emption right to one thousand acres more adjoining, to be secured by a land office warrant. **1826** *Whitten Letter* Others has after July to give $1 an acre for all vacant land he takes up. **1953** Hall *Coll* (Bryson City NC) Land was so cheap [after the Civil War]. My grandfather had taken up six hundred acres. He protected his new title by possession. Then my grandfather came down here and entered—took up—lands at twelve and a half cents an acre. The tract he lived on was bought from an old man named Culberson. **1969** GSMNP-42:9 Seems like he said they got it for a dollar a acre, took it up from the state. **1973** GSMNP-87:1:6 You didn't have to buy [land]. You took it up back then. **1983** *Dark Corner OHP*-9A One of my great-great-grandfathers, took up a section of land in Gowan's Gap. That's just a little gap on the other side of Hogback.

4 Of a school day, school term, or church service: to begin, go into session; of a congregation: to begin (a church service). See also **take in, turn out.**

1913 Morley *Carolina Mts* 221 Nor can one blame those parents who prefer to keep the children at home rather than send them miles, it may be, through the forest and over rushing streams, to the schoolhouse where school "takes up" for only a few weeks in the year, and where the teacher, like the rest of the people, knows little more than how to be kind. **1935** Sheppard *Cabins in Laurel* 209 When "preachin' takes up" and the singing begins, the loiterers by the road move to the upper flight of steps. **1965** West *Time Was* 53 Meeting was already taking up, and the last talkers were straggling through the front door of the little weather-boarded church. **1972** GSMNP-69:31 They let all the other schools go through their season. Then this [subscription] school would take up right after the other school were out, so we actually got six months schooling by changing back and forth. **1974** Fink *Bits Mt Speech* 26 Has meeting *took up* yet? **1989** Landry *Smoky Mt Interviews* 181 He come early one morning before time for school to take up. **1995** McCauley *Mt Religion* 82 "Taking up" church or beginning the church service depends on when enough people have gathered. The time is not rigidly punctual but flexible, even up to a half hour or more beyond the usual gathering time. **2014** Williams *Coll* What time does church take up?

[DARE *take up* v phr 2 especially Midland, West]

5 To assume residence, lodge.

1942 (in **1987** Perdue *Outwitting Devil* 72) He went back to the house an' took up. **1955** Ritchie *Singing Family* 95 They'd take up nights at whatever house they happened closest to when dark came. **1968** Miller *Pigeon's Roost* (Aug 8) This farmer wanted this to be made plain that he would rather have one black snake take up at his barn to stay as to have a half dozen cats around it. **1979** Melton *'Pon My Honor* 46 For some reason Dave had gone to the

Copelands when he was just a tad of a boy and took up. So Granny Copeland had raised him as her own.

[DARE *take up* v phr 5 chiefly South Midland]

6 See 1957 citation.

1900 Harben *N GA Sketches* 292–93 "Mary," she asked, "have you put on the supper?" "Yes'm; but it hain't tuk up yit." **1957** Broaddus *Vocab Estill Co KY* 78 = to remove food from the stove and put it on the table.

[DARE *take up* v phr 1 scattered, but chiefly South, South Midland]

take up a serpent *verb phrase* As practiced in some Pentecostal churches, to pick up a poisonous snake and handle it, in conformity to the Gospel according to Mark 16:17: "And these signs shall follow them that believe; in my name they shall cast out devils; they shall speak with new tongues. They shall take up serpents" (KJV).

1997 Johnson *Melungeon Heritage* 42 I have never believed in "taking up a serpent." However, I have no doubt now, and I had no doubt then, of the faith of those who do and did believe.

take up books See **books A**.

take up with *verb phrase* To become attached to, especially to become enamored with and cohabit with (someone).

1931–33 (in **1987** Oliver and Oliver *Sketches* 23 Soon after the war he took up with a young lady whose name was Lurena Frazier. **1937** Hall Coll (Cosby Creek TN) That man must like you the way he tuck up with you. **1963** Medford *Mt People* 66 "Oh, I guess the ol' 'oman an' kids would run me off if I went back 'thout that little mare," returned Barnes, "they're so took up with 'er." **1972** AOHP/LJC-104 That was my mother's brother. He took up with that show. **1977** Norman *Kinfolks* 101 If Cindy was looking for something worthless to take up with, she sure found it. **1985** Irwin *Alex Stewart* 170 Maude Bell and her man, they took up with the Holiness and she could handle them snakes anyway she wanted to, but one finally bit her. **1999** Russell and Barnett *Granny Curse* 28 He took up with Trulie Jane Lawson within a year after Mavis was buried.

[DARE (at *take up* v phr 8) chiefly South, especially Louisiana]

take with *verb phrase*

1 To put up with, tolerate. See also **hold with**, **take to 2**.

1939 Hall Coll (Bradley Fork NC) They wanted to drive me out of the settlement because I wouldn't take with their ways. That was no place to raise a family. They was livin' like hogs.

2 To contract, become ill with (an infection or a disease).

1832 McLean *Diary* 9 William Triplet took with a Cold. **1908** Johnson *Life KY Mts* 177 Before he was seven years old he took with diphtheria, which he caught at school, and became its victim after an illness of only a few days. **1949** Arnow *Hunter's Horn* 138 He'd seemed puny, sniffling around and not eating so good, but he'd never got bad sick until last night when he took with something like distemper, but what his wife said was just like pneumonia in a baby.

talcum powder *noun* Construed as a count noun; hence plural form *talcum powders*. For similar forms, see **powder A**.

1968 *Faith Healing* 63 I just draw the fire out of [the wound] and take common old baby powders—talcum powders they used t'call 'em—baby powders that they used t'put on a baby.

tale *noun* An account of little or no credibility or worth, a piece of gossip. See also **tale bearing**, **tale-idle**.

1862 L Jones *CW Letters* (Nov 20) I will say to you as many tales as has went to camps abowt me marrying I ante married yet nor I dont exspect to be soon. **1913** Kephart *Our Sthn High* 296 Tale always means an idle or malicious report. **1994–97** Montgomery Coll (known to ten consultants from the Smoky Mountains). **2007** Preece *Leavin' Sandlick* 24 I git carried away sometimes with them thar big tales I tell and tell them they were the truth when I knows they haint.

tale bearer See **tale bearing**.

tale bearing (also *tale telling*) *verbal noun* Spreading self-serving, spurious, or malicious reports about another person; hence *tale bearer* = one who spreads such reports. See also **pack tales**.

1867 Harris *Sut Lovingood* 50 Ole Bullin dun hit, an' I'll hev tu kill him yet, the cussed, infernel ole talebarer! **1913** Kephart *Our Sthn High* 272 Sometimes a man is "churched" for breaking the Sabbath, "cussin'," "tale-bearin'"; but sins of the flesh are rarely punished, being regarded as amiable frailties of mankind. **1994–98** Montgomery Coll: *tale bearing* (known to eight consultants from the Smoky Mountains); *tale bearer* (known to Cardwell); *tale telling* (known to Ellis).

tale-idle *noun* A false report, story with little credibility or foundation. See also **tale**.

1931 Combs *Lg Sthn High* 1305 Hit's nary a thing but a tale-idle. **c1945** Haun *Hawk's Done* 242 She was just not going to believe it, saying it was a tale-idle—like she was having to argue with herself about it. **1957** Combs *Lg Sthn High: Word List*99 = gossip, a false, malicious report, hearsay. [**1995** Montgomery Coll (unknown to consultants from the Smoky Mountains).]

[inversion of *idle tale*; DARE *tale-idle* n especially southern] Appalachians]

tale packer *noun* See citation. See also **pack tales**.

1939 Farr *TN Mt Regions* 92 = gossiper: "That old woman's a tale packer."

talk *verb* To engage in courtship, discuss marriage; in phrase *talk to* = to court, keep company with. See also **spark**.

1895 Edson and Fairchild *TN Mts* 374 Judge Jackson's son has been *talkin' to* my daughter nigh on a year. **1915** Pollard *TN Mts* 243 *talk to* = to court, woo. **1921** Campbell *Sthn Highlander* 145 A young man "talking to" a young woman in the Highlands is not giving her a scolding as he might be understood to be doing, were he so rash. **1924** Raine *Saddlebags* 98 When young folk in love with each other make serious plans, they are said to be *talking*. The same word is used by Regan in *King Lear*. **1935** Sheppard *Cabins in Laurel* 172 When a mountain boy slips up beside the girl he likes after "preachin' has broke" and escorts her up the road home, her friends say she is "talkin' to him." **1961** Williams *Content Mt Speech* 16 When Lil an' that-ar man o' hern fust started sparkin', jist when they was beginnin' talkin' together. **1967** Jones *Peculiarities Mtneers* 55 In [former] days a boy never went "courting." He went to "talk to" or to "set up with a girl"—usually on a Saturday night. **1974** Fink *Bits Mt Speech* 26 *talking to* = courting. "Jim's been *talking* to Arminty nigh onto three years." **1984** Woods *WV Was Good* 228 For courting, there were three standard expressions: (1) *talking to*, (2) *going to see*, and (3) *keeping company with*. **1989** *Matewan OHP-102* Of course I've talked with two or three [boys] before ever I met him. **1993** Weaver *Scotch-Irish Speech* 16 Also, expressions such as "sparking" (dating), "courting" (dating with serious intent), and "talking" (contemplating marriage), very distinct in meaning in West Virginia, were used interchangeably in the Carolinas.

[CUD *talk to* (at *talk* v 2) "court (a girl)"; DARE *talk* v 1 chiefly South Midland]

talk fire out *verb phrase* To relieve pain (of a burn) by repeating a verbal charm over it. See also **blow fire**, **burn doctor**, **draw B3**, **take out a burn**.

2006 *Encycl Appalachia* 868 Burn doctors "talked the fire" out of burns and promoted quick healing by moving a hand across and slightly above the burn while reciting the following: "There came an angel from the east bringing fire and frost. In frost, out fire, in the name of the Father, the Son, and the Holy Ghost."

talk hard *verb phrase* To speak harshly or unkindly.

1856 *Elijoy Church Minutes* 89 Brother Davis acknowl that he had talked too hard about Brother [Burnett]. **1998** Montgomery *Coll* I don't want to talk too hard about it, but you need to know the truth (Cardwell).

talkified *adjective* Talkative, prone to talk.

1930 Armstrong *This Day and Time* 38 Doke's jest so talkified. **1942** Hall *Phonetics Smoky Mts* 61. **1997** Montgomery *Coll* (known to Adams, Bush, Cardwell, Ledford, Norris, Weaver).

talkingest *adjective* Most inclined to talk. See also **-est 1** and Grammar and Syntax §3.4.1.

1895 Edson and Fairchild *TN Mts* 374 She is the *talkenest* woman I ever saw. **1925** Furman *Glass Window* 33 Now you, Tutt, being the main-oldest man here next to me and one of the talkingest, lead [sic] off. **1943** Hannum *Mt People* 148 With even more fanciful flux, verbs transfer into adjectives: "the travelin'est hosses; the talkin'est woman; the workin'est man." **1955** Washburn *Country Doctor* 68 He's the talkin'es' man in two states, an' it don't matter one bit whether he knows what he's talkin' erbout or not.

talk poor mouth See **poor-mouth**.

talk proud *verb phrase* See citation.

2013 House *Own Country* 196 All my life I've been told to not trust people who "talk proud," a colloquialism for speaking with a northern accent. I was raised to believe that folks who spoke that way had gotten above their raising (the ultimate sin in Appalachian culture), thought they were better than me, were trying to act as if they had money.

talk short *verb phrase* See citation.

c1960 Wilson *Coll* = to speak angrily.

talk to See **talk**.

talk to one's plate *verb phrase* To say a prayer at the beginning of a meal.

1911 Shearin *E KY Word-List* 540 = to "say grace," return thanks at the table, e.g., "Stranger, talk to your plate." **1957** Combs *Lg Sthn High: Word List* 99 *talk to one's plate* = to return thanks. **1962** Williams *Mtneers Mind Manners* 22 If there is a guest in the house at mealtime, the father of the house might ask him whether he "talks to his plate." If he does, the children stop eating and sit gravely while the blessing is being asked.

tall See **taw**.

tallar, taller See **tallow**.

tallest pole takes the persimmon *phrase* See citation.

1881 Pierson *In the Brush* 8 When many persons were striving for the same object, or where there were rival aspirants for the heart and hand of the same lady, they said of the successful one, "The tallest pole takes the persimmon."

tallow *noun* Variant forms *tallar*, *taller*.

1862 *Barkley CW Letter* (Feb 26) tell mother to send me a peace of tallar to greese my shoes with. **1863** *Copenhaver CW Letters* (Jan 12) I want some taller to greas my boots & a cake of sope. **1867** Harris *Sut Lovingood* 217 He wer gwine tu ride ontu the prongs ove that ar pitch-fork, dripin now wif the burnin taller ofen Seize's ribs, strait tu whar all quacks go. **1937** Hall *Coll* (Upper Cosby Creek TN) To cure the flux, drink a tea of sweet gum bark, or take some mutton taller melted. **1969** Hannum *Look Back* 62 Fried onions with goat "taller" poured over them made a salve that could be rubbed on the throat of child with croup. **1981** Whitener *Folk-Ways* 37 [The Balm of Gilead] was produced from the buds of balsam poplar tree and used with mutton tallow (taller), which when heated together on the back of the old wood-burning cook stove produced a salve which was used for chapped hands and other medical purposes. **1985** Irwin *Alex Stewart* 31 Most people had to keep what little grease they had to season their food with. They wouldn't ever waste a bit of beef taller.

tallow dip *noun* A primitive candle made by dipping a wick into hot liquid tallow and then letting it cool and harden, with the action repeated until the candle has the thickness desired. See also **grease lamp**, **slut**.

1889 Murfree *Broomsedge Cove* 80 Wall, sir, eatin' supper by a tallow dip—whoever hearn the beat? **1901** Harben *Westerfelt* 232 In a corner dimly lighted by a tallow-dip, and surrounded by pans, pots, and cooking utensils, Bradley stood washing dishes. **1930** Smith *Reminiscences* 8 [During the Civil War] if our tallow dips gave out for light at night, we would take a rag and lay it in a saucer of fried grease. **1957** Parris *My Mts* 5 He grew up when tallow-dips furnished light. **1995–97** Montgomery Coll (known to Brown, Shields).

tallow nut *noun* The oilnut (*Pyrularia pubera*), a parasitic shrub from which an oil is derived for use in small lamps and fashioned into primitive candles. Also called **buffalo nut**, **colic ball**, **rabbit wood**.

1791 Bartram *Journey through Carolina* 114–15 Near the river, on this high shore, grew Corypha palma . . . and the beautiful evergreen shrub called Wild lime or Tallow nut. This last shrub grows six or eight feet high, many erect rising from a root; Page leaves are lanciolate and intire, two or three inches in length and one in breadth, of a deep green colour, and polished; at the foot of each leaf grows a stiff, sharp thorn; the flowers are small and in clusters, of a greenish yellow colour, and sweet scented; they are succeeded by a large oval fruit, of the consistence and taste of an ordinary plumb, of a fine yellow colour when ripe, a soft sweet pulp covers a nut which has a thin shell, enclosing a white kernel somewhat of the consistence and taste of the sweet Almond, but more oily and very much like hard tallow, which induced my father when he first observed it, to call it the Tallow nut. **1982** Stupka *Wildflowers* 22 This is a common shrub in the southern Appalachian forest, especially where oaks are dominant at elevations up to 4,000 feet. . . . One botanist claims that the fruit are so oily it would burn like a candle if a wick were drawn through it. "Tallow-nut" and "buffalo-nut" are other names for it. **1997** Montgomery Coll = used to produce a wick in which a candle was put (Cardwell).

tally man *noun* See citation.

1994 Farwell and Buchanan *Logging Terms* = in logging, a man who kept records showing grades of boards and number of feet of each grade.

tanbark *noun* The bark of any tree (but especially a swamp chestnut oak, *Quercus prinus*) containing tannin, used to treat animal hides; this bark was pulled and sold to tanneries. See also **acid timber**, **tan oak**.

1913 Morley *Carolina Mts* 283 At the narrowest places you meet loaded tanbark wagons. **1964** Stupka *Trees Shrubs Vines* 50 Lambert remarked that during the logging era the chestnut oak was the largest contributor to the tanbark industry in the Southern Appalachian area. **1979** *Smokies Heritage* 277 Tanbark was gathered in the spring of the year when the sap was "up." "Tanbark" oaks were felled and trimmed of the smaller branches. **1982** Ginns *Snowbird Gravy* 78 In the spring, we'd peel tanbark. We'd cut the trees down and peel the bark off of them. Cut it all up around 'em, you know, and dry it. It wasn't so awfully hard to peel 'em. It would slip off at the right time, early in the spring. Tanbark trees, we called 'em. Just chestnut oak. Stack the bark up around, you know. Then we'd pull it off of the top of the mountain on brushes, down to where we could get it on a sled. Then we'd get it on a sled and bring it on down to where we could get it on a wagon. **1983** Aiken *Mt Ways* 148 Tanbark was any species of tree bark rich in tannic acid and the wood itself was often called "acid wood" when being worked for the bark.

tangle-foot (also *tangle-foot whiskey*, *tangle-leg whiskey*) *noun* Illegally distilled whiskey.

1864 Gilmore *Down in TN* 185 They obtain plentiful supplies of a vile fluid, which is compounded of log-wood, strychnine, juniper berries, and alcohol, and "circulates" among them under the appropriate names of "Tangle-foot," "Blue-ruin," "Red-eye," "Bust-head," and "Knock-'em-stiff." **1867** Harris *Sut Lovingood* 113 I got *two* par ove boots, an' ole tangle-foot whisky enuf tu fill 'em. *Ibid.* 129 They'se mity good things, too, fur a feller tu straiten up on, fur a fresh start, when he's layin off the wum ove a fence, onder a deckload ove tangle-laig whisky. **1981** Morrell *Mirth* 29 No narrative of the Great Smokies would be complete without at least one story about "Moonshine" whiskey, also known as "Splo," "panther sweat," "tangle-foot," and "block and tackle liquor." **1990** Oliver *Cooking Hazel Creek* 12 It would not be fair to leave corn without mentioning one more use for it, the making of moonshine, or as it was sometimes called, among many other names, tanglefoot or scorpion juice.

tangle-gut *noun* An edible wild green.

1969 Newell *Genus Joinvillea* 555 (DARE) In parts of West Virginia, *Claytonia caroliniana* is known as "tangle-gut." **1982** Slone *How We Talked* 47 [In a list of "salet" plants:] Tangle gut.

[DARE *tangle-gut* n 2 especially southern Appalachians]

tangle-legs *noun* Same as **hobblebush**.

1860 Curtis *Plants NC* 91 = a small straggling shrub found in cold damp places in the Mountains. The branches spread upon the ground, and, taking root, at their ends, form well secured loops for tripping the feet of inexperienced way-farers. **1901** Lounsberry *Sthn Wild Flowers* 478 *Tangle-legs* . . . Along the slopes of the high mountains in North Carolina, often where deep shadows fall, this viburnum is most conspicuous among the shrubbery.

tangle-leg whiskey See **tangle-foot**.

tan oak *noun* Any oak from which **tanbark** is taken, especially the swamp chestnut oak (*Quercus prinus*). See also **acid timber**, **tanbark**.

1939 Hall Coll (Cataloochee Creek NC) The tan oak is used for getting tan bark off of.

tant See **taunt**.

tap hand *noun* A children's chasing game.

1982 Powers and Hannah *Cataloochee* 167 We'd play Tap-Hand up there in the old Field. Tap-Hand, one of those old games. Hold hands around this way in a big circle, and one fellow'd tap and went around the ring, and the other'n see if he could catch him. The old Tap Hand Ring. The boys would tap the girls. And the girls would tap the boys.

[DARE *tap hand* n chiefly southern Appalachians]

tar See **tire.**

tar baby *noun* A native of North Carolina, especially one who fought in the Civil War.

1932 Strong *Great Smokies* 232 You boys there, get all the field-guns and cannons from these here tar babies and put 'em by that tree next to Stan. **1997** Montgomery *Coll* = a North Carolina soldier in the Civil War period, a term still in limited use today (Brown).

taring See **tear B.**

tarment, tarmint See **torment.**

tarnal (also *tornel*) *adjective* Infernal, unending (used as a mild oath).

1864 Hill *CW Letters* (March 16) I can make more [money] at home in the bushes amakeing brooms than I can here in this tornel war. **1883** Zeigler and Grosscup *Heart of Alleghanies* 61 The tarnal thing war gone, an' thar war me without a weepin' big enough to skin a boomer. **1913** Kephart *Our Sthn High* 119 Hit's all 'tarnal foolishness, the notions some folks has! **1939** Hall *Coll* (Eagle Creek NC) Those tarnal devilish things! (said of panthers).

[alteration of *eternal*, with the vowel in the accented syllable preserving earlier pronunciation of the word; DARE *tarnal* adj chiefly New England, less frequent South Midland]

tarnashus See **tarnatious.**

tarnation *interjection, noun, adverb* Used as a euphemism for *damnation, damned*.

1904 Fox *Christmas Eve* 135 Abe was a-havin' sech a tarnation good time with his devilmint he jes didn't want to run no risk o' havin' hit stopped. **1939** Hall *Coll* (Jefferson City TN) = mild oath. **1956** McAtee *Some Dial NC* 45 = euphemistic swear-word and general-purpose intensifier. *Ibid.* 46 = exclamation of annoyance. **1979** Melton *'Pon My Honor* 26 Patsy heard the commotion and run out the door to see what in tarnation was going on. **1997** Montgomery *Coll* (known to nine consultants from the Smoky Mountains).

[variant of *darnation, damnation*, perhaps influenced by *tarnal*; OED3 n chiefly U.S. 1790→; EDD *tarnation* sb 1 in general dialect use in Scot, Irel, Engl; Web3 *tarnation* n dialect]

tarnatious (also *tarnashus*) *adjective, adverb* Fearsome(ly), outlandish(ly), extreme(ly).

1859 Taliaferro *Fisher's River* 44 In all the "tight fits" and "tarnatious snarls" he got into, he would outfight, outquarrel, or outwit. **1964** Williams *Prep Mt Speech* 54 She has "laid off for to ricollect not to whup so tarnashus all-fard hard."

tarpin See **terrapin.**

tarpole wagon *noun* A wagon covered with a tarpaulin, a covered wagon.

1939 Hall *Coll* (Gumstand TN) The axle-tree of tarpole wagons [was] made out of hickory [with] no skeins [skinz] over it. **1991** Thomas *Sthn Appal* 126 Poppa ewst t'have these ol' tar-pole waggins. He bought 'im one; I guess it'uz th' first new'un he ever bought.

[*tarpole* probably folk etymology for *tarpaulin*; DARE *tarpole wagon* n chiefly Midland, Southwest]

tarripin See **terrapin.**

taste *verb* Variant third-singular form of two syllables: *taste-es*. See also **-es**[2].

1973 *Foxfire Interviews* A-73-43 Chew that there and see if it taste-es like that other one. **1973** GSMNP-79:22 He always seems to think it tastes so good. **1974** Fink *Bits Mt Speech* 26 *tastes* (2 syllables).

[DARE *taste* v, n A 2 especially South, South Midland]

tasted *adjective* Tasting.

1937 Hyatt *Kiverlid* 80 With tree-sugar sweet'nin' hits better tasted than coffee. **c1960** Wilson *Coll*: *tasted*: a suffix, meaning tasting or to the taste, used extensively: good-tasted, sweet-tasted, bitter-tasted.

[DARE *tasted* adj chiefly South Midland]

taste of *verb phrase* To try by tasting. See also **of 3.**

1937 Hall *Coll* (Bradley Fork NC) I've tasted of it [= sassafras tea], but I don't like to drink it. **1939** Hall *Coll* (Smokemont NC) He said he tasted of everything he ever killed, ever' varmint, even a buzzard. **1941** Stuart *Men of Mts* 235 "Better than honey," he says "you fellars get up and taste o' one." **1976** Carter *Little Tree* 65 Said he set some fresh whiskey back and let it set for a week and when he tasted of it, it didn't taste one lick damn different from all the other whiskey he made. **1978** Montgomery *White Pine Coll* III-2 I just throwed it in there and tasted of it, to see how it tasted. **1997** Montgomery *File* I've never tasted of it (60-year-old man, Maggie Valley NC).

tastes See **taste.**

tater See **potato.**

taterbug *noun* A type of mandolin featured in string bands.

1979 Irwin *Musical Instruments* 91 The mandolin was seldom even heard of in the mountains until well into the 20th century. This one . . . is shown here with the well-made European type mandolin known in this region as a "tater bug." **2000** Miller *Looneyville* 74 Looneyville people never bought into the idea that a mandolin was pear shaped. And why would they? The mandolin was only half-pear shaped to them. Its body was like a Colorado potato beetle: "That taterbug makes some of the finest music on this earth." **2018** Malone and Laird *Country Music* 33 The mandolin's early "tater bug" construction (a bulging, striped back) may have inhibited both its sound and the ability of musicians to hold it comfortably, but when Lloyd Loar fashioned his slim, finely crafted F5 for the Gibson Company in 1919, he devised an instrument that fit readily into the string bands of the day.

tater chunk *noun* A short distance.

2007 Homan *Turkey Tracks* 86 Only tater chunks and hoot and a holler had plurals: two tater chunks down the road, a couple of hoots and a holler (never a hoot and a couple of hollers). I never heard anyone say two yonders, three pieces, or four fer pieces. It just wasn't done.... Based upon the folks I talked to—an admittedly small and much older than average sample—I compiled five alternative measures of Appalachian distance. The smallest component was tater chunk, as in "you're real close, it's just another tater chunk down the road." Following tater chunk in progression were yonder, hoot and a holler, a piece, and a fer piece.

tater fritter *noun* A pastry made with potato rather than flour or meal.

1986 Pederson et al. *LAGS* (Rockdale Co GA, Hall Co GA). **2007** McMillon *Notes*.

tater hole See **potato hole.**

tater noodling *noun* See 1997 citation. See also **noodling.**

1961 Seeman *Arms of Mt* 52 We're havin' 'tater noodlins. **1997** Montgomery *Coll* = balls of cornbread cooked in potato and ham broth (Andrews).

tater-patch *verb* To deal with on equal terms.

1919 Combs *Word-List South* 35 = used as a verb: "He ain't got nothin' on me, I'll tater-patch with ary man in this county" [Knott Co. KY].

tater riffle *noun* See citation.

1952 Wilson *Folk Speech NC* 598 = light bread.

tater rose *noun* See citation.

c1982 Young *Colloquial Appal* 22 = dahlia.

tater slip *noun* Same as **sweet potato slip.**

1920 Ridley *Sthn Mtneer* 87 I'm jist obliged to set out a few tater slips.

tatoe See **potato.**

taunt *verb* Variant forms *tant*, *taynt*.

1933 Thomas *Traipsin' Woman* 37 "Git a pair eye specs! You fool!" he taynted. **1978** Hiser *Quare Do's* 128 Singing about the gal that went ting-a-ling at her true lover's door when he was a-marrying up with a dark skinned gal and tanting her about her skin.

taw (also *tall*, *tawl*) *noun* A large shooting marble in the children's game.

1916 Combs *Old Early English* 296 Games at "marvles" (marbles) . . . such as . . . "long taw(l)." **1964** Banks *Back to Mts* 22 Some "taws" were treated with talismatic regard, endowed by their owners with personality and showered with special care and affection. **1982** Slone *How We Talked* 93 *tall* = the marble used to "shoot" with (hit the other marbles). **1983** Broaddus *Estill Co KY Word List* 59 *tawl* = the only pronunciation I ever heard as a child. **1984** Head *Brogans* 37 Each player had a favorite marble he shot with, called a "taw." **1984** Smith *Enduring Memories* 7 Many of the boys would return from recess to the classroom with dirty knees and knuckles from playing marbles. Every marble player had his favorite "taw" or shooting marble and he would prize it highly, shine it often and never would he play for keeps with his "taw." **1993** Page and Smith *Foxfire Toys and Games* 49 Most players had a favorite shooting marble, usually a larger marble, referred to as a taw. Some players used steel ball bearings as taws, especially in tournaments.

taynt See **taunt.**

tea *noun* Any medicinal drink made from the bark, roots, or other part of a wild plant. See also **black snakeroot, ginger tea, life everlasting, root tea.**

1939 Hall *Coll* (Big Creek NC) We treated the best we can. We could use teas of all kinds and make tea, pour in them and sweat them. *Ibid.* (Cosby TN) We could use teas of all kinds. An' make teas, pour it in [sick people] ... Bone-set tea, fever-weed tea. Get you a beadwood bark, make hit fer tea . . . Yeah, Indian physic tea. It's good. **1969** Hannum *Look Back* 61 They have hurried to the nearest she-balsam, cut off a hunk of bark, and brewed it into a kidney tea. **1975** *GSMNP-62:15* They'd go and chop out some chips and bark off a sycamore and make a tea out of it, and they'd drink it, and it would break them measles out. **2005** Williams *Gratitude* 530 = not black, pekoe, etc. as is commonly known. In the mountains, *tea* is just about anything put in hot water and drunk. Medicinal herbs, bark or roots are infused, or steeped, and the resulting liquid is called tea, usually adding a generous portion of corn likker unless it is for the younguns. Some teas are: birch bark, boneset, calamus root (calomel root), ginger, ground ivy, mountain birch, mint, peach bark, sassafras, spignet, spicewood and yaller root.

teach *verb* Principal parts.

1 Variant past-tense form *teached*.

1924 Spring *Lydia Whaley* 1 Had no edication [sic] hisself but wanted his chilurn to have it. He "professed religion and he possessed it." He teached his chilurn to read the Bible and do right. **1941** Stuart *Men of Mts* 208 Pap jest never teached us like that. **1956** Hall *Coll* (Big Bend NC) Miss Ogle teached school down there. **1957** Broaddus *Vocab Estill Co KY* 79 *teached* = past tense of *teach*. **1962** Williams *Verbs Mt Speech* 17 The past and past participle of ... *teach* become *teached*. **1971** *AOHP/ALC-33* One teacher teached all the grades, from the first grade to the eighth. **1973** Miller *English Unicoi Co* 141 *teached* (as past tense) attested by 3 of 6 speakers. **1978** Reese *Speech NE Tenn* 181 = attested by 6/12 (50%) speakers. **1980** Miles *Verbs in Haywood Co* 86 They teached different things than they do now. **1985** Irwin *Alex Stewart* 51 There was several of us boys that studied out of that book, and the teacher, she borrowed it and teached from it.

2 Variant past-participle forms *teach, teached*.

1937 Hall *Coll* (Cades Cove TN) Our dog has been teached to run the cattle. **1954** *GSMNP*-19:23b My daddy had teach me how to find these wild bee trees. [See **1962** in **1**.] **1975** *We Sing* 20 Our sounds went direct to Tokyo, Japan, and was teached to the Japanese. **1996** Isbell *Last Chivaree* 58 I was pretty good and civilized and was teached the Bible by my mama.

[cf SND *teachit* past-tense and past-participle form]

teached See **teach 1, 2.**

teach up *verb phrase* Usually of a parent with regard to his or her children: to raise properly.

1924 Raine *Saddlebags* 99 The mountain man uses *kill up* as Shakespeare does, and also *live up*, and *teach up*, as in teach up children to have good manners. **1931** Combs *Lg Sthn High* 1302 The pupils are not taught to discard their dialect and their grammatical irregularities, because their teachers employ so much of it themselves. However, when a boy or girl goes away to school to be "taught up," he usually returns with a different manner of speech. **1997** Montgomery *Coll* (known to Bush); You should teach up the children to have manners (Cardwell).

tear *verb*

A Variant past-participle forms *tore, tored, tourned*.

1862 *Ingram CW Letters* (Sept 12) they are pittiful looking persons shure to see armes legs shoulders tore so with the Ball. **1863** *Lister CW Letters* (Nov 18) this redgment is mitely tore up at this time. **1864** *Joyce CW Letters* (Aug 19) he tourned them [= letters] up for fear the yankeys wold get them. **1867** Harris *Sut Lovingood* 268 The tupentine lit up a bright road ahine him, kivered wif broke down an' tore up briars. **1939** Hall *Coll* (Cataloochee NC) He didn't have a thing on, only his shirt, only just his shirt collar. [The bear] had tore everything off of him and the blood just a-flying out of him. **1956** Hall *Coll* (Big Bend NC) Next mornin', when we got up, the old hog had tore the pen down and was gone. **1975** *GSMNP*-59:16 The store's tore down now. It was right where that big brick church was in there. **1979** *Big South Fork OHP*-27 They told me that hit had broke once and had tored everything up down there. **1980** Miles *Verbs in Haywood Co* 100 He was really tore up. **2007** Preece *Leavin' Sandlick* 27 Their courtship had been a rocky one, though, for Anna Belle stayed tored between Eddie Lee Washington and Ernest Brown.

B To move or act with excitement, speed, or abandon; hence participial adjective *taring*.

1867 Harris *Sut Lovingood* 137 She wer a tarin gal enyhow. Luved kissin, wrastlin, an' biled cabbige, an' hated tile clothes, hot weather, an' suckit-riders. **1903** Fox *Little Shepherd* 174 "He come tearin' up behind me 'bout an hour ago, like a house afire." **1935** Murray *Schoolhouse* 78 I tore loose to runnin'. **1941** Stuart *Men of Mts* 233 [They] loaded the bees on the wagon and run two big black horses hard as they could tear up the road with all his bees in the back end of the wagon. **c1950** Adams *Grandpap* 27 When he done that, she just broke an' went a-tearin' off through the woods just as hard as she could go. *Ibid.* 39 The old woman was so mad that she didn't know what to do. Oh, she was just a-rearin' and a-tearin'! **1967** Hall *Coll* (Cades Cove TN) This old bear tore into the calf, you know, and killed it and then took it right back across the road from where I lived. **1974** Roberts *Sang Branch* 201 She give him a piece [of bread] and he went out. Come back just a-tearing. **2005** Williams *Gratitude* 533 She tore in the house and tore into him with both fists. When she tore loose to cussin' and them dogs tore out to barkin', he run like a scalded dog.

tear down

A *verb phrase* To ruin, damage, mutilate; hence participial adjective *tearing down* = of an occasion: riotous, boisterous, wild. See also **tear up, torn down.**

1858 *Webb Letter* 109 We had one tareing down [dancing party] last night at Pine Lawson. **c1950** (in **2000** Oakley *Roamin' Man* 64) [We] had a good chicken dinner that night and went to the Wiley Shop and had a tearin down time listenin to the mountain music. **1986** Pederson et al. *LAGS* (Sullivan Co TN) a tearing down good time. **1995** Montgomery *Coll*: *tear down* (known to Bush, Norris).

B *noun* A great commotion, boisterous argument.

1925 (in **1935** Edwards *NC Novels* 96) *tear-down*. **1982** *Foxfire VII* 203 They had a tear-down over there in the Methodist Church. **1989** *Matewan OHP*-1 Just like in the movies, oh it was a regular tear down and knock down and drag out affair there.

tearing down See **tear down.**

tear up See also **tear down.**

A *verb phrase* To break, ruin, damage (a machine or tool); to discourage, disturb, or exhaust (a person); hence participial adjective *tore up* = upset, discouraged, damaged.

1862 *Kendrick CW Letters* (July 28) we ar undear marching ordars and ar all tor up we dont no whear we ar going too. **1864** *Confederate Coll* (May 22) i thouht that i Could rite you a good letter but my mind got tore up so that it is badly done. **1925** Dargan *Highland Annals* 264 Nathe wuz so tore up I reckon he couldn't think o' pickin' his way. **1940** Haun *Hawk's Done* 107 I was so tore up I didn't care what washed away. **1946** Matthias *Speech Pine Mt* 191 = to break: "Don't set in thet cha'r. One o' hits legs is tore up." **1949** Arnow *Hunter's Horn* 278 I was all raggedy an my hair all tore up, an I hated fer him to see me. **c1960** Wilson *Coll* = to disarrange. **1969** *DARE Survey* (Sawyer KY) Somebody hit us in the back, tore his car up. **1975** Chalmers *Better* 66 One who is discouraged is clean out of heart, his nerves may be all tore up, or he is merely tired and whupped out. **1990** Bailey *Draw Up Chair* 13 For example an engine that has stopped running, or an appliance that has gone dead, is "tore up." The remedy may be a whole new transmission in one case, or simply a spark plug in the other, but the fact remains,

"Hit's tore up." **1997** Montgomery *Coll* (known to eight consultants from the Smoky Mountains). **2007** Farr *My Appalachia* 122 Edna Mae is just tore up something awful about it. **2007** Preece *Leavin' Sandlick* 16 I am mighty tore up myself, and the children don't know which way to turn either.

[DARE *tear up* v phr 3 chiefly South, South Midland]

B *noun* A rampage, great commotion.

1931 Goodrich *Mt Homespun* 56 "It's a regular tare-up of a meetin'," said Hannah, keen for excitement. **1997** Montgomery *Coll* (known to Bush, Weaver).

tear up jack *verb phrase* To cause a commotion or disturbance, do damage, "raise hell." See also **cut up jack, jack**[1].

1862 Lockmiller *CW Letters* (March 22) the linkernts [i.e. Lincolnites] is rangen sec Skuatchey [i.e. Sequatchie] valey taring up jack. **1915** Dingus *Word-List VA* 191 The boys was just tearin' up jack when the teacher come. **1923** Montague *Today Tomorrow* 159 Well then, one day, that little feller he tuck down sick, and when Tony got the word of it, he jest fa'rly tore up Jack till he got aholt of the finest doctor in the county. **c1960** Wilson *Coll* = to cause a disturbance, raise hell. **2005** Williams *Gratitude* 533 = to go at something roughly and wholeheartedly; do some damage. At a wild party, sometimes things got out of hand, and they just *tear up jack*. **2009** Benfield *Mt Born* 162 = to wantonly destroy.

[DARE cf *tear up jack* (at *jack* n[1] 14) chiefly South, Midland]

tear up the patch *verb phrase* See citation.

1911 Shearin *E KY Word-List* 540 = to rant.

tech See **touch**.

teched See **touched**.

techous See **touchous**.

teder (also *titter*) *noun* See citations.

1919 Combs *Word-List South* 35 *titter* = tetter, the disease of the hands [Knott Co]. **1990** Cavender *Folk Medical Lex* 32 *teder* = a scaly, red skin rash.

[DARE (at *tetter* n) formerly widespread, now chiefly South, South Midland, TX]

tedious *adjective* Variant forms *teejus, tegious, tegus, tejus*.

1863 Hundley *CW Letters* (May 25) ande rinels ande agreate meny mor oF my [aquantances] too tegus to mensho[n]. **1864** Chapman *CW Letters* (April 4) it is to tegious to wright to Every one. **1904–20** Kephart *Notebooks* 2:642 You needn't take it so tejus as to axe ary man you meet on Stecoah what his name is. Jist say, "Hello, Mr Crisp." **1942** Hall *Phonetics Smoky Mts* 96. **1950** Bray *Disappearing Dialect* 285 An old-time mountaineer may tell stories which are "tejus" (tedious) to his grandchildren. **2005** Williams *Gratitude* 530 *teejus*. **2016** *Blind Pig* (Nov 26) Tejus and tedious are not the same word. Not even close. Almost opposites; Tedious is long, boring and tiring. Tejus is delicate, extricate [sic] and complicated; Tedious is digging a ditch. Tejus is tatting lace or tying dry flies; Tedious is hoeing a long corn row. Tejus is fixing a watch.

teejus See **tedious**.

teenincey (also *teeninecy, teeniney*) *adjective* Extremely small.

1939 *FWP Guide NC* 98 The "arm baby" is also the "least 'un," the "teeniney," or "teeny chap," her youngest. **1973** McCarthy *Child of God* 98 I'd say it would fit her unless she's just teeninecy. **2005** Williams *Gratitude* 56 Some folks had little tee-nincey bottles a smellin' salts. **2012** *Blind Pig* (Jan 11) There's some little yellow flowers growing on a vine at the mailbox. They look like tee-niney Jonquills.

[DARE (at *tee-nincy* adj) chiefly South, South Midland]

teeninecy, teeniney See **teenincey**.

teester *noun* A bed canopy.

1998–99 Montgomery *Coll* I don't have any use for those old teesters (Bush), = the structure set on top of the bed four posts made of wood slats that holds the canopy in place (Wilson).

[OED3 variant of *tester* n[2]; DARE (at *tester* n) chiefly South, South Midland]

teetotal *adjective, adverb* Absolute(ly), complete(ly), entire(ly).

1977 Still *Wonder Beans* 8 Sow them and they will feed your life tee-total. **1986** Helton *Around Home* 381. **2011** Thompson *Just Men* 110 Teetotal prohibition was never a stated Primitive Baptist goal.

[reduplication of *total* (originally pertaining to abstinence); OED *teetotal* adj 2 dialect, 1840→]

teetotally (also *teetotely*) *adverb* Completely, entirely, utterly.

1862 Epperly *CW Letters* (May 16) every thing is tetoley destroid in this part of the State. **1895** Dromgoole *Logan's Courtship* 147 [That heifer] will eat your saddle flaps teetotally off if you leave your mare out there. **1939** Hall *Coll* (Cataloochee NC) My daddy, he hollered for mother, says, "Mother, come here," he says, "confound it, that cussed old cat scratched my hoss, and he's teetotally ruined." **1963** Edwards *Gravel* 104 It was gone, plumb tee-totally gone! **1974–75** McCracken *Logging* 5:61 That branch is hopelessly and teetotally dry. **1978** Montgomery *White Pine Coll* III-2 No wonder the girls at these stands was give out teetotally. *Ibid.* X-2 You didn't get no rest. [You were] just wore teetotally plumb out. **1982** Slone *How We Talked* 30 *tee-tote-ly* = exactly. **1985** Irwin *Alex Stewart* 273 I noticed that these bottoms down here was tee-totally covered with this old yellow dock.

teetotely See **teetotally**.

tee-whitey, to a (also *to a tee-wonk-tum, to a T-witey*) *adverbial phrase* To exactness or perfection.

1941 (in **1944** Wentworth *ADD* 670) (eWV) = a "T": "It fits to a T-witey." **1969** *DARE Survey* (Rome GA) [done] *to a tee-whitey* = to perfection. **1982** Slone *How We Talked* 38 *to fit to a tee-wonk-tum* (exactly).

tee-wonk-tum See **tee-whitey, to a**.

tegious, **tegus**, **tejus** See **tedious**.

tel See **till**.

telegram pole *noun* A timber suitable for a telephone or telegraph pole.

1939 Hall *Coll* (Indian Creek NC) During a hard crop year the Champion Fiber Company] would allow us to get out acid wood, telegram poles, and railroad ties. **1969** *GSMNP-37:2:5* You had to have something to live on, you see. I've peeled bark, got out crossties, telegram poles, hauled them to Bryson City and down at mouth of the creek there.

telephone loafer *noun* A lurker on a telephone party line.

1963 Edwards *Gravel* 37 This [information] was grist for the mill of the telephone loafers, and they made excellent telephone capital of it.

tell[1] See **till**.

tell[2] *verb*

A Variant past-tense forms *telled*, *tolt*.

1914 Furman *Sight* 56 She tolt me what to do, and I follered it, and, lo! The meracle was performed. **1933** Carpenter *Sthn Mt Dialect* 24 In parts of southwestern Virginia, Kentucky and North Carolina certain words have [t] in place of [d]. SECOND is *secont*, TOLD, *tolt*, and HUSBAND, *husbant*. **1940** Bowman *KY Mt Stories* 248 *tell'd* = told. **1985** Williams *Role of Folklore* 220 He grabbed me by the back of the hair and punched me in the back and telled me he'd blow me in two.

B To report, give an account (usually followed by a complement clause). See also **hear tell**, **tell on**.

1862 *Durham CW Letters* (April 22) I have heard that Whits worth who deserted & left ous has got home & told that we was all kild. **1938** Justus *No-End Hollow* 24 They even tell that he takes it along when goes to plow his field. **1940** Haun *Hawk's Done* 18 Basil butted in and told that Tiny started it. **1955** Ritchie *Singing Family* 59 Mammy Sally and Pap and t'others seemed like they had a good time talking to him and listening to him tell, but I couldn't open my mouth to save me. **1959** Hall *Coll* (Roaring Fork TN) That's what they told, but I don't know. **1969** *Burton-Manning Coll-93A* That's what the telegram told from the government. **1989** *Matewan OHP-1* The word got out. One of the chambermaids down at the hotel told that she overheard them. **1997** King *Mt Folks* 45 He told that, "no," he had not; he had concocted the entire story so he could keep his five dollars.

tell howdy See **howdy B**.

tell off on *verb phrase* To inform on, "tattle on."

1963 Edwards *Gravel* 22 Wes rolled under the bed and she couldn't find him. So Uncle Jeems told off on him.

[DARE (at *tell* v C4) chiefly South, South Midland]

tell on *verb phrase* To report or claim about (someone). See also **tell**[2] **B**.

1985 Irwin *Alex Stewart* 249 They's a whole lot told on them that wasn't right—according to what my granddaddy told me. **1998** *Dante OHP-61* He'd arrest them and take that there gallon of liquor and sell it again. Now that's been told on him. **2000** Morgan *Mts Remember* 89 She never was sick in her mind really, like they told it on her.

tell the hanging of one's granny *verb phrase* See citation.

2014 Williams *Coll* = to tell everything one knows about a subject: "You'd tell the hanging of your granny."

temp *verb* See citation. See also **temping bottle**.

1974 Maurer and Pearl *KY Moonshine* 126 = to test the bead on liquor by shaking it in a bottle in order to ascertain whether or not the liquor must be "tempered" by the addition of water or backings. If the liquor does not hold a bead, higher proof distillate must be added.

temping bottle *noun* See citation. See also **temp**.

1949 Maurer *Argot of Moonshiner* 13 = a bottle in which a sample of liquor is placed and shaken to test the formation of beads indicating the proof of the liquor: "Here, take that temping bottle and see how this stuff beads."

tender *verb* To pamper, make (one) delicate.

1979 Carpenter *Walton War* 149 "Women folks hain't much account now-a-days, they have tendered themselves too much." How better to say someone has "gone soft"? Said by an old lady who had always worked hard and thought the younger generation was lazy. **1995–97** Montgomery *Coll* (known to Brown, Bush).

[OED3 *tender* v[2] 2c, now dialect]

tender beans *noun* See citation.

1949 McDavid *Grist* 114 (Rabun Co GA) = string beans.

Tenesy See **Tennessee**.

Tennessee (also *Tenesy*, *Tennessy*) *noun* Variant form reflecting stress on the first syllable: *TEN-nes-see*.

1829 (in **1938** Read *Pronunciation on Frontier* 264) Tennessee is accented on the last syllable, but with a strong disposition to throw the accent back to the first. Ten'ne-sy is not an unusual sound. **1883** Zeigler and Grosscup *Heart of Alleghanies* 259 "Tenesy," answered the man, giving the accent on the first syllable, a pronunciation peculiar to the uneducated natives. **1895** Edson and Fairchild *TN Mts* 375 = with initial stress. **1931** Goodrich *Mt Homespun* 54 Maw wants you should go with her tomorrow to her aunts' in Tennessy. **1942** Hall *Phonetics Smoky Mts* 55 *Tennessee*, usually now [tɛnə'si], but the older ['tɪnə̣si] is still fairly common. **1966** Wilson *Coll*: Tennessee, among older people in southern Kentucky and northern Tennessee, is often ['tɪnə̣si]. Five generations of my family lived there and called it thus.

[DARE *Tennessee* n (pronc) chiefly South, South Midland]

Tennessee pearl *noun* A pearl found in the shell of a mussel, a freshwater mollusk native to large streams of northeastern Tennessee and nearby areas. See also **gut pearl**.

1940 Still *River of Earth* 122–23 You've never seed a pretty like this, Child. A Tennessee pearl. Growed in a river mussel shell. **1941** Still *Proud Walkers* 112 I'd give a Tennessee pearl to see you atop a twenty-foot ladder potting nails. **1981** Henry *Alex Stewart* 48 Alex has owned and operated three sawmills, invented the mussel box, an aid in finding Tennessee pearls, and with his foot-powered spring-pole lathe, he has turned out countless chairs, spinning wheels, and rolling-pins. *Ibid.* 55 Other river stories describe mussels and the search for Tennessee pearls. Mussels are fresh water mollusks. Back when our rivers were free-flowing and clean they thrived in all our large streams. In the past thirty or forty years, however, dams and industrial pollution have all but wiped out the mussels. **2009** TN *Encycl* The legislature of Tennessee has officially adopted additional symbols to represent the State through the years. They include . . . the official gem (1979) as the Tennessee pearl.

Tennessy See **Tennessee.**

tent *noun* A simple log cabin used for temporary residence at a **camp meeting**.

1982 *Foxfire VII* 270 I remember when people would come in their wagons to camp out. Back then, most all of the service goers would camp out the entire week here. Many built small, simple log cabins or "tents" to camp in from year to year. "Tents" like these, are still in existence today with many being permanently owned by the regulars of the camp meeting faithful.

terbaccer, terbacker, terbacky See **tobacco**.

terectly See **directly**.

terrapin *noun* Variant forms *tarpin*, *tarripin*.

1883 Zeigler and Grosscup *Heart of Alleghanies* 52 This kind never misses fire an' rain never teches hit, fer this 'ere kiver, ter put over the pan, keeps hit as dry as a tarripin hull. **1937** Haun *Cocke Co* 3 [Girls] mosey around over the hills like tarpins, are skeery of snakes when they see them quiled up, and they and lambs are supposed to be seely. **1967** *DARE Survey* (Maryville TN) *tarpin*.

terrectly See **directly**.

terrible

A Variant forms *turbil* [see **1863** in **B**], *turble*, *turrible*.

1942 Hall *Phonetics Smoky Mts* 62 For *terrible*, many old-timers say ['tɝbəl], a pronunciation which illustrates the tendency toward obscuration and loss of the vowel. *Ibid.* 64 *turble*. **1946** Matthias *Speech Pine Mt* 190 She's fell off somethin' turrible, last two-three months.

[DARE *terrible* adj, adv (pronc) especially South, South Midland, New England]

B *adjective* Extraordinary, prodigious.

1862 *Kiracofe CW Letters* (Dec 17) they say it was a turble Slaughter upon the enemy. **1863** *Reese CW Letters* (Jan 10) thair has Bin A turbil time dow hear the fite Comenst the day Be fore new years. **1956** Hall *Coll* (Raccoon Creek NC) This man was also a coon hunter, and he was a terrible fool about sauerkraut. **1961** *Coe Ridge OHP-343A* Yeah, he was a terrible banjo picker. **1973** GSMNP-88 I was a terrible feller to eat ramps. **1978** *American Chestnut* 255 He has a terrible crop of them each summer, more than he can sell. **1978** Montgomery *White Pine Coll* IX-1 It means a big crowd. It was a terrible crowd. *Ibid.* IX-4 Eddie's a terrible Republican. **1985** Irwin *Alex Stewart* 172 Old man Lou Trent down here, that's Margie's granddaddy, kept fox hounds all the time and he was a terrible feller to fox hunt.

C *adverb* Extremely, immensely, terribly.

1913 Kephart *Our Sthn High* 78 Thar come one turrible vyg'rous blow that jist nacherally lifted the ground. **1930** Armstrong *This Day and Time* 184 I thank ye terrible, but you-all 'ull best stay fer dinner. **1939** Hall *Coll* Some of that country is terrible rough. **1941** Still *Troublesome Creek* 102 For a host o' folks, they're terrible quiet. **c1950** (in **2000** Oakley *Roamin' Man* 92) That means you are turble mad or angry so don't use God's name in vain. **1985** Irwin *Alex Stewart* 105 There was a terrible big crowd, and nobody didn't bid on him much. **1991** Thomas *Sthn Appal* 197 I'z abused terrible by some of th' teachers. **2004** House *Coal Tattoo* 31 I miss them terrible bad.

[OED3 *terrible* adv now chiefly regional and U.S.; HT *terrible* adv "extremely"]

terrible to *adjective phrase* Having an extreme tendency to (do something). See also **bad to.**

1973 GSMNP-88:30 I was a terrible fellow to eat ramps. **1985** Irwin *Alex Stewart* 172 Old man Lou Trent down here, that's Margie's granddaddy, kept fox hounds all the time and he was a terrible feller to fox hunt.

test *noun* Variant plural forms of two syllables: *test-es*, *testis*.

1998 *Dante OHP-71* He took testes, but they put him in the mines as a engineer. **2000** Lowry *Folk Medical Term* I want to know what you think about my husband's testes. **2013** DeLozier and Jourdan *Back Seat* 125 They say you're smart. They say you do good on them testis.

testament *noun* Variant form with secondary stress on the last syllable. For similar forms, see **-ment A**.

1942 Hall *Phonetics Smoky Mts* 71 The suffixes *-dent* and *-ment* (except in *independent*) in most instances have secondary stress: *accident, confident, devilment, instrument, monument, payment, settlement, testament*, etc.

tester See **teester**.

testes See **test**.

testimony meeting *noun* A church gathering (or part of a service), often held at a revival, in which individuals testify about their personal spiritual experience.

1974 GSMNP-50:2:6 On Wednesday night we would meet and sing for thirty minutes, and then we would have a prayer meeting. Someone would conduct a prayer meeting, and he would have a prayer. Then he would have a song, a prayer and a song, prayer and song, till it got kind of through, and usually it would end up with a testimony meeting. **1998** Montgomery *Coll* = this minister might say at the beginning of a revival service, as "I'd like to start off with a testimony meeting" (Cardwell). **2005** Morgan *Old Time Religion* 12 During Sunday schools and the two preaching services per month, there were never any "testimony meetings" such as those held often in unaffiliated churches today and even less often in mainline churches. These old mountaineers were reticent to "perform," as it were, in public. Besides, they didn't like to be put in positions where they felt pressured to do anything because everything must be at the undeniable unction of the Spirit.

testis See **test.**

tetch See **touch.**

tetched See **touched.**

tetcheous, **tetcherous**, **tetchified**, **tetchious**, **tetchous**, **tetchus** See **touchous.**

tetchsome *adjective* Touchy.

1966 Dakin *Vocab Ohio River Valley* 468 *Tetchsome* appears only once in the Mountains [of KY].

tetter See **teder.**

text *noun* Variant plural form as two syllables: *text-es.*

1891 Primer *Studies in WV* 168 One minister, a hard-shell Baptist, or Ironsides as they call this sect there, spoke of the textes from which he preached his sermon. **1921** Campbell *Sthn Highlander* 16 "Textes" and "nestes" and similar plurals bring to mind the Pilgrims to Canterbury. *Ibid.* 178 The Scriptures are the source from which arguments are drawn for every important discussion of Church or State, or of life in general. To bolster up a cause or an opinion the Highlander is able to quote disassociated texts—"textes" as he would say—and often, too often, the Book of Books becomes a cudgel for the head of an opponent rather than a "lamp unto the feet."

[DARE *text* n chiefly South, South Midland]

thaing See **thing.**

than *conjunction*

1 Following an adjective or adverbial phrase superlative in form but comparative in interpretation (thus, *most of* = more of).

1939 Hall *Coll* (Waynesville NC) I was scared the worst than any other time. **1956** Miller *Pigeon's Roost* (Nov 15) It is reported there has been the least work this autumn by prospectors searching for mineral ore in the Pigeon Roost section than there has been in a long time. **1966** *Ibid.* (Jan 27) I remember one song that she sung most for him than any other song, but I can only now recall a very few words to the song. **2003** Smith *Orlean Puckett* 104 I thought the most of that old dress than anything in the world.

2 As.

1975–76 Wolfram/Christian *WV Coll* 31 My old woman in there has made as good of biscuits than you ever stuck [in] your mouth.

thang See **thing.**

thankee *phrase* See citation.

1976 Garber *Mountain-ese* 92 = thank you.

than what *conjunctive phrase* Than is the case that.

1864 *Watkins CW Letters* (June 9) I think if times gits no worse then what they are we will git to come home about whet cutin time on a furlow or some way. **1964** Roberts *Hell-Fer-Sartin* 85 I've still got a better bag now than what I had before. **1971** *AOHP/ALC-183* They got a lot of different ways of getting to school now than what they had in my day. *Ibid.* The community was altogether different than what it was before that time and it's never been back like it was. **1987** (in **2015** Yarrow *Voices* 25–26) A loose rock's bigger than what you think it's gonna be. **1998** *Dante OHP-71* You could go to Mister Mac's store down there and get stuff cheaper than what you could out of the Dante store.

thar, **thare** See **there.**

tharen See **theirn.**

tharsefs See **theirself.**

that

A *pronoun, conjunction, adjective* Variant forms *at, 'at.*

1862 *Matthews CW Letters* (Sept 26) Tell Farther & the galls at i Heant for got them. **1925** (in **1935** Edwards *NC Novels* 46) *'at.* **1939** Hall *Coll* (Deep Creek NC) We had some old trained bear hounds 'at turned off in the roughs, the laurel on the Bear Creek side, and picked up a cold trail. **1953** Hall *Coll* (Plott Creek NC) That's a place where . . . nothin' but a bear or somep'n like 'at can go. **1961** *Coe Ridge OHP-343A* At's about the oldest one that I remember was Aunt —— Coe. **1970** *Hunting Stories* 33 Don't you see 'at turkey. **1972** *AOHP/ALC-342* I forget what his name was, that fellow at was running for president of the union. **1973** *Flu Epidemic* 104 Sometimes we'd make 'em some kind a'tea, y'know; boneset, and stuff like'at. **1976** GSMNP-113:2 Yes, siree, yeah 'at's my mother. **1994** McCarthy *Jack Two Worlds* 11 She couldn't be got out of it till somebody broke 'at. **2005** Williams *Gratitude* 134 At's where th' littlest younguns set. **2007** Preece *Leavin' Sandlick* 19 It just ain't right when people do lik at.

[DARE *that* pron, conj, adv, art A 1a especially South, South Midland]

B *relative pronoun* See also **thats** and Grammar and Syntax §2.9.

1 Who, which (in a nonrestrictive clause, following a proper name).

1910 Cooke *Power and Glory* 60 Miss Baird, that taught the school I went to over at Rainy Gap, had a herbarium. **1927** Furman *Lonesome Road* 62 A few [books] came down from my paw, that was a learned man and a school-teacher. **1939** Hall Coll (Sugarlands TN) This is Steve Cole, that lives in the Sugarlands near Gatlinburg in the park, been a-living here ever since the park was established. **1961** *Coe Ridge* OHP-334A He wasn't near as tall as Mitchell that works for me down here. **1973** GSMNP-61:4 The Queen family was all of them good to sing, and Mister Wilson Queen, that lived there at the campground, why he was a song leader when I was a little girl. **1973** GSMNP-79:5 Miss Hathaway, that lives here now in Gatlinburg, she taught the older children up there when I went to school. **1974** Ogle *Memories* 4 There was one preacher, Brad Ogle that stayed at our house so much. **1984** Gibson *Remembering* [addendum] 2 There was Wesley Huskey, and Ephraim Ogle, that owned the store in Gatlinburg, where the post office used to be in the back of the store. **1989** *Matewan* OHP-39 We lived at the end of Blackberry Bridge, that goes over into Blackberry Creek. *Ibid.* Bill had come out and he'd caught Number Three passenger train, that comes through there about midnight.

2 Who (in a restrictive clause).

1863 *W L Brown CW Letters* (Nov 20) Mager Catlet will start home in the moring and a good meny others men that has no famley. **1953** Hall Coll (Bryson City NC) Bill Cope and Little John Cable was just the two that had the dogs. **1961** *Coe Ridge* OHP-343A He had some children that's pretty bright. **1989** *Matewan* OHP-23 He has two daughters and a son-in-law that's members and goes there now. **1998** *Dante* OHP-25 The man that was with me was a preacher.

C *conjunction*

1 Used to introduce a relative clause that is formally like that of an independent sentence.

1969 *Burton-Manning Coll*-93A She's the one that her husband won't let her work. **1972** AOHP/LJC-104 I had an uncle, William Caudill, that he lived right back over here on the bank. **1973** Kahn *Hillbilly Women* 191 [We had] one of them old toilets that the water run all the time in it. **1979** *Big South Fork* OHP-1 We had some friends that one of the girls still lives in Oneida. Her daddy was an engineer on the train. **1989** Landry *Smoky Mt Interviews* 181 There was a couple of brothers that they had a moonshine still. **1989** *Matewan* OHP-1 My grandmother was a type of person that I only knew what she wanted me to know. *Ibid.* 94 They was a little old tipple that the trucks went up on this ramp and dumped the coal. **1990** *Matewan* OHP-73 They was several men that we knowed that I just can't think of their names right off. **1991** Thomas *Sthn Appal* 131 Take a machine—we had a machine here 'at we could quilt saddle-seats with it—an' go right on. *Ibid.* 248 I had an old crippled shepherd dog, that I thought me an' that dog would handle enny bears. *Ibid.* 260 I was in another runaway, that I was blamed partly for the runaway. **1997** *Dante* OHP-14 They was a fence up on the spur from where we lived that nobody didn't live up there.

[OED3 *that* pron² 3 c888→; "very common down to 16c→; now arch. and poetic"]

2 Added redundantly to form phrases, as **because that, before that, how that, if that, unless that, when that, whenever that, where that, why that.** See Grammar and Syntax §15.4.

[DARE *that* conj C 2 chiefly South, South Midland]

D *adverb* So.

1864 *Stepp CW Letters* (May 7) i am that tired and Sleepy i cant hardly rite. **1898** Dromgoole *Cinch* 31 I have laid 'wake nights in the corral long o' the horses, with the stars shinin' down on me, that lonesome that I actually cried. **1900** Harben *N GA Sketches* 303 We are all that excited we don't know which way to turn. **1916** Combs *Old Early English* 291 He is that blind that he can't read. **1925** Furman *Glass Window* 52 I'm that consarned to keep a breath of air from getting to her. **1957** Combs *Lg Sthn High: Syntax* 9 = sometimes used for *so, such . . . that*: "He is *that* ignorant *that* he cain't vote." **1970** *Foxfire Interviews* A-70-5 I was that glad it [= a stroke] didn't stop my tongue. **1975** AOHP/LJC-384 I wore that dress. She [= my mother] kept it that long that I wore it.

[DARE *that* adv B chiefly South, South Midland]

that ar See **that there**.

thataway *adverb* In that direction or manner, like that. See also **thisaway**.

1862 *Robinson CW Letters* (June 7) I have to come home that away. **1863** *Watkins CW Letters* (Oct 18) I dont like for no boddy to talk about mee that a way when I cant help my self. **1895** Edson and Fairchild *TN Mts* 374 Ef the world's as big every way as she is *that-a-'way*, she's a whopper. **1903** Fox *Little Shepherd* 25 I'm a-goin' thataway. **1913** Kephart *Our Sthn High* 160 Hit was thataway in my Pa's time, and in Gran'sir's, too. **1924** Spring *Lydia Whaley* 2 [She] saw a star in the sky for three months. . . . After a while it turned to goin' thataway. **1939** Hall Coll (Smokemont NC) They were poor chances then for us young fellows a-growin' up to get any chance much of schoolin', and it remained that-a-way for a good long while before we had any better advantages. **1956** Hall Coll (Roaring Fork TN) You go thataway, and I'll go thisaway, and we'll whip them boys that are trying to scare us. **1961** *Coe Ridge* OHP-342A He dropped his gun down thataway, but he come back up with it and throwed his arms around thataway. **1978** Montgomery *White Pine Coll* VIII-2 When you're coming down thataway, they ain't many places to stop. **1979** *Big South Fork* OHP-1 We don't work ataway no more. **1985** Irwin *Alex Stewart* 271 Wind won't hurt timber much. It will just spring thisaway and thataway.

[OED3 *that-a-way* adv 1, 2 chiefly dialect and U.S.; Web3 *thataway* adv dialect]

that dog won't hunt *phrase* That plan or idea won't work.

2001 Montgomery Coll (known to Cardwell).

that don't make me never no mind See **never no mind**.

thats (also **that's**) *relative pronoun* Whose.

1961 *Coe Ridge* OHP-340B Is he the one thats wife was back there in town now? **1986** Montgomery *File* We need to remember a woman thats child has died (50-year-old man). **1999** Morgan

Gap Creek 130 I didn't sob like a little girl that's heart was broke. **2004** Adams *Old True Love* 12 I've knowed some that's passion for each other turned to hate after they'd been married awhile. **2012** *Blind Pig* (June 27) I know a man thats kids work harder than he does. **2017** *Blind Pig* (Nov 17) He told us the story of a friend that's family grew these beans for generations.

[< Scots, formed from *that his*, later taken as a possessive form analogous with *whose*]

that thar See **that there.**

that there See also **them there, this here.**

A *Variant forms at air, that air* [see **1978** in **C**], *that ar* [see **1867** in **B**], *that thar* [see **1875** in **B**], *that thir* [see **1864** in **C**].

1957 Broaddus *Vocab Estill Co KY* 4 *at air.*

B *pronoun phrase* That.

1867 Harris *Sut Lovingood* 30 Plant yersef ontu that ar log, an' I'll tell ef I kin, but hit's a'mos beyant tellin. **1875** Davis *Qualla* 579 "For it don't stand to reason," said one old man, arguing the matter, "that God 'ud make two such fiends as that thar in one generation." **1931** Owens *Speech Cumberlands* 94 That-air dommer rooster belongs to me. **1939** Hall *Coll* (Cades Cove TN) Then you make up the mash, and that there kept. Pour hot water on it and stir it up and make it up . . . and put a little sugar in it. **1956** *GSMNP*-22:30 That there's Tom's boy, I guess. **1973** *Foxfire Interviews* A-73-43 When I dug that there right there, I was digging through that and I found lots of great big bunches [of ginseng]. **1973** *GSMNP*-88 That there's the way this here changed hands right along then. **1974** *Instrument Makers* 181 "It's got a finer, mellower tone than that there," he said, pointing to my factory-made banjo. **1989** Giardina *Storming Heaven* 7 "Our people allays lived hard," Dillon replied. "That there is what makes us."

C *adjective phrase* That.

1845 (in **1974** Harris *High Times* 48) Bill Jones, quit a smashin that ar cat's tail! **1864** *Dalton CW Letters* (June 4) I wrot A let ter to that thir girl you know who but I dont know whether I will get A anser. **1908** Fox *Lonesome Pine* 21 Hitch that 'ar post to yo' hoss and come right in. **1927** Bird *Among Highlanders* 27 Did that there boy ask you to marry him? **1954** *GSMNP*-19:8 They just tied a knot in the road, and they made that there loop bridge. **1957** *GSMNP*-23:1:15 My daddy owned in time of Civil War, he owned that there Trentham property over above Fork of the River. **1961** Williams *Content Mt Speech* 16 When Lil an' that ar man o' hern fust started sparkin', jist when they was beginnin' talkin' together, I met Lil one evenin' about dusky dark. **1969** *GSMNP*-42:12 That there first little mill had a little overshot [waterwheel]. **1975** *GSMNP*-62:11 That there sawmill I worked at was there before I married. **1978** Hiser *Quare Do's* 145 Hit's done like that air homebrew we uset to make back yander; hit's done swole up and done busted. **1998** *Dante OHP*-61 That there coal dust gets in your lungs and just settles across it and coats your lungs till you can't breathe, just blocks your breathing off and you get short of breath.

[OED3 (at *that* demonstrative adj B2b) dialect and vulgar]

that thir See **that there.**

that'un (also *that'un*) *pronoun* That one. See also **one 1.**

1942 Hall *Phonetics Smoky Mts* 86. **1976** *Bear Hunting* 262 He beat that'uns's brains out with a pine knot. **1980** *GSMNP*-115:50 Before ever that'un was built up yander I quit school. **1997** Landry *Coll* We'll try another'un, being that'un paid off. **2005** Williams *Gratitude* 50 She was careful about them big latch pins. As she took it out of the diaper, she'd pin one through her dress and latch it, an'en pin the other'ns through that'n. **2007** McMillon *Notes* This'un's better ner that'un.

thaw up *verb phrase* Of something frozen: to unfreeze; to cause (something or someone) to unfreeze.

1942 (in **1987** Perdue *Outwitting Devil* 28–29) He said all right, an' Jack took his rod and passed it about the place and everything thawed up an' he poured Jack out some beer and told him to go to a certain place and hide himself on the bank of the river and he'd see the daughters of King Morock when they come to wash. **1961** *Coe Ridge OHP*-334B [They] wrapped him up in yarn blankets and wallowed him in that spring I don't know how long and thawed him up. **1974** *GSMNP*-50:2:18 When it thawed up again, [the maple syrup] would start running again. **1979** *Preacher Cook* 199 When [the snake] got warm, it thawed up and bit him. **1997** Montgomery *Coll* (known to Adams, Bush, Jones, Ledford, Norris, Weaver); The ground thawed up along about March (Cardwell).

thay See **there.**

the *definite article*

1 Used in place-names.

1861 *Griffin CW Letters* (Nov 2) I must quit this is the last leter that I will write from the Hot springs prehaps it is the last one that I will ever wright. **1862** *Mangum CW Letters* (June 16) I am a bout 300 miles fom home by the railrod and right by the foot of the look out mountain a bout one half a mile from Chattanooga. **1863** *Reese CW Letters* (Jan 13) I found John hier at the straw berry plains 15 miles from knoxville. **1915** Hall *Autobiog Claib Jones* 28 We reached Beech mountain, stayed all night with an old sager. We laid in our bread and hired him and his horse to take us to the Beech mountain. **1937** Hall *Coll* (Cosby TN) People was beginnin' to settle the Smoky. . . . That happened afore I left the Smoky. *Ibid.* (White Oak NC) "The Smoky" usually means the top of the Great Smoky Mountains. **1939** Hall *Coll* (Tuckaleechee Cove TN) Me and my brother-in-law one time left the White Oak. *Ibid.* (Gatlinburg TN) We went to the Newfound Gap and built a trail from Newfound Gap to LeConte. *Ibid.* (Hazel Creek NC) It's been called the Rowan Branch ever since I was a young'un. **1969** *Burton-Manning Coll*-93A I come from Bakersville, North Carolina, up above the Roan Mountain. **1972** *AOHP/ALC*-276 You go right up here to the Shelby Gap, and you can go right across that road and go up on top. **1983** *Dark Corner OHP*-9A I don't remember exactly where it was at, around the Spartanburg somewhere. **1991** Thomas *Sthn Appal* 103 From there, ye go up, an' ye cross th' stone Mount'n, down over in over to Beaver Dam country. *Ibid.* 144 They ewst to dig a little of that miker back up in under th' Roan Mount'n. **2016**

Blind Pig (March 30) If you look right straight to your right, you're looking right up the Walnut Cove.

2 In phrase *in the bed*. See **bed A**.

3 Used with a superlative. See **(the) best**.

4 In phrases *the old lady, the old woman, the wife, the woman* = one's wife; *the daughter* = one's daughter.

1913 Kephart *Our Sthn High* 257 "The woman," as every wife is called, has her kingdom within the house. **1939** Hall Coll (Bradley Fork NC) Finally I lost the old lady seven year ago last January. **c1951** Chapman *Speech Confusing* A mountain wife, though still in her teens, is called "the old woman" by her youthful husband. She likewise calls him "my old man," regardless of his age. **1979** Carpenter *Walton War* 68 We've et but the wife'll get you some supper. **1995** Montgomery Coll I sent the daughter to borrow Frank's tooth drawers (Cardwell).

[EDD *the* II.1 Scot, nEngl; SND *the* 2]

5 In phrase *the most*. See also **the best**.

1813 Hartsell *Memora* 103 the most of the men was melted into teeres under the sermont. **1845** *McLean Diary* 93 the waters has Bin froosing for the Most of the month. **1861** *Hileman CW Letters* (Aug 23) It has been Raining down here the most of the time sience you were down. **1862** *Patton CW Letters* (Dec 11) we have been travling about the most of our time. **1922** *TN CW Ques* 9 The most of the schools was privat scools. **1939** Hall Coll (Gatlinburg TN) I always made the feathers fly, but the trouble was the meat went with it the most of the time. **1969** *Burton-Manning Coll*-89B The most of them thought she ought to be killed. **1973** GSMNP-4:1:21 I think that's where the most of the trouble came from was the people coming in there from them logging companies. **1989** Landry *Smoky Mt Interviews* 194 Old man Sparks, he spent the most of his life on that mountain. **1998** *Dante OHP*-51 I knew the most of them. **2008** *Rosie Hicks* 4 The most of them, I think they just come to listen.

6 In phrase *the both*.

1940 Haun *Hawk's Done* 21 I can nigh see them now—the both of them setting there, either one thinking of tothern. **1979** *Big South Fork OHP*-11 He just grabbed up a big whip and went to whooping the both of us. **1983** *Dark Corner OHP*-26A We met Jel and Hugh Reed coming out with the both of them. **2002** Rash *Foot in Eden* 26 I'm going to talk to the both of them.

[OED3 *both* B dialect or obsolete; CUD *the both* (at *the* def art (i))]

7 With the name of a disease or physical ailment. See also **fever, sugar 2**. [Editor's note: The article is standard before some diseases or ailments, as *the flu, the measles*.]

1833 *McLean Diary* 20 [I] Worked at the Cort house Susanna sick with the tooth ake. **1862** *Reese CW Letters* (Nov 10) thair is A heep of Sickness hear with the Brane feaver. **1862** *Sutton CW Letters* (Nov 8) We lost one man out of our Co., John Martain. He died with the fever. **1863** *Penland CW Letters* (March 2) I have the bad cold very bad. **1864** *Revis CW Letters* (Dec 7) I herd he had the sore thrat. **1930** Armstrong *This Day and Time* 121 I taken the headache awhile back. **1937** Hall Coll (Cosby TN) A sight of people died of the fever [= typhoid] on this branch twenty-five or thirty year ago. . . . To cure the croup and the phthisic, straighten a sourwood stick behind the back and head, cut it off even with the top of the head, and hide it where it'll never be found. *Ibid.* (Upper Cosby Creek TN) To cure the flux, drink a tea of sweet gum bark or take some mutton taller melted. **1941** Stuart *Men of Mts* 247 I heard that he had the consumption. **1954** Arnow *Dollmaker* 59 I'll have to cook with butter, an butter seasonen gives me th sick headache. **1972** *AOHP/LJC*-104 They would [have] sickness such as the flux and the typhoid fever. **1977** *Jake Waldroop* 172 Our littlest girl, that was Ruth, she was the one that died with the cancer. **1989** *Matewan OHP*-28 [The smoke] would give you the headache, or they called [it] a sick headache. You'd vomick and everything. **1996** Cavender *Bold Hives* 18 It is common in parts of the American South, including Appalachia, to attach the definite article the to the descriptor. This grammatical form often appears today in illness discourse (e.g., "My baby has *the* colic," "He's got *the* cancer," "She's just now getting over the measles"). **1999** Hodges *Tough Customers* 67 I know it's just going to be like this from now on, one thing happening after another, now you got the sugar and all.

[EDD *the* II.1 Scot, nEngl; SND *the* 4]

8 In phrase *the one* = the same.

1924 Montague *Betsy Beaver* 221 They's all of a size, like they'd been hatched outer the one cone, and all going up the ridge one right behind the tother.

9 In phrases *the old man, the widow* + surname.

1834 *McLean Diary* (Aug 7) [I] made a coffin for the widow Clark price 6.50. **1977** Shackelford et al. *Our Appalachia* 253 He was killed that night and he was very highly respected, the old man Tom Blackburn was.

10 Miscellaneous use.

2009 Holbrook *Upheaval* 11 I've not had to go on the welfare.

the back See **back of 1**.

the best See **(the) best**.

the best in the world See **(the) best kind**.

the best kind See **(the) best kind**.

the best upon earth See **(the) best kind**.

the finest kind See **(the) finest kind**.

the first See **first B**.

theft *verb* To steal.

c1940 Simms Coll His chickens were thefted.

their *pronoun* Variant forms *they, thur*.

1975 *AOHP/ALC*-1128 [If] they knowed some kids in they school, they want to go down and play with them. **1991** Thomas *Sthn Appal* 50 Some foaks ewst to cook thur cabbage ha'f a day. *Ibid.* 102 They had overseers, over th' fellers that'uz workin'—gittin' in thur six days a year.

theirn (also *tharen, their'n*) *pronoun* Theirs. For similar forms, see Grammar and Syntax §2.2.

1862 *Lockmiller CW Letters* (Sept 25) our fokes ar whopen thern ever whars and i hope that pas will be mad. **1862** *Shifflet CW Letters* (March 18) I want you to right to me whether enny of the rest of the woman gits tharen and if the do I will Rase pertictler thunder with them when I git home. **1934–47** *LAMSAS Appal* (Madison Co NC, Swain Co NC). **c1945** Haun *Hawk's Done* 268 Mallie just kept on wanting me to go on and get my meal sifted so she could take it home with her, said a hole had come in theirn. **1964** Roberts *Hell-Fer-Sartin* 128 That night two more men come in to stay all night and put their'n up. **1979** *Big South Fork OHP-2* The other boys were leading theirn [= mules]. **1991** Haynes *Haywood Home* 77 Jut would say far (firc), tar (tire), yander (yonder), her'n (hers), his'n (his), their'n (theirs). **1997** Montgomery *Coll* The colts is theirn (Brown).

[historically *their* + n by analogy with *my/mine*; now sometimes construed ahistorically as from *their* + *one*; OED3 theirn pron English midland and southern dialect form of theirs, on analogy with *ourn, yourn, hisn, hern*, c1425→; EDD *theirn* pron 1; *their'un* represents false analysis, mEngl, sEngl; DARE *theirn* pron especially New England, South, South Midland]

their own self, their own selfs See **their own selves.**

their own selves (also *their own self, their own selfs*) *pronoun phrase* Themselves. See also **own B.**

1931 Goodrich *Mt Homespun* 62 The men-folks would go off once a year to the settlements to get their corn ground, packing it on mule-back or toting it their own selves. **1939** Hall *Coll* (Catons Grove TN) People doctored their own selfs. **1969** *GSMNP-28:10* Everybody took care of their own self.

theirs all See **they all.**

theirself (also *tharsefs, theirselfs, theirselve, theirselves, therself, therselfs, therselves, theyself, theyselves*) *pronoun* Themselves. For similar forms, see Grammar and Syntax §2.3.3.

1813 Hartsell *Memora* 122 Last evning General Cock went to the Deferent Companeys in Colonel Waires Ridgement to See how maney men would volenteere ther Selves for Twenty Days longer to goo to join General Jacksons armey. **1863** (in **1992** Heller and Heller *Confederacy* 93) a bout one thousand women arm[ed] ther self with axes and clubs and firearms and march[ed] in to the citty and broak open stoers grocers and comassary's took what every tha[y] wanted in spite of milatary or sivel authority. **1863** *Walker CW Letters* (May 22) there was 7 yankeys Comes in an give there selves up an they sed that rosey was not agoing to give figt. **1866** *Elijoy Church Minutes* 108 the Church agrees to receive no other then p[u]blic acknowledgment for public crime & that the offender be notyfied to attend & answer for their selves the charge specifyed in the notice. **1867** Harris *Sut Lovingood* 77 Oh, hits jis' no use in thar talkin, an' groanin, an' sweatin tharsefs about hit. **1883** Murfree *Old Sledge* 550 Ef they scorches theyselves with this hyar coal o' fire from hell . . . it air Tom an' him a-blowin' on it ez hev kep' it a-light. **1900** Harben *N GA Sketches* 98 It'u'd look more decent ef you'd leave 'em to the'rselves, Alf. **1922** *TN CW Ques* 1009 (Sullivan Co TN) Slaveholders seemed to think their selves a little better [than] the people that didn't own slaves. *Ibid.* 1129 Men that had slaves seemed to think ther self better than them that didn't have any. . . . [They] done it ther selfs. **1934–47** *LAMSAS Appal*: *theirself* = attested by 7/148 speakers (4.7%) from WV, 2/20 (10%) from VA, and 15/37 (40.5%) from NC; *theirselves* = attested by 40/148 speakers (27.0%) from WV, 4/20 (20%) from VA, 21/37 (66.8%) from NC, 1/14 (7.1%) from SC, and 7/12 (58.3%) from GA. **1939** Walker *Mtneer Looks* 9 Down inside o' theirselves they're a-sayin' that ye ain't nothin' but a ol' dirty hillbilly. **1954** *GSMNP-19:25* Sometimes [the cattle] fall out of the pasture field because it was too steep. Once in a while they kill theirself. **1961** *Coe Ridge OHP-337A* They had the law to let them have guns to protect theyself. **1972** *AOHP/ALC-241* They'd just cover theirself someway. **1973** *AOHP/ASU-149* There wasn't nothing for young ones much to have fun out of, only just something they could do with theirselve. **1973** *GSMNP-1:36* I halfway believe that the people had it done theirselves. **1978** Montgomery *White Pine Coll* VI-2 The county went to furnishing them theirself. **1989** *Matewan OHP-33* He wouldn't give them nothing, just let them live theirself the best way they could. **2006** Childs *Texana* 32 The other one [was] so scared to go by theyself.

[OED3 at *theirselves* pron plural 1520→; EDD *theirselves* pron in general dialect use in Scot, Irel, Engl; DARE *theirselves* pron chiefly northern New England, South, South Midland]

theirselfs, theirselve, theirselves See **theirself.**

their'uns *pronoun* Their ones.

1976 Lindsay *Grassy Balds* 200 They kept their'uns up there [at] Hall Cabin, but they come back up to Silers Meadows too.

the last See **last² B.**

the like See **like C.**

them

A *demonstrative pronoun* Those, they.

1835 Crockett *Account* 99 The old saying, "them that don't work should not eat," don't apply to them. **1845** (in **1974** Harris *High Times* 52) Them that was sober enuff went home, and them that was *wounded* staid whar they fell. **1862** *Carter CW Letters* (May 9) bee good children and mind your mother for them is the sort that the good man loves. **1864** *Epperly CW Letters* (March 12) I think them that has worked hard to mak grain ort to have the good of it. **1901** Harben *Westerfelt* 101 Them's Cohutta men a-talkin'; you kin bet yore sweet life. **1913** Kephart *Our Sthn High* 17 Them's the outlandish. **1916** Combs *Old Early English* 290 *Them* is often used for *they*, as in "*Them's* the kind I like." **1922** *TN CW Ques* 72 (McMinn Co TN) Them that had slaves was idle and did no work. **1937** Hall *Coll* (Cosby Creek TN) Them's not peerch. Them's bass. **1952** Giles *40 Acres* 49 Them's the purtiest shoes . . . I wisht I had me a pair. **1961** Williams *Content Mt Speech* 15 "Them's gospel words," says Pol.

1973 GSMNP-79:1:24 You know, them looks a whole lot steeper and taller than they did in my young days. **1983** *Dark Corner OHP-4A* Them's mine in a way, and they're Dean's in a way. **1985** Irwin *Alex Stewart* 51 I was about eight or nine years old . . . and them was the first school books that ever I had. **1989** *Matewan OHP-9* [All] my granddaddy had to buy was sugar, coffee, and salt, and flour. Them's the only four things he had to buy. **2001** House *Clay's Quilt* 236 How long till them are done, Easter?

[DARE *them* pron B1 chiefly South, South Midland; also New England]

B *demonstrative adjective* Those.

1774 *Dunmore's War* 143 Them Stragling little partys will do Abundance of Damage. **1799** (in **2008** Ellison *High Vistas* 39) In so obscure a place that but few knows of it & them few only knows it as the paint rock. **1826** Royall *Sketches* 58 [They say] "put them *cheers*" (chairs) out of the road. **1847** (in **1870** Drake *Pioneer Life KY* 64) The new soils of Kentucky were not good for wheat, and the weevil, moreover, in "them days" (to speak in the dialect of the field), "done" great injury to that grain. **1861** (in **1980** Clark *Civil War Diary* 29) In capturing of them Yankeys we got 12 fine peices of artillery and a large amount of commissary's. **1863** *Sexton CW Letters* (Nov 12) you rote to me to send you a name for them children. **1884** Smith *Arp Scrap Book* 79 I would give a quarter to paddle them boys. **1939** Hall *Coll* (Deep Creek NC) They was just enough of us to fill them three benches. **1953** Hall *Coll* (Gatlinburg TN) The ones that went the other way into the mountain, they'd killed them turkeys. **1961** *Coe Ridge OHP-343A* He was killed in bed, in that house, right at the head of them steps. **1971** *AOHP/ALC-147* He got a yellow one of them old pack saddles on him once. He got stung with it. **1973** *Church of God* 13 Them pinto beans, they got a lot of acid in them. **1989** Landry *Smoky Mt Interviews* 194 I've went up over them rocks a many a time. **1992** Gabbard *Thunder Road* 36 So, when them son-of-a-guns checked me, I had to pay taxes on all that money. **1998** *Dante OHP-11* She used to come and belonged to my church. Yeah, I knew all of them people.

[OED3 *them* 8, regional and nonstandard; DARE *them* adj C 1 scattered, but chiefly South, South Midland; also New England]

C *pronoun* Used reflexively as indirect object (the so-called personal dative) = (for) themselves.

1953 Hall *Coll* (Bryson City NC) During the day, he said, a gang of turkeys come around in sight of the house, and he run his gun through a crack of the camp and killed one of them so's't they'd have them some turkey meat. **1961** *Coe Ridge OHP-333A* They bought this little tract, you know, the little one to have them a home. **1969** GSMNP-37:2:1 Well, they'd get them a preacher and let him preach a while. Then they'd change and get them another. **1972** *Hide Tanning* 183 [They would] then lay'em maybe a big rock on there an' let it lay there till it dried out. **1975** *Another Look* 140 If there's anything there, they'll take 'em a drink. **1979** GSMNP-118:19 They'd get 'em out honey. **1985** Irwin *Alex Stewart* 244 They'd take them an old basket in the fall of the year and go out in the woods and gather wild grapes. **1989** *Matewan OHP-28* He told them to buy them some clothes [so] that the shame of their nakedness didn't appear. **1990** *Matewan OHP-73* When they got to get them a charter and form them a union, they was tickled to death. **1993** Page and Smith *Foxfire Toys and Games* 49 I reckon every house where there were children had 'em a little ol' course laid out where you'd go [to shoot marbles]. **1998** *Dante OHP-71* He told the church to hunt them another pastor. **2005** Preece *I Grew* 85 They'd put them a quilt or two down on the concrete driveway that ran up beside the porch of the house to the kitchen.

[DARE *them* pron B 2 especially South, South Midland]

them air See **them there.**

them all *pronoun phrase* All of them.

1976 Miller *Mts within Me* 84 Double-barrelled pronouns—perhaps the most universally recognized mountain usage is the adding of suffixes of "uns" and "all" to pronouns; hence, we-uns, us-uns, you-uns, we-all, you-all, them-all.

them ar See **them there.**

them days *adverb phrase* At that time, (in) those days. See also **them times.**

1895 Dromgoole *Humble Advocate* 323 I ware not accounted a bad-lookin' gal nuther, them days. **1953** Shelton *Autobiog II* 6 We never met folks on roads or trails them days like we do nowadays. **1961** *Coe Ridge OHP-333A* Back them days five hundred dollars was a whole lot of money. **1972** *AOHP/LJC-104* They didn't have living rooms them days. **1989** *Matewan OHP-28* Back them days if you done wrong, they whipped you with a switch. *Ibid.* 33 We didn't have no union back them days awful they'd be the awfullest lot of people, right when you come through that underpass, right. **2003** Smith *Orlean Puckett* 36 He farmed the land, jus' like people did back them days.

the most See **the 5.**

themself (also *themselfs*) *pronoun* Themselves. See also **theirself.** For similar forms, see Grammar and Syntax §2.3.2.

1862 *Robinson CW Letters* (June 7) there has [b]in 2 of our Ridge ment shot them self on picket. **1864** *Chapman CW Letters* (n.d.) that is all the crope they hav in to them self. **1939** Hall *Coll* (Hazel Creek NC) They'd all go and enjoy themself. **1978** Montgomery *White Pine Coll* II-3 These arbitrary rules that people set up for themself, that's something else I don't like. *Ibid.* IX-4 I like to see young people try to make something of themselfs.

[OED3 *themself* now chiefly U.S. nonstandard, c1250→]

them there

A Variant forms *them air* [see **1996** in **B**], *them ar* [see **1867** in **B**], *them thar* [see **1923** in **B**].

B *adjective phrase* Those. See also **that there, this here.**

1864 *Chapman CW Letters* (April 13) I would like to see them ther foalk is all well. **1867** Harris *Sut Lovingood* 170 In three minits an' a 'alf arter I finish'd my 'sistin ove em by pullin them ar strings, hit wer all over scept the swellin, hurtin, an' gittin home. **1923** Greer-Petrie *Angeline Steppin' Out* 2 I must be on the lookout fur to see when every body got thoo eatin', and go out to the kitchen and wash up all them thar deeshes fur her. **1925** Furman *Glass Window* 130 Now hain't hit a picter, people? Look a-there at them-air blue eyes and rosy jaws and yaller curls. Hit's too pretty to live! **1963** Watkins and Watkins *Yesterday* 119 Give me some of them-air pills so's I can be a-chawing on em while you're biling the tea. **1969** GSMNP-37:2:5 Him and his brother, them there fellows come through here, stealing horses and things. c**1975** Lunsford *It Used to Be* 157 Two words often used together are "them there," such as: "Listen to them there youngins," or "Pass me some of them there molasses." **1983** *Dark Corner OHP*-5A The road was so muddy all them there lieutenants and captains would ride up to the side of that porch. **1996** Woodring *Times Gone By* 29 They'd ordered them air wolf biscuits, they called em, and put em around in bird's nestes and things and dogs ud get em and get poisoned. It'd kill em. **1998** *Dante OHP*-61 [The coal] run across air tables, them there tables that shook like that.

them times *adverb phrase* In those times. See also **them days.**

1970 *Burton-Manning Coll*-93B We wove, spun, and made, carded and spun and made our cloth with looms them times what we had to wear. **1975** *AOHP/ALC*-1128 It'd be real hard when the miners got killed back them times.

them'uns *pronoun* Those ones, them.

1918 Steadman *NC Word List* 19 = them. Probably due to analogy to *we'uns, you'uns*, which are much more common than themuns. **1969** Doran *Folklore White Co* 115 *them'uns* = those.

[cf SND *them yins* (at *yin* pron/adj 3)]

the one See **the 7.**

there *adverb*

A Variant forms *air, thar, thare* [ðaɚ], *thay, they* (the last two only to introduce a clause).

1801 (in **1956** Eliason *Tarheel Talk* 319) (Caldwell Co NC) *they*. **1861** (in **1980** Clark *Civil War Diary* 17) We got thare that night. **1862** *Watters-Curtis CW Letters* (Feb 15) We ar here at lebanon yet but thay is aprospect of us leving. *Ibid.* (Aug 22) we ar going to hav him Sent home if thar is any chance. **1890** Fruit *KY Words* 69 *thar*. **1895** Edson and Fairchild *TN Mts* 375 *thar*. **1913** Kephart *Our Sthn High* 12 Stop thar! Whut's you-unses name? **1937** Hall *Coll* (Ravensford NC) They used to be a puncheon floor in it, but my father tuck it up. **1939** Hall *Coll* (Proctor NC) [Did you organize a party for a hunt?] Yeah, we'd all just fix us up a sack of rations . . . and every feller would take his rations up thar. **1942** Hall *Phonetics Smoky Mts* 24–25 A number of old people, and a few others, still say [ðaɚ] *there*, a form which is preserved as a kind of fossil in [ovɚ'aɚ] *over there*, heard on Cosby Creek. **1961** *Coe Ridge OHP*-336A He stayed around thar so long, and he couldn't rest and he come back to this country. **1971** *AOHP/ALC*-260 He'd have plenty of visitors thare, and he could talk to them and get some votes. **1972** *AOHP/ALC*-241 My daddy I reckon come from air too. **1981** GSMNP-117:6–7 When he tuck a notion to whup a boy, he'd bring him up thar, and talk about the dust a-flyin', he'd whup the tar out of him. **1985** Irwin *Alex Stewart* 69 That Spring they come a demand for tanbark. **1998** *Dante OHP*-71 They had a farm, just a level farm thar up on that hill, but you couldn't get a car up in thar. c**1999** Sutton *Me and Likker* 31 I told him I couldn't do that or they would be a whole bunch of people after my ass for not saving them a jar of it.

[*they* Scottish form; cf SND (at *there* adv); CUD *they*[1]; HT "there"; DARE *there* adv, adj, pron A2 (pronc) chiefly South, South Midland]

B Syntax. See also Grammar and Syntax §16.

1 *they* used to introduce clauses, especially in form *they's* = there is, there has, there was (often regardless of the number of the subject or tense of the verb).

1774 *Dunmore's War* 99 These men tells me they are fresh Signs of Indians Seen Every Morning about the plantation at Forbes. **1863** *Councill CW Letters* (April 27) I am a fraide that They is somc-thing the matter in the famley. **1929** (in **1952** Mathes *Tall Tales* 99) Why, they's turpentine, balsam ile, an' corn liquor. **1937** Hall *Coll* (Mingus Creek NC) They never was but two doctors in my father's house. **1939** Hall *Coll* (Hazel Creek NC) They's a lot of hunting that's done in this country now. *Ibid.* (Little Cataloochee NC) They's been from twenty to twenty-five murdered people there. *Ibid.* (Smokemont NC) They come a big rain and washed the old foot bridge plumb into the hallway between the two barns. **1969** GSMNP-37:2:31 He was about the oldest man they was in here. **1978** Montgomery *White Pine Coll* VIII-1 They were lots of people carrying knifes and carrying steel bars to school. **1991** Thomas *Sthn Appal* 216 Well, they come a diphtheria outbreak through here one time, an' killed all th' children, nearly, in th' country. **1997** *Dante OHP*-14 The company had a dray, you know. They's mules, I believe, and somebody drove that dray and they'd bring our stuff.

2 *there, they* To introduce an existential clause that includes a singular form of a verb and a plural subject. See **be D2, have B3.**

the recipe See **(the) recipe.**

thereckly See **directly.**

therself, therselfs, therselves See **theirself.**

these here See **this here.**

these'ns (also *thesens*) *pronoun* These ones. See also **one 1.**

1936 Skidmore *Lift Up Eyes* 38 Four is bout all we can take care of times like these'ns. **1973** McCarthy *Child of God* 131 Is them all the watches you got? Just them three is all. Here. Hand him thesens back.

the Smoky, (the) Smoky Mountain See **(the) Smoky.**

the snubs See **snub.**

the sugar See **sugar 2.**

the t'other See **t'other 1**.

thew, th'ew See **through**.

the wife, the woman See **the 4**.

the worst See **(the) worst**.

the worst in the world See **(the) worst**.

they[1] See **there A, B1, B2**.

they[2] See **their**.

they[3] *interjection* Used as an exclamation of exasperation, surprise, or consternation. See also **eh la, la**.

1961 Williams *Content Mt Speech* 15 Thay, Lord! That little witty was as purty a baby up till hit was a set-along child as I ever laid eyes on. **1969** Doran *Folklore White Co* 98 When friends come, [a White Countian] may greet them in the driveway, if he has time to get there, saying, "Git right out of there and come in." If he knows visitors very well, he may say, "They, look what the cat drug in." **1971** *Granny Women* 261 I was might'near froze t'death when I got there. And th'wind a'blowin'—they, my goodness! **1973** *Flu Epidemic* 102 They, Lord. Now that's th'truth if ever I've said it. **1976** Thompson *Touching Home* 17 *they Lord* = a cry of surprise. **1981** Williams *Storytelling* "They Lord 'a mercy, there that there thing comes right behind us" (incidentally, *they* there means "thou"). **1992** Morgan *Potato Branch* 39 They lordy me. Them bulls tore down that fence and liked to kill each other. **1997** Frazier *Cold Mountain* 126 He soon stumbled over an old man sitting on a low stool and knocked him onto the floor. The man on the floor said, They damn. **2000** Carden *Mason Jars* 31 They, hush your mouth. **2005** Williams *Gratitude* 531 = an exclamation to express surprise or amazement, as: "They!" "They, gosh!" or "They, Lordymercy!" **2007** McMillon *Notes* They, good Lord. **2016** *Blind Pig* (March 30) It was also common to hear the expression of "they law" as a response to hearing something unbelievable or astounding.

[DARE *they* exclam especially NC, GA]

they all *pronoun phrase* [with stress on *they*] All of them (possessive form *theirs all*). For other forms with *all*, see Grammar and Syntax §2.7.1.

1969 GSMNP-42:10 Old man Lon and Will all, they all went with him.

[DARE *they-all* pron southern Appalachians, Ozarks]

they's See **there B1**.

theyself, theyselves See **theirself**.

they'uns *pronoun* Those ones. See also **one 1, us'uns, we'uns, you'uns**. [Editor's note: This form does not occur in ATASC.]

1895 Dromgoole *Fiddling to Fame* 47 They'uns flocked ter me lik crows flockin' ter a corn-field. **c1982** Young *Colloquial Appal* 28 They uns live back beyance Heartburn Hill. **1996** Montgomery *Coll* (known to Cardwell).

[DARE *they-uns* pron especially southern Appalachians]

thick as fiddlers in hell, as *adjective phrase* Crowded, close; chummy, intimate.

1967 Combs *Folk-Songs* 91–92 The simile "as thick as fiddlers in hell" is sometimes heard in the Highlands. A young Highlander initiated me into the mystery of its interpretation: "So thick that they can't move their bows back and forth." **1977** Wolfe *TN Strings* 17 The common expression "as thick as fiddlers in hell" ("so thick they couldn't move their bows back and forth") reflects an all-too-common reaction of southern Protestants toward fiddling: fiddling was equated with laziness, and laziness with sin. **1999** Montgomery *Coll* (known to Cardwell).

thick as four in a bed See **thick as two in a bed**.

thick as two in a bed (also *thick as four in a bed*) *adjective phrase* Of people: being very close or fast companions.

1942 Clark *Kentucky* 114 When a man says men are intimate friends, he says, "They are as thick as four in a bed." **c1945** Haun *Hawk's Done* 302 They always seemed to be about as thick as two in a bed. Pa always took up for him.

thick blood *noun* A folk medical diagnosis that a person has an excessive volume of morbid matter in the blood, a diagnosis based on the theory of humoral pathology, about which see 1992 citation and the entry "Folk Medicine" (pp. 866–68) in **2006** *Encycl Appalachia*. See also **high blood, low blood, thin blood**.

1992 Cavender *Folk Hematology* 28 It is believed that people with abnormally thick blood are more prone than others to having a heart attack or a stroke. According to folk theory, *thick blood* is more viscous due to having accumulated a lot of waste products, such as "fatty stuff" and other undefinable substances that the body, for various reasons, has not evacuated. Since the blood is laden with waste, it is greater in weight and, in some informants' view, greater in volume by displacement. Abnormally thick blood places stress on the heart and the circulatory system because its heaviness makes it more difficult to pump through the body. **2000** Lowry *Folk Medical Term* = blood that clots too quickly after a cut.

thicketty See **thickety**.

thickety (also *thicketty*) *adjective* Of a place: full of thickets, overgrown or tangled with vegetation; also used in place-names (see 1968 citation).

1925 Dargan *Highland Annals* 102 Jed Weaver had told me that old trail had got so thicketty a man would have to tie his eyeballs in if he come down it an' didn't lose 'em. **1939** Hall *Coll* The cave is hard to git to, hit's in such a thickety place. **1940** Still *River of Earth* 148 I saw the thickety slopes of Lean Neck Valley glisten in the morning sun. **1968** Powell *NC Gazetteer* 491 Thickety Creek rises in e Haywood Co and flows s[outh] into Pigeon River. **1974** Dabney *Mt Spirits* 13 If you can get a revenuer in a thickety place, it's no trouble to get away. **1982** Rives *Blue Ridge* 22 Sometimes one comes upon a lilac, now grown into a "thickety bush," a reminder of a mountain woman long ago who planted this bit of color and fragrance near her door.

[*thicket* + *-y*; cf *snaky*, *talky*]

thieving rod *noun* See citation.

1980 Riggleman *WV Mtneer* 126–27 [Loggers] usually had nicknames for everybody and everything around the camp. . . . A log scale was called a "thieving rod."

thiglum See **metheglin**.

thimbleberry *noun* The purple-flowering raspberry (*Rubus* spp).

1978 *Smokies Heritage* 169 Another berry member of the rose family is the raspberry, also known as the thimble-berry to early Smokies settlers. This strange nickname is derived from the raspberry's appearance, for it is a firm, seedy fruit that surrounds a hollow core, almost large enough to place on a person's thumb like a thimble.

thin blood *noun* A folk medical diagnosis that a person's blood is too thin and hence weak, a diagnosis based on the theory of humoral pathology. See citation and the entry "Folk Medicine" (pp. 866–68) in **2006** *Encycl Appalachia*. See also **high blood**, **low blood**, **thick blood**.

1992 Cavender *Folk Hematology* 31 According to most informants, old and young alike, *thin blood* was defined as having a watery consistency and lacking in essential properties. As with low blood, however, most informants were unsure as to what these essential properties are. Some said "red blood cells," some said "white blood cells," but most said simply they did not know. While they were uncertain as to what properties were lacking, there was near uniform agreement as to the symptoms of thin blood. In contrast to one who has abnormally thick blood, a thin blooded individual has a frail, emaciated body and pallid complexion.

thing *noun* Variant forms *thaing*, *thang*.

1861 *Dalton CW Letters* (Sept 31) mother idont no as I nead enny thaing at present If i nead enny thaing it was a blanket. **1862** *Carter CW Letters* (Aug 9) I wish I was thare to eat peachs and aples pies and other good thangs. **1935** (in **2009** Powell *Shenandoah Letters* 43) I'm very much surprised to get a thang like that. **c1950** (in **2000** Oakley *Roamin' Man* 80) They both have a big head and can bite like one thang. **1963** Edwards *Gravel* 7 He can't any more escape it than he can avoid saying "Thang" when he means "Thing." **1964** Williams *Prep Mt Speech* 53 *A* is sometimes used for what would seem to be rhythmical purposes: "and me a not a-knowin' a thang about it and a nuver a-cyurin' much." **1991** Thomas *Sthn Appal* 215 When one ov us 'ud take a cold, mother thought that'uz the best thang fer a cold that ever wuz, wuz cuckleburr tea.

[DARE *thing* n (pronc) especially South, South Midland]

(a) thing in the world *noun phrase* Anything at all.

1953 Hall *Coll* (Bryson City NC) So we went out the next day and run several bear and nobody killed a thing in the world. **1956** Hall *Coll* (Newport TN) The old woman, she was accused of being a witch. [She said] he wouldn't catch a thing in the world [on a hunting trip].

thingydo *noun* See citation.

2007 McMillon *Notes*: = an object unnamed.

think *verb*

A Forms.

1 Variant past-tense forms *thort*, *thunk* (usually jocular).

1861 *Griffin CW Letters* (Aug 3) I thort you had for goten us but you have not. **1867** Harris *Sut Lovingood* 33 I now thort I wer ded, an' hed died ove rhumatics ove the hurtines' kind. **1976** Garber *Mountain-ese* 94 I thunk about it fer a long time and finally made up my mind. **1997** Montgomery *Coll*: *thunk* (known to Bush, Cardwell, Jones, Ledford, Weaver). **1999** Montgomery *File* I thunk me a thought (85-year-old man, Gatlinburg TN).

[DARE *think* v B 2a chiefly South, South Midland]

2 Variant past-participle form *thunk* (usually jocular).

1991 Still *Wolfpen Notebooks* 51 I'd bet that in his head many a thought has been thunk.

[DARE *think* v B 2a chiefly South, South Midland]

B Variant first-person-singular form *thinks*, used in relating narrative action in the past (especially vicariously).

1866 Smith *So Called* 119 Thinks, says I to myself, this is a big thing certain, and I will invest my bottom dollar in this kind of money. **1973** *Carpenter* 122 I thinks t'm'self, "She don't need t'read such junk." **1974** Roberts *Sang Branch* 53 I thinks to myself, "Old fellow, if you come on up here, I'll drop you right there." **1985** Irwin *Alex Stewart* 156 I thinks to myself, "Now he's a gonna pull something on me."

C To remind (one).

1913 Kephart *Our Sthn High* 297 You think me of it in the mornin'. **1952** Wilson *Folk Speech NC* 600 = to remind one. "Jim, think me to go by your grandma's and get that pig." **1997** Montgomery *Coll* (known to Cardwell, Oliver).

[DARE *think* v C 1 South, South Midland]

think hard *verb phrase* See also **talk hard**.

1 To resent.

1814 Hartsell *Memora* 139 Judge White rote to Colonel Lillard that he hoped that he wold not think heard to Stay a few Days Longer. **1999** Montgomery *Coll* = to resent (known to Cardwell).

2 In phrases *think hard of*, *think hard on* = to view (someone) harshly or unkindly.

1863 *D B Walker CW Letters* (Aug 3) I think hard of him that he dont see to me geting letters. **1899** Fox *Mt Europa* 129 "I hope ye won't think hard on me," he continued; "I hev had a hard fight with the devil as long as I can ricolect." **1955** Ritchie *Singing Family* 82 She kept her a bottle of corn likker on her mantelpiece. Called it her tonic and she tuck her tonic regular every morning after breakfast. But nobody ever thought hard of her for that. **1999**

Montgomery Coll = to resent, think ill or unkindly of another person (Cardwell).

thinkingest *adjective* Pondering or thinking the most. See also **-est 1** and Grammar and Syntax §3.4.1.

1940 Haun *Hawk's Done* 43 Ad said Barshia was the thinkin'est boy in the world.

think on *verb phrase* To think of. See also **on B3**.

1883 Zeigler and Grosscup *Heart of Alleghanies* 61 I never hed no objections ter meetin' a varmint in a squar, stan'up fight,—his nails agin my knife, ye know; so without wunct thinkin' on gittin' outer the way, I retched fer my sticker. **1940** Haun *Hawk's Done* 5 Maybe it's because I've thought a heap on Letitia. *Ibid.* 6 It makes me feel peaceable as a full kitten just to set here and look at the Family Record page and think on all the names. **1954** Arnow *Dollmaker* 115 I told him everthing I could think on. **1976** Still *Pattern of Man* 33 "Knock and beat and battle is all you think on," she snorted.

[EDD *think* v 8 with *on* "to recollect, to bear in mind"]

think the sun rises and sets in *verb phrase* To admire, prize (someone).

1940 Haun *Hawk's Done* 29 She thought the sun riz and set in Amy.

third (also *third down*) *verb, verb phrase* To divide a **run** of homemade whiskey into three parts (the first being pure alcohol, the second ordinary whiskey, and the third **backings**) and then to blend the three into a more consistently potable product.

1956 Hall Coll (Mt Sterling NC) We'd third it down. Third it means cut it, you know, make it about a hundred proof. *Ibid.* (Hazelwood NC) They cleaned their still out real good. Then they thirded this liquid that they'd get, which was alcohol, whiskey, and backings.

third down See **third**.

this *adjective* These (before a quantifier).

1774 *Dunmore's War* 104 I keep the Scouts out continualy and has Seen no fresh Signs this four or five days. **1863** *Watters-Curtis CW Letters* (Summer) [I] hope and trust that this Few lins will find you and the Little Boy all well and in gouen Helth and all rite. **1936** Coleman *Dial N GA* 24 These phrases are of common usage . . . "this twenty year."

[OED3 *this* demonstrative determiner 5f; SND *this* adj II]

thisaway *adverb* (In) this direction or manner. See also **thataway.**

1861 Rogers *CW Letters* (June 24) Direct your letter this a way John Rogers Camp Davis LinchBurg VA Incear of Captain Higgins. **1863** *Lee CW Letters* (May 15) it is reported here that tha[y] is two hundred Thousan yankeys advansen on this A way. **1900** Harben *N GA Sketches* 186 "I kin see you think I'm a sight to behold," she laughed, merrily. "Sally fixed me up this-a-way." **1910** Weeks *Barbourville Word List* 457 *that-a, this-a* = that, this. "You should not talk that-a way." **1913** Kephart *Our Sthn High* 122 Jest thisaway. **1934–47** *LAMSAS Appal* = attested by 55/148 speakers (37.1%) from WV, 18/20 (90%) from VA, 31/37 (83.8%) from NC, 4/14 (28.6%) from SC, and 4/12 (33.3%) from GA. **1939** Hall Coll (Cataloochee NC) Old Uncle Steve Woody says, "I'll go around down thisaway below him and you go down in on him." **1956** Hall Coll (Roaring Fork TN) You go thataway and I'll go thisaway, and we'll whip them boys that are trying to scare us. **1969** GSMNP-27:9 I was a-laying on the bank watching them bees just out thisaway from where the mud hole was. **1985** Irwin *Alex Stewart* 271 wind won't hurt timber much. It will just spring thisaway and thataway. **1998** *Dante OHP-61* They had a vibrator on them, and they'd jump up and down and they had ridges across them thisaway.

[OED3 *this-a-way* adv 1, 2 dialect and U.S.; Web3 *thisaway* adv dialect; DARE *thisaway* adv scattered, but more frequent Atlantic, South, South Midland, TX]

this day a year *adverb phrase* One year from this day.

1942 Thomas *Blue Ridge* 327 I'll finish school this day a year. **1997** Montgomery Coll (known to Bush, Weaver).

this here (plural form *these here*) See also **that there.**

A *pronoun phrase* This.

1939 Burnett *Gap o' Mountains* 39 "I don't want to do it," Joe moaned, "and I hate to be hung, but this here is forced on me and I caint hep mysef." **1939** Hall Coll (Nine Mile TN) This here's the old residenter bear hunter, Fonze Cable. **1969** GSMNP-42:12 These here was on the inside there. **1973** *Foxfire Interviews* A-73-43 They get on this here here [sic] or something or other and cause this here to blight. **1991** Thomas *Sthn Appal* 136 He'uz a vet'inary doctor. But not registered like these here is now.

[OED3 (at *this* demonstrative determiner II 5i), now dialect or vulgar; EDD (at *this* demonstrative pron II.1.2)]

B *adjective phrase* This.

1867 Harris *Sut Lovingood* 173 The shakin an' jumblin ove this yere war ove ourn, hes fotch up tu the top ove the groun a new kine ove pisonus reptile. **1895** Edson and Fairchild *TN Mts* 372 These 'ere make-dos are no 'count. **1923** (in **1952** Mathes *Tall Tales* 3) The old man came with no soft gospel of compromise or tolerance toward the "onscriptural teachin's of these here Methodis' people up the creek." **1930** Armstrong *This Day and Time* 24 You ain't a-goin' to raw-hide these here knobs whilst I'm here. **1939** Hall Coll (Big Creek NC) This here beadwood bark, make hit for tea. Poke bark, they make hit for tea, for a bowel complaint. *Ibid.* (Cataloochee NC) We was in a laurel thicket, and Jack, he had a gun. He had one of these here hog rifles. Hit was a good'un too. **1967** Hall Coll (Townsend TN) This here'un is made out of metal. **1973** *Foxfire Interviews* A-73-43 Look here at this here'un. **1975** Chalmers *Better* 37 How true is the old saying in the mountains that "Men and dogs has it kindly easy in these here parts, but wimmen and steers has it mighty hard." **1979** Smith *White Rock* 12 There shore is strength in this here chicken broth. **1991** Thomas *Sthn Appal* 24 Then stir this 'yer buckwheat, ground, ur rye, in there with them cooked punkins.

this'un (also *this'n*) *pronoun* This one. See also **one 1**, **that'un**.

1901 Harben *Westerfelt* 18 Shorely he'll do a little some'n' in a case like this un. **1973** GSMNP-88 He came here in eighteen and seventeen and built another cabin and lived there, and then built this'un in later years. **1978** *Horsetrading* 46 Those other fellows up there had another big ol' bay horse that this'un would match. **1978** Montgomery *White Pine Coll* VI-2 Them old circuit riders had seven or eight churches, them Methodists did. Maybe this'un had preaching first, and then they'd have Sunday school, and then he'd go down here and preach. **2012** Jourdan *Medicine Men* 114 Boy, you have done took the cake with this'n.

thole *verb* To endure patiently, tolerate.

1940 Haun *Hawk's Done* 41 I would put a dip of snuff in my mouth and go and thole it the best I could. *Ibid.* 163 I thought I couldn't thole it when Ad and Linus first started selling off my stuff. **1944** Wentworth *ADD* 639 (WV) Can you thole the pain? [**1995** Montgomery *Coll* (unknown to consultants from the Smoky Mountains).]

[OED3 *thole* v 2 < Old English *þolian* "to suffer, hold out, endure" (Sweet), now northern dialect or archaic; EDD *thole* v 1 Scot, nEngl; SND (from Old Scots *thoill*) *thole* v 1; CUD *thole* v 1 "bear, endure"; HT *thole* "endure pain"; Web3 *thole* v chiefly dialect]

Thomson's eyewater See **eyewater**.

thoo See **through**.

thort See **think A1**.

those there See **that there**.

thoughted *adjective* Thoughtful, attentive. See also **unthoughted**.

1913 Kephart *Our Sthn High* 285 A verb may serve as an adverb [sic]: "If I'd a-been thoughted enough." **1994–97** Montgomery *Coll*: *thoughted* (known to Brown, Cardwell).

thoughty *adjective* Thoughtful, attentive.

1952 Justus *Children* 38 Uncle Bildad nodded in a thoughty manner. **1952** Wilson *Folk Speech NC* 601 = thoughtful, kind. **1975** Chalmers *Better* 66 Others were right thoughty about the ways of the country.

[EDD *thoughty* adj Scot; SND *tho(u)chty* (at *thocht* n 1.6); Web3 *thoughty* adj chiefly dialect; DARE *thoughty* adj 1 chiefly South Midland]

thousand-legged worm (also *thousand-leg(s)*) *noun* A millipede or centipede.

1929 Duncan and Duncan *Sayings* 235 See ah thousand leg: sign uv rain. **1957** Combs *Lg Sthn High: Word List* 101 *thousand-legged worm* = centipede. **1967** Wilson *Folkways Mammoth Cave* 42 If you see a millipede or thousand-legs, be sure to keep your mouth closed, for the critter might see and count your teeth and thus make them fall out. **1995** Adams *Come Go Home* 2 We had a run-in with a huge thousand-legs. Granny capped her hand over my mouth when we saw the thousand-legs, because if you show them your teeth, they'll every one rot out.

[DARE *thousand-legs* n scattered, but especially frequent South, Midland]

thout, thoutn See **without**.

thouten See **withouten**.

thow See **throw**.

thraish See **thrush**.

thrash See **thresh**, **thrush**.

thrash beans *noun* Beans dried in the pod so that they become easily separated from it.

2008 Salsi *Ray Hicks* 113 We just knowed we was a workin' our fingers to the bone tryin' to stay alive on what we growed. It was mostly 'taters, cabbage, squash, punkin, corn, apples, and thrash beans we dried for leather britches.

thrash doctor See **thrush doctor**

thrashers' day *noun* In the late 19th and early 20th centuries, a day on which a steam-driven engine came to a community to thrash each farmer's wheat in turn, providing an occasion to socialize and enjoy watching the machine at work.

1963 Medford *Mt People* 68 This occasion was the delight of every boy in the neighborhood; and it was just too bad if one had to go to school on the "thrashers' day."

thrash rock *noun* See citation.

1983 Broaddus *Estill Co KY Word List* 59 = a large, flat rock for threshing wheat. The wheat was piled on the rock where a horse trod on it.

three-foot(ed) plow *noun* A type of **bull tongue** plow. See also **foot B1**.

1986 Pederson et al. *LAGS* = attested by 3/60 interviewees (5%) from E TN; 3/3 of all LAGS interviewees (100%) attesting term were from Appalachia. **2003** LaLone et al. *Farming Life* 321 They had what they called three-footed plow, with these three little prongs that went through. The horse pulled. . . . What the three-footed plow didn't get out we had to go back and chop and pull around the corn.

three holer *noun* An outhouse with three seats. See also **one holer**, **two holer**.

1997 Montgomery *Coll* Bill has a three holer for his large family (Brown).

three pink kisses *noun phrase* See citation. See also **snake A1**.

1943 Korson *Coal Dust* 74 The miners applied humorous nicknames to marks which the different companies used to indicate indebtedness in payments. Some companies placed three red crosses where the statement read "balance due," and the miners called them "three pink kisses." When two lines were drawn straight down the statement to convey the same sad message, they referred to them as "a pair of rails," but if the lines spiraled, they were known as "snakes" or "corkscrews."

thresh *verb* Variant forms *thrash, thrush.*

1862 *Lockmiller CW Letters* (June 22) Hiram L miller is to thrush the Rye for the seventh part of hit. **1864** *Hill CW Letters* (Aug 6) you stated in the letter that you was still well and was Gitting along verry well and has got yor wheat thrashed. **1922** *TN CW Ques* 1386 (Wilkes Co NC) I worke on the farm plowing . . . thrashing with a frail braking flax. **1942** Hall *Phonetics Smoky Mts* 20 *Thresh* and *wrestle* are uniformly pronounced with [æ].

thrifty *adjective* Flourishing, thriving, fleshy.

1978 Hiser *Quare Do's* 2 We walked out to the stable, and he looked the cow over. The poor thing didn't look thrifty the way Pap's stock generally did. **2013** Reed *Medical Notes* = fleshy.

thrin *noun* One of a set of triplets.

1978 Hiser *Quare Do's* "We've got thrins," that Huze hollered as soon as he got close enough. None of us younguns had ever heard of a thrin, didn't even know what one was, and Grandpa was gone off in the War so we couldn't ask him. . . . "Yes, sir," he told us proudly, "yore granny fetched us three little wild babies, boys, over to our place Saturday night: Billman, Tillman, and Willman, the woman named them: and we thought she done such a good deed we give her a fowl for each little feller, and a shoat for the whole bunch. First thrins ever was borned in the whole country fur as I can hear tell of." "What's a thrin?" I asked. "You know what a twin is," Granny said, taking her apron down off the peg and tying it around her waist, "when two of them are born together, one of them is a twin. Well, when three comes at once, one is a thrin. Yes, Deb Neace birthed thrins a Saturday night."

[Web3 *thrin* n dialect]

throan See **throw 2**.

throde See **throw 3**.

throng *adjective* Occupied, busy.

1924 Raine *Saddlebags* 101 I've been very throng today.

[DARE *throng* adj especially PA]

through

A Variant forms *thew, th'ew, thoo, th'ough, th'u.*

1862 *Hawn CW Letters* (July 7) we marched very hard the day marched up thew [the] valey at night. **1891** Brown *Dialect in TN* 171 S'rink is used for shrink, and th'ough for through. **1923** Greer-Petrie *Angeline Steppin' Out* 1 The keenest spitter that ever lived couldn't spit thoo four doors all jined together and whirlin' round at onct. **1942** Hall *Phonetics Smoky Mts* 90. **1956** Hall *Coll* (Townsend TN) They had a shootin' match down there at Lizzie Penfield's. Lizzie's boy Dan shot Bill Hedges, blowed a hole right th'u him. **1984** Burns *Cold Sassy* 35 If'n she don't pull th'ew, I ain't go'n say it was Thy will. **1996** GSMNPCOHP-1:4 There's trees over there that's two foot th'u.

[DARE *through* adv, prep 1 (pronc) chiefly South, South Midland]

B *adverb* See **break through**, **come through**, **pray through**, **pull through**.

C *noun*

1 In phrases *cut a through, have a through, take a big through* = to experience a spate or fit of emotion or sensation, especially of religious euphoria at a revival meeting.

1861 *Patton CW Letters* (Sept 14) Our company has had a prety good threw of the chills for the last week or too. **1905** Miles *Spirit of Mts* 3 Confinement for an hour or two, with songs and the imminent expectation of somebody's "takin' a big through" of religious excitement to break the monotony, is not supportable. **1913** Kephart *Our Sthn High* 283 Nance tuk the biggest through at meetin'! **1917** Kephart *Word-List* 418 = spasm. "I take a big *through* o' sneezin' every day." **c1945** Haun *Hawk's Done* 240 He fussed if she made big biscuits, and he cut a through if she made little biscuits. **1976** Dwyer *Southern Sayin's* 25 = ungovernable shouting, ecstasy, bodily contortions. "She took the biggest through at the church." **1994–97** Montgomery *Coll*: *through* (known to Adams, Brown, Bush, Cardwell, Jones). **1996** Dykeman *Memories* What if I was to cut a through like that at preachin' again and dropped my bean seed?

[DARE *through* n 2 southern Appalachians]

2 A trip or pass from one end of a field to the other in harvesting grain.

1862 *L Jones CW Letters* (Aug 9) [I] dont no when I will get out of the ware for it goes slow for it is A big throug[h] to wead and wee cant get along fast with it shore. **1890** Fruit *KY Words* 66 = the number of rows worked by a set of hands through a tobacco field. To illustrate: Seven hands will take fourteen rows at a through, working from one side of a field to the other: "Did you finish that last through?" **1941** Stuart *Men of Mts* 179 Twenty men gathered to hoe Wilburn's corn. We took twenty rows of corn at a time . . . "Twenty rows of corn at a through," said Uncle Hankas. **1992** Jones and Miller *Sthn Mt Speech* 114 He cut two rows of corn at a through. **1995–97** Montgomery *Coll* (known to Brown, Cardwell, Jones).

3 Same as **dogtrot**.

1927 Furman *Lonesome Road* 106 In the open "through" between the two big front rooms or "houses" was a table, and on it a bucket holding what Jared first supposed to be water, but, on raising some of it to his lips in the gourd, he spat it out hurriedly; it was the finest and fieriest of corn-liquor.

through cut *noun* A short cut. See also **cut C1**, **near cut**, **nigh cut**.

1957 GSMNP-23:1:9 My daddy used to come through here. They had a through cut, a road through there.

throw *verb* Principal parts

1 Variant infinitive/base forms *thow, th'ow.*

1862 *Robinson CW Letters* (June 22) we had to pack our nap Sacks before that & was orderd to thow away ever thing but 2 paire pants 2 Slips 2 Shirts &1 blanket. **1890** Fruit *KY Words* 69 He can't th'ow any distance. **1936** (in **1952** Mathes *Tall Tales* 206) I'll he'p you-uns th'ow this tree an' then I want both of ye to he'p me. **1939** Hall *Coll* (Cataloochee NC) That's the nature of a turkey, to th'ow its head up. **1942** Hall *Phonetics Smoky Mts* 90. **1973** Miller *English Unicoi Co* 82 = attested by 4 of 6 speakers. **1998** *Dante OHP-61* He'd pull [the coal cars] back up above the switch and thow the switch and take them back to Spark Track on the side track.

[DARE *throw* v A1 chiefly South, South Midland]

2 Variant past-tense forms *thowed, throan, throwd, throwed.*

1834 (in **2003** *TN Petitions II* 208) They throwed down my house from over my property turnd my family out off doors exposed my property to the weather in my absence. **1861** *Carden CW Letter* (Oct 6) We lost one man out of our Co., John Martain. He died with the fever. there cannons throwed Afew bums. **1862** *Dalton CW Letters* (Feb 21) we throan on Hour coutrements and fel in And march about a half a mile And forme aline of battle. **1862** *Robinson CW Letters* (June 28) I exspect tha[y] thowd part of my clothes away. **1873** Smith *Arp Peace Papers* 111 [He] throwd mud on him, and drug him about and rubbed sand in his eyes. **1901** Harben *Westerfelt* 58 Then Toot laughed an' thowed it down and shook his fists at 'im. **1913** Kephart *Our Sthn High* 284 In many cases a weak preterite supplants the proper strong one: . . . drawed, growed, knowed, throwed. **1931–33** (in **1987** Oliver and Oliver *Sketches* 24) He told her that he had found the Lord and was happy and that he wanted her to seek the Lord and be happy too and throwed his arms around her. **1934–47** *LAMSAS Appal* (Madison Co NC, Swain Co NC). **1939** Hall *Coll* (Little Cataloochee NC) They drug them out just a few steps from the trail and throwed them in a sink hole. **1940** Oakley *Roamin'/Restin'* 52 I throwed the razor away. **1961** *Coe Ridge OHP-339A* He throwed his daddy down, and his daddy beat him to the house. **1971** *AOHP/ALC-107* [He] took this coal and shoveled this coal up, thowed up and built me a wall and then building that wall up there. **1978** Montgomery *White Pine Coll* VIII-2 [The creature] has thowed a stick at us before, for disturbing it. **1979** *Big South Fork OHP-18* That boy killed him and drug him off and throwed him over a little clift. **1989** *Matewan OHP-7* I played [baseball] until I throwed my arm out of circulation.

3 Variant past-participle forms *threw, throde, throwed.*

1861 (in **1938** Taliaferro *Carolina Humor* 19) Lazy Ephraim will be throwed sky high off uv his back, *co-whallop*, ah! **1863** Wilson *Confederate Private* 26 (July 12) I had rote a leter for you at glade springs and throde of the rong leter. **1973** *GSMNP-84*:29 They was an old abandoned house, an old big log house down here in an old big field, great big farm, that had been throwed out and growed up. **1978** Montgomery *White Pine Coll* VIII-1 One year a brick got threw through somebody's windshield. *Ibid.* X-2 Maybe it had been throwed off down there or something. **1980** Miles *Verbs in Haywood Co* 91 That's just one that's throwed together. **2010** Owenby *Trula Ownby* 17 Somebody had threw a cigar butt down and he had picked it up and smoked it.

throwd See **throw 2.**

throw down *verb phrase* To relinquish, give (something) up.

1993 Cunningham *Sthn Talk* 160 I use to be the biggest drunkard there ever was, but I throwed it down. **1997** Montgomery *Coll* (known to Bush, Weaver).

throwed See **throw 2, 3.**

-throwed *participial adjective* Used in compound adjectives **horse-throwed, wind-throwed,** etc.

1904–20 Kephart *Notebooks* 2:475 He was horse-throwed, and lit on a stob, and hurt his shoulder. **1913** Kephart *Our Sthn High* 77 Several trees has been wind-throwed and busted to kindlin'. **1974** Fink *Bits Mt Speech* 29 All the big trees was *wind throwed.* **1994–97** Montgomery *Coll: horse-throwed* (known to Brown, Cardwell, Ellis, Oliver, Weaver); *wind-throwed* (known to Cardwell).

throw it over the hill *verb phrase* To go home.

1997 Montgomery *Coll* It's time for me to throw it over the hill (Norris).

throw knives *verb phrase* See citation.

c1960 Wilson *Coll* = to exchange knives, "sight unseen."

throw off on *verb phrase* To belittle, ridicule, speak disparagingly of (someone).

1915 Pollard *TN Mts* 243 = to make fun of; also, to say uncomplimentary things about. He threw off on me something awful when I wore them. **1921** Campbell *Sthn Highlander* 111 If I get into trouble, even if I am not to blame, there is no use of going to law if the judge is kin to the other side, or if the lawyer has succeeded in getting his own men on the jury, it doesn't make any difference what the evidence is, the case goes the way they want it to go. Then there is nothing for me to do but to accept, and let them throw off on me as a coward, if I stay in the country. **1937** Hall *Coll* (Big Creek NC) She was throwing off on me. **1939** Bond *Appal Dialect* 111 = to slander; speak poorly of someone. **1951** Miller *Pigeon's Roost* (May 31) This is not written to throw off on anybody, as I do read all the news the paper contains, but I first look for Sinclair Conley and Ethel Edwards' writing. **c1959** Weals *Hillbilly Dict* 8 = ridicule, make fun of. "They throwed off on her somethin' awful for wearin' sich a mini dress." **1967** *DARE Survey* (Gatlinburg TN) = to say uncomplimentary things about another person. **1973** Kahn *Hillbilly Women* 97 It was sort of hard when I first moved here cause people was all the time calling me a hillbilly or throwing off on the way I talked. **1989** *Matewan OHP-18* I don't preach at these other preachers. I don't throw off on them. That's up to them and God, I get along with all these preachers. **2008** McKinley *Bear Mt* 92 They'd "throw off" on Mrs. Trussell and say she must be "awful trifling" to sleep the day away like that—and told everybody just how "no good" she was!

[DARE *throw off* v phr 4 South, South Midland]

throw one's hoe over in the weeds *verb phrase* To put aside one's work in favor of having a meal.

1987 Young *Lost Cove* 35 Most of the no-counts and others who frowned on hard work had already *thrown their hoes over in the weeds* and got in line for free vittles.

throw over *verb phrase* To abandon, quit (as a job or a suitor).

1956 Still *Burning of Waters* 55 Father had thrown over his job, bought steel traps and gun shells and provisions, including a hundred-pound sack of pinto beans. **c1960** Wilson *Coll* = to jilt.

throw the hatchet *verb phrase* To tell a lie, exaggerate the truth.

c1940 Aswell *Glossary TN Idiom* 18 = to lie. "He can't open his mouth without *throwing the hatchet*." **1984** Wilder *You All Spoken* 116 = exaggerate; tell lies; extend the truth. **1996–97** Montgomery *Coll* (known to Brown, Cardwell).

[DARE *throw the hatchet* v phr especially southern Appalachians]

throw up (also *throw up to*) *verb phrase* To mention (especially in a spiteful way).

1901 Harben *Westerfelt* 241 He has deliberately insulted you by throwing up a delicate matter to you, which God knows you couldn't help. **1930** Armstrong *This Day and Time* 141 You'd best be a-lookin' atter your own affairs, place o' throwin' up Uncle Abel to me. **1940** Haun *Hawk's Done* 50 He throwed it up to Marthy that she didn't try to get things for him. *Ibid.* 144 Anywhere else their youngons would have had it throwed up to them that their pa had been in the penitentiary. **1957** Neel *Backwoodsman* 43 = to remind one of shady dealings or actions in the past, usually in hot argument: "I throwed it up to him how he usta do!" **c1960** Wilson *Coll* = to recall spitefully what someone said or did. **1997** Montgomery *Coll* (known to nine consultants from the Smoky Mountains). **2001** House *Clay's Quilt* 186 You throwing it up to me that I never kilt him?

thrush *noun* See also **thresh**.

A Variant forms *thrash* [see **1935** in **B**].

B A fungal infection of the mouth (specifically oral moniliasis) in infants, which according to traditional belief could be cured only by a **thrush doctor**. See 1970 citation. Also called **baby mouth**, **white mouth**.

1897 Pederson *Mtneers Madison Co* 828 To cure white thrush in a baby's mouth, let someone who never saw its father blow in its mouth. **1935** Farr *Riddles and Superstitions* 330 A baby will never have thrash if he is carried over water before he is three days old. **1961** Seeman *Arms of Mt* 34 Pity the puny infant with the "thrash." **1970** Adams *Appal Revisit* 43 It was a common superstition to believe that certain people had the power to blow in a baby's mouth and cure the "thrash" or mouth sores. A posthumous person had this power if he was born without seeing his father; that is, born after the death of his father. The seventh son borne by a woman in seven years had this power. Many mothers took their children to certain people and had them blow in the mouth to cure the thrash and other ailments. **1981** Brewer *Wonderment* 29 One day she had met a woman who had taken her baby far up the branch to have a man blow in its mouth to cure the "thrash." **2005** Williams *Gratitude* 53 The thrash (thrush) [is] a fungal infection where a white coatin' forms in patches on the inside of the mouth and back of the throat.

thrush doctor *noun* A folk healer who can purportedly cure **thrush** in an infant by blowing into the infant's mouth.

1968 *Faith Healing* 18 Doctors tell [that] everybody goes to 'em with a baby with th' thrash t'go hunt'em up a thrash doctor. **1972** Cooper *NC Mt Folklore* 17 Thrush Doctors were men who had never seen their fathers, and they blew their breaths into a baby's mouth to cure the thrush. If no real Thrush Doctors were available, it was thought that the baby's drinking a few drops of water from the shoe of a blackeyed young man would work a cure. **1997** Montgomery *Coll* (known to Cardwell, Ledford, Norris, Weaver), = could also be a woman (Bush), = tradition was that the seventh son of a seventh son had this power (Jones), = said to be cured by a man who was born with a cowl [= caul] over his face blowing down the throat of the infant (Oliver). **2003** Cavender *Folk Medicine* 120 Various individuals were thought to have an inherent power to cure thrash by blowing into the baby's mouth. These "thrash doctors" came to their healing role by being a seventh son or daughter, the son of a seventh son, or someone who "never looked into the eyes of his father."

th'u See **through A.**

thug *noun* An armed guard hired to police a coal camp, sometimes deputized by local authorities. Same as **gun thug**. See also **Baldwin thug**.

1973 Kahn *Hillbilly Women* 31 The thugs made my mind up for me right off, which side I was on. *Ibid.* 91–92 Sometimes after that he'd have to go off up there in the mountains with the other miners. The thugs would try to catch them and make them come out.

thump See **thump barrel**.

thump barrel (also *thump*, *thump chest*, *thumper*, *thumping chest*, *thump keg*, *thump tank*) *noun* In distilling, a second **condenser** added to a whiskey **still** between the **cooker** and the **coil**, eliminating the need to run liquor through a second time to strengthen it. Also called **doubler**. See also **doubling**, **singling(s)**.

1912 Mason *Raiding Moonshiners* 199 Some cut wood, others stirred mash, while one well-known desperate character plastered the "thumper" and retort ready for business. **1913** Kephart *Our Sthn High* 136–38 It is possible to make an inferior whiskey at one distillation, by running the singlings through a steam-chest commonly known as a "thumpin' chist." . . . Two and a half gallons is all that can be got out of a bushel [of corn] by blockaders' methods, even with the aid of a "thumpin'-chist." **1939** Hall *Coll* To turn fermented mash into steam, which is condensed in a cooling tank into liquor, the first run is known as "singlin's": the second is "doublin's." The second run is by-passed by the use of the "thump tank." *Ibid.* (Cades Cove TN) I don't like a thump a-tall . . . I would rather have singlin's than doublin's. *Ibid.* (Emerts Cove TN) That thump keg, it takes the place of the . . . singling and doubling. The old times didn't have that. **1949** Maurer *Argot of Moonshiner* 13 The term thumper or thump keg derives from the putt-putt thumping noise caused by steam in the keg. **1969** DARE

Survey (Dillard GA) The thump barrel was also known as the doubling barrel or the doubler. . . . The thump barrel sets between your condenser and your still—it doubles the whiskey; you put backings or beer in this barrel. **1972** Carr *Oldest Profession* 104 The thump keg or doubler became the moonshiner's pride and joy, although the remark is still heard to this day from some of the old moonshiners: "I don't want nary a thing to do with that new-fangled thumper keg, I'd druther do hit the ole' way." **1972** *Foxfire I* 323 Perhaps the most revolutionary addition was the thump barrel. Steam bubbling up through the fresh beer in this barrel was automatically doubled thus removing forever the necessity of saving the singlings and running them through again to double their strength. *Ibid.* 325 From this barrel . . . the steam moves into the long thump rod . . . which carries it to the bottom of the fifty-gallon thump barrel . . . and releases it to bubble up through the fresh beer . . . Picked up again at the top by the short thump rod . . . the steam moves into the heater box. **1974** Dabney *Mt Spirits* xxv *thump barrel* = also known as the doubler, thumper, or thump keg. This container is charged with fresh beer or backings. Vapors from the pot bubble through, giving a second distillation called "thump likker." *Ibid.* 110 [By the 1920s] someone in the hills had already invented the "thumper" keg, which eliminated the time-consuming second distilling step. The thumper, usually fifty gallons in size, is placed between the cooking pot and the condenser, and filled with beer. Hot water sent vapors bubbling up from the pot through a thumper. Beer produced a second distillation in the keg along with a rhythmic thumping sound. *Ibid.* 125 You just emptied it [= the beer] from the pot into the heater box . . . and in not over two minutes the thumper would go to thumpin' and the whiskey would start flowin' from the worm. **1985** Dabney *More Mt Spirits* 169 Just about the most common addition is the "thump keg," or thumper (sometimes called the "thump chest" or doubler), usually a 55-gallon barrel or steel drum, which is placed between the distilling kettle and the condenser. It thumps like crazy at the beginning of a run. By filling this keg partway up with distiller's beer, or low-proof whiskey called "backins" from a previous run, the thumper serves as a "doubler," giving the whiskey a second distillation, making it "doubled" whiskey without a second run. **2007** Rowley *Moonshine!* 163 *thump keg* = an airtight container sometimes placed between a boiler and condenser of a pot still that increases the proof of a single run, eliminating the need to do a double run. The thump keg is charged with beer, feints, or backins. Hot vapors enter from under the beer's surface, heat it, and produce higher proof vapors that exit to the condenser. **2013** Pierce *Corn in Jar* 47–48 In addition to the aggregation of small stills and the increasing size of some blockade operations, local and state prohibition brought in the early 20th century led to at least one significant change in the whiskey-making process: the addition of the "thump keg." The "thump keg," or "doubler," was a barrel or keg placed between the still and the condenser. Fresh beer and/or backings were poured into the thump keg and the alcohol vapor from the still ran by pipe to the bottom of the barrel where it bubbled up through the beer and out the top through another pipe and into the condenser.

[DARE *thump barrel* n chiefly southern Appalachians]

thump chest, thumper, thumping chest, thump keg See **thump barrel.**

thump liquor (also *thump whiskey*) *noun* See 1974 citation. Same as **doubling 2.**

1968 *End of Moonshining* 101 Names given moonshine include . . . thump whiskey. **1974** Dabney *Mt Spirits* xxv [The thump barrel] container is charged with fresh beer or backings. Vapors from the pot bubble through, giving a second distillation called "thump likker."

thump post (also *thump rod*) *noun* The pipe conveying steam to the bottom of the **thump barrel.**

1972 *Foxfire I* 325 From this barrel . . . the steam moves into the long thump rod . . . which carries it to the bottom of the fifty-gallon thump barrel . . . and releases it to bubble up through the fresh beer . . . Picked up again at the top by the short thump rod . . . the steam moves into the heater box. **1985** Dabney *More Mt Spirits* 113 One-inch holes must be bored on each side of the top of this [= thump keg], one for the insertion of the "thump post" and the other for insertion of the "headache piece." A ½-inch hole should be bored in the side of the bottom to draw the "feints" out, after a run. **c1999** Sutton *Me and Likker* 106 = a pipe that goes down in the thump keg with a notch cut out to let the steam through. You put about 4 or 5 gallon of backins in the thump keg for vapors to filter through on the first run. You have to use still beer but after that you run you some extra backins to charge the thump keg with. It makes the likker come out more clear if you use backins.

thump rod See **thump post.**

thump tank See **thump barrel.**

thump whiskey See **thump liquor.**

thunder and lightning and the dogs a-barking *noun* The "fireworks" in a hard-run political campaign.

1963 Hooper *Unwanted Boy* 75 The Regular Democratic Organization [in Oct 1910], having revamped its ticket, determined to put on what the Germans now call a blitzkrieg. As the mountain folks sometimes say, they figured on having "thunder and lightnin' and the dogs a-barkin'."

thunderation

A *interjection* Used as a mild oath to express annoyance or vexation.

1936 Carpenter *WV Expletives* 347 Vexation for many, many years has manifested itself in West Virginia in: Thunderation; Murderation; Shucks. **1956** McAtee *Some Dial NC* 46 = exclamation of annoyance. **1962** Wilson *Folkways Mammoth Cave* 44 Substitutes for *hell* and its idea [included] *thunderation.*

B *noun* See citation.

1989 Still *Rusties and Riddles* [94] = loud talk.

thunderbuster *noun* A thunderstorm.

1997 Johnson *Melungeon Heritage* 13 Our parents didn't know it, but sometimes I prayed lustily for a "thunder-buster" so we wouldn't have to work in the terrible heat.

thunder dog (also *thunderslut*) *noun* A type of large salamander. Same as **waterdog**.

1982 Slone *How We Talked* 111 (or *water dog*) = a small, worm-like animal that lives in the water. We were told that if one bites you, it would not let go until it thundered or a cow bawled. I don't think they bit at all. **1997–98** Montgomery *Coll* = a large salamander. It was believed that they came to the surface after a thunderstorm. A more common term than *water dog* (Bush), = so called because it made a loud splash where entering the water (Cardwell). **2001** Liftig *Lessons* 15 I learned many of the most fundamental concepts of biology, botany, hydrology, and geology—though we didn't have the scientific vocabulary to go with them. No, we learned the names Granny and Mommy taught us, like "waterdogs," "thundersluts," and "snake doctors" . . . "Don't catch salamanders and hold them because if they bite you, they won't turn you loose until it thunders—so folks up and down Ganderbill called them thundersluts."

[DARE *thunder dog* n southern Appalachians]

thunderheads *noun* Large cumulus clouds that portend a storm. See also **boil C**, **bread wagon**.

1937 Hall *Coll* (Cades Cove TN) Hear them thunderheads a-bilin'. **1939** Hall *Coll* (White Oak NC) Look at them thunderheads a-bilin' up. **1966–68** *DARE Survey* (Brasstown NC, Cherokee NC, Spruce Pine NC, Gatlinburg TN, Maryville TN) = big clouds that roll up high before a rainstorm.

thunder mug (also *thunder pot*) *noun* A chamber pot for night-time toileting use.

c1950 (in **2000** Oakley *Roamin' Man*) 51 Heare was the order my dady [sic] give me, 2 pounds of Arbuckle green coffee, 5 pounds of sugar, 15 cts. box of matches and a thunder pot with lid. **1957** Neel *Backwoodsman* 43 = euphemism for chamber pot. **2004** Myers and Boyer *Walker Sisters* 32 If a family member or their guests found it necessary to answer nature's call during the night, he or she used a yellow (yaller) "thunder mug." Since families did not have indoor plumbing, a thunder mug was a necessity. **2013** Patton *Go Back* 5 I want to see the yaller "thundermugs" drying in the sun back of the kitchen. **2015** *Blind Pig* (Nov 12) When he was a little boy he always had to clean out the thunder pot. He's so weak stomached he'd gag all the way outside and back.

thunder pot See **thunder mug**.

thunder road *noun* A route taken by **bootleggers** on their way to deliver a load of **moonshine**, speeding in high-powered cars and often at night with headlights off to evade law-enforcement officers. For an account of the original route, see 2016 citation.

1992 Gabbard *Thunder Road* 81 After the war, '45 and '46 Fords, followed by the much sleeker '49 and '50 Fords, saw so much duty on southern highways as moonshine vehicles that they gave rise to the term "thunder road" for the roads they were used on. **2005** McCrumb *St. Dale* 393 After all, stock car racing started on Thunder Road in western North Carolina and eastern Tennessee. **2009** Pipes *Free People* 2 The trip to one of the highest points on the east coast began on Gay Street in Knoxville [and] then across the Henley Street bridge and down Chapman Highway (known locally as the famed "thunder road"). **2016** Simmons *Legends & Lore* 61 "Thunder Road" was the real code name given by the feds to an overall operation to shut down moonshiners and bootlegging ridge-runners in the Appalachian Mountains. Locals used the term to refer to a route that originated in Harlan County, Kentucky, and then made its way through Claiborne and Union Counties in Tennessee on into the city of Knoxville.

thunderslut See **thunder dog**.

thunderwood *noun* A poison sumac (*Toxicodendron vernix*).

1986 Pederson et al. *LAGS* = attested by 3/35 (8.6%) from N GA; 3/17 of all LAGS interviewees (17.6%) attesting term were from Appalachia; Franklin Co GA, Gwinnett Co GA, Rockdale Co GA.

[DARE *thunderwood* n 1 South, especially GA]

thunk See **think A1**, **A2**.

thur See **their**.

tick *noun* The heavy fabric casing of a mattress or pillow, filled with straw, corn husks, feathers, leaves, or other resilient material that is replaced or cleaned periodically; sometimes the casing and the material within it. Same as **bed tick**. See also **featherbed tick**, **flock tick**, **shuck bed**, **straw tick**, **ticking**.

1883 Jones *Highlands N Carol* 379 Our beds are striped ticks filled with straw, and, as we drop into sound refreshing slumber as soon as we retire, we have never perceived that they are not woven wire or curled hair. **1948** Dick *Dixie Frontier* 301 Ticks were filled with cattails or oak leaves until enough corn or wheat was raised to fill them with shucks or straw. **1951** Hodges *Handicrafts* 7 Ropes to form a support for the "tick," or mattress were made out of the tough outer fiber or flax they raised. **1955** Dykeman *French Broad* 51 Some [settlers] came on horseback, but where there was a family, it was rare that all could ride, although a few necessities—on the pack horse—were added . . . bedding, maybe, blankets and empty ticks which could be filled with leaves or, later, straw and feathers—a froe, an extra skillet of iron, eating utensils, hoes and plowpoints and an auger. **1977** Shields *Cades Cove* 22 All the old straw was dumped out and the bed tick was washed and dried and stuffed anew with the fresh straw. **1977** Stanley *Tough* 33 The tick, we called it, which was the same thing as a mattress in this day—you take a large piece of material, sew it up and make a sack out of it. And then you could fill that either with feathers or straw [oat or rye straw]. Some people filled them with corn shucks. And then you would put this tick on those ropes. It didn't make a good bed at all. It was lumpy. **1979** Slone *My Heart* 52 = a large cloth bag filled with corn shucks, was a mattress. **1989** Oliver *Hazel Creek* 18 Bed ticks were filled with, at first, dry grass and later with corn shucks (noisy and lumpy) or with straw.

1997 King *Mt Folks* 93 Making beds in earlier years was no easy task. Ogle tells that some of the beds they made had a tick filled with straw for the bottom mattress and one filled with feathers on the top to make the mattresses more comfortable for the next night's sleep. Every day the straw was stirred by hand and her mother beat the feather mattress with a broom. . . . In the spring and fall, women emptied the straw ticks. "We'd dump the straw and wash the ticks and head to the big straw stack (to fill them up again)," Ogle said.

tick bag *noun* A small bag made of heavy fabric material.

2008 Salsi *Ray Hicks* 21 The tiniest scraps of fabric was put into a tick bag to use for patchin' up clothes or for makin' quilts.

ticket *noun* A slip of paper on which a Bible verse and the name of an accused person are written, used to counter a spell. See citations.

2007 Milnes *Signs Cures Witches* 78 The spells might be curses or other forms of hexing (German for witching) put on innocent people by witches. Dovie's methods are forms of imitative magic. A "ticket," for instance, is prepared and harmed in some way, and this, through this thought process, causes harm to the perpetrator. (A ticket is simply a piece of paper on which a certain Bible verse is written along with the accused person's name, if known. It is always finished with an invocation of the Father, Son, and Holy Ghost.) . . . "Now, the best way to get rid of a witch is to write you a ticket and go to the white oak tree and bore you a hole. Put that in there and take an iron rod, push in there and [slaps her hand on an imaginary rod]. It'll hurt 'em. If it don't kill 'em, it'll hurt 'em. Now that's what [a man] done to [a baby]. And [a woman's] daddy was the one puttin' the spell on the baby. It wasn't, I think about three days, he died. [The man] just [by following this formula] knocked him flat." *Ibid.* 82 Dovie says that to make a ticket one need only have a scrap of paper on which you write a Bible verse: Get thee behind me, Satan: thou art an offense unto me: for thou savourist not the things that are of God, but those that be of men (Matt. 16:23). Then, she says, you write the person's name and "Father, Son, and Holy Ghost," referred to as the "three highest names." Once written, some physical harm is done to the ticket.

ticking *noun* The coarse fabric used to make a **tick**; the material (straw, feathers, etc.) encased to form a mattress. [Editor's note: This term and **tick** are apparently used interchangeably by some speakers.]

1796 Dunlap *Will* Allow my wife to have the loom and tickings, and they are to be at her disposal. **1931** Greve *Tradition Gatlinburg* 71 Some of the older men today tell of helping their mothers break the flax in their childhood; it was macerated in water until soft, the tough, outer fiber stripped and twisted into rope, the next layer, not quite so coarse, woven into stout material for meal bags and ticking for the beds, while the fine inner parts were spun into soft thread for weaving sheets and dresses and other articles of clothing. **1977** Arnow *Old Burnside* 115 Mama gave Elizabeth and me the job—ordinarily done in April and November—of taking the feathers out of the pillows used in the winter and putting them into clean ticks. **1984** Smith *Enduring Memories* 19 Before the introduction of cotton mattresses, most of the rural homes in the Upper Cumberland used straw placed in a heavy twill cloth (called ticking) for mattresses. The ticking cloth could be purchased from dry goods stores and would last several years. In the summer, when the wheat was harvested and wheat straw was available, mother would gather all the straw mattresses, empty them of their straw, wash the mattress cloth, and refill them with the fresh clean wheat straw. The cloth was sewn together in the shape of a mattress with one hole left open about the size of a gallon bucket. That hole was used to take old straw out and place new straw in the mattress. **1989** Oliver *Hazel Creek* 18 Beds were simple affairs with the ticking or mattress held up with ropes stretched across the bedframes. **1992** Bush *Dorie* 90 Ma kept her feathers in clean ticking until she had enough to make a plump, soft pillow.

tickle-bone *noun* The "funny bone" on the elbow; figuratively, a sense of humor.

1946 Stuart *Plum Grove Hills* 121 "Now, Lizzie, that's not all you's laughin' about," Grandpa said. "I know you too well. I know the things that touch your tickle bone." **1966–70** *DARE Survey* (Spruce Pine NC, Dayton TN, Laurel Fork VA) = the place in the elbow that gives you a strange feeling if you hit it against something. **1967** Wilson *Folkways Mammoth Cave* 32 = the elbow bone, which feels funny when struck accidentally.

[DARE *tickle-bone* n chiefly South, South Midland]

ticktack night *noun phrase* See citation.

1982 Slone *How We Talked* 36 = Halloween.

tide

A *noun* A surge of water sometimes over the banks of a river or stream after sudden or heavy rainfall, occurring mainly in spring, sometimes prolonged by melting snow upstream, and used to float logs downstream to a mill. See also **boat tide**, **flash tide**, **fresh B1**, **freshet**, **high tide**, **ice tide**, **May fresh**, **raft tide**, **spring fresh**.

1892 Doak *Wagonauts Abroad* 249 The river runs, now smooth, now broad, shallow and rippling, now boiling, foaming, and roaring in tumultuous cascades over among and around great granite boulders, now plunging down in long rapids. All along we can see lodged sawlogs among the rocks, log slides on the opposite bank, and great piles of logs, got down too late for the last "tide." **1904** Fox *Christmas Eve* 178–79 It takes eight yoke of oxen, sometimes, to drag the heart of a monarch to the chute, and there the logs are "rafted"—as the mountaineer calls the work; that is, they are rolled with hand-spikes into the water and lashed side by side with split saplings—length-wise in the broad Big Sandy, broadside in the narrow Kentucky. Every third or fourth log is a poplar, because that wood is buoyant and will help float the chestnut and the oak. At bow and stem, a huge long limber oar is rigged on a turning stile, the raft is anchored to a tree with a cable of rope or grapevine, and there is a patient wait for a "tide." Some day in March or April—sometimes not until May—mist and clouds loose the rain in torrents, the neighbors gather, the cable is slipped, and the raft swings out the mouth of the creek on its long way to the land of which, to this day, the average mountaineer knows hardly less than that land knows of him. **1913** Kephart *Our Sthn High* 21 The only roads follow the beds of tortuous and rock-strewn water courses, which may be nearly dry when you start out in the morning, but within an hour may be raging torrents . . . A spring "tide" will stop all travel, even from neighbor to neighbor, for a day or two at a time. **1924** Raine *Saddlebags* 24 The most sudden tides are the result of heavy rains back in the mountains, when there are a few inches of snow. Then, overnight, creeks will swell to ten times their volume of water and rush down, a strong sullen stream. **1953** Hall *Coll* (Bryson City NC) The streams was rough, and later on then, years later, they built what they called splash dams and made the splash flood to run these logs out that way and run them into the river, and then the natural tides took them down the river, and they'd raft them up down the river and pull them down into Chattanooga with a little old tugboat, down the Tennessee River. . . . [We had to wait] for the storm to bring on a tide, and it wouldn't last but a few hours or a day, and there would be some time before you would ever get another one. So that was a pretty slow process of gitting lumber out. **1957** Broaddus *Vocab Estill Co KY* 80 = a flooding of the river caused by rains toward the source. **1958** Wood *Words from TN* 17 When enough rain fell to cause the river to rise to a stage that the rafts [of recently cut logs] lying on its banks would float—that was a tide. **1963** Arnow *Flowering* 139 We on the Cumberland, though the mouth of our river was a thousand miles from the sea, also had tides until the water was dammed; there were little tides and big tides, spring tides, and Christmas tides—these last to the old people did not mean tides that came at Christmas but a fall tide early enough so the little steamboats could get up from Nashville with candy and other good things for Christmas—but only when the Cumberland rolled over Burnside did we have a flood tide. **1975** *AOHP/LJC-384* He bought up a lot of walnut timber and it come a big tide and he lost it all. **1982** Eller *Miners* 90 Families who lived close to the larger streams, therefore, often chose to tie their logs together into long rafts that were ridden with spring "tides" into the slow-moving streams to sawmills. **1993** Montell *Cumberland Country* 14 [Miners] dumped coal into wooden barges that were sent downstream to Burnside when rains afforded the [Cumberland] river with a "coal boat tide." **2000** Goode *Being Appalachian* 84 The coal company had bought [the building] and used it as a police building. Later, coal sludge covered it during one of the high spring "tides."

[DARE *tide* n chiefly southern Appalachians]

B *verb* Of a church bell: to signal.

c1940 Simms *Coll* I heared the church bell a-tidin' a death this morning.

tierpole (also *tierstick*) *noun* See citations.

1944 Dingus *Tobacco Words* 72 *tier-pole, tier-stick* = one of several wooden beams upon which the smaller "loaded" sticks of tobacco are hung. **1969** Miller *Raising Tobacco* 34 These casing houses were equipped with tierpoles so tobacco could be brought there in low case (moist enough to handle if you were careful, but not moist enough to work off) and brought into higher case. **2009** Wingfield *Franklin Co VA* 53 Tobacco sticks, riven from oak or chestnut trees, and about five feet long, were laden with six or eight tobacco plants each, and placed in these rooms, each end of the stick resting on a tier pole. These tier poles had to be nearly as large as the logs from which the barn was built, so they would not spring, when men stood on them to hoist the tobacco in its place, nor sway under the great weight of the green tobacco.

tierstick See **tierpole**.

tiger spit *noun phrase* Homemade whiskey of poor quality.

1974 Dabney *Mt Spirits* 24 Frontiersmen of the 1700s and 1800s referred to corn whiskey as "tiger spit," "black betsy," and "forty-rod."

till See also **until**.

A Variant forms *tel, tell, twell, twill*.

1790 *Lenoir Papers* a Wednesday [I] went to George Davidsons and stayd there tell Friday. **1813** Hartsell *Memora* 103 as I pased throw the horses nickered for my cane tell my hart aked for them. **1845** (in **1956** Eliason *Tarheel Talk* 319) (Caldwell Co NC) *tell*. **1862** *Shifflet CW Letters* (Jan) I hope that you will Still do well tell I come home. **1864** *Misemer CW Letters* (April 11) our Officers say they wont furlow us tel we draw money so that we can take it home to our familyes. **1891** Brown *Dialect in TN* 172 On the other hand, *e* is used for i: *tell* for *till* (until). **1895** *Mt Baptist Sermon* 12 Ef yer don't believe hit, you jest take down yer Bible an' hunt twell yer fine hit. **1915** Dingus *Word-List VA* 191 *tell*, variant of *till*. **1927** Montague *Hog's Eye* 196 I never got really acquainted with that hog twill he was ham. **1965** *Dict Queen's English* 17 *tell* = till, until. "We'll be there *tell* morning." **1967** Williams *Subtlety Mt Speech* 15 He was a-wonderin at that, too, twill all of a suddent hit struck him betwixt the eyes. **1997** Montgomery *Coll*: *twell* (known to Cardwell).

[DARE *tell* (at *till* prep, conj A1) chiefly South, South Midland; *twell, twill* (at *till* prep, conj A2) especially South, South Midland]

B *conjunction*

1 So that, with the result or consequence that, in such a way that.

1847 McLean *Diary* 102 Snow Storm till the Earth is Covered. **1862** *Martin CW Letters* (July 18) the wether is So hot that A fellow gets weeken down in one Day till he hardly Can walk. **1863** *Revis CW Letters* (Feb 10) we air all lousey and smoked til you cold not tell whether we was a bacon side or a human. **1865** *Hill CW Letters* (Feb 25) I think if I was at home I could walk rite well in pertickler if I could get a little brandy tel I would begin to turn red. **1898** Elliott *Durket Sperret* 77 She's mad tell she's sick; an' thet's the jig they're dancin' to now. **1922** *TN CW Ques* 378 (Hancock Co TN) My mind is week [sic] till I cant think of lots of things has past. **1939** Hall *Coll* (Hazel Creek NC) I'd have my mustache to freeze [in the cold weather] till I could hardly get my breath. *Ibid.* (Tuckaleechee Cove TN) They had tied silk cords around a jack's leg till he couldn't walk. **1946** Stuart *Plum Grove Hills* 59 I can't write my name till you can read it. **1956** Hall *Coll* (Indian Camp Creek NC) They told her that somebody was a-witching the cows till they couldn't churn the milk. **1969** *GSMNP-25:2:5* Most of the farms, they was straight up and down almost or just hillsidey, till it was actually hard farming. **1973** *AOHP/ASU-111* They changed [the mail route] over there now till they's not but very few lives on this upper end. **1977** Shackelford et al. *Our Appalachia* 128 We'd pad ourselves till the goose couldn't bite us. **1984** Gibson *Remembering* ii If you get this would you drop me a card till I'll know you did get it. **1989** *Matewan OHP-2* I was trying to get him to go and get my car, till I'd get out of there. **1991** Thomas *Sthn Appal* 213 I never seen 'im a-drankin' till you could tell it. **1993** Page and Smith *Foxfire Toys and Games* 4 You fixed them till they'd all look the same. **1998** *Dante OHP-61* He built a box till they wouldn't fill that up. **2012** Milnes *Signs Cures Witchery* They heard the clicking, clicking sound of knitting needles till they couldn't sleep.

[SND *till* conj 3 "implying purpose, in order that"; DHE *till*; CUD *till* conj "in order that"; cf HT *tae*[1] "in order that"; DARE *till* conj C1 chiefly South]

2 That (following an adverb expressing degree, such as with *so* or *enough*).

1956 Hall *Coll* (Gatlinburg TN) The bean beetle got so bad till we stopped growing them here. *Ibid.* (Roaring Fork TN) He liked it so strong till you could slice it. **1996** Harrell *Fetch It* 230 These observers were people who lived close enough to the river till from their residences they could look out on the river.

3 By the time that, before. See also **until B1**.

1862 Lockmiller *CW Letters* (July 21) yew must Bee good Boys and mind your Mother and dont bee Sassey till I come home. **1863** Click *CW Letters* (March 21) I want to now if gorge has got me a saddle yet and if he ant to tell him to get it till I come home. **1864** Tesh *CW Letters* (Jan 26) Bet said she was Feeding her Chickens to mak them fat till Billy come home. **1949** Kurath *Word Geog East US* 34 Another expression that has its focus in central Pennsylvania is *till the time* ... for *by the time (I get there)*. The use of *till* is found between the Alleghenies and the Great Valley, including part of the bilingual German area, and in scattering fashion on the upper reaches of the Potomac in West Virginia ... [the form] *till* is almost certainly of Ulster Scots origin. The Pennsylvania Germans adopted it as a convenient rendering of *bis* in such phrases as *bis er kommt* "by the time he comes," since in their German *bis* had the same range of meanings as the Northern English *till*, as exemplified in *till sundown*. **1950** Bray *Disappearing Dialect* 282 Wash the dishes till I sweep the floor.

[calque of Pennsylvania German *bis*; DARE *till* conj C2 PA German area]

C *preposition*

1 Until.

1862 Shifflet *CW Letters* (Oct 26) we was on a march and didnt hav time to right to you tell this morning. **1956** Hall *Coll* (Gatlinburg TN) [I] went to school till about the eighth grade.

2 To (used to indicate segments of time between the half-hour and the hour).

1949 Kurath *Word Geog East US* 30 In the greater part of the Midland the phrase *quarter till eleven* is current. In south-central Pennsylvania and the entire Midland area lying to the south of Pennsylvania *till* is the usual preposition in this phrase. **1966** Cox *Dialect Scott Co TN* 69 Fifteen till eleven. **1966** Dakin *Vocab Ohio River Valley* 17 The Kentucky Mountains and Knobs, Indiana south of the Vincennes Trace, and the interior Illinois counties north of the Shawnee Hills have *till* almost exclusively. It is the predominate [sic] term throughout the rest of Kentucky except for the Bluegrass. **1967** *DARE Survey* (Gatlinburg TN, Maryville TN) *quarter till eleven.* **1978** Reese *Speech NE Tenn* 36 *quarter till* = attested by 9/12 (75%) speakers. **1986** Pederson et al. *LAGS* (Cocke Co TN, Jefferson Co TN, Sevier Co TN). **1989** *Matewan OHP-33* I'm interviewing Charlie Elliott on July the tenth at a quarter till four in the afternoon.

[ultimately < Old Norse *til* "to"; this is an older form than *until*, but is now often construed as a shortened form of it]

3 By, before.

1863 Tesh *CW Letters* (Dec 5) Tell bet and Fanny They must bake me a sweet cake and send it to me Till Christmas.

[DARE *till* adv B4 especially PA German area]

timber *verb* To harvest and sell trees from (a piece of land); to harvest trees.

1939 Hall *Coll* (Cataloochee NC) [The old settlers on this creek] bought lots of this speculation land and timbered it. **1993** Ison and Ison *Whole Nother Lg* 67 = to cut trees for a sawmill and possibly deliver them.

timber doodle *noun*

1 The pileated woodpecker (*Dryocopus pileatus*).

1952 (in **2018** Montgomery *File*) The Woodcock, or Timber Doodle, as country folks are often wont to call this strange bird, is active during the twilight and early evening. In the daylight it may appear as sleepy and as stupid as an owl. But its habit of not flushing until the last instant, then fluttering quickly up and over the tops of brush and undergrowth, only to drop again almost immediately into another hiding place, rates it high as a game bird. **1980** Brewer *Hit's Gettin'* A woodcock sometimes is a "timber doodle" in both places [i.e. the Smokies and the Ozarks]. **1996–97** Montgomery *Coll* (known to Brown, Cardwell, Oliver).

2 See citation.

2005 Ellison *Mt Passages* 7 When the splash dams on the creeks in the Smokies were released, lumber-herders ran along the banks to clear jams. Some few, like Cathey, were known as timber doodles because they had the agility and courage to ride the logs down the creek while standing up, ducking branches and risking sure death in the event of a miscue.

timberhick *noun* See citation.

2006 *WV Encycl* 809 The origin of the term is probably self-explanatory. Loggers were looked upon as unsophisticated persons working in the woods, and since at least the 16th century the word "hick" has meant an ignorant country person. Perhaps it was for this reason West Virginia woodworkers were called woodhicks or timberhicks.

time about *adverb phrase* At an alternating interval, by turns or in rotation; in phrases *give time about, take time about* = to take turns. See also **weekends about.**

1838 *Paw Paw Hollow Church Minutes* 84 the male members agree to git wine time about. **c1841** Shane (in **1998** Perkins *Border Life* 200) The first meeting house was built in 1785. Mr. Rankin gave us time about with Lexington. **1862** *Robinson CW Letters* (July 13) you & Mrs Kircus must put your letters to gether & pay time about that is the way me & W P is doing. **1863** *Whitaker CW Letters* (May 8) Scott turned his pistol from welch & Shot at dave wounding him in the arm I supose they then shot time about Scott is badly wounded. **1969** Roberts *Greasybeard* 40 We took time about sawing till we had his head off. **1974** Fink *Bits Mt Speech* 27 – alternately. "They go to her church and his'n, *time about.*" **1978** Montgomery *White Pine Coll* IX-1 I think they take it time about.

[cf OED3 *about* adv A3 "in turn, in succession . . . alternately" now U.S. regional; DARE *time about* adv phr (Scots, nEngl dial) chiefly South Midland, especially southern Appalachians]

time boss *noun* See citation.

1994 Farwell and Buchanan *Logging Terms* = an employee of a logging company who collected and kept records of the time the men worked; he went from camp to camp and issued scrip for use in the company store or commissary.

tin-bill *noun* A hired armed guard at a coal camp. Same as **gun thug.**

1975 Screven *John B Wright* 13 Then those tin-bills, I call them—thugs and whatever you call it—was a-working the post, you know, with them guns and was guarding and everything, trying to keep them out.

tinkerbell *noun* The red or wild columbine (*Aquilegia canadensis*).

1980 *Smokies Heritage* 153 [My father Wiley Oakley] told them the flower names that local people used, such as ivy for laurel, tinkerbell for columbine and so forth. **1983** Patterson *Spring Wildflower* 18 Lucinda and her late husband Earnest hiked local trails, gathering specimens like "Tinker Bell," "Doll's Eye," "Dog Hobble," "Fairy Wand," and "Black-Eyed Trillium."

tinsey (also *tinsy*) *adjective* See citations.

1936 Farr *Folk Speech Mid TN* 276 *tinsey* = tiny or small: "She's a tinsey bantling." **1936** Morehouse *Rain on Just* 13 Even for nine Dolly was uncommon tinsy.

[DARE *tinesy* adj chiefly South, South Midland]

tip *verb* To touch.

1946 Dudley *KY Words* 272 = to touch: "Just tip the mule with your whip and he'll go right along." **1976** Still *Pattern of Man* 48 Nowadays young'uns won't tip hard work. **1977** Still *Wonder Beans* 28 When Jack tipped the ground he halloed to his mam, "Fetch the ax!" **2007** Shelby *Molly Whuppie* 10 "I never tipped you," he said, "and you better not say I did!"

tipple *noun* An apparatus or an area near the entrance of a coal mine used to load (sometimes to wash and sort) and unload coal by rail.

1973 Preston *Bituminous Term* 57 = the largest surface building in a bituminous coal mining operation which takes the loaded mine cars and dumps them into graders, screeners, trucks, or piles. **c1975** *Miners' Jargon* 8 = facility where coal is received from underground and prepared for shipment on the surface. **2000** Norman *Consciousness* 150 Around us all day, every working day, was the roar of the tipple as it processed the coal before dropping it into the great gon[dola]s below, filling them one by one to make a train. **2002** Armstead *Black Days* 247 = [an] elevated structure outside a mine shaft or entrance where coal is dumped or "tipped" in from mine cars or a conveyor system and is then washed.

tire *verb, noun* Variant form *tar.*

1862 *Sutton CW Letters* (Nov 8) I am giting tard of riting. **1942** Hall *Phonetics Smoky Mts* 44. **1991** Haynes *Haywood Home* 77 Jut would say far (fire), tar (tire). **2006** Ledford *Survivals* 1014 The Appalachian tendency for r to modify the pronunciation of the preceding vowel (*tar* "tire," . . .) is similar to phonetic spellings found in colonial writings.

[DARE *tire* v, n chiefly South Midland]

tirectly See **directly.**

tissic See **phthisic.**

tisswood (also *tizwood*) *noun* A common deciduous tree (*Halesia carolina*) in the region. Same as **peawood.**

1910 Guerrant *Galax Gatherers* 105 Among these I found a rare tree of most beautiful white and pink, bell-shaped flowers, and called by the natives the Tizwood. I had never seen it before. It blooms alongside the dogwood, but has a more beautiful flower. **1913** Gibson *Amer Forest Trees* 602 In the Great Smoky mountains in Tennessee, where the species [= Mohrodendron carolinum] reaches its greatest development, it bears a variety of names, among them being tisswood, peawood, bellwood, and chittamwood. **1981** *Smokies Heritage* 31:3 Trilliums flower in the spring along with serviceberry and Carolina silverbells (in this area sometimes known as "tiz-wood"). **1982** Powers and Hannah *Cataloochee* 339 The house was built . . . using native stone and timber which were abundant in the area hemlock, poplar, chestnut, locust, and tizwood (or silverbell).

[DARE *tisswood* n 2 chiefly western NC, east TN]

titter See **teder.**

titty *noun* See citation.

1915 Dingus *Word-List VA* 192 = breast milk.

[DARE *titty* n^2 chiefly South, South Midland]

tizic, tizicky See **phthisic.**

tizic tree *noun* Apparently a tree from which a medicine is made to treat phthisic.

1949 Arnow *Hunter's Horn* 286 Deb's tizic tree had done but poorly in the hot dry summer, and now he was taller than the measure of his head last year—that could mean he was going to die, outgrowing his tree like that.

tizwood See **tisswood.**

tizzick, tizzy See **phthistic.**

to *preposition*

1 Compared with.

1862 *Copeland CW Letters* (Oct 5) I thought I seed hard times when I wase at home but I did not see any thing to Whate I see here. **1864** *Chapman CW Letters* (May 27) it is Lone som times now to what it use to bee when the Rebbles was hear. **1908** Smith *Reminiscences* 434 There ain't no game here to what there used to be. **1930** Smith *Reminiscences* 30 The life of the brakeman now is comfortable to what it was in the early days of the [rail]road. **1939** Hall Coll (Cades Cove TN) Yeah, [the old-timers] worked hard to what we do now. **1960** McCaulley *Cades Cove* It's a paradise to what I'm a-living in now. **1975–76** Wolfram/Christian *WV Coll* 83 I sure was young then to what I am now. **1977** Norman *Kinfolks* 47 He was a little thin to what he was the last time I had seen him.

[cf SND *tae* prep 6(3) "compared with"]

2 In phrase *to one's age* = in comparison to the norm for one's age.

1937 Hall Coll (Emerts Cove TN) Aunt Sis Henry is stout to her age. *Ibid.* (Emerts Cove TN) That bear was small to his age. **1967** Miller *Pigeon's Roost* (April 13) He said he put the calf drinking milk out of a bucket and now the calf is the prettiest calf that he ever seen to its age and it is the biggest pet. **1991** Thomas *Sthn Appal* 170 I was a big boy, I was big to my age.

[DARE *to* prep B15 Gulf States, southern Appalachians]

3 In.

1939 Hall Coll (Wears Cove TN) Ever' bone [of the body of a man allegedly murdered some years before] was to its place but one. **2008** *Rosie Hicks* 6 That's the way we used to make gravy to the mountains.

4 Of (expressing familial or other close relationship), especially in phrases *brother to, sister to.*

1957 GSMNP-23:2:9 He wasn't a brother to us, but a friend. **1961** *Coe Ridge OHP*-333A Wasn't she a sister to Uncle John? **1962** Hall Coll (Cades Cove TN) Uncle Jim Cable, brother to Aunt Becky Cable, and Julius Gregg herded cattle one summer. **1969** GSMNP-25 She was sister to Ephraim Bales. **1974** GSMNP-50:2:10 He was a brother to my grandpa Whaley. **1975** *"Last Chance" School* 42 She was cousin to us. **1979** *Big South Fork OHP*-4 A woman told me here a few years back that her mother was the sister to the board member. **1989** *Matewan OHP*-1 Sailor's wife was a sister to R. W., or she was a sister to Meldy Buskirk. **2002** Nelson *Turn Back* 117 Cumi was a sister to Dr. Boyd Owen's father (Charlie Owen). **2015** *Blind Pig* (Sept 9) An older neighbor to my mom used the term to describe a fellow she had no use for.

[cf SND *tae* prep 6(5)(ii) "expressing family relationship . . ." somewhat obsolete (in Scots), now obsolete or archaic in English]

5 At. See also **all to once, to home.**

1861 *Odell CW Letters* (Oct 11) tell Adline & marget shiply that wee wood like to be to the quilten. **1862** *Spainhourd CW Letters* (July 7) I landed to Sailsbury Sunday morning a bout half past one Saft as a Juge. **1910** Cooke *Power and Glory* 10 They ain't got no baby to their house. **1935** Sheppard *Cabins in Laurel* 52 We'd made a house full if we'd all been home to one time, but of course some of the big ones had gone off by themselves and settled when there was still little ones comin'. **1953** Hall Coll (Bryson City NC) Later on, in a few weeks or months after that, they found a dead pant'er in across at the river bluffs down to the end of the Smoky Mountain in there. **1972** *AOHP/ALC*-355 He's buried over to town, back on a high hill back there. **1973** GSMNP-80:12 You know where it was at? Up to Leon's. **1976** Lindsay *Grassy Balds* 117 No, Jim Russell, he stayed down t'home. **1997** *Dante OHP*-53 Why're you not trading down to the store? **2008** *Rosie Hicks* 1 He come in and sit to the arm of the bed . . . *Ibid.* 1 Mister Marshall come and told us to come to school that fall, and it's out here to Cool Springs.

6 From.

1956 Hall Coll (Roaring Fork TN) They were men to the community.

toad frog (also *toadyfrog*) *noun* A toad. See also **ground frog.**

1913 Kephart *Our Sthn High* 295 In the Smokies a toad is called a frog or a toad-frog, and a toadstool is a frog-stool. **1929** Rainey *Animal Plant Lore* 13 I never knew of a toad-frog till I came to Kentucky. I had heard of bull-frogs and leopard frogs and tree frogs and frogs, but toad-frog was new to me. And I am still uncertain whether it is a frog or a toad. **1940** Haun *Hawk's Done* 17 Both of them swelled up like toad frogs. **1963** Edwards *Gravel* 102 I don't know what causes warts, but I don't believe a toad frog does. **1966** Dakin *Vocab Ohio River Valley* 389–91 The Southern and South Midland term is *toad-frog*. This name is regular and invariable among the oldest generation of Kentuckians and usual among most of the relatively younger. **1975** Dwyer *Thangs* 4 = a toad, sometimes *toadyfrogs*. **1991** Still *Wolfpen Notebooks* 94 I figure you know it's the worst kind of bad luck to kill a toady-frog.

[DARE *toad frog* n 1 chiefly South, South Midland]

toadhide (also *toadie, toadskin*) *noun* Paper currency, a dollar bill. Also called **frogskin, green frog.**

1941 Hall Coll (Cataloochee NC) *toadskin*. **1943** Korson *Coal Dust* 73 United States greenbacks were referred to as "toadhides," and on those rare occasions when miners could afford to wait for the semi-monthly payday without drawing scrip they were said to be waiting for their wages to "grow green." **1968** *DARE Survey* (Burnsville NC) = nickname for a dollar bill. **1997** Montgomery Coll (known to Brown). **2013** Montgomery *File*: *toadie* = a dollar bill (41-year-old woman, Robbinsville NC).

toad hole *noun* See citation.

2004 *Early Mines* 34 (as of 1902) Only one man survived the explosion. He had crawled out a toad hole. A toad hole is another entrance to the mine other than the main pit-mouth. **2010** Mann and Keeling *Nurses on Line* 76 A second rescue crew was sent into Mine 8 around 4:00 pm. after moaning was heard by a rescuer coming from a ventilation shaft, also known as a "toad hole."

toadie, toadskin See **toadhide.**

toad strangler *noun* A sudden, heavy rain. Same as **frog drowner.**

1958 Newton *Dialect Vocab* (Happy Valley TN). **1966** Dakin *Vocab Ohio River Valley* 22 *Toad strangler* [occurs] once [in the] Kentucky Mountains.

[DARE *toad-strangler* n chiefly Gulf States, South Midland]

toadyfrog See **toad frog.**

to a fare-thee-well, to a fare-ye-well, to a fare-you-well See **fare-thee-well.**

to a tee-whitey, to a tee-wonk-tum, to a T-witey See **tee-whitey, to a.**

tobacco *noun* Variant forms *bacca, baccer, baccow, baccy, backer, backie, terbaccer, terbacker, terbacky, tobaccy, tobakker.*

1864 (May 24) you must Let B F masingo have two or three Leaves of this baccow to rop up his sore toe. **1884** Smith *Arp Scrap Book* 73 [He] chaws tobakker like a gentleman. **1917** Kephart *Word-List* 414 = unless. "Men don't do nothing for amusement, *lessun* they chew terbacky." **c1926** Cox *Cullowhee Wordlist* Have a cud of baccy, ma'am. **1941** Stuart *Men of Mts* 235 I've got to work in the terbacker field today. **1956** Hall *Coll* (Big Bend NC) That's about all the chance I have of makin' a livin'—from the cattle and the 'baccer in the fall. *Ibid.* (Del Rio TN) He would steal a chaw of terbacker out of your mouth an' you a-lookin' at him. **1961** Williams *R in Mt Speech* 6 Frequently *r* is inserted in other words . . . *breakferst, terbaccer, rurnt* (ruined). **1969** GSMNP-37:2:3 They used to be some big bacca barns. **1981** Henry *Alex Stewart* 56 Alex says, "Store bought 'backer don't do me a bit of good." So he raises his own, cures it, twists it, and hangs it on a string behind the kitchen stove. **1982** Powers and Hannah *Cataloochee* 349 He had some trouble eating, but later contented himself with his 'baccy. **1989** Giardina *Storming Heaven* 132 "I put in a little patch of tobaccy, first time ever," Ben said. **2000** Miller *Looneyville* 37 Most older men carried home-grown and home-made twists of *bacca/backer* [while] the faint-of-heart and younger people carried a store-bought pouch of chewing tobacco: "Here, Henry, fill that *whopper-jaw* of yours full of my twist backer. It will put some hair on your chest." **2007** McMillon *Notes*: *backie* = jocular term for *tobacco.*

[DARE *tobacco* n A 1 (pronc) chiefly South, South Midland]

tobacco heart *noun* Weakening of the heart purportedly caused by indulgence in tobacco.

c1910 Frost *Success* 20 The doctor said if he had not been broken down by his tobacco habit he might have recovered. But he had a "tobacco heart" and so this wound which needn't have killed him proved fatal.

tobacco spitter *noun* A grasshopper.

1966 *DARE Survey* (Cherokee NC) = a grasshopper. **1998** Montgomery *Coll* (known to eight consultants from the Smoky Mountains).

tobacco weed *noun* Same as **rabbit tobacco.**

1997 Montgomery *Coll* = so called because it was chewed by children to mimic adults (Cardwell).

tobacco worm *noun* See citation.

1968 Clarke *Stuart's Kentucky* 160 The habit of chewing gave rise to the epithet terbacker worms for those who were really addicted to the habit.

tobaccy, tobakker See **tobacco.**

toboggan *noun*

A Variant forms *boggan* [see **c1960** in **B**], *'boggin* [see **2005** in **B**].

B (also *toboggan cap*) A knitted cap worn in cold or icy weather.

1942 Hall *Phonetics Smoky Mts* 57 = a knit cap with a tassel. **c1960** Wilson *Coll* = a knitted cap, often just *boggan* or *toboggan cap.* **1977** Stanley *Tough* 32 My mother then would use the yarn to make sweaters and socks, stockings and mittens, gloves and toboggans, and that type of thing. We used our sheep for this particular purpose. **1983** Jones *Sin-Eater* 7 John quickly put on a heavy coat and toboggan and hurried out into the worsening weather. **2005** Williams *Gratitude* 44 They shore did pull them 'boggins a way down over their yeres (ears).

[DARE *toboggan* n 1 chiefly South, South Midland; also Inland North]

toboggan cap See **toboggan.**

toddick *noun*

A Variant forms *taddick* [see **c1960** in **B**], *taddle* [see **1995–97** in **B**].

B A small measuring vessel; hence a small portion, as of grain given a miller in payment for grinding one's corn (often one gallon from each bushel of ground corn). See also **toll[2] A.**

1913 Kephart *Our Sthn High* 292 When a farmer goes to one of our little tub-mills . . . he leaves a portion of the meal as toll. This he measures out in a toll-dish or toddick or taddle (the name varies with the locality) which the mill-owner left for that purpose. Toddick, then, is a small measure. **1917** Kephart *Word-List* 418 *toddick* = a small amount. "I won't take a full turn o' meal but jist a *toddick.*" **1943** Hannum *Mt People* 149 Women borrow a "toddick" of wool, as they did in *The Winter's Tale.* **1952** Wilson *Folk Speech NC* 601 *toddick* = a small amount. **c1960** Wilson *Coll*: *taddick* = a small quantity, as a left-over of food. **1974** Fink *Bits Mt Speech* 27 = small measuring vessel used in taking toll at a grist mill; hence small amount. **1995–97** Montgomery *Coll*: *taddle* (known to Brown, Bush, Hooper).

[Web3 *toddick* n 1a/1b South; DARE *toddick* n chiefly NC]

to-do *noun* [with stress on both syllables] A social affair of unusual show, size, or formality. See also **doings**.

1961 *Coe Ridge OHP-336B* They was going to have a march down there and put on a big to-do. **1978** Hiser *Quare Do's* 126 All the beasties waked up and come runnin into the room. They let inst to caper around and make a big to-do. **1996** Montgomery *Coll* (known to Ledford).

[Web3 *to do* n 2 dialect]

toe, toe-eetch See **toe-itch.**

toe dancing *noun* See citation.

2009 Benfield *Mt Born* 47 Clogging is also called "toe dancing" and, if performed by a man, "buck dancing."

toe-itch (also *toe-eetch*) *noun* See citations. See also **dew poison, ground itch, mud poison.**

1929 Kephart *Smoky Mt Magic* 10 We call it toe-eetch. You walk into it in your bare feet and you'll git a lot o' leetle prickles atween your toes that'll eetch like flea-bites. **c1960** Wilson *Coll* = dew poison, ringworm, hookworm, ground itch. **1963** Watkins and Watkins *Yesterday* 123 Athlete's foot, which the country people called toe "eatch" or toe itch, was treated with a poultice of cow manure, preferably hot from the cow. **1968** Wilson *Folklore Mammoth Cave* 36 = an infection of the toes, now known to be connected with hookworm; also called *toe (-eetch)*.

[DARE *toe itch* n 1 chiefly South, South Midland]

toe jam *noun* See 2005 citation.

2005 Williams *Gratitude* 532 = the soft accumulation of malodorous dead skin and sweat between the toes, caused from not keeping the feet clean. **2008** Salsi *Ray Hicks* 78 We'd get excited and get the toe jam outta our stockin' afore puttin' it aside the fireplace.

toe sack See **tow sack.**

tofore *conjunction* Before.

1916 Combs *Old Early English* 288 It rained tofore we had a chance to plow. **1997** Montgomery *Coll* (known to Cardwell, Weaver).

[ultimately < Old English *toforan*; OED3 *tofore* conj Cb obsolete; Web3 *tofore* adv obsolete; DARE *tofore* prep, adv especially South Midland]

tohind *preposition, adverb* Behind.

1911 Shearin *E KY Word-List* 540 = behind (adv. and prep.). **1944** Wilson *Word-List* 50 Look t'hind ye, and ye'll see the snake. **1957** Combs *Lg Sthn High: Word List* 102 = behind, adv. and prep. **1996–97** Montgomery *Coll* (known to Brown, Bush, Cardwell).

[DARE *tohind* prep, adv especially southern Appalachians]

to home *adverb phrase* At home. See also **to 5**.

1924 Spring *Lydia Whaley* 1 When son was in the camp he got the measles, red and black. "He'd always scouted from the measles ter home." **1964** Roberts *Hell-Fer-Sartin* "Get right up here to the fire, Bill, you fellers, and make yourselves to home." **1973** *AOHP/ASU-178* The mothers used to stay to home with [the children]. **1979** *Smokies Heritage* 34 "Is Wes to home?" It was James Nell, a neighbor of ours from down the way.

[OED3 *to* prep A(1)4 regional (chiefly U.S.)]

token *noun*

1 An omen, apparition.

1924 Raine *Saddlebags* 197 Then, after prolonged and sometimes intense wrestling in prayer, he "comes through," receiving assurance of salvation, preferably by some notable or strange token. **1940** Haun *Hawk's Done* 60 Then she thought she heard something. A horse. Enzor's horse. She thought it was a token, maybe. **1968** Clarke *Stuart's Kentucky* 27 One of the old men in "300 Acres of Elbow Room" had heard it said that tokens "told people things": ". . . they come like headless men or in the forms of light, and they speak to people. I've heard of them comin' in the form of a shepherd dog at night or a pig that run across the road and squealed." **1975** Montell *Ghosts Cumberland* 220 = synonym for omen, but especially of wide popularity in the Eastern Pennyroyal of Kentucky. [**1995** Montgomery *Coll* (unknown to consultants from the Smoky Mountains).] **2007** Milnes *Signs Cures Witches* 130 They learned that he had come down with the flu. One evening, after a week or so, they heard his loud hoot salute them again and were happy to know he was getting back to normal. However, Robert said, his eyes welling up with tears, the hoot was just "a token"; they soon learned he had died about the time they heard his last call.

[DARE *token* n chiefly South Midland]

2 See citation.

2006 Farwell *Logging Term* 1021 Men were paid in "scrip," or "dougaloo," and dropped "tokens," small company coins, into a pail before each meal.

tolable, tolble See **tolerable.**

tole (also *toll*) *verb* To entice or lure (a person or animal) often in order to deceive or capture.

1863 *Gilley CW Letters* (Nov 22) they come in the day time and carried of[f] the shetter of my Barn doer told my sheep out of the Parster and Cild my big ho[r]ned sheep. **1866** Smith *So Called* 8 They are . . . tolling [the laborers] off to parts unknown under false pretenses. **1895** Dromgoole *Fiddling to Fame* 55 "Ilin' [= Oiling] up" meant gettin' my fiddle ready an' callin' the boys tergether in a committee-room or somewher's, an' tollin' 'em inter measures with "Rabbit in the Pea Patch," "Chicken in the Bread Tray," an' some o' the other mount'n tunes. **1917** Kephart *Word-List* 418 *tole* = to lure, entice. "I could *tole* that pig around anywhere." **c1926** Cox *Cullowhee Wordlist*: *tole* = to lead by feeding, as hogs or wild turkeys. **1966** Dykeman *Far Family* 82 When he left her that night, he said, "You really tolled me on, pretty girl." **1974** Fink *Bits Mt Speech* 27 = entice, lure. "They took some corn to *tole* the turkeys in." **1994** Montgomery *Coll* I know he was toling me on (Cardwell).

[OED3 toll, tole v[1] 2 now dialect and U.S.; EDD toll v[2] 1 chiefly sEngl; CUD *tole* v "entice, allure"; DARE *toll* v 1 chiefly New England, South, South Midland]

tolerabel, tolerabele, tolerabl See **tolerable.**

tolerable

A Variant forms *tolable* [see **1965** in **B**], *tolble, tolble, tolerabel* [see **1863** in **B**], *tolerabele* [see **1814** in **C**], *tolerabl* [see **1836** in **C**], *tollable* [see **1989** in **B**], *tollarble* [see **1863** in **B**], *tollebl* [see **1864** in C], *tolerable* [see **1790** in **C**].

1890 Fruit *KY Words* 69 "I'm tol'ble well."

B *adjective* Especially of one's health: passable, fair, moderate.

1815 (in **1920** DeWitt *Sevier Journal* 60) (Sept 9) There is some tolerable land on Culluha Creek & about Hawkins old place. **1834** (in **1996** Edmondson *Crawford Memoirs* 127) Andrew's health is but tolerable. **1863** Gilliland *CW Letters* (May 1) I am in the tolerabel helth & i am tollarble well satisfide as mutch so as could be expected. **c1863** (in **1992** Jackson *Surry Co Soldiers* 238) We get tolerable plenty of meat and bread to eat. **1952** Wilson *Folk Speech NC* 601 *tolerable* = fairly well, fairly satisfactory. **c1959** Weals *Hillbilly Dict* 8 ["How are you?"] "Jus' tol'ble." It's a reply that can cover a wide range of conditions. **1965** *Dict Queen's English* 17 = fairly well. "When asked how he was feeling, the old man replied, 'Tolable, thank ye.'" **1989** Landry *Smoky Mt Interviews* 181 We used to say the times were only tolerable then. **1989** Nicholson *Field Guide* 54 *tollable* = not any better than just okay. **2003** Carter *Mt Home* 208 I'm tolable, jest tolable, not even fair to middlin'.

[DARE *tolerable* adj, adv B chiefly South, South Midland, also New England]

C *adverb* Somewhat, passably, moderately (the interpretation depends on the context, with the senses of the term ranging from "rather" to "barely"). Same as **tolerably.**

1790 *Lenoir Papers* I am still in hopes that I shall Learn Tollerable well. **1800** (in **1920** DeWitt *Sevier Journal* 30) (Nov 5) Tolerable good land here and at spring rich. **1814** Hartsell *Memora* 143 all of my men is tolerabele well. **1836** (in **2004** *Bowman's Ms* 59) John Fisher Cashier at the Bank of Westminster had a tolerabl large white sow called The Bonnets. **1855** *Mitchell Letter* There has been some sickness here this winter and some tollerable fatal. **1861** Shipman *CW Letters* (Sept 24) Blesingane Struck him With A suord and hurt him tolerable Bad. **1864** Chapman *CW Letters* (March 5) the helth of our campany is tollebl good. **1895** Edson and Fairchild *TN Mts* 375 It's a *tolerable* hot day. **1939** Hall *Coll* My family done tolerable well. **1969** GSMNP-46 Get your chain under the log and pull it up tolerable tight and run it through the ring. **1988** Russell *It Happened* 36 Other expressions that I remember are . . . "Reckon I'm tolerable pwert [sic]." **1997** Montgomery *Coll* I feel tolble well today (Brown).

[EDD *tolerable* adj and adv 3; Web3 *tolerable* adv dialect]

tolerably *adverb* Somewhat, passably, fairly. Same as **tolerable C.**

1815 (in **1920** DeWitt *Sevier Journal* 59–60) (Sept 7) We traveled through pretty good levell land, and tolerably watered & lodged at an old village (evacuated) 12 miles from F. Jackson. **1826** Whitten *Letter* Springs also are tolerably scarce. **1861** *Odell CW Letters* (Nov 9) Owen Brice is tolerably sick and talks of coming home provided he can get a lieve of absence. **1878** *Tuckaleechee Cove Church Minutes* 40 Then met the Primitive Baptist Church of Christ in Tuckaleechee Cove. Only tolerably good representation.

toll[1] See **tole.**

toll[2]

A *noun* The portion of corn or meal charged by a miller. See also **toddick.**

1937 Hall *Coll* (Mingus Creek NC) = 1/2 gallon per bushel of meal. **1939** Hall *Coll* (Bradley Fork NC) I didn't take any toll off orphans nor widows. **1956** GSMNP-22:15 A bushel of corn you took out one quart of cornmeal and that was the toll. That's what they paid for having their corn ground, and we'd take out this little toll, and then they'd take their sack on their back of cornmeal and go home, and we'd lock up the old mill and go back to the house. **1982** Powers and Hannah *Cataloochee* 304 He charged one gallon of meal out of eight ground as his toll. The toll corn was then frequently sold to renters and tenants in the area. **2007** Ball *Tub Mills* 10 After the corn was ground, the miller would take a tolling scoop or bucket and remove his "toll" (payment) if he was milling a neighbor's corn.

[OED3 *toll* n[1] 2a(b) obsolete or dialect]

B *verb*

1 Of a miller: to take a portion of corn or meal as a fee for grinding one's corn.

1862 Fuller *CW Letters* (Nov 7) caldonia tolled the sugar corn and put it in the garner and I saw hime and he told me that he reckon he would grind it. **1973** GSMNP-78:26 He tolled the corn. He would take his part out before he would grind, although if he was short of meal, possibly he would grind hisn and take it out then. But usually he would grind your meal, put it in the sack, tie the sack, and put it on your back. He'd head you home. Then he'd grind his part of the meal. **c1975** Lunsford *It Used to Be* 22 The man who owns and operates one of the water mills gets his support from toling [sic] each man's turn of meal which was brought to the mill.

2 Of a bell: to announce the death of a person by being rung that person's years of age.

1997 GSMNPCOHP-3:13 You'd just start counting when that bell started tolling, one time for each year old that person was. Maybe Uncle John was eighty-nine years old and he'd been sick and the bell tolled eighty-nine times. That was a pretty good indication. You could hear that bell all over the cove there. You could tell which church it was at. . . . Everybody left what they were doing and they went and started digging the grave, and John McCaulley or whoever started building the coffin quick as they could.

tollable, tollarble See **tolerable.**

toll dish *noun* A dish or box, generally quart-sized, to remove the toll (see **toll**[2] **A**) from a bushel of ground meal. See also **toddick.**

1889 Mooney *Folk Carolina Mts* 97 Among these are tolldish, a measure equivalent to one fourth of a peck, and so called because this is the amount deducted as toll by the miller from a bushel of grain. **1913** Kephart *Our Sthn High* 292 When a farmer goes to one of our little tub-mills . . . he leaves a portion of the meal as toll. This he measures out in a toll-dish or toddick or taddle (the name varies with the locality) which the mill-owner left for that purpose. **1944** Hayes *Word-List NC* 37 = a measure holding one-eighth of a bushel, used at corn mills to measure the miller's share. **1975** Jackson *Unusual Words* 152 One old timer, explaining the operation of his mill and discussing the days when he used to grind corn for other farmers in the area, noted that the taking of a toll of the meal was pay for the miller's work; in fact, "They'd law ya if you tuk more than two toll dishes full for a bushel of corn," a toll dish being a small wooden box.

tollebl, **tollerable** See **tolerable.**

toll the bell *verb phrase* See citation.

1994 Crissman *Death and Dying* 26 When communities began to develop in the central Appalachian Mountains, "tolling the bell," in addition to announcing an ailing resident, also notified those within hearing distance that a fellow mountaineer had died.

tomater See **tomato.**

tomato *noun* Variant forms *mater, matoe, matter, mortas, tomater*. See also **tommytoe.**

1915 Dingus *Word-List VA* 185 *mortases*, n. pl. Tomatoes. **1925** (in **1935** Edwards *NC Novels* 88) *'maters*. **1956** Hall *Coll* (Big Bend NC) I raised corn, raised hogs, tomaters, beans and cabbage and all vegetables like that. **c1959** Weals *Hillbilly Dict* 5 We like maters 'n' taters. **1970** *Hillard Green* 136 You tell'em I'm puttin' up 'maters for th'winter. **1977** Shackelford et al. *Our Appalachia* 326 In the country instead of saying "tomato" you'd say "mater." **1982** Slone *How We Talked* 26 *matoes, matters* = tomatoes. **1997** Andrews *Mountain Vittles* 31 The last of the maters had to be canned and a few more jars of vegetable soup mix, too. **1997** Landry *Coll* I canned four dozen mater quarts last year.

[DARE *mater, matoe, tomater* (at *tomato* n A 4 (pronc)) chiefly South, South Midland]

tomato sore *noun* See citations.

1964 Wright *Mt Medicine* 9 There was a lot of impetigo. It went by such names as "Tomato Sores," and "Fall Sores," and "Weed Sores." **1998** Montgomery *Coll* (known to Adams, Brown).

tomb grave *noun* See citation.

2004 Finch *Ashes to Ashes* 67–68 Graveyards of the Cumberland region are noteworthy for the variety of covered graves that have been found here. Even before the profession of stonecutting became established in the Highland Rim–Cumberland Plateau region, a distinctive style of grave covering had made its appearance. In Overton County's Roaring River Cemetery, a rough-hewn squarish block of sandstone dated 1822 stands at the head of two long slabs of the same rock. These slabs lean together like the sides of a puptent or the comb of a roof, covering the grave of J. H. Bilbery. This is the earliest noted example of what the old timers call a "tomb grave."

tomb rock *noun* A gravestone. See also **grave rock.**

1942 Campbell *Cloud-Walking* 168 He painted all the home made tomb rocks in the graveyard blue to match Sam's grave house. **1973** GSMNP-88:82 No, they always ordered the tomb rocks and had 'em brought in here, and they'd have it already cut and engraved what they wanted on it. **1997** Montgomery *Coll* (known to Adams, Bush, Cardwell, Jones, Weaver). **2004** Finch *Ashes to Ashes* 66 "Tomb rocks"—a folk expression that can still be heard among old timers in the Upper Cumberland region—can be very telling of a region's people and their social development. . . . [Early] tomb rocks bear no inscriptions, and serve only to indicate the grave locations. *Ibid.* 67 The overall favorite source of tomb rocks was the widely available sandstone now known to geologists as the Hartselle Formation.

[DARE *tomb rock* n chiefly South Midland]

tomcat (around) *verb, verb phrase*; hence verbal noun *tomcatting*. See citations. Also called **cat around.** See also **wild-hog.**

1937 Hall *Coll* (Emerts Cove TN) = to make a visit to the ladies. **1939** Hall *Coll* (Cataloochee NC) [Wild hogging is] when they get on one of these big drunks and go to these honky-tonks. It's the same as tomcattin'. Both wild hoggin' and tomcattin' mean to look for a woman especially. **1952** Wilson *Folk Speech NC* 601 = to call on the ladies at night. **2002** Rash *Foot in Eden* 32 Mrs. Winchester says Holland was tomcating around with your Missus.

[DARE *tomcat* v, hence vbl n *tomcatting* Also with *around* widespread, but especially frequent South, South Midland]

tomcatting See **tomcat (around).**

tommytoe *noun* A small salad tomato, cherry tomato.

1957 Broaddus *Vocab Estill Co KY* 80 *tommytoe* = a variety of tomatoes that are approximately 1½ inches in diameter when ripe. **1976** Garber *Mountain-ese* 94 = tiny bell tomato. "We raised a bushel of tommy-toes on jist one vine in the garden." **1981** Dumas *Appal Glossary* 18 = a cherry or plum tomato. **1986** Pederson et al. LAGS = attested by 37/60 interviewees (61.7%) from E TN and 8/35 (22.7%) from N GA; 45/183 of all LAGS interviewees (24.5%) attesting term were from Appalachia. **1990** Oliver *Cooking Hazel Creek* 15 Originally, [tomatoes] were small, like salad tomatoes or "tommy toes" of today, with tough ribs and not very much pulp. **1996–97** Montgomery *Coll* (known to Adams, Brown, Cardwell, Jones, Ledford, Norris, Oliver). **2007** Farr *My Appalachia* 71 Every year we would find tomatoes growing in the places where a tomato had rotted, or tomato peel and seed had been dumped. These we called "Tommy Toes," and it was incredible how strong and vigorous the plants were and how the small, round tomatoes would be bursting with flavor. Today at the farmers market I buy cherry tomatoes. But they never taste as good as the sweet, sound flesh of the Tommy Toes in our garden.

[DARE *tommytoe* n now chiefly South, South Midland]

tommy walkers See **tom walkers**.

tomorrow *adverb* Variant forms *tomorry, tomor.*

1915 Dingus *Word-List VA* 192 *tomor.* **1941** Still *Troublesome Creek* 74 It's the contrary season to gather herbs, yit a kettle o' tonic's got to be brewed ere I set off tomorry.

tom walkers (also *tommy walkers*) *noun* Makeshift stilts fashioned by children from forked branches, small trees, or poles. Also known as **johnny walkers, walkers.**

1978 Montgomery *White Pine Coll* V-3 We had a place to play baseball. We'd play that and also tom walkers. You've heard of them, or stilts they call 'em now. You've not heard of that? Well, it's a stick. You go in the woods and get a stick about the size of your arm with a fork on it. So you'd cut it off and leave the fork up about two or three feet on the side of the stick and set your foot on that fork in each one, one in each hand. Hold it with your hand, and feet in down there and it'd put you way up like a circus, you know, tall man [that] walks around. And you'd walk around way up in the air, see. It was a skill and an art to it, and so we enjoyed that. **1979** *Tom Walkers* 203 Tom Walkers are a great deal like stilts except they come from the woods and are not manufactured with fine materials. [To make a pair] Clyde finds two small trees that are similar in shape and structure . . . he has taken care to find ones that have natural and strong limbs near the bottom. Of course, these will be used to hold one's feet. **1993** Page and Smith *Foxfire Toys and Games* 141 We used to make what we called Tommy Walkers. We'd make those things and walk around. Those were usually made with little forked saplings. Cut off a little fork. **1996** Parton *Mt Memories* 262 At the end of the day on the way home we'd cut forked limbs for pairs of stilts, or "tommy walkers," which always blistered our feet and gave us stone bruises as we hobbled back to the house. **2013** Pack *Toys and Games* 29 Tom Walkers were actually gifts given to children by Mother Nature herself. The trick to owning a pair of these prized "walkin' crutches" or "stilts" was having a good eye for forked tree limbs or saplings while trekking through the woods. Naturally, the Tom Walkers worked best if the two forked limbs were shaped alike and the fork was cut at about the same distance from the ground. The object of playing with Tom Walkers was to place one's feet in the forks.

[DARE *tom walkers* n pl chiefly South, South Midland]

ton *noun* Variant plural form without -*s* following a numeral; see Grammar and Syntax §1.1.

1973 *AOHP/EH-73* I guess that there was around a thousand ton a day. **1975** Woolley *We Be Here* 56 I made about four and a half ton of candy a day.

tone the bell *verb phrase* To temper the sound of a church bell in respect for the deceased person for whom it is rung. See 1998 citation.

1937 Hall *Coll* (Catons Grove TN) Aunt Tildie Caton was the first the bell was toned for [in honor of the woman who had collected money for the bell]. Bells [were] toned down for funerals. **1998** Montgomery *Coll* = the bell was rung so its clapper hit the bell softly. Sometimes the clapper was covered with cloth or burlap to tone down the sound (Brown).

[DARE (at *tone* v) chiefly South]

tongue *noun*

1 Same as **sheep's tongue.**

1982 Maples *Memories* 74 The mountain people called [the flower] tongue or sheep's tongue. It was real bright yellow with spotted green leaves.

2 See citation.

2007 Plott *Story Plott Hound* 184 = sometimes used to describe hounds barking or baying on the game trail.

tonic

A *noun* See citation. See also **spring tonic.**

1975 Dwyer *Thangs* 34 Springtime in the mountains was synonymous with tonics for everybody in the mountain family. "Purifiers" they were called. Cherry bark bitters mixed with whiskey was not one of the favorites, along with a host of other bitter teas. Red sassafras tea was one purifier and blood-thinner that stood out from all others and was usually relished by the family when sweetened with honey or sugar. Some preferred spicewood tea but sassafras was the favorite, and some drank it year-round.

B *verb* To treat with a potion intended to relieve or rejuvenate; hence verbal noun *tonicking.*

1937 Hyatt *Kiverlid* 38 I allus say when abody gits fevered up, hit takes a lot of tonnickin' on good yarb tea and sich, and aplenty of it, to bring 'em out. **1998** Montgomery *Coll* (known to eight consultants from the Smoky Mountains).

tonicky *adjective* Having the effects of a tonic.

1925 Dargan *Highland Annals* 46 A body ought to put up a lot of grapes. They're so tonicky. An' they make the nicest jelly there is for the sick. **1997** Montgomery *Coll* (known to Bush, Oliver).

[*tonic* n + -*y* adj forming suffix]

tonic root *noun* Same as **goldenseal.**

1963 Edwards *Gravel* 171 I thought I'd dig fer some o' that tonic root down along the branch thar. **1968** *Sang Signs* 15 Best known as sang-sign is . . . the golden seal (Hydrastis canadensis). Other names for Hydrastis include . . . tonic-root.

took See **take A2.**

tooken See **take A1, A2.**

to one's age See **to 2.**

toothache medicine *noun* Homemade whiskey.

1939 Hall *Coll.*

toothache tree *noun* An ash tree (*Zanthoxylum* spp), from whose bark a medicinal tea is made. Same as **prickly ash.**

1960 Price *Root Digging in Appal* 9 The common names more often suggest medicinal uses, among them ague bark, quinine tree, cancer jalap, kidneyroot, asthma weed, emetic herb, eyebright, feverwort, birthroot, toothache tree, nerveroot, coughweed, cramp-bark tree, soldier's-woundwort, and maiden's relief. And there are many more. **2006** *WV Encycl* 568 People chewed the inner bark of the prickly ash or toothache tree to numb aching teeth, and willow bark, which contains salicin (from which aspirin was later derived), to cure aches and pains.

toothbrush *noun*

1 A twig, usually a birch or sweetgum tree, chewed to a fray on one end, used to apply snuff to the gum of the mouth. Also called **chaw stick, dip stick, snuff mop**.

1895 Edson and Fairchild *TN Mts* 375 = snuff-stick (used in "dipping"). **1913** Kephart *Our Sthn High* 244 The narrow mantel-shelf holds pipes and snuff and various other articles of frequent use, among them a twig or two of sweet birch that has been chewed to shreds at one end and is clearly discolored with something brown (this is what the mountain woman calls her "toothbrush," a snuffstick, understand). **1921** Campbell *Sthn Highlander* 136 So fond a husband was he that we had to climb to the top of the mountain for mountain birch, whose twigs are especially suitable for "tooth brushes" which he wished to take to his own little old woman who was, he said, "sure the dearest lover of snuff he ever did see." **1935** Sheppard *Cabins in Laurel* 183 The snuff is brushed on the gums inside the lower lip with a twig frayed out at one end and called a "tooth brush." **1974** Fink *Bits Mt Speech* 27 = twig with one end chewed into a rude brush, used in dipping snuff. **1975** Dwyer *Thangs* 36 Black gum twigs, cut about four inches long, also provided mountain folks with "chaw sticks" or tooth brushes. The stick chews up well into a little brush at the end and was used to dip snuff. It was dipped into the snuff then rubbed up and down along "teeth gums." Not only did older women dip snuff, but the fairest of the young mountain girls, as well. On some festive occasions the girls provided the snuff and the men, the whiskey. **2007** Myers *Smoky Mt Remedies* 33–34 We brushed our teeth with toothbrushes made from tender birch sticks approximately five inches long. We removed one inch of bark from one end of the wood and chewed that end of the stick until the fiber broke apart. When the fiber broke into a circle, we used the circular fiber for our toothbrushes.

[DARE *toothbrush* n 1 chiefly South, South Midland]

2 See citation.

1968 *End of Moonshining* 50 Swab stick or Toothbrush—a hickory stick half as thick as your arm and long enough to reach from the top to the bottom of the still. One end is beaten up well so that it frazzles and makes a fibrous swab. This is used to stir the beer in the still while waiting for it to come to a boil, thus preventing it from sticking to the sides of the still, or settling to the bottom and burning.

tooth dentist (also *tooth doctor*) *noun* A dentist. See also **doctor dentist, tooth jumper.**

1943 Hannum *Mt People* 147 Shapes of phrases repeat themselves and the same sounds re-echo, giving, oddly enough, vividness rather than monotony—as in their use of double words: "down-log; sulphur-match; man-person; flower-thing; mother-woman; storm of rain; tooth-dentist; neighbor-people; ocean-sea; ham-meat; cookin'-pan; belly-empty; biscuit-bread; rifle-gun; ridin'-critter; cow-brute; preacher-man; granny-woman; we-uns; chanty-song." **1966–68** *DARE Survey* (Brasstown NC, Cherokee NC, Gatlinburg TN) *tooth doctor* = joking term for dentist. **1974** Betts and Walser *NC Folklore* 264 The tooth-puller and the tooth-jumper were known as Tooth Doctors. Decayed and aching teeth were usually tolerated for a long time before most persons overcame their timidity sufficiently to have them extracted. **1975** Chalmers *Better* 34 The big chair, a left-over from the days when the "tooth-dentist" from Knoxville held monthly clinics, held the patients one by one. **1985** Irwin *Alex Stewart* 150 Back then we didn't have a tooth dentist anywhere in this whole country, and if you had a tooth to hurt you bad enough, why he had to come out.

[DARE *tooth dentist* n chiefly South, South Midland, *tooth doctor* n scattered, but chiefly South, Midland]

tooth doctor See **tooth dentist.**

tooth drawers (also *tooth pullers*) *noun* A pair of pliers used to extract aching teeth.

1913 Kephart *Our Sthn High* 34 He also owned the only "tooth pullers" in the settlement; a pair of universal forceps that he designed, forged, fired out, and wielded with barbaric grit. **1921** Campbell *Sthn Highlander* 214 The teeth, too, usually need attention, the only attention indeed commonly given them in very rural districts being to pull them out when they ache. In past days this was accomplished by means of crude home-made "tooth-pullers" wielded by some man who had obtained a reputation for skill along this and other "surgical" lines. **1964** Cooper *History Avery Co* 30 Teeth were extracted by "tooth pullers," who had fashioned for themselves in blacksmith shops crude, but serviceable forceps. Often the patient was made to lie on the floor or ground while the "tooth puller" straddled him and extracted the aching tooth. **1982** Slone *How We Talked* 104 *tooth drawers, tooth pullers* = a kind of pliers made in the blacksmith shop. Mountain people endured a lot of pain, and had to. Each community had someone who owned a pair of tooth-pullers. I remember my father had some and kept them in the drawers of the sewing machine. Every few weeks someone would come with an aching tooth. Father would sit him down in a straight back chair, give him a good "swig" of whiskey, take one himself, and pull the tooth. The patient would wash out with another mouthful of moonshine, and they both went back to work. **1994–97** Montgomery *Coll* I sent the daughter to borrow Frank's tooth drawers (Cardwell); *tooth pullers* (known to Adams, Brown, Cardwell, Jones, Norris, Weaver).

tooth jumper *noun* An amateur dentist who uses a hammer and a nail to extract or cause a tooth to jump out; also verbal noun *tooth jumping*. See also **doctor dentist, tooth dentist.**

[**1913** Kephart *Our Sthn High* 228 "I have heard of tooth-jumping," said I, "and reported it to dentists back home, but they laughed at me." "Well, they needn't laugh; for it's so. Some men git to be as experienced at it as tooth-dentists are at pullin'. They cut around the gum, and then put the nail at jest sich an angle, slantin' downward for an upper tooth, or upwards for a lower one, and hit one lick."] **1961** Seeman *Arms of Mt* 35 Imagine going to a mountain "tooth-jumper," who was armed with hammer and nail and kept a pair of home-forged pliers handy! **1972** Parris *Storied Mts* 77 The tooth-jumper has given way to a science that saves a tooth which in Grandpa's day came out when it started acting up. And nobody uses a hammer and a chisel any more. **2004** Mays *Passion* 23 Raymond Huggins was a farmer, a preacher, and a blacksmith. Most of all, though, he was known far and wide for his skill as a first-class tooth-jumper. One of Huggins's descendants claims that Rev. Dr. Raymond Huggins was far more than a mere primitive dentist who used pain-producing pliers or pinchers to extract a tooth. His talent and expertise lay in his skillful use of a hammer and a chisel, the instruments employed by the tooth-jumpers of the era.

[DARE *tooth jumper* n southern Appalachians, Ozarks]

tooth pullers See **tooth drawers.**

top

A *noun*

1 A mountain summit, high point on a mountain ridge; also used in place-names, as in *Chestnut Top* (TN) and *Rocky Top* (NC/TN). See 1956, 1968 citations. Also called **big top**, **high top**.

1943 Peattie *Indian Days* 40 The word peak is found on our maps and might be understood in this region but it is really not native to it. The equivalent is top, or knob; high top and high knob indicate lofty peaks. **1956** Hall *Coll* (Byrds Creek NC) I operated a camp for six years on Fuzzy Top away up on top of Smoky Mountain. I did about ten mile of [logging] railroad up there. **1968** Powell *NC Gazetteer* Canadian Top (w Haywood Co NC in the park), Hall Top (Haywood Co NC on Chestnut Ridge), Flat Top (Buncombe Co NC), Cedar Top (Graham Co NC), Round Top Knob (Haywood County in the park), Sharp Top (Tennesseans' name for White Rock, on the state line in the park), Rocky Top (in Thunderhead TN area). **1999** McNeil *Purchase Knob* 55 Low land might be called "bottoms" and high land "tops."

[DARE *top* n 1 southern Appalachians]

2 (as *top fodder, tops*) The portion of a corn plant on the stalk above the ears, cut or broken off in the fall for feeding to cattle during the winter as **fodder**. See also **blade fodder, cut tops B**.

1931 Goodrich *Mt Homespun* 54 The children were in the fields, stripping off the lower leaves of the corn for "blade fodder" while the larger boys and the men were "topping" the stalks; cutting the "top fodder" with a quick, dexterous slash of the knife. **1973** GSMNP-78:19 They would use corn stovers or tops we called it to cut the corn off above the ear, and they'd tie that up in a bundle and call it tops. Well, they'd pull the fodder off then, the rest of it, and use it in the fodder . . . the fodder was better feed than the tops because the tops had the stalk in it. **1975** *Used to Farm* 31 Every bit of the corn plant was used—from the ear up was referred to as "tops" and from the ear down "fodder."

B *verb*

1 To cut or break off (the top of a tobacco plant or the top of a cornstalk) for use as **fodder**. See also **cut tops**.

[See **1931** in **A2**.] **1985** Irwin *Alex Stewart* 267 I was working down here for John Miser topping corn and Lloyd was following along behind me pulling the fodder.

2 To use dynamite to shear off the surface of a mountain to strip off exposed seams of coal in the process often called "mountaintop removal."

1997 Hufford *American Ginseng* 16 Mountaintop removal is a method of mining that shears off the top of a mountain, allowing the efficient recovery of multiple seams of coal. When the "topped" mountains are rigorously reclaimed under the terms of the Surface Mining Control and Reclamation Act of 1977, the rich soils essential to ginseng and hardwood cove forests are gone, and with them the multigenerational achievement of the commons.

top fodder See **top A2**.

top off *verb phrase* To fatten (a hog) in an enclosed area before selling or butchering it.

1984 Page and Wigginton *Foxfire Cookery* 117 We always fattened our hogs in a floored pen and topped them off on corn. Of course, they could get fat in the mountains eating chestnuts, but the meat from chestnuts could be streaky and flabby. We didn't like it. So we would always catch our hogs and bring them in and pen them and top them off on corn. **1995** Trout *Historic Buildings* 56 Entry into the pen was a one-way trip for the pig. There he was "topped off," or fattened for a while on corn and chestnuts. Limiting his movement hastened weight gain.

top of Smoky (also *top of Smoky Mountain*) *noun phrase* The main chain or ridge of the Great Smoky Mountains, which runs along the TN/NC state border. Same as **(the) Smoky**. See also **Big Smokies**.

1927 Thornburgh *Tramping* 466 Looking out over an unended sea of mountains tumbled and massed confusingly, I suddenly realized that "Top of Smoky" as the main divide is affectionately called by the mountain people, is literally the tops of many high ridges, which branch off into North Carolina and Tennessee and are connected by other mountains or narrow ridges. **1939** Hall *Coll* (Deep Creek NC) The hounds was a-fighting right in under, to the right of the Clingmans Dome. They was in three hundred yards of the top of Smoky fighting. *Ibid.* (Hazel Creek NC) [The panther] took right up to the top of the bald and right up to the top of Smoky, right up to the top. . . . Top of Smoky was the line, the state line, between Tennessee and North Carolina. . . . Well, I herded lots right on the top of Smoky, lots of cattle. **1953** Hall *Coll* (Bryson City NC) That's a house that I had to live in on top of Smoky Mountain. *Ibid.* (Walland TN) [I] worked at logging for several years, mostly in this county . . . I worked on Smoky some, the foothills. Some of the finest timber was in Aunt Becky Cable's Sugar Cove. Most of the timber at the top of Smoky is scrubby. **1975** GSMNP-59:15 My father took it on top of Smoky Mountain at the head of what we call Locust Ridge.

top out *verb phrase* To reach the crest of a ridge or summit of a mountain.

1922 Kephart *Our Sthn High* 212 At a few minutes past 3 p.m., we "topped out" in the Gap. **1930** Fink *Trails* 69 Let the clothes be stout, to resist the dense underbrush that often intrudes on the trail, and preferably of wool, to guard against chill after a drenching in an unexpected shower or when, after a strenuous climb, one "tops out" on a high ridge to face the searching breezes of the upper levels. **1939** Hall *Coll* (Deep Creek NC) I went on and topped out at the Bear Pen Gap that's at the far winter range, at the back of Round Top. Well, when I topped out, the hounds was a-fighting right in under, to the right of the Clingmans Dome. **1970** Broome *Earth Man* 74 After two more miles, you "top out" on the Stateline. **1986** Rader *Mt Legacy* 22 Just before we topped out on the main lead of the mountain top, we passed through a small natural bench covered with small poplars on one end and sheltered by its saucer-like topography.

top over *verb phrase* To cross over a ridge or mountain crest.

1915 Bohannon *Bear Hunt* 464 As Old Sharpnose was only a few yards ahead of the dogs when she topped over, the dogs were soon hot on her trail down the Tennessee side and within a few minutes they were baying her far down the mountain-side.

tops See **fodder**, **top A2**.

tore See **tear A**.

tore down See **torn down**.

tore up See **tear up**.

Torey See **tory**.

torge See **towards**.

torment

A Variant forms *tarment* [see **1865** in **B**], *tarmint*.

1928 (in **1952** Mathes *Tall Tales* 60) Fer five year he's been in a endurin' tarmint. **1942** Hall *Phonetics Smoky Mts* 33.

B *verb* To exasperate, annoy, tease (someone).

1865 *Larue CW Letters* (Jan 5) I hope we wont be tarmented with them a gain. . . . [I]t appeares thos tarmenting Rebes are constantly Tarrying up the Rail Rod ever chance thay get. **1913** Kephart *Our Sthn High* 78 I had one tormentin' time findin' my hat. **1957** Broaddus *Vocab Estill Co KY* 81 = to annoy, tease. **1994–97** Montgomery *Coll* (known to Adams, Brown, Cardwell, Jones, Weaver).

C *noun* Hell.

1892 Dromgoole *War of Roses* 492 He couldn't fetch that note, not ter save his soul from torment. **1923** Greer-Petrie *Angeline Doin' Society* 2 Hit would sarve her right if'n she landed in the hottest part of torment and sizzled thar fur alluz! **1930** Armstrong *This Day and Time* 33 I reckon I've died an' went to torment. **1976** Still *Pattern of Man* 57 There's even a woman on the ticket, with about as much chance as a snowball in Torment. **1977** Shackelford et al. *Our Appalachia* 285 I thought shore I's bound fer tarment and couldn't shun it. **1991** Thomas *Sthn Appal* 238 People's a-gittin' too high-ish . . . in sa-siety, honey. Honey, that's th' reason 'at everthang's a-goin' to th' torment, jist as fast as it can. **2005** Williams *Gratitude* 533 *torment* = hell.

[DARE *torment* n chiefly South, South Midland]

torn down (also *tore down*) *adjective phrase* Hence participial adjective superlative forms *torn-downdest*, *torn-downest*.

1 Of a person: disreputable, dissolute, unruly.

1913 Kephart *Our Sthn High* 169 One day I asked a mountain man, "How about the revenue officers? What sort of men are they?" "Torn-down scoundrels, every onc." *Ibid.* 285 Peculiar adjectives are formed from verbs . . . "That Thunderhead is the torn-downdest place!" **1927** Woofter *Dialect from WV* 366 = worthless. "He is the most torn-down man in this neighborhood." **1944** Williams *Word-List Mts* 31 *torn down* = mischievous. "What can a body do with a gang of torn-down younguns under her feet?" **1944** Wilson *Word-List* 50 *torn downdest* = wildest, most destructive, most full of life. "I was one of the *torn downdest* tomboys you ever hear of." **1997** Montgomery *Coll*: She ain't nothing but a tore-down woman [i.e. morally bankrupt] (Andrews).

[cf Web3 *torn-down* n "an unruly person" dialect]

2 Of a place: dilapidated.

1974 Fink *Bits Mt Speech* 27 = dilapidated, messed up, etc. "That's the *torn-downdest* house I ever seen."

3 Of an occasion: wild, riotous, wonderful.

1986 Pederson et al. *LAGS* (Sullivan Co TN) A torn-down good time. **2007** McMillon *Notes*: *torn-down* = wonderful, great; thus *torn-downest* = best, wonderfullest, greatest, etc.

[OED3 *torn down* past-part/adj (at *torn* adj c(b)) "rough, riotous, boisterous" dialect and U.S.; Web3 *torn-down* adj "riotous, rough, unruly, violent" dialect]

tornel See **tarnal**.

tor(r)eckly See **directly**.

tory (also *torey*) *noun* A renegade soldier during the Civil War, usually one of Unionist sympathies who resisted Confederate conscription by hiding in the hills and preying on local citizenry; also used as a derogatory term for someone with such sympathies. See also **bee hunter**, **bushwhacker**, **jayhawker**, **outlier**, **scout C**.

1861 *Rector CW Letters* (Dec 8) I tell you we have had hot times down heare with the toryes we be gan to think we would have fighting right at home but they ware to[o] big couards to fight. **1862** *Bell CW Letters* (Jan 30) I suppose my boy[s] is having some difficulty in arresting those traitors & Deserters the Maj. will write Lieut Bird this evening & if these toreys resest ther arest he will send force enough to wipe out the overt act. **1862** *Haggard CW Letters* (Feb) I had the pleaserue of Seeing old Jeneral F. K. Zolakoffer the old tory after he was killed in the battle and not only him but ma[n]y others of his mates. **1862** *Patton CW Letters* (Jan 6)

I understand the tories have broke out in madison again and that our men has killed about forty. **1863** *Revis CW Letters* (May 13) we cotch a tory as we came on and kild him and the tories shot at our boys and shot one threw the hat. **1864** *Love CW Letters* (Jan 8) I here the torys and yanks are near asheville now. **1953** Bryan *Confederate GA* 152 In the fall of 1864 bands of Tories were plundering northeast Georgia. **1988** Bryan *Tories amidst Rebels* 4 Ironically, the policies adopted by Confederate authorities in dealing with East Tennessee "Tories" were similar to those used when their enemy occupied the South. Loyalty oaths, mass arrests of people on suspicion of treason, reconstruction of civil government, and at times, harsh treatment of civilians were no less hallmarks of the Confederate occupation of East Tennessee than they were of Union occupation of the South.

[originally "one of the dispossessed Irish, who became outlaws, subsisting by plundering and killing the English settlers and soldiers" (**2005** Crowley *War of Words*); OED3 Anglicized spelling of Irish **tóraidhe, -aighe* . . . "pursuer"]

tosel See **tossel.**

toss *verb* past-tense and past-participle form of two syllables: *tos(s)-ted*.

1924 Raine *Saddlebags* 96 They try to follow the modern trend, making a regular past tense end in *ed*. So they say . . . "He tosted us the hay." **1957** Combs *Lg Sthn High: Word List* 103 *tossted* = past-tense and past participle of *toss*. **1978** Burns *Our Sthn Mtneers* 12 On the other hand, they follow the modern trend and say "throwed," "growed," and "knowed," or go out of their way to be proper and say "borned" in June, "tosted" in the hay, or he "yelded" loud. **2009** Miller *Nigh Gone* 95 Double past tense of regular verbs or adding an extra "ed" to past tense verbs—"drowneded" instead of drowned, "tosseded" instead of tossed, and "yelleded" instead of yelled, etc. This is due largely to the mountain tendency to substitute a "t" or a "d" for the final consonant in a present tense verb ending in double "s" or double "l." Thus, in the mountain vernacular, toss would become "tost" and then be put into the past tense as a regular verb resulting in "tosted," or yell would become "yeld" and then "yelded."

tossel (also *tosel*) *noun* Variant form of *tassel*.

1862 *CW Soldiers' Letters* (June 28) the Boy has got the whet holed up and stack and wee have silkes and tosels the potatoes lokes finely. **1948** Chase *Grandfather Tales* 190 You couldn't see the tossel on it even with a spy-glass. **1966–68** *DARE Survey* (Brasstown NC, Spruce Pine NC). **1973** Miller *English Unicoi Co* 91 *tossel* attested by 5 of 6 speakers. **1999** *Montgomery Coll* (known to Cardwell). **2002** Morgan *Mt Born* 164 *tossel*.

tossted, tosted See **toss.**

totch See **touch B.**

tote *verb* Of a person: to carry (usually something heavy). See also **carry 1, pack B1.**

1834 Crockett *Narrative* 63 I would have taken her up, and toated her, if it hadn't been that I wanted her where I could see her all the time. **1847** (in **1870** Drake *Pioneer Life KY* 59) We, of course, went on foot, and I "toted" the peck of corn on my back. **1858** (in **1974** Harris *High Times* 134) I hearn them say "tote him to the Horsespital." **1862** *Dalton CW Letters* (Feb 5) wee have to toat wood about A half amile and mud I never Saw the like. **1864** *Reese CW Letters* (May 31) tha[y] giv mee a gun to tote But this morning colonel weaver had it turned over so I hav no gun to tote. **1883** Zeigler and Grosscup *Heart of Alleghanies* 298 You'd better die in the snow a peaceful death than be toted away by hants. **1889** Mooney *Folk Carolina Mts* 97 *Gwine* and *obleeged*, *tote* and *holp*, are universally used, and many words obsolete or almost unknown in other sections of the country are still retained here. **1929** (in **1952** Mathes *Tall Tales* 135) "Git out thar, Jake, an' tote the little-un in the house," Uncle Hamp ordered. **1939** *Hall Coll* (Big Creek NC) They'd th'ow [the bridegroom] a-straddle of a rail and tote him around. **1953** *Hall Coll* (Bryson City NC) First started huntin' at age fourteen, when I was big enough to tote a gun, with an old-fashioned rifle, killed squirrels and turkeys. . . . It was too heavy. Cope couldn't tote it. John couldn't tote it. **1974** Fink *Bits Mt Speech* 27 How much can you *tote*? **1979** *Smokies Heritage* 361 He fotched in all the wood he could "tote." **1983** *Dark Corner OHP-10A* That's our job when we were real little was toting slabs we called it. We didn't know "carry" then, so it was "toting," and we'd carry them as far as from here to the garden down there.

[OED3 *tote* v[1] says "origin unascertained. There is no foundation for an alleged origin in the black slave communities of the Southern States (and ultimately Africa); the quot. 1677 at sense **a** from Virginia does not refer to slaves; later the word is found well-established in the New England States; evidence for an Indian origin is also wanting"; DARE *tote* v A 1 widespread, but somewhat more frequent South, South Midland]

tote fair *verb phrase* To deal honestly with, carry one's fair share.

1866 Smith *So Called* 147 I don't think you tote fair. **1917** Kephart *Word-List* 418 *tote fair with* = to deal fairly with. **c1960** *Wilson Coll*: *tote fair* = to do one's own part honestly and willingly. **1974** Fink *Bits Mt Speech* 27 *tote fair* = deal honestly. "He'll *tote fair* in a trade." **1995** *Montgomery Coll*: *tote fair with* (known to Brown, Cardwell).

[DARE (at *tote* v B 2) chiefly South, South Midland]

tote-road *noun* A crude trail for transporting goods.

1917 Kephart *Camping & Woodcraft* 2:64 Once the old lumber-camp site is reached, even though it be long deserted, the signs of an old "tote-road" can be discerned, leading to a settlement from which supplies can be transported.

tote the mail *verb phrase* See citation. See also **rock B1.**

c1975 Lunsford *It Used to Be* 167 "Tote the mail" is a term used to say of a fellow who gets in a hurry. You say, "I made him tote the mail," and it means I made him run. A boy sometimes, maybe a stranger in the community and not acquainted so well in the community, maybe accompanies some young lady home up the creek.

The boys will get together and get along on the side of the road somewhere in the pines where they know he'll come back by, and they will throw a few rocks his way,—toss first one or two over in behind him on the road and he backs up. They throw some more and, of course, as he goes on they throw quite a number in his direction, and their report is, "Boys we made him tote the mail." You speak to a fellow and tell him, "Tote the mail pumpus."

[DARE (at *tote* v B 6) especially South]

t'other (also *tother*) *pronoun, adjective* See also **another'un, other'un, tothern.**

1 (also *the t'other*) Other.

1831 (in **1956** Eliason *Tarheel Talk* 301) (Rutherford Co NC) The whole town were putting on their "tother clothes." **1834** Crockett *Narrative* 31 I was trying to get as far the t'other way as possible. **1924** Montague *Betsy Beaver* 221 They's all of a size, like they'd been hatched outer the one cone, and all going up the ridge one right behind the tother. **1937** Hall *Coll* (Cades Cove TN) The fer mountains [are on] the t'other side of the cove. **1939** Hall *Coll* (Copeland Creek TN) When one's gone, the t'other's proud of it. **1967** Hall *Coll* (Townsend TN) I remember him just the same as it a-being the tother day.

[Web3 *tother* adj chiefly dialect]

2 (also *tuther*) The other. See also **tother house.**

1849 Lanman *Alleghany Mts* 49 Old Vandever is an illiterate man, and when I asked him to give me his opinion of President Polk, he replied: "I never seed the Governor of this State; for, when he came to this country some years ago, I was off on 'tother side of the ridge, shooting deer." **1862** *Bradshaw CW Letters* (March 30) [You] have fur gotton me one or tother. **1862** *Lockmiller CW Letters* (Oct 30) I have Seen aheape of my cind folks in the armey wee past william vincent tother Side of the mountin. **1867** Harris *Sut Lovingood* 24 Every now an' then he'd fan the side ove his hed, fust wif wun fore laig an' then tuther. **1898** Elliott *Durket Sperret* 133 T'other night they hearn a great miration in the chicken house, an' they ketched two critters eatin' jest ever'thing. **1913** Kephart *Our Sthn High* 81 T'other way, no hound'll raelly fight a bar—hit takes a big severe dog to do that. **1924** Spring *Lydia Whaley* 3 There were two brothers in the Burg—one loafered, tother one was in a notion of marryin'. **1941** Stuart *Men of Mts* 268 I seen a big rat runnin' out'n here t' other day. **1954** Arnow *Dollmaker* 87 She didn't come with t'others that Sunday about a week ago. **1963** Edwards *Gravel* 13 I tole Ma tother day this might happen just anytime. **1974** GSMNP-50:1:16 One or t'other of them whupped the other one. **1976** Ogle and Nixon *If Only* We always called it this house and "tother" house.

[*the tother* represents an incorrect division of Middle English *thet other* < Old English *þæt oþer* "the other"; OED3 *tother* pron/adj now Scot, nEngl; EDD (at *tother* indef pron) Scot, nIrel, Engl; cf SND *tither* pron/adj; CUD *tother* pron "the other"; HT *tither*[1] adj "other"; Web3 *tother* pron chiefly dialect; DARE *tother* pron, adj chiefly New England, South, South Midland]

tother house *noun* The smaller room of a two-room dwelling.

1927 Furman *Lonesome Road* 12 Across the front of the home were two large rooms, "main-house" and "tuther-house," with "kitchen-house" in their rear.

tothern (also *t'othern, t'other'n, t'other'un*) *pronoun* The other one. See also **another'un, other'un, t'other.**

1923 Greer-Petrie *Angeline Doin' Society* 8 One of 'em was a-blowin' a saxyfone, as the Jedge called hit, and t'other'n a trumbone. **1940** Haun *Hawk's Done* 21 I can nigh see them now—the both of them setting there, either one thinking of tothern. **1954** Arnow *Dollmaker* 116 They's no need fer neither a ye tu give in tu t'othern. **1981** Williams *Storytelling* He started out, a-swinging his little budget in one hand and a-pulling his drag sled with t'other'un. **1986** Ogle *Lucinda* 48 The second log cabin was referred to as this house and "tothern." *Ibid.* 223 She would put two forked sticks into the ground and put the kittel on a stick that retch from one fork to tothern. **1995** South *What It Is* 34 [The sandwich]'uz a whole fish, 'twixt two slices whitebread, with the head stickin' out-a one side, and the tail out t'other'n.

t'othern, t'other'n, t'other'un See **tothern.**

to the side of *conjunctive phrase* See citation.

2005 Williams *Gratitude* 533 = compared to. "It was a nice house *to the side of* the one they'd been living in."

toting papers *noun* An arrest warrant.

1952 Wilson *Folk Speech NC* 602 The sheriff was here looking for you. He had *toting papers* for you. **1996–97** Montgomery *Coll* (known to Brown, Bush, Cardwell).

touch

A *noun, verb* Variant forms *tech, tetch.*

1859 Taliaferro *Fisher's River* 64–67 I could smash bucks anywhar and any time, but that sassy rascal, I couldn't tech a har on him. **1863** *Tesh CW Letters* (Nov 1) I got to camp without Tetching My butter or molasses I tell You it goes splendid now and it was a sight to see me eat it and Think who cooked it and how good it was. **1905** Miles *Spirit of Mts* 43 We're all tired of 'em; I put 'em on the table and they ain't tetched. **1940** Haun *Hawk's Done* 193 Number 2 grabbed the pillow and throwed it at Ma, but the pillow landed over on the floor and appeared to have gone right through Ma without ever teching her. **1957** Parris *My Mts* 256 "Come with me boy," he said. "Reckon you could do with a tetch of whiskey." **1961** Kurath and McDavid *Pron Engl Atl Sts* 146 *Touch* . . . commonly has the vowel . . . of *fetch* in the folk speech of the South and the South Midland. **1974** Roberts *Sang Branch* 293 When he tetched them all they every one of them turned into rocks.

[DARE *touch* v, n (pronc) chiefly South, South Midland]

B *verb* Variant past-tense form *totch.*

1867 Harris *Sut Lovingood* 59 Then he totch ontu me; sed I wer a livin proof ove the hell-desarvin nater ove man. **1942** Hall *Phonetics Smoky Mts* 40 = *old-fashioned.*

[DARE *touch* v, n B chiefly South, South Midland]

touched *adjective* Variant forms *teched*, *tetched*.

1936 Ogden *Rescue Work* One mountaineer lamented, "She must be a leetle grain teched." **1974** Fink *Bits Mt Speech* 26 = feeble-minded or slightly deranged. "Their least boy is sorter *tetched*." **2000** Lowry *Folk Medical Term* = mentally unbalanced. "He is tetched in the head."

touch-me-not *noun* A wildflower (*Impatiens* spp) with a seedpod that bursts open when touched. See also **jewel flower**, **snapweed**, **water weed**.

1961 Douglas *My Wilderness* 173 We found the touch me not in seed. I learned that its seed pods are under tension. For when I touched one, it would burst, sending its seeds out in a radius of eighteen inches or more. Its appropriate scientific name is *Impatiens*. **1962** Brewer *Hiking* 34 [A flower] that's numerous in late summer is the touch-me-not, ranging in color from yellow to nearly white.

touchous *adjective*

A Variant forms *tetcheous* [see **1933** in **B2**], *tetcherous* [see **1976** in **B2**], *tetchified* [see **1957** citations in **B2**], *tetchious* [see **1913** in **B2**], *tetchous* [see **1966** in **B2**], *tetchus* [see **1867** in **B2**].

B Senses.

1 Physically tender or sensitive, sore or painful to touch, delicate.

1990 Cavender *Folk Medical Lex* 33 = painfully sensitive to movement or touch. "This toe is so touchous I can hardly walk." **1994** Montgomery *Coll*: *touchous* (known to Cardwell, Ogle). **1997** Dante *OHP-53* [The job] was touchous, but I was young and had just come back.

[DARE *touchous* adj 2 South, South Midland]

2 Easily offended, irritable, sensitive.

1867 Harris *Sut Lovingood* 96 Now haint hit strange how tetchus they [are], on the subjick ove bees? **1913** Kephart *Our Sthn High* 294 A choleric or fretful person is tetchious. **1933** Thomas *Traipsin' Woman* 19–20 When we had passed on quite a distance I heard Still Tongue mumbling, "The Trivitts is a tetcheous race." **1957** Combs *Lg Sthn High: Word List* 99 *tetchified*, *tetchious* = choleric, fretful. **1966** Dakin *Vocab Ohio River Valley* 466 Old variants [of *tetchy*] both of these terms, *touchous* and *tetchous*, are usual in the Mountains (*tetchous* in the south) and southern Kentucky and fairly common among older speakers everywhere in this state. Only the younger and more educated in the Mountains and the south have abandoned this old form in favor of the standard touchy. **1966** Dykeman *Far Family* 202 We won't mention anything to the others about Nye Blankenship having been in prison. He might be touchous about it. **1974** Fink *Bits Mt Speech* 26 She's powerful *tetchous* these days. **1976** Garber *Mountain-ese* 92 Tetcherous . . . touchy, edgy—She's mighty tetcherous about that subject so don't mention it to her. **1986** Pederson et al. *LAGS*: *touchous* = attested by 17/60 interviewees (28.3%) from E TN and 1/35 (2.9%) from N GA; 18/77 of all LAGS interviewees (23.3%) attesting term were from Appalachia. **1990** Cavender *Folk Medical Lex* 33 = [having] an irritable disposition. "She gets so touchous when you talk about politics." **1994** Montgomery *Coll* (known to Cardwell, Ogle). **1998** Hyde *My Home* 46 If a person was highly fretful, the word to describe that person was "tetchious," probably from "toucheous," meaning not wanting to be touched.

[OED3 *touchous* adj dialect; Web3 *touchous* adj "touchy" chiefly dialect; DARE *touchous* adj 1 chiefly South, South Midland]

touch up *verb phrase* Of medicine: to invigorate.

1968 Stubbs *Mountain-Wise* (April–May) 10 Doc looked in his satchel an' got him out some energizin' medicine to tech him up.

tough jack *noun* Molasses candy. Same as **molasses candy**.

1957 Combs *Lg Sthn High Word-List* 103 = a tough candy made by boiling molasses at a "candy pulling." **1969** *DARE Survey* (Honeybee KY) = molasses candy, old-fashioned. **1983** Farr *More Moonshine* 193 We always called molasses candy "Tough Jack"—I was never sure why, unless it was hard work pulling, doubling back, twisting, and pulling again until the candy was taffy colored and firm.

[DARE *tough jack* n especially KY]

tough row of stumps *noun phrase* A path difficult to clear or manage. See citation.

1984 Woods *WV Was Good* 14 It is from this phase of clearing new land and growing corn on the newground that we get the old expression, "a tough row of stumps." Also, "a hard row to hoe."

tourister *noun* A tourist (a facetious term introduced to the mountains in recent times).

1975 Dwyer *Thangs* 5 We don't advise touristers to go galavantin' around the mountains callin' natives "hillbillies." **1997** Montgomery *Coll* (known to Adams, Bush, Cardwell, Jones, Ledford, Oliver, Weaver). **2005** Jones and Wheeler *Laughter in Appalachia* 85 This tourister came along driving a big black Cadillac and asked me if I'd like a ride.

[DARE *tourister* n chiefly South, South Midland]

touron *noun* See citation.

2000 Brown *Far East* 215 In any given day behind the counter at the Sugarlands Visitor Center [of Great Smoky Mountains National Park], park rangers still hear visitors ask where Sugarcreek is. With a map containing the correct names laid in front of them, tourists wonder aloud about "Kingmans Doom" (Clingmans Dome) or "Codes Cave" (Cades Cove). Although proper park etiquette in the 1950s and 1960s required park rangers to call every traveler a "visitor," privately they joked about individual "tourons" (a combination of tourist and moron). **2006** *Encycl Appalachia* 890 In the Smokies, the quintessential tourists are "Maud and Henry," whose antics are preserved by park rangers in both oral narratives and in notebooks. Maud and Henry are the folks who want to know if they will see giraffes on the Cades Cove loop road or ask if there is anything to see besides mountains in the park. More generically, there are "tourons," the especially moronic tourists that rangers and local people encounter.

towards *preposition* Variant forms *torge, towardge, to warge, twarge, tworge.*

1862 *Shifflet CW Letters* (July 13) we ar a gardin a rail rode and helpin bild bridges betwixt Chattanooga and nashville we ar a comin to warge nashville. **1937** Hyatt *Kiverlid* 87 Oncet a pant'er run Gran'pap an' another feller mor'n a mile, as they lit out one night goin' torge home. **1944** Williams *Word-List Mts* 32 *towardge.* **1963** Edwards *Gravel* 16 That's what Old Dom was asaying out round the barn lot and down the little sandy road twarge the spring. *Ibid.* 100 She looked up tworge the mountain, and it was all black with shadder.

[DARE *torge, towardge, twarge* (at *toward* prep) especially South Midland]

tow bag See **tow sack.**

to where *conjunction* To or at the point that.

1953 Hall Coll (Bryson City NC) The coons, they was hung up to where they froze up and was all right. **1973** GSMNP-4:1:12 The CCC was beginning to work on [the roads], you know, at that time and put gravel and clean out to where you could travel then pretty good. **1975** *Richard and Margaret* 10 People are selling out their land even to where their children couldn't have anywhere to live. **1978** Montgomery *White Pine Coll* III-1 They've gotten it under control now to where they have a pretty good drainage on that. *Ibid.* VIII-2 I got to where I like to hear stuff like that. **1984** Page and Wigginton *Foxfire Cookery* 270 He put that thing together, put a head on it and fixed it to where it'd hold water. **1995** Adams *Come Go Home* 91 Cas used to say that he had ridden on Inez's hip enough to where he felt like he ought to be one of her young'uns. **2006** Childs *Texana* 39 Finally Peter woke up and he came out and got Cooper to where I could go into the house.

town ball *noun* A simplified form of baseball played with homemade bats and balls. See also **blind cat, bull pen, cat 1, two-eyed cat.**

1813 Hartsell *Memora* 134 Several of the Majors and Several of the Docters and my Selfe Commenced the game Coled town ball, for to heave It to Day we had no other Sport for acrismass frolic. **1892** Smith *Farm and Fireside* 267 Base-ball has grown out of town-ball; it is no improvement. The pitcher used to belong to the ins and threw the best ball he could, for he wanted it hit . . . but now he belongs to the outs and wants it missed. We used to throw at a boy to stop him running to another base, and we hit him if we could, but these modern balls are hard and heavy and dangerous. **1904** (in **2002** Gibson *Gibson Remembers*) 15 The boys played baseball and the girls played "town-ball" with balls made of yarn, and batted with a bat, then run to first base. If the ball was thrown between them and the base, they were out. **1915** Dingus *Word-List VA* 192 = of two kinds—straight-town and round-town—according to the position of the bases. **1959** Wilgus *Down Our Way* 1 To set forth the rules of town ball or even to describe the game as played in Kentucky is difficult. In fact, it would be accurate to say that is the name applied to any game of base-ball—and some games that are not baseball—not played with regulation equipment and according to the standard rules. Most historians of baseball identify town ball . . . as an adult form of rounders that developed in New England before 1850 and had as its distinguishing feature a sixty-foot square playing field, with the batter's station midway between "first" and "home." **1976** Miller *Mts within Me* 39 A favorite game was "town ball." It was played with a rubber ball and a broomstick. You were out if you struck at the ball and the catcher caught it on the first bounce or if you hit it and the fielder caught it on the first bounce. The most exciting way to be put out was by the pitcher's hitting the runner between bases with the ball. Some pitchers would try to hit the skirts of girl runners and make them fly up with resulting threats of "If you don't stop that, I'm going to tell the Principal." **1984** Smith *Enduring Memories* 7 Town ball was played with a soft rubber ball and any type of bat we could find, round or flat. The rules were similar to softball except the team in the field could also get an out by throwing the ball in front of the baserunner as he or she advanced on the bases. **1985** *Schools and Pastimes* 43 I have no idea where the game "town ball" got its name. It was played with any kind of ball and bat, the ball usually homemade by winding yarn around a buckeye or marble and a bat whittled out of a short, thick board. At the beginning of the game two of the older boys would choose sides in this manner: one tossed the bat or stick through the air to the other who caught it somewhere near the bottom. Then they grasped it fist over fist until there was no room at the top. The one whose fist ended up on top got the privilege of choosing the first player. Then they alternately chose one after another until all the players were on one side or the other. Each captain designated a pitcher and catcher. Everyone took a turn at bat and ran the bases as they do in baseball, but a player was called "out" when the ball was fielded and thrown across in front of him as he ran between bases; "crossing out" it was called. **1987** Carver *Regional Dialects* 172 Perhaps a more common pastime, especially among boys, is *town ball*, a bat-and-ball game resembling baseball but with fewer players. *DeWitt's Base-Ball Guide* noted that "nearly forty years ago [this] species of base-ball . . . was in vogue." It was called town ball because it was played whenever a town meeting was held. **1993** Page and Smith *Foxfire Toys and Games* 6 Apparently every community played its own version of ball, sometimes using different names. Field-ball is a variant of Catball, sometimes under the same name—the most common being Townball. There are common elements: pitcher, catcher, batters, bases, and, of course, ball and bat. (We did find one variant, Bullpen, described by Ernest Rogers, that does not use a bat.) Most were played with homemade balls and homemade bats. Games usually ended when it got dark. Baseball and Softball, with their standardized rules, replaced Town-ball, Catball, and Fieldball, with their adjustable rules and local adaptations. Store-bought, manufactured balls and bats replaced homemade. *Ibid.* 9 Ray Hicks: Townball was generally played like baseball, but in Townball you had to get every member of the batting team out before the opposite team went up to bat. And when you got them all out you had what we called "town"—that was the opportunity to have a round at bat. Three of the fastest runners were placed on first base. They'd throw the batter the ball, he'd hit it, and the first runner would go around the bags [bases]. If the batter didn't knock it too hard, the pitcher got the ball, and he hit the runner [with the ball]. 'Course the runner would stop and lurk; he would get half way home and somebody from the other team would get behind him and catch the ball while the catcher threw it. They'd try to make a run successfully home without being tagged out. If the runners made three safe runs, then the whole in-team got another chance at bat.

[Web3 *townball* n "a ball game preceding and resembling baseball" so called from the fact that it was played during the time of town meetings; DARE *town ball* n 1 chiefly South, South Midland]

town dood See **town dude.**

town dude (also *town dood*) *noun* See citations.

1967–69 DARE *Survey* (Rome GA, Gatlinburg TN) = nickname for a citified person. **2005** Williams *Gratitude* 169 Some of the outdoor games I remember us a-playin' was Whoopee Hide, which the town doods at school called "Hide And Seek."

townified *adjective* Having characteristics of being from a town of city.

1966 DARE *Survey* (Burnsville NC) = nickname for a city person. **1998** Montgomery *Coll* (known to Cardwell), = mountaineers often make adjectives/adverbs from practically any noun or other part of speech by simply adding "fied." A person who is argumentative may be said to be "argufied," or a fish market might be said to smell "fishified." It would not be uncommon for a person who exhibited characteristics of a town resident to be called "townified" (Ledford).

tow of logs See **trail of logs.**

tow sack (also *toe sack, tow bag*) *noun* A large, heavy bag made from tow, used to carry farm produce and other commodities, a gunny sack. Also called **chopsack, coffee sack, crocus bag, grass sack.**

1913 Kephart *Our Sthn High* 21 In many districts the only means of transportation is with saddle-bags on horseback, or with a "tow sack" afoot. **1934–47** LAMSAS *Appal* (Madison Co NC, Swain Co NC) *tow sack*. **1949** Kurath *Word Geog East US* 57 *Tow sack* is the North Carolina term [for the coarse loose-woven sack in which potatoes and other farm produce are shipped]. It is common throughout the state and rare outside of it, except around Norfolk, Virginia. **1952–57** (in **1973** McDavid and McDavid *Vocab E KY* 156) *tow sack* = attested by 8/52 (15.3%) of E KY speakers for the Linguistic Atlas of the North Central States. **1958** Newton *Dialect Vocab*: *tow sack* = common term in E TN mountains, as opposed to *burlap bag, crocus/croker sack, tow bag*. **1966** DARE *Survey* (Cherokee NC) *tow sack* = a cloth container for feed, a container of rough brown cloth, commonly used for potatoes. **1973** GSMNP-79:19 On the weekends way back I've heard them talk about riding the horses to the ramp patches, filling the tow sacks. **1984** Smith *Enduring Memories* 26 We would shell a large sack, (burlap) that we called a "toe sack," full of corn and take it to one of the mills with the wagon and mules. The mill owner would measure out his share in a tall bucket and then pour the rest of the shelled corn in the hopper and place our meal sack over the opening where the fresh ground meal would come out. When the corn was completely ground into meal we would take the meal back home and pour it into a large wooden chest, called the meal chest, and Mother would use it as needed. **1986** Ogle *Lucinda* 59 They would pay us twenty-five cents a tow sack full of Galax leaves and ground pine. **1986** Pederson et al. *LAGS tow sack* = attested by 40/60 interviewees (66.7%) from E TN and 11/35 (31.4%) from N GA; 51/315 of all LAGS interviewees (16.1%) attesting term were from Appalachia. **1996** Johnson *Lexical Change* 138 *tow bag* = statistically more common in the mountains of South Carolina and Georgia than in the Piedmont and Coastal Plain c1990. **1997** King *Mt Folks* 1 The dried peas are placed in a tow sack (a sack made from yarn spun from coarse tow fibers).

[DARE *tow bag* n formerly widespread, now especially NC; *tow sack* n chiefly South, South Midland, TX, OK]

to yonder See **yonder D3.**

trace *noun*

1 A path or trail across rough terrain, as one made originally by animals or indigenous peoples and later by hunters and settlers marking trees; a crude trail usually passable only on foot or by horse.

1925 Furman *Glass Window* 197 At the head of the hollow, a slight trail or "trace" tacked up the mountainside to the gap above. Reaching this gap, they looked down into steeply sloping valleys on both sides, and from thence followed nothing more than what was a cowpath along the narrow comb of the ridge. **1972** Alderman *Big Bald* 16 The buffalo was a trail-breaker. He has been dubbed the engineer of the animal world. His instinct guided routes of least resistance from feeding grounds to salt licks. The creeks and river valleys, covered with thick cane brakes, furnished much of his winter food. A good sized herd would soon demolish a meadow of cane and then move on to another valley. Somehow the cane would grow back to furnish food for another day. The herds traveled single file through the mountain passes and across fordable spots in the riverbeds. In many places the three foot wide trail would be packed two or three feet below the ground surface. The Indians of the Mound Building period were known to use these traces in going from tribe to tribe. The traces became their trails of communication and war paths to battle. The Great Indian War Path, running from the south northward, is thought to have once been a buffalo trace. **1977** Shields *Cades Cove* 10 During this period the only access to the cove was by way of the old Indian traces. **1983** Montell *Don't Go Up* 201 = hand-blazed, rough trail, designed for horseback or ox-cart travel. **1998** Montgomery *Coll* = a trail from Cosby Tn. to the Cherokee nation is still called by some the "Moonshine Trace" because much moonshine whiskey was carried over this trail (Brown). **2000** Morgan *Mts Remember* 6 There wasn't hardly a road up Saluda mountain and through the gap except the little wagon trace down through Gap Creek. **2005** Hicks *Blood and Bone* 69 I heard the mule / on the trace, bearing Mama and her black bag of relief. **2013** Lyon *Voice-*

place 186 I saw a historical marker pointing to a part of the buffalo trace you can still walk on, so I set off into the woods.

[OED3 *trace* n[1] 5b "a beaten path through a wild or unenclosed region" U.S.; Web3 *trace* n 2c "a marked or blazed trail through woods or over open land"]

2 A branch of a stream.

1924 Raine *Saddlebags* 5–6 In one day's journey you may ford the river a hundred times; or you may "take up" a "branch" or "fork" or "trace" to its source in a spring near the top of a ridge, then follow the trail across the ridge, through the "gap," till on the other side you come upon another little brooklet, which you follow down till it empties into a larger stream. **1997** Montgomery *Coll* (known to Bush, Cardwell, Jones).

trace up (also *track up*) *verb phrase* To trace, track down.

1939 Hall *Coll* (Smokemont NC) He went back into the laurel hung with this trap, and finally we traced him up. **1940** Oakley *Roamin'/Restin'* 109 He wanted to know why I was so far from home and up in the Mountains so I said I was out trying to track up Rack coons and Oposams in the snow.

track up See **trace up.**

track walker *noun* In logging, a worker who patrols a section of railway and inspects it for problems.

1991 Weals *Last Train* 39 The big activity in that part of the Smokies then was with the Little River Lumber Co. Shelton's several jobs with the company included one as a "track walker" and later as a track maintenance foreman on the railroad.

trade *verb*

1 To engage in a business.

1939 Hall *Coll* (Bradley Fork NC) I went in that area to trade, and I went in the milling business, mill company. I learned my trade.

2 To shop for goods, buy things; hence verbal noun *trading* = shopping, making purchases, doing business with.

1864 *Chapman CW Letters* (May 13) I shal Start to Williamsberg to morrow or nex day To mail this Letter and To trade some. **1913** Morley *Carolina Mts* 162 Another stranger fed a mountain woman, who, having come to town to "trade," stopped at the door tired and hungry, to sell her butter. **1940** Oakley *Roamin'/Restin'* 62 One Summer day Mrs. Wiley had gone to Gatlinburg to do some trading while I keep house and look after the boys. **c1950** Adams *Grandpap* 56 He went on into town an' done his tradin' an' started back home. **1967** Fetterman *Stinking Creek* 69 He does all the family "trading" in small stores, and on occasion can be found in Barbourville, twenty miles from his house, arguing politics or watching the cattle sell under the auctioneer's chant at the stockyard. **1971** *AOHP/ALC-4* On an average [the prices at the company store] were a little high, but the most of people traded there. **1975** Purkey *Madison Co* 80 We got our mail on Saturday when we went to town to trade. **1989** *Matewan OHP-1* My grandmother traded at the private stores a lot. **1998** *Dante OHP-61* I'd go to the store of the morning and trade for three people before I'd go to school. **2008** McKinley *Bear Mt* 183 (also *trade with*) = [to] buy from or do business with.

trade howdy See **howdy B.**

trade last *noun* See citation. See also **last go trade.**

c1960 Wilson *Coll* = a compliment in trade or return for one.

trading See **trade 2.**

traffic about (also *traffic around*) *verb* To loaf, to walk or wander aimlessly.

1913 Kephart *Our Sthn High* 203 Jist traffickin' about. **1994** Montgomery *Coll*: *traffic around* (known to Cardwell).

[EDD *traffic(k)* v 8 "to walk about aimlessly, to trespass on another's property"; DARE at *traffic* v especially southern Appalachians]

trafling See **trifling.**

trail *verb*

1 Of cattle: to drag (felled timber).

1977 *Foxfire IV* 271 If you was on steep ground, you could take six head of cattle and in places trail as many as fifteen logs behind them. Just looked like a freight train.

2 (also *trail out*) To follow a path.

1926 Hunnicutt *Twenty Years* 46 Old Muse trailed out to the head of Little Cove. *Ibid.* 51 Old Muse trailed up the creek to the falls and there she got bothered very badly. **1939** Hall *Coll* (Proctor NC) That old dog we had with us, an old hound, he struck somep'n's track, and he trailed on up that creek till I guess he trailed two mile, every bit of it.

trail dog (also *trailer*) *noun* A hunting dog especially skilled in following a scent and trailing game. See also **cold trailer.**

1955 Parris *Roaming Mts* 175 Some of 'em are trailers and some of 'em are only fighters. **1995** Montgomery *Coll* (known to Cardwell, Ledford, Shields). **2007** Neufeld *History W NC* 23 Fallen snow had already smothered bear tracks and scent, but the dogs sniffed fur-brushed bushes until a trail dog scratched his way under a pile of tree tops heaped up by a lumber company.

trailer See **trail dog.**

trail grab See **trail of logs.**

trail of logs (also *trail grab*) *noun phrase* A line of logs for cattle to drag down a slope. See also **trail together.**

1964 Clarkson *Lumbering in WV* 373 *trail of logs, tow of logs.* **1979** Carpenter *Walton War* 123 His story is an excursion into the past; for now, for better or worse, machinery has done away with the era of the double-bit ax, the crosscut saw and "trail grabs" of up to 20 big logs being "skidded" out of the mountains behind teams of horses, oxen, or mules.

trail out See **trail 2**.

trail together (also *trail up*) *verb phrase* To line up (logs) preparatory to having cattle drag them. See also **trail of logs**.

1977 *Foxfire IV* 271 Whenever I got them logs all trailed up together, I wouldn't have to do nothing only just get the slack all pulled out of them. *Ibid.* 272 Take half a day to get'em. Maybe be two o'clock before you got'em all trailed together and ready to go out with'em.

tramp *verb*

A Variant form *tromp*. See also **tromp**.

1891 Brown *Dialect in TN* 171 We very frequently hear stomp for stamp. . . . Similarly we have tromp for tramp. **1915** Dingus *Word-List VA* 192 *tromp*. **1927** Montague *Hog's Eye* 193 'Fore he seen it, Big Henry tromped down on the thing, and mashed it right inter Kingdom Come! **1935** Sheppard *Cabins in Laurel* 89 You just had to take your chance of tromping on [snakes] and bear away from where you heard 'em sing. **1939** Hall *Coll* I've tromped all over these mountains. **1960** McCaulley *Cades Cove* Agin you'd put five hundred head of cattle in there, they'd have what little grass there was tromped up. **1973** *Carpenter* 123 He got t'hearin' things a'trompin' an' he thought it was a horse. **2003** Onchuck *Mud Pie Memories* 99 They tromped through the fields and brush making all sorts of gyrations and silly motions, which each follower would then mimic.

B (also *tramp snow*) Of a fire in the fireplace: to signal approaching snow by crackling in an unusual manner.

1937 Wilson *Folklore SE KY* 14 When the fire is "tromping snow," it will snow (known to 8/31 speakers in Bell Co KY and 16/31 speakers in Blount Co TN). **1949** Arnow *Hunter's Horn* 362 His old daddy, Enoch, had smelled more snow in the air the day before, and all night the fire had tramped snow, and sure enough it had started snowing before they'd gone five mile. *Ibid.* 383 Something else could maybe make that noise; lots a times when it's turnen colder they's funny noises in trees an rocks; mebbe it's th fire trampen snow in a new kind a way we don't know about. **1962** Wilson *Folkways Mammoth Cave* 22 When the fire in the fireplace makes strange noises, that is called *tramping* /tromping/ snow; that is, there will soon be enough snow to make noises when you *tromp* on it. **2009** Miller *Nigh Gone* 58 If the fire "tramped" or made a soft, sputtering sound, snow could be expected soon.

[DARE *tramp snow* v phr especially South, South Midland]

trash *noun*

1 A grade of leaf from near the bottom of a tobacco stalk.

1968 Guthrie *Tobacco* 41 The grades most often made were, beginning at the bottom of the stalk, dog-trash, trash, lugs, bright-leaf, red-leaf, and tips. Sometimes these six grades were further sub-divided on the basis of length of leaf.

[DARE *trash* n chiefly South Midland, especially KY]

2 Used as a derogatory term for a white person from Appalachia. [Editor's note: This usage is more common in the Deep South.]

1997 Miller *Brier Poems* 70 They said we were trash, said we were Briers.

trash mover *noun*

1 A sudden heavy rainfall.

1934–47 *LAMSAS Appal* = attested by 5/14 speakers (35.7%) from SC. **1986** Pederson et al. *LAGS* = attested by 2/60 interviewees (3.3%) from E TN and 3/35 interviewees (8.6%) from N GA; 5/11 of all LAGS interviewees (45.4%) attesting term were from Appalachia.

[DARE *trash mover* n 1 chiefly Mid and South Atlantic, Lower Mississippi Valley]

2 An energetic person.

1966 *DARE Survey* (Boone NC) = a very able and energetic person who gets things done. **1984** Wilder *You All Spoken* 121 Rat killin's nowadays are gatherings of ardent and fun-loving political partisans—political workers known with affection as "trash-movers." **2005** Williams *Gratitude* 315 Artie was an older woman, and her children were older than me, but she could sure turn out the work. She was a regular "trash mover."

[DARE *trash mover* 2 Southeast, especially NC, SC]

traveler *noun* See citations.

1939 Farr *TN Mt Regions* 92 *travelers* = head lice. "The baby's head is full of travelers." **1957** Combs *Lg Sthn High Word-List* 103 = louse.

travelingest *adjective* Traveling the most, best able or suited to travel. See also **-est 1** and Grammar and Syntax §3.4.1.

1913 Kephart *Our Sthn High* 285 Them was the travellin'est horses you ever did see. **1994** Montgomery *Coll* (known to Cardwell).

tread *verb* Of a male bird, especially poultry: to copulate with (a hen); of people: to cohabit.

1931 Combs *Lg Sthn High* 1322 "Tread" is also a dangerous word in highland speech, meaning to cohabit. **1939** Hall *Coll* (Emerts Cove TN) I saw a rooster treadin' a chicken.

[DARE *tread* v 2 "to cohabit" chiefly Ozarks, southern Appalachians]

tread-save (also *tread-saft*) *noun* A nettle (*Cnidoscolus stimulosus/texanus*) with medicinal uses.

1884 Smith *Arp Scrap Book* 72 Then there is briars and nettles and tread safts and smartweed. **1972** *Foxfire 1* 240 [For hives] take any of a variety of teas to break them out. These teas include . . . a tea made from the mashed up berries of the tread-save, red alder leaves, raw alder bark scraped uphill, or a tea from cockle burrs.

[DARE *tread-soft(ly)* n 1 South Atlantic, Gulf States]

tree *verb*

1 Of a hunted animal: to seek refuge, especially but not necessarily in a tree. See also **bark tree(d)**, **take tree**.

1913 Kephart *Our Sthn High* 81 Finally [the bear] gits so tired and het up that he trees to rest hisself. **1939** Hall *Coll* (Sugarlands TN) Me and my first cousin follered it down there and finally [the bear] treed, went up a tree. *Ibid.* (Del Rio TN) "He'll tree" = common expression applied to a dog adept at treeing. *Ibid.* (Smokemont NC) He went up to the river with his two dogs, and they struck, went across the river, and he treed agin a cliff, he said.

The bear went down, and the dogs whupped the bear back up. **1953** Hall *Coll* (Deep Creek NC) A bear will tree just as quick as a possum at night. **1955** Parris *Roaming Mts* 177 He'll tree when he's crowded, and the dogs will bunch at the base of the tree and howl in rage. **1960** Burnett *My Valley* 31 Daddy, from his Pinnacle outlook, yelled out that the dogs had treed just under Rainbow Gap. **1970** *Hunting* 16 A hunter would . . . follow his dogs as best he could when they "struck," and when they had "treed" (which could be in any place from a hole in the ground to a rock cliff to the top of a real tree) he'd hurry to the spot, call the dogs off, and make his kill. **1982** Ginns *Snowbird Gravy* 138 When it takes a notion to tree, it'll go in the hole.

2 Of a hunter or hunting dog: to corner or drive (a hunted animal) to seek refuge, especially but not necessarily in a tree, and to guard (it); to force a hunted animal to seek refuge.

1847 (in **1870** Drake *Pioneer Life KY* 52) When I went into the woods he would "tree" squirrels for me; and when I was out after dark he kept by my side. **1865** *Hill CW Letters* (Jan 6) tel dock he must lern his dog to tree possoms and Squirles So that me and him can go hunting when I get home. **1926** Hunnicutt *Twenty Years* 30 I said no, Print, they are treed in a bear den and they are in the den now . . . *Ibid.* 118 We let our dogs loose and they got after an otter and treed in the bank of the creek. **1939** Hall *Coll* (Deep Creek NC) He treed a coon in the cliff. After a while we treed in the ground, we caught a skunk . . . [then] we went to our dogs, and they treed in the ground, and we dug in and got [a possum]. **1963** Miller *Pigeon's Roost* (March 7) I guess that there is now about as many groundhogs that is treed by a dog that never could be caught as those that are caught. **1968** Vincent *Best Stories* 47 One time the dogs chased him and treed him in a cave. **1976** *Bear Hunting* 296 One of these dogs was so well trained that he had found where these two cubs went up a tree, so he treed them. *Ibid.* 300 They came back to the highest part [of the cliff] and treed that bear in a hole. **1984** Wilder *You All Spoken* 58 = to bark and hit a tree with front paws, indicating that a coon is up the tree. **2018** *Blind Pig* (June 16) We used to always have a good snake dog around when we would go blackberry picking. A dog can smell a snake and "tree" it.

[DARE *tree* v 3 especially South, South Midland]

tree bark (also *tree yelp*) *noun* A hunting dog's distinctive bark signaling that an animal has been cornered. See also **bark tree(d)**.

1923 Williams *After Bruin* We heard the furious race, the well-known tree bark, and Mark's shots. **1939** Hall *Coll* (Deep Creek NC) [The dogs] stopped, bayed, and commenced barking the tree bark. **1960** Burnett *My Valley* 31 As soon as Fan and Glass, Lead, Sooner, and Ring got their second breath, they settled down to their coarse tree bark. **1969** *DARE Survey* (Ball Ground GA) We'd hear him give the tree yelp. That tree bark was entirely different because in making it, the dog would point his head upward and it would be a entirely different sound. So by the second time Old Riley'd made his tree bark, Sam would say he's treed.

tree dog *noun* A dog trained to corner game, especially an animal that seeks refuge in a tree. See also **Plott, Walker**.

1926 Hunnicutt *Twenty Years* 27 I knew this dog was not a tree dog. **1949** Hall *Coll* (Del Rio TN) Mix a red bone and a feist, and he'll make a good tree dog . . . A beagle hound is a hound dog. A hound dog is a good hunter, a tree dog. A red bone hound is a tree dog, runs foxes, but not like Walkers. **1957** Broaddus *Vocab Estill Co KY* 81 = a dog trained to hunt animals such as coons, possums, etc. that take refuge in trees.

treeing feist *noun* A type of small hunting dog especially skilled in driving squirrels up a tree. See also **feist B, mountain feist, penny feist.**

2006 *Encycl Appalachia* 872 Treeing feists, another breed, are now synonymous with squirrel hunting, while Brittany spaniels are the preferred dog for hunting ruffed grouse.

treeing Walker *noun* A type of small hunting dog especially skilled in driving animals up a tree. See also **Walker.**

2006 *Encycl Appalachia* 1373 Good hunting dogs often cost thousands of dollars. Among recognized bear-hunting breeds are Black and Tans, Plotts, Blue Ticks, and Treeing Walkers. **2006** Skipper *Tear Down* 73 This dog wouldn't run anything but coon. He's a pureabread [sic] Treeing Walker.

tree lap *noun* See citations. Same as **lap[1] A.**

1951 Giles *Harbin's Ridge* 74 By the light we could tell we were in a blowdown, with tree laps all around us. **c1960** Wilson *Coll* = part of a tree cut for lumber that is not usable for logs. **1978** Reese *Speech NE Tenn* 46 = branches left after a tree is timbered. **1987** Young *Lost Cove* 28 While he was up there he might as well drag down some dead tree laps for Vista to chop and use in the cook stove.

tree molasses (also *tree 'lasses, tree sugar, tree sugar sweetening, tree sweeting, tree syrup*) *noun* Maple syrup, made by boiling the sap of the sugar maple tree. Also called **maple molasses.**

1937 Hyatt *Kiverlid* 80 KY With tree-sugar sweet'nin' hits better tasted than coffee. **1952** Wilson *Folk Speech NC* 602 *tree sugar* = maple sugar. **1974** Fink *Bits Mt Speech* 27 *tree sugar* = sugar made by boiling down the sweet sap of hard maple. Also called *tree syrup* and *tree molasses.* **1978** Parris *Mt Cooking* 210 White sugar was scarce. Folks had to look for substitutes. And usually, you would find on the table tree sweeting, bee sweeting, and sorghum—that is, maple sugar, honey, and molasses. **1982** Ginns *Snowbird Gravy* 39 Bore a hole in a tree with a bit. Then drive a elder spout in there for the water to run out. Catch it in a trough. Carry it in and make tree sugar out of it. Boil it down. **1985** Irwin *Alex Stewart* 193 Tree molasses, or maple molasses, is just a little thicker than tree syrup. That's all. You just let them boil a little longer. **1998** Montgomery *Coll*: *tree sugar* (known to Adams, Bush, Cardwell, Weaver). **2006** *Encycl Appalachia* 930 To preserve the skills of tapping maple trees (also known as gathering "tree sugar" or "tree 'lasses"), Monterey, Virginia, hosts an early spring Highland Maple Festival.

[DARE *tree sugar* n chiefly South Midland, *tree syrup* especially South Midland]

tree sugar, tree sugar sweetening, tree sweeting, tree syrup See **tree molasses.**

tree toad *noun* The gray tree frog (*Hyla versicolor/chrysocelis*).

1939 King *Herpetology* 567 The tree toad is well known by local residents in the Great Smoky Mountains.

tree yelp See **tree bark.**

tremendous

A *adjective* Variant forms *tremendeous, tremendious, tremenjious, tremenstrous.*

1841 Donaldson (in **1934** Smith *Tennessean's Pronunciation* 263) *tremendious.* **1846** McLean *Diary* 96 a Tremendeous S[n]ow Storm with High winds. **1907** Dugger *Balsam Groves* 130 He made a tremenstrous effort to steel Mr. Clippersteel's purty gal, an' jis' tol' ye that fur spite 'kase he couldn't git 'ur. **1927** Mason *Lure of Smokies* 207 I begun to gnaw the bush an' paw the log sump'n tremenjious. **1944** Hayes *Word-List NC* 37 *tremendious.*

B *adverb* Very greatly, tremendously.

1864 *Epperly CW Letters* (March 25) I sopose they ar cheaper then they ar thair every thing is tremendious hi here. **1885** *Bayless Letters* 118 I know it has been tremendous cold out there this winter and you have lost one of your ears smooth off.

trepster *noun* See citation.

1987 Young *Lost Cove* 216 = thief or vandal.

trestle *noun*

A Variant forms *trussle, trustle.*

1891 Brown *Dialect in TN* 172 *Trustle* is the usual pronunciation of *trestle*, and *d'ruther* for *had rather* is a common contraction and mispronunciation. **1942** Hall *Phonetics Smoky Mts* 20. **1953** Hall Coll (Bryson City NC) I started to cross a railroad trussle, an old grade in there, and I got about a half way, and the trussle had broken in two. **1973** *AOHP/ASU-166* He said he was going to fill up some trussles over here at Minneapolis, and he asked me if I wouldn't want to go back to work.

B A type of sawhorse.

1973 Miller *English Unicoi Co* 155 *trussle* = a sawhorse. **1986** Pederson et al. *LAGS* (Hawkins Co TN, Johnson Co TN) = A-frame sawhorse.

[DARE *trestle* B especially Central Atlantic, Midland]

trick *noun*

1 A small article or personal belonging.

1862 *Neves CW Letters* (Jan 9) I woold be glad to see you & hear you tell some of your christmas trick as you have taken it wher you did never beforure. **1864** *Hill CW Letters* (Sept 30) I got a pocket book with dollars of green back and a nap sack and a blanket and a good oil chloth and pare of boots and severl other little tricks. **1886** Smith *Sthn Dialect* 343 *tricks* = little ornaments, etc. **1924** Raine *Saddlebags* 12 He's been off workin' at public works and got a leetle money for gittin' some tricks and fixin's for the house. **1958** Campbell *Tales* 242 She just said she reckoned the younguns needed learning more than they needs tricks and fixings to wear. **1981** Henry *Alex Stewart* 52 Show him that other trick you've got in there, that pipe. **2007** Shelby *Molly Whuppie* 2 Into the kitchen marched Molly Whuppie, with her bonnet tied around her neck and her tricks packed in a poke. "I aim to go, too," she announced.

[DARE *trick* n 2 chiefly South, South Midland]

2 A small child or woman.

1911 Shearin *E KY Word-List* 540 = a small child. **1951** Giles *Harbin's Ridge* 7 She [= a woman] was a little trick of a person.

[DARE *trick* n 3 especially South Midland]

triddler *noun* See citation.

1936 Farr *Folk Speech* 276 = a woman gossiper: "The old triddler is busy."

[cf EDD *triddler* adj "talking nonsense"]

trifeling See **trifling.**

trifling *adjective*

1 (also *trafling, trifeling*) Especially of a person: worthless, lazy, despicable.

1863 *Vance Papers* (May 7) they persons that have the corn stilled hire people to still it that are so trifeling that the good Citizans think it unnesissary to take them to Court, as non but the stiller suffers according to the act of the legislature on stilling. **1864** *Joyce CW Letters* (June 18) the trafling yankes Jest tars up evry thing whare thay go thay Destroy all the propety thay can find. **1901** Harben *Westerfelt* 7 I'd be above lettin' any triflin' man know I was that bad off. **1927** Mason *Lure of Smokies* 41 The matter 'th a plenty of 'em is they're jest too lazy an' triflin' to take the trouble. **1940** Haun *Hawk's Done* 84 Effena said she felt so trifling she thought she needed to be away from everybody—especially Linus. **1955** Parris *Roaming Mts* 29 Why, I know the time when a feller was considered trifling if he didn't have a dozen or so [bee] gums. **1963** Edwards *Gravel* 109 We thought she married because she was lonely for Ada more so than because she loved that trifling Lonnie. **1971** Thornburgh *Great Smoky Mts* 162 That writer-man hunted up the triflinest, the most no-countest family he could find to write up. **1975** Chalmers *Better* 66 Good shoes will wear stout even for this trifling generation. **1975** Purkey *Madison Co* 54 Chewin' and smokin' are triflin' habits. *Ibid.* 66 In our cove a "banjer picker" was considered "plain triflin'." **1986** Pederson et al. *LAGS* = attested by 3/60 interviewees (5%) from E TN; 3/14 of all LAGS interviewees (21.4%) attesting term were from Appalachia. **2007** McMillon *Notes* = won't work.

[DARE *trifling* adj 1 chiefly South, Midland]

2 Of a person: tired, lacking energy, "under the weather."

1892 *DARE File* She hev been sort o' puny 'n' triflin' o' late, but I reckon she 'll be all right ag'in in a day or two. **2009** Fields *Growing Up* 330 *trifling* = not feeling well; ill or getting sick.

[DARE *trifling* adj 2 South, South Midland]

trigger

A *noun* See citation. See also **splash dam.**

1984 High *Titan Rock* 32 Workers constructed splash dams by building pens on both sides of the tributary, filling in between with tree trunks, branches, stones, and mud. Water backed up into a pool, which would be filled with mud. Usually a crew waited until after a soaking rain or when a "tide" or flood rose in the river. Then they knocked out the "key log" or "trigger," which released the logs and carried them toward the river.

B *verb*

1 (with *around*) To tinker, putter.

1923 Greer-Petrie *Angeline Steppin' Out* 8 He's always a triggerin' round, a-fixin' sticks fur the neighbors.

[DARE *trigger* v 1 chiefly Midland]

2 (with *up*) To dress up; hence; hence participial adjective phrase *triggered up*.

1950 Stuart *Hie Hunters* 207 I jest want to see if I'd know old Sparkie all triggered-up in a new suit!

[DARE *trigger* v 2 chiefly Midland]

trim *verb* To castrate (a mature animal, especially a hog). See also **alter**, **change**, **cut B2**.

1934–47 *LAMSAS Appal* (Swain Co NC). **1961** *Coe Ridge OHP-340B* On the new of the moon, I mean, when a moon news, that the sign runs in the legs and down to the feet, it's when we do our work, I mean, you know, trimming. **1966** Dakin *Vocab Ohio River Valley* 245 *Trim* . . . is fairly common (but no less so than other terms) in the Mountains but rare farther west in Kentucky and unused west of the Kentucky River. **1966** *DARE Survey* (Cherokee NC) = word for castrating an animal. **1967** Hall Coll (Townsend TN) We put this old hog in there, and we worked on him and trimmed this hog. **1975** *GSMNP-62:3* We'd go out here and we caught a male hog. We'd trim him and turn him loose and when he got well, he got fat. We'd kill him in the woods. **1982** Slone *How We Talked* 119 Hogs were "trimmed," also called "changed" (castrated). **1985** Irwin *Alex Stewart* 106 He tied his head up to the wall good, and I just went over there, grabbed him by the sac and pulled it right down to where he couldn't kick me and I stood there and trimmed him, standing up.

[DARE *trim* v 2 chiefly Midland, Mid Atlantic]

trimmer *noun* See citation.

1994 Farwell and Buchanan *Logging Terms* = a member of a logging crew who cut bark off boards and removed blemishes such as knots.

trinkle *verb* To drip, trickle.

1924 Raine *Saddlebags* 114 Don't you see my own heart's blood / Come trinkling down my knee? **1940** Oakley *Roamin'/Restin'* I like to hear the water trinkling down the mountain all night long so I can sleep well. **1976** Garber *Mountain-ese* 96 I watched the water trinkle off the house when the snow melted.

trip *noun* See citations. See also **mantrip**.

1900 *Treatise Coal Mining* 60 A trip of empty [coal] cars is coming in at the siding. . . . Cars are lowered to the siding D and empty cars are taken up from the siding—while a trip of empty cars is coming into the siding. **2002** Armstead *Black Days* 247 = a succession of coal cars moved at one time by a mine locomotive. **2004** *Early Mines* 27 (as of 1902) A "trip" was the term to denote a number of coupled-together cars.

tripper (also *moonshine tripper*) *noun* One who hauls a load of **moonshine** to distributors, usually in high-powered cars. See also **runner**, **shine runner**.

1974 Dabney *Mt Spirits* 151 The usual method of the trippers, they'd come around a curve and see the road blocked, and they'd jump out and high-tail it and leave the car and the liquor. **1981** Dart *Thunder Road* 4B Howell said he sold his whiskey for a dime-a-gallon every night to a tripper who drove it to cities, cut it and more than doubled his money. **2005** Good *Racing in Appalachia* 3 Tradition often proclaims that stock car racing owes its heritage to the bootleggers and whiskey runners (or trippers) in and around the southern Appalachian mountains . . . of them in southern Appalachia. Soon, the chase was on between the moonshine trippers and pursuing merit "revenuers."

tripping (also *whiskey tripping*) *verbal noun* Hauling a load of **moonshine** to distributors, sometimes in high-powered cars with high-speed pursuit by law-enforcement officers.

1974 Dabney *Mt Spirits* 149 In the saga of corn whiskey in America's Appalachians, the "tripping" of the liquid contraband has left an indelible mark. **2002** Lacey *Amazing NC* What started as moonshine running (or whiskey tripping) in automobiles racing to escape "revenuers" became the billion-dollar industry known as stock car racing.

tri-weekly *noun* See citation. See also **hand mill**, **hominy pounder**, **lazy Jim**, **pounding mill**, **quern**, **slow John**.

1953 Wilburn *Pounding Mill* Fifteen years ago, when I first came into the Southern mountains, I heard at times of a mysterious machine whereby a pestle was worked up and down by waterpower. This was called a pounding-mill, or facetiously, a "lazy-John" or "tri-weekly." The descriptions given by old settlers were certainly genuine; and yet I could not get through my head how such a thing would work. Then, last summer, I found a real pounding-mill, within six miles of my residence, Bryson City. It is at the home of Telitha Bumgarner, on a branch of Deep Creek, and was made by her son, Jim.

trod *verb* To tread.

c1960 Wilson Coll (as base form) "Don't trod on the grass."

troft See **trough**.

tromp *verb* See citation. See also **tramp**.

1969 Miller *Raising Tobacco* 28 More often, a farmer would *tromp* instead of tramp; that is, beginning at one end of the bed, he would press the seeds into the soil by stepping on every inch of the bed, letting his tracks overlap a little. One of my earliest memories is of being taken to a clearing where a tobacco bed was in preparation and seeing my grandfather's tracks, hundreds of them, on the smooth expanse of the bed. After the seeds were sown and *tromped*, the bed was covered with *tobacco canvas* (cheesecloth) stretched over the bed and tacked to poles.

tromple *verb* Variant form of *trample*.

1892 Fruit *KY Words* 234 *trompled on*. **1905** Miles *Spirit of Mts* 178 Your children's a-whuppin' my children, and they're all about to tromple the life out of our children! **1927** Montague *Funny Bone* 332 Paul was milling 'round in the cloud, trompling on it and teasing it, making the thing so mad that it was gitting blacker and blacker. **1943** Chase *Jack Tales* 11.4 Why, no, and the ground ain't trompled none, neither. **1997** Montgomery Coll (known to Cardwell, Jones, Oliver, Weaver).

trot *noun*

1 A covered, open-ended passageway connecting the two sections of a **dogtrot** house.

1990 Morgan *Log House E TN* 31 The third method of enlargement also consisted of construction of a second pen adjacent to the gable-end opposite the chimney of the original pen. In this method, however, an open passageway or "trot" was left between the two pens. This type of double-pen dwelling is referred to as a "dogtrot" house.

2 A narrow trail worn by the passage of animals.

2000 Carden *Mason Jars* 171 "Do guineas trot?" said Bug. "No, honey, they run just like a chicken. But, like hogs, cows, and chickens, they made a little trail across the ridge, and a trail is called a 'trot.'"

trouble stick (also *troubling stick*) *noun* Same as **battle A**. See also **troubling**.

1999 Morgan *Gap Creek* 60 I dumped the dirty long handles in and stirred them with the troubling stick, then let them boil for a minute and lifted them out with the stick and dumped them smoking on the wash table. **2000** Morgan *Mts Remember* 40 A woman stood over a washpot beside the cabin, working her trouble stick in the column of smoke and steam, in the early morning chill.

troubling *verbal noun* Washing clothes by dashing them in a pot of boiling water using a stick. See also **trouble stick**.

2000 Morgan *Mts Remember* 71 I'm the one that did the troubling in the pot and rubbed the clothes on that old washboard on the coldest days, even after he did get in the pumplogs that brung water into the yard.

troubly *adjective* See citation.

1958 Combs *Archaic English in KY* 45 = cloudy: "The day was troubly."

[OED3 *troubly* adj 1 obsolete]

trough *noun* Variant *troft*, *trought*.

1863 Hogg *CW Letters* (July 2) John Adams Randals sone fell in to a hot troft of Still Slop and burnt him so he dide [= died] in some three weaks after. **1864** *Watkins CW Letters* (July 10) me and pegy wadkins went up to ans last sadurday to se about That leather but John sed he had not tuck it out of the tan troft yeat. **1915** Dingus *Word-List VA* 192 *troft*. **1917** Kephart *Word-List* 418 *troft*. **1931–33** (in **1987** Oliver and Oliver *Sketches* 280) Their shoes likewise were homemade over homemade lasts. The leather [was] tanned in large trofts [troughs] by themselves. **1942** Hall *Phonetics Smoky Mts* 92 Many speakers pronounce the following words with excrescent final t: Cliff, trough. **1971** *AOHP/ALC-260* We had a big troft that was hewed out and [a] hole bored on the bottom of it, and a peg went up in there just to stop that water running out, and on the end of it was flat, and she'd dip them clothes down in that water in that troft and lay them up there. **1973** Miller *English Unicoi Co* 85 *troft* attested by 4 of 6 speakers. **1983** Broaddus *Estill Co KY Word List* 59 *trought* = a gutter. **1994** Montgomery Coll (known to Cardwell).

[*trough* + excrescent *t*; DARE (at *trough* n A 1) (pronc) scattered, but especially South, Midland]

trought See **trough**.

trouser worm See **stung by a trouser worm**.

trout *noun* Variant plural form *trouts*.

1937 Hall Coll (Groundhog Creek TN) I caught a mess of trouts today.

trout fish *noun* A trout.

1929 Kephart *Smoky Mt Magic* 5 I've obleeged to be plumb keerful not to git damp in ary water dingier than trout-fish swim in. **1960** McCaulley *Cades Cove* I could step out from my house as a kid and in two hours get a nice mess of trout fish for supper.

[DARE *trout-fish* n formerly widespread, now especially South, South Midland]

trout lily *noun* A dogtooth violet (*Erythronium americanum/albidum*). Same as **lamb('s) tongue**.

1964 Campbell *Great Smoky Wildflowers* 72 = *Erythronium americanum*. The mottling of the 6- to 8-inch leaves suggests the speckled trout of the mountain streams.... Cherokee Indians regarded the flowering of this lily as the time to fish for trout. **1981** Brewer *Wonderment* 22 Lamb's tongue, Randy said, is trout lily. Or dogtooth violet, or adder's tongue, or fawn lily.

truck *noun*

1 Garden vegetables grown for barter or sale. See also **farm stuff**, **garden salad**, **salad B**, **sauce B2**, **stuff**, **truck patch**.

1862 *Huntley CW Letters* (Jan 17) I Waunt you to make all the truck you can this coming year for it will Be Worth something. **c1950** Adams *Grandpap* 217 We got to keep all of the tops and blade fodder, as well as all of the beans and other truck that we'd raised, rentfree. **1966** Dakin *Vocab Ohio River Valley* 353 *Truck* (and *garden truck*) also has some currency [in KY] in the Knobs and the Mountain Margin south of the Bluegrass. **1974** Roberts *Sang Branch* 20 There were fruit trees all about the place, and all around the house were rank cabbages, beets, onions, and other truck.

2 Provisions, supplies, small material goods, miscellaneous items.

1860 *Week in Smokies* 122 I mind I was powerful sick then, and I do believe, Mister, I should 'a' died but for some truck the Gineral gave me, God bless him! **1862** *Hampton CW Letters* (Sept 27) if you cold come out and fetch a teem and load of butter chees and brandy and such truck and get you a load of Salt I think you wold doo well as Salt is plenty heair. **1864** *Chapman CW Letters* (May 3) I hav some other little truk to plant yet such as cotten seed & cane pach. **1867** Harris *Sut Lovingood* 97d [sic] I tuck off the Doctor's squar bodied saddil bags an sarched em, an tuck all the docterin truck outen the vials an boxes. **1900** Harben *N GA Sketches* 172 "Seems to me," remarked the old maid, "that you've got a sight more truck here than you'll have any need fer." **1971** Thornburgh *Great Smoky Mts* 154 There'll be furriners larnin' my children a lot o' truck that won't do 'em a mite o' good.

truck garden See **truck patch**.

truckle *verb* To go in haste.

1859 Taliaferro *Fisher's River* 126 I seen a passel ov men com trucklin' to me, rockin' along, see-saw one side, then see-saw t'other side. *Ibid.* 133 My old inimy were perfectly satisfied with me, and let me truckle off and save my bacon, so fur as he were consarned. **1998** Montgomery *Coll* He truckled up the mountain to see if he could kill a squirrel (Cardwell).

truck mine (also *truck mines*) *noun* A small mine from which coal is hauled away by truck.

1975 *AOHP/ALC-903* We had a truck mine up here, me and some fellows a-gang working. **1975** Woolley *We Be Here* 12 I went into the mines when I was thirteen years old. It was a little truck mines over in Virginia. **1989** *Matewan OHP-7* I worked for Elliott Hatfield in a truck mine.

truck patch (also *truck garden*) *noun* A vegetable garden. See also **sass patch**.

1824 (in **1912** Doddridge *Notes on Settlement* 88) Every family, besides the little garden for the vegetables which they cultivated, had another small enclosure containing from half an acre to an acre, which they called a truck patch, in which they raised corn for roasting ears, pumpkins, squashes, beans, and potatoes. **1832** *McLean Diary* 12 [I] fenced my truck patch. **1847** (in **1870** Drake *Pioneer Life KY* 47) For several years our chief article of cultivation was Indian corn, but in the center of the field, in some spot not easily found by trespassers, was a "truck patch"; in which water melons and musk melons were planted, while in some corner we had a turnip patch. **1861** *Zimmerman CW Letters* (June 1) you wrote and that the Garden and truck patches looked flourishing. **1864** *Chapman CW Letters* (May 29) next weak we air going to work over our little truck patches. **1911** Shearin *E KY Word-List* 540 = garden. **1936** (in **2009** Powell *Shenandoah Letters* 86) I am writing to you as it is time to plant my garden and truck patches and I aint heard any thing from you about it. **1957** Broaddus *Vocab Estill Co KY* 81 = a vegetable garden for home use. **c1960** Wilson *Coll* = an extension of the garden, for such things as cucumbers, watermelons, sweet potatoes, Irish potatoes, squash, etc. i.e. things requiring space. **1966** Dakin *Vocab Ohio River Valley* 354 *Truck garden/patch* is used in Kentucky in the same sections that have truck "vegetables." **1979** Slone *My Heart* 9 Then the garden, or "truck patch" was planted all around the cabin. **1996** *GSMNPCOHP-1:2* Everybody had his garden and some small patches they called truck patches close around the house, such as that. **2008** McCaulley *Cove Childhood* 61 There was a gate across the road into the property, and much of what is now wooded was open land, with large gardens and "truck patches" behind the cabin.

[DARE *truck patch* n chiefly Midland, Lower Mississippi Valley]

true-vineness *noun* See citation.

1996 Dorgan *Baptist Diversity* 11 Nevertheless, the small number of adherents and limited geographic distribution of many of these groups do not discourage them from asserting that they are the direct and true descendants of the Church of St. Paul, to claim what the Old Baptists call "true-vineness."

trunk Baptist *noun* A person whose membership in a Baptist church is verified by a certificate rather than by participation, the implication being that one is either inactive in churchgoing or reluctant to join a new congregation due to an attachment to a former one, though possessing a letter of dismissal and attending a new church regularly.

1992 Bush *Dorie* 45 Ma always said they were "trunk Baptists." She explained that they were called trunk Baptists because she kept their letter of membership in the big trunk beside her bed. **1997** Montgomery *Coll* If Clon ever ceased being a trunk Baptist, we'll get him active in the church (Cardwell). **2014** Montgomery *Doctrine* 196 One who keeps their church membership in their suitcase or trunk. This would transpire when people relocated; they would ask for a letter of dismissal and then never find a church. Thus the letter went into the proverbial trunk.

trunk trading *noun* The exchange or sale of goods brought and displayed in an automobile.

1987 Wear *Sevierville* 40 The cars filled the street where the families settled all day with packed lunches and "trunk trading" of home grown foods and goods.

trussle, trustle See **trestle**.

try *verb* To bite.

1915 Pollard *TN Mts* 243 A copperhead tried me. **1998** Montgomery *Coll* (known to Adams, Brown, Bush).

tub *noun* See citation.

1939 Hall *Coll* (Hazel Creek NC) = container for fermenting mash for distilling [liquor].

tubercles *noun* Tuberculosis.

1930 Armstrong *This Day and Time* 147 Hit were the tubercles kilt your mammy.

tub mill *noun* A small grist mill with a horizontally operated waterwheel attached to a vertical shaft that turns the stone for grinding corn or wheat. See also **tub wheel**.

1824 (in **1912** Doddridge *Notes on Settlement* 112) Our first water mills were of that description denominated tub mills. It consists of a perpendicular staff, to the lower end of which an horizontal wheel of about four or five feet diameter is attached; the upper end passes through the bedstone and carries the runner, after the manner of a trundlehead. **1853** Ramsey *Annals* 719 If the grain is to be converted into meal, a simple tub-mill answers the purpose best, as the meal least perfectly ground is always preferred. **1913** Kephart *Our Sthn High* 132 About every fourth or fifth farmer has a tiny tub mill of his own. **1924** Raine *Saddlebags* 80 When a man lives on a branch or a prong of the creek, whar the water's lasty and thar's a right smart trickle all the time, he puts him in a tub mill, and lets the water grind fer him. . . . Ye take a log and hew it till hit's kindly like a tub with a long spindle rising right out'n the midst of it. Run your water in a trough so it'll hit right in the tub and as fast as hit turns o' course the spindle turns too. Then ye fasten your grindin' stone on the top o' your spindle, and thar's your mill. Of course ye make a roof and walls, and put a floor in, and thar's a leetle room for grinding, up above the tub. The spindle goes up through the floor. **1965** Shields *Cades Cove* 7 Grist mills served the populace [of Cades Cove], turning corn and wheat into bread materials. The first were "tub" (turbine) mills. These were replaced by overshot wheel structures in the 1840's. **1969** Madden and Jones *Alfred Reagan* 15 The grist mill was a turbine or "tub" mill, the most common type found in the mountains. Water was channeled to strike a primitive horizontal wooden turbine wheel, which turned and provided direct drive power to the mill stones. **1977** Shields *Cades Cove* 25 Mills to prepare the grains were an early necessity. The first were probably simple tub mills. The tub mill operates from the weight of a column of water or from the velocity of a directed stream striking a fly-wheel attached to the bottom of a shaft. Its drive shaft is vertical, in contrast to overshot or undershot wheels. **1990** *Smokies Guide* (Summer) 13 A notch up from the pounding mill was the tub mill. There were probably hundreds of these operating in the Smokies a century ago. They were small, fairly simple mechanisms used for grinding one or two families' grain crops. Because they operate best powered by small, fast streams, they were perfectly suited for the Smokies. Tub mills saved farmers the toll they would have to pay at the large commercial mills and were something of a status symbol in these parts. **2000** Strutin *Gristmills* 13 Used in Europe and Asia for centuries, this type of mill was called a tub mill because the wooden wheel with its angled blades was originally housed in a tublike frame. The sides of the tub directed splashing water back onto the blades of the wheel, upping efficiency slightly. Still, tubmills were usually less than 30 percent efficient. By the time Smokies residents began building tubmills, in the early 1800s, the frame was long gone, but the name stuck. **2002** Oliver *Cooking and Living* 14 The next step in the evolution of the mill in the Smokies was the construction of tub mills. In some places it had a wooden tub-like enclosure around the wheel, hence its name. Tub mills were small, and except for the millstones, could be built by any settler, some of whom could also cut millstones. These little mills usually stood on a high bank with 2 legs in the water and 2 on the ground. Since these mills ground, rather than pounded grain, they had to have 2 millstones. Made with blades radiating out from the center, the tub wheel resembled an electric fan laid face down. Water was directed against the blades of the wheel which turned the lower millstone which was revolved a fraction of an inch below the upper, stationary stone. Corn was poured into a hopper which slowly channeled it between the stones which ground it into cornmeal which moved outward to the edge, whereupon it poured into a chute and into a bucket or sack. **2007** Ball *Tub Mills* 3–5 The "wheel" which drove the mill was neither more nor less than a primitive turbine carved (when possible) from a suitably sized monolithic section of a large tree trunk which was mounted horizontally rather than vertically to the flow of water. When viewed from overhead, the "wheel" roughly resembled a thick hub with a series of outwardly radiating "spokes" (vanes or paddles). To better utilize the motive force of the water, the "wheel" was frequently set in a cylindrical container made of wood or masonry which resembled a tub, hence the name of the mill—or so we are told. For purposes of clarification, it should be noted that few early European mills were constructed with the hallmark "tub," and while they should appropriately be termed a horizontal mill, American molinologists persist in referring to them generically as "tub mills" although this designation is technically incorrect. The timeframe in which the "tub" was added to the configuration of these mills remains uncertain but . . . the earliest recorded use of the term "tub mill" in America dates to 1744 and it may reasonably be presumed that this feature was well known prior to that time. In point of fact, the origin of the term "tub mill" is both obscure and conjectural . . . this term is applied to two distinctly configured wheels: (1) a wheel nestled within a separately constructed enclosure; and (2) those with a circular enclosure affixed to the wheel itself. *Ibid.* 28 Mann observed that within Madison County, North Carolina, such mills were variously referred to as a "tub mill," "corn mill," "blockade mill," or "Willis wheel." **2017** *BearPaw* 13 No one seems to know for sure, but tub mills are probably named for the tub-like appearance of the horizontal water wheel that turns the stone. Much simpler in design than larger grist mills the spinning water wheel rotates a spindle directly connected to the millstone above.

[DARE *tub mill* n especially southern Appalachians]

tub wheel *noun* See citations. See also **tub mill**.

1995 Trout *Historic Buildings* 73 The tiny little tub mills once found all through the Smokies were powered by a horizontal "tub wheel," whose vanes were struck by fast-moving water. They were family-owned, and could grind a small amount of cornmeal or crack a little chicken feed. **2006** *Encycl Appalachia* 936 Some mills housed horizontal wheels inside, where they were called turbines or "tub" wheels.

tuck See **take A1**, **A2**.

Tuckahoe *noun* See citations.

1817 (in **1975** Higgs and Manning *Voices* 65) This snug little rivalry is beginning to bud vigorously in Virginia. The people of whom I am now writing call those east of the mountain Tuckahoes, and their country Old Virginia. They themselves are the Cohees, and their country New Virginia. **1902** Chamberlain *Algonkian Words* 263–64 The name of several vegetable substances used for food by the Indians of the southern and middle Atlantic States,—the "Virginia wake-robin" . . . the "golden club." . . . The name is also applied to a sort of fungus called also "Virginia truffle," "Indian bread," "Indian loaf,"—various species of *Pachyma*, *Lycoperdon*, etc. The Indian word seems to have had a generic meaning and to have been applied to a variety of bulbous roots. The origin of *tuckahoe* is seen in the Lenâpé *p'tuckqueu*, "something round, rounded." . . . A secondary meaning of *tuckahoe* is "an inhabitant of Lower Virginia." **1929** Phillips *Life and Labor* 354 J. K. Paulding noted while in the Shenandoah about 1815: "The people of whom I am now writing call those east of the mountain Tuckahoes, and their country Old Virginia. They themselves are the Cohees, and their country New Virginia" (*Letters from the South*, I, 1ll). He set forth at some length the contrasting cults of elegance by the one and plainness by the other. The name Tuckahoe was derived somehow from the Indian designation. **1972** Cooper *NC Mt Folklore* 123 Tuckahoe was the name given by the American Indian to an edible tuberous vegetable or underground fungus that grows in Eastern North Carolina and is small, knotty and inferior to other potatoes. In the Carolina mountains, the appelation [sic] was given to a person who was lazy, shiftless and lack[ed] sufficient ambition to improve his economic condition to the point of raising his standard of living. [**1984** Woods *WV Was Good* 223 In West Virginia this word referred to a person from Virginia who spoke with a Virginia accent more pronounced than in the speech of local people.] [**1995** Montgomery *Coll* (unknown to consultants from the Smoky Mountains).]

tucking comb *noun* A comb to fasten the hair at the top or back of the head. See also **reddening comb.**

1891 Moffat *Mtneers Middle TN* 317 The older girls wear theirs "roached" (combed back straight), and fastened in a loose knot at the back of the head with a "tucking comb"—a back comb without a top. **1915** Dingus *Word-List VA* 192 = a comb used in fastening up the hair. [**c1960** Wilson *Coll* The comb was fastened in the knot of hair, the "biscuit" or bun.] **1985** Irwin *Alex Stewart* 268 Pap made what they called a tucking comb. Women drew their hair up on top of their head in a ball, and they'd use this comb to hold it.

[DARE at *tucking comb* n chiefly South Midland]

tulip poplar (also *tulip tree*) *noun* A large deciduous tree (*Liriodendron tulipifera*) with large, tulip-like flowers. Same as **yellow poplar.**

1928 Galyon *Plant Naturalist* 5 The king of the Smokies is the tulip tree; on the moist mountain slopes this tree reaches 10 feet in diameter, and 190 feet in height. The trunks are straight and free of branches for 100 feet. The trunks of the tulip tree are unsurpassed in grandeur of column by those of any eastern tree. . . . Forest stands of tulip tree do not obtain, but many individuals grow thickly scattered throughout the range. **1941** Walker *Story of Mt* 66 The tulip-tree, or yellow poplar, is one of the most dignified and majestic trees growing . . . contrary to general belief, this tree is not a true poplar but belongs to the magnolia family. **1975** *GSMNP-62:11* Walnut's high priced logs and all that always was higher than any other kind excepting tulip poplar. [**1982** Stupka *Wildflowers* 38 The specific names, *tulipifera*, "tulip-bearing," is appropriate, since this tree bears great quantities of tuliplike flowers.]

[DARE *tulip poplar* n chiefly Midland, Mid and Central Atlantic]

tumblebug

A *noun* A small beetle that forms and rolls balls of dung into holes, laying eggs in them for the hatched larvae to feed on.

1867 Harris *Sut Lovingood* 242–43 Then nail hit on toe aind foremos', bein led by me, looks sorter like a plum tree barin tumil bug-balls, but hit wer jis' so. **1988** Lincoln *Avenue* 259 (DARE) When the eagle screams . . . the coo-koo knocks off from his foolishness and rolls hisself up like a tumblebug!

[DARE *tumblebug* n 1 scattered, but especially South, Midland]

B *verb* See citation.

1966 Stubbs *Mountain-Wise* (Feb–March) 13 They's four ways of gittin' big logs out of the woods. . . . Another way is fer a feller to tumble-bug 'em out. (He explained this process as lifting the logs, and walking them from end to end.)

tumbleset *noun* A somersault. Same as **somerset.**

1967 *DARE Survey* (Gatlinburg TN). **1986** Pederson et al. *LAGS* (Floyd Co GA, Habersham Co GA, Watton Co GA).

[DARE *tumbleset* n, v chiefly Southeast, Gulf States; also Northeast]

tune *noun* Variant form *chune.*

1923 Greer-Petrie *Angeline Doin' Society* 8 Sich quick an' dev'lish chunes. **1928** Justus *Betty Lou* 185 Following this came songs without words, "chunes," as they were called. "The Cacklin' Hen," "Sourwood Mountain," and "The Fox Race" being the liveliest of these.

tune bow (also *tuning bow*) *noun* Same as **Jew's harp, mouth bow, music bow.**

1979 Irwin *Musical Instruments* 59 I have found more people in Hancock County, Tennessee, than elsewhere who were familiar with the mouth bow—also called the music bow and the tuning bow. **1980** Wigginton *Foxfire VI* 91 In Madison County, North Carolina, they make a "tune bow" out of split hemlock tobacco-curing sticks and wire string.

tuning bow See **tune bow.**

tunnel bed *noun* A trundle bed.

1977 Ginns *Rough Weather* 24 The "tunnel bed," well, every day you'd make it up and push it under the big bed.

[DARE *tunnel bed* n especially South Midland]

turble See **terrible.**

turf *verb* To make tufts in (a piece of fabric).

1937 Eaton *Handicrafts* 226 The tufted, or "turfed" as some of the old-timers call the operation, and the knotted spreads are not new to the Southern Highlands. **1940** Haun *Hawk's Done* 149 I bought meal from Arwoods. Turfed and pieced quilts to pay for it.

turkentine *noun* Turpentine.

1939 Hall Coll. **1996–97** Montgomery Coll (known to Brown, Cardwell, Oliver).

turkey *noun*

A Variant plural form *turkey*.

1939 Hall Coll (Deep Creek NC) I've killed lots of deer and lots of turkey and catched lots of fish.

B A small bundle of clothing or personal effects tied up in a garment and to the end of a stick or slung across one's shoulder (as if one were carrying a slain turkey).

1938 Stuart *Dark Hills* 316 He carried his little bag of belongings thrown over his back in "turkey" fashion. **1941** Stuart *Men of Mts* 312 I carried my turkey of clothes tied to my ax handle across my shoulder. **1964** Clarkson *Lumbering in WV* 374 = a bag containing a lumberjack's personal belongings. **1993** Stuart *Daughter* 238 = a bundle tied to a long stick, containing a person's belongings. The outer wrapping of the bundle was often a shirt, coat, or other garment. Men working away from home, peddlers or homeless people often carried turkeys across the shoulder. **1997** Farwell *Logging* = in logging: the bag containing woodhicks' personal belongings.

turkey bean (also *turkey craw bean*) *noun* A type of green bean.

1980 *Smokies Heritage* 297 Settlers hereabouts tell a tale of how the "turkey bean" came to the mountains. It seems a flock of wild turkeys once wandered into the Jones Cove community, and consequently ended up as the main course for several Sunday dinners. But something strange had been discovered when the people killed and dressed the wild turkeys: in each bird's craw lay a handful of bean seeds. Not being wasteful, people put the seeds by and sowed them the following Spring. What grew as a result were a special type of bean with a flat hull and tiny, pea-like seeds inside. The delicious beans came to be called "turkey beans," for they had first appeared in the wild turkey's craw. **1996** Montgomery Coll: *turkey craw bean* = string bean (Cardwell).

turkey buzzard *noun* A turkey vulture (*Cathartes aura*).

1961 Miller *Pigeon's Roost* (Sept 28) We always call the chimney swift birds the chimney sweepers. The towhees, jorees; phoebee, pewees; turkey vultures, turkey buzzards; nighthawks, bullbats; and wood thrush, wood thrashers.

turkey corn *noun* The corn-like tuber of the bleeding heart plant (*Dicentra canadensis*). Same as **squirrel corn**.

c1982 Young *Colloquial Appal* 23 = root of a wild forest plant.

turkey craw bean See **turkey bean**.

turkey-foot mustard (also *turkey mustard*) *noun* An early spring edible wild green, a toothwort (*Cardamine diphylla*). Same as **crowsfoot.**

1967 *Food Gathering* 23 Among those plants gathered in the spring and eaten fresh or boiled were . . . "Turkey Mustard" (Dentaria diphylla), Sachon, Heucheram, Shepherds Purse, Creases, ramps (Allium), "Beargrass" (Tradescantia virginiana), and Indian cucumber. **1973** *Foxfire II* 81 Dentaria laciniata [= Cardamine concatenata], crowfoot or turkeyfoot, has leaves divided into narrow segments. . . . Peeled roots or young leaves add flavoring to salads, but a very little goes a long way. **1981** *Smokies Heritage* 26:4 Bishop's cap has a tall, slender stem, upon which are born tiny white flowers that resemble bells; toothwort, in contrast, has more noticeable flowers growing above its edible leaves which settlers once called turkey foot mustard. **1991** Weals *Last Train* 15 The cattle relished the first greens of spring—the ramps, bear lettuce, turkey mustard, lamb's tongue, and crow's foot—after their winter diet of hay.

[DARE *turkey mustard* n southern Appalachians]

turkey hunt *verb phrase* To go hunting for turkeys; hence verbal noun *turkey hunting*; for similar compounds, see **hunt B.**

1967 Hall Coll (Townsend TN) John McCaulley, he'd turkey hunt. He'd find the turkeys. **1989** Landry *Smoky Mt Interviews* 194 I never went a-turkey hunting in my life. I never went a-deer hunting in my life.

turkey hunting See **turkey hunt.**

turkey mustard See **turkey-foot mustard**.

turkey pen *noun* A large enclosure built to entrap wild turkeys.

1939 Hall Coll (Cataloochee NC) How to build a turkey pen: You just build a square pen out of ten foot fence rails, and when you get the wall built, you build it up about three feet high, and then you cover the pen over with fence rails laid close together all over it, and then you go out back a distance from the pen, start a trench, shallow at first, and the deeper you go, get under the rail of the pen. Why, it's deep enough for a turkey to walk under the bottom rail, but the trench then sloped out, up from the middle of the pen, and the turkey walks through there, and they get inside this pen. They raise up and see where they're at. They get so excited that they don't notice the hole down there to go out back outside.

turkey rifle *noun* See citation.

1941 Kendall *Rifle-Making* 22 The calibre of the mountain rifles deserves a word of mention. Strictly speaking, these rifles had no calibre in the ordinary sense of the word. Usually, however, four kinds of rifles were made: one of about .35 calibre (0.35 inch) which was called a squirrel gun; one about .40 calibre (0.40 inch) called a turkey rifle; one about .45 calibre (0.45 inch) called a deer rifle; and one of approximately .50 calibre (0.50 inch) called a bear gun.

turkey shoot *noun* A marksmanship competition to shoot the head off a turkey, the winner of which is awarded the bird as the prize. See also **beef shoot, chicken shoot.**

1939 *FWP Guide TN* 132 A unique sport . . . is the "turkey shoots" of the mountain people stemming from the rifle contests of pioneer times. Scorning modern breech loaders, the contestants use long-barreled cap and ball "hog" rifles, patterned after the famous guns of the frontiersmen. **1972** Cooper *NC Mt Folklore* 36 Beef and turkey shoots and rooster fights were great recreational events. **1978** Parris *Mt Cooking* 12 Back then we had real live turkey shoots. We'd cut a hole in the top of a box and put the turkey in there with his head and neck sticking out of the box and shoot at it. The feller that shot its head off got to take the turkey home. **1997** Montgomery *Coll* = turkey (and ham) shoots were common . . . beef shoots were usually conducted with rifles, while modern turkey shoots usually are conducted with shot guns. The rules and methods of scoring are also different (Ellis). **2013** *Blind Pig* (Dec 23) Though not as common as they once were Turkey Shoots still occur in Swain County. In the early seventies these were a social event used by many civic organizations to raise revenue.

turkey's paw *noun* Same as **ground pine.**

1999 Morgan *Gap Creek* 206 What I was looking for was turkey's paw, what some people call ground pine. It's [a] kind of club moss and grows in thickets, and on the north sides in damp shady places. It grows along a vine that runs under leaves and litter and lifts up yellow green leaves that look like turkey's feet. It's the perfect decoration for hanging along mantels and over doorways.

turkey-tail *verb* Of a watercourse: to divide or branch out in a fan-like pattern.

1913 Kephart *Our Sthn High* 282 The creek away up thar turkey tails out into numerous leetle forks. **1975** Jackson *Unusual Words* 152 The pattern of shortening a phrase is evident. . . . "The creek turkey-tails farther down the mountain." **1992** Jones and Miller *Sthn Mt Speech* 116 = of a watercourse: to spread out. "That creek turkey tails out into forks." **1996–97** Montgomery *Coll* (known to Brown, Cardwell, Jones, Oliver).

[DARE *turkey-tail* v southern Appalachians]

turkey track (also *turkey trail*) *verb phrase* Of a stream: to follow a meandering path similar to that left by a turkey's tracks.

1931 Combs *Lg Sthn High* 1320 The road turkey-trails up the creek. **1957** Combs *Lg Sthn High: Word List* 104 *turkey trail* = to wind or meander, as of a small stream. Ex.: "Possum Trot turkey-trails right up from Troublesome Creek." **2007** Homan *Turkey Tracks* 87 "I know exactly where that tree is; I've been walking past it for fifty years. The hemlock you're looking for is to the right where the creek turkey tracks." That was all he said, but it was good as a National Geographic map. I was walking upstream and had seen many of the three-toed turkey tracks on past rambles, so I knew what to look for. After a little more than a mile I came to the obvious spot, the place where three narrow runs braided around two flood-wracked islands before flowing back toward each other with the precise splay of a turkey track. The mountaineer's eight-word directions—to the right where the creek turkey tracks—proved to be both creative and accurate.

turkey trail See **turkey track.**

turkey trot *noun* Same as **dogtrot.**

1992 Jones and Miller *Sthn Mt Speech* 76. **1995–97** Montgomery *Coll* (known to Cardwell, Jones, Weaver). **2003** Cavender *Folk Medicine* 20 Some families lived in small single-room log or clapboard houses with a half-story loft. Most families, however, lived in houses partitioned into two "pens" (rooms). Some of these houses had an exposed hallway, known as a "dogtrot" or "turkey trot," separating the pens. A chimney was located at the inside center of the house or on one or both gable ends, and many houses had a rear addition that often served as a kitchen.

[DARE *turkey trot* n 4 chiefly South Midland]

turkey wax *noun* Turpentine.

1996 Montgomery *Coll* (known to Cardwell).

turkil, turkle See **turtle.**

turkle dove *noun* A turtle dove.

1937 Haun *Cocke Co* 3 Turkle doves build their nestes between two jints of a limb. **1949** Hall *Coll* (Del Rio TN) When you kill a turkle dove and look in the end of your gun, it looks like you. Some people link a turkle dove with death. Lots of people claim it's a sin to kill a turkle dove.

[DARE *turtledove* n now especially Mississippi Valley, South]

turmick See **turnip.**

turn

A *verb* Principal parts.

1 Variant past-tense forms *turnded, turnt.*

1914 Furman *Sight* 36–37 That whole funeral meeting kotch its breath at them awful words, and sot there rooted and grounded; and she turnt and looked around defiant-like. **1957** Combs *Lg Sthn High: Word List* 104 *turnt* = past-tense and past participle of turn. **1977** McGreevy *Breathitt KY Grammar* 93 *turnded* = attested by 1 speaker. **2005** Williams *Gratitude* 138 When you got out what ye wanted, ye turnt the leever loose.

2 Variant past-participle form *turnt* [see **1957** in **A1**].

B *verb*

1 Of milk: to sour or curdle. Same as **clabber C1.**

1978 Slone *Common Folks* 209 Aunt Nance hated it when she heard her milk had "turned," but I was tickled. I loved clabbered milk. **1982** Slone *How We Talked* 7 For milk to turn . . . milk was put in a crock or churn and set before the fire or in the sun so the warmth would cause it to ferment, or become sour. **2005** Williams *Gratitude* 143 When it first started to turn (sour), it was called blinked milk, then it set up thick and clabbered.

2 To approach and prompt (a squirrel) to retreat to the other side of a tree, where a second hunter can shoot it.

1961 *Coe Ridge OHP-336B* You stand right there now, and I'll walk around the bottom of that tree and turn the squirrel for you. **1972** Parris *Storied Mts* 116 I "turned squirrels" for him. Huh? Turning squirrels? Why, that's getting the squirrels to move from one side of the tree to the other so the fellow that's got the gun can get a shot at 'em.

C *noun*

1 A disposition, distinct personal character, nature, or inclination.

1923 Greer-Petrie *Angeline Doin' Society* 15 That feller had a distant turn . . . and jest play'd shet mouth. **1937** Hall Coll (Emerts Cove TN) She has a nice turn. **1939** Hall Coll (Sevierville TN) I don't like his turn. **1946** Dudley *KY Words* 272 = disposition, distinct personal character, nature, or inclination: "He said I was the most hateful turned girl he ever met." **1955** Dykeman *French Broad* 333 I waited on two or three doctors at different times while I was growing up—everybody always said I had the turn to be a nurse—and after a while women started sending for me if they couldn't get the doctor, and pretty soon some of them wanted just me, wouldn't hear to a doctor looking after them. **1984** Wilder *You All Spoken* 15 = a talent, manner, or instinct for, as "Bob Scott an' Pat Taylor have a turn for doin' the right thing—almost ever' time near 'bout." **1998** *Dante OHP-61* She had, I think, the best turn. Everybody thought the world of her.

[EDD *turn* sb 14 Scot, nEngl; DARE *turn* n 3 South Midland]

2 The amount of meal, wood, corn, or other material one can carry at a time; figuratively = a measure of anything. See also **armload, grist B.**

1863 *Martin CW Letters* (July 13) there is Men plenty in the Cuntry that is Surrounded with Ever thing plenty and wont help apore woman to one hands turn. **1863** *Robinson CW Letters* (Jan 6) if you git off 3 or 4 miles from the Mill & you have to pay 50 cents for every turn you have took to Mill you will Soon find out that you wont git along So well. **1913** Kephart *Our Sthn High* 292 A turn of meal is so called because "each man's corn is ground in turn—he waits his turn." **1931** *Professor Learns* "Here, I brought you a turn of fresh water-ground meal," he said. "I've been up Buffalo fishing and got it at the Laytown mill. Bake you a hoe-cake out of it. It's so fresh it will taste like gritty-bread." **1934–47** *LAMSAS Appal* (Madison Co NC, Swain Co NC); *turn of corn*; (Madison Co NC) *turn of wood*. **1939** Hall Coll (Emerts Cove TN) A turn of corn is the amount of corn you would take to mill—no special measure. **1949** Kurath *Word Geog East US* 43 *Turn of corn* as a synonym for the Midland *grist of corn* is found only in the Piedmont of Virginia and in the part of the South Midland lying to the south of the Kanawha and the Roanoke. **1966** Dakin *Vocab Ohio River Valley* 145 It appears (insofar as data are available) that the *grist* of the North and North Midland areas predominates in Ohio, but that to the west of this state it loses out to the *turn* of the South Midland and Virginia Piedmont—the term which also predominates in Kentucky. **1973** GSMNP-78:25 The turn of the corn was the amount that the boy thought he could carry. It wasn't no certain amount. **1986** Pederson et al. *LAGS*: *turn of corn* = attested by 17/60 interviewees (28.3%) from E TN and 6/35 (17.4%) from N GA; 23/139 of all LAGS interviewees (16.5%) attesting term were from Appalachia. **1993** Ison and Ison *Whole Nother Lg* 71 = a sack of grain ready to go to the mill to be ground into flour or meal. **1999** Morgan *Gap Creek* 5 Took us all day to get down the mountain, wait for the turn of corn to be ground, while the men eyed us and told jokes.

3 See citation.

1964 Clarkson *Lumbering in WV* 374 = a single trip and return made by one team in skidding logs.

turnded See **turn A1**.

turn down *verb phrase* In a spelling match, to displace (a fellow student) by spelling correctly a word the latter has missed. See also **spell down A.**

1848 (in **1870** Drake *Pioneer Life KY* 147) When the time for "letting out" was at hand, the whole school were called up to spell, and then came the strife of glory—the turning down and going up head. **1905** Miles *Spirit of Mts* 8 Some Friday afternoon he will turn Cliff down, and then we can soon challenge the school yon side the creek to spell against us. **c1930** (in **2014** Oliver *Cades Cove* 80) Every word was repeated until it was spelled. The student spelling a word missed by others was moved ahead in the line to the point it was first missed. This was called "turning down," or moving ahead of the person or persons who missed the word. When, by this process, the student reached the head of the line, and successfully spelled the next word, he or she crossed over to the other side, and in doing so called out his or her side number, i.e., "Side Number 1" or "Side Number 2." This crossover was a "talley." One student was the tallier, recording on the blackboard when a student achieved a crossover. **1968** Wilson *Folklore Mammoth Cave* 43 A merit mark [was] given the child who stood, at the end of the class, at the head of the spelling line; then, the next day, he went to the foot of the class and worked his way back to the head by *turning down* the one above him who missed a word. **1969** Foust *Kingdom of Wilkes* 62–63 It was the custom on Friday afternoons for the teacher to select the pupil who was supposed to be the best speller, and he was allowed to choose his opponent, and the two of them took "turns" choosing "sides" until all the students both great and small, were lined up in two rows extending the length of the room. Then the teacher, standing or sitting, between these two mighty heads started "giving out" easy words at the foot of the lines, gradually calling longer and more difficult words. The first to miss a word took his seat, and so on until all were "turned down" except the head of one of the lines, and he was declared the winner of the day's match. **1977** Shields *Cades Cove* 47 The successful pupil would "turn down" those who had missed [the correct spelling].

[DARE *turn down* v phr chiefly South Midland]

turn-down man *noun* See citation. See also **off-bearer.**

1994 Farwell and Buchanan *Logging Terms* = a member of a logging crew who kept slabs moving away from the carriage and from the board being cut [and] transferred slabs to a chain drive.

turned *adjective* Having a certain natural inclination or disposition (used especially in compounds, as **mild-turned**, **puny-turned**, **smart-turned**, **well-turned**).

1867 Harris *Sut Lovingood* 73 I seed a-cummin, a ole widder, what wer a pow'ful pius turn'd pusson. **1910** Weeks *Barbourville Word List* 457 = to look like or to be like: "Mary is turned like her mother." **1931** Goodrich *Mt Homespun* 68 I'll not say it's not a worrisome job, but if a body's turned that way, like I am, there's a heap of satisfaction in it. **1937** Hall *Coll* (Emerts Cove TN) She's a mild-turned girl. **1939** Hall *Coll* (White Oak NC, in speaking of a certain trait in his and his brother's personalities) That's the way we're turned. *Ibid.* (White Oak NC) They are turned different than she is. **1946** Dudley *KY Words* 272 He said I was the most hateful turned girl he ever met. **1955** Ritchie *Singing Family* 203 I don't know whatever made me turned like that. I couldn't stand for anyone to think that I liked the boys. **1976** Thompson *Touching Home* 17 = to have a certain type of personality: "He was turned like his dad." **1976** Weals *It's Owin'* She's turned like her mother—sorta droll (whimsical). **c1982** Young *Colloquial Appal* 18 *quare-turned* = strange or odd personality.

[DARE *turned* adj 1 chiefly South Midland, especially KY]

turner (also *turner plow, turning plow, turnover, turn plow*) *noun* A plow whose mechanism (a plowshare for cutting the soil or a moldboard for turning the soil over) can be reversed so that a farmer can more effectively follow the contour of a hillside. Same as **hillside plow 1**. See also **buzzard wing**, **landside plow**, **left-hand plow**, **right-hand plow**.

1901 Harben *Westerfelt* 59 [He] has been ploughin' a two-hoss turnover [plow]. **1956** Hall *Coll* (Big Creek NC) Farming was a hard go back when I was a boy. We plowed a steer, didn't have no turnin' plow. We had what we called a bull tongue. **1957** Broaddus *Vocab Estill Co KY* 82 *turning plow* = a plow with a big blade used for the first plowing in the Spring. **1973** GSMNP-4:10 I've plowed that with a bull tongue plow, all of it, with one horse, and raised a crop with what they call a bull tongue plow. It wasn't a turning plow, you know. It's just a straight, most people call layoff plow now. **1973** GSMNP-92:3 We just started plowing early in the spring with a horse and a single plow. The ground was so rough you couldn't use a turn plow, so we just used a single plow. **1977** Shackelford et al. *Our Appalachia* 124 I done a lot of plowing myself. I've plowed a big old-fashioned turning plow that you had to kick with your foot every time you got to the end of a row. We plowed straight around the hill. **1981** Whitener *Folk-Ways* 11 I learned to plow with the big turning plow as well as the shovel plow, both pulled by mule. **1986** Pederson et al. *LAGS*: *turner* = attested by 3/60 interviewees (5%) from E TN and 2/35 (5.7%) from N GA; 5/11 of all LAGS interviewees (45.4%) attesting term were from Appalachia; *turner plow* (Gordon Co GA, Habersham Co GA); *turning plow* = attested by 3/60 interviewees (5%) from E TN and 4/35 (11.4%) from N GA; 7/11 of all LAGS interviewees (63.6%) attesting term were from Appalachia. **1998** *Dante OHP-24* I plowed and I wasn't but about nineteen years old, eighteen or nineteen, and plowing with a old horse and plow, turn plow. **2003** LaLone et al. *Farming Life* 321 We had what they called turning plows, which turned the ground over with horses, and of course it took all day long to plow a little bitty place.

[DARE *turning plow* n chiefly South, South Midland, TX, *turn plow* chiefly South Atlantic, Gulf States, WV]

turn go *verb phrase* See citation.

1915 Dingus *Word-List VA* 192 = to set free, turn loose.

[DARE (at *turn* v C4) chiefly South, South Midland]

turn in *verb phrase*

1 (+ *and* or *to* + *verbal noun*) To apply oneself to a task; to set about, begin. See also Grammar and Syntax §7.2.

1834 Crockett *Narrative* 79 They had bows and arrows, and I turned in to shooting with their boys by a pine light. *Ibid.* 154 We turned in and cleared a field, and planted our corn. **1853** Kennedy *Blackwater Chronicle* 52 The hostler also was absent; and finding no representative of that very important individual, we turned in and groomed our own horses. **1923** Furman *Mothering* 247 Then when his bath night come, he turnt in and pintly scrubbed the hide off his years, in and out. **1937** Hall *Coll* (Copeland Creek TN) They was turned in to drinkin'. **1939** Hall *Coll* (Sugarlands TN) We turned in to shooting at the limb under it where it was kind of weak and finally got it weak enough till the limb broke with the bear and fell down. **1959** Hall *Coll* (Cataloochee NC) Folks liked one another on Cataloochee. They was just like one family. When one got sick, they all turned in and did his work. **c1960** Wilson *Coll* = to begin: "He turned in and planted his corn in April." **1967** *Grandmother Cherokee* 75 They turned in and shaved that thing [= a pig] all over. **1979** *Big South Fork OHP-4* He'd got married a day or two before, and they all got at him to buy them something, and he turned in and bought them all a necktie apiece.

[DARE *turn in* v phr 1 chiefly Midland]

2 Of measles: to affect the internal organs, resist treatment.

1962 Dykeman *Tall Woman* 213 During days and nights of their fretfulness and fever, she gave the sick children hot brews Aunt Tildy had taught her would "bring out" the measles and keep them from "turning in." **2002** Reid *Hall's Top* 22 Spicewood tea kept the Measles from "turning in."

3 To drive (livestock) into a field to feed. See also **turning on the range**, **turn up**.

1862 *Epperly CW Letters* (July 10) I want you to turn our hogs up at the other plase in the granfields after you get the grain out and if it hant worth cuting turn the hogs in and let them eat what they will of it. **1941** Stuart *Men of Mts* 156 The cows have been brought in from the high hill pasture and turned in on the meadow weeds that have grown up after the last cutting.

turning on the range *verbal noun* Freeing livestock to range beyond fenced-in crops in the summer. See also **open range**, **turn in 3**, **turn up**.

1997 Davis *Cataloochee Valley* 20 Turning on the range was taking the cattle out on the grassy balds to pasture for the summer. The stock range law was in effect for about 125 years. In many sections of our county, it was voted out in favor of the "stock laws" in the early 1890s. But in certain sections like Cataloochee and Big Creek, Hurricane and White Oak, it was kept well into the present century. It was a much prized privilege because, from an economical standpoint in our county and throughout this entire region, turning on the range meant fully half the living. It was free ranging. No one had to pay for the summer pasture.

turning out time See **turn out 1**.

turning plow See **turner**.

turning-row *noun* See citation.

1890 Fruit *KY Words* 66 = a row unplanted in a corn or tobacco field, where the horses turn around in plowing.

[DARE (at *turnrow* n) chiefly South, South Midland]

turning the baby *verbal noun* See citation. See also **liver bound**.

2003 Cavender *Folk Medicine* 205 = an exercise performed on an infant to prevent a livergrown condition. The exercise involved holding the baby upside down by one leg and then grasping an arm and rotating the child to an upright position.

turn in one's checks See **check**[2] **3**.

turn in to See **turn in 1**.

turnip *noun*

A Variant form *turmick*.

1966 West *Dialect Sthn Mts* 32 "This here is a mess of turmick (turnip) sallet (greens)," he would have said.

B Senses.

1 A pocket watch.

1941 Stuart *Men of Mts* 54 My old turnip says it's ten minutes till eleven. **1957** Broaddus *Vocab Estill Co KY* 82 = a nickname for a pocket watch.

2 (also *turnip bottom, turnip still*) A type of **moonshine still**.

1972 Carr *Oldest Profession* 183 The pot still is the oldest of all the designs and is the mother Still of moonshining. It is occasionally called the "turnip bottom" still if it is made in the shape of a turnip (rounded bottom with tapering neck). **1985** Dabney *More Mt Spirits* 154 The copper pot "mother still" is found in three configurations—the "turnip," round and fat; the "half turnip," and the upright copper pot, shaped like a metal drum and placed vertically in the furnace. It is also called the Buccaneer, the Blockade Still and the "mountain teapot." The American copper pot is very similar to the "poit du" (black pot) stills on display in the Highland Folk Museum in Scotland and the Poteen stills in Ireland. **2009** Webb et al. *Moonshining* 329 Before World War I, southern moonshiners used "turnip stills," a turnip-shaped setup whose main parts are wooden "mash boxes," in which the grain mash mixtures fermented before distilling; the large, round copper "pot" or "cooker," in which the mash is heated; the copper "bulb" or cap, placed over the mouth of the pot; and the "worm," a coiled length of copper pipe immersed in water in a wooden box. **2014** Joyce *Moonshine* 150 Traditionally, moonshine has been made in copper pot stills. Sometimes called turnip stills, these devices get their name from the distinctive rounded shape of the boiler. They're the kinds of whiskey stills used by America's Scots-Irish settlers and their early descendants, and they're still used by distillers today.

turnip hole *noun* See also **potato hole**.

c1975 Lunsford *It Used to Be* 13 Then there was the turnip hole,—they hole up the turnips and hole up the potatoes.

turnip kraut *noun* Turnip tops shredded and pickled like **sauerkraut**.

1925 Dargan *Highland Annals* 75 I give her some pickled beets, an' turnip-kraut, an' 'tater salad made with that blackberry vinegar. **1986** Pederson et al. *LAGS* (Roane Co TN). **1997** Montgomery *Coll* = bits of turnip pickled with cabbage (Brown), = made like cabbage kraut with shredded turnips (Jones).

turnip still See **turnip B2**.

turn off *verb phrase*

1 To drink (an entire cup of liquor) at one time.

1913 Combs *Kentucky Highlander* 25 The story is told in Knott County of a man who "turned off" a whole cup of moonshine before taking the cup from his head.

2 To fail to accommodate, forsake, send (someone) away.

c1950 Adams *Grandpap* 76 The old woman an' the baby girl—the only one left at home—they allowed it would be a sin to turn him off. **1967** Fetterman *Stinking Creek* 76 Nobody can turn their own young'uns off, can they?

3 To perform, execute (work).

1938 Stuart *Dark Hills* 197 You certainly can turn off the work. **1962** Dykeman *Tall Woman* 133 Afore you get down to making the journey in fact you'd best turn off a mite of work at home. **1963** Edwards *Gravel* 122 Nope, I ain't got the knack of turnin off work like I used to do. **1977** Ross *Come Go* 109 He turned off a powerful lot of work.

4 Of weather: to become.

1984 Burns *Cold Sassy* 295 Mr. Nolly thinks it's go'n turn off cold t'night. **1985** Irwin *Alex Stewart* 216 It turned off cold and started to snow and she didn't have no shoes and just a very few clothes and she was about to freeze. **1991** Thomas *Sthn Appal* 47 You could set [beans] out-side, set 'um around on th' south side of th' house. An' then, bring 'um in, if it rained . . . or turned off bad.

[DARE *turn off* v phr 2 scattered, but especially South, Midland]

5 To produce, harvest.

1835 *McLean Diary* 33 [I] turned off Som [maple] Sugar to Day.

turn of the night *noun phrase* See citation.

1915 Dingus *Word-List VA* 192 = passing midnight: "We heard you slip in toward the turn of the night."

turn out *verb phrase*

1 Of a school day or school term, or a church service: to adjourn, be interrupted or dismissed; hence verbal noun *turning out*. See also **take up 4**.

c1890 Job *Diary* 5 It was study from morning till noon, then an hour for our playtime, and study from 1 o'clock till turning out time. **1940** Bowman *KY Mt Stories* 14 As soon as school "turns out" in the spring, every high school girl must necessarily get out and hoe in the fields of corn and tobacco. **1941** Justus *Kettle Creek* 30 It was customary for the school on Little Twin to turn out for two weeks during this season so that the children could help with the harvesting. **1949** Arnow *Hunter's Horn* 18 Old Andrew, poor fellow, was getting so old that sometimes he never got there till the day was half over, or he went to sleep at morning recess and the whole school ran away to the woods and stayed till time to turn out books. **1973** *AOHP/ASU*-160 Sometimes they'd have to call on them to stay in after school turned out. They'd give them a talking. **1974** Fink *Bits Mt Speech* 27 = dismiss. "Has school *turned out* yet?" **1976** GSMNP-114:4 [The teacher] had to turn school out to go home and get dry clothes. **1986** Pederson et al. *LAGS* = attested by 15/60 interviewees (25%) from E TN and 10/35 (28.6%) from N GA; 25/166 of all LAGS interviewees (15.1%) attesting term were from Appalachia.

[DARE *turn out* v phr 2 chiefly South, South Midland]

2 To expel from a church congregation for violating a standard of conduct; in phrase *turn out of* = to expel from (a church). See also **church 1, 2**.

1847 *Zion Church Minutes* 31 Church Conference find all in fellowship that was present. Case of William Bennett was taking up and he was turned out. Wee are no more accountable for his conduct. **1931–33** (in **1987** Oliver and Oliver *Sketches* 27) If they did not come and make their acknowledgements they were turned out of the church. **1963** Watkins and Watkins *Yesterday* 33 Mrs. Reece was turned out of the church, but she continued to attend, and finally she was accepted again as a member. **1973** *AOHP/ASU*-69 [If] you just didn't [attend the weekly church service] because you didn't want to go, they'd tell you "now next meeting time, if you ain't there, we're going to turn you out," and if you ain't there, out you went. You see how strict them rules was back then [in the Baptist church]. If we used them now, why, they wouldn't be nobody in the church, would they? **1994** McCarthy *Jack Two Worlds* 71 They turned Counce Harmon outta the church two or three times 'cause he told these stories. **1996** Cole *Forney's Creek* 69 Daddy got turned out of the church one time for fightin' and cussin' a horse. Somebody brought charges against him and they turned him out of the church. I don't know how long he stayed out of the church before he made his acknowledgments and rejoined the church. But when he made his acknowledgments, they forgave him and let him rejoin the church. **2002** Myers *Best Yet Stories* 43 If a member of the congregation committed any one of those "forbidden sins" while failing to apologize or confess his sin, he or she was "churched" or "turned out," meaning that fellowship or membership was withdrawn.

3 To let (land) lie fallow.

1915 Dingus *Word-List VA* 192 = of land: to let (it) lie fallow. [DARE *turn out* v phr 1 chiefly South]

turnover See **turner.**

turn over *verb phrase* See citation.

c1982 Young *Colloquial Appal* 23 = reform.

turnpike (also *turnpike road*) *noun* Originally a road with a turnstile, gate, or other barrier built and maintained by a company or agent collecting tolls from all passersby (i.e. vehicles, pedestrians, herded animals) that were used to keep the road in good repair. The agent often lived along the road. Later the term referred to a substantial through road (see 1973, 1974 citations) and more recently to a broad, commercial road. Two well-known early examples in NC were the Cataloochee Turnpike and the Buncumbe Turnpike. See also **pike**.

1819 (in **2003** *TN Petitions II* 205) There is probably about— miles of said road which your petitioners are of the opinion would be of a public good to be kept up by a turnpike. **1862** *Gilley CW Letters* (July 13) we have moved on this side of James river an camped near drurys bluff b[e]twen Richmond an petburg on the turnpik road. **1941** Stuart *Men of Mts* 30 He's just rid along the turnpikes and stopped at the houses. **1973** Wellman *Kingdom of Madison* 38 Toll gates and toll houses would be set up at intervals of about ten miles, to collect fees for travel on this turnpike. A six-horse wagon or a four-wheeled "pleasure carriage" must pay $2.50 for the entire route. Charge for a four-horse wagon was set at $2.00, and for a two- or three-horse wagon or a "peddler's" cart, $1.50. A two-wheeled gig or sulky would pay $1.00, a two-wheeled "road cart" 50 cents, a horse and rider 20 cents. Those great herds of stock would also be placed under toll—6 1/4 cents per head for horses, mules, and beef cattle, and 3 cents for hogs and sheep. **1974** Underwood *Madison Co* 18 To relieve the congestion which had developed on this "Wagon Road," the North Carolina General Assembly of 1824 created the Buncombe Turnpike Corporation and granted it full authority to build a toll road from the Tennessee state line by way of the French Broad River to the mouth of Big Ivy and from there to the South Carolina line. By 1827 the new turnpike was said to be the finest in the state. . . . This turnpike served until 1882 as the major trade route through the mountains of Western North Carolina. Stock driving had grown to tremendous proportions by the time the turnpike was completed. Tollgate records indicate that from 150,000 to 200,000 Tennessee hogs were driven up the French Broad every year. **1984** Dykeman and Stokely *At Home* 25 During the spring and fall, all able-bodied men were "warned out" for six days—eight if there had been washout rains—to keep up what had become the well-used Cataloochee Turnpike. **1997** Davis *Cataloochee Valley* 47 The toll road led from the right hand prong of Cove Creek, above the Davis place (where the toll gate was) to the Cataloochee Creek, and was called "Cataloochee Turnpike." Allison was made keeper of the toll gate. He was to have the gate fees as his for keeping said road in good repair and etc. Here are the stated fees Allison was to collect: For a man and a horse 18-3/4 cents For an extra pack horse 6-1/2 cents For each head of hogs, 1 cent each For cattle, 2 cents per head. No fees for vehicles were mentioned whatsoever, because we suppose it was entirely impassible for such, except possibly a half sled.

turn plow See **turner.**

turn thanks See **return thanks over the table.**

turn up *verb phrase* To free (livestock) to range beyond fenced-in crops in the summer. See also **turn in 3**, **turning on the range.**

1862 *Epperly CW Letters* (July 10) I want you to turn our hogs up at the other plase in the granfields after you get the grain out and if it hant worth cuting turn the hogs in and let them eat what they will of it.

turn up one's toes *verb phrase* To die.

1961 Medford *History Haywood Co* 202 "Turned up his toes." Means he died, or something caused him to die.

turrible See **terrible.**

tursh, turshes See **tusk A.**

turtle *noun* Variant forms *turkil, turkle.*

1834 Crockett *Narrative* 33 I was certain his anger would hang onto him like a turkle does to a fisherman's toe. **1867** Harris *Sut Lovingood* 83 I liked his moshuns onder a skeer rite well; he made that dodge jis' like a mud-turkil draps ofen a log when a big steamboat cums tarin a-pas'. **1934–47** *LAMSAS Appal* (Swain Co NC). **1942** Hall *Phonetics Smoky Mts* 82. **1969** Roberts *Greasybeard* 39 Then we saw what it was. It wa'n't no big cat a tall but a big turkle. **1985** Irwin *Alex Stewart* 195 I've seed a lot of turkles but I never saw one any bigger than that one. **1991** Still *Wolfpen Notebooks* 66 John M. went turkle hunting on Carr Creek yesterday. **1995** *Montgomery Coll* (known to Shields). **2007** McMillon *Notes* I saw me a turkle.

[DARE (at *turtle* n A) chiefly South, South Midland]

tush, tushes See **tusk A.**

tush hog *noun* A wild hog with long, protruding, highly destructive cuspids or **tusks**; also used figuratively.

c1959 Weals *Hillbilly Dict* 8 *tush hog* = a fighter, relentless, savage; figuratively = a man having such qualities. Sometimes also applied to a man who is relentless in the pursuit and conquest of women. A "tush hog" gets his name from the wild boar that roams the mountains and rips his adversaries with his long teeth, or tusks, or "tushes." **1982** *Smokies Heritage* 67 = a wild boar (because of its long, protruding tusks). **2013** DeLozier and Jourdan *Back Seat* 34 *Tush hogs*, as they're called in the Smokies, had killed people and animals of all sizes, including a lot of famous warriors in history, even well-armed noblemen and kings.

[DARE (at *tush hog* n 1) South, South Midland]

tushies See **tusk A.**

tusk *noun*

A Variant singular forms *tursh, tush*; variant plural forms *turshes, tushes, tushies.*

1934–47 *LAMSAS Appal* (Madison Co NC, Swain Co NC) *tush.* **1967** *Hall Coll* (Townsend TN) [The hog] stuck a tursh right in this heel right here, and he cut a hole right there. **1970** *Burton-Manning Coll*-93A They dug down that night and cut her [= an elephant] tushies off. She had long tushies. **2013** DeLozier and Jourdan *Back Seat* 34 I'd seen the trophies hunters made of their [= wild hogs'] long, curved, razor-sharp tusks, called *tushes* in the local dialect.

[DARE *tursh* (at *tush* A1) chiefly Southeast, southern Appalachians]

B A long, protruding, highly destructive cuspid (especially a lower one) of a bear or wild hog. See also **tush hog.**

1913 Kephart *Our Sthn High* 81 [The bear] gits so mad you can hear his tushes pop half a mile away. **1941** *Hall Coll* (Dellwood NC) Elephants and hogs have tushes. Snakes has fangs. **1966** Stubbs *Mountain-Wise* (Feb–March) 12 A local hog-farmer had a fine, but very large Hampshire boar that had become so vicious that he had to get rid of him: that his "tushes" were long and sharp and that he could easily kill either man or dog that got in his way. **1971** Hutchins *Hidden Valley* 112 Both males and females [= pigs] have greatly elongated canine teeth called "tusks," located in both upper and lower jaws. **1976** *Bear Hunting* 306 [The bear's] old tushes was about two and a quarter inches long.

[cf OED3 *tush* n^1 1a now chiefly archaic or dialect]

tussle *verb* To carry (a heavy object) awkwardly.

1913 Kephart *Our Sthn High* 123 Whar one o' our leetle sleds can't go, we haffter pack on mule-back or tussle it on our own wethers. **1994–97** *Montgomery Coll* (known to Brown, Bush, Cardwell, Cypher, Hooper, Oliver).

tuther See **t'other.**

tutor *verb*

1 To cure (meat).

1904–20 Kephart *Notebooks* 2:361 I b'lieve I can make a hundred pound o' pork out o' that pig—tutor it jist right. **1931** Combs *Lg Sthn High* 1304 Tutor hit up jist right, this old Ned (bacon) orter last a good span.

2 See citation.

1983 Broaddus *Estill Co KY Word List* 60 = to spoil (a child).

[cf EDD *tutor* v "to manage, handle; to humor, coax"; DARE *tutor* v both senses especially southern Appalachians, Ozarks]

twan't (also *twarn't, tweren't, twusn't*) contractions of *it wasn't* or *it weren't*. See also **twer.**

1908 Fox *Lonesome Pine* 15 "'Twusn't no joke," he said shortly. **1913** Kephart *Our Sthn High* 130 'Twa'n't (so and so), for he hain't got no squar'-headed hobnails. **1927** Mason *Lure of Smokies* 167 'Twa'n't no fun firin' a crazy gun. **c1960** *Wilson Coll*: *Twan't* =

it wasn't. **1963** Edwards *Gravel* 128 Tweren't long till they was plumb familiar, and finally got so I'd get em out of their cage of a mornin and they'd run about the place all day, but when night came back into their cage they'd go, just like a hoss to his stable. **1972** Cooper *NC Mt Folklore* 96 *'twant nothing* = amounted to nothing. **1974** Fink *Bits Mt Speech* 27 *Twarn't* me. **1984** Smith *Oral History* 41 Twerent natural, no moren a snow in July. **1986** Helton *Around Home* 379 *twarn't* = it was not.

twarge See **towards.**

twarn't See **twan't.**

tweedle *verb* See citation.

1982 Slone *How We Talked* 29 *tweedle someone* = talk them into believing something.

twell See **till.**

twer *phrase* It was. See also **twan't.**

1984 Smith *Oral History* 37 I can't say twer ary surprise.

tweren't See **twan't.**

twice *adverb* Variant forms *twicet, twict, twist, twiste*, pronounced as one syllable.

1824 Knight *Letter from KY* 106 The Phraseology in this state is sometimes novel. . . . Many from habit, like the Virginians, tuck a t at the end of such words as onct, twict, skifft. **1862** Epperly *CW Letters* (April 7) wee hant dooing any thing here onley drill a little twist aday. **1864** *Watters-Curtis CW Letters* (July 18) I have had the triall of it twist and maby has parted forever. **1867** Harris *Sut Lovingood* 241 He walk'd clean roun hit twiste, never takin his eyes ofen hit. **1891** Brown *Dialect in TN* 172 In *oncet, twicet, acrost, dost*, and *clost*, we have a final t added. **1913** Kephart *Our Sthn High* 107 I had to fire twiste afore he tumbled. **1939** Walker *Mtneer Looks* 4 A final t is sometimes added to words ending in the sound of *s-* of *twicet, oncet*. **1942** Hall *Phonetics Smoky Mts* 92 Many speakers pronounce the following words with excrescent final t . . . *twice, orphan, vermin*. **1961** Kurath and McDavid *Pron Engl Atl Sts* 179 An added /t/ occurs in *once* and *twice* throughout the Midland and the South. . . . Though most common in folk speech, it is widely used by middle-class speakers, especially in the South Midland. **1973** GSMNP-57:63 That's [the] only time you see a car then, about twicet a year. **1989** *Matewan OHP-1* McGinnis was so good to me, he come down here at least twicet a week. **1998** *Dante OHP-25* Uncle Wilbur Hale was brother-in-laws twicet, so all them Hales and my mother was double first cousins, just a mixed-up bunch.

[*twice* + excrescent t; DARE *twice* adv, adj (pronc) chiefly South, South Midland]

twice out of sight *adverb phrase* Beyond visibility over the horizon.

1960 Allen *Land of Sky* 43 Up yonder, things are hidden twice out of sight. **1976** Garber *Mountain-ese* 97 = twice as far as you can see—They's a store down the road jist twice out uv sight. **1982** Plowman *Out of Sight* 120 I want to remember these beautiful mountains and the people as we found them . . . when we were "Twice Out of Sight."

[DARE *twice out of sight* adv phr southern Appalachians]

twicet, twict See **twice.**

twichet *noun* The female genitalia.

1944 Combs *Word-List Sthn High* 21 = Pudenda muliebria.

[DARE *twitchet* n 1 chiefly Mid Atlantic, southern Appalachians]

twill See **till.**

twinkle *noun* A pine needle.

1913 Kephart *Our Sthn High* 285 In some places pine needles are called twinkles. **1929** Chapman *Homeplace* 313 *twinkles* = pine or spruce needles; balsam leaves. **1957** Combs *Lg Sthn High: Word List* 105 *twinkles* = pine needles. [**1992** Montgomery *Coll* (unknown to consultants from the Smoky Mountains).]

twist[1]

A *verb, noun* Variant plural form and variant third-singular present-tense verb form of two syllables: *twist-es*.

1864 *Watkins CW Letters* (July 12) I wood be glad for you to send me 5 or 6 twistes of tobacco. **1924** Raine *Saddlebags* 97 The rope twistes all up. **2007** McMillon *Notes* There's so many turns and twistes between here and there.

B *noun* Tobacco leaves braided into a thick rope before being cured to be chewed or smoked.

1863 *Poteet CW Letters* (Feb 4) I sent you somthing to eat by Marion Higins five pies and five ginger Cakes one doz unions two custerds 1 ham of Meat and three twists of tobacco. **1864** *Watkins CW Letters* (July 12) I wood be glad for you to send me 5 or 6 twistes of tobacco. **1913** Kephart *Our Sthn High* 39 Generally some tobacco is grown for family consumption, the strong "twist" being smoked or chewed indifferently. **1973** GSMNP-79:22 He'd make [the tobacco] up in these fancy little twistes of tobacco, you know, with the golden looking colors. **1989** *Matewan OHP-56* He smoked what they called a twist, a shoe peg twist. **2003** Carter *Mt Home* 13 He chawed burley, too, and when he could get it, he chawed store boughten twist. **2006** *Encycl Appalachia* 433 Tobacco was an important cash crop in some parts of the Appalachian region. Tobacco was also grown for personal use and made into "twist" for chewing and crumbled for pipe tobacco.

[DARE *twist* n 1 chiefly Midland, South, Southwest]

C See **double.**

twist[2], **twiste** See **twice.**

twister (also *twister plow*) *noun* A type of **turner** plow.

1884 Smith *Arp Scrap Book* 66 My farmer boy stripped the vines . . . Then ran a one-horse twister on each side. **1973** *Gardening* 233

Later they had turnin' plows, an' shovel or [a] lay-off plow for layin' off rows, an' twister plows for hilling your dirt.

[DARE *twister* n 1 South, South Midland]

twistes See **twist**[1].

twistification *noun* A country dance or dancing game with partners in facing lines. See also **civil party, play.**

1904 Johnson *Highways South* 101 For Twistification we all gets in line, boys on one side, girls on the other, with room for a couple to march up between us in dancing step. At the end of the line they swing and we all promenade. Then we form the line and start again. **1913** Kephart *Our Sthn High* 263 Wherever the church has not put its ban on "twistifications" the country dance is the chief amusement of young and old. **1932** Strong *Great Smokies* 163 As for the gals, the most fun they have is a twistification in the schoolhouse fer them what's courtin'. **c1940** Simms *Coll* Old-time dancing at arm's length distance from one's partner [was] not considered sinful—"that's just prancin' and cavortin'; the dancin's what's sinful, is whare you go into the clinch and do the twistification."

[Web3 *twistification* n 2 "a dancing game in which each couple in turn weaves in and out among others who stand in two lines" South and Midland; DARE *twistification* n southern Appalachians, GA, AL]

twixt See **betwixt.**

two-dollar stove See **smoke like a two-dollar stove.**

two-eyed cat *noun* A rudimentary form of baseball played by children. See also **blind cat, bull pen, cat, town ball.**

1976 Braden *Grandma Was Girl* 84–85 Sometimes we went to the pasture field near Grandpa's and played baseball or "two-eyed cat." This latter game was played with two batters about 50 feet apart, and a hindcatcher behind each batter, and any number of players on the field. The catcher threw the ball to the opposite batter. If he missed the ball with his bat and the hindcatcher caught it, the catcher took the batter's place. If the batter hit the ball, the batters had to change bases. If one of the catchers or someone in the field could get the ball and throw it in front of the running batter, he and a mate could take the batters' places.

[DARE *two-eyed cat* n especially South, South Midland]

two holer *noun* An outhouse with two seats. See also **one holer, three holer.**

1994–96 Montgomery *Coll* (known to Adams, Cardwell, Jones, Shields). **2004** Purkey *Home Revisited* vii I can remember visits to relatives who survived with two-holers and wood burning stoves. **2009** Wiles and Wiles *Location* 16–17 The new house was a two-holer with special ventilation. Behind each hole was a 6 inch by 6 inch wooden boxing which rose on the inside to meet with a horizontal boxing across the back of the building. This was ventilated on both sides to carry away odors from the facility.

Two-Seed in the Spirit *noun* See citation.

1996 Dorgan *Baptist Diversity* 9 These last questions influenced the formation of the "Two-Seed" doctrine in the early 19th century, that deterministic position held by Two-Seed in the Spirit Predestinarian Baptists. Under this set of beliefs, an all-good God can create no evil, but an all-evil Satan can and does.

two whoops and a holler See **whoop and a holler.**

twusn't See **twan't.**

typhoid fever *noun* (often *the typhoid fever*) Typhoid. Also called **mountain fever.** See also **fever.**

1939 Hall *Coll* (Catons Grove TN) Boneset's a good remedy for typhoid fever and flu and all sorts of fevers, colds. **1966** Dykeman *Far Family* 264 "Yes. Only Kin's had a bad sickness," she said. "Last fall we nearly didn't bring him through the typhoid fever." **1969** GSMNP-44:14 Why, he took typhoid fever.

tyrollick *verb* See citation.

1957 Combs *Lg Sthn High: Idioms* 8 [He's] tyrollickin' (He's feeling fine).

U

ugly *adjective* Of a person: bad-tempered, mean, misbehaving.

1992 Brooks *Sthn Stuff* 20 *act ugly* = misbehave. "My ma would beat the livin' daylights out of me if Ah acted ugly when cump'ny came." **1994** Rash *New Jesus* 37 Larry has gone out of his way to be as ugly as possible to me. **2017** *Blind Pig* (March 31) "Don't be ugly," meaning don't be sassy or mean.

[DARE *ugly* B1 chiefly Northeast, South, South Midland]

ugly as a mud fence (also *ugly as homemade sin*, and variants) *phrase* Usually of a woman: having unattractive, unsightly looks.

1937 Wilson *Folklore SE KY* 16–17 *ugly as homemade sin* (known to 27/31 speakers in Bell Co KY and 28/31 speakers in Blount Co TN); *ugly as a mud fence* (known to 24/31 speakers in Bell Co KY and 16/31 speakers in Blount Co TN); *ugly as a mud fence after a hail storm* (known to 14/31 speakers in Bell Co KY and 19/31 speakers in Blount Co TN). **1940** Haun *Hawk's Done* 62 He told her she was ugly as a mud fence daubed with tadpoles—throwed that up to her one time when he was mad. *Ibid.* 156 That old dirty gal was ugly as home-made sin. **1965** West *Git Tard* When he says that Hill Anderson's wife is "as ugly as a mud fence daubed with chinquapins," the reader gets the impression that that's some kind of ugly. **1989** Giardina *Storming Heaven* 46 "Big for his britches, ain't he?" Ila Mae said. "And him ugly as a mud pie."

uh *interjection* Same as **ah**. See also **ha**, **holy tone**, **huh**.

1943 Korson *Coal Dust* 46 I have listened to these local preachers in the coal camps of the Appalachian region. . . . They could be spotted by common characteristics: frequent allusions to the Bible, a sing-song drone, and that peculiar, long-drawn-out sound "uh" which they made at regular intervals in the course of their harangues.

(the) ujinctum *noun* Hell.

1919 Combs *Word-List South* 35 = hell (Knott Co [KY]). **1944** Combs *Word-List Sthn High* 21 = hell (used with the definite article): "You ought to be in the ujinctum!" **1992** Brooks *Sthn Stuff* 166 = a hell-like place. "If he doesn't mend his ways, he's headed straight for the ujinctum."

umberel, umbrel See **umbrella**.

umbrella *noun* Variant forms *umberel*, *umbrel*.

1923 Greer-Petrie *Angeline Doin' Society* 25 [There was] a long, slim table with some lamps a-settin' on hit that look'd like pink umbrels. **1944** Williams *Word-List Mts* 32 *umbrel*. **1957** Wise *Mt Speech* 307 umberel' for umbrella.

umbrella magnolia See **umbrella tree**.

umbrella plant *noun* Same as **mayapple**.

1966 *DARE Survey* (Cherokee NC) = mayapple.

umbrella tree (also *umbrella magnolia*) *noun* A large deciduous tree (*Magnolia* spp). See also **cucumber tree**, **Indian bitter 2**, **mountain magnolia**, **wahoo 2**, **yellow linn**.

1901 Lounsberry *Sthn Wild Flowers* 165 Umbrella tree, or elkwood, also bears very large leaves which, however, are ovate-lanceolate in outline, pointed at the apex and distinctively wedge-shaped at the base. . . . At the end of the branches these leaves grow in clusters in a way very suggestive of the ribs of an umbrella. **1913** Morley *Carolina Mts* 21 There are several varieties of these "cucumber" and "umbrella" trees, as the people call them. **1964** Stupka *Trees Shrubs Vines* 61 In rich soils at low altitudes, chiefly along streams, the umbrella magnolia is a fairly common tree.

umer See **humor**.

ummern See **woman A**.

umor See **humor**.

'un See **one 1**.

un- *prefix* In-; used with adjectives and verbs. See also **in-**, **on-**.

1971 Dwyer *Dict for Yankees* 32 I hope we didn't unconvenience you. **1997** Montgomery *Coll* ([*unconvenient*] known to Bush, Cardwell, Jones, Ledford, Oliver, Weaver).

unbeknowing, **unbeknowingest**, **unbeknowin's**, **unbeknowns** See **unbeknownst**.

unbeknownst *adjective*

A Variant forms *onbeknowenst*, *onbeknownst*, *onbenowen*, *unbeknowing*, *unbeknowingest*, *unbeknowin's*, *unbeknowns*.

1942 Hall *Phonetics Smoky Mts* 58 *onbeknownst*.

B Senses.

1 Happening without notice, warning, or one's knowledge or awareness.

1867 Harris *Sut Lovingood* 53 When he wer a-ravin ontu his tip-toes, an' a-poundin the pulpit wif his fis'—onbeknowenst to enybody, I ontied my bag ove reptiles, put the mouf ove hit onder the bottim ove his britches-laig, an' sot intu pinchin thar tails. *Ibid.* 117 They crawl'd up onbenowen tu enybody inter the lof, an' clar tu the tuther aind furthest frum the lodge room, an' trap-door, an' lay pow'ful low, waitin fur night an' the masons. **1941** Stuart *Men of Mts* 84 We like to do things together like takin a little snort unbeknowns to your Ma. **c1950** Adams *Grandpap* 230 Will had seed the girl an' he'd talked to her. The fact is, all unbeknowin's to the King, he'd been a-sparkin' her a little. **1960** Hall *Smoky Mt Folks* 9 He "clim" the tree "ferninst" the place where the animal was clinging, and "onbeknownst" to the bear, prepared to shoot it. **1974** Fink *Bits Mt Speech* 28 = without notice or warning. "He left *unbeknownst* to anybody." **1983** Mull and Boger *Recollections* 77 Mr. A went coon-hunting one night and "unbeknowingest" to him, the family pet by the name of Trip had followed the other coon to the woods. **1998** Montgomery *Coll* Unbeknowing to Bob, the squirrel slipped down the other side of the tree (Brown).

2 Ignorant, unaware.

1998 Montgomery *Coll* Unbeknowing of the facts, he asked about her father (Cardwell).

unbelonging *adjective* Not belonging.

1940 Still *River of Earth* 192 I allus wanted to bring up my chaps honest, never taking a thing unbelonging to them, never taking a grain they didn't earn.

uncertain See **on- 1**.

unchurch *verb* Of a church congregation. to dismiss (a person from membership) for violating a standard of conduct. See also **church 1, 2**.

1966 Frome *Strangers* 252 The worst fate that could befall a man was to be "unchurched"; he might accept it philosophically, as a license to live his own life, but to his neighbors, for one to be "unchurched," it meant that he could not possibly be saved. **1987** Wear *Sevierville* 101 Many were "unchurched" for going against the rules, especially for drinking and making whiskey. **1997** Montgomery *Coll* (known to Adams, Bush, Ledford). [redundant prefix]

uncle *noun* Used as a quasi-honorific name or title to express courtesy, familiarity, or respect for an older man in the community not necessarily related to the speaker, often preceded by *old* or followed by a man's name; used to address or in third-person reference. See also **aunt B**, **dad**, **granny A1**, **old uncle**.

1899 Crozier *White-Caps* 176 "Old Uncle Andy," as he was familiarly known, lived in the Henderson Spring neighborhood and was one of the oldest and best citizens in Sevier county. **c1950** Adams *Grandpap* 19 Uncle Jonathan Richmond was not my real uncle. As far as I know he was not a blood-uncle to anybody. But he was old. He was also one of the richest men in Letcher County. So, out of respect for his age and money, everybody called him uncle. Other honorary uncles in our neighborhood were Will Sexton, Tom Collins, Lige Breeding, Sam Caudill and Peter Adkins. **1957** GSMNP-23:1:18 I used to prowl these mountains all over, me and old Uncle Eph Reagan. That's my brother-in-law. We would always go out in fall of the year. We'd made our crops. **1960** Justus *Right House* 20–22 Uncle Josh was no real kin to the Turners, but everyone called him Uncle out of respect for his age. He claimed to be over ninety years old, but he was spry as a squirrel, and was noted as a great talker and a teller of tall tales. **1962** Williams *Mtneers Mind Manners* 21 Children address by first names contemporaries of their parents, but they address people belonging to the generation of their grandparents as aunt and uncle without regard for blood kinship. **1973** GSMNP-48:8 I was taught to respect elderly people, and we were to refer to them as aunt or uncle one, if they were old. **1985** Wear *Lost Communities* 4 He was not my real uncle, but for respect we children were taught to call all old people uncle and aunt. **1991** Haynes *Haywood Home* 70 He was not really our uncle. He was no kin to us that I know of. But the young of my time were taught to address older people as uncle or aunt whether they were any kin or not. It was respectful. **2005** Williams *Gratitude* 13 Back then, it was a sign of respect to call older folks "Aunt" and "Uncle," when they were friends too close to be called "Mister" and "Missus." **2017** *Blind Pig* (Oct 12) When I first went to a country church in my community (almost fifty years ago), my friend was introducing me to different people like "Aunt Hilda," "Uncle Clea," "Aunt Bessie," etc. I thought she was kin to every person in the congregation. *Ibid.* When I was young, adults were Aunt and Uncle if they were close to the family or neighbors, otherwise Miz and Mr.

[OED3 *uncle* n 2b local and U.S.; DARE *uncle* n 1a now chiefly South, South Midland]

uncle finger *noun* Apparently the middle finger.

1941 Still *Troublesome Creek* 76 "I'll get your pay," he said, and fetched a bottle out of the mill, a bottle no taller than my uncle-finger.

uncommon

A *adjective* Variant form *oncommon*.

1885 Murfree *Prophet* 306 "That ain't nuthin' oncommon," said the old man.

B *adverb* Unusually, quite.

1937 Hyatt *Kiverlid* 56 "Well, Granny," said Nancy, picking up the ball of gray stocking yarn, "this 'u'd be uncommon purty yarn fer jeans." **1955** Ritchie *Singing Family* 114 That's right uncommon interesting because it talks about some of our people. **1997** Montgomery *Coll* (known to eight consultants from the Smoky Mountains).

[OED3 *uncommon* adj/adv 6 colloquial or dialect; Web3 *uncommon* adv chiefly dialect]

unconvenience, **unconvenient** See **un-**.

underbit *noun* A **mark** cut into the bottom edge of a domestic animal's ear to identify its owner. See also **overbit**, **smooth crop**, **split B1**, **swallowfork**.

1890 (in **1975** *Foxfire III* 86) His stock mark is as follows. A Smooth crop and an under bit in the right ear, and a [sic] under half crop in the left ear. **1915** Dingus *Word-List VA* 185 = a triangular cut from the lower side [of an animal's ear]. **1923** Greer-Petrie *Angeline Steppin' Out* 3 He would jest go to the trouble of cuttin' his mark in thar years, say under bit in the left and a slit in the right. **1972** *Raising Sheep* 92 She explained what an overbit looked like: "It's a notch on the top of the ear. If it's on the underside, it's an 'underbit.'"

[DARE (at *under* adj) chiefly South, South Midland, TX]

underbody *noun* An article of women's underwear. See also **body 2**.

1949 Arnow *Hunter's Horn* 70 Ruby with her dress falling down and her purple outing underbody showing. **1992** Brooks *Sthn Stuff* 167 = a woman's lightweight undershirt. **1993** Ison and Ison *Whole Nother Lg* 72 = bra, usually homemade. **1997** Montgomery *Coll* = a corset cover (Bush).

[OED3 *underbody* n dialect "a garment (as a petticoat, corset cover, or slip) worn under an outer garment"; DARE *underbody* n South, South Midland]

undercut *verb* In coal mining, to use a pick to make a slit in the bottom of (the **face** of a coal seam), from which coal is then blasted free, to be loaded into a car to haul out of the mine; hence noun = such a section of coal. See citations.

1982 Eller *Miners* 177 At the coal face, the miner and his helper or loader began work by undercutting the coal seam. This he accomplished by making a horizontal or wedge-shaped slit with his pick at the bottom of the seam, so that the coal would fall when blasted from above. The miner would do most of his undercutting lying on his side swinging with a short-handled pick into the coal seam. . . . After taking two or three hours to make the undercut, the miner then drilled holes in the undercut, loaded the holes with black powder, and fired them, bringing down the undercut coal. **2002** Armstead *Black Days* 247 = [the] first step in hand-loading and conventional coal mining, historically done by hand with a pick, removing a section of the coal at the bottom of the coal face.

underpending *noun* See citation.

1976 Thompson *Touching Home* 17 = underwear.

undershot wheel *noun* The wheel of an undershot grist mill, driven by water passing across the bottom. See also **overshot waterwheel**.

1940 McNeil *Mt Folk* These water powered corn mills, as found in the North Carolina mountains, are of two principal types—the undershot wheel and the overshot wheel—the overshot type being far more prevalent. . . . In the undershot wheel type a comparatively large dam is required, dry seasons may limit grinding time to three or four hours a day, and a more complicated structure is called for in the mechanical arrangements. **1983** Montell *Don't Go Up* 201 = wheel that is powered clockwise by the weight of water passing beneath the wheel. **2006** *Encycl Appalachia* 936 Other mills had vertical waterwheels on the outside. These vertical wheels could be either "overshot" or "undershot." The overshot wheel was turned when water spilling from the end of a flume above it filled a bucket or trough at the top of the wheel's rotation and then spilled into the buckets below, slowly rotating the wheel. In the undershot wheel, the lower part of the wheel rested in a trough of flowing water; the force of the water striking the wheel's evenly spaced baffles turned it.

under the hill *adverbial phrase* In a coal mine.

2006 *Encycl Appalachia* 162 A coal-camp family's economic well-being depended on the shifting fortunes of the coal industry, over which mining families had no control. What men could do to affect the family's economic situation was to go to work "under the hill" and work hard.

unern See **onion**.

unfellowship *noun* A state of dismissal from membership and suspension of participation in a church congregation. See also **church 1**, **unchurch**.

1800 *Globe Creek Church Minutes* 8 therefore we declare an on fellowship with S:d W:m [sic] Humphries.

unfitten *adjective* Unfit, unqualified.

1900 Harben *N GA Sketches* 261 Ab Calihan is either fitten or unfitten, one ur t'other. **c1940** Aswell *Glossary TN Idiom* 19 = unfit. "He's just unfitten to do the work." **1944** Justus *Lizzie* 5 A fairly unfitten way it was for barefoot folk, she was thinking. **1996** Montgomery *Coll* (known to eight consultants from the Smoky Mountains).

[perhaps influenced by *unfitting*; Web3 *un-* + *fitten* past participle of *fit*; DARE *unfitten* adj especially southern Appalachians]

ungyern See **onion**.

unionalls *noun*

1 (also *unionhalls*) Overalls. See also **coverhauls**, **overhalls**.

1940 Haun *Hawk's Done* 121 He had on new unionalls and they suited him. **c1960** Wilson *Coll*: *unionalls* = coveralls, overalls. **1968** *DARE Survey* (Brasstown NC). **1998** Montgomery *Coll* (known to Brown, Bush); *unionhalls* = overalls with black and white stripes having no suspenders over the shoulders (Cardwell).

2 (also *union suit*) Long underwear. See also **long handles**.

c1982 Young *Colloquial Appal* 24 *unionalls* = heavy underwear, long johns. **1984** Burns *Cold Sassy* 298 I just pulled off down to my union suit. **1998** Montgomery *Coll*: Even girls wore unionalls in the winter, which consisted of cotton knit with long sleeves and long legs with a "trap door" in the back (Norris). **2005** Williams *Gratitude* 534 *union suit* = a man's long sleeved, one-piece knit winter underwear. Some of them had a drop seat and some had a split seat. "A man was liable to git in a bind if he come down with the bowel complaint with a *union suit* on." **2016** *Blind Pig* (Jan 21) Every time I put that red union suit on one of the girls to sleep in, I thought they were the cutest thing I ever saw.

unionhalls See **unionalls 1**.

union meeting *noun*

1 An interdenominational church service or reception, as one shared by Baptists, Methodists, etc.

1891 Davidson *Reminiscences* 8 Then they came together and held what they called "Union Meetings" under arbors made with poles and brush, or at the private residence of some good citizen, often at my father's home.

2 See citation.

1995 McCauley *Mt Religion* 69 Setting aside the periodic Fifth Sunday for what is called "union meetings" when local, as well as farther away, Old Regular Baptist churches will all worship together.

union suit See **unionalls 2**.

unknowenst *adjective* Beyond belief or knowledge.

c1954 Adams *Word-List* Isn't that the unknowenst thing?

unless *conjunction*

A Variant forms *less, onless.*

1774 *Dunmore's War* 99 Onless you Send Some men down the Case will be Bad So that I must stay with not more then Six men unless I kill part and tye the Other. **1861** (in **1938** Taliaferro *Carolina Humor* 15) They . . . made preachers, who won't be satisfied onless they are on the backs o' the peepul ridin inter popularity and great wealth. **1913** Kephart *Our Sthn High* 102 A bear allers dies flat on his back, onless he's trapped. **1932** Strong *Great Smokies* 27 Onless those folks hev changed more'n I think, ye'll stay up thar jest as long as they want ye ter, an' no longer. **1939** Burnett *Gap o' Mountains* 12 I warn you that onless we gyard the ballot in whuch our manhood and freedom air wropped—we will all be slaves. **2002** Rash *Foot in Eden* 87 It wasn't no bruising grip but sure enough not to let me leave less he allowed it.

B Without it happening that.

1964 Roberts *Hell-Fer-Sartin* 88 She couldn't think of any way to get rid of her unless the neighbors would know about it. **1973** *Carpenter* 119 Ain't nobody gonna slip in here an' put stuff around unless I find it.

unlessen *conjunction* Unless. See also **lessen**.

1977 Yeager *Mostly Work* 9 We didn't have to go out unlessen we just wanted to. **1988** Smith *Fair and Tender* 188 I thought I would not mention to Oakley about it being a burying quilt unlessen of course he was to ask me flat out. **1997** Montgomery *Coll* No one will come unlessen Paul does (Cardwell).

[DARE *unlessen* conj chiefly South, South Midland]

unless that *conjunctive* Unless; for similar forms with *that*, see **that C** and Grammar and Syntax §15.4.

1989 *Matewan OHP-102* They [= doctors] wouldn't come to the house, only in emergency, unless that hit was something that we couldn't take care of.

untel, untell See **until**.

untelling *adjective*

A Variant form *ontelling* [see **1941** in **B**].

B Untellable, beyond description, belief, conjecture, or comprehension. See also **unknowenst**.

1916 Combs *Old Early English* There's a man say it's untellin'. **1925** Furman *Glass Window* 123 Hit's too much to hope that they'll get past Christmas without busting-out, and ontelling what they'll do. **1941** Still *Troublesome Creek* 10 I say it's ontelling what a ton o' coal will sell for. **1952** Giles *40 Acres* 4 If one is uncertain about the length of time since an occurrence, it is "untelling" how long it has been. **1955** Ritchie *Singing Family* 33 Lordie mercy, why it's untelling what he'll do and him so franzy like that. **1979** Carpenter *Walton War* 158 What I have seed in my time is untelling. **1981** Henry *Alex Stewart* 52 I let him have that pipe for a quart of chestnuts. And I've thought that if that preacher didn't get forgiven for that, that he's just as sure for hell as a fat hog is the meathouse. If I had it today it's untelling what it'd bring me. **1995** Montgomery *Coll* (known to Adams, Brown); *it's ontelling* [i.e. there's no telling] (Cardwell), = wonderful (Oliver). **1998** Joslin *Living Heritage* 13 Horse talk has turned to talk of rock walls, as they discuss how the "untelling" number of rocks in the fields had to be gathered into piles to clear the way for cultivation. **2007** McMillon *Notes* = anybody's guess. **2009** Holbrook *Upheaval* 32 It's untelling which one would be worse off.

[OED3 *untelling* present-part/adj 2, northern, Scot[tish] and U.S. dialect; EDD *untelling* ppl adj Scot "impossible to tell, beyond words, past reckoning"; SND *untellin* adj "past reckoning, impossible to tell"; DARE *untelling* ppl adj 1 chiefly southern Appalachians]

unthoughted See also **thoughted, unthoughtedly**.

A *adjective* Thoughtless, without thinking, spontaneous, impromptu. See also **unthoughtless**.

1915 Dingus *Word-List VA* 192 = thoughtless (also adverb). **1937** Hyatt *Kiverlid* 97 "Well, I was unthoughted not to a drawed hit back an' pinned hit better," said Nancy. **1975** Chalmers *Better* 32 Reckon I was jest unthoughted. **1989** Buxton and Burns *Blowing Rock* 112 The girls are eager to learn and to try, but they are so "unthoughted," as they express carelessness.

[Web3 *unthoughted* adj 2 dialect; DARE *unthoughted* adj chiefly South, South Midland]

B *adverb* Unexpectedly, unintentionally, uncontrollably.

1925 Furman *Glass Window* 5 'Pears like I think of 'em unthoughted, paw. **1942** Hall *Phonetics Smoky Mts* 58 It happened so quick and unthoughted.

unthoughtedly *adverb*

A Variant form *onthoughtedly* [see **1867** in **B**].

B Unthinkingly, unintentionally, absentmindedly. See also **unthoughted B**.

1867 (in **1974** Harris *High Times* 188) The sight ove the dorg [= dog], sot me to hummin' sorter onthoughtedly. **1924** Raine *Saddlebags* 101 He did it unthoughtedly. **c1975** Lunsford *It Used to Be* 32 He was there, and they very unthoughtedly, possibly, didn't let him know the ladies were out there.

[EDD *unthoughtedly* adv "without thinking" Yorkshire and America]

unthoughtless

A *adjective* Careless.

1927 Woofter *Dialect from WV* 366 = very careless. "It was so unthoughtless of me to walk in on sister and her beau."

B *adverb* Most unthinkingly, carelessly. See also **unthoughted A, unthoughtedly B**.

1904–20 Kephart *Notebooks* 4:749 I run into them turkeys the unthoughtless of anything I ever done. **1957** Combs *Lg Sthn High: Word List* 106 = superl[ative] of *thoughtlessly*. Ex.: "The unthoughtless of anything he ever done wuz to bounce into that yaller-jacket's nest." **1995–97** Montgomery *Coll* (known to Brown, Bush, Cypher, Ledford).

unthoughty

A *adjective* Unthinking. See also **thoughty**.

1998 Montgomery *Coll* (known to Brown, Bush, Jones); She's an unthoughty person. That's why she's so clumsy (Cardwell).

[DARE (at *thoughty* adj 1) chiefly South Midland]

B *adverb* Unthinkingly, unintentionally.

1982 Ginns *Snowbird Gravy* 98 "I wouldn't do you a wrong if I knowed it with my mind," and I said, "Or I'd just do it unthoughty if I did."

until See also **till**.

A Variant forms *ontel, ontell, ontil, untel, untell, untill* [see **1863** in **B1**].

1813 Hartsell *Memora* 132 he hoped that the Volenteers from east Tennessee wold not Leave him untell he Recived a reinforcement of men to go on to the hickrey ground. **1858** (in **1974** Harris *High Times* 154) I listened ontil hit guv me the toothake, an I had a sour taste in my mouf. **1861** *Hanes CW Letters* (June 16) if you havent writen to me yet you needent to untel I get to garyesburge. **1862** *Councill CW Letters* (Dec 21) I remain your Cousin ontel death. Rite soon and give me all the nuse. **1862** *Sutton CW Letters* (Nov 8) you need not rit to me any moure untell I rit to you. **1923** Greer-Petrie *Angeline Doin' Society* 3 He didn't aim to go back home ontell he got a good sight of one of them thar vampyures. **1953** Hall *Coll* (Bryson City NC) [When] the spring of the year come, why he went to plowing and planting his corn and beans, potatoes and things. He'd take care of that ontil he got through and got his crop laid by.

B *conjunction*

1 By the time that. See also **till B3**.

1862 *Click CW Letters* (Jan 16) give my love to all the girls and tell them to get reddy to get married untell this ware is at and end. **1863** *Hundley CW Letters* (Jan 7) tell toody and sis they must not forget me and they must be smart untill I come home.

2 (Up) to the point or time that, to the extent that.

1923 Greer-Petrie *Angeline Steppin' Out* 14 He let his temper git the upper hand of him ontell he was plum beside hisse'f. **1926** Hunnicutt *Twenty Years* 65 She has been tied up until her feet are tender. **1938** Hall *Coll* (Cades Cove TN) It has just rained all summer until people can't get to do any work much. **1941** Stuart *Men of Mts* 230 Sweat is streaming in my eyes until I can't see the path. **1961** *Coe Ridge OHP-334B* She didn't stay too long down South until she came back to this country. **1972** Foster *Walker Valley* 5:10 It made enough of noise until the snake went out and out the window over there. **1973** Kahn *Hillbilly Women* 141 I've fell lots of times. The spirit'll just hit you until you black out. **1984** Harmon *Falling Leaves* 37 Today the nature of the hen has been taken away from her until now most of them cannot now perform in the natural way. **2000** Montgomery *File* I've done this [labeling] until they could take and interpret the pictures (70-year-old woman, Walland TN). **2007** Preece *Leavin' Sandlick* 28 Her sister said she was grievin' too hard until it was makin' her sick.

up

A *adverb*

1 Used to extend or intensify the action of a verb or to show completeness of action. See Grammar and Syntax §14.4.

1863 *Bartlett CW Letters* (March 12) if I could get orders to Tenn it would revive me up considerable I would feel like a new man. **1863** *Vance Papers* (May 11) I live in Transylvania on french Broad and is A Mill Rite and the people wants Mee to Come and Repair up Mills if I am A lowd to. **1924** Bacheller *Happiest Person* 98 In the mountains Mrs. Gentry had been known as "the revenoo lady" because she and another woman had tramped back in the wilderness and located a wild still which had been "spoilin' up the boys." **1939** Hall *Coll* They've got [the town] renewed up . . . She's improved up a bit. *Ibid.* (Smokemont NC) He [= a bear] went back into the laurel hung with this trap, and finally we traced him up. **1961** Seeman *Arms of Mt* 57 [He] murdered up a man fer four dollars! **1973** *AOHP/ASU-111* He [was] just scared to plant it [in tobacco], so he planted up a patch and planted it in sugar corn up there. **1974** Roberts *Sang Branch* 55 We made whiskey along a little 'cause it was about the only way we had to collect up any money to keep ourselves in clothing and ever'thing. **1980** Wigginton *Foxfire VI* 153 When he got vexed up, he'd say what he thought and it didn't make no difference. **1997** Montgomery *Coll* Fetch up a pail of water (Brown). **2008** Salsi *Ray Hicks* 74 All the while, she was actin' innocent and foolin' up the adults.

2 In phrasal prepositions. See **up in** and Grammar and Syntax §14.5.

3 With ellipsis of a following locative preposition.

1975 Kroeger *WV Farm Life* 8 You can drive turkeys, and now that was real, for they have roosted a time or two up home. **1978** Montgomery *White Pine Coll* III-2 My Dad's brother that lives up Del Rio in Cocke County, he had about twenty or twenty-five beestands. We called it, gums of bees. **1989** *Matewan OHP-23* That was up Newtown above Red Jacket. *Ibid.* 88 My brother Carlos, the one that lives up Cape Cod. **1998** *Dante OHP-29* I was living up Morefield then. *Ibid.* 71 Let's go up Mister Moore's house. **2007** (in **2012** McQuaid *Interface* 269) He was working up the school with her with the young'uns.

B *verb* To prepare, move quickly in anticipation. See also **up and**.

1939 Hall *Coll* (Cataloochee NC) I up with this here big old hog rifle, cap and ball gun, and I took good bead at him, and I hit him right where I missed him before.

up agin it *adjective phrase* Facing a tight situation, especially a financial one.

1937 Hall *Coll* (Cades Cove TN) [I used to plow with oxen] when I was up agin it. I had two yokes of oxens. **1982** Ginns *Snowbird Gravy* 101 Well, a fellow who was out there stealing in the daytime, he ain't really a-stealing. He maybe was just up agin it in the olden time. **2008** Salsi *Ray Hicks* 163 I was up agin it a tryin' to find a girl that weren't kin to me.

up and *auxiliary verb phrase*

A Variant past-tense form *upped and*.

1941 Justus *Kettle Creek* 81 "You needn't get miffed," Matt said, "because I upped and asked you a point-blank question." **c1945** Haun *Hawk's Done* 261 I got to thinking maybe she didn't know it, so I upped and told her that night.

B Used to convey rising or starting movement, accompanied by quick, sudden, or unanticipated action. See also **on B**.

1938 Bowman *High Horizons* 42 Nigh sundown she up an' died, but her body stayed limp as a rag ontil her baby, 'twar a leetle gal, died 'bout midnight—hit's a shore sign I reckon. **1943** Justus *Bluebird* 102 Let's up and surprise Miss Judy on our next speaking day with some of these funny songs—the ones you are making the tunes for. **1969** Medford *Finis* 85 "Nothin' a'tall," Mrs. Cason, testified; "I was jist cookin' breakfast—when he up an' slapped me down with his hand or fist." **1972** *AOHP/ALC-355* Somebody told me, but I'll not up and remember now what it was . . . I'd have to up and count that. I don't know how many there was of them now. **1973** *GSMNP-79:25* My leg all swelled up and had these big red lines run all the way up my leg. Well, they didn't up and take me and run to the doctor. **1983** *Dark Corner OHP-27A* Somebody up and went into running it [= a store].

upards, up'ards See **upwards**.

up-headed *adjective*

1 Carrying the head high.

1917 Kephart *Word-List* 418 A fine lookin', *upheaded* gal. **1994–97** Montgomery *Coll* (known to Brown, Bush, Cardwell).

2 Shrewd, self-confident; arrogant, conceited.

1919 Combs *Word-List South* 35 = shrewd, intelligent. **1925** Furman *Glass Window* 47 Sary was a up-headed woman, I hain't denying hit, and her pride maybe needed some setback. **1997** Montgomery *Coll* (known to Brown, Bush, Jones).

upheadiness (also *upheadyness*) *noun* Conceit, arrogance.

1963 Williams *Metaphor Mt Speech II* 53 The mountain woman who, after moving to the county seat, begins to achieve social standing and "thank she's sumpin on a stick," loses the respect of her country cousins for her "upheadyness." **1995** Montgomery *Coll* (known to Cardwell).

upheadyness See **upheadiness**.

uphold (also *uphold for*) *verb, verb phrase* To defend (someone); to take a position of defense for.

1938 (in **2009** Powell *Shenandoah Letters* 149) I am not trying to uphold them for doing wrong. **1938** Stuart *Dark Hills* 343 I don't uphold for one of my children in the wrong.

up home *noun* One's native or ancestral area. See also **down home, homeland.**

2016 Lundy and Autry *Victuals* 19 We moved to the city, Louisville, so my father could find work. Like most who migrated in the many hillbilly diasporas brought on by the regional economic crashes of the 20th century, my parents continued to call Corbin [KY] "up home" and to take me there whenever they had a chance.

up in *phrasal preposition* See also **in A1**.

1 (+ *adverb*)

1855 *Mitchell Letter* Commerce in this country ("up in here," as the natives say) is mostly carried on by barter, and the prices of produce are little affected by Sebastopol, or Mark Lane, or Wall Street; but mainly by a good or bad season.

2 (also *up out*) (+ *prepositional phrase*)

1938 Bowman *High Horizons* 43–44 Hit war showed me like a "pitcher" that the babe wuz asleep up in under a log like, on the side of a ridge that I knowed whar hit be by hits size and shape. **1939** Hall *Coll* (Smokemont NC) In the Ace Cove, we went up out on top Hughes Ridge, come back to the bald. **1982** Powers and Hannah *Cataloochee* 376 Sure 'nough, there come one right up in above where he lived over there on Catalooch'! **1997** Montgomery *Coll* The old tomcat went up in under the chair (Brown). **2014** *Blind Pig* (March 31) We used to go grabbling for catfish upinunder the rocks in the Little Tennessee. *Ibid.* Where I come from the bear would have been way back up in above Pap's house and the earring would have been way back upinunder the bed.

up jumped the Devil *phrase* See citation.

2017 *Blind Pig* (Oct 20) = said after a mischievous or mean act has taken place or when someone who is disliked suddenly shows up.

upland *noun* See citation. Same as **bench 1**.

1939 Hall *Coll* (Proctor NC) = a piece of land that lays flat up on a hill, also called a bench. Most people would call it a bench. There can be a bench also in a flat, wooded area. You don't hear upland used so very much. You hear bench much more.

upling block See **upping block**.

upon my honor (also *my honor, pon my honor, upon my word*) *interjection*

1 Honestly! This is the truth! I give you my word!

1921 Greer-Petrie *Angeline at Seelbach* 2 'Pon my honor, that door whirled around like a merry-go-round. **1936** Skidmore *Lift Up Eyes* 21 Pon my honor, boy, yore cutten down more'n yore leavin up. **1973** *AOHP/LJC-317* Let's see, 'pon my honor, I don't actually know where the first post office was there in Haddix. **1985** Irwin *Alex Stewart* 100 Upon my honor, that beats anything ever I seed. **1993** Ison and Ison *Whole Nother Lg* 51 *pon my honor* = this is correct, I give you my word on this. May be used as an exclamation also. **1997** Montgomery *Coll*: *upon my honor* (known to Brewer, Bush, Cardwell, Jones, Ledford); *upon my word* (known to Bush, Cardwell, Jones, Weaver). **1999** Milnes *Play of Fiddle* 94 Another common oral tradition in West Virginia is the byword. Most tale tellers mimic the actual speaking voices of the characters, including the identifying byword(s) interjected throughout the tale. For instance, Eddie Hammons's byword was "Upon my honor," with which he apparently started almost every sentence. In most tellings, this gets shortened to just "'Pon my honor," or, "My honor."

2 See citation.

1997 Johnson *Melungeon Heritage* 61 "'Pon my honor" was used to express amazement or disbelief.

up out See **up in 2**.

uppards See **upwards**.

upper *adjective* Situated at a higher elevation; hence *upperest* = farthest or highest up, especially at the head of a stream.

1919 Combs *Word-List South* 35 = the house farthest up, or on the head of a stream. **1929** Kephart *Smoky Mt Magic* 38 "Which way d' he go?" "The upperest trail." **1956** Hall *Coll* (Big Creek NC) Turkey George Palmer was in the upperest house on Indian Creek. **1969** GSMNP-25:2:22 Swaggerty I believe was the one built the big house now that we lived in on, that was the upperest house up Roaring Fork. That was just after you come through Spruce Flats. The Clabo family lived at that time on the very upperest house. **1980** GSMNP-115:4 He had a boy named Mid, Uncle Aaron did, lived on the Middle Fork that built that upperest house up there.

upper dogtrot *noun* See citation. See also **dogtrot**.

1968 Clarke *Stuart's Kentucky* 183 The typical house had a lean-to kitchen, separated from the main part of the house by a dog-trot, which aided ventilation; in some two-story log houses, an upper dogtrot served the same purpose.

upperds See **upwards**.

upperest See **upper**.

upping block (also *upling block*) *noun* A block used especially by women as a step to mount a horse.

1883 Smith *Southernisms* 55 *Upping-block*, a "horse-block," [is] in common use in West Virginia. **1896** *Word-List* 426 *uppin' block* = horse-block. **1923** (in **1952** Mathes *Tall Tales* 6) It was near sundown on Saturday before the fifth Sunday of May when he drew rein at the "uppin' block" in front of Nath Walker's "tub mill." **1952** Wilson *Folk Speech NC* 603 *upping block* = a block used by ladies to mount a horse. **1972** Carson and Vick *Cookin* 2 6 When I got older, they'd let me ride Lucy to the mill. I'd get on an upling block to make the saddle. **1977** Hamilton *Mt Memories* 26 There was an "upping block" between the road and river. It was a block of wood set in the ground with a lower block for a step. This contrivance was used for the women to get on a horse. **2002** Myers *Best Yet Stories* 227 Many early homes had an "upping block" used especially by women to mount their horses or mules. It was usually located in the front yard near the home. Side saddles and very long dresses with lots of petticoats made the upping blocks a necessity.

[EDD *upping block* mEngl, sEngl; DARE *upping block* n chiefly Midland]

upscuddle *noun* A quarrel. Also called **rupscud**.

1913 Kephart *Our Sthn High* 294 If they quarrel, it is a ruction, a rippit, a jower, or an upscuddle—so be it there are no fatalities which would amount to a real fray. **1941** Justus *Kettle Creek* 51 "If I had any notion who took'em—" he doubled up his fists and swung out his arms—"there'd be an upscuddle, all right!" **1981** Whitener *Folk-Ways* 40 They was a regular upscuddle at the schoolhouse. **1997** Montgomery *Coll* (known to Adams).

[DARE *upscuddle* n chiefly southern Appalachians]

upset *verb* Variant past-tense and past-participle form *upsot*.

1867 Harris *Sut Lovingood* 97h [sic] He had *hellfire harness on*, an he run over my hosses an upsot the waggin, en tuck thru my camp fire, makin the chunks, an sparks, an ashes fly es high es the trees, an out ove site in a minit. **1924** Montague *Betsy Beaver* 226 Tony was skeered he mought be right badly upsot if he was to ketch a glimpse of what it was like sure 'nough. **1971** Dwyer *Dict for Yankees* 32 = upset. "She got so upsot when the soup was upsot." **1997** Montgomery *Coll* (known to Bush, Cardwell, Norris, Weaver).

[DARE (at *upsot* v) scattered, but especially South Midland, New England]

upside (also *upside of, up the side of*) *preposition, phrasal preposition* Against, upon (a vertical surface).

1983 *Dark Corner OHP-5A* They'd throw [the can], just pick it up, get it out of them boxes, hit their horse up side the head with it, try to make them get up out of the road. **1998** *Dante OHP-61* I'll put this geography book up the side of your head. **1999** Morgan *Gap Creek* 262 Hank swung the chair and hit Timmy upside of the head. **2000** Morgan *Mts Remember* 143 I want to hit him up the side of his fence. **2009** Burton *Beech Mt Man* 59 What's all that paint upside your car and pieces of wood hangin' down from under it?

[DARE *upside* prep 1a especially South]

upside of See **upside**.

upsot See **upset**.

up the country *adverb phrase* Up or out in the country.

1865 *Leigh CW Letters* (Jan 15) I Just got back from oup the country we had a bad time of it. **1883** Bonner *Dialect Tales* 178 The captain was up the country on a moonshine raid. **2007** McMillon *Notes* = an indefinite distance from one's own area.

up the mountain See **mountain C**.

up the side of See **upside**.

uptrip *verb* See citation.

1941 (in **1944** Wentworth *ADD*) = to trip one up.

[DARE *uptrip* v chiefly South Midland, especially KY]

upwards *adverb* Variant forms *upards, up'ards, uppards, upperds*.

1862 *Click CW Letters* (Sept 18) we have bin on this trip upperds of 5 weaks and we have had know chance to write untill we got here. **1867** Harris *Sut Lovingood* 252 He flung hit up'ards, an' es hit cum down, hit met one ove of Wirt's boots. **1885** Murfree *Prophet* 150 Him an' me run a sour mash still on the top of the mounting in the light o' day up'ards o' twenty year, an' never hearn o' no raider. **1927** Furman *Lonesome Road* 40 Study on 'em, backards and forrards, upards and downards. **1931** Combs *Lg Sthn High* 1318 W is elided in several words: "awkard," . . . "upards." **1954** Roberts *Bought a Dog* 12 I'll turn this bucket bottom uppards on the tater hill.

[DARE *upwards* adv scattered, but especially South, South Midland]

upwards in See **in A1**.

urban holler *noun* See citation.

2006 *Encycl Appalachia* 904 Sizable Appalachian neighborhoods such as Uptown (Chicago), Lower Price Hill (Cincinnati), and "Hazeltucky" (Hazel Park, Michigan) have been called cultural islands or "urban hollers" because their people continue traditional community and family-centered lifestyles, folkways, regional dialects, and codes of neighborliness and hospitality that define them as Appalachian.

us *pronoun* See also **us'uns**.

1 Used reflexively as indirect object (the so-called personal dative) = (for) ourselves.

1862 *Robinson CW Letters* (Dec 4) we have cleaned off us a place to stay this winter. **1863** *Mangum CW Letters* (Dec 10) we have no tents a tall Sam and me taken our old blankets and put them together and made us a very good little tente. **1922** *TN CW Ques* 1317 (Sullivan Co TN) As I come we stoped at wood yard and got us a friring [sic] pan and made a fire and fried us some meat. **1939** *Hall Coll* (Proctor NC) We'd all just fix us up a sack of rations, you know, and every fellow would take his rations up there. *Ibid.* (Sugarlands TN) We had us a big fire made up at the root of the tree. **1972** *AOHP/ALC-355* [We'd] get out and bend us down some trees in the woods and ride them up and down. **1973** *Foxfire Interviews* A-73-43 You just furnish the place, and me and you'll grow us a bunch of gourds. **1979** *Gamecock* 162 Me and Bill went around and picked us out the game cock first. **1989** *Matewan OHP-28* We'd take us a little jar of milk and butter. **1991** *Thomas Sthn Appal* 105 We went out here to a feller, Mister Lowell Nance, an' bought us five turkeys—we paid seb'mty-five cents apiece for those turkeys. **2008** *Rosie Hicks* 3 We got us all on stage.

2 As part of a compound subject (thus *us and them* = we and they). See also **her 1**, **him 1**.

1998 *Dante OHP-58*. Us and Papaw and them had the first cars in the neighborhood.

use *verb*

1 Of an animal: to visit habitually, make a home at or around, frequent, resort to a place regularly for feeding, grazing, bedding down, etc.; to become habituated to a place; to leave a **sign** while feeding.

1878 Coale *Wilburn Waters* 44 Wilburn asked Blevins if his was a good region for wolves. On being informed that any number "used in those parts," as well as bears and all sorts of wild animals, he at once determined to go there and try his luck. **1895** Edson and Fairchild *TN Mts* 375 These chickens *uses* round the place. **1904–20** Kephart *Notebooks* 4:749 The bears are usin' on the south side of the mts now. **1926** Hunnicutt *Twenty Years* 65 There is a fox using on Sharp Top. **1939** Hall Coll (Cataloochee NC) We located the big bear and found where he was a-using. *Ibid.* (Proctor NC) "A bear's usin' in the head of this cove" means the bear's feedin' there, eatin' berries or whatever he can find there. You could say "the hogs are usin' up in the head of this cove," but not of cattle. For them you'd say, "They're grazin' in that field." [The term is] mostly employed of bears and hogs. **1949** Hall Coll (Del Rio TN) Bear, deer, wild hog, groundhog, squirrels, quail, pheasants, and turkeys all feed in the same place, use in the same boundary. Wild cat, he stays there to catch 'em. **1953** Hall Coll (Plott Creek NC) These bears was using in a apple orchard there. **1982** Powers and Hannah *Cataloochee* 337 One could see tracks in the dust of the dirt floor where deer and raccoon had been "usin'." **1996** Harrell *Fetch It* 167 In our hiking, we came across considerable black bear signs. We passed an apple tree or two, and the bear had eaten an apple or two. They had bedded down there, and they had left claw marks on the trunk of the apple tree where they had climbed up and down. These signs were fairly fresh, meaning they were "using" there at the time.

[EDD *use* v 7; Web3 *use* v 1d chiefly dialect; DARE *use* v B chiefly South, South Midland]

2 To treat.

1852 *Carson Letter* 147 I shall always think well of Polley and Gum for the way they used me on the road.

used to See also **usen**, **will B**.

A *adverb phrase* Formerly (preceding the subject in clauses with a past-tense or present-perfect verb).

1931 Goodrich *Mt Homespun* 72 Used to when we was little, we'd make us horses out of cornstalks. **1965** Miller *Pigeon's Roost* (Jan 7) Used to, all beefs was fixed that way, too. **1973** *AOHP/ASU-111* Used to parents raised the children, and if they were good parents they tried to teach the children morals and things like that. **1973** *GSMNP-78:3* That branch that comes off that you'uns lives in is the Holy Butt Branch, used to, I've been up squirrel hunting. Used to I've been up in there lots of times back my young days, a-hunting. **1978** Montgomery *White Pine Coll* IV-2 Used to, you know, there wasn't very much working on Sundays. *Ibid.* VIII-3 Used to, once in a while they'd have some kind of a frolic up at White Pine. **1984** Page and Wigginton *Foxfire Cookery* 85 Used to, when we made slaw we'd take the thick cream of the milk and mix it and vinegar together and pour it over the cabbage. **2001** Montgomery *File* Used to, when she came through town we would always have dinner (60-year-old man, Blount Co TN).

B *auxiliary verb phrase*

1 In phrases *used to could* = formerly was/were able to; *used to couldn't* = formerly was/were not able to.

1863 *Dalton CW Letters* (May 16) so mutch smoake And snow hit has Ruin my eyese I have got so that i cante see one bit at night & about Half as good as I use too Cood. **1884** Smith *Arp Scrap Book* 66 I used to could plow, but it looks like I have lost the lick [= skill]. **1891** Brown *Dialect in TN* 174 *Could* is frequently used as an infinitive, as "I can't play the fiddle now, but I used to could." **1961** *Coe Ridge OHP-333A* I can't recollect things like I used to could, now I'm a old lady I just forget people's names that I know. **1967**

Miller *Pigeon's Roost* (Nov 9) Now all sawmills is run by electricity or motors that burns fuel oil and the sawmills can saw more lumber in a day now than they used to could, but the cost of getting the lumber sawed is much higher. **1984** Gibson *Remembering* 15 You used to could look from Grandpa's door to the graveyard and the church house where we attended church. **1986** Pederson et al. LAGS (Sevier Co TN) [I] used to couldn't slaughter [hogs]; (Johnson Co TN) I used to could work all day. **1988** Smith *Fair and Tender* 122 You know we used to could see it from Sugar Fork.

[CUD *used to could* (at *use* v)]

2 In phrases *used to did* = formerly did; *used to didn't* = formerly did not.

1960 McCaulley *Cades Cove* I don't expect I could quote very many of [the songs] now there, but I used to did. **1963** Miller *Pigeon's Roost* (June 27) For some reason or another, it seems like that a large congregation don't never assemble out at the decorations like they used to did. **1971** *AOHP/ALC-260* We have our gas in running church houses that we used to didn't have. **1983** Page and Wigginton *Aunt Arie* 156 Y'know, you use t'didn't have much of a bank. **1998** *Dante OHP-65* Nowadays people don't get together like they used to did then. **2001** Lowry *Expressions* 18 It came out like it used to did.

[DARE *used to* v phr C 2a chiefly South, South Midland]

3 In phrases *used to was/were* (also *useter war*) = formerly was; *used to wasn't* (also *ust to wasn't*) = formerly was not.

1866 Smith *So Called* 30 As General Byron said, "I ain't now what I used to was." **1931** Combs *Lg Sthn High* 1319 "It useter war (were)" means "It used to be." **1940** Stuart *Trees of Heaven* 251 It ust to wasn't like this. [**1966** See **2**]. **2001** Lowry *Expressions* 15 I thought I was going to get like I used to was.

[DARE *used to* v phr C 2a chiefly South, South Midland]

4 In phrases *used to would* = formerly was/were accustomed or able to, *used to wouldn't* = formerly was/were not accustomed or able to.

1891 Brown *Dialect in TN* 174 He used to wouldn't dance. **1968** *Faith Healing* 62 Now they's a few old women used t'wouldn't learn but three. **1978** Montgomery *White Pine Coll* VI-1 A dollar used to would go a week, but now it takes a kid twenty dollars. *Ibid.* VI-3 The children used to would kind of stay in the background. **1986** Pederson et al. LAGS (Claiborne Co TN) I used to would have said I'm going to perk a pot of coffee.

usen *verb* To accustom; hence participial adjective *usen* accustomed.

1886 Smith *Sthn Dialect* 350 A language might deteriorate any time from such causes in the way of such forms as . . . *usen* . . . bear the stamp of antiquity. **1896** Fox *Vendetta* 106 It act'ally looks like lots o' decent young folks hev got usen to the idee [of killing] thar's so much of it goin' on. **1913** Kephart *Our Sthn High* 288 Afore, atwixt, awar, heap o' folks, peart, up and done it, usen for used, all these everyday expressions of the backwoods were contemporary with the *Canterbury Tales*. **1952** Wilson *Folk Speech NC* 603 *usen* = past participle of *use*, be accustomed to. "Pass me the beans; I want something to eat I'm *usen* to." **1994–97** Montgomery *Coll*: *usen* (known to Brown, Cardwell.

[past participle of *use*; Web3 *usen* dialect variant of *used*; DARE *usen* v chiefly South, South Midland]

usens See **us'uns.**

useter war See **used to B3.**

use to didn't See **used to B2.**

ust to wasn't See **used to B3.**

usually always *adverb phrase* Customarily, regularly. See citations.

1973 *Holidays* 327 We usually always had a big fat hen f'Easter. **1975** *Another Look* 139 Usually always you take and leave one of the jugs or whatever you carry it out in. **1975** Dwyer *Thangs* 17 Words used in the mountains to name something that can be adequately named by one—probably used for emphasis and to be "sure an' certain of clarity" . . . usually always.

us'uns (also *usens*) *pronoun* Us; we. See also **one 1**, **they'uns**, **we'uns**, **you'uns.**

1940 Bowman *KY Mt Stories* 249 = us. **1976** Miller *Mts within Me* 84 Double-barrelled pronouns—perhaps the most universally recognized mountain usage is the adding of suffixes of "uns" and "all" to pronouns; hence, we-uns, us-uns, you-uns, we-all, you-all, them-all. **1977** Shackelford et al. *Our Appalachia* 326 Instead of saying "yellow" you'd say "yeller," "usens" instead of "we." **1996–97** Montgomery *Coll* (known to Adams, Brewer, Bush, Cardwell, Jones, Oliver).

[cf SND *us yins* (at *yin* pron/adj 3); cf HT *iz yins* (at *yin*)]

V

vagrous See **vigorous.**

valley fill *noun* See citation.

2006 Mooney *Lg Coal Mining* 1028 In "mountaintop removal mining," the tops of mountains are removed to expose the coal seams below, and the overburden is pushed into an adjacent hollow, creating a "valley fill."

vallyble *adjective* Valuable.

1927 Mason *Lure of Smokies* 228 I mought bring down game a heap sight more vallyble, mebbe!

vapors *noun* See citations.

1990 Cavender *Folk Medical Lex* 31 = fainting spells; mental depression. **1994** *Montgomery Coll* = fainting spells, mental depression, sometimes epilepsy (Ogle).

varment See **vermin.**

varminous See **verminous.**

varmint dog *noun* Same as **feist A.**

1992 *Montgomery Coll* (known to Shields).

varmit, varmont See **vermin.**

vasty *adjective* See citation.

1957 Combs *Lg Sthn High: Word List* 107 = vast. [Cf.] "I can call spirits from the vasty deep."—I Henry IV, III, i, 52.

vaunty *adjective* Boastful, vain.

1997 *Montgomery Coll* (known to Cardwell, Weaver).

[OED3 *vaunty* adj dialect except in Scot; CUD *vauntie* adj "boastful," *vantie* "vain; proud"; Web3 *vaunty* adj Scottish]

veil *noun* A caul. The person born with one purportedly has the capacity to see ghosts and to exercise other powers.

1959 *Hall Coll* (Newport TN) Mother was born with a veil over her face, and she could tell you when somethin' was a-goin' to happen. When Mother said somethin' was a-goin' to happen, you'd better not go.

velvet-plant *noun* The common mullein, a tall biennial wild plant (*Verbascum thapsus*) from which a medicinal tea is made. Same as **feltwort.**

[**1971** Krochmal et al. *Medicinal Plants Appal* 264 A tea made from the leaves is used in Appalachia for colds.] **1982** Stupka *Wildflowers* 102 Of its many local names, ones like "flannel-leaf," "velvet plant," and "feltwort" refer to its exceptionally dense wooliness.

veneral *adjective* Venereal.

1944 Hayes *Word-List NC* 37.

venomous worm *noun* Same as **worm 1.**

1906 Haney *Mt People KY* 67 The voice of the people is always heard against him, and the near future will see the last "copper kettle" destroyed, the last "venomous worm" dead and the last moonshiner . . . surrender to authority.

ventur *noun, verb* A venture; to venture.

1924 Raine *Saddlebags* 99 The dialect writers pounce with derisive hilarity upon such awkward, slovenly slips as *ventur, natur.*

vermin *noun*

A Variant forms *varment* [see **1834** in **B1**], *varmint, varmit* [see **1979** in **B1**], *varmont.*

1824 Knight *Letter from KY* 106–7 Some words are used, even by genteel people, from their imperfect education, in a new sense; and others, by the lower classes in society, pronounced very uncouthly . . . varmont for vermin. **1942** Hall *Phonetics Smoky Mts* 92 Many speakers pronounce the following words with excrescent final t . . . *vermin* ['varmənt].

[originally *vermin* + excrescent t]

B Senses.

1 Any bothersome, mean, troublesome wild creature, especially one that preys on chickens or other farm animals.

1834 Crockett *Narrative* 154 There was no stock, however, or anything else to disturb our corn, except for wild varments. **1883** Zeigler and Grosscup *Heart of Alleghanies* 48 His yard had been entered the last past night by some "varmint," and a fine hundred-pound hog (otherwise known as a mountain shad) killed and eaten within the pig-pen. **1895** Edson and Fairchild *TN Mts* 375 "He lay out among the *varmints*"—of one hiding from recruiting officers during the war. **1913** Kephart *Our Sthn High* 81 My dogs can foller ary trail, same's a hound; but they'll run right in on the varmint (bear), snappin' and chawin' and worryin' him till he gits so mad you can hear his tushes pop half a mile. **1924** Raine *Saddlebags* 212 Every family has chickens, but the hawks and the "varmints" (minks, weasels, skunks, and rats) get a large share of them. **1939** *Hall Coll* (Smokemont NC) He said he tasted of everything he had ever killed, every varment, even a buzzard. **1953** *Hall Coll* (Plott Creek NC) There was varmints. There was bear, panther, wolves, bob-cats, and all kinds of animals that was detrimental to both stock and poultry. And the dogs kind of cleaned out the varmints. At night, the stock had to be brought in and kept in lots, heavy fences that kept the varmints out. **1967** Wilson *Folkways Mammoth Cave* 23 = animals that prey upon a farmer's poultry. **1979** Slone *My Heart* 13 I don't believe God would have wasted his time to create any plants or varmit or anything at all if it did not have some use or purpose. **1991** Thomas *Sthn Appal* 87 Back when I'z a boy, if ye lived out in th' country, ye kepp two ur three dogs. Ye had to, to hunt th' varmits an' keep um' scared off. **2005** Williams *Gratitude* 534 = an animal that ain't no use to nobody for nuthin', and goes around destroying or ruining things; the lowest form of critter. "A possum or a muskrat is a *varment* that kills your chickens." **2011** *Blind Pig* (Nov 13) I am in the process of teaching 3 young grandsons that our people eat what we shoot other than varmints.

2 A low-class, contemptible, or untrustworthy person, one who lives in disrepute.

1937 Hall *Coll* (Cades Cove TN) [He] is a varmint, for he lived for a time with his sister [and had children by her]. **1975** Gainer *Speech Mtneer* 18 = an unwanted creature, sometimes a human being. "Some varmint stole three of my chickens."

[the stressed vowel in *varment/varmint* reflects the older pronunciation; Web3 1c *varmint* "esp. an animal or bird considered as a pest or nuisance"]

verminous *adjective*

A Variant form *varminous* [see **1883** in **B**].

B Wild, malicious, having the character of a **vermin**; foul with vermin.

1883 Zeigler and Grosscup *Heart of Alleghanies* 77 Traps is good fer 'em ez hunts rabbits, an' rabbit huntin' is good fer boys; but fer me gim me my ole flint-lock shootin'-iron, an' let a keen pack o' lean hounds be hoppin' on ahead; an' of all sports, the master sport is follerin' their music over the mountings, an' windin' up, with bullet or sticker, a varminous ole bar! **1997** Montgomery *Coll* (known to Bush, Cardwell), = also to have body lice on oneself (Weaver).

very *adverb* See citation. See also **very well**.

1931 Combs *Lg Sthn High* 1309 In highland speech "very" has lost its superlative significance, and means "ordinarily" in the expression "very well."

very well *adverb phrase* Very much, the most. See also **mighty well**, **very**.

1862 *Patton CW Letters* (May 1) I am coming home if I live next fall and see my friends I would like to see you all very well. **1862** *Watters-Curtis CW Letters* (Jan 17) [I] woud like to Come home very well and iam agoen to come Jest as soon as ican get off.

vest *noun* Variant plural form *vest-es*.

1939 Hall *Coll*.

V-harrow *noun* See citations.

c1960 Wilson *Coll* = a home-made harrow shaped like the capital A. Sometimes it is called a V-harrow, looked at from the other direction. **1986** Pederson et al. *LAGS* (Bradley Co TN) = has 28 teeth.

vigorous

A Variant forms *vagrous* [see **1961** in **C**], *vigrus* [see **1915** in **B**], *vygerus* [see **1937** in **B**], *vygorous* [see **1917** in **B**], *vygrous* [see **1939** in **B**].

1942 Hall *Phonetics Smoky Mts* 17. **1974** Fink *Bits Mt Speech* 28 = vigorous. "He's plumb *vigrus* these days."

B *adjective* Vicious, fierce, angry.

1915 Dingus *Word-List VA* 192 *vigrus* = angry, vicious—of animals or humans: "That dog looked vigrus at me and I got afraid." **1917** Kephart *Word-List* 419 *vygorous* = vigorously. "The pig squealed *vygorous*." **1928** (in **1952** Mathes *Tall Tales* 79) He's allus makin' out like he's a turrible vygrous feller, but he ain't. Why, he's jes' as saft-hearted as a gal! **1934–47** *LAMSAS Appal* (Swain Co NC) = in fighting condition. **1937** Hyatt *Kiverlid* 89 Yer Gran'pap had the bear dawgs an' had fed 'em on hog hastlets an' gun powder to make 'em plumb fierce an' vygerus. **1939** Hall *Coll* (White Oak NC) Watch that dog. He's vygrous. **1952** Wilson *Folk Speech NC* 604 = angry, out of sorts. **1962** Hall *Coll* (Cataloochee NC) The panther was so vygrous and mad, hit took each piece and tore it up. She tore all her clothes off and finally made it home start naked.

[DARE (at *vigrous* adj) South, South Midland]

C (also *vigrously*) *adverb* Viciously, fiercely, vigorously.

1937 Hall *Coll* (Mt Sterling NC) Hit was intentioned to bite me. I never heared a snake sing so vygrous. **1952** Wilson *Folk Speech NC* 604 *vigrously* = angrily, testily. **1961** Williams *Rhythm and Melody* 9 Hit's been so wet a body couldn't afford to rurn his ground a-workin' it, and the weeds a-gittin' vagrouser an' vagrouser ever' day.

vigrous, **vigrously**, **vigrus** See **vigorous**.

villain *noun* Variant forms *villion*, *vilyun*.

1936 Coleman *Dial N GA* 27 "Villion" [is used] for "villain." **1997** Montgomery *Coll*: *vilyun* (known to Bush, Cardwell, Ellis, Jones, Oliver, Weaver).

[DARE *villain* n chiefly South, South Midland]

villion, **vilyun** See **villain**.

vine up *verb phrase* To regain life.

2007 Farr *My Appalachia* 40 I heard Aunt Bertha say, "Children, keep praying; she might 'vine' up again." How could a poor, sick woman "vine" up, I wondered. Years later I realized that she had meant that Aunt Martha Jane might revive.

viper snake *noun* A hognose snake.

1975 Dwyer *Thangs* 17 Words used in the mountains to name something that can be adequately named by one—probably used for emphasis and to be "sure an' certain of clarity" . . . viper-snake.

visit *verb* To spend time with someone as a social ritual, with no definite objective in mind.

1929 Kephart *Smoky Mt Magic* 87 Kit "visited" for some time, after the mountain manner, talking about anything except what was on his mind. Then gradually he led up to it and talked about Matlock's quest.

vitles, vittels, vittils See **vittles**.

vittles

A (also *vitles*, *vittels*, *vittils*) *noun* Food (sometimes including drink), provisions.

1863 *Huntley CW Letters* (Aug 6) Father is A fixing to start in the morning and Mother is A fixing vitles to send to him. **1864** *Apperson CW Letters* (Jan 6) I ante had no warme vittels sents I have bin her to eate. **1867** Harris *Sut Lovingood* 93 Now, the smashin ove delf, an' the mixin ove vittils begun. **1923** Greer-Petrie *Angeline Doin' Society* 5 If the comp-ny has cleaned up the platter, or she's a-savin' her vittles back for tomorrow, I can make out fine with a glass of butter milk. **1934–47** *LAMSAS Appal* (Madison Co NC, Swain Co NC). **1960** *Hall Coll* (Cataloochee NC) Now you take up the vittles and I'll wash the dishes. **1974** Fink *Bits Mt Speech* 12 She het up the vittles. **1997** *Montgomery Coll* I come along for the vittles (Brown). **2009** Benfield *Mt Born* 73 "Vittles" is the correct pronunciation of the word "victuals." It is an ancient word meaning food or provisions.

B (as *vittle*) *verb* To eat a meal.

1994 *Montgomery Coll* Have you already vittled? (Cardwell).

[*vittle* represents the historic form and its more prevalent pronunciation since the 16th century, with *victual* being a later development; cf Web3 *victuals* n alteration of ME *vitaile*, influenced by Late Latin *victuallis*]

volunteer

A *noun*

1 Often used attributively: an unsown plant or crop of vegetables or grain that comes up from old seeds either late in the season, after harvest, or before planting in the spring; hence adverb *volunteer* = spontaneously.

1915 Dingus *Word-List VA* 192 = a plant growing without being purposely sown: "The volunteer oats was good." **1957** Broaddus *Vocab Estill Co KY* 83 *volunteer crop* = plants that come up the following year from seed dropped, or plants left standing at harvest time; *volunteer onion* = onion that keeps coming up every year. **1957** Combs *Lg Sthn High: Word List* 107 = a vegetable or plant that has come up in a garden or field without having been planted or sown; that is, from seed or root that has lain there from the previous season. **1963** Miller *Pigeon's Roost* (July 25) The writer has mole beans growing in the garden again this year. But I don't have to plant them anymore. They just come up volunteer. **1966–68** *DARE Survey* (Burnsville NC, Spruce Pine NC, Gatlinburg TN) = a crop that springs up and grows by itself from old seed. **1973** *Foxfire Interviews* A-73-43 The last one [= gourd plant] I had out there come up a volunteer. I didn't plant it. I didn't mean for it to come up, but one come up and I just let it grow up on my clothesline there. **1992** Brooks *Sthn Stuff* 170 = plants grown from seeds not planted or tended in the usual way, but transported and dropped by birds or the wind. **1992** Morgan *Potato Branch* 8 Then he walked to the little volunteer peach tree near the can house and cut off a limb covered with leaves. **1997** *Montgomery Coll* (known to Brown, Cardwell, Ellis, Ledford, Norris, Oliver, Weaver). **2014** Hicks *Driving* 26 The odd volunteer vegetable flourishes amid the ragweed.

[DARE *volunteer* 1a widespread except Northeast]

2 An illegitimate child.

1986 Pederson et al. *LAGS* (Sullivan Co TN).

B *verb* Of a crop: to grow spontaneously after the first crop has been harvested.

1915 Dingus *Word-List VA* 192 = to grow as a "volunteer": "So much wheat volunteered that I let it stand." **2012** *Blind Pig* (Jan 11) We've got things blooming that should have been killed by a cold snap and/or shouldn't be up til late spring. For heaven's sakes, there's a second crop of lettuce volunteering in the garden.

vomic, vomick See **vomit**.

vomit *verb*

A Variant form *vomic, vomick, vommick*.

1904–20 Kephart *Notebooks* 2:475 It made me vomic. **1927** Woofter *Dialect from WV* 366 Run your finger down your throat and it will vommick you. **1934–47** *LAMSAS Appal* (Madison Co NC, Swain Co NC). **1961** Seeman *Arms of Mt* 94 When he clim' out, all red and swellin', he vomicked and vomicked. **1966** Dakin *Vocab Ohio River Valley* 483 The variant *vomick* is scattered throughout Kentucky in the speech of the less educated simple folk of the oldest generation but is not common. **1968** *DARE Survey* (Brasstown NC). **1974** Fink *Bits Mt Speech* 28. **1989** *Matewan OHP-28* [The smoke] would give you the headache, or they called a sick headache. You'd vomick and everything.

[DARE *vomit* n, v (pronc) chiefly South, South Midland]

B Past-tense form *vomit*.

2009 Burton *Beech Mt Man* 93 I vomit for two hours over it.

vommick See **vomit**.

vordegrease *noun*

A Variant form *bardy grease* [see **1968** in **B**].

[folk etymology for *verdigris*; DARE (at *bardy grease* n) southern Appalachians]

B In distilling, a poisonous substance (i.e. fusel oil produced by the action of acetic acid on copper that must be filtered out of the process). See also **fire chunk**.

1956 *Hall Coll* (Del Rio TN) Vordegrease comes from the copper still. It comes from the pot ordinarily, which is very poisonous. *Ibid.* (Waynesville NC) You had a rag and put fire coals in there and strain it through them fire coals, take the vordegrease off. **1968** *Best Was Made* 105 A funnel should be inserted in the container which is lined with a clean, fine white cloth on the bottom, a yarn cloth on top of that, and a double handful of washed hickory coals on top of that. The coals remove the "bardy grease" (it shows up as an oil slick on top of the whiskey if not drained off) which can make one very ill. **1976** Carter *Little Tree* 68 Where it come out, we had hickory coals to strain off the bardy grease which would make you sick if you drank it.

vow and declare *verb phrase* To attest, swear.

1944 Justus *Billy and Bones* 47 "I vow and declare," she cried, "you're a handy person to have around." **1959** Justus *Bring Banjo* 32 "I vow and declare," he muttered, "seems like I just can't think how [the song] goes on from there."

vygorous, vygrous See **vigorous**.

wag *verb* To lug, haul, carry with difficulty.

1931 Owens *Speech Cumberlands* 99 Vicey's too puney to wag that big young'un aroun'. **1941** Stuart *Men of Mts* 255 I just wagged the baby right in the church house. **1952** Wilson *Folk Speech NC* 604 = to carry: "I got tired of wagging that big young un on my hip." **1969** Doran *Folklore White Co* 115 = to carry. **1972** *AOHP/LJC*-259 I don't see how they wagged it [= a peddler's sack]. **1986** Pederson et al. *LAGS*: *wag it* = (Holston Valley TN) = of a heavy suitcase up a hill.

[Web3 *wag*[1] vt 1b dialect; DARE *wag* v South, South Midland]

wagon mine *noun* Same as **doghole**.

1943 Korson *Coal Dust* 4 Some farmers . . . operated small mines variously called "country banks," "wagon mines," "dog holes," "gopher holes," or "father-and-son" mines. **1973** Kahn *Hillbilly Women* 96 We lived in Tennessee for a while and Dad worked in a wagon mine, where they use mules to haul the coal out.

wahoo *noun*

1 A burning bush shrub (*Euonymus atropurpureus*). Also called **Indian bitter**. See also **hearts bustin', spindle bush, strawberry bush**.

1937 Thornburgh *Great Smoky Mts* 25 The seeds of some shrubs are more spectacular than their flowers. This is true of one of the showiest shrubs in the Great Smokies, the euonymous, wahoo or spindlebush. It is especially lovely in October when its seed-pod bursts open, displaying orange-colored seeds in its glowing red heart. It has many descriptive local names—swamp willow, strawberry bush, catspaw, jewel-box, but most descriptive of all is the name given by a mountain man of, "Heart's-bustin'-with-love." This shrub has been adopted by the Smoky Mountains Hiking Club, whose greeting is, "Wahoo, wahoo!" and whose signature [is], "Heart's-bustin-with-love." **1970** Campbell et al. *Smoky Mt Wildflowers* 102 Common names include strawberry bush, swamp dogwood, spindle bush, arrowwood, wahoo, and a dozen others.

2 A large deciduous tree (*Magnolia* spp). See also **cucumber tree, Indian bitter 2, mountain magnolia, umbrella tree, yellow linn.**

1883 Zeigler and Grosscup *Heart of Alleghanies* 49 A tree called the wahoo, grows here as well as on many of the ranges. It bears a white lily-shaped flower in the summer. **1974–75** McCracken *Logging* 10:24 They were one that was in here that we called him a wahoo. . . . He was a big tree, and he had a small cucumber on him just about the size of your thumb. **1981** High *Coll* (*DARE*) = commonly used in the Gorge as a name for the cucumber magnolia (Magnolia acuminata) instead of as a term for the winged elm (Ulmus alata), though both trees grow in the area.

[DARE *wahoo* n[1] c NC, TN, KY, VA]

waist baby *noun* See citation.

1952 Wilson *Folk Speech NC* 604 = a baby tall enough to reach one's waist.

waiter *noun* A wedding attendant, especially the best man or maid of honor.

1937 Hyatt *Kiverlid* 104 She was one o' my waiters when I married Jeems. **1939** Hall *Coll* (Emerts Cove TN) = the gentleman that would sit by the side of the one that was a-going to be married. They would be a lady sit by the side of the woman that was a-going to be married. That was called the waiters. **1942** Thomas *Blue Ridge* 151 How happy the young couple were as they stood before the elder, the groom with his waiter at his side, and the bride with her waiter beside her. **1949** Kurath *Word Geog East US* 40 Other expressions that are used throughout the South and the South Midland are *pallet*, *waiter*, *branch*, and the well-known *you-all* . . . *Waiter* . . . is the common folk term for the best man and the bridesmaid in Virginia and the Carolinas . . . it is not common in West Virginia, but scattered instances of it occur even as far north as the Monongahela. **1952** Wilson *Folk Speech NC* 604 = a man or woman attendant for the groom or bride at a wedding. **1966** Dakin *Vocab Ohio River Valley* 499 The bridegroom's principal attendant is usually called the *best man* everywhere in the Ohio Valley . . . older speakers in eastern and southwestern Kentucky still say *waiter*. As among simple folk south of the Potomac in the East, this term is usually used for both male or [sic] female attendants (best man and bridesmaid or maid of honor). **1996** Montgomery *Coll* = only an attendant (Brown), = best man (Cardwell).

[OED3 *waiter* n 6b obsolete except U.S. dialect or historical; Web3 *waiter* n 2b "attendant of the bride or groom at a wedding," South; DARE *waiter* n chiefly South, South Midland]

wait on *verb phrase*

1 To court (a woman).

1974 Fink *Bits Mt Speech* 29 = court, woo. "John's *waitin' on* that new gal." **1996–97** Montgomery *Coll* (known to Adams, Brown, Bush, Cardwell, Hooper).

[DARE *wait on* v phr 1 chiefly Northeast, South]

2 To await the approach or arrival of.

1862 *Shipman CW Letters* (June 19) I have bin wating on you for an answer. **1901** Harben *Westerfelt* 33 The preacher promised me this mornin' he'd wait on me an' my folks. **1939** Hall *Coll* (Deep Creek NC) I was supposed to wait on this fellow at the forks of the creek where we heard the dogs a-barking when I left him. **1940** Oakley *Roamin'/Restin'* 148 Time dont wait on no one. **1969** *GSMNP*-27:8 They would follow us all day long, and we would have to stop and wait on them. **1978** Montgomery *White Pine Coll* IV-4 I just didn't have time to wait on the sign. . . . If you're waiting on the moon, and you're needing to plant corn, it would probably be wet when the moon was right. **1989** Smith *Flyin' Bullets* 30 They made it up with a woman to have her a'standin' there, a'waitin' on him to come by. **1998** *Dante OHP*-25 I'll be at the door a-waiting on you.

[EDD (at *on* prep II.10) "wait for"; SND (at *wait* v 1 (3)); DARE (at *on* prep 3a) widespread, but more frequent South, Midland]

3 To minister to, care for (one who is sick or incapacitated); hence verbal noun *waiting on*.

1862 *Hancock CW Letters* (July 24) he has been in Richmond several days waiting on his son henry poor ben and henry they will kneed no more waiting on. . . . Henry died in a few days afterwards. **1862** *Love CW Letters* (Aug 13) he is purty bad of with relaps of mesels woody went to wate on him. **1901** Harben *Westerfelt* 193 I thought may be I could persuade you now to come back to your room at the hotel, where mother and I could wait on you. **1953** Shelton *Autobiog II* 4 Then the family, taking its turn about among the older ones, went to sit up and help wait on Mother until it came the turn of one of my older half-brothers. **1971** *AOHP/ALC-33* They would go to one and another's houses and help them to hoe their corns out or either come at sickness in the family, and then they would help out and do all the work and their washing and cooking and waiting on sick people. **1973** *Flu Epidemic* 105 Doc Neville was a'waitin' on us an' a'carin' for us. **1989** *Matewan OHP-102* Everyone in our family had it [= the flu] . . . [but] usually they'd be one that would get better enough till they can wait on the other group of the family. **1991** Thomas *Sthn Appal* 214 I always laid in th' bed nine ur ten days. Have somebody to wait on me. **1998** *Dante OHP-25* We had Janice in a wheelchair, had to wait on her.

wait on the table *verb phrase* To say the blessing at the beginning of a meal.

1911 Shearin *E KY Word-List* 540 = to say grace. **1913** Combs *KY Highlander* 18 Don't be surprised, if at the breakfast table [the mountaineer] asks you to wait on the table; for he is very reverent if he thinks you have a mind to return thanks. **1921** Weeks *Speech of KY Mtneer* 13 If you are a pious looking youth, you may be asked to wait on the table. **1939** Hall *Coll.* **1998** Montgomery *Coll* (known to Bush).

[DARE *wait on the table* v phr southern Appalachians]

wake

A *verb* Principal parts.

1 Variant past-tense forms *waked, woked.*

1979 *Big South Fork OHP-4* One night at midnight I waked up, and I could hear glass a-breaking. **1983** *Dark Corner OHP-11A* One night we waked up and this cow was yelling in the barn. **1997** Montgomery *Coll*: *woked* (known to Brown, Norris, Oliver, Weaver); I woked up when the rooster started crowing (Cardwell).

[DARE *waked* (at *wake* v 1b) formerly widespread; now scattered, but chiefly South, South Midland, Texas; *woked* (at *wake* v 1c) especially South, South Midland]

2 Variant past-participle forms *woke, woked.*

1961 *Coe Ridge OHP-336B* If they had woke up, he'd have killed them. **1973** *GSMNP-90:26* I've woked up a many a time and seen [the revenue men] laying all over the floor. **1997** Montgomery *Coll* (known to Brown, Norris, Oliver, Weaver).

B *noun* An all-night vigil held at the home of a deceased person before the burial. The occasion is often a time of socializing and family reunion. According to consultants from the Smoky Mountains, the traditional mountain term for this event is **setting up**; most consultants from the Smoky Mountains say that *wake* is used by outsiders or is a book term rarely if ever used by mountain people.

1940 Mathes *Jeff Howell* 20 The keening of the women at the "wake" that night was made more harrowing by the foreboding of mothers, sisters, and wives over what was likely to happen at the burying on the morrow. **1970** Mull *Mt Yarns* 115 When a good Baptist died in the hill country, they just didn't bury him right off but had a "wake" before the funeral. **1976** *Sevier Co Saga* 17 The custom of holding "wakes" when someone died gave the people a chance to meet in the home of the deceased and sit up all night with the corpse. Proper respect was not paid the departed one if someone did not sit up all night. The mourners talked in whispers and tiptoed from room to room, always seeing that there was plenty of coffee brewing on the stove to be sipped while eating the cakes and pies of various kinds sent in by kind neighbors. **1995** Adams *Come Go Home* 34 I wish the old-fashioned wake still took place here in the mountains. Used to be when a person died, the family took them to the funeral home located in the county seat. After the departed loved one was fixed up, he or she was hauled back home and set up there to await burial. During this waiting period friends and family would come to sit up with the body. Lots of times a wake took on the air of a family reunion. Of course, there was grief and mourning, but it was an open, cleansing kind of mourning, and what better place than with loving friends and relatives?

wake robin *noun* The erect trillium (*Trillium erectum*), whose roots have medicinal uses. Also called **beth root**, **brown Beth**, **rattlesnake root 3**, **stinking Willie**.

[**1901** Lounsberry *Sthn Wild Flowers* 62 The mountain people, especially those of the Cumberlands and Alleghanies, find, however, more efficacious results from the use of this species of trillium in the treatment of nervous diseases than from any other one.] **1971** Hutchins *Hidden Valley* 55–57 Here beside the road I discover another trillium, this one a wake-robin (*Trillium erectum*). Its three petals are deep-purple red and the plant has a most unpleasant smell, which is the reason it is often known as "stinking Willie." [**1971** Krochmal et al. *Medicinal Plants Appal* 256 The Indians of Appalachia cooked pieces of the root in food as an aphrodisiac.]

walded See **wall**.

walink See **wallink**.

walk *verb* Of a wild animal, especially a bear or panther: to go about its range or domain, prowl, stalk, stride.

1859 Taliaferro *Fisher's River* 76 I looked up in a post-oak-tree right dab over me, and there sot the biggest painter that uver walked the Blue Ridge. **1939** Hall *Coll* (Deep Creek NC) When we got into the cabin to the light, why he noticed the blood all over me, and John Edwards says to me, "Man, you've killed a bear." "Well," I said, "yes, I've killed the biggest bear that ever walked the Smokies, Johnny." *Ibid.* (Nine Mile TN) The bear fell down, rolled over once. He got up then and walked around the hill.

Walker (also *Walker hound*) *noun* See citations. See also **treeing Walker.**

1949 Hall Coll (Del Rio TN) A Walker or Walker hound is a fox hunter and is generally the fastest dog we can get in this country. A Walker keeps on walking even after the fox is tired out and goes right on. **1991** Haynes *Haywood Home* 54 Most men kept four or five dogs for fox hunting. Most of the fox dogs were Walker Hounds that could be used to hunt all game. **2009** Prewitt *Coon Hounds* 273 Nowadays, the black and tan, the redbone, the bluetick, the English, the treeing Walker, and the Plott are among the standard breeds that hunters say can potentially make good coon hounds.

[DARE *Walker hound* n chiefly South, South Midland]

Walker hound See **Walker.**

walkers *noun* Same as **tom walkers.**

2018 *Blind Pig* (Aug 14) Remember what happened when you encountered soft ground? You kept walking but your Walkers [= stilts] stubbed up and wouldn't move.

walking the farm *verbal noun* See citation.

2004 Rehder *Appal Folkways* 74 As generations of families occupied a land that had such uncertain boundaries, "walking the farm" became a tradition. At a selected time of the year, usually in the early winter when the leaves were off the trees, the father or grandfather—the patriarch of the clan—would take his family along the bounds of their land and point out landmarks and boundary points along the way. To the youngsters, it was a joyous walk in the woods, but to those in line to inherit, the walk was meant to imprint the critical landmarks that marked the family's property line, no matter how inconspicuous they might be.

walk the aisle (also *walk the benches*) *verb phrase* Of a person in a state of spiritual bliss at the close of a worship service: to step along a church pew, enthusiastically shaking hands with fellow worshippers. See also **run the benches.**

1984 Head *Brogans* 156 At the conclusion of the Saturday night singing, the pastor gave an "altar call" and invited people to join the church and usually someone "walked the aisle." If it was somebody well known, it brought on another round of shouting! **2005** Morgan *Old Time Religion* 113–14 Another custom of old time religion services, although it is rarely employed now, was "walking the benches." This custom faded out as larger churches were constructed and/or congregations dwindled. Visions of people recklessly running along the tops of the backrests of the pews are what are usually envisioned when one first hears this term. But, in keeping with these folks' unemotional, sincere beliefs about worship, it turned out to be another very beautiful expression of their love for their fellowmen and praise to the Lord. During the latter parts of services when the congregation was standing and people, usually older folks, were being spiritually blessed with their emotions overflowing with tears of joy, some of these elderly folk, usually men, and I don't really know why ladies did not often engage in this activity, perhaps it was considered unseemly, usually would begin at the front of the sanctuary and shake hands with everyone standing in front of the first pew on which they had been sitting. Then they would step up on the seat part of the first pew and walk the length of it, shaking hands with the people standing behind the first pew who had been sitting on the second pew. Next, they stepped upon the second pew seat and proceeded down the length of this pew shaking hands with those of the third pew. They continued thusly until they had walked all of the benches in the entire church and had shaken hands with everyone present.

wall *verb*

A Variant past-tense form *walded.*

1919 Combs *Word-List South* 36 *walded* = preterit of the verb *wall.* Other examples are *attacted, drownded,* etc.

B In phrase *wall/waul the eyes* = to roll one's eyes.

1883 Smith *Southernisms* 55 = to roll the eyes, that is, so as to show the white. **1952** Wilson *Folk Speech NC* 604 *wall, waul, the eyes* = to roll the eye towards one without any or much movement of the head, generally indicative of dislike or contempt. **2011** Woodall *Not My Mt* 26 Dad walled his eyes in disgust, counted his loss, and bought another cow.

[DARE *wall* v South, South Midland]

waller See **wallow.**

wallink (also *walink*) *noun* A creeping perennial vine (*Veronica americana*) with medicinal uses.

1960 Hall *Smoky Mt Folks* 51 (R. Caton) For croup and phthisic she often used a tea made of ground ivy, which she called "wallink." **1963** Arnow *Flowering* 67 Many of these teas—walink (walking leaf)[,] catnip, watermelon seed, rattleroot were some of the most common—are still used in the hills for babies.

[DARE *wallink* n 2 South Midland, especially KY]

wallow *noun, verb* Variant form *waller.* See also **bear wallow, hen wallow, hog wallow.**

1867 Harris *Sut Lovingood* 160 They hed hawl'd straw untill hit cum up ni ontu levil wi' the tops ove the bainches, tu git happy in, an' du thar huggin an' wallerin on. **2005** Williams *Gratitude* 148 Them chickens liked to git up inunder the porch and fluff up and waller in th' dust.

[DARE *wallow* n, v (pronc) scattered, but more frequent South, South Midland]

wall the eyes See **wall B.**

walnut *noun* Variant forms *warnet, warnit, warnut, wernet, wornet.*

1824 (in **1956** Eliason *Tarheel Talk* 320) (Caldwell Co NC) *warnet.* **1862** *Lockmiller CW Letters* (Oct 30) I want yewns to Save mee Some wornets. **1867** Harris *Sut Lovingood* 115 Yu's drunk, ur yure sham'd tu tell hit, an' so yu tries tu put us al asleep wif a mess ove durn'd nonsince, 'bout echo's an' grapes, an' warnit trees; oh, yu be durn'd. **1890** Fruit *KY Words* 69 *warnut.* **1911** Shearin *E KY Word-List* 540 *warnet.* **c1940** Simms Coll Walnuts are called "wernets" by the mountain people. **1942** Hall *Phonetics Smoky Mts* 32 ['wɔə-nət]. **1974** Roberts *Sang Branch* 24 Mother had about three colors she would generally prepare. She'd take warnut roots, skin the bark off, boil it, and make yaller color.

[DARE *walnut* n (pronc) chiefly South, South Midland]

wampus (also *wampus cat*) *noun*

A Variant forms *whompus* [see **1967** in **B**], *wompus* [see **1984–85** in **B**].

B An imaginary, large, fearsome, cat-like figure that is the subject of folk stories and is used to warn children to behave; also, a panther. See also **catawampus**[1], **saugus cat**. For legends, see 1984–85 citation.

1967 *DARE Survey* (Maryville TN) *whompus* = imaginary animal or monster that people tell tales about, especially to tease greenhorns: "Anything can be a whompus if ye don't know and are a-wonderin'"; "They's a whompus a-usin' around here." **1980** Brewer *Hit's Gettin'* Both [East Tennessee and the Ozarks] have had "wampus-cats," bloodthirsty critters that usually are more rumor than truth. **1984–85** *Sevier Settler* 3:24 The "Wompus Cat" is probably one of the most unusual legends to come out of Sevier County. The Wompus Cat was supposed to be a black shaggy-haired thing about the size of a dog with a long, pointed nose that glowed like a cigar. The Wompus Cat could stand on its hind legs and was also a nuisance to lone riders on deserted roads. It was said that the Wompus Cat would jump out of an overhanging tree onto the back of the horse pulling the weary traveler's buggy and scare the horse into a panic.... Not only was the Wompus Cat a nuisance, it is said to be indestructible. Every farmer or hunter who shot at it claimed its fur repelled the bullets as a duck's feather repels water. **1985** Edwards *Folksy Sketches* 71–72 The area appeared to serve as a harboring place for wampus cats. "It's a wonder you hadn't been attacked by one before the night was over," Jase said. He then told about Dr. Alec Mason's boy Harley, who experienced a frightening race with a wampus cat coming out of these woods.... Well, the wampus cat got after young Harley, and he was so frightened that he allowed nothing to get in his way. He didn't even look for a path or a road to follow home. He just split right through the briars, bushes, and other undergrowth or whatever stood in his way. When he came to the tall gate at his home he just cleared it and forgot how high it was supposed to be. **1995** Montgomery *Coll* (known to Cardwell). **2016** Simmons *Legends & Lore* 103 The description of the beast tells of it having the build of a mountain lion with short tan fur while walking upright on its two hind legs like a human. It is said to have two pointy cat-like ears with paws rather than feet, as well as a long tail. The Wampus Cat is said to have long, sharp fangs, which it flashes menacingly while hissing at anyone who comes in contact with it. Its eyes glow in the dark with a bright-yellow color. **2019** *Blind Pig* (Feb 22) I've heard wampus cat used as a common name for cougars.

[shortening or inversion of *catawampus*; DARE *wampus* n[1] 1 scattered, but especially South, South Midland]

wampy-jawed See **whopper-jawed**.

want[1] *verb* To desire, wish earnestly.

1 With ellipsis of following *that*, followed by a dependent clause containing the auxiliary verb *should*.

1862 Robinson *CW Letters* (June 1) I want you should Rite on all the paper you send. **1927** Woofter *Dialect from WV* 366 = wish that he should. "I want he should sell me his team." **1931** Goodrich *Mt Homespun* 49 They want you should use the hickory on some of them rough boys. *Ibid.* 54 Maw wants you should go with her tomorrow to her aunts' in Tennessy. **1953** Wharton *Dr Woman Cumberlands* 41 Mammy wants you should come he'p her. **1975** Chalmers *Better* 59 Pink's wife's been took bad, and Doc wants you should come and he'p him.

2 (+ *preposition or adverbial*) With ellipsis of the infinitive of a verb of motion (as in phrases *want away*, *want back*, *want home*, *want in*, *want off*, *want out*). See also **need 3**.

1914 Arthur *Western NC* 267 [We] claim that when we "want in," we generally manage to "get" in, whether we say "get" or not. **1915** Pollard *TN Mts* 243 = used without an infinitive following; as, "I *wanted* out. I was *wantin'* home. I'm just a *wantin'* in a higher grade." **1934–47** *LAMSAS Appal* (Madison Co NC, Swain Co NC) *want off*. **1939** Hall *Coll* (Wears Cove TN) All the people that left the mountains is a-wanting back. **1949** Kurath *Word Geog East US* 79 [I]n the common speech of the Midland, the shorter *I want off* is widely used. One hears it on the Susquehanna and from there westward to the Ohio Valley and southward all through the Appalachians. The preservation in the Midlands of this older English construction in which an adverb is joined directly to *want* may in part be due to German influence (cf *ich will hinaus*). **1951** Barnwell *Our Mt Speech* He does not use come or go for entering or leaving a house, but, "I want in, I want out." **1954** Arnow *Dollmaker* 39 Take her out, Mom. It's Sunday—she wants out. **1966** *DARE Survey* (Cherokee NC) *want in*, *want off*. **1986** Pederson et al. *LAGS* = attested by 28/60 interviewees (46.7%) from E TN; 28/112 of all LAGS interviewees (25%) attesting term were from E TN. **1991** Still *Wolfpen Notebooks* 97 They wanted on the payroll and some of them couldn't hardly read or write. **2004** Adams *Old True Love* 18 In a voice sharper than it needed to be, I called out, "Come on, Larkin!" And then I wanted away from that place. **2004** Fisher *Kettle Bottom* 18 [He] wanted in with them men with the pockets.

[SND *want* v 6; CUD (at *in* prep and at *want* v 5); cf HT *wish hame* (in, out, etc.) "wish to go home (in, out, etc.)"]

3 (+ *past participle*) With ellipsis of a following infinitive (as in phrase *want done*, etc.). See also **need 1**.

1863 Shipman *CW Letters* (July 25) Liet Henery wants to no what you want don with Alberts Horse. **1863** *Watters-Curtis CW Letters* (April 22) you must write what you want done to the grave or whether you are comeing after his corpse or not. **1939** Hall *Coll* (Cataloochee NC) We set it on the fire and put our meat in it or beans or anything we wanted boiled. **1943** Justus *Jerry Jake* 16 What do you think he might want fixed? **1959** Roberts *Up Cutshin* 101 If she wanted to scare us, or if we wanted scared, she would get into them ghost and witch tales. **1999** McNeil *Purchase Knob* Just tell me what you want done.

[DARE *want* v C3 chiefly Midland, especially wPA]

4 As a progressive verb. See also **know B**.

1931 Stuart *Yarb Doctor* 5 Sonny, here air a shore sign to live and die by if ye ain't wantin' no toothache. **1939** Hall *Coll* Was you wantin' to go to town? *Ibid.* What was you wantin' to say? (a polite request to repeat something not heard). **1952** Giles *40 Acres* 58 What would you be wantin' with two? **1974** Roberts *Sang Branch* 17 The weight of the whole ridge above you was wanting to come down. **1989** *Matewan OHP-56* I was wanting to know why that they wasn't getting no support. **2005** Joslin *Handcrafters* 44 I'm not sure if they're wanting to do it like this one, or get a vinyl copy made. **2011** *Blind Pig* (Sept 22) He said he was wantin somebody to take him to town to buy some cigarettes.

[CUD *want* v 2]

5 In construction *want that* = to desire that.

1920 Ridley *Sthn Mtneer* 42 Jake, I want that we shall sit down here on the roadside and have a little talk, if you have time. **1928** Justus *Betty Lou* 91 I want that ye should come back an' go to meetin' with us.

want², **wan't**, **wa'nt**, **wa'n't** See **be E1**.

want away, **want back**, **want home**, **want in**, **want off**, **want out** See **want**¹ **2**.

war¹ See **be F1**.

war² *noun* A violent feud between extended families persisting one or more generations.

1896 Fox *Vendetta* 168 The citizens air gittin' tired o' these wars. **1921** Campbell *Sthn Highlander* 113 While feuds have existed in many parts of the mountain country, the most extensive and widely known have taken place in Kentucky. The name commonly applied to the feud in Kentucky is "war," and the principle upon which it was carried on was the principle of warfare—to do as much harm to the enemy as possible while incurring the least risk oneself. . . . However much the brutality of such early encounters may be deplored, there was a certain code of honor observed. They were, however, affairs of man to man, and as a rule not family, clique, nor clan matters fought under the principle of warfare. **1922** Cobb *KY Mt Rhymes* 43 Make one family of the King and Howard bands? . . . "Kings and Howards hev quit their War." **1933** Thomas *Traipsin' Woman* 13–14 The frightened creature told Mother, when they brought her in, how, after seeing her own blood-kin handcuffed and shot before her very eyes, she had walked across the mountain to get away from the "war,"—the "feud," as outlanders would say. **1941** Stuart *Men of Mts* 94 I've had enough of that damn war over a line fence. **1957** Combs *Lg Sthn High: Word List* 108 = feud, vendetta. Some of the principal "wars" in the Kentucky Highlands have been: the French-Eversole War; the McCoy-Hatfield War; the Rowan County War; the Baker-Howard War; the Hargis-Callahan War; the Jones-Hays War. **1973** *AOHP/LJC-350* That was right along among this other feud, and this French and Eversole War. They had a pure war, the French and Eversole. **1985** Irwin *Alex Stewart* 261 They was a war over here at Mulberry Gap that went on for years between the Collins and Brewers. Somebody would get bushwacked over there every little bit. **1989** *Matewan OHP-2* Most of them's dead now, all the Hatfields that was in that Hatfield-McCoy war. **1991** Still *Wolfpen Notebooks* 61 Several wars were going on during my young days. The killings have stopped now and there are many tales about how they got started in the first place. Yet if it was your grandpaw or an uncle or any of your folks who got killed back then it's hard to forget.

War between the Democrats and Republicans, **War between the North and South** See **War between the States.**

War between the States (also *War between the Democrats and Republicans, War between/of the North and the South*) *noun* The American Civil War. [Editor's note: For a century or more after the conflict, *War between the States* was a widely used designation for the conflict in much of the South, preferred on the grounds that Confederate states sought to withdraw from the union and not to engage in a war to vanquish and annex northern states; of the 95 speakers in Appalachian areas (E TN, N GA) surveyed by the Linguistic Atlas of the Gulf States, 30 (31.6%) attested *War between the States.*] Also called **Confederate War**, **Great War**, **Old War 2**, **Revolution War**, **Silver War**, **Sixty-Five War**, **War of the Revolution**.

c1960 Wilson *Coll*: *War between the States* is a very rare usage [in south-central KY]; the regular term is *Civil War*. After all, most of the men [in south-central KY] capable of bearing arms in the 1860's were in the Union Army. **1963** Edwards *Gravel* 93 That was the War Betwixt the States; some people called it the Civil War, you know. Maybe your school books does. **1966** Dakin *Vocab Ohio River Valley* 516 *The War between* (sometimes *of*) *the North and the South* is also occasional in eastern Kentucky. These terms are not heard only in Kentucky. **1986** Pederson et al. *LAGS*: *War between the Democrats and Republicans* (Meigs Co TN); *War between the North and the South* (Hawkins Co TN, Knox Co TN); *War between the States* = attested by 20/60 interviewees (33.3%) from E TN and 10/35 (28.6%) from N GA. **2007** McMillon *Notes*: *War between the Democrats and Republicans* = Civil War.

[DARE *War between the States* n chiefly South, South Midland]

wardrobe *noun* A storage closet, especially for clothes, built into the wall. [Editor's note: This term referring to a movable clothes closet is widespread in the US.]

1966 Dakin *Vocab Ohio River Valley* 45 In the southern Mountain counties [of KY] and the southern Knobs region, *wardrobe* is fairly common as the only word used or is used in addition to *closet*. **1986** Pederson et al. *LAGS* = attested by 17/60 interviewees (28.3%) from E TN; 17/22 of all LAGS interviewees (77%) attesting term were from E TN.

ware See **be F1**, **where**.

warm house *noun* A cellar.

1983 Broaddus *Estill Co KY Word List* 60 = a root cellar. **1991** Still *Wolfpen Notebooks* 163 = cellar.

warn (also *warn in, warn out*) *verb, verb phrase* To notify or summon (a man) to perform legally required maintenance work on local roads. See citations.

1912 Perrow *Songs and Rhymes* 142 If you should pass a group of men who, having been "warned" to work the road, were "putting in their time" on the highway, you would hear them continually breaking into song as they swung the pick, handled the shovel, or drove the steel drill into some projecting rock. **1977** Blackmun *Western NC* 177 The highway was marked off into sections with one man assigned to oversee the construction and upkeep of each section. His crew consisted of "warned in" citizens, ordered by the county court to work a certain number of days. **1984** Dykeman and Stokely *At Home* 25 During the spring and fall, all able-bodied men were "warned out" for six days—eight if there had been washout rains—to keep up what had become the well-used Cataloochee Turnpike. **1988** Brown *Beech Creek* 57–58 Before Work Projects Administration road work began every man was expected to contribute a number of days each year to "working the roads." A "foreman" on the creek was appointed by the county judge, and he "warned the hands" of certain days they were to appear for work. If they failed to come, they could be fined.

warnet See **walnut.**

warn in See **warn.**

warnit See **walnut.**

warn out See **warn.**

warnut See **walnut.**

War of the North and South See **War between the States.**

War of the Revolution *noun phrase* The American Civil War. Same as **War between the States.**

1966 Dakin *Vocab Ohio River Valley* 516–17 Some older speakers in the Mountains [of KY]—and a few scattered elsewhere—also seem to say *The War of the Revolution* or (more common) *The Revolution War.*

[DARE (at *Revolution* n South, South Midland]

warp *verb*

1 (also *wharp*) To strike, beat, thrash. See also **swarp B1, wharping stick.**

1845 (in **1974** Harris *High Times* 51) We had it head-and-tails fur a very long time, all over the house, but the truth must come and shame my kin, he warped me nice. **1959** Roberts *Up Cutshin* 123 The old giant come back with a big frail, and the first lick he warped the sack. **1990** Clouse *Wilder* 20 Soon as she'd get 'em [= children] real close she'd haul off and warp 'em a good one with her cane. **1997** Montgomery *Coll* (known to Adams, Bush, Ellis, Jones, Ledford, Oliver, Weaver); I warped him over the head (Cardwell). **2005** Williams *Gratitude* 535 He wharped his hat against his pants leg. **2012** Still *Hills Remember* 365 If I hadn't sworn not to, I'd warp you one.

2 To stagger. See also **swarp B3.**

1939 Hall *Coll* He came a-warpin' along.

[perhaps alteration of *whop*]

warpen *participial adjective* See citation.

1927 Woofter *Dialect from WV* 366 = warped. "Those boards are warpen."

warrant *verb*

1 To indict, have a warrant issued against (someone); to arrest (someone).

1911 Shearin *E KY Word-List* 540 = to indict; e.g., "The grand jury warranted him for stealing." **1960** Westover *Highland Lg* 21 *warranted* = arrested. **1992** Jones and Miller *Sthn Mt Speech* 117 = to be arrested on a warrant. "I've raised five sons, and none of them were ever warranted." **1996–97** Montgomery *Coll* (known to Brown, Bush, Cardwell, Hooper, Jones).

[DARE *warrant* v chiefly South, South Midland]

2 To guarantee.

1931 Stuart *Yarb Doctor* 5 I'll warrant ye ain't bothered with that thar tooth no more. **2001** Montgomery *Coll* I'll warrant I'll be there by nine o'clock (Cardwell).

warsh See **wash.**

warsp, warspers See **wasp 2.**

wart conjurer (also *wart doctor, wart witch*) *noun* A folk healer purportedly skilled in casting spells or otherwise being able to remove warts. See also **charm doctor, conjure doctor, faith doctor, fever doctor, Indian doctor, power doctor, witch doctor.**

1964 Cooper *History Avery Co* 30 Warts were removed by wart conjurors; cancers were thought to be cured by the incantations of seventh sons of seventh sons. A good many wart conjurors are still doing business in Avery County. **1965** Cooper *Witches Roamed* Strangely, those who practiced sorcery and magic, such as wart-conjurers; seventh sons of seventh sons, who attempted to cure skin cancer; and those who cured the thrush of babies by virtue of having been born after the death of their fathers, were never accused of being witches, but were considered to be helpful members of society. **1967** Wilson *Folkways Mammoth Cave* 43 The *wart-doctor* is just born with this power [of healing]. **2003** Cavender *Folk Medicine* 106 Should these or many of the other wart remedies fail, one sought a "wart doctor" who had the ability to conjure warts off by rubbing them with a hand and murmuring "You grow and you go" or some other secret charm. **2006** Thompson and Moser *Folklife* 145 Wart removal is another problem that has many folk cures, including being in the presence of a "wart witch."

wart doctor, wart witch See **wart conjurer.**

was See **be E.**

was a week See **week 2.**

wash

A *verb, noun* Variant form *warsh.*

1922 *TN CW Ques* 8 my mother [did] all kinds of hous work such as cooking warshing weaving making quilts cuting and making clothes for the family. **1933** Carpenter *Sthn Mt Dialect* 25 In parts of the mountains in certain words "r" is added where it does not belong. Among these are WASH, HUSH, and MUSH, which become warsh, hursh, and mursh. These are particularly noticeable in southern West Virginia and eastern Kentucky. **1942** Hall *Phonetics Smoky Mts* 32. **1963** Edwards *Gravel* 97 She warshed her face and hands and started to cook breakfast, but she felt plumb quare. **1972** *AOHP/ALC-276* That's how we made soap and how we warshed back in my days. **1973** Miller *English Unicoi Co* 76 *warsh* attested by 5 of 6 speakers. **1989** *Matewan OHP-102* They called it a warsh place because there was plenty of water there, and the whole neighborhood come to this place and warshed [their clothes]. **2008** McCaulley *Cove Childhood* 28 After the new house was built up on the hillside, Maw continued to do the "warsh" down in the flatter area near the old house.

[DARE *wash* n, v (pronc) widespread but especially frequent Midland]

B *verb* in phrase *go in washing* = to go swimming.

1892 Fruit *KY Words* 233 *to go in washin'* = to go in bathing. **1991** Still *Wolfpen Notebooks* 13 I seemed not to be doing anything that summer except picking blackberries and going in "washing," as we called it, swimming.

[DARE *wash* v B South, South Midland]

C *noun* See 1963 citation. See also **washout.**

1963 Lord *Blue Ridge* 6D Wash Creek, like many headwater streams draining Pisgah Ledge, swells into a freshet or "wash" during heavy rains. **1996–97** Montgomery *Coll* (known to Adams, Brown, Cardwell, Norris).

washing hole *noun* See citation.

1945 Wilson *Passing Institutions* 142 Other parts of the world may call a hole in the creek a "swimming hole," but our name for it was "washing hole." Swimming was not necessarily part of the Saturday-afternoon dip in the creek.

washing powder (also *wash powder*) *noun* Laundry detergent in powdered form (construed as a count noun; hence plural form *washing powders*). Same as **laundry powder.** For similar forms, see **powder 1.**

1930 Armstrong *This Day and Time* 90 I 'ull jest take a nickel's worth o' washin'-powders an' the balance that's comin' to me in snuff. **1954** Arnow *Dollmaker* 208 I did see him passen out some washen powders and soap. **1989** *Matewan OHP-102* Some [= World War II coupons] was for coffee and sugar and canned fruits and different kinds of food and wash powders. You had to have a coupon to buy that . . . I've shared wash powders with my mother. She couldn't hardly get wash powders. **2005** Williams *Gratitude* 34 Mom put a few washin' powders in th' tub.

wash off *verb phrase* Of a flood: to carry (a large object) away.

1982 Slone *How We Talked* 26 Something carried away by the flood waters; "He got warshed off," meant his house was carried away by the creek or river. **1990** *Matewan OHP-73* The seventy-seven flood washed all the houses off but one row up there.

washout *noun*

1 A flash flood after a rain. See also **wash C.**

c1960 Wilson *Coll* = a sudden flood. **1966** Dakin *Vocab Ohio River Valley* 21 *Washout* [is] common [in] Kentucky Mountains; . . . *water spout* [occurs in] extreme southern Kentucky, Mountains to Mississippi. **1966** *DARE Survey* (Spruce Pine NC) = a sudden rush of water coming from a rain that causes a landslide. **1971** Foster *Walker Valley* 4:18 It was pretty narrey at the time and then they had that washout back in twenty. **1982** Slone *How We Talked* 20 *wash out* = flood waters. When rain caused the creeks to rise and overflow their banks.

2 A gully or ravine resulting from erosion. See citations.

c1960 Wilson *Coll* = deep gully. **1967** *DARE Survey* (Maryville TN) = deep place cut in sloping ground by running water. **2002** Rash *Foot in Eden* 150 Sheriff Alexander's law car bumped down the washout.

3 See citation.

c1975 *Miners' Jargon* 8 = absence of coal in the rock sequence.

wash powder See **washing powder.**

washtub bass *noun* Same as **gut bucket.**

2005 Ebel *Orville Hicks* 115 When instruments were not available, folks on the mountain improvised. Orville shows his miniature version of the gut bucket, so named for the materials used to make it. "Folks couldn't afford a string bass," Orville says, "so they made these gut buckets, or washtub basses, as some people call them." Orville plucks the single string. In years past, the string would have been gut, or sinew.

wasp *noun*

1 Variant singular forms *wasper, wast, wausper, waust, wawst.*

1949 Watkins *Mtneers' Archaic English* 222 The mountaineer changes the p of *wasp* to a t. **1957** Broaddus *Vocab Estill Co KY* 84 *wasper* = a wasp. **1976** Still *Pattern of Man* 48 [He was] a master boy, smart as a wasper. **2002** Morgan *Mt Born* 163 *wausper, wast.* **2015** *Blind Pig* (May 5) I grew up with the word "wasper/s" and still hear it. It has a softer sound than wasp and requires less effort. *Ibid.* "Waust and waustes" is how we pronounced them. My buddy Beanie said "wausper." The *au* in either was pronounced like *awe. Ibid.* My grandpa called them all "wawsts."

[DARE *wasper* n chiefly South Midland]

2 Variant plural forms *warsp, warspers, wasp, wasper, waspers, waspes, wast, waustes, wawsts.*

1917 (in **1944** Wentworth *ADD* 694) (sWV) *waspes.* **1934–47** *LAMSAS Appal* (Madison Co NC) *waspers.* **1949** McDavid *Grist* 114 (Fannin Co GA) *warspers* = wasps. **1973** Miller *English Unicoi Co* 93 *waspers* attested by 3 of 6 speakers, *wasp* by 2 of 6, *warsp* by 1 of 6. **1974** Fink *Bits Mt Speech* 29 *waspes* or *waspers.* **1986** Pederson et al.

LAGS = attested by 6/60 interviewees (10%) from E TN; 6/13 of all LAGS interviewees (46%) attesting term were from E TN. **1996** Montgomery *Coll*: *wasper* (known to Cardwell, Oliver). [See **2015** in **1**.]

wasper See **wasp 1**, **2**.

waspers, **waspes** See **wasp 2**.

wast See **wasp 1**, **2**.

waste

A *verb*

1 To deplete (a supply), spend (money).

1924 Raine *Saddlebugs* 100 "I've wasted it." Which means used or spent, not squandered. **1931** Owens *Speech Cumberlands* 91 = to spend, use up: "Whar's that last load of coal gone? I've wasted hit." **1936** Coleman *Dial N GA* 16 "Wasted" means "used or spent" to the mountaineer as it did to Shakespeare, when Celia said in "As You Like It," "I like this place and willingly would waste my time in it." **1960** Westover *Highland Lg* 21 *wasted* = used. **1997** Montgomery *Coll* (known to Bush, Norris).

[Web3 *waste* v 3b archaic]

2 Of fruit: to spoil.

1864 Poteet *CW Letters* (Aug 30) he sed that the apels was wasted Roten that tha[y] wasant no acount.

[OED3 *waste* v 6 obsolete, rare]

3 See citation.

1946 Matthias *Speech Pine Mt* 192 = to have a hemorrhage, especially from the uterus. "Go git the doctor quick, an' tell him Maw's a-wastin'."

B *noun* See citation.

2009 House and Howard *Something* 1 This destructive method of mining requires large areas for disposal of the resulting overburden, or "waste"—topsoil, dirt, rocks, trees (almost never harvested so the coal can be extracted as quickly as possible)—which is then pushed into the valleys below, burying the streams, trees, and animals. This activity is neatly described as "valley fills."

waste house *noun* An unoccupied dwelling that has fallen to ruin.

c1950 Adams *Grandpap* 128 They come to an old waste house that nobody'd lived in for a long time an' they decided to go in an' lay out in it. **1985** Irwin *Alex Stewart* 173 They got to talking to Uncle Boone and he felt sorry for them and he took pity sakes on them and let them move into an old waste house he had.

watch and care See **watch care**.

watch care (also *watch and care*) *noun* Scrutiny and monitoring of a new convert by a church congregation to ascertain and ensure his/her reformation and growth as a believer.

1990 Bush *Ocona Lufta Baptist* 4 In earlier times people were "churched" or removed from the body of the church if there was no reconciliation between the factions or if the board found enough evidence to call for dismissal or exclusion. At times, leaders or members of other Baptist churches came in to give impartial judgements on the complaints. Some of the offenders were put under the "watch care" of the church members. **2002** Morgan *Mt Born* 40 When the message had been concluded, the pastor called all of the new Christians to come and stand at the front of the sanctuary. The pastor questioned each one of these people concerning their beliefs of certain scriptural essentials pertaining to salvation. This constituted their public professions of faith. A voice vote was taken of the congregation whether or not these new converts should be placed "under the watch and care of the church" for one year, during which time their daily lives could be observed to discern, as much as it is possible, if their conversion was indeed genuine.

watch night (also *night watch*) *noun* A church service, especially of prayer, on New Year's Eve to observe the advent of the new year.

1833 (in **1984** Tipps *McKendree Church* 65) [The church] was dedicated, twice in December 1833, and on the last night of the year he conducted a Watch Night Service. **c1960** Wilson *Coll* = a ceremony on the last night of the year, often observed in churches. **1991** Montell *Singing Glory* 158 [In addition] to funerals, singings are also scheduled at church homecomings, revival services, "all-night sings," and Watch Night services on New Year's Eve. **1995** McCauley *Mt Religion* 195 I attended a "night watch" service for praying in the new year at Crank's Holiness Church in Harlan County Kentucky. ("Night watch" is a common word-order inversion for the tradition of the watch-night service going back most recently to plain-folk camp meeting religion and earlier still to Baptist revival culture.) **1995** McCauley *Mt Religion* 179 Foot-washing and "sacrament" (communion) may occur during the New Year's Eve watch night service.

watch one's bees *verb phrase* See citation. See also **bees swarm**, **mind one's bees**.

1939 Hall *Coll* (Saunook NC) "Minding his bees" or "watching his bees" is used of a man whose wife is expecting a baby. Sometimes he stays home for this reason.

watercreases *noun* Watercress.

1996 GSMNPCOHP-1:2 One old green was what you might say was a wild herb. It was called watercreases.

water doctor *noun* One with the gift of dowsing for water using a divining rod. See also **power doctor**, **water witch A1**.

1927 Montague *Funny Bone* 333 With that he breaks off a switch from a witch-hazel bush like what you've seen a water doctor use, and gives it to the young-un to whip through the spring fer a spell.

waterdog *noun* A type of large salamander. Same as **thunder dog**.

1911 Shearin *Superstitions Cumberland* 319 If a turtle or a "water-dog," a species of fresh-water newt, lay hold of one's toe, it will not release it until thunder is heard. **1996–97** Montgomery *Coll* (known to Brown, Hooper), = large, black salamander 12–20 inches long, also known as *thunder dog* or *mud puppy* (Cardwell).

water dunk *verb phrase* To baptize by immersion.

1997 Montgomery *Coll* He's been water dunked so many times even the fish know him (Brown).

water dunker *noun* A Baptist; one who baptizes by immersion.

1997 Montgomery *Coll* (known to Brown).

water gap (also *water gate*) *noun* The point at which a fence reaches a watercourse, with a swinging contrivance constructed across it to prevent livestock from wading in and passing.

1859 (in **1992** Murray-Woolley *Rock Fences* 58) (DARE) The best water gaps are pillars made of stone, with stone wall wings. . . . A good shutter is a common horse rack, suspended by hinges or wooden hooks upon a pole resting on the pillars. **1949** Stuart *Thread* 31 A water-gap fence spanned the creek. **1957** Combs *Lg Sthn High: Word List* 109 *water gap* = a paling stretched across a stream in lieu of a fence. **c1960** Wilson *Coll*: *water gap*: *water gate* = a swinging panel of fence across a stream, which can rise or fall with the water and thus keep the stock out.

[DARE *water gap* n 1 chiefly South, South Midland, especially KY]

water gravy *noun* Gravy made from water rather than milk.

1982 Slone *How We Talked* 55 Water gravy was only used when there was no milk available.

[DARE *water gravy* n especially South, South Midland]

water jack

A *noun* A boy tasked with having a bucket of fresh water at hand, usually to refresh loggers or workers in the field.

1930 Pendleton *Wood-Hicks Speak* 89 = water boy. **1952** Wilson *Folk Speech NC* 605 = a man or boy who brings water to workmen. **1969** Miller *Raising Tobacco* 29 Behind the setter came the *waterjack* or *waterboy* with bucket and longhandled dipper or gourd, watering the plants. **c1975** Lunsford *It Used to Be* 164 "Waterjack" is a boy who carries water to the field. It's also used on public works where they have to send for water and sometimes a fellow in changing or quitting his work will stop in the middle of it and say "waterjack." If the boy doesn't have water he has to go get it. **1983** Weals *Waterjacking* Pete was a *waterjack* carrying drinking water to the men who worked on no. 4 skidder.

[DARE *water jack* n especially South, South Midland]

B *verb phrase* To carry water to a logging crew.

1974–75 McCracken *Logging* 5:56 I was a-water jackin' on a section when this set.

water mash *noun* See citation.

1949 Maurer *Argot of Moonshiner* 13 = the first mash made in a stilling operation: this is mixed with water, since there is no spent stillage available. "We never got much turnout on the water mash."

watermelon *noun* Variant forms *watermilion*, *watermillion*, *watermillon*, *watermilon*.

1857 *Knoxville Register* (Sept 9) We noticed one beautiful girl off by herself with an exceedingly melancholy [look], and fearing it was on account of her being neglected in the general treat [of fresh watermelons], we were about to invest some loose change for her benefit, when she stopped our generosity by screaming out at the top of her lung power, "Jeems, fetch me a watermillion." **1862** *Love CW Letters* (Aug 21) we got plenty to eat chickens rosenyears [= roasting ears] to eat water milons to eat. **1863** *Warrick CW Letters* (Aug 2) evry thing is so hy her that ther is no use of talking about it water millons is worth from ten to twenty dollars a pies. **1864** *Councill CW Letters* (July 20) we ar geting plenty of Bred and meat to eat. and we Can Steel as many watermilions as we want so the 6 Cav. will not starve while eney Body els has eney thing to eat. **1929** Duncan and Duncan *Sayings* 235 Plant yar water millions in full moon in May. **1969** Doran *Folklore White Co* 115 *watermillion*.

watermilion, **watermillion**, **watermillon**, **watermilon** See **watermelon.**

water moccasin *noun* The northern water snake (*Nerodia sipedon*). [Editor's note: This term referring to *Agkistrodon piscivorus* is widespread in the US.]

1967 Huheey and Stupka *Amphibians and Reptiles* 56 Here, as in many parts of its range, the Northern Water Snake is known as "Water Moccasin," the latter (*Agkistrodon piscivorus*) being a venomous species that it resembles. Habitats wherein the Water Moccasin or Cottonmouth might be expected do not exist in or near Great Smoky Mountains National Park.

water oak *noun* An oak found near water, especially *Quercus phellos*, the willow oak.

1917 Kephart *Camping & Woodcraft* 2:205 Our first choice for clapboards is "mountain oak," when we can find one that splits well . . . Otherwise we take white, black, red, or water oak. **1967** *DARE Survey* (Gatlinburg TN). **1974–75** McCracken *Logging* 3:15 Then when you got on up in your higher elevations, you got what they call water oak. **1997** Montgomery *Coll* = same as river oak (Cardwell).

[DARE *water oak* n 1 chiefly South, South Midland]

water of life See **elixir of life.**

water out *verb phrase* To extinguish (a fire) using water.

1900 Carter *NC Sketches* 106 Before we went we watered out the fire . . . ; so it weren't that as sot the fire. **1966–69** *DARE Survey* (Rome GA, Brasstown NC, Highlands NC) *water out* (the fire).

water permillion See **permillion.**

water sandwich *noun* See citation.

1943 Korson *Coal Dust* 68 Bread was the staff of life [in coal camps]. Sometimes it was the only food consumed. In hard times miners carried what they called a "water sandwich" in their dinner pails. It consisted of stale bread soaked in lard and water, upon which they subsisted all day in the mines.

water shelf *noun* A shelf, as at a school, on which are kept buckets that hold fresh water for drinking and washing or contain the lunches of schoolchildren.

1853 Ramsey *Annals* 716 The whole furniture, of the one apartment, answering in these primitive times, the purpose of the kitchen, the dining-room, the nursery and the dormitory, were a plain home-made bedstead or two . . . a water shelf and a bucket . . . and sometimes a loom. **1941** Justus *Kettle Creek* 8 Mat was sent outside to the dog-trot to slick down his hair . . . and for several minutes they heard him sloshing about at the water shelf. **1949** Arnow *Hunter's Horn* 83 He sat and waited while the fourteen pupils, followed by the hounds, ran noisily to the row of lard buckets on the water shelf, pried off the lids with a great clattering, seized biscuits and baked sweet potatoes. **1950** Justus *Luck for Lihu* 46 She went over to the water shelf. "Drat the luck," she muttered, "dry as a bone." **2004** Myers and Boyer *Walker Sisters* 18 The large kitchen shared a large table, with benches, chairs, two cookstoves, a work table, water shelf, jelly box, salt gum, cupboard, and meal and flour bins made from hollow gum logs.

[DARE *water shelf* n South, South Midland]

waterspout *noun* A very local violent rainstorm, as one accompanied by a tornado or causing a flash flood.

1849 Lanman *Alleghany Mts* 53–54 Among the matters touched upon in our conversation was a certain mysterious "water-spout," of which I had heard a great deal among the people in my journeying, and which was said to have fallen upon Trail Mountain. I again inquired into the particulars, and Major Williams replied as follows: "This water-spout story has always been a great botheration to me. The circumstance occurred several years ago. A number of hunters were spending the night in the very ravine where this shanty now stands, where, about midnight, they heard a tremendous roaring in the air, and a large torrent of water fell upon their camp and swept it, with all of its effects and inmates, about a dozen yards from the spot where they had planted their poles. There were three hunters, and one of them was severely injured on the head by the water, and all of them completely drenched. They were of course much alarmed at the event, and concluded that a spring farther up the mountain had probably broken away; but when morning came they could find no evidence of a spring, and every where above their camping place the ground was perfectly dry, while on the lower side it was completely saturated. They were now perplexed to a marvellous degree, and returned to a lower country impressed with the idea that a water-spout had burst over their heads." I of course attempted no explanation of this phenomenon, but Mr. Hubbard gave it as his opinion that if the affair did occur, it originated from a whirlwind, which might have taken up the water from some neighboring river, and dashed it by the merest accident upon the poor hunters. **1939** Hall *Coll* (Deep Creek NC) They had came a water spout in time and drifted in a big lot of timber, spruce, and hemlock and stuff. . . . They'd been a water spout a cloud bust put there in time and run in, just a awful lot of spruce and timber. **1970** Miller *Pigeon's Roost* (Oct 22) Hundreds of farms on uplands are scarred up with slides or water spouts. **1986** Pederson et al. *LAGS* (Sullivan Co TN) = a very heavy rain. **2002** Myers *Best Yet Stories* 199 When we played in the river (ice cold to me today) our parents warned us to listen for a "roar" in the water. Many times water spouts would hit high up in the mountains while the sun might be shining at our place. This caused the water to rise rapidly and dangerously for us.

water swift *noun* See citations.

1966 *DARE Survey* (Spruce Pine NC) = where water falls over rocks. **1998** Montgomery *Coll* (known to Bush).

water weed *noun* Same as **jewel flower**.

1982 Slone *How We Talked* 49 *Water weed* (also called "Jewelweed"). **1984** High *Titan Rock* 42 Folk remedies for snake bite seem to abound almost as plentifully as snakes themselves. . . . Concoctions with water weed (*Impatiens capenses*, also called jewelweed or wild touch-me-not) were thought to be helpful against poison ivy as well as snake bite.

water witch

A *noun*

1 One who has the gift of dowsing for underground water using a divining stick. See also **power doctor**, **water doctor**.

1912 Perrow *Songs and Rhymes* 140 Scarcely any one will dig a well without consulting a water-witch, who with his peach-tree fork, together with a good supply of native judgment, usually succeeds in locating a stream. **1962** Woosley *Water Witching* 138 A house called for a well, and a well called for a water witch. **1985** Irwin *Alex Stewart* 228 He had him a water witch and he found water for people. **1994** Thomas *Come Go* 7 He wouldn't have a well dug, without he knowed where the water was. He'd want a water witch. He wouldn't do it hisself. Ye see, nobody except one person in a family, gener'ly, could do that.

2 A forked stick used to dowse for underground water, a divining rod. Same as **witching stick**.

1972 Carson and Vick *Cookin 2* 61 Willer, peach and apple twigs make the best water witches if you're a-goin to dig a well.

B *verb phrase* To dowse for underground water using a divining stick; hence verbal noun *water witching*, noun *water witcher*. Same as **switch**.

1955 Rogers *Switching* 108 The majority of persons claiming to possess the power of "water witching" suggests that the forked twig be cut from any kind of growing tree which produces a fruit bearing a stone. The order of preference therefore seems to be a peach tree, plum, dogwood, and apple. **1962** Woosley *Water Witching* 137 No skepticism is voiced by a large number of people on Big Reedy when water witching is mentioned. The reason is clearly explainable. The same large number of people believe that water witchers do exist, are accurate, and still go about making the ground yield water that has heretofore remained hidden. **2007** *DARE File* Back in the 70's we were taught how to water witch at Girl Scout camp in northeast Tennessee. **2013** Osborne *Raisin' Cane* 215 Since digging a well is a difficult chore, folks in Appalachia always wanted to make sure that the location of the dig had a good chance of having plenty of water. Many folks used a special technique, called water witching.

[DARE *water witch* v phr scattered, but chiefly Mississippi-Ohio Valleys, West]

waul See **wall B.**

wausper, waust See **wasp 1.**

waustes See **wasp 2.**

wave *verb* Variant past-tense form *wove.*

1996 Landry Coll He retch out and wove at me. **1999** GSMNPCOHP-1:5 I poked my hand out the window and wove at you.

wawst See **wasp 1.**

wawsts See **wasp 2.**

wax *noun* Chewing gum.

c1960 Wilson *Coll* = the former name for chewing gum. **1983** Broaddus *Estill Co KY Word List* 60 = chewing gum.

[DARE *wax* n 3 especially South Midland]

way *adverb* Very much, far, at a distance (preceding another adverb). See also **away, way yonder.**

1937 Hall Coll (Little Greenbrier TN) [There are] lots of wild cat here.... Panter is more of a dog specie, a lot bigger and way longer than a wild cat. **c1950** Adams *Grandpap* 26 Hit kept on till way long in the night. **1975** Woolley *We Be Here* 81 We had a strike then. Way long years ago. **1989** Landry *Smoky Mt Interviews* 181 She was way away from Greenbrier.

ways *noun*

1 A distance. See also **little piece, piece 1.**

1863 *Hall CW Letters* (Feb 7) I want you to rite to me as often as you can and let me here the nuse as I am a long ways from hom and very lonesom. **1863** *Revis CW Letters* (March 31) I am along ways from you but I hav not fer got you. **1926** Hunnicutt *Twenty Years* 62 Just a little ways up the hill, the dogs will trail it up in the morning if you have killed it. **1939** Hall Coll (Cataloochee NC) He followed the noise of the bear down a ways as far down as he heared it. **1973** GSMNP-2:5 During them days if they got five miles away, they was a long ways from home. **1978** Montgomery *White Pine Coll* VIII-2 It was a long ways to them woods. **1998** *Dante OHP*-71 It [= a rock] broke loose up the road there a little ways. **2004** House *Coal Tattoo* 107 She could see it coming from a long ways off.

2 A period of time, especially an indefinite one.

1997 Montgomery Coll (known to Adams, Bush, Oliver).

[< Middle English *wayes,* genitive of *way*]

way yonder *adverb phrase*

1 Far away (in distance). See also **way, yonder B3.**

1964 Roberts *Hell-Fer-Sartin* 14 I see three robbers way yonder, countin' their money. **1969** GSMNP-37:2:2 Thad Watson, he lived way yonder on Mingus Creek. **1985** Edwards *Folksy Sketches* 46 You see that cleared space way yonder on the ridge?

2 Considerably, far and away.

1930 Armstrong *This Day and Time* 154 Birch twigs, to chew 'em, is way yonder better to clean a body's teeth. **1939** Bond *Appal Dialect* 112 = considerably: "I'm way yonder smarter than what I was." **1971** *Kenny Runnion* 137 A woman's got way yonder better a chance, and a man don't stand none. **1975–76** Wolfram/Christian *WV Coll* 22 This world is way yonder worse now than when we was growing up. **1993** Cunningham *Sthn Talk* 170 They're already gittin' way yonder more [money] than they ort to fer jist playin'.

[DARE (at *yonder* B 4) chiefly South, South Midland]

weak as stump water See **stump water 3.**

weak jerks (also *weak trembles*) *noun* Tremor, general weakness of the body, as from hunger or worry.

1913 Kephart *Our Sthn High* 227–28 Old Uncle Neddy Cyarter went to jump one of his own teeth out, one time, and missed the nail and mashed his nose with the hammer. He had the weak trembles. **1943** Justus *Bluebird* 21 When the old man went to the woods or the field to work for a good while he always took along a bite to eat, not because he got hungry, he said, but to keep his stomach from getting the "weak trembles" as he called them. [**1952** Wilson *Folk Speech NC* 605 *have the weak trembles* = to be worried.] **1983** Page and Wigginton *Aunt Arie* 79 It scared me s'bad it give me th'weak jerks. **1984** Wilder *You All Spoken* 205 *weak trembles* = weak and wobbly because of hunger or apprehension. **1990** Cavender *Folk Medical Lex* 33 *weak trembles* = a feeling of general weakness associated with mild trembles of the body. **1994–97** Montgomery Coll: *weak trembles* (known to ten consultants from the Smoky Mountains).

[DARE *weak trembles* n chiefly South Midland]

weakly *adjective* Weak.

1920 De Long *Fiddler John* She's hearty, but weakly—a stout, well-built chunk of a heavy woman. **1939** Hall Coll (Deep Creek NC) He was a little weakly, delicate fellow, I tried to keep him from going in the [hunting] party. **1988** Brown *Beech Creek* 86 She had epilepsy, and several seizures as a young child alarmed her parents and encouraged them to be even more protective of their "weakly" child.

we all *pronoun phrase* All of us. See also **we'uns.** For other forms with *all,* see Grammar and Syntax §2.7.1.

1864 *Joyce CW Letters* (July 5) we all conscripes has to start to Ralegh on the 15th of July. **1886** Smith *Sthn Dialect* 345 You-all and we-all (just a little better than *you-uns* and *we-uns,* and the same thing in effect). **1960** Hall *Smoky Mt Folks* 64 We all have more time than money. **1976** Miller *Mts within Me* 84 Double-barrelled pronouns—perhaps the most universally recognized mountain usage is the adding of suffixes of "un" and "all" to pronouns; hence, we-uns, us-uns, you-uns, we-all, you-all, them-all.

[DARE *we-all* pron 1 chiefly South, South Midland]

weaner (also *weaner cabin, weaning house*) *noun* A small cabin serving as a temporary dwelling for a newly married couple, usually located on land belonging to the husband's parents. See also **honeymoon house, marriage house.**

1960 Westover *Highland Lg* 21 *weaning house* = house built for the oldest son (he moves into on the day of his marriage). **1965** Shields *Cades Cove* 6 Later [the house] was used as a "weaner" by the Shields family. When one of the boys married, he occupied the house until he could get his own dwelling built, or was weaned from the family group, as it was called. **1975** Brewer *Valley So Wild* 117–18 A smaller house on Fed's farm became known as the "weaner cabin." When any of Fed's several sons married, he and his bride lived in the "weaner cabin" while he was being "weaned" away from home. He soon built a house of his own, freeing the "weaner cabin" for the next brother who needed it. **1975** Montell *Ghosts Cumberland* 220 *weaning house* = small dwelling built adjacent to the parents' home for newlyweds who are apprehensive of an immediate total break from safety and security of parental care and guidance. **1979** *Smokies Heritage* 308 When the oldest son (about eighteen years) decided to get married they built him a smaller log cabin and barn at the back of the Flats about half a mile away—This cabin was called the weaner cabin or Honeymoon house. **1982** Slone *How We Talked* Some parents had a small, one-room house close by where the newlyweds first lived, while waiting to build a house of their own. This house was called a "weaning house" and was used over and over again as each child got married. **1993** Montell *Cumberland Country* 54 Living adjacent to parents or grandparents on the same parcel of land was also typical. Young marrieds were encouraged to settle down and build homes close to their parents. The term "weaning house" was sometimes applied to these nearby dwellings, especially in Russell and Wayne counties, Kentucky. **1995** Montgomery *Coll* (known to Cardwell).

[DARE (at *weaner house* n) chiefly South Midland]

wear *verb*

1 Variant past-tense forms *weared, wored.*

1970 *Foxfire Interviews* A-70-5 I think I wored out old Mister Fripps. **1991** Thomas *Sthn Appal* 222 I'll tell ye: [the cloth] never weared out, hardly ever.

2 Variant past-participle forms *wor, wore, wored, worned.*

1864 Hill *CW Letters* (Feb 25) you Sed your shous was wore out tel Emoline She must look a round and try and get you Some. **1864** *Walker CW Letters* (May 31) we air wor out at this time. **1901** Harben *Westerfelt* 57 Since then Toot has al'ays wore his hat at dances. **1953** Atwood *Verbs East US* 25 *Wore* . . . in the M[iddle] A[tlantic] S[tates] and the S[outh] A[tlantic] S[tates] its frequency . . . varies from about two thirds (Pa.) to more than nine tenths (N.C.) **1969** GSMNP-46:9 I have got some old ones here that has been wore. **1971** *AOHP/ALC*-226 I'd never worned a bathing suit and one of my girlfriends invited me to go to the beach. **1973** GSMNP-4:41 I've wore out a lot of pair of britches playing marbles. **1978** Slone *Common Folks* 229 That's a piece of wored out flag. **1986** Pederson et al. *LAGS* (Sevier Co TN). **2000** Morgan *Mts Remember* 5 It wasn't until I was milking the cow by lantern-light I seen how rough my hands had wore. **2008** Salsi *Ray Hicks* 7 I started rememberin' Sunday afternoons on the front porch with fiddle playin' and me buck dancin' across the wored-out floorboards.

wear out *verb phrase* To whip thoroughly, spank (usually a misbehaving child).

1921 Campbell *Sthn Highlander* 124–25 [The child] has, however, neither training nor example in self-control. At times his father, equally undisciplined, "whups" him in a fit of furious temper; or the weary and exasperated mother puts into execution her frequent threat to "wear him out with a hickory." **1929** Kephart *Smoky Mt Magic* 194 If you stir up a polecat, damn you, I'll wear you out with a hick'ry. **1949** Arnow *Hunter's Horn* 83 If your pop knowed how you was misbehaven, he'd wear you out; he was a good boy in school an got his lessons. **1989** *Matewan OHP*-28 They'd go out and cut a switch off of a bush and just wear you out with it. **1997** *Dante OHP*-14 Our daddy said, "If I ever hear tell of y'all making fun of anybody, I'll wear you out." **2005** Williams *Gratitude* 535 = give somebody a good thrashin'.

[DARE (at *wear* v C1) chiefly South, South Midland]

wearry See **worry.**

wear the bells *verb phrase* To act like a fool.

1931 Hannum *Thursday April* 225 You cain't fault me jest 'cause Joe in his old age tuk the notion to wear the bells.

wear the britches (also *have the britches, wear the pants*) *verb phrase* Usually of a wife with respect to her husband: to exercise authority in the family, be the boss.

1936 Stuart *Head of Hollow* 36 My wife Symanthia and my boy Isiah wears the pants. **1952** Wilson *Folk Speech NC* 523 = to act the male, to be the boss; said especially of a woman. **1988** Brown *Beech Creek* 78 He just played shut-mouth and let Nancy Ann wear the breeches. **1995** Montgomery *Coll* She wears the britches (Cardwell); She's got the britches in the family (Shields). **1999** Morgan *Gap Creek* 111 "Hank," she said, "you've got to show who's wearing the britches in this house."

[DARE *wear the britches* v phr chiefly South, South Midland]

wear the hatching jacket *verb phrase* See citation.

1967 *DARE Survey* (Gatlinburg TN) = used by women for another woman who is about to have a baby.

weary *verb* To tire. See also **worry.**

c1900 (in **1997** Stoddart *Quare Women* 126) That hill worried me (meaning wearied).

weary along *verb phrase* To persevere.

1864 *Carson CW Letters* (Oct 16) I want you to keepe in good harte werey along Sum how alitel longer.

weasel *noun* The runt of a litter; a malnourished or undersized animal. See also **weasly.**

1996 Montgomery *Coll* (known to Cardwell).

weasley See **weasly.**

weasly (also *weasley*) *adjective* Of a person: withered, wrinkled, unhealthy. See also **weasel.**

1967–69 *DARE Survey* (Gatlinburg TN) = too small to be worth much; (Dillard GA, Rome GA) = when a person doesn't look healthy, or looks as if he hadn't been well for some time. **1974** Fink *Bits Mt Speech* 29 = wizened. "Looks sorter *weasley*, don't he?" **1986** Helton *Around Home* 377 *weasly* = aged and wrinkled. **1995–96** Montgomery *Coll* (known to Brown, Cardwell, Jones, Ledford, Norris, Oliver).

[DARE *weasly* adj chiefly South, South Midland]

weather

A *noun* See citation.

2007 Milnes *Signs Cures Witches* 77 Old people have told me that a warm day in the cold season is a "weather."

B (also *weather up*) *verb, verb phrase* To rain, storm, sleet, etc.

1929 Kephart *Smoky Mt Magic* 94 Haven't you heard the mountaineers say "the el-e-ments looks like rain—hit's goin' to weather"? **1930** Armstrong *This Day and Time* 46 Apt as not hit'll weather afore night. **1940** Still *River of Earth* 44 "When it 'gins to blow around the north points of a morning," Father said, "sign it's going to weather." **1944** Hayes *Word-List NC* 37 = to rain, snow, sleet, or blow. **1957** Broaddus *Vocab Estill Co KY* 84 = to precipitate, any form. **1966** Dykeman *Far Family* 181 I'm going to have heaps and heaps of wood ahead, enough for a whole year or more, and when it snows or rains or weathers up any way a-tall, I'll just build me the biggest blaze I can and be warm and cozy, knowing there's all the wood I'll ever need waiting to be used. **1988** Kosier *Maggie* 112 Grandpa would watch the sky. "Looks like it's gonna weather-up!" when dark clouds moved into the area. **1995–97** Montgomery *Coll*: *weather up* (known to Brown, Cardwell, Ellis, Ledford).

[DARE *weather, weather up* v South, South Midland]

weatherboard (collectively *weatherboarding*) *noun* House siding; hence verb *weatherboard* = to cover (a house) with such siding.

1967–69 *DARE Survey* (Clayhole KY, Owingsville KY). **1973** *AOHP/ASU-97* I done all of it, the weather boarding and everything. **1974** *AOHP/ALC-334* They was ceiled with an old-time ceiling, weather boarding on the outside of them. [**1975** *Shenandoah OHC* 121 We had a weatherboard house. It wasn't a modern house like you see today, and it wasn't as warm as the houses now.] **1990** Williams *Pride and Prejudice* 220 You take a board house—take the board—they ain't got framing in it. They just built the whole plate around and nail the board down here up. And just slat it over. See, a frame house, it got two by fours in it, put the weatherboarding on the outside like this and ceiling on the inside. **1994** Thomas *Come Go* 12 Part of it is the o-o-old original logs. Course, it's been weatherboarded.

[DARE (at *weatherboard* n) chiefly South, Midland]

weather breeder *noun* A period of mild weather in winter.

1824 (in **1912** Doddridge *Notes on Settlement* 55) We commonly had an open spell of weather during the latter part of February denominated by some powwowwing days and by others weather breeders. **1960** Miller *Pigeon's Roost* (Feb 4) We noticed the cattle lying around in the fields basking in the warm sunshine. The older people called those warm days "weather breeders." That's why the cold weather seemed so pinching coming right on the heels of the warm spell. **1984** Wilder *You All Spoken* 140 = warm spells in the midst of cold.

weatherish *adjective* See citation. See also **weather B.**

c1960 Wilson *Coll* = boding a storm.

weather prophet *noun* A traditional weather forecaster predicting conditions by watching the sky, the behavior of animals, and so on.

1963 Medford *Mt People* 100 After all, these old-time "weather prophets"—with nothing more to guide them than the old "signs," often had about as many "misses" as "hits." **1974** Cate et al. *Sthn Appal Heritage* 83 Almost every community had its weather prophet. However, some weather signs were known by almost everybody. Many of these have been passed from generation to generation. **2002** Myers *Best Yet Stories* 192 Our mountain weather prophets counted the number of heavy fogs in August to determine the number of measurable snows in the winter time. The number of snows was supposed to be the same as the number of fogs.

weather swan *noun* See citation.

2002 Myers *Best Yet Stories* 236 The "Weather Swan" (a glass barometer—a bulb-shaped body with an open-ended spout) was filled with water. In a low-pressure system the water is pushed down in the main body and up in the spout. If a high-pressure system is approaching, the water returns to the main body of the swan indicating good weather.

weather up See **weather B.**

weathery *adjective* Characterized by inclement weather. See also **weather B.**

1939 Hall *Coll* (White Oak NC) There's no need of you going out. It's so weathery.

weave *verb*

1 Variant past-tense form *weaved.*

1971 *AOHP/ALC-137* She weaved all the clothes. Yeah, she weaved cloth, clothes, beautiful. She'd color a chain. **1979** *Big South Fork OHP-1* They both had looms and weaved carpets and stuff like that.

2 Variant past-participle form *wove.*

1939 Hall *Coll* (Big Creek NC) I've wove many a day, made cloth. **1973** *GSMNP-79:1:21* She's wove for years and years for the Pi Beta Phi school. **1981** Whitener *Folk-Ways* 10 I've got a chair in my house that was wove over sixty years ago and it's still strong.

[DARE *wove* as past participle (*weave* v Aa) especially South, South Midland]

Webster's blue back speller See **blue back(ed) speller**.

wed See **weed A**.

weddinger *noun* A member of a wedding party; the party itself, including bride and groom.

1823 Doddridge *Logan* 44 (DARE) Your wedners are as still as mice I dont like it; marriage commonly comes but once in a body's life and there ought to be some fun about it. **1895** Edson and Fairchild *TN Mts* 375 = the bride and the groom, with the wedding party. **1952** Wilson *Folk Speech NC* 605 = member of a wedding party. [**1995** Montgomery *Coll* (unknown to consultants from the Smoky Mountains).]

[OED3 *weddinger* n dialect; EDD *weddinger* sb Scot, Irel, Engl; CUD *weddiner* 2 (at *wed*[1]) "a member of the wedding-party"]

weed

A *verb* Principal parts. [Editor's note: These forms do not occur in ATASC.]

1 Variant past-tense form *wed*.

1840 McLean *Diary* 69 Rain and warm [I] Wed my oats. **1913** Kephart *Our Sthn High* 284 There are many corrupt forms of the verb, such as . . . wed (weeded). **1930** Thomas *Death Knell* Verbs especially have undergone many changes for the worse, such as seed for saw and seen, cotch (in all tenses) for catch, fotch, chaw, clem, wed (weeded), bile, borned, and drempt. **1952** Wilson *Folk Speech NC* 605 = past tense and past-participle of *weed*: "I *wed* my tobacco last week." **2007** McMillon *Notes*: *wed*.

2 Variant past-participle form *wed*.

1904–20 Kephart *Notebooks* 2:350 Did you'uns git them weeds wed out yit? [**1952** in **A1**.]

B (also *weeded*, *weed in the breast*) *noun* Mastitis. Same as **milk weed**.

1930 Armstrong *This Day and Time* 66 Don't ketch ye a cold an' git ye the weed. Hain't nothin' worse 'an a bealed breast. **1955** Washburn *Country Doctor* 74, 74–75 "Doc," he said, "Carrie's got the weed this time. I'uz a-feared she'd get it. She got erlong well till yestiddy, an' this mornin' she 'gun ter run fever." . . . Not knowing what the "weed" might be, I contented myself with examining the patient. I could hardly believe my findings were correct. Her pulse, temperature, and respiration were normal, and except for weakness there was nothing wrong with her. I was much perplexed . . . it was not until I visited Cousin Dovie Freeman, about two weeks later, that I learned that "weed" is an engorgement of the breasts due to delayed lactation,—a condition usually brought on by the mother getting up too soon after confinement and catching cold. **1982** Slone *How We Talked* 103 *weed in the breast* = mastitis. **2000** Lowry *Folk Medical Term* = mastitis, especially during the time a newborn is nursed. **2003** Cavender *Folk Medicine* 205 *weeded* = inflammation of the breast, mastitis.

[SND n[3]; CUD *weed* n 1 "a fever suffered by women after giving birth or when breast-feeding"; DARE *weed* n now chiefly southern Appalachians]

weeded See **weed B**.

weedely *noun* See citation. See also **biddy**, **deedie**, **dibbler**, **diddle**[2] **A**, **widdie**.

1984 Woods *WV Was Good* 221 Little weedelies—chickens newly hatched.

weed in the breast See **weed B**.

weed monkey (also *weed mule*) *noun* See citation.

1949 Maurer *Argot of Moonshiner* 13 (or *weed mule*) = the old car or truck used to haul supplies and to transport liquor. Mostly Tennessee usage. "Take that old weed monkey and go get the meal."

weed mule See **weed monkey**.

weed one's own road/row *verb phrase* To take care of oneself.

1859 Taliaferro *Fisher's River* 28 He "axed nobody no boot, and could weed his own row." **1963** Edwards *Gravel* 61 Every man must weed his own row; he must face and master his fate.

[DARE *weed one's own row* v phr chiefly South, South Midland]

weed sore *noun* Impetigo.

1964 Wright *Mt Medicine* 9 There was a lot of impetigo. It went by such names as "Tomato Sores," and "Fall Sores," and "Weed Sores." **1999** Montgomery *Coll* (known to Cardwell).

weedy *adjective* Of milk: tasting of a plant a cow has eaten. See also **bitter A**, **bitterweed milk**.

c1960 Wilson *Coll* = taste of milk from cows that have eaten some plants not normally on their diet. **1968** *DARE Survey* (Brasstown NC) = milk that has a taste from something the cow ate in the pasture. **1998** Montgomery *Coll* (known to Cardwell).

[DARE *weedy* adj chiefly South, South Midland, West]

week *adverb*

1 (also *a week*) Seven days before or after the day cited, as *Sunday week* (with primary stress on *week*).

1784 (in **1956** Eliason *Tarheel Talk* 304) I shall . . . leave this Detested place . . . this day week. **1842** *Richardson Letter* 35 he was to make a big talk to the whole Nation last Thursday week. I have not heard the result. **1862** Robinson *CW Letters* (May 25) I Shal look fur a letter in ansur to this tomorrow weak. **1864** *Poteet CW Letters* (Feb 4) there has bin several deaths in the last two or three weeks your Aunt Barbry died last sunday week. **1874** Swearingen *Letters* 165 our School for last year closed yesterday will reopen Sunday week. **1933** Thomas *Traipsin' Woman* 188 Come to the apple peelin' and play party tomorrow night a week. **1937** Hall *Coll* (Cosby Creek TN) I reckon school commences next Monday a week. **c1960** Wilson *Coll*: *Friday week* = usually past (but may be future).

[DARE *week* n[1] Ba chiefly South, South Midland]

2 In phrase *was a week* = a week ago [from the day cited].

1849 Lanman *Alleghany Mts* 22 I do not believe you ever heard of a snake fight. I saw one, Monday was a week, between a black-racer and a rattlesnake. **1862** *Robinson CW Letters* (June 6) I havent got eny letter from you cense last monday nite was a weak. **1863** *Warrick CW Letters* (May 4) Lieut Hannon got back last Sunday was a week. **1900** Harben *N GA Sketches* 92 I seed 'er thar soap-bilin' as I driv by last Tuesday was a week. **1930** Armstrong *This Day and Time* 84 She would have me an' Enoch to stay fer supper, Tuesday was a week.

[DARE *week* n[1] Bb South, South Midland]

weekends about *adverb phrase* On alternating weekends, (by) turn or in rotation. See also **time about.**

1979 *Big South Fork OHP-4* The two younger boys would take it weekends about to get the truck.

[cf OED3 *about* adv A3 "in turn, in succession . . . alternately" now U.S. regional]

weep *verb* Variant past-tense form *wopt.*

1955 Washburn *Country Doctor* 42 *wopt* = wept.

we'erunses See **we'uns B1.**

wee-waw (also *wee-wow) adjective* See citation.

c1954 Adams *Word-List: wee-waw* (also *wee-wow*) = wobbly or shaky.

welcome bread *noun* Homemade bread.

1925 Dargan *Highland Annals* 58 I says to that girl when you're at home you're eatin' welcome bread, and when you're out in the world you don't know what you're eatin'. **1996–97** Montgomery *Coll* (known to Bush, Cardwell).

well *interjection*

1 See citation.

1976 Van Nest *Gillis Ridge* 308 There is, too, a certain ritualistic way of approaching a delicate subject. A direct, frank approach is put aside in favor of a more elaborate chassé. A "dreaded" subject has to be surrounded by an aura of the ordinary, locked securely within the concerns that keep Gillis folk where they are, before it can be attempted. To simply blurt out what everyone knows the discussion is really about violates decorum. Gillises often subtly warn a stranger that he is going too quickly to the heart of the matter: if asked for an awkward "yes" or "no" by someone unfamiliar with Gillis rhetoric and pace, a ridgeman will merely say "well" to such a direct thrust. There is a "well" that trails off to denote a slightly negative feeling; there is a "well" intoned in a far-off, pathetically lost way; there is a "well" with a slight surge of affirmation at the end; there is a "well" exhaled in exhaustion, and many more. None of them, of course, comes to the point, and all of them let the listener in on only one secret—the pace at which a Gillis approaches conclusions.

2 All right! Okay! (used as a single-word response to close a conversation or another's account or explanation).

c1950 Adams *Grandpap* 89 [In response] she said, "Well!" An' he took her by the arm an' led her in the house an' set by her till meetin' broke up. **1961** *Coe Ridge OHP-337B* [Speaker A:] You could see a dog and a man a-walking, but I don't believe it because I've traveled it too much, I didn't see it. [Speaker B:] Well. **1963** Edwards *Gravel* 160 "Next time you see her tell her I said stop and get this chair," said Uncle Jed, and Spud said, "Well." **1964** Roberts *Hell-Fer-Sartin* 84 The king told him, says, "Well, you can have my daughter and all I own here, if you will spare my life." That soldier said, "Well." *Ibid.* 106 Her mother's cotton begin to get ripe and she said, "Mother, why don't we have a cotton pickin' and invite Jack and his master?" She said, "Well." **1976** *Bear Hunting* 310 He said, "Whatever you do, don't step on a stick or nothing to make a racket. Scare it," he says, "[and] it'll be gone." And I told him, "Well." **2001** House *Clay's Quilt* 159 When she'd finished, he had said, "She always sung songs from the radio to me. Do you know any of them?" "No, all I know is church songs, baby." "Well," he had said with finality. **2008** *Rosie Hicks* 1 Juanita said, "Mama, I got you some colored apple. That might be a little stronger than the white," and I said, "Well."

well as common *adjective phrase* With reference to an individual's health or well-being: as well as usual (as in response to the query "How are you today?"). See also **common 1.**

1834 (in **1996** Edmondson *Crawford Memoirs* 127) I seen Thomas Reynolds last week. They are all well as common. **1852** *Carson Letter* 146 by 2 o'clock I felt as well as common and thought it was nothing but the common headache. **1861** *Odell CW Letters* (Nov 9) Bro. John is also well as common. **1864** *Chapman CW Letters* (Feb 13) I can inform you that I am well as common at presant. **1898** Elliott *Durket Sperret* 75 I'm well as common, Miss Agnes, but Granny's sick. **1914** Arthur *Western NC* 267 Being, in our own estimation, at least, "as well as common," in this respect as in many others, "we still manage to understand and to be understood." **1940** Haun *Hawk's Done* 102 [How are you and Mos?] As well as common, I reckon. **1956** Hall *Coll* (Gatlinburg TN) Lord, just as well as common [in response to a query if she was feeling well].

well box (also *well gum*) *noun* The box or section of hollow log enclosing the top of a well.

1941 Stuart *Men of Mts* 93 Here is the well box and the big sassafras tree by the well box in our kitchen yard. *Ibid.* 257 I went in Lima's yard to draw me a drink of water and right by the well-gum stood Rister and Lima. **c1960** Wilson *Coll: well gum* = a hollow log used to enclose a spring. **1997** Montgomery *Coll: well gum* (known to Brown, Cardwell).

[DARE (at *gum* n[2] 3d) especially Appalachians]

well gum See **well box.**

well tickled *adjective phrase* Thoroughly amused.

1963 Edwards *Gravel* 20 Patty got so well tickled she got a bread crumb hung in her windpipe and Ma had to beat her back till she was as red in the face as a pickle beet before it would come loose. **1998** Montgomery *Coll* (known to Adams, Brown, Bush, Cardwell, Jones, Oliver).

well-turned *adjective* Having a pleasing or proper character. See also **turn B1**.

1962 Drukker *Lg By-Ways* 51 A citizen or neighbor whose disposition is amiable and who gets on well with others is "well turned." **1962** Dykeman *Tall Woman* 14 "Ah, Hamilton's a well-turned boy, and the Nelsons are good livers," she had said when he brought Lydia home once from a sociable at the Burkes'.

wellup, welp See **welt**.

welt *noun, verb* Variant forms *wellup, welp, whelk, whelp*.

1957 Broaddus *Vocab Estill Co KY* 85 *whelk* = a welt. **1960** Westover *Highland Lg* 21 *whelk, whelp*. **c1960** Wilson Coll: *whelk* = a welt or bump on the skin. **1962** Clark *Folk Speech NC* 324 *whelp* = welt. **1977** (in **2011** Hurst and Lewis *Roaring Fork* 15) It'd welp your arm up after you got stung. I was stung by 'em [= packsaddles] many a time. **1982** Slone *How We Talked* 27 *whelps* = ridges or raised places on the body, caused by a slight blow; as, "Where he whipped him, it raised big whelps." **1985** Sienkneckt *Rheumatic Diseases* 184 *wellup* = localized swelling of subcutaneous tissue.

wen *noun* A cyst.

1864 *Mangum CW Letters* (March 21) tel M B to have his wen cut out and stay at home til it gets well. **1974** Roberts *Sang Branch* 75 What caused old Charles to die, he had a wen to come on his side and he operated on it. **2013** Reed *Medical Notes* = a noncancerous tumor or a sebaceous cyst.

[DARE *wen* n chiefly North, North Midland, especially northern OH]

we'ns See **we'uns**.

went See **go A3**.

we ones See **we'uns**.

were See **be F**.

wernet See **walnut**.

werry See **worry**.

wet or dry *phrase* "Heads or tails" (in a children's ritual to decide who has first privilege).

1982 Slone *How We Talked* 17 *throw up wet or dry* = just like tossing a coin for heads or tails, our folks used a small stone. They made one side wet by spitting on it. Leaving the other side dry, they tossed it up in the air to see which side came up on top, the dry or the wet. **1993** Page and Smith *Foxfire Toys and Games* 5 "Wet or dry?" Instead of "Heads or tails."

we'uns *pronoun* We. [Editor's note: This term was not observed by Joseph Hall in the Smoky Mountains in the late 1930s, indicating its marked lower currency than that of the analogous form **you'uns**.] See also **one 1**, **they'uns**, **us'uns**, **we all**.

A Variant forms *we-erunses* [see **1957** in **B1**], *we'ns* [see **1988** in **B1**], *we ones* [see **1973** in **B1**], *we-uns* [see **1913** in **B1**], *we wones* [see **1861** in **B1**], *w'uns* [see **1949** in **B1**].

B Senses.

1 Both of us, all of us.

1861 (in **1992** Heller and Heller *Confederacy* 27) owning to the sicness that has bin in our regement and caren off prisnours whitch 100 of our reg has bin engage in the gard duty has bin heavy on us we wones. **1881** Atkinson *After Moonshiners* 114 Powerful fine weather we'uns are havin'! **1892** Smith *Farm and Fireside* 10 How they got to using such twisted language as you'uns and we'uns and inguns and mout and gwine and all sich is not known, nor was such talk universal. **1904–20** Kephart *Notebooks* 4:723 We'uns don't foller takin' in strangers. **1913** Kephart *Our Sthn High* 286 Let's we-uns all go over to youerunses house. **1915** Bradley *Hobnobbing* 96 "The reason why we-uns knows so much more than you-uns," said an old mountain woman, "is because we cain't *read* so much. So we *think* more." **c1940** Simms Coll A mountain man wanted to know, Who and what give the outlanders the idee (idea) that we'uns (the mountain people) air a lot ov hell-goin' trouble-raisers? **1949** Arnow *Hunter's Horn* 314 Whyn't you an your two oldest come along with w'uns? **1957** Combs *Lg Sthn High: Syntax* 8 Highland speech has preserved some earlier pronominal forms (*hisself, theirselfs*, etc.), and has also coined a few new ones: *we-erunses, you-erunses*, etc. The last two are of course longer forms of *we-uns* and *you-uns*, although they are corrupt forms of *we-uns* and *you-uns*. **1972** *Raising Sheep* 93 We had to feed'em fodder 'cause we'uns didn't have no hay back then. **1973** GSMNP-76:22 We ones [will] see you tomorrow. **1979** Slone *My Heart* 17 Paw always gets better after we'uns get the corn laid by. **1988** Mashburn *Mt Summer* 55 As they started to shovel the dirt in on top, Sam struggled to his feet and said, "Don't you fellers think we'ns ought ter say a few words over that poor ol' cow afore you kiver her up?" **1996–97** Montgomery Coll (known to Cardwell, Jones, Norris, Oliver); We'uns had a mess of poke sallet (Brown). **2008** Salsi *Ray Hicks* 32 Atter growin' and puttin' food away, we'uns had to go out and pull leaves of all kinds.

[contraction of *we* + *ones*; DARE *we-uns* pron chiefly South Midland]

2 Possessive form *we'uns's*.

1898 Dromgoole *Cinch* 37 It ain't been locked sence Bragg busted it open . . . ter git we-uns's meat out fur the rebels ter feed on.

whack *noun*

1 A portion, especially a large one.

c1940 Aswell *Glossary TN Idiom* 19 = a large quantity. "I'm going to make a *whack* of money out of this deal." **1996–97** Montgomery Coll (known to Brown, Cardwell, Oliver).

[OED3 *whack* n 2 "a portion, share"; SND *whack* n 3]

2 A lie.

1956 McAtee *Some Dial NC* 50 = a lie: "He told some of the biggest whacks." **1957** Broaddus *Vocab Estill Co KY* 84 = a lie.

[DARE *whack* n 2 South, South Midland]

3 A deal, agreement.

1911 Shearin E KY *Word-List* 540 = an agreement, a "go," e.g. "That's a whack!" **1957** Combs *Lg Sthn High: Word List* 109 = bargain, agreement: "That's a whack; we're agreed."

[Web3 *whack* n 3 Midland]

whang[1] (also *whang string*) *noun* A strip, especially one used for a shoelace, cut from an animal's tanned hide; hence *whang leather*.

1824 (in **1912** Doddridge *Notes on Settlement* 114) [Moccasins] were sewed together and patched with deer skin thongs, or whangs as they were commonly called. **1914** Arthur *Western NC* 265 Smaller skins were tanned in the same way, and those of dogs, coons, ground hogs, etc., were used for "whang" leather—that is, they were cut into strings for sewing other leather with. **1917** Kephart *Camping & Woodcraft* 2:315 Woodchuck skins are proverbially tough, and are good for whangs or shoe strings.... Whang-leather is prepared just like rawhide, but the thongs are cut out before softening. **1952** Wilson *Folk Speech NC* 606 = tough rawhide cut into strips and used to sew shoes or belting. **c1975** Lunsford *It Used to Be* 163 "Whang leather" is a tough rawhide leather suitable for making shoe strings. You cut it into fine strips for tying the rough boots or shoes. **1984** Woods *WV Was Good* 229 A *whang-string* meant a stout leather string cut from a groundhog hide or tanned cowhide. **1985** Irwin *Alex Stewart* 108 We'd make whangs (leather thongs) to sew harness with. **1991** Haynes *Haywood Home* 37 Each [brogan] shoe had four eyelets for the rawhide strings that came with them. When the rawhide strings wore out, new strings were cut from tanned groundhog hides. We called these strings "whang" strings. **1995** Montgomery *Coll* (known to Adams, Cardwell).

[< Middle English *thwang*, from which *thong* also derives; DARE *whang* n[1] 2 Scots, nIr, dial var of *thong*]

whang[2]

A *verb* See citation.

1969 Doran *Folklore White Co* 115 = to beat.

B *noun* See citation.

c1982 Young *Colloquial Appal* 24 = slap.

whang[3] (also *whang up*) *verb, verb phrase* To sew up hurriedly.

1939 Farr *TN Mt Regions* 92 = to sew up roughly: "She whanged up the ripped place." **1946** Woodard *Word-List VA/NC* 32 = to patch or repair a garment hurriedly. **1991** Thomas *Sthn Appal* 129 Repairin' th' [horse] collar, you'd use an awl an' thread. We gener'ly got a calfskin an' cut a little strang—sump'n 'at's tough—an' whanged 'um up.

[DARE (at *whang* v) chiefly Midland]

whang[4] *noun* A distinctive taste.

1968 *End of Moonshining* 107 It makes "pretty" whiskey which holds a good bead, but has a funny "whang" flavor. **1973** *Gardening* 240 If it's not good an' sweet, it'll have a kind of bitter whang. **1991** Still *Wolfpen Notebooks* 107 Reach me one more little horn o' that likker. Hit's got a whang to it tha[t] I like. **2005** Williams *Gratitude* 535 = a slightly different taste than what you'd expect, as: "It had a little sour *whang* to it."

[CUD *whang*[2] n 1 "a rancid taste in milk or butter"; DARE *whang* n[3] chiefly South, South Midland]

whangdoodle *noun* See citations.

c1960 Wilson *Coll* = an imaginary animal that lives far away and mourns for its first born. [**1974** Betts and Walser *NC Folklore* 18 He is about the length of a cow, but only as high as a goat. He has gray hair all over him. His ears are as big as a mule. He creeps about like a mountain panther. He comes in the middle of the night, moaning loud like this, "Yee-ee-ee-ow-ow-ow!" He goes to the hog pen to fill his huge stomach . . . most of the time the beast escapes, with a hog in its mouth.]

whang leather, whang string See **whang**[1].

whang up See **whang**[3].

whanker, out of *adjective phrase* Out of line, askew.

1976 Still *Pattern of Man* 80 A grandson of mine climbed a tower in Italy called Pisa, and to hear him tell it it was out of whanker, leaning on air.

whar, whare See **where**.

wharp See **warp 1**.

wharping stick *noun* See citation.

1997 Montgomery *Coll* (known to Bush, Cardwell, Weaver), = a five to six feet long hardwood stick, hand shaped or cut as a growing sprout, approximately two inches in diameter on one end and sloping to one inch at the other end. It was used to kill snakes or to prod livestock or as a walking stick (Brown).

what

A *relative pronoun* That, who, whom. [Editor's note: This usage is apparently marginal in the region's speech, there being only one example from Joseph Hall's 1939 material. Citations come mainly from print. For other relative pronouns, see Grammar and Syntax §2.9.]

1861 *Patton CW Letters* (July 15) we received a leter from sam a few days since what stated that he was geting along finely. **1862** *Watters-Curtis CW Letters* (July 29) I am cuming to eat that chicken yet what you sed that you would cook. **1926** Montague *Big Music* 423 Thar was a little feller in camp what all the hands called Fiddling Jimmy, 'count of him allus playing tunes on his fiddle. **1939** Hall *Coll* I knowed the White Caps what done the murder. **1957** Combs *Lg Sthn High: Word List* 109 = used personally for *who* and *that*. Ex.: "He's the man what I saw." **1961** Williams *Rhythm and Melody* 8 *What* as a relative pronoun referring to persons, although sometimes placed in the mouths of mountain folk by novelists, is practically unknown in the entire mountain region. **1971** *AOHP/ALC-137* They built [a school] on Puritan along Pine Creek, a bunch of Starborn and Listey what done the work. **1979** *Big South Fork OHP-4* She had a sister what came from . . . a place called Robbinstown. **1989** *Matewan OHP-7* Pauli Vince, he was the first one, of course, what brought it on. **2003** LaLone et al. *Farming Life* 251 All what's happening in Riner is that they're still rezoning and letting subdivisions and things come in. **2009** Burton *Beech Mt Man* 61 I showed the copy what she sent me.

B *pronoun* Whoever.

1967 Fetterman *Stinking Creek* 33 What don't work is drawin'.... They draw welfare checks or commodities or both.

C *conjunction* Used redundantly in phrase *as what*. See also **but B1**.

1863 Gilliland *CW Letters* (June 14) it has relieved mi mind a grate eal to here that your wheat looked well & that you was gitting a long every way as well as what you are. **1864** Poteet *CW Letters* (June 16) I feel very thankfull that it is as well with you as what it is. **1971** *AOHP/ALC-139* There was always work, because I'd have to help in the fields as what I could.

what all *pronoun phrase* All of what, everything.

1 (also *what all that*) What—with redundant *all* to emphasize a wide range of options; see citations.

1862 *Warrick CW Letters* (July 4) I dont [k]now what all to Say at this time. **1863** Wilson *Confederate Private* 2 (Feb 1) you must let mee no what all you want in the way of clothing. **1905** Miles *Spirit of Mts* 106 If the moon knowed what all you-uns hold hit responsible fur hit'd git scared and fall down out o' the sky. **1961** *Coe Ridge OHP-333A* I don't know what all they would do. **1971** *AOHP/ALC-160* We growed the most of what all we was living on on the farm. **1971** *AOHP/ALC-260* I don't know what all that he had there to sell. **1973** *GSMNP-5:8* I can play Oh My Darling, Nelly Gray, and I don't know what all, quite a few. **1978** Montgomery *White Pine Coll* X-2 That's just about what all I've done. **1986** Pederson et al. *LAGS* (Jefferson Co TN) I don't know what all happened to him. **1999** *GSMNPCOHP-1:5* I can remember what all happened, but I can't remember how old I was.

2 Used similarly in a direct interrogative.

c1950 Adams *Grandpap* 225 What all did you do on New Year's Day? **1971** *AOHP/ALC-703* What all was it you had to furnish? **1986** Pederson et al. *LAGS* (Cocke Co TN) What all did they see?

3 Used attributively in a direct interrogative.

1956 *Hall Coll* (Waynesville NC) What all kinds of herbs do you have on your porch? **1973** *AOHP/ASU-111* Well, what all jobs have you worked at during your life?

what all that *conjunctive phrase* What; for similar forms with *that*, see **that C**.

1971 *AOHP/ALC-260* I don't know what all that he had there to sell.

what and all (also *what in all*) *pronoun phrase* All that, everything that. See also **what all, where in all, who and all**.

1948 Chase *Grandfather Tales* 59 She told the old lady about what-'n-all happened. **1959** Roberts *Up Cutshin* 104 [She] started walking down the road to see where it went to and what and all she could see down there. **2004** Adams *Old True Love* 47 I just had to wander over there to see what and all was going on. **2014** *Williams Coll*: *what in all*.

[DARE *what and all* pron 1a chiefly South, South Midland]

whatever that *conjunctive phrase* Whatever; for similar forms with *that*, see **that C** and Grammar and Syntax §15.4.

1985 Williams *Role of Folklore* 299 [He was] pickin' up them aluminum cans and bottles an' whatever that you can get some money out of.

what for

A *adverb phrase* Why, for what purpose, with what object. See also **for why, why for.** [Editor's note: The usage of the two elements of this phrase when separated (as in "what did they do that for?") is widespread in the US.]

1916 Combs *Old Early English* 289 *For* is also used in such expressions as, e.g. "*What fer* did you do that?" **1931** Goodrich *Mt Homespun* 45 While Mrs. Fox had stepped outside on some errand, little Opal said to her sister, "What for did you tell me Paw warn't at home?" **1937** Thornburgh *Great Smoky Mts* 134 I couldn't think what fur he's been talkin' to me about grasshoppers. **c1950** (in **2000** Oakley *Roamin' Man* 84) What fur I don't know but I guess the bear couldnt read. **1979** Slone *My Heart* 35 "Isom," she asked in a very concerned voice, "what fer are ye all dressed up in your Sunday go to meetin' clothes and it be a weekday?"

[OED3 (at *what* 11a) Scot and north dialect; CUD *what for* (at *what* interrog pron); DARE *what for* adv phr 1 chiefly South, South Midland]

B *adjective phrase* What kind of.

1863 *Sexton CW Letters* (Dec 20) write how all of my connection is coming on and what for times there is in Ashe. **1864** *Zimmerman CW Letters* (Oct 10) I should be glad to here from you all and what for cropp you made. **1895** Edson and Fairchild *TN Mts* 375 What fer a country is it? **1927** Woofter *Dialect from WV* 366 = what sort of man is he? "Did you want to know what for man he is?" **1939** Eastridge *Folklore Adair Co* 134 "What for meeting did you have?" = Was it a good church service?; "What for time did you have?" = Did you have a good time? **1952** Wilson *Folk Speech NC* 606 = what kind of. "*What for* man is your new boss." **c1960** *Wilson Coll* What for time did you have at the party?

C *noun phrase* A deserved scolding or whipping.

1979 Melton *'Pon My Honor* 41 When he heard that the 8th Tennessee Infantry was going south following the battle of Perryville, he was bent and determined to join up with what was left of his old friends and neighbors [to] help them give them Yankees some more what-fer. **2009** Benfield *Mt Born* 203 *give someone what for* = this is a strict scolding. You have let a person know, in no uncertain terms, what you think of them and, most likely, all their relatives. A severe scolding has taken place. **2016** *Blind Pig* (March 9) That burned me up! I went right down there and told him what for, and I made sure he understood that it better not ever happen again.... Giving someone what for is like giving them a scolding but in a more fierce manner.

what in all See **what and all.**

what in tarnation See tarnation.

what in the nation See **nation 2.**

whear See **whether.**

wheat *noun* A farmer hired to mine coal only in colder months.

1943 Korson *Coal Dust* 4–5 Farmers and farm-hands also hired themselves out to coal operators as miners during the winter season. Since digging and loading coal was only temporary work for them, they were less likely to be interested in efforts to raise wages and improve working conditions than professional miners. . . . Full-time miners naturally resented them and expressed their distrust by calling them . . . "wheats."

wheat bread *noun* Any bread made from flour, especially biscuits, sometimes without yeast. See also **flour bread, light bread, loaf bread.**

1937 Hall *Coll* (Big Creek NC) Wheat bread on Sundays, corn bread and potatoes during the week. **1957** Combs *Lg Sthn High: Word List* 109 = biscuits. By analogy with *corn-bread*. "Pass the wheat-bread, please." **1990** Fisher *Preacher Stories* 25 In the economy of the mountains, most people ate cornbread at least twice a day. "Wheatbread," as it was sometimes called, was usually reserved for breakfast and many times only for special occasions, especially if it had yeast in it, in which case it was called "light bread."

wheat cradle (also *wheat reap*) *noun* Same as **cradle A.**

1930 Smith *Reminiscences* 7–8 My mother could do any kind of work in the field except to handle a wheat cradle. In the early [eighteen] fifties the cradle had just come into use. I remember having seen men cutting wheat with the sickle. **c1940** Simms *Coll* Sam A. King, from Roaring Fork, came to inquire whether the Museum could use a "wheat-reap"—a hook for reaping wheat. **1997** Nelson *Country Folklore* 146 There were wheat cradles, sickle blades, and mowing blades.

wheat mill *noun* Any mill capable of grinding wheat into flour.

1969 GSMNP-43:4 They had quit growing wheat. He didn't run the wheat mill at all. He just run the corn mill, and then the old man Floyd put this one up over here, and they brought their wheat over here then.

wheat reap See **wheat cradle.**

wheedle-dee (also *wheelspindle, whittle-ding*) *noun* A wood thrush (*Hylocichla mustelina*).

1940 Still *River of Earth* 37 I caught a wheedle-dee throwing his voice once, him setting in one tree, making out he was in another'n, and me looking my eyeballs out trying to see him. **1955** Ritchie *Singing Family* 91 Marthe was singing a high part-like, just sweet and cler as a whittle-ding. **1998** Still *Appal Mother Goose* 14 Wheelspindle, wheelspindle, is this so?

[DARE *wheedle-dee* n KY]

whee-hawed *adverb* See citation.

1927 Woofter *Dialect from WV* 366 = crooked. "That picture hangs all wheehawed."

wheel *noun* See citation.

1972 Cooper *NC Mt Folklore* 89 = a silver dollar.

wheelhorse *noun* One who does the hard work in an operation, a trusted and dependable assistant.

1901 Harben *Westerfelt* 278 God bless 'im, Mitch is a wheel-hoss. **1973** McCarthy *Child of God* 165 One man with a little guts stood up to em and that was Tom Davis. He was a wheelhorse. **1976** Garber *Mountain-ese* 100 Ask Charlie about that, he's the boss' wheel-horse. **1990** Merriman *Moonshine Rendezvous* 67 You know the blond, her brother is my wheel hoss at the still.

[DARE *wheelhorse* n chiefly South Midland, TX]

wheelspindle See **wheedle-dee.**

whelk, whelp See **welt.**

whenever *conjunction* When. See also **evern, everwhen, whenevern.**

1 In reference to a single, nonhypothetical event or action in the past: occurring at the very moment or time when.

1939 Hall *Coll* (Smokemont NC) What did they do with you whenever you killed that man two or three year ago? **1940** Haun *Hawk's Done* 88 Little Murf would be black too whenever he come into the world. **1958** Campbell *Tales* 246 Whenever she came out and aimed to lock up the door, the key turned red hot, and it stayed that-a-way. **1970** *Hillard Green* 139 My momma died whenever I'uz only eighteen months old. **1978** Montgomery *White Pine Coll* IV-2 Whenever she passed away, she had pneumonia. . . . I was just eight whenever she died. **1983** Pyle *CCC 50th Anniv* A:2:9 Whenever we come in, he said, "Boy," he said, "Am I glad to see you fellows." **1989** *Matewan OHP*-33 Whenever she died, she give her the house, and she got a beauty shop in it. **1994** Schmidt and Hooks *Whistle* 145 [At the time the logging operation closed,] they had a ceremony there whenever they brought the last logs into the mill. . . . Everybody that lived around Townsend was there whenever they rolled them logs off of the train. . . . Whenever they sent that log up the chute into the mill there they was grown men that had worked on the lumber yard and around there, that was a-standin' there a-cryin' because they didn't think there was anyplace else to work. **1997** Hufford *American Ginseng* 12 It [= ginseng] accumulated and accumulated, and whenever I got married and left, why the whole back of that hill was ginseng. **1998** Bushyhead *Cherokee Lg* 169 Whenever the community saw [the messenger] coming, a great shout of joy went up as he came into the gate and came into the chief. *Ibid.* 175 Now then whenever [Sequoyah] was accepted, the Cherokee people were very interested [in learning to read Cherokee]. **2007** (in **2012** McQuaid *Interface* 274) Terry got his back hurt whenever he was working at Maymead.

[OED3 *whenever* 2 "at the very time or moment when" now only in Scottish and Irish use; DARE *whenever* conj a South, South Midland, western PA]

2 Used in reference to a single prospective or hypothetical punctual event or action: as soon as, at the earliest moment when.

1836 (in **2007** Davis *Co Line Baptist* 115) Him and his [family] is Dismiss when Ever he Joines any other Baptist Church. **1861** *Martin CW Letters* (Oct 13) [I] want you to go to walhalla & get your salt when ever it gets their. **1864** *Chapman CW Letters* (May 15) I may want to by [the filly] if she suits me and you will sell her when ever I come home. **1955** Ritchie *Singing Family* 194 I know this ain't the last skimmin', I'll finish filling it whenever you skim her for the main last time. **1973** GSMNP-4:1:48 That's Little Cataloochee, and then just across the mountain is Big Catalooch, and then whenever you get to Big Catalooch, it's just across the mountain to Caldwell Fork, and then whenever you get to Caldwell Fork, it's just across the mountain to Hemphill. **1994** Schmidt and Hooks *Whistle* 18 They told him that they'd received the holes and whenever they got the soppers for the holes they'd pay for the lumber. **2001** Montgomery *File* They's a lot of artifacts that needs to be gathered before this lady is gone. Whenever she dies they'll go up for sale (72-year-old woman, Bryson City NC). **2011** *COROH* (Brannon) David's not here, but I'll tell him whenever he gets home.

3 Used in reference to a process or an extended period of time in the past: during or within the time that.

1971 *AOHP/ALC*-33 I'd spin nightly whenever I was a girl. . . . Whenever I was small-like, I don't know how [teachers] got [certification] then. **1973** GSMNP-4:1:39 They were real good religious people, I mean, whenever I'd knowed them. *Ibid.* 50–51 I'd say a good team of mules, whenever I was just a small boy, would bring in five hundred dollars. . . . Maybe one automobile in three months would go through that country whenever I was a boy. **1975–76** Wolfram/Christian *WV Coll* 83 Whenever Earl was a-living, they'd always go somewhere every Saturday, and that dog knowed just as well as humans when Sunday come. **1978** Montgomery *White Pine Coll* IV-2 Whenever I went to school, we was all alike. . . . My mother, whenever she was living, she just told you one time [to do something]. **1984** Page and Wigginton *Foxfire Cookery* 156 Whenever I was growing up we'd go to the field and get just regular old field corn.

[EDD *whenever* conj Scot and Irel "as soon as"; SND *whanever* (at *whan* "as soon as, at the very moment when"; CUD *whenever* conj 3 "as soon as"; Web3 chiefly Scot; DARE *whenever* conj b South, South Midland]

whenevern *conjunction* See also **evern**, **everwhen**, **whenever**.

1 Of a recurring or intermittent event: when, at any point in time that.

1960 McCaulley *Cades Cove* He'd come up there with his book and put all them cattle down, how many they was, how many steers, how many heifers, how many cows, and what the mark was. Well, then whenevern he got that done, why, they'd turn them cattle over to him. **1974–75** McCracken *Logging* 15:7 I'll describe it to you then how a big cove looked like whenevern they got through logging. *Ibid.* 16:36 Whenevern it was snowin', you couldn't get half the logs out of that brush. **1978** Burton *Ballad Folks* 52 I'd say whenevern you sing these new songs, the words is good, but the tune ain't no 'count. **1983** Pyle *CCC 50th Anniv* A:2:19 There were three in the saw crew whenevern you cut trees.

[DARE *whenevern* conj 1 South Midland]

2 Of a single event: as soon as.

1974–75 McCracken *Logging* 15:16 Whenevern we got married, we went on back to Marks Cove. **1983** Pyle *CCC 50th Anniv* A:2:11 I jumped up and run plumb out of the shack and way down in the field with that hose up my britches leg, and whenevern I seen what it was, why I went back to the shack.

3 Of a process or duration of time in the past: through or during the period that.

1991 Thomas *Sthn Appal* 204 When-ever'n I was a right young man . . . they'ud have some of the awfulest times.

[perhaps *whenever* + *-en* by analogy with *iffen*; DARE *whenevern* conj 2 South Midland]

whenever that *conjunctive phrase* Whenever; for similar forms with *that*, see **that C** and Grammar and Syntax §15.4.

1971 *AOHP/ALC*-137 Whenever that any of us would get sick that way of a cold, why she would always make a tea of old field pennyrile and catnip together and mullein.

whensomever *conjunction* Whenever.

1938 Bowman *High Horizons* 41 "Whensomever a dead body don't git stiff right off, there's goin' to be 'nother death in the family," my granny said, an' she orter knowed fur she washed and laid out nigh onto ever woman corpse in these here hills fur forty year or more. **1997** Montgomery *Coll* (known to Bush, Cardwell, Norris, Oliver, Weaver).

[OED3 *whensomever* adv/conj now dialect or vulgar; Web3 alteration of *whensoever*, influenced by *whatsomever*, chiefly dialect; DARE *whensomever* conj especially South, South Midland]

whenst *conjunction* When, while.

1895 Murfree *Phantoms* 259 That thar fiddle 'minds me o' how unexpected 'twar whenst I met up with Lee-yander hyar. **1957** Combs *Lg Sthn High: Word List* 109 = when, while, whilst.

when that *conjunctive phrase* When; for similar forms with *that*, see **that C** and Grammar and Syntax §15.4.

1957 Combs *Lg Sthn High: Word List* 109 = when. Especially common in Primitive Baptist sermons. Use of the redundant conjunction, that, is common in the metrical romances, and antedates Chaucer's famous first line in the Canterbury Tales: "When that Aprile," etc. In the romances one may also note: yif that, what that, etc. In the Paston Letters (1477): "Yf that ye cowde be content," etc. And a line in Julius Caesar will be recalled: "When that the poor have cried, Caesar hath wept." **1978** Montgomery

White Pine Coll X-2 I don't remember exactly when that they started building in White Pine. **2007** McMillon *Notes* I don't know when 'at they come back. **2014** *Blind Pig* (Jan 10) Do you know when that they are going to start moving over to the new store?

where

A Variant forms *ware* [see **1919** in **B**], *whar, whare, whirr, whor, whur*. See also **whether**.

1834 (in **1956** Eliason *Tarheel Talk* 320) (Burke Co NC) *whar*. **1863** Wilson *Confederate Private* 4 (Feb 7) you must let me no when you hurd from B huddle and whor he is. **1895** *Mt Baptist Sermon* 15 They found me in the mornin' an' come to whar I war by them ahearin' me asingin'. **1913** Kephart *Our Sthn High* 201 Stranger—meanin' no harm—*whar* are ye gwine? **1937** Thornburgh *Great Smoky Mts* 133 I left whar I was and went up whar the men wuz. **1942** Hall *Phonetics Smoky Mts* 24 *whare* [hwær]. **1969** Dial *Dialect Appal People* 486 You can hear many characteristic Scottish pronunciations. *Whar, thar, dar* (*where, there,* and *dare*) are typical. **c1975** Whitehead *E TN Accent*: *whirr* = at what place. "Let me know whirr you're at." **1991** Thomas *Sthn Appal* 5 [Daniel Boone] made it through here an' down here on th' head of Boone Creek whur he killed that bear. *Ibid.* 71 They wuz a turkey got to roostin' in a big pine right close to whor we lived, there.

[DARE *where* adv, conj, pron A 1, 2 chiefly South, South Midland]

B *relative pronoun* Who, that. [Editor's note: This usage does not occur in ATASC.]

1917 (in **1944** Wentworth *ADD* 703, eastern WV). **1919** Combs *Word-List South* 19 *ware, where* = who, whom, as relatives: "The man where I saw is gone." **1930** Armstrong *This Day and Time* 31 I hain't got no stomick to eat victuals where's been fingered over. *Ibid.* 102 Hit 'ull take all her pap kin rake an' scrape to git Wash outen the trouble where's on him. **1937** (in **2009** Powell *Shenandoah Letters* 101) It is so hard on my husband an my son too where works on the Ditch work at skyland. *Ibid.* 102 I thought [that] the Relief would help to keep people going at got sick and needed help where has bin working on it for Sevral years. **1941** (in **1944** Wentworth *ADD* 703, Berkeley Co WV) "The book where I bought . . ." = the book that I bought.

[DARE *where* pron B southern Appalachians]

where all *phrase* All the places (that). See also **where in all**. For other forms with *all*, see Grammar and Syntax §2.7.2.

1973 GSMNP-90:23 I don't know where all he sold it at, but Papa used to always keep honey and sell to the people that come.

[DARE *where-all* adv scattered, but more frequent South, South Midland]

where in all *pronoun phrase* To what places—used as an interrogative. For other forms with *all*, see Grammar and Syntax §2.7.2.

2014 Williams *Coll* Where 'n all did you go?

where that *conjunctive phrase* Where; for similar forms with *that*, see **that C** and Grammar and Syntax §15.4.

1967 *Grandmother Cherokee* 78 He told me right where that th'Indians took up camp when they was drivin'em out'a here. **1978** Montgomery *White Pine Coll* III-2 That's where that I went to school. **1979** *Big South Fork OHP*-27 Dirt Rock House is on a little further from where that the church house was. **1984** GSMNP-153:45 He brought him out, down to where that they could get him in a car. **1989** *Matewan OHP*-102 [Looters] tried to steal, you know, would try to go in houses where that they was anything left. **1998** *Dante OHP*-12 This lumber was loaded pretty close to where that hit was sawed. . . . [In] this home they had a big extra room, and that's where that I went to school.

where the wool was short *noun phrase* An awkward situation.

1987 Young *Lost Cove* 118 The older sons now realized that matters were getting where the wool was short and forgot all about the picture as they placed their pappy back in his coffin.

whet *noun* A while, period of time or work.

1859 Taliaferro *Fisher's River* 84 I piked fur home with my pigeons, and we made uvry pan and pot stink with 'um fur one whet. **1915** Dingus *Word-List VA* 192 = a turn or "spell" of work. **1940** Haun *Hawk's Done* 34 I set there till it was a right smart whet after dark and I heard Ad snoring out on the back porch. **1956** McAtee *Some Dial NC* 50 = a considerable period of time: "She's staying away quite a whet."

[DARE *whet* n South, South Midland]

whet a banter *verb phrase* See citation. See also **banter B.**

1927 Woofter *Dialect from WV* 366 = to challenge for a contest in mowing by the manner of whetting the scythe. "John whet a banter just then."

whether *conjunction* Variant forms *wheare, where, whur, whurr, whuther*.

1862 *Love CW Letters* (Sept 10) I dont now wheare you got it [= a letter] or not. **1930** Armstrong *This Day and Time* 5 I don't know whurr he's dead or alive. **c1950** Adams *Grandpap* 28 He couldn't think where he'd rather have her with him or not. **c1960** Wilson *Coll*: *whether* is often [*whur*]. **1972** *AOHP/LJC*-104 I don't know where it's the blue-back or not. **1974** Fink *Bits Mt Speech* 29 I don't know *whur* to go or not. **1991** Thomas *Sthn Appal* 14 She never did know whuther they ever got into th' war, or whuther somebody killed 'um first. **2003** Carter *Mt Home* 33 Ila Mae ask[ed] the kindly doctor that helped it be born where it was a boy or a girl.

[DARE *whether* conj 2 South, South Midland]

whether that *conjunctive phrase* Whether; for similar forms with *that*, see **that C** and Grammar and Syntax §15.4.

1862 *Warrick CW Letters* (Aug 31) you mus write me word what you have done, and where you have moved to and also state whether the Conscripts have got Ab. Wideman or not, and whether R. Thornton has gone to his company or not, and also state whether or not that Father got Henry's cloths.

whetrock *noun* A whetstone, usually smaller than a **grinding rock**. See c1975 citation.

1913 Kephart *Our Sthn High* 297 A mountaineer . . . sharpens tools on a grindin'-rock or whet-rock. **1915** Dingus *Word-List VA* 192 = whetstone. **1934–47** *LAMSAS Appal* (Madison Co NC, Swain Co NC). **c1975** Lunsford *It Used to Be* 16 They had a long whetrock about a foot long, and they'd stand the scythe and cradle on the tip of the sneed, put the arm over the cradle and it would rest on the blade. They would whet it by a motion—rub the whetrock down on one side and then on the other side. Of course, it made a ringing sound and when four would be whetted at the same time, it would sound rather unusual to me. **1994–97** Montgomery *Coll* (known to nine consultants from the Smoky Mountains), = smaller than a grindstone, which is larger and rounder (Ledford).

[Web3 South; DARE (at *rock* n[1] 4b) chiefly South, South Midland]

which

A *relative pronoun* In a nonrestrictive clause with a human antecedent. For other relative pronouns, see Grammar and Syntax §2.9.

1969 *GSMNP-25:2:20* His other son Giles, which was a-working at it that time, got caught in the mill somehow or another and cut his leg off. **1975** *Shenandoah OHC* 121 He worked for Mister Pollock for years, and he had two sons, which is Cecil Taylor, that lives in Sperryville . . . and Bernie Taylor.

[DARE *which* pron 1 South, South Midland]

B *conjunction* See also **and which, that C2.**

1 Followed by an anaphoric pronoun (as **1982** citation), anaphoric adverb (as **1961** citation), or parallel form (as **1998** citation).

1859 Taliaferro *Fisher's River* 76 I nuver tuck time to ondress him, which his skin would have been wuth a right smart uv ammernition. **1924** Bacheller *Happiest Person* 7 A'ter a while my sister broke down an' I tuk her five little uns 'gin she got better, which she never done. **1928** (in **1952** Mathes *Tall Tales* 72) He was brung up on the ol'-time hawg rifle, which it took a coon's age to load the blame thing, an' he jest had to git his b'ar the fust shot. **1957** Combs *Lg Sthn High: Syntax* 9 Which is smetimes redundant, or used without construction: "Which I hope that he'll do this." **1960** Miller *Pigeon's Roost* (Sept 22) One farmer said that he noticed it to be a certain sign that if it rained on the 8th day of June which he said it rained on that day this year, that there would be no grapes that year. **1961** Williams *Content Mt Speech* 16 They's not a cow brute on his place, which he's got a good little piece of crappin' land there. **1965** Miller *Pigeon's Roost* (March 25) McCoury has kept a daily record of the weather for the last four years at his place which he has named "Dog Flat Hollow," but he has no one to take up where he left off while he is away which he expects to be in the hospital for a week. *Ibid.* (Aug 26) They was especially interested in the old timey key-winding wall clocks which they seen the kind the writer owns. **1979** *Big South Fork OHP-10* In the smoke boxes [on the train engine] we had a screen, a netting up there, which the smoke and everything comes through there before it comes out the stack. **1982** Ginns *Snowbird Gravy* 26 They'd save the [coffee] grounds. . . . Then they'd go back and make it again. Which it got very weak toward the last of it. **1984** *GSMNP-154* He went by a man's house, which I'll not call his name, and picked up a little bottle of whiskey. **1989** *Matewan OHP-56* We'd go to [the] Protestant church, which the Catholics wasn't supposed to do that then. *Ibid.* 56 The ninth [grade] was in the high school building, which it was just kindly down below it. **1994** Montgomery *Coll* (known to Cardwell). **1998** *Dante OHP-71* Doctor Davis was up in the hollow at his house in the head of the hollow delivering their baby, which Cotton had a little girl and his wife was named Maggie. **2004** Fisher *Kettle Bottom* 33 Roger Coyle raises his hand, which, he don't never say nothing. **2008** *Rosie Hicks* Sometimes she might use just applesauce, you know, to put on it, which that was good too.

[DARE *which* conj chiefly South, South Midland]

2 Followed by no anaphoric, parallel form. See also **and which.**

1859 Taliaferro *Fisher's River* 92 [I] got on a log where I could see a leetle, which the laurel and ivy was monstrous thick. **1862** *Patton CW Letters* (Dec 15) I received a letter from you dated 6th and one from Jane dated the 28th which I was glad to heare from you. **1863** *Kendrick CW Letters* (June 4) I receivd your kind letr to day which I was glad to hur from you all. **1976** Wolfram and Christian *Appal Speech* 121 I remember the doctor comin' and deliverin' the baby, which we were in the other room. **1989** *Matewan OHP-23* They loaded him up and hauled him back in a wagon, which they didn't have any cars or trucks. *Ibid.* 56 I'd generally come to Bert Shannon's or the grocery stores here in Matewan, which Bert was the one that I always remember. **1997** *Dante OHP-53* They all started with Laborn and they spread out, which Robert J. was my great-grandfather. **2008** *Rosie Hicks* 1 [We] thought there was no oranges until, you know, Christmas time, and maybe bananas too, which I don't guess we didn't get many bananas.

C *interrogative pronoun* See citations.

1915 Bradley *Hobnobbing* 100 You ask a Kentucky mountaineer a question he does not quite grasp, and he says "How?" A Tennessean, in like case, exclaims "Which?" **1921** Weeks *Speech of KY Mtneer* 17 In the Alleghany mountains we bluntly say "What?" when we fail to understand; in the Cumberlands, we never, but we politely ask "Which?"

[DARE *which* pron 2 South, South Midland]

whichaway *adverb* (In) which direction or manner. See also **a**[3], **any which way, every which away.**

1948 Chase *Grandfather Tales* 20 She took out and ran around the house till she saw which-a-way the girl's tracks went. **1956** McAtee *Some Dial NC* 50 *whichaway* = in what manner or direction. "I don't know whichaway would be best." **1977** *Jake Waldroop* 159 Lawrence, do you have any idea which a way you went?

[DARE *whichaway(s)* adv scattered, but more frequent South, Midland, TX, North Central]

which from the other (also *which from t'other*) *pronoun phrase* One from another.

1915 Dingus *Word-List VA* 192 *which from t'other* = [used] with *tell, know*, etc., in comparing things: "Them twins so much alike, you can't tell which from t'other." **1997** Montgomery *Coll*: *which from the other* (known to Bush, Jones, Norris, Oliver, Weaver); These twins look so much alike that I can't tell which from the other (Cardwell).

which from t'other See **which from the other.**

which nor whether *noun phrase* Anything at all.

1931 Combs *Lg Sthn High* 1305 She hain't a-carin' which ner whuther about it.

which'n See **which'un.**

which'un (also *which'n*) *pronoun* Which one.

1929 Duncan and Duncan *Sayings* 235 Which'un (parent) a first child favors, ull die fust. **1984** Burns *Cold Sassy* 28 "We never knowed which'n he meant," Granny said . . . I knew which'n. It was Granny. **2005** Williams *Gratitude* 148 We'd put 'em [= eggs] in some water to figger out whichuns was rurnt.

whicker (also *whimper*) *verb*

1 Of a horse: to whinny; hence participial adjective *whickering*. See also **nicker.**

1859 Taliaferro *Fisher's River* 83 The way he whickered were a fact, when I spoke to him. **1934–47** *LAMSAS Appal* (Madison Co NC); *whicker, whimper*. **1941** Hall *Coll* (White Oak NC) Nicker, whimper—these are the common expressions around the White Oak. Some say neigh. **1949** Kurath *Word Geog East US* 42 *Whicker* is the usual expression along the coast from southern Delaware to Georgia and in the greater part of the Carolina Piedmont. **1995** Adams *Come Go Home* 28 Kate pulled her head back in the stall, and Pete made his peculiar whickering sound. **1998** Montgomery *Coll*: *whicker* (known to Jones, Oliver); *whimper* (known to Oliver). **2007** McMillon *Notes*: *whicker* = to whinny.

[imitative; OED3 *whicker* v 2 dialect and U.S.; EDD *whicker* v 1 sEngl; DARE *whicker* n[1], v chiefly Southeast, Mid Atlantic]

2 See citation.

1940 Bowman *KY Mt Stories* 249 = [to] cheat.

whilest (also *whils*) *conjunction* While.

1895 Dromgoole *Humble Advocate* 328 She jest doctored herse'f on corn whiskey whiles't she ware waitin' on the rattlesnake's-master. **1967** Williams *Subtlety Mt Speech* 14 Don't ye be a-openin' that thar poke whilest I'm gone. **2007** Preece *Leavin' Sandlick* 37 My Ma and Pa was on assistance, and whils I was growing up.

whimmy-diddle *noun* A nameless contraption or imaginary object. See also **gee-haw whimmy-diddle 1.**

1941 (in **1944** Wentworth *ADD* 705) (eWV) = thingemajig. **1968** *DARE Survey* (Wytheville VA) = [an implement] used to grind smoke.

[DARE *whimmy-diddle* n chiefly southern Appalachians]

whimper See **whicker 1.**

whimpus *noun* See citation.

1910 Cox *Fearsome Creatures* 33 (DARE) According to woodsmen who have been "looking" timber in eastern Tennessee, the whimpus . . . has a gorilla-shaped head and body and enormous front feet. Its unique method of obtaining food is to station itself upon a trail, where it stands on its diminutive hind legs and whirls. The speed is increased until the animal is invisible. Any creature coming along the trail . . . is almost certain to walk into the danger zone and become instantly deposited in the form of syrup or varnish upon the huge paws of the whimpus.

whindle (also *whinnel, whinnle*) *verb* To whine, whimper.

1886 Smith *Southernisms* 45 To whindle or whinnel, "to cry peevishly, to whimper" (used of a child) is very common in East Tennessee. **1917** Kephart *Word-List* 419 = to whine. "I never did cry but wunst; I *whinnled* a little endurin' the war." **1949** Arnow *Hunter's Horn* 63 The talk and laughter and whindling of the babies was like a blanket between her and her troubles. **1957** Neel *Backwoodsman* 48 *whindle* = to whine or fret (said of children). **1995–97** Montgomery *Coll*: *whindle* (known to Adams, Brown), = to half cry, as "Don't come whinnling around me" (Norris).

[DARE *whindle* v South, South Midland]

whinnel, whinnle See **whindle.**

whinny owl *noun* See citation.

1949 McDavid *Grist* 114 (Rabun Co GA) = screech owl ("lives in pines").

whip See also **whip off.**

A *verb, noun* Variant forms *hwup, whoop, whop* [see **1941** in **B1**], *whope* [see **1913** in **B1**], *whup*.

1862 *Lockmiller CW Letters* (Sept 25) our fokes ar whopen thern ever whars and i hope that pas [i.e. peace] will be mad so that you all can git home one time more. **1890** Fruit *KY Words* 69 = often pronounced *hwup*. **1915** Dingus *Word-List VA* 192 *whup*. **1942** Hall *Phonetics Smoky Mts* 17 [hwʊp]. **1961** *Coe Ridge OHP-335B* Grandpa'd say, "I'm going to whoop her if she goes." **1971** *AOHP/ALC-107* I'd get just as much as one whooping per year. That's about all the whoopings I'd get, much as one whooping per year. **1983** *Dark Corner OHP-26A* They knew it was the man that come back to whoop him about his boys, but they never could, you know, just confirm it. **1999** McNeil *Purchase Knob* 36 They didn't always understand his vocabulary and that "whupped" meant "whipped" and "fur piece" a goodly distance.

[DARE *whoop, whup* (at *whip* v, n A1 (pronc)) chiefly South, South Midland]

B Senses.

1 To thrash, beat (up), defeat (an adversary), drive, exhaust; hence participial adjective *whipped* = worn out, verbal nouns *whipping, whooping* = a thrashing, beating.

1861 *Patton CW Letters* (Sept 14) the yankees have not landed any place yet close about here nor we do not intend for them to come about without a whiping. **1864** Wilson *Confederate Private* 74 (Nov 29) our sharp shuters whuped them back & kild several yanks & a good meny horses. **c1900** (in **1997** Stoddart *Quare Women* 88) Many sad stories we heard, how the father drank and "whooped" the mother or of some member of the family who was in the penitentiary or had been murdered. **1913** Kephart *Our Sthn High* 91 She made off on her legs like the devil whoppin' out fire. *Ibid.* 284 Whope is sometimes used in the present tense, but whup is more common. **1939** Hall *Coll* (Nine Mile TN) I looked up the tree. I allowed [the mother bear] might have had some cubs there and whooped them up a tree. **1941** Stuart *Men of Mts* 99 They might kill 'im but they won't whop 'im. **1966** *DARE Survey* (Cherokee NC) *whipped* = very tired. **1972** *AOHP/ALC-298* He didn't whup me much for fighting. **1974** *AOHP/ALC-728* He give me a good whooping for it. **1979** *Big South Fork OHP-11* He just grabbed up a big whip and went to whooping the both of us. **1985** Irwin *Alex Stewart* 56 I jerked loose and whupped all three of them. **1989** *Matewan OHP-39* I heard him say, "I'll whip that fellow in the morning," and sure enough, he did. He broke his nose all to pieces. **2005** Bailey *Henderson County* 32 "I jist got me a hick'ry out o' that apple tree yonder an' I whopped her," the woman said, using the familiar local connotation of the word "hick'ry."

2 To win.

1941 Still *Troublesome Creek* 20 We'll larn which roosters whooped. *Ibid.* 104 Allus ago we fit, and nary a one could whoop.

3 In phrase *whip down* = to fatigue, exhaust.

1935 Sheppard *Cabins in Laurel* 90 I was young and rested directly, but Ma would be whipped down. *Ibid.* 284 She panted as she climbed the steep steps to the porch and admitted that she was "fair whipped down." **1984** Wilder *You All Spoken* 206 *whipped down* = debilitated.

4 In phrase *whip out*.

a (also *whup out*) To defeat (one's intention), outdo (another), punish; to fatigue; hence participial adjective *whipped out* = fatigued, defeated, punished.

1861 *Carden CW Letter* (Oct 6) Jackson has whiped them out on cheat mountain. **1862** *Haggard CW Letters* (Feb) you ought to see the toryes throw down their guns and run we whiped them out and taken all they had. **1863** *Hundley CW Letters* (June 16) We Whooped the yankes out & takin Winchester & We gaind a great victory hear. **1923** Furman *Mothering* 117 This morning at recess I seed him whup out five-at-a-time. Yes, sir, five was on him, and by Ned if he didn't lay out the last one. **1927** Shearin *Speech of Fathers* 7 We argued a long time but he finally whupped me out. **1956** Hall *Coll* (Big Bend NC) [The hog] whupped their dogs out. **1960** Burnett *My Valley* 24 If a bear whips out one pack of say eight to 12, a fresh pack of equal number is ready to take up the conflict with the already tired animal. **1973** *Ethel Corn* 262 I have backslid, but God'll whup ye out when you do. **1975** Chalmers *Better* 66 One who is discouraged is clean out of heart, his nerves may be all tore up, or he is merely tired and whupped out. **1990** Cavender *Folk Medical Lex* 34 *whipped out* = tired, fatigued. **1994** Montgomery *Coll* (known to Cardwell, Ogle).

[DARE (at *whip* v B2) chiefly South, South Midland]

b See citation.

1931 Combs *Lg Sthn High* 1306 Well, I'm fexatially (or fexatiously) whipped out. (That is, completely surprised, or astonished.)

whip-crack *noun* A children's game. See citation.

2006 Shearer *Wilder Days* 161 [We] played whip-crack. All line up and hold hands and sling 'em around.

[DARE (at *whip-cracker* 1) chiefly South Midland]

whip down See **whip B3**.

whip off *verb phrase*

1 To rush off.

1939 Hall *Coll* (Nine Mile TN) One of the old dogs seen me and whupped off under the hill and went to hollerin'.

2 To drive (dogs) off.

1894 Wingfield *Big Buck* 400 I am satisfied that he [= a buck deer] had whipped the dogs off when they came to me in the woods and led the way back to the deer.

whip out See **whip B4**.

whippoorwill pea *noun* A pea speckled like a whippoorwill's egg.

1941 Justus *Kettle Creek* 98 The dried corn, the shucky beans, the whippoorwill peas, which took longer to cook, had all been put in a good while before. **1997** Montgomery *Coll* = a clay pea, farmers grew fields of them as a money crop in the fall (Adams).

[DARE *whippoorwill pea* n chiefly South, South Midland]

whippoorwill squall See **whippoorwill winter**.

whippoorwill's shoes *noun* An orchid (*Cypripedium* spp). See also **lady('s) slipper**.

1951 Barnwell *Our Mt Speech* The dainty, little lady's slipper is "whippoorwill's shoes."

whippoorwill storm See **whippoorwill winter**.

whippoorwill winter (also *whippoorwill squall*, *whippoorwill storm*) *noun* A frost or cold spell in spring about the time whippoorwills are first heard. For terms describing a similar phenomenon, see **blackberry winter**.

c1960 Wilson *Coll*: *whippoorwill squall* (or *whippoorwill storm*) = one of the early spring cold spells. **1962** Dykeman *Tall Woman* 14 After the cold spell, when dogwoods bloomed, there would be whippoorwill winter and blackberry winter. **1995** Montgomery *Coll*: *whippoorwill winter* (known to Cardwell).

[DARE *whippoorwill winter* n South, South Midland]

whipstitch *noun* A moment, brief interval of time. [Editor's note: This term with the meaning of a broad stitch to hem a garment is widespread in the US.]

1999 Montgomery *Coll* I'll be there in a whipstitch (Cardwell).

[DARE *whipstitch* n 1 scattered, but chiefly South, South Midland]

whip the devil around the stump *verb phrase*

1 See citations.

1967 *DARE Survey* (Gatlinburg TN) = to avoid giving a definite answer. **1982** Slone *How We Talked* 23 Don't whip the devil around the stump = to pretend to be honest about something, while all the time you are not, or to use one excuse for doing something, yet you really have another cause for doing it.

[DARE (at *devil* n B2) now chiefly South, South Midland]

2 See citation.

c1960 Wilson *Coll* = to overcome someone by using his own tricks.

[DARE (at *devil* n B2) now chiefly South, South Midland]

whip up *verb phrase* To repair (a hole in a garment) quickly.

1968 *DARE Survey* (Brasstown NC) = to sew or repair in a hurry. **1997** Montgomery *Coll* Give me that skirt and I'll whip up the hole (Norris).

whirligust See **whirlygust**.

whirlygust (also *whirligust*) *noun* A whirlwind.

1859 Taliaferro *Fisher's River* 138 Away went the bar like a whirlygust uv woodpeckers were arter it. **1864** Gilmore *Down in TN* 87 When ye gits thar, pike off like lightnin' chasin' a whirlygust (hurricane). **1970** Clark *NC Beliefs* 55 When whirligusts, called devil dancers and little whirlwinds, are seen along roads, it is a sure sign of rain.

[DARE *whirlygust* n especially NC, TN]

whirr See **where**.

whiskey scrape *noun* A fight involving one or more intoxicated participants. Same as **licker scrape**. See also **scrape A**.

1901 Harben *Westerfelt* 219 You know he swore pa out of a big whiskey scrape in Atlanta, and since then pa and him has been mighty thick.

whiskey still *noun* Same as **still B**.

1949 Maurer *Argot of Moonshiner* 13 = the smaller still in contrast to the beer still, in which spirits are redistilled to get whisky: "This little pot is big enough for a whisky still."

whiskey tree *noun* See citation.

1991 Still *Wolfpen Notebooks* 86 We call these hard maples either "whiskey trees" or "sugar trees," depending on what you need them for. Sugar trees if you're up to boiling down the sap for sweetening. Whiskey trees to make charcoal to use at the still.

whiskey tripping See **tripping**.

whistle hog See **whistle pig**.

whistle pig (also *whistle hog*) *noun* A woodchuck (*Marmota monax*), so called from its shrill whistle when excited or frightened. Same as **groundhog A1**. See 1971 citation.

1917 Kephart *Word-List* 419. **1937** Thornburgh *Great Smoky Mts* 36–37 Woodchucks . . . are also called groundhogs, and locally whistle-pigs. **1940** Oakley *Roamin'/Restin'* 147 City people calls a ground hog a woodchuck but mountain people calls them whistle pigs or ground hogs. **1961** Seeman *Arms of Mt* 159 Ground hogs are called "whistle pigs" because of the shrill, burbling whistle they give when excited or alarmed. **1971** Linzey and Linzey *Mammals of Smoky* 23 Locally, the Wood-chuck is known as the "whistle-pig," because of the piercing whistle it occasionally emits before disappearing into its burrow. **1982** Powers and Hannah *Cataloochee* 472 The groundhog, known locally as a "whistlepig," was eaten as a delicacy, particularly the very young fat ones, though one had to make sure that the proper underforeleg glands were removed before eating. **1997** Andrews *Mountain Vittles* 82 Some folks called the little varmints whistle pigs a'cause of the noise they make. **1997** Montgomery *Coll*: *whistle hog* (known to Bush, Cardwell).

[DARE *whistle pig* n 1 chiefly Appalachians]

whistle punk *noun* In logging, a man or boy who sends signals between members of a yarding crew.

1964 Clarkson *Lumbering in WV* 374 = the man who rings signals for a steam skidding crew. This was originally done with a whistle[,] later with a bell. **1975** GSMNP-56:21 They sometimes called [choker bosses] "whistle punks" [or] "bell boys."

White Cap

A *noun* A member of a self-appointed, lawless group of men in Sevier Co TN who in the 1890s attempted to enforce local public order and morality by intimidating or punishing alleged offenders; also *White Caps*, the group itself. Sworn to secrecy and active at night, they were so called from their white hoods. Their violent excesses led to formation of the officially sanctioned **Blue Bills** to counter and eradicate them. [Editor's note: This group had no affiliation or relation to the Ku Klux Klan, nor did it apparently target members of any minority or ethnic group.]

1899 Crozier *White-Caps* 7 A few good citizens of Sevier county, desirous of ridding the county of a certain lawless element, and disgruntled at the dilatoriness of legal methods, determined to take the law into their own hands, and by summary punishment eradicate the crime or exterminate the criminal. This desire led to the formation of the order called "White-caps." The object of this organization made it popular with some of the better element, who aided and abetted the movement. But, lawless in its inception, it was soon dominated by the lawless element against which it was formed. The good citizens, instead of restoring law and order, became the servants and tools of disorder and mob violence. After two years of white-capism, another organization was formed to "down" the "White-caps," called "Blue Bills." **1937** Hall *Coll* (Copeland Creek TN) The White Caps got to doin' all sorts of meanness. **1939** Hall *Coll* (Copeland Creek TN) They was scared to death about the White Caps, so they got in under the floor in the cellar, and they stayed there . . . I never did say anything about this at all till after the White Caps was done put out. The Blue Bills cut them out. *Ibid.* (Mt Sterling NC) He received a note from the White Caps, but he paid it no attention. *Ibid.* (Waldens Creek TN) That was desperate times. They never did bother me, [but] the White Caps was the cause of a man and woman bein' hung. I heard the trial and saw them hung. [It was in] ninety-five or ninety-six. The White Caps come here of a night, beat them up, beat people with buggy whips. [The trouble] must have lasted a year. **1985** *Sevier Settler* 4:16 There were from six hundred to fifteen hundred White-Caps in Sevier County, but there were only approximately two hundred Blue Bills. **1989** Trent *Sequel to Lore* 77 In 1892, there was formed a secret organization of church members known as the "White Caps." Their intended purpose was to rid the community of prostitution, gamblers, and bootleggers by placing a bundle of switches at their door. The organization was soon infiltrated by hoodlums and criminals who terrorized [Sevier County TN] with a series of beatings, murders, and robberies, until a special act of the Tennessee Legislature and the appointment of a fearless judge and prosecutor from adjoining Knox County. The ring was broken up in 1896.

B *verb phrase* Of such a group: to engage in organized, often violent vigilante activities (intimidation, tarring and feathering, etc.) against purported offenders, such as prostitutes and moonshiners; hence verbal noun *White-Capping*.

1899 Crozier *White-Caps* 85 White-capping in Sevier county first began in Emert's Cove, but ceased as abruptly as it began. **1976** *Sevier Co Saga* 19 Certain communities around [Sevier County] had become infested with lewd characters. After repeated but unsuccessful efforts by legal forces to punish these evil-doers in the courts, the citizens became disheartened and began considering other methods of getting rid of the immoral characters. This was the beginning of "white capping." While these citizens realized they would be violating the law, they considered it necessary to right an existing evil. **1984–85** *Sevier Settler* 3:15 By the time Sheriff Maples' second term of office expired in 1898, white-capping in Sevier County was a thing of the past and many other members of the organization who were found guilty of related crimes had been tried and found guilty.

White-Capping See **White Cap B**.

white corn (also *white corn liquor*) *noun* Homemade whiskey.

1961 Murry *Salt* 112 It was a quart bottle of white corn, which he hospitably extended to us! **2013** Pierce *Corn in Jar* 5 No other product is more iconic and more associated with traditional life in the Great Smoky Mountains than illegally distilled, un-aged, white corn liquor.

white damp *noun* See citations.

c1975 *Miners' Jargon* 8 = carbon monoxide gas underground [in a coal mine]. **2007** *Mining Terms* = carbon monoxide, CO. A gas that may be present in the afterdamp of a gas- or coal-dust explosion, or in the gases given off by a mine fire; also one of the constituents of the gases produced by blasting. Rarely found in mines under other circumstances. It is absorbed by the hemoglobin of the blood to the exclusion of oxygen. One-tenth of 1% (.001) may be fatal in 10 minutes.

white dog *noun* Homemade whiskey.

2013 Pierce *Corn in Jar* 5 White lightning, corn squeezin's, mountain dew, white mule, splo', white dog! Whatever you call it, no other product is more iconic and more associated with traditional life in the Great Smoky Mountains than illegally distilled, un-aged, white corn liquor.

white-eye

A *verb* To falter or fail, quit working before finishing because of heat prostration or exhaustion; to quit (on one); hence participial adjective *white-eyed* = exhausted.

1911 Shearin *E KY Word-List* 540 = to desert, abandon: e.g., "He white-eyed on us." **1928** (in **1952** Mathes *Tall Tales* 76) Ye ain't no dawg o' mine if ye go an' white-eye on me now! **1936** Neitzel *TN Expressions* 373 = to be overcome, usually by heat, as "I nearly *white-eyed*, digging in that ditch." **1952** Matthias *Wordcatcher* 24 What are you studyin' to do—white-eye on me? **1957** Neel *Backwoodsman* 48 = to give up before a task is finished, either from exhaustion or lack of courage. **1966** Medford *Ol' Starlin* 66 To "peter out" or "white-eye" means to fail, fall out or quit. **1974** Roberts *Sang Branch* 14 You talk about white-eyeing on the job—I come in a pea of doing it on my first job in the mines. **1992** Brooks *Sthn Stuff* 174 = to be overcome from heat prostration or some other condition, until one is near fainting, causing one's eyes to roll back. **1994–96** Montgomery *Coll* = to overwork, till one almost falls (Adams), = to give up, give out, lose strength, "I worked till I was white eyed" (Cardwell). **1998** Brewer *Don't Scrouge* "White-eyed" is one [word that's not heard much anymore]. I believe it began as a description of one who became faint from fieldwork in the sun and gets pale around the eyes and mouth.

[DARE *white-eye* v 1 chiefly southern Appalachians, especially eastern KY; *white-eyed* adj 1 chiefly southern Appalachians]

B *noun* See 1990 citation. Same as **wide-eye 2**.

1990 Cavender *Folk Medical Lex* 34 = severe exhaustion. **1994–97** Montgomery *Coll* (known to Brown, Cardwell, Ogle).

white-eyed See **white-eye A**.

white gravy (also *white sop*) *noun* Chicken or other light-colored gravy made with unbrowned flour. See also **sop A**.

1960 Hall *Smoky Mt Folks* 60 *white sop*. **1986** Pederson et al. *LAGS* (Johnson Co TN) *white sop* = gravy made of white meat. **1997** Montgomery *Coll*: *white sop* = a thin white sauce served over boiled potatoes (Ellis). **2006** *Encycl Appalachia* 934 The majority of the common gravies are starch-bound, using either flour or cornmeal as a thickener. Most are also "white" as opposed to "brown" gravies, using milk instead of meat broth or stock as their liquid component.

white hat *noun* A member of a private security force organized to police a convention of the United Mine Workers of America.

1975 Woolley *We Be Here* 61 The "White Hats," as the enforcers were named because of the white miner's hat they wore.

white Indian *noun* See citations.

1939 Hall *Coll* (Smokemont NC) = a person with at least one-sixteenth Indian blood who lives in the Qualla Reservation, on Tow String Creek. **1943** Gilbert *Eastern Cherokees* 210 Some 12 families out of the 50 families at Big Cove are "white Indians," or persons showing no perceptible Indian characteristics either in physique or culture. Some white families have even been admitted into the tribe by the act of adopting a Cherokee child, others by the marriage of a relative to an Indian man or woman. The "white Indians" tend to take up all of the best land. The purebloods retain small holdings of steep hillside land, rocky and forested. The average Indian holding is 30 acres, and of this hardly more than six is cultivated as a rule. There is nothing to prevent the buying up or inheriting of land beyond the 30-acre limit. In the Adam's Creek district of Birdtown the same situation exists, namely the white Indians occupying all the low-lying level and fertile areas while the purer bloods occupy the rim of the valley. Again in the rich Soco bottoms, an immense amount of white invasion has taken place and intermarriage with the Indians occurred. **1965** Kupferer *Eastern Cherokee* 128 Just as there is genetic diversity among the Cherokee, so is there social and cultural diversity. It is, however, somewhat doubtful that all the Cherokees see the subtle differences. Although everyone knows his degree of Indian inheritance, the most frequent distinction made between the people is "full blood" and "white" Indian. A "full blood" is one who looks like an Indian; a "white" Indian is one who usually has less than 1/4 Indian inheritance and who looks white. The term "full blood" tends to imply people who are traditionally oriented. **1991** Neely *Snowbird Cherokees* 49 Those Cherokees who make little effort to limit certain types of interactions with whites and, from the point of view of fullbloods, step over boundaries separating Indians from non-Indians, become classified as white Indians, people who are viewed as Indian in a legal sense only. Although white Indians usually look more white than Indian, the term is also sometimes used to refer to very Indian-looking people who fail to act as cultural traditionalists in certain situations. Families who have crossed these boundaries are those who for generations have married whites or other "white Indians"; shown a preference for the English language over Cherokee; permanently left the Cherokee area; elected to practice the Protestant Ethic over the Indian Harmony Ethic. **1998** Montgomery *Coll* = a Cherokee Indian who has adopted white culture (Brown), = a person with at least one-sixteenth Indian blood, who lives in the Qualla Reservation (Bush).

white laurel *noun* Same as **rosebay rhododendron** (*Rhododendron maximum*).

1937 Hall *Coll* (Cosby Creek TN) We have red laurels and white laurels here in the mountains.

white lightning *noun* Homemade whiskey. Also called **lightning**.

1921 Campbell *Sthn Highlander* 109 Here is the recipe for the latest North Carolina "temperance tipple" called "white lightning": "One bushel corn meal, 100 pounds of sugar, two boxes of lye, four plugs of tobacco, four pounds of poke root berries, two pounds of soda. Water to measure and distill." This recipe is for fourteen and one-half gallons of the "third rail" liquor. **1955** Parris *Roaming Mts* 84 The whiskey is uncolored. And that's how it got its name—white whiskey, or white lightening [sic]. **c1975** Lunsford *It Used to Be* 156 There's an expression called "bust head." That means whiskey . . . And what you take is a "snort," that's a dram. Or, you say, "Let me have a shot of that" and "Give me a swig of that." If you use the term "swig" it has an idea that you feel what you're getting is a little better than just "bust head" or "white lightning." **1978** Montgomery *White Pine Coll* VII-3 All that white lightning and everything, you know they got into it somehow. **1988** Kosier *Maggie* 26 Young and old alike participated in these "hoedowns," with a nip of corn liquor (white lightning) in the barn loft livening up the social event even more for the men. **2013** Pierce *Corn in Jar* 5 White lightning . . . whatever you call it, no other product is more iconic and more associated with traditional life in the Great Smoky Mountains than illegally distilled, un-aged, white corn liquor.

[DARE *white lightning* n scattered, but chiefly South, Midland, Southwest]

white line *noun* See citation.

1980 Riggleman *WV Mtneer* 126–27 [Loggers] usually had nicknames for everybody and everything around the camp. . . . Milk was "cow" or "white line."

white liniment *noun* Homemade whiskey.

1969 GSMNP-28:63 I thought it [= moonshine] was white liniment up until I was eighteen years old.

white liquor *noun* Homemade whiskey.

1915 Buck *Code of Mts* 116 Saturday is a day for gathering at the county seat and for drinking white liquor. **1961** Murry *Salt* 25 I didn' want to let h'it go, so that feller pulls out a quart bottle of white likker, and we takes us a dram. **1973** GSMNP-13:26 There wasn't much white liquor made over there in those days. **1995** Montgomery *Coll* (known to Ledford). **2009** Burton *Beech Mt Man* 109 I knowed all these guys was goin' up 'ere buying white liquor off the sheriff.

[DARE *white liquor* n chiefly South, South Midland]

white-livered *adjective* See 2002 citation.

1991 Still *Wolfpen Notebooks* 65 They told her that the man she was marrying had already buried three wives which proves he had a white liver. Women don't live long with white-livered husbands. **2002** Cavender and Crowder *White-Livered Women* 139 The most common meaning [of the term] revealed in informant interviews . . . is a sexual disorder involving an abnormally powerful or insatiable sexual drive. The notion is that people affected with "white liver" incapacitate or kill a spouse, or perhaps significant other, by literally draining them of their vital essence through inveterate coitus.

[cf EDD *white liver(ed)* (at *white* adj 1.54.(b) and 55.(a)); cf SND *white liver* (at *white* adj I.(39)); cf DARE *white liver* n "a presumed condition of the liver characterized by an abnormally powerful sexual drive and the death of sexual partners" especially South, South Midland]

white man bread *noun* See citation.

1966 DARE *Survey* (Cherokee NC) = bread that is not made at home.

white mouth *noun* Same as **thrush B**.

1990 Cavender *Folk Medical Lex* 34 = thrush.

white mule *noun* Homemade whiskey.

1929 (in **1952** Mathes *Tall Tales* 145) Hit's what a heap o' people calls white mule. Hit's made out o' corn. **c1960** Wilson *Coll* = moonshine with a milky color. **1962** Williams *Metaphor Mt Speech I* 12 "White mule" will make "a rabbit twist a rattlesnake's tail" and "a tomcat spit in a bulldog's eye," but good "mountain dew," the kind made by expert hands and aged in a charred white oak keg, will make "a preacher lay his Bible down," "a man wink at his mother-in-law," and "the lamb and the lion lay down together." **c1970** Handlon *Ol' Smoky* 8 You know, mountain people don't call liquor moonshine. They name it mountain dew or white mule. **1974** Dabney *Mt Spirits* 24 It [= corn whiskey] is called "white mule" in areas of Kentucky and Tennessee, apparently due to its kick.

[probably from the beverage's "kick"; DARE *white mule* n scattered but, especially frequent Midland, West]

whitening (also *face whitening*) *noun* See citations. See also **face powder**.

1936 Farr *Folk Speech* 276 *whitening* = face powder: "She uses too much whitening." **1983** Broaddus *Estill Co KY Word List* 60 *whitening* = women's face powder. **1992** Brooks *Sthn Stuff* 48 *face whitenin'* = face powder.

[DARE *whitening* n South, South Midland]

white oak *noun* A large deciduous tree (*Quercus alba*) whose bark is made into a medicinal tea and produces a dye. See also **white oak splint**.

1939 Hall *Coll* (Catons Grove TN) White oak bark tea is real good for diarrhea. **1967** Jones *Peculiarities Mtneers* 69 Wild artichoke tea and white oak bark tea were other remedies for "flux." [**1971** Krochmal et al. *Medicinal Plants Appal* 212 In Appalachia, a bark tea is used to treat burns and sore mouth. A chartreuse dye is obtained from the bark.] **1975** GSMNP-62:15 For diarrhea, they'd go and peel a white oak. They'd skin it down, get that inside bark and make a tea out of it, and that would check the bowels for us. **c1984** Dennis *Smoky Mt Heritage* 7 Boil the white oak bark, making tea, used as a gargle for tonsillitis.

white oak splint See **white oak split**.

white oak split (also *white oak splint*) *noun* A ribbon of wood sliced from a white oak or hickory log to be interwoven with others to make a basket, a chair bottom, or other object. See also **split B2**, **split basket**.

1937 Eaton *Handicrafts* 151 The woods used [by chairmakers] principally are sugar maple or ash for the posts, hickory for the rounds, and either white oak splints or hickory bark for the seats. **1937** Wilburn *Notes* Chairs [were] made of hickory or oak bottomed with white oak splits or basswood bark. **1977** Ross *Come Go* 28 Little Elkins and her family would gather on a big flat rock in back of her home and rive the white oak splits and weave baskets. **1995** Williams *Smoky Mts Folklife* 84 They . . . go into the woods and cut white oak and drag long pieces, you know, and they'd split it up and make splits and bottom chairs with them splits. . . . Yeah, and she made them baskets out of white oak splits. **2007** Alexander *Moonshiners Gone* 44 A farmer sitting by the flickering fireplace would use a knife or a broken shard of glass to scrape splinters and roughness from half inch wide, one-sixteenth inch thick white oak "splits" with which to bottom household chairs or weave baskets to store apples.

white oak winter *noun* A spring frost or cold spell when the white oak begins to bloom. For terms describing a similar phenomenon, see **blackberry winter**.

1995 Montgomery *Coll* When the white oak winter is over, you can plant your corn (Cardwell).

white poplar *noun* Same as **tulip poplar**.

1893 Bergen *Plant Names II* 136 = yellow or hickory poplar.

[DARE *white poplar* n 2 chiefly South Midland, especially KY]

whites *noun* See citation.

2000 Lowry *Folk Medical Term* = severe vaginal moniliasis or yeast infection.

white snakeroot *noun* A **boneset** (*Eupatorium* spp) that causes **milk sick** when consumed by cattle or by humans who drink their milk. See also **staggerweed 3**.

1982 Stupka *Wildflowers* 119 Fatal cases of "milk sickness" in man have been traced to the use of milk from cows that had eaten white snakeroot. It is sometimes poisonous to cattle. **1999** Montgomery *Coll* = since it is a poisonous plant, death usually followed. The poison is soluble in milk and easily transmitted to a person who drank the milk and developed a condition known as milk sickness (Cardwell).

white sop See **white gravy**.

white sucker *noun* Same as **hog fish**.

1939 Hall *Coll* (Waldens Creek TN) The creek was full of fish—bass, white suckers, silversides, red horses, hog mollies in the creek.

white swelling *noun* Inflammation and swelling of a joint.

1845 (in **2003** *TN Petitions I* 131) He was grieveously afflicted by Providence by a white swelling in his hip, which so disabled him that he cannot walk a step without the aid of crutches. **1864** Chapman *CW Letters* (June 11) Tell Wm Mc Culy his sister Jane has got the White sweling and is verry bad off. **1939** Hall *Coll* (Little Cataloochee NC) My father got crippled after about the third year after he came down here. He got his leg hurt, took the rheumatiz, and got a white swellin'. Never could get to do anything much. **1941** Stuart *Men of Mts* 102 Uncle Charlie was shot in the leg. He's got white swellin in his leg now and he hast to drag it along. **1997** Nelson *Country Folklore* 42 Grandpa was crippled, something called "white swelling." This didn't stop him from performing his many duties.

white walnut *noun* The butternut (*Juglans cineria*), a deciduous tree of medium height whose bark has medicinal uses.

1927 Thornburgh *Tramping* 466 He also told me that the mountain people call hemlock "spruce pine," the black spruce "he-balsam," the Fraser balsam "she-balsam," the sumac "shumake," the butternut "white walnut," while cucumber is humorously called "cowcumber." [**1971** Krochmal et al. *Medicinal Plants Appal* 148 In Appalachia, a tea made from the bark is used as a laxative.]

whiteweed *noun* A common field daisy (*Chrysanthemum leucanthemum*). Same as **ox-eye daisy**.

1978 *Smokies Heritage* 234 Despite its beauty and its use as an ornamental flower for bouquets, the ox-eye daisy can be a bad weed for many farmers, who call the flower "whiteweed."

white whiskey *noun* Homemade whiskey.

1883 Bonner *Dialect Tales* 158 We tasted the Cumberland punch. . . . It was sugarless, lemonless, waterless. It was smoky, strong, and brought tears to the eyes. In short, it was white whiskey mixed with white whiskey. **1955** Parris *Roaming Mts* 84 The whiskey is uncolored. And that's how it got its name—white whiskey, or white lightening [sic]. **1975** Brewer *Valley So Wild* 265 I've poured out many a gallon of white whiskey bootleggers tried to sneak into Fontana and there were a lot of stills operating in the hills. **1995–97** Montgomery *Coll* (known to Brown, Cardwell, Ellis, Ledford).

[DARE *white whiskey* n South, South Midland]

whitlow-wort *noun* See citation.

1941 Walker *Story of Mt* 47 On top of the rocks at High Point, which had the loftiest altitude of Lookout Mountain [TN], being 2,392 high, is found whitlow-wort. The plant was formerly employed for curing a finger and toe disease known as whitlow.

whittle-ding See **wheedle-dee**.

whittlety whet *adjective phrase* Of a race: neck and neck.

1890 Fruit *KY Words* 66 When two are running a race, we say, "It is whittlety-whet who will get there first."

whiz *noun* Used in comparisons to intensify adjectives; also adverb *whizzing* = extremely.

1960 Hall *Smoky Mt Folks* 63 As mad as whiz. **1982** Powers and Hannah *Cataloochee* 417 Mark still writes of winters in Maggie Valley . . . as "whizzin' cold" or "cold as whiz."

[DARE *whiz* n chiefly South Midland, *whizzing* adv chiefly South, South Midland]

whiz oak *noun* A kind of oak.

1966 *DARE Survey* (Linville NC). **2007** Hardy *Remembering Avery Co* 16 It don't pay to be stingy with wood on a morning like this, specially if your [sic] burning whiz oak or sourwood.

whizzing See **whiz**.

whoa back *interjection* Back up! (used as a call to a horse). Also called **ho back**. See also **back C**.

1941 Stuart *Men of Mts* 85 Finn says: "Get up there, Barnie. Whoa back, Barnie." And the mule creeps out along the furrow. **1967–68** *DARE Survey* (Brasstown NC, Gatlinburg TN) = call to make the horse go backward. **1996** Montgomery *Coll* (known to Cardwell).

who all *pronoun phrase* Who, whom—used as an indefinite pronoun to indicate a group of people. See also **who all's**, **who and all**. For other forms with *all*, see Grammar and Syntax §2.7.2.

1 In an embedded clause.

1861 (in **1992** Heller and Heller *Confederacy* 41) I want to know who all went in Boggsis Co. **1862** *Parris CW Letters* (July 3) parker did not [k]now hoo all was mising. **c1950** Adams *Grandpap* 184 Mammy told Granny about who all she'd seen at the meeting; who looked pert and who was ailing. **1952** Wilson *Folk Speech NC* 607 The use of *all* in this phrase is an attempt to make an indefinite pronoun. It means "who in general?" **1969** GSMNP-38:123 A number of people taught. I don't know who all. **1973** GSMNP-78:16 I know not too many, maybe one or two people that could pretty well give you who all is buried here. **1989** *Matewan OHP*-56 I'm trying to think of who all else they was. **2009** Holbrook *Upheaval* 38 I begin to think about who-all has handled [the phone] before me.

2 In a main clause.

1986 Pederson et al. *LAGS* (Cocke Co TN) Who all was there? **1998** *Dante OHP*-78 Who all is going to church?

[OED3 *who all* pron U.S. dialect; CUD *who all* (at all) "who (plural)"; HT *who a'* (at a') "exactly who, all those who"; DARE *who-all* pron 1a scattered, but chiefly South, South Midland]

who all's *pronoun phrase* Whose. See also **who all**.

1952 Wilson *Folk Speech NC* 607 The use of *all* in this phrase [i.e. *who all*] may be used in the possessive: "Who alls' [sic] house is that?"

who and all (also *who in all*) *pronoun phrase* Who—used as an indefinite pronoun to indicate a group of people. See also **what and all**, **where in all**, **who all**.

1982 *Foxfire VII* 203 I don't know who in all and those women just threw that snuff winding. **2007** McMillon *Notes* Who and all went to the store? **2014** Williams *Coll*: *who in all*.

whole hominy See **big hominy**.

whole push See **push 1**.

whomper-jawed, **whompy-jawed** See **whopper-jawed 2**.

whomp up *verb phrase* To prepare (a meal) on short notice. Same as **scare up 2**.

1972 Carson and Vick *Cookin* 2 18 A person could whomp up a meal for comp'ny downright quick by robbin a hen's nest and pickin a fat old hen. **1992** Brooks *Sthn Stuff* 174 whomp up. To stir up, or throw things together. "He could whomp up a roe-mance between two dead people."

whompus See **wampus**.

whoodle *verb* Of a young chicken or goose: to call to be fed.

1962 Williams *Verbs Mt Speech* 18 The farmer's wife may complain that the "biddies" and goslings around the kitchen door might' nigh drive her crazy with their "infernal and everlastin' whoodling" because she has "disremembered" to feed them.

whooie, pig, pig, pig, pig! *interjection* See citation.

1983 Broaddus *Estill Co KY Word List* 60 = a call to make the pigs come.

whoop See **whip A**.

whoop and a holler (also *whoop and a hollo*) *noun phrase* Hearing distance; figuratively, a short but indefinite distance or period of time. Same as **hoot and a holler**.

1919 Combs *Word-List South* 36 = a short distance. As far as the combined sounds of "two whoops and a holler" would carry? **1952** Wilson *Folk Speech NC* 607 = a short distance; a short time. "He lives a *whoop and a hollo* from my house." **1961** Williams *Content Mt Speech* 14 The next cabin up the creek is a "whoop and a holler away." **c1982** Young *Colloquial Appal* 25 *whoop and a holler* = hearing distance. **1997** Montgomery *Coll*: *whoop and a holler* (known to eight consultants from the Smoky Mountains). **2009** Benfield *Mt Born* 207 = a term identifying a place within hearing distance. If you live within a whoop and a holler of your neighbor, then he can hear you whoop and holler.

[DARE (at *whoop* n C1) chiefly South, South Midland]

whoop and hide (also *hoop hide*, *hoopie hide*, *hoopy hide*, *hoot-and-hide*, *whoopee hide*, *whooping hide*, *whoop 'n hide*, *whoopy hide*) *noun* The children's game hide and (go) seek; sometimes also the call used to start the game. Also called **hide and whoop**.

1915 Dingus *Word-List VA* 192 *whooping hide* = variant of *whoop and hide*, a children's game. **1939** Walker *Mtneer Looks* 7 The game called "Hoopie-Hide" in Tuckaleechee is just plain "Hide-and-Seek" in Happy Valley. **1952** Brewster *Games and Rhymes* 39 *whoopy hide* = this is another form of "Hide and Seek." Players announce by whoops that they are hidden. The counter follows the whoops, often being misled by the players, who change their locations after they have whooped. As a rule, this changing of position is regarded as "no fair," but, as in most cases of controversy, the decision is against the child who is "It." **1957** Broaddus *Vocab Estill Co KY* 85 *whoop 'n hide* = hide and seek. **1966–69** *DARE Survey* (Dillard GA, Hardshell KY, Boone NC, Burnsville NC, Gatlinburg TN, Jonesborough TN, Maryville TN, Rogersville TN, Big Stone Gap VA) *(w)hoopy-hide*; (Viper KY) *hoop-hide* = old-fashioned; (Tompkinsville KY) *hoot-and-hide*. **1973** GSMNP-74:25 We'd call it whoopyhide, but [they] call it hide and seek now. **1980** Wigginton *Foxfire VI* 288 We would hide and then holler, "Hoopie Hide" and somebody would have to come hunt for us. If they caught you before you got back to your home base, they got to hide in the next game. If they didn't catch you, you got to hide again. **1996** Montgomery *Coll*: *whoopy hide* (known to Cardwell, Jones, Ledford, Norris, Oliver). **2003** Cooper *Gathering Memories* 30 In the game of Whoopee Hide, a home base was agreed upon, and one player was chosen to be the keeper of the base. This selection was made by repeating the rhyme: "Wire, briar, limber lock: Three geese in a flock: one flew east, one flew west; one flew over the cuckoo's nest. O-U-T out goes he." After the keeper was chosen, the players would run to hide while he counted to one hundred. After he finished counting, the keeper would say, "Bushel of wheat, bushel of rye, all not ready holler I." If anyone hollered "I," then the counting was repeated. Soon followed, "Bushel of wheat, bushel of clover, all not ready can't hide over. Bum, bum, bum, here I come." When "it" found the hider, they would race to be the first back to home base. If the keeper lost, the winner could hide again. The last one found had the privilege of being "it" the next time. **2005** Williams *Gratitude* 169 Some of the outdoor games I remember us a-playin' was Whoopee Hide, which the town doods at school called "Hide And Seek."

[perhaps from the caller's cry when beginning to search for those hiding; DARE *whoop-and-hide* n 1 chiefly South Midland, South Atlantic]

whoop and stave *verb phrase* To rage, throw a fit. Same as **rip and stave**.

1981 Williams *Storytelling* Muts Mag begun to whoop and stave and make a lot of noise, but it didn't do no good.

whoopee hide See **whoop and hide**.

whooping See **whip B1**.

whooping hide, **whoop 'n hide**, **whoopy hide** See **whoop and hide**.

whop, **whope** See **whip**.

whopper-jawed *adjective*

1 (also *wampy-jawed*, *wopper-jawed*) Having a large, protruding, or crooked lower jaw. See also **jimber-jawed**, **lantern-jawed**.

1915 Dingus *Word-List VA* 192 *whopper-jawed* = having very large (usually distorted) jaws. **1930** (in **1952** Mathes *Tall Tales* 167) Ye're sorty wopper-jawed anyway, an' a beard would set right well on ye till ye git fleshed up some. **1992** Brooks *Sthn Stuff* 172 *wampy-jawed* = of a jaw: out of line or protrudes.

[DARE cf *whomper-jawed* adj 1 chiefly Central Atlantic, Middle Atlantic, Southeast, North Central]

2 (also *whomper-jawed, whompy-jawed, whopper-jawed, wompy-jawed, woppy-jawed*) Lopsided, out of proper shape or proportion, crooked. Also called **lopper-jawed.**

1957 Neel *Backwoodsman* 48 = crooked or uneven. **1966** *DARE Survey* (Spruce Pine NC) *whomper-jawed* = out of proper shape. **1997** Montgomery *Coll*: *whomper-jawed* (known to Brewer, Bush, Ellis, Jones, Ledford, Weaver); *whompy-jawed* (known to Ellis); *whopper-jawed* (known to Adams, Ellis, Jones, Ledford, Oliver). **2005** Williams *Gratitude* 536 *whopper-jawed* = out of square, uneven, crooked; catty-cornered. **2007** McMillon *Notes*: *wompy-jawed, woppy-jawed* = out of line.

[DARE *whomper-jawed* adj 2 chiefly Midland, South, TX]

3 See citation.

2015 *Blind Pig* (Dec 16) = stunned. "When Pap saw what I had done to his truck with a can of red paint and a brush, he was whopper-jawed."

whopping See **whip B1.**

whopping the cap *verbal noun* See citation.

1972 Carr *Oldest Profession* 78 The moonshiner weights down the still cap, after tapping it with a stick to determine the pressure buildup taking place. He is skilled at this and can tell, by the sound his tapping makes, the degree of pressure build-up or reduction. This operation is called "whoppin' the cap."

whor See **where.**

who-shot (also *who-shot-John*) *noun* Homemade whiskey, usually of a low grade.

1929 (in **2011** Shearer *Moonshine Trade* 85) On June 6, 1929, the newspaper reported that the first "Who-Shot-John" moonshine still was captured by raiders near Blowing Rock Gap. **1963** Williams *Metaphor Mt Speech II* 52 He'd take and go off to the woods some'eres and make hisself a little run o' who-shot-John. **1976** Still *Pattern of Man* 113 Nobody made such spirits any more. All you could find was who-shot. **1998** Still *Appal Mother Goose* 21 Who-shot with turpentine / That's what gave me / A nose that glows.

who that *conjunctive phrase* Who; for similar forms with *that*, see **that C** and Grammar and Syntax §15.4.

1989 *Matewan OHP-102* We usually agreed on who that we thought would be the best person and voted.

who'uns *pronoun* Who. See also **one 1.**

1932 Strong *Great Smokies* 61 Ma, guess who'uns this is. **1997–98** Montgomery *Coll* (known to Brown, Bush, Cardwell, Jones); Who'uns is at the door? (Oliver).

[contraction of *who* + *ones*]

whup See **whip A.**

whup out See **whip B4.**

whur See **where, whether.**

whurr, whuther See **whether.**

why all *conjunctive phrase* All the reasons why, exactly why. For other forms with *all*, see Grammar and Syntax §2.7.2.

1955 Ritchie *Singing Family* 93 Don't know for shore why-all I do it, but child when you get to be eighty-nine year old you'll set fore the fire and rub your old eyes out, too, and you won't know why.

why come *conjunction* Why.

1984 Burns *Cold Sassy* 125 Why come Granny hadn't given all that to Mama when I was born? *Ibid.* 241 Why come you hate Hosie, Will?

why for, why . . . for *adverb phrase* Why. See also **for why, what for A.**

1962 Justus *Smoky Sampler* 14 Folks do say [witches] talk to cattle; though what for and why for I never did hear anybody say. **1972** *AOHP/ALC-388* She said "Why do you'uns a-want to be in the hall so much for?" **1973** *AOHP/LJC-350* Why did they hang him for? Did he kill somebody? **1989** *Matewan OHP-1* Why do you want to go to Hot Springs for? **2009** Burton *Beech Mt Man* 32 Why they kept it for, I don't know.

why that *conjunctive phrase* Why; for similar forms with *that*, see **that C** and Grammar and Syntax §15.4.

1864 McGill *CW Letters* (May 29) Robert wrote a letter to you at Home and wants to know why that you did not write to him. **1956** Hall *Coll* (Del Rio TN) Maybe you can explain then why that it does do that. **1961** *Coe Ridge OHP-340B* That's why that they live a longer life. **1973** *AOHP/ALC-154* That's the reason why that I can't see why they wanted to take the reading of the Scripture for two or three minutes out of the school when there's scripture that will discipline the children better than any other way. **1989** *Matewan OHP-56* I was wanting to know why that they wasn't getting no support. **1997** *Dante OHP-53* They didn't have the ventilation, and that's why that they shut that mines down. **1999** Montgomery *File* I can see why that that would be so. **2014** *Blind Pig* (Jan 10) I don't know why that he thinks he can get away with that.

widder See **widow.**

widderman See **widowman.**

widderwoman See **widow woman.**

widdie (also *widdy*) *noun* A baby chicken; hence interjection *widdie! widdie!* = come! (used as a call to chickens). See also **biddy, deedie, dibbler, diddle[2] A, weedely.**

1904–20 Kephart *Notebooks* 2:371 Come, widdy, widdy. **1936** Morehouse *Rain on Just* 20 His young bitch Drum had been . . . sucking eggs from under Aunt Largey Drake's setting hen, and the little widdies all but pecking through their shells. **1975** Purkey

Madison Co 75–76 Mama mixed a little cornmeal dough and ran out into the back yard calling: "Widdie, widdie." And when all the chickens flocked around her, picking up the dough, she nabbed the fattest one in the bunch and wrung its neck off. **1997** Montgomery *Coll* (known to Ledford).

[DARE *widdie* interj chiefly South Midland, especially NC]

widdy See **widdie**.

widdy man See **widowman**.

widdy woman See **widow woman**.

wide-eye *noun*

1 See citation.

1990 Cavender *Folk Medical Lex* 34 = severe exhaustion.

2 See citation. Same as **white-eye**.

1990 Cavender *Folk Medical Lex* 34 = insomnia.

widow *noun*

A Variant form *widder*.

1853 (in **1956** Eliason *Tarheel Talk* 320) (Caldwell Co NC) *widder*. **1867** Harris *Sut Lovingood* 141 I be dod rabbited ef a man can't 'propriate happiness by the skinful ef he is in contack wif sumbody's widder, an' is smart. **1910** Cooke *Power and Glory* 10 I'm a widder, and I never look to wed again. **1974** Fink *Bits Mt Speech* 23 Henry's settin' up to the widder Brown.

[DARE *widow* n (pronc) chiefly South, South Midland]

B A widower. Same as **widowman B**.

1915 Dingus *Word-List VA* 192 *widder*, variant of *widow* and used also in the sense "widower." **1972** *AOHP/LJC*-104 He had been a widow for seventeen years. **1982** Slone *How We Talked* 36 both men and women were called "widders."

[cf EDD *widow* sb 1(5) "widower"; DARE *widow* n B 2 scattered, but especially South, South Midland]

widow maker *noun*

1 See citations.

1939 Hall *Coll* (Proctor NC) = a limb of a tree that's being felled. **1964** Clarkson *Lumbering in WV* 374 = a broken limb hanging loose in the top of a tree.

2 Homemade whiskey, especially if high in lead content.

1974 Dabney *Mt Spirits* 25 The names [= for corn whiskey] go on ... "widow makers." **1992** Bush *If Life* 21 If the beverage is grayish color, it is ... rot-gut booze, white mule, widow maker, or any corn squeezin's made in a galvanized still. **1997** Montgomery *File* (known to 65-year-old man, Maggie Valley NC).

widowman *noun*

A Variant forms *widder man* [see **1961** in **B**], *widdy man* [see **1930** in **B**].

B A widower. Also called **widow B**.

1892 Fruit *KY Words* 233 = widower. **1917** Kephart *Word-List* 419 = widower. **1921** Campbell *Sthn Highlander* 132 The mother [of an illegitimate child] quite generally marries—an older man, often, or a "widder man" with children—and her husband provides for the child of her unmarried state as for his own. **1930** Armstrong *This Day and Time* 48 I am a poor widdy man. **1941** Still *Troublesome Creek* 87 I knew he was the Law, and a widow-man. **1961** Murry *Salt* 20 He were a widder man, didn' have no woman, hunted an' fished a heap, done a little farmin'. **1967** *DARE Survey* (Gatlinburg TN) *widowman*. **1994** Montgomery *Coll*: *widowman* (known to Cardwell).

[DARE *widowman* n scattered, but chiefly South, South Midland]

widow woman *noun*

A Variant forms *widderwoman*, *widdy woman* [see **1930** in **B**].

1972 *AOHP/ALC*-342 Anyone that wasn't able to work might have needed stuff, like a widder woman with a few chillern.

B A widow.

1796 Cunningham *Letter* Jas. Cunningham is living on the Cataba River yet, and is maried to a mighty clever widow woman and is right ful in the world. **1864** *Chapman CW Letters* (April) I am well at this time and doing the best I can for myself and all of the widow women around mee. **1892** Fruit *KY Words* 233 = widow. **1908** Smith *Reminiscences* 421 Even in the dialect of the people one is often reminded of Homeric speech. For example, the mountaineer says not simply "doctor" or "widow," but "doctor-man," "widow-woman," "cow-brute," "apple-fruit," just as the Homeric man three thousand years ago spoke of a "healer-man," a "widow-woman," a "lady-mistress," a "master-lord." **1930** Armstrong *This Day and Time* 37 I heerd you was workin' fer a rich widdy woman. **1937** Hall *Coll* (Cataloochee NC) An old widow woman lives at the Major Woody place. **1977** Weals *Cove Folk* We looked after them folks. If it was a widow woman, she was took care of. If we seed that, she was took care of.

[OED3 (at *widow* n[1] C1a usually archaic or dialect); EDD (at *widow* sb 1(10); DARE *widow woman* n formerly widespread, now especially Midland, South]

wif See **with**.

(the) wife See **the 4**.

wife woman *noun* A wife.

1943 Hannum *Mt People* 140 There were the great puncheons to be hewn for the floor boards—leaving a few of them loose, so the wife-woman could store the preserves and pickles and jars of wild huckleberries and gooseberries underneath. **1972** GSMNP-71:15 Then the wife woman scrubbed the floor.

wiggletail (also *wiggleworm*) *noun* A mosquito larva.

1861 *Estes CW Letter* (Sept 29) The water we have is the very worst of water. Such as you never Drank in your Life the wigeltails is as thick as Bees in gum. **1862** *Robinson CW Letters* (Sept 24) we have to drink wate[r] thick with mud & wigeltails. **1979** Melton *'Pon My Honor* 19 He was as full of jokes about preachers as a rain barrel is of wiggletails. **1983** Broaddus *Estill Co KY Word List* 61 *wiggle worm* = a mosquito larva. **1999** Perry *Clinch River* Water for washing was caught in rain barrels placed along under the eaves of the house, in summertime wiggle tails were a problem in the rain barrels.

[DARE *wiggletail* n 1 chiefly South, South Midland, TX, OK, *wiggleworm* chiefly Midland]

wild alum *noun* The hairy alumroot plant (*Heuchera villosa*), the roots of which are boiled to make a tea to treat diarrhea and stomach ailments.

1939 Hall *Coll* (Catons Grove TN) Wild alum, that's the best thing I ever saw used for cholera marvus and diarrhea.

wild apricot (also *apricot, apricot vine*) *noun* A tall vine (*Passiflora incarnata*) with large, flesh-colored flowers, edible yellow fruit, and medicinal uses. Same as **maypop**, **molly pop**, **passion flower**. See also **molly pop**.

1913 Morley *Carolina Mts* 68 In some parts of the mountains the people call the maypops "apricots" and eat them, though they belong principally to the age of childhood. **1937** Thornburgh *Great Smoky Mts* 22–23 The strange, symbolic purple passion flower, the former state flower of Tennessee, grows in profusion and its fruit is prized by the mountain children who call it wild apricot. **1970** Campbell et al. *Smoky Mt Wildflowers* 66 Also known as wild apricot and maypop, [the passion flower] is a vine up to ten feet in length. [**1971** Krochmal et al. *Medicinal Plants Appal* This plant . . . has been used to reduce blood pressure and to increase the rate of respiration.] **1982** Stupka *Wildflowers* 69 The fruit is a many-seeded berry the shape of a lemon. When ripe it is yellow and edible. The fruit accounts for the alternate names "wild apricot" and "maypop." **1996** Montgomery *Coll* = passion flower, the fruit of which was sometimes made into preserves (Cardwell).

[from resemblance of the fruit to an apricot; DARE *wild apricot* n chiefly South Midland]

wild baby *noun* An illegitimate child.

1978 Hiser *Quare Do's* 34 When a little wild baby was to be born in the neighborhood (and they was a God's plenty, believe me) people'd get her for a midwife.

wild Bill *noun* See citation.

1892 Allen *Cumberland Gap* 257–58 A "wild Bill" is a bed made by boring auger-holes into a log, driving sticks into these, and overlaying them with hickory bark and sedge-grass—a favorite couch.

wildcat *adjective* Especially of a distillery: operated beyond the bounds of the law; hence verbal noun *wildcatting* = operating a distillery in such a fashion, and noun = the product of such an operation (i.e. illegal whiskey).

1892 Crutcher *Spurrier with Wildcats* 105–6 George little dreamed when he first laid his plans for wildcatting that his hopes and anticipations should so soon come to an end, and he landed in prison. But so it was. Soon after starting his wildcat business, it was reported to the authorities, and a posse of men were detailed to look into the matter and bring to justice the offender. **1914** Wilson *Sthn Mtneers* 49 To assume that, because "wildcat" illicit distilling is done in some places in the mountains, the favorite occupation of the mass of the mountaineers is "moonshine" is absurd. **1968** *DARE Survey* (Brasstown NC) = illegally made whiskey. **2007** Rowley *Moonshine!* 162 A wildcat sale is a purchase of questionable moonshine from an irregular or undesirable source. Wildcat may refer simply to an unregistered still. Wildcatter refers to moonshiners who operate such stills. The latter two imply merely "illicit" and do not carry the negative undertones of wildcat sale.

wildcatter *noun* See citation. See also **moonshiner**.

1895 Wiltse *Moonshiners* 8 They are known by several other names, and "moonshiner" is the most euphonious term that is ever applied to them. They are sometimes called "moonlighters," sometimes "wildcatters," sometimes "blockaders," sometimes "contrabanders."

wildcatting See **wildcat**.

wild cherry *noun* The black cherry tree (*Prunus* spp); a flavoring and a medicinal tea are made from its bark. See also **lung balm**.

1939 Hall *Coll* (Catons Grove TN) Wild cherry bark is good for the blood and for coughs, really good. [**1940** Haun *Hawk's Done* 31 Right then I knowed what was wrong. "Hit is mountain fever," I said. Me and Amy made plenty of cherry bark tea. That is the first time I ever seen it fail to cure the fever.] **1971** Krochmal et al. *Medicinal Plants Appal* 210 The bark is used primarily as a flavoring agent. The drug is an excellent expectorant. Appalachian wild cherry bark tea is used for coughs, colds, and cholera. **1980** *Smokies Heritage* 118 Fruit is only the beginning of the wild cherry's virtues. Mountain people have always known it as the "lung balm" tree, a source of medicine for the cold of highland winters. A tea of its bark, sometimes mixed with honey or whiskey, was given many a sufferer to still his cough.

wild cucumber tree *noun* Same as **cucumber tree**.

1940 Bandy *Folklore Macon Co TN* 57 Macon County people call a magnolia a "wild cucumber tree."

wildfire *noun* Erysipylas.

2007 Milnes *Signs Cures Witches* 75 Dovie . . . started talking about cures that sat squarely in the occult vein. She talked about a disease she called "wildfire" and went on to tell how it could be cured with the topical application of blood from a black chicken. *Ibid.* 101 Dovie noted that the disease wildfire starts as a small red spot on the skin and increases in size: It'd start just in a little red place and it just starts keepin' a-goin', getting bigger and bigger, bigger and bigger, bigger and bigger. And old people claim—wildfire—they claim if it got big enough to cover your heart, it'd kill you. . . . Wildfire is the skin disease erysipelas, a streptococcal infection characterized by inflammation and redness of the skin in round or oval patches. In Germany it was also known as St. Anthony's fire, or *Das versegnt*, but also wildfire. Dovie's Randolph County cure specifies that a black chicken be used. In Pendleton County another clearly magical cure for erysipelas/wildfire was known. The afflicted person had to strip off all clothing, kneel down in front of a fireplace, and face away from it. Nine matches were struck in groups of three and then thrown over the shoulder into the fireplace while the afflicted person said, "In the name of the Father, Son, and Holy Ghost" for each group of three.

[<Pennsylvania German *wildfeier*]

wildfish *noun* Same as **dry-land fish**.

1985 Irwin *Alex Stewart* 190 Law, at the wildfish [mushroom] in the woods this spring. They grow to about the size of your arm, and the end is right blunt, just like you'd broke it off. They come out early in the spring, just about the time trees start putting out their leaves. When they get to turning a sort of grey color, you need to get them.... You just split them open and fry them like you was frying a potato.... They taste just like fish, only better. I'd like to have a mess of wildfish today.

wild-hog *verb* To have a riotous, debauched time, often when consuming alcohol; to behave wildly, especially in going into town and visiting places of doubtful repute; hence verbal noun *wild-hogging*. See also **tomcat (around)**.

1939 Hall *Coll* (Cataloochee NC) = when they get on one of these big drunks and go to these honky-tonks. It's the same as tomcattin'. Both wild hoggin' and tomcattin' mean to look for a woman especially. *Ibid.* (Sugarlands TN) They must have been out wild hogging around last night. **1940** Hall *Coll* (Spring Creek NC) Their drinking and wild hogging would come to an end. **1952** Wilson *Folk Speech NC* 608 = to live a life of debauchery, to be wild. **1967** *DARE Survey* (Gatlinburg TN) *wild hogging* = a party at which there is considerable drinking. **1994** Montgomery *File* We used to go into Gatlinburg and wild hog on the weekends (82-year-old man, Gatlinburg TN).

[DARE *wild-hog* v phr southern Appalachians]

wild hog tale *noun* An account of an encounter with a wild hog, especially an exaggerated or fantastic account. See also **panther tale**, **snake tale**.

1956 Hall *Coll* (Big Bend NC) She could really tell wild hog tales. Her and pap and Aunt Nance and Uncle Merritt went over to Slick Rock Branch and catched a big wild male hog once. They tied him and put him on a pole and started out up the mountain, and her foot slipped, and she busted him right on the nose.

wild honeysuckle *noun* A wild azalea or pinkster bush (especially *Rhododendron periclymenoides*). Also called **flame azalea**, **honeysuckle**.

1901 Lounsberry *Sthn Wild Flowers* 378–79 Pinkster-flower, wild honeysuckle, or pink azalea, which is mostly branched near its summit, grows on the contrary in woods and thickets and opens its blooms at the same time, or a little before its leaves. Its pink and white flowers have not as intense a fragrance as those of the swamp honeysuckle, and their tube is pubescent but very slightly glandular. **1970** Campbell et al. *Smoky Mt Wildflowers* 42 Deciduous *Rhododendron* (*calendulaceum*) is known to mountain people as wild honeysuckle.

[DARE *wild honeysuckle* n 1 chiefly South, South Midland]

wild indigo *noun* A perennial wildflower (*Baptisia* spp) with medicinal uses.

1937 Thornburgh *Great Smoky Mts* 29 Other herbs and roots used by the old folks in various ways are ... horse mint, butterfly root.... wild indigo, yellow fringed orchid or rattlesnake master. **1939** Hall *Coll* (Chestnut Branch NC) They was a weed that they call wild indigo. You can take hit, and it'll stop blood poison. Take the roots and beat it up, put sweet milk in it, and put it on it, and it'll draw it white and cure it up. [**1971** Krochmal et al. *Medicinal Plants Appal* 72 Most authorities agree that the herb has value as a febrifuge, tonic, purgative, and antiseptic.]

wild oat *noun* See citations.

1968 *DARE Survey* (Romney WV, Westover WV) = an illegitimate child. **1997** Montgomery *Coll* = an illegitimate child (Brown).

wild onion milk *noun* Milk that tastes of onions that a milk-giving cow has consumed. See also **bitterweed milk**, **ragweed milk**, **weedy**.

1996 Montgomery *Coll* Come on and have supper with us, but our cow's been giving wild onion milk (Cardwell).

wild pork *noun* Bear meat.

2001 Montgomery *Coll* (known to Cardwell).

wild salad *noun*

A Variant forms *wild salat* [see **1905** in **B**], *wild sallet* [see **1963** in **B**].

B Wild greens. See also **salad B**.

1905 Miles *Spirit of Mts* 33 Into the skillet are [put] thickly sliced potatoes to be half-fried, half-stewed; the earliest cucumbers and onions are sliced raw and salted; perhaps a pot of "wild salat" has been boiling for some time already, seasoned with a generous cube of fat pork, for "people that buy their meat by the quarter's worth can't eat pokeweed in their greens." **1940** Haun *Hawk's Done* 112 It started that day I sent her up yonder to Arwood's branch to pick a mess of wild sallet. **1956** Hall *Coll* (Gatlinburg TN) = wild greens in the spring: mustard greens, poke sallet, wild turnip greens, pepper grass in old fields, old field creases.... Put poke in boiling grease, break eggs in it an' stir. Crows feet are good boiled or fried in grease. Other plants that can be picked at random are lambs quarters, plaintain, dock. **1963** Wilson *Regional Words* 80 *Greens* is distinctly a modern word; *sallet* is the standard word among older people, with such prefixes as *mustard*, *turnip*, or *wild*. *Wild sallet* represents a whole slice of botany, with polk, narrow-leaved dock, lamb's quarters, peppergrass, wild mustard, dandelions, and many other plants included.

wild spinach *noun* Same as **lamb's quarter(s)**.

1978 Parris *Mt Cooking* 162 I've heard some folks call lamb's quarters wild spinach.

will *auxiliary verb*

A *will*.

1 Variant negative forms *want*, *wunt*.

1913 Kephart *Our Sthn High* 122 The law wunt let us have liquor shipped to us from anywhars in the State. **1936** (in **2009** Powell *Shenandoah Letters* 94) We Been wating all the spring and He want put them [= the hogs] up.

2 Contracted to *'ll* in a negative context.

1901 Harben *Westerfelt* 181 He'll not try it tonight. **1931** Goodrich *Mt Homespun* 68 I'll not say it's not a worrisome job. **1941** Stuart *Men of Mts* 96 You'll not be able to stand many more bullets in your body. **1949** Still *Master Time* 45 He batted an eye at us, "We'll not be outsharped." **1973** *Foxfire Interviews* A-73-43 I'll not go over there and check. **1977** Prichard *Teams and Teamsters* 23 We'll not eat here. We'll not pay for the food you've fixed for us, nor for the horses' feed. **1980** GSMNP-115:28 If you don't jine a church and be baptized this time, I'll not never get to see you baptized. **1981** Nicholas *Appal Speech* 4 In Jackson County, North Carolina, the mountain county where I live and work, exhibit a marked tendency to contract a subject pronoun with the auxiliary, as Shakespeare would have done, rather than to adopt the more recent alternative of contracting the auxiliary with the negative—so that *I'll not do it* competes with *I won't do it*. **1984** GSMNP-154 He went by a man's house, which I'll not call his name, and picked up a little bottle of whiskey. **1989** Landry *Smoky Mt Interviews* 181 You'll not find no John [Ogle] blood around Maryville. **2002** Rash *Foot in Eden* 105 I'll not let you go out in such weather.

3 Inverted with the subject in a negative clause.

1930 Armstrong *This Day and Time* 67 Won't no man stand fer that. **1961** Williams *Rhythm and Melody* 9 Let a chicken git in the gyarden, an' ye can howl yer head off fer a dog, but won't nary one on the place come a-nigh ye. **1964** Roberts *Hell-Fer-Sartin* 35 "That place is hainted." Says, "Won't nobody live up there." **1973** Kahn *Hillbilly Women* 81 Won't none of them go unless they've got fifty or seventy-five men. **1988** Smith *Fair and Tender* 199 Danny's grave is sunk in now and covered all over in violets, but won't nothing grow on Babe's. **2004** Fisher *Kettle Bottom* 48 Won't nobody be able to tell her different.

4 In combination with following *can*.

1930s (in **1944** Wentworth *ADD* 92) (WV) "He'll not kin go".... Always in combination *'ll not kin* or *'ll never kin*: "She'll never kin catch a mouse now." Said when a pet cat became crippled.

B *would*.

1 Variant negative forms *wouldn't, woutn't, wutn't*.

1962 Williams *Verbs Mt Speech* 17 The mountaineer's preference for *t* over *d* in conjunction with nasal sounds sometimes results in *wutn't, cutn't,* and *shutn't*. **1978** Hiser *Quare Do's* 91 We'll have other children, he tried to console me. I know in my heart we wouldn't. **2005** Williams *Gratitude* 527 A person who was too lazy to work at anything *woutn't strike a lick*.

2 Contracted to *'d* before *not*.

1898 Elliott *Durket Sperret* 15 If you hed any grit we'd not be pushed. **c1936** (in **2005** Ballard and Chung *Arnow Stories* 113) I figgered they'd not git back 'fore dark. **c1950** Adams *Grandpap* 39 He knowed if they killed his bull that he'd not get anything more to eat an' that would soon be the end of him. **1962** (in **2014** McCarter *Memories of Boy* 22) If you were coming east that was it, and they'd not see you again. **1983** McDermitt *Boy Named Jack* 8 I wouldn't have been a-livin a-probably if I'd not been Jack's friend. **1992** Offutt *KY Straight* 139 I'd not do that. **2002** Rash *Foot in Eden* 17 If he was here he'd not let me get up there without him helping me.

3 Inverted with the subject in a negative clause.

1955 Ritchie *Singing Family* 243 Wouldn't a day pass after that but what five or six big long trainloads of coal would rumble by. **1976** Wolfram and Christian *Appal Speech* 113 It had this room that wouldn't hardly nobody stay in. **1984** Smith *Oral History* 44 Wouldn't nothing cure it. **1989** Giardina *Storming Heaven* 5 Wouldn't no good come of it, he said.

willer tea *noun* A switching, whipping, one administered with a branch taken from a willow tree. See also **birch tea**, **hickory B2**, **peach-tree-limb tea**.

2007 Preece *Leavin' Sandlick* 34 I'll break a switch off'n one of them willer trees and I'll whup both of ye. Do we want a little willer tea?

wilt *verb* Same as **kill B**. See also **wilted salad**.

1982 Slone *How We Talked* 62 Some of the greens we used were not cooked, but eaten raw. They were "looked" (checked for bugs and rotting spots), washed, sprinkled with salt and wilted or "killed" by pouring real hot pork grease over them. **1997** Andrews *Mountain Vittles* 15 Gather, wash, eat raw with salt or cook by wilting.

wilted salad *noun* Same as **killed salad**. See also **wilt**.

1997 Montgomery Coll (known to Adams, Brewer, Bush, Ledford, Norris, Oliver), = made from torn pieces of lettuce and diced onions with hot sizzling grease poured over it (Cardwell), = made by pouring hot bacon grease on it (Jones). **2007** McMillon *Notes* = any greens such as branch lettuce or leaf lettuce that scalding grease or oil is poured over.

wimmen See **women A2**.

win *verb*

1 Variant past-tense form *winned*.

1941 Stuart *Men of Mts* 43 They'd be there to see if their man winned. **1962** Williams *Verbs Mt Speech* 17 Certain persistent perversities in the use of verbs are also widespread. Strong verbs are often weakened, irregular verbs made regular. The past and past participle of. . . . win [become] winned. **1973** *AOHP/ASU*-149 By one vote we winned to have schools prolonged. **1989** *Matewan OHP*-33 He winned fifty thousand dollars while he was down there, winned fifty thousand dollars, a sweepstake. **2002** McGowan *Beech Mt Tales* 111 He watched and winned that time and got their nickel.

2 Variant past-participle form *winned*.

1946 Stuart *Plum Grove Hills* 121 Tell about fights you've winned. [See **1962** in **1**.]

[DARE *win* v 1 especially South, South Midland]

wind *verb* To winnow.

1967–69 *DARE Survey* (Tompkinsville KY, Gatlinburg TN).

[OED3 *wind* v³ dialect; DARE *wind* v scattered, but especially Mid and South Atlantic]

windblow *noun* A very strong wind, perhaps a tornado.

1963 Lord *Blue Ridge* 19D Years ago, perhaps beyond the memory of anyone living, a tremendous "wind-blow" knocked down much of the spruce forest covering the ridge. **1997** Montgomery Coll (known to Brown, Bush).

winder *noun* (rhymes with *hinder*) A window.

1867 Harris *Sut Lovingood* 158 Sich kerryins on hesn't been seed since ole Tam Shadrick wer a-seein the witches a-dansin thru the ole chu'ch winders what yu narrated tuther nite. **1901** Harben *Westerfelt* 190 We could see 'em frum the kitchen winder. **1940** Bowman *KY Mt Stories* 18 Many of the dialect forms are merely mispronunciations but they are important enough to be mentioned from the fact that their spelling has been affected by the persistent mispronunciation. [Schoolchildren] insist on spelling "window" as "winder" because that is the way it is pronounced. **1963** Edwards *Gravel* 95 He could hear the sigh of the wind in the tree outside the winder. **1989** *Matewan OHP-33* They went there and shot their winders out, buddy, and shot some of them. **2006** Ledford *Survivals* 1014 In present-day Appalachia there are still survivals from colonial pronunciation. A final *r* in such mountain terms as *winder* "window" and *piller* "pillow" have their counterparts in colonial writings.

wind hole *noun* See citation.

1978 Hiser *Quare Do's* 40 [The school] hadn't no windows, only holes cut in the logs walls with wooden shutters to close when it got bitter weather, wind holes, they was called.

winding (also *a-winding*) *adverb* Sideways, askew, cockeyed.

1930 Greer-Petrie *Angeline Outsmarts* 3 He keerlessly jobbed his elbow agin that lookin' glass, knockin' hit a-windin', and bustin' hit. **1950** Bray *Disappearing Dialect* 280 He slapped her a-windin'. **1963** Edwards *Gravel* 154 Willis would. . . . raise one of his big feet. . . . and kick Fido winding and yell, "Get away from here dog." **1982** *Foxfire VII* 203 Those women just threw that snuff winding. **1983** Broaddus *Estill Co KY Word List* 46 *knock winding* = to give a staggering blow to. **2009** Benfield *Mt Born* 191 *slap you winding* = getting ready to deliver [definite punishment that will send the tormentor spinning. This is most often used as a threat. "Woody, you try to kiss me, and I'll slap you winding."

[DARE *winding* adv South, South Midland]

window door *noun* A half-door that can be opened at the top.

1940 Haun *Hawk's Done* 104 I opened the window door and kept it open, even if the lightning did scare me. **1998** Montgomery Coll (known to Bush), = a door designed to keep out dogs and to let in light (Brown).

window glass (also *window light*) *noun* A windowpane.

1941 Stuart *Men of Mts* 99 I could see eyes peepin from the winder glasses at me. **1943** Hannum *Mt People* 130 There was no glass in the windows as yet. "Window lights" cost cash money, and that was slow to accumulate. **c1959** Weals *Hillbilly Dict* 9 = window panes, or glass. "The boys got rambunctious and broke out all my windowlights." **1965** Hall Coll (Cataloochee NC) They shot out sixteen holes in the house [and] knocked out the window lights. **1971** *AOHP/ALC-137* [We had] a little log schoolhouse and big winters out in it and no lights, no window lights, and a big hole cut out of there. **1997** *Dante OHP-14* [The church] is still around, but the window lights is all broke out. **1997** Landry Coll Don't shoot them window lights out.

windrow

A *noun* Hay raked into a row or ridge before being pitched or rolled into stacks.

1957 Broaddus *Vocab Estill Co KY* 86 = a row of hay raked together to dry before putting it into stacks. **1984** Smith *Enduring Memories* 16 After the hay was cut and allowed to dry, it was raked onto wind-rows, and the real fun would begin. With one person on the wagon and two or more persons on the ground we would use pitch forks to throw the hay from the wind-rows upon the wagon. The person on the wagon was responsible for placing it so that a good load of hay could be hauled without falling off the wagon. **1995** Montgomery Coll (known to Cardwell).

B *verb* To rake (hay) into a row or ridge before stacking it.

1978 Montgomery *White Pine Coll* III-2 They go through there and leave the straw in a row, and then they go along and windrow that straw.

windshake *noun* A crack or twisted grain in timber apparently produced by high wind or a freeze. See also **windshaken**.

1925 Dargan *Highland Annals* 22 I could'a' cast out the snirly blocks, but it was the wind-shake that finally ruined me. **1969** Sorden *Lumber Lingo* 141 = a crack in timber due to frost or high wind. **1996** Montgomery Coll (known to Jones).

windshaken (also *windshook*) *participial adjective* Of timber: having developed cracks from high winds or extreme cold. See also **windshake**.

1977 Arnow *Old Burnside* 53 They were "wind-shook" or had some other defect that ruined them for lumber. **1985** Irwin *Alex Stewart* 271 I've heard that many a time way back yonder. I've been out in the woods on right cold times and heard the timber a popping and cracking, but it was winter back then. We don't have the winters nothing like we used to have. [Does that damage the trees?] Yeah, it hurts them a sight. It causes them to be what they call windshaken. *Ibid.* 272 There was 30 or 40 hickories on it that was two and three feet thick. We'd cut them and they'd just fall apart. They was windshook and they weren't fit for anything. Once a tree gets windshook it stays that way. It won't grow back. Hit's no account.

windshook See **windshaken**.

windsplitter *noun* Same as **razorback**.

1969 Wall *History Davie Co* 39 (DARE) Chickens were kept, and hogs, "razor-back" or "wind splitter" species, were raised in large numbers.

wind-sucker *noun* Same as **stump sucker.**

1939 Hall Coll (Cataloochee NC) My daddy. . . . was an awful horse trader. He had an old wind sucker. **1952** Wilson *Folk Speech NC* 608 = a lean, runty pig that is supposed to stand in a corner and suck wind; by transference, a thin weak person, generally a child.

wind-throwed *adjective phrase* Blown down by wind. See also **-throwed.**

1913 Kephart *Our Sthn High* 77 Several trees has been wind-throwed and busted to kindlin'. **1974** Fink *Bits Mt Speech* 29 = blown over by wind. "All the big trees was *wind throwed.*" **1994** Montgomery Coll (known to Cardwell).

wind tumor *noun* See citation.

1990 Cavender *Folk Medical Lex* 34 = hernia in the groin area near the small bowel.

wind work *noun* See citation.

1995 Montgomery Coll We got to do the wind work first [i.e. We have to talk about it first, in order to get in the right frame of mind to get started] (Cardwell).

windy *adjective* (first syllable rhymes with *kind*) Of a road: curvy, winding.

2006 Logan and Jackson *Wytheville* v I grew up in Knoxville, Tennessee, some 180 miles southwest of Wytheville, Virginia, on pre-Interstate, twisty, windy roads, literally worlds away from the epidemic that Wytheville was experiencing in 1950. **2008** Salsi *Ray Hicks* 7 Then, by habit and want, I taken one last look at the big ol' white house, just one more time afore headin' down the windy narrow dirt road.

wingle *verb* To wind and twist, meander.

1913 Kephart *Our Sthn High* 30 All roads and trails "wingled and wiggled around" so that some families were several miles from a neighbor. *Ibid.* 100 I girded myself and ran, "wiggling and wingling" myself along the main divide. **1994** Montgomery Coll (known to Cardwell, but not to other consultants from the Smoky Mountains).

[perhaps alteration of *wiggle*, but cf EDD *wingle* "to bend and twist" Shetland/Orkney; DARE *wingle* v especially southern Appalachians]

winned See **win 1, 2.**

winter *verb* To serve as feed for (livestock) in wintertime.

1962 Williams *Verbs Mt Speech* 17 The mountain farmer talks of raising enough corn to "bread" his family and enough "roughness" to "winter" his brutes.

wintercress *noun* A variety of **cress** (*Barbarea vulgaris*).

1975 Dwyer *Thangs* 13 Winter cress [is] often found in old fields and along roadsides. Young leaves are good all year, except during summer.

winter digger *noun* A farmer hired to mine coal only in colder months.

1943 Korson *Coal Dust* 4–5 Farmers and farm-hands also hired themselves out to coal operators as miners during the winter season. Since digging and loading coal was only temporary work for them, they were less likely to be interested in efforts to raise wages and improve working conditions than professional miners. . . . Full-time miners naturally resented them and expressed their distrust by calling them "winter diggers."

winter fever *noun* See citation.

1957 Broaddus *Vocab Estill Co KY* 86 = the old name for pneumonia.

wintergreen *noun* The teaberry, a low evergreen shrub (*Gaultheria procumbens*) that produces bright berries in the fall and winter and whose oil is used as a flavoring and as medicine. Same as **mountain tea.**

1970 Campbell et al. *Smoky Mt Wildflowers* 80 Other common names [of the teaberry] are checkerberry, wintergreen, and mountain tea. **1982** Stupka *Wildflowers* 83 Teaberry, often called "wintergreen" or "checkerberry," is an old-time remedy, used as a diuretic.

winter school *noun* Formerly, a **subscription school** held in winter months. See citations.

1975 *AOHP/LJC-384* He'd send us to winter school. You'd have winter school. You'd have people to come there and teach. **1987** Davenport *Pine Grove* 40 The public school program at that time provided for a school term of only five months, during the spring and fall. For those parents who wished to enhance the quality of education for their children, there were private schools of three months during the winter. Those "winter schools," as they were called, were taught by regular teachers and a tuition fee was paid directly to them.

wish *verb* Variant forms *wisht, wusht.* For their derivation, see 1975 citation.

1891 Brown *Dialect in TN* 172 We also say *all of a suddent, wisht* for the present tense of *wish, skift* for *skiff,* and *take holt of* for *take hold of,* etc. **1901** Harben *Westerfelt* 25 I wisht you'd hand me a switch, John. **1939** Hall Coll I wisht I had a ballet of that song. **1939** Walker *Mtneer Looks* 4 A final *t* is sometimes added to words ending in the sound of *s*. . . . *Wish* is usually *wisht* or *wusht.* **1954** Arnow *Dollmaker* 90 I wisht she'd set on that sled an ride. **1964** Stokely *Harvest* 153 [I w]isht I could find some way to git a-holt of some money. **1975** Schrock *Exam of Dialect* 467 *Wisht,* in "I wisht he hadn't 'a saw fit," at first glance, appears to be a past-tense verb where present tense is expected, but upon close examination, we find that it is an assimilated form of *wish that*. It occurs only before a relative [sic] clause before which the relative has been omitted. **1980** GSMNP-115:45 I wisht I could remember 'em. I should have wrote 'em down way back then when I was a girl.

wish and want book See **wish book**.

wish book (also *wish and want book*) *noun* A large mail-order catalog, usually distributed prior to Christmas. This term most often refers to the *Sears Wish Book*, first produced by Sears Roebuck and Company in 1933, and sometimes to its predecessor produced by Montgomery Ward and Company. Montgomery Ward and Company was the first major mail-order retailer, issuing its first catalog in 1872. The term was later broadened to include other, similar catalogs.

1949 Justus *Toby Has Dog* 14 Father was wearing his new blue wish-book britches with shirt and necktie to match. **1982** Slone *How We Talked* 36 *wish book* (also *wish and want book*) = [mail-order] catalog. **1997** Montgomery Coll (known to nine consultants from the Smoky Mountains). **2003** Strutin *Hikes of Smokies* 13 With more cash [paid to men for logging] came store-bought clothes, kerosene lamps, and many other amenities via "wish books," such as the Sears and Roebuck catalog, and the general stores that had popped up in each mountain community.

wishee *noun* A type of mushroom.

2010 Montgomery File The Cherokees harvest "wishees" and "slicks," two different types of mushrooms from the [western NC] region. **2015** Long *Ethnic Food* 439 Mushrooms, especially sautéed morels, wishee, hickory chicken (hen of the woods), Owl's heads, and even puffballs, supplemented Woodland diets during times of plenty and famine alike.

wisht See **wish**.

witch *verb*

1 To bewitch, cast a spell on (someone).

1956 Hall Coll (Big Bend NC) They said Granpap's sister. . . . was a witch. She witched her brother when he was a small kid. He tore a board off the top of the house and dropped a rock down and skinned her head all over for witchin' him. *Ibid.* (Gatlinburg TN) The witches over there in North Carolina would witch everything you had. A witch had my uncle near dead. A witch doctor drawed a picture of the witch and nailed it back of the door, druv a nail in her heart, and then she died. Now witches can do you dirt. *Ibid.* (Jones Cove TN) I had an uncle to witch people. *Ibid.* (Newport TN) She thought her son was witched—bewitched. She said she was witched into a black cat and hauled miles and miles and miles.

2 To dowse for water preparatory to digging (a well).

1952 Giles *40 Acres* 96 Here on the ridge we don't dig a well until we have it witched. Of course we know that there's water anywhere if you dig deep enough. But when you're going to spring-pole a well by hand, you certainly don't want to have to spring-pole halfway to China to find water. It's much easier to have a water witch come and locate a stream and tell you exactly where to put your well. **1962** Woosley *Water Witching* 138 Taking his shovel and peach tree limb, grandpap set out to witch some water. **1993** Montell *Cumberland Country* 37–38 Almost without exception dowsers were used to "witch" wells dug in the region before the 1930s. A dowser, or "water witch," is a person perceived to have a skill for discovering underground water with the use of a divining rod, usually a small, forked limb cut from any fruit-bearing tree or willow.

witch ball *noun* See citation. See also **conjure ball**, **hair ball**.

2007 Milnes *Signs Cures Witches* 167 Witch balls and/or hairballs are an unusual but fairly widely known supernatural phenomenon in the Appalachians. There are two very different classifications of a witch ball. The first kind, also called a hairball, is believed to be sent to people supernaturally as a curse. The second is made of glass and is commonly used for divination.

witch doctor (also *witch master*) *noun* One who uses incantations, herbal remedies, Bible verses, etc. to either carry out or counter magic spells. See 1972 citation. See also **conjure doctor**, **herb doctor**, **Indian doctor**, **power doctor**, **wart conjurer**.

1824 (in **1912** Doddridge *Notes on Settlement* 126) Wizards were men supposed to possess the same mischievous power as the witches; but these were seldom exercised for bad purposes. The powers of the wizards were exercised almost exclusively for the purpose of counteracting the malevolent influence of the witches of the other sex. I have known several of those witch masters, as they were called, who made a public profession of curing the diseases inflicted by the influence of witches, and I have known respectable physicians who had no greater portion of business in the line of their profession than many of these witch masters had in theirs. **1894** Porter *Folklore Mt Whites* 113 The key to a place from which something has been stolen, placed by a competent "witch doctor" in the Bible, its covers tied together, and the whole held by the loser while he guesses at the culprit's name, will fall out when his surmise is correct. **1924** Raine *Saddlebags* 77 When ordinary means fail, a Mountaineer may consult a witch-doctor instead of an agricultural expert when "the cow gives quar milk, and the butter won't come." **1943** Korson *Coal Dust* 55 In Wise County, Virginia, which is old mining country, miners consulted "witch doctors." Picturesque old codgers they were, wearing long hair, flowing whiskers, and moccasins. **1956** Hall Coll (Gatlinburg TN) A witch doctor drawed a picture of the witch and nailed it back of the door, druv a nail in her heart, and then she died. **1963** Parris *Witches* You never of hear of witches any more. But in grandpa's day and time the woods were full of them. There was hardly a community that didn't have its witchdoctor. **1972** Cooper *NC Mt Folklore* 17 In his day, the Witch Doctor was an exalted and very important personality, for it was he who was always ready to combat the wickedness of the witches of his area, either by removing their witchery on beast or human beings, or by punishing them as severely as their misdeeds warranted. **1974** GSMNP-51:22

This family lived across there, and they claimed this boy'd been bewitched by somebody, and they'd sent and got a witch doctor. He could take this spell off.

witch hobble *noun* Same as **hobblebush**.

1943 Stupka *Through the Year* 283 The hobblebush or witch hobble [is] an abundant high-mountain shrub whose large roundish leaves reach their color peak in September. The hiker will encounter this plant along all the trails which take him through forests of spruce and fir. **2013** DeLozier and Jourdan *Back Seat* 20 The bad news was that we were nearly surrounded by an impenetrable thicket of leucothe shrubs. The locals called them *dog hobble* and *witch hobble*.

witching stick *noun* A forked stick used to dowse for underground water, a divining rod. Also called **charm stick, water witch A2**.

1955 Rogers *Switching* 109 He used a peach tree "witching stick" cut in the usual manner of a fork. The stick begins to turn downward when one is over water, and points straight down at the place where the water is nearest the surface. **1968** Wilson *Folklore Mammoth Cave* 25 *witching stick* = a forked stick or switch—usually from a peachtree—used to locate underground water. There are several noted water-witches in the region.

witch marks *noun* See citation.

2007 McMillon *Notes* = stars and symbols drawn at points of entrance to homes.

witch master See **witch doctor**.

witch's light *noun* See citations.

1966 *DARE Survey* (Burnsville NC) = a small light that seems to dance or flicker over a marsh at night. **1998** Montgomery *Coll* (known to Brown, Bush).

witch stick *noun* A stick used in divining message from the stars.

1933 Thomas *Traipsin' Woman* 123 He claimed he saw signs in the stars; anyway, with the witch stick and the cedar box [of hair balls] he sped across the mountain in the dead of night to Tacketts' to break the spell on Nordie.

witch tale *noun* A memorable story about an encounter with a witch.

1956 Hall *Coll* (Townsend TN) My mother heared them old witch tales. She was afeared she'd see a witch.

witch woman *noun* A woman who practices witchcraft.

1964 Roberts *Hell-Fer-Sartin* 112 When she come back to unhitch him, why, he slipped that bridle on that woman, on that witch-woman, and he traveled two or three days. **1978** Hiser *Quare Do's* 122 The old witch woman told her the same as she had before, that the fair fine prince would come the next day and get the youngest gal Alafair.

[redundant form]

with *preposition*

A Variant form *wif*.

1867 Harris *Sut Lovingood* 70 [They] got him wide enuf awake tu bleve that he wer threatened wif sum orful pussonal calamerty. **2007** McMillon *Notes* He tuck up wif old man Bennett's girl.

[DARE *with* prep A4 (pronc) chiefly South, South Midland]

B Senses.

1 By (expressing agency).

1973 Carpenter *Mid-Appal* 35 Frequently a statement such as, "I got kicked with a mule" may be heard. When a husband tells a doctor, "Doc, my wife got kicked with a cow, and I would like for you to come over to see what you can do," he does not mean that his wife and cow both were kicked.

2 Because of.

1971 *AOHP/ALC-129* He was crying with his head. [I] never put my hand [on] a person's head hotter in my life. **1973** *Serpents* 36 He had t'go t'th'doctor with it.

withdraw *verb* Variant past-tense form *withdrawed*.

1792 *Richland Church Minutes* 187 Brother Richard Megee with Drawd from the church for which the church Doth Refuse him their fellowship.

withey (also *withy*) *adjective* Of a person: sinewy, wirey, tough.

1913 Kephart *Our Sthn High* 92 The stamina of these "withey" little men was even more remarkable than their endurance of cold. **1917** Kephart *Word-List* 419 = sinewy. "He's a *withey* little devil in a bear fight." **1994** Montgomery *Coll* (known to Cardwell, Jones, Oliver, Weaver). **1995** Stone *Smoky Mt Women* 69 She was "a withy (a mountain expression meaning small and slender but strong and tough) little woman," Ogle said.

[< *withe* "a slender, flexible branch or twig" + *-y*; DARE *withy* adj 2 especially New England, South Midland]

without

A Variant forms *athout, thout*.

1863 *Griffin CW Letters* (May 9) maby I will git a leter from home this eaving if I dont I will hafter do athout. **1883** Murfree *Old Sledge* 552 [It is] a blessin' that I hev got it agin, for't would hev been mighty ill convenient 'round hyur 'thout it. **1901** Harben *Westerfelt* 56 That left jest Lum Evans facin' 'im 'thout a thing in his hands. **1924** Raine *Saddlebags* 29 [He] sat down by the fire and warmed himself 'thout sayin' nothin'. **1954** Arnow *Dollmaker* 89 I've got to learn to manage this store thout a man. **2007** Preece *Leavin' Sandlick* 18 I don't know how I'm goina live athout him.

[DARE *athout, thout* (at *without* prep, adv, conj A1) chiefly South, South Midland, New England]

B *conjunction* Unless, except it is the case that. Also called **withouten C**.

1793 (in **1919** DeWitt *Sevier Journal* 163) (Oct 14) It is ordered from this time forward that no person presume to set on fire any Indian Hutt or town in which there is corn or provision without there is orders from me to do the same. **1806** (in **2011** *Cocke Co TN Petitions* 145) Your Petitioner further advines that he will be considerably injured without your Honble body grants the priveledge he prays for. **1863** *Warrick CW Letters* (Oct 29) It looks like a bad chance for me ever to git home without I runaway. **1895** Edson and Fairchild *TN Mts* 376 I never seen nary 'thout that wasn't one. **1911** Shearin *E KY Word-List* 540 = unless; e.g., "I won't try it without you help me." **1937** Hall *Coll* (Cataloochee NC) You couldn't cow him without you whipped him. *Ibid.* (Cosby TN) A dog won't stay 'thout he's fenced. **1972** GSMNP-71:33 You've never lived without you rode a bulger wagon off of the Hickham Hill. **1982** Powers and Hannah *Cataloochee* 232 He.... stayed at home pretty well all the time without he wasn't in the mountains. **1989** *Matewan OHP*-45 Hit wouldn't do for a stranger to go up there without he had somebody that they knowed with him.

[OED3 *without* conj B chiefly U.S. dialect use: DARE *without* prep, conj B chiefly Northeast, South, South Midland]

withouten

A Variant forms *thouten* [see **1952** in **B**], *thoutn*.

1931 Combs *Lg Sthn High* 1317 "thoutn" (without).

B *preposition* Without.

1886 Smith *Sthn Dialect* 350 A language might deteriorate any time from such causes in the way of such forms as.... withouten. **1917** Burelbach *After Bruin* 316 We'll be a-leavin' here in the mornin' and will have 'nough to pack withouten it. **1939** Walker *Mtneer Looks* 9 I seed 'im throw a steer oncet an' tie 'im up withouten any help. **1940** Still *River of Earth* 39 'Pon my word and honor, you can't stretch your arms withouten knocking flower pots over. **1952** Wilson *Folk Speech NC* 601 I won't go 'thouten him. **1963** Edwards *Gravel* 139 [We] went on then withouten the least sign of a bite until purt nigh milkin time, an I finely sez to Bob, "Bob, reckin we hadn't orter go home? Hit's a gittin clost to milkin time."

C *conjunction* Unless. Same as **without B**.

1952 Wilson *Folk Speech NC* 601 I won't go *'thouten* you go. **1974** Fink *Bits Mt Speech* 29 I won't go *withouten* you do.

[< Middle English *withouten* < *wiþútan*, from *wiþ* "with" prep + *útan* "outen" (adv); EDD *withouten* prep, north Britain; DARE *withouten* prep, conj chiefly South, South Midland, especially southern Appalachians]

with socks on *adjective phrase* Of coffee: with milk or cream added. See also **barefoot**.

1944 Wentworth *ADD* 43 (WV) Investigation revealed that the people in that section drank their coffee "barefooted" or "with socks on," meaning with or without cream. **2001** Montgomery *Coll* I'll have my coffee with socks on (Cardwell).

withy See **withey**.

witness *noun* A wedding attendant.

1966 Dakin *Vocab Ohio River Valley* 499 Among some Mountain speakers [in KY] it is apparently a common practice to call such attendants *witness*—a term which of course designates their actual legal function and purpose but which is recorded nowhere else.

witness tree *noun* See citation.

1939 Hall *Coll* (Smokemont NC) = a tree used to mark the corner of a farm.

witty

A *adjective* See citations.

c1960 Wilson *Coll* = intelligent or clever. **1967** Giles *40 Acres* 4 A man who is able or capable is said to be "witty" or "clever."

B *noun* A half-wit, simpleton.

1940 Still *River of Earth* 179 "Sometimes I fair think Jolly is a witty," Aunt Rilla said. **1962** Dykeman *Tall Woman* 27 Then she had known that the witty understood more than people ever realized. He knew his position; the wretchedness of his life was real and raw to him. **1976** Still *Pattern of Man* 87 Witties are granted compassion, lackers of knowledge a season to catch up. **1989** Still *Rusties and Riddles* [26] = a simpleton.

wobble water *noun* Homemade whiskey.

1994 Montgomery *File* (known to 82-year-old man, Gatlinburg TN).

woke, woked See **wake A**.

wolf (also *wool*) *noun* A swelling beneath the skin of cattle and other animals caused by the parasitic larva of a fly; the larva itself.

1917 Kephart *Word-List* 419 *wolf* = the warble that appears in summer in the backs of rabbits and squirrels. **1944** Combs *Word-List Sthn High* 22 *wolves* = bots or warbles in the backs of cows [or rabbits and squirrels], caused supposedly by sprinkling salt on the cows' backs. **1982** Slone *How We Talked* 118 *wools in the back* = the large "horse fly" laid its eggs under the skin on the back of the cows.... When they hatched the larva were called "wools." Very painful. **2009** Wiles and Wiles *Location* 42 Besides being a farmer, he was known to have cures for ailing farm animals. The most notable treatment was administered to cattle when the symptoms didn't really indicate any particular ailment, in those cases, the disease had to be caused by "wolf in the tail."

[DARE chiefly South, South Midland]

wolfing the tail *verbal noun phrase* See citation.

2007 Milnes *Signs Cures Witches* 81 In southern West Virginia, Kent Lilly described a method of removing a curse from a farm through a magical procedure. Several cows on a local farm got the "hollow tail," a condition in which the tail goes limp or flaccid. Kent said they tried to cure them by a method [called] "wolfin' the tail." The tail is split open and has salt and pepper poured into it.

wolf pit *noun* A type of trap to catch wolves.

1949 Hall *Coll* (Del Rio TN) They dug wolf pits on Cosby [Creek]. They'd throw meat in there. Wolves would get caught in them. **1962** Hall *Coll* (Newport TN) Old man Tommy Webb had a wolf pit.... He had a plank fixed, put a sheep's head on the end of it, sheep's head nailed to the plank. Plank would go down and drop the wolf off and then go back up for another one. Uncle Tom would go every morning and catch two or three and sometimes eight, ten, or twelve. [Wolves] couldn't climb any more than a dog.

wolf tree *noun* A large, often bent tree with branches approaching the ground, thereby covering undergrowth and depriving it of sunlight. It is often of little value as timber.

1969 Sorden *Lumber Lingo* 142 = a large tree overtopping and smothering the young growth, often a limby, low-value specimen. **1974–75** McCracken *Logging* 21:24 A wolf tree has branches almost down to the ground. It takes up so much space. **1997** Hufford *Stalking* Some people call beeches "wolf trees" because they gobble up all the nutrients. [But] I like to leave four or five, if they're not too close together, for game. **1999** Montgomery *Coll* = any species of tree that is very limby and undesirable for timber, especially one with many knots in the wood (Pittillo).

wolf whiskey *noun* Homemade whiskey.

1974 Dabney *Mt Spirits* 25 The names [for corn whiskey include].... wolf whiskey.

woman *noun*

A Forms.

1 Variant singular forms *dummern, oman, omern, ummern, wimmen, womern.*

1845 (in **1974** Harris *High Times* 48) "You, Jake Snyder, don't holler so!" says the old oman—"Why, you are worse nor a painter." **1884** Smith *Arp Scrap Book* 73 Over 200 [Hens] now respond to my old 'oman's call every mornin. **1913** Kephart *Our Sthn High* 279 In Mi[t]chell County, North Carolina, we hear the extraordinary forms ummern and dummern ("La! Look at them dummernses a-comin'!") **1944** Wilson *Word-List* 38 That 'omern's above her own kinnery. **1978** Williams *Appal Speech* 175 The sound of *r* is also inserted in many words in mountain speech: "woman," "womern." **1982** Slone *How We Talked* 36 *womern.* **2006** Shelby *Appal Studies* 39 Old womern, you talk too much!

[DARE *oman, omern, ummern* (at *woman* n A1) chiefly South, South Midland; *womern* (at *woman* n A2) especially southern Appalachians, Central Atlantic]

2 Variant plural forms *dummernses* [see **1913** in **A1**], *womens.*

1971 *AOHP/ALC-160* Back at that time the womens, they didn't work in factories in this part of the country like they do today. **1971** *Granny Women* 247 Most of th'old womens in those days smoked cobbed pipes. **1979** *Big South Fork OHP-4* The womens all works to town and they buy that kind of stuff down there. **2008** *Rosie Hicks* 6 It seem like the womens wouldn't tell the kids like they did.

[DARE *woman* n Bb South, South Midland]

B See **the 4**.

C A female spouse or companion (used often by a man in reference to his own).

1791 *Richland Church Minutes* 102 Church Confess ther falt Receiving John Burnett and his woman into their Fellowship. **1913** Kephart *Our Sthn High* 197–98 If the man of the house has misgivings as to the state of the larder, he will say: "I'll ax the woman gin she can give you a bite." *Ibid.* 257 "The woman," as every wife is called, has her kingdom within the house. **1927** Furman *Lonesome Road* 25 I's Cindy Stoll—Preacher Jared Stoll's woman—from over on Stoll's Branch. **1939** Hall *Coll* (Hazel Creek NC) We went over there a-chestnut hunting and took our women with us, leave them there. **1979** Carpenter *Walton War* 69 "Now, Ellie," said Tome angrily, "I ain't goin' to take that kind of talk from my woman." **2005** Williams *Gratitude* 536 = a wife; old lady; ol' woman. "Him and his *woman* has been married for forty year."

woman doctor *noun* One skilled in obstetrics or midwifery.

1973 *GSMNP-76*:30 Lincoln Whaley, he was a good woman doctor. **1975** Jackson *Unusual Words* 154 The midwife was a *woman doctor* or a *granny woman*, who would come in the old days and stay a week after delivering the baby for the grand sum of one dollar.

woman-person *noun* A woman.

c1940 Padelford *Notes* A woman-person's ways. **1952** Justus *Children* 45 There was no woman person in their home since Mrs. Harris had died the year before. **1975** Chalmers *Better* 65–66 He drug the ground and ruke the leaves, while his woman-person shuk the rug and rinsed the clothes by splunging them in the creek, or the branch, or the fork or the prong.

[redundant form; DARE *woman-person* n chiefly South, South Midland]

womenfolk(s) *noun* Women collectively, the female members of a family or group.

1869 (in **1974** Harris *High Times* 216) The wimmen folks seems to think [kissing is] something worth fightin for so we must sorter "let on." **1913** Kephart *Our Sthn High* 285–86 Pleonasms are abundant.... Everywhere in the mountains we hear of biscuit-bread.... women-folks. **1940** Oakley *Roamin'/Restin'* 15 As the war was growing strong at the time father said he would visit the mountain peoples homes and sometimes carry in wood and help out the women folks as the most of the men was gone to war. **1969** Medford *Finis* 82 Often the women folk in this way took the "turns" of corn to the grist-mills and the produce to market. **1974** Fink *Bits Mt Speech* 29 The *women folks* had all gone to meeting. **1979** Slone *My Heart* 121 That was another code of the hills. No female was allowed to go far from home without the protection of some male of the same family. They had this respect and reverence for their "womenfolks," even when they were very young. **1988** Russell *It Happened* 13 Much preserving and canning of food was done by the women folks. **1995** Adams *Come Go Home* 21 [The men] would often play in someone's barn until the womenfolk found out where they were playing, and then they would take their blanket and move somewhere else.

womens See **woman A2**.

womern See **women A1**.

wompus cat See **wampus**.

wompy-jawed See **whopper-jawed**.

wonder *verb*

1 In phrase *I wonder me* = I wonder.

1943 Hannum *Mt People* 146 Their phrasing has a rhythm to it, such as. . . . "I wonder me if." **1960** Cooper *Jularker Bussed* I wonder me if she can bake biscuit bread.

[OED3 *wonder* v 1f obsolete or dialect]

2 To cause to marvel, amaze (especially in phrase *it wonders me*).

1921 Combs *KY Items* 119 It wonders me what that boy's about. **1952** Wilson *Folk Speech NC* 608 = to cause to wonder. "It *wonders* me how that bear ever climbed that tree." **1979** Carpenter *Walton War* 172 Hit wonders me how time can go on as far as everything has got, and I have pondered on hit a sight. **1997** Montgomery *Coll*: *it wonders me* (known to Adams, Bush, Cardwell, Oliver).

[OED3 *wonder* v 4 obsolete; perhaps influenced by German; Web3 dialect]

3 Followed by an embedded yes/no question that maintains inversion of the subject and verb (thus *wonder can you* = wonder whether/if you can). See also **ask B1**, **know C1**, **see B1**.

1982 Abell *Better Felt* 18 There's where a lot of people wonder can a man be lost after he was once saved.

4 Followed by an embedded *wh*-question that maintains inversion of the subject and verb (thus *wonder how can you* = wonder how you can). See also **know C2**, **see B2**.

1972 *AOHP/LJC-259* I just wondered how did we get along.

wonderful

A *adjective* Extreme, unusual, surprising.

1831 *McLean Diary* 1 friday and a Wonderful storm of wind and snow. **1904–20** Kephart *Notebooks* 4:855 My woman, she's given me a wonderful sight o' trouble. **1913** Kephart *Our Sthn High* 174 It was wonderful how soon that room was emptied! **1979** Carpenter *Walton War* 80 The story is that his young wife once got a terrific toothache—hurting something wonderful, as they sometimes said in the hills—and no dentist was available.

B *adverb* Extremely, unusually, surprisingly.

1940 Bowman *KY Mt Stories* 18 The use of "wonderful" instead of "very"—as: "The room was wonderful dirty"—surely must be a carry-over from the seventeenth century, used in the sense of "enough to excite surprise." **1969** Medford *Finis* 66 "Jim orter a-made a good moonshiner, if he hadn't a been so skeery," said Jess Abbotts, "since he could see and hear so wonderful well."

[OED3 *wonderful* adv B now dialect; EDD *wonderful* adj and adv 3]

wonderly *adjective* Wonderful.

1925 Furman *Glass Window* 11 You air young, and have seed sech a sight of this wonderly world. **1936** Justus *Honey Jane* 108 I have been thinking what a wonderly sight it will be to sit by the fire and look at the snow through all them new glass winders! **1943** Justus *Bluebird* 60 A wonderly thing it was indeed that they would all stick together even with the apple-butter filling. **1997** Montgomery *Coll* (known to Cardwell, Weaver).

[OED3 *wonderly* adj obsolete]

wonest, wonst See **once**.

won't quit See **quit**.

woodchuck *noun* A woodpecker, commonly the pileated woodpecker (*Dryocopus pileatus*). See also **chuckwood**, **peckerwood 1**, **sapsucker**, **woodcock**.

1934–47 *LAMSAS Appal* (Madison Co NC). **1966** Dakin *Vocab Ohio River Valley* 395 In the mountains and the eastern Knobs [of KY] older speakers commonly say *woodchuck* (once *chuckwood* in Johnson City). **1968** *DARE Survey* (London KY) = pileated woodpecker: "I've seen 'em down in the bottoms; some of 'em got mighty near as big as a small banty hen"; (Brasstown NC) = type of woodpecker. **1986** Pederson et al. *LAGS* (Blount Co TN, Greene Co TN, Washington Co TN).

[DARE *woodchuck* n 2a chiefly South, South Midland]

woodcock (also *woodhen*) *noun* The pileated woodpecker (*Dryocopus pileatus*). See also **woodchuck**.

1913 Kephart *Our Sthn High* 295 The giant woodpecker (here still a common bird) is known as a woodcock or woodhen. **1934–47** *LAMSAS Appal* (Swain Co NC) *wood hen*. **1939** Hall *Coll* (White Oak NC) *woodhen* = a red-headed peckerwood. **1961** Seeman *Arms of Mt* 132 The mountain people say that when the "old wood hen" changes sides of the mountain, the weather is going to change. **1981** Alderman *Tilson Mill* 16 He paid attention to the cackle of the pileated woodhens predicting snow, the moaning sound of the rain crow, the fierce winds trailing the high ridges, the message of high winds roaring around and across the top of Big Bald Mountain. **1994–97** Montgomery *Coll*: *wood cock* (known to Brown, Cardwell, Jones, Oliver); *wood hen* (known to Cardwell, Ellis).

[DARE *wood hen* n 2 chiefly South Midland]

wood cutting *noun* Formerly, a neighborhood work activity in the fall to help families, often in rotation, to cut firewood for the coming winter. See also **wood getting**.

1937 Haun *Cocke Co* 11 The same thing happens at fall wood cutting, among those who cut enough wood in the fall to last them all winter. Everybody helps everybody else. They cut at one man's house one day and at another's the next. There is usually one especially good tale-teller or riddler or singer in the crowd, and much use is made of his talents.

woodfish *noun* Same as **dry-land fish**.

2006 *DARE File* "You have to get up in the woods to find them," he said of woodfish mushrooms, more commonly known as morel mushrooms. *Ibid*. Locals call them [= morels] "woodfish" here in VA. **2007** McMillon *Notes* = dry-land fish.

[DARE *woodfish* especially VA, TN]

wood getting *noun* Formerly, a neighborhood work activity in the fall to help families, often in rotation, to gather firewood for the coming winter. See also **wood cutting**.

2003 Smith *Orlean Puckett* 28 As summer turned to autumn, wood gettin's brought the community together to frolic, feast, and gossip while preparing for the coming, unforgiving weather. Chopping wood was always hard work, but the load was lifted when the neighbors joined together to complete the chore. Like corn huskin's, wood gettin's were festive occasions complete with food, cider, music, games, and dancing. With all that teamwork, enough wood to last a family through the winter could be chopped and split in one afternoon. **2008** Salsi *Ray Hicks* 4 Sometimes, we'd help to shuck corn or stir molasses. We might have a wood getting. Anytime people'd swap back and forth helpin' one another, it was time for eatin', talkin', and music.

woodhammer *noun* An unspecified type of woodpecker.

1934–47 *LAMSAS Appal* (Swain Co NC). **1986** Pederson et al. *LAGS* (Scott Co TN). **1997** Montgomery *Coll* (known to Bush, Jones).

wood harp *noun* In logging, a crosscut saw.

2004 *BearPaw* The photos show the transformation from tree to board feet—men cut massive trees with crosscut saws ("misery whips" or "wood harps"), moved the logs with skidders, overhead cables, mules, or greased chutes (some a mile long), loaded them on train cars, dumped them in mill ponds (where "pond monkeys" with spiked boots rolled them around), and fed them into sawmills.

woodhen *noun*

1 See **woodcock.**

2 The northern flicker (*Colaptes auratus*), a medium-sized woodpecker. See also **yellow hammer.**

1992 Joslin *Mt People II* 97 Instead, a pair of Northern Flickers, locally known as yellowhammers or wood hens, had been doing some remodeling to a dead fork of the tree.

woodhick *noun*

1 (also *woodpecker*) A lumberjack, sometimes an itinerant one. See also **hick, timberhick.**

1930 Pendleton *Wood-Hicks Speak* 88 How the "Wood Hicks" Speak.... Hick (sometimes "wood hick"), a lumber jack, a worker in the woods. **1941** *FWP Guide WV* 369 Steel rails, log roads, steam engines, band saws, and other machinery marred the grandeur of the region; but the lumberjack, or wood-hick, was the human instrument of this ruthless drive. **1967** Parris *Mt Bred* 132 A wood-hick, he explained, is the mountain term for lumberjack or logger. **1976** Tyler *Man's Work* 28 It was some of this heroin. A lot of the old wood hicks used it. **1978** Hall *Yarns and Tales* 19 No longer is Gatlinburg, Tennessee, a town of "wood hicks" and "mountain hoosiers." **1991** Weals *Last Train* 53 "Wood hicks" was their name for themselves, for all those men who worked in the woods, Roy M. Myers said. **1996** Cole *Forney's Creek* 63 While many of the loggers worked strictly for Norwood, several roamed from job to job. According to Jerry Ledford, these roamers were commonly known as "wood hicks." Many of them wore large floppy brimmed hats and each day that they worked they would cut a notch in the brim. When it came time to be paid, they would present their hat at the company office, collect their pay for the indicated number of days, and trim the notches from the brim. This process sometimes continued until there was little left but the crown of the hat. **2006** Farwell *Logging Term* 1021 Derogatory terms for loggers—such as *woodhicks* and *woodpeckers*—are no longer used, nor is *ridgerunner* applied to a farmer who logs part time. **2006** *WV Encycl* 809 The origin of the term is probably self-explanatory. Loggers were looked upon as unsophisticated persons working in the woods, and since at least the 16th century the word "hick" has meant an ignorant country person. Perhaps it was for this reason West Virginia woodworkers were called woodhicks or timberhicks.

[DARE *wood hick* n Appalachians]

2 See citation.

1937 Hall *Coll* = a Kentucky term for a Tennessee mountaineer.

wood horse *noun* See citation.

1986 Pederson et al. *LAGS* (Gordon Co GA) = an A-frame [trestle].

wooding *verbal noun* Cutting timber.

1974–75 McCracken *Logging* 23:4 When they went to wooding, I went to working in the woods instead of logging. *Ibid.* 23:32 We started wooding there, along not far from Polls Gap and a-going back in on toward Heintoga, behind the timber cutting.

wood lot *noun* See citations. Woodland on a farm set aside for its timber to be harvested for domestic use.

c1960 Wilson *Coll* = grove of trees left to grow. **1977** Shields *Cades Cove* 32 Most farms had a section of forest reserved as the wood lot, to be cut for this purpose [i.e. of providing firewood].

[DARE *woodlot* n widespread, but especially North, Midland]

woodpeck *noun* A woodpecker.

1934–47 *LAMSAS Appal* (Swain Co NC). **1997** Montgomery *Coll* (known to Bush).

woodpecker *noun*

1 See **woodhick 1.**

2 One who is a poor chopper of wood.

1964 Clarkson *Lumbering in WV* 374 = a poor chopper. **1998** Robbins *Logging Terms.*

wood pretty (also *woods pretty*) *noun* See citations.

1937 Eaton *Handicrafts* 233 In wandering through the mountains it is not uncommon to come across women and children gathering the seeds, pods, berries, acorns, leaves, and cones in which the Highlands abound and arranging them in attractive and interesting forms. The natives call these "wood pretties." **1971** Stevens *Mountain Craftsmen* 5 There are wood carvings, wooden bowls, handmade furniture, wreaths of "woods pretties," vegetable-dyed wools, and hand-woven materials, some of them in patterns hundreds of years old. **1976** *Sevier Co Saga* 22 Many craft items were made in [Sevier County], and Arrowmont was soon selling "coverlets," woven scarves, yard goods, table mats, baskets, whittlings and carvings, small wood items, small furniture, brooms, articles made of corn shuck and "wood pretties," toys and dolls.

[DARE *wood pretty* n especially southern Appalachians]

wood rack *noun* A **sawbuck** with X-shaped endpieces.

1952–57 (in **1973** McDavid and McDavid *Vocab E KY* 160) = saw buck. **1983** Broaddus *Estill Co KY Word List* 61 = a saw rack.

wood sawyer *noun* See citation.

1966 *DARE Survey* (Cherokee NC) = worm used for bait.

woods boss *noun* A logging superintendent.

1979 Carpenter *Walton War* 123 There was a "Woods Boss"—sometimes called the "Bull-of-the-Woods," who was in charge of all the work.

woods' chap See **woods colt 2**.

woods colt *noun*

1 A horse unintentionally bred, one of unknown paternity.

1966 *DARE Survey* (Spruce Pine NC) = a horse that was not intentionally bred, or bred by accident. **1997** Montgomery *Coll* (known to Bush, Weaver).

[DARE *woods colt* n 1 chiefly South, South Midland, TX]

2 (also *woods' chap*) An illegitimate child.

1895 *Word-Lists* 395 = a foundling (Winchester, Ky.). **1903** Fox *Little Shepherd* 93 The boy had said, with amazing frankness and without a particle of shame, that he was a waif—a "woodscolt." **1913** Kephart *Our Sthn High* 294 A bastard is a woods-colt or an outsider. **1926** Wilson *Cullowhee Wordlist*: *woods' chap* = bastard. **1935** Sheppard *Cabins in Laurel* 172 Perhaps he overpersuades her and they "plant their corn before they build their fence"; if he fails to marry her, the child she bears out of wedlock will be a "woods-colt." **1949** Kurath *Word Geog East US* 77 *Woods colt* is current in the Carolinas, the southern Appalachians, and the Ohio Valley from Wheeling downstream. **1964** Reynolds *Born of Mts* 82 In the mountains a child born out of wedlock was once referred to as a woods colt, a colt born out in the woods far from the field nearby. **1966–68** *DARE Survey* (Brasstown NC, Burnsville NC, Spruce Pine NC, Gatlinburg TN) = joking name for a child with unwed parents. **1982** Powers and Hannah *Cataloochee* 262 Often bastards or "woods colts" were given the names of their fathers to soften the impact later in life. **1985** Jones *Growing Up* 176 A woods colt is a person who doesn't know who his father is. **1996–97** Montgomery *Coll* (known to Adams, Brown, Cardwell, Jones, Ledford, Oliver, Weaver).

[DARE *woods colt* n 2 chiefly South, South Midland]

wood shamrock *noun* Same as **mountain shamrock**.

1962 Brewer *Hiking* 29 A low-growing flower you'll see under thick stands of spruce and fir is mountain sorrel (Oxalis montana), sometimes called wood shamrock.

woods loafer *noun* See 1998 citation.

1961 Seeman *Arms of Mt* 47 The people on our creek call the Haney family over in the Ripshin Gap "woods loafers." **1998** Montgomery *Coll* = a person who lived in the woods and survived by hunting, fishing, and gathering, but [was] thought to lack industry by the rest of society (Brown).

woods pretty See **wood pretty**.

woods rabbit *noun* The New England cottontail rabbit (*Silvilagus transitionalis*).

1938 Komarek and Komarek *Mammals* 160 Local people asserted that two kinds of rabbits are found in the park and that one of these found in the higher region is called the "woods rabbit."

wood thrasher *noun* A wood thrush, perhaps the brown thrush (*Hylocichla mustelina*).

1961 Miller *Pigeon's Roost* (Sept 28) We always call the chimney swift birds the chimney sweepers. The towhees, jorees; phoebee, pewees;. . . . and wood thrush, wood thrashers.

wool

A See **wolf**.

B *verb*

1 To play with, rub, or handle, as a baby, puppy, or kitten.

c1960 Wilson *Coll* = to tousle, muss up. **1963** Edwards *Gravel* 21 He reached down and wooled my head so hard that he made my head hot. . . . "I wisht I had me a boy like you, Tad," he said. **1982** Slone *How We Talked* 24 = to fondle or handle a baby gently, to play with it. **1983** Broaddus *Estill Co KY Word List* 61 = to fondle somewhat roughly, as in fondling a little pup, or handling a baby. **2014** *WV Talk* = to handle or pet excessively. "You're going to wool that kitten to death."

[DARE *wool* v 3 chiefly South Midland]

2 Of a hunting dog: to snap or bite at (a game animal shot and killed) as a reflex in the aftermath of the kill.

1976 *Bear Hunting* 274 We let them dogs wool the bear for about five minutes [after it has been killed]. Then we get the dogs off.

wooley breeches See **woollen breeches**.

wool gather *verb phrase* To bewilder.

1987 Young *Lost Cove* 34 How the voices could travel so far in the air woolgathered the oldtimers no end.

[cf DARE *wool-gathered* adj "muddled, bewildered, distracted" especially South, South Midland]

wool hat *noun* A man's plain, rounded felt hat with a shapeless brim; hence a rustic person, resident of the hills.

1952 Callahan *Smoky Mt Country* 87 In the other months, shapeless, rounded black felts gave their wearers the name of "wool hats." **1957** Parris *My Mts* 155 Back in the jeans-britches and wool-hat era when the corncob pipe was all the go. **1997** Montgomery *Coll* (known to Bush).

[DARE *wool hat* n chiefly South, South Midland, especially South Atlantic]

woolies *noun* Long winter underwear. See also **long handles**.

1976 Garber *Mountain-ese* 103 = winter underwear: "It's time to put on your woolies."

woolie worm See **wooly worm**.

woollen breeches (also *wooley breeches, woolly britches, wooly-breeches*) *noun* An edible green.

1818 Barton *Vegetable Materia Medica* 2.xiii (DARE) I send you a plant, vulgarly known in Ohio, Kentucky, and Tennessee, by the name of Woollen-breeches. The young shoots are eaten in the spring, as a sallad. . . . The plant in question proves. . . . to be Hydrophyllum appendiculatum. **1937** Hyatt *Kiverlid* 79 We picked wild mustard an'. . . . wooly-breeches. **1952** McCall *Cherokees and Pioneers* 100 The pinch comes in late winter when "leather breeches" (green beans strung on thread to dry), dried fruit, and holed-up potatoes begin to give out, and when poke, dandelions, "wooley breeches," and other "greens" have not yet "put out." **1999** Perry *Clinch River* Nobody in our family said greens or land-cress, it was Sallet. I especially like the homey names of plants Granny taught me to recognize, Narrow dock, speckled Dick, woolly britches.

woolly britches See **woollen breeches**.

woolly bug See **wooly worm**.

wooly

A *adjective* Overgrown with rhododendron and other dense vegetation.

1996 Montgomery *Coll* I want to walk somewhere it's not wooly, so I can see if there's any snakes (Adams).

B (also *wooly back, wooly head, wooly patch*) *noun* See citations. Same as **laurel bed**. See also **wooly ridge, wooly top, yellow patch**.

1913 Kephart *Our Sthn High* 301 A "hell" or "slick" or "wooly-head" or "yaller patch" is a thicket of laurel or rhododendron, impassable save where the bears have bored out trails. **1933** McCoy and Masa *Smoky Guide* 94 A number of persons, unfamiliar with the region, have been lost in these wildernesses, colloquially known as "slicks," "hells," or "woolyheads," and have wandered for days over dim and ever-crossing bear-trails searching for some way out. **1956** Fink *That's Why* 4 [Tangles] of low rhododendron or kalmia. . . . are also called woolies or woolly patches. **1976** *Bear Hunting* 281 [The bear might] be laying up in a wooly head up a ridge. **1996** Montgomery *Coll*: *wooly back* (known to Adams, Cardwell, Oliver).

[DARE *woolly head* n 2 especially southern Appalachians]

wooly back See **wooly B**.

wooly booger *noun* An imaginary ragged, unkempt, frightful-looking figure. See also **booger A1**.

1997 Montgomery *Coll* = anything or anyone frightful looking, as "He looked like a wooly booger with that long hair and ragged clothes" (Norris). **2009** Benfield *Mt Born* 207 = rather like a boogerman, but with wild hair projecting from all sorts of body parts. A frightful apparition. **2013** DeLozier and Jourdan *Back Seat* 6 The one named April wore a homemade sweater of purple yarn that hung big on her. The one named Portia had leather patches across the shoulders of her sweater, like she was on a submarine. They both had big wild hair. Mamaw said they looked like woolyboogers. **2014** Ellis *Coll* = very common when I was growing up [in the 1950s]. "You look like a wooly booger." Parents or grandparents might say "You better look out—a wooly booger might get you."

wooly-breeches, wooly britches See **woollen breeches**.

wooly bug See **wooly worm**.

wooly head, wooly patch See **wooly B**.

wooly ridge *noun* A mountain ridge covered with a dense thicket or **slick**; also used in place-names, as in *Wooly Ridge* (NC). See also **wooly B**.

1960 Hall *Smoky Mt Folks* 59 = laurel bed, lettuce bed, rough, slick, woolly (as in woolly head, woolly ridge, woolly top), yellow patch, and hell (as in Huggin's Hell).

wooly top *noun* Same as **heath bald**. See also **wooly B**.

1979 Horton *Natural Heritage* 27 Shrub balds, also called wooly tops, laurel slicks, or laurel hells, usually contain many species of shrubs, but often the best represented family is the heath family which contains rhododendrons, azaleas, laurel or ivy, and many less well-known types of shrub. **1989** Oliver *Hazel Creek* 25 [The balds] are of two types: shrub balds, called wooly tops, laurel slicks or laurel hells (Huggins Hell on Welch Ridge), and grassy balds or fields a little lower. **1994** Montgomery *Coll* = often very extensive, covering hundreds of acres, having small deciduous tracts, making it look wooly in the wintertime (from loss of leaves); these tend to be higher in the mountains (Shields).

wooly worm (also *woolie worm, woolly bug, wooly bug*) *noun* A large, hairy caterpillar, the larva of a moth of the family *Arctiidae*, whose width of colored bands and behavior purportedly foretell the duration and severity of the oncoming winter.

1940 Haun *Hawk's Done* 24 When I got close to it, I felt like wooly bugs were crawling all over me. **1970** *Weather Signs* 7 It will be a hard winter if. . . . there are a lot of wooly worms traveling about, or heading south. The same worm also tells of a bad winter if he is crawling before the first frost, or if he has an especially heavy coat. The more black than brown the wooly worm's coat is, and/or the wider the black stripe, the harder the winter will be. **1982** Slone *How We Talked* 100 Wooly worms tell what kind of winter there will be: light color—snow; dark color—wet; multi-colored—varied. **1997** Montgomery *Coll*: *woolly bug* (known to Adams, Andrews, Bush, Cardwell, Weaver). **2003** Howell *Folklife*

Big South Fork 40 If most of the woolie worms seem to be headed southward, it will be a bad winter.

[DARE *woolly worm* n scattered, but chiefly west Midland, Mississippi-Ohio Valleys, TX]

wopper-jawed See **whopper-jawed 1**.

word with the bark on it *noun phrase* A blunt statement.

1892 Fruit *KY Words* 233 = for emphasis: "That is the word with the bark on it; you better mind out."

[DARE *word with the bark on (it)* n phr chiefly South Midland]

wore See **wear**.

wore out See **wear out**.

work-brickle See **work-brittle**.

work-brittle *adjective*

A Variant form *work brickle* [see **1927** in **B1**; **1952** in **B2**].

B Senses.

1 Energetic, eager and willing to work, industrious.

1927 Woofter *Dialect from WV* 36 *work brickle* = anxious to work. "What makes you so work brickle all at once?" **1940** Bowman *KY Mt Stories* 250 *work brickle* = eager for work. **1966–67** *DARE Survey* (Spruce Pine NC, Gatlinburg TN) = feeling ambitious and eager to work. **1974** Fink *Bits Mt Speech* 29 *work-brittle* = industrious. **1992** Jones and Miller *Sthn Mt Speech* 119 *work brittle (brickle)* = to like to work, have a great capacity to work. **1995–97** Montgomery *Coll*: *work brittle* = describes a person who works well at a number of jobs, knows how to achieve, needs no supervision (Cardwell).

[OED3 *work brittle* adj "eager to work" English regional and U.S. regional; DARE *work-brittle* adj 1 chiefly Midland, especially Indiana]

2 Unaccustomed or unwilling to work.

1952 Wilson *Folk Speech NC* 609 *work brickle* = unaccustomed to working. **1995–97** Montgomery *Coll*: *work brittle* = detesting work of any kind, as "He's work brittle; a little work could break him" (Bush), = fragile, hesitant (Jones). **2007** McMillon *Notes*: *work brittle* = said of one who is lazy and dislikes or won't do work.

[DARE *work-brittle* adj 2 chiefly southern Appalachians]

work cow *noun* See citation.

1957 Broaddus *Vocab Estill Co KY* 89 = an ox.

work frolic (also *working party*) *noun* Formerly, a gathering of young people for partying after participating in a **working**.

1959 Hall *Coll* (Hartford TN) For social life back in the mountains when I was very young, it was mostly confined to working parties. We would have the apple peeling, the berry canning, the molasses making, and corn husking. . . . these seasonal affairs that the older people would let the younger people gather and do the seasonal canning or processing of food and promise them that afterward they could have a little social life in the form of doing the buckwing or the hoedown. **1998** Dabney *Smokehouse Ham* 38 "Work frolics" became the great social event. They began on the frontier, when raising a house required quick, communal action in the face of unfriendly Indians. But popularity of the "workings" went well beyond the end of the Indian wars.

workhorse *noun* See citation.

1983 Broaddus *Estill Co KY Word List* 61 = a saw horse.

[DARE *workhorse* n chiefly South, South Midland]

workified *adjective* Having much work experience, working very hard.

c1945 Haun *Hawk's Done* 297 "You look stout and workified in it," he said. **1990** Bailey *Draw Up Chair* 14 If a person working unusually hard is said to be "workified," logically one suffering from spells or fits is "fittified." **1997** Montgomery *Coll* (known to Bush, Cardwell). **2005** Bailey *Henderson County* 30 Unimpressed by the extra hours of duty for which her friend had volunteered, a woman laughed and said, "I ain't all that workified."

working *noun*

1 Traditionally, a gathering of neighbors to perform a communal task or to help a family perform or complete a particular task, such as a **house raising** or **corn shucking**, with the labor usually followed by a party or **frolic**; the gathering might also be held to undertake a public works project or help a destitute family. See also **work frolic**.

1921 Campbell *Sthn Highlander* 129–30 In the democratic life of the remote Highlands distinctions are not strongly marked, and legitimate social events, such as singings and "workings" where a large crowd may be present, are attended by all who wish to come, regardless of difference in social or moral status. **1931** Goodrich *Mt Homespun* 41 Her children made frequent visits, and she was called on as a matter of course to help whenever there was a "working"; whether "fodder pulling," "corn shucking," or "grubbing"; for no one else could superintend as she could the cooking of a big dinner. **1936** Stuart *Head of Hollow* 27 We had to get together and have workins and put the fence back. We had to put some barns back and two houses. **1937** White *Highland Heritage* 37 There used to be logrollings and house-raisings to get new couples started, but they are not common any more. There may, however, be a working on a new church or school building. **1957** GSMNP-23:2:27 My neighbors come in and holped me raise [the house], and we put that up in a day. . . . We call it a working, and they come up there, and we put the rafters on that, and they got it ready to cover in a day. **1968** Clarke *Stuart's Kentucky* 92 Workin's, which had been of vital importance in the truly pioneer period, were largely social affairs by Stuart's lifetime. **1973** GSMNP-74:33 That there now is the way that a lot of the folks had to do that come to this country, and they wasn't no houses. They'd go and they'd cut down timber and they'd hew the logs flat on each side, and they'd put a notch in them so that they could put them up, and they'd get enough cut to build that house. Then they called a working. They'd ask the men, the neighbors to come in and help them. And they'd come in and help lift those logs, and they'd build that day, you see, put it up. **1976** Braden *Grandma Was Girl* 86 The men had their "workings" too. Maybe a man needed a new field cleared, and his friends would come to help. They would cut the trees, grub out the bushes, and burn the brush. Some of the wives came to help with the dinner and visit. Some of them brought their children. Sometimes somebody would have a barn raising, and the man's friends would come in to help with the heavy work. **1979** *Preacher Cook* 195 They'd have workings and they'd clean off land, great fields of land. **1991** Thomas *Sthn Appal* 175 A typical response to loss suffered by one family in the community was some form of "working," as in rebuilding a house, barn or fence. To help a disabled person with his farm crops, neighbors would assemble for planting, plowing, hoeing, crop-gathering—or perhaps a man would send his son with a horse and plow for a few days. **1995** *Smokies Guide* (Autumn) 1 In autumn farmers gathered for group "workings," such as corn shuckings, sorghum molasses making, and hog-butchering—labors that were blended with music, dancing, eating, courting, and general socializing to make them activities that were savored rather than dreaded. **1995** Weber *Rugged Hills* 14 When someone is injured or sick, neighbors have "a workin'" and put up his hay or cut his tobacco or put a new roof on a widow's house as they recently did for Ruby Noah.

[DARE *working* n chiefly South, South Midland]

2 In a coal mine, an area or chamber from which coal is being extracted.

1971 *AOHP/ALC-66* We'd get in these old workings that had been worked out for several years. **2002** Armstead *Black Days* 241 = [a] ventilated area in a coal mine where miners and/or machines work or travel. **2004** *Early Mines* 31 (as of 1902) A mine car was pushed into the working by a man whose job was to distribute cars. . . . When the car was full, the men in the working would push it to the main line.

working alive *adjective phrase* Especially of animals: plentiful, swarming.

1862 *Warrick CW Letters* (June 13) I can in form you that I neve seen so meney men Since God made me the woulds [= woods] is working alive for about fore miles Square. **c1950** Adams *Grandpap* 155 That was when I was a-gatherin' up these sheep. Oh, that river is just a-workin' alive with 'em! **1969** Roberts *Greasybeard* 37 The river was just naturally working alive with all kinds of fish when I was growing up. **1999** Montgomery *Coll* = used especially with reference to bees, yellow jackets, ants, etc. (Cardwell).

workingest *adjective* Working the most or best. See 1998 citation. See also **-est 1** and Grammar and Syntax §3.4.1.

1913 Kephart *Our Sthn High* 285 Peculiar adjectives are formed from verbs. . . . "She's the workin'est woman!" **1921** Weeks *Speech of KY Mtneer* 18 We like to give the superlative degree to our present participles. My friend says, "Hits a sight in the world how that boy works! He's the workingest boy I've got." **1939** Walker *Mtneer Looks* 2–3 There are few words so characteristic as *beatin'est* and *workin'est*, which in politer society would be *strangest* and *most industrious*. **1943** Hannum *Mt People* 148 With even more fanciful flux, verbs transfer into adjectives: "the travelin'est hosses; the talkin'est woman; the workin'est man." **1963** Edwards *Gravel* 51 Brad Green was a worker; Sara could see that, and even Mark exclaimed: "That's the workinest man in forty states." **1973** *AOHP/ASU-106* He's got a farm, the workingest fellow you've ever saw hit the ground. **1998** Montgomery *Coll* (consultants from the Smoky Mountains interpret this form in the following ways: eight as "works more than anyone else," five as "works better than anyone else," and eight as "enjoys working more than anyone else").

working face *noun* Same as **face 1**.

c1975 *Miners' Jargon* 3 *face* = in any tunnel, slope, chamber room, or entry [of a coal mine], the end at which work is progressing or was last done. Also called *working face*.

working match *noun* See citation.

1983 Smith *Recollections of Blue Ridge* 44 Machinery could not be brought into the mountains, nor could it be used profitably in the rocky, sloping fields. What the mountaineers used instead was manpower. They excelled at an activity called a "working match." In these matches, men did not lift rocks to prove their strength, but lifted building logs, or wielded scyths and hand-reapers.

working off See **work off**.

working party See **work frolic**.

work off *verb phrase* To ferment; hence *working off* = fermentation. See citations.

1967 Williams *Moonshining* 14 After fermentation ("working off") is complete, the beer is ready to run. **1982** Slone *How We Talked* 67 *working off* = the process of fermenting the mixture of sugar, water and mash. **1995** Montgomery *Coll* The kraut is working off (Cardwell). **c1999** Sutton *Me and Likker* xi It takes 30 days for a barrel of apples to work off in the summer time. In the winter time, it takes 90 days or more. This makes apple brandy.

work out *verb phrase*

1 To labor sufficiently to finish (a task) or accrue (a reward).

1931 Norbeck *Lure of Hills* 97 The mother had done what she could to provide for the children the summer preceding by "working out a crap," as she termed it. **1948** Chase *Grandfather Tales* 153 He went back [to work] on the county roads again till he worked out a twenty-four-pound poke of flour. **1969** GSMNP-42:11 Lon Floyd now, he worked out enough money to come to Knoxville over here on the train. **1977** Shackelford et al. *Our Appalachia* 207 That was my money, I worked it out, and I have the right to trade it where I want to trade it. **1987** Young *Lost Cove* 38 By the end of June, Clem had *worked out* forty dollars hoeing corn, clipping pastures and fixing fences. **1989** *Matewan OHP-9* Some of us had worked out a little money [so] that we bought it.

2 To complete one cycle of hoeing (a crop or garden).

1960 McCaulley *Cades Cove* Let's go in down here on Monday morning and work that crop out. **1974** GSMNP-51:8–9 The treasurer wasn't a-paying nothing. They didn't have no salary set whatever for a preacher. If he sometimes got in trouble, they would go and work out his crop, or got sick or come down, you would give him a sack of flour or ham or something, you know, for him to live on, and that's the way they paid the preachers. **2005** Williams *Gratitude* 537 = used to describe finishing a (one time) hoeing of a field or garden. "They *worked out* the garden."

worm *noun*

1 In distilling, the long, bent or coiled copper pipe attached to the **cap** of a **still** or **cooker** and then submerged in cold water, causing vaporized alcohol inside to condense. See c1975 citation. Also called **coil B**, **condenser**, **venomous worm**.

1883 Zeigler and Grosscup *Heart of Alleghanies* 362 The men worked in the light of the furnace fire, and talked in loud tones above the noise of the running water flowing down troughs into the hogshead, through which wound the worm from the copper still. **1914** Arthur *Western NC* 273 When a sufficient quantity has been produced, the mash is removed from the still, and it is washed out, after which the "singlings" are poured into the still and evaporated, passing through the worm a second time, thus becoming "doublings," or high proof whiskey. **1939** Hall *Coll* (Emerts Cove TN) The beer, they'd run hit off, put it in a still, run it out without any. They didn't have any worm or any thumb keg at that time. . . . The old times didn't have that, you know, and they run it twice, made the singling and doubling. This thump keg, it goes between the still and the condenser or worm, whichever you use. **1967** Williams *Moonshining* 13 A copper coil made of tubing or retrieved from an old-fashioned water heater is a suitable "worm." **1969** GSMNP-37:23 I've used both. I've used a condenser and I've used a worm, same, just the same. They both run through the thump keg. You had to have something to cool them. **1974** Roberts *Sang Branch* 49 We'll put a worm in it if we're making the old-fashioned way—we'll take our worm then and put it in the other end of the arm, and we'll daub her in there good. And of course if we're making it with a crooked worm, we'll have a barrel to put that worm in, and if we're making with a straight worm, we'll have a trough made, and a hole bored in each end of it, and the worm would run through it for the water to pour in on. **c1975** Lunsford *It Used to Be* 79 The worm is the copper pipe crooked around, possibly ten feet long. They bend it around a log or something to give it the proper curve. It's about eight to ten inches across and stands up about two and one-half feet high in a coil. The worm is put down in a keg and it is run out the bottom of the keg at the cover end. There is a spout that carries the water from a nearby branch or spring to pour into this keg to keep that worm cool. The worm is attached to the shank that's fastened to the cap of the still, and this cap is set on the still. **c1999** Sutton *Me and Likker* 106 = a copper coil usually 48 feet long if you are running a big rig—a big rig is a still that will hold anywhere from 300 to 600 gallons. **2011** Shearer *Moonshine Trade* 53 On top of that pot you put something that looks like a wooden churn. . . . At the top of that churn you drill a hole and you take a copper pipe and you fit it into that hole. That copper pipe is called the worm.

[DARE *worm* n 2 chiefly South, South Midland, especially southern Appalachians]

2 (also *fence worm*, *worm rail*) The course of rails laid down in the construction of a **worm fence**, including the first rail (frequently *worms* = the bottom or ground rails collectively). Also called **ground worm**. See also **worm fence**.

1867 Harris *Sut Lovingood* 129 They'se mity good things, too, fur a feller tu straiten up on, fur a fresh start, when he's layin off the wum ove a fence, onder a deckload ove tangle-laig whisky. **1905** Miles *Spirit of Mts* 106 Even a "fence-worm" if laid in the wrong time of the year is a failure; with frost and thawing the rails will surely sink into the ground. **1915** Dingus *Word-List VA* 193 *worm rail* = the bottom rail of a worm fence. **1957** Combs *Lg Sthn High: Word List* 112 *worm rail* = the ground or bottom rail, in the old-time rail fence. **1975** *Rail Fences* 124 First Millard put strings along the fence's path so we could stay on course. Then, using the string as a guide, he helped us lay the first zig-zag course which is called "laying the worm." Then we put a rock under the ends of each rail so that no rails would touch the ground and rot. **1983** Broaddus *Estill Co KY Word List* 61 Laying the bottom rail of a worm fence is called "laying the worm." **1995** Trout *Historic Buildings* 23 His father always laid the "worm" or outline of a split rail fence in the dark of the moon, otherwise this first rail would rot. The other rails could be laid any other time. **1997** Montgomery *Coll*: *fence worm* (known to Brown, Bush). **2006** *WV Encycl* 235 Split-rail fences [were] found in the pastures, with now and then a gate or a bar of poles. For the most part the chestnut timber was felled and split. There was art or what the natives called a "sleight" in this, as there was art in laying the worm for the fence—the first line of rails, each corner on a stone, upon which the structure of the fence was to be erected; after which it was finished with a stake and rider.

[DARE *worm* n 1 chiefly South, South Midland]

wormafuge (also *wormyfuge*) *noun* See c1959 citation.

1843 *McLean Diary* 81 Jain Sick Got a vial of worm a fuge. **1939** Hall *Coll*: *wormyfuge*. **c1959** Weals *Hillbilly Dict* 10 *wormyfuge* = a medicine concocted of herbs; taken to rid the intestinal tract of worms.

[folk etymologies for *vermifuge*]

worm bender *noun* A device to twist a metal pipe in a fashion to form a **worm 1**.

c1999 Sutton *Me and Likker* 38 Me and Tim are going to twist 2 worms here shortly. Me and Tim are the only ones that have a worm bender. . . . Mine is all steel handle and all. Tim's has wooden handles on it.

worm candy *noun* A vermifuge made into a candy to be more palatable.

1967 Wilson *Folkways Mammoth Cave* 45 Usually a tea combined with one or more of these [plants] was combined with sugar or molasses to make candy. Dozens of people recall eating *worm candy* every spring.

worm eater *noun* See citation.

1939 Farr *TN Mt Regions* 92 = tobacco chewer. "He's an eternal worm eater."

worm fence (also *worm fencing*) *noun* A fence made of horizontal wooden **rails** and usually vertical posts, constructed in zigzag fashion. Also called **crooked rail fence**, **galloping fence**, **snake fence**, **zigzag fence**. See also **worm 2**.

1915 Dingus *Word-List VA* 192 *worm-fence* = a rail fence built in zigzag fashion, one rail lying over another. **1949** Kurath *Word Geog East US* 31 *Worm fence* is a distinctive Midland term for a rail fence laid zigzag fashion, which is simply known as a *rail fence* in the North and the South. [**1978** Dykeman and Stokely *Highland Homeland* 19–20 [In constructing a worm fence], the ground-rails were put down, end-on-end, alternating the lengths—first a long rail and then a short one—and so on through. Anyone who has seen a rail fence knows that the rails were laid end-on-end at angles—not at right angles, but nearly so.] **1986** Pederson et al. *LAGS*: *worm fence* = attested by 3/60 interviewees (5%) from E TN; 3/11 of all LAGS interviewees (27.3%) attesting term were from E TN; *worms* = attested by 6/60 interviewees (5%) from E TN; 6/15 of all LAGS interviewees (40%) attesting term were from E TN. **1995** *Smokies Guide* (Summer) 13 Although there were several types of rail fence used in the Smokies, the most common was the worm or "snake" fence. The zig-zag style of construction was among the most common and aesthetically pleasing in the mountains. One big advantage of the worm fence was that it was portable. Since there were usually no posts, they could be picked up and moved whenever a new field was created. Also, since there were no posts, no post holes had to be dug, an enormous consideration on rocky terrain. American chestnut was the preferred building material for worm fences. It resists rot, is relatively light, and was a common species prior to the chestnut blight. Black locust is also rot-resistant, but its weight makes it difficult to work with. Worm fences were generally built eight to ten rails high and some were propped up at the corners with rocks to decrease contact with the ground. Some worm fence builders believed it was important to lay the fence during the proper moon phase in order to discourage rot and to encourage the fence to hold together. A drawback of this style of fence was that it required lots of split wood. To build a mile of worm fence takes approximately 8,000 rails.

[DARE *worm fence* n scattered, but chiefly Central Atlantic, Appalachians]

worm-grass *noun* A small perennial plant (*Spigelia marilandica*) whose roots and leaves have medicinal uses, especially for a tea drunk as a vermifuge. Also called **Indian pink**, **pink-root**, **star-bloom**.

[**1971** Krochmal et al. *Medicinal Plants Appal* 240 The root is used as a vermifuge, anthelmintic, and cathartic. In Appalachia, a tea made from the leaves is used to aid digestion.] **1982** Stupka *Wildflowers* 87 [Indian pink] is also called "pink-root," "star-bloom," and "worm-grass"—the last a reference to the use of the root by pioneers for expelling or destroying intestinal worms.

worm rail See **worm 2**.

worm syrup *noun* A purported remedy taken to rid the body of intestinal worms.

1968 *Remedies* 14 For Worms: 1. Take "worm syrup" which is made by boiling Jerusalem Oak and Pink Root together. 2. Mix Jerusalem Oak seeds with any kind of syrup to make a candy. Feed this to the afflicted person. **1983** Walker *Tales Civil War* 73 (as of 1863) During the War Between the States, i.e. the Civil War, my wife's grandmother, Mrs. Lovina Fleener, who lived on the land now owned by her great grandchildren, Mack Rader and his sister, Mrs. Charlsie [sic] Robeson, had four or five children that she decided were wormy so she gathered a lot of the worm weed leaves and made a batch of strong tea and sweetened it with sorghum and set it out on the back porch to cool. While it was cooling a lot of Rebel soldiers came up and demanded to be fed. So she decided to bake them some bread and feed them and maybe she could get rid of them. While she was baking the bread, the soldiers found the worm syrup and tasted it and decided it was honey. When she got the bread baked, the soldiers wanted some spoons to eat that good honey she had out on the back porch. She told them that it was not honey, that it was worm syrup. They said, "Oh, you are lying, we know what it is." She told them to go ahead and eat it if it was so good, that if they had any worms in their guts she would guarantee them they wouldn't have any by day after tomorrow.

worm tree *noun* A catalpa tree (*Catalpa* spp).

1991 Still *Wolfpen Notebooks* 88 Plant a worm tree if you want a quick shade. The worm critters that feed on the leaves make good fish bait, but when they bloom—hello, brother!

[DARE *worm tree* n South]

wormwood *noun* Same as **Jerusalem oak**.

2003 Cavender *Folk Medicine* 91 Jerusalem oak seed (also called wormweed. . . .) was a favored remedy [for pinworms and roundworm in children].

wormy chestnut *noun* Also called **bug-wood**.

1985 *Schools and Pastimes* 50 When the trees were no longer plentiful, wormy chestnut lumber and paneling suddenly became stylish, especially for dens and recreation rooms. Soon the price was as much as twenty times what it was earlier. **1991** Haynes *Haywood Home* 51 Most of the blighted dead [chestnut] trees have fallen and rotted where they lay, but some of the logs were gotten out and sawed into lumber. At least some timber was salvaged and wormy chestnut is a highly prized and expensive decorative lumber today.

wormyfuge See **wormafuge**.

wornet See **walnut**.

worn out See **wear out**.

worriation *noun* Worry, worrying.

c1940 Simms *Coll* = worry. **1949** Arnow *Hunter's Horn* 150 I've got too much time and trouble and money worriation in th things ever to git out what I've put in. **1997** Montgomery *Coll* (known to

Bush, Weaver); Worriation has never been one of her problems (Cardwell).

[DARE *worriation* n chiefly Mid Atlantic, especially SC, NC]

worrit See **worry B**.

worrited See **worry C**.

worry

A *noun, verb* Variant forms *weary, wearry, werry* ['wɛrɪ]. See also **weary**.

1936 Stuart *Head of Hollow* 236 All this trouble and all this weary. It worries me just to think about it. **1940** Bowman *KY Mt Stories* 249 *wearry* = to worry. **1942** Hall *Phonetics Smoky Mts* 42 ['wɛrɪ]. **c1979** Chiles *Glossary* 7 *werry*.

[DARE *worry* v, n A1 chiefly South Midland]

B *verb* Variant past-tense form *worrit*.

1962 Williams *Verbs Mt Speech* 17 The -*d* and -*ed* endings of past forms of verbs are frequently pronounced -t. . . . A few such examples are *worried*, worrit. **1984** Smith *Oral History* 59 He was worrit because of how it was with Eli.

C *verb*

1 (also *worry out*) *verb, verb phrase* To exhaust, tire (someone); hence participial adjective form *worrited*.

1898 Elliott *Durket Sperret* 39 She's been worrited an' onsettled all day, mad 'bout Lizer a-goin. **1913** Kephart *Our Sthn High* 294 When a man is tired he likely will call it worried. **1926** Hunnicutt *Twenty Years* 180 The fish did some jumping and pulling. . . . I worried it down and landed it on the bank of the creek. **1930** (in **1952** Mathes *Tall Tales* 182) I've had to chop the wood, tend to the beastes, plow the corn an' tobacker an' mow the br'ars till I'm naterly werried an' wore out. **1965** *Dict Queen's English* 17 *worried* = tired. "He has worked all day and is all *worried out*." **1994–97** Montgomery *Coll* (known to Adams, Brown, Cardwell, Jones, Norris, Oliver). **1998** Hyde *My Home* 46 In describing a man in a hurry, my folks would say that he was "worried."

[OED3 *worry* v 5e "to afflict with physical fatigue or distress," U.S.]

2 In phrase *worry with* = to struggle with.

c1950 Adams *Grandpap* 84 That evening, after Pap had worried with the old mare awhile, we all went over to Grandpap's and Granny's house.

worry out See **worry C1**.

worry with See **worry C2**.

worse *verb* To worsen. See also **(the) worst B**.

1994 Huskey *County Squire* 14 Some bettered and some worsed theirselves.

[OED3 *worse* v obsolete; Web3 *worse* v archaic]

worser See **bad A**.

worsest See **bad B**.

(the) worst (also *the worst in the world, the worst that*) *adverb phrase* As bad as. See also **bad B**.

A *adverb* In phrase *the worst in the world* = as bad as can be.

1861 Martin *CW Letters* (Nov 15) I want to see you the worst in the world. **1862** Warrick *CW Letters* (April 30) I have had the Meezels the worst that ever you seen in your life but I am som beter. I waunt to see you and the 2 children the worst in the world. **1864** *Reese CW Letters* (May 1) I want to see you and the Childrn the worst I Ever did in my life.

B *verb* To make worse, defeat, get the better of (one). See also **worse**.

1861 Kendrick *CW Letters* (Dec 20) This is a pore pine ridge bough for the purpes of State troups & I candid belive that we cant worst it by camping on it. **1862** *Warrick CW Letters* (Nov 2) Some of our boys looked right badly worsted after they got back from Kentucky; and others looked as well as ever. **1863** *Revis CW Letters* (June 6) that trip to caintuck worsted all the boys. **1937** Hall *Coll* (Tobes Creek NC) I have a toothache today, but I don't guess that'll worst me.

[EDD *worse* v 2 "to get worse"; Web3 chiefly archaic]

worst in the world See **(the) worst A**.

worst to See **bad to**.

would See **will B**.

wouldn't See **be E1**.

woultn't, woutn't See **will B1**.

wove See **wave, weave**.

wrap *verb* Principal parts.

1 Variant infinitive/base forms *rop, wrop*.

1864 *Chapman CW Letters* (May 24) you must Let B F masingo have two or three Leaves of this [to]baccow to rop up his sore toe. **1915** Dingus *Word-List VA* 193 *wrop*. **1939** Hall *Coll* (Deep Creek NC) They had to take and cut wood, build a big fire for him, and take off all their mackinaws and duck backs and wrop him up, keep him from freezing to death. **1942** Hall *Phonetics Smoky Mts* 26 [rɑp], [rɒp].

2 Variant past-tense forms *wropped, wropt*.

1936 Stuart *Head of Hollow* 25 That black snake wropped around the rattler so quick it would make your head swim. **1978** Burns *Our Sthn Mtneers* 12 Strong preterites like "clum," "dug," "wropt," "holp" and "fotch" are common even as Shakespeare, Chaucer, and the King James Bible are used. **1981** Williams *Storytelling* They got out and sopped all the liquor out of the bottom of the pot and wropped their johnny cakes up in a towel.

3 Variant past participle and past-participial adjective forms *roped, wropped*.

1864 *Chapman CW Letters* (May 13) the nife you sent your father it dont soot him at all for he keeps it Roped up in a rag and in his pocket and dont use it Send him a barlow that he will use.

1904–20 Kephart *Notebooks* 2:475 He went around with his thumb wropped up. **1923** Furman *Mothering* 257 It would be pure cruelty to keep her here and get her all wropped up in me again, only to face a' eternal parting. **1961** Seeman *Arms of Mt* 27 Little Ivy clutched a grubby potato doll, with a stick stuck in it for a handle and a bit of rag wropped around it for a dress. **1996** Houk *Foods & Recipes* 18 The meat was "wropped" in brown paper and put in cloth seed and flour sacks.

wrastle See **wrestle**.

wren-bird See **-bird**.

wrestle *verb* Variant forms *rassel, rassell, wrastle.*

1867 Harris *Sut Lovingood* 137 She wer a tarin gal enyhow. Luved kissin, wrastlin, an' biled cabbige, an' hated tile clothes, hot weather, an' suckit-riders. **1891** Brown *Dialect in TN* 172 The old form *wrastle* is still very common and is heard in everyday language much more frequently than *wrestle*. **1904–20** Kephart *Notebooks* 4:860 The boys was jist wrastlin', at fust, but they got het up. **1915** Dingus *Word-List VA* 188 *rassel*. **1942** Hall *Phonetics Smoky Mts* 20 Thresh and *wrestle* are uniformly pronounced with [æ]. **1972** GSMNP-93:2:4 They rasseled around there and fit a while. **1982** Maples *Memories* 67 We rasselled all the laurel bushes down back there after we had a few drinks of his whiskey, didn't we?

wrinkledy *adjective* Wrinkled.

1997 Montgomery *Coll* (known to nine consultants from the Smoky Mountains). **2008** McKinley *Bear Mt* 90 Not only did Grandpa prefer nicely ironed clothes, Granny wouldn't have wanted him to look all "wrinkledy" and "half-seen about" like he was "batching."

[DARE *wrinkledy* adj especially South, South Midland]

wrist *noun* Variant plural form of two syllables: *wrist-es.*

2005 Williams *Gratitude* 36 Yer wristes got awful sore. **2009** Burton *Beech Mt Man* 64 She took a knife and cut both her wristes, and cut across her throat.

writ See **write 1, 2.**

write *verb* Principal parts.

1 Variant past-tense forms *rit, riten, writ, writen, written.*

1863 *D B Walker CW Letters* (Nov 29) Mary Jane Walker rit theas few lines becas I for goten to rit about you coming out her. **1863** *Epperly CW Letters* (May 12) the last leter I writen to you was dated the 2 of the present month. *Ibid.* (May 12) the last leter I writen to you was dated the 2 of the present month. **1901** Harben *Westerfelt* 42 As soon as you writ the price you wus willin' to give in a lumpin' sum, Luke set to scheming. **1913** Kephart *Our Sthn High* 284 In many cases a weak preterite supplants the proper strong one: div, driv, fit, gi'n or give, rid, rive, riz, writ. **1922** *TN CW Ques* 45 (Hawkins Co TN) He nevr riten eney Book. **1935** (in **2009** Powell *Shenandoah Letters* 65) I did not want him to cut over on me is why I written. **1939** Burnett *Gap o' Mountains* 102 I wonder to my soul who writ me that letter. **1976** Garber *Mountain-ese* 34 Hand me my git-box and I'll pick you a little tune I writ myself.

[DARE *write* v B1a chiefly South, South Midland]

2 Variant past participle forms *rit, rot, rote, writ, wrote.*

1774 *Dunmore's War* 208–9 I have Rote to my Sergent to take what Men is in my Company Out Amedeate protection and shall Go amedeately my Self to Carrolinia. **1791** *Bent Creek Church Minutes* 11 the reason [is] to be inserted in a letter appointed to be wrote to her by br. John Murphy. **1861** *Watson CW Letters* I have red 4 leters from you and has rot you 2. **1862** (in **1999** *Davis CW Letters* 77) I have wrote so much, I hardly know what to write to interest you. **1864** *Walker CW Letters* (Sept 12) I hav rit severl lettrs to you and this is the first I hav got. **1901** Harben *Westerfelt* 218 I thought maybe he had wrote back to you. **1924** (in **1952** Mathes *Tall Tales* 31) Hit's writ in some kind of writin' that nobody in Dry Cove can't read hit. **1940** Haun *Hawk's Done* 6 The pokeberry ink is faded till it looks like the name is writ with catnip tea. **1953** Atwood *Verbs East US* 26 Outside of N. Eng. *wrote* predominates in Type I [i.e. older speakers with little formal education] everywhere, the proportion ranging from about three fifths (N.Y.) to well over nine tenths (N.C.). **1954** Arnow *Dollmaker* Your sister Meg has been so good an kind; she's writ me so many letters. **1961** *Coe Ridge OHP*-340B We might get it all together by the time you come back again and get it writ down. **1973** GSMNP-80:13 I'd wrote that down this morning myself just before we left. **1978** Reese *Speech NE Tenn* 182 *wrote* = attested by 7/12 (58.3%) speakers. **1980** Miles *Verbs in Haywood Co* 99 I never did get it wrote. **1998** *Dante OHP*-12 I should have had them wrote down.

[DARE *write* v B2a, 2b especially South, South Midland]

writen See **write 1.**

write off *verb phrase* To write out.

1933 Thomas *Traipsin' Woman* 252 "You've got my ballets all writ off now," he said proudly, as I packed up my paper and the portable [typewriter].

writing *noun* A written document, text.

1974 Fink *Bits Mt Speech* 29 = something written, a letter, etc. "They give him a *writin'* to take to the jedge." **1995–97** Montgomery *Coll* (known to Brown, Bush, Cardwell, Hooper).

writing school *noun* Formerly, a short-term school charging a small fee for instruction in the rudiments of penmanship, often conducted by an itinerant teacher. See 1970 citation. See also **arithmetic school, singing school, subscription school.**

1922 *TN CW Ques* 1302 (Grainger Co TN) We also had the ten days writing school, sometimes a ten days singing school and we also had an occasional ten days arithmetic school. **1939** Hall *Coll* (Hartford TN) I went to a writing school about a couple of days. I got some copy and I kept fooling with them copies till I could begin to write, and I got so I could write a pretty good hand. **1960** McCaulley *Cades Cove* We had lots of services there such as church,

singings and singing schools and writing schools and things like that. **1970** Mull *Mt Yarns* 11 In some sections a two-week "writing" school would be held where, for a small fee, children and adults would be taught to write. **1982** Slone *How We Talked* 79 Each summer there would be a few weeks of school just to teach anyone that wanted to, to learn to write. It was called "writing school."

writing spider *noun* A garden spider (*Argiope aurantia*) whose webs are imagined to resemble the letters of words forming a messages.

2002 Rash *Foot in Eden* 122 "No good will come from such a sight as that," said Grandma when she saw a letter in a writing spider's web.

[DARE *writing spider* chiefly South, South Midland]

written See **write 1**.

wrongous *adjective* Wrong.

1991 Still *Wolfpen Notebooks* 57 [His grandmother] wanted a Bible to read in. So he stole her one. Was that too wrongous? Not by my counts.

wrop, **wropped**, **wropt** See **wrap**.

wrote See **write 2**.

wudden, **wuddent** See **be E1**.

w'uns See **we'uns**.

wunst See **once**.

wusht See **wisht**.

wusp See **wasp 1**.

wuss, **wusser** See **bad A**.

wust See **bad B**.

wutn't See **be E1**.

Y

-y *suffix* Added to an adjective to form an adjective. See also **checkedy**, **flowerdy**, **mingledy**, **splotchedy**, **streakedy**, **stripedy**.

1916 Combs *Old Early English* 295 The suffix [-y] is found with adjectives which in modern English do not require it, as in steepy. **2014** *Blind Pig* (Oct 4) Personally I was never much for flowerdy or stripedy. I am more of a checkerdy type myself. **2017** *Blind Pig* (Feb 16) These [adjectives ending in *-y*] are the words one searches for when most words won't describe exactly as we wish. It seems I have heard them preceded mostly by kinda. For instance, my most becoming colors are kinda mingledy.

[DARE *-y* suff[1] 2 chiefly South, South Midland]

yagger *verb* To find fault, complain.

1922 Cobb *KY Mt Rhymes* 45 Times I would sull up like a possum while / The travelers would yagger to theirselves. **1957** Combs *Lg Sthn High: Word List* 113 = cavil. Ex.: "O, I wouldn't yagger about a little thing like that."

[DARE *yagger* v especially KY]

yahoo *noun* See citations.

1915 Dingus *Word-List VA* 193 = an uncouth backwoodsman. **1986** Pederson et al. *LAGS* (Sullivan Co TN) = person from the country.

[DARE *yahoo* n widespread, but somewhat more frequent South, South Midland]

yairb See **herb**.

y'all *pronoun* All of you; both of you. See also Grammar and Syntax §2.7.1.

1 Nominative or objective form.

1862 *Martin CW Letters* (Aug 5) I am Sorry to Say to yall that William is Dead he Died this morning about one o clock. **1900** Harben *N GA Sketches* 107 I'll call y'all in to supper directly. **1915** Dingus *Word-List VA* 193 = short for *you all*. **1925** Dargan *Highland Annals* 154 When we find where he is, y'all stretch 'round above us, an' I'll go in an' sic up the dogs. **1934–47** *LAMSAS Appal* (Madison Co NC, Swain Co NC) *y'all*. **1942** Hall *Phonetics Smoky Mts* 39 The pronoun of the second person plural, *you-ones* ['juənz] maintains its vitality in familiar use among speakers of all ages and classes. Some very well-bred mountain people have been observed to say it. Steadily encroaching upon it, however, is ['jụɔl] or [jɔl] (more familiar), as in [*y'all come back*] (hospitable invitation to return). **1956** Hall *Coll* (Hurricane Creek NC) I played that night some for y'all and we went to bed. **1971** *AOHP/ALC-101* Y'all got a early start. **1979** *Big South Fork OHP-9* That's where y'all lived, wasn't it? **1989** Giardina *Storming Heaven* 15 "Yall, lookee here," I said. "I got a surprise treat for after supper." **1994** Parton *Dolly* 14 Y'all get dressed. We're going over to Aunt Marth's house. **1997** *Dante OHP-14* If I ever hear tell of y'all making fun of anybody, I'll wear you out. [**2007** McMillon *Notes* = I never heard y'all spoken by old-time mountain folk unless they were self-conscious in the presence of outsiders, and even then it was you all, not y'all. You-uns, you-unses, yournses, and according to the area (especially Tennessee) yerns took the place of y'all between the Yadkin-Catawba basins to the Cumberlands in Tennessee.]

[cf DARE *you-all* pron, adj chiefly South, South Midland]

2 Possessive form *y'all's*. See also **your all's A**.

1968 *Faith Healing* 65–66 If 'ere's anything 'at I'm a'gonna' do that's again y'all's way of doin. . . . say so, and le'me do it like you. **1973** *AOHP/ASU-106* How many people was a-living in y'all's family during the Depression? **1989** *Matewan OHP-28* Did your mother make y'all's clothes? **2004** Larimore *Bryson Seasons* 54 I did receive a strange phone call last night. I'd be interested in y'all's advice about it.

yaller See **yellow**.

yaller bell See **yellow bell**.

yaller hound See **yellow hound**.

yaller janders See **yellow jaundice**.

yaller patch See **yellow patch**.

y'all's See **y'all 2**.

yan See **yon**.

yanaway *adverb* That way, in that direction. See also **a**[3], **thataway**, **yon way** (at **yon B**).

1974–75 McCracken *Logging* 8:26 It had to be set where it would pull off from a forty-five, off yanaway, off this way.

yander, yandering See **yonder**.

yankee dime (also *yankee nickel*) *noun* A kiss or hug, usually given to a child for performing a small favor such as a household chore.

c1960 Wilson *Coll*: *Yankee dime* = a kiss, usually a stolen one. **1978** Ball *Speech Knox Co* 141 *Yankee nickel*, *Yankee dime* = a hug and a kiss, respectively. **1984** Wilder *You All Spoken* 105 *Yankee dime* = payment by a kiss for a small favor. **1989** Hannah *Reflections* 22 I'll bet you a Yankee dime you'll be seeing your own shoe. **1995–97** Montgomery *Coll*: *Yankee dime* (known to Adams, Brewer, Jones, Ledford, Weaver); If you'll carry my books, I'll give you a Yankee dime (Ledford), = also *Yankee nickel* (known to Norris). **1997** Johnson *Melungeon Heritage* 21 Dad would promise us a "Yankee dime" if we would say words correctly, and we found out that a Yankee dime was a kiss on the cheek.

[DARE *Yankee dime* n chiefly South, South Midland, especially Alabama]

yan side See **yon B**.

yarb See **herb**.

yarb doctor See **herb doctor**.

yarb tea See **herb tea**.

yarbwoman See **herb granny**.

yard *noun* A measurement of three feet; variant unmarked plural without *-s* following a numeral.

1939 Hall *Coll* (Cable Branch NC) They just stove right out at it, and there it was up on a hill about fifty yard and went to barking.

yard ax *noun* An untrained lay preacher.

1986 Pederson et al. *LAGS* (Sullivan Co TN) = an untrained preacher.

yard baby *noun* See citation.

c1975 Lunsford *It Used to Be* 179 A "yard baby" is one large enough to run around in the yard.

yard broom *noun* See citation.

1983 Broaddus *Estill Co KY Word List* 62 = a brush broom.

[DARE *yard broom* n chiefly South, South Midland]

yard grass *noun* See citation.

1983 Broaddus *Estill Co KY Word List* 62 = blue grass.

[DARE *yard grass* n 2 especially South Midland]

yarming *verbal noun* See citation.

1976 Dwyer *Southern Sayin's* 26 = complaining: "Quit your yarmin'."

yarth See **earth**.

yawl *verb* To howl.

c1950 Adams *Grandpap* 58 The dog he come back to the house, just a-yelpin' an' a-yawlin' like ever' breath would be the last, an' run under the bed.

[OED3 *yawl* v 1a now dialect]

ye See **you B1**.

ye all See **you all A**.

year[1] See **ear**.

year[2] *noun* Variant plural form without *-s* following a numeral; see Grammar and Syntax §1.1.

1863 *Owens CW Letters* (April 26) The yankes say that we shant have no confedersy they say they will fite 20 year longer. **1864** *Councill CW Letters* (Nov 30) I dont think that I will Stay in this Cruel war more than forty year longer. **1867** Harris *Sut Lovingood* 74 Now yu cudent guess in ten year what he then went an' did. **1904** Fox *Christmas Eve* 117 I hain't been a-raftin' logs down to the settlemints o' Kaintuck fer nigh on to twenty year fer nothin'. **1922** *TN CW Ques* 231 (Knox Co TN) In this cuntry land was cheap 50 year ago. **1939** Hall Coll (Bradley Fork NC) Just after the [Civil] war a few year I was married. *Ibid.* (Proctor NC) I guess it's been ten or fifteen year. *Ibid.* (Deep Creek NC) I plowed a steer for several year till I got able to get a horse. *Ibid.* (Smokemont NC) I've been living on Tow String a couple of year. **1969** GSMNP-46:25 I am nearly ten year older than my brother right over there. **1979** *Big South Fork OHP-2* I spent two year right out on top of the hill there from Wolf River where the incline went. **1989** *Matewan OHP-102* We stayed up there for thirty year in it at least in this one house. **1998** *Dante OHP-12* I worked thirty year in mines.

[OED3 *year* n 1b now chiefly regional; DARE *year* n B chiefly South, South Midland]

yearb See **herb.**

yearling *noun*

1 Any of various younger animals (not necessarily one year old).

1939 Hall Coll (Cataloochee NC) They was two old she's and three yearlin's [= bears]. Well, the next'un come out was one of the yearlin's. **1963** Wilson *Regional Words* 81 = a male of the cattle family was, only among men, a bull; elsewhere he was a *yearling* (regardless of his age), an *old animal*, a *steer*, or a *male-cow* (by very modest people).

2 A young boy (used attributively).

1969 Miller *Raising Tobacco* 29 Yearling boys could carry big buckets of water up from the branch or from the sled or truck, placing them at stations in the patch where smaller boys and girls with smaller buckets could fill up and go behind the *setter*, pouring a dipper of water into the hole.

yearly *adjective* Early ['jɚrli].

1924 Abernethy *Moonshine* 118 Next mornin' bright an' yearly, I tuk my mule an' rid over to Lang Thomson's to git his kivvered buggy so as to go in some sorter style. **1997** Montgomery Coll (known to Bush, Weaver).

yearn, yearnt See **earn.**

yearth See **earth.**

yeast *noun* Variant form *east*.

1863 *Gilley CW Letters* (Dec 13) pleas send me some east to make light bred if you have got enny. **1891** Brown *Dialect in TN* 175 Ear is called *year*, but *yeast* is called *east*. **1892** Fruit *KY Words* 234 *east*. **1961** Kurath and McDavid *Pron Engl Atl Sts* 174 In the Midland and the South. . . . /ist/ is the most common pronunciation of *yeast*. It is in almost exclusive use in Virginia and in adjoining parts of Maryland, West Virginia, and North Carolina. **1966** *DARE Survey* (Spruce Pine NC). **1973** Miller *English Unicoi Co* 86 *east* attested by 4 of 6 speakers.

yeast bread *noun* Leavened bread made from flour.

1984 Gibson *Remembering* 17 Mama baked homemade yeast bread and I can almost smell again how delicious it smelled and tasted every bit as good. **1986** Pederson et al. *LAGS* = attested by 8/60 interviewees (13.3%) from E TN and 10/35 (28.6%) from N GA; 18/77 of all LAGS interviewees (23.3%) attesting term were from Appalachia.

yeathen See **heathen.**

yeep (also *yep*) *noun* The sound made by a fowl.

1925 Dargan *Highland Annals* 191 All at onct there come a "yeep" like a slit—you know how different a duck's "yeep" is from a chicken's—an' when that hen heard it she jumped off the nest an' flew fer a smart stretch a-squawkin' like she wuz skeered crazy. **1997** Montgomery Coll: *yep* (known to Andrews).

yelded see **yell A.**

yelke *noun* The yolk of an egg.

1990 Bailey *Draw Up Chair* 11 The word "yelke" is an example still heard from old-timers too accustomed to it to set it aside for "yolk."

[variant of *yolk*; cf EDD *yelk* sb mEngl, sEngl]

yell *verb*

A Variant past-tense forms *yelded*, *yelt*.

c1950 Haun *When the Wind* 12 "Hit's a God-damned lie and you know it," Bob yelt again. **1978** Burns *Our Sthn Mtneers* 12 On the other hand, they follow the modern trend and say "throwed," "growed," and "knowed," or go out of their way to be proper and say "borned" in June, "tosted" in the hay, or he "yelded" loud. **1996** Montgomery Coll: *yelt* (known to Ledford).

B Of a hunting dog: to bark and yelp on finding a hot trail of game.

1939 Hall Coll (Smokemont NC) Atter a while we hit a bear track. The dogs went to yellin'. We turned 'em loose.

yeller See **yellow A.**

yellow

A Variant forms *yaller*, *yeller*.

1862 *Love CW Letters* (Sept 28) they have got the yaller feever and smallpocks both in wilmington. **1866** Smith *So Called* 35 Flowers have bloomed sweetly. . . . dog fennel has yallered the ground. **1913** Kephart *Our Sthn High* 98 "Doc" Jones opined that it "looked yaller," and he even affirmed that it "tasted yaller." **1928** Justus *Betty Lou* 207 Maybe your hair is too yaller to go with it. **1974** Roberts *Sang Branch* 24 She would take mulberry roots and make another color, on a yaller color but more darker. **1977** Shackelford et al. *Our Appalachia* 76 Onion hulls made yeller dye. **1997** *Dante OHP-12* The foreman. . . . wore a pair of khaki britches, yaller khaki britches. **2006** Shelby *Appal Studies* 23 The well blew up. And the creek turned yaller.

[DARE *yeller* (at *yellow* adj, n A 1 (pronc)) scattered, but especially frequent South, South Midland]

B *verb* Of tobacco: to turn yellow; to cause (tobacco) to turn yellow.

c1975 Lunsford *It Used to Be* 28 For the first few days you'd keep the fire very slow, and allow the tobacco to "yaller," meaning for it to turn yellow. They let it yaller, say, a few days, until they got it kind of wilted, then they'd run the heat on it. At the time they're running the heat, they'd have to stay up all night. They could yaller it if they put the tobacco in on Friday and let it yaller over to Monday. On Tuesday they'd run the heat on it. They'd run the heat on it by making it very hot,—I've forgotten the exact degree. You could yaller it at about 90 degrees, but to cure it the heat had to be far above that.

yellow bell *noun* Forsythia (*Forsythia viridissima*). Same as **Easter bush**.

2004 *Reminder of Dwellings* 39 Forsythia—still called "yaller-bells" by some old-time mountain women—has prospered without human care along creek banks and other damp areas.

yellow cur (also *yellow dog*, *yellow hound*) *noun* A dog whose cowardice is attributed to mixed ancestry; hence a cowardly or despicable person.

1928 (in **1952** Mathes *Tall Tales* 68) I'll admit I do think a right smart of that thar dawg, but if he's got enough yaller cur in him so's he won't tussle Ol' Lucky today, I hope he'll git hisself plumb teetotally et up! **1929** (in **1952** Mathes *Tall Tales* 146) "Ye infernal yaller hound!" he roared, and made a motion toward the wagon, where his rifle lay beneath the fodder under the seat. **1998** Montgomery *Coll*: *yellow cur* (known to Brown, Bush, Jones, Norris, Weaver); He lied like a yellow dog (Cardwell); *yellow hound* (known to Brown, Weaver), He's as sneaky as a yellow hound (Cardwell).

yellow daisy *noun* A black-eyed Susan wildflower (*Rudbeckia fulgida/hirta*). Same as **black-eyed Susie**.

1982 Stupka *Wildflowers* 126 [Black-eyed Susan] is also called "yellow daisy."

yellow dock *noun* A perennial plant (*Rumex crispus*) whose root is used to make a tea drunk for medicinal purposes, especially as a tonic. See also **dock**, **narrow dock**, **speckled dick**.

[**1971** Krochmal et al. *Medicinal Plants Appal* 218 In Appalachia the root is placed in vinegar and the wash is used to treat ringworm; the leaves are used in a poultice to treat hives. The Indians used the root for a yellow dye.] **1972** Cooper *NC Mt Folklore* 12 Yellow dock, mandrake, poke root, blood root and black cohosh were used as alternatives to tone up the system and establish a healthy condition. **1991** Haynes *Haywood Home* 66 Goldenseal Root tea was a good heart tonic while Yellow Dock Root tea was good for circulation. **2008** *Rosie Hicks* 6 The yellow dock, it was said, it toned up the entire system.

yellow dog See **yellow cur**.

yellow-dog contract *noun* See citation.

2006 *WV Encycl* 188 In 1907, he issued a sweeping temporary injunction against the UMW to prevent organizing, claiming that the union violated Hitchman's individual employment contracts, the so-called "yellow-dog contracts" which forbade employees to join a union. He further ruled that the union was an unlawful organization because it was a monopoly in violation of the Sherman Antitrust Act.

yellow eye *noun*

1 Hepatitis.

1990 Cavender *Folk Medical Lex* 34 = hepatitis. **1994** Montgomery *Coll* (known to Ogle).

2 Jaundice. Same as **yellow jaundice**.

1994 Montgomery *Coll* (known to Cardwell, Ogle).

yellow hammer *noun* The northern flicker bird (*Colaptes* spp). See also **woodhen 2**.

1901 Harben *Westerfelt* 134 In my day an' time I've been on all sorts o' hunts, from bear an' deer down to yaller-hammers. **1939** Hall *Coll* (Saunook NC) In a dead tree from which the top and branches have fallen off or been broken off by the elements, a yellow hammer pecks out a hole in a snag and builds him a nest. **1980** Brewer *Hit's Gettin'* A yellow-billed cuckoo is a "rain crow" both [in E TN] and [the Ozarks] just as is a flicker a "yellow hammer." **1982** Powers and Hannah *Cataloochee* 480 The flickers, or yellow hammers, as the old timers called 'em, made nests up in the attic. **1982** Slone *How We Talked* 46 *yaller hammer* = wood hen. **1992** Joslin *Mt People II* 97 Instead, a pair of Northern Flickers, locally known as yellowhammers or wood hens, had been doing some remodeling to a dead fork of the tree. **1995** Montgomery *Coll* = yellow flicker (Cardwell).

[DARE *yellowhammer* n 1 widespread, but especially frequent South]

yellow hound See **yellow cur**.

yellow jack *noun* Yellow fever.

2003 Cavender *Folk Medicine* 23 In 1875 a physician and civic leader in Knoxville, which had several mineral spring spas located nearby, promoted the idea of developing the town as a retreat for those seeking refuge from "yellow jack."

yellow jacket soup *noun* See citation.

1951 Ulmer and Beck *Cherokee Cooklore* 56 Hunt for ground-dwelling yellowjackets either in the early morning or in the late afternoon. Gather the whole comb. Place the comb over the fire or on the stove with the right side up to loosen the grubs that are not covered. Remove all the uncovered grubs. Place the comb now over the fire or on the stove upside down until the paper-like covering parches. Remove the comb from the heat, pick out the yellowjackets and place in the oven to brown. Make the soup by boiling the browned yellowjackets in a pot of water with salt and grease added if you like. **1997** French *Counseling Indians* 91 Other traditional foods preserved by the Cherokee female elders during these cultural interactions were fish soups and fish dishes and yellow jacket soup. Yellow jacket soup requires that the bees be gathered in the winter when they are not active.

yellow jaundice *noun* (usually *the yellow jaundice*) Variant forms *yaller janders, yeller janders.* Also called **janders, yellow eye 2.**

1862 *Sexton CW Letters* (Oct 24) [I] have got the yaller janders and the liver complaint. **1863** *Chapman CW Letters* (Dec 10) I have had a spell of the yellow janders but I have fortunally recovered. **1881** Atkinson *After Moonshiners* 152 One of the gals in the neighborhood was sick with the breast complaint, and another was down with the yaller janders. **1939** *Hall Coll* (Jonathans Creek NC) I caught the yeller janders because of my irregular life there. **1966** Frome *Strangers* 79 A combination of "sowbugs," found under the hearth rocks in the chimney, and 'lasses was prescribed for yellow jaundice, or "yaller janders." **1967** *DARE Survey* (Maryville TN) *yeller janders.* **1967** Jones *Peculiarities Mtneers* 72 Jaundice, usually called "yaller janders," was treated with good stiff doses of saffron tea.

yellow linn *noun* A large deciduous tree (*Magnolia* spp). See also **cucumber tree, Indian bitter 2, mountain magnolia, wahoo 2.**

1893 Bergen *Plant Names II* 136 = *Magnolia acuminata* = yellow linn.

[DARE *yellow linn* n chiefly WV]

yellow patch *noun* Same as **laurel bed.**

1913 Kephart *Our Sthn High* 301 A "hell" or "slick" or "woolyhead" or "yaller patch" is a thicket of laurel or rhododendron, impassable save where the bears have bored out trails. **1915** Bohannon *Bear Hunt* 462 Lying grounds, you must know, are, in this country, always on the north or Tennessee side of the mountains, where are those laurel growths known variously as "woolly heads," "slicks," "roughs" and "yellow patches".... At certain seasons of the year the leaves turn yellow, so "yellow patches." **1939** *Hall Coll* (White Oak NC) = where it's been growed up, where it's so thick you can't get through it. **1960** Hall *Smoky Mt Folks* 59 = laurel bed, lettuce bed, rough, slick, woolly (as in woolly head, woolly ridge, woolly top).... and hell.

[DARE *yellow patch* n southern Appalachians]

yellow poplar *noun* A large deciduous tree (*Liriodendron tulipifera*) ranging up to seven feet in diameter. Also called **tulip poplar, white poplar.**

1926 Schantz *Beyond the Haze* The giant of the forest is the tulip or yellow poplar—Liriodendron tulipifera—whose clean boles, showing scarcely any taper for seventy-five or eighty feet, appear like graceful columns supporting the forest roof. **1937** Thornburgh *Great Smoky Mts* 28 Hemlock is "spruce pine," mountain magnolia is "cucumber" and the tulip tree is "yellow poplar." **1941** Walker *Story of Mt* 66 The tulip-tree, or yellow poplar, is one of the most dignified and majestic trees growing.... contrary to general belief, this tree is not a true poplar but belongs to the magnolia family. **1964** Stupka *Trees Shrubs Vines* 61 From the lowest altitudes to approximately 4000 ft., in all except the driest situations, the yellow-poplar is one of the most abundant trees in the park. **1970** Campbell et al. *Smoky Mt Wildflowers* 40 Although frequently called yellow poplar, or just poplar, this big tree of the Smokies is related to the magnolia and is not a true poplar. **1981** Powell *Gracie* 37 The mighty tulip tree [is] known in the Smokies as yellow poplar.

yellowroot *noun* Same as **goldenseal.**

1951 Giles *Harbin's Ridge* 7 She knew that goldenseal, what we hereabouts call yaller-root, was good for stomach trouble, or sore mouth, or heart burn. **1967** Fetterman *Stinking Creek* 120 [He] moved north—to find himself a city and a job and a place where you don't have to take yaller root for ulcers. **1970** Vincent *More of Best* 41 He brews it from wild "yarbs" around there, yellowroot, sarsaparilla, rat's bane, heart leaf, burdock, poplar bark, wild cherry bark, scaly hickory bark and slippery elm. **1973** GSMNP-5:18 You boil it and make a tea for sore mouth. It's as good a thing as you can use, yellowroot. **1985** Irwin *Alex Stewart* 145 Now they ain't nothing that beats yellow root, that's the same as goldenseal, for doctoring sore eyes. You dig the roots and boil them till you get a good thick brew. Then just take you a cloth and bathe your eyes with that every two or three hours. **2011** Lix *Medicine Women* 27 They call it yellow root tonic. It's made from *Xanthoriza simplicissima*, a leafy, low-growing plant that favors creek banks and sandy soils. Cherokee and European-American settlers boiled its namesake bright yellow roots in water and used the bitter infusion as a treatment for curing mouth sores and stomach ulcers, settling nerves, and as an ingredient in a "blood purifier."

yellowwood *noun* A deciduous tree (*Cladrastis lutea/kentukea*) that grows at middle elevations of the mountains. Its wood is bright yellow when first exposed, but later turns brown. Also called **chittam, gopherwood.**

1928 Galyon *Plant Naturalist* 5 The rarest of our eastern trees—the yellow-wood, *Cladrastis* spp, is found in the Smokies. . . . Yellow-wood may be found growing on the banks of the west fork of the Little Pigeon River, a tributary to the Tennessee. The trees are large with trunks cleft nearly to the base; the large branches droop, giving them the appearance of extreme flexibility. The compound leaves and panicles of green pods sometimes present a rather feathery, graceful appearance, which serves to distinguish it at some distance. **1932** Bennett *Majestic Smokies* Here grows the rare yellowwood, with its fragrant, showy white flowers—the tree from which Noah built the Ark, if we may rely upon tradition.

yelt See **yell A.**

yens See **you'uns 1.**

yenses' See **you'uns 3.**

yep See **yeep.**

yerb See **herb.**

yere See **here A.**

yerk *verb* To pull, jerk.

1867 Harris *Sut Lovingood Yarns* 297 He yerk'd back a littil es the lick cum, an' hit went thru the dubil ove the hide.

[DARE *yerk* v, n especially South, South Midland]

yerker *noun* A child.

1964 Roberts *Hell-Fer-Sartin* 193 When he come he told us little yerkers to get in the house and not to peep out anytime.

yern See **yourn 1**.

yerns See **you'uns 1**.

yerth See **earth**.

yesterday *adverb* Variant forms *yestiddy, yestidy, yisterday, yistiddy*.

1862 Gilley *CW Letters* (July 13) I received you letter yestidy and was glad to hear from you all. **1864** *Watkins CW Letters* (Aug 8) Cab Chitwood got Shot threw the hand yisterday morning & hea will come home in a few days. **1891** Brown *Dialect in TN* 175 *Yesterday* becomes *yestiddy*. **1915** Dingus *Word-List VA* 193 *yisterday*. **1923** (in **1952** Mathes *Tall Tales* 8) I mind it jest like hit was yisterday. **1961** Murry *Salt* 29 He died out yestiddy. **1963** Edwards *Gravel* 16 Oh, you orter have been here yisterday! **1969** Doran *Folklore White Co* 116 *yistiddy*.

[DARE *yesterday* adv, n chiefly South, South Midland, occasionally Northeast]

yestiddy, yestidy See **yesterday**.

yet *adverb*

A Variant form *yit*.

1915 Dingus *Word-List VA* 193 *yit*. **1937** Hall *Coll* (Tight Run Branch NC) [My brothers] were on the rebel side, and I'm a rebel yit. **1942** Hall *Phonetics Smoky Mts* 19. **1957** Combs *Lg Sthn High: Word List* 8 That's the bangest nag I ever yit seed. **1967** Fetterman *Stinking Creek* 61 I ain't through lookin' around yit. **1991** Thomas *Sthn Appal* 113 Everthang is sold yit on terms.

[DARE *yet* adv, conj (pronc) chiefly South, South Midland]

B At or up to the present or other specified time (in affirmative sentences, sometimes co-occurring with *still*, which always precedes it).

1823 (in **2007** Dunkerly *Kings Mt* 117) Had it not been for Campbell and his Virginians, Ferguson would have been on that mountain yet, had he chosen to stay there. **1836** *Sullivan Co Soldiers* Our company is altogether yet but one Charles Shely left us at Athens and is discharged from the service. **1861** (in **1980** Clark *Civil War Diary* 24) To day the 25th we are still in camps yet and have no orders to march on yet. **1862** *Sexton CW Letters* (July 12) he dide [= died] on the 27 day of June 186[2] but i am Spared yit. **1864** *Warrick CW Letters* (Aug 4) I hant got eny news to Rite you we are still fitting the yankes yet. **1922** *TN CW Ques* 9 (Jefferson Co TN) [I] still work at the business yet when I am able to work. **1939** Hall *Coll* (Emerts Cove TN) They's one man living there yet, though that man was a man born when I was just a little boy. **1957** GSMNP-23:1:14 The rocks is still there yet. They ain't moved. **1969** GSMNP-46:4 I have got the old collar up there yet that I used on him. **1978** Montgomery *White Pine Coll* III-2 Some people still might use the signs yet. *Ibid.* IX-1 I believe that old good book will do to live by yet. **1989** *Matewan OHP*-9 We got an old log church house over in Washington County. The inside of it yet has the old logs. **2008** *Rosie Hicks* 1 We're kindly up on that hill yet. Still our house is, didn't blow away.

yet and still *adverb phrase* Nevertheless.

1930 Armstrong *This Day and Time* 247 Turkey is dry eatin', but yet an' still it's good.

[DARE (at *yet* adv 3) chiefly South, South Midland]

yeth See **earth**.

ye'uns, yewns See **you'uns 1**.

yew pine *noun* The red spruce tree (*Picea rubens*). See also **he-balsam**.

1927 Cox *Yew Pine Mts* 226 The *yew pine* is a term widely used in West Virginia for the *red spruce*. The *Yew Pine Mountains* are located in Nicholas County up in above Richwood. **1952** Strausbaugh and Core *Flora WV* 46 (DARE) P[icea] *rubens* = sometimes called Yew Pine in West Virginia.

[DARE *yew pine* n 1 chiefly WV]

yieldy *adjective* Of land: productive; of a crop: abundant.

1924 Raine *Saddlebags* 102 Hits good wheat, but not very *yieldy* on the ground. **1937** Haun *Cocke Co* 2 Folks still tote their turns of meal to mill in pokes and aim on raising a yieldy crap of corn next year. **1976** Dykeman *Time to Build* "Yieldy"—used as an adjective. It means abundant in quantity, as when a farmer says, "That creekbottom was always yieldy." **1997** Montgomery *Coll* (known to Adams, Bush, Cardwell, Jones, Ledford, Weaver).

[DARE *yieldy* adj Midland]

yince See **you'uns 1**.

yisterday See **yesterday**.

yit See **yet**.

yo See **ewe**.

yon See also **yonder**.

A Variant form *yan* [jæn]. See also citations at **B**.

1934–47 *LAMSAS Appal* (Swain Co NC).

[DARE (at *yon* adj, pron, adv, n (pronc)) especially South, South Midland]

B *adjective* The other, the far or farther (especially in phrases *yan side, yon side, yon way*). See also **yonder C**.

1910 Norman *English of Mtneers* 276 A few of them have never seen "yon side" of the cove where they were born. **1931** *Professor Learns* Of course he says reckon, and right smart, and you all and quietus, and pizen, and yon-side. **1937** Thornburgh *Great Smoky Mts* 131 Just yan side of Bluff Mountain must be Sevierville. **1939** Hall *Coll* (Big Creek NC) Middlesboro is on yan side of Cumberland Gap. **1951** Giles *Harbin's Ridge* 2 There's one right good-sized mountain at yon end of the ridge. **1958** GSMNP-110:14 [They] logged all that big poplar timber out up from the bridge yon way up to that flat with a groundhog skidder. **1967** Hall Coll (Townsend TN) Hit's yan side of the Brier Ridge. **1974–75** McCracken *Logging* 15:2 You can see the boards in there yet on the yan part of it. **1982** Powers and Hannah *Cataloochee* 382 They'd be way at the other end. They'd ring their bells. Well, he'd go yan (yon) way. **2005** Williams *Gratitude* 538 He's gone yonways. **2008** Terrell *Mt Lingo* In the old days, they would say such things as "the fur side of the mountain," meaning the other side, or they might call it the "yander side," or, shorter and simpler still, the "yan side."

C *adverb*

1 (Over) there.

1913 Kephart *Our Sthn High* 112 She's in the field, up yan, gittin' roughness. *Ibid.* 122 Yan's my field of corn. **1939** Hall Coll (Copeland Creek TN) I says, "Yon's the White Caps now." **1974** Fink *Bits Mt Speech* 18 They live over yan.

2 Exactly this.

1942 Hall *Phonetics Smoky Mts* 29 I saw a fish yon [that] long. . . . *Ibid.* I caught a fish yan big.

[DARE *yon* adj, pron, adv, n chiefly South, South Midland, especially southern Appalachians]

yonder See also **yon**.

A Variant forms *hyanner, hyonder, yander, yandering, yon'er.*

1964 Roberts *Hell-Fer-Sartin* 121 They's a little gray house hanging way down hyonder on a beech limb. **1966** West *Dialect Sthn Mts* 31 I had the same vocabulary, learned from my father, until school displaced it. I remember vividly the day my teacher forced me to substitute yonder for yander. **1983** Broaddus *Estill Co KY Word List* 44 *hyanner* = yonder. **2007** McMillon *Notes: hyonder.*

[DARE *yander* (at *yonder* adv, adj, n A1 (pronc)) chiefly South, South Midland; *hyonder* (at *yonder* A5) South, South Midland, *yanner* (at *yonder* A6) chiefly South]

B *adverb*

1 (Over) there, at or to that place.

1863 Tesh *CW Letters* (Sept 2) yander goes Wily Cumbo with a load of water melons. **1867** Harris *Sut Lovingood* 109 We camp't jist tuther side that high pint yu see yander. **1913** Kephart *Our Sthn High* 78 About half an hour later, I lit spang in the mud, way down yander in Tuckaleechee Cove. **1937** Thornburgh *Great Smoky Mts* 94 She's buried in the corpse-yard yander. **c1950** Adams *Grandpap* 100 Yon'er comes King John an' all his hounds! **1964** Roberts *Hell-Fer-Sartin* 121 They's a little gray house hanging way down hyonder on a beech limb. **1974** GSMNP-50:2:14 They was some trees that stood all up here and yonder about in the orchard. **1977** Shackelford et al. *Our Appalachia* 326 We say, "Let's go over yonder and see that movie"; they say "Do you mean you want to go 'over there'?" **1980** GSMNP-115:2 A girl about my age, Lola Whaley, was brought here and buried right up yander. **1989** Landry *Smoky Mt Interviews* 194 [Bears] come off the mountain right here and went on down yander. . . . Our land went through yander and down to the picnic grounds.

[DARE *yander* (at *yonder* adv, adj, n B1) widespread, but more frequent South, South Midland; *hyonder* (at *yonder* A5 South, South Midland), *yanner* (at *yonder* A6) chiefly South]

2 Long ago, far in the past (as in phrase *back yonder*).

1941 Stuart *Men of Mts* 115 [I] wished they'd never made that agreement back yander between old Bill Dingus and Pap not to have fit with knives. **1957** GSMNP-23:2:17 North Carolina, my God, took all this country way back yonder. **1969** GSMNP-37:2:26 I just plain forgot. It was away back yander. **1972** AOHP/ALC-76 People don't know nothing about how peoples lived back yonder. **1985** Irwin *Alex Stewart* 120 I could shore play back yonder, but I've lost my teeth and I can't play half so good. **1993** Burleson *Aunt Keziah* 11 We never had no balloons to play with back yander. **1999** Hoyle *Handed Down* 22 "Way back yonder" was referred to as being when the older person telling the story was young.

3 In phrases *away yander, away yonder, off out yander, way yonder* = far away, far off.

1961 Williams *Content Mt Speech* 16 Lil jist got her head turned because Abe had been off out yander to the ocean-see, er sommers. **1963** Edwards *Gravel* 94 They was a driving along. . . . somers away yander, somers near the Calinder line. **1969** GSMNP-69 Thad Watson, he lived away yonder on Mingus's Creek. **1973** GSMNP-88 See them trees away yonder? We owned all that. **1991** Still *Wolfpen Notebooks* 155 Two days ago they hired four new miners, fellers from away yander.

C *adjective* The other, the far or farther. See also **yon B**.

1927 Woofter *Dialect from WV* 367 He is down in yandering field. **1948** Chase *Grandfather Tales* 21 She went right yonder way. **1981** GSMNP-122:20 You cross the big bridge goin' in yander way right there.

D *noun*

1 A relatively short distance.

2007 Homan *Turkey Tracks* 86, 87 Based upon the folks I talked to—an admittedly small and much older than average sample—I compiled five alternative measures of Appalachian distance. The smallest component was tater chunk, as in "you're real close, it's just another tater chunk down the road." Following tater chunk in progression were yonder, hoot and a holler, a piece, and a fer piece.

2 In phrase *in yonder* = in that place.

1969 GSMNP-27:7 My daddy worked in yander on Freezeland, and he just come home about every two or three weeks. **1974** AOHP/ALC-228 He had a little garage back out in yonder, and he kept his car in there. **1989** *Matewan OHP-2* We'd go from here to up in yonder and around.

[DARE (at *yonder* adv, adj, n Da) chiefly South]

3 In phrase *to yonder* = to that place.

1961 *Coe Ridge OHP-341B* They knowed, see, that sound when it crossed from here to yonder, and these other places.

[DARE (at *yonder* adv, adj, n Db) chiefly South, South Midland, West]

E *verb* See citation.

1997 Montgomery Coll (known to Bush), = to go or move about without a destination (Brown).

yons See **you'uns 1**.

yon side, yon way See **yon B**.

yore'n See **yourn 1**.

you *pronoun* See also **y'all**, **you all**, **you'uns**, **yous**, and Grammar and Syntax §2.1.

A Variant forms *ye* [jɪ, ji] (used primarily in unstressed positions, singular or plural), *yer*.

1861 *Gilley CW Letters* (Nov 8) I now drop ye an all a few lines that I am well at the present time. **1864** *Chapman CW Letters* (May 3) maby tha[y] will furlow you home untell ye get able for serves. **1908** Smith *Reminiscences* 414 Strangers, who are ye? **1913** Kephart *Our Sthn High* 84 I knowed I couldn't roust ye no other way. **1939** Hall *Coll* Get ye chairs. *Ibid.* (Deep Creek NC) If you call [a turkey] too much, you'll never get one to ye. *Ibid.* Here's ye (sing.) a light. **1940** Bowman *KY Mt Stories* 250 *yer* = you (to you) Used objectively. **1942** Hall *Phonetics Smoky Mts* 39 *Ye* for *you* is very common in older speakers. **1950** Bray *Disappearing Dialect* 282 [*Ye*] is more apt to occur in a question: "Did ye?" or as an objective: "I love ye so good." **1957** *GSMNP-23:2:28* [If] a neighbor wouldn't help ye, he wasn't considered a neighbor. **1965** West *Git Tard* The "ye" for "you" is an interesting elision with such expressions as "tell 'ye [sic]," "see 'ye [sic]," "tax ye." The sound is not "yee," but "yi" (the "i" pronounced as in "it"). **1973** *GSMNP-80:4* When did you move from there to Bullhead then? How old was ye? **1980** *GSMNP-122* I can't see to tell ye these back'uns [in reference to identifying older grave sites in a cemetery]. **1997** *Dante OHP-53* Your dad would tell ye, "Don't get the caps close to the powder."

[OED3 (at *ye* pron A II 4) in objective case c1405→; SND (at *ye* pron A) "the original nominative has been retained in Scotland. . . . and has also been transferred to use as the objective case"; CUD *ye*; HT *ye* (unstressed) "you"; DARE *ye* (at *you* pron[1] A2) chiefly South, South Midland]

B Grammar.

1 Used reflexively, often pleonastically (= *yourself/-selves*).

a As a direct object.

1956 Hall *Coll* (Roaring Fork TN) You'uns better get you in a tree. Old mammy bear will come direckly.

b Used as an indirect object.

1913 Kephart *Our Sthn High* 298 Set down and eat you some supper. **1939** Hall *Coll* (Chestnut Branch NC) Get you a sourwood switch and then have it a-standing up at the door and measure your stick, and if the young one grows, why, hit'll cure it. **1964** Roberts *Hell-Fer-Sartin* 5 Come on around, you boys, and get you a chear. **1971** *AOHP/ALC-260* Would you mind to work a couple hours more on a day and make you a little more money? **1973** *GSMNP-4:44* You could kill you a mess of meat any time you wanted it. **1979** *Gamecock* 163 You might have you a can of whole kernel corn. **1983** *Dark Corner OHP-5A* If you want to just plain old salt [the ham], get you a big old box and just put you down a layer of salt, put your meat in there and cover it up good. **1989** Smith *Flyin' Bullets* 59 Son, always carry ye a pen-knife. . . . Ye never know when ye'll have ta leave it a'stickin' in somebody! **1998** *Dante OHP-24* You drilled you a hole and made you a shot and put it in. **2012** Milnes *Signs Cures Witchery* Take you an iron rod and the hammer [and] put the iron rod in there.

[DARE *you* pron[1] B 1b especially South, South Midland]

2 Used as an ethical dative, to indicate that the advantage of the person(s) addressed is concerned.

1939 Hall *Coll* Here's ye (sing.) a light. **1946** Dudley *KY Words* 271 Here's you some money. . . . Here's you a nice easy one. **1966** *DARE Survey* (Highlands NC) Some of 'em [= trout] really puts you up a good fight. **2009** House and Howard *Something* 136 Here's ye a paycheck.

[DARE *you* pron[1] B2 chiefly South Midland]

you all *pronoun phrase*

A Variant form *ye all* [see **c1900** in **B1**].

B All of you, both of you [Editor's note: For currency in the Smoky Mountains in the late 1930s, see 1942 citation.] (For other forms with *all*, see Grammar and Syntax §2.7.1.) See also **y'all**, **you**, **you'uns**. [Editor's note: The forms below come from letters and other contexts in which multiple individuals can be inferred as addressees and thus the plurality of their reference.]

1 Nominative or objective form *you all*.

1826 *Whitten Letter* She frets a good deal about you all and the distance she is from you all. **1836** *Sullivan Co Soldiers* White sends his best respects to you all also. Elcany Millard sends his best respects to you all. Timoty Millard sends his best respect to you all. **1861** *Martin CW Letters* (Dec 22) I wish this war would end so you all soldiers could get home one more time to enjoy your selfes if you wish to. **1863** *Lance CW Letters* (March 1) I Re ceived your kind Letter Last male I was truly glad to here from you all. **1865** *Bailey CW Letters* (Jan 8) I recievd a letter from you last night which give me grate Sadisfaction to hear from you all. **c1900** (in **1997** Stoddart *Quare Women* 62) I never seed any quare wimmen like ye all before and I have seed such a good time today. **1929** (in **1952** Mathes *Tall Tales* 116) And you-all may be needn't [sic] it one o' these days. **1935** (in **2009** Powell *Shenandoah Letters* 42) He told me to write you all and get you all to get your all part of the fence. **1942** Hall *Phonetics Smoky Mts* 39 The pronoun of the second person plural, *you-ones* [ˈjuənz] maintains its vitality in familiar use among speakers of all ages and classes. Some very well-bred mountain people have been observed to say it. Steadily encroaching upon it, however, is [ˈju̯ɔl] or [jɔl] (more familiar), as in [*y'all come back*] (hospitable invitation to return). **1949** Kurath *Word Geog East US* 40 In the South Midland the distinctive Midland plural form *you'ns* survives. . . . by the side of the more common *you-all*. **1967** Wilson *Folkways Mammoth Cave* 21 *You-all* as the plural of *you* is universal now, but a few old people recall having heard *you-uns* not too many years ago. **1974** Fink *Bits Mt Speech* 30 = sometimes heard in mountain speech, but regarded as an intrusion from Deep South. **1976** Weals *Two Minus*: *You all* is not a mountain expression. It never appears in the speech of older inhabitants of the Smokies, those who have lived here all their lives. **1998** *Dante OHP-24* I told him about you all getting married. **2002** Rash *Foot in Eden* 28 I think maybe you and your husband know where he is. . . . It's going to be easier on everybody if you all admit it.

[DARE *you-all* pron, adj chiefly South, South Midland]

2 Possessive form *you all's*. See also **y'all's** (at **y'all 2**), **your all's**.

1976 Garber *Mountain-ese* 104 You-all's dog stayed over at our house last night. **1989** *Matewan OHP-56* Did you all's family ever talk about the feud when you were growing up?

[DARE *you-all's* adj, pron² South, South Midland]

you all's See **you all B2**.

you come See **you'uns come**.

youenst See **you'uns 1**.

youerunses See **yourns's**.

youngern, **youngin**, **young'n** See **young one**.

young one *noun*

A Variant forms *young'en* [see **2003** in **B**], *youngern* [see **1939** in **B**], *youngin* [see **1984** in **B**], *young'n* [see **1962** in **B**], *young'un* [see **1859** in **B**].

B A child. See also **grandyoungun**, **grown'un**, **least one B2**, **little one**.

1859 Taliaferro *Fisher's River* 114 With the "young'uns" it was a generation from one Christmas to another. **1910** Cooke *Power and Glory* 114 If you can make a cotton mill healthy for young-uns, you can do more than God A'mighty. **1931** Goodrich *Mt Homespun* 63 [She was] quite unfit to take up the battle of life for herself and the three "young-uns" clinging to her skirts. **1937** Hall *Coll* (Mingus Creek NC) [Did you see many armies [in the Civil War] go through here?] No, we young'uns would shy 'em. **1939** Hall *Coll* (Jefferson City TN) You youngerns, get in here. *Ibid.* (Chestnut Branch NC) Get you a sourwood switch and then have it a-standing up at the door and measure your stick, and if the young one grows, why, hit'll cure it. **1955** Ritchie *Singing Family* 3 Mom had my brother Wilmer when she was forty, and she settled back to raise her thirteen young uns without any more interference. **1962** Dykeman *Tall Woman* 112 Go out and tend to the young'ns. **1972** *AOHP/ALC-241* Them two churches was about all I know of when I was a young'un a-growing up. **1984** Six *Hill 'n Holler* 10 It's comin up Christmas, don't you youngins be prusin none in the press. **1989** *Matewan OHP-89* Every one of their young'uns is in Matewan now. **1997** Montgomery *Coll* He is forever talking about how sorry his young'uns are (Andrews). **2003** Williams *Coming of Age* 118 The little young'ens would have better hearts for travel in the cold night. **2007** (in **2012** McQuaid *Interface* 269) He was working up the school with her with the young'uns.

[DARE *young one* n especially South, South Midland]

young'un See **young one**.

you ones See **you'uns 1**.

your all's See also *y'all's* (at **y'all 2**), *you all's* (at **you all B2**). (For other forms with *all*, see Grammar and Syntax §2.7.1.)

A (also *your all*, *your alls*) *adjective phrase* Your.

1935 (in **2009** Powell *Shenandoah Letters* 42) He told me to write you all and get you all to get your all part of the fence.... It is your alls place to fix your part of the fence. **1989** Kingsolver *Homeland* 173 He lived next door to us for a while there. Next to your-all's house on Polk Street.

B *pronoun phrase* Yours (plural).

1977 Norman *Kinfolks* 45 Why our climate is a hundred per cent better than your all's here. **1998** Montgomery *Coll* Is this table your all's? (Ledford).

[DARE *your-all's* adj, pron South, South Midland]

yourenses See **yourns's**.

your'n See **yourn 1**.

yourn *pronoun*

1 Variant forms *yore'n* [see **1901** in **2**], *your'n* [see **1845** in **2**].

2 Yours. For similar forms, see Grammar and Syntax §2.2.

1845 (in **1974** Harris *High Times* 48) Misses Spraggins drive out these dratted tow-headed brats of your'n—give room! **1860** *Week in Smokies* 125 Why, mister, my old man there knows more about bees, in one day, than them book men of yourn in all their lives. **1862** Shifflet *CW Letters* (Jan) when george open his letter I found yourn and I soon red it and the was a few tears fell from my eys. **1864** Poteet *CW Letters* (Nov 2) if the war dont stop there will be moor children that will perish besids yourn. **1901** Harben *Westerfelt* 133 [I] thought I'd halt an' ax about that cut o' yore'n. **1929** (in **1952** Mathes *Tall Tales* 138) You tend to yourn an' he'll look atter hisn. **1939** Hall *Coll* (Wears Cove TN) I says, "Cut loose, I'll take care of myself, and you take care of yourn." **1946** Cleaves *King's English* 35 "Ourn," "hern," "hisn," and "yourn" represent an attempt at uniformity. Since the forms "my" and "mine" developed from a common Teutonic source, a similar inflection was created to distinguish between the adjectival and substantive uses for the remaining personal pronouns. **1971** *AOHP/ALC-129* "Hit's yourn" [I] says, "you can have it." **1976** Lindsay *Grassy Balds* 208 Yeah, well I found your'n too; your'n was with mine. **1989** Smith *Flyin' Bullets* 13 I was mad at them deputies of yorn, not you! **2000** Wilkinson *Blackberries* 133 [I] always did think you was pretty, with that long, lean neck of yourn.

3 Used in attributive position.

1862 Carter *CW Letters* (May 6) hits a painful thing to my poor heart to be away from you and the children but I intend to contend for yourn and my childrens Rights.

[historically *your* + *n* by analogy with *my/mine*, now sometimes construed ahistorically as from *your* + *one*; EDD *yourn* pron mEngl, sEngl; DARE *yourn* pron especially New England, South, South Midland]

yourns *pronoun*

1 (also *your uns*) Your people.

1864 (in **1952** Wiley *Life Billy Yank* 64) The rebs.... when they see our guns they say "no wonder yourns shoot so fast, if weuns had such guns we'd fight longer." **1983** *Dark Corner OHP-5A* They'd give you a pig and you'd raise a gang for them, and you give another boy a pig, you know, and that don't cost you. You get yourns free then. **1990** Clouse *Wilder* 196 Word is the whole bunch of yourns sure does stick together. **1993** Weaver *Scotch-Irish Speech* 14 With appropriate sons and daughters, sometimes "your uns" become "our uns," as "we uns" become "you uns."

[DARE *yourns* pron chiefly South, South Midland]

yournses See **yourns's**.

yourns's (also *yornses, youerunses, yourenses, yournses, yourunses, yurnses*) *adjective, pronoun* Your, yours (used in reference to more than one person).

1913 Kephart *Our Sthn High* 286 Let's we-uns all go over to youerunses house. **1939** Hall *Coll* What did you-uns do with yourunses? **1952** Wilson *Folk Speech NC* 610 *yourunses* = yours. **1956** Hall *Coll* (Roaring Fork TN) I saw a bear cross into yourenses woodland. **1957** Combs *Lg Sthn High: Syntax* 8 Highland speech has preserved some earlier pronominal forms (*hisself, theirselfs*, etc.), and has also coined a few new ones: *we-erunses, you-erunses*, etc. The last two are of course longer forms of *we-uns* and *you-uns*, although they are corrupt forms of *we-ones* and *you-ones*. **1976** Garber *Mountain-ese* 105 This calf don't belong to usenses so it must be yournses. **2005** Williams *Gratitude* 538 *yornses', yurnses'* = possessive form of your (belonging to the whole bunch of yuns). Examples: "*Yurnses'* clothes is still a-hangin' on the line." "*Yornses'* cow is in the cornfield." **2007** McMillon *Notes* The boundary is yournses.

your own self See **own B**.

yours *interjection* You're welcome!

1936 Farr *Folk Speech* 276 = reply to "thank you" for a favor.

yourself *pronoun* Yourselves. For similar forms, see Grammar and Syntax §2.3.2.

1973 GSMNP-76:5 I said, "Dang you ones. If you want them out, get in and get them yourself."

yourunses See **yourns's**.

yous (also *you's, yous all*) *pronoun* You (plural). See also **y'all, you all, you'uns**.

1863 *Copenhaver CW Letters* (June 24) this leves all well hop it may find yous all well. **1864** *Love CW Letters* (Jan 8) I am uneasy for yous for they will Steal any thing that they lay hans on. **1979** *Big South Fork OHP-11* I'll see yous boys one at a time. **1982** Slone *How We Talked* 5 "We'uns will pay you's": when these words were used, with a handshake by a mountain man, it was more binding than any contract drawn up by a lawyer, or a treaty between countries.

you's, yous all See **yous**.

you'un See **you'uns 2**.

you'uns *pronoun* You. See also **one 1, they'uns, us'uns, we'uns, y'all, you all, yous.**

1 (also *yens, yerns, ye'uns, yewns, yince, yons, youens, youenst, youns, you'ns, younse, you'unses, yunce, yuns*) Used as nominative or objective plural form in reference to more than one person, sometimes used to include one or more persons associated with the addressee but not present (see 2008 Terrell citation).

1861 *Lance CW Letters* (Nov 10) I thought of youns at home and me here on the lonesom Sea Side and did not know what minute the yankies mite come. **1862** *Lockmiller CW Letters* (Aug 14) I want yew to tell mee whether yewns have bin good boy[s] ornot. **c1863** (in **1957** Monaghan *CW Slang* 129) The neat uniforms of the Indiana 58th appeared so dressed up to the Tennessee mountaineers that one of them told a soldier, "youens look like meetin' folks." **1863** Wilson *Confederate Private* 1 (Feb 1) everybody ses the best youens could a dun wod a bin to turn rown and come home the next day. **1881** Atkinson *After Moonshiners* 108 "They're expecting you'uns," was the prompt reply, "and they're hidin' in the woods, or else watchin' for you at the still houses." **1892** Doak *Wagonauts Abroad* 56 He'll take you-uns fer the "revenues," but I reckon I kin keep him from shootin'. **1910** Smith *Tramping in Mts* 2 10 *You-uns* we heard, of course, all through the mountains, but never of one person [i.e. used as a singular]. **1913** Kephart *Our Sthn High* 118 I reckon you'uns would find a United States court purty hard to convince. **c1936** (in **2005** Ballard and Chung *Arnow Stories* 57) Ye'uns shorely ain't got th' best teacher we've ever had out a cuttin' wood. **1939** Hall *Coll* (Mt Sterling NC) You'uns is talking about rough country. [**1942** Hall *Phonetics Smoky Mts* 39 The pronoun of the second person plural, *you-ones* ['juənz] maintains its vitality in familiar use among speakers of all ages and classes. Some very well-bred mountain people have been observed to say it. Steadily encroaching upon it, however, is ['ju̜ɔl] or [jɔl] (more familiar).] **c1945** Haun *Hawk's Done* 205 George said they wouldn't a-kept on rocking them till they made everybody run if you'ns hadn't brought your guns along. **1949** Kurath *Word Geog East US* 31 The simple folk of the Midland employ *you'ns* as the plural of *you*. This usage is common in Pennsylvania from the middle of the Susquehanna westward and in northern West Virginia. . . . In the South Midland *you'ns* is being replaced by the Southern *you-all*, which has already eliminated this term in the Valley of Virginia and on the upper reaches of the Potomac in West Virginia. **1956** Hall *Coll* (Roaring Fork TN) You'uns better get you in a tree. Old mammy bear will come direckly. **1966** Dakin *Vocab Ohio River Valley* 307–9 In Kentucky *you'ns* is obviously an old expression which has been supplanted by Southern *you-all*. In common with a number of other relics, it is used commonly enough to be elicited only in the conservative Mountain region. **1967** Wilson *Folkways Mammoth Cave* 21 *You-all* as the plural of *you* is universal now, but a few old people recall having heard *you-uns* not too many years ago. **1969** GSMNP-37:2:28 He knows you'uns and you'uns knows him. **1972** *Foxfire I* 26 Now if I live, and you'ns lives, an' you'ns comes t'eat with me any time this winter, I'll open a can a'souse. **1973** GSMNP-77:10 I 'preciate ever' one of you'uns here. **1973** Jones *Cades Cove TN* 71 = common plural for *you*. **1976** Weals *Two Minus* You all is not a mountain expression. It never appears in the speech of the older inhabitants of the Smokies, those who have lived here all their lives. You'ns, which had a sensible beginning centuries ago as a shortening of "you ones," can still be heard in mountain neighborhoods. **1981** GSMNP-117:23 She said, "You'uns stay at home till the scent of ramps leaves you." **1982** Young *Colloquial Appal* 25 *youenst* = you folks. **1988** Kosier *Maggie* 84 The mountain talk was strange to their ears. They heard all about "kin-folks" and "you'uns." They missed the "yawls" they heard so often in Texas. **1995** Adams *Come Go Home* 89 Younse is gonna have to help me. **2000** Joyner *Magic Mts* 147 As I had passed a corner of Lexington and College I overheard a mountain woman tell another, "You-unses come see us when you-unses can." **2005** Williams *Gratitude* 537 *yens*, *yuns* = more than one person. Them Yankees says we say, "you'uns," two syllables with the emphasis on you, or "y'all," one, but the way we say it is with one syllable—yuns, or yens, meaning ever'body, or all of yuns in the whole crowd—ever last one of yens. To us, the word you is one single solitary person. **2007** McMillon *Notes* You-uns, you-unses, yournses, and according to the area (especially Tennessee) yerns took the place of y'all between the Yadkin-Catawba basins to the Cumberlands in Tennessee. **2007** Rogers *Carson-Newman* 2 Most of the speakers mentioned "y'all" as a word they associate with the South. . . . and some also added "you'uns" as a uniquely Appalachian synonym. **2008** Terrell *Mt Lingo* If a man and his wife wanted a couple to come and visit with them, the wife would say, "You'uns come," and if she wanted the others to bring their family, she would pluralize the invitation by saying, "You'unses come." **2008** Williams *Dialect Scott Co TN* We also use the word you'uns, but we pronounce it as yons. **2009** Benfield *Mt Born* 210 Have you'unses got shet of them trashy neighbors? **2012** Montgomery *File* = reported to be common among students at Carson-Newman University, Jefferson City, TN.

[cf SND *you yins* (at *yin* pron/adj 3); HT *yous yins* (at *yin*); DARE *you-uns* pron[1] 1 chiefly Midland]

2 (also *you'un*) Used as a singular form.

1889 *Hogs* Them snaikes is gettin' purty thick, but you'un needn't be afearred. They won't bite less they're cornered. *Ibid.* I forgot you'uns don't [know] nothin' of Timberlake's razorbacks. **1913** Kephart *Our Sthn High* 286 Whar's you-uns a-goin' ter? **1971** *AOHP/ALC-33* You just learnt that book from the first beginning to the back, and you knowed it by heart, and then they would just turn you'un in to another book.

3 (also *yenses'*, *you'unses*, *you'uns's*) Used as a possessive plural form.

1913 Kephart *Our Sthn High* 12 Whut's you-unses name? **1934–47** LAMSAS *Appal* (Swain Co NC) *you'unses*. **1963** Watkins and Watkins *Yesterday* 148 Ma come out there and stopped us and said, "You ought to be ashamed of youunses selves, treating that terrapin thataway." **1975** Chalmers *Better* 66 I taken you-uns potion, for I had a misery, but now I am fitten to circulate around again. **1981** GSMNP-117:27 You'uns get a permit from you'uns's parents and let them write me a note tellin' me to let you'uns go up there and go in swimmin'. **1996** Isbell *Last Chivaree* 35 Is that you'un's ox up there in the field? **2005** Williams *Gratitude* 537 *yenses'* = your (plural). "Git *yenses'* feet washed and git in the bed."

[DARE *you-uns'* adj, pron especially South Midland]

4 Used as a reflexive (the so-called personal dative) = (for) yourselves.

2008 *Rosie Hicks* 4 Carry the wood in and help gather the stuff to cook, and when we cook, you'uns is going to get you'uns a plate and get you'uns some food.

you'uns come (also *you come*, *you'uns come and see us*) *imperative phrase* Come see us! (Used as a leave-taking pleasantry.) See also **come and go home with me**, **go home with us**.

1937 Hall *Coll* (Del Rio TN) You come. **1939** Hall *Notebooks* 13:1 (White Oak NC) You'uns come and see us. **1955** Ritchie *Singing Family* 199 Some of the older folks had begun to stir around to go home; they gathered their buckets and their little children and lit their lanterns. They said, "Go home with us why don't you?" and "Can't tonight, I reckon. You'ns come," to each other, and pretty soon their lights were fading this way and that way through the hills. **1976** Weals *Two Minus* A polite thing to say upon parting is, "You'ns come." Translated it means, "You come see us." **1990** Bailey *Draw Up Chair* 15 We spared them the confusion of an alternative "You'uns come!" belonging strictly to mountain folks. **1998** Hyde *My Home* 125 "Youns come," he said, as he sauntered over the loft and down the steps. We didn't answer. He had disappeared from sight.

you'uns come and see us See **you'uns come**.

you'unses See **you'uns 1**, **3**.

you'uns's See **you'uns 3**.

you'uns self (also *you'unses selves*) *pronoun* Yourselves.

1939 Hall *Coll* Step up here, boys, and he'p you'uns se'f. **1963** Watkins and Watkins *Yesterday* 148 Ma come out there and stopped us and said, "You ought to be ashamed of youunses selves, treating that terrapin thataway."

yowe See **ewe**.

yumor See **humor**.

yuns See **you'uns 1**.

yurnses See **yourns's**.

Z

Zeke *noun* A member of a biracial group in Cumberland County, Kentucky.

1961 *Coe Ridge OHP-334A* I said "You always said you'd like to see a Zeke". . . . We call Zekes.

ziggerboo *noun* Same as **gee-haw whimmy diddle 1**.

1968 Connelly *Discover Appal* 131 Several unique hand toys have seen a rebirth. The gee-haw-whimmydiddle dates back to early Central Europe and to Sweden and China. In Tennessee this toy is called a ziggerboo, in Georgia a geehaw, and by the Unaka Cherokee, a hoodoo. **1972** Cooper *NC Mt Folklore* 34 For many decades and until stores became plentiful, the children's Christmas toys and gifts were mainly homemade. There were dolls, yarn balls, whistles, geehaw whimmydiddles or ziggerboos, rattle traps, noisemakers or bull roars and flipperdingers. [**1995** Montgomery *Coll* (unknown to consultants from the Smoky Mountains).]

zigzag fence *noun* Same as **worm fence**.

1907 Dugger *Balsam Groves* 31 The zigzag fence was ten rails high, and each angle was propped with two small logs, which leaned against it from opposite directions, and crossed each other just over the top rail.

zip *noun* See citation.

1964 Banks *Back to Mts* 71 Generally we got plenty of good crisp biscuit[s]. Buttered, those biscuit[s] went exceptionally well with the homemade sugar syrup that was always in plentiful supply. It was known among us as "zip."

zizz wheel *noun* A child's toy. See citation.

1989 Still *Rusties and Riddles* [9] = a twirling button operated by strings.

zonies alive *interjection* Used as a mild oath. See also **great zonies**.

2000 Montgomery *Coll* Zonies alive, I don't believe it (Cardwell).

Chronological List of Works Cited with Abbreviated Titles

This bibliography provides a chronological list of the sources for every citation within the dictionary. Each item consists of three parts. The first is a citation header, which is an abbreviated version of the full bibliographical information of the source in question. Each begins with the year of publication or creation in bold type, followed by the last name(s) of the author(s) or editor(s), and ends with an italicized (and usually abbreviated) title. When a date is approximate, the notation c, indicating "circa," is prefixed to the date. Many sources have no known author or editor, and in such cases the title follows the date. Other sources (especially archival collections of manuscripts, recordings, or other materials) span multiple years. In such cases the source is listed at the earliest year cited. Thus, **1937–87** Hall Coll refers to the large Joseph Sargent Hall Collection at the Archives of Appalachia at East Tennessee State University, a collection that includes materials from a span of several decades.

The second part gives bibliographic details of each source in a consistent reference style. The third part consists of a bracketed label indicating the geographic region from which most items come, providing the part of a state and, if possible, the county of origin. Geographical information is not always available, so not every entry includes a bracketed label.

Some entries for manuscripts held by libraries and archives, especially those from the Civil War, follow a variety of formats, which reflect the original repository. Sources with no page numbers either consist of a single page or lack a known page number. It is important to note that some publications below have been retitled in recent years and that some repositories have relocated.

A number of sources are collections whose items span a range of years. In these cases, the individual citations within entry paragraphs will contain a single year, but in this section such sources will be represented by their span of dates, rather than each individual year.

Adams Tales. See **1939–42** Adams Tales

Alexander CW Letters. See **1862–65** Alexander CW Letters

AOHP/ALC. See **1971–75** AOHP/ALC

AOHP/ASU. See **1973–74** AOHP/ASU

AOHP/EH. See **1971–75** AOHP/EH

AOHP/LJC. See **1972–75** AOHP/LJC

Apperson CW Letters. See **1862–64** Apperson CW Letters

Asheville Citizen-Times. See **1952–84** Asheville Citizen-Times

Bailey CW Letters. See **1864–65** Bailey CW Letters

Bartlett CW Letters. See **1863–64** Bartlett CW Letters

Bayless Letters. See **1884–86** Bayless Letters

BearPaw. See **1996–2017** BearPaw

Bell CW Letters. See **1862–63** Bell CW Letters

Bent Creek Church. See **1785–96** Bent Creek Church Minutes

Big Pigeon Church. See **1789–98** Big Pigeon Church Minutes

Blind Pig. See **2010–19** Blind Pig

Bradshaw CW Letters. See **1862–63** Bradshaw CW Letters

Brown CW Letters. See **1863–65** Brown CW Letters

Burton-Manning Coll. See **1969–70** Burton-Manning Coll

Carpenter Diary I. See **1842–77** Carpenter Diary I

Carson CW Letters. See **1857–65** Carson CW Letters

Carter CW Letters. See **1861–69** Carter CW Letters

Chapman CW Letters. See **1852–67** Chapman CW Letters

Click CW Letters. See **1861–63** Click CW Letters

Coggin CW Letters. See **1862–63** Coggin CW Letters

Cole Letters. See **1888–1905** Cole Letters

Copeland CW Letters. See **1862–64** Copeland CW Letters

Copenhaver CW Letters. See **1861–65** Copenhaver CW Letters

Councill CW Letters. See **1862–64** Councill CW Letters

Crosby Journal. See **1842–45** Crosby Journal/Account Book

CW Soldiers' Letters. See **1862–63** CW Soldiers' Letters

Dalton CW Letters. See **1861–64** Dalton CW Letters

Dante OHP. See **1997–98** Dante OHP

DARE File. See **1871–2013** DARE File

DARE Survey. See **1965–70** DARE Survey

Davis CW Letters. See **1861–62** Davis CW Letters

DSAE Internet File. See **2008–19** DSAE Internet File

Earnest CW Diary. See **1862–63** Earnest CW Diary

Edmonston/Kelly CW Letters. See **1862–64** Edmonston/Kelly CW Letters

Elijoy Church. See **1834–77** Elijoy Church Minutes

Epperly CW Letters. See **1862–65** Epperly CW Letters

Foster Walker Valley. See **1970–74** Foster Walker Valley

Foxfire Interviews. See **1970–73** Foxfire Interviews

French Broad Petitions. See **1784–89** French Broad Petitions

French Broad Church. See **1793–98** French Broad Church Minutes

Fuller CW Letters. See **1861–65** Fuller CW Letters

Gilley CW Letters. See **1861–63** Gilley CW Letters

Globe Creek Church. See **1797–1812** Globe Creek Church Minutes

Griffin CW Letters. See **1861–64** Griffin CW Letters

GSMNP. See **1954–84** GSMNP

GSMNPCOHP. See **1996–99** GSMNPCOHP

Hall Coll. See **1937–87** Hall Coll

Hall CW Letters. See **1863–70** Hall CW Letters

Hancock CW Letters. See **1862–64** Hancock CW Letters

Hanes CW Letters. See **1861–64** Hanes CW Letters

Hartsell Memora. See **1813–14** Hartsell Memora

Hawn CW Letters. See **1862–63** Hawn CW Letters

Hedgecock Diary. See **1861–62** Hedgecock Diary

Heinmiller Coll. See **2010–19** Heinmiller Coll

Hill CW Letters. See **1863–65** Hill CW Letters

House Spotlight. See **2012–13** House Spotlight

Hundley CW Letters. See **1862–65** Hundley CW Letters

Huntley CW Letters. See **1861–63** Huntley CW Letters

Huskey Rogers Papers. See **1801–8** Huskey Rogers Papers

Ingram CW Letters. See **1862–63** Ingram CW Letters

Jamison Jubilant Spirit. See **1993–94** Jamison Jubilant Spirit

Jefferson Co Wills I. See **1793–1804** Jefferson Co Wills I

Jefferson Co Wills II. See **c1796–98** Jefferson Co Wills II

Joyce CW Letters. See **1862–65** Joyce CW Letters

Kendrick CW Letters. See **1861–68** Kendrick CW Letters

Kephart Notebooks. See **1904–20** Kephart Notebooks

Kiracofe CW Letters. See **1861–65** Kiracofe CW Letters

Knoxville Register. See **1843–57** Knoxville Register

LAMSAS Appal. See **1934–47** LAMSAS Appal

Lance CW Letters. See **1861–64** Lance CW Letters

Landry Coll. See **1988–97** Landry Coll

Landry Smoky Mt Interviews. See **1989–99** Landry Smoky Mt Interviews

Leigh CW Letters. See **1861–65** Leigh CW Letters

Lister CW Letters. See **1862–64** Lister CW Letters

Love CW Letters. See **1860–65** Love CW Letters

Mangum CW Letters. See **1862–64** Mangum CW Letters

Martin CW Letters. See **1861–65** Martin CW Letters

Matewan OHP. See **1989–90** Matewan OHP

McCracken Logging. See **1974–75** McCracken Logging

McFee CW Letters. See **1862–63** McFee CW Letters

McLean Diary. See **1831–47** *McLean Diary*

Miller Pigeon's Roost. See **1950–73** *Miller Pigeon's Roost*

Misemer CW Letters. See **1863–65** *Misemer CW Letters*

Montgomery Coll. See **1992–2002** *Montgomery Coll*

Montgomery File. See **1975–2018** *Montgomery File*

Neves CW Letters. See **1861–63** *Neves CW Letters*

Odell CW Letters. See **1861–64** *Odell CW Letters*

Oliver Fifty Years. See **1938–46** *Oliver Fifty Years*

Oliver Sketches. See **1931–34** *Oliver Sketches*

Owens CW Letters. See **1863–64** *Owens CW Letters*

Parris CW Letters. See **1862** *Parris CW Letters*

Patton CW Letters. See **1861–63** *Patton CW Letters*

Paw Paw Hollow Church. See **1803–70** *Paw Paw Hollow Church Minutes*

Penland CW Letters. See **1862–63** *Penland CW Letters*

Poe Family Papers. See **1862–65** *Poe Family Papers*

Poteet CW Letters. See **1861–65** *Poteet CW Letters*

Proffit CW Letters. See **1861–64** *Proffit CW Letters*

Providence Church. See **1829–32** *Providence Church Minutes*

Rector CW Letters. See **1861–63** *Rector CW Letters*

Reese CW Letters. See **1862–64** *Reese CW Letters*

Revis CW Letters. See **1862–65** *Revis CW Letters*

Richland Church. See **1791–92** *Richland Church Minutes*

Robinson CW Letters. See **1861–63** *Robinson CW Letters*

Rogers CW Letters. See **1861–64** *Rogers CW Letters*

Sevier Settler. See **1984–86** *Sevier Settler*

Sexton CW Letters. See **1862–64** *Sexton CW Letters*

Shenandoah OHC. See **1975–79** *Shenandoah OHC*

Shifflet CW Letters. See **1861–63** *Shifflet CW Letters*

Shipman CW Letters. See **1861–63** *Shipman CW Letters*

Simms Coll. See **1934–40** *Simms Coll*

Sinking Creek Church. See **1787–99** *Sinking Creek Church Minutes*

Six Hill 'n Holler. See **1984** *Six Hill 'n Holler*

Smith CW Letters. See **1862–65** *Smith CW Letters*

Smokies Guide. See **1980–2013** *Smokies Guide*

Smokies Heritage. See **1978–82** *Smokies Heritage*

Smoky Mt News. See **2002–18** *Smoky Mt News*

Smoky Vistas. See **1977–79** *Smoky Vistas*

Still Moving. See **1940–41** *Still Moving*

Stubbs Mountain-Wise. See **1959–71** *Stubbs Mountain-Wise*

Sutton CW Letters. See **1861–62** *Sutton CW Letters*

Swearingen Letters. See **1874–96** *Swearingen Letters*

Tesh CW Letters. See **1862–64** *Tesh CW Letters*

Thompson CW Letters. See **1861–63** *Thompson CW Letters*

Tuckaleechee Cove Church. See **1870–78** *Tuckaleechee Cove Church Minutes*

Vance Papers. See **1862–64** *Vance Papers*

Walker CW Letters. See **1863–65** *Walker CW Letters*

Warrick CW Letters. See **1862–65** *Warrick CW Letters*

Watkins CW Letters. See **1862–64** *Watkins CW Letters*

Watson CW Letters. See **1861–62** *Watson CW Letters*

Watters-Curtis CW Letters. See **1861–64** *Watters-Curtis CW Letters*

Wesson CW Letters. See **1861–65** *Wesson CW Letters*

Whitaker CW Letters. See **1863–64** *Whitaker CW Letters*

W H Wesson CW Letters. See **1861–65** *W H Wesson CW Letters*

Wilburn Notes. See **1937–39** *Wilburn Notes*

Williams Coll. See **2012–14** *Williams Coll*

Wilson Coll. See **c1960–68** *Wilson Coll*

Wilson Confederate Private. See **1863–65** *Wilson Confederate Private*

Wiseman CW Letters. See **1861–65** *Wiseman CW Letters*

Wolfram/Christian WV Coll. See **1975–83** *Wolfram/Christian WV Coll*

Wright CW Letters. See **1862–64** *Wright CW Letters*

W Walker CW Letters. See **1862–63** *W Walker CW Letters*

Zimmerman CW Letters. See **1861–64** *Zimmerman CW Letters*

Zion Church. See **1838–64** *Zion Church Minutes*

1774 *Dunmore's War* = Thwaites, Reuben Gold, and Louise Phelps Kellogg, eds. 1905. *Documentary history of Dunmore's War 1774*. Madison: Wisconsin Historical Society. [southwestern VA]

1780 *Donelson Journal* = Donelson, John. 1779–80. Journal. MS in Tennessee State Library and Archives. Published in J. G. M. Ramsey, *The annals of Tennessee to the end of the eighteenth century*, 197–203. Charleston, SC: Walker and James, 1853. Repr., Knoxville: East Tennessee Historical Society, 1967. [east TN]

1783 *Washington Co Petition* = Petition from Washington County relative to the division whereof Washington Bill. 2002. *Watauga Association of Genealogists Bulletin* 31: 39. [northeast TN]

1784–89 *French Broad Petitions* = Petitions to the North Carolina General Assembly from inhabitants south of the French Broad. 2001. Transcribed by Cherel Bolin Henderson. *Tennessee Ancestors* 17: 208–27. [central east TN]

1785–96 *Bent Creek Church Minutes* = *Bent Creek Baptist Church Minutes, 1785–1844*. 1938. Historical Records Project 465-44-3-115, WPA. Transcribed copy on deposit at Calvin M. McClung Historical Collection, Knox County Public Library, Knoxville. [Hamblen County, central east TN]

1787–99 *Sinking Creek Church Minutes* = *Sinking Creek Baptist Church Minutes*. 1787–99. Historical Records Project 465-44-3-115, WPA, 1938. Transcribed copy on deposit at Calvin M. McClung Historical Collection, Knox County Public Library, Knoxville. [Carter County, northeast TN]

1788 *Greene Petition* = Petition from the inhabitants of Greene County. 2002. *Watauga Association of Genealogists Bulletin* 31: 9–10. [Greene County, northeast TN]

1789–98 *Big Pigeon Church Minutes* = *Minutes of the Big Pigeon Baptist Church, 1787–1874*. Transcribed copy on deposit at Calvin M. McClung Historical Collection, Knox County Public Library, Knoxville. [Cocke County, central east TN]

1790 *Lenoir Papers* = [William Lenoir letter, March 25, to Father]. Lenoir Family Papers. Collection 426, Southern Historical Collection, Wilson Library, University of North Carolina at Chapel Hill. [central western NC]

1791 *Bartram Journey through Carolina* = Bartram, William. 1791. *Travels through North & South Carolina, Georgia, East & West Florida, the Cherokee country, the extensive territories of the Muscogulges, or Creek Confederacy, and the country of the Chactaws; containing an account of the soil and natural productions of those regions, together with observations on the manners of the Indians*. Philadelphia: James and Johnson.

1791–92 *Richland Church Minutes* = *Richland Baptist Church, Grainger County, Tennessee Minutes, April 11, 1791–August 8, 1795*. 1987. *Tennessee Ancestors* 3: 89–100. [Grainger County, northeast TN]

1793–98 *French Broad Church Minutes* = *French Broad River Baptist Church minutes. 1786–1859*. Historical Records Project 65-44-1466, WPA. 1933. Transcribed copy on deposit at Calvin M. McClung Historical Collection, Knox County Public Library, Knoxville, Tennessee. [Jefferson County, central east TN]

1793–1804 *Jefferson Co Wills I* = Jefferson County, Tennessee, will book 1, 1792–1810, part 1. 2001. *East Tennessee Roots* 9(1): 35–49. [Jefferson County, central east TN]

1796 *Cunningham Letter* = Cunningham, Paul. 1796. [Letter to Brother and Sister and Cozens from Knox County, TN]. Typescript on deposit at Tennessee State Library and Archives, Nashville.

1796 Dunlap Will = Some early Blount County wills. 2002. *Blount Journal: A Tennessee Genealogical Magazine* 49(1): 6. [Blount County, central east TN]

c1796–98 *Jefferson Co Wills II* = Jefferson County, Tennessee, will book 1,

1792–1810, part 2. 2001. *East Tennessee Roots* 9(3): 231–41. [Jefferson County, central east TN]

1797–1812 *Globe Creek Church Minutes* = Church Book for the Globe Creek Baptist Church. 1797–1812. Collection 2308. Southern Historical Collection, Wilson Library, University of North Carolina at Chapel Hill. [Caldwell County, northwestern NC]

1797 Imlay *Western Terr* = Imlay, Gilbert. 1797. *A topographical description of the western territory of North America*. 3rd ed. London: J. Debrett. [KY]

1801–8 Huskey *Rogers Papers* = Huskey, Allan. 1990. *The Joseph Rogers papers, compiled and transcribed by Allan Huskey*. Copy on deposit at Calvin M. McClung Historical Collection, Knox County Public Library, Knoxville. [Hawkins County, northeast TN]

1803–70 *Paw Paw Hollow Church Minutes* = *Paw Paw Hollow Baptist Church, Sevier County, Tennessee: Minutes, Dec. 1802–May 1880*. Transcribed copy on deposit at Calvin M. McClung Historical Collection, Knox County Public Library, Knoxville. [Sevier County, central east TN]

1813–14 Hartsell *Memora* = Hartsell, Jacob. 1939–40. The J. Hartsell Memora: The journal of a Tennessee captain in the War of 1812. Edited by Mary Harden McCown. *East Tennessee Historical Society Publication* 11: 93–115; 12: 118–46. [northeast TN]

1818 Barton *Vegetable Materia Medica* = Barton, William P. C. 1818. *Vegetable materia medica of the United States or medical botany: Containing a botanical, general, and medical history of medicinal plants indigenous to the United States*. Boston: Boston Book Company.

1818 Fearon *Sketches* = Fearon, Henry Bradshaw. 1818. *Sketches of America*. London: Longman et al. [KY]

1823 Doddridge *Logan* = Doddridge, Joseph. 1823. *Logan*. Buffaloe Creek, VA: Solomon Sala. [WV]

1824 Knight *Letter from KY* = Knight, Henry C. 1824. Letter from Kentucky. In *Letters from the south and west*, 83–108. Boston: Richardson and Lord. [KY]

1826 Royall *Sketches* = Royall, Anne Newport. 1826. *Sketches of history, life, and manners in the United States: By a traveller*. New Haven, CT: Privately published. [WV]

1826 *Whitten Letter* = Whitten letter. 1826. Transcribed and published in *Upper Cumberland Genealogical Association* 15 (1990): 154. [Greenville District, northwestern SC]

1829–32 *Providence Church Minutes* = *Minutes of Providence Primitive Baptist Church, 1829–1881*. Historical Records Project No. 465-44-3-115, WPA. 1933. Transcribed copy on deposit at Calvin M. McClung Historical Collection, Knox County Public Library, Knoxville. [Cocke County, central east TN]

c1830 Benson *Rev Pension Letter* = [William W. Benson, Revolutionary War pension application, c1830]. In Dockter, Albert W., Jr. 1987. Some Revolutionary War soldiers. *Blount Journal* 3: 38. [Blount County, central east TN]

1831–47 *McLean Diary* = *The George McLean diary, February 27, 1831–April 15, 1848*. 1966. Elkins, WV: Randolph County Historical Society. [east central WV]

1832 Rafinesque *Atlantic Journal* = Rafinesque, Constantine Samuel. 1832–33. *Atlantic journal and friend of knowledge*. Philadelphia. [KY]

1834 Caruthers *Kentuckian in NY* = Caruthers, William Alexander. 1834. *The Kentuckian in New-York*. New York: Harper & Sons.

1834 Crockett *Narrative* = Crockett, David. 1834. *Narrative of the life of David Crockett of the state of Tennessee*. Baltimore: Cary, Hart and Company. Facsimile ed., Knoxville: University of Tennessee Press, 1973. [east TN]

1834–77 *Elijoy Church Minutes* = *Elijoy Church (Baptist) Blount County (Arm of Miller's Cove Church on Elijoy) records, 1818–1878*. Transcribed copy on deposit at Calvin M. McClung Historical Collection, Knox County Public Library, Knoxville. [Blount County, central east TN]

1834 *Seal Letter* = [Letter from John and Margaret Seal]. 1985. *Distant Crossroads* 1(1): 49. [White County, central TN]

1835 Click *Departed Voice* = Click, Temperance. 1835. A long-departed voice from Red Hill, Alabama. Transcribed and published in *Greene County Pioneer* 8(80) (1992). [Greene County, northeast TN]

1835 Crockett *Account* = Crockett, David. 1835. *An account of Col. Crockett's tour to the north and down-east in the year of our Lord one-thousand eight-hundred and thirty-four*. Philadelphia: Grey and Hart. [east TN]

1836 *Sullivan Co Soldiers* = Sullivan County Tennessee soldiers in the Cherokee removal—the Trail of Tears. 1836. Transcribed and published in *Holston Pastfinder* 13 (1995): 32. [Sullivan County, northeast TN]

1838–64 *Zion Church Minutes* = Zion Baptist Church, Yancey Co., NC: Minutes, 1834–80. 2007. In *The heritage of the Toe River Valley*, vol. 6, edited by Lloyd Richard Bailey Sr., 19–89. Marceline, MO: Walsworth. [Yancey County, northwestern NC]

1842–77 Carpenter *Diary I* = Carpenter, Jacob. c1845–1920. [Diary excerpts.] In Hannum, Alberta Pierson. 1943. The mountain people. In *The Great Smokies and the Blue Ridge*, edited by Roderick Peattie, 73–151. New York: Vanguard. Other excerpts in Horton Cooper 1972, 148–49. [northwestern NC]

1842–45 Crosby *Journal/Account Book* = Journal and account book of George Crosby, Feb. 1842–Oct. 1846. 1995. *East Tennessee Roots* 7(3): 101–10. [Jefferson County, central east TN]

1842 *Richardson Letter* = What a find: 154 year-old Richardson letter. 1996. *Campbell Countian* 7: 35–36. [Campbell County, northeast TN]

1843–57 *Knoxville Register* = Dulaney, Miriam Fink. 1991. *Humor, rumor and romance in old Jonesborough*. Johnson City, TN: Overmountain. [northeast TN]

c1844 Beckner *Shane Interview* = Beckner, Lucien. 1934. Rev. John Dabney Shane Interview with Mrs. Sarah Graham of Bath County. *Filson Club History Journal* 9: 224–41. [KY]

1844 *Broyles Letter* = Letter to Amos Broyles, Sparta, White County, Tennessee. 1844. Transcribed and published in *Upper Cumberland Genealogical Association* 15 (1990): 113. [central TN]

1844 Willnotah *Ms* = Willnotah. 1844. The life and memory & death; Of my brother Yona Gus Kah. Transcribed and published in *Bone Rattler* 11(2) (1995): 15–16.

c1845 *Coffee Co TN Letters* = Letters of the era and the area. 1989. *Coffee County Historical Society Quarterly* 19(3–4): 76–77. [Coffee County, southeast TN]

1845 Johnston v. Shelton = Johnston v. Shelton, 39 NC 85. 1845. https://casetext.com/case/johnston-v-shelton.

1845 *Millsaps Letters* = Adly M. Millsaps letters. 1845. Transcribed and published in *Roane County Roots* 10 (2006): 2–3. [Roane County, central east TN]

1845 *Sevier Co Court* = Sevier County Court: Two deeds transcribed by Pollyanna Creekmore. 1997. *Smoky Mountain Historical Society Journal and Newsletter* 23: 14–15. [Sevier County, central east TN]

1845 *Wyrick Letter* = Wyrick, Nathaniel. 1845. [Letter to Lewis Atkins in Grainger County, TN, dated April 13]. Transcribed and published in *Claiborne County Historical Society Reflections* 16 (1997): 3–4. [Grainger County, northeast TN]

1848 Gray *Illustrations* = Gray, Asa. 1848. Chloris Boreali-Americana: Illustrations of New, Rare, or otherwise Interesting North American Plants, selected chiefly from those recently brought into Cultivation at the Botanic Garden of Harvard University, Cambridge. Decade I, *Memoirs of the American Academy of Arts and Sciences*, n.s., 3: 1–56. [western NC]

1849 Anon *Melungeons* = Anonymous. 1849. The Melungeons. *Littell's Living Age* 20: 618–19. [Hancock County, northeast TN]

1849 Lanman *Alleghany Mts* = Lanman, Charles. 1849. *Letters from the Alleghany Mountains*. New York: Putnam.

1852 *Carson Letter* = Big John Ross Carson. 1852. [Letter]. Transcribed and published in *Watauga Association of Genealogists Bulletin* 20 (1991): 145–47. [Washington County, northeast TN]

1852–67 *Chapman CW Letters* = Chapman Family Letters, 1848–1881. MS 69-1853, Tennessee State Library and Archives, Nashville. [Campbell County, northeast TN and Russell County, southwestern VA.

1853 Kennedy *Blackwater Chronicle* = Kennedy, Philip Pendleton. 1853. The Blackwater chronicle: A narrative of an expedition into the land of Canaan, in Randolph County. New York: Redfield. [east central WV]

1853 Ramsey *Annals* = Ramsey, J. G. M. 1853. *The annals of Tennessee to the end of the eighteenth century*. Charleston, SC: Walker and James. Reprinted 1967. Knoxville: East Tennessee Historical Society. [east TN]

1855 *Mitchell Letter* = Letter to Lewis Mitchell from brother, Morris Mitchell. 1988. *Distant Crossroads* 5(3): 70. [Blount County, central east TN]

1856 *Athens Post* = *Athens Post*. 1856. [Untitled newspaper article]. July 4. [TN]

1857–65 *Carson CW Letters* = Carson Family Papers. Georgia Department of Archives and History, Atlanta. [Bradley County, southeast TN]

1857 *Knoxville Register* = *Knoxville Register*. 1857. [Untitled newspaper article]. 9 September.

1858 *Webb Letter* = Webb, Samuel. 1858. [Letter]. Transcribed and published in *Distant Crossroads* 24 (2007): 109–10. [Hawkins County, northeast TN]

1859 Colton *Mt Scenery* = Colton, Henry E. 1859. *Mountain scenery*. Raleigh: W. L. Pomeroy. [western NC]

1859 Taliaferro *Fisher's River* = Taliaferro, H[arden E.]. 1859. *Fisher's River (North Carolina) scenes and characters*. New York: Harper and Brothers. [Surry County, northwestern NC, in the 1820s]

1860 Curtis *Plants NC* = Curtis, Moses Ashley. 1860. *Geological and natural history survey of North Carolina: Part III, Botany containing a catalogue of the indigenous and naturalized plants of the state*. Raleigh: NC Institution for the Deaf and Dumb and the Blind.

1860 *Foust CW Letters* = Foust Family. 1860–65. [Letters]. Private collection.

1860–65 *Love CW Letters* = Mathew N. Love Papers, 1827–1868. David M. Rubenstein Rare Book and Manuscript Library, Duke University, Durham, NC. [Henderson County, southwestern NC]

1860 Olmsted *Back Country* = Olmsted, Frederick Law. 1860. *A journey in the back country in the winter of 1853–4*. London: Low, Son and Company.

1860 Taliaferro *Ducktown* = Taliaferro, H. E. 1860. Ducktown. *Southern Literary Messenger* 31 (November): 337–42. [Surry County, northwestern NC]

1860 *Toe Valley Church Minutes* = Toe Valley Church. 2007. [Selected minutes]. In *The heritage of the Toe River Valley Volume VI*, edited by Lloyd Richard Bailey Sr., 48. Marceline, MO: Walsworth. [Yancey County, northwestern NC]

1860 *Week in Smokies* = A week in the Smoky Mountains. 1860. *Southern Literary Messenger* 31 (August): 117–31. [Sevier County, central east TN]

1861 *Carden CW Letter* = Carden, William. [Letter to William Beezly, October 6, 1861]. William Bryant Carden Civil War Letters, Hunter Library Special Collections, Western Carolina University, Cullowhee, NC. [Macon County, southwestern NC]

1861–69 *Carter CW Letters* = Chillon C. Carter Papers. MSS 122, Manuscripts and Folklife Archives, Western Kentucky University, Bowling Green. [Monroe County, south central KY]

1861–63 *Click CW Letters* = Jacob B. Click Papers, 1861–1867. David M. Rubenstein Rare Book and Manuscript Library, Duke University, Durham, NC. [Augusta County, central western VA]

1861–65 *Copenhaver CW Letters* = Copenhaver, Andrew J. 1861–65. Andrew J. Copenhaver Papers. Accession 39717, Library of Virginia Archives, Richmond.

1861 *Cushwa CW Letters* = Cushwa, Daniel G. 1850–91. Daniel G. Cushwa Papers. MSS 2C9597b, Virginia Museum of History and Culture, Richmond.

1861–64 *Dalton CW Letters* = Dalton Family. 1861–64. [Selected letters]. Dalton Family Papers, 1839–1904. South Caroliniana Library, University of South Carolina, Columbia. [Greenville District, northwestern SC]

1861–62 *Davis CW Letters* = H. J. Davis to Christian Davis. 1861–62. WPA Civil War Transcriptions. Tennessee State Library and Archives, Nashville. [Yadkin County, northwestern NC]

1861 *Estes CW Letter* = A Civil War letter. 1997. *Bone Rattler* 13(1): 34–35. [Jackson County, southwestern NC]

1861–65 *Fuller CW Letters* = Fuller Family. 1861–65. [Letters]. Private collection.

1861–63 *Gilley CW Letters* = Joseph K. Gilley, *Letters to Home, the Civil War Letters of Daniel Haywood Gilley*. Williamsburg, VA: Joseph K. Gilley, 1999. [Henry County, southwestern VA]

1861–64 *Griffin CW Letters* = Griffin, Clarence W. 1861–64. Clarence W. Griffin Letters, Lorraine Griffin Letters. PC 153, State Archives of North Carolina, Raleigh. [Rutherford County, southwestern NC]

1861 *Hampton CW Letters* = Hampton, Ezekiel H. 1861–64. [Letters]. Bailey Family Letters. Civil War Document Collection, US Army Military History Institute, Carlisle, PA.

1861–64 *Hanes CW Letters* = Harrison H. Hanes Papers, 1861–1864. David M. Rubenstein Rare Book and Manuscript Library, Duke University, Durham, NC. [Davie County, northwestern NC]

1861–62 Hedgecock *Diary* = Hedgecock, W. E. 1861–63. W. E. Hedgecock Civil War diary record: Diary which I kept while in the Army against the rebellion, 1861–1863. *Tennessee Ancestors* 16: 99–114. [Knox County, central east TN]

1861 *Hileman CW Letters* = Hileman Family. 1861. [Letters]. Lewis Leigh Collection, US Army Military History Institute, Carlisle, PA. [Rockbridge County, central western VA]

1861–63 *Huntley CW Letters* = George Job Huntley Papers, 1861–1863. Hunter Library Special Collections, Western Carolina University, Cullowhee, NC. [Rutherford County, southwestern NC]

1861 *J Love CW Letter* = Love, John C. 1996. A Civil War letter. *Bone Rattler* 12(4): 32–34.

1861–68 *Kendrick CW Letters* = Larkin S. Kendrick Papers. PC 1921, State Archives of North Carolina, Raleigh. [Cleveland County, southwestern NC]

1861–65 *Kiracofe CW Letters* = Kiracofe Family. 1861–65. [Letters]. Private collection.

1861–64 *Lance CW Letters* = Samuel J. Lance Papers. MSS 616, Louisiana and Lower Mississippi Valley Collection, Louisiana State University Libraries, Baton Rouge. [Buncombe County, central western NC]

1861–65 *Leigh CW Letters* = Leigh Family. 1861–65. [Letters]. Private collection.

1861–65 *Martin CW Letters* = William T. Martin Papers, 1816 (1861–1865). Collection No. 466, Stuart A. Rose Manuscript, Archives, and Rare Book Library, Emory University, Atlanta. [Pickens District, northwestern SC]

1861 *Mason CW Letter* = Johnson, Kenneth R. 1971. The early Civil War in south Kentucky as experienced by a Confederate sympathizer. *Register of the Kentucky Historical Society* 69: 177–80. [southern KY]

1861 *Mingus Letters* = Letters of the Mingus family, 1850–62. 1988. *Bone Rattler* 4(2): 25–32. [Haywood County, central western NC]

1861–63 *Neves CW Letters* = Neves Family Papers. South Caroliniana Library, University of South Carolina, Columbia. [Greenville District, northwestern SC]

1861–64 *Odell CW Letters* = Odell Family. 1861–64. [Letters]. *The Civil War in Tennessee*, Tennessee State Library and Archives, Nashville, http://sos.tn.gov/tsla/looking-back-civil-war-tennessee. [Sullivan County, northeast TN]

1861 *Odum CW Letter* = Odum, J. W. 1861. [Letter]. WPA Civil War Transcriptions. Tennessee State Library and Archives, Nashville. [Hamilton County, southeast TN]

1861 *Painter CW Letters* = Painter, James Barney. 1861. Letters of

James Barney Painter. MSS 10661, University of Virginia Library, Charlottesville. [Botetourt County, central western VA]

1861–63 *Patton CW Letters* = Patton Family Papers, 1860–1864. Collection 581, Southern Historical Collection, Wilson Library, University of North Carolina, Chapel Hill. [Buncombe County, central western NC]

1861–65 *Poteet CW Letters* = Poteet-Dickson Papers. 1861–64. State Archives of North Carolina, Raleigh. [McDowell County, northwestern NC]

1861–64 *Proffit CW Letters* = Proffit Family Letters, 1860–1865. Collection 3408. Southern Historical Collection, Wilson Library, University of North Carolina, Chapel Hill. [Wilkes County, northwestern NC]

1861–63 *Rector CW Letters* = Rector, W. S. 1861–63. [Letters]. Washington Swisher Rector Papers, 1837, 1860–1906. Dolph Briscoe Center for American History, University of Texas at Austin. [Rhea County, southeast TN]

1861–63 *Robinson CW Letters* = Henry W. Robinson Letters. 1861–63. MSS 392, Stuart A. Rose Manuscript, Archives, and Rare Book Library, Emory University, Atlanta. [Jackson County, northeast GA]

1861–64 *Rogers CW Letters* = Reece Rogers Letters. 1861–64. Confederate Miscellany Collection, MSS 20. Stuart A. Rose Manuscript and Rare Book Library, Emory University, Atlanta. [DeKalb County, northeast AL]

1861–63 *Shifflet CW Letters* = Collection of Hillory Shifflet. 1861–63. Gilder Lehrman Collection 02174, New York, NY; also Hillory Shifflet Letters, Missouri Historical Society, St. Louis. [Madison County, southeastern KY]

1861–63 *Shipman CW Letters* = Shipman Family Correspondence, MSN/CW 5043. Hesburgh Libraries, Rare Books and Special Collections, University of Notre Dame, South Bend, IN. [Henderson County, southwestern NC]

1861–62 *Sutton CW Letters* = Sutton, Solomon. 1997. [Letters to brother James Solomon, November 17, 1861, and November 8, 1862]. *Bone Rattler* 13(3): 40–42. [western NC]

1861–63 *Thompson CW Letters* = Thompson, Gordon. 1861–63. [Letters]. MSS 2T3735b, Virginia Historical Society, Richmond. [Mercer County, southern WV]

1861–62 *Watson CW Letters* = James Watson Collection. Hunter Library Special Collections, Western Carolina University, Cullowhee, NC. [Jackson County, southwestern NC]

1861–64 *Watters-Curtis CW Letters* = Watters-Curtis Family Papers. MSS A V345, Filson Historical Society, Special Collections, Louisville, KY. [Estill County, southeastern KY]

1861–65 *Wesson CW Letters* = Wesson Family. 1861–65. [Letters]. Private collection.

1861–65 *W H Wesson CW Letters* = Wesson, William H. 1861–65. William H. Wesson Papers. Accession 41008, Miscellaneous reel 4368, Library of Virginia Archives, Richmond.

1861–65 *Wiseman CW Letters* = Wiseman Family. 1861–65. [Letters]. Private collection.

1861–64 *Zimmerman CW Letters* = James C. Zimmerman Papers, 1779–1910. David M. Rubenstein Rare Book and Manuscript Library, Duke University, Durham, NC. [Forsyth Co NC]

1862–65 *Alexander CW Letters* = Alexander Family. 1862–65. [Letters]. Private collection.

1862–64 *Apperson CW Letters* = Apperson Family Papers. Virginia Polytechnic Institute and State University, Blacksburg. [Franklin County, southwestern VA]

1862 *Baggarly CW Letters* = Tilmon F. Baggarly Papers, 1860–1879. David M. Rubenstein Rare Book and Manuscript Library, Duke University, Durham, NC. [Alexander County, northwestern NC]

1862 *Barkley CW Letters* = Barkley Family. 1861–64. [Letters]. Barkley Family Papers. Collection 3032. Southern Historical Collection, Wilson Library, University of North Carolina, Chapel Hill. [Anderson District, northwestern SC]

1862–63 *Bell CW Letters* = Thomas A. Bell Letters, 1861–1863. David M. Rubenstein Rare Book and Manuscript Library, Duke University, Durham, NC. [Augusta County, central western VA]

1862 *Black CW Letters* = Black, John H. 1862. John H. Black Letters. University of Virginia Library, Charlottesville.

1862–63 *Bradshaw CW Letters* = Jonas A. Bradshaw Papers, 1855–1864. David M. Rubenstein Rare Book and Manuscript Library, Duke University, Durham, NC. [Alexander County, northwestern NC]

1862–63 *Coggin CW Letters* = Coggin, E. B. 1862–63. E. B. Coggin Papers. Alabama Department of Archives and History, Montgomery.

1862–64 *Copeland CW Letters* = Copeland, Isaac. 1862–64. [Letters]. Isaac Copeland Papers. Civil War Collection, Miscellaneous Military Collection, State Archives of North Carolina, Raleigh. [Surry County, northwestern NC]

1862 *Couch CW Letters* = Couch, Jackson. 1862. Jackson Couch Letters. Confederate Miscellany, box 2, folder 1, Stuart A. Rose Manuscript and Rare Book Library, Emory University, Atlanta. [Murray County, north GA]

1862–64 *Councill CW Letters* = Mary A. (Horton) Councill Papers, 1862–1864. David M. Rubenstein Rare Book and Manuscript Library, Duke University, Durham, NC. [Watauga County, northwestern NC]

1862 *Cunningham CW Letters* = Cunningham Family. 1862. Cunningham Letters, 1861–62. PC 1455, State Archives of North Carolina, Raleigh. [Haywood County, central western NC]

1862–63 *CW Soldiers' Letters* = Civil War soldiers' letters. 1862–63. Miscellaneous letters and diaries written by Civil War soldiers whose names are unknown. In editor's private collection.

1862 *Durham CW Letters* = Durham Civil War Letter Collection. 1864. [Letter dated April 22]. Private collection.

1862–63 *Earnest CW Diary* = Earnest, John Guilford. 2005. *All right let them come: The Civil War diary of an East Tennessee Confederate, John Guilford Earnest.* Edited by Charles Swift Northen. Knoxville: University of Tennessee Press.

1862–64 *Edmonston/Kelly CW Letters* = Edmonston/Kelly Families. 1860–65. [Letters]. Edmonston/Kelly Families Collection. Box MSS 95-5, Hunter Library Special Collections, Western Carolina University, Cullowhee, NC. [Haywood County, central western NC]

1862 *Enloe CW Letter* = Enloe, B. F. 1862. [Civil War letter]. Transcribed and published in *The heritage of Swain County North Carolina*, vol. 14 (1988). Winston-Salem, NC: Hunter. [Swain County, southwestern NC]

1862–65 *Epperly CW Letters* = Epperly, C. M. 1862–65. [Letters]. Christian Marion Epperly Papers. Gilder Lehrman Collection 2715, New York, NY. [Floyd County, southwestern VA]

1862 *Ferguson CW Letter* = Ferguson, Thomas. 1862. [Civil War letter]. Transcribed and published in *The heritage of Swain County North Carolina*, vol. 14 (1988). Winston-Salem, NC: Hunter. [Swain County, southwestern NC]

1862 *Fitch CW Letters* = Fitch Family. 1861–65. [Letters]. Private collection.

1862 *Gatlin Immortal Hero* = Gatlin, Radford. 1862. *The parentage, birth, nativity and exploits of the immortal hero Jack Keelan, who successfully defended the bridge at Strawberry Plains, and alone, put to flight fifteen Lincolnites on the night of the eighth of November, 1861.* Atlanta: Daily Intelligencer Print. [east TN]

1862 *Haggard CW Letters* = Haggard Family. 1862. [Letters]. Tennessee in the Civil War (online), http://www.tn.gov/tsla/cwtn/index.htm, Tennessee State Library and Archives, Nashville. [Anderson County, central east TN]

1862 *Hamblen CW Letters* = Cozart, Arl. 1989. Letters written during the Civil War. *Hamblen Heritage* 4: 63–66. [Hamblen County, northeast TN]

1862–64 *Hancock CW Letters* = William Hancock Letters. Federal Collection, box 22, folder 17, Tennessee State Library and Archives, Nashville. [Sevier County, central east TN]

1862–63 *Hawn CW Letters* = Elisha A. Hawn Letters, Special Collections,

University of Tennessee Library, Knoxville. [Morgan County, central east TN]

1862 *Hitt CW Letters* = David M. Hitt Letters. Confederate Miscellany, MSS 20, box 3, Stuart A. Rose Manuscript and Rare Book Library, Emory University, Atlanta. [Cherokee County, north central GA]

1862–65 *Hundley CW Letters* = Hundley Family Papers. Collection 4971, Southern Historical Collection, Wilson Library, University of North Carolina, Chapel Hill. [Stokes County, northwestern NC]

1862 *Hynds CW Letters* = Samuel H. Hynds Letter. *The Civil War in Tennessee*, Tennessee State Library and Archives, Nashville, http://sos.tn.gov/tsla/looking-back-civil-war-tennessee. [Jefferson County, central east TN]

1862–63 *Ingram CW Letters* = John Ingram Papers, 1852–1863. David M. Rubenstein Rare Book and Manuscript Library, Duke University, Durham, NC. [Forsyth County, northwestern NC]

1862–65 *Joyce CW Letters* = John W. Joyce Papers. Harrisburg Civil War Round Table, box 4, US Army Military History Institute, Carlisle, PA. [Stokes County, northwestern NC]

1862–64 *Lister CW Letters* = Lister Family Papers. South Caroliniana Library, University of South Carolina, Columbia. [Greenville District, northwestern SC]

1862 *L Jones CW Letters* = Lewis J. Jones Papers. Small Manuscripts Collection, section A, box 75, items 1–7, David M. Rubenstein Rare Book and Manuscript Library, Duke University, Durham, NC.

1862 *Lockmiller CW Letters* = Lockmiller Family Papers, 1862–1863. MSS 815, Stuart A. Rose Manuscript and Rare Book Library, Emory University, Atlanta. [Meigs County, southeast TN]

1862–64 *Mangum CW Letters* = William P. Mangum Papers. MS 3416, Hargrett Rare Book and Manuscript Library, University of Georgia, Athens. [Jackson County, northeast GA]

1862 *Matthews CW Letters* = Matthews, Hardy. 1862. [Letters]. McLeod Letters Collection. Southern Historical Collection, Wilson Library, University of North Carolina, Chapel Hill.

1862–63 *McFee CW Letters* = John E. and Jeptha C. McFee Letters, Stones River National Battlefield, Murfreesboro, TN. [Buncombe County, central western NC]

1862 *Merriman CW Letters* = W. H. Merriman Letters. *The Civil War in Tennessee*, Tennessee State Library and Archives, Nashville, http://sos.tn.gov/tsla/looking-back-civil-war-tennessee. [Hawkins County, northeast TN]

1862 *Parris CW Letters* = Major Wiley Parris Civil War Letters. Hunter Library Special Collections, Western Carolina University, Cullowhee, NC. [Jackson County, southwestern NC]

1862–63 *Penland CW Letters* = Penland, William C. 1862–63. The William C. Penland Letters from East Tennessee 1862–63. Penland Historical Society, Inc.

1862–65 *Poe Family Papers* = Poe Family. 1862–65. [Letters and documents]. Private collection.

1862–64 *Reese CW Letters* = John W. Reese Papers, 1862–1874. David M. Rubenstein Rare Book and Manuscript Library, Duke University, Durham, NC. [Buncombe County, central western NC]

1862–65 *Revis CW Letters* = Daniel W. Revis Letters, PC 1914, State Archives of North Carolina, Raleigh. [Henderson County, southwestern NC]

1862 *Roddie CW Letter* = Roddie Family. 1862. [Letter]. John H. Crawford Papers. Archives of Appalachia, East Tennessee State University, Johnson City. [Washington County, northeast TN]

1862 *Rudasil CW Letters* = H. F. Rudasil Letters. Confederate Miscellany Collection. MSS 20. Stuart A. Rose Manuscript and Rare Book Library, Emory University, Atlanta. [Davie County, northwestern NC]

1862–64 *Sexton CW Letters* = Thornton Sexton Letters, 1861–1864. David M. Rubenstein Rare Book and Manuscript Library, Duke University, Durham, NC. [Ashe County, northwestern NC]

1862 *Shockley CW Letters* = W. S. Shockley Papers, 1861–1864. David M. Rubenstein Rare Book and Manuscript Library, Duke University, Durham, NC. [Jackson County, northwest GA]

1862–65 *Smith CW Letters* = William D. Smith Papers, 1862–1865. David M. Rubenstein Rare Book and Manuscript Library, Duke University, Durham, NC. [Davie County, northwestern NC]

1862 *Spainhourd CW Letters* = Robert Spainhourd Papers, 1862. David M. Rubenstein Rare Book and Manuscript Library, Duke University, Durham, NC. [Forsyth County, northwestern NC]

1862 *Sullivan Co in CW I* = Sullivan Countians in the Civil War. 1995. *Holston Pastfinder* 13(51): 32–33. [Sullivan County, northeast TN]

1862–64 *Tesh CW Letters* = William A. Tesh Papers, 1858–1864. David M. Rubenstein Rare Book and Manuscript Library, Duke University, Durham, NC. [Yadkin County, northwestern NC]

1862–64 *Vance Papers* = [Letters to North Carolina Governor Zebulon Vance]. Zebulon Vance Papers. State Archives of North Carolina, Raleigh. [various counties, western NC]

1862–65 *Warrick CW Letters* = Thomas Warrick Papers. SPR420, Alabama Department of Archives and History, Montgomery. [Coosa County, east central AL]

1862–64 *Watkins CW Letters* = James W. Watkins Papers, 1861–1864. MSS 413, Stuart A. Rose Manuscript, Archives, and Rare Book Library, Emory University, Atlanta. [Franklin County, northeast GA]

1862 *West CW Letters* = West Family Letters. South Caroliniana Library, University of South Carolina, Columbia. [Spartanburg District, northwestern SC]

1862 *Williams CW Letters* = Williams, James. 1861–65. James Williams Letters. Accession 25920, Library of Virginia Archives, Richmond.

1862 *Willis CW Letters* = Willis Family. 1861–65. [Letters]. Private collection.

1862–64 *Wright CW Letters* = Bryant Wright Papers, 1859–1864. MS 5916, David M. Rubenstein Rare Book and Manuscript Library, Duke University, Durham, NC. [Tallapoosa County, east central AL]

1863 *A B Walker CW Letters* = Walker Family Papers. Tennessee State Library and Archives, Nashville. [Knox County, central east TN]

1863 *Averett Letters* = Averett, Harris Hardin. 1863. Correspondence, 1854–63. SPR 422. Alabama Department of Archives and History, Montgomery.

1863–64 *Bartlett CW Letters* = Bartlett Letters. Tennessee State Library and Archives, Nashville. http://www.tn.gov/tsla/cwtn/index.htm [Claiborne County, northeast Tennessee]

1863–65 *Brown CW Letters* = Brown Family Papers. Archives of Appalachia, East Tennessee State University, Johnson City. [Knox County, central east TN]

1863 *Cathey CW Letter* = Cathey Family Papers. Hunter Library Special Collections, Western Carolina University, Cullowhee, NC. [Haywood County, central western NC]

1863–64 *Confederate Coll* = Miscellaneous letters and documents written by Confederate Civil War soldiers. Confederate Civil War Collection. Tennessee State Library and Archives, Nashville.

1863 *D B Walker CW Letters* = Daniel B. Walker Letters, 1855–1889. Manuscripts Collection, Filson Historical Society, Louisville, KY. [McMinn County, southeast TN]

1863 *Gilliland CW Letters* = Gilliland Family. 1863. Gilliland Civil War Letters. MS.54-136, Mississippi Valley Collection, University of Memphis, TN.

1863–70 *Hall CW Letters* = Hall, Elijah. 1863–1870. Civil War Letters of Elijah Hall, Bell Irvin Wiley Collection, Stuart A. Rose Manuscript, Archives, and Rare Book Library, Emory University, Atlanta. [Morgan County, central east TN]

1863–65 *Hill CW Letters* = Jesse Hill Letters, 1864–1865. PC 1888, State Archives of North Carolina, Raleigh. [Forsyth County, northwestern NC]

1863 *Hogg CW Letters* = Hiram Hogg Letters, 1863. SC 986, Kentucky Historical Society, Frankfort. [Letcher County, southeastern KY]

1863 *Jones CW Letters* = George W. Jones Letter. *The Civil War in Tennessee*, Tennessee State Library and Archives, Nashville, http://sos.tn.gov/tsla/looking-back-civil-war-tennessee. [Sullivan County, northeast TN]

1863 *Karnes CW Letters* = J. A. and E. A. Karnes Letters. 1863. Civil War Collection: Confederate and Federal 1861–1865, Confederate Collection, box C8, folder 5, Tennessee State Library and Archives, Nashville. [Mercer County, southern WV]

1863 *Kinsland CW Letter* = Kinsland, Mary. 1863. [Letter]. MS 872, Hargrett Rare Book and Manuscript Library, University of Georgia, Athens. [Haywood County, central western NC]

1863 *Lee CW Letters* = William Henry Harrison Lee Papers, 1862–1863. South Caroliniana Library, University of South Carolina, Columbia. [Greenville District, northwestern SC]

1863 *Levi CW Letters* = Levi Letters, 1863. Tennessee State Library and Archives, Nashville. [Hamilton County, southeast TN]

1863 *Matthews CW Letters* = Matthews Family Papers, 1856–1910. MS 81-11, State Archives of Florida, Tallahassee. [Cherokee County, northeast AL]

1863–65 *Misemer CW Letters* = Henry Marshall Misemer Family Letters, 1861-[1863–1865]-1878 (Microfilm 2008). Tennessee State Library and Archives, Nashville. [Monroe County, central east TN]

1863–64 *Owens CW Letters* = Owens Family. 1863–64. [Letters]. Confederate Papers, Collection 172, Southern Historical Collection, Wilson Library, University of North Carolina, Chapel Hill. [Wilkes County, northwestern NC]

1863 *Phillips CW Letters* = Phillips, Sarah. 1862–63. D. W. Phillips Letters. MS 1751, Hargrett Rare Book and Manuscript Library, University of Georgia.

1863 Smith *Battle of Rome* = Smith, Charles Henry. 1863. The battle of Rome—official. *Southern Confederacy* (Atlanta). May 9. [northwest GA]

1862–65 *Walker CW Letters* = Walker Family Papers. 1863–65. Confederate Collection, box 11, folder 35a, Tennessee State Library and Archives, Nashville. [Knox County, central east TN]

1863–64 *Whitaker CW Letters* = Stephen Whitaker Papers. PC 26, State Archives of North Carolina, Raleigh. [Cherokee County, southwestern NC]

1863–65 Wilson *Confederate Private* = Wilson, James. 2004. *Letters of a Confederate private: Thomas O. Wilson, Company F, 51st Virginia Infantry, Whartons Brigade.* Blacksburg, VA: Pocahantas. [Bland County, southwestern VA]

1863 *Woody CW Letters* = Green B. Woody letter. Confederate Miscellany, MSS 20, Stuart A. Rose Manuscript, Archives, and Rare Book Library, Emory University, Atlanta. [Yancey County, northwestern NC]

1863 *W Robinson CW Letter* = W. M. Robinson letter. http://www.jcncgs.com. [Jackson County, southwestern NC]

1864–65 *Bailey CW Letters* = Bailey Family Papers, 1827–1871. MSS 2B1565B, Virginia Historical Society, Richmond. [Mercer County, southern WV]

1864 *Blair CW Letters* = Blair Letters, 1838–1884, PC 1206, State Archives of North Carolina, Raleigh. [Caldwell County, northwestern NC]

1864 *C A Walker CW Letters* = William Walker Papers. Hunter Library Special Collections, Western Carolina University, Cullowhee, NC. [Cherokee County, southwestern NC]

1864 *Conley CW Letter* = Conley Family. 1864. [Letter]. Civil War Soldiers' Letters. LPR78, box 1, folder 11, Alabama Department of Archives and History, Montgomery. [Jackson County, southwestern NC]

1864 *Cooper CW Letter* = Cooper, R. 1864. Robert Cooper Letter. WPA Civil War Transcriptions, Tennessee State Library and Archives, Nashville. [Hawkins County, northeast TN]

1864 *D Walker CW Letters* = Letters of Daniel B. Walker, Manuscripts Collection, Filson Historical Society, Louisville, KY. [McMinn County, southeast TN]

1864 *Forgotten Ancestors* = Frank, Elisha A. 1864. [Letter to wife]. *Letters from Forgotten Ancestors.* https://www.tngenweb.org/tnletters/jeff.htm [Jefferson County, east TN]

1864 Gilmore *Down in TN* = Gilmore, James R. 1864. *Down in Tennessee, and back by way of Richmond.* New York: Carleton. [north central TN]

1864 *Harrill CW Letters* = Letters of A. S. Harrill. WPA Civil War Transcriptions. Tennessee State Library and Archives, Nashville. [Rutherford County, southwestern NC]

1864 *Houston CW Letter* = Robert L. Houston Letter. WPA Civil War Transcriptions, Tennessee State Library and Archives, Nashville. [Blount County, central east TN]

1864 *McGill CW Letters* = McGill-Thatcher Family Papers, 1818–1979. Mf 1844, box 1, folder 6, Tennessee State Library and Archives, Nashville. [Hamilton County, southeast TN

1864 *Millican CW Letter* = Frank M. Millican Letter. WPA Civil War Transcriptions, Tennessee State Library and Archives, Nashville. [Roane County, central east TN]

1864 *Stepp CW Letters* = Stepp, S. H. 1864. [Letters]. Silas H. Stepp Civil War Letters. M2004.4.1, Special Collections, University of North Carolina at Asheville. [Buncombe County, central western NC]

1864 *Sullivan Co in CW II* = Sullivan Countians in the Civil War. 1995. *Holston Pastfinder* 13(52): 32–33. [Sullivan County, northeast TN]

1864 *Teague CW Letter* = John Teague Letters. *The Civil War in Tennessee,* Tennessee State Library and Archives, Nashville, http://sos.tn.gov/tsla/looking-back-civil-war-tennessee. [McMinn County, southeast TN]

1864 *Wester Letters* = Wester, Thomas C. 1864. Thomas C. Wester Papers, 1864–65. State Archives of North Carolina, Raleigh.

1864 *Williams CW Letters* = Williams, James. 1861–65. James Williams Letters, Accession 25920, Library of Virginia Archives, Richmond.

1865 *Larue CW Letters* = Larue Family Papers. *The Civil War in Tennessee,* Tennessee State Library and Archives, Nashville, http://sos.tn.gov/tsla/looking-back-civil-war-tennessee. [Knox County, central east TN]

1865 *Morrison CW Letters* = Morrison, Ralph B. 1895. Civil War letters of Thomas Lafayette Morrison. *Burke Journal* 4: 7–16. [Burke County, central western NC]

1865 *Parlier CW Letters* = Military Collection, Civil War, box 85, folder 28, State Archives of North Carolina, Raleigh. [Wilkes County, northwestern NC]

1865 *Smith Letter* = Andrew T. Smith's letter home at the end of the Civil War. 2000. *Pellissippian* 21: 10–11. [Anderson County, east TN]

1865 *Wax Letter* = [Letter from H. G. Wax]. 1865. Transcribed and published in *Distant Crossroads* 1(1) (1985): 39–41. [Hawkins County, northeast TN]

1866 Smith *So Called* = Smith, Charles Henry. 1866. *Bill Arp, so called: A side show of the southern side of the war.* New York: Metropolitan Record Office. [northwest GA]

1867 Harris *Sut Lovingood* = Harris, George Washington. 1867. *Sut Lovingood: Yarns spun by a nat'ral bornd durn'd fool.* Facsimile ed., edited by M. Thomas Inge. Memphis, TN: St. Lukes, 1987. [east TN]

1870 Drake *Pioneer Life KY* = Drake, Daniel. 1870. *Pioneer life in Kentucky, 1785–1800.* Cincinnati: R. Clarke. [northeastern KY]

1870–78 *Tuckaleechee Cove Church Minutes* = *Records of the Primitive Baptist Church of Christ in Tuckaleechee Cove, Tennessee, April 1870 through August 1912.* 1988. Transcribed by Betty R. Davis. On deposit at Calvin M. McClung Historical Collection, Knox County Public Library, Knoxville. [Blount County, central east TN]

1873 Harney *Strange Land* = Harney, Will Wallace. 1873. A strange land and a peculiar people. *Lippincott's* 12: 429–38. [southwestern VA]

1873 May *Journal* = May, John. 1873. *Journal and letters of Col. John May, of Boston, relative of two journeys to the Ohio country in 1788 and '89.* Cincinnati: Clarke. [WV]

1873 Smith *Arp Peace Papers* = Smith, Charles Henry. 1873. *Bill Arp's peace papers.* New York: Carleton. [northwest GA]

1874 Collins *Hist Sketches KY* = Collins, Lewis. 1874. *Collins' historical sketches of Kentucky.* 2 vols. Covington, KY: Collina. [KY]

1874–96 Swearingen *Letters* = Swearingen, Janelle. 1994. Letters from home. *Tennessee Ancestors* 10: 163–68. [Monroe and Bradley Counties, southeast TN]

1875 Davis *Qualla* = Davis, Rebecca Harding. 1875. Qualla. *Lippincott's* 16: 576–86. [central western NC]

1875 King *Great South* = King, Edward. 1875. *The great South*. Edited by W. McGruder Drake and Robert R. Jones. Hartford, CT: American Publishing Company. Repr., Baton Rouge: Louisiana State University Press, 1972.

1875 Reid *Land of Sky* = Reid, Christian. 1875. *Land of the sky; or, adventures in mountain by-ways*. New York: Appleton. [Buncombe County, central western NC]

1878 Coale *Wilburn Waters* = Coale, Charles B. 1878. *The life and adventures of Wilburn Waters, the famous hunter and trapper of White Top Mountain*. Richmond: G. W. Gray & Co. [southwestern VA]

1878 Guild *Old Times TN* = Guild, Joseph Conn. 1878. *Old times in Tennessee*. Nashville, TN: Tavel, Eastman & Howell.

1879 Jones *Backwoods Carolina* = Jones, Louise Coffin. 1879. In the backwoods of Carolina. *Lippincott's* 24: 747–56. [western NC]

1881 Atkinson *After Moonshiners* = Atkinson, George W. 1881. *After the moonshiners: A book of thrilling, but truthful narratives*. Wheeling, WV: Frew and Campbell.

1881 *Cincinnati Enquirer* = *Cincinnati Enquirer*, October 18, 1881, 2/1.

1881 Draper *Kings Mt* = Draper, Lyman C. 1881. *King's Mountain and its heroes: History of the battle of King's Mountain, October 7th, 1780, and the events that led to it*. Cincinnati: Thomson.

1881 Pierson *In the Brush* = Pierson, Hamilton W. 1881. *In the brush*. New York: D. Appleton & Co. [KY]

1882 Winstadt *Letter* = Winstadt, Jacob. 1993. [Letter]. *Distant Crossroads* 10 (January): 4. [northeast TN]

1883 Bonner *Dialect Tales* = Bonner, Sherwood. 1883. *Dialect tales*. New York: Harper and Brothers. [Putnam County, central TN]

1883 Jones *Highlands N Carol* = Jones, Louise Coffin. 1883. In the highlands of North Carolina. *Lippincott's* 32: 378–86. [western NC]

1883 Murfree *Old Sledge* = Craddock, Charles Egbert [Mary Murfree]. 1883. A-playin' of Old Sledge at the settlemint. *Atlantic Monthly* 52: 544–57.

1883 Smith *Southernisms* = Smith, Charles Forster. 1883. On southernisms. *Transactions of the American Philological Association* 14: 42–56. [east TN]

1883 Zeigler and Grosscup *Heart of Alleghanies* = Zeigler, Wilbur Gleason, and Benn S. Grosscup. 1883. *The heart of the Alleghanies: or, Western North Carolina; comprising its topography, history, resources, people, narratives, incidents, and pictures in travel, hunting and fishing, and legends of its wildernesses*. Raleigh: Williams and Company. [western NC]

1884–86 *Bayless Letters* = Bayless letters. 1991. *Watauga Association of Genealogists Bulletin* 20: 117–20. [Carter County, northeast TN]

1884 Milliken and Vertrees *Code of TN* = Milliken, W. A., and John J. Vertrees. 1884. *The code of Tennessee, being a compilation of the statute laws of the state of Tennessee, of a general nature, in force June 1, 1884*. Nashville, TN: Marshall and Bruce.

1884 Murfree *In TN Mts* = Craddock, Charles Egbert [Mary Murfree]. 1884. *In the Tennessee mountains*. Boston: Houghton Mifflin.

1884 Scott *Visit* = Scott, A. E. 1884. A visit to Mitchell and Roan Mountains. *Appalachia* 4: 112–20. [western NC]

1884 Smith *Arp Scrap Book* = Smith, Charles Henry. 1884. *Bill Arp's scrap book: Humor and philosophy*. Atlanta: J. P. Harrison. [northwest GA]

1885 Baine *Among Moonshiners* = Baine, Donald A. 1885. Among the moonshiners. *Dixie* 1: 9–14. [north GA]

1885 Murfree *Down Ravine* = Craddock, Charles Egbert [Mary Noailles Murfree]. 1885. *Down the ravine*. Boston: Houghton Mifflin.

1885 Murfree *Prophet* = Craddock, Charles Egbert [Mary Murfree]. 1885. *The prophet of the Great Smoky Mountains*. Boston: Houghton Mifflin.

1886 Murfree *In the Clouds* = Craddock, Charles Egbert [Mary Murfree]. 1886. *In the clouds*. Boston: Houghton Mifflin.

1886 Smith *History KY* = Smith, Zachariah Frederick. 1886. *The history of Kentucky from its earliest discovery and settlement, to the present date*. Louisville, KY: Courier-Journal Job Printing. [KY]

1886 Smith *Southernisms* = Smith, Charles Forster. 1886. On southernisms. *Transactions of the American Philological Association* 17: 34–46. [east TN]

1886 Smith *Sthn Dialect* = Smith, Charles F[orster]. 1886. Southern dialect in life and literature. *Southern Bivouac* 4: 343–50. [east TN]

1887 Goode *Amer Fishes* = Goode, George Brown. 1887. *American fishes*. Boston: Estes and Lauriat.

1888 Alexander *Hiking Big Smokies* = Alexander, Eben. 1888. Hiking through the Big Smokies: Graphic description by Prof. Alexander. *Knoxville Journal*, July 7, 1929, originally published in *New York Evening Post*, August 4, 1888.

1888 Brown *Peculiar People* = Brown, William Perry. 1888. A peculiar people. *Overland Monthly*, 2nd ser. (November), 505–8.

1888–1905 Cole *Letters* = Jesse Cole: The murder's other victim. 1993. *Tennessee Folklore Society Bulletin* 64: 70–80. [Cocke County, central east TN]

1888 *Congress Record* = *Congressional Record*. 1888. 19(4): 3587, May 1. [KY]

1888 *Greene Letters* = Greene letters. 1987. *Watauga Association of Genealogists Bulletin* 16: 151–52. [Roane County, central east TN]

1888 Meriwether *Mt Life in TN* = Meriwether, Lee. 1888. Mountain life in Tennessee. *Cosmopolitan* 5: 456–60. [TN]

1889 Brown *Dialect Survivals in TN* = Brown, Calvin S. 1889. Dialectal survivals in Tennessee. *Modern Language Notes* 4: 205–9. [TN]

1889 Burnett *Note Melungeons* = Burnett, Swan M. 1889. A note on the Melungeons. *American Anthropologist* 2: 347–50. [Hancock County, northeast TN]

1889 *Hogs* = Hogs against serpents. 1889. *Lexington (NC) Ledger*, October 31. [Swain County, southwestern NC]

1889 Mooney *Folk Carolina Mts* = Mooney, James. 1889. Folk-lore of the Carolina mountains. *Journal of American Folk-lore* 2: 95–104. [central western NC]

1889 Murfree *Broomsedge Cove* = Craddock, Charles Egbert [Mary Murfree]. 1889. *The despot of Broomsedge Cove*. Boston: Houghton-Mifflin.

1889 Phelan *History of TN* = Phelan, James. 1889. *History of Tennessee: The making of a state*. Boston: Houghton, Mifflin and Company. [TN]

1890 Carpenter *Thunderhead Peak* = Carpenter, Frank O. 1890. The Great Smoky Mountains and Thunderhead Peak. *Appalachia* 6: 138–46. [central east TN]

1890 Fruit *KY Words* = Fruit, John P. 1890. Kentucky words and phrases. *Dialect Notes* 1: 63–69. [south central KY]

c1890 Job *Diary* = Job, Joshua. c1890. *Diary*. [Excerpted in Inez Burns. 1978. Our southern mountaineers. *Smoky Mountain Historical Society Newsletter* 4(2): 10–13]. [Blount County, central east TN]

1890 Mooney *Cherokee Ball Play* = Mooney, James. 1890. The Cherokee ball play. *American Anthropologist* 3: 105–32. [Swain County, southwestern NC]

1890 Rush *Fishery* = Rush. 1890. River and sea fishery. *Forest and Stream* 35: 276–77.

1891 Brown *Dialect in TN* = Brown, Calvin S. 1891. Other dialectal forms in Tennessee. *Publications of the Modern Language Association* 6: 171–75. [TN]

1891 Davidson *Reminiscences* = Davidson, Allen T. 1891. Reminiscences of western North Carolina. *Lyceum* 1(8): 4–13. [western NC]

1891 Moffat *Mtneers Middle TN* = Moffat, Adeline. 1891. The mountaineers of middle Tennessee. *Journal of American Folk-lore* 4: 314–20. [south central TN]

1891 Murfree *Stranger People* = Craddock, Charles Egbert [Mary Murfree]. 1891. *In the stranger people's country*. New York: Harper and Brothers.

1891 Primer *Studies in WV* = Primer, Sylvester. 1891. Dialectical studies in West Virginia. *Publications of the Modern Language Society* 6(3): 161–70. [WV]

1892 Allen *Cumberland Gap* = Allen, James Lane. 1892. Through Cumberland Gap on horseback. In *The blue-grass region of Kentucky: And other Kentucky articles*, 229–68. New York: Harper & Brothers. [southeastern KY]

1892 Bergen *Plant Names I* = Bergen, Fanny D. 1892. Popular American plant-names. *Journal of American Folk-lore* 5: 89–106. [northwestern NC]

1892 Crutcher *Spurrier with Wildcats* = Crutcher, T. P. 1892. *Spurrier with the wildcats and moonshiners*. Nashville, TN: University. [central TN]

1892 Cushing *Story of Post Office* = Cushing, Marshal. 1892. *Story of our post office*. Boston: A. M. Thayer. [WV]

1871–2013 DARE File = [Miscellaneous oral and written material published in the *Dictionary of American Regional English*]

1892 Doak *Wagonauts Abroad* = Doak, Henry Melvil. 1892. *The Wagonauts abroad*. Nashville, TN: Southwestern. [east TN]

1892 Dromgoole *Dan to Beersheba* = Dromgoole, Will Allen. 1892. From Dan to Beersheba. *Arena* 5: 77–88.

1892 Dromgoole *War of Roses* = Dromgoole, Will Allen. 1892. The War of the Roses. *Arena* 5: 481–93.

1892 Edwards *Waste-Basket* = Edwards, Charles. 1892. Waste-basket of words. *Journal of American Folklore* 5: 236. [TN]

1892 Fruit *KY Words* = Fruit, John P. 1892. Kentucky words. *Dialect Notes* 1: 229–34. [south central KY]

1892 Smith *Farm and Fireside* = Smith, Charles Henry. 1892. *The farm and the fireside: Sketches of domestic life in war and peace*. Atlanta: Constitution. [northwest GA]

1893 Bergen *Plant Names II* = Bergen, Fanny D. 1893. Popular American plant-names, II. *Journal of American Folk-lore* 6: 135–42. [northwestern NC]

1893 Bolton *Waste-Basket* = Bolton, H. Carrington. 1893. Waste-basket of words. *Journal of American Folk-lore* 6: 143. [western VA]

1893 Wells *Superstitions* = Wells, J. C. 1893. Weather and moon superstitions in Tennessee. *Journal of American Folk-lore* 6: 298–300. [TN]

1894 *Alexandria Gaz* = *Alexandria Gazette*. 1894. [Untitled article]. In DARE File. [VA]

1894 Bergen *Plant Names III* = Bergen, Fanny D. 1894. Popular American plant-names, III. *Journal of American Folk-lore* 7: 89–104. [northwestern NC]

1894 Lanier *Wild Turkey* = Lanier, Charles Day. 1894. On the trail of the wild turkey. *Harper's New Monthly* 89: 881–89.

1894 Murfree *Vanished Star* = Craddock, Charles Egbert [Mary Murfree]. 1894. *His vanished star*. Boston: Houghton-Mifflin.

1894 Porter *Folklore Mt Whites* = Porter, J. Hampton. 1894. Notes on the folk-lore of the mountain whites of the Alleghanies. *Journal of American Folk-lore* 7: 105–17.

1894 Wingfield *Big Buck* = Wingfield, A. B. 1894. The big buck of Walden's Ridge. *Forest and Stream* 43: 399–400. [TN]

1895 Dromgoole *Fiddling to Fame* = Dromgoole, Will Allen. 1895. Fiddling his way to fame. In *The heart of Old Hickory and other stories of Tennessee*, 39–72. Boston: Estes and Lauriat.

1895 Dromgoole *Humble Advocate* = Dromgoole, Will Allen. 1895. A humble advocate. *Arena* 12: 322–33.

1895 Dromgoole *Logan's Courtship* = Dromgoole, Will Allen. 1895. Ole Logan's courtship. In *The heart of Old Hickory and other stories of Tennessee*, 133–56. Boston: Estes and Lauriat.

1895 Dromgoole *Old Hickory* = Dromgoole, Will Allen. 1895. The heart of Old Hickory. In *The heart of Old Hickory and other stories*, 1–38. Boston: Estes and Lauriat.

1895 Edson and Fairchild *TN Mts* = Edson, H. A., and Edith M. Fairchild. 1895. Tennessee mountains in word lists. *Dialect Notes* 1: 370–77. [southeastern KY, northeast TN, northwestern NC]

1895 *Mt Baptist Sermon* = A mountain Baptist sermon. 1895. *Berea Quarterly* 1(1): 12–15. [east TN]

1895 Murfree *Phantoms* = Craddock, Charles Egbert [Mary Noailles Murfree]. 1895. *The phantoms of the foot-bridge, and other stories*. New York: Harper and Row.

1895 Murfree *Witch-Face* = Craddock, Charles Egbert [Mary Murfree]. 1895. *The mystery of witch-face mountain*. Boston: Houghton-Mifflin.

1895 Wiltse *Moonshiners* = Wiltse, Henry M. 1895. *The moonshiners*. Chattanooga: Times.

1895 *Word-Lists* = General list A. 1895. *Dialect Notes* 1: 384–95.

1896 Fox *Last Stetson* = Fox, John, Jr. 1896. The last Stetson. In *A Cumberland vendetta and other stories*, 178–215. New York: Harper and Brothers.

1896 Fox *Vendetta* = Fox, John, Jr. 1896. A Cumberland vendetta. In *A Cumberland vendetta and other stories*, 1–177. New York: Harper and Brothers.

1896 Frost *Education Program* = Frost, William Goodell. 1896. An educational program for Appalachian America. *Berea Quarterly* 1(4): 5–13.

1896 *NC State Board of Resources* = North Carolina State Board of Agriculture. 1896. *North Carolina and its resources*. Winston, NC: M. I. & J. C. Stewart, Public Printers and Binders.

1896 Pool *In Buncombe Co* = Pool, Maria Louise. 1896. *In Buncombe County*. Chicago: Stone. [Buncombe County, central western NC]

1896 Radford *Block Houses* = Radford, P. M. 1896. Block houses. *American Historical Magazine* 1: 247–52.

1896 *Word-List* = Word-list. 1896. *Dialect Notes* 1: 411–27. [southwestern NC]

1897 Barton *Truth about Trouble* = Barton, William E. 1897. *The truth about the trouble at Roundstone*. Boston: Pilgrim. [southeastern KY]

1897 Brown *Dialectal Survivals* = Brown, Calvin S. 1897. Dialectal survivals from Chaucer. *Dial* 22: 139–41. [TN]

1897 *Incidents* = Incidents. 1897. *Berea Quarterly* 2(4): 27. [eastern KY]

1897 Murfree *Juggler* = Craddock, Charles Egbert [Mary Noailles Murfree]. 1897. The juggler. *Atlantic Monthly* 80: 241–63.

1897 Pederson *Mtneers Madison Co* = Pederson, D. L. 1897. The mountaineers of Madison County, North Carolina. *Missionary Review of the World* 20 (November): 821–31. [central western NC]

1897 Skelton *Last Soldiers* = Skelton, William Henry. 1897. The last three soldiers. St. *Nicholas* 24: 367–71. [east TN]

1898 Dromgoole *Cinch* = Dromgoole, Will Allen. 1898. *Cinch and other tales and stories of Tennessee*. Boston: Estes and Company.

1898 Elliott *Durket Sperret* = Elliott, Sarah Barnwell. 1898. *The Durket sperret*. New York: Henry Holt.

1898 *Incidents* = Incidents. 1898. *Berea Quarterly* 3(1): 31. [eastern KY]

1899 Crozier *White-Caps* = Crozier, E. W. 1899. *The White-Caps: A history of the organization in Sevier County*. Knoxville: Bean, Warters and Gaut. [Sevier County, central east TN]

1899 Fox *Mt Europa* = Fox, John, Jr. 1899. *A mountain Europa*. New York: Harper & Brothers.

1899 Frost *Ancestors* = Frost, William Goodell. 1899. Our contemporary ancestors in the southern mountains. *Atlantic Monthly* 83(March): 311–19. [eastern KY]

1899 Frost *Sthn Mts* = Frost, William Goodell. 1899. In the southern mountains. *Berea Quarterly* 4(2): 9–12. [eastern KY]

1899 Green *VA Word-Book* = Green, Bennett Wood. 1899. *Word book of Virginia folk-speech*. Richmond: W. E. Jones' Sons.

1899 Temple *E TN Civil War* = Temple, Oliver P. 1899. *East Tennessee and the Civil War*. Cincinnati: R. Clarke. [east TN]

1899 *US Comm Fish & Fisheries* = United States Commission of Fish & Fisheries. 1899. Report of the Commissioner for 1897–1898. Washington, DC: Government Printing Office.

1900 Carter *NC Sketches* = Carter, Mary Nelson. 1900. *North Carolina sketches: Phases of life where the galax grows*. Chicago: McClurg.

1900 Harben *N GA Sketches* = Harben, William Nathaniel. 1900. *Northern Georgia sketches*. Chicago: McClung.

1900 *NY Journal* = Hawthorne, Julian. 1900. Mountain votes spoil Huntington's revenge. *New York Journal*, April 23.

1900 *Treatise Coal Mining* = *A treatise on coal mining*. 1900. 2nd ed. Scranton, PA: Colliery Engineer Company.

1901 Harben *Westerfelt* = Harben, William Nathaniel. 1901. *Westerfelt*. New York: Harper & Brothers.

1901 Lounsberry *Sthn Wild Flowers* = Lounsberry, Alice. 1901. *Southern wild flowers and trees*. New York: Stokes.

1901 McClintock *KY Mts* = McClintock, S. S. 1901. The Kentucky mountains and their feuds I: The people and their country. *American Journal of Sociology* 7: 1–28. [eastern KY]

1901 Price *KY Folk-Lore* = Price, Sadie F. 1901. Kentucky folk-lore. *Journal of American Folk-lore* 14: 30–38. [eastern KY]

1902 Chamberlain *Algonkian Words* = Chamberlain, Alexander F. 1902. Algonkian words in American English: A study in the contact of the white man and the Indian. *Journal of American Folklore* 15: 240–67.

1902 Grime *Middle TN Baptists* = Grime, John H. 1902. History of middle Tennessee Baptists. Nashville, TN: Baptist and Reflector. [central TN]

1902 Harben *Abner Daniel* = Harben, William Nathaniel. 1902. *Abner Daniel*. New York: Harper & Row.

1902 Hubbard *Moonshiner at Home* = Hubbard, Leonidas, Jr. 1902. The moonshiner at home. *Atlantic Monthly* 90: 234–41. [north GA]

1903 Beddow *Oracle of Bend* = Beddow, Elizabeth Russell. 1903. *The oracle of Moccasin Bend: A story of Lookout Mountain*. Washington, DC: Neale.

1903 Fox *Little Shepherd* = Fox, John, Jr. 1903. *The little shepherd of Kingdom Come*. New York: Charles Scribner's Sons.

1904 Fox *Christmas Eve* = Fox, John, Jr. 1904. *Christmas Eve on Lonesome, and other stories*. New York: Charles Scribner's Sons.

1904 Harben *Georgians* = Harben, William Nathaniel. 1904. *The Georgians*. New York: Harper.

1904 Johnson *Highways South* = Johnson, Clifton. 1904. *Highways and byways of the South*. New York: Macmillan.

1904–20 Kephart *Notebooks* = Kephart, Horace. 1904–20. Horace Kephart's Journals. Horace Kephart Collection, Hunter Library Special Collections, Western Carolina University, Cullowhee, NC. [unpaginated, undated observations and clippings, southwestern NC]

1905 Ayres and Ashe *Appal Forests* = Ayres, Horace Beemer, and William Willard Ashe. 1905. *The southern Appalachian forests*. Washington, DC: US Geological Survey.

1905 Miles *Spirit of Mts* = Miles, Emma Bell. 1905. *The spirit of the mountains*. New York: James Pott & Company. [southeast TN]

1905 Pinchot *Logging Terms* = Pinchot, Gifford. 1905. *Terms used in forestry and logging*. US Department of Agriculture Bureau of Forestry Bulletin 61. Washington, DC: Government Printing Office.

1905 *Pittsburgh Post* = *Pittsburgh Post*. 1905. Strange, picturesque words in the lumberjack's vocabulary. March 26, 32.

1906 Haney *Mt People KY* = Haney, William H. 1906. *The mountain people of Kentucky*. Cincinnati: Robert Clarke. [eastern KY]

1906 Harben *Ann Boyd* = Harben, William Nathaniel. 1906. *Ann Boyd, a novel*. New York: Harper & Brothers.

1906 Weir *Hot Springs* = Weir, Sally Royce. 1906. *Hot Springs, past and present*. Knoxville: F. E. Newman. [central western NC]

1907 *Dogwood Winter* = Squaw winter, Indian winter, dogwood winter. 1907. *Journal of American Folk-lore* 20: 235–36.

1907 Dugger *Balsam Groves* = Dugger, Shepherd M. 1907. *The balsam groves of the Grandfather Mountain: A tale of the western North Carolina mountains*. Banner Elk, NC: Shepherd M. Dugger. [northwestern NC]

1907 Parker *Folk-Lore of NC* = Parker, Haywood. 1907. Folk-lore of the North Carolina mountains. *Journal of American Folk-lore* 20: 241–50. [western NC]

1908 Britton *N Amer Trees* = Britton, Nathaniel Lord. 1908. *North American trees*. New York: H. Holt. [northwestern NC, southwestern VA, WV]

1908 Fox *Lonesome Pine* = Fox, John, Jr. 1908. *The trail of the lonesome pine*. New York: Charles Scribner's Sons.

1908 Johnson *Life KY Mts* = Johnson, Samuel. 1908. Life in the Kentucky mountains. *Independent* 65 (July 9), 72–82. Repr. in *Appalachian images in folk and popular culture*, edited by W. K. McNeil, 175–85. Knoxville: University of Tennessee Press, 1989. [eastern KY]

1908 *Mt Life* = Mountain life as it is. 1908. *Berea Quarterly* 12(8): 5–10 [eastern KY]

1908 Smith *Reminiscences* = Smith, Charles Forster. 1908. *Reminiscences and sketches*. Nashville, TN: Methodist Episcopal Church, South. [TN]

1909 Bascom *Ballads and Songs* = Bascom, Louise Rand. 1909. Ballads and songs of western North Carolina. *Journal of American Folklore* 22: 238–50. [western NC]

1909 Godfrey *Autobiog* = Godfrey, W. B. 1909. *Autobiography of W. B. Godfrey*. Cincinnati: Revivalist Press.

1910 Bolton *Scotch-Irish Pioneers* = Bolton, Charles K. 1910. *Scotch-Irish pioneers in Ulster and America*. Boston: Bacon and Brown. Repr., Baltimore: Genealogical Publishing Company, 1967.

1910 Cooke *Power and Glory* = Cooke, Grace MacGowan. 1910. *The power and the glory*. New York: Doubleday Page.

1910 Cox *Fearsome Creatures* = Cox, William T. 1910. *Fearsome creatures of the lumberwoods*. Washington, DC: Judd and Detweiler.

1910 Essary *TN Mtneers* = Essary, J. T. 1910. *Tennessee mountaineers in type: A collection of stories*. New York: Cochrane. [east TN]

c1910 Frost *Success* = Frost, William Goodell. c1910. The ladder of success. [Speech for the] Educational Rally at Big Stone Gap [Virginia], *Citizen* reprint No. 10 [Special Correspondence to the *Citizen*]. [southwestern VA]

1910 Guerrant *Galax Gatherers* = Guerrant, Edward O. 1910. *The galax gatherers: The gospel among the highlanders*. Richmond: Upward. [central western NC]

1910 Norman *English of Mtneers* = Norman, Henderson Daingerfield. 1910. The English of the mountaineer. *Atlantic Monthly* 105: 276–78.

1910 Smith *Tramping in Mts 1* = Smith, Charles Forster. 1910. Tramping in the mountains—the Great Smokies and Thunder Head. *Christian Advocate*, September 23, 10–12. [east TN]

1910 Smith *Tramping in Mts 2* = Smith, Charles Forster. 1910. Tramping in the mountains, no. 2. *Christian Advocate*, October 23, 10–11. [east TN]

1910 Thompson *Highlanders* = Thompson, Samuel H. 1910. *The highlanders of the South*. New York: Eaton and Mains.

1910 Weeks *Barbourville Word List* = Weeks, Abigail. 1910. A word list from Barbourville, Kentucky. *Dialect Notes* 3: 456–57. [south central KY]

1911 Shearin *E KY Word-List* = Shearin, Hubert G. 1911. An eastern Kentucky dialect word-list. *Dialect Notes* 3: 537–40. [eastern KY]

1911 Shearin *Superstitions Cumberland* = Shearin, Hubert Gibson. 1911. Some superstitions in the Cumberland Mountains. *Journal of American Folklore* 24: 319–22. [eastern KY]

1912 Chalkley *Augusta Co VA* = Chalkley, Lyman. 1912. *Chronicles of the Scotch-Irish settlement in Virginia, extracted from the original court records of Augusta County 1745–1800*. Baltimore: Genealogical Publishing Company. [Augusta County, central western VA]

1912 De Long *Troublesome* = De Long, Ethel. 1912. Doings on Troublesome. *Smith Alumnae Quarterly*, July 11. [southeastern KY]

1912 Doddridge *Notes on Settlement* = Doddridge, Joseph. 1824. *Notes on the settlement and Indian wars of the western parts of Virginia & Pennsylvania: From the year 1763 until the year 1783 inclusive; together with a view, of the state of society and manners of the first settlers of the western country*. Wellsburgh, VA, printed at the office of the *Gazette*, for the author. Repr., Pittsburgh: Ritenour and Lindsey, 1912. [WV]

1912 Mason *Raiding Moonshiners* = Mason, Robert Lindsay. 1912. Raiding moonshiners in Tennessee. *Recreation* 35(5): 197–99. [east TN]

1912 Perrow *Songs and Rhymes* = Perrow, E. C. 1912. Songs and rhymes from the South. *Journal of American Folklore* 25: 137–53.

1913 Bruce *Terms from TN* = Bruce, J. Douglas. 1913. Terms from Tennessee. *Dialect Notes* 4: 58. [TN]

1913 Combs *KY Highlander* = Combs, Josiah. 1913. *The Kentucky highlander from a native mountaineer's viewpoint*. Lexington, KY: Richardson and Company. [southeastern KY]

1913 Gibson *Amer Forest Trees* = Gibson, Henry H. 1913. *American forest trees*. Chicago: Hardwood Record. [east TN]

1913 Kephart *Our Sthn High* = Kephart, Horace. 1913. *Our southern highlanders*. New York: Macmillan. [southwestern NC]

1913 Morley *Carolina Mts* = Morley, Margaret. 1913. *The Carolina mountains.* Boston: Houghton Mifflin. [western NC]

1914 Arthur *Western NC* = Arthur, John Preston. 1914. *Western North Carolina: A history.* Raleigh: Edwards and Broughton. [western NC]

1914 Beeson *Spirit of Adventure* = Beeson, D. C. 1994. *In the spirit of adventure—a hike in the Great Smoky Mountains, August 28–September 4, 1914.* Edited by Norma Myers et al. Seymour, TN: Panther Press. [northeast TN]

1914 Bryant *Logging* = Bryant, Ralph Clement. 1914. *Logging: The principles and general methods of operation in the United States.* New York: John Wiley & Sons.

1914 Combs *Magic in KY Mts* = Combs, Josiah H. 1914. Sympathetic magic in the Kentucky mountains. *Journal of American Folklore* 27: 328–30. [southeastern KY]

1914 Crain *Life Story* = Crain, J. Dean. 1914. *A mountain boy's life story.* Greenville, SC: Baptist Courier Company.

1914 Furman *Sight* = Furman, Lucy. 1914. *Sight to the blind.* New York: Macmillan. [southeastern KY]

1914 Harben *New Clarion* = Harben, Will[iam] N[athaniel]. 1914. *The new Clarion.* New York: Harpers.

1914 Morton *Monroe Co WV* = Morton, Oren Frederick. 1914. *A history of Monroe County, West Virginia.* Kingwood, WV: Journal Publishing. [southwes VA]

1914 Wilson *Sthn Mtneers* = Wilson, Samuel Tyndale. 1914. *The southern mountaineers.* New York: Presbyterian Home Missions.

1915 Bohannon *Bear Hunt* = Bohannon, J. S. 1915. A bear hunt in the Great Smoky Mountains. *National Sportsman* (October): 461–65. [central east TN, central western NC]

1915 Bradley *Hobnobbing* = Bradley, Francis Aspenwall. 1915. Hobnobbing with hill-billies. *Harper's* 93 (December): 91–103.

1915 Buck *Code of Mts* = Buck, Charles Neville. 1915. *The code of the mountains.* New York: Grosset & Dunlap.

1915 Campbell *Songs and Ballads* = Campbell, Olive Dame. 1915. Songs and ballads of the southern mountains. *The Survey* 33 (January 2): 371–74.

1915 Dingus *Word-List VA* = Dingus, L. R. 1915. A word-list from Virginia. *Dialect Notes* 4: 177–93. [southwestern VA]

1915 Hall *Autobiog Claib Jones* = Hall, J. W. 1915. *The Autobiography of old Claib Jones.* Whitesburg, KY: Eagle. [eastern KY]

1915 Masters *Baptist Missions* = Masters, Victor. 1915. *Baptist missions in the South: Century of the saving impact of a great spiritual body on society in the southern states.* Atlanta: Townley and Co.

1915 Pollard *TN Mts* = Pollard, Mary O. 1915. Terms from the Tennessee mountains. *Dialect Notes* 4: 242–43. [Sevier County, central east TN]

1916 Canby *Top Smoky* = Canby, Henry Seidel. 1916. Top o' Smoky. *Harper's Monthly* 132 (March): 783–93. [central east TN, central western NC]

1916 Combs *Old Early English* = Combs, Josiah H. 1916. Old, early, and Elizabethan English in the southern mountains. *Dialect Notes* 4: 283–97. [southeastern KY]

1916 Schockel *KY Mts* = Schockel, B. H. 1916. Changing conditions in the Kentucky mountains. *Scientific Monthly*, August, 105–31. [eastern KY]

1917 Burelbach *After Bruin* = Burelbach, M. J. 1917. After bruin in the big Smokies. *Field and Stream* 22 (February): 314–17. [Blount County, central east TN]

1917 Campbell and Sharp *Engl Folk Songs* = Campbell, Olive Dame, and Cecil Sharp. 1917. *English folk songs from the southern Appalachians, comprising 122 songs and ballads, and 323 tunes.* New York: G. P. Putnam's.

1917 Davis *A Bornin'* = Davis, Clara M. 1917. A bornin'. *American Journal of Nursing* 17: 704–7. [southeastern KY]

1917 Goddard *Thirty Years* = Goddard, Charles H. 1917. *Thirty years of southern upbuilding.* New York: Colish.

1917 Kephart *Camping & Woodcraft* = Kephart, Horace. 1917. *Camping & woodcraft: A handbook for vacation campers and for travelers in the wilderness.* New York: Macmillan. [southwestern NC]

1917 Kephart *Word-List* = Kephart, Horace. 1917. A word-list from the mountains of western North Carolina. *Dialect Notes* 4: 407–19. [southwestern NC]

1918 Hartt *Lost Tribes* = Hartt, Rollin Lynde. 1918. The mountaineers: Our own lost tribes. *Century* 95: 395–404.

1918 Steadman *NC Word List* = Steadman, J. M. 1918. North Carolina word list. *Dialect Notes* 5: 18–20. [NC]

1918 *Story* = The story of a mountain girl. 1918. *Mountain Herald* 18: 4–5, 17–21. [northeast TN]

1919 Combs *Word-List South* = Combs, Josiah H. 1919. A word-list from the South. *Dialect Notes* 5: 31–40. [east TN, southeastern KY, western NC]

1919 DeWitt *Sevier Journal* = DeWitt, John H. 1919. Journal of Governor John Sevier (1789–1815). *Tennessee Historical Magazine* 5: 156–94. [east TN]

1919 Pearson et al. *Birds NC* = Pearson, T. Gilbert, C. S. Brimley, and H. H. Brimley. 1919. *Birds of North Carolina.* Vol. 4 of *North Carolina Geological and Economic Survey.* Raleigh: Edwards and Broughton. [western NC]

1919 Wilson *Welfare* = Wilson, Isabella Chilton. 1919. Welfare in a mining town. *Journal of Home Economics* 11: 21–23. [WV]

1920 De Long *Fiddler John* = De Long, Ethel. 1920. Fiddler John. *Notes from the Pine Mountain Settlement School* 1(5) (November). [southeastern KY]

1920 DeWitt *Sevier Journal* = DeWitt, John H. 1920. Journal of Governor John Sevier. *Tennessee Historical Magazine* 6: 18–68. [east TN]

1920 Ridley *Sthn Mtneer* = Ridley, Caleb A. c1920. *The southern mountaineer.* N.p.: n.p.

1921 Campbell *Sthn Highlander* = Campbell, John C. 1921. *The southern highlander and his homeland.* New York: Russell Sage Foundation.

1921 Combs *KY Items* = Combs, Josiah H. 1921. Kentucky items. *Dialect Notes* 5: 118–19. [southeastern KY]

1921 Combs *Slang Survivals* = Combs, Josiah H. 1921. Early English slang survivals in the mountains of Kentucky. *Dialect Notes* 5: 115–17. [southeastern KY]

1921 Fink *Week in Smoky Range* = Fink, Paul [M.]. 1921. A week in the Great Smoky range. *Appalachia* 15: 140–53. [Blount County, Sevier County, central east TN]

1921 Greer-Petrie *Angeline at Seelbach* = Greer-Petrie, Cordia. 1921. *Angeline at the Seelbach.* Louisville, KY: Angeline. [eastern KY]

1921 Holton *Robber's Creek* = Holton, Celia Cathcart. 1921. Funeralizing on Robber's Creek. *Outlook* 127 (April): 588–89.

1921 Kirkland *Mt Music* = Kirkland, Winifred. 1921. Mountain music. https://pinemountainsettlement.net/?page_id=14397. [southeastern KY]

1921 Spalding *Hills o' Ca'liny* = Spalding, Arthur W. 1921. *The hills o' Ca'liny.* Washington, DC: Review and Herald. [western KY]

1921 Weeks *Speech of KY Mtneer* = Weeks, Abigail E. 1921. The speech of the Kentucky mountaineer as I know it. MA thesis, Teachers College, Columbia University. [eastern KY]

1922 Cobb *KY Mt Rhymes* = Cobb, Ann. 1922. *Kinfolks: Kentucky mountain rhymes.* Boston: Riverside. [eastern KY]

1922 Kephart *Our Sthn High* = Kephart, Horace. 1922. *Our southern highlanders.* 2nd ed. New York: Macmillan. [southwestern NC]

1922 *TN CW Ques* = Dyer, Gustavus W., et al., eds. 1985. *Tennessee Civil War veterans questionnaire* [typed reproductions of responses to a 43-item survey of Civil War veterans, conducted under the auspices of the Tennessee State Library]. 5 vols. Easley, SC: Southern Historical Press.

1922 West *Songs of Mtneers* = West, Roy Andrew. 1922. The songs of the mountaineers. MA thesis, George Peabody College, Nashville, TN.

1922 Wolfe *Buck Gavin* = Wolfe, Thomas. 1922. The return of Buck Gavin. In *Carolina folk-plays*, edited by Frederick H. Koch, 33–44. New York: Holt. [western NC]

1923 Combs *Addenda KY* = Combs, Josiah H. 1923. Addenda from Kentucky. *Dialect Notes* 5: 242–43. [southeastern KY]

1923 Furman *Mothering* = Furman, Lucy. 1923. *Mothering on the Perilous.* New York: Macmillan. [southeastern KY]

1923 Greer-Petrie *Angeline Doin' Society* = Greer-Petrie, Cordia. 1923. *Angeline doin' society*. Louisville, KY: Angeline. [eastern KY]

1923 Greer-Petrie *Angeline Steppin' Out* = Greer-Petrie, Cordia. 1923. *Angeline steppin' out*. Louisville, KY: Angeline. [eastern KY]

1923 Montague *Today Tomorrow* = Montague, Margaret Prescott. 1923. The to-day to-morrow. *Atlantic Monthly* 132 (February): 159–67. [WV]

1923 Williams *After Bruin* = Williams, Wayne W. 1923. After bruin in the Great Smokies. *National Sportsman*, March. [Swain County, central western NC]

1924 Abernethy *Moonshine* = Abernethy, Arthur Talmage. 1924. *Moonshine, being Appalachia's Arabian nights*. Asheville, NC: Dixie.

1924 Bacheller *Happiest Person* = Bacheller, Irving. 1924. The happiest person I ever knew. *American Magazine* (March), 5–7, 98, 100. [central western NC]

1924 Buffum *Shakespearean Survivals* = Buffum, Vryling W. 1924. Shakespearean survivals in the mountains. *Mountain Herald* 28(2): 14–17. [northeast TN]

1924 Greer-Petrie *Angeline Gits Eyeful* = Greer-Petrie, Cordia. 1924. *Angeline gits an eyeful*. Louisville, KY: Angeline. [eastern KY]

1924 Montague *Betsy Beaver* = Montague, Margaret Prescott. 1924. Miss Betsy Beaver. *Atlantic Monthly* 133 (February): 221–29. [WV]

1924 *Notes Pine Mt* = *Notes from the Pine Mountain Settlement School*. 1924. 2(2) (May): 1–3. [southeastern KY]

1924 Raine *Saddlebags* = Raine, James Watt. 1924. *Land of saddle-bags: A study of the mountain people of Appalachia*. New York: Council of the Women for Home Missions and Missionary Education Movement of the United States and Canada. [eastern KY]

1924 Raine *Speech of Land* = Raine, James Watt. 1924. The speech of the land of saddle-bags. *Quarterly Journal of Speech* 10(3): 230–37.

1924 Spring *Lydia Whaley* = Spring, Agnes Wright. 1924. Rough outline of visit with Aunt Lydia Whaley. Typescript consulted at Library, Great Smoky Mountains National Park, Gatlinburg, TN. [Blount County, central east TN]

1924 Vollmer *Sun-Up* = Vollmer, Lula. 1924. *Sun-up: A play in three acts*. New York: Brentano's.

1925 Carter *Mt White Tales* = Carter, Isabel. 1925. Mountain white folk-tales from the southern Blue Ridge. *Journal of American Folklore* 38: 340–74. [western NC, east TN]

1925 Combs *Folk-Songs* = Combs, Josiah H. 1925. *Folk-songs du Midi des États-Unis*. Doctoral thesis, Université Paris-Sorbonne. Translated by D. K. Wilgus as *Folk-songs of the Southern United States* and published by the University of Tennessee Press, 1961. [southeastern KY]

1925 Dargan *Highland Annals* = Dargan, Olive Tilford. 1925. *Highland annals*. New York: Scribner's Sons.

1925 Davis *KY Mts* = Davis, H. D. 1925. The changing role of the Kentucky mountains and the passing of the Kentucky mountaineer. *Journal of Geography* 24(February): 41–52. [eastern KY]

1925 Furman *Glass Window* = Furman, Lucy. 1925. *The glass window: A story of the quare women*. Boston: Little, Brown. [southeastern KY]

1925 Greer-Petrie *Angeline Hill Country* = Greer-Petrie, Cordia. 1925. *Angeline of the hill country*. New York: Crowell. [eastern KY]

c1926 Bird *Cullowhee Wordlist* = Bird, William. c1926. Wordlist compiled at Cullowhee, North Carolina. Horace Kephart Collection, Hunter Library Special Collections, Western Carolina University, Cullowhee, NC. [southwestern NC]

1926 Bird *Spirit of W NC* = Bird, W. E., ed. 1926. *The spirit of western North Carolina (a pageant)*. Cullowhee, NC: Cullowhee State Normal School Department of English. [southwestern NC]

c1926 Cox *Cullowhee Wordlist* = Cox, Tom. c1926. Wordlist compiled at Cullowhee, North Carolina. Horace Kephart Collection, Hunter Library Special Collections, Western Carolina University, Cullowhee, NC. [southwestern NC]

1926 Ganier *Summer Birds* = Ganier, Albert F. 1926. Summer birds of the Great Smoky Mountains. *Journal of the Tennessee Academy of Sciences* 1(2): 31–40. [central east TN, central western NC]

1926 Harris *WV Hand Book* = Harris, Robert T. 1926. *West Virginia legislative hand book and manual and official register*. Charleston, WV: Tribune. [WV]

1926 Hunnicutt *Twenty Years* = Hunnicutt, Samuel J. 1926. *Twenty years hunting and fishing in the Great Smoky Mountains*. Knoxville: Newman. [western NC]

1926 Lunsford *Folk-Lore* = Lunsford, Bascom Lamar. 1926. Folk-lore in western North Carolina. *Southern Tourist* (April): 13–14. [western NC]

1926 Montague *Big Music* = Montague, Margaret Prescott. 1926. Big music. *The Forum* 76: 420–33. [WV]

1926 Morgan *Smoky Mts* = Morgan, F. B. 1926. Rediscovering the Great Smoky Mountains. *National Magazine* 54(11): 401–2.

1926 Reinhardt *Speech and Balladry* = Reinhardt, J. M. 1926. Speech and balladry of the southern highlands. *Quarterly Journal of the University of North Dakota* 16: 139–47.

1926 Roberts *Time of Man* = Roberts, Elizabeth Madox. 1926. *The time of man: A novel*. New York: Viking.

1926 Schantz *Beyond the Haze* = Schantz, Orpheus Moyer. 1926. Beyond the haze in the high Smokies. *Country Life in America* (August): 60–61. [central east TN, central western NC]

1926 Shaver *Flowers of Smokies* = Shaver, Jesse M. 1926. Flowers of the Great Smokies. *Journal of the Tennessee Academy of Sciences* 1: 17–20. [central east TN, central western NC]

1926 Thomas *Hills and Mts of KY* = Thomas, William Roscoe. 1926. *Life among the hills and mountains of Kentucky*. Louisville, KY: Standard Printing Co. Press. [eastern KY]

1926 Willy *Great Smoky Natl Park* = Willy, John. 1926. Ten days in the proposed Great Smoky Mountains National Park. *Hotel Monthly* (September): 44–58. [Sevier County, central east TN]

1926 Wilson *Cullowhee Wordlist* = Wilson, Mrs. Eddie W. 1926. Wordlist compiled at Cullowhee, North Carolina. Horace Kephart Collection, Hunter Library Special Collections, Western Carolina University, Cullowhee, NC. [southwestern NC]

1927 Axley *Larrows* = Axley, Lowry. 1927. Larrows to catch meddlers. *American Speech* 2: 408–9. [western NC]

1927 Bird *Among Highlanders* = Bird, W. E., ed. 1927. *Among the highlanders yesterday and today: A pageant of western North Carolina*. Cullowhee, NC: Cullowhee State Normal School. [western NC]

1927 Bolton *Mt Girl Speaks* = Bolton, Irene. 1927. A mountain girl speaks. *Mountain Herald* 30(1): 4–5. [northeast TN]

1927 Camak *June of Hills* = Camak, David English. 1927. *June of the hills: The Junaluska prize novel; A tale of the southern mountains with Lake Junaluska as the center of action*. Lake Junaluska, NC: Junaluska Women's Club. [western NC]

1927 Cox *Yew Pine Mts* = Cox, John Harrington. 1927. The Yew Pine Mountains: A "John Hardy" ballad. *American Speech* 3: 225–26. [WV]

1927 Dingus *Appal Mt Words* = Dingus, L. R. 1927. Appalachian mountain words. *Dialect Notes* 5: 468–71. [eastern KY]

1927 Furman *Lonesome Road* = Furman, Lucy. 1927. *The lonesome road*. Boston: Little, Brown. [eastern KY]

1927 Justus *Peter Pocket* = Justus, May. 1927. *Peter Pocket: A little boy of the Cumberland Mountains*. Garden City, NY: Doubleday. [east TN]

1927 *Louisville Courier-Journal* = *Louisville Courier-Journal*. 1927. [Untitled article]

1927 Mason *Lure of Smokies* = Mason, Robert [Lindsay]. 1927. *Lure of the Great Smokies*. Boston: Houghton Mifflin. [central east TN, central western NC]

1927 Montague *Funny Bone* = Montague, Margaret Prescott. 1927. The world's funny bone. *Atlantic Monthly* 10: 327–36. [WV]

1927 Montague *Hog's Eye* = Montague, Margaret Prescott. 1927. Hog's eye and human. *The Forum* 78: 190–203. [WV]

1927 Shearin *Speech of Fathers* = Shearin, Hubert. 1927. The speech of our fathers. *Kentucky Folk-lore and Poetry Magazine* 2: 6–7. [eastern KY]

1927 Thornburgh *Tramping* = Thornburgh, Laura [published under the name Laura Thornborough]. 1927. Tramping in the Great Smokies. *American Forests and Forest Life* 33 (August): 463–66, 512. [central east TN]

1927 Woofter *Dialect from WV* = Woofter, Carey. 1927. Dialect words and phrases from west-central West Virginia. *American Speech* 2: 347–67. [WV]

1928 Busbee *Elizabethan Settlements* = Busbee, Jacques. 1928. Elizabethan settlements in North Carolina. *Mentor* 16(7): 21–22.

1928 Chapman *Happy Mt* = Chapman, Maristan. 1928. *The happy mountain.* New York: Literary Guild.

1928 Galyon *Plant Naturalist* = Galyon, Willa Love. 1928. The Smoky Mountains and the plant naturalist. *Journal of the Tennessee Academy of Sciences* 3(3): 3–13. [central east TN, central western NC]

1928 Ivey *Mt Whites* = Ivey, Majel. 1928. Mountain whites. *Charlotte Observer*, March 25. [western NC]

1928 Justus *Betty Lou* = Justus, May. 1928. *Betty Lou of Big Log Mountain.* Garden City, NY: Sun. [east TN]

1928 Thornburgh *Americans Forgot* = Thornburgh, Laura [published under the name Laura Thornborough]. 1928. Americans the twentieth century forgot. *Travel* 50 (April): 25–28, 42.

1929 Carpenter *Evolution of Dialect* = Carpenter, Charles. 1929. The evolution of our dialect. *West Virginia Review* 7: 9, 28. [WV]

1929 Chapman *Homeplace* = Chapman, Maristan. 1929. *Homeplace.* New York: Viking.

1929 Chapman *Speech Sthn Highlands* = Chapman, Maristan. 1929. American speech as practiced in the southern highlands. *Century* 117: 617–23.

1929 Duncan and Duncan *Sayings* = Duncan, Hannibal Gerald, and Winnie Leah Duncan. 1929. Superstitions and sayings among the southern highlanders. *Journal of American Folklore* 42: 233–37.

1929 *Fastnesses* = Fastnesses of Great Smokies explored. 1929. *New York Times Magazine*, August 4. [central east TN, central western NC]

1929 Kephart *Smoky Mt Magic* = Kephart, Horace. (1929) 2009. *Smoky Mountain magic.* Gatlinburg, TN: Great Smoky Mountains Association.

1929 Phillips *Life and Labor* = Phillips, Ulrich Bonnell. 1929. *Life and labor in the old South.* Boston: Little, Brown, and Company.

1929 Rainey *Animal Plant Lore* = Rainey, Fran L. 1929. Animal and plant lore. *Kentucky Folk-Lore and Poetry Magazine* 4: 8–15. [eastern KY]

1929 Sanders *Medical Lore* = Sanders, Myra. 1929. Some medical lore. *Kentucky Folk-Lore and Poetry Magazine* 1: 10–11. [eastern KY]

1929 Summers *Annals SW VA* = Summers, Lewis Preston. 1929. *Annals of southwest Virginia, 1769–1800.* Abingdon, VA: L. P. Summers. [southwestern VA]

1929 Wolfe *Look Homeward* = Wolfe, Thomas. 1929. *Look homeward, angel: A story of the buried life.* New York: Scribner's.

1930 Armstrong *This Day and Time* = Armstrong, Anne W. 1930. *This day and time.* New York: Alfred A. Knopf.

1930 *Charleston Daily Mail* = *Charleston (WV) Daily Mail.* 1930. [Untitled article]. September 29.

1930 Edgerton and Mattoon *Sthn Forest Study* = Edgerton, Daisy Priscilla Smith, and W. R. Mattoon. 1930. *First steps in southern forest study.* New York: Rand McNally.

1930 Fink *Trails* = Fink, Paul M. 1930. Trails of the Great Smokies. *Appalachia* 18(1): 63–69. [central east TN]

c1930 Goff *Dialects Sthn Mtneers* = Goff, John Hedges. c1930. Ballads and dialects of the southern mountaineers. MA thesis, Oglethorpe University, Atlanta.

1930 Greer-Petrie *Angeline Outsmarts* = Greer-Petrie, Cordia. 1930. *Angeline outsmarts her man.* Louisville, KY: Angeline. [eastern KY]

1930 *Herald-Advertiser* = *Herald-Advertiser.* 1930. Huntingdon, WV, November 30. [WV]

1930 Justus *Foot Windy Low* = Justus, May. 1930. *At the foot of Windy Low.* New York: P. F. Volland. [east TN]

1930 Justus *Pocket's Luck* = Justus, May. 1930. *Peter Pocket's luck.* Garden City, NY: Doubleday, Doran and Company. [east TN]

1930 Pendleton *Wood-Hicks Speak* = Pendleton, Paul E. 1930. How the "wood hicks" speak. *Dialect Notes* 6: 86–89. [Upshur County, central WV]

1930 Perry *Handicraft Art* = Perry, Jo Ruth. 1930. Handicraft art in the Great Smokies. *Knoxville News-Sentinel*, March 23, C1.

1930 Schantz *Hill Dwellers* = Schantz, O. M. 1930. Hill dwellers of the Smokies are rare types. *Christian Science Monitor*, June 2: 1, 3.

1930 Smith *Reminiscences* = Smith, Captain Ross. 1930. *Reminiscences of an old-timer.* [Jonesborough, TN]: Privately published.

1930 Thomas *Death Knell* = Thomas, Monroe. 1930. Highways and schools sounding death knell of mountain dialect. *Asheville Citizen*, September 30. [central western NC]

1931 Burns *Coves Blount Co* = Burns, Inez. 1931. Settlement and early history of the coves of Blount County, Tennessee. *East Tennessee Historical Society Publication* 3: 44–67. [Blount County, central east TN]

1931 Combs *Lg Sthn High* = Combs, Josiah [H.]. 1931. Language of the southern highlanders. *Publications of the Modern Language Association* 46: 1302–22. [southeastern KY]

1931 Goodrich *Mt Homespun* = Goodrich, Frances Louisa. 1931. *Mountain homespun.* New Haven, CT: Yale University Press. [western NC]

1931 Greve *Tradition Gatlinburg* = Greve, Jeannette. 1931. Traditions of Gatlinburg. *East Tennessee Historical Society Publication* 3: 62–77. [Sevier County, central east TN]

1931 Hannum *Thursday April* = Hannum, Alberta. 1931. *Thursday April.* New York: Harper and Brothers. [northwestern NC]

1931 Malone *Any More* = Malone, Kemp. 1931. Any more in the affirmative. *American Speech* 6: 460. [southern WV]

1931 Norbeck *Lure of Hills* = Norbeck, Mildred E. 1931. *The lure of the hills: A tale of the mountains of Kentucky.* Oakdale, KY: Revivalist Press.

1931–34 Oliver *Sketches* = Oliver, William Howell. 1931–34. Sketches of the Olivers. Typescript consulted at Library, Great Smoky Mountains National Park, Gatlinburg, TN. [Blount County, central east TN]

1931 Owens *Speech Cumberlands* = Owens, Bess Alice. 1931. Folk speech of the Cumberlands. *American Speech* 7: 89–95. [southeastern KY]

1931 *Professor Learns* = Professor learns about Carolina mountain dialect. 1931. *Charlotte News and Observer*, October 8. [western NC]

1931 Stuart *Yarb Doctor* = Stuart, Jesse. 1931. The yarb doctor. *Kentucky Folk-Lore and Poetry Magazine* 6: 4–10. [northeastern KY]

1931 Thomas *Ditties* = Thomas, Jean. 1931. *Devil's ditties: Being the stories of the Kentucky mountain people told by Jean Thomas with the songs they sing.* Chicago: W. Wilbur Hatfield. [northeastern KY]

1932 Bennett *Majestic Smokies* = Bennett, Hugh Hammond. 1932. The majestic Smokies. *Holland's* 51(4): 12–13, 57, 61. [Sevier County, central east TN]

1932 Cox *Affirm Any More* = Cox, John Harrington. 1932. [Affirmative *any more*]. *American Speech* 7: 236.

1932 Creal *Quaint Speech* = Creal, Katherine. 1932. Mountaineers of south have quaint speech. *Asheville Citizen*, April 17. [central western NC]

1932 Dargan *Call Home* = Dargan, Olive Tilford. 1932. *Call home the heart.* London: Longmans.

1932 Dugger *War Trails* = Dugger, Shepherd M. 1932. *War trails of the Blue Ridge.* Banner Elk, NC: Self-published. [northwestern NC]

1932 Hines *Wildflowers Appal* = Hines, Linda C. 1932. Wildflowers of the Appalachians. *Country Life* 62(5): 65–67.

1932 Poole *Nurses Horseback* = Poole, Ernest. 1932. *Nurses on horseback.* New York: Macmillan. [eastern KY]

1932 Sharp *Folk Songs* = Sharp, Cecil. 1932. Introduction. In *English folk-songs from the southern Appalachians*, by Cecil Sharp and Olive Campbell, xxi–xxxvii. London: Oxford University Press.

1932 Strong *Great Smokies* = Strong, Paschal Neilson. 1932. *Behind the Great Smokies.* Boston: Little, Brown.

1933 Carpenter *Sthn Mt Dialect* = Carpenter, Charles. 1933. Variation in the southern mountain dialect. *American Speech* 8(1): 22–25.

1933 Chapman *Glen Hazard* = Chapman, Maristan. 1933. *Glen hazard*. New York: Knopf.

1933 Fink *Early Explorers* = Fink, Paul M. 1933. Early explorers in the Great Smokies. *East Tennessee Historical Society Publication* 5: 55–68. [central east TN]

1933 Hooker *Religion in Highlands* = Hooker, Elizabeth R. 1933. *Religion in the highlands: Native churches and missionary enterprises in the southern Appalachian area*. New York: Home Mission Council.

1933 Jackson *White Spirituals* = Jackson, George Pullen. 1933. *White spirituals of the southern uplands: The story of the fasola folk, their songs, singings, and buckwheat notes*. Chapel Hill: University of North Carolina Press. [upper South]

1933 McCoy and Masa *Smoky Guide* = McCoy, George W., and George Masa. 1933. *A guide to the Great Smoky Mountains National Park*. Asheville, NC: Inland Press. [central east TN, central western NC]

1933 Miller *Healing Gods* = Miller, Joseph. 1933. The healing gods or medical superstition. *West Virginia Medical Journal* 29: 465–78. [WV]

1933 Thomas *Jilson Setters* = Thomas, Jean. 1933. Jilson Setters: Singin' fiddler of Lost Hope Hollow. *American Speech* 8(2): 28–30. [northeastern KY]

1933 Thomas *Traipsin' Woman* = Thomas, Jean. 1933. *The traipsin' woman*. New York: Dutton.

1934 Carpenter *Archaic English in WV* = Carpenter, Charles. 1934. Remnants of archaic English in West Virginia. *West Virginia Review* 12: 77–79, 94–95. [WV]

1934 Carter *Mt White Riddles* = Carter, Isabel. 1934. Mountain white riddles. *Journal of American Folklore* 47: 76–80. [western NC, east TN]

1934 Cushman *Swing Mountain Gal* = Cushman, Rebecca. 1934. *Swing your mountain gal: Sketches of life in the southern highlands*. Boston: Houghton Mifflin.

1934–47 *LAMSAS Appal* = Linguistic Atlas of the Middle and South Atlantic States. 1934–47. [Field notebooks of interviews conducted for the Linguistic Atlas of the Middle and South Atlantic States, covering northeastern Florida to New York State. Data from Appalachian counties of West Virginia (148), Virginia (20), North Carolina (37), South Carolina (12), and Georgia (12), conducted between 1934 and 1947, are presented either in summarized fashion (as available online at us.english.uga.edu) or for specific counties in NC bordering the Smoky Mountains, as available on microfilm of the original field notebooks completed by Guy S. Lowman]

1934 Parke *Bear Hunt* = Parke, Robert. 1934. Our southern highlanders [part 1]. *The Bison: University of Buffalo Magazine*, 10–12. Repr., 2011, *Smoky Mountain Historical Society Journal and Newsletter* 37(2): 7–13. [Sevier County, east central TN]

1934 Parke *Sthn Highlander* = Parke, Robert. 1934. Our southern highlanders [part 2]. *The Bison: University of Buffalo Magazine*. Repr., 1977, *Smoky Mountain Historical Society Newsletter* 3(4): 8–12.

1934–40 Simms *Coll* = Simms, Edna Lynn. 1934–40. Edna Lynn Simms Collection [typed 3-by-5-inch citation cards created by Ms. Simms of Gatlinburg, TN, for a prospective museum, later given to Berea College, Berea, KY, for its permanent archives]. [Sevier County, central east TN]

1934 Smith *Tennessean's Pronunciation* = Smith, Rebecca W. 1934. A Tennessean's pronunciation in 1841. *American Speech* 9: 262–63. [Jefferson County, central east TN]

1934 Wilson *Bog Plants* = Wilson, Eddie W. 1934. Odd bog plants kill insects, help man in Smoky Mountains park. *Asheville Citizen*, July 8. [western NC]

1935 Allen *Annals Haywood Co* = Allen, W. C. 1935. *Annals of Haywood county*. N.p.: n.p. [Haywood County, central western NC]

1935 Edwards *NC Novels* = Edwards, Dorothy E. 1935. The dialect of the southern highlander as recorded in North Carolina novels. MA thesis, University of Rochester. [western NC]

1935 Farr *Riddles and Superstitions* = Farr, T. J. 1935. Riddles and superstitions from middle Tennessee. *Journal of American Folklore* 48: 318–36. [east central TN]

1935 Kenny *To in WV* = Kenny, Hamill. 1935. "To" in West Virginia. *American Speech* 10: 135–36. [WV]

1935 Murray *Schoolhouse* = Murray, Lena Davis. 1935. *Schoolhouse in the foothills*. New York: Simon and Schuster. [east TN]

1935 Sheppard *Cabins in Laurel* = Sheppard, Muriel E. 1935. *Cabins in the laurel*. Chapel Hill: University of North Carolina Press. [northwestern NC]

1935 Stuart *KY Mt People* = Stuart, Jesse. 1935. Kentucky mountain people. *Kentucky Progress* 6: 256–63. [northeastern KY]

1935 Thomas *Song Festival* = Thomas, Jean. 1935. The American Folk Song Festival. *American Speech* 10: 36–37.

1936 Arnow *Mt Path* = Arnow, Harriette Louisa Simpson. 1936. *Mountain path*. New York: Little and Ives.

1936 Carpenter *WV Expletives* = Carpenter, Charles. 1936. West Virginia expletives. *West Virginia Review* 13: 346–47. [WV]

1936 Coleman *Dial N GA* = Coleman, Wilma. 1936. Mountain dialect of north Georgia. MA thesis, University of Georgia. [north GA]

1936 Farr *Folk Speech* = Farr, T. J. 1936. Folk speech of middle Tennessee. *American Speech* 11: 275–76. [east central TN]

1936 Farrier *Few Of* = Farrier, P. H. 1936. "Few of" and "few bit." *American Speech* 11: 278–79. [Giles County, southwestern VA]

1936 Hench *Gleanings* = Hench, Atcheson. 1936. Gleanings. *American Speech* 11: 104. [southern WV]

1936 Justus *Honey Jane* = Justus, May. 1936. *Honey Jane*. Garden City, NY: Doubleday. [east TN]

1936 Lyman *WV Idioms* = Lyman, Dean B. 1936. Idioms in West Virginia. *American Speech* 11: 63. [WV]

1936 Maupin *Pittman Center* = Maupin, Juanita. 1936. A study of the living conditions in the Pittman Center community, 1934–1935. MA thesis, University of Tennessee. [Sevier County, central east TN]

1936 McCutshan *VA Expressions* = McCutshan, J. Wilson. 1936. Virginia expressions. *American Speech* 11: 372–73. [western VA]

1936 McDowell *Background* = McDowell, L. L. 1936. A background of folklore. *Tennessee Folklore Society Bulletin* 2: 1–8.

1936 Morehouse *Rain on Just* = Morehouse, Kathleen Moore. 1936. *Rain on the just*. New York: Furman.

1936 Neitzel *TN Expressions* = Neitzel, Stuart. 1936. Tennessee expressions. *American Speech* 11: 373. [Hamilton County, southeast TN]

1936 Ogden *Rescue Work* = Ogden, Warner. 1936. "Rescue work" is responsible for museum at Gatlinburg that tells life story of mountaineers of the Smokies. *Knoxville News-Sentinel*, July 10. [Sevier County, central east TN]

1936 Skidmore *Lift Up Eyes* = Skidmore, Hubert. 1936. *I will lift up mine eyes*. Garden City, NY: Doubleday.

1936–37 Still *Defeated Creek* = Still, James. 1936–37. On Defeated Creek. *Frontier and Midland* 17: 120–24.

1936 Still *Horse Doctor* = Still, James. 1936. Horse doctor. *Frontier and Midland* 17: 25–28.

1936 Still *One Leg* = Still, James. 1936. One leg gone to judgment. *Mountain Life and Work* 12(3): 9–10.

1936 Stuart *Head of Hollow* = Stuart, Jesse. 1936. *Head o' W-Hollow*. New York: Dutton.

1936 Stuart *Lonesome Waters* = Stuart, Jesse, 1936. Lonesome waters. *Esquire* 5: 32–33. [northeastern KY]

1937 Campbell *KY Mt Community* = Campbell, Marie. 1937. The folklife of a Kentucky mountain community. MA thesis, George Peabody College, Nashville, TN. [southeastern KY]

1937 Conner *Ms* = Conner, Edward C. 1937. [The Conner manuscript]. Typescript consulted at Library of Great Smoky Mountains National Park, Gatlinburg, TN. [central east TN]

1937 Eaton *Handicrafts* = Eaton, Allen. 1937. *Handicrafts of the southern highlands.* New York: Russell Sage.

1937–87 Hall *Coll* = Hall, Joseph S. 1937–87. [Recorded interviews and other material, on deposit in Joseph Sargent Hall Collection, Archives of Appalachia, East Tennessee State University, Johnson City; includes items recorded or noted in speech or from personal letters]

1937 Haun *Cocke Co* = Haun, Mildred. 1937. Cocke County ballads and songs. MEd thesis, George Peabody College, Nashville, TN. [Cocke County, central east TN]

1937 Hyatt *Kiverlid* = Hyatt, Rebecca Dougherty. 1937. *Marthy Lou's kiverlid: A sketch of mountain life.* Morristown, TN: Triangle.

1937 Leybourne *Urban Adjustments* = Leybourne, Grace G. 1937. Urban adjustments of migrants from the southern Appalachian plateaus. *Social Forces* 16: 238–46.

1937 Hall *Notebooks* = Hall, Joseph S. 1937, 1939. [Pocket-sized notebooks of random observations of mountain speech, on deposit at Archives of Appalachia, East Tennessee State University, Johnson City]

1937 Still *Brother to Methusalem* = Still, James. 1937. Brother to Methusalem. *Story* 11(64): 45–52.

1937 Still *Egg Tree* = Still, James. 1937. The egg tree. *Yale Review* 27: 100–109.

1937 Still *Quare Day* = Still, James. 1937. The quare day. *Household Magazine* 37: 36.

1937 Thornburgh *Great Smoky Mts* = Thornburgh, Laura [published under the name Laura Thornborough]. 1937. *The Great Smoky Mountains.* New York: Crowell. [Rev. and enlarged eds. were published in many years, including 1956 and 1971, by University of Tennessee Press.] [central east TN]

1937 White *Highland Heritage* = White, Edwin E. 1937. *Highland heritage: The southern mountains and the nation.* New York: Friendship.

1937–39 Wilburn *Notes* = Wilburn, Hiram C. 1937–39. [Notes from the first historian of Great Smoky Mountains National Park, collected by Joseph Sargent Hall]. [central east TN, central western NC]

1937 Wilson *Folklore SE KY* = Wilson, Gypsy Vera. 1937. Folklore in southeastern Kentucky. MA thesis, George Peabody College, Nashville, TN. [southeastern KY]

1938 Bowman *High Horizons* = Bowman, Elizabeth Skaggs. 1938. *Land of high horizons: An intimate interpretation of the Great Smokies.* Kingsport, TN: Southern. [central east TN, central western NC]

1938 *Facts and Legends of Cullowhee* = Western Carolina Teachers College. 1938. *Facts and legends of the Cullowhee region.* Cullowhee, NC: Western Carolina Teachers College. [southwestern NC]

1938 Justus *No-End Hollow* = Justus, May. 1938. *The house in No-End Hollow.* Garden City, NY: Doubleday. [east TN]

1938 Komarek and Komarek *Mammals* = Komarek, E. V., and R. Komarek. 1938. *Mammals of the Great Smoky Mountains.* Chicago: Bulletin of the Chicago Academy of Sciences. [central east TN, central western NC]

1938 Maxwell *Valhalla* = Maxwell, Philip H. 1938. *Valhalla in the Smokies.* Cleveland: Exline.

1938–46 Oliver *Fifty Years* = Oliver, John W. 1938–46. Fifty years of Cades Cove. Typescript consulted at Library, Great Smoky Mountains National Park, Gatlinburg, TN. [Blount County, central east TN]

1938 Read *Pronunciation on Frontier* = Read, Allen Walker. The pronunciation of names on the frontier, 1829–30. *American Speech* 13: 263–67. [TN]

1938 Still *Bat Flight* = Still, James. 1938. Bat flight. *Saturday Evening Post* 211(10): 12–13.

1938 Still *Mole-Bane* = Still, James. 1938. Mole-bane. *Atlantic Monthly* 161: 372–74.

1938 Stuart *Dark Hills* = Stuart, Jesse. 1938. *Beyond dark hills.* New York: Dutton. [northeastern KY]

1938 Taliaferro *Carolina Humor* = Taliaferro, Harden E. 1938. *Carolina humor: Sketches by Harden E. Taliaferro* [stories from the *Southern Literary Messenger*, originally published 1860–63]. Richmond: Dietz. [northwestern NC]

1939–42 Adams *Tales* = Adams, James Taylor. c1939–42. http://www2.ferrum.edu/applit/.

1939 Bond *Appal Dialect* = Bond, George Foot. 1939. A study of an Appalachian dialect. MA thesis, University of Florida. [Rutherford County, southwestern NC]

1939 Burnett *Gap o' Mountains* = Burnett, G. L. 1939. *Gap o' the mountains.* Knoxville: Newman. [east TN]

1939 Campbell *Play Party* = Campbell, Marie. 1939. Play party. *Tennessee Folklore Society Bulletin* 5: 17–48. [southeastern KY]

1939 Eastridge *Folklore Adair Co* = Eastridge, Nancy Emilia. 1939. A study of folklore in Adair County, Kentucky. MA thesis, George Peabody College, Nashville, TN. [Adair County, south central KY]

1939 *English in Mts* = English in the mountains. 1939. *Chattanooga Times*, September 30.

1939 Farr *TN Mt Regions* = Farr, T. J. 1939. The language of the Tennessee mountain regions. *American Speech* 14: 89–92. [east central TN]

1939 *FWP Guide KY* = Federal Writers' Program. 1939. *A guide to the bluegrass state.* New York: Harcourt, Brace. [KY]

1939 *FWP Guide NC* = Federal Writers' Program. 1939. *A guide to the old north state.* Chapel Hill: University of North Carolina Press. [NC]

1939 *FWP Guide TN* = Federal Writers' Program. 1939. *A guide to Tennessee.* New York: Viking. [TN]

1939 Hall *Notebooks* = Hall, Joseph S. 1937, 1939. [Pocket-sized notebooks of random observations of mountain speech. Manuscripts on deposit at Archives of Appalachia, East Tennessee State University, Johnson City]

1939 Hall *Recording Speech* = Hall, Joseph S. 1939. Recording speech in the Great Smokies. *Regional Review* 3(4–5): 3–8. [central east TN, central western NC]

1939 Jennison *Flora Great Smokies* = Jennison, Harry Milliken. 1939. Flora of the Great Smokies. *Journal of the Tennessee Academy of Science* 14: 266–98. [central east TN, central western NC]

1939 King *Herpetology* = King, Willis. 1939. *A survey of the herpetology of Great Smoky Mountains National Park.* South Bend, IN: University of Notre Dame Press. [central east TN, central western NC]

1939 Krumpelmann *WV Peculiarities* = Krumpelmann, John T. 1939. West Virginia peculiarities. *American Speech* 14: 155–56. [WV]

1939 McIlwaine *Southern Poor-Whites* = McIlwaine, Shields. 1939. *Southern poor-whites.* Norman: University of Oklahoma Press.

1939 Siler *Cherokee Lore* = Siler, Margaret L. 1939. *Cherokee Indian lore and Smoky Mountain stories.* Bryson City, NC: Bryson City Times. [Swain County, southwestern NC]

1939 Still *Ploughing* = Still, James. 1939. The ploughing. *Atlantic Monthly* 164(6): 776–78.

1939 Still *Sugar in Gourd* = Still, James. 1939. Sugar in a gourd. *Prairie Schooner* 13: 99–104.

1939 Still *Twelve Pears* = Still, James. 1939. Twelve pears hanging high. *Mountain Life and Work* 15(1): 14–18.

1939 Still *Two Eyes* = Still, James. 1939. Two eyes, two pennies. *Saturday Evening Post* 211(40): 12–13, 94–95, 97.

1939 Walker *Mtneer Looks* = Walker, Raphy S. 1939. A mountaineer looks at his own speech. *Tennessee Folklore Society Bulletin* 5: 1–13. [central east TN]

1940 Adams *Coll* = *Adams Collection.* 1940. Documents in editors' private collection.

c1940 Aswell *Glossary TN Idiom* = Aswell, James. c1940. Brief glossary of Tennessee idiom. Prepared under auspices of the WPA. Typescript on deposit at Tennessee State Library and Archives, Nashville. [TN]

1940 Bandy *Folklore Macon Co TN* = Bandy, Lewis D. 1940. Folklore of Macon County, Tennessee. MA thesis, George Peabody College, Nashville, TN. [Macon County, north central TN]

1940 Bowman *KY Mt Stories* = Bowman, Blanche Sappenfield. 1940. Study of the dialect employed by the people of the Kentucky mountains and presented through a group of original short stories. MS thesis, Kansas State College. [eastern KY]

1940 Caton *Wildflowers of Smokies* = Caton, Joseph. 1940. *Wildflowers of the Great Smokies.* Knoxville: J. L. Caton. [central east TN, central western NC]

1940 *Charleston Gaz* = *Charleston (WV) Gazette.* 1940. [Untitled article]. [WV]

1940 Farr *More TN Expressions* = Farr, T. J. 1940. More Tennessee expressions. *American Speech* 15: 446–48. [east central TN]

1940 Fitzpatrick *Lg Tobacco Market* = Fitzpatrick, Robert J. 1940. Language of the tobacco market. *American Speech* 15: 132–35.

1940 *FWP Guide GA* = Federal Writers' Program. 1940. *Georgia: A guide to its towns and countryside.* Athens: University of Georgia Press. [GA]

1940 *FWP Guide VA* = Federal Writers' Program. 1940. *Virginia: A guide to the Old Dominion, compiled by workers of the Writers' Project of the Work Projects Administration in the state of Virginia.* New York: Oxford University Press. [VA]

1940 Haun *Hawk's Done* = Haun, Mildred. (1940) 1968. *The hawk's done gone and other stories.* Edited by Hershel Gower. [Previously published stories, pp. 1–197]. Nashville, TN: Vanderbilt University Press. [Cocke County, central east TN]

1940 Mathes *Jeff Howell* = Mathes, Charles Hodge. 1940. Jeff Howell's buryin'. *Tennessee Folklore Society Bulletin* 7(2): 19–22. [east TN]

1940 McJimsey *Topo Terms in VA* = McJimsey, George Davis. 1940. Topographic terms in Virginia. *American Speech* 15: 149–79, 262–300, 381–419. [western VA]

1940 McNeil *Mt Folk* = McNeil, Kin. 1940. Mountain folk still "tote" corn to mill. *Asheville Citizen,* April 29. [central western NC]

1940 Mims *Swagerty Family* = Mims, Cora Massey. 1940. The Swagerty family. *Pioneer personalities, prominent people, pleasant places: Excerpts from historical sketches* [consulted at Calvin M. McClung Collection, Knox County Public Library, Knoxville]. [Cocke County, central east TN]

c1940 *Newport (TN) Plain Citizen* = *Newport (TN) Plain Citizen.* c1940. [Story from *Newport (TN) Plain Citizen* newspaper, of unknown date, in collections of Joseph Sargent Hall]. [Cocke County, central east TN]

1940 Oakley *Roamin'/Restin'* = Oakley, Wiley. 1940. *Roamin' & restin' with the roamin' man of the Smoky Mountains.* Sevierville, TN: Oakley Enterprises. [Sevier County, central east TN]

c1940 Padelford *Notes* = Padelford, Ida. c1940. [Notes on the Smoky Mountains, collected by Joseph Sargent Hall from a librarian in Asheville NC; on deposit in Joseph Sargent Hall Collection, Archives of Appalachia, East Tennessee State University, Johnson City]. [central western NC]

1940 Perry *Pronoun Hit* = Perry, Louise Sublette. 1940. A study of the pronoun hit in Grassy Branch, North Carolina. MA thesis, Louisiana State University, Baton Rouge. [western NC]

1940 Pyle *Roving Reporter* = Pyle, Ernie. 1940. Roving reporter. *Knoxville News-Sentinel,* October 23. [east TN]

1940 Simms *Wiley Oakley* = Simms, Edna Lynn. 1940. *The roamin' man of the mountains: A sketch of Wiley Oakley, native guide, naturalist, philosopher of Gatlinburg, Tennessee in the Great Smoky Mountains.* N.p.: Privately published. [Sevier County, central east TN]

1940 Still *Love Rooster* = Still, James. 1940. I love my rooster. *Saturday Evening Post* 212(40): 16–17, 62, 64, 70.

1940–41 Still *Moving* = Still, James. 1940–41. The moving. *North Georgia Review* 5(3–4): 18–20.

1940 Still *River of Earth* = Still, James. 1940. *River of earth.* New York: Viking.

1940 Still *Snail Pie* = Still, James. 1940. Snail pie. *American Mercury* 50: 209–14.

1940 Stuart *Trees of Heaven* = Stuart, Jesse. 1940. *Trees of heaven.* New York: Dutton.

1940 Vincent *Us Mt Folks* = Vincent, Bert. 1940. *Us mountain folks.* Knoxville: Walters. [central east TN]

1941 Dearden *Word Geog S Atl Sts* = Dearden, Elizabeth Jeannette. 1941. A word geography of the South Atlantic states. MA thesis, Brown University, Providence, RI.

1941 *FWP Guide WV* = Writers' Program of the Work Projects Administration in the State of West Virginia. 1941. *West Virginia: A guide to the mountain state.* New York: Oxford University Press. [WV]

1941 Hall *Ballads and Songs* = Hall, Joseph S. 1941. Great Smokies ballads and songs. *American Poet* 1(9): 18–23. [central east TN, central western NC]

1941 Hall *Party Games* = Hall, Joseph S. 1941. Some party-games of the Great Smoky Mountains. *Journal of American Folklore* 54: 68–71. [central east TN, central western NC]

1941 Harper *Way We Said* = Harper, Francis. 1941. The way we said it. *North Georgia Review* 6: 129–30. [north GA]

1941 Justus *Kettle Creek* = Justus, May. 1941. *Cabin on Kettle Creek.* New York: Lippincott. [east TN]

1941 Kendall *Rifle-Making* = Kendall, Arthur I. 1941. Rifle making in the Great Smoky Mountains. *National Park Service Popular Study Series, History no. 13.* Washington, DC: US Department of the Interior. [central east TN, central western NC]

1941 Korson *Black Land* = Korson, George Gershon. 1941. *Black land: The way of life in the coal fields.* Evanston, IL: Row, Peterson and Co.

1941 *Land of Breathitt* = Works Projects Administration. 1941. *In the land of Breathitt.* New York: Bacon, Percy, and Daggett. [southeastern KY]

1941 Rothert *McDowell Letters* = Rothert, Otto A. 1941. Samuel McDowell's letters to Andrew Reid. *Filson Club History Quarterly* 16: 172–86. [KY]

1941 Still *Proud Walkers* = Still, James. 1941. Proud walkers. *Saturday Evening Post* 213(45): 111–14.

1941 Still *Stir-Off* = Still, James. 1941. The stir-off. *Mountain Life and Work* 17(3): 1–7.

1941 Still *Troublesome Creek* = Still, James. 1941. *On Troublesome Creek.* New York: Viking.

1941 Stuart *Men of Mts* = Stuart, Jesse. 1941. *Men of the mountains.* New York: Dutton. [northeastern KY]

1941 Walker *Story of Mt* = Walker, Robert Sparks. 1941. *Lookout: The story of a mountain.* Kingsport, TN: Southern. [southeast TN]

1941 *Words* = Words words words. 1941. *American Speech* 16: 41. [western NC]

1942 Campbell *Cloud-Walking* = Campbell, Marie. 1942. *Cloud-walking.* New York: Farrar and Rinehart. [southeastern KY]

1942 Clark *Kentucky* = Clark, Joseph D. 1942. *The Kentucky.* New York: Rinehart. [KY]

1942 Hall *Phonetics Smoky Mts* = Hall, Joseph S. 1942. *The phonetics of Great Smoky Mountain speech.* American Speech reprints and monograph no. 4. New York: King's Crown. [central east TN, central western NC]

1942 Justus *Step Along* = Justus, May. 1942. *Step Along and Jerry Jake.* Chicago: Whitman. [east TN]

1942 Posey *Frontier Baptist* = Posey, Walter B. 1942. The frontier Baptist ministry. *East Tennessee Historical Society Publication* 14: 3–10. [east TN]

1942 Robertson *Red Hills* = Robertson, Ben. 1942. *Red hills and cotton: An upcountry memory.* New York: Knopf. [northwestern SC]

1942 Thomas *Blue Ridge* = Thomas, Jean. 1942. *Blue Ridge country.* New York: Duell, Sloan and Pearce.

1943 Bandy *Witchcraft* = Bandy, Lewis D. 1943. Witchcraft and divination in Macon County. *Tennessee Folklore Society Bulletin* 9: 1–13. [Macon County, north central TN]

1943 Bewley *Picturesque Speech* = Bewley, Irene. 1943. Picturesque speech. *Tennessee Folklore Society Bulletin* 9(3): 4. [Greene County, northeast TN]

1943 Chase *Jack Tales* = Chase, Richard. 1943. *The Jack tales.* Boston: Houghton Mifflin.

1943 Erskine *Adventures* = Erskine, Ralph. 1943. Adventures among the mountain craftsmen. In *The Great Smokies and the Blue Ridge,* edited by Roderick Peattie, 201–16. New York: Vanguard.

1943 Gilbert *Eastern Cherokees* = Gilbert, William Harlen. 1943. *The eastern Cherokees.* Washington, DC: GPO. [Swain County, southwestern NC]

1943 Goerch *Down Home* = Goerch, Carl. 1943. *Down home.* Raleigh: Edwards and Broughton. [NC]

1943 Hannum *Mt People* = Hannum, Alberta Pierson. 1943. The mountain people. In *The Great Smokies and the Blue Ridge*, edited by Roderick Peattie, 73–151. New York: Vanguard. [western NC, south central VA]

1943 Justus *Bluebird* = Justus, May. 1943. *Bluebird, fly up!* New York: Lippincott. [east TN]

1943 Justus *Jerry Jake* = Justus, May. 1943. *Jerry Jake carries on*. Chicago: Whitman and Company. [east TN]

1943 Korson *Coal Dust* = Korson, George. 1943. *Coal dust on the fiddle: Songs and stories of the bituminous industry*. Philadelphia: University of Pennsylvania Press.

1943 Niles *Folk Ballad* = Niles, John Jacob. 1943. Folk ballads and carols. In *The Great Smokies and the Blue Ridge*, edited by Roderick Peattie, 217–38. New York: Vanguard.

1943 Peattie *Great Smokies* = Peattie, Roderick, ed. 1943. *The Great Smokies and the Blue Ridge*. New York: Vanguard.

1943 Peattie *Indian Days* = Peattie, Daniel Culross. 1943. Indian days and the coming of the white man. In *The Great Smokies and the Blue Ridge*, edited by Roderick Peattie, 15–72. New York: Vanguard.

1943 Peattie *Men Mt Trees* = Peattie, Donald Culross. 1943. Men, mountains and trees. In *The Great Smokies and the Blue Ridge*, edited by Roderick Peattie, 152–71. New York: Vanguard.

1943 Peattie *Wild Flowers* = Peattie, Donald Culross. 1943. Blue Ridge wild flowers. In *The Great Smokies and the Blue Ridge*, edited by Roderick Peattie, 172–99. New York: Vanguard.

1943 Stuart *Private Tussie* = Stuart, Jesse. 1943. *Taps for Private Tussie*. New York: Dutton. [northeastern KY]

1943 Stupka *Through the Year* = Stupka, Arthur. 1943. Through the year in the Great Smoky Mountains National Park. In *The Great Smokies and the Blue Ridge*, edited by Roderick Peattie, 263–89. New York: Vanguard. [central east TN, central western NC]

1944 Blair *Tall Tale America* = Blair, Walter. 1944. *Tall tale America: A legendary history of our humorous heroes*. New York: Coward-McCann.

1944 Combs *Word-List Sthn High* = Combs, Josiah [H.]. 1944. A word-list from the southern highlands. *Publication of the American Dialect Society* 2: 17–23. [southeastern KY]

1944 Dennis *Word-List* = Dennis, Leah A. 1944. A word-list from Alabama and some other southern states. *Publication of the American Dialect Society* 2: 6–16.

1944 Dingus *Tobacco Words* = Dingus, L. R. 1944. Tobacco words. *Publication of the American Dialect Society* 2: 63–72. [KY, VA]

1944 Hayes *Word-List NC* = Hayes, Francis C. 1944. A word-list from North Carolina. *Publication of the American Dialect Society* 2: 32–37. [northwestern NC]

1944 Justus *Billy and Bones* = Justus, May. 1944. *Banjo Billy and Mr. Bones*. Chicago: Albert Whitman and Company. [east TN]

1944 Justus *Lizzie* = Justus, May. 1944. Lizzie. Chicago: Albert Whitman and Company.

1944 Laughlin *Word-List Buncombe Co* = Laughlin, Hugh C. 1944. A word-list from Buncombe County, North Carolina. *Publication of the American Dialect Society* 2: 24–27. [Buncombe County, central western NC]

1944 *Picturesque Speech* = Picturesque speech. 1944. *Tennessee Folklore Society Bulletin* 10: 9–12.

1944 Wentworth *ADD* = Wentworth, Harold. 1944. *American dialect dictionary*. New York: Crowell. [various locales as specified at individual citations]

1944 Williams *Word-List Mts* = Williams, Cratis D. 1944. A word-list from the mountains of Kentucky and North Carolina. *Publication of the American Dialect Society* 2: 28–31. [northeastern KY, northwestern NC]

1944 Wilson *Word-List* = Wilson, George. 1944. A word-list from Virginia and North Carolina. *Publication of the American Dialect Society* 2: 38–52. [western NC]

1944 Wright *Query* = Wright, Nathalia. 1944. Query. *Tennessee Folklore Society Bulletin* 10(2): 10. [Blount County, central east TN]

c1945 Haun *Hawk's Done* = Haun, Mildred. 1968. *The hawk's done gone and other stories*. Edited by Hershel Gower. [Previously unpublished stories, pp. 201–354]. Nashville, TN: Vanderbilt University Press. [Cocke County, central east TN]

1945 McAtee *Nomina Arbitera* = McAtee, W. L. 1945. *Nomina arbitera*. N.p.: Privately published.

1945 McNeer *Sthn Highlands* = McNeer, May. 1945. *The story of the southern highlands*. New York: Harper and Brothers.

1945 O'Dell *Old Mills* = O'Dell, Ruth Webb. 1945. Old mills. *Tennessee Folklore Society Bulletin* 11(3): 1–4. [Cocke County, central east TN]

1945 Stewart *Names on Land* = Stewart, George. 1945. *Names on the land*. New York: Random House.

1945 Still *Mrs Razor* = Still, James. 1945. Mrs. Razor. *Atlantic* 176(1): 52–53.

1945 Thomas *Mt Folk* = Thomas, Jean. 1945. The changing mountain folk. *American Mercury* 63: 43–49.

1945 Vincent *Here in TN* = Vincent, Bert. 1945. *Here in Tennessee*. Knoxville: Walters. [central east TN]

1945 Williams *Comment* = Williams, Cratis [D.] 1945. [Comment on cuckold]. *Publication of the American Dialect Society* 3: 9–10. [northeastern KY]

1945 Wilson *Passing Institutions* = Wilson, Gordon. 1945. *Passing institutions*. Cynthiana, KY: Hobson. [south central KY]

1946 Burnett *Shingle Making* = Burnett, Edmund Cody. 1946. Shingle making on the lesser waters of the Big Creek of the French Broad River. *Agricultural History* 20(4): 225–35. [central western NC]

1946 Cleaves *King's English* = Cleaves, Mildred P. 1946. King's English reigns in the Kentucky Knobs. *In Kentucky* 10(3): 35. [KY]

1946 Dudley *KY Words* = Dudley, Fred A. 1946. "Swarp" and some other Kentucky words. *American Speech* 21: 270–73. [northeastern KY]

1946 Lassiter *Games Played* = Lassiter, James. 1946. Games we played. *Tennessee Folklore Society Bulletin* 12: 17–22.

1946 Maloney *Time Stood* = Maloney, John. 1946. Time stood still in the Smokies. *Saturday Evening Post* 218 (April 27): 16–17, 82, 84–85. [central east TN, central western NC]

1946 Matthias *Speech Pine Mt* = Matthias, Virginia P. 1946. Folk speech of Pine Mountain, Kentucky. *American Speech* 21: 188–92. [Harlan County, southeastern KY]

1946 Moore *Affirm Any More* = Moore, Arthur K. 1946. New light on affirmative "any more." *American Speech* 21: 301–2.

1946 Nixon *Glossary VA Words* = Nixon, Phyllis J. 1946. A glossary of Virginia words. *Publication of the American Dialect Society* 5: 3–43. [western VA]

1946 O'Dell *Moonshine* = O'Dell, Ruth Webb. 1946. Moonshine in the Tennessee mountains. *Tennessee Folklore Society Bulletin* 12(3): 1–5. [Cocke County, central east TN]

1946 Pendleton *Illicit Whiskey* = Pendleton, Charles. 1946. Illicit whiskey making. *Tennessee Folklore Society Bulletin* 12: 1–16.

1946 *Shore Sign* = Shore sign: A play based on the superstitions of the Cumberland mountain folk. 1946. *Tennessee Folklore Society Bulletin* 12(4): 3–7. [east central TN]

1946 Still *Pattern of Man* = Still, James. 1946. Pattern of a man. *Yale Review* 36: 93–100.

1946 Stuart *Foretaste Glory* = Stuart, Jesse. 1946. *Foretaste of glory*. New York: Dutton.

1946 Stuart *Plum Grove Hills* = Stuart, Jesse. 1946. *Tales from the Plum Grove Hills*. New York: Dutton. [northeastern KY]

1946 Wilson *Fidelity Folks* = Wilson, Gordon. 1946. *Fidelity folks*. Cynthiana, KY: Hobson. [south central KY]

1946 Woodard *Word-List VA/NC* = Woodard, C. M. 1946. A word-list from Virginia and North Carolina. *Publication of the American Dialect Society* 6: 4–43.

1947 Dunlap and Weslager *Tri-racial Groups* = Dunlap, A. R., and C. A. Weslager. 1947. Trends in the naming of tri-racial mixed-blood groups in the eastern United States. *American Speech* 22: 81–87.

1947 Gamble *Heritage* = Gamble, Margaret Elizabeth. 1947. The heritage and folk music of Cades Cove, Tennessee. MA thesis, University of Southern California, Los Angeles. [Blount County, central east TN]

1947 Read *Pickering Vocabulary* = Read, Allen Walker. 1947. The collections for Pickering's "Vocabulary." *American Speech* 22: 271–86. [KY, NC]

1947 Steed *KY Tobacco Patch* = Steed, Virgil S. 1947. *Kentucky tobacco patch.* Indianapolis: Bobbs-Merrill. [KY]

1947 Stuart *Corn Cuttin'* = Stuart, Jesse, 1947. Corn cuttin's pretty work. *Farm Journal* 7(1): 22–23. [northeastern KY]

1948 Baldwin *Big Trees* = Baldwin, S. G. 1948. Big trees of the Great Smokies. *Southern Lumberman* 177 (December 15): 172–78. [central east TN, central western NC]

1948 Chase *Grandfather Tales* = Chase, Richard. 1948. *Grandfather tales.* New York: Houghton Mifflin.

1948 Dick *Dixie Frontier* = Dick, Everett. 1948. *The Dixie frontier.* New York: Knopf. [upper South]

1948 Gasque *Hunting Fishing* = Gasque, Jim. 1948. *Hunting & fishing in the Great Smokies.* New York: Knopf. [central east TN]

1948 Still *Nest* = Still, James. 1948. The nest. *Prairie Schooner* 22: 53–56.

1949 Arnow *Hunter's Horn* = Arnow, Harriette Louisa Simpson. 1949. *Hunter's horn.* New York: Macmillan.

1949 Hornsby *Lonesome Valley* = Hornsby, Henry. 1949. *Lonesome valley.* New York: Sloane. [KY]

1949 Justus *Toby Has Dog* = Justus, May. 1949. *Toby has a dog.* Chicago: Whitman and Company. [east TN]

1949 Kurath *Word Geog East US* = Kurath, Hans. 1949. *Word geography of the eastern United States.* Ann Arbor: University of Michigan Press.

1949 Marshall *Squire Jim* = Marshall, Robert K. 1949. *Little Squire Jim.* New York: Duel, Sloan, and Pearce. [western NC]

1949 Maurer *Argot of Moonshiner* = Maurer, David W. 1949. The argot of the moonshiner. *American Speech* 24: 3–13.

1949 McDavid *Grist* = McDavid, Raven I., Jr. 1949. Grist from the Atlas mill. *American Speech* 24: 105–14. [northeast GA, northwestern SC]

1949 Sharpe *Lowgap Man* = Sharpe, Bill. 1949. Lowgap man is ginsenging: Waxy leaves provide big business. *Roanoke Times* (VA), June 31.

1949 Still *Master Time* = Still, James. 1949. A master time. *Atlantic Monthly* 183: 43–46.

1949 Stuart *Thread* = Stuart, Jesse. 1949. *The thread that runs so true.* New York: Scribner's Sons. [northeastern KY]

1949 Turner *Africanisms* = Turner, Lorenzo Dow. 1949. *Africanisms in the Gullah dialect.* Chicago: University of Chicago Press.

1949 Watkins *Mtneers' Archaic English* = Watkins, Floyd. 1949. The southern mountaineers' archaic English. *Georgia Review* 3: 219–25. [north central GA]

c1950 Adams *Grandpap* = Adams, James Taylor. 1950. *Grandpap told me tales.* Manuscript stories collected and edited by Fletcher Dean. Big Stone Gap, VA: F. Dean. [southwestern VA]

1950 Bray *Disappearing Dialect* = Bray, Rose Altizer. 1950. Disappearing dialect. *Antioch Review* 10: 279–88.

1950 Dalton *Wordlist Sthn KY* = Dalton, Alford P. 1950. A wordlist from southern Kentucky. *Publication of the American Dialect Society* 15: 22–23. [southern KY]

c1950 Haun *When the Wind* = Haun, Mildred. 1993. When the wind blows. In *Mossy Creek Reader*, edited by Jeff Daniel Marion, 3–18. Jefferson City, TN: Carson-Newman College. [Cocke County, central east TN]

c1950 Henderson *Ebenezer Mission* = Henderson, Mary O. c1950. Ebenezer Mission in Cocke County, Tennessee "as I knew it." Typescript loaned to the editor by Cherel Henderson. [Cocke County, central east TN]

1950 Justus *Luck for Lihu* = Justus, May. 1950. *Luck for little Lihu.* New York: Aladdin. [east TN]

1950 King and Stupka *Geology and Natural History* = King, Philip B., and Arthur Stupka. 1950. The Great Smoky Mountains: Their geology and natural history. *Science Monthly* 71: 31–43. [central east TN, central western NC]

c1950 Matthews *Smokey Hills* = Matthews, Fred Decatur. c1950. *Them Smokey Hills is "hypoed": Tales and legends of the Great Smoky Mountains as gathered by Fred Matthews* [consulted at Library, Great Smoky Mountains National Park, Gatlinburg, TN]. N.p.: n.p.

1950–73 Miller *Pigeon's Roost* = Miller, Harvey J. 1974. *News from Pigeon's Roost.* Rabun Gap, GA: Foxfire. [Mitchell County, northwestern NC]

1950 Stuart *Hie Hunters* = Stuart, Jesse. 1950. *Hie to the hunters.* New York: Harcourt, Brace and World. [northeastern KY]

c1950 Whaley *Aunt Lydia* = Whaley, Sam. c1950. "Aunt Lydia" living in shadow of LeConte, typifies mountain woman of earlier days; is Bible student [clipping from unidentified newspaper consulted at Library, Great Smoky Mountains National Park, Gatlinburg, TN]

c1950 Wilburn *Quern* = Wilburn, H. C. c1950. Quern, a grinding device, dates from ancient days. *Asheville Citizen.* [central western NC]

1950 Wood *Sure of Life* = Wood, Violet. 1950. *So sure of life.* New York: Friendship. [Sevier County, central east TN]

1950 Woody *Cataloochee Homecoming* = Woody, Robert H. 1950. Cataloochee homecoming. *South Atlantic Quarterly* 49: 8–17. [Haywood County, central western NC]

1951 Barnwell *Our Mt Speech* = Barnwell, Lila Ripley. 1951. Our mountain speech. *Asheville Citizen*, January 4. [central western NC]

c1951 Chapman *Speech Confusing* = Chapman, Ashton. c1951. Speech of WNC mountain people is often confusing to newcomers. *Asheville Citizen*, undated. [central western NC]

1951 Craig *Singing Hills* = Craig, Lillian K. 1951. *The singing hills.* New York: Crowell.

1951 Giles *Harbin's Ridge* = Giles, Janice Holt. 1951. *Harbin's ridge.* Boston: Houghton Mifflin. [southeastern KY]

1951 Hodges *Handicrafts* = Hodges, Sidney Cecil. 1951. Handicrafts in Sevier County, Tennessee. MS thesis, University of Tennessee, Knoxville. [Sevier County, central east TN]

1951 Justus *Lucky Penny* = Justus, May. 1951. *Lucky penny.* New York: Aladdin. [east TN]

1951 McAtee *Bird Names* = McAtee, W. L. 1951. Bird names connected with weather, seasons, and hours. *American Speech* 26: 268–77.

1951 McAtee *Names for Plants* = McAtee, W. L. 1951. Some folk and scientific names for plants. *Publication of the American Dialect Society* 15: 3–25.

1951 Pyle *Gatlinburg* = Pyle, Ernest T. 1951. *Gatlinburg and the Great Smokies.* Gatlinburg, TN: Mountain Press. [Sevier County, central east TN]

1951 Still *Short Dog* = Still, James. 1951. A ride on the short dog. *Atlantic Monthly* 188: 55–58.

1951 Ulmer and Beck *Cherokee Cooklore* = Ulmer, Mary, and Samuel E. Beck. 1951. *Cherokee cooklore.* Sylva, NC: Privately published. [Swain County, southwestern NC]

1952–84 *Asheville Citizen-Times* = [Miscellaneous articles and clippings from the *Asheville Citizen* and *Asheville Citizen-Times* newspapers, consulted at Pack Memorial Library, Asheville, NC]

1952 Beck *Herpetol Lore* = Beck, H. P. 1952. Herpetological lore from the Blue Ridge. *Midwest Folklore* 2: 141–50. [WV]

1952 Breckinridge *Neighborhoods* = Breckinridge, Mary C. 1952. *Wide neighborhoods: A story of the Frontier Nursing Service.* New York: Harper and Brothers. [southeastern KY]

1952 Brewster *Games and Rhymes* = Brewster, Paul G., ed. 1952. Children's games and rhymes. In *The Frank C. Brown Collection of North Carolina folklore*, edited by Newman Ivey White et al., vol. 1, 29–220. Durham, NC: Duke University Press. [NC]

1952 Brown *NC Folklore* = Brown, Frank C., ed. 1952. *The Frank C. Brown collection of North Carolina folklore.* 6 vols. Durham, NC: Duke University Press. [NC]

1952 Callahan *Smoky Mt Country* = Callahan, North. 1952. *Smoky mountain country.* Sevierville, TN: Smoky Mountain Historical Society. [southeast TN]

1952 Chase *Hindman Pageant* = Chase, Richard. 1952. The Hindman Pageant. *Mountain Life and Work* 28(2): 19. [southeastern KY]

1952 Giles *40 Acres* = Giles, Janice Holt. 1952. *40 acres and no mule*. Philadelphia: Westminster. [southeastern KY]

1952 Huffman *Mt Memories* = Huffman, Alza. 1952. *My mountain memories: The outstanding incidents and ideas of my eighty-five years*. Philadelphia: Dorrance and Company. [WV]

1952 Justus *Children* = Justus, May. 1952. *Children of the Great Smoky Mountains*. New York: Dutton and Company. [east TN]

1952 Law *Some Folklore* = Law, Harry. 1952. Some folklore of Macon County, Tennessee. *Tennessee Folklore Society Bulletin* 18: 97–100. [Macon County, north central TN]

1952 Mathes *Tall Tales* = Mathes, Charles Hodge. 1952. *Tall tales from old Smoky*. Kingsport, TN: Southern. [east TN]

1952 Mathews *Matters Lexicographical* = Mathews, Mitford M. 1952. Of matters lexicographical. *American Speech* 27: 124–27. [east TN]

1952 Matthias *Wordcatcher* = Matthias, Virginia P. 1952. A wordcatcher asks your help. *Mountain Life and Work* 28(3): 23–24.

1952 McCall *Cherokees and Pioneers* = McCall, William A. 1952. *Cherokees and pioneers*. Asheville, NC: Stephens. [western NC]

1952 Ritchie and Pickow *Swapping Song* = Ritchie, Jean, and George Pickow. 1952. *The swapping song book*. New York: Oxford University Press. [eastern KY]

1952 Strausbaugh and Core *Flora WV* = Strausbaugh, Perry Daniel, and Earl L. Core. 1952. *Flora of West Virginia*, part 1. Morgantown, WV: n.p. [WV]

1952 Stuart *Christmas in Valley* = Stuart, Jesse. 1952. Christmas in the valley. *Ladies Home Journal* 69 (December): 38–39, 81–83.

1952 Taylor and Whiting *Proverbs and Sayings* = Taylor, Archer, and Bartlett Jere Whiting. 1952. *Modern proverbs and proverbial sayings*. Cambridge, MA: Harvard University Press.

1952 Wiley *Life Billy Yank* = Wiley, Bell Irvin. 1952. *The life of Billy Yank: The common soldier of the Union*. Garden City, NY: Doubleday.

1952 Wilson *Folk Speech NC* = Wilson, George. 1952. Folk speech. In *The Frank C. Brown collection of North Carolina folklore*, edited by Newman Ivey White et al., vol. 1, 505–618. Durham, NC: Duke University Press. [western NC]

1953 Atwood *Verbs East US* = Atwood, E. Bagby. 1953. *A survey of verb forms in the eastern United States*. Ann Arbor: University of Michigan Press.

1953 Boshears *Shivaree* = Boshears, Frances. 1953. The shivaree. *Tennessee Folklore Society Bulletin* 19: 65–67. [Scott and Morgan Counties, east central TN]

1953 Brewster *Amer Nonsinging Games* = Brewster, Paul. 1953. *American nonsinging games*. Norman: University of Oklahoma Press.

1953 Bryan *Confederate GA* = Bryan, Thomas Conn. 1953. *Confederate Georgia*. Athens: University of Georgia Press.

1953 Chapman *Decoration Day* = Chapman, Ashton. 1953. Decoration day custom dates from early days in the mountains. *Asheville Citizen*, May 31. [central western NC]

1953 Davison *Word-List Appal* = Davison, Zeta C. 1953. A word-list from the Appalachians and the Piedmont area of North Carolina. *Publication of the American Dialect Society* 19: 8–14. [NC, KY, TN]

1953 Greene and Blomquist *Flowers South* = Greene, Wilhemina F., and Hugo L. Blomquist. 1953. *Flowers of the South*. Chapel Hill: University of North Carolina Press.

1953 Shelton *Autobiog I* = Shelton, James. 1953. Autobiography. Typescript consulted at Library, Great Smoky Mountains National Park, Gatlinburg, TN. [Sevier County, central east TN]

1953 Shelton *Autobiog II* = Shelton, James. 2004. Autobiography of James Shelton. *Smoky Mountain Historical Society Journal and Newsletter* 30(4): 3–6. [expanded version of the preceding item; Sevier County, central east TN]

1953 Stuart *Good Spirit* = Stuart, Jesse. 1953. *The good spirit of Laurel Ridge*. New York: McGraw-Hill.

1953 Wharton *Dr Woman Cumberlands* = Wharton, May Cravath. 1953. *Doctor woman of the Cumberlands: The autobiography of May Cravath Wharton, M.D.* Pleasant Hill, TN: Uplands. [Cumberland County, east central TN]

1953 Wilburn *Pounding Mill* = Wilburn, H. C. 1953. Pounding-mill is remarkable machine. *Asheville Citizen*, August 2. [central western NC]

c1954 Adams *Word-List* = Adams. 1954. *Word-List*. [Document part of author's private collection.]

1954 Arnow *Dollmaker* = Arnow, Harriette Louisa Simpson. 1954. *The dollmaker*. New York: Macmillan.

1954 Blackhurst *Riders of Flood* = Blackhurst, W. E. 1954. *Riders of the flood*. Parsons, WV: McClain. [WV]

1954–84 GSMNP = Great Smoky Mountains National Park interviews. 1954–84. [Recorded interviews and provisional transcripts consulted at Library, Great Smoky Mountains National Park, Gatlinburg, TN, with citations giving the page number of those transcripts for ease of consulting before they were revised and improved for this book.] [central east TN, central western NC]

1954 Medford *Waynesv* = Medford, W. Clark. 1954. [Untitled article]. *Waynesville Mountaineer*, June 17. [central western NC]

1954 Roberts *Bought a Dog* = Roberts, Leonard. 1954. *I bought me a dog*. Berea, KY: Council of the Southern Mountains. [southeastern KY]

1954 *Tennessean* = *The Tennessean*. 1954. [Untitled newspaper article]

1954 *Waynesville Mtneer* = *Waynesville Mountaineer*. 1954. [Untitled newspaper article]. August 2. [central western NC]

1954 Weals *Lost Gold Mine* = Weals, Vic. 1954. Lost gold mine in Big Greenbrier. *Knoxville Journal*, May 11. [Sevier County, central east TN]

1955 Boone *Folk Names* = Boone, Laura Phipps. 1955. Folk names for blooming plants. *Southern Folklore Quarterly* 19: 230–36.

1955 Dykeman *French Broad* = Dykeman, Wilma. 1955. *The French Broad*. New York: Holt, Rinehart and Winston.

1955 Justus *Peter Pocket* = Justus, May. 1955. *Surprise for Peter Pocket*. New York: Henry Holt. [east TN]

1955 Parris *Roaming Mts* = Parris, John. 1955. *Roaming the mountains with John Parris*. Asheville, NC: Citizen-Times. [central western NC]

1955 Ritchie *Singing Family* = Ritchie, Jean. 1955. *Singing family of the Cumberlands*. New York: Oxford University Press. [eastern KY]

1955 Rogers *Switching* = Rogers, E. G. 1955. Switching for water. *Tennessee Folklore Society Bulletin* 21: 108–11. [central TN]

1955 Washburn *Country Doctor* = Washburn, Benjamin Earl. 1955. *A country doctor in the South Mountains*. Asheville, NC: Stephens Press. [Rutherford County, southwestern NC]

1955 Wiley *Put-Togethers* = Put-together(s). *American Speech* 30: 154. [WV]

1955 Zelinsky *Place-Name Generics* = Zelinsky, Wilbur. 1955. Some problems in the distribution of generic terms in the place-names of the northeastern United States. *Annals of the Association of American Geographers* 41: 319–49. [eastern KY, western VA, WV]

1956 Carter *Methodists in TN* = Carter, Cullen Tuller. 1956. *History of the Tennessee Conference: And a brief summary of the general conferences, the Methodist Church, from the frontier in middle Tennessee to the present time*. N.p.: Self-published. [central TN]

1956 Chapman *Folk Retain* = Chapman, Ashton. 1956. Folk retain "old English." *Winston-Salem Journal*, January 9, 8. [western NC]

1956 Eliason *Tarheel Talk* = Eliason, Norman E. 1956. *Tarheel talk: An historical study of the English language in North Carolina to 1860*. Chapel Hill: University of North Carolina Press. [western NC]

1956 Fink *That's Why* = Fink, Paul M. 1956. *That's why they call it: Names and lore of the Great Smokies*. Jonesboro, TN: Privately published. [central east TN, central western NC]

1956 Freel *Cherokee Co* = Freel, Margaret Walker. 1956. *Our heritage: The people of Cherokee County, North Carolina 1540–1955*. Asheville, NC: Miller. [Cherokee County, southwestern NC]

1956 McAtee *Some Dial NC* = McAtee, W. L. 1956. *Some dialect of North Carolina*. Chapel Hill, NC: Privately published. [central western NC]

1956 Medford *Big Bend* = Medford, W. Clark. 1956. Once rough, Big Bend now rests in peaceful solitude. *Asheville Citizen-Times*, July 1. [central western NC]

1956 Settle *Beulah Land* = Settle, Mary Lee. 1956. *O Beulah Land*. New York: Viking Press.

1956 Still *Burning of Waters* = Still, James. 1956. The burning of the waters. *Atlantic Monthly* 188: 55–60.

1956 Stuart *Year Rebirth* = Stuart, Jesse. 1956. *The year of my rebirth*. New York: McGraw-Hill.

1957 Baughan *Tarheel Talk* = Baughan, Denver Ewing. 1957. Review of *Tarheel Talk* by Norman Eliason. *American Speech* 32: 283–85. [western NC]

1957 Broaddus *Vocab Estill Co KY* = Broaddus, James. 1957. The folk vocabulary of Estill County, Kentucky. MA thesis, University of Kentucky. [Estill County, eastern KY]

1957 Chiles and Trotter *Mt Makin's* = Chiles, Mary Ruth, and Mrs. William P. Trotter. 1957. *Mountain makin's in the Smokies: A cookbook*. Asheville, NC: Stephens.

1957 Combs *Lg Sthn High: Idioms* = Combs, Josiah H. 1957. Idioms. *Language of the southern highlanders*. Typescript on deposit at Berea College Library Appalachian Collection, Berea, KY. [southeastern KY]

1957 Combs *Lg Sthn High: Syntax* = Combs, Josiah H. 1957. Syntax. *Language of the southern highlanders*. Typescript on deposit at Berea College Library Appalachian Collection, Berea, KY. [southeastern KY]

1957 Combs *Lg Sthn High: Word List* = Combs, Josiah H. 1957. Word list. *Language of the southern highlanders*. Typescript on deposit at Berea College Library Appalachian Collection, Berea, KY. [southeastern KY]

1957 Garred *History of Garreds* = Garred, Ulysses Victoria. 1957. *A history and genealogy of the Garreds, Jarretts of Kentucky, and many related families*. Whiting, IA: J. Holmes.

1957 Hall *Bear Stories* = Hall, Joseph S. 1957. Bear-hunting stories from the Great Smokies. *Tennessee Folklore Society Bulletin* 23: 67–75. [central east TN, central western NC]

1957 Hewes *Boxcar* = Hewes, Laurence. 1957. *Boxcar in the Sand*. New York: Knopf.

1957 Justus *Other Side* = Justus, May. 1957. *The other side of the mountain*. New York: Hastings House. [east TN]

1957 McDavid *American Dialects* = McDavid, Raven I., Jr. 1957. American English dialects. In *The structure of American English*, by W. Nelson Francis, 480–543. New York: Ronald.

1957 McMeekin *Old KY Country* = McMeekin, Clark. 1957. *Old Kentucky country*. New York: Duell, Sloan and Pearce. [KY]

1957 Monaghan *CW Slang* = Monaghan, Jay. 1957. Civil War slang and humor. *Civil War History* 3: 125–33.

1957 Neel *Backwoodsman* = Neel, Marvin H. 1957. *The word-book of a backwoodsman*. Ceres, VA: Backwoods Press.

1957 Parris *My Mts* = Parris, John. 1957. *My mountains, my people*. Asheville, NC: Citizen-Times. [central western NC]

1957 Weals *Sary Parker* = Weals, Vic. 1957. A bridge for Sary Parker. *Knoxville Journal*, May 12, 12D. [central east TN]

1957 Wise *Mt Speech* = Wise, Claude Merton. 1957. Mountain English. In *Applied phonetics*, 303–21. Englewood Cliffs, NJ: Prentice Hall.

1957 Woodbridge *Hunting Terms* = Woodbridge, Hensley C. 1957. Some unrecorded hunting terms found in Kentucky. *Kentucky Folklore Record* 3: 153–58. [KY]

1958 Campbell *Tales* = Campbell, Marie. 1958. *Tales from the cloud walking country*. Bloomington: Indiana University Press. [southeastern KY]

1958 Combs *Archaic English in KY* = Combs, Mona. 1958. Archaic English words used in north eastern Kentucky. MEd thesis, Morehead State College. [northeastern KY]

1958 Morgan *Gift from Hills* = Morgan, Lucy. 1958. *Gift from the hills: Miss Lucy Morgan's story with Lebette Blythe*. Indianapolis: Bobbs-Merrill. [northwestern NC]

1958 Newton *Dialect Vocab* = Newton, Mary Catherine. 1958. A comparative study of the dialect vocabularies of east Tennessee and western North Carolina using selected words. Senior thesis, Maryville College, Maryville, TN. [east TN, western NC]

1958 Sanderson *County Scott* = Sanderson, Esther Sharp. 1958. *County Scott and its mountain folk*. Huntsville, TN: Privately published. [northeast TN]

1958 Stuart *Plowshare* = Stuart, Jesse. 1958. *Plowshare to heaven*. New York: McGraw-Hill.

1958 Wood *Words from TN* = Wood, Gordon [R.]. 1958. A list of words from Tennessee. *Publication of the American Dialect Society* 29: 3–18. [TN]

1959 Chapman *Flower for Suds* = Chapman, Ashton. 1959. Early settlers used flower for suds to wash and bathe. *Asheville Citizen-Times*, August 9. [central western NC]

1959 Cooper *Corpse Could Sleep* = Cooper, Horton. 1959. Only a corpse could sleep at a wake. *Charlotte News and Observer*, March 2. [western NC]

1959 Forest *Jessie's* = Forest, Herman. 1959. *Jessie's children*. New York: Vanguard.

1959 Justus *Bring Banjo* = Justus, May. 1959. *Barney, bring your banjo*. New York: Henry Holt and Company. [east TN]

1959 Pearsall *Little Smoky* = Pearsall, Marion. 1959. *Little Smoky Ridge: The natural history of a southern Appalachian neighborhood*. Tuscaloosa: University of Alabama Press.

1959 Roberts *Up Cutshin* = Roberts, Leonard W. 1959. *Up Cutshin and down Greasy: Folkways of a Kentucky family*. Lexington: University Press of Kentucky. [southeastern KY]

1959–71 Stubbs *Mountain-Wise* = Stubbs, Thomas B. 1959–71. Mountain-wise [bimonthly column]. *Georgia Magazine*. [Rabun County, northeast GA]

c1959 Weals *Hillbilly Dict* = Weals, Vic. c1959. *Hillbilly dictionary: An edifying collection of mountain expressions*. Gatlinburg, TN: Weals. [east TN]

1959 Wilgus *Down Our Way* = Wilgus, D. K. 1959. Down our way: Who's in town? *Kentucky Folklore Record* 5: 1–8. [KY]

1960 Allen *Land of Sky* = Allen, Martha Norburn. 1960. *Land of the sky*. Charlotte: Heritage House. [western NC]

1960 Arnow *Seedtime* = Arnow, Harriette Louisa Simpson. 1960. *Seedtime on the Cumberland*. New York: Macmillan. [southeastern KY]

1960 Burnett *My Valley* = Burnett, Fred M. 1960. *This was my valley*. Ridgecrest, NC: n.p. [east TN]

1960 Campbell *Birth* = Campbell, Carlos C. 1960. *Birth of a national park in the Great Smoky Mountains*. Knoxville: University of Tennessee Press. [central east TN, central western NC]

1960 Cooper *Jularker Bussed* = Cooper, Horton. 1960. The jularker bussed his jusem-sweet. *Charlotte News and Observer*, July 31. [western NC]

1960 Hall *Smoky Mt Folks* = Hall, Joseph S. 1960. *Smoky Mountain folks and their lore*. Asheville, NC: Cataloochee. [central east TN, central western NC]

1960 Justus *Right House* = Justus, May. 1960. *The right house for Rowdy*. New York: Holt, Rinehart and Winston. [east TN]

1960 Mason *Memoir* = Mason, Henry McGilbert. 1960. The memoir of a southern Appalachian mountaineer. Typescript consulted at Library, Great Smoky Mountains National Park, Gatlinburg, TN.

1960 McCaulley *Cades Cove* = McCaulley, John. 1960. [Audio interview recorded by Vic Weals]. [Blount County, central east TN]

1960 Price *Root Digging in Appal* = Price, Edward T. 1960. Root digging in the Appalachians: The geography of botanical drugs. *Geographical Review* 50: 1–20. [WV]

1960 Schwarz *Ordeal by Serpents* = Schwarz, Berthold E. 1960. Ordeal by serpent, fire, and strychnine: A study of some provocative psychosomatic phenomena. *Psychiatric Quarterly* 31: 405–29.

1960 Stuart *God's Oddling* = Stuart, Jesse. 1960. *God's oddling*. New York: McGraw-Hill. [northeastern KY]

1960 Stupka *Great Smoky Mts* = Stupka, Arthur. 1960. *Great Smoky Mountains National Park North Carolina and Tennessee*. Natural history handbook series, no. 5. Washington, DC: US National Park Service. [central east TN, central western NC]

1960 Sutherland *Folk Speech* = Sutherland, E. J. 1960. Folk speech on frying pan. *Mountain Life and Work* 36(2): 11–14. [eastern KY]

1960 Westover *Highland Lg* = Westover, J. Huston. 1960. Highland language of the Cumberland coal country. *Mountain Life and Work* 36(2): 18–21. [eastern KY]

c1960–68 Wilson *Coll* = Wilson, Gordon. c1960, 1966, 1968. [Unpublished dialect materials from the area of Mammoth Cave in Edmonson County, south central KY, donated to the *Dictionary of American Regional English* project, consulted at the DARE office (1994, 1997) and through its first five published volumes] [south central KY]

1961 *Coe Ridge OHP* = Coe Ridge Oral History Project. 1961. [Selected audio interviews from Michael Montgomery's dissertation fieldwork, transcribed for this book]. Indiana and Kentucky, William Lynwood Montell Collection, Archives of Traditional Music, Indiana University, Bloomington. [Monroe and Cumberland Counties, south central KY]

c1961 Cooper *Nairy a Word* = Cooper, Horton. 1961. Nairy a word. [Undated news clipping, western NC]

1961 Douglas *My Wilderness* = Douglas, William O. 1961. *My wilderness: East to Katahdin*. New York: Doubleday.

1961 Kurath and McDavid *Pron Engl Atl Sts* = Kurath, Hans, and Raven I. McDavid Jr. 1961. *Pronunciation of English in the Atlantic states*. Ann Arbor: University of Michigan Press.

1961 Lambert *Little River* = Lambert, Robert S. 1961. Logging on Little River, 1890–1940. *East Tennessee Historical Society Publication* 33: 32–42. [Sevier County, central east TN]

1961 Lambert *Logging in Smokies* = Lambert, Robert S. 1961. Logging in Great Smokies, 1880–1930. *Tennessee Historical Quarterly* 21: 350–63. [central east TN, central western NC]

1961 Medford *History Haywood Co* = Medford, W. Clark. 1961. *The early history of Haywood County*. Asheville, NC: Miller. [central western NC]

1961 Murry *Salt* = Murry, Howard. 1961. *Salt o' life*. Winston-Salem, NC: Blair.

1961 Niles *Ballad Book* = Niles, John Jacob. 1961. *The ballad book of John Jacob Niles*. Lexington: University Press of Kentucky. [eastern KY]

1961 Seeman *Arms of Mt* = Seeman, Elizabeth. 1961. *In the arms of the mountain: An intimate journal of the Great Smokies*. New York: Crown. [southeast TN]

1961 Williams *Content Mt Speech* = Williams, Cratis D. 1961. The content of mountain speech. *Mountain Life and Work* 37(4): 13–17.

1961 Williams *Rhythm and Melody* = Williams, Cratis D. 1961. Rhythm and melody in mountain speech. *Mountain Life and Work* 37(3): 7–10.

1961 Williams *R in Mt Speech* = Williams, Cratis D. 1961. The "r" in mountain speech. *Mountain Life and Work* 37(1): 5–8.

1962 Brewer *Hiking* = Brewer, Carson. 1962. *Hiking in the Great Smokies*. Knoxville: Holston. [central east TN, central western NC]

1962 Clark *Folk Speech NC* = Clark, Joseph D. 1962. Folk speech from North Carolina. *Southern Folklore Quarterly* 26: 301–25. [NC]

1962 Drukker *Lg By-Ways* = Drukker, Raymond. 1962. Language by-ways. *Mountain Life and Work* 38 (Summer): 50–52. [eastern KY]

1962 Dykeman *Tall Woman* = Dykeman, Wilma. 1962. *The tall woman*. Newport, TN: Wakestone.

1962 Hunter *Folk Remedies* = Hunter, Earl D. 1962. Folk remedies on man and beasts. *Kentucky Folklore Record* 8: 97–108. [KY]

1962 Justus *Smoky Sampler* = Justus, May. 1962. *Smoky Mountain sampler*. New York: Abingdon. [east TN]

1962 Krutch *More Lives* = Krutch, Joseph Wood. 1962. *More lives than one*. New York: Sloane. [east TN]

1962 Rouse *Colorful Tint* = Rouse, J. Michael. 1962. Language at Stoney Point spoken with colorful tint. *Asheville Citizen-Times*, April 29. [central western NC]

1962 Smith *Dancing and Singing* = Smith, Frank. 1962. Dancing and singing games. In *The Southern Appalachian region: A survey*, edited by Thomas R. Ford, 271–78. Lexington: University Press of Kentucky.

1962 Weatherford and Brewer *Life and Religion* = Weatherford, Willis Duke, and Earl D. C. Brewer. 1962. *Life and religion in southern Appalachia*. New York: Friendship Press.

1962 Williams *Metaphor Mt Speech I* = Williams, Cratis D. 1962. Metaphor in mountain speech. *Mountain Life and Work* 38(4): 9–12.

1962 Williams *Mtneers Mind Manners* = Williams, Cratis D. 1962. Mountaineers mind their manners. *Mountain Life and Work* 38(2): 19–25.

1962 Williams *Verbs Mt Speech* = Williams, Cratis D. 1962. Verbs in mountain speech. *Mountain Life and Work* 38(2): 15–19.

1962 Wilson *Folkways Mammoth Cave* = Wilson, Gordon. 1962. *Folkways of the Mammoth Cave region*. Bowling Green, KY: Self-published. [south central KY]

1962 Woosley *Water Witching* = Woosley, Glenda Janice. 1962. Water witching Big Reedy style. *Kentucky Folklore Record* 8: 137–40. [KY]

1963 Arnow *Flowering* = Arnow, Harriette Louisa Simpson. 1963. *Flowering of the Cumberland*. New York: Macmillan. [southeastern KY]

1963 Berry *Almost White* = Berry, Brewton. 1963. *Almost white*. New York: Macmillan. [southeastern KY, northeast TN, southwestern VA]

1963 Carson *History Bourbon* = Carson, Gerald. 1963. *The social history of bourbon: An unhurried account of our star-spangled American drink*. New York: Dodd, Mead.

1963 Corey *Folk Toys* = Corey, John. 1963. Folk toys disregard space age. *Christian Science Monitor*, April 26.

1963 Edwards *Gravel* = Edwards, Lawrence. 1963. *Gravel in my shoe*. Montevallo, AL: Times. [northeast TN]

1963 Glassie *Appal Log Cabin* = Glassie, Henry. 1963. The Appalachian log cabin. *Mountain Life and Work* 39(4): 5–14. [western VA]

1963 Hooper *Unwanted Boy* = Hooper, Ben W. 1963. *The unwanted boy: The autobiography of Governor Ben W. Hooper*. Edited by Everett Robert Boyce. Knoxville: University of Tennessee Press.

1963 Lord *Blue Ridge* = Lord, William G. 1963. *The Blue Ridge guide: From Asheville N.C. to Great Smoky Mountains National Park N.C.* Asheville, NC: Stephens. [western NC]

1963 Medford *Mt People* = Medford, W. Clark. 1963. *Mountain people, mountain times*. Asheville, NC: Miller. [Haywood County, central western NC]

1963 Parris *Witches* = Parris, John. 1963. Witches and witchdoctors once flourished. *Asheville Citizen-Times*, August 13. [central western NC]

1963 Ritchie *Dulcimer Book* = Ritchie, Jean. 1963. *The dulcimer book*. New York: Oak.

1963 Watkins and Watkins *Yesterday* = Watkins, Floyd C., and Charles Hubert Watkins. 1963. *Yesterday in the hills*. Athens: University of Georgia Press. [north central GA]

1963 Weals *Oldtimers* = Weals, Vic. 1963. Oldtimers. *Knoxville Journal*, January 28, 12. [central east TN]

1963 White *Marbles E KY* = White, Edward M. 1963. The vocabulary of marbles in eastern Kentucky. *Kentucky Folklore Record* 9: 57–74. [eastern KY]

1963 Williams *Metaphor* = Williams, Cratis. 1963. Metaphor in mountain speech. *Mountain Life and Work* 39(1): 51–53.

1963 Williams *Metaphor Mt Speech II* = Williams, Cratis D. 1963. Metaphor in mountain speech. *Mountain Life and Work* 39(2): 53–55.

1963 Wilson *Regional Words* = Wilson, Gordon. 1963. Studying folklore in a small region IV: Regional words. *Tennessee Folklore Society Bulletin* 29: 79–86. [south central KY]

1964 Banks *Back to Mts* = Banks, Gabriel Conklyn. 1964. *Back to the mountains: Autobiography of Gabriel Conklyn Banks*. N.p.: Gabriel C. Banks. [eastern KY]

1964 Campbell *Great Smoky Wildflowers* = Campbell, Carlos C. 1964. *Great Smoky Mountains wildflowers*. Knoxville: University of Tennessee Press. [central east TN, central western NC]

1964 Clarke *Stuart's Writings* = Clarke, Mary Washington. 1964. Jesse Stuart's writings preserve passing folk idiom. *Southern Folklore Quarterly* 28: 157–98. [northeastern KY]

1964 Clarkson *Lumbering in WV* = Clarkson, Roy B. 1964. *Tumult on the mountains: Lumbering in West Virginia, 1770–1920*. Parsons, WV: McClain. [WV]

1964 Cooper *History Avery Co* = Cooper, Horton. 1864. *History of Avery County*. Asheville, NC: Biltmore. [Avery County, northwestern NC]

1964 Glassie *Mt Jack Tales* = Glassie, Henry. 1964. Three southern mountain Jack tales. *Tennessee Folklore Society Bulletin* 30: 88–102. [southwestern VA]

1964 Greve *Story of Gatlinburg* = Greve, Jeanette Sterling. 1964. *The story of Gatlinburg*. Gatlinburg, TN: Mangrum. [Sevier County, central east TN]

1964 La Barre *Snake-Handling* = La Barre, Weston. 1964. The snake-handling cult of the American South. In *Cultural anthropology*, edited by Ward Goodenough, 309–33. New York: McGraw-Hill.

1964 Reynolds *Born of Mts* = Reynolds, T. W. 1964. *Born of the mountains*. [Highlands, NC]: n.p. [western NC]

1964 Reynolds *High Lands* = Reynolds, T. W. 1964. *High lands*. N.p.: n.p. [western NC]

1964 Roberts *Hell-Fer-Sartin* = Roberts, Leonard W. 1964. *South from Hell-fer-Sartin*. Berea, KY: Council of the Southern Mountains.

1964 Smith et al. *Germans of Valley* = Smith, Elmer Lewis, John G. Stewart, and M. Ellsworth Kyger. 1964. *The Pennsylvania Germans of the Shenandoah Valley*. Vol. 26. Allentown, PA: Pennsylvania German Folklore Society. [eastern WV]

1964 Stokely *Harvest* = Stokely, Janie May Jones. 1964. *Years of harvest: Poems and tales from the Smoky foothills*. Newport, TN: n.p. [Cocke County, central east TN]

1964 Stupka *Trees Shrubs Vines* = Stupka, Arthur. 1964. *Trees, shrubs, and woody vines of Great Smoky Mountains National Park*. Knoxville: University of Tennessee Press. [central east TN, central western NC]

1964 Thomas and Kob *Ballad Makin'* = Thomas, Jean, and Walter Kob. 1964. *Ballad makin' in the mountains of Kentucky*. New York: Oak. [northeastern KY]

1964 Williams *Prep Mt Speech* = Williams, Cratis D. 1964. Prepositions in mountain speech. *Mountain Life and Work* 40(1): 53–55.

1964 Wilson *Plants and Animals* = Wilson, Gordon. 1964. Words relating to plants and animals in the Mammoth Cave region. *Publication of the American Dialect Society* 42: 11–25. [south central KY]

1964 Wright *Mt Medicine* = Wright, Lillian Mayfield. 1964. Mountain medicine. *North Carolina Folklore* 12: 7–12. [western NC]

1965 Clarke *Proverbs of Stuart* = Clarke, Mary Washington. 1965. Proverbs, proverbial phrases, and proverbial comparisons in the writings of Jesse Stuart. *Southern Folklore Quarterly* 29: 142–63. [northeastern KY]

1965 Cooper *Witches Roamed* = Cooper, Horton. 1965. Witches once thought to have roamed N.C. hills. *Charlotte Observer*, October 31. [western NC]

1965–70 *DARE Survey* = [Responses to interviews conducted by the *Dictionary of American Regional English* project. Field notebooks consulted in DARE office, University of Wisconsin at Madison, in 1994 and 1997, and through its first five published volumes]

1965 Davis *Summer Land* = Davis, Burke. 1965. *Summer land*. New York: Random House.

1965 *Dict Queen's English* = *A dictionary of the Queen's English*. 1965. Raleigh: North Carolina Department of Natural and Economic Resources. [NC]

1965 Ferrell *Bear Tales* = Ferrell, Dorothy. 1965. *Bear tales and panther tracks*. Vol. 1. Atlanta: Appalachian. [north GA]

1965 Glassie *Old Barns* = Glassie, Henry. 1965. Old barns of Appalachia. *Mountain Life and Work* 40(2): 21–30. [western VA]

1965 Green *Hillbilly Music* = Green, Archie. 1965. Hillbilly music: Source and symbol. *Journal of American Folklore* 78: 204–28.

1965 Grossman *Jenkins Cabin* = Grossman, Charles S. 1965. *Historic structures report part I and II: The Chandler Jenkins cabin bldg #147 and pig pen, Indian Camp Truck Trail*. Washington, DC: US National Park Service. [Cocke County, central east TN]

1965 Kupferer *Eastern Cherokee* = Kupferer, Harriet J. 1965. The isolated eastern Cherokee. *Midcontinent American Studies Journal* 6: 124–34. [Swain County, southwestern NC]

1965 Shelton *Pioneer Comforts* = Shelton, Ferne. 1965. *Pioneer comforts and kitchen remedies: Oldtimey highland secrets from the Blue Ridge and Great Smoky Mountains*. High Point, NC: Hutcraft. [central east TN, central western NC]

1965 Shields *Cades Cove* = Shields, A. Randolph. 1965. Cades Cove in the Great Smoky Mountains National Park. *Tennessee Historical Quarterly* 24(3): 3–20. [Blount County, central east TN]

1965 Weller *Yesterday's People* = Weller, Jack E. 1965. *Yesterday's people: Life in contemporary Appalachia*. Lexington: University Press of Kentucky. [WV]

1965 West *Git Turd* = West, John Foster. 1965. They git tard in the hills but hit ain't from talkin'. *Charlotte Observer*, March 21. [western NC]

1965 West *Time Was* = West, John Foster. 1965. *Time was*. New York: Random House. [northwestern NC]

1966 Adams *Mt LeConte* = Adams, Paul J. 1966. *Mt. LeConte*. Knoxville: Holston. [Sevier County, central east TN]

1966 Boykin *Study of Harris* = Boykin, Carol D. 1966. A study of the phonology, morphology, and vocabulary of George Washington Harris' *Sut Lovingood Yarns*. MA thesis, University of Tennessee, Knoxville. [east TN]

1966 Caudill *My Appalachia* = Caudill, Rebecca. 1966. *My Appalachia: A reminiscence*. New York: Holt, Rinehart and Winston. [southeastern KY]

1966 Cox *Dialect Scott Co TN* = Cox, Ellen Duncan. 1966. A study of dialect peculiarities of Scott County, Tennessee secondary school students. MS thesis, University of Tennessee, Knoxville. [Scott County, north central TN]

1966 Dakin *Vocab Ohio River Valley* = Dakin, Robert F. 1966. *The dialect vocabulary of the Ohio River Valley*. 3 vols. PhD diss., University of Michigan, Ann Arbor. [This dictionary cites only the second volume and only for the subregion of eastern KY]

1966 Dykeman *Far Family* = Dykeman, Wilma. 1966. *The far family*. Newport, TN: Wakestone.

1966 Frome *Strangers* = Frome, Michael. 1966. *Strangers in high places: The story of the Great Smoky Mountains*. Garden City, NY: Doubleday. [central east TN, central western NC]

1966 Guthrie *Corn* = Guthrie, Charles S. 1966. Corn: The mainstay of the Cumberland Valley. *Kentucky Folklore Record* 13: 87–91.

1966 Hayes *Greene Co CW* = Hayes, Carl N. 1966. *Neighbor against neighbor, brother against brother: Greene County in the Civil War*. N.p.: Privately published. [Greene County, northeast TN]

1966 Kniffen and Glassie *Building in Wood* = Kniffen, Fred, and Henry Glassie. 1966. Building in wood in the eastern United States: A time-place perspective. *Geographical Review* 56: 40–66.

1966 Medford *Ol' Starlin* = Medford, W. Clark. 1966. *Great Smoky Mountain stories and sun over ol' Starlin*. Waynesville, NC: Miller. [Haywood County, central western NC]

1966 Parris *Time to Go* = Parris, John. 1966. Spring is the time to go gummin'. *Asheville Citizen-Times*, March 17. [central western NC]

1966 West *Dialect Sthn Mts* = West, John Foster. 1966. Dialect of the southern mountains. *North Carolina Folklore* 14: 31–34. [western NC]

1966 Wilson *Coll* = [see c1960 Wilson]

1967 Brewer *Park Creepers* = Brewer, Carson. 1967. Park creepers, crawlers listed in new Smoky book. *Knoxville News-Sentinel*, October 15. [central east TN]

1967 Campbell *Memories of Smoky* = Campbell, Carlos C. 1967. *Memories of old Smoky*. Typescript consulted at Library, Great Smoky Mountains National Park, Gatlinburg, TN. [central east TN, central western NC]

1967 Combs *Folk-Songs* = Combs, Josiah H. 1967. *Folk-songs of the southern*

United States. Edited by D. K. Wilgus. Austin: University of Texas Press. [southeastern KY]

1967 Fetterman *Stinking Creek* = Fetterman, John. 1967. *Stinking Creek*. New York: Dutton. [southeastern KY]

1967 *Food Gathering* = Food gathering. 1967. *Foxfire Magazine* 1(3): 21–24. [Macon County, southwestern NC]

1967 Giles *40 Acres* = Giles, Janice Holt. 1967. Prologue. In *40 acres and no mule* [addition to reprint of 1952 edition]. Philadelphia: Westminster. [southeastern KY]

1967 *Grandmother Cherokee* = My grandmother was a Cherokee and . . . 1967. *Foxfire Magazine* 1(3): 75–81.

1967 Huheey and Stupka *Amphibians and Reptiles* = Huheey, James E., and Arthur Stupka. 1967. *Amphibians and reptiles of Great Smoky Mountains National Park*. Knoxville: University of Tennessee Press. [central east TN, central western NC]

1967 Jones *Peculiarities Mtneers* = Jones, Ora L. 1967. *Peculiarities of the mountaineer: A summary of legends, traditions, signs and superstitions that are almost forgotten*. Detroit: Harlo. [western NC]

1967 Justus *Growing Up* = Justus, May. 1967. Growing up in the Great Smokies. *Appalachian South* 2 (Fall/Winter): 16. [east TN]

1967 Key *Tobacco Vocab* = Key, Mary Ritchie. 1967. Tobacco vocabulary. Typescript on deposit at office of *Dictionary of American Regional English* project, Madison WI. [KY, TN]

1967 Parris *Mt Bred* = Parris, John. 1967. *Mountain bred*. Asheville, NC: Citizen-Times. [central western NC]

1967 *Revival* = Anatomy of a revival. 1967. *Foxfire Magazine* 1(2): 9–12, 47–52. [Rabun County, northeast GA]

1967 Stuart *New Wine* = Stuart, Jesse. 1967. New wine in old bottles. *Kentucky Folklore Record* 13: 20–24. [northeastern KY]

1967 Williams *Moonshining* = Williams, Cratis D. 1967. Moonshining in the mountains. *North Carolina Folklore* 15: 11–17.

1967 Williams *Subtlety Mt Speech* = Williams, Cratis D. 1967. Subtlety in mountain speech. *Mountain Life and Work* 43(1): 14–16.

1967 Wilson *Folkways Mammoth Cave* = Wilson, Gordon. 1967. *Folkways of the Mammoth Cave region*. No. 2. N.p.: National Park Concessions. [south central KY]

1968 *Best Was Made* = How the best of the best was made. 1968. *Foxfire Magazine* 2(3–4): 102–6.

1968 Birch et al. *Sorghum* = Birch, George, Judy Brown, and David Wilson. 1968. Sorghum: Home-grown syrup. *Foxfire Magazine* 2(3–4): 26–29.

1968 *Busthaid* = Busthaid Blockade Popskull. 1968. *Foxfire Magazine* 2(3–4): 100–101.

1968 Clarke *Stuart's Kentucky* = Clarke, Mary Washington. 1968. *Jesse Stuart's Kentucky*. New York: McGraw-Hill. [northeastern KY]

1968 Comstock *Hillbilly* = Whittaker, Otto, ed. 1968. *Best of "Hillbilly": A prize collection of 100 percent writing from Jim Comstock's West Virginia hillbilly*. Anderson, SC: Droke. [WV]

1968 Connelly *Discover Appal* = Connelly, Thomas L. 1968. *Discovering the Appalachians: What to look for from the past and in the present along America's eastern frontier*. Harrisburg, PA: Stackpole.

1968 *Crafts* = Crafts: Making and weaving your own white oak splints. 1968. *Foxfire Magazine* 2(2): 7–11. [Rabun County, northeast GA and Macon County, southwestern NC

1968 *End of Moonshining* = The end of moonshining as a fine art. 1968. *Foxfire Magazine* 2(3–4): 35–56, 89–110.

1968 *Expressions* = Expressions. 1968. *Foxfire Magazine* 2(3–4): 23–25. [northeast GA]

1968 *Faith Healing* = Faith healing. 1968. *Foxfire Magazine* 2(1): 15–24, 61–70.

1968 Ferrell *Bear Tales* = Ferrell, Dorothy. 1968. *Bear tales and panther tracks*. Vol. 2. Atlanta: Appalachian. [north GA]

1968 Glassie *Material Folk Cult* = Glassie, Henry. 1968. *Pattern in the material folk culture in the eastern United States*. Philadelphia: University of Pennsylvania Press.

1968 Grimm *Flowering Plants* = Grimm, William Carey. 1968. *How to recognize flowering wild plants*. New York: Castle Books.

1968 Guthrie *Tobacco* = Guthrie, Charles S. 1968. Tobacco: Cash crop of the Cumberland Valley. *Kentucky Folklore Record* 14: 38–43.

1968 Justus *It Happened* = Justus, May. 1968. *It happened in No-End Hollow*. Champaign, IL: Garrard. [east TN]

1968 Powell *NC Gazetteer* = Powell, William S. 1968. *The North Carolina gazetteer*. Chapel Hill: University of North Carolina Press. [NC]

1968 *Raised Up* = This is the way I was raised up. 1968. *Foxfire Magazine* 2(1): 8–9.

1968 *Remedies* = Home remedies. 1968. *Foxfire Magazine* 2(1): 10–14.

1968 *Sang Season* = Sang season. 1968. *Foxfire Magazine* 2(1): 28–32, 72–77. [Rabun County, northeast GA]

1968 *Sang Signs* = Sang signs. 1968. *Foxfire Magazine* 2(2): 15, 17–52. [Rabun County, northeast GA]

1968 Sharp and Karpeles *Songs Sthn Appal* = Sharp, Cecil J., and Maud Karpeles. 1968. *Eighty English folk songs from the southern Appalachians*. Cambridge, MA: MIT Press

1968 Vincent *Best Stories* = Vincent, Bert. 1968. *The best stories of Bert Vincent*. Maryville, TN: Brazos. [central east TN]

1968 Wilson *Folklore Mammoth Cave* = Wilson, Gordon. 1968. *Folklore of the Mammoth Cave region*. Bowling Green, KY: Kentucky Folklore Society. [south central KY]

1968 Wilson *Local Plants* = Wilson, Gordon. 1968. Local plants in folk remedies in the Mammoth Cave region. *Southern Folklore Quarterly* 32: 320–27. [south central KY]

1969–70 *Burton-Manning Coll* = Burton-Manning Collection. 1969–70. [Selected audio interviews, transcribed for this book]. Thomas Burton-Ambrose Manning Collection. Archives of Appalachia, East Tennessee State University, Johnson City. [northeast TN, northwestern NC]

1969 *DARE FW Addit* = [interview addenda and notes collected by interviewers for the *Dictionary of American English* project, located at the University of Wisconsin]. 1969. Madison: University of Wisconsin.

1969 Dial *Dialect Appal People* = Dial, Wylene. 1969. The dialect of the Appalachian people. *West Virginia History* 30: 463–71. [WV]

1969 Doran *Folklore White Co* = Doran, Edwina Bean. 1969. Folklore in White County, Tennessee. PhD diss., George Peabody College, Nashville, TN. [central TN]

1969 Ferrell *Bear Tales* = Ferrell, Dorothy. 1969. *Bear tales and panther tracks*. Vol. 3. Atlanta: Appalachian. [north GA]

1969 Foust *Kingdom of Wilkes* = Foust, Clora McNeill. 1969. *Horse and buggy days in the "Kingdom of Wilkes."* N.p.: Privately published. [Wilkes County, northwestern NC]

1969 Hannum *Look Back* = Hannum, Alberta Pierson. 1969. *Look back with love*, 29–33. New York: Vanguard. [northwestern NC, south central VA]

1969 Justus *Eben and Rattlesnake* = Justus, May. 1969. *Eben and the rattlesnake*. Champaign, IL: Garrard. [east TN]

1969 Lee *Bloodletting* = Lee, Howard B. 1969. *Bloodletting in Appalachia: The story of West Virginia's four major mine wars and other thrilling incidents of the coal fields*. Morgantown: West Virginia University Press. [WV]

1969 Madden and Jones *Alfred Reagan* = Madden, Robert R., and T. Russell Jones. 1969. *Alfred Reagan house and tub mill: Historic structures report, Great Smoky Mountains National Park, historic data section*. Washington, DC: US National Park Service. [Sevier County, central east TN]

1969 Madden and Jones *Walker Sisters* = Madden, Robert R., and T. Russell Jones. 1969. *Walker Sisters Home: Historic structures report part II and furnishings, Great Smoky Mountains National Park, historic data section*. Washington, DC: US National Park Service. [Sevier County, central east TN]

1969 Medford *Finis* = Medford, W. Clark. 1969. *Finis and farewell*. Waynesville, NC: Privately published. [central western NC]

1969 Miller *Raising Tobacco* = Miller, Jim Wayne. 1969. The vocabulary and methods of raising burley tobacco in western North Carolina. *North Carolina Folklore* 17: 27–38.

1969 *Mize Dulcimers* = Mize, Robert. 1969. Dulcimers. *Foxfire Magazine* 3(1): 5–8. [Rabun County, northeast GA]

1969 *Mt Recipes* = Mountain recipes. 1969. *Foxfire Magazine* 3(3): 25–26, 58–61. [Rabun County, northeast GA]

1969 Newell *Genus Joinvillea* = Newell, Thomas. 1969. A study of the genus Joinvillea (Flagellariaceae). *Journal of the Arnold Arboretum* 50: 527–54. [WV]

1969 *Own Log Cabin* = Building your own log cabin. 1969. *Foxfire Magazine* 3(2): 9–32.

1969 Parris *Hard Likker* = Parris, John. 1969. Soft water, hard likker. *Asheville Citizen-Times*, January 15. [central western NC]

1969 Parris *Uncle Smart Carter* = Parris, John. 1969. Uncle Smart Carter was feared conjurin' man. *Asheville Citizen-Times*, April 21. [central western NC]

1969 Roberts *Greasybeard* = Roberts, Leonard W. 1969. *Old Greasybeard: Tales from the Cumberland Gap.* Detroit: Folklore Associates. [southeastern KY]

1969 Royall *Letters from AL* = Royall, Anne Newport. 1969. *Letters from Alabama, 1817–1822.* Biographical introduction and notes by Lucille Griffith. Tuscaloosa: University of Alabama Press. [northern AL]

1969 *Something Human* = A quilt is something human. 1969. *Foxfire Magazine* 3(3): 5–7, 44–49. [Rabun County, northeast GA]

1969 Sorden *Lumber Lingo* = Sorden, L. G. 1969. *Lumberjack lingo.* Spring Green, WI: Wisconsin House.

1969 *Sunday Gazette Mail* = *Charleston (WV) Gazette.* 1969. [Untitled article]. May 11. In DARE File. [WV]

1969 Wall *History Davie Co* = Wall, Robert W. 1969. *History of Davie County in the forks of the Yadkin.* Mocksville, NC: Davie County Historical Publishing. [Davie County, northwestern NC]

1969 Weslager *Log Cabin in America* = Weslager, C. A. 1969. *The log cabin in America.* New Brunswick, NJ: Rutgers University Press.

1970 Adams *Appal Revisit* = Adams, Frazier B. 1970. *Appalachia revisited: How people lived fifty years ago.* Ashland, KY: Economy.

1970 *Aunt Airy* = Aunt Airy. 1970. *Foxfire Magazine* 4(1–2): 4–7, 86–95. [Macon County, southwestern NC]

1970 Broome *Earth Man* = Broome, Harvey. 1970. *Harvey Broome, earth man: Some miscellaneous writings.* Knoxville: Greenbrier. [east TN]

1970 Campbell et al. *Smoky Mt Wildflowers* = Campbell, Carlos C., W. F. Hudson, and A. J. Sharp. 1970. *Great Smoky Mountains wildflowers.* Knoxville: University of Tennessee Press. [central east TN, central western NC]

1970 Clark *NC Beliefs* = Clark, Joseph D. 1970. North Carolina popular beliefs and superstitions. *North Carolina Folklore* 18(1): 9–34. [NC]

1970 Drake *Federal Union* = Drake, Richard B. 1970. The Appalachians and the federal union. In *An Appalachian reader*, 46–66. Berea, KY: Richard Drake.

1970 *Dressing and Cooking* = Dressing and cooking game. 1970. *Foxfire Magazine* 4(1–2): 18–26.

1970–74 Foster *Walker Valley* = Foster, Lloyd. 1970–74. *History of Walker Valley* [interviews transcribed by Mary Ruth Chiles]. Typescript consulted at Library, Great Smoky Mountains National Park, Gatlinburg, TN. [Sevier County, central east TN]

1970–73 *Foxfire Interviews* = [Selected audio interviews, transcribed for this book]. 1970–73. Foxfire Project, Rabun Gap, GA. [Rabun County, northeast GA, Macon County, southwestern NC]

1970 Hall *Witchlore* = Hall, Joseph S. 1970. Witchlore and ghostlore in the Great Smokies. *Tennessee Folklore Society Bulletin* 36(1): 1–6; 36(2): 31–36. [central east TN, central western NC]

c1970 Handlon *Ol' Smoky* = Handlon, Anne Emily. c1970. *Ol' Smoky* [consulted at Library, Great Smoky Mountains National Park, Gatlinburg, TN]. N.p.: n.p. [Sevier County, central east TN]

1970 *Hillard Green* = Hillard Green. 1970. *Foxfire Magazine* 4(3): 134–44. [Macon County, southwestern NC]

1970 *Hunting* = Hunting: Training dogs and hunting techniques. 1970. *Foxfire Magazine* 4(1–2): 8–17, 70–76.

1970 *Hunting Stories* = Hunting stories. 1970. *Foxfire Magazine* 4(1–2): 28–35, 77–86.

1970 Jones *Oliver Barn* = Jones, Russell. 1970. *Leige Oliver barn and corn crib: Historic structures report architectural data.* Washington, DC: US National Park Service.

1970 Justus *Holidays* = Justus, May. 1970. *Holidays in No-End Hollow.* Champaign, IL: Garrard. [east TN]

1970 Justus *Tales* = Justus, May. 1970. *Tales from near-side and far.* Champaign, IL: Garrard. [east TN]

1970 Lombard *Hills of Home* = Lombard, Frances Baumgarner. 1970. *From the hills of home in western North Carolina.* N.p.: n.p. [western NC]

1970 Madden and Jones *Ephraim Bales* = Madden, Robert R., and T. Russell Jones. 1970. *Ephraim Bales wood shed and meat house historic structures report.* Washington, DC: US National Park Service. [Sevier County, central east TN]

1970 Mead *Handbook Denominations* = Mead, Frank S. 1970. *Handbook of denominations.* Nashville: Abingdon.

1970 Montell *Coe Ridge* = Montell, Lynwood. 1970. *The saga of Coe Ridge: A study in oral history.* Knoxville: University of Tennessee Press. [Monroe and Cumberland Counties, south central KY]

1970 Mull *Mt Yarns* = Mull, J. Alexander. 1970. *Mountain yarns, legends, and lore.* Banner Elk, NC: Pudding Stone. [western NC]

1970 Roberts and Roberts *Time Stood Still* = Roberts, Bruce, and Nancy Roberts. 1970. *Where time stood still: A portrait of Appalachia.* New York: Crowell-Collier.

1970 *Slaughtering* = Slaughtering, curing and cooking hog. 1970. *Foxfire Magazine* 4(1–2): 36–48, 65–69.

1970 Smith *Folk Customs* = Smith, Marilyn. 1970. Folk customs of Jefferson County, Tennessee. In *A collection of folklore by undergraduate students at East Tennessee State University*, edited by Thomas G. Burton and Ambrose N. Manning, 54–57. Johnson City: East Tennessee State University. [Jefferson County, central east TN]

1970 *Snake Lore* = Snake lore. 1970. *Foxfire Magazine* 4(3): 166–77.

1970 *Valuable Possession* = My most valuable possession. 1970. *Foxfire Magazine* 4(4): 242–45.

1970 Vincent *More of Best* = Vincent, Bert. 1970. *More of the best stories of Bert Vincent.* Maryville, TN: Mangrum. [east TN]

1970 *Weather Signs* = Weather signs. 1970. *Foxfire Magazine* 4(4): 206–9.

1971–75 AOHP/ALC = [Selected audio interviews, transcribed for this book]. 1971–75. Appalachian Oral History Project, Alice Lloyd College Library, Pippa Passes, KY. [various counties, southeastern KY]

1971 *Arie's Egg Custard* = Aunt Arie's recipe for egg custard (cooked on a wood stove). 1971. *Foxfire Magazine* 5(1–2): 95. [Macon County, southwestern NC]

1971 *Beekeeping* = Beekeeping. 1971. *Foxfire Magazine* 5(3): 161–73.

1971 *Boogers* = Boogers, witches, and haints. 1971. *Foxfire Magazine* 5(1–2): 28–48, 65–79.

1971 Brewer *Your Community* = Brewer, Carson. 1971. This is your community. *Knoxville News-Sentinel*, November 1. [east TN]

1971 Chapman *Uses for Sumac* = Chapman, Ashton. 1971. Early settlers found many uses for sumac. *Asheville Citizen-Times*, October 25. [western NC]

1971 *Corn Shuckin's* = Corn shuckin's house raisin's quiltin's pea thrashin's singin's log rollin's candy pullin's and . . . 1971. *Foxfire Magazine* 5(1–2): 96–108.

1971 Costner *Song of Life* = Costner, Ella V. 1971. *Song of life in the Smokies: Stories of mine own people and sketches of life as it was lived in the mountains before the park took over.* Maryville, TN: Brazos. [Cocke County, central east TN]

1971 Diehl *Stripping Myths* = Diehl, Rick. 1971. Stripping away the myths. *Peoples Appalachia*, September/October, 5–10.

1971 *Dowdle* = Happy Dowdle: An interview with Happy Dowdle and his wife. 1971. *Foxfire Magazine* 5(1–2): 10–27. [Macon County, southwestern NC]

1971 Dwyer *Dict for Yankees* = Dwyer, Paul. 1971. *Dictionary for Yankees and other uneducated people.* Highlands, NC: Merry Mountaineers.

1971 Fetterman *People Cumberland Gap* = Fetterman, John. 1971. The people of Cumberland Gap. *National Geographic* 140: 591–620. [southeastern KY, northeast TN]

1971 Fox *Mouth of Mtneer* = Fox, Ruby O. 1971. *From the mouth of the mountaineer.* N.p.: Privately published.

1971 Gordon *Moonshining in GA* = Gordon, John. 1971. Slingings and high shots: Moonshining in the Georgia mountains. In *The not so solid South*, edited by Kenneth Morland, 56–64. Athens: University of Georgia Press. [north GA]

1971 *Granny Women* = Midwives and granny women. 1971. *Foxfire Magazine* 5(4): 238–62.

1971 Hutchins *Hidden Valley* = Hutchins, Ross E. 1971. *Hidden valley of the Smokies with a naturalist in the Great Smoky Mountains.* New York: Dodd, Mead. [east TN]

1971 Justus *Jumping Johnny* = Justus, May. 1971. *Jumping Johnny outwits Skedaddle.* Champaign, IL: Garrard. [east TN]

1971 *Kenny Runnion* = Kenny Runnion. 1971. *Foxfire Magazine* 5(3): 128–41.

1971 Krochmal et al. *Medicinal Plants Appal* = Krochmal, Arnold, Russell Walters, and Richard M. Doughty. 1971. *A guide to medicinal plants of Appalachia.* Washington, DC: US Forest Service.

1971 Lee *My Appalachia* = Lee, Howard B. 1971. *My Appalachia.* Charleston, WV: McClain. [southern WV]

1971 Linzey and Linzey *Mammals of Smoky* = Linzey, A. V., and D. W. Linzey. 1971. *Mammals of Great Smoky Mountains National Park.* Knoxville: University of Tennessee Press. [central east TN, central western NC

1971 Stevens *Mountain Craftsmen* = Stevens, Bernice. 1971. *Our mountain craftsmen.* Gatlinburg, TN: Buckhorn. [east TN]

1971 *Sunday with Arie* = Sunday with Aunt Arie. 1971. *Foxfire Magazine* 5(1–2): 80–87. [Macon County, southwestern NC]

1971 Thornburgh *Great Smoky Mts* = Thornburgh, Laura [published under the name Laura Thornborough]. 1971. *The Great Smoky Mountains.* Rev. and enlarged ed. of 1937 original. Knoxville: University of Tennessee Press. [central east TN]

1971 Wood *Vocab Change* = Wood, Gordon Reid. 1971. *Vocabulary change.* Carbondale: Southern Illinois University Press.

1972–75 *AOHP/EH* = [Selected audio interviews, transcribed for this book]. 1972–75. Appalachian Oral History Project, Emory & Henry College Library, Emory, VA. [western VA]

1972 Alderman *Big Bald* = Alderman, Pat. 1972. *In the shadow of Big Bald: About the Appalachians and their people.* Mars Hill, NC: Bald Mountain Development Corporation. [northeast TN]

1972 *Anna Howard* = Anna Howard. 1972. *Foxfire Magazine* 6(1): 50–55. [Macon County, southwestern NC]

1972–75 *AOHP/LJC* = [Selected audio interviews, transcribed for this book]. 1972–75. Appalachian Oral History Project, Lees Junior College Library, Jackson, KY. [various counties, southeastern KY]

1972 *Burial Customs* = Old-time burial customs. 1972. *Foxfire Magazine* 6(1): 8–25.

1972 Carr *Oldest Profession* = Carr, Jess. 1972. *The second oldest profession: An informal history of moonshining in America.* Englewood Cliffs, NJ: Prentice Hall.

1972 Carson and Vick *Hillbilly Cookin* = Carson, Sam, and A. W. Vick. 1972. *Hillbilly cookin.* Thorn Hill, TN: Clinch Mountain Lookout.

1972 Carson and Vick *Cookin 2* = Carson, Sam, and A. W. Vick. 1972. *Hillbilly cookin 2.* Thorn Hill, TN: Clinch Mountain Lookout.

1972 Clarke *Dance in Trough* = Clarke, Mary Washington. 1972. To dance in a hog trough. *Kentucky Folklore Record* 18: 68–69. [northeastern KY]

1972 Cooper *NC Mt Folklore* = Cooper, Horton. 1972. *North Carolina mountain folklore and miscellany.* Murfreesboro, NC: Johnson. [northwestern NC]

1972 Davis *Christmas* = Davis, Hubert J. 1972. *Christmas in the mountains: Southwest Virginia Christmas customs and their origins.* Murfreesboro, NC: Johnson. [southwestern VA]

1972 Ensor *Tales of Supernatural* = Ensor, Wanda. 1972. Tales of the supernatural collected in Mitchell and Yancey Counties, northwestern North Carolina. *Tennessee Folklore Society Bulletin* 38: 61–71. [northwestern NC]

1972 *Foxfire I* = Wigginton, Eliot, ed. 1972. *Foxfire 1: The Foxfire book: Hog dressing; log cabin building; mountain crafts and foods; planting by the signs; snake lore, hunting tales, faith healing; moonshining; and other affairs of plain living.* New York: Doubleday.

1972 *Graham County* = *Graham County centennial, 1872–1972.* 1972. Robbinsville, NC: Graham County Centennial, Inc. [southwestern NC]

1972 Hall *Sayings* = Hall, Joseph S. 1972. *Sayings from old Smoky.* Asheville, NC: Cataloochee. [central east TN, central western NC]

1972 *Hide Tanning* = Hide tanning. 1972. *Foxfire Magazine* 6(3): 178–92.

1972 *Kelly* = Ada Kelly. 1972. *Foxfire Magazine* 6(2–3): 80–87.

1972 Parris *Storied Mts* = Parris, John. 1972. *These storied mountains.* Asheville, NC: Citizen-Times. [central western NC]

1972 *Raising Sheep* = "I've been raising sheep for forty years." 1972. *Foxfire Magazine* 6(2–3): 88–101.

1972 Walls and Stephenson *Appal in Sixties* = Walls, David S., and John B. Stephenson, eds. 1972. *Appalachia in the sixties: Decade of reawakening.* Lexington: University Press of Kentucky.

1972 Williams *Sthn Mtneers* = Williams, Cratis D. 1972. Who are the southern mountaineers? *Appalachian Journal* 4: 174–81.

1973–74 *AOHP/ASU* = [Selected audio interviews, transcribed for this book]. 1973–74. Appalachian Oral History Project, 1965–79, Eury Appalachian Collection, Belk Library, Appalachian State University, Boone, NC. [northwestern NC]

1973 Brower *Split-Rail Fence* = Brower, Nancy. 1973. The split-rail fence: David Webb revives art. *Asheville Times*, October 29. [western NC]

1973 *Carpenter* = Mary Carpenter. 1973. *Foxfire Magazine* 7(2): 118–30. [Rabun County, northeast GA]

1973 Carpenter *Mid-Appal* = Carpenter, Charles. 1973. Pronunciation and grammar of mid-Appalachia. *Journal of the Alleghenies* 9: 31–35. [WV]

1973 Cate *Molasses Making* = Cate, Herma. 1973. Molasses making. *Maryville-Alcoa Daily Times*, October 10. [Blount County, central east TN]

1973 *Church of God* = A church of God. 1973. *Foxfire Magazine* 7(1): 5–13.

1973 *Corn Shocks* = Corn shocks. 1973. *Foxfire Magazine* 7(4): 325.

c1973 Crabtree *Rememberin'* = Crabtree, Margaret Stinnett. c1973. Rememberin' the Little Greenbriar School and Primitive Baptist Church. Typescript consulted at Library, Great Smoky Mountains National Park, Gatlinburg, TN. [Blount County, central east TN]

1973 Davis *'Pon My Honor* = Davis, Hubert J. 1973. *'Pon my honor, hit's the truth: Tall tales from the mountains.* Murfreesboro, NC: Johnson.

1973 *Dipper Gourds* = Dipper gourds. 1973. *Foxfire Magazine* 7(4): 280–85. [Rabun County, northeast GA]

1973 *Ethel Corn* = Ethel Corn. 1973. *Foxfire Magazine* 7(4): 260–67. [Rabun County, northeast GA]

1973 *Florence and Lawton* = Florence and Lawton. 1973. *Foxfire Magazine* 7(3): 192–208. [Jackson County, southwestern NC]

1973 *Flu Epidemic* = The flu epidemic. 1973. *Foxfire Magazine* 7(2): 100–11. [Rabun County, northeast GA, and Jackson County, southwestern NC]

1973 *Foxfire II* = Wigginton, Eliot, ed. 1973. *Foxfire 2: Ghost stories, spring wild plant foods, spinning and weaving, midwifing, burial customs, corn shuckin's, wagon making and more affairs of plain living.* Garden City, NY: Anchor.

1973 Ganier *Wildlife First Met* = Ganier, Albert. 1973. The wildlife met by Tennessee's first settlers. *The Migrant* 44: 58–72. [east TN]

1973 *Gardening* = Gardening. 1973. *Foxfire Magazine* 7(3): 228–52.

1973 *Garland Willis* = Garland Willis. 1973. *Foxfire Magazine* 7(1): 76–82. [Macon County, southwestern NC]

1973 *Gathered Together* = For where two or three are gathered together in my name, there am I in the midst of them. 1973. *Foxfire Magazine* 7(1): 14–30.

1973 *Hair Singed* = Nor was a hair of their head singed. 1973. *Foxfire Magazine* 7(1): 48–51.

1973 *Holidays* = Holidays. 1973. *Foxfire Magazine* 7(4): 326–38.

1973 Irwin *Arnwine* = Irwin, John Rice. 1973. *A brief history of the Arnwine Cabin and the pioneer artifacts it contains: One of thirteen such structures located in the Museum of Appalachia*. Norris, TN: Museum of Appalachia. [east TN]

1973 Joines *Twister Tales* = Joines, Jerry. 1973. Twister tall tales from Wilkes County. *North Carolina Folklore Journal* 20: 3–11. [Wilkes County, northwestern NC]

1973 Jones *Cades Cove TN* = Jones, Jean. 1973. The regional English of the former inhabitants of Cades Cove in the Great Smoky Mountains. PhD diss., University of Tennessee, Knoxville. [Blount County, central east TN]

1973 Kahn *Hillbilly Women* = Kahn, Kathy. 1973. *Hillbilly women*. New York: Doubleday.

1973 *Lay Hands* = They shall lay hands on the sick, and they shall recover. 1973. *Foxfire Magazine* 7(1): 52–58.

1973 McCarthy *Child of God* = McCarthy, Cormac. 1973. *Child of God*. New York: Random House.

1973 McDavid and McDavid *Vocab E KY* = McDavid, Raven I., Jr., and Virginia G. McDavid. 1973. The folk vocabulary of eastern Kentucky. In *Lexicography and dialect geography*, edited by Harald Scholler and John Reidy, 147–64. Wiesbaden: Steiner Verlag. [eastern KY]

1973 McKamey *Park VIP* = McKamey, Jeannine. 1973. Park VIP works to save history. *Gatlinburg Press*, March 1, A3. [Sevier County, central east TN]

1973 Medford *Long Hard Road* = Medford, W. Clark. 1973. *The long hard road*. Waynesville, NC: Privately published. [central western NC]

1973 Miller *English Unicoi Co* = Miller, Tracey R. 1973. An investigation of the regional English of Unicoi County. PhD diss., University of Tennessee, Knoxville. [northeast TN]

1973 Mullins *Herbs KY Highlands* = Mullins, Gladys. 1973. Herbs of the southern highlands and their medicinal uses. *Kentucky Folklore Record* 19: 36–41. [eastern KY]

1973 Preston *Bituminous Term* = Preston, Dennis R. 1973. Bituminous coal mining vocabulary of the eastern United States. *Publication of the American Dialect Society* 59.

1973 Primack *ARC* = Primack, Phil. ARC: In case you were wondering about ARC but didn't know where to look. *Mountain Life and Work* 49(3): 6–9.

1973 Schulman *Logging Terms* = Schulman, Steven A. 1973. Logging terms from the Upper Cumberland River. *Tennessee Folklore Society Bulletin* 39: 35–36. [south central KY]

1973 *Serpents* = They shall take up serpents. 1973. *Foxfire Magazine* 7(1): 31–47.

1973 Van Noppen *Western NC* = Van Noppen, Ina. 1973. *Western North Carolina since the Civil War*. Boone, NC: Appalachian Consortium Press. [western NC]

1973 Watkins and Watkins *Yesterday* = Watkins, Floyd C., and Charles Hubert Watkins. 1973. *Yesterday in the hills* [revised version of 1963 original]. Athens: University of Georgia Press. [Cherokee County, north central GA]

1973 Wellman *Kingdom of Madison* = Wellman, Manly Wade. 1973. *The kingdom of Madison: A southern mountain fastness and its people*. Chapel Hill: University of North Carolina Press. [Madison County, central western NC]

1973 *Words & Expressions* = Words and expressions. 1973. *Foxfire Magazine* 7(2): 133–38.

1974 Aiken *Offield CW Letters* = Aiken, Leona Taylor. 1974. Letters of the Offield brothers, Confederate soldiers from upper East Tennessee. *East Tennessee Historical Society Publication* 46: 116–25. [northeast TN]

1974 Betts and Walser *NC Folklore* = Betts, Leonidas, and Richard Walser. 1974. *Gateway to North Carolina folklore*. Raleigh: North Carolina State University School of Education. [western NC]

1974 Brewer *Your Community 1* = Brewer, Carson. 1974. This is your community. *Knoxville News-Sentinel*, July 28. [east TN]

1974 Brewer *Your Community 2* = Brewer, Carson. 1974. This is your community. *Knoxville News-Sentinel*, October 10. [east TN]

1974 Bruce *Sang Hallelujah* = Bruce, Dickson R., Jr. 1974. *And they all sang Hallelujah: Plain-folk, camp-meeting religion, 1800–1845*. Knoxville: University of Tennessee Press.

1974 Cate *Winter Food Supply* = Cate, Herma. 1974. Winter food supply. *Maryville-Alcoa Daily Times*. November 6. [Blount County, central east TN]

1974 Cate et al. *Sthn Appal Heritage* = Cate, Herma, Clyde Ussery, and Randy Armstrong. 1974. *Our southern Appalachian heritage*. Kingsport, TN: Holston. [Blount County, central east TN]

1974 *Cornshuck Dolls* = Cornshuck dolls. 1974. *Foxfire Magazine* 8(1): 78–81. [Rabun County, northeast GA]

1974 Dabney *Mt Spirits* = Dabney, Joseph E. 1974. *Mountain spirits: A chronicle of corn whiskey from King James' Ulster plantation to America's Appalachians and the moonshine life*. New York: Scribner's Sons. [north GA]

1974 *Death and Burial* = Death and burial in the mountains. 1974. *Appalachian Heritage* 2 (Winter): 57–63.

1974 Dwyer and Dwyer *Mt Cookin'* = Dwyer, Louise, and Bil Dwyer. 1974. *Mountain cookin'*. Highlands, NC: Merry Mountaineers.

1974 Fink *Bits Mt Speech* = Fink, Paul [M.]. 1974. *Bits of mountain speech*. Boone, NC: Appalachian Consortium Press. [northeast TN, northwestern NC]

1974 Harris *High Times* = Harris, George Washington. 1974. *High times and hard times*. Edited by M. Thomas Inge. Nashville, TN: Vanderbilt University Press. [east TN]

1974 *Instrument Makers* = A special issue devoted to instrument makers. 1974. *Foxfire Magazine* 8(3): 177–240.

1974 Jones *Preface* = Jones, Loyal. 1974. Preface. In *A right good people*, by Harold F. Warren. Boone, NC: Appalachian Consortium Press.

1974 Maurer and Pearl *KY Moonshine* = Maurer, David W., and Quinn Pearl. 1974. *Kentucky moonshine*. Lexington: University Press of Kentucky.

1974–75 McCracken *Logging* = McCracken, Weaver H., III. 1974–75. [Interviews about logging in Great Smoky Mountains. 24 vols. of transcripts made by Mary Ruth Chiles, consulted at Library, Great Smoky Mountains National Park, Gatlinburg, TN] [central east TN]

1974 Moore *Dr. Mac* = Moore, Iva McMahan. 1974. *"Dr. Mac": A beloved physician* [consulted at Library, Great Smoky Mountains National Park, Gatlinburg, TN]. N.p.: n.p. [Sevier County, central east TN]

1974 Murray *Down to Earth* = Murray, Kenneth. 1974. *Down to earth: People of Appalachia*. Boone, NC: Appalachian Consortium Press. [southeastern KY]

1974 *No Sang* = One of these days there ain't gonna be no sang. 1974. *Foxfire Magazine* 8(1): 4–24.

1974 Ogle *Memories* = Ogle, Philip. 1974. Memories by Maggie Clabough Ogle. Typescript consulted at Library, Great Smoky Mountains National Park, Gatlinburg, TN. [Sevier County, central east TN]

1974 Raulston and Livingood *Sequatchie* = Raulston, J. Leonard, and James W. Livingood. 1974. *Sequatchie: A story of the southern Cumberlands*. Knoxville: University of Tennessee Press. [Sequatchie County, southeast TN]

1974 Roberts *Sang Branch* = Roberts, Leonard. 1974. *Sang Branch settlers: Folksongs and tales of a Kentucky mountain family*. Austin: University of Texas Press. [southeastern KY]

1974 Russell *Hillbilly* = Russell, Gladys Trentham. 1974. *Call me hillbilly: A personal account of growing up in the Smokies near Gatlinburg*. Alcoa, TN: Russell. [Sevier County, central east TN]

1974 Underwood *Madison Co* = Underwood, Jinsie. 1974. *This is Madison County*. N.p.: Privately published. [Madison County, central western NC]

1974 Warren *Good People* = Warren, Harold F. 1974. *A right good people*. Boone, NC: Appalachian Consortium Press. [western NC]

1974 Wood *Mt Memories* = Wood, Lawrence Edward. 1974. *Mountain memories*. Franklin, NC: Privately published. [southwestern NC]

1975 *Another Look* = Another look at moonshining. 1975. *Foxfire Magazine* 9(2–3): 132–44.

1975 Brewer *Valley So Wild* = Brewer, Alberta, and Carson Brewer. 1975. *Valley so wild: A folk history*. Knoxville: East Tennessee Historical Society. [southeast TN]

1975 Broome *Out under Smokies* = Broome, Harvey. 1975. *Out under the sky of the Great Smokies: A personal journal*. Knoxville: Greenbrier. [central east TN, central western NC]

1975 Carawan and Carawan *Voices from Mt* = Carawan, Guy, and Candie Carawan. 1975. *Voices from the mountain*. New York: Knopf.

1975 Carter *Gospel Truth* = Carter, Ted. 1975. It's the gospel truth. *Asheville Citizen-Times*, December 11. [western NC]

1975 Chalmers *Better* = Chalmers, Marjorie. 1975. *"Better I stay": An invitation in the Great Smokies*. Gatlinburg, TN: Crescent. [Sevier County, central east TN]

1975 *Change in Lifestyle* = Change: A difference in lifestyle. 1975. *Foxfire Magazine* 9(1): 45–51. [Rabun County, northeast GA and Jackson County, southwestern NC]

1975 *Cucumber Doll* = Making a cucumber doll. 1975. *Foxfire Magazine* 9(4): 376–78. [Rabun County, northeast GA]

1975 Dial *Yesterday's Lg* = Dial, Wylene. 1975. Yesterday's language. In *Mountain heritage*, edited by Beryl Blake Maurer, 92–93. Ripley, WV: Mountain State Art and Craft Fair. [WV]

1975 Doolittle *Sthn Appal* = Doolittle, Jerome. 1975. *The southern Appalachians*. New York: Time-Life Books.

1975 Duncan *Mt Sayens* = Duncan, Mary Lou. 1975. Mountain sayens: "Dog days" to "dogwood winter." *Mountain Call* 2(1): 31.

1975 Dwyer *Thangs* = Dwyer, Paul. 1975. Thangs Yankees don' know: Dialect, lawin', greens, recipes, squar' dancin', beauty aids, wild life, remedies, signs, stills, and folks. Highlands, NC: Merry Mountaineers.

1975 *Fiddle Making* = Fiddle making. 1975. *Foxfire Magazine* 9(4): 307–23. [Macon County, southwestern NC, Yancey County, northwestern NC]

1975 Fink *Backpacking* = Fink, Paul [M.]. 1975. *Backpacking was the only way*. Johnson City: East Tennessee State University. [central east TN]

1975 Fink *Foreword* = Fink, Paul [M.]. 1975. Foreword. In *Home in Madison County*, by Lena Penland Purkey. Johnson City: East Tennessee State University.

1975 *Foxfire III* = Wigginton, Eliot, ed. 1975. *Foxfire 3: Animal care, banjos and dulcimers, hide tanning, summer and fall wild plant foods, butter churns, ginseng, and still more affairs of plain living*. Garden City, NY: Anchor.

1975 Gainer *Speech Mtneer* = Gainer, Patrick W. 1975. Speech of the mountaineers. In *Witches, ghosts and signs: Folklore of the southern Appalachians*, 1–18. Morgantown, WV: Seneca. [WV]

1975 Gainer *Witches Ghosts Signs* = Gainer, Patrick. 1975. *Witches, ghosts and signs: Folklore of the southern Appalachians*. Morgantown, WV: Seneca. [WV]

1975 *Grist Mill* = The grist mill. 1975. *Foxfire Magazine* 9(1): 18–21. [Rabun County, northeast GA]

1975 Hamel and Chiltoskey *Cherokee Plants* = Hamel, Paul D., and Mary Ulmer Chiltoskey. 1975. *Cherokee plants and their use*. Sylva, NC: Herald. [Swain County, southwestern NC]

1975 *Hartley I* = Charlie Ross Hartley (part 1). 1975. *Foxfire Magazine* 9(2–3): 166–76. [Watauga County, northwestern NC]

1975 *Hartley II* = Charlie Ross Hartley (part 2). 1975. *Foxfire Magazine* 9(4): 379–91. [Watauga County, northwestern NC]

1975 Higgs and Manning *Voices* = Higgs, Robert J., and Ambrose N. Manning, eds. 1975. *Voices from the hills: Selected readings of Southern Appalachia*. New York: Ungar.

1975 *Hopper Family* = The Hopper family. 1975. *Foxfire Magazine* 9(1): 13–17. [Rabun County, northeast GA]

1975 Jackson *Unusual Words* = Jackson, Sarah E. 1975. Unusual words, expressions, and pronunciations in a North Carolina mountain community. *Appalachian Journal* 2: 148–60. [western NC]

1975 Kroeger *WV Farm Life* = Kroeger, Mildred. 1975. Central West Virginia farm life between 1893 and 1970: Interview with Mrs. Anna Hopkins. *Goldenseal* 1(1): 3–8, 39. [WV]

1975 *"Last Chance" School* = The "Last Chance" school. 1975. *Foxfire Magazine* 9(1): 41–44.

1975 *Logging* = Logging. 1975. *Foxfire Magazine* 9(1): 37–40. [Rabun County, northeast GA]

c1975 Lunsford *It Used to Be* = Lunsford, Bascom Lamar. 1975. *"It used to be": Memories of Bascom Lamar Lunsford*. Edited by Mildred Frances Thomas. Typescript on deposit at Appalachian Collection, Belk Library, Appalachian State University, Boone, NC. [northwestern NC]

c1975 *Miners' Jargon* = *Coal miners' jargon*. c1975. Big Stone Gap, VA: Madisonville Community College.

1975 Montell *Ghosts Cumberland* = Montell, William Lynwood. 1975. *Ghosts along the Cumberland*. Knoxville: University of Tennessee Press. [south central KY]

1975–2018 Montgomery File = [Observations by Michael Montgomery of usages by natives of east Tennessee and western North Carolina]

1975 Mull *Old Burke* = Mull, J. Alex. 1975. *Tales from old Burke*. Morganton, NC: News Herald. [central western NC]

1975 Purkey *Madison Co* = Purkey, Lena. 1975. *Home in Madison County*. Johnson City: East Tennessee State University. [Madison County, central western NC]

1975 *Rail Fences* = Split rail fences. 1975. *Foxfire Magazine* 9(2–3): 124–25. [Rabun County, northeast GA]

1975 *Richard and Margaret* = Richard and Margaret. 1975. *Foxfire Magazine* 9(1): 4–12. [Rabun County, northeast GA]

1975 Riedl *House Customs* = Riedl, Norbert. 1975. House customs and beliefs in east Tennessee. *Tennessee Folklore Society Bulletin* 41: 47–56. [east TN]

1975 Schrock *Exam of Dialect* = Schrock, Earl F., Jr. 1975. An examination of the dialect in *This Day and Time* [by Anne W. Armstrong]. In *Voices from the hills: Selected readings from southern Appalachia*, edited by Robert J. Higgs and Ambrose N. Manning, 459–73. New York: Ungar. [east TN]

1975 Screven *John B Wright* = Screven, Tom. 1975. John B. Wright: Retired coal miner and self-taught artist. *Goldenseal* 1(1): 11–16. [WV]

1975–79 *Shenandoah OHC* = [Interview transcripts from the Shenandoah National Park Oral History Collection.] 1975–79. https://www.lib.jmu.edu/special/manuscripts/sdarchsnp/. [western VA]

1975 *Used to Farm* = Used to farm. 1975. *Foxfire Magazine* 9(1): 30–36. [Rabun County, northeast GA]

1975 *We Sing* = We sing about life and what it means to us: A conversation with Everett Lilly. *Goldenseal* 1(2): 14–20. [WV]

c1975 Whitehead *E TN Accent* = Whitehead, Don. c1975. On what's an East Tennessee accent. *Knoxville News-Sentinel*, undated.

1975–83 Wolfram/Christian *WV Coll* = Wolfram, Walt, and Donna Christian. 1975–83. [Transcriptions of interviews conducted in Mercer and Monroe Counties, southern WV, in 1975 for the authors' book *Appalachian Speech* (1976) and for later research]

1975 Woolley *We Be Here* = Woolley, Bryan. 1975. *We be here when the morning comes*. Lexington: University Press of Kentucky. [southeastern KY]

1976 Anderson *Fairy Crosses* = Anderson, R. 1976. Fairy crosses. In *Touching home: A collection of folklore from the Copper Basin, Fannin County area*, edited by Kathy Thompson, 25–27. Orlando, FL: Daniels. [southeast TN]

1976 *Bear Hunting* = Bear hunting in the Appalachians. 1976. *Foxfire Magazine* 10(4): 259–318. [Haywood County, central western NC]

1976 Braden *Grandma Was Girl* = Braden, Beulah Brummett. 1976. *When grandma was a girl*. Oak Ridge, TN: Oak Ridger. [central east TN]

1976 Brandes and Brewer *Dialect Clash* = Brandes, Paul D., and Jeutonne

Brewer. 1976. Appalachian Amerenglish. In *Dialect clash in America: Issues and answers*, 251–311. Metuchen, NJ: Scarecrow.

1976 Bullard *Crafts TN Mts* = Bullard, Helen. 1976. *Crafts and craftsmen of the Tennessee mountains*. Falls Church, VA: Summit. [east TN]

1976 Carroll and Pulley *Little Cataloochee* = Carroll, Roy, and Raymond H. Pulley. 1976. Historic structures report: Little Cataloochee, North Carolina. Boone, NC: Appalachian State University. [Haywood County, central western NC]

1976 *Carrying Mail* = Carrying the mail. 1976. *Foxfire Magazine* 10(2): 99–110. [Rabun County, northeast GA]

1976 Carter *Little Tree* = Carter, Forrest. 1976. *The education of Little Tree*. New York: Delacorte. [western NC]

c1976 Cate *Cattle Herder* = Cate, Herma. c1976. Cattle herder. *Maryville-Alcoa Daily Times*. [Blount County, central east TN]

c1976 Cate *Ginseng Digger* = Cate, Herma. c1976. Ginseng digger. *Maryville-Alcoa Daily Times*. [Blount County, central east TN]

1976 Clarkson *Logging in Appal* = Clarkson, Roy B. 1976. Mountain logging in the southern Appalachians at the turn of the century. *Southern Lumberman* 233: 117–22. [WV]

1976 Daugherty *Serpent-Handling* = Daugherty, Mary Lee. 1976. Serpent-handling as sacrament. *Theology Today* 33: 232–43. [WV]

1976 *Digging Well* = Digging a well. 1976. *Foxfire Magazine* 10(2): 125–37.

1976 Dillon *They Died* = Dillon, Lacy A. 1974. *They died in the darkness*. Parsons, WV: McClain.

1976 Dumas *Smoky Mt Speech* = Dumas, Bethany. 1976. Smoky mountain speech. In *Pioneer spirit 76*, edited by Dolly Berthelot, 24–29. Knoxville: Berthelot. [central east TN]

1976 Durrance and Shamblin *Appal Ways* = Durrance, Jill, and William Shamblin, eds. 1976. *Appalachian ways*. Washington, DC: Appalachian Regional Commission.

1976 Dwyer *Southern Sayin's* = Dwyer, Paul. 1976. *Southern sayin's for Yankees and other immigrants*. Highlands, NC: Merry Mountaineers.

1976 Dykeman *Additions* = Dykeman, Wilma. 1976. Additions to the Appalachian vocabulary. *Knoxville News-Sentinel*, December 5, C-2. [east TN]

1976 Dykeman *Time to Build* = Dykeman, Wilma. 1976. Time to build your Appalachian vocabulary. *Knoxville News-Sentinel*, October 17, C-2. [east TN]

1976 Ferrell *Tweetsie Country* = Ferrell, Mallory Hope. 1976. *Tweetsie country: The East Tennessee & Western North Carolina Railroad*. Boulder, CO: Pruett. [southwestern NC]

1976 Garber *Mountain-ese* = Garber, Aubrey. 1976. *Mountain-ese: Basic grammar for Appalachia*. Radford, VA: Commonwealth. [southwestern VA]

1976 *Hartley III* = Charlie [Charley] Ross Hartley (part 3). 1976. *Foxfire Magazine* 10(1): 4–10. [Watauga County NC]

1976 Lawson *Hammontrees Fight* = Lawson, Lewis A. 1976. The Hammontrees fight the Civil War: Letters from the Fifth East Tennessee Infantry. *Lincoln Herald* 78: 117–22. [Blount County, central east TN]

1976 Ledford *Folk Vocabulary* = Ledford, Ted Roland. 1976. Folk vocabulary of western North Carolina: Some recent changes. *Appalachian Journal* 3: 277–84. [northwestern NC]

1976 Lindsay *Grassy Balds* = Lindsay, Mary. 1976. History of the grassy balds in the Great Smoky Mountains. Management report no. 4. NPS southeast regional uplands field research laboratory, Great Smoky Mountains National Park. Typescript consulted at Library, Great Smoky Mountains National Park, Gatlinburg, TN. [central east TN]

1976 Maloney *Appal Culture* = Maloney, Michael. 1976. *Appalachian culture: A guide to students and teachers*. Edited by Peggy Celeste and Ann Hill. Columbus: Ohio State University Research Foundation.

1976 Mathias *Briars* = Mathias, Frank. 1976. Briars. *Mountain Review* 2(3): 1–3.

1976 Miller *Mts within Me* = Miller, Zell. 1976. *The mountains within me*. Toccoa, GA: Commercial. [north central GA]

1976 Ogle and Nixon *If Only* = Ogle, Lucinda, and Emily Nixon. 1976. If only these walls could talk. *Sevier County Times*, September 26, B7. [Sevier County, central east TN]

1976 Padgett *Clay Co NC* = Padgett, Guy. 1976. *A history of Clay County North Carolina*. Hayesville, NC: Clay County Bicentennial Committee. [Clay County, southwestern NC]

1976 *Sevier Co Saga* = *Sevier County saga*. 1976. Sevierville, TN: Sevier County American Revolution Bicentennial Celebration Commission. [Sevier County, central east TN]

1976 Smith and Smith *Sthn Words* = Smith, Fabia Rue, and Charles Rayford Smith. 1976. *Southern words and sayings*. Jackson, MS: Office Supply Company.

1976 Still *Pattern of Man* = Still, James. 1976. *Pattern of a man and other stories*. Lexington, KY: Gnomon.

1976 Thompson *Touching Home* = Thompson, Kathy, ed. 1976. *Touching home: A collection of history and folklore from the Copper Basin, Fannin County area*. Orlando, FL: Daniels. [north central GA]

1976 Tyler *Man's Work* = Tyler, Alicia. 1976. Benjamin Matheny: "Doin' a man's work": Logging in central and southern counties between 1918 and 1930. *Goldenseal* 2(3): 26–30. [central and southern WV]

1976 Van Nest *Gillis Ridge* = Van Nest, R. J. 1976. Gillis Ridge. *Appalachian Journal* 3: 307–10.

1976 Weals *Funky Offends* = Weals, Vic. 1976. Funky offends mountain ears (and noses). *Knoxville Journal*, September 27. [central east TN]

1976 Weals *It's Owin'* = Weals, Vic. 1976. It's owin' to how a word is used. *Knoxville Journal*, September 6, 9. [central east TN]

1976 Weals *Mountaineer* = Weals, Vic. 1976. Mountaineer asks us to "mind" our language. *Knoxville Journal*, June 28, 9. [central east TN]

1976 Weals *Plenty Water* = Weals, Vic. 1976. Plenty of water, but nothing to eat in the "gant" lot. *Knoxville Journal*, December 13, 11. [central east TN]

1976 Weals *Two Minus* = Weals, Vic. 1976. Two minus two equals nary. *Knoxville Journal*, July 19, 12. [central east TN]

1976 Weals *Words Stay* = Weals, Vic. 1976. Words stay "alive" with oldtimers. *Knoxville Journal*, July 26, 7. [central east TN]

1976 Wigginton *Stanley Hicks* = Wigginton, Eliot, ed. 1976. Stanley Hicks, Sugar Grove, North Carolina. In *"I wish I could give my son a wild raccoon,"* 353–66. Garden City, NY: Anchor. [northwestern NC]

1976 Wolfram and Christian *Appal Speech* = Wolfram, Walt, and Donna Christian. 1976. *Appalachian speech*. Arlington, VA: Center for Applied Linguistics. [Mercer and Monroe Counties, southern WV]

1976 *Wooden Sleds* = Wooden sleds. 1976. *Foxfire Magazine* 10(2): 147–64.

1977 Adams *Remembering* = Adams, Inez McCaulley. 1977. Remembering: A trip back to grandpa's house. In *The Cades Cove story*, by A. Randolph Shields, 92–99. Gatlinburg, TN: Great Smoky Mountains Natural History Association. [Blount County, central east TN]

1977 Arnow *Old Burnside* = Arnow, Harriette Louisa Simpson. 1977. *Old Burnside*. Lexington: University Press of Kentucky. [southeastern KY]

1977 *Ben Chappell* = Don't call me Mr. Chappell, call me Uncle Ben. 1977. *Foxfire Magazine* 11: 226–33. [Rabun County, northeast GA]

1977 Blackmun *Western NC* = Blackmun, Ora. 1977. *Western North Carolina: Its mountains and its people to 1880*. 2nd ed. Boone, NC: Appalachian Consortium Press. [western NC]

1977 *Blacksmithing* = Blacksmithing. 1977. *Foxfire Magazine* 11(3): 185–225. [Macon County, southwestern NC]

1977 Brookman *Veterinary Diseases* = Brookman, Rosemary. 1977. Folk veterinary medicine in upper east Tennessee. *Tennessee Folklore Society Bulletin* 43: 140–48. [northeast TN]

1977 Coon *Useful Plants* = Coon, Nelson. 1977. *The dictionary of useful plants*. Emmaus, PA: Rodale.

1977 Douglas and McClellan *Fiddler* = Douglas, Wilson, and Jancy McClellan. 1977. How I came to be a fiddler. *Goldenseal* 3(1): 21–23. [WV]

1977 Farthing *Food Customs* = Farthing, Mary Ann. 1977. Appalachian food customs. *North Carolina Folklore Journal* 25: 36–44. [western NC]

1977 Foxfire IV = Wigginton, Eliot, ed. 1977. *Foxfire 4: Water systems, fiddle making, logging, gardening, sassafras tea, wood carving and further affairs of plain living*. Garden City, NY: Anchor.

1977 Ginns Rough Weather = Ginns, Patsy Moore. 1977. *Rough weather makes good timber*. Chapel Hill: University of North Carolina Press. [northwestern NC]

1977 Hamilton Mt Memories = Hamilton, Alice McGuire. 1977. *Blue Ridge mountain memories: The true story of a mountain girl at the turn of the century*. Atlanta: Conger.

1977 Howard Fifty Years = Howard, Martha C. 1977. Fifty years later and less: Loss of dialect in central West Virginia. Paper presented at American Dialect Society meeting. [WV]

1977 Hurst and Lewis Roaring Fork = Hurst, Sharon, and Laura Lewis. 1977. Roaring Fork School—fifty years ago: As told by Herb Clabo. *Smoky Mountain Historical Society Newsletter* 3(6): 22–24. [Sevier County, central east TN]

1977 Jake Waldroop = Jake Waldroop. 1977. *Foxfire Magazine* 11(2): 142–76. [Macon County, southwestern NC]

1977 King Her Story = King, Eva Samples. 1977. Eva Samples King: Her story. *Goldenseal* 3(1): 24–26. [WV]

1977 Madden and Jones Mt Home = Madden, Robert R., and T. Russell Jones. 1977. *Mountain home: The Walker family farmstead*. Washington, DC: US National Park Service. [Sevier County, central east TN]

1977 Maurer Mt Heritage = Maurer, B. B. 1977. *Mountain heritage*. Parsons, WV: McClain. [WV]

1977 McClelland Wilson Douglas = McClelland, Nancy. 1977. Wilson Douglas: Mountain man and mountain musician. *Goldenseal* 3(1): 15–20. [WV]

1977 McGreevy Breathitt KY Grammar = McGreevy, John Charles. 1977. Breathitt County, Kentucky grammar. PhD diss., Illinois Institute of Technology, Chicago. [Breathitt County, southeastern KY]

1977 Moore Jenks = Moore, J. Roderick. 1977. Mack Jenks, Union bard: 1971 interview with McDowell County coal miner and musician. *Goldenseal* 3(2): 25–34. [WV]

1977 Moser Friday = Moser, Joan. 1977. Friday at Parhams'. In *An Appalachian symposium: Essays written in honor of Cratis D. Williams*, edited by J. W. Williamson, 206–14. Boone, NC: Appalachian State University.

1977 Nevell Time to Dance = Nevell, Richard. 1977. *A time to dance: American country dancing from hornpipes to hot hash*. New York: St. Martin's.

1977 Norman Kinfolks = Norman, Gurney. 1977. *Kinfolks: The Wilgus stories*. Frankfort, KY: Gnomon.

1977 Parris Mt Idiom = Parris, John. 1977. Mountain idiom getting to be rare. *Asheville Citizen*, May 27, 3. [central western NC]

1977 Pederson Dugout = Pederson, Lee A. 1977. The dugout dairy. *Tennessee Folklore Society Bulletin* 43: 88–89. [northeast TN]

1977 Pederson Randy Sons = Pederson, Lee. 1977. The randy sons of Nancy Whisky. *American Speech* 52: 112–21. [northeast TN]

1977 Prichard Teams and Teamsters = Prichard, Arthur. 1977. Teams and teamsters in the Mannington oil and gas fields. *Goldenseal* 3(4): 21–24. [WV]

1977 Ross Come Go = Ross, Smith G. 1977. *Come, go with me: How to be independent and enjoy rural living*. Pine Knot, KY: Kentucky Hills Industries. [southeastern KY]

1977 Shackelford et al. Our Appalachia = Shackelford, Laurel, Bill Weinberg, and Donald R. Anderson. 1977. *Our Appalachia: An oral history*. New York: Hill and Wang. [eastern KY]

1977 Shields Cades Cove = Shields, A. Randolph. 1977. *The Cades Cove story*. Gatlinburg, TN: Great Smoky Mountains Natural History Association. [Blount County, central east TN]

1977 Simpkins Culture = Simpkins, O. Norman. 1977. Culture. In *Mountain heritage*, edited by B. B. Maurer, 29–51. Parsons, WV: McClain. [WV]

1977–79 Smoky Vistas = *Smoky Vistas*. 1977–79. [Magazine published by the Great Smoky Mountains Natural History Association]. [central east TN, central western NC]

1977 Stanley Tough = Stanley, Bonnie G. 1977. But we were tough and hardy. *Goldenseal* 3(1): 30–34. [WV]

1977 Stephenson Basketry Appal Mts = Stephenson, Sue H. 1977. *Basketry of the Appalachian mountains*. New York: Van Nostrand.

1977 Still Wonder Beans = Still, James. 1977. *Jack and the wonder beans*. New York: Putnam's Sons.

1977 Stratton Grassy Cove = Stratton, Cora. S. 1977. *And this is Grassy Cove*. Crossville, TN: BK Enterprises. [Cumberland County, east central TN]

1977 Weals Cove Folk = Weals, Vic. 1977. Cove folk knew a stranger by his factory-made track. *Knoxville Journal*, January 17, 7. [central east TN]

1977 Weals Logger = Weals, Vic. 1977. Logger past saving but friends did try. *Knoxville Journal*, January 31. [central east TN]

1977 Wolfe TN Strings = Wolfe, Charles K. 1977. *Tennessee strings*. Knoxville: University of Tennessee Press. [TN]

1977 Yeager Mostly Work = Yeager, Barbara. 1977. Mostly work: Making a home in Widen. *Goldenseal* 3(1): 7–10. [WV]

1978 American Chestnut = Memories of the American chestnut. 1978. *Foxfire Magazine* 12(3): 240–60. [Rabun County, northeast GA and Macon County, southwestern NC]

1978 Ball Speech Knox Co = Ball, Donald B. 1978. Notes on the slang and folk speech of Knoxville, Knox County. *Tennessee Folklore Society Bulletin* 44: 134–42. [Knox County, central east TN]

1978 Bird Traps = Bird traps. 1978. *Foxfire Magazine* 12(1): 73–76.

1978 Burns Our Sthn Mtneers = Burns, Inez. 1978. Our southern mountaineers. *Smoky Mountain Historical Society Newsletter* 4(2): 10–13.

1978 Burton Ballad Folks = Burton, Thomas G. 1978. *Some ballad folks*. Johnson City: East Tennessee State University Research Development Committee. [northeast TN, northwestern NC]

1978 Cohn Courtship and Marriage = Cohn, Philip W. 1978. Traditional courtship and marriage customs of the Appalachian South. In *Glimpses of southern Appalachian folk culture*, edited by Charles H. Faulkner and Carol K. Buckles, 34–42. Chattanooga: Tribute.

1978 Dykeman and Stokely Highland Homeland = Dykeman, Wilma, and James Stokely. 1978. *Highland homeland: The people of the Great Smokies*. Washington, DC: US National Park Service. [central east TN, central western NC]

1978 Evans Palen Fence = Evans, E. Raymond. 1978. The palen fence: An example of Appalachian folk culture. *Tennessee Anthropologist* 3: 93–99. [southeast TN]

1978 Glassie Sthn Mt Cabin = Glassie, Henry. 1978. The types of the southern mountain cabin. In *The study of American folklore*, edited by Jan Brunvand, 391–420. New York: Norton. [western VA]

1978 Gourd Bean = A gourd bean? 1978. *Foxfire Magazine* 12(3): 226–27.

1978 Hall Yarns and Tales = Hall, Joseph S. 1978. *Yarns and tales from the Great Smokies: Some narratives from the southern Appalachians*. Asheville, NC: Cataloochee. [central east TN, central western NC]

1978 Head Mt Moments = Head, Maynard. 1978. Mountain moments. *Newport (TN) Plain Talk*, July 1, September 7.

1978 Hiser Quare Do's = Hiser, Berniece. 1978. *Quare do's in Appalachia: East Kentucky legends and memorats*. Pikeville, KY: Pikeville College Press. [eastern KY]

1978 Horn New Harp of Columbia = Horn, Dorothy D. 1978. Introduction. In *The new harp of Columbia: A system of musical notation*, by M. L. Swan, vii–xvii. Knoxville: University of Tennessee Press.

1978 Horsetrading = Horsetrading. 1978. *Foxfire Magazine* 12(1): 40–71.

1978 Montgomery White Pine Coll = Montgomery, Michael. 1978. Interviews conducted in White Pine TN, analyzed in the author's 1979 University of Florida PhD diss., *A discourse analysis of Appalachian English*. In the dictionary, interviews are referenced according to the list of speakers on page 163 of that work. [Jefferson County, central east TN]

1978 Morton Superstitions = Morton, Joan. 1978. Superstitions and beliefs concerning babies in southern Appalachia. In *Glimpses of southern Appalachian folk culture*, edited by Charles H. Faulkner and Carol K. Buckles, 1–19. Chattanooga: Tribute.

1978 *Parris Mt Cooking* = Parris, John. 1978. *Mountain cooking*. Asheville, NC: Asheville Citizen-Times. [western NC]

1978 Petersen and Phillips *New Harp of Columbia* = Petersen, Ron, and Candra Phillips. 1978. East Tennessee harp singing. In *The new harp of Columbia: A system of musical notation*, edited by M. L. Swan, xvii–xxx. Knoxville: University of Tennessee Press.

1978 Reese *Dialects in E Tenn* = Reese, James Robert. 1978. Randomly distributed dialects in Appalachian English: Syntactic and phonological variation in east Tennessee. *SECOL Bulletin* 2: 67–76. [northeast TN]

1978 Reese *Speech NE Tenn* = Reese, James Robert. 1978. Variation in Appalachian English: A study of the speech of elderly, rural natives of east Tennessee. PhD diss., University of Tennessee, Knoxville. [northeast TN]

1978 Slone *Common Folks* = Slone, Verna Mae. 1978. *Common folks*. Pippa Passes, KY: Alice Lloyd College. [Knott County, southeastern KY]

1978–82 *Smokies Heritage* = *Our Smokies heritage*. 1978–82. [Monthly magazine published by Crescent Printing, Gatlinburg, TN]. [mainly Sevier County, central east TN]

c1978 Trout and Watson *Piece of Smokies* = Trout, Ed, and Olin Watson. c1978. *A piece of the Smokies: A pictorial history of life in the Smoky Mountains*. Maryville, TN: Printers. [central east TN, central western NC]

1978 Weals *Loggers Wrote* = Weals, Vic. 1978. Loggers wrote own ballad. *Knoxville Journal*, July 27. [central east TN]

1978 Weals *Mules* = Weals, Vic. 1978. Mules. *Knoxville Journal*. [central east TN]

1978 Weals *Two Locomotives* = Weals, Vic. 1978. Two locomotives. *Knoxville Journal*. [central east TN]

1978 White *Champ Ferguson* = White, Linda C. 1978. Champ Ferguson: A legacy of blood. *Tennessee Folklore Society Bulletin* 44: 66–70. [north central TN]

1978 Williams *Appal Speech* = Williams, Cratis [D.] 1978. Appalachian speech. *North Carolina Historical Review* 55: 174–79.

1979 *Big South Fork OHP* = Big South Fork Oral History Project. 1979. [Selected audio interviews, transcribed for this book]. Folk life along the Big South Fork of the Cumberland River Oral History Collection. Special Collections Department, University of Kentucky, Lexington. [McCreary County, southeastern KY, Fentress County and Pickett County, TN]

1979 Brewer *Morels* = Brewer, Carson. 1979. Morels springing up all over. *Knoxville News-Sentinel*, May 13, C-4. [east TN]

1979 Cantu *Great Smoky Mts* = Cantu, Rita. 1979. *Great Smoky Mountains: The story behind the scenery*. Las Vegas, NV: KC Publications. [central east TN, central western NC]

1979 Carpenter *Walton War* = Carpenter, Cal. 1979. *The Walton war and tales of the Great Smoky Mountains*. Lakemont, GA: Copple House. [southwestern NC]

1979 Cash *Among Klediments* = Cash, June Carter. 1979. *Among my klediments*. Grand Rapids, MI: Zondervan.

c1979 Chiles *Glossary* = Chiles, Mary Ruth. c1979. [Glossary to accompany Lloyd Foster, *History of Walker Valley*, 1970–74; consulted at Library, Great Smoky Mountains National Park, Gatlinburg, TN] [central east TN, central western NC]

1979 *Cockfighting I* = Cockfighting I. 1979. *Foxfire Magazine* 13(1): 50–68.

1979 *Cockfighting II* = Cockfighting II. 1979. *Foxfire Magazine* 13(3): 151–59.

1979 Cook *Mt Grown* = Cook, O. Dathan. 1979. *Mountain grown*. N.p.: Self-published.

1979 *Daddy Oakley* = Daddy Oakley. 1979. *Foxfire Magazine* 13(3): 173–81.

1979 Dressman *Redd Up* = Dressman, Michael R. 1979. "Redd up." *American Speech* 54: 141–45.

1979 *Drive Cattle* = "Just give me the money; I'll drive the cattle." 1979. *Foxfire Magazine* 13(1): 73–75.

1979 *Gamecock* = A gamecock is the gamest thing on earth. 1979. *Foxfire Magazine* 13(3): 160–72.

1979 *God Put Herbs* = God put the herbs here to heal the nation. 1979. *Foxfire Magazine* 13(1): 8–11.

1979 Horton *Natural Heritage* = Horton, James H. 1979. Our natural heritage. In *Our cultural heritage: Essays on the natural & cultural history of western North Carolina*, 9–33. Lakemont, GA: CSA. [western NC]

1979 Irwin *Musical Instruments* = Irwin, James Rice. 1979. *Musical instruments of the southern Appalachian Mountains*. Norris, TN: Museum of Appalachia.

1979 Melton *'Pon My Honor* = Melton, Carrie Myers. 1979. *'Pon my honor: Folk tales from the Upper Cumberland*. N.p.: n.p. [north central TN]

1979 Parris *Logging by Cable* = Parris, John. 1979. Logging by cable is nothing new, oldtimer says. *Asheville Citizen-Times*, December 30. [central western NC]

1979 *Preacher Cook* = Preacher Ben Cook. 1979. *Foxfire Magazine* 13(3): 190–202.

1979 *Raising Dogs* = Raising dogs. 1979. *Foxfire Magazine* 13(3): 182–89.

1979 Slone *My Heart* = Slone, Verna Mae. 1979. *What my heart wants to tell*. Washington, DC: New Republic. [Knott County, southeastern KY]

1979 Smith *White Rock* = Smith, Mary Bell. 1979. *In the shadow of the white rock*. Morristown, TN: Privately published.

1979 *Swapped That Dog* = I swapped that dog even for that ole T-Model. 1979. *Foxfire Magazine* 13(1): 42–43.

1979 *Tom Walkers* = Tom walkers. 1979. *Foxfire Magazine* 13(3): 203–5.

1980 Berry and Repass *Grandpa Says* = Berry, Pearlleen D., and Mary Eva Repass. 1980. *Grandpa says: Superstitions and sayings from eastern Kentucky*. Fredericksburg, VA: Foxhound. [eastern KY]

1980 Bledsoe *Just Folks* = Bledsoe, Jerry. 1980. *Just folks: Visitin' with Carolina people*. Asheboro, NC: Down Home. [northwestern SC]

1980 Brewer *Hit's Gettin'* = Brewer, Carson. 1980. Hit's gettin' to be a sight what outlanders are sayin'. *Knoxville News-Sentinel*, February 24, C-4. [east TN]

c1980 Campbell *Memories of Smoky* = Campbell, Carlos C. c1980. Memories of old Smoky: A collection of experiences, observations, and information from the early years of the Great Smoky Mountains National Park and from several pre-park years. Typescript on deposit at Library, Great Smoky Mountains National Park, Gatlinburg, TN. [central east TN, central western NC]

1980 Chiles *Logging Lingo* = Chiles, Mary Ruth. 1980. Logging lingo [compilation from oral history recordings and otherwise as noted, based mainly on 1974–75 McCracken Logging; consulted at Library, Great Smoky Mountains National Park, Gatlinburg, TN] [central east TN, central western NC]

1980 Clark *Civil War Diary* = Clark, Darius. 1980. The Civil War diary of Darius Clark of White County, TN, Co. G, 16th Tennessee Infantry, Confederate States of America. Transcribed by James Joseph Betterton. Copy on deposit in Tennessee State Library and Archives, Nashville. [central TN]

1980 Crewdson *Revenuers* = Crewdson, John M. 1980. Revenuers (and their TNT) sweep land of corn liquor. *New York Times*, January 22, A12. [north GA]

1980 Matthews *Appal Physician* = Matthews, Hugh A. 1980. *Leaves from the notebook of an Appalachian physician*. Cullowhee, NC: Privately published. [Jackson County, southwestern NC]

1980 Miles *Verbs in Haywood Co* = Miles, Celia H. 1980. Selected verb features in Haywood County, North Carolina: A generational study. PhD diss., Indiana University of Pennsylvania, Indiana, PA. [Haywood County, central western NC]

1980 Ogle *Joy and Sorrow* = Ogle, Una Kate Price. 1980. *The joy and sorrow of teaching in the Great Smoky Mountains of Tennessee*. Gatlinburg, TN: Crescent.

1980 Riggleman *WV Mtneer* = Riggleman, Homer F. 1980. *A West Virginia mountaineer remembers*. Parsons, WV: McClain. [WV]

1980 Rinzler and Sayers *N GA Potters* = Rinzler, Ralph, and Robert Sayers. 1980. *The Meaders family, north Georgia potters*. Washington, DC: Smithsonian. [north GA]

c1980 Roberts *Olden Times* = Roberts, Harry B. c1980. *Olden times in Greene County*. N.p.: H. B. Roberts. [Scrapbook on deposit at Calvin M. McClung Historical Collection, Knox County Public Library, Knoxville]. [Greene County, northeast TN]

1980–2013 *Smokies Guide* = *Smokies Guide: Official newsletter of Great Smoky Mountains National Park*. 1977–96. [central east TN, central western NC]

1980 Still *Run for Elbertas* = Still, James. 1980. *The run for the Elbertas*. Lexington: University Press of Kentucky.

1980 Weals *Dunn Early* = Weals, Vic. 1980. Dunn Early, lone ranger in forests, parks. *Knoxville Journal*, June 19. [central east TN]

1980 Weals *Strangers* = Weals, Vic. 1980. Strangers on mountain trail wary of knocking on doors. *Knoxville Journal*, April 3. [central east TN]

1980 Wigginton *Foxfire V* = Wigginton, Eliot, ed. 1980. *Foxfire 5: Ironmaking, blacksmithing, flintlock rifles, bear hunting and other affairs of plain living*. Originally published 1979; reprinted in 1980 as part of multivolume set. Garden City, NY: Anchor.

1980 Wigginton *Foxfire VI* = Wigginton, Eliot, ed. 1980. *Foxfire 6: Shoemaking, gourd banjos, and songbows, one hundred toys and games, wooden locks, a water powered sawmill, and other affairs of just plain living*. 1980. Garden City, NY: Anchor.

1981 Alderman *Tilson Mill* = Alderman, Pat. 1981. *Tilson grist mill: Mountain folklore genealogy*. Johnson City, TN: Overmountain. [northeast TN]

1981 Brewer *Wonderment* = Brewer, Carson. 1981. *A wonderment of mountains: The Great Smokies*. Knoxville: Tenpenny. [central east TN]

1981 Dart *Thunder Road* = Dart, Bob. 1981. Thunder Road fades. *Atlanta Journal Constitution*, October 31, 4B. [north GA]

1981 Daugneaux *Separate Place* = Daugneaux, Christine B. 1981. *Appalachia: A separate place, a unique people*. Parsons, WV: McClain.

1981 Dumas *Appal Glossary* = Dumas, Bethany. 1981. Appalachian glossary. In *An encyclopedia of east Tennessee*, edited by Jim Stokely and Jeff D. Johnson, 16–18. Oak Ridge, TN: Children's Museum. [east TN]

1981 Eiler et al. *Blue Ridge Harvest* = Eiler, Lyntha Scott, Terry Eiler, and Carl Fleischhauer, eds. 1981. *Blue Ridge harvest: A region's folklife in photographs*. Washington, DC: American Folklife Center, Library of Congress.

1981 Henry *Alex Stewart* = Henry, Bill. 1981. Alex Stewart: A personal reminiscence. *Tennessee Folklore Society Bulletin* 47: 48–66. [Hancock County, northeast TN]

1981 High *Coll* = [Material donated to the *Dictionary of American Regional English* project by Ellesa Clay High]. [east central KY, as of c1950]

1981 Irwin *Arnwine Cabin* = Irwin, John Rice. 1981. *The Arnwine cabin: A history of this pioneer dwelling and its contents located at the Museum of Appalachia, Norris, Tennessee*. Norris, TN: Museum of Appalachia. [east TN]

1981 Morrell *Mirth* = Morrell, John. 1981. *The mirth of a national park*. N.p.: Privately published. [east TN]

1981 Nicholas *Appal Speech* = Nicholas, J. Karl. 1981. Some features of present-day Appalachian English. Paper presented at the Modern Language Association meeting, New York, December. [Jackson County, southwestern NC]

1981 Philliber et al. *Invisible Minority* = Philliber, William W., Clyde B. McCoy, and Harry C. Dillingham, eds. *The Invisible minority, urban Appalachians*

1981 Powell *Gracie* = Powell, Emilie Ervin. 1981. *Gracie and the mountain*. Chattanooga: Target. [Sevier County, central east TN]

1981 Roth *Greenbrier Early Days* = Roth, Margaret Ann. 1981. Greenbrier in the early days. *Smoky Mountain Historical Society Newsletter* 7(1): 7–13. [Sevier County, central east TN]

1981 Stokely and Johnson *Encycl E TN* = Stokely, Jim, and Jeff D. Johnson. 1981. *An encyclopedia of east Tennessee*. Oak Ridge, TN: Children's Museum.

1981 Weals *Becky Rewards* = Weals, Vic. 1981. Becky rewards family coffinmaker. *Knoxville Journal*, December 31, 3. [Blount County, central east TN]

1981 Weals *Farmers* = Weals, Vic. 1981. Farmers made hay on top of Smoky. *Knoxville Journal*, December 3, A8. [central east TN]

1981 Weals *Fire Towers* = Weals, Vic. 1981. Falling fire towers end era of adventure. *Knoxville Journal*, December 24, A8. [central east TN]

1981 Weals *Older Cows* = Weals, Vic. 1981. Older cows eager to summer atop mountain. *Knoxville Journal*, October 15, D3. [central east TN]

1981 Weals *Rocky Top* = Weals, Vic. 1981. Rocky Top. *Knoxville Journal*. [central east TN]

1981 Weals *Root-Hogs* = Weals, Vic. 1981. Root-hogs unwelcome on high cattle range. *Knoxville Journal*, December 10, C12. [central east TN]

1981 Whitener *Folk-Ways* = Whitener, Rogers. 1981. Selections from "Folk-ways and folk speech." *North Carolina Folklore Journal* 29: 1–86. [northwestern NC]

1981 Williams *Storytelling* = Williams, Cratis D. 1981. [Typescript of lecture delivered at the conference Language Variety in the South: Perspectives in Black and White, Columbia, SC, October 2]

1982 Abell *Better Felt* = Abell, Troy D. 1982. *Better felt than said: The Holiness-Pentecostal movement in southern Appalachia*. Waco, TX: Markham. [northwestern NC]

1982 Absher *Wilkes County* = Absher, Mrs. W. O. 1982. *The heritage of Wilkes county*. North Wilkesboro, NC: Wilkes Genealogical Society. [Wilkes County, northwestern NC]

1982 DeArmond *So High* = DeArmond, Nora. 1982. *So high the sun*. Knoxville: Jostens. [east TN]

1982 Eller *Miners* = Eller, Ronald D. 1982. *Miners, millhands, and mountaineers: Industrialization of the Appalachian South, 1880–1930*. Knoxville: University of Tennessee Press.

1982 *Foxfire VII* = Gillespie, Paul F., ed. 1982. *Foxfire 7*. Garden City, NY: Anchor.

1982 Ginns *Snowbird Gravy* = Ginns, Patsy Moore. 1982. *Snowbird gravy and dishpan pie: Mountain people recall*. Chapel Hill: University of North Carolina Press. [northwestern North Carolina]

1982 Hurst *Appal Words* = Hurst, Sharon Elaine. 1982. Appalachian words. *Our Smokies heritage*, 98–99. Gatlinburg, TN: Crescent. [mainly Sevier County, central east TN]

1982 Irwin *Baskets* = Irwin, John Rice. 1982. *Baskets and basket makers in southern Appalachia*. Exton, PA: Schiffer. [east TN]

1982 Maples *Memories* = Maples, Alie Newman. 1982. *Memories of my mountains* [consulted at Library, Great Smoky Mountains National Park, Gatlinburg, TN]. N.p.: n.p. [Sevier County, central east TN]

1982 Plowman *Out of Sight* = Plowman, Roscoe E. 1982. *Twice out of sight*. Berea, KY: Kentucke Imprints.

1982 Powers and Hannah *Cataloochee* = Powers, Elizabeth D., and Mark E. Hannah. 1982. *Cataloochee: Lost settlement of the Smokies*. Charleston, SC: Blazer. [Haywood County, central western NC]

1982 Rives *Blue Ridge* = Rives, Margaret Rose. 1982. *The Blue Ridge Parkway: The story behind the scenery*. Las Vegas, NV: KC Publications.

1982 Slone *How We Talked* = Slone, Verna Mae. 1982. *How we talked*. Pippa Passes, KY: Pippa Valley Printing. [Knott County, southeastern KY]

1982 *Smokies Heritage Book 1* = *Our Smokies heritage book 1*. 1982. Gatlinburg, TN: Crescent. [central east TN, central western NC]

1982 Stupka *Wildflowers* = Stupka, Arthur. 1982. *Wildflowers in color*. New York: HarperCollins.

1982 Weals *Andy Greer* = Weals, Vic. 1981. Andy Greer's slow oxen died, quick as lightning, in storm at top of Smoky. *Knoxville Journal*, July 22, A15. [central east TN]

1982 Weals *Cove Lumber* = Weals, Vic. 1982. Cove lumber plentiful—road to market steep. *Knoxville Journal*, January 7, B8. [Blount County, central east TN]

1982 Weals *Hog or Cow Brute* = Weals, Vic. 1982. Hog or cow brute safe with silent Dan. *Knoxville Journal*, July 15, B5. [central east TN]

1982 Wells *Remarkable Flora* = Wells, B. W. 1982. *The remarkable flora of the Great Smoky Mountains.* Asheville: North Carolina National Park Commission. [central east TN, central western NC]

c1982 Young *Colloquial Appal* = Young, Malone. c1982. One thousand colloquialisms from deep Appalachia. Typescript on deposit at Berea College Library, Appalachian Center Unprocessed Materials, log 400, box 1, Southern Appalachian Archives, Berea, KY.

1983 Aiken *Mt Ways* = Aiken, Gene. 1983. *Mountain ways: An album of the Smokies.* Gatlinburg, TN: Buckhorn. [Sevier County, central east TN]

1983 Belt *Chattooga Country* = Belt, Don. 1983. Chattooga River country. *National Geographic* 163 (April): 458–77. [northeast GA]

1983 Broaddus *Estill Co KY Word List* = Broaddus, James. 1983. An annotated Estill county, Kentucky word list. *Midwestern Journal of Language and Folklore* 9: 24–62. [Estill County, eastern KY]

1983 *CW Harlan Co* = Civil War in Harlan: The Harlan County Battalion. 1983. *Harlan Footprints: Genealogical Society of Harlan County* 1(4): 19–26. [Harlan County, southeastern KY]

1983 *Dark Corner OHP* = [Selected audio interviews transcribed for this book]. Tales from the Dark Corner: Documenting the oral tradition (Bernard Zaidman, project director), South Caroliniana Library, University of South Carolina, Columbia. [Greenville County, northwestern SC]

1983 Davis *Lucky Day* = Davis, Donald. 1983. *My lucky day: Tales from a southern Appalachian storyteller.* Murfreesboro, NC: Johnson. [western NC]

1983 Davis *Multi-lingual Mule* = Davis, Hubert J. 1983. *The multi-lingual mule and other short stories.* Radford, VA: Commonwealth. [southwestern VA]

1983 DeLozier *Work and Play* = DeLozier, Mary Jean. 1983. The good old days? Work and play in the Upper Cumberland. In *Lend an ear: Heritage of the Tennessee Upper Cumberland*, edited by Calvin Dickinson, Larry Whiteaker, and Leo McGee, 59–76. Lanham, MD: University Press of America. [north central TN]

1983 Farr *More Moonshine* = Farr, Sidney Saylor. 1983. *More than moonshine: Appalachian recipes and recollections.* Pittsburgh: University of Pittsburgh Press. [eastern KY]

1983 Forester *Harlan KY* = Forester, William D. 1983. *Before we forget: Harlan County 1920 through 1930 with background dating further in time.* Harlan, KY: Self-published. [southeastern KY]

1983 Helsly *Country Doctor* = Helsly, Mrs. Wilford W. 1983. *The country doctor and his people, 1910–1923.* Knoxville: Privately published.

1983 Irwin *Guns and Gun-Making* = Irwin, John Rice. 1983. *Guns and gun-making tools of southern Appalachia: The story of the Kentucky rifle.* 2nd ed. Exton, PA: Schiffer.

1983 Jones *Sin-Eater* = Jones, James Gay. 1980. *A wayfaring sin-eater and other Appalachian tales.* Parsons, WV: McClain.

1983 Matthews *Cutting a Dido* = Matthews, Gail V. S. 1983. Cutting a dido: A dancer's eye view of mountain dance in Haywood County, N.C. MA thesis, Indiana University, Bloomington, IN. [Haywood County, central western NC]

1983 McDermitt *Boy Named Jack* = McDermitt, Barbara. 1983. Storytelling and a boy named Jack. *North Carolina Folklore Journal* 31: 3–22. [Avery County, northwestern NC]

1983 Montell *Don't Go Up* = Montell, William Lynwood. 1983. *Don't go up Kettle Creek: Verbal legacy of the Upper Cumberland.* Knoxville: University of Tennessee Press. [south central KY]

1983 Mull and Boger *Recollections* = Mull, J. Alexander, and Gordon Boger. 1983. *Recollections of the Catawba Valley.* Boone, NC: Appalachian Consortium Press. [central western NC]

1983 Page and Wigginton *Aunt Arie* = Page, Linda Garland, and Eliot Wigginton. 1983. Aunt Arie: *A Foxfire portrait.* New York: Dutton. [Macon County, southwestern NC]

1983 Patterson *Cooking* = Patterson, Virginia. 1983. Cooking . . . mountain style: The greens of spring. *In the Smokies* 1(1): 20.

1983 Patterson *Spring Wildflower* = Patterson, Virginia. 1983. Spring wildflower pilgrimage. *In the Smokies* 1(1): 18.

1983 Pederson *East TN Folk Speech* = Pederson, Lee. 1983. East Tennessee folk speech: A synopsis. *Bamberger beitrage zur Englischen sprachwissenschaft* 12. Frankfurt/Main: Peter Lang. [east TN]

1983 Pyle *CCC 50th Anniv* = Pyle, Charlotte. 1983. CCC fiftieth anniversary interviews. Typescript consulted at Library, Great Smoky Mountains National Park, Gatlinburg TN. 3 vols. [central east TN, central western NC]

1983 Ridings *Cades Cove* = Ridings, Gladys Oliver. 1983. *Cades Cove and parts of the Great Smoky Mountains.* N.p.: Privately published. [Blount County, central east TN]

1983 Smith *Recollections of Blue Ridge* – Smith, Dorothy Noble. 1983. *Recollections: The people of the Blue Ridge remember.* Edited by James F. Gorman. Verona, VA: McClure.

1983 Walker *Tales Civil War* = Walker, Edward R. III. 1983. *Tales from the Civil War.* Cosby, TN: Busy Bee. [Cocke County, central east TN]

1983 Weals *Ball-Hooting* = Weals, Vic. 1983. Ball-hooting, log-nosing days remembered. *Knoxville Journal*, October 20, A10. [Blount County, central east TN]

1983 Weals *Len Cogdill* = Weals, Vic. 1983. Len Cogdill recalls hills full of timber, Republicans. *Knoxville Journal*, November 3, B11. [central east TN]

1983 Weals *Waterjacking* = Weals, Vic. 1983. Waterjacking a dangerous job, as Peter McCarter discovered. *Knoxville Journal*, September 8, B10. [central east TN]

1983 Whisnant *Native & Fine* = Whisnant, David E. 1983. *All that is native & fine: The politics of culture in an American region.* Chapel Hill: University of North Carolina Press.

1983 Whiteaker *Enemy Is Brother* = Whiteaker, Larry. 1983. "The enemy is my brother": The Civil War in the Upper Cumberland. In *Lend an ear: Heritage of the Tennessee Upper Cumberland*, edited by Calvin Dickinson, Larry Whiteaker, and Leo McGee, 33–44. Lanham, MD: University Press of America. [north central TN]

1984 Allison *Character Notes* = Allison, Junius. 1984. Orphan character notes in Appalachia. *North Carolina Folklore Journal* 32: 82–90.

1984 *Asheville Citizen-Times* = *Asheville Citizen-Times*. 1984. [Untitled article in vertical file of Pack Memorial Library, Asheville, NC]

1984 Burns *Cold Sassy* = Burns, Olive Ann. 1984. *Cold Sassy tree.* New York: Ticknor & Fields. [north GA]

c1984 Dennis *Smoky Mt Heritage* = Dennis, Delmar. c1984. *Smoky Mountain heritage: A treasury of old time mountain photos.* Sevierville, TN: Nandel. [Sevier County, central east TN]

1984 Dykeman and Stokely *At Home* = Dykeman, Wilma, and James Stokely. 1984. *At home in the Smokies: A history handbook for Great Smoky Mountains National Park: North Carolina and Tennessee* [revision of Dykeman and Stokely 1978]. Washington, DC: US Department of the Interior. [central east TN, central western NC]

1984 Garber *Old Harp* = Garber, Anna. 1984. Old harp singing. *In the Smokies* 2(3): 30–31.

1984 Gibson *Remembering* = Gibson, Flora Carr. 1984. Remembering my Smoky Mountain home. Typescript consulted at Library, Great Smoky Mountains National Park, Gatlinburg, TN. [Sevier County, central east TN]

1984 Gray *Hazel Creek* = Gray, Sam. 1984. *Hazel Creek: Patterns of life on an Appalachian watershed.* Knoxville: TVA Division of Land and Forest Resources. [Swain County, southwestern NC]

1984 Harmon *Falling Leaves* = Harmon, Bertha Cox. 1984. *Falling leaves of Appalachia: Memories of yesterday.* N.p.: Snapp.

1984 Head *Brogans* = Head, Maynard. 1984. *Brogans, clothespins, and a twist of tobacco.* West Allis, WI: Pinetree. [eastern KY, east TN]

1984 High *Titan Rock* = High, Ellesa Clay. 1984. *Past Titan Rock: Journeys* *into an Appalachian valley*. Lexington: University Press of Kentucky. [east central KY]

1984 *History of Beth-Car* = *History of Beth-Car United Methodist Church and cemetery*. 1984. N.p.: Privately published. [Jefferson County, central east TN]

1984 Martin *Hollybush* = Martin, Charles E. 1984. *Hollybush: Folk building and social change in an Appalachian community*. Knoxville: University of Tennessee Press. [southeastern KY]

1984 Morgan *Log Barns* = Morgan, John. 1984. The log barns of Blount County, Tennessee. *Tennessee Anthropologist* 9: 85–103. [Blount County, central east TN]

1984 Page and Wigginton *Foxfire Cookery* = Page, Linda Garland, and Eliot Wigginton, eds. 1984. *The Foxfire book of Appalachian cookery*. New York: Gramercy.

1984 Roth *Reminiscences* = Roth, Margaret Ann. 1984. Reminiscences. *Smoky Mountain Star*, June 21. [Sevier County, central east TN]

1984–86 *Sevier Settler* = *Sevier Settler*. 1984–86. [Quarterly magazine with local history, legends, and reminiscences; Sevier County, central east TN]

1984 Six *Hill 'n Holler* = Six, S. Dean. 1984. *Hill 'n holler expressions: A dictionary of West Virginia hillbilly talk*. Cairo, WV: Little Pink Pig. [WV]

1984 Smith *Enduring Memories* = Smith, Flavious Joseph, Sr. 1984. *Enduring memories: Growing up in Dry Valley, the heart of the Upper Cumberland*. N.p.: n.p. [north central TN]

1984 Smith *Oral History* = Smith, Lee. 1984. *Oral history*. New York: Ballantine.

1984 Tipps *McKendree Church* = Tipps, Henry Thurston. 1984. *A history of McKendree Church*. Nashville, TN: Parthenon. [north GA]

1984 Trout *Gatlinburg* = Trout, Ed. 1984. *Gatlinburg: Cinderella city*. Pigeon Forge, TN: Griffin. [Sevier County, central east TN]

1984 Wilder *You All Spoken* = Wilder, Roy. 1984. *You all spoken here*. New York: Viking.

1984 Wilson *Train Ride* = Wilson, Veta. 1984. A train ride into Elkmont's colorful past. *Mountain Press*, June 13, 5, 7. [Sevier County, central east TN]

1984 Woods *WV Was Good* = Woods, Cloe. 1984. *West Virginia was good*. Charleston, WV: Mountain State Press. [WV]

1984 Yeatts *Old Mayberry* = Yeatts, John H. 1984. *Remembering old Mayberry*. Charlotte: Delmar. [northwestern NC]

1985 Dabney *More Mt Spirits* = Dabney, Joseph E. 1985. *More mountain spirits: The continuing chronicle of moonshine life and corn whiskey, wines, ciders & beers in America's Appalachians*. Asheville, NC: Bright Mountain. [north GA]

1985 Edwards *Folksy Sketches* = Edwards, Funson. 1985. *Folksy sketches from Appalachia*. Knoxville: Privately published. [northeast TN]

1985 Irwin *Alex Stewart* = Irwin, John Rice. 1985. *Alex Stewart, portrait of a pioneer*. West Chester, PA: Schiffer. [Hancock County, northeast TN]

1985 Jones *Growing Up* = Jones, G. C. 1985. Growing up hard in Harlan County. Lexington: University Press of Kentucky. [southeastern KY]

1985 Jones *Travail* = Jones, Loyal. 1985. Grandpa's travail. *Appalachian Heritage* 13(3): 21–23.

1985 Kiser *Life and Times* = Kiser, Mabel. 1985. *The life of a girl from the land of utopia: The hill country*. N.p.: n.p. [western NC]

1985 Pittman *Comm* = *Pittman Community Center: A mountain mission*. 1985. Gatlinburg, TN: Buckhorn. [Sevier County, central east TN]

1985 Reagan *Sugarlands* = Reagan, Charles Aaron. 1985. Life in the Sugarlands before the Great Smokies Park. Typescript consulted at Library, Great Smoky Mountains National Park, Gatlinburg, TN. [Sevier County, central east TN]

1985 *Schools and Pastimes* = Country schools and pastimes. 1985. *North Carolina Folklore Journal* 33: 34–50. [western NC]

1985 Sienkneckt *Rheumatic Diseases* = Sienknecht, Charles. 1985. A primer in the rheumatic diseases for east Tennessee. *American Journal of Medicine* 78(2): 182–84. [east TN]

1985 *Smokies Anniv Book* = *Great Smoky Mountains National Park golden anniversary commemorative book, 1934–1984*. 1985. Gatlinburg, TN: Oakley Enterprises. [central east TN, central western NC]

1985 *Walker Bible Record* = Bible record of Hester Jane Walker. 1985. *Watauga Association of Genealogists Bulletin* 14: 60–61.

1985 Wear *Lost Communities* = Wear, Jerry, ed. 1985. *Lost communities of Sevier County Tennessee: Greenbrier*. Sevierville, TN: Sevierville Heritage Committee. [Sevier County, central east TN]

1985 Williams *Better Man* = Williams, Cratis D. 1985. *William H. Vaughn: A better man than I ever wanted to be*. Morehead, KY: Appalachian Development Center.

1985 Williams *Role of Folklore* = Williams, John Rodger. 1985. Appalachian migrants in Cincinnati, Ohio: The role of folklore in the reinforcement of ethnic identity. PhD diss., Indiana University, Bloomington.

1985 Wiseman *Autobiography* = Wiseman, Scott G. 1985. Wiseman's view: The autobiography of Skyland Scotty Wiseman. *North Carolina Folklore Journal* 33: 1–90. [western NC]

1986 Aiken *Mt Ways Two* = Aiken, Gene. 1986. *Mountain ways two: An album of the Smokies*. Gatlinburg, TN: Buckhorn. [Sevier County, central east TN]

1986 *Back Home Blount Co* = *Back home in Blount County*. 1986. Maryville, TN: Blount County Historic Trust. [Blount County, central east TN]

1986 Helton *Around Home* = Helton, William W. 1986. In a manner of speaking. *Around home in Unicoi County*, 373–81. Johnson City, TN: Overmountain. [Unicoi County, northeast TN]

1986 Huskey *Sugarlands* = Huskey, Charles Aaron. 1986. Life in the Sugarlands. In *Sugarlands: A lost community of Sevier county*, edited by Jerry L. Wear, 2–9. Sevierville, TN: Sevierville Heritage Committee. [Sevier County, central east TN]

1986 Ivey *Damned Brier* = Ivey, Mike. 1986. A rose by another name is a damned brier. *Appalachian Heritage* 14(3): 54–55.

1986 Lauterer *Runnin' on Rims* = Lauterer, Jock. 1986. *Runnin' on rims: Appalachian profiles*. Chapel Hill, NC: Algonquin. [western North Carolina]

1986 Lewelling *White Caps Sevier Co* = Lewelling, Joseph C. 1986. The White Caps of Sevier County: Economic and cultural perspectives. *Tennessee Anthropologist* 11: 156–71. [Sevier County, central east TN]

1986 McDavid and McDavid *KY Verb Forms* = McDavid, Raven I., Jr., and Virginia G. McDavid. 1986. Kentucky verb forms. In *Language variety in the South: Perspectives in black and white*, edited by Michael Montgomery and Guy Bailey, 264–93. University: University of Alabama Press. [eastern KY]

1986 Noonkesser *Crossing* = Noonkesser, David. 1986. *The crossing: A history of White Pine, Tennessee*. Rogersville: East Tennessee Printing. [Jefferson County, central east TN]

1986 Ogle *Lucinda* = Ogle, Lucinda Oakley. 1986. Lucinda Oakley Ogle and early settlers. In *Sugarlands: A lost community of Sevier County*, edited by Jerry L. Wear, 37–77. Sevierville, TN: Sevierville Heritage Committee. [Sevier County, central east TN]

1986 Ogle *My Valley* = Ogle, Lucinda Oakley. 1986. My valley . . . in the Smokies. *In the Smokies* 4(2): 39. [Sevier County, central east TN]

1986 Page *Daughter of Hills* = Page, Mira. 1986. *Daughter of the hills: A woman's part in the coal miners' struggle*. New York: Feminist Press of CUNY. [eastern KY]

1986 Pederson et al. *LAGS* = Pederson, Lee, et al. 1986. *Linguistic atlas of the Gulf States: Basic materials*. Ann Arbor, MI: University Microfilms. [Responses to interviews conducted by the Linguistic Atlas of the Gulf States project at Emory University, Atlanta, from 1968 to 1983. Responses in this book include all 60 speakers from the East Tennessee sector and 35 of the 87 speakers from the North Georgia sector]

1986 Rader *Mt Legacy* = Rader, Ron. 1986. A mountain legacy. In *Sugarlands: A lost community of Sevier County*, edited by Jerry L. Wear, 17–22. Sevierville, TN: Sevierville Heritage Committee. [Sevier County, central east TN]

1986 Scott and Scott *Beyond Beauty* = Scott, Dorothy, and Billy Scott. 1986. Beyond beauty: The Great Smoky Mountains, their people and cemeteries. N.p.: n.p. [Consulted at Library, Great Smoky Mountains National Park, Gatlinburg, TN] [central east TN, central western NC]

1986 Smith and Eye *Hardwood Stands* = Smith, H. Clay, and Maxine C. Eye. 1986. *Guidelines for managing immature Appalachian hardwood stands.* Morgantown: West Virginia University College of Agriculture and Forestry. [WV]

1986 Still *Wolfpen Poems* = Still, James. 1986. *The Wolfpen poems.* Berea, KY: Berea College Press.

1986 Tyson *Reflections* = Tyson, Lona Parton. 1986. *Reflections of the pinnacle: The story of the Parton roots.* Gatlinburg, TN: Crescent. [Sevier County, central east TN]

1986 Watts *Same Block* = Watts, Monteen Keener. 1986. *Chips off the same block.* Tiger, GA: J & M.

1986 Wear *Sugarlands* = Wear, Jerry L. 1986. *Sugarlands: A lost community of Sevier County.* Sevierville, TN: Sevierville Heritage Committee. [Sevier County, central east TN]

1987 Bruce *Wolfe Stories* = Bruce, Sally. 1987. Old Catawbans and "mountain grill": The Appalachian in Thomas Wolfe's short stories. *Contemporary Appalachia: In search of a usable past: Proceedings of the ninth annual Appalachian Studies Conference*, 37–48. Boone, NC: Appalachian Consortium Press. [western NC]

1987 Carver *Regional Dialects* = Carver, Craig M. 1987. *American regional dialects: A word geography.* Ann Arbor: University of Michigan Press.

1987 Davenport *Pine Grove* = Davenport, L. Theodore. 1987. *The rise and decline of Pine Grove: The story of a rural community in Sevier County.* Maryville, TN: BGA. [Sevier County, central east TN]

1987 Dorgan *Glory to God* = Dorgan, Howard. 1987. *Giving glory to God in Appalachia: Worship practices of six Baptist subdenominations.* Knoxville: University of Tennessee Press.

1987 Elingburg *Mt Breed* = Elingburg, Sandra. 1987. W. Amos Abrams prize co-winner: Mountain breed western North Carolina tales. *North Carolina Folklore Journal* 34: 52–60. [western NC]

1987 *Hewing Crossties* = Hewing crossties. 1987. *Foxfire Magazine* 21(3–4): 210.

1987 Irwin *Museum Appalachia* = Irwin, John Rice. 1987. *The museum of Appalachia story.* West Chester, PA: Schiffer. [east TN]

1987 Kytle *Voices* = Kytle, Elizabeth. 1987. *The voices of Robby Wilde.* New York: Pocket Books.

1987 Obermiller *Labeling* = Obermiller, Philip J. 1987. Labeling urban Appalachians. In *Too few tomorrows: Urban Appalachians in the 1980's*, edited by Philip J. Obermiller and William W. Philliber. Boone, NC: Appalachian Consortium Press.

1987 Oliver and Oliver *Sketches* = Oliver, Hugh Russell, and Margaret Thomas Oliver. 1987. *Sketches of the Olivers: A family history, 1726–1966.* Pinehurst, NC: H. R. Oliver. [Blount County, central east TN]

1987 Perdue *Outwitting Devil* = Perdue, Charles L., Jr. 1987. *Outwitting the devil: Jack tales from Wise County, Virginia.* Santa Fe, NM: Ancient City. [southwestern VA]

1987 Smalling *Watauga Co* = Smalling, Curtis. 1987. *The heritage of Watauga County, North Carolina.* Vol. 2. Boone, NC: Southern Appalachian Historical Association. [Watauga County, northwestern NC]

1987 Trent *Yesteryear* = Trent, Emma Dean Smith. 1987. *East Tennessee's lore of yesteryear.* Whitesburg, TN: Privately published. [northeast TN]

1987 Wear *Sevierville* = Wear, Jerry L. 1987. *Sevierville 1795–1986: A homecoming look at our past, present, and future.* Kingsport, TN: Kingsport Press. [Sevier County, central east TN]

1987 Williams *Rethinking House* = Williams, Michael Ann. 1987. Rethinking the house: Interior space and social change. *Appalachian Journal* 14: 174–82. [southwestern NC]

1987 Young *Lost Cove* = Young, Malone. 1987. *Latchpins of the Lost Cove.* Johnson City, TN: Latchpin Press. [northeast TN]

1988 *Augusta Heritage* = Augusta Heritage Center. 1960–88. Documents, video, and audio recordings of the Augusta Heritage Center, Augusta Collection of Folk Culture in Booth Library, Davis & Elkins College.

1988 Brown *Beech Creek* = Brown, James S. 1988. *Beech Creek: A study of a Kentucky mountain neighborhood.* Berea, KY: Berea College Press. [eastern KY]

1988 Bryan *Tories amidst Rebels* = Bryan, Charles F. 1988. "Tories" amidst Rebels: Confederate occupation of east Tennessee, 1861–1863. *East Tennessee Historical Society Publication* 60: 3–22. [east TN]

1988 Carden *Looking Out* = Carden, Gary. 1988. Inside looking out. *Now & Then* 5(2): 7–8. [western NC]

1988 Collins *Decoration Day* = Collins, Bobbie L. 1988. Decoration day in Unicoi County. *Tennessee Folklore Society Bulletin* 54: 82–90. [northeast TN]

1988 Dickey and Bake *Wayfarer* = Dickey, James, and William A. Bake. 1988. *Wayfarer: A voice from the southern mountains.* Birmingham, AL: Oxmoor House.

1988 Dunn *Cades Cove* = Dunn, Durwood. 1988. *Cades Cove: The life and death of a southern Appalachian community 1818–1937.* Knoxville: University of Tennessee Press. [Blount County, central east TN]

1988 Dyer *Farmstead Yards* = Dyer, Delce. 1988. The farmstead yards at Cades Cove: Restoration and management alternatives for the domestic landscape of the southern Appalachian mountaineer. MS thesis, University of Georgia. [Blount County, central east TN]

1988 Houk *Exploring Smokies* = Houk, Rose. 1988. *Exploring the Smokies.* Gatlinburg, TN: Great Smoky Mountains Natural History Association. [central east TN, central western NC]

1988 Jackson *Commodities* = Jackson, Dot. 1988. A lesson in commodities. *Now & Then* 5(3): 31–32.

1988 Jones *Modesty* = Jones, Loyal. 1988. Modesty. *Appalachian Heritage* 16(2–3): 82–86.

1988 Kingsolver *Bean Trees* = Kingsolver, Barbara. 1988. *The bean trees.* New York: Harper & Row.

1988 Kosier *Maggie* = Kosier, Patty Pylant. 1988. *Maggie of Maggie Valley, N.C.* Corpus Christi, TX: Privately published. [Haywood County, central western NC]

1988 Lambert *Kinfolks* = Lambert, Walter N. 1988. *Kinfolks and custard pie: Recollections and recipes from east Tennessee.* Knoxville: University of Tennessee Press. [east TN]

1988–97 Landry *Coll* = Landry, Bill. 1988–97. Interviews conducted for the Heartland television series, on deposit at WBIR-TV, Knoxville. [east TN]

1988 Lincoln *Avenue* = Lincoln, Charles Eric. 1988. *The avenue.* Garden City, NY: William Morrow. [Buncombe County, central western NC]

1988 Mashburn *Mt Summer* = Mashburn, William H. 1988. *Mountain summer.* Blacksburg, VA: Pocahantas. [western NC]

1988 Moore *Emergence* = Moore, John Hebron. 1988. *The emergence of the cotton kingdom in the Old Southwest.* Baton Rouge: Louisiana State University Press.

1988 Moore *Mt Voices* = Moore, Warren. 1988. *Mountain voices: A legacy of the Blue Ridge and Great Smokies.* Chester, CT: Globe Pequot. [western NC]

1988 Moore *Roadside Guide* = Moore, Harry L. 1988. *A roadside guide to the geology of Great Smoky Mountains National Park.* Knoxville: University of Tennessee Press. [central east TN, central western NC]

1988 Russell *It Happened* = Russell, Gladys Trentham. 1988. *It happened in the Smokies: A mountaineer's memories of happenings in the Smoky Mountains in pre-park days.* Alcoa, TN: Russell. [Sevier County, central east TN]

1988 Russell and Barnett *Ghost Stories* = Russell, Randy, and Janet Barnett. 1988. *Mountain ghost stories and curious tales of western North Carolina.* Winston-Salem, NC: Blair. [western NC]

1988 Smith *Fair and Tender* = Smith, Lee. 1988. *Fair and tender ladies.* New York: Putnam.

1988 Still *Hunting Hindman* = Still, James. 1988. Hunting for Hindman: An exercise in the use of the vernacular. *Appalachian Heritage* 21: 13–14. [southeastern KY]

1988 Stipe *Smokies Man* = Stipe, Sylvia. 1988. Glenn Cardwell: Smokies man of the year. *In the Smokies* 6(5): 16–19. [Sevier County, central east TN]

1988 Trotter *Bushwhackers!* = Trotter, William R. 1988. *Bushwhackers! The Civil War in North Carolina: The mountains*. Winston-Salem, NC: Blair.

1989 Aiken *Tragedy* = Aiken, Gene. 1989. Tragedy in the forest. *The Star*, February 2. [Sevier County, central east TN]

1989 Alvey *KY Folklore* = Alvey, R. Gerald. 1989. *Kentucky folklore*. Lexington: University Press of Kentucky. [KY]

1989 Bryson *City Centennial* = Bryson City Centennial Committee. 1989. *100 years of progress: Bryson City, N.C. centennial*. Bryson City, NC: Swain County Genealogical and Historical Society. [Swain County, southwestern NC]

1989 Buxton and Burns *Blowing Rock* = Buxton, Barry M., and Jerry W. Burns. 1989. *A village tapestry: The history of Blowing Rock*. Boone, NC: Appalachian Consortium Press. [northwestern North Carolina]

1989 Carson *Nobody Yet* = Carson, Jo. 1989. *Stories I ain't told nobody yet*. New York: Orchard.

1989 Cheek *Go Home* = Cheek, Pauline B. 1989. You can't go home if you haven't been away. *Now & Then* 6(2): 9–10.

1989 Dorgan *Regular Baptists* = Dorgan, Howard. 1989. *The Old Regular Baptists of central Appalachia: Brothers and sisters in hope*. Knoxville: University of Tennessee Press. [eastern KY]

1989 Fink *Jonesborough* = Fink, Paul M. 1989. *Jonesborough: The first century of Tennessee's first town, 1776–1876*. Johnson City, TN: Overmountain. [Washington County, northeast TN]

1989 Friedland *Old Time Dancing* = Friedland, Lee Ellen. 1989. Introduction. In *Old time dancing in the Appalachian mountains*, 3–4. Johnson City: East Tennessee State University Center for Appalachian Studies and Services.

1989 Giardina *Storming Heaven* = Giardina, Denise. 1989. *Storming heaven: A novel*. New York: Ballantine.

1989 Hannah *Reflections* = Hannah, Mark E. 1989. *Smoky Mountain reflections*. N.p.: Sev-Hannah. [Haywood County, central western NC]

1989 Kingsolver *Homeland* = Kingsolver, Barbara. 1989. *Homeland and other stories*. New York: Harper & Row.

1989–99 Landry *Smoky Mt Interviews* = Landry, Bill. 1989, 1997, 1999. [Audio and video interviews conducted under the auspices of the Great Smoky Mountains National Park, consulted at the Library, Great Smoky Mountains National Park, Gatlinburg, TN]. [central east TN, central western NC]

1989–90 *Matewan OHP* = [Selected audio interviews, transcribed for this book]. Matewan Development Center Oral History Project. Special Collections, Marshall University Library, Huntingdon, WV. [southwestern WV]

1989 Miller *Newfound* = Miller, Jim Wayne. 1989. *Newfound: A novel*. New York: Orchard.

1989 Millner *Letcher* = Millner, Sondra. 1989. Letcher. *Now & Then* 6(2): 11–15. [southeastern KY]

1989 Nicholson *Field Guide* = Nicholson, Charles. 1989. *A field guide to southern speech*. Little Rock, AR: August House.

1989 Oliver *Hazel Creek* = Oliver, Duane. 1989. *Hazel Creek from then to now*. N.p.: Privately published. [Swain County, southwestern NC]

1989 Ownby *Forks Little Pigeon* = Ownby, Harold. 1989. *Forks of Little Pigeon Church: Bicentennial history, First Baptist Church Sevierville Tennessee*. N.p.: Privately published. [Sevier County, central east TN]

1989 Smith *Flyin' Bullets* = Smith, Era Rhea Noland. 1989. *Flyin' bullets and resplendent badge*. Sevierville, TN: Nandel. [central east TN]

1989 Still *Rusties and Riddles* = Still, James. 1989. *Rusties and riddles & gee-haw whimmy-diddles*. Lexington: University Press of Kentucky. [southeastern KY]

1989 Trent *Sequel to Lore* = Trent, Emma Dean Smith. 1989. *A sequel to East Tennessee's lore of yesteryear*. Whitesburg, TN: Privately published. [northeast TN]

1989 Woodside *Hungry for Dance* = Woodside, Jane Harris. 1989. The Cherokee: Hungry for the dance. *Now & Then* 6(3): 22–25. [western NC]

1990 Aiken *Stories* = Aiken, Gene. 1990. *Stories from the Great Smoky Mountains*. Gatlinburg, TN: Buckhorn. [Sevier County, central east TN]

1990 Aiken *Wiley Oakley* = Aiken, Gene. 1990. Wiley Oakley: Roaming man of the mountains. *The Star*, April 13. [Sevier County, central east TN]

1990 Bailey *Draw Up Chair* = Bailey, Louise Howe. 1990. *Draw up a chair*. Skyland, NC: Hickory Printing. [Henderson County, southwestern NC]

1990 Brown *Oldest Camp Meeting* = Brown, Kenneth O. 1990. Finding America's oldest camp meeting. *Methodist History* 20(4): 252–54.

1990 Bush *Maize* = Bush, Florence Cope. 1990. Amazing maize. *Smoky Mountain Historical Society Newsletter* 16(2): 29–31.

1990 Bush *Ocona Lufta Baptist* = Bush, Florence Cope. 1990. *Ocona Lufta Baptist: Pioneer church of the Smokies, 1836–1939*. Concord, TN: Misty Cove. [Swain County, southwestern NC]

c1990 *Cataloochee Auto Tour* = *Cataloochee Auto Tour*. c1990. Gatlinburg, TN: Great Smoky Mountains Natural History Association. [Haywood County, central western NC]

1990 Cavender *Folk Medical Lex* = Cavender, Anthony. 1990. *A folk medical lexicon of south central Appalachia*. Johnson City: East Tennessee State University. [northeast TN]

1990 Clouse *Wilder* = Clouse, Lolketta. 1990. *Wilder*. Nashville, TN: Rutledge Hill Press.

1990 Davis *Homeplace* = Davis, Don. 1990. Homeplace geography. *Now & Then* 7(1): 18–19. [western NC]

1990 Fisher *Preacher Stories* = Fisher, Ben C. 1990. *Mountain preacher stories: Laughter among the trumpets*. Boone, NC: Appalachian Consortium Press.

1990 Kline *Cherokee Songs and Ceremonies* = Kline, Michael. 1990. Where the ravens roost: Songs and ceremonies of Big Cove. *Old Herald* 2(5): 24–28. [Swain County, southwestern NC]

1990 Merriman *Moonshine Rendezvous* = Merriman, Stony. 1990. *Midnight moonshine rendezvous: Secrets of Luke Alexander Denny's moonshine running adventures (1930s–1960s)*. Smithville, TN: Privately published. [central TN]

1990 Moore *Pittston Strike* = Moore, Marat. 1990. Women's stories from the Pittston Strike. *Now & Then* 7(3): 6–12, 32–35.

1990 Morgan *Log House E TN* = Morgan, John. 1990. *The log house in east Tennessee*. Knoxville: University of Tennessee Press. [east TN]

1990 Ogle *That's Why* = Ogle, Lucinda Oakley. 1990. That's why I thought me a thought. *In the Smokies* 9(1): 18–19. [Sevier County, central east TN]

1990 Oliver *Cooking Hazel Creek* = Oliver, Duane. 1990. *Cooking on Hazel Creek: The best of southern mountain cooking*. Hazelwood, NC: Privately published. [southwestern NC]

1990 Speer *Appal Photographs* = Speer, Jean Haskell. 1990. *The Appalachian photographs of Earl Palmer*. Lexington: University Press of Kentucky.

1990 Whitener *Thrice-Told* = Whitener, Rogers. 1990. *Thrice-told tales*. Boone, NC: Whitener and Miller. [northwestern NC]

1990 Wigginton *Foxfire Christmas* = Wigginton, Eliot. 1990. *A Foxfire Christmas*. New York: Doubleday.

1990 Williams *Pride and Prejudice* = Williams, Michael Ann. 1990. Pride and prejudice: The Appalachian boxed house in southwestern North Carolina. *Winterthur Portfolio* 25: 217–30. [southwestern NC]

1991 Alsop *Birds of Smokies* = Alsop, Fred J. 1991. *Birds of the Smokies*. Gatlinburg, TN: Great Smoky Mountains Natural History Association. [central east TN, central western NC]

1991 Alvic *Weavers of Highlands* = Alvic, Philis. 1993. *Weavers in the highlands: The early years in Gatlinburg*. Murray, KY: Privately published. [Sevier County, central east TN]

1991 Beverley *Old Mt Idiom* = Beverley, Robert. 1991. A few examples of the old mountain idiom. In *The western North Carolina almanac and book of facts*, 146–47. Franklin, NC: Sanctuary Press. [western NC]

1991 Bible *Bent Twigs* = Bible, Jean. 1991. *Bent twigs in Jefferson County*. Rogersville: East Tennessee Printing. [Jefferson County, central east TN]

1991 Conant and Collins *Field Guide* = Conant, R., and J. T. Collins. 1991. *A field guide to reptiles and amphibians: Eastern and central North America*. 3rd ed. Boston: Houghton Mifflin.

1991 Egerton *Dispatches* = Egerton, John. 1991. *Shades of gray: Dispatches from the modern South*. Baton Rouge: Louisiana State University Press.

1991 Finger *Cherokee Americans* = Finger, John R. 1991. *Cherokee Americans: The Eastern Band of the Cherokees in the twentieth century*. Lincoln: University of Nebraska Press. [Swain County, southwestern NC]

1991 Haynes *Haywood Home* = Haynes, Alice Hawkins. 1991. *Haywood home: Memories of a mountain woman*. Tallahassee: Rose. [Haywood County, central western NC

1991 Headrick *Headrick's Chapel* = Headrick, Lena. 1991. Headrick's Chapel, Sevier County Tennessee, and old harp singing. *Tennessee Ancestors* 7: 205–7. [Sevier County, central east TN]

1991 Joslin *Mt People I* = Joslin, Michael, and Ruth Joslin. 1991. *Mountain people, places and ways: A southern Appalachian sampler*. Johnson City, TN: Overmountain. [northwestern NC]

1991 Law and Taylor *Oak Basketmaking* = Law, Rachel Nash, and Cynthia Wieboldt Taylor. 1991. *Appalachian white oak basketmaking: Handing down the basket*. Knoxville: University of Tennessee Press.

1991 LeMaster *Jesse Stuart* = LeMaster, J. R. 1991. *Jesse Stuart on education*. Lexington: University Press of Kentucky. [northeastern KY]

1991 Miller *Revenuers and Moonshiners* = Miller, Wilbur R. 1991. *Revenuers and moonshiners: Enforcing federal liquor law in the mountain South, 1865–1900*. Chapel Hill: University of North Carolina Press.

1991 Montell *Singing Glory* = Montell, William Lynwood. 1991. *Singing the glory down: Amateur gospel music in south central Kentucky, 1900–1990*. Lexington: University Press of Kentucky. [south central KY]

1991 Neely *Snowbird Cherokees* = Neely, Sharlotte. 1991. *Snowbird Cherokees: People of persistence*. Athens: University of Georgia Press. [Graham County, southwestern NC]

1991 Reeder and Reeder *Shenandoah Secrets* = Reeder, Carolyn, and Jack Reeder. 1991. *Shenandoah's Secrets: The story of the park's hidden past*. Vienna, VA: Potomac Appalachian Trail Club. [western VA]

1991 Rennicke *Black Bear* = Rennicke, Jeff. 1991. *The Smoky Mountain black bear: Spirit of the hills*. Gatlinburg, TN: Great Smoky Mountains Natural History Association. [central east TN, central western NC]

1991 Shifflett *Coal Towns* = Shifflett, Crandall. *Coal towns: Life, work, and culture in coal mining towns of southern Appalachia, 1880–1960*. Knoxville: University of Tennessee Press.

1991 Still *Wolfpen Notebooks* = Still, James. 1991. *The Wolfpen notebooks*. Lexington: University Press of Kentucky.

1991 Thomas *Sthn Appal* = Thomas, Roy Edwin. 1991. *Southern Appalachia, 1885–1915: Oral histories from residents of the state corner area of North Carolina*. Jefferson, NC: McFarland. [northwestern NC]

1991 Walker *Great Smoky* = Walker, Steven L. 1991. *Great Smoky Mountains: Splendor of the southern Appalachians*. Scottsdale, AZ: Camelback/Elan Venture. [central east TN, central western NC]

1991 Weals *Last Train* = Weals, Vic. 1991. *Last train to Elkmont: A look back at life on Little River in the Great Smoky Mountains*. Knoxville: Olden. [Blount County, central east TN]

1991 Williams *Homeplace* = Williams, Michael Ann. 1991. *Homeplace: The social use and meaning of the folk dwelling in southwestern North Carolina*. Athens: University of Georgia Press. [southwestern NC]

1992 Austin *Vanishing Art* = Austin, Ben. 1992. The vanishing art of cooking table-grade sorghum molasses. *Tennessee Folklore Society Bulletin* 55: 101–7. [White County, central TN]

1992 Brooks *Sthn Stuff* = Brooks, Mildred Jordan. 1992. *Southern stuff, down-home talk and bodacious lore from deep in the heart of Dixie*. New York: Avon.

1992 Bush *Dorie* = Bush, Florence Cope. 1992. *Dorie: Woman of the mountains*. Knoxville: University of Tennessee Press. [Blount County, central east TN]

1992 Bush *If Life* = Bush, Florence Cope. 1992. *If life gives you scraps, make a quilt: Short stories from the Smoky Mountains*. Concord, TN: Misty Cove.

1992 Cavender *Folk Hematology* = Cavender, Anthony. 1992. Folk hematology in the Appalachian South. *Journal of Folklore Research* 29: 23–36. [northeast TN]

1992 Davis *Jack Tales* = Davis, Donald. 1992. *Southern Jack tales*. Little Rock, AR: August House. [central western NC]

1992 Farwell *Stonewall* = Farwell, Byron. 1992. *Stonewall: A biography of General Thomas J. Jackson*. New York: Norton.

1992 Gabbard *Thunder Road* = Gabbard, Alex. 1992. Return to Thunder Road: The story behind the legend. Lenoir City, TN: Gabbard. [east TN]

1992 Giardina *Unquiet Earth* = Giardina, Denise. 1992. *The unquiet earth*. New York: Norton.

1992 Heller and Heller *Confederacy* = Heller, J. Roderick III, and Carolyn Ayres Heller. 1992. *The Confederacy is on her way up the spout: Letters to South Carolina, 1861–1864*. Athens: University of Georgia Press. [northwestern SC]

1992 Jackson *Surry Co Soldiers* = Jackson, Hester Bartlett, ed. 1992. *Surry County soldiers in the Civil War*. Charlotte: Delmar. [Surry County, northwestern NC]

1992 Jones and Miller *Sthn Mt Speech* = Jones, Loyal, and Jim Wayne Miller. 1992. Glossary of mountain speech. *Southern mountain speech*, 63–120. Berea, KY: Berea College Press.

1992 Joslin *Mt People II* = Joslin, Michael, and Ruth Joslin. 1992. *Mountain people, places and ways: Another southern Appalachian sampler*. Johnson City, TN: Overmountain. [northwestern NC]

1992 Miller *CW Campbell Co* = Miller, George K. 1992. *The Civil War and Campbell County, Tennessee*. Jackson, TN: Action. [Campbell County, northeast TN]

1992–2002 Montgomery *Coll* = Montgomery Collection. 1992–2002. Observations and responses by consultants to queries, collected by Michael Montgomery for the *Dictionary of Smoky Mountain English* (2004).

1992 Morgan *Potato Branch* = Morgan, Joe Richard. 1992. *Potato Branch: Sketches of mountain memories*. Asheville, NC: Bright Mountain. [western NC]

1992 Murray-Woolley *Rock Fences* = Murray-Woolley, Carolyn, and Karl B. Raitz. 1992. *Rock fences of the Bluegrass*. Lexington: University Press of Kentucky. [eastern KY]

1992 Offutt *KY Straight* = Offutt, Chris. 1992. *Kentucky straight*. New York: Vintage.

1992 Oxford *Ray Hicks* = Oxford, Cheryl. 1992. The storyteller as shaman: Ray Hicks telling his Jack tales. *North Carolina Folklore Journal* 38: 75–120. [Avery County, northwestern NC]

1992 Sabol *Sacred Harp* = Sabol, Steven. 1992. Sacred harp: History & tradition. Typescript in editor's possession.

1992 Seeger *Talking Feet* = Seeger, Mike. 1992. *Talking feet: Buck, flatfoot and tap: Solo southern dance of the Appalachian, Piedmont, and Blue Ridge Mountain regions*. Berkeley, CA: North Atlantic.

1992 Toops *Great Smoky Mts* = Toops, Connie. 1992. *Great Smoky Mountains*. Stillwater, MN: Voyageur. [central east TN, central western NC]

1993 Bansemer *Mts in Mist* = Bansemer, Roger. 1993. *Mountains in the mist: Impressions of the Great Smokies*. Dallas, TX: Taylor. [central east TN, central western NC]

1993 Brewer *Great Smoky Mts* = Brewer, Carson. 1993. *The Great Smoky Mountains*. Portland, OR: Graphic Arts. [central east TN]

1993 Burchill et al. *Ghosts and Haunts* = Burchill, James V., Linda J. Crider, Peggy Kendrick, and Marcia Wright Bonner. 1993. *Ghosts and haunts from the Appalachian foothills: Stories and legends*. Nashville, TN: Rutledge Hill Press.

1993 Burleson *Aunt Keziah* = Burleson, Bertie. 1993. *According to Aunt Keziah: Christmas mem'rys*. Newland, NC: Avery Journal. [Avery County, northwestern NC]

1993 Burton *Take Up Serpents* = Burton, Thomas. 1993. *They shall take up serpents*. Knoxville: University of Tennessee Press.

1993 Cunningham *Sthn Talk* = Cunningham, Ray. 1993. *Southern talk: A disappearing language*. Asheville, NC: Bright Mountain.

1993 Farwell and Nicholas *Smoky Mt Voices* = Farwell, Harold, and J. Karl Nicholas. 1993. *Smoky Mountain voices: A lexicon of southern Appalachian speech.* Lexington: University Press of Kentucky. [Swain County, southwestern NC]

1993 *Foxfire X* = Reynolds, George P., Susan Walker, et al., eds. 1993. *Foxfire 10: Railroad lore, boardinghouses, Depression-era Appalachia, chair making, whirligigs, snakes, canes, and gourd art.* New York: Doubleday.

1993 Howze *Schoolhouse* = Howze, Tom P. 1993. And not a single arm rotted off: Memories of a one-room schoolhouse. *Now & Then* 10(1): 31–32.

1993 Ison and Ison *Whole Nother Lg* = Ison, Isaac, and Anna H. Ison. 1993. *A whole 'nother language: Our personal collection of Appalachian expressions.* N.p.: Privately published. [eastern KY]

1993 Jacobs *Elbert Childress* = Jacobs, Scott Allan. 1993. Board of Education: An interview with Elbert Childress. *Now & Then* 10(1): 28–30. [WV]

1993–94 Jamison *Jubilant Spirit* = Jamison, Philip. 1993–94. "A jubilant spirit within me": Buckdance, flatfoot, or clogging? *Old-Time Herald*, Winter, 14–17, 51. [western NC]

1993 Mason *Feather Crowns* = Mason, Bobbie Ann. 1993. *Feather crowns.* New York: HarperCollins.

1993 Moffett and Wodehouse *E TN Barns* = Moffett, Marian, and Lawrence Wodehouse. 1993. *East Tennessee cantilever barns.* Knoxville: University of Tennessee Press. [east TN]

1993 Montell *Cumberland Country* = Montell, William Lynwood. 1993. *Upper Cumberland country.* Jackson: University Press of Mississippi. [south central KY, north central TN]

1993 Moore *Dark and Deep* = Moore, Marat. 1993. Because the earth is dark and deep. *American Voice* 22: 73–88.

1993 Page and Smith *Foxfire Toys and Games* = Page, Linda Garland, and Hilton Smith. 1993. *The Foxfire book of Appalachian toys and games.* Chapel Hill: University of North Carolina Press.

1993 Parris *Folklore* = Parris, John. 1993. Folklore and folkways. In *The history of Jackson County*, edited by Max R. Williams, 469–516. Sylva, NC: Jackson County Historical Society. [Jackson County, western NC]

1993 Sobol *Growing Up with Jack* = Sobol, Joseph Daniel. 1993. Growing up with Jack in Haywood County: The background and development of Donald Davis's storytelling. *North Carolina Folklore Journal* 40: 80–113. [Haywood County, central western NC]

1993 Soesbee *Wordlist* = Soesbee, Mary Lou. 1993. Wordlist [manuscript provided to the editor]. [western NC]

1993 *Stories 'neath Roan* = *Stories 'neath the Roan: Memories of the people of Yancey, Mitchell and Avery Counties at the foot of Roan Mountain, North Carolina.* 1993. Little Switzerland, NC: Blue Ridge Reading Team. [Mitchell and Yancey Counties, northwestern NC]

1993 Stuart *Daughter* = Stuart, Jesse. 1993. *Daughter of the legend.* Edited by John H. Spurlock. Ashland, KY: Jesse Stuart Foundation.

c1993 *Tremont Logging* = *Tremont Logging Camp Auto Tour.* n.d. Gatlinburg, TN: Great Smoky Mountains Natural History Association.

1993 Weaver *Scotch-Irish Speech* = Weaver, Jack. 1993. Sociolinguistics of Scotch-Irish speech in Appalachia. *Irish Studies Working Papers* 93: 12–19.

1994 Bluestein *Poplore* = Bluestein, Gene. 1994. *Poplore: Folk and pop in American culture.* Amherst: University of Massachusetts Press.

1994 Carden and Anderson *Buzzards* = Carden, Gary, and Nina Anderson. 1994. *Buzzards, hucksters, and grieving specters.* Asheboro, NC: Down Home.

1994 Crissman *Death and Dying* = Crissman, James. 1994. *Death and dying in central Appalachia.* Urbana: University of Illinois Press. [eastern KY]

1994 Dorgan *Liquid Graves* = Dorgan, Howard. 1994. Liquid graves and dripping saints. *Now & Then* 11(3): 10–12. [KY, NC, VA]

1994 Dumas *Care To* = [comment on the American Dialect Society listserv, October 6, 1994]

1994 Dumas *Hope How Soon* = [comment on the American Dialect Society listserv, November 16, 1994]

1994 Farwell and Buchanan *Logging Terms* = Farwell, Harold, and Paul Buchanan. 1994. [Paper presented at Appalachian Studies Association meeting, Blacksburg, VA, based on Buchanan's recollections from the 1920s]. [western NC]

1994 Garza *Matchbox Mt* = Garza, Amy Ammons. 1994. *Matchbox mountains: Stories based on a mountain childhood.* Asheville, NC: Bright Mountain. [western NC]

1994 Holbrook *First* = Holbrook, Chris. 1994. First of the month. *Now & Then* 11(2): 18–21.

1994 Huskey *County Squire* = Huskey, Conley. 1994. *Memories of a county squire.* Sevierville, TN: Nandel. [Sevier County, central east TN]

1994 Jones *Appal Values* = Jones, Loyal. 1994. *Appalachian values.* Ashland, KY: Jesse Stuart Foundation.

1994 Lambert *Sawmills* = Lambert, Carol Glenn. 1994. Sawmills and railroads. *Bone Rattler* 10(4): 44–48. [western NC]

1994 Martin *Stock Car Legends* = Martin, Ronda Jackson. 1994. *Stock car legends: The laughs, practical jokes, and fun stories from racing's greats.* Nashville, TN: Premium Press America.

1994 McCarthy *Jack Two Worlds* = McCarthy, William B. 1994. *Jack in two worlds: Contemporary North American tales and their tellers.* Chapel Hill: University of North Carolina Press.

1994 Morgan *Hinterlands* = Morgan, Robert. 1994. *The hinterlands: A mountain tale in three parts.* Chapel Hill, NC: Algonquin.

1994 Mullins *Coaley Creek* = Mullins, Denvil. 1994. *The cornfields of Coaley Creek.* Johnson City, TN: Overmountain. [southwestern VA]

1994 Mullins *Echoes Appal* = Mullins, Denvil. 1994. *Echoes of Appalachia.* Johnson City, TN: Overmountain. [southwestern VA]

1994 Parton *Dolly* = Parton, Dolly. 1994. *Dolly: My life and other unfinished business.* New York: HarperCollins. [Sevier County, central east TN]

1994 Rash *New Jesus* = Rash, Ron. 1994. *The night the new Jesus fell to earth and other stories from Cliffside, North Carolina.* Columbia, SC: Bench.

1994 Schmidt and Hooks *Whistle* = Schmidt, Ronald G., and William S. Hooks. 1994. *Whistle over the mountain: Timber, track and trails in the Tennessee Smokies.* Yellow Springs, OH: Graphicom. [Blount and Sevier Counties, central east TN]

1994 Speer *Power to Create* = Speer, Jean Haskell. 1994. The power to create identity. *Now & Then* 10(3): 2.

1994 Thomas *Come Go* = Thomas, Roy Edwin. 1994. *Come go with me: Old-timer stories from the southern mountains.* New York: Farrar, Straus and Giroux. [northwestern NC]

1994 Walker *Life History* = Walker, Cas. 1994. *My life history: A book of true stories.* N.p.: Privately published. [Sevier County, central east TN]

1994 Weals *Coll* = [observations, news clippings, and other material collected by the editor from Vic Weals] [central east TN]

1995 Adams *Come Go Home* = Adams, Sheila Kay. 1995. *Come go home with me.* Chapel Hill: University of North Carolina Press. [Haywood County, central western NC]

1995 Alexander *Mt Fever* = Alexander, Tom. 1995. *Mountain fever.* Edited by Tom Alexander Jr. and Jane Alexander. Asheville, NC: Bright Mountain. [Haywood County, central western NC]

1995 Andrews *Jes' Broguin'* = Andrews, Scottie. 1995. *Jes' a' broguin' about.* Waynesville, NC: Broguin' About Books. [Haywood County, central western NC]

1995 Brewer *Cow Flats* = Brewer, Carson. 1995. Cow Flats, Zenith are old names of Smokies. *Knoxville News-Sentinel*, January 5. [east TN]

c1995 *Cades Cove* = *Cades Cove.* c1995. Gatlinburg, TN: Great Smoky Mountains Natural History Association. [Blount County, central east TN]

1995 Cheek *Appal Scrapbook* = Cheek, Pauline B. 1995. *Appalachian scrapbook: An A-B-C of growing up in the mountains.* Johnson City, TN: Overmountain.

1995 Creekmore *TN Extracts* = Creekmore, Pollyanna. 1995. Tennessee newspaper extracts and abstracts: Marriage, death, and other items of genealogical/historical interest: *The Knoxville Press, vol. 1816–1830.* Knoxville: Clinchdale. [east TN]

1995 Elliott *Wild Roots* = Elliott, Doug. 1995. *Wild roots*. New York: Healing Arts Press.

1995 Harrison *Smoke Rings* = Harrison, Deane Bell. 1995. *Smoke rings*. Rogersville: East Tennessee Printing. [Jefferson County, central east TN]

1995 Higgs et al. *Inside Out* = Higgs, Robert J., Ambrose N. Manning, and Jim Wayne Miller, eds. 1995. *Appalachia inside out*. Knoxville: University of Tennessee Press.

1995 Horrell and Russell *Coal Portfolio* = Horrell, C. William, and Herbert K. Russell. 1995. *Southern Illinois coal: A portfolio*. Carbondale: Southern Illinois University Press.

1995 Jones *Early Sevier Archit* = Jones, Robbie D. 1995. The early architecture of Sevier County, Tennessee. *Smoky Mountain Historical Society Journal and Newsletter* 21: 4–23. [Sevier County, central east TN]

1995 McCauley *Mt Religion* = McCauley, Deborah Vansau. 1995. *Appalachian mountain religion: A history*. Urbana: University of Illinois Press.

1995 Milnes *Old Christmas* = Milnes, Gerald. 1995. Old Christmas and belsnickles: Our early holiday traditions. *Goldenseal* 21(4): 26–31. [WV]

c1995 *Mingus Mill* = *Mingus Mill*. c1995. Gatlinburg, TN: Great Smoky Mountains Natural History Association. [Blount County, central east TN]

1995 Minick *Groundhogs* = Minick, Jim. 1995. Groundhogs. *Now & Then* 12(1): 15–16.

1995 Moffett *Cantilever Barns* = Moffett, Marian. 1995. East Tennessee cantilever barns. *Smoky Mountain Historical Society Journal and Newsletter* 21(1): 12–25. [east TN]

1995 Montieth *Tall Tales* = Montieth, David. 1995. Tall tales of the mountains. *Bone Rattler* 10(3): 10–12. [western NC]

1995 Mullins *Road Back* = Mullins, Denvil. 1995. *The road back home: Tales of Appalachia*. Johnson City, TN: Overmountain.

1995 Olson *Walker Calhoun* = Olson, Ted. 1995. An interview with Walker Calhoun. *Appalachian Journal* 23(1): 70–77. [Swain County, southwestern NC]

1995 Parce *Twice-Told* = Parce, Mead. 1995. *Twice-told true tales of the Blue Ridge and Great Smokies*. Hendersonville, NC: Harmon Den.

1995 Patterson *Sound of Dove* = Patterson, Beverly Bush. 1995. *The sound of the dove: Singing in Appalachian Primitive Baptist churches*. Urbana: University of Illinois Press.

1995 Peterson *Ginseng Hunter* = Peterson, Ronan K. 1995. Sanging in Poplar, NC: Zelotes Peterson, ginseng hunter. *North Carolina Folklore Journal* 42: 52–61. [western NC]

c1995 *Pioneer Farmstead* = *Pioneer farmstead*. c1995. Gatlinburg, TN: Great Smoky Mountains Natural History Association. [Swain County, southwestern NC]

1995 Prince *Quill Rose* = Prince, Pete. 1995. Quill Rose—famous moonshiner. *Bone Rattler* 11(3): 27–30. [Swain County, southwestern NC]

c1995 *Roaring Fork* = *Roaring Fork auto tour*. c1995. Gatlinburg, TN: Great Smoky Mountains Natural Historical Association. [Sevier County, central east TN]

1995 South *What It Is* = South, Stanley. 1995. *What it is, boss man?* Columbia, SC: Wine Cellar Press. [northwestern NC]

1995 Stone *Smoky Mt Women* = Stone, Mary O. 1995. *Confidence courage spunk: Smoky mountain women*. Sevierville, TN: Mountain Press. [central east TN, central western NC]

1995 Suter *Shenandoah Folklife* = Suter, Scott Hamilton. 1995. *Shenandoah Valley folklife*. Jackson: University Press of Mississippi. [western VA]

1995 Trout *Historic Buildings* = Trout, Ed. 1995. *Historic buildings of the Smokies*. Gatlinburg, TN: Great Smoky Mountains Natural History Association. [central east TN, central western NC]

1995 Weber *Rugged Hills* = Weber, William J. 1995. *Rugged hills, gentle folk: My friends and neighbors in the Big Pine Valley*. Glendale, WI: Reiman. [western NC]

1995 Williams *Become Teacher* = Williams, Cratis D. 1995. I become a teacher: A memoir of one-room school life in eastern Kentucky. Ashland, KY: Jesse Stuart Foundation.

1995 Williams *Smoky Mts Folklife* = Williams, Michael Ann. 1995. *Great Smoky Mountains folklife*. Jackson: University Press of Mississippi. [central east TN, central western NC]

1996 Bailey *Mizriz* = Bailey, Lucille M. 1996. The persistence of /mɪzrɪz/ among younger speakers in Kentucky. *SECOL Review* 20: 154–63. [KY]

1996–2017 *BearPaw* = *BearPaw* (Great Smoky Mountains Association newsletter). 1996–2013. Gatlinburg, TN: Great Smoky Mountains Natural History Association and Great Smoky Mountains Association. [central east TN, central western NC]

1996 Casada *Gospel Hook* = Casada, Jim. 1996. Caught by the gospel hook. *Bone Rattler* 12(4): 24–27. [Swain County, southwestern NC]

1996 Cavender *Bold Hives* = Cavender, Anthony. 1996. A note on the origin and meaning of bold hives in the American South. *Southern Folklore* 53: 17–24. [northeast TN]

1996 Cole *Forney's Creek* = Cole, David. 1996. A social history of Forney's Creek, North Carolina. *Bone Rattler* 12(3): 59–71. [Swain County, southwestern NC]

1996 Dorgan *Baptist Diversity* = Dorgan, Howard. 1996. Baptist diversity in Appalachia. *Now & Then* 13(3): 8–11.

1996 Dorgan *Review* = Dorgan, Howard. 1996. Review of *The sound of the dove: Singing in Appalachian Primitive Baptist churches*, by Beverly Bush Patterson. *Now & Then* 13(3): 36–37.

1996 Dykeman *Memories* = Dykeman, Wilma. 1996. Memories of Smokies park remain. *Knoxville News-Sentinel*, December 15. [east TN]

1996 Edmondson *Crawford Memoirs* = Edmondson, Kenneth L. 1996. Hugh Forgey Crawford: Family memoirs, letters, and New Year's notes. *Tennessee Ancestors* 12: 125–37.

1996–99 *GSMNPCOHP* = University of Tennessee / Great Smoky Mountains National Park Cooperative Oral History Project. 1996–99. [Recorded interviews consulted at Library, Great Smoky Mountains National Park, Gatlinburg, TN]. [central east TN, central western NC]

1996 Gump *Amis Ledger* = Gump, Lucy. 1996. *Amis ledger B (1782–1794): Interpretive transcription of an east Tennessee business record book*. Johnson City, TN: Privately published. [northeast TN]

1996 Harrell *Fetch It* = Harrell, A. D. 1996. *Fetch it, Rusty!* Burnsville, NC: Celo Valley. [northwestern NC]

1996 Houk *Foods & Recipes* = Houk, Rose. 1996. *Foods & recipes of the Smokies*. Gatlinburg, TN: Great Smoky Mountains Natural History Association. [central east TN, central western NC]

1996 Hughes *Swain County* = Hughes, Walter. 1996. Swain County. *Bone Rattler* 12(1): 12–21. [Swain County, southwestern NC]

1996 Huheey *Variant Names* = Huheey, James E. 1996. Variant names for Smoky Mountain reptiles and amphibians. Typescript provided to the editor. [central east TN, central western NC]

1996 Isbell *Last Chivaree* = Isbell, Robert. 1996. *The last chivaree: The Hicks family of Beech Mountain*. Chapel Hill: University of North Carolina Press. [Avery County, northwestern NC]

1996 Isserman *People in Appal* = Isserman, Andrew. 1996. Do people in Appalachia know they're Appalachians? *Now & Then* 13(2): 14.

1996 Johnson *Lexical Change* = Johnson, Ellen. 1996. *Lexical change and variation in the southeastern United States, 1930–1990*. Tuscaloosa: University of Alabama Press. [north GA, northwestern SC]

1996 Leonard *Ministering* = Leonard, Bill J. 1996. Ministering in Appalachia. *Now & Then* 13(3): 12–14.

1996 Lewis *People in Appal* = Lewis, Helen M. 1996. Do people in Appalachia know they're Appalachians? *Now & Then* 13(2): 14.

1996 Linn *West Fork* = Linn, Beulah. 1996. The west fork of the Little Pigeon River. *Smoky Mountain Historical Society Journal and Newsletter* 22(2): 3–4. [Sevier County, central east TN]

1996 Pardue *Recollections* = Pardue, Paul. 1996. Recollections of a somewhat early childhood. *Smoky Mountain Historical Society Journal and Newsletter* 22(3): 16–17. [Sevier County, central east TN]

1996 Parton *Mt Memories* = Parton, Willadeene. 1996. *Smoky Mountain memories: Stories from the hearts of Dolly Parton's family*. Nashville, TN: Rutledge Hill Press. [Sevier County, central east TN]

1996 South *Never Killed* = South, Stanley. 1996. *I never killed a man didn't need killing*. Columbia, SC: Wine Cellar Verse. [Watauga County, northwestern NC]

1996 Spurlock *Glossary* = Spurlock, John H. 1996. Glossary to accompany *Beyond Dark Hills*, by Jesse Stuart, 389–414. Ashland, KY: Jesse Stuart Foundation. [northeastern KY]

1996 Thompson *Link in Chain* = Thompson, Mary Rado. 1996. A link in a chain. *Now & Then* 13(3): 17–20.

1996 White et al. *Wildflowers* = White, Peter, T. Condon, J. Rock, and C. A. McCormick. 1996. *Wildflowers of the Smokies*. Gatlinburg, TN: Great Smoky Mountains Association. [central east TN, central western NC]

1996 Woodring *Times Gone By* = Woodring, Howard. 1996. *A window to times gone by: Tales and songs*. Transcribed and published by Stanley South. Columbia, SC: Privately published. [Watauga County, northwestern NC]

1997 Andrews *Mountain Vittles* = Andrews, Scottie. 1997. *Dude's mountain vittles: Country food mountain style*. Waynesville, NC: Old Style Printing. [western NC]

1997 Axtell *Hog Wild* = Axtell, Nathaniel H. 1997. Hog wild: Exotic boars keep Smokies staff jumping. *Appalachian Voice* (Spring): 3, 19.

1997 Blaustein *Pelznickel* = Blaustein, Richard. 1997. Harvey Miller and the Pelznickel: Exploring a survival of German folk culture in southern Appalachia. Paper presented at the Appalachian Studies Association conference, Cincinnati.

1997 Brown *Listening* = Brown, Fred. 1997. Listening to the men of the mountain: Glenn Cardwell speaks with the knowledge of the past. *Knoxville News-Sentinel*, October 26. Repr., *Smoky Mountain Historical Society Journal and Newsletter* 23(3): 22–23. [Sevier County, central east TN]

1997–98 *Dante OHP* = Dante Oral History Project. 1997–98. [Selected audio interviews, transcribed for this book]. Dante Oral History Project Records. Archives of Appalachia, East Tennessee State University, Johnson City. [southwestern VA]

1997 Davis *Cataloochee Valley* = Davis, Hattie Caldwell. 1997. *Cataloochee Valley: Vanished settlements of the Great Smoky Mountains*. Alexander, NC: WorldComm. [Haywood County, central western NC]

1997 Dorgan *Happy God* = Dorgan, Howard. 1997. *In the hands of a happy God: The no-hellers of central Appalachia*. Knoxville: University of Tennessee Press. [southeastern KY]

1997 Farwell *Logging* = Farwell, Harold. 1997. The language of Smoky Mountain loggers. Paper presented at the Dictionary Society of North America meeting, Madison, WI. [Haywood County, central western NC]

1997 Frazier *Cold Mountain* = Frazier, Charles. 1997. *Cold Mountain*. New York: Vintage.

1997 French *Counseling Indians* = French, Lawrence. 1997. *Counseling American Indians*. Lanham, MD: University Press of America.

1997 Hufford *American Ginseng* = Hufford, Mary. 1997. American ginseng and the idea of the commons. *Folklife Center News* 19(1–2): 3–18. https://www.loc.gov/collections/folklife-and-landscape-in-southern-west-virginia/articles-and-essays/american-ginseng-and-the-idea-of-the-commons/ginseng-and-the-future-of-the-commons/. [southern WV]

1997 Hufford *Stalking* = Hufford, Mary. 1997. Stalking the mother forest: Voices beneath the canopy. https://www.loc.gov/collections/folklife-and-landscape-in-southern-west-virginia/articles-and-essays/stalking-the-mother-forest-voices-beneath-the-canopy/. [southern WV]

1997 Johnson *Melungeon Heritage* = Johnson, Mattie Ruth. 1997. *My Melungeon heritage: A story of life on Newman's Ridge*. Johnson City, TN: Overmountain. [northeast TN]

c1997 Jones *Why They Talk* = Jones, Patricia S. c1997. Why they talk that way: Language factors in migrant Appalachians adaptations. Paper presented at the Appalachian Studies Association conference, Cincinnati, and copy provided to the editor. [Morgan County, eastern KY]

1997 King *Mt Folks* = King, Veta Wilson. 1997. *Mountain folks of old Smoky*. Sevierville, TN: Back Home. [Sevier County, central east TN]

1997 Miller *Brier Poems* = Miller, Jim Wayne. 1997. *The brier poems*. Frankfort, KY: Gnomon.

1997 Morgan *Barn in SW VA* = Morgan, John. 1997. The cantilever barn in southwest Virginia. In *Diversity and accommodation: Essays on the cultural composition of the Virginia frontier*, edited by Michael J. Puglisi, 275–92. Knoxville: University of Tennessee Press. [southwestern VA]

1997 Nelson *Country Folklore* = Nelson, Louise K. 1997. *Country folklore 1920s & 1930s and that's the way it was*. Alexander, NC: WorldComm. [western NC]

1997 Ownby *Big Greenbrier* = Ownby, Evolena. 1997. Memories of Big Greenbrier, Sevier County, Tennessee. *Smoky Mountain Historical Society Journal and Newsletter* 23(2): 15–25. [Sevier County, central east TN]

1997 Roe *Teaching Stories* = Roe, Betty D. 1997. *Teaching through stories: Yours, mine, and theirs*. Norwood, MA: Christopher Gordon.

1997 Smith *Dulcimer Traditions* = Smith, Ralph Lee. 1997. *Appalachian dulcimer traditions*. Lanham, MD: Scarecrow.

1997 Stoddart *Quare Women* = Stoddart, Jess, ed. 1997. *The quare women's journals: May Stone and Katherine Pettit's summers in the Kentucky mountains and the founding of the Hindman Settlement School*. Ashland, KY: Jesse Stuart Foundation. [southeastern KY]

1997 Watkins *Photographers* = Watkins, Charles Alan. Why have there been no Great Appalachian Photographers? *Now & Then* 14(2): 21–25.

1998 Brewer *Don't Scrouge* = Brewer, Carson. 1998. Don't scrouge: There's plenty of room for mountain lingo. *Knoxville News-Sentinel*, March 5, B1. [east TN]

1998 Brewer *Words of Past* = Brewer, Carson. 1998. Words of the past bring a mess of mail. *Knoxville News-Sentinel*, April 9, B1. [east TN]

1998 Buchanan *Logging Terms* = Buchanan, Paul. 1998. [Typescript compilation of logging terms provided to editor by Harold Farwell]. [western NC]

1998 Bueker *Head Letters* = Bueker, Terese Bland. 1998. Head family letters. *Tennessee Ancestors* 14: 13–18.

1998 Bushyhead *Cherokee Lg* = Bushyhead, Robert. 1998. Cherokee language. In *Living stories of the Cherokee*, edited by Barbara K. Duncan and Davey Arch, 145–49. Chapel Hill: University of North Carolina Press. [Swain County, southwestern NC]

1998 Dabney *Smokehouse Ham* = Dabney, Joseph E. 1998. *Smokehouse ham, spoon bread, and scuppernong wine*. Nashville, TN: Cumberland.

1998 Farwell *Logging Terms* = Farwell, Harold. 1998. [Typescript compilation of logging terms provided to the editor]. [western NC]

1998 Giardina *No Scapin* = Giardina, Denise. 1998. No scapin the booger man. In *Bloodroot: Reflections on place by Appalachian women writers*, edited by Joyce Dyer, 128–31. Lexington: University Press of Kentucky.

1998 Hamby *Grassy Creek* = Hamby, Zetta Barker. 1998. *Memoirs of Grassy Creek: Growing up in the mountains on the Virginia–North Carolina line*. Jefferson, NC: MacFarland. [southwestern VA, northwestern NC]

1998 Hyde *My Home* = Hyde, Herbert. 1998. *My home is in the Smoky Mountains*. Alexander, NC: WorldComm. [western NC]

1998 Joslin *Living Heritage* = Joslin, Michael. 1998. *Our living heritage*. Johnson City, TN: Overmountain. [northwestern NC]

1998 Miller and Sharpless *Kingdom of Coal* = Miller, Donald L., and Richard E. Sharpless. 1998. *The kingdom of coal: Work, enterprise, and ethnic communities in the mine fields*. Easton, PA: Canal History and Technology Press.

1998 Olson *Blue Ridge Folklife* = Olson, Ted. 1998. *Blue Ridge folklife*. Jackson: University Press of Mississippi.

1998 Olszewski *Old Harp* = Olszewski, Larry. 1998. Comments on old harp. *Old harp: The new harp of Columbia newsletter* 21: 12–13.

1998 Ownby *Big Greenbrier* = Ownby, Evolena. 1998. Life after Big Greenbrier. *Smoky Mountain Historical Society Journal and Newsletter* 24(1): 4–13. [Sevier County, central east TN]

1998 Perkins *Border Life* = Perkins, Elizabeth A. 1998. *Border life: Experience and memory in the Revolutionary Ohio Valley*. Chapel Hill: University of North Carolina Press.

1998 Robbins *Logging Terms* = Robbins, Tom. 1998. [Typescript compilation of logging terms provided to the editor]. [western NC]

1998 Still *Appal Mother Goose* = Still, James. 1998. *Appalachian Mother Goose*. Lexington: University Press of Kentucky.

1999 Axtell *Moonshine Making* = Axtell, Nathaniel H. 1999. Moonshine making "still" thriving in Appalachia. *Appalachian Voice* (Winter): 3, 18.

1999 Bishir et al. *Archit W NC* = Bishir, Catherine W., Michael Southern, and Jennifer F. Martin. 1999. *A guide to the historic architecture of western North Carolina*. Chapel Hill: University of North Carolina Press. [western NC]

1999 Brewer *Appal Lg* = Brewer, Carson. 1999. Author privy to Appalachian language. *Knoxville News-Sentinel*, January 28. [east TN]

1999 Carver *Branch Water Tales* = Carver, Bill. 1999. *Branch water tales*. Andrews, NC: Mountain Voice. [southwestern NC]

1999 Coggins *Place Names Smokies* = Coggins, Allen R. 1999. *Place names in the Smokies*. Gatlinburg, TN: Great Smoky Mountains Association. [central east TN, central western NC]

1999 Collins et al. *Foxfire XI* = Collins, Kaye Carver, Lacy Hunter, et al., eds. 1999. *Foxfire 11: The old homeplace, wild plant uses, preserving and cooking food, hunting stories, fishing, and more affairs of plain living*. New York: Anchor.

1999 Davis *CW Letters* = Davis, Hattie Caldwell. 1999. *Civil War letters and memories from the Great Smoky Mountains*. Maggie Valley, NC: Privately published. [Haywood County, central western NC]

1999 DeRozier *Creeker* = DeRozier, Linda Scott. 1999. *Creeker: A woman's journey*. Lexington: University Press of Kentucky. [eastern KY]

1999 Dumas *Sthn Mt English* = Dumas, Bethany. 1999. Southern mountain English: The language of the Ozarks and southern Appalachia. In *The workings of language from prescriptives to perspectives*, edited by Rebecca S. Wheeler, 67–79. Westport, CT: Praeger.

1999 Fisher *Stepchild* = Fisher, Stephen L. 1999. Appalachian stepchild. In *Confronting Appalachian stereotypes: Back talk from an American region*, edited by Dwight Billings, Katherine Ledford, and Gurney Norman, 187–90. Lexington: University Press of Kentucky. [southern WV]

1999 Fulcher *Raising Cane* = Fulcher, Bob. 1999. Raising cane in Tennessee. *Tennessee Conservationist* (July/August): 11–15. [east TN]

1999 Gilley *Letters* = Gilley, Joseph K. 1999. *Letters to home, the Civil War letters of Daniel Haywood Gilley*. Williamsburg, VA: Joseph K. Gilley. [Henry County, southwestern VA]

1999 Goodman and Burgin *Daughters* = Goodman, Linda, and Raymond Burgin. 1999. *Daughters of the Appalachians: Six unique women*. Johnson City, TN: Overmountain.

1999 Green and Fernandez *Native N America* = Green, Rayna, and Melanie Fernandez, eds. 1999. *The British Museum encyclopedia of native North America*. London: British Museum Press.

1999 Hodges *Tough Customers* = Hodges, Mary Bozeman. 1999. *Tough customers*. Ashland, KY: Jesse Stuart Foundation. [east TN]

1999 House *Elements Appal Lit* = House, Silas. 1999. Elements most often found in Appalachian literature. *Now & Then* 16(2): 2.

1999 Hoyle *Handed Down* = Hoyle, Joy Phillips. 1999. *Handed down then passed around*. Whittier, NC: Ammons. [western NC]

1999 Isbell *Keepers* = Isbell, Robert. 1999. *The keepers: Mountain folk holding on to old skills and talents*. Winston-Salem, NC: Blair. [western NC]

1999 Lane *Chattooga* = Lane, John. 1999. *Chattooga: Descending into the myth of Deliverance River*. Athens: University of Georgia Press. [northeast GA]

1999 McNeil *Purchase Knob* = McNeil, Kathryn K. 1999. *Purchase Knob: Essays from a mountain notebook*. Santa Barbara, CA: Fithian.

1999 Milnes *Play of Fiddle* = Milnes, Gerald. 1999. *Play of a fiddle: Traditional music, dance, and folklore in West Virginia*. Lexington: University Press of Kentucky. [WV]

1999 Morgan *Gap Creek* = Morgan, Robert. 1999. *Gap Creek*. Chapel Hill, NC: Algonquin.

1999 Nelson *Aroma and Memories* = Nelson, Louise K. 1999. *Aroma and memories of grandma's and mama's kitchen*. Alexander, NC: WorldComm. [western NC]

1999 Offutt *Out of Woods* = Offutt, Chris. 1999. *Out of the woods*. New York: Simon & Schuster.

1999 Perry *Clinch River* = Perry, Virgie Brewer. 1999. Memories along Clinch River. www.tngenweb.org/union/history/Memories-Along-Clinch-River.pdf. [northeast TN]

1999 Postell *Traditions* = Postell, Lesa W. 1999. *Appalachian traditions: Mountain ways of canning, pickling & drying*. Whittier, NC: Ammons. [western NC]

1999 Russell and Barnett *Granny Curse* = Russell, Randy, and Janet Barnett. 1999. *The granny curse and other ghosts and legends from east Tennessee*. Winston-Salem, NC: Blair. [east TN]

1999 Schwartz *Holiness Believers* = Schwartz, Scott W. 1999. *Faith, serpents, and fire: Images of Kentucky Holiness believers*. Jackson: University Press of Mississippi.

1999 Spencer *Memory Lane* = Spencer, Ezalee Kear. 1999–2000. Down memory lane [parts 1 and 2 of 3]. *Smoky Mountain Historical Society Journal and Newsletter* 25(3): 6–10; 25(4): 2–11. [Sevier County, central east TN]

c1999 Sutton *Me and Likker* = Sutton, Popcorn. c1999. *Me and my likker: The story of a mountain moonshiner*. Maggie Valley, NC: Privately published. [Cocke County, central east TN and Haywood County, central western NC]

1999 Wilkinson *Being Country* = Wilkinson, Crystal E. 1999. On being "country": One Affrilachian woman's return home. In *Confronting Appalachian stereotypes: Back talk from an American region*, edited by Dwight E. Billings, Gurney Norman, and Katherine Ledford, 184–86. Lexington: University Press of Kentucky. [south central KY]

1999 Williams *Come to Boone* = Williams, Cratis D. 1999. *I come to Boone*. Boone, NC: Appalachian Consortium Press.

1999 Wilson and Haas *Memory Quilt* = Wilson, Jane, and Michaele Haas. 1999. *MeeMa's memory quilt: Treasured stories of Watauga County history*. Boone, NC: Parkway. [Watauga County, northwestern NC]

2000 Bailey *Price of Assimilation* = Bailey, Rebecca J. 2000. I never thought of my life as history: A story of the "hillbilly" exodus and the price of assimilation. In *Appalachian migration*, edited by Philip J. Obermiller, Thomas E. Wagner, and E. Bruce Tucker, 27–38. Westport, CT: Praeger.

2000 Berry *Sthn Migrants* = Berry, Chad. 2000. *Southern migrants, Northern exiles*. Champaign: University of Illinois Press.

2000 Brown *Far East* = Brown, Margaret Lynn. 2000. *The far east: A biography of the Great Smoky Mountains*. Gainesville: University Press of Florida. [central east TN, central western NC]

2000 Carden *Mason Jars* = Carden, Gary. 2000. *Mason jars in the flood and other stories*. Boone, NC: Parkway. [Jackson County, southwestern NC]

2000 Clark *Don't Mess* = Clark, Amy. 2000. Can't pronounce *Appalachia*? Then don't mess with us. *Now & Then* 17(2): 29–30.

2000 Eller *Lost and Found* = Eller, Ron. 2000. The education of a hillbilly. In *One hundred years of Appalachian visions, 1897–1996*, edited by Bill Best, 125–30. Berea, KY: Appalachian Imprints. [WV]

2000 Ellis *KY River* = Ellis, William E. 2000. *The Kentucky River*. Lexington: University Press of Kentucky. [eastern KY]

2000 Fisher *Stepchild* = Fisher, Steve. 2000. Appalachian stepchild. In *One hundred years of Appalachian visions, 1897–1996*, edited by Bill Best, 157–60. Berea, KY: Appalachian Imprints. [southern WV]

2000 Goode *Being Appalachian* = Goode, James B. 2000. Taking stock of being Appalachian. In *One hundred years of Appalachian visions, 1897–1996*, edited by Bill Best, 81–84. Berea, KY: Appalachian Imprints. [Harlan County, southeastern KY]

2000 Higgs *Two Pappies* = Higgs, Robert J. 2000. Two hills and two pappies. In *One hundred years of Appalachian visions, 1897–1996*, edited by Bill Best, 53–56. Berea, KY: Appalachian Imprints. [south central TN]

2000 Inscoe *Appalachians and Race* = Inscoe, John C. 2000. *Appalachians and race: The mountain South from slavery to segregation*. Lexington: University Press of Kentucky.

2000 Joyner *Magic Mts* = Joyner, Nancy. 2000. The magic mountains. In *One hundred years of Appalachian visions, 1897–1996*, edited by Bill Best, 145–48. Berea, KY: Appalachian Imprints. [northwestern SC]

2000 Lewis *Appal Countryside* = Lewis, Ronald L. 2000. *Transforming the Appalachian countryside: Railroads, deforestation, and social change in West Virginia, 1880–1920*. Chapel Hill: University of North Carolina Press. [WV]

2000 Lowry *Folk Medical Term* = Lowry, Houston. 2000. Folk medical terminology as remembered from my practice. Typescript provided to the editor. [Monroe County, southeast TN]

2000 Lyon *Growing Up* = Lyon, George Ella. 2000. Growing up in Harlan County. In *One hundred years of Appalachian visions, 1897–1996*, edited by Bill Best, 85–86. Berea, KY: Appalachian Imprints. [Harlan County, southeastern KY]

2000 Miller *Ignorant People* = Miller, Judy. 2000. Only Ignorant people. In *One hundred years of Appalachian visions, 1897–1996*, edited by Bill Best, 71–72. Berea, KY: Appalachian Imprints.

2000 Miller *Looneyville* = Miller, Jake. 2000. *Looneyville zip code 25259 lore: Appalachian mountain folklore, popular etymology, colloquial speech*. Philadelphia: Xlibris. [WV]

2000 Morgan *Mts Remember* = Morgan, Robert. 2000. *The mountains won't remember us, and other stories*. New York: Scribner.

2000 Norman *Consciousness* = Norman, Gurney. 2000. An "other" consciousness. In *One hundred years of Appalachian visions, 1897–1996*, edited by Bill Best, 149–56. Berea, KY: Appalachian Imprints. [eastern KY, WV]

2000 Oakley *Roamin' Man* = Oakley, Harvey. 2000. *Rememberin' the roamin' man of the mountains, Wiley Oakley*. Gatlinburg, TN: Oakley Books. [Sevier County, central east TN]

2000 Puckett *Pronunciation* = Puckett, Anita. 2000. On the pronunciation of Appalachia. *Now & Then* 17(2): 25–29.

2000 Puckett *Seldom Ask* = Puckett, Anita. 2000. *Seldom ask, never tell: Labor and discourse in Appalachia*. New York: Oxford University Press. [southeastern KY]

2000 Robbins *Mt Museum* = Robbins, Tom. 2000. *Mountain farm museum*. Gatlinburg, TN: Great Smoky Mountains Association. [Swain County, southwestern NC]

2000 Spencer *Memory Lane* = Spencer, Ezalee Kear. 1999–2000. Down memory lane [part 3 of 3]. *Smoky Mountain Historical Society Journal and Newsletter* 26(1): 2–8. [Sevier County, central east TN]

2000 Strutin *Gristmills* = Strutin, Michael. 2000. *Gristmills*. Gatlinburg, TN: Great Smoky Mountains Association. [central east TN, central western NC]

2000 Tipton *CW in Greasy Cove* = Tipton, A. Christine. 2000. *Civil War in the mountains: Greasy Cove, Tennessee*. Erwin, TN: Shining Mountain. [northeast TN]

2000 Venable *Mt Hands* = Venable, Sam. 2000. *Mountain hands: A portrait of southern Appalachia*. Knoxville: University of Tennessee Press. [east TN]

2000 Walker *Affrilachia* = Walker, Frank X. 2000. *Affrilachia: Poems by Frank X Walker*. Lexington, KY: Old Cove Press.

2000 Wilcox *Shaped Notes* = Wilcox, Patricia. 2000. *Shaped notes: Stories of twentieth century Georgia*. Binghamton, NY: Pageant Press. [northwest GA]

2000 Wilkinson *Blackberries* = Wilkinson, Crystal. 2000. *Blackberries, blackberries*. London: Toby. [south central KY]

2001 Cooper and Cooper *New River* = Cooper, Land, and Mary Lee Cooper. 2001. *The people of the New River: Oral histories from the Ashe, Alleghany, and Watauga Counties of North Carolina*. West Jefferson, NC: McFarland. [northwestern NC]

2001 House *Clay's Quilt* = House, Silas. 2001. *Clay's quilt*. New York: Ballantine.

2001 Hoyle *Call Home* = Hoyle, Vernon J. 2001. *A place to call home: Memoirs of J. Vernon Hoyle a mountain man*. Sylva, NC: Jackson County Historical Association. [Jackson County, southwestern NC]

2001 Joslin *Appal Bounty* = Joslin, Michael. 2001. *Appalachian bounty: Nature's gifts from the mountains: A collection of essays and photographs*. Johnson City, TN: Overmountain. [northwestern NC]

2001 Liftig *Lessons* = Liftig, Inez. 2001. Fugate: Lessons from Ganderbill Holler. *Now & Then* 18(1): 13–17. [eastern KY]

2001 Lowry *Expressions* = Lowry, Houston. 2001. Expressions, sayings, descriptions of patients in my practice: Notes sporadically made from about 1965 through 1998. Typescript provided to the editor. [Monroe County, southeast TN]

2001 Tilley and Huheey *Reptiles & Amphibians* = Tilley, Stephen G., and James E. Huheey. 2001. *Reptiles & amphibians of the Great Smokies*. Gatlinburg, TN: Great Smoky Mountains Association. [central east TN, central western NC]

2001 Wilson *Textile Art* = Wilson, Kathleen Curtis. 2001. *Textile art from southern Appalachia: The quiet work of women*. 2001. Johnson City, TN: Overmountain.

2002 Armstead *Black Days* = Armstead, Robert. 2002. *Black days, black dust: The memories of an African American coal miner*. Knoxville: University of Tennessee Press. [southern WV]

2002 *Cades Cove Preserv* = *Recipes, remedies & rumors: Volume 1*. 2002. Maryville, TN: Cades Cove Preservation Association. [Blount County, central east TN]

2002 Carter *Chaney Creek* = Carter, Clyde William. 2002. *Life on Chaney Creek*. Emory, VA: Clinch Mountain. [southwestern VA]

2002 Cavender and Crowder *White-Livered Women* = Cavender, Anthony, and Steve Crowder. 2002. White-livered women and bad-blooded men: Folk illness and sexual disorder in southern Appalachia. *Journal of the History of Sexuality* 11(4): 637–49.

2002 Davis *Step Back* = Davis, Hattie Caldwell. 2002. *Step back in time: See historic Cataloochee Valley of the elk*. Maggie Valley, NC: Privately published. [Haywood County, central western NC]

2002 Gibson *Gibson Remembers* = Gibson, Gertrude Andrews. 2002. Gertrude Andrews Gibson remembers. *Smoky Mountain Historical Society Journal and Newsletter* 28(1): 13–16. [Sevier County, central east TN]

2002 Goff *Sthn Gospel* = Goff, James R., Jr. 2002. *Close harmony: A history of southern gospel*. Chapel Hill: University of North Carolina Press.

2002 Hayler *Sound Wormy* = Hayler, Nicole, ed. 2002. *Sound wormy: Memoir of Andrew Gennett, lumberman*. Athens: University of Georgia Press. [north GA]

2002 Jones *Leicester Luminist* = Jones, Loyal. 2002. Leicester Luminist lighted local language and lore. *Appalachian Heritage* 30(1): 18–25. [western NC]

2002 Jones *Minstrel* = Jones, Loyal. 2002. *Minstrel of the Appalachians: The story of Bascom Lamar Lunsford*. Lexington: University Press of Kentucky. [western NC]

2002 Lacey *Amazing NC* = Lacey, Theresa Jensen. 2002. *Amazing North Carolina: Fascinating facts, entertaining tales, bizarre happenings, and historical oddities from the Tarheel State*. Nashville, TN: Rutledge Hill Press. [western NC]

2002 McGowan *Beech Mt Tales* = McGowan, Thomas, ed. 2002. Four Beech Mountain Jack tales. *North Carolina Folklore Journal* 49: 69–115. [Avery County, northwestern NC]

2002 Mitchell *Popcorn* = Mitchell, Henry H. 2002. Popcorn Sutton comments on local moonshine tradition. http://www.victorianvilla.com/sims-mitchell/local/vis/suttonp, accessed August 15, 2007.

2002 Morgan *Mt Born* = Morgan, Larry G. 2002. *Mountain born, mountain molded*. Boone, NC: Parkway. [western NC]

2002 Myers *Best Yet Stories* = Myers, Bonnie Trentham. 2002. *Best yet stories.* Gatlinburg, TN: Privately published. [central east TN]

2002 Nelson *Turn Back* = Nelson, Louise K. 2002. *Turn back the pages of time: Early mountain living.* Waynesville, NC: Privately published. [western NC]

2002 Ogle *Remembrances* = Ogle, Lucinda Oakley. 2002. *Remembrances of my past 93 years: Growing up in the Great Smoky Mountains.* Gatlinburg, TN: Privately published. [Sevier County, central east TN]

2002 Oliver *Cooking and Living* = Oliver, Duane. 2002. *Cooking and living along Hazel Creek.* Hazelwood, NC: Privately published. [Swain County, southwestern NC]

2002 Powell *Writing Geography* = Powell, Katrina M. 2002. Writing the geography of the Blue Ridge Mountains: How displacement recorded the land. *Biography* 25: 73–94. [central western Virginiannn]

2002 Quasha *Draw Georgia* = Quasha, Jennifer. 2002. *How to draw Georgia's sights and symbols (a kid's guide to drawing America).* N.p.: Powerkids Press.

2002 Rash *Foot in Eden* = Rash, Ron. 2002. *One foot in Eden.* Charlotte: Novello Festival Press.

2002 Reid *Hall's Top* = Reid, Juanita. 2002. Hall's Top remembered. *Smoky Mountain Historical Society Journal and Newsletter* 28(1): 22–24. [Cocke County, central east TN]

2002–18 *Smoky Mt News* = *Smoky Mt. News* (Bryson City, NC). 2002–18. [Miscellaneous articles from daily newspaper for Swain County]. [central western NC]

2002 Tate *Log Houses* = Tate, Bryan. 2002. Appalachian pioneers and log houses. *Journal of Alabama Archaeology* 48: 1–18.

2002 Weals *Legends* = Weals, Vic. 2002. *Legends of Cades Cove and the Smokies beyond.* Knoxville: Olden. [Blount County, central east TN]

2002 Williams *Appalachia* = Williams, John Alexander. 2002. *Appalachia: A history.* Chapel Hill: University of North Carolina Press.

2003 *Appal Journal* = Cozzo, David. 2003. Beyond tall tales: Ray Hicks and mountain herbalism. *Appalachian Journal* 30(4): 284–301.

2003 Blaustein *Thistle and Brier* = Blaustein, Richard. 2003. *The thistle and the brier: Historical links and cultural parallels between Scotland and Appalachia.* Jefferson, NC: McFarland.

2003 Carter *Mt Home* = Carter, Betty L. 2003. *My little mountain home (and me).* Victoria, BC: Trafford.

2003 Cavender *Folk Medicine* = Cavender, Anthony. 2003. *Folk medicine in southern Appalachia.* Chapel Hill: University of North Carolina Press. [northeast TN, southwestern VA]

2003 Cooper *Gathering Memories* = Cooper, Ann Goode. 2003. *Gathering up memories: A collection of Appalachian stories.* Boone, NC: Parkway. [western NC]

2003 Duncan and Riggs *Cherokee Trails* = Duncan, Barbara, and Brett Riggs. 2003. *Cherokee Heritage Trails guidebook.* Chapel Hill: University of North Carolina Press. [central western NC]

2003 Gibson *Sthn Mt Dialect* = Gibson, Dan. 2003. Southern mountain dialect. http://www.angelfire.com/tn2/ScottCoTnMemories/SouthernMountainDialect.html, accessed January 5, 2010. [Scott County, north central TN]

2003 Howell *Folklife Big South Fork* = Howell, Benita J. 2003. *Folklife along the Big South Fork of the Cumberland River.* Knoxville: University of Tennessee Press. [north central TN, southeastern KY]

2003 Jordan-Byshkov *Upland South* = Jordan-Byshkov, Terry G. 2003. *The upland South: The making of an American folk region.* Sante Fe, NM: Center for American Places.

2003 Josheff *Craft Traditions* = Josheff, Nicole. 2003. *Craft traditions: The Southern Highland Craft Guild collection.* [Asheville, NC]: Folk Arts Center.

2003 LaLone et al. *Farming Life* = LaLone, Mary B., Peg Wimmer, and Reva K. Spence. 2003. *Appalachian farming life: Memories and perspectives on family farming in Virginia's New River Valley.* N.p.: Brightside Press. [southwestern VA]

2003 Onchuck *Mud Pie Memories* = Onchuck, Sandra Young. 2003. *Mud pie memories: A scrapbook of an Appalachian childhood.* Philips, WI: Asaph. [southwestern NC]

2003 Smith *Orlean Puckett* = Smith, Karen Cecil. 2003. *Orlean Puckett: The life of a mountain midwife, 1844–1939.* Boone, NC: Parkway.

2003 Strutin *Hikes of Smokies* = Strutin, Michael. 2003. *History hikes of the Smokies.* Gatlinburg, TN: Great Smoky Mountains Association. [central east TN, central western NC]

2003 *TN Petitions I* = Index and examples of petitions to the Tennessee legislature. 2003. *Tennessee Ancestors* 19: 113–35. [east TN]

2003 *TN Petitions II* = Examples of petitions to the Tennessee legislature: Various counties. 2003. *Tennessee Ancestors* 19: 196–208. [east TN]

2003 Triplett *Mt Roots* = Triplett, George R. 2003. *Our proud mountain roots and heritage.* Elkins, WV: Self-published. [eastern WV]

2003 Watford *Civil War in NC* = Watford, Christopher M., ed. 2003. *The Civil War in North Carolina: Soldiers' and civilians' letters and diaries, 1861–1865*, vol. 2: *The mountains.* Jefferson, NC: McFarland. [western NC]

2003 Williams *Coming of Age* = Williams, Cratis. 2003. *Tales from sacred wind: Coming of age in Appalachia. The Cratis Williams Chronicle.* Boone, NC: Appalachian State University. [northeastern KY]

2003 Wolfram et al. *Mt Talk* = Wolfram, Walt, James W. Clark, Neal Hutcheson, and Gary Carden. 2003. *Mountain talk: A journey to the heart of southern Appalachia.* DVD. Raleigh: North Carolina Language and Life Project, North Carolina State University, Humanities Extension. [southwestern North Carolina]

2004 Adams *Old True Love* = Adams, Sheila Kay. 2004. *My old true love.* Chapel Hill, NC: Algonquin.

2004 *Bowman's Ms* = John Hoss Bowman's manuscript of travels to the North. 2004. *Watauga Association of Genealogists Bulletin* 33: 54–61.

2004 Burton *In Memoriam* = Burton, Thomas. 2004. Ray Hicks: A man who became a name. *Appalachian Journal* 31: 138–43. [Avery County, northwestern NC]

2004 Curry *The Sticks* = Curry, Janet. 2004. From the sticks: Growing up on the other side of the tracks. *Tradition: A Journal of West Virginia Folklife and Educational Awareness* 1: 39–40. [WV]

2004 Dodd *Amphibians Smoky Mts* = Dodd, C. Kenneth. 2004. *The amphibians of Great Smoky Mountains National Park.* Knoxville: University of Tennessee Press. [central east TN, central western NC]

2004 *Early Mines* = Early mines and mining methods in Monongah. 2004. *Tradition: A Journal of West Virginia Folklife and Educational Awareness* 1: 27–34. [WV]

2004 Finch *Ashes to Ashes* = Finch, Richard C. 2004. Ashes to ashes: Burial Upper Cumberland style. In *Rural life and culture in the Upper Cumberland*, edited by Michael E. Birdwell and W. Calvin Dickinson, 66–72. Lexington: University Press of Kentucky. [eastern KY]

2004 Fisher *Kettle Bottom* = Fisher, Diane Gilliam. 2004. *Kettle bottom.* Florence, MA: Perugia.

2004 *Foxfire XII* = Collins, Kaye Carver, Angie Cheek, et al., eds. 2004. *Foxfire 12: War stories, Cherokee traditions, summer camps, square dancing, crafts, and more affairs of plain living.* New York: Anchor.

2004 House *Coal Tattoo* = House, Silas. 2004. *The coal tattoo.* Chapel Hill, NC: Algonquin.

2004 Johnson *Camp Memories* = Coal camp memories: An interview with Johnnie Johnson. 2004. *Tradition: A Journal of West Virginia Folklife* 1: 22–25. [WV]

2004 Larimore *Bryson Seasons* = Larimore, Walt. 2004. *Bryson City seasons: More tales of a doctor's practice in the Smoky Mountains.* Grand Rapids, MI: Zondervan. [Swain County, southwestern NC]

2004 Maynard *Churches of Smokies* = Maynard, Charles. 2004. *Churches of the Smokies.* Gatlinburg, TN: Great Smoky Mountains Association. [central east TN, central western NC]

2004 Mays *Passion* = Mays, Carl. 2004. *People of passion: Spotlighting Southern Appalachia, representing America.* Johnson City, TN: Overmountain. [east TN]

2004 McGee *Blues* = McGee, Jim. 2004. Coal camp blues: Coalfield struggle. *Tradition: A Journal of West Virginia and Educational Awareness* 1: 45–46. [southwestern WV]

2004 Myers and Boyer *Walker Sisters* = Myers, Bonnie Trentham, and Linda Myers Boyer. 2004. *The Walker Sisters: Spirited women of the Smokies*. Maryville, TN: Myers and Myers. [Sevier County, central east TN]

2004 Purkey *Home Revisited* = Purkey, Lena Penland. 2004. *Home to Madison County revisited: To the descendants*. Edited by Shirley Purkey Hendrix. N.p.: Privately published. [Madison County, central western NC]

2004 Rash *Saints at River* = Rash, Ron. 2004. *Saints at the river*. New York: Henry Holt.

2004 Rehder *Appal Folkways* = Rehder, John. 2004. *Appalachian folkways*. Baltimore: Johns Hopkins University Press.

2004 *Reminder of Dwellings* = A reminder of dwellings from not so long ago. 2004. *Smoky Mountain News* (March 24–30), 39.

2004 Snodgrass *Kitchen History* = Snodgrass, Mary Ellen, ed. 2004. *Encyclopedia of kitchen history*. New York: Routledge.

2004 TN *Petitions III* = Index and examples of petitions to the Tennessee legislature. 2004. *Tennessee Ancestors* 20: 23–54. [east TN]

2004 West *Lonesome Road* = West, Don. 2004. *No lonesome road*. Edited by Jeff Biggers and George Brosi. Urbana: University of Illinois Press.

2004 Whitaker *Saints Sinners* = Whitaker, Larry. 2004. Saints, sinners, and dinners on the grounds: The religious legacy of the Upper Cumberland. In *Rural life and culture in the Upper Cumberland*, edited by Michael E. Birdwell and W. Calvin Dickinson, 49–65. Lexington: University Press of Kentucky. [north central TN]

2005 Bailey *Henderson County* = Bailey, Louise Howe. 2005. *Remembering Henderson County: A legacy of lore*. Charleston, SC: History Press. [Henderson County, southwestern NC]

2005 Ball *Gravehouse Origins* = Ball, Donald S. 2005. Observations on gravehouse origins in the upper south. *Tennessee Folklore Society Bulletin* 56(2): 17–30.

2005 Ballard and Chung *Arnow Stories* = Ballard, Sandra L., and Haeja K. Chung. 2005. *The collected short stories of Harriette Simpson Arnow*. East Lansing: Michigan State University Press.

2005 Cantrell *Clingman's Dome* = Cantrell, Geoff. 2005. *Clingman's Dome*. Gatlinburg, TN: Great Smoky Mountains Association.

2005 Crowley *War of Words* = Crowley, Tony. 2005. *Wars of words: The politics of language in Ireland, 1537–2004*. Oxford: Oxford University Press.

2005 Ebel *Orville Hicks* = Ebel, Julia Taylor. 2005. *Orville Hicks: Mountain stories—mountain roots*. Boone, NC: Parkway. [northwestern NC]

2005 Ellison *Mt Passages* = Ellison, George. 2005. *Mountain passages: Natural and cultural history of western North Carolina and the Great Smoky Mountains*. Charleston, SC: History Press. [western NC]

2005 Fisher *CW in Smokies* = Fisher, Noel. 2005. *The Civil War in the Smokies*. Gatlinburg, TN: Great Smoky Mountains Association. [central east TN, central western NC]

2005 Friend *Maysville Road* = Friend, Craig Thompson. 2005. *Along the Maysville Road: The early American republic in the trans-Appalachian West*. Knoxville: University of Tennessee Press. [northeastern KY]

2005 Good *Racing in Appalachia* = Good, Don. 2005. Racing in Appalachia. *Now & Then* 25(2): 3–4.

2005 Hicks *Blood and Bone* = Hicks, Jane. 2005. *Blood and bone remember*. Ashland, KY: Jesse Stuart Foundation.

2005 Houk *Walker Sisters* = Houk, Rose. 2005. *The Walker sisters of Little Greenbrier*. Gatlinburg, TN: Great Smoky Mountains Association. [Sevier County, central east TN]

2005 *Jefferson Co TN Petitions* = Index and examples of petitions to the Tennessee legislature: Jefferson County. 2005. *Tennessee Ancestors* 21: 172–216. [Jefferson County, central east TN]

2005 Jones and Wheeler *Laughter in Appalachia* = Jones, Loyal, and Billy Edd Wheeler. 2005. *Laughter in Appalachia: A festival of southern humor*. Little Rock, AR: August House.

2005 Joslin *Handcrafters* = Joslin, Michael. 2005. *Highland handcrafters: Appalachian craftspeople*. Boone, NC: Parkway. [northwestern NC]

2005 McCrumb *St. Dale* = McCrumb, Sharyn. 2005. St. Dale. New York: Kensington.

2005 Morgan *Old Time Religion* = Morgan, Larry G. 2005. *Old time religion in the southern Appalachians*. Boone, NC: Parkway. [western NC]

2005 Preece *I Grew* = Preece, Mary Ellen Goble. 2005. *In this valley I grew: Life on Backlog and Happy Hollow*. Baltimore: PublishAmerica. [eastern KY]

2005 Rains *Appal Mt Stories* = Rains, David. 2005. *The Shaman's daughter: Appalachian mountain stories*. New York: iUniverse.

2005 Sparks *Famous Preacher* = Sparks, John. 2005. *Raccoon John Smith: Frontier Kentucky's most famous preacher*. Lexington: University Press of Kentucky.

2005 Starnes *Land of Sky* = Starnes, Richard. 2005. *Creating the Land of the Sky: Tourism and society in western North Carolina*. Tuscaloosa: University of Alabama Press. [western NC]

2005 Williams *Gratitude* = Williams, Cleo Hicks. 2005. *Gratitude for shoes: Growing up poor in the Smokies*. New York: Universe. [Graham County, southwestern NC, as of 1940s]

2006 Awiakta *Abiding Appal* = Awiakta, Marilou. 2006. *Abiding Appalachia: Where mountain and atom meet*. Blacksburg, VA: Pocahontas.

2006 Burton *Serpent Handling* = Burton, Thomas G. 2006. Serpent handling. In *Encyclopedia of Appalachia*, edited by Rudy Abramson and Jean Haskell, 1350–52. Knoxville: University of Tennessee Press.

2006 Cavender *Medical Term* = Cavender, Anthony. 2006. Medical and health terminology. In *Encyclopedia of Appalachia*, edited by Rudy Abramson and Jean Haskell, 1021–22. Knoxville: University of Tennessee Press.

2006 Childs *Texana* = Texana Committee on Community History and Preservation. 2006. *Voices of Texana*. Raleigh: Barefoot Press. [Cherokee County, southwestern NC]

2006 Davis *Homeplace Geography* = Davis, Donald Edward. 2006. *Homeplace geography: Essays for Appalachia*. Macon, GA: Mercer University Press. [northwest GA]

2006 Ellison *Nature Journal* = Ellison, George, and Elizabeth Ellison. 2006. *Blue Ridge nature journal: Reflections on the Appalachians in essays and art*. Charleston, SC: History Press. [western NC]

2006 *Encycl Appalachia* = Abramson, Rudy, and Jean Haskell, eds. 2006. *Encyclopedia of Appalachia*. Knoxville: University of Tennessee Press.

2006 Farwell *Logging Term* = Farwell, Harold. 2006. Logging terminology. In *Encyclopedia of Appalachia*, edited by Rudy Abramson and Jean Haskell, 1020–21. Knoxville: University of Tennessee Press.

2006 *Foxfire 40th Anniv* = *The Foxfire 40th anniversary book: Faith, family, and the land*. 2006. Mountain City, GA: Foxfire Fund.

2006 Gary *Hogs Problems* = Gary, Lisa Byerley. 2006. Big hogs, big problems: Park control of wild hogs protects fragile ecosystems. *Sightline* 2(1). http://eerc.ra.utk.edu/sightline/InvasionsV2N1.html.

2006 Hicks *Mt Legacy* = Hicks, Enoch E. 2006. *Mountain legacy*. Dayton, OH: Wingspan and DreamPower.

2006 Howell *Medicinal Plants* = Howell, Patricia Kyritsi. 2006. *Medicinal plants of the southern Appalachians*. Mountain City, GA: Botanologos.

2006 Hufford *Headwaters* = Hufford, Mary. c2006. Landscapes and history at the headwaters of the Big Coal River Valley: An overview [excerpt]. Library of Congress. https://www.loc.gov/collections/folklife-and-landscape-in-southern-west-virginia/articles-and-essays/landscape-and-history-at-the-headwaters-of-the-big-coal-river/. [southern WV]

2006 Hufford *Ramp Suppers* = Hufford, Mary. 2006. Ramp suppers, biodiversity, and the integrity of the mountains. In *Cornbread nation III: The best writing about foods of the mountain South*, edited by Ronni Lundy, 108–17. Chapel Hill: University of North Carolina Press. [southern WV]

2006 Johannsen *Ginseng Dreams* = Johannsen, Kristin. 2006. *Ginseng dreams: The secret life of America's most valuable plant*. Lexington: University Press of Kentucky.

2006 Lalone *Coal Camps* = Lalone, Mary B. 2006. *Life in the coal camps of Wise County: In honor of Wise County sesquicentennial.* Wise, VA: Lonesome Pine Office of Youth. [southwestern VA]

2006 Lang *Conversations* = Lang, John, ed. 2006. *Appalachia and beyond: Conversations with writers from the mountain South.* Knoxville: University of Tennessee Press.

2006 Ledford *Survivals* = Ledford, Ted Roland. 2006. Colonial survivals in Appalachian English. In *Encyclopedia of Appalachia*, edited by Rudy Abramson and Jean Haskell, 1014. Knoxville: University of Tennessee Press.

2006 Logan and Jackson *Wytheville* = Logan, Linda, and Stevan Jackson. 2006. *A summer without children: An oral history of Wytheville Virginia's 1950 polio epidemic.* Wytheville, VA: Wordsprint. [southwestern VA]

2006 Montgomery *Ulster to America* = Montgomery, Michael. 2006. *From Ulster to America: The Scotch-Irish heritage of American English.* Belfast: Ulster Historical Foundation.

2006 Mooney *Lg Coal Mining* = Mooney, Stephen D. 2006. Coal mining terminology. In *Encyclopedia of Appalachia*, edited by Rudy Abramson and Jean Haskell, 1028–29. Knoxville: University of Tennessee Press.

2006 Puckett *Melungeon* = Puckett, Anita. 2006. Melungeon. In *Encyclopedia of Appalachia*, edited by Rudy Abramson and Jean Haskell, 1022–23. Knoxville: University of Tennessee Press. [Hancock County, northeast TN]

2006 Sauceman *Place Setting* = Sauceman, Fred W. 2006. The place setting. *Timeless tastes of the mountain south, from Bright Hope to Frog Level.* Macon, GA: Mercer University Press. [northeast TN]

2006 Shearer *Wilder Days* = Shearer, Kathy. 2006. *Wilder days: Coal town life on Dumps Creek.* Emory, VA: Clinch Mountain Press. [southwestern VA]

2006 Shelby *Appal Studies* = Shelby, Anne. 2006. *Appalachian studies: Poems.* Nicholasville, KY: Wind.

2006 Shumate *Bridge Crew* = Shumate, Samuel. 2006. *The bridge crew: Growing up in the Blue Ridge Mountains in the 1940s and 50s.* Boone, NC: Parkway. [western NC]

2006 Skipper *Tear Down* = Skipper, Roger Alan. 2006. *Tear down the mountain: An Appalachian love story.* New York: Soft Skull Press.

2006 Sohn *Whistlin' and Crowin'* = Sohn, Katherine Kelleher. 2006. *Whistlin' and crowin' women of Appalachia: Literacy practices since college.* Carbondale: Southern Illinois University Press. [eastern KY]

2006 Thompson and Moser *Folklife* = Thompson, Debra, and Irene Moser. 2006. Appalachian folklore. In *A handbook of Appalachia: An introduction to the region*, edited by Grace Toney Edwards, JoAnn Asbury, and Ricky Cox, 143–72. Knoxville: University of Tennessee Press.

2006 Vande Brake *They Shine* = Vande Brake, Katherine. 2006. *How they shine.* Macon, GA: Mercer University Press. [northeast TN]

2006 *WV Encycl* = *The West Virginia encyclopedia.* 2006. Charleston: West Virginia Humanities Council.

2007 Albala *Bean History* = Albala, Ken. 2007. *Beans: A history.* New York: Berg.

2007 Alexander *Forgotten Basket* = Alexander, Bill. 2007. The forgotten basket of the Smoky Mountains. *Smoky Mountain Historical Society Journal and Newsletter* 33(2): 7–9. [east TN]

2007 Alexander *Moonshiners Gone* = Alexander, John L. 2006. *Where have all our moonshiners gone?* Seneca, SC: Privately published. [northeast GA, northwestern SC]

2007 Baldridge *E KY Railway* = Baldridge, Terry L. 2007. *Eastern Kentucky Railway.* Charleston, SC: Arcadia. [eastern KY]

2007 Ball *Tub Mills* = Ball, Donald B. 2007. The history and use of tub mills in southern Appalachia. *Tennessee Folklore Society Bulletin* 63(1–2): 3–56.

2007 Ballard and Weinstein *Neighbor* = Ballard, Sandra L., and Leila E. Weinstein, eds. 2007. *Neighbor to neighbor: A memoir of family, community, and Civil War in Appalachian North Carolina.* Boone, NC: Appalachian State University Center for Appalachian Studies. [northwestern NC]

2007 Barksdale *Radford* = Barksdale, John W. 2007. *Radford.* Charleston, SC: Arcadia. [southwestern VA]

2007 Cave *Recollections* = Cave, Kent. 2007. [Personal notes shared with the editor]. [Surry County, northwestern NC]

2007 Davis *Co Line Baptist* = Davis, Matt. 2007. County Line Baptist Church Hawkins Grainger [part 1 of 2]. *Tennessee Ancestors* 23: 37–56, 102–16. [Grainger and Hawkins Counties, northeast TN]

2007 Dunkerly *Kings Mt* = Dunkerly, Robert M. 2007. *The battle of King's Mountain: Eyewitness accounts.* Charleston, SC: History Press.

2007 Ellison *Dandelions* = Ellison, George. 2007. Persecution of the dandelion. *Smoky Mountain News*, May 2. [western NC]

2007 Farr *My Appalachia* = Farr, Sidney Saylor. 2007. *My Appalachia: A memoir.* Lexington: University Press of Kentucky. [eastern KY]

2007 Hardy *Remembering Avery Co* = Hardy, Michael C. 2007. *Remembering Avery County.* Charleston, SC: History Press. [Avery County, northwestern NC]

2007 Homan *Turkey Tracks* = Homan, Tim. 2007. Where the creek turkey tracks: Wild land and language. *Appalachian Heritage* 35: 83–88. [northeast GA]

2007 Joslin *Sang Season* = Joslin, Michael. 2007. Sang season: Diggin' spirit-frisking ginseng. *Now & Then* 23(1): 57–60.

2007 Kerns *Mountaintop Removal* = Kerns, Megan Jewell. The geography of sorrow: Mountaintop removal in Appalachia. *Now & Then* 23(1): 6–8.

2007 McMillon *Notes* = McMillon, Bobby. 2007. [Notes and observations on the speech of the Tennessee–North Carolina border, including manuscripts loaned to the editor]. [east TN, western NC]

2007 Milnes *Signs Cures Witches* = Milnes, Gerald. 2007. *Signs, cures and witches: German Appalachian folklore.* Knoxville: University of Tennessee Press. [eastern WV]

2007 *Mining Terms* = Glossary of mining terms. 2007. http://www.coaleducation.org/glossary.htm, accessed January 24, 2011.

2007 *Music of Coal* = Wright, Jack. 2007. *Music of coal: Mining songs from the Appalachian coalfields.* Big Stone Gap, VA: Lonesome Records & Publishing.

2007 Myers *Smoky Mt Remedies* = Myers, Bonnie Trentham. 2007. *Smoky Mountain remedies.* Maryville, TN: Myers and Myers. [central east TN, central western NC]

2007 Neufeld *History W NC* = Neufeld, Rob. 2007. *A popular history of western North Carolina: Mountains, heroes & hootnoggers.* Charleston, SC: History Press. [western NC]

2007 Plott *Story Plott Hound* = Plott, Bob. 2007. *The story of the Plott hound: Strike & stay.* Charleston, SC: History Press. [southwestern NC]

2007 Preece *Leavin' Sandlick* = Preece, Mary Ellen Goble. 2007. *Leavin' Sandlick and speakin' Appalachian.* Baltimore: PublishAmerica.

2007 Rogers *Carson-Newman* = Rogers, Courtney. 2007. A study of Appalachian dialects in the Carson-Newman community. Paper presented at Appalachian Studies Association meeting. [east TN]

2007 Rose *Games Mt Children* = Rose, Sharon. 2007. Games of mountain children. *Smoky Mountain Historical Society Journal and Newsletter* 33(4): 15–17.

2007 Rowley *Moonshine!* = Rowley, Matthew B. 2007. *Moonshine! Recipes, tall tales, drinking songs, historical stuff, knee-slappers, how to make it, how to drink it, pleasin' the law, recoverin' the next day.* New York: Lark Crafts.

2007 Shelby *Molly Whuppie* = Shelby, Anne. 2007. *The adventures of Molly Whuppie and other Appalachian folktales.* Chapel Hill: University of North Carolina Press.

2007 Stryk *Groundhog Brood* = Stryk, Dan. 2007. Meditation on a groundhog brood. *Now & Then* 23(1): 42–43.

2008 Bailey *Matewan* = Bailey, Rebecca. 2008. *Matewan before the massacre: Politics, coal, and the roots of violence in a West Virginia mining community.* Morgantown: West Virginia University Press. [southwestern WV]

2008 Cain *Wake Forest* = Cain, Morgan Rochelle. 2008. Wake Forest: Voices that tell of a faith community. Senior thesis, Virginia Tech University, Blacksburg. [southwestern VA]

2008 Cobb *Vacation Time* = Cobb, Margaret Ogle. 2008. Vacation time. *Smoky Mountain Historical Society Journal and Newsletter* 34(1–2): 15–23. [Sevier County, central east TN]

2008–19 *DSAE Internet File* = *Dictionary of Southern Appalachian English Internet File*. 2008–19. Observations, notes, and miscellany collected from various online sources by Michael Montgomery and Jennifer Heinmiller for the *Dictionary of Southern Appalachian English*.

2008 Ellison *High Vistas* = Ellison, George. 2008. *High vistas: An anthology of nature writing from western North Carolina and the Great Smoky Mountains, 1694–1900*. Charleston, SC: History Press. [western NC]

2008 Eskew *Sacred Harp* = Eskew, Harry. 2008. Sacred harp. In *New encyclopedia of southern culture*, vol. 12: *Music*, edited by Bill C. Malone, 128–33. Chapel Hill: University of North Carolina Press.

2008 Goan *Nursing Service* = Goan, Melanie Beals. 2008. *Mary Breckinridge: The Frontier Nursing Service and rural health in Appalachia*. Chapel Hill: University of North Carolina Press. [eastern KY]

2008 Hunter *Porch Sit* = Hunter, Elizabeth. 2008. The great bandana porch sit. *Now & Then* 24(2): 10.

2008 Joyner *Dulcimer* = Joyner, Charles W. 2008. Dulcimer. In *New encyclopedia of southern culture*, vol. 12: *Music*, edited by Bill C. Malone, 223–24. Chapel Hill: University of North Carolina Press.

2008 Malone *All-Day Singings* = Malone, Bill C. 2008. All-day singings. In *New encyclopedia of southern culture*, vol. 12: *Music*, edited by Bill C. Malone, 162–63. Chapel Hill: University of North Carolina Press.

2008 McCaulley *Cove Childhood* = McCaulley, Margaret. 2008. *A Cades Cove childhood*. Charleston, SC: History Press. [Blount County, central east TN]

2008 McKinley *Bear Mt* = McKinley, Janie Mae Jones. 2008. *The legacy of Bear Mountain*. Sylva, NC: Catch the Spirit of Appalachia. [Jackson County, southwestern NC]

2008 Miller *Curse of Collar* = Miller, John W. 2008. *The curse of Satan's collar*. N.p.: Alibris.

2008 *Newfound Gap Road* = *Newfound Gap Road*. 2008. Gatlinburg, TN: Great Smoky Mountains Association.

2008 Plott *Hunting in Smokies* = Plott, Bob. 2008. *A history of hunting in the Great Smoky Mountains*. Charleston, SC: History Press. [southwestern NC]

2008 Reed et al. *Cornbread Nation IV* = Reed, Dale Volberg, John Shelton Reed, and John T. Edge. 2008. *Cornbread nation 4: The best of southern food writing*. Athens: University of Georgia Press.

2008 Riddle *All There Is* = Riddle, Rita Sizemore. 2008. *All there is to keep: Poems*. Oak Ridge, TN: Iris.

2008 *Rosie Hicks* = [Audio interviews recorded by Donnie Shedlarz, transcribed for this book]. 2008. Thomas G. Burton Collection, Archives of Appalachia, East Tennessee State University, Johnson City. [Avery County, northwestern NC]

2008 Salsi *Ray Hicks* = Salsi, Lynn. 2008. *The life and times of Ray Hicks*. Knoxville: University of Tennessee Press. [Avery County, northwestern NC]

2008 Sharp *Country Doctor* = Sharp, Roland. 2008. *Roland Sharp, country doctor: Memories of a life well lived*. Dunmore, WV: Parsons. [WV]

2008 Shirley *Raisen'* = Shirley, Hoke. 2008. *Raisen'*. Clayton, GA: Laurel Mountain Press. [northeast GA]

2008 Terrell *Mt Lingo* = Terrell, Bob. 2008. Mountain lingo. *Smoky Mountain Living*, June 8. http://www.smliv.com/features/mountain-lingo/. [western NC]

2008 West *Country Boy* = West, Lawrence Edward. 2008. *The life of a good ole country boy*. Beeson, WV: Self-published. [WV]

2008 Williams *Dialect Scott Co TN* = Williams, Barbara. 2008. [Email to the editor, April 1]. [Scott County, north central TN]

2009 Applegate and Miller *Lake Cumberland* = Applegate, Kris, and Jarenda Miller. 2009. *Around Lake Cumberland*. Charleston, SC: Arcadia.

2009 Aubrey *Pig Pickin'* = Aubrey, Amanda P. 2009. A southwest Virginia pig pickin'. *Now & Then* 25(1): 39–41.

2009 Benfield *Mt Born* = Benfield, Jean Boone. 2009. *Mountain born: A recollection of life and language in western North Carolina*. Spartanburg, SC: Reprint Company. [central western NC]

2009 Blackwell *Rough Place* = Blackwell, Joshua Beau. 2009. *"Used to be a rough place in them hills": Moonshine, the Dark Corner, and the new South*. Bloomington, IN: AuthorHouse. [Greenville County, northwestern SC]

2009 Burton *Beech Mt Man* = Burton, Thomas. 2009. *Beech Mountain man*. Knoxville: University of Tennessee Press. [Avery County, northwestern NC]

2009 Callahan *Work and Faith* = Callahan, Richard J. 2009. *Work and faith in the Kentucky coal fields: Subject to dust*. Bloomington: Indiana University Press.

2009 Ebel and Hicks *Jack Tales* = Ebel, Julia Taylor, and Orville Hicks. 2009. *Jack tales and mountain yarns*. Boone, NC: Parkway. [Avery County, northwestern NC]

2009 Fields *Growing Up* = Fields, Truman. 2009. *Remembering the 40's: Growing up in the heart of Appalachia*. Bloomington, IN: AuthorHouse. [Perry County, southeastern KY]

2009 Fulcher *Rolley Hole* = Fulcher, Bobby. 2009. Rolley hole. In *New encyclopedia of southern culture*, vol. 14: *Folklife*, edited by Glenn Hinson and William Ferris, 360–62. Chapel Hill: University of North Carolina Press.

2009 *Hard Life* = "It was a hard life": Growing up on the Pendleton County poor farm. 2009. *Goldenseal* 35(2): 38–43. [eastern WV]

2009 Holbrook *Upheaval* = Holbrook, Chris. 2009. *Upheaval: Stories*. Lexington: University Press of Kentucky.

2009 House and Howard *Something* = House, Silas, and Jason Howard. 2009. *Something's rising: Appalachians fighting mountaintop removal*. Lexington: University Press of Kentucky.

2009 Jabbour *Decoration Day* = Jabbour, Alan. 2009. Decoration Day. In *New encyclopedia of southern culture*, vol. 14: *Folklife*, edited by Glenn Hinson and William Ferris, 278–81. Chapel Hill: University of North Carolina Press. [Swain County, southwestern NC]

2009 Koontz *Guide to Smokies* = Koontz, Katy. 2009. *Insiders' guide to the Great Smoky Mountains*. Guilford, CT: Globe Pequot Press. [central east TN, central western NC]

2009 Lloyd *Tremont* = Lloyd, Jeremy. 2009. Tremont: Company town. *Smokies Life* 3(1): 30–37. [Blount County, central east TN]

2009 Lloyd *Walker Valley* = Lloyd, Jeremy. 2009. *A home in Walker Valley*. Gatlinburg, TN: Great Smoky Mountains Association. [Sevier County, central east TN]

2009 McNeely *Unlikely Flour* = McNeely, Renee. 2009. An unlikely source of flour. *Now & Then* 25(1): 14.

2009 Miller *Nigh Gone* = Miller, Zell. 2009. *Purt nigh gone*. Macon, GA: Stroud and Hall. [north GA]

2009 Morgan *October Crossing* = Morgan, Robert. 2009. *October crossing: Poems*. Frankfort, KY: Broadstone.

2009 Mould *Ginseng* = Mould, Tom. 2009. Ginseng. In *New encyclopedia of southern culture*, vol. 14: *Folklife*, edited by Glenn Hinson and William Ferris, 298–300. Chapel Hill: University of North Carolina Press.

2009 Pipes *Free People* = Pipes, Chase Earl Alexander. 2009. To the free people of America. *Smoky Mountain Historical Society Journal and Newsletter* 35(3): 2–5.

2009 Plott *Legendary Hunters* = Plott, Bob. 2009. *Legendary hunters of the southern highlands: A century of sport and survival in the Great Smoky Mountains*. Charleston, SC: History Press. [western NC]

2009 Powell *Shenandoah Letters* = Powell, Katrina M., ed. 2009. *"Answer at once": Letters of mountain families in Shenandoah National Park, 1934–1938*. Charlottesville: University of Virginia Press. [central western VA]

2009 Prewitt *Coon Hounds* = Prewitt, Wiley. 2009. Coon hounds. In *New encyclopedia of southern culture*, vol. 14: *Folklife*, edited by Glenn Hinson and William Ferris, 273–75. Chapel Hill: University of North Carolina Press.

2009 Reed *Preface* = Reed, John Shelton. 2009. Preface. In *Beech Mountain man* by Thomas Burton, xiii–xv. Knoxville: University of Tennessee Press.

2009 Roberts *Outbuildings* = Roberts, Katherine. 2009. Outbuildings. In *New encyclopedia of southern culture, vol. 14: Folklife*, edited by Glenn Hinson and William Ferris, 334–36. Chapel Hill: University of North Carolina Press.

2009 Roebuck *Dinner on Grounds* = Roebuck, David G. 2009. Dinner on the grounds. In *New encyclopedia of southern culture*, vol. 14: *Folklife*, edited by Glenn Hinson and William Ferris, 283–85. Chapel Hill: University of North Carolina Press.

2009 Sanders *Breakfast* = Sanders, Randy. 2009. A breakfast platter. *Now & Then* 25(1): 44–46.

2009 Shelton *Gritty Bread* = Shelton, Susan. 2009. Cove Creek gritty bread. *Now & Then* 25(1): 28–29.

2009 Skipper *Billy Bean* = Skipper, Roger Alan. 2009. *The baptism of Billy Bean*. Berkeley, CA: Counterpoint.

2009 Sohn *Appal Home Cooking* = Sohn, Mark. 2009. *Appalachian home cooking: History, cultures, and recipes*. Lexington: University Press of Kentucky.

2009 Sutton *Me and Likker II* = Sutton, Popcorn. 2009. *Me and my likker*. Rev. ed. Maggie Valley, NC: Self-published. [west central NC]

2009 Thompson *Driving with Devil* = Thompson, Neal. 2009. *Driving with the devil: Southern moonshine, Detroit wheels, and the birth of NASCAR*. New York: Broadway.

2009 *TN Encycl* = *Tennessee encyclopedia of history and culture*. 2009. Rev. ed. https://tennesseeencyclopedia.net/. Originally published in book form by Rutledge Hill Press, Nashville, TN.

2009 Waldvogel *Bark Baskets* = Waldvogel, Merikay. 2009. Bark baskets and buckets: Made on the spot of what you've got. *Smokies Life* 2(1): 18–21. [east TN]

2009 Webb et al. *Moonshining* = Webb, Vaughan, Andrew Pauly, and Roddy Moore. 2009. Moonshining. In *New encyclopedia of southern culture, vol. 14: Folklife*, edited by Glenn Hinson and William Ferris, 328–31. Chapel Hill: University of North Carolina Press.

2009 Whaley *Stoney Creek* = Whaley, Martha. 2009. The Stoney Creek Primitive Baptist Associational meeting and dinner on the ground. *Now & Then* 25(1): 59–60.

2009 Wiles and Wiles *Location* = Wiles, Bill, and Mary Wiles. 2009. *Up on Location: The story of a West Virginia farm, a road and the people who lived there*. Parsons, WV: McClain. [central WV]

2009 Williams *Maw Surry* = Williams, Tiffany M. 2009. Maw Surry. http://www.stilljournal.net/tiffany-williams-fiction.php.

2009 Wingfield *Franklin Co VA* = Wingfield, Marshall. 2009. *Franklin County, Virginia: A history*. Baltimore: Clearfield. [southwestern VA]

2010–19 *Blind Pig* = [Installments of the blog *Blind Pig and the Acorn*]. https://www.blindpigandtheacorn.com/. [east TN, western NC]

2010 Fugate *Found Me* = Fugate, Crystal. 2010. *I found me: Appalachian stories from a lost hillbilly girl*. N.p.: lulu.com. [eastern KY]

2010–19 Heinmiller *Coll* = Heinmiller, Jennifer K. N. 2010–19. [Selected items from Heinmiller's fieldwork]

2010 House *Opening* = House, Silas. 2010. At the opening of *Coal Miner's Daughter*, Corbin, Kentucky, March 27, 1980. In *The southern poetry anthology*, vol. 3: *Contemporary Appalachia*, edited by Jesse Graves et al., 99. Huntsville: Texas Review Press.

2010 Jabbour *North Shore Assn* = Jabbour, Alan. 2010. Helen Cable Vance and the North Shore Historical Association. *North Carolina Folklore Journal* 57(2): 22–28. [Swain County, southwestern NC]

2010 Jabbour and Jabbour *Decoration Day* = Jabbour, Alan, and Karen Singer Jabbour. 2010. *Decoration Day in the mountains: Traditions of cemetery decoration in the southern Appalachians*. Chapel Hill: University of North Carolina Press. [Swain County, southwestern NC]

2010 Mann and Keeling *Nurses on Line* = Wall, Barbara Mann, and Arlene W. Keeling. 2010. *Nurses on the front line: When disaster strikes, 1878–2010*. New York: Springer.

2010 Neal *Bio* = Patricia Neal: A biography. 2010. https://www.patneal.org/patricia-neal-a-biography/.

2010 Owenby *Trula Ownby* = Owenby, Robert C. 2010. Trula Cole Ownby. *Smoky Mountain Historical Society Journal and Newsletter* 36(4): 6–19. [Sevier County, central east TN]

2010 Smith *Mother's Love* = Smith, Tony. 2010. *An Appalachian mother's love*. N.p.: AuthorHouse.

2010 Still *Bare-Bones* = Still, James. 2010. Bare-bones. *Appalachian Heritage* 38(4): 21–24.

2010 Whisnant and Whisnant *Parkway Came* = Whisnant, Anne Mitchell, and David Whisnant. 2010. *When the parkway came*. Chapel Hill, NC: Primary Source. [northwestern NC]

2011 Baker *Pickles* = Baker, Katie. 2011. Bread and butter pickles: A green southern treat. *Now & Then* 27(1): 30–31. [northeast TN]

2011 Best *Bean Terminology* = Best, Bill. 2011. Southern Appalachian heirloom bean terminology. http://www.heirlooms.org/terminology.html, accessed November 2, 2011. [KY]

2011 *Cocke Co TN Petitions* = Blomquist, Ann K., and Cherel Bolin Henderson, transcribers. 2011. Index and petitions to the Tennessee legislature: Cocke County, Tennessee. *Tennessee Ancestors* 27: 143–90. [Cocke County, central east TN]

2011 Coonfield *Varmits* = Coonfield, Ted. 2011. *The Varmits: Living with Appalachian outlaws*. N.p.: AuthorHouse. [southeast OH]

2011 *COROH* (Brannon) = Center for Oak Ridge Oral History. 2011. [Transcription of audio interview with Robert Brannon]. Oak Ridge Oral History Project records, stored at Oak Ridge Public Library, Oak Ridge, TN. [east TN]

2011 Garretson *Barefoot Hillbillies* = Garretson, Lauren. 2011. Why are we still seen as "barefoot hillbillies"? *Loyal Jones Appalachian Center Newsletter* (Berea College) 39(2): 4.

2011 Hague *Spring* = Hague, Richard. 2011. The spring. *Now & Then* 27(1): 11–12.

2011 Houk *Quilts* = Houk, Rose. 2011. *Quilts and coverlets of the Smokies*. Gatlinburg, TN: Great Smoky Mountains Association. [central east TN, central western NC]

2011 Hurst and Lewis *Roaring Fork* = Hurst, Sharon, and Laura Lewis. 2011. Roaring Fork School—fifty years ago [reprint of Hurst and Lewis 1977]. *Smoky Mountain Historical Society Journal and Newsletter* 37(2): 14–16. [Sevier County, central east TN]

2011 Lix *Medicine Women* = Lix, Courtney. 2011. Smoky Mountain medicine women. *Smokies Life* 5(1): 26–35. [central east TN, central western NC]

2011 *Massey Report* = *Report to the governor, Governor's independent investigation panel, the April 5, 2010, explosion: A failure of basic coal mine safety practices, Upper Big Branch*. [WV]

2011 McAteer *Upper Big Branch* = McAteer, J. Davitt, et al. 2011. Upper Big Branch—the April 5, 2010, explosion: A failure of basic coal mine safety practices. In *Report to the governor, Governor's Independent Investigation Panel*, 19. https://www.nrc.gov/docs/ML1206/ML12069A003.pdf. [WV]

2011 Powers *Haints Cave* = Powers, Ginny. 2011. *Haints Cave: An Appalachian tale*. N.p.: Alibris.

2011 Richmond *Appal Folklore* = Richmond, Nancy. 2011. *Appalachian folklore: Omens, signs and superstitions*. N.p.: CreateSpace.

2011 Shearer *Moonshine Trade* = Shearer, Kathy. 2011. *Tales from the moonshine trade*. Emory, VA: Clinch Mountain Press. [southwestern VA]

2011 *Smoky Mt Times* = *Smoky Mountain Times* (Bryson City, NC). 2011. [Miscellaneous newspaper articles]

2011 Spriggs *Walker Exemplar* = Spriggs, Bianca. 2011. Frank X. Walker: Exemplar of Affrilachia. *Appalachian Heritage* 39(3): 21–25.

2011 Tabler *Hillbilly Highway* = Tabler, Dave. 2011. Where the Hillbilly Highway ends. http://appalachianalliance.com/tag/dayton-oh/, accessed March 26, 2012.

2011 Thompson *Just Men* = Thompson, Charles D. 2011. *Spirits of just men:*

Mountaineers, liquor bosses, and lawmen in the moonshine capital of the world. Urbana: University of Illinois Press. [southwestern VA]

2011 Woodall *Not My Mt* = Woodall, Barbara Taylor. 2011. *It's not my mountain anymore.* Sylva, NC: Catch the Spirit of Appalachia, Inc.

2012 Houk *Weaving in Smokies* = Houk, Rose. 2012. Weaving a livelihood in the Smokies. *Smokies Life* 6(1): 38–45. [central east TN, central western NC]

2012–13 House *Spotlight* = House, Silas. 2012–13. Membership spotlight. *Appalachian Voices* (December–January): 26.

2012 Jourdan *Medicine Men* = Jourdan, Carolyn. 2012. *Medicine men: Extreme Appalachian doctoring.* N.p.: Jourdain-Michael. [east TN]

2012 McQuaid *Interface* = McQuade, Goldie Ann. 2012. Variation at the morphology-phonology interface in Appalachian English. PhD diss., Georgetown University, Washington, DC. [northeast TN]

2012 Milnes *Signs Cures Witchery* = Milnes, Gerry. 2012. *Signs, cures & witchery: German Appalachian folklore.* Elkins, WV: Augusta Heritage Center. [DVD; eastern WV]

2012 Pittman *Proud Creekers* = Pittman, Margie J. 2012. *Coal camp kinds: Proud creekers.* Bloomington, IN: AuthorHouse. [southern WV]

2012 Portelli *They Say* = Portelli, Alessandro. 2012. *They say in Harlan County: An oral history.* New York: Oxford University Press. [southeastern KY]

2012 Still *Hills Remember* = Still, James. 2012. *The hills remember: The complete short stories of James Still.* Edited by Ted Olson and Teresa Perry Reynolds. Lexington: University Press of Kentucky.

2012 *White Baneberry* = White baneberry. 2009. Wildflowers of the southeastern US. http://2bnthewild.com/plants/H110.htm.

2012–14 Williams *Coll* = Williams, Tiffany M. 2012–14. [Notes and observations regarding Letcher County, southeastern KY]

2013 Beaver and Ballard *Voices* = Beaver, Patricia D., and Sandra L. Ballard. 2013. *Voices from the headwaters: Stories from Meat Camp (Pottertown) & Sutherland, North Carolina.* Boone, NC: Appalachian State University. [northwestern NC]

2013 Byers *Mt Mother Goose* = Byers, Judith Prozzillo. 2013. *Mountain Mother Goose: Child lore of West Virginia.* Fairmont: West Virginia Folklife Center.

2013 Crawford *Mt Memories* = Crawford, Joe Cobb. 2013. *Mountain shadow memories.* Clayton, GA: Laurel Mountain Press.

2013 DeLozier and Jourdan *Back Seat* = DeLozier, Kim, and Carolyn Jourdan. 2013. *Bear in the back seat: Adventures of a wildlife ranger in the Great Smoky Mountains National Park.* Vol. 1. Gatlinburg, TN: Great Smoky Mountains Association. [central east TN, central western NC]

2013 Dodson *Mt-Keeper* = Dodson, Willie. 2013. Moutain-keeper: Larry Gibson remembered. *Loyal Jones Appalachian Center Newsletter* (Berea College) 41(1): 6–7.

2013 *Harp Singing* = Sacred Harp Singing. http://home.olemiss.edu/~mudws/harp.html, consulted March 5, 2019.

2013 Hicks *Perception* = **Hicks, Jane. 2013.** A matter of perception. In *Talking Appalachian: Voice, identity, and community,* edited by Amy D. Clark and Susan M. Hayward, 209–14. Lexington: University Press of Kentucky.

2013 House *Own Country* = House, Silas. 2013. In my own country. In *Talking Appalachian: Voice, identity, and community,* edited by Amy D. Clark and Nancy M. Hayward, 193–204. Lexington: University Press of Kentucky.

2013 Landry *Tellin' It* = Landry, Bill. 2013. *Tellin' it for the truth.* Knoxville: Celtic Cat. [east TN]

2013 Loop *Shadow of Appal* = Loop, Cowboy. 2013. *In the shadow of the Appalachians.* N.p.: Alibris.

2013 Lyon *Voiceplace* = Lyon, George Ella. 2013. Voiceplace. In *Talking Appalachian: Voice, identity, and community,* edited by Amy D. Clark and Nancy Hayward, 185–92. Lexington: University Press of Kentucky. [eastern KY]

2013 McMahan *Lem Ownby* = McMahan, F. Carroll. 2013. *Elkmont's Uncle Lem Ownby: Sage of the Smokies.* Charleston, SC: History Press. [Sevier County, central east TN]

2013 Osborne *Raisin' Cane* = Osborne, David. 2013. *Raisin' cane in Appalachia.* N.p.: Trafford. [southeastern KY]

2013 Pack *Toys and Games* = Pack, Linda Hager. 2013. *Appalachian toys and games.* Lexington: University Press of Kentucky.

2013 Patton *Go Back* = Patton, E. E. 2013. I want to go back. *Smoky Mountain Historical Society Journal and Newsletter* 39(2): 4–5.

2013 Pierce *Corn in Jar* = Pierce, Daniel S. 2013. *Corn in a jar: Moonshine in the Great Smoky Mountains.* Gatlinburg, TN: Great Smoky Mountains Association. [central east TN, central western NC]

2013 Reed *Medical Notes* = Reed, Paulette. 2013. [Notes on medical terminology]. Typescript provided to the editor. [Hancock County, northeast TN]

2013 Salsi *Jack and Giants* = Salsi, Lynn. 2013. *Jack and the giants.* Terra Alta, WV: Headline.

2013 Shedlarz *Rosa Hicks* = Shedlarz, Donnie. 2013. *Rosa Hicks and her recipe book.* N.p.: LandaBooks. [Avery County, northwestern NC]

2013 Smith and Kraig *Food and Drink* = Smith, Andrew, and Bruce Kraig. 2013. *The Oxford encyclopedia of food and drink in America.* New York: Oxford University Press.

2013 Venable *How to Tawlk* = Venable, Sam. 2013. *How to tawlk and rite good: A guide to the language of southern Appalachia.* North Charleston, SC: CreateSpace. [east TN]

2014 Burns *Remembrances* = Burns, Inez. 2014. Remembrances of the past. *Smoky Mountain Historical Society Journal and Newsletter* 40(1): 6–8.

2014 Cardwell *Yule Log* = Cardwell, R. Glenn. 2014. Pittman Center Yule log. *Smoky Mountains Historical Society Journal and Newsletter* 15(3): 2–6.

2014 Ellis *Coll* = Ellis, Michael E. 2014. [Comments on unpublished draft of this book]

2014 Finch *TN Comb Graves* = Finch, Richard C. 2014. Tennessee comb grave traditions. *Tennessee Folklore Society Bulletin* 70(1–2): 1–98. [central TN]

2014 Funderberg *Bootleggers* = Funderburg, Anne. 2014. *Bootleggers and beer barons of the Prohibition Era.* Jefferson, NC: McFarland.

2014 Graves *Basin Ghosts* = Graves, Jesse. 2014. *Basin ghosts.* Huntsville, TX: Texas Review Press.

2014 Hicks *Driving* = Hicks, Jane. 2014. *Driving with the dead: Poems.* Lexington: University Press of Kentucky.

2014 House *Talking About* = House, Silas. 2014. The matter is you don't know what you're talking about. http://silashouseblog.blogspot.com/2014/07/the-matter-is-you-dont-know-what-youre.html.

2014 Joyce *Moonshine* = Joyce, Jaime. 2014. *Moonshine: A cultural history of America's infamous liquor.* Minneapolis: Zenith.

2014 McCarter *Memories of Boy* = McCarter, Pinckney J. 2014. Memories of a boy. *Smoky Mountain Historical Society Journal and Newsletter* 40(1): 20–25. [central east TN]

2014 Miles and Cox *I Had Wings* = Miles, Emma Bell, and Steven Cox. 2014. *Once I too had wings: The journals of Emma Bell Miles, 1908–1918.* Athens: Ohio University Press. [southeast TN]

2014 Montgomery *Doctrine* = Montgomery, David. 2014. *Doctrine for dummies.* N.p.: lulu.com.

2014 Oliver *Cades Cove* = Oliver, William Wayne. 2014. *Cades Cove: A personal history.* Gatlinburg, TN: Great Smoky Mountains Association. [Blount County, central east TN]

2014 Sauceman *Buttermilk* = Sauceman, Fred. 2014. *Buttermilk & Bible burgers: More stories from the kitchens of Appalachia.* Macon, GA: Mercer University Press.

2014 Spalding *Appal Dance* = Spalding, Susan Eike. 2014. *Appalachian dance: Creativity and continuity in six communities.* Urbana: University of Illinois Press.

2014 *WV Talk* = Smith-Carroll, Eva. 2014. *West Virginia talk: Words & phrases from the Mountain State.* https://wva.homestead.com/WVaTalk.html.

2015 Dykeman *Family of Earth* = Dykeman, Wilma. 2015. *Family of earth.* Chapel Hill: University of North Carolina Press. [east TN, western NC]

2015 Garrison *N GA Moonshine* = Garrison, Judith. 2015. *North Georgia moonshine: A history of the Lovells & other liquor makers*. Charleston, SC: History Press. [north GA]

2015 Holbrook *Something* = Holbrook, Chris. 2015. Something to tell. In *Appalachia now: Short stories of contemporary Appalachia*, edited by Larry Smith and Charles Dodd White, 143–59. Huron, OH: Bottom Dog Press.

2015 *Imitator Salamander* = Imitator salamanders that don't imitate. 2015. *BearPaw* (Spring/Summer): 4.

2015 Jamison *Hoedowns* = Jamison, Phil. 2015. *Hoedowns, reels, and frolics: Roots and branches of southern Appalachian dance*. Urbana: University of Illinois Press. [western NC]

2015 Jones *In Memoriam* = Jones, Loyal. 2015. In memoriam: Jean Ritchie. *Appalachian Heritage* 43(3): 8–9.

2015 Jones *Tintagel* = Jones, Loyal. 2015. Tintagel. *Appalachian Heritage* 43(3): 54.

2015 Kidd and Hankins *Baptists in Amer* = Kidd, Thomas S., and Barry Hankins. 2015. *Baptists in America: A History*. New York: Oxford University Press.

2015 Long *Ethnic Food* = Long, Lucy M., ed. 2015. *Ethnic American food*. Lanham, MD: Rowman and Littlefield. [central western NC]

2015 Robbins *Land Sled* = Robbins, Tom. 2015. Wagons without wheels: The humble land sled. *Smokies Life* 9(2): 8–15. [western NC]

2015 Seidl *New Roots* = Seidl, Carla. 2015. Chestnuts: A traditional Cherokee food source puts down new roots in WNC. https://mountainx.com/food/chestnuts-a-traditional-cherokee-food-source-puts-down-new-roots-in-wnc/, accessed April 2, 2018.

2015 Waters *Swinging Bridges* = Waters, John B., Jr. 2015. Swinging bridges in Sevier County. *Smoky Mountain Historical Society Journal and Newsletter* 41(1): 20–21. [Sevier County, central east TN]

2015 Yarrow *Voices* = Yarrow, Mike. 2015. *Voices from the coalfields: Found poems*. Huron, OH: Bottom Dog Press.

2016 Ellison *Excursions* = Ellison, George. 2016. *Literary excursions in the southern highlands: Essays on natural history*. Charleston, SC: History Press. [central western NC]

2016 Gipe *Gone to Water* = Gipe, Robert. 2016. Gone to water. *Appalachian Heritage* 44(4): 39–48.

2016 Grimm *Moonville* = Grimm, Mary. 2016. Going to Moonville. *Appalachian Heritage* 44(2): 8–34.

2016 Houk *Vampires* = Houk, Rose. 2016. Vampires and zombies of the flora kind. *Smokies Life* 10(2): 58–63. [central east TN]

2016 Lundy and Autry *Victuals* = Lundy, Ronni, and Johnny Autry. 2016. *Victuals: An Appalachian journey, with recipes*. New York: Crown.

2016 McCarroll *On and On* = McCarroll, Meredith. 2016. On and on: Appalachian accent and academic power. *Southern Cultures* 26: 45–48. [northwestern NC]

2016 Netherland *Appal Cooking* = Netherland, Robert G. 2016. *Southern Appalachian farm cooking: A memoir of food and family*. Knoxville: University of Tennessee Press.

2016 Simmons *Legends & Lore* = Simmons, Shane S. 2016. *Legends & lore of east Tennessee*. Charleston, SC: History Press. [east TN]

2016 Winkler *About Melungeons* = Winkler, Wayne. 2016. About the Melungeons. October 14. http://melungeon.org/2016/10/14/about-the-melungeons-by-wayne-winkler-2004-article/.

2017 Blankenship *Songs of Whippoorwill* = Blankenship, John. 2017. *Songs of the whippoorwill: An Appalachian odyssey*. Vol. 1. N.p.: Lulu.com.

2017 Corbin *Battle Branch* = Corbin, Wilford. 2017. *The boys of Battle Branch: How growing up in Appalachia shaped our lives*. Cullowhee, NC: Western Carolina University Print Shop. [southwestern NC]

2017 *Johnson City Press* = Holloway, Maynard "PePaw" obituary. 2017. *Johnson City (TN) Press*, July 27.

2017 Kinsler *Take Girl* = Kinsler, Jennifer. 2017. *You can take the girl out of the mountains but you can't take the mountains out of the girl*. N.p.: CreateSpace. [northeast TN]

2017 Lufkart *Comfort Zone* = Lufkart, Kenneth A. 2017. *The comfort zone: Growing up in Appalachia*. N.p.: Xulon. [WV]

2017 *Salyersville Independent* = *Salyersville Independent*. 2017. [Untitled newspaper article]. [eastern KY]

2017 Williams *Murmuration* = Williams, Tiffany M. 2017. Murmuration. *Appalachian Heritage* 45(2): 9–17.

2018 *Davenport Survey* = Davenport made survey through Great Smokies in 1821. 2018. *Smoky Mountain Historical Society Journal and Newsletter* 44: 18–19.

2018 Malone and Laird *Country Music* = Malone, Bill C., and Tracey Laird. 2018. *Country music USA: 50th anniversary edition*. Austin: University of Texas Press.

Alphabetical List of Works Cited

Abell, Troy D. 1982. *Better felt than said: The Holiness-Pentecostal movement in southern Appalachia*. Waco, TX: Markham. [northwestern NC]

Abernethy, Arthur Talmage. 1924. *Moonshine, being Appalachia's Arabian nights*. Asheville, NC: Dixie.

Abramson, Rudy, and Jean Haskell, eds. 2006. *Encyclopedia of Appalachia*. Knoxville: University of Tennessee Press.

Absher, Mrs. W. O. 1982. *The heritage of Wilkes County*. North Wilkesboro, NC: Wilkes Genealogical Society. [Wilkes County, northwestern NC]

Ada Kelly. 1972. *Foxfire Magazine* 6(2–3): 80–87.

Adams. 1954. *Word-List*. [Document part of author's private collection.]

Adams, Frazier B. 1970. *Appalachia revisited: How people lived fifty years ago*. Ashland, KY: Economy.

Adams, Inez McCaulley. 1977. Remembering: A trip back to grandpa's house. In *The Cades Cove story*, by A. Randolph Shields, 92–99. Gatlinburg, TN: Great Smoky Mountains Natural History Association. [Blount County, central east TN]

Adams, James Taylor. c1939–42. http://www2.ferrum.edu/applit/.

———. 1950. *Grandpap told me tales*. Manuscript stories collected and edited by Fletcher Dean. Big Stone Gap, VA: F. Dean. [southwestern VA]

Adams, Paul J. 1966. *Mt. LeConte*. Knoxville: Holston. [Sevier County, central east TN]

Adams, Sheila Kay. 1995. *Come go home with me*. Chapel Hill: University of North Carolina Press. [Haywood County, central western NC]

———. 2004. *My old true love*. Chapel Hill, NC: Algonquin.

Adams Collection. 1940. Documents housed in editors' private collection.

Adly M. Millsaps letters. 1845. Transcribed and published in *Roane County Roots* 10 (2006): 2–3. [Roane County, central east TN]

Aiken, Gene. 1983. *Mountain ways: An album of the Smokies*. Gatlinburg, TN: Buckhorn. [Sevier County, central east TN]

———. 1986. *Mountain ways two: An album of the Smokies*. Gatlinburg, TN: Buckhorn. [Sevier County, central east TN]

———. 1989. Tragedy in the forest. *The Star*, February 2. [Sevier County, central east TN]

———. 1990. *Stories from the Great Smoky Mountains*. Gatlinburg, TN: Buckhorn. [Sevier County, central east TN]

———. 1990. Wiley Oakley: Roaming man of the mountains. *The Star*, April 13. [Sevier County, central east TN]

Aiken, Leona Taylor. 1974. Letters of the Offield brothers, Confederate soldiers from upper East Tennessee. *East Tennessee Historical Society Publication* 46: 116–25. [northeast TN]

Albala, Ken. 2007. *Beans: A history*. New York: Berg.

Alderman, Pat. 1972. *In the shadow of Big Bald: About the Appalachians and their people*. Mars Hill, NC: Bald Mountain Development Corporation. [northeast TN]

———. 1981. *Tilson grist mill: Mountain folklore genealogy*. Johnson City, TN: Overmountain. [northeast TN]

Alexander, Bill. 2007. The forgotten basket of the Smoky Mountains. *Smoky Mountain Historical Society Journal and Newsletter* 33(2): 7–9. [east TN]

Alexander, Eben. 1888. Hiking through the Big Smokies: Graphic description by Prof. Alexander. *Knoxville Journal*, July 7, 1929, originally published in *New York Evening Post*, August 4, 1888.

Alexander, John L. 2006. *Where have all our moonshiners gone?* Seneca, SC: Privately published. [northeast GA, northwestern SC]

Alexander, Tom. 1995. *Mountain fever*. Edited by Tom Alexander Jr. and Jane Alexander. Asheville, NC: Bright Mountain. [Haywood County, central western NC]

Alexander Family. 1862–65. [Letters]. Private collection.

Alexandria Gazette. 1894. [Untitled article]. In *DARE File*.

Allen, James Lane. 1892. Through Cumberland Gap on horseback. In *The blue-grass region of Kentucky: And other Kentucky articles*, 229–68. New York: Harper & Brothers. [southeastern KY]

Allen, Martha Norburn. 1960. *Land of the sky*. Charlotte: Heritage House. [western NC]

Allen, W. C. 1935. *Annals of Haywood County*. N.p.: n.p. [Haywood County, central western NC]

Allison, Junius. 1984. Orphan character notes in Appalachia. *North Carolina Folklore Journal* 32: 82–90.

Alsop, Fred J. 1991. *Birds of the Smokies*. Gatlinburg, TN: Great Smoky Mountains Natural History Association. [central east TN, central western NC]

Alvey, R. Gerald. 1989. *Kentucky folklore*. Lexington: University Press of Kentucky. [KY]

Alvic, Philis. 1993. *Weavers in the highlands: The early years in Gatlinburg*. Murray, KY: Privately published. [Sevier County, central east TN]

Anatomy of a revival. 1967. *Foxfire Magazine* 1(2): 9–12, 47–52. [Rabun County, northeast GA]

Anderson, R. 1976. Fairy crosses. In *Touching home: A collection of folklore from the Copper Basin, Fannin County area*, edited by Kathy Thompson, 25–27. Orlando, FL: Daniels. [southeast TN]

Andrews, Scottie. 1995. *Jes' a' broguin' about*. Waynesville, NC: Broguin' About Books. [Haywood County, central western NC]

———. 1997. *Dude's mountain vittles: Country food mountain style*. Waynesville, NC: Old Style Printing. [western NC]

Andrew T. Smith's letter home at the end of the Civil War. 2000. *Pellissippian* 21: 10–11. [Anderson County, east TN]

Anna Howard. 1972. *Foxfire Magazine* 6(1): 50–55. [Macon County, southwestern NC]

Anonymous. 1849. The Melungeons. *Littell's Living Age* 20: 618–19. [Hancock County, northeast TN]

Another look at moonshining. 1975. *Foxfire Magazine* 9(2–3): 132–44.

Appalachian Oral History Project (Alice Lloyd College). 1971–75. [Selected audio interviews, transcribed for this book]. Appalachian Oral History Project, Alice Lloyd College Library, Pippa Passes, KY. [various counties, southeastern KY]

Appalachian Oral History Project (Emory & Henry College). 1972–75. [Selected audio interviews, transcribed for the present volume]. Appalachian Oral History Project, Emory & Henry College Library, Emory, VA. [western VA]

Appalachian Oral History Project (Lees Junior College). 1972–75. [Selected audio interviews, transcribed for this book]. Appalachian Oral History Project, Lees Junior College Library, Jackson, KY. [various counties, southeastern KY]

Appalachian Oral History Project (Appalachian State University). 1973–74. [Selected audio interviews, transcribed for this book]. Appalachian Oral History Project, 1965–79. Eury Appalachian Collection, Belk Library, Appalachian State University, Boone, NC. [northwestern NC]

Apperson Family. 1862–64. [Letters]. Apperson Family Papers. Virginia Polytechnic Institute and State University, Blacksburg. [Franklin County, southwestern VA]

Applegate, Kris, and Jarenda Miller. 2009. *Around Lake Cumberland*. Charleston, SC: Arcadia.

Armstead, Robert. 2002. *Black days, black dust: The memories of an African*

American coal miner. Knoxville: University of Tennessee Press. [southern WV]

Armstrong, Anne W. 1930. *This day and time*. New York: Alfred A. Knopf.

Arnow, Harriette Louisa Simpson. 1936. *Mountain path*. New York: Little and Ives.

———. 1949. *Hunter's horn*. New York: Macmillan.

———. 1954. *The dollmaker*. New York: Macmillan.

———. 1960. *Seedtime on the Cumberland*. New York: Macmillan. [southeastern KY]

———. 1963. *Flowering of the Cumberland*. New York: Macmillan. [southeastern KY]

———. 1977. *Old Burnside*. Lexington: University Press of Kentucky. [southeastern KY]

Arthur, John Preston. 1914. *Western North Carolina: A history*. Raleigh: Edwards and Broughton. [western NC]

Asheville Citizen-Times. 1952–84. [Miscellaneous articles and clippings from the *Asheville Citizen* and *Asheville Citizen-Times* newspapers, consulted at Pack Memorial Library, Asheville, NC]

———. 1984. [Untitled article in vertical file of Pack Memorial Library, Asheville, NC]

Aswell, James. c1940. Brief glossary of Tennessee idiom. Prepared under auspices of the WPA. Typescript on deposit at Tennessee State Library and Archives, Nashville. [TN]

Athens Post. 1856. [Untitled newspaper article]. July 4. [TN]

Atkinson, George W. 1881. *After the moonshiners: A book of thrilling, but truthful narratives*. Wheeling, WV: Frew and Campbell.

Atwood, E. Bagby. 1953. *A survey of verb forms in the eastern United States*. Ann Arbor: University of Michigan Press.

Aubrey, Amanda P. 2009. A southwest Virginia pig pickin'. *Now & Then* 25(1): 39–41.

Augusta Heritage Center. 1960–88. Documents, video, and audio recordings of the Augusta Heritage Center. Augusta Collection of Folk Culture in Booth Library, Davis & Elkins College.

Aunt Arie's recipe for egg custard (cooked on a wood stove). 1971. *Foxfire Magazine* 5(1–2): 95. [Macon County, southwestern NC]

Aunt Airy. 1970. *Foxfire Magazine* 4(1–2): 4–7, 86–95. [Macon County, southwestern NC]

Austin, Ben. 1992. The vanishing art of cooking table-grade sorghum molasses. *Tennessee Folklore Society Bulletin* 55: 101–7. [White County, central TN]

Averett, Harris Hardin. 1863. Correspondence, 1854–63. SPR 422. Housed at the Alabama Department of Archives and History, Montgomery.

Awiakta, Marilou. 2006. *Abiding Appalachia: Where mountain and atom meet*. Blacksburg, VA: Pocahontas.

Axley, Lowry. 1927. Larrows to catch meddlers. *American Speech* 2: 408–9. [western NC]

Axtell, Nathaniel H. 1997. Hog wild: Exotic boars keep Smokies staff jumping. *Appalachian Voice* (Spring): 3, 19.

———. 1999. Moonshine making "still" thriving in Appalachia. *Appalachian Voice* (Winter): 3, 18.

Ayres, Horace Beemer, and William Willard Ashe. 1905. *The southern Appalachian forests*. Washington, DC: US Geological Survey.

Bacheller, Irving. 1924. The happiest person I ever knew. *American Magazine* (March), 5–7, 98, 100. [central western NC]

Back home in Blount County. 1986. Maryville, TN: Blount County Historic Trust. [Blount County, central east TN]

Baggarly, Tilmon F. 1862. [Letters]. Tilmon F. Baggarly Papers, 1860–1879. David M. Rubenstein Rare Book and Manuscript Library, Duke University, Durham, NC. [Alexander County, northwestern NC]

Bailey, Louise Howe. 1990. *Draw up a chair*. Skyland, NC: Hickory Printing. [Henderson County, southwestern NC]

———. 2005. *Remembering Henderson County: A legacy of lore*. Charleston, SC: History Press. [Henderson County, southwestern NC]

Bailey, Lucille M. 1996. The persistence of /mɪzrɪz/ among younger speakers in Kentucky. *SECOL Review* 20: 154–63. [KY]

Bailey, Rebecca. 2008. *Matewan before the massacre: Politics, coal, and the roots of violence in a West Virginia mining community*. Morgantown: West Virginia University Press. [southwestern WV]

Bailey, Rebecca J. 2000. I never thought of my life as history: A story of the "hillbilly" exodus and the price of assimilation. In *Appalachian migration*, edited by Philip J. Obermiller, Thomas E. Wagner, and E. Bruce Tucker, 27–38. Westport, CT: Praeger.

Bailey Family. 1864–65. [Letters.] Bailey Family Papers, 1827–1871. MSS 2B1565B, Virginia Historical Society, Richmond. [Mercer County, southern WV]

Baine, Donald A. 1885. Among the moonshiners. *Dixie* 1: 9–14. [north GA]

Baker, Katie. 2011. Bread and butter pickles: A green southern treat. *Now & Then* 27(1): 30–31. [northeast TN]

Baldridge, Terry L. 2007. *Eastern Kentucky Railway*. Charleston, SC: Arcadia. [eastern KY]

Baldwin, S. G. 1948. Big trees of the Great Smokies. *Southern Lumberman* 177 (December 15): 172–78. [central east TN, central western NC]

Ball, Donald B. 1978. Notes on the slang and folk speech of Knoxville, Knox County. *Tennessee Folklore Society Bulletin* 44: 134–42. [Knox County, central east TN]

———. 2007. The history and use of tub mills in southern Appalachia. *Tennessee Folklore Society Bulletin* 63(1–2): 3–56.

Ball, Donald S. 2005. Observations on gravehouse origins in the upper South. *Tennessee Folklore Society Bulletin* 56(2): 17–30.

Ballard, Sandra L., and Haeja K. Chung. 2005. *The collected short stories of Harriette Simpson Arnow*. East Lansing: Michigan State University Press.

Ballard, Sandra L., and Leila E. Weinstein, eds. 2007. *Neighbor to neighbor: A memoir of family, community, and Civil War in Appalachian North Carolina*. Boone, NC: Appalachian State University Center for Appalachian Studies. [northwestern NC]

Bandy, Lewis D. 1940. Folklore of Macon County, Tennessee. MA thesis, George Peabody College, Nashville, TN. [Macon County, north central TN]

———. 1943. Witchcraft and divination in Macon County. *Tennessee Folklore Society Bulletin* 9: 1–13. [Macon County, north central TN]

Banks, Gabriel Conklyn. 1964. *Back to the mountains: Autobiography of Gabriel Conklyn Banks*. N.p.: Gabriel C. Banks. [eastern KY]

Bansemer, Roger. 1993. *Mountains in the mist: Impressions of the Great Smokies*. Dallas, TX: Taylor. [central east TN, central western NC]

Barkley Family. 1861–64. [Letters]. Barkley Family Papers. Collection 3032, Southern Historical Collection, Wilson Library, University of North Carolina, Chapel Hill. [Anderson District, northwestern SC]

Barksdale, John W. 2007. *Radford*. Charleston, SC: Arcadia. [southwestern VA]

Barnwell, Lila Ripley. 1951. Our mountain speech. *Asheville Citizen*, January 4. [central western NC]

Bartlett Family. 1863–64. [Letters]. Bartlett Letters. Tennessee State Library and Archives, Nashville. http://www.tn.gov/tsla/cwtn/index.htm [Claiborne County, northeast Tennessee]

Barton, William E. 1897. *The truth about the trouble at Roundstone*. Boston: Pilgrim. [southeastern KY]

Barton, William P. C. 1818. *Vegetable materia medica of the United States or medical botany: Containing a botanical, general, and medical history of medicinal plants indigenous to the United States*. Boston: Boston Book Company.

Bartram, William. 1791. *Travels through North & South Carolina, Georgia, East & West Florida, the Cherokee country, the extensive territories of the Muscogulges, or Creek Confederacy, and the country of the Chactaws; containing an account of the soil and natural productions of those regions, together with observations on the manners of the Indians*. Philadelphia: James and Johnson.

Bascom, Louise Rand. 1909. Ballads and songs of western North Carolina. *Journal of American Folklore* 22: 238–50. [western NC]

Baughan, Denver Ewing. 1957. Review of *Tarheel Talk* by Norman Eliason. *American Speech* 32: 283–85. [western NC]

Bayless letters. 1991. *Watauga Association of Genealogists Bulletin* 20: 117–20. [Carter County, northeast TN]

Bear hunting in the Appalachians. 1976. *Foxfire Magazine* 10(4): 259–318. [Haywood County, central western NC]

BearPaw (Great Smoky Mountains Association newsletter). 1996–2013. Gatlinburg, TN: Great Smoky Mountains Natural History Association and Great Smoky Mountains Association. [central east TN, central western NC]

Beaver, Patricia D., and Sandra L. Ballard. 2013. *Voices from the headwaters: Stories from Meat Camp (Pottertown) & Sutherland, North Carolina*. Boone, NC: Appalachian State University. [northwestern NC]

Beck, H. P. 1952. Herpetological lore from the Blue Ridge. *Midwest Folklore* 2: 141–50. [WV]

Beckner, Lucien. c1844. Rev. John Dabney Shane interview with Mrs. Sarah Graham of Bath County. Transcribed and published in *Filson Club History Journal* 9 (1934): 224–41. [KY]

Beddow, Elizabeth Russell. 1903. *The oracle of Moccasin Bend: A story of Lookout Mountain*. Washington, DC: Neale.

Beekeeping. 1971. *Foxfire Magazine* 5(3): 161–73.

Beeson, D. C. 1994. *In the spirit of adventure: A hike in the Great Smoky Mountains, August 28–September 4, 1914*. Edited by Norma Myers et al. Seymour, TN: Panther Press. [northeast TN]

Bell, Thomas A. 1862–63. [Letters]. Thomas A. Bell Letters, 1861–1863. David M. Rubenstein Rare Book and Manuscript Library, Duke University, Durham, NC. [Augusta County, central west VA]

Belt, Don. 1983. Chattooga River country. *National Geographic* 163 (April): 458–77. [northeast GA]

Benfield, Jean Boone. 2009. *Mountain born: A recollection of life and language in western North Carolina*. Spartanburg, SC: Reprint Company. [central western NC]

Bennett, Hugh Hammond. 1932. The majestic Smokies. *Holland's* 51(4): 12–13, 57, 61. [Sevier County, central east TN]

Benson, William W. c1830. [Revolutionary War pension application]. In Dockter, Albert W., Jr. 1987. Some Revolutionary War soldiers. *Blount Journal* 3: 38.

Bent Creek Baptist Church Minutes, 1785–1844. 1938. Historical Records Project 465-44-3-115, WPA. Transcribed copy on deposit at Calvin M. McClung Historical Collection, Knox County Public Library, Knoxville. [Hamblen County, central east TN]

Bergen, Fanny D. 1892. Popular American plant-names. *Journal of American Folk-lore* 5: 89–106. [northwestern NC]

———. 1893. Popular American plant-names, II. *Journal of American Folk-lore* 6: 135–42. [northwestern NC]

———. 1894. Popular American plant-names, III. *Journal of American Folk-lore* 7: 89–104. [northwestern NC]

Berry, Brewton. 1963. *Almost white*. New York: Macmillan. [southeastern KY, northeast TN, southwestern VA]

Berry, Chad. 2000. *Southern migrants, Northern exiles*. Champaign: University of Illinois Press.

Berry, Pearlleen D., and Mary Eva Repass. 1980. *Grandpa says: Superstitions and sayings from eastern Kentucky*. Fredericksburg, VA: Foxhound. [eastern KY]

Best, Bill. 2011. Southern Appalachian heirloom bean terminology. http://www.heirlooms.org/terminology.html, accessed November 2, 2011. [KY]

Betts, Leonidas, and Richard Walser. 1974. *Gateway to North Carolina folklore*. Raleigh: North Carolina State University School of Education. [western NC]

Beverley, Robert. 1991. A few examples of the old mountain idiom. In *The western North Carolina almanac and book of facts*, 146–47. Franklin, NC: Sanctuary Press. [western NC]

Bewley, Irene. 1943. Picturesque speech. *Tennessee Folklore Society Bulletin* 9(3): 4. [Greene County, northeast TN]

Bible, Jean. 1991. *Bent twigs in Jefferson County*. Rogersville: East Tennessee Printing. [Jefferson County, central east TN]

Bible record of Hester Jane Walker. 1985. *Watauga Association of Genealogists Bulletin* 14: 60–61.

Big John Ross Carson. 1852. [Letter]. Transcribed and published in *Watauga Association of Genealogists Bulletin* 20 (1991): 145–47. [Washington County, northeast TN]

Big South Fork Oral History Project. 1979. [Selected audio interviews, transcribed for this book]. Folk life along the Big South Fork of the Cumberland River Oral History Collection. Special Collections Department, University of Kentucky, Lexington. [McCreary County, southeastern KY; Fentress County and Pickett County, TN]

Birch, George, Judy Brown, and David Wilson. 1968. Sorghum: Home-grown syrup. *Foxfire Magazine* 2(3–4): 26–29.

Bird, W. E., ed. 1926. *The spirit of western North Carolina (a pageant)*. Cullowhee, NC: Cullowhee State Normal School Department of English. [southwestern NC]

———. 1927. *Among the highlanders yesterday and today: A pageant of western North Carolina*. Cullowhee, NC: Cullowhee State Normal School. [western NC]

Bird, William. c1926. Wordlist compiled at Cullowhee, North Carolina. Horace Kephart Collection, Hunter Library Special Collections, Western Carolina University, Cullowhee, NC. [southwestern NC]

Bird traps. 1978. *Foxfire Magazine* 12(1): 73–76.

Bishir, Catherine W., Michael Southern, and Jennifer F. Martin. 1999. *A guide to the historic architecture of western North Carolina*. Chapel Hill: University of North Carolina Press. [western NC]

Black, John H. 1862. John H. Black Letters. University of Virginia Library, Charlottesville.

Blackhurst, W. E. 1954. *Riders of the flood*. Parsons, WV: McClain. [WV]

Blackmun, Ora. 1977. *Western North Carolina: Its mountains and its people to 1880*. 2nd ed. Boone, NC: Appalachian Consortium Press. [western NC]

Blacksmithing. 1977. *Foxfire Magazine* 11(3): 185–225. [Macon County, southwestern NC]

Blackwell, Joshua Beau. 2009. *"Used to be a rough place in them hills": Moonshine, the Dark Corner, and the new South*. Bloomington, IN: AuthorHouse. [Greenville County, northwestern SC]

Blair, Walter. 1944. *Tall tale America: A legendary history of our humorous heroes*. New York: Coward-McCann.

Blair Family. 1864. [Letters]. Blair Letters, 1838–1884, PC 1206, State Archives of North Carolina, Raleigh. [Caldwell County, northwestern NC]

Blankenship, John. 2017. *Songs of the whippoorwill: An Appalachian odyssey*. Vol. 1. N.p.: Lulu.com.

Blaustein, Richard. 1997. Harvey Miller and the Pelznickel: Exploring a survival of German folk culture in southern Appalachia. Paper presented at the Appalachian Studies Association conference, Cincinnati.

———. 2003. *The thistle and the brier: Historical links and cultural parallels between Scotland and Appalachia*. Jefferson, NC: McFarland.

Bledsoe, Jerry. 1980. *Just folks: Visitin' with Carolina people*. Asheboro, NC: Down Home. [northwestern SC]

Blind Pig and Acorn. 2010–19. [Installments of the blog *Blind Pig and the Acorn*]. https://www.blindpigandtheacorn.com/. [east TN, western NC]

Blomquist, Ann K., and Cherel Bolin Henderson, transcribers. 2011. Index and petitions to the Tennessee legislature: Cocke County, Tennessee. *Tennessee Ancestors* 27: 143–90. [Cocke County, central east TN]

Bluestein, Gene. 1994. *Poplore: Folk and pop in American culture*. Amherst: University of Massachusetts Press.

Bohannon, J. S. 1915. A bear hunt in the Great Smoky Mountains. *National Sportsman* (October): 461–65. [central east TN, central western NC]

Bolton, Charles K. 1910. *Scotch-Irish pioneers in Ulster and America.* Boston: Bacon and Brown. Repr., Baltimore: Genealogical Publishing Company, 1967.

Bolton, H. Carrington. 1893. Waste-basket of words. *Journal of American Folk-lore* 6: 143. [western VA]

Bolton, Irene. 1927. A mountain girl speaks. *Mountain Herald* 30(1): 4–5. [northeast TN]

Bond, George Foot. 1939. A study of an Appalachian dialect. MA thesis, University of Florida. [Rutherford County, southwestern NC]

Bonner, Sherwood. 1883. *Dialect tales.* New York: Harper and Brothers. [Putnam County, central TN]

Boogers, witches, and haints. 1971. *Foxfire Magazine* 5(1–2): 28–48, 65–79.

Boone, Laura Phipps. 1955. Folk names for blooming plants. *Southern Folklore Quarterly* 19: 230–36.

Boshears, Frances. 1953. The shivaree. *Tennessee Folklore Society Bulletin* 19: 65–67. [Scott and Morgan Counties, east central TN]

Bowman, Blanche Sappenfield. 1940. Study of the dialect employed by the people of the Kentucky mountains and presented through a group of original short stories. MS thesis, Kansas State College. [eastern KY]

Bowman, Elizabeth Skaggs. 1938. *Land of high horizons: An intimate interpretation of the Great Smokies.* Kingsport, TN: Southern. [central east TN, central western NC]

Boykin, Carol D. 1966. A study of the phonology, morphology, and vocabulary of George Washington Harris' *Sut Lovingood Yarns.* MA thesis, University of Tennessee, Knoxville. [east TN]

Braden, Beulah Brummett. 1976. *When Grandma was a girl.* Oak Ridge, TN: Oak Ridger. [central east TN]

Bradley, Francis Aspenwall. 1915. Hobnobbing with hill-billies. *Harper's* 93 (December): 91–103.

Bradshaw, Jonas A. 1862–63. [Letters]. Jonas A. Bradshaw Papers, 1855–1864. David M. Rubenstein Rare Book and Manuscript Library, Duke University, Durham, NC. [Alexander County, northwestern NC]

Brandes, Paul D., and Jeutonne Brewer. 1976. Appalachian Amerenglish. In *Dialect clash in America: Issues and answers,* 251–311. Metuchen, NJ: Scarecrow.

Bray, Rose Altizer. 1950. Disappearing dialect. *Antioch Review* 10: 279–88.

Breckinridge, Mary C. 1952. *Wide neighborhoods: A story of the Frontier Nursing Service.* New York: Harper and Brothers. [southeastern KY]

Brewer, Alberta, and Carson Brewer. 1975. *Valley so wild: A folk history.* Knoxville: East Tennessee Historical Society. [southeast TN]

Brewer, Carson. 1962. *Hiking in the Great Smokies.* Knoxville: Holston. [central east TN, central western NC]

———. 1967. Park creepers, crawlers listed in new Smoky book. *Knoxville News-Sentinel,* October 15. [central east TN]

———. 1971. This is your community. *Knoxville News-Sentinel,* November 1. [east TN]

———. 1974. This is your community. *Knoxville News-Sentinel,* July 28. [east TN]

———. 1974. This is your community. *Knoxville News-Sentinel,* October 10. [east TN]

———. 1979. Morels springing up all over. *Knoxville News-Sentinel,* May 13, C-4. [east TN]

———. 1980. Hit's gettin' to be a sight what outlanders are sayin'. *Knoxville News-Sentinel,* February 24, C-4. [east TN]

———. 1981. *A wonderment of mountains: The Great Smokies.* Knoxville: Tenpenny. [central east TN]

———. 1993. *The Great Smoky Mountains.* Portland, OR: Graphic Arts. [central east TN]

———. 1995. Cow Flats, Zenith are old names of Smokies. *Knoxville News-Sentinel,* January 5. [east TN]

———. 1998. Don't scrouge: There's plenty of room for mountain lingo. *Knoxville News-Sentinel,* March 5, B1. [east TN]

———. 1998. Words of the past bring a mess of mail. *Knoxville News-Sentinel,* April 9, B1. [east TN]

———. 1999. Author privy to Appalachian language. *Knoxville News-Sentinel,* January 28. [east TN]

Brewster, Paul. 1953. *American nonsinging games.* Norman: University of Oklahoma Press.

Brewster, Paul G., ed. 1952. Children's games and rhymes. In *The Frank C. Brown collection of North Carolina folklore,* edited by Newman Ivey White et al., vol. 1, 29–220. Durham, NC: Duke University Press. [NC]

Britton, Nathaniel Lord. 1908. *North American trees.* New York: H. Holt. [northwestern NC, southwestern VA, WV]

Broaddus, James. 1957. The folk vocabulary of Estill County, Kentucky. MA thesis, University of Kentucky. [Estill County, eastern KY]

———. 1983. An annotated Estill County, Kentucky word list. *Midwestern Journal of Language and Folklore* 9: 24–62. [Estill County, eastern KY]

Brookman, Rosemary. 1977. Folk veterinary medicine in upper east Tennessee. *Tennessee Folklore Society Bulletin* 43: 140–48. [northeast TN]

Brooks, Mildred Jordan. 1992. *Southern stuff, down-home talk and bodacious lore from deep in the heart of Dixie.* New York: Avon.

Broome, Harvey. 1970. *Harvey Broome, earth man: Some miscellaneous writings.* Knoxville: Greenbrier. [east TN]

———. 1975. *Out under the sky of the Great Smokies: A personal journal.* Knoxville: Greenbrier. [central east TN, central western NC]

Brower, Nancy. 1973. The split-rail fence: David Webb revives art. *Asheville Times,* October 29. [western NC]

Brown, Calvin S. 1889. Dialectal survivals in Tennessee. *Modern Language Notes* 4: 205–9. [TN]

———. 1891. Other dialectal forms in Tennessee. *Publications of the Modern Language Association* 6: 171–75. [TN]

———. 1897. Dialectal survivals from Chaucer. *Dial* 22: 139–41. [TN]

Brown, Frank C., ed. 1952. *The Frank C. Brown collection of North Carolina folklore.* 6 vols. Durham, NC: Duke University Press. [NC]

Brown, Fred. 1997. Listening to the men of the mountain: Glenn Cardwell speaks with the knowledge of the past. *Knoxville News-Sentinel,* October 26. Repr., *Smoky Mountain Historical Society Journal and Newsletter* 23(3): 22–23. [Sevier County, central east TN]

Brown, James S. 1988. *Beech Creek: A study of a Kentucky mountain neighborhood.* Berea, KY: Berea College Press. [eastern KY]

Brown, Kenneth O. 1990. Finding America's oldest camp meeting. *Methodist History* 20(4): 252–54.

Brown, Margaret Lynn. 2000. *The far east: A biography of the Great Smoky Mountains.* Gainesville: University Press of Florida. [central east TN, central western NC]

Brown, William Perry. 1888. A peculiar people. *Overland Monthly,* 2nd ser. (November), 505–8.

Brown Family. 1863–65. [Letters]. Brown Family Papers, Archives of Appalachia, East Tennessee State University, Johnson City. [Knox County, central east TN]

Bruce, Dickson R., Jr. 1974. *And they all sang Hallelujah: Plain-folk, camp-meeting religion, 1800–1845.* Knoxville: University of Tennessee Press.

Bruce, J. Douglas. 1913. Terms from Tennessee. *Dialect Notes* 4: 58. [TN]

Bruce, Sally. 1987. Old Catawbans and "mountain grill": The Appalachian in Thomas Wolfe's short stories. *Contemporary Appalachia: In search of a usable past: Proceedings of the ninth annual Appalachian Studies Conference,* 37–48. Boone, NC: Appalachian Consortium Press. [western NC]

Bryan, Charles F. 1988. "Tories" amidst Rebels: Confederate occupation of east Tennessee, 1861–1863. *East Tennessee Historical Society Publication* 60: 3–22. [east TN]

Bryan, Thomas Conn. 1953. *Confederate Georgia.* Athens: University of Georgia Press.

Bryant, Ralph Clement. 1914. *Logging: The principles and general methods of operation in the United States.* New York: John Wiley & Sons.

Bryson City Centennial Committee. 1989. *100 years of progress: Bryson*

City, N.C. centennial. Bryson City, NC: Swain County Genealogical and Historical Society. [Swain County, southwestern NC]

Buchanan, Paul. 1998. [Typescript compilation of logging terms provided to editor by Harold Farwell]. [western NC]

Buck, Charles Neville. 1915. *The code of the mountains*. New York: Grosset & Dunlap.

Bueker, Terese Bland. 1998. Head family letters. *Tennessee Ancestors* 14: 13–18.

Buffum, Vryling W. 1924. Shakespearean survivals in the mountains. *Mountain Herald* 28(2): 14–17. [northeast TN]

Building your own log cabin. 1969. *Foxfire Magazine* 3(2): 9–32.

Bullard, Helen. 1976. *Crafts and craftsmen of the Tennessee mountains*. Falls Church, VA: Summit. [east TN]

Burchill, James V., Linda J. Crider, Peggy Kendrick, and Marcia Wright Bonner. 1993. *Ghosts and haunts from the Appalachian foothills: Stories and legends*. Nashville, TN: Rutledge Hill Press.

Burelbach, M. J. 1917. After bruin in the big Smokies. *Field and Stream* 22 (February): 314–17. [Blount County, central east TN]

Burleson, Bertie. 1993. *According to Aunt Keziah: Christmas mem'rys*. Newland, NC: Avery Journal. [Avery County, northwestern NC]

Burnett, Edmund Cody. 1946. Shingle making on the lesser waters of the Big Creek of the French Broad River. *Agricultural History* 20(4): 225–35. [central western NC]

Burnett, Fred M. 1960. *This was my valley*. Ridgecrest, NC: n.p. [east TN]

Burnett, G. L. 1939. *Gap o' the mountains*. Knoxville: Newman. [east TN]

Burnett, Swan M. 1889. A note on the Melungeons. *American Anthropologist* 2: 347–50. [Hancock County, northeast TN]

Burns, Inez. 1931. Settlement and early history of the coves of Blount County, Tennessee. *East Tennessee Historical Society Publication* 3: 44–67. [Blount County, central east TN]

———. 1978. Our southern mountaineers. *Smoky Mountain Historical Society Newsletter* 4(2): 10–13.

———. 2014. Remembrances of the past. *Smoky Mountain Historical Society Journal and Newsletter* 40(1): 6–8.

Burns, Olive Ann. 1984. *Cold Sassy tree*. New York: Ticknor & Fields. [north GA]

Burton, Thomas. 1993. *They shall take up serpents*. Knoxville: University of Tennessee Press.

———. 2004. Ray Hicks: A man who became a name. *Appalachian Journal* 31: 138–43. [Avery County, northwestern NC]

———. 2009. *Beech Mountain man*. Knoxville: University of Tennessee Press. [Avery County, northwestern NC]

Burton, Thomas G. 1978. *Some ballad folks*. Johnson City: East Tennessee State University Research Development Committee. [northeast TN, northwestern NC]

———. 2006. Serpent handling. In *Encyclopedia of Appalachia*, edited by Rudy Abramson and Jean Haskell, 1350–52. Knoxville: University of Tennessee Press.

Burton-Manning Collection. 1969–70. [Selected audio interviews, transcribed for this book]. Thomas Burton-Ambrose Manning Collection. Archives of Appalachia, East Tennessee State University, Johnson City. [northeast TN, northwestern NC]

Busbee, Jacques. 1928. Elizabethan settlements in North Carolina. *Mentor* 16(7): 21–22.

Bush, Florence Cope. 1990. Amazing maize. *Smoky Mountain Historical Society Newsletter* 16(2): 29–31.

———. 1990. *Ocona Lufta Baptist: Pioneer church of the Smokies, 1836–1939*. Concord, TN: Misty Cove. [Swain County, southwestern NC]

———. 1992. *Dorie: Woman of the mountains*. Knoxville: University of Tennessee Press. [Blount County, central east TN]

———. 1992. *If life gives you scraps, make a quilt: Short stories from the Smoky Mountains*. Concord, TN: Misty Cove.

Bushyhead, Robert. 1998. Cherokee language. In *Living stories of the Cherokee*, edited by Barbara K. Duncan and Davey Arch, 145–49. Chapel Hill: University of North Carolina Press. [Swain County, southwestern NC]

Busthaid Blockade Popskull. 1968. *Foxfire Magazine* 2(3–4): 100–101.

Buxton, Barry M., and Jerry W. Burns. 1989. *A village tapestry: The history of Blowing Rock*. Boone, NC: Appalachian Consortium Press. [northwestern North Carolina]

Byers, Judith Prozzillo. 2013. *Mountain Mother Goose: Child lore of West Virginia*. Fairmont: West Virginia Folklife Center.

Cades Cove. c1995. Gatlinburg, TN: Great Smoky Mountains Natural History Association. [Blount County, central east TN]

Cain, Morgan Rochelle. 2008. Wake Forest: Voices that tell of a faith community. Senior thesis, Virginia Tech University, Blacksburg. [southwestern VA]

Callahan, North. 1952. *Smoky Mountain country*. Sevierville, TN: Smoky Mountain Historical Society. [southeast TN]

Callahan, Richard J. 2009. *Work and faith in the Kentucky coal fields: Subject to dust*. Bloomington: Indiana University Press.

Camak, David English. 1927. *June of the hills: The Junaluska prize novel; A tale of the southern mountains with Lake Junaluska as the center of action*. Lake Junaluska, NC: Junaluska Women's Club. [western NC]

Campbell, Carlos C. 1960. *Birth of a national park in the Great Smoky Mountains*. Knoxville: University of Tennessee Press. [central east TN, central western NC]

———. 1964. *Great Smoky Mountains wildflowers*. Knoxville: University of Tennessee Press. [central east TN, central western NC]

———. 1967. *Memories of old Smoky*. Typescript consulted at Library, Great Smoky Mountains National Park, Gatlinburg, TN. [central east TN, central western NC]

———. c1980. Memories of old Smoky: A collection of experiences, observations, and information from the early years of the Great Smoky Mountains National Park and from several pre-park years. Typescript on deposit at Library, Great Smoky Mountains National Park, Gatlinburg, TN. [central east TN, central western NC]

Campbell, Carlos C., W. F. Hudson, and A. J. Sharp. 1970. *Great Smoky Mountains wildflowers*. Knoxville: University of Tennessee Press. [central east TN, central western NC]

Campbell, John C. 1921. *The southern highlander and his homeland*. New York: Russell Sage Foundation.

Campbell, Marie. 1937. The folklife of a Kentucky mountain community. MA thesis, George Peabody College, Nashville, TN. [southeastern KY]

———. 1939. Play party. *Tennessee Folklore Society Bulletin* 5: 17–48. [southeastern KY]

———. 1942. *Cloud-walking*. New York: Farrar and Rinehart. [southeastern KY]

———. 1958. *Tales from the cloud walking country*. Bloomington: Indiana University Press. [southeastern KY]

Campbell, Olive Dame. 1915. Songs and ballads of the southern mountains. *The Survey* 33 (January 2): 371–74.

Campbell, Olive Dame, and Cecil Sharp. 1917. *English folk songs from the southern Appalachians, comprising 122 songs and ballads, and 323 tunes*. New York: G. P. Putnam's.

Canby, Henry Seidel. 1916. Top o' Smoky. *Harper's Monthly* 132 (March): 783–93. [central east TN, central western NC]

Cantrell, Geoff. 2005. *Clingman's Dome*. Gatlinburg, TN: Great Smoky Mountains Association.

Cantu, Rita. 1979. *Great Smoky Mountains: The story behind the scenery*. Las Vegas, NV: KC Publications. [central east TN, central western NC]

Carawan, Guy, and Candie Carawan. 1975. *Voices from the mountain*. New York: Knopf.

Carden, Gary. 1988. Inside looking out. *Now & Then* 5(2): 7–8. [western NC]

———. 2000. *Mason jars in the flood and other stories*. Boone, NC: Parkway. [Jackson County, southwestern NC]

Carden, Gary, and Nina Anderson. 1994. *Buzzards, hucksters, and grieving specters*. Asheboro, NC: Down Home.

Carden, William. 1861. [Letter to William Beezly, October 6, 1861]. William Bryant Carden Civil War Letters. Hunter Library Special Collections, Western Carolina University, Cullowhee, NC. [Macon County, southwestern NC]

Cardwell, R. Glenn. 2014. Pittman Center Yule log. *Smoky Mountains Historical Society Journal and Newsletter* 15(3): 2–6.

Carpenter, Cal. 1979. *The Walton war and tales of the Great Smoky Mountains*. Lakemont, GA: Copple House. [southwestern NC]

Carpenter, Charles. 1929. The evolution of our dialect. *West Virginia Review* 7: 9, 28. [WV]

———. 1933. Variation in the southern mountain dialect. *American Speech* 8(1): 22–25.

———. 1934. Remnants of archaic English in West Virginia. *West Virginia Review* 12: 77–79, 94–95. [WV]

———. 1936. West Virginia expletives. *West Virginia Review* 13: 346–47. [WV]

———. 1973. Pronunciation and grammar of mid-Appalachia. *Journal of the Alleghenies* 9: 31–35. [WV]

Carpenter, Frank O. 1890. The Great Smoky Mountains and Thunderhead Peak. *Appalachia* 6: 138–46. [central east TN]

Carpenter, Jacob. c1845–1920. [Diary excerpts.] In Hannum, Alberta Pierson. 1943. The mountain people. In *The Great Smokies and the Blue Ridge*, edited by Roderick Peattie, 73–151. New York: Vanguard. Other excerpts in Horton Cooper 1972, 148–49. [northwestern NC]

Carr, Jess. 1972. *The second oldest profession: An informal history of moonshining in America*. Englewood Cliffs, NJ: Prentice Hall.

Carroll, Roy, and Raymond H. Pulley. 1976. Historic structures report: Little Cataloochee, North Carolina. Boone, NC: Appalachian State University. [Haywood County, central western NC]

Carrying the mail. 1976. *Foxfire Magazine* 10(2): 99–110. [Rabun County, northeast GA]

Carson, Gerald. 1963. *The social history of bourbon: An unhurried account of our star-spangled American drink*. New York: Dodd, Mead.

Carson, Jo. 1989. *Stories I ain't told nobody yet*. New York: Orchard.

Carson, Sam, and A. W. Vick. 1972. *Hillbilly cookin*. Thorn Hill, TN: Clinch Mountain Lookout.

———. 1972. *Hillbilly cookin 2*. Thorn Hill, TN: Clinch Mountain Lookout.

Carson Family. 1857–65. Carson Family Papers. Georgia Department of Archives and History, Atlanta. [Bradley County, southeast TN]

Carter, Betty L. 2003. *My little mountain home (and me)*. Victoria, BC: Trafford.

Carter, Chillon C. 1861–69. [Selected letters]. Chillon C. Carter Papers. MSS 122, Manuscripts and Folklife Archives, Western Kentucky University, Bowling Green. [Monroe County, south central KY]

Carter, Clyde William. 2002. *Life on Chaney Creek*. Emory, VA: Clinch Mountain. [southwestern VA]

Carter, Cullen Tuller. 1956. *History of the Tennessee Conference: And a brief summary of the general conferences, the Methodist Church, from the frontier in middle Tennessee to the present time*. N.p.: self-published. [central TN]

Carter, Forrest. 1976. *The education of Little Tree*. New York: Delacorte. [western NC]

Carter, Isabel. 1925. Mountain white folk-tales from the southern Blue Ridge. *Journal of American Folklore* 38: 340–74. [western NC, east TN]

———. 1934. Mountain white riddles. *Journal of American Folklore* 47: 76–80. [western NC, east TN]

Carter, Mary Nelson. 1900. *North Carolina sketches: Phases of life where the galax grows*. Chicago: McClurg.

Carter, Ted. 1975. It's the gospel truth. *Asheville Citizen-Times*, December 11. [western NC]

Caruthers, William Alexander. 1834. *The Kentuckian in New-York*. New York: Harper & Sons.

Carver, Bill. 1999. *Branch water tales*. Andrews, NC: Mountain Voice. [southwestern NC]

Carver, Craig M. 1987. *American regional dialects: A word geography*. Ann Arbor: University of Michigan Press.

Casada, Jim. 1996. Caught by the gospel hook. *Bone Rattler* 12(4): 24–27. [Swain County, southwestern NC]

Cash, June Carter. 1979. *Among my klediments*. Grand Rapids, MI: Zondervan.

Cataloochee Auto Tour. c1990. Gatlinburg, TN: Great Smoky Mountains Natural History Association. [Haywood County, central western NC]

Cate, Herma. 1973. Molasses making. *Maryville-Alcoa Daily Times*, October 10. [Blount County, central east TN]

———. 1974. Winter food supply. *Maryville-Alcoa Daily Times*. November 6. [Blount County, central east TN]

———. c1976. Cattle herder. *Maryville-Alcoa Daily Times*. [Blount County, central east TN]

———. c1976. Ginseng digger. *Maryville-Alcoa Daily Times*. [Blount County, central east TN]

Cate, Herma, Clyde Ussery, and Randy Armstrong. 1974. *Our southern Appalachian heritage*. Kingsport, TN: Holston. [Blount County, central east TN]

Cathey Family. 1863. [Letter]. Cathey Family Papers. Hunter Library Special Collections, Western Carolina University, Cullowhee, NC. [Haywood County, central western NC]

Caton, Joseph. 1940. *Wildflowers of the Great Smokies*. Knoxville: J. L. Caton. [central east TN, central western NC]

Caudill, Rebecca. 1966. *My Appalachia: A reminiscence*. New York: Holt, Rinehart and Winston. [southeastern KY]

Cave, Kent. 2007. [Personal notes shared with the editor]. [Surry County, northwestern NC]

Cavender, Anthony. 1990. *A folk medical lexicon of south central Appalachia*. Johnson City: East Tennessee State University. [northeast TN]

———. 1992. Folk hematology in the Appalachian South. *Journal of Folklore Research* 29: 23–36. [northeast TN]

———. 1996. A note on the origin and meaning of bold hives in the American South. *Southern Folklore* 53: 17–24. [northeast TN]

———. 2003. *Folk medicine in southern Appalachia*. Chapel Hill: University of North Carolina Press. [northeast TN, southwestern VA]

———. 2006. Medical and health terminology. In *Encyclopedia of Appalachia*, edited by Rudy Abramson and Jean Haskell, 1021–22. Knoxville: University of Tennessee Press.

Cavender, Anthony, and Steve Crowder. 2002. White-livered women and bad-blooded men: Folk illness and sexual disorder in southern Appalachia. *Journal of the History of Sexuality* 11(4): 637–49.

Center for Oak Ridge Oral History. 2011. [Transcription of audio interview with Robert Brannon]. Oak Ridge Oral History Project records, stored at Oak Ridge Public Library, Oak Ridge, TN. [east TN]

Chalkley, Lyman. 1912. *Chronicles of the Scotch-Irish settlement in Virginia, extracted from the original court records of Augusta County 1745–1800*. Baltimore: Genealogical Publishing Company. [Augusta County, central west VA]

Chalmers, Marjorie. 1975. *"Better I stay": An invitation in the Great Smokies*. Gatlinburg, TN: Crescent. [Sevier County, central east TN]

Chamberlain, Alexander F. 1902. Algonkian words in American English: A study in the contact of the white man and the Indian. *Journal of American Folklore* 15: 240–67.

Change: A difference in lifestyle. 1975. *Foxfire Magazine* 9(1): 45–51. [Rabun County, northeast GA; Jackson County, southwestern NC]

Chapman, Ashton. c1951. Speech of WNC mountain people is often confusing to newcomers. *Asheville Citizen*, undated. [central western NC]

———. 1953. Decoration day custom dates from early days in the mountains. *Asheville Citizen*, May 31. [central western NC]

———. 1956. Folk retain "old English." *Winston-Salem Journal*, January 9, 8. [western NC]

———. 1959. Early settlers used flower for suds to wash and bathe. *Asheville Citizen-Times*, August 9. [central western NC]
———. 1971. Early settlers found many uses for sumac. *Asheville Citizen-Times*, October 25. [western NC]
Chapman, Maristan. 1928. *The happy mountain*. New York: Literary Guild.
———. 1929. American speech as practiced in the southern highlands. *Century* 117: 617–23.
———. 1929. *Homeplace*. New York: Viking.
———. 1933. *Glen hazard*. New York: Knopf.
Chapman Family. 1848–81. Chapman Family Letters, 1848–1881. MS 69-1853, Tennessee State Library and Archives, Nashville. [Campbell County, northeast TN; Russell County, southwestern VA]
Charleston (WV) Daily Mail. 1930. [Untitled article]. September 29. [WV]
Charleston (WV) Gazette. 1940. [Untitled article]. [WV]
———. 1969. [Untitled article]. May 11. In DARE File. [WV]
Charlie Ross Hartley (part 1). 1975. *Foxfire Magazine* 9(2–3): 166–76. [Watauga County, northwestern NC]
Charlie Ross Hartley (part 2). 1975. *Foxfire Magazine* 9(4): 379–91. [Watauga County, northwestern NC]
Charlie [Charley] Ross Hartley (part 3). 1976. *Foxfire Magazine* 10(1): 4–10. [Watauga County NC]
Chase, Richard. 1943. *The Jack tales*. Boston: Houghton Mifflin.
———. 1948. *Grandfather tales*. New York: Houghton Mifflin.
———. 1952. The Hindman Pageant. *Mountain Life and Work* 28(2): 19. [southeastern KY]
Cheek, Pauline B. 1989. You can't go home if you haven't been away. *Now & Then* 6(2): 9–10.
———. 1995. *Appalachian scrapbook: An A-B-C of growing up in the mountains*. Johnson City, TN: Overmountain.
Chiles, Mary Ruth. c1979. [Glossary to accompany Lloyd Foster, *History of Walker Valley*, 1970–74; consulted at Library, Great Smoky Mountains National Park, Gatlinburg, TN]. [central east TN, central western NC]
———. 1980. Logging lingo [compilation from oral history recordings and otherwise as noted, based mainly on 1974–75 McCracken *Logging*; consulted at Library, Great Smoky Mountains National Park, Gatlinburg, TN]. [central east TN, central western NC]
Chiles, Mary Ruth, and Mrs. William P. Trotter. 1957. *Mountain makin's in the Smokies: A cookbook*. Asheville, NC: Stephens.
Church Book for the Globe Creek Baptist Church. 1797–1812. Collection 2308. Southern Historical Collection, Wilson Library, University of North Carolina at Chapel Hill. [Caldwell County, northwestern NC]
A church of God. 1973. *Foxfire Magazine* 7(1): 5–13.
Civil War in Harlan: The Harlan County Battalion. 1983. *Harlan Footprints: Genealogical Society of Harlan County* 1(4): 19–26. [Harlan County, southeastern KY]
A Civil War letter. 1997. *Bone Rattler* 13(1): 34–35. [Jackson County, southwestern NC]
Civil War soldiers' letters. 1862–63. Miscellaneous letters and diaries written by Civil War soldiers whose names are unknown. In editor's private collection.
Clark, Amy. 2000. Can't pronounce *Appalachia*? Then don't mess with us. *Now & Then* 17(2): 29–30.
Clark, Darius. 1980. The Civil War diary of Darius Clark of White County, TN, Co. G, 16th Tennessee Infantry, Confederate States of America. Transcribed by James Joseph Betterton. Copy on deposit in Tennessee State Library and Archives, Nashville. [central TN]
Clark, Joseph D. 1942. *The Kentucky*. New York: Rinehart. [KY]
———. 1962. Folk speech from North Carolina. *Southern Folklore Quarterly* 26: 301–25. [NC]
———. 1970. North Carolina popular beliefs and superstitions. *North Carolina Folklore* 18(1): 9–34. [NC]
Clarke, Mary Washington. 1964. Jesse Stuart's writings preserve passing folk idiom. *Southern Folklore Quarterly* 28: 157–98. [northeastern KY]
———. 1965. Proverbs, proverbial phrases, and proverbial comparisons in the writings of Jesse Stuart. *Southern Folklore Quarterly* 29: 142–63. [northeastern KY]
———. 1968. *Jesse Stuart's Kentucky*. New York: McGraw-Hill. [northeastern KY]
———. 1972. To dance in a hog trough. *Kentucky Folklore Record* 18: 68–69. [northeastern KY]
Clarkson, Roy B. 1964. *Tumult on the mountains: Lumbering in West Virginia, 1770–1920*. Parsons, WV: McClain. [WV]
———. 1976. Mountain logging in the southern Appalachians at the turn of the century. *Southern Lumberman* 233: 117–22. [WV]
Cleaves, Mildred P. 1946. King's English reigns in the Kentucky Knobs. *In Kentucky* 10(3): 35. [KY]
Click, Jacob B. 1861–67. [Selected letters]. Jacob B. Click Papers, 1861–1867. David M. Rubenstein Rare Book and Manuscript Library, Duke University, Durham, NC. [Augusta County, central west VA]
Click, Temperance. 1835. A long-departed voice from Red Hill, Alabama. Transcribed and published in *Greene County Pioneer* 8(80) (1992). [Greene County, northeast TN]
Clouse, Lolketta. 1990. *Wilder*. Nashville, TN: Rutledge Hill Press.
Coal camp memories: An interview with Johnnie Johnson. 2004. *Tradition: A Journal of West Virginia Folklife* 1: 22–25. [WV]
Coale, Charles B. 1878. *The life and adventures of Wilburn Waters, the famous hunter and trapper of White Top Mountain*. Richmond: G. W. Gray & Co. [southwestern VA]
Coal miners' jargon. c1975. Big Stone Gap, VA: Madisonville Community College.
Cobb, Ann. 1922. *Kinfolks: Kentucky mountain rhymes*. Boston: Riverside. [eastern KY]
Cobb, Margaret Ogle. 2008. Vacation time. *Smoky Mountain Historical Society Journal and Newsletter* 34(1–2): 15–23. [Sevier County, central east TN]
Cockfighting I. 1979. *Foxfire Magazine* 13(1): 50–68.
Cockfighting II. 1979. *Foxfire Magazine* 13(3): 151–59.
Coe Ridge Oral History Project. 1961. [Selected audio interviews from Michael Montgomery's dissertation fieldwork, transcribed for this book]. Indiana and Kentucky, William Lynwood Montell Collection, Archives of Traditional Music, Indiana University, Bloomington. [Monroe and Cumberland Counties, south central KY]
Coggin, E. B. 1862–63. E. B. Coggin Papers. Alabama Department of Archives and History, Montgomery.
Coggins, Allen R. 1999. *Place names in the Smokies*. Gatlinburg, TN: Great Smoky Mountains Association. [central east TN, central western NC]
Cohn, Philip W. 1978. Traditional courtship and marriage customs of the Appalachian South. In *Glimpses of southern Appalachian folk culture*, edited by Charles H. Faulkner and Carol K. Buckles, 34–42. Chattanooga: Tribute.
Cole, David. 1996. A social history of Forney's Creek, North Carolina. *Bone Rattler* 12(3): 59–71. [Swain County, southwestern NC]
Coleman, Wilma. 1936. Mountain dialect of north Georgia. MA thesis, University of Georgia. [north GA]
Collins, Bobbie L. 1988. Decoration day in Unicoi County. *Tennessee Folklore Society Bulletin* 54: 82–90. [northeast TN]
Collins, Kaye Carver, Angie Cheek, et al., eds. 2004. *Foxfire 12: War stories, Cherokee traditions, summer camps, square dancing, crafts, and more affairs of plain living*. New York: Anchor.
Collins, Kaye Carver, Lacy Hunter, et al., eds. 1999. *Foxfire 11: The old homeplace, wild plant uses, preserving and cooking food, hunting stories, fishing, and more affairs of plain living*. New York: Anchor.
Collins, Lewis. 1874. *Collins' historical sketches of Kentucky*. 2 vols. Covington, KY: Collina. [KY]
Colton, Henry E. 1859. *Mountain scenery*. Raleigh: W. L. Pomeroy. [western NC]
Combs, Josiah [H.]. 1913. *The Kentucky highlander from a native mountaineer's viewpoint*. Lexington, KY: Richardson and Company. [southeastern KY]

———. 1914. Sympathetic magic in the Kentucky mountains. *Journal of American Folklore* 27: 328–30. [southeastern KY]

———. 1916. Old, early, and Elizabethan English in the southern mountains. *Dialect Notes* 4: 283–97. [southeastern KY]

———. 1919. A word-list from the South. *Dialect Notes* 5: 31–40. [east TN, southeastern KY, western NC]

———. 1921. Early English slang survivals in the mountains of Kentucky. *Dialect Notes* 5: 115–17. [southeastern KY]

———. 1921. Kentucky items. *Dialect Notes* 5: 118–19. [southeastern KY]

———. 1923. Addenda from Kentucky. *Dialect Notes* 5: 242–43. [southeastern KY]

———. 1925. *Folk-songs du Midi des États-Unis*. Doctoral thesis, Université Paris-Sorbonne. Translated by D. K. Wilgus as *Folk-songs of the Southern United States* and published by the University of Tennessee Press, 1961. [southeastern KY]

———. 1931. Language of the southern highlanders. *Publications of the Modern Language Association* 46: 1302–22. [southeastern KY]

———. 1944. A word-list from the southern highlands. *Publication of the American Dialect Society* 2: 17–23. [southeastern KY]

———. 1957. Idioms. *Language of the southern highlanders*. Typescript on deposit at Berea College Library Appalachian Collection, Berea, KY. [southeastern KY]

———. 1957. Syntax. *Language of the southern highlanders*. Typescript on deposit at Berea College Library Appalachian Collection, Berea, KY. [southeastern KY]

———. 1957. Word list. *Language of the southern highlanders*. Typescript on deposit at Berea College Library Appalachian Collection, Berea, KY. [southeastern KY]

———. 1967. *Folk-songs of the southern United States*. Edited by D. K. Wilgus. Austin: University of Texas Press. [southeastern KY]

Combs, Mona. 1958. Archaic English words used in north eastern Kentucky. MEd thesis, Morehead State College. [northeastern KY]

Conant, R., and J. T. Collins. 1991. *A field guide to reptiles and amphibians: Eastern and central North America*. 3rd ed. Boston: Houghton Mifflin.

Confederate Civil War Collection. 1861–65. Miscellaneous letters and documents written by Confederate Civil War soldiers. Tennessee State Library and Archives, Nashville.

Congressional Record. 1888. 19(4): 3587, May 1. [KY]

Conley Family. 1864. [Letter]. Civil War Soldiers' Letters. LPR78, box 1, folder 11, Alabama Department of Archives and History, Montgomery. [Jackson County, southwestern NC]

Connelly, Thomas L. 1968. *Discovering the Appalachians: What to look for from the past and in the present along America's eastern frontier*. Harrisburg, PA: Stackpole.

Conner, Edward C. 1937. [The Conner manuscript]. Typescript consulted at Library of Great Smoky Mountains National Park, Gatlinburg, TN. [central east TN]

Cook, O. Dathan. 1979. *Mountain grown*. N.p.: Self-published.

Cooke, Grace MacGowan. 1910. *The power and the glory*. New York: Doubleday Page.

Coon, Nelson. 1977. *The dictionary of useful plants*. Emmaus, PA: Rodale.

Coonfield, Ted. 2011. *The Varmits: Living with Appalachian outlaws*. N.p.: AuthorHouse. [southeast OH]

Cooper, Ann Goode. 2003. *Gathering up memories: A collection of Appalachian stories*. Boone, NC: Parkway. [western NC]

Cooper, Horton. 1864. *History of Avery County*. Asheville, NC: Biltmore. [Avery County, northwestern NC]

———. 1959. Only a corpse could sleep at a wake. *Charlotte News and Observer*, March 2. [western NC]

———. 1960. The jularker bussed his jusem-sweet. *Charlotte News and Observer*, July 31. [western NC]

———. 1961. Nairy a word. [Undated news clipping, western NC]

———. 1965. Witches once thought to have roamed N.C. hills. *Charlotte Observer*, October 31. [western NC]

———. 1972. *North Carolina mountain folklore and miscellany*. Murfreesboro, NC: Johnson. [northwestern NC]

Cooper, Land, and Mary Lee Cooper. 2001. *The people of the New River: Oral histories from the Ashe, Alleghany, and Watauga Counties of North Carolina*. West Jefferson, NC: McFarland. [northwestern NC]

Cooper, R. 1864. Robert Cooper Letter. WPA Civil War Transcriptions, Tennessee State Library and Archives, Nashville. [Hawkins County, northeast TN]

Copeland, Isaac. 1862–64. [Letters]. Isaac Copeland Papers. Civil War Collection, Miscellaneous Military Collection, State Archives of North Carolina, Raleigh. [Surry County, northwestern NC]

Copenhaver, Andrew J. 1861–65. Andrew J. Copenhaver Papers. Accession 39717, Library of Virginia Archives, Richmond.

Corbin, Wilford. 2017. *The boys of Battle Branch: How growing up in Appalachia shaped our lives*. Cullowhee, NC: Western Carolina University Print Shop. [southwestern NC]

Corey, John. 1963. Folk toys disregard space age. *Christian Science Monitor*, April 26.

Corn shocks. 1973. *Foxfire Magazine* 7(4): 325.

Cornshuck dolls. 1974. *Foxfire Magazine* 8(1): 78–81. [Rabun County, northeast GA]

Corn shuckin's house raisin's quiltin's pea thrashin's singin's log rollin's candy pullin's and . . . 1971. *Foxfire Magazine* 5(1–2): 96–108.

Costner, Ella V. 1971. *Song of life in the Smokies: Stories of mine own people and sketches of life as it was lived in the mountains before the park took over*. Maryville, TN: Brazos. [Cocke County, central east TN]

Couch, Jackson. 1862. Jackson Couch Letters. Confederate Miscellany, box 2, folder 1, Stuart A. Rose Manuscript and Rare Book Library, Emory University, Atlanta. [Murray County, north GA]

Councill, M. A. 1862–64. [Letters]. Mary A. (Horton) Councill Papers, 1862–1864. David M. Rubenstein Rare Book and Manuscript Library, Duke University, Durham, NC. [Watauga County, northwestern NC]

Country schools and pastimes. 1985. *North Carolina Folklore Journal* 33: 34–50. [western NC]

Cox, Ellen Duncan. 1966. A study of dialect peculiarities of Scott County, Tennessee secondary school students. MS thesis, University of Tennessee, Knoxville. [Scott County, north central TN]

Cox, John Harrington. 1927. The Yew Pine Mountains: A "John Hardy" ballad. *American Speech* 3: 225–26. [WV]

———. 1932. [Affirmative *any more*]. *American Speech* 7: 236.

Cox, Tom. c1926. Wordlist compiled at Cullowhee, North Carolina. Horace Kephart Collection, Hunter Library Special Collections, Western Carolina University, Cullowhee, NC. [southwestern NC]

Cox, William T. 1910. *Fearsome creatures of the lumberwoods*. Washington, DC: Judd and Detweiler.

Cozart, Arl. 1989. Letters written during the Civil War. *Hamblen Heritage* 4: 63–66. [Hamblen County, northeast TN]

Cozzo, David. 2003. Beyond tall tales: Ray Hicks and mountain herbalism. *Appalachian Journal* 30(4): 284–301.

Crabtree, Margaret Stinnett. c1973. Rememberin' the Little Greenbriar School and Primitive Baptist Church. Typescript consulted at Library, Great Smoky Mountains National Park, Gatlinburg, TN. [Blount County, central east TN]

Craddock, Charles Egbert [Mary Murfree]. 1883. A-playin' of Old Sledge at the settlemint. *Atlantic Monthly* 52: 544–57.

———. 1884. *In the Tennessee mountains*. Boston: Houghton Mifflin.

———. 1885. *The prophet of the Great Smoky Mountains*. Boston: Houghton Mifflin.

———. 1886. *In the clouds*. Boston: Houghton Mifflin.

———. 1889. *The despot of Broomsedge Cove*. Boston: Houghton-Mifflin.

———. 1891. *In the stranger people's country*. New York: Harper and Brothers.

———. 1894. *His vanished star.* Boston: Houghton-Mifflin.
———. 1895. *The mystery of witch-face mountain.* Boston: Houghton-Mifflin.
Craddock, Charles Egbert [Mary Noailles Murfree]. 1885. *Down the ravine.* Boston: Houghton Mifflin.
———. 1895. *The phantoms of the foot-bridge, and other stories.* New York: Harper and Row.
———. 1897. The juggler. *Atlantic Monthly* 80: 241–63.
Crafts: Making and weaving your own white oak splints. 1968. *Foxfire Magazine* 2(2): 7–11. [Rabun County, northeast GA and Macon County, southwestern NC]
Craig, Lillian K. 1951. *The singing hills.* New York: Crowell.
Crain, J. Dean. 1914. *A mountain boy's life story.* Greenville, SC: Baptist Courier Company.
Crawford, Joe Cobb. 2013. *Mountain shadow memories.* Clayton, GA: Laurel Mountain Press.
Creal, Katherine. 1932. Mountaineers of south have quaint speech. *Asheville Citizen,* April 17. [central western NC]
Creekmore, Pollyanna. 1995. Tennessee newspaper extracts and abstracts: Marriage, death, and other items of genealogical/historical interest: *The Knoxville Press, vol. 1816–1830.* Knoxville: Clinchdale. [east TN]
Crewdson, John M. 1980. Revenuers (and their TNT) sweep land of corn liquor. *New York Times,* January 22, A12. [north GA]
Crissman, James. 1994. *Death and dying in central Appalachia.* Urbana: University of Illinois Press. [eastern KY]
Crockett, David. 1834. *Narrative of the life of David Crockett of the state of Tennessee.* Baltimore: Cary, Hart and Company. Facsimile ed., Knoxville: University of Tennessee Press, 1973. [east TN]
———. 1835. *An account of Col. Crockett's tour to the north and down-east in the year of our Lord one-thousand eight-hundred and thirty-four.* Philadelphia: Grey and Hart. [east TN]
Crowley, Tony. 2005. *Wars of words: The politics of language in Ireland, 1537–2004.* Oxford: Oxford University Press.
Crozier, E. W. 1899. *The White-Caps: A history of the organization in Sevier County.* Knoxville: Bean, Warters and Gaut. [Sevier County, central east TN]
Crutcher, T. P. 1892. *Spurrier with the wildcats and moonshiners.* Nashville, TN: University. [central TN]
Cunningham, Paul. 1796. [Letter to Brother and Sister and Cozens from Knox County, TN]. Typescript on deposit at Tennessee State Library and Archives, Nashville.
Cunningham, Ray. 1993. *Southern talk: A disappearing language.* Asheville, NC: Bright Mountain.
Cunningham Family. 1862. [Letters]. Cunningham Letters, 1861–62. PC 1455, State Archives of North Carolina, Raleigh. [Haywood County, central western NC]
Curry, Janet. 2004. From the sticks: Growing up on the other side of the tracks. *Tradition: A Journal of West Virginia Folklife and Educational Awareness* 1: 39–40. [WV]
Curtis, Moses Ashley. 1860. *Geological and natural history survey of North Carolina: Part III, Botany containing a catalogue of the indigenous and naturalized plants of the state.* Raleigh: NC Institution for the Deaf and Dumb and the Blind.
Cushing, Marshal. 1892. *Story of our post office.* Boston: A. M. Thayer. [WV]
Cushman, Rebecca. 1934. *Swing your mountain gal: Sketches of life in the southern highlands.* Boston: Houghton Mifflin.
Cushwa, Daniel G. 1850–91. Daniel G. Cushwa Papers. MSS 2C9597b, Virginia Museum of History and Culture, Richmond.
Dabney, Joseph E. 1974. *Mountain spirits: A chronicle of corn whiskey from King James' Ulster plantation to America's Appalachians and the moonshine life.* New York: Scribner's Sons. [north GA]
———. 1985. *More mountain spirits: The continuing chronicle of moonshine life and corn whiskey, wines, ciders & beers in America's Appalachians.* Asheville, NC: Bright Mountain. [north GA]
———. 1998. *Smokehouse ham, spoon bread, and scuppernong wine.* Nashville, TN: Cumberland.
Daddy Oakley. 1979. *Foxfire Magazine* 13(3): 173–81.
Dakin, Robert F. 1966. *The dialect vocabulary of the Ohio River Valley.* 3 vols. PhD diss., University of Michigan, Ann Arbor. [This dictionary cites only the second volume and only for the subregion of eastern KY]
Dalton, Alford P. 1950. A wordlist from southern Kentucky. *Publication of the American Dialect Society* 15: 22–23. [southern KY]
Dalton Family. 1861–64. [Selected letters]. Dalton Family Papers, 1839–1904. South Caroliniana Library, University of South Carolina, Columbia. [Greenville District, northwestern SC]
Dante Oral History Project. 1997–98. [Selected audio interviews, transcribed for this book]. Dante Oral History Project Records. Archives of Appalachia, East Tennessee State University, Johnson City. [southwestern VA]
DARE Survey. 1965–70. [Responses to interviews conducted by the *Dictionary of American Regional English* project. Field notebooks consulted at the DARE office, University of Wisconsin at Madison, in 1994 and 1997, and through its first five published volumes]
Dargan, Olive Tilford. 1925. *Highland annals.* New York: Scribner's Sons.
———. 1932. *Call home the heart.* London: Longmans.
Dark Corner Oral History Project. 1983. [Selected audio interviews transcribed for this book]. Tales from the dark corner: Documenting the oral tradition (Bernard Zaidman, project director), South Caroliniana Library, University of South Carolina, Columbia. [Greenville County, northwestern SC]
Dart, Bob. 1981. "Thunder Road" fades. *Atlanta Journal-Constitution,* October 31, 4B. [north GA]
Daugherty, Mary Lee. 1976. Serpent-handling as sacrament. *Theology Today* 33: 232–43. [WV]
Daugneaux, Christine B. 1981. *Appalachia: A separate place, a unique people.* Parsons, WV: McClain.
Davenport, L. Theodore. 1987. *The rise and decline of Pine Grove: The story of a rural community in Sevier County.* Maryville, TN: BGA. [Sevier County, central east TN]
Davenport made survey through Great Smokies in 1821. 2018. *Smoky Mountain Historical Society Journal and Newsletter* 44: 18–19.
Davidson, Allen T. 1891. Reminiscences of western North Carolina. *Lyceum* 1(8): 4–13. [western NC]
Davis, Burke. 1965. *Summer land.* New York: Random House.
Davis, Clara M. 1917. A bornin'. *American Journal of Nursing* 17: 704–7. [southeastern KY]
Davis, Don. 1990. Homeplace geography. *Now & Then* 7(1): 18–19. [western NC]
Davis, Donald. 1983. *My lucky day: Tales from a southern Appalachian storyteller.* Murfreesboro, NC: Johnson. [western NC]
———. 1992. *Southern Jack tales.* Little Rock, AR: August House. [central western NC]
Davis, Donald Edward. 2006. *Homeplace geography: Essays for Appalachia.* Macon, GA: Mercer University Press. [northwest GA]
Davis, H. D. 1925. The changing role of the Kentucky mountains and the passing of the Kentucky mountaineer. *Journal of Geography* 24(February): 41–52. [eastern KY]
Davis, H. J. 1861–62. [Letters to Christian Davis]. WPA Civil War Transcriptions. Tennessee State Library and Archives, Nashville. [Yadkin County, northwestern NC]
Davis, Hattie Caldwell. 1997. *Cataloochee Valley: Vanished settlements of the Great Smoky Mountains.* Alexander, NC: WorldComm. [Haywood County, central western NC]
———. 1999. *Civil War letters and memories from the Great Smoky Mountains.* Maggie Valley, NC: Privately published. [Haywood County, central western NC]

———. 2002. *Step back in time: See historic Cataloochee Valley of the elk*. Maggie Valley, NC: Privately published. [Haywood County, central western NC]

Davis, Hubert J. 1972. *Christmas in the mountains: Southwest Virginia Christmas customs and their origins*. Murfreesboro, NC: Johnson. [southwestern VA]

———. 1973. *'Pon my honor, hit's the truth: Tall tales from the mountains*. Murfreesboro, NC: Johnson.

———. 1983. *The multi-lingual mule and other short stories*. Radford, VA: Commonwealth. [southwestern VA]

Davis, Matt. 2007. County Line Baptist Church Hawkins Grainger [part 1 of 2]. *Tennessee Ancestors* 23: 37–56, 102–16. [Grainger and Hawkins Counties, northeast TN]

Davis, Rebecca Harding. 1875. Qualla. *Lippincott's* 16: 576–86. [central western NC]

Davison, Zeta C. 1953. A word-list from the Appalachians and the Piedmont area of North Carolina. *Publication of the American Dialect Society* 19: 8–14. [NC, KY, TN]

Dearden, Elizabeth Jeannette. 1941. A word geography of the South Atlantic states. MA thesis, Brown University, Providence, RI.

DeArmond, Nora. 1982. *So high the sun*. Knoxville: Jostens. [east TN]

Death and burial in the mountains. 1974. *Appalachian Heritage* 2 (Winter): 57–63.

Dell, Ruth Webb. 1946. Moonshine in the Tennessee mountains. *Tennessee Folklore Society Bulletin* 12(3): 1–5. [Cocke County, central east TN]

De Long, Ethel. 1912. Doings on Troublesome. *Smith Alumnae Quarterly*, July 11. [southeastern KY]

———. 1920. Fiddler John. *Notes from the Pine Mountain Settlement School* 1(5) (November). [southeastern KY]

DeLozier, Kim, and Carolyn Jourdan. 2013. *Bear in the back seat: Adventures of a wildlife ranger in the Great Smoky Mountains National Park*. Vol. 1. Gatlinburg, TN: Great Smoky Mountains Association. [central east TN, central western NC]

DeLozier, Mary Jean. 1983. The good old days? Work and play in the Upper Cumberland. In *Lend an ear: Heritage of the Tennessee Upper Cumberland*, edited by Calvin Dickinson, Larry Whiteaker, and Leo McGee, 59–76. Lanham, MD: University Press of America. [north central TN]

Dennis, Delmar. c1984. *Smoky Mountain heritage: A treasury of old time mountain photos*. Sevierville, TN: Nandel. [Sevier County, central east TN]

Dennis, Leah A. 1944. A word-list from Alabama and some other southern states. *Publication of the American Dialect Society* 2: 6–16.

DeRozier, Linda Scott. 1999. *Creeker: A woman's journey*. Lexington: University Press of Kentucky. [eastern KY]

DeWitt, John H. 1919. Journal of Governor John Sevier (1789–1815). *Tennessee Historical Magazine* 5: 156–94. [east TN]

———. 1920. Journal of Governor John Sevier. *Tennessee Historical Magazine* 6: 18–68. [east TN]

Dial, Wylene. 1969. The dialect of the Appalachian people. *West Virginia History* 30: 463–71. [WV]

———. 1975. Yesterday's language. In *Mountain heritage*, edited by Beryl Blake Maurer, 92–93. Ripley, WV: Mountain State Art and Craft Fair. [WV]

Dick, Everett. 1948. *The Dixie frontier*. New York: Knopf. [upper South]

Dickey, James, and William A. Bake. 1988. *Wayfarer: A voice from the southern mountains*. Birmingham, AL: Oxmoor House.

Dictionary of American Regional English (DARE). 1892–2008. [Miscellaneous oral and written material published in the *Dictionary of American Regional English*, ed. Frederic G. Cassidy et al., 6 vols. (Cambridge, MA: Belknap Press of Harvard University Press, 1985–2013)]

Dictionary of American Regional English (DARE) File. 1969. [Interview addenda and notes collected by interviewers for the DARE project, located at the University of Wisconsin at Madison]

Dictionary of Southern Appalachian English Internet File. 2008–19. Observations, notes, and miscellany collected from various online sources by Michael Montgomery and Jennifer Heinmiller for the *Dictionary of Southern Appalachian English*.

A dictionary of the Queen's English. 1965. Raleigh: North Carolina Department of Natural and Economic Resources. [NC]

Diehl, Rick. 1971. Stripping away the myths. *Peoples Appalachia*, September/October, 5–10.

Digging a well. 1976. *Foxfire Magazine* 10(2): 125–37.

Dillon, Lacy A. 1974. *They died in the darkness*. Parsons, WV: McClain.

Dingus, L. R. 1915. A word-list from Virginia. *Dialect Notes* 4: 177–93. [southwestern VA]

Dingus, L. R. 1927. Appalachian mountain words. *Dialect Notes* 5: 468–71. [eastern KY]

Dingus, L. R. 1944. Tobacco words. *Publication of the American Dialect Society* 2: 63–72. [KY, VA]

Dipper gourds. 1973. *Foxfire Magazine* 7(4): 280–85. [Rabun County, northeast GA]

Doak, Henry Melvil. 1892. *The Wagonauts abroad*. Nashville, TN: Southwestern. [east TN]

Dockter, Albert W., Jr. 1987. Some Revolutionary War soldiers. *Blount Journal* 3: 38. [Blount County, central east TN]

Dodd, C. Kenneth. 2004. *The amphibians of Great Smoky Mountains National Park*. Knoxville: University of Tennessee Press. [central east TN, central western NC]

Doddridge, Joseph. 1823. *Logan*. Buffaloe Creek, VA: Solomon Sala. [WV]

———. 1824. *Notes on the settlement and Indian wars of the western parts of Virginia & Pennsylvania: From the year 1763 until the year 1783 inclusive; together with a view, of the state of society and manners of the first settlers of the western country*. Wellsburgh, VA, printed at the office of the *Gazette*, for the author. Repr., Pittsburgh: Ritenour and Lindsey, 1912. [WV]

Dodson, Willie. 2013. Moutain-keeper: Larry Gibson remembered. *Loyal Jones Appalachian Center Newsletter* (Berea College) 41(1): 6–7.

Donelson, John. 1779–80. Journal. Manuscript in Tennessee State Library and Archives. Published in J. G. M. Ramsey, *The annals of Tennessee to the end of the eighteenth century*, 197–203. Charleston, SC: Walker and James, 1853. Repr., Knoxville: East Tennessee Historical Society, 1967. [east TN]

Don't call me Mr. Chappell, call me Uncle Ben. 1977. *Foxfire Magazine* 11: 226–33. [Rabun County, northeast GA]

Doolittle, Jerome. 1975. *The southern Appalachians*. New York: Time-Life Books.

Doran, Edwina Bean. 1969. Folklore in White County, Tennessee. PhD diss., George Peabody College, Nashville, TN. [central TN]

Dorgan, Howard. 1987. *Giving glory to God in Appalachia: Worship practices of six Baptist subdenominations*. Knoxville: University of Tennessee Press.

———. 1989. *The Old Regular Baptists of central Appalachia: Brothers and sisters in hope*. Knoxville: University of Tennessee Press. [eastern KY]

———. 1994. Liquid graves and dripping saints. *Now & Then* 11(3): 10–12. [KY, NC, VA]

———. 1996. Baptist diversity in Appalachia. *Now & Then* 13(3): 8–11.

———. 1996. Review of *The sound of the dove: Singing in Appalachian Primitive Baptist churches*, by Beverly Bush Patterson. *Now & Then* 13(3): 36–37.

———. 1997. *In the hands of a happy God: The no-hellers of central Appalachia*. Knoxville: University of Tennessee Press. [southeastern KY]

Douglas, William O. 1961. *My wilderness: East to Katahdin*. New York: Doubleday.

Douglas, Wilson, and Jancy McClellan. 1977. How I came to be a fiddler. *Goldenseal* 3(1): 21–23. [WV]

Drake, Daniel. 1870. *Pioneer life in Kentucky, 1785–1800*. Cincinnati: R. Clarke. [northeastern KY]

Drake, Richard B. 1970. The Appalachians and the federal union. In *An Appalachian reader*, 46–66. Berea, KY: Richard Drake.

Draper, Lyman C. 1881. *King's Mountain and its heroes: History of the battle of King's Mountain, October 7th, 1780, and the events that led to it*. Cincinnati: Thomson.

Dressing and cooking game. 1970. *Foxfire Magazine* 4(1–2): 18–26.
Dressman, Michael R. 1979. "Redd up." *American Speech* 54: 141–45.
Dromgoole, Will Allen. 1892. From Dan to Beersheba. *Arena* 5: 77–88.
———. 1892. The War of the Roses. *Arena* 5: 481–93.
———. 1895. Fiddling his way to fame. In *The heart of Old Hickory and other stories of Tennessee*, 39–72. Boston: Estes and Lauriat.
———. 1895. The heart of Old Hickory. In *The heart of Old Hickory and other stories*, 1–38. Boston: Estes and Lauriat.
———. 1895. A humble advocate. *Arena* 12: 322–33.
———. 1895. Ole Logan's courtship. In *The heart of Old Hickory and other stories of Tennessee*, 133–56. Boston: Estes and Lauriat.
———. 1898. *Cinch and other tales and stories of Tennessee*. Boston: Estes and Company.
Drukker, Raymond. 1962. Language by-ways. *Mountain Life and Work* 38 (Summer): 50–52. [eastern KY]
Dudley, Fred A. 1946. "Swarp" and some other Kentucky words. *American Speech* 21: 270–73. [northeastern KY]
Dugger, Shepherd M. 1907. *The balsam groves of the Grandfather Mountain: A tale of the western North Carolina mountains*. Banner Elk, NC: Shepherd M. Dugger. [northwestern NC]
———. 1932. *War trails of the Blue Ridge*. Banner Elk, NC: Self-published. [northwestern NC]
Dulaney, Miriam Fink. 1991. *Humor, rumor and romance in old Jonesborough*. Johnson City, TN: Overmountain. [northeast TN]
Dumas, Bethany. 1976. Smoky mountain speech. In *Pioneer spirit 76*, edited by Dolly Berthelot, 24–29. Knoxville: Berthelot. [central east TN]
———. 1981. Appalachian glossary. In *An encyclopedia of east Tennessee*, edited by Jim Stokely and Jeff D. Johnson, 16–18. Oak Ridge, TN: Children's Museum. [east TN]
———. 1999. Southern mountain English: The language of the Ozarks and southern Appalachia. In *The workings of language from prescriptives to perspectives*, edited by Rebecca S. Wheeler, 67–79. Westport, CT: Praeger.
Duncan, Barbara, and Brett Riggs. 2003. *Cherokee Heritage Trails guidebook*. Chapel Hill: University of North Carolina Press. [central western NC]
Duncan, Hannibal Gerald, and Winnie Leah Duncan. 1929. Superstitions and sayings among the southern highlanders. *Journal of American Folklore* 42: 233–37.
Duncan, Mary Lou. 1975. Mountain sayens: "Dog days" to "dogwood winter." *Mountain Call* 2(1): 31.
Dunkerly, Robert M. 2007. *The battle of King's Mountain: Eyewitness accounts*. Charleston, SC: History Press.
Dunlap, A. R., and C. A. Weslager. 1947. Trends in the naming of tri-racial mixed-blood groups in the eastern United States. *American Speech* 22: 81–87.
Dunn, Durwood. 1988. *Cades Cove: The life and death of a southern Appalachian community 1818–1937*. Knoxville: University of Tennessee Press. [Blount County, central east TN]
Durham Civil War Letter Collection. 1864. [Letter dated April 22]. Private collection.
Durrance, Jill, and William Shamblin, eds. 1976. *Appalachian ways*. Washington, DC: Appalachian Regional Commission.
Dwyer, Louise, and Bil Dwyer. 1974. *Mountain cookin'*. Highlands, NC: Merry Mountaineers.
Dwyer, Paul. 1971. *Dictionary for Yankees and other uneducated people*. Highlands, NC: Merry Mountaineers.
———. 1975. Thangs Yankees don' know: Dialect, lawin', greens, recipes, squar' dancin', beauty aids, wild life, remedies, signs, stills, and folks. Highlands, NC: Merry Mountaineers.
———. 1976. *Southern sayin's for Yankees and other immigrants*. Highlands, NC: Merry Mountaineers.
Dyer, Delce. 1988. The farmstead yards at Cades Cove: Restoration and management alternatives for the domestic landscape of the southern Appalachian mountaineer. MS thesis, University of Georgia. [Blount County, central east TN]
Dyer, Gustavus W., et al., eds. 1985. *Tennessee Civil War veterans questionnaire* [typed reproductions of responses to a 43-item survey of Civil War veterans, conducted under the auspices of the Tennessee State Library]. 5 vols. Easley, SC: Southern Historical Press.
Dykeman, Wilma. 1955. *The French Broad*. New York: Holt, Rinehart and Winston.
———. 1962. *The tall woman*. Newport, TN: Wakestone.
———. 1966. *The far family*. Newport, TN: Wakestone.
———. 1976. Additions to the Appalachian vocabulary. *Knoxville News-Sentinel*, December 5, C-2. [east TN]
———. 1976. Time to build your Appalachian vocabulary. *Knoxville News-Sentinel*, October 17, C-2. [east TN]
———. 1996. Memories of Smokies park remain. *Knoxville News-Sentinel*, December 15. [east TN]
———. 2015. *Family of earth*. Chapel Hill: University of North Carolina Press. [east TN, western NC]
Dykeman, Wilma, and James Stokely. 1978. *Highland homeland: The people of the Great Smokies*. Washington, DC: US National Park Service. [central east TN, central western NC]
———. 1984. *At home in the Smokies: A history handbook for Great Smoky Mountains National Park: North Carolina and Tennessee* [revision of Dykeman and Stokely 1978]. Washington, DC: US Department of the Interior. [central east TN, central western NC]
Early mines and mining methods in Monongah. 2004. *Tradition: A Journal of West Virginia Folklife and Educational Awareness* 1: 27–34. [WV]
Earnest, John Guilford. 2005. *All right let them come: The Civil War diary of an East Tennessee Confederate, John Guilford Earnest*. Edited by Charles Swift Northen. Knoxville: University of Tennessee Press.
Eastridge, Nancy Emilia. 1939. A study of folklore in Adair County, Kentucky. MA thesis, George Peabody College, Nashville, TN. [Adair County, south central KY]
Eaton, Allen. 1937. *Handicrafts of the southern highlands*. New York: Russell Sage.
Ebel, Julia Taylor. 2005. *Orville Hicks: Mountain stories—mountain roots*. Boone, NC: Parkway. [northwestern NC]
Ebel, Julia Taylor, and Orville Hicks. 2009. *Jack tales and mountain yarns*. Boone, NC: Parkway. [Avery County, northwestern NC]
Edgerton, Daisy Priscilla Smith, and W. R. Mattoon. 1930. *First steps in southern forest study*. New York: Rand McNally.
Edmondson, Kenneth L. 1996. Hugh Forgey Crawford: Family memoirs, letters, and New Year's notes. *Tennessee Ancestors* 12: 125–37.
Edmonston/Kelly Families. 1860–65. [Letters]. Edmonston/Kelly Families Collection. Box MSS 95-5, Hunter Library Special Collections, Western Carolina University, Cullowhee, NC. [Haywood County, central western NC]
Edson, H. A., and Edith M. Fairchild. 1895. Tennessee mountains in word lists. *Dialect Notes* 1: 370–77. [southeastern KY, northeast TN, northwestern NC]
Edwards, Charles. 1892. Waste-basket of words. *Journal of American Folklore* 5: 236. [TN]
Edwards, Dorothy E. 1935. The dialect of the southern highlander as recorded in North Carolina novels. MA thesis, University of Rochester. [western NC]
Edwards, Funson. 1985. *Folksy sketches from Appalachia*. Knoxville: Privately published. [northeast TN]
Edwards, Lawrence. 1963. *Gravel in my shoe*. Montevallo, AL: Times. [northeast TN]
Egerton, John. 1991. *Shades of gray: Dispatches from the modern South*. Baton Rouge: Louisiana State University Press.
Eiler, Lyntha Scott, Terry Eiler, and Carl Fleischhauer, eds. 1981. *Blue Ridge*

harvest: A region's folklife in photographs. Washington, DC: American Folklife Center, Library of Congress.

Eliason, Norman E. 1956. *Tarheel talk: An historical study of the English language in North Carolina to 1860.* Chapel Hill: University of North Carolina Press. [western NC]

Elijoy Church (Baptist) Blount County [arm of Miller's Cove Church on Elijoy] *records, 1818–1878.* Transcribed copy on deposit at Calvin M. McClung Historical Collection, Knox County Public Library, Knoxville. [Blount County, central east TN]

Elingburg, Sandra. 1987. W. Amos Abrams prize co-winner: Mountain breed western North Carolina tales. *North Carolina Folklore Journal* 34: 52–60. [western NC]

Eller, Ron. 2000. The education of a hillbilly. In *One hundred years of Appalachian visions, 1897–1996,* edited by Bill Best, 125–30. Berea, KY: Appalachian Imprints. [WV]

Eller, Ronald D. 1982. *Miners, millhands, and mountaineers: Industrialization of the Appalachian South, 1880–1930.* Knoxville: University of Tennessee Press.

Elliott, Doug. 1995. *Wild roots.* New York: Healing Arts Press.

Elliott, Sarah Barnwell. 1898. *The Durket sperret.* New York: Henry Holt.

Ellis, Michael E. 2014. [Comments on unpublished draft of this book]

Ellis, William E. 2000. *The Kentucky River.* Lexington: University Press of Kentucky. [eastern KY]

Ellison, George. 2005. *Mountain passages: Natural and cultural history of western North Carolina and the Great Smoky Mountains.* Charleston, SC: History Press. [western NC]

———. 2007. Persecution of the dandelion. *Smoky Mountain News,* May 2. [western NC]

———. 2008. *High vistas: An anthology of nature writing from western North Carolina and the Great Smoky Mountains, 1694–1900.* Charleston, SC: History Press. [western NC]

———. 2016. *Literary excursions in the southern highlands: Essays on natural history.* Charleston, SC: History Press. [central western NC]

Ellison, George, and Elizabeth Ellison. 2006. *Blue Ridge nature journal: Reflections on the Appalachians in essays and art.* Charleston, SC: History Press. [western NC]

The end of moonshining as a fine art. 1968. *Foxfire Magazine* 2(3–4): 35–56, 89–110.

English in the mountains. 1939. *Chattanooga Times,* September 30.

Enloe, B. F. 1862. [Civil War letter]. Transcribed and published in *The heritage of Swain County North Carolina,* vol. 14 (1988). Winston-Salem, NC: Hunter. [Swain County, southwestern NC]

Ensor, Wanda. 1972. Tales of the supernatural collected in Mitchell and Yancey Counties, northwestern North Carolina. *Tennessee Folklore Society Bulletin* 38: 61–71. [northwestern NC]

Epperly, C. M. 1862–65. [Letters]. Christian Marion Epperly Papers. Gilder Lehrman Collection 2715, New York, NY. [Floyd County, southwestern VA]

Erskine, Ralph. 1943. Adventures among the mountain craftsmen. In *The Great Smokies and the Blue Ridge,* edited by Roderick Peattie, 201–16. New York: Vanguard.

Eskew, Harry. 2008. Sacred harp. In *New encyclopedia of southern culture,* vol. 12: *Music,* edited by Bill C. Malone, 128–33. Chapel Hill: University of North Carolina Press.

Essary, J. T. 1910. *Tennessee mountaineers in type: A collection of stories.* New York: Cochrane. [east TN]

Ethel Corn. 1973. *Foxfire Magazine* 7(4): 260–67. [Rabun County, northeast GA]

Evans, E. Raymond. 1978. The palen fence: An example of Appalachian folk culture. *Tennessee Anthropologist* 3: 93–99. [southeast TN]

Examples of petitions to the Tennessee legislature: Various counties. 2003. *Tennessee Ancestors* 19: 196–208. [east TN]

Expressions. 1968. *Foxfire Magazine* 2(3–4): 23–25. [northeast GA]

Faith healing. 1968. *Foxfire Magazine* 2(1): 15–24, 61–70.

Farr, Sidney Saylor. 1983. *More than moonshine: Appalachian recipes and recollections.* Pittsburgh: University of Pittsburgh Press. [eastern KY]

———. 2007. *My Appalachia: A memoir.* Lexington: University Press of Kentucky. [eastern KY]

Farr, T. J. 1935. Riddles and superstitions from middle Tennessee. *Journal of American Folklore* 48: 318–36. [east central TN]

———. 1936. Folk speech of middle Tennessee. *American Speech* 11: 275–76. [east central TN]

———. 1939. The language of the Tennessee mountain regions. *American Speech* 14: 89–92. [east central TN]

———. 1940. More Tennessee expressions. *American Speech* 15: 446–48. [east central TN]

Farrier, P. H. 1936. "Few of" and "few bit." *American Speech* 11: 278–79. [Giles County, southwestern VA]

Farthing, Mary Ann. 1977. Appalachian food customs. *North Carolina Folklore Journal* 25: 36–44. [western NC]

Farwell, Byron. 1992. *Stonewall: A biography of General Thomas J. Jackson.* New York: Norton.

Farwell, Harold. 1997. The language of Smoky Mountain loggers. Paper presented at the Dictionary Society of North America meeting, Madison, WI. [Haywood County, central western NC]

———. 1998. [Typescript compilation of logging terms provided to the editor]. [western NC]

———. 2006. Logging terminology. In *Encyclopedia of Appalachia,* edited by Rudy Abramson and Jean Haskell, 1020–21. Knoxville: University of Tennessee Press.

Farwell, Harold, and Paul Buchanan. 1994. [Paper presented at Appalachian Studies Association meeting, Blacksburg, VA, based on Buchanan's recollections from the 1920s]. [western NC]

Farwell, Harold, and J. Karl Nicholas. 1993. *Smoky Mountain voices: A lexicon of southern Appalachian speech.* Lexington: University Press of Kentucky. [Swain County, southwestern NC]

Fastnesses of Great Smokies explored. 1929. *New York Times Magazine,* August 4. [central east TN, central western NC]

Fearon, Henry Bradshaw. 1818. *Sketches of America.* London: Longman et al. [KY]

Federal Writers' Program. 1939. *A guide to Tennessee.* New York: Viking. [TN]

———. 1939. *A guide to the bluegrass state.* New York: Harcourt, Brace. [KY]

———. 1939. *A guide to the old north state.* Chapel Hill: University of North Carolina Press. [NC]

———. 1940. *Georgia: A guide to its towns and countryside.* Athens: University of Georgia Press. [GA]

———. 1940. *Virginia: A guide to the Old Dominion, compiled by workers of the Writers' Project of the Work Projects Administration in the state of Virginia.* New York: Oxford University Press. [VA]

Ferguson, Thomas. 1862. [Civil War letter]. Transcribed and published in *The heritage of Swain County North Carolina,* vol. 14 (1988). Winston-Salem, NC: Hunter. [Swain County, southwestern NC]

Ferrell, Dorothy. 1965. *Bear tales and panther tracks.* Vol. 1. Atlanta: Appalachian. [north GA]

———. 1968. *Bear tales and panther tracks.* Vol. 2. Atlanta: Appalachian. [north GA]

———. 1969. *Bear tales and panther tracks.* Vol. 3. Atlanta: Appalachian. [north GA]

Ferrell, Mallory Hope. 1976. *Tweetsie country: The East Tennessee & Western North Carolina Railroad.* Boulder, CO: Pruett. [southwestern NC]

Fetterman, John. 1967. *Stinking Creek.* New York: Dutton. [southeastern KY]

———. 1971. The people of Cumberland Gap. *National Geographic* 140: 591–620. [southeastern KY, northeast TN]

Fiddle making. 1975. *Foxfire Magazine* 9(4): 307–23. [Macon County, southwestern NC, Yancey County, northwestern NC]

Fields, Truman. 2009. *Remembering the 40's: Growing up in the heart of*

Appalachia. Bloomington, IN: AuthorHouse. [Perry County, southeastern KY]

Finch, Richard C. 2004. Ashes to ashes: Burial Upper Cumberland style. In *Rural life and culture in the Upper Cumberland*, edited by Michael E. Birdwell and W. Calvin Dickinson, 66–72. Lexington: University Press of Kentucky. [eastern KY]

———. 2014. Tennessee comb grave traditions. *Tennessee Folklore Society Bulletin* 70(1–2): 1–98. [central TN]

Finger, John R. 1991. *Cherokee Americans: The Eastern Band of the Cherokees in the twentieth century*. Lincoln: University of Nebraska Press. [Swain County, southwestern NC]

Fink, Paul [M.]. 1921. A week in the Great Smoky range. *Appalachia* 15: 140–53. [Blount County, Sevier County, central east TN]

———. 1930. Trails of the Great Smokies. *Appalachia* 18(1): 63–69. [central east TN]

———. 1933. Early explorers in the Great Smokies. *East Tennessee Historical Society Publication* 5: 55–68. [central east TN]

———. 1956. *That's why they call it: Names and lore of the Great Smokies*. Jonesboro, TN: Privately published. [central east TN, central western NC]

———. 1974. *Bits of mountain speech*. Boone, NC: Appalachian Consortium Press. [northeast TN, northwestern NC]

———. 1975. *Backpacking was the only way*. Johnson City: East Tennessee State University. [central east TN]

———. 1975. Foreword. In *Home in Madison County*, by Lena Penland Purkey. Johnson City: East Tennessee State University.

———. 1989. *Jonesborough: The first century of Tennessee's first town, 1776–1876*. Johnson City, TN: Overmountain. [Washington County, northeast TN]

Fisher, Ben C. 1990. *Mountain preacher stories: Laughter among the trumpets*. Boone, NC: Appalachian Consortium Press.

Fisher, Diane Gilliam. 2004. *Kettle bottom*. Florence, MA: Perugia.

Fisher, Noel. 2005. *The Civil War in the Smokies*. Gatlinburg, TN: Great Smoky Mountains Association. [central east TN, central western NC]

Fisher, Stephen L. 1999. Appalachian stepchild. In *Confronting Appalachian stereotypes: Back talk from an American region*, edited by Dwight Billings, Katherine Ledford, and Gurney Norman, 187–90. Lexington: University Press of Kentucky. [southern WV]

Fisher, Steve. 2000. Appalachian stepchild. In *One hundred years of Appalachian visions, 1897–1996*, edited by Bill Best, 157–60. Berea, KY: Appalachian Imprints. [southern WV]

Fitch Family. 1861–65. [Letters]. Private collection.

Fitzpatrick, Robert J. 1940. Language of the tobacco market. *American Speech* 15: 132–35.

Florence and Lawton. 1973. *Foxfire Magazine* 7(3): 192–208. [Jackson County, southwestern NC]

The flu epidemic. 1973. *Foxfire Magazine* 7(2): 100–11. [Rabun County, northeast GA, and Jackson County, southwestern NC]

Food gathering. 1967. *Foxfire Magazine* 1(3): 21–24. [Macon County, southwestern NC]

Forest, Herman. 1959. *Jessie's children*. New York: Vanguard.

Forester, William D. 1983. *Before we forget: Harlan County 1920 through 1930 with background dating further in time*. Harlan, KY: Self-published. [southeastern KY]

For where two or three are gathered together in my name, there am I in the midst of them. 1973. *Foxfire Magazine* 7(1): 14–30.

Foster, Lloyd. 1970–74. *History of Walker Valley* [interviews transcribed by Mary Ruth Chiles]. Typescript consulted at Library, Great Smoky Mountains National Park, Gatlinburg, TN. [Sevier County, central east TN]

Foust, Clora McNeill. 1969. *Horse and buggy days in the "Kingdom of Wilkes."* N.p.: Privately published. [Wilkes County, northwestern NC]

Foust Family. 1861–65. [Letters]. Private collection.

Fox, John, Jr. 1896. A Cumberland vendetta. In *A Cumberland vendetta and other stories*, 1–177. New York: Harper and Brothers.

———. 1896. The last Stetson. In *A Cumberland vendetta and other stories*, 178–215. New York: Harper and Brothers.

———. 1899. *A mountain Europa*. New York: Harper & Brothers.

———. 1903. *The little shepherd of Kingdom Come*. New York: Charles Scribner's Sons.

———. 1904. *Christmas Eve on Lonesome, and other stories*. New York: Charles Scribner's Sons.

———. 1908. *The trail of the lonesome pine*. New York: Charles Scribner's Sons.

Fox, Ruby O. 1971. *From the mouth of the mountaineer*. N.p.: Privately published.

The Foxfire 40th anniversary book: Faith, family, and the land. 2006. Mountain City, GA: Foxfire Fund.

Foxfire interviews. 1970–73. [Selected audio interviews, transcribed for this book]. Foxfire Project, Rabun Gap, GA. [Rabun County, northeast GA; Macon County, southwestern NC]

Frazier, Charles. 1997. *Cold Mountain*. New York: Vintage.

Freel, Margaret Walker. 1956. *Our heritage: The people of Cherokee County, North Carolina 1540–1955*. Asheville, NC: Miller. [Cherokee County, southwestern NC]

French, Lawrence. 1997. *Counseling American Indians*. Lanham, MD: University Press of America.

French Broad River Baptist Church minutes. 1786–1859. Historical Records Project 65-44-1466, WPA. 1933. Transcribed copy on deposit at Calvin M. McClung Historical Collection, Knox County Public Library, Knoxville. [Jefferson County, central east TN]

Friedland, Lee Ellen. 1989. Introduction. In *Old time dancing in the Appalachian mountains*, 3–4. Johnson City: East Tennessee State University Center for Appalachian Studies and Services.

Friend, Craig Thompson. 2005. *Along the Maysville Road: The early American republic in the trans-Appalachian West*. Knoxville: University of Tennessee Press. [northeastern KY]

Frome, Michael. 1966. *Strangers in high places: The story of the Great Smoky Mountains*. Garden City, NY: Doubleday. [central east TN, central western NC]

Frost, William Goodell. 1896. An educational program for Appalachian America. *Berea Quarterly* 1(4): 5–13.

———. 1899. In the southern mountains. *Berea Quarterly* 4(2): 9–12. [eastern KY]

———. 1899. Our contemporary ancestors in the southern mountains. *Atlantic Monthly* 83(March): 311–19. [eastern KY]

———. c1910. The ladder of success. [Speech for the] Educational Rally at Big Stone Gap [Virginia], *Citizen* reprint No. 10 [Special Correspondence to the *Citizen*]. [southwestern VA]

Fruit, John P. 1890. Kentucky words and phrases. *Dialect Notes* 1: 63–69. [south central KY]

———. 1892. Kentucky words. *Dialect Notes* 1: 229–34. [south central KY]

Fugate, Crystal. 2010. *I found me: Appalachian stories from a lost hillbilly girl*. N.p.: lulu.com. [eastern KY]

Fulcher, Bob. 1999. Raising cane in Tennessee. *Tennessee Conservationist* (July/August): 11–15. [east TN]

Fulcher, Bobby. 2009. Rolley hole. In *New encyclopedia of southern culture*, vol. 14: *Folklife*, edited by Glenn Hinson and William Ferris, 360–62. Chapel Hill: University of North Carolina Press.

Fuller Family. 1861–65. [Letters]. Private collection.

Funderburg, Anne. 2014. *Bootleggers and beer barons of the Prohibition Era*. Jefferson, NC: McFarland.

Furman, Lucy. 1914. *Sight to the blind*. New York: Macmillan. [southeastern KY]

———. 1923. *Mothering on the Perilous*. New York: Macmillan. [southeastern KY]

———. 1925. *The glass window: A story of the quare women*. Boston: Little, Brown. [southeastern KY]

———. 1927. *The lonesome road*. Boston: Little, Brown. [eastern KY]

Gabbard, Alex. 1992. *Return to Thunder Road: The story behind the legend*. Lenoir City, TN: Gabbard. [east TN]

Gainer, Patrick. 1975. *Witches, ghosts and signs: Folklore of the southern Appalachians*. Morgantown, WV: Seneca. [WV]

Gainer, Patrick W. 1975. Speech of the mountaineers. In *Witches, ghosts and signs: Folklore of the southern Appalachians*, 1–18. Morgantown, WV: Seneca. [WV]

Galyon, Willa Love. 1928. The Smoky Mountains and the plant naturalist. *Journal of the Tennessee Academy of Sciences* 3(3): 3–13. [central east TN, central western NC]

Gamble, Margaret Elizabeth. 1947. The heritage and folk music of Cades Cove, Tennessee. MA thesis, University of Southern California, Los Angeles. [Blount County, central east TN]

A gamecock is the gamest thing on earth. 1979. *Foxfire Magazine* 13(3): 160–72.

Ganier, Albert. 1973. The wildlife met by Tennessee's first settlers. *The Migrant* 44: 58–72. [east TN]

Ganier, Albert F. 1926. Summer birds of the Great Smoky Mountains. *Journal of the Tennessee Academy of Sciences* 1(2): 31–40. [central east TN, central western NC]

Garber, Anna. 1984. Old harp singing. *In the Smokies* 2(3): 30–31.

Garber, Aubrey. 1976. *Mountain-ese: Basic grammar for Appalachia*. Radford, VA: Commonwealth. [southwestern VA]

Gardening. 1973. *Foxfire Magazine* 7(3): 228–52.

Garland Willis. 1973. *Foxfire Magazine* 7(1): 76–82. [Macon County, southwestern NC]

Garred, Ulysses Victoria. 1957. *A history and genealogy of the Garreds, Jarretts of Kentucky, and many related families*. Whiting, IA: J. Holmes.

Garretson, Lauren. 2011. Why are we still seen as "barefoot hillbillies"? *Loyal Jones Appalachian Center Newsletter* (Berea College) 39(2): 4.

Garrison, Judith. 2015. *North Georgia moonshine: A history of the Lovells & other liquor makers*. Charleston, SC: History Press. [north GA]

Gary, Lisa Byerley. 2006. Big hogs, big problems: Park control of wild hogs protects fragile ecosystems. *Sightline* 2(1). http://eerc.ra.utk.edu/sightline/InvasionsV2N1.html.

Garza, Amy Ammons. 1994. *Matchbox mountains: Stories based on a mountain childhood*. Asheville, NC: Bright Mountain. [western NC]

Gasque, Jim. 1948. *Hunting & fishing in the Great Smokies*. New York: Knopf. [central east TN]

Gatlin, Radford. 1862. *The parentage, birth, nativity and exploits of the immortal hero Jack Keelan, who successfully defended the bridge at Strawberry Plains, and alone, put to flight fifteen Lincolnites on the night of the eighth of November, 1861*. Atlanta: Daily Intelligencer Print. [east TN]

General list A. 1895. *Dialect Notes* 1: 384–95.

The George McLean diary, February 27, 1831–April 15, 1848. 1966. Elkins, WV: Randolph County Historical Society. [east central WV]

Giardina, Denise. 1989. *Storming heaven: A novel*. New York: Ballantine.

———. 1992. *The unquiet earth*. New York: Norton.

———. 1998. No scapin the booger man. In *Bloodroot: Reflections on place by Appalachian women writers*, edited by Joyce Dyer, 128–31. Lexington: University Press of Kentucky.

Gibson, Dan. 2003. Southern mountain dialect. http://www.angelfire.com/tn2/ScottCoTnMemories/SouthernMountainDialect.html, accessed January 5, 2010. [Scott County, north central TN]

Gibson, Flora Carr. 1984. Remembering my Smoky Mountain home. Typescript consulted at Library, Great Smoky Mountains National Park, Gatlinburg, TN. [Sevier County, central east TN]

Gibson, Gertrude Andrews. 2002. Gertrude Andrews Gibson remembers. *Smoky Mountain Historical Society Journal and Newsletter* 28(1): 13–16. [Sevier County, central east TN]

Gibson, Henry H. 1913. *American forest trees*. Chicago: Hardwood Record. [east TN]

Gilbert, William Harlen. 1943. *The eastern Cherokees*. Washington, DC: GPO. [Swain County, southwestern NC]

Giles, Janice Holt. 1951. *Harbin's ridge*. Boston: Houghton Mifflin. [southeastern KY]

———. 1952. *40 acres and no mule*. Philadelphia: Westminster. [southeastern KY]

———. 1967. Prologue. In *40 acres and no mule* [addition to reprint of 1952 edition]. Philadelphia: Westminster. [southeastern KY]

Gillespie, Paul F., ed. 1982. *Foxfire 7*. Garden City, NY: Anchor.

Gilley, Joseph K. 1999. *Letters to home, the Civil War letters of Daniel Haywood Gilley*. Williamsburg, VA: Joseph K. Gilley. [Henry County, southwestern VA]

Gilliland Family. 1863. [Letters]. Gilliland Civil War Letters. MS.54-136, Mississippi Valley Collection, University of Memphis, TN.

Gilmore, James R. 1864. *Down in Tennessee, and back by way of Richmond*. New York: Carleton. [north central TN]

Ginns, Patsy Moore. 1977. *Rough weather makes good timber*. Chapel Hill: University of North Carolina Press. [northwestern NC]

———. 1982. *Snowbird gravy and dishpan pie: Mountain people recall*. Chapel Hill: University of North Carolina Press. [northwestern North Carolina]

Gipe, Robert. 2016. Gone to water. *Appalachian Heritage* 44(4): 39–48.

Glassie, Henry. 1963. The Appalachian log cabin. *Mountain Life and Work* 39(4): 5–14. [western VA]

———. 1964. Three southern mountain Jack tales. *Tennessee Folklore Society Bulletin* 30: 88–102. [southwestern VA]

———. 1965. Old barns of Appalachia. *Mountain Life and Work* 40(2): 21–30. [western VA]

———. 1968. *Pattern in the material folk culture in the eastern United States*. Philadelphia: University of Pennsylvania Press.

———. 1978. The types of the southern mountain cabin. In *The study of American folklore*, edited by Jan Brunvand, 391–420. New York: Norton. [western VA]

Glossary of mining terms. 2007. http://www.coaleducation.org/glossary.htm, accessed January 24, 2011.

Goan, Melanie Beals. 2008. *Mary Breckinridge: The Frontier Nursing Service and rural health in Appalachia*. Chapel Hill: University of North Carolina Press. [eastern KY]

Goddard, Charles H. 1917. *Thirty years of southern upbuilding*. New York: Colish.

Godfrey, W. B. 1909. *Autobiography of W. B. Godfrey*. Cincinnati: Revivalist Press.

God put the herbs here to heal the nation. 1979. *Foxfire Magazine* 13(1): 8–11.

Goerch, Carl. 1943. *Down home*. Raleigh: Edwards and Broughton. [NC]

Goff, James R., Jr. 2002. *Close harmony: A history of southern gospel*. Chapel Hill: University of North Carolina Press.

Goff, John Hedges. c1930. Ballads and dialects of the southern mountaineers. MA thesis, Oglethorpe University, Atlanta.

Good, Don. 2005. Racing in Appalachia. *Now & Then* 25(2): 3–4.

Goode, George Brown. 1887. *American fishes*. Boston: Estes and Lauriat.

Goode, James B. 2000. Taking stock of being Appalachian. In *One hundred years of Appalachian visions, 1897–1996*, edited by Bill Best, 81–84. Berea, KY: Appalachian Imprints. [Harlan County, southeastern KY]

Goodman, Linda, and Raymond Burgin. 1999. *Daughters of the Appalachians: Six unique women*. Johnson City, TN: Overmountain.

Goodrich, Frances Louisa. 1931. *Mountain homespun*. New Haven, CT: Yale University Press. [western NC]

Gordon, John. 1971. Slingings and high shots: Moonshining in the Georgia mountains. In *The not so solid South*, edited by Kenneth Morland, 56–64. Athens: University of Georgia Press. [north GA]

A gourd bean? 1978. *Foxfire Magazine* 12(3): 226–27.

Graham County centennial, 1872–1972. 1972. Robbinsville, NC: Graham County Centennial, Inc. [southwestern NC]

Graves, Jesse. 2014. *Basin ghosts*. Huntsville: Texas Review Press.

Gray, Asa. 1848. Chloris Boreali-Americana: Illustrations of New, Rare, or otherwise Interesting North American Plants, selected chiefly from those recently brought into Cultivation at the Botanic Garden of Harvard University, Cambridge. Decade I, *Memoirs of the American Academy of Arts and Sciences*, n.s., 3: 1–56. [western NC]

Gray, Sam. 1984. *Hazel Creek: Patterns of life on an Appalachian watershed*. Knoxville: TVA Division of Land and Forest Resources. [Swain County, southwestern NC]

Great Smoky Mountains National Park golden anniversary commemorative book, 1934–1984. 1985. Gatlinburg, TN: Oakley Enterprises. [central east TN, central western NC]

Great Smoky Mountains National Park interviews. 1954–84. [Recorded interviews and provisional transcripts consulted at Library, Great Smoky Mountains National Park, Gatlinburg, TN, with citations giving the page number of those transcripts for ease of consulting before they were revised and improved for this book]. [central east TN, central western NC]

Green, Archie. 1965. Hillbilly music: Source and symbol. *Journal of American Folklore* 78: 204–28.

Green, Bennett Wood. 1899. *Word book of Virginia folk-speech*. Richmond: W. E. Jones' Sons.

Green, Rayna, and Melanie Fernandez, eds. 1999. *The British Museum encyclopedia of native North America*. London: British Museum Press.

Greene, Wilhemina F., and Hugo L. Blomquist. 1953. *Flowers of the South*. Chapel Hill: University of North Carolina Press.

Greene letters. 1987. *Watauga Association of Genealogists Bulletin* 16: 151–52. [Roane County, central east TN]

Greer-Petrie, Cordia. 1921. *Angeline at the Seelbach*. Louisville, KY: Angeline. [eastern KY]

———. 1923. *Angeline doin' society*. Louisville, KY: Angeline. [eastern KY]

———. 1923. *Angeline steppin' out*. Louisville, KY: Angeline. [eastern KY]

———. 1924. *Angeline gits an eyeful*. Louisville, KY: Angeline. [eastern KY]

———. 1925. *Angeline of the hill country*. New York: Crowell. [eastern KY]

———. 1930. *Angeline outsmarts her man*. Louisville, KY: Angeline. [eastern KY]

Greve, Jeanette Sterling. 1964. *The story of Gatlinburg*. Gatlinburg, TN: Mangrum. [Sevier County, central east TN]

Greve, Jeannette. 1931. Traditions of Gatlinburg. *East Tennessee Historical Society Publication* 3: 62–77. [Sevier County, central east TN]

Griffin, Clarence W. 1861–64. Clarence W. Griffin Letters, Lorraine Griffin Letters. PC 153, State Archives of North Carolina, Raleigh. [Rutherford County, southwestern NC]

Grime, John H. 1902. History of middle Tennessee Baptists. Nashville, TN: Baptist and Reflector. [central TN]

Grimm, Mary. 2016. Going to Moonville. *Appalachian Heritage* 44(2): 8–34.

Grimm, William Carey. 1968. *How to recognize flowering wild plants*. New York: Castle Books.

The grist mill. 1975. *Foxfire Magazine* 9(1): 18–21. [Rabun County, northeast GA]

Grossman, Charles S. 1965. *Historic structures report part I and II: The Chandler Jenkins cabin bldg #147 and pig pen, Indian Camp Truck Trail*. Washington, DC: US National Park Service. [Cocke County, central east TN]

Guerrant, Edward O. 1910. *The galax gatherers: The gospel among the highlanders*. Richmond: Upward. [central western NC]

Guild, Joseph Conn. 1878. *Old times in Tennessee*. Nashville, TN: Tavel, Eastman & Howell.

Gump, Lucy. 1996. *Amis ledger B (1782–1794): Interpretive transcription of an east Tennessee business record book*. Johnson City, TN: Privately published. [northeast TN]

Guthrie, Charles S. 1966. Corn: The mainstay of the Cumberland Valley. *Kentucky Folklore Record* 13: 87–91.

———. 1968. Tobacco: Cash crop of the Cumberland Valley. *Kentucky Folklore Record* 14: 38–43.

Haggard Family. 1862. [Letters]. Tennessee in the Civil War (online), http://www.tn.gov/tsla/cwtn/index.htm, Tennessee State Library and Archives, Nashville. [Anderson County, central east TN]

Hague, Richard. 2011. The spring. *Now & Then* 27(1): 11–12.

Hall, Elijah. 1863–70. [Letters]. Civil War Letters of Elijah Hall, Bell Irvin Wiley Collection, Stuart A. Rose Manuscript, Archives, and Rare Book Library, Emory University, Atlanta. [Morgan County, central east TN]

Hall, J. W. 1915. *The Autobiography of old Claib Jones*. Whitesburg, KY: Eagle. [eastern KY]

Hall, Joseph S. 1937–87. [Recorded interviews and other material, on deposit in Joseph Sargent Hall Collection, Archives of Appalachia, East Tennessee State University, Johnson City; includes items recorded or noted in speech or from personal letters]

———. 1937, 1939. [Pocket-sized notebooks of random observations of mountain speech, on deposit at Archives of Appalachia, East Tennessee State University, Johnson City]

———. 1939. Recording speech in the Great Smokies. *Regional Review* 3(4–5): 3–8. [central east TN, central western NC]

———. 1941. Great Smokies ballads and songs. *American Poet* 1(9): 18–23. [central east TN, central western NC]

———. 1941. Some party-games of the Great Smoky Mountains. *Journal of American Folklore* 54: 68–71. [central east TN, central western NC]

———. 1942. *The phonetics of Great Smoky Mountain speech*. American Speech reprints and monograph no. 4. New York: King's Crown. [central east TN, central western NC]

———. 1957. Bear-hunting stories from the Great Smokies. *Tennessee Folklore Society Bulletin* 23: 67–75. [central east TN, central western NC]

———. 1960. *Smoky Mountain folks and their lore*. Asheville, NC: Cataloochee. [central east TN, central western NC]

———. 1970. Witchlore and ghostlore in the Great Smokies. *Tennessee Folklore Society Bulletin* 36(1): 1–6; 36(2): 31–36. [central east TN, central western NC]

———. 1972. *Sayings from old Smoky*. Asheville, NC: Cataloochee. [central east TN, central western NC]

———. 1978. *Yarns and tales from the Great Smokies: Some narratives from the southern Appalachians*. Asheville, NC: Cataloochee. [central east TN, central western NC]

Hamby, Zetta Barker. 1998. *Memoirs of Grassy Creek: Growing up in the mountains on the Virginia–North Carolina line*. Jefferson, NC: MacFarland. [southwestern VA, northwestern NC]

Hamel, Paul D., and Mary Ulmer Chiltoskey. 1975. *Cherokee plants and their use*. Sylva, NC: Herald. [Swain County, southwestern NC]

Hamilton, Alice McGuire. 1977. *Blue Ridge mountain memories: The true story of a mountain girl at the turn of the century*. Atlanta: Conger.

Hampton, Ezekiel H. 1861–64. [Letters]. Bailey Family Letters. Civil War Document Collection, US Army Military History Institute, Carlisle, PA.

Hancock, William. 1862–64. [Letters]. William Hancock Letters. Federal Collection, box 22, folder 17, Tennessee State Library and Archives, Nashville. [Sevier County, central east TN]

Handlon, Anne Emily. c1970. *Ol' Smoky* [consulted at Library, Great Smoky Mountains National Park, Gatlinburg, TN]. N.p.: n.p. [Sevier County, central east TN]

Hanes, Harrison H. 1861–64. Harrison H. Hanes Papers. David M. Rubenstein Rare Book and Manuscript Library, Duke University, Durham, NC. [Davie County, northwestern NC]

Haney, William H. 1906. *The mountain people of Kentucky*. Cincinnati: Robert Clarke. [eastern KY]

Hannah, Mark E. 1989. *Smoky Mountain reflections*. N.p.: Sev-Hannah. [Haywood County, central western NC]

Hannum, Alberta. 1931. *Thursday April*. New York: Harper and Brothers. [northwestern NC]

Hannum, Alberta Pierson. 1943. The mountain people. In *The Great Smokies and the Blue Ridge*, edited by Roderick Peattie, 73–151. New York: Vanguard. [western NC, south central VA]

———. 1969. *Look back with love*, 29–33. New York: Vanguard. [northwestern NC, south central VA]

Happy Dowdle: An interview with Happy Dowdle and his wife. 1971. *Foxfire Magazine* 5(1–2): 10–27. [Macon County, southwestern NC]

Harben, William Nathaniel. 1900. *Northern Georgia sketches*. Chicago: McClung.

———. 1901. *Westerfelt*. New York: Harper & Brothers.

———. 1902. *Abner Daniel*. New York: Harper & Row.

———. 1904. *The Georgians*. New York: Harper.

———. 1906. *Ann Boyd, a novel*. New York: Harper & Brothers.

———. 1914. *The new Clarion*. New York: Harpers.

Hardy, Michael C. 2007. *Remembering Avery County*. Charleston, SC: History Press. [Avery County, northwestern NC]

Harmon, Bertha Cox. 1984. *Falling leaves of Appalachia: Memories of yesterday*. N.p.: Snapp.

Harney, Will Wallace. 1873. A strange land and a peculiar people. *Lippincott's* 12: 429–38. [southwestern VA]

Harper, Francis. 1941. The way we said it. *North Georgia Review* 6: 129–30. [north GA]

Harrell, A. D. 1996. *Fetch it, Rusty!* Burnsville, NC: Celo Valley. [northwestern NC]

Harrill, A. C. 1864. [Letters]. Letters of A. S. Harrill. WPA Civil War Transcriptions. Tennessee State Library and Archives, Nashville. [Rutherford County, southwestern NC]

Harris, George Washington. 1867. *Sut Lovingood: Yarns spun by a nat'ral bornd durn'd fool*. Facsimile ed., edited by M. Thomas Inge. Memphis, TN: St. Lukes, 1987. [east TN]

———. 1974. *High times and hard times*. Edited by M. Thomas Inge. Nashville, TN: Vanderbilt University Press. [east TN]

Harris, Robert T. 1926. *West Virginia legislative hand book and manual and official register*. Charleston, WV: Tribune. [WV]

Harrison, Deane Bell. 1995. *Smoke rings*. Rogersville: East Tennessee Printing. [Jefferson County, central east TN]

Hartsell, Jacob. 1939–40. The J. Hartsell Memora: The journal of a Tennessee captain in the War of 1812. Edited by Mary Harden McCown. *East Tennessee Historical Society Publication* 11: 93–115; 12: 118–46. [northeast TN]

Hartt, Rollin Lynde. 1918. The mountaineers: Our own lost tribes. *Century* 95: 395–404.

Haun, Mildred. 1937. Cocke County ballads and songs. MEd thesis, George Peabody College, Nashville, TN. [Cocke County, central east TN]

———. (1940) 1968. *The hawk's done gone and other stories*. Edited by Hershel Gower. [Previously published stories, pp. 1–197]. Nashville, TN: Vanderbilt University Press. [Cocke County, central east TN]

———. 1968. *The hawk's done gone and other stories*. Edited by Hershel Gower. [Previously unpublished stories, pp. 201–354]. Nashville, TN: Vanderbilt University Press. [Cocke County, central east TN]

———. 1993. When the wind blows. In *Mossy Creek Reader*, edited by Jeff Daniel Marion, 3–18. Jefferson City, TN: Carson-Newman College. [Cocke County, central east TN]

Hawn, Elisha A. 1862–63. Elisha A. Hawn Letters, Special Collections, University of Tennessee Library, Knoxville. [Morgan County, central east TN]

Hawthorne, Julian. 1900. Mountain votes spoil Huntington's revenge. *New York Journal*, April 23.

Hayes, Carl N. 1966. *Neighbor against neighbor, brother against brother: Greene County in the Civil War*. N.p.: Privately published. [Greene County, northeast TN]

Hayes, Francis C. 1944. A word-list from North Carolina. *Publication of the American Dialect Society* 2: 32–37. [northwestern NC]

Hayler, Nicole, ed. 2002. *Sound wormy: Memoir of Andrew Gennett, lumberman*. Athens: University of Georgia Press. [north GA]

Haynes, Alice Hawkins. 1991. *Haywood home: Memories of a mountain woman*. Tallahassee: Rose. [Haywood County, central western NC]

Head, Maynard. 1978. Mountain moments. *Newport (TN) Plain Talk*, July 1, September 7.

———. 1984. *Brogans, clothespins, and a twist of tobacco*. West Allis, WI: Pinetree. [eastern KY, east TN]

Headrick, Lena. 1991. Headrick's Chapel, Sevier County Tennessee, and old harp singing. *Tennessee Ancestors* 7: 205–7. [Sevier County, central east TN]

Hedgecock, W. E. 1861–63. W. E. Hedgecock Civil War diary record: Diary which I kept while in the Army against the rebellion, 1861–1863. *Tennessee Ancestors* 16: 99–114. [Knox County, central east TN]

Heinmiller, Jennifer K. N. 2010–19. [Selected items from Heinmiller's fieldwork]

Heller, J. Roderick III, and Carolyn Ayres Heller. 1992. *The Confederacy is on her way up the spout: Letters to South Carolina, 1861–1864*. Athens: University of Georgia Press. [northwestern SC]

Helsly, Mrs. Wilford W. 1983. *The country doctor and his people, 1910–1923*. Knoxville: Privately published.

Helton, William W. 1986. In a manner of speaking. *Around home in Unicoi County*, 373–81. Johnson City, TN: Overmountain. [Unicoi County, northeast TN]

Hench, Atcheson. 1936. Gleanings. *American Speech* 11: 104. [southern WV]

Henderson, Mary O. c1950. Ebenezer Mission in Cocke County, Tennessee "as I knew it." Typescript loaned to the editor by Cherel Henderson. [Cocke County, central east TN]

Henry, Bill. 1981. Alex Stewart: A personal reminiscence. *Tennessee Folklore Society Bulletin* 47: 48–66. [Hancock County, northeast TN]

Herald-Advertiser. 1930. Huntingdon, WV, November 30. [WV]

Hewes, Laurence. 1957. *Boxcar in the sand*. New York: Knopf.

Hewing crossties. 1987. *Foxfire Magazine* 21(3–4): 210.

Hicks, Enoch E. 2006. *Mountain legacy*. Dayton, OH: Wingspan and DreamPower.

Hicks, Jane. 2005. *Blood and bone remember*. Ashland, KY: Jesse Stuart Foundation.

———. 2013. A matter of perception. In *Talking Appalachian: Voice, identity, and community*, edited by Amy D. Clark and Susan M. Hayward, 209–14. Lexington: University Press of Kentucky.

———. 2014. *Driving with the dead: Poems*. Lexington: University Press of Kentucky.

Hide tanning. 1972. *Foxfire Magazine* 6(3): 178–92.

Higgs, Robert J. 2000. Two hills and two pappies. In *One hundred years of Appalachian visions, 1897–1996*, edited by Bill Best, 53–56. Berea, KY: Appalachian Imprints. [south central TN]

Higgs, Robert J., and Ambrose N. Manning, eds. 1975. *Voices from the hills: Selected readings of Southern Appalachia*. New York: Ungar.

Higgs, Robert J., Ambrose N. Manning, and Jim Wayne Miller, eds. 1995. *Appalachia inside out*. Knoxville: University of Tennessee Press.

High, Ellesa Clay. 1984. *Past Titan Rock: Journeys into an Appalachian valley*. Lexington: University Press of Kentucky. [east central KY]

High Collection. 1981. [Material donated to the *Dictionary of American Regional English* project by Ellesa Clay High]. [east central KY, as of c1950]

Hileman Family. 1861. [Letters]. Lewis Leigh Collection, US Army Military History Institute, Carlisle, PA. [Rockbridge County, central west VA]

Hill, Jesse. 1863–65. [Letters]. Jesse Hill Letters, 1864–1865. PC 1888, State Archives of North Carolina, Raleigh. [Forsyth County, northwestern NC]

Hillard Green. 1970. *Foxfire Magazine* 4(3): 134–44. [Macon County, southwestern NC]

Hines, Linda C. 1932. Wildflowers of the Appalachians. *Country Life* 62(5): 65–67.

Hiser, Berniece. 1978. *Quare do's in Appalachia: East Kentucky legends and memorats*. Pikeville, KY: Pikeville College Press. [eastern KY]

History of Beth-Car United Methodist Church and cemetery. 1984. N.p.: Privately published. [Jefferson County, central east TN]

Hitt, David M. 1862. [Letter]. David M. Hitt Letters. Confederate Miscellany, MSS 20, box 3, Stuart A. Rose Manuscript and Rare Book Library, Emory University, Atlanta. [Cherokee County, north central GA]

Hodges, Mary Bozeman. 1999. *Tough customers*. Ashland, KY: Jesse Stuart Foundation. [east TN]

Hodges, Sidney Cecil. 1951. Handicrafts in Sevier County, Tennessee. MS thesis, University of Tennessee, Knoxville. [Sevier County, central east TN]

Hogg, Hiram. 1863. [Letters]. Hiram Hogg Letters, 1863. SC 986, Kentucky Historical Society, Frankfort. [Letcher County, southeastern KY]

Hogs against serpents. 1889. *Lexington (NC) Ledger*, October 31. [Swain County, southwestern NC]

Holbrook, Chris. 1994. First of the month. *Now & Then* 11(2): 18–21.

———. 2009. *Upheaval: Stories*. Lexington: University Press of Kentucky.

———. 2015. Something to tell. In *Appalachia now: Short stories of contemporary Appalachia*, edited by Larry Smith and Charles Dodd White, 143–59. Huron, OH: Bottom Dog Press.

Holidays. 1973. *Foxfire Magazine* 7(4): 326–38.

Holloway, Maynard "PePaw" obituary. 2017. *Johnson City (TN) Press*, July 27.

Holton, Celia Cathcart. 1921. Funeralizing on Robber's Creek. *Outlook* 127 (April): 588–89.

Homan, Tim. 2007. Where the creek turkey tracks: Wild land and language. *Appalachian Heritage* 35: 83–88. [northeast GA]

Home remedies. 1968. *Foxfire Magazine* 2(1): 10–14.

Hooker, Elizabeth R. 1933. *Religion in the highlands: Native churches and missionary enterprises in the southern Appalachian area*. New York: Home Mission Council.

Hooper, Ben W. 1963. *The unwanted boy: The autobiography of Governor Ben W. Hooper*. Edited by Everett Robert Boyce. Knoxville: University of Tennessee Press.

The Hopper family. 1975. *Foxfire Magazine* 9(1): 13–17. [Rabun County, northeast GA]

Horn, Dorothy D. 1978. Introduction. In *The new harp of Columbia: A system of musical notation*, by M. L. Swan, vii–xvii. Knoxville: University of Tennessee Press.

Hornsby, Henry. 1949. *Lonesome valley*. New York: Sloane. [KY]

Horrell, C. William, and Herbert K. Russell. 1995. *Southern Illinois coal: A portfolio*. Carbondale: Southern Illinois University Press.

Horsetrading. 1978. *Foxfire Magazine* 12(1): 40–71.

Horton, James H. 1979. Our natural heritage. In *Our cultural heritage: Essays on the natural & cultural history of western North Carolina*, 9–33. Lakemont, GA: CSA. [western NC]

Houk, Rose. 1988. *Exploring the Smokies*. Gatlinburg, TN: Great Smoky Mountains Natural History Association. [central east TN, central western NC]

———. 1996. *Foods & recipes of the Smokies*. Gatlinburg, TN: Great Smoky Mountains Natural History Association. [central east TN, central western NC]

———. 2005. *The Walker sisters of Little Greenbrier*. Gatlinburg, TN: Great Smoky Mountains Association. [Sevier County, central east TN]

———. 2011. *Quilts and coverlets of the Smokies*. Gatlinburg, TN: Great Smoky Mountains Association. [central east TN, central western NC]

———. 2012. Weaving a livelihood in the Smokies. *Smokies Life* 6(1): 38–45. [central east TN, central western NC]

———. 2016. Vampires and zombies of the flora kind. *Smokies Life* 10(2): 58–63. [central east TN]

House, Silas. 1999. Elements most often found in Appalachian literature. *Now & Then* 16(2): 2.

———. 2001. *Clay's quilt*. New York: Ballantine.

———. 2004. *The coal tattoo*. Chapel Hill, NC: Algonquin.

———. 2010. At the opening of *Coal Miner's Daughter*, Corbin, Kentucky, March 27, 1980. In *The southern poetry anthology*, vol. 3: *Contemporary Appalachia*, edited by Jesse Graves et al., 99. Huntsville: Texas Review Press.

———. 2012–13. Membership spotlight. *Appalachian Voices* (December–January): 26.

———. 2013. In my own country. In *Talking Appalachian: Voice, identity, and community*, edited by Amy D. Clark and Nancy M. Hayward, 193–204. Lexington: University Press of Kentucky.

———. 2014. The matter is you don't know what you're talking about. http://silashouseblog.blogspot.com/2014/07/the-matter-is-you-dont-know-what-youre.html.

House, Silas, and Jason Howard. 2009. *Something's rising: Appalachians fighting mountaintop removal*. Lexington: University Press of Kentucky.

Houston, R. L. 1864. [Letter]. Robert L. Houston Letter. WPA Civil War Transcriptions, Tennessee State Library and Archives, Nashville. [Blount County, central east TN]

Howard, Martha C. 1977. Fifty years later and less: Loss of dialect in central West Virginia. Paper presented at American Dialect Society meeting. [WV]

Howell, Benita J. 2003. *Folklife along the Big South Fork of the Cumberland River*. Knoxville: University of Tennessee Press. [north central TN, southeastern KY]

Howell, Patricia Kyritsi. 2006. *Medicinal plants of the southern Appalachians*. Mountain City, GA: Botanologos.

How the best of the best was made. 1968. *Foxfire Magazine* 2(3–4): 102–6.

Howze, Tom P. 1993. And not a single arm rotted off: Memories of a one-room schoolhouse. *Now & Then* 10(1): 31–32.

Hoyle, Joy Phillips. 1999. *Handed down then passed around*. Whittier, NC: Ammons. [western NC]

Hoyle, Vernon J. 2001. *A place to call home: Memoirs of J. Vernon Hoyle a mountain man*. Sylva, NC: Jackson County Historical Association. [Jackson County, southwestern NC]

Hubbard, Leonidas, Jr. 1902. The moonshiner at home. *Atlantic Monthly* 90: 234–41. [north GA]

Huffman, Alza. 1952. *My mountain memories: The outstanding incidents and ideas of my eighty-five years*. Philadelphia: Dorrance and Company. [WV]

Hufford, Mary. 1997. American ginseng and the idea of the commons. *Folklife Center News* 19(1–2): 3–18. https://www.loc.gov/collections/folklife-and-landscape-in-southern-west-virginia/articles-and-essays/american-ginseng-and-the-idea-of-the-commons/ginseng-and-the-future-of-the-commons/. [southern WV]

———. 1997. Stalking the mother forest: Voices beneath the canopy. https://www.loc.gov/collections/folklife-and-landscape-in-southern-west-virginia/articles-and-essays/stalking-the-mother-forest-voices-beneath-the-canopy/. [southern WV]

———. c2006. Landscapes and history at the headwaters of the Big Coal River Valley: An overview [excerpt]. Library of Congress. https://www.loc.gov/collections/folklife-and-landscape-in-southern-west-virginia/articles-and-essays/landscape-and-history-at-the-headwaters-of-the-big-coal-river/. [southern WV]

———. 2006. Ramp suppers, biodiversity, and the integrity of the mountains. In *Cornbread nation III: The best writing about foods of the mountain South*, edited by Ronni Lundy, 108–17. Chapel Hill: University of North Carolina Press. [southern WV]

Hughes, Walter. 1996. Swain County. *Bone Rattler* 12(1): 12–21. [Swain County, southwestern NC]

Huheey, James E. 1996. Variant names for Smoky Mountain reptiles and amphibians. Typescript provided to the editor. [central east TN, central western NC]

Huheey, James E., and Arthur Stupka. 1967. *Amphibians and reptiles of Great Smoky Mountains National Park*. Knoxville: University of Tennessee Press. [central east TN, central western NC]

Hundley Family. 1862–65. Hundley Family Papers. Collection 4971, Southern Historical Collection, Wilson Library, University of North Carolina, Chapel Hill. [Stokes County, northwestern NC]

Hunnicutt, Samuel J. 1926. *Twenty years hunting and fishing in the Great Smoky Mountains*. Knoxville: Newman. [western NC]

Hunter, Earl D. 1962. Folk remedies on man and beasts. *Kentucky Folklore Record* 8: 97–108. [KY]

Hunter, Elizabeth. 2008. The great bandana porch sit. *Now & Then* 24(2): 10.

Hunting: Training dogs and hunting techniques. 1970. *Foxfire Magazine* 4(1–2): 8–17, 70–76.

Hunting stories. 1970. *Foxfire Magazine* 4(1–2): 28–35, 77–86.

Huntley, George Job. 1861–63. [Letters]. George Job Huntley Papers, 1861–1863. Hunter Library Special Collections, Western Carolina University, Cullowhee, NC. [Rutherford County, southwestern NC]

Hurst, Sharon, and Laura Lewis. 1977. Roaring Fork School—fifty years ago: As told by Herb Clabo. *Smoky Mountain Historical Society Newsletter* 3(6): 22–24. [Sevier County, central east TN]

———. 2011. Roaring Fork School—fifty years ago [reprint of Hurst and Lewis 1977]. *Smoky Mountain Historical Society Journal and Newsletter* 37(2): 14–16. [Sevier County, central east TN]

Hurst, Sharon Elaine. 1982. Appalachian words. *Our Smokies heritage*, 98–99. Gatlinburg, TN: Crescent. [mainly Sevier County, central east TN]

Huskey, Allan. 1990. *The Joseph Rogers papers, compiled and transcribed by Allan Huskey*. Copy on deposit at Calvin M. McClung Historical Collection, Knox County Public Library, Knoxville. [Hawkins County, northeast TN]

Huskey, Charles Aaron. 1986. Life in the Sugarlands. In *Sugarlands: A lost community of Sevier county*, edited by Jerry L. Wear, 2–9. Sevierville, TN: Sevierville Heritage Committee. [Sevier County, central east TN]

Huskey, Conley. 1994. *Memories of a county squire*. Sevierville, TN: Nandel. [Sevier County, central east TN]

Hutchins, Ross E. 1971. *Hidden valley of the Smokies with a naturalist in the Great Smoky Mountains*. New York: Dodd, Mead. [east TN]

Hyatt, Rebecca Dougherty. 1937. *Marthy Lou's kiverlid: A sketch of mountain life*. Morristown, TN: Triangle.

Hyde, Herbert. 1998. *My home is in the Smoky Mountains*. Alexander, NC: WorldComm. [western NC]

Hynds, Samuel H. 1862. Samuel H. Hynds Letter. *The Civil War in Tennessee*, Tennessee State Library and Archives, Nashville, http://sos.tn.gov/tsla/looking-back-civil-war-tennessee, accessed January 20, 2020. [Jefferson County, central east TN]

Imitator salamanders that don't imitate. 2015. *BearPaw* (Spring/Summer): 4.

Imlay, Gilbert. 1797. *A topographical description of the western territory of North America*. 3rd ed. London: J. Debrett. [KY]

Incidents. 1897. *Berea Quarterly* 2(4): 27. [eastern KY]

Incidents. 1898. *Berea Quarterly* 3(1): 31. [eastern KY]

Index and examples of petitions to the Tennessee legislature. 2003. *Tennessee Ancestors* 19: 113–35. [east TN]

Index and examples of petitions to the Tennessee legislature. 2004. *Tennessee Ancestors* 20: 23–54. [east TN]

Index and examples of petitions to the Tennessee legislature: Jefferson County. 2005. *Tennessee Ancestors* 21: 172–216. [Jefferson County, central east TN]

Ingram, John. 1862–63. [Letters]. John Ingram Papers, 1852–1863. David M. Rubenstein Rare Book and Manuscript Library, Duke University, Durham, NC. [Forsyth County, northwestern NC]

Inscoe, John C. 2000. *Appalachians and race: The mountain South from slavery to segregation*. Lexington: University Press of Kentucky.

Irwin, James Rice. 1979. *Musical instruments of the southern Appalachian Mountains*. Norris, TN: Museum of Appalachia.

Irwin, John Rice. 1973. *A brief history of the Arnwine Cabin and the pioneer artifacts it contains: One of thirteen such structures located in the Museum of Appalachia*. Norris, TN: Museum of Appalachia. [east TN]

———. 1981. *The Arnwine cabin: A history of this pioneer dwelling and its contents located at the Museum of Appalachia, Norris, Tennessee*. Norris, TN: Museum of Appalachia. [east TN]

———. 1982. *Baskets and basket makers in southern Appalachia*. Exton, PA: Schiffer. [east TN]

———. 1983. *Guns and gun-making tools of southern Appalachia: The story of the Kentucky rifle*. 2nd ed. Exton, PA: Schiffer.

———. 1985. *Alex Stewart, portrait of a pioneer*. West Chester, PA: Schiffer. [Hancock County, northeast TN]

———. 1987. *The museum of Appalachia story*. West Chester, PA: Schiffer. [east TN]

Isbell, Robert. 1996. *The last chivaree: The Hicks family of Beech Mountain*. Chapel Hill: University of North Carolina Press. [Avery County, northwestern NC]

———. 1999. *The keepers: Mountain folk holding on to old skills and talents*. Winston-Salem, NC: Blair. [western NC]

Ison, Isaac, and Anna H. Ison. 1993. *A whole 'nother language: Our personal collection of Appalachian expressions*. N.p.: Privately published. [eastern KY]

Isserman, Andrew. 1996. Do people in Appalachia know they're Appalachians? *Now & Then* 13(2): 14.

I swapped that dog even for that ole T-Model. 1979. *Foxfire Magazine* 13(1): 42–43.

"It was a hard life": Growing up on the Pendleton County poor farm. 2009. *Goldenseal* 35(2): 38–43. [eastern WV]

"I've been raising sheep for forty years." 1972. *Foxfire Magazine* 6(2–3): 88–101.

Ivey, Majel. 1928. Mountain whites. *Charlotte Observer*, March 25. [western NC]

Ivey, Mike. 1986. A rose by another name is a damned brier. *Appalachian Heritage* 14(3): 54–55.

Jabbour, Alan. 2009. Decoration Day. In *New encyclopedia of southern culture*, vol. 14: Folklife, edited by Glenn Hinson and William Ferris, 278–81. Chapel Hill: University of North Carolina Press. [Swain County, southwestern NC]

———. 2010. Helen Cable Vance and the North Shore Historical Association. *North Carolina Folklore Journal* 57(2): 22–28. [Swain County, southwestern NC]

Jabbour, Alan, and Karen Singer Jabbour. 2010. *Decoration Day in the mountains: Traditions of cemetery decoration in the southern Appalachians*. Chapel Hill: University of North Carolina Press. [Swain County, southwestern NC]

Jackson, Dot. 1988. A lesson in commodities. *Now & Then* 5(3): 31–32.

Jackson, George Pullen. 1933. *White spirituals of the southern uplands: The story of the fasola folk, their songs, singings, and buckwheat notes*. Chapel Hill: University of North Carolina Press. [upper South]

Jackson, Hester Bartlett, ed. 1992. *Surry County soldiers in the Civil War*. Charlotte: Delmar. [Surry County, northwestern NC]

Jackson, Sarah E. 1975. Unusual words, expressions, and pronunciations in a North Carolina mountain community. *Appalachian Journal* 2: 148–60. [western NC]

Jacobs, Scott Allan. 1993. Board of Education: An interview with Elbert Childress. *Now & Then* 10(1): 28–30. [WV]

Jake Waldroop. 1977. *Foxfire Magazine* 11(2): 142–76. [Macon County, southwestern NC]

Jamison, Phil. 2015. *Hoedowns, reels, and frolics: Roots and branches of southern Appalachian dance*. Urbana: University of Illinois Press. [western NC]

Jamison, Philip. 1993–94. "A jubilant spirit within me": Buckdance, flatfoot, or clogging? *Old-Time Herald*, Winter, 14–17, 51. [western NC]

Jefferson County, Tennessee, will book 1, 1792–1810, part 1. 2001. *East Tennessee Roots* 9(1): 35–49. [Jefferson County, central east TN]

Jefferson County, Tennessee, will book 1, 1792–1810, part 2. 2001. *East Tennessee Roots* 9(3): 231–41. [Jefferson County, central east TN]

Jennison, Harry Milliken. 1939. Flora of the Great Smokies. *Journal of the Tennessee Academy of Science* 14: 266–98. [central east TN, central western NC]

Jesse Cole: The murder's other victim. 1993. *Tennessee Folklore Society Bulletin* 64: 70–80. [Cocke County, central east TN]

Job, Joshua. c1890. *Diary*. Excerpted in Inez Burns 1978. [Blount County, central east TN]

Johannsen, Kristin. 2006. *Ginseng dreams: The secret life of America's most valuable plant*. Lexington: University Press of Kentucky.

John Hoss Bowman's manuscript of travels to the North. 2004. *Watauga Association of Genealogists Bulletin* 33: 54–61.

Johnson, Clifton. 1904. *Highways and byways of the South*. New York: Macmillan.

Johnson, Ellen. 1996. *Lexical change and variation in the southeastern United States, 1930–1990*. Tuscaloosa: University of Alabama Press. [north GA, northwestern SC]

Johnson, Kenneth R. 1971. The early Civil War in south Kentucky as experienced by a Confederate sympathizer. *Register of the Kentucky Historical Society* 69: 177–80. [southern KY]

Johnson, Mattie Ruth. 1997. *My Melungeon heritage: A story of life on Newman's Ridge*. Johnson City, TN: Overmountain. [northeast TN]

Johnson, Samuel. 1908. Life in the Kentucky mountains. *Independent* 65 (July 9), 72–82. Repr. in *Appalachian images in folk and popular culture*, edited by W. K. McNeil, 175–85. Knoxville: University of Tennessee Press, 1989. [eastern KY]

Johnston v. Shelton, 39 NC 85. 1845. https://casetext.com/case/johnston-v-shelton.

Joines, Jerry. 1973. Twister tall tales from Wilkes County. *North Carolina Folklore Journal* 20: 3–11. [Wilkes County, northwestern NC]

Jones, G. C. 1985. Growing up hard in Harlan County. Lexington: University Press of Kentucky. [southeastern KY]

Jones, George W. 1863. George W. Jones Letter. *The Civil War in Tennessee*, Tennessee State Library and Archives, Nashville, http://sos.tn.gov/tsla/looking-back-civil-war-tennessee. [Sullivan County, northeast TN]

Jones, James Gay. 1980. *A wayfaring sin-eater and other Appalachian tales*. Parsons, WV: McClain.

Jones, Jean. 1973. The regional English of the former inhabitants of Cades Cove in the Great Smoky Mountains. PhD diss., University of Tennessee, Knoxville. [Blount County, central east TN]

Jones, Lewis J. 1862–64. Lewis J. Jones Papers. Small Manuscripts Collection, section A, box 75, items 1–7, David M. Rubenstein Rare Book and Manuscript Library, Duke University, Durham, NC.

Jones, Louise Coffin. 1879. In the backwoods of Carolina. *Lippincott's* 24: 747–56. [western NC]

———. 1883. In the highlands of North Carolina. *Lippincott's* 32: 378–86. [western NC]

Jones, Loyal. 1974. Preface. In *A right good people*, by Harold F. Warren. Boone, NC: Appalachian Consortium Press.

———. 1985. Grandpa's travail. *Appalachian Heritage* 13(3): 21–23.

———. 1988. Modesty. *Appalachian Heritage* 16(2–3): 82–86.

———. 1994. *Appalachian values*. Ashland, KY: Jesse Stuart Foundation.

———. 2002. Leicester Luminist lighted local language and lore. *Appalachian Heritage* 30(1): 18–25. [western NC]

———. 2002. *Minstrel of the Appalachians: The story of Bascom Lamar Lunsford*. Lexington: University Press of Kentucky. [western NC]

———. 2015. In memoriam: Jean Ritchie. *Appalachian Heritage* 43(3): 8–9.

———. 2015. Tintagel. *Appalachian Heritage* 43(3): 54.

Jones, Loyal, and Jim Wayne Miller. 1992. Glossary of mountain speech. *Southern mountain speech*, 63–120. Berea, KY: Berea College Press.

Jones, Loyal, and Billy Edd Wheeler. 2005. *Laughter in Appalachia: A festival of southern humor*. Little Rock, AR: August House.

Jones, Ora L. 1967. *Peculiarities of the mountaineer: A summary of legends, traditions, signs and superstitions that are almost forgotten*. Detroit: Harlo. [western NC]

Jones, Patricia S. c1997. Why they talk that way: Language factors in migrant Appalachians adaptations. Paper presented at the Appalachian Studies Association conference, Cincinnati, and copy provided to the editor. [Morgan County, eastern KY]

Jones, Robbie D. 1995. The early architecture of Sevier County, Tennessee. *Smoky Mountain Historical Society Journal and Newsletter* 21: 4–23. [Sevier County, central east TN]

Jones, Russell. 1970. *Leige Oliver barn and corn crib: Historic structures report architectural data*. Washington, DC: US National Park Service.

Jordan-Byshkov, Terry G. 2003. *The upland South: The making of an American folk region*. Sante Fe, NM: Center for American Places.

Josheff, Nicole. 2003. *Craft traditions: The Southern Highland Craft Guild collection*. [Asheville, NC]: Folk Arts Center.

Joslin, Michael. 1998. *Our living heritage*. Johnson City, TN: Overmountain. [northwestern NC]

———. 2001. *Appalachian bounty: Nature's gifts from the mountains: A collection of essays and photographs*. Johnson City, TN: Overmountain. [northwestern NC]

———. 2005. *Highland handcrafters: Appalachian craftspeople*. Boone, NC: Parkway. [northwestern NC]

———. 2007. Sang season: Diggin' spirit-frisking ginseng. *Now & Then* 23(1): 57–60.

Joslin, Michael, and Ruth Joslin. 1991. *Mountain people, places and ways: A southern Appalachian sampler*. Johnson City, TN: Overmountain. [northwestern NC]

———. 1992. *Mountain people, places and ways: Another southern Appalachian sampler*. Johnson City, TN: Overmountain. [northwestern NC]

Jourdan, Carolyn. 2012. *Medicine men: Extreme Appalachian doctoring*. N.p.: Jourdain-Michael. [east TN]

Journal and account book of George Crosby, Feb. 1842–Oct. 1846. 1995. *East Tennessee Roots* 7(3): 101–10. [Jefferson County, central east TN]

Joyce, Jaime. 2014. *Moonshine: A cultural history of America's infamous liquor*. Minneapolis: Zenith.

Joyce, John W. 1862–65. [Letters]. John W. Joyce Papers. Harrisburg Civil War Round Table, box 4, US Army Military History Institute, Carlisle, PA. [Stokes County, northwestern NC]

Joyner, Charles W. 2008. Dulcimer. In *New encyclopedia of southern culture*, vol. 12: *Music*, edited by Bill C. Malone, 223–24. Chapel Hill: University of North Carolina Press.

Joyner, Nancy. 2000. The magic mountains. In *One hundred years of Appalachian visions, 1897–1996*, edited by Bill Best, 145–48. Berea, KY: Appalachian Imprints. [northwestern SC]

"Just give me the money; I'll drive the cattle." 1979. *Foxfire Magazine* 13(1): 73–75.

Justus, May. 1927. *Peter Pocket: A little boy of the Cumberland Mountains*. Garden City, NY: Doubleday. [east TN]

———. 1928. *Betty Lou of Big Log Mountain*. Garden City, NY: Sun. [east TN]

———. 1930. *At the foot of Windy Low*. New York: P. F. Volland. [east TN]

———. 1930. *Peter Pocket's luck*. Garden City, NY: Doubleday, Doran and Company. [east TN]

———. 1936. *Honey Jane*. Garden City, NY: Doubleday. [east TN]

———. 1938. *The house in No-End Hollow*. Garden City, NY: Doubleday. [east TN]

———. 1941. *Cabin on Kettle Creek*. New York: Lippincott. [east TN]

———. 1942. *Step Along and Jerry Jake*. Chicago: Whitman. [east TN]

———. 1943. *Bluebird, fly up!* New York: Lippincott. [east TN]

———. 1943. *Jerry Jake carries on*. Chicago: Whitman and Company. [east TN]

———. 1944. *Banjo Billy and Mr. Bones*. Chicago: Albert Whitman and Company. [east TN]

———. 1944. Lizzie. Chicago: Albert Whitman and Company.

———. 1949. *Toby has a dog*. Chicago: Whitman and Company. [east TN]

———. 1950. *Luck for little Lihu*. New York: Aladdin. [east TN]

———. 1951. *Lucky penny*. New York: Aladdin. [east TN]

———. 1952. *Children of the Great Smoky Mountains*. New York: Dutton and Company. [east TN]

———. 1955. *Surprise for Peter Pocket*. New York: Henry Holt. [east TN]

———. 1957. *The other side of the mountain*. New York: Hastings House. [east TN]

———. 1959. *Barney, bring your banjo*. New York: Henry Holt and Company. [east TN]

———. 1960. *The right house for Rowdy*. New York: Holt, Rinehart and Winston. [east TN]

———. 1962. *Smoky Mountain sampler*. New York: Abingdon. [east TN]

———. 1967. Growing up in the Great Smokies. *Appalachian South* 2 (Fall/Winter): 16. [east TN]

———. 1968. *It happened in No-End Hollow*. Champaign, IL: Garrard. [east TN]

———. 1969. *Eben and the rattlesnake*. Champaign, IL: Garrard. [east TN]

———. 1970. *Holidays in No-End Hollow*. Champaign, IL: Garrard. [east TN]

———. 1970. *Tales from near-side and far*. Champaign, IL: Garrard. [east TN]

———. 1971. *Jumping Johnny outwits Skedaddle*. Champaign, IL: Garrard. [east TN]

Kahn, Kathy. 1973. *Hillbilly women*. New York: Doubleday.

Karnes, J. A., and E. A. Karnes. 1863. [Letters]. Civil War Collection: Confederate and Federal 1861–1865, Confederate Collection, box C8, folder 5, Tennessee State Library and Archives, Nashville. [Mercer County, southern WV]

Kendall, Arthur I. 1941. *Rifle making in the Great Smoky Mountains*. National Park Service Popular Study Series, History no. 13. Washington, DC: US Department of the Interior. [central east TN, central western NC]

Kendrick, Larkin S. 1861–68. [Letters]. Larkin S. Kendrick Papers. PC 1921, State Archives of North Carolina, Raleigh. [Cleveland County, southwestern NC]

Kennedy, Philip Pendleton. 1853. The Blackwater chronicle: A narrative of an expedition into the land of Canaan, in Randolph County. New York: Redfield. [east central WV]

Kenny, Hamill. 1935. "To" in West Virginia. *American Speech* 10: 135–36. [WV]

Kenny Runnion. 1971. *Foxfire Magazine* 5(3): 128–41.

Kephart, Horace. 1904–20. Horace Kephart's Journals. Horace Kephart Collection, Hunter Library Special Collections, Western Carolina University, Cullowhee, NC. [unpaginated, undated observations and clippings, southwestern NC]

———. 1913. *Our southern highlanders*. New York: Macmillan. [southwestern NC]

———. 1917. *Camping & woodcraft: A handbook for vacation campers and for travelers in the wilderness*. New York: Macmillan. [southwestern NC]

———. 1917. A word-list from the mountains of western North Carolina. *Dialect Notes* 4: 407–19. [southwestern NC]

———. 1922. *Our southern highlanders*. 2nd ed. [used for three chapters (pp. 191–264) added to the 1913 edition]. New York: Macmillan. [southwestern NC]

———. (1929) 2009. *Smoky Mountain magic*. Gatlinburg, TN: Great Smoky Mountains Association.

Kerns, Megan Jewell. The geography of sorrow: Mountaintop removal in Appalachia. *Now & Then* 23(1): 6–8.

Key, Mary Ritchie. 1967. Tobacco vocabulary. Typescript on deposit at office of *Dictionary of American Regional English* project, Madison WI. [KY, TN]

Kidd, Thomas S., and Barry Hankins. 2015. *Baptists in America: A History*. New York: Oxford University Press.

King, Edward. 1875. *The great South*. Edited by W. McGruder Drake and Robert R. Jones. Hartford, CT: American Publishing Company. Repr., Baton Rouge: Louisiana State University Press, 1972.

King, Eva Samples. 1977. Eva Samples King: Her story. *Goldenseal* 3(1): 24–26. [WV]

King, Philip B., and Arthur Stupka. 1950. The Great Smoky Mountains: Their geology and natural history. *Science Monthly* 71: 31–43. [central east TN, central western NC]

King, Veta Wilson. 1997. *Mountain folks of old Smoky*. Sevierville, TN: Back Home. [Sevier County, central east TN]

King, Willis. 1939. *A survey of the herpetology of Great Smoky Mountains National Park*. South Bend, IN: University of Notre Dame Press. [central east TN, central western NC]

Kingsolver, Barbara. 1988. *The bean trees*. New York: Harper & Row.

———. 1989. *Homeland and other stories*. New York: Harper & Row.

Kinsland, Mary. 1863. [Letter]. MS 872, Hargrett Rare Book and Manuscript Library, University of Georgia, Athens. [Haywood County, central western NC]

Kinsler, Jennifer. 2017. *You can take the girl out of the mountains but you can't take the mountains out of the girl*. N.p.: CreateSpace. [northeast TN]

Kiracofe Family. 1861–65. [Letters]. Private collection.

Kirkland, Winifred. 1921. Mountain music. https://pinemountainsettlement.net/?page_id=14397. [southeastern KY]

Kiser, Mabel. 1985. *The life of a girl from the land of utopia: The hill country*. N.p.: n.p. [western NC]

Kline, Michael. 1990. Where the ravens roost: Songs and ceremonies of Big Cove. *Old Herald* 2(5): 24–28. [Swain County, southwestern NC]

Kniffen, Fred, and Henry Glassie. 1966. Building in wood in the eastern United States: A time-place perspective. *Geographical Review* 56: 40–66.

Knight, Henry C. 1824. Letter from Kentucky. In *Letters from the south and west*, 83–108. Boston: Richardson and Lord. [KY]

Knoxville Register. 1857. [Untitled newspaper article]. 9 September.

Komarek, E. V., and R. Komarek. 1938. *Mammals of the Great Smoky Mountains*. Chicago: Bulletin of the Chicago Academy of Sciences. [central east TN, central western NC]

Koontz, Katy. 2009. *Insiders' guide to the Great Smoky Mountains*. Guilford, CT: Globe Pequot Press. [central east TN, central western NC]

Korson, George. 1943. *Coal dust on the fiddle: Songs and stories of the bituminous industry*. Philadelphia: University of Pennsylvania Press.

Korson, George Gershon. 1941. *Black land: The way of life in the coal fields*. Evanston, IL: Row, Peterson and Co.

Kosier, Patty Pylant. 1988. *Maggie of Maggie Valley, N.C.* Corpus Christi, TX: Privately published. [Haywood County, central western NC]

Krochmal, Arnold, Russell Walters, and Richard M. Doughty. 1971. *A guide to medicinal plants of Appalachia*. Washington, DC: US Forest Service.

Kroeger, Mildred. 1975. Central West Virginia farm life between 1893 and 1970: Interview with Mrs. Anna Hopkins. *Goldenseal* 1(1): 3–8, 39. [WV]

Krumpelmann, John T. 1939. West Virginia peculiarities. *American Speech* 14: 155–56. [WV]

Krutch, Joseph Wood. 1962. *More lives than one*. New York: Sloane. [east TN]

Kupferer, Harriet J. 1965. The isolated eastern Cherokee. *Midcontinent American Studies Journal* 6: 124–34. [Swain County, southwestern NC]

Kurath, Hans. 1949. *Word geography of the eastern United States*. Ann Arbor: University of Michigan Press.

Kurath, Hans, and Raven I. McDavid Jr. 1961. *Pronunciation of English in the Atlantic states*. Ann Arbor: University of Michigan Press.

Kytle, Elizabeth. 1987. *The voices of Robby Wilde*. New York: Pocket Books.

La Barre, Weston. 1964. The snake-handling cult of the American South. In *Cultural anthropology*, edited by Ward Goodenough, 309–33. New York: McGraw-Hill.

Lacey, Theresa Jensen. 2002. *Amazing North Carolina: Fascinating facts, entertaining tales, bizarre happenings, and historical oddities from the Tarheel State*. Nashville, TN: Rutledge Hill Press. [western NC]

Lalone, Mary B. 2006. *Life in the coal camps of Wise County: In honor of Wise County sesquicentennial*. Wise, VA: Lonesome Pine Office of Youth. [southwestern VA]

LaLone, Mary B., Peg Wimmer, and Reva K. Spence. 2003. *Appalachian farming life: Memories and perspectives on family farming in Virginia's New River Valley*. N.p.: Brightside Press. [southwestern VA]

Lambert, Carol Glenn. 1994. Sawmills and railroads. *Bone Rattler* 10(4): 44–48. [western NC]

Lambert, Robert S. 1961. Logging in Great Smokies, 1880–1930. *Tennessee Historical Quarterly* 21: 350–63. [central east TN, central western NC]

———. 1961. Logging on Little River, 1890–1940. *East Tennessee Historical Society Publication* 33: 32–42. [Sevier County, central east TN]

Lambert, Walter N. 1988. *Kinfolks and custard pie: Recollections and recipes from east Tennessee*. Knoxville: University of Tennessee Press. [east TN]

Lance, Samuel J. 1861–64. [Letters]. Samuel J. Lance Papers. MSS 616, Louisiana and Lower Mississippi Valley Collection, Louisiana State University Libraries, Baton Rouge. [Buncombe County, central western NC]

Landry, Bill. 1988–97. Interviews conducted for the *Heartland* television series, on deposit at WBIR-TV, Knoxville. [east TN]

———. 1989, 1997, 1999. [Audio and video interviews conducted under the auspices of the Great Smoky Mountains National Park, consulted at the Library, Great Smoky Mountains National Park, Gatlinburg, TN]. [central east TN, central western NC]

———. 2013. *Tellin' it for the truth*. Knoxville: Celtic Cat. [east TN]

Lane, John. 1999. *Chattooga: Descending into the myth of Deliverance River*. Athens: University of Georgia Press. [northeast GA]

Lang, John, ed. 2006. *Appalachia and beyond: Conversations with writers from the mountain South*. Knoxville: University of Tennessee Press.

Lanier, Charles Day. 1894. On the trail of the wild turkey. *Harper's New Monthly* 89: 881–89.

Lanman, Charles. 1849. *Letters from the Alleghany Mountains*. New York: Putnam.

Larimore, Walt. 2004. *Bryson City seasons: More tales of a doctor's practice in the Smoky Mountains*. Grand Rapids, MI: Zondervan. [Swain County, southwestern NC]

Larue Family. 1865. [Letters]. Larue Family Papers. *The Civil War in Tennessee*, Tennessee State Library and Archives, Nashville, http://sos.tn.gov/tsla/looking-back-civil-war-tennessee. [Knox County, central east TN]

Lassiter, James. 1946. Games we played. *Tennessee Folklore Society Bulletin* 12: 17–22.

The "Last Chance" school. 1975. *Foxfire Magazine* 9(1): 41–44.

Laughlin, Hugh C. 1944. A word-list from Buncombe County, North Carolina. *Publication of the American Dialect Society* 2: 24–27. [Buncombe County, central western NC]

Lauterer, Jock. 1986. *Runnin' on rims: Appalachian profiles*. Chapel Hill, NC: Algonquin. [western North Carolina]

Law, Harry. 1952. Some folklore of Macon County, Tennessee. *Tennessee Folklore Society Bulletin* 18: 97–100. [Macon County, north central TN]

Law, Rachel Nash, and Cynthia Wieboldt Taylor. 1991. *Appalachian white oak basketmaking: Handing down the basket*. Knoxville: University of Tennessee Press.

Lawson, Lewis A. 1976. The Hammontrees fight the Civil War: Letters from the Fifth East Tennessee Infantry. *Lincoln Herald* 78: 117–22. [Blount County, central east TN]

Ledford, Ted Roland. 1976. Folk vocabulary of western North Carolina: Some recent changes. *Appalachian Journal* 3: 277–84. [northwestern NC]

———. 2006. Colonial survivals in Appalachian English. In *Encyclopedia of Appalachia*, edited by Rudy Abramson and Jean Haskell, 1014. Knoxville: University of Tennessee Press.

Lee, Howard B. 1969. *Bloodletting in Appalachia: The story of West Virginia's four major mine wars and other thrilling incidents of the coal fields*. Morgantown: West Virginia University Press. [WV]

———. 1971. *My Appalachia*. Charleston, WV: McClain. [southern WV]

Lee, W. H. H. 1863. [Letter]. William Henry Harrison Lee Papers, 1862–1863. South Caroliniana Library, University of South Carolina, Columbia. [Greenville District, northwestern SC]

Leigh Family. 1861–65. [Letters]. Private collection.

LeMaster, J. R. 1991. *Jesse Stuart on education*. Lexington: University Press of Kentucky. [northeastern KY]

Lenoir, William. 1790. [Letter dated March 25, to Father]. Lenoir Family Papers. Collection 426, Southern Historical Collection, Wilson Library, University of North Carolina at Chapel Hill. [central western NC]

Leonard, Bill J. 1996. Ministering in Appalachia. *Now & Then* 13(3): 12–14.

Letters of the era and the area. 1989. *Coffee County Historical Society Quarterly* 19(3–4): 76–77. [Coffee County, southeast TN]

Letters of the Mingus family, 1850–62. 1988. *Bone Rattler* 4(2): 25–32. [Haywood County, central western NC]

Letter to Amos Broyles, Sparta, White County, Tennessee. 1844. Transcribed and published in *Upper Cumberland Genealogical Association* 15 (1990): 113. [central TN]

Levi Family. 1863. [Letters]. Levi Letters, 1863. Tennessee State Library and Archives, Nashville. [Hamilton County, southeast TN]

Lewelling, Joseph C. 1986. The White Caps of Sevier County: Economic and cultural perspectives. *Tennessee Anthropologist* 11: 156–71. [Sevier County, central east TN]

Lewis, Helen M. 1996. Do people in Appalachia know they're Appalachians? *Now & Then* 13(2): 14.

Lewis, Ronald L. 2000. *Transforming the Appalachian countryside: Railroads, deforestation, and social change in West Virginia, 1880–1920*. Chapel Hill: University of North Carolina Press. [WV]

Leybourne, Grace G. 1937. Urban adjustments of migrants from the southern Appalachian plateaus. *Social Forces* 16: 238–46.

Liftig, Inez. 2001. Fugate: Lessons from Ganderbill Holler. *Now & Then* 18(1): 13–17. [eastern KY]

Lincoln, Charles Eric. 1988. *The avenue*. Garden City, NY: William Morrow. [Buncombe County, central western NC]

Lindsay, Mary. 1976. History of the grassy balds in the Great Smoky Mountains. Management report no. 4. NPS southeast regional uplands field research laboratory, Great Smoky Mountains National Park. Typescript consulted at Library, Great Smoky Mountains National Park, Gatlinburg, TN. [central east TN]

Linguistic Atlas of the Middle and South Atlantic States. 1934–47. [Field notebooks of interviews conducted for the Linguistic Atlas of the Middle and South Atlantic States, covering northeastern Florida to New York State. Data from Appalachian counties of West Virginia (148), Virginia (20), North Carolina (37), South Carolina (12), and Georgia (12), conducted between 1934 and 1947, are presented either in summarized fashion (as available online at us.english.uga.edu) or for specific counties in NC bordering the Smoky Mountains, as available on microfilm of the original field notebooks completed by Guy S. Lowman]

Linn, Beulah. 1996. The west fork of the Little Pigeon River. *Smoky Mountain Historical Society Journal and Newsletter* 22(2): 3–4. [Sevier County, central east TN]

Linzey, A. V., and D. W. Linzey. 1971. *Mammals of Great Smoky Mountains National Park*. Knoxville: University of Tennessee Press. [central east TN, central western NC]

Lister Family. 1862–64. [Letters]. Lister Family Papers. South Caroliniana Library, University of South Carolina, Columbia. [Greenville District, northwestern SC]

Lix, Courtney. 2011. Smoky Mountain medicine women. *Smokies Life* 5(1): 26–35. [central east TN, central western NC]

Lloyd, Jeremy. 2009. *A home in Walker Valley*. Gatlinburg, TN: Great Smoky Mountains Association. [Sevier County, central east TN]

Lloyd, Jeremy. 2009. Tremont: Company town. *Smokies Life* 3(1): 30–37. [Blount County, central east TN]

Lockmiller Family. 1862. [Letters]. Lockmiller Family Papers, 1862–1863. MSS 815, Stuart A. Rose Manuscript and Rare Book Library, Emory University, Atlanta. [Meigs County, southeast TN]

Logan, Linda, and Stevan Jackson. 2006. *A summer without children: An oral history of Wytheville Virginia's 1950 polio epidemic*. Wytheville, VA: Wordsprint. [southwestern VA]

Logging. 1975. *Foxfire Magazine* 9(1): 37–40. [Rabun County, northeast GA]

Lombard, Frances Baumgarner. 1970. *From the hills of home in western North Carolina*. N.p.: n.p. [western NC]

Long, Lucy M., ed. 2015. *Ethnic American food*. Lanham, MD: Rowman and Littlefield. [central western NC]

Loop, Cowboy. 2013. *In the shadow of the Appalachians*. N.p.: Alibris.

Lord, William G. 1963. *The Blue Ridge guide: From Asheville N.C. to Great Smoky Mountains National Park N.C.* Asheville, NC: Stephens. [western NC]

Lounsberry, Alice. 1901. *Southern wild flowers and trees*. New York: Stokes.

Louisville Courier-Journal. 1927. [Untitled article]

Love, John C. 1996. A Civil War letter. *Bone Rattler* 12(4): 32–34.

Love, Mathew N. 1860–65. Mathew N. Love Papers, 1827–1868. David M. Rubenstein Rare Book and Manuscript Library, Duke University, Durham, NC. [Henderson County, southwestern NC]

Lowry, Houston. 2000. Folk medical terminology as remembered from my practice. Typescript provided to the editor. [Monroe County, southeast TN]

———. 2001. Expressions, sayings, descriptions of patients in my practice: Notes sporadically made from about 1965 through 1998. Typescript provided to the editor. [Monroe County, southeast TN]

Lufkart, Kenneth A. 2017. *The comfort zone: Growing up in Appalachia*. N.p.: Xulon. [WV]

Lundy, Ronni, and Johnny Autry. 2016. *Victuals: An Appalachian journey, with recipes*. New York: Crown.

Lunsford, Bascom Lamar. 1926. Folk-lore in western North Carolina. *Southern Tourist* (April): 13–14. [western NC]

———. 1975. *"It used to be": Memories of Bascom Lamar Lunsford*. Edited by Mildred Frances Thomas. Typescript on deposit at Appalachian Collection, Belk Library, Appalachian State University, Boone, NC. [northwestern NC]

Lyman, Dean B. 1936. Idioms in West Virginia. *American Speech* 11: 63. [WV]

Lyon, George Ella. 2000. Growing up in Harlan County. In *One hundred years of Appalachian visions, 1897–1996*, edited by Bill Best, 85–86. Berea, KY: Appalachian Imprints. [Harlan County, southeastern KY]

———. 2013. Voiceplace. In *Talking Appalachian: Voice, identity, and community*, edited by Amy D. Clark and Nancy Hayward, 185–92. Lexington: University Press of Kentucky. [eastern KY]

Madden, Robert R., and T. Russell Jones. 1969. *Alfred Reagan house and tub mill: Historic structures report, Great Smoky Mountains National Park, historic data section*. Washington, DC: US National Park Service. [Sevier County, central east TN]

———. 1969. *Walker Sisters Home: Historic structures report part II and furnishings, Great Smoky Mountains National Park, historic data section*. Washington, DC: US National Park Service. [Sevier County, central east TN]

———. 1970. *Ephraim Bales wood shed and meat house historic structures report*. Washington, DC: US National Park Service. [Sevier County, central east TN]

———. 1977. *Mountain home: The Walker family farmstead*. Washington, DC: US National Park Service. [Sevier County, central east TN]

Making a cucumber doll. 1975. *Foxfire Magazine* 9(4): 376–78. [Rabun County, northeast GA]

Malone, Bill C. 2008. All-day singings. In *New encyclopedia of southern culture*, vol. 12: *Music*, edited by Bill C. Malone, 162–63. Chapel Hill: University of North Carolina Press.

Malone, Bill C., and Tracey Laird. 2018. *Country music USA: 50th anniversary edition*. Austin: University of Texas Press.

Malone, Kemp. 1931. Any more in the affirmative. *American Speech* 6: 460. [southern WV]

Maloney, John. 1946. Time stood still in the Smokies. *Saturday Evening Post* 218 (April 27): 16–17, 82, 84–85. [central east TN, central western NC]

Maloney, Michael. 1976. *Appalachian culture: A guide to students and teachers*. Edited by Peggy Celeste and Ann Hill. Columbus: Ohio State University Research Foundation.

Mangum, William P. 1862–64. [Letters]. William P. Mangum Papers. MS 3416, Hargrett Rare Book and Manuscript Library, University of Georgia, Athens. [Jackson County, northeast GA]

Maples, Alie Newman. 1982. *Memories of my mountains* [consulted at Library, Great Smoky Mountains National Park, Gatlinburg, TN]. N.p.: n.p. [Sevier County, central east TN]

Marshall, Robert K. 1949. *Little Squire Jim*. New York: Duel, Sloan, and Pearce. [western NC]

Martin, Charles E. 1984. *Hollybush: Folk building and social change in an Appalachian community*. Knoxville: University of Tennessee Press. [southeastern KY]

Martin, Ronda Jackson. 1994. *Stock car legends: The laughs, practical jokes, and fun stories from racing's greats*. Nashville, TN: Premium Press America.

Martin, William T. 1861–65. William T. Martin Papers, 1816 (1861–1865). Collection No. 466, Stuart A. Rose Manuscript, Archives, and Rare Book Library, Emory University, Atlanta. [Pickens District, northwestern SC]

Mary Carpenter. 1973. *Foxfire Magazine* 7(2): 118–30. [Rabun County, northeast GA]

Mashburn, William H. 1988. *Mountain summer*. Blacksburg, VA: Pocahantas. [western NC]

Mason, Bobbie Ann. 1993. *Feather crowns*. New York: HarperCollins.

Mason, Henry McGilbert. 1960. The memoir of a southern Appalachian mountaineer. Typescript consulted at Library, Great Smoky Mountains National Park, Gatlinburg, TN.

Mason, Robert [Lindsay]. 1927. *Lure of the Great Smokies*. Boston: Houghton Mifflin. [central east TN, central western NC]

Mason, Robert Lindsay. 1912. Raiding moonshiners in Tennessee. *Recreation* 35(5): 197–99. [east TN]

Masters, Victor. 1915. *Baptist missions in the South: Century of the saving impact of a great spiritual body on society in the southern states*. Atlanta: Townley and Co.

Matewan Oral History Project. 1989–90. [Selected audio interviews, transcribed for this book]. Matewan Development Center Oral History Project. Special Collections, Marshall University Library, Huntingdon, WV. [southwestern WV]

Mathes, Charles Hodge. 1940. Jeff Howell's buryin'. *Tennessee Folklore Society Bulletin* 7(2): 19–22. [east TN]

———. 1952. *Tall tales from old Smoky*. Kingsport, TN: Southern. [east TN]

Mathews, Mitford M. 1952. Of matters lexicographical. *American Speech* 27: 124–27. [east TN]

Mathias, Frank. 1976. Briars. *Mountain Review* 2(3): 1–3.

A matter of perception. 2013. In *Talking Appalachian: Voice, identity, and community*, edited by Amy D. Clark and Susan M. Hayward, 209–14. Lexington: University Press of Kentucky.

Matthews, Fred Decatur. c1950. *Them Smokey Hills is "hypoed": Tales and legends of the Great Smoky Mountains as gathered by Fred Matthews* [consulted at Library, Great Smoky Mountains National Park, Gatlinburg, TN]. N.p.: n.p.

Matthews, Gail V. S. 1983. Cutting a dido: A dancer's eye view of mountain dance in Haywood County, N.C. MA thesis, Indiana University, Bloomington, IN. [Haywood County, central western NC]

Matthews, Hardy. 1862. [Letters]. McLeod Letters Collection. Southern Historical Collection, Wilson Library, University of North Carolina, Chapel Hill.

Matthews, Hugh A. 1980. *Leaves from the notebook of an Appalachian physician*. Cullowhee, NC: Privately published. [Jackson County, southwestern NC]

Matthews Family. 1863. [Letters]. Matthews Family Papers, 1856–1910. MS 81-11, State Archives of Florida, Tallahassee. [Cherokee County, northeast AL]

Matthias, Virginia P. 1946. Folk speech of Pine Mountain, Kentucky. *American Speech* 21: 188–92. [Harlan County, southeastern KY]

———. 1952. A wordcatcher asks your help. *Mountain Life and Work* 28(3): 23–24.

Maupin, Juanita. 1936. A study of the living conditions in the Pittman Center community, 1934–1935. MA thesis, University of Tennessee. [Sevier County, central east TN]

Maurer, B. B. 1977. *Mountain heritage*. Parsons, WV: McClain. [WV]

Maurer, David W. 1949. The argot of the moonshiner. *American Speech* 24: 3–13.

Maurer, David W., and Quinn Pearl. 1974. *Kentucky moonshine*. Lexington: University Press of Kentucky.

Maxwell, Philip H. 1938. *Valhalla in the Smokies*. Cleveland: Exline.

May, John. 1873. *Journal and letters of Col. John May, of Boston, relative of two journeys to the Ohio country in 1788 and '89*. Cincinnati: Clarke. [WV]

Maynard, Charles. 2004. *Churches of the Smokies*. Gatlinburg, TN: Great Smoky Mountains Association. [central east TN, central western NC]

Mays, Carl. 2004. *People of passion: Spotlighting Southern Appalachia, representing America*. Johnson City, TN: Overmountain. [east TN]

McAtee, W. L. 1951. Bird names connected with weather, seasons, and hours. *American Speech* 26: 268–77.

———. 1945. *Nomina arbitera*. N.p.: Privately published.

———. 1951. Some folk and scientific names for plants. *Publication of the American Dialect Society* 15: 3–25.

———. 1956. *Some dialect of North Carolina*. Chapel Hill, NC: Privately published. [central western NC]

McAteer, J. Davitt, et al. 2011. Upper Big Branch—the April 5, 2010, explosion: A failure of basic coal mine safety practices. In *Report to the governor, Governor's Independent Investigation Panel*, 19. https://www.nrc.gov/docs/ML1206/ML12069A003.pdf. [WV]

McCall, William A. 1952. *Cherokees and pioneers*. Asheville, NC: Stephens. [western NC]

McCarroll, Meredith. 2016. On and on: Appalachian accent and academic power. *Southern Cultures* 26: 45–48. [northwestern NC]

McCarter, Pinckney J. 2014. Memories of a boy. *Smoky Mountain Historical Society Journal and Newsletter* 40(1): 20–25. [central east TN]

McCarthy, Cormac. 1973. *Child of God*. New York: Random House.

McCarthy, William B. 1994. *Jack in two worlds: Contemporary North American tales and their tellers*. Chapel Hill: University of North Carolina Press.

McCauley, Deborah Vansau. 1995. *Appalachian mountain religion: A history*. Urbana: University of Illinois Press.

McCaulley, John. 1960. [Audio interview recorded by Vic Weals]. [Blount County, central east TN]

McCaulley, Margaret. 2008. *A Cades Cove childhood*. Charleston, SC: History Press. [Blount County, central east TN]

McClelland, Nancy. 1977. Wilson Douglas: Mountain man and mountain musician. *Goldenseal* 3(1): 15–20. [WV]

McClintock, S. S. 1901. The Kentucky mountains and their feuds I: The people and their country. *American Journal of Sociology* 7: 1–28. [eastern KY]

McCoy, George W., and George Masa. 1933. *A guide to the Great Smoky Mountains National Park*. Asheville, NC: Inland Press. [central east TN, central western NC]

McCracken, Weaver H., III. 1974–75. [Interviews about logging in Great Smoky Mountains. 24 vols. of transcripts made by Mary Ruth Chiles, consulted at Library, Great Smoky Mountains National Park, Gatlinburg, TN]. [central east TN]

McCrumb, Sharyn. 2005. *St. Dale*. New York: Kensington.

McCutshan, J. Wilson. 1936. Virginia expressions. *American Speech* 11: 372–73. [western VA]

McDavid, Raven I., Jr. 1949. Grist from the Atlas mill. *American Speech* 24: 105–14. [northeast GA, northwestern SC]

———. 1957. American English dialects. In *The structure of American English*, by W. Nelson Francis, 480–543. New York: Ronald.

McDavid, Raven I., Jr., and Virginia G. McDavid. 1973. The folk vocabulary of eastern Kentucky. In *Lexicography and dialect geography*, edited by Harald Scholler and John Reidy, 147–64. Wiesbaden: Steiner Verlag. [eastern KY]

———. 1986. Kentucky verb forms. In *Language variety in the South: Perspectives in black and white*, edited by Michael Montgomery and Guy Bailey, 264–93. University: University of Alabama Press. [eastern KY]

McDermitt, Barbara. 1983. Storytelling and a boy named Jack. *North Carolina Folklore Journal* 31: 3–22. [Avery County, northwestern NC]

McDowell, L. L. 1936. A background of folklore. *Tennessee Folklore Society Bulletin* 2: 1–8.

McFee, John E., and Jeptha C. McFee. 1862–63. John E. and Jeptha C. McFee Letters, Stones River National Battlefield, Murfreesboro, TN. [Buncombe County, central western NC]

McGee, Jim. 2004. Coal camp blues: Coalfield struggle. *Tradition: A Journal of West Virginia and Educational Awareness* 1: 45–46. [southwestern WV]

McGill Family. 1864. [Letters]. McGill-Thatcher Family Papers, 1818–1979. Mf 1844, box 1, folder 6, Tennessee State Library and Archives, Nashville. [Hamilton County, southeast TN]

McGowan, Thomas, ed. 2002. Four Beech Mountain Jack tales. *North Carolina Folklore Journal* 49: 69–115. [Avery County, northwestern NC]

McGreevy, John Charles. 1977. Breathitt County, Kentucky grammar. PhD diss., Illinois Institute of Technology, Chicago. [Breathitt County, southeastern KY]

McIlwaine, Shields. 1939. *Southern poor-whites*. Norman: University of Oklahoma Press.

McJimsey, George Davis. 1940. Topographic terms in Virginia. *American Speech* 15: 149–79, 262–300, 381–419. [western VA]

McKamey, Jeannine. 1973. Park VIP works to save history. *Gatlinburg Press*, March 1, A3. [Sevier County, central east TN]

McKinley, Janie Mae Jones. 2008. *The legacy of Bear Mountain*. Sylva, NC: Catch the Spirit of Appalachia. [Jackson County, southwestern NC]

McMahan, F. Carroll. 2013. *Elkmont's Uncle Lem Ownby: Sage of the Smokies*. Charleston, SC: History Press. [Sevier County, central east TN]

McMeekin, Clark. 1957. *Old Kentucky country*. New York: Duell, Sloan and Pearce. [KY]

McMillon, Bobby. 2007. [Notes and observations on the speech of the Tennessee–North Carolina border, including manuscripts loaned to the editor]. [east TN, western NC]

McNeely, Renee. 2009. An unlikely source of flour. *Now & Then* 25(1): 14.

McNeer, May. 1945. *The story of the southern highlands*. New York: Harper and Brothers.

McNeil, Kathryn K. 1999. *Purchase Knob: Essays from a mountain notebook*. Santa Barbara, CA: Fithian.

McNeil, Kin. 1940. Mountain folk still "tote" corn to mill. *Asheville Citizen*, April 29. [central western NC]

McQuade, Goldie Ann. 2012. Variation at the morphology-phonology interface in Appalachian English. PhD diss., Georgetown University, Washington, DC. [northeast TN]

Mead, Frank S. 1970. *Handbook of denominations*. Nashville: Abingdon.

Medford, W. Clark. 1954. [Untitled article]. *Waynesville Mountaineer*, June 17. [central western NC]

———. 1956. Once rough, Big Bend now rests in peaceful solitude. *Asheville Citizen-Times*, July 1. [central western NC]

———. 1961. *The early history of Haywood County*. Asheville, NC: Miller. [central western NC]

———. 1963. *Mountain people, mountain times.* Asheville, NC: Miller. [Haywood County, central western NC]

———. 1966. *Great Smoky Mountain stories and sun over ol' Starlin.* Waynesville, NC: Miller. [Haywood County, central western NC]

———. 1969. *Finis and farewell.* Waynesville, NC: Privately published. [central western NC]

———. 1973. *The long hard road.* Waynesville, NC: Privately published. [central western NC]

Melton, Carrie Myers. 1979. *'Pon my honor: Folk tales from the Upper Cumberland.* N.p.: n.p. [north central TN]

Memories of the American chestnut. 1978. *Foxfire Magazine* 12(3): 240–60. [Rabun County, northeast GA; Macon County, southwestern NC]

Meriwether, Lee. 1888. Mountain life in Tennessee. *Cosmopolitan* 5: 456–60. [TN]

Merriman, Stony. 1990. *Midnight moonshine rendezvous: Secrets of Luke Alexander Denny's moonshine running adventures (1930s–1960s).* Smithville, TN: Privately published. [central TN]

Merriman, W. H. 1862. [Letters]. W. H. Merriman Letters. *The Civil War in Tennessee*, Tennessee State Library and Archives, Nashville, http://sos.tn.gov/tsla/looking-back-civil-war-tennessee. [Hawkins County, northeast TN]

Midwives and granny women. 1971. *Foxfire Magazine* 5(4): 238–62.

Miles, Celia H. 1980. Selected verb features in Haywood County, North Carolina: A generational study. PhD diss., Indiana University of Pennsylvania, Indiana, PA. [Haywood County, central western NC]

Miles, Emma Bell. 1905. *The spirit of the mountains.* New York: James Pott & Company. [southeast TN]

Miles, Emma Bell, and Steven Cox. 2014. *Once I too had wings: The journals of Emma Bell Miles, 1908–1918.* Athens: Ohio University Press. [southeast TN]

Miller, Donald L., and Richard E. Sharpless. 1998. *The kingdom of coal: Work, enterprise, and ethnic communities in the mine fields.* Easton, PA: Canal History and Technology Press.

Miller, George K. 1992. *The Civil War and Campbell County, Tennessee.* Jackson, TN: Action. [Campbell County, northeast TN]

Miller, Harvey J. 1974. *News from Pigeon's Roost.* Rabun Gap, GA: Foxfire. [Mitchell County, northwestern NC]

Miller, Jake. 2000. *Looneyville zip code 25259 lore: Appalachian mountain folklore, popular etymology, colloquial speech.* Philadelphia: Xlibris. [WV]

Miller, Jim Wayne. 1969. The vocabulary and methods of raising burley tobacco in western North Carolina. *North Carolina Folklore* 17: 27–38.

———. 1989. *Newfound: A novel.* New York: Orchard.

Miller, Jim Wayner. 1997. *The brier poems.* Frankfort, KY: Gnomon.

Miller, John W. 2008. *The curse of Satan's collar.* N.p.: Alibris.

Miller, Joseph. 1933. The healing gods or medical superstition. *West Virginia Medical Journal* 29: 465–78. [WV]

Miller, Judy. 2000. Only ignorant people. In *One hundred years of Appalachian visions, 1897–1996*, edited by Bill Best, 71–72. Berea, KY: Appalachian Imprints.

Miller, Tracey R. 1973. An investigation of the regional English of Unicoi County. PhD diss., University of Tennessee, Knoxville. [northeast TN]

Miller, Wilbur R. 1991. *Revenuers and moonshiners: Enforcing federal liquor law in the mountain South, 1865–1900.* Chapel Hill: University of North Carolina Press.

Miller, Zell. 1976. *The mountains within me.* Toccoa, GA: Commercial. [north central GA]

———. 2009. *Purt nigh gone.* Macon, GA: Stroud and Hall. [north GA]

Millican, F. M. 1864. [Letters]. Frank M. Millican Letter. WPA Civil War Transcriptions. Tennessee State Library and Archives, Nashville. [Roane County, central east TN]

Milliken, W. A., and John J. Vertrees. 1884. *The code of Tennessee, being a compilation of the statute laws of the state of Tennessee, of a general nature, in force June 1, 1884.* Nashville, TN: Marshall and Bruce.

Millner, Sondra. 1989. Letcher. *Now & Then* 6(2): 11–15. [southeastern KY]

Milnes, Gerald. 1995. Old Christmas and belsnickles: Our early holiday traditions. *Goldenseal* 21(4): 26–31. [WV]

———. 1999. *Play of a fiddle: Traditional music, dance, and folklore in West Virginia.* Lexington: University Press of Kentucky. [WV]

———. 2007. *Signs, cures and witches: German Appalachian folklore.* Knoxville: University of Tennessee Press. [eastern WV]

Milnes, Gerry, dir. 2012. *Signs, cures & witchery: German Appalachian folklore.* DVD. Elkins, WV: Augusta Heritage Center. [eastern WV]

Mims, Cora Massey. 1940. The Swagerty family. *Pioneer personalities, prominent people, pleasant places: Excerpts from historical sketches* [consulted at Calvin M. McClung Collection, Knox County Public Library, Knoxville]. [Cocke County, central east TN]

Mingus Mill. c1995. Gatlinburg, TN: Great Smoky Mountains Natural History Association. [Blount County, central east TN]

Minick, Jim. 1995. Groundhogs. *Now & Then* 12(1): 15–16.

Minutes of Providence Primitive Baptist Church, 1829–1881. Historical Records Project No. 465-44-3-115, WPA. 1933. Transcribed copy on deposit at Calvin M. McClung Historical Collection, Knox County Public Library, Knoxville. [Cocke County, central east TN]

Minutes of the Big Pigeon Baptist Church, 1787–1874. Transcribed copy on deposit at Calvin M. McClung Historical Collection, Knox County Public Library, Knoxville. [Cocke County, central east TN]

Misemer, H. M. 1863–65. [Letters]. In Henry Marshall Misemer Family Letters, 1861–1878 (Microfilm 2008). Tennessee State Library and Archives, Nashville. [Monroe County, central east TN]

Mitchell, Henry H. 2002. Popcorn Sutton comments on local moonshine tradition. http://www.victorianvilla.com/sims-mitchell/local/vis/suttonp, accessed August 15, 2007.

Mitchell, Morris. 1855. [Letter to Lewis Mitchell]. Transcribed and published in *Distant Crossroads* 5(3) (1988): 70. [Blount County, central east TN]

Mize, Robert. 1969. Dulcimers. *Foxfire Magazine* 3(1): 5–8. [Rabun County, northeast GA]

Moffat, Adeline. 1891. The mountaineers of middle Tennessee. *Journal of American Folk-lore* 4: 314–20. [south central TN]

Moffett, Marian. 1995. East Tennessee cantilever barns. *Smoky Mountain Historical Society Journal and Newsletter* 21(1): 12–25. [east TN]

Moffett, Marian, and Lawrence Wodehouse. 1993. *East Tennessee cantilever barns.* Knoxville: University of Tennessee Press. [east TN]

Montague, Margaret Prescott. 1923. The to-day to-morrow. *Atlantic Monthly* 132 (February): 159–67. [WV]

———. 1924. Miss Betsy Beaver. *Atlantic Monthly* 133 (February): 221–29. [WV]

———. 1926. Big music. *The Forum* 76: 420–33. [WV]

———. 1927. Hog's eye and human. *The Forum* 78: 190–203. [WV]

———. 1927. The world's funny bone. *Atlantic Monthly* 10: 327–36. [WV]

Montell, Lynwood. 1970. *The saga of Coe Ridge: A study in oral history.* Knoxville: University of Tennessee Press. [Monroe and Cumberland Counties, south central KY]

Montell, William Lynwood. 1975. *Ghosts along the Cumberland.* Knoxville: University of Tennessee Press. [south central KY]

———. 1983. *Don't go up Kettle Creek: Verbal legacy of the Upper Cumberland.* Knoxville: University of Tennessee Press. [south central KY]

———. 1991. *Singing the glory down: Amateur gospel music in south central Kentucky, 1900–1990.* Lexington: University Press of Kentucky. [south central KY]

———. 1993. *Upper Cumberland country.* Jackson: University Press of Mississippi. [south central KY, north central TN]

Montgomery, David. 2014. *Doctrine for dummies.* N.p.: lulu.com.

Montgomery, Michael. 1975–2013. [Personal observations recorded in notebooks by Michael Montgomery of usages by natives of east Tennessee and western North Carolina]

———. 1978. Interviews conducted in White Pine, TN, analyzed in *A discourse analysis of Appalachian English*, the author's 1979 University of Florida PhD diss. In the dictionary, interviews are referenced according to the list of speakers on p. 163 of that work. [Jefferson County, central east TN]

———. 2006. *From Ulster to America: The Scotch-Irish heritage of American English*. Belfast: Ulster Historical Foundation.

Montgomery Collection. 1992–2002. Observations and responses by consultants to queries, collected by Michael Montgomery for the *Dictionary of Smoky Mountain English* (2004).

Montieth, David. 1995. Tall tales of the mountains. *Bone Rattler* 10(3): 10–12. [western NC]

Mooney, James. 1889. Folk-lore of the Carolina mountains. *Journal of American Folk-lore* 2: 95–104. [central western NC]

———. 1890. The Cherokee ball play. *American Anthropologist* 3: 105–32. [Swain County, southwestern NC]

Mooney, Stephen D. 2006. Coal mining terminology. In *Encyclopedia of Appalachia*, edited by Rudy Abramson and Jean Haskell, 1028–29. Knoxville: University of Tennessee Press.

Moore, Arthur K. 1946. New light on affirmative "any more." *American Speech* 21: 301–2.

Moore, Harry L. 1988. *A roadside guide to the geology of Great Smoky Mountains National Park*. Knoxville: University of Tennessee Press. [central east TN, central western NC]

Moore, Iva McMahan. 1974. *"Dr. Mac": A beloved physician* [consulted at Library, Great Smoky Mountains National Park, Gatlinburg, TN]. N.p.: n.p. [Sevier County, central east TN]

Moore, J. Roderick. 1977. Mack Jenks, Union bard: 1971 interview with McDowell County coal miner and musician. *Goldenseal* 3(2): 25–34. [WV]

Moore, John Hebron. 1988. *The emergence of the cotton kingdom in the Old Southwest*. Baton Rouge: Louisiana State University Press.

Moore, Marat. 1990. Women's stories from the Pittston Strike. *Now & Then* 7(3): 6–12, 32–35.

———. 1993. Because the earth is dark and deep. *American Voice* 22: 73–88.

Moore, Warren. 1988. *Mountain voices: A legacy of the Blue Ridge and Great Smokies*. Chester, CT: Globe Pequot. [western NC]

Morehouse, Kathleen Moore. 1936. *Rain on the just*. New York: Furman.

Morgan, F. B. 1926. Rediscovering the Great Smoky Mountains. *National Magazine* 54(11): 401–2.

Morgan, Joe Richard. 1992. *Potato Branch: Sketches of mountain memories*. Asheville, NC: Bright Mountain. [western NC]

Morgan, John. 1984. The log barns of Blount County, Tennessee. *Tennessee Anthropologist* 9: 85–103. [Blount County, central east TN]

———. 1990. *The log house in east Tennessee*. Knoxville: University of Tennessee Press. [east TN]

———. 1997. The cantilever barn in southwest Virginia. In *Diversity and accommodation: Essays on the cultural composition of the Virginia frontier*, edited by Michael J. Puglisi, 275–92. Knoxville: University of Tennessee Press. [southwestern VA]

Morgan, Larry G. 2002. *Mountain born, mountain molded*. Boone, NC: Parkway. [western NC]

———. 2005. *Old time religion in the southern Appalachians*. Boone, NC: Parkway. [western NC]

Morgan, Lucy. 1958. *Gift from the hills: Miss Lucy Morgan's story with Lebette Blythe*. Indianapolis: Bobbs-Merrill. [northwestern NC]

Morgan, Robert. 1994. *The hinterlands: A mountain tale in three parts*. Chapel Hill, NC: Algonquin.

———. 1999. *Gap Creek*. Chapel Hill, NC: Algonquin.

———. 2000. *The mountains won't remember us, and other stories*. New York: Scribner.

———. 2009. *October crossing: Poems*. Frankfort, KY: Broadstone.

Morley, Margaret. 1913. *The Carolina mountains*. Boston: Houghton Mifflin. [western NC]

Morrell, John. 1981. *The mirth of a national park*. N.p.: Privately published. [east TN]

Morrison, Ralph B. 1895. Civil War letters of Thomas Lafayette Morrison. *Burke Journal* 4: 7–16. [Burke County, central western NC]

Morton, Joan. 1978. Superstitions and beliefs concerning babies in southern Appalachia. In *Glimpses of southern Appalachian folk culture*, edited by Charles H. Faulkner and Carol K. Buckles, 1–19. Chattanooga: Tribute.

Morton, Oren Frederick. 1914. *A history of Monroe County, West Virginia*. Kingwood, WV: Journal Publishing. [southwestern VA]

Moser, Joan. 1977. Friday at Parhams'. In *An Appalachian symposium: Essays written in honor of Cratis D. Williams*, edited by J. W. Williamson, 206–14. Boone, NC: Appalachian State University.

Mould, Tom. 2009. Ginseng. In *New encyclopedia of southern culture*, vol. 14: *Folklife*, edited by Glenn Hinson and William Ferris, 298–300. Chapel Hill: University of North Carolina Press.

A mountain Baptist sermon. 1895. *Berea Quarterly* 1(1): 12–15. [east TN]

Mountain life as it is. 1908. *Berea Quarterly* 12(8): 5–10 [eastern KY]

Mountain recipes. 1969. *Foxfire Magazine* 3(3): 25–26, 58–61. [Rabun County, northeast GA]

Mull, J. Alex. 1975. *Tales from old Burke*. Morganton, NC: News Herald. [central western NC]

Mull, J. Alexander. 1970. *Mountain yarns, legends, and lore*. Banner Elk, NC: Pudding Stone. [western NC]

Mull, J. Alexander, and Gordon Boger. 1983. *Recollections of the Catawba Valley*. Boone, NC: Appalachian Consortium Press. [central western NC]

Mullins, Denvil. 1994. *The cornfields of Coaley Creek*. Johnson City, TN: Overmountain. [southwestern VA]

———. 1994. *Echoes of Appalachia*. Johnson City, TN: Overmountain. [southwestern VA]

———. 1995. *The road back home: Tales of Appalachia*. Johnson City, TN: Overmountain.

Mullins, Gladys. 1973. Herbs of the southern highlands and their medicinal uses. *Kentucky Folklore Record* 19: 36–41. [eastern KY]

Murfree, Mary. *See* Craddock, Charles Egbert.

Murfree, Mary Noailles. *See* Craddock, Charles Egbert.

Murray, Kenneth. 1974. *Down to earth: People of Appalachia*. Boone, NC: Appalachian Consortium Press. [southeastern KY]

Murray, Lena Davis. 1935. *Schoolhouse in the foothills*. New York: Simon and Schuster. [east TN]

Murray-Woolley, Carolyn, and Karl B. Raitz. 1992. *Rock fences of the Bluegrass*. Lexington: University Press of Kentucky. [eastern KY]

Murry, Howard. 1961. *Salt o' life*. Winston-Salem, NC: Blair.

Myers, Bonnie Trentham. 2002. *Best yet stories*. Gatlinburg, TN: Privately published. [central east TN]

———. 2007. *Smoky Mountain remedies*. Maryville, TN: Myers and Myers. [central east TN, central western NC]

Myers, Bonnie Trentham, and Linda Myers Boyer. 2004. *The Walker Sisters: Spirited women of the Smokies*. Maryville, TN: Myers and Myers. [Sevier County, central east TN]

My grandmother was a Cherokee and . . . 1967. *Foxfire Magazine* 1(3): 75–81.

My most valuable possession. 1970. *Foxfire Magazine* 4(4): 242–45.

Neely, Sharlotte. 1991. *Snowbird Cherokees: People of persistence*. Athens: University of Georgia Press. [Graham County, southwestern NC]

Neitzel, Stuart. 1936. Tennessee expressions. *American Speech* 11: 373. [Hamilton County, southeast TN]

Nelson, Louise K. 1997. *Country folklore 1920s & 1930s and that's the way it was*. Alexander, NC: WorldComm. [western NC]

———. 1999. *Aroma and memories of grandma's and mama's kitchen*. Alexander, NC: WorldComm. [western NC]

———. 2002. *Turn back the pages of time: Early mountain living*. Waynesville, NC: Privately published. [western NC]

Netherland, Robert G. 2016. *Southern Appalachian farm cooking: A memoir of food and family*. Knoxville: University of Tennessee Press.

Neufeld, Rob. 2007. *A popular history of western North Carolina: Mountains, heroes & hootnoggers*. Charleston, SC: History Press. [western NC]

Nevell, Richard. 1977. *A time to dance: American country dancing from hornpipes to hot hash*. New York: St. Martin's.

Neves Family. 1861–63. [Letters]. Neves Family Papers. South Caroliniana Library, University of South Carolina, Columbia. [Greenville District, northwestern SC]

Newell, Thomas. 1969. A study of the genus *Joinvillea (Flagellariaceae)*. *Journal of the Arnold Arboretum* 50: 527–54. [WV]

Newfound Gap Road. 2008. Gatlinburg, TN: Great Smoky Mountains Association.

Newport (TN) Plain Citizen. c1940. [Story from *Newport (TN) Plain Citizen* newspaper, of unknown date, in collections of Joseph Sargent Hall]. [Cocke County, central east TN]

Newton, Mary Catherine. 1958. A comparative study of the dialect vocabularies of east Tennessee and western North Carolina using selected words. Senior thesis, Maryville College, Maryville, TN. [east TN, western NC]

Nicholas, J. Karl. 1981. Some features of present-day Appalachian English. Paper presented at the Modern Language Association meeting, New York, December. [Jackson County, southwestern NC]

Nicholson, Charles. 1989. *A field guide to southern speech*. Little Rock, AR: August House.

Niles, John Jacob. 1943. Folk ballads and carols. In *The Great Smokies and the Blue Ridge*, edited by Roderick Peattie, 217–38. New York: Vanguard.

———. 1961. *The ballad book of John Jacob Niles*. Lexington: University Press of Kentucky. [eastern KY]

Nixon, Phyllis J. 1946. A glossary of Virginia words. *Publication of the American Dialect Society* 5: 3–43. [western VA]

Noonkesser, David. 1986. *The crossing: A history of White Pine, Tennessee*. Rogersville: East Tennessee Printing. [Jefferson County, central east TN]

Norbeck, Mildred E. 1931. *The lure of the hills: A tale of the mountains of Kentucky*. Oakdale, KY: Revivalist Press.

Norman, Gurney. 1977. *Kinfolks: The Wilgus stories*. Frankfort, KY: Gnomon.

———. 2000. An "other" consciousness. In *One hundred years of Appalachian visions, 1897–1996*, edited by Bill Best, 149–56. Berea, KY: Appalachian Imprints. [eastern KY, WV]

Norman, Henderson Daingerfield. 1910. The English of the mountaineer. *Atlantic Monthly* 105: 276–78.

North Carolina State Board of Agriculture. 1896. *North Carolina and its resources*. Winston, NC: M. I. & J. C. Stewart, Public Printers and Binders.

Nor was a hair of their head singed. 1973. *Foxfire Magazine* 7(1): 48–51.

Notes from the Pine Mountain Settlement School. 1924. 2(2) (May): 1–3. [southeastern KY]

Oakley, Harvey. 2000. *Rememberin' the roamin' man of the mountains, Wiley Oakley*. Gatlinburg, TN: Oakley Books. [Sevier County, central east TN]

Oakley, Wiley. 1940. *Roamin' & restin' with the roamin' man of the Smoky Mountains*. Sevierville, TN: Oakley Enterprises. [Sevier County, central east TN]

Obermiller, Philip J. 1987. Labeling urban Appalachians. In *Too few tomorrows: Urban Appalachians in the 1980's*, edited by Philip J. Obermiller and William W. Philliber. Boone, NC: Appalachian Consortium Press.

O'Dell, Ruth Webb. 1945. Old mills. *Tennessee Folklore Society Bulletin* 11(3): 1–4. [Cocke County, central east TN]

Odell Family. 1861–64. [Letters]. *The Civil War in Tennessee*, Tennessee State Library and Archives, Nashville, http://sos.tn.gov/tsla/looking-back-civil-war-tennessee. [Sullivan County, northeast TN]

Odum, J. W. 1861. [Letter]. WPA Civil War Transcriptions. Tennessee State Library and Archives, Nashville. [Hamilton County, southeast TN]

Offutt, Chris. 1992. *Kentucky straight*. New York: Vintage.

———. 1999. *Out of the woods*. New York: Simon & Schuster.

Ogden, Warner. 1936. "Rescue work" is responsible for museum at Gatlinburg that tells life story of mountaineers of the Smokies. *Knoxville News-Sentinel*, July 10. [Sevier County, central east TN]

Ogle, Lucinda Oakley. 1986. Lucinda Oakley Ogle and early settlers. In *Sugarlands: A lost community of Sevier County*, edited by Jerry L. Wear, 37–77. Sevierville, TN: Sevierville Heritage Committee. [Sevier County, central east TN]

———. 1986. My valley . . . in the Smokies. *In the Smokies* 4(2): 39. [Sevier County, central east TN]

———. 1990. That's why I thought me a thought. *In the Smokies* 9(1): 18–19. [Sevier County, central east TN]

———. 2002. *Remembrances of my past 93 years: Growing up in the Great Smoky Mountains*. Gatlinburg, TN: Privately published. [Sevier County, central east TN]

Ogle, Lucinda, and Emily Nixon. 1976. If only these walls could talk. *Sevier County Times*, September 26, B7. [Sevier County, central east TN]

Ogle, Philip. 1974. Memories by Maggie Clabough Ogle. Typescript consulted at Library, Great Smoky Mountains National Park, Gatlinburg, TN. [Sevier County, central east TN]

Ogle, Una Kate Price. 1980. *The joy and sorrow of teaching in the Great Smoky Mountains of Tennessee*. Gatlinburg, TN: Crescent.

Old-time burial customs. 1972. *Foxfire Magazine* 6(1): 8–25.

Oliver, Duane. 1989. *Hazel Creek from then to now*. N.p.: Privately published. [Swain County, southwestern NC]

———. 1990. *Cooking on Hazel Creek: The best of southern mountain cooking*. Hazelwood, NC: Privately published. [southwestern NC]

———. 2002. *Cooking and living along Hazel Creek*. Hazelwood, NC: Privately published. [Swain County, southwestern NC]

Oliver, Hugh Russell, and Margaret Thomas Oliver. 1987. *Sketches of the Olivers: A family history, 1726–1966*. Pinehurst, NC: H. R. Oliver. [Blount County, central east TN]

Oliver, John W. 1938–46. Fifty years of Cades Cove. Typescript consulted at Library, Great Smoky Mountains National Park, Gatlinburg, TN. [Blount County, central east TN]

Oliver, William Howell. 1931–34. Sketches of the Olivers. Typescript consulted at Library, Great Smoky Mountains National Park, Gatlinburg, TN. [Blount County, central east TN]

Oliver, William Wayne. 2014. *Cades Cove: A personal history*. Gatlinburg, TN: Great Smoky Mountains Association. [Blount County, central east TN]

Olmsted, Frederick Law. 1860. *A journey in the back country in the winter of 1853–4*. London: Low, Son and Company.

Olson, Ted. 1995. An interview with Walker Calhoun. *Appalachian Journal* 23(1): 70–77. [Swain County, southwestern NC]

———. 1998. *Blue Ridge folklife*. Jackson: University Press of Mississippi.

Olszewski, Larry. 1998. Comments on old harp. *Old harp: The new harp of Columbia newsletter* 21: 12–13.

Onchuck, Sandra Young. 2003. *Mud pie memories: A scrapbook of an Appalachian childhood*. Philips, WI: Asaph. [southwestern NC]

One of these days there ain't gonna be no sang. 1974. *Foxfire Magazine* 8(1): 4–24.

Osborne, David. 2013. *Raisin' cane in Appalachia*. N.p.: Trafford. [southeastern KY]

Our Smokies heritage. 1978–82. [Monthly magazine published by Crescent Printing, Gatlinburg, TN]. [mainly Sevier County, central east TN]

Our Smokies heritage book 1. 1982. Gatlinburg, TN: Crescent. [central east TN, central western NC]

Owenby, Robert C. 2010. Trula Cole Ownby. *Smoky Mountain Historical Society Journal and Newsletter* 36(4): 6–19. [Sevier County, central east TN]

Owens, Bess Alice. 1931. Folk speech of the Cumberlands. *American Speech* 7: 89–95. [southeastern KY]

Owens Family. 1863–64. [Letters]. Confederate Papers, Collection 172,

Southern Historical Collection, Wilson Library, University of North Carolina, Chapel Hill. [Wilkes County, northwestern NC]

Ownby, Evolena. 1997. Memories of Big Greenbrier, Sevier County, Tennessee. *Smoky Mountain Historical Society Journal and Newsletter* 23(2): 15–25. [Sevier County, central east TN]

———. 1998. Life after Big Greenbrier. *Smoky Mountain Historical Society Journal and Newsletter* 24(1): 4–13. [Sevier County, central east TN]

Ownby, Harold. 1989. *Forks of Little Pigeon Church: Bicentennial history, First Baptist Church Sevierville Tennessee.* N.p.: Privately published. [Sevier County, central east TN]

Oxford, Cheryl. 1992. The storyteller as shaman: Ray Hicks telling his Jack tales. *North Carolina Folklore Journal* 38: 75–120. [Avery County, northwestern NC]

Pack, Linda Hager. 2013. *Appalachian toys and games.* Lexington: University Press of Kentucky.

Padelford, Ida. c1940. [Notes on the Smoky Mountains, collected by Joseph Sargent Hall from a librarian in Asheville NC; on deposit in Joseph Sargent Hall Collection, Archives of Appalachia, East Tennessee State University, Johnson City]. [central western NC]

Padgett, Guy. 1976. *A history of Clay County North Carolina.* Hayesville, NC: Clay County Bicentennial Committee. [Clay County, southwestern NC]

Page, Linda Garland, and Hilton Smith. 1993. *The Foxfire book of Appalachian toys and games.* Chapel Hill: University of North Carolina Press.

Page, Linda Garland, and Eliot Wigginton. 1983. *Aunt Arie: A Foxfire portrait.* New York: Dutton. [Macon County, southwestern NC]

———, eds. 1984. *The Foxfire book of Appalachian cookery.* New York: Gramercy.

Page, Mira. 1986. *Daughter of the hills: A woman's part in the coal miners' struggle.* New York: Feminist Press of CUNY. [eastern KY]

Painter, James Barney. 1861. Letters of James Barney Painter. MSS 10661, University of Virginia Library, Charlottesville. [Botetourt County, central west VA]

Parce, Mead. 1995. *Twice-told true tales of the Blue Ridge and Great Smokies.* Hendersonville, NC: Harmon Den.

Pardue, Paul. 1996. Recollections of a somewhat early childhood. *Smoky Mountain Historical Society Journal and Newsletter* 22(3): 16–17. [Sevier County, central east TN]

Parke, Robert. 1934. Our southern highlanders [part 1]. *The Bison: University of Buffalo Magazine*, 10–12. Repr., 2011, *Smoky Mountain Historical Society Journal and Newsletter* 37(2): 7–13. [Sevier County, east central TN]

———. 1934. Our southern highlanders [part 2]. *The Bison: University of Buffalo Magazine.* Repr., 1977, *Smoky Mountain Historical Society Newsletter* 3(4): 8–12.

Parker, Haywood. 1907. Folk-lore of the North Carolina mountains. *Journal of American Folk-lore* 20: 241–50. [western NC]

Parlier Family. 1865. [Letters]. Military Collection, Civil War, Box 85, Folder 28, State Archives of North Carolina, Raleigh. [Wilkes County, northwestern NC]

Parris, John. 1955. *Roaming the mountains with John Parris.* Asheville, NC: Citizen-Times. [central western NC]

———. 1957. *My mountains, my people.* Asheville, NC: Citizen-Times. [central western NC]

———. 1963. Witches and witchdoctors once flourished. *Asheville Citizen-Times*, August 13. [central western NC]

———. 1966. Spring is the time to go gummin'. *Asheville Citizen-Times*, March 17. [central western NC]

———. 1967. *Mountain bred.* Asheville, NC: Citizen-Times. [central western NC]

———. 1969. Soft water, hard likker. *Asheville Citizen-Times*, January 15. [central western NC]

———. 1969. Uncle Smart Carter was feared conjurin' man. *Asheville Citizen-Times*, April 21. [central western NC]

———. 1972. *These storied mountains.* Asheville, NC: Citizen-Times. [central western NC]

———. 1977. Mountain idiom getting to be rare. *Asheville Citizen*, May 27, 3. [central western NC]

———. 1978. *Mountain cooking.* Asheville, NC: Citizen-Times. [western NC]

———. 1979. Logging by cable is nothing new, oldtimer says. *Asheville Citizen-Times*, December 30. [central western NC]

———. 1993. Folklore and folkways. In *The history of Jackson County*, edited by Max R. Williams, 469–516. Sylva, NC: Jackson County Historical Society. [Jackson County, western NC]

Parris, Wiley. 1862. [Letters]. Major Wiley Parris Civil War Letters. Hunter Library Special Collections, Western Carolina University, Cullowhee, NC. [Jackson County, southwestern NC]

Parton, Dolly. 1994. *Dolly: My life and other unfinished business.* New York: HarperCollins. [Sevier County, central east TN]

Parton, Willadeene. 1996. *Smoky Mountain memories: Stories from the hearts of Dolly Parton's family.* Nashville, TN: Rutledge Hill Press. [Sevier County, central east TN]

Patricia Neal: A biography. 2010. https://www.patneal.org/patricia-neal-a-biography/, accessed July 1, 2016.

Patterson, Beverly Bush. 1995. *The sound of the dove: Singing in Appalachian Primitive Baptist churches.* Urbana: University of Illinois Press.

Patterson, Virginia. 1983. Cooking . . . mountain style: The greens of spring. *In the Smokies* 1(1): 20.

———. 1983. Spring wildflower pilgrimage. *In the Smokies* 1(1): 18.

Patton, E. E. 2013. I want to go back. *Smoky Mountain Historical Society Journal and Newsletter* 39(2): 4–5.

Patton Family. 1861–63. [Letters]. Patton Family Papers, 1860–1864. Collection 581, Southern Historical Collection, Wilson Library, University of North Carolina, Chapel Hill. [Buncombe County, central western NC]

Paw Paw Hollow Baptist Church, Sevier County, Tennessee: Minutes, Dec. 1802–May 1880. Transcribed copy on deposit at Calvin M. McClung Historical Collection, Knox County Public Library, Knoxville. [Sevier County, central east TN]

Pearsall, Marion. 1959. *Little Smoky Ridge: The natural history of a southern Appalachian neighborhood.* Tuscaloosa: University of Alabama Press.

Pearson, T. Gilbert, C. S. Brimley, and H. H. Brimley. 1919. *Birds of North Carolina.* Vol. 4 of *North Carolina Geological and Economic Survey.* Raleigh: Edwards and Broughton. [western NC]

Peattie, Daniel Culross. 1943. Blue Ridge wild flowers. In *The Great Smokies and the Blue Ridge*, edited by Roderick Peattie, 172–99. New York: Vanguard.

———. 1943. Indian days and the coming of the white man. In *The Great Smokies and the Blue Ridge*, edited by Roderick Peattie, 15–72. New York: Vanguard.

———. 1943. Men, mountains and trees. In *The Great Smokies and the Blue Ridge*, edited by Roderick Peattie, 152–71. New York: Vanguard.

Peattie, Roderick, ed. 1943. *The Great Smokies and the Blue Ridge.* New York: Vanguard.

Pederson, D. L. 1897. The mountaineers of Madison County, North Carolina. *Missionary Review of the World* 20 (November): 821–31. [central western NC]

Pederson, Lee A. 1977. The dugout dairy. *Tennessee Folklore Society Bulletin* 43: 88–89. [northeast TN]

———. 1977. The randy sons of Nancy Whisky. *American Speech* 52: 112–21. [northeast TN]

———. 1983. East Tennessee folk speech: A synopsis. *Bamberger beitrage zur Englischen sprachwissenschaft* 12. Frankfurt am Main: Peter Lang. [east TN]

———, et al. 1986. *Linguistic atlas of the Gulf States: Basic materials* [responses to interviews conducted by the Linguistic Atlas of the Gulf States project at Emory University, Atlanta, from 1968 to 1983. Responses in the present volume include all 60 speakers from the East Tennessee sector and 35 of the 87 speakers from the North Georgia sector]. Ann Arbor, MI: University Microfilms.

Pendleton, Charles. 1946. Illicit whiskey making. *Tennessee Folklore Society Bulletin* 12: 1–16.

Pendleton, Paul E. 1930. How the "wood hicks" speak. *Dialect Notes* 6: 86–89. [Upshur County, central WV]

Penland, William C. (1862–63) 1987. The William C. Penland Letters from East Tennessee 1862–63. Penland Historical Society, Inc.

Perdue, Charles L., Jr. 1987. *Outwitting the devil: Jack tales from Wise County, Virginia.* Santa Fe, NM: Ancient City. [southwestern VA]

Perkins, Elizabeth A. 1998. *Border life: Experience and memory in the Revolutionary Ohio Valley.* Chapel Hill: University of North Carolina Press.

Perrow, E. C. 1912. Songs and rhymes from the South. *Journal of American Folklore* 25: 137–53.

Perry, Jo Ruth. 1930. Handicraft art in the Great Smokies. *Knoxville News-Sentinel*, March 23, C1.

Perry, Louise Sublette. 1940. A study of the pronoun *hit* in Grassy Branch, North Carolina. MA thesis, Louisiana State University, Baton Rouge. [western NC]

Perry, Virgie Brewer. 1999. Memories along Clinch River. http://www.tngenweb.org/union/history/Memories-Along-Clinch-River.pdf. [northeast TN]

Petersen, Ron, and Candra Phillips. 1978. East Tennessee harp singing. In *The new harp of Columbia: A system of musical notation*, edited by M. L. Swan, xvii–xxx. Knoxville: University of Tennessee Press.

Peterson, Ronan K. 1995. Sanging in Poplar, NC: Zelotes Peterson, ginseng hunter. *North Carolina Folklore Journal* 42: 52–61. [western NC]

Petition from the inhabitants of Greene County. 1788. Transcribed and published in *Watauga Association of Genealogists Bulletin* 31 (2002): 9–10. [Greene County, northeast TN]

Petition from Washington County relative to the division whereof Washington Bill. 1783. Transcribed and published in *Watauga Association of Genealogists Bulletin* 31 (2002): 39. [northeast TN]

Petitions to the North Carolina General Assembly from inhabitants south of the French Broad. 1784–89. Transcribed by Cherel Bolin Henderson for *Tennessee Ancestors* 17 (2001): 208–27. [central east TN]

Phelan, James. 1889. *History of Tennessee: The making of a state.* Boston: Houghton, Mifflin and Company. [TN]

Philliber, William W., Clyde B. McCoy, and Harry C. Dillingham, eds. 1981. *The Invisible minority, urban Appalachians.*

Phillips, Sarah. 1862–63. D. W. Phillips Letters. MS 1751, Hargrett Rare Book and Manuscript Library, University of Georgia.

Phillips, Ulrich Bonnell. 1929. *Life and labor in the old South.* Boston: Little, Brown, and Company.

Picturesque speech. 1944. *Tennessee Folklore Society Bulletin* 10: 9–12.

Pierce, Daniel S. 2013. *Corn in a jar: Moonshine in the Great Smoky Mountains.* Gatlinburg, TN: Great Smoky Mountains Association. [central east TN, central western NC]

Pierson, Hamilton W. 1881. *In the brush.* New York: D. Appleton & Co. [KY]

Pinchot, Gifford. 1905. *Terms used in forestry and logging.* US Department of Agriculture Bureau of Forestry Bulletin 61. Washington, DC: Government Printing Office.

Pioneer farmstead. c1995. Gatlinburg, TN: Great Smoky Mountains Natural History Association. [Swain County, southwestern NC]

Pipes, Chase Earl Alexander. 2009. To the free people of America. *Smoky Mountain Historical Society Journal and Newsletter* 35(3): 2–5.

Pittman, Margie J. 2012. *Coal camp kinds: Proud creekers.* Bloomington, IN: AuthorHouse. [southern WV]

Pittman Community Center: A mountain mission. 1985. Gatlinburg, TN: Buckhorn. [Sevier County, central east TN]

Pittsburgh Post. 1905. Strange, picturesque words in the lumberjack's vocabulary. March 26, 32.

Plott, Bob. 2007. *The story of the Plott hound: Strike & stay.* Charleston, SC: History Press. [southwestern NC]

———. 2008. *A history of hunting in the Great Smoky Mountains.* Charleston, SC: History Press. [southwestern NC]

———. 2009. *Legendary hunters of the southern highlands: A century of sport and survival in the Great Smoky Mountains.* Charleston, SC: History Press. [western NC]

Plowman, Roscoe E. 1982. *Twice out of sight.* Berea, KY: Kentucke Imprints.

Poe Family. 1862–65. [Letters and documents]. Private collection.

Pollard, Mary O. 1915. Terms from the Tennessee mountains. *Dialect Notes* 4: 242–43. [Sevier County, central east TN]

Pool, Maria Louise. 1896. *In Buncombe County.* Chicago: Stone. [Buncombe County, central western NC]

Poole, Ernest. 1932. *Nurses on horseback.* New York: Macmillan. [eastern KY]

Portelli, Alessandro. 2012. *They say in Harlan County: An oral history.* New York: Oxford University Press. [southeastern KY]

Porter, J. Hampton. 1894. Notes on the folk-lore of the mountain whites of the Alleghanies. *Journal of American Folk-lore* 7: 105–17.

Posey, Walter B. 1942. The frontier Baptist ministry. *East Tennessee Historical Society Publication* 14: 3–10. [east TN]

Postell, Lesa W. 1999. *Appalachian traditions: Mountain ways of canning, pickling & drying.* Whittier, NC: Ammons. [western NC]

Poteet-Dickson Papers. 1861–64. State Archives of North Carolina, Raleigh. [McDowell County, northwestern NC]

Powell, Emilie Ervin. 1981. *Gracie and the mountain.* Chattanooga: Target. [Sevier County, central east TN]

Powell, Katrina M. 2002. Writing the geography of the Blue Ridge Mountains: How displacement recorded the land. *Biography* 25: 73–94. [central western VA]

———, ed. 2009. *"Answer at once": Letters of mountain families in Shenandoah National Park, 1934–1938.* Charlottesville: University of Virginia Press. [central western VA]

Powell, William S. 1968. *The North Carolina gazetteer.* Chapel Hill: University of North Carolina Press. [NC]

Powers, Elizabeth D., and Mark E. Hannah. 1982. *Cataloochee: Lost settlement of the Smokies.* Charleston, SC: Blazer. [Haywood County, central western NC]

Powers, Ginny. 2011. *Haints Cave: An Appalachian tale.* N.p.: Alibris.

Preacher Ben Cook. 1979. *Foxfire Magazine* 13(3): 190–202.

Preece, Mary Ellen Goble. 2005. *In this valley I grew: Life on Backlog and Happy Hollow.* Baltimore: PublishAmerica. [eastern KY]

———. 2007. *Leavin' Sandlick and speakin' Appalachian.* Baltimore: PublishAmerica.

Preston, Dennis R. 1973. Bituminous coal mining vocabulary of the eastern United States. *Publication of the American Dialect Society* 59.

Prewitt, Wiley. 2009. Coon hounds. In *New encyclopedia of southern culture*, vol. 14: *Folklife*, edited by Glenn Hinson and William Ferris, 273–75. Chapel Hill: University of North Carolina Press.

Price, Edward T. 1960. Root digging in the Appalachians: The geography of botanical drugs. *Geographical Review* 50: 1–20. [WV]

Price, Sadie F. 1901. Kentucky folk-lore. *Journal of American Folk-lore* 14: 30–38. [eastern KY]

Prichard, Arthur. 1977. Teams and teamsters in the Mannington oil and gas fields. *Goldenseal* 3(4): 21–24. [WV]

Primack, Phil. 1973. ARC: In case you were wondering about ARC but didn't know where to look. *Mountain Life and Work* 49(3): 69.

Primer, Sylvester. 1891. Dialectical studies in West Virginia. *Publications of the Modern Language Society* 6(3): 161–70. [WV]

Prince, Pete. 1995. Quill Rose—famous moonshiner. *Bone Rattler* 11(3): 27–30. [Swain County, southwestern NC]

Professor learns about Carolina mountain dialect. 1931. *Charlotte News and Observer*, October 8. [western NC]

Proffit Family. 1860–65. [Letters]. Collection 3408. Southern Historical Collection, Wilson Library, University of North Carolina, Chapel Hill. [Wilkes County, northwestern NC]

Program of the Work Projects Administration in the State of West Virginia. 1941. *West Virginia: A guide to the mountain state*. New York: Oxford University Press. [WV]

Puckett, Anita. 2000. On the pronunciation of *Appalachia*. *Now & Then* 17(2): 25–29.

———. 2000. *Seldom ask, never tell: Labor and discourse in Appalachia*. New York: Oxford University Press. [southeastern KY]

———. 2006. Melungeon. In *Encyclopedia of Appalachia*, edited by Rudy Abramson and Jean Haskell, 1022–23. Knoxville: University of Tennessee Press. [Hancock County, northeast TN]

Purkey, Lena Penland. 1975. *Home in Madison County*. Johnson City: East Tennessee State University. [Madison County, central western NC]

———. 2004. *Home to Madison County revisited: To the descendants*. Edited by Shirley Purkey Hendrix. N.p.: Privately published. [Madison County, central western NC]

Put-together(s). 1955. *American Speech* 30: 154. [WV]

Pyle, Charlotte. 1983. CCC fiftieth anniversary interviews. Typescript consulted at Library, Great Smoky Mountains National Park, Gatlinburg TN. 3 vols. [central east TN, central western NC]

Pyle, Ernest T. 1951. *Gatlinburg and the Great Smokies*. Gatlinburg, TN: Mountain Press. [Sevier County, central east TN]

Pyle, Ernie. 1940. Roving reporter. *Knoxville News-Sentinel*, October 23. [east TN]

Quasha, Jennifer. 2002. *How to draw Georgia's sights and symbols (a kid's guide to drawing America)*. N.p.: Powerkids Press.

A quilt is something human. 1969. *Foxfire Magazine* 3(3): 5–7, 44–49. [Rabun County, northeast GA]

Rader, Ron. 1986. A mountain legacy. In *Sugarlands: A lost community of Sevier County*, edited by Jerry L. Wear, 17–22. Sevierville, TN: Sevierville Heritage Committee. [Sevier County, central east TN]

Radford, P. M. 1896. Block houses. *American Historical Magazine* 1: 247–52.

Rafinesque, Constantine Samuel. 1832–33. *Atlantic journal and friend of knowledge*. Philadelphia. [KY]

Raine, James Watt. 1924. *Land of saddle-bags: A study of the mountain people of Appalachia*. New York: Council of the Women for Home Missions and Missionary Education Movement of the United States and Canada. [eastern KY]

———. 1924. The speech of the land of saddle-bags. *Quarterly Journal of Speech* 10(3): 230–37.

Rainey, Fran L. 1929. Animal and plant lore. *Kentucky Folk-Lore and Poetry Magazine* 4: 8–15. [eastern KY]

Rains, David. 2005. *The shaman's daughter: Appalachian mountain stories*. New York: iUniverse.

Raising dogs. 1979. *Foxfire Magazine* 13(3): 182–89.

Ramsey, J. G. M. 1853. *The annals of Tennessee to the end of the eighteenth century*. Charleston, SC: Walker and James. Repr., Knoxville: East Tennessee Historical Society, 1967. [east TN]

Rash, Ron. 1994. *The night the new Jesus fell to earth and other stories from Cliffside, North Carolina*. Columbia, SC: Bench.

———. 2002. *One foot in Eden*. Charlotte: Novello Festival Press.

———. 2004. *Saints at the river*. New York: Henry Holt.

Raulston, J. Leonard, and James W. Livingood. 1974. *Sequatchie: A story of the southern Cumberlands*. Knoxville: University of Tennessee Press. [Sequatchie County, southeast TN]

Read, Allen Walker. 1938. The pronunciation of names on the frontier, 1829–30. *American Speech* 13: 263–67. [TN]

———. 1947. The collections for Pickering's "Vocabulary." *American Speech* 22: 271–86. [KY, NC]

Reagan, Charles Aaron. 1985. Life in the Sugarlands before the Great Smokies Park. Typescript consulted at Library, Great Smoky Mountains National Park, Gatlinburg, TN. [Sevier County, central east TN]

Recipes, remedies & rumors: Volume I. 2002. Maryville, TN: Cades Cove Preservation Association. [Blount County, central east TN]

Records of the Primitive Baptist Church of Christ in Tuckaleechee Cove, Tennessee, April 1870 through August 1912. 1988. Transcribed by Betty R. Davis. On deposit at Calvin M. McClung Historical Collection, Knox County Public Library, Knoxville. [Blount County, central east TN]

Rector, W. S. 1861–63. [Letters]. Washington Swisher Rector Papers, 1837, 1860–1906. Dolph Briscoe Center for American History, University of Texas at Austin. [Rhea County, southeast TN]

Reed, Dale Volberg, John Shelton Reed, and John T. Edge. 2008. *Cornbread nation 4. The best of southern food writing*. Athens: University of Georgia Press.

Reed, John Shelton. 2009. Preface. In *Beech Mountain man*, by Thomas Burton, xiii–xv. Knoxville: University of Tennessee Press.

Reed, Paulette. 2013. [Notes on medical terminology]. Typescript provided to the editor. [Hancock County, northeast TN]

Reeder, Carolyn, and Jack Reeder. 1991. *Shenandoah's secrets: The story of the park's hidden past*. Vienna, VA: Potomac Appalachian Trail Club. [western VA]

Reese, James Robert. 1978. Randomly distributed dialects in Appalachian English: Syntactic and phonological variation in east Tennessee. *SECOL Bulletin* 2: 67–76. [northeast TN]

———. 1978. Variation in Appalachian English: A study of the speech of elderly, rural natives of east Tennessee. PhD diss., University of Tennessee, Knoxville. [northeast TN]

Reese, John W. 1862–64. [Letters]. John W. Reese Papers, 1862–1874. David M. Rubenstein Rare Book and Manuscript Library, Duke University, Durham, NC. [Buncombe County, central western NC]

Rehder, John. 2004. *Appalachian folkways*. Baltimore: Johns Hopkins University Press.

Reid, Christian. 1875. *Land of the sky; or, Adventures in mountain by-ways*. New York: Appleton. [Buncombe County, central western NC]

Reid, Juanita. 2002. Hall's Top remembered. *Smoky Mountain Historical Society Journal and Newsletter* 28(1): 22–24. [Cocke County, central east TN]

Reinhardt, J. M. 1926. Speech and balladry of the southern highlands. *Quarterly Journal of the University of North Dakota* 16: 139–47.

A reminder of dwellings from not so long ago. 2004. *Smoky Mountain News*, March 24–30, 39.

Rennicke, Jeff. 1991. *The Smoky Mountain black bear: Spirit of the hills*. Gatlinburg, TN: Great Smoky Mountains Natural History Association. [central east TN, central western NC]

Revis, Daniel W. 1862–65. [Letters]. Daniel W. Revis Letters. PC 1914, State Archives of North Carolina, Raleigh. [Henderson County, southwestern NC]

Reynolds, George P., Susan Walker, et al., eds. 1993. *Foxfire 10: Railroad lore, boardinghouses, Depression-era Appalachia, chair making, whirligigs, snakes, canes, and gourd art*. New York: Doubleday.

Reynolds, T. W. 1964. *Born of the mountains*. [Highlands, NC]: n.p. [western NC]

Richard and Margaret. 1975. *Foxfire Magazine* 9(1): 4–12. [Rabun County, northeast GA]

Richland Baptist Church, Grainger County, Tennessee Minutes, April 11, 1791–August 8, 1795. 1987. *Tennessee Ancestors* 3: 89–100. [Grainger County, northeast TN]

Richmond, Nancy. 2011. *Appalachian folklore: Omens, signs and superstitions*. N.p.: CreateSpace.

Riddle, Rita Sizemore. 2008. *All there is to keep: Poems*. Oak Ridge, TN: Iris.

Ridings, Gladys Oliver. 1983. *Cades Cove and parts of the Great Smoky Mountains*. N.p.: Privately published. [Blount County, central east TN]

Ridley, Caleb A. c1920. *The southern mountaineer.* N.p.: n.p.

Riedl, Norbert. 1975. House customs and beliefs in east Tennessee. *Tennessee Folklore Society Bulletin* 41: 47–56. [east TN]

Riggleman, Homer F. 1980. *A West Virginia mountaineer remembers.* Parsons, WV: McClain. [WV]

Rinzler, Ralph, and Robert Sayers. 1980. *The Meaders family, north Georgia potters.* Washington, DC: Smithsonian. [north GA]

Ritchie, Jean. 1955. *Singing family of the Cumberlands.* New York: Oxford University Press. [eastern KY]

———. 1963. *The dulcimer book.* New York: Oak.

Ritchie, Jean, and George Pickow. 1952. *The swapping song book.* New York: Oxford University Press. [eastern KY]

Rives, Margaret Rose. 1982. *The Blue Ridge Parkway: The story behind the scenery.* Las Vegas, NV: KC Publications.

Roaring Fork auto tour. c1995. Gatlinburg, TN: Great Smoky Mountains Natural Historical Association. [Sevier County, central east TN]

Robbins, Tom. 1998. [Typescript compilation of logging terms provided to the editor]. [western NC]

———. 2000. *Mountain farm museum.* Gatlinburg, TN: Great Smoky Mountains Association. [Swain County, southwestern NC]

———. 2015. Wagons without wheels: The humble land sled. *Smokies Life* 9(2): 8–15. [western NC]

Roberts, Bruce, and Nancy Roberts. 1970. *Where time stood still: A portrait of Appalachia.* New York: Crowell-Collier.

Roberts, Elizabeth Madox. 1926. *The time of man: A novel.* New York: Viking.

Roberts, Harry B. c1980. *Olden times in Greene County* [scrapbook on deposit at Calvin M. McClung Historical Collection, Knox County Public Library, Knoxville]. N.p.: H. B. Roberts. [Greene County, northeast TN]

Roberts, Katherine. 2009. Outbuildings. In *New encyclopedia of southern culture*, vol. 14: *Folklife*, edited by Glenn Hinson and William Ferris, 334–36. Chapel Hill: University of North Carolina Press.

Roberts, Leonard W. 1954. *I bought me a dog.* Berea, KY: Council of the Southern Mountains. [southeastern KY]

———. 1959. *Up Cutshin and down Greasy: Folkways of a Kentucky family.* Lexington: University Press of Kentucky. [southeastern KY]

———. 1969. *Old Greasybeard: Tales from the Cumberland Gap.* Detroit: Folklore Associates. [southeastern KY]

———. 1974. *Sang Branch settlers: Folksongs and tales of a Kentucky mountain family.* Austin: University of Texas Press. [southeastern KY]

Robertson, Ben. 1942. *Red hills and cotton: An upcountry memory.* New York: Knopf. [northwestern SC]

Robinson, H. W. 1861–63. Henry W. Robinson Letters, MSS 392. Stuart A. Rose Manuscript, Archives, and Rare Book Library, Emory University, Atlanta. [Jackson County, northeast GA]

Robinson, W. M. 1863. [Letter]. W. M. Robinson letter. http://www.jcncgs.com. [Jackson County, southwestern NC]

Roddie Family. 1862. [Letter]. John H. Crawford Papers. Archives of Appalachia, East Tennessee State University, Johnson City. [Washington County, northeast TN]

Roe, Betty D. 1997. *Teaching through stories: Yours, mine, and theirs.* Norwood, MA: Christopher Gordon.

Roebuck, David G. 2009. Dinner on the grounds. In *New encyclopedia of southern culture*, vol. 14: *Folklife*, edited by Glenn Hinson and William Ferris, 283–85. Chapel Hill: University of North Carolina Press.

Rogers, Courtney. 2007. A study of Appalachian dialects in the Carson-Newman community. Paper presented at Appalachian Studies Association meeting. [east TN]

Rogers, E. G. 1955. Switching for water. *Tennessee Folklore Society Bulletin* 21: 108–11. [central TN]

Rogers, Reece. 1861–64. [Letters]. Reece Rogers Letters, 1861–1864. Confederate Miscellany Collection, MSS 20, Stuart A. Rose Manuscript and Rare Book Library, Emory University, Atlanta. [DeKalb County, northeast AL]

Rose, Sharon. 2007. Games of mountain children. *Smoky Mountain Historical Society Journal and Newsletter* 33(4): 15–17.

Ross, Smith G. 1977. *Come, go with me: How to be independent and enjoy rural living.* Pine Knot, KY: Kentucky Hills Industries. [southeastern KY]

Roth, Margaret Ann. 1981. Greenbrier in the early days. *Smoky Mountain Historical Society Newsletter* 7(1): 7–13. [Sevier County, central east TN]

———. 1984. Reminiscences. *Smoky Mountain Star*, June 21. [Sevier County, central east TN]

Rothert, Otto A. 1941. Samuel McDowell's letters to Andrew Reid. *Filson Club History Quarterly* 16: 172–86. [KY]

Rouse, J. Michael. 1962. Language at Stoney Point spoken with colorful tint. *Asheville Citizen-Times*, April 29. [central western NC]

Rowley, Matthew B. 2007. *Moonshine: Recipes, tall tales, drinking songs, historical stuff, knee-slappers, how to make it, how to drink it, pleasin' the law, recoverin' the next day.* New York: Lark Crafts.

Royall, Anne Newport. 1826. *Sketches of history, life, and manners in the United States: By a traveller.* New Haven, CT: Privately published. [WV]

———. 1969. *Letters from Alabama, 1817–1822.* Biographical introduction and notes by Lucille Griffith. Tuscaloosa: University of Alabama Press. [northern AL]

Rudasil, H. F. 1862. [Letters]. H. F. Rudasil Letters. Confederate Miscellany Collection, MSS 20, Stuart A. Rose Manuscript and Rare Book Library, Emory University, Atlanta. [Davie County, northwestern NC]

Rush. 1890. River and sea fishery. *Forest and Stream* 35: 276–77.

Russell, Gladys Trentham. 1974. *Call me hillbilly: A personal account of growing up in the Smokies near Gatlinburg.* Alcoa, TN: Russell. [Sevier County, central east TN]

———. 1988. *It happened in the Smokies: A mountaineer's memories of happenings in the Smoky Mountains in pre-park days.* Alcoa, TN: Russell. [Sevier County, central east TN]

Russell, Randy, and Janet Barnett. 1988. *Mountain ghost stories and curious tales of western North Carolina.* Winston-Salem, NC: Blair. [western NC]

———. 1999. *The granny curse and other ghosts and legends from east Tennessee.* Winston-Salem, NC: Blair. [east TN]

Sabol, Steven. 1992. Sacred harp: History & tradition. Typescript in editor's possession.

Sacred Harp Singing. 2013. http://home.olemiss.edu/~mudws/harp.html, accessed March 5, 2019.

Salsi, Lynn. 2008. *The life and times of Ray Hicks.* Knoxville: University of Tennessee Press. [Avery County, northwestern NC]

———. 2013. *Jack and the giants.* Terra Alta, WV: Headline.

Salyersville Independent. 2017. [Untitled newspaper article]. [eastern KY]

Sanders, Myra. 1929. Some medical lore. *Kentucky Folk-Lore and Poetry Magazine* 1: 10–11. [eastern KY]

Sanders, Randy. 2009. A breakfast platter. *Now & Then* 25(1): 44–46.

Sanderson, Esther Sharp. 1958. *County Scott and its mountain folk.* Huntsville, TN: Privately published. [northeast TN]

Sang season. 1968. *Foxfire Magazine* 2(1): 28–32, 72–77. [Rabun County, northeast GA]

Sang signs. 1968. *Foxfire Magazine* 2(2): 15, 47–52. [Rabun County, northeast GA]

Sauceman, Fred W. 2006. The place setting. *Timeless tastes of the mountain South, from Bright Hope to Frog Level.* Macon, GA: Mercer University Press. [northeast TN]

———. 2014. *Buttermilk & Bible burgers: More stories from the kitchens of Appalachia.* Macon, GA: Mercer University Press.

Schantz, O. M. 1930. Hill dwellers of the Smokies are rare types. *Christian Science Monitor*, June 2: 1, 3.

Schantz, Orpheus Moyer. 1926. Beyond the haze in the high Smokies. *Country Life in America* (August): 60–61. [central east TN, central western NC]

Schmidt, Ronald G., and William S. Hooks. 1994. *Whistle over the mountain:*

Timber, track and trails in the Tennessee Smokies. Yellow Springs, OH: Graphicom. [Blount and Sevier Counties, central east TN]

Schockel, B. H. 1916. Changing conditions in the Kentucky mountains. *Scientific Monthly*, August, 105–31. [eastern KY]

Schrock, Earl F., Jr. 1975. An examination of the dialect in *This Day and Time* [by Anne W. Armstrong]. In *Voices from the hills: Selected readings from southern Appalachia*, edited by Robert J. Higgs and Ambrose N. Manning, 459–73. New York: Ungar. [east TN]

Schulman, Steven A. 1973. Logging terms from the Upper Cumberland River. *Tennessee Folklore Society Bulletin* 39: 35–36. [south central KY]

Schwartz, Scott W. 1999. *Faith, serpents, and fire: Images of Kentucky Holiness believers*. Jackson: University Press of Mississippi.

Schwarz, Berthold E. 1960. Ordeal by serpent, fire, and strychnine: A study of some provocative psychosomatic phenomena. *Psychiatric Quarterly* 31: 405–29.

Scott, A. E. 1884. A visit to Mitchell and Roan Mountains. *Appalachia* 4: 112–20. [western NC]

Scott, Dorothy, and Billy Scott. 1986. Beyond beauty: The Great Smoky Mountains, their people and cemeteries [consulted at Library, Great Smoky Mountains National Park, Gatlinburg, TN]. N.p.: n.p. [central east TN, central western NC]

Screven, Tom. 1975. John B. Wright: Retired coal miner and self-taught artist. *Goldenseal* 1(1): 11–16. [WV]

Seal, John, and Margaret Seal. 1834. Letter. Transcribed and published in *Distant Crossroads* 1(1) (1985): 49. [White County, central TN]

Seeger, Mike. 1992. *Talking feet: Buck, flatfoot and tap. Solo southern dance of the Appalachian, Piedmont, and Blue Ridge Mountain regions*. Berkeley, CA: North Atlantic.

Seeman, Elizabeth. 1961. *In the arms of the mountain: An intimate journal of the Great Smokies*. New York: Crown. [southeast TN]

Seidl, Carla. 2015. Chestnuts: A traditional Cherokee food source puts down new roots in WNC. https://mountainx.com/food/chestnuts-a-traditional-cherokee-food-source-puts-down-new-roots-in-wnc/, accessed April 2, 2018.

Settle, Mary Lee. 1956. *O Beulah land*. New York: Viking.

Sevier County Court: Two deeds transcribed by Pollyanna Creekmore. 1997. *Smoky Mountain Historical Society Journal and Newsletter* 23: 14–15. [Sevier County, central east TN]

Sevier County saga. 1976. Sevierville, TN: Sevier County American Revolution Bicentennial Celebration Commission. [Sevier County, central east TN]

Sevier Settler. 1984–86. [Quarterly magazine with local history, legends, and reminiscences]. [Sevier County, central east TN]

Sexton, Thornton. 1862–64. [Letters]. Thornton Sexton Letters, 1861–1864. David M. Rubenstein Rare Book and Manuscript Library, Duke University, Durham, NC. [Ashe County, northwestern NC]

Shackelford, Laurel, Bill Weinberg, and Donald R. Anderson. 1977. *Our Appalachia: An oral history*. New York: Hill and Wang. [eastern KY]

Sharp, Cecil. 1932. Introduction. In *English folk-songs from the southern Appalachians*, by Cecil Sharp and Olive Campbell, xxi–xxxvii. London: Oxford University Press.

Sharp, Cecil J., and Maud Karpeles. 1968. *Eighty English folk songs from the southern Appalachians*. Cambridge, MA: MIT Press.

Sharp, Roland. 2008. *Roland Sharp, country doctor: Memories of a life well lived*. Dunmore, WV: Parsons. [WV]

Sharpe, Bill. 1949. Lowgap man is ginsenging: Waxy leaves provide big business. *Roanoke Times*, June 31. [VA]

Shaver, Jesse M. 1926. Flowers of the Great Smokies. *Journal of the Tennessee Academy of Sciences* 1: 17–20. [central east TN, central western NC]

Shearer, Kathy. 2006. *Wilder days: Coal town life on Dumps Creek*. Emory, VA: Clinch Mountain Press. [southwestern VA]

———. 2011. *Tales from the moonshine trade*. Emory, VA: Clinch Mountain Press. [southwestern VA]

Shearin, Hubert. 1927. The speech of our fathers. *Kentucky Folk-lore and Poetry Magazine* 2: 6–7. [eastern KY]

Shearin, Hubert G. 1911. An eastern Kentucky dialect word-list. *Dialect Notes* 3: 537–40. [eastern KY]

Shearin, Hubert Gibson. 1911. Some superstitions in the Cumberland Mountains. *Journal of American Folklore* 24: 319–22. [eastern KY]

Shedlarz, Donnie. 2008. [Audio interviews recorded by Donnie Shedlarz, transcribed for this book]. Thomas G. Burton Collection, Archives of Appalachia, East Tennessee State University, Johnson City. [Avery County, northwestern NC]

———. 2013. *Rosa Hicks and her recipe book*. N.p.: LandaBooks. [Avery County, northwestern NC]

Shelby, Anne. 2006. *Appalachian studies: Poems*. Nicholasville, KY: Wind.

———. 2007. *The adventures of Molly Whuppie and other Appalachian folktales*. Chapel Hill: University of North Carolina Press.

Shelton, Ferne. 1965. *Pioneer comforts and kitchen remedies: Oldtimey highland secrets from the Blue Ridge and Great Smoky Mountains*. High Point, NC: Hutcraft. [central east TN, central western NC]

Shelton, James. 1953. Autobiography. Typescript consulted at Library, Great Smoky Mountains National Park, Gatlinburg, TN. [Sevier County, central east TN]

———. 2004. Autobiography of James Shelton [expanded version of the preceding item]. *Smoky Mountain Historical Society Journal and Newsletter* 30(4): 3–6. [Sevier County, central east TN]

Shelton, Susan. 2009. Cove Creek gritty bread. *Now & Then* 25(1): 28–29.

Shenandoah Oral History Collection. 1975–79. [Interview transcripts from the Shenandoah National Park Oral History Collection.] https://www.lib.jmu.edu/special/manuscripts/sdarchsnp/. [western VA]

Sheppard, Muriel E. 1935. *Cabins in the laurel*. Chapel Hill: University of North Carolina Press. [northwestern NC]

Shields, A. Randolph. 1965. Cades Cove in the Great Smoky Mountains National Park. *Tennessee Historical Quarterly* 24(3): 3–20. [Blount County, central east TN]

———. 1977. *The Cades Cove story*. Gatlinburg, TN: Great Smoky Mountains Natural History Association. [Blount County, central east TN]

Shifflet, Hillory. 1861–63. [Letters]. Collection of Hillory Shifflet, 1861–63. Gilder Lehrman Collection 02174, New York, NY; also Hillory Shifflet Letters, Missouri Historical Society, St. Louis. [Madison County, southeastern KY]

Shifflett, Crandall. 1991. *Coal towns: Life, work, and culture in coal mining towns of southern Appalachia, 1880–1960*. Knoxville: University of Tennessee Press.

Shipman Family. 1861–63. [Letters]. Shipman Family Correspondence, MSN/CW 5043. Hesburgh Libraries, Rare Books and Special Collections, University of Notre Dame, South Bend, IN. [Henderson County, southwestern NC]

Shirley, Hoke. 2008. *Raisen'*. Clayton, GA: Laurel Mountain Press. [northeast GA]

Shockley, W. S. 1862. [Letters]. W. S. Shockley Papers, 1861–1864. David M. Rubenstein Rare Book and Manuscript Library, Duke University, Durham, NC. [Jackson County, northwest GA]

Shore sign: A play based on the superstitions of the Cumberland mountain folk. 1946. *Tennessee Folklore Society Bulletin* 12(4): 3–7. [east central TN]

Shumate, Samuel. 2006. *The bridge crew: Growing up in the Blue Ridge Mountains in the 1940s and 50s*. Boone, NC: Parkway. [western NC]

Sienknecht, Charles. 1985. A primer in the rheumatic diseases for east Tennessee. *American Journal of Medicine* 78(2): 182–84. [east TN]

Siler, Margaret L. 1939. *Cherokee Indian lore and Smoky Mountain stories*. Bryson City, NC: Bryson City Times. [Swain County, southwestern NC]

Simmons, Shane S. 2016. *Legends & lore of east Tennessee*. Charleston, SC: History Press. [east TN]

Simms, Edna Lynn. 1934–40. Edna Lynn Simms Collection [typed 3-by-

5-inch citation cards created by Ms. Simms of Gatlinburg, TN, for a prospective museum, later given to Berea College, Berea, KY, for its permanent archives]. [Sevier County, central east TN]

———. 1940. *The roamin' man of the mountains: A sketch of Wiley Oakley, native guide, naturalist, philosopher of Gatlinburg, Tennessee in the Great Smoky Mountains*. N.p.: Privately published. [Sevier County, central east TN]

Simpkins, O. Norman. 1977. Culture. In *Mountain heritage*, edited by B. B. Maurer, 29–51. Parsons, WV: McClain. [WV]

Sinking Creek Baptist Church Minutes. 1787–99. Historical Records Project 465-44-3-115, WPA, 1938. Transcribed copy on deposit at Calvin M. McClung Historical Collection, Knox County Public Library, Knoxville. [Carter County, northeast TN]

Six, S. Dean. 1984. *Hill 'n holler expressions: A dictionary of West Virginia hillbilly talk*. Cairo, WV: Little Pink Pig. [WV]

Skelton, William Henry. 1897. The last three soldiers. *St. Nicholas* 24: 367–71. [east TN]

Skidmore, Hubert. 1936. *I will lift up mine eyes*. Garden City, NY: Doubleday.

Skipper, Roger Alan. 2006. *Tear down the mountain: An Appalachian love story*. New York: Soft Skull.

———. 2009. *The baptism of Billy Bean*. Berkeley, CA: Counterpoint.

Slaughtering, curing and cooking hog. 1970. *Foxfire Magazine* 4(1–2): 36–48, 65–69.

Slone, Verna Mae. 1978. *Common folks*. Pippa Passes, KY: Alice Lloyd College. [Knott County, southeastern KY]

———. 1979. *What my heart wants to tell*. Washington, DC: New Republic. [Knott County, southeastern KY]

———. 1982. *How we talked*. Pippa Passes, KY: Pippa Valley Printing. [Knott County, southeastern KY]

Smalling, Curtis. 1987. *The heritage of Watauga County, North Carolina*. Vol. 2. Boone, NC: Southern Appalachian Historical Association. [Watauga County, northwestern NC]

Smith, Andrew, and Bruce Kraig. 2013. *The Oxford encyclopedia of food and drink in America*. New York: Oxford University Press.

Smith, Captain Ross. 1930. *Reminiscences of an old-timer*. [Jonesborough, TN]: Privately published.

Smith, Charles Forster. 1883. On southernisms. *Transactions of the American Philological Association* 14: 42–56. [east TN]

———. 1886. On southernisms. *Transactions of the American Philological Association* 17: 34–46. [east TN]

———. 1886. Southern dialect in life and literature. *Southern Bivouac* 4: 343–50. [east TN]

———. 1908. *Reminiscences and sketches*. Nashville, TN: Methodist Episcopal Church, South. [TN]

———. 1910. Tramping in the mountains—the Great Smokies and Thunder Head. *Christian Advocate*, September 23, 10–12. [east TN]

———. 1910. Tramping in the mountains, no. 2. *Christian Advocate*, October 23, 10–11. [east TN]

Smith, Charles Henry. 1863. The battle of Rome—official. *Southern Confederacy* (Atlanta). May 9. [northwest GA]

———. 1866. *Bill Arp, so called: A side show of the southern side of the war*. New York: Metropolitan Record Office. [northwest GA]

———. 1873. *Bill Arp's peace papers*. New York: Carleton. [northwest GA]

———. 1884. *Bill Arp's scrap book: Humor and philosophy*. Atlanta: J. P. Harrison. [northwest GA]

———. 1892. *The farm and the fireside: Sketches of domestic life in war and peace*. Atlanta: Constitution. [northwest GA]

Smith, Dorothy Noble. 1983. *Recollections: The people of the Blue Ridge remember*. Edited by James F. Gorman. Verona, VA: McClure.

Smith, Era Rhea Noland. 1989. *Flyin' bullets and resplendent badge*. Sevierville, TN: Nandel. [central east TN]

Smith, Fabia Rue, and Charles Rayford Smith. 1976. *Southern words and sayings*. Jackson, MS: Office Supply Company.

Smith, Flavious Joseph, Sr. 1984. *Enduring memories: Growing up in Dry Valley, the heart of the Upper Cumberland*. N.p.: n.p. [north central TN]

Smith, Frank. 1962. Dancing and singing games. In *The Southern Appalachian region: A survey*, edited by Thomas R. Ford, 271–78. Lexington: University Press of Kentucky.

Smith, H. Clay, and Maxine C. Eye. 1986. *Guidelines for managing immature Appalachian hardwood stands*. Morgantown: West Virginia University College of Agriculture and Forestry. [WV]

Smith, Karen Cecil. 2003. *Orlean Puckett: The life of a mountain midwife, 1844–1939*. Boone, NC: Parkway.

Smith, Lee. 1984. *Oral history*. New York: Ballantine.

———. 1988. *Fair and tender ladies*. New York: Putnam.

Smith, Marilyn. 1970. Folk customs of Jefferson County, Tennessee. In *A collection of folklore by undergraduate students at East Tennessee State University*, edited by Thomas G. Burton and Ambrose N. Manning, 54–57. Johnson City: East Tennessee State University. [Jefferson County, central east TN]

Smith, Mary Bell. 1979. *In the shadow of the white rock*. Morristown, TN: Privately published.

Smith, Ralph Lee. 1997. *Appalachian dulcimer traditions*. Lanham, MD: Scarecrow.

Smith, Rebecca W. 1934. A Tennessean's pronunciation in 1841. *American Speech* 9: 262–63. [Jefferson County, central east TN]

Smith, Tony. 2010. *An Appalachian mother's love*. N.p.: AuthorHouse.

Smith, William D. 1862–65. [Letters]. William D. Smith Papers, 1862–1865. David M. Rubenstein Rare Book and Manuscript Library, Duke University, Durham, NC. [Davie County, northwestern NC]

Smith, Zachariah Frederick. 1886. *The history of Kentucky from its earliest discovery and settlement, to the present date*. Louisville, KY: Courier-Journal Job Printing. [KY]

Smith-Carroll, Eva. 2014. *West Virginia talk: Words & phrases from the Mountain State*. https://wva.homestead.com/WVaTalk.html.

Smokies Guide: Official newsletter of Great Smoky Mountains National Park. 1977–96. [central east TN, central western NC]

Smoky Mountain Times (Bryson City, NC). 2011. [Miscellaneous newspaper articles]

Smoky Mt. News (Bryson City, NC). 2002–18. [Miscellaneous articles from daily newspaper for Swain County]. [central western NC]

Smoky Vistas. 1977–79. [Magazine published by the Great Smoky Mountains Natural History Association]. [central east TN, central western NC]

Snake lore. 1970. *Foxfire Magazine* 4(3): 166–77.

Snodgrass, Mary Ellen, ed. 2004. *Encyclopedia of kitchen history*. New York: Routledge.

Sobol, Joseph Daniel. 1993. Growing up with Jack in Haywood County: The background and development of Donald Davis's storytelling. *North Carolina Folklore Journal* 40: 80–113. [Haywood County, central western NC]

Soesbee, Mary Lou. 1993. Wordlist [manuscript provided to the editor]. [western NC]

Sohn, Katherine Kelleher. 2006. *Whistlin' and crowin' women of Appalachia: Literacy practices since college*. Carbondale: Southern Illinois University Press. [eastern KY]

Sohn, Mark. 2009. *Appalachian home cooking: History, cultures, and recipes*. Lexington: University Press of Kentucky.

Some early Blount County wills. 2002. *Blount Journal: A Tennessee Genealogical Magazine* 49(1): 6. [Blount County, central east TN]

Sorden, L. G. 1969. *Lumberjack lingo*. Spring Green, WI: Wisconsin House.

South, Stanley. 1995. *What it is, boss man?* Columbia, SC: Wine Cellar Press. [northwestern NC]

———. 1996. *I never killed a man didn't need killing*. Columbia, SC: Wine Cellar Verse. [Watauga County, northwestern NC]

Spainhourd, Robert. 1862. [Letters]. Robert Spainhourd Papers, 1862.

David M. Rubenstein Rare Book and Manuscript Library, Duke University, Durham, NC. [Forsyth County, northwestern NC]

Spalding, Arthur W. 1921. *The hills o' Ca'liny*. Washington, DC: Review and Herald. [western KY]

Spalding, Susan Eike. 2014. *Appalachian dance: Creativity and continuity in six communities*. Urbana: University of Illinois Press.

Sparks, John. 2005. *Raccoon John Smith: Frontier Kentucky's most famous preacher*. Lexington: University Press of Kentucky.

A special issue devoted to instrument makers. 1974. *Foxfire Magazine* 8(3): 177–240.

Speer, Jean Haskell. 1990. *The Appalachian photographs of Earl Palmer*. Lexington: University Press of Kentucky.

———. 1994. The power to create identity. *Now & Then* 10(3): 2.

Spencer, Ezalee Kear. 1999–2000. Down memory lane [in 3 parts]. *Smoky Mountain Historical Society Journal and Newsletter* 25(3): 6–10; 25(4): 2–11; 26(1): 2–8. [Sevier County, central east TN]

Split rail fences. 1975. *Foxfire Magazine* 9(2–3): 124–25. [Rabun County, northeast GA]

Spriggs, Bianca. 2011. Frank X. Walker: Exemplar of Affrilachia. *Appalachian Heritage* 39(3): 21–25.

Spring, Agnes Wright. 1924. Rough outline of visit with Aunt Lydia Whaley. Typescript consulted at Library, Great Smoky Mountains National Park, Gatlinburg, TN. [Blount County, central east TN]

Spurlock, John H. 1996. Glossary to accompany *Beyond Dark Hills*, by Jesse Stuart, 389–414. Ashland, KY: Jesse Stuart Foundation. [northeastern KY]

Squaw winter, Indian winter, dogwood winter. 1907. *Journal of American Folk-lore* 20: 235–36.

Stanley, Bonnie G. 1977. But we were tough and hardy. *Goldenseal* 3(1): 30–34. [WV]

Starnes, Richard. 2005. *Creating the Land of the Sky: Tourism and society in western North Carolina*. Tuscaloosa: University of Alabama Press. [western NC]

Steadman, J. M. 1918. North Carolina word list. *Dialect Notes* 5: 18–20. [NC]

Steed, Virgil S. 1947. *Kentucky tobacco patch*. Indianapolis: Bobbs-Merrill. [KY]

Stephenson, Sue H. 1977. *Basketry of the Appalachian mountains*. New York: Van Nostrand.

Stepp, S. H. 1864. [Letters]. Silas H. Stepp Civil War Letters. M2004.4.1, Special Collections, University of North Carolina at Asheville. [Buncombe County, central western NC]

Stevens, Bernice. 1971. *Our mountain craftsmen*. Gatlinburg, TN: Buckhorn. [east TN]

Stewart, George. 1945. *Names on the land*. New York: Random House.

Still, James. 1936. Horse doctor. *Frontier and Midland* 17: 25–28.

———. 1936. One leg gone to judgment. *Mountain Life and Work* 12(3): 9–10.

———. 1936–37. On Defeated Creek. *Frontier and Midland* 17: 120–24.

———. 1937. Brother to Methusalem. *Story* 11(64): 45–52.

———. 1937. The egg tree. *Yale Review* 27: 100–109.

———. 1937. The quare day. *Household Magazine* 37: 36.

———. 1938. Bat flight. *Saturday Evening Post* 211(10): 12–13.

———. 1938. Mole-bane. *Atlantic Monthly* 161: 372–74.

———. 1939. The ploughing. *Atlantic Monthly* 164(6): 776–78.

———. 1939. Sugar in a gourd. *Prairie Schooner* 13: 99–104.

———. 1939. Twelve pears hanging high. *Mountain Life and Work* 15(1): 14–18.

———. 1939. Two eyes, two pennies. *Saturday Evening Post* 211(40): 12–13, 94–95, 97.

———. 1940. I love my rooster. *Saturday Evening Post* 212(40): 16–17, 62, 64, 70.

———. 1940. *River of earth*. New York: Viking.

———. 1940. Snail pie. *American Mercury* 50: 209–14.

———. 1940–41. The moving. *North Georgia Review* 5(3–4): 18–20.

———. 1941. *On Troublesome Creek*. New York: Viking.

———. 1941. Proud walkers. *Saturday Evening Post* 213(45): 111–14.

———. 1941. The stir-off. *Mountain Life and Work* 17(3): 1–7.

———. 1945. Mrs. Razor. *Atlantic* 176(1): 52–53.

———. 1946. Pattern of a man. *Yale Review* 36: 93–100.

———. 1948. The nest. *Prairie Schooner* 22: 53–56.

———. 1949. A master time. *Atlantic Monthly* 183: 43–46.

———. 1951. A ride on the short dog. *Atlantic Monthly* 188: 55–58.

———. 1956. The burning of the waters. *Atlantic Monthly* 188: 55–60.

———. 1976. *Pattern of a man and other stories*. Lexington, KY: Gnomon.

———. 1977. *Jack and the wonder beans*. New York: Putnam's Sons.

———. 1980. *The run for the Elbertas*. Lexington: University Press of Kentucky.

———. 1986. *The Wolfpen poems*. Berea, KY: Berea College Press.

———. 1988. Hunting for Hindman: An exercise in the use of the vernacular. *Appalachian Heritage* 21: 13–14. [southeastern KY]

———. 1989. *Rusties and riddles & gee-haw whimmy-diddles*. Lexington: University Press of Kentucky. [southeastern KY]

———. 1991. *The Wolfpen notebooks*. Lexington: University Press of Kentucky.

———. 1998. *Appalachian Mother Goose*. Lexington: University Press of Kentucky.

———. 2010. Bare-bones. *Appalachian Heritage* 38(4): 21–24.

———. 2012. *The hills remember: The complete short stories of James Still*. Edited by Ted Olson and Teresa Perry Reynolds. Lexington: University Press of Kentucky.

Stipe, Sylvia. 1988. Glenn Cardwell: Smokies man of the year. *In the Smokies* 6(5): 16–19. [Sevier County, central east TN]

Stoddart, Jess, ed. 1997. *The quare women's journals: May Stone and Katherine Pettit's summers in the Kentucky mountains and the founding of the Hindman Settlement School*. Ashland, KY: Jesse Stuart Foundation. [southeastern KY]

Stokely, Janie May Jones. 1964. *Years of harvest: Poems and tales from the Smoky foothills*. Newport, TN: n.p. [Cocke County, central east TN]

Stokely, Jim, and Jeff D. Johnson. 1981. *An encyclopedia of east Tennessee*. Oak Ridge, TN: Children's Museum.

Stone, Mary O. 1995. *Confidence courage spunk: Smoky mountain women*. Sevierville, TN: Mountain Press. [central east TN, central western NC]

Stories 'neath the Roan: Memories of the people of Yancey, Mitchell and Avery Counties at the foot of Roan Mountain, North Carolina. 1993. Little Switzerland, NC: Blue Ridge Reading Team. [Mitchell and Yancey Counties, northwestern NC]

The story of a mountain girl. 1918. *Mountain Herald* 18: 4–5, 17–21. [northeast TN]

Stratton, Cora. S. 1977. *And this is Grassy Cove*. Crossville, TN: BK Enterprises. [Cumberland County, east central TN]

Strausbaugh, Perry Daniel, and Earl L. Core. 1952. *Flora of West Virginia, part 1*. Morgantown, WV: n.p. [WV]

Strong, Paschal Neilson. 1932. *Behind the Great Smokies*. Boston: Little, Brown.

Strutin, Michael. 2000. *Gristmills*. Gatlinburg, TN: Great Smoky Mountains Association. [central east TN, central western NC]

———. 2003. *History hikes of the Smokies*. Gatlinburg, TN: Great Smoky Mountains Association. [central east TN, central western NC]

Stryk, Dan. 2007. Meditation on a groundhog brood. *Now & Then* 23(1): 42–43.

Stuart, Jesse. 1931. The yarb doctor. *Kentucky Folk-Lore and Poetry Magazine* 6: 4–10. [northeastern KY]

———. 1935. Kentucky mountain people. *Kentucky Progress* 6: 256–63. [northeastern KY]

———. 1936. *Head o' W-Hollow*. New York: Dutton.

———. 1936. Lonesome waters. *Esquire* 5: 32–33. [northeastern KY]

———. 1938. *Beyond dark hills*. New York: Dutton. [northeastern KY]

———. 1940. *Trees of heaven*. New York: Dutton.

———. 1941. *Men of the mountains*. New York: Dutton. [northeastern KY]

———. 1943. *Taps for Private Tussie*. New York: Dutton. [northeastern KY]

———. 1946. *Foretaste of glory*. New York: Dutton.

———. 1946. *Tales from the Plum Grove Hills*. New York: Dutton. [northeastern KY]

———. 1947. Corn cuttin's pretty work. *Farm Journal* 7(1): 22–23. [northeastern KY]

———. 1949. *The thread that runs so true*. New York: Scribner's Sons. [northeastern KY]

———. 1950. *Hie to the hunters*. New York: Harcourt, Brace and World. [northeastern KY]

———. 1952. Christmas in the valley. *Ladies Home Journal* 69 (December): 38–39, 81–83.

———. 1953. *The good spirit of Laurel Ridge*. New York: McGraw-Hill.

———. 1956. *The year of my rebirth*. New York: McGraw-Hill.

———. 1958. *Plowshare to heaven*. New York: McGraw-Hill.

———. 1960. *God's oddling*. New York: McGraw-Hill. [northeastern KY]

———. 1967. New wine in old bottles. *Kentucky Folklore Record* 13: 20–24. [northeastern KY]

———. 1993. *Daughter of the legend*. Edited by John H. Spurlock. Ashland, KY: Jesse Stuart Foundation.

Stubbs, Thomas B. 1959–71. Mountain-wise [bimonthly column]. *Georgia Magazine*. [Rabun County, northeast GA]

Stupka, Arthur. 1943. Through the year in the Great Smoky Mountains National Park. In *The Great Smokies and the Blue Ridge*, edited by Roderick Peattie, 263–89. New York: Vanguard. [central east TN, central western NC]

———. 1960. *Great Smoky Mountains National Park North Carolina and Tennessee*. Natural history handbook series, no. 5. Washington, DC: US National Park Service. [central east TN, central western NC]

———. 1964. *Trees, shrubs, and woody vines of Great Smoky Mountains National Park*. Knoxville: University of Tennessee Press. [central east TN, central western NC]

———. 1982. *Wildflowers in color*. New York: HarperCollins.

Sullivan Countians in the Civil War. 1995. *Holston Pastfinder* 13(51): 32–33. [Sullivan County, northeast TN]

Sullivan Countians in the Civil War. 1995. *Holston Pastfinder* 13(52): 32–33. [Sullivan County, northeast TN]

Sullivan County Tennessee soldiers in the Cherokee removal—the Trail of Tears. 1836. Transcribed and published in *Holston Pastfinder* 13 (1995): 32. [Sullivan County, northeast TN]

Summers, Lewis Preston. 1929. *Annals of southwest Virginia, 1769–1800*. Abingdon, VA: L. P. Summers. [southwestern VA]

Sunday with Aunt Arie. 1971. *Foxfire Magazine* 5(1–2): 80–87. [Macon County, southwestern NC]

Suter, Scott Hamilton. 1995. *Shenandoah Valley folklife*. Jackson: University Press of Mississippi. [western VA]

Sutherland, E. J. 1960. Folk speech on frying pan. *Mountain Life and Work* 36(2): 11–14. [eastern KY]

Sutton, Popcorn. c1999. *Me and my likker: The story of a mountain moonshiner*. Maggie Valley, NC: Privately published. [Cocke County, central east TN, and Haywood County, central western NC]

———. 2009. *Me and my likker*. Rev. ed. Maggie Valley, NC: Self-published. [central western NC]

Sutton, Solomon. 1997. [Letters to brother James Solomon, November 17, 1861, and November 8, 1862]. *Bone Rattler* 13(3): 40–42. [western NC]

Swearingen, Janelle. 1994. Letters from home. *Tennessee Ancestors* 10: 163–68. [Monroe and Bradley Counties, southeast TN]

Tabler, Dave. 2011. Where the Hillbilly Highway ends. http://appalachianalliance.com/tag/dayton-oh/, accessed March 26, 2012.

Taliaferro, H[arden E.]. 1859. *Fisher's River (North Carolina) scenes and characters*. New York: Harper and Brothers. [Surry County, northwestern NC, in the 1820s]

———. 1860. Ducktown. *Southern Literary Messenger* 31 (November): 337–42. [Surry County, northwestern NC]

———. 1938. *Carolina humor: Sketches by Harden E. Taliaferro* [stories from the *Southern Literary Messenger*, originally published 1860–63]. Richmond: Dietz. [northwestern NC]

Tate, Bryan. 2002. Appalachian pioneers and log houses. *Journal of Alabama Archaeology* 48: 1–18.

Taylor, Archer, and Bartlett Jere Whiting. 1952. *Modern proverbs and proverbial sayings*. Cambridge, MA: Harvard University Press.

Teague, John. 1864. [Letters]. John Teague Letters. *The Civil War in Tennessee*, Tennessee State Library and Archives, Nashville, http://sos.tn.gov/tsla/looking-back-civil-war-tennessee. [McMinn County, southeast TN]

Temple, Oliver P. 1899. *East Tennessee and the Civil War*. Cincinnati: R. Clarke. [east TN]

The Tennessean. 1954. [Untitled newspaper article]

Tennessee encyclopedia of history and culture. 2009. Rev. ed. https://tennesseeencyclopedia.net/. Originally published in book form by Rutledge Hill Press, Nashville, TN.

Terrell, Bob. 2008. Mountain lingo. *Smoky Mountain Living*, June 8. http://www.smliv.com/features/mountain-lingo/. [western NC]

Tesh, William A. 1862–64. [Letters]. William A. Tesh Papers, 1858–1864. David M. Rubenstein Rare Book and Manuscript Library, Duke University, Durham, NC. [Yadkin County, northwestern NC]

Texana Committee on Community History and Preservation. 2006. *Voices of Texana*. Raleigh: Barefoot Press. [Cherokee County, southwestern NC]

They shall lay hands on the sick, and they shall recover. 1973. *Foxfire Magazine* 7(1): 52–58.

They shall take up serpents. 1973. *Foxfire Magazine* 7(1): 31–47.

This is the way I was raised up. 1968. *Foxfire Magazine* 2(1): 8–9.

Thomas, Jean. 1931. *Devil's ditties: Being the stories of the Kentucky mountain people told by Jean Thomas with the songs they sing*. Chicago: W. Wilbur Hatfield. [northeastern KY]

———. 1933. Jilson Setters: Singin' fiddler of Lost Hope Hollow. *American Speech* 8(2): 28–30. [northeastern KY]

———. 1933. *The traipsin' woman*. New York: Dutton.

———. 1935. The American Folk Song Festival. *American Speech* 10: 36–37.

———. 1942. *Blue Ridge country*. New York: Duell, Sloan and Pearce.

———. 1945. The changing mountain folk. *American Mercury* 63: 43–49.

Thomas, Jean, and Walter Kob. 1964. *Ballad makin' in the mountains of Kentucky*. New York: Oak. [northeastern KY]

Thomas, Monroe. 1930. Highways and schools sounding death knell of mountain dialect. *Asheville Citizen*, September 30. [central western NC]

Thomas, Roy Edwin. 1991. *Southern Appalachia, 1885–1915: Oral histories from residents of the state corner area of North Carolina*. Jefferson, NC: McFarland. [northwestern NC]

———. 1994. *Come go with me: Old-timer stories from the southern mountains*. New York: Farrar, Straus and Giroux. [northwestern NC]

Thomas, William Roscoe. 1926. *Life among the hills and mountains of Kentucky*. Louisville, KY: Standard Printing Co. Press. [eastern KY]

Thompson, Charles D. 2011. *Spirits of just men: Mountaineers, liquor bosses, and lawmen in the moonshine capital of the world*. Urbana: University of Illinois Press. [southwestern VA]

Thompson, Debra, and Irene Moser. 2006. Appalachian folklore. In *A handbook of Appalachia: An introduction to the region*, edited by Grace Toney Edwards, JoAnn Asbury, and Ricky Cox, 143–72. Knoxville: University of Tennessee Press.

Thompson, Gordon. 1861–63. [Letters]. MSS 2T3735b, Virginia Historical Society, Richmond. [Mercer County, southern WV]

Thompson, Kathy, ed. 1976. *Touching home: A collection of history and folklore from the Copper Basin, Fannin County area*. Orlando, FL: Daniels. [north central GA]

Thompson, Mary Rado. 1996. A link in a chain. *Now & Then* 13(3): 17–20.

Thompson, Neal. 2009. *Driving with the devil: Southern moonshine, Detroit wheels, and the birth of NASCAR*. New York: Broadway.

Thompson, Samuel H. 1910. *The highlanders of the South*. New York: Eaton and Mains.

Thornburgh, Laura [published under the name Laura Thornborough]. 1927. Tramping in the Great Smokies. *American Forests and Forest Life* 33 (August): 463–66, 512. [central east TN]

——— [published under the name Laura Thornborough]. 1928. Americans the twentieth century forgot. *Travel* 50 (April): 25–28, 42.

——— [published under the name Laura Thornborough]. 1937. *The Great Smoky Mountains*. New York: Crowell. [Rev. and enlarged eds. were published in many years, including 1956 and 1971, by University of Tennessee Press.] [central east TN]

——— [published under the name Laura Thornborough]. 1971. *The Great Smoky Mountains*. Rev. and enlarged ed. of 1937 original. Knoxville: University of Tennessee Press. [central east TN]

Thwaites, Reuben Gold, and Louise Phelps Kellogg, eds. 1905. *Documentary history of Dunmore's War 1774*. Madison: Wisconsin Historical Society. [southwestern VA]

Tilley, Stephen G., and James E. Huheey. 2001. *Reptiles & amphibians of the Great Smokies*. Gatlinburg, TN: Great Smoky Mountains Association. [central east TN, central western NC]

Tipps, Henry Thurston. 1984. *A history of McKendree Church*. Nashville, TN: Parthenon. [north GA]

Tipton, A. Christine. 2000. *Civil War in the mountains: Greasy Cove, Tennessee*. Erwin, TN: Shining Mountain. [northeast TN]

Toe Valley Church. 2007. [Selected minutes]. In *The heritage of the Toe River Valley, Volume VI*, 48. Berwyn Heights, MD: County Heritage Books. [northwestern NC]

Tom walkers. 1979. *Foxfire Magazine* 13(3): 203–5.

Toops, Connie. 1992. *Great Smoky Mountains*. Stillwater, MN: Voyageur. [central east TN, central western NC]

A treatise on coal mining. 1900. 2nd ed. Scranton, PA: Colliery Engineer Company.

Tremont Logging Camp Auto Tour. n.d. Gatlinburg, TN: Great Smoky Mountains Natural History Association.

Trent, Emma Dean Smith. 1987. *East Tennessee's lore of yesteryear*. Whitesburg, TN: Privately published. [northeast TN]

———. 1989. *A sequel to East Tennessee's lore of yesteryear*. Whitesburg, TN: Privately published. [northeast TN]

Triplett, George R. 2003. *Our proud mountain roots and heritage*. Elkins, WV: Self-published. [eastern WV]

Trotter, William R. 1988. *Bushwhackers! The Civil War in North Carolina: The mountains*. Winston-Salem, NC: Blair.

Trout, Ed. 1984. *Gatlinburg: Cinderella city*. Pigeon Forge, TN: Griffin. [Sevier County, central east TN]

———. 1995. *Historic buildings of the Smokies*. Gatlinburg, TN: Great Smoky Mountains Natural History Association. [central east TN, central western NC]

Trout, Ed, and Olin Watson. c1978. *A piece of the Smokies: A pictorial history of life in the Smoky Mountains*. Maryville, TN: Printers. [central east TN, central western NC]

Turner, Lorenzo Dow. 1949. *Africanisms in the Gullah dialect*. Chicago: University of Chicago Press.

Tyler, Alicia. 1976. Benjamin Matheny: "Doin' a man's work": Logging in central and southern counties between 1918 and 1930. *Goldenseal* 2(3): 26–30. [central and southern WV]

Tyson, Lona Parton. 1986. *Reflections of the pinnacle: The story of the Parton roots*. Gatlinburg, TN: Crescent. [Sevier County, central east TN]

Ulmer, Mary, and Samuel E. Beck. 1951. *Cherokee cooklore*. Sylva, NC: Privately published. [Swain County, southwestern NC]

Underwood, Jinsie. 1974. *This is Madison County*. N.p.: Privately published. [Madison County, central western NC]

United States Commission of Fish & Fisheries. 1899. Report of the Commissioner for 1897–1898. Washington, DC: Government Printing Office.

University of Tennessee / Great Smoky Mountains National Park Cooperative Oral History Project. 1996–99. [Recorded interviews consulted at Library, Great Smoky Mountains National Park, Gatlinburg, TN]. [central east TN, central western NC]

Used to farm. 1975. *Foxfire Magazine* 9(1): 30–36. [Rabun County, northeast GA]

Vance, Zebulon. 1962–64. [Letters to North Carolina Governor Zebulon Vance]. Zebulon Vance Papers. State Archives of North Carolina, Raleigh. [various counties, western NC]

Vande Brake, Katherine. 2006. *How they shine*. Macon, GA: Mercer University Press. [northeast TN]

Van Nest, R. J. 1976. Gillis Ridge. *Appalachian Journal* 3: 307–10.

Van Noppen, Ina. 1973. *Western North Carolina since the Civil War*. Boone, NC: Appalachian Consortium Press. [western NC]

Venable, Sam. 2000. *Mountain hands: A portrait of southern Appalachia*. Knoxville: University of Tennessee Press. [east TN]

———. 2013. *How to tawlk and rite good: A guide to the language of southern Appalachia*. North Charleston, SC: CreateSpace. [east TN]

Vincent, Bert. 1940. *Us mountain folks*. Knoxville: Walters. [central east TN]

———. 1945. *Here in Tennessee*. Knoxville: Walters. [central east TN]

———. 1968. *The best stories of Bert Vincent*. Maryville, TN: Brazos. [central east TN]

———. 1970. *More of the best stories of Bert Vincent*. Maryville, TN: Mangrum. [east TN]

Vollmer, Lula. 1924. *Sun-up: A play in three acts*. New York: Brentano's.

Waldvogel, Merikay. 2009. Bark baskets and buckets: Made on the spot of what you've got. *Smokies Life* 2(1): 18–21. [east TN]

Walker, A. B. 1863. [Letters]. Walker Family Papers. Tennessee State Library and Archives, Nashville. [Knox County, central east TN]

Walker, C. A. 1864. [Letter]. William Walker Papers. Hunter Library Special Collections, Western Carolina University, Cullowhee, NC. [Cherokee County, southwestern NC]

Walker, Cas. 1994. *My life history: A book of true stories*. N.p.: Privately published. [Sevier County, central east TN]

Walker, Daniel B. 1863. [Letters]. Daniel B. Walker Letters, 1855–1889. Manuscripts Collection, Filson Historical Society, Louisville, KY. [McMinn County, southeast TN]

Walker, Edward R. III. 1983. *Tales from the Civil War*. Cosby, TN: Busy Bee. [Cocke County, central east TN]

Walker, Frank X. 2000. *Affrilachia: Poems by Frank X Walker*. Lexington, KY: Old Cove Press.

Walker, Raphy S. 1939. A mountaineer looks at his own speech. *Tennessee Folklore Society Bulletin* 5: 1–13. [central east TN]

Walker, Robert Sparks. 1941. *Lookout: The story of a mountain*. Kingsport, TN: Southern. [southeast TN]

Walker, Steven L. 1991. *Great Smoky Mountains: Splendor of the southern Appalachians*. Scottsdale, AZ: Camelback/Elan Venture. [central east TN, central western NC]

Walker Family. 1823–65. [Letters]. Walker Family Papers. Confederate Collection, box 11, folder 35a, Tennessee State Library and Archives, Nashville. [Knox County, central east TN]

Wall, Barbara Mann, and Arlene W. Keeling. 2010. *Nurses on the front line: When disaster strikes, 1878–2010*. New York: Springer.

Wall, Robert W. 1969. *History of Davie County in the forks of the Yadkin*. Mocksville, NC: Davie County Historical Publishing. [Davie County, northwestern NC]

Walls, David S., and John B. Stephenson, eds. 1972. *Appalachia in the sixties: Decade of reawakening*. Lexington: University Press of Kentucky.

Warren, Harold F. 1974. *A right good people*. Boone, NC: Appalachian Consortium Press. [western NC]

Warrick, Thomas. 1862–65. [Letters]. Thomas Warrick Papers. SPR420, Alabama Department of Archives and History, Montgomery. [Coosa County, east central AL]

Washburn, Benjamin Earl. 1955. *A country doctor in the South Mountains*. Asheville, NC: Stephens Press. [Rutherford County, southwestern NC]

Waters, John B., Jr. 2015. Swinging bridges in Sevier County. *Smoky Mountain Historical Society Journal and Newsletter* 41(1): 20–21. [Sevier County, central east TN]

Watford, Christopher M., ed. 2003. *The Civil War in North Carolina: Soldiers' and civilians' letters and diaries, 1861–1865*, vol. 2: *The mountains*. Jefferson, NC: McFarland. [western NC]

Watkins, Charles Alan. Why have there been no Great Appalachian Photographers? *Now & Then* 14(2): 21–25.

Watkins, Floyd. 1949. The southern mountaineers' archaic English. *Georgia Review* 3: 219–25. [north central GA]

Watkins, Floyd C., and Charles Hubert Watkins. 1963. *Yesterday in the hills*. Athens: University of Georgia Press. [north central GA]

———. 1973. *Yesterday in the hills* [revised version of 1963 original]. Athens: University of Georgia Press. [Cherokee County, north central GA]

Watkins, James W. 1862–64. [Letters]. James W. Watkins Papers, 1861–1864. MSS 413, Stuart A. Rose Manuscript, Archives, and Rare Book Library, Emory University, Atlanta. [Franklin County, northeast GA]

Watson, James. 1861–62. [Letters]. James Watson Collection. Hunter Library Special Collections, Western Carolina University, Cullowhee, NC. [Jackson County, southwestern NC]

Watters-Curtis Family. 1861–64. [Letters]. Watters-Curtis Family Papers. MSS A V345, Filson Historical Society, Special Collections, Louisville, KY. [Estill County, southeastern KY]

Watts, Monteen Keener. 1986. *Chips off the same block*. Tiger, GA: J & M.

Wax, H. G. 1865. [Letter from H. G. Wax]. Transcribed and published in *Distant Crossroads* 1(1) (1985): 39–41. [Hawkins County, northeast TN]

Waynesville Mountaineer. 1954. [Untitled newspaper article]. August 2. [central western NC]

Weals, Vic. 1954. Lost gold mine in Big Greenbrier. *Knoxville Journal*, May 11. [Sevier County, central east TN]

———. 1957. A bridge for Sary Parker. *Knoxville Journal*, May 12, 12D. [central east TN]

———. c1959. *Hillbilly dictionary: An edifying collection of mountain expressions*. Gatlinburg, TN: Weals. [east TN]

———. 1963. Oldtimers. *Knoxville Journal*, January 28, 12. [central east TN]

———. 1976. Funky offends mountain ears (and noses). *Knoxville Journal*, September 27. [central east TN]

———. 1976. It's owin' to how a word is used. *Knoxville Journal*, September 6, 9. [central east TN]

———. 1976. Mountaineer asks us to "mind" our language. *Knoxville Journal*, June 28, 9. [central east TN]

———. 1976. Plenty of water, but nothing to eat in the "gant" lot. *Knoxville Journal*, December 13, 11. [central east TN]

———. 1976. Two minus two equals nary. *Knoxville Journal*, July 19, 12. [central east TN]

———. 1976. Words stay "alive" with oldtimers. *Knoxville Journal*, July 26, 7. [central east TN]

———. 1977. Cove folk knew a stranger by his factory-made track. *Knoxville Journal*, January 17, 7. [central east TN]

———. 1977. Logger past saving but friends did try. *Knoxville Journal*, January 31. [central east TN]

———. 1978. Loggers wrote own ballad. *Knoxville Journal*, July 27. [central east TN]

———. 1978. Mules. *Knoxville Journal*. [central east TN]

———. 1978. Two locomotives. *Knoxville Journal*. [central east TN]

———. 1980. Dunn Early, lone ranger in forests, parks. *Knoxville Journal*, June 19. [central east TN]

———. 1980. Strangers on mountain trail wary of knocking on doors. *Knoxville Journal*, April 3. [central east TN]

———. 1981. Andy Greer's slow oxen died, quick as lightning, in storm at top of Smoky. *Knoxville Journal*, July 22, A15. [central east TN]

———. 1981. Becky rewards family coffinmaker. *Knoxville Journal*, December 31, 3. [Blount County, central east TN]

———. 1981. Falling fire towers end era of adventure. *Knoxville Journal*, December 24, A8. [central east TN]

———. 1981. Farmers made hay on top of Smoky. *Knoxville Journal*, December 3, A8. [central east TN]

———. 1981. Older cows eager to summer atop mountain. *Knoxville Journal*, October 15, D3. [central east TN]

———. 1981. Rocky Top. *Knoxville Journal*. [central east TN]

———. 1981. Root-hogs unwelcome on high cattle range. *Knoxville Journal*, December 10, C12. [central east TN]

———. 1982. Cove lumber plentiful—road to market steep. *Knoxville Journal*, January 7, B8. [Blount County, central east TN]

———. 1982. Hog or cow brute safe with silent Dan. *Knoxville Journal*, July 15, B5. [central east TN]

———. 1983. Ball-hooting, log-nosing days remembered. *Knoxville Journal*, October 20, A10. [Blount County, central east TN]

———. 1983. Len Cogdill recalls hills full of timber, Republicans. *Knoxville Journal*, November 3, B11. [central east TN]

———. 1983. Waterjacking a dangerous job, as Peter McCarter discovered. *Knoxville Journal*, September 8, B10. [central east TN]

———. 1991. *Last train to Elkmont: A look back at life on Little River in the Great Smoky Mountains*. Knoxville: Olden. [Blount County, central east TN]

———. 2002. *Legends of Cades Cove and the Smokies beyond*. Knoxville: Olden. [Blount County, central east TN]

Wear, Jerry, ed. 1985. *Lost communities of Sevier County Tennessee: Greenbrier*. Sevierville, TN: Sevierville Heritage Committee. [Sevier County, central east TN]

Wear, Jerry L. 1986. *Sugarlands: A lost community of Sevier County*. Sevierville, TN: Sevierville Heritage Committee. [Sevier County, central east TN]

———. 1987. *Sevierville 1795–1986: A homecoming look at our past, present, and future*. Kingsport, TN: Kingsport Press. [Sevier County, central east TN]

Weatherford, Willis Duke, and Earl D. C. Brewer. 1962. *Life and religion in southern Appalachia*. New York: Friendship Press.

Weather signs. 1970. *Foxfire Magazine* 4(4): 206–9.

Weaver, Jack. 1993. Sociolinguistics of Scotch-Irish speech in Appalachia. *Irish Studies Working Papers* 93: 12–19.

Webb, Samuel. 1858. [Letter]. Transcribed and published in *Distant Crossroads* 24 (2007): 109–10. [Hawkins County, northeast TN]

Webb, Vaughan, Andrew Pauly, and Roddy Moore. 2009. Moonshining. In *New encyclopedia of southern culture*, vol. 14: *Folklife*, edited by Glenn Hinson and William Ferris, 328–31. Chapel Hill: University of North Carolina Press.

Weber, William J. 1995. *Rugged hills, gentle folk: My friends and neighbors in the Big Pine Valley*. Glendale, WI: Reiman. [western NC]

A week in the Smoky Mountains. 1860. *Southern Literary Messenger* 31 (August): 117–31. [Sevier County, central east TN]

Weeks, Abigail. 1910. A word list from Barbourville, Kentucky. *Dialect Notes* 3: 456–57. [south central KY]

Weeks, Abigail E. 1921. The speech of the Kentucky mountaineer as I know it. MA thesis, Teachers College, Columbia University. [eastern KY]

Weir, Sally Royce. 1906. *Hot Springs, past and present*. Knoxville: F. E. Newman. [central western NC]

Weller, Jack E. 1965. *Yesterday's people: Life in contemporary Appalachia*. Lexington: University Press of Kentucky. [WV]

Wellman, Manly Wade. 1973. *The kingdom of Madison: A southern mountain fastness and its people*. Chapel Hill: University of North Carolina Press. [Madison County, central western NC]

Wells, B. W. 1982. *The remarkable flora of the Great Smoky Mountains*. Asheville: North Carolina National Park Commission. [central east TN, central western NC]

Wells, J. C. 1893. Weather and moon superstitions in Tennessee. *Journal of American Folk-lore* 6: 298–300. [TN]

Wentworth, Harold. 1944. *American dialect dictionary*. New York: Crowell. [various locales as specified at individual citations]

We sing about life and what it means to us: A conversation with Everett Lilly. 1975. *Goldenseal* 1(2): 14–20. [WV]

Weslager, C. A. 1969. *The log cabin in America*. New Brunswick, NJ: Rutgers University Press.

Wesson, William H. 1861–65. William H. Wesson Papers. Accession 41008, Miscellaneous reel 4368, Library of Virginia Archives, Richmond.

Wesson Family. 1861–65. [Letters]. Private collection.

West, Don. 2004. *No lonesome road*. Edited by Jeff Biggers and George Brosi. Urbana: University of Illinois Press.

West, John Foster. 1965. They git tard in the hills but hit ain't from talkin'. *Charlotte Observer*, March 21. [western NC]

———. 1965. *Time was*. New York: Random House. [northwestern NC]

———. 1966. Dialect of the southern mountains. *North Carolina Folklore* 14: 31–34. [western NC]

West, Lawrence Edward. 2008. *The life of a good ole country boy*. Beeson, WV: Self-published. [WV]

West, Roy Andrew. 1922. The songs of the mountaineers. MA thesis, George Peabody College, Nashville, TN.

Wester, Thomas C. 1864. Thomas C. Wester Papers, 1864–65. State Archives of North Carolina, Raleigh.

Western Carolina Teachers College. 1938. *Facts and legends of the Cullowhee region*. Cullowhee, NC: Western Carolina Teachers College. [southwestern NC]

West Family. 1862. [Letters]. West Family Letters. South Caroliniana Library, University of South Carolina, Columbia. [Spartanburg District, northwestern SC]

Westover, J. Huston. 1960. Highland language of the Cumberland coal country. *Mountain Life and Work* 36(2): 18–21. [eastern KY]

The West Virginia encyclopedia. 2006. Charleston: West Virginia Humanities Council.

Whaley, Martha. 2009. The Stoney Creek Primitive Baptist Associational meeting and dinner on the ground. *Now & Then* 25(1): 59–60.

Whaley, Sam. c1950. "Aunt Lydia" living in shadow of LeConte, typifies mountain woman of earlier days; is Bible student [clipping from unidentified newspaper consulted at Library, Great Smoky Mountains National Park, Gatlinburg, TN]

Wharton, May Cravath. 1953. *Doctor woman of the Cumberlands: The autobiography of May Cravath Wharton, M.D.* Pleasant Hill, TN: Uplands. [Cumberland County, east central TN]

What a find: 154 year-old Richardson letter. 1996. *Campbell Countian* 7: 35–36. [Campbell County, northeast TN]

Whisnant, Anne Mitchell, and David Whisnant. 2010. *When the parkway came*. Chapel Hill, NC: Primary Source. [northwestern NC]

Whisnant, David E. 1983. *All that is native & fine: The politics of culture in an American region*. Chapel Hill: University of North Carolina Press.

Whitaker, Larry. 2004. Saints, sinners, and dinners on the grounds: The religious legacy of the Upper Cumberland. In *Rural life and culture in the Upper Cumberland*, edited by Michael E. Birdwell and W. Calvin Dickinson, 49–65. Lexington: University Press of Kentucky. [north central TN]

Whitaker, Stephen. 1863–64. [Letters]. Stephen Whitaker Papers. PC 26, State Archives of North Carolina, Raleigh. [Cherokee County, southwestern NC]

White, Edward M. 1963. The vocabulary of marbles in eastern Kentucky. *Kentucky Folklore Record* 9: 57–74. [eastern KY]

White, Edwin E. 1937. *Highland heritage: The southern mountains and the nation*. New York: Friendship.

White, Linda C. 1978. Champ Ferguson: A legacy of blood. *Tennessee Folklore Society Bulletin* 44: 66–70. [north central TN]

White, Peter, T. Condon, J. Rock, and C. A. McCormick. 1996. *Wildflowers of the Smokies*. Gatlinburg, TN: Great Smoky Mountains Association. [central east TN, central western NC]

Whiteaker, Larry. 1983. "The enemy is my brother": The Civil War in the Upper Cumberland. In *Lend an ear: Heritage of the Tennessee Upper Cumberland*, edited by Calvin Dickinson, Larry Whiteaker, and Leo McGee, 33–44. Lanham, MD: University Press of America. [north central TN]

White baneberry. 2009. Wildflowers of the southeastern US. http://2bnthewild.com/plants/H110.htm.

Whitehead, Don. c1975. On what's an East Tennessee accent. *Knoxville News-Sentinel*, undated.

Whitener, Rogers. 1981. Selections from "Folk-ways and folk speech." *North Carolina Folklore Journal* 29: 1–86. [northwestern NC]

———. 1990. *Thrice-told tales*. Boone, NC: Whitener and Miller. [northwestern NC]

Whittaker, Otto, ed. 1968. *Best of "Hillbilly": A prize collection of 100 percent writing from Jim Comstock's West Virginia hillbilly*. Anderson, SC: Droke. [WV]

Whitten letter. 1826. Transcribed and published in Upper Cumberland *Genealogical Association* 15 (1990): 154. [Greenville District, northwestern SC]

Wigginton, Eliot, ed. 1972. *The Foxfire book: Hog dressing; log cabin building; mountain crafts and foods; planting by the signs; snake lore, hunting tales, faith healing; moonshining; and other affairs of plain living*. New York: Doubleday.

———. 1973. *Foxfire 2: Ghost stories, spring wild plant foods, spinning and weaving, midwifing, burial customs, corn shuckin's, wagon making and more affairs of plain living*. Garden City, NY: Anchor.

———. 1975. *Foxfire 3: Animal care, banjos and dulcimers, hide tanning, summer and fall wild plant foods, butter churns, ginseng, and still more affairs of plain living*. Garden City, NY: Anchor.

———. 1976. Stanley Hicks, Sugar Grove, North Carolina. In *"I wish I could give my son a wild raccoon,"* 353–66. Garden City, NY: Anchor. [northwestern NC]

———. 1977. *Foxfire 4: Water systems, fiddle making, logging, gardening, sassafras tea, wood carving and further affairs of plain living*. Garden City, NY: Anchor.

———. 1980. *Foxfire 5: Ironmaking, blacksmithing, flintlock rifles, bear hunting and other affairs of plain living*. Originally published 1979; reprinted in 1980 as part of multivolume set. Garden City, NY: Anchor.

———. 1980. *Foxfire 6: Shoemaking, gourd banjos, and songbows, one hundred toys and games, wooden locks, a water powered sawmill, and other affairs of just plain living*. 1980. Garden City, NY: Anchor.

———. 1990. *A Foxfire Christmas*. New York: Doubleday.

Wilburn, H. C. c1950. Quern, a grinding device, dates from ancient days. *Asheville Citizen*. [central western NC]

———. 1953. Pounding-mill is remarkable machine. *Asheville Citizen*, August 2. [central western NC]

Wilburn, Hiram C. 1937–39. [Notes from the first historian of Great Smoky Mountains National Park, collected by Joseph Sargent Hall]. [central east TN, central western NC]

Wilcox, Patricia. 2000. *Shaped notes: Stories of twentieth century Georgia*. Binghamton, NY: Pageant Press. [northwest GA]

Wilder, Roy. 1984. *You all spoken here*. New York: Viking.

Wiles, Bill, and Mary Wiles. 2009. *Up on Location: The story of a West Virginia farm, a road and the people who lived there*. Parsons, WV: McClain. [central WV]

Wiley, Bell Irvin. 1952. *The life of Billy Yank: The common soldier of the Union*. Garden City, NY: Doubleday.

Wilgus, D. K. 1959. Down our way: Who's in town? *Kentucky Folklore Record* 5: 1–8. [KY]

Wilkinson, Crystal E. 1999. On being "country": One Affrilachian woman's return home. In *Confronting Appalachian stereotypes: Back talk from an American region*, edited by Dwight E. Billings, Gurney Norman, and Katherine Ledford, 184–86. Lexington: University Press of Kentucky. [south central KY]

———. 2000. *Blackberries, blackberries*. London: Toby. [south central KY]

Williams, Barbara. 2008. [Email to the editor, April 1]. [Scott County, north central TN]

Williams, Cleo Hicks. 2005. *Gratitude for shoes: Growing up poor in the Smokies*. New York: Universe. [Graham County, southwestern NC, as of 1940s]

Williams, Cratis D. 1944. A word-list from the mountains of Kentucky and North Carolina. *Publication of the American Dialect Society* 2: 28–31. [northeastern KY, northwestern NC]

———. 1945. [Comment on *cuckold*]. *Publication of the American Dialect Society* 3: 9–10. [northeastern KY]

———. 1961. The content of mountain speech. *Mountain Life and Work* 37(4): 13–17.

———. 1961. Rhythm and melody in mountain speech. *Mountain Life and Work* 37(3): 7–10.

———. 1961. The "r" in mountain speech. *Mountain Life and Work* 37(1): 5–8.

———. 1962. Metaphor in mountain speech. *Mountain Life and Work* 38(4): 9–12.

———. 1962. Mountaineers mind their manners. *Mountain Life and Work* 38(2): 19–25.

———. 1962. Verbs in mountain speech. *Mountain Life and Work* 38(2): 15–19.

———. 1963. Metaphor in mountain speech. *Mountain Life and Work* 39(1): 51–53.

———. 1963. Metaphor in mountain speech. *Mountain Life and Work* 39(2): 53–55.

———. 1964. Prepositions in mountain speech. *Mountain Life and Work* 40(1): 53–55.

———. 1967. Moonshining in the mountains. *North Carolina Folklore* 15: 11–17.

———. 1967. Subtlety in mountain speech. *Mountain Life and Work* 43(1): 14–16.

———. 1972. Who are the southern mountaineers? *Appalachian Journal* 4: 174–81.

———. 1978. Appalachian speech. *North Carolina Historical Review* 55: 174–79.

———. 1981. [Typescript of lecture delivered at the conference Language Variety in the South: Perspectives in Black and White, Columbia, SC, October 2]

———. 1985. *William H. Vaughn: A better man than I ever wanted to be*. Morehead, KY: Appalachian Development Center.

———. 1995. I become a teacher: A memoir of one-room school life in eastern Kentucky. Ashland, KY: Jesse Stuart Foundation.

———. 1999. *I come to Boone*. Boone, NC: Appalachian Consortium Press.

———. 2003. *Tales from sacred wind: Coming of age in Appalachia. The Cratis Williams Chronicle*. Boone, NC: Appalachian State University. [northeastern KY]

Williams, James. 1861–65. James Williams Letters. Accession 25920, Library of Virginia Archives, Richmond.

Williams, John Alexander. 2002. *Appalachia: A history*. Chapel Hill: University of North Carolina Press.

Williams, John Rodger. 1985. Appalachian migrants in Cincinnati, Ohio: The role of folklore in the reinforcement of ethnic identity. PhD diss., Indiana University, Bloomington.

Williams, Michael Ann. 1987. Rethinking the house: Interior space and social change. *Appalachian Journal* 14: 174–82. [southwestern NC]

———. 1990. Pride and prejudice: The Appalachian boxed house in southwestern North Carolina. *Winterthur Portfolio* 25: 217–30. [southwestern NC]

———. 1991. *Homeplace: The social use and meaning of the folk dwelling in southwestern North Carolina*. Athens: University of Georgia Press. [southwestern NC]

———. 1995. *Great Smoky Mountains folklife*. Jackson: University Press of Mississippi. [central east TN, central western NC]

Williams, Tiffany M. 2009. Maw Surry. http://www.stilljournal.net/tiffany-williams-fiction.php.

———. 2012–14. [Notes and observations regarding Letcher County, southeastern KY]

———. 2017. Murmuration. *Appalachian Heritage* 45(2): 9–17.

Williams, Wayne W. 1923. After bruin in the Great Smokies. *National Sportsman*, March. [Swain County, central western NC]

Willis Family. 1861–65. [Letters]. Private collection.

Willnotah. 1844. The life and memory & death; Of my brother Yona Gus Kah. Transcribed and published in *Bone Rattler* 11(2) (1995): 15–16.

Willy, John. 1926. Ten days in the proposed Great Smoky Mountains National Park. *Hotel Monthly* (September): 44–58. [Sevier County, central east TN]

Wilson, Eddie W. 1934. Odd bog plants kill insects, help man in Smoky Mountains park. *Asheville Citizen*, July 8. [western NC]

Wilson, George. 1944. A word-list from Virginia and North Carolina. *Publication of the American Dialect Society* 2: 38–52. [western NC]

———. 1952. Folk speech. In *The Frank C. Brown collection of North Carolina folklore*, edited by Newman Ivey White et al., vol. 1, 505–618. Durham, NC: Duke University Press. [western NC]

Wilson, Gordon. 1945. *Passing institutions*. Cynthiana, KY: Hobson. [south central KY]

———. 1946. *Fidelity folks*. Cynthiana, KY: Hobson. [south central KY]

———. c1960, 1966, 1968. [Unpublished dialect materials from the area of Mammoth Cave in Edmonson County, south central KY, donated to the *Dictionary of American Regional English* project, consulted at the DARE office (1994, 1997) and through its first five published volumes]. [south central KY]

———. 1962. *Folkways of the Mammoth Cave region*. Bowling Green, KY: Self-published. [south central KY]

———. 1963. Studying folklore in a small region IV: Regional words. *Tennessee Folklore Society Bulletin* 29: 79–86. [south central KY]

———. 1964. Words relating to plants and animals in the Mammoth Cave region. *Publication of the American Dialect Society* 42: 11–25. [south central KY]

———. 1967. *Folkways of the Mammoth Cave region*. No. 2. N.p.: National Park Concessions. [south central KY]

———. 1968. *Folklore of the Mammoth Cave region*. Bowling Green, KY: Kentucky Folklore Society. [south central KY]

———. 1968. Local plants in folk remedies in the Mammoth Cave region. *Southern Folklore Quarterly* 32: 320–27. [south central KY]

Wilson, Gypsy Vera. 1937. Folklore in southeastern Kentucky. MA thesis, George Peabody College, Nashville, TN. [southeastern KY]

Wilson, Isabella Chilton. 1919. Welfare in a mining town. *Journal of Home Economics* 11: 21–23. [WV]

Wilson, James. 2004. *Letters of a Confederate private: Thomas O. Wilson, Company F, 51st Virginia Infantry, Whartons Brigade*. Blacksburg, VA: Pocahantas. [Bland County, southwestern VA]

Wilson, Jane, and Michaele Haas. 1999. *MeeMa's memory quilt: Treasured stories of Watauga County history*. Boone, NC: Parkway. [Watauga County, northwestern NC]

Wilson, Kathleen Curtis. 2001. *Textile art from southern Appalachia: The quiet work of women*. 2001. Johnson City, TN: Overmountain.

Wilson, Mrs. Eddie W. 1926. Wordlist compiled at Cullowhee, North Carolina. Horace Kephart Collection, Hunter Library Special Collections, Western Carolina University, Cullowhee, NC. [southwestern NC]

Wilson, Samuel Tyndale. 1914. *The southern mountaineers*. New York: Presbyterian Home Missions.

Wilson, Veta. 1984. A train ride into Elkmont's colorful past. *Mountain Press*, June 13, 5, 7. [Sevier County, central east TN]
Wiltse, Henry M. 1895. *The moonshiners*. Chattanooga: Times.
Wingfield, A. B. 1894. The big buck of Walden's Ridge. *Forest and Stream* 43: 399–400. [TN]
Wingfield, Marshall. 2009. *Franklin County, Virginia: A history*. Baltimore: Clearfield. [southwestern VA]
Winkler, Wayne. 2016. About the Melungeons. October 14. http://melungeon.org/2016/10/14/about-the-melungeons-by-wayne-winkler-2004-article/.
Winstadt, Jacob. 1993. [Letter]. *Distant Crossroads* 10 (January): 4. [northeast TN]
Wise, Claude Merton. 1957. Mountain English. In *Applied phonetics*, 303–21. Englewood Cliffs, NJ: Prentice Hall.
Wiseman, Scott G. 1985. Wiseman's view: The autobiography of Skyland Scotty Wiseman. *North Carolina Folklore Journal* 33: 1–90. [western NC]
Wiseman Family. 1861–65. [Letters]. Private collection.
Wolfe, Charles K. 1977. *Tennessee strings*. Knoxville: University of Tennessee Press. [TN]
Wolfe, Thomas. 1922. The return of Buck Gavin. In *Carolina folk-plays*, edited by Frederick H. Koch, 33–44. New York: Holt. [western NC]
———. 1929. *Look homeward, angel: A story of the buried life*. New York: Scribner's.
Wolfram, Walt, and Donna Christian. 1975–83. [Transcriptions of interviews conducted in Mercer and Monroe Counties, southern WV, in 1975 for the authors' book *Appalachian speech* (1976) and for later research]
———. 1976. *Appalachian speech*. Arlington, VA: Center for Applied Linguistics. [Mercer and Monroe Counties, southern WV]
Wolfram, Walt, James W. Clark, Neal Hutcheson, and Gary Carden. 2003. *Mountain talk: A journey to the heart of southern Appalachia*. DVD. Raleigh: North Carolina Language and Life Project, North Carolina State University, Humanities Extension. [southwestern North Carolina]
Wood, Gordon [R.]. 1958. A list of words from Tennessee. *Publication of the American Dialect Society* 29: 3–18. [TN]
Wood, Gordon Reid. 1971. *Vocabulary change*. Carbondale: Southern Illinois University Press.
Wood, Lawrence Edward. 1974. *Mountain memories*. Franklin, NC: Privately published. [southwestern NC]
Wood, Violet. 1950. *So sure of life*. New York: Friendship. [Sevier County, central east TN]
Woodall, Barbara Taylor. 2011. *It's not my mountain anymore*. Sylva, NC: Catch the Spirit of Appalachia, Inc.
Woodard, C. M. 1946. A word-list from Virginia and North Carolina. *Publication of the American Dialect Society* 6: 4–43.
Woodbridge, Hensley C. 1957. Some unrecorded hunting terms found in Kentucky. *Kentucky Folklore Record* 3: 153–58. [KY]
Wooden sleds. 1976. *Foxfire Magazine* 10(2): 147–64.
Woodring, Howard. 1996. *A window to times gone by: Tales and songs*. Transcribed and published by Stanley South. Columbia, SC: Privately published. [Watauga County, northwestern NC]
Woods, Cloe. 1984. *West Virginia was good*. Charleston, WV: Mountain State Press. [WV]
Woodside, Jane Harris. 1989. The Cherokee: Hungry for the dance. *Now & Then* 6(3): 22–25. [western NC]
Woody, G. B. 1863. Green B. Woody letters. Confederate Miscellany, MSS 20, Stuart A. Rose Manuscript, Archives, and Rare Book Library, Emory University, Atlanta. [Yancey County, northwestern NC]
Woody, Robert H. 1950. Cataloochee homecoming. *South Atlantic Quarterly* 49: 8–17. [Haywood County, central western NC]
Woofter, Carey. 1927. Dialect words and phrases from west-central West Virginia. *American Speech* 2: 347–67. [WV]
Woolley, Bryan. 1975. *We be here when the morning comes*. Lexington: University Press of Kentucky. [southeastern KY]
Woosley, Glenda Janice. 1962. Water witching Big Reedy style. *Kentucky Folklore Record* 8: 137–40. [KY]
Word-list. 1896. *Dialect Notes* 1: 411–27. [southwestern NC]
Words and expressions. 1973. *Foxfire Magazine* 7(2): 133–38.
Words words words. 1941. *American Speech* 16: 41. [western NC]
Works Projects Administration. 1941. *In the land of Breathitt*. New York: Bacon, Percy, and Daggett. [southeastern KY]
Wright, Bryant. 1862–64. [Letters]. Bryant Wright Papers, 1859–1864. MS 5916, David M. Rubenstein Rare Book and Manuscript Library, Duke University, Durham, NC. [Tallapoosa County, east central AL]
Wright, Jack. 2007. *Music of coal: Mining songs from the Appalachian coalfields*. Big Stone Gap, VA: Lonesome Records & Publishing.
Wright, Lillian Mayfield. 1964. Mountain medicine. *North Carolina Folklore* 12: 7–12. [western NC]
Wright, Nathalia. 1944. Query. *Tennessee Folklore Society Bulletin* 10(2): 10. [Blount County, central east TN]
Wyrick, Nathaniel. 1845. [Letter to Lewis Atkins in Grainger County, TN, dated April 13]. Transcribed and published in *Claiborne County Historical Society Reflections* 16 (1997): 3–4. [Grainger County, northeast TN]
Yarrow, Mike. 2015. *Voices from the coalfields: Found poems*. Huron, OH: Bottom Dog Press.
Yeager, Barbara. 1977. Mostly work: Making a home in Widen. *Goldenseal* 3(1): 7–10. [WV]
Yeatts, John H. 1984. *Remembering old Mayberry*. Charlotte: Delmar. [northwestern NC]
Young, Malone. 1987. *Latchpins of the Lost Cove*. Johnson City, TN: Latchpin Press. [northeast TN]
———. c1982. One thousand colloquialisms from deep Appalachia. Typescript on deposit at Berea College Library, Appalachian Center Unprocessed Materials, log 400, box 1, Southern Appalachian Archives, Berea, KY.
Zeigler, Wilbur Gleason, and Benn S. Grosscup. 1883. *The heart of the Alleghanies: or, Western North Carolina; comprising its topography, history, resources, people, narratives, incidents, and pictures in travel, hunting and fishing, and legends of its wildernesses*. Raleigh: Williams and Company. [western NC]
Zelinsky, Wilbur. 1955. Some problems in the distribution of generic terms in the place-names of the northeastern United States. *Annals of the Association of American Geographers* 41: 319–49. [eastern KY, western VA, WV]
Zimmerman, James C. 1861–64. [Letters]. James C. Zimmerman Papers, 1779–1910. David M. Rubenstein Rare Book and Manuscript Library, Duke University, Durham, NC. [Forsyth Co NC]
Zion Baptist Church, Yancey Co., NC: Minutes, 1834–1880. 2007. In *The heritage of the Toe River Valley*, vol. 6, edited by Lloyd Richard Bailey Sr., 19–89. Marceline, MO: Walsworth. [Yancey County, northwestern NC]